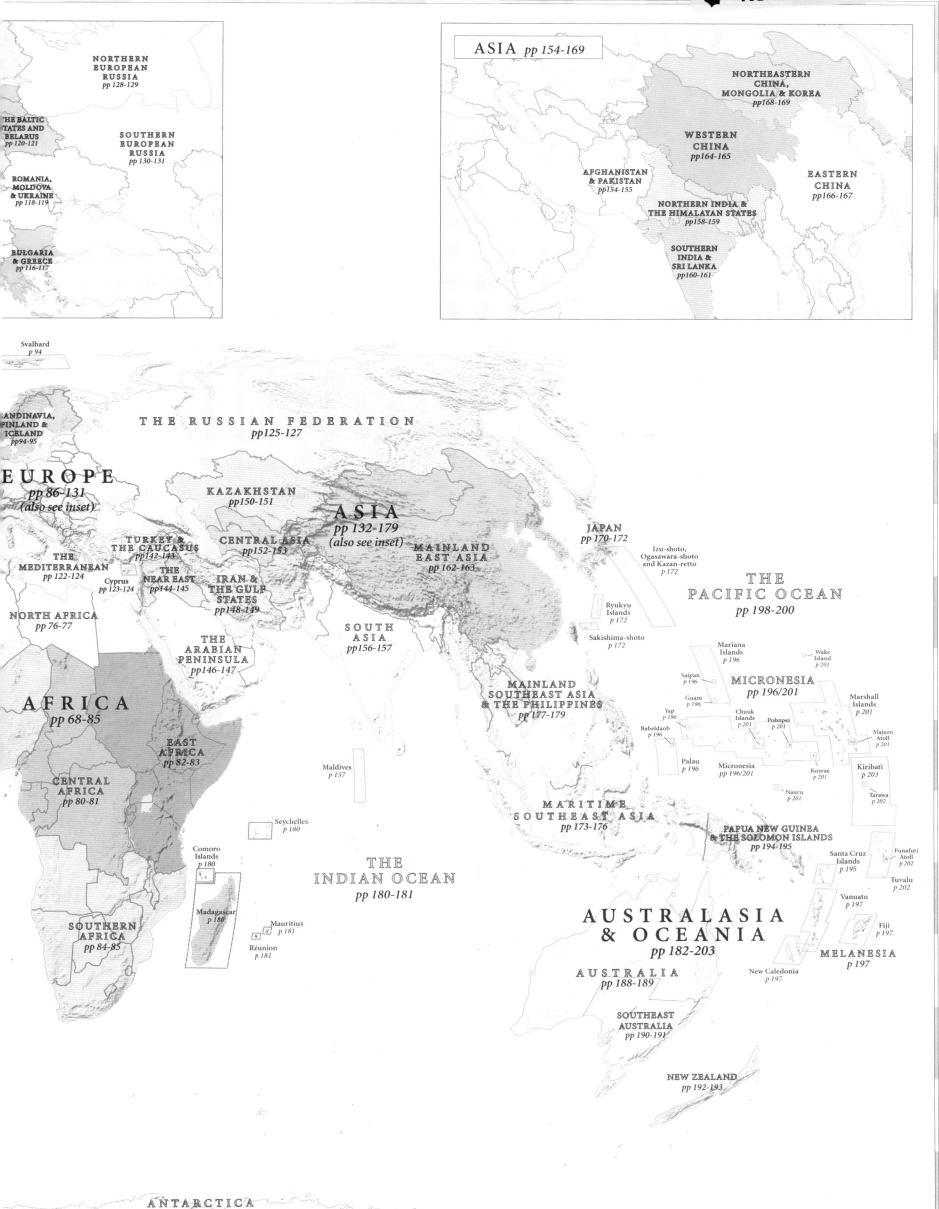

REFERENCE
ATLAS
of the
WORLD

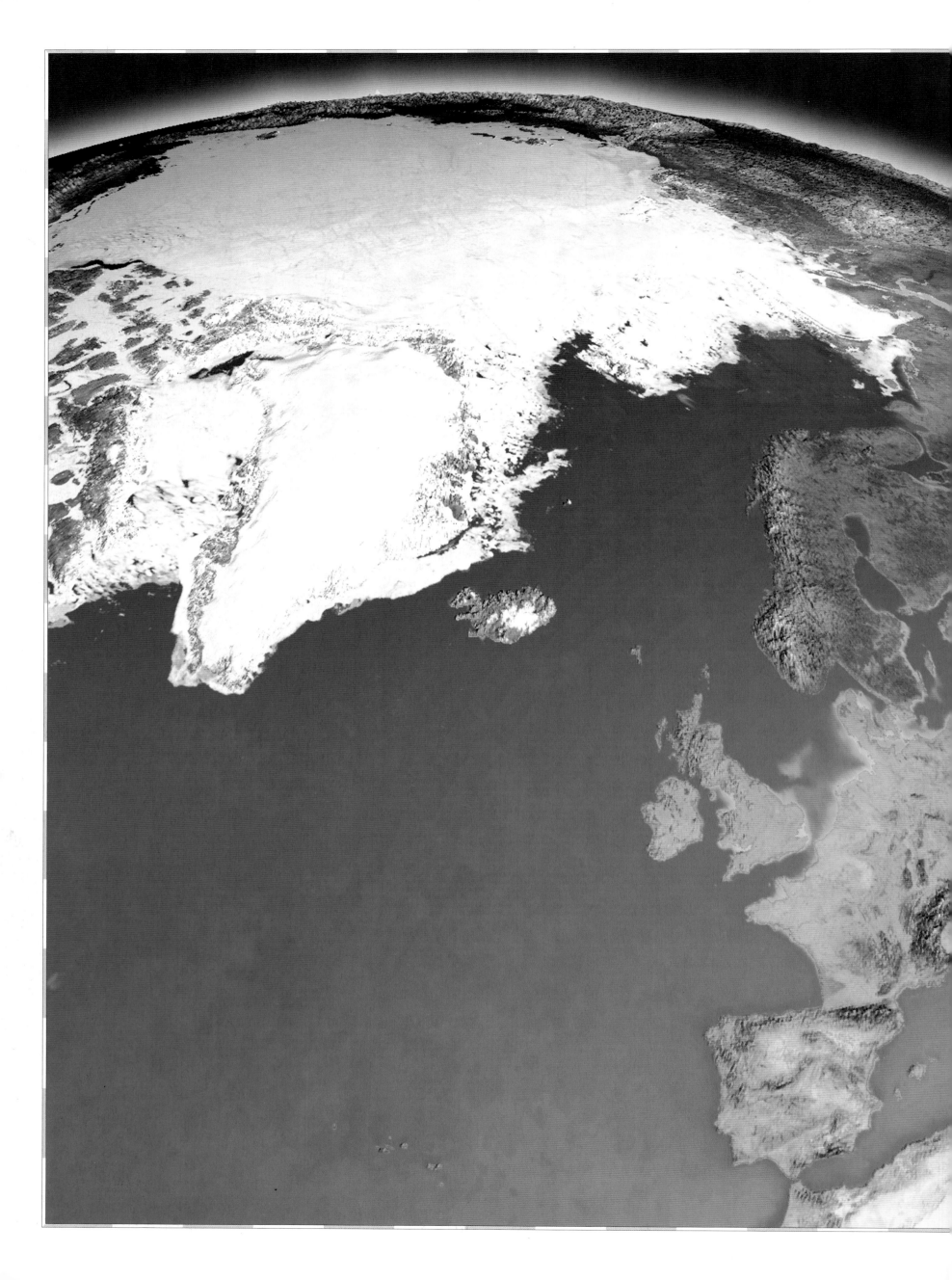

DORLING KINDERSLEY

REFERENCE
ATLAS
of the
WORLD

A Dorling Kindersley Book

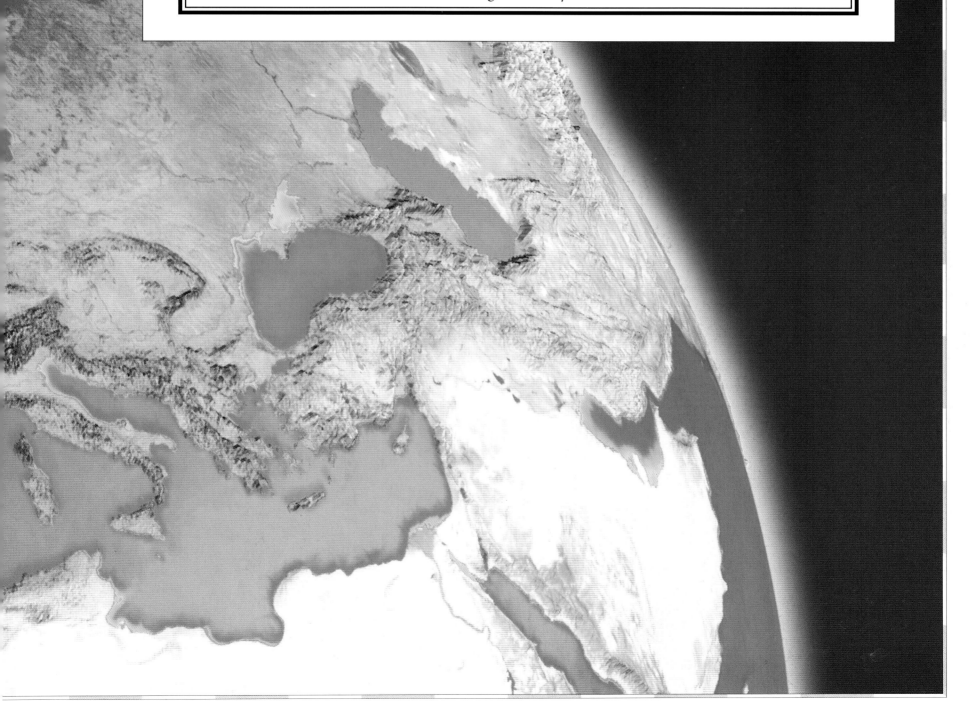

Dorling DK Kindersley

LONDON, NEW YORK, SYDNEY, DELHI, PARIS, MUNICH AND JOHANNESBURG

GENERAL GEOGRAPHICAL CONSULTANTS

PHYSICAL GEOGRAPHY • Denys Brunsden, Emeritus Professor, Department of Geography, King's College, London

HUMAN GEOGRAPHY • Professor J Malcolm Wagstaff, Department of Geography, University of Southampton

PLACE NAMES • Caroline Burgess, Permanent Committee on Geographical Names, London

BOUNDARIES • International Boundaries Research Unit, Mountjoy Research Centre, University of Durham

DIGITAL MAPPING CONSULTANTS

DK Cartopia developed by George Galfalvi and XMap Ltd, London

Professor Jan-Peter Muller, Department of Photogrammetry and Surveying, University College, London

Cover globes, planets and information on the Solar System provided by Philip Eales and Kevin Tildsley, Planetary Visions Ltd, London

REGIONAL CONSULTANTS

NORTH AMERICA • Dr David Green, Department of Geography, King's College, London
Jim Walsh, Head of Reference, Wessell Library, Tufts University, Medford, Massachussetts

SOUTH AMERICA • Dr David Preston, School of Geography, University of Leeds

EUROPE • Dr Edward M Yates, formerly of the Department of Geography, King's College, London

AFRICA • Dr Philip Amis, Development Administration Group, University of Birmingham
Dr Ieuan Ll Griffiths, Department of Geography, University of Sussex
Dr Tony Binns, Department of Geography, University of Sussex

CENTRAL ASIA • Dr David Turnock, Department of Geography, University of Leicester

SOUTH AND EAST ASIA • Dr Jonathan Rigg, Department of Geography, University of Durham

AUSTRALASIA AND OCEANIA • Dr Robert Allison, Department of Geography, University of Durham

ACKNOWLEDGEMENTS

Digital terrain data created by Eros Data Center, Sioux Falls, South Dakota, USA. Processed by GVS Images Inc, California, USA and Planetary Visions Ltd, London, UK
• CIRCA Research and Reference Information, Cambridge, UK • Digitization by Robertson Research International, Swanley, UK • Peter Clark
British Isles maps generated from a dataset supplied by Map Marketing Ltd/European Map Graphics Ltd in combination with DK Cartopia copyright data

FOR THE SECOND EDITION

EDITOR-IN-CHIEF
Andrew Heritage

SENIOR CARTOGRAPHIC MANAGER
David Roberts

MANAGING CARTOGRAPHER   SENIOR CARTOGRAPHIC EDITOR
Roger Bullen   Simon Mumford

DIGITAL MAPPING SUPPLIERS
Encompass Graphics

CARTOGRAPHERS
Tony Chambers • Jan Clark •John Plumer • Rob Stokes • Julie Turner • Iorwerth Watkins • Peter Winfield

SENIOR EDITOR   SENIOR MANAGING ART EDITOR
Debra Clapson   Philip Lord

EDITORS   DESIGNERS
Wim Jenkins • Sam Atkinson   Karen Gregory, Carol Ann Davis, David Douglas

SYSTEMS COORDINATOR   INDEX GAZETTEER
Phil Rowles   Margaret Hynes

PRODUCTION
Michelle Thomas

DORLING KINDERSLEY CARTOGRAPHY

EDITOR-IN-CHIEF
Andrew Heritage

MANAGING CARTOGRAPHER   SENIOR CARTOGRAPHIC EDITOR
David Roberts   Roger Bullen

CARTOGRAPHERS
Pamela Alford • James Anderson • Sarah Baker-Ede • Caroline Bowie • Dale Buckton • Tony Chambers • Jan Clark • Bob Croser • Martin Darlison • Claire Ellam
Sally Gable • Jeremy Hepworth • Geraldine Horner • Chris Jackson • Christine Johnston • Julia Lunn • Michael Martin • James Mills-Hicks • Simon Mumford • John Plumer
John Scott • Ann Stephenson • Julie Turner • Jane Voss • Scott Wallace • Iorwerth Watkins • Bryony Webb • Alan Whitaker • Peter Winfield

DIGITAL MAPS CREATED IN DK CARTOPIA BY   PLACENAMES DATABASE TEAM
Tom Coulson • Thomas Robertshaw   Natalie Clarkson • Ruth Duxbury • Caroline Falce • John Featherstone • Dan Gardiner
Philip Rowles • Rob Stokes   Ciárán Hynes • Margaret Hynes • Helen Rudkin • Margaret Stevenson • Annie Wilson

DATABASE MANAGER
Simon Lewis

MANAGING EDITOR   SENIOR MANAGING ART EDITOR
Lisa Thomas   Philip Lord
EDITORS   DESIGNERS
Thomas Heath • Wim Jenkins • Jane Oliver   Scott David • Carol Ann Davis • David Douglas
Siobhán Ryan • Elizabeth Wyse   Rhonda Fisher • Karen Gregory • Nicola Liddiard • Paul Williams
EDITORIAL RESEARCH   ILLUSTRATIONS
Helen Dangerfield • Andrew Rebeiro-Hargrave   Ciárán Hughes • Advanced Illustration, Congleton, UK
ADDITIONAL EDITORIAL ASSISTANCE   PICTURE RESEARCH
Debra Clapson • Robert Damon • Ailsa Heritage • Constance Novis • Jayne Parsons • Chris Whitwell   Melissa Albany • James Clarke • Anna Lord • Christine Rista • Sarah Moule • Louise Thomas

EDITORIAL DIRECTION • Louise Cavanagh   ART DIRECTION • Chez Picthall

First published in Great Britain in 1997 as the DK World Atlas *by Dorling Kindersley Limited, 80 Strand, London WC2R 0RL. Reprinted with revisions 1998, 1999.*

Copyright © 1997, 1998, 1999, 2001 Dorling Kindersley Limited, London
see our complete catalogue at www.dk.com

This book is supported by a website. For the most up-to-date information, visit:
www.dk.com/world-desk-reference

Reproduction by Colourscan, Singapore. Printed and bound by Mondadori, Italy.

INTRODUCTION

FOR MANY, THE OUTSTANDING LEGACY OF THE TWENTIETH CENTURY was the way in which the Earth shrank. As we enter the third millennium, it is increasingly important for us to have a clear vision of the World in which we live. The human population has increased fourfold since 1900. The last scraps of *terra incognita* – the polar regions and ocean depths – have been penetrated and mapped. New regions have been colonized, and previously hostile realms claimed for habitation. The advent of aviation technology and mass tourism allows many of us to travel further, faster and more frequently than ever before. In doing so we are given a bird's-eye view of the Earth's surface denied to our forebears.

AT THE SAME TIME, the amount of information about our World has grown enormously. Telecommunications can span the greatest distances in fractions of a second: our multi-media environment hurls uninterrupted streams of data at us, on the printed page, through the airwaves and across our television and computer screens; events from all corners of the globe reach us instantaneously, and are witnessed as they unfold. Our sense of stability and certainty has been eroded; instead, we are aware that the World is in a constant state of flux and change. Natural disasters, man-made cataclysms and conflicts between nations remind us daily of the enormity and fragility of our domain.

OUR CURRENT 'GLOBAL' CULTURE has made the need greater than ever before for everyone to possess an atlas. The *DK Reference Atlas of the World* has been conceived to meet this need. At its core, like all atlases, it seeks to define where places are, to describe their main characteristics, and to locate them in relation to other places. Every attempt has been made to make the information on the maps as clear and accessible as possible. In addition, each page of the atlas provides a wealth of further information, bringing the maps to life. Using photographs, diagrams, 'at-a-glance' maps, introductory texts and captions, the atlas builds up a detailed portait of those features – cultural, political, economic and geomorphological – which make each region unique, and which are also the main agents of change.

THIS SECOND EDITION INCORPORATES thousands of revisions and updates affecting every map and every page, and features a new typographic design for the maps; a further addition is the provision of longitude and latitude co-ordinates for every site in the Index-Gazetteer. Since its first publication in 1997 the book has proved extremely popular – going into 22 editions around the world – and has been translated into 13 languages, including Greek and Russian.

ANDREW HERITAGE
EDITOR-IN-CHIEF

CONTENTS

THE WORLD TODAY

THE BRITISH ISLES

ATLAS OF THE WORLD

NORTH AMERICA

SOUTH AMERICA

AFRICA

EUROPE

ASIA

AUSTRALASIA AND OCEANIA

INDEX–GAZETTEER

KEY TO REGIONAL MAPS

PHYSICAL FEATURES

elevation

	6000m / 19,686ft
	4000m / 13,124ft
	3000m / 9843ft
	2000m / 6562ft
	1000m / 3281ft
	500m / 1640ft
	250m / 820ft
	100m / 328ft
	sea level
	below sea level

△ elevation above sea level (mountain height)

▲ volcano

✕ pass

▽ elevation below sea level (depression depth)

	sand desert
	lava flow
	coastline
	reef
	atoll

sea depth

	sea level
	-250m / -820ft
	-500m / -1640ft
	-1000m / -3281ft
	-2000m / -6562ft
	-3000m / -9843ft

▲ seamount / guyot symbol

▽ undersea spot depth

DRAINAGE FEATURES

main river
secondary river
tertiary river
minor river
main seasonal river
secondary seasonal river
canal
waterfall
rapids
dam
perennial lake
seasonal lake
perennial salt lake
seasonal salt lake
reservoir
salt flat / salt pan
marsh / salt marsh
mangrove
wadi
spring / well / waterhole / oasis

ICE FEATURES

ice cap / sheet
ice shelf
glacier / snowfield
summer pack ice limit
winter pack ice limit

COMMUNICATIONS

motorway / highway
motorway / highway (under construction)
major road
minor road
tunnel (road)
main line
minor line
tunnel (rail)
✈ international airport

BORDERS

full international border
undefined international border
disputed *de facto* border
disputed territorial claim border
indication of country extent (Pacific only)
indication of dependent territory extent (Pacific only)
demarcation/ cease fire line
autonomous / federal region border
2nd order internal administrative border
3rd order internal administrative border

SETTLEMENTS

built up area

settlement population symbols

■ more than 5 million
◉ 1 million to 5 million
◉ 500,000 to 1 million
◎ 100,000 to 500,000
⊕ 50,000 to 100,000
○ 10,000 to 50,000
○ fewer than 10,000

■ ● ● country/dependent territory capital city

■ ● ● autonomous / federal region / 2nd order internal administrative centre

■ ● ● 3rd order internal administrative centre

MISCELLANEOUS FEATURES

▭▭▭▭ ancient wall
◇ site of interest
○ scientific station

GRATICULE FEATURES

lines of latitude and longitude / Equator
Tropics / Polar circles
45° degrees of longitude / latitude

TYPOGRAPHIC KEY

PHYSICAL FEATURES

landscape features ..   *Namib Desert*
    Massif Central
    ANDES

headland ....   *Nordkapp*

elevation / volcano / pass ....   Mount Meru 4556 m

drainage features....   *Lake Rudolf*

rivers / canals spring / well / waterhole / oasis / waterfall / rapids / dam ....   *Mekong*

ice features ....   *Vatnajökull*

sea features............   *Golfe de Lion*
    Andaman Sea
    INDIAN OCEAN

undersea features ...   *Barracuda Fracture Zone*

REGIONS

country.................   **ARMENIA**

dependent territory with parent state......   NIUE (to NZ)

region outside feature area...........   ANGOLA

autonomous / federal region........   MINAS GERAIS

2nd order internal administrative region..................   MINSKAYA VOBLASTS'

3rd order internal administrative region ....   Vaucluse

cultural region.......   New England

SETTLEMENTS

capital city............   **BEIJING**

dependent territory capital city............   FORT-DE-FRANCE

other settlements....   Chicago
    Adana
    Tizi Ozou
    Yonezawa
    Farnham

MISCELLANEOUS

sites of interest / miscellaneous........   *Valley of the Kings*

Tropics / Polar circles..........   *Antarctic Circle*

HOW TO USE THIS ATLAS

THE ATLAS IS ORGANIZED BY CONTINENT, moving eastwards from the International Dateline. The opening section describes the world's structure, systems and its main features. The Atlas of the World which follows, is a continent-by-continent guide to today's world, starting with a comprehensive insight into the physical, political and economic structure of each continent, followed by integrated mapping and descriptions of each region or country.

THE WORLD

THE INTRODUCTORY SECTION of the Atlas deals with every aspect of the planet, from physical structure to human geography, providing an overall picture of the world we live in. Complex topics such as the landscape of the Earth, climate, oceans, population and economic patterns are clearly explained with the aid of maps and diagrams drawn from the latest information.

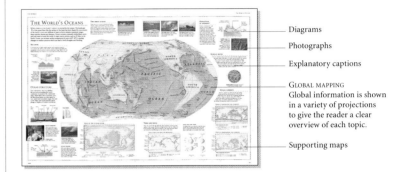

Diagrams
Photographs
Explanatory captions
GLOBAL MAPPING
Global information is shown in a variety of projections to give the reader a clear overview of each topic.
Supporting maps

THE POLITICAL CONTINENT

THE POLITICAL PORTRAIT of the continent is a vital reference point for every continental section, showing the position of countries relative to one another, and the relationship between human settlement and geographic location. The complex mosaic of languages spoken in each continent is mapped, as is the effect of communications networks on the pattern of settlement.

Locator map
Introductory text
Communications map
Population map
POLITICAL MAP
All the countries in each continent are shown, with their political capitals and most populous cities.
Languages map

CONTINENTAL RESOURCES

THE EARTH'S RICH NATURAL RESOURCES, including oil, gas, minerals and fertile land, have played a key role in the development of society. These pages show the location of minerals and agricultural resources on each continent, and how they have been instrumental in dictating industrial growth and the varieties of economic activity across the continent.

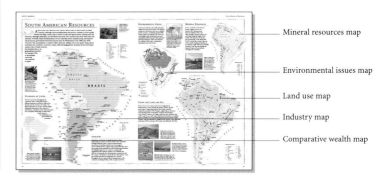

Mineral resources map
Environmental issues map
Land use map
Industry map
Comparative wealth map

THE PHYSICAL CONTINENT

THE ASTONISHING VARIETY of landforms, and the dramatic forces that created and continue to shape the landscape, are explained in the continental physical spread. Cross-sections, illustrations and terrain maps highlight the different parts of the continent, showing how nature's forces have produced the landscapes we see today.

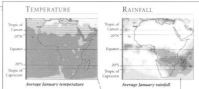

CLIMATE CHARTS
Rainfall and temperature charts clearly show the continental patterns of rainfall and temperature.

CLIMATE MAP
Climatic regions vary across each continent. The map displays the differing climatic regions, as well as daily hours of sunshine at selected weather stations.

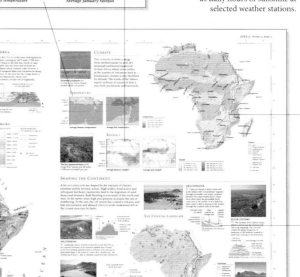

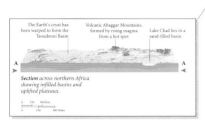

CROSS-SECTIONS
Detailed cross-sections through selected parts of the continent show the underlying geomorphic structure.

LANDFORM DIAGRAMS
The complex formation of many typical landforms is summarized in these easy-to-understand illustrations.

MAIN PHYSICAL MAP
Detailed satellite data has been used to create an accurate and visually striking picture of the surface of the continent.

PHOTOGRAPHS
A wide range of beautiful photographs bring the world's regions to life.

LANDSCAPE EVOLUTION MAP
The physical shape of each continent is affected by a variety of forces which continually sculpt and modify the landscape. This map shows the major processes which affect different parts of the continent.

REGIONAL MAPPING

THE MAIN BODY of the Atlas is a unique regional map set, with detailed information on the terrain, the human geography of the region and its infrastructure. Around the edge of the map, additional 'at-a-glance' maps, give an instant picture of regional industry, land use and agriculture. The detailed terrain map (shown in perspective), focuses on the main physical features of the region, and is enhanced by annotated illustrations, and photographs of the physical structure.

TRANSPORT NETWORK
The differing extent of the transport network for each region is shown here, along with key facts about the transport system.

REGIONAL LOCATOR
This small map shows the location of each country in relation to its continent.

KEY TO MAIN MAP
A key to the population symbols and land heights accompanies the main map.

WORLD LOCATOR
This locates the continent in which the region is found on a small world map.

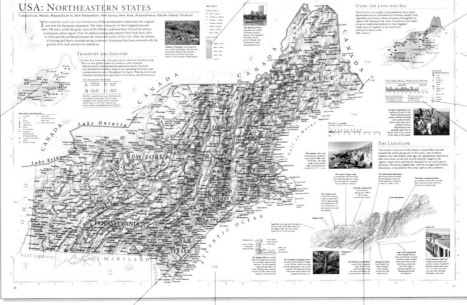

LAND USE MAP
This shows the different types of land use which characterize the region, as well as indicating the principal agricultural activities.

GRID REFERENCE
The framing grid provides a location reference for each place listed in the Index.

MAP KEYS
Each supporting map has its own key.

TRANSPORT AND INDUSTRY MAP
The main industrial areas are mapped, and the most important industrial and economic activities of the region are shown.

THE URBAN/RURAL POPULATION DIVIDE	
urban 78%	rural 22%
POPULATION DENSITY	TOTAL LAND AREA
306 people per sq mile (118 people per sq km)	161,096 sq miles (417,222 sq km)

URBAN/RURAL POPULATION DIVIDE
The proportion of people in the region who live in urban and rural areas, as well as the overall population density and land area are clearly shown in these simple graphics.

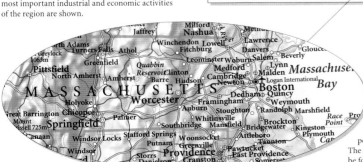

CONTINUATION SYMBOLS
These symbols indicate where adjacent maps can be found.

MAIN REGIONAL MAP
A wealth of information is displayed on the main map, building up a rich portrait of the interaction between the physical landscape and the human and political geography of each region. The key to the regional maps can be found on page viii.

LANDSCAPE MAP
The computer-generated terrain model accurately portrays an oblique view of the landscape. Annotations highlight the most important geographic features of the region.

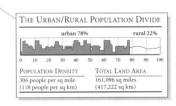

JUPITER

- ⊖ **Diameter:** 88,846 miles (142,984 km)
- ⊙ **Mass:** 1,900,000 million million million tons
- ○ **Temperature:** -153°C (extremes not available)
- ◗◖ **Distance from Sun:** 483 million miles (778 million km)
- ◑ **Length of day:** 9.84 hours
- ◐ **Length of year:** 11.86 earth years
- ⊖ **Surface gravity:** 1 kg = 2.53 kg

MARS

- ⊖ **Diameter:** 4217 miles (6786 km)
- ⊙ **Mass:** 642 million million million tons
- ○ **Temperature:** -137 to 37°C
- ◗◖ **Distance from Sun:** 142 million miles (228 million km)
- ◑ **Length of day:** 24.623 hours
- ◐ **Length of year:** 1.88 earth years
- ⊖ **Surface gravity:** 1 kg = 0.38 kg

EARTH

- ⊖ **Diameter:** 7926 miles (12,756 km)
- ⊙ **Mass:** 5976 million million million tons
- ○ **Temperature:** -70 to 55°C
- ◗◖ **Distance from Sun:** 93 million miles (150 million km)
- ◑ **Length of day:** 23.92 hours
- ◐ **Length of year:** 365.25 earth days
- ⊖ **Surface gravity:** 1 kg = 1 kg

VENUS

- ⊖ **Diameter:** 7520 miles (12,102 km)
- ⊙ **Mass:** 4870 million million million tons
- ○ **Temperature:** 457°C (extremes not available)
- ◗◖ **Distance from Sun:** 67 million miles (108 million km)
- ◑ **Length of day:** 243.01 earth days
- ◐ **Length of year:** 224.7 earth days
- ⊖ **Surface gravity:** 1 kg = 0.88 kg

MERCURY

- ⊖ **Diameter:** 3031 miles (4878 km)
- ⊙ **Mass:** 330 million million million tons
- ○ **Temperature:** -173 to 427°C
- ◗◖ **Distance from Sun:** 36 million miles (58 million km)
- ◑ **Length of day:** 58.65 earth days
- ◐ **Length of year:** 87.97 earth days
- ⊖ **Surface gravity:** 1 kg = 0.38 kg

THE SOLAR SYSTEM

NINE MAJOR PLANETS, their satellites, and countless minor planets (asteroids) orbit the Sun to form the Solar System. The Sun, our nearest star, creates energy from nuclear reactions deep within its interior, providing all the light and heat which make life on Earth possible. The Earth is unique in the Solar System in that it supports life: its size, gravitational pull and distance from the Sun have all created the optimum conditions for the evolution of life. The planetary images seen here are composites derived from actual spacecraft images (not shown to scale).

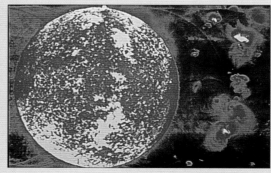

THE SUN

- ⊖ **Diameter:** 864,948 miles (1,392,000 km)
- ⊙ **Mass:** 1990 million million million million tons

THE SUN was formed when a swirling cloud of dust and gas contracted, pulling matter into its centre. When the temperature at the centre rose to 1,000,000°C, nuclear fusion – the fusing of hydrogen into helium, creating energy – occurred, releasing a constant stream of heat and light.

Solar flares are sudden bursts of energy from the Sun's surface. They can be 125,000 miles (200,000 km) long.

THE FORMATION OF THE SOLAR SYSTEM

The cloud of dust and gas thrown out by the Sun during its formation cooled to form the Solar System. The smaller planets nearest the Sun are formed of minerals and metals. The outer planets were formed at lower temperatures, and consist of swirling clouds of gases.

THE MILANKOVITCH CYCLE

The amount of radiation from the Sun which reaches the Earth is affected by variations in the Earth's orbit and the tilt of the Earth's axis, as well as by 'wobbles' in the axis. These variations cause three separate cycles, corresponding with the durations of recent ice ages.

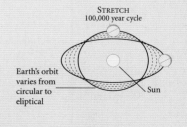

STRETCH 100,000 year cycle

Earth's orbit varies from circular to eliptical

Sun

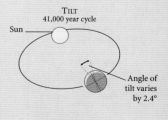

TILT 41,000 year cycle

Sun

Angle of tilt varies by 2.4°

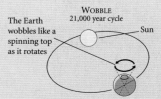

WOBBLE 21,000 year cycle

The Earth wobbles like a spinning top as it rotates

Sun

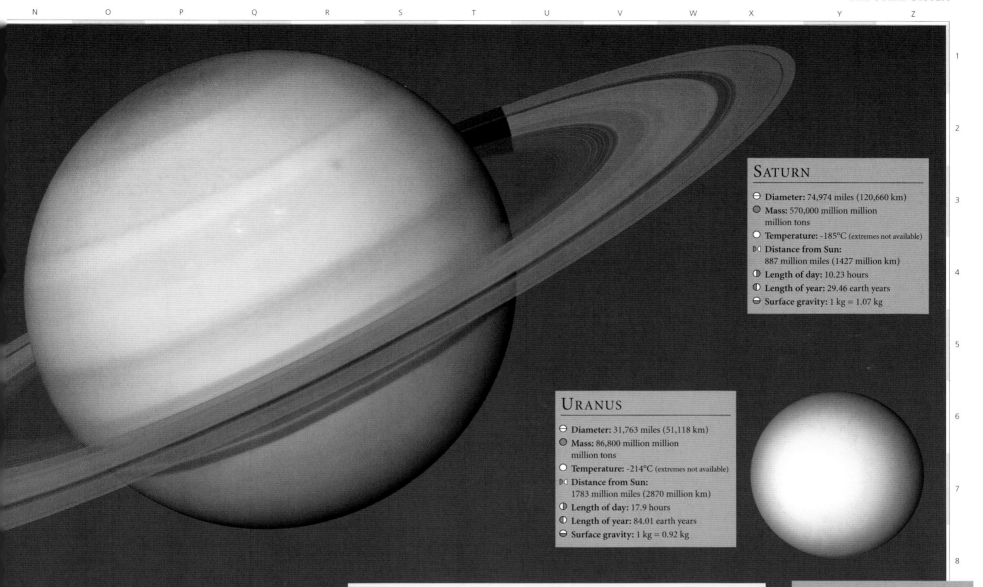

SATURN

- Diameter: 74,974 miles (120,660 km)
- Mass: 570,000 million million million tons
- Temperature: -185°C (extremes not available)
- Distance from Sun: 887 million miles (1427 million km)
- Length of day: 10.23 hours
- Length of year: 29.46 earth years
- Surface gravity: 1 kg = 1.07 kg

URANUS

- Diameter: 31,763 miles (51,118 km)
- Mass: 86,800 million million million tons
- Temperature: -214°C (extremes not available)
- Distance from Sun: 1783 million miles (2870 million km)
- Length of day: 17.9 hours
- Length of year: 84.01 earth years
- Surface gravity: 1 kg = 0.92 kg

NEPTUNE

- Diameter: 30,775 miles (49,528 km)
- Mass: 102,000 million million million tons
- Temperature: -225°C (extremes not available)
- Distance from Sun: 2794 million miles (4497 million km)
- Length of day: 19.2 hours
- Length of year: 164.79 earth years
- Surface gravity: 1 kg = 1.18 kg

PLUTO

- Diameter: 1429 miles (2300 km)
- Mass: 13 million million million tons
- Temperature: -236°C (extremes not available)
- Distance from Sun: 3666 million miles (5900 million km)
- Length of day: 6.39 hours
- Length of year: 248.54 earth years
- Surface gravity: 1 kg = 0.30 kg

SPACE DEBRIS

MILLIONS OF OBJECTS, remnants of planetary formation, circle the Sun in a zone lying between Mars and Jupiter: the asteroid belt. Fragments of asteroids break off to form meteoroids, which can reach the Earth's surface. Comets, composed of ice and dust, originated outside our Solar System. Their elliptical orbit brings them close to the Sun and into the inner Solar System.

Meteor Crater in Arizona is 4200 ft (1300 m) wide and 660 ft (200 m) deep. It was formed over 10,000 years ago.

METEOROIDS

Meteoroids are fragments of asteroids which hurtle through space at great velocity. Although millions of meteoroids enter the Earth's atmosphere, the vast majority burn up on entry, and fall to the Earth as a meteor or shooting star. Large meteoroids travelling at speeds of 155,000 mph (250,000 kmph) can sometimes withstand the atmosphere and hit the Earth's surface with tremendous force, creating large craters on impact.

POSSIBLE AND ACTUAL METEORITE CRATERS

Map key
- Possible impact craters
- Meteorite impact craters

The orbit of Halley's Comet brings it close to the Earth every 76 years. It last visited in 1986.

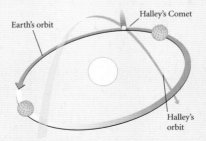

Earth's orbit

Halley's Comet

Halley's orbit

ORBIT OF HALLEY'S COMET AROUND THE SUN

THE EARTH'S ATMOSPHERE

DURING THE EARLY STAGES of the Earth's formation, ash, lava, carbon dioxide and water vapour were discharged onto the surface of the planet by constant volcanic eruptions. The water formed the oceans, while carbon dioxide entered the atmosphere or was dissolved in the oceans. Clouds, formed of water droplets, reflected some of the Sun's radiation back into space. The Earth's temperature stabilized and early life forms began to emerge, converting carbon dioxide into life-giving oxygen.

It is thought that the gases that make up the Earth's atmosphere originated deep within the interior, and were released many millions of years ago during intense volcanic activity, similar to this eruption at Mount St. Helens.

ORDER AND RELATIVE DISTANCE FROM THE SUN OF PLANETS

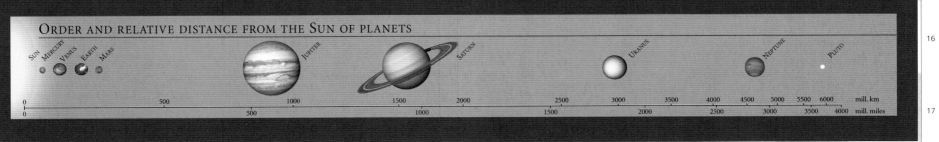

THE PHYSICAL WORLD

THE EARTH'S SURFACE is constantly being transformed: it is uplifted, folded and faulted by tectonic forces; weathered and eroded by wind, water and ice. Sometimes change is dramatic, the spectacular results of earthquakes or floods. More often it is a slow process lasting millions of years. A physical map of the world represents a snapshot of the ever-evolving architecture of the Earth. This terrain map shows the whole surface of the Earth, both above and below the sea.

THE WORLD IN SECTION

These cross-sections around the Earth, one in the northern hemisphere; one straddling the Equator, reveal the limited areas of land above sea level in comparison with the extent of the sea floor. The greater erosive effects of weathering by wind and water limit the upward elevation of land above sea level, while the deep oceans retain their dramatic mountain and trench profiles.

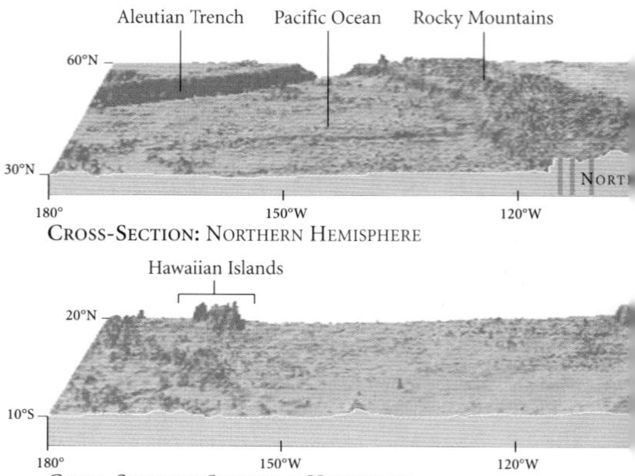

Aleutian Trench Pacific Ocean Rocky Mountains
60°N
30°N
180° 150°W 120°W
CROSS-SECTION: NORTHERN HEMISPHERE

Hawaiian Islands
20°N
10°S
180° 150°W 120°W
CROSS-SECTION: SOUTHERN HEMISPHERE

MAP KEY

GEOGRAPHICAL REGIONS

- ice
- tundra
- needleleaf forest
- broadleaf forest
- cultivated land
- hot desert
- cold desert
- tropical grassland
- tropical rainforest
- mountain
- submarine regions

SCALE 1:60,000,000
(projection: Wagner VII)

Km
0 250 500 1,000 1,500 2,000
Miles
0 250 500 1,000 1,500 2,000

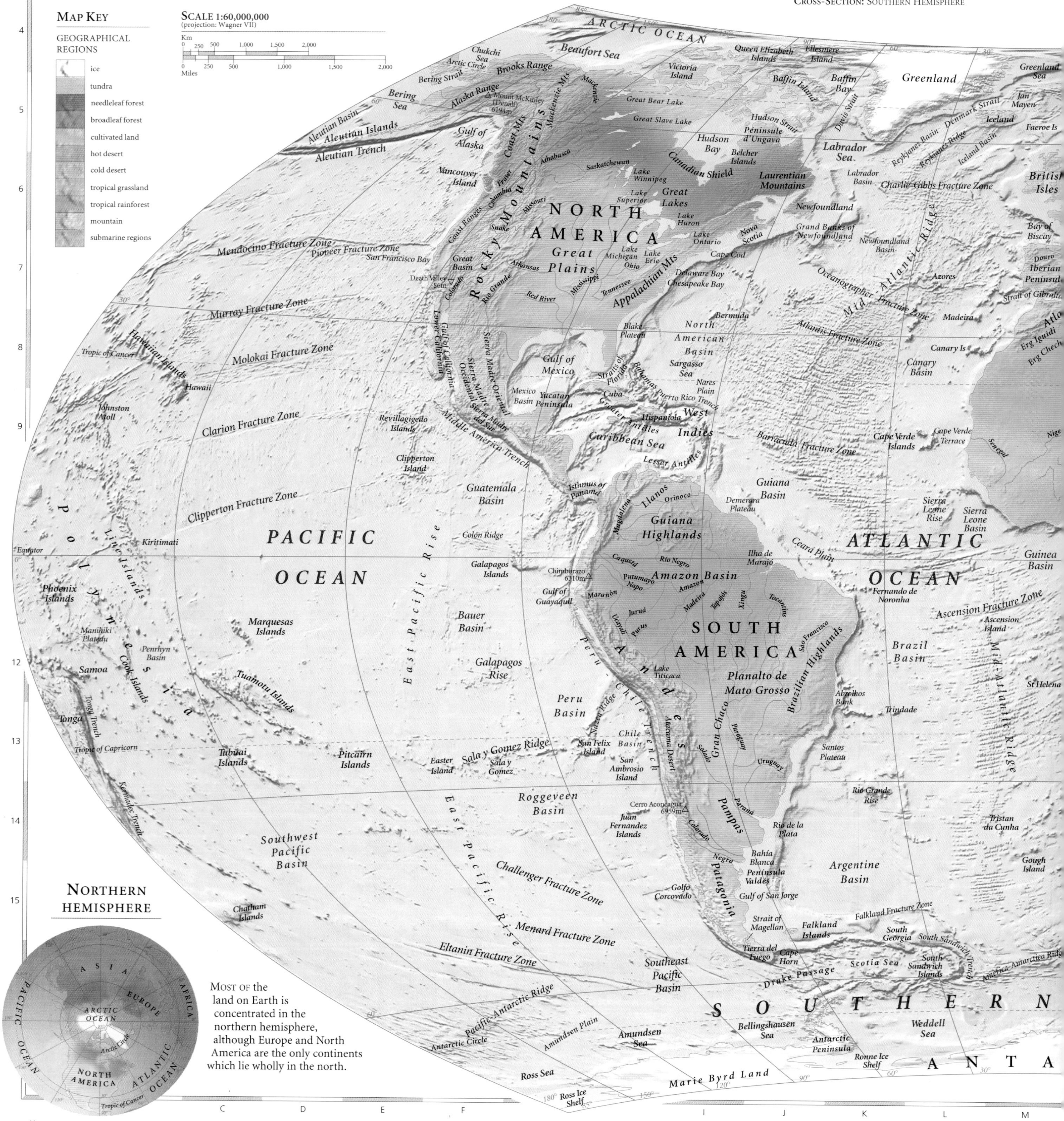

NORTHERN HEMISPHERE

MOST OF the land on Earth is concentrated in the northern hemisphere, although Europe and North America are the only continents which lie wholly in the north.

ASIA
EUROPE
AFRICA
PACIFIC OCEAN
ARCTIC OCEAN
Arctic Circle
ATLANTIC OCEAN
NORTH AMERICA
Tropic of Cancer

Map labels

ARCTIC OCEAN
Chukchi Sea
Beaufort Sea
Brooks Range
Arctic Circle
Bering Strait
Bering Sea
Aleutian Basin
Aleutian Islands
Aleutian Trench
Gulf of Alaska
Alaska Range
Mount McKinley (Denali) (6194m)
Coast Mts
Mackenzie Mts
Mackenzie
Victoria Island
Queen Elizabeth Islands
Ellesmere Island
Greenland
Greenland Sea
Jan Mayen
Iceland
Faeroe Is
Denmark Strait
Reykjanes Ridge
Reykjanes Basin
Iceland Basin
British Isles
Baffin Island
Baffin Bay
Hudson Strait
Péninsule d'Ungava
Belcher Islands
Hudson Bay
Great Bear Lake
Great Slave Lake
Athabasca
Saskatchewan
Lake Winnipeg
Canadian Shield
Laurentian Mountains
Labrador Sea
Labrador Basin
Charlie-Gibbs Fracture Zone
Vancouver Island
Columbia
Fraser
Coast Ranges
Rocky Mountains
Great Lakes
Lake Superior
Lake Michigan
Lake Huron
Lake Erie
Lake Ontario
Newfoundland
Grand Banks of Newfoundland
Newfoundland Basin
NORTH AMERICA
Great Plains
Snake
Great Basin
Mendocino Fracture Zone
Pioneer Fracture Zone
San Francisco Bay
Death Valley 86m
Colorado
Rio Grande
Arkansas
Red River
Tennessee
Ohio
Mississippi
Missouri
Appalachian Mts
Delaware Bay
Chesapeake Bay
Cape Cod
Nova Scotia
Bermuda
Azores
Iberian Peninsula
Strait of Gibraltar
Madeira
Oceanographer Fracture Zone
Mid Atlantic Ridge
Bay of Biscay
Douro
Murray Fracture Zone
Molokai Fracture Zone
Hawaiian Islands
Hawaii
Tropic of Cancer
Johnston Atoll
North American Basin
Atlantis Fracture Zone
Canary Is
Canary Basin
Erg Iguidi
Erg Chech
Blake Plateau
Sierra Madre Oriental
Sierra Madre Occidental
Sierra Madre del Sur
Mexico Basin
Yucatan Peninsula
Gulf of Mexico
Gulf of California
Lower California
Straits of Florida
Bahamas Banks
Cuba
Nares Plain
Puerto Rico Trench
Hispaniola
West Indies
Greater Antilles
Sargasso Sea
Middle America Trench
Revillagigedo Islands
Clarion Fracture Zone
Clipperton Island
Clipperton Fracture Zone
Guatemala Basin
Colón Ridge
Caribbean Sea
Lesser Antilles
Isthmus of Panama
Barracuda Fracture Zone
Cape Verde Islands
Cape Verde Terrace
Senegal
Niger
Magdalena
Llanos
Orinoco
Guiana Highlands
Guiana Basin
Demerara Plateau
Sierra Leone Rise
Sierra Leone Basin
ATLANTIC OCEAN
Galapagos Islands
Galapagos Rise
Bauer Basin
PACIFIC OCEAN
East Pacific Rise
Equator
Polynesia
Line Islands
Kiritimati
Phoenix Islands
Manihiki Plateau
Penrhyn Basin
Marquesas Islands
Samoa
Cook Islands
Tonga
Tonga Trench
Tubuai Islands
Tuamotu Islands
Pitcairn Islands
Easter Island
Sala y Gomez Ridge
Sala y Gomez
San Felix Island
San Ambrosio Island
Chimborazo 6310m
Gulf of Guayaquil
Marañón
Napo
Putumayo
Caquetá
Río Negro
Amazon
Amazon Basin
Madeira
Juruá
Purus
Ucayali
Tapajós
Xingu
Tocantins
São Francisco
Ilha de Marajó
Ceará Plain
SOUTH AMERICA
Planalto de Mato Grosso
Brazilian Highlands
Brazil Basin
Fernando de Noronha
Ascension Fracture Zone
Ascension Island
Guinea Basin
St Helena
Mid Atlantic Ridge
Peru Basin
Andes
Peru-Chile Trench
Nazca Ridge
Lake Titicaca
Chile Basin
Atacama Desert
Gran Chaco
Paraguay
Paraná
Uruguay
Santos Plateau
Río Grande Rise
Roggeveen Basin
Cerro Aconcagua 6959m
Juan Fernandez Islands
Pampas
Colorado
Negro
Río de la Plata
Bahía Blanca
Peninsula Valdés
Argentine Basin
Tristan da Cunha
Gough Island
Southwest Pacific Basin
Chatham Islands
Kermadec Trench
East Pacific Rise
Challenger Fracture Zone
Menard Fracture Zone
Eltanin Fracture Zone
Golfo Corcovado
Patagonia
Gulf of San Jorge
Strait of Magellan
Falkland Islands
Falkland Fracture Zone
South Georgia
South Sandwich Islands
South Sandwich Trench
Mid Atlantic Ridge
Tierra del Fuego
Cape Horn
Scotia Sea
Drake Passage
Southeast Pacific Basin
Pacific-Antarctic Ridge
Antarctic Circle
Amundsen Plain
Amundsen Sea
Bellingshausen Sea
Antarctic Peninsula
Weddell Sea
Ronne Ice Shelf
American-Antarctic Ridge
SOUTHERN
Ross Sea
Ross Ice Shelf
Marie Byrd Land
ANTARCTICA

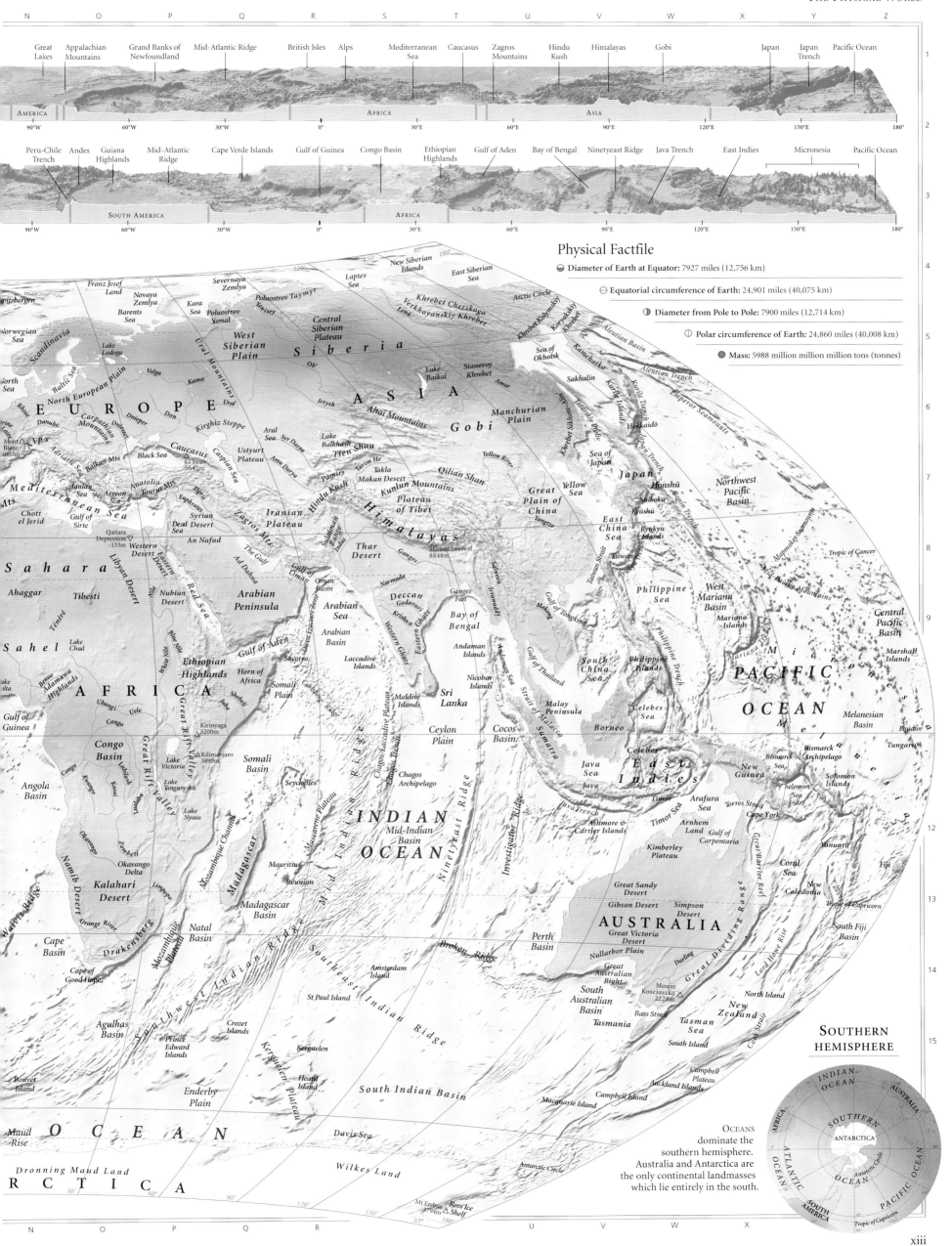

N O P Q R S T U V W X Y Z

Great Lakes | Appalachian Mountains | Grand Banks of Newfoundland | Mid-Atlantic Ridge | British Isles | Alps | Mediterranean Sea | Caucasus | Zagros Mountains | Hindu Kush | Himalayas | Gobi | Japan | Japan Trench | Pacific Ocean

AMERICA   AFRICA   ASIA

90°W   60°W   30°W   0°   30°E   60°E   90°E   120°E   150°E   180°

Peru-Chile Trench | Andes | Guiana Highlands | Mid-Atlantic Ridge | Cape Verde Islands | Gulf of Guinea | Congo Basin | Ethiopian Highlands | Gulf of Aden | Bay of Bengal | Ninetyeast Ridge | Java Trench | East Indies | Micronesia | Pacific Ocean

SOUTH AMERICA   AFRICA

90°W   60°W   30°W   0°   30°E   60°E   90°E   120°E   150°E   180°

Physical Factfile

- Diameter of Earth at Equator: 7927 miles (12,756 km)
- Equatorial circumference of Earth: 24,901 miles (40,075 km)
- Diameter from Pole to Pole: 7900 miles (12,714 km)
- Polar circumference of Earth: 24,860 miles (40,008 km)
- Mass: 5988 million million million tons (tonnes)

SOUTHERN HEMISPHERE

OCEANS dominate the southern hemisphere. Australia and Antarctica are the only continental landmasses which lie entirely in the south.

STRUCTURE OF THE EARTH

THE EARTH AS IT IS TODAY is just the latest phase in a constant process of evolution which has occurred over the past 4.5 billion years. The Earth's continents are neither fixed nor stable; over the course of the Earth's history, propelled by currents rising from the intense heat at its centre, the great plates on which they lie have moved, collided, joined together, and separated. These processes continue to mould and transform the surface of the Earth, causing earthquakes and volcanic eruptions and creating oceans, mountain ranges, deep ocean trenches and island chains.

INSIDE THE EARTH

THE EARTH'S HOT INNER CORE is made up of solid iron, while the outer core is composed of liquid iron and nickel. The mantle nearest the core is viscous, whereas the rocky upper mantle is fairly rigid. The crust is the rocky outer shell of the Earth. Together, the upper mantle and the crust form the lithosphere.

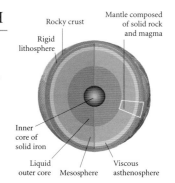

Rocky crust
Mantle composed of solid rock and magma
Rigid lithosphere
Inner core of solid iron
Liquid outer core
Mesosphere
Viscous asthenosphere

THE DYNAMIC EARTH

THE EARTH'S CRUST is made up of eight major (and several minor) rigid continental and oceanic tectonic plates, which fit closely together. The positions of the plates are not static. They are constantly moving relative to one another. The type of movement between plates affects the way in which they alter the structure of the Earth. The oldest parts of the plates, known as shields, are the most stable parts of the Earth and little tectonic activity occurs here.

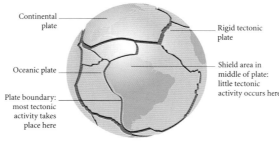

Continental plate
Oceanic plate
Plate boundary: most tectonic activity takes place here
Rigid tectonic plate
Shield area in middle of plate: little tectonic activity occurs here

Inner core
Outer core
Subduction zone
Ocean crust
Movement of plate
Mid-ocean ridge
Lithosphere
Asthenosphere
Mesosphere
Continental crust

CONVECTION CURRENTS

DEEP WITHIN THE EARTH, at its inner core, temperatures may exceed 8100°F (4500°C). This heat warms rocks in the mesosphere which rise through the partially molten mantle, displacing cooler rocks just below the solid crust, which sink, and are warmed again by the heat of the mantle. This process is continually repeated, creating convection currents which form the moving force beneath the Earth's crust.

PLATE BOUNDARIES

THE BOUNDARIES BETWEEN THE PLATES are the areas where most tectonic activity takes place. Three types of movement occur at plate boundaries: the plates can either move towards each other, move apart, or slide past each other. The effect this has on the Earth's structure depends on whether the margin is between two continental plates, two oceanic plates or an oceanic and continental plate.

MID-OCEAN RIDGES

Mid-ocean ridges are formed when two adjacent oceanic plates pull apart, allowing magma to force its way up to the surface, which then cools to form solid rock. Vast amounts of volcanic material are discharged at these mid-ocean ridges which can reach heights of 10,000 ft (3000 m).

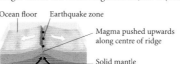

Ocean floor
Earthquake zone
Magma pushed upwards along centre of ridge
Solid mantle

FORMATION OF A MID-OCEAN RIDGE

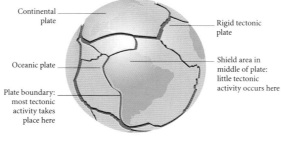

The Mid-Atlantic Ridge rises above sea level in Iceland, producing geysers and volcanoes.

Mount Pinatubo is an active volcano, lying on the Pacific 'Ring of Fire'.

OCEAN PLATES MEETING

Oceanic crust is denser and thinner than continental crust; on average it is 3 miles (5 km) thick, while continental crust averages 18–24 miles (30–40 km). When oceanic plates of similar density meet, the crust is contorted as one plate overrides the other, forming deep sea trenches and volcanic island arcs above sea level.

Overriding plate
Chain of islands
Ocean trench
Diving plate
Volcanic activity

OCEAN PLATES MEETING TO FORM AN ISLAND ARC

Tectonic Activity

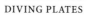

- - - - - uncertain plate boundary
▲ volcanic zone
● earthquake zone
● hot spot
ⅤⅤⅤⅤ rift valley

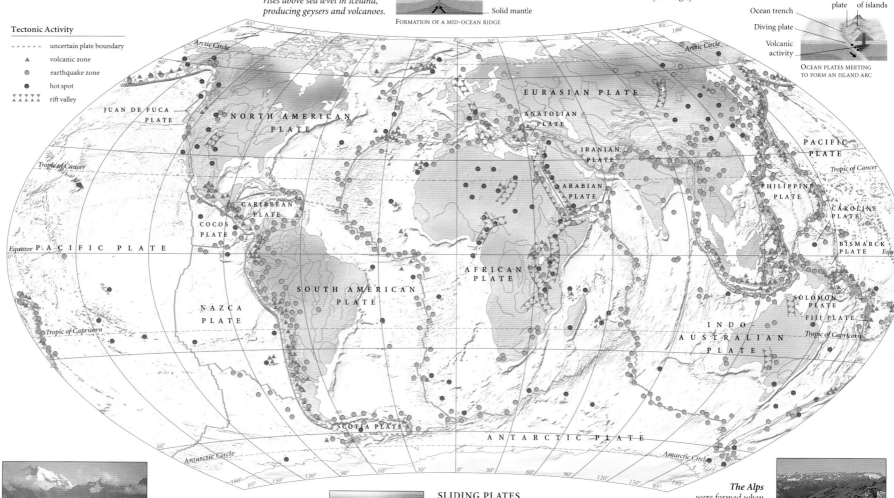

Arctic Circle
EURASIAN PLATE
ANATOLIAN PLATE
JUAN DE FUCA PLATE
NORTH AMERICAN PLATE
IRANIAN PLATE
PACIFIC PLATE
Tropic of Cancer
ARABIAN PLATE
PHILIPPINE PLATE
CARIBBEAN PLATE
CAROLINE PLATE
COCOS PLATE
BISMARCK PLATE
Equator PACIFIC PLATE
Equator
AFRICAN PLATE
SOUTH AMERICAN PLATE
SOLOMON PLATE
NAZCA PLATE
FIJI PLATE
INDO-AUSTRALIAN PLATE
Tropic of Capricorn
Tropic of Capricorn
SCOTIA PLATE
ANTARCTIC PLATE
Antarctic Circle
Antarctic Circle

DIVING PLATES

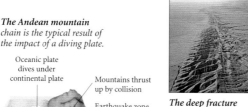

When an oceanic and a continental plate meet, the denser oceanic plate is driven underneath the continental plate, which is crumpled by the collision to form mountain ranges. As the ocean plate plunges downward, it heats up, and molten rock (magma) is forced up to the surface.

The Andean mountain chain is the typical result of the impact of a diving plate.

Oceanic plate dives under continental plate
Mountains thrust up by collision
Earthquake zone
Continental plate

DIVING PLATE

The deep fracture caused by the sliding plates of the San Andreas Fault can be clearly seen in parts of California.

SLIDING PLATES

When two plates slide past each other, friction is caused along the fault line which divides them. The plates do not move smoothly, and the uneven movement causes earthquakes.

Plate
Plate
Fault line
Earthquake zone

SLIDING PLATES

The Alps were formed when the African plate collided with the Eurasian Plate, about 65 million years ago.

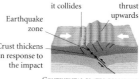

Plate buckles as it collides
Mountains thrust upwards
Earthquake zone
Crust thickens in response to the impact

CONTINENTAL PLATES COLLIDING TO FORM A MOUNTAIN RANGE

COLLIDING PLATES

When two continental plates collide, great mountain chains are thrust upwards as the crust buckles and folds under the force of the impact.

CONTINENTAL DRIFT

ALTHOUGH THE PLATES which make
up the Earth's crust move only
a few centimetres in a year, over
the millions of years of the Earth's
history, its continents have moved
many thousands of kilometres,
to create new continents,
oceans and mountain chains.

1: CAMBRIAN PERIOD

*570–510 million years ago. Most continents
are in tropical latitudes. The supercontinent
of Gondwanaland reaches the South Pole.*

2: DEVONIAN PERIOD

*408–362 million years ago. The continents
of Gondwanaland and Laurentia
are drifting northwards.*

3: CARBONIFEROUS PERIOD

*362–290 million years ago. The Earth is
dominated by three continents; Laurentia,
Angaraland and Gondwanaland.*

4: TRIASSIC PERIOD

*245–208 million years ago. All three major
continents have joined to form the supercontinent of Pangea.*

5: JURASSIC PERIOD

*208–145 million years ago. The super-
continent of Pangea begins to break up,
causing an overall rise in sea levels.*

6: CRETACEOUS PERIOD

*145–65 million years ago. Warm shallow
seas cover much of the land: sea levels are
about 80 ft (25 m) above present levels.*

7: TERTIARY PERIOD

*65–2 million years ago. Although the
world's geography is becoming more
recognizable, major events such as the
creation of the Himalayan mountain chain,
are still to occur during this period.*

CONTINENTAL SHIELDS

THE CENTRES OF THE EARTH'S CONTINENTS, known
as shields, were established between 2500 and
500 million years ago; some contain rocks over
three billion years old. They were formed by
a series of turbulent events: plate movements,
earthquakes and volcanic eruptions. Since the
Pre-Cambrian period, over 570 million years
ago, they have experienced little tectonic activity,
and today, these flat, low-lying slabs of solidified
molten rock form the stable centres of the
continents. They are bounded or covered by
successive belts of younger sedimentary rock.

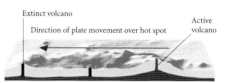

CREATION OF THE HIMALAYAS

BETWEEN 10 AND 20 MILLION YEARS AGO, the Indian subcontinent,
part of the ancient continent of Gondwanaland, collided with
the continent of Asia. The Indo-Australian Plate continued to
move northwards, displacing continental crust and uplifting the
Himalayas, the world's highest mountain chain.

MOVEMENTS OF INDIA

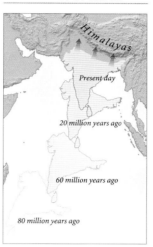

Present day

20 million years ago

60 million years ago

80 million years ago

Force of collision
pushes up mountains

CROSS-SECTION THROUGH
THE HIMALAYAS

*The Himalayas were uplifted
when the Indian subcontinent
collided with Asia.*

THE HAWAIIAN ISLAND CHAIN

A HOT SPOT lying deep beneath the Pacific Ocean
pushes a plume of magma from the Earth's
mantle up through the Pacific Plate to form
volcanic islands. While the hot spot remains
stationary, the plate on which the islands sit is
moving slowly. A long chain of islands has been
created as the plate passes over the hot spot.

Extinct volcano

Direction of plate movement over hot spot

Active
volcano

CROSS-SECTION THROUGH THE HAWAIIAN ISLANDS

EVOLUTION OF THE HAWAIIAN ISLANDS

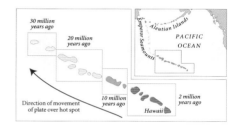

*30 million
years ago*

*20 million
years ago*

PACIFIC
OCEAN

Direction of movement
of plate over hot spot

*10 million
years ago*

*2 million
years ago*

Hawaii

THE EARTH'S GEOLOGY

THE EARTH'S ROCKS are created in
a continual cycle. Exposed rocks
are weathered and eroded by wind,
water and chemicals and deposited
as sediments. If they pass into the
Earth's crust they will be transformed
by high temperatures and pressures
into metamorphic rocks or they will
melt and solidify as igneous rocks.

SANDSTONE

8   Sandstones are
sedimentary rocks
formed mainly in
deserts, beaches and
deltas. Desert sandstones are
formed of grains of quartz which have
been well rounded by wind erosion.

*Rock stacks of desert sandstone, at
Bryce Canyon National Park, Utah, USA.*

*Extrusive
igneous rocks
are formed
during volcanic
eruptions, as
here in Hawaii.*

ANDESITE

7   Andesite is an
extrusive igneous rock
formed from magma
which has solidified on the
Earth's crust after a volcanic eruption.

GNEISS

1   Gneiss is a metamorphic
rock made at great depth
during the formation of
mountain chains, when intense
heat and pressure transform
sedimentary or igneous rocks.

*Gneiss formations in
Norway's Jotunheimen Mountains.*

*Basalt columns
at Giant's Causeway,
Northern Ireland, UK.*

BASALT

2   Basalt is an igneous rock,
formed when small quantities
of magma lying close to the
Earth's surface cool rapidly.

LIMESTONE

3   Limestone is a sedimentary
rock, which is formed
mainly from the calcite
skeletons of marine
animals which have
been compressed
into rock.

Limestone hills, Guilin, China.

CORAL

4   Coral reefs
are formed from
the skeletons
of millions of
individual corals.

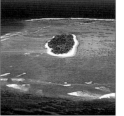

Great Barrier Reef, Australia.

THE WORLD'S MAJOR GEOLOGICAL REGIONS

Geological Regions
- continental shield
- sedimentary cover
- coral formation
- igneous rock types

Mountain Ranges
- Alpine (new)
- Hercynian (old)
- Caledonian (ancient)

SCHIST

6   Schist is a metamorphic rock formed
during mountain building,
when temperature and
pressure are comparatively
high. Both mudstones and
shales reform into schist
under these conditions.

*Schist formations in the
Atlas Mountains, northwestern Africa.*

GRANITE

5   Granite is an intrusive igneous
rock formed from magma
which has solidified deep
within the Earth's crust.
The magma cools
slowly, producing a
coarse-grained rock.

*Namibia's Namaqualand
Plateau is formed of granite.*

SHAPING THE LANDSCAPE

THE BASIC MATERIAL OF THE EARTH'S SURFACE is solid rock: valleys, deserts, soil and sand are all evidence of the powerful agents of weathering, erosion and deposition which constantly shape and transform the Earth's landscapes. Water, either flowing continually in rivers or seas, or frozen and compacted into solid sheets of ice, has the most clearly visible impact on the Earth's surface. But wind can transport fragments of rock over huge distances and strip away protective layers of vegetation, exposing rock surfaces to the impact of extreme heat and cold.

WATER

LESS THAN 2% of the world's water is on the land, but it is the most powerful agent of landscape change. Water, as rainfall, groundwater and rivers, can transform landscapes through both erosion and deposition. Eroded material carried by rivers forms the world's most fertile soils.

Waterfalls such as the Iguaçu Falls on the border between Argentina and southern Brazil, erode the underlying rock, causing the falls to retreat.

COASTAL WATER

THE WORLD'S COASTLINES are constantly changing; every day, tides deposit, sift and sort sand and gravel on the shoreline. Over longer periods, powerful wave action erodes cliffs and headlands and carves out bays.

A low, wide sandy beach on South Africa's Cape Peninsula is continually re-shaped by the action of the Atlantic waves.

The sheer chalk cliffs at Seven Sisters in southern England are constantly under attack from waves.

GROUNDWATER

IN REGIONS where there are porous rocks such as chalk, water is stored underground in large quantities; these reservoirs of water are known as aquifers. Rain percolates through topsoil into the underlying bedrock, creating an underground store of water. The limit of the saturated zone is called the water table.

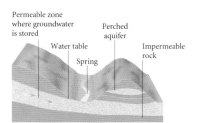

Permeable zone where groundwater is stored
Water table
Perched aquifer
Spring
Impermeable rock

STORAGE OF GROUNDWATER IN AN AQUIFER

World river systems

drainage basin

World river systems:
Sediment deposited annually per drainage basin

tons per sq mile per year
9120
6080
2400
1600
1520
760
400
200 and less
tonnes per sq km per year

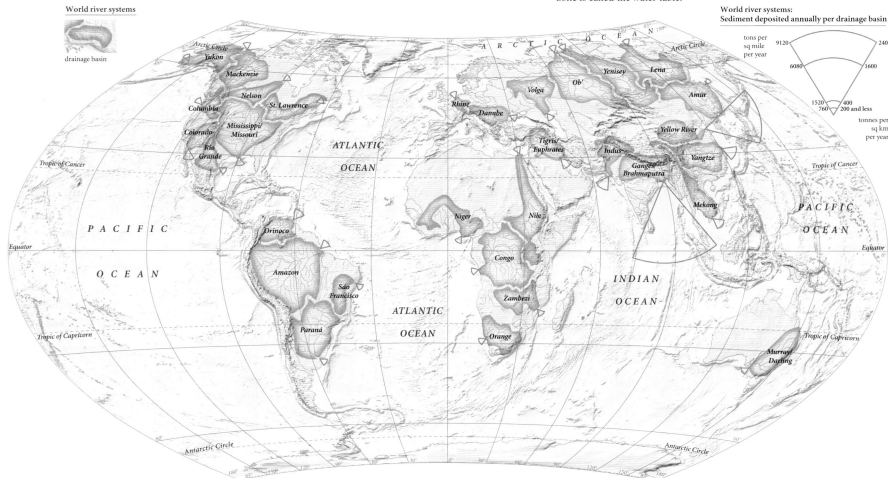

Arctic Circle
Yukon
Mackenzie
Nelson
Columbia
St. Lawrence
Mississippi/Missouri
Colorado
Rio Grande
Tropic of Cancer
ATLANTIC OCEAN
PACIFIC OCEAN
Equator
Orinoco
Amazon
São Francisco
Paraná
Tropic of Capricorn
ATLANTIC OCEAN
Antarctic Circle
ARCTIC OCEAN
Rhine
Danube
Volga
Ob'
Yenisey
Lena
Amur
Yellow River
Tigris/Euphrates
Indus
Yangtze
Ganges/Brahmaputra
Mekong
Niger
Nile
Congo
Zambezi
Orange
INDIAN OCEAN
PACIFIC OCEAN
Tropic of Cancer
Equator
Tropic of Capricorn
Murray/Darling
Arctic Circle
Antarctic Circle

RIVERS

RIVERS ERODE THE LAND by grinding and dissolving rocks and stones. Most erosion occurs in the river's upper course as it flows through highland areas. Rock fragments are moved along the river bed by fast-flowing water and deposited in areas where the river slows down, such as flat plains, or where the river enters seas or lakes.

RIVER VALLEYS

Over long periods of time rivers erode uplands to form characteristic V-shaped valleys with smooth sides.

Resistant rock
River
Chemical erosion cuts valley in softer rock

RIVER VALLEY EROSION

DELTAS

When a river deposits its load of silt and sediment (alluvium) on entering the sea, it may form a delta. As this material accumulates, it chokes the mouth of the river, forcing it to create new channels to reach the sea.

The Nile forms a broad delta as it flows into the Mediterranean.

DRAINAGE BASINS

The drainage basin is the area of land drained by a major trunk river and its smaller branch rivers or tributaries. Drainage basins are separated from one another by natural boundaries known as watersheds.

Watershed
Major trunk river
Alps
Apennines
Tributary river
Delta
River mouth
Po Valley
Dolomites

The drainage basin of the Po River, northern Italy.

MEANDERS

In their lower courses, rivers flow slowly. As they flow across the lowlands, they form looping bends called meanders.

The Mississippi River forms meanders as it flows across the southern USA.

The meanders of Utah's San Juan River have become deeply incised.

DEPOSITION

When rivers have deposited large quantities of fertile alluvium, they are forced to find new channels through the alluvium deposits, creating braided river systems.

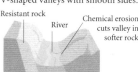

Mud is deposited by China's Yellow River in its lower course.

LANDSLIDES

Heavy rain and associated flooding on slopes can loosen underlying rocks, which crumble, causing the top layers of rock and soil to slip.

A huge landslide in the Swiss Alps has left massive piles of rocks and pebbles called scree.

GULLIES

In areas where soil is thin, rainwater is not effectively absorbed, and may flow overland. The water courses downhill in channels, or gullies, and may lead to rapid erosion of soil.

A deep gully in the French Alps caused by the scouring of upper layers of turf.

ICE

DURING ITS LONG HISTORY, the Earth has experienced a number of glacial episodes when temperatures were considerably lower than today. During the last Ice Age, 18,000 years ago, ice covered an area three times larger than it does today. Over these periods, the ice has left a remarkable legacy of transformed landscapes.

GLACIERS

GLACIERS ARE FORMED by the compaction of snow into 'rivers' of ice. As they move over the landscape, glaciers pick up and carry a load of rocks and boulders which erode the landscape they pass over, and are eventually deposited at the end of the glacier.

A massive glacier advancing down a valley in southern Argentina.

POST-GLACIAL FEATURES

WHEN A GLACIAL EPISODE ENDS, the retreating ice leaves many features. These include depositional ridges called moraines, which may be eroded into low hills known as drumlins; sinuous ridges called eskers; kames which are rounded hummocks; depressions known as kettle holes; and windblown loess deposits.

GLACIAL VALLEYS

GLACIERS CAN ERODE much more powerfully than rivers. They form steep-sided, flat-bottomed valleys with a typical U-shaped profile. Valleys created by tributary glaciers, whose floors have not been eroded to the same depth as the main glacial valley floor, are called hanging valleys.

The U-shaped profile and piles of morainic debris are characteristic of a valley once filled by a glacier.

A series of hanging valleys high up in the Chilean Andes.

The profile of the Matterhorn has been formed by three cirques lying 'back-to-back'.

PAST AND PRESENT WORLD ICE-COVER AND GLACIAL FEATURES

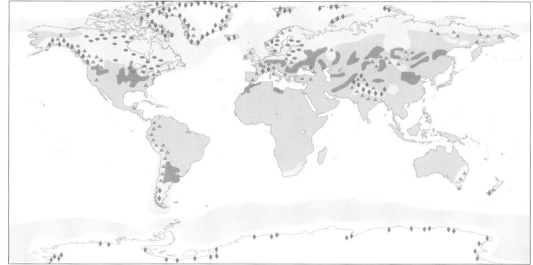

POST-GLACIAL LANDSCAPE FEATURES

Kame terrace
Kettle hole
Esker
Braided river
Windblown loess
Retreating glacier
Drumlin
Terminal moraine
Glacial till
Bedrock

Past and present world ice cover and glacial features

extent of last Ice Age	present day ice cover
loess deposits	glacial field
post-glacial feature	
glacial feature	

ICE SHATTERING

Water drips into fissures in rocks and freezes, expanding as it does so. The pressure weakens the rock, causing it to crack, and eventually to shatter into polygonal patterns.

Irregular polygons show through the sedge-grass tundra in the Yukon, Canada.

CIRQUES

Cirques are basin-shaped hollows which mark the head of a glaciated valley. Where neighbouring cirques meet, they are divided by sharp rock ridges called arêtes. It is these arêtes which give the Matterhorn its characteristic profile.

FJORDS

Fjords are ancient glacial valleys flooded by the sea following the end of a period of glaciation. Beneath the water, the valley floor can be 4000 ft (1300 m) deep.

A fjord fills a former glacial valley in southern New Zealand.

PERIGLACIATION

Periglacial areas occur near to the edge of ice sheets. A layer of frozen ground lying just beneath the surface of the land is known as permafrost. When the surface melts in the summer, the water is unable to drain into the frozen ground, and so 'creeps' downhill, a process known as solifluction

WIND

STRONG WINDS can transport rock fragments great distances, especially where there is little vegetation to protect the rock. In desert areas, wind picks up loose, unprotected sand particles, carrying them over great distances. This powerfully abrasive debris is blasted at the surface by the wind, eroding the landscape into dramatic shapes.

PREVAILING WINDS AND DUST TRAJECTORIES

Arctic Circle
Tropic of Cancer
Equator
Tropic of Capricorn
Antarctic Circle

Prevailing winds
northeast trade
southeast trade
westerly
westerly
polar easterly
polar easterly

Dust trajectories
trajectory of aeolian dust

DEPOSITION

THE ROCKY, STONY FLOORS of the world's deserts are swept and scoured by strong winds. The smaller, finer particles of sand are shaped into surface ripples, dunes, or sand mountains, which rise to a height of 650 ft (200 m). Dunes usually form single lines, running perpendicular to the direction of the prevailing wind. These long, straight ridges can extend for over 100 miles (160 km).

Barchan dunes in the Arabian Desert.

Complex dune system in the Sahara.

DUNES

Dunes are shaped by wind direction and sand supply. Where sand supply is limited, crescent-shaped barchan dunes are formed.

wind direction

— TYPES OF DUNE —

Transverse dune
Barchan dune
Linear dune
Star dune

TEMPERATURE

HOT AND COLD DESERTS

Arctic Circle
Tropic of Cancer
Equator
Tropic of Capricorn
Antarctic Circle

Main desert types
hot arid
semi-arid
cold polar

MOST OF THE WORLD'S deserts are in the tropics. The cold deserts which occur elsewhere are arid because they are a long way from the rain-giving sea. Rock in deserts is exposed because of lack of vegetation and is susceptible to changes in temperature; extremes of heat and cold can cause both cracks and fissures to appear in the rock.

HEAT

FIERCE SUN can heat the surface of rock, causing it to expand more rapidly than the cooler, underlying layers. This creates tensions which force the rock to crack or break up. In arid regions, the evaporation of water from rock surfaces dissolves certain minerals within the water, causing salt crystals to form in small openings in the rock. The hard crystals force the openings to widen into cracks and fissures.

The cracked and parched floor of Death Valley, California. This is one of the hottest deserts on Earth.

DESERT ABRASION

Abrasion creates a wide range of desert landforms from faceted pebbles and wind ripples in the sand, to large-scale features such as yardangs (low, streamlined ridges), and scoured desert pavements.

Wind abrasion
Faceted rock
Wind direction
Desert pavement
Gravel
Sand desert
Wind rippling
Thermal fracturing

FEATURES OF A DESERT SURFACE

This dry valley at Ellesmere Island in the Canadian Arctic is an example of a cold desert. The cracked floor and scoured slopes are features also found in hot deserts.

The World's Oceans

Two-thirds of the Earth's surface is covered by the oceans. The landscape of the ocean floor, like the surface of the land, has been shaped by movements of the Earth's crust over millions of years to form volcanic mountain ranges, deep trenches, basins and plateaux. Ocean currents constantly redistribute warm and cold water around the world. A major warm current, such as El Niño in the Pacific Ocean, can increase surface temperature by up to 46°F (8°C), causing changes in weather patterns which can lead to both droughts and flooding.

The great oceans

There are five oceans on Earth: the Pacific, Atlantic, Indian and Southern oceans, and the much smaller Arctic Ocean. These five ocean basins are relatively young, having evolved within the last 80 million years. One of the most recent plate collisions, between the Eurasian and African plates, created the present-day arrangement of continents and oceans.

***The Indian Ocean** accounts for approximately 20% of the total area of the world's oceans.*

Sea level

If the influence of tides, winds, currents and variations in gravity were ignored, the surface of the Earth's oceans would closely follow the topography of the ocean floor, with an underwater ridge 3000 ft (915 m) high producing a rise of up to 3 ft (1 m) in the level of the surface water.

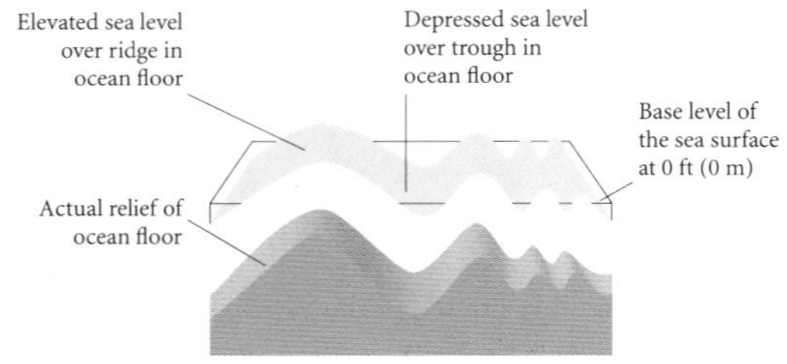

Elevated sea level over ridge in ocean floor
Depressed sea level over trough in ocean floor
Base level of the sea surface at 0 ft (0 m)
Actual relief of ocean floor

How surface waters reflect the relief of the ocean floor

***The low relief** of many small Pacific islands such as these atolls at Huahine in French Polynesia makes them vulnerable to changes in sea level.*

Ocean structure

The continental shelf is a shallow, flat sea-bed surrounding the Earth's continents. It extends to the continental slope, which falls to the ocean floor. Here, the flat abyssal plains are interrupted by vast, underwater mountain ranges, the mid-ocean ridges, and ocean trenches which plunge to depths of 35,828 ft (10,920 m).

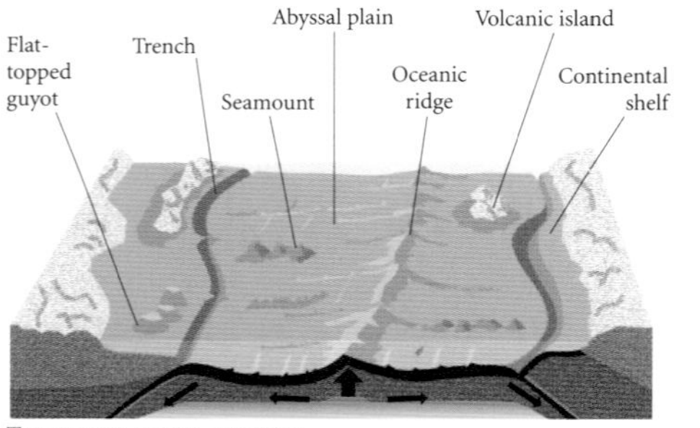

Flat-topped guyot
Trench
Seamount
Abyssal plain
Oceanic ridge
Volcanic island
Continental shelf

Typical sea-floor features

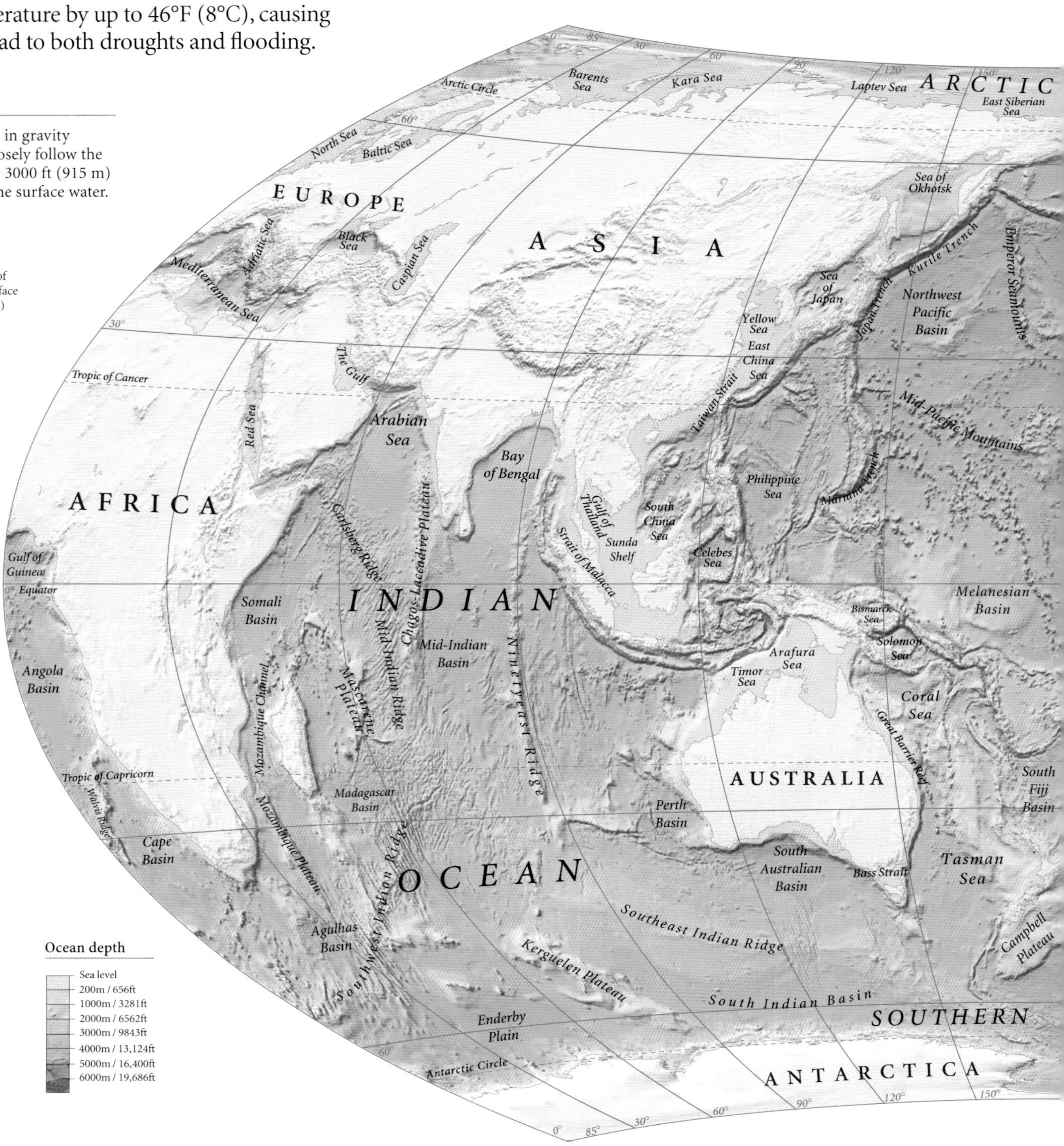

Arctic Circle
Barents Sea
Kara Sea
Laptev Sea
ARCTIC
East Siberian Sea
North Sea
Baltic Sea
EUROPE
Sea of Okhotsk
Black Sea
Adriatic Sea
Caspian Sea
Mediterranean Sea
ASIA
Sea of Japan
Kurile Trench
Emperor Seamounts
Northwest Pacific Basin
Japan Trench
Yellow Sea
East China Sea
Tropic of Cancer
The Gulf
Red Sea
Arabian Sea
Taiwan Strait
Mid-Pacific Mountains
Bay of Bengal
Philippine Sea
Mariana Trench
AFRICA
Carlsberg Ridge
Chagos-Laccadive Plateau
Gulf of Thailand
South China Sea
Sunda Shelf
Strait of Malacca
Gulf of Guinea
Equator
Celebes Sea
Somali Basin
INDIAN
Melanesian Basin
Bismarck Sea
Solomon Sea
Mid-Indian Basin
Mid-Indian Ridge
Ninetyeast Ridge
Mascarene Plateau
Mozambique Channel
Angola Basin
Arafura Sea
Timor Sea
Coral Sea
Great Barrier Reef
Tropic of Capricorn
Walvis Ridge
AUSTRALIA
South Fiji Basin
Madagascar Basin
Mozambique Plateau
Perth Basin
Cape Basin
OCEAN
South Australian Basin
Bass Strait
Tasman Sea
Southwest Indian Ridge
Agulhas Basin
Southeast Indian Ridge
Campbell Plateau
Kerguelen Plateau
South Indian Basin
SOUTHERN
Enderby Plain
Antarctic Circle
ANTARCTICA
Ocean depth
Sea level
200m / 656ft
1000m / 3281ft
2000m / 6562ft
3000m / 9843ft
4000m / 13,124ft
5000m / 16,400ft
6000m / 19,686ft

Black smokers

These vents in the ocean floor disgorge hot, sulphur-rich water from deep in the Earth's crust. Despite the great depths, a variety of lifeforms have adapted to the chemical-rich environment which surrounds black smokers.

***A black smoker** in the Atlantic Ocean.*

***Surtsey, near Iceland**, is a volcanic island lying directly over the Mid-Atlantic Ridge. It was formed in the 1960s following intense volcanic activity nearby.*

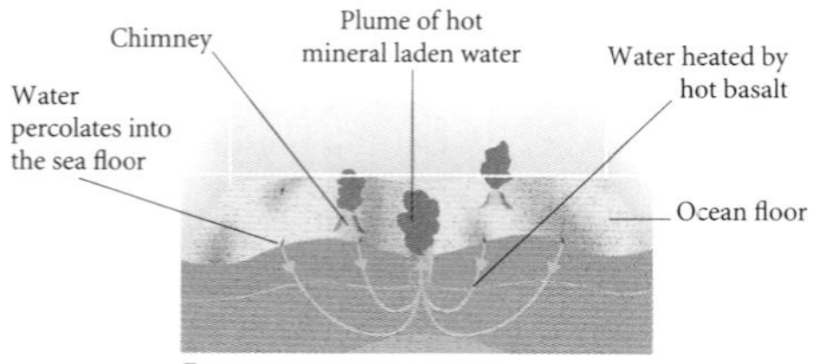

Chimney
Plume of hot mineral laden water
Water heated by hot basalt
Water percolates into the sea floor
Ocean floor

Formation of black smokers

Ocean floors

Mid-ocean ridges are formed by lava which erupts beneath the sea and cools to form solid rock. This process mirrors the creation of volcanoes from cooled lava on the land. The ages of sea floor rocks increase in parallel bands outwards from central ocean ridges.

Ages of the ocean floor

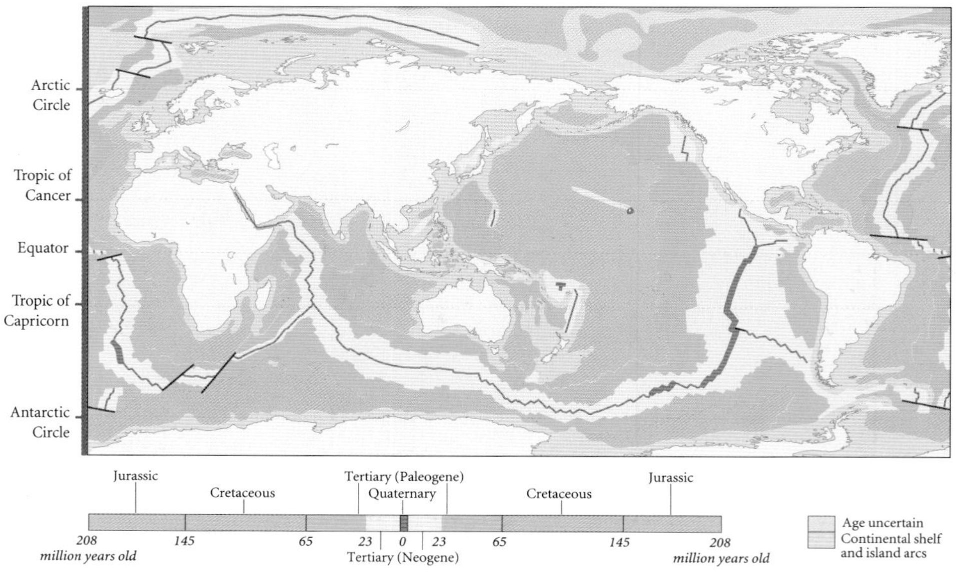

Arctic Circle
Tropic of Cancer
Equator
Tropic of Capricorn
Antarctic Circle
Jurassic
Cretaceous
Tertiary (Paleogene)
Quaternary
Cretaceous
Jurassic
208 million years old
145
65
23
0
23
65
145
208 million years old
Tertiary (Neogene)
Age uncertain
Continental shelf and island arcs

Currents in the Southern Ocean are driven by some of the world's fiercest winds, including the Roaring Forties, Furious Fifties and Shrieking Sixties.

The Pacific Ocean is the world's largest and deepest ocean, covering over one-third of the surface of the Earth.

The Atlantic Ocean was formed when the landmasses of the eastern and western hemispheres began to drift apart 180 million years ago.

DEPOSITION OF SEDIMENT

STORMS, EARTHQUAKES, and volcanic activity trigger underwater currents known as turbidity currents which scour sand and gravel from the continental shelf, creating underwater canyons. These strong currents pick up material deposited at river mouths and deltas, and carry it across the continental shelf and through the underwater canyons, where it is eventually laid down on the ocean floor in the form of fans.

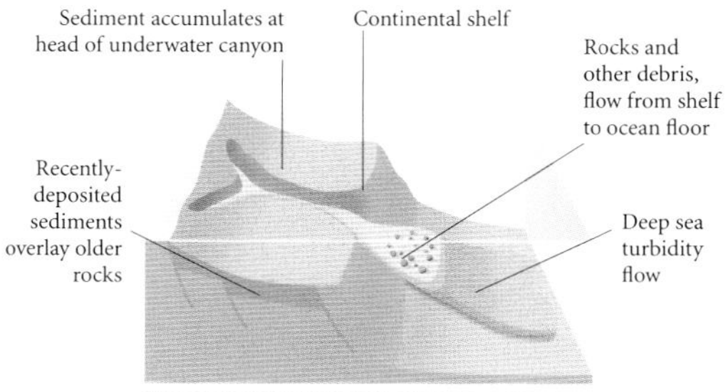

Sediment accumulates at head of underwater canyon — Continental shelf — Rocks and other debris, flow from shelf to ocean floor

Recently-deposited sediments overlay older rocks — Deep sea turbidity flow

HOW SEDIMENT IS DEPOSITED ON THE OCEAN FLOOR

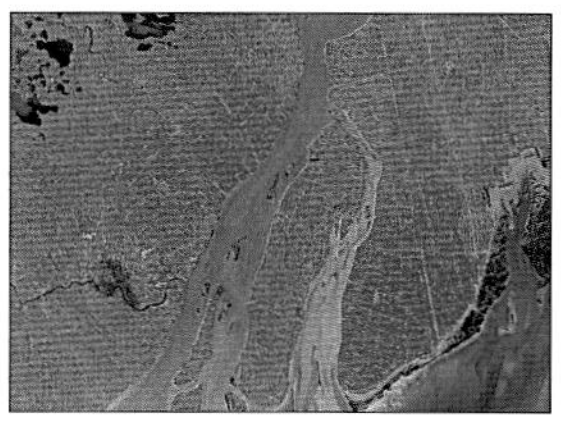

Satellite image of the Yangtze (Chang Jiang) Delta, in which the land appears red. The river deposits immense quantities of silt into the East China Sea, much of which will eventually reach the deep ocean floor.

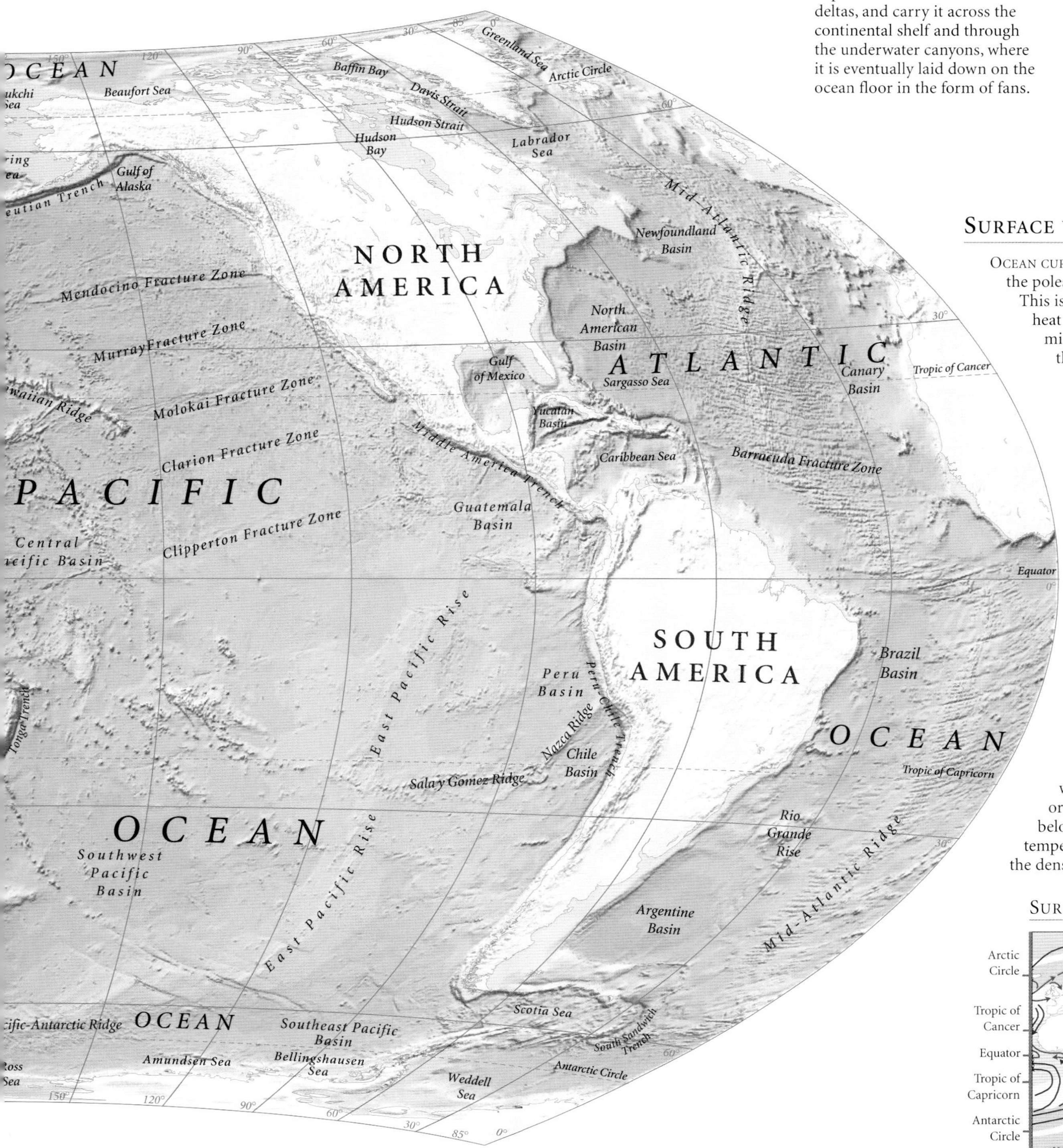

SURFACE WATER

OCEAN CURRENTS move warm water away from the Equator towards the poles, while cold water is, in turn, moved towards the Equator. This is the main way in which the Earth distributes surface heat and is a major climatic control. Approximately 4000 million years ago, the Earth was dominated by oceans and there was no land to interrupt the flow of the currents, which would have flowed as straight lines, simply influenced by the Earth's rotation.

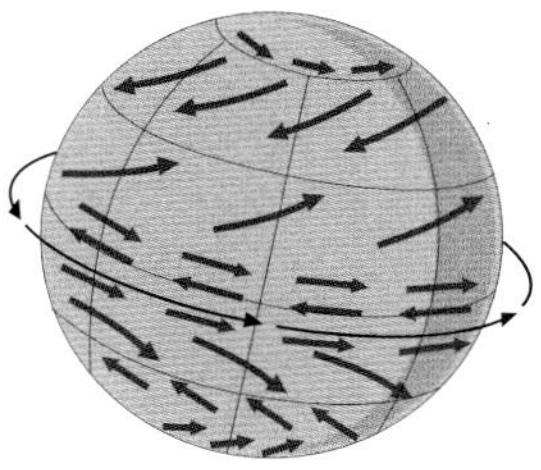

Idealized globe showing the movement of water around a landless Earth.

OCEAN CURRENTS

SURFACE CURRENTS are driven by the prevailing winds and by the spinning motion of the Earth, which drives the currents into circulating whirlpools, or gyres. Deep sea currents, over 330 ft (100 m) below the surface, are driven by differences in water temperature and salinity, which have an impact on the density of deep water and on its movement.

Map labels (main ocean map)

OCEAN • Beaufort Sea • Bering Sea • Chukchi Sea • Gulf of Alaska • Aleutian Trench • Baffin Bay • Davis Strait • Hudson Strait • Hudson Bay • Labrador Sea • Greenland Sea • Arctic Circle • Mid-Atlantic Ridge • NORTH AMERICA • Mendocino Fracture Zone • Murray Fracture Zone • Hawaiian Ridge • Molokai Fracture Zone • Clarion Fracture Zone • Newfoundland Basin • North American Basin • Gulf of Mexico • Sargasso Sea • ATLANTIC • Canary Basin • Tropic of Cancer • Yucatan Basin • Caribbean Sea • Barracuda Fracture Zone • PACIFIC • Central Pacific Basin • Clipperton Fracture Zone • Middle America Trench • Guatemala Basin • Equator • OCEAN • Tonga Trench • East Pacific Rise • Peru Basin • Nazca Ridge • Sala y Gomez Ridge • Chile Basin • SOUTH AMERICA • Brazil Basin • Tropic of Capricorn • Rio Grande Rise • Southwest Pacific Basin • Argentine Basin • Mid-Atlantic Ridge • East Pacific Rise • Pacific-Antarctic Ridge • OCEAN • Ross Sea • Amundsen Sea • Southeast Pacific Basin • Bellingshausen Sea • Scotia Sea • South Sandwich Trench • Weddell Sea • Antarctic Circle

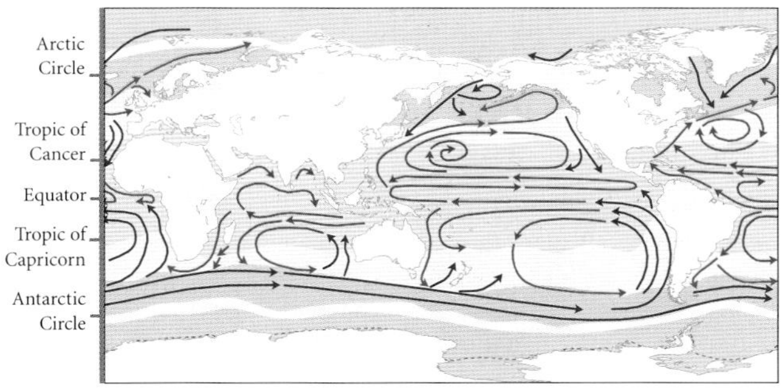

TIDES AND WAVES

TIDES ARE CREATED by the pull of the Sun and Moon's gravity on the surface of the oceans. The levels of high and low tides are influenced by the position of the Moon in relation to the Earth and Sun. Waves are formed by wind blowing over the surface of the water.

HIGH AND LOW TIDES

The highest tides occur when the Earth, the Moon and the Sun are aligned *(below left)*. The lowest tides are experienced when the Sun and Moon align at right angles to one another *(below right)*.

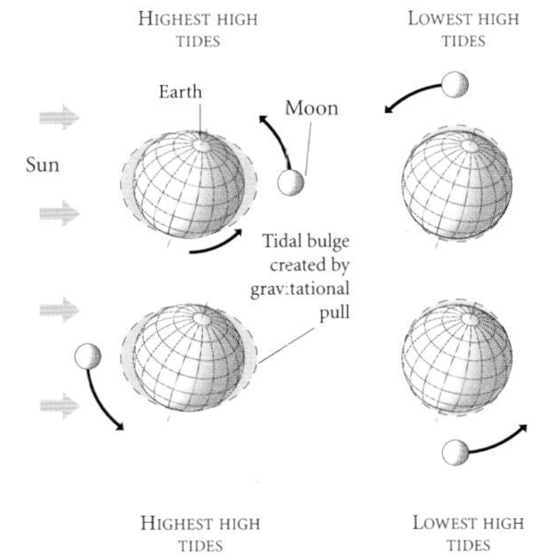

TIDAL RANGE AND WAVE ENVIRONMENTS

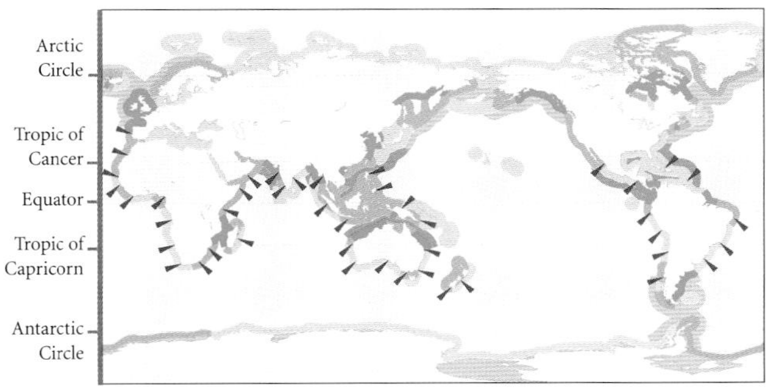

Arctic Circle • Tropic of Cancer • Equator • Tropic of Capricorn • Antarctic Circle

Tidal range and wave environments
- less than 2m / 7ft
- 2–4m / 7–13ft
- greater than 4m / 13ft
- east coast swell
- west coast swell
- tropical cyclone
- storm wave
- ice-shelf

HIGHEST HIGH TIDES — LOWEST HIGH TIDES

Earth • Moon • Sun • Tidal bulge created by gravitational pull

HIGHEST HIGH TIDES — LOWEST HIGH TIDES

SURFACE TEMPERATURE AND CURRENTS

Arctic Circle • Tropic of Cancer • Equator • Tropic of Capricorn • Antarctic Circle

Surface temperature and currents
- Ice-shelf (below 0°C / 32°F)
- Sea-ice* (average) below -2°C / 28°F
- Sea-water -2–0°C / 28–32°F
- * Sea-water freezes at -1.9°C / 28.4°F
- 0–10°C / 32–50°F
- 10–20°C / 50–68°F
- 20–30°C / 68–86°F
- → warm current
- → cold current

DEEP SEA TEMPERATURE AND CURRENTS

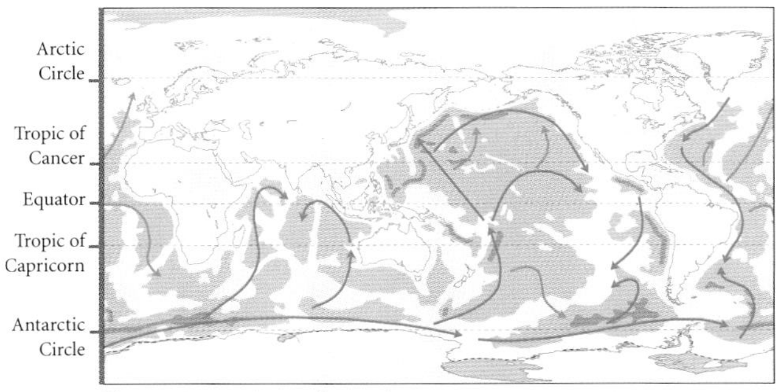

Arctic Circle • Tropic of Cancer • Equator • Tropic of Capricorn • Antarctic Circle

Deep sea temperature and currents
- Ice-shelf (below 0°C / 32°F)
- Sea-water -2–0°C / 28–32°F (below 5000m / 16,400ft)
- Sea-water 0–5°C / 32–41°F (below 4000m / 13,120ft)
- → Primary currents
- → Secondary currents

THE GLOBAL CLIMATE

THE EARTH'S CLIMATIC TYPES CONSIST of stable patterns of weather conditions averaged out over a long period of time. Different climates are categorized according to particular combinations of temperature and humidity. By contrast, weather consists of short-term fluctuations in wind, temperature and humidity conditions. Different climates are determined by latitude, altitude, the prevailing wind and circulation of ocean currents. Longer-term changes in climate, such as global warming or the onset of ice ages, are punctuated by shorter-term events which comprise the day-to-day weather of a region, such as frontal depressions, hurricanes and blizzards.

THE ATMOSPHERE, WIND AND WEATHER

THE EARTH'S ATMOSPHERE has been compared to a giant ocean of air which surrounds the planet. Its circulation patterns are similar to the currents in the oceans and are influenced by three factors; the Earth's orbit around the Sun and rotation about its axis, and variations in the amount of heat radiation received from the Sun. If both heat and moisture were not redistributed between the Equator and the poles, large areas of the Earth would be uninhabitable.

Heavy fogs, as here in southern England, form as moisture-laden air passes over cold ground.

TEMPERATURE

THE WORLD CAN BE DIVIDED into three major climatic zones, stretching like large belts across the latitudes: the tropics which are warm; the cold polar regions and the temperate zones which lie between them. Temperatures across the Earth range from above 30°C (86°F) in the deserts to as low as -55°C (-70°F) at the poles. Temperature is also controlled by altitude; because air becomes cooler and less dense the higher it gets, mountainous regions are typically colder than those areas which are at, or close to, sea level.

AVERAGE JANUARY TEMPERATURES

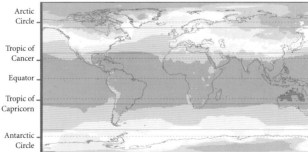

AVERAGE JULY TEMPERATURES

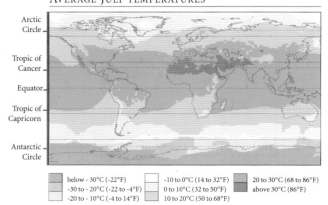

below - 30°C (-22°F)	-10 to 0°C (14 to 32°F)	20 to 30°C (68 to 86°F)
-30 to 20°C (-22 to -4°F)	0 to 10°C (32 to 50°F)	above 30°C (86°F)
-20 to - 10°C (-4 to 14°F)	10 to 20°C (50 to 68°F)	

GLOBAL AIR CIRCULATION

AIR DOES NOT SIMPLY FLOW FROM THE EQUATOR TO THE POLES, it circulates in giant cells known as Hadley and Ferrel cells. As air warms it expands, becoming less dense and rising; this creates areas of low pressure. As the air rises it cools and condenses, causing heavy rainfall over the tropics and slight snowfall over the poles. This cool air then sinks, forming high pressure belts. At surface level in the tropics these sinking currents are deflected polewards as the westerlies and towards the Equator as the trade winds. At the poles they become the polar easterlies.

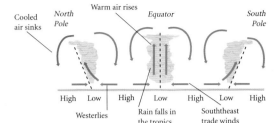

The Antarctic pack-ice expands its area by almost seven times during the winter as temperatures drop and surrounding seas freeze.

CLIMATIC CHANGE

THE EARTH IS CURRENTLY IN A WARM PHASE between ice ages. Warmer temperatures result in higher sea levels as more of the polar ice caps melt. Most of the world's population lives near coasts, so any changes which might cause sea levels to rise, could have a potentially disastrous impact.

This ice fair, painted by Pieter Brueghel the Younger in the 17th century, shows the Little Ice Age which peaked around 300 years ago.

THE GREENHOUSE EFFECT

Gases such as carbon dioxide are known as 'greenhouse gases' because they allow shortwave solar radiation to enter the Earth's atmosphere, but help to stop longwave radiation from escaping. This traps heat, raising the Earth's temperature. An excess of these gases, such as that which results from the burning of fossil fuels, helps trap more heat and can lead to global warming.

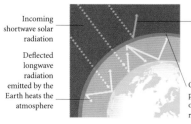

Incoming shortwave solar radiation

Deflected shortwave solar radiation

Deflected longwave radiation emitted by the Earth heats the atmosphere

Greenhouse gases prevent the escape of longwave radiation

The islands of the Caribbean, Mexico's Gulf coast and the southeastern USA are often hit by hurricanes formed far out in the Atlantic.

OCEANIC WATER CIRCULATION

IN GENERAL, OCEAN CURRENTS parallel the movement of winds across the Earth's surface. Incoming solar energy is greatest at the Equator and least at the poles. So, water in the oceans heats up most at the Equator and flows polewards, cooling as it moves north or south towards the Arctic or Antarctic. The flow is eventually reversed and cold water currents move back towards the Equator. These ocean currents act as a vast system for moving heat from the Equator towards the poles and are a major influence on the distribution of the Earth's climates.

In marginal climatic zones years of drought can completely dry out the land and transform grassland to desert.

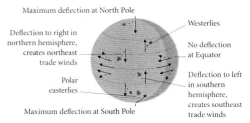

The wide range of environments found in the Andes is strongly related to their altitude, which modifies climatic influences. While the peaks are snow-capped, many protected interior valleys are semi-tropical.

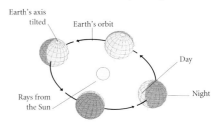

TILT AND ROTATION

The tilt and rotation of the Earth during its annual orbit largely control the distribution of heat and moisture across its surface, which correspondingly controls its large-scale weather patterns. As the Earth annually rotates around the Sun, half its surface is receiving maximum radiation, creating summer and winter seasons. The angle of the Earth means that on average the tropics receive two and a half times as much heat from the Sun each day as the poles.

Earth's axis tilted / Earth's orbit / Day / Night / Rays from the Sun

THE CORIOLIS EFFECT

The rotation of the Earth influences atmospheric circulation by deflecting winds and ocean currents. Winds blowing in the northern hemisphere are deflected to the right and those in the southern hemisphere are deflected to the left, creating large-scale patterns of wind circulation, such as the northeast and southeast trade winds and the westerlies. This effect is greatest at the poles and least at the Equator.

Maximum deflection at North Pole / Westerlies / Deflection to right in northern hemisphere, creates northeast trade winds / No deflection at Equator / Polar easterlies / Deflection to left in southern hemisphere, creates southeast trade winds / Maximum deflection at South Pole

MAP KEY

Climate zones

 ice cap
subarctic
tundra
continental
temperate
warm temperate
 mediterranean
semi-arid
arid
hot humid
humid equatorial
tropical

Ocean currents
warm
cold

Prevailing winds
→ warm
→ cold

Local winds
→ warm
→ cold
→ seasonal*
* (seasonal winds which can either be warm or cold)

PRECIPITATION

WHEN WARM AIR EXPANDS, it rises and cools, and the water vapour it carries condenses to form clouds. Heavy, regular rainfall is characteristic of the equatorial region, while the poles are cold and receive only slight snowfall. Tropical regions have marked dry and rainy seasons, while in the temperate regions rainfall is relatively unpredictable.

Monsoon rains, which affect southern Asia from May to September, are caused by sea winds blowing across the warm land.

Heavy tropical rainstorms occur frequently in Papua New Guinea, often causing soil erosion and landslides in cultivated areas.

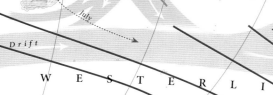

(Map labels: EASTERLIES, Arctic Circle, January, July, Buran, Mistral, Föhn, Bora, Etesian, June-October, Sirocco, Khamsin, Haboob, Southwest Monsoon, Monsoon Drift, Equatorial Counter Current, Doldrums, Northeast Monsoon October-March, South Equatorial Current, SOUTH EAST TRADES, Benguela Current, West Australian Current, West Wind Drift, WESTERLIES, EASTERLIES, Antarctic Circle, Kuro-Siwo Current, North Equatorial Current, NORTH EAST TRADES, Equatorial Counter Current, Doldrums, Equator, Southeast Monsoon October-March, South Equatorial Current, Typhoon July-October, April-September, Willy Willies January, Queensland, Hurricanes January, Tropic of Cancer, Tropic of Capricorn)

AVERAGE JANUARY RAINFALL

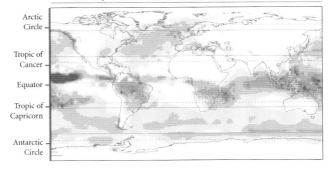

Arctic Circle / Tropic of Cancer / Equator / Tropic of Capricorn / Antarctic Circle

AVERAGE JULY RAINFALL

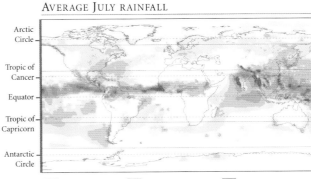

Arctic Circle / Tropic of Cancer / Equator / Tropic of Capricorn / Antarctic Circle

0–25 mm (0–1 in) / 25–50 mm (1–2 in) / 50–100 mm (2–4 in) / 100–200 mm (4–8 in) / 200–300 mm (8–12 in) / 300–400 mm (12–16 in) / 400–500 mm (16–20 in) / above 500 mm (20 in)

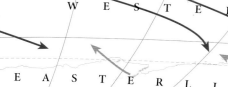

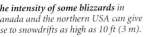

The intensity of some blizzards in Canada and the northern USA can give rise to snowdrifts as high as 10 ft (3 m).

The Atacama Desert in Chile is one of the driest places on Earth, with an average rainfall of less than 2 inches (50 mm) per

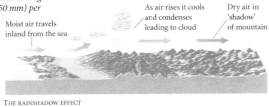

Violent thunderstorms occur along advancing cold fronts, when cold, dry air masses meet warm, moist air, which rises rapidly, its moisture condensing into thunderclouds. Rain and hail become electrically charged, causing lightning.

THE RAINSHADOW EFFECT

When moist air is forced to rise by mountains, it cools and the water vapour falls as precipitation, either as rain or snow. Only the dry, cold air continues over the mountains, leaving inland areas with little or no rain. This is called the rainshadow effect and is one reason for the existence of the Mojave Desert in California, which lies east of the Coast Ranges.

As air rises it cools and condenses leading to cloud / Dry air in 'shadow' of mountain / Moist air travels inland from the sea

THE RAINSHADOW EFFECT

LIFE ON EARTH

A UNIQUE COMBINATION of an oxygen-rich atmosphere and plentiful water is the key to life on Earth. Apart from the polar ice caps, there are few areas which have not been colonized by animals or plants over the course of the Earth's history. Plants process sunlight to provide them with their energy, and ultimately all the Earth's animals rely on plants for survival. Because of this reliance, plants are known as primary producers, and the availability of nutrients and temperature of an area is defined as its primary productivity, which affects the quantity and type of animals which are able to live there. This index is affected by climatic factors – cold and aridity restrict the quantity of life, whereas warmth and regular rainfall allow a greater diversity of species.

BIOGEOGRAPHICAL REGIONS

THE EARTH CAN BE DIVIDED into a series of biogeographical regions, or biomes, ecological communities where certain species of plant and animal co-exist within particular climatic conditions. Within these broad classifications, other factors including soil richness, altitude and human activities such as urbanization, intensive agriculture and deforestation, affect the local distribution of living species within each biome.

POLAR REGIONS
A layer of permanent ice at the Earth's poles covers both seas and land. Very little plant and animal life can exist in these harsh regions.

TUNDRA
A desolate region, with long, dark freezing winters and short, cold summers. With virtually no soil and large areas of permanently frozen ground known as permafrost, the tundra is largely treeless, though it is briefly clothed by small flowering plants in the summer months.

NEEDLELEAF FORESTS
With milder summers than the tundra and less wind, these areas are able to support large forests of coniferous trees.

BROADLEAF FORESTS
Much of the northern hemisphere was once covered by deciduous forests, which occurred in areas with marked seasonal variations. Most deciduous forests have been cleared for human settlement.

TEMPERATE RAINFORESTS
In warmer wetter areas, such as southern China, temperate deciduous forests are replaced by evergreen forest.

DESERTS
Deserts are areas with negligible rainfall. Most hot deserts lie within the tropics; cold deserts are dry because of their distance from the moisture-providing sea.

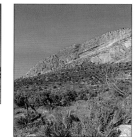

MEDITERRANEAN
Hot, dry summers and short winters typify these areas, which were once covered by evergreen shrubs and woodland, but have now been cleared by humans for agriculture.

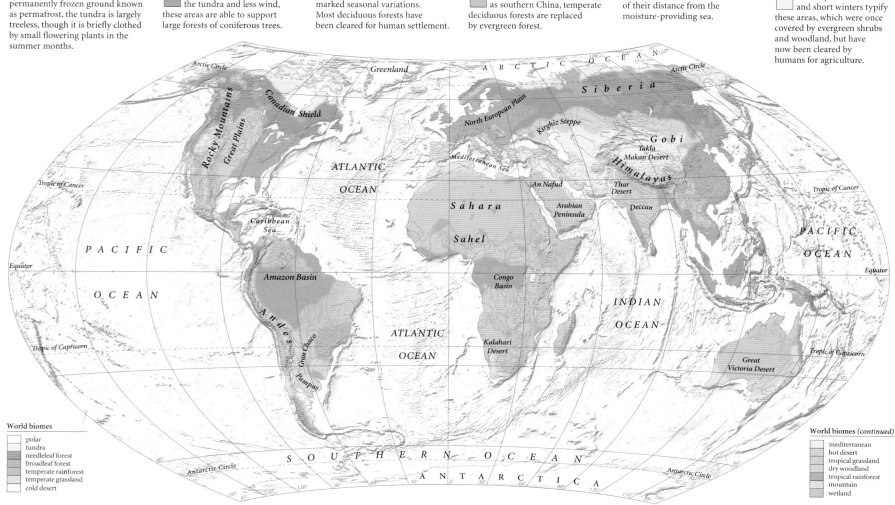

World biomes
- polar
- tundra
- needleleaf forest
- broadleaf forest
- temperate rainforest
- temperate grassland
- cold desert

World biomes (continued)
- mediterranean
- hot desert
- tropical grassland
- dry woodland
- tropical rainforest
- mountain
- wetland

TROPICAL AND TEMPERATE GRASSLANDS
The major grassland areas are found in the centres of the larger continental landmasses. In Africa's tropical savannah regions, seasonal rainfall alternates with drought. Temperate grasslands, also known as *steppes* and *prairies* are found in the northern hemisphere, and in South America, where they are known as the *pampas*.

DRY WOODLANDS
Trees and shrubs, adapted to dry conditions, grow widely spaced from one another, interspersed by savannah grasslands.

TROPICAL RAINFORESTS
Characterized by year-round warmth and high rainfall, tropical rainforests contain the highest diversity of plant and animal species on Earth.

MOUNTAINS
Though the lower slopes of mountains may be thickly forested, only ground-hugging shrubs and other vegetation will grow above the tree line which varies according to both altitude and latitude.

WETLANDS
Rarely lying above sea level, wetlands are marshes, swamps and tidal flats. Some, with their moist, fertile soils, are rich feeding grounds for fish and breeding grounds for birds. Others have little soil structure and are too acidic to support much plant and animal life.

BIODIVERSITY

THE NUMBER OF PLANT AND ANIMAL SPECIES, and the range of genetic diversity within the populations of each species, make up the Earth's biodiversity. The plants and animals which are endemic to a region – that is, those which are found nowhere else in the world – are also important in determining levels of biodiversity. Human settlement and intervention have encroached on many areas of the world once rich in endemic plant and animal species. Increasing international efforts are being made to monitor and conserve the biodiversity of the Earth's remaining wild places.

ANIMAL ADAPTATION

THE DEGREE OF AN ANIMAL'S ADAPTABILITY to different climates and conditions is extremely important in ensuring its success as a species. Many animals, particularly the largest mammals, are becoming restricted to ever-smaller regions as human development and modern agricultural practices reduce their natural habitats. In contrast, humans have been responsible – both deliberately and accidentally – for the spread of some of the world's most successful species. Many of these introduced species are now more numerous than the indigenous animal populations.

POLAR ANIMALS

The frozen wastes of the polar regions are able to support only a small range of species which derive their nutritional requirements from the sea. Animals such as the walrus *(left)* have developed insulating fat, stocky limbs and double-layered coats to enable them to survive in the freezing conditions.

DIVERSITY OF ANIMAL SPECIES

DESERT ANIMALS

Many animals which live in the extreme heat and aridity of the deserts are able to survive for days and even months with very little food or water. Their bodies are adapted to lose heat quickly and to store fat and water. The Gila monster *(above)* stores fat in its tail.

AMAZON RAINFOREST

The vast Amazon Basin is home to the world's greatest variety of animal species. Animals are adapted to live at many different levels from the treetops to the tangled undergrowth which lies beneath the canopy. The sloth *(below)* hangs upside down in the branches. Its fur grows from its stomach to its back to enable water to run off quickly.

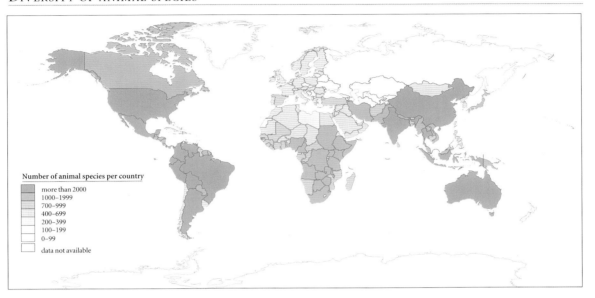

Number of animal species per country
- more than 2000
- 1000–1999
- 700–999
- 400–699
- 200–399
- 100–199
- 0–99
- data not available

MARINE BIODIVERSITY

The oceans support a huge variety of different species, from the world's largest mammals like whales and dolphins down to the tiniest plankton. The greatest diversities occur in the warmer seas of continental shelves, where plants are easily able to photosynthesize, and around coral reefs, where complex ecosystems are found. On the ocean floor, nematodes can exist at a depth of more than 10,000 ft (3000 m) below sea level.

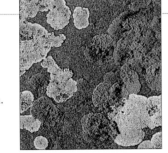

HIGH ALTITUDES

Few animals exist in the rarefied atmosphere of the highest mountains. However, birds of prey such as eagles and vultures *(above)*, with their superb eyesight can soar as high as 23,000 ft (7000 m) to scan for prey below.

URBAN ANIMALS

The growth of cities has reduced the amount of habitat available to many species. A number of animals are now moving closer into urban areas to scavenge from the detritus of the modern city *(left)*. Rodents, particularly rats and mice, have existed in cities for thousands of years, and many insects, especially moths, quickly develop new colouring to provide them with camouflage.

ENDEMIC SPECIES

Isolated areas such as Australia and the island of Madagascar, have the greatest range of endemic species. In Australia, these include marsupials such as the kangaroo *(below)*, which carry their young in pouches on their bodies. Destruction of habitat, pollution, hunting, and predators introduced by humans, are threatening this unique biodiversity.

PLANT ADAPTATION

ENVIRONMENTAL CONDITIONS, particularly climate, soil type and the extent of competition with other organisms, influence the development of plants into a number of distinctive forms. Similar conditions in quite different parts of the world create similar adaptations in the plants, which may then be modified by other, local, factors specific to the region.

COLD CONDITIONS

In areas where temperatures rarely rise above freezing, plants such as lichens *(left)* and mosses grow densely, close to the ground.

RAINFORESTS

Most of the world's largest and oldest plants are found in rainforests; warmth and heavy rainfall provide ideal conditions for vast plants like the world's largest flower, the rafflesia *(left)*.

HOT, DRY CONDITIONS

Arid conditions lead to the development of plants whose surface area has been reduced to a minimum to reduce water loss. In cacti *(above)*, which can survive without water for months, leaves are minimal or not present at all.

ANCIENT PLANTS

Some of the world's most primitive plants still exist today, including algae, cyclads and many ferns *(above)*, reflecting the success with which they have adapted to changing conditions.

RESISTING PREDATORS

A great variety of plants have developed devices including spines *(above)*, poisons, stinging hairs and an unpleasant taste or smell to deter animal predators.

DIVERSITY OF PLANT SPECIES

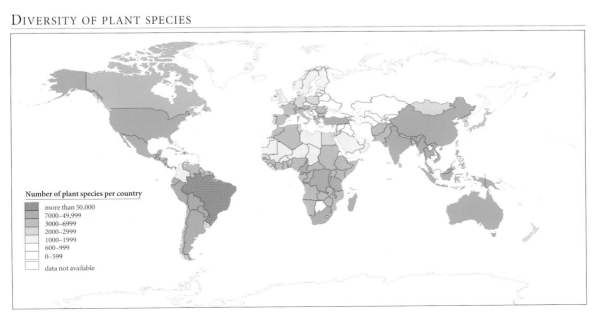

Number of plant species per country
- more than 50,000
- 7000–49,999
- 3000–6999
- 2000–2999
- 1000–1999
- 600–999
- 0–599
- data not available

WEEDS

Weeds such as bindweed *(above)* are fast-growing, easily dispersed, and tolerant of a number of different environments, enabling them to quickly colonize suitable habitats. They are among the most adaptable of all plants.

POPULATION AND SETTLEMENT

THE EARTH'S POPULATION IS PROJECTED to rise from its current level of about 5.5 billion to reach some 10 billion by 2025. The global distribution of this rapidly growing population is very uneven, and is dictated by climate, terrain and natural and economic resources. The great majority of the Earth's people live in coastal zones, and along river valleys. Deserts cover over 20% of the Earth's surface, but support less than 5% of the world's population. It is estimated that over half of the world's population live in cities – most of them in Asia – as a result of mass migration from rural areas in search of jobs. Many of these people live in the so-called 'megacities', some with populations as great as 40 million.

PATTERNS OF SETTLEMENT

THE PAST 200 YEARS have seen the most radical shift in world population patterns in recorded history.

NOMADIC LIFE

ALL THE WORLD'S PEOPLES were hunter-gatherers 10,000 years ago. Today nomads, who live by following available food resources, account for less than 0.0001% of the world's population. They are mainly pastoral herders, moving their livestock from place to place in search of grazing land.

Nomadic population

▨ Nomadic population area

THE GROWTH OF CITIES

IN 1900 there were only 14 cities in the world with populations of more than a million, mostly in the northern hemisphere. Today, as more and more people in the developing world migrate to towns and cities, there are 29 cities whose population exceeds 5 million, and around 200 million-cities.

MILLION-CITIES IN 1900

Million-cities in 1900

• Cities over 1 million population

MILLION-CITIES IN 1995

Million-cities in 1995

• Cities over 1 million population

NORTH AMERICA

THE EASTERN AND WESTERN SEABOARDS of the USA, with huge expanses of interconnected cities, towns and suburbs, are vast, densely-populated megalopolises. Central America and the Caribbean also have high population densities. Yet, away from the coasts and in the wildernesses of northern Canada the land is very sparsely settled.

Vancouver on Canada's west coast, grew up as a port city. In recent years it has attracted many Asian immigrants, particularly from the Pacific Rim.

North America's central plains, the continent's agricultural heartland, are thinly populated and highly productive.

EUROPE

WITH ITS TEMPERATE CLIMATE, and rich mineral and natural resources, Europe is generally very densely settled. The continent acts as a magnet for economic migrants from the developing world, and immigration is now widely restricted. Birth rates in Europe are generally low, and in some countries, such as Germany, the populations have stabilized at zero growth, with a fast-growing elderly population.

Many European cities, like Siena, once reflected the 'ideal' size for human settlements. Modern technological advances have enabled them to grow far beyond the original walls.

Within the densely-populated Netherlands the reclamation of coastal wetlands is vital to provide much-needed land for agriculture and settlement.

Population density (inhabitants per sq km)

■ More than 200
■ 101–200
■ 51–100
■ 21–50
□ 11–20
□ 6–10
□ 1–5
□ Less than 1

NORTH AMERICA

Population 9%   World land area 17%

EUROPE

Population 14%   World land area 7.1%

AFRICA

Population 12%   World land area 20.2%

SOUTH AMERICA

Population 5.5%   World land area 11.8%

SOUTH AMERICA

MOST SETTLEMENT IN SOUTH AMERICA is clustered in a narrow belt in coastal zones and in the northern Andes. During the 20th century, cities such as São Paulo and Buenos Aires grew enormously, acting as powerful economic magnets to the rural population. Shanty towns have grown up on the outskirts of many major cities to house these immigrants, often lacking basic amenities.

Many people in western South America live at high altitudes in the Andes, both in cities and in villages such as this one in Bolivia.

Venezuela is the most highly urbanized country in South America, with more than 90% of the population living in cities such as Caracas.

AFRICA

THE ARID CLIMATE of much of Africa means that settlement of the continent is sparse, focusing in coastal areas and fertile regions such as the Nile Valley. Africa still has a high proportion of nomadic agriculturalists, although many are now becoming settled, and the population is predominantly rural.

Cities such as Nairobi (above), Cairo and Johannesburg have grown rapidly in recent years, although only Cairo has a significant population on a global scale.

Traditional lifestyles and homes persist across much of Africa, which has a higher proportion of rural or village-based population than any other continent.

ASIA

MOST ASIAN SETTLEMENT originally centred around the great river valleys such as the Indus, the Ganges and the Yangtze. Today, almost 60% of the world's population lives in Asia, many in burgeoning cities – particularly in the economically-buoyant Pacific Rim countries. Even rural population densities are high in many countries; practices such as terracing in Southeast Asia making the most of the available land.

Many of China's cities are now vast urban areas with populations of more than 5 million people.

This stilt village in Bangladesh is built to resist the regular flooding. Pressure on land, even in rural areas, forces many people to live in marginal areas.

POPULATION STRUCTURES

POPULATION PYRAMIDS are an effective means of showing the age structures of different countries, and highlighting changing trends in population growth and decline. The typical pyramid for a country with a growing, youthful population, is broad-based *(left)*, reflecting a high birth rate and a far larger number of young rather than elderly people. In contrast, countries with populations whose numbers are stabilizing have a more balanced distribution of people in each age band, and may even have lower numbers of people in the youngest age ranges, indicating both a high life expectancy, and that the population is now barely replacing itself *(right)*. The Russian Federation *(centre)* still bears the scars of the Second World War, reflected in the dramatically lower numbers of men than women in the 60–80+ age range.

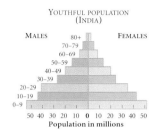

YOUTHFUL POPULATION
(INDIA)

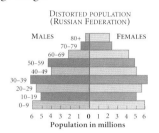

DISTORTED POPULATION
(RUSSIAN FEDERATION)

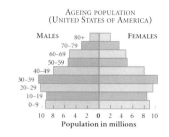

AGEING POPULATION
(UNITED STATES OF AMERICA)

POPULATION GROWTH

IMPROVEMENTS IN FOOD SUPPLY and advances in medicine have both played a major role in the remarkable growth in global population, which has increased five-fold over the last 150 years. Food supplies have risen with the mechanization of agriculture and improvements in crop yields. Better nutrition, together with higher standards of public health and sanitation, have led to increased longevity and higher birth rates.

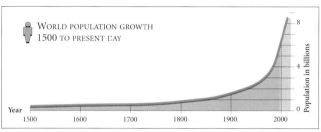

WORLD POPULATION GROWTH
1500 TO PRESENT DAY

WORLD NUTRITION

TWO-THIRDS OF THE WORLD'S food supply is consumed by the industrialized nations, many of which have a daily calorific intake far higher than is necessary for their populations to maintain a healthy body weight. In contrast, in the developing world, about 800 million people do not have enough food to meet their basic nutritional needs.

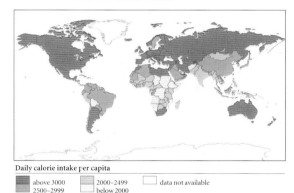

Daily calorie intake per capita

■ above 3000	2000–2499	data not available
2500–2999	below 2000	

WORLD LIFE EXPECTANCY

IMPROVED PUBLIC HEALTH and living standards have greatly increased life expectancy in the developed world, where people can now expect to live twice as long as they did 100 years ago. In many of the world's poorest nations, inadequate nutrition and disease, means that the average life expectancy still does not exceed 45 years.

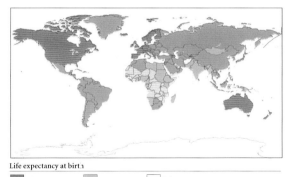

Life expectancy at birth

■ above 75 years	55–64 years	below 44 years
65–74 years	45–54 years	data not available

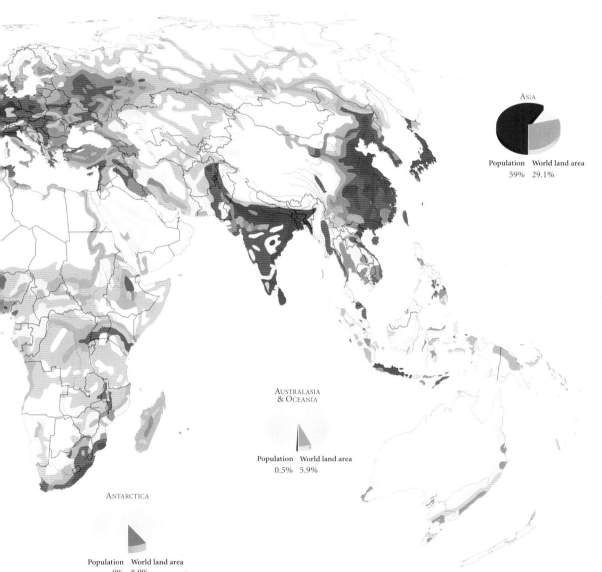

Asia

Population   World land area
59%   29.1%

AUSTRALASIA
& OCEANIA

Population   World land area
0.5%   5.9%

ANTARCTICA

Population   World land area
0%   8.9%

AUSTRALASIA & OCEANIA

THIS IS THE WORLD'S most sparsely settled region. The peoples of Australia and New Zealand live mainly in the coastal cities, with only scattered settlements in the arid interior. The Pacific islands can only support limited populations because of their remoteness and lack of resources.

Brisbane, on Australia's Gold Coast is the most rapidly expanding city in the country. The great majority of Australia's population lives in cities near the coasts.

The remote highlands of Papua New Guinea are home to a wide variety of peoples, many of whom still subsist by traditional hunting and gathering.

AVERAGE WORLD BIRTH RATES

BIRTH RATES ARE MUCH HIGHER in Africa, Asia and South America than in Europe and North America. Increased affluence and easy access to contraception are both factors which can lead to a significant decline in a country's birth rate.

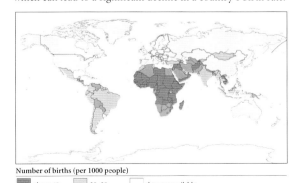

Number of births (per 1000 people)

■ above 40	20–29	data not available
30–39	below 20	

WORLD INFANT MORTALITY

IN PARTS OF THE DEVELOPING WORLD infant mortality rates are still high; access to medical services such as immunization, adequate nutrition and the promotion of breast-feeding have been important in combating infant mortality.

World infant mortality rates (deaths per 1000 live births)

■ above 125	35–74	below 15
75–124	15–43	data not available

THE ECONOMIC SYSTEM

THE WEALTHY COUNTRIES OF THE DEVELOPED WORLD, with their aggressive, market-led economies and their access to productive new technologies and international markets, dominate the world economic system. At the other extreme, many of the countries of the developing world are locked in a cycle of national debt, rising populations and unemployment. The state-managed economies of the former communist bloc began to be dismantled during the 1990s, and China is emerging as a major economic power following decades of isolation.

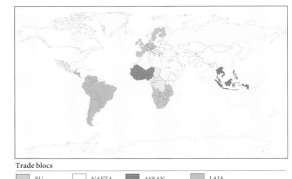

Trade blocs

EU		NAFTA		ASEAN		LAIA
CACM		SADC		ECOWAS		CEEAC

TRADE BLOCS

INTERNATIONAL TRADE BLOCS are formed when groups of countries, often already enjoying close military and political ties, join together to offer mutually preferential terms of trade for both imports and exports. Increasingly, global trade is dominated by three main blocs: the EU, NAFTA, and ASEAN. They are supplanting older trade blocs such as the Commonwealth, a legacy of colonialism.

INTERNATIONAL TRADE FLOWS

WORLD TRADE acts as a stimulus to national economies, encouraging growth. Over the last three decades, as heavy industries have declined, services – banking, insurance, tourism, airlines and shipping – have taken an increasingly large share of world trade. Manufactured articles now account for nearly two-thirds of world trade; raw materials and food make up less than a quarter of the total.

SHIPPING
Ships carry 80% of international cargo, and extensive container ports, where cargo is stored, are vital links in the international transport network.

MULTINATIONALS
Multinational companies are increasingly penetrating inaccessible markets. The reach of many American commodities is now global.

PRIMARY PRODUCTS
Many countries, particularly in the Caribbean and Africa, are still reliant on primary products such as rubber and coffee, which makes them vulnerable to fluctuating prices.

SERVICE INDUSTRIES
Service industries such as banking, tourism and insurance were the fastest-growing industrial sector in the last half of the 20th century. Lloyds of London is the centre of the world insurance market.

Countries reliant on a single export
- bananas
- coffee
- oil/petroleum
- copper

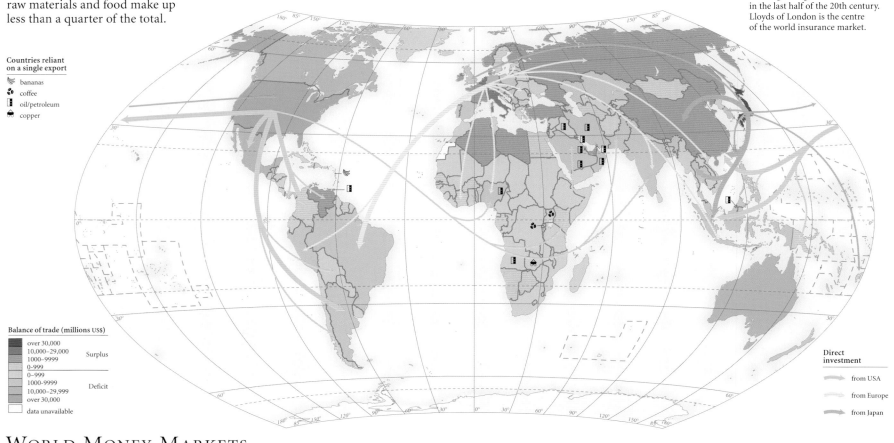

Balance of trade (millions US$)

over 30,000	
10,000–29,000	
1000–9999	Surplus
0–999	
0–999	
1000–9999	Deficit
10,000–29,999	
over 30,000	
data unavailable	

Direct investment

- from USA
- from Europe
- from Japan

WORLD MONEY MARKETS

THE FINANCIAL WORLD has traditionally been dominated by three major centres – Tokyo, New York and London, which house the headquarters of stock exchanges, multinational corporations and international banks. Their geographic location means that, at any one time in a 24-hour day, one major market is open for trading in shares, currencies and commodities. Since the late 1980s, technological advances have enabled transactions between financial centres to occur at ever-greater speed, and new markets have sprung up throughout the world.

NEW STOCK MARKETS

NEW STOCK MARKETS are now opening in many parts of the world, where economies have recently emerged from state controls. In Moscow and Beijing, and several countries in eastern Europe, newly-opened stock exchanges reflect the transition to market-driven economies.

THE DEVELOPING WORLD

INTERNATIONAL TRADE in capital and currency is dominated by the rich nations of the northern hemisphere. In parts of Africa and Asia, where exports of any sort are extremely limited, home-produced commodities are simply sold in local markets.

MAJOR MONEY MARKETS

London
New York
Tokyo

Location of major stock markets
- Major stock markets

The Tokyo Stock Market crashed in 1990, leading to a slow-down in the growth of the world's most powerful economy, and a refocusing on economic policy away from export-led growth and towards the domestic market.

Dealers at the Calcutta Stock Market. The Indian economy has been opened up to foreign investment and many multinationals now have bases there.

Markets have thrived in communist Vietnam since the introduction of a liberal economic policy.

WORLD WEALTH DISPARITY

A GLOBAL ASSESSMENT of Gross Domestic Product (GDP) by nation reveals great disparities. The developed world, with only a quarter of the world's population, has 80% of the world's manufacturing income. Civil war, conflict and political instability further undermine the economic self-sufficiency of many of the world's poorest nations.

Cities such as Detroit have been badly hit by the decline in heavy industry.

URBAN DECAY

ALTHOUGH THE USA still dominates the global economy, it faces deficits in both the federal budget and the balance of trade. Vast discrepancies in personal wealth, high levels of unemployment, and the dismantling of welfare provisions throughout the 1980s have led to severe deprivation in several of the inner cities of North America's industrial heartland.

BOOMING CITIES

SINCE THE 1980s the Chinese government has set up special industrial zones, such as Shanghai, where foreign investment is encouraged through tax incentives. Migrants from rural China pour into these regions in search of work, creating 'boomtown' economies.

Foreign investment has encouraged new infrastructure development in cities like Shanghai.

URBAN SPRAWL

CITIES ARE EXPANDING all over the developing world, attracting economic migrants in search of work and opportunities. In cities such as Rio de Janeiro, housing has not kept pace with the population explosion, and squalid shanty towns *(favelas)* rub shoulders with middle-class housing.

The favelas of Rio de Janeiro sprawl over the hills surrounding the city.

COMPARATIVE WORLD WEALTH

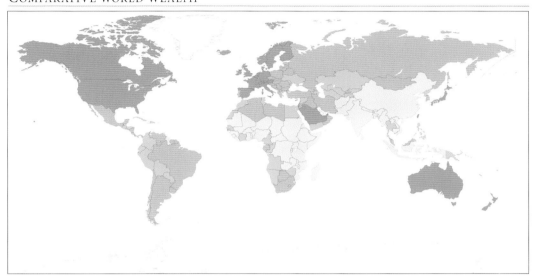

World economies

- high income
- upper-middle income
- lower-middle income
- low income
- data unavailable

ECONOMIC 'TIGERS'

THE ECONOMIC 'TIGERS' of the Pacific Rim – Taiwan, Singapore, and South Korea – have grown faster than Europe and the USA over the last decade. Their export- and service-led economies have benefited from stable government, low labour costs, and foreign investment.

Hong Kong, with its fine natural harbour, is one of the most important ports in Asia.

AGRICULTURAL ECONOMIES

IN PARTS OF THE DEVELOPING WORLD, people survive by subsistence farming – only growing enough food for themselves and their families. With no surplus product, they are unable to exchange goods for currency, the only means of escaping the poverty trap. In other countries, farmers have been encouraged to concentrate on growing a single crop for the export market. This reliance on cash crops leaves farmers vulnerable to crop failure and to changes in the market price of the crop.

The Ugandan uplands are fertile, but poor infrastructure hampers the export of cash crops.

A shopping arcade in Paris displays a great profusion of luxury goods.

THE AFFLUENT WEST

THE CAPITAL CITIES of many countries in the developed world are showcases for consumer goods, reflecting the increasing importance of the service sector, and particularly the retail sector, in the world economy. The idea of shopping as a leisure activity is unique to the western world. Luxury goods and services attract visitors, who in turn generate tourist revenue.

TOURISM

IN 1995, THERE WERE 567 million tourists worldwide. Tourism is now the world's biggest single industry, employing 127 million people, though frequently in low-paid unskilled jobs. While tourists are increasingly exploring inaccessible and less-developed regions of the world, the benefits of the industry are not always felt at a local level. There are also worries about the environmental impact of tourism, as the world's last wildernesses increasingly become tourist attractions.

Botswana's Okavango Delta is an area rich in wildlife. Tourists make safaris to the region, but the impact of tourism is controlled.

MONEY FLOWS

FOREIGN INVESTMENT in the developing world during the 1970s led to a global financial crisis in the 1980s, when many countries were unable to meet their debt repayments. The International Monetary Fund (IMF) was forced to reschedule the debts and, in some cases, write them off completely. Within the developing world, austerity programmes have been initiated to cope with the debt, leading in turn to high unemployment and galloping inflation. In many parts of Africa, stricken economies are now dependent on international aid.

In rural Southeast Asia, babies are given medical checks by UNICEF as part of a global aid programme sponsored by the un.

TOURIST ARRIVALS

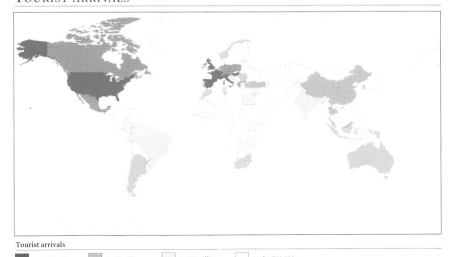

Tourist arrivals

- over 20 million
- 10–20 million
- 5–10 million
- 2.5–5 million
- 1–2.5 million
- 700,000–999,000
- under 700,000
- data unavailable

INTERNATIONAL DEBT: DONORS AND RECEIVERS

International debt (as percentage of GNP)

- over 100%
- 70–90%
- 50–69%
- 30–49%
- below 30
- negligible
- data unavailable

A B C D E F G H I J K L M

THE POLITICAL WORLD

THERE ARE 192 INDEPENDENT COUNTRIES in the world today. With the exception of Antarctica, where territorial claims have been deferred by international treaty, every land area of the Earth's surface either belongs to, or is claimed by, one country or another. The largest country in the world is the Russian Federation, the smallest is Vatican City. Some 60 overseas dependent territories remain, administered variously by France, Australia, Denmark, New Zealand, Norway, Portugal, the UK, the USA and the Netherlands.

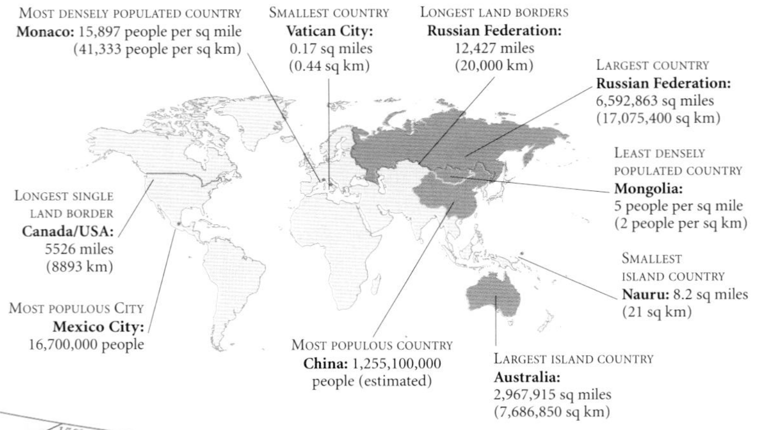

INTERNATIONAL BORDERS

THE MAP SHOWS three main types of boundary between states. Full borders represent internationally agreed and recognized territorial boundaries. Undefined borders exist where no fixed boundary between states has been demarcated; the boundaries indicated in this way show approximate areas of sovereignty. A disputed border is indicated where a *de facto* territorial boundary exists, which is not agreed or is subject to arbitration.

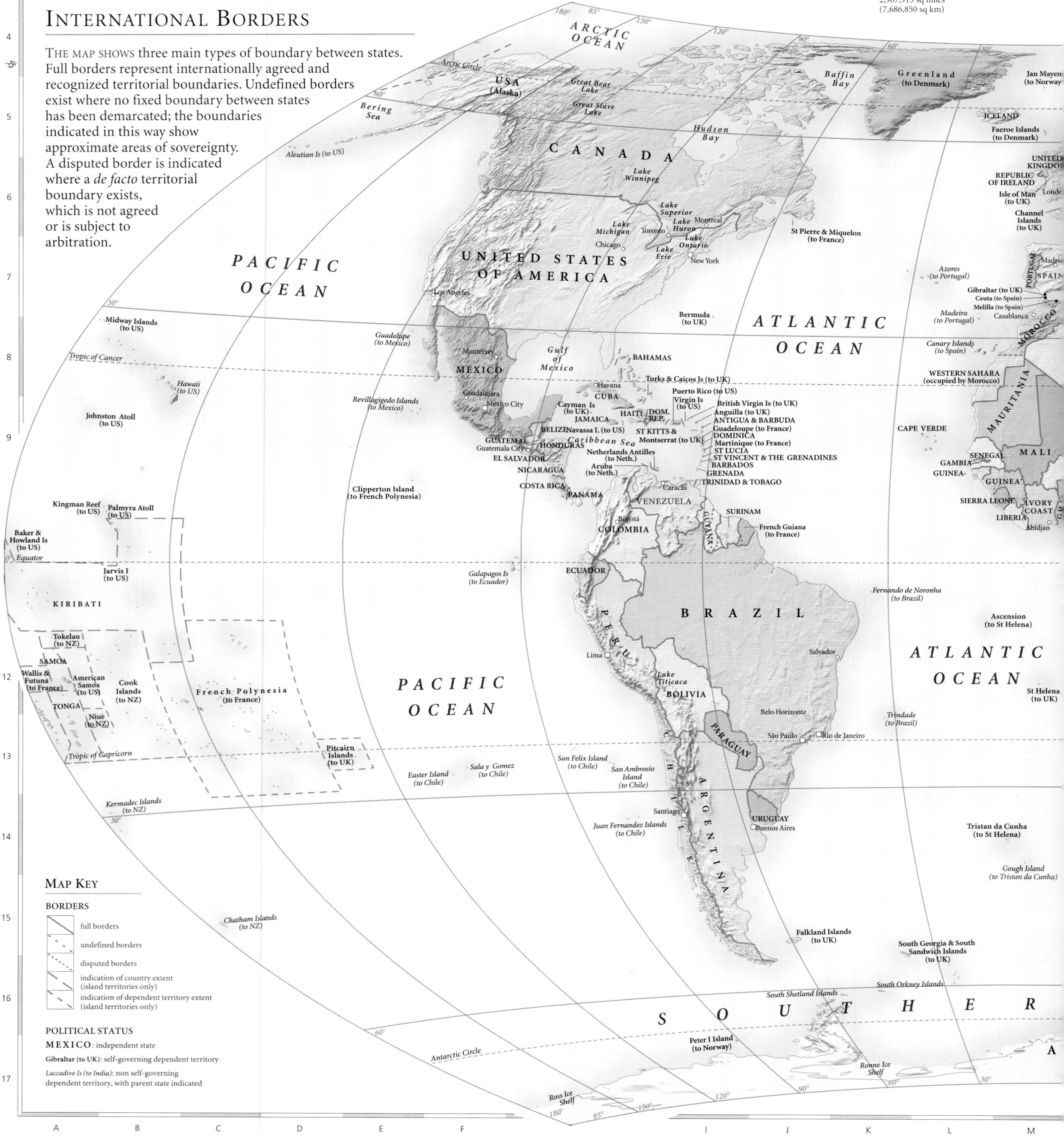

MOST DENSELY POPULATED COUNTRY
Monaco: 15,897 people per sq mile
(41,333 people per sq km)

SMALLEST COUNTRY
Vatican City:
0.17 sq miles
(0.44 sq km)

LONGEST LAND BORDERS
Russian Federation:
12,427 miles
(20,000 km)

LARGEST COUNTRY
Russian Federation:
6,592,863 sq miles
(17,075,400 sq km)

LEAST DENSELY POPULATED COUNTRY
Mongolia:
5 people per sq mile
(2 people per sq km)

SMALLEST ISLAND COUNTRY
Nauru: 8.2 sq miles
(21 sq km)

LONGEST SINGLE LAND BORDER
Canada/USA:
5526 miles
(8893 km)

MOST POPULOUS CITY
Mexico City:
16,700,000 people

MOST POPULOUS COUNTRY
China: 1,255,100,000
people (estimated)

LARGEST ISLAND COUNTRY
Australia:
2,967,915 sq miles
(7,686,850 sq km)

MAP KEY

BORDERS

- full borders
- undefined borders
- disputed borders
- indication of country extent (island territories only)
- indication of dependent territory extent (island territories only)

POLITICAL STATUS

MEXICO: independent state
Gibraltar (to UK): self-governing dependent territory
Laccadive Is (to India): non self-governing dependent territory, with parent state indicated

N O P Q R S T U V W X Y Z

THE WORLD IN 1914

THE EARLY YEARS OF the 20th century saw the mainly European colonial empires reaching their greatest extents by 1914. Two world wars inaugurated their disintegration, but even in 1950 there were only 82 independent countries. Since then, over 100 have gained their independence, culminating in the breakup of the Soviet Union and former Yugoslavia in the early 1990s.

PERCENTAGE OF EARTH'S LAND SURFACE
CONTROLLED BY COLONIAL EMPIRES IN 1914

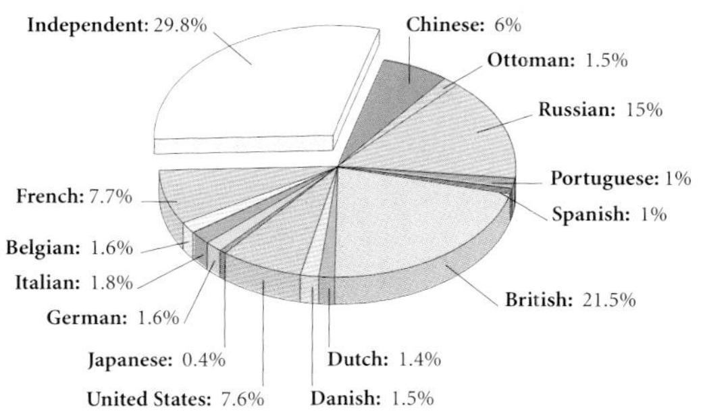

Independent: 29.8%
Chinese: 6%
Ottoman: 1.5%
Russian: 15%
Portuguese: 1%
Spanish: 1%
British: 21.5%
French: 7.7%
Belgian: 1.6%
Italian: 1.8%
German: 1.6%
Japanese: 0.4%
Dutch: 1.4%
United States: 7.6%
Danish: 1.5%

COLONIAL EMPIRES IN 1914

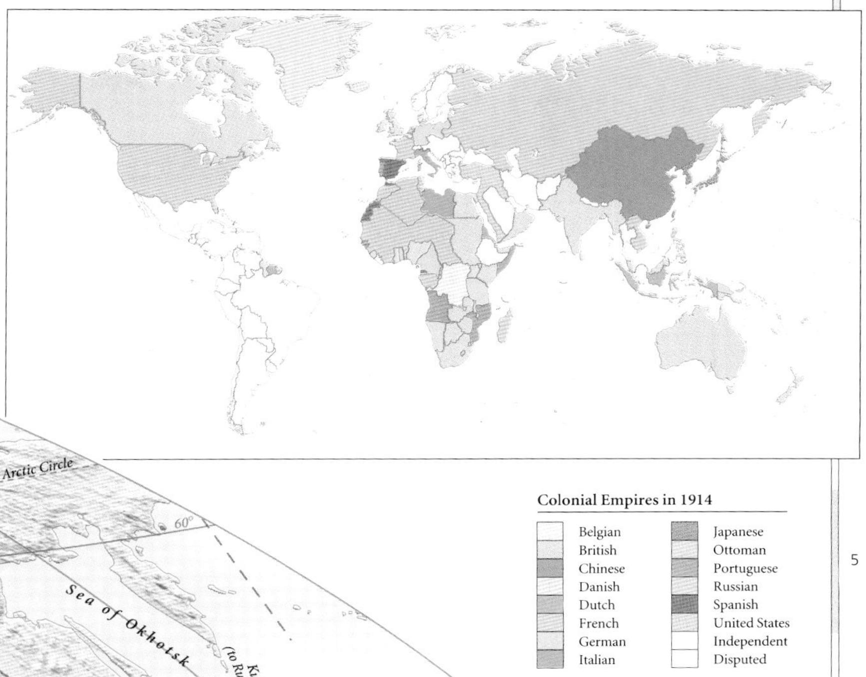

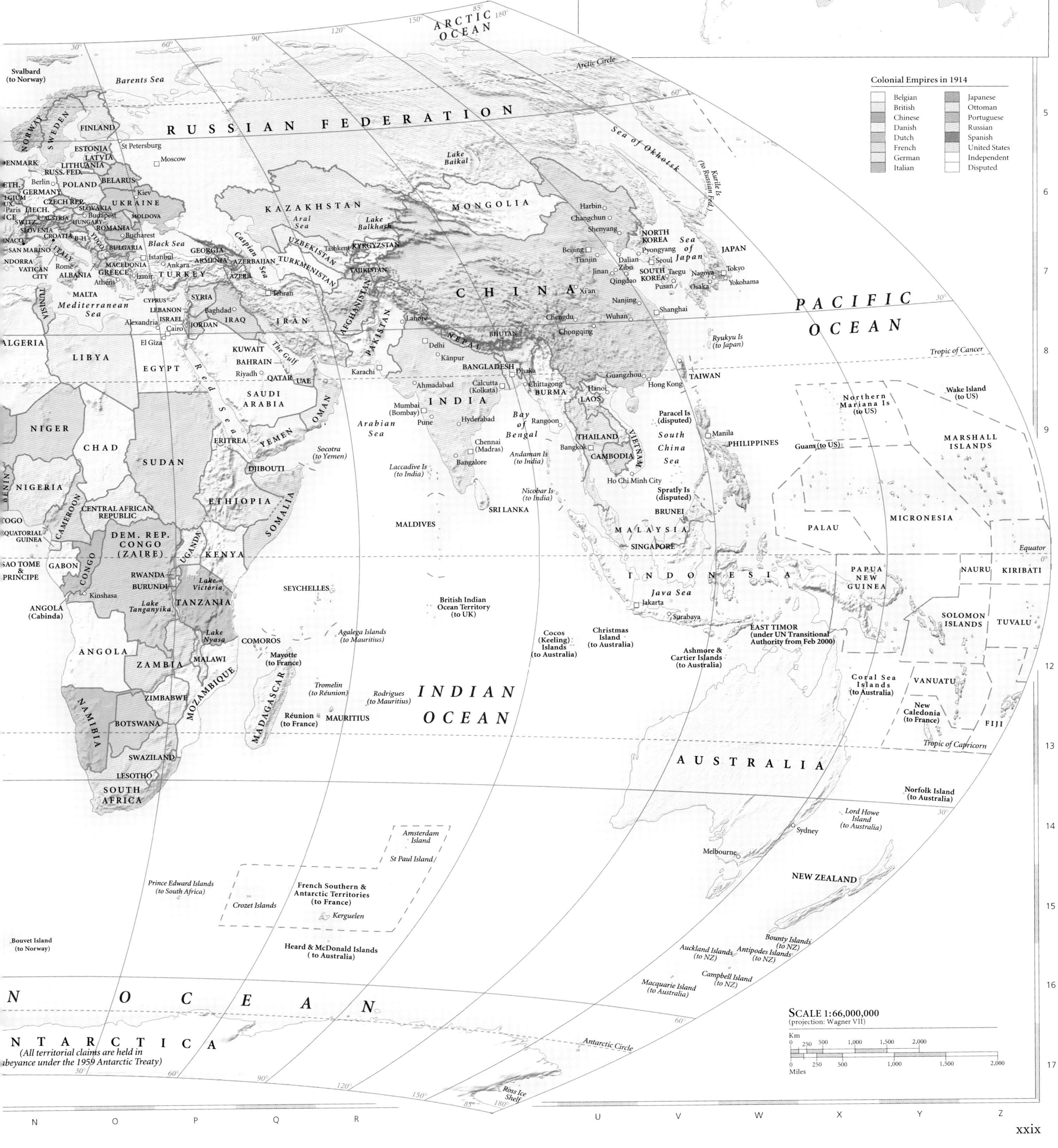

Colonial Empires in 1914

Belgian	Japanese
British	Ottoman
Chinese	Portuguese
Danish	Russian
Dutch	Spanish
French	United States
German	Independent
Italian	Disputed

SCALE 1:66,000,000
(projection: Wagner VII)

Km
0 250 500 1,000 1,500 2,000

Miles
0 250 500 1,000 1,500 2,000

STATES AND BOUNDARIES

THERE ARE OVER 190 SOVEREIGN STATES in the world today; in 1950 there were only 82. Over the last half-century national self-determination has been a driving force for many states with a history of colonialism and oppression. As more borders are added to the world map, the number of international border disputes increases.

In many cases, where the impetus towards independence has been religious or ethnic, disputes with minority groups have also caused violent internal conflict. While many newly-formed states have moved peacefully towards independence, successfully establishing government by multi-party democracy, dictatorship by military regime or individual despot is often the result of the internal power-struggles which characterize the early stages in the lives of new nations.

THE NATURE OF POLITICS

Democracy is a broad term: it can range from the ideal of multiparty elections and fair representation to, in countries such as Singapore and Indonesia, a thin disguise for single-party rule. In despotic regimes, on the other hand, a single, often personal authority has total power; institutions such as parliament and the military are mere instruments of the dictator.

The stars and stripes of the US flag are a potent symbol of the country's status as a federal democracy.

Types of government

- Multiparty democracy for more than 10 yrs
- Multiparty/transitional democracy within last 10 yrs
- Single-party government
- Military regime
- Theocracy
- Absolute monarchy
- ⚑ Current civil unrest

THE CHANGING WORLD MAP

DECOLONIZATION

In 1950, large areas of the world remained under the control of a handful of European countries (*page xxviii*). The process of decolonization had begun in Asia, where, following the Second World War, much of south and southeast Asia sought and achieved self-determination. In the 1960s, a host of African states achieved independence, so that by 1965, most of the larger tracts of the European overseas empires had been substantially eroded. The final major stage in decolonization came with the break-up of the Soviet Union and the Eastern bloc after 1990. The process continues today as the last toeholds of European colonialism, often tiny island nations, press increasingly for independence.

Iran is one of the world's true theocracies; Islam has an impact on every aspect of political life.

Saddam Hussein overthrew his predecessor in 1979. Since then he has promoted an extreme personality cult, with autocratic control over 21.8 million Iraqis.

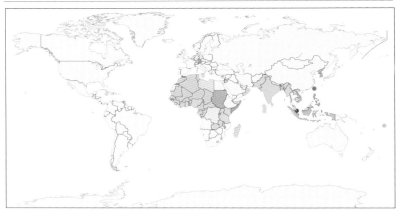

NEW NATIONS 1945–1965

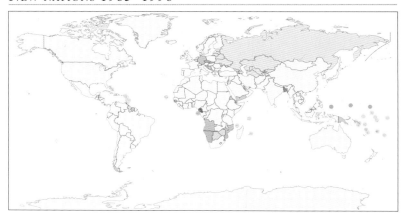

NEW NATIONS 1965–1996

Icons of communism, including statues of former leaders such as Lenin and Stalin, were destroyed when the Soviet bloc was dismantled in 1989, creating several new nations.

North Korea is an independent communist republic. Power is concentrated in the hands of Kim Jong Il.

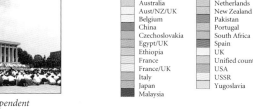

South Africa became a democracy in 1994, when elections ended over a century of white minority rule.

Administration at the time of independence

Australia	Netherlands
Aust/NZ/UK	New Zealand
Belgium	Pakistan
China	Portugal
Czechoslovakia	South Africa
Egypt/UK	Spain
Ethiopia	UK
France	Unified country
France/UK	USA
Italy	USSR
Japan	Yugoslavia
Malaysia	

In Brunei the Sultan has ruled by decree since 1962; power is closely tied to the royal family. The Sultan's brothers are responsible for finance and foreign affairs.

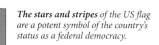

LINES ON THE MAP

THE DETERMINATION OF INTERNATIONAL BOUNDARIES can use a variety of criteria. Many of the borders between older states follow physical boundaries; some mirror religious and ethnic differences; others are the legacy of complex histories of conflict and colonialism, while others have been imposed by international agreements or arbitration.

POST-COLONIAL BORDERS

WHEN THE EUROPEAN COLONIAL EMPIRES IN AFRICA were dismantled during the second half of the 20th century, the outlines of the new African states mirrored colonial boundaries. These boundaries had been drawn up by colonial administrators, often based on inadequate geographical knowledge. Such arbitrary boundaries were imposed on people of different languages, racial groups, religions and customs. This confused legacy often led to civil and international war.

Dates from which current
boundaries have existed

1990–1993
1966–1989
1946–1965
1915–1945
1850–1914
1800–1849
Pre-1800

The conflict that has plagued many African countries since independence has caused millions of people to become refugees.

PHYSICAL BORDERS

MANY OF THE WORLD'S COUNTRIES are divided by physical borders: lakes, rivers, mountains. The demarcation of such boundaries can, however, lead to disputes. Control of waterways, water supplies and fisheries are frequent causes of international friction.

ENCLAVES

THE SHIFTING POLITICAL MAP over the course of history has frequently led to anomalous situations. Parts of national territories may become isolated by territorial agreement, forming an enclave. The West German part of the city of Berlin, which until 1989 lay several hundred kilometres within East German territory, was a famous example.

Since the independence of Lithuania and Belarus, the peoples of the Russian enclave of Kaliningrad have become physically isolated.

ANTARCTICA

WHEN ANTARCTIC EXPLORATION began a century ago, seven nations, Australia, Argentina, Britain, Chile, France, New Zealand and Norway, laid claim to the new territory. In 1961 the Antarctic Treaty, signed by 39 nations, agreed to hold all territorial claims in abeyance.

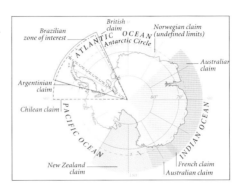

GEOMETRIC BORDERS

STRAIGHT LINES and lines of longitude and latitude have occasionally been used to determine international boundaries; and indeed the world's longest international boundary, between Canada and the USA follows the 49th Parallel for over one-third of its course. Many Canadian, American and Australian internal administrative boundaries are similarly determined using a geometric solution.

Different farming techniques in Canada and the USA clearly mark the course of the international boundary in this satellite map.

WORLD BOUNDARIES

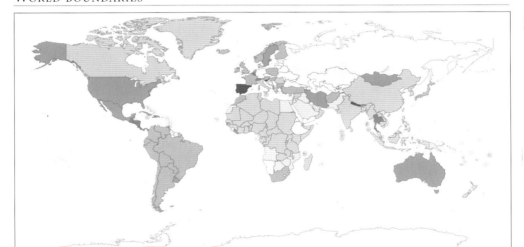

LAKE BORDERS
Countries which lie next to lakes usually fix their borders in the middle of the lake. Unusually the Lake Nyasa border between Malawi and Tanzania runs along Tanzania's shore.

Complicated agreements between colonial powers led to the awkward division of Lake Nyasa.

RIVER BORDERS
Rivers alone account for one-sixth of the world's borders. Many great rivers form boundaries between a number of countries. Changes in a river's course and interruptions of its natural flow can lead to disputes, particularly in areas where water is scarce. The centre of the river's course is the nominal boundary line.

The Danube forms all or part of the border between nine European nations.

MOUNTAIN BORDERS
Mountain ranges form natural barriers and are the basis for many major borders, particularly in Europe and Asia. The watershed is the conventional boundary demarcation line, but its accurate determination is often problematic.

The Pyrenees form a natural mountain border between France and Spain.

SHIFTING BOUNDARIES – POLAND

BORDERS BETWEEN COUNTRIES can change dramatically over time. The nations of eastern Europe have been particularly affected by changing boundaries. Poland is an example of a country whose boundaries have changed so significantly that it has literally moved around Europe. At the start of the 16th century, Poland was the largest nation in Europe. Between 1772 and 1795, it was absorbed into Prussia, Austria and Russia, and it effectively ceased to exist. After the First World War, Poland became an independent country once more, but its borders changed again after the Second World War following invasions by both Soviet Russia and Nazi Germany.

In 1634, Poland was the largest nation in Europe, its eastern boundary reaching towards Moscow.

From 1772–1795, Poland was gradually partitioned between Austria, Russia and Prussia. Its eastern boundary receded by over 100 miles (160 km).

Following the First World War, Poland was reinstated as an independent state, but it was less than half the size it had been in 1634.

After the Second World War the Baltic Sea border was extended westwards, but much of the eastern territory was annexed by Russia.

INTERNATIONAL DISPUTES

THERE ARE MORE THAN 60 DISPUTED BORDERS or territories in the world today. Although many of these disputes can be settled by peaceful negotiation, some areas have become a focus for international conflict. Ethnic tensions have been a major source of territorial disagreement throughout history, as has the ownership of, and access to, valuable natural resources. The turmoil of the post-colonial era in many parts of Africa is partly a result of the 19th century 'carve-up' of the continent, which created potential for conflict by drawing often arbitrary lines through linguistic and cultural areas.

JAMMU AND KASHMIR

DISPUTES OVER JAMMU AND KASHMIR have caused three serious wars between India and Pakistan since 1947. Pakistan wishes to annex the largely Muslim territory, while India refuses to cede any territory or to hold a referendum, and also lays claim to the entire territory. Most international maps show the 'line of control' agreed in 1972 as the *de facto* border. In addition, both Pakistan and India have territorial disputes with neighbouring China. The situation is further complicated by a Kashmiri independence movement, active since the late 1980s.

Indian army troops maintain their positions in the mountainous terrain of northern Kashmir.

NORTH AND SOUTH KOREA

SINCE 1953, the *de facto* border between North and South Korea has been a ceasefire line which straddles the 38th Parallel and is designated as a demilitarized zone. Both countries have heavy fortifications and troop concentrations behind this zone.

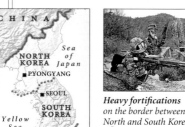

Heavy fortifications on the border between North and South Korea.

CYPRUS

CYPRUS WAS PARTITIONED in 1974, following an invasion by Turkish troops. The south is now the Greek Cypriot Republic of Cyprus, while the self-proclaimed Turkish Republic of Northern Cyprus is recognized only by Turkey.

The so-called 'green line' divides Cyprus into Greek and Turkish sectors.

TURKISH REPUBLIC OF NORTHERN CYPRUS

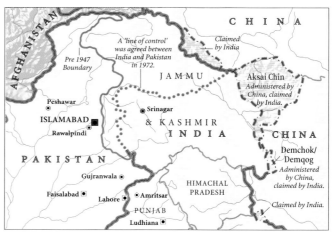

THE FALKLAND ISLANDS

THE BRITISH DEPENDENT TERRITORY of the Falkland Islands was invaded by Argentina in 1982, sparking a full-scale war with the UK. In 1995, the UK and Argentina reached an agreement on the exploitation of oil reserves around the islands.

British warships in Falkland Sound during the 1982 war with Argentina.

ISRAEL

ISRAEL WAS CREATED IN 1948 following the 1947 UN Resolution (147) on Palestine. Until 1979 Israel had no borders, only ceasefire lines from a series of wars in 1948, 1967 and 1973. Treaties with Egypt in 1979 and Jordan in 1994 led to these borders being defined and agreed. Negotiations over Israeli settlements in disputed territories such as the West Bank, and the issue of self-government for the Palestinians, continue.

- ■ Israeli settlement
- ● Major settlement
- △ Palestinian settlement
- ▨ Area under Palestinian control

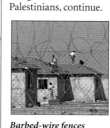

Barbed-wire fences surround a settlement in the Golan Heights.

YUGOSLAVIA

FOLLOWING THE DISINTEGRATION in 1991 of the communist state of Yugoslavia, the breakaway states of Croatia and Bosnia-Herzegovina came into conflict with the 'parent' state (consisting of Serbia and Montenegro). Warfare focused on ethnic and territorial ambitions in Bosnia. The tenuous Dayton Accord of 1995 sought to recognize the post-1990 borders, whilst providing for ethnic partition and required international peace-keeping troops to maintain the terms of the peace.

▨ Republika Srpska
▨ Federacija Bosna i Hercegovina

THE SPRATLY ISLANDS

THE SITE OF POTENTIAL OIL and natural gas reserves, the Spratly Islands in the South China Sea have been claimed by China, Vietnam, Taiwan, Malaysia and the Philippines since the Japanese gave up a wartime claim in 1951.

Most claimant states have small military garrisons on the Spratly Islands.

- ● Occupied by Taiwan
- ● Occupied by Philippines
- ● Occupied by Malaysia
- ● Occupied by China
- ● Occupied by Vietnam

Disputed territories and borders

- Countries involved in active territorial or border disputes
- Disputed borders
- Undefined borders
- Disputed territories

THE
BRITISH ISLES

LYING IN THE NORTH ATLANTIC OCEAN,
the British Isles were once joined to continental
Europe. Rugged mountains in the north and west
are the continuation of a Scandinavian mountain
chain. Chalk landscapes in southern England
were formed over 80 million years ago
when flooding seas deposited a thick
layer of chalk in the region. The British
Isles also bear the imprint of the
last Ice Age, which ended
10,000 years ago. Ice sheets
eroded highlands, carved
deep valleys and indented
the Scottish coastline.

Glen Coe, in the western Scottish
highlands, is a U-shaped valley. It is
typical of the northern and western
parts of the British Isles, where glaciers
shaped much of the landscape.

The South Downs in southeast England are a range of
chalk hills formed when the region was below sea level,
over 80 million years ago. The region boasts some of
the last remaining chalk grasslands in northern Europe
and is a designated Area of Outstanding Beauty.

**The wild and
mountainous** scenery
of southwest Ireland
bears testimony
to its glacial history.

SCALE 1:3,800,000
(projection: Lambert Conformal Conic)

Km
0 10 20 30 40 50 60 70

Miles
0 10 20 30 40 50 60 70

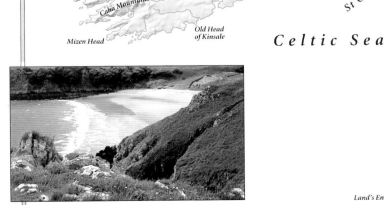

Wales has natural boundaries on three sides, with the
shores of Liverpool Bay to the north, the Irish Sea and
St George's Channel to the west, and the Bristol Channel
and the river Severn's estuary in the south.

Map labels

Herma Ness
Unst
Yell
Mainland *Shetland Islands*
Sumburgh Head

Orkney Islands
Westray
Sanday
Stronsay
Mainland
Hoy
Pentland Firth
Dunnet Head

Outer Hebrides
Butt of Lewis
Isle of Lewis
Harris
North Uist
South Uist
Sea of the Hebrides
Isle of Skye
Rhum
Barra Head
Coll
Tiree
Isle of Mull
Colonsay
Jura
Islay
Sound of Jura
Inner Hebrides

Cape Wrath
The Minch
The Little Minch

North West Highlands
Beinn Dearg 1084m
Moray Firth
Buchan Ness
Loch Ness
Cairngorm Mountains
Ben Macdui 1309m
Dee
Grampian Mountains
Ben Nevis 1343m
Loch Ericht
Glen Coe
Loch Awe
Loch Tay
Tay
Sidlaw Hills
Firth of Tay
Firth of Lorn
Ochil Hills
Loch Lomond
Firth of Forth
Isle of Arran
Firth of Clyde
Kintyre
Clyde
Pentland Hills
Tweed
St Abb's Head
Holy Island

Southern Uplands
Merrick 843m
Cheviot Hills
Dee
Solway Firth
Esk
Eden
Tyne
Wear
NORTH SEA

Malin Head
Bloody Foreland
Lough Foyle
Sperrin Mtns
Sawel 683m
Blue Stack Mtns
Sperrin Mtns
Inishowen Mountains
Lough Neagh
North Channel
Donegal Bay
Dartry Mtns
Lower Lough Erne
Upper Lough Erne
Strangford Lough
Ballyquintin Point
Point of Ayre
St Bees Head
Scafell Pike 977m
Cumbrian Mtns
Ullswater
Lake District
North York Moors
Flamborough Head
Erris Head
Slieve Gamph
Iron Mtns
Mourne Mtns
Slieve Donard 852m
Calf of Man
Isle of Man
Lake Windermere
Yorkshire Dales
Swale
The Wolds
Dundalk Bay
Derwent
Partry Mtns
Lough Mask
Lough Corrib
Lough Ree
Liffey
Dublin Bay
Irish Sea
Morecambe Bay
Wharfe
Pennines
Ribble
Ouse
Spurn Head
Connemara
Slyne Head
Galway Bay
Burren
Liscannor Bay
Slieve Aughty Mtns
Lough Derg
Slieve Bloom Mtns
Wicklow Mountains
Lugnaquillia Mountain 926m
Wicklow Head
Holy Island
Anglesey
Liverpool Bay
Mersey
Peak District
Dee
Don
Trent
Derwent
The Wolds
Humber

Ireland

Loop Head
Nore
Barrow
Suir
Shannon
Galty Mtns
Blackwater
Boggeragh Mtns
Carrauntoohil 1038m
Macgillycuddy's Reeks
Caha Mountains
Dingle Bay
Mizen Head
Old Head of Kinsale

Wexford Bay
Carnsore Point
St George's Channel
St David's Head
Cardigan Bay
Snowdonia
Snowdon 1085m
Cadair Idris 893m
Cambrian Mountains

Britain

Trent
Nene
Welland
Rutland Water
The Wash
The Broads
Yare
East Anglia
Witham
The Fens
Great Ouse
Avon
Malvern Hills
Severn
Cotswold Hills
Thames
Chiltern Hills
Thames
Isle of Sheppey
North Foreland
Brecon Beacons Pen y Fan 886m
Black Mtns
Wye
Gower
Avon
Mendip Hills
Kennet
North Downs
The Weald
Dungeness
Strait of Dover
Lundy
Bristol Channel
Hartland Point
Exmoor
Quantock Hills
Salisbury Plain
South Downs
New Forest
The Solent
Selsey Bill
Beachy Head
High Willhays 621m
Dartmoor
Exe
Lyme Bay
Portland Bill
Isle Of Wight
Bodmin Moor
Tor Bay
Start Point
Land's End
Falmouth Bay
Isles of Scilly
Lizard Point

Celtic Sea
ATLANTIC OCEAN
English Channel

Guernsey
Channel Islands
Jersey

POLITICAL BRITISH ISLES

THE UNITED KINGDOM'S SYSTEM OF GOVERNMENT has evolved over a long period, uninterrupted by any successful foreign invasion since 1066. Democracy takes the form of a constitutional monarchy, in which the monarch is a passive figurehead. The identity of the UK is being challenged by the prospect of a federal Europe, by the establishment of national assemblies in Scotland and Wales and by the introduction of an assembly in Northern Ireland which represents Unionist and Republican views. The Republic of Ireland grew out of the Irish Free State, established in 1921, and has become an independent democracy with membership of the UN and the EU. The Anglo-Irish Accord of 1985 established a permanent cabinet-level channel for dialogue between Britain and Ireland.

1 CENTRAL SCOTLAND

CLACKMANNANSHIRE · WEST DUNBARTONSHIRE · EAST DUNBARTONSHIRE · NORTH LANARKSHIRE · FALKIRK · INVERCLYDE · GLASGOW · WEST LOTHIAN · EDINBURGH · RENFREWSHIRE · EAST RENFREWSHIRE · MIDLOTHIAN

2 THE NORTHEAST

NORTH TYNESIDE · NEWCASTLE UPON TYNE · SOUTH TYNESIDE · GATESHEAD · SUNDERLAND

3 TEESSIDE

HARTLEPOOL · STOCKTON-ON-TEES · DARLINGTON · MIDDLESBROUGH · REDCAR AND CLEVELAND

4 THE NORTHWEST

ROCHDALE · BURY · OLDHAM · BOLTON · WIGAN · SALFORD · TAMESIDE · SEFTO[N] · ST HELENS · TRAFFORD · MANCHESTER · STOCKPORT · KNOWSLEY · LIVERPOOL · WIRRAL

UK ADMINISTRATIVE REGIONS
The UK radically reformed its administrative structure in the mid-1990s. A single-tier system of unitary authorities for local government was introduced for Scotland and Wales and the most densely-populated parts of England. The traditional two-tier system of counties subdivided into districts remains in the more rural parts of England. Northern Ireland has had a system of unitary authorities since 1972, although the county names are still commonly used.

SCALE 1:4,200,000
(projection: Lambert Conformal Conic)

Km
0 5 10 20 30 40 50 60 70 80

Miles
0 5 10 20 30 40 50 60 70 80

REPUBLIC OF IRELAND ADMINISTRATIVE REGIONS
The Republic of Ireland has been divided into 26 counties since independence in 1921. When the six counties of Northern Ireland were included, the island could be divided into the four historic provinces of Ulster, Connaught, Leinster and Munster (see map of Ireland on page xliv), although these have little or no administrative function today.

5 SOUTH WALES

MERTHYR TYDFIL · BLAENAU GWENT · TORFAEN · NEATH PORT TALBOT · RHONDDA CYNON TAFF · CAERPHILLY · SWANSEA · NEWPORT · BRIDGEND · CARDIFF · THE VALE OF GLAMORGAN

6 THE WEST MIDLANDS

WOLVERHAMPTON · WALSALL · DUDLEY · SANDWELL · BIRMINGHAM · SOLIHULL · COVENTRY

GUERNSEY (British Crown dependency)

JERSEY (British Crown dependency)

GREATER LONDON ADMINISTRATIVE REGIONS
London is divided into 32 boroughs (plus the Corporation of the City of London), which effectively have the same status as other unitary authorities in the UK. Until the Mayor of London elections in 2000, London had not had a directly elected council since the abolition of the Greater London Council (GLC) in 1986.

7 GREATER LONDON

1. HAMMERSMITH & FULHAM
2. KENSINGTON & CHELSEA
3. WESTMINSTER
4. ISLINGTON
5. HACKNEY
6. CITY OF LONDON
7. TOWER HAMLETS
8. SOUTHWARK
9. WANDSWORTH

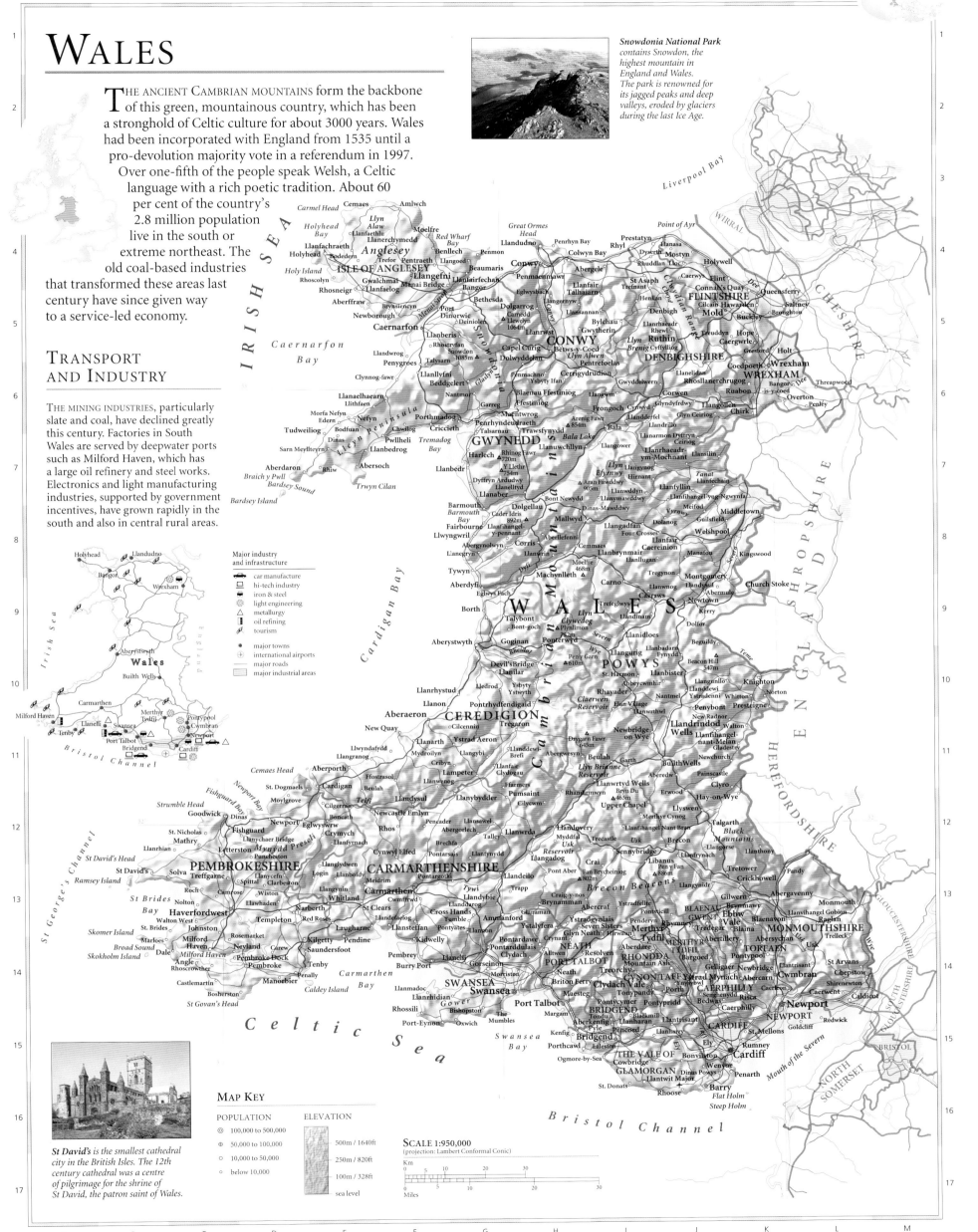

WALES

THE ANCIENT CAMBRIAN MOUNTAINS form the backbone of this green, mountainous country, which has been a stronghold of Celtic culture for about 3000 years. Wales had been incorporated with England from 1535 until a pro-devolution majority vote in a referendum in 1997. Over one-fifth of the people speak Welsh, a Celtic language with a rich poetic tradition. About 60 per cent of the country's 2.8 million population live in the south or extreme northeast. The old coal-based industries that transformed these areas last century have since given way to a service-led economy.

TRANSPORT AND INDUSTRY

THE MINING INDUSTRIES, particularly slate and coal, have declined greatly this century. Factories in South Wales are served by deepwater ports such as Milford Haven, which has a large oil refinery and steel works. Electronics and light manufacturing industries, supported by government incentives, have grown rapidly in the south and also in central rural areas.

Snowdonia National Park contains Snowdon, the highest mountain in England and Wales. The park is renowned for its jagged peaks and deep valleys, eroded by glaciers during the last Ice Age.

St David's is the smallest cathedral city in the British Isles. The 12th century cathedral was a centre of pilgrimage for the shrine of St David, the patron saint of Wales.

Major industry and infrastructure
- car manufacture
- hi-tech industry
- iron & steel
- light engineering
- metallurgy
- oil refining
- tourism
- major towns
- international airports
- major roads
- major industrial areas

MAP KEY

POPULATION
- 100,000 to 500,000
- 50,000 to 100,000
- 10,000 to 50,000
- below 10,000

ELEVATION
- 500m / 1640ft
- 250m / 820ft
- 100m / 328ft
- sea level

SCALE 1:950,000
(projection: Lambert Conformal Conic)

Km 0 5 10 20 30
Miles 0 5 10 20 30

SOUTHERN ENGLAND

SOUTHERN ENGLAND is the most affluent part of the British Isles, benefiting from close proximity to Europe, fertile agricultural land, and the capital, London, as a focus of wealth, political power and population. The physical landscape varies dramatically from the bleak uplands of the southwestern Cornish peninsula through the rolling Cotswold Hills to the flat, often marshy, expanses of Essex.

The southeast of England is the most densely populated region of the UK, and the growth of industries such as communications and financial services since the 1980s, has put considerable strain on transport and housing provision, with the building of new infrastructure becoming an issue of political controversy in the 1990s.

The city of Bath is built on the site of the Roman spa, Aquae Sulis. It is one of the most architecturally distinguished of British cities, noted for its elegant Georgian crescents built from the distinctive honey-coloured local stone.

MAP KEY

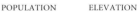

POPULATION

- ■ above 5 million
- ◼ 1 million to 5 million
- ◉ 500,000 to 1 million
- ◎ 100,000 to 500,000
- ⊕ 50,000 to 100,000
- ○ 10,000 to 50,000
- ∘ below 10,000

ELEVATION

- 500m / 1640ft
- 250m / 820ft
- 100m / 328ft
- sea level

Clifton Suspension Bridge, which spans the Avon Gorge, was designed by the great Victorian engineer, Isambard Kingdom Brunel and completed in 1864. It served as an important transport link for Bristol's then growing import and export trade in meat, tobacco and fruit.

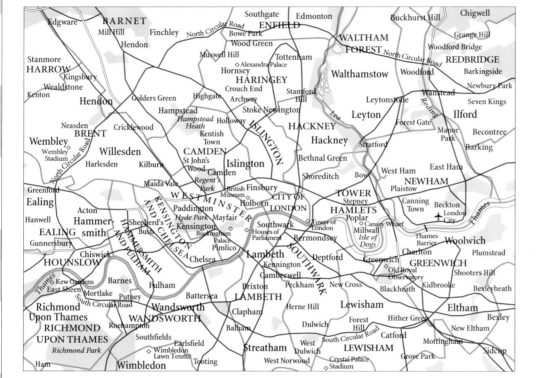

LONDON

SCALE 1:230,000

0 ————— 5 Km

0 ————— 5 Miles

The cliffs of north Devon bear the full force of the Atlantic Ocean. The entire British land mass is gradually tilting, with uplift continuing on the west coast, while the east faces the increasing threat of flooding by the sea.

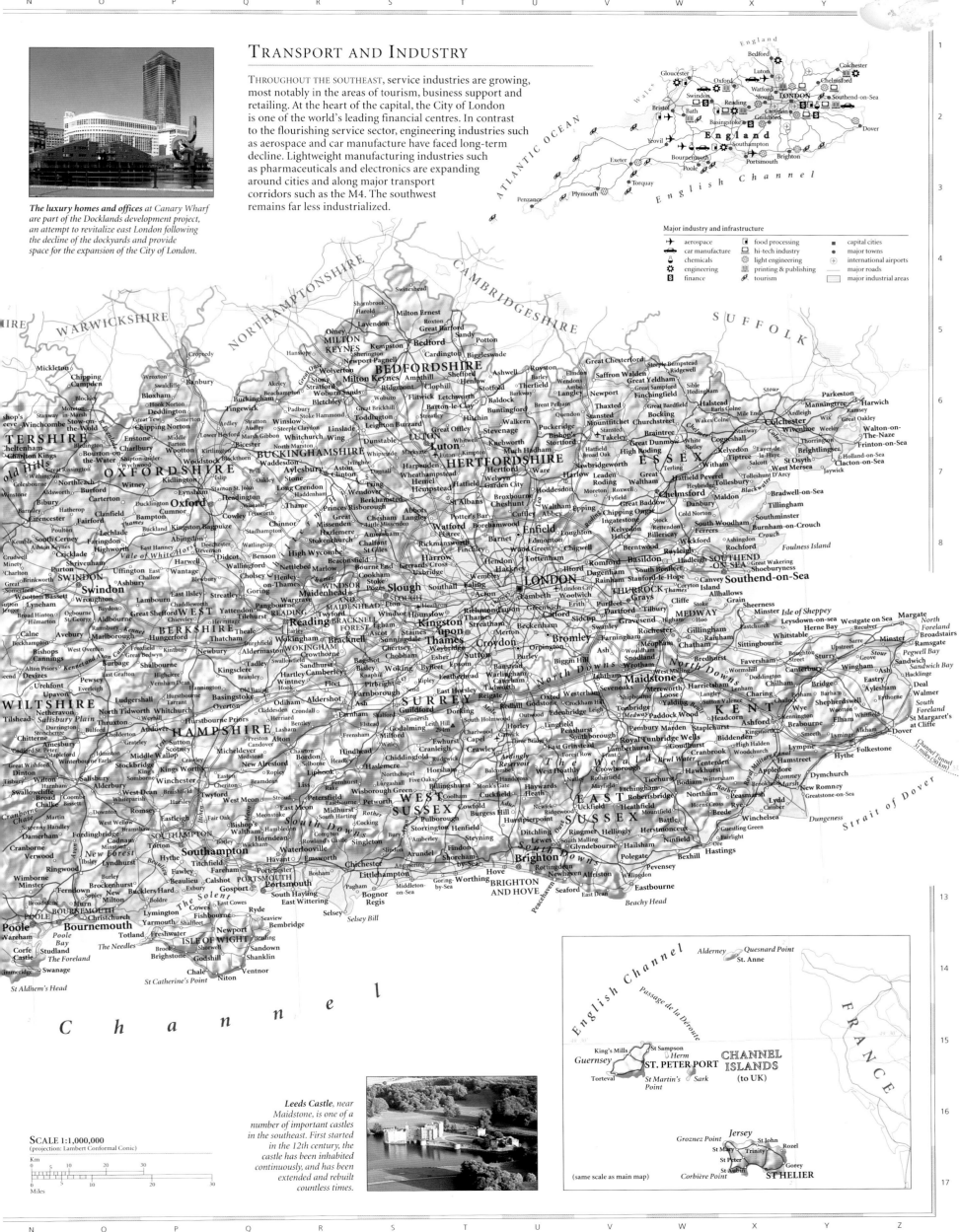

TRANSPORT AND INDUSTRY

THROUGHOUT THE SOUTHEAST, service industries are growing, most notably in the areas of tourism, business support and retailing. At the heart of the capital, the City of London is one of the world's leading financial centres. In contrast to the flourishing service sector, engineering industries such as aerospace and car manufacture have faced long-term decline. Lightweight manufacturing industries such as pharmaceuticals and electronics are expanding around cities and along major transport corridors such as the M4. The southwest remains far less industrialized.

The luxury homes and offices at Canary Wharf are part of the Docklands development project, an attempt to revitalize east London following the decline of the dockyards and provide space for the expansion of the City of London.

Major industry and infrastructure

- ✈ aerospace
- 🚗 car manufacture
- chemicals
- ⚙ engineering
- Ⓢ finance
- food processing
- hi-tech industry
- light engineering
- printing & publishing
- tourism
- ■ capital cities
- ● major towns
- ✛ international airports
- major roads
- major industrial areas

Leeds Castle, near Maidstone, is one of a number of important castles in the southeast. First started in the 12th century, the castle has been inhabited continuously, and has been extended and rebuilt countless times.

CHANNEL ISLANDS (to UK)

(same scale as main map)

SCALE 1:1,000,000
(projection: Lambert Conformal Conic)

CENTRAL ENGLAND

THE INDUSTRIAL REGIONS around Birmingham, Coventry and the Potteries of Stoke-on-Trent, the dramatic hills of the Derbyshire's Peak District, and the windy fenlands of Lincolnshire and Norfolk, all illustrate the great diversity of England's central counties. Many of the most important developments of the Industrial Revolution occurred in this area, including the construction of the canal system. The traditional industrial heartland remains the most populous part of this region with far lower densities in East Anglia, although counties such as Cambridgeshire have recently seen large influxes of people from the crowded southeast.

TRANSPORT AND INDUSTRY

THE MASS PRODUCTION of iron and steel, ceramics and textiles was important in this region from the end of the 18th century onwards. This great industrial base provided an ideal location for automotive manufacturing throughout much of the 20th century, particularly around Coventry and Birmingham. In recent years, the growth of hi-tech and service industries, particularly in and around Cambridge, has attracted new investment, while agriculture remains important in both Hereford and the East Anglian counties.

Major industry and infrastructure

- ✈ aerospace
- 🍺 brewing
- 🚗 car manufacture
- ceramics
- chemicals
- engineering
- fish processing
- 🍴 food processing
- △ metallurgy
- 💊 pharmaceuticals
- printing & publishing
- textiles
- hi-tech industry
- major towns
- ✈ international airports
- major roads
- major industrial areas

THE WEST MIDLANDS

SCALE 1:560,000

0   5   10 Km
0   5   10 Miles

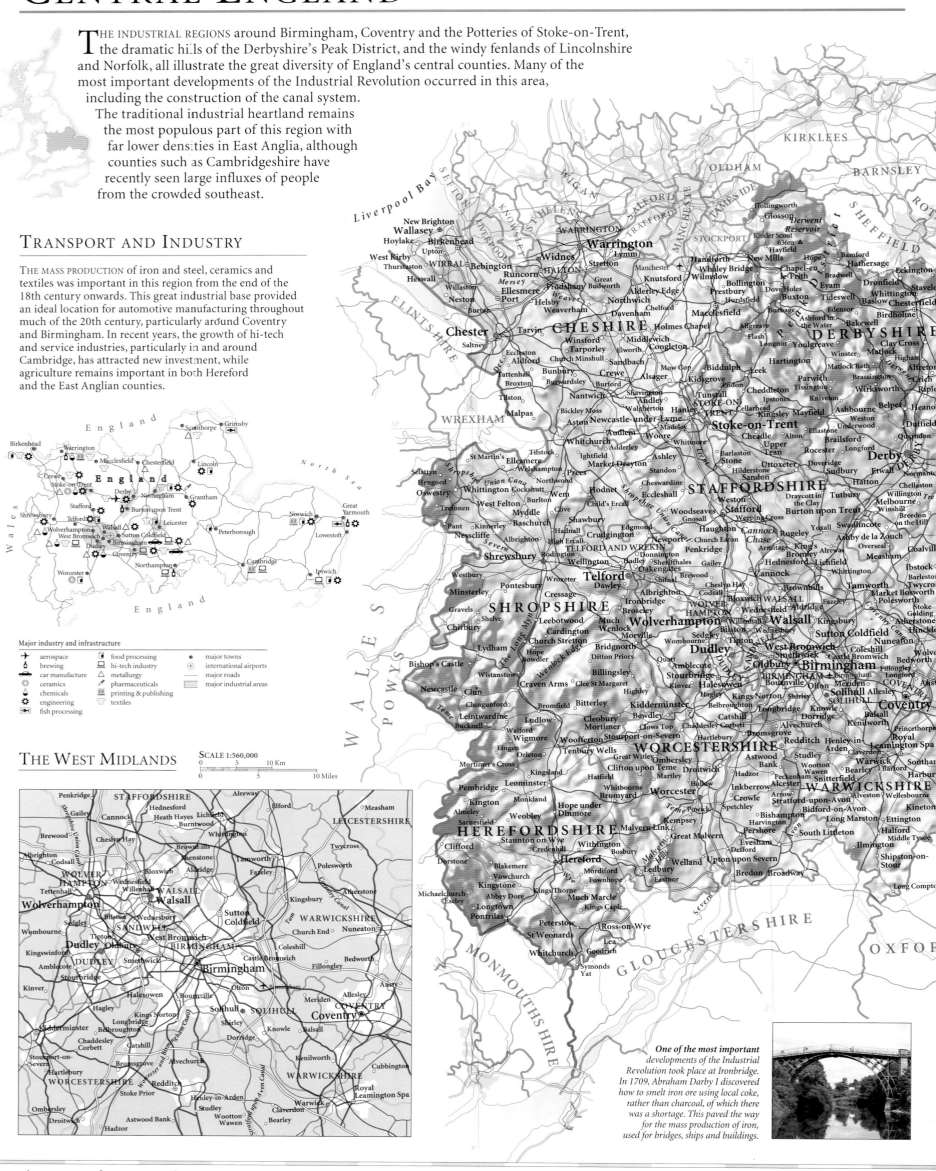

One of the most important developments of the Industrial Revolution took place at Ironbridge. In 1709, Abraham Darby I discovered how to smelt iron ore using local coke, rather than charcoal, of which there was a shortage. This paved the way for the mass production of iron, used for bridges, ships and buildings.

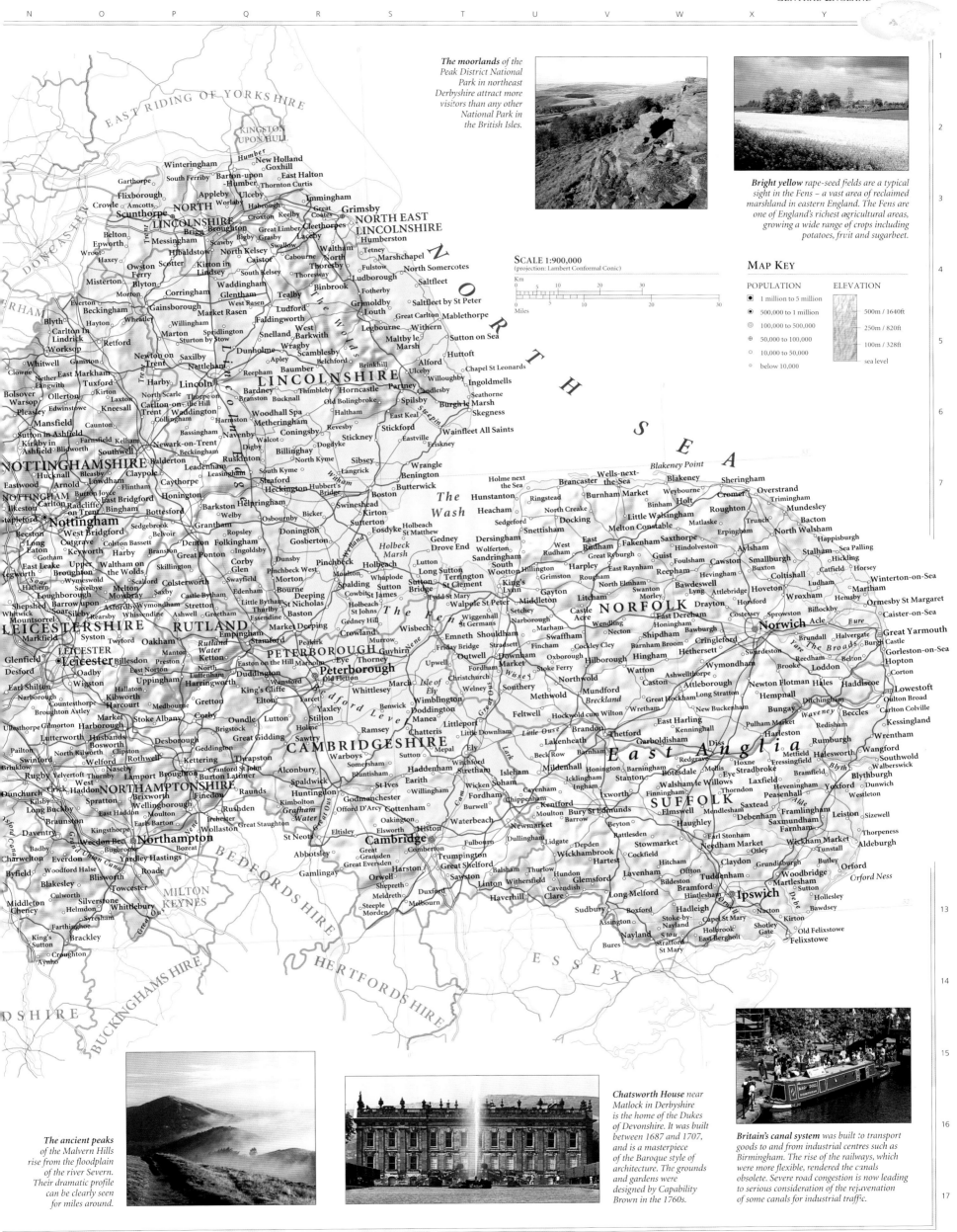

The moorlands of the Peak District National Park in northeast Derbyshire attract more visitors than any other National Park in the British Isles.

Bright yellow rape-seed fields are a typical sight in the Fens – a vast area of reclaimed marshland in eastern England. The Fens are one of England's richest agricultural areas, growing a wide range of crops including potatoes, fruit and sugarbeet.

SCALE 1:900,000
(projection: Lambert Conformal Conic)

Km
0   5   10   20   30

Miles
0   10   20   30

MAP KEY

POPULATION
- 1 million to 5 million
- 500,000 to 1 million
- 100,000 to 500,000
- 50,000 to 100,000
- 10,000 to 50,000
- below 10,000

ELEVATION
- 500m / 1640ft
- 250m / 820ft
- 100m / 328ft
- sea level

The ancient peaks of the Malvern Hills rise from the floodplain of the river Severn. Their dramatic profile can be clearly seen for miles around.

Chatsworth House near Matlock in Derbyshire is the home of the Dukes of Devonshire. It was built between 1687 and 1707, and is a masterpiece of the Baroque style of architecture. The grounds and gardens were designed by Capability Brown in the 1760s.

Britain's canal system was built to transport goods to and from industrial centres such as Birmingham. The rise of the railways, which were more flexible, rendered the canals obsolete. Severe road congestion is now leading to serious consideration of the rejuvenation of some canals for industrial traffic.

A B C D E F G H I J K L M

NORTHERN ENGLAND

THE DRAMATIC PENNINE RANGE provides a central upland spine for northern England's fine and varied landscape, flanked to the west by the famous Lake District. The modern world's first industrial cities, including Manchester, Sheffield and Bradford, rose to greatness across this region from the mid 18th century, fuelled by local coal fields, with each specializing in particular trades including textiles, metal products and shipbuilding. The decline of manufacturing – particularly in the heavy industries – in the 20th century hit northern England hard, leading to prolonged economic depression. However, following major economic restructuring in the late 1980s, the north has been highly successful in attracting foreign investment. The great industrial cities such as Manchester, Liverpool, Leeds and Newcastle have maintained their position at the centre of northern England's cultural and economic life.

***Blackpool's famous tower**, built in 1895, stands as a testament to the rise of the tourist industry in late 19th century Britain, as workers from the nearby Lancashire cotton mills and Yorkshire woollen mills flocked to the town on their annual holidays. Blackpool remains a popular tourist resort today.*

TRANSPORT AND INDUSTRY

ONCE THE CENTRE of heavy manufacturing, service industries now dominate the northern economy, following a difficult period of transition. Massive inward investment by multinational companies has helped northern England retain a majority share of current manufacturing activity in the UK. New light engineering and car production plants have developed in and around the region's cities, alongside more traditional industries such as iron and steel, and textiles.

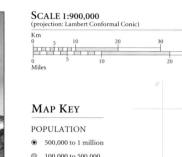

***The Laxey Wheel** on the Isle of Man – 72 ft (22 m) high is the largest waterwheel in the world. During the 19th century it was used to pump water from the nearby iron ore mines. The 'Three Legs of Man' on the front of the wheel is an ancient symbol, first thought to have been used by the Vikings.*

SCALE 1:900,000
(projection: Lambert Conformal Conic)

Km 0 5 10 20 30
Miles 0 5 10 20 30

MAP KEY

POPULATION

- 500,000 to 1 million
- 100,000 to 500,000
- 50,000 to 100,000
- 10,000 to 50,000
- below 10,000

ELEVATION

- 500m / 1640ft
- 250m / 820ft
- 100m / 328ft
- sea level

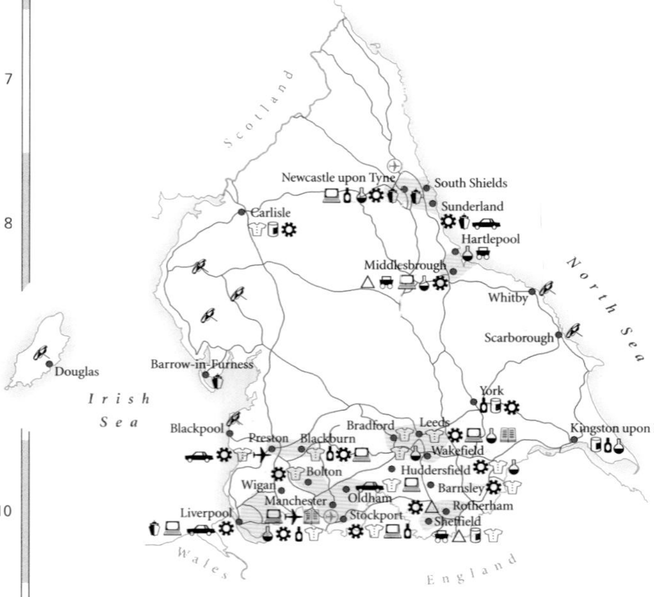

Major industry and infrastructure

aerospace	iron & steel	major towns
brewing	metallurgy	international airports
car manufacture	printing & publishing	major roads
chemicals	shipbuilding	major industrial areas
engineering	textiles	
food processing	tourism	
hi-tech industry		

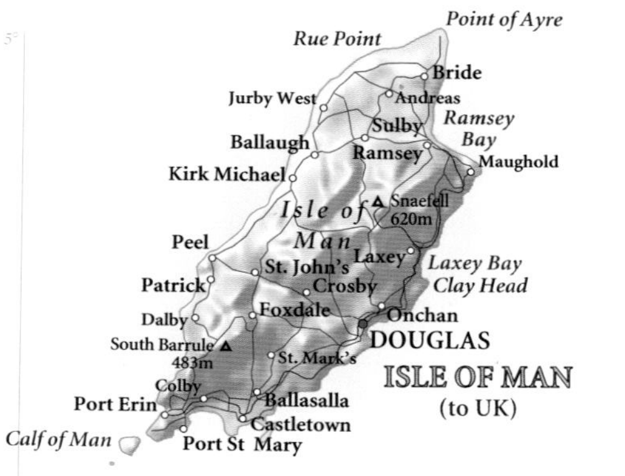

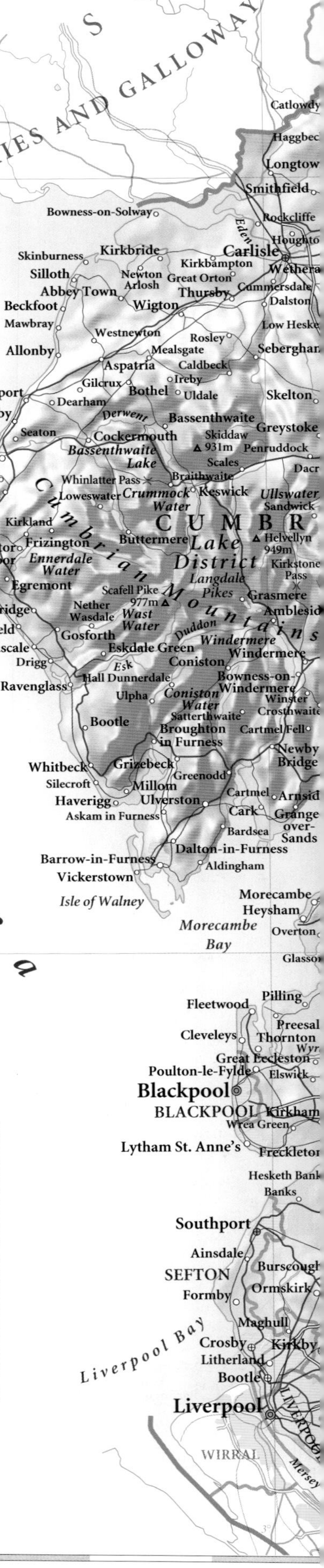

THE NORTHWEST

SCALE 1:560,000
0 5 10 Km
0 5 10 Miles

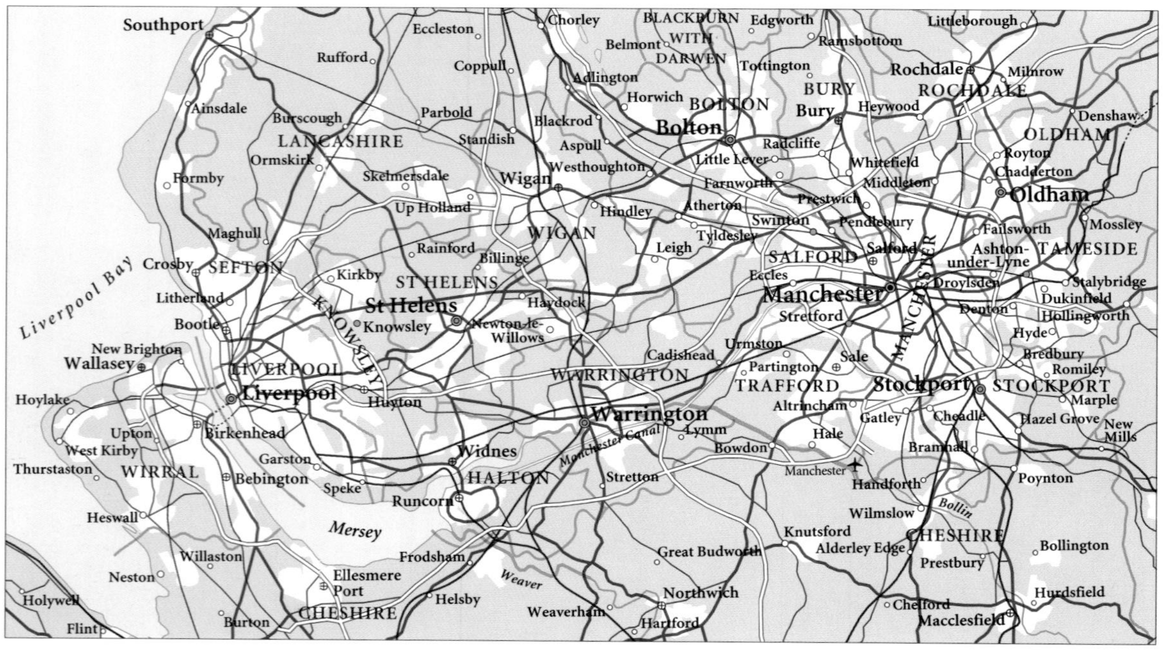

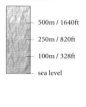

***The spectacular gothic-revival** architecture of Manchester Town Hall recalls the great wealth and civic pride of the city at the height of the Industrial Revolution.*

A B C D E F G H I J K L M

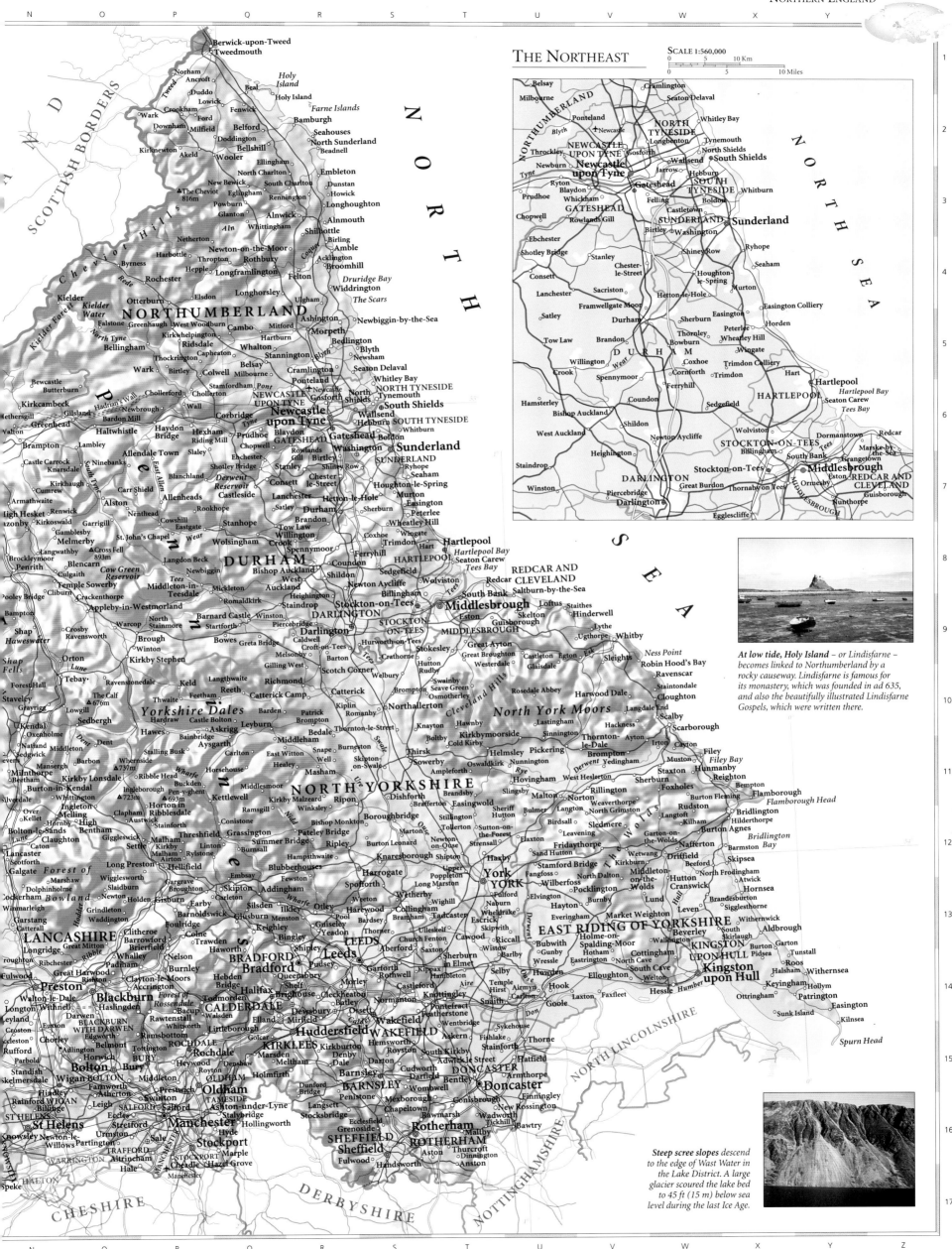

At low tide, Holy Island – or Lindisfarne – becomes linked to Northumberland by a rocky causeway. Lindisfarne is famous for its monastery, which was founded in ad 635, and also the beautifully illustrated Lindisfarne Gospels, which were written there.

Steep scree slopes descend to the edge of Wast Water in the Lake District. A large glacier scoured the lake bed to 45 ft (15 m) below sea level during the last Ice Age.

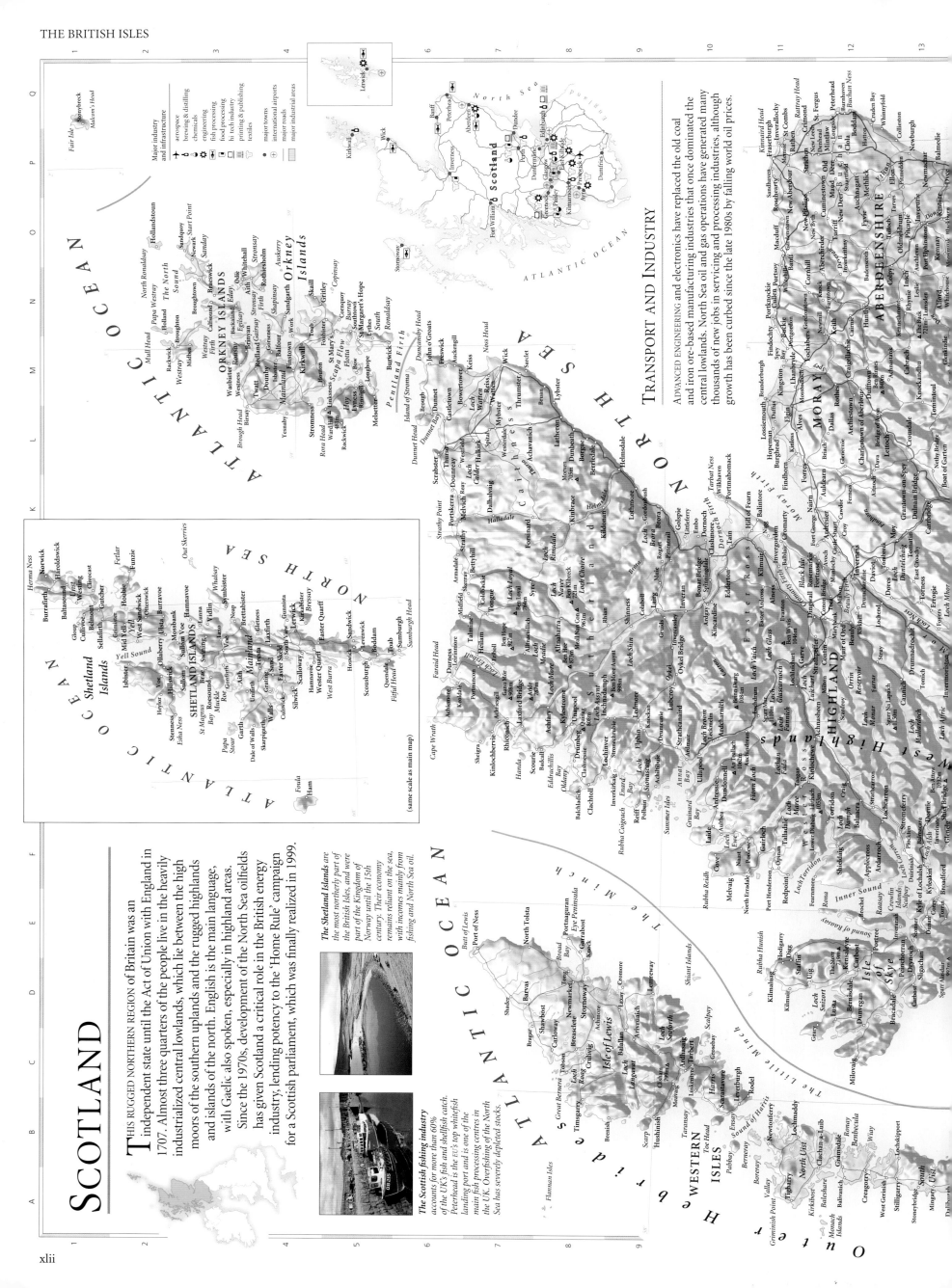

SCOTLAND

THIS RUGGED NORTHERN REGION of Britain was an independent state until the Act of Union with England in 1707. Almost three quarters of the people live in the heavily industrialized central lowlands, which lie between the high moors of the southern uplands and the rugged highlands and islands of the north. English is the main language, with Gaelic also spoken, especially in highland areas. Since the 1970s, development of the North Sea oilfields has given Scotland a critical role in the British energy industry, lending potency to the 'Home Rule' campaign for a Scottish parliament, which was finally realized in 1999.

The Shetland Islands are the most northerly part of the British Isles, and were part of the Kingdom of Norway until the 15th century. Their economy remains reliant on the sea, with incomes mainly from fishing and North Sea oil.

The Scottish fishing industry accounts for more than 60% of the UK's fish and shellfish catch. Peterhead is the EU's top whitefish landing port and is one of the main fish processing centres in the UK. Overfishing of the North Sea has severely depleted stocks.

TRANSPORT AND INDUSTRY

ADVANCED ENGINEERING and electronics have replaced the old coal and iron ore-based manufacturing industries that once dominated the central lowlands. North Sea oil and gas operations have generated many thousands of new jobs in servicing and processing industries, although growth has been curbed since the late 1980s by falling world oil prices.

Major industry and infrastructure
- aerospace
- brewing & distilling
- chemicals
- engineering
- fish processing
- food processing
- hi tech industry
- printing & publishing
- textiles
- major towns
- international airports
- major roads
- major industrial areas

(same scale as main map)

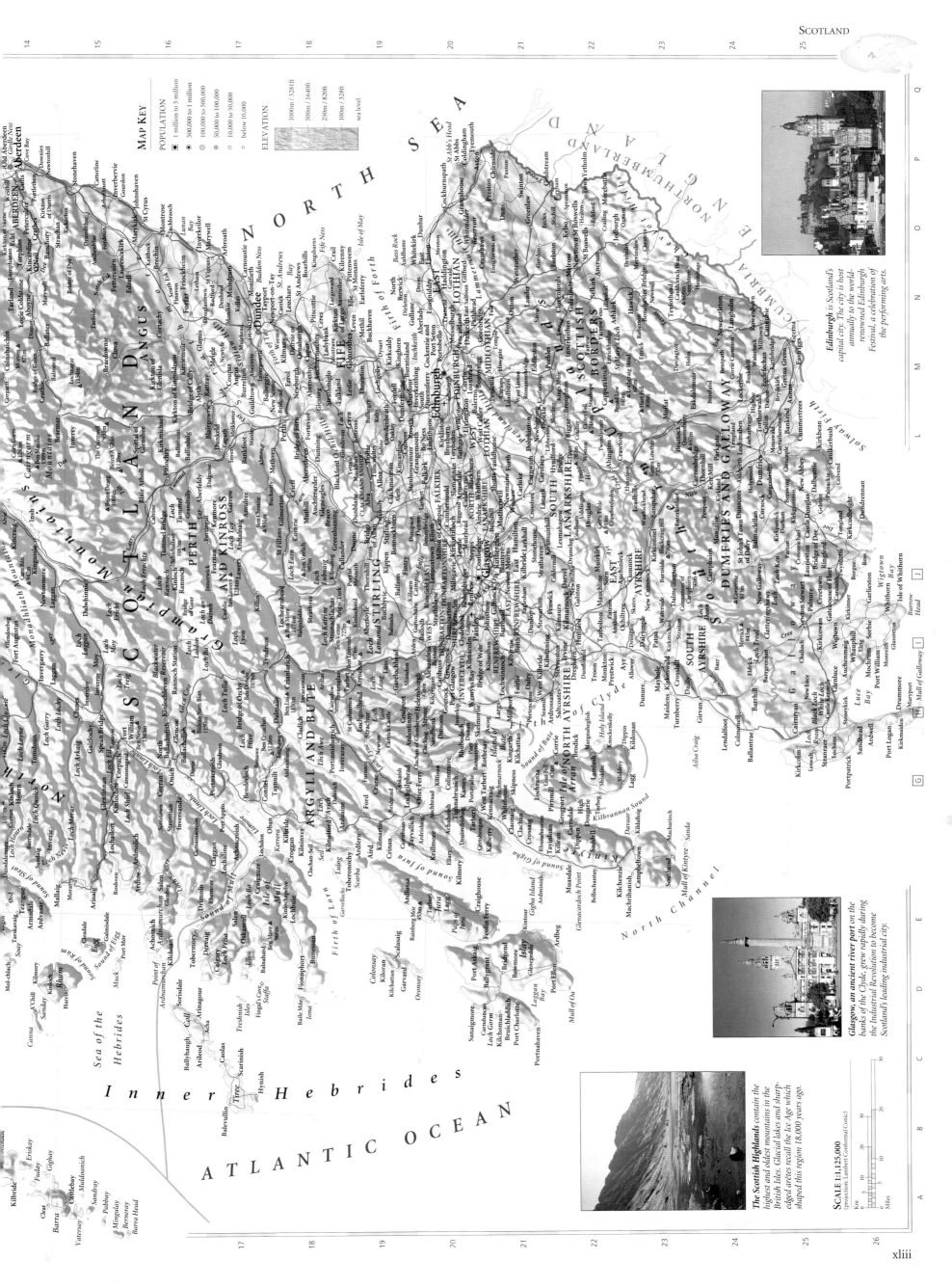

MAP KEY

POPULATION
- 1 million to 5 million
- 500,000 to 1 million
- 100,000 to 500,000
- 50,000 to 100,000
- 10,000 to 50,000
- below 10,000

ELEVATION
- 1000m / 3281ft
- 500m / 1640ft
- 250m / 820ft
- 100m / 328ft
- sea level

Edinburgh is Scotland's capital city. The city is host annually to the world-renowned Edinburgh Festival, a celebration of the performing arts.

Glasgow, an ancient river port on the banks of the Clyde, grew rapidly during the Industrial Revolution to become Scotland's leading industrial city.

The Scottish Highlands contain the highest and oldest mountains in the British Isles. Glacial lakes and sharp-edged arêtes recall the Ice Age which shaped this region 18,000 years ago.

SCALE 1:1,125,000
(Projection: Lambert Conformal (Conic))

IRELAND

THE UNSPOILT SCENERY and folk culture of Ireland reflect its remote position on the western fringe of Europe, and contrast with the so-called 'troubles' which have long hindered its development. The Republic of Ireland emerged from British rule as a free state in 1921 and is separated from Northern Ireland by the UK's only land border. Coastal hill ranges encircle a central undulating plain, strewn with many lakes and bogs. The Republic has benefited from EU grants since the 1980s, which have contributed to the growth of industry and infrastructure.

MAP KEY

POPULATION

◉ 100,000 to 500,000
⊕ 50,000 to 100,000
○ 10,000 to 50,000
○ below 10,000

ELEVATION

1000m / 3281ft
500m / 1640ft
250m / 820ft
100m / 328ft
sea level

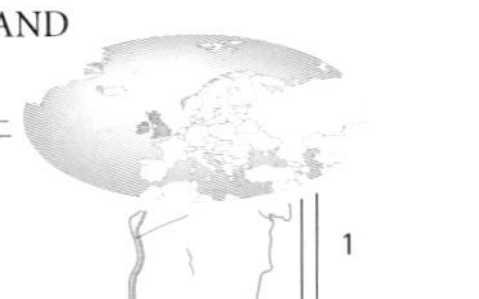

The Campanile in Trinity College, Dublin, was built by Sir Charles Lanyon, architect of Queen's College, Belfast. It is 98 ft (30 m) high.

The Burren is a massive limestone plateau in the northwest of County Clare. A wide range of Mediterranean and Alpine plants flourish in the pastures, near shallow lakes and in the cracks in the limestone pavement.

SCALE 1:1,600,000
(projection: Lambert Conformal Conic)

Km
0 10 20 30 40 50

Miles
0 10 20 30 40 50

TRANSPORT AND INDUSTRY

NORTHERN IRELAND'S industries are concentrated in Belfast, once a great textiles and shipbuilding centre which has faced chronic recession since the 1970s. Industrialization in the Republic of Ireland began properly in the 1950s. A broad range of goods are now produced for export near Dublin, and in many other larger towns.

Major industry and infrastructure

- ✈ aerospace
- 🍺 brewing
- chemicals
- ⚙ engineering
- food processing
- 🖥 hi-tech industry
- textiles
- tourism

- capital cities
- major towns
- ⊕ international airports
- major roads
- major industrial areas

Northern Ireland

REPUBLIC OF IRELAND

INDEX – BRITISH ISLES & IRELAND

THE PLACE NAMES OF THE BRITISH ISLES reflect the languages of both the present and the past. The distribution of these settlement names on maps indicates where these languages are now, and where they were once spoken. The early inhabitants of the British Isles were Celts. Their names now survive in the west; the region to which they were driven by successive invasions of Romans, Anglo-Saxons and Norwegian Vikings. The most immediately recognisable of these names are Welsh names. These are found both in north Wales, where the language is still the mother tongue of more than half a million people, and in the south, where the language generally spoken is now English. The familiar initial elements Llan– (church) and Aber– (river mouth, confluence) are found throughout Wales and many anglicised names on maps and signposts are now accompanied by their original Welsh forms: Cardiff (Caerdydd), Swansea (Abertawe), Carmarthen (Caerfyrddin).

Less than 100,000 people in Scotland still speak Gaelic. They are found principally in the Hebrides and the northwest highlands. Surviving Gaelic names are more widely dispersed throughout western Scotland as a whole. Some physical feature names are preserved in their Gaelic spelling, for example, Sgurr a 'Choire Ghlais – but most settlement names, and the names of prominent features such as Oban and Ben Nevis, have long been anglicised. However as in Wales, there is now increasing recognition of Gaelic spellings: Benbecula (Beinn na Faoghlia) and North Uist (Uibhist a'Tuath).

Most of the Irish Gaelic names in Ireland were systematically anglicised during the years of British rule and the language itself all but disappeared; barely 60,000 people in the western extremities of the country still speak Irish as their mother tongue. Since independence in 1922, the Irish government has tried to remedy this situation by decreeing Irish the official national language and making it a compulsory subject in schools. As a result, over half a million people in the island of Ireland now claim to be able to speak some Irish. A commission has also been set up by the Irish government to determine the true Irish form of every place name in the country and many of these are now being given recognition on maps, for example, Dublin (Baile Átha Cliath), Cork (Corcaigh) and Limerick (Luimneach). Very few names exist in Irish only. Examples are Dun Laoghaire (formerly Kingstown) and Cobh (formerly Queenstown). Typical anglicised Irish elements in place names are Bally- (Town) and Inish- (island).

Two lesser Celtic languages, both now dead, survive in a few place names: Cornish, with names beginning with Tre- (Village), and Manx with names prefaced by Balla-.

Little place name evidence remains of the Roman occupation of Britain. Though the Romans latinized the mainly Celtic names they found throughout the country, these soon disappeared as later Anglo-Saxon and Norwegian newcomers imposed their own names. Old Sarum is a rare example of a surviving Latin name. The Language continued to be used occasionally; Magna (big), Parva (little) and Super-Mare (on the sea) were added to place names to differentiate villages of the same name.

Anglo-Saxons began their invasion of southern Britain only thirty years after the Romans left in AD 410. Norwegian Viking invasions of Scotland and northern Britain followed in the late eighth and early ninth centuries. Thus it came about that Norwegian and Anglo-Saxon place names spread across the country from Shetland in the north, to Hampshire in the south and westwards to the Celtic fringe. These are the names that survive today, though their spellings are very different from the Old English forms recorded in the Domesday Book of 1086. The dividing line between the two linguistic strands is geographically complex but as a general rule it can be stated that names ending in –by and –thorpe are Norwegian in origin, while those with –ham and –ton are Anglo-Saxon.

The Norman Invasion of 1066 brought the French language with it. French, therefore, contributed in a minor way to the formation of place names in southern England; names with Beau- and Bel- (beautiful) being the most conspicuous. Norman French prepositions survive in such names as Ashby de la Zouch and Chapel en le Frith.

GLOSSARY OF ABBREVIATIONS

This glossary provides a guide to the abbreviations used in this Index.
For a full glossary and the main index please refer to page 215

anc. ancient	**N** north
C central	**prev.** previous
E east	**S** south
Fr. French	**UK** United Kingdom
hist. historical	**var.** variant
Ir. Irish	**W** west
Lat. Latin	**Wel.** Welsh

Symbol key		
◆ COUNTRY	◆ ADMINISTRATIVE REGION	▲ MOUNTAIN	◎ LAKE
◆ COUNTRY CAPITAL	○ DEPENDENT TERRITORY	✖ INTERNATIONAL AIRPORT	▲▲ MOUNTAIN RANGE	◎ RESERVOIR	❧ RIVER
○ DEPENDENT TERRITORY CAPITAL		

◆ COUNTRY ◇ DEPENDENT TERRITORY ◈ ADMINISTRATIVE REGION ▲ MOUNTAIN ◎ LAKE
● COUNTRY CAPITAL ○ DEPENDENT TERRITORY CAPITAL ✕ INTERNATIONAL AIRPORT ▲▲ MOUNTAIN RANGE ⊞ RESERVOIR ≈ RIVER

Broad Hinton – Colesbourne

xxxvii N9 **Broad Hinton** Wiltshire, S England, UK
xliii L22 **Broad Law** ▲ S Scotland, UK
xxxvi L14 **Broadmayne** Dorset, S England, UK
xxxv B14 **Broad Sound** *sound* SW Wales, UK
xxxvii Z10 **Broadstairs** Kent, SE England, UK
xxxix Y9 **Broads, The** *wetland* E England, UK
xxxvii N13 **Broadstone** Poole, S England, UK
xxxvi J13 **Broadway** Somerset, SW England, UK
xxxviii L14 **Broadway** Worcestershire, W England, UK
xxxvi L14 **Broadwey** Dorset, S England, UK
xxxvi K13 **Broadwindsor** Dorset, S England, UK
xlii E12 **Brochel** Highland, NW Scotland, UK
xxxvii O13 **Brockenhurst** Hampshire, S England, UK
xli N8 **Brockleymoor** Cumbria, NW England, UK
xliii G21 **Brodick** North Ayrshire, W Scotland, UK
xxxviii H11 **Bromfield** Shropshire, W England, UK
xxxvii U9 **Bromley** Bromley, SE England, UK
xxxiv L17 **Bromley** ◐ *London borough* SE England, UK
xli V11 **Brompton** North Yorkshire, N England, UK
xli S11 **Brompton** North Yorkshire, N England, UK
xxxvi I12 **Brompton Ralph** Somerset, SW England, UK
xxxvi H12 **Brompton Regis** Somerset, SW England, UK
xxxviii B16 **Bromsgrove** Worcestershire, W England, UK
xxxviii I12 **Bromyard** Herefordshire, W England, UK
xxxvii P14 **Brook** Isle of Wight, S England, UK
xxxix X10 **Brooke** Norfolk, E England, UK
xxxvii X12 **Brookland** Kent, SE England, UK
xli R4 **Broomhill** Northumberland, N England, UK
xlii G10 **Broom, Loch** *inlet* NW Scotland, UK
xlii K9 **Brora** Highland, N Scotland, UK
xlii J9 **Brora** ≈ N Scotland, UK
xlii K9 **Brora, Loch** ◎ N Scotland, UK
xxxviii I10 **Broseley** Shropshire, W England, UK
xliv D12 **Brosna** Kerry, SW Ireland
xliv I9 **Brosna** ≈ Westmeath, C Ireland
xli O9 **Brough** Cumbria, NW England, UK
xlii L6 **Brough** Highland, N Scotland, UK
xlii L3 **Brough Head** *island* N Scotland, UK
xliv L3 **Broughshane** Ballymena, NE Northern Ireland, UK
xli N14 **Broughton** Lancashire, NW England, UK
xxxix P11 **Broughton** Northamptonshire, C England, UK
xxxix P3 **Broughton** North Lincolnshire, N England, UK
xli P13 **Broughton** North Yorkshire, N England, UK
xlii M2 **Broughton** Orkney Islands, N Scotland, UK
xliii L21 **Broughton** The Borders, S Scotland, UK
xxxv K5 **Broughton** Flintshire, N Wales, UK
xxxix N10 **Broughton Astley** Leicestershire, C England, UK
xl L11 **Broughton in Furness** Cumbria, NW England, UK
xlii N3 **Broughtown** Orkney Islands, N Scotland, UK
xxxviii C13 **Brownhills** Walsall, C England, UK
xxxvi D14 **Brown Willy** *hill* SW England, UK
xxxvii T8 **Broxbourne** Hertfordshire, E England, UK
xliii L20 **Broxburn** City of Edinburgh, E Scotland, UK
xxxviii H7 **Broxton** Cheshire, W England, UK
xlii M7 **Bruan** Highland, N Scotland, UK
xxxvi J11 **Brue** ≈ SW England, UK
xliv F12 **Bruff** Limerick, SW Ireland
xliii D20 **Bruichladdich** Argyll and Bute, W Scotland, UK
xxxix Y9 **Brundall** Norfolk, E England, UK
xliv F12 **Bruree** Limerick, SW Ireland
xxxvi L12 **Bruton** Somerset, SW England, UK
xliii M24 **Brydekirk** Dumfries and Galloway, SW Scotland, UK
xxxv H13 **Brynamman** Carmarthenshire, S Wales, UK
xxxv I12 **Bryn Du** *hill* E Wales, UK
xxxv J13 **Brynmawr** Blaenau Gwent, SE Wales, UK
xxxv F5 **Brynsiencyn** Isle of Anglesey, NW Wales, UK
xli U14 **Bubwith** East Riding of Yorkshire, N England, UK
xlii Q12 **Buchan Ness** *headland* NE Scotland, UK
xliii K17 **Buchanty** Perth and Kinross, C Scotland, UK
xliii J19 **Buchlyvie** Stirling, C Scotland, UK
xli P11 **Buckden** North Yorkshire, N England, UK
xxxvi G15 **Buckfastleigh** Devon, SW England, UK
xliii M18 **Buckhaven** Fife, E Scotland, UK
xxxvi F5 **Buckhurst Hill** Redbridge, SE England, UK
xlii M11 **Buckie** Moray, NE Scotland, UK
xxxvii Q6 **Buckingham** Buckinghamshire, C England, UK
xxxvii Q7 **Buckinghamshire** ◐ *county* SE England, UK
xxxvii O8 **Buckland** Oxfordshire, C England, UK
xxxvi F12 **Buckland Brewer** Devon, SW England, UK
xxxvii P13 **Bucklers Hard** Hampshire, S England, UK
xxxv K5 **Buckley** Flintshire, N Wales, UK
xxxix R6 **Bucknall** Lincolnshire, E England, UK
xxxviii G12 **Bucknell** Shropshire, W England, UK
xlii P13 **Bucksburn** City of Aberdeen, NE Scotland, UK
xxxvi E12 **Buck's Cross** Devon, SW England, UK
xlii M13 **Buck, The** ▲ N Scotland, UK
xliii N17 **Buddon Ness** *headland* E Scotland, UK
xxxvi E13 **Bude** Cornwall, SW England, UK
xxxvi D13 **Bude Bay** *bay* SW England, UK
xxxvi I14 **Budleigh Salterton** Devon, SW England, UK
xxxix O12 **Bugbrooke** Northamptonshire, C England, UK
xxxvi D16 **Bugle** Cornwall, SW England, UK
xxxv J11 **Builth Wells** Powys, E Wales, UK
xxxvii O11 **Bulford** Wiltshire, S England, UK
xliv A15 **Bull, The** *island* S Ireland
xli U12 **Bulmer** North Yorkshire, N England, UK
xliv G2 **Bunbeg** Donegal, N Ireland
xxxviii H7 **Bunbury** Cheshire, W England, UK
xliv K11 **Bunclody** Wexford, SE Ireland
xliv I2 **Buncrana** *Ir.* Bun Cranncha. Donegal, NW Ireland
xliv G5 **Bundoran** *Ir.* Bun Dobhráin. Donegal, NW Ireland
xliii D18 **Bunessan** Argyll and Bute, W Scotland, UK
xxxix Y10 **Bungay** Suffolk, E England, UK
xliv I13 **Bunmahon** Waterford, S Ireland
xliv F10 **Bunnaglass** Galway, W Ireland
xliv F11 **Bunratty** Clare, W Ireland
xxxvii U6 **Buntingford** Hertfordshire, SE England, UK
xxxviii K6 **Burbage** Derbyshire, C England, UK
xxxvii O10 **Burbage** Wiltshire, S England, UK
xxxix Y9 **Bure** ≈ E England, UK
xxxix V14 **Bures** Essex, E England, UK
xxxviii I7 **Burfard** Cheshire, C England, UK
xxxvii O7 **Burford** Oxfordshire, C England, UK
xxxvii T12 **Burgess Hill** West Sussex, SE England, UK
xxxix Y9 **Burgh Castle** Norfolk, E England, UK
xlii L11 **Burghead** Moray, N Scotland, UK
xxxvii Q10 **Burghfield** West Berkshire, S England, UK
xxxix T6 **Burgh le Marsh** Lincolnshire, E England, UK
xxxvii O13 **Burley** Hampshire, S England, UK
xxxviii H8 **Burlton** Shropshire, W England, UK
xli V13 **Burnby** East Riding of Yorkshire, N England, UK
xli R11 **Burneston** North Yorkshire, N England, UK
xxxix V7 **Burnham Market** Norfolk, E England, UK
xxxvii X8 **Burnham-on-Crouch** Essex, SE England, UK
xxxvi J11 **Burnham-on-Sea** Somerset, SW England, UK
xlii Q12 **Burnhaven** Aberdeenshire, NE Scotland, UK
xli F14 **Burnley** Lancashire, NW England, UK
xli Q12 **Burnsall** North Yorkshire, N England, UK
xliii J23 **Burnside** East Ayrshire, W Scotland, UK
xliii M19 **Burntisland** Fife, E Scotland, UK
xxxviii C13 **Burntwood** Staffordshire, C England, UK
xlii J1 **Burrafirth** Shetland Islands, NE Scotland, UK
xlii I2 **Burravoe** Shetland Islands, NE Scotland, UK
xlii N5 **Burray** *island* NE Scotland, UK
xliii M17 **Burrelton** Perth and Kinross, C Scotland, UK
xliv E9 **Burren** Clare, W Ireland
xliv E10 **Burren** *physical region* W Ireland
xliii I26 **Burrow Head** *headland* SW Scotland, UK
xxxv F14 **Burry Port** Carmarthenshire, S Wales, UK
xl M15 **Burscough** Lancashire, NW England, UK
xl B17 **Burton** Cheshire, W England, UK
xli W12 **Burton Agnes** East Riding of Yorkshire, N England, UK
xxxvi K14 **Burton Bradstock** Dorset, S England, UK
xli W11 **Burton Fleming** East Riding of Yorkshire, N England, UK
xli N11 **Burton-in-Kendal** Cumbria, NW England, UK
xxxix O7 **Burton Joyce** Nottinghamshire, C England, UK
xxxix P11 **Burton Latimer** Northamptonshire, C England, UK
xli S12 **Burton Leonard** North Yorkshire, N England, UK
xli X14 **Burton Pidsea** East Riding of Yorkshire, N England, UK
xliv G3 **Burtonport** Donegal, N Ireland
xxxviii L9 **Burton upon Trent** *var.* Burton on Trent, Burton-upon-Trent. Staffordshire, C England, UK
xxxviii H7 **Burwardsley** Cheshire, W England, UK
xxxix T12 **Burwell** Cambridgeshire, E England, UK
xlii M5 **Burwick** Orkney Islands, N Scotland, UK
xl G14 **Bury** Bury, NW England, UK
xxxvii S13 **Bury** West Sussex, SE England, UK
xl F14 **Bury** ◐ *unitary authority* NW England, UK
xxxix U12 **Bury St Edmunds** *hist.* Beodericsworth. Suffolk, E England, UK
xliv K2 **Bushmills** Moyle, N Northern Ireland, UK
xliii G20 **Bute, Island of** *island* SW Scotland, UK
xliii G21 **Bute, Sound of** *sound* W Scotland, UK
xxxvi K12 **Butleigh** Somerset, SW England, UK
xxxix Y13 **Butley** Suffolk, SW England, UK
xli O6 **Butterburn** Cumbria, NW England, UK
xl L9 **Buttermere** Cumbria, NW England, UK
xxxix S7 **Butterwick** Lincolnshire, E England, UK
xliv F13 **Buttevant** Cork, S Ireland
xxxviii K6 **Buxton** Derbyshire, C England, UK
xxxix X8 **Buxton** Norfolk, E England, UK
xxxix N13 **Byfield** Northamptonshire, C England, UK
xxxvii S10 **Byfleet** Surrey, SE England, UK
xxxv I5 **Bylchau** Conwy, N Wales, UK
xli O4 **Byrness** Northumberland, N England, UK

C

xxxix Q4 **Cabourne** Lincolnshire, E England, UK
xlii M13 **Cabrach** Moray, N Scotland, UK
xxxv H8 **Cader Idris** ▲ NW Wales, UK
xl F15 **Cadishead** Salford, NW England, UK
xxxvii O13 **Cadnam** Hampshire, S England, UK
xxxv K5 **Caergwrle** Flintshire, N Wales, UK
xxxv K14 **Caerleon** Newport, SE Wales, UK
xxxv F5 **Caernarfon** *var.* Caernarvon, Carnarvon. Gwynedd, NW Wales, UK
xxxv D5 **Caernarfon Bay** *bay* NW Wales, UK
xxxv J15 **Caerphilly** Caerphilly, S Wales, UK
xxxv J14 **Caerphilly** ◐ *unitary authority* S Wales, UK
xxxv I9 **Caersws** Powys, C Wales, UK
xxxv L14 **Caerwent** Monmouthshire, SE Wales, UK
xxxv J4 **Caerwys** Flintshire, N Wales, UK
xliv C14 **Caha Mountains** *Ir.* An Cheacha. ▲▲ SW Ireland
xliv H12 **Caher** *Ir.* An Cathair. Tipperary, S Ireland
xliv B13 **Caherciveen** *Ir.* Cathair Saidhbhín. Kerry, SW Ireland
xliv B14 **Caherdaniel** Kerry, SW Ireland
xliv L12 **Cahore Point** *Ir.* Rinn Chathóir. *headland* SE Ireland
xliii F19 **Cairnbaan** Argyll and Bute, W Scotland, UK
xliii H18 **Cairndow** Argyll and Bute, W Scotland, UK
xliii L14 **Cairn Gorm** ▲ C Scotland, UK
xliii L14 **Cairngorm Mountains** ▲▲ C Scotland, UK
xlii N12 **Cairnie** Aberdeenshire, NE Scotland, UK
xliii H24 **Cairnryan** Dumfries and Galloway, SW Scotland, UK
xliii J23 **Cairnsmore of Carsphairn** ▲ SW Scotland, UK
xliii K22 **Cairn Table** ▲ C Scotland, UK
xliii L15 **Cairnwell, The** ▲ C Scotland, UK
xxxix Z9 **Caister-on-Sea** Norfolk, E England, UK
xxxix Q4 **Caistor** Lincolnshire, E England, UK
xl M8 **Caldbeck** Cumbria, NW England, UK
xli R15 **Calder** ≈ N England, UK
xl K10 **Calder Bridge** Cumbria, NW England, UK
xliii K20 **Caldercruix** North Lanarkshire, C Scotland, UK
xli P15 **Calderdale** ◐ *unitary authority* N England, UK
xlii K6 **Calder, Loch** ◎ N Scotland, UK
xliii J21 **Caldermill** South Lanarkshire, C Scotland, UK
xxxv D14 **Caldey Island** *island* SW Wales, UK
xxxv L14 **Caldicot** Monmouthshire, SE Wales, UK
xli R9 **Caldwell** North Yorkshire, N England, UK
xl F12 **Calf of Man** *island* SW Isle of Man
xlii N3 **Calfsound** Orkney Islands, N Scotland, UK
xli O10 **Calf, The** ▲ NW England, UK
xliii D16 **Calgary** Argyll and Bute, W Scotland, UK
xliv I12 **Callan** *Ir.* Callain. Kilkenny, S Ireland
xliii J18 **Callander** Stirling, C Scotland, UK
xxxvi E15 **Callington** Cornwall, SW England, UK
xxxvii N9 **Calne** Wiltshire, S England, UK
xxxvii P13 **Calshot** Hampshire, S England, UK
xliv G8 **Caltra** Galway, W Ireland
xliii K15 **Calvine** Perth and Kinross, C Scotland, UK
xxxix T12 **Cam** ≈ E England, UK
xliii F16 **Camasnacroise** Highland, NW Scotland, UK
xxxvii X12 **Camber** East Sussex, SE England, UK
xxxvii R10 **Camberley** Surrey, SE England, UK
xxxvi D8 **Camberwell** Southwark, SE England, UK
xli Q5 **Cambo** Northumberland, N England, UK
xxxvi B17 **Camborne** Cornwall, SW England, UK
xxxv H11 **Cambrian Mountains** ▲▲ C Wales, UK
xxxix S12 **Cambridge** *Lat.* Cantabrigia. Cambridgeshire, E England, UK
xxxix Q11 **Cambridgeshire** ◐ *county* E England, UK
xxxiv K16 **Camden** ◐ *London borough* SE England, UK
xxxvi C7 **Camden** Camden, SE England, UK
xxxvi D15 **Camel** ≈ SW England, UK
xxxvi D14 **Camelford** Cornwall, SW England, UK
xliii P14 **Cammachmore** Aberdeenshire, NE Scotland, UK
xliv C12 **Camp** Kerry, SW Ireland
xliii F22 **Campbeltown** Argyll and Bute, W Scotland, UK
xliii J19 **Campsie Fells** ▲▲ Stirling, C Scotland, UK
xxxv C13 **Camrose** Pembrokeshire, SW Wales, UK
xliii G15 **Camusnagaul** Highland, NW Scotland, UK
xxxix S6 **Candlesby** Lincolnshire, E England, UK
xliii C14 **Canna** *island* NW Scotland, UK
xlii H12 **Cannich** Highland, NW Scotland, UK
xxxvi J11 **Cannington** Somerset, SW England, UK
xxxvi F7 **Canning Town** Newham, SE England, UK
xxxviii B13 **Cannock** Staffordshire, C England, UK
xxxviii K9 **Cannock Chase** *forest* C England, UK
xliii N24 **Canonbie** Dumfries and Galloway, SW Scotland, UK
xxxvii X10 **Canterbury** *hist.* Cantwaraburh, *anc.* Durovernum, *Lat.* Cantuaria. Kent, SE England, UK
xxxvii W9 **Canvey Island** Essex, SE England, UK
xliii C16 **Caolas** Argyll and Bute, W Scotland, UK
xxxvii T11 **Capel** Surrey, SE England, UK
xxxv H5 **Capel Curig** Conwy, N Wales, UK
xxxix W13 **Capel St Mary** Suffolk, E England, UK
xli Q5 **Capheaton** Northumberland, N England, UK
xliii M22 **Cappercleuch** The Borders, S Scotland, UK
xliv H13 **Cappoquin** Waterford, S Ireland
xliii L17 **Caputh** Perth and Kinross, C Scotland, UK
xxxvi L16 **Carbis Bay** Cornwall, SW England, UK
xlii D13 **Carbost** Highland, NW Scotland, UK
xlii D12 **Carbost** Highland, NW Scotland, UK
xliv J9 **Carbury** Kildare, E Ireland
xxxv J15 **Cardiff** ◐ *unitary authority* S Wales, UK
xxxv K15 **Cardiff** *Wel.* Caerdydd. *national region capital* Cardiff, S Wales, UK
xxxv E11 **Cardigan** *Wel.* Aberteifi. Ceredigion, SW Wales, UK
xxxv E10 **Cardigan Bay** *bay* W Wales, UK
xxxviii H10 **Cardington** Shropshire, W England, UK
xxxvii T6 **Cardington** Bedfordshire, C England, UK
xliii I19 **Cardross** Argyll and Bute, W Scotland, UK
xxxv D14 **Carew** Pembrokeshire, SW Wales, UK
xliii L24 **Cargenbridge** Dumfries and Galloway, SW Scotland, UK
xl M11 **Cark** Cumbria, NW England, UK
xliv H3 **Cark Mountain** *hill* N Ireland
xli P13 **Carleton** North Yorkshire, N England, UK
xliv L6 **Carlingford** Louth, NE Ireland
xliv L6 **Carlingford Lough** *inlet* Ireland/Northern Ireland, UK
xl M7 **Carlisle** *anc.* Caer Luel, Luguvallium, Luguvallum. Cumbria, NW England, UK
xliii L20 **Carlops** The Borders, S Scotland, UK
xliv J11 **Carlow** *Ir.* Ceatharlach. Carlow, SE Ireland
xliv J11 **Carlow** *Ir.* Cheatharlach. ◐ *county* SE Ireland
xlii C8 **Carloway** Western Isles, NW Scotland, UK
xli U14 **Carlton** North Yorkshire, N England, UK
xli Q11 **Carlton** North Yorkshire, N England, UK
xxxix N7 **Carlton** Nottinghamshire, C England, UK
xxxix Z10 **Carlton Colville** Suffolk, E England, UK
xxxix N5 **Carlton in Lindrick** Nottinghamshire, C England, UK
xxxix P6 **Carlton-on-Trent** Nottinghamshire, C England, UK
xliii K21 **Carluke** South Lanarkshire, C Scotland, UK
xxxv F13 **Carmarthen** Carmarthenshire, SW Wales, UK
xxxv E14 **Carmarthen Bay** *bay* S Wales, UK
xxxv E13 **Carmarthenshire** ◐ *unitary authority* S Wales, UK
xxxv E3 **Carmel Head** *headland* NW Wales, UK
xliv C9 **Carna** Galway, W Ireland
xliii J14 **Carn Bàn** ▲ NW Scotland, UK
xliv I2 **Carndonagh** *Ir.* Carn Domhnach. Donegal, NW Ireland
xliii D20 **Carnduncan** Argyll and Bute, W Scotland, UK
xxxv G5 **Carnedd Llywelyn** ▲ NW Wales, UK
xlii H13 **Carn Eige** ▲ N Scotland, UK
xliv K11 **Carnew** Wicklow, E Ireland
xliv F5 **Carney** Sligo, N Ireland
xliv L3 **Carnlough** Larne, E Northern Ireland, UK
xxxv I9 **Carno** Powys, C Wales, UK
xliii N17 **Carnoustie** Angus, E Scotland, UK
xliv K13 **Carnsore Point** *Ir.* Ceann an Chairn. *headland* SE Ireland
xliii L21 **Carnwath** South Lanarkshire, C Scotland, UK
xliii F21 **Carradale** Argyll and Bute, W Scotland, UK
xliv E7 **Carra, Lough** ◎ NW Ireland
xliv D9 **Carraroe** Galway, W Ireland
xliv C13 **Carrauntoohil** *Ir.* Carrantual, Carrauntohil, Corrán Tuathail. ▲ SW Ireland
xlii K13 **Carrbridge** Highland, NW Scotland, UK
xliii N17 **Carrick** Fife, E Scotland, UK
xliv F4 **Carrick** Donegal, N Ireland
xliv H2 **Carrickart** *var.* Carrigart, *Ir.* Carraig Airt. Donegal, N Ireland
xliii H19 **Carrick Castle** Argyll and Bute, W Scotland, UK
xliv M4 **Carrickfergus** ◐ *district* E Northern Ireland, UK
xliv M4 **Carrickfergus** *Ir.* Carraig Fhearghais. Carrickfergus, NE Northern Ireland, UK
xliv J6 **Carrickmacross** *Ir.* Carraig Mhachaire Rois. Monaghan, N Ireland
xliv J4 **Carrickmore** Omagh, W Northern Ireland, UK
xliv G7 **Carrick-on-Shannon** *Ir.* Cora Droma Rúisc. Leitrim/Roscommon, NW Ireland
xliv I12 **Carrick-on-Suir** *Ir.* Carraig na Siúire. Tipperary, S Ireland
xliv E14 **Carrigadrohid Reservoir** ⊡ S Ireland
xliv C11 **Carrigaholt** Clare, W Ireland
xliv G10 **Carrigahorig** Tipperary, S Ireland
xliv F14 **Carrigaline** Cork, S Ireland
xliv H7 **Carrigallen** Leitrim, N Ireland
xliv I3 **Carrigans** Donegal, N Ireland
xlii H10 **Carron** ≈ NW Scotland, UK
xliii K23 **Carronbridge** Dumfries and Galloway, SW Scotland, UK
xlii F12 **Carron, Loch** *inlet* NW Scotland, UK
xliv J2 **Carrowkeel** *var.* Kerrykeel. Donegal, N Ireland
xliv D5 **Carrowmore Lake** ◎ NW Ireland
xli O7 **Carr Shield** Northumberland, N England, UK
xliii L24 **Carrutherstown** Dumfries and Galloway, SW Scotland, UK
xliv L5 **Carryduff** Castlereagh, E Northern Ireland, UK
xliii J25 **Carsluith** Dumfries and Galloway, SW Scotland, UK
xliii J23 **Carsphairn** Dumfries and Galloway, SW Scotland, UK
xliii K21 **Carstairs** South Lanarkshire, C Scotland, UK
xxxvii O8 **Carterton** Oxfordshire, C England, UK
xl M11 **Cartmel** Cumbria, NW England, UK
xl M11 **Cartmel Fell** Cumbria, NW England, UK
xliv C9 **Cashel** Galway, W Ireland
xliv H12 **Cashel** *Ir.* Caiseal. Tipperary, S Ireland
xliv D12 **Cashen** ≈ SW Ireland
xliii I17 **Cashlie** Perth and Kinross, C Scotland, UK
xxxix V9 **Castle Acre** Norfolk, E England, UK
xliv E7 **Castlebar** *Ir.* Caisleán an Bharraigh. Mayo, W Ireland
xliii A14 **Castlebay** Western Isles, NW Scotland, UK
xliv K7 **Castlebellingham** Louth, NE Ireland
xliv K6 **Castleblayney** *Ir.* Baile na Lorgan. Monaghan, N Ireland
xli Q10 **Castle Bolton** North Yorkshire, N England, UK
xliv K12 **Castlebridge** Wexford, SE Ireland
xxxviii D15 **Castle Bromwich** Birmingham, C England, UK
xxxix Q9 **Castle Bytham** Lincolnshire, E England, UK
xli N7 **Castle Carrock** Cumbria, NW England, UK
xxxvi L12 **Castle Cary** Somerset, SW England, UK
xxxvi M9 **Castle Combe** Wiltshire, S England, UK
xliv I11 **Castlecomer** Kilkenny, SE Ireland
xliv B14 **Castlecove** Kerry, SW Ireland
xliii L21 **Castlecraig** The Borders, S Scotland, UK
xliv K3 **Castledawson** Magherafelt, C Northern Ireland, UK
xliv I4 **Castlederg** Strabane, W Northern Ireland, UK
xliv J10 **Castledermot** Kildare, E Ireland
xliii K25 **Castle Douglas** Dumfries and Galloway, S Scotland, UK
xliv K12 **Castleellis** Wexford, SE Ireland
xliv I3 **Castlefinn** *Ir.* Caisleán na Finne. Donegal, NW Ireland
xli S14 **Castleford** Wakefield, N England, UK
xliv C12 **Castlegregory** Kerry, SW Ireland
xliv D12 **Castleisland** *Ir.* Oileán Ciarral. Kerry, SW Ireland
xliii H25 **Castle Kennedy** Dumfries and Galloway, SW Scotland, UK
xliv C13 **Castlemaine** Kerry, SW Ireland
xxxv C14 **Castlemartin** Pembrokeshire, SW Wales, UK
xliv G14 **Castlemartyr** Cork, S Ireland
xliv I8 **Castlepollard** Westmeath, C Ireland
xliv F7 **Castlerea** *Ir.* An Caisleán Riabhach. Roscommon, W Ireland
xliv L4 **Castlereagh** *Ir.* An Caisleán Riabhach. Castlereagh, N Northern Ireland, UK
xliv L4 **Castlereagh** ◐ *district* E Northern Ireland, UK
xliv J2 **Castlerock** Coleraine, N Northern Ireland, UK
xli Q7 **Castleside** Durham, N England, UK
xlii J12 **Castle Stuart** Highland, NW Scotland, UK
xli U9 **Castleton** North Yorkshire, N England, UK
xl F12 **Castletown** SE Isle of Man
xli W3 **Castletown** Sunderland, NE England, UK
xlii L6 **Castletown** Highland, N Scotland, UK
xliv C14 **Castletown Bere** Cork, S Ireland
xliv F13 **Castletownroche** Cork, S Ireland
xliv D15 **Castletownshend** Cork, S Ireland
xliv L6 **Castlewellan** Down, E Northern Ireland, UK
xxxix V10 **Caston** Norfolk, E England, UK
xxxvii U10 **Caterham** Surrey, SE England, UK
xxxix Y8 **Catfield** Norfolk, E England, UK
xxxvi F9 **Catford** Lewisham, SE England, UK
xl M5 **Catlowdy** Cumbria, NW England, UK
xli N12 **Caton** Lancashire, NW England, UK
xliii J22 **Catrine** East Ayrshire, SW Scotland, UK
xxxviii B16 **Catshill** Worcestershire, W England, UK
xli N13 **Catterall** Lancashire, NW England, UK
xli R10 **Catterick** North Yorkshire, N England, UK
xli R10 **Catterick Camp** North Yorkshire, N England, UK
xliii N23 **Cauldcleuch Head** ▲ S Scotland, UK
xliii L25 **Caulkerbush** Dumfries and Galloway, SW Scotland, UK
xxxix O6 **Caunton** Nottinghamshire, C England, UK
xliv I7 **Cavan** *Ir.* Cabhán. Cavan, N Ireland
xliv I6 **Cavan** *Ir.* An Cabhán. ◐ *county* N Ireland
xxxix U13 **Cavendish** Suffolk, E England, UK
xxxix U11 **Cavenham** Suffolk, E England, UK
xli T14 **Cawood** North Yorkshire, N England, UK
xxxix W8 **Cawston** Norfolk, E England, UK
xxxix P7 **Caythorpe** Lincolnshire, E England, UK
xli W11 **Cayton** North Yorkshire, N England, UK
xliv K9 **Celbridge** Kildare, E Ireland
xxxviii K7 **Cellarhead** Staffordshire, C England, UK
xxxv E3 **Cemaes** Isle of Anglesey, NW Wales, UK
xxxv D11 **Cemaes Head** *headland* SW Wales, UK
xxxv H8 **Cemmaes** Powys, C Wales, UK
xxxv F10 **Ceredigion** ◐ *unitary authority* W Wales, UK
xliii M18 **Ceres** Fife, E Scotland, UK
xxxvi L13 **Cerne Abbas** Dorset, S England, UK
xxxv I6 **Cerrigydrudion** Conwy, N Wales, UK
xl H14 **Chadderton** Oldham, NW England, UK
xxxviii B16 **Chaddesley Corbett** Worcestershire, W England, UK
xxxvii P9 **Chaddleworth** West Berkshire, S England, UK
xxxvi G14 **Chagford** Devon, SW England, UK
xxxvii P14 **Chale** Isle of Wight, S England, UK
xxxvii S8 **Chalfont St Giles** Buckinghamshire, C England, UK
xxxvi G11 **Challacombe** Devon, SW England, UK
xliii I24 **Challoch** Dumfries and Galloway, SW Scotland, UK
xxxvii X10 **Challock** Kent, SE England, UK
xxxvii X15 **Channel Islands** *Fr.* Îles Normandes. *island group* S English Channel
xxxvii Z11 **Channel Tunnel** *tunnel* France/UK
xxxviii K5 **Chapel-en-le-Frith** Derbyshire, C England, UK
xxxix T5 **Chapel St Leonards** Lincolnshire, E England, UK
xli S16 **Chapeltown** Sheffield, N England, UK
xxxvi K13 **Chard** Somerset, SW England, UK
xxxvi J13 **Chardstock** Devon, SW England, UK
xxxvii X11 **Charing** Kent, SE England, UK
xxxvii P7 **Charlbury** Oxfordshire, C England, UK
xlii M12 **Charlestown of Aberlour** Moray, N Scotland, UK
xliv F6 **Charlestown** Mayo, NW Ireland
xxxvi F8 **Charlton** Greenwich, SE England, UK
xxxvii N9 **Charlton** Wiltshire, S England, UK
xxxvii N7 **Charlton Kings** Gloucestershire, C England, UK
xxxvii T11 **Charlwood** Surrey, SE England, UK
xxxvi K14 **Charmouth** Dorset, S England, UK
xxxix N12 **Charwelton** Northamptonshire, C England, UK
xxxvii W10 **Chatham** Kent, SE England, UK
xxxix S11 **Chatteris** Cambridgeshire, E England, UK
xxxvi G13 **Chawleigh** Devon, SW England, UK
xxxvii Q11 **Chawton** Hampshire, S England, UK
xxxviii K7 **Cheadle** Staffordshire, C England, UK
xli P17 **Cheadle** Stockport, NW England, UK
xxxvi K11 **Cheddar** Somerset, SW England, UK
xxxviii K7 **Cheddleton** Staffordshire, C England, UK
xl G17 **Chelford** Cheshire, W England, UK
xxxviii M8 **Chellaston** City of Derby, C England, UK
xxxvii W7 **Chelmer** ≈ E England, UK
xxxvii W8 **Chelmsford** Essex, E England, UK
xxxvi C8 **Chelsea** Kensington and Chelsea, SE England, UK
xxxvi M7 **Cheltenham** Gloucestershire, C England, UK
xxxv M14 **Chepstow** Monmouthshire, SE Wales, UK
xxxvii Q12 **Cheriton** Hampshire, S England, UK
xxxvi H13 **Cheriton Fitzpaine** Devon, SW England, UK
xxxvii S10 **Chertsey** Surrey, SE England, UK
xxxvii S8 **Chesham** Buckinghamshire, C England, UK
xl H17 **Cheshire** ◐ *county* C England, UK
xxxvii U8 **Cheshunt** Hertfordshire, SE England, UK
xxxviii B13 **Cheslyn Hay** Staffordshire, C England, UK
xxxviii G6 **Chester** *Wel.* Caerleon; *hist.* Legaceaster, *Lat.* Deva, Devana Castra. Cheshire, C England, UK
xxxviii M6 **Chesterfield** Derbyshire, C England, UK
xli R7 **Chester-le-Street** Durham, N England, UK
xliii O22 **Chesters** The Borders, S Scotland, UK
xxxviii I8 **Cheswardine** Shropshire, W England, UK
xxxvi L13 **Chetnole** Dorset, S England, UK
xliii O23 **Cheviot Hills** *hill range* England/Scotland, UK
xli P3 **Cheviot, The** ▲ NE England, UK
xxxvi L10 **Chew Magna** Bath and North East Somerset, SW England, UK
xxxvi L11 **Chewton Mendip** Somerset, SW England, UK
xxxvii R13 **Chichester** West Sussex, SE England, UK
xxxvi L14 **Chickerell** Dorset, S England, UK
xxxvii S11 **Chiddingfold** Surrey, SE England, UK
xxxvi K14 **Chideock** Dorset, S England, UK
xxxvii P9 **Chieveley** West Berkshire, S England, UK
xxxvi G5 **Chigwell** Essex, SE England, UK
xxxviii I8 **Child's Ercall** Shropshire, W England, UK
xxxvii Y10 **Chilham** Kent, SE England, UK
xxxvi F14 **Chillaton** Devon, SW England, UK
xxxvii R8 **Chiltern Hills** *hill range* S England, UK
xxxvii R8 **Chinnor** Oxfordshire, C England, UK
xxxix U12 **Chippenham** Cambridgeshire, E England, UK
xxxvi M9 **Chippenham** Wiltshire, S England, UK
xxxvii N6 **Chipping Campden** Gloucestershire, C England, UK
xxxvii O7 **Chipping Norton** Oxfordshire, C England, UK
xxxvii V8 **Chipping Ongar** Essex, SE England, UK
xxxvi M9 **Chipping Sodbury** South Gloucestershire, SW England, UK
xxxviii G10 **Chirbury** Shropshire, W England, UK
xxxv K6 **Chirk** Wrexham, NE Wales, UK
xliii P20 **Chirnside** The Borders, S Scotland, UK
xxxvi B8 **Chiswick** Hounslow, SE England, UK
xxxvii N11 **Chitterne** Wiltshire, S England, UK
xxxvi G12 **Chittlehampton** Devon, SW England, UK
xxxvii S10 **Chobham** Surrey, SE England, UK
xlii J8 **Choire, Loch** ◎ NW Scotland, UK
xxxvii O11 **Cholderton** Wiltshire, S England, UK
xli P6 **Chollerford** Northumberland, N England, UK
xli P6 **Chollerton** Northumberland, N England, UK
xxxvii Q9 **Cholsey** Oxfordshire, C England, UK
xli Q7 **Chopwell** Gateshead, NE England, UK
xli N15 **Chorley** Lancashire, NW England, UK
xxxix T10 **Christchurch** Cambridgeshire, E England, UK
xxxvii O14 **Christchurch** Dorset, S England, UK
xxxvi H14 **Chudleigh** Devon, SW England, UK
xxxvi G13 **Chulmleigh** Devon, SW England, UK
xxxvi M7 **Churchdown** Gloucestershire, C England, UK
xxxviii J9 **Church Eaton** Staffordshire, C England, UK
xli T14 **Church Fenton** North Yorkshire, N England, UK
xxxviii H6 **Church Minshull** Cheshire, W England, UK
xxxv K9 **Church Stoke** Powys, C Wales, UK
xxxviii H10 **Church Stretton** Shropshire, W England, UK
xliv K13 **Churchtown** Wexford, SE Ireland
xliv J13 **Churchtown** Wexford, SE Ireland
xxxv F6 **Chwilog** Gwynedd, NW Wales, UK
xxxv J5 **Cilcain** Flintshire, N Wales, UK
xxxv G11 **Cilcennin** Ceredigion, W Wales, UK
xxxv E12 **Cilgerran** Pembrokeshire, SW Wales, UK
xxxv H12 **Cilycwm** Carmarthenshire, S Wales, UK
xxxvi L7 **Cinderford** Gloucestershire, C England, UK
xxxvii N8 **Cirencester** *anc.* Corinium, Corinium Dobunorum. Gloucestershire, C England, UK
xliii H19 **Clachaig** Argyll and Bute, W Scotland, UK
xliii F21 **Clachan** Argyll and Bute, W Scotland, UK
xlii A11 **Clachan-a-Luib** Western Isles, NW Scotland, UK
xliii G19 **Clachan of Glendaruel** Argyll and Bute, W Scotland, UK
xliii F18 **Clachan-Seil** Argyll and Bute, W Scotland, UK
xlii G8 **Clachtoll** Highland, NW Scotland, UK
xliii K19 **Clackmannan** Clackmannan, C Scotland, UK
xliii K18 **Clackmannan** ◐ *unitary authority* C Scotland, UK
xxxvii Y7 **Clacton-on-Sea** *var.* Clacton. Essex, E England, UK
xliii H18 **Cladich** Argyll and Bute, W Scotland, UK
xxxv H10 **Claerwen Reservoir** ⊡ E Wales, UK
xliii F16 **Claggan** Highland, NW Scotland, UK
xliv K9 **Clane** Kildare, E Ireland
xxxvii O8 **Clanfield** Oxfordshire, C England, UK
xliii G20 **Claonaig** Argyll and Bute, W Scotland, UK
xxxvi D9 **Clapham** Lambeth, SE England, UK
xli O12 **Clapham** North Yorkshire, N England, UK
xxxv D13 **Clarbeston** Pembrokeshire, SW Wales, UK
xxxix V13 **Clare** Suffolk, E England, UK
xliv E10 **Clare** *Ir.* An Clár. ◐ *county* W Ireland
xliv F8 **Clare** ≈ W Ireland
xliv E10 **Clarecastle** Clare, W Ireland
xliv H10 **Clareen** Offaly, C Ireland
xliv E9 **Claregalway** Galway, W Ireland
xliv C7 **Clare Island** *Ir.* Cliara. *island* W Ireland
xliv E7 **Claremorris** *Ir.* Clár Chlainne Mhuiris. Mayo, W Ireland
xliv F9 **Clarinbridge** Galway, W Ireland
xlii J10 **Clashmore** Highland, NW Scotland, UK
xlii G8 **Clashnessie** Highland, NW Scotland, UK
xliii J24 **Clatteringshaws Loch** ◎ SW Scotland, UK
xliv J3 **Claudy** Londonderry, NW Northern Ireland, UK
xli N12 **Claughton** Lancashire, NW England, UK
xxxviii D17 **Claverdon** Warwickshire, C England, UK
xxxvi E13 **Clawton** Devon, SW England, UK
xxxviii M6 **Clay Cross** Derbyshire, C England, UK
xxxix W13 **Claydon** Suffolk, E England, UK
xl G11 **Clay Head** *headland* C Isle of Man
xxxix P7 **Claypole** Lincolnshire, E England, UK
xli O14 **Clayton-le-Moors** Lancashire, NW England, UK
xliii E15 **Cleadale** Highland, NW Scotland, UK
xliv C15 **Clear, Cape** *var.* The Bill of Cape Clear, *Ir.* Ceann Cléire. *headland* SW Ireland
xliv D15 **Clear Island** *island* S Ireland
xliii A14 **Cleat** Western Isles, NW Scotland, UK
xl K9 **Cleator Moor** Cumbria, NW England, UK
xli R14 **Cleckheaton** Kirklees, N England, UK
xxxviii H11 **Clee St Margaret** Shropshire, W England, UK
xxxix R3 **Cleethorpes** North East Lincolnshire, E England, UK
xxxviii I11 **Cleobury Mortimer** Shropshire, W England, UK
xxxvi K10 **Clevedon** North West Somerset, SW England, UK
xli T10 **Cleveland Hills** *hill range* N England, UK
xl M13 **Cleveleys** Lancashire, NW England, UK
xliv C7 **Clew Bay** *Ir.* Cuan Mó. *inlet* W Ireland
xli N9 **Cliburn** Cumbria, NW England, UK
xxxvii Q11 **Cliddesden** Hampshire, S England, UK
xliv C8 **Clifden** *Ir.* An Clochán. Galway, W Ireland
xxxvii W9 **Cliffe** Kent, SE England, UK
xxxviii G13 **Clifford** Herefordshire, W England, UK
xxxviii I12 **Clifton upon Teme** Worcestershire, W England, UK
xxxix O11 **Clipston** Northamptonshire, C England, UK
xlii C9 **Clisham** ▲ NW Scotland, UK
xli O13 **Clitheroe** Lancashire, NW England, UK
xxxviii H9 **Clive** Shropshire, W England, UK
xlii J1 **Clivocast** Shetland Islands, NE Scotland, UK
xliv H3 **Cloghan** Donegal, N Ireland
xliv H9 **Cloghan** Offaly, C Ireland
xliv G12 **Clogheen** Tipperary, S Ireland
xliv I5 **Clogher** Dungannon, C Northern Ireland, UK
xliv L7 **Clogher Head** *headland* E Ireland
xliv L7 **Clogherhead** Louth, NE Ireland
xliv M5 **Cloghy** Ards, E Northern Ireland, UK
xliv L3 **Clog Mills** Ballymena, NE Northern Ireland, UK
xlii P12 **Clola** Aberdeenshire, NE Scotland, UK
xliv E15 **Clonakilty** *Ir.* Cloich na Coillte. Cork, SW Ireland
xliv E15 **Clonakilty Bay** *bay* S Ireland
xliv I9 **Clonaslee** Laois, C Ireland
xliv F8 **Clonbern** Galway, W Ireland
xliv D8 **Clonbur** Galway, W Ireland
xliv K9 **Clondalkin** *Ir.* Cluain Dolcáin. Dublin, E Ireland
xliv I13 **Clonea Bay** *bay* S Ireland
xliv I5 **Clones** *Ir.* Cluain Eois. Monaghan, N Ireland
xliv G9 **Clonfert** Galway, W Ireland
xliv H9 **Clonmacnoise** Offaly, C Ireland
xliv H12 **Clonmel** *Ir.* Cluain Meala. Tipperary, S Ireland
xliv K12 **Clonroche** Wexford, SE Ireland
xliv J6 **Clontibret** Monaghan, NE Ireland
xliv E8 **Cloonboo** Galway, W Ireland
xliv F11 **Cloonlara** Clare, W Ireland
xliv G10 **Cloonoon** Galway, W Ireland
xliv F9 **Cloonymorris** Galway, W Ireland
xxxvii S6 **Clophill** Bedfordshire, C England, UK
xli W10 **Cloughton** North Yorkshire, N England, UK
xliii M15 **Clova** Angus, E Scotland, UK
xxxvi E12 **Clovelly** Devon, SW England, UK
xliii N21 **Clovenfords** The Borders, S Scotland, UK
xxxix N5 **Clowne** Derbyshire, C England, UK
xxxviii J11 **Clows Top** Worcestershire, W England, UK
xlii G13 **Cluanie, Loch** ◎ NW Scotland, UK
xxxviii G11 **Clun** Shropshire, W England, UK
xliii H14 **Clunes** Highland, NW Scotland, UK
xxxviii G11 **Clungunford** Shropshire, W England, UK
xxxvi L10 **Clutton** Bath and North East Somerset, SW England, UK
xxxv J4 **Clwyd** ≈ N Wales, UK
xxxv J4 **Clwydian Range** ▲▲ N Wales, UK
xxxv H14 **Clydach** Swansea, S Wales, UK
xxxv I14 **Clydach Vale** Rhondda Cynon Taff, S Wales, UK
xliii K22 **Clyde** ≈ W Scotland, UK
xliii I20 **Clydebank** West Dunbartonshire, W Scotland, UK
xliii H20 **Clyde, Firth of** *inlet* S Scotland, UK
xxxv F6 **Clynnog-fawr** Gwynedd, NW Wales, UK
xxxv K11 **Clyro** Powys, C Wales, UK
xxxvi I13 **Clyst** ≈ SW England, UK
xxxvi I14 **Clyst St Mary** Devon, SW England, UK
xxxv I9 **Clywedog, Llyn** *var.* Clywedog Reservoir. ⊡ E Wales, UK
xliv E14 **Coachford** Cork, S Ireland
xliii K21 **Coalburn** South Lanarkshire, C Scotland, UK
xliv K4 **Coalisland** Dungannon, C Northern Ireland, UK
xxxviii M9 **Coalville** Leicestershire, C England, UK
xliii K20 **Coatbridge** North Lanarkshire, S Scotland, UK
xliv G14 **Cobh** *Ir.* An Cóbh; *prev.* Cove of Cork, Queenstown. Cork, SW Ireland
xliii O20 **Cockburnspath** The Borders, S Scotland, UK
xliii N19 **Cockenzie and Port Seton** East Lothian, SE Scotland, UK
xli N13 **Cockerham** Lancashire, NW England, UK
xl K8 **Cockermouth** Cumbria, NW England, UK
xxxix V12 **Cockfield** Suffolk, E England, UK
xxxvii R12 **Cocking** West Sussex, SE England, UK
xxxix U9 **Cockley Cley** Norfolk, E England, UK
xxxviii H8 **Cockshutt** Shropshire, W England, UK
xxxvii N11 **Codford St Peter** Wiltshire, S England, UK
xxxviii J10 **Codsall** Staffordshire, C England, UK
xxxv K5 **Coedpoeth** Wrexham, NE Wales, UK
xxxvii W7 **Coggeshall** Essex, SE England, UK
xlii F9 **Coigeach, Rubha** *headland* NW Scotland, UK
xlii I9 **Colaboll** Highland, NW Scotland, UK
xl F12 **Colby** S Isle of Man
xxxvii X7 **Colchester** *hist.* Colneceaste, *anc.* Camulodunum. Essex, E England, UK
xlii J7 **Coldbackie** Highland, N Scotland, UK
xliii P20 **Coldingham** The Borders, S Scotland, UK
xli T11 **Cold Kirby** North Yorkshire, N England, UK
xxxvii W8 **Cold Norton** Essex, SE England, UK
xliii P21 **Coldstream** The Borders, SE Scotland, UK
xxxvi L8 **Coleford** Gloucestershire, C England, UK
xliv K2 **Coleraine** *Ir.* Cúil Raithin. Coleraine, N Northern Ireland, UK
xliv J2 **Coleraine** ◐ *district* N Northern Ireland, UK
xxxvii N7 **Colesbourne** Gloucestershire, C England, UK

◆ Country
● Country Capital
◇ Dependent Territory
○ Dependent Territory Capital
◐ Administrative Region
✕ International Airport
▲ Mountain
▲▲ Mountain Range
◎ Lake
⊡ Reservoir
≈ River

xlvii

COLESHILL – EASTINGTON

xxxviii D15 **Coleshill** Warwickshire, C England, UK
xliii G20 **Colintraive** Argyll and Bute, W Scotland, UK
xlii C16 **Coll** *island* W Scotland, UK
xlii P12 **Collieston** Aberdeenshire, NE Scotland, UK
xxxvi E15 **Colliford Reservoir** ⊞ SW England, UK
xliii L24 **Collin** Dumfries and Galloway, SW Scotland, UK
xli S13 **Collingham** Leeds, N England, UK
xxxix P6 **Collingham** Nottinghamshire, C England, UK
xliv K7 **Collon** Louth, NE Ireland
xliv F6 **Collooney** *Ir.* Cúil Mhuine. Sligo, NW Ireland
xliii H24 **Colmonell** South Ayrshire, W Scotland, UK
xlii M13 **Colnabaichin** Aberdeenshire, NE Scotland, UK
xli P13 **Colne** Lancashire, NW England, UK
xxxvii X7 **Colne** ~ SE England, UK
xliii D19 **Colonsay** *island* W Scotland, UK
xlii N12 **Colpy** Aberdeenshire, NE Scotland, UK
xxxix P8 **Colsterworth** Lincolnshire, E England, UK
xxxix O8 **Colston Bassett** Nottinghamshire, C England, UK
xxxix X8 **Coltishall** Norfolk, E England, UK
xliii K25 **Colvend** Dumfries and Galloway, SW Scotland, UK
xli P5 **Colwell** Northumberland, N England, UK
xxxv H4 **Colwyn Bay** Conwy, N Wales, UK
xxxvi J14 **Colyford** Devon, SW England, UK
xxxvi J14 **Colyton** Devon, SW England, UK
xxxvi G11 **Combe Martin** Devon, SW England, UK
xliv M5 **Comber** *Ir.* An Comar. Ards, E Northern Ireland, UK
xxxix S12 **Comberton** Cambridgeshire, E England, UK
xxxvi J13 **Combe St Nicholas** Somerset, SW England, UK
xliv H12 **Comeragh Mountains** ▲▲ S Ireland
xxxvii R12 **Compton** West Sussex, SE England, UK
xliii K17 **Comrie** Perth and Kinross, C Scotland, UK
xliv E8 **Cong** Mayo, NW Ireland
xxxviii I6 **Congleton** Cheshire, W England, UK
xxxvi K10 **Congresbury** North West Somerset, SW England, UK
xxxix R6 **Coningsby** Lincolnshire, E England, UK
xli T16 **Conisbrough** Doncaster, N England, UK
xl M10 **Coniston** Cumbria, NW England, UK
xli Q12 **Conistone** North Yorkshire, N England, UK
xl L10 **Coniston Water** ◎ NW England, UK
xliv G13 **Conna** Cork, S Ireland
xxxv K5 **Connah's Quay** Flintshire, N Wales, UK
xliv D7 **Connaught** *var.* Connacht, *Ir.* Chonnacht, Cúige. *province* W Ireland
xliii G17 **Connel** Argyll and Bute, W Scotland, UK
xliv C8 **Connemara** *Ir.* Conamara. *physical region* W Ireland
xliv E6 **Conn, Lough** *Ir.* Loch Con. ◎ W Ireland
xlii I11 **Conon Bridge** Highland, NW Scotland, UK
xli U4 **Consett** Durham, N England, UK
xlii I11 **Contin** Highland, NW Scotland, UK
xxxv H4 **Conwy** Conwy, N Wales, UK
xxxv H5 **Conwy** ◈ *unitary authority* N Wales, UK
xxxv H5 **Conwy** ~ N Wales, UK
xxxvii R9 **Cookham** Windsor and Maidenhead, S England, UK
xliv K4 **Cookstown** *Ir.* An Chorr Chríochach. Cookstown, C Northern Ireland, UK
xliv J4 **Cookstown** ◈ *district* C Northern Ireland, UK
xliv G10 **Coolbaun** Tipperary, S Ireland
xxxvii T12 **Coolham** West Sussex, SE England, UK
xliv C13 **Coomacarrea** ▲ SW Ireland
xxxvii N12 **Coombe Bissett** Wiltshire, S England, UK
xliv J6 **Cootehill** *Ir.* Muinchille. Cavan, N Ireland
xliv M4 **Copeland Island** *island* E Northern Ireland, UK
xlii N5 **Copinsay** *island* N Scotland, UK
xxxvi G13 **Copplestone** Devon, SW England, UK
xl D13 **Coppull** Lancashire, N England, UK
xli R4 **Coquet** ~ N England, UK
xxxvi W17 **Corbiere Point** *headland* Jersey, Channel Islands
xli Q6 **Corbridge** Northumberland, N England, UK
xxxix P10 **Corby** Northamptonshire, C England, UK
xxxix Q8 **Corby Glen** Lincolnshire, E England, UK
xxxvi J12 **Corfe** Somerset, SW England, UK
xxxvi N14 **Corfe Castle** Dorset, S England, UK
xlii M13 **Corgarff** Aberdeenshire, NE Scotland, UK
xliv F14 **Cork** *Ir.* Corcaigh. Cork, S Ireland
xliv F13 **Cork** *Ir.* Corcaigh. ◈ *county* SW Ireland
xliv F14 **Cork** ✕ Cork, SW Ireland
xliv G14 **Cork Harbour** *Ir.* Cuan Chorcaí. *inlet* SW Ireland
xli W5 **Cornforth** Durham, N England, UK
xlii N11 **Cornhill** Aberdeenshire, NE Scotland, UK
xlii N5 **Cornquoy** Orkney Islands, N Scotland, UK
xxxvi C16 **Cornwall** ◈ *county* SW England, UK
xxxvi L16 **Cornwall, Cape** *headland* SW England, UK
xlii G15 **Corpach** Highland, NW Scotland, UK
xlii F14 **Corran** Highland, NW Scotland, UK
xlii G16 **Corran** Highland, NW Scotland, UK
xliv D8 **Corrib, Lough** *Ir.* Loch Coirib. ◎ W Ireland
xliii G21 **Corrie** North Ayrshire, W Scotland, UK
xliii M24 **Corrie Common** Dumfries and Galloway, SW Scotland, UK
xxxix P4 **Corringham** Lincolnshire, E England, UK
xxxv H8 **Corris** Gwynedd, NW Wales, UK
xliv E10 **Corrofin** Clare, W Ireland
xlii E13 **Corry** Highland, NW Scotland, UK
xlii J24 **Corserine** ▲ SW Scotland, UK
xxxvi M10 **Corsham** Wiltshire, S England, UK
xliii K24 **Corsock** Dumfries and Galloway, SW Scotland, UK
xliii M16 **Cortachy** Angus, E Scotland, UK
xxxix Z10 **Corton** Suffolk, E England, UK
xxxv J6 **Corwen** Denbighshire, N Wales, UK
xxxvii W9 **Coryton** Essex, SE England, UK
xliv D9 **Costelloe** Galway, W Ireland
xxxix X9 **Costessey** Norfolk, E England, UK
xxxix O8 **Cotgrave** Nottinghamshire, C England, UK
xxxvii N7 **Cotswold Hills** *var.* Cotswolds. *hill range* S England, UK
xxxix S12 **Cottenham** Cambridgeshire, E England, UK
xli W14 **Cottingham** East Riding of Yorkshire, N England, UK
xliii H19 **Coulport** Argyll and Bute, W Scotland, UK
xliii L21 **Coulter** South Lanarkshire, C Scotland, UK
xliv H13 **Coumfea** ▲ S Ireland
xli R8 **Coundon** Durham, N England, UK
xxxix N10 **Countesthorpe** Leicestershire, C England, UK
xliii M17 **Coupar Angus** Perth and Kinross, C Scotland, UK
xliv F15 **Courtmacsherry** Cork, S Ireland
xliv L11 **Courtown** *var.* Courtown Harbour. Wexford, SE Ireland
xliii H19 **Cove** Argyll and Bute, W Scotland, UK
xlii F10 **Cove** Highland, NW Scotland, UK
xlii P14 **Cove Bay** City of Aberdeen, NE Scotland, UK
xxxviii F15 **Coventry** *anc.* Couentrey. Coventry, C England, UK
xxxviii E15 **Coventry** ◈ *unitary authority* C England, UK
xxxviii E14 **Coventry Canal** *canal* C England, UK
xxxvi C17 **Coverack** Cornwall, SW England, UK
xxxix R9 **Cowbit** Lincolnshire, E England, UK
xxxv I15 **Cowbridge** The Vale of Glamorgan, S Wales, UK
xliii L19 **Cowdenbeath** Fife, E Scotland, UK
xxxvii P13 **Cowes** Isle of Wight, S England, UK
xxxvii T12 **Cowfold** West Sussex, SE England, UK
xli O8 **Cow Green Reservoir** ⊞ NW England, UK
xxxvii Q8 **Cowley** Oxfordshire, S England, UK
xli P8 **Cowshill** Durham, N England, UK
xli S8 **Coxhoe** Durham, N England, UK
xlii K13 **Coylumbridge** Highland, NW Scotland, UK
xli O9 **Crackenthorpe** Cumbria, NW England, UK
xxxvi C14 **Crackington Haven** Cornwall, SW England, UK
xxxv I13 **Crai** Powys, C Wales, UK
xlii G12 **Craig** Highland, NW Scotland, UK
xliv K5 **Craigavon** Craigavon, C Northern Ireland, UK
xliv K5 **Craigavon** ◈ *district* C Northern Ireland, UK
xlii M12 **Craigellachie** Moray, N Scotland, UK
xliii E20 **Craighouse** Argyll and Bute, W Scotland, UK
xliii F17 **Craignure** Argyll and Bute, W Scotland, UK
xxxv H13 **Craig-y-nos** Powys, C Wales, UK
xliii N18 **Crail** Fife, E Scotland, UK
xliii O22 **Crailing** The Borders, S Scotland, UK
xli R5 **Cramlington** Northumberland, N England, UK
xxxvii N13 **Cranborne** Dorset, S England, UK
xxxvii N13 **Cranborne Chase** *hill range* S England, UK
xxxvii W11 **Cranbrook** Kent, SE England, UK
xxxix P11 **Cranford St John** Northamptonshire, C England, UK
xxxvii S11 **Cranleigh** Surrey, SE England, UK
xliii O20 **Cranshaws** The Borders, S Scotland, UK
xliii G19 **Crarae** Argyll and Bute, W Scotland, UK
xlii O14 **Crathes** Aberdeenshire, NE Scotland, UK
xlii M14 **Crathie** Aberdeenshire, NE Scotland, UK
xli S10 **Crathorne** North Yorkshire, N England, UK
xliv F9 **Craughwell** Galway, W Ireland
xxxviii H11 **Craven Arms** Shropshire, W England, UK
xliii L22 **Crawford** South Lanarkshire, C Scotland, UK
xliii K22 **Crawfordjohn** South Lanarkshire, C Scotland, UK
xxxvii P11 **Crawley** Hampshire, S England, UK
xxxvii T11 **Crawley** West Sussex, SE England, UK
xlii E12 **Crawlin Islands** *island group* NW Scotland, UK
xlii A12 **Creagorry** Western Isles, NW Scotland, UK
xxxviii H13 **Credenhill** Herefordshire, W England, UK
xxxvi H13 **Crediton** Devon, SW England, UK
xliii I24 **Cree** ~ SW Scotland, UK
xliv D11 **Creegh** Clare, W Ireland
xliv F2 **Creeslough** Donegal, N Ireland
xliii I25 **Creetown** Dumfries and Galloway, SW Scotland, UK
xliv J4 **Creggan** Omagh, W Northern Ireland, UK
xliv C7 **Cregganbaun** Mayo, NW Ireland
xxxviii H10 **Cressage** Shropshire, W England, UK
xliii F20 **Cretshengan** Argyll and Bute, W Scotland, UK
xxxviii I7 **Crewe** Cheshire, C England, UK
xxxvi K13 **Crewkerne** Somerset, SW England, UK
xliii I17 **Crianlarich** Stirling, C Scotland, UK
xxxv G11 **Cribyn** Ceredigion, W Wales, UK
xxxv F6 **Criccieth** Gwynedd, NW Wales, UK
xxxviii M7 **Crich** Derbyshire, C England, UK
xxxix N11 **Crick** Northamptonshire, C England, UK
xxxv K13 **Crickhowell** Powys, C Wales, UK
xxxvi N8 **Cricklade** Wiltshire, S England, UK
xxxvi B6 **Cricklewood** Brent, SE England, UK
xliii K17 **Crieff** Perth and Kinross, C Scotland, UK
xlii P11 **Crimond** Aberdeenshire, NE Scotland, UK
xliii F19 **Crinan** Argyll and Bute, W Scotland, UK
xxxix X9 **Cringleford** Norfolk, E England, UK
xliv D7 **Croagh Patrick** *Ir.* Cruach Phádraig. ▲ W Ireland
xxxvii U11 **Crockham Hill** Kent, SE England, UK
xli R9 **Croft-on-Tees** Darlington, N England, UK
xliii F17 **Croggan** Argyll and Bute, W Scotland, UK
xlii J11 **Cromarty** Highland, N Scotland, UK
xlii J11 **Cromarty Firth** *inlet* N Scotland, UK
xlii L13 **Cromdale** Highland, NW Scotland, UK
xxxix X7 **Cromer** Norfolk, E England, UK
xlii D9 **Cromore** Western Isles, NW Scotland, UK
xxxvii R11 **Crondall** Hampshire, S England, UK
xli R8 **Crook** Durham, N England, UK
xli P2 **Crookham** Northumberland, N England, UK
xliv C15 **Crookhaven** Cork, S Ireland
xliv E14 **Crookstown** Cork, S Ireland
xliv F12 **Croom** Limerick, SW Ireland
xxxvii P6 **Cropredy** Oxfordshire, C England, UK
xl G11 **Crosby** C Isle of Man
xl B15 **Crosby** *var.* Great Crosby. Sefton, NW England, UK
xli N9 **Crosby Ravensworth** Cumbria, NW England, UK
xliv E8 **Cross** Mayo, NW Ireland
xliii F21 **Crossaig** Argyll and Bute, W Scotland, UK
xli O8 **Cross Fell** ▲ N England, UK
xliii K21 **Crossford** South Lanarkshire, C Scotland, UK
xliv M5 **Crossgar** Down, E Northern Ireland, UK
xxxv G13 **Cross Hands** Carmarthenshire, S Wales, UK
xliv G14 **Crosshaven** Cork, S Ireland
xliii I23 **Crosshill** South Ayrshire, W Scotland, UK
xliv K6 **Crossmaglen** Newry and Mourne, S Northern Ireland, UK
xliii K24 **Crossmichael** Dumfries and Galloway, SW Scotland, UK
xliv D6 **Crossmolina** Mayo, NW Ireland
xl M11 **Crosthwaite** Cumbria, NW England, UK
xli N15 **Croston** Lancashire, NW England, UK
xxxvii X8 **Crouch** ~ E England, UK
xxxvi D6 **Crouch End** Haringey, SE England, UK
xxxix N14 **Croughton** Northamptonshire, C England, UK
xxxvii V12 **Crowborough** East Sussex, SE England, UK
xxxix R9 **Crowland** Lincolnshire, E England, UK
xxxix O3 **Crowle** North Lincolnshire, N England, UK
xxxviii K13 **Crowle** Worcestershire, W England, UK
xxxvii R10 **Crowthorne** Bracknell Forest, S England, UK
xxxix Q3 **Croxton** North Lincolnshire, N England, UK
xlii K12 **Croy** Highland, NW Scotland, UK
xxxvi F11 **Croyde** Devon, SW England, UK
xxxvii U10 **Croydon** Croydon, SE England, UK
xxxiv L17 **Croydon** ◈ *London borough* SE England, UK
xlii P12 **Cruden Bay** Aberdeenshire, NE Scotland, UK
xxxviii I9 **Crudgington** Shropshire, W England, UK
xxxvii N8 **Crudwell** Wiltshire, S England, UK
xlii C8 **Crulivig** Western Isles, NW Scotland, UK
xliv L4 **Crumlin** Antrim, NE Northern Ireland, UK
xl L9 **Crummock Water** ◎ NW England, UK
xliv E10 **Crusheen** Clare, W Ireland
xxxv E12 **Crymych** Pembrokeshire, SW Wales, UK
xxxv H14 **Crynant** Neath Port Talbot, S Wales, UK
xxxviii F16 **Cubbington** Warwickshire, C England, UK
xxxvii U12 **Cuckfield** West Sussex, SE England, UK
xli S15 **Cudworth** Barnsley, N England, UK
xxxviii U8 **Cuffley** Hertfordshire, E England, UK
xliv J2 **Culdaff** Donegal, N Ireland
xli N8 **Culgaith** Cumbria, NW England, UK
xlii N11 **Cullen** Moray, N Scotland, UK
xliv E6 **Cullin, Lough** ◎ NW Ireland
xlii I1 **Cullivoe** Shetland Islands, NE Scotland, UK
xxxvi I13 **Cullompton** Devon, SW England, UK
xliv K3 **Cullybackey** Ballymena, NE Northern Ireland, UK
xliv I3 **Culmore** Donegal, N Ireland
xxxvi I13 **Culmstock** Devon, SW England, UK
xliii L19 **Culross** Fife, E Scotland, UK
xlii H4 **Culswick** Shetland Islands, NE Scotland, UK
xliii L22 **Culter Fell** ▲ C Scotland, UK
xlii P14 **Cults** City of Aberdeen, NE Scotland, UK
xxxix N13 **Culworth** Northamptonshire, C England, UK
xliii K20 **Cumbernauld** North Lanarkshire, S Scotland, UK
xl L8 **Cumbria** ◈ *county* NW England, UK
xl L9 **Cumbrian Mountains** ▲▲ NW England, UK
xlii O11 **Cuminestown** Aberdeenshire, NE Scotland, UK
xl M7 **Cummersdale** Cumbria, NW England, UK
xliii L24 **Cummertrees** Dumfries and Galloway, SW Scotland, UK
xliii J22 **Cumnock** East Ayrshire, W Scotland, UK
xxxvii P8 **Cumnor** Oxfordshire, C England, UK
xli N7 **Cumrew** Cumbria, NW England, UK
xliii M18 **Cupar** Fife, E Scotland, UK
xliv J9 **Curragh, The** *physical region* E Ireland
xliv B14 **Currane, Lough** ◎ SW Ireland
xliii M20 **Currie** City of Edinburgh, SE Scotland, UK
xliv C6 **Cushcamcarragh** ▲ NW Ireland
xliv L3 **Cushendall** Moyle, N Northern Ireland, UK
xliv L2 **Cushendun** Moyle, N Northern Ireland, UK
xliv F10 **Cutra, Lough** ◎ W Ireland
xxxv K13 **Cwmbran** *Wel.* Cwmbrân. Torfaen, SW Wales, UK
xxxv F13 **Cwmffrwd** Carmarthenshire, S Wales, UK
xxxv I5 **Cyffylliog** Denbighshire, N Wales, UK
xxxv I6 **Cynwyd** Denbighshire, N Wales, UK
xxxv F12 **Cynwyl Elfed** Carmarthenshire, S Wales, UK

D

xl M8 **Dacre** Cumbria, NW England, UK
xxxvii V9 **Dagenham** Barking and Dagenham, SE England, UK
xxxvii S7 **Dagnall** Buckinghamshire, C England, UK
xliii H23 **Dailly** South Ayrshire, W Scotland, UK
xliii I16 **Daimh, Loch an** ◎ C Scotland, UK
xliv I9 **Daingean** Offaly, C Ireland
xliii N18 **Dairsie** Fife, E Scotland, UK
xliii G18 **Dalavich** Argyll and Bute, W Scotland, UK
xliii K25 **Dalbeattie** Dumfries and Galloway, SW Scotland, UK
xl F12 **Dalby** W Isle of Man
xlii H13 **Dalchreichart** Highland, NW Scotland, UK
xxxv C14 **Dale** Pembrokeshire, SW Wales, UK
xlii H3 **Dale of Walls** Shetland Islands, NE Scotland, UK
xliii L16 **Dalguise** Perth and Kinross, C Scotland, UK
xlii K7 **Dalhalvaig** Highland, N Scotland, UK
xlii A13 **Daliburgh** Western Isles, NW Scotland, UK
xliii M20 **Dalkeith** Midlothian, SE Scotland, UK
xliv L9 **Dalkey** Dublin, E Ireland
xlii L11 **Dallas** Moray, N Scotland, UK
xliii H17 **Dalmally** Argyll and Bute, W Scotland, UK
xliii I23 **Dalmellington** East Ayrshire, W Scotland, UK
xliii I21 **Dalry** North Ayrshire, W Scotland, UK
xliii I22 **Dalrymple** South Ayrshire, W Scotland, UK
xl M7 **Dalston** Cumbria, NW England, UK
xliii L24 **Dalton** Dumfries and Galloway, SW Scotland, UK
xl L12 **Dalton-in-Furness** Cumbria, NW England, UK
xliii J15 **Dalwhinnie** Highland, NW Scotland, UK
xxxvi J13 **Dalwood** Devon, SW England, UK
xxxvii N12 **Damerham** Hampshire, S England, UK
xlii F12 **Damph, Loch** ◎ NW Scotland, UK
xxxvii W8 **Danbury** Essex, SE England, UK
xli S16 **Darfield** Barnsley, N England, UK
xli W7 **Darlington** Darlington, N England, UK
xli R9 **Darlington** ◈ *unitary authority* N England, UK
xxxvi H15 **Dart** ~ SW England, UK
xxxvii V9 **Dartford** Kent, SE England, UK
xxxvi H15 **Dartington** Devon, SW England, UK
xxxvi G15 **Dartmoor** *moorland* SW England, UK
xxxvi H16 **Dartmouth** Devon, SW England, UK
xli S15 **Darton** Barnsley, N England, UK
xliv G5 **Dartry Mountains** ▲▲ N Ireland
xliii J21 **Darvel** East Ayrshire, W Scotland, UK
xli O15 **Darwen** Lancashire, NW England, UK
xlii L12 **Dava** Moray, N Scotland, UK
xliii F22 **Davaar** *island* W Scotland, UK
xxxviii I6 **Davenham** Cheshire, W England, UK
xxxix N12 **Daventry** Northamptonshire, C England, UK
xliii M23 **Davington** Dumfries and Galloway, SW Scotland, UK
xlii J12 **Daviot** Highland, NW Scotland, UK
xxxviii I10 **Dawley** Shropshire, W England, UK
xxxvi I15 **Dawlish** Devon, SW England, UK
xliv F3 **Dawros Head** *headland* N Ireland
xxxvii Z10 **Deal** Kent, SE England, UK
xxxviii L8 **Dean, Forest of** *forest* C England, UK
xl K8 **Dearham** Cumbria, NW England, UK
xxxix X13 **Deben** ~ E England, UK
xxxix X12 **Debenham** Suffolk, E England, UK
xxxvii P6 **Deddington** Oxfordshire, C England, UK
xxxv K4 **Dee** *Wel.* Afon Dyfrdwy. ~ England/Wales, UK
xliii J25 **Dee** ~ S Scotland, UK
xlii N14 **Dee** ~ NE Scotland, UK
xliv E11 **Deel** ~ W Ireland
xxxix Q9 **Deeping St Nicholas** Lincolnshire, E England, UK
xliv I8 **Deeravaragh, Lough** ◎ C Ireland
xxxviii J13 **Defford** Worcestershire, W England, UK
xxxv G5 **Deiniolen** Gwynedd, NW Wales, UK
xxxvi D14 **Delabole** Cornwall, SW England, UK
xliv D8 **Delphi** Mayo, NW Ireland
xliv J8 **Delvin** Westmeath, C Ireland
xxxv I5 **Denbigh** *Wel.* Dinbych. Denbighshire, NE Wales, UK
xxxv I5 **Denbighshire** ◈ *unitary authority* N Wales, UK
xli R15 **Denby Dale** Kirklees, N England, UK
xlii N16 **Denhead** Aberdeenshire, NE Scotland, UK
xliii P11 **Denhead** Angus, E Scotland, UK
xliii N22 **Denholm** The Borders, S Scotland, UK
xliii K19 **Denny** Falkirk, C Scotland, UK
xli Q15 **Denshaw** Oldham, NW England, UK
xli O11 **Dent** Cumbria, NW England, UK
xli O11 **Dent** ~ NW England, UK
xxxix P8 **Denton** Lincolnshire, E England, UK
xli H15 **Denton** Tameside, NW England, UK
xxxix U12 **Depden** Suffolk, E England, UK
xxxvi E8 **Deptford** Lewisham, SE England, UK
xxxviii M8 **Derby** City of Derby, C England, UK
xxxviii M8 **Derby, City of** ◈ *unitary authority* C England, UK
xxxviii L6 **Derbyshire** ◈ *county* C England, UK
xliv I4 **Derg** ~ Ireland/Northern Ireland, UK
xliv F10 **Derg, Lough** *Ir.* Loch Deirgeirt. ◎ W Ireland
xliv H4 **Derg, Lough** ◎ N Ireland
xxxvii W14 **Déroute, Passage de la** *strait* Channel Islands/France
xliv C14 **Derreendarragh** Kerry, SW Ireland
xliv G2 **Derrybeg** Donegal, N Ireland
xliv H5 **Derrygonnelly** Fermanagh, W Northern Ireland, UK
xliv K2 **Derrykeighan** Ballymoney, N Northern Ireland, UK
xliv I6 **Derrylin** Fermanagh, W Northern Ireland, UK
xliv H6 **Derrynacreeve** Cavan, N Ireland
xliv G3 **Derryveagh Mountains** ▲▲ N Ireland
xxxix U8 **Dersingham** Norfolk, E England, UK
xliii D16 **Dervaig** Argyll and Bute, W Scotland, UK
xl L8 **Derwent** ~ NW England, UK
xli U13 **Derwent** ~ N England, UK
xxxviii L4 **Derwent Reservoir** ⊞ C England, UK
xli Q7 **Derwent Reservoir** ⊞ N England, UK
xxxix P11 **Desborough** Northamptonshire, C England, UK
xxxix N10 **Desford** Leicestershire, C England, UK
xlii N12 **Deveron** ~ NE Scotland, UK
xxxv H10 **Devil's Bridge** Ceredigion, W Wales, UK
xxxvi N10 **Devizes** Wiltshire, S England, UK
xxxvi G14 **Devon** ◈ *county* SW England, UK
xli R15 **Dewsbury** Kirklees, N England, UK
xxxvii P9 **Didcot** Oxfordshire, C England, UK
xxxix Q7 **Digby** Lincolnshire, E England, UK
xlii D11 **Digg** Highland, NW Scotland, UK
xxxv E7 **Dinas** Gwynedd, NW Wales, UK
xxxv D12 **Dinas** Pembrokeshire, SW Wales, UK
xxxv H8 **Dinas-Mawddwy** Gwynedd, NW Wales, UK
xxxv J15 **Dinas Powys** The Vale of Glamorgan, S Wales, UK
xliv B13 **Dingle** *Ir.* An Daingean. Kerry, SW Ireland
xliv B13 **Dingle Bay** *Ir.* Bá an Daingin. *bay* SW Ireland
xlii I11 **Dingwall** Highland, N Scotland, UK
xliii N14 **Dinnet** Aberdeenshire, NE Scotland, UK
xli T17 **Dinnington** Rotherham, N England, UK
xxxvi N12 **Dinton** Wiltshire, S England, UK
xliii F21 **Dippen** Argyll and Bute, W Scotland, UK
xliii G22 **Dippin** North Ayrshire, W Scotland, UK
xliii N19 **Dirleton** East Lothian, SE Scotland, UK
xli S12 **Dishforth** North Yorkshire, N England, UK
xxxix W11 **Diss** Norfolk, E England, UK
xl K9 **Distington** Cumbria, NW England, UK
xxxix Y10 **Ditchingham** Norfolk, E England, UK
xxxvii U12 **Ditchling** East Sussex, SE England, UK
xxxvi H16 **Dittisham** Devon, SW England, UK
xxxviii I11 **Ditton Priors** Shropshire, W England, UK
xxxvi E15 **Dobwalls** Cornwall, SW England, UK
xxxix U8 **Docking** Norfolk, E England, UK
xxxix S10 **Doddington** Cambridgeshire, E England, UK
xxxvii X10 **Doddington** Kent, SE England, UK
xli P2 **Doddington** Northumberland, N England, UK
xxxv K5 **Dodleston** Flintshire, N Wales, UK
xxxvi D17 **Dodman Point** *headland* SW England, UK
xxxix R6 **Dogdyke** Lincolnshire, E England, UK
xxxv J8 **Dolanog** Powys, C Wales, UK
xxxv J9 **Dolfor** Powys, C Wales, UK
xxxv H5 **Dolgarrog** Conwy, N Wales, UK
xxxv H7 **Dolgellau** Gwynedd, NW Wales, UK
xliv G11 **Dolla** Tipperary, S Ireland
xliii L18 **Dollar** Clackmannan, C Scotland, UK
xliii L21 **Dolphinton** The Borders, S Scotland, UK
xxxvi F13 **Dolton** Devon, SW England, UK
xxxv H6 **Dolwyddelan** Conwy, N Wales, UK
xli U14 **Don** ~ N England, UK
xlii O13 **Don** ~ NE Scotland, UK
xliv M4 **Donaghadee** Ards, E Northern Ireland, UK
xli T16 **Doncaster** *anc.* Danum. Doncaster, N England, UK
xli T15 **Doncaster** ◈ *unitary authority* N England, UK
xliv G4 **Donegal** *Ir.* Dún na nGall. Donegal, NW Ireland
xliv H3 **Donegal** *Ir.* Dún na nGall. ◈ *county* NW Ireland
xliv H4 **Donegal Bay** *Ir.* Bá Dhún na nGall. *bay* NW Ireland
xliv C11 **Donegal Point** *headland* W Ireland
xxxix R8 **Donington** Lincolnshire, E England, UK
xxxviii I9 **Donnington** Shropshire, W England, UK
xliv F13 **Donoughmore** Cork, S Ireland
xliv C6 **Dooagh** Mayo, NW Ireland
xliv C6 **Doogort** *var.* Dugort. Mayo, NW Ireland
xliv C6 **Doohooma** Mayo, NW Ireland
xliv G11 **Doon** Limerick, SW Ireland
xliv D11 **Doonbeg** ~ W Ireland
xliii I23 **Doon, Loch** ◎ W Scotland, UK
xli N13 **Dophinholme** Lancashire, NW England, UK
xxxvi M14 **Dorchester** *anc.* Durnovaria. Dorset, S England, UK
xxxvii Q8 **Dorchester** Oxfordshire, C England, UK
xlii J12 **Dores** Highland, NW Scotland, UK
xxxvii T11 **Dorking** Surrey, SE England, UK
xli Y6 **Dormanstown** Redcar and Cleveland, N England, UK
xlii F13 **Dornie** Highland, NW Scotland, UK
xlii J10 **Dornoch** Highland, N Scotland, UK
xlii J10 **Dornoch Firth** *inlet* N Scotland, UK
xxxviii D16 **Dorridge** Solihull, C England, UK
xxxvi L13 **Dorset** ◈ *county* S England, UK
xxxviii G13 **Dorstone** Herefordshire, W England, UK
xliii G21 **Dougarie** North Ayrshire, W Scotland, UK
xliv F14 **Douglas** Cork, S Ireland
xl G12 **Douglas** ○ (Isle of Man) E Isle of Man
xliii K22 **Douglas** South Lanarkshire, C Scotland, UK
xliii N16 **Douglastown** Angus, E Scotland, UK
xlii M4 **Dounby** Orkney Islands, N Scotland, UK
xliii J18 **Doune** Stirling, C Scotland, UK
xlii K6 **Dounreay** Highland, NW Scotland, UK
xxxviii K5 **Dove Holes** Derbyshire, C England, UK
xxxvii Z11 **Dover** *Fr.* Douvres; *Lat.* Dubris Portus. Kent, SE England, UK
xxxviii L8 **Doveridge** Derbyshire, C England, UK
xxxvii Z12 **Dover, Strait of** *var.* Straits of Dover, *Fr.* Pas de Calais. *strait* England, UK/France
xliv M5 **Down** ◈ *district* SE Northern Ireland, UK
xli P2 **Downham** Northumberland, N England, UK
xxxix T10 **Downham Market** Norfolk, E England, UK
xlii P14 **Downies** Aberdeenshire, NE Scotland, UK
xliv M5 **Downpatrick** *Ir.* Dún Pádraig. Down, SE Northern Ireland, UK
xxxvii O12 **Downton** Wiltshire, S England, UK
xliv H6 **Dowra** Leitrim, N Ireland
xliv K4 **Draperstown** Magherafelt, C Northern Ireland, UK
xxxviii L8 **Draycott in the Clay** Staffordshire, C England, UK
xxxix X9 **Drayton** Norfolk, E England, UK
xliv C12 **Dreenagh** Kerry, SW Ireland
xliii I21 **Dreghorn** North Ayrshire, W Scotland, UK
xliii N19 **Drem** East Lothian, SE Scotland, UK
xli W12 **Driffield** East Riding of Yorkshire, N England, UK
xl K10 **Drigg** Cumbria, NW England, UK
xlii E16 **Drimnin** Highland, NW Scotland, UK
xliv D15 **Drimoleague** Cork, S Ireland
xliv K7 **Drogheda** *Ir.* Droichead Átha. Louth, NE Ireland
xliv J9 **Droichead Nua** *var.* An Droichead Nua, Newbridge, C Ireland
xxxviii B17 **Droitwich** Worcestershire, W England, UK
xliv G5 **Dromahair** Leitrim, N Ireland
xliv L5 **Dromara** Banbridge, SE Northern Ireland, UK
xliv E12 **Dromcolliher** Limerick, SW Ireland
xliv G10 **Dromineer** Tipperary, S Ireland
xliv H7 **Dromod** Leitrim, N Ireland
xliv L5 **Dromore** *Ir.* Droim Mór. Banbridge, SE Northern Ireland, UK
xliv I4 **Dromore** Omagh, W Northern Ireland, UK
xliv F5 **Dromore West** Sligo, N Ireland
xxxviii L5 **Dronfield** Derbyshire, C England, UK
xliii I22 **Drongan** East Ayrshire, W Scotland, UK
xl H15 **Droylsden** Tameside, NW England, UK
xliii F20 **Druimdrishaig** Argyll and Bute, W Scotland, UK
xliv I3 **Drumahoe** Londonderry, NW Northern Ireland, UK
xlii G8 **Drumbeg** Highland, NW Scotland, UK
xliv K6 **Drumbilla** Louth, NE Ireland
xlii J12 **Drumchardine** Highland, NW Scotland, UK
xliv G5 **Drumcliff** Sligo, N Ireland
xliii J21 **Drumclog** South Lanarkshire, C Scotland, UK
xlii E13 **Drumfearn** Highland, NW Scotland, UK
xliv I2 **Drumfree** Donegal, N Ireland
xliv G6 **Drumkeeran** Leitrim, N Ireland
xliv H7 **Drumlish** Longford, C Ireland
xlii O15 **Drumlithie** Aberdeenshire, NE Scotland, UK
xliii H26 **Drummore** Dumfries and Galloway, SW Scotland, UK
xlii I13 **Drumnadrochit** Highland, NW Scotland, UK
xliv I4 **Drumquin** Omagh, W Northern Ireland, UK
xlii H9 **Drumrunie** Highland, NW Scotland, UK
xliv H7 **Drumshanbo** Leitrim, N Ireland
xliv H7 **Drumsna** Leitrim, N Ireland
xli R4 **Druridge Bay** *bay* N England, UK
xxxv I11 **Drygarn Fawr** ▲ E Wales, UK
xlii D13 **Drynoch** Highland, NW Scotland, UK
xliv L9 **Dublin** *Ir.* Baile Átha Cliath; *anc.* Eblana. ● (Ireland) Dublin, E Ireland
xliv K9 **Dublin** *Ir.* Baile Átha Cliath; *anc.* Eblana. ◈ *county* E Ireland
xliv L8 **Dublin** ✕ Dublin, E Ireland
xliv L9 **Dublin Bay** *bay* E Ireland
xxxvii P8 **Ducklington** Oxfordshire, C England, UK
xxxix Q10 **Duddington** Northamptonshire, C England, UK
xli P1 **Duddo** Northumberland, N England, UK
xl L10 **Duddon** ~ NW England, UK
xxxviii B15 **Dudley** Dudley, C England, UK
xxxviii J11 **Dudley** ◈ *unitary authority* C England, UK
xxxviii M7 **Duffield** Derbyshire, C England, UK
xlii M12 **Dufftown** Moray, N Scotland, UK
xlii M11 **Duffus** Moray, N Scotland, UK
xlii F13 **Duirinish** Highland, NW Scotland, UK
xlii F13 **Duisdalemore** Highland, NW Scotland, UK
xl H15 **Dukinfield** Tameside, NW England, UK
xxxix U12 **Dullingham** Cambridgeshire, E England, UK
xlii K13 **Dulnain Bridge** Highland, NW Scotland, UK
xxxvi H12 **Dulverton** Somerset, SW England, UK
xxxvi E9 **Dulwich** Southwark, SE England, UK
xliii I19 **Dumbarton** West Dunbartonshire, W Scotland, UK
xliii L24 **Dumfries** Dumfries and Galloway, SW Scotland, UK
xliii J24 **Dumfries and Galloway** ◈ *unitary authority* SW Scotland, UK
xliii H20 **Dunan** Argyll and Bute, W Scotland, UK
xlii E13 **Dunan** Highland, NW Scotland, UK
xliv L7 **Dunany Point** *headland* NE Ireland
xliii O19 **Dunbar** East Lothian, SE Scotland, UK
xlii L8 **Dunbeath** Highland, N Scotland, UK
xliii K18 **Dunblane** Stirling, C Scotland, UK
xliv K8 **Dunboyne** Meath, E Ireland
xliv J13 **Duncannon** Wexford, SE Ireland
xlii M6 **Duncansby Head** *headland* N Scotland, UK
xxxix N11 **Dunchurch** Warwickshire, C England, UK
xliv K13 **Duncormick** Wexford, SE Ireland
xliv K7 **Dundalk** *Ir.* Dún Dealgan. Louth, NE Ireland
xliv L7 **Dundalk Bay** *Ir.* Cuan Dhún Dealgan. *bay* NE Ireland
xliii M17 **Dundee** City of Dundee, E Scotland, UK
xliii M17 **Dundee, City of** ◈ *unitary authority* E Scotland, UK
xliii I22 **Dundonald** South Ayrshire, W Scotland, UK
xlii G10 **Dundonnell** Highland, NW Scotland, UK
xliii K25 **Dundrennan** Dumfries and Galloway, SW Scotland, UK
xliv G11 **Dundrum** Tipperary, S Ireland
xliv M5 **Dundrum** Down, E Northern Ireland, UK
xliv M6 **Dundrum Bay** *Ir.* Cuan Dhún Droma. *inlet* NW Irish Sea
xlii O13 **Dunecht** Aberdeenshire, NE Scotland, UK
xliv H2 **Dunfanaghy** *Ir.* Dún Fionnachaidh. Donegal, NW Ireland
xliii L19 **Dunfermline** Fife, C Scotland, UK
xli R16 **Dunford Bridge** Barnsley, N England, UK
xliv J5 **Dungannon** *Ir.* Dún Geanainn. Dungannon, C Northern Ireland, UK
xliv J5 **Dungannon** ◈ *district* C Northern Ireland, UK
xliv H13 **Dungarvan** *Ir.* Dun Garbháin. Waterford, S Ireland
xxxvii Y12 **Dungeness** *headland* SE England, UK
xliv J3 **Dungiven** Limavady, N Northern Ireland, UK
xliv G3 **Dunglow** *var.* Dungloe, *Ir.* An Clochán Liath. NW Ireland
xxxix Q5 **Dunholme** Lincolnshire, E England, UK
xliii K19 **Dunipace** Falkirk, C Scotland, UK
xliii L16 **Dunkeld** Perth and Kinross, C Scotland, UK
xxxvi H11 **Dunkery Beacon** ▲ SW England, UK
xliv L9 **Dún Laoghaire** *Eng.* Dunleary; *prev.* Kingstown. Dublin, E Ireland
xliv K10 **Dunlavin** Wicklow, E Ireland
xliv K7 **Dunleer** Louth, NE Ireland
xliii I21 **Dunlop** East Ayrshire, W Scotland, UK
xliv C15 **Dunmanus Bay** *bay* S Ireland
xliv E14 **Dunmanway** *Ir.* Dún Mánmhaí. Cork, SW Ireland
xliv F8 **Dunmore** Galway, W Ireland
xliv J13 **Dunmore East** Waterford, S Ireland
xliv L5 **Dunmurry** Lisburn, E Northern Ireland, UK
xliv I3 **Dunnamanagh** Strabane, W Northern Ireland, UK
xlii L6 **Dunnet** Highland, N Scotland, UK
xlii L6 **Dunnet Bay** *bay* N Scotland, UK
xlii L6 **Dunnet Head** *headland* N Scotland, UK
xliii L18 **Dunning** Perth and Kinross, C Scotland, UK
xliii H20 **Dunoon** Argyll and Bute, W Scotland, UK
xliv B13 **Dunquin** Kerry, SW Ireland
xliii O20 **Duns** The Borders, SE Scotland, UK
xxxix Q8 **Dunsby** Lincolnshire, E England, UK
xliii K24 **Dunscore** Dumfries and Galloway, SW Scotland, UK
xxxvi H14 **Dunsford** Devon, SW England, UK
xliv K8 **Dunshaughlin** Meath, E Ireland
xxxvii S7 **Dunstable** *Lat.* Durocobrivae. Bedfordshire, E England, UK
xli R3 **Dunstan** Northumberland, N England, UK
xxxvi I11 **Dunster** Somerset, SW England, UK
xlii J12 **Duntelchaig, Loch** ◎ NW Scotland, UK
xliii H22 **Dunure** South Ayrshire, W Scotland, UK
xlii D12 **Dunvegan** Highland, NW Scotland, UK
xxxix Y11 **Dunwich** Suffolk, E England, UK
xxxvi M14 **Durdle Door** *natural arch* S England, UK
xli V4 **Durham** *hist.* Dunholme. Durham, N England, UK
xli Q8 **Durham** ◈ *county* N England, UK
xlii I6 **Durness** Highland, N Scotland, UK
xlii G16 **Duror** Highland, NW Scotland, UK
xxxvi O11 **Durrington** Wiltshire, S England, UK
xliv I10 **Durrow** Laois, C Ireland
xliv D15 **Durrus** Cork, S Ireland
xliv B15 **Dursey Head** *Ir.* Ceann Baoi. *headland* S Ireland
xliv B15 **Dursey Island** *Ir.* Oileán Baoi. *island* SW Ireland
xxxvi L8 **Dursley** Gloucestershire, C England, UK
xxxix T13 **Duxford** Cambridgeshire, E England, UK
xlii P13 **Dyce** City of Aberdeen, NE Scotland, UK
xxxv G7 **Dyffryn Ardudwy** Gwynedd, NW Wales, UK
xxxv H8 **Dyfi** ~ W Wales, UK
xxxvii Y12 **Dymchurch** Kent, SE England, UK
xxxvi L6 **Dymock** Gloucestershire, C England, UK
xliii M19 **Dysart** Fife, E Scotland, UK
xxxv I4 **Dyserth** Denbighshire, N Wales, UK

E

xliii J21 **Eaglesham** East Renfrewshire, W Scotland, UK
xxxvi A7 **Ealing** Ealing, SE England, UK
xxxiv K16 **Ealing** ◈ *London borough* SE England, UK
xli P13 **Earby** Lancashire, NW England, UK
xxxix S11 **Earith** Cambridgeshire, E England, UK
xxxvii R9 **Earley** Reading, S England, UK
xxxix P12 **Earls Barton** Northamptonshire, C England, UK
xxxvii W6 **Earls Colne** Essex, SE England, UK
xliii N18 **Earlsferry** Fife, E Scotland, UK
xxxvi C9 **Earlsfield** Wandsworth, S England, UK
xxxix N10 **Earl Shilton** Leicestershire, C England, UK
xliii N21 **Earlston** The Borders, S Scotland, UK
xxxix W12 **Earl Stonham** Suffolk, E England, UK
xliii K17 **Earn** ~ N Scotland, UK
xliii J17 **Earn, Loch** ◎ C Scotland, UK
xxxvii R12 **Easebourne** West Sussex, SE England, UK
xli W4 **Easington** Durham, N England, UK
xli Y14 **Easington** East Riding of Yorkshire, N England, UK
xli X4 **Easington Colliery** Durham, N England, UK
xli T12 **Easingwold** North Yorkshire, N England, UK
xliv F5 **Easky** Sligo, N Ireland
xli P7 **East Allen** ~ N England, UK
xxxix V11 **East Anglia** *physical region* E England, UK
xliii I22 **East Ayrshire** ◈ *unitary authority* W Scotland, UK
xxxix W14 **East Bergholt** Suffolk, E England, UK
xxxvii V13 **Eastbourne** East Sussex, SE England, UK
xxxvi J11 **East Brent** Somerset, SW England, UK
xxxix O7 **East Bridgford** Nottinghamshire, C England, UK
xxxvii P9 **East Challow** Oxfordshire, C England, UK
xxxvi L13 **East Chinnock** Somerset, SW England, UK
xxxvii X9 **Eastchurch** Kent, SE England, UK
xxxvii P13 **East Cowes** Isle of Wight, S England, UK
xlii J13 **East Croachy** Highland, NW Scotland, UK
xxxvii V13 **East Dean** East Sussex, SE England, UK
xxxix W9 **East Dereham** Norfolk, E England, UK
xliii I19 **East Dunbartonshire** ◈ *unitary authority* C Scotland, UK
xlii J11 **Easter Ardross** Highland, NW Scotland, UK
xlii M14 **Easter Balmoral** Aberdeenshire, NE Scotland, UK
xlii I4 **Easter Quarff** Shetland Islands, NE Scotland, UK
xlii H4 **Easter Skeld** Shetland Islands, NE Scotland, UK
xli P8 **Eastgate** Durham, N England, UK
xxxvi O10 **East Grafton** Wiltshire, S England, UK
xxxvii U11 **East Grinstead** West Sussex, SE England, UK
xxxix O12 **East Haddon** Northamptonshire, C England, UK
xxxix Q3 **East Halton** North Lincolnshire, N England, UK
xxxvi F7 **East Ham** Newham, SE England, UK
xxxvii P8 **East Hanney** Oxfordshire, C England, UK
xxxix W11 **East Harling** Norfolk, E England, UK
xxxvii T10 **East Horsley** Surrey, SE England, UK
xxxvii P9 **East Ilsley** West Berkshire, S England, UK
xxxvi M8 **Eastington** Gloucestershire, C England, UK

◆ Country ● Country Capital ◇ Dependent Territory ○ Dependent Territory Capital ◈ Administrative Region ✕ International Airport ▲ Mountain ▲▲ Mountain Range ◎ Lake ⊞ Reservoir ~ River

◆ COUNTRY ◇ DEPENDENT TERRITORY ◆ ADMINISTRATIVE REGION ▲ MOUNTAIN ◎ LAKE
● COUNTRY CAPITAL ○ DEPENDENT TERRITORY CAPITAL ✕ INTERNATIONAL AIRPORT ▲ MOUNTAIN RANGE ▢ RESERVOIR ∿ RIVER

xlix

GREAT SHEFFORD – KERRY

xxxvii P9 **Great Shefford** West Berkshire, S England, UK
xxxix T13 **Great Shelford** Cambridgeshire, E England, UK
xxxvii N9 **Great Somerford** Wiltshire, S England, UK
xxxix R12 **Great Staughton** Cambridgeshire, E England, UK
xxxvii Y12 **Greatstone-on-Sea** Kent, SE England, UK
xxxvii P7 **Great Tew** Oxfordshire, C England, UK
xxxvi F12 **Great Torrington** Devon, SW England, UK
xxxvii X9 **Great Wakering** Essex, SE England, UK
xxxvii W7 **Great Waltham** Essex, SE England, UK
xxxvii N11 **Great Wishford** Wiltshire, S England, UK
xxxviii I12 **Great Witley** Worcestershire, W England, UK
xxxix Z9 **Great Yarmouth** *var.* Yarmouth. Norfolk, E England, UK
xxxvii V6 **Great Yeldham** Essex, SE England, UK
xliv J2 **Greencastle** Donegal, N Ireland
xliv L6 **Greencastle** Newry and Mourne, S Northern Ireland, UK
xxxvi A7 **Greenford** Ealing, SE England, UK
xli O5 **Greenhaugh** Northumberland, N England, UK
xli N6 **Greenhead** Northumberland, N England, UK
xliii O21 **Greenlaw** The Borders, S Scotland, UK
xliii K18 **Greenloaning** Perth and Kinross, C Scotland, UK
xliii K22 **Green Lowther** ▲ C Scotland, UK
xliii H19 **Greenock** Inverclyde, W Scotland, UK
xl M11 **Greenodd** Cumbria, NW England, UK
xliv L13 **Greenore Point** *headland* SE Ireland
xxxiv L16 **Greenwich** ⬖ *London borough* SE England, UK
xxxvii U9 **Greenwich** hist. Grenawic. Greenwich, SE England, UK
xxxix P9 **Greetham** Rutland, C England, UK
xli S16 **Grenoside** Sheffield, N England, UK
xxxv K5 **Gresford** Wrexham, NE Wales, UK
xli Q9 **Greta Bridge** Durham, N England, UK
xliii M24 **Gretna** Dumfries and Galloway, SW Scotland, UK
xliii M24 **Gretna Green** Dumfries and Galloway, SW Scotland, UK
xxxix P10 **Gretton** Northamptonshire, C England, UK
xliv M5 **Greyabbey** Ards, E Northern Ireland, UK
xl M8 **Greystoke** Cumbria, NW England, UK
xliv L10 **Greystones** *Ir.* Na Clocha Liatha. Wicklow, E Ireland
xlii A11 **Griminish Point** *headland* NW Scotland, UK
xlii I2 **Grimister** Shetland Islands, NE Scotland, UK
xxxix S5 **Grimoldby** Lincolnshire, E England, UK
xxxix R3 **Grimsby** *prev.* Great Grimsby. North East Lincolnshire, E England, UK
xxxix U8 **Grimston** Norfolk, E England, UK
xli O13 **Grindleton** Lancashire, NW England, UK
xlii N4 **Gritley** Orkney Islands, N Scotland, UK
xl L11 **Grizebeck** Cumbria, NW England, UK
xliii F21 **Grogport** Argyll and Bute, W Scotland, UK
xlii C10 **Grosebay** Western Isles, NW Scotland, UK
xxxvii Y10 **Grove** Kent, SE England, UK
xxxvi F9 **Grove Park** Lewisham, SE England, UK
xxxvii W16 **Groznez Point** *headland* Jersey, Channel Islands
xlii I9 **Gruids** Highland, NW Scotland, UK
xlii F10 **Gruinard Bay** *bay* NW Scotland, UK
xxxix X13 **Grundisburgh** Suffolk, E England, UK
xlii H4 **Gruting** Shetland Islands, NE Scotland, UK
xxxiv H16 **Guernsey** *off.* Bailiwick of Guernsey. ◇ *UK crown dependency* NW Europe
xxxvii V15 **Guernsey** *island* Channel Islands, NW Europe
xxxvii W12 **Guestling Green** East Sussex, SE England, UK
xxxvii S11 **Guildford** Surrey, SE England, UK
xliii L17 **Guildtown** Perth and Kinross, C Scotland, UK
xxxv K8 **Guilsfield** Powys, C Wales, UK
xli T9 **Guisborough** Redcar and Cleveland, N England, UK
xli R13 **Guiseley** Leeds, N England, UK
xxxix W8 **Guist** Norfolk, E England, UK
xliii N19 **Gullane** East Lothian, SE Scotland, UK
xli U14 **Gunby** East Riding of Yorkshire, N England, UK
xxxvi A8 **Gunnersbury** Hounslow, SE England, UK
xxxvi F15 **Gunnislake** Cornwall, SW England, UK
xlii I4 **Gunnista** Shetland Islands, NE Scotland, UK
xxxvi B17 **Gunwalloe** Cornwall, SW England, UK
xlii I1 **Gutcher** Shetland Islands, NE Scotland, UK
xxxix S9 **Guyhirn** Cambridgeshire, E England, UK
xxxv F4 **Gwalchmai** Isle of Anglesey, NW Wales, UK
xliv F3 **Gweebarra Bay** *Ir.* Béal an Bheara. *inlet* W Ireland
xliv G2 **Gweedore** *Ir.* Gaoth Dobhair. Donegal, NW Ireland
xxxv J6 **Gwyddelwern** Denbighshire, N Wales, UK
xxxv G7 **Gwynedd** ⬖ *unitary authority* NW Wales, UK
xxxv H5 **Gwytherin** Conwy, N Wales, UK

H

xxxix Q3 **Habrough** North East Lincolnshire, E England, UK
xxxvii Z10 **Hacklinge** Kent, SE England, UK
xli V10 **Hackness** North Yorkshire, N England, UK
xxxvi E6 **Hackney** Hackney, SE England, UK
xxxiv L16 **Hackney** ⬖ *London borough* SE England, UK
xxxvii R8 **Haddenham** Buckinghamshire, C England, UK
xxxix T11 **Haddenham** Cambridgeshire, E England, UK
xliii N19 **Haddington** East Lothian, SE Scotland, UK
xxxix Y10 **Haddiscoe** Norfolk, E England, UK
xxxvii W9 **Hadleigh** Essex, SE England, UK
xxxix W13 **Hadleigh** Suffolk, E England, UK
xxxviii I9 **Hadley** Shropshire, W England, UK
xxxviii H9 **Hadnall** Shropshire, W England, UK
xli O6 **Hadrian's Wall** *ancient wall* N England, UK
xxxviii B17 **Hadzor** Worcestershire, W England, UK
xl M6 **Haggbeck** Cumbria, NW England, UK
xxxviii B15 **Hagley** Worcestershire, W England, UK
xliv D10 **Hag's Head** *Ir.* Ceann Caillí. *headland* W Ireland
xxxvii V13 **Hailsham** East Sussex, SE England, UK
xli O17 **Hale** Trafford, NW England, UK
xxxix Y10 **Hales** Norfolk, E England, UK
xxxviii B15 **Halesowen** Dudley, C England, UK
xxxix Y11 **Halesworth** Suffolk, E England, UK
xxxviii M13 **Halford** Warwickshire, C England, UK
xli Q14 **Halifax** Calderdale, N England, UK
xlii L6 **Halkirk** Highland, N Scotland, UK
xlii K7 **Halladale** ∽ N Scotland, UK
xxxix P10 **Hallaton** Leicestershire, C England, UK
xl L10 **Hall Dunnerdale** Cumbria, NW England, UK
xxxviii J13 **Hallow** Worcestershire, W England, UK
xxxvi H17 **Hallsands** Devon, SW England, UK
xxxvi D14 **Hallworthy** Cornwall, SW England, UK
xli X14 **Halsham** East Riding of Yorkshire, N England, UK
xxxvii W6 **Halstead** Essex, SE England, UK
xxxix R6 **Haltham** Lincolnshire, E England, UK
xl D16 **Halton** ⬖ *unitary authority* NW England, UK
xli O6 **Haltwhistle** Northumberland, N England, UK
xxxix Y9 **Halvergate** Norfolk, E England, UK
xxxvi H16 **Halwell** Devon, SW England, UK
xxxvi F13 **Halwill** Devon, SW England, UK
xxxvi A9 **Ham** Richmond upon Thames, SE England, UK
xlii G4 **Ham** Shetland Islands, NE Scotland, UK
xxxvii Q12 **Hambledon** Hampshire, S England, UK
xli T14 **Hambleton** North Yorkshire, N England, UK
xliii J20 **Hamilton** South Lanarkshire, S Scotland, UK
xxxvi A7 **Hammersmith** *London borough capital* Hammersmith and Fulham, SE England, UK
xxxiv K16 **Hammersmith and Fulham** ⬖ *London borough* SE England, UK
xlii I3 **Hamnavoe** Shetland Islands, NE Scotland, UK
xlii I4 **Hamnavoe** Shetland Islands, NE Scotland, UK
xxxvii P11 **Hampshire** ⬖ *county* S England, UK
xxxvi C6 **Hampstead** Camden, SE England, UK
xli R12 **Hampsthwaite** North Yorkshire, N England, UK
xli U5 **Hamsterley** Durham, N England, UK
xxxvii X11 **Hamstreet** Kent, SE England, UK
xlii G7 **Handa Island** *island* NW Scotland, UK
xxxvii T12 **Handcross** West Sussex, SE England, UK
xl G16 **Handforth** Cheshire, W England, UK
xli S17 **Handsworth** Rotherham, N England, UK
xxxviii J7 **Hanley** City of Stoke-on-Trent, C England, UK
xxxvii Q10 **Hannington** Hampshire, S England, UK
xxxvii R6 **Hanslope** Milton Keynes, C England, UK
xxxvi A7 **Hanwell** Ealing, SE England, UK
xxxix Y8 **Happisburgh** Norfolk, E England, UK
xli P4 **Harbottle** Northumberland, N England, UK
xxxviii M12 **Harbury** Warwickshire, C England, UK
xxxix O8 **Harby** Leicestershire, C England, UK
xxxix P6 **Harby** Nottinghamshire, C England, UK
xli P10 **Hardrow** North Yorkshire, N England, UK
xli S13 **Harewood** Leeds, N England, UK
xxxiv K16 **Haringey** ⬖ *London borough* SE England, UK
xxxv G7 **Harlech** Gwynedd, NW Wales, UK
xxxvi B7 **Harlesden** Brent, SE England, UK
xxxix X11 **Harleston** Norfolk, E England, UK
xxxvii U7 **Harlow** Essex, E England, UK
xxxix P6 **Harmston** Lincolnshire, E England, UK
xxxvii N12 **Harnham** Wiltshire, S England, UK
xxxvii S5 **Harold** Bedfordshire, C England, UK
xlii J1 **Haroldswick** Shetland Islands, NE Scotland, UK
xxxvii S7 **Harpenden** Hertfordshire, E England, UK
xxxix U8 **Harpley** Norfolk, E England, UK
xxxvii W10 **Harrietsham** Kent, SE England, UK
xxxix P10 **Harringworth** Northamptonshire, C England, UK
xliii D14 **Harris** Highland, NW Scotland, UK
xlii C10 **Harris** *physical region* NW Scotland, UK
xlii B10 **Harris, Sound of** *strait* NW Scotland, UK
xli S12 **Harrogate** North Yorkshire, N England, UK
xxxvii T8 **Harrow** Harrow, SE England, UK
xxxiv K16 **Harrow** ⬖ *London borough* SE England, UK
xxxix S13 **Harston** Cambridgeshire, E England, UK
xli S8 **Hart** Hartlepool, N England, UK
xli Q5 **Hartburn** Northumberland, N England, UK
xxxix V12 **Hartest** Suffolk, E England, UK
xliii L22 **Hart Fell** ▲ SW Scotland, UK
xl E17 **Hartford** Cheshire, C England, UK
xxxviii L6 **Hartington** Derbyshire, C England, UK
xxxvi E12 **Hartland** Devon, SW England, UK
xxxvi D12 **Hartland Point** *headland* SW England, UK
xxxviii A16 **Hartlebury** Worcestershire, W England, UK
xli Y5 **Hartlepool** Hartlepool, N England, UK
xli X5 **Hartlepool** ⬖ *unitary authority* NE England, UK
xli T8 **Hartlepool Bay** *bay* N England, UK
xxxvii R10 **Hartley Wintney** Hampshire, S England, UK
xxxvi M7 **Hartpury** Gloucestershire, C England, UK
xxxviii K13 **Harvington** Worcestershire, W England, UK
xxxvii P9 **Harwell** Oxfordshire, C England, UK
xxxvii Y6 **Harwich** Essex, E England, UK
xli V10 **Harwood Dale** North Yorkshire, N England, UK
xxxvii S12 **Haslemere** Surrey, SE England, UK
xli O15 **Haslingden** Lancashire, NW England, UK
xxxvii W13 **Hastings** East Sussex, SE England, UK
xxxvi J12 **Hatch Beauchamp** Somerset, SW England, UK
xli U15 **Hatfield** Doncaster, N England, UK
xxxviii I12 **Hatfield** Herefordshire, W England, UK
xxxvii T7 **Hatfield** Hertfordshire, E England, UK
xxxvii V7 **Hatfield Broad Oak** Essex, SE England, UK
xxxvii W7 **Hatfield Peverel** Essex, SE England, UK
xxxvi F13 **Hatherleigh** Devon, SW England, UK
xxxix N9 **Hathern** Leicestershire, C England, UK
xxxvii N8 **Hatherop** Gloucestershire, C England, UK
xxxviii L5 **Hathersage** Derbyshire, C England, UK
xxxviii L8 **Hatton** Derbyshire, C England, UK
xlii P12 **Hatton** Aberdeenshire, NE Scotland, UK
xxxix W12 **Haughley** Suffolk, E England, UK
xxxviii J9 **Haughton** Staffordshire, C England, UK
xxxvii R13 **Havant** Hampshire, S England, UK
xxxv C13 **Haverfordwest** Pembrokeshire, SW Wales, UK
xxxix U13 **Haverhill** Suffolk, E England, UK
xl K11 **Haverigg** Cumbria, NW England, UK
xxxiv M16 **Havering** ⬖ *London borough* SE England, UK
xxxv K5 **Hawarden** Flintshire, N Wales, UK
xli P11 **Hawes** North Yorkshire, N England, UK
xli N9 **Haweswater** ◎ NW England, UK
xliii N22 **Hawick** The Borders, SE Scotland, UK
xxxvii W12 **Hawkhurst** Kent, SE England, UK
xli T11 **Hawnby** North Yorkshire, N England, UK
xli Q14 **Haworth** Bradford, N England, UK
xli T12 **Haxby** York, N England, UK
xxxix O4 **Haxey** North Lincolnshire, N England, UK
xl D15 **Haydock** St Helens, NW England, UK
xli P6 **Haydon Bridge** Northumberland, N England, UK
xxxviii K5 **Hayfield** Derbyshire, C England, UK
xxxvi M16 **Hayle** Cornwall, SW England, UK
xxxvi M16 **Hayle** ∽ SW England, UK
xxxv K12 **Hay-on-Wye** Powys, E Wales, UK
xli V13 **Hayton** East Riding of Yorkshire, N England, UK
xxxix O5 **Hayton** Nottinghamshire, C England, UK
xxxvii U12 **Haywards Heath** West Sussex, SE England, UK
xxxvi L13 **Hazelbury Bryan** Dorset, S England, UK
xli P17 **Hazel Grove** Stockport, NW England, UK
xxxvii R8 **Hazlemere** Buckinghamshire, SE England, UK
xxxix U7 **Heacham** Norfolk, E England, UK
xxxvii W11 **Headcorn** Kent, SE England, UK
xliv E8 **Headford** Galway, W Ireland
xxxvii Q8 **Headington** Oxfordshire, S England, UK
xxxvii R11 **Headley** Hampshire, S England, UK
xli R11 **Healey** North Yorkshire, N England, UK
xxxviii M7 **Heanor** Derbyshire, C England, UK
xxxvi H15 **Heathfield** Devon, SW England, UK
xxxvii V12 **Heathfield** East Sussex, SE England, UK
xxxviii C13 **Heath Hayes** Staffordshire, C England, UK
xxxvii S9 **Heathrow** ✕ (London) SE England, UK
xli R6 **Hebburn** South Tyneside, NE England, UK
xli Q14 **Hebden Bridge** Calderdale, N England, UK
xliii C15 **Hebrides, Sea of the** *sea* NW Scotland, UK
xxxix Q7 **Heckington** Lincolnshire, E England, UK
xxxviii C13 **Hednesford** Staffordshire, C England, UK
xli R9 **Heighington** Darlington, N England, UK
xlii I7 **Heilam** Highland, NW Scotland, UK
xliii O21 **Heiton** The Borders, S Scotland, UK
xliii H19 **Helensburgh** Argyll and Bute, W Scotland, UK
xli P13 **Hellifield** North Yorkshire, N England, UK
xxxvii V13 **Hellingly** East Sussex, SE England, UK
xxxix N13 **Helmdon** Northamptonshire, C England, UK
xlii L9 **Helmsdale** Highland, N Scotland, UK
xlii K8 **Helmsdale** ∽ N Scotland, UK
xli T11 **Helmsley** North Yorkshire, N England, UK
xxxix Q7 **Helpringham** Lincolnshire, E England, UK
xl D17 **Helsby** Cheshire, W England, UK
xxxvi B17 **Helston** Cornwall, SW England, UK
xl M9 **Helvellyn** ▲ NW England, UK
xliv H13 **Helvick Head** *headland* S Ireland
xxxvii S8 **Hemel Hempstead** Hertfordshire, E England, UK
xxxix X10 **Hempnall** Norfolk, E England, UK
xxxix Y9 **Hemsby** Norfolk, E England, UK
xli S15 **Hemsworth** Wakefield, N England, UK
xxxvi B6 **Hendon** Barnet, SE England, UK
xxxvii T12 **Henfield** West Sussex, SE England, UK
xxxviii G8 **Hengoed** Shropshire, W England, UK
xxxviii D17 **Henley-in-Arden** Warwickshire, C England, UK
xxxvii Q9 **Henley-on-Thames** Oxfordshire, C England, UK
xxxv I5 **Henllan** Conwy, N Wales, UK
xxxvii T6 **Henlow** Bedfordshire, C England, UK
xxxvi L12 **Henstridge** Somerset, SW England, UK
xli P4 **Hepple** Northumberland, N England, UK
xxxviii H13 **Hereford** Herefordshire, W England, UK
xxxvi K6 **Herefordshire** ⬖ *unitary authority* W England, UK
xliii N20 **Heriot** The Borders, S Scotland, UK
xxxvii W15 **Herm** *island* Channel Islands
xlii J1 **Herma Ness** *headland* NE Scotland, UK
xxxvii P9 **Hermitage** West Berkshire, S England, UK
xliii N23 **Hermitage** The Borders, S Scotland, UK
xxxvii Y10 **Herne Bay** Kent, SE England, UK
xxxvi D9 **Herne Hill** Southwark, SE England, UK
xxxvii Q11 **Herriard** Hampshire, S England, UK
xxxvii V12 **Herstmonceux** East Sussex, SE England, UK
xxxvii T7 **Hertfordshire** ⬖ *county* E England, UK
xl M15 **Hesketh Bank** Lancashire, NW England, UK
xli W14 **Hessle** East Riding of Yorkshire, N England, UK
xl B16 **Heswall** Wirral, NW England, UK
xxxix X9 **Hethersett** Norfolk, E England, UK
xl M6 **Hethersgill** Cumbria, NW England, UK
xli W4 **Hetton-le-Hole** Sunderland, NE England, UK
xxxix Y11 **Heveningham** Suffolk, E England, UK
xxxix X8 **Hevingham** Norfolk, E England, UK
xli Q6 **Hexham** Northumberland, N England, UK
xxxvii W8 **Heybridge** Essex, SE England, UK
xlii H2 **Heylor** Shetland Islands, NE Scotland, UK
xl M12 **Heysham** Lancashire, NW England, UK
xxxvi M11 **Heytesbury** Wiltshire, S England, UK
xli P15 **Heywood** Rochdale, NW England, UK
xxxix P4 **Hibaldstow** North Lincolnshire, N England, UK
xxxix Y8 **Hickling** Norfolk, E England, UK
xxxviii M6 **Higham** Derbyshire, C England, UK
xxxvii W9 **Higham** Kent, SE England, UK
xxxvi F13 **Highampton** Devon, SW England, UK
xli O12 **High Bentham** North Yorkshire, N England, UK
xxxvi J11 **Highbridge** Somerset, SW England, UK
xxxvii P10 **Highclere** Hampshire, S England, UK
xxxviii I9 **High Ercall** Shropshire, W England, UK
xxxvi I17 **Higher Town** Isles of Scilly, SW England, UK
xxxvi C6 **Highgate** Haringey, SE England, UK
xxxvii X11 **High Halden** Kent, SE England, UK
xl K8 **High Harrington** Cumbria, NW England, UK
xl M7 **High Hesket** Cumbria, NW England, UK
xlii H12 **Highland** ⬖ *unitary authority* NW Scotland, UK
xxxviii I11 **Highley** Shropshire, W England, UK
xxxvii V7 **High Roding** Essex, SE England, UK
xliii L24 **Hightae** Dumfries and Galloway, SW Scotland, UK
xxxvi G14 **High Willhays** ▲ SW England, UK
xxxvii O8 **Highworth** Swindon, S England, UK
xxxvii R8 **High Wycombe** *prev.* Chepping Wycombe, Chipping Wycombe. Buckinghamshire, SE England, UK
xxxix V10 **Hilborough** Norfolk, E England, UK
xxxviii J8 **Hilderstone** Staffordshire, C England, UK
xli X12 **Hilderthorpe** East Riding of Yorkshire, N England, UK
xxxiv K16 **Hillingdon** ⬖ *London borough* SE England, UK
xxxix U8 **Hillington** Norfolk, E England, UK
xlii K10 **Hill of Fearn** Highland, N Scotland, UK
xliv L5 **Hillsborough** Lisburn, E Northern Ireland, UK
xlii H2 **Hillswick** Shetland Islands, NE Scotland, UK
xliv L6 **Hilltown** Newry and Mourne, S Northern Ireland, UK
xxxvii N9 **Hilmarton** Wiltshire, S England, UK
xxxviii M10 **Hinckley** Leicestershire, C England, UK
xli U9 **Hinderwell** North Yorkshire, N England, UK
xxxvii R11 **Hindhead** Surrey, SE England, UK
xli N16 **Hindley** Wigan, NW England, UK
xxxix W8 **Hindolveston** Norfolk, E England, UK
xxxvi M12 **Hindon** Wiltshire, S England, UK
xxxix W10 **Hingham** Norfolk, E England, UK
xxxix W13 **Hintlesham** Suffolk, E England, UK
xxxv I7 **Hirnant** Powys, C Wales, UK
xxxv I14 **Hirwaun** Rhondda Cynon Taff, S Wales, UK
xxxix S12 **Histon** Cambridgeshire, E England, UK
xxxix W13 **Hitcham** Suffolk, E England, UK
xxxvii T6 **Hitchin** Hertfordshire, E England, UK
xxxvi F9 **Hither Green** Lewisham, SE England, UK
xxxix U10 **Hockwold cum Wilton** Norfolk, E England, UK
xli O13 **Hodder** ∽ NW England, UK
xxxvii U8 **Hoddesdon** Hertfordshire, SE England, UK
xxxviii I8 **Hodnet** Shropshire, W England, UK
xxxix S8 **Holbeach** Lincolnshire, E England, UK
xxxix S9 **Holbeach St Johns** Lincolnshire, E England, UK
xxxix S8 **Holbeach St Matthew** Lincolnshire, E England, UK
xxxix S8 **Holbeck Marsh** *physical region* E England, UK
xxxvi D7 **Holborn** Camden, SE England, UK
xxxix X13 **Holbrook** Suffolk, E England, UK
xxxvi I12 **Holcombe Rogus** Devon, SW England, UK
xli O13 **Holden** Lancashire, NW England, UK
xxxvi I11 **Holford** Somerset, SW England, UK
xlii M2 **Holland** Orkney Islands, N Scotland, UK
xxxvii Y7 **Holland-on-Sea** Essex, SE England, UK
xlii O2 **Hollandstoun** Orkney Islands, N Scotland, UK
xxxix Y13 **Hollesley** Suffolk, E England, UK
xl I15 **Hollingworth** Tameside, NW England, UK
xxxvi C6 **Holloway** Islington, SE England, UK
xli Y14 **Hollym** East Riding of Yorkshire, N England, UK
xliv E7 **Hollymount** Mayo, NW Ireland
xliv K10 **Hollywood** Wicklow, E Ireland
xliii M23 **Holm** Dumfries and Galloway, SW Scotland, UK
xxxix R10 **Holme** Cambridgeshire, E England, UK
xxxix U7 **Holme next the Sea** Norfolk, E England, UK
xli U13 **Holme on Spalding Moor** East Riding of Yorkshire, N England, UK
xxxviii I6 **Holmes Chapel** Cheshire, W England, UK
xli R15 **Holmfirth** Kirklees, N England, UK
xxxvi E13 **Holsworthy** Devon, SW England, UK
xxxix W7 **Holt** Norfolk, E England, UK
xxxv L5 **Holt** Wrexham, NE Wales, UK
xliv H11 **Holycross** Tipperary, S Ireland
xxxv E4 **Holyhead** *Wel.* Caer Gybi. Isle of Anglesey, NW Wales, UK
xxxv E4 **Holyhead Bay** *bay* NW Wales, UK
xli Q1 **Holy Island** Northumberland, N England, UK
xli Q1 **Holy Island** *island* NE England, UK
xliii H22 **Holy Island** *island* W Scotland, UK
xxxv D4 **Holy Island** *island* NW Wales, UK
xxxvi L13 **Holywell** Dorset, S England, UK
xl A17 **Holywell** Flintshire, N Wales, UK
xliii L24 **Holywood** Dumfries and Galloway, SW Scotland, UK
xxxix W9 **Honingham** Norfolk, E England, UK
xxxix P7 **Honington** Lincolnshire, E England, UK
xxxix V11 **Honington** Suffolk, E England, UK
xxxvi J13 **Honiton** Devon, SW England, UK
xxxvii W9 **Hoo** Kent, SE England, UK
xli U14 **Hook** East Riding of Yorkshire, N England, UK
xxxvii R10 **Hook** Hampshire, S England, UK
xliv J13 **Hook Head** *Ir.* Rinn Duáin. *headland* SE Ireland
xxxvii P6 **Hook Norton** Oxfordshire, C England, UK
xxxviii L5 **Hope** Derbyshire, C England, UK
xxxv K5 **Hope** Flintshire, N Wales, UK
xxxviii H10 **Hope Bowdler** Shropshire, W England, UK
xlii L11 **Hopeman** Moray, N Scotland, UK
xxxvi H15 **Hope's Nose** *headland* SW England, UK
xxxviii H13 **Hope under Dinmore** Herefordshire, W England, UK
xxxix Z10 **Hopton** Norfolk, E England, UK
xli X4 **Horden** Durham, N England, UK
xxxvii U11 **Horley** Surrey, SE England, UK
xli N12 **Hornby** Lancashire, NW England, UK
xxxix R6 **Horncastle** Lincolnshire, E England, UK
xxxvii Q13 **Horndean** Hampshire, S England, UK
xliv H2 **Horn Head** *headland* N Ireland
xxxvii W12 **Horns Cross** East Sussex, SE England, UK
xli X13 **Hornsea** East Riding of Yorkshire, E England, UK
xxxvi C5 **Hornsey** Haringey, SE England, UK
xxxvi F15 **Horrabridge** Devon, SW England, UK
xli Q11 **Horsehouse** North Yorkshire, N England, UK
xliv H9 **Horseleap** Westmeath, C Ireland
xxxix Y8 **Horsey** Norfolk, E England, UK
xxxix X9 **Horsford** Norfolk, E England, UK
xxxvii T12 **Horsham** West Sussex, SE England, UK
xxxvi M8 **Horsley** Gloucestershire, C England, UK
xli P12 **Horton in Ribblesdale** North Yorkshire, N England, UK
xli O15 **Horwich** Bolton, NW England, UK
xlii I5 **Hoswick** Shetland Islands, NE Scotland, UK
xli V14 **Hotham** East Riding of Yorkshire, N England, UK
xlii J2 **Houbie** Shetland Islands, NE Scotland, UK
xl M7 **Houghton** Cumbria, NW England, UK
xli S7 **Houghton-le-Spring** Sunderland, NE England, UK
xxxvii S9 **Hounslow** Hounslow, SE England, UK
xxxiv K16 **Hounslow** ⬖ *London borough* SE England, UK
xliii F14 **Hourn, Loch** *inlet* NW Scotland, UK
xlii M4 **Houton** Orkney Islands, N Scotland, UK
xxxvii T13 **Hove** Brighton and Hove, SE England, UK
xxxix X9 **Hoveton** Norfolk, E England, UK
xli U11 **Hovingham** North Yorkshire, N England, UK
xli U14 **Howden** East Riding of Yorkshire, N England, UK
xliii M20 **Howgate** Midlothian, SE Scotland, UK
xli R3 **Howick** Northumberland, N England, UK
xliv L9 **Howth** Dublin, E Ireland
xxxix X11 **Hoxne** Suffolk, E England, UK
xlii L5 **Hoy** *island* N Scotland, UK
xl A16 **Hoylake** Wirral, NW England, UK
xxxix R7 **Hubbert's Bridge** Lincolnshire, E England, UK
xxxix N7 **Hucknall** Nottinghamshire, C England, UK
xli R15 **Huddersfield** Kirklees, N England, UK
xxxvi I17 **Hugh Town** Isles of Scilly, SW England, UK
xxxvi I12 **Huish Champflower** Somerset, SW England, UK
xli W13 **Hull** ∽ N England, UK
xxxvi M9 **Hullavington** Wiltshire, S England, UK
xli W14 **Humber** *estuary* E England, UK
xxxix R4 **Humberston** North East Lincolnshire, E England, UK
xxxix U13 **Hundon** Suffolk, E England, UK
xxxvii P10 **Hungerford** West Berkshire, S England, UK
xliv C14 **Hungry Hill** ▲ SW Ireland
xlii D11 **Hunish, Rubha** *headland* NW Scotland, UK
xli W11 **Hunmanby** North Yorkshire, N England, UK
xxxix U7 **Hunstanton** Norfolk, E England, UK
xxxix R12 **Huntingdon** Cambridgeshire, E England, UK
xxxvi L7 **Huntley** Gloucestershire, C England, UK
xlii N12 **Huntly** Aberdeenshire, NE Scotland, UK
xxxvi J11 **Huntspill** Somerset, SW England, UK
xl H17 **Hurdsfield** Cheshire, C England, UK
xliii I21 **Hurlford** East Ayrshire, W Scotland, UK
xxxvii N13 **Hurn** Dorset, S England, UK
xxxvii P12 **Hursley** Hampshire, S England, UK
xxxvii P11 **Hurstbourne Priors** Hampshire, S England, UK
xxxvii P11 **Hurstbourne Tarrant** Hampshire, S England, UK
xxxvii U12 **Hurstpierpoint** West Sussex, SE England, UK
xli R9 **Hurworth-on-Tees** Darlington, N England, UK
xxxix O11 **Husbands Bosworth** Leicestershire, C England, UK
xlii B9 **Hushinish** Western Isles, NW Scotland, UK
xxxix T5 **Huttoft** Lincolnshire, E England, UK
xli W13 **Hutton Cranswick** East Riding of Yorkshire, N England, UK
xli S10 **Hutton Rudby** North Yorkshire, N England, UK
xl C16 **Huyton** Knowsley, NW England, UK
xli P16 **Hyde** Tameside, NW England, UK
xliii K21 **Hyndford Bridge** South Lanarkshire, C Scotland, UK
xliii B17 **Hynish** Argyll and Bute, W Scotland, UK
xxxvii P13 **Hythe** Hampshire, S England, UK
xxxvii Y11 **Hythe** Kent, SE England, UK

I

xxxvii O13 **Ibsley** Hampshire, S England, UK
xxxviii M9 **Ibstock** Leicestershire, C England, UK
xxxix U11 **Icklingham** Suffolk, E England, UK
xxxvi H15 **Ideford** Devon, SW England, UK
xxxvii O11 **Idmiston** Wiltshire, S England, UK
xxxviii H8 **Ightfield** Shropshire, W England, UK
xxxvii V10 **Ightham** Kent, SE England, UK
xxxvi K12 **Ilchester** Somerset, SW England, UK
xxxvi G6 **Ilford** Redbridge, SE England, UK
xxxvi F11 **Ilfracombe** Devon, SW England, UK
xxxix N7 **Ilkeston** Derbyshire, C England, UK
xli R13 **Ilkley** Bradford, N England, UK
xxxviii L13 **Ilmington** Warwickshire, C England, UK
xxxvi K13 **Ilminster** Somerset, SW England, UK
xxxix R3 **Immingham** North East Lincolnshire, E England, UK
xliv E10 **Inagh** Clare, W Ireland
xliv C13 **Inch** Kerry, SW Ireland
xliii O16 **Inchbraoch** Angus, E Scotland, UK
xliv E14 **Inchigeelagh** Cork, S Ireland
xliii M19 **Inchkeith** *island* C Scotland, UK
xliii G20 **Inchmarnock** *island* W Scotland, UK
xlii H8 **Inchnadamph** Highland, NW Scotland, UK
xxxvii V8 **Ingatestone** Essex, SE England, UK
xxxix V11 **Ingham** Suffolk, E England, UK
xli O11 **Ingleborough** ▲ N England, UK
xli O12 **Ingleton** North Yorkshire, N England, UK
xxxix T6 **Ingoldmells** Lincolnshire, E England, UK
xxxix Q8 **Ingoldsby** Lincolnshire, E England, UK
xliv F14 **Inishannon** Cork, S Ireland
xliv B8 **Inishark** *island* W Ireland
xliv B7 **Inishbofin** *Ir.* Inis Bó Finne. *island* W Ireland
xliv D10 **Inisheer** *var.* Inishere, *Ir.* Inis Oírr. *island* W Ireland
xliv B6 **Inishkea North** *island* NW Ireland
xliv B6 **Inishkea South** *island* NW Ireland
xliv C9 **Inishmaan** *Ir.* Inis Meáin. *island* W Ireland
xliv D9 **Inishmore** *Ir.* Árainn. *island* W Ireland
xliv F5 **Inishmurray** *island* N Ireland
xliv J2 **Inishowen Head** *headland* N Ireland
xliv J1 **Inishtrahull** *Ir.* Inis Trá Tholl. *island* NW Ireland
xliv I1 **Inishtrahull Sound** *sound* N Ireland
xliv B8 **Inishturk** *Ir.* Inis Toirc. *island* W Ireland
xliv J12 **Inistioge** Kilkenny, SE Ireland
xxxviii K12 **Inkberrow** Worcestershire, W England, UK
xliii B17 **Inner Hebrides** *island group* W Scotland, UK
xliii M21 **Innerleithen** The Borders, S Scotland, UK
xlii E12 **Inner Sound** *strait* NW Scotland, UK
xliii J16 **Innerwick** Perth and Kinross, C Scotland, UK
xliv E5 **Inniscrone** Sligo, N Ireland
xliv B14 **Inny** ∽ SW Ireland
xlii N12 **Insch** Aberdeenshire, NE Scotland, UK
xliii K14 **Insh** Highland, NW Scotland, UK
xxxvi F12 **Instow** Devon, SW England, UK
xliii I18 **Invararnan** Stirling, C Scotland, UK
xliv G4 **Inver** Donegal, N Ireland
xliii L17 **Inver** Perth and Kinross, C Scotland, UK
xlii P11 **Inverallochy** Aberdeenshire, NE Scotland, UK
xliv D9 **Inveran** Galway, W Ireland
xlii I9 **Inveran** Highland, NW Scotland, UK
xliii H18 **Inveraray** Argyll and Bute, W Scotland, UK
xlii E12 **Inverarish** Highland, NW Scotland, UK
xliii O15 **Inverbervie** Aberdeenshire, NE Scotland, UK
xlii I9 **Invercassley** Highland, NW Scotland, UK
xliii H20 **Inverclyde** ⬖ *unitary authority* C Scotland, UK
xliii L14 **Inverey** Aberdeenshire, NE Scotland, UK
xliii H14 **Invergarry** Highland, NW Scotland, UK
xliii H15 **Invergloy** Highland, NW Scotland, UK
xlii J11 **Invergordon** Highland, N Scotland, UK
xliii M17 **Invergowrie** City of Dundee, E Scotland, UK
xliii F14 **Inverie** Highland, NW Scotland, UK
xlii G13 **Inverinate** Highland, NW Scotland, UK
xliii O16 **Inverkeilor** Angus, E Scotland, UK
xliii L19 **Inverkeithing** Fife, E Scotland, UK
xlii N12 **Inverkeithny** Aberdeenshire, NE Scotland, UK
xliii H20 **Inverkip** Inverclyde, W Scotland, UK
xlii G8 **Inverkirkaig** Highland, NW Scotland, UK
xlii I13 **Invermoriston** Highland, NW Scotland, UK
xlii J12 **Inverness** Highland, N Scotland, UK
xliii H15 **Inverroy** Highland, NW Scotland, UK
xliii G16 **Inversanda** Highland, NW Scotland, UK
xliii I18 **Inveruglas** Argyll and Bute, W Scotland, UK
xlii O13 **Inverurie** Aberdeenshire, NE Scotland, UK
xliii D18 **Iona** *island* W Scotland, UK
xxxviii K7 **Ipstones** Staffordshire, C England, UK
xxxix X13 **Ipswich** *hist.* Gipeswic. Suffolk, E England, UK
xxxix P12 **Irchester** Northamptonshire, C England, UK
xl L8 **Ireby** Cumbria, NW England, UK
xliv F8 **Ireland, Republic of** *off.* Republic of Ireland, *var.* Ireland, *Ir.* Éire. ◆ *republic* NW Europe
xxxvi L9 **Iron Acton** South Gloucestershire, SW England, UK
xxxviii I10 **Ironbridge** The Wrekin, W England, UK
xliv I8 **Iron, Lough** ◎ C Ireland
xliv H6 **Iron Mountains** ▲▲ N Ireland
xli W11 **Irton** North Yorkshire, N England, UK
xliii I21 **Irvine** North Ayrshire, W Scotland, UK
xliv I5 **Irvinestown** Fermanagh, W Northern Ireland, UK
xlii M4 **Isbister** Orkney Islands, N Scotland, UK
xlii I2 **Isbister** Shetland Islands, NE Scotland, UK
xliii L17 **Isla** ∽ C Scotland, UK
xliii D21 **Islay** *island* SW Scotland, UK
xxxix U11 **Isleham** Cambridgeshire, E England, UK
xxxv E4 **Isle of Anglesey** ⬖ *unitary authority* NW Wales, UK
xl G12 **Isle of Man** ◇ *UK crown dependency* NW Europe
xliii I26 **Isle of Whithorn** Dumfries and Galloway, SW Scotland, UK
xxxvii P14 **Isle of Wight** ⬖ *unitary authority* S England, UK
xxxiv L16 **Islington** ⬖ *London borough* SE England, UK
xxxvi D7 **Islington** *London borough capital* Islington, SE England, UK
xxxvii P7 **Islip** Oxfordshire, C England, UK
xxxvii P12 **Itchen** ∽ S England, UK
xxxvii S7 **Ivinghoe** Buckinghamshire, C England, UK
xxxvi G16 **Ivybridge** Devon, SW England, UK
xxxix V11 **Ixworth** Suffolk, E England, UK

J

xli W2 **Jarrow** South Tyneside, NE England, UK
xxxvii Y7 **Jaywick** Essex, SE England, UK
xliii O22 **Jedburgh** The Borders, SE Scotland, UK
xxxiv I16 **Jersey** ◇ *UK crown dependency* NW Europe
xxxvii X16 **Jersey** *island* NW Europe
xlii M6 **John o'Groats** Highland, N Scotland, UK
xliii O15 **Johnshaven** Aberdeenshire, NE Scotland, UK
xxxv C13 **Johnston** Pembrokeshire, SW Wales, UK
xliii I20 **Johnstone** Renfrewshire, W Scotland, UK
xliv H11 **Johnstown** Kilkenny, SE Ireland
xliii E19 **Jura** *island* SW Scotland, UK
xliii E20 **Jura, Paps of** ▲▲ W Scotland, UK
xliii E20 **Jura, Sound of** *strait* W Scotland, UK
xl G10 **Jurby West** NW Isle of Man

K

xliii G20 **Kames** Argyll and Bute, W Scotland, UK
xliv E13 **Kanturk** *Ir.* Ceann Toirc. Cork, SW Ireland
xliii I18 **Katrine, Loch** ◎ C Scotland, UK
xliv G6 **Keadew** Roscommon, C Ireland
xliv K5 **Keady** Armagh, S Northern Ireland, UK
xxxix R3 **Keelby** Lincolnshire, E England, UK
xxxix N8 **Kegworth** Leicestershire, C England, UK
xli Q13 **Keighley** Bradford, N England, UK
xliii F19 **Keillmore** Argyll and Bute, W Scotland, UK
xliii K23 **Keir Mill** Dumfries and Galloway, SW Scotland, UK
xlii M6 **Keiss** Highland, N Scotland, UK
xlii M11 **Keith** Moray, NE Scotland, UK
xliii N15 **Keithock** Angus, E Scotland, UK
xli P10 **Keld** North Yorkshire, N England, UK
xxxix O6 **Kelham** Nottinghamshire, C England, UK
xliii N17 **Kellas** Angus, E Scotland, UK
xliv I12 **Kells** Kilkenny, S Ireland
xliv J7 **Kells** *Ir.* Ceanannas. Meath, E Ireland
xliii O21 **Kelso** The Borders, SE Scotland, UK
xliii L19 **Kelty** Fife, E Scotland, UK
xxxvii W7 **Kelvedon** Essex, SE England, UK
xxxvii V8 **Kelvedon Hatch** Essex, SE England, UK
xxxvii N8 **Kemble** Gloucestershire, C England, UK
xlii O13 **Kemnay** Aberdeenshire, NE Scotland, UK
xxxviii J13 **Kempsey** Worcestershire, W England, UK
xxxvii S6 **Kempston** Bedfordshire, E England, UK
xli N11 **Kendal** Cumbria, NW England, UK
xxxv H15 **Kenfig** Bridgend, S Wales, UK
xxxviii E16 **Kenilworth** Warwickshire, C England, UK
xliii J24 **Ken, Loch** ◎ SW Scotland, UK
xliv D14 **Kenmare** *Ir.* Neidín. Kerry, S Ireland
xliv B14 **Kenmare River** *Ir.* An Ribhéar. *inlet* NE Atlantic Ocean
xliii K16 **Kenmore** Perth and Kinross, C Scotland, UK
xliii F20 **Kennacraig** Argyll and Bute, W Scotland, UK
xxxvii O10 **Kennet** ∽ S England, UK
xxxvii O10 **Kennet and Avon Canal** *canal* S England, UK
xlii N12 **Kennethmont** Aberdeenshire, NE Scotland, UK
xxxvi H14 **Kennford** Devon, SW England, UK
xxxix W11 **Kenninghall** Norfolk, E England, UK
xxxvii X11 **Kennington** Kent, SE England, UK
xxxvi D8 **Kennington** Lambeth, SE England, UK
xlii D12 **Kensaleyre** Highland, NW Scotland, UK
xxxvi C7 **Kensington** *London borough capital* Kensington and Chelsea, SE England, UK
xxxiv K16 **Kensington and Chelsea** *var.* Royal Borough of Kensington and Chelsea. ⬖ *London borough* SE England, UK
xxxvii W11 **Kent** ⬖ *county* SE England, UK
xl M10 **Kent** ∽ NW England, UK
xxxix U11 **Kentford** Suffolk, E England, UK
xxxvi G11 **Kentisbury** Devon, SW England, UK
xxxvi C6 **Kentish Town** Camden, SE England, UK
xxxvi A6 **Kenton** Harrow, SE England, UK
xlii H6 **Keoldale** Highland, NW Scotland, UK
xliii F17 **Kerrera** *island* W Scotland, UK
xxxv J9 **Kerry** Powys, C Wales, UK

1

◆ COUNTRY
● COUNTRY CAPITAL
◇ DEPENDENT TERRITORY
○ DEPENDENT TERRITORY CAPITAL
⬖ ADMINISTRATIVE REGION
✕ INTERNATIONAL AIRPORT
▲ MOUNTAIN
▲▲ MOUNTAIN RANGE
◎ LAKE
⊠ RESERVOIR
∽ RIVER

◆ COUNTRY   ◇ DEPENDENT TERRITORY   ✦ ADMINISTRATIVE REGION   ▲ MOUNTAIN   ⊚ LAKE
● COUNTRY CAPITAL   ○ DEPENDENT TERRITORY CAPITAL   ✕ INTERNATIONAL AIRPORT   ▲▲ MOUNTAIN RANGE   ▣ RESERVOIR   ～ RIVER

M

N

◆ COUNTRY   ◇ DEPENDENT TERRITORY   ◆ ADMINISTRATIVE REGION   ▲ MOUNTAIN
● COUNTRY CAPITAL   ○ DEPENDENT TERRITORY CAPITAL   ✈ INTERNATIONAL AIRPORT   ▲▲ MOUNTAIN RANGE   ◎ LAKE   ☒ RESERVOIR   ♒ RIVER

◆ COUNTRY ◇ DEPENDENT TERRITORY ✦ ADMINISTRATIVE REGION ▲ MOUNTAIN ⦵ LAKE
● COUNTRY CAPITAL ○ DEPENDENT TERRITORY CAPITAL ✕ INTERNATIONAL AIRPORT ▲▲ MOUNTAIN RANGE ⊡ RESERVOIR ⬨ RIVER

REDRUTH – SOWERBY

xxxvi B17 **Redruth** Cornwall, SW England, UK
xxxv F4 **Red Wharf Bay** bay N Wales, UK
xxxv L15 **Redwick** Newport, SE Wales, UK
xxxix Y10 **Reedham** Norfolk, E England, UK
xliv H8 **Ree, Lough** Ir. Loch Rí. ◎ C Ireland
xliv E12 **Reens** Limerick, SW Ireland
xxxix Q5 **Reepham** Lincolnshire, E England, UK
xxxix W8 **Reepham** Norfolk, E England, UK
xli Q10 **Reeth** North Yorkshire, N England, UK
xlii E10 **Reidh, Rubha** headland NW Scotland, UK
xlii G9 **Reiff** Highland, NW Scotland, UK
xxxvii T11 **Reigate** Surrey, SE England, UK
xli W11 **Reighton** North Yorkshire, N England, UK
xli M7 **Reiss** Highland, N Scotland, UK
xliii J20 **Renfrew** Renfrewshire, W Scotland, UK
xliii H20 **Renfrewshire** ◐ unitary authority W Scotland, UK
xli R3 **Rennington** Northumberland, N England, UK
xliii I19 **Renton** West Dunbartonshire, W Scotland, UK
xli N7 **Renwick** Cumbria, NW England, UK
xxxv H14 **Resolven** Neath Port Talbot, S Wales, UK
xxxix O5 **Retford** Nottinghamshire, C England, UK
xxxvii W8 **Rettendon** Essex, SE England, UK
xxxix R6 **Revesby** Lincolnshire, E England, UK
xxxv H11 **Rhandirmwyn** Carmarthenshire, S Wales, UK
xxxv I10 **Rhayader** Powys, C Wales, UK
xxxv G10 **Rheidol** ≈ W Wales, UK
xliii E16 **Rhemore** Highland, NW Scotland, UK
xxxv J5 **Rhewl** Denbighshire, N Wales, UK
xlii I8 **Rhian** Highland, NW Scotland, UK
xlii H7 **Rhiconich** Highland, NW Scotland, UK
xxxv G7 **Rhinog Fawr** ▲ NW Wales, UK
xxxv E7 **Rhiw** Gwynedd, NW Wales, UK
xliv I9 **Rhode** Offaly, E Ireland
xxxv I14 **Rhondda Cynon Taff** ◐ unitary authority S Wales, UK
xxxv J16 **Rhoose** The Vale of Glamorgan, S Wales, UK
xxxv F12 **Rhos** Carmarthenshire, S Wales, UK
xxxv E4 **Rhoscolyn** Isle of Anglesey, NW Wales, UK
xxxv C14 **Rhoscrowther** Pembrokeshire, SW Wales, UK
xxxv K6 **Rhosllanerchrugog** Wrexham, NE Wales, UK
xxxv E4 **Rhosneigr** Isle of Anglesey, NW Wales, UK
xxxv F15 **Rhossili** Swansea, S Wales, UK
xxxv F5 **Rhostryfan** Gwynedd, NW Wales, UK
xliii G20 **Rhubodach** Argyll and Bute, W Scotland, UK
xxxv I4 **Rhuddlan** Denbighshire, N Wales, UK
xliii D14 **Rhum** var. Rum. island W Scotland, UK
xliii F21 **Rhunahaorine** Argyll and Bute, W Scotland, UK
xxxv J7 **Rhydycroesau** Powys, C Wales, UK
xxxv I4 **Rhyl** Denbighshire, NE Wales, UK
xxxv J13 **Rhymney** Caerphilly, S Wales, UK
xlii N13 **Rhynie** Aberdeenshire, NE Scotland, UK
xli O14 **Ribble** ≈ NW England, UK
xli O11 **Ribble Head** North Yorkshire, N England, UK
xli O14 **Ribchester** Lancashire, NW England, UK
xli U13 **Riccall** North Yorkshire, N England, UK
xliv K5 **Richhill** Armagh, S Northern Ireland, UK
xli R10 **Richmond** North Yorkshire, N England, UK
xxxvi A9 **Richmond upon Thames** Richmond upon Thames, SE England, UK
xxxiv K16 **Richmond upon Thames** var. Richmond-upon-Thames. ◐ London borough SE England, UK
xliii O14 **Rickarton** Aberdeenshire, NE Scotland, UK
xxxvii S8 **Rickmansworth** Hertfordshire, SE England, UK
xxxvii W6 **Ridgewell** Essex, SE England, UK
xxxvii U12 **Ridgewood** East Sussex, SE England, UK
xxxvii S6 **Ridgmont** Bedfordshire, C England, UK
xli P6 **Riding Mill** Northumberland, N England, UK
xli P5 **Ridsdale** Northumberland, N England, UK
xliii K20 **Riggend** North Lanarkshire, C Scotland, UK
xli V11 **Rillington** North Yorkshire, N England, UK
xlii J8 **Rimsdale, Loch** ◎ N Scotland, UK
xliv G14 **Ringaskiddy** Cork, S Ireland
xliii J25 **Ringford** Dumfries and Galloway, SW Scotland, UK
xxxvii U13 **Ringmer** East Sussex, SE England, UK
xliv K3 **Ringsend** Coleraine, N Northern Ireland, UK
xxxix U7 **Ringstead** Norfolk, E England, UK
xxxvi O13 **Ringwood** Dorset, S England, UK
xlii M5 **Rinnigill** Orkney Islands, N Scotland, UK
xxxviii M7 **Ripley** Derbyshire, C England, UK
xli R12 **Ripley** North Yorkshire, N England, UK
xxxvii S10 **Ripley** Surrey, SE England, UK
xli R12 **Ripon** North Yorkshire, N England, UK
xxxv K14 **Risca** Caerphilly, S Wales, UK
xli O14 **Rishton** Lancashire, NW England, UK
xliv F14 **Riverstown** Cork, S Ireland
xxxix O13 **Roade** Northamptonshire, C England, UK
xxxvi F14 **Roadford Reservoir** ▣ SW England, UK
xlii C8 **Roag, Loch** inlet NW Scotland, UK
xliv C15 **Roaringwater Bay** bay S Ireland
xliii N22 **Roberton** The Borders, S Scotland, UK
xxxvii W12 **Robertsbridge** East Sussex, SE England, UK
xliv J9 **Robertstown** Kildare, E Ireland
xli V10 **Robin Hood's Bay** North Yorkshire, N England, UK
xxxvi F13 **Roborough** Devon, SW England, UK
xxxviii K8 **Rocester** Staffordshire, C England, UK
xxxv C13 **Roch** Pembrokeshire, SW Wales, UK
xl G13 **Rochdale** Rochdale, NW England, UK
xli P14 **Rochdale** ◐ unitary authority NW England, UK
xxxvii V10 **Rochester** anc. Durobrivae. Kent, SE England, UK
xli O4 **Rochester** Northumberland, N England, UK
xxxvii X8 **Rochford** Essex, SE England, UK
xliv I8 **Rochfortbridge** Westmeath, C Ireland
xxxvi I14 **Rockbeare** Devon, SW England, UK
xliv E12 **Rockchapel** Cork, S Ireland
xl M6 **Rockcliffe** Cumbria, NW England, UK
xliv J6 **Rockcorry** Monaghan, NE Ireland
xlii B10 **Rodel** Western Isles, NW Scotland, UK
xxxvi V8 **Roding** ≈ SE England, UK
xxxviii H9 **Rodington** Shropshire, W England, UK
xliv J3 **Roe** ≈ N Northern Ireland, UK
xxxvi B9 **Roehampton** Wandsworth, SE England, UK
xlii H3 **Roesound** Shetland Islands, NE Scotland, UK
xlii J9 **Rogart** Highland, NW Scotland, UK
xli Q9 **Romaldkirk** Durham, N England, UK
xli S10 **Romanby** North Yorkshire, N England, UK
xliii L21 **Romannobridge** The Borders, S Scotland, UK
xxxvii V9 **Romford** Havering, SE England, UK
xl H15 **Romiley** Stockport, NW England, UK
xxxvii X12 **Romney Marsh** physical region SE England, UK
xxxvii O12 **Romsey** Hampshire, S England, UK
xlii E11 **Rona** island NW Scotland, UK
xlii B12 **Ronay** island NW Scotland, UK
xli P7 **Rookhope** Durham, N England, UK
xli X14 **Roos** East Riding of Yorkshire, N England, UK
xliv H7 **Roosky** Roscommon, C Ireland
xxxvii Q12 **Ropley** Hampshire, S England, UK
xxxix Q8 **Ropsley** Lincolnshire, E England, UK
xlii L4 **Rora Head** headland N Scotland, UK
xliv H2 **Rosapenna** Donegal, N Ireland
xliv G8 **Roscommon** Ir. Ros Comáin. Roscommon, C Ireland
xliv F7 **Roscommon** Ir. Ros Comáin. ◐ county C Ireland
xliv H10 **Roscrea** Ir. Ros Cré. Tipperary, C Ireland
xli U10 **Rosedale Abbey** North Yorkshire, N England, UK
xlii P11 **Rosehearty** Aberdeenshire, NE Scotland, UK
xxxv C14 **Rosemarket** Pembrokeshire, SW Wales, UK
xlii J11 **Rosemarkie** Highland, NW Scotland, UK
xliii F15 **Roshven** Highland, NW Scotland, UK
xl M7 **Rosley** Cumbria, NW England, UK
xliii J25 **Ross** Dumfries and Galloway, SW Scotland, UK
xliv F4 **Rossan Point** headland N Ireland
xliv E15 **Ross Carbery** Cork, S Ireland
xli P14 **Rossendale, Forest of** forest N England, UK
xliv G2 **Rosses Bay** bay N Ireland
xliv F5 **Rosses Point** Sligo, N Ireland
xliv K13 **Rosslare** Ir. Ros Láir. Wexford, SE Ireland
xliv K13 **Rosslare Harbour** Wexford, SE Ireland
xliv K12 **Rosslare Point** headland SE Ireland
xliv J6 **Rosslea** Fermanagh, W Northern Ireland, UK
xxxviii I14 **Ross-on-Wye** Herefordshire, W England, UK
xliv L6 **Rostrevor** Newry and Mourne, S Northern Ireland, UK
xli L19 **Rosyth** Fife, E Scotland, UK
xli Q4 **Rothbury** Northumberland, N England, UK
xxxvii S12 **Rother** ≈ S England, UK
xxxvii X12 **Rother** ≈ SE England, UK
xxxvii V12 **Rotherfield** East Sussex, SE England, UK
xli S16 **Rotherham** Rotherham, N England, UK
xli S16 **Rotherham** ◐ unitary authority N England, UK
xlii M12 **Rothes** Moray, N Scotland, UK
xliii H20 **Rothesay** Argyll and Bute, W Scotland, UK
xlii N4 **Rothiesholm** Orkney Islands, N Scotland, UK
xli S14 **Rothwell** Leeds, N England, UK
xxxix P11 **Rothwell** Northamptonshire, C England, UK
xxxvii U13 **Rottingdean** Brighton and Hove, SE England, UK
xxxix V8 **Rougham** Norfolk, E England, UK
xxxix X7 **Roughton** Norfolk, E England, UK
xliv C8 **Roundstone** Galway, W Ireland
xliv L10 **Roundwood** Wicklow, E Ireland
xlii M3 **Rousay** island N Scotland, UK
xliii N24 **Rowanburn** Dumfries and Galloway, SW Scotland, UK
xxxvii R13 **Rowland's Castle** Hampshire, S England, UK
xli R6 **Rowlands Gill** Gateshead, NE England, UK
xxxvii T5 **Roxton** Bedfordshire, C England, UK
xxxvii V8 **Roxwell** Essex, SE England, UK
xliv H8 **Royal Canal** Ir. An Chanáil Ríoga. canal C Ireland
xxxviii E17 **Royal Leamington Spa** var. Leamington, Leamington Spa. Warwickshire, C England, UK
xxxvii X12 **Royal Military Canal** canal SE England, UK
xxxvii V11 **Royal Tunbridge Wells** var. Tunbridge Wells. Kent, SE England, UK
xli S15 **Royston** Barnsley, N England, UK
xxxvii U6 **Royston** Hertfordshire, E England, UK
xli P15 **Royton** Oldham, NW England, UK
xxxvi X16 **Rozel** Jersey, Channel Islands
xxxv K6 **Ruabon** Wrexham, NE Wales, UK
xxxvi B17 **Ruan Minor** Cornwall, SW England, UK
xxxvii S11 **Rudgwick** West Sussex, SE England, UK
xli W12 **Rudston** East Riding of Yorkshire, N England, UK
xl G10 **Rue Point** headland N Isle of Man
xli N15 **Rufford** Lancashire, NW England, UK
xxxviii M11 **Rugby** Warwickshire, C England, UK
xxxviii K9 **Rugeley** Staffordshire, C England, UK
xxxix Y11 **Rumburgh** Suffolk, E England, UK
xxxv K15 **Rumney** Cardiff, S Wales, UK
xliii D15 **Rùm, Sound of** strait NW Scotland, UK
xliv L2 **Runabay Head** headland N Northern Ireland, UK
xl D16 **Runcorn** Cheshire, C England, UK
xliv L8 **Rush** Ir. An Ros. Dublin, E Ireland
xxxix Q12 **Rushden** Northamptonshire, C England, UK
xxxix Q7 **Ruskington** Lincolnshire, E England, UK
xliii J20 **Rutherglen** City of Glasgow, C Scotland, UK
xxxv J5 **Ruthin** Wel. Rhuthun. Denbighshire, NE Wales, UK
xxxix P9 **Rutland** ◐ unitary authority C England, UK
xxxix P9 **Rutland Water** ◎ C England, UK
xliii G25 **Ryan, Loch** inlet SW Scotland, UK
xxxvii X12 **Rye** East Sussex, SE England, UK
xli T11 **Rye** ≈ N England, UK
xli S7 **Ryhope** Sunderland, NE England, UK
xli P12 **Rylstone** North Yorkshire, N England, UK
xli U2 **Ryton** Gateshead, NE England, UK

S

xli V4 **Sacriston** Durham, N England, UK
xliii F22 **Saddell** Argyll and Bute, W Scotland, UK
xli G13 **Saddle, The** ▲ NW Scotland, UK
xxxvii V6 **Saffron Walden** Essex, SE England, UK
xliii P20 **St Abbs** The Borders, S Scotland, UK
xliii P20 **St Abb's Head** headland SE Scotland, UK
xxxvi B16 **St Agnes** Cornwall, SW England, UK
xxxvi I17 **St Agnes** island SW England, UK
xxxvii T8 **St Albans** anc. Verulamium. Hertfordshire, E England, UK
xxxvii N15 **St Alban's Head** var. St Aldhelm's Head. headland S England, UK
xliii N18 **St Andrews** Fife, E Scotland, UK
xliii N17 **St Andrews Bay** bay E Scotland, UK
xxxvii X14 **St Anne** Alderney, N Guernsey
xxxv L14 **St Arvans** Monmouthshire, SE Wales, UK
xxxv I4 **St Asaph** Denbighshire, N Wales, UK
xxxvii X17 **St Aubin** Jersey, Channel Islands
xxxvi D16 **St Austell** Cornwall, SW England, UK
xxxvi D16 **St Austell Bay** bay SW England, UK
xl K9 **St Bees** Cumbria, NW England, UK
xl J9 **St Bees Head** headland NW England, UK
xxxvi D16 **St Blazey** Cornwall, SW England, UK
xliii N21 **St Boswells** The Borders, S Scotland, UK
xxxvi K8 **St Briavels** Gloucestershire, C England, UK
xxxv C13 **St Brides** Pembrokeshire, SW Wales, UK
xxxv B13 **St Brides Bay** inlet SW Wales, UK
xliii H18 **St Catherines** Argyll and Bute, W Scotland, UK
xxxvii P15 **St Catherine's Point** headland S England, UK
xxxv E13 **St Clears** Carmarthenshire, S Wales, UK
xxxvi C15 **St Columb Major** Cornwall, SW England, UK
xlii P11 **St Combs** Aberdeenshire, NE Scotland, UK
xliii O15 **St Cyrus** Aberdeenshire, NE Scotland, UK
xxxv B13 **St David's** Pembrokeshire, SW Wales, UK
xxxv A12 **St David's Head** headland SW Wales, UK
xxxvi B17 **St Day** Cornwall, SW England, UK
xxxvi C16 **St Dennis** Cornwall, SW England, UK
xxxv E11 **St Dogmaels** Ceredigion, W Wales, UK
xxxv I16 **St Donats** The Vale of Glamorgan, S Wales, UK
xli P11 **St Fergus** Aberdeenshire, NE Scotland, UK
xliv M5 **Saintfield** Down, E Northern Ireland, UK
xliii J17 **St Fillans** Perth and Kinross, C Scotland, UK
xxxvi E16 **St Germans** Cornwall, SW England, UK
xxxv C14 **St Govan's Head** headland SW Wales, UK
xxxv I10 **St Harmon** Powys, C Wales, UK
xl D15 **St Helens** St Helens, NW England, UK
xli N16 **St Helens** ◐ unitary authority NW England, UK
xxxvii X17 **St Helier** ○ (Jersey) S Jersey, Channel Islands
xxxvi C15 **St Issey** Cornwall, SW England, UK
xxxix S11 **St Ives** Cambridgeshire, E England, UK
xxxvi L16 **St Ives** Cornwall, SW England, UK
xxxvi M16 **St Ives Bay** bay SW England, UK
xxxvii X16 **St John** Jersey, Channel Islands
xl F11 **St John's** C Isle of Man
xli P8 **St John's Chapel** Durham, N England, UK
xliv F4 **St John's Point** headland N Ireland
xliv M6 **St John's Point** headland E Northern Ireland, UK
xliv I3 **St Johnstown** Donegal, N Ireland
xliii J24 **St John's Town of Dalry** Dumfries and Galloway, SW Scotland, UK
xxxvi C7 **St John's Wood** Westminster, SE England, UK
xxxvi L16 **St Just** Cornwall, SW England, UK
xxxvi C17 **St Keverne** Cornwall, SW England, UK
xli H3 **St Magnus Bay** bay N Scotland, UK
xxxvii Z11 **St Margaret's at Cliffe** Kent, SE England, UK
xlii M5 **St Margaret's Hope** Orkney Islands, NE Scotland, UK
xl G12 **St Mark's** S Isle of Man
xxxvii X17 **St Mary** Jersey, Channel Islands
xli M5 **St Mary's** Orkney Islands, N Scotland, UK
xxxvi I17 **St Mary's** island SW England, UK
xliii M22 **St Mary's Loch** ◎ S Scotland, UK
xxxvi C17 **St Mawes** Cornwall, SW England, UK
xxxvi C15 **St Mawgan** Cornwall, SW England, UK
xxxvi F15 **St Mellion** Cornwall, SW England, UK
xxxv K15 **St Mellons** Cardiff, S Wales, UK
xxxvi C15 **St Minver** Cornwall, SW England, UK
xliii N18 **St Monans** Fife, E Scotland, UK
xxxvi E15 **St Neot** Cornwall, SW England, UK
xxxix R12 **St Neots** Cambridgeshire, E England, UK
xxxv C12 **St Nicholas** Pembrokeshire, SW Wales, UK
xxxvi Y7 **St Osyth** Essex, SE England, UK
xxxvii X17 **St Peter** Jersey, Channel Islands
xxxvii V15 **St Peter Port** ○ (Guernsey) C Guernsey, Channel Islands
xxxvii W15 **St Sampson** Guernsey, Channel Islands
xxxvi D14 **St Teath** Cornwall, SW England, UK
xliii O16 **St Vigeans** Angus, E Scotland, UK
xxxvi C15 **St Wenn** Cornwall, SW England, UK
xxxviii H14 **St Weonards** Herefordshire, W England, UK
xxxvi G17 **Salcombe** Devon, SW England, UK
xxxvii X7 **Salcott** Essex, SE England, UK
xli P16 **Sale** Trafford, NW England, UK
xliii E17 **Salen** Argyll and Bute, W Scotland, UK
xliii F16 **Salen** Highland, NW Scotland, UK
xl G15 **Salford** Salford, NW England, UK
xli O15 **Salford** ◐ unitary authority NW England, UK
xliii L19 **Saline** Fife, E Scotland, UK
xxxvii O12 **Salisbury** var. New Sarum. Wiltshire, S England, UK
xxxvii N11 **Salisbury Plain** plain S England, UK
xxxvi E16 **Saltash** Cornwall, SW England, UK
xli U9 **Saltburn-by-the-Sea** Redcar and Cleveland, N England, UK
xliii H21 **Saltcoates** North Ayrshire, W Scotland, UK
xliv K13 **Saltee Islands** island group SE Ireland
xxxix S4 **Saltfleet** Lincolnshire, E England, UK
xxxix S4 **Saltfleet by St Peter** Lincolnshire, E England, UK
xxxvi L10 **Saltford** Bath and North East Somerset, SW England, UK
xxxviii G6 **Saltney** Cheshire, W England, UK
xxxvi I13 **Sampford Peverell** Devon, SW England, UK
xliii D20 **Sanaigmore** Argyll and Bute, W Scotland, UK
xli I4 **Sand** Shetland Islands, NE Scotland, UK
xliii F23 **Sanda** island W Scotland, UK
xliii F14 **Sandaig** Highland, NW Scotland, UK
xliii C14 **Sanday** island NW Scotland, UK
xlii O3 **Sanday** island NE Scotland, UK
xxxviii I6 **Sandbach** Cheshire, W England, UK
xliii H19 **Sandbank** Argyll and Bute, W Scotland, UK
xxxvi K10 **Sandford** North West Somerset, SW England, UK
xlii N4 **Sandgarth** Orkney Islands, N Scotland, UK
xlii P11 **Sandhaven** Aberdeenshire, NE Scotland, UK
xliii H25 **Sandhead** Dumfries and Galloway, SW Scotland, UK
xxxvii R10 **Sandhurst** Bracknell Forest, S England, UK
xli U12 **Sand Hutton** North Yorkshire, N England, UK
xxxviii K8 **Sandon** Staffordshire, C England, UK
xxxvii Q14 **Sandown** Isle of Wight, S England, UK
xxxvi E16 **Sandplace** Cornwall, SW England, UK
xlii O2 **Sandquoy** Orkney Islands, N Scotland, UK
xliii A15 **Sandray** island NW Scotland, UK
xxxix U8 **Sandringham** Norfolk, E England, UK
xxxviii B14 **Sandwell** ◐ unitary authority C England, UK
xxxvi Z10 **Sandwich** Kent, SE England, UK
xxxvii Z10 **Sandwich Bay** bay SE England, UK
xl M9 **Sandwick** Cumbria, NW England, UK
xli I5 **Sandwick** Shetland Islands, NE Scotland, UK
xxxvii T5 **Sandy** Bedfordshire, C England, UK
xliii K23 **Sanquhar** Dumfries and Galloway, SW Scotland, UK
xli M7 **Sarclet** Highland, N Scotland, UK
xxxvii W15 **Sark** Fr. Sercq. island Channel Islands
xxxviii G13 **Sarnesfield** Herefordshire, W England, UK
xxxv E7 **Sarn Meyllteyrn** Gwynedd, NW Wales, UK
xxxvii Y10 **Sarre** Kent, SE England, UK
xli Q7 **Satley** Durham, N England, UK
xl M11 **Satterthwaite** Cumbria, NW England, UK
xliii N23 **Saughtree** The Borders, S Scotland, UK
xxxv D14 **Saundersfoot** Pembrokeshire, SW Wales, UK
xxxvii U7 **Sawbridgeworth** Hertfordshire, SE England, UK
xliv J3 **Sawel** ▲ C Northern Ireland, UK
xxxix T13 **Sawston** Cambridgeshire, E England, UK
xxxix R11 **Sawtry** Cambridgeshire, E England, UK
xxxix P9 **Saxby** Leicestershire, C England, UK
xxxix O9 **Saxelbye** Leicestershire, C England, UK
xxxix P5 **Saxilby** Lincolnshire, E England, UK
xxxix Y12 **Saxmundham** Suffolk, E England, UK
xxxix X12 **Saxtead** Suffolk, E England, UK
xxxix W8 **Saxthorpe** Norfolk, E England, UK
xli S14 **Saxton** North Yorkshire, N England, UK
xl L10 **Scafell Pike** ▲ NW England, UK
xliii D19 **Scalasaig** Argyll and Bute, W Scotland, UK
xli W10 **Scalby** North Yorkshire, N England, UK
xl M9 **Scales** Cumbria, NW England, UK
xxxix O8 **Scalford** Leicestershire, C England, UK
xlii I4 **Scalloway** Shetland Islands, N Scotland, UK
xlii C10 **Scalpay** island NW Scotland, UK
xlii E13 **Scalpay** island NW Scotland, UK
xxxix R5 **Scamblesby** Lincolnshire, E England, UK
xlii M5 **Scapa Flow** sea basin N Scotland, UK
xli B10 **Scarastavore** Western Isles, NW Scotland, UK
xliii E18 **Scarba** island W Scotland, UK
xli W10 **Scarborough** North Yorkshire, N England, UK
xlii H12 **Scardroy** Highland, NW Scotland, UK
xliv A14 **Scariff Island** island SW Ireland
xliii C17 **Scarinish** Argyll and Bute, W Scotland, UK
xliii B9 **Scarp** island NW Scotland, UK
xliv F10 **Scarriff** Clare, W Ireland
xli R4 **Scars, The** headland N England, UK
xxxix P4 **Scawby** North Lincolnshire, N England, UK
xliii J16 **Schiehallion** ▲ C Scotland, UK
xliv D15 **Schull** Cork, S Ireland
xxxvi I17 **Scilly, Isles of** island group SW England, UK
xlii E13 **Sconser** Highland, NW Scotland, UK
xli R10 **Scotch Corner** North Yorkshire, N England, UK
xli N12 **Scotforth** Lancashire, NW England, UK
xliii H15 **Scotland** national region Scotland, UK
xliii F16 **Scotstown** Highland, NW Scotland, UK
xxxix P4 **Scotter** Lincolnshire, E England, UK
xlii G7 **Scourie** Highland, NW Scotland, UK
xli I5 **Scousburgh** Shetland Islands, NE Scotland, UK
xlii L6 **Scrabster** Highland, N Scotland, UK
xliv H8 **Scramoge** Roscommon, C Ireland
xliv D8 **Screeb** Galway, W Ireland
xxxix P3 **Scunthorpe** North Lincolnshire, E England, UK
xxxvii V13 **Seaford** East Sussex, SE England, UK
xlii C9 **Seaforth, Loch** inlet NW Scotland, UK
xli S7 **Seaham** Durham, N England, UK
xli R2 **Seahouses** Northumberland, N England, UK
xliii H21 **Seamill** North Ayrshire, W Scotland, UK
xxxix Y8 **Sea Palling** Norfolk, E England, UK
xl K10 **Seascale** Cumbria, NW England, UK
xxxix T6 **Seathorne** Lincolnshire, E England, UK
xl K8 **Seaton** Cumbria, NW England, UK
xxxvi J14 **Seaton** Devon, SW England, UK
xli T8 **Seaton Carew** Hartlepool, N England, UK
xli R5 **Seaton Delaval** Northumberland, N England, UK
xli T10 **Seave Green** North Yorkshire, N England, UK
xxxvii Q14 **Seaview** Isle of Wight, S England, UK
xl M8 **Sebergham** Cumbria, NW England, UK
xli O10 **Sedbergh** Cumbria, NW England, UK
xxxix P8 **Sedgebrook** Lincolnshire, E England, UK
xli S8 **Sedgefield** Durham, N England, UK
xxxix U8 **Sedgeford** Norfolk, E England, UK
xxxviii A14 **Sedgley** Dudley, C England, UK
xli N11 **Sedgwick** Cumbria, NW England, UK
xxxvi M10 **Seend** Wiltshire, S England, UK
xl L15 **Sefton** ◐ unitary authority NW England, UK
xliii F18 **Seil** island W Scotland, UK
xxxviii G8 **Selattyn** Shropshire, W England, UK
xxxvii R11 **Selborne** Hampshire, S England, UK
xli T14 **Selby** North Yorkshire, N England, UK
xliii N22 **Selkirk** SE Scotland, UK
xl K10 **Sellafield Station** Cumbria, NW England, UK
xli I1 **Sellafirth** Shetland Islands, NE Scotland, UK
xxxvii R14 **Selsey** West Sussex, SE England, UK
xxxvii R14 **Selsey Bill** headland S England, UK
xxxvi M10 **Semington** Wiltshire, S England, UK
xxxvii S10 **Send** Surrey, SE England, UK
xxxv J14 **Senghenydd** Caerphilly, S Wales, UK
xxxvi L16 **Sennen** Cornwall, SW England, UK
xxxv I12 **Sennybridge** Powys, C Wales, UK
xxxix U9 **Setchey** Norfolk, E England, UK
xli P12 **Settle** North Yorkshire, N England, UK
xxxvi G6 **Seven Kings** Redbridge, SE England, UK
xxxvii U10 **Sevenoaks** Kent, SE England, UK
xxxv H13 **Seven Sisters** Neath Port Talbot, S Wales, UK
xxxvi J10 **Severn, Mouth of the** estuary England/Wales, UK
xlii D13 **Sgurr Alasdair** ▲ NW Scotland, UK
xlii H11 **Sgurr Mor** cliff NW Scotland, UK
xlii H12 **Sgurr Na Lapaich** ▲ Highland, NW Scotland, UK
xlii D7 **Shader** Western Isles, NW Scotland, UK
xxxvi M12 **Shaftesbury** Dorset, S England, UK
xxxvi O10 **Shalbourne** Wiltshire, S England, UK
xxxvii P14 **Shalfleet** Isle of Wight, S England, UK
xxxvii S11 **Shalford** Surrey, SE England, UK
xliii H19 **Shandon** Argyll and Bute, W Scotland, UK
xxxvii Q14 **Shanklin** Isle of Wight, S England, UK
xliv E14 **Shanlaragh** Cork, S Ireland
xliv E11 **Shannon** Clare, W Ireland
xliv G9 **Shannon** Ir. Ant Sionainn. ≈ W Ireland
xliv E11 **Shannon** ✕ Clare, W Ireland
xliv G9 **Shannonbridge** Offaly, C Ireland
xliv H6 **Shannon Erne Waterway** canal N Ireland
xliv C11 **Shannon, Mouth of the** estuary W Ireland
xli N9 **Shap** Cumbria, NW England, UK
xli N10 **Shap Fells** ▲▲ NW England, UK
xliii N4 **Shapinsay** island NE Scotland, UK
xxxix S13 **Sharnbrook** Bedfordshire, C England, UK
xxxvi L8 **Sharpness** Gloucestershire, C England, UK
xxxviii I7 **Shavington** Cheshire, W England, UK
xlii C7 **Shawbost** Western Isles, NW Scotland, UK
xxxviii H9 **Shawbury** Shropshire, W England, UK
xxxvi F13 **Shebbear** Devon, SW England, UK
xliv I7 **Sheelin, Lough** ◎ C Ireland
xliv H2 **Sheep Haven** Ir. Cuan na gCaorach. inlet N Ireland
xliv B15 **Sheep's Head** headland S Ireland
xxxvi F13 **Sheepwash** Devon, SW England, UK
xxxvii X9 **Sheerness** Kent, SE England, UK
xli S17 **Sheffield** Sheffield, N England, UK
xli R17 **Sheffield** ◐ unitary authority N England, UK
xxxvii T6 **Shefford** Bedfordshire, C England, UK
xli H7 **Sheigra** Highland, NW Scotland, UK
xli Q14 **Shelf** Bradford, N England, UK
xxxviii G10 **Shelve** Shropshire, W England, UK
xxxvi B7 **Shepherd's Bush** Hammersmith and Fulham, SE England, UK
xxxvii Y11 **Shepherdswell** Kent, SE England, UK
xxxvii X9 **Sheppey, Isle of** island SE England, UK
xxxix S13 **Shepreth** Cambridgeshire, E England, UK
xxxix N9 **Shepshed** Leicestershire, C England, UK
xxxvi L11 **Shepton Mallet** Somerset, SW England, UK
xxxvi L12 **Sherborne** Dorset, S England, UK
xli W4 **Sherburn** Durham, N England, UK
xli V11 **Sherburn** North Yorkshire, N England, UK
xli T14 **Sherburn in Elmet** North Yorkshire, N England, UK
xliv J6 **Shercock** Cavan, N Ireland
xxxviii I9 **Sheriffhales** Shropshire, W England, UK
xli T12 **Sheriff Hutton** North Yorkshire, N England, UK
xxxix X7 **Sheringham** Norfolk, E England, UK
xxxvi R6 **Sherington** Milton Keynes, C England, UK
xliv D15 **Sherkin Island** island S Ireland
xxxvi M9 **Sherston** Wiltshire, S England, UK
xli H3 **Shetland Islands** ◐ unitary authority NE Scotland, UK
xli H1 **Shetland Islands** island group NE Scotland, UK
xliii D10 **Shiant Islands** island group NW Scotland, UK
xliii G13 **Shiel Bridge** Highland, NW Scotland, UK
xliii F12 **Shieldaig** Highland, NW Scotland, UK
xliii F15 **Shiel, Loch** ◎ N Scotland, UK
xxxviii I9 **Shifnal** Shropshire, W England, UK
xli R3 **Shilbottle** Northumberland, N England, UK
xli R8 **Shildon** Durham, N England, UK
xliv K11 **Shillelagh** Wicklow, E Ireland
xxxvi M13 **Shillingstone** Dorset, S England, UK
xli S7 **Shiney Row** Sunderland, NE England, UK
xli I9 **Shin, Loch** ◎ N Scotland, UK
xli I9 **Shinness** Highland, NW Scotland, UK
xliv H10 **Shinrone** Offaly, C Ireland
xxxvii V10 **Shipbourne** Kent, SE England, UK
xxxix V9 **Shipdham** Norfolk, E England, UK
xli R13 **Shipley** Bradford, N England, UK
xxxviii M13 **Shipston on Stour** Warwickshire, C England, UK
xli T12 **Shipton** North Yorkshire, N England, UK
xxxvii O7 **Shipton-under-Wychwood** Oxfordshire, C England, UK
xxxv L14 **Shirenewton** Monmouthshire, SE Wales, UK
xxxviii D16 **Shirley** Solihull, C England, UK
xliii G22 **Shiskine** North Ayrshire, W Scotland, UK
xxxvii X9 **Shoeburyness** Southend-on-Sea, SE England, UK
xxxvi G8 **Shooters Hill** Greenwich, SE England, UK
xxxvi E7 **Shoreditch** Hackney, SE England, UK
xxxvii S13 **Shoreham-by-Sea** West Sussex, SE England, UK
xxxvii P14 **Shorwell** Isle of Wight, S England, UK
xli Q7 **Shotley Bridge** Durham, N England, UK
xxxix X13 **Shotley Gate** Suffolk, E England, UK
xliii K20 **Shotts** North Lanarkshire, C Scotland, UK
xxxix U9 **Shouldham** Norfolk, E England, UK
xxxviii H9 **Shrewsbury** hist. Scrobesbyrig'. Shropshire, W England, UK
xxxvii O9 **Shrivenham** Oxfordshire, C England, UK
xxxviii G10 **Shropshire** ◐ county W England, UK
xxxviii B13 **Shropshire Union Canal** canal W England, UK
xxxvi J14 **Shute** Devon, SW England, UK
xxxvii W6 **Sible Hedingham** Essex, SE England, UK
xxxix S7 **Sibsey** Lincolnshire, E England, UK
xxxvi I14 **Sidbury** Devon, SW England, UK
xxxvi G9 **Sidcup** Bexley, SE England, UK
xliii M17 **Sidlaw Hills** ▲▲ E Scotland, UK
xxxvi J14 **Sidmouth** Devon, SW England, UK
xli W13 **Sigglesthorne** East Riding of Yorkshire, N England, UK
xxxix N9 **Sileby** Leicestershire, C England, UK
xl K11 **Silecroft** Cumbria, NW England, UK
xl K7 **Silloth** Cumbria, NW England, UK
xli Q13 **Silsden** Bradford, N England, UK
xli N11 **Silverdale** Lancashire, NW England, UK
xliv G11 **Silvermine Mountains** hill range Tipperary, C Ireland
xxxix O13 **Silverstone** Northamptonshire, C England, UK
xxxvi H13 **Silverton** Devon, SW England, UK
xli H4 **Silwick** Shetland Islands, NE Scotland, UK
xxxvi G11 **Simonsbath** Somerset, SW England, UK
xxxvii R13 **Singleton** West Sussex, SE England, UK
xli U11 **Sinnington** North Yorkshire, N England, UK
xli G9 **Sionascaig, Loch** ◎ NW Scotland, UK
xliv I3 **Sion Mills** Strabane, W Northern Ireland, UK
xxxvii X10 **Sittingbourne** Kent, SE England, UK
xliv F11 **Sixmilebridge** Clare, W Ireland
xxxvii N12 **Sixpenny Handley** Dorset, S England, UK
xxxix Y12 **Sizewell** Suffolk, E England, UK
xlii N4 **Skaill** Orkney Islands, N Scotland, UK
xliii J22 **Skares** East Ayrshire, W Scotland, UK
xli H4 **Skarpigarth** Shetland Islands, NE Scotland, UK
xxxix T6 **Skegness** Lincolnshire, E England, UK
xli N16 **Skelmersdale** Lancashire, NW England, UK
xliii H20 **Skelmorlie** North Ayrshire, W Scotland, UK
xl M8 **Skelton** Cumbria, NW England, UK
xli U9 **Skelton** Redcar and Cleveland, N England, UK
xlii J6 **Skerray** Highland, N Scotland, UK
xliv L8 **Skerries** Ir. Na Sceirí. Dublin, E Ireland
xliv D15 **Skibbereen** Ir. An Sciobairín. Cork, SW Ireland
xl L8 **Skiddaw** ▲ NW England, UK
xxxix P8 **Skillington** Lincolnshire, E England, UK
xl K7 **Skinburness** Cumbria, NW England, UK
xliii G20 **Skipness** Argyll and Bute, W Scotland, UK
xli X12 **Skipsea** East Riding of Yorkshire, N England, UK
xli Q13 **Skipton** North Yorkshire, N England, UK
xli S11 **Skipton-on-Swale** North Yorkshire, N England, UK
xli T13 **Skipwith** North Yorkshire, N England, UK
xliii L21 **Skirling** The Borders, S Scotland, UK
xxxv A14 **Skokholm Island** island SW Wales, UK
xxxv A13 **Skomer Island** island SW Wales, UK
xlii D12 **Skye, Isle of** island NW Scotland, UK
xli O13 **Slaidburn** Lancashire, NW England, UK
xli P7 **Slaley** Northumberland, N England, UK
xliii K20 **Slamannan** Falkirk, C Scotland, UK
xliv K7 **Slane** Meath, E Ireland
xliv K11 **Slaney** Ir. An tSláine. ≈ SE Ireland
xxxvi H16 **Slapton** Devon, SW England, UK
xxxix Q7 **Sleaford** Lincolnshire, E England, UK
xliv B13 **Slea Head** Ir. Ceann Sléibhe. headland SW Ireland
xliii F14 **Sleat, Sound of** strait NW Scotland, UK
xli V12 **Sledmere** East Riding of Yorkshire, N England, UK
xli V10 **Sleights** North Yorkshire, N England, UK
xliii G22 **Sliddery** North Ayrshire, W Scotland, UK
xliv F9 **Slieve Aughty Mountains** ▲▲ W Ireland
xliv H10 **Slieve Bloom Mountains** ▲▲ C Ireland
xliv D6 **Slieve Car** ▲ NW Ireland
xliv L6 **Slieve Donard** ▲ SE Northern Ireland, UK
xliv G11 **Slievefelim Mountains** ▲▲ C Ireland
xliv F6 **Slieve Gamph** var. Ox Mountains. ▲▲ N Ireland
xliv G11 **Slievekimalta** ▲ C Ireland
xliv C13 **Slieve Mish Mountains** ▲▲ SW Ireland
xliv H12 **Slievenamon** ▲ S Ireland
xliv I2 **Slieve Snaght** ▲ N Ireland
xliii E13 **Sligachan** Highland, NW Scotland, UK
xliv G5 **Sligo** Ir. Sligeach. Sligo, NW Ireland
xliv F6 **Sligo** Ir. Sligeach. ◐ county NW Ireland
xliv F5 **Sligo Bay** Ir. Cuan Shligigh. inlet NW Ireland
xxxvii S13 **Slindon** West Sussex, SE England, UK
xli T11 **Slingsby** North Yorkshire, N England, UK
xxxvii S9 **Slough** Slough, S England, UK
xxxvii S9 **Slough** ◐ unitary authority S England, UK
xliv B8 **Slyne Head** Ir. Ceann Léime. headland W Ireland
xxxix Y8 **Smallburgh** Norfolk, E England, UK
xxxvii Y11 **Smeeth** Kent, SE England, UK
xxxviii B15 **Smethwick** Sandwell, C England, UK
xl M6 **Smithfield** Cumbria, NW England, UK
xl G11 **Snaefell** ▲ C Isle of Man
xli T14 **Snaith** East Riding of Yorkshire, N England, UK
xli R11 **Snape** North Yorkshire, N England, UK
xliv C14 **Sneem** Kerry, SW Ireland
xxxix Q5 **Snelland** Lincolnshire, E England, UK
xxxix U8 **Snettisham** Norfolk, E England, UK
xxxviii L12 **Snitterfield** Warwickshire, C England, UK
xlii D11 **Snizort, Loch** inlet NW Scotland, UK
xxxvii W10 **Snodland** Kent, SE England, UK
xxxv G5 **Snowdon** ▲ NW Wales, UK
xxxv G5 **Snowdonia** ▲▲ NW Wales, UK
xxxix N8 **Soar** ≈ C England, UK
xliii D14 **Soay** island NW Scotland, UK
xxxix T11 **Soham** Cambridgeshire, E England, UK
xxxvii P13 **Solent, The** channel S England, UK
xxxviii D15 **Solihull** Solihull, C England, UK
xxxviii L11 **Solihull** ◐ unitary authority C England, UK
xxxv C13 **Solva** Pembrokeshire, SW Wales, UK
xxxvi J12 **Somerset** ◐ county SW England, UK
xxxix S11 **Somersham** Cambridgeshire, E England, UK
xxxvii P7 **Somerton** Oxfordshire, C England, UK
xxxvi K12 **Somerton** Somerset, SW England, UK
xxxvii O13 **Sopley** Hampshire, S England, UK
xliii I25 **Sorbie** Dumfries and Galloway, SW Scotland, UK
xliii D16 **Sorisdale** Argyll and Bute, W Scotland, UK
xliii J22 **Sorn** East Ayrshire, W Scotland, UK
xxxvi T9 **Southall** Ealing, SE England, UK
xxxviii M12 **Southam** Warwickshire, C England, UK
xxxvii P13 **Southampton** hist. Hamwih, Lat. Clausentum. City of Southampton, S England, UK
xxxvii P12 **Southampton, City of** ◐ unitary authority S England, UK
xliii H23 **South Ayrshire** ◐ unitary authority W Scotland, UK
xli U9 **South Bank** Redcar and Cleveland, N England, UK
xl F12 **South Barrule** hill S Isle of Man
xxxvii W9 **South Benfleet** Essex, SE England, UK
xxxvii V11 **Southborough** Kent, SE England, UK
xxxvi G16 **South Brent** Devon, SW England, UK
xli V14 **South Cave** East Riding of Yorkshire, N England, UK
xxxvii N8 **South Cerney** Gloucestershire, C England, UK
xli R3 **South Charlton** Northumberland, N England, UK
xxxvii R12 **South Downs** hill range SE England, UK
xliii F23 **Southend** Argyll and Bute, W Scotland, UK
xxxvii X9 **Southend-on-Sea** Essex, E England, UK
xxxvii W9 **Southend-on-Sea** ◐ unitary authority SE England, UK
xii-xiii **Southern Ocean** ocean
xliii K23 **Southern Uplands** ▲▲ S Scotland, UK
xxxix T10 **Southery** Norfolk, E England, UK
xliii N16 **South Esk** ≈ E Scotland, UK
xxxix P3 **South Ferriby** North Lincolnshire, N England, UK
xxxvi B9 **Southfields** Wandsworth, SE England, UK
xxxvii Z11 **South Foreland** headland SE England, UK
xxxvi D5 **Southgate** Enfield, SE England, UK
xxxvi L8 **South Gloucestershire** ◐ unitary authority W England, UK
xxxvii R12 **South Harting** West Sussex, SE England, UK
xxxvii Q13 **South Hayling** Hampshire, S England, UK
xxxvii T11 **South Holmwood** Surrey, SE England, UK
xxxix Q4 **South Kelsey** Lincolnshire, E England, UK
xli S15 **South Kirkby** Wakefield, N England, UK
xxxix R7 **South Kyme** Lincolnshire, E England, UK
xliii J21 **South Lanarkshire** ◐ unitary authority C Scotland, UK
xxxviii K13 **South Littleton** Worcestershire, C England, UK
xxxvii U13 **South Malling** East Sussex, SE England, UK
xxxvii X8 **Southminster** Essex, SE England, UK
xxxvi G12 **South Molton** Devon, SW England, UK
xxxvi K12 **South Petherton** Somerset, SW England, UK
xl B13 **Southport** Sefton, NW England, UK
xliii L19 **South Queensferry** City of Edinburgh, SE Scotland, UK
xli N5 **South Ronaldsay** island NE Scotland, UK
xli W2 **South Shields** South Tyneside, NE England, UK
xli W13 **South Skirlaugh** East Riding of Yorkshire, N England, UK
xliv D10 **South Sound** sound W Ireland
xli N5 **Southtown** Orkney Islands, N Scotland, UK
xli O7 **South Tyne** ≈ N England, UK
xli S6 **South Tyneside** ◐ unitary authority NE England, UK
xlii A13 **South Uist** island NW Scotland, UK
xlii I4 **South View** Shetland Islands, NE Scotland, UK
xxxvi L16 **Southwark** ◐ London borough SE England, UK
xxxvi D8 **Southwark** London borough capital Southwark, SE England, UK
xxxix O7 **Southwell** Nottinghamshire, C England, UK
xxxix Z11 **Southwold** Suffolk, E England, UK
xxxvii W8 **South Woodham Ferrers** Essex, E England, UK
xxxix T8 **South Wootton** Norfolk, E England, UK
xxxvi G14 **South Zeal** Devon, SW England, UK
xli S11 **Sowerby** North Yorkshire, N England, UK

◆ Country ● Country Capital ◇ Dependent Territory ○ Dependent Territory Capital ◐ Administrative Region ✕ International Airport ▲ Mountain ▲▲ Mountain Range ◎ Lake ▣ Reservoir ≈ River

Spalding – Walsall

xxxix R8 **Spalding** Lincolnshire, E England, UK
xxxix R11 **Spaldwick** Cambridgeshire, E England, UK
xliv D10 **Spanish Point** *headland* W Ireland
xxxvi L12 **Sparkford** Somerset, SW England, UK
xliii H15 **Spean Bridge** Highland, NW Scotland, UK
xl M17 **Speke** Liverpool, NW England, UK
xli R8 **Spennymoor** Durham, N England, UK
xliv J3 **Sperrin Mountains** ▲▲ N Northern Ireland, UK
xxxviii J13 **Spetchley** Worcestershire, W England, UK
xlii M11 **Spey** ≈ NE Scotland, UK
xlii M11 **Spey Bay** Moray, N Scotland, UK
xliv E9 **Spiddle** Galway, W Ireland
xxxix S6 **Spilsby** Lincolnshire, E England, UK
xliii J10 **Spinningdale** Highland, NW Scotland, UK
xliii L7 **Spital** Highland, N Scotland, UK
xxxv D13 **Spittal** Pembrokeshire, SW Wales, UK
xliii L15 **Spittal of Glenshee** Perth and Kinross, C Scotland, UK
xli R13 **Spofforth** North Yorkshire, N England, UK
xxxix O12 **Spratton** Northamptonshire, C England, UK
xxxix Q5 **Spridlington** Lincolnshire, E England, UK
xliii O21 **Sprouston** The Borders, S Scotland, UK
xxxix X9 **Sprowston** Norfolk, E England, UK
xli Y15 **Spurn Head** *headland* E England, UK
xliv L10 **Sraghmore** Wicklow, E Ireland
xlii J4 **Stack Skerry** *island* N Scotland, UK
xxxvii Q8 **Stadhampton** Oxfordshire, C England, UK
xliii D17 **Staffa** *island* W Scotland, UK
xlii E11 **Staffin** Highland, NW Scotland, UK
xxxviii J9 **Stafford** Staffordshire, C England, UK
xxxviii C13 **Staffordshire** ◐ *county* C England, UK
xli Q9 **Staindrop** Durham, N England, UK
xxxvi S9 **Staines** Surrey, SE England, UK
xli T15 **Stainforth** Doncaster, N England, UK
xli P12 **Stainforth** North Yorkshire, N England, UK
xli W10 **Staintondale** North Yorkshire, N England, UK
xli U9 **Staithes** Redcar and Cleveland, N England, UK
xxxvi L12 **Stalbridge** Dorset, S England, UK
xxxix Y8 **Stalham** Norfolk, E England, UK
xli P11 **Stalling Busk** North Yorkshire, N England, UK
xl Q16 **Stalybridge** Tameside, NW England, UK
xxxix Q9 **Stamford** Lincolnshire, E England, UK
xli U12 **Stamford Bridge** East Riding of Yorkshire, N England, UK
xli Q6 **Stamfordham** Northumberland, N England, UK
xxxvi D6 **Stamford Hill** Hackney, SE England, UK
xli N15 **Standish** Wigan, NW England, UK
xxxviii J8 **Standon** Staffordshire, C England, UK
xxxvii W9 **Stanford-le-Hope** Essex, SE England, UK
xli Q8 **Stanhope** Durham, N England, UK
xliii L22 **Stanhope** The Borders, S Scotland, UK
xli Q7 **Stanley** Durham, N England, UK
xliii L17 **Stanley** Perth and Kinross, C Scotland, UK
xxxvi A5 **Stanmore** Harrow, SE England, UK
xli R5 **Stannington** Northumberland, N England, UK
xxxvii V7 **Stansted** ✕ (London) Essex, E England, UK
xxxvii V7 **Stansted Mountfitchet** Hertfordshire, E England, UK
xxxix V11 **Stanton** Suffolk, E England, UK
xxxvii Q8 **Stanton St John** Oxfordshire, C England, UK
xxxvii X7 **Stanway** Essex, SE England, UK
xxxvii N6 **Stanway** Gloucestershire, C England, UK
xxxvi J12 **Staple Fitzpaine** Somerset, SW England, UK
xxxix N8 **Stapleford** Nottinghamshire, C England, UK
xxxvii N11 **Stapleford** Wiltshire, S England, UK
xxxvii W11 **Staplehurst** Kent, SE England, UK
xxxvi J14 **Starcross** Devon, SW England, UK
xxxvi H16 **Start Bay** *bay* SW England, UK
xli Q9 **Startforth** Durham, N England, UK
xxxvi H17 **Start Point** *headland* SW England, UK
xlii O3 **Start Point** *headland* N Scotland, UK
xxxvii M7 **Staunton** Gloucestershire, C England, UK
xxxvii K7 **Staunton** Gloucestershire, C England, UK
xxxviii G13 **Staunton on Wye** Herefordshire, W England, UK
xli N10 **Staveley** Cumbria, NW England, UK
xxxviii M5 **Staveley** Derbyshire, C England, UK
xxxvii M7 **Staverton** Gloucestershire, C England, UK
xli W11 **Staxton** North Yorkshire, N England, UK
xxxvi J10 **Steep Holm** *island* S England, UK
xxxix S6 **Steeping** ≈ E England, UK
xxxvii W6 **Steeple Bumpstead** Essex, SE England, UK
xxxvii R7 **Steeple Claydon** Buckinghamshire, C England, UK
xxxix R13 **Steeple Morden** Cambridgeshire, E England, UK
xliii K19 **Stenhousemuir** Falkirk, C Scotland, UK
xlii H2 **Stenness** Shetland Islands, NE Scotland, UK
xliii O19 **Stenton** East Lothian, SE Scotland, UK
xxxvi E7 **Stepney** Tower Hamlets, SE England, UK
xliii J20 **Stepps** North Lanarkshire, C Scotland, UK
xxxvii T7 **Stevenage** Hertfordshire, E England, UK
xliii I21 **Stevenston** North Ayrshire, W Scotland, UK
xxxvii P8 **Steventon** Oxfordshire, C England, UK
xliii I21 **Stewarton** East Ayrshire, W Scotland, UK
xxxvii T13 **Steyning** West Sussex, SE England, UK
xxxvi F13 **Stibb Cross** Devon, SW England, UK
xliii O21 **Stichill** The Borders, S Scotland, UK
xxxix S6 **Stickford** Lincolnshire, E England, UK
xxxix S6 **Stickney** Lincolnshire, E England, UK
xlii A12 **Stilligarry** Western Isles, NW Scotland, UK
xli T12 **Stillington** North Yorkshire, N England, UK
xxxix R10 **Stilton** Cambridgeshire, E England, UK
xliii H23 **Stinchar** ≈ W Scotland, UK
xliii K19 **Stirling** Stirling, C Scotland, UK
xliii I19 **Stirling** ◐ *unitary authority* C Scotland, UK
xxxvi B17 **Stithians** Cornwall, SW England, UK
xxxvii W8 **Stock** Essex, SE England, UK
xxxvii P11 **Stockbridge** Hampshire, S England, UK
xxxvi J13 **Stockland** Devon, SW England, UK
xl H16 **Stockport** Stockport, NW England, UK
xli P16 **Stockport** ◐ *unitary authority* NW England, UK
xli R16 **Stocksbridge** Sheffield, N England, UK
xli X6 **Stockton-on-Tees** *var.* Stockton on Tees. Stockton-on-Tees, N England, UK
xli S9 **Stockton-on-Tees** ◐ *unitary authority* NE England, UK
xxxvii W9 **Stoke** Kent, SE England, UK
xxxix P10 **Stoke Albany** Northamptonshire, C England, UK
xxxix W13 **Stoke-by-Nayland** Suffolk, E England, UK
xxxix U10 **Stoke Ferry** Norfolk, E England, UK
xxxvi H16 **Stoke Fleming** Devon, SW England, UK
xxxviii M10 **Stoke Golding** Leicestershire, C England, UK
xxxvii R7 **Stoke Hammond** Buckinghamshire, C England, UK
xxxvii R8 **Stokenchurch** Buckinghamshire, C England, UK
xxxvi D6 **Stoke Newington** Hackney, SE England, UK
xxxviii J7 **Stoke-on-Trent** *var.* Stoke. City of Stoke-on-Trent, C England, UK
xxxviii J7 **Stoke-on-Trent, City of** ◐ *unitary authority* C England, UK
xxxvii S9 **Stoke Poges** Buckinghamshire, C England, UK
xxxviii B17 **Stoke Prior** Worcestershire, W England, UK
xli T9 **Stokesley** North Yorkshire, N England, UK
xxxvii R7 **Stone** Buckinghamshire, C England, UK
xxxvi L8 **Stone** Gloucestershire, C England, UK
xxxviii J8 **Stone** Staffordshire, C England, UK
xliii P14 **Stonehaven** Aberdeenshire, NE Scotland, UK
xxxvii N11 **Stonehenge** *ancient monument* Wiltshire, S England, UK
xliii J21 **Stonehouse** South Lanarkshire, C Scotland, UK
xlii A13 **Stoneybridge** Western Isles, NW Scotland, UK
xliii H25 **Stoneykirk** Dumfries and Galloway, SW Scotland, UK
xlii Q1 **Stonybreck** Shetland Islands, NE Scotland, UK
xxxvii R6 **Stony Stratford** Milton Keynes, C England, UK
xlii D8 **Stornoway** Western Isles, NW Scotland, UK
xxxvii S12 **Storrington** West Sussex, S England, UK
xli E12 **Storr, The** ▲ NW Scotland, UK
xxxix T6 **Stotfold** Bedfordshire, E England, UK
xxxix W13 **Stour** ≈ E England, UK
xxxvi L12 **Stour** ≈ S England, UK
xxxvii Z10 **Stour** ≈ SE England, UK
xxxviii B15 **Stourbridge** Dudley, C England, UK
xxxviii A16 **Stourport-on-Severn** Worcestershire, W England, UK
xliii N21 **Stow** The Borders, S Scotland, UK
xxxix W12 **Stowmarket** Suffolk, E England, UK
xxxvii N7 **Stow-on-the-Wold** Gloucestershire, C England, UK
xliv I3 **Strabane** *Ir.* An Srath Bán. Strabane, W Northern Ireland, UK
xliv I3 **Strabane** ◐ *district* W Northern Ireland, UK
xliii O14 **Strachan** Aberdeenshire, NE Scotland, UK
xliii H18 **Strachur** Argyll and Bute, W Scotland, UK
xliv J10 **Stradbally** Laois, C Ireland
xxxix X11 **Stradbroke** Suffolk, E England, UK
xliv I6 **Stradone** Cavan, N Ireland
xxxix U9 **Stradsett** Norfolk, E England, UK
xliii I23 **Straiton** South Ayrshire, W Scotland, UK
xliv F5 **Strandhill** Sligo, N Ireland
xliv M5 **Strangford** Down, E Northern Ireland, UK
xliv M5 **Strangford Lough** *Ir.* Loch Cuan. *inlet* E Northern Ireland, UK
xliv H3 **Stranorlar** *Ir.* Srath an Urláir. Donegal, NW Ireland
xliii H25 **Stranraer** Dumfries and Galloway, S Scotland, UK
xxxvi E6 **Stratford** Newham, SE England, UK
xxxix W14 **Stratford St Mary** Suffolk, E England, UK
xxxviii K13 **Stratford-upon-Avon** *var.* Stratford. Warwickshire, C England, UK
xxxviii D17 **Stratford upon Avon Canal** *canal* C England, UK
xliii J21 **Strathaven** South Lanarkshire, C Scotland, UK
xliii J19 **Strathblane** Stirling, C Scotland, UK
xlii H9 **Strathcanaird** Highland, NW Scotland, UK
xlii G12 **Strathcarron** Highland, NW Scotland, UK
xlii M13 **Strathdon** Aberdeenshire, NE Scotland, UK
xliii M18 **Strathmiglo** Fife, E Scotland, UK
xlii I11 **Strathpeffer** Highland, NW Scotland, UK
xlii K6 **Strathy** Highland, N Scotland, UK
xlii J6 **Strathy Point** *headland* N Scotland, UK
xliii J18 **Strathyre** Stirling, C Scotland, UK
xxxvi E13 **Stratton** Cornwall, SW England, UK
xxxvii Q7 **Stratton Audley** Oxfordshire, C England, UK
xxxvi D9 **Streatham** Lambeth, SE England, UK
xxxvii S6 **Streatley** Bedfordshire, C England, UK
xxxvii Q9 **Streatley** West Berkshire, S England, UK
xxxvi K11 **Street** Somerset, SW England, UK
xli T12 **Strensall** York, N England, UK
xl P16 **Stretford** Trafford, NW England, UK
xxxix T11 **Stretham** Cambridgeshire, E England, UK
xl E16 **Stretton** Cheshire, W England, UK
xxxix Q9 **Stretton** Rutland, C England, UK
xlii P11 **Strichen** Aberdeenshire, NE Scotland, UK
xliv G7 **Strokestown** Roscommon, C Ireland
xlii I6 **Stroma, Island of** *island* N Scotland, UK
xlii F12 **Stromeferry** Highland, N Scotland, UK
xlii L4 **Stromness** Orkney Islands, N Scotland, UK
xliii I18 **Stronachlachar** Stirling, C Scotland, UK
xliii H19 **Strone** Argyll and Bute, W Scotland, UK
xlii H8 **Stronechrubie** Highland, NW Scotland, UK
xlii N3 **Stronsay** *island* NE Scotland, UK
xlii N3 **Stronsay Firth** *inlet* N Scotland, UK
xliii F16 **Strontian** Highland, NW Scotland, UK
xxxvi M8 **Stroud** Gloucestershire, C England, UK
xxxvii R12 **Stroud** Hampshire, S England, UK
xxxv C12 **Strumble Head** *headland* SW Wales, UK
xlii I12 **Struy** Highland, NW Scotland, UK
xlii P12 **Stuartfield** Aberdeenshire, NE Scotland, UK
xxxvii N14 **Studland** Dorset, S England, UK
xxxviii C17 **Studley** Warwickshire, C England, UK
xxxvii M13 **Sturminster Newton** Dorset, S England, UK
xxxvii Y10 **Sturry** Kent, SE England, UK
xxxix P5 **Sturton by Stow** Lincolnshire, E England, UK
xliv G8 **Suck** ≈ C Ireland
xxxviii L8 **Sudbury** Derbyshire, C England, UK
xxxix V13 **Sudbury** Suffolk, E England, UK
xxxix W12 **Suffolk** ◐ *county* E England, UK
xliv H12 **Suir** *Ir.* An tSiúir. ≈ S Ireland
xl G11 **Sulby** N Isle of Man
xlii J4 **Sule Skerry** *island* N Scotland, UK
xlii I2 **Sullom** Shetland Islands, NE Scotland, UK
xlii I5 **Sumburgh** Shetland Islands, NE Scotland, UK
xlii I6 **Sumburgh Head** *headland* NE Scotland, UK
xli R12 **Summer Bridge** North Yorkshire, N England, UK
xxxvi C16 **Summercourt** Cornwall, SW England, UK
xlii F9 **Summer Isles** *island group* NW Scotland, UK
xliii F16 **Sunart, Loch** *inlet* NW Scotland, UK
xli X3 **Sunderland** *var.* Wearmouth. Sunderland, NE England, UK
xli W3 **Sunderland** ◐ *unitary authority* NE England, UK
xli X15 **Sunk Island** East Riding of Yorkshire, N England, UK
xxxvii S10 **Sunningdale** Surrey, SE England, UK
xxxvii S11 **Surrey** ◐ *county* SE England, UK
xxxix R8 **Sutterton** Lincolnshire, E England, UK
xxxix S11 **Sutton** Cambridgeshire, E England, UK
xxxix Y13 **Sutton** Suffolk, E England, UK
xxxvii T10 **Sutton** Sutton, SE England, UK
xxxvi K17 **Sutton** ◐ *London borough* SE England, UK
xxxvi M9 **Sutton Benger** Wiltshire, S England, UK
xxxix T8 **Sutton Bridge** Lincolnshire, E England, UK
xxxviii D14 **Sutton Coldfield** Birmingham, C England, UK
xxxix N6 **Sutton in Ashfield** Nottinghamshire, C England, UK
xxxix T5 **Sutton on Sea** Lincolnshire, E England, UK
xli T12 **Sutton-on-the-Forest** North Yorkshire, N England, UK
xxxix S5 **Sutton St James** Lincolnshire, E England, UK
xxxvii P11 **Sutton Scotney** Hampshire, S England, UK
xxxviii W11 **Sutton Valence** Kent, SE England, UK
xxxviii L9 **Swadlincote** Derbyshire, C England, UK
xxxix V9 **Swaffham** Norfolk, E England, UK
xli S10 **Swainby** North Yorkshire, N England, UK
xxxvi M10 **Swainswick** Bath and North East Somerset, SW England, UK
xxxvii P6 **Swalcliffe** Oxfordshire, C England, UK
xli S11 **Swale** ≈ N England, UK
xliv H6 **Swalinbar** Cavan, N Ireland
xxxix Q4 **Swallow** Lincolnshire, E England, UK
xxxvii N12 **Swallowcliffe** Wiltshire, S England, UK
xxxvii R10 **Swallowfield** Wokingham, S England, UK
xxxvii N14 **Swanage** Dorset, S England, UK
xxxvii V9 **Swanley** Kent, SE England, UK
xxxv G14 **Swansea** *Wel.* Abertawe. Swansea, S Wales, UK
xxxv G14 **Swansea** ◐ *unitary authority* S Wales, UK
xxxv G15 **Swansea Bay** *bay* S Wales, UK
xxxix W9 **Swanton Morley** Norfolk, E England, UK
xxxix X10 **Swardeston** Norfolk, E England, UK
xxxix Q8 **Swayfield** Lincolnshire, E England, UK
xlii H3 **Swilly** ≈ N Ireland
xliv I2 **Swilly, Lough** *Ir.* Loch Súilí. *inlet* N Ireland
xxxvi G12 **Swimbridge** Devon, SW England, UK
xxxvii O9 **Swindon** Thamesdown, S England, UK
xxxvii N9 **Swindon** ◐ *unitary authority* S England, UK
xxxvii S5 **Swineshead** Bedfordshire, C England, UK
xxxix R7 **Swineshead** Lincolnshire, E England, UK
xliv E6 **Swinford** Mayo, NW Ireland
xxxix N11 **Swinford** Leicestershire, C England, UK
xlii I3 **Swining** Shetland Islands, NE Scotland, UK
xl O16 **Swinton** Salford, NW England, UK
xliii P21 **Swinton** The Borders, S Scotland, UK
xliv L8 **Swords** *Ir.* Sord; Sórd Choluim Chille. Dublin, E Ireland
xli T15 **Sykehouse** Doncaster, N England, UK
xlii I3 **Symbister** Shetland Islands, NE Scotland, UK
xxxviii H15 **Symonds Yat** Herefordshire, W England, UK
xlii J7 **Syre** Highland, N Scotland, UK
xxxix O13 **Syresham** Northamptonshire, C England, UK
xxxix O9 **Syston** Leicestershire, C England, UK

T

xli S13 **Tadcaster** North Yorkshire, N England, UK
xxxvii Q10 **Tadley** Hampshire, S England, UK
xxxvii T11 **Tadworth** Surrey, SE England, UK
xxxv J15 **Taff** ≈ SE Wales, UK
xliv K12 **Taghmon** Wexford, SE Ireland
xlii J10 **Tain** Highland, N Scotland, UK
xxxvii V7 **Takeley** Essex, SE England, UK
xxxv J12 **Talgarth** Powys, C Wales, UK
xlii F11 **Talladale** Highland, NW Scotland, UK
xliv L9 **Tallaght** Dublin, E Ireland
xxxv G12 **Talley** Carmarthenshire, S Wales, UK
xliv G13 **Tallow** Waterford, S Ireland
xlii I6 **Talmine** Highland, N Scotland, UK
xxxv G6 **Talsarnau** Gwynedd, NW Wales, UK
xxxv G9 **Talybont** Ceredigion, W Wales, UK
xxxv F6 **Talysarn** Gwynedd, NW Wales, UK
xxxviii D14 **Tam** ≈ C England, UK
xxxvi E14 **Tamar** ≈ SW England, UK
xxxvi F15 **Tamerton Foliot** Devon, SW England, UK
xli P16 **Tameside** ◐ *unitary authority* NW England, UK
xxxviii D13 **Tamworth** Staffordshire, C England, UK
xxxv J7 **Tanat** ≈ E Wales, UK
xliv K5 **Tandragee** Armagh, S Northern Ireland, UK
xli B9 **Taransay** *island* NW Scotland, UK
xlii K10 **Tarbat Ness** *headland* N Scotland, UK
xliv D11 **Tarbert** Kerry, SW Ireland
xliii G20 **Tarbert** Argyll and Bute, W Scotland, UK
xliii E19 **Tarbert** Argyll and Bute, W Scotland, UK
xlii C10 **Tarbert** Western Isles, NW Scotland, UK
xliii I18 **Tarbet** Argyll and Bute, W Scotland, UK
xliii I22 **Tarbolton** South Ayrshire, W Scotland, UK
xlii N15 **Tarfside** Angus, E Scotland, UK
xliii N14 **Tarland** Aberdeenshire, NE Scotland, UK
xxxviii I6 **Tarporley** Cheshire, W England, UK
xliii E14 **Tarskavaig** Highland, NW Scotland, UK
xxxviii H6 **Tarvin** Cheshire, W England, UK
xxxviii H6 **Tattenhall** Cheshire, W England, UK
xxxvi J12 **Taunton** Somerset, SW England, UK
xxxvi F15 **Tavistock** Devon, SW England, UK
xxxvi F15 **Tavy** ≈ SW England, UK
xxxvi G12 **Taw** ≈ SW England, UK
xliv F7 **Tawnyinah** Mayo, NW Ireland
xliii I17 **Tay** ≈ C Scotland, UK
xliii M17 **Tay, Firth of** *inlet* E Scotland, UK
xliii F21 **Tayinloan** Argyll and Bute, W Scotland, UK
xliii J17 **Tay, Loch** ◎ C Scotland, UK
xliii G17 **Taynuilt** Argyll and Bute, W Scotland, UK
xliii N17 **Tayport** Fife, E Scotland, UK
xliii F19 **Tayvallich** Argyll and Bute, W Scotland, UK
xxxix R4 **Tealby** Lincolnshire, E England, UK
xliii E14 **Teangue** Highland, NW Scotland, UK
xli N10 **Tebay** Cumbria, NW England, UK
xxxvi G14 **Tedburn St Mary** Devon, SW England, UK
xli R9 **Tees** ≈ N England, UK
xli T8 **Tees Bay** *bay* N England, UK
xxxv E12 **Teifi** *var.* River Teif. ≈ SW Wales, UK
xxxv H14 **Teign** ≈ SW England, UK
xxxvi H15 **Teignmouth** Devon, SW England, UK
xxxviii I9 **Telford** Shropshire, W England, UK
xxxviii J13 **Teme** ≈ England/Wales, UK
xliv H11 **Templemore** Tipperary, S Ireland
xliii L24 **Templand** Dumfries and Galloway, SW Scotland, UK
xxxvi D15 **Temple** Cornwall, SW England, UK
xliii M20 **Temple** Midlothian, SE Scotland, UK
xxxvi L12 **Templecombe** Somerset, SW England, UK
xli T14 **Temple Hirst** North Yorkshire, N England, UK
xliv L4 **Templepatrick** Antrim, NE Northern Ireland, UK
xli N8 **Temple Sowerby** Cumbria, NW England, UK
xxxv D13 **Templeton** Pembrokeshire, SW Wales, UK
xxxviii I12 **Tenbury Wells** Worcestershire, W England, UK
xxxv E14 **Tenby** Pembrokeshire, SW Wales, UK
xxxvii X11 **Tenterden** Kent, SE England, UK
xxxvii W7 **Terling** Essex, SE England, UK
xliv H2 **Termon** Donegal, N Ireland
xxxix T8 **Terrington St Clement** Norfolk, E England, UK
xxxvii P11 **Test** ≈ S England, UK
xxxvi M8 **Tetbury** Gloucestershire, C England, UK
xxxix S4 **Tetney** Lincolnshire, E England, UK
xxxvii Q8 **Tetsworth** Oxfordshire, C England, UK
xxxviii A14 **Tettenhall** Wolverhampton, C England, UK
xliii M23 **Teviot** ≈ SE Scotland, UK
xliii N23 **Teviothead** The Borders, S Scotland, UK
xxxvi M6 **Tewkesbury** Gloucestershire, C England, UK
xxxvii Q8 **Thame** Oxfordshire, C England, UK
xxxvii T9 **Thames** ≈ S England, UK
xxxvii P10 **Thatcham** West Berkshire, S England, UK
xxxvii V6 **Thaxted** Essex, SE England, UK
xxxvii Q10 **Theale** West Berkshire, S England, UK
xliii M22 **The Borders** ◐ *unitary authority* S Scotland, UK
xxxvii V9 **The Medway Towns** ◐ *unitary authority* SE England, UK
xxxv G15 **The Mumbles** Swansea, S Wales, UK
xxxvii U6 **Therfield** Hertfordshire, SE England, UK
xxxix V11 **Thetford** Norfolk, E England, UK
xxxv I15 **The Vale of Glamorgan** ◐ *unitary authority* S Wales, UK
xxxviii H9 **The Wrekin** ◐ *unitary authority* C England, UK
xxxix R6 **Thimbleby** Lincolnshire, E England, UK
xli S11 **Thirsk** North Yorkshire, N England, UK
xli P5 **Thockrington** Northumberland, N England, UK
xliv G8 **Thomas Street** Roscommon, C Ireland
xliv I12 **Thomastown** Kilkenny, SE Ireland
xxxix R4 **Thoresway** Lincolnshire, E England, UK
xli X7 **Thornaby on Tees** Middlesbrough, NE England, UK
xxxvi L9 **Thornbury** South Gloucestershire, SW England, UK
xxxix O11 **Thornby** Northamptonshire, C England, UK
xxxvi K13 **Thorncombe** Dorset, S England, UK
xxxix W12 **Thorndon** Suffolk, E England, UK
xli U15 **Thorne** Doncaster, N England, UK
xli S13 **Thorner** Leeds, N England, UK
xxxix R9 **Thorney** Cambridgeshire, E England, UK
xliii K23 **Thornhill** Dumfries and Galloway, S Scotland, UK
xliii J18 **Thornhill** Stirling, C Scotland, UK
xli Q7 **Thornley** Durham, N England, UK
xl M13 **Thornton** Lancashire, NW England, UK
xliii M18 **Thornton** Fife, E Scotland, UK
xxxix Q3 **Thornton Curtis** North Lincolnshire, N England, UK
xli V11 **Thornton Dale** North Yorkshire, N England, UK
xli S11 **Thornton-le-Street** North Yorkshire, N England, UK
xxxix Y12 **Thorpeness** Suffolk, E England, UK
xxxix P6 **Thorpe on the Hill** Lincolnshire, E England, UK
xxxvii Y7 **Thorrington** Essex, SE England, UK
xxxvi H13 **Thorverton** Devon, SW England, UK
xxxix Q11 **Thrapston** Northamptonshire, C England, UK
xxxvii U11 **Three Bridges** West Sussex, S England, UK
xli P12 **Threshfield** North Yorkshire, N England, UK
xli U2 **Throckley** Newcastle upon Tyne, NE England, UK
xli Q4 **Thropton** Northumberland, N England, UK
xlii M7 **Thrumster** Highland, N Scotland, UK
xxxvii O11 **Thruxton** Hampshire, S England, UK
xli T16 **Thurcroft** Rotherham, N England, UK
xxxix Q9 **Thurlby** Lincolnshire, E England, UK
xliv H11 **Thurles** *Ir.* Durlas. Tipperary, S Ireland
xxxvi G16 **Thurlestone** Devon, SW England, UK
xxxix U13 **Thurlow** Suffolk, E England, UK
xxxviii V9 **Thurrock** ◐ *unitary authority* SE England, UK
xl M7 **Thursby** Cumbria, NW England, UK
xlii L6 **Thurso** Highland, N Scotland, UK
xlii K7 **Thurso** ≈ NW Scotland, UK
xl B16 **Thurstaston** Wirral, NW England, UK
xli P10 **Thwaite** North Yorkshire, N England, UK
xxxvi L7 **Tibberton** Gloucestershire, C England, UK
xxxviii W12 **Ticehurst** East Sussex, SE England, UK
xli T16 **Tickhill** Doncaster, N England, UK
xxxvi K8 **Tidenham** Gloucestershire, C England, UK
xxxviii L5 **Tideswell** Derbyshire, C England, UK
xli A11 **Tigharry** Western Isles, NW Scotland, UK
xliii G20 **Tighnabruaich** Argyll and Bute, W Scotland, UK
xxxvii V9 **Tilbury** Essex, SE England, UK
xxxvii Q9 **Tilehurst** Reading, S England, UK
xliii K19 **Tillicoultry** Clackmannan, C Scotland, UK
xxxvii X8 **Tillingham** Essex, SE England, UK
xxxvii N11 **Tilshead** Wiltshire, S England, UK
xxxviii H8 **Tilstock** Shropshire, W England, UK
xxxviii H7 **Tilston** Cheshire, W England, UK
xliii K15 **Tilt** ≈ C Scotland, UK
xliv E15 **Timoleague** Cork, S Ireland
xlii B8 **Timsgarry** Western Isles, NW Scotland, UK
xliv K11 **Tinahely** Wicklow, E Ireland
xxxvii Q6 **Tingewick** Buckinghamshire, C England, UK
xxxvi D14 **Tintagel** Cornwall, SW England, UK
xliii L21 **Tinto** ▲ C Scotland, UK
xliii K22 **Tinto Hills** ▲▲ South Lanarkshire, C Scotland, UK
xliv G12 **Tipperary** *Ir.* Tiobraid Árann. Tipperary, S Ireland
xliv G11 **Tipperary** *Ir.* Tiobraid Árann. ◐ *county* S Ireland
xxxviii B14 **Tipton** Sandwell, C England, UK
xxxvii X7 **Tiptree** Essex, SE England, UK
xliii B17 **Tiree** *island* W Scotland, UK
xxxvii N12 **Tisbury** Wiltshire, S England, UK
xxxviii L7 **Tissington** Derbyshire, C England, UK
xxxvii Q13 **Titchfield** Hampshire, S England, UK
xxxvi I13 **Tiverton** Devon, SW England, UK
xlii N4 **Toab** Orkney Islands, N Scotland, UK
xlii I5 **Toab** Shetland Islands, NE Scotland, UK
xliv F6 **Tobercurry** Sligo, N Ireland
xliii E16 **Tobermory** Argyll and Bute, W Scotland, UK
xliii F18 **Toberonochy** Argyll and Bute, W Scotland, UK
xlii C8 **Tobson** Western Isles, NW Scotland, UK
xxxvi S6 **Toddington** Bedfordshire, C England, UK
xli P14 **Todmorden** Calderdale, N England, UK
xliv D15 **Toe Head** *headland* SW Ireland
xlii B10 **Toe Head** *headland* NW Scotland, UK
xli T12 **Tollerton** North Yorkshire, N England, UK
xxxvii X7 **Tollesbury** Essex, SE England, UK
xxxvii X7 **Tolleshunt d'Arcy** Essex, SE England, UK
xlii K13 **Tomatin** Highland, NW Scotland, UK
xlii J12 **Tombreck** Highland, NW Scotland, UK
xlii H14 **Tomdoun** Highland, NW Scotland, UK
xliv F10 **Tomgraney** Clare, W Ireland
xlii H13 **Tomich** Highland, NW Scotland, UK
xlii L13 **Tomintoul** Moray, N Scotland, UK
xxxvii V11 **Tonbridge** Kent, SE England, UK
xxxv I15 **Tondu** Bridgend, S Wales, UK
xlii D8 **Tong** Western Isles, NW Scotland, UK
xliii J25 **Tongland** Dumfries and Galloway, SW Scotland, UK
xlii J7 **Tongue** Highland, N Scotland, UK
xxxv I14 **Tonypandy** Rhondda Cynon Taff, S Wales, UK
xliv C8 **Toombeola** Galway, W Ireland
xliv K4 **Toome Bridge** Antrim, NE Northern Ireland, UK
xliv G10 **Toomyvara** Tipperary, S Ireland
xliv C15 **Toormore** Cork, S Ireland
xxxvi C9 **Tooting** Wandsworth, SE England, UK
xxxvi I14 **Topsham** Devon, SW England, UK
xxxvi H16 **Tor Bay** *bay* SW England, UK
xxxvi H15 **Torbay** ◐ *unitary authority* SW England, UK
xliii G22 **Torbeg** North Ayrshire, W Scotland, UK
xxxvi H16 **Torcross** Devon, SW England, UK
xlii J11 **Tore** Highland, NW Scotland, UK
xxxv K14 **Torfaen** ◐ *unitary authority* SE Wales, UK
xxxvi M9 **Tormarton** South Gloucestershire, SW England, UK
xlii J13 **Torness** Highland, NW Scotland, UK
xliii L20 **Torphichen** West Lothian, SE Scotland, UK
xliii N14 **Torphins** Aberdeenshire, NE Scotland, UK
xxxvi F16 **Torpoint** Cornwall, SW England, UK
xxxvi H15 **Torquay** Devon, SW England, UK
xxxvi F12 **Torridge** ≈ SW England, UK
xlii F11 **Torridon** Highland, NW Scotland, UK
xlii F11 **Torridon, Loch** *inlet* NW Scotland, UK
xlii E13 **Torrin** Highland, NW Scotland, UK
xxxvii V16 **Torteval** Guernsey, Channel Islands
xliii L24 **Torthorwald** Dumfries and Galloway, SW Scotland, UK
xliv G2 **Tory Island** *Ir.* Toraigh. *island* NW Ireland
xliv G2 **Tory Sound** *sound* N Ireland
xxxvii P14 **Totland** Isle of Wight, S England, UK
xxxvi H15 **Totnes** Devon, SW England, UK
xxxvi D5 **Tottenham** Haringey, SE England, UK
xl O15 **Tottington** Bury, NW England, UK
xxxvii P13 **Totton** Hampshire, S England, UK
xxxix O13 **Towcester** Northamptonshire, C England, UK
xxxiv L16 **Tower Hamlets** ◐ *London borough* SE England, UK
xli Q8 **Tow Law** Durham, N England, UK
xliii O22 **Town Yetholm** The Borders, S Scotland, UK
xl O17 **Trafford** ◐ *unitary authority* NW England, UK
xliv C12 **Tralee** *Ir.* Trá Lí. Kerry, SW Ireland
xliv C12 **Tralee Bay** *Ir.* Bá Thrá Lí. *bay* SW Ireland
xliv I13 **Tramore** *Ir.* Tráigh Mhór, Trá Mhór. Waterford, S Ireland
xliii N20 **Tranent** East Lothian, SE Scotland, UK
xxxv G13 **Trapp** Carmarthenshire, S Wales, UK
xli P14 **Trawden** Lancashire, NW England, UK
xxxv H6 **Trawsfynydd** Gwynedd, NW Wales, UK
xxxv I12 **Trecastle** Powys, C Wales, UK
xxxv J13 **Tredegar** Blaenau Gwent, SE Wales, UK
xxxvi L17 **Treen** Cornwall, SW England, UK
xxxv I9 **Trefeglwys** Powys, C Wales, UK
xxxv C13 **Treffgarne** Pembrokeshire, SW Wales, UK
xxxv I4 **Trefnant** Denbighshire, N Wales, UK
xxxviii G8 **Trefonen** Shropshire, W England, UK
xxxv F4 **Trefor** Isle of Anglesey, NW Wales, UK
xxxv H11 **Tregaron** Ceredigion, W Wales, UK
xxxvi C16 **Tregony** Cornwall, SW England, UK
xxxv J8 **Tregynon** Powys, C Wales, UK
xliii H15 **Treig, Loch** ◎ NW Scotland, UK
xxxv L14 **Trelleck** Monmouthshire, SE Wales, UK
xxxv F7 **Tremadog Bay** *bay* NW Wales, UK
xxxvi L12 **Trent** Somerset, SW England, UK
xxxviii M8 **Trent** ≈ C England, UK
xxxv I14 **Treorchy** Rhondda Cynon Taff, S Wales, UK
xxxvi I17 **Tresco** *island* SW England, UK
xliii D17 **Treshnish Isles** *island group* W Scotland, UK
xxxvi C16 **Tresillian** Cornwall, SW England, UK
xlii I4 **Tresta** Shetland Islands, NE Scotland, UK
xxxv J13 **Tretower** Powys, C Wales, UK
xxxv K5 **Treuddyn** Flintshire, N Wales, UK
xxxvi B15 **Trevose Head** *headland* SW England, UK
xliv J8 **Trim** *Ir.* Baile Átha Troim. Meath, E Ireland
xli S8 **Trimdon** Durham, N England, UK
xli X5 **Trimdon Colliery** Durham, N England, UK
xxxix X7 **Trimingham** Norfolk, E England, UK
xxxvii S7 **Tring** Hertfordshire, SE England, UK
xxxvii X17 **Trinity** Jersey, Channel Islands
xliii I24 **Trool, Loch** ◎ Dumfries and Galloway, SW Scotland, UK
xliii H22 **Troon** South Ayrshire, W Scotland, UK
xxxvi M10 **Trowbridge** Wiltshire, S England, UK
xxxix T12 **Trumpington** Cambridgeshire, E England, UK
xxxix X8 **Trunch** Norfolk, E England, UK
xxxvi C16 **Truro** Cornwall, SW England, UK
xliv G5 **Truskmore** ▲ N Ireland
xxxv E7 **Trwyn Cilan** *headland* NW Wales, UK
xliv F8 **Tuam** *Ir.* Tuaim. Galway, W Ireland
xxxix X13 **Tuddenham** Suffolk, E England, UK
xxxv E6 **Tudweiliog** Gwynedd, NW Wales, UK
xliv F10 **Tulla** Clare, W Ireland
xliii H16 **Tulla, Loch** ◎ W Scotland, UK
xliv I9 **Tullamore** *Ir.* Tulach Mhór. Offaly, C Ireland
xliii K19 **Tullibody** Clackmannan, C Scotland, UK
xlii O12 **Tulloch** Aberdeenshire, NE Scotland, UK
xliv J11 **Tullow** *Ir.* An Tullach. Carlow, SE Ireland
xliv H5 **Tully** Fermanagh, SW Northern Ireland, UK
xliv G7 **Tulsk** Roscommon, C Ireland
xxxv G13 **Tumble** Carmarthenshire, S Wales, UK
xlii K16 **Tummel** ≈ C Scotland, UK
xlii K16 **Tummel Bridge** Perth and Kinross, C Scotland, UK
xliii K16 **Tummel, Loch** ◎ C Scotland, UK
xxxviii J7 **Tunstall** City of Stoke-on-Trent, C England, UK
xli X14 **Tunstall** East Riding of Yorkshire, N England, UK
xxxix Y12 **Tunstall** Suffolk, E England, UK
xliii H23 **Turnberry** South Ayrshire, W Scotland, UK
xlii O11 **Turriff** Aberdeenshire, NE Scotland, UK
xxxviii L8 **Tutbury** Staffordshire, C England, UK
xxxix O6 **Tuxford** Nottinghamshire, C England, UK
xlii M4 **Twatt** Orkney Islands, N Scotland, UK
xliii P21 **Tweed** ≈ England/Scotland, UK
xli P1 **Tweedmouth** Northumberland, N England, UK
xliii L22 **Tweedsmuir** The Borders, S Scotland, UK
xliv C8 **Twelve Pins, The** ▲▲ W Ireland
xxxvi A9 **Twickenham** Richmond upon Thames, SE England, UK
xxxvi G15 **Two Bridges** Devon, SW England, UK
xxxviii E13 **Twycross** Leicestershire, C England, UK
xxxvii P12 **Twyford** Hampshire, S England, UK
xxxix O9 **Twyford** Leicestershire, C England, UK
xxxvii R9 **Twyford** Wokingham, S England, UK
xliii J25 **Twynholm** Dumfries and Galloway, SW Scotland, UK
xxxix S9 **Tydd St Mary** Lincolnshire, E England, UK
xliv J5 **Tyholland** Monaghan, NE Ireland
xl E14 **Tyldesley** Wigan, NW England, UK
xliii I17 **Tyndrum** Stirling, C Scotland, UK
xli Q6 **Tyne** ≈ N England, UK
xli S6 **Tynemouth** North Tyneside, NE England, UK
xxxv G13 **Tywi** ≈ S Wales, UK
xxxv G8 **Tywyn** Gwynedd, W Wales, UK

U

xxxvii U12 **Uckfield** East Sussex, SE England, UK
xliii K21 **Uddingston** South Lanarkshire, C Scotland, UK
xxxvi I13 **Uffculme** Devon, SW England, UK
xxxvii O9 **Uffington** Oxfordshire, C England, UK
xli U9 **Ugthorpe** North Yorkshire, N England, UK
xlii D11 **Uig** Highland, N Scotland, UK
xxxix S5 **Ulceby** Lincolnshire, E England, UK
xxxix Q3 **Ulceby** North Lincolnshire, N England, UK
xl L8 **Uldale** Cumbria, NW England, UK
xxxvi M8 **Uley** Gloucestershire, C England, UK
xli R4 **Ulgham** Northumberland, N England, UK
xlii G10 **Ullapool** Highland, N Scotland, UK
xli T13 **Ulleskelf** North Yorkshire, N England, UK
xxxix N11 **Ullesthorpe** Leicestershire, C England, UK
xl M9 **Ullswater** ◎ NW England, UK
xl L10 **Ulpha** Cumbria, NW England, UK
xlii I2 **Ulsta** Shetland Islands, NE Scotland, UK
xliv H4 **Ulster** *province* Northern Ireland, UK/Ireland
xliv J5 **Ulster Canal** *canal* Ireland/Northern Ireland, UK
xliii D17 **Ulva** *island* W Scotland, UK
xl L11 **Ulverston** Cumbria, NW England, UK
xlii H8 **Unapool** Highland, NW Scotland, UK
xlii H3 **Unifirth** Shetland Islands, NE Scotland, UK
xlii J1 **Unst** *island* NE Scotland, UK
xxxvii N10 **Upavon** Wiltshire, S England, UK
xl D14 **Up Holland** Lancashire, NW England, UK
xxxvi J13 **Upottery** Devon, SW England, UK
xxxix O8 **Upper Broughton** Nottinghamshire, C England, UK
xxxv J12 **Upper Chapel** Powys, C Wales, UK
xliv H5 **Upper Lough Erne** ◎ SW Northern Ireland, UK
xli T13 **Upper Poppleton** York, N England, UK
xxxviii K8 **Upper Tean** Staffordshire, C England, UK
xxxix P10 **Uppingham** Rutland, C England, UK
xxxvii Y10 **Upstreet** Kent, SE England, UK
xl B16 **Upton** Wirral, NW England, UK
xxxviii J13 **Upton upon Severn** Worcestershire, W England, UK
xxxix T10 **Upwell** Cambridgeshire, E England, UK
xxxvii N10 **Urchfont** Wiltshire, S England, UK
xli R11 **Ure** ≈ N England, UK
xliv H11 **Urlingford** Kilkenny, SE Ireland
xl O16 **Urmston** Salford, NW England, UK
xxxv L14 **Usk** Monmouthshire, SE Wales, UK
xxxv L14 **Usk** *Wel.* Wysg. ≈ SE Wales, UK
xxxv H12 **Usk Reservoir** ⊡ S Wales, UK
xxxviii K8 **Uttoxeter** Staffordshire, C England, UK
xxxvii S9 **Uxbridge** Hillingdon, SE England, UK

V

xlii H10 **Vaich, Loch** ◎ NW Scotland, UK
xliv A13 **Valencia Island** *Ir.* Dairbhre. *island* SW Ireland
xlii A11 **Vallay** *island* NW Scotland, UK
xliii A14 **Vatersay** *island* NW Scotland, UK
xxxvii Q14 **Ventnor** Isle of Wight, S England, UK
xxxvii P10 **Vernham Dean** Hampshire, S England, UK
xxxvii N13 **Verwood** Dorset, S England, UK
xxxvi C17 **Veryan** Cornwall, SW England, UK
xl L12 **Vickerstown** Cumbria, NW England, UK
xlii I3 **Vidlin** Shetland Islands, NE Scotland, UK
xliv J7 **Virginia** Cavan, N Ireland
xlii I3 **Voe** Shetland Islands, NE Scotland, UK
xlii H2 **Voe** Shetland Islands, NE Scotland, UK
xxxviii G14 **Vowchurch** Herefordshire, W England, UK
xxxv J8 **Vyrnwy** *Wel.* Afon Efyrnwy. ≈ E Wales, UK

W

xxxvii R7 **Waddesdon** Buckinghamshire, C England, UK
xxxix Q4 **Waddingham** Lincolnshire, E England, UK
xli O13 **Waddington** Lancashire, NW England, UK
xxxix Q6 **Waddington** Lincolnshire, E England, UK
xxxvi D15 **Wadebridge** Cornwall, SW England, UK
xli T16 **Wadworth** Doncaster, N England, UK
xxxix T6 **Wainfleet All Saints** Lincolnshire, E England, UK
xli S15 **Wakefield** Wakefield, N England, UK
xli R15 **Wakefield** ◐ *unitary authority* N England, UK
xxxix X6 **Wakes Colne** Essex, SE England, UK
xxxix Z11 **Walberswick** Suffolk, E England, UK
xxxix Q6 **Walcot** Lincolnshire, E England, UK
xxxv H9 **Wales** *Wel.* Cymru. *national region* Wales, UK
xxxviii G12 **Walford** Herefordshire, W England, UK
xxxviii I7 **Walgherton** Cheshire, W England, UK
xxxvii T7 **Walkern** Hertfordshire, SE England, UK
xli V14 **Walkington** East Riding of Yorkshire, N England, UK
xli P6 **Wall** Northumberland, N England, UK
xl B15 **Wallasey** Wirral, NW England, UK
xxxvii Q9 **Wallingford** Oxfordshire, C England, UK
xlii H4 **Walls** Shetland Islands, NE Scotland, UK
xli R6 **Wallsend** North Tyneside, NE England, UK
xxxvii Z10 **Walmer** Kent, SE England, UK
xl L12 **Walney, Isle of** *island* NW England, UK
xxxix T9 **Walpole St Peter** Norfolk, E England, UK
xxxviii C14 **Walsall** Walsall, C England, UK

◆ Country ● Country Capital ◇ Dependent Territory ○ Dependent Territory Capital ◐ Administrative Region ✕ International Airport ▲ Mountain ▲▲ Mountain Range ◎ Lake ⊡ Reservoir ≈ River

Y

◆ Country ◇ Dependent Territory ◈ Administrative Region ▲ Mountain ◎ Lake
● Country Capital ○ Dependent Territory Capital × International Airport ▲▲ Mountain Range ⊡ Reservoir ≈ River

ATLAS
OF THE
WORLD

THE MAPS IN THIS ATLAS ARE ARRANGED CONTINENT BY CONTINENT, STARTING FROM
THE INTERNATIONAL DATE LINE, AND MOVING EASTWARDS. THE MAPS PROVIDE A
UNIQUE VIEW OF TODAY'S WORLD, COMBINING TRADITIONAL CARTOGRAPHIC TECHNIQUES
WITH THE LATEST REMOTE-SENSED AND DIGITAL TECHNOLOGY.

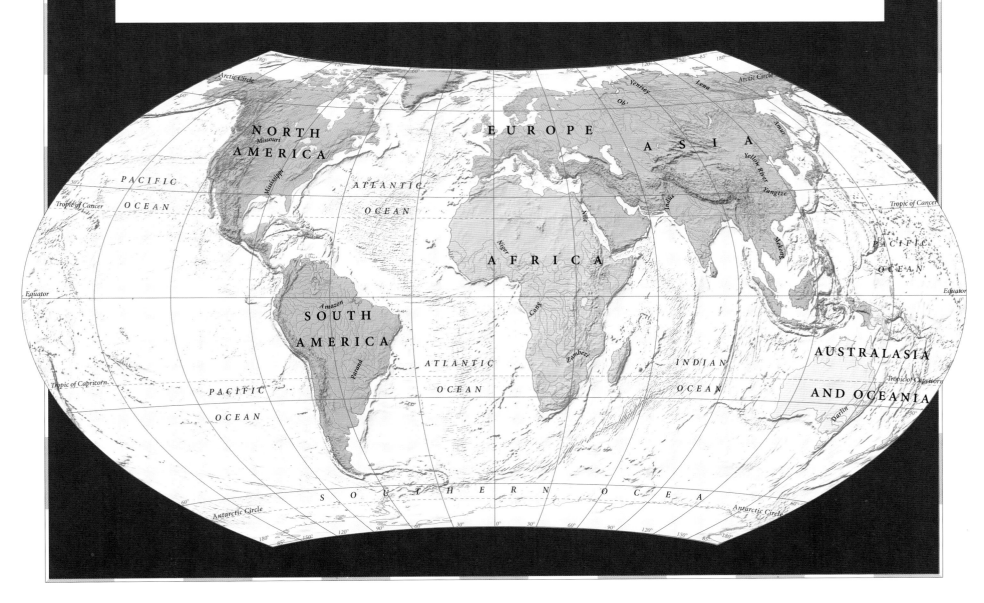

EURASIAN PLATE
NORTH AMERICAN PLATE

ARCTIC OCEAN

Franz Josef Land

North Pole

Nordøstrundingen

Sea of
Okhotsk

East Siberian
Sea

Khrebet Cherskogo

Khrebet Kolymsky

Kamchatka

Kanchalan

Koryakskoye Nagor'ye

Anandyrskiy
Zaliv

Cape Prince
of Wales

Chukchi
Sea

Point Barrow

Beaufort Sea

Kap
Morris Jesup

Greenland Sea

Norwegian Sea

Greenland

King Frederik
VIII Land

Iceland

Denmark Strait

Kurit Trench

Northwest Pacific
Basin

Aleutian Islands

Bowers Ridge

Aleutian
Basin

Bering
Sea

Nunivak
Island

St Lawrence
Island

Seward
Peninsula

Bering Strait

Norton
Sound

Brooks Range

Coville

Kuskokwim

Yukon

McClure Strait

Banks Island

Parry Islands

Jones Sound

Prince
Patrick
Island

Viscount Melville Sound

Lancaster Sound

Queen
Elizabeth Islands

Ellesmere
Island

Queen
Elizabeth Islands

King Christian X Land

Baffin Bay

Baffin Island

Davis Strait

Aleutian Trench

NORTH AMERICAN PLATE

PACIFIC PLATE

Gulf of
Alaska

Alaska Peninsula

Kodiak
Island

Kenai
Mountains

Alaska Range

Bristol
Bay

Kuskokwim Bay

Mackenzie
Bay

Mackenzie

Anderson

Amundsen Gulf

Victoria
Island

Great Bear Lake

Coppermine

Coronation Gulf

Queen Maud
Gulf

Boothia
Peninsula

Gulf
of Boothia

Foxe
Basin

Foxe Channel

Southampton
Island

Hudson Strait

Frobisher Bay

Cumberland
Sound

Nettilling Lake

King Frederik
VI Coast

Labrador
Sea

Patton Seamount

Cobb Seamount

Giacomini Seamount

Queen Charlotte Islands

Dickins
Seamount

Union Seamount

Morton Seamount

Vancouver
Island

Cascadia
Basin

Delgada
Fan

Gorda Ridge

JUAN DE FUCA PLATE

PACIFIC PLATE

NORTH AMERICAN PLATE

Hecate
Strait

Peace

Fraser

Great Slave Lake

Back

Thelon

Dubawnt Lake

Kazan

Baker Lake

Garry Lake

Arctic Circle

Wollaston Lake

Lake Athabasca

Reindeer Lake

Coats Island

Mansel
Island

Ross Welcome Sound

Hudson Bay

Belcher
Islands

Péninsule
d'Ungava

Rivière
aux Feuilles
Rivière
aux Mélèzes

Ungava Bay

Arnaud

George

Mendocino Fracture Zone

Pioneer Fracture Zone

Murray Fracture Zone

Maurice
Seamounts

Molokai Fracture Zone

Tropic of Cancer

Clarion Fracture Zone

PACIFIC OCEAN

Astoria
Fan

Coast Mountains

Cascade Range

Coast Ranges

Columbia

Mount Rainier
4392m

Mount St Helens 2549m

Columbia
Plateau

Harney Basin

Snake

Yellowstone

ROCKY
Mountains

Canadian Shield

NORTH

AMERICA

Missouri

Churchill

Nelson

Lake Winnipeg

Severn

Lake Manitoba

Winnipeg

Lake of the Woods

Lake Nipigon

Lake Superior

Great Lakes

Lake Michigan

Lake Huron

Lake Nipissing

Attawapiskat

Albany

James
Bay

Moose

Lac Mistassini

Ottawa

St Lawrence

La Grande Rivière

Laurentian
Mountains

Saguenay

Lake Champlain

Columbia
Plateau

San Joaquin

Great Basin

Sierra Nevada

Coast Ranges

Mount Whitney 4418m

Death Valley

Mojave
Desert

Great Salt Lake

Lake Powell

Lake Mead

Grand
Canyon

Colorado
Plateau

Painted Desert

Mount Elbert 4399m

Colorado

Arkansas

Cheyenne

North Platte

South Platte

Platte

Niobrara

Black Hills

Lake Oahe

Missouri

Des Moines

Minnesota

Wisconsin

Illinois

Mississippi

Ohio

Lake
St Clair

Lake Erie

Niagara
Falls

Lake Ontario

Allegheny Mountains

Appalachian Mountains

Cumberland Plateau

Tennessee

Blue Ridge

Mount Mitchell 2037m

Roanoke

Long Island

Delaware Bay

Chesapeake Bay

Cape Hatteras

Cape Lookout

Great Plains

Kansas

Arkansas

Red River

Canadian

Mississippi

Arkansas

Pecos

Colorado

Rio Grande

Sonoran
Desert

Gila

Baldy Peak 3476m

Humphreys
Peak 3851m

San Francisco Bay

Monterey Bay

Islas Alijos

Revillagigedo
Islands

Mathematicians
Seamounts

Clipperton Fracture Zone

Clipperton
Island

Seamounts

Siqueiros Fracture Zone

Orozco Fracture Zone

COCOS PLATE

PACIFIC PLATE

East Pacific Rise

Albatross
Plateau

Guatemala
Basin

Colón Ridge

Cocos Ridge

Middle America Trench

Tehuantepec Ridge

Gulf of
Tehuantepec

Golfo de
Fonseca

COCOS PLATE

NORTH AMERICAN PLATE

CARIBBEAN PLATE

Berlanga Rise

Cabo San
Lucas

Lower California

Gulf of
California

Sierra Madre Occidental

Sierra Madre Oriental

Sierra Madre del Sur

Lago de Chapala

Popocatépetl
5452m

Citlaltepetl
5700m

Nevado de
Toluca

Río Grande de Santiago

Mexico
Basin

Gulf of Mexico

Mississippi
Delta

Galveston Bay

Mississippi Fan

Sigsbee Escarpment

Campeche Bank

Bay of
Campeche

Yucatan
Peninsula

Yucatan
Channel

Yucatan Basin

Cayman Trench

Apalachee
Bay

Alabama

Chattahoochee

Savannah

Apalachicola

Tampa Bay

Lake Okeechobee

The
Everglades

Cape Canaveral

Blake
Plateau

Straits of Florida

Great Bahama Bank

Blake-Bahama Ridge

Cuba

Bahamas

Windward Passage

Jamaica

Greater

Nicaraguan
Rise

Gulf of Honduras

Lake Managua

Lake Nicaragua

Mosquito
Gulf

Gulf of Darién

Isthmus of Panama

Gulf of
Panama

Peninsula
de Azuero

Panama
Basin

Mosquito Coast

Caribbean

Peninsula
de la Guajira

Colombian
Basin

Cordillera Occidental

Cordillera Central

Cordillera Oriental

Magdalena

Cauca

Maracaibo

NORTH AMERICA

NORTH AMERICA IS THE WORLD'S THIRD LARGEST CONTINENT WITH A
TOTAL AREA OF 9,358,340 SQ MILES (24,238,000 SQ KM) INCLUDING
GREENLAND AND THE CARIBBEAN ISLANDS. IT LIES WHOLLY
WITHIN THE NORTHERN HEMISPHERE.

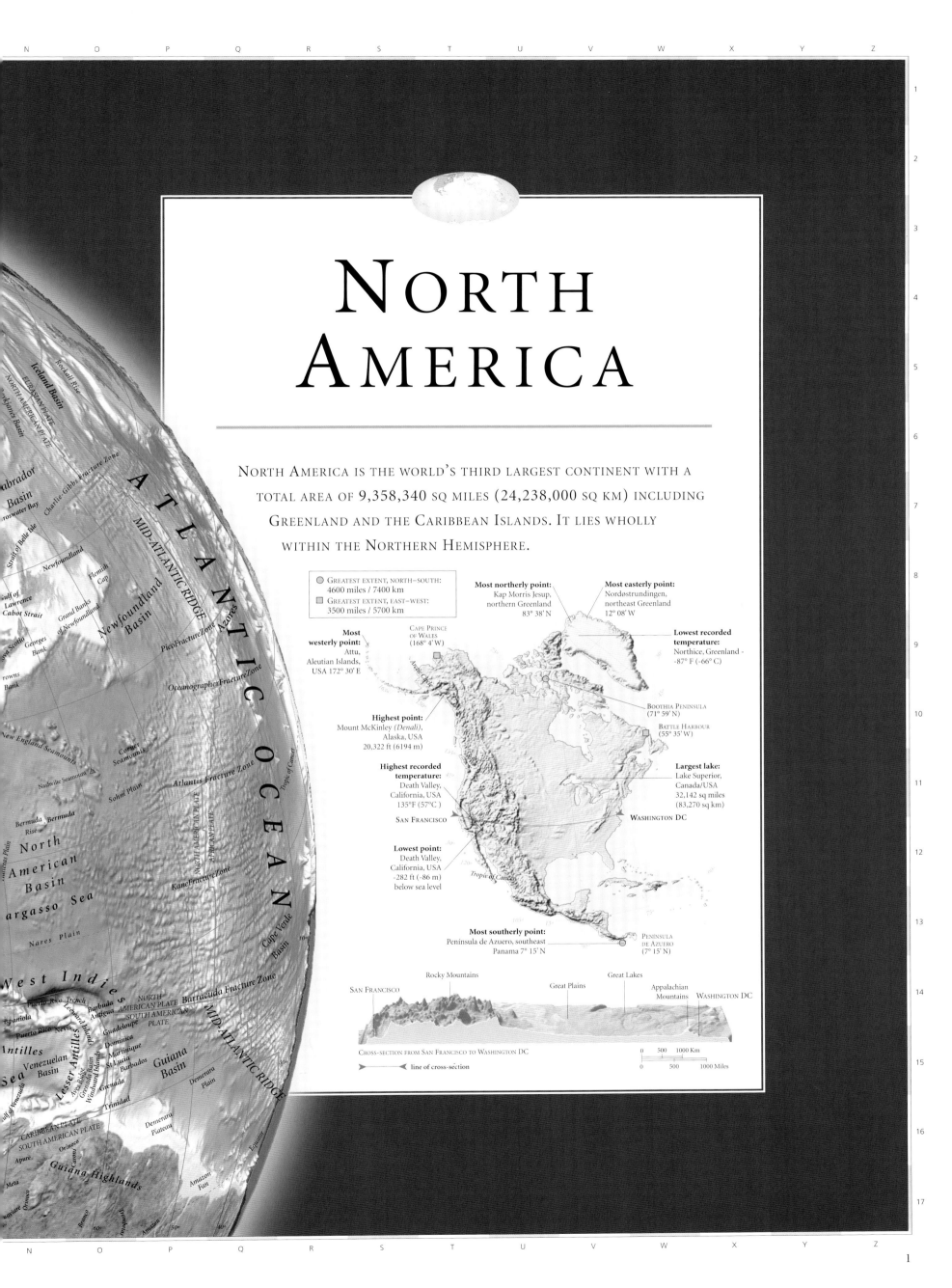

⬤ GREATEST EXTENT, NORTH–SOUTH:
4600 miles / 7400 km
⬛ GREATEST EXTENT, EAST–WEST:
3500 miles / 5700 km

Most northerly point:
Kap Morris Jesup,
northern Greenland
83° 38' N

Most easterly point:
Nordøstrundingen,
northeast Greenland
12° 08' W

**Most
westerly point:**
Attu,
Aleutian Islands,
USA 172° 30' E

CAPE PRINCE
OF WALES
(168° 4' W)

**Lowest recorded
temperature:**
Northice, Greenland -
-87° F (-66° C)

Highest point:
Mount McKinley *(Denali)*,
Alaska, USA
20,322 ft (6194 m)

BOOTHIA PENINSULA
(71° 59' N)

BATTLE HARBOUR
(55° 35' W)

**Highest recorded
temperature:**
Death Valley,
California, USA
135°F (57°C)

Largest lake:
Lake Superior,
Canada/USA
32,142 sq miles
(83,270 sq km)

SAN FRANCISCO

WASHINGTON DC

Lowest point:
Death Valley,
California, USA
-282 ft (-86 m)
below sea level

Tropic of Cancer

Most southerly point:
Península de Azuero, southeast
Panama 7° 15' N

PENÍNSULA
DE AZUERO
(7° 15' N)

SAN FRANCISCO
Rocky Mountains
Great Plains
Great Lakes
Appalachian
Mountains
WASHINGTON DC

CROSS-SECTION FROM SAN FRANCISCO TO WASHINGTON DC

◄— line of cross-section

| 0 | 500 | 1000 Km |
| 0 | 500 | 1000 Miles |

Globe map labels (Atlantic Ocean region):

Iceland Basin
Rockall Rise
EURASIAN PLATE
NORTH AMERICAN PLATE
Reykjanes Basin
Labrador
Basin
Charlie-Gibbs Fracture Zone
Stroswater Bay
Strait of Belle Isle
Newfoundland
Flemish
Cap
Gulf of
Lawrence
Cabot Strait
Grand Banks
of Newfoundland
Newfoundland
Basin
MID-ATLANTIC RIDGE
Pico Fracture Zone
Azores
owa Scotia
Georges
Bank
Oceanographer Fracture Zone
Tropic of Cancer
New England Seamounts
crowns
Bank
Corner
Seamounts
Atlantis Fracture Zone
Bermuda
Bermuda
Rise
Nashville Seamount
Sohm Plain
North
American
Basin
NORTH AMERICAN PLATE
AFRICAN PLATE
Kane Fracture Zone
argasso Sea
Nares plain
Cape Verde
Basin
hadeus Plain
West Indies
Puerto Rico Trench
Barbuda
Antigua
NORTH
AMERICAN PLATE
Barracuda Fracture Zone
ispaniola
Leeward Islands
SOUTH AMERICAN
PLATE
Puerto Rico
Nevis
Guadeloupe
Dominica
Antilles
Grenada Basin
Martinique
St Lucia
Venezuelan
Basin
Lesser Antilles
Aves Ridge
Windward Islands
Barbados
Guiana
Basin
Trinidad
Grenada
Demerara
Plain
Sea
CARIBBEAN PLATE
SOUTH AMERICAN PLATE
Demerara
Plateau
MID-ATLANTIC RIDGE
Apure
Meta
Orinoco
Guiana Highlands
Amazon
Fan
Equator
Amazon

PHYSICAL NORTH AMERICA

T HE NORTH AMERICAN CONTINENT can be divided into a number of major structural areas: the Western Cordillera, the Canadian Shield, the Great Plains and Central Lowlands, and the Appalachians. Other smaller regions include the Gulf Atlantic Coastal Plain which borders the southern coast of North America from the southern Appalachians to the Great Plains. This area includes the expanding Mississippi Delta. A chain of volcanic islands, running in an arc around the margin of the Caribbean Plate, lie to the east of the Gulf of Mexico.

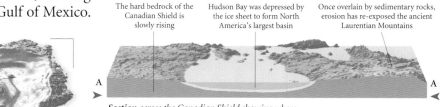

THE CANADIAN SHIELD

SPANNING NORTHERN CANADA and Greenland, this geologically stable plain forms the heart of the continent, containing rocks over two billion years old. A long history of weathering and repeated glaciation has scoured the region, leaving flat plains, gentle hummocks, numerous small basins and lakes, and the bays and islands of the Arctic.

The hard bedrock of the Canadian Shield is slowly rising

Hudson Bay was depressed by the ice sheet to form North America's largest basin

Once overlain by sedimentary rocks, erosion has re-exposed the ancient Laurentian Mountains

A — A

Section across the Canadian Shield showing where the ice sheet has depressed the underlying rock and formed bays and islands.

0 100 200 Km
0 100 200 Miles

THE WESTERN CORDILLERA

ABOUT 80 MILLION YEARS ago the Pacific and North American plates collided, uplifting the Western Cordillera. This consists of the Aleutian, Coast, Cascade and Sierra Nevada mountains, and the inland Rocky Mountains. These run parallel from the Arctic to Mexico.

The weight of the ice sheet, 1.8 miles (3 km) thick, has depressed the land to 0.6 miles (1 km) below sea level

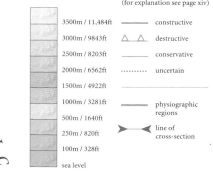

This computer-generated view shows the ice-covered island of Greenland without its ice cap.

Strata have been thrust eastward along fault lines

The Rocky Mountain Trench is the longest linear fault on the continent

B — B

Volcanic rock

Cross-section through the Western Cordillera showing direction of mountain building.

0 50 100 Km
0 50 100 Miles

MAP KEY

ELEVATION

	3500m / 11,484ft
	3000m / 9843ft
	2500m / 8203ft
	2000m / 6562ft
	1500m / 4922ft
	1000m / 3281ft
	500m / 1640ft
	250m / 820ft
	100m / 328ft
	sea level

PLATE MARGINS
(for explanation see page xiv)

———— constructive
△ △ destructive
———— conservative
·········· uncertain

———— physiographic regions

◄►— line of cross-section

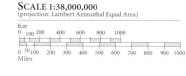

SCALE 1:38,000,000
(projection: Lambert Azimuthal Equal Area)

Km
0 100 200 400 600 800 1000
0 50 100 200 300 400 500 600 700 800 900 1000
Miles

THE GREAT PLAINS & CENTRAL LOWLANDS

DEPOSITS LEFT by retreating glaciers and rivers have made this vast flat area very fertile. In the north this is the result of glaciation, with deposits up to one mile (1.7 km) thick, covering the basement rock. To the south and west, the massive Missouri/Mississippi river system has for centuries deposited silt across the plains, creating broad, flat flood plains and deltas.

THE APPALACHIANS

THE APPALACHIAN MOUNTAINS, uplifted about 400 million years ago, are some of the oldest in the world. They have been lowered and rounded by erosion and now slope gently towards the Atlantic across a broad coastal plain.

Horizontal strata

Sedimentary strata folded and faulted into ridges and valleys

Softer strata has been crumpled against the harder basement rock

Hard basement rock

C — C

Cross-section through the Appalachians showing the numerous folds, which have subsequently been weathered to create a rounded relief.

0 50 100 Km
0 50 100 Miles

Sedimentary layers overlay domed basement rock

Upland rivers drain south towards the Mississippi Basin

Confluence of the Missouri and Mississippi rivers

D — D

Section across the Great Plains and Central Lowlands showing river systems and structure.

0 200 400 Km
0 200 400 Miles

Map labels

ASIA
Bering Strait
Aleutian Islands
Bering Sea
Beaufort Sea
Brooks Range
Mackenzie Delta
Mount McKinley 6194m
Mackenzie Mountains
Aleutian Range, Alaska Range
Gulf of Alaska
PACIFIC PLATE
NORTH AMERICAN PLATE
Coast Mountains
Great Bear Lake
Great Slave Lake
Lake Athabasca
Reindeer Lake
WESTERN CORDILLERA
ROCKY MOUNTAINS
CANADIAN SHIELD
CENTRAL LOWLANDS
GREAT PLAINS
Mount Rainier 4392m
Mount St Helens 2549m
Cascade Range
Coast Ranges
San Joaquin
Sierra Nevada
Great Basin
Great Salt Lake
San Andreas Fault
Death Valley 86m
Mojave Desert
Grand Canyon
Colorado Plateau
Colorado
Sonoran Desert
PACIFIC OCEAN
Lower California
Gulf of California
Sierra Madre Occidental
Sierra Madre del Sur
Volcán Pico de Orizaba 5700m
Rio Grande
Missouri
Arkansas
Mississippi
GULF ATLANTIC COASTAL PLAIN
Mississippi Delta
Gulf of Mexico
Yucatan Peninsula
Lake Nicaragua
Sierra Madre Oriental
Isthmus of Panama
COCOS PLATE
CARIBBEAN PLATE
Caribbean Sea
NORTH AMERICAN PLATE
SOUTH AMERICAN PLATE
SOUTH AMERICA
Lesser Antilles
Greater Antilles
West Indies
ATLANTIC OCEAN
Greenland
Baffin Bay
Baffin Island
Davis Strait
Foxe Basin
Hudson Strait
Labrador Sea
Hudson Bay
Laurentian Mountains
Newfoundland
Nova Scotia
St Lawrence
Cape Cod
Appalachian Mountains
APPALACHIANS
Lake Winnipeg
Lake Manitoba
Lake Superior
Lake Huron
Lake Ontario
Lake Michigan
Lake Erie
Great Lakes
Ohio

N O P Q R S T U V W X Y

CLIMATE

NORTH AMERICA'S climate includes extremes ranging from freezing Arctic conditions in Alaska and Greenland, to desert in the southwest, and tropical conditions in southeastern Florida, the Caribbean and Central America. Central and southern regions are prone to severe storms including tornadoes and hurricanes.

'Tornado alley' in the Mississippi Valley suffers frequent tornadoes.

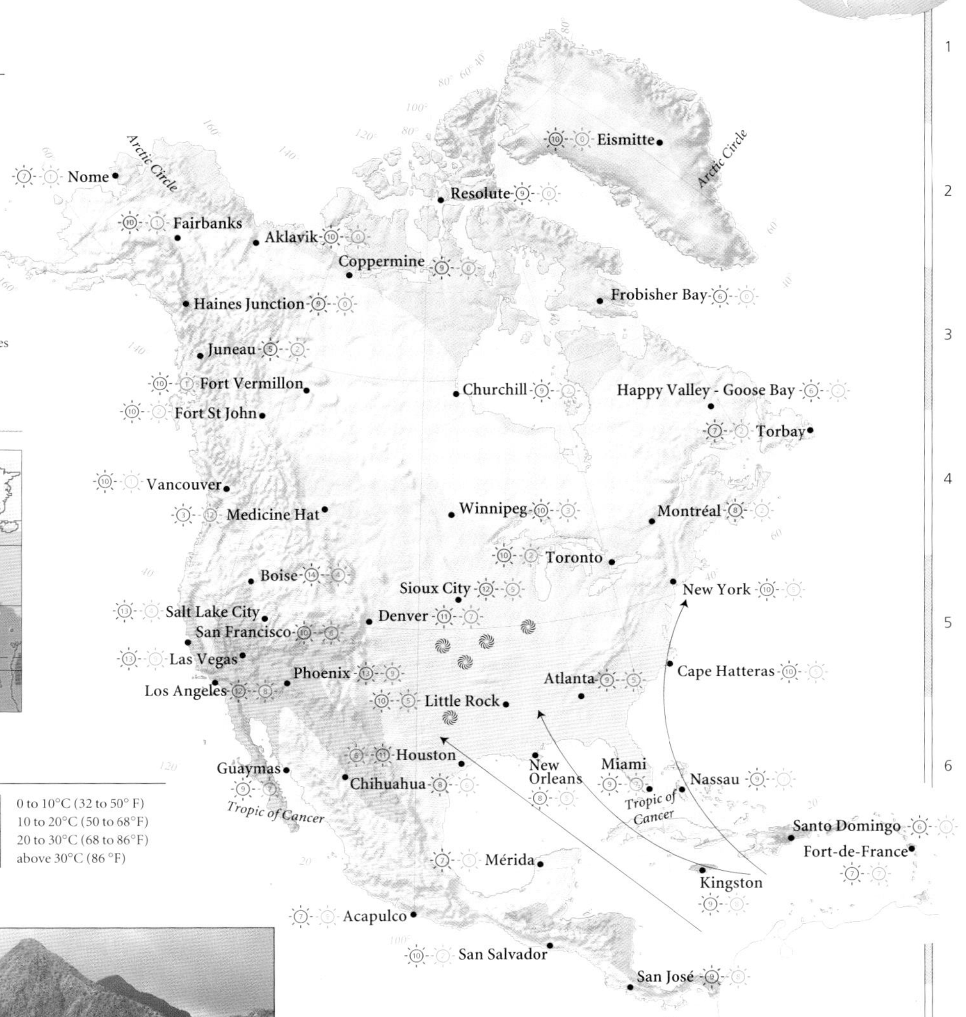

Much of the southwest is semi-desert; receiving less than 12 inches (300 mm) of rainfall a year.

Climate

- ice cap
- tundra
- subarctic
- cool continental
- warm humid
- semi-arid
- arid
- humid equatorial
- tropical
- ☀ daily hours of sunshine, January
- ☀ daily hours of sunshine, July
- → direction of hurricanes
- ◎ tornado zones

TEMPERATURE

Arctic Circle
60° N
40° N
Tropic of Cancer
20° N

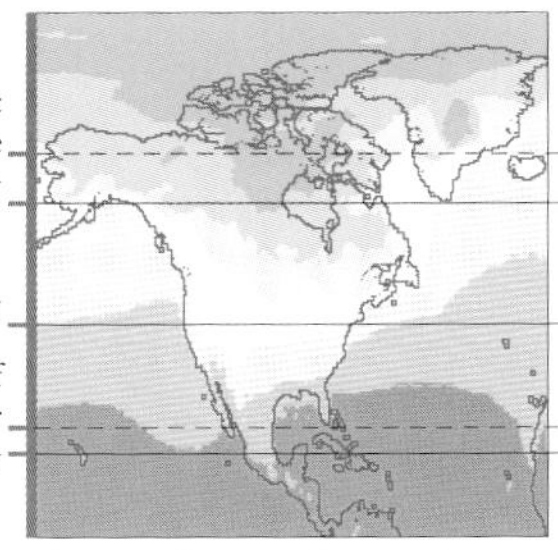

Average January temperature

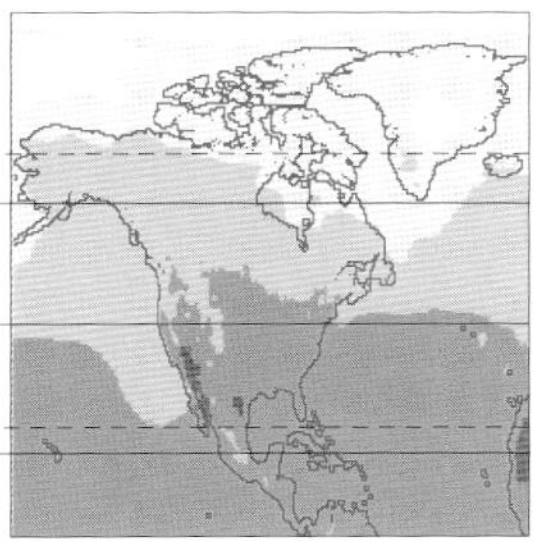

Average July temperature

Temperature

below -30°C (-22°F)	0 to 10°C (32 to 50° F)
-30 to -20°C (-22 to -4°F)	10 to 20°C (50 to 68° F)
-20 to -10°C (-4 to 14°F)	20 to 30°C (68 to 86° F)
-10 to 0°C (14 to 32°F)	above 30°C (86° F)

RAINFALL

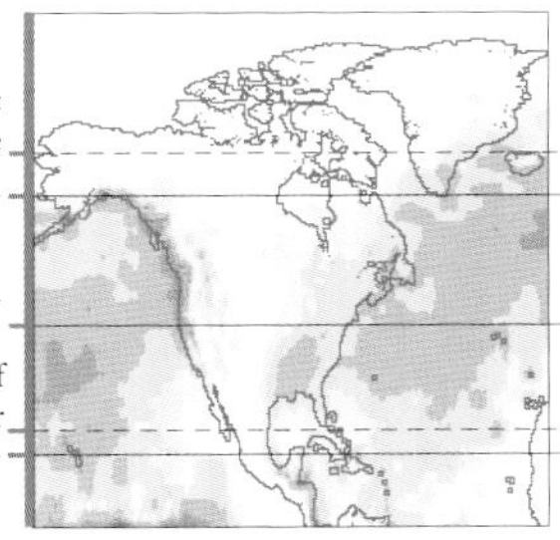

Arctic Circle
60° N
40° N
Tropic of Cancer
20° N

Average January rainfall

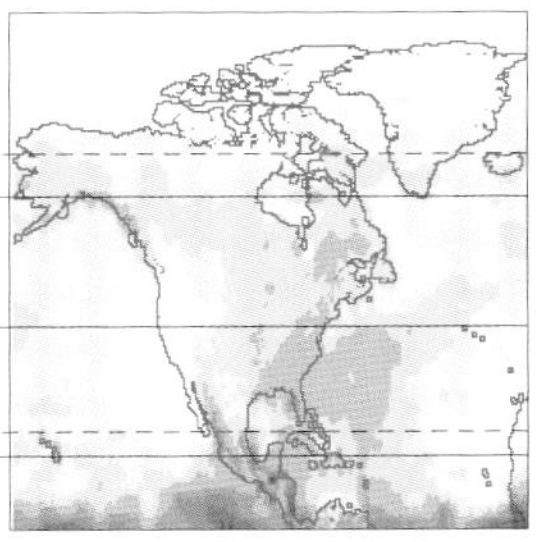

Average July rainfall

Rainfall

- 0–25 mm (0–1 in)
- 25–50 mm (1–2 in)
- 50–100 mm (2–4 in)
- 100–200 mm (4–8 in)
- 200–300 mm (8–12 in)
- 300–400 mm (12–16 in)
- 400–500 mm (16–20 in)
- more than 500 mm (20 in)

The lush, green mountains of the Lesser Antilles receive annual rainfalls of up to 360 inches (9000 mm).

Cities (map labels): Nome, Fairbanks, Aklavik, Coppermine, Resolute, Eismitte, Frobisher Bay, Haines Junction, Juneau, Churchill, Happy Valley - Goose Bay, Fort Vermillon, Torbay, Fort St John, Vancouver, Winnipeg, Montréal, Medicine Hat, Toronto, Boise, New York, Salt Lake City, Sioux City, Denver, San Francisco, Cape Hatteras, Las Vegas, Phoenix, Atlanta, Los Angeles, Little Rock, Houston, Miami, Guaymas, New Orleans, Nassau, Chihuahua, Santo Domingo, Fort-de-France, Mérida, Kingston, Acapulco, San José, San Salvador

Arctic Circle, Tropic of Cancer

SHAPING THE CONTINENT

GLACIAL PROCESSES affect much of northern Canada, Greenland and the Western Cordillera. Along the western coast of North America, Central America and the Caribbean, underlying plates moving together lead to earthquakes and volcanic eruptions. The vast river systems, fed by mountain streams, constantly erode and deposit material along their paths.

VOLCANIC ACTIVITY

1 Mount St Helens volcano (right) in the Cascade Range erupted violently in May 1980, killing 57 people and levelling large areas of forest. The lateral blast filled a valley for 15 miles (25 km) with debris.

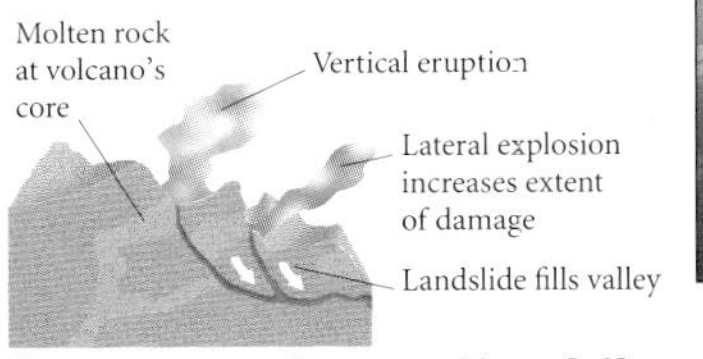

- Molten rock at volcano's core
- Vertical eruption
- Lateral explosion increases extent of damage
- Landslide fills valley

VOLCANIC ACTIVITY: ERUPTION OF MOUNT ST HELENS

SEISMIC ACTIVITY

5 The San Andreas Fault (above) places much of the North America's west coast under constant threat from earthquakes. It is caused by the Pacific Plate grinding past the North American Plate at a faster rate, though in the same direction.

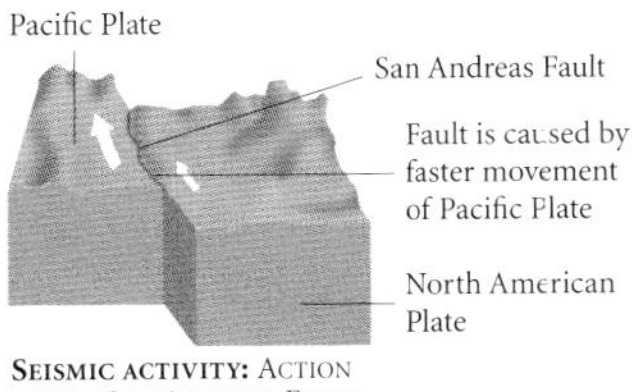

- Pacific Plate
- San Andreas Fault
- Fault is caused by faster movement of Pacific Plate
- North American Plate

SEISMIC ACTIVITY: ACTION OF THE SAN ANDREAS FAULT

RIVER EROSION

6 The Grand Canyon (above) in the Colorado Plateau was created by the downward erosion of the Colorado River, combined with the gradual uplift of the plateau, over the past 30 million years. The contours of the canyon formed as the softer rock layers eroded into gentle slopes, and the hard rock layers into cliffs. The depth varies from 3855–6560 ft (1175–2000 m).

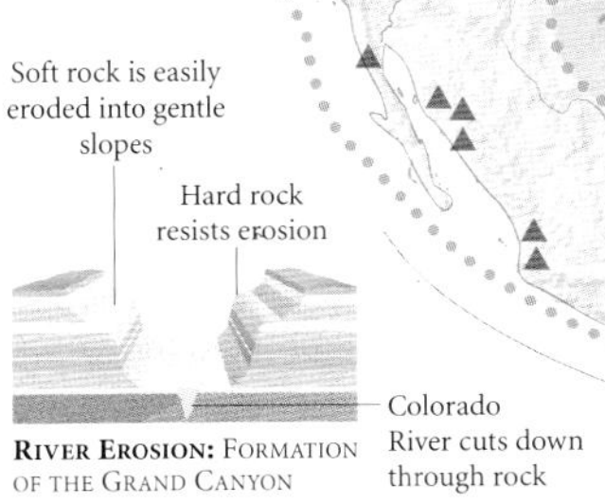

- Soft rock is easily eroded into gentle slopes
- Hard rock resists erosion
- Colorado River cuts down through rock

RIVER EROSION: FORMATION OF THE GRAND CANYON

PERIGLACIATION

2 The ground in the far north is nearly always frozen: the surface thaws only in summer. This freeze-thaw process produces features such as pingos (left); formed by the freezing of groundwater. With each successive winter ice accumulates producing a mound with a core of ice.

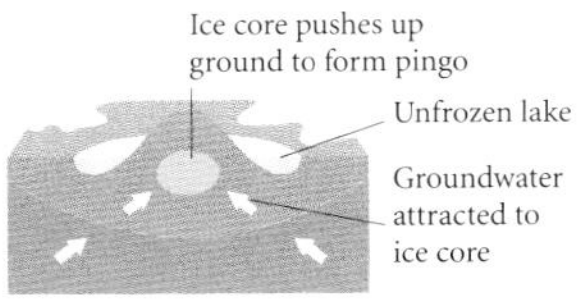

- Ice core pushes up ground to form pingo
- Unfrozen lake
- Groundwater attracted to ice core

PERIGLACIATION: FORMATION OF A PINGO IN THE MACKENZIE DELTA

THE EVOLVING LANDSCAPE

Landscape

- limestone region
- sinking land
- stable land
- uplifting land

- ▲ active volcano
- ⋯ area of tectonic activity
- – – limit of permafrost
- —— maximum limit of glaciation
- → ocean current

POST-GLACIAL LAKES

3 A chain of lakes from Great Bear Lake to the Great Lakes (above) was created as the ice retreated northwards. Glaciers scoured hollows in the softer lowland rock. Glacial deposits at the lip of the hollows, and ridges of harder rock, trapped water to form lakes.

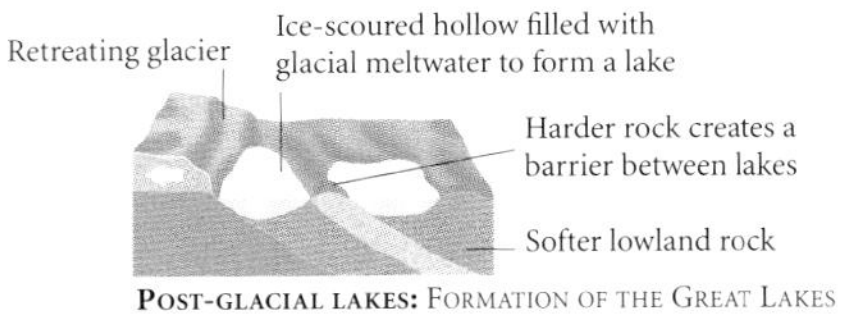

- Retreating glacier
- Ice-scoured hollow filled with glacial meltwater to form a lake
- Harder rock creates a barrier between lakes
- Softer lowland rock

POST-GLACIAL LAKES: FORMATION OF THE GREAT LAKES

WEATHERING

4 The Yucatan Peninsula is a vast, flat limestone plateau in southern Mexico. Weathering action from both rainwater and underground streams has enlarged fractures in the rock to form caves and hollows, called sinkholes (above).

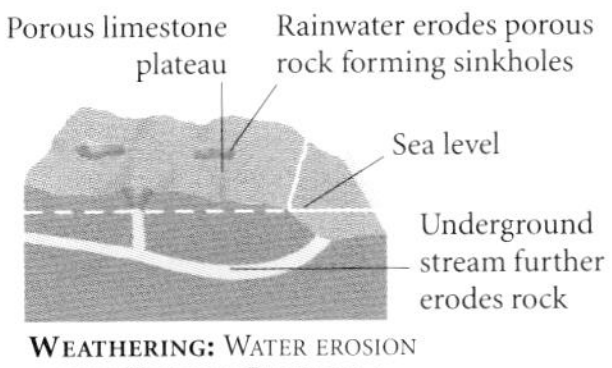

- Porous limestone plateau
- Rainwater erodes porous rock forming sinkholes
- Sea level
- Underground stream further erodes rock

WEATHERING: WATER EROSION ON THE YUCATAN PENINSULA

N O P Q R S T U V W X Y Z

POLITICAL NORTH AMERICA

DEMOCRACY IS WELL ESTABLISHED in some parts of the continent but is a recent phenomenon in others. The economically dominant nations of Canada and the USA have a long democratic tradition but elsewhere, notably in the countries of Central America, political turmoil has been more common. In Nicaragua and Haiti, harsh dictatorships have only recently been superseded by democratically-elected governments. North America's largest countries, Canada, Mexico and the USA have federal state systems, sharing political power between national and state governments. The USA has intervened militarily on several occasions in Central America and the Caribbean to protect its strategic interests.

TRANSPORT

IN THE 19TH CENTURY, railways were used to open up the North American continent. Air transport is now more common for long distance passenger travel, although railways are still extensively used for bulk freight transport. Waterways, like the Mississippi River, are important for the transport of bulk materials, and the Panama Canal is a vital link between the Pacific Ocean and the Caribbean. In the 20th century, road transport increased massively in North America, with the introduction of cheap, mass-produced motor cars and extensive highway construction.

This busy suburban interchange in Los Angeles is part of the USA's Interstate freeway system. Construction of the 55,000 mile (88,500 km) freeway network began in the 1950s, and it now connects most major cities, and carries one-fifth of the USA's road traffic.

Transport
- major roads and motorways
- major railways
- major canals
- international borders
- transport intersections
- international airports
- major ports

The 40 mile (65 km) long Panama Canal cuts through the Isthmus of Panama, a narrow strip of land connecting North and South America. Opened in 1914, the canal reduced the journey between the Atlantic and Pacific oceans by almost 8000 nautical miles (14,800 km).

Low-density housing developments such as this one on the outskirts of Phoenix, Arizona, reflect the USA's abundance of land and a dispersed population, dependent on the motor car for personal mobility.

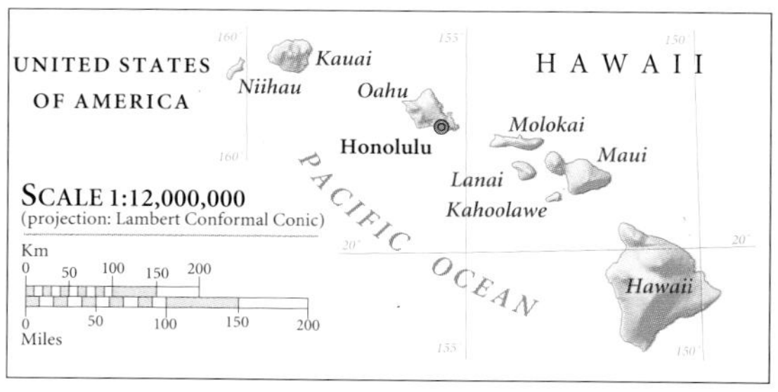

UNITED STATES OF AMERICA

HAWAII

SCALE 1:12,000,000
(projection: Lambert Conformal Conic)

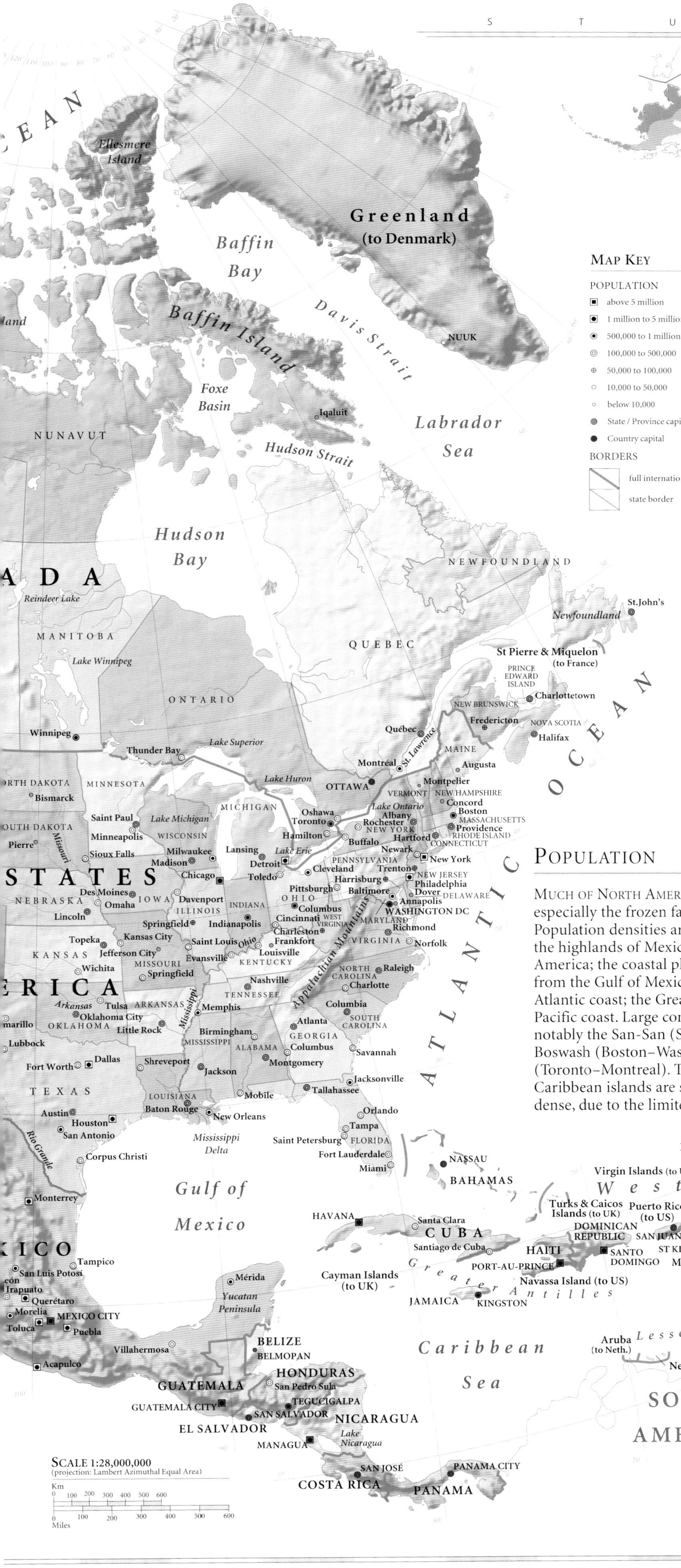

S T U V Y Z

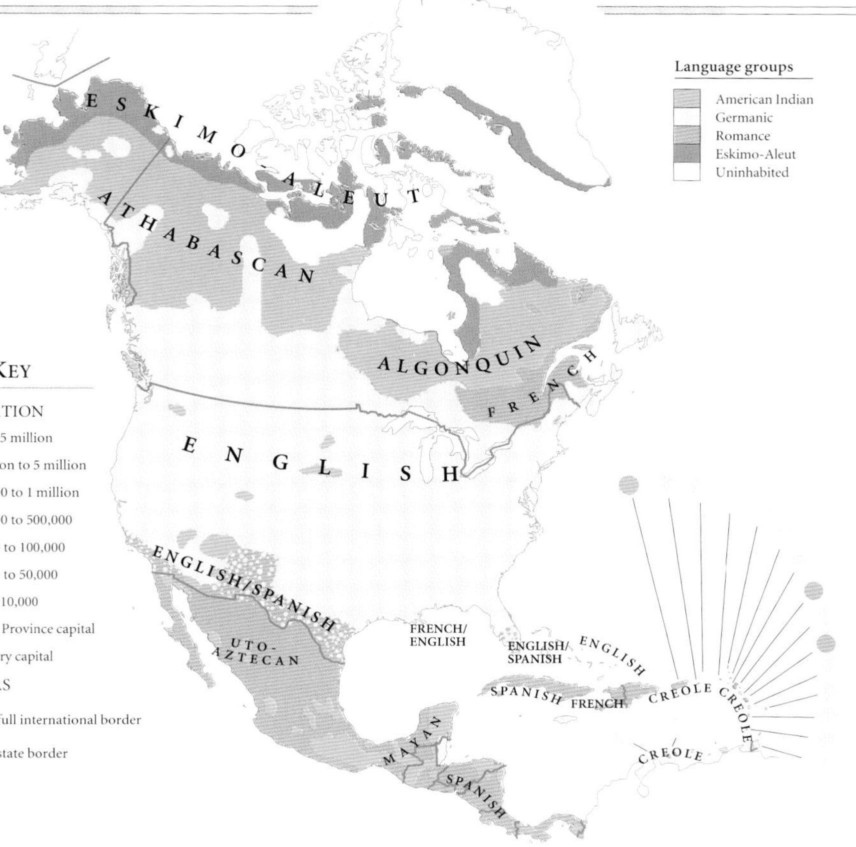

Language groups

- American Indian
- Germanic
- Romance
- Eskimo-Aleut
- Uninhabited

Greenland
(to Denmark)

Ellesmere Island

Baffin Bay

NUUK

Davis Strait

Baffin Island

Foxe Basin

Labrador Sea

Hudson Strait

Hudson Bay

NUNAVUT

ESKIMO-ALEUT

ATHABASCAN

ALGONQUIN

FRENCH

ENGLISH

ENGLISH/SPANISH

UTO-AZTECAN

FRENCH/ENGLISH

ENGLISH/SPANISH

ENGLISH

SPANISH FRENCH

CREOLE CREOLE

CREOLE

MAYAN

SPANISH

MAP KEY

POPULATION
- ■ above 5 million
- ▣ 1 million to 5 million
- ◉ 500,000 to 1 million
- ◎ 100,000 to 500,000
- ⊕ 50,000 to 100,000
- ○ 10,000 to 50,000
- ∘ below 10,000
- ● State / Province capital
- ● Country capital

BORDERS
- full international border
- state border

Reindeer Lake

MANITOBA

NEWFOUNDLAND

ADA

QUEBEC

Newfoundland

St.John's

St Pierre & Miquelon
(to France)

PRINCE EDWARD ISLAND

Lake Winnipeg

ONTARIO

NEW BRUNSWICK

Charlottetown

Québec

Fredericton

NOVA SCOTIA

Halifax

Winnipeg

Thunder Bay

Lake Superior

MAINE

Montréal

St.Lawrence

Augusta

RTH DAKOTA

MINNESOTA

MICHIGAN

Lake Huron

VERMONT

NEW HAMPSHIRE

Montpelier

Concord

Bismarck

Oshawa

Lake Ontario

Albany

Boston

OUTH DAKOTA

Saint Paul

Lake Michigan

Toronto

Rochester

MASSACHUSETTS

Pierre

Minneapolis

WISCONSIN

Hamilton

Buffalo

NEW YORK

Hartford

Providence

RHODE ISLAND

CONNECTICUT

Sioux Falls

Madison

Milwaukee

Lansing

Lake Erie

Newark

New York

NEBRASKA

IOWA

Chicago

Detroit

PENNSYLVANIA

Trenton

NEW JERSEY

Lincoln

Des Moines

ILLINOIS

INDIANA

Toledo

Cleveland

Pittsburgh

Harrisburg

Philadelphia

Dover

DELAWARE

Omaha

OHIO

Columbus

Baltimore

STATES

Davenport

Indianapolis

Cincinnati

WEST VIRGINIA

MARYLAND

WASHINGTON DC

Topeka

Kansas City

Saint Louis

Frankfort

Richmond

ERICA

KANSAS

Jefferson City

MISSOURI

Ohio

Charleston

VIRGINIA

Norfolk

Wichita

Springfield

Evansville

Louisville

KENTUCKY

Arkansas

Tulsa

ARKANSAS

Nashville

Raleigh

NORTH CAROLINA

amarillo

Oklahoma City

TENNESSEE

Charlotte

Columbia

Lubbock

OKLAHOMA

Little Rock

Memphis

Mississippi

Appalachian Mountains

ATLANTIC OCEAN

Fort Worth

Dallas

Birmingham

Atlanta

SOUTH CAROLINA

GEORGIA

Columbus

Savannah

Austin

TEXAS

LOUISIANA

Shreveport

Jackson

MISSISSIPPI

ALABAMA

Montgomery

Houston

Baton Rouge

Mobile

Jacksonville

San Antonio

New Orleans

Mississippi Delta

Orlando

Tampa

Tallahassee

FLORIDA

Corpus Christi

Saint Petersburg

Fort Lauderdale

Gulf of Mexico

Miami

NASSAU

BAHAMAS

West Indies

British Virgin Islands (to UK)

Virgin Islands (to US)

Anguilla (to UK)

Monterrey

HAVANA

Santa Clara

Turks & Caicos Islands (to UK)

Puerto Rico (to US)

ANTIGUA & BARBUDA

Rio Grande

SAN JUAN

DOMINICAN REPUBLIC

Guadeloupe (to France)

MICO

Tampico

CUBA

Santiago de Cuba

HAITI

SANTO DOMINGO

DOMINICA

Martinique (to France)

ST KITTS & NEVIS

San Luis Potosí

cón

Irapuato

Mérida

Cayman Islands (to UK)

PORT-AU-PRINCE

Greater Antilles

Montserrat (to UK)

ST LUCIA

BARBADOS

Querétaro

Yucatan Peninsula

JAMAICA

KINGSTON

Navassa Island (to US)

ST VINCENT & THE GRENADINES

Morelia

MEXICO CITY

Puebla

GRENADA

Toluca

Lesser Antilles

TRINIDAD & TOBAGO

Villahermosa

BELIZE

Aruba (to Neth.)

PORT-OF-SPAIN

Acapulco

BELMOPAN

Caribbean Sea

Netherlands Antilles (to Neth.)

GUATEMALA

HONDURAS

San Pedro Sula

SOUTH AMERICA

GUATEMALA CITY

TEGUCIGALPA

SAN SALVADOR

NICARAGUA

EL SALVADOR

MANAGUA

Lake Nicaragua

SAN JOSÉ

PANAMA CITY

COSTA RICA

PANAMA

SCALE 1:28,000,000
(projection: Lambert Azimuthal Equal Area)

Km
0 100 200 300 400 500 600

Miles
0 100 200 300 400 500 600

LANGUAGES

THE THREE MAJOR official languages of North America are of European origin, brought by settlers in the 16th century. In Canada, French and English are spoken; in the USA, English is the main language, with large Spanish-speaking areas in the southwest; Mexicans are Spanish-speaking; while the Caribbean islands use French, English and Spanish as well as the hybrid Creole tongues. In isolated areas, languages of the indigenous peoples still exist, such as Inuit in the far north of the continent.

Land in northern Canada has been set aside for Inuit reserves, allowing the Inuit and other Native American groups to maintain their traditional practices and culture.

POPULATION

MUCH OF NORTH AMERICA is almost empty, especially the frozen far north. Population densities are highest in the highlands of Mexico and Central America; the coastal plain stretching from the Gulf of Mexico along the Atlantic coast; the Great Lakes area; and the Pacific coast. Large conurbations have developed, notably the San-San (San Francisco–San Diego), Boswash (Boston–Washington) and Main Street (Toronto–Montreal). The populations of the Caribbean islands are small, but settlement is dense, due to the limited amount of land available.

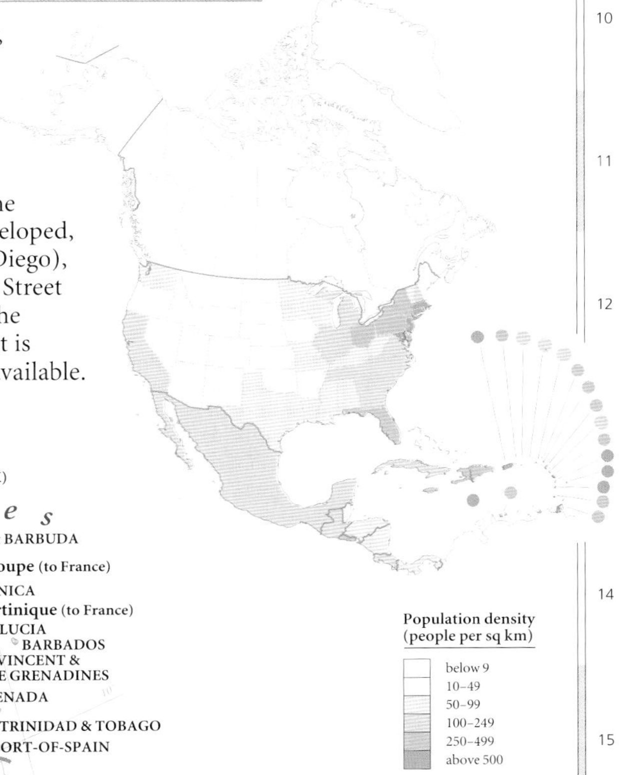

Population density
(people per sq km)
- below 9
- 10–49
- 50–99
- 100–249
- 250–499
- above 500

Mexico City is one of the world's largest and highest cities. Fresh water supplies are dwindling, while air pollution regularly creates thick smog.

N O P Q R S T U V W X Y Z

5

NORTH AMERICAN RESOURCES

THE TWO NORTHERN COUNTRIES of Canada and the USA are richly endowed with natural resources which have helped to fuel economic development. The USA is the world's largest economy, although today it is facing stiff competition from the Far East. Mexico has relied on oil revenues but there are hopes that the North American Free Trade Agreement (NAFTA), will encourage trade growth with Canada and the USA. The poorer countries of Central America and the Caribbean depend largely on cash crops and tourism.

STANDARD OF LIVING

THE USA AND CANADA have one of the highest overall standards of living in the world. However, many people still live in poverty, especially in inner city ghettos and some rural areas. Central America and the Caribbean are markedly poorer than their wealthier northern neighbours. Haiti is the poorest country in the western hemisphere.

Standard of Living
(UN Human Development Index)

high

low

INDUSTRY

THE MODERN, INDUSTRIALIZED economies of the USA and Canada contrast sharply with those of Mexico, Central America and the Caribbean. Manufacturing is especially important in the USA; vehicle production is concentrated around the Great Lakes, while electronic and hi-tech industries are increasingly found in the western and southern states. Mexico depends on oil exports and assembly work, taking advantage of cheap labour. Many Central American and Caribbean countries rely heavily on agricultural exports.

After its purchase from Russia in 1867, Alaska's frozen lands were largely ignored by the USA. Oil reserves similar in magnitude to those in eastern Texas were discovered in Prudhoe Bay, Alaska in 1968. Freezing temperatures and a fragile environment hamper oil extraction.

Fish such as cod, flounder and plaice are caught in the Grand Banks, off the Newfoundland coast, and processed in many North Atlantic coastal settlements.

South of San Francisco, 'Silicon Valley' is both a national and international centre for hi-tech industries, electronic industries and research institutions.

Multinational companies rely on cheap labour and tax benefits to assemble vehicles in Mexican factories.

The twin towers of the World Trade Center dominate the Manhattan skyline. New York is one of the world's leading trade and finance centres.

Industry

Symbol	Industry
✈	aerospace
▲	brewing
🚗	car/vehicle manufacture
⚗	chemicals
🛡	defence
▦	electronics
⚙	engineering
🎬	film industry
$	finance
▣	food processing
▭	hi-tech industry
▦	iron & steel
🔬	pharmaceuticals
🖶	printing & publishing
☢	research & development
⚓	shipbuilding
▼	sugar processing
▼	textiles
🌲	timber processing
🌿	tobacco processing
◆	coal
◯	oil
◗	gas
•	industrial cities
▨	major industrial areas

GNP per capita (US$)

Colour	Range
	0–1999
	2000–4999
	5000–9999
	10,000–19,999
	20,000–24,999
	25,000+

ARCTIC OCEAN

Bering Strait

RUSS. FED.

Bering Sea

Beaufort Sea

Prudhoe Bay

USA

Gulf of Alaska

Greenland (to Denmark)

Baffin Bay

Labrador Sea

Hudson Strait

Hudson Bay

CANADA

PACIFIC OCEAN

Vancouver
Calgary
Seattle
Winnipeg
Portland
Montréal

UNITED STATES OF AMERICA

Minneapolis
Milwaukee
Toronto
Buffalo
Albany
Detroit
Cleveland
New York
Chicago
Pittsburgh
Philadelphia
Dayton
Baltimore
Boston
San Francisco
Denver
Kansas City
Saint Louis
Cincinnati
Wichita
Nashville
Greensboro
Charlotte
Los Angeles
Tulsa
Phoenix
Birmingham
Atlanta
San Diego
Dallas
Tijuana
Ciudad Juárez
El Paso
Jacksonville
Houston
New Orleans
Orlando
Tampa
Miami

ATLANTIC OCEAN

Monterrey

Gulf of Mexico

Havana
CUBA
BAHAMAS

West Indies

Virgin Islands (to US)
British Virgin Islands (to UK)
Anguilla (to UK)
Turks & Caicos Islands (to UK)
ST KITTS & NEVIS
ANTIGUA & BARBUDA
Puerto Rico (to US)
Montserrat (to UK)
Guadeloupe (to France)
San Juan
DOMINICA
HAITI
DOMINICAN REPUBLIC
Port-au-Prince
Santo Domingo
ST LUCIA
BARBADOS
ST VINCENT & THE GRENADINES
JAMAICA
Greater Antilles
GRENADA
Cayman Islands (to UK)
Navassa Island (to US)
TRINIDAD & TOBAGO
Port-of-Spain
Lesser Antilles
Aruba (to Neth.)
Netherlands Antilles (to Neth.)
Caribbean Sea
Guadalajara
MEXICO
Mexico City
BELIZE
VENEZUELA
GUATEMALA
Guatemala City
HONDURAS
Tegucigalpa
EL SALVADOR
San Salvador
NICARAGUA
Managua
COSTA RICA
San José
Panama City
PANAMA
COLOMBIA

ENVIRONMENTAL ISSUES

MANY FRAGILE ENVIRONMENTS ARE UNDER THREAT throughout the region. In Haiti, all the primary rainforest has been destroyed, while air pollution from factories and cars in Mexico City is amongst the worst in the world. Elsewhere, industry and mining pose threats, particularly in the delicate arctic environment of Alaska where oil spills have polluted coastlines and decimated fish stocks.

MINERAL RESOURCES

FOSSIL FUELS ARE EXPLOITED in considerable quantities throughout the continent. Coal mining in the Appalachians is declining but vast open pits exist further west in Wyoming. Oil and natural gas are found in Alaska, Texas, the Gulf of Mexico, and the Canadian West. Canada has large quantities of nickel, while Jamaica has considerable deposits of bauxite, and Mexico has large reserves of silver.

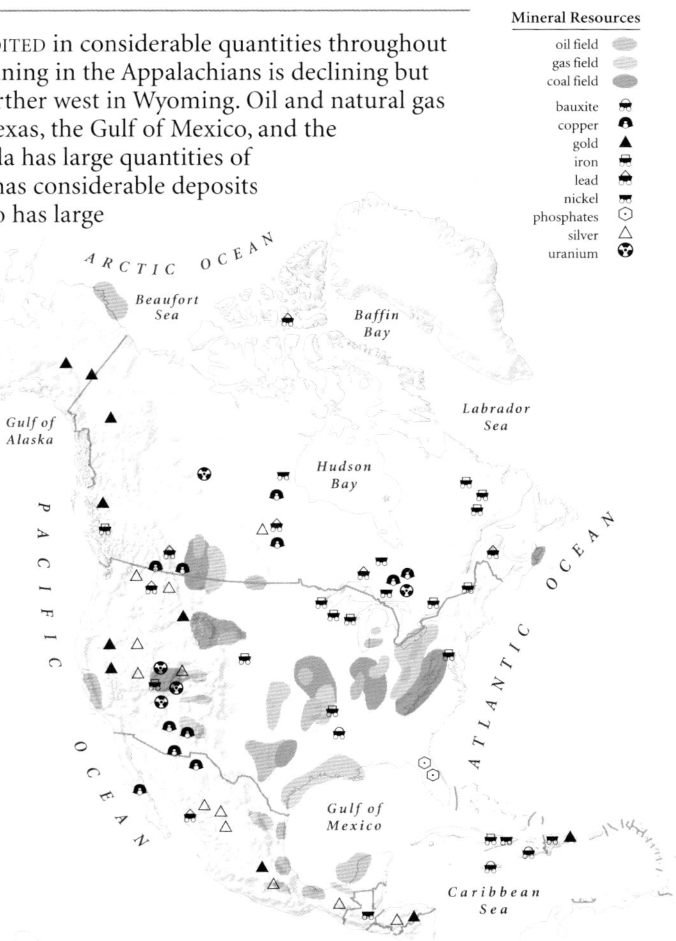

Mineral Resources
- oil field
- gas field
- coal field
- bauxite
- copper
- gold
- iron
- lead
- nickel
- phosphates
- silver
- uranium

Environmental Issues
- national parks
- acid rain
- tropical forest
- forest destroyed
- desert
- desertification
- polluted rivers
- radioactive contamination
- marine pollution
- heavy marine pollution
- poor urban air quality

In addition to fossil fuels, North America is also rich in exploitable metallic ores. This vast, mile-deep (1.6 km) pit is a copper mine in New Mexico.

Wild bison graze in Yellowstone National Park, the world's first national park. Designated in 1872, geothermal springs and boiling mud are among its natural spectacles, making it a major tourist attraction.

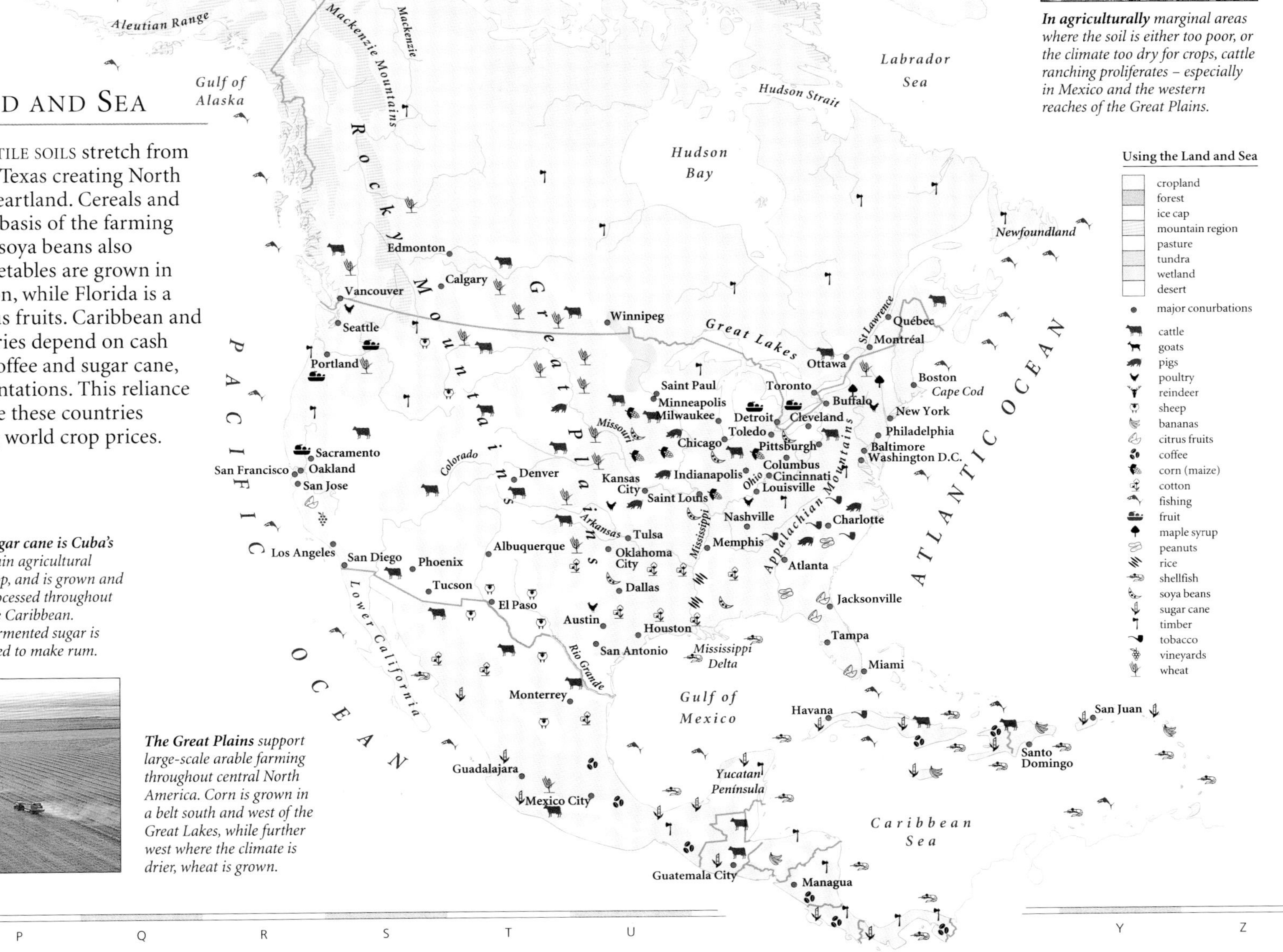

In agriculturally marginal areas where the soil is either too poor, or the climate too dry for crops, cattle ranching proliferates – especially in Mexico and the western reaches of the Great Plains.

USING THE LAND AND SEA

ABUNDANT LAND AND FERTILE SOILS stretch from the Canadian prairies to Texas creating North America's agricultural heartland. Cereals and cattle ranching form the basis of the farming economy, with corn and soya beans also important. Fruit and vegetables are grown in California using irrigation, while Florida is a leading producer of citrus fruits. Caribbean and Central American countries depend on cash crops such as bananas, coffee and sugar cane, often grown on large plantations. This reliance on a single crop can leave these countries vulnerable to fluctuating world crop prices.

Sugar cane is Cuba's main agricultural crop, and is grown and processed throughout the Caribbean. Fermented sugar is used to make rum.

The Great Plains support large-scale arable farming throughout central North America. Corn is grown in a belt south and west of the Great Lakes, while further west where the climate is drier, wheat is grown.

Using the Land and Sea
- cropland
- forest
- ice cap
- mountain region
- pasture
- tundra
- wetland
- desert
- major conurbations
- cattle
- goats
- pigs
- poultry
- reindeer
- sheep
- bananas
- citrus fruits
- coffee
- corn (maize)
- cotton
- fishing
- fruit
- maple syrup
- peanuts
- rice
- shellfish
- soya beans
- sugar cane
- timber
- tobacco
- vineyards
- wheat

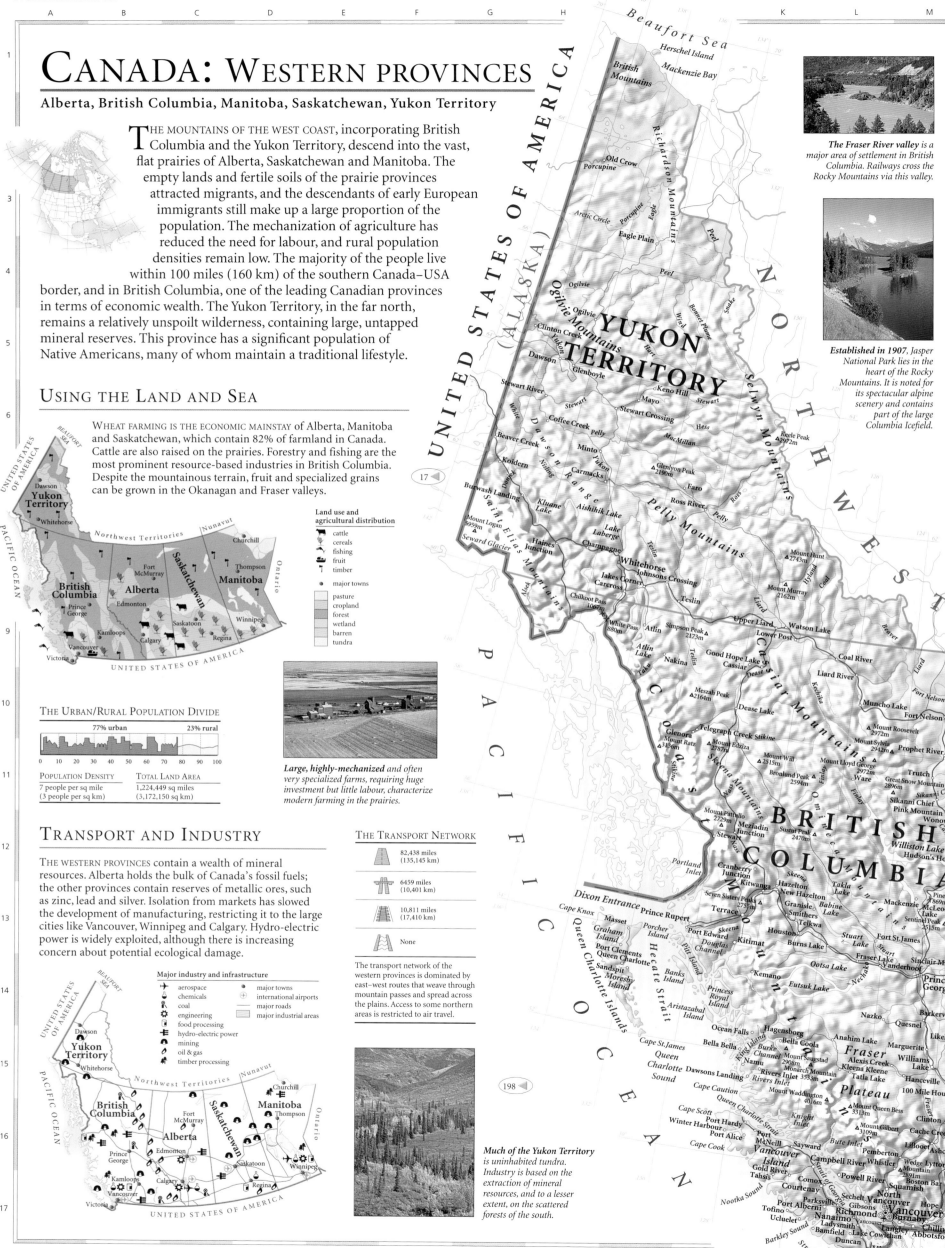

CANADA: WESTERN PROVINCES

Alberta, British Columbia, Manitoba, Saskatchewan, Yukon Territory

THE MOUNTAINS OF THE WEST COAST, incorporating British Columbia and the Yukon Territory, descend into the vast, flat prairies of Alberta, Saskatchewan and Manitoba. The empty lands and fertile soils of the prairie provinces attracted migrants, and the descendants of early European immigrants still make up a large proportion of the population. The mechanization of agriculture has reduced the need for labour, and rural population densities remain low. The majority of the people live within 100 miles (160 km) of the southern Canada–USA border, and in British Columbia, one of the leading Canadian provinces in terms of economic wealth. The Yukon Territory, in the far north, remains a relatively unspoilt wilderness, containing large, untapped mineral reserves. This province has a significant population of Native Americans, many of whom maintain a traditional lifestyle.

USING THE LAND AND SEA

WHEAT FARMING IS THE ECONOMIC MAINSTAY of Alberta, Manitoba and Saskatchewan, which contain 82% of farmland in Canada. Cattle are also raised on the prairies. Forestry and fishing are the most prominent resource-based industries in British Columbia. Despite the mountainous terrain, fruit and specialized grains can be grown in the Okanagan and Fraser valleys.

Land use and agricultural distribution

- cattle
- cereals
- fishing
- fruit
- timber
- major towns
- pasture
- cropland
- forest
- wetland
- barren
- tundra

Large, highly-mechanized and often very specialized farms, requiring huge investment but little labour, characterize modern farming in the prairies.

THE URBAN/RURAL POPULATION DIVIDE

77% urban   23% rural

0 10 20 30 40 50 60 70 80 90 100

POPULATION DENSITY	TOTAL LAND AREA
7 people per sq mile (3 people per sq km)	1,224,449 sq miles (3,172,150 sq km)

TRANSPORT AND INDUSTRY

THE WESTERN PROVINCES contain a wealth of mineral resources. Alberta holds the bulk of Canada's fossil fuels; the other provinces contain reserves of metallic ores, such as zinc, lead and silver. Isolation from markets has slowed the development of manufacturing, restricting it to the large cities like Vancouver, Winnipeg and Calgary. Hydro-electric power is widely exploited, although there is increasing concern about potential ecological damage.

THE TRANSPORT NETWORK

- 82,438 miles (135,145 km)
- 6459 miles (10,401 km)
- 10,811 miles (17,410 km)
- None

The transport network of the western provinces is dominated by east–west routes that weave through mountain passes and spread across the plains. Access to some northern areas is restricted to air travel.

Major industry and infrastructure

- aerospace
- chemicals
- coal
- engineering
- food processing
- hydro-electric power
- mining
- oil & gas
- timber processing
- major towns
- international airports
- major roads
- major industrial areas

Much of the Yukon Territory is uninhabited tundra. Industry is based on the extraction of mineral resources, and to a lesser extent, on the scattered forests of the south.

The Fraser River valley is a major area of settlement in British Columbia. Railways cross the Rocky Mountains via this valley.

Established in 1907, Jasper National Park lies in the heart of the Rocky Mountains. It is noted for its spectacular alpine scenery and contains part of the large Columbia Icefield.

N O P Q R S T U V W X Y

THE LANDSCAPE

THE MASSIVE ROCKY MOUNTAINS form a continental divide between rivers flowing eastward and westward. East of the mountains, stretching from the Arctic Circle south into the USA, lie the interior plains. Covered with glacial deposits from the last Ice Age, these are interspersed with hilly regions and long, steep escarpments.

MAP KEY

POPULATION

⊙ 500,000 to 1 million
◎ 100,000 to 500,000
⊕ 50,000 to 100,000
○ 10,000 to 50,000
∘ below 10,000

ELEVATION

6000m / 19,686ft
4000m / 13,124ft
3000m / 9843ft
2000m / 6562ft
1000m / 3281ft
500m / 1640ft
250m / 820ft
100m / 328ft
sea level

SCALE 1:7,500,000
(projection: Lambert Conformal Conic)

Km
0 25 50 100 150 200 250

Miles
0 50 100 150 200 250

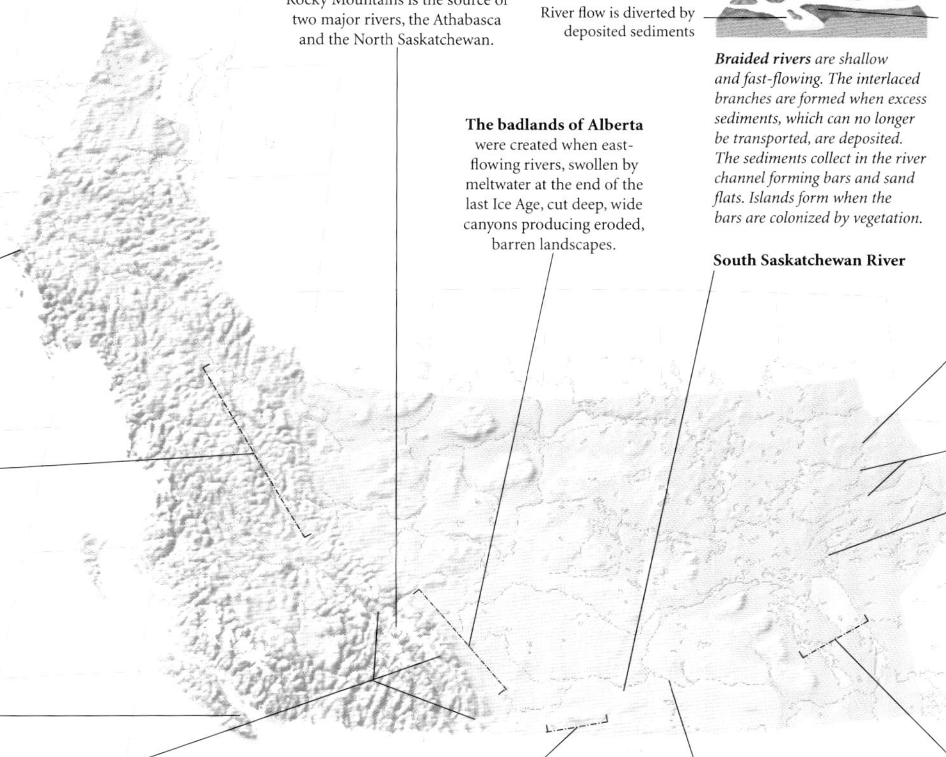

Mount Logan rises 19,551 ft (5959 m). It is the highest peak in Canada.

The Rocky Mountain Trench is the longest linear fault in the world. It has formed a straight, flat-bottomed valley between 2–9 miles (4–15 km) wide, and up to 3280 ft (1000 m) deep.

Hundreds of islands dot the fjord-indented coast of British Columbia; the largest is Vancouver Island.

Three major passes cut through the Rocky Mountains: Yellowhead, Kicking Horse and Crowsnest. They are all used as transport routes through the mountains.

The Cypress Hills rise to 4806 ft (1465 m) above the surrounding plain. Having escaped the last glaciation they contain unique plant and animal life. The silvery lupine, bunchberry and lodgepole pine all grow in the cool, moist climate of the hills.

The Columbia Icefield in the Rocky Mountains is the source of two major rivers, the Athabasca and the North Saskatchewan.

The badlands of Alberta were created when east-flowing rivers, swollen by meltwater at the end of the last Ice Age, cut deep, wide canyons producing eroded, barren landscapes.

South Saskatchewan River

Vegetated island
River flow is diverted by deposited sediments
Bar
Sand flat

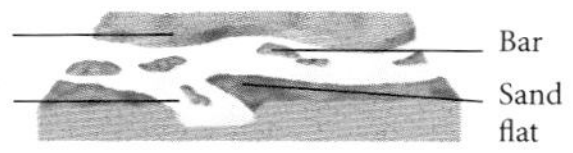

Braided rivers are shallow and fast-flowing. The interlaced branches are formed when excess sediments, which can no longer be transported, are deposited. The sediments collect in the river channel forming bars and sand flats. Islands form when the bars are colonized by vegetation.

Across the tundra of northern Manitoba, widespread permafrost inhibits water from permeating the soil. This causes rivers like the Churchill to flow in many channels, which can be frozen for up to six months during the winter.

The Nelson and Churchill rivers drain northward across the Canadian Shield to Hudson Bay. The shield covers three-fifths of Saskatchewan.

Setting Lake

Ancient granite outcrops, part of the Canadian Shield, rise above the surface of Setting Lake, which was initially formed by meltwater from the last Ice Age.

The Alberta and Saskatchewan plains bear strong testament to past glaciations. The Assiniboine, Saskatchewan and Qu'Appelle rivers occupy flat-bottomed, steep-sided valleys eroded during the last Ice Age by glacial meltwater.

The lowlands of Manitoba are a basin that once held the vast post-glacial Lake Agassiz, remnants of which include Lake Winnipeg, Lake Winnipegosis and Lake Manitoba.

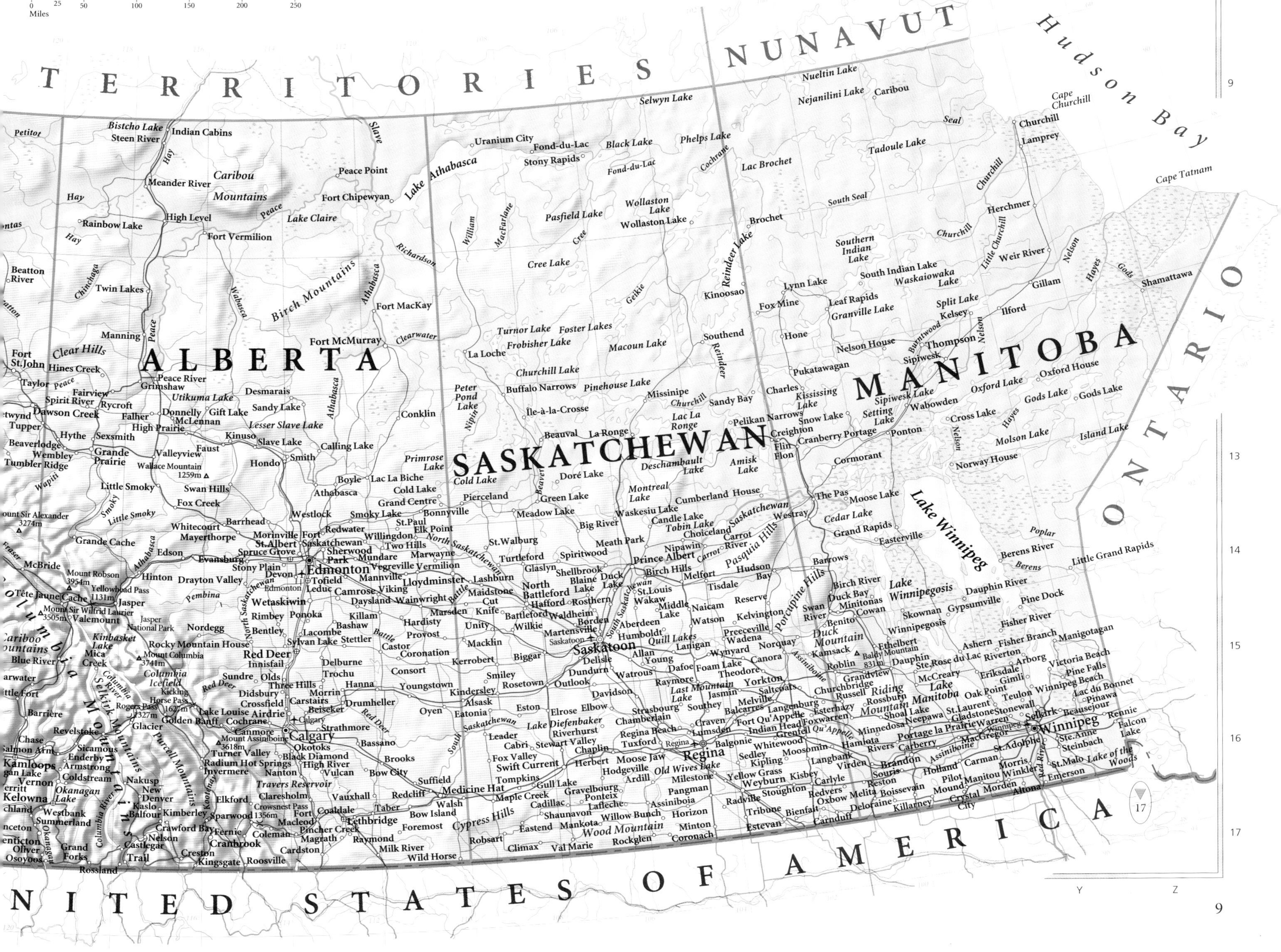

[Map labels — provinces and territories]

TERRITORIES — NUNAVUT — Hudson Bay

ALBERTA — SASKATCHEWAN — MANITOBA — ONTARIO

UNITED STATES OF AMERICA

[Selected map place names]

Petitot, Bistcho Lake, Indian Cabins, Steen River, Hay, Meander River, Caribou Mountains, Peace Point, Slave, Selwyn Lake, Nueltin Lake, Cape Churchill, Churchill, Lamprey

Hay, Rainbow Lake, High Level, Lake Claire, Fort Chipewyan, Lake Athabasca, Uranium City, Fond-du-Lac, Black Lake, Phelps Lake, Stony Rapids, Cochrane, Lac Brochet, Tadoule Lake, Cape Tatnam

Hay, Fort Vermilion, Peace, William, MacFarlane, Pasfield Lake, Wollaston Lake, Brochet, South Seal, Herchmer

Beatton River, Twin Lakes, Chinchaga, Wabasca, Athabasca, Richardson, Cree, Cree Lake, Wollaston Lake, Reindeer Lake, Southern Indian Lake, Churchill, Little Churchill

Fort St.John, Clear Hills, Hines Creek, Manning, Birch Mountains, Fort MacKay, Clearwater, Geikie, Kinoosao, Lynn Lake, Fox Mine, Leaf Rapids, Split Lake, Gillam, Hayes, Weir River, Shamattawa

Taylor, Peace, Fairview, Grimshaw, Peace River, Desmarais, Utikuma Lake, Turnor Lake, Foster Lakes, La Loche, Frobisher Lake, Macoun Lake, Southend, Reindeer, Hone, Nelson House, Granville Lake, Waskaiowaka Lake, South Indian Lake, Ilford, Goods

ALBERTA, Spirit River, Rycroft, Falher, Donnelly, Gift Lake, Sandy Lake, Conklin, Churchill Lake, Buffalo Narrows, Pinehouse Lake, Île-à-la-Crosse, Missinipe, Churchill, Sandy Bay, Pelican Narrows, Snow Lake, Wabowden, Thompson, Sipiwesk, Oxford House, Gods Lake

Dawson Creek, McLennan, High Prairie, Lesser Slave Lake, Slave Lake, Kinuso, Calling Lake, Beauval, La Ronge, Lac La Ronge, Kississing, Cranberry Portage, Creighton, Flin Flon, Ponton, Cross Lake, Molson Lake, Island Lake

Tumbler Ridge, Grande Prairie, Wembley, Beaverlodge, Hythe, Sexsmith, Valleyview, Wallace Mountain 1259m, Hondo, Faust, Smith, Swan Hills, Fox Creek, Primrose Lake, Cold Lake, Doré Lake, Deschambault Lake, Amisk Lake, Cormorant, Norway House

SASKATCHEWAN, MANITOBA, Lake Winnipeg, Berens River, Little Grand Rapids, Poplar, Berens

Boyle, Lac La Biche, Cold Lake, Barrhead, Westlock, Grand Centre, Bonnyville, Pierceland, Green Lake, Meadow Lake, Big River, Waskesiu Lake, Candle Lake, Montreal Lake, Cumberland House, The Pas, Moose Lake, Cedar Lake, Grand Rapids, Easterville, Barrows

Whitecourt, Mayerthorpe, Morinville, Fort Saskatchewan, St.Paul, Elk Point, Willingdon, North Saskatchewan, St.Walburg, Turtleford, Glaslyn, Spiritwood, Shellbrook, Prince Albert, Nipawin, Carrot, Pasquia Hills, Westray, Birch River, Swan River, Minitonas, Benito, Skownan, Gypsumville, Pine Dock, Fisher River

Grande Cache, St.Albert, Spruce Grove, Stony Plain, Edmonton, Sherwood Park, Mundare, Vegreville, Vermilion, Lloydminster, Lashburn, Blaine Lake, North Battleford, Battleford, Hafford, Rosthern, Melfort, Tisdale, Hudson Bay, Reserve, Kelvington, Preeceville, Swan, Duck Mountain, Roblin, Kamsack, Dauphin, Sclater, Grandview, Ethelbert, Winnipegosis, Dauphin River, Fisher Branch, Ashern

Hinton, Edson, Evansburg, Drayton Valley, Devon, Leduc, Camrose, Viking, Wainwright, Marwayne, Maidstone, St.Louis, Wakaw, Naicam, Watson, Wadena, Quill Lakes, Wynyard, Norquay, Lake Winnipegosis, Cowan, Winnipegosis, Gladstone, Stonewall

Mount Robson 3954m, Tête Jaune Cache 1131m, Yellowhead Pass, Jasper, Mount Sir Wilfrid Laurier 3505m, Valemount, Jasper National Park, Nordegg, Wetaskiwin, Tofield, Mannville, Daysland, Killam, Hardisty, Marsden, Unity, Borden, Saskatoon, Aberdeen, Allan, Young, Lanigan, Foam Lake, Theodore, Yorkton, Saltcoats, Canora, Melville, Esterhazy, Langenburg, Russell, Riding Mountain, McCreary, Neepawa, Minnedosa, Shoal Lake, Birtle, Ste.Rose du Lac, Eriksdale, Teulon, Winnipeg Beach

McBride, Rimbey, Ponoka, Lacombe, Bashaw, Bentley, Sylvan Lake, Stettler, Castor, Coronation, Provost, Macklin, Biggar, Delisle, Dundurn, Dafoe, Raymore, Jasmin, Last Mountain Lake, Strasbourg, Southey, Balcarres, Fort Qu'Appelle, Indian Head, Grenfell, Qu'Appelle, Wolseley, Hamiota, Rivers, Brandon, Carberry, Minnedosa, Oak Point, Winnipeg, Selkirk, Lac du Bonnet

Cariboo Mountains, Kinbasket Lake, Mica, Columbia, Rocky Mountain House, Red Deer, Innisfail, Sundre, Olds, Three Hills, Trochu, Hanna, Kindersley, Rosetown, Outlook, Davidson, Watrous, Lumsden, Regina Beach, Balgonie, Sedley, Kipling, Moosomin, Virden, Oak Lake, Souris, Boissevain, Melita, Deloraine, Killarney

Columbia Icefield, Kicking Horse Pass, Banff, Lake Louise, Golden, Canmore, Mount Assiniboine 3618m, Calgary, Strathmore, Bassano, Brooks, Oyen, Eston, Elrose, Elbow, Lake Diefenbaker, Chamberlain, Riverhurst, Chaplin, Tuxford, Moose Jaw, Regina, Weyburn, Stoughton, Carlyle, Redvers, Oxbow

Revelstoke, Glacier, Radium Hot Springs, Turner Valley, Black Diamond, Okotoks, High River, Vulcan, Bow City, Suffield, Medicine Hat, Leader, Fox Valley, Swift Current, Herbert, Gull Lake, Hodgeville, Gravelbourg, Ponteix, Assiniboia, Weyburn, Milestone, Yellow Grass, Radville, Tribune, Carnduff, Estevan, Bienfait

Chase, Sicamous, Enderby, Vernon, Coldstream, Nakusp, New Denver, Westbank, Balfour, Kimberley, Sparwood, Claresholm, Nanton, Vauxhall, Taber, Coaldale, Foremost, Maple Creek, Cadillac, Shaunavon, Eastend, Willow Bunch, Horizon, Minton, Wood Mountain, Rockglen, Coronach

Kelowna, Okanagan Lake, Summerland, Penticton, Nelson, Castlegar, Elkford, Elko, Fernie, Crowsnest Pass 1356m, Pincher Creek, Coleman, Magrath, Cardston, Raymond, Milk River, Robsart, Val Marie, Climax

Grand Forks, Rossland, Trail, Creston, Kingsgate, Roosville, Lethbridge, Macleod, Wild Horse, Cypress Hills

17

9

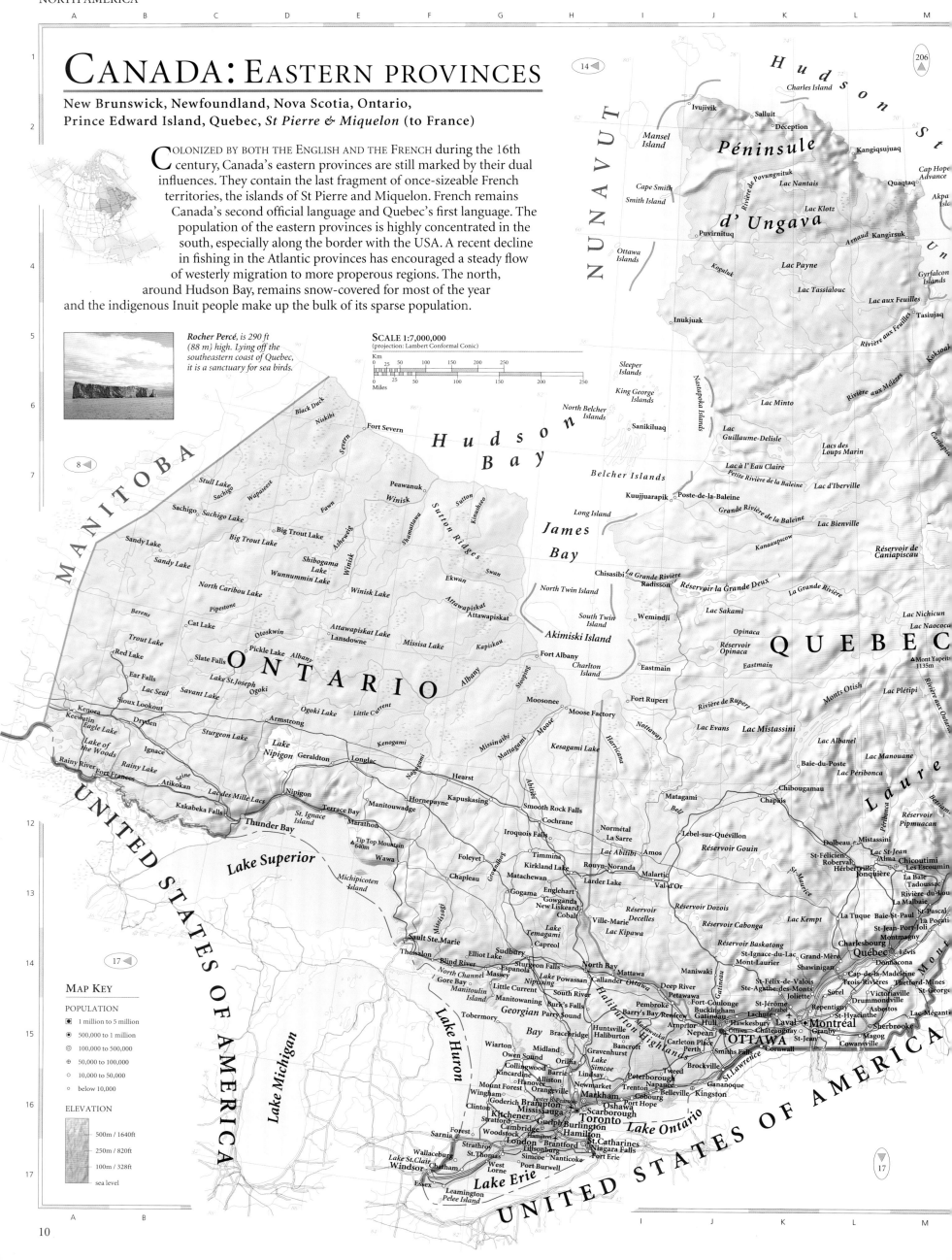

CANADA: EASTERN PROVINCES

New Brunswick, Newfoundland, Nova Scotia, Ontario,
Prince Edward Island, Quebec, *St Pierre & Miquelon* (to France)

COLONIZED BY BOTH THE ENGLISH AND THE FRENCH during the 16th century, Canada's eastern provinces are still marked by their dual influences. They contain the last fragment of once-sizeable French territories, the islands of St Pierre and Miquelon. French remains Canada's second official language and Quebec's first language. The population of the eastern provinces is highly concentrated in the south, especially along the border with the USA. A recent decline in fishing in the Atlantic provinces has encouraged a steady flow of westerly migration to more properous regions. The north, around Hudson Bay, remains snow-covered for most of the year and the indigenous Inuit people make up the bulk of its sparse population.

Rocher Percé, is 290 ft (88 m) high. Lying off the southeastern coast of Quebec, it is a sanctuary for sea birds.

SCALE 1:7,000,000
(projection: Lambert Conformal Conic)

MAP KEY

POPULATION

- ▣ 1 million to 5 million
- ◉ 500,000 to 1 million
- ◉ 100,000 to 500,000
- ⊕ 50,000 to 100,000
- ◉ 10,000 to 50,000
- ○ below 10,000

ELEVATION

- 500m / 1640ft
- 250m / 820ft
- 100m / 328ft
- sea level

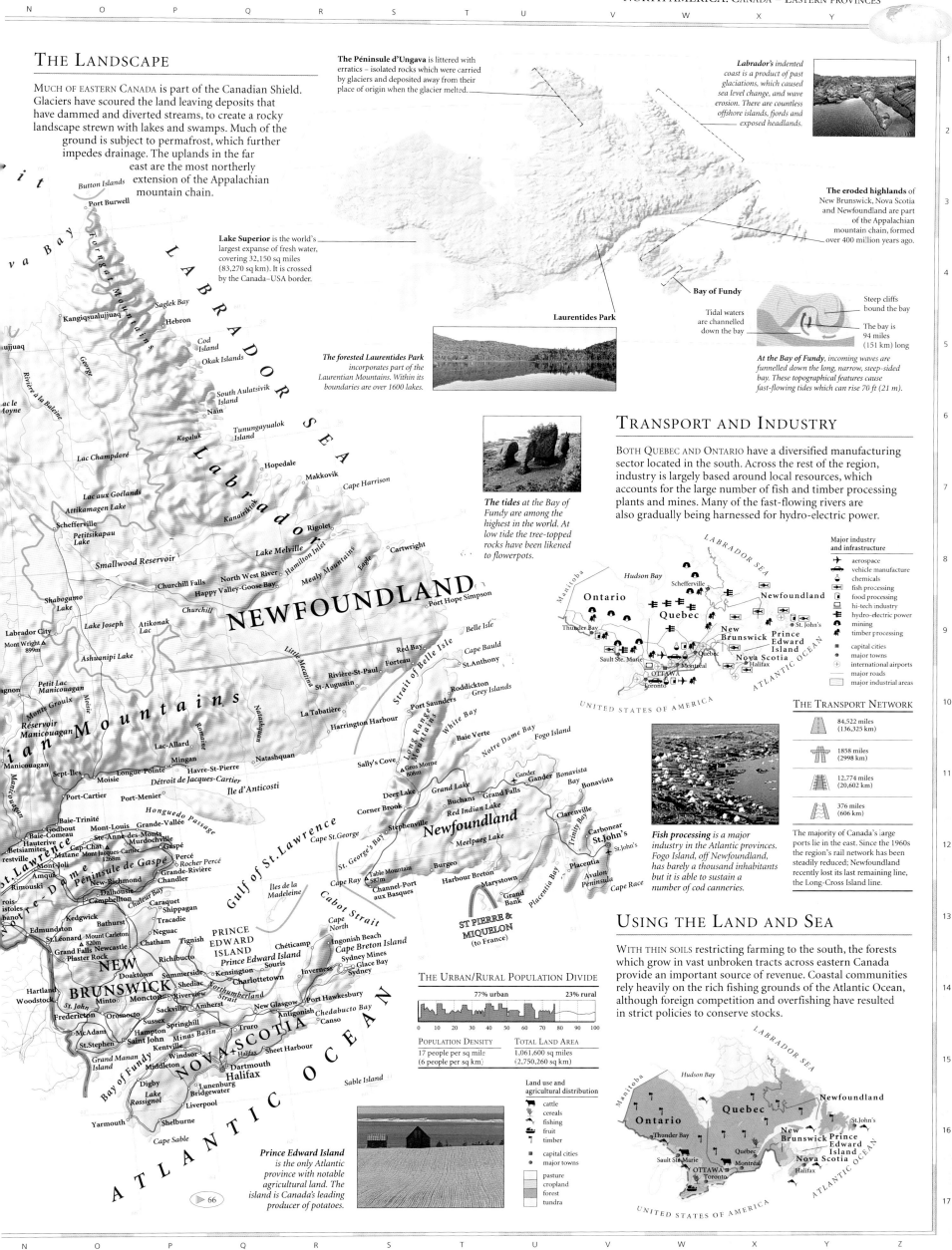

THE LANDSCAPE

MUCH OF EASTERN CANADA is part of the Canadian Shield. Glaciers have scoured the land leaving deposits that have dammed and diverted streams, to create a rocky landscape strewn with lakes and swamps. Much of the ground is subject to permafrost, which further impedes drainage. The uplands in the far east are the most northerly extension of the Appalachian mountain chain.

The Péninsule d'Ungava is littered with erratics – isolated rocks which were carried by glaciers and deposited away from their place of origin when the glacier melted.

Labrador's indented coast is a product of past glaciations, which caused sea level change, and wave erosion. There are countless offshore islands, fjords and exposed headlands.

The eroded highlands of New Brunswick, Nova Scotia and Newfoundland are part of the Appalachian mountain chain, formed over 400 million years ago.

Lake Superior is the world's largest expanse of fresh water, covering 32,150 sq miles (83,270 sq km). It is crossed by the Canada–USA border.

Bay of Fundy

Tidal waters are channelled down the bay

Steep cliffs bound the bay

The bay is 94 miles (151 km) long

Laurentides Park

The forested Laurentides Park incorporates part of the Laurentian Mountains. Within its boundaries are over 1600 lakes.

At the Bay of Fundy, incoming waves are funnelled down the long, narrow, steep-sided bay. These topographical features cause fast-flowing tides which can rise 70 ft (21 m).

The tides at the Bay of Fundy are among the highest in the world. At low tide the tree-topped rocks have been likened to flowerpots.

TRANSPORT AND INDUSTRY

BOTH QUEBEC AND ONTARIO have a diversified manufacturing sector located in the south. Across the rest of the region, industry is largely based around local resources, which accounts for the large number of fish and timber processing plants and mines. Many of the fast-flowing rivers are also gradually being harnessed for hydro-electric power.

Major industry and infrastructure

- aerospace
- vehicle manufacture
- chemicals
- fish processing
- food processing
- hi-tech industry
- hydro-electric power
- mining
- timber processing
- capital cities
- major towns
- international airports
- major roads
- major industrial areas

THE TRANSPORT NETWORK

- 84,522 miles (136,325 km)
- 1858 miles (2998 km)
- 12,774 miles (20,602 km)
- 376 miles (606 km)

The majority of Canada's large ports lie in the east. Since the 1960s the region's rail network has been steadily reduced; Newfoundland recently lost its last remaining line, the Long-Cross Island line.

Fish processing is a major industry in the Atlantic provinces. Fogo Island, off Newfoundland, has barely a thousand inhabitants but it is able to sustain a number of cod canneries.

USING THE LAND AND SEA

WITH THIN SOILS restricting farming to the south, the forests which grow in vast unbroken tracts across eastern Canada provide an important source of revenue. Coastal communities rely heavily on the rich fishing grounds of the Atlantic Ocean, although foreign competition and overfishing have resulted in strict policies to conserve stocks.

THE URBAN/RURAL POPULATION DIVIDE

77% urban   23% rural

POPULATION DENSITY
17 people per sq mile
(6 people per sq km)

TOTAL LAND AREA
1,061,600 sq miles
(2,750,260 sq km)

Land use and agricultural distribution
- cattle
- cereals
- fishing
- fruit
- timber
- capital cities
- major towns
- pasture
- cropland
- forest
- tundra

Prince Edward Island is the only Atlantic province with notable agricultural land. The island is Canada's leading producer of potatoes.

66

SOUTHEASTERN CANADA

Southern Ontario, Southern Quebec

The SOUTHERN PARTS of Quebec and Ontario form the economic heart of Canada. The two provinces are divided by their language and culture; in Quebec, French is the main language, whereas English is spoken in Ontario. Separatist sentiment in Quebec has led to a provincial referendum on the question of a sovereignty association with Canada. The region contains Canada's capital, Ottawa and its two largest cities: Toronto, the centre of commerce and Montréal, the cultural and administrative heart of French Canada.

Niagara Falls lies on the border between Canada and the USA. It comprises a system of two falls: American Falls, in New York, is separated from Horseshoe Falls, in Ontario, by Goat Island. Horseshoe Falls, seen here, plunges 184 ft (56 m) and is 2500 ft (762 m) wide.

The port at Montréal is situated on the St. Lawrence Seaway. A network of 16 locks allows sea-going vessels access to routes once plied by fur-trappers and early settlers.

TRANSPORT AND INDUSTRY

The CITIES OF SOUTHERN QUEBEC AND ONTARIO, and their hinterlands, form the heart of Canadian manufacturing industry. Toronto is Canada's leading financial centre, and Ontario's motor and aerospace industries have developed around the city. A major centre for nickel mining lies to the north of Toronto. Most of Quebec's industry is located in Montréal, the oldest port in North America. Chemicals, paper manufacture and the construction of transport equipment are leading industrial activities.

Major industry and infrastructure

🚗 car manufacture	textiles
⚙ chemicals	paper industry
⚙ engineering	timber processing
$ finance	■ capital cities
food processing	major towns
hi-tech industry	+ international airports
mining	major roads
iron & steel	major industrial areas

THE TRANSPORT NETWORK

The opening of the St. Lawrence Seaway in 1959 finally allowed ocean-going ships (up to 24,000 tons (tonnes)) access to the interior of Canada, creating a vital trading route.

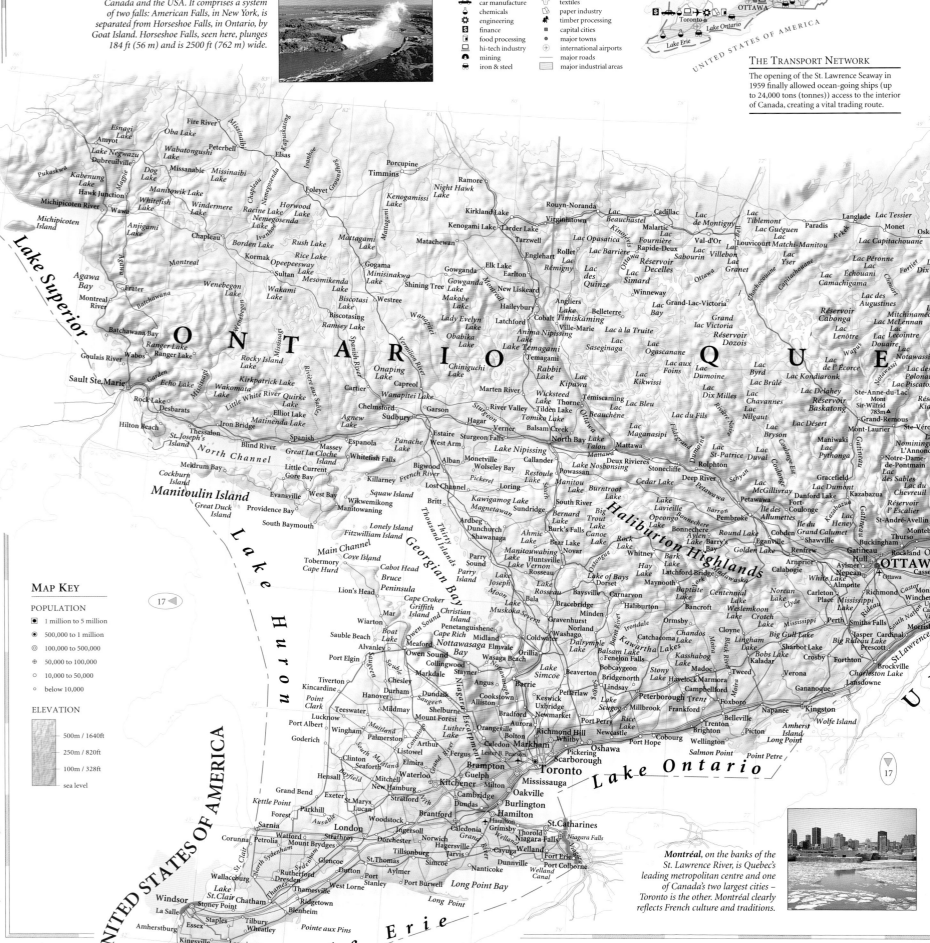

MAP KEY

POPULATION

▣	1 million to 5 million
◉	500,000 to 1 million
⊙	100,000 to 500,000
⊕	50,000 to 100,000
○	10,000 to 50,000
○	below 10,000

ELEVATION

	500m / 1640ft
	250m / 820ft
	100m / 328ft
	sea level

USING THE LAND AND SEA

THE PRODUCTIVE NIAGARA 'FRUIT BELT' on the shores of Lake Erie and Lake Ontario is a major farming region, although available farmland is being challenged by urban expansion. Quebec is Canada's leading producer of maple syrup and dairy products. In the north, farmland gives way to extensive areas of forest, partly used for commercial logging. Fishing occurs in Atlantic waters and in the Great Lakes.

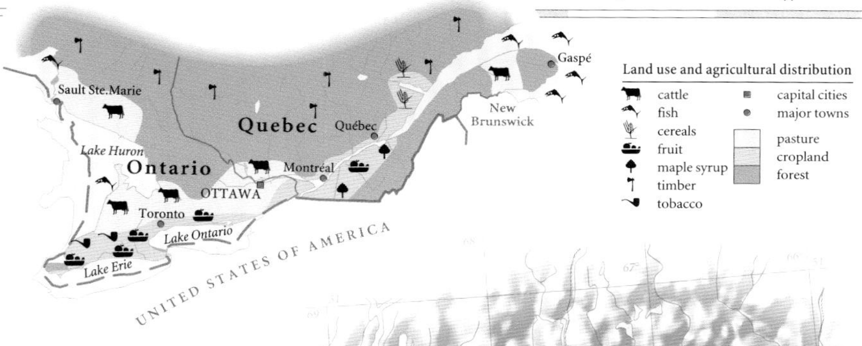

THE URBAN/RURAL POPULATION DIVIDE

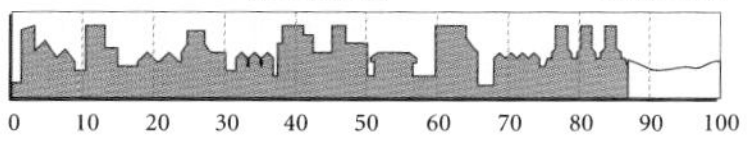

urban 87%   rural 13%

0 10 20 30 40 50 60 70 80 90 100

POPULATION DENSITY	TOTAL LAND AREA
64 people per sq mile (25 people per sq km)	214,230 sq miles (555,000 sq km)

Land use and agricultural distribution

- cattle
- fish
- cereals
- fruit
- maple syrup
- timber
- tobacco
- ■ capital cities
- • major towns
- pasture
- cropland
- forest

Pumpkins are just one of the crops grown in the Niagara 'fruit belt'. The mild climate, moderated by the lakes, allows the cultivation of a wide range of fruit and vegetables, including cherries, apples, peaches, grapes and asparagus. Fruit and vegetable growing is confined to southern Canada, due to the colder climate and short growing season of the northern regions.

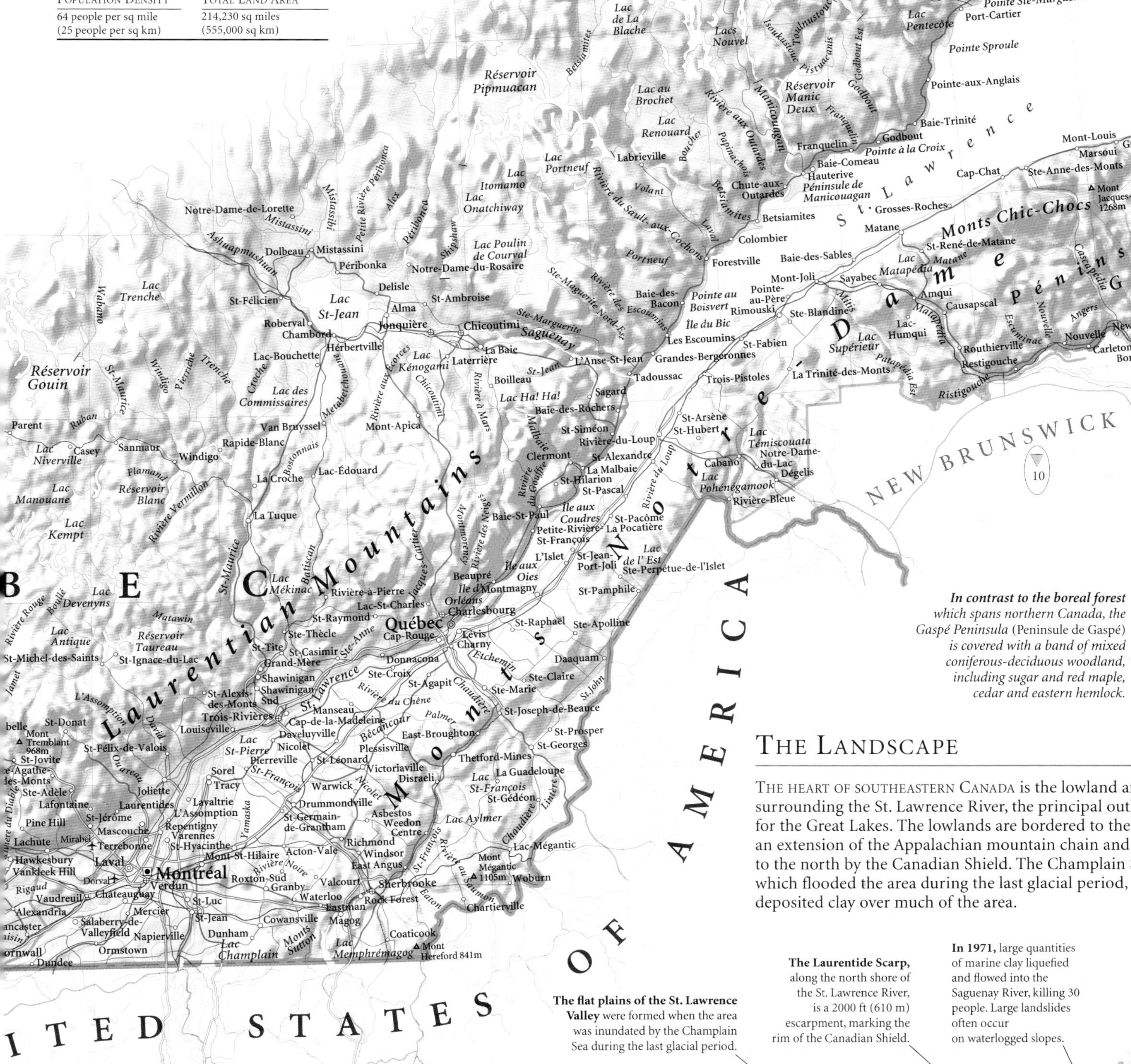

In contrast to the boreal forest which spans northern Canada, the Gaspé Peninsula (Peninsule de Gaspé) is covered with a band of mixed coniferous-deciduous woodland, including sugar and red maple, cedar and eastern hemlock.

THE LANDSCAPE

THE HEART OF SOUTHEASTERN CANADA is the lowland area surrounding the St. Lawrence River, the principal outlet for the Great Lakes. The lowlands are bordered to the east by an extension of the Appalachian mountain chain and to the north by the Canadian Shield. The Champlain Sea, which flooded the area during the last glacial period, deposited clay over much of the area.

The wooded Gaspé Peninsula (Peninsule de Gaspé) includes the Notre Dame and Shickshock mountains (Monts Chic-Chocs). These are a northerly outcrop of the Appalachian mountain chain.

The flat plains of the St. Lawrence Valley were formed when the area was inundated by the Champlain Sea during the last glacial period.

The Laurentide Scarp, along the north shore of the St. Lawrence River, is a 2000 ft (610 m) escarpment, marking the rim of the Canadian Shield.

In 1971, large quantities of marine clay liquefied and flowed into the Saguenay River, killing 30 people. Large landslides often occur on waterlogged slopes.

SCALE 1:3,000,000
(projection: Lambert Conformal Conic)

Km
0 5 10 20 30 40 50 60 70 80

Miles
0 5 10 20 30 40 50 60 70 80

Point Pelee is a world-famous site for bird migration. Over 250 species of bird have been sighted on the sandspit which forms the southern tip of the Canadian mainland.

Lake Superior

Lake Huron

Lake Erie

Lake Ontario

The Great Lakes moderate the climate of the area surrounding the St. Lawrence River. Their water, which cools more slowly than the land, acts as a reservoir for warmth, extending the growing season into the early autumn.

Mount Royal, around which the city of Montréal has developed, is the result of an igneous intrusion which occurred between 135 and 65 million years ago.

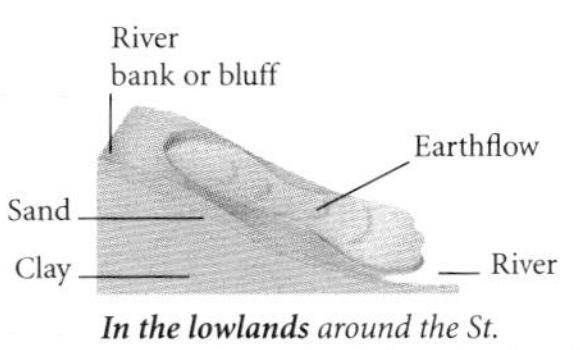

River bank or bluff

Earthflow

Sand

Clay

River

In the lowlands around the St. Lawrence, earthflows have developed along gentle river banks where sand overlies clay, making the surface layers very unstable. When the slope's natural equilibrium is disturbed, an earthflow can occur.

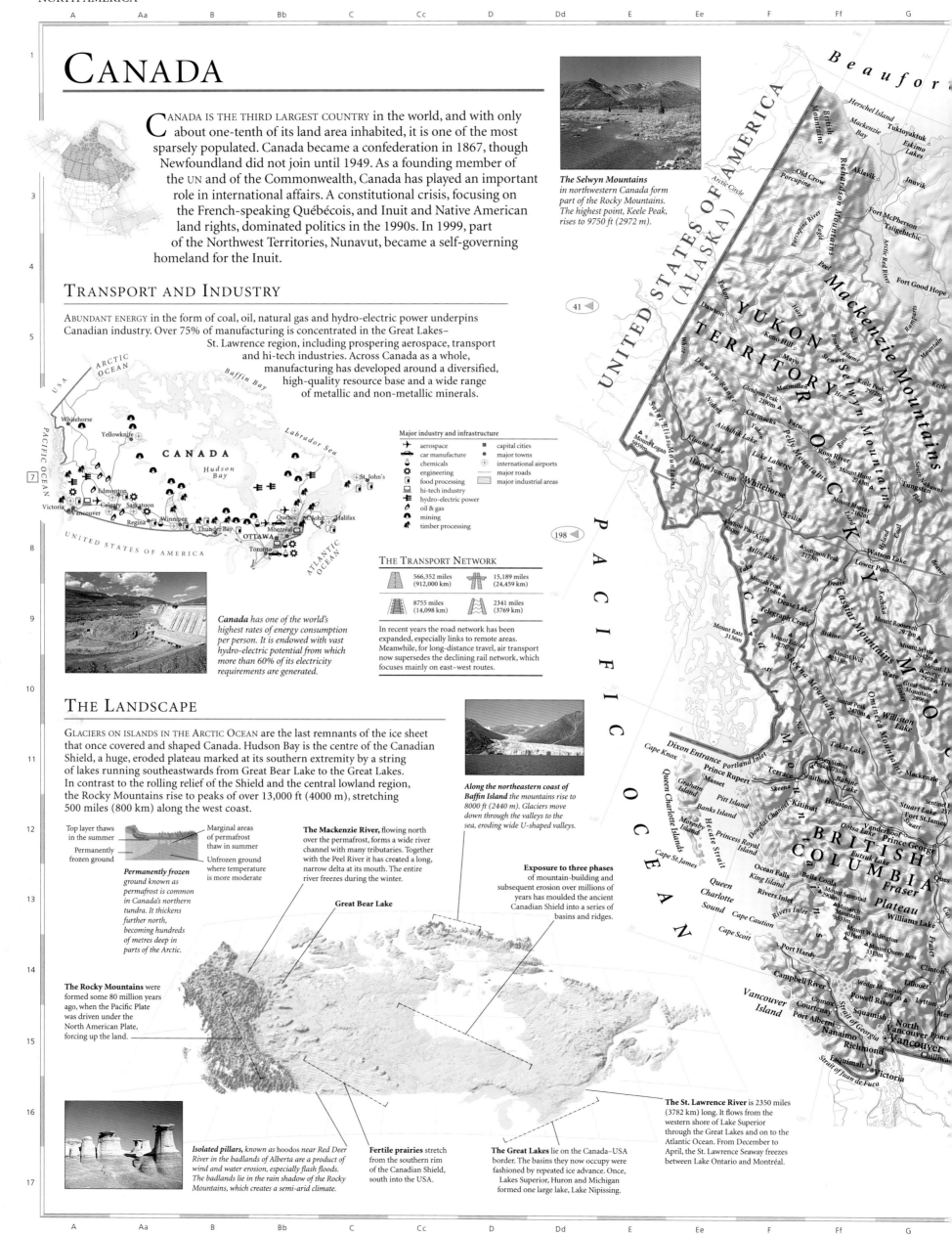

CANADA

CANADA IS THE THIRD LARGEST COUNTRY in the world, and with only about one-tenth of its land area inhabited, it is one of the most sparsely populated. Canada became a confederation in 1867, though Newfoundland did not join until 1949. As a founding member of the UN and of the Commonwealth, Canada has played an important role in international affairs. A constitutional crisis, focusing on the French-speaking Québécois, and Inuit and Native American land rights, dominated politics in the 1990s. In 1999, part of the Northwest Territories, Nunavut, became a self-governing homeland for the Inuit.

The Selwyn Mountains in northwestern Canada form part of the Rocky Mountains. The highest point, Keele Peak, rises to 9750 ft (2972 m).

TRANSPORT AND INDUSTRY

ABUNDANT ENERGY in the form of coal, oil, natural gas and hydro-electric power underpins Canadian industry. Over 75% of manufacturing is concentrated in the Great Lakes–St. Lawrence region, including prospering aerospace, transport and hi-tech industries. Across Canada as a whole, manufacturing has developed around a diversified, high-quality resource base and a wide range of metallic and non-metallic minerals.

Major industry and infrastructure

- aerospace
- car manufacture
- chemicals
- engineering
- food processing
- hi-tech industry
- hydro-electric power
- oil & gas
- mining
- timber processing
- capital cities
- major towns
- international airports
- major roads
- major industrial areas

Canada has one of the world's highest rates of energy consumption per person. It is endowed with vast hydro-electric potential from which more than 60% of its electricity requirements are generated.

THE TRANSPORT NETWORK

566,352 miles (912,000 km)	15,189 miles (24,459 km)
8755 miles (14,098 km)	2341 miles (3769 km)

In recent years the road network has been expanded, especially links to remote areas. Meanwhile, for long-distance travel, air transport now supersedes the declining rail network, which focuses mainly on east–west routes.

THE LANDSCAPE

GLACIERS ON ISLANDS IN THE ARCTIC OCEAN are the last remnants of the ice sheet that once covered and shaped Canada. Hudson Bay is the centre of the Canadian Shield, a huge, eroded plateau marked at its southern extremity by a string of lakes running southeastwards from Great Bear Lake to the Great Lakes. In contrast to the rolling relief of the Shield and the central lowland region, the Rocky Mountains rise to peaks of over 13,000 ft (4000 m), stretching 500 miles (800 km) along the west coast.

Along the northeastern coast of Baffin Island the mountains rise to 8000 ft (2440 m). Glaciers move down through the valleys to the sea, eroding wide U-shaped valleys.

Top layer thaws in the summer
Permanently frozen ground

Marginal areas of permafrost thaw in summer
Unfrozen ground where temperature is more moderate

Permanently frozen ground known as permafrost is common in Canada's northern tundra. It thickens further north, becoming hundreds of metres deep in parts of the Arctic.

The Mackenzie River, flowing north over the permafrost, forms a wide river channel with many tributaries. Together with the Peel River it has created a long, narrow delta at its mouth. The entire river freezes during the winter.

Great Bear Lake

Exposure to three phases of mountain-building and subsequent erosion over millions of years has moulded the ancient Canadian Shield into a series of basins and ridges.

The Rocky Mountains were formed some 80 million years ago, when the Pacific Plate was driven under the North American Plate, forcing up the land.

The St. Lawrence River is 2350 miles (3782 km) long. It flows from the western shore of Lake Superior through the Great Lakes and on to the Atlantic Ocean. From December to April, the St. Lawrence Seaway freezes between Lake Ontario and Montréal.

Isolated pillars, known as hoodoos near Red Deer River in the badlands of Alberta are a product of wind and water erosion, especially flash floods. The badlands lie in the rain shadow of the Rocky Mountains, which creates a semi-arid climate.

Fertile prairies stretch from the southern rim of the Canadian Shield, south into the USA.

The Great Lakes lie on the Canada–USA border. The basins they now occupy were fashioned by repeated ice advance. Once, Lakes Superior, Huron and Michigan formed one large lake, Lake Nipissing.

41 ◄

198 ◄

A   Aa   B   Bb   C   Cc   D   Dd   E   Ee   F

THE UNITED STATES OF AMERICA

CONTERMINOUS USA (FOR ALASKA AND HAWAII SEE PAGES 40-41)

THE USA'S PROGRESSION FROM FRONTIER TERRITORY to economic and political superpower has taken less than 200 years. The 48 conterminous states, along with the outlying states of Alaska and Hawaii, are part of a federal union, held together by the guiding principles of the US Constitution, which enshrines the ideals of democracy and liberty for all. Abundant fertile land and a rich resource-base fuelled and sustained the USA's economic development. With the spread of agriculture and the growth of trade and industry came the need for a larger workforce, which was supplied by millions of immigrants, many seeking an escape from poverty and political or religious persecution. Immigration continues today, particularly from Central America and Asia.

Mount Rainier is a dormant volcano in the Cascade Range, Washington. This 14,090 ft (4392 m) peak is flanked by the most extensive glacier outside Alaska.

TRANSPORT AND INDUSTRY

THE USA HAS BEEN THE INDUSTRIAL POWERHOUSE of the world since the Second World War, pioneering mass-production and the consumer lifestyle. Initially, heavy engineering and manufacturing in the northeast led the economy. Today, heavy industry has declined and the USA's economy is driven by service and financial industries, with the most important being defence, hi-tech and electronics.

Washington DC was established as the site for the nation's capital in 1790. It is home to the seat of national government, on Capitol Hill, as well as the President's official residence, the White House.

198

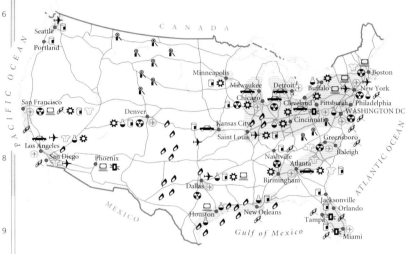

Major industry and infrastructure

- aerospace
- car manufacture
- chemicals
- coal
- electronics
- engineering
- food processing
- hi-tech industry
- oil & gas
- research & development
- textiles
- tourism
- capital cities
- major towns
- international airports
- major roads
- major industrial areas

THE TRANSPORT NETWORK

3,875,040 miles (6,240,000 km)	52,388 miles (84,361 km)
148,308 miles (235,238 km)	25,467 miles (41,009 km)

Transport in the USA is dominated by the car which, with the extensive Interstate Highway system, allows great personal mobility. Today, internal air flights between major cities provide the most rapid cross-country travel.

198

THE LANDSCAPE

THE HIGH, RUGGED MOUNTAIN RANGES of the west are about 80 million years old, geologically young compared to the old, eroded, Appalachian mountain chain, which dates from when North America and Europe were joined together as part of the supercontinent Pangaea, 400 million years ago. In contrast, the Great Plains and Mississippi Basin have a low relief and fertile soils.

Devils Tower, in Wyoming is a 1280 ft (390 m) intrusion of basalt rock, which cooled to form octagonal pillars. In 1906 it became the first US National Monument.

The massive drainage basin of the Mississippi covers 1,250,000 sq miles (3,200,000 sq km). It includes all areas drained by the Mississippi and its chief tributaries, the Missouri and Ohio rivers, and drains the entire region from the Appalachians to the Rockies.

Mount Rainier

Hells Canyon running through part of Idaho and Oregon, is North America's deepest gorge. It was formed by the down-cutting of the Snake River through the thick basalt rocks of the Columbia–Snake Plateau.

The Rocky Mountains form the backbone of the USA, running from Alaska to New Mexico. They contain the USA's highest mountains and many active volcanoes.

The Hudson-Mohawk Gap, lying at the point where the two rivers join, allows passage from the Atlantic Ocean to the continental interior.

The Great Lakes

Death Valley, California, 282 ft (86 m) below sea level, is the lowest point in the western hemisphere, and one of the hottest places on Earth. Temperatures of 190° F (88° C) have been recorded here.

Niagara Falls

Barrier beaches, bars and spits are typical of the Atlantic coast. These sand formations around Cape Hatteras stretch along the coast for 200 miles (320 km).

The Great Smoky Mountains, part of the ancient Appalachian mountain chain, formed a natural barrier to early settlers attempting to penetrate the country's interior.

Monument Valley's striking sandstone spires and pillars (buttes) have been formed by the action of wind, water, heat and cold.

Volcanically heated water erupts every 40-80 minutes from Old Faithful geyser in Yellowstone National Park, Wyoming. The 170 ft (50 m) column of water and steam persists for 4 minutes.

The deep gullies of South Dakota's badlands are created by periodic, torrential rainfall, which erodes the soft soils and rocks. Their form has been greatly affected by changes in land use.

Great Plains

Most of the USA is drained by the great Mississippi River system. At its mouth, where levées are breached, floodwaters are carried to the swamps through a series of channels. This region is known as the bayou.

The USA's Gulf Coast is seriously affected by hurricane erosion which reshapes its beaches and sandbanks.

The Everglades are a vast area of saw-grass swamp covering 4000 sq miles (10,300 sq km) of southern Florida.

A   Aa   B   Bb   C   Cc   D   Dd   E   Ee   F   Ff

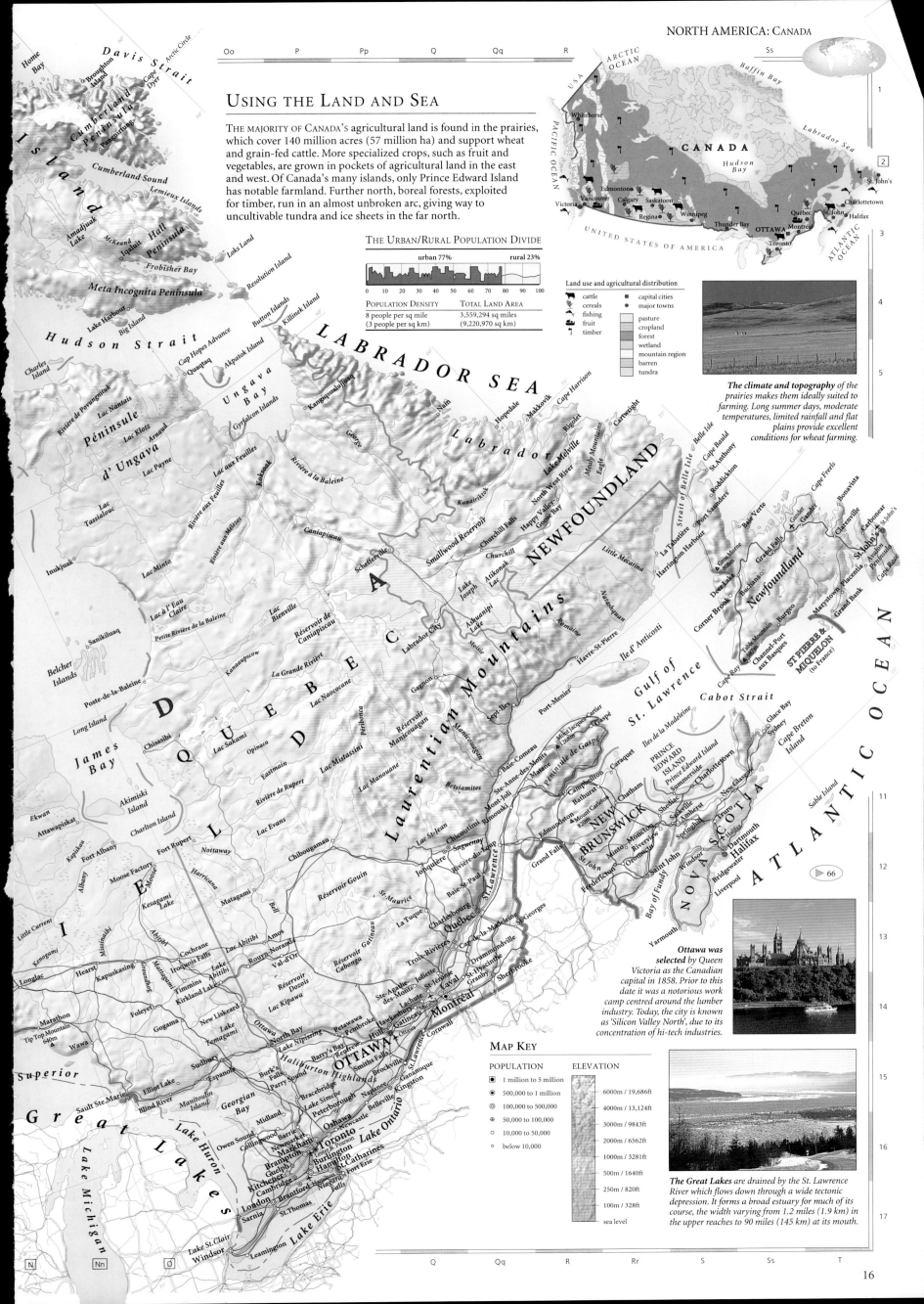

USING THE LAND AND SEA

THE MAJORITY OF CANADA'S agricultural land is found in the prairies, which cover 140 million acres (57 million ha) and support wheat and grain-fed cattle. More specialized crops, such as fruit and vegetables, are grown in pockets of agricultural land in the east and west. Of Canada's many islands, only Prince Edward Island has notable farmland. Further north, boreal forests, exploited for timber, run in an almost unbroken arc, giving way to uncultivable tundra and ice sheets in the far north.

THE URBAN/RURAL POPULATION DIVIDE

urban 77% rural 23%

0 10 20 30 40 50 60 70 80 90 100

POPULATION DENSITY	TOTAL LAND AREA
8 people per sq mile (3 people per sq km)	3,559,294 sq miles (9,220,970 sq km)

Land use and agricultural distribution

- cattle
- cereals
- fishing
- fruit
- timber
- ■ capital cities
- • major towns

pasture
cropland
forest
wetland
mountain region
barren
tundra

The climate and topography of the prairies makes them ideally suited to farming. Long summer days, moderate temperatures, limited rainfall and flat plains provide excellent conditions for wheat farming.

MAP KEY

POPULATION
- ⊡ 1 million to 5 million
- ⊙ 500,000 to 1 million
- ◎ 100,000 to 500,000
- ⊕ 50,000 to 100,000
- ⊙ 10,000 to 50,000
- ○ below 10,000

ELEVATION
- 6000m / 19,686ft
- 4000m / 13,124ft
- 3000m / 9843ft
- 2000m / 6562ft
- 1000m / 3281ft
- 500m / 1640ft
- 250m / 820ft
- 100m / 328ft
- sea level

Ottawa was selected by Queen Victoria as the Canadian capital in 1858. Prior to this date it was a notorious work camp centred around the lumber industry. Today, the city is known as 'Silicon Valley North', due to its concentration of hi-tech industries.

The Great Lakes are drained by the St. Lawrence River which flows down through a wide tectonic depression. It forms a broad estuary for much of its course, the width varying from 1.2 miles (1.9 km) in the upper reaches to 90 miles (145 km) at its mouth.

▶ 66

The Sonoran Desert in southwestern Arizona stretches into Mexico and merges to the northwest with California's Mojave Desert. Much of the southwest is very arid, especially the 'rain-starved' areas between the Coast Ranges and the Rocky Mountains.

MAP KEY

POPULATION
- ■ above 5 million
- ▣ 1 million to 5 million
- ◉ 500,000 to 1 million
- ◎ 100,000 to 500,000
- ⊕ 50,000 to 100,000
- ○ 10,000 to 50,000
- · below 10,000

ELEVATION
- 4000m / 13,124ft
- 3000m / 9843ft
- 2000m / 6562ft
- 1000m / 3281ft
- 500m / 1640ft
- 250m / 820ft
- 100m / 328ft
- sea level

SCALE 1: 8,750,000
(projection: Lambert Azimuthal Equal Area)

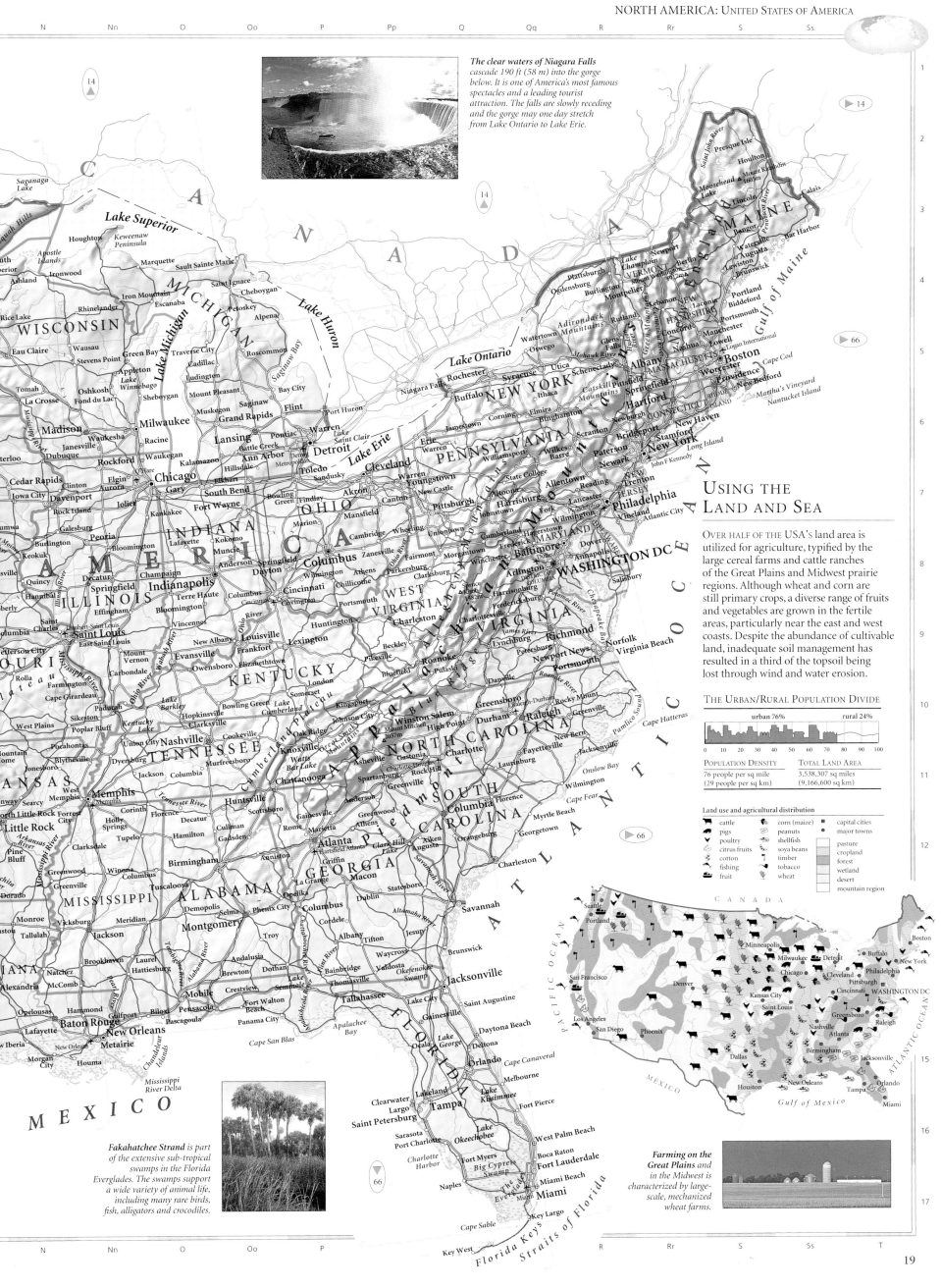

The clear waters of Niagara Falls cascade 190 ft (58 m) into the gorge below. It is one of America's most famous spectacles and a leading tourist attraction. The falls are slowly receding and the gorge may one day stretch from Lake Ontario to Lake Erie.

USING THE LAND AND SEA

OVER HALF OF THE USA's land area is utilized for agriculture, typified by the large cereal farms and cattle ranches of the Great Plains and Midwest prairie regions. Although wheat and corn are still primary crops, a diverse range of fruits and vegetables are grown in the fertile areas, particularly near the east and west coasts. Despite the abundance of cultivable land, inadequate soil management has resulted in a third of the topsoil being lost through wind and water erosion.

THE URBAN/RURAL POPULATION DIVIDE

urban 76%   rural 24%

0 10 20 30 40 50 60 70 80 90 100

POPULATION DENSITY
76 people per sq mile
(29 people per sq km)

TOTAL LAND AREA
3,538,307 sq miles
(9,166,600 sq km)

Land use and agricultural distribution

cattle	corn (maize)
pigs	peanuts
poultry	shellfish
citrus fruits	soya beans
cotton	timber
fishing	tobacco
fruit	wheat

capital cities
major towns

pasture
cropland
forest
wetland
desert
mountain region

Fakahatchee Strand is part of the extensive sub-tropical swamps in the Florida Everglades. The swamps support a wide variety of animal life, including many rare birds, fish, alligators and crocodiles.

Farming on the Great Plains and in the Midwest is characterized by large-scale, mechanized wheat farms.

USA: Northeastern states

Connecticut, Maine, Massachusetts, New Hampshire, New Jersey, New York, Pennsylvania, Rhode Island, Vermont

THE INDENTED COAST AND VAST WOODLANDS of the northeastern states were the original core area for European expansion. The rustic character of New England prevails after 390 years, while the great cities of the Atlantic seaboard have formed an almost continuous urban region. Over 20 million immigrants entered New York from 1855 to 1924 and the northeast became the industrial centre of the USA. After the decline of mining and heavy manufacturing, economic dynamism has been restored with the growth of hi-tech and service industries.

Chelsea in Vermont, surrounded by trees in their fall foliage. Tourism and agriculture dominate the economy of this self-consciously rural state, where no town exceeds 30,000 people.

MAP KEY

POPULATION
- above 5 million
- 1 million to 5 million
- 500,000 to 1 million
- 100,000 to 500,000
- 50,000 to 100,000
- 10,000 to 50,000
- below 10,000

ELEVATION
- 1000m / 3281ft
- 500m / 1640ft
- 250m / 820ft
- 100m / 328ft
- sea level

TRANSPORT AND INDUSTRY

THE PRINCIPAL SEABOARD CITIES grew up on trade and manufacturing. They are now global centres of commerce and corporate administration, dominating the regional economy. Research and development facilities support an expanding electronics and communications sector throughout the region. Pharmaceutical and chemical industries are important in New Jersey and Pennsylvania.

THE TRANSPORT NETWORK

340,090 miles (544,144 km)	4813 miles 7700 km
12,872 miles (20,592 km)	2108 miles (3389 km)

New York's commercial success is tied historically to its transport connections. The Erie Canal, completed in 1825, opened up the Great Lakes and the interior to New York's markets and carried a stream of immigrants into the Midwest.

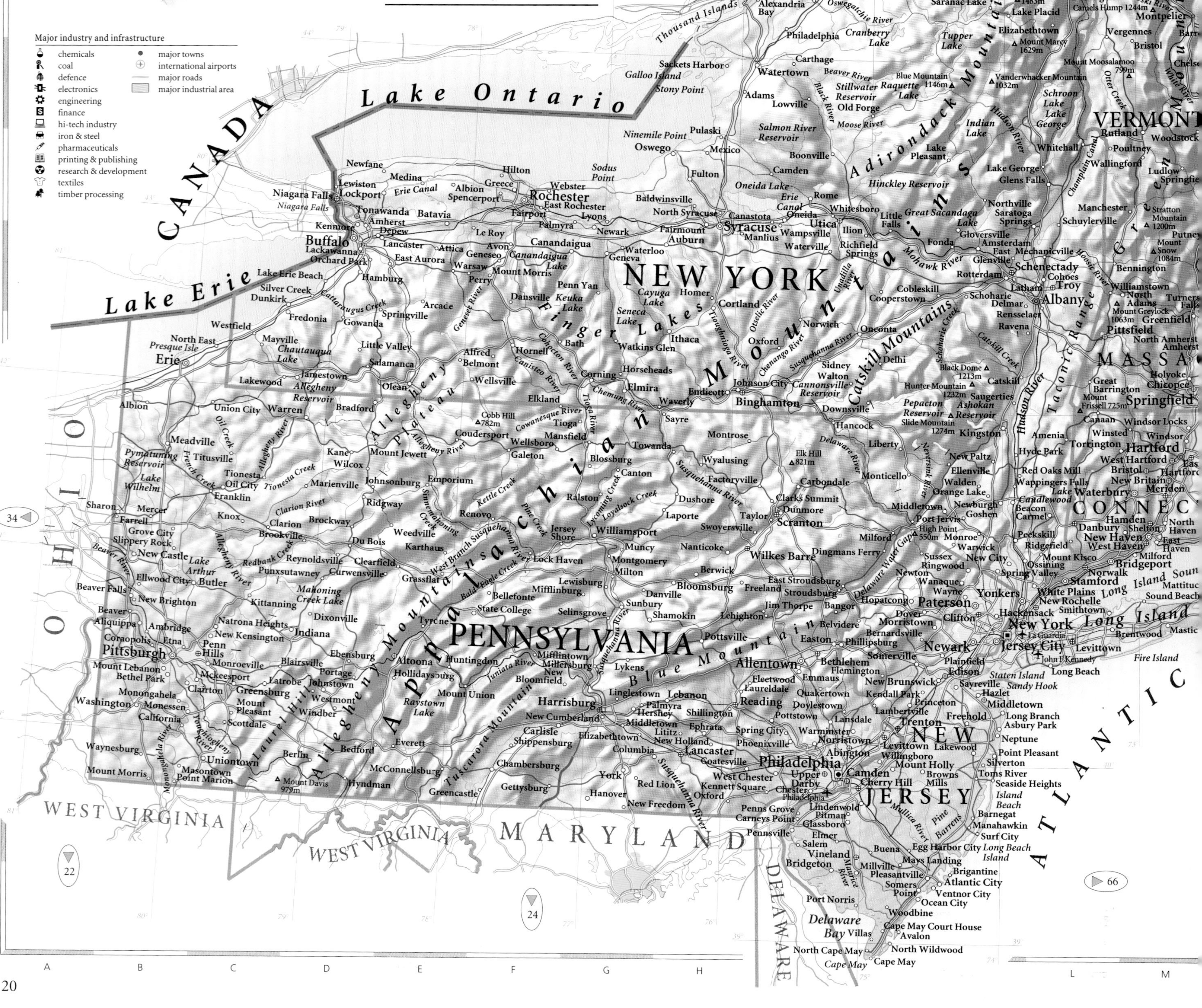

Major industry and infrastructure
- chemicals
- coal
- defence
- electronics
- engineering
- finance
- hi-tech industry
- iron & steel
- pharmaceuticals
- printing & publishing
- research & development
- textiles
- timber processing
- major towns
- international airports
- major roads
- major industrial area

(Map labels include: Lake Ontario, Lake Erie, CANADA, Saint Lawrence River, Lake Champlain, Adirondack Mountains, Catskill Mountains, Appalachian Mountains, Allegheny Plateau, Finger Lakes, NEW YORK, PENNSYLVANIA, NEW JERSEY, VERMONT, MASSACHUSETTS, CONNECTICUT, OHIO, WEST VIRGINIA, MARYLAND, DELAWARE, ATLANTIC OCEAN, and numerous cities including Buffalo, Rochester, Syracuse, Albany, Pittsburgh, Harrisburg, Philadelphia, New York, Newark, Trenton, Atlantic City, Scranton, Binghamton, and others.)

The Hancock Tower dominates the skyline of Boston's business district. New England's principal city has grown through land reclamation within Massachusetts Bay.

USING THE LAND AND SEA

PENNSYLVANIA HAS a large rural population and a major agribusiness sector dominated by livestock-raising. Fruit, vegetables and nursery plants are grown throughout the region, with fishing on the coast. Cranberries and maple syrup are traditional products in New England. Large areas of cropland in the north were returned to forest in the 20th century.

Land use and agricultural distribution

- cattle
- poultry
- cranberries
- fishing
- fodder
- fruit
- maple syrup
- timber
- major towns
- pasture
- cropland
- forest

THE URBAN/RURAL POPULATION DIVIDE

urban 78%   rural 22%

0 10 20 30 40 50 60 70 80 90 100

POPULATION DENSITY
306 people per sq mile
(118 people per sq km)

TOTAL LAND AREA
161,096 sq miles
(417,222 sq km)

Foreign competition and depletion of stocks in the Atlantic fishing grounds caused a decline in fishing in the seaboard states. Recent years have seen a gradual recovery; Massachusetts now annually ranks third or fourth in the USA in terms of the value of fish landed.

SCALE 1:2,750,000
(projection: Lambert Conformal Conic)

Km
0 5 10 20 30 40 50 60 70 80 90 100
Miles

The islands, inlets and promontories of Maine's coast extend 3500 miles (5630 km). The tidal range is particularly high, varying between 12 and 24 ft (3.7–7.3 m).

THE LANDSCAPE

THE MARSHY LOWLANDS of the Atlantic Coastal Plain dwindle towards the north, giving way to the rocky coast of Maine. Uplifted over 400 million years ago, the Appalachian Mountains have since been carved into several discrete ranges by the region's main rivers and heavily denuded by successive glacial advances. This broad upland belt, with the younger Adirondack Mountains, is bounded by the Great Lakes in the northwest.

The narrow Finger Lakes of northwestern New York State were formed by glaciers cutting into deep deposits of material from an earlier ice advance.

The Adirondack Mountains were formed when the deeply buried basement rocks were forced upwards in a dome by as much as 2 miles (3 km).

The lower Connecticut River has cut down into the flat, clay valley floor, which previously formed the bed of an ice-dammed lake.

Deposits of glacial till from the last Ice Age are up to 1000 ft (300 m) deep around Lake Ontario.

The Genesee river in New York State has eroded a canyon 800 ft (240 m) deep through the Appalachians. The river continued to cut downwards as the land was uplifted.

Green Mountains

Niagara Falls

Lake Erie, receiving water flowing from the rest of the Great Lakes, drains via the Niagara Falls, into Lake Ontario, which lies 325 ft (99 m) below.

Cape Cod

Resistant rock
Force of water continues to undercut cliffs
River fed by water from the Great Lakes
Softer rock is eroded more quickly

The Niagara Falls were created where the Niagara River reached an escarpment capped by hard limestone. This was gradually eroded exposing softer rock strata. Plunging water continues to erode the softer strata causing the falls to recede upstream.

The waterfalls at Dingmans Ferry are typical of those found in villages on the 'Fall-line', where rivers drop from the Appalachians to the coastal lowlands. These locations provide water power and are often at the navigable head of the river.

Dingmans Ferry

The Atlantic Coastal Plain is part of the continental shelf, which extends several hundred miles out to sea, providing a rich environment for marine life.

Rising sea levels have flooded river valleys along the coast, creating rias such as Long Island Sound.

Cape Cod, Long Island and the islands between them mark the top of a great terminal moraine, formed at the front of the ice sheet which once covered the land. This ridge of deposited material was subsequently flooded by rising seas.

Cape Cod

At Provincetown, Cape Cod, complex and powerful ocean currents continue to modify the shoreline, washing away some 3 ft (1 m) of the lower cape each year, while extending the beaches in the north.

USA: MID-EASTERN STATES

Delaware, District of Columbia, Kentucky, Maryland, North Carolina,
South Carolina, Tennessee, Virginia, West Virginia

KEY EVENTS IN THE HISTORY OF THE USA took place in this diverse region, which became the front line in the Civil War of 1861–65 between North and South. Strong regional contrasts exist between the fertile coastal plains, the isolated upcountry of the Appalachian Mountains and the cotton-growing areas of the Mississippi lowlands to the west. Whilst coal mining, a traditional industry in the Appalachians, has declined in recent years leaving much rural poverty, service industries elsewhere have increased, especially in the US federal capital, Washington DC.

MAP KEY

POPULATION
- 500,000 to 1 million
- 100,000 to 500,000
- 50,000 to 100,000
- 10,000 to 50,000
- below 10,000

ELEVATION
- 6000m / 19,686ft
- 4000m / 13,124ft
- 3000m / 9843ft
- 2000m / 6562ft
- 1000m / 3281ft
- 500m / 1640ft
- 250m / 820ft
- 100m / 328ft
- sea level

SCALE 1:3,000,000
(projection: Lambert Conformal Conic)

The Bluegrass region of Kentucky centres on the town of Lexington. This exceptionally fertile rolling plain is well known for its thoroughbred horse-breeding ranches.

TRANSPORT AND INDUSTRY

IN THE URBANIZED NORTHEAST, manufacturing remains important, alongside a burgeoning service sector. North Carolina is a major centre for industrial research and development. Traditional industries include Tennessee whiskey, and textiles in South Carolina. The decline of open-cast coal mining in the Appalachians has been hastened by environmental controls, although adventure-tourism is a flourishing new industry.

Major industry and infrastructure
- adventure-tourism
- car manufacture
- coal
- electronics
- engineering
- finance
- food processing
- hi-tech industry
- mining
- research & development
- textiles
- capital cities
- major towns
- international airports
- major roads
- major industrial areas

THE TRANSPORT NETWORK
- 452,218 miles (723,548 km)
- 5737 miles (8267 km)
- 18,336 miles (29,503 km)
- 4404 miles (7081 km)

Tennessee's rivers are part of an important inland bulk-transport network. Memphis is connected with New Orleans in the south, and with cities as distant as Minneapolis, Sioux City, Chicago and Pittsburgh, via the Mississippi and its tributaries.

THE LANDSCAPE

THE EASTERN TRIBUTARIES OF THE MISSISSIPPI drain the interior lowlands. The Cumberland Plateau and the parallel ranges of the Appalachians have been successively uplifted and eroded over time, with the eastern side reduced to a series of foothills known as the Piedmont. The broad coastal plain gradually falls away into salt marshes, lagoons and offshore bars, broken by flooded estuaries along the shores of the Atlantic.

The Mammoth Cave is part of an extensive cave system in the limestone region of southwestern Kentucky. It stretches for over 300 miles (485 km) on five different levels and contains three rivers and three lakes.

The Mississippi River and its tributary the Ohio River form the western border of the region.

Natural Bridge in eastern Kentucky is an arch 78 ft (26 m) long and 65 ft (20 m) high. It has been shaped from resistant sandstone by gradual weathering processes, which removed the softer rock lying underneath.

The Allegheny Mountains form the northwestern edge of the Appalachian mountain chain. Continuous folding has formed rich seams of bituminous coal.

Appalachian Mountains

Farmland on the eastern shores of Chesapeake Bay is sustained by artificial drainage. The area also provides refuge for a variety of waterfowl.

The many inlets of Chesapeake Bay are the flooded tributaries of the main river valley, which have been inundated by rising sea levels.

Salt marshes such as Great Dismal Swamp, develop where the coast is sheltered. Vast areas of such marshland have been reclaimed for farmland and settlement.

Cape Hatteras is the easternmost point of an offshore barrier island; a wave-deposited sand-bar which has become permanent, establishing its own vegetation.

Barrier islands

- Tidal inlet
- Barrier island

These intertidal mudflats become submerged at high tide

Barrier islands are common along the coasts of North and South Carolina. As sea levels rise, wave action builds up ridges of sand and pebbles parallel to the coast, separated by lagoons or intertidal mudflats, which are flooded at high tide.

The Cumberland Plateau is the most southwesterly part of the Appalachians. Big Black Mountain at 4180 ft (1274 m) is the highest point in the range.

The Great Smoky Mountains *form the western escarpment of the Appalachians. The region is heavily forested, with over 130 species of tree.*

The Blue Ridge Mountains are a steep ridge, culminating in Mount Mitchell, the highest point in the Appalachians, at 6684 ft (2037 m).

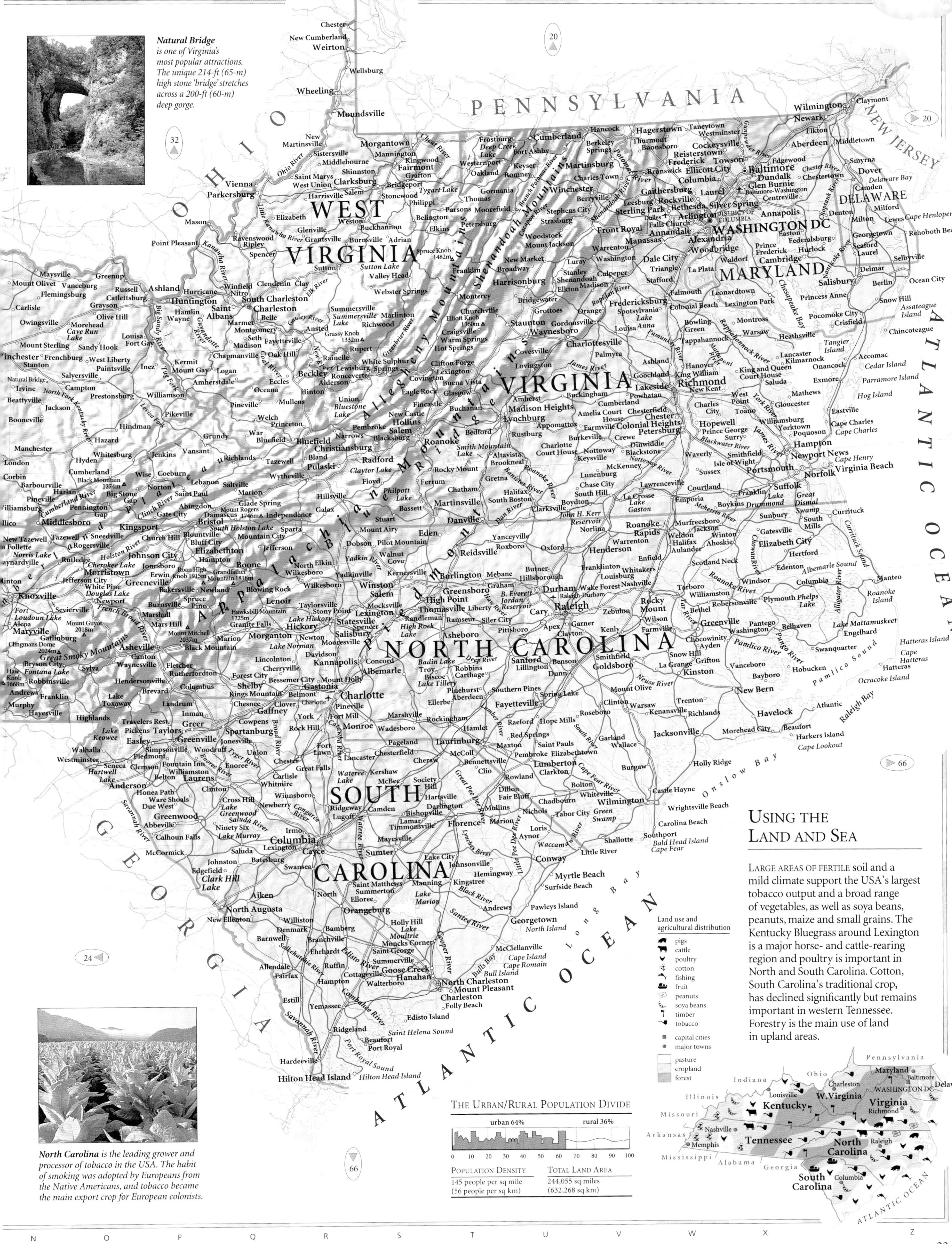

Natural Bridge
is one of Virginia's
most popular attractions.
The unique 214-ft (65-m)
high stone 'bridge' stretches
across a 200-ft (60-m)
deep gorge.

OHIO

PENNSYLVANIA

NEW JERSEY

WEST VIRGINIA

DELAWARE

WASHINGTON DC

MARYLAND

VIRGINIA

Appalachian Mountains

Allegheny Mountains

Shenandoah Mountains

Piedmont

Blue Ridge Mountains

NORTH CAROLINA

SOUTH CAROLINA

GEORGIA

ATLANTIC OCEAN

North Carolina is the leading grower and
processor of tobacco in the USA. The habit
of smoking was adopted by Europeans from
the Native Americans, and tobacco became
the main export crop for European colonists.

USING THE LAND AND SEA

LARGE AREAS OF FERTILE soil and a
mild climate support the USA's largest
tobacco output and a broad range
of vegetables, as well as soya beans,
peanuts, maize and small grains. The
Kentucky Bluegrass around Lexington
is a major horse- and cattle-rearing
region and poultry is important in
North and South Carolina. Cotton,
South Carolina's traditional crop,
has declined significantly but remains
important in western Tennessee.
Forestry is the main use of land
in upland areas.

Land use and agricultural distribution

- pigs
- cattle
- poultry
- cotton
- fishing
- fruit
- peanuts
- soya beans
- timber
- tobacco
- capital cities
- major towns
- pasture
- cropland
- forest

THE URBAN/RURAL POPULATION DIVIDE

urban 64%   rural 36%

0 10 20 30 40 50 60 70 80 90 100

POPULATION DENSITY
145 people per sq mile
(56 people per sq km)

TOTAL LAND AREA
244,055 sq miles
(632,268 sq km)

23

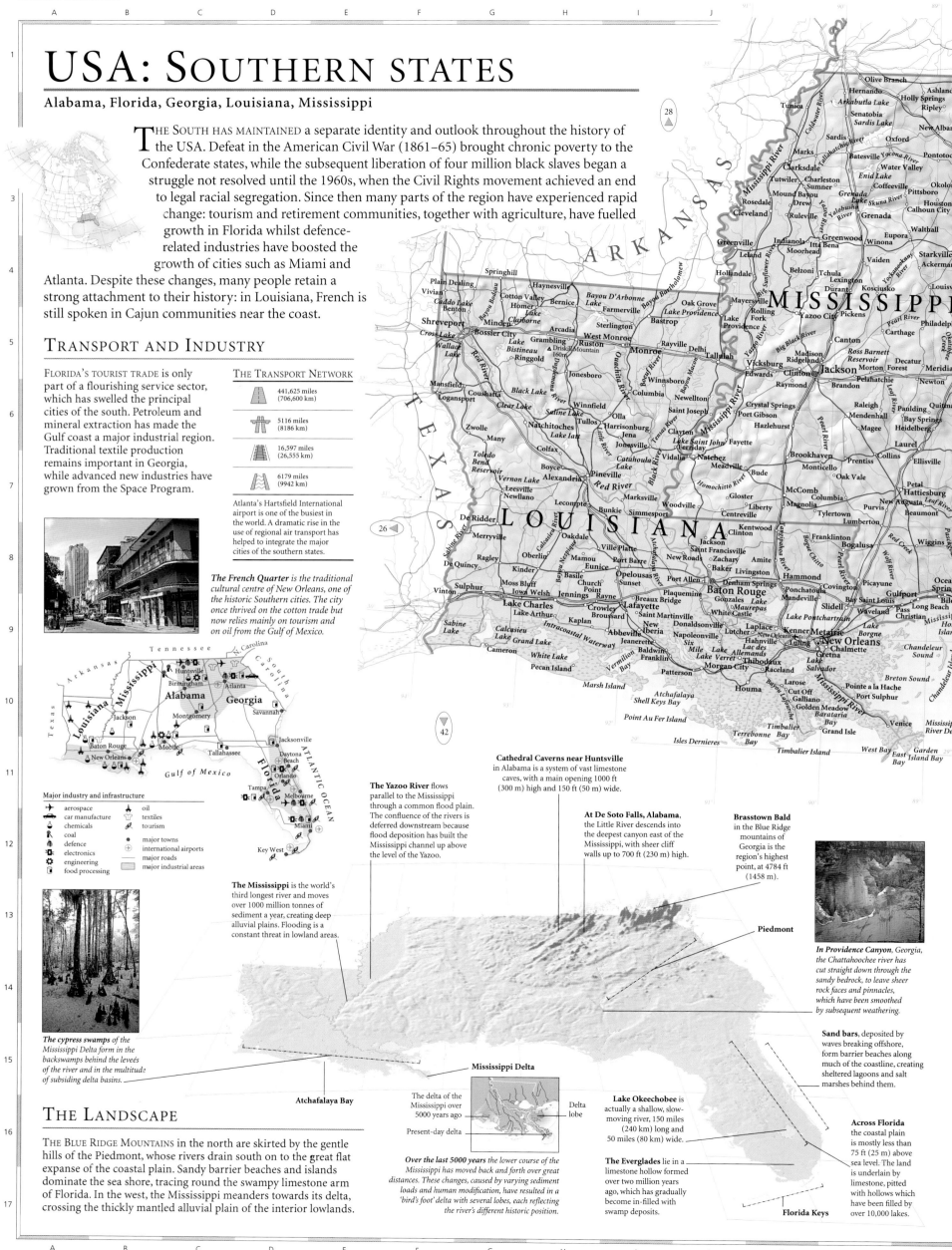

USA: SOUTHERN STATES

Alabama, Florida, Georgia, Louisiana, Mississippi

THE SOUTH HAS MAINTAINED a separate identity and outlook throughout the history of the USA. Defeat in the American Civil War (1861–65) brought chronic poverty to the Confederate states, while the subsequent liberation of four million black slaves began a struggle not resolved until the 1960s, when the Civil Rights movement achieved an end to legal racial segregation. Since then many parts of the region have experienced rapid change: tourism and retirement communities, together with agriculture, have fuelled growth in Florida whilst defence-related industries have boosted the growth of cities such as Miami and Atlanta. Despite these changes, many people retain a strong attachment to their history: in Louisiana, French is still spoken in Cajun communities near the coast.

TRANSPORT AND INDUSTRY

FLORIDA'S TOURIST TRADE is only part of a flourishing service sector, which has swelled the principal cities of the south. Petroleum and mineral extraction has made the Gulf coast a major industrial region. Traditional textile production remains important in Georgia, while advanced new industries have grown from the Space Program.

THE TRANSPORT NETWORK

441,625 miles (706,600 km)

5116 miles (8186 km)

16,597 miles (26,555 km)

6179 miles (9942 km)

Atlanta's Hartsfield International airport is one of the busiest in the world. A dramatic rise in the use of regional air transport has helped to integrate the major cities of the southern states.

The French Quarter is the traditional cultural centre of New Orleans, one of the historic Southern cities. The city once thrived on the cotton trade but now relies mainly on tourism and on oil from the Gulf of Mexico.

The cypress swamps of the Mississippi Delta form in the backswamps behind the leveés of the river and in the multitude of subsiding delta basins.

Major industry and infrastructure

- ✈ aerospace
- 🚗 car manufacture
- chemicals
- coal
- defence
- electronics
- engineering
- food processing
- oil
- textiles
- tourism
- • major towns
- ✈ international airports
- — major roads
- major industrial areas

THE LANDSCAPE

THE BLUE RIDGE MOUNTAINS in the north are skirted by the gentle hills of the Piedmont, whose rivers drain south on to the great flat expanse of the coastal plain. Sandy barrier beaches and islands dominate the sea shore, tracing round the swampy limestone arm of Florida. In the west, the Mississippi meanders towards its delta, crossing the thickly mantled alluvial plain of the interior lowlands.

The Yazoo River flows parallel to the Mississippi through a common flood plain. The confluence of the rivers is deferred downstream because flood deposition has built the Mississippi channel up above the level of the Yazoo.

The Mississippi is the world's third longest river and moves over 1000 million tonnes of sediment a year, creating deep alluvial plains. Flooding is a constant threat in lowland areas.

Cathedral Caverns near Huntsville in Alabama is a system of vast limestone caves, with a main opening 1000 ft (300 m) high and 150 ft (50 m) wide.

At De Soto Falls, Alabama, the Little River descends into the deepest canyon east of the Mississippi, with sheer cliff walls up to 700 ft (230 m) high.

Brasstown Bald in the Blue Ridge mountains of Georgia is the region's highest point, at 4784 ft (1458 m).

Piedmont

In Providence Canyon, Georgia, the Chattahoochee river has cut straight down through the sandy bedrock, to leave sheer rock faces and pinnacles, which have been smoothed by subsequent weathering.

Sand bars, deposited by waves breaking offshore, form barrier beaches along much of the coastline, creating sheltered lagoons and salt marshes behind them.

Atchafalaya Bay

Mississippi Delta

The delta of the Mississippi over 5000 years ago

Present-day delta

Delta lobe

Over the last 5000 years the lower course of the Mississippi has moved back and forth over great distances. These changes, caused by varying sediment loads and human modification, have resulted in a 'bird's foot' delta with several lobes, each reflecting the river's different historic position.

Lake Okeechobee is actually a shallow, slow-moving river, 150 miles (240 km) long and 50 miles (80 km) wide.

The Everglades lie in a limestone hollow formed over two million years ago, which has gradually become in-filled with swamp deposits.

Across Florida the coastal plain is mostly less than 75 ft (25 m) above sea level. The land is underlain by limestone, pitted with hollows which have been filled by over 10,000 lakes.

Florida Keys

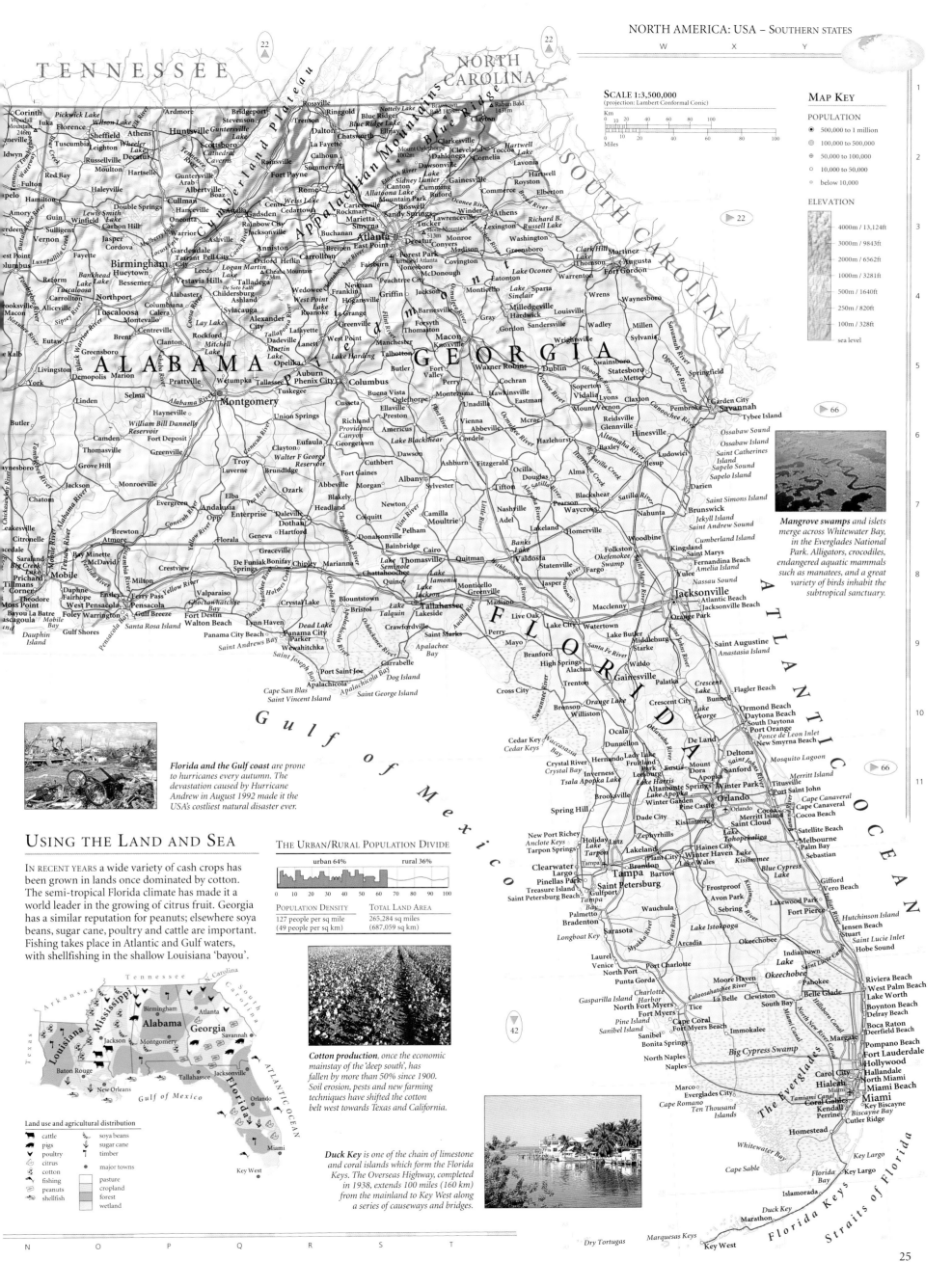

SCALE 1:3,500,000
(projection: Lambert Conformal Conic)

MAP KEY

POPULATION
- 500,000 to 1 million
- 100,000 to 500,000
- 50,000 to 100,000
- 10,000 to 50,000
- below 10,000

ELEVATION
- 4000m / 13,124ft
- 3000m / 9843ft
- 2000m / 6562ft
- 1000m / 3281ft
- 500m / 1640ft
- 250m / 820ft
- 100m / 328ft
- sea level

Mangrove swamps and islets merge across Whitewater Bay, in the Everglades National Park. Alligators, crocodiles, endangered aquatic mammals such as manatees, and a great variety of birds inhabit the subtropical sanctuary.

Florida and the Gulf coast are prone to hurricanes every autumn. The devastation caused by Hurricane Andrew in August 1992 made it the USA's costliest natural disaster ever.

USING THE LAND AND SEA

IN RECENT YEARS a wide variety of cash crops has been grown in lands once dominated by cotton. The semi-tropical Florida climate has made it a world leader in the growing of citrus fruit. Georgia has a similar reputation for peanuts; elsewhere soya beans, sugar cane, poultry and cattle are important. Fishing takes place in Atlantic and Gulf waters, with shellfishing in the shallow Louisiana 'bayou'.

THE URBAN/RURAL POPULATION DIVIDE

urban 64%   rural 36%

POPULATION DENSITY	TOTAL LAND AREA
127 people per sq mile (49 people per sq km)	265,284 sq miles (687,059 sq km)

Cotton production, once the economic mainstay of the 'deep south', has fallen by more than 50% since 1900. Soil erosion, pests and new farming techniques have shifted the cotton belt west towards Texas and California.

Duck Key is one of the chain of limestone and coral islands which form the Florida Keys. The Overseas Highway, completed in 1938, extends 100 miles (160 km) from the mainland to Key West along a series of causeways and bridges.

Land use and agricultural distribution
- cattle
- pigs
- poultry
- citrus
- cotton
- fishing
- peanuts
- soya beans
- sugar cane
- timber
- major towns
- pasture
- cropland
- forest
- wetland

USA: TEXAS

First explored by Spaniards moving north from Mexico in search of gold, Texas was controlled by Spain and then Mexico, before becoming an independent republic in 1836, and joining the Union of States in 1845. During the 19th century, many of the migrants who came to Texas raised cattle on the abundant land; in the 20th century, they were joined by prospectors attracted by the promise of oil riches. Today, although natural resources, especially oil, still form the basis of its wealth, the diversified Texan economy includes thriving hi-tech and finance industries. The major urban centres, home to 80% of the population, lie in the south and east, and include Houston, the 'oil-city', and Dallas–Fort Worth. Hispanic influences remain strong, especially in the south and west.

Dallas was founded in 1841 as a prairie trading post and its development was stimulated by the arrival of railroads. Cotton and then oil funded the town's early growth. Today, the modern, high-rise skyline of Dallas reflects the city's position as a leading centre of banking, insurance and the petroleum industry in the southwest.

USING THE LAND

Cotton production and livestock-raising, particularly cattle, dominate farming, although crop failures and the demands of local markets have led to some diversification. Following the introduction of modern farming techniques, cotton production spread out from the east to the plains of western Texas. Cattle ranches are widespread, while sheep and goats are raised on the dry Edwards Plateau.

Land use and agricultural distribution
- cattle
- goats
- sheep
- cereals
- cotton
- • major towns

pasture
cropland
forest
barren

THE URBAN/RURAL POPULATION DIVIDE

urban 80%   rural 20%

0 10 20 30 40 50 60 70 80 90 100

38 ◀

POPULATION DENSITY
73 people per sq mile
(28 people per sq km)

TOTAL LAND AREA
267,338 sq miles
(692,402 sq km)

The huge cattle ranches of Texas developed during the 19th century when land was plentiful and could be acquired cheaply. Today, more cattle and sheep are raised in Texas than in any other state.

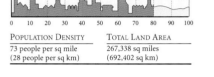
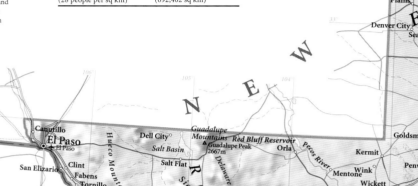

THE LANDSCAPE

Texas is made up of a series of massive steps descending from the mountains and high plains of the west and northwest to the coastal lowlands in the southeast. Many of the state's borders are delineated by water. The Rio Grande flows from the Rocky Mountains to the Gulf of Mexico, marking the border with Mexico.

Cap Rock Escarpment juts out from the plains, running 200 miles (320 km) from north to south. Its height varies from 300 ft (90 m) rising to sheer cliffs up to 1000 ft (300 m).

42 ◀

The Llano Estacado or Staked Plain in northern Texas is known for its harsh environment. In the north, freezing winds carrying ice and snow sweep down from the Rocky Mountains, and to the south, sandstorms frequently blow up, scouring anything in their paths. Flash floods, in the wide, flat river beds that remain dry for most of the year, are another hazard.

The Guadalupe Mountains lie in the southern Rocky Mountains. They incorporate Guadalupe Peak, the highest in Texas, rising 8749 ft (2667 m).

The Rio Grande flows from the Rocky Mountains through semi-arid land, supporting sparse vegetation. The river actually shrinks along its course, losing more water through evaporation and seepage than it gains from its tributaries and rainfall.

Big Bend National Park

The Red River flows for 1300 miles (2090 km), marking most of the northern border of Texas. A dam and reservoir along its course provide vital irrigation and hydro-electric power to the surrounding area.

Sabine River

Extensive forests of pine and cypress grow in the eastern corner of the coastal lowlands where the average rainfall is 45 inches (1145 mm) a year. This is higher than the rest of the state and over twice the average in the west.

In the coastal lowlands of southeastern Texas the Earth's crust is warping, causing the land to subside and allowing the sea to invade. Around Galveston, the rate of downward tilting is 6 inches (15 cm) per year. Erosion of the coast is also exacerbated by hurricanes.

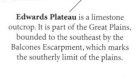
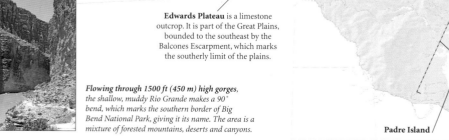

Edwards Plateau is a limestone outcrop. It is part of the Great Plains, bounded to the southeast by the Balcones Escarpment, which marks the southerly limit of the plains.

Flowing through 1500 ft (450 m) high gorges, the shallow, muddy Rio Grande makes a 90° bend, which marks the southern border of Big Bend National Park, giving it its name. The area is a mixture of forested mountains, deserts and canyons.

Laguna Madre in southern Texas has been almost completely cut off from the sea by Padre Island. This sand bank was created by wave action, carrying and depositing material along the coast. The process is known as longshore drift.

Padre Island

Oil deposits

Oil trapped by fault

Oil deposits migrate through reservoir rocks such as shale

Oil accumulates beneath impermeable cap rock

Impermeable rock strata

Salt dome

Oil deposits are found beneath much of Texas. They collect as oil migrates upwards through porous layers of rock until it is trapped, either by a cap of rock above a salt dome, or by a fault line which exposes impermeable rock through which the oil cannot rise.

TRANSPORT AND INDUSTRY

INDUSTRY IN THE 20TH CENTURY was largely concentrated on the processing of local raw materials, especially oil – deposits were discovered under 65% of the state's area. The technological demands of the oil industry and defence-related institutions, particularly NASA, have stimulated the development of numerous electronics and hi-tech firms which, alongside many national corporate headquarters, are based in Dallas–Fort Worth and Houston.

Major industry and infrastructure

- chemicals
- defence
- engineering
- finance
- food processing
- gas
- hi-tech industry
- mining
- oil
- textiles
- major towns
- international airports
- major roads
- major industrial areas

THE TRANSPORT NETWORK

293,509 miles (496,614 km)	3229 miles (5166 km)
10,681 miles (17,089 km)	845 miles (1359 km)

The sheer size of Texas promoted the development of an extensive road and rail network. The highway system, although well-developed, is concentrated in the east.

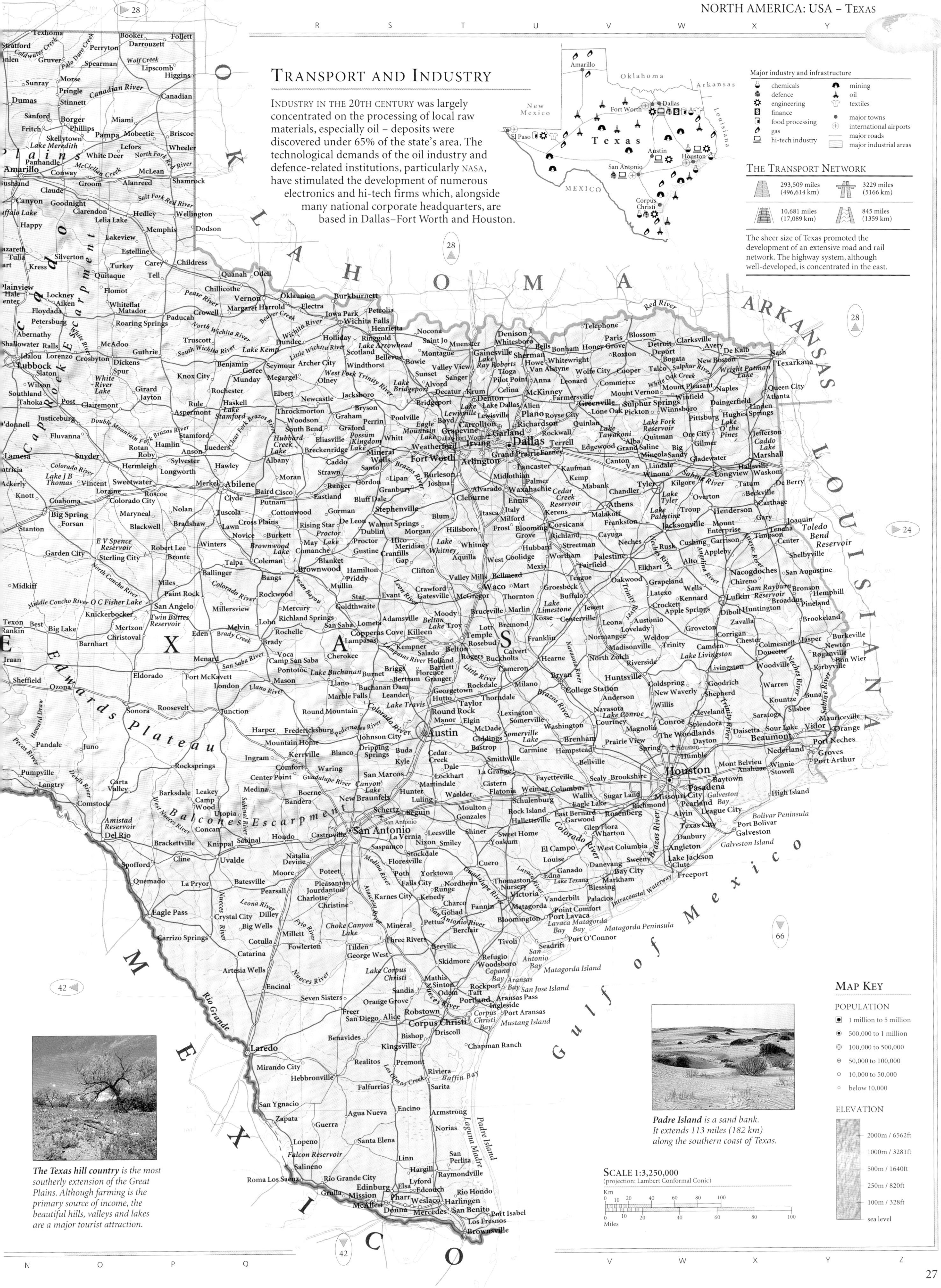

The Texas hill country is the most southerly extension of the Great Plains. Although farming is the primary source of income, the beautiful hills, valleys and lakes are a major tourist attraction.

Padre Island is a sand bank. It extends 113 miles (182 km) along the southern coast of Texas.

SCALE 1:3,250,000
(projection: Lambert Conformal Conic)

Km 0 10 20 40 60 80 100
Miles 0 20 40 60 80 100

MAP KEY

POPULATION

- 1 million to 5 million
- 500,000 to 1 million
- 100,000 to 500,000
- 50,000 to 100,000
- 10,000 to 50,000
- below 10,000

ELEVATION

- 2000m / 6562ft
- 1000m / 3281ft
- 500m / 1640ft
- 250m / 820ft
- 100m / 328ft
- sea level

USA: SOUTH MIDWESTERN STATES

Arkansas, Kansas, Missouri, Oklahoma

THE EXPANSION OF THE USA focused on this region in the mid-19th century. Settlers spread from the confluence of the Missouri and Mississippi rivers up onto the Great Plains. This treeless expanse, which early explorers had called the 'Great American Desert', was turned into one of the world's richest agricultural regions; but periodic droughts, coupled with over-intensive farming, led to the 'Dustbowl' soil erosion crisis of the 1930s, the abandonment of many farms, and a mass exodus to the west coast. The land has since recovered, although the mechanization of agriculture has led to a decline in the rural population. In recent years, suburban residential development has spread rapidly across the wooded Ozark Plateau in the east of the region.

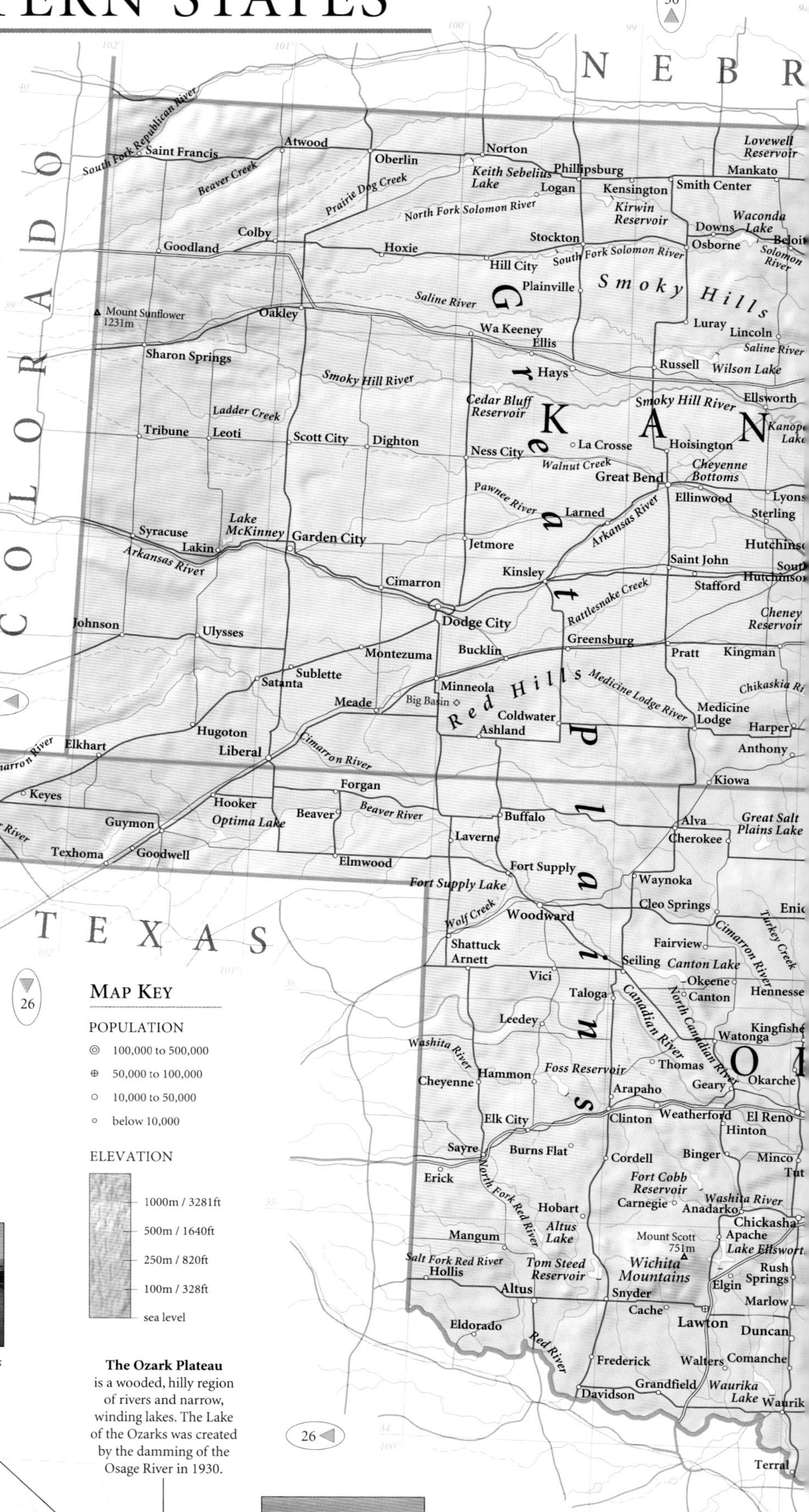

TRANSPORT AND INDUSTRY

THE PROCESSING OF AGRICULTURAL PRODUCTS, such as brewing and meat packing, has been traditionally important in these states. In Kansas and Oklahoma, diversified manufacturing now supplements income from fossil fuels; Wichita has become a world centre for aeronautical engineering, an industry which also employs many people in neighbouring Missouri.

Major industry and infrastructure

- ✈ aerospace
- ⚙ engineering
- ⑤ finance
- 🏭 food processing
- ◊ gas
- ⛏ mining
- 🛢 oil
- 🚗 vehicle manufacture
- • major towns
- ⊕ international airports
- — major roads
- major industrial areas

Agricultural produce from the plains is moved by barges along the Mississippi. The river now carries a far greater tonnage of freight than any other waterway system in the USA.

THE LANDSCAPE

MOST OF THE REGION consists of high, treeless plains, which gradually descend east from the Rocky Mountains. Drainage follows this slope, with rivers flowing towards the alluvial lowlands of the Mississippi in the southeast. Between the plains and the lowlands lie various ranges of wooded hills, including the deeply incised Ozark Plateau.

Collapsed limestone caverns led to the formation of Big Basin in Kansas; a depression 100 ft (33 m) deep and 1 mile (1.6 km) wide.

The Great Salt Plains of northern Oklahoma cover 45 sq miles (116 sq km). The arid, white flats were left by the gradual evaporation of an ancient salt lake.

Underground water reserves

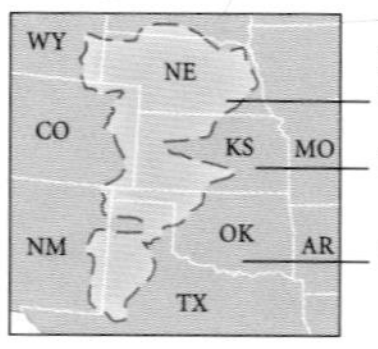

The Ogallala Aquifer, beneath the Great Plains, is the largest known source of underground water in the world. There is concern about the rapid depletion of this finite water supply by irrigation schemes.

Flint Hills is the region's easternmost major escarpment. Steep, grassy uplands are interspersed with rocky, wooded ravines and outcrops of limestone and chert.

Red River

Devil's Den is a dry badland area. The rugged landscape, strewn with large boulders, is the eroded remnant of a spur extending from the Arbuckle mountains to the west.

Ouachita Mountains

THE TRANSPORT NETWORK

380,307 miles (608,491 km)	4068 miles (6508 km)
16,185 miles (25,896 km)	1994 miles (3208 km)

The Arkansas River and its tributaries allow access to over half of the USA's navigable inland waterways. A system of locks and dams along the river provides Tulsa in Oklahoma with a navigable water route to the Gulf of Mexico.

MAP KEY

POPULATION

- ◉ 100,000 to 500,000
- ⊕ 50,000 to 100,000
- ○ 10,000 to 50,000
- ○ below 10,000

ELEVATION

- 1000m / 3281ft
- 500m / 1640ft
- 250m / 820ft
- 100m / 328ft
- sea level

The Ozark Plateau is a wooded, hilly region of rivers and narrow, winding lakes. The Lake of the Ozarks was created by the damming of the Osage River in 1930.

The Mississippi, North America's longest river, is joined by the Missouri, its main tributary, on a flood plain which spreads south to the Gulf of Mexico.

Missouri River

Lake Ouachita, in Arkansas is one of a number of irregularly-shaped lakes found among the ridges of the Ouachita Mountains.

Mississippi river

Crowleys Ridge is a long, sandy ridge, rising from the Mississippi flood plain. It was formed over thousands of years by the deposition of sand blown eastwards from the Great Plains.

SCALE 1:3,000,000
(projection: Lambert Conformal Conic)

Km
0 5 10 20 30 40 50 60 70

Miles
0 5 10 20 30 40 50 60 70

The landscape of northeast Kansas is interlaced by rivers which have cut broad wooded valleys through the gentle hills. All the rivers in Kansas form part of the massive Missouri/Mississippi drainage basin.

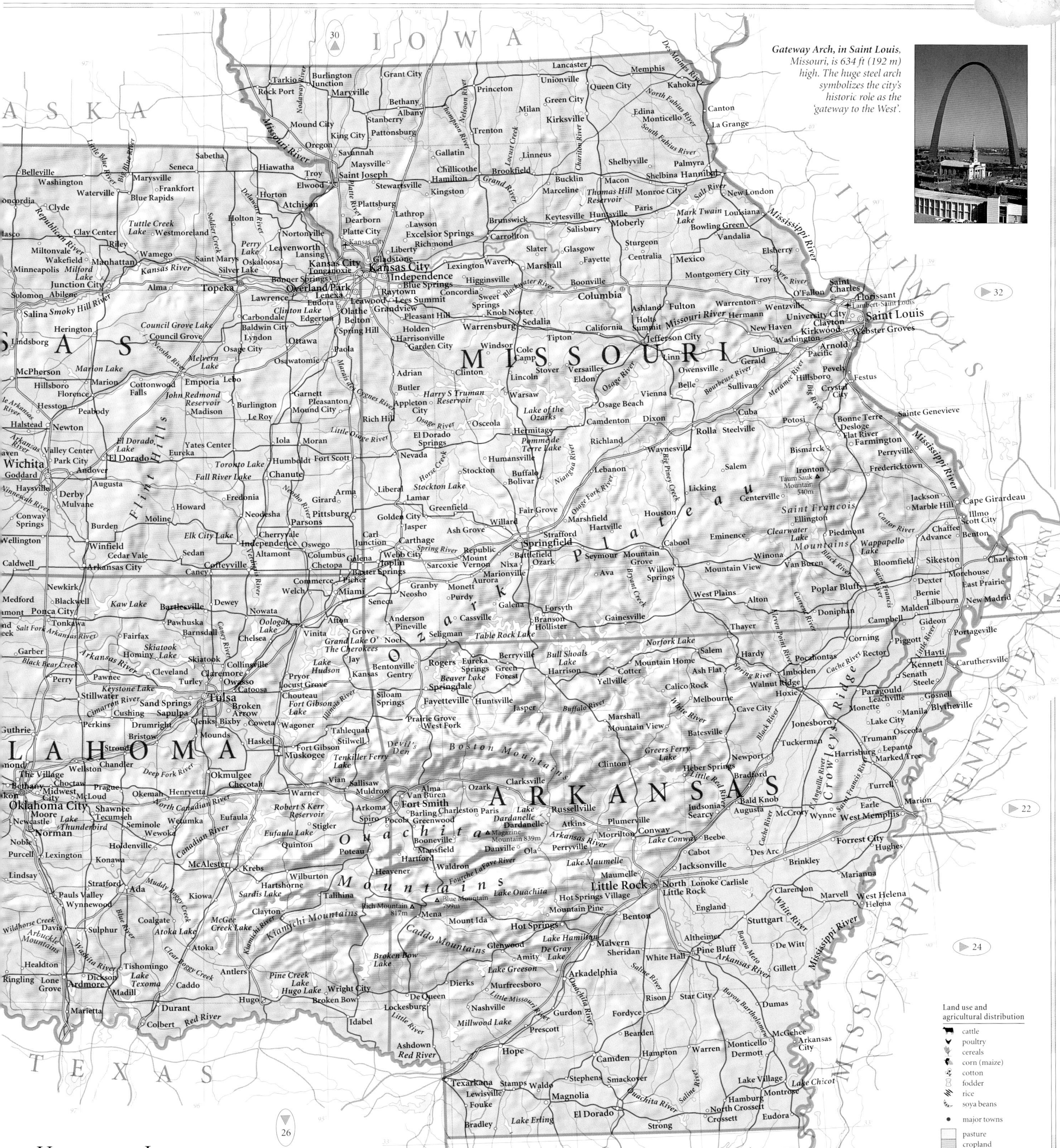

IOWA

NEBRASKA

KANSAS

MISSOURI

OKLAHOMA

ARKANSAS

TEXAS

LOUISIANA

ILLINOIS

KENTUCKY

TENNESSEE

Gateway Arch, in Saint Louis, Missouri, is 634 ft (192 m) high. The huge steel arch symbolizes the city's historic role as the 'gateway to the West'.

USING THE LAND

THE PROBLEMS of a harsh continental climate, with severe winters and hot, dry summers, are partially offset by the rich soils of the plains. Kansas is a major cereal producer, ranking first in the USA for the production of wheat and sorghum. Rainfall increases towards the east, favouring the cultivation of soya beans, cotton and rice, with corn concentrated in Missouri. Huge herds of cattle are raised in Oklahoma, Kansas and Missouri.

A combine harvester works the land on the great plains. A hundred years ago this region, also known as the prairies – the French word for pasture – was covered with tall, wild grasses.

THE URBAN/RURAL POPULATION DIVIDE

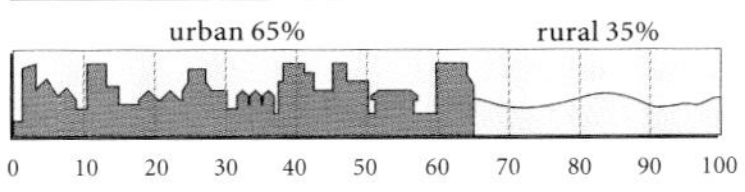

urban 65%   rural 35%

POPULATION DENSITY	TOTAL LAND AREA
50 people per sq mile (19 people per sq km)	274,900 sq miles (712,177 sq km)

Land use and agricultural distribution
- cattle
- poultry
- cereals
- corn (maize)
- cotton
- fodder
- rice
- soya beans
- • major towns
- pasture
- cropland
- forest

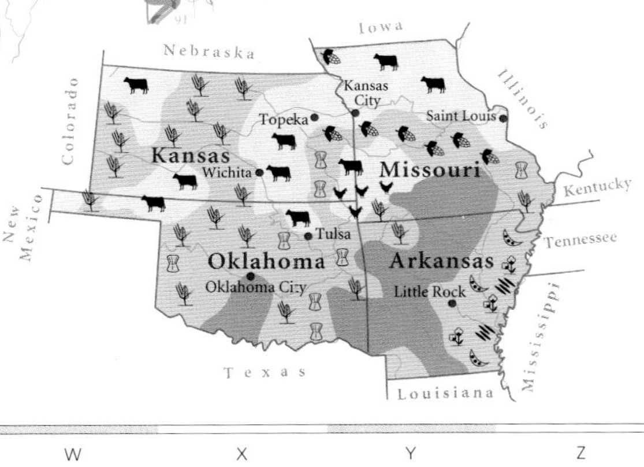

USA: NORTH MIDWESTERN STATES

C

Iowa, Minnesota, Nebraska, North Dakota, South Dakota

LYING AT THE VERY HEART of the North American continent, much of this region was acquired from France as part of the Louisiana Purchase in 1803. The area was largely by-passed by the early waves of westward migrants. When Europeans did settle, during the 19th century, they displaced the Native Americans who lived on the plains. The settlers planted arable crops and raised cattle on the immensely fertile prairie land, founding an agrarian tradition which flourishes today. Most of this region remains rural; of the five states, only in Minnesota has there been significant diversification away from agriculture and resource-based industries into the hi-tech and service sectors.

USING THE LAND

THE POPULAR IMAGE of these states as agricultural is entirely justified; prairies stretch uninterrupted across most of the area. Croplands fall into two regions: the wheat belt of the plains, and the corn belt of the central USA. Cash crops, such as soya beans, are grown to supplement incomes. Livestock, particularly pigs and cattle, are raised throughout this region.

Dark, fertile prairie soils in the southeast provide Minnesota's most productive farmland. Hot, humid summers create a long growing season for corn cultivation.

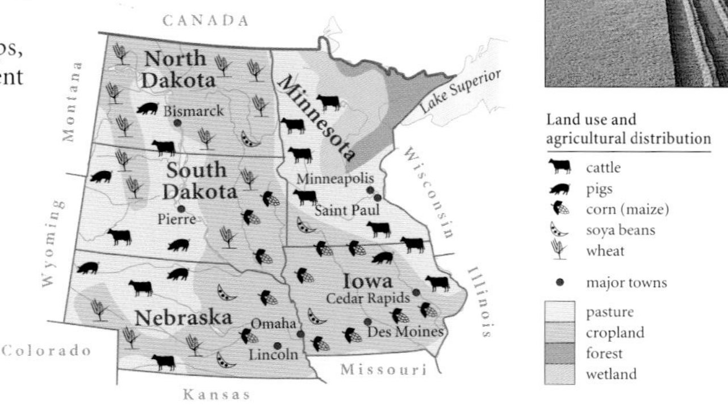

THE URBAN/RURAL POPULATION DIVIDE

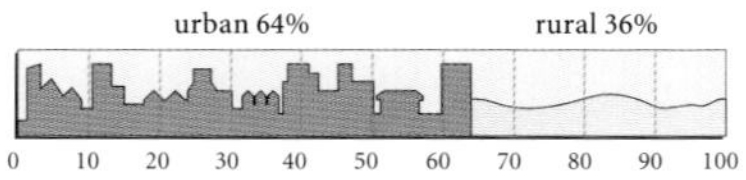

urban 64%   rural 36%

0 10 20 30 40 50 60 70 80 90 100

POPULATION DENSITY	TOTAL LAND AREA
29 people per sq mile (11 people per sq km)	365,287 sq miles (946,056 sq km)

Land use and agricultural distribution
- cattle
- pigs
- corn (maize)
- soya beans
- wheat
- major towns
- pasture
- cropland
- forest
- wetland

TRANSPORT AND INDUSTRY

FOOD PROCESSING and the production of farm machinery are supported by the large agricultural sector. Mineral exploitation is also an important activity: gold is mined in the ore-rich Black Hills of South Dakota, and both North Dakota and Nebraska are emerging as major petroleum producers.

Water erosion along the Little Missouri River has carried away sedimentary deposits, creating rugged landscapes known as badlands.

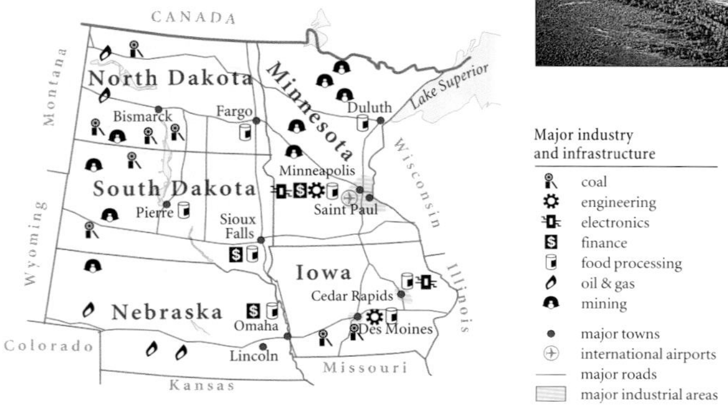

THE TRANSPORT NETWORK

504,522 miles (807,235 km)		3422 miles (5475 km)	
16,940 miles (27,104 km)		683 miles (1098 km)	

Nebraska's central location has made it an important transport artery for east–west traffic. Minnesota's road network radiates out from the hub of the twin cities, Minneapolis–Saint Paul.

Major industry and infrastructure
- coal
- engineering
- electronics
- finance
- food processing
- oil & gas
- mining
- major towns
- international airports
- major roads
- major industrial areas

THE LANDSCAPE

THESE STATES STRADDLE the Great Plains and the lowlands of the central USA, with Minnesota lying in a transition zone between the eastern forests and the prairies. The region was shaped by repeated ice advances and retreats, leaving a flat relief, broken only by the numerous lakes and broad river networks which drain the prairies.

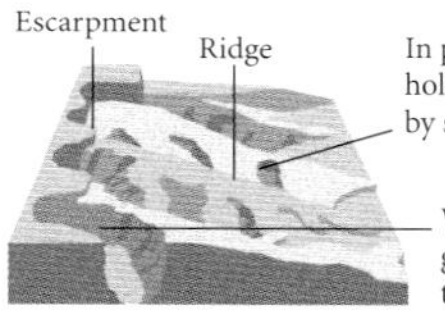

Escarpment   Ridge

In permeable strata hollows are formed by small mudslides

Water flowing into gullies erodes back the escarpment

Badlands are formed by stormwater run-off which flows down the impermeable strata of the escarpment and saturates the permeable strata leading to mudslides and the formation of gullies.

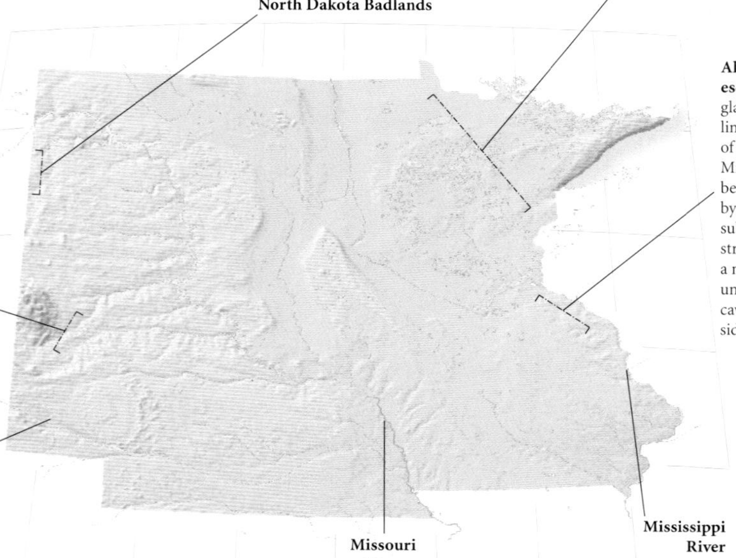

North Dakota Badlands

The Minnesota landscape contains many post-glacial features, including its numerous lakes, boulder-strewn hills and mineral-rich deposits.

Although it escaped the last glaciation, the limestone bedrock of southeastern Minnesota has been eroded by surface and subterranean streams, leaving a network of underground caverns and steep-sided valleys.

In the badlands of North and South Dakota, horizontal layers of sandstone have been eroded by rivers, leaving a landscape of narrow gullies, sharp crests and pinnacles.

South Dakota Badlands

Chimney Rock is a remnant of an ancient land surface, eroded by the North Platte River. The tip of its spire stands 500 ft (150 m) above the plain.

Missouri River

Mississippi River

In northeastern Iowa, the Mississippi and its tributaries have deeply incised the underlying bedrock creating a hilly terrain, with bluffs standing 300 ft (90 m) above the valley.

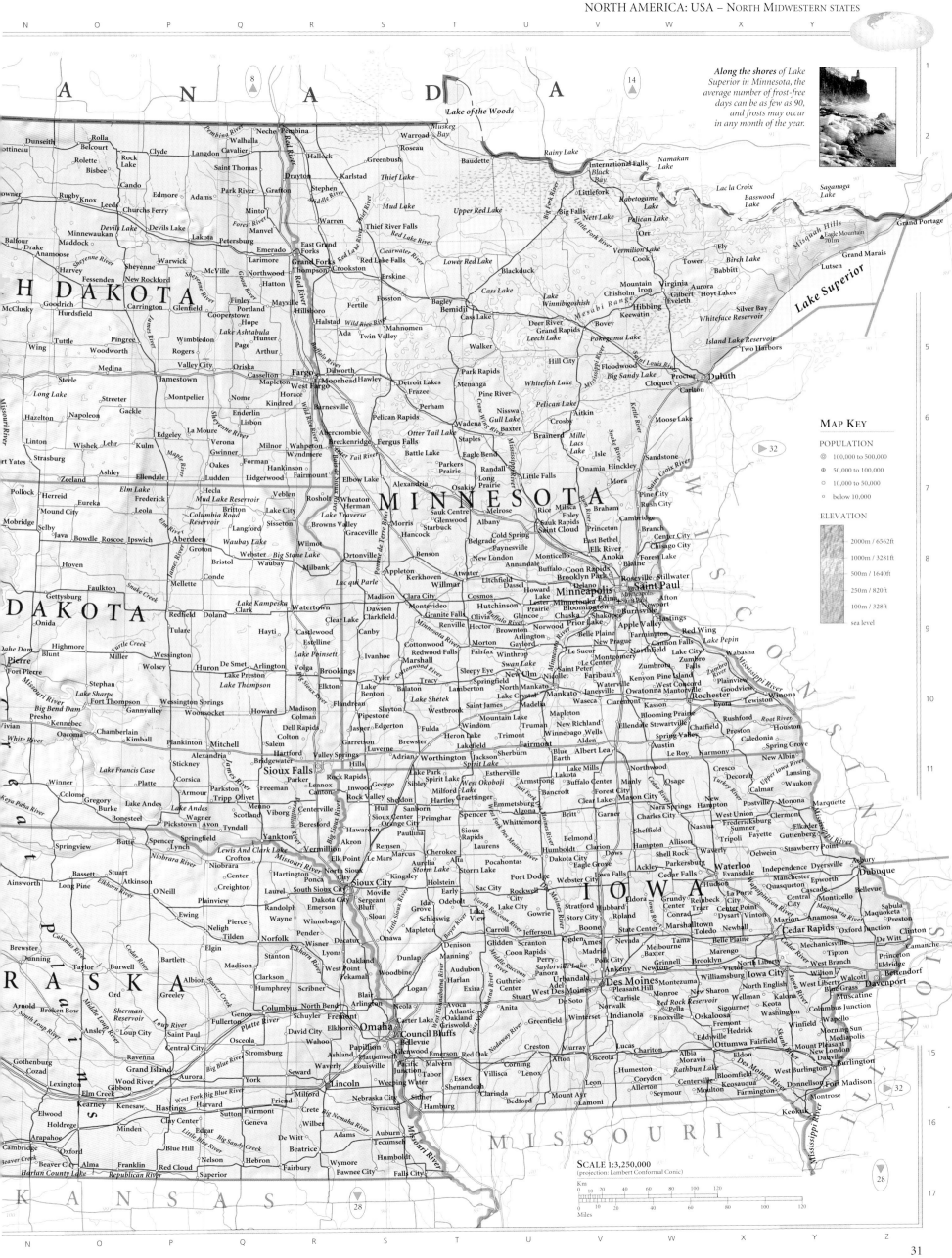

Along the shores of Lake Superior in Minnesota, the average number of frost-free days can be as few as 90, and frosts may occur in any month of the year.

USA: GREAT LAKES STATES

Illinois, Indiana, Michigan, Ohio, Wisconsin

THE STATES BORDERING THE GREAT LAKES developed rapidly in the second half of the 19th century as a result of improvements in communications: rail to the west and waterways to the south and east. Fertile land and good links with growing eastern seaboard cities encouraged the development of agriculture and food processing. Migrants from Europe and other parts of the USA flooded into the region and for much of the 20th century the region's economy boomed. However, in recent years heavy industry has declined, earning the region the unwanted label the 'Rustbelt'.

TRANSPORT AND INDUSTRY

THE GREAT LAKES REGION IS THE CENTRE of the USA's car industry. Since the early part of the 20th century, its prosperity has been closely linked to the fortunes of automobile manufacturing. Iron and steel production has expanded to meet demand from this industry. In the 1970s, nationwide recession, cheaper foreign competition in the automobile sector, pollution in and around the Great Lakes and the collapse of the meat-packing industry, centred on Chicago, forced these states to diversify their industrial base. New industries have emerged, notably electronics, service and finance industries.

THE TRANSPORT NETWORK

540,682 miles (865,091 km)	6550 miles (10,480 km)
24,928 miles (39,884 km)	2330 miles (3748 km)

Few areas of the USA have a comparable transport system. Chicago is a principal transport terminus with a dense network of roads, railways and Interstate freeways radiating from the city.

Ever since Ransom Olds and Henry Ford started mass-producing automobiles in Detroit early in the 20th century, the city's name has become synonymous with the American automotive industry.

Major industry and infrastructure

- car manufacture
- coal
- electronics
- engineering
- finance
- food processing
- iron & steel
- oil
- research & development
- textiles
- major towns
- international airports
- major roads
- major industrial areas

THE LANDSCAPE

MUCH OF THIS REGION shows the impact of glaciation which lasted until about 10,000 years ago, and extended as far south as Illinois and Ohio. Although the relief of the region slopes towards the Great Lakes, because the ice sheets blocked northerly drainage, most of the rivers today flow southwards, forming part of the massive Mississippi/Missouri drainage basin.

The dunes near Sleeping Bear Point rise 400 ft (120 m) from the banks of Lake Michigan. They are constantly being resculpted by wind action.

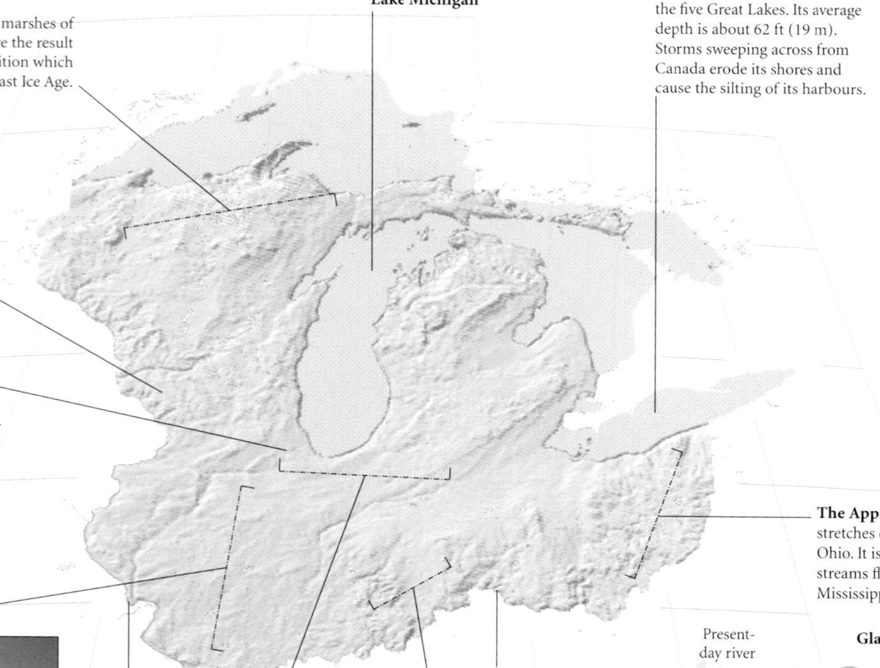

Lake Michigan

Lake Erie is the shallowest of the five Great Lakes. Its average depth is about 62 ft (19 m). Storms sweeping across from Canada erode its shores and cause the silting of its harbours.

The many lakes and marshes of Wisconsin and Michigan are the result of glacial erosion and deposition which occurred during the last Ice Age.

Southwestern Wisconsin is known as a 'driftless' area. Unlike most of the region, low hills protected it from erosion by the advancing ice sheet.

Most of the water used in northern Illinois is pumped from underground reservoirs. Due to increased demand, many areas now face a water shortage. Around Joliet, the water table was lowered by more than 700 ft (210 m) over the last century.

Illinois plains

The plains of Illinois are characteristic of drift landscapes, scoured and flattened by glacial erosion and covered with fertile glacial deposits.

Mississippi River

Relict landforms from the last glaciation, such as shallow basins and ridges, cover all but the south of this region. Ridges, known as moraines, up to 300 ft (100 m) high, lie to the south of Lake Michigan.

Ohio River

Unlike the level prairie to the north, southern Indiana is relatively rugged. Limestone in the hills has been dissolved by water, producing features such as sinkholes and underground caves.

The Appalachian plateau stretches eastward from Ohio. It is dissected by streams flowing west into the Mississippi and Ohio rivers.

Glacial till

- Present-day river or stream
- Channels caused by outwash from melting glacier
- Most recent till deposits
- Older till sheet
- Bedrock

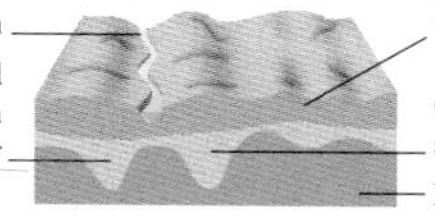

As a result of successive glacial depositions, the total depth of till along the former southern margin of the Laurentide ice sheet can exceed 1300 ft (400 m).

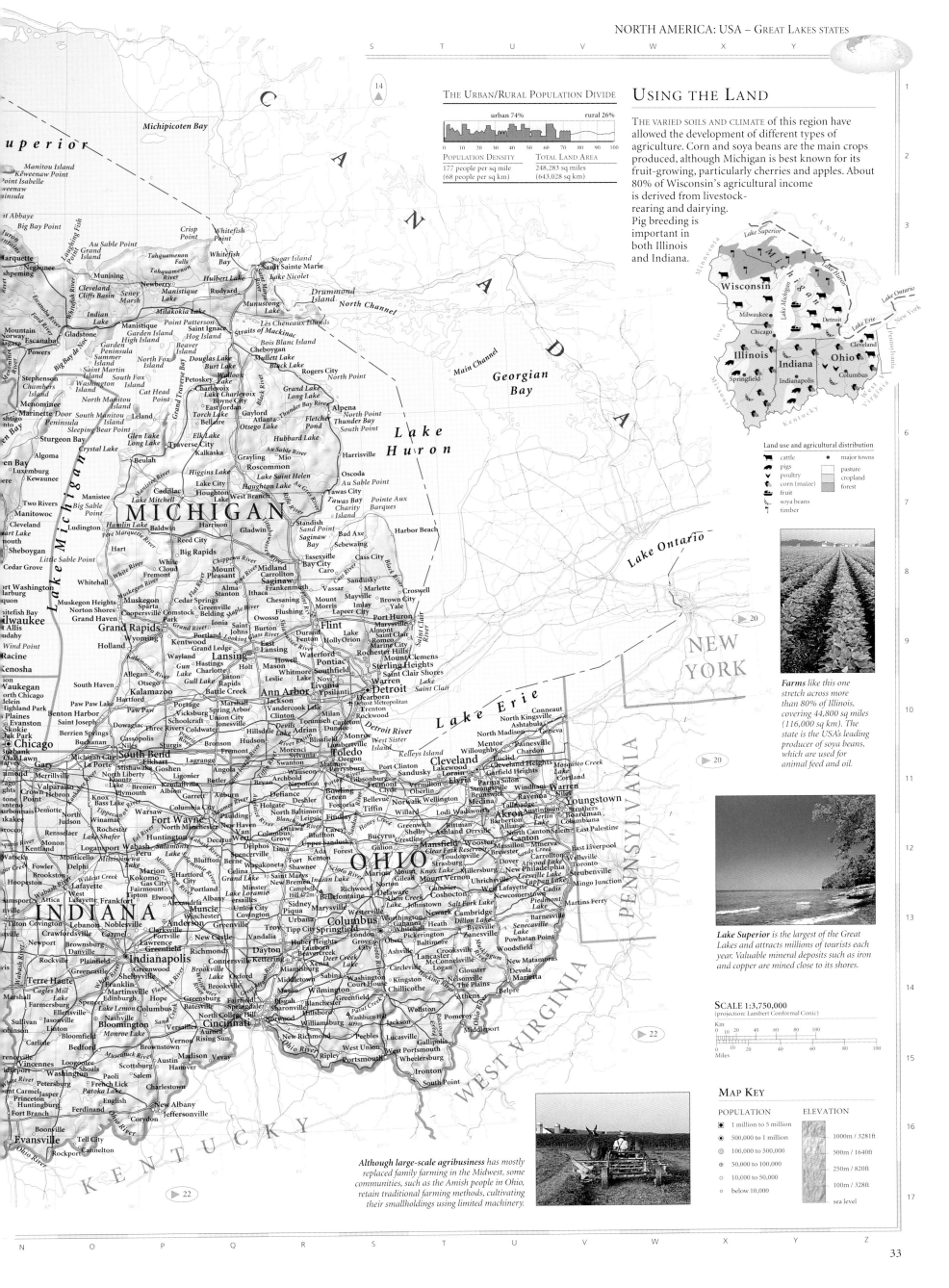

THE URBAN/RURAL POPULATION DIVIDE

urban 74%   rural 26%

POPULATION DENSITY	TOTAL LAND AREA
177 people per sq mile (68 people per sq km)	248,283 sq miles (643,028 sq km)

USING THE LAND

THE VARIED SOILS AND CLIMATE of this region have allowed the development of different types of agriculture. Corn and soya beans are the main crops produced, although Michigan is best known for its fruit-growing, particularly cherries and apples. About 80% of Wisconsin's agricultural income is derived from livestock-rearing and dairying. Pig breeding is important in both Illinois and Indiana.

Land use and agricultural distribution

- cattle
- pigs
- poultry
- corn (maize)
- fruit
- soya beans
- timber
- major towns
- pasture
- cropland
- forest

Farms like this one stretch across more than 80% of Illinois, covering 44,800 sq miles (116,000 sq km). The state is the USA's leading producer of soya beans, which are used for animal feed and oil.

Lake Superior is the largest of the Great Lakes and attracts millions of tourists each year. Valuable mineral deposits such as iron and copper are mined close to its shores.

SCALE 1:3,750,000

(projection: Lambert Conformal Conic)

MAP KEY

POPULATION

- 1 million to 5 million
- 500,000 to 1 million
- 100,000 to 500,000
- 50,000 to 100,000
- 10,000 to 50,000
- below 10,000

ELEVATION

- 1000m / 3281ft
- 500m / 1640ft
- 250m / 820ft
- 100m / 328ft
- sea level

Although large-scale agribusiness has mostly replaced family farming in the Midwest, some communities, such as the Amish people in Ohio, retain traditional farming methods, cultivating their smallholdings using limited machinery.

USA: NORTH MOUNTAIN STATES

Idaho, Montana, Oregon, Washington, Wyoming

THE REMOTENESS OF THE NORTHWESTERN STATES, coupled with the rugged landscape, ensured that this was one of the last areas settled by Europeans in the 19th century. Fur-trappers and gold-prospectors followed the Snake River westwards as it wound its way through the Rocky Mountains. The states of the northwest have pioneered many conservationist policies, with the USA's first national park opened at Yellowstone in 1872. More recently, the Cascades and Rocky Mountains have become havens for adventure tourism. The mountains still serve to isolate the western seaboard from the rest of the continent. This isolation has encouraged west coast cities to expand their trade links with countries of the Pacific Rim.

The Snake River has cut down into the basalt of the Columbia Basin to form Hells Canyon, the deepest in the USA, with cliffs up to 7900 ft (2408 m) high.

MAP KEY

POPULATION
- ⊙ 500,000 to 1 million
- ◎ 100,000 to 500,000
- ⊕ 50,000 to 100,000
- ○ 10,000 to 50,000
- ○ below 10,000

ELEVATION
- 4000m / 13,124ft
- 3000m / 9843ft
- 2000m / 6562ft
- 1000m / 3281ft
- 500m / 1640ft
- 250m / 820ft
- 100m / 328ft
- sea level

Fine-textured, volcanic soils in the hilly Palouse region of eastern Washington are susceptible to erosion.

USING THE LAND

WHEAT FARMING IN THE EAST gives way to cattle ranching as rainfall decreases. Irrigated farming in the Snake River valley produces large yields of potatoes and other vegetables. Dairying and fruit-growing take place in the wet western lowlands between the mountain ranges.

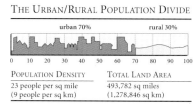

THE URBAN/RURAL POPULATION DIVIDE

urban 70%   rural 30%

0 10 20 30 40 50 60 70 80 90 100

POPULATION DENSITY
23 people per sq mile
(9 people per sq km)

TOTAL LAND AREA
493,782 sq miles
(1,278,846 sq km)

SCALE 1:3,750,000
(projection: Lambert Conformal Conic)

Km 0 10 20 40 60 80 100
Miles 0 20 40 60 80 100

Land use and agricultural distribution

- cattle
- poultry
- cereals
- fruit
- potatoes
- timber
- major towns

- pasture
- cropland
- forest

198 ◀

TRANSPORT AND INDUSTRY

MINERALS AND TIMBER are extremely important in this region. Uranium, precious metals, copper and coal are all mined, the latter in vast open-cast pits in Wyoming; oil and natural gas are extracted further north. Manufacturing, notably related to the aerospace and electronics industries, is important in western cities.

THE TRANSPORT NETWORK

- 347,857 miles (556,571 km)
- 4200 miles (6720 km)
- 12,354 miles (19,766 km)
- 1108 miles (1782 km)

Major industry and infrastructure
- adventure tourism
- aerospace
- coal
- chemicals
- electronics
- food processing
- mining
- oil & gas
- timber processing
- major towns
- international airports
- major roads
- major industrial areas

The Union Pacific Railroad has been in service across Wyoming since 1867. The route through the Rocky Mountains is now shared with the Interstate 80, a major east–west highway.

Seattle lies in one of Puget Sound's many inlets. The city receives oil and other resources from Alaska, and benefits from expanding trade across the Pacific.

Crater Lake, Oregon, is 6 miles (10 km) wide and 1800 ft (600 m) deep. It marks the site of a volcanic cone, which collapsed after an eruption within the last 7000 years.

THE LANDSCAPE

THE ROCKY MOUNTAINS are flanked by lower parallel ranges, which spread onto the Great Plains in the east and surmount the broad lava plateau which extends westwards. The Cascade Range divides the Columbia Basin from the coastlands, where the low areas skirting Puget Sound are broken by the steep, volcanic Olympic Mountains and the wooded hills of the Coast Ranges.

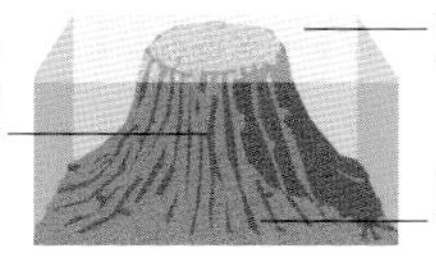

Glacial valleys on the seaward side of the Olympic Mountains receive about 142 inches (3600 mm) of rain per year, supporting the only true rainforest of the northern hemisphere.

The Cascades are glacially scoured volcanic mountains, the highest of which is Mount Rainier, a dormant volcano at 14,409 ft (4392 m).

Mount St Helens erupted in 1980, killing 57 people and devastating a huge area.

Puget Sound

Columbia Basin

Grand Coulee and the lesser *coulées* (ravines) were cut by cataclysmic floods, from the release of an ice-dammed lake, at the end of the last ice age.

The Continental Divide, or watershed, crosses the Lewis Range. From here, rivers flow east to Hudson Bay, south to the Gulf of Mexico and west to the Pacific Ocean.

Piney Buttes are the remnants of an older, higher land surface gradually weathered and eroded into isolated outcrops with flat tops and steep sides.

Molten rock cools, forming parallel columns

Surrounding strata eroded away

Molten rock wells up from the Earth's core

Coast Ranges

Great Plains

Devil's Tower

Devil's Tower in Wyoming is an igneous intrusion, formed below the Earth's surface. Molten rock intruded through cracks in the overlying strata and cooled. Over time, the softer rock layers have been eroded away, leaving only the tower standing.

The plateaux of the Columbia and Snake rivers represent one of the world's largest accumulations of lava. Over 5 million years ago, successive flows of molten basalt buried the existing land surface by up to 450 ft (150 m).

The contorted rock shapes at 'Craters of the Moon' National Monument in Idaho were left 2000 years ago by the sporadic upwelling of viscous lava from fissures in the basalt plateau.

Rocky Mountains

Water from the hot springs in Yellowstone National Park deposits minerals as it cools in rock pools. Long periods of deposition have created these rock terraces.

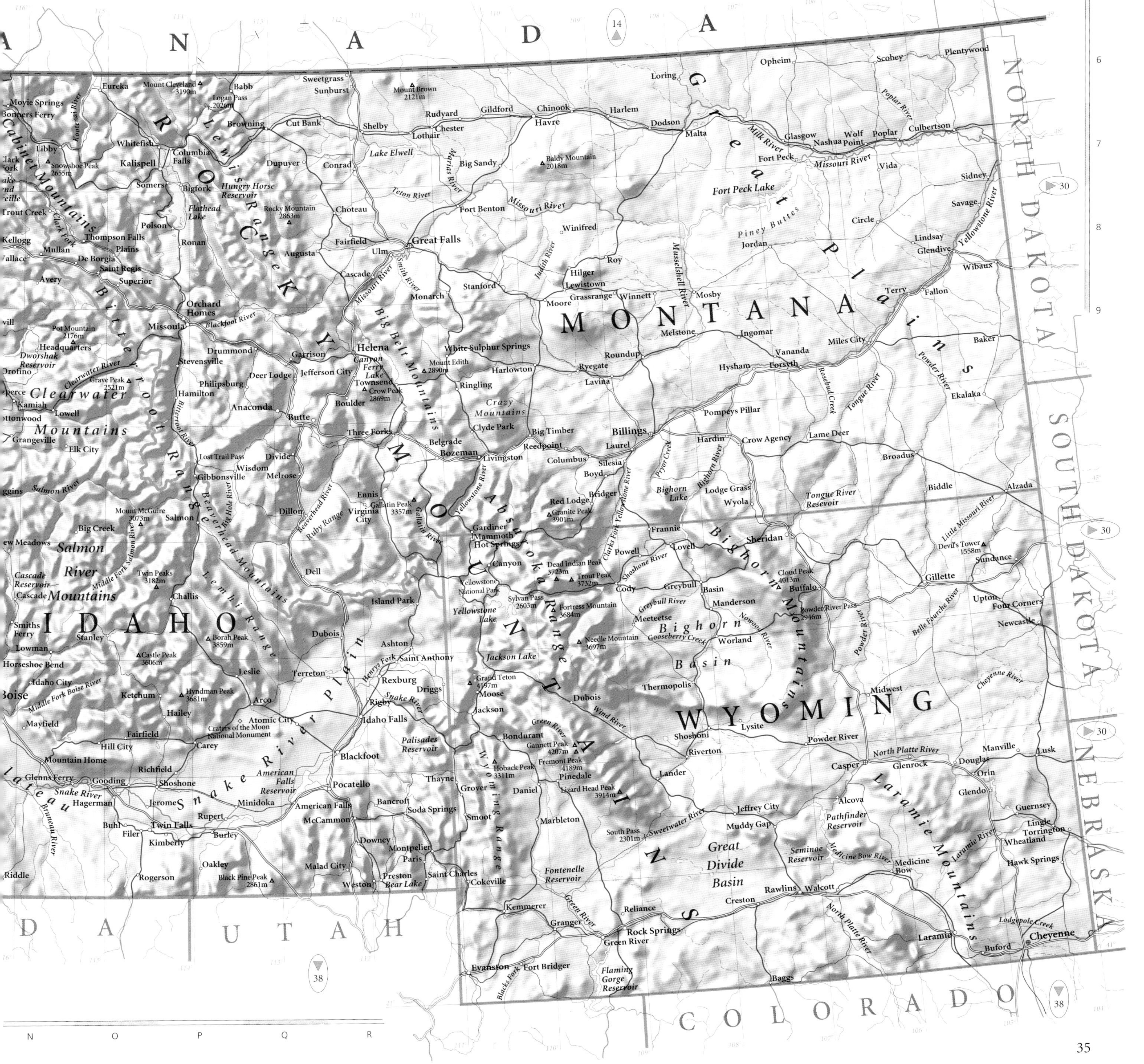

USA: California & Nevada

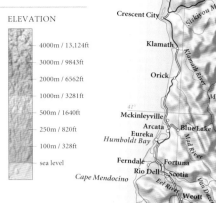

THE 'GOLD RUSH' of 1849 attracted the first major wave of European settlers to the USA's west coast. The pleasant climate, beautiful scenery and dynamic economy continue to attract immigrants – despite the ever-present danger of earthquakes – and California has become the USA's most populous state. The overwhelmingly urban population is concentrated in the vast conurbations of Los Angeles, San Francisco and San Diego; new immigrants include people from South Korea, the Philippines, Vietnam and Mexico. Nevada's arid lands were initially exploited for minerals; in recent years, revenue from mining has been superseded by income from the tourist and gambling centres of Las Vegas and Reno.

MAP KEY

POPULATION
- 1 million to 5 million
- 500,000 to 1 million
- 100,000 to 500,000
- 50,000 to 100,000
- 10,000 to 50,000
- below 10,000

ELEVATION
- 4000m / 13,124ft
- 3000m / 9843ft
- 2000m / 6562ft
- 1000m / 3281ft
- 500m / 1640ft
- 250m / 820ft
- 100m / 328ft
- sea level

SCALE 1:3,000,000
(projection: Lambert Conformal Conic)

Km 0 5 10 20 30 40 50 60 70 80

Miles 0 5 10 20 30 40 50 60 70 80

TRANSPORT AND INDUSTRY

NEVADA'S RICH MINERAL RESERVES ushered in a period of mining wealth which has now been replaced by revenue generated from gambling. California supports a broad set of activities including defence-related industries and research and development facilities. 'Silicon Valley', near San Francisco, is a world leading centre for micro-electronics, while tourism and the Los Angeles film industry also generate large incomes.

Gambling was legalized in Nevada in 1931. Las Vegas has since become the centre of this multi-million dollar industry.

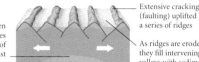

Major industry and infrastructure
- ✈ aerospace
- 🚗 car manufacture
- defence
- 🎬 film industry
- $ finance
- food processing
- gambling
- hi-tech industry
- mining
- pharmaceuticals
- research & development
- textiles
- tourism
- • major towns
- ✈ international airports
- major roads
- major industrial areas

THE TRANSPORT NETWORK
- 211,459 miles (338,334 km)
- 2944 miles (4710 km)
- 7872 miles (12,595 km)
- 190 miles (306 km)

In California, the motor vehicle is a vital part of daily life, and an extensive freeway system runs throughout the state, which has a greater *per capita* car ownership than anywhere else in the world.

THE LANDSCAPE

THE BROAD CENTRAL VALLEY divides California's coastal mountains from the Sierra Nevada. The San Andreas Fault, running beneath much of the state, is the site of frequent earth tremors and sometimes more serious earthquakes. East of the Sierra Nevada, the landscape is characterized by the basin and range topography with stony deserts and many salt lakes.

Rising molten rock causes stretching of the Earth's crust

Extensive cracking (faulting) uplifted a series of ridges

As ridges are eroded they fill intervening valleys with sediments

Molten rock (magma) welling up to form a dome in the Earth's interior, causes the brittle surface rocks to stretch and crack. Some areas were uplifted to form mountains (ranges), while others sunk to form flat valleys (basins).

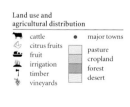

The General Sherman sequoia tree in Sequoia National Park is 3000 years old and at 275 ft (84 m) is one of the largest living things on earth.

Most of California's agriculture is confined to the fertile and extensively irrigated Central Valley, running between the Coast Ranges and the Sierra Nevada. It incorporates the San Joaquin and Sacramento valleys

The dramatic granitic rock formations of Half Dome and El Capitan, and the verdant coniferous forests, attract millions of visitors annually to Yosemite National Park in the Sierra Nevada.

Sierra Nevada

The Great Basin dominates most of Nevada's topography containing large open basins, punctuated by eroded features such as *buttes* and *mesas*. River flow tends to be seasonal, dependent upon spring showers and winter snow melt.

USING THE LAND

CALIFORNIA is the USA's leading agricultural producer, although low rainfall makes irrigation essential. The long growing season and abundant sunshine allow many crops to be grown in the fertile Central Valley including grapes, citrus fruits, vegetables and cotton. Almost 17 million acres (6.8 million hectares) of California's forests are used commercially. Nevada's arid climate and poor soil are largely unsuitable for agriculture; 85% of its land is state owned and large areas are used for underground testing of nuclear weapons.

Wheeler Peak is home to some of the world's oldest trees, bristlecone pines, which live for up to 5000 years.

When the Hoover Dam across the Colorado River was completed in 1936, it created Lake Mead, one of the largest artificial lakes in the world, extending for 115 miles (285 km) upstream.

Land use and agricultural distribution
- cattle
- citrus fruits
- fruit
- irrigation
- timber
- vineyards
- • major towns
- pasture
- cropland
- forest
- desert

The San Andreas Fault is a transverse fault which extends for 650 miles (1050 km) through California. Major earthquakes occur when the land either side of the fault moves at different rates. San Francisco was devastated by an earthquake in 1906.

Death Valley

Named by migrating settlers in 1849, Death Valley is the driest, hottest place in North America, as well as being the lowest point on land in the western hemisphere, at 282 ft (86 m) below sea level.

The sparsely populated Mojave Desert receives less than 8 inches (200 mm) of rainfall a year. It is used extensively for weapons-testing and military purposes.

The Salton Sea was created accidentally between 1905 and 1907 when an irrigation channel from the Colorado River broke out of its banks and formed this salty 300 sq mile (777 sq km), land-locked lake.

Amargosa Desert

The Sierra Nevada create a 'rainshadow', preventing rain from reaching much of Nevada. Pacific air masses, passing over the mountains, are stripped of their moisture.

Without considerable irrigation, this fertile valley at Palm Springs would still be part of the Sonoran Desert. California's farmers account for about 80% of the state's total water usage.

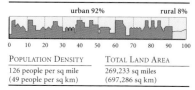

THE URBAN/RURAL POPULATION DIVIDE
urban 92%   rural 8%

0 10 20 30 40 50 60 70 80 90 100

POPULATION DENSITY	TOTAL LAND AREA
126 people per sq mile (49 people per sq km)	269,233 sq miles (697,286 sq km)

198 ◀

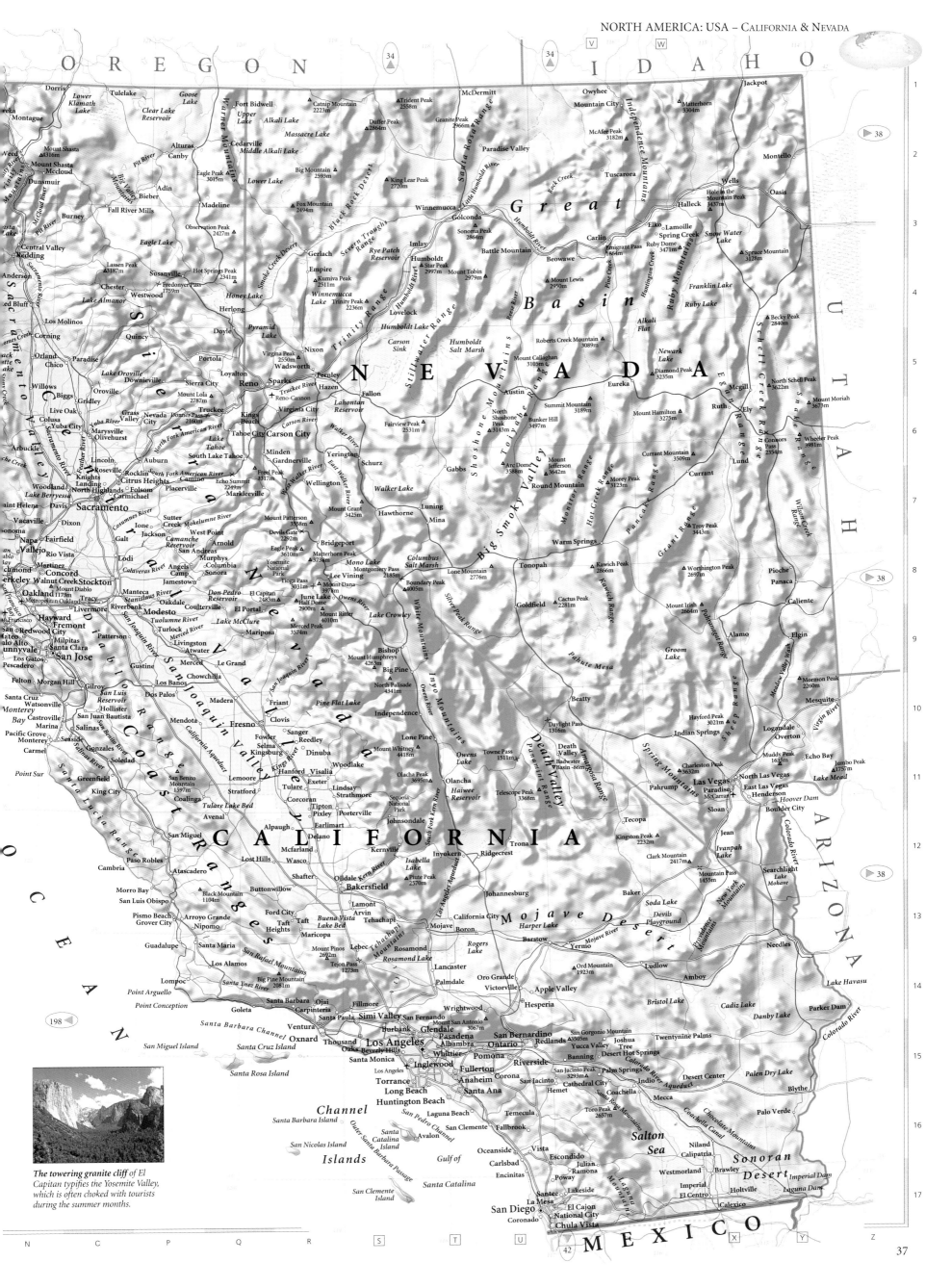

The towering granite cliff of El Capitan typifies the Yosemite Valley, which is often choked with tourists during the summer months.

USA: South Mountain States

Arizona, Colorado, New Mexico, Utah

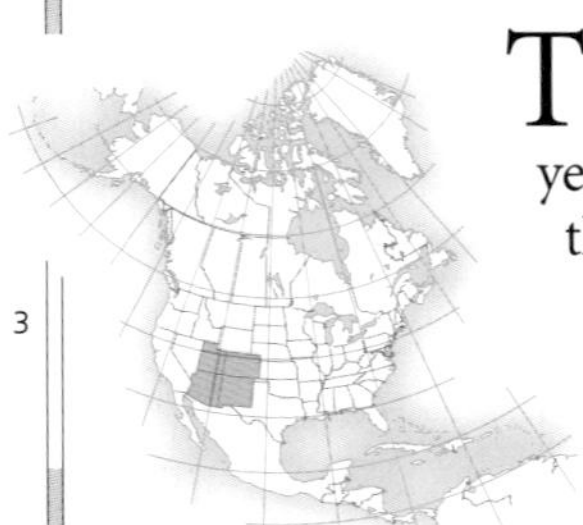

This arid region, characterized by expansive plateaux and spectacular canyons is home to several distinct peoples. The ruins of cliff dwellings built a thousand years ago by the Anasazi people still exist today, and native Americans own one-third of the land in Arizona. Spanish and Mexican conquest and settlement left a Hispanic presence which is strongest in New Mexico. The Mormons, who came to the Great Salt Lake seeking religious freedom in 1847, were among the earliest Anglo-American settlers and now make up over 70% of Utah's population. The region's mineral wealth drove rapid development in the 20th century, yet the constraints of a fragile environment, including widespread water shortages, may limit prospects for growth.

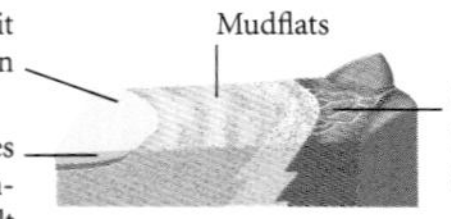

When water evaporates it leaves a salt pan
Mudflats
Water level of lake varies according to quantity of run-off received from snow melt
Lake is fed by seasonal snow melt

The Great Salt Lake is an ephemeral lake; it can remain dry for extended periods, leaving a pan of evaporated mineral salts in its centre.

The Landscape

The arid, rocky expanse of the Colorado Plateau is dissected by immense canyons of the Colorado River. Desert lies to the north and south and branches of the Rocky Mountains run to the east and west. The Great Salt Lake and Desert lie within the Great Basin, a barren region of parallel mountain ranges which extends into Arizona.

Over 13 million years of weathering has created thousands of spires and pinnacles from the alternating rock strata of Bryce Canyon.
Lake Powell
The Rio Grande has its source in several meltwater streams, which have cut deep valleys into the platform of the San Juan mountains.
The parallel basins and ridges, which run north–south along the Great Basin, reflect a major series of block-faults in the underlying bedrock.
Sand dunes, 600 ft (180 m) high, have been deposited in San Luis Valley, by winds funnelled through the San Juan and Sangre de Cristo mountains in the Rockies.
Parts of the Grand Canyon, which cuts through the Colorado Plateau, are 16 miles (25 km) wide. The Colorado River has cut down 6262 ft (2000 m), exposing rock strata more than 2 billion years old.
Rainbow Bridge is the world's largest natural arch. The 309 ft (94 m) span probably began to grow when the sandstone spur of a meandering creek was breached during a flash flood.
The striking colour effects seen in the Painted Desert come from minerals such as gypsum and haematite, combined with ambient heat and dust.
Petrified Forest
Shifting gypsum sands produce a constantly changing land surface, overwhelming plants and any other obstacles in Tularosa Valley.
Carlsbad Caverns

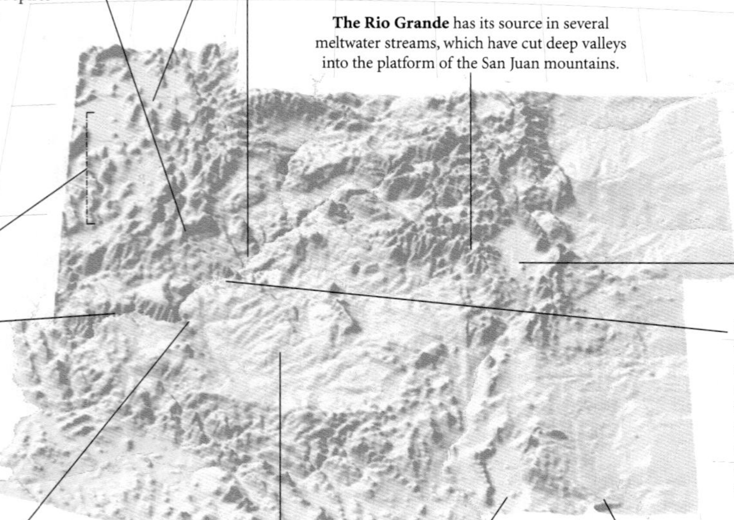

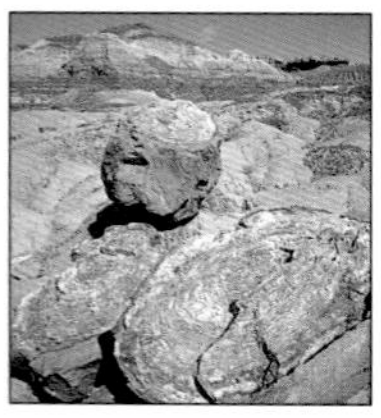

In the arid landscape of Petrified Forest National Park in Arizona, the grain of prehistoric trees has been preserved as a fossil imprint in the rocks. The bog-preserved trees were gradually turned to stone by seeping mineral-rich water.

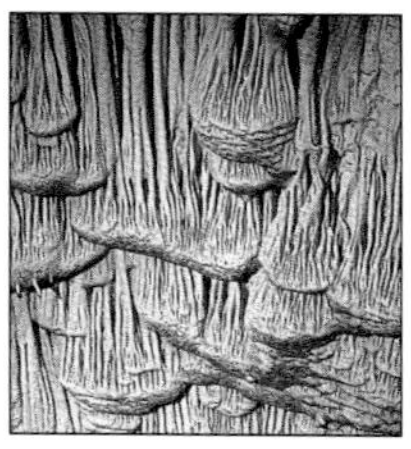

The intricate stalactites of Carlsbad Caverns have grown with the seepage of calcium-rich water, over the last 100,000 years. The huge caves are home to around 100,000 Mexican freetail bats.

Transport and Industry

New industries have helped reduce the region's dependence on the extraction of minerals and fossil fuels. Precision manufacture has grown rapidly, particularly in Arizona and Colorado. Salt Lake City and Denver are well-established financial centres and New Mexico, the USA's major producer of uranium, is a prominent region for nuclear research. Colorado is the USA's most important centre for winter sports.

The Transport Network

232,434 miles (373,986 km)	4059 miles (6515 km)
8627 miles (13,881 km)	none

The Colorado Rockies are crossed by 32 mountain passes, some as high as 12,183 ft (3713 m). The Eisenhower Tunnel west of Denver carries Interstate Highway 70 straight through the Continental Divide.

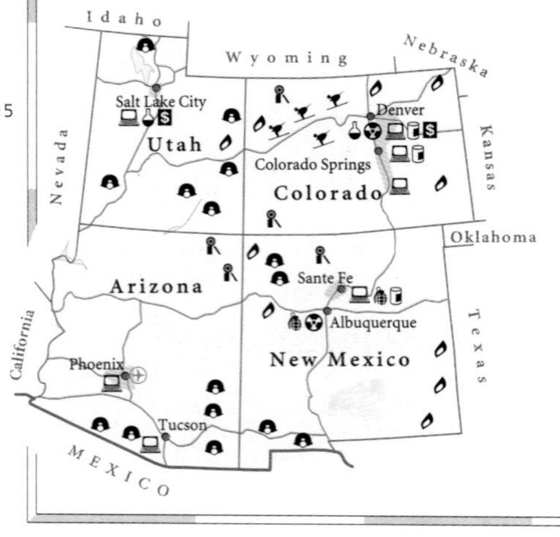

Idaho
Wyoming
Nebraska
Nevada
Utah
Salt Lake City
Denver
Colorado Springs
Colorado
Kansas
Oklahoma
Arizona
Santa Fe
Albuquerque
New Mexico
Texas
California
Phoenix
Tucson
MEXICO
Major industry and infrastructure
chemicals
coal
defence
finance
food processing
hi-tech industry
oil & gas
mining
research & development
winter sports
major towns
international airports
major roads
major industrial areas

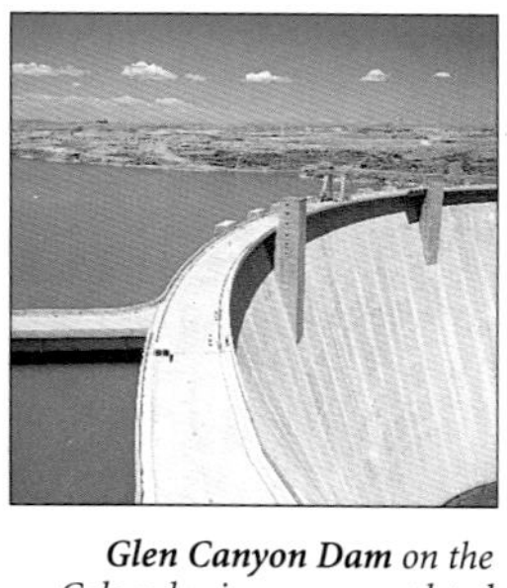

Glen Canyon Dam on the Colorado river was completed in 1964. it provides hydro-electric power and irrigation water as part of a long-term federal project to harness the river.

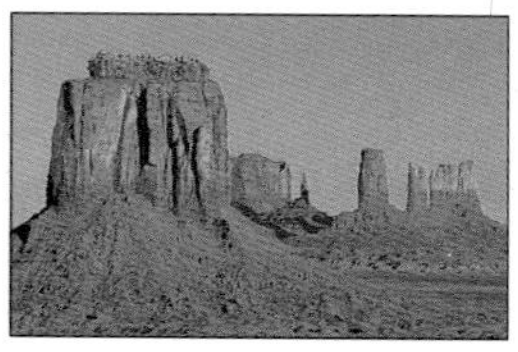

The flat tablelands (mesas), and the isolated pinnacles (buttes) which rise from the floor of Monument Valley are the resistant remnants of an earlier land surface, gradually cut back by erosion under arid conditions.

IDAHO
NEVADA
UTAH
ARIZONA
CALIFORNIA
MEXICO
Great Salt Lake
Great Salt Lake Desert
Great Basin
Salt Lake City
Ogden
Provo
Sevier Lake
Colorado Plateau
Grand Canyon
Lake Powell
Lake Mead
Lake Mohave
Lake Havasu City
Kingman
Flagstaff
Prescott
Phoenix
Tempe
Mesa
Tucson
Yuma
Sonoran Desert
Colorado River
Gila River
Painted Desert
Kaibab Plateau
Coconino Plateau
Saint George
Cedar City
Kanab
Page
Glen Canyon Dam
Nogales

34
36
36
42

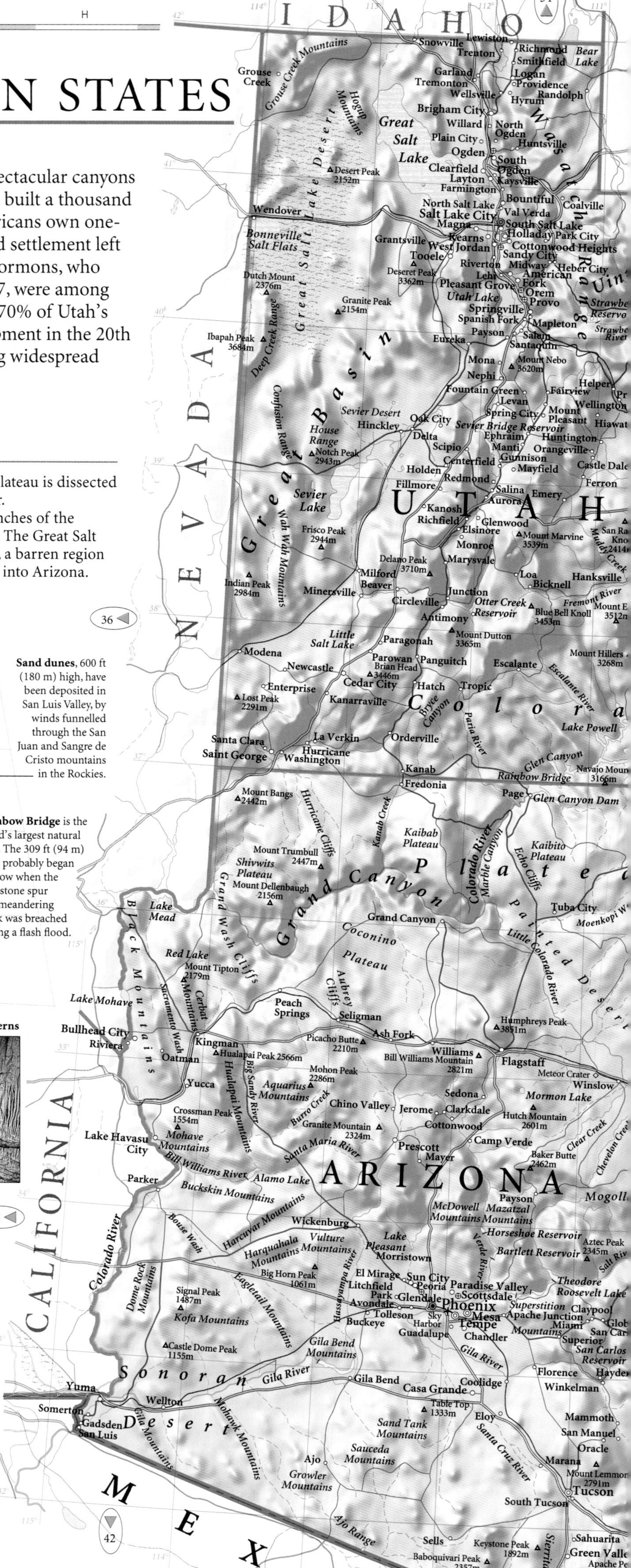

*The **Bonneville Salt Flats** are in the Great Salt Lake. Sodium chloride (salt), magnesium, and other minerals are commercially extracted from these flats.*

SCALE 1:3,500,000
(projection: Lambert Conformal Conic)

Km
0 20 40 60 80 100

Miles
0 20 40 60 80 100

MAP KEY

POPULATION

- ⊙ 500,000 to 1 million
- ⊚ 100,000 to 500,000
- ⊕ 50,000 to 100,000
- ⊙ 10,000 to 50,000
- ∘ below 10,000

ELEVATION

- 4000m / 13124ft
- 3000m / 9843ft
- 2000m / 6562ft
- 1000m / 3281ft
- 500m / 1640ft
- 250m / 820ft
- 100m / 328ft
- sea level

A glacially-eroded valley in Rocky Mountain National Park, Colorado. There are 1500 peaks exceeding 10,000 ft (3000 m) within the state, six times the number of major mountains found in the Swiss Alps.

USING THE LAND

LIVESTOCK, PARTICULARLY cattle-ranching, is the main source of agricultural income. The region has a long growing season and areas of rich soil, but depends heavily on water for irrigation. Crops include corn and wheat in eastern areas, and chilli peppers, fruit and cotton aided by additional irrigation.

Land use and agricultural distribution

- cattle
- cereals
- cotton
- fruit
- irrigation
- major towns
- pasture
- cropland
- forest
- desert

THE URBAN/RURAL POPULATION DIVIDE

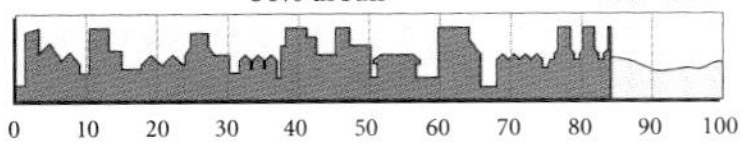

84% urban   16% rural

0 10 20 30 40 50 60 70 80 90 100

POPULATION DENSITY	TOTAL LAND AREA
29 people per sq mile	424,738 sq miles
(11 people per sq km)	(1,100,028 sq km)

Cattle-ranching was introduced to New Mexico via Texas in the 19th century, and has become the principal agricultural land use across this region.

State and country labels (map)

WYOMING · NEBRASKA · KANSAS · COLORADO · OKLAHOMA · NEW MEXICO · TEXAS · MEXICO

ROCKY MOUNTAINS · Sangre de Cristo Mountains · San Juan Mountains · Sacramento Mountains

▷ 30
▷ 28
▷ 28
▷ 26
▽ 42

USA: Hawaii

T HE 122 ISLANDS of the Hawaiian archipelago – which are part of Polynesia – are the peaks of the world's largest volcanoes. They rise approximately 6 miles (9.7 km) from the floor of the Pacific Ocean. The largest, the island of Hawaii, remains highly active. Hawaii became the USA's 50th state in 1959. A tradition of receiving immigrant workers is reflected in the islands' ethnic diversity, with peoples drawn from around the rim of the Pacific. Only 2% of the current population are native Polynesians.

The island of Molokai is formed from volcanic rock. Mature sand dunes cover the rocks in coastal areas.

USING THE LAND AND SEA

THE ICE-FREE COASTLINE of Alaska provides access to salmon fisheries and more than 5.5 million acres (2.2 million ha) of forest. Most of Alaska is uncultivable, and around 90% of food is imported. Barley, hay and hothouse products are grown around Anchorage, where dairy farming is also concentrated.

THE URBAN/RURAL POPULATION DIVIDE

urban 68%   rural 32%

0 10 20 30 40 50 60 70 80 90 100

POPULATION DENSITY	TOTAL LAND AREA
1 person per sq mile (0.4 people per sq km)	586,412 sq miles (1,518,800 sq km)

A raft of timber from the Tongass forest is hauled by a tug, bound for the pulp mills of the Alaskan coast between Juneau and Ketchikan.

TRANSPORT AND INDUSTRY

TOURISM DOMINATES the economy, with over half of the population employed in services. The naval base at Pearl Harbor is also a major source of employment. Industry is concentrated on the island of Oahu and relies mostly on imported materials, while agricultural produce is processed locally.

Major industry and infrastructure

- food processing
- military base
- textiles
- tourism
- major towns
- international airports
- major roads
- major industrial areas

THE TRANSPORT NETWORK

4102 miles (6600 km)	43 miles (69 km)
none	none

Hawaii relies on ocean-surface transportation. Honolulu is the main focus of this network, bringing foreign trade and the markets of mainland USA to Hawaii's outer islands.

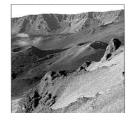

Haleakala's extinct volcanic crater is the world's largest. The giant caldera, containing many secondary cones, is 2000 ft (600 m) deep and 20 miles (32 km) in circumference.

SCALE 1:3,500,000
(projection: Lambert Conformal Conic)

Km
0 10 20 40 60 80 100

Miles
0 10 20 40 60 80 100

MAP KEY

POPULATION

- 100,000 to 500,000
- 50,000 to 100,000
- 10,000 to 50,000
- below 10,000

ELEVATION

- 4000m / 13,124ft
- 3000m / 9843ft
- 2000m / 6562ft
- 1000m / 3281ft
- 500m / 1640ft
- 250m / 820ft
- 100m / 328ft
- sea level

USING THE LAND AND SEA

THE VOLCANIC SOILS are extremely fertile and the climate hot and humid on the lower slopes, supporting large commercial plantations growing sugar cane, bananas, pineapples and other tropical fruit, as well as nursery plants and flowers. Some land is given to pasture, particularly for beef and dairy cattle.

Land use and agricultural distribution

- cattle
- fishing
- fruit
- sugar cane
- major towns
- pasture
- cropland
- forest
- mountain region

The island of Kauai is one of the wettest places in the world, receiving some 450 inches (11,500 mm) of rain a year.

THE URBAN/RURAL POPULATION DIVIDE

urban 89%   rural 11%

0 10 20 30 40 50 60 70 80 90 100

POPULATION DENSITY	TOTAL LAND AREA
183 people per sq mile (71 people per sq km)	6,423 sq miles (16,636 sq km)

MAP KEY

POPULATION

- 100,000 to 500,000
- 50,000 to 100,000
- 10,000 to 50,000
- below 10,000

ELEVATION

- 4000m / 13,124ft
- 3000m / 9843ft
- 2000m / 6562ft
- 1000m / 3281ft
- 500m / 1640ft
- 250m / 820ft
- 100m / 328ft
- sea level

SCALE 1:8,000,000
(projection: Lambert Conformal Conic)

Km
0 25 50 100 150 200 250

Miles
0 50 100 150 200 250

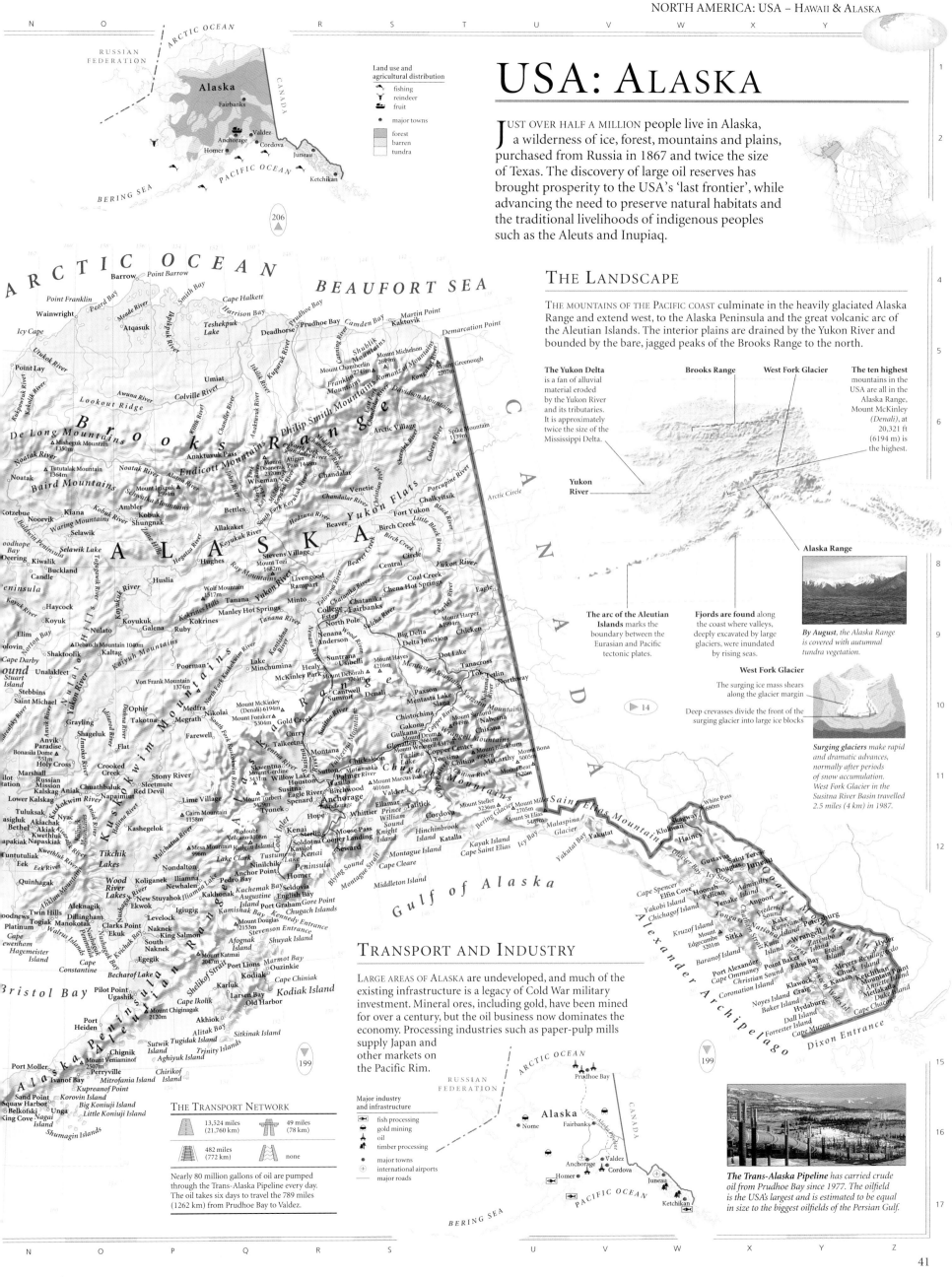

USA: ALASKA

JUST OVER HALF A MILLION people live in Alaska, a wilderness of ice, forest, mountains and plains, purchased from Russia in 1867 and twice the size of Texas. The discovery of large oil reserves has brought prosperity to the USA's 'last frontier', while advancing the need to preserve natural habitats and the traditional livelihoods of indigenous peoples such as the Aleuts and Inupiaq.

THE LANDSCAPE

THE MOUNTAINS OF THE PACIFIC COAST culminate in the heavily glaciated Alaska Range and extend west, to the Alaska Peninsula and the great volcanic arc of the Aleutian Islands. The interior plains are drained by the Yukon River and bounded by the bare, jagged peaks of the Brooks Range to the north.

The Yukon Delta is a fan of alluvial material eroded by the Yukon River and its tributaries. It is approximately twice the size of the Mississippi Delta.

Brooks Range

West Fork Glacier

The ten highest mountains in the USA are all in the Alaska Range, Mount McKinley (*Denali*), at 20,321 ft (6194 m) is the highest.

Yukon River

Alaska Range

By August, the Alaska Range is covered with autumnal tundra vegetation.

The arc of the Aleutian Islands marks the boundary between the Eurasian and Pacific tectonic plates.

Fjords are found along the coast where valleys, deeply excavated by large glaciers, were inundated by rising seas.

West Fork Glacier

The surging ice mass shears along the glacier margin

Deep crevasses divide the front of the surging glacier into large ice blocks

Surging glaciers make rapid and dramatic advances, normally after periods of snow accumulation. West Fork Glacier in the Susitna River Basin travelled 2.5 miles (4 km) in 1987.

TRANSPORT AND INDUSTRY

LARGE AREAS OF ALASKA are undeveloped, and much of the existing infrastructure is a legacy of Cold War military investment. Mineral ores, including gold, have been mined for over a century, but the oil business now dominates the economy. Processing industries such as paper-pulp mills supply Japan and other markets on the Pacific Rim.

THE TRANSPORT NETWORK

13,524 miles (21,760 km)

49 miles (78 km)

482 miles (772 km)

Nearly 80 million gallons of oil are pumped through the Trans-Alaska Pipeline every day. The oil takes six days to travel the 789 miles (1262 km) from Prudhoe Bay to Valdez.

Major industry and infrastructure
- fish processing
- gold mining
- oil
- timber processing
- major towns
- international airports
- major roads

The Trans-Alaska Pipeline has carried crude oil from Prudhoe Bay since 1977. The oilfield is the USA's largest and is estimated to be equal in size to the biggest oilfields of the Persian Gulf.

Land use and agricultural distribution
- fishing
- reindeer
- fruit
- major towns
- forest
- barren
- tundra

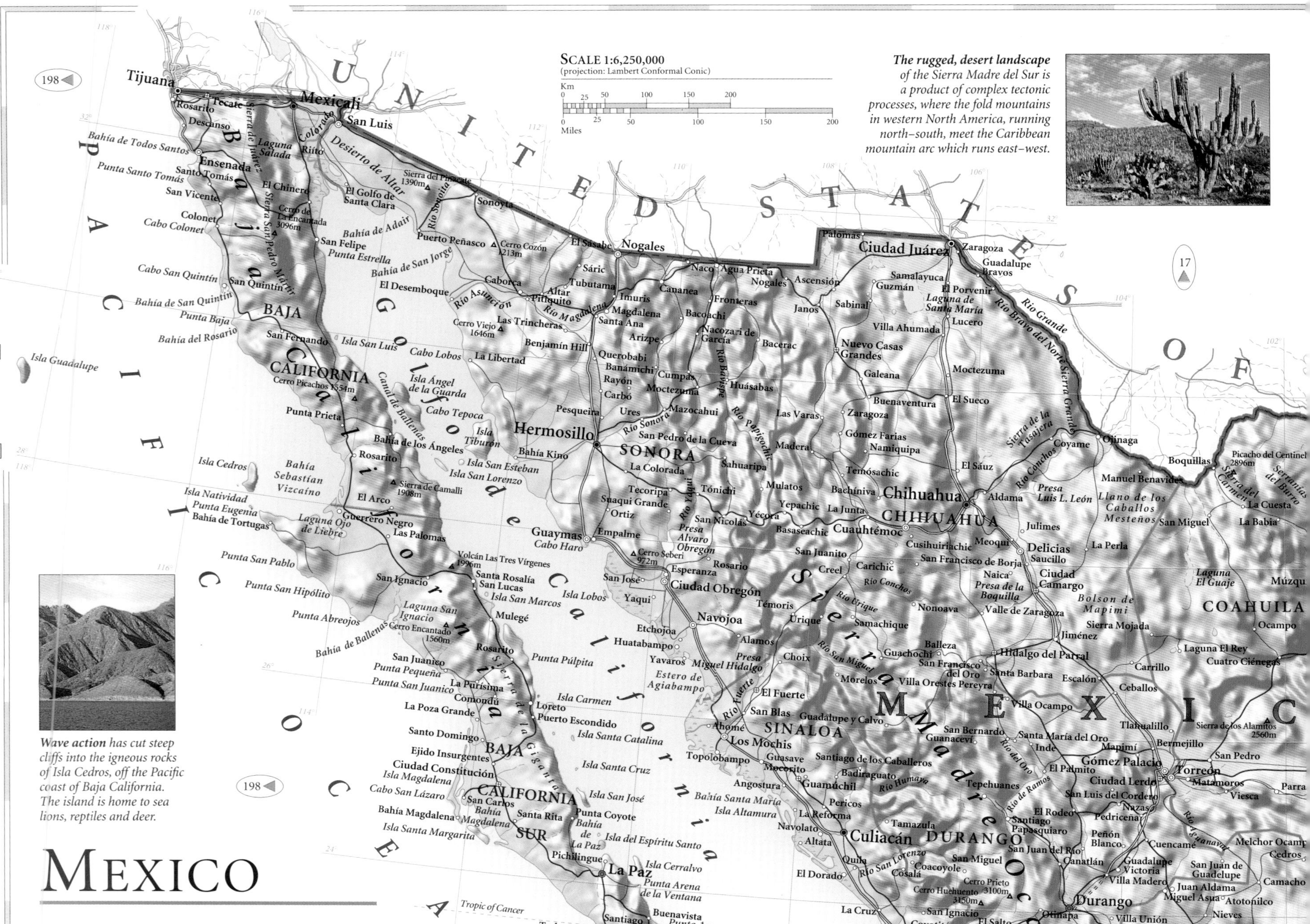

The rugged, desert landscape of the Sierra Madre del Sur is a product of complex tectonic processes, where the fold mountains in western North America, running north–south, meet the Caribbean mountain arc which runs east–west.

SCALE 1:6,250,000
(projection: Lambert Conformal Conic)

Wave action has cut steep cliffs into the igneous rocks of Isla Cedros, off the Pacific coast of Baja California. The island is home to sea lions, reptiles and deer.

MEXICO

MEXICO POSSESSES rich mineral resources, limited agricultural land and the world's largest and fastest growing Spanish-speaking population. Most Mexicans are *mestizo*, although Amerindian communities still exist in the south, 400 years after Spain destroyed the Aztec empire at its height. Much of the arid north is sparsely inhabited, while Mexico City is becoming the world's most populous city. Conflict with the USA has long overshadowed Mexico's development, but the North American Free Trade Agreement offers the chance for a more benign relationship, which may help to offset Mexico's problems of hyperinflation, foreign debt, unequal wealth distribution and political instability.

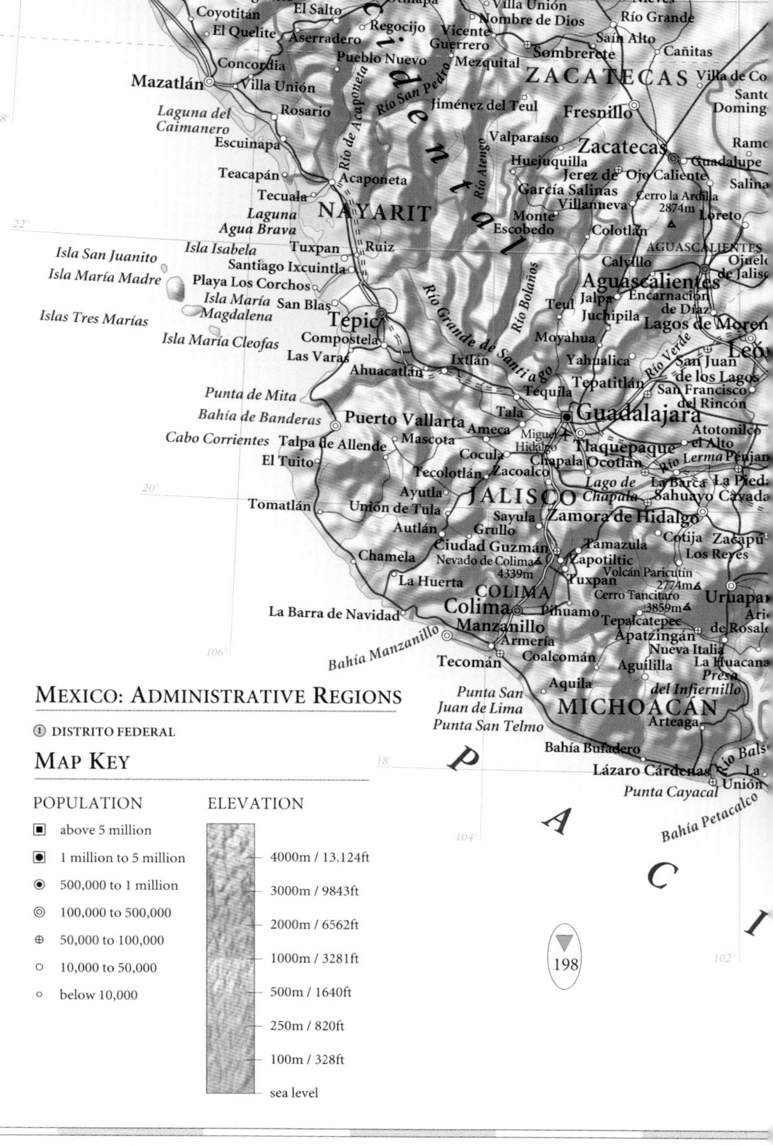

USING THE LAND AND SEA

CORN OCCUPIES much of the cultivated area. Commercial plantations of coffee, sugar, vanilla and cotton are found along the Gulf coastal plain and in irrigated parts of the arid north, which is otherwise used for extensive ranching. Fishing is important, particularly shellfish for export. A soaring population has created the need for grain imports since 1980.

THE URBAN/RURAL POPULATION DIVIDE

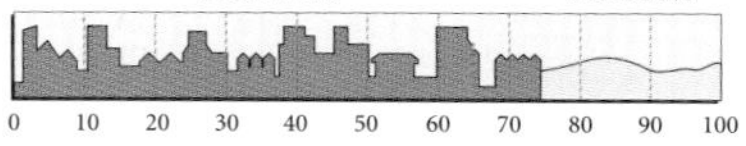

urban 74%   rural 26%

0 10 20 30 40 50 60 70 80 90 100

POPULATION DENSITY	TOTAL LAND AREA
130 people per sq mile	755,865 sq miles
(50 people per sq km)	(1,958,200 sq km)

Land use and agricultural distribution

- cattle
- coffee
- corn (maize)
- cotton
- fishing
- shellfish
- sugar cane
- timber
- vanilla

- capital cities
- major towns

pasture
cropland
forest
desert

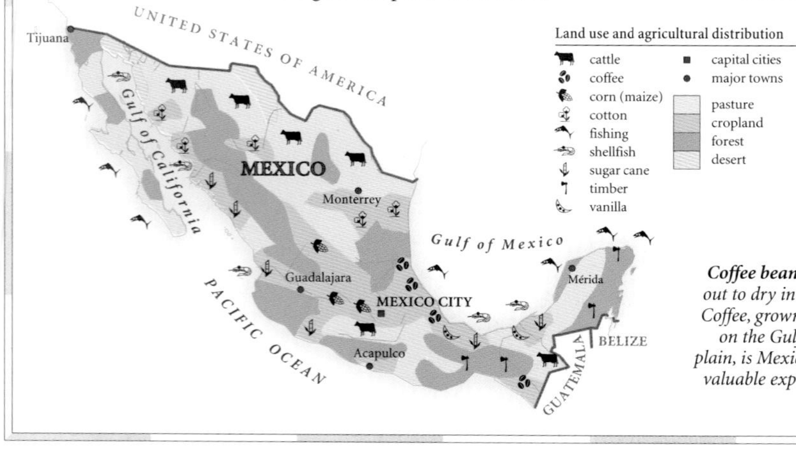

Coffee beans spread out to dry in the sun. Coffee, grown mainly on the Gulf coastal plain, is Mexico's most valuable export crop.

MEXICO: ADMINISTRATIVE REGIONS

⊕ DISTRITO FEDERAL

MAP KEY

POPULATION

- ▣ above 5 million
- ▪ 1 million to 5 million
- ◎ 500,000 to 1 million
- ⊕ 100,000 to 500,000
- ○ 50,000 to 100,000
- ∘ 10,000 to 50,000
- · below 10,000

ELEVATION

- 4000m / 13,124ft
- 3000m / 9843ft
- 2000m / 6562ft
- 1000m / 3281ft
- 500m / 1640ft
- 250m / 820ft
- 100m / 328ft
- sea level

THE LANDSCAPE

THE GREAT CENTRAL PLATEAU rises gently southwards from the Rio Grande, isolated from the coastal plains by the Sierra Madre Oriental and Occidental. The two ranges converge from east and west respectively, culminating in high volcanic peaks around Mexico City. Further ranges of the Sierra Madre rise to the south of the Balsas Basin, skirted by the low-lying Isthmus of Tehuantepec (*Istmo de Tehuantepec*) and Yucatan Peninsula.

The long, narrow, extremely arid peninsula of Baja (lower) California is an elongated granite block, separated from the mainland by the flooded rift valley of the Gulf of California (*Golfo de California*).

Wave action has constructed sand bars which shelter lagoons along the shore of the Gulf coastal plain.

Sierra Madre Oriental

Rio Grande

The dormant cone of Volcán Pico de Orizaba is, at 18,700 ft (5700 m), the highest peak in Mexico. In North America, only Mount McKinley and Mount Logan are taller.

Tropical rainforest abounds in the Yucatan Peninsula, a broad, low limestone shelf. Rivers are rare due to the porous nature of limestone, so the forest is mostly fed by streams and underground water.

The heavily-forested Isthmus of Tehuantepec (*Istmo de Tehuantepec*) is a *graben*; a low-lying trough created by downward movement of the bedrock between two fault lines.

Formation of the Gulf of California

Direction of plate movement
Baja California
Gulf of California
Transform fault
Spreading oceanic ridge
Edge of continental crust

The Gulf of California (Golfo de California) began to open out about 4 million years ago as a result of rifting and plate displacement along transform faults.

Sierra Madre Occidental

Popocatépetl is a dormant volcano, part of the Pacific 'Rim of Fire'. The crater is over half a mile (1 km) wide.

Río Balsas

Popocatépetl

The unstable, earthquake-prone, upland basin around Mexico City was once a region of shallow lakes. Flood control measures and domestic consumption over the last four centuries have caused the virtual disappearance of this surface water.

The highlands of Chiapas are a series of *horsts*, blocks of land thrust upwards between two fault lines. Volcanic cones have developed where lava has flowed out from the faults.

TRANSPORT AND INDUSTRY

OIL AND GAS ON THE GULF COAST are Mexico's main sources of export income. Metal mining has declined but the country remains a leading global producer of silver. Manufacturing is heavily concentrated around the Mexico City metropolitan area, while the duty-free movement of goods in the USA border region, under the *Maquiladora* (twin plant) scheme, has created new hi-tech and service growth centres.

Major industry and infrastructure

brewing		oil & gas	
car manufacture		textiles	
chemicals		capital cities	
electronics		major towns	
fish processing		international airports	
maquiladoras		major roads	
mining		major industrial areas	

THE TRANSPORT NETWORK

55,021 miles (88,601 km)	
4186 miles (6740 km)	
16,422 miles (26,445 km)	
1801 miles (2900 km)	

Fast, modern highways or *autopistas* now link Mexico City with Toluca, Puebla and other satellite cities, yet distant centres like Chihuahua are still served by narrow roads and an outdated rail network.

A stone figure reclines by the Temple of Warriors, within the Mayan city of Chichén-Itzá. The Maya civilization flourished across the Yucatan Peninsula between 200 and 900 ad.

43

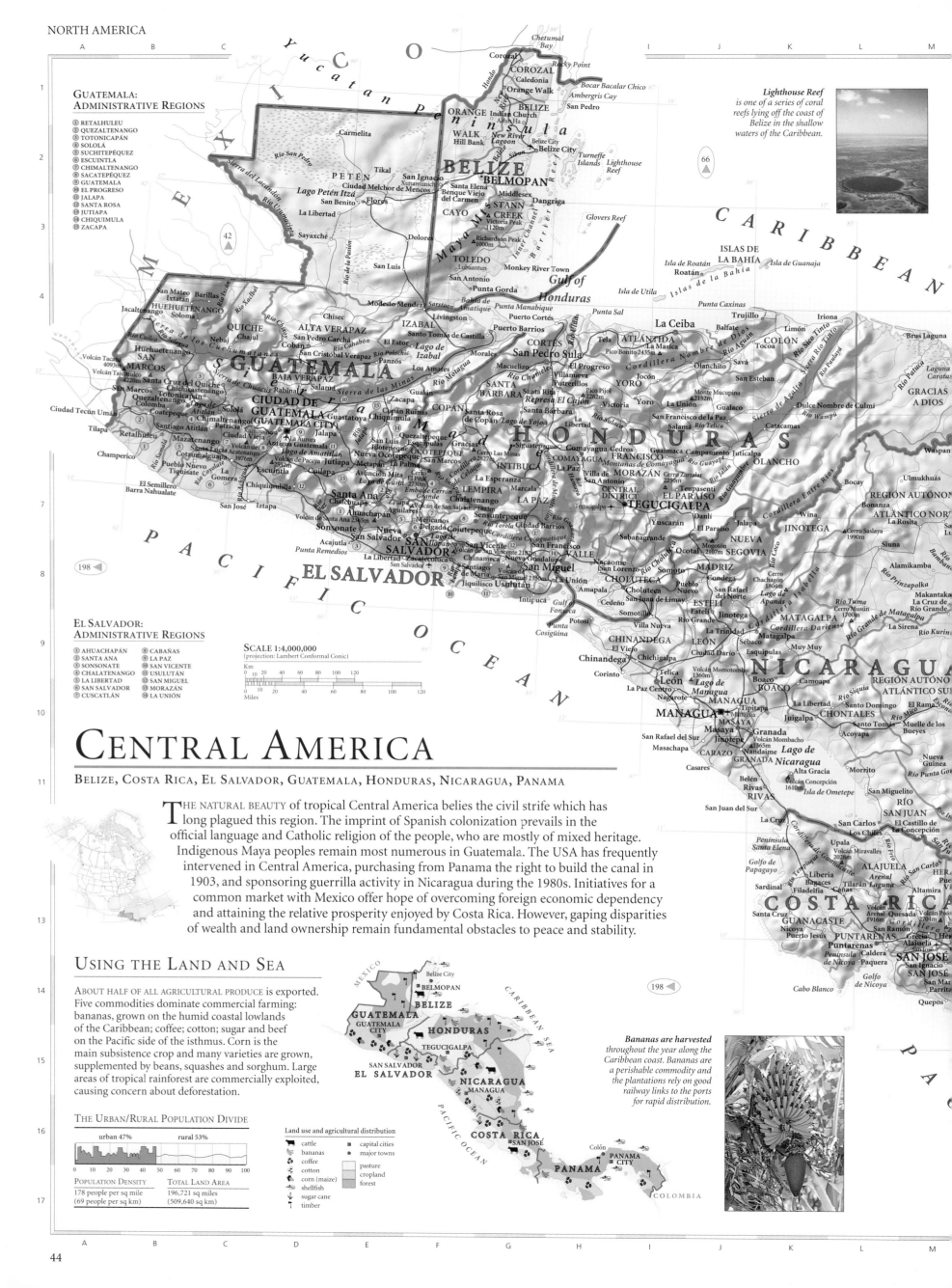

GUATEMALA: ADMINISTRATIVE REGIONS

1 RETALHULEU
2 QUEZALTENANGO
3 TOTONICAPÁN
4 SOLOLÁ
5 SUCHITEPÉQUEZ
6 ESCUINTLA
7 CHIMALTENANGO
8 SACATEPÉQUEZ
9 GUATEMALA
10 EL PROGRESO
11 JALAPA
12 SANTA ROSA
13 JUTIAPA
14 CHIQUIMULA
15 ZACAPA

EL SALVADOR: ADMINISTRATIVE REGIONS

1 AHUACHAPÁN
2 SANTA ANA
3 SONSONATE
4 CHALATENANGO
5 LA LIBERTAD
6 SAN SALVADOR
7 CUSCATLÁN
8 CABAÑAS
9 LA PAZ
10 SAN VICENTE
11 USULUTÁN
12 SAN MIGUEL
13 MORAZÁN
14 LA UNIÓN

SCALE 1:4,000,000
(projection: Lambert Conformal Conic)

Lighthouse Reef is one of a series of coral reefs lying off the coast of Belize in the shallow waters of the Caribbean.

CENTRAL AMERICA

BELIZE, COSTA RICA, EL SALVADOR, GUATEMALA, HONDURAS, NICARAGUA, PANAMA

THE NATURAL BEAUTY of tropical Central America belies the civil strife which has long plagued this region. The imprint of Spanish colonization prevails in the official language and Catholic religion of the people, who are mostly of mixed heritage. Indigenous Maya peoples remain most numerous in Guatemala. The USA has frequently intervened in Central America, purchasing from Panama the right to build the canal in 1903, and sponsoring guerrilla activity in Nicaragua during the 1980s. Initiatives for a common market with Mexico offer hope of overcoming foreign economic dependency and attaining the relative prosperity enjoyed by Costa Rica. However, gaping disparities of wealth and land ownership remain fundamental obstacles to peace and stability.

USING THE LAND AND SEA

ABOUT HALF OF ALL AGRICULTURAL PRODUCE is exported. Five commodities dominate commercial farming: bananas, grown on the humid coastal lowlands of the Caribbean; coffee; cotton; sugar and beef on the Pacific side of the isthmus. Corn is the main subsistence crop and many varieties are grown, supplemented by beans, squashes and sorghum. Large areas of tropical rainforest are commercially exploited, causing concern about deforestation.

THE URBAN/RURAL POPULATION DIVIDE

urban 47%   rural 53%

POPULATION DENSITY
178 people per sq mile
(69 people per sq km)

TOTAL LAND AREA
196,721 sq miles
(509,640 sq km)

Land use and agricultural distribution
- cattle
- bananas
- coffee
- cotton
- corn (maize)
- shellfish
- sugar cane
- timber
- capital cities
- major towns
- pasture
- cropland
- forest

Bananas are harvested throughout the year along the Caribbean coast. Bananas are a perishable commodity and the plantations rely on good railway links to the ports for rapid distribution.

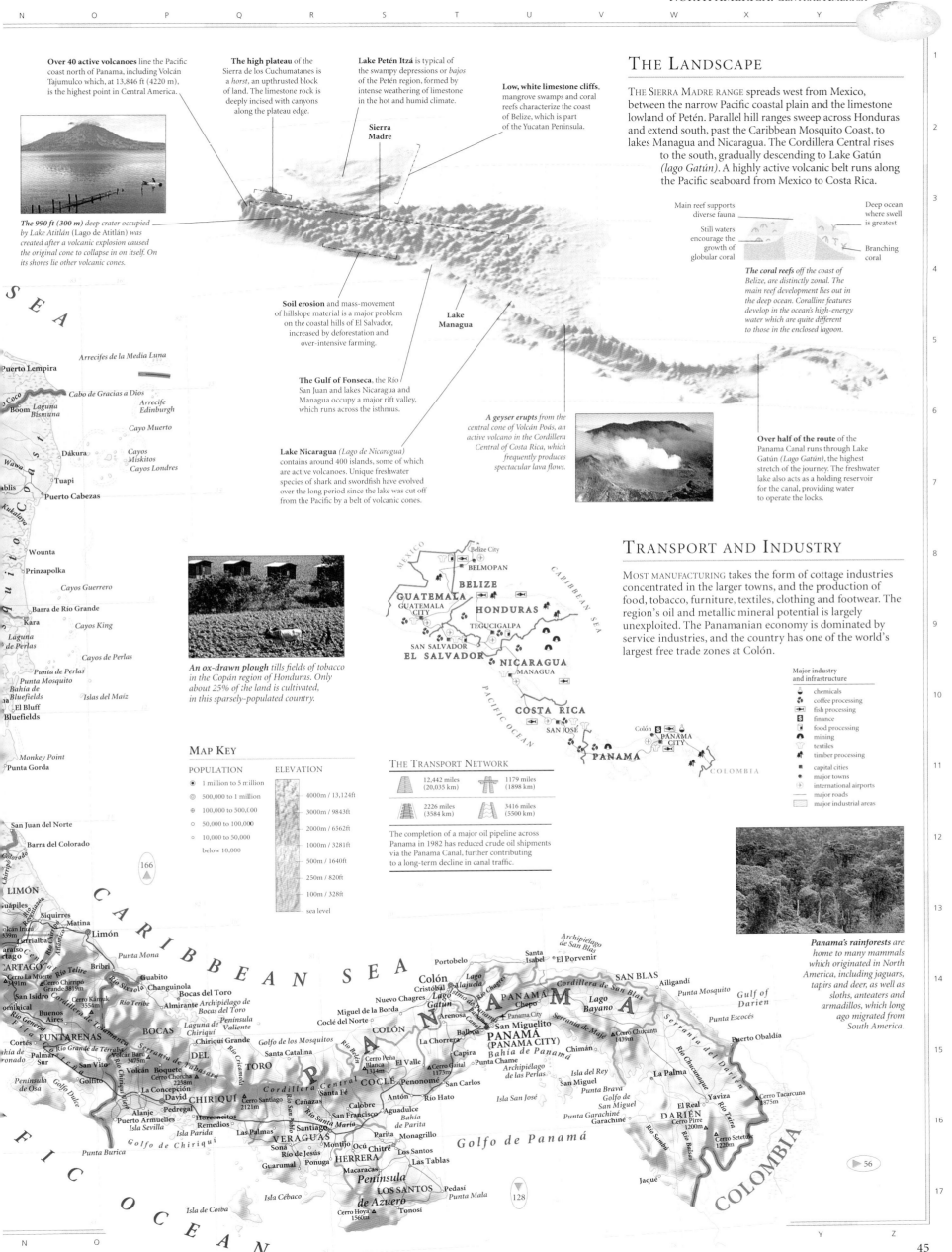

Over 40 active volcanoes line the Pacific coast north of Panama, including Volcán Tajumulco which, at 13,846 ft (4220 m), is the highest point in Central America.

The high plateau of the Sierra de los Cuchumatanes is a *horst*, an upthrusted block of land. The limestone rock is deeply incised with canyons along the plateau edge.

Lake Petén Itzá is typical of the swampy depressions or *bajos* of the Petén region, formed by intense weathering of limestone in the hot and humid climate.

Low, white limestone cliffs, mangrove swamps and coral reefs characterize the coast of Belize, which is part of the Yucatan Peninsula.

Sierra Madre

The 990 ft (300 m) deep crater occupied by Lake Atitlán (Lago de Atitlán) was created after a volcanic explosion caused the original cone to collapse in on itself. On its shores lie other volcanic cones.

Soil erosion and mass-movement of hillslope material is a major problem on the coastal hills of El Salvador, increased by deforestation and over-intensive farming.

Lake Managua

The Gulf of Fonseca, the Río San Juan and lakes Nicaragua and Managua occupy a major rift valley, which runs across the isthmus.

Lake Nicaragua (*Lago de Nicaragua*) contains around 400 islands, some of which are active volcanoes. Unique freshwater species of shark and swordfish have evolved over the long period since the lake was cut off from the Pacific by a belt of volcanic cones.

A geyser erupts from the central cone of Volcán Poás, an active volcano in the Cordillera Central of Costa Rica, which frequently produces spectacular lava flows.

THE LANDSCAPE

THE SIERRA MADRE RANGE spreads west from Mexico, between the narrow Pacific coastal plain and the limestone lowland of Petén. Parallel hill ranges sweep across Honduras and extend south, past the Caribbean Mosquito Coast, to lakes Managua and Nicaragua. The Cordillera Central rises to the south, gradually descending to Lake Gatún (*lago Gatún*). A highly active volcanic belt runs along the Pacific seaboard from Mexico to Costa Rica.

Main reef supports diverse fauna

Deep ocean where swell is greatest

Still waters encourage the growth of globular coral

Branching coral

The coral reefs off the coast of Belize, are distinctly zonal. The main reef development lies out in the deep ocean. Coralline features develop in the ocean's high-energy water which is quite different to those in the enclosed lagoon.

Over half of the route of the Panama Canal runs through Lake Gatún (*Lago Gatún*), the highest stretch of the journey. The freshwater lake also acts as a holding reservoir for the canal, providing water to operate the locks.

TRANSPORT AND INDUSTRY

MOST MANUFACTURING takes the form of cottage industries concentrated in the larger towns, and the production of food, tobacco, furniture, textiles, clothing and footwear. The region's oil and metallic mineral potential is largely unexploited. The Panamanian economy is dominated by service industries, and the country has one of the world's largest free trade zones at Colón.

An ox-drawn plough tills fields of tobacco in the Copán region of Honduras. Only about 25% of the land is cultivated, in this sparsely-populated country.

MEXICO
Belize City
BELMOPAN
BELIZE
GUATEMALA
GUATEMALA CITY
HONDURAS
TEGUCIGALPA
CARIBBEAN SEA
SAN SALVADOR
EL SALVADOR
NICARAGUA
MANAGUA
PACIFIC OCEAN
COSTA RICA
SAN JOSÉ
Colón
PANAMA CITY
PANAMA
COLOMBIA

Major industry and infrastructure
- chemicals
- coffee processing
- fish processing
- finance
- food processing
- mining
- textiles
- timber processing
- capital cities
- major towns
- international airports
- major roads
- major industrial areas

MAP KEY

POPULATION
- ◉ 1 million to 5 million
- ◎ 500,000 to 1 million
- ⊕ 100,000 to 500,000
- ○ 50,000 to 100,000
- ○ 10,000 to 50,000

ELEVATION
- 4000m / 13,124ft
- 3000m / 9843ft
- 2000m / 6562ft
- 1000m / 3281ft
- 500m / 1640ft
- 250m / 820ft
- 100m / 328ft
- sea level

166

THE TRANSPORT NETWORK

12,442 miles (20,035 km)		1179 miles (1898 km)
2226 miles (3584 km)		3416 miles (5500 km)

The completion of a major oil pipeline across Panama in 1982 has reduced crude oil shipments via the Panama Canal, further contributing to a long-term decline in canal traffic.

Panama's rainforests are home to many mammals which originated in North America, including jaguars, tapirs and deer, as well as sloths, anteaters and armadillos, which long ago migrated from South America.

Map labels

SEA

Arrecifes de la Media Luna

Puerto Lempira
Cabo de Gracias a Dios
Río Coco
Boom
Laguna Bismuna
Arrecife Edinburgh
Cayo Muerto
Dákura
Cayos Miskitos
Cayos Londres
Wawa
Tuapi
Puerto Cabezas
Kukalaya
Wounta
Prinzapolka
Cayos Guerrero
Barra de Río Grande
Kara
Cayos King
Laguna de Perlas
Cayos de Perlas
Punta de Perlas
Punta Mosquito
Bahía de Bluefields
Islas del Maíz
El Bluff
Bluefields
Monkey Point
Punta Gorda
San Juan del Norte
Barra del Colorado

LIMÓN
Guápiles
Siquirres
Matina
Turrialba
Cerro Irazú
Limón
Punta Mona
Bribri
CARTAGO
Cerro La Muerte
Río Telire
Guabito
Cerro Chirripó Grande 3819m
Changuinola
Bocas del Toro
San Isidro
Cordillera de Talamanca
Río Sixaola
Nuevo Chagres
Río Teribe
Almirante
Archipiélago de Bocas del Toro
Miguel de la Borda
Buenos Aires
Coclé del Norte
Cortés
Laguna de Chiriquí
Chiriquí Grande
Arenosa
La Chorrera
PUNTARENAS
Río Grande de Térraba
BOCAS DEL TORO
Santa Catalina
Balboa
Palmar Sur
Volcán Barú 3475m
Serranía de Tabasará
Golfo de los Mosquitos
Río Belén
Cerro Peña Blanca 1314m
San Miguelito
Peninsula de Osa
Volcán Boquete
Cerro Chorcha 2238m
La Concepción
Chiriquí Grande
Río Cricamola
El Valle
Capira
PANAMÁ (PANAMA CITY)
Golfito
David
CHIRIQUÍ
Cerro Gaital 1173m
Punta Chame
Horconcitos
Remedios
Alanje
Pedregal
Cañazas
Río Santa María
San Francisco
Río San Pablo
Santiago
Santa Fé
Calobre
Aguadulce
Penonomé
Antón
San Carlos
Río Hato
Puerto Armuelles
Isla Sevilla
Isla Parida
Las Palmas
VERAGUAS
Río de Jesús
Calovebora
Montijo
Divisa
Parita
Chitré
Monagrillo
Los Santos
Golfo de Chiriquí
Punta Burica
Soná
Guarumal
Ponuga
Macaracas
HERRERA
Ocú
Las Tablas
Isla Cébaco
Peninsula de Azuero
LOS SANTOS
Pedasí
Punta Mala
Isla de Coiba
Cerro Hoya 1560m
Tonosí

CARIBBEAN SEA
Portobelo
Santa Isabel
El Porvenir
Colón
Lago Alajuela
SAN BLAS
Ailigandi
Punta Mosquito
Cordillera de San Blas
Cristóbal
Lago Gatún
Lago Bayano
Gulf of Darien
PANAMA
Chepo
Serranía de Majé
Cerro Chucanti 1439m
Puerto Obaldía
Bahía de Panamá
Chimán
Archipiélago de las Perlas
Isla del Rey
San Miguel
La Palma
Punta Brava
Golfo de San Miguel
Punta Garachiné
Garachiné
DARIÉN
El Real
Cerro Pirre 1200m
Cerro Tacarcuna 1875m
Serranía del Darién
Río Tuira
Río Chucunaque
Río Sambú
Cerro Setetule 1220m
Golfo de Panamá
Jaqué
COLOMBIA

56
128

PACIFIC OCEAN

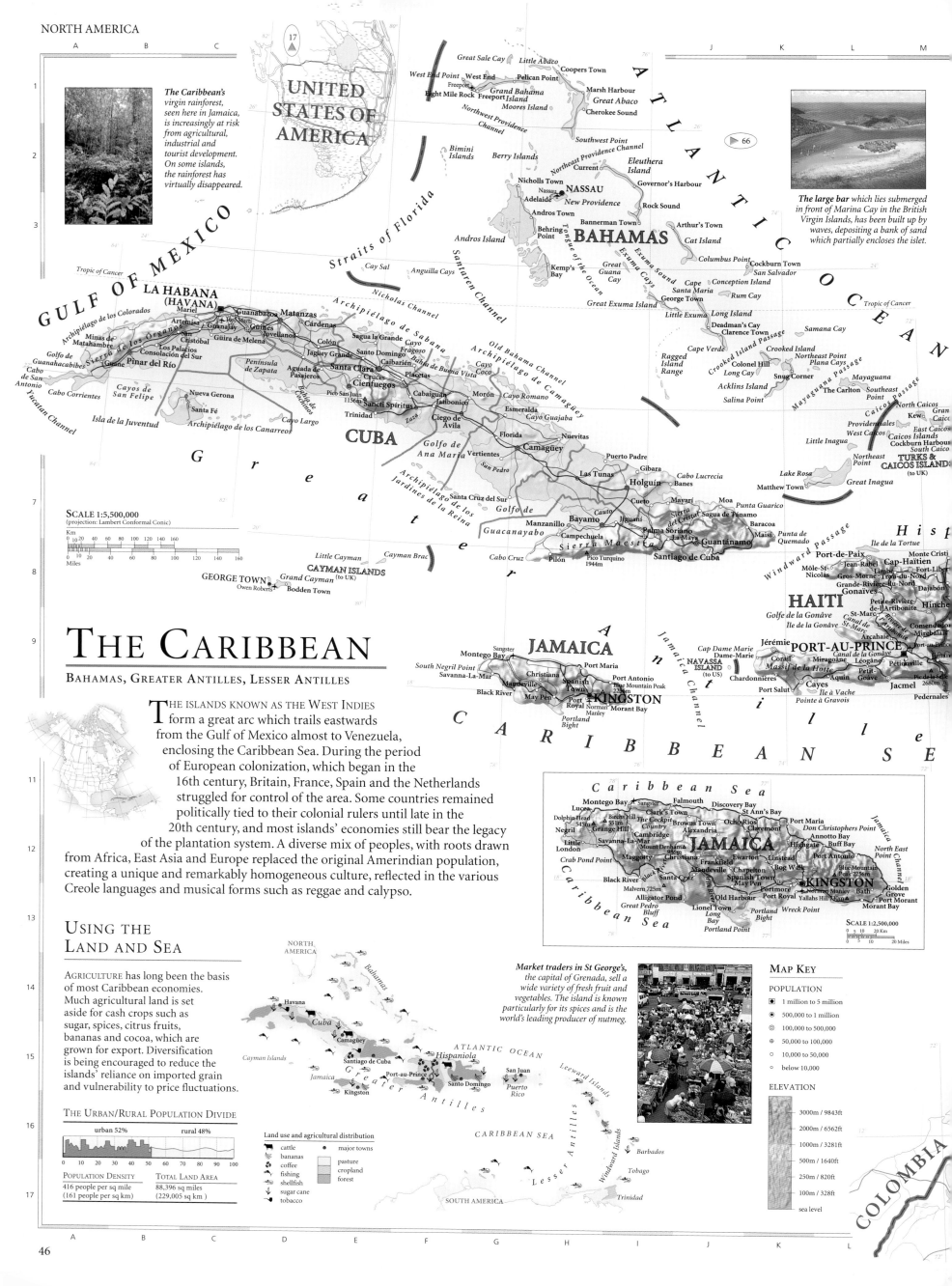

The Caribbean's virgin rainforest, seen here in Jamaica, is increasingly at risk from agricultural, industrial and tourist development. On some islands, the rainforest has virtually disappeared.

UNITED STATES OF AMERICA

The large bar which lies submerged in front of Marina Cay in the British Virgin Islands, has been built up by waves, depositing a bank of sand which partially encloses the islet.

ATLANTIC OCEAN

GULF OF MEXICO

BAHAMAS

CUBA

CAYMAN ISLANDS (to UK)

HAITI

JAMAICA

CARIBBEAN SEA

TURKS & CAICOS ISLANDS (to UK)

NAVASSA ISLAND (to US)

PORT-AU-PRINCE

THE CARIBBEAN

BAHAMAS, GREATER ANTILLES, LESSER ANTILLES

THE ISLANDS KNOWN AS THE WEST INDIES form a great arc which trails eastwards from the Gulf of Mexico almost to Venezuela, enclosing the Caribbean Sea. During the period of European colonization, which began in the 16th century, Britain, France, Spain and the Netherlands struggled for control of the area. Some countries remained politically tied to their colonial rulers until late in the 20th century, and most islands' economies still bear the legacy of the plantation system. A diverse mix of peoples, with roots drawn from Africa, East Asia and Europe replaced the original Amerindian population, creating a unique and remarkably homogeneous culture, reflected in the various Creole languages and musical forms such as reggae and calypso.

USING THE LAND AND SEA

AGRICULTURE has long been the basis of most Caribbean economies. Much agricultural land is set aside for cash crops such as sugar, spices, citrus fruits, bananas and cocoa, which are grown for export. Diversification is being encouraged to reduce the islands' reliance on imported grain and vulnerability to price fluctuations.

THE URBAN/RURAL POPULATION DIVIDE

urban 52%   rural 48%

POPULATION DENSITY
416 people per sq mile
(161 people per sq km)

TOTAL LAND AREA
88,396 sq miles
(229,005 sq km)

Land use and agricultural distribution
- cattle
- bananas
- coffee
- fishing
- shellfish
- sugar cane
- tobacco
- major towns
- pasture
- cropland
- forest

Market traders in St George's, the capital of Grenada, sell a wide variety of fresh fruit and vegetables. The island is known particularly for its spices and is the world's leading producer of nutmeg.

JAMAICA

SCALE 1:5,500,000
(projection: Lambert Conformal Conic)

MAP KEY

POPULATION
- 1 million to 5 million
- 500,000 to 1 million
- 100,000 to 500,000
- 50,000 to 100,000
- 10,000 to 50,000
- below 10,000

ELEVATION
- 3000m / 9843ft
- 2000m / 6562ft
- 1000m / 3281ft
- 500m / 1640ft
- 250m / 820ft
- 100m / 328ft
- sea level

COLOMBIA

TRANSPORT AND INDUSTRY

CARIBBEAN INDUSTRY remains, with few exceptions, agricultural and export-led, or service-based, supporting the flourishing tourist industry. However, several countries including Jamaica, Barbados, Trinidad and Tobago and Puerto Rico have developed important mineral industries, and Cuba is attempting to diversify its economy by importing capital goods to start up new manufacturing businesses.

Major industry and infrastructure

- fish processing
- finance
- mining
- oil refining
- sugar refining
- tourism
- major towns
- international airports
- major roads
- major industrial areas

Cruise ships, such as this one moored at Castries in St Lucia, have become a popular way for tourists to travel round the Caribbean islands, stopping off at several islands for sightseeing and shopping.

THE TRANSPORT NETWORK

21,197 miles (34,133 km)		369 miles (627 km)	
9100 miles (14,654 km)		211 miles (340 km)	

Air links are well-developed between most of the Caribbean islands. The importance of the tourist trade has recently encouraged many countries to upgrade their paved roads.

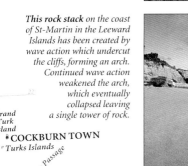

This rock stack on the coast of St-Martin in the Leeward Islands has been created by wave action which undercut the cliffs, forming an arch. Continued wave action weakened the arch, which eventually collapsed leaving a single tower of rock.

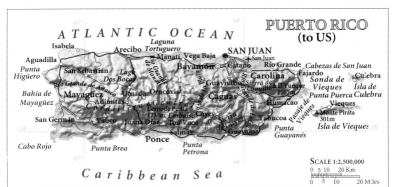

PUERTO RICO (to US)

SCALE 1:2,500,000

GUADELOUPE (to France)

SCALE 1:2,500,000

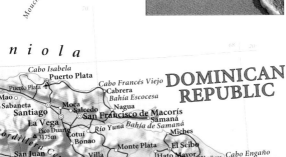

DOMINICAN REPUBLIC

PUERTO RICO (to US)

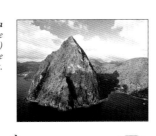

The Pitons in St Lucia are two volcanic domes; the tallest is 2620 ft (798 m) high. Their steep slopes are covered in thick forest.

DOMINICA

SCALE 1:2,000,000

MARTINIQUE (to France)

SCALE 1:2,500,000

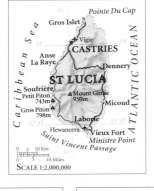

ST LUCIA

SCALE 1:2,000,000

Trinidad

SCALE 1:2,500,000

BARBADOS

SCALE 1:2,000,000

ST VINCENT

SCALE 1:2,000,000

GRENADA

SCALE 1:2,000,000

SOUTH AMERICA

REACHING FROM THE HUMID TROPICS DOWN INTO THE COLD SOUTH ATLANTIC, SOUTH AMERICA HAS AN AREA OF 6,886,000 SQ MILES (17,835,000 SQ KM). THERE ARE 12 SEPARATE COUNTRIES, WITH THE LARGEST, BRAZIL, COVERING ALMOST HALF THE CONTINENT.

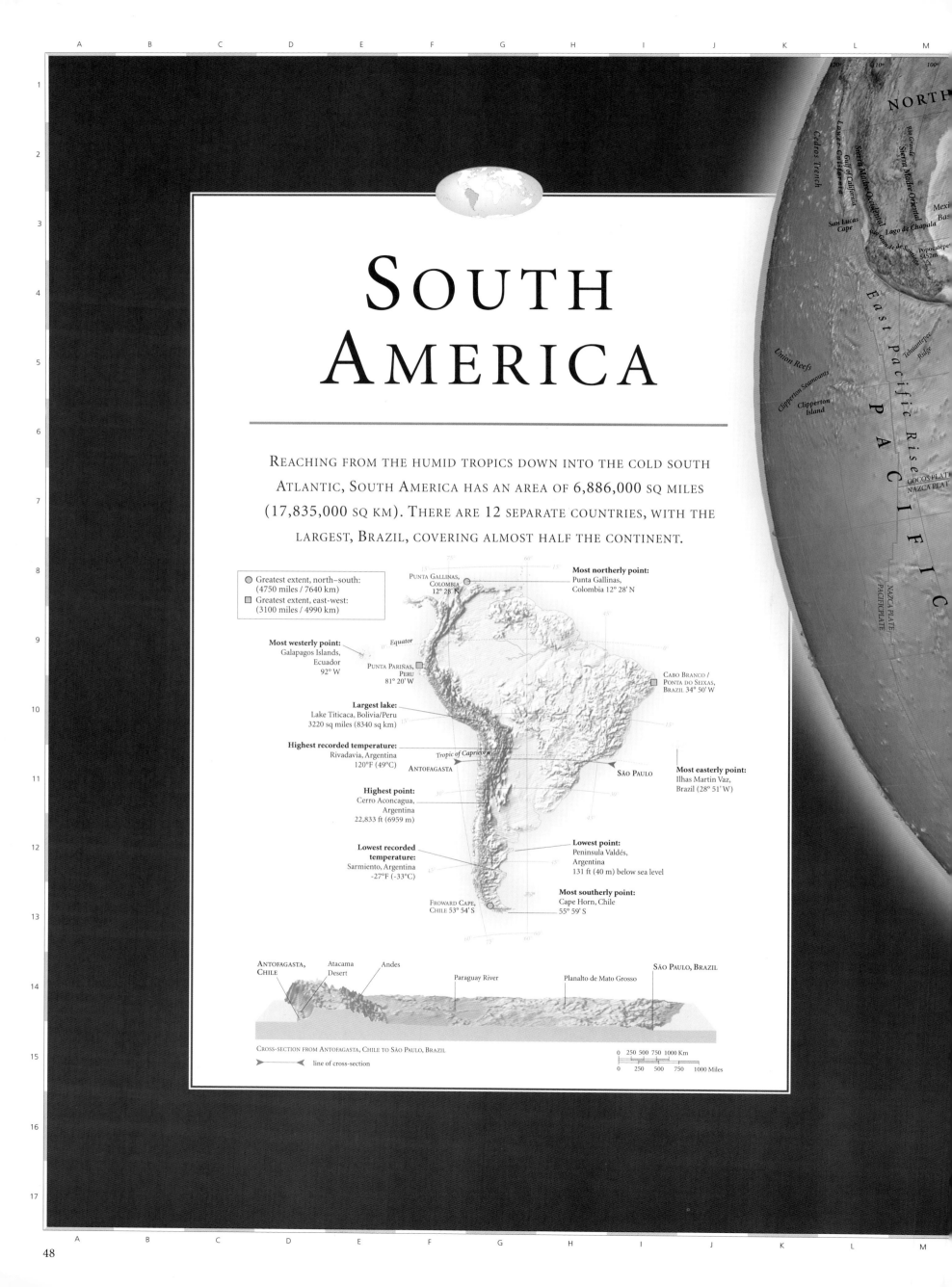

● Greatest extent, north–south:
(4750 miles / 7640 km)
■ Greatest extent, east-west:
(3100 miles / 4990 km)

Most northerly point:
Punta Gallinas,
Colombia 12° 28' N

PUNTA GALLINAS,
COLOMBIA
12° 28' N

Most westerly point:
Galapagos Islands,
Ecuador
92° W

Equator

PUNTA PARIÑAS,
PERU
81° 20' W

CABO BRANCO /
PONTA DO SEIXAS,
BRAZIL 34° 50' W

Largest lake:
Lake Titicaca, Bolivia/Peru
3220 sq miles (8340 sq km)

Highest recorded temperature:
Rivadavia, Argentina
120°F (49°C)

Tropic of Capricorn

ANTOFAGASTA

SÃO PAULO

Most easterly point:
Ilhas Martin Vaz,
Brazil (28° 51' W)

Highest point:
Cerro Aconcagua,
Argentina
22,833 ft (6959 m)

Lowest point:
Peninsula Valdés,
Argentina
131 ft (40 m) below sea level

Lowest recorded temperature:
Sarmiento, Argentina
-27°F (-33°C)

FROWARD CAPE,
CHILE 53° 54' S

Most southerly point:
Cape Horn, Chile
55° 59' S

ANTOFAGASTA,
CHILE

Atacama
Desert

Andes

Paraguay River

Planalto de Mato Grosso

SÃO PAULO, BRAZIL

CROSS-SECTION FROM ANTOFAGASTA, CHILE TO SÃO PAULO, BRAZIL.

▶——◀ line of cross-section

0 250 500 750 1000 Km

0   250   500   750   1000 Miles

AMERICA

Cape Canaveral

Apalachee Bay

Lake Okeechobee

Sargasso
Sea

Nares Plain

Tropic of Cancer

Cape Verde
Basin

Cape Verde
Islands

Mississippi Fan

gbee Escarpment

Gulf of Mexico

Straits of Florida

Great Bahama Bank

Bahamas

Hatteras plain

West Indies

Puerto Rico Trench

NORTH AMERICAN PLATE
SOUTH AMERICAN PLATE

MID-ATLANTIC RIDGE

ATLANTIC

Yucatan
Peninsula

Cuba

Yucatan
Basin

Greater

Cayman Trough

Jamaica

Windward Passage

Hispaniola

Leeward Islands

Puerto Rico   Nevis

Barbuda
Antigua
Guadeloupe

Dominica

Gambia
Plain

Antilles

Cayman Trough

NORTH AMERICAN
PLATE

Gulf of
Honduras

CARIBBEAN
PLATE

Sierra
Madre del Sur

Gulf of
Fonseca

Middle America Trench

Guatemala
Basin

Colón Ridge

Mosquito Coast

Lake
Nicaragua

Mosquito
Gulf

Isthmus of Panama

Gulf of Panama

Gulf of
Darién

Panama
Basin

Caribbean Sea

Punta
Gallinas

Peninsula
de la Guajira

Lesser Antilles

Isla de
Margarita

Martinique

Saint Lucia

Barbados

Grenada

Tobago

Trinidad

Aruba
Curaçao

Bonaire

Gulf of Venezuela

Cordillera de la Costa

AFRICAN PLATE

Doldrums Fracture Zone

Demerara
Plain

Guiana

Basin

Four North Fracture Zone   Saint Paul Fracture Zone

Equator

Lake
Maracaibo

CARIBBEAN PLATE

SOUTH AMERICAN
PLATE

Cordillera Oriental

Orinoco

Apure

Arauca

Meta

Llanos

Guaviare

Vichada

Caquetá

Caroni

Orinoco

Caura

Guiana Highlands

Serra
Parima

Branco

Urariçoera

Tumuc-Humac Mountains

Araguari

Ceará Plain

Amazon Fan

Baía de
Marajó

Baía de
São Marcos

Atol
das Rocas

Fernando
de Noronha

Cabo de
São Roque

Galapagos
Islands

Colombian
Basin

Peninsula
de Azuero

Cordillera Occidental

Cordillera Central

Putumayo

Napo

Uaupés

Rio Negro

Japurá

Içá

Jutaí

Jauaperi

Represa
Balbina

Amazon

Purus

Juruá

Negro   Viruá   Iriri

Xingu

Tapajós

Tocantins

Represa
de Tucuruí

Itapicuru

Mearim

Serra Grande

Parnaíba

Planalto da
Borborema

Cabo Branco

Represa de
Itaparica

Pernambuco
Plain

Chimborazo
6310m

Gulf of
Guayaquil

Punta
Parinas

Cordillera Real

Amazon Basin

SOUTH

AMERICA

Amazon

Purus

Madre de Dios

Roosevelt

Aripuanã

Juruena

Serra do Cachimbo

Serra do Roncador

Teles Pires   Xingu

Araguaia

Chapada das
Mangabeiras

Represa de
Sobradinho

São Francisco

Chapada Diamantina

Brazilian Highlands

Serra do Espinhaço

Brazil

Basin

Peru
Basin

Mendaña Fracture Zone

ANDES

Marañón

Ucayali

Guaporé

Beni

Mamoré

Madeira

Chapada dos Parecis

Pôrto

Serra Formosa

Serra Geral
de Goiás

Planalto de

Mato Grosso

Cuiabá

Aporé

Paranaíba

Rio Grande

Serra da Mantiqueira

Doce

Paraguai

Baía de
Todos os Santos

Jequitinhonha

Abrolhos
Bank

Trindade Spur

Tropic of Capricorn

Chile
Basin

Nazca Ridge

Islas de los
Desventurados

Sala y Gomez Fracture Zone

Cordillera Oriental

Altiplano

Yungas

Lake
Titicaca

Lago Poopó

Pilcomayo

Gran Chaco

Paraguay

Pantanal

Taquari

Paraná

Iguaçu

Represa
de Itaipú

Uruguay

Serra do
Paranapiacaba

Serra do Mar

Ilha de
São Sebastião

Santos
Plateau

Rio Grande
Rise

Easter
Island

Roggeveen
Basin

Juan Fernandez
Islands

Peru–Chile Trench

Atacama Desert

Aconcagua
6960m

Sierra de Córdoba

Mar Chiquita

Laguna
Mar Chiquita

Pampas

Mesopotamia

Paraná

Embalse
de Río Negro

Río
Negro

Cuchilla Grande

Mirim
Lagoon

Lagoa
dos Patos

Ilha de
São Francisco

Argentine

Basin

East Pacific Rise

NAZCA PLATE

ANTARCTIC PLATE

Neuquén

Colorado
Río Negro

Limay

Bahía
Blanca

Golfo San Matías

Argentine
Plain

Falkland Escarpment

Maurice Ewing
Bank

South Sandwich Trench

Chubut

Gulf of
San Jorge

Bahía
Grande

Falkland
Plateau

Falkland Islands

South Georgia

South Georgia Ridge

South
Sandwich
Islands

Lago
Buenos
Aires

Chico

Deseado

Lago Corcovado

Archipiélago
de los Chonos

Golfo Corcovado

Strait of Magellan

Tierra
del Fuego

Cape Horn

Scotia Ridge

SOUTH AMERICAN PLATE

SCOTIA PLATE

Scotia
Sea

SCOTIA PLATE

ANTARCTIC PLATE

Antarctic Circle

ANTARCTIC PLATE
PACIFIC PLATE

South Shetland Trough

South Shetland
Islands

South Orkney
Islands

Weddell
Sea

ANTARCTICA

A B C D E F G H I J K L M

PHYSICAL SOUTH AMERICA

THREE MAJOR PHYSIOGRAPHIC REGIONS characterize South America. The oldest, the ancient Brazilian Shield and the smaller Guyana and Patagonian shields, form the stable core of the continent. Stretching along the entire west coast are the younger Andean fold mountains with many summits rising to 20,000 ft (6100 m). These two diverse regions are separated by a number of sedimentary basins carrying South America's large river systems to the sea. These include the massive Amazon Basin and the basin of the Gran Chaco.

THE AMAZON BASIN AND GUYANA SHIELD

THE RIVER AMAZON occupies a large depression in the Earth's crust, formed by the uplift of the Andes. It is covered by thick volcanic deposits and layers of alluvium – these have been laid down by the Amazon's many tributaries. To the north is the smaller Guyana Shield.

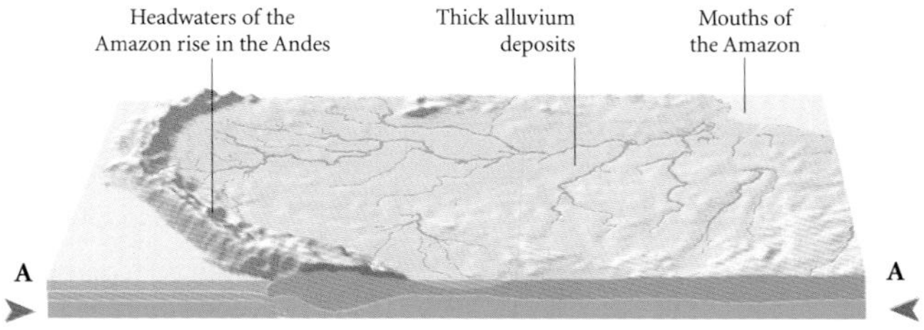

Headwaters of the Amazon rise in the Andes — Thick alluvium deposits — Mouths of the Amazon

A ———— A

Section across northern South America showing Amazon Basin and its drainage pattern.

0 500 1000 Km
0 500 1000 Miles

SCALE 1:27,500,000
(projection: Lambert Azimuthal Equal Area)

Km
0 100 200 400 600 800
Miles
0 100 200 400 600 800

THE ANDEAN UPLANDS

THE ANDEAN UPLANDS run along the west coast of South America. They are being uplifted as the Nazca Plate is subducted beneath the South American Plate. They contain some of the world's largest volcanoes, such as Cotopaxi, and Lake Titicaca which occupies a dormant site. The far south has many large ice-sheets and a fragmented coastline.

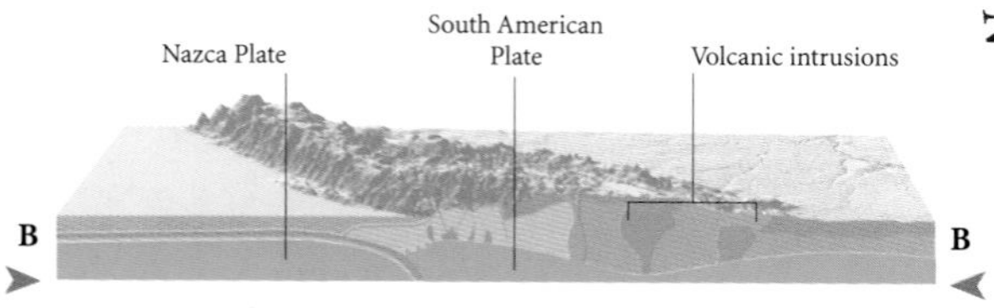

Nazca Plate — South American Plate — Volcanic intrusions

B ———— B

Cross-section through the Andes showing the subduction of the Nazca Plate beneath the South American Plate.

0 200 400 Km
0 200 400 Miles

THE BRAZILIAN SHIELD AND GRAN CHACO

THE IMMENSE BRAZILIAN SHIELD underlies more than one-third of South America. It is pitted with numerous volcanic intrusions, and a large basaltic plateau exists between the Paraná River and the Atlantic Ocean. The flat Gran Chaco lies to the west of the shield, covered by sedimentary deposits eroded from the Andes, and transported by South America's mighty rivers.

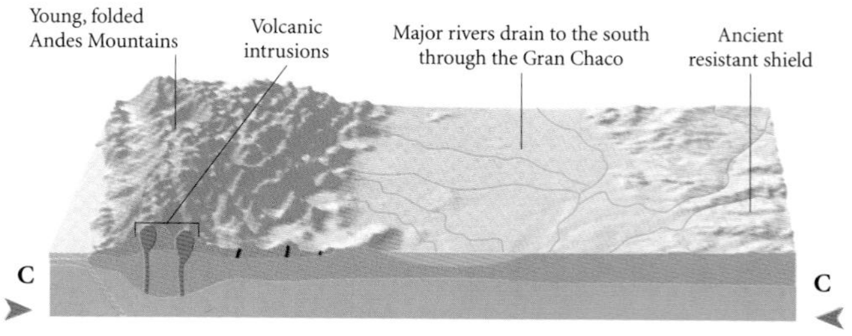

Young, folded Andes Mountains — Volcanic intrusions — Major rivers drain to the south through the Gran Chaco — Ancient resistant shield

C ———— C

Section across central South America showing the flat basin of the Gran Chaco and the ancient Brazilian Shield.

0 200 400 Km
0 200 400 Miles

MAP KEY

ELEVATION

6000m / 19,686ft
4000m / 13,124ft
3000m / 9843ft
2000m / 6562ft
1500m / 4922ft
1000m / 3281ft
500m / 1640ft
250m / 820ft
100m / 328ft
sea level

PLATE MARGINS
(for explanation see page xiv)

———— constructive
△ △ destructive
———— conservative
.... uncertain

———— physiographic regions
► line of cross-section

Map labels

Punta Gallinas
Gulf of Venezuela
Lake Maracaibo
Gulf of Darien
Gulf of Panama
Cauca
Magdalena
Cordillera Occidental
Cordillera Central
Cordillera Oriental
Llanos
Orinoco
Pakaraima Mountains
GUYANA SHIELD
Guiana Highlands
Tumuc-Humac Mountains
Río Negro
Branco
Japurá
Amazon
Represa Balbina
Ilha de Marajó
Cabo de São Roque
COCOS PLATE
NAZCA PLATE
Cordillera Real
Cotopaxi 5897m
Chimborazo 6310m
Putumayo
Amazon
Javirí
Purus
Madeira
Tapajós
Xingu
Serra dos Carajás
Araguaia
Tocantins
Planalto da Borborema
Gulf of Guayaquil
Marañón
Ucayali
SUB-ANDEAN
Serra do Cachimbo
BRAZILIAN
Represa de Sobradinho
Punta Negra
Nevado Huascarán 6768m
Chapada dos Parecis
Guaporé
Madre de Dios
Serra Formosa
Serra do Roncador
Serra Dourada
São Francisco
SHIELD
Brazilian Highlands
Serra do Espinhaço
Lake Titicaca
Planalto de Mato Grosso
Pantanal
SOUTH AMERICAN PLATE
NAZCA PLATE
ANDEAN SYSTEM
Altiplano
Lago Poopó
Serra do Caiapó
Serra de Maracaju
Pilcomayo
Gran Chaco
Paraná
Serra Geral
Serra do Mar
Serra da Mantiqueira
PACIFIC OCEAN
ATLANTIC OCEAN
Cerro Ojos del Salado 6880m
Paraguay
Mesopotamia
Uruguay
Lagoa dos Patos
Cerro Aconcagua 6959m
Salado
Pampas
Mirim Lagoon
Paraná
Río de la Plata
Isla de Chiloé
Colorado
Río Negro
Península Valdés
PATAGONIAN SHIELD
Chico
Lago Colhué Huapi
Gulf of San Jorge
Patagonia
Deseado
Golfo de Peñas
Bahía Grande
Falkland Islands
ANTARCTIC PLATE
Strait of Magellan
Tierra del Fuego
SOUTH AMERICAN PLATE
SCOTIA PLATE
Cape Horn

CLIMATE

THE CLIMATE OF SOUTH AMERICA is influenced by three principal factors: the seasonal shift of high pressure air masses over the tropics, cold ocean currents along the western coast, affecting temperature and precipitation, and the mountain barrier produced by the Andes, which creates a rain shadow over much of the south.

Mild winters and cool summers typify the extensive Pampas grasslands of Argentina.

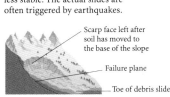

Chile's hyper-arid Atacama Desert is renowned as one of the driest places on Earth.

Climate
- tundra
- cool continental
- warm humid
- semi-arid
- arid
- humid equatorial
- tropical
- daily hours of sunshine, January
- daily hours of sunshine, July
- → cold wind

TEMPERATURE

Average January temperature

Average July temperature

Temperature
- below -30°C (-22°F)
- -30 to -20°C (-22 to -4°F)
- -20 to -10°C (-4 to 14°F)
- -10 to 0°C (14 to 32°F)
- 0 to 10°C (32 to 50°F)
- 10 to 20°C (50°F)
- 20 to 30°C (68 to 86°F)
- above 30°C (86°F)

RAINFALL

Average January rainfall

Average July rainfall

Rainfall
- 0–25 mm (0–1 in)
- 25–50 mm (1–2 in)
- 50–100 mm (2–4 in)
- 100–200 mm (4–8 in)
- 200–300 mm (8–12 in)
- 300–400 mm (12–16 in)
- 400–500 mm (16–20 in)
- more than 500 mm (20 in)

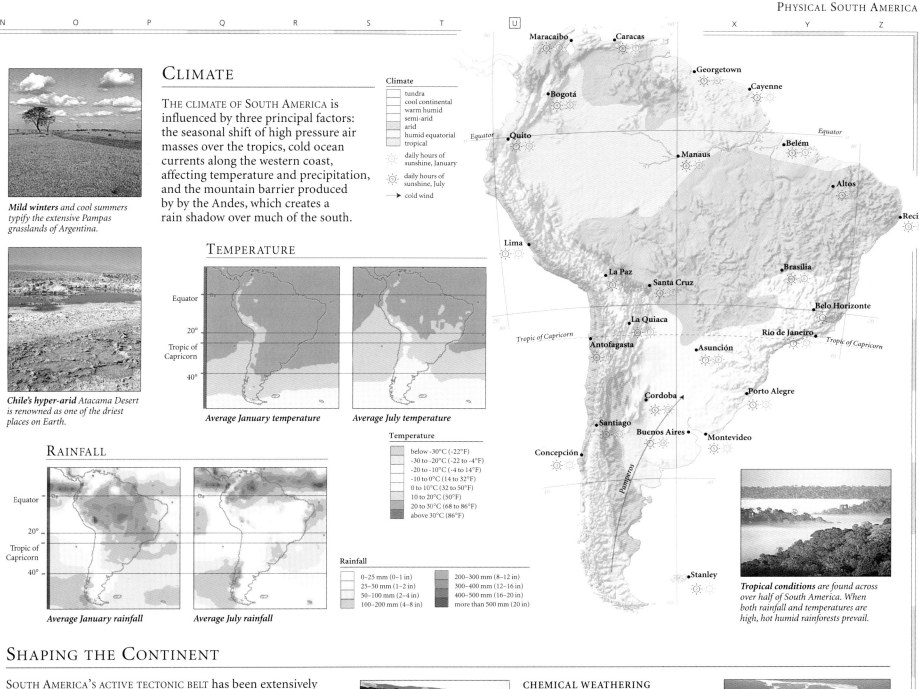

Tropical conditions are found across over half of South America. When both rainfall and temperatures are high, hot humid rainforests prevail.

SHAPING THE CONTINENT

SOUTH AMERICA'S ACTIVE TECTONIC BELT has been extensively folded over millions of years; landslides are still frequent in the mountains. The large river systems that erode the mountains flow across resistant shield areas, depositing sediment. Present-day glaciation affects the distinctive landscape of the far south.

MASS MOVEMENT

6 Debris slides are common in the highlands of South America *(left)*. They occur where soil on a slope is saturated by rainwater and therefore less stable. The actual slides are often triggered by earthquakes.

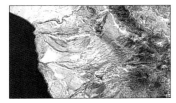

- Scarp face left after soil has moved to the base of the slope
- Failure plane
- Toe of debris slide

MASS MOVEMENT: A SECTION OF A DEBRIS SLIDE

CHEMICAL WEATHERING

1 Table mountains *(left)* are the eroded remnants of an ancient upland. As water percolates along cracks in these high, flat-topped mountains it forms intricate cave systems. Chemical weathering also isolates large blocks which then collapse, accumulating as rockfalls at the foot of scarp slopes.

- Smooth summit dissected by deep gorges
- Rainfall
- Run-off surges down caverns as waterfalls

CHEMICAL WEATHERING: EROSION OF THE GUYANA SHIELD

THE EVOLVING LANDSCAPE

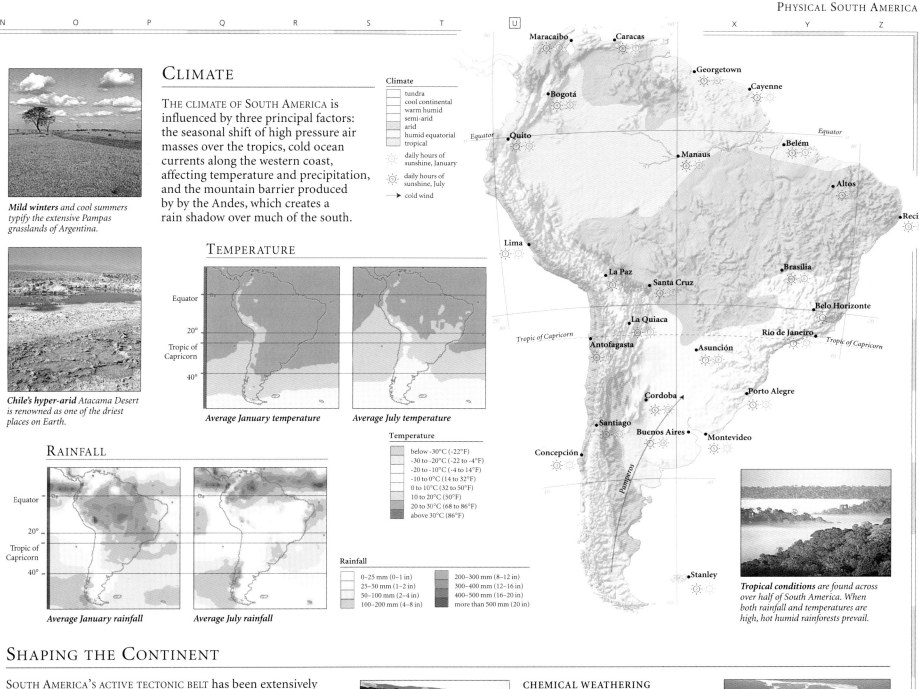

RIVER SYSTEMS

2 Along the Amazon *(above)* there is a great variation in rates of erosion. As the headwaters of the Amazon flow down from the Andes, they erode and transport vast quantities of sediment, and are known as whitewaters. Across the shield areas erosion rates are very low. These rivers, carrying rotting vegetation, are called blackwaters.

- Whitewater river
- Blackwater river
- Little erosion in shield areas
- Confluence of whitewater with blackwater

RIVER SYSTEMS: SUSPENDED SEDIMENTS IN THE AMAZON

FOLDING

5 Folding occurs beneath the surface under high temperatures and pressures. Rocks become sufficiently malleable to flow and not fracture as tectonic plates collide. In the Valley of the Moon in Chile *(above)*, anticlines (or upfolds) and synclines (or troughs) have been exploited by erosion.

- Fold axis
- Anticline
- Syncline
- Fold axis

FOLDING: SYNCLINES AND ANTICLINES

DEPOSITION

4 Large alluvial fans are found extensively across South America *(above)*. Confined mountain rivers, carrying large quantities of eroded material, emerge from a mountain gorge onto the plains, where they deposit their load in huge fans.

- Mountain front
- Subsequent fan
- Confined stream in the mountains
- Fan forms as stream emerges onto the plain

DEPOSITION: FORMATION OF AN ALLUVIAL FAN

Landscape
- uplifting land
- stable land
- sinking land
- glacier
- → ocean current
- alluvial fan
- inselberg
- river

- Unstable front in deep water, where ice is fracturing
- Original extent of glacier
- Icebergs
- Stable front
- Glacier was grounded against a shoal

GLACIATION: RETREATING GLACIER IN PATAGONIA

GLACIATION

3 As fjord glaciers in Patagonia *(above)* retreat, they become grounded on shoals. In deeper water the base of the glacier becomes unstable, and icebergs break off (calve) until the glacier snout grounds once more.

POLITICAL SOUTH AMERICA

MODERN SOUTH AMERICA'S POLITICAL BOUNDARIES have their origins in the territorial endeavours of explorers during the 16th century, who claimed almost the entire continent for Portugal and Spain. The Portuguese land in the east later evolved into the federal states of Brazil, while the Spanish vice-royalties eventually emerged as separate independent nation-states in the early 19th century. South America's growing population has become increasingly urbanized, with the expansion of coastal cities into large conurbations like Rio de Janeiro and Buenos Aires. In Brazil, Argentina, Chile and Uruguay, a succession of military dictatorships has given way to fragile, but strengthening, democracies.

Europe retains a small foothold in South America. Kourou in French Guiana was the site chosen by the European Space Agency to launch the Ariane rocket. As a result of its status as a French overseas department, French Guiana is actually part of the European Union.

SCALE 1:21,500,000
(projection: Lambert Azimuthal Equal Area)

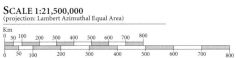

TRANSPORT

MOST MAJOR ROAD AND RAIL ROUTES are confined to the coastal regions by the forbidding natural barriers of the Andes Mountains and the Amazon Basin. Few major cross-continental routes exist, although Buenos Aires serves as a transport centre for the main rail links to La Paz and Valparaíso, while the construction of the Trans-Amazon and Pan-American Highways have made direct road travel possible from Recife to Lima and from Puerto Montt up the coast into central America. A new waterway project is proposed to transform the River Paraguay into a major shipping route, although it involves considerable wetland destruction.

South America's most extensive rail network is centred on the Argentinian capital, Buenos Aires. The construction of new rail lines from this important port, allowed the colonization of the Pampas lands for agriculture.

LANGUAGES

PRIOR TO EUROPEAN EXPLORATION in the 16th century, a diverse range of indigenous languages were spoken across the continent. With the arrival of Iberian settlers, Spanish became the dominant language, with Portuguese spoken in Brazil, and Native American languages such as Quechua and Guaraní, becoming concentrated in the continental interior. Today this pattern persists, although successive European colonization has led to Dutch being spoken in Surinam, English in Guyana, and French in French Guiana, while in large urban areas, Japanese and Chinese are increasingly common.

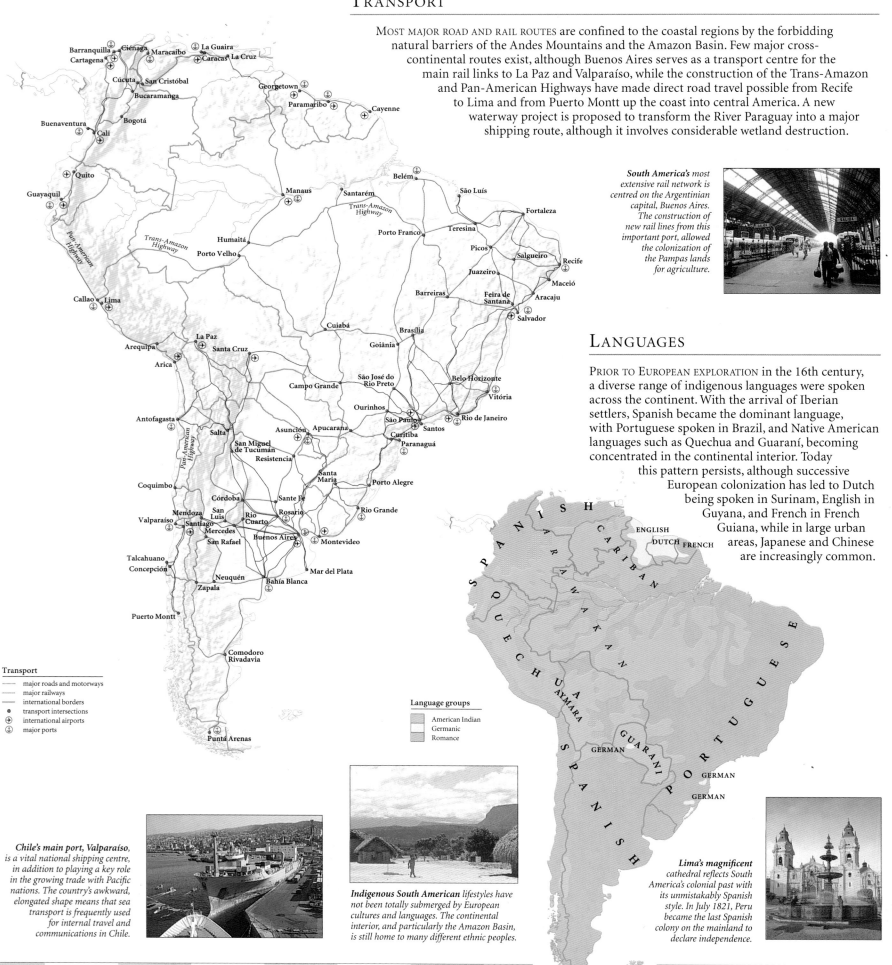

Transport
- major roads and motorways
- major railways
- international borders
- transport intersections
- international airports
- major ports

Language groups
- American Indian
- Germanic
- Romance

Chile's main port, Valparaíso, is a vital national shipping centre, in addition to playing a key role in the growing trade with Pacific nations. The country's awkward, elongated shape means that sea transport is frequently used for internal travel and communications in Chile.

Indigenous South American lifestyles have not been totally submerged by European cultures and languages. The continental interior, and particularly the Amazon Basin, is still home to many different ethnic peoples.

Lima's magnificent cathedral reflects South America's colonial past with its unmistakably Spanish style. In July 1821, Peru became the last Spanish colony on the mainland to declare independence.

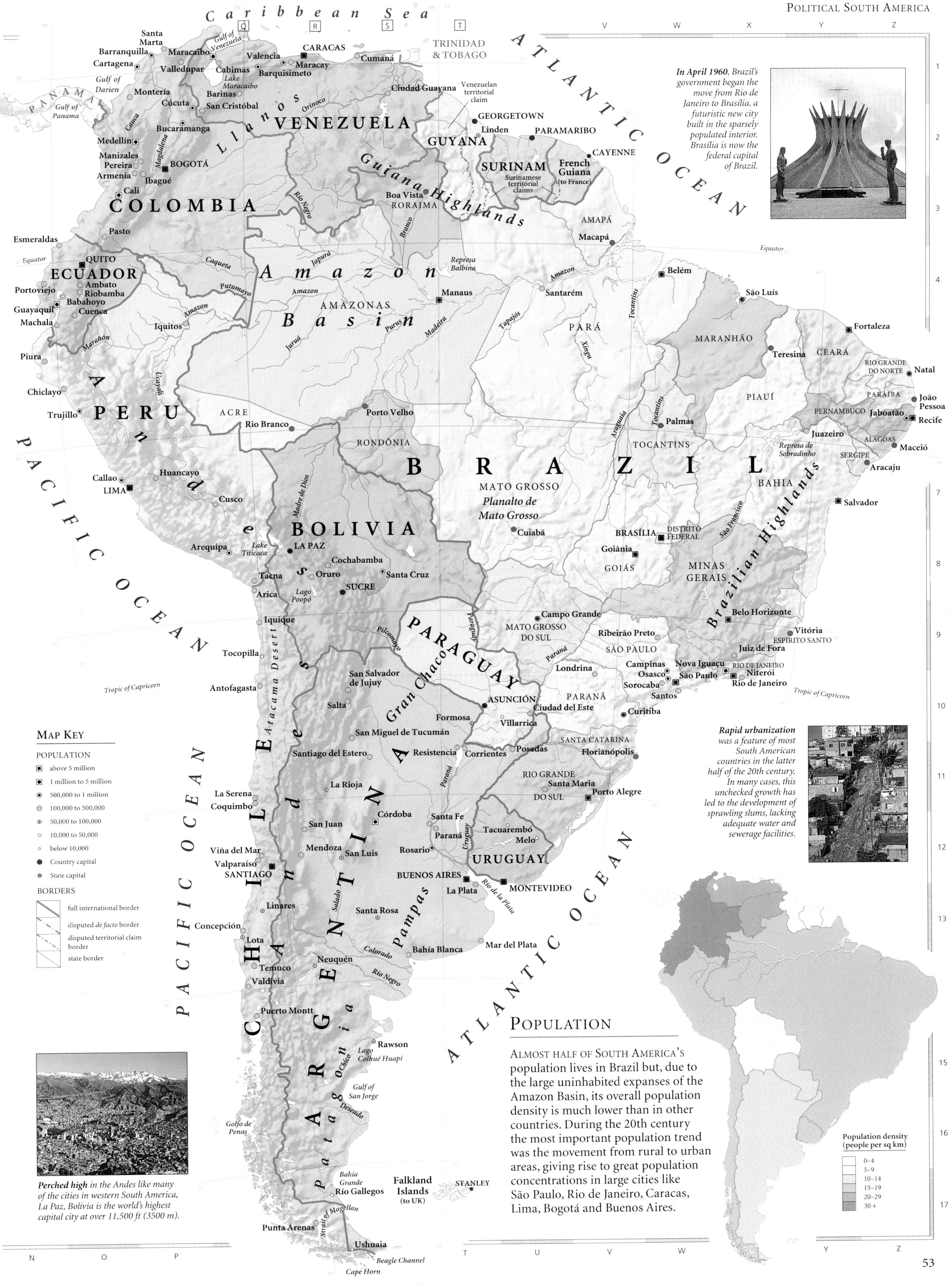

Caribbean Sea

ATLANTIC OCEAN

TRINIDAD & TOBAGO

Santa Marta
Barranquilla
Cartagena
Maracaibo
Valledupar
Cabimas
Valencia
Maracay
CARACAS
Cumaná
Barquisimeto
Montería
Cúcuta
Barinas
San Cristóbal
Ciudad Guayana
GEORGETOWN
Linden
PARAMARIBO
CAYENNE

VENEZUELA
GUYANA
SURINAM
French Guiana (to France)

Bucaramanga
Medellín
Manizales
Pereira
Armenia
Ibagué
BOGOTÁ
Cali
Pasto
Boa Vista
RORAIMA

COLOMBIA

Guiana Highlands

Esmeraldas
QUITO
ECUADOR
Portoviejo
Ambato
Riobamba
Babahoyo
Guayaquil
Cuenca
Machala
Piura
Chiclayo
Trujillo
Iquitos

AMAPÁ
Macapá
Belém
Santarém
São Luís
MARANHÃO
Fortaleza
Teresina
CEARÁ
Natal
RIO GRANDE DO NORTE
PARAÍBA
João Pessoa
Jaboatão
Recife
PERNAMBUCO
ALAGOAS
Maceió
SERGIPE
Aracaju

Amazon Basin
AMAZONAS
Manaus

PERU
Huancayo
Callao
LIMA
Cusco
Arequipa
Tacna
Arica
Iquique
Tocopilla
Antofagasta

BRAZIL
MATO GROSSO
Planalto de Mato Grosso
Cuiabá
BRASÍLIA
DISTRITO FEDERAL
Goiânia
GOIÁS
Palmas
TOCANTINS
BAHIA
Salvador
Brazilian Highlands
MINAS GERAIS
Belo Horizonte
Vitória
ESPÍRITO SANTO

BOLIVIA
LA PAZ
Cochabamba
Oruro
Santa Cruz
SUCRE
Campo Grande
MATO GROSSO DO SUL
Ribeirão Preto
SÃO PAULO
Campinas
Osasco
Sorocaba
São Paulo
Santos
Nova Iguaçu
Niterói
Rio de Janeiro
RIO DE JANEIRO
Juiz de Fora
Londrina

PARAGUAY
ASUNCIÓN
Ciudad del Este
Villarrica
PARANÁ
Curitiba
Florianópolis
SANTA CATARINA
RIO GRANDE DO SUL
Santa Maria
Porto Alegre

Gran Chaco
San Salvador de Jujuy
Salta
San Miguel de Tucumán
Santiago del Estero
Resistencia
Corrientes
Posadas
Formosa
La Rioja
San Juan
Córdoba
Santa Fe
Paraná
Rosario
Tacuarembó
Melo
URUGUAY
MONTEVIDEO

CHILE
ARGENTINA
La Serena
Coquimbo
Viña del Mar
Valparaíso
SANTIAGO
Mendoza
San Luis
Linares
Concepción
Lota
Temuco
Valdivia
Puerto Montt
BUENOS AIRES
La Plata
Santa Rosa
Bahía Blanca
Mar del Plata
Pampas
Neuquén
Rawson
Río Gallegos
Punta Arenas
Ushuaia

Falkland Islands (to UK)
STANLEY

PACIFIC OCEAN
ATLANTIC OCEAN

In April 1960, Brazil's government began the move from Rio de Janeiro to Brasília, a futuristic new city built in the sparsely populated interior. Brasília is now the federal capital of Brazil.

MAP KEY

POPULATION
- above 5 million
- 1 million to 5 million
- 500,000 to 1 million
- 100,000 to 500,000
- 50,000 to 100,000
- 10,000 to 50,000
- below 10,000
- Country capital
- State capital

BORDERS
- full international border
- disputed de facto border
- disputed territorial claim border
- state border

Rapid urbanization was a feature of most South American countries in the latter half of the 20th century. In many cases, this unchecked growth has led to the development of sprawling slums, lacking adequate water and sewerage facilities.

Perched high in the Andes like many of the cities in western South America, La Paz, Bolivia is the world's highest capital city at over 11,500 ft (3500 m).

POPULATION

ALMOST HALF OF SOUTH AMERICA'S population lives in Brazil but, due to the large uninhabited expanses of the Amazon Basin, its overall population density is much lower than in other countries. During the 20th century the most important population trend was the movement from rural to urban areas, giving rise to great population concentrations in large cities like São Paulo, Rio de Janeiro, Caracas, Lima, Bogotá and Buenos Aires.

Population density (people per sq km)
- 0–4
- 5–9
- 10–14
- 15–19
- 20–29
- 30 +

SOUTH AMERICAN RESOURCES

AGRICULTURE STILL PROVIDES THE LARGEST SINGLE FORM OF EMPLOYMENT in South America, although rural unemployment and poverty continue to drive people towards the huge coastal cities in search of jobs and opportunities. Mineral and fuel resources, although substantial, are distributed unevenly; few countries have both fossil fuels and minerals. To break industrial dependence on raw materials, boost manufacturing, and improve infrastructure, governments borrowed heavily from the World Bank in the 1960s and 1970s. This led to the accumulation of massive debts which are unlikely ever to be repaid. Today, Brazil dominates the continent's economic output, followed by Argentina. Recently, the less-developed western side of South America has benefited due to its geographical position; for example Chile is increasingly exporting raw materials to Japan.

Ciudad Guayana is a planned industrial complex in eastern Venezuela, built as an iron and steel centre to exploit the nearby iron ore reserves.

Industry

aerospace	pharmaceuticals
brewing	printing & publishing
car/vehicle manufacture	shipbuilding
chemicals	sugar processing
electronics	textiles
engineering	timber processing
finance	tobacco processing
fish processing	wine
food processing	oil
hi-tech industry	gas
iron & steel	
meat processing	industrial cities
metal refining	major industrial areas
narcotics	

The cold Peru Current flows north from the Antarctic along the Pacific coast of Peru, providing rich nutrients for one of the world's largest fishing grounds. However, over-exploitation has severely reduced Peru's anchovy catch.

STANDARD OF LIVING

WEALTH DISPARITIES throughout the continent create a wide gulf between affluent landowners and those afflicted by chronic poverty in inner-city slums. The illicit production of cocaine, and the hugely influential drug barons who control its distribution, contribute to the violent disorder and corruption which affect northwestern South America, de-stabilizing local governments and economies.

Standard of Living
(UN Human Development Index)
low
high

Both Argentina and Chile are now exploring the southernmost tip of the continent in search of oil. Here in Punta Arenas, a drilling rig is being prepared for exploratory drilling in the Strait of Magellen.

GNP per capita (US$)
0–499
500–999
1000–1499
1500–2999
3000–5999
6000+

INDUSTRY

ARGENTINA AND BRAZIL are South America's most industrialized countries and São Paulo is the continent's leading industrial centre. Long-term government investment in Brazilian industry has encouraged a diverse industrial base; engineering, steel production, food processing, textile manufacture and chemicals predominate. The illegal production of cocaine is economically significant in the Andean countries of Colombia and Bolivia. In Venezuela, the oil-dominated economy has left the country vulnerable to world oil price fluctuations. Food processing and mineral exploitation are common throughout the less industrially developed parts of the continent, including Bolivia, Chile, Ecuador and Peru.

ENVIRONMENTAL ISSUES

THE AMAZON BASIN is one of the last great wilderness areas left on Earth. The tropical rainforests which grow there are a valuable genetic resource, containing innumerable unique plants and animals. The forests are increasingly under threat from new and expanding settlements and 'slash and burn' farming techniques, which clear land for the raising of beef cattle, causing land degradation and soil erosion.

Clouds of smoke billow from the burning Amazon rainforest. Over 25,000 sq miles (60,000 sq km) of virgin rainforest are being cleared annually, destroying an ancient, irreplaceable, natural resource and biodiverse habitat.

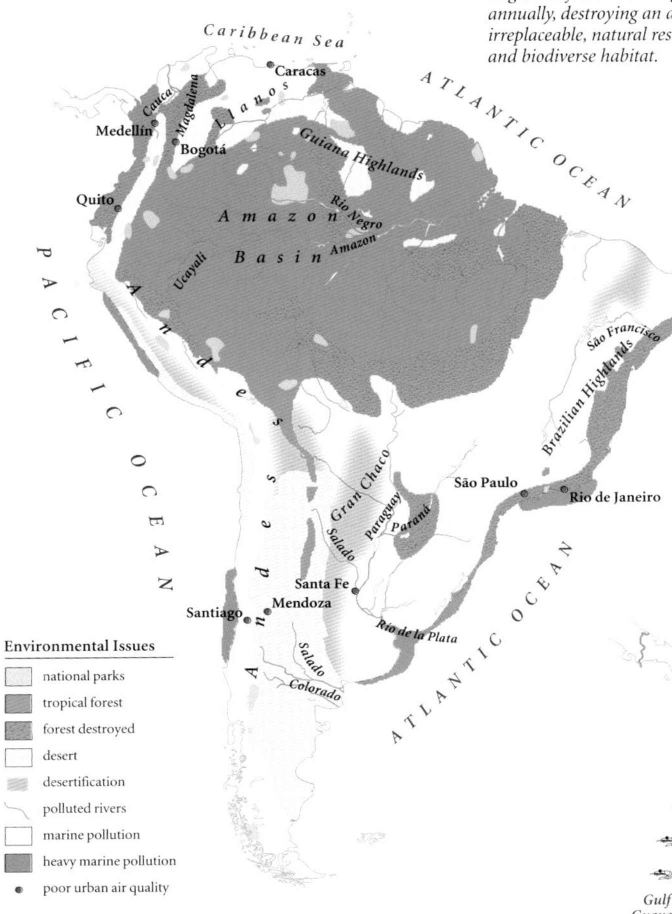

Environmental Issues

- national parks
- tropical forest
- forest destroyed
- desert
- desertification
- polluted rivers
- marine pollution
- heavy marine pollution
- poor urban air quality

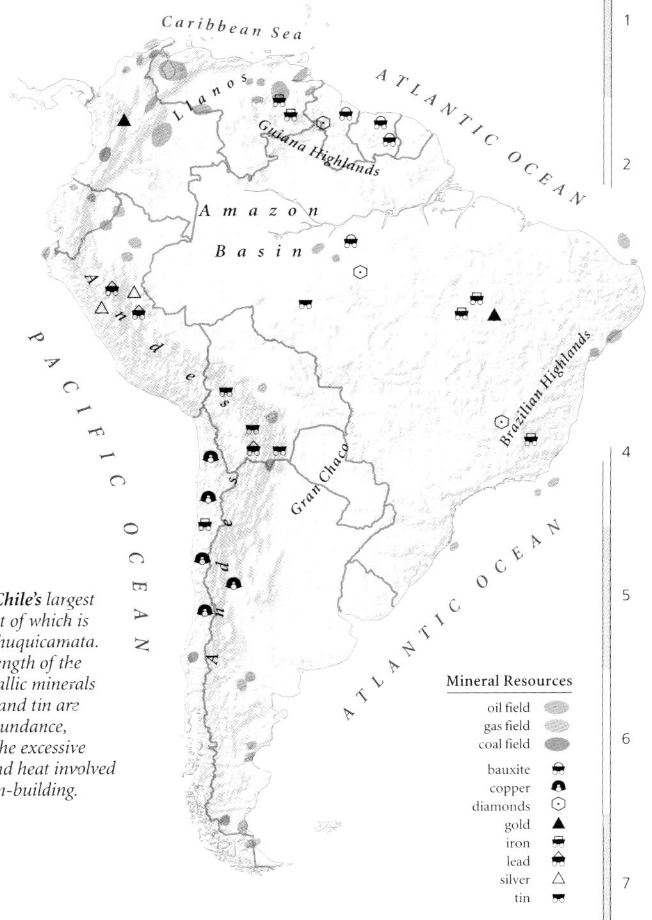

USING THE LAND AND SEA

MANY FOODS NOW COMMON WORLDWIDE originated in South America. These include the potato, tomato, squash, and cassava. Today, large herds of beef cattle roam the temperate grasslands of the Pampas, supporting an extensive meat-packing trade in Argentina, Uruguay and Paraguay. Corn (maize) is grown as a staple crop across the continent and coffee is grown as a cash crop in Brazil and Colombia. Coca plants grown in Bolivia, Peru and Colombia provide most of the world's cocaine. Fish and shellfish are caught off the western coast, especially anchovies off Peru, shrimps off Ecuador and pilchards off Chile.

South America, and Brazil in particular, now leads the world in coffee production, mainly growing Coffea Arabica in large plantations. Coffee beans are harvested, roasted and brewed to produce the world's second most popular drink, after tea.

The Pampas region of southeast South America is characterized by extensive, flat plains, and populated by cattle and ranchers (gauchos). Argentina is a major world producer of beef, much of which is exported to the USA for use in hamburgers.

High in the Andes, hardy alpacas graze on the barren land. Alpacas are thought to have been domesticated by the Incas, whose nobility wore robes made from their wool. Today, they are still reared and prized for their soft, warm fleeces.

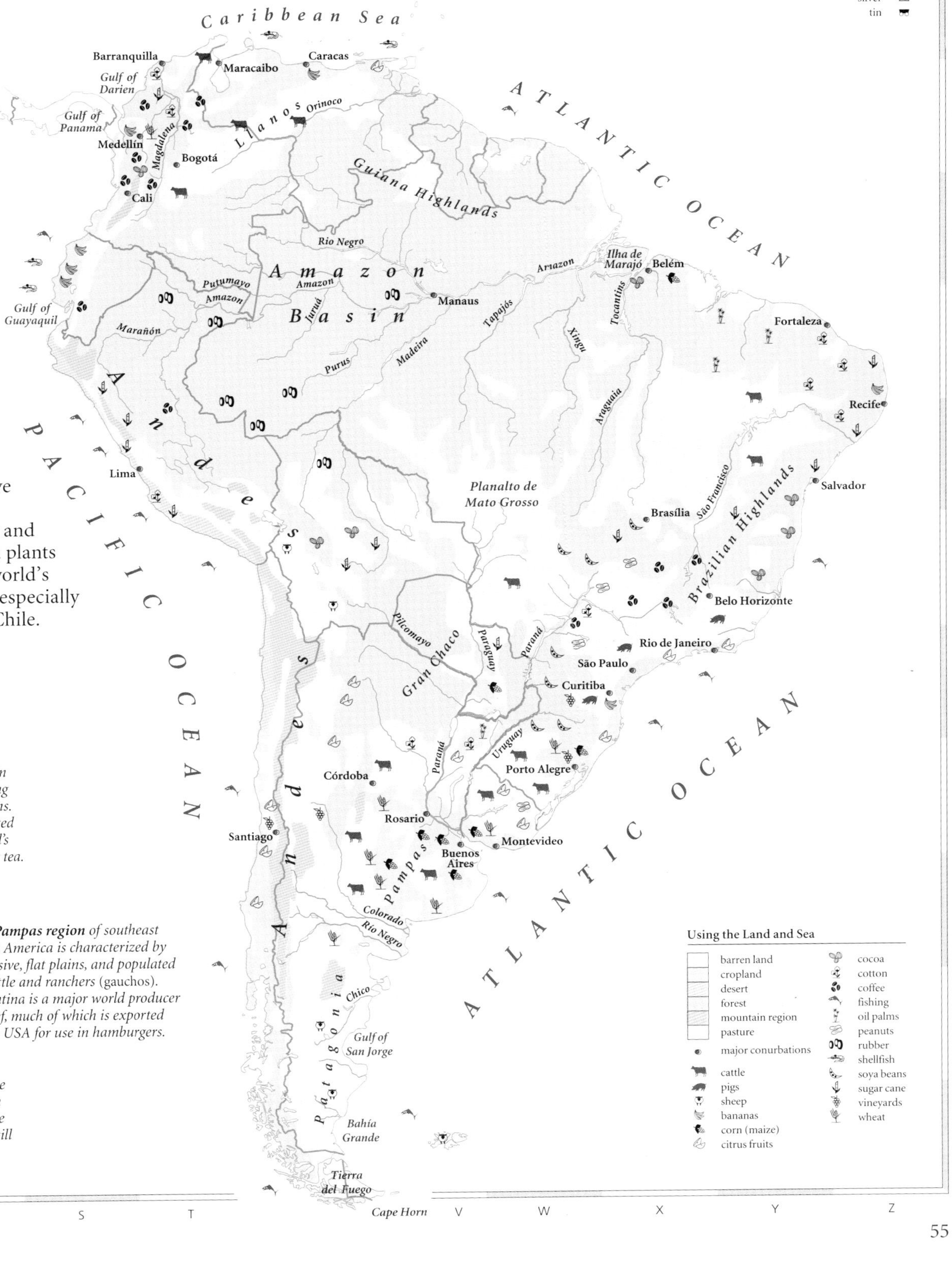

MINERAL RESOURCES

OVER A QUARTER OF THE WORLD's known copper reserves are found at the Chuquicamata mine in northern Chile, and other metallic minerals such as tin are found along the length of the Andes. The discovery of oil and gas at Venezuela's Lake Maracaibo in 1917 turned the country into one of the world's leading oil producers. In contrast, South America is virtually devoid of coal, the only significant deposit being on the peninsula of Guajira in Colombia.

Copper is Chile's largest export, most of which is mined at Chuquicamata. Along the length of the Andes, metallic minerals like copper and tin are found in abundance, formed by the excessive pressures and heat involved in mountain-building.

Mineral Resources

- oil field
- gas field
- coal field
- bauxite
- copper
- diamonds
- gold
- iron
- lead
- silver
- tin

Using the Land and Sea

- barren land
- cropland
- desert
- forest
- mountain region
- pasture
- major conurbations
- cattle
- pigs
- sheep
- bananas
- corn (maize)
- citrus fruits
- cocoa
- cotton
- coffee
- fishing
- oil palms
- peanuts
- rubber
- shellfish
- soya beans
- sugar cane
- vineyards
- wheat

NORTHERN SOUTH AMERICA

COLOMBIA, GUYANA, SURINAM, VENEZUELA, *French Guiana* (to France)

Fringed by the Pacific and Atlantic oceans and the Caribbean Sea, South America's northern region has a rich range of natural resources, some exploited for centuries by colonial powers including the Spanish, French, Dutch and British, others still to be fully explored.

The prospects for further economic development in Colombia, Guyana and Surinam are blighted by drug-related violence and political instability. Venezuela, despite huge incomes from its oil reserves, remains less developed in other industrial sectors.

French Guiana is an overseas *département* of France, now seeking greater autonomy. Most of the major population centres, such as Bogotá, have grown up in the temperate conditions of the high Andes or, like Caracas, at strategic points along the Caribbean coast.

Flowers grown in Colombia are exported all over the world, and include fine carnations and roses. Here, workers are cutting roses which have been grown in plastic greenhouses.

MAP KEY

POPULATION

- ▣ 1 million to 5 million
- ◉ 500,000 to 1 million
- ◎ 100,000 to 500,000
- ⊕ 50,000 to 100,000
- ⊙ 10,000 to 50,000
- ○ below 10,000

ELEVATION

- 4000m / 13,124ft
- 3000m / 9843ft
- 2000m / 6562ft
- 1000m / 3281ft
- 500m / 1640ft
- 250m / 820ft
- 100m / 328ft
- sea level

SCALE 1:6,500,000
(projection: Lambert Azimuthal Equal Area)

Km
0   50   100   150   200

Miles
0   50   100   150   200

Large open squares like the Plaza Bolívar in Bogotá are characteristic of many cities founded by the Spanish.

Scattered farms and villages have grown up on the gentle slopes of this Colombian river valley, utilizing the fertile soils for farming.

The Orinoco River flows from its source in the southern Guiana Highlands to form a broad delta on Venezuela's Atlantic coast. One of its distributary channels opens into a wide bay called the Serpent's Mouth.

56

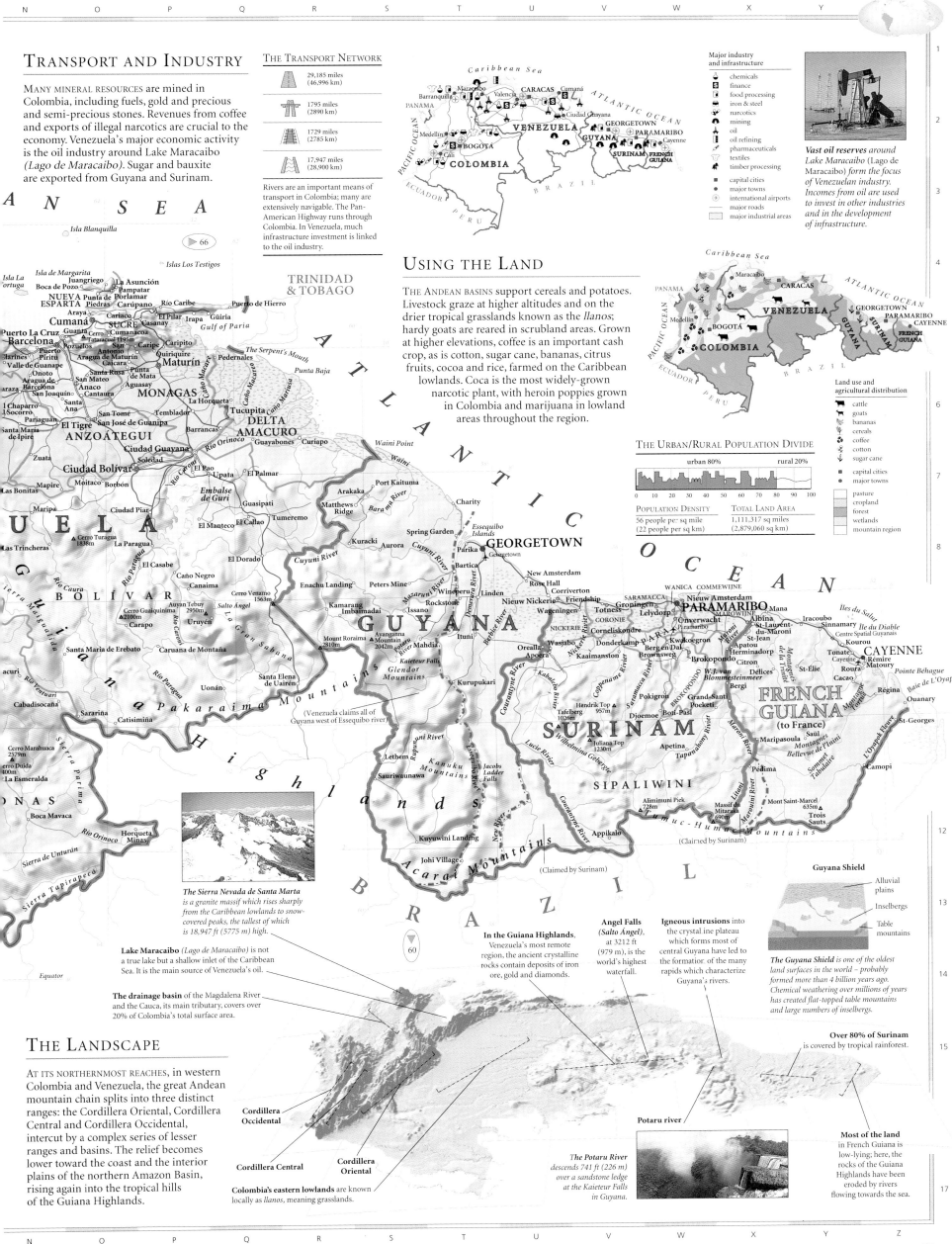

TRANSPORT AND INDUSTRY

MANY MINERAL RESOURCES are mined in Colombia, including fuels, gold and precious and semi-precious stones. Revenues from coffee and exports of illegal narcotics are crucial to the economy. Venezuela's major economic activity is the oil industry around Lake Maracaibo *(Lago de Maracaibo)*. Sugar and bauxite are exported from Guyana and Surinam.

THE TRANSPORT NETWORK

🛣	29,185 miles (46,996 km)
🛤	1795 miles (2890 km)
🚂	1729 miles (2785 km)
✈	17,947 miles (28,900 km)

Rivers are an important means of transport in Colombia; many are extensively navigable. The Pan-American Highway runs through Colombia. In Venezuela, much infrastructure investment is linked to the oil industry.

Major industry and infrastructure
- chemicals
- finance
- food processing
- iron & steel
- narcotics
- mining
- oil
- oil refining
- pharmaceuticals
- textiles
- timber processing
- ■ capital cities
- major towns
- ✈ international airports
- major roads
- major industrial areas

Vast oil reserves around Lake Maracaibo (Lago de Maracaibo) form the focus of Venezuelan industry. Incomes from oil are used to invest in other industries and in the development of infrastructure.

USING THE LAND

THE ANDEAN BASINS support cereals and potatoes. Livestock graze at higher altitudes and on the drier tropical grasslands known as the *llanos*; hardy goats are reared in scrubland areas. Grown at higher elevations, coffee is an important cash crop, as is cotton, sugar cane, bananas, citrus fruits, cocoa and rice, farmed on the Caribbean lowlands. Coca is the most widely-grown narcotic plant, with heroin poppies grown in Colombia and marijuana in lowland areas throughout the region.

THE URBAN/RURAL POPULATION DIVIDE

urban 80%   rural 20%

0 10 20 30 40 50 60 70 80 90 100

POPULATION DENSITY
56 people per sq mile
(22 people per sq km)

TOTAL LAND AREA
1,111,317 sq miles
(2,879,060 sq km)

Land use and agricultural distribution
- 🐄 cattle
- 🐐 goats
- 🍌 bananas
- 🌾 cereals
- ☕ coffee
- cotton
- sugar cane
- ■ capital cities
- • major towns
- pasture
- cropland
- forest
- wetlands
- mountain region

THE LANDSCAPE

AT ITS NORTHERNMOST REACHES, in western Colombia and Venezuela, the great Andean mountain chain splits into three distinct ranges: the Cordillera Oriental, Cordillera Central and Cordillera Occidental, intercut by a complex series of lesser ranges and basins. The relief becomes lower toward the coast and the interior plains of the northern Amazon Basin, rising again into the tropical hills of the Guiana Highlands.

The Sierra Nevada de Santa Marta is a granite massif which rises sharply from the Caribbean lowlands to snow-covered peaks, the tallest of which is 18,947 ft (5775 m) high.

Lake Maracaibo (Lago de Maracaibo) is not a true lake but a shallow inlet of the Caribbean Sea. It is the main source of Venezuela's oil.

The drainage basin of the Magdalena River and the Cauca, its main tributary, covers over 20% of Colombia's total surface area.

Cordillera Occidental
Cordillera Central
Cordillera Oriental

Colombia's eastern lowlands are known locally as *llanos*, meaning grasslands.

In the Guiana Highlands, Venezuela's most remote region, the ancient crystalline rocks contain deposits of iron ore, gold and diamonds.

Angel Falls *(Salto Ángel)*, at 3212 ft (979 m), is the world's highest waterfall.

Igneous intrusions into the crystalline plateau which forms most of central Guyana have led to the formation of the many rapids which characterize Guyana's rivers.

Guyana Shield
- Alluvial plains
- Inselbergs
- Table mountains

The Guyana Shield is one of the oldest land surfaces in the world – probably formed more than 4 billion years ago. Chemical weathering over millions of years has created flat-topped table mountains and large numbers of inselbergs.

Over 80% of Surinam is covered by tropical rainforest.

The Potaru River descends 741 ft (226 m) over a sandstone ledge at the Kaieteur Falls in Guyana.

Potaru river

Most of the land in French Guiana is low-lying; here, the rocks of the Guiana Highlands have been eroded by rivers flowing towards the sea.

57

WESTERN SOUTH AMERICA

BOLIVIA, ECUADOR, PERU

THE THREE STATES OF WESTERN SOUTH AMERICA share a similar geography and recent history. Dominated by the Inca empire until Spanish conquest in the 16th century, they achieved independence from Spain in the early 19th century. The precipitous terrain of the Andes presents severe difficulties for overland transport and continues to be a barrier to national unity and stability. Although Ecuador is now a relatively stable democracy, the military is highly influential in Peru and Bolivia, while the drug trade and associated corruption discourages external aid and economic progress. Wealth and power are still largely concentrated in the hands of a small elite of families, who attained their position during the Spanish colonial period. Land rights and political recognition for the indigenous peoples are becoming increasingly important issues, particularly in Ecuador.

THE LANDSCAPE

BOLIVIA, PERU AND ECUADOR each possess a high Andean mountain region and an eastern region consisting of tropical lowlands and the Andean slope leading down to them. Towards the south of the region, the mountains widen to form the high plateau of the Altiplano. Peru and Ecuador also have fertile, lowland coastal plains. A wide variety of environments include *selva* (tropical rainforest), *montaña* (mountain forest) and grassland.

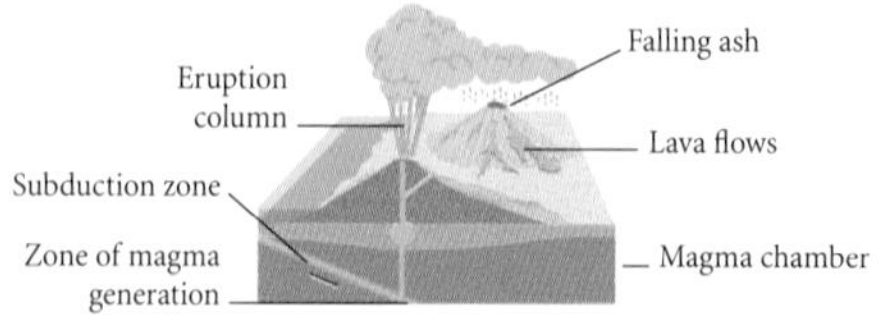

There are many large and active volcanoes in the Andes. Magma generated in the heart of the volcano erupts in a huge cloud of ash. Ash-fall deposits are common throughout the Andes and the rock produced is known as andesite. This is rapidly soaked by heavy rain, causing massive debris flows.

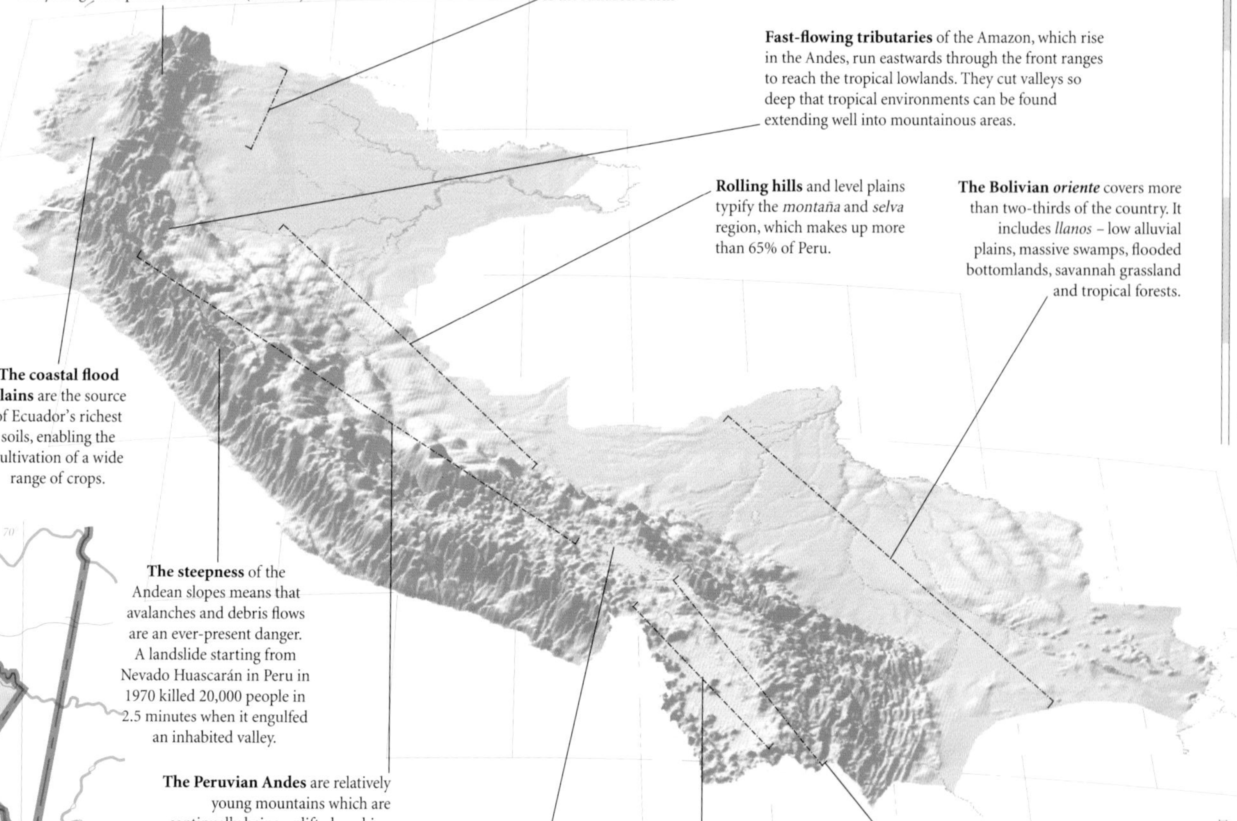

Falling ash
Lava flows
Magma chamber
Eruption column
Subduction zone
Zone of magma generation

Fast-flowing tributaries of the Amazon, which rise in the Andes, run eastwards through the front ranges to reach the tropical lowlands. They cut valleys so deep that tropical environments can be found extending well into mountainous areas.

The Bolivian *oriente* covers more than two-thirds of the country. It includes *llanos* – low alluvial plains, massive swamps, flooded bottomlands, savannah grassland and tropical forests.

Much of eastern Ecuador is covered by the tropical rainforest of the Amazon Basin.

Rolling hills and level plains typify the *montaña* and *selva* region, which makes up more than 65% of Peru.

Cotopaxi is the world's highest active volcano, with a peak 19,347 ft (5897 m) high. A massive eruption in 1877 caused a mudflow which destroyed everything in its path for 150 miles (240 km).

The coastal flood plains are the source of Ecuador's richest soils, enabling the cultivation of a wide range of crops.

The steepness of the Andean slopes means that avalanches and debris flows are an ever-present danger. A landslide starting from Nevado Huascarán in Peru in 1970 killed 20,000 people in 2.5 minutes when it engulfed an inhabited valley.

The Peruvian Andes are relatively young mountains which are continually being uplifted, making the area very unstable, with frequent earthquakes. The transport difficulties that they present continue to form a barrier to national unity.

Ecuador's capital city, Quito, lies high in the Andes, nestling between snow-capped peaks. At 9350 ft (2850 m), Quito is the second highest capital in the world – La Paz in Bolivia is the highest.

Bolivian Andes

Nevado de Illampu and Nevado de Ancohuma, at 21,275 ft (6485 m) and 21,490 ft (6550 m) respectively, form Illampu, the highest mountain in the Bolivian Andes.

The Altiplano is a flat, high plateau lying between the Cordillera Oriental and the Cordillera Occidental at a height of up to 12,500 ft (3800 m). At its margins lie many spurs and alluvial fans.

Lake Titicaca

Lake Titicaca, which forms part of the border between Peru and Bolivia, is the largest lake in South America and the highest significant body of water in the world at an altitude of 12,507 ft (3812 m).

SCALE 1:7,750,000
(projection: Lambert Azimuthal Equal Area)

MAP KEY

POPULATION
- above 5 million
- 1 million to 5 million
- 500,000 to 1 million
- 100,000 to 500,000
- 50,000 to 100,000
- 10,000 to 50,000
- below 10,000

ELEVATION
- 6000m / 19,686ft
- 4000m / 13,124ft
- 3000m / 9843ft
- 2000m / 6562ft
- 1000m / 3281ft
- 500m / 1640ft
- 250m / 820ft
- 100m / 328ft
- sea level

ECUADOREAN ADMINISTRATIVE REGIONS

① CARCHI
② TUNGURAHUA
③ BOLÍVAR
④ CHIMBORAZO
⑤ ZAMORA CHINCHIPE

COLOMBIA

ECUADOR

PERU

BRAZIL

Llamas, with alpacas and vicuñas, are indigenous to South America. They thrive in Andean conditions and their wool is both exported and used in the manufacture of local textiles.

BOLIVIA'S TWO CAPITALS

LA PAZ – legislative and administrative capital
SUCRE – legal capital

THE URBAN/RURAL POPULATION DIVIDE

urban 64%   rural 36%

POPULATION DENSITY	TOTAL LAND AREA
44 people per sq mile	1,019,515 sq miles
(17 people per sq km)	(2,641,230 sq km)

Clearance of the forest in coca-growing regions is encouraged by the Bolivian government. The inaccessible terrain makes policing the growers very difficult. Coca is a popular crop because it is simple to grow and to transport, and is very profitable when illegally processed as cocaine.

USING THE LAND AND SEA

THE COASTAL REGIONS support a variety of cash crops including rice, sugar cane, bananas, coffee and cocoa, watered by rainfall or by irrigation schemes. The grasslands of the high *sierra* are used mainly for grazing a wide range of livestock; cattle and sheep are reared, along with pigs, and the indigenous llama and alpaca. Subsistence crops, especially potatoes and cereals, are grown lower down the mountain flanks. Despite government incentives to grow alternative crops, coca, used for cocaine, is the Bolivian and Peruvian *oriente's* most profitable commercial crop.

Land use and agricultural distribution

capital cities · major towns · pasture · cropland · forest · mountain region · desert · wetlands

cattle · sheep · bananas · cereals · cocoa · coffee · fishing · rubber · sugar cane

The ancient city of Machupicchu, in the Peruvian Andes was built prior to the Inca period. Its impressive ruins reflect a culture which had developed a high degree of sophistication.

The Galápagos Islands are mainly composed of lava, with very little vegetation near to the coasts, although the wetter inland slopes are mantled with forest.

A colony of marine iguanas basks on the rocks of Isla Fernandina in the Galápagos Islands. Charles Darwin's theory of evolution was inspired by the differences he found between the animal species on neighbouring islands in the Galápagos.

Galápagos Islands
(Archipiélago de Colón)

GALÁPAGOS
(to Ecuador)

(same scale as main map)

TRANSPORT AND INDUSTRY

THE MOUNTAIN REGIONS are rich in minerals including lead, copper, silver, gold, zinc and tungsten, though high production and transport costs have meant that they are expensive to extract and vulnerable to price collapses. Foreign debt remains a major burden, hampering industrial development. Manufacturing tends to be small-scale and concentrates on products for local needs, including textiles, food processing and pharmaceuticals. Narcotics are an important, though illegal, export.

Major industry and infrastructure

car manufacture · chemicals · engineering · fish processing · food processing · iron & steel · mining · narcotics · oil · pharmaceuticals · shipbuilding · capital cities · major towns · international airports · major roads · major industrial areas

THE TRANSPORT NETWORK

50,274 miles	1860 miles
(80,956 km)	(2995 km)
3940 miles	14,966 miles
(6344 km)	(24,100 km)

A trans-continental highway is under construction to link Ilo, on Peru's Pacific coast, to Porto Esperança in Brazil, via Puerto Suárez in Bolivia. Establishing port facilities on the Pacific coast is crucial to landlocked Bolivia's further development.

At Potosí in Bolivia, silver has been mined for over 400 years.

59

BRAZIL

B RAZIL IS THE LARGEST COUNTRY in South America, with a population of
over 165 million – greater than the combined total for the whole of the
rest of the continent. The 26 states which make up the federal republic of
Brazil are administered from the purpose-built capital, Brasília. Tropical
rainforest, covering more than one-third of the country, contains rich natural
resources, but great tracts are sacrificed to agriculture, industry and urban
expansion on a daily basis. Most of Brazil's multi-ethnic population now live in
cities, some of which are vast areas of urban sprawl; São Paulo is one of the world's
biggest conurbations, with more than 17 million inhabitants. Although prosperity
is a reality for some, many people still live in great poverty, and mounting foreign debts
continue to damage Brazil's prospects of economic advancement.

USING THE LAND

BRAZIL HAS IMMENSE NATURAL RESOURCES, including minerals and
hardwoods, many of which are found in the fragile rainforest.
Brazil is the world's leading coffee grower and a major producer
of livestock, sugar and orange juice concentrate. Soya beans for
animal feed, particularly for poultry feed, have become the
country's most significant crop.

Land use and
agricultural distribution

- cattle
- pigs
- sheep
- citrus fruits
- coffee
- cotton
- soya beans
- sugar cane
- timber

- capital cities
- major towns

- pasture
- cropland
- forest

THE LANDSCAPE

THE AMAZON BASIN, containing the largest area of
tropical rainforest on Earth, covers nearly half of Brazil.
It is bordered by two shield areas: in the south by the
Brazilian Highlands, and in the north by the Guiana
Highlands. The east coast is dominated by a great
escarpment which runs for 1600 miles (2565 km).

Brazil's highest mountain is the Pico
da Neblina which was only discovered
in 1962. It is 9888 ft (3014 m) high.

The flood plains which
border the Amazon River
are made up of a variety
of different features
including shallow lakes
and swamps, mangrove
forests in the tidal
delta area and fertile
levees on river banks
and point bars.

Guiana Highlands

*The fecundity of parts of
Brazil's rainforest results
from exceptionally high
levels of rainfall and the
quantities of silt deposited
by the Amazon river system.*

*The Pantanal region in the
south of Brazil is an extension
of the Gran Chaco plain. The
swamps and marshes of this area
are renowned for their beauty,
and abundant and unique
wildlife, including wildfowl and
these caimans, a type of crocodile.*

Pantanal swamps

*The Iguaçu River surges over the
spectacular Iguaçu Falls (Saltos do
Iguaçu) towards the Paraná River.
Falls like these are increasingly under
pressure from large-scale hydro-electric
projects such as that at Itaipú.*

The ancient Brazilian Highlands have a
varied topography. Their plateaux, hills and deep
valleys are bordered by highly-eroded mountains
containing important mineral deposits. They are
drained by three great river systems, the Amazon,
the Paraguay–Paraná and the São Francisco.

The São Francisco Basin has a climate unique
in Brazil. Known as the 'drought polygon', it
has almost no rain during the dry season,
leading to regular disastrous droughts.

The northeastern scrublands
are known as the *caatinga*, a
virtually impenetrable thorny
woodland, sometimes intermixed
with cacti where water is scarce.

**The famous Sugar Loaf
Mountain** (*Pão de Açúcar*)
which overlooks Rio de
Janeiro is a fine example
of a volcanic plug a domed
core of solidified lava left
after the slopes of the original
volcano have eroded away.

Deep natural harbours
such as Baia de Guanabara were
created where the steep slopes
of the Serra da Mantiqueira
plunge directly into the ocean.

The Amazon Basin is the largest river basin
in the world. The Amazon River and over
a thousand tributaries drain an area of
2,375,000 sq miles (6,150,000 sq km)
and carry one-fifth of the world's
fresh water out to sea.

Hillslope gullying

Direction of
growth

Overland
water flow

Gully

Rainfall

Water seeps
through
hillslope

*Large-scale gullies
are common in Brazil,
particularly on hillslopes from
which vegetation has been
removed. Gullies grow
headwards (up the slope),
aided by a combination
of erosion through water
seepage and rainwater runoff.*

THE URBAN/RURAL POPULATION DIVIDE

urban 78%   rural 22%

TOTAL LAND AREA
3,286,472 sq miles
(8,511,970 sq km)

POPULATION DENSITY
50 people per sq mile
(19 people per sq km)

MAP KEY

POPULATION

- ■ above 5 million
- ■ 1 million to 5 million
- ⊙ 500,000 to 1 million
- ⊕ 100,000 to 500,000
- ⊙ 50,000 to 100,000
- ○ 10,000 to 50,000
- ○ below 10,000

ELEVATION

- 3000m / 9843ft
- 2000m / 6562ft
- 1000m / 3281ft
- 500m / 1640ft
- 250m / 820ft
- 100m / 328ft
- sea level

Map place names

ATLANTIC OCEAN

Equator

Recife do Silva
Recife Manuel Luís
Ilha de São Luís
Ilha do Caju
Itapecuru-Mirim
Chapadinha
Sobral
Acaraú
Camocim
Parnaíba
Cuceia
Aracati
Itapipoca
Camocim

São Luís
Turiaçu
Carutapera
Viseu
São João de Côrtes
Castanhal Capanema
Vigia
Tomé-Açu
Belém
Portel
Ilha de Marajó
Ilha Grande
de Gurupá
Breves
Mouths of the Amazon
Ilha Mexiana
Ilha Caviana de Fora
Ilha de Maruda
Ilha do Caruá
Ilha Baília
Sucuriju

Cabo Orange
Oiapoque
Calçoene
Amapá
Macapá
Porto de Moz

FRENCH
GUIANA
(to France)

Rio Oiapoque
Rio Iari
Rio Paru
AMAPÁ
Monte Dourado
Almeirim
Óbidos Alenquer
Santarém
Altamira
Planalto
Maracanaquará

SURINAM

Tumuc Humac Mountains
Acarai Mountains
Rio Trombetas
Rio Paru de Oeste
Rio Mapuera
Oriximiná
Itacoatiara
Uruará

Serra do Iatapu
Rio Iatapu
Rio Uatumã

GUYANA
Guiana Highlands

Mount Roraima
2810m
Pakaraima Mts
Normandia
Conceição
do Maú
Santa Rosa
Uraricoera
Boa Vista
RORAIMA
Caracaraí
Catrimani
Rio Catrimani
Rio Branco
Boiaçu
Novo Airão

Manaus
Represa
Balbina
Manacapuru
Codajás
Anori
Caapiranga
A m a z o n a s
B r a s i l

Rio Negro
Rio Solimões
Tefé
Coari

VENEZUELA
Serra Parima
Mount Roraima
2810m

COLOMBIA

Rio Içá
Santo Antônio
do Içá
Tonantins
Amaturá
Fonte Boa
Jutaí
Juruá
Carauari

Vista Alegre
São Marcelino
Içana
Rio Içana
Santa Isabel
do Rio Negro
Barcelos
Moura

São Joaquim
Rio Japurá
Japurá
Maraã
Fonte Boa
Alvarães

Pico da Neblina
3014m

PERU

BOLIVIA
PARAGUAY
URUGUAY
ARGENTINA

BRASÍLIA
Belo Horizonte
São Paulo
Rio de Janeiro
Curitiba
Porto Alegre
Salvador
Fortaleza
Recife
Belém
Manaus
Carajás

ATLANTIC OCEAN

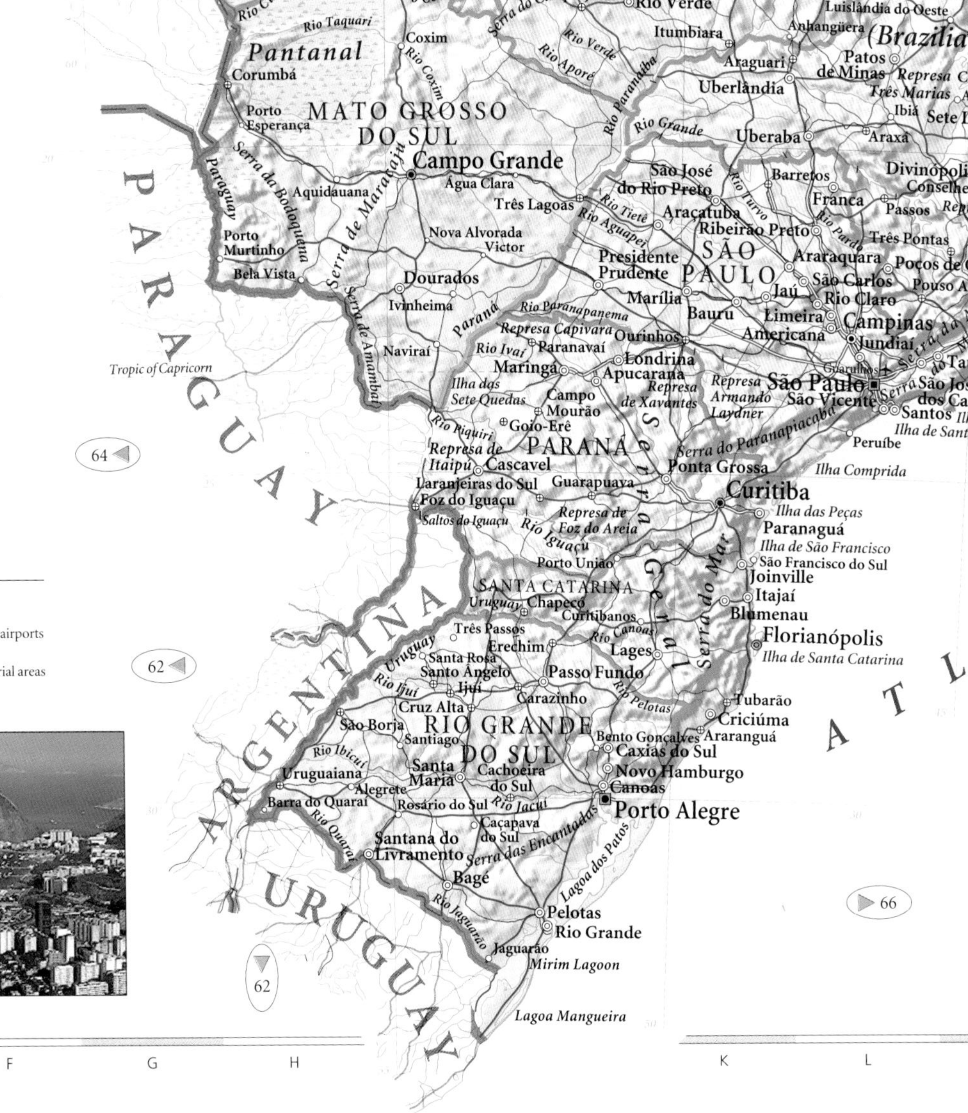

Picinguaba Beach lies in Serra do Mar State Park in São Paulo state. São Paulo's beaches stretch for 386 miles (622 km) along the Atlantic coast.

A gaucho in traditional costume herds beef cattle on the grasslands of the Rio Grande do Sul in southern Brazil.

TRANSPORT AND INDUSTRY

BRAZILIAN INDUSTRY is diverse and well developed, in part as a result of past government incentives, including the prohibition of imports. Industries which have benefited include car manufacture, petrochemicals and micro-electronics. Textiles, clothing and footwear are among Brazil's most successful exports. The country's services and tourism sectors are also expanding rapidly.

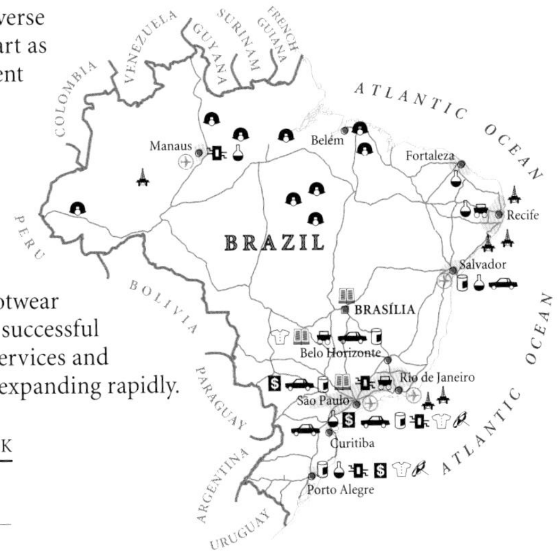

THE TRANSPORT NETWORK

139,351 miles (224,397 km)	
3105 miles (5000 km)	
18,865 miles (30,379 km)	
31,050 miles (50,000 km)	

An extensive new road network is being built to link Brazil's main centres. Investment is needed to update the antiquated railway system. In São Paulo, the subway system is being extended to accommodate the expanding population.

SCALE 1:12,750,000
(projection Lambert Azimuthal Equal Area)

Brazil's urban population has grown by over 6% per year since the mid-1970s – at current population levels a rate of nearly 6 million people annually. In Rio de Janeiro prosperous neighbourhoods exist alongside over 450 shanty towns or favelas, some of which house as many as 250,000 people.

Major industry and infrastructure

car manufacture
chemicals
electronics
finance
food processing
iron & steel
mining
oil
printing & publishing
textiles
timber processing
tourism

capital cities
major towns
international airports
major roads
major industrial areas

BRAZIL

ATLANTIC OCEAN

Manaus · Belém · Fortaleza · Recife · Salvador · Brasília · Belo Horizonte · São Paulo · Rio de Janeiro · Curitiba · Porto Alegre

EASTERN SOUTH AMERICA

URUGUAY, NORTHEAST ARGENTINA, SOUTHEAST BRAZIL

THE VAST CONURBATIONS OF RIO DE JANEIRO, São Paulo and Buenos Aires form the core of South America's highly-urbanized eastern region. São Paulo state, with almost 35 million inhabitants, is among the world's 20 most powerful economies, and São Paulo is the fastest growing city on the continent. Rio de Janeiro and Buenos Aires, transformed in the last hundred years from port cities to great metropolitan areas each with more than 10 million inhabitants, typify the unstructured growth and wealth disparities of South America's great cities. In Uruguay, over half of the population lives in the capital, Montevideo, which faces Buenos Aires across the River Plate (*Rio de la Plata*). Immigration from the countryside has created severe pressure on the urban infrastructure, particularly on available housing, leading to a profusion of crowded shanty settlements (*favelas or barrios*).

USING THE LAND

MOST OF URUGUAY and the Pampas of northern Argentina are devoted to the rearing of livestock, especially cattle and sheep, which are central to both countries' economies. Soya beans, first produced in Brazil's Rio Grande do Sul, are now more widely grown for large-scale export, as are cereals, sugar cane and grapes. Subsistence crops, including potatoes, corn and sugar beet, are grown on the remaining arable land.

Land use and agricultural distribution

- cattle
- sheep
- cereals
- fruit
- coffee
- soya beans
- sugar cane
- major cities
- major towns

- pasture
- cropland
- forest
- wetlands
- barren land

The rolling grasslands of Uruguay are ideally suited to the rearing of cattle, which are concentrated in great herds throughout the region.

TRANSPORT AND INDUSTRY

SOUTHEAST BRAZIL IS HOME TO MUCH of the important motor and capital goods industry, largely based around São Paulo; iron and steel production is also concentrated in this region. Uruguay's economy continues to be based mainly on the export of livestock products including meat and leather goods. Buenos Aires is Argentina's chief port, and the region has a varied and sophisticated economic base including service-based industries such as finance and publishing, as well as primary processing.

Major industry and infrastructure

- car manufacture
- chemicals
- engineering
- finance
- food processing
- iron & steel
- meat processing
- printing & publishing
- shipbuilding
- textiles
- timber processing
- capital cities
- major towns
- international airports
- major roads
- major industrial areas

MAP KEY

POPULATION
- above 5 million
- 1 million to 5 million
- 500,000 to 1 million
- 100,000 to 500,000
- 50,000 to 100,000
- 10,000 to 50,000
- below 10,000

ELEVATION
- 2000m / 6562ft
- 1000m / 3281ft
- 500m / 1640ft
- 250m / 820ft
- 100m / 328ft
- sea level

SCALE 1:6,250,000
(projection: Lambert Azimuthal Equal Area)

Soya beans are harvested, pressed, and processed into soya cake, which is used as animal feed. The cake is fed mainly to chickens on large-scale factory farms, and the growth in soya production has been an important factor in the expansion of the Brazilian poultry trade.

THE TRANSPORT NETWORK

Throughout the region, road networks need to be expanded to cope with urban development. Plans are underway to build a bridge over the River Plate (*Rio de la Plata*) to link Colonia and Buenos Aires.

The Itaipú dam on the Paraná River is one of the largest hydro-electric projects in the world, jointly financed by Brazil and Paraguay.

Rio de Janeiro's annual carnival, Mardi Gras, which ushers in the start of Lent, is an extravagant five-day parade through the city, characterized by fantastically decorated floats, exuberant dancing and samba music.

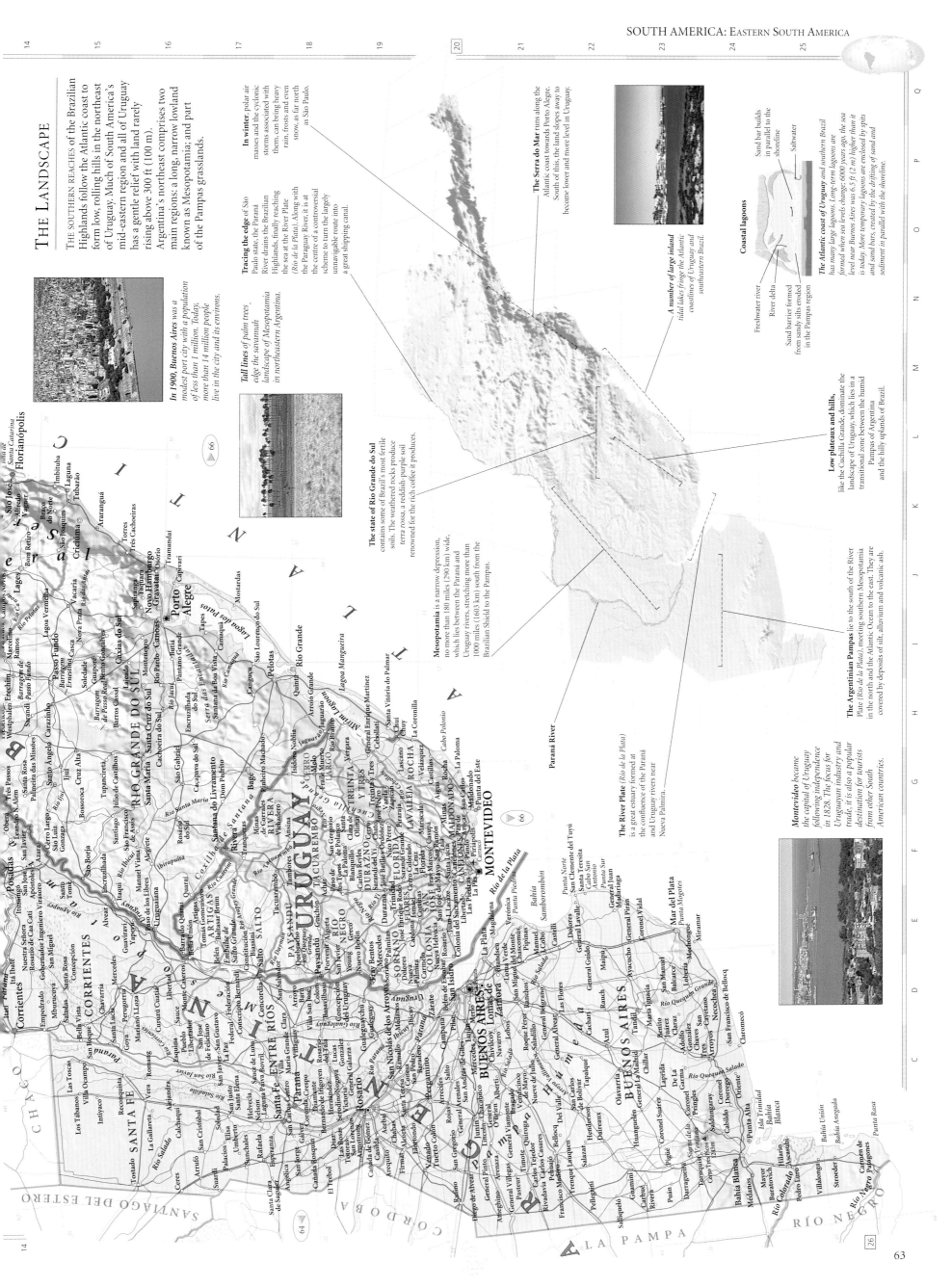

THE LANDSCAPE

THE SOUTHERN REACHES of the Brazilian Highlands follow the Atlantic coast to form low, rolling hills in the northeast of Uruguay. Much of South America's mid-eastern region and all of Uruguay has a gentle relief with land rarely rising above 300 ft (100 m). Argentina's northeast region comprises two main regions: a long, narrow lowland known as Mesopotamia; and part of the Pampas grasslands.

In winter, polar air masses and the cyclonic storms associated with them, can bring heavy rain, frosts and even snow, as far north as São Paulo.

Tracing the edge of São Paulo state, the Paraná River drains the Brazilian Highlands, finally reaching the sea at the River Plate (Rio de la Plata). Along with the Paraguay River, it is at the centre of a controversial scheme to turn the largely unnavigable route into a great shipping canal.

The Serra do Mar runs along the Atlantic coast towards Porto Alegre. South of this, the land slopes away to become lower and more level in Uruguay.

Coastal lagoons

Sand bar builds in parallel to the shoreline

Saltwater

Freshwater river

River delta

Sand barrier formed from sandy silts eroded in the Pampas region

The Atlantic coast of Uruguay and southern Brazil has many large lagoons. Long-term lagoons are formed when sea levels change: 6000 years ago, the sea level near Buenos Aires was 6.5 ft (2 m) higher than it is today. More temporary lagoons are enclosed by spits and sand bars, created by the drifting of sand and sediment in parallel with the shoreline.

In 1900, Buenos Aires was a modest port city with a population of less than 1 million. Today, more than 14 million people live in the city and its environs.

Tall lines of palm trees edge the savannah landscape of Mesopotamia in northeastern Argentina.

A number of large inland tidal lakes fringe the Atlantic coastlines of Uruguay and southeastern Brazil.

Low plateaux and hills, like the Cuchilla Grande, dominate the landscape of Uruguay, which lies in a transitional zone between the humid Pampas of Argentina and the hilly uplands of Brazil.

The state of Rio Grande do Sul contains some of Brazil's most fertile soils. The weathered rocks produce terra rossa, a reddish-purple soil renowned for the rich coffee it produces.

Mesopotamia is a narrow depression, no more than 180 miles (290 km) wide, which lies between the Paraná and Uruguay rivers, stretching more than 1000 miles (1603 km) south from the Brazilian Shield to the Pampas.

The Argentinian Pampas lie to the south of the River Plate (Rio de la Plata), meeting southern Mesopotamia in the north and the Atlantic Ocean to the east. They are covered by deposits of silt, alluvium and volcanic ash.

Paraná River

The River Plate (Rio de la Plata) is a great estuary formed at the confluence of the Paraná and Uruguay rivers near Nueva Palmira.

Montevideo became the capital of Uruguay following independence in 1828. The focus for Uruguayan industry and trade, it is also a popular destination for tourists from other South American countries.

SOUTHERN SOUTH AMERICA

ARGENTINA, CHILE, PARAGUAY

SOUTH AMERICA'S CONE-SHAPED SOUTHERN REGION IS shared by Argentina and Chile, two overwhelmingly urbanized nations whose populations live mainly in or around the capital cities, Buenos Aires and Santiago. The people are largely *mestizo* or of European origin; in the early 20th century Argentina absorbed waves of new European immigrants, many from Italy and Germany. Paraguay is far less urbanized than its neighbours, with a homogeneous population of mixed Spanish and Guaraní origin, who retain their Indian roots through the Guaraní language. Though most Paraguayans live in the southeast, near Asunción, the indigenous Indians live in the sparsely populated Gran Chaco. The Gran Chaco is also home to some of Argentina's minority indigenous peoples, who otherwise live mainly in Andean regions. Chile's estimated 800,000 Mapuche Indians live almost exclusively in the south.

TRANSPORT AND INDUSTRY

FOOD PROCESSING AND AGRICULTURAL EXPORTS remain a fundamental part of Argentina's economy. The growth of manufacturing is regularly hampered by hyper-inflation and massive foreign debts. The world's most important copper-producer and one of the top ten gold producers, Chile also has a thriving wine and grape industry. Most Paraguayan exports involve primary processing, although domestic goods are produced for home markets.

Floodwaters cover the land in the Gran Chaco, partly submerging its vegetation of fan palms and hyacinths.

Boiling water and steam emerge from a volcanic vent, one of the Tatio geysers which lie at the foot of Cerro de Tocorpuri near Chile's border with Bolivia.

Chuquicamata copper mine, lies on a desert plateau near Calama in the Andes of northern Chile. It is the world's largest open-cast copper mine.

THE TRANSPORT NETWORK

Argentina's state transport system is undergoing privatization, though the outmoded rail network requires updating. Paraguay requires foreign investment to upgrade its roads and railways. Essential internal air routes, especially across the Andes, are well developed in all three countries.

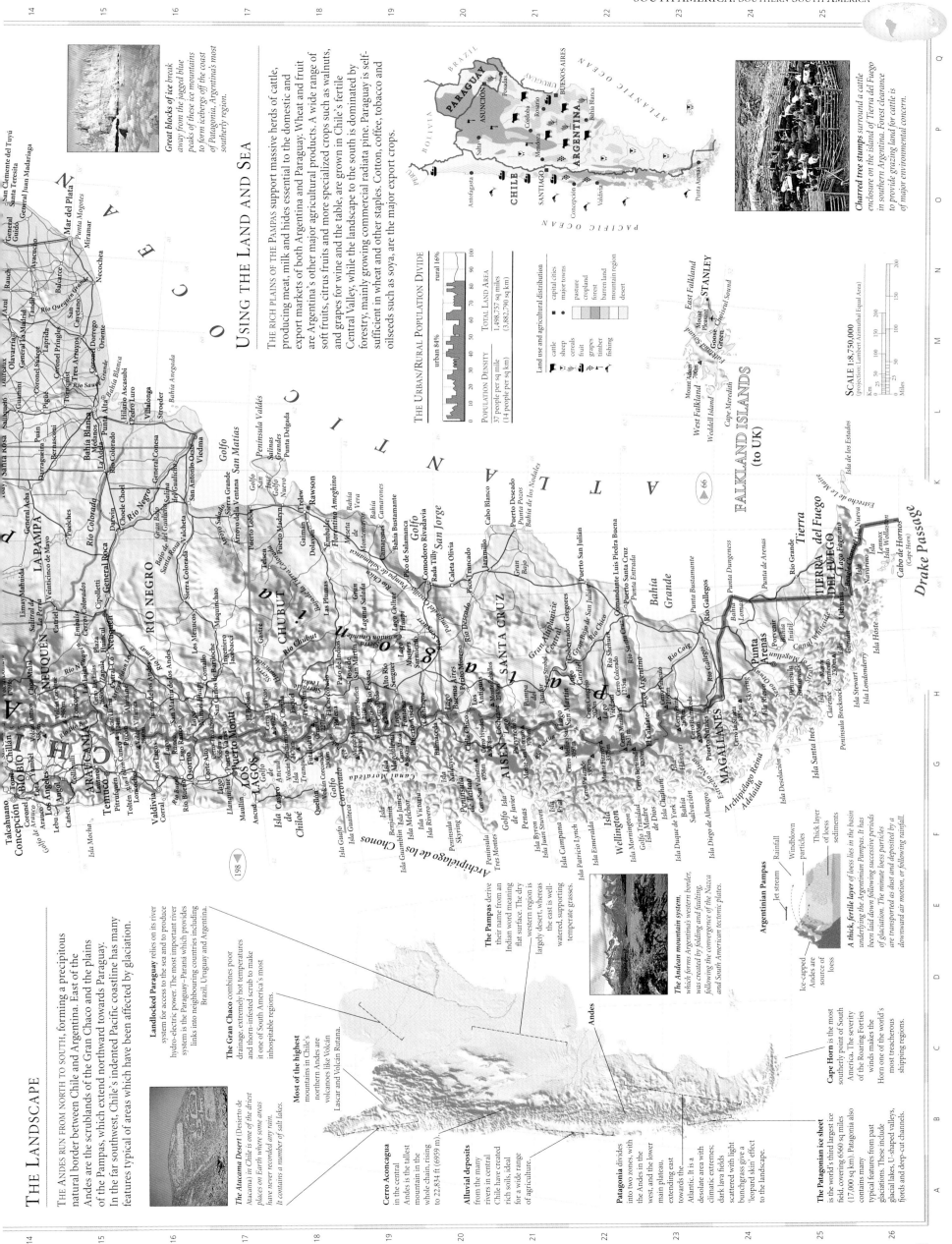

The Landscape

The Andes run from north to south, forming a precipitous natural border between Chile and Argentina. East of the Andes are the scrublands of the Gran Chaco and the plains of the Pampas, which extend northward towards Paraguay. In the far southwest, Chile's indented Pacific coastline has many features typical of areas which have been affected by glaciation.

Great blocks of ice break away from the jagged blue peaks of these ice mountains to form icebergs off the coast of Patagonia, Argentina's most southerly region.

The Atacama Desert (Desierto de Atacama) in Chile is one of the driest places on Earth where some areas have never recorded any rain. It contains a number of salt lakes.

Cerro Aconcagua in the central Andes is the tallest mountain in the whole chain, rising to 22,834 ft (6959 m).

Alluvial deposits from the many rivers in central Chile have created rich soils, ideal for a wide range of agriculture.

Most of the highest mountains in Chile's northern Andes are volcanoes like Volcán Lascar and Volcán Rutana.

The Gran Chaco combines poor drainage, extremely hot temperatures and thorn-infested scrub to make it one of South America's most inhospitable regions.

Landlocked Paraguay relies on its river system for access to the sea and to produce hydro-electric power. The most important river system is the Paraguay–Paraná which provides links into neighbouring countries including Brazil, Uruguay and Argentina.

The Pampas derive their name from an Indian word meaning flat surface. The dry western region is largely desert, whereas the east is well-watered, supporting temperate grasses.

The Andean mountain system, which forms Argentina's western border, was created by folding and faulting, following the convergence of the Nazca and South American tectonic plates.

Argentinian Pampas

Rainfall
Jet stream
Windblown particles
Thick layer of loess sediments
Ice-capped Andes are source of loess

A thick, fertile layer of loess lies in the basin underlying the Argentinian Pampas. It has been laid down following successive periods of glaciation. The minute loess particles are transported as dust and deposited by a downward air motion, or following rainfall.

Patagonia divides into two zones, with the Andes in the west, and the lower main plateau, extending east towards the Atlantic. It is a desolate area with climatic extremes; dark lava fields scattered with light bunchgrass give a "leopard skin" effect to the landscape.

The Patagonian ice sheet is the world's third largest ice field, covering 6560 sq miles (17,000 sq km). Patagonia also contains many typical features from past glaciations. These include glacial lakes, U-shaped valleys, fjords and deep-cut channels.

Cape Horn is the most southerly point of South America. The severity of the Roaring Forties winds makes the Horn one of the world's most treacherous shipping regions.

Using the Land and Sea

The rich plains of the Pampas support massive herds of cattle, producing meat, milk and hides essential to the domestic and export markets of both Argentina and Paraguay. Wheat and fruit are Argentina's other major agricultural products. A wide range of soft fruits, citrus fruits and more specialized crops such as walnuts, and grapes for wine and the table, are grown in Chile's fertile Central Valley, while the landscape to the south is dominated by forestry, mainly growing commercial radiata pine. Paraguay is self-sufficient in wheat and other staples. Cotton, coffee, tobacco and oilseeds such as soya, are the major export crops.

Charred tree stumps surround a cattle enclosure on the island of Tierra del Fuego in southern Argentina. Forest clearance to provide grazing land for cattle is of major environmental concern.

The Urban/Rural Population Divide

urban 84% / rural 16%

Total Land Area
1,498,757 sq miles
(3,882,790 sq km)

Population Density
37 people per sq mile
(14 people per sq km)

Land use and agricultural distribution
- cattle
- sheep
- fruit
- grapes
- timber
- fishing
- capital cities
- major towns
- pasture
- cropland
- forest
- barren land
- mountain region
- desert

SCALE 1:8,750,000
(projection: Lambert Azimuthal Equal Area)

The Atlantic Ocean

The Atlantic is the youngest of the world's oceans, formed about 180 million years ago when the landmasses of the eastern and western hemispheres separated. Its underwater topography is dominated by the Mid-Atlantic Ridge, a huge mountain system running north to south along the centre of the ocean. Although most of the ridge's peaks lie below the sea, some emerge as volcanic islands, like Iceland and the Azores. The Atlantic contains a wealth of resources, including substantial oil and gas reserves and rich fishing grounds. Until the 1950s, the north Atlantic was the world's busiest shipping route; cheaper air transport and alternative routes have shifted patterns of world trade.

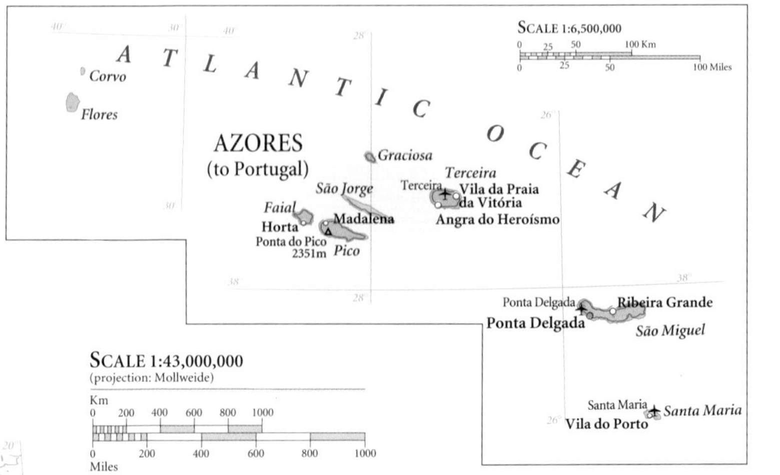

RESOURCES

Development of the oil and gas reserves in the Atlantic began in the 1940s around the Gulf of Mexico. Since then other areas have been exploited, including the North Sea, the west coast of Africa and the area east of Newfoundland and Nova Scotia. There is also extensive mining of sand, gravel and shell deposits by the USA and UK. For centuries, the north Atlantic's fishing grounds have been utilized more heavily than other oceans, leading to a serious decline in many fish stocks.

Resources (including wildlife)
- fish
- whales
- aggregates
- oil & gas
- major towns
- major ports

Fishing in the seas around northwestern Europe dates back over 1500 years. The high nutrient content of the seas makes them ideal breeding grounds for many species of fish.

Surtsey near Iceland, lies on the Mid-Atlantic Ridge. The island was formed in 1963 following a volcanic eruption caused by sea-floor spreading.

SCALE 1:43,000,000
(projection: Mollweide)

On 5 January 1993, the oil tanker Braer ran aground in the Shetland Islands, spilling 83,660 tons (85,000 tonnes) of light crude oil into the ocean, devastating the local marine ecosystem.

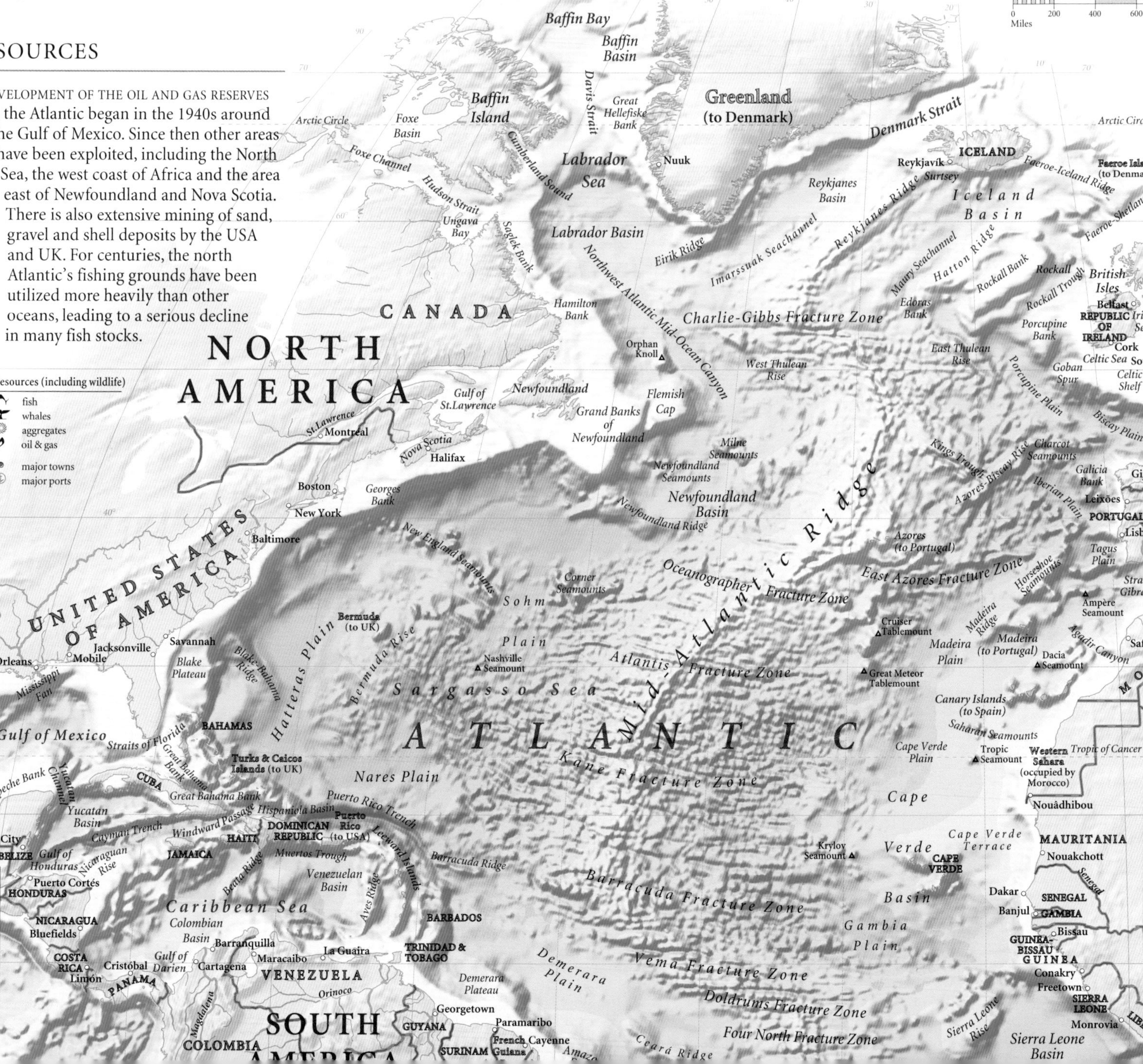

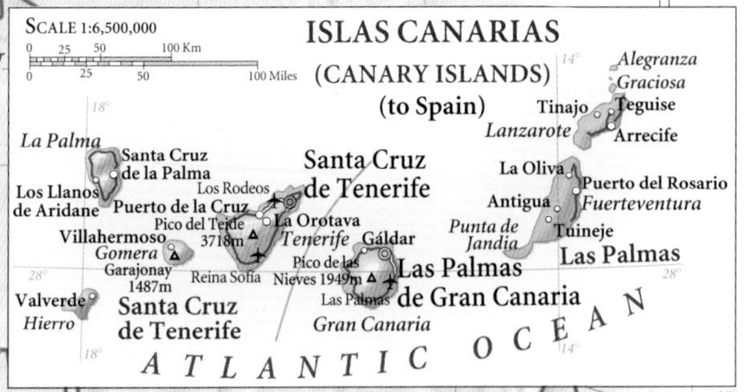

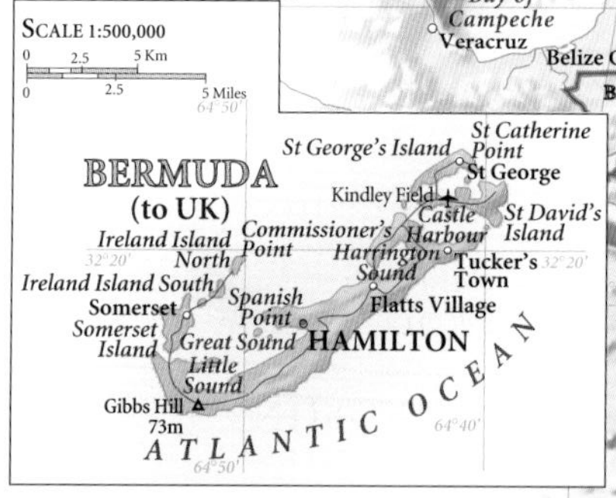

AZORES
(to Portugal)

SCALE 1:6,500,000

Corvo
Flores
Graciosa
Terceira
São Jorge
Faial
Pico
Horta
Ponta do Pico 2351m
Madalena
Angra do Heroísmo
Vila da Praia da Vitória
Ribeira Grande
São Miguel
Ponta Delgada
Santa Maria
Vila do Porto

ATLANTIC OCEAN

MADEIRA
(to Portugal)

SCALE 1:2,500,000

Camacha
Porto Santo
Porto Santo
Ilhéu de Baixo
Ponta do Pargo
Porto do Moniz
Madeira (to Portugal)
São Vicente
Pico Ruivo de Santana 1861m
Calheta
Ribeira Brava
Câmara de Lobos
Machico
Funchal
Santa Cruz
Ilhas Desertas
Deserta Grande
Bugio

ISLAS CANARIAS
(CANARY ISLANDS)
(to Spain)

SCALE 1:6,500,000

Alegranza
Graciosa
Arrecife
Lanzarote
La Oliva
Puerto del Rosario
Fuerteventura
Antigua
Tinajo
Las Palmas
Teguise
La Palma
Los Llanos de Aridane
Santa Cruz de la Palma
Puerto de la Cruz
Orotava
Gáldar
de Gran Canaria
Las Palmas de Gran Canaria
Gomera
Reina Sofía
Nueva 1949m
Pico del Teide 3718m
Santa Cruz de Tenerife
Valverde
Hierro 1467m
Teror
ATLANTIC OCEAN

BERMUDA
(to UK)

SCALE 1:500,000

Ireland Island North
Ireland Island South
Somerset
Little Sound
Great Sound
Gibbs Hill 73m
Spanish Point
St Catherine Point
Kindley Field
St David's Island
St George's Island
St George
Castle Harbour
Harrington Sound
Flatts Village
Tucker's Town
HAMILTON

Map Labels

ARCTIC OCEAN
EUROPE
AFRICA
NORTH AMERICA
SOUTH AMERICA
ATLANTIC OCEAN
ANTARCTICA
Reykjavik
Rotterdam
New York
Gibraltar
New Orleans
Sargasso Sea
Caribbean Sea
Cristobal
Rio de Janeiro
La Guaira
Buenos Aires
Cape Town
Lagos
Scotia Sea
Weddell Sea

Greenland (to Denmark)
ICELAND
Arctic Circle
Denmark Strait
Reykjavik
Reykjanes Ridge
Reykjanes Basin
Faeroe Islands (to Denmark)
Faeroe-Iceland Ridge
Shetland Islands
North Sea
UNITED KINGDOM
Rotterdam
EUROPE
Milford Haven
Southampton
English Channel
FRANCE
Nantes
Bordeaux
Bay of Biscay
Biscay Plain
Bilbao
Gijón
SPAIN
PORTUGAL
Lisbon
Tagus
Tagus Plain
Guadiana
Gibraltar
Strait of Gibraltar
Casablanca
Safi
MOROCCO
ALGERIA
AFRICA
Western Sahara (occupied by Morocco)
Tropic of Cancer
Nouâdhibou
MAURITANIA
Nouakchott
SENEGAL
Dakar
Banjul
GAMBIA
GUINEA-BISSAU
Bissau
GUINEA
Conakry
SIERRA LEONE
Freetown
LIBERIA
Monrovia
IVORY COAST
Abidjan
GHANA
TOGO
BENIN
NIGERIA
Lagos
CAMEROON
Douala

CANADA
Baffin Bay
Baffin Basin
Baffin Island
Davis Strait
Great Hellefisk Bank
Labrador Sea
Labrador Basin
Nuuk
Eirik Ridge
Hudson Strait
Ungava Bay
Foxe Channel
Foxe Basin
Cumberland Sound
Saglek Bank
Hamilton Bank
Newfoundland
Grand Banks of Newfoundland
Flemish Cap
Orphan Knoll
Newfoundland Ridge
Newfoundland Basin
Gulf of St. Lawrence
Halifax
Nova Scotia
St. Lawrence
Montreal
Boston
New York
Baltimore
Washington
UNITED STATES OF AMERICA
NORTH AMERICA
Savannah
Jacksonville
Mobile
New Orleans
Gulf of Mexico
Straits of Florida
Blake Plateau
Blake-Bahama Ridge
BAHAMAS
CUBA
Great Bahama Bank
TURKS & CAICOS ISLANDS (to UK)
HAITI
DOMINICAN REPUBLIC
Puerto Rico (to USA)
Windward Passage
Leeward Islands
JAMAICA
Caribbean Sea
Colombian Basin
Venezuelan Basin
Aves Ridge
Windward Islands
BARBADOS
TRINIDAD & TOBAGO
MEXICO
Tampico
Veracruz
Bay of Campeche
Campeche Bank
Yucatán Channel
Yucatán Basin
Cayman Trench
Nicaraguan Rise
Belize City
BELIZE
HONDURAS
Gulf of Honduras
Puerto Cortés
GUATEMALA
Bluefields
NICARAGUA
COSTA RICA
Limón
Cristóbal
Darién
PANAMA
Gulf of Panama
Maracaibo
COLOMBIA
Barranquilla
Cartagena
VENEZUELA
Caracas
La Guaira
Orinoco
Magdalena
GUYANA
Georgetown
Paramaribo
SURINAM
French Guiana
Cayenne
SOUTH AMERICA
Demerara Plain
Demerara Plateau

Arctic Circle
Iceland Basin
Hatton Bank
Hatton-Rockall Basin
Rockall Bank
Rockall Plateau
Porcupine Bank
Porcupine Plain
Porcupine Seabight
Goban Spur
Celtic Sea
Celtic Shelf
British Isles
IRELAND
REPUBLIC OF IRELAND
Irish Sea
Cork
Iberian Plain
Iberian Basin
Azores-Biscay Rise
Galicia Bank
Charcot Seamounts
Josephine Seamount
Ampère Seamount
Gettysburg
Coral Patch Seamount
Madeira (to Portugal)
Madeira Plain
Seine Plain
Canary Islands (to Spain)
Canary Basin
Cape Verde Plain
Dacia Seamount
Essaouira Seamount
Agadir Canyon
Seamount
Tropic of Cancer
Cape Verde
Cape Verde Terrace
CAPE VERDE
Cape Verde Basin
Gambia Plain
Gambia Basin
Sierra Leone Basin
Sierra Leone Rise
Guinea Plain

Greenland Sea
Norwegian Sea
Jan Mayen Ridge
Jan Mayen Fracture Zone
Mid-Atlantic Ridge
Kolbeinsey Ridge
Maury Seachannel
Maury Channel
Hatton Basin
West Thulean Rise
East Thulean Rise
Rockall Trough
Feni Ridge
Gardar Ridge

MID-ATLANTIC RIDGE
ATLANTIC
Sargasso Sea
Charlie-Gibbs Fracture Zone
Northwest Atlantic Mid-Ocean Canyon
Milne Seamounts
New England Seamounts
Bermuda (to UK)
Bermuda Rise
Nares Plain
Hatteras Plain
Puerto Rico Trench
Sohm Plain
Nashville Seamount
Nares Abyssal Plain
Corner Seamounts
Atlantis Fracture Zone
Atlantis Seamount
Azores Fracture Zone
Azores (to Portugal)
East Azores Fracture Zone
Great Meteor Tablemount
Oceanographer Fracture Zone
Kane Fracture Zone
Kane Seamount
Krylov Seamount
Barracuda Fracture Zone
Vema Fracture Zone
Doldrums Fracture Zone
Four North Fracture Zone
Fifteen-Twenty Fracture Zone

Tropic of Cancer

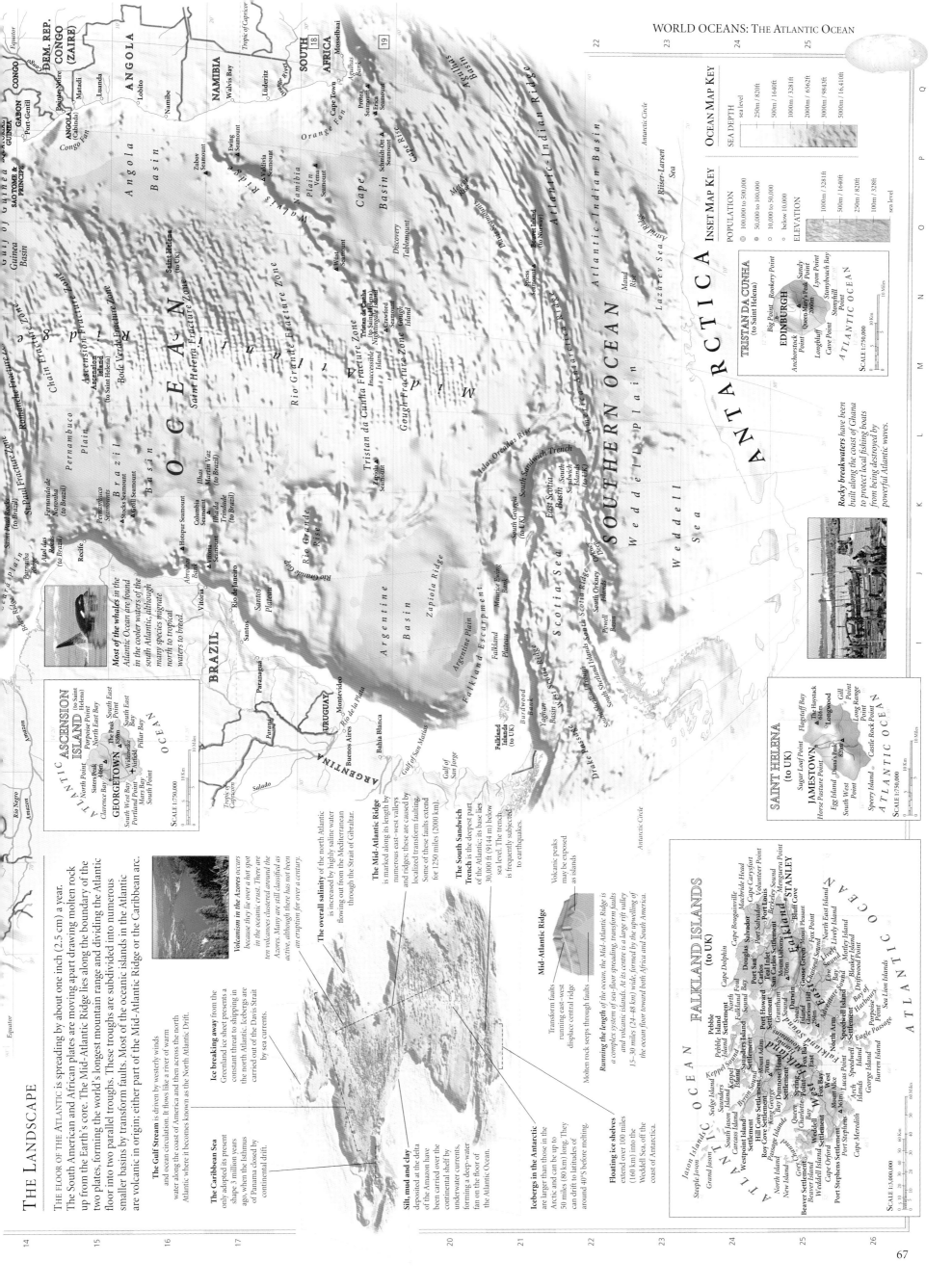

THE LANDSCAPE

THE FLOOR OF THE ATLANTIC is spreading by about one inch (2.5 cm) a year. The South American and African plates are moving apart drawing molten rock up from the Earth's core. The Mid-Atlantic Ridge lies along the boundary of the two plates, forming the world's longest mountain range and dividing the Atlantic floor into two parallel troughs. These troughs are subdivided into numerous smaller basins by transform faults. Most of the oceanic islands in the Atlantic are volcanic in origin; either part of the Mid-Atlantic Ridge or the Caribbean arc.

The Gulf Stream is driven by westerly winds and ocean circulation. It flows like a river of warm water along the coast of America and then across the north Atlantic where it becomes known as the North Atlantic Drift.

The Caribbean Sea only adopted its present shape 3 million years ago, when the Isthmus of Panama closed by continental drift.

Ice breaking away from the Greenland ice sheet presents a constant threat to shipping in the north Atlantic. Icebergs are carried out of the Davis Strait by sea currents.

Silt, mud and clay deposited at the delta of the Amazon have been carried over the continental shelf by underwater currents, forming a deep-water fan on the floor of the Atlantic Ocean.

Icebergs in the Antarctic are larger than those in the Arctic and can be up to 50 miles (80 km) long. They can drift to latitudes of around 40°S before melting.

Floating ice shelves extend over 100 miles (160 km) into the Weddell Sea, off the coast of Antarctica.

Volcanism in the Azores occurs because they lie over a hot spot in the oceanic crust. There are ten volcanoes clustered around the Azores. Many are still classified as active, although there has not been an eruption for over a century.

The overall salinity of the north Atlantic is increased by highly saline water flowing out from the Mediterranean through the Strait of Gibraltar.

The Mid-Atlantic Ridge is marked along its length by numerous east-west valleys and ridges; these are caused by localized transform faulting. Some of these faults extend for 1250 miles (2000 km).

The South Sandwich Trench is the deepest part of the Atlantic; its base lies 30,000 ft (9144 m) below sea level. The trench is frequently subjected to earthquakes.

Volcanic peaks may be exposed as islands.

Mid-Atlantic Ridge

Transform faults running east-west displace central ridge

Molten rock seeps through faults

Running the length of the ocean, the Mid-Atlantic Ridge is a complex system of sea-floor spreading, transform faults and volcanic islands. At its centre is a large rift valley 15–30 miles (24–48 km) wide, formed by the upwelling of the ocean floor toward both Africa and South America.

Most of the whales in the Atlantic Ocean are found in the cooler waters of the south Atlantic, although many species migrate north to tropical waters to breed.

Rocky breakwaters have been built along the coast of Ghana to protect local fishing boats from being destroyed by powerful Atlantic waves.

OCEAN MAP KEY

SEA DEPTH
- sea level
- 250m / 820ft
- 500m / 1640ft
- 1000m / 3281ft
- 2000m / 6562ft
- 3000m / 9843ft
- 5000m / 16,410ft

INSET MAP KEY

POPULATION
- ⬤ 100,000 to 500,000
- ⊕ 50,000 to 100,000
- ⊙ 10,000 to 50,000
- ○ below 10,000

ELEVATION
- 1000m / 3281ft
- 500m / 1640ft
- 250m / 820ft
- 100m / 328ft
- sea level

TRISTAN DA CUNHA
(to Saint Helena)

Big Point Rookery Point
Sandy Point
EDINBURGH Lyon Point
Queen Mary's Peak 2060m
Stonybeach Bay
Anchorstock Stonyhill
Longbluff Cave Point
ATLANTIC OCEAN
SCALE 1:750,000
0   5   10 Miles
0   5   10 Km

SAINT HELENA
(to UK)

Sugar Loaf Point Flagstaff Bay
The Haystack
Horse Pasture Point **JAMESTOWN**
Longwood
Egg Island Diana's Peak Gill Point
South West 820m Long Range Point
Point
Speery Island Castle Rock Point
ATLANTIC OCEAN
SCALE 1:750,000
0   5   10 Miles
0   5   10 Km

FALKLAND ISLANDS
(to UK)

Jason Islands C.
Steeple Jason Grand Jason
Keppel Island
Pebble Cape Bougainville
Saunders Island Settlement Cape Dolphin
South Jason North Macbride Head
Carcass Island Keppel Sound Cape Carysfort
Westpoint Saunders Island Falkland Sound Douglas Salvador Port Salvador
Settlement Port Louis Volunteer Point
Roy Cove Settlement Port San Carlos
King George Teal Inlet Berkeley Sound
Passage Islands Port Howard **STANLEY**
North Island Settlement Estancia Settlement Mengeara Point
New Island Mount Adam Carlos Bluff Cove
700m Mount Usborne
Darwin 705m Fox Point
Swan Goose Green Mount Pleasant
Island Mount Low
Beaver Settlement Spring Point Fox Bay
Weddell Island Charlotte Adventure Sound
Weddell Island Settlement East Bleaker Island
George North Arm Low Motley Island
Island West Bay Lively Island
Port Stephens Settlement Sound Driftwood Point
363m Lucas Point Eagle Passage
Arch Speedwell Sea Lion Islands
Islands Island
Port Stephens George Island
Cape Meredith Barren Island
SCALE 1:3,000,000
ATLANTIC OCEAN

ASCENSION ISLAND
(to Saint Helena)

North Point
The Peak 859m South East Point
Widewake South East Bay
GEORGETOWN Airfield
South West Bay Porpoise Point
Sisters Peak 446m North East Bay
Portland Point
Clarence Bay Mars Bay
South Point
ATLANTIC OCEAN
SCALE 1:750,000
0   5   10 Miles
0   5   10 Km

Map labels

DEM. REP. CONGO (ZAIRE)
CONGO
Pointe-Noire
GABON Matadi
Port-Gentil
SÃO TOMÉ & PRÍNCIPE
Gulf of Guinea
Guinea Basin
Equator
ANGOLA
Cabinda
Luanda
Lobito
Namibe
NAMIBIA
Walvis Bay
Lüderitz
SOUTH AFRICA
Cape Town
Mossel Bay
Agulhas Bank
Tropic of Capricorn

Angola Basin
Congo Fan
Orange Fan
Walvis Ridge
Namibia Plain
Cape Basin
Agulhas Basin
Cape Rise
Ewing Seamount
Valdivia Seamount
Zubov Seamount
Schmidt-Ott Seamount
Discovery Tablemount
Meteor Seamount
Wust Seamount
Spiess Seamount
Crawford Seamount
Atlantic-Indian Ridge
Atlantic-Indian Basin
Bouvet Island (to Norway)
Maud Rise
Riiser-Larsen Sea
Lazarev Sea
Antarctic Circle

ATLANTIC OCEAN
Saint Paul Rocks (to Brazil)
Romanche Fracture Zone
Chain Fracture Zone
St. Paul Fracture Zone
Ascension Fracture Zone
Bode Verde Fracture Zone
Ascension Island (to Saint Helena)
Fernando de Noronha (to Brazil)
Barrachia Ridge
Pernambuco Plain
Pernambuco Seamounts
Recife
Brazil Basin
Atol das Rocas (to Brazil)
Stocks Seamount
Grill Seamount
Hotspur Seamount
Columbia Seamount
Martin Vaz (to Brazil)
Ilha da Trindade (to Brazil)
Vitória Seamount
Abrolhos Bank
Saint Helena (to UK)
Saint Helena Fracture Zone
Rio Grande Fracture Zone
Tristan da Cunha Fracture Zone
Gough Fracture Zone
Tristan da Cunha (to Saint Helena)
Inaccessible Island
Nightingale Island
Gough Island (to UK)
Rio Grande Rise
Rio Grande Gap
Zapiola Seamount
Zapiola Ridge
Vitória
Rio de Janeiro
Santos
Santos Plateau
BRAZIL
Paranaguá
URUGUAY
Montevideo
Río de la Plata
Buenos Aires
Bahía Blanca
ARGENTINA
Salado
Paraná
Tropic of Capricorn
Argentine Basin
Argentine Plain
Falkland Escarpment
Falkland Plateau
Maurice Ewing Bank
Gulf of San Matías
Gulf of San Jorge
Burdwood Bank
Falkland Islands (to UK)
Islas Orcadas Rise
South Georgia (to UK)
South Sandwich Trench
South Sandwich Islands (to UK)
East Scotia Basin
West Scotia Basin
Scotia Sea
North Scotia Ridge
South Scotia Ridge
South Orkney Islands
Powell Basin
South Shetland Islands
South Sandwich Trench
Drake Passage
Yaghan Basin
Orkney Deep
SOUTHERN OCEAN
ANTARCTICA
Weddell Plain
Weddell Sea
Antarctic Peninsula
American-Antarctic Ridge
Antarctic Circle

AFRICA

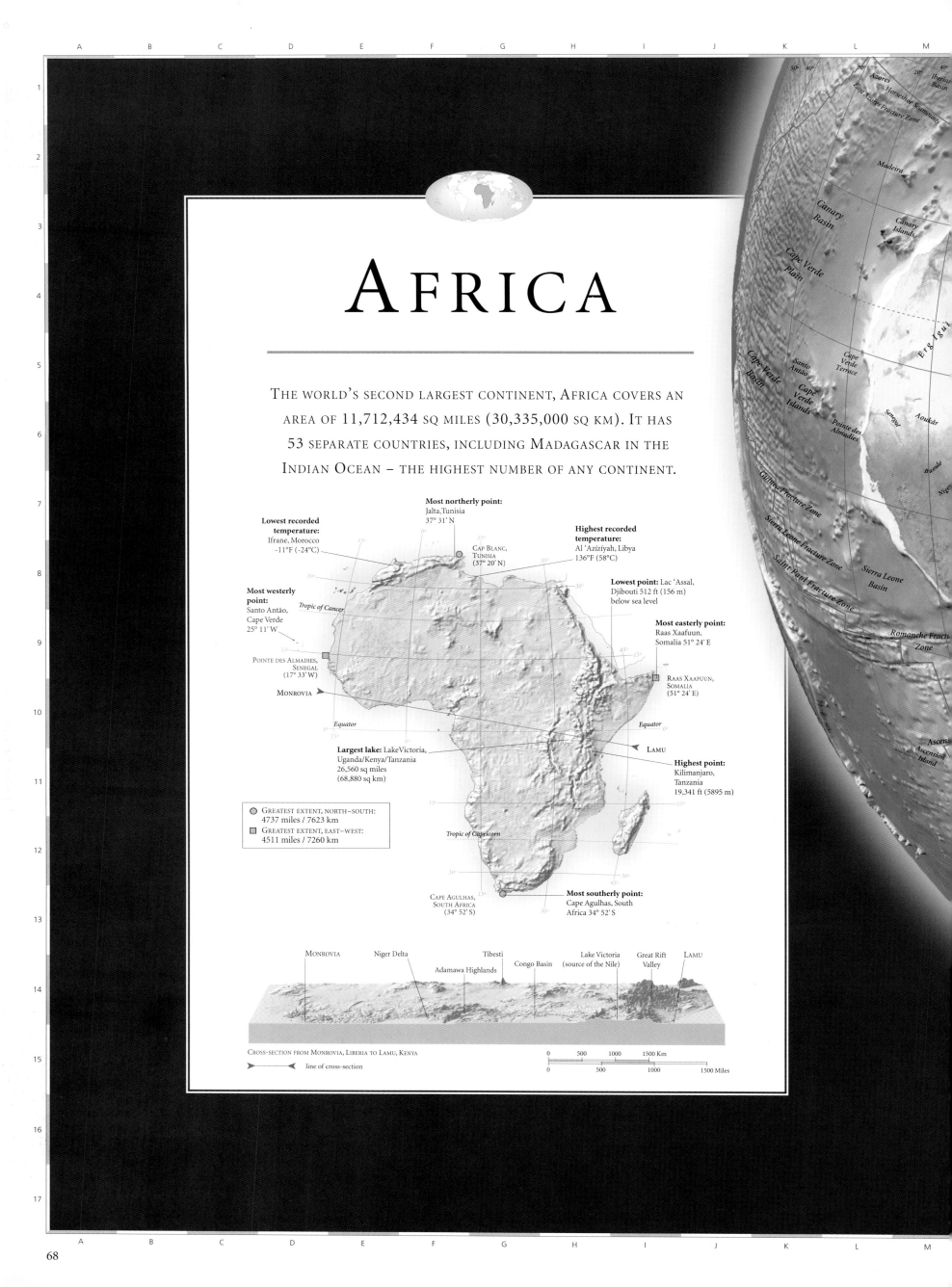

THE WORLD'S SECOND LARGEST CONTINENT, AFRICA COVERS AN
AREA OF 11,712,434 SQ MILES (30,335,000 SQ KM). IT HAS
53 SEPARATE COUNTRIES, INCLUDING MADAGASCAR IN THE
INDIAN OCEAN – THE HIGHEST NUMBER OF ANY CONTINENT.

Most northerly point:
Jalta, Tunisia
37° 31' N

CAP BLANC,
TUNISIA
(37° 20' N)

**Lowest recorded
temperature:**
Ifrane, Morocco
-11°F (-24°C)

**Highest recorded
temperature:**
Al 'Azízíyah, Libya
136°F (58°C)

Lowest point: Lac 'Assal,
Djibouti 512 ft (156 m)
below sea level

**Most westerly
point:**
Santo Antão,
Cape Verde
25° 11' W

Tropic of Cancer

POINTE DES ALMADIES,
SENEGAL
(17° 33' W)

MONROVIA

Most easterly point:
Raas Xaafuun,
Somalia 51° 24' E

RAAS XAAFUUN,
SOMALIA
(51° 24' E)

Equator

Equator

LAMU

Largest lake: LakeVictoria,
Uganda/Kenya/Tanzania
26,560 sq miles
(68,880 sq km)

Highest point:
Kilimanjaro,
Tanzania
19,341 ft (5895 m)

⊙ GREATEST EXTENT, NORTH–SOUTH:
4737 miles / 7623 km
▢ GREATEST EXTENT, EAST–WEST:
4511 miles / 7260 km

Tropic of Capricorn

CAPE AGULHAS,
SOUTH AFRICA
(34° 52' S)

Most southerly point:
Cape Agulhas, South
Africa 34° 52' S

MONROVIA | Niger Delta | Tibesti | Congo Basin | Lake Victoria (source of the Nile) | Great Rift Valley | LAMU

Adamawa Highlands

CROSS-SECTION FROM MONROVIA, LIBERIA TO LAMU, KENYA

line of cross-section

| 0 | 500 | 1000 | 1500 Km |
| 0 | 500 | 1000 | 1500 Miles |

Azores
Horseshoe Seamounts
Iberian
Basin
East Azores Fracture Zone
Madeira
Canary
Basin
Canary
Islands
Cape Verde
Plain
Ergʻ Iguïdi
Cape Verde
Basin
Santo
Antão
Cape
Verde
Terrace
Cape
Verde
Islands
Pointe des
Almadies
Sénégal
Aoukâr
Baoulé
Niger
Guinea Fracture Zone
Sierra Leone Fracture Zone
Saint Paul Fracture Zone
Sierra Leone
Basin
Romanche Fracture
Zone
Ascension
Island
Ascension

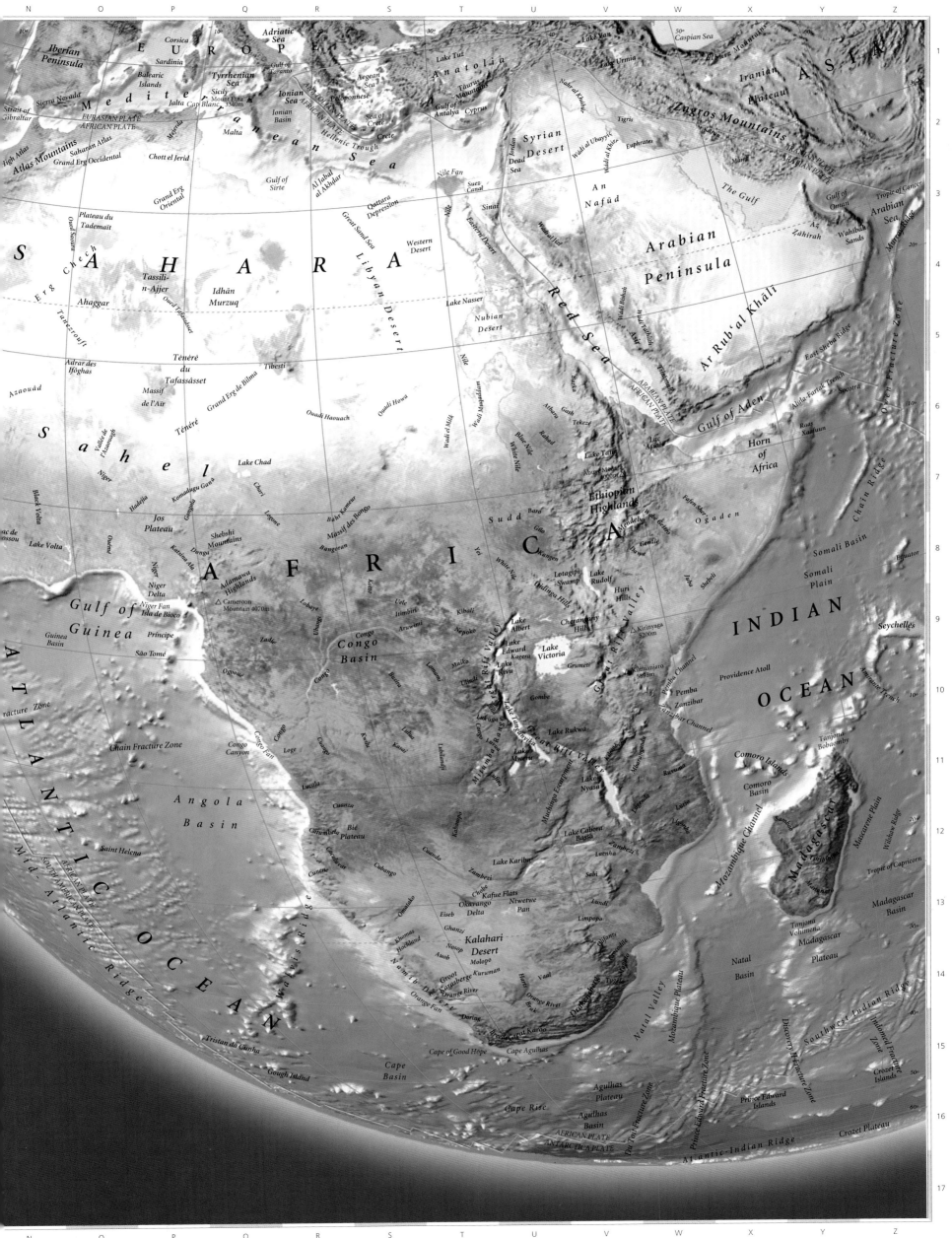

1
2
3
4
5
6
7
8
9
10
11
12
13
14
15
16
17

EUROPE

Iberian Peninsula
Corsica
Adriatic Sea
Sardinia
Balearic Islands
Tyrrhenian Sea
Sicily
Sierra Nevada
Mount Etna 3340m
Malta
Cap Blanc
Jalta
Gulf of Taranto
Aegean Sea
Ionian Sea
Ionian Basin
Hellenic Trough
Peloponnese
Sea of Crete
Crete
Anatolia
Lake Tuz
Taurus Mountains
Gulf of Antalya
Cyprus
Lake Van
Elburz Mountains
Caspian Sea

ASIA

Iranian Plateau
Zagros Mountains
Strait of Gibraltar
Mediterranean
EURASIAN PLATE
AFRICAN PLATE
Atlas Mountains
Saharan Atlas
Grand Erg Occidental
Migda
Plateau du Tademaït
Grand Erg Oriental
Chott el Jerid
Gulf of Sirte
Al Jabal al Akhdar
Qattara Depression
Nile Fan
Suez Canal
Sinai
Eastern Desert
Nile
Dead Sea
Syrian Desert
Nahr al Khabur
Jordan
Wadi al Ubayyic
Tigris
Euphrates
Karış
Mand
IRANIAN PLATE
ARABIAN PLATE
Gulf of Oman
Arabian Sea
Murray Ridge
Tropic of Cancer

SAHARA

Tigh Atlas
Oued Saoura
Erg Chech
Tassili-n-Ajjer
Idhān Murzuq
Great Sand Sea
Western Desert
Lake Nasser
Nubian Desert
An Nafūd
Az Zāhirah
Wahibah Sands
Arabian Peninsula
Ar Rub' al Khālī
Ahaggar
Oued Tafassasset
Erg Chech
Tanezrouft
Adrar des Ifôghas
Ténéré du Tafassâsset
Massif de l'Aïr
Ténéré
Grand Erg de Bilma
Tibesti
Ouadi Howa
Red Sea
ARABIAN PLATE
AFRICAN PLATE
East Sheba Ridge
Gulf of Aden
Alula-Fartak Trench
Socotra
Owen Fracture Zone
Azouâd
Grand Erg de Bilma
Ouadi Haouach
Wadi el Milk
Barka
Gulf of Aden
Raas Xaafuun
Valée de l'Azaouagh
Niger
Hadejia
Komadugu Gana
Chari
Logone
Bahr Keunar
Wadi Muqaddam
White Nile
Blue Nile
Arbara
Rahad
Tekeze
Gash
Lac Assal
Lake Tana
Abuye Meda 4000m
Horn of Africa
Sahel
Black Volta
Lake Chad
Sudd
Baro
Gilo
Ethiopian Highlands
Mendeba
Wabe Gestro
Genale
Dawa
Ogaden
Fafen Shet Valley
Somali Basin
Equator

AFRICA

Jos Plateau
Shebshi Mountains
Danga
Massif des Bongo
Bangoran
Yei
Kangen
Lotagipi Swamp
Lodinga Hills
Lake Rudolf
Huri Hills
Jubba
Shebeli
Somali Plain
Lake Volta
Ouémé
Katsina Ala
Niger Delta
Adamawa Highlands
Zabaye
Uele
Ubangi
Itimbiri
Aruwimi
Nepoko
Kibali
Maiko
White Nile
Cheranganiy Hills
Lake Albert
Kirinyaga 5200m
Seychelles
Niger Fan
Isla de Bioco
Cameroon Mountain 4070m
Congo Basin
Zanza
Lumami
Lindi
Lake Edward
Lake Kivu
Lake Kagera
Lake Victoria
Grumeti
Kilimanjaro 5893m
INDIAN
Gulf of Guinea
Guinea Basin
Príncipe
São Tomé
Ogooué
Congo
Lulonga
Uluhi
Lake Kivu
Lake Tanganyika
Gombe
Pemba
Zanzibar
Providence Atoll
OCEAN
ATLANTIC
Congo Fan
Congo Canyon
Loge
Kwilu
Kasai
Lulonga
Luhlamba
Lake Mweru
Zanzibar Channel
Chain Fracture Zone
Lucela
Lake Rukwa
Muchinga Escarpment
Mbarangandu
Ruvuma
Comoro Islands
Tanjona Bobaomby
Fracture Zone
Angola Basin
Cuango
Cuanza
Bié Plateau
Lake Nyasa
Ugenza
Loico
Laura
Comoro Basin
Saint Helena
Cuito
Cutumbela
Cubango
Lake Cabora Bassa
Luenha
Ugenza
Madagascar
Mascarene Plain
Mid-Atlantic Ridge
Cuanavale
Cuando
Zambezi
Lake Kariba
Zambezi
Sabi
Mozambique Channel
Tropic of Capricorn
Mascarene Plain
Wilkins Ridge
Choke
Kafue Flats
Ntwetwe Pan
Lundi
Madagascar Basin
Okavango Delta
Eiseb
Omaako
Ghanzi
Kalahari Desert
Molopo
Limpopo
Olifants
Tanjona Vohimena
Madagascar Plateau
Walvis Ridge
Khomas Hochland
Nosop
Auob
Kurasberge
Kuruman
Harts
Crocodile
Namib Desert
Groot
Orange River
Vaal
Orange River
Natal Basin
Dording
Orange Fan
Brak
Tugela
Natal Valley
Southwest Indian Ridge
SOUTH AMERICAN PLATE
AFRICAN PLATE
Tristan da Cunha
Great Escarpment Karoo
Drakensberg
Mozambique Plateau
Discovery II Fracture Zone
Indomed Fracture Zone
Gough Island
Cape of Good Hope
Cape Agulhas
Cape Basin
Prince Edward Islands
Crozet Islands
Cape Rise
Agulhas Plateau
Agulhas Basin
Prince Edward Fracture Zone
Crozet Plateau
AFRICAN PLATE
ANTARCTICA PLATE
Du Toit Fracture Zone
Atlantic-Indian Ridge

PHYSICAL AFRICA

THE STRUCTURE OF AFRICA was dramatically influenced by the break up of the supercontinent Gondwanaland about 160 million years ago and, more recently, rifting and hot spot activity. Today, much of Africa is remote from active plate boundaries and comprises a series of extensive plateaux and deep basins, which influence the drainage patterns of major rivers. The relief rises to the east, where volcanic uplands and vast lakes mark the Great Rift Valley. In the far north and south sedimentary rocks have been folded to form the Atlas Mountains and the Great Karoo.

EAST AFRICA

THE GREAT RIFT VALLEY is the most striking feature of this region, running for 4475 miles (7200 km) from Lake Nyasa to the Red Sea. North of Lake Nyasa it splits into two arms and encloses an interior plateau which contains Lake Victoria. A number of elongated lakes and volcanoes lie along the fault lines. To the west lies the Congo Basin, a vast, shallow depression, which rises to form an almost circular rim of highlands.

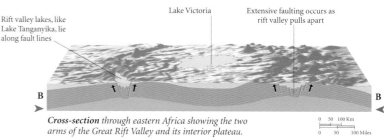

Rift valley lakes, like Lake Tanganyika, lie along fault lines

Lake Victoria

Extensive faulting occurs as rift valley pulls apart

Cross-section through eastern Africa showing the two arms of the Great Rift Valley and its interior plateau.

NORTHERN AFRICA

NORTHERN AFRICA COMPRISES a system of basins and plateaux. The Tibesti and Ahaggar are volcanic uplands, whose uplift has been matched by subsidence within large surrounding basins. Many of the basins have been infilled with sand and gravel, creating the vast Saharan lands. The Atlas Mountains in the north were formed by convergence of the African and Eurasian plates.

The Earth's crust has been warped to form the Taoudenni Basin

Volcanic Ahaggar Mountains, formed by rising magma from a hot spot

Lake Chad lies in a sand-filled basin

Section across northern Africa showing infilled basins and uplifted plateaux.

SCALE 1:36,000,000
(projection: Lambert Azimuthal Equal Area)

Km
0 100 200   400   600   800

Miles
0   100   200   400   600   800

MAP KEY

ELEVATION

5000m / 16,405ft
4000m / 13,124ft
3000m / 9843ft
2000m / 6562ft
1000m / 3281ft
500m / 1640ft
250m / 820ft
100m / 328ft
sea level
below sea level

PLATE MARGINS
(for explanation see page xiv)

—— constructive
△ △ destructive
—— conservative
······ uncertain
►— line of cross-section

SOUTHERN AFRICA

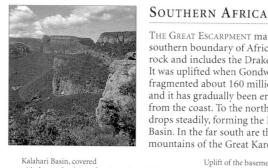

THE GREAT ESCARPMENT marks the southern boundary of Africa's basement rock and includes the Drakensberg range. It was uplifted when Gondwanaland fragmented about 160 million years ago and it has gradually been eroded back from the coast. To the north, the relief drops steadily, forming the Kalahari Basin. In the far south are the fold mountains of the Great Karoo.

Kalahari Basin, covered with the sandy plains of the Kalahari Desert

Boundary of the Great Escarpment

Uplift of the basement rock created a raised plateau

Drakensberg

Cross-section through southern Africa showing the boundary of the Great Escarpment.

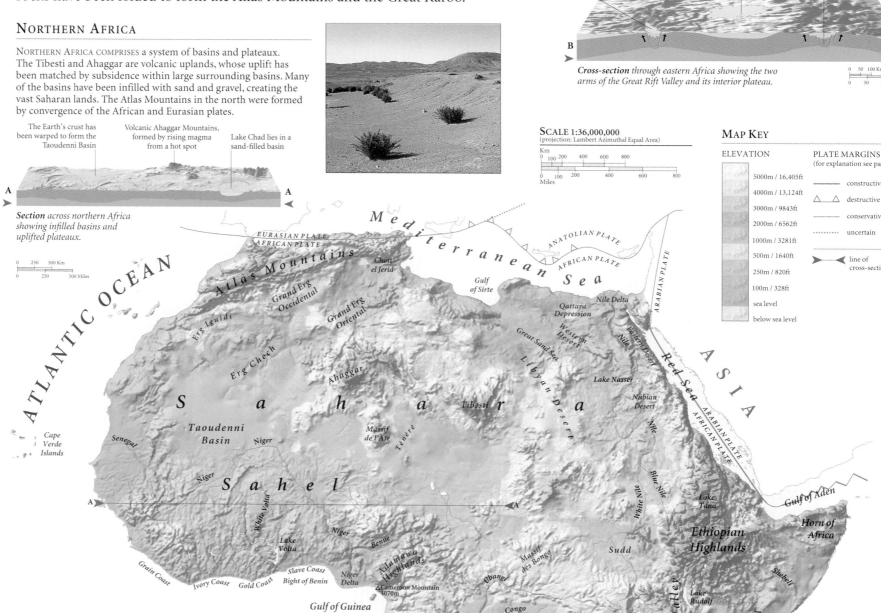

ATLANTIC OCEAN

Mediterranean Sea

EURASIAN PLATE
AFRICAN PLATE

ANATOLIAN PLATE

AFRICAN PLATE

ARABIAN PLATE

Atlas Mountains

Chott el Jerid

Gulf of Sirte

Grand Erg Occidental

Grand Erg Oriental

Qattara Depression

Nile Delta

ASIA

Erg Iguidi

Erg Chech

Ahaggar

Great Sand Sea

Western Desert

Libyan Desert

Eastern Desert

Red Sea

ARABIAN PLATE
AFRICAN PLATE

Sahara

Tibesti

Lake Nasser

Nubian Desert

Cape Verde Islands

Senegal

Taoudenni Basin

Massif de l'Aïr

Ténéré

Nile

Blue Nile

Lake Tana

Gulf of Aden

Niger

Sahel

White Volta

Niger

Benue

Lake Volta

Niger

Sudd

White Nile

Ethiopian Highlands

Horn of Africa

Shebeli

Grain Coast

Ivory Coast

Gold Coast

Slave Coast

Bight of Benin

Niger Delta

Adamawa Highlands

△Cameroon Mountain 4070m

Ubangi

Massif des Bongo

Lake Rudolf

Juba

Gulf of Guinea

São Tomé

Congo

Congo Basin

Congo

Lake Albert
Lake Victoria

△Kilimanjaro 5895m

Great Rift Valley

Seychelles

Bié Plateau

Lake Tanganyika

Pemba Island
Zanzibar

Mitumba Mts

Zambezi

Lake Nyasa

Comoro Islands

Zambezi

Mozambique Channel

Madagascar

Mauritius
Réunion

Bié Plateau

Okavango Delta

Kalahari Basin

Kalahari Desert

Namib Desert

Limpopo

ATLANTIC OCEAN

INDIAN OCEAN

Orange River

Great Karoo

Drakensberg

Cape of Good Hope

CLIMATE

THE CLIMATES OF AFRICA range
from mediterranean to arid, dry
savannah and humid equatorial.
In East Africa, where snow settles
at the summit of volcanoes such as
Kilimanjaro, climate is also modified
by altitude. The winds of the Sahara
export millions of tonnes of dust a
year both northwards and eastwards.

*Savannah grasslands run
in a belt across Africa; limited
rainfall inhibits tree growth.*

TEMPERATURE

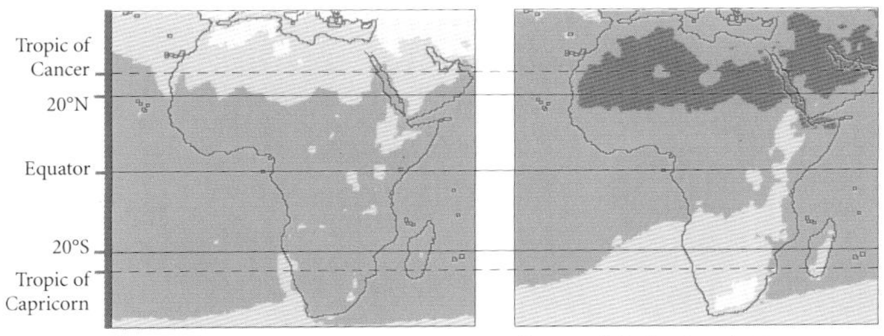

Average January temperature

Average July temperature

Temperature	
	0 to 10°C (32 to 50° F)
	10 to 20°C (50 to 68°F)
	20 to 30°C (68 to 86°F)
	above 30°C (86°F)

RAINFALL

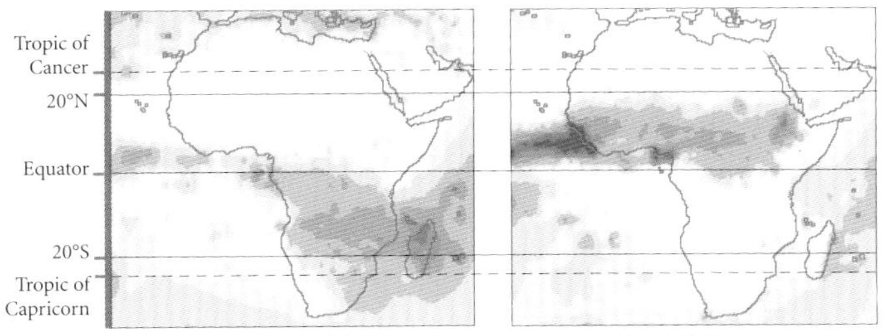

Average January rainfall

Average July rainfall

Rainfall		
0–25 mm (0–1 in)		200–300 mm (8–12 in)
25–50 mm (1–2 in)		300–40`3 mm (12–16 in)
50–100 mm (2–4 in)		400–500 mm (16–20 in)
100–200 mm (4–8 in)		more than 500 mm (20 in)

*The hot, equatorial basin of the
Congo River receives over 48 inches
(1200 mm) of rainfall per year.*

Climate	
	arid
	humid equatorial
	mediterranean
	semi-arid
	tropical
	warm humid
	daily hours of sunshine, January
	daily hours of sunshine, July
	cold wind
	hot wind

SHAPING THE CONTINENT

AFRICAN LANDSCAPES are shaped by the intensity of climatic
extremes and by tectonic action. High aridity, wind action and
infrequent but heavy rainstorms, lead to the migration of sand
dunes and dramatic flash flooding across much of the north and
west. In the wetter areas, high precipitation increases the rate of
weathering. To the east, the rift system has created a volcanic and
lake environment and allowed rivers to erode weaknesses left in
the crustal structure by faults.

GROUNDWATER

1 Oases are found in desert areas such
as the Sahara *(left)*. Groundwater migrates
through permeable rock strata. confined
between two impermeable layers. Oases
form either when the permeable rocks
come near to the surface, or at a fault line,
when water is able to seep up to the surface
through the crushed rocks at the fault.

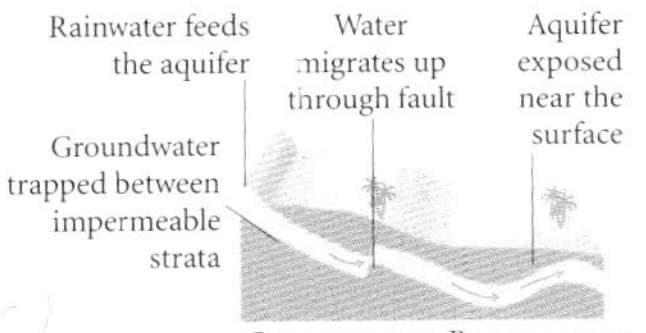

GROUNDWATER: REPLENISHMENT OF AN OASIS

RIVER SYSTEMS

2 The Zambezi River *(above)* drops
360 ft (110 m) over the Victoria Falls
into a zig-zag gorge. The river has
eroded the gorge along lines of
weakness in the bedrock, created by
fault lines running in two directions.

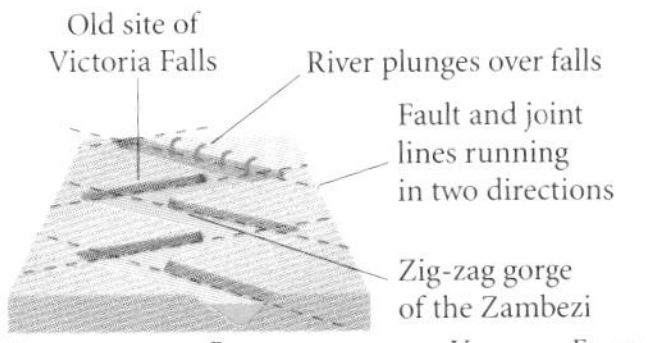

RIVER SYSTEMS: RETREATING OF THE VICTORIA FALLS

THE EVOLVING LANDSCAPE

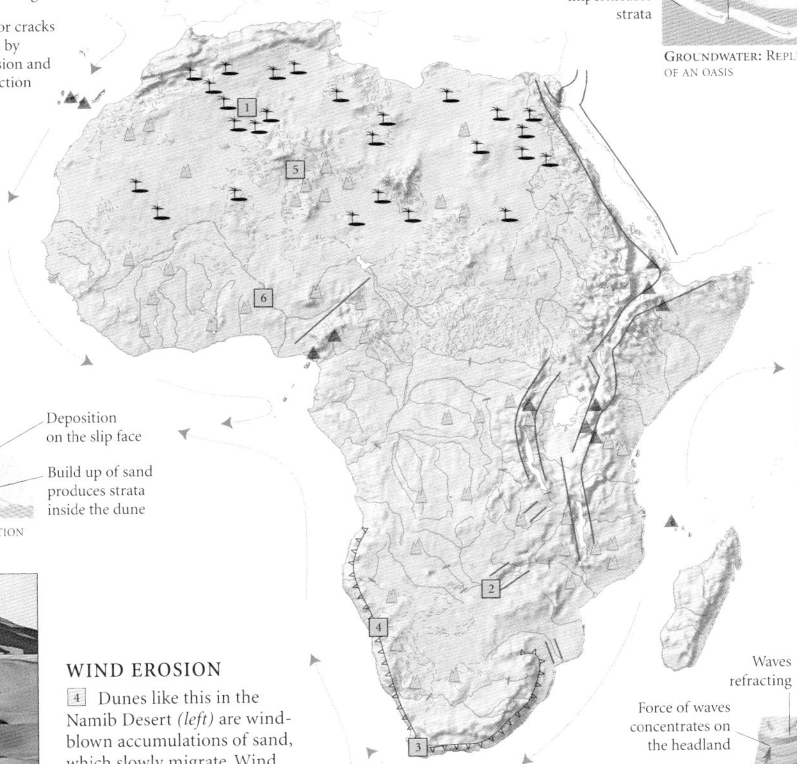

WEATHERING

6 Inselbergs *(above)*, found extensively across West Africa,
are exposed remnants of an extensive upland area. Erosion
of the surrounding uplands leaves a resistant rock outcrop. Its
spheroidal shape is the result of 'onion-skin' weathering – the
exfoliating layers – due to repeated expansion and contraction.

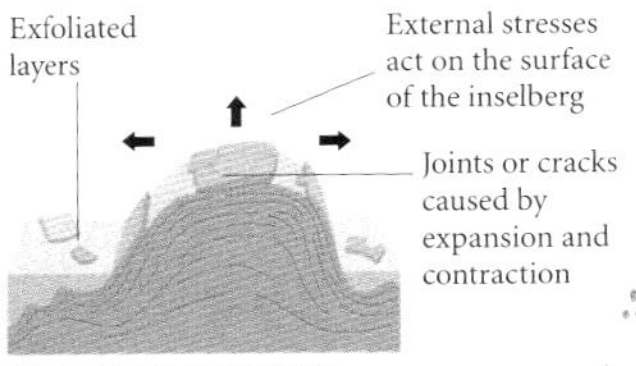

WEATHERING: FORMATION OF AN INSELBERG

EPHEMERAL CHANNELS

5 Wadis *(above)* drain much of
northern Africa. These drybed courses
are flooded only after infrequent, but
intense, storms in the uplands cause
water to surge along their channels.

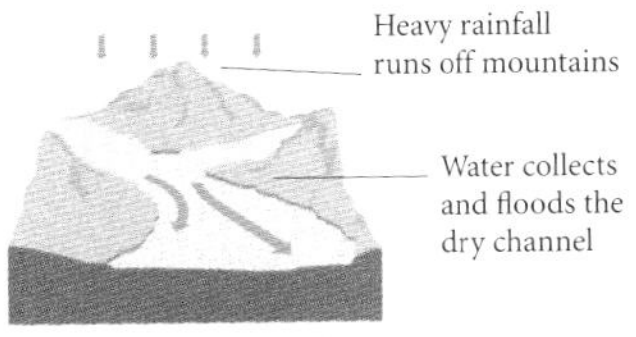

EPHEMERAL CHANNELS: FLASH FLOODING OF A WADI

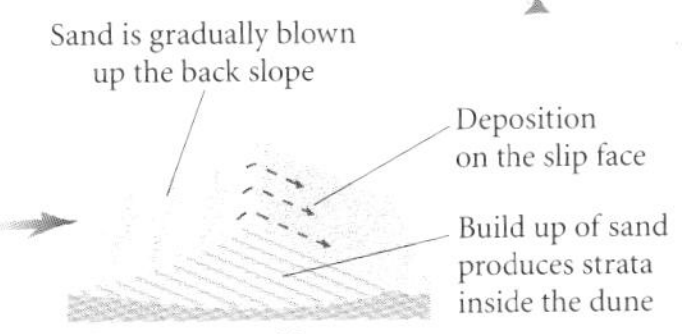

WIND EROSION

4 Dunes like this in the
Namib Desert *(left)* are wind-
blown accumulations of sand,
which slowly migrate. Wind
action moves sand up the
shallow back slope; when the
sand reaches the crest of the dune
it is deposited on the slip face.

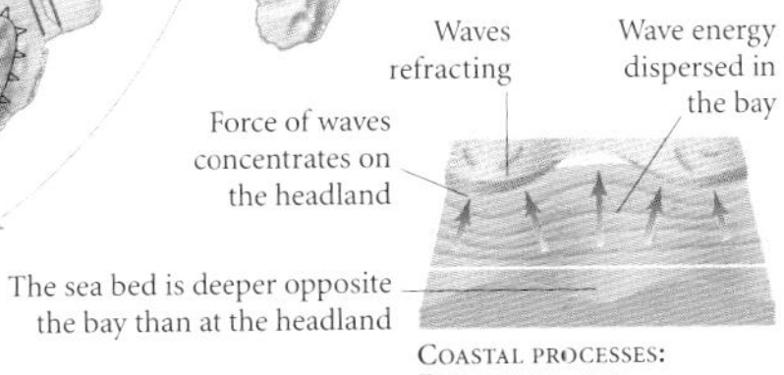

WIND EROSION: MIGRATION OF A DUNE

Landscape	
	sinking land
	stable land
	uplifting land
	escarpment
	ocean current
	rift
	active volcano
	inselberg
	oasis
	river
	wadi
	waterfall

COASTAL PROCESSES

3 Houtbaai *(above)*, in
southern Africa, is constantly being
modified by wave action.
As waves approach the indented
coastline, they reach the shallow
water of the headland, slowing
down and reducing in length.
This causes them to bend or
refract, concentrating their
erosive force at the headlands.

COASTAL PROCESSES: EROSION OF A BAY

A B C D E F G H I J K L

POLITICAL AFRICA

THE POLITICAL MAP OF MODERN AFRICA only emerged following the end of the Second World War. Over the next half-century, all of the countries formerly controlled by European powers gained independence from their colonial rulers – only Liberia and Ethiopia were never colonized. The post-colonial era has not been an easy period for many countries, but there have been moves towards multi-party democracy in much of West Africa, and in Zambia, Tanzania and Kenya. In South Africa, democratic elections replaced the internationally-condemned apartheid system only in 1994. Other countries have still to find political stability; corruption in government and ethnic tensions are serious problems. National infrastructures, based on the colonial transport systems built to exploit Africa's resources, are often inappropriate for independent economic development.

LANGUAGES

THREE MAJOR WORLD LANGUAGES act as *lingua francas* across the African continent: Arabic in North Africa; English in southern and eastern Africa and Nigeria; and French in Central and West Africa, and in Madagascar. A huge number of African languages are spoken as well – over 2000 have been recorded, with more than 400 in Nigeria alone – reflecting the continuing importance of traditional cultures and values. In the north of the continent, the extensive use of Arabic reflects Middle Eastern influences while Bantu is widely-spoken across much of southern Africa.

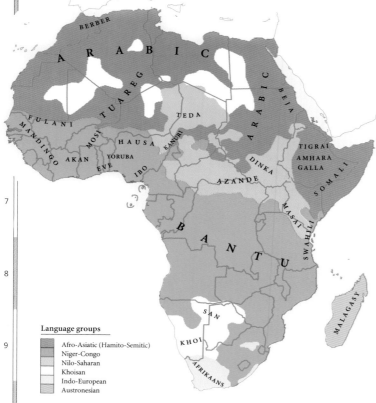

Language groups
- Afro-Asiatic (Hamito-Semitic)
- Niger-Congo
- Nilo-Saharan
- Khoisan
- Indo-European
- Austronesian

OFFICIAL AFRICAN LANGUAGES

Official languages
- French
- English
- Arabic
- Portuguese
- Swahili
- Amharic
- Spanish
- French/English
- French/Arabic
- French/Malagasay
- English/Swahili
- Arabic/Somali

Islamic influences are evident throughout North Africa. The Great Mosque at Kairouan, Tunisia, is Africa's holiest Islamic place.

In northeastern Nigeria, people speak Kanuri – a dialect of the Saharan language group.

TRANSPORT

AFRICAN RAILWAYS WERE BUILT to aid the exploitation of natural resources, and most offer passage only from the interior to the coastal cities, leaving large parts of the continent untouched – five land-locked countries have no railways at all. The Congo, Nile and Niger river networks offer limited access to land within the continental interior, but have a number of waterfalls and cataracts which prevent navigation from the sea. Many roads were developed in the 1960s and 1970s, but economic difficulties are making the maintenance and expansion of the networks difficult.

South Africa has the largest concentration of railways in Africa. Over 20,000 miles (32,000 km) of routes have been built since 1870.

Traditional means of transport, such as the camel, are still widely used across the less accessible parts of Africa.

The Congo River, though not suitable for river transport along its entire length, forms a vital link for people and goods in its navigable inland reaches.

Transport
- major roads and motorways
- major railways
- major canal
- international borders
- transport intersections
- international airports
- major ports

MOROCCO
Casablanca
Safi
Marrakech
Agadir
Canary Islands (to Spain)
Madeira (to Portugal)

LAÂYOUNE
Western Sahara (Occupied by Morocco)

Tropic of Cancer

MAURITANIA
NOUAKCHOTT

CAPE VERDE
PRAIA

Senegal

SENEGAL
DAKAR
Kaolack
BANJUL
GAMBIA
GUINEA-BISSAU
BISSAU
BAMAKO
Niger
GUINEA
CONAKRY
Koidu
FREETOWN
SIERRA LEONE
YAMOUSSOUKRO
MONROVIA
IVORY COAST
LIBERIA

Ceuta (to Spain)
Tanger
Rabat
Casablanca
Oran
Algiers
Skikda
Tunis
Agadir
Tripoli

Nouâdhibou
Nouakchott
Dakar
Banjul
Bissau
Conakry
Freetown
Monrovia
Abidjan
Bamako
Ouagadougou
Niamey
Kano
Maiduguri
Agadez
Tamanrasset
Accra
Lomé
Lagos
Warri
Cotonou
Douala
Malabo
Yaoundé
Libreville
Port-Gentil
Bangui
Kisangani

Alexandria
Port Said
Suez Canal
Cairo
Suez
Aswân
Wadi Halfa
Port Sudan
Massawa
Khartoum
Assab
Djibouti
Addis Ababa
Nyala
Ndjamena
Mogadishu
Kampala
Nairobi
Bukavu
Mombasa
Brazzaville
Kinshasa
Kananga
Kalemie
Dodoma
Dar es Salaam
Pointe-Noire
Matadi
Mbeya
Luanda
Lubumbashi
Lobito
Nampula
Namibe
Lusaka
Livingstone
Harare
Antananarivo
Toamasina
Tsumeb
Bulawayo
Beira
Walvis Bay
Windhoek
Keetmanshoop
Pretoria
Maputo
Johannesburg
Durban
Cape Town
Port Elizabeth

72

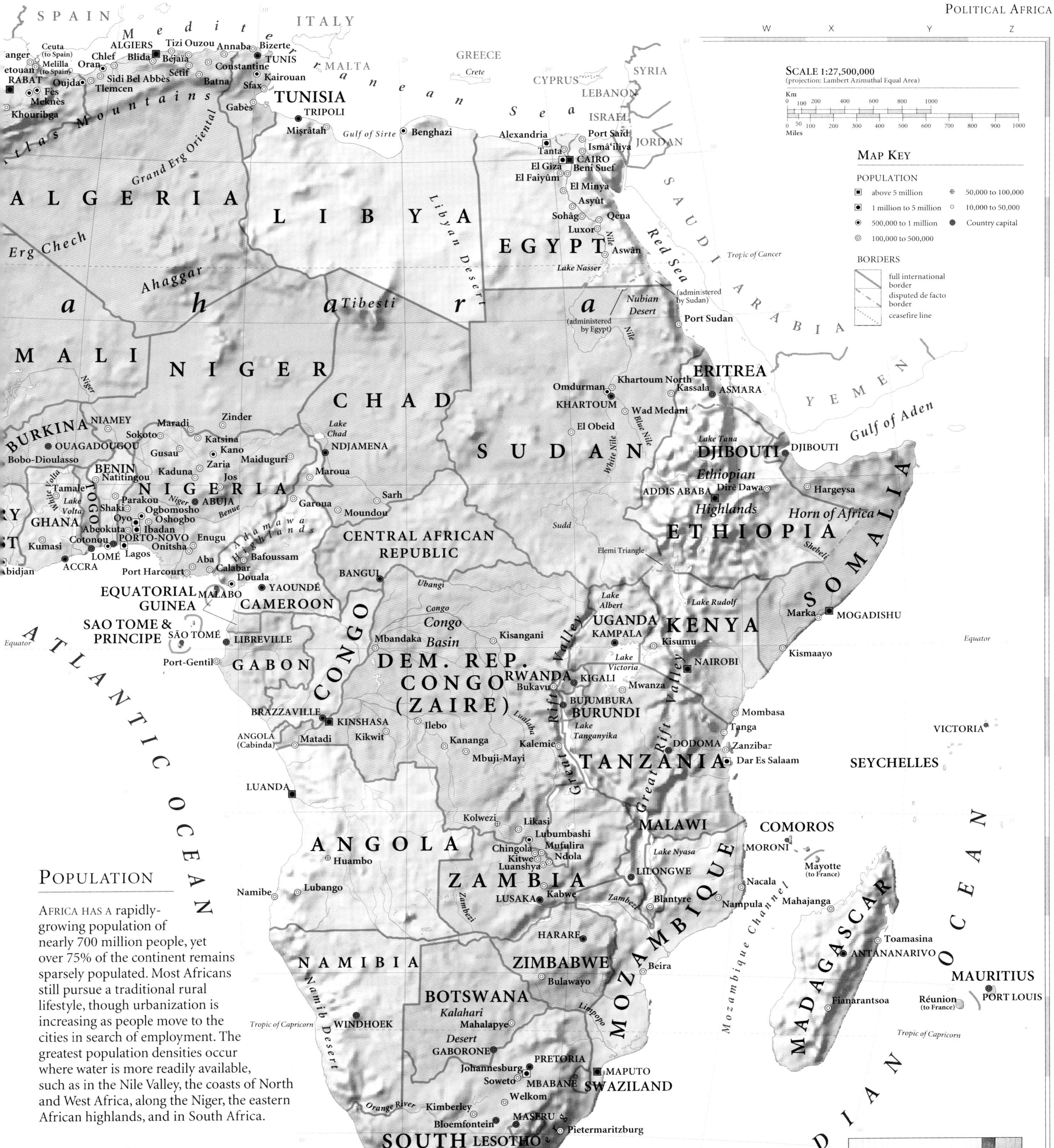

Map Key

SCALE 1:27,500,000
(projection: Lambert Azimuthal Equal Area)

POPULATION

- ■ above 5 million
- ■ 1 million to 5 million
- ◉ 500,000 to 1 million
- ◎ 100,000 to 500,000
- ⊕ 50,000 to 100,000
- ○ 10,000 to 50,000
- ● Country capital

BORDERS

- full international border
- disputed de facto border
- ceasefire line

POPULATION

AFRICA HAS A rapidly-growing population of nearly 700 million people, yet over 75% of the continent remains sparsely populated. Most Africans still pursue a traditional rural lifestyle, though urbanization is increasing as people move to the cities in search of employment. The greatest population densities occur where water is more readily available, such as in the Nile Valley, the coasts of North and West Africa, along the Niger, the eastern African highlands, and in South Africa.

Population density
(people per sq km)
- below 49
- 50–99
- 100–149
- 150–199
- 200–299
- above 300

A thin layer of smog blankets the dusty streets of Cairo, Africa's most populous city and home to over six million people. In the 1990s Cairo grew at a rate of about 1500 people per day.

Thriving street markets in Gambia's capital, Banjul, trade a variety of locally-grown produce. Africa's population is still predominantly rural-based.

73

AFRICAN RESOURCES

THE ECONOMIES OF MOST AFRICAN COUNTRIES are dominated by subsistence and cash crop agriculture, with limited industrialization. Manufacturing industry is largely confined to South Africa. Many countries depend on a single resource, such as copper or gold, or a cash crop, such as coffee, for export income, which can leave them vulnerable to fluctuations in world commodity prices. In order to diversify their economies and develop a wider industrial base, investment from overseas is being actively sought by many African governments.

INDUSTRY

MANY AFRICAN INDUSTRIES concentrate on the extraction and processing of raw materials. These include the oil industry, food processing, mining and textile production. South Africa accounts for over half of the continent's industrial output with much of the remainder coming from the countries along the northern coast. Over 60% of Africa's workforce is employed in agriculture.

The unspoilt natural splendour of wildlife reserves, like the Serengeti National Park in Tanzania, attract tourists to Africa from around the globe. The tourist industry in Kenya and Tanzania is particularly well developed, where it accounts for almost 10% of GNP.

STANDARD OF LIVING

SINCE THE 1960s most countries in Africa have seen significant improvements in life expectancy, healthcare and education. However, 18 of the 20 most deprived countries in the world are African, and the continent as a whole lies well behind the rest of the world in terms of meeting many basic human needs.

Standard of Living
(UN Human Development Index)
- high
- low

GNP per capita (US$)
- 0–199
- 200–399
- 400–599
- 600–899
- 900–1999
- 2000+

Industry
- brewing
- car/vehicle manufacture
- cement
- chemicals
- coffee processing
- electronics
- engineering
- finance
- fish processing
- food processing
- iron & steel
- mining
- palm oil processing
- peanut processing
- pharmaceuticals
- rice milling
- shipbuilding
- sugar processing
- tea processing
- textiles
- timber processing
- tobacco processing
- coal
- oil
- gas
- industrial cities
- major industrial areas

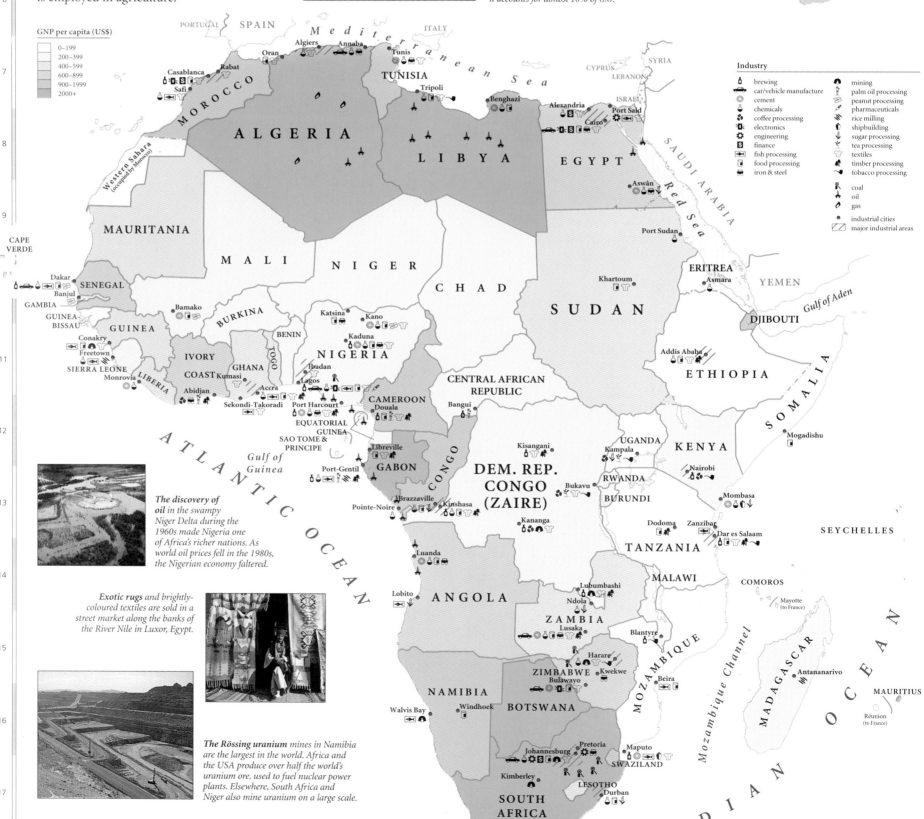

The discovery of **oil** in the swampy Niger Delta during the 1960s made Nigeria one of Africa's richer nations. As world oil prices fell in the 1980s, the Nigerian economy faltered.

Exotic rugs *and brightly-coloured textiles are sold in a street market along the banks of the River Nile in Luxor, Egypt.*

The Rössing uranium mines in Namibia are the largest in the world. Africa and the USA produce over half the world's uranium ore, used to fuel nuclear power plants. Elsewhere, South Africa and Niger also mine uranium on a large scale.

ENVIRONMENTAL ISSUES

ONE OF AFRICA'S most serious environmental problems occurs in marginal areas such as the Sahel where scrub and forest clearance, often for cooking fuel, combined with overgrazing, are causing desertification. Game reserves in southern and eastern Africa have helped to preserve many endangered animals, although the needs of growing populations have led to conflict over land use, and poaching is a serious problem.

Environmental Issues
- national parks
- tropical forest
- forest destroyed
- desert
- desertification
- polluted rivers
- radioactive contamination
- marine pollution
- heavy marine pollution
- poor urban air quality

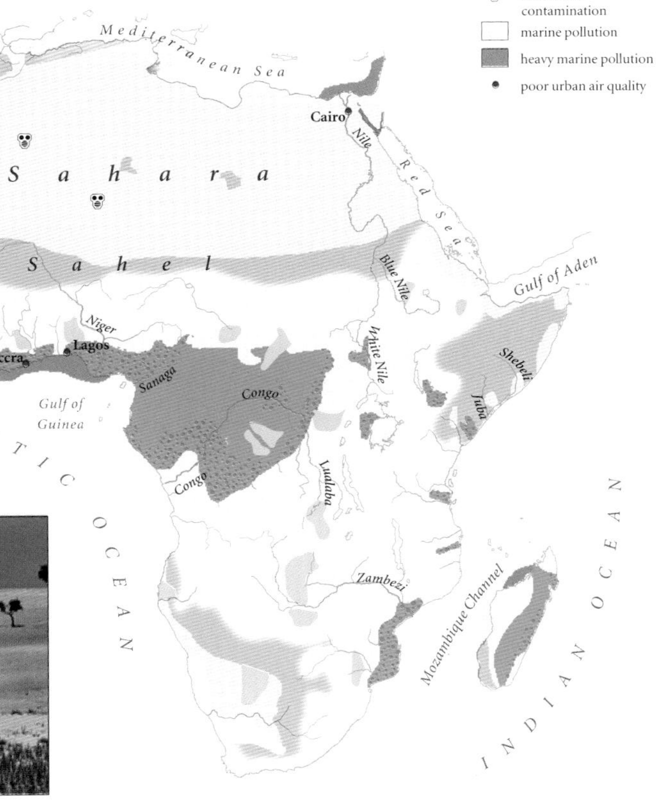

The Sahel's delicate natural equilibrium is easily destroyed by the clearing of vegetation, drought and overgrazing. This causes the Sahara to advance south, engulfing the savannah grasslands.

MINERAL RESOURCES

AFRICA'S ANCIENT PLATEAUX contain some of the world's most substantial reserves of precious stones and metals. About 30% of the world's gold is mined in South Africa; Zambia has great copper deposits; and diamonds are mined in Botswana, Dem. Rep. Congo (Zaire) and South Africa. Oil has brought great economic benefits to Algeria, Libya and Nigeria.

Mineral Resources
- oil field
- gas field
- coal field
- bauxite
- copper
- diamonds
- gold
- iron
- phosphates
- tin
- uranium

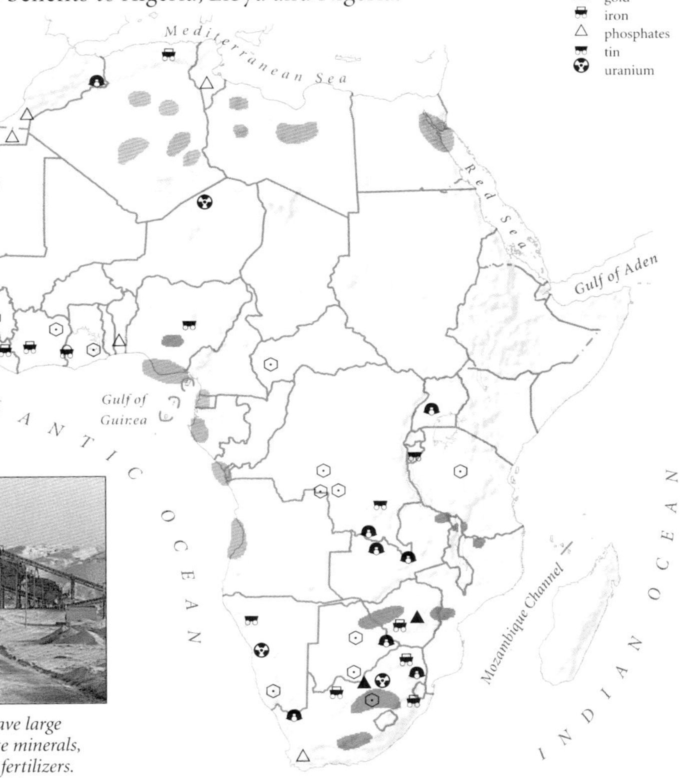

North and West Africa have large deposits of white phosphate minerals, which are used in making fertilizers. Morocco, Senegal, and Tunisia are the continent's leading producers.

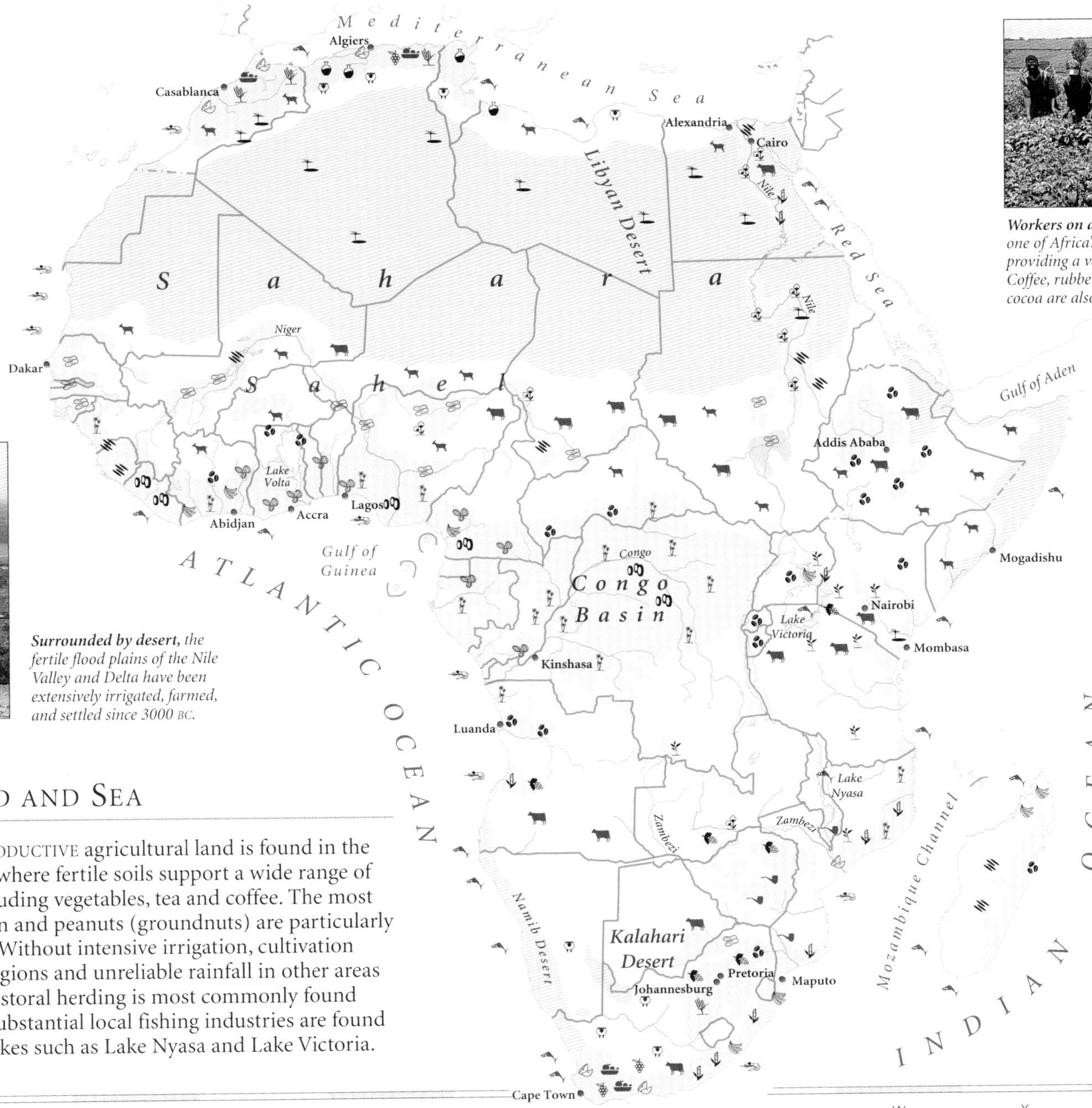

Workers on a tea plantation gather one of Africa's most important cash crops, providing a valuable source of income. Coffee, rubber, bananas, cotton and cocoa are also widely grown as cash crops.

Surrounded by desert, the fertile flood plains of the Nile Valley and Delta have been extensively irrigated, farmed, and settled since 3000 BC.

USING THE LAND AND SEA

SOME OF AFRICA'S MOST PRODUCTIVE agricultural land is found in the eastern volcanic uplands, where fertile soils support a wide range of valuable export crops including vegetables, tea and coffee. The most widely-grown grain is corn and peanuts (groundnuts) are particularly important in West Africa. Without intensive irrigation, cultivation is not possible in desert regions and unreliable rainfall in other areas limits crop production. Pastoral herding is most commonly found in these marginal lands. Substantial local fishing industries are found along coasts and in vast lakes such as Lake Nyasa and Lake Victoria.

Using the Land and Sea
- cropland
- desert
- forest
- pasture
- wetland
- major conurbations
- cattle
- goats
- cereals
- sheep
- bananas
- corn (maize)
- citrus fruits
- cocoa
- cotton
- coffee
- dates
- fishing
- fruit
- oil palms
- olives
- peanuts
- rice
- rubber
- shellfish
- sugar cane
- tea
- tobacco
- vineyards
- wheat

NORTH AFRICA

ALGERIA, EGYPT, LIBYA, MOROCCO, TUNISIA, WESTERN SAHARA

FRINGED BY THE MEDITERRANEAN along the northern coast and by the arid Sahara in the south, North Africa reflects the influence of many invaders, both European and, most importantly, Arab, giving the region an almost universal Islamic flavour and a common Arabic language. The countries lying to the west of Egypt are often referred to as the Maghreb, an Arabic term for 'west'. Today, Morocco and Tunisia exploit their culture and landscape for tourism, while rich oil and gas deposits aid development in Libya and Algeria, despite political turmoil. Egypt, with its fertile, Nile-watered agricultural land and varied industrial base, is the most populous nation.

THE LANDSCAPE

THE ATLAS MOUNTAINS, which extend across much of Morocco, northern Algeria and Tunisia, are part of the fold mountain system which also runs through much of southern Europe. They recede to the south and east, becoming a steppe landscape before meeting the Sahara desert which covers more than 90% of the region. The sediments of the Sahara overlie an ancient plateau of crystalline rock, some of which is more than four billion years old.

These rock piles in Algeria's Ahaggar Mountains are the result of weathering caused by extremes of temperature. Great cracks or joints appear in the rocks, which are then worn and smoothed by the wind.

MAP KEY

POPULATION
- ■ above 5 million
- ◉ 1 million to 5 million
- ◎ 500,000 to 1 million
- ⊚ 100,000 to 500,000
- ⊕ 50,000 to 100,000
- ○ 10,000 to 50,000
- ○ below 10,000

ELEVATION
- 4000m / 13,124ft
- 3000m / 9843ft
- 2000m / 6562ft
- 1000m / 3281ft
- 500m / 1640ft
- 250m / 820ft
- 100m / 328ft
- sea level

The town of Tiznit, Morocco, lies in an oasis in the desert. Crops and trees grow on the fertile land surrounding the town.

SCALE 1:11,000,000
(projection: Lambert Azimuthal Equal Area)

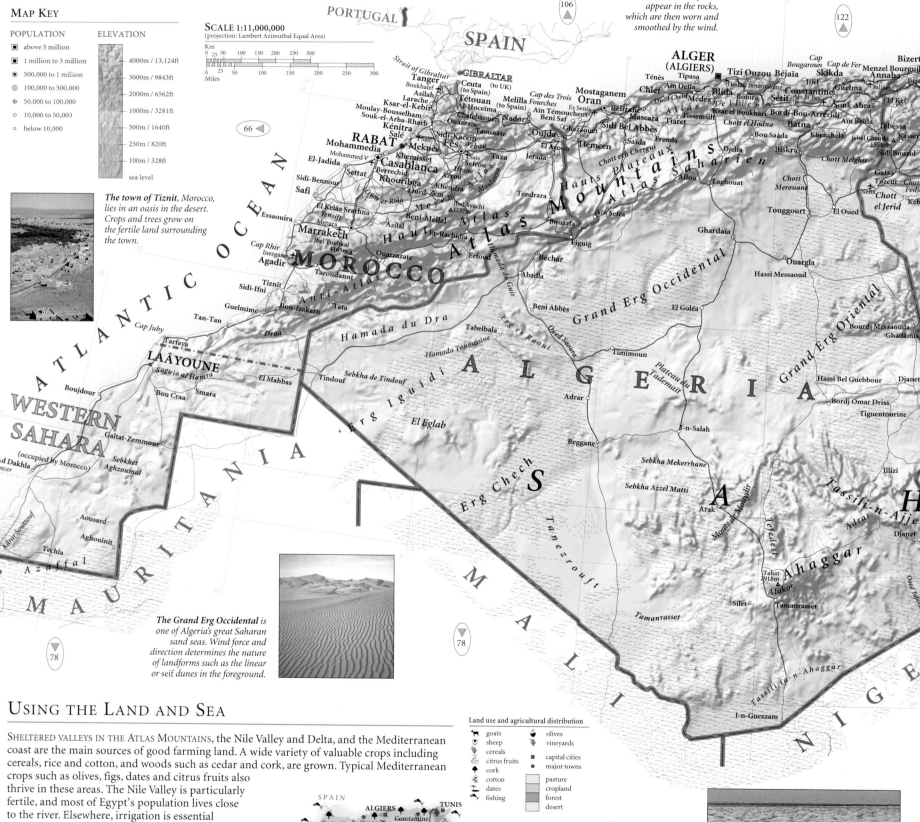

The Grand Erg Occidental is one of Algeria's great Saharan sand seas. Wind force and direction determines the nature of landforms such as the linear or seif dunes in the foreground.

USING THE LAND AND SEA

SHELTERED VALLEYS IN THE ATLAS MOUNTAINS, the Nile Valley and Delta, and the Mediterranean coast are the main sources of good farming land. A wide variety of valuable crops including cereals, rice and cotton, and woods such as cedar and cork, are grown. Typical Mediterranean crops such as olives, figs, dates and citrus fruits also thrive in these areas. The Nile Valley is particularly fertile, and most of Egypt's population lives close to the river. Elsewhere, irrigation is essential to improve crop yields on the desert margins.

Land use and agricultural distribution
- goats
- sheep
- cereals
- citrus fruits
- cork
- cotton
- dates
- fishing
- olives
- vineyards
- ■ capital cities
- ● major towns
- pasture
- cropland
- forest
- desert

THE URBAN/RURAL POPULATION DIVIDE

urban 50%   rural 50%

0 10 20 30 40 50 60 70 80 90 100

POPULATION DENSITY
62 people per sq mile
(24 people per sq km)

TOTAL LAND AREA
2,215,020 sq miles
(5,738,394 sq km)

Many North African nomads, such as the Bedouin, maintain a traditional pastoral lifestyle on the desert fringes, moving their herds of sheep, goats and camels from place to place – crossing country borders in order to find sufficient grazing land.

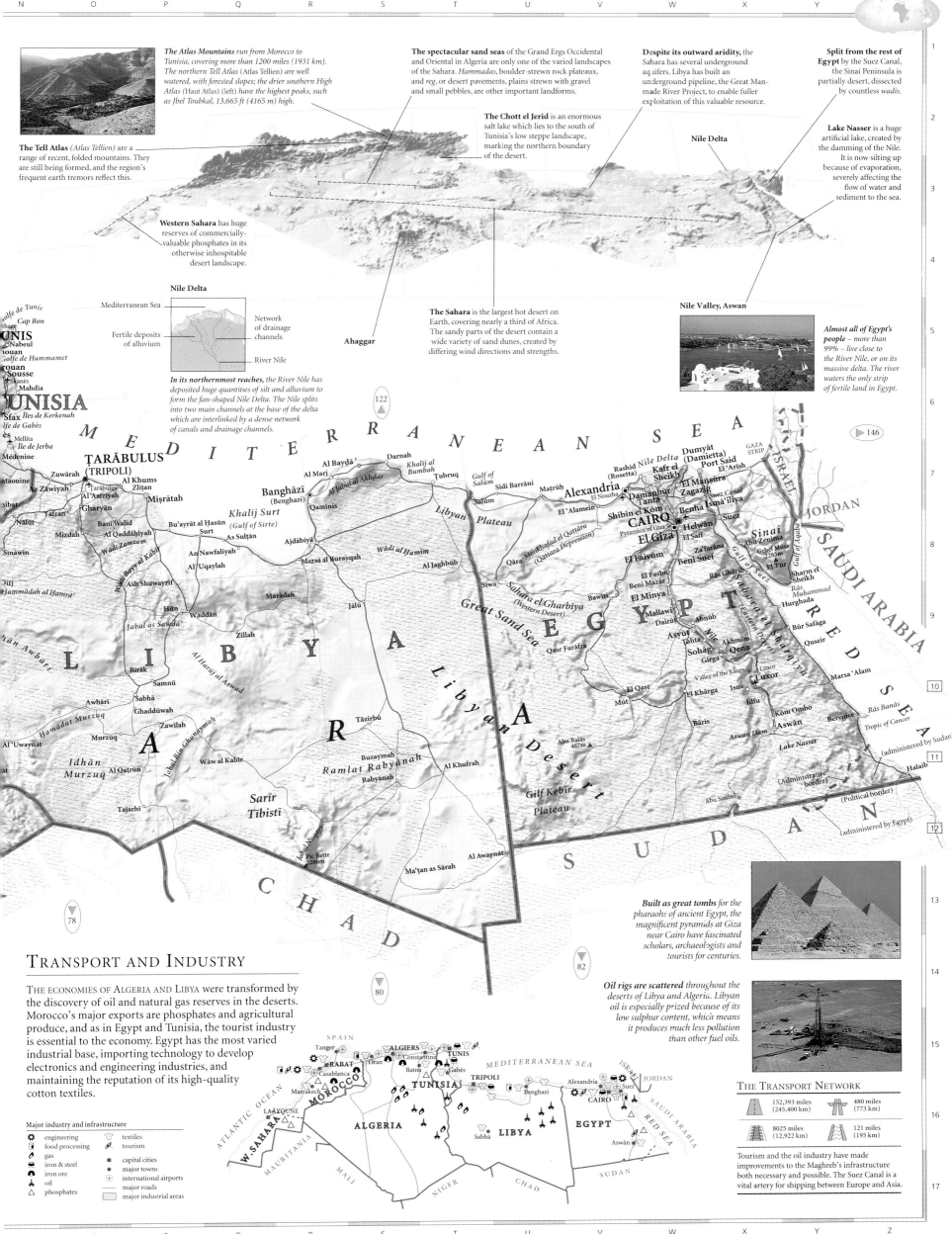

The Atlas Mountains run from Morocco to Tunisia, covering more than 1200 miles (1931 km). The northern Tell Atlas (Atlas Tellien) are well watered, with forested slopes; the drier southern High Atlas (Haut Atlas) (left) have the highest peaks, such as Jbel Toubkal, 13,665 ft (4165 m) high.

The spectacular sand seas of the Grand Ergs Occidental and Oriental in Algeria are only one of the varied landscapes of the Sahara. *Hammadas*, boulder-strewn rock plateaux, and *reg*, or desert pavements, plains strewn with gravel and small pebbles, are other important landforms.

Despite its outward aridity, the Sahara has several underground aquifers. Libya has built an underground pipeline, the Great Man-made River Project, to enable fuller exploitation of this valuable resource.

Split from the rest of Egypt by the Suez Canal, the Sinai Peninsula is partially desert, dissected by countless *wadis*.

The Tell Atlas (Atlas Tellien) are a range of recent, folded mountains. They are still being formed, and the region's frequent earth tremors reflect this.

The Chott el Jerid is an enormous salt lake which lies to the south of Tunisia's low steppe landscape, marking the northern boundary of the desert.

Nile Delta

Lake Nasser is a huge artificial lake, created by the damming of the Nile. It is now silting up because of evaporation, severely affecting the flow of water and sediment to the sea.

Western Sahara has huge reserves of commercially-valuable phosphates in its otherwise inhospitable desert landscape.

Nile Delta

Mediterranean Sea

Network of drainage channels

Fertile deposits of alluvium

River Nile

Ahaggar

The Sahara is the largest hot desert on Earth, covering nearly a third of Africa. The sandy parts of the desert contain a wide variety of sand dunes, created by differing wind directions and strengths.

Nile Valley, Aswan

Almost all of Egypt's people – more than 99% – live close to the River Nile, or on its massive delta. The river waters the only strip of fertile land in Egypt.

In its northernmost reaches, the River Nile has deposited huge quantities of silt and alluvium to form the fan-shaped Nile Delta. The Nile splits into two main channels at the base of the delta which are interlinked by a dense network of canals and drainage channels.

Built as great tombs for the pharaohs of ancient Egypt, the magnificent pyramids at Giza near Cairo have fascinated scholars, archaeologists and tourists for centuries.

Oil rigs are scattered throughout the deserts of Libya and Algeria. Libyan oil is especially prized because of its low sulphur content, which means it produces much less pollution than other fuel oils.

TRANSPORT AND INDUSTRY

THE ECONOMIES OF ALGERIA AND LIBYA were transformed by the discovery of oil and natural gas reserves in the deserts. Morocco's major exports are phosphates and agricultural produce, and as in Egypt and Tunisia, the tourist industry is essential to the economy. Egypt has the most varied industrial base, importing technology to develop electronics and engineering industries, and maintaining the reputation of its high-quality cotton textiles.

Major industry and infrastructure

⚙ engineering
▯ food processing
⬤ gas
⬥ iron & steel
⬢ iron ore
✈ oil
△ phosphates

✣ textiles
🛈 tourism

■ capital cities
● major towns
✈ international airports
— major roads
▒ major industrial areas

THE TRANSPORT NETWORK

152,393 miles (245,400 km)		480 miles (773 km)	
8025 miles (12,922 km)		121 miles (195 km)	

Tourism and the oil industry have made improvements to the Maghreb's infrastructure both necessary and possible. The Suez Canal is a vital artery for shipping between Europe and Asia.

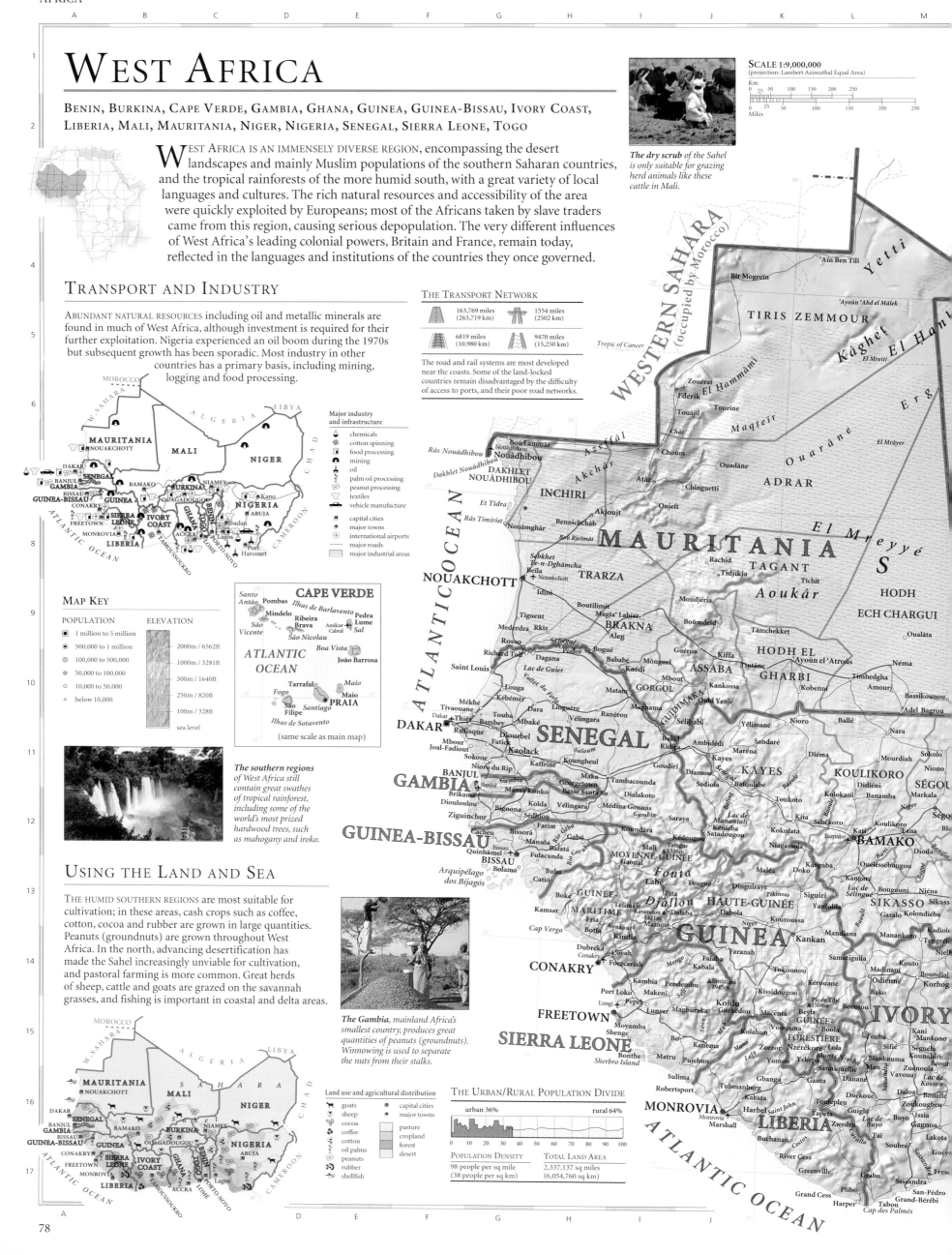

WEST AFRICA

Benin, Burkina, Cape Verde, Gambia, Ghana, Guinea, Guinea-Bissau, Ivory Coast, Liberia, Mali, Mauritania, Niger, Nigeria, Senegal, Sierra Leone, Togo

West Africa is an immensely diverse region, encompassing the desert landscapes and mainly Muslim populations of the southern Saharan countries, and the tropical rainforests of the more humid south, with a great variety of local languages and cultures. The rich natural resources and accessibility of the area were quickly exploited by Europeans; most of the Africans taken by slave traders came from this region, causing serious depopulation. The very different influences of West Africa's leading colonial powers, Britain and France, remain today, reflected in the languages and institutions of the countries they once governed.

TRANSPORT AND INDUSTRY

Abundant natural resources including oil and metallic minerals are found in much of West Africa, although investment is required for their further exploitation. Nigeria experienced an oil boom during the 1970s but subsequent growth has been sporadic. Most industry in other countries has a primary basis, including mining, logging and food processing.

THE TRANSPORT NETWORK

163,769 miles (263,719 km)	1554 miles (2502 km)
6819 miles (10,980 km)	9470 miles (15,250 km)

The road and rail systems are most developed near the coasts. Some of the land-locked countries remain disadvantaged by the difficulty of access to ports, and their poor road networks.

Major industry and infrastructure:
- chemicals
- cotton spinning
- food processing
- mining
- oil
- palm oil processing
- peanut processing
- textiles
- vehicle manufacture
- capital cities
- major towns
- international airports
- major roads
- major industrial areas

The dry scrub of the Sahel is only suitable for grazing herd animals like these cattle in Mali.

SCALE 1:9,000,000
(projection: Lambert Azimuthal Equal Area)

MAP KEY

POPULATION
- 1 million to 5 million
- 500,000 to 1 million
- 100,000 to 500,000
- 50,000 to 100,000
- 10,000 to 50,000
- below 10,000

ELEVATION
- 2000m / 6562ft
- 1000m / 3281ft
- 500m / 1640ft
- 250m / 820ft
- 100m / 328ft
- sea level

CAPE VERDE
(same scale as main map)

The southern regions of West Africa still contain great swathes of tropical rainforest, including some of the world's most prized hardwood trees, such as mahogany and iroko.

USING THE LAND AND SEA

The humid southern regions are most suitable for cultivation; in these areas, cash crops such as coffee, cotton, cocoa and rubber are grown in large quantities. Peanuts (groundnuts) are grown throughout West Africa. In the north, advancing desertification has made the Sahel increasingly unviable for cultivation, and pastoral farming is more common. Great herds of sheep, cattle and goats are grazed on the savannah grasses, and fishing is important in coastal and delta areas.

The Gambia, mainland Africa's smallest country, produces great quantities of peanuts (groundnuts). Winnowing is used to separate the nuts from their stalks.

Land use and agricultural distribution
- goats
- sheep
- cocoa
- coffee
- cotton
- oil palms
- peanuts
- rubber
- shellfish
- capital cities
- major towns
- pasture
- cropland
- forest
- desert

THE URBAN/RURAL POPULATION DIVIDE
urban 36% — rural 64%

POPULATION DENSITY
98 people per sq mile
(38 people per sq km)

TOTAL LAND AREA
2,337,137 sq miles
(6,054,760 sq km)

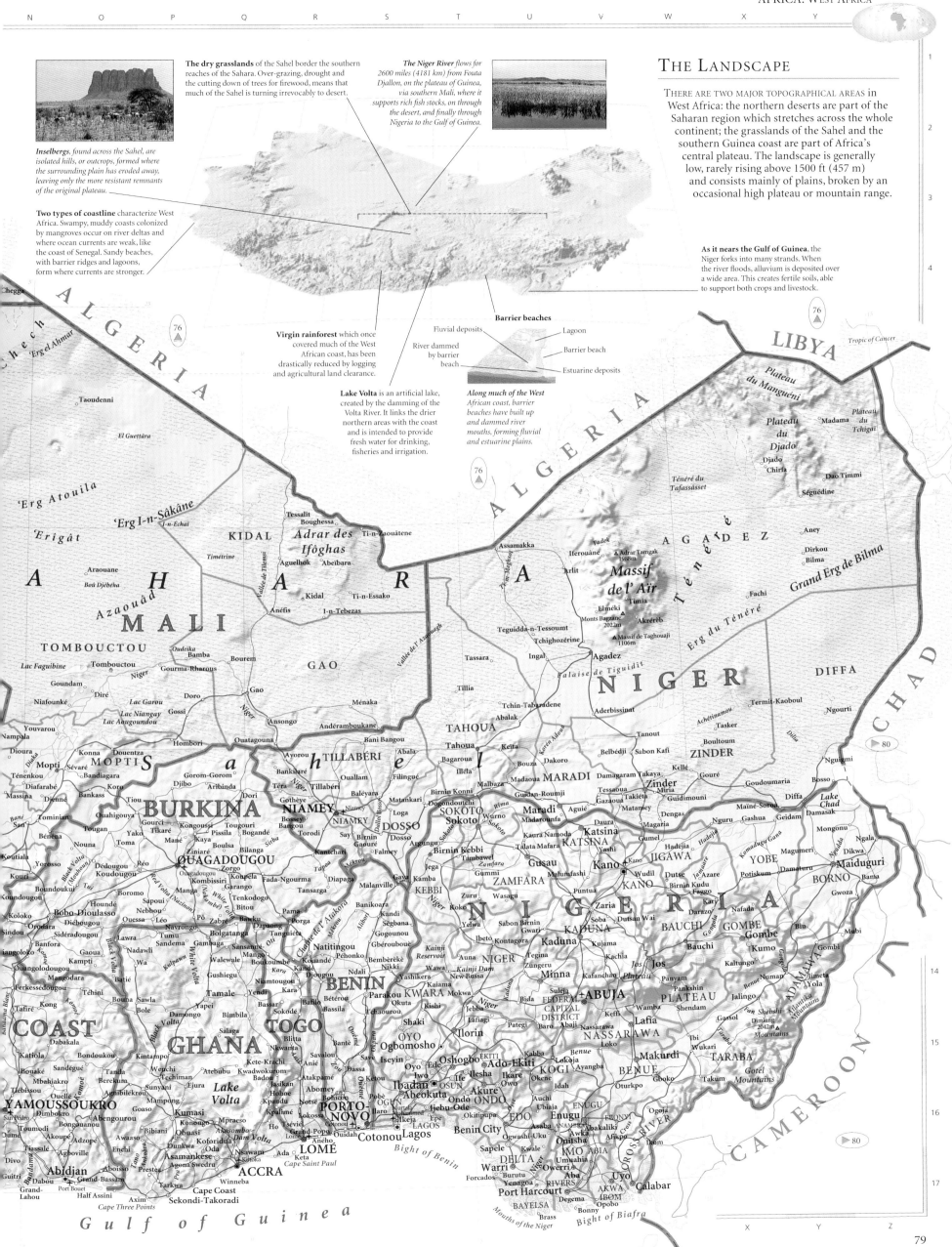

THE LANDSCAPE

THERE ARE TWO MAJOR TOPOGRAPHICAL AREAS in West Africa: the northern deserts are part of the Saharan region which stretches across the whole continent; the grasslands of the Sahel and the southern Guinea coast are part of Africa's central plateau. The landscape is generally low, rarely rising above 1500 ft (457 m) and consists mainly of plains, broken by an occasional high plateau or mountain range.

Inselbergs, found across the Sahel, are isolated hills, or outcrops, formed where the surrounding plain has eroded away, leaving only the more resistant remnants of the original plateau.

The dry grasslands of the Sahel border the southern reaches of the Sahara. Over-grazing, drought and the cutting down of trees for firewood, means that much of the Sahel is turning irrevocably to desert.

The Niger River flows for 2600 miles (4181 km) from Fouta Djallon, on the plateau of Guinea, via southern Mali, where it supports rich fish stocks, on through the desert, and finally through Nigeria to the Gulf of Guinea.

Two types of coastline characterize West Africa. Swampy, muddy coasts colonized by mangroves occur on river deltas and where ocean currents are weak, like the coast of Senegal. Sandy beaches, with barrier ridges and lagoons, form where currents are stronger.

Virgin rainforest which once covered much of the West African coast, has been drastically reduced by logging and agricultural land clearance.

Lake Volta is an artificial lake, created by the damming of the Volta River. It links the drier northern areas with the coast and is intended to provide fresh water for drinking, fisheries and irrigation.

As it nears the Gulf of Guinea, the Niger forks into many strands. When the river floods, alluvium is deposited over a wide area. This creates fertile soils, able to support both crops and livestock.

Barrier beaches
Fluvial deposits — Lagoon
River dammed by barrier beach — Barrier beach
— Estuarine deposits

Along much of the West African coast, barrier beaches have built up and dammed river mouths, forming fluvial and estuarine plains.

CENTRAL AFRICA

CAMEROON, CENTRAL AFRICAN REPUBLIC, CHAD, CONGO,
DEM. REP. CONGO (ZAIRE), EQUATORIAL GUINEA, GABON,
SAO TOME & PRINCIPE

THE GREAT RAINFOREST BASIN of the Congo River embraces most of remote Central Africa. The interior was largely unknown to Europeans until late in the 19th century, when its tribal kingdoms were split – principally between France and Belgium – with Sao Tome and Principe the lone Portuguese territory, and Equatorial Guinea controlled by Spain. Open democracy and regional economic integration are important goals for these nations – several of which have only recently emerged from restrictive regimes – and investment is needed to improve transport infrastructures. Many of the small, but fast-growing and increasingly urban population, speak French, the regional *lingua franca*, along with several hundred Pygmy, Bantu and Sudanic dialects.

TRANSPORT AND INDUSTRY

LARGE RESERVES OF VALUABLE MINERALS are found in Central Africa: copper, cobalt, zinc and tin are mined in Dem. Rep. Congo (Zaire) and Cameroon; diamonds in the Central African Republic, and manganese in Gabon. Congo, Cameroon, Gabon, and Dem. Rep. Congo (Zaire) have oil deposits and oil has also been recently discovered in Chad. Goods such as palm oil and rubber are processed for export.

The ancient rocks of Dem. Rep. Congo (Zaire) hold immense and varied mineral reserves. This open pit copper mine is at Kolwezi in the far south.

Major industry
and infrastructure
- brewing
- chemicals
- cobalt
- copper
- diamonds
- food processing
- manganese
- oil
- palm oil processing
- textiles
- tin
- capital cities
- major towns
- international airports
- major roads
- major industrial areas

THE TRANSPORT NETWORK

124,349 miles (200,240 km)	342 miles (550 km)
3830 miles (6167 km)	15,261 miles (24,575 km)

The Trans-Gabon railway, which began operating in 1987, has opened up new sources of timber and manganese. Elsewhere, much investment is needed to update and improve road, rail and water transport.

THE LANDSCAPE

LAKE CHAD LIES IN a desert basin bounded by the volcanic Tibesti Mountains in the north, plateaux in the east and, in the south, the broad watershed of the Congo Basin. The vast circular depression of the Congo is isolated from the coastal plain by the granite Massif du Chaillu. To the northwest, the volcanoes and fold mountains of the Cameroon Ridge (*Dorsale Camerounaise*) extend as islands into the Gulf of Guinea. The high fold mountains fringing the east of the Congo Basin fall steeply to the lakes of the Great Rift Valley.

A plug of resistant lava, at the southwestern end of the Cameroon Ridge (Dorsale Camerounaise), is all that remains of an eroded volcano.

The Tibesti Mountains are the highest in the Sahara. They were pushed up by the movement of the African Plate over a hot spot, which first formed the northern Ahaggar Mountains and is now thought to lie under the Great Rift Valley.

The Congo River is second only to the Amazon in the volume of water it carries, and in the size of its drainage basin.

Lake Tanganyika, the world's second deepest lake, is the largest of a series of linear ribbon lakes occupying a trench within the Great Rift Valley.

Rich mineral deposits in the 'Copper Belt' of Dem. Rep. Congo (Zaire) were formed under intense heat and pressure when the ancient African Shield was uplifted to form the region's mountains.

Virgin tropical rainforest covers the Ruwenzori range on the borders of Dem. Rep. Congo and Uganda.

The lake-like expansion of the Congo River at Stanley Pool is the lowest point of the interior basin, although the river still descends more than 1000 ft (300 m) to reach the sea.

Waterfalls and cataracts

Submarine canyon

Broad, shallow basin

The Congo River flows sluggishly through the rainforest of the interior basin. Towards the coast, the river drops steeply in a series of waterfalls and cataracts. At this point, the erosional power of the river becomes so great that it has formed a deep submarine canyon offshore.

The vast sand flats surrounding Lake Chad were once covered by water. Changing climatic patterns caused the lake to shrink, and desert now covers much of its previous area.

Lake Chad is the remnant of an inland sea, which once occupied much of the surrounding basin. A series of droughts since the 1970s has reduced the area of this shallow freshwater lake to about 1000 sq miles (2599 sq km).

The volcanic massif of Cameroon Mountain occupies an area which remains volcanically active.

Gulf of Guinea

Massif du Chaillu

MAP KEY

POPULATION
- ■ 1 million to 5 million
- ◉ 500,000 to 1 million
- ⊚ 100,000 to 500,000
- ⊕ 50,000 to 100,000
- ⊙ 10,000 to 50,000
- ⊙ below 10,000

ELEVATION
- 4000m / 13,124ft
- 3000m / 9843ft
- 2000m / 6562ft
- 1000m / 3281ft
- 500m / 1640ft
- 250m / 820ft
- 100m / 328ft
- sea level

SCALE 1:9,500,000
(projection: Lambert Azimuthal Equal Area)

Map labels

LIBYA

SUDAN

C H A D

NIGER

NIGERIA

Tropic of Cancer

Massif d'Abo
Aozou
Bardaï
Zouar
Sherda
Yebbi-Bou
Tibesti
Emi Koussi 3415m

BORKOU-ENNEDI-TIBESTI

Erdi
Redi Ma
Redi Ma
Ouadi Howa

Depression du Mourdi
Eninedi
Fada
Monou

Ouadi Haouach

Ouaddaï Howa

Gouro
Faya

Erg du Djourab

Koro Toro

Bodélé

Harar-Djombo

Arada
Biltine
Guéréda
Iriba
Massif du Kapka
Abéché

BILTINE

OUADDAÏ

Aïn Dam
Goz-Beïda
Adré

Birao

VAKAGA

Gordil
Ouanda Djallé

KANEM

Nokou
Salal

Djédaa
Ati

BATHA

Oum-Hadjer

Mongo
Bitkine
Melfi

GUÉRA

Am Timan
Zakouma
Abou-Deïa

SALAMAT

Gordil
Singako
Garba
Ndélé

BAMINGUI-BANGORAN

Big-Rig
Mao

LAC

Ngouri
Bol

Massakory
Ngoura
Moussoro

Bokoro
Moyto

Massaguet

NDJAMENA

CHARI-BAGUIRMI

Bousso
Ba Illi

Gounou-Gaya

MOYEN-CHARI

Sarh

Lake Chad

Koumra
Doba

TANDJILÉ

Lai

Bongor

Logone

MAYO-KEBBI

Garoua

Léré
Pala

Kousseri
Mora
Maroua

EXTRÊME-NORD

Kaélé

Guider

NORD

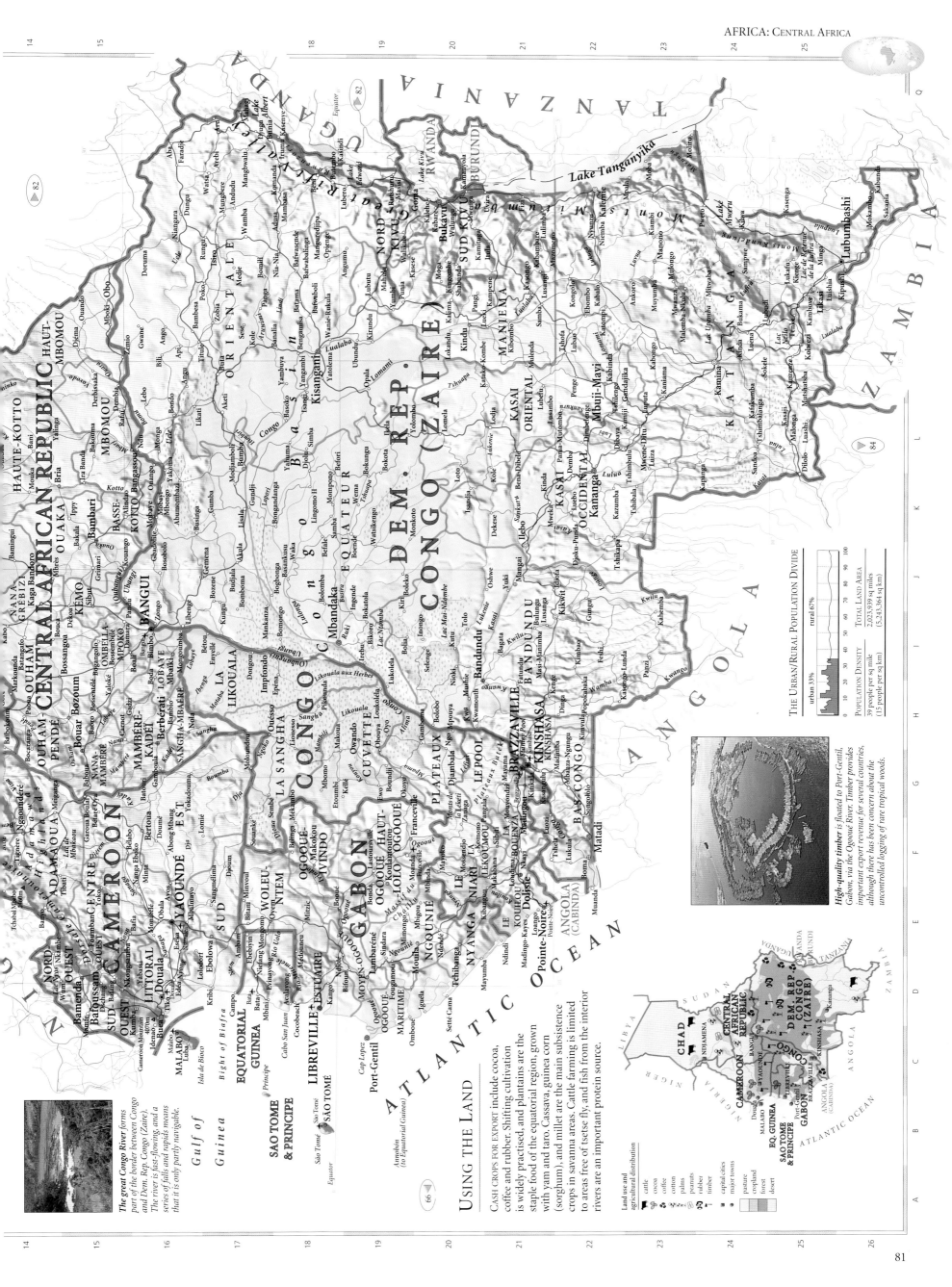

The great Congo River forms part of the border between Congo and Dem. Rep. Congo (Zaire). The river is fast-flowing, and a series of falls and rapids means that it is only partly navigable.

USING THE LAND

CASH CROPS FOR EXPORT include cocoa, coffee and rubber. Shifting cultivation is widely practised, and plantains are the staple food of the equatorial region, grown with yam and taro. Cassava, guinea corn (sorghum), and millet are the main subsistence crops in savanna areas. Cattle farming is limited to areas free of tsetse fly, and fish from the interior rivers are an important protein source.

High-quality timber is floated to Port-Gentil, Gabon, via the Ogooué River. Timber provides important export revenue for several countries, although there has been concern about the uncontrolled logging of rare tropical woods.

Land use and agricultural distribution
- cattle
- cocoa
- coffee
- cotton
- palms
- peanuts
- rubber
- timber

- capital cities
- major towns

- pasture
- cropland
- forest
- desert

THE URBAN/RURAL POPULATION DIVIDE

urban 33%   rural 67%

POPULATION DENSITY	TOTAL LAND AREA
39 people per sq mile	2,023,939 sq miles
(15 people per sq km)	(5,243,364 sq km)

EAST AFRICA

BURUNDI, DJIBOUTI, ERITREA, ETHIOPIA, KENYA, RWANDA, SOMALIA, SUDAN, TANZANIA, UGANDA

THE COUNTRIES OF EAST AFRICA divide into two distinct cultural regions. Sudan and the 'Horn' nations have been influenced by the Middle East; Ethiopia was the home of one of the earliest Christian civilizations, and Sudan reflects both Muslim and Christian influences, while the southern countries share a closer cultural affinity with other sub-Saharan nations. Some of Africa's most densely populated countries lie in this region, and the needs of a growing number of people have put pressure on marginal lands and fragile environments. Although most East African economies remain strongly agricultural, Kenya has developed a varied industrial base.

THE LANDSCAPE

EAST AFRICA'S MOST SIGNIFICANT landscape feature is the Great Rift Valley, which formed during the most recent phase of continental movement when the rigid basement rocks cracked and buckled. Great blocks of land were raised and lowered, creating huge flat-bottomed valleys and steep escarpments, sometimes covered by volcanic extrusions in highland areas.

This dome at Gonder, in Ethiopia, is a volcanic intrusion, formed when molten rock pushed up the surface of the Earth and then solidified, leaving an outcrop of igneous rock.

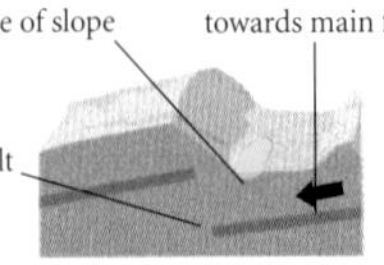

Ephemeral lake forms at far edge of slope

Boundary fault

Central block slopes towards main fault

The eastern arm of the Great Rift Valley is gradually being pulled apart; however the forces on one side are greater than the other causing the land to slope. This affects regional drainage which migrates down the slope.

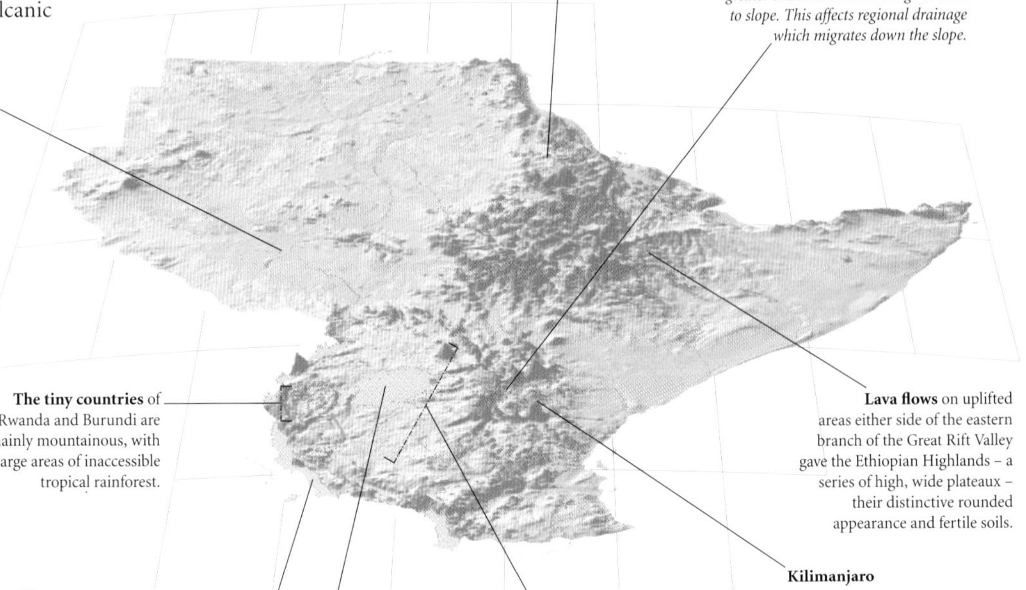

Lava flows on uplifted areas either side of the eastern branch of the Great Rift Valley gave the Ethiopian Highlands – a series of high, wide plateaus – their distinctive rounded appearance and fertile soils.

Kilimanjaro

An extinct volcano, Kilimanjaro is Africa's highest mountain, rising 19,340 ft (5895 m). It is one of the few places in Africa where snow settles, allowing glacier ice to form.

A vast plateau lies between the eastern and western rift valleys in Kenya, Uganda and western Tanzania. It has been levelled by long periods of erosion to form a peneplain, but is dotted with inselbergs – outcrops of more resistant rocks.

Lake Victoria occupies a vast basin between the two arms of the Great Rift Valley. It is the world's second largest lake in terms of surface area, extending 26,560 sq miles (68,880 sq km). The lake contains numerous islands and coral reefs.

Lake Tanganyika lies 8202 ft (2500 m) above sea level. It has a depth of nearly 4700 ft (1435 m). The lake traces the valley floor for some 400 miles (644 km) of the western arm of the Great Rift Valley.

The tiny countries of Rwanda and Burundi are mainly mountainous, with large areas of inaccessible tropical rainforest.

Much of northern Sudan is covered by desert. However, in the tropical wetlands of the southern Sudd region, annual rainfall can sometimes exceed 40 inches (1000 mm).

The Kassala region in eastern Sudan is watered by the Atbara River, an important tributary of the Nile. Most of the population is engaged in agriculture, growing cotton and cereals.

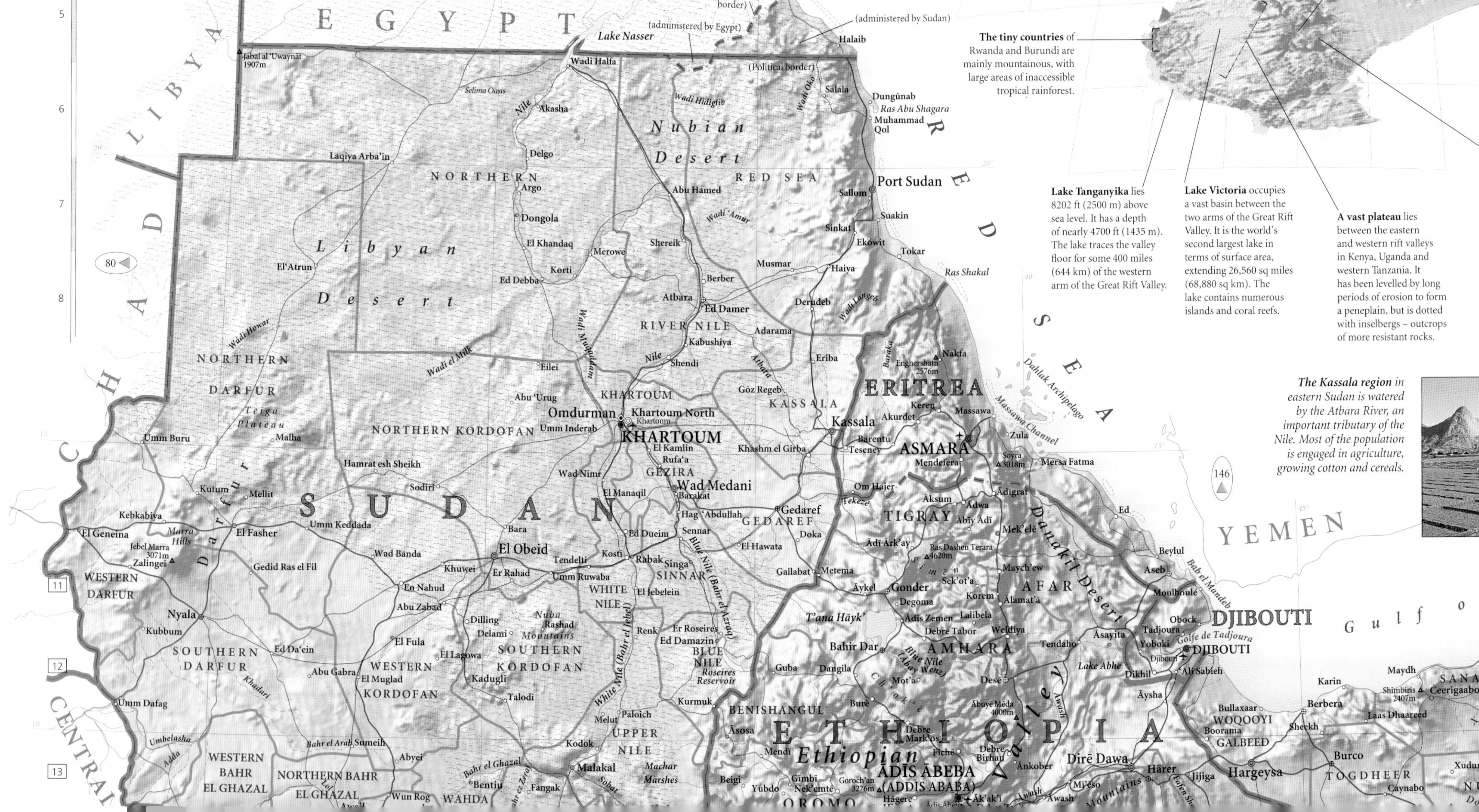

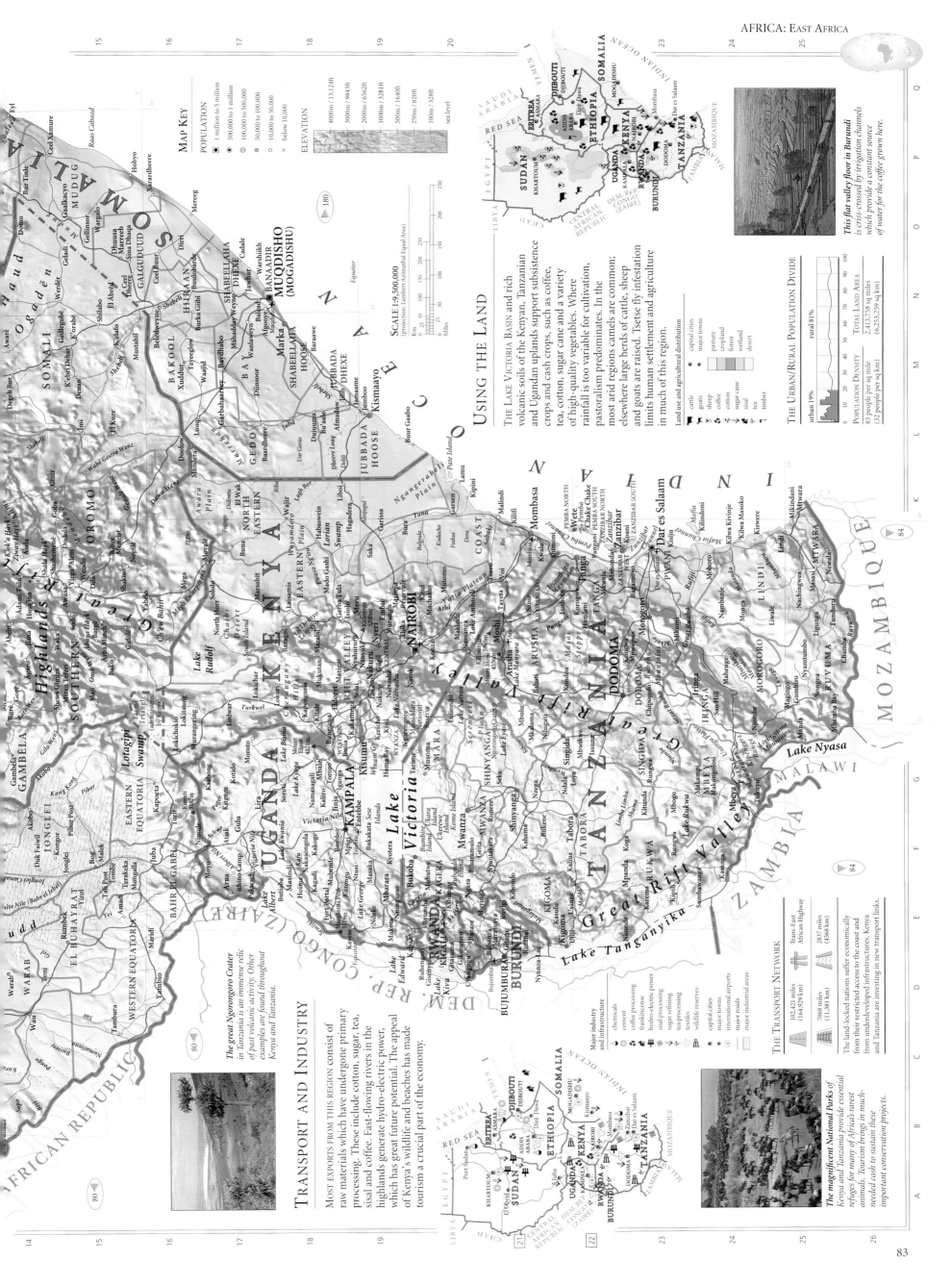

USING THE LAND

THE LAKE VICTORIA BASIN and rich volcanic soils of the Kenyan, Tanzanian and Ugandan uplands support subsistence crops and cash crops, such as coffee, tea, cotton, sugar cane and a variety of high-quality vegetables. Where rainfall is too variable for cultivation, pastoralism predominates. In the most arid regions camels are common; elsewhere large herds of cattle, sheep and goats are raised. Tsetse fly infestation limits human settlement and agriculture in much of this region.

Land use and agricultural distribution

cattle
goats
sheep
coffee
cotton

pasture
cropland
forest
wetland
desert

sugar cane
sisal
tea
timber

THE URBAN/RURAL POPULATION DIVIDE

urban 19%
rural 81%

POPULATION DENSITY	TOTAL LAND AREA
83 people per sq mile	2,413,758 sq miles
(32 people per sq km)	(6,253,259 sq km)

This flat valley floor in Burundi is criss-crossed by irrigation channels which provide a constant source of water for the coffee grown here.

TRANSPORT AND INDUSTRY

MOST EXPORTS FROM THIS REGION consist of raw materials which have undergone primary processing. These include cotton, sugar, tea, sisal and coffee. Fast-flowing rivers in the highlands generate hydro-electric power, which has great future potential. The appeal of Kenya's wildlife and beaches has made tourism a crucial part of the economy.

The great Ngorongoro Crater in Tanzania is an immense relic of past volcanic activity. Other examples are found throughout Kenya and Tanzania.

Major industry and infrastructure

chemicals
cement
coffee processing
frankincense
hydro-electric power
sugar refining
tea processing
textiles
wildlife reserves
capital cities
major towns
international airports
major roads
major industrial areas

THE TRANSPORT NETWORK

Trans-East African Highway		102,421 miles (164,929 km)
		2837 miles (4568 km)
		7068 miles (11,381 km)

The land-locked nations suffer economically from their restricted access to the coast and from underdeveloped infrastructures. Kenya and Tanzania are investing in new transport links.

The magnificent National Parks of Kenya and Tanzania provide essential refuges for many of Africa's rarest animals. Tourism brings in much-needed cash to sustain these important conservation projects.

MAP KEY

POPULATION
● 1 million to 5 million
◎ 500,000 to 1 million
⊕ 100,000 to 500,000
⊙ 50,000 to 100,000
○ 10,000 to 50,000
∘ below 10,000

ELEVATION
400m/13,124ft
3000m/9843ft
2000m/656ft
1000m/328ft
500m/1640ft
250m/820ft
100m/328ft
sea level

SCALE 1:9,500,000
(Projection: Lambert Azimuthal Equal Area)

SOUTHERN AFRICA

ANGOLA, BOTSWANA, LESOTHO, MALAWI, MOZAMBIQUE, NAMIBIA, SOUTH AFRICA, SWAZILAND, ZAMBIA, ZIMBABWE

A FRICA'S VAST SOUTHERN PLATEAU has been a contested homeland for disparate peoples for many centuries. The European incursion began with the slave trade and quickened in the 19th century, when the discovery of enormous mineral wealth secured South Africa's regional economic dominance. The struggle against white minority rule led to strife in Namibia, Zimbabwe, and the former Portuguese territories of Angola and Mozambique. South Africa's notorious apartheid laws, which denied basic human rights to more than 75% of the people, led to the state being internationally ostracized until 1994, when the first fully democratic elections inaugurated a new era of racial justice.

TRANSPORT AND INDUSTRY

SOUTH AFRICA, the world's largest exporter of gold, has a varied economy which generates about 75% of the region's income and draws migrant labour from neighbouring states. Angola exports petroleum; Botswana and Namibia rely on diamond mining; and Zambia is seeking to diversify its economy to compensate for declining copper reserves.

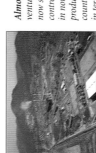

Almost all new mining ventures in Zimbabwe are now subject to government control. This mine at Bindura in northeastern Zimbabwe produces nickel, one of the country's top three minerals in terms of economic value.

THE LANDSCAPE

MOST OF SOUTHERN AFRICA rests on a concave plateau comprising the Kalahari basin and a mountainous fringe, skirted by a coastal plain which widens out in Mozambique. The plateau extends north, towards the Planalto de Bié in Angola, the Congo Basin region is drained by the Zambezi and Limpopo rivers, and the Orange is the major western river.

Thousands of years of evaporating water have produced the Etosha Pan, one of the largest salt flats in the world. Lake and river sediments in the area indicate that the region was once less arid.

Finger Rock, near Khorixas, Namibia is a remnant of a former land surface, which has been denuded by erosion over the last 5 million years. These occasional stacks of partially weathered rocks interrupt the plains of the dry southern interior.

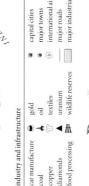

Following a series of droughts, this baobab tree in Zimbabwe now stands alone in a field once filled by sugar cane. The thick trunk and small leaves of the baobab help it to conserve water, enabling it to survive even in drought conditions.

At Victoria Falls, the Zambezi River has cut a spectacular gorge taking advantage of large joints in the basalt, which were first formed as the lava cooled and contracted.

The fast-flowing Zambezi River cuts a deep, wide channel as it flows along the Zimbabwe/Zambia border.

The Okavango/Cubango River flows from the Planalto de Bié to the swamplands of the Okavango Delta, one of the world's largest inland deltas, where it divides into countless distributary channels, feeding out into the desert.

Lake Nyasa occupies one of the deep troughs of the Great Rift Valley, where the land has been displaced downwards by as much as 3000 ft (920 m).

Great Rift Valley

Bushveld intrusion

Limpopo River

Volcanic lava, over 250 million years old, caps the peaks of the Drakensberg range, which lie on the mountainous rim of southern Africa's interior plateau.

Broad, flat-topped mountains characterize the Great Karoo, which have been cut from level rock strata under extremely arid conditions.

The mountains of the Little Karoo are composed of sedimentary rocks which have been substantially folded and faulted.

Planalto de Bié

Khorixas, Namibia

Namib Desert

The Kalahari Desert is the largest continuous sand surface in the world. Iron oxide gives a distinctive red colour to the windblown sand, which, in eastern areas, covers the bedrock by over 200 ft (60 m).

The Orange River, one of the longest in Africa, rises in Lesotho and is the only major river in the south which flows westward, rather than to the east coast.

THE TRANSPORT NETWORK

84,213 miles (135,609 km)	746 miles (1202 km)
23,208 miles (37,372 km)	3815 miles (6144 km)

Southern Africa's Cape-gauge rail network is by far the largest in the continent. About two-thirds of the 20,000 mile (32,000 km) system lies within South Africa. Lines such as the Harare–Bulawayo route have become corridors for industrial growth.

MAP KEY

POPULATION

- ■ 1 million to 5 million
- ◉ 500,000 to 1 million
- ⦿ 100,000 to 500,000
- ⊕ 50,000 to 100,000
- ⊙ 10,000 to 50,000
- ○ below 10,000

ELEVATION

- 3000m / 9843ft
- 2000m / 6562ft
- 1000m / 3281ft
- 500m / 1640ft
- 250m / 820ft
- 100m / 328ft
- sea level

Bushveld intrusion

- Granite
- Chromite
- Gabbro and peridotite
- Magnetite
- Platinum minerals

The Bushveld intrusion lies on South Africa's high 'veld'. Molten magma intruded into the Earth's crust creating a saucer-shaped feature, more than 180 miles (300 km) across, containing regular layers of precious minerals, overlain by a dome of granite.

SOUTH AFRICA'S THREE CAPITALS

PRETORIA – administrative capital
CAPE TOWN – legislative capital
BLOEMFONTEIN – judicial capital

SCALE 1:9,500,000

(projection: Lambert Azimuthal Equal Area)

Major industry and infrastructure

- car manufacture
- coal
- copper
- diamonds
- gold
- oil
- textiles
- uranium
- wildlife reserves
- food processing

- capital cities
- major towns
- international airports
- major roads
- major industrial areas

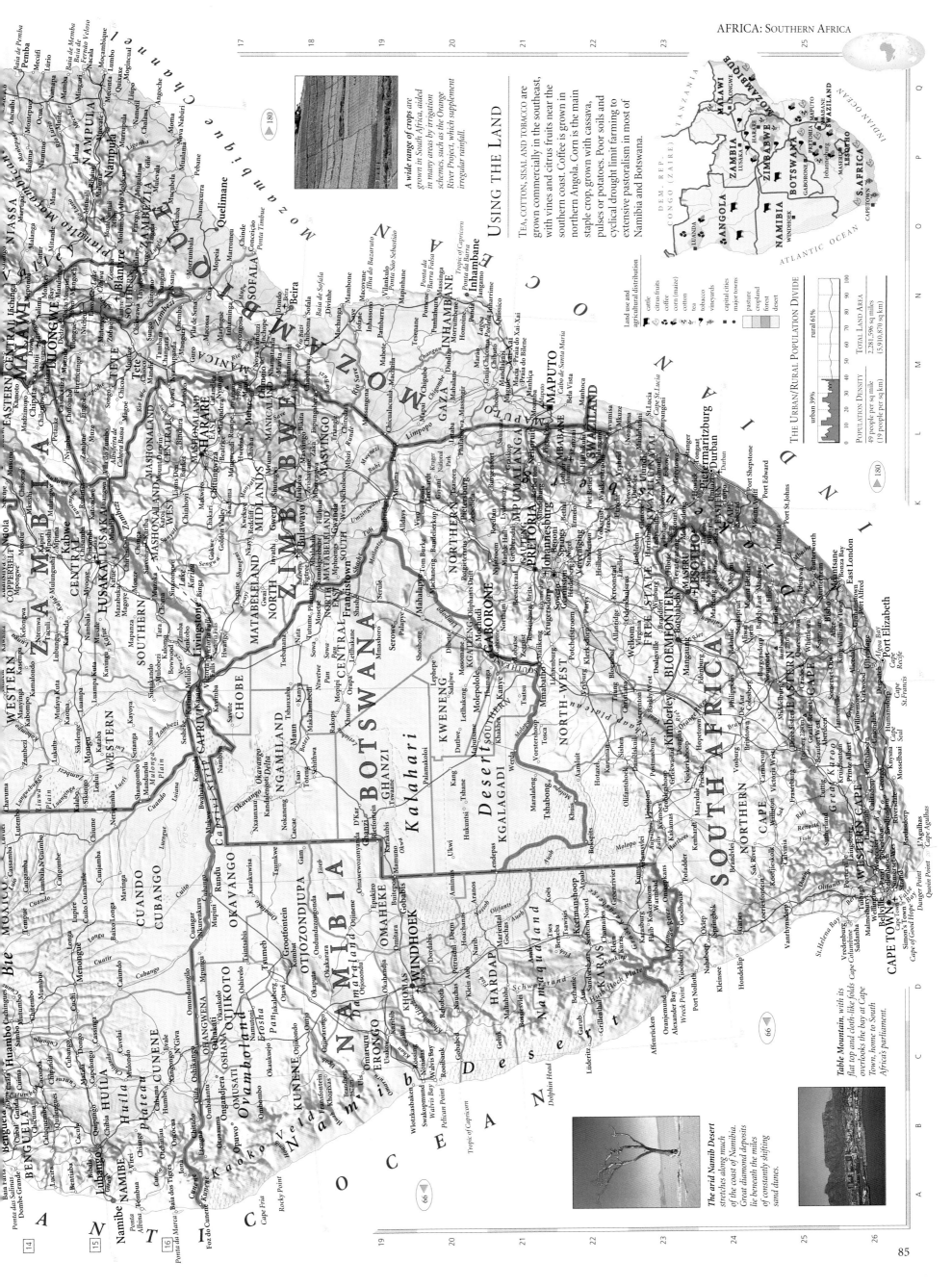

A wide range of crops are grown in South Africa, aided in many areas by irrigation schemes, such as the Orange River Project, which supplement irregular rainfall.

USING THE LAND

TEA, COTTON, SISAL AND TOBACCO are grown commercially in the southeast, with vines and citrus fruits near the southern coast. Coffee is grown in northern Angola. Corn is the main staple crop, grown with cassava, pulses or potatoes. Poor soils and cyclical drought limit farming to extensive pastoralism in most of Namibia and Botswana.

Land use and agricultural distribution

- cattle
- citrus fruits
- coffee
- corn (maize)
- cotton
- tea
- tobacco
- vineyards
- capital cities
- major towns

pasture
cropland
forest
desert

THE URBAN/RURAL POPULATION DIVIDE

urban 39%   rural 61%

TOTAL LAND AREA
2,281,596 sq miles
(5,910,870 sq km)

POPULATION DENSITY
49 people per sq mile
(19 people per sq km)

Table Mountain, with its flat top and cloth-like folds overlooks the bay at Cape Town, home to South Africa's parliament.

The arid Namib Desert stretches along much of the coast of Namibia. Great diamond deposits lie beneath the miles of constantly shifting sand dunes.

ARCTIC OCEAN
North Pole

Ellesmere Island

Greenland

King Frederik VIII Land

King Christian X Land

Greenland Sea

Spitsbergen

Jan Mayen Fracture Zone
Jan Mayen Ridge
Jan Mayen

Arctic Circle

Denmark Strait
Kolbeinsey Ridge

Bjargtangar

Iceland Plateau

Reykjanes Ridge

Iceland
Vatnajökull

Iceland Basin

Faeroe-Iceland Ridge

Rockall Rise

Hatton Ridge

Feni Ridge

Rockall Trough

Bill Baileys Bank

Faeroe-Shetland Trough

Faeroe Islands

Shetland Islands

Viking Bank

Orkney Islands

Outer Hebrides

Ben Nevis 1344m
Grampian Mountains

North Channel

Ireland

Shannon

Irish Sea

British Isles

Snowdon 1085m

St. George's Channel

Celtic Sea

Celtic Shelf

Bristol Channel

Land's End

Channel Islands

Britain

The Fens

Thames

Severn

Trent

Pennines

Strait of Dover

English Channel

NORWEGIAN SEA

Norwegian Basin

Vøring Plateau

Tromsøflaket
North Cape Nordkinn
Fugløya Bank

Vesterålen

Lofoten

Traena Bank

Kebnekaise 2117m

Scandinavia

Kölen

Galdhøpiggen 2469m

Glåma

Ljungan

Ljusnan

Vänern

Vättern

Norwegian Trench

Jutland Bank

Skagerrak

Kattegat

North Sea

Great Fisher Bank

Dogger Bank

Jylland

Sjælland

Frisian Islands

Elbe

Oder

Harz

ATLANTIC OCEAN

Porcupine Plain

Charcot Seamounts

Biscay Plain

Bay of Biscay

Theta Gap

Galicia Bank

Iberian Plain

Cordillera Cantabrica

Iberian Peninsula

Duero

Douro

Sistema Central

Sistema Iberico

Aragón

Ebro

Azores-Biscay Rise

Gorringe Ridge

Horseshoe Seamounts

Cape Saint Vincent

Cabo da Roca

Tagus

Guadiana

Sierra Morena

Guadalquivir

Tagus Plain

Ampère Seamount

Seine Plain

Seine Seamount

Madeira

Dacia Seamount

Canary Islands

Agadir Canyon

Punta de Tarifa

Strait of Gibraltar

Alborán Sea

Rif

Sebou

Oum er Rbia

Moulouya

Oum er Rbia

Middle Atlas

High Atlas

Atlas Mountains

Tell Atlas

Oued Chelif

Saharan Atlas

Chott el Jerid

Erg Iguidi

Grand Erg Occidental

Erg Chech

SAHARA

Grand Erg Oriental

AFRICA

Seine

Marne

Loire

Vienne

Cher

Ardennes

Meuse

Moselle

Vosges

Saône

Black Forest

Massif Central

Dordogne

Lot

Cévennes

Garonne

Rhône

Mont Blanc 4810m

Lake Geneva

Lake Constance

Danube

ALPS

Lake Garda

Po

Gran Paradiso 4061m

Apennines

Ligurian Sea

Gulf of Lion

Corsica

Strait of Bonifacio

Sardinia

Balearic Islands

Gulf of Valencia

Júcar

Segura

Sistemas Béticos

Sierra Nevada

Algerian Basin

Mediterranean Sea

EURASIAN PLATE
AFRICAN PLATE

Tyrrhenian Sea

Tyrrhenian Basin

Corno Grande 2912m

Adriatic Sea

Adriatic Basin

Gulf of Taranto

Strait of Otranto

Mount Etna 3340m

Sicily

Strait of Messina

Ionian Sea

Malta

Ionian Basin

Gulf of Sirte

EUROPE

North European Plain

Vistula

Warta

Bug

Pripet Marshes

Desna

Dnieper Lowlands

Kiev Reservoir

Dniester

Podil's'ka Vysochina

Pivdennyy Buh

Kremenchuk Reservoir

Dnieper

Carpathian Mountains

Tisza

Bakony

Lake Balaton

Great Hungarian Plain

Drava

Sava

Tisza

Transylvanian Alps

Danube

Dinaric Alps

Balkan Mountains

Maritsa

Rhodope Mountains

Lake Scutari

Lake Ohrid

Lake Prespa

Pindus Mountains

Peloponnese

Mirtoan Sea

Aegean Sea

Sea of Marmara

Bosporus

Dardanelles

Sea of Crete

Crete

Gavdos

Mediterranean Ridge

Levantine Basin

Black Sea Lowland

Sea of Azov

Crimea

Kerch Strait

Kuban

Black Sea

EURASIAN PLATE
ANATOLIAN PLATE

Anatolia

Lake Tuz

Taurus Mountains

Gulf of Antalya

Rhodes

Karpathos

Cyprus

Cyprus Basin

ARABIAN PLATE

Dead Sea

Suez Canal

Nile Fan

Sinai

Gulf of Suez

Qattara Depression -133m

Western Desert

Libyan Desert

A S I A

Ural Mountains

West Siberian Plain

Ob

Barents Sea

Kara Sea

Poluostrov Taymyr

Laptev Sea

Severnaya Zemlya

Ostrov Rudolfa

Franz Josef Land

Novaya Zemlya

Poluostrov Yamal

Baydaratskaya Guba

Gulf of Ob

Kara Strait

Ostrov Kolguyev

Poluostrov Kanin

Pechora

Mezen

Northern Dvina

Timanskiy Kryazh

Gora Narodnaya

Tobol

White Sea

Onega Bay

Ozero Vygozero

Lake Onega

Ozero Beloye

Lake Ladoga

Åland

Gulf of Finland

Lake Peipus

Lake Ilmen

Lake Pskov

Gulf of Riga

Gotland

Baltic Sea

Neman

Byerazino

Byarezina

Western Dvina

Moskva

Central Russian Upland

Don

Donets

Seym

Volga Upland

Sea of Azov

Tsimlyansk Reservoir

Don

Manych

Yergeni

Caspian

Volga

Kirghiz Steppe

Ural

Barents Trough

Murmansk Rise

Kola Peninsula

Ozero Imandra

Oulujoki

Umeälven

Inarijärvi

Torneälven

Indalsälven

Kemijoki

Kemi

Ivalojoki

Gulf of Bothnia

EUROPE

EUROPE IS THE WORLD'S SECOND SMALLEST CONTINENT, COVERING 4,053,309 SQ MILES (10,498,000 SQ KM). IT COMPRISES 44 SEPARATE COUNTRIES, INCLUDING TURKEY AND THE RUSSIAN FEDERATION, ALTHOUGH THE GREATER PARTS OF THESE NATIONS LIE IN ASIA.

○ GREATEST EXTENT, NORTH–SOUTH:
2700 miles / 4300 km
□ GREATEST EXTENT, EAST–WEST:
3500 miles / 5600 km

Most northerly point:
Ostrov Rudol'fa,
Russian Federation
81° 47' N

Most easterly point:
Mys Flissingskiy,
Novaya Zemlya,
Russian Federation
69° 03' E

N URAL
MOUNTAINS,
RUSSIAN
FEDERATION
(66° 12' E)

Most westerly point:
Bjargtangar,
Iceland
24° 33' W

Arctic Circle

NORDKINN,
NORWAY
(71° 08' N)

**Lowest recorded
temperature:**
Ust 'Shchugor,
Russian Federation
-67°F (-55°C)

Largest lake:
Lake Ladoga,
Russian Federation
7100 sq miles
(18,390 sq km)

URAL MOUNTAINS

CABO DA ROCA,
PORTUGAL
(9° 32' W)

CAPE SAINT
VINCENT

PUNTA DE TARIFA,
SPAIN (36° 01' N)

Lowest point:
Caspian Depression,
Russian Federation
92 ft (28 m) below sea level

Highest point: El'brus,
Russian Federation
18,510 ft (5642 m)

**Highest recorded
temperature:**
Seviile, Spain
122°F (50°C)

Most southerly point:
Gávdos, Greece 34° 51' N

CAPE SAINT VINCENT   British Isles   Carpathian   Scandinavia   Baltic Sea   North   URAL MOUNTAINS
Pyrenees   Massif   Alps   Mountains   European Plain
Central
Iberian
Peninsula

CROSS-SECTION FROM CAPE SAINT VINCENT, PORTUGAL TO THE URAL MOUNTAINS, RUSSIAN FEDERATION

◄—— line of cross-section

0   200   400 Km

0   200   400 Miles

Altai Mountains
Ozero Balkhash
Aral Sea
Syr Darya
Kara Tau
Tien Shan
Kyzyl Kum
Amu Darya
Depression
Ustyurt Plateau
Kara Kum
Caspian Sea
Caucasus
Elbrus
Mt Ararat
Lake Van
Lake Urmia
EURASIAN PLATE
IRANIAN PLATE
ARABIAN PLATE
INDO-AUSTRALIAN PLATE
Iranian Plateau
Dasht-e Kavir
Dasht-e Lut
Zagros Mountains
Euphrates
Tigris
Syrian Desert
An Nafud
Arabian
Ad Dahna
The Gulf
Oman
Peninsula
Ar Rub' al Khali
Tropic of Cancer

PHYSICAL EUROPE

THE PHYSICAL DIVERSITY of Europe belies its relatively small size. To the northwest and south it is enclosed by mountains. The older, rounded Atlantic Highlands of Scandinavia and the British Isles lie to the north and the younger, rugged peaks of the Alpine Uplands to the south. In between lies the North European Plain, stretching 2485 miles (4000 km) from The Fens in England to the Ural Mountains in Russia. South of the plain lies a series of gently folded sedimentary rocks separated by ancient plateaux, known as massifs.

THE NORTH EUROPEAN PLAIN

RISING LESS THAN 1000 ft (300 m) above sea level, the North European Plain strongly reflects past glaciation. Ridges of both coarse moraine and finer, wind-blown deposits have accumulated over much of the region. The ice sheet also diverted a number of river channels from their original courses.

Section across the North European Plain showing its low relief and drainage.

Glacial lakes
Rivers were diverted from their original course by the ice sheet
A layer of glacial sediments covers the North European Plain

THE ATLANTIC HIGHLANDS

THE ATLANTIC HIGHLANDS were formed by compression against the Scandinavian Shield during the Caledonian mountain-building period over 500 million years ago. The highlands were once part of a continuous mountain chain, now divided by the North Sea and a submerged rift valley.

The Atlantic Highlands continue in the British Isles
Rift valley buried by sediments
North Sea
Atlantic Highlands in Norway
Rocks affected by ancient mountain-building
Scandinavian Shield

Cross-section through northeastern Europe showing the continuous mountain chain and rift valley system.

SCALE 1:23,000,000
(projection: Lambert Azimuthal Equal Area)

MAP KEY
ELEVATION

4000m / 13,124ft
3000m / 9843ft
2000m / 6562ft
1000m / 3281ft
500m / 1640ft
250m / 820ft
100m / 328ft
sea level

PLATE MARGINS
(for explanation see page xiv)

constructive
destructive
conservative
uncertain

physiographic regions
line of cross-section

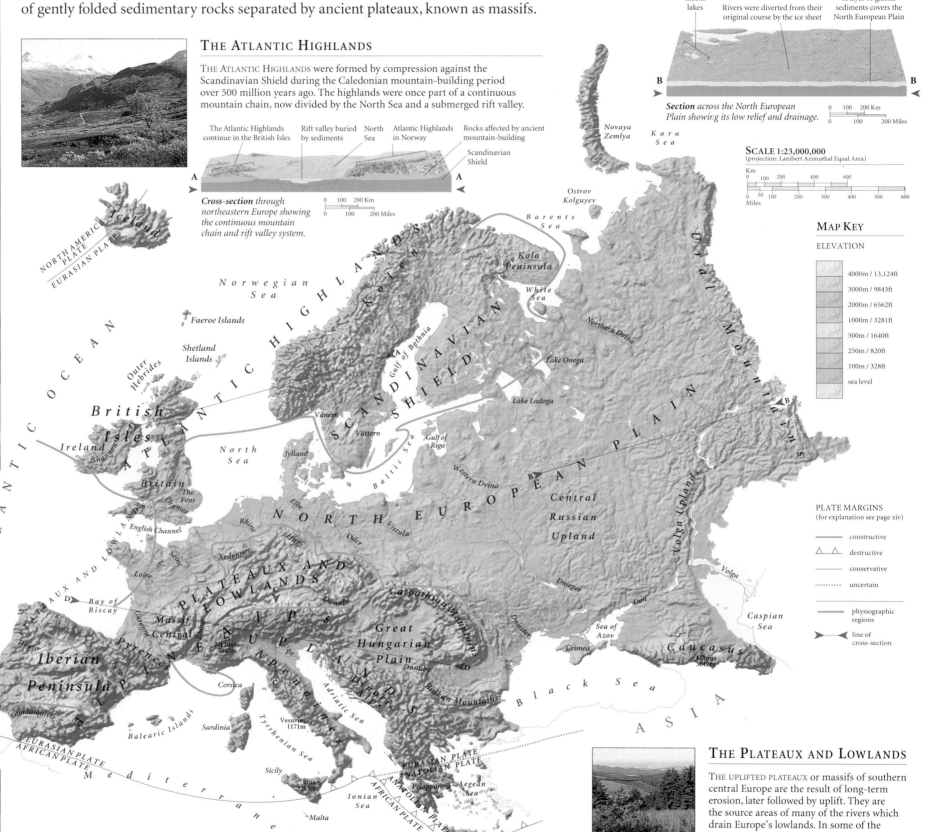

THE PLATEAUX AND LOWLANDS

THE UPLIFTED PLATEAUX or massifs of southern central Europe are the result of long-term erosion, later followed by uplift. They are the source areas of many of the rivers which drain Europe's lowlands. In some of the higher reaches, fractures have enabled igneous rocks from deep in the Earth to reach the surface.

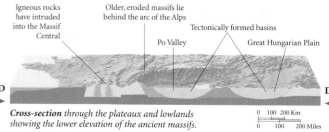

Igneous rocks have intruded into the Massif Central
Older, eroded massifs lie behind the arc of the Alps
Tectonically formed basins
Po Valley
Great Hungarian Plain

Cross-section through the plateaux and lowlands showing the lower elevation of the ancient massifs.

THE ALPINE UPLANDS

THE COLLISION OF the African and European continents, which began about 65 million years ago, folded and then uplifted a series of mountain ranges running across southern Europe and into Asia. Two major lines of folding can be traced: one includes the Pyrenees, the Alps and the Carpathian Mountains; the other incorporates the Apennines and the Dinaric Alps.

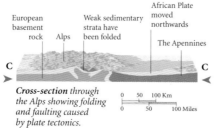

European basement rock
Alps
Weak sedimentary strata have been folded
African Plate moved northwards
The Apennines

Cross-section through the Alps showing folding and faulting caused by plate tectonics.

CLIMATE

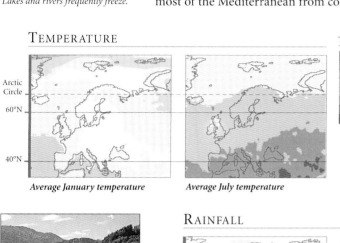

Frost grips northern and eastern Europe during the long cold winters. Lakes and rivers frequently freeze.

EUROPE EXPERIENCES few extremes in either rainfall or temperature, with the exception of the far north and south. Along the west coast, the warm currents of the North Atlantic Drift moderate temperatures. Although east–west air movement is relatively unimpeded by relief, the Alpine Uplands halt the progress of north–south air masses, protecting most of the Mediterranean from cold, north winds.

TEMPERATURE

Average January temperature

Average July temperature

Temperature
- below -30°C (-22°F)
- -30 to -20°C (-22 to -4°F)
- -20 to -10°C (-4 to 14°F)
- -10 to 0°C (14 to 32°F)
- 0 to 10°C (32 to 50°F)
- 10 to 20°C (50 to 60°F)
- 20 to 30°C (68 to 86°F)
- above 30°C (86°F)

RAINFALL

Average January rainfall

Average July rainfall

Rainfall
- 0–25 mm (0–1 in)
- 25–50 mm (1–2 in)
- 50–100 mm (2–4 in)
- 100–200 mm (4–8 in)
- 200–300 mm (8–12 in)
- 300–400 mm (12–16 in)
- 400–500 mm (16–20 in)
- more than 500 mm (20 in)

Mild temperatures and frequent rainfall contribute to the fertile farming land found over much of northwestern Europe.

Dusty Sirocco winds from Africa help create the semi-arid scrubland common across the Mediterranean coastlands of southern Europe.

Climate
- tundra
- subarctic
- cool continental
- warm humid
- mediterranean
- semi-arid
- daily hours of sunshine, January
- daily hours of sunshine, July
- cold wind
- hot wind

SHAPING THE CONTINENT

SUCCESSIVE ICE AGES have left many relict landforms across Europe. Present glaciers continue to carve peaks and valleys in the northern Atlantic Highlands and Alpine Uplands. Tectonic activity, both past and present, has shaped southern Europe and Iceland. Active volcanoes and earthquakes still occur in Italy and Greece. Europe's extensive coastline, particularly in the northwest, is constantly modified by wave action and fluvial deposits.

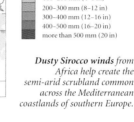

GLACIATION

1 Valley glaciers, such as this one *(left)* in Iceland, form in hollows at the top of valleys and flow downwards, drawn by gravity. Their growth is dynamic; new snowfall constantly accumulates at the head of the glacier, while the snout melts, depositing material eroded and carried by the glacier.

Snow accumulates at the head of glacier

Glacier movement erodes valley

Glacier snout melts depositing eroded debris

GLACIATION: DEVELOPMENT OF A GLACIER

RIVER SYSTEMS

2 Rivers are continuously transporting eroded material towards the sea. Slow-moving, low-gradient rivers, like this one in western Russia *(above)*, deposit their alluvium load, infilling valleys creating a flood plain. Subsequent climatic and tectonic fluctuations may erode the flood plain to form terraces.

Terrace created by erosion

Flood plain

Deposited alluvium

River channel

RIVER SYSTEMS: FORMATION OF A FLOOD PLAIN AND TERRACES

COASTAL PROCESSES

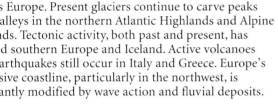

5 Spits are narrow bands of sand or shingle, formed by longshore drift; a process whereby waves carry material along the beach. They usually form where the coastline changes direction, and their growth is then halted by an opposing river current, as at Spurn Head, in the British Isles *(left)*. Coastal features such as these are constantly being created and destroyed.

Sand and shingle spit

Original coastline

Opposing river current

Waves breaking at an angle

COASTAL PROCESSES: FORMATION OF A SPIT

THE EVOLVING LANDSCAPE

Landscape
- uplifting land
- stable land
- sinking land
- limestone region
- glacier
- ▲ active volcano
- → ocean current
- area of tectonic activity
- maximum limit of glaciation

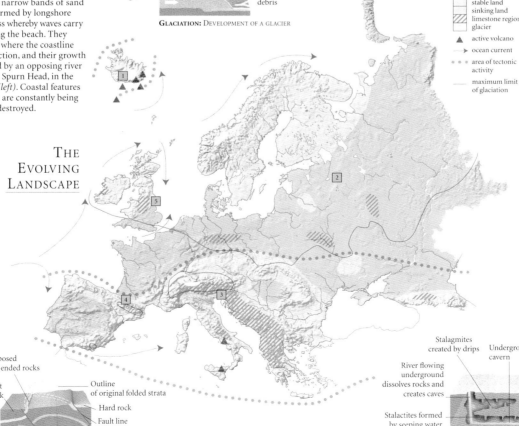

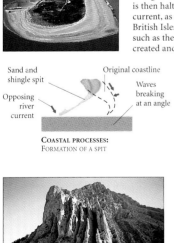

EROSION AND WEATHERING

4 Much of Europe was once subjected to folding and faulting, exposing hard and soft rock layers. Subsequent erosion and weathering has worn away the softer strata, leaving up-ended layers of hard rock as in the French Pyrenees *(above)*.

Exposed up-ended rocks

Soft rock

Outline of original folded strata

Hard rock

Fault line

Folded rock strata

EROSION AND WEATHERING: MODIFICATION OF A FOLD

Stalagmites created by drips

Underground cavern

River flowing underground dissolves rocks and creates caves

Stalactites formed by seeping water

WEATHERING: FORMATION OF A CAVE

WEATHERING

3 As surface water filters through permeable limestone, the rock dissolves to form underground caves, like Postojna in the Karst region of Slovenia *(above)*. Stalactites grow downwards as lime-enriched water seeps from roof fractures; stalagmites grow upwards where drips splash down.

POLITICAL EUROPE

THE POLITICAL BOUNDARIES OF EUROPE have changed many times, especially during the 20th century in the aftermath of two world wars, the break-up of the empires of Austria-Hungary, Nazi Germany and, towards the end of the century, the collapse of communism in eastern Europe. The fragmentation of Yugoslavia has again altered the political map of Europe, highlighting a trend towards nationalism and devolution. In contrast, economic federalism is growing. In 1958, the formation of the European Economic Community (now the European Union or EU) started a move towards economic and political union.

The Brandenburg Gate in Berlin is a potent symbol of German reunification. From 1961, the road beneath it ended in a wall, built to stop the flow of refugees to the West. It was opened again in 1989 when the wall was destroyed and East and West Germany were reunited.

POPULATION

EUROPE IS A DENSELY POPULATED, urbanized continent; in Belgium over 90% of people live in urban areas. The highest population densities are found in an area stretching east from southern Britain and northern France, into Germany. The northern fringes are only sparsely populated.

Demand for space in densely populated European cities like London has led to the development of high-rise offices and urban sprawl.

Population density
(people per sq km)

below 49
50–99
100–149
150–199
200–299
above 300

Traditional lifestyles still persist in many remote and rural parts of Europe, especially in the south, east, and in the far north.

MAP KEY

POPULATION

■ above 5 million
▣ 1 million to 5 million
◉ 500,000 to 1 million
◎ 100,000 to 500,000
⊕ 50,000 to 100,000
○ 10,000 to 50,000
● Country capital

BORDERS

⟋ full international border

SCALE 1:15,500,000
(projection: Lambert Azimuthal Equal Area)

Km
0 50 100 200 300 400 500 600 700 800 900 1000
Miles
0 50 100 200 300 400 500 600 700

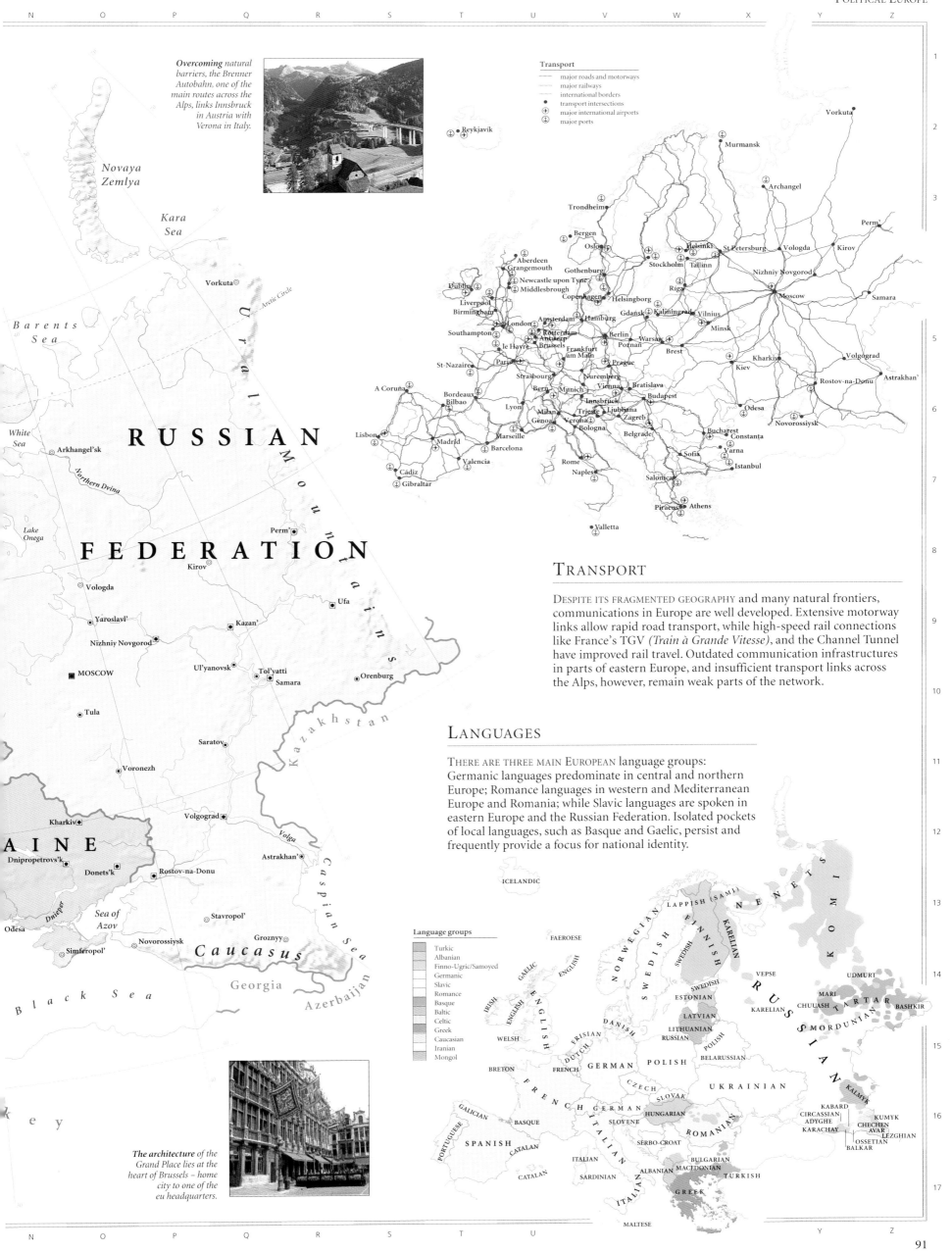

Overcoming natural barriers, the Brenner Autobahn, one of the main routes across the Alps, links Innsbruck in Austria with Verona in Italy.

Transport

– – – major roads and motorways
– – – major railways
——— international borders
• transport intersections
⊕ major international airports
⊕ major ports

Novaya Zemlya

Kara Sea

Barents Sea

White Sea

Lake Onega

Arctic Circle

Vorkuta

Vorkuta

Murmansk

Archangel

Trondheim

Bergen

Oslo

Helsinki

St Petersburg

Vologda

Kirov

Perm'

Aberdeen
Grangemouth
Newcastle upon Tyne
Middlesbrough
Dublin
Liverpool
Birmingham
Southampton
le Havre
St-Nazaire
Paris
A Coruña
Bordeaux
Bilbao
Lisbon
Madrid
Valencia
Cádiz
Gibraltar
Marseille
Barcelona
Rome
Naples
Valletta
Piraeus
Athens

Gothenburg
Stockholm
Copenhagen
Helsingborg
Helsingør
Riga
Gdańsk
Kaliningrad
Vilnius
Minsk
Brest
Hamburg
Berlin
Poznań
Warsaw
Kiev
Kharkiv
Amsterdam
Rotterdam
Antwerp
Brussels
London
Frankfurt am Main
Strasbourg
Nuremberg
Prague
Bern
Munich
Lyon
Milan
Trieste
Ljubljana
Genoa
Verona
Zagreb
Bologna
Belgrade
Innsbruck
Vienna
Bratislava
Budapest
Salonica

Tallinn
Nizhniy Novgorod
Moscow
Samara
Volgograd
Rostov-na-Donu
Astrakhan'
Odesa
Novorossiysk
Bucharest
Constanţa
Varna
Sofia
Istanbul
Reykjavík

RUSSIAN FEDERATION

Ural Mountains

Vologda
Kirov
Perm'
Yaroslavl'
Nizhniy Novgorod
Kazan'
Ufa
Ul'yanovsk
Tol'yatti
Samara
Orenburg
MOSCOW
Tula
Saratov
Voronezh
Volgograd
Astrakhan'

Kazakhstan

AINE

Kharkiv
Dnipropetrovs'k
Donets'k
Rostov-na-Donu
Stavropol'
Groznyy
Novorossiysk
Simferopol'
Odesa

Sea of Azov

Black Sea

Caspian Sea

Volga

Dnieper

Caucasus

Georgia

Azerbaijan

key

The architecture of the Grand Place lies at the heart of Brussels – home city to one of the EU headquarters.

Transport

Despite its fragmented geography and many natural frontiers, communications in Europe are well developed. Extensive motorway links allow rapid road transport, while high-speed rail connections like France's TGV *(Train à Grande Vitesse)*, and the Channel Tunnel have improved rail travel. Outdated communication infrastructures in parts of eastern Europe, and insufficient transport links across the Alps, however, remain weak parts of the network.

Languages

There are three main European language groups: Germanic languages predominate in central and northern Europe; Romance languages in western and Mediterranean Europe and Romania; while Slavic languages are spoken in eastern Europe and the Russian Federation. Isolated pockets of local languages, such as Basque and Gaelic, persist and frequently provide a focus for national identity.

Language groups

Turkic
Albanian
Finno-Ugric/Samoyed
Germanic
Slavic
Romance
Basque
Baltic
Celtic
Greek
Caucasian
Iranian
Mongol

ICELANDIC
FAEROESE
LAPPISH (SAMI)
NORWEGIAN
SWEDISH
SWEDISH
FINNISH
KARELIAN
NENETS
KOMI
GALLIC
ENGLISH
ENGLISH
IRISH
WELSH
ENGLISH
VEPSE
UDMURT
MARI
CHUUASH
TARTAR
BASHKIR
KARELIAN
VEPSE
FRISIAN
DANISH
ESTONIAN
LATVIAN
LITHUANIAN
RUSSIAN
MORDVINIAN
DUTCH
GERMAN
POLISH
BELARUSSIAN
RUSSIAN
BRETON
FRENCH
GERMAN
CZECH
SLOVAK
UKRAINIAN
GALICIAN
BASQUE
SLOVENE
HUNGARIAN
ROMANIAN
KALMYK
PORTUGUESE
SPANISH
CATALAN
ITALIAN
SERBO-CROAT
KABARD
CIRCASSIAN
ADYGHE
KARACHAY
CHECHEN
AVAR
KUMYK
LEZGHIAN
OSSETIAN
BALKAR
ITALIAN
SARDINIAN
CATALAN
BULGARIAN
MACEDONIAN
TURKISH
ALBANIAN
GREEK
MALTESE

EUROPEAN RESOURCES

EUROPE'S LARGE TRACTS OF FERTILE, accessible land, combined with its generally temperate climate, have allowed a greater percentage of land to be used for agricultural purposes than in any other continent. Extensive coal and iron ore deposits were used to create steel and manufacturing industries during the 19th and 20th centuries. Today, although natural resources have been widely exploited, and heavy industry is of declining importance, the growth of hi-tech and service industries has enabled Europe to maintain its wealth.

INDUSTRY

EUROPE'S WEALTH WAS GENERATED by the rise of industry and colonial exploitation during the 19th century. The mining of abundant natural resources made Europe the industrial centre of the world. Adaptation has been essential in the changing world economy, and a move to service-based industries has been widespread except in eastern Europe, where heavy industry still dominates.

Countries like Hungary are still struggling to modernize inefficient factories left over from extensive, centrally-planned industrialization during the communist era.

Other power sources are becoming more attractive as fossil fuels run out; 16% of Europe's electricity is now provided by hydro-electric power.

Frankfurt am Main is an example of a modern service-based city. The skyline is dominated by headquarters from the worlds of banking and commerce.

STANDARD OF LIVING

LIVING STANDARDS IN WESTERN EUROPE are among the highest in the world, although there is a growing sector of homeless, jobless people. Eastern Europeans have lower overall standards of living – a legacy of stagnated economies.

Standard of Living
(UN Human Development Index)

low

high

Skiing brings millions of tourists to the slopes each year, which means that even unproductive, marginal land is used to create wealth in the French, Swiss, Italian and Austrian Alps.

GNP per capita (US$)

below 1999
2000–4999
5000–9999
10,000–19,999
20,000–24,999
above 25,000

Industry

aerospace	food processing
brewing	hi-tech industry
car/vehicle manufacture	iron & steel
chemicals	pharmaceuticals
defence	printing & publishing
electronics	shipbuilding
engineering	textiles
finance	timber processing

wine
coal
oil
gas
industrial cities
major industrial areas

ICELAND
Reykjavík

Novaya Zemlya

Ostrov Kolguyev

Barents Sea

Murmansk

Archangel

RUSSIAN FEDERATION

Perm'

Kazan'

Ufa

Cherepovets

Yaroslavl'

Ivanovo

Nizhniy Novgorod

Moscow

Tol'yatti

Samara

Ryazan'

Tula

Saratov

Volgograd

Voronezh

Kursk

KAZAKHSTAN

Faeroe Islands
(to Denmark)

Norwegian Sea

Trondheim

Bergen

Oslo

Stockholm

Gothenburg

Helsinki

Turku

Tallinn

St Petersburg

FINLAND

Gulf of Bothnia

Glasgow
Belfast
Newcastle upon Tyne

REPUBLIC OF IRELAND

Dublin
Isle of Man (to UK)
Liverpool
Manchester

UNITED KINGDOM

Cardiff
Birmingham

London

Channel Islands (to UK)

North Sea

DENMARK

Copenhagen

Malmö

Hamburg

Gdańsk

Baltic Sea

Riga

LATVIA

LITHUANIA

Vilnius

RUSS. FED. (Kaliningrad)

ESTONIA

Minsk

BELARUS

Kiev

UKRAINE

Kharkiv

Dnipropetrovs'k

Donets'k

Kryvyy Rih

Rostov-na-Donu

Amsterdam
NETH.
Rotterdam
Antwerp
BELG.
Brussels
Liège
Cologne
Essen

GERMANY

Berlin

Poznań

Łódź

Warsaw

POLAND

Leipzig

Dresden

Wrocław

Lille
Rouen
Paris

FRANCE

Nantes

Metz
LUX.
Strasbourg

Frankfurt am Main

Stuttgart

Munich

Zürich
LIECH.
SWITZ.

Linz
Vienna

AUSTRIA

Budapest

HUNGARY

CZECH REP.
Prague
Katowice
Kraków

SLOVAKIA
Bratislava

Kursk

MOLDOVA

ROMANIA

Ploești

Bucharest

Constanța

Odesa

Black Sea

GEORGIA

AZERBAIJAN

Caspian Sea

A Coruña
Porto

Bilbao

Bordeaux

Toulouse

Bay of Biscay

SPAIN

Lisbon

PORTUGAL

Madrid

ANDORRA

Seville

Gibraltar (to UK)

Ceuta (to Spain)

Melilla (to Spain)

MOROCCO

Lyon

Turin
Milan
Genoa
Bologna

ITALY

Marseille

MONACO

Corsica

Barcelona

Balearic Islands

Sardinia

Mediterranean Sea

Venice
SLVN.

Zagreb

CROATIA

BOSNIA & HERZ.

SAN MARINO

VATICAN CITY
Rome

Naples

Taranto

Palermo

Sicily

MALTA

Tyrrhenian Sea

Adriatic Sea

YUGOSLAVIA

Belgrade

Sofia

BULGARIA

Varna

ALBANIA

MACED.

Salonica

GREECE

Piraeus

Athens

Crete

Aegean Sea

Ionian Sea

Istanbul

TURKEY

Atlantic Ocean

Environmental Issues (legend)

- national parks
- acid rain
- polluted rivers
- radioactive contamination
- marine pollution
- heavy marine pollution
- poor urban air quality

MINERAL RESOURCES

FOSSIL FUELS ARE EUROPE'S main mineral resource, although fuel demand far outstrips production. Sizeable coal reserves remain in the Donbass in Ukraine, Germany's Ruhr Valley, Poland, and in the British Isles. Oil and gas reserves are found mainly in the North Sea, and in the Volga Basin.

Mineral Resources (legend)
- oil field
- gas field
- coal field
- bauxite
- iron
- lead
- mercury
- potassium
- uranium
- zinc

The valuable oil and gas reserves in the North Sea were first discovered in the early 1960s, and are exploited by the UK, Denmark, Germany and Norway.

ENVIRONMENTAL ISSUES

THE PARTIALLY ENCLOSED WATERS of the Baltic and Mediterranean seas have become heavily polluted, while the Barents Sea is contaminated with spent nuclear fuel from Russia's navy. Acid rain, caused by emissions from factories and power stations, is actively destroying northern forests. As a result, pressure is growing to safeguard Europe's natural environment and prevent further deterioration.

Coniferous forest covers vast swathes of northern Scandinavia and the Russian Federation. Pollutants from other parts of Europe mixing with rainfall are causing defoliation and serious damage to many forests.

The Camargue in the Rhône Delta, southern France, is a protected wetland area, famous for its native population of white horses, and unique bird and plant life.

USING THE LAND AND SEA

EUROPE'S SWELLING URBAN POPULATION and the outward expansion of many cities has created acute competition for land. Despite this, European resourcefulness has maximized land potential, and over half of Europe's land is still used for a wide variety of agricultural purposes. Land in northern Europe is used for cattle-rearing, pasture, and arable crops. Towards the Mediterranean, the mild climate allows the growing of grapes for wine; olives, sunflowers, tobacco and citrus fruits. EU subsidies, however, have resulted in massive overproduction and a land 'set-aside' policy has been introduced.

Using the Land and Sea (legend): cropland, forest, ice cap, mountain region, pasture, tundra, wetland, major conurbations, cattle, goats, pigs, poultry, reindeer, sheep, cereals, citrus fruits, cotton, fishing, fodder, fruit, olive oil, potatoes, rice, root crops, roses, shellfish, sunflowers, timber, tobacco, vineyards

Bulgarian roses are one of the many diverse crops grown in Europe. Rose oil, extracted from the petals, is used in perfume making.

Lowland pastures are used for dairy farming. Good transport links and refrigeration allow fresh milk to be distributed throughout Europe.

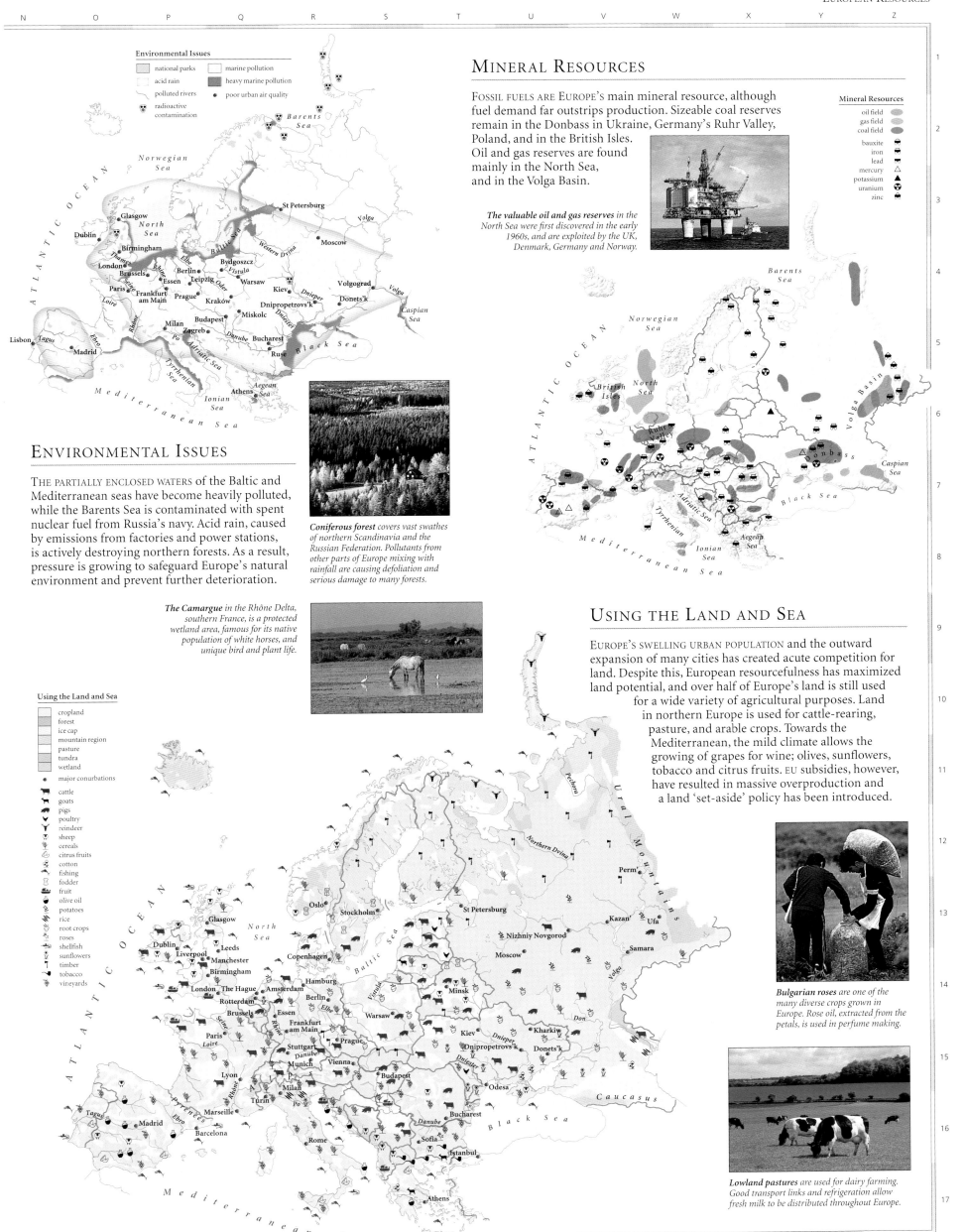

SCANDINAVIA, FINLAND & ICELAND

DENMARK, NORWAY, SWEDEN, FINLAND, ICELAND

JUTTING INTO THE ARCTIC CIRCLE, this northern swathe of Europe has some of the continent's harshest environments, but benefits from great reserves of oil, gas and natural evergreen forests. While most early settlers came from the south, migrants to Finland came from the east, giving it a distinct language and culture. Since the late 19th century, the Scandinavian states have developed strong egalitarian traditions. Today, their welfare benefits systems are among the most extensive in the world, and standards of living are high. The Lapps, or Sami, maintain their traditional lifestyle in the northern regions of Norway, Sweden and Finland.

THE LANDSCAPE

GLACIERS UP TO 10,000 ft (3000 m) deep covered most of Scandinavia and Finland during the last Ice Age. The effects of glaciation mark the entire landscape, from the mountains to the lowlands, across the tundra landscape of Lapland, and the lake districts of Sweden and Finland.

Geysers are a by-product of Iceland's volcanic activity. Geysir, Iceland's largest spring, gives them their name.

The fjords on the western coast of Norway were once gentle river valleys. Their deep floors and steep sides were carved out by glaciers during the last Ice Age, and they were later flooded by the sea.

Fjords

The Lofoten Islands were one of the first areas exposed as the ice sheet melted.

Lapland, north of the Arctic Circle, is an area of undulating fells and plains known as tundra. The subsoil is permanently frozen and therefore impermeable. There are many peat bogs. Pools reappear in the summer when the surface thaws.

Halti Mountain is Finland's highest point, at 4356 ft (1328 m).

Finland's landscape was fashioned by ice action. Glaciers gouged out its distinctive shallow lake basins, such as Oulujärvi, and left debris called moraines in their wake.

Oulujärvi

On the coast of Sjælland, these cliffs have been eroded by the sea, exposing layers of chalk and limestone.

Sjælland coast

Scandinavia is still recovering from the last Ice Age, when ice depressed the land by 2000 ft (600 m). This gradual uplift is known as isostatic rebound.

Area of maximum yearly uplift 0.3 in/yr (9 mm/yr)

Slower rates of uplift 0.1 in/yr (3 mm/yr)

USING THE LAND AND SEA

THE COLD CLIMATE, short growing season, poorly developed soil, steep slopes, and exposure to high winds across northern regions means that most agriculture is concentrated, with the population, in the south. Most of Finland and much of Norway and Sweden are covered by dense forests of pine, spruce and birch, which supply the timber industries.

Land use and agricultural distribution

- capital cities
- major towns

- pasture
- cropland
- forest
- mountain region
- tundra

- fishing
- pigs
- reindeer
- sheep
- timber

- cereals

THE URBAN/RURAL POPULATION DIVIDE

rural 23%
urban 77%

POPULATION DENSITY	TOTAL LAND AREA
20 people per sq mile (51 people per sq km)	473,970 sq miles (1,227,610 sq km)

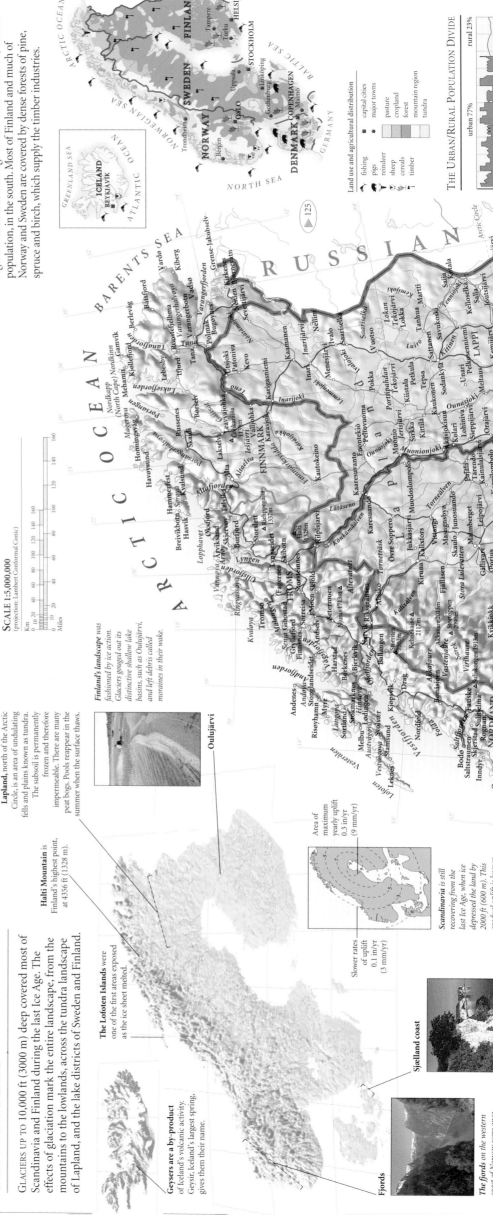

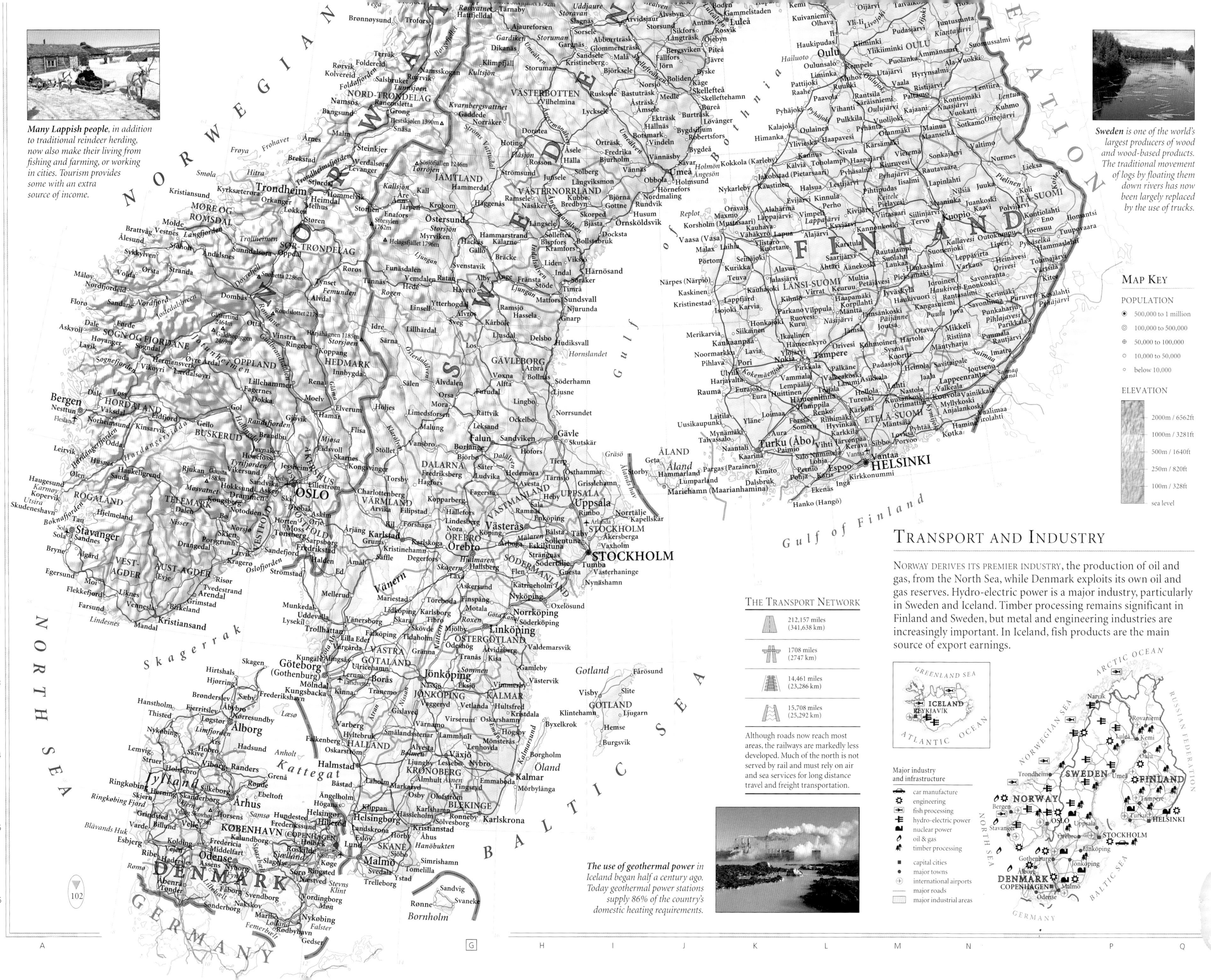

Sweden is one of the world's largest producers of wood and wood-based products. The traditional movement of logs by floating them down rivers has now been largely replaced by the use of trucks.

MAP KEY

POPULATION

- ◉ 500,000 to 1 million
- ◎ 100,000 to 500,000
- ⊕ 50,000 to 100,000
- ⊕ 10,000 to 50,000
- • below 10,000

ELEVATION

- 2000m / 6562ft
- 1000m / 3281ft
- 500m / 1640ft
- 250m / 820ft
- 100m / 328ft
- sea level

TRANSPORT AND INDUSTRY

NORWAY DERIVES ITS PREMIER INDUSTRY, the production of oil and gas, from the North Sea, while Denmark exploits its own oil and gas reserves. Hydro-electric power is a major industry, particularly in Sweden and Iceland. Timber processing remains significant in Finland and Sweden, but metal and engineering industries are increasingly important. In Iceland, fish products are the main source of export earnings.

THE TRANSPORT NETWORK

212,157 miles (341,638 km)	1708 miles (2747 km)
14,461 miles (23,286 km)	15,708 miles (25,292 km)

Although roads now reach most areas, the railways are markedly less developed. Much of the north is not served by rail and must rely on air and sea services for long distance travel and freight transportation.

The use of geothermal power in Iceland began half a century ago. Today geothermal power stations supply 86% of the country's domestic heating requirements.

Major industry and infrastructure:
- car manufacture
- engineering
- fish processing
- hydro-electric power
- nuclear power
- oil & gas
- timber processing
- capital cities
- major towns
- international airports
- major roads
- major industrial areas

Many Lappish people, in addition to traditional reindeer herding, now also make their living from fishing and farming, or working in cities; tourism provides some with an extra source of income.

NORTH SEA

102

95

SOUTHERN SCANDINAVIA

SOUTHERN NORWAY, SOUTHERN SWEDEN, DENMARK

SCANDINAVIA'S ECONOMIC AND POLITICAL HUB is the more habitable and accessible southern region. Many of the area's major cities are on the southern coasts, including Oslo and Stockholm, the capitals of Norway and Sweden. In Denmark, most of the population and the capital, Copenhagen, are located on its many islands. A cultural unity links the three Scandinavian countries. Their main languages, Danish, Swedish and Norwegian, are mutually intelligible, and they all retain their monarchies, although the parliaments have legislative control.

USING THE LAND

AGRICULTURE IN SOUTHERN SCANDINAVIA is highly mechanized although farms are small. Denmark is the most intensively farmed country and its western pastureland is used mainly for pig farming. Cereal crops including wheat, barley and oats, predominate in eastern Denmark and in the far south of Sweden. Southern Norway and Sweden have large tracts of forest which are exploited for logging.

Land use and agricultural distribution

- cattle
- pigs
- sheep
- cereals
- fodder
- root crops
- timber
- ● capital cities
- • major towns
- pasture
- cropland
- forest
- mountain region

THE URBAN/RURAL POPULATION DIVIDE

urban 87%   rural 13%

POPULATION DENSITY	TOTAL LAND AREA
152 people per sq mile	173,487 sq miles
(61 people per sq km)	(456,564 sq km)

THE LANDSCAPE

SOUTHERN SCANDINAVIA, with the exception of Norway, has a flatter terrain than the rest of the region. Denmark and southern Sweden are both extensions of the North European Plain. In this area, because of glacial deposition rather than erosion, the soils are deeper and more fertile.

In the past, glaciers such as this one in Olden, Norway, were much larger. Today, many are retreating to yield the spectacular glacial scenery.

Olden

Acid rain, caused by industrial pollution carried north from elsewhere in Europe, harms plant and animal life in Scandinavian forests and lakes. The region's surface rocks lack lime to neutralize the acid, so making the problem more serious.

Limestone pillars eroded by the sea dot the coast of Gotland and surrounding islands.

Distinctive low ridges, called eskers, are found across southern Sweden. They are formed from sand and gravel deposits left by retreating glaciers.

The peak of Glittertind in the Jotunheimen Mountains is 8044 ft (2452 m) high.

The lakes of southern Sweden remain from a period when the land was completely flooded. As the ice melted, the land rose, leaving lakes in shallow, ice-scoured depressions. Sweden has over 90,000 lakes.

Vänern in Sweden is the largest lake in Scandinavia. It covers an area of 2080 sq miles (5390 sq km).

Denmark's flat and fertile soils are formed on glacial deposits between 100–160 ft (30–50 m) deep.

When the ice retreated the valley was flooded by the sea / Old valley floor

Erosion by glaciers deepened existing river valleys / Sea level

Sognefjorden is the deepest of Norway's many fjords. It drops to 4291 ft (1308 m) below sea level.

Sognefjorden

MAP KEY

POPULATION
- ● 500,000 to 1 million
- ◉ 100,000 to 500,000
- ⊕ 50,000 to 100,000
- ⊙ 10,000 to 50,000
- • below 10,000

ELEVATION
- 2000m / 6562ft
- 1000m / 3281ft
- 500m / 1640ft
- 250m / 820ft
- 100m / 328ft
- sea level

SCALE 1:2,900,000
(projection: Lambert Conformal Conic)

In Norway winters are longer and colder inland than in coastal areas, where the warm current of the North Atlantic Drift moderates the climate.

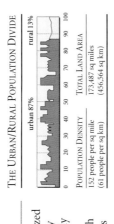

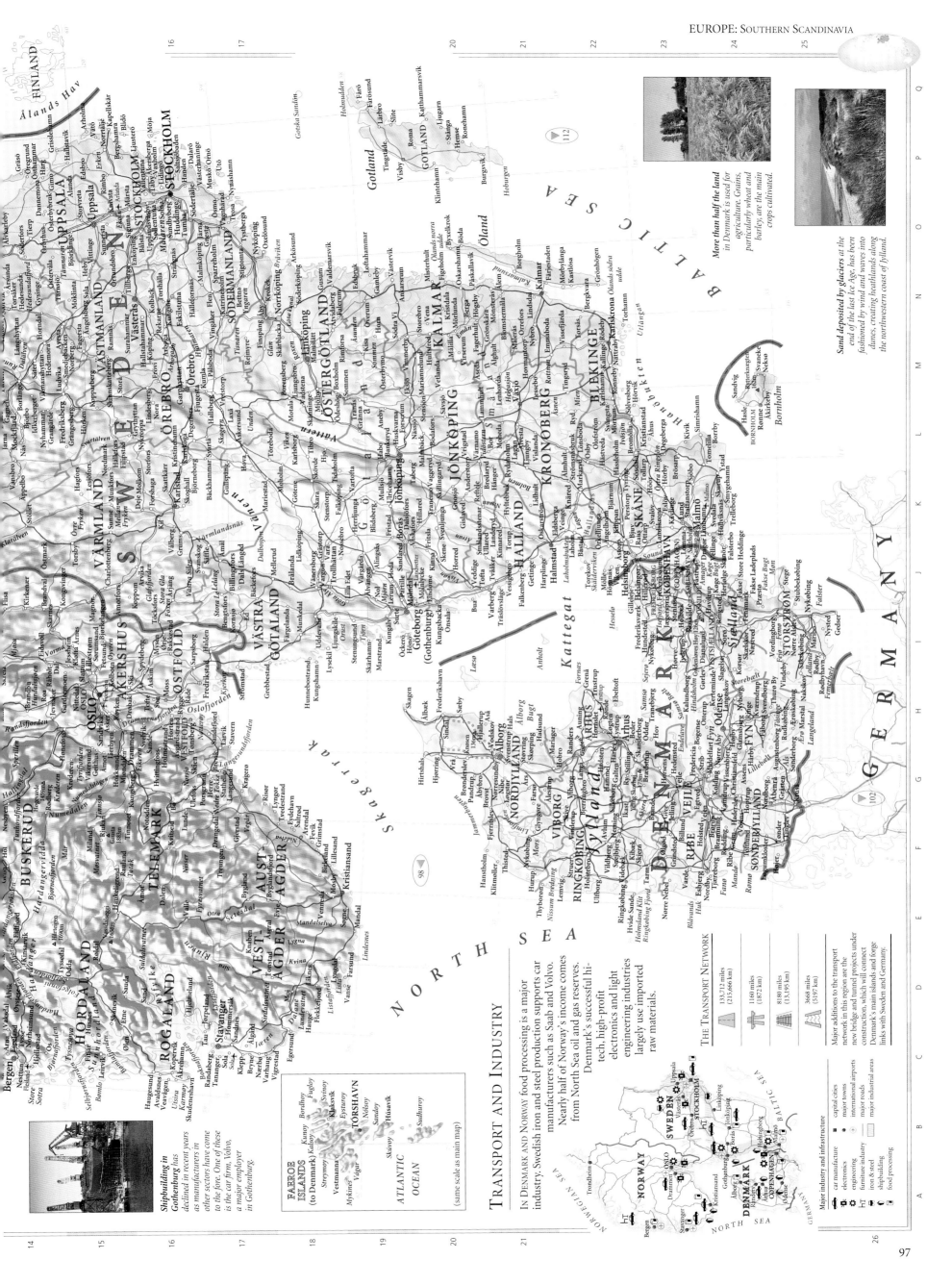

More than half the land in Denmark is used for agriculture. Grains, particularly wheat and barley, are the main crops cultivated.

Sand deposited by glaciers at the end of the last Ice Age, has been fashioned by wind and waves into dunes, creating heathlands along the northwestern coast of Jylland.

Shipbuilding in Gothenburg has declined in recent years as manufacturers in other sectors have come to the fore. One of these is the car firm, Volvo, a major employer in Gothenburg.

FAEROE ISLANDS (to Denmark)
Kunoy, Bordhoy, Fugloy
Streymoy, Kalsoy, Svinoy
Vestmanna, Viðoy, Kaksvik
Eysturoy
Mykines, Vágar, Nólsoy
Sandoy, Husavik
TÓRSHAVN
Skúvoy, Suðuroy
ATLANTIC OCEAN
(same scale as main map)

TRANSPORT AND INDUSTRY

IN DENMARK AND NORWAY food processing is a major industry. Swedish iron and steel production supports car manufacturers such as Saab and Volvo. Nearly half of Norway's income comes from North Sea oil and gas reserves. Denmark's successful hi-tech, high-profit electronics and light engineering industries largely use imported raw materials.

THE TRANSPORT NETWORK

133,712 miles (215,666 km)	
1160 miles (1872 km)	
8180 miles (13,195 km)	
3668 miles (5197 km)	

Major additions to the transport network in this region are the new bridge and tunnel projects under construction, which will connect Denmark's main islands and forge links with Sweden and Germany.

Major industry and infrastructure
- capital cities
- major towns
- international airports
- major roads
- major industrial areas

- car manufacture
- electronics
- engineering
- furniture industry
- iron & steel
- shipbuilding
- food processing

THE BRITISH ISLES

UNITED KINGDOM, REPUBLIC OF IRELAND

THE BRITISH ISLES have for centuries played a central role in European and world history. England, Wales, Scotland and Northern Ireland together form the United Kingdom (UK), while the southern portion of Ireland is an independent country, self-governing since 1921. Although England has tended to be the politically and economically dominant partner in the UK, the Scots, Welsh and Irish maintain independent cultures, distinct national identities and languages. Southeastern England is the most densely populated part of this crowded region, with over nine million people living in and around the London area.

The valley of Glen Coe in the Scottish Highlands is a U-shaped valley, typical of the north and west of the British Isles, where glaciers shaped much of the landscape.

TRANSPORT AND INDUSTRY

THE BRITISH ISLES' INDUSTRIAL BASE was founded primarily on coal, iron and textiles, based largely in the north. Today, the most productive sectors include hi-tech industries clustered mainly in southeastern England, chemicals, finance and the service sector, particularly tourism.

Major industry and infrastructure

- car manufacture
- chemicals
- engineering
- hi-tech industry
- iron & steel
- tourism

- ▪ capital cities
- ▪ major towns
- ✈ international airports
- major roads
- major industrial areas

THE TRANSPORT NETWORK

288,330 miles (464,300 km)	2046 miles (3295 km)
11,874 miles (19,121 km)	3806 miles (6129 km)

The UK's congested roads have become a major focus of environmental concern in recent years. No longer an island, the UK was finally linked to continental Europe by the Channel Tunnel in 1994.

Clew Bay in western Ireland, is characteristic of the heavily indented west coast, where deep wide-mouthed bays separate the mountains of Mayo, Donegal and Kerry as they thrust out into the Atlantic Ocean.

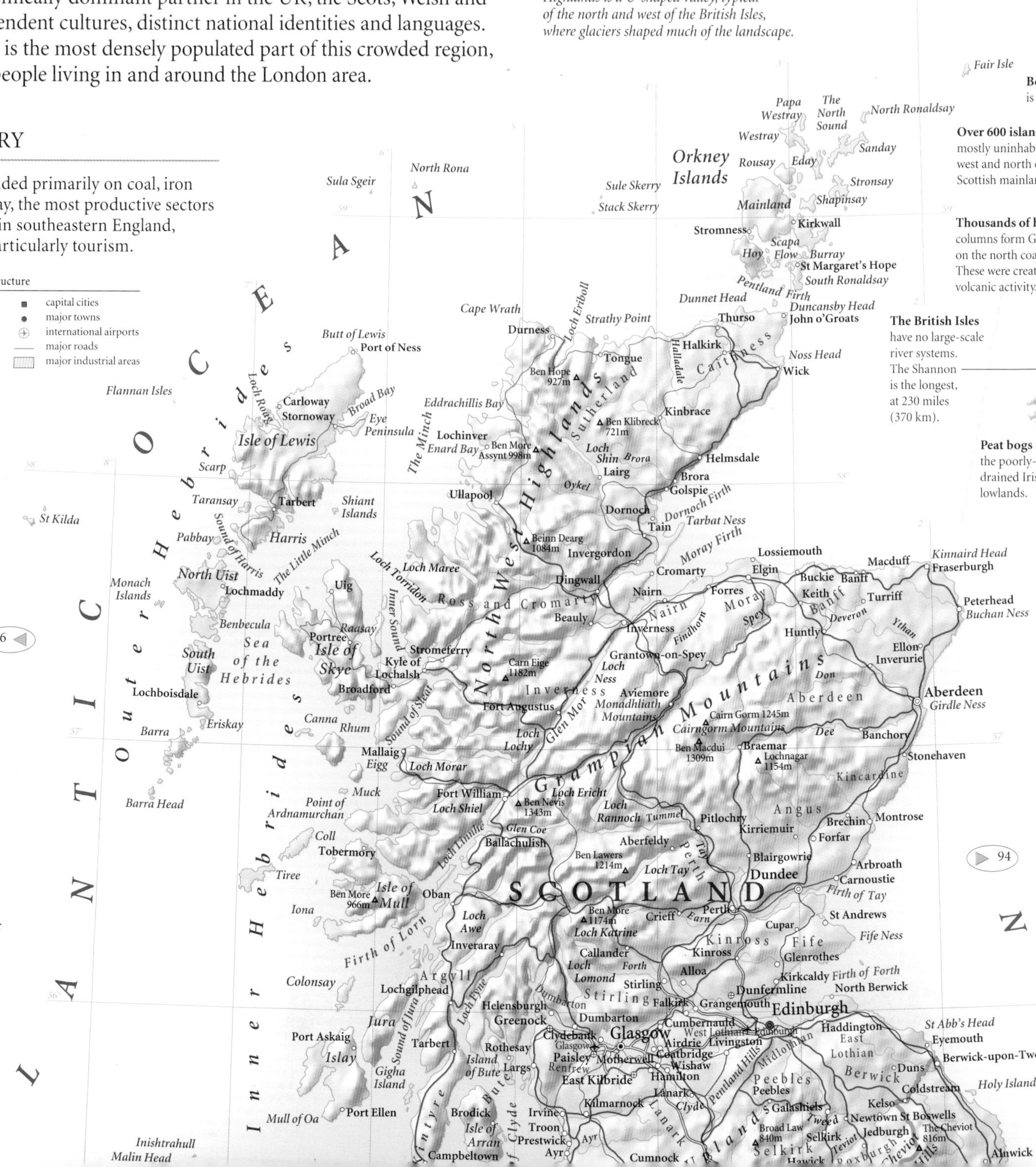

THE LANDSCAPE

RUGGED UPLANDS dominate the landscape of Scotland, Wales and northern England. All the peaks in the British Isles over 4000 ft (1219 m) lie in highland Scotland. Lowland England rises into several ranges of rolling hills, including the older Mendips, and the Cotswolds and the Chilterns, which were formed at the same time as the Alps in southern Europe.

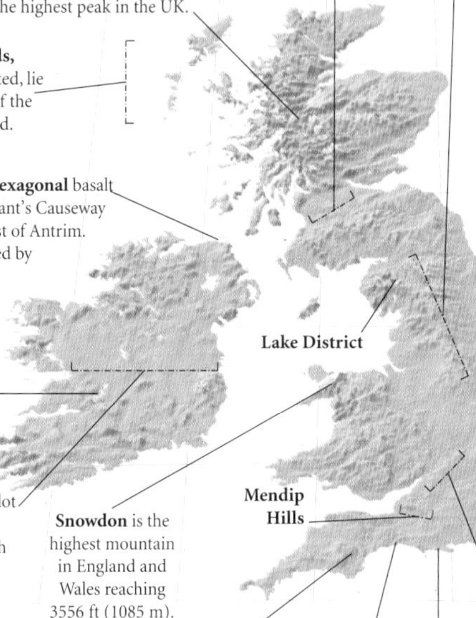

Ullswater in the Lake District fills a deep valley formed by glacial erosion.

The Fens are a low-lying area reclaimed from the sea.

The Pennines, sometimes called 'the backbone of England' are formed of limestones and grits.

Chiltern Hills

The Cotswold Hills are characterized by a series of limestone ridges overlooking clay vales.

Durdle Door

Coastal erosion around the British Isles forms striking features such as this limestone arch, Durdle Door in Dorset.

The lowlands of Scotland, drained by the Tay, Forth and Clyde rivers, are centred on a rift valley. The region contains valuable coal reserves.

Lake District

Mendip Hills

Ben Nevis at 4409 ft (1343 m) is the highest peak in the UK.

Snowdon is the highest mountain in England and Wales reaching 3556 ft (1085 m).

Over 600 islands, mostly uninhabited, lie west and north of the Scottish mainland.

Thousands of hexagonal basalt columns form Giant's Causeway on the north coast of Antrim. These were created by volcanic activity.

Peat bogs dot the poorly-drained Irish lowlands.

The British Isles have no large-scale river systems. The Shannon is the longest, at 230 miles (370 km).

Dartmoor, studded with tors, is an exposed part of a vast granite dome, formed when molten rock intruded into the Earth's crust.

Black Ven, Lyme Regis

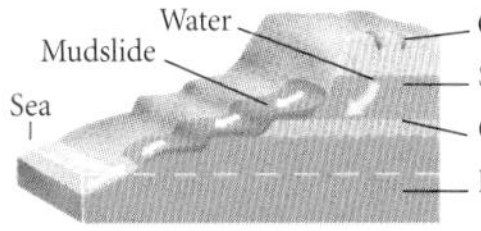

Much of the south coast is subject to landslides. Following rain, porous sandstones feed water into the underlying, less permeable clays which then crumble and slide into the sea.

- Cracks
- Sandstone
- Clay
- Limestone
- Water
- Mudslide
- Sea

MAP KEY

POPULATION
- ▪ above 5 million
- ▪ 1 million to 5 million
- ▪ 500,000 to 1 million
- ◉ 100,000 to 500,000
- ⊕ 50,000 to 100,000
- ⊙ 10,000 to 50,000
- ∘ below 10,000

ELEVATION
- 1000m / 3281ft
- 500m / 1640ft
- 250m / 820ft
- 100m / 328ft
- sea level

Shetland Islands

Herma Ness
Unst
Fedlar
Yell
Yell Sound
Hillswick
St Magnus Bay
Sullom Voe
Out Skerries
Whalsay
Mainland
Lerwick
Bressay
Papa Stour
Scalloway
West Burra
Foula
Fitful Head
Sumburgh Head

Fair Isle

Orkney Islands

North Ronaldsay
Sanday
Stronsay
Westray
The North Sound
Papa Westray
Rousay
Eday
Shapinsay
Stromness
Mainland
Kirkwall
Burray
Hoy
Scapa
St Margaret's Hope
South Ronaldsay
Sule Skerry
Stack Skerry
Pentland Firth
Dunnet Head
Duncansby Head
John o'Groats
Noss Head
Thurso
Wick
Halkirk
Hallodale

North Rona
Sula Sgeir

Cape Wrath
Durness
Loch Eriboll
Strathy Point
Tongue
Ben Hope 927m
Loch Hope
Ben Loyal
Allen Kilbreck 721m
Kinbrace
Brora
Golspie
Dornoch
Dornoch Firth
Tarbat Ness
Tain
Lairg
Loch Shin
Ben More Assynt 998m
Oykel
Helmsdale

Butt of Lewis
Port of Ness
Eye Peninsula
Stornoway
Isle of Lewis
Loch Roag
Scarp
Tarbert
Harris
Taransay
Sound of Harris
North Uist
Benbecula
South Uist
Lochboisdale
Eriskay
Barra
Barra Head
Monach Islands
Flannan Isles
St Kilda

Eldrachillis Bay
Lochinver
Enard Bay
Assynt
Ullapool
Ben Wyvis 1046m
Cromarty
Beauly
Inverness
Moray Firth
Nairn

Eddrachillis Bay
The Minch
Inner Sound
Raasay
Portree
Isle of Skye
Broadford
Kyle of Lochalsh
Kyleakin
Glen Affric
Glen More
Loch Ness
Fort Augustus
Loch Lochy
Loch Oich
Grantown-on-Spey
Aviemore
Cairn Gorm 1245m
Braemar
Lochnagar
1155m

Shiant Islands
Stromeferry
Loch Carron
Loch Torridon
Loch Maree
Ross and Cromarty

Ben Macdui 1309m
Cairngorm Mountains

Canna
Rhum
Eigg
Point of Ardnamurchan
Muck
Coll
Tiree
Mallaig
Loch Morar
Fort William
Ben Nevis 1343m
Loch Shiel
Loch Linnhe
Glen Coe
Ballachulish

Tobermory
Ben More 966m
Isle of Mull
Iona
Sound of Mull
Oban
Loch Awe
Inveraray
Loch Fyne

Colonsay
Jura
Port Askaig
Islay
Port Ellen
Mull of Oa
Gigha Island
Campbeltown
Mull of Kintyre

Argyll
Lochgilphead
Loch Lomond
Ben More 1174m

Inner Hebrides
Outer Hebrides

Kinnaird Head
Fraserburgh
Peterhead
Buchan Ness
Aberdeen
Girdle Ness
Stonehaven
Macduff
Banff
Buckie
Turriff
Elgin
Lossiemouth
Keith
Forres
Huntly
Inverurie
Ellon
Cairn Gorm
Ben Rinnes
Dee
Bennachie 1733m
Kincardine
Montrose
Brechin
Forfar
Arbroath
Carnoustie
St Andrews
Fife Ness
Dundee
Firth of Tay
Perth
Aberfeldy
Pitlochry
Blairgowrie
Loch Tummel
Loch Rannoch
Loch Tay
Crieff
Kinross
Loch Leven
Alloa
Stirling
Callander
Loch Katrine
Dunfermline
Firth of Forth
Kirkcaldy
Edinburgh
Livingston
Grangemouth
Falkirk
Airdrie
Motherwell
Hamilton
Wishaw
Lanark
Cumbernauld
Glasgow
Paisley
East Kilbride
Kilmarnock

Berwick-upon-Tweed
Holy Island
St Abb's Head
Eyemouth
Duns
Coldstream
Kelso
Jedburgh
Berwick
Selkirk
Peebles
Galashiels
Hawick

Dumbarton
Greenock
Helensburgh
Rothesay
Isle of Bute
Brodick
Isle of Arran
Largs
Irvine
Troon
Prestwick
Ayr

SCOTLAND

North West Highlands
Grampian Mountains
Angus

ATLANTIC OCEAN

Inishtrahull
Malin Head

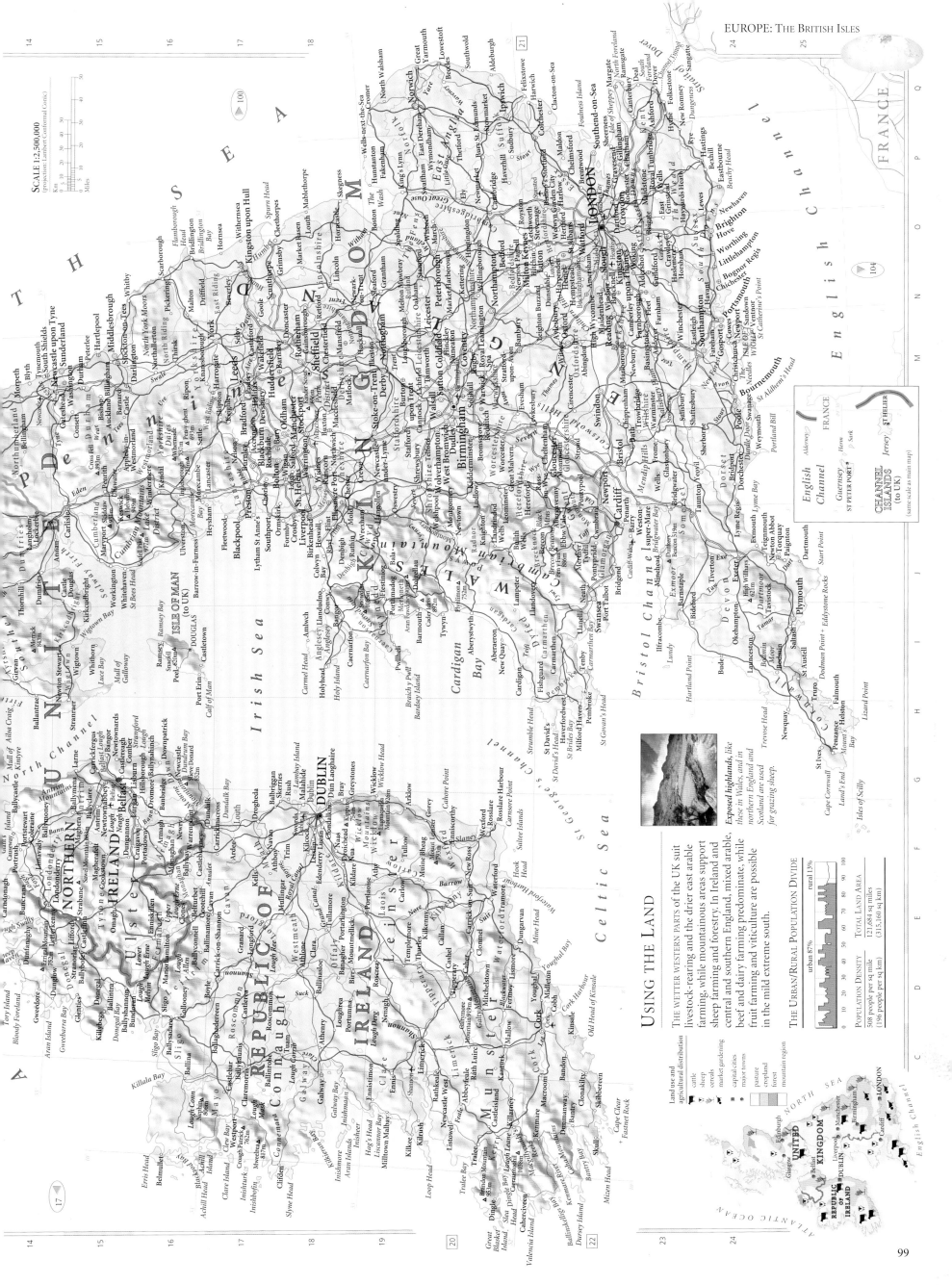

USING THE LAND

THE WETTER WESTERN PARTS of the UK suit livestock-rearing and the drier east arable farming, while mountainous areas support sheep farming and forestry. In Ireland and central and southern England, mixed arable, beef and dairy farming predominate, while fruit farming and viticulture are possible in the mild extreme south.

Exposed highlands, like these in Wales, and in northern England and Scotland are used for grazing sheep.

THE URBAN/RURAL POPULATION DIVIDE

urban 87%   rural 13%

POPULATION DENSITY
508 people per sq mile
(196 people per sq km)

TOTAL LAND AREA
121,684 sq miles
(315,160 sq km)

land use and agricultural distribution
- cattle
- sheep
- cereals
- market gardening
- capital cities
- major towns
- pasture
- cropland
- forest
- mountain region

SCALE 1:2,500,000
(projection: Lambert Conformal Conic)

THE LOW COUNTRIES

BELGIUM, LUXEMBOURG, NETHERLANDS

O NE OF NORTHWESTERN EUROPE'S strategic crossroads, the Low Countries are united by a common history in which they have often been a battleground in European wars. For over a thousand years they were ruled by foreign powers. Even after they achieved independence, the three countries maintained close links, later forming the world's first totally free labour and goods market, the Benelux Economic Union, which became the core of the European Community (now the European Union or EU). These states have remained at the forefront of wider European co-operation; Brussels, The Hague and Luxembourg are hosts to major institutions of the EU.

THE LANDSCAPE

THE MAIN GEOGRAPHICAL REGIONS of the Netherlands are the northern glacial heathlands, the low-lying lands of the Rhine and Maas/Meuse, the reclaimed polders, and the dune coast and islands. Belgium includes part of the Ardennes, together with the coalfields on its northern flanks, and the fertile Flanders Plain.

Since the Middle Ages the people of the Netherlands have used ditches and drainage dykes to reclaim land from the sea. These reclaimed areas are known as polders.

Extensive sand dune systems along the coast have prevented flooding of the land. Behind the dunes, marshy land is drained to form polders, usable land suitable for agriculture.

Sand dunes

Sea
Dune system
Polder
Drainage ditch

The loess soils of the Flanders Plain in western Belgium provide excellent conditions for arable farming.

Uplifted and folded 220 million years ago, the Ardennes have since been reduced to relatively level plateaux, then sharply incised by rivers such as the Maas/Meuse.

Ardennes

Hautes Fagnes is the highest part of Belgium. The bogs and streams in this upland region result from high rainfall and low temperatures.

Schoorl

Heathlands, like these at Schoorl, are found along the coast of the Netherlands. Much of the coast was breached by the sea in the 5th century, creating its distinctive inlets and islands.

One-third of the Netherlands lies below sea level and flooding is a constant threat. Barrages have been built across the mouths of many rivers to contain floodwaters.

The parallel valleys of the Maas/Meuse and Rhine rivers were created when the Rhine was deflected from its previous course by the ice sheet which formed during the last Ice Age.

Silts and sands eroded by the Rhine throughout its course are deposited to form a delta on the west coast of the Netherlands.

TRANSPORT AND INDUSTRY

IN THE WESTERN NETHERLANDS, a massive, sprawling industrialized zone encompasses many new hi-tech and service industries. Belgium's central region has emerged as the country's light manufacturing and services centre. Luxembourg city is home to more than 160 banks and the European headquarters of many international companies.

THE TRANSPORT NETWORK

280,630 miles (451,900 km)
2536 miles (4083 km)
4037 miles (6501 km)
4366 miles (7031 km)

The Low Countries hold a key position on the North Sea, containing Europe's two largest ports, Rotterdam and Antwerp, which are connected to a comprehensive system of inland waterways.

Major industry and infrastructure

aerospace
finance
engineering
hi-tech industry
pharmaceuticals
textiles
capital cities
major towns
international airports
major roads
major industrial areas

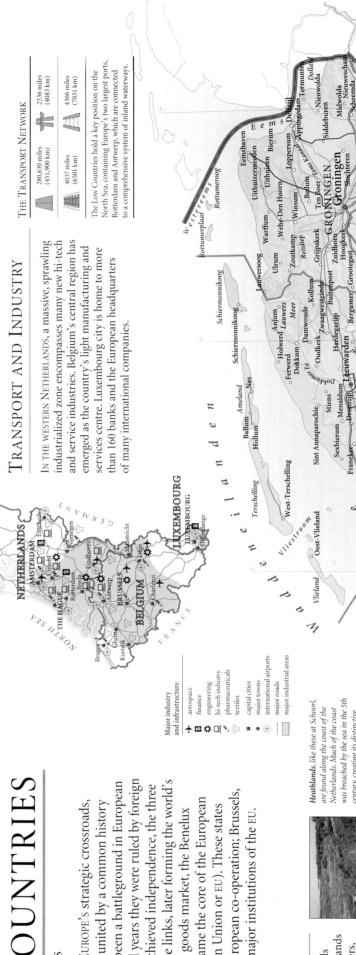

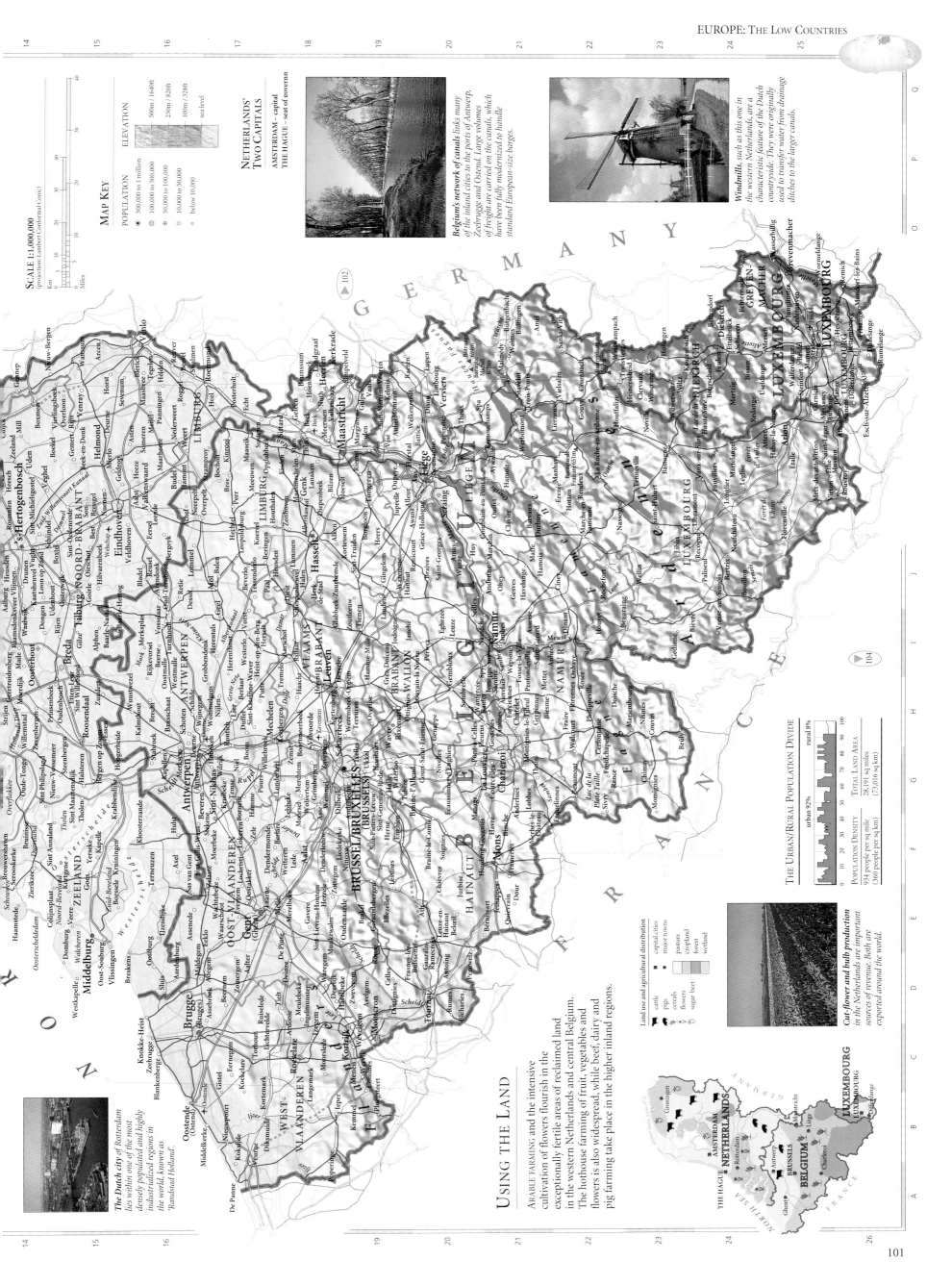

SCALE 1:1,000,000
(projection: Lambert Conformal Conic)

MAP KEY

ELEVATION
- 500m / 1640ft
- 250m / 820ft
- 100m / 328ft
- sea level

POPULATION
- ● 500,000 to 1 million
- ◉ 100,000 to 500,000
- ⊕ 50,000 to 100,000
- ⊙ 10,000 to 50,000
- ○ below 10,000

**NETHERLANDS'
TWO CAPITALS**

AMSTERDAM – capital
THE HAGUE – seat of govern

Belgium's network of canals links many of the inland cities to the ports of Antwerp, Zeebrugge and Ostend. Large volumes of freight are carried on the canals, which have been fully modernized to handle standard European-size barges.

Windmills, such as this one in the western Netherlands, are a characteristic feature of the Dutch countryside. They were originally used to transfer water from drainage ditches to the larger canals.

USING THE LAND

ARABLE FARMING and the intensive cultivation of flowers flourish in the exceptionally fertile areas of reclaimed land in the western Netherlands and central Belgium. The hothouse farming of fruit, vegetables and flowers is also widespread, while beef, dairy and pig farming take place in the higher inland regions.

The Dutch city of Rotterdam lies within one of the most densely populated and highly industrialized regions in the world, known as 'Randstad Holland'.

Land use and agricultural distribution
- cattle
- pigs
- cereals
- flowers
- sugar beet
- ■ capital cities
- ● major towns
- pasture
- cropland
- forest
- wetland

Cut-flower and bulb production in the Netherlands are important sources of revenue. Both are exported around the world.

THE URBAN/RURAL POPULATION DIVIDE

	urban 92%	rural 8%

POPULATION DENSITY	TOTAL LAND AREA
934 people per sq mile	28,191 sq miles
(360 people per sq km)	(73,016 sq km)

101

GERMANY

D ESPITE THE DEVASTATION of its industry and infrastructure during the Second World War and its separation from eastern Germany during the Cold War, West Germany made a rapid recovery in the following generation to become Europe's most formidable economic power. When the Berlin Wall was dismantled in 1989, the two halves of Germany were politically united for the first time in 40 years. Complete social and economic unity remain a longer term goal, as East German industry and society adapt to a free market. Germany has been a key player in the creation of the European Union (EU) and in moves toward a single European currency.

USING THE LAND

G ERMANY HAS a large, efficient agricultural sector, and produces more than three-quarters of its own food. The major crops grown are cereals and sugar beet on the more fertile soils, and root crops, rye, oats and fodder on the poorer soils of the northern plains and central uplands. Southern Germany is also a principal producer of high quality wines. Vineyards cover the slopes surrounding the Rhine and its tributaries.

Land use and agricultural distribution
- cattle
- pigs
- cereals
- sugar beet
- vineyards
- major cities
- major towns
- pasture
- cropland
- forest

THE URBAN/RURAL POPULATION DIVIDE

urban 87%   rural 13%

POPULATION DENSITY	TOTAL LAND AREA
598 people per sq mile (231 people per sq km)	13,804 sq miles (356,910 sq km)

The Moselle River flows through the Rhine State Uplands (Rheinisches Schiefergebirge). During a period of uplift, pre-existing river meanders were deeply incised, to form its present dramatic contours.

THE LANDSCAPE

T HE PLAINS OF NORTHERN GERMANY, the volcanic plateaux and mountains of the central uplands, and the Bavarian Alps are the three principal geographic regions in Germany. North to south the land rises steadily from barely 300 ft (90 m) in the plains to 6500 ft (2000 m) in the Bavarian Alps, which are a small but distinct region in the far south.

The heathlands of northern Germany are covered by glacial deposits of sandy outwash soil which makes them largely infertile. They support only sheep and solitary trees.

Lüneburg Heath (*Lüneburger Heide*)

Müritz lake covers 45 sq miles (117 sq km), but is only 108 ft (33 m) deep. It lies in a shallow valley formed by meltwater flowing out from a retreating ice sheet. These valleys are known as *Urstromtäler.*

Much of the landscape of northern Germany has been shaped by glaciation. During the last Ice Age, the ice sheet advanced as far as the northern slopes of the central uplands.

Fault lines

Rhine

Downfaulted block

Part of the floor of the Rhine Rift Valley was let down between two parallel faults in the Earth's crust.

Rhine Rift Valley

The Harz Mountains were formed 300 million years ago. They are block-faulted mountains, formed when a section of the Earth's crust was thrust up between two faults.

Elbe River

The Elbe flows in wide meanders across the north German plain to the North Sea. At its mouth it is 10 miles (16 km) wide.

The Rhine is Germany's principal waterway and one of Europe's longest rivers, flowing 820 miles (1320 km).

The Danube rises in the Black Forest (*Schwarzwald*) and flows east, across a wide valley, on its course to the Black Sea.

Zugspitze, the highest peak in Germany at 9719 ft (2962 m), was formed during the Alpine mountain-building period, 30 million years ago.

SCALE 1:2,250,000
(projection: Lambert Conformal Conic)

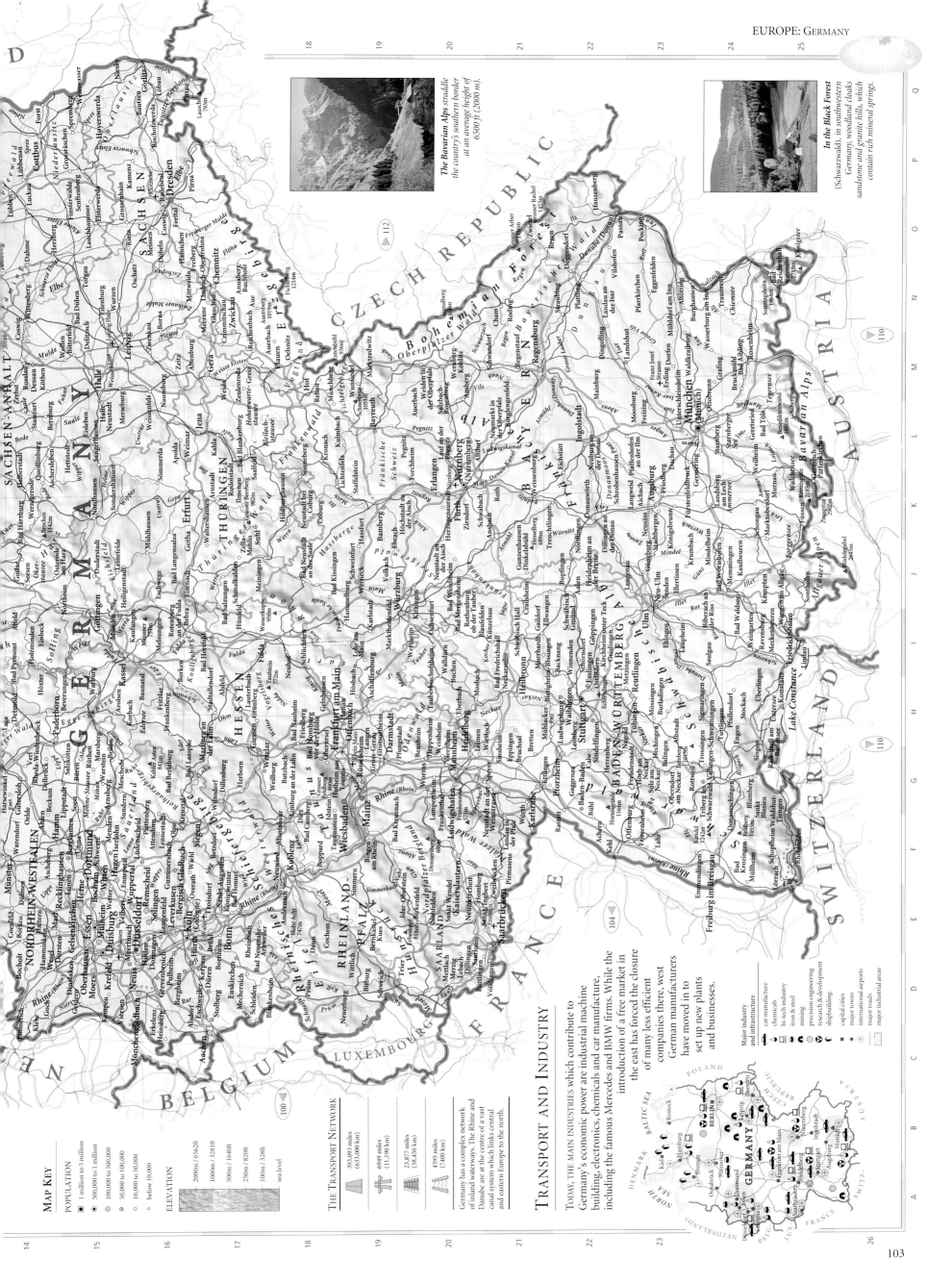

The Bavarian Alps straddle the country's southern border at an average height of 6500 ft (2000 m).

In the Black Forest (Schwarzwald), in southwestern Germany, woodland cloaks sandstone and granite hills, which contain rich mineral springs.

MAP KEY

POPULATION

- 1 million to 5 million
- 500,000 to 1 million
- 100,000 to 500,000
- 50,000 to 100,000
- 10,000 to 50,000
- below 10,000

ELEVATION

2000m/6562ft
1000m/3281ft
500m/1640ft
250m/820ft
100m/328ft
sea level

THE TRANSPORT NETWORK

393,093 miles (633,000 km)

6949 miles (11,190 km)

23,877 miles (38,450 km)

4595 miles (7400 km)

Germany has a complex network of inland waterways. The Rhine and Danube are at the centre of a vast canal system which links central and eastern Europe to the north.

TRANSPORT AND INDUSTRY

TODAY, THE MAIN INDUSTRIES which contribute to Germany's economic power are industrial machine building, electronics, chemicals and car manufacture, including the famous Mercedes and BMW firms. While the introduction of a free market in the east has forced the closure of many less efficient companies there, west German manufacturers have moved in to set up new plants and businesses.

Major industry and infrastructure

- car manufacture
- chemicals
- hi-tech industry
- iron & steel
- mining
- precision engineering
- research & development
- shipbuilding
- capital cities
- major cities
- major towns
- international airports
- major roads
- major industrial areas

103

FRANCE

FRANCE, MONACO

A MAJOR CENTRE OF CULTURE AND FASHION, and a leading producer of both industrial and agricultural goods, France is a key player in the push towards European unity. The founder of modern Republican government in the 18th century, France has been closely involved in European events for many centuries. The Paris Basin is the most highly populated area; Île de France is home to over nine million people. Large parts of rural France remain thinly populated, particularly the mountainous Massif Central, Pyrennees and southern Alps.

The chalk cliffs of Normandy (Normandie) and southeastern England form part of a single geological region, now divided in two by the English Channel.

THE LANDSCAPE

FRANCE'S LANDSCAPE was fashioned by two phases of mountain-building. The northwestern peninsula, the Massif Central and the Vosges date from 220 million years ago. The complex folds of the Alps and Pyrenees, the gently-folded Jura, and the low-lying sedimentary areas of the Paris, Garonne and Rhône basins started to form 65 million years ago.

The coast of Brittany (Bretagne) is highly indented where deep valleys in the northwestern peninsula were drowned by the sea.

The Normandy (Normandie) coastline is characterized by high chalk cliffs.

The coastline of France is 2141 miles (3427 km) long.

The Paris Basin consists of a layered sequence of sedimentary rocks. Fertile soils over much of the area make good agricultural land.

The gently rounded summits of the Vosges are over 200 million years old.

The Biscay coast, like the Mediterranean, is characterized by flat sandy beaches, interspersed with lagoons.

Garonne Basin

The folded Jura form low ridges and long narrow valleys.

The Alps were forced up during several phases of mountain-building beginning 65 million years ago.

The Dordogne region contains spectacular examples of limestone scenery including caves and gorges.

The Pyrenees form a natural border between France and Spain.

The ancient Massif Central, disturbed by the formation of the Alps, was subject to volcanism that only ceased during the last 10,000 years.

Rhône Basin

Rhône Delta

Rhône

Delta plain

The marshes of the Camargue

Corsica's northeastern peninsula has dramatic cliffs of folded limestone.

The volcanic landscape of the Auvergne where the cones of its extinct volcanoes have worn away to leave 'plugs' of lava.

Deposition in the Rhône Delta is wave-dominated. Sea currents carry river sediments extending the delta plain westwards.

TRANSPORT AND INDUSTRY

TODAY THE MAIN FRENCH GROWTH INDUSTRIES are hi-tech, including micro-electronics, telecommunications and aerospace. Other important sectors are the nuclear industry, only rivalled in scale by that of the USA, car manufacture, dominated by the giants Renault and Peugeot and a highly diversified tourist industry.

Major industry and infrastructure

- aerospace industry
- car manufacture
- chemicals
- engineering
- hi-tech industry
- nuclear power
- tourism
- capital cities
- major towns
- international airports
- major roads
- major industrial areas

THE TRANSPORT NETWORK

599,017 miles (964,600 km)

5900 miles (9500 km)

19,761 miles (31,821 km)

5279 miles (8500 km)

The French TGV (*Train à Grande Vitesse*) leads the world in high-speed train technology, and provides a service which is faster, door-to-door, than air travel.

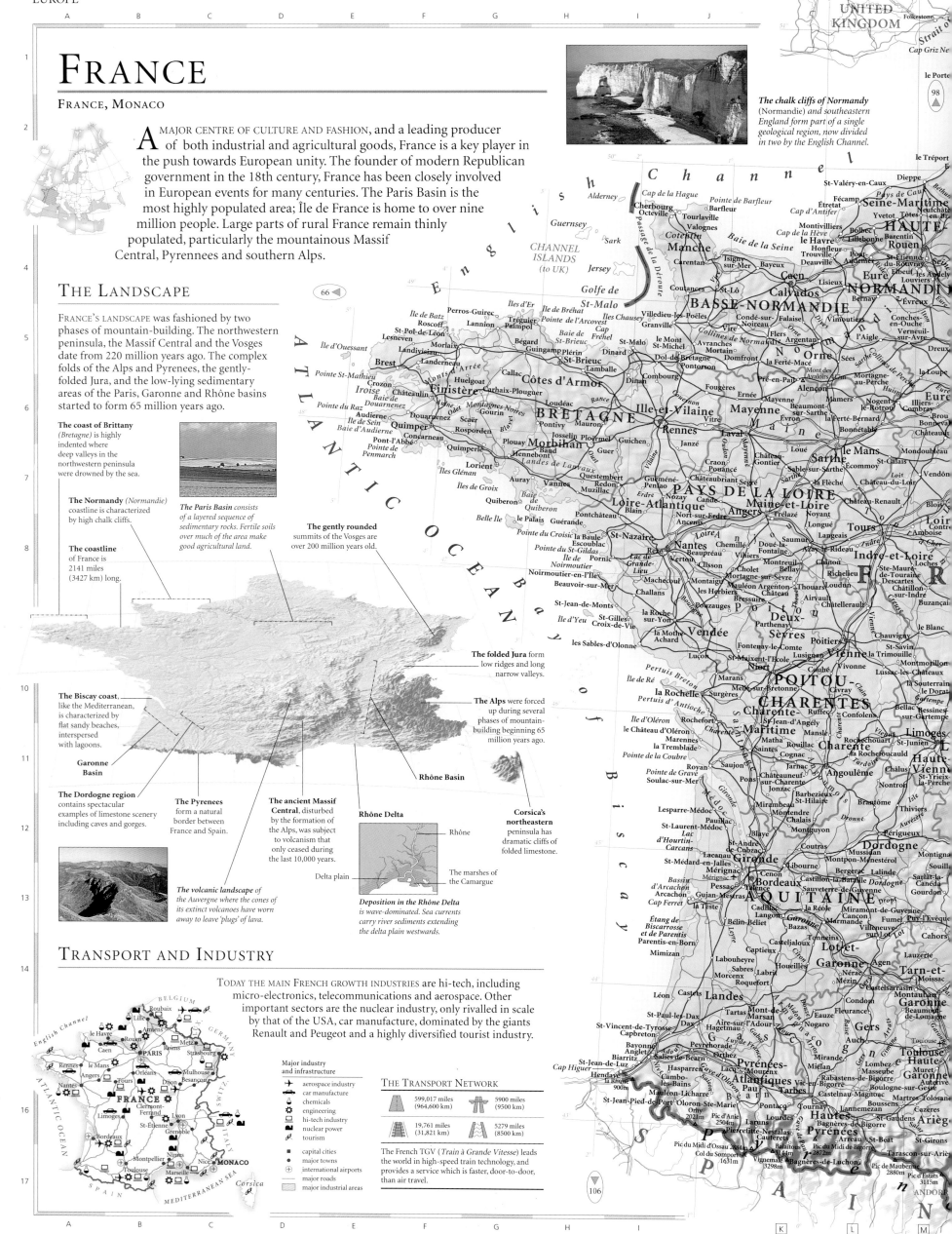

USING THE LAND

FRANCE IS WESTERN EUROPE's leading agricultural producer, and benefits from high levels of EU subsidy. The variation in climate and soils across the country provides great potential for agriculture and forestry, reflected in the range of products cultivated, including cereals, olives, herbs, and grapes for its famous wines.

Land use and agricultural distribution
- cattle
- cereals
- market gardening
- sugar beet
- vineyards
- capital cities
- major towns
- pasture
- cropland
- forest
- mountain region

The Romans first introduced wine-making to France when they occupied the region. Traditional vineyards can be found all over France, producing many of the world's classic wines.

THE URBAN/RURAL POPULATION DIVIDE

urban 73%   rural 27%

0 10 20 30 40 50 60 70 80 90 100

POPULATION DENSITY	TOTAL LAND AREA
276 people per sq mile (106 people per sq km)	212,930 sq mile (551,500 sq km)

The rugged hills and cliffs of Corsica were uplifted when the African and Eurasian plates collided. Frost action during the Ice Age created their present form.

In the sunny climate of southern France olives, vines, peppers, garlic and lavender now grow in place of the forests that once covered much of the area.

SCALE 1:2,750,000
(projection: Lambert Conformal Conic)

Km
0 5 10 20 30 40 50 60 70 80

Miles
0 5 10 20 30 40 50 60 70 80

MAP KEY

POPULATION
- above 5 million
- 1 million to 5 million
- 500,000 to 1 million
- 100,000 to 500,000
- 50,000 to 100,000
- 10,000 to 50,000
- below 10,000

ELEVATION
- 4000m / 13,124ft
- 3000m / 9843ft
- 2000m / 6562ft
- 1000m / 3281ft
- 500m / 1640ft
- 250m / 820ft
- 100m / 328ft
- sea level

Corse (Corsica)
(same scale as main map)

THE IBERIAN PENINSULA

ANDORRA, GIBRALTAR, PORTUGAL, SPAIN (Azores, Canary Islands, Madeira on p.66)

THE IBERIAN PENINSULA is separated from the rest of Europe by the Pyrenees, and at its most southerly point is only 5 miles (8 km) from North Africa. The location of Iberia has been central to its diverse history. The Greeks, Carthaginians, Romans, Visigoths and most recently the Moors, invaded Iberia at various times. For much of the 20th century, both Spain and Portugal were governed by right-wing dictators. Since the establishment of democratic governments in the mid-1970s, modernization has been rapid and both countries are now among the most popular of European holiday destinations.

USING THE LAND

THE PRINCIPAL CROPS grown in Iberia are cereals, especially wheat and barley. Both countries are major wine producers, most notably of Rioja, sherry and port. Sheep are kept throughout the region, and citrus fruits thrive on the Mediterranean coast. The successful forest industry in Iberia produces two-thirds of the world's cork.

The steep, terraced slopes of the Douro Valley in northern Portugal, are used to cultivate vines. The grapes harvested produce Portugal's famous port wine.

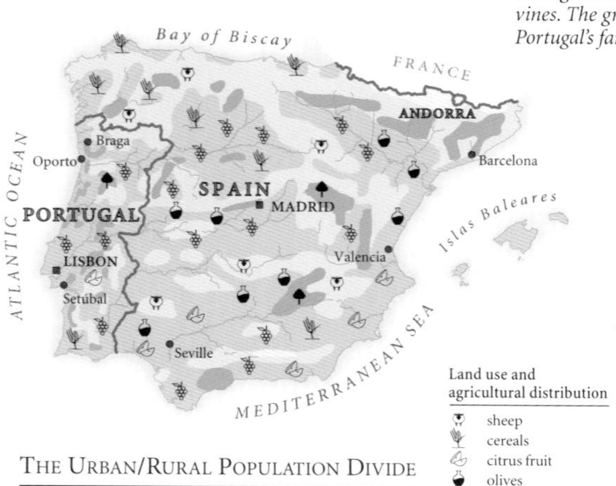

Land use and agricultural distribution

- sheep
- cereals
- citrus fruit
- olives
- vineyards
- cork
- capital cities
- major towns
- pasture
- cropland
- forest
- mountain region

THE URBAN/RURAL POPULATION DIVIDE

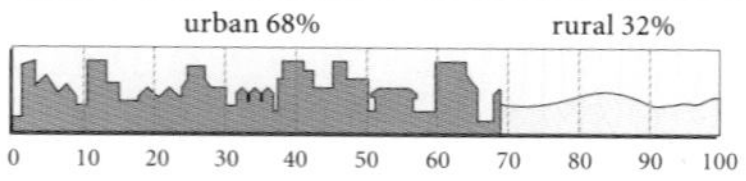

urban 68%   rural 32%

0 10 20 30 40 50 60 70 80 90 100

POPULATION DENSITY	TOTAL LAND AREA
215 people per sq mile (83 people per sq km)	230,569 sq miles (597,170 sq km)

TRANSPORT AND INDUSTRY

SINCE THE 1970s, the economies of Spain and Portugal have expanded and diversified. In both countries, tourism has outstripped agriculture in economic importance. Spain's resource base is varied, including coal, iron and the world's largest reserves of mercury. Portugal is a leading producer of tungsten ore.

Major industry and infrastructure

- car manufacture
- chemicals
- engineering
- fish processing
- mining
- textiles
- tourism
- capital cities
- major towns
- international airports
- major roads
- major industrial areas

THE TRANSPORT NETWORK

241,720 miles (388,990 km)	1552 miles (2529 km)
11,793 miles (18,979 km)	1159 miles (1865 km)

Radiating from Madrid, the road network in Spain dates from the 18th century, but now includes many motorways. Portugal's road system has been completely modernized in recent years.

The eroded cliffs of the Algarve in southern Portugal were carved by Atlantic waves. The numerous rocky bays and beaches, and the region's pleasant climate, have made it a popular tourist destination.

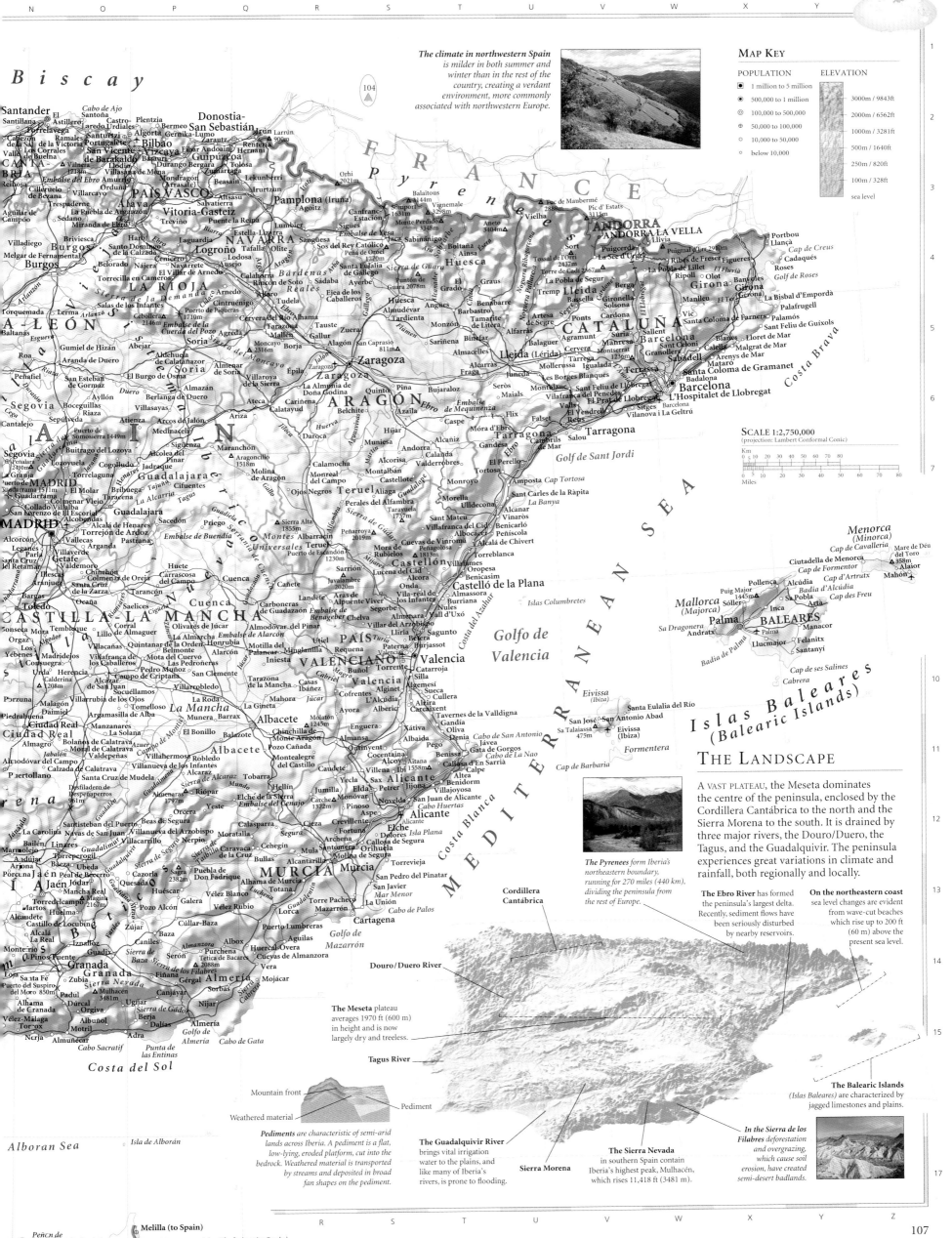

The climate in northwestern Spain is milder in both summer and winter than in the rest of the country, creating a verdant environment, more commonly associated with northwestern Europe.

MAP KEY

POPULATION

- ■ 1 million to 5 million
- ◉ 500,000 to 1 million
- ⊕ 100,000 to 500,000
- ⊕ 50,000 to 100,000
- ⊕ 10,000 to 50,000
- ○ below 10,000

ELEVATION

- 3000m / 9843ft
- 2000m / 6562ft
- 1000m / 3281ft
- 500m / 1640ft
- 250m / 820ft
- 100m / 328ft
- sea level

SCALE 1:2,750,000
(projection: Lambert Conformal Conic)

Km
Miles

THE LANDSCAPE

A VAST PLATEAU, the Meseta dominates the centre of the peninsula, enclosed by the Cordillera Cantábrica to the north and the Sierra Morena to the south. It is drained by three major rivers, the Douro/Duero, the Tagus, and the Guadalquivir. The peninsula experiences great variations in climate and rainfall, both regionally and locally.

The Pyrenees form Iberia's northeastern boundary, running for 270 miles (440 km), dividing the peninsula from the rest of Europe.

The Ebro River has formed the peninsula's largest delta. Recently, sediment flows have been seriously disturbed by nearby reservoirs.

On the northeastern coast sea level changes are evident from wave-cut beaches which rise up to 200 ft (60 m) above the present sea level.

Cordillera Cantábrica

Douro/Duero River

The Meseta plateau averages 1970 ft (600 m) in height and is now largely dry and treeless.

Tagus River

Mountain front
Pediment
Weathered material

Pediments are characteristic of semi-arid lands across Iberia. A pediment is a flat, low-lying, eroded platform, cut into the bedrock. Weathered material is transported by streams and deposited in broad fan shapes on the pediment.

The Guadalquivir River brings vital irrigation water to the plains, and like many of Iberia's rivers, is prone to flooding.

Sierra Morena

The Sierra Nevada in southern Spain contain Iberia's highest peak, Mulhacén, which rises 11,418 ft (3481 m).

The Balearic Islands (Islas Baleares) are characterized by jagged limestones and plains.

In the Sierra de los Filabres deforestation and overgrazing, which cause soil erosion, have created semi-desert badlands.

THE ITALIAN PENINSULA

ITALY, SAN MARINO, VATICAN CITY

THE ITALIAN PENINSULA is a land of great contrasts. Until unification in 1861, Italy was a collection of independent states, whose competitiveness during the Renaissance resulted in the architectural and artistic magnificence of cities such as Rome, Florence and Venice. The majority of Italy's population and economic activity is concentrated in the north, centred on the sophisticated industrial city of Milan. Southern Italy, the *Mezzogiorno*, has a harsh and difficult terrain, and remains far less developed than the north. Attempts to attract industry and investment in the south are frequently deterred by the entrenched network of organized crime and corruption.

THE LANDSCAPE

THE MAINLY MOUNTAINOUS and hilly Italian peninsula took its present form following a collision between the African and Eurasian tectonic plates. The Alps in the northwest rise to a high point of 15,772 ft (4807 m) at Mont Blanc (*Monte Bianco*) on the French border, while the Apennines (*Appennino*) form a rugged backbone, running along the entire length of the country.

The island of Sardinia is an ancient land mass; an uplifted section of very old igneous rocks. Its rugged mountainous regions provide pasture for sheep and goats, while its valleys support some agriculture.

Costa Smeralda

Mont Blanc (*Monte Bianco*)

The Dolomites (*Alpi Dolomitiche*) are formed of thick limestones, overlying weaker marine strata. They have distinctive serrated peaks and many massive landslides occur.

The distinctive square shape of the Gulf of Taranto (*Golfo di Taranto*) was defined by numerous block faults. Earthquakes are common in this region.

Vesuvius (*Vesuvio*)

The Pontine Marshes (*Agro Pontino*) are bounded by low sand hills which prevent natural drainage.

The Apennines (*Appennino*) are the source of most of Italy's rivers. They run 823 miles (1324 km) down the length of the peninsula.

The Po Valley once formed part of the Adriatic Sea. Sediments of gravel, sand and clay washed down from the Alps gradually filling the bay and forming a broad, cultivable plain.

The Strait of Messina (*Stretto di Messina*) is between 2 and 12 miles (3–19 km) wide, and is a rich fishing ground.

Sicily is the largest island in the Mediterranean at 9926 sq miles (25,708 sq km).

The southwestern tip of Sicily lies 95 miles (152 km) from the north African mainland and is part of the same geological region.

Sardinia is the second largest island in the Mediterranean Sea. The highest point is Punta La Marmora at 6017 ft (1834 m).

Vesuvius (*Vesuvio*)

Present-day crater has developed within the old crater of Monte Somma

Old crater

Monte Somma

Old crater

There have been four volcanoes on the site of Vesuvius since volcanic activity began here more than 10,000 years ago.

USING THE LAND

ITALY PRODUCES 95% of its own food. The best farming land is in the Po Valley in northern Italy, where soft wheat and rice are grown. Irrigation is essential to agriculture in much of the south. Italy is a major producer and exporter of citrus fruits, olives, tomatoes and wine.

THE URBAN/RURAL POPULATION DIVIDE

urban 67%   rural 33%

POPULATION DENSITY
492 people per sq mile
(190 people per sq km)

TOTAL LAND AREA
116,320 sq miles
(301,270 sq km)

Land use and agricultural distribution

cattle · capital cities
cereals · major towns
citrus fruits · pasture
olive oil · cropland
rice · forest
vineyards · mountain region

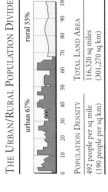
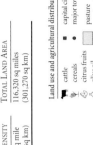
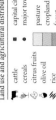

ITALY
ROME
SAN MARINO
Milan
Turin
Genoa
Florence
Bologna
Naples
Bari
Palermo
Catania
Sicily
Sardinia
Cagliari
Sassari

AUSTRIA
SLOVENIA
CROATIA
SWITZERLAND
FRANCE

Adriatic Sea
Tyrrhenian Sea
Ionian Sea
MEDITERRANEAN SEA

SCALE 1:2,500,000
(projection: Lambert Conformal Conic)

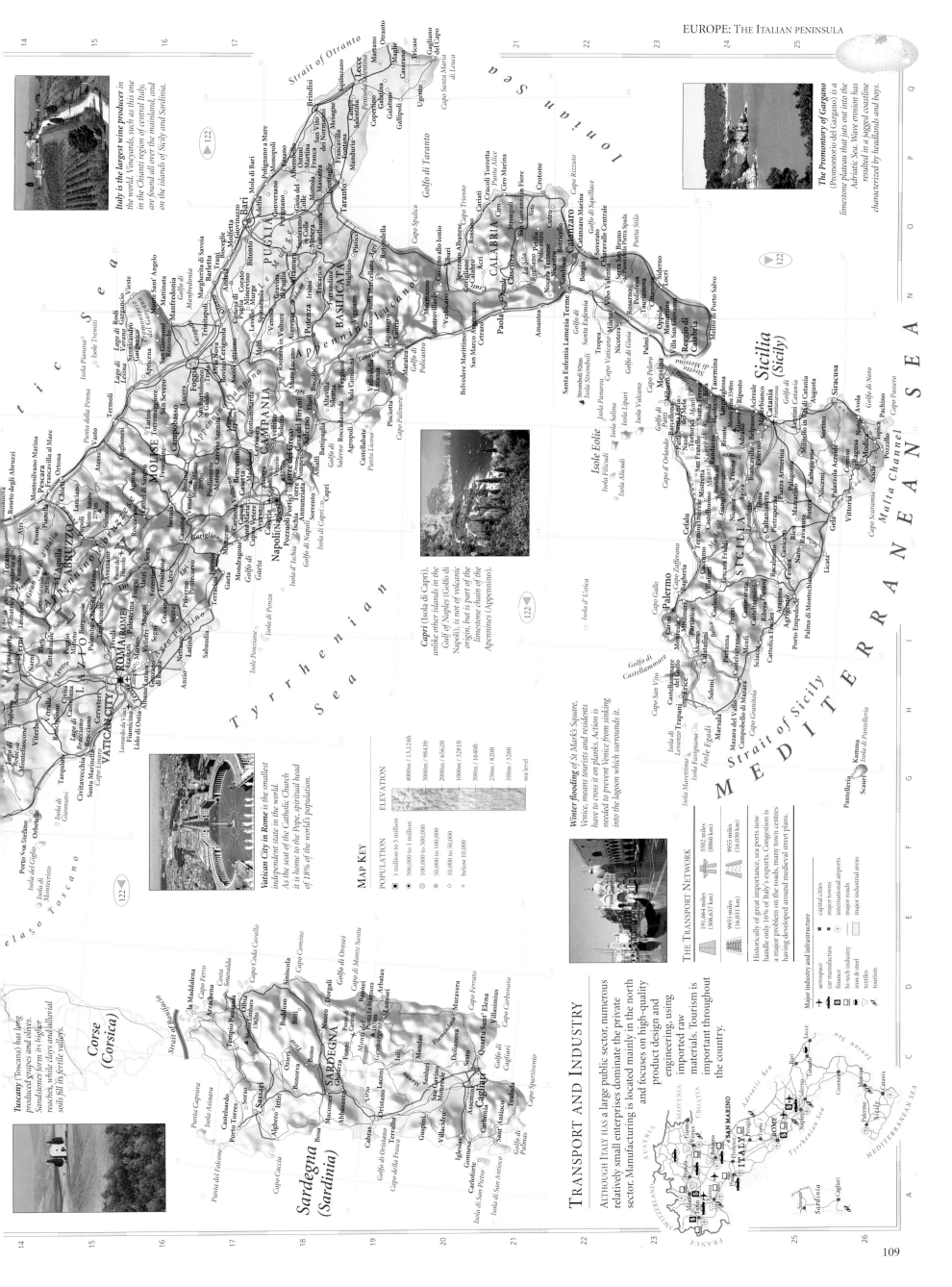

Italy is the largest wine producer in the world. Vineyards, such as this one in the Chianti region of central Italy, are found all over the mainland, and on the islands of Sicily and Sardinia.

The Promontory of Gargano (Promontorio del Gargano) is a limestone plateau that juts out into the Adriatic Sea. Wave erosion has resulted in a jagged coastline characterized by headlands and bays.

Tuscany (Toscana) has long produced grapes and olives. Sandstones form its higher reaches, while clays and alluvial soils fill its fertile valleys.

Capri (Isola di Capri), unlike other islands in the Gulf of Naples (Golfo di Napoli), is not of volcanic origin, but is part of the limestone chain of the Apennines (Appennino).

Vatican City in Rome is the smallest independent state in the world. As the seat of the Catholic Church it is home to the Pope, spiritual head of 18% of the world's population.

Winter flooding of St Mark's Square, Venice, means tourists and residents have to cross it on planks. Action is needed to prevent Venice from sinking into the lagoon which surrounds it.

MAP KEY

ELEVATION

	4000m / 13,124ft
	3000m / 9843ft
	2000m / 6562ft
	1000m / 3281ft
	500m / 1640ft
	250m / 820ft
	100m / 328ft
	sea level

POPULATION

- ■ 1 million to 5 million
- ● 500,000 to 1 million
- ◉ 100,000 to 500,000
- ⊕ 50,000 to 100,000
- ○ 10,000 to 50,000
- ○ below 10,000

THE TRANSPORT NETWORK

191,664 miles (308,457 km)	5592 miles (8860 km)
9955 miles (16,031 km)	9955 miles (16,030 km)

Historically of great importance, sea ports now handle only 16% of Italy's exports. Congestion is a major problem on the roads, many town centres having developed around medieval street plans.

- ● capital cities
- ○ major towns
- ✈ international airports
- major roads
- major industrial areas

TRANSPORT AND INDUSTRY

ALTHOUGH ITALY HAS a large public sector, numerous relatively small enterprises dominate the private sector. Manufacturing is located mainly in the north and focuses on high-quality product design and engineering, using imported raw materials. Tourism is important throughout the country.

Major industry and infrastructure

- ✈ aerospace
- 🚗 car manufacture
- S finance
- hi-tech industry
- iron & steel industry
- textiles
- tourism

109

THE ALPINE STATES

AUSTRIA, LIECHTENSTEIN, SLOVENIA, SWITZERLAND

THE ALPINE COUNTRIES of Austria, Switzerland, Liechtenstein and Slovenia form a narrow strip across western Europe's geographical core, lying on the main north–south trading routes across the Alps. Switzerland, politically neutral since 1815, is an important international meeting place and houses one of the headquarters of the United Nations, although not itself a member. Austria, once at the heart of the great Habsburg Empire has been a fully independent nation since 1955, and maintains a deserved reputation as an international centre of culture. Slovenia declared independence from the former Yugoslavia in 1991 and despite initial economic hardship, is now starting to achieve the prosperity enjoyed by its Alpine neighbours.

USING THE LAND

THE ALPINE REGION'S mountainous terrain discourages cultivation over much of the land area. The primary agricultural activity is the raising of dairy and beef cattle on the pasture land of the lower mountain slopes. Austria is self-supporting in grains, and crops such as wheat, barley and grapes are grown on the east Austrian lowlands. Woodlands are more prevalent in the eastern Alps; both Austria and Slovenia have large tracts of forest.

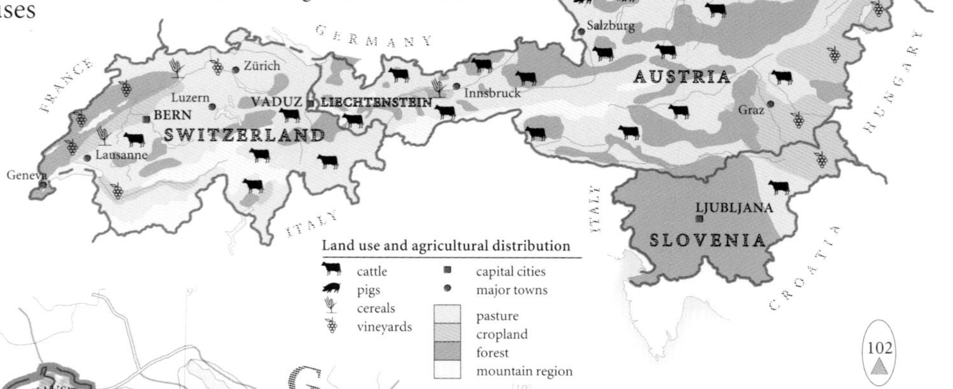

Land use and agricultural distribution

- cattle
- pigs
- cereals
- vineyards
- capital cities
- major towns
- pasture
- cropland
- forest
- mountain region

The Matterhorn, on the Swiss-Italian border, is one of the highest mountains in the Alps, at 14,692 ft (4478 m). The term 'horn' refers to its distinctive peak, formed by three glaciers eroding hollows, known as cirques, in each of its sides.

THE LANDSCAPE

THE ALPS OCCUPY THREE-FIFTHS OF SWITZERLAND, most of southern Austria and the northwest of Slovenia. They were formed by the collision of the African and Eurasian tectonic plates, which began 65 million years ago. Their complex geology is reflected in the differing heights and rock types of the various ranges. The Rhine flows along Liechtenstein's border with Switzerland, creating a broad flood plain in the north and west of Liechtenstein. In the far northeast and east are a number of lowland regions, including the Vienna Basin, Burgenland and the plain of the Danube. Slovenia's major rivers flow across the lower eastern regions; in the west, the rivers flow underground through the limestone Karst region.

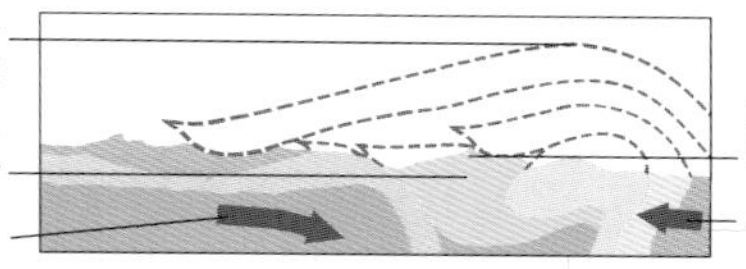

Original height after uplift and folding

Folded strata are overturned creating a *nappe*

Eurasian Plate

Present-day height of Alps

African Plate

The convergence of the African and Eurasian plates compressed and folded huge masses of rock strata. As the plates continued to move together, the folded strata were overturned, creating complex nappes. Much of the rock strata has since been eroded, resulting in the current topography of the Alps.

Constricted as it cuts through ridges in the Alps, the Danube meanders across the lowlands, where uplift combined with river erosion has deepened meanders.

The Vienna Basin lies mainly below 390 ft (120 m). It gradually subsided and filled with sediment as the Alps were uplifted.

Neusiedler See straddles the border of Austria and Hungary; the area around it provides some of the best wine-growing land in Austria.

The mountains of the Jura form a natural border between Switzerland and France. Their marine limestones date from over 200 million years ago. When the Alps were formed the Jura were folded into a series of parallel ridges and troughs.

Tectonic activity has resulted in dramatic changes in land height over very short distances. Lake Geneva, lying at 1221 ft (372 m) is only 43 miles (70 km) away from the 15,772 ft (4807 m) peak of Mont Blanc, on the France–Italy border.

The Bernese Alps (Berner Alpen) contain the Aletsch, which at 15 miles (24 km) is the longest Alpine glacier.

The Rhine, like other major Alpine rivers, follows a broad, flat trough between the mountains. Along part of its course, the Rhine forms the boundary between Switzerland and Liechtenstein.

The deep, blue lakes of the Karst region are part of a drainage network which runs largely underground through this limestone area.

The first road through the Brenner Pass was built in 1772, although it has been used as a mountain route since Roman times. It is the lowest of the main Alpine passes at 4298 ft (1374 m).

Karst region

The limestone cave system at Postojna extends for more than 10 miles (16 km) and includes caverns reaching 125 ft (40 m) in height and width.

The Austrian Alps comprise three distinct mountain ranges, separated by deep trenches. The northern and southern ranges are rugged limestones, while the Tauern range is formed of crystalline rocks.

The Tauern range in the central Austrian Alps contains the highest mountain in Austria, the towering Grossglockner, rising 12,461 ft (3798 m).

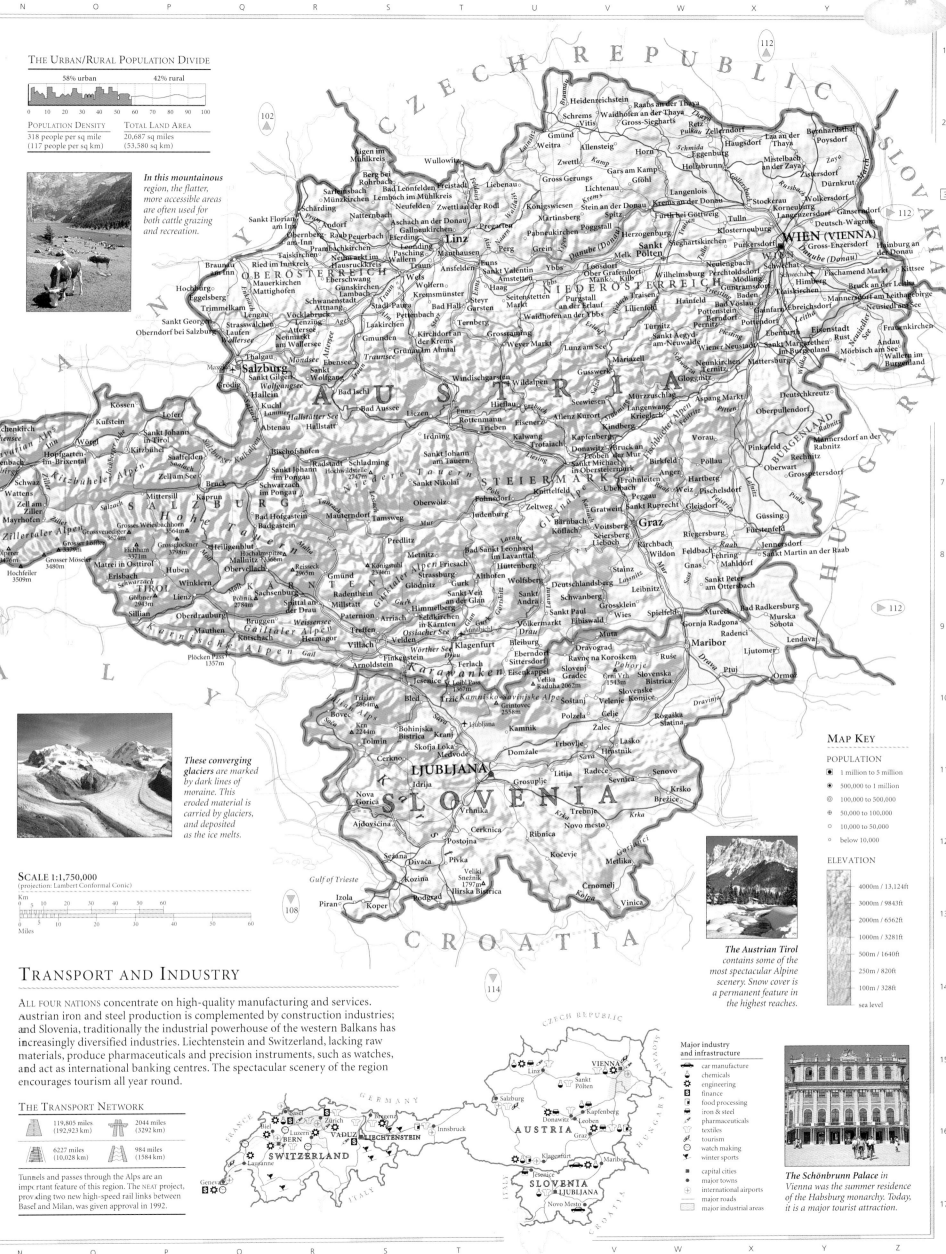

THE URBAN/RURAL POPULATION DIVIDE

58% urban   42% rural

POPULATION DENSITY
318 people per sq mile
(117 people per sq km)

TOTAL LAND AREA
20,687 sq miles
(53,580 sq km)

In this mountainous region, the flatter, more accessible areas are often used for both cattle grazing and recreation.

These converging glaciers are marked by dark lines of moraine. This eroded material is carried by glaciers, and deposited as the ice melts.

SCALE 1:1,750,000
(projection: Lambert Conformal Conic)

Km 0 10 20 30 40 50 60
Miles 0 10 20 30 40 50 60

MAP KEY

POPULATION
- 1 million to 5 million
- 500,000 to 1 million
- 100,000 to 500,000
- 50,000 to 100,000
- 10,000 to 50,000
- below 10,000

ELEVATION
4000m / 13,124ft
3000m / 9843ft
2000m / 6562ft
1000m / 3281ft
500m / 1640ft
250m / 820ft
100m / 328ft
sea level

The Austrian Tirol contains some of the most spectacular Alpine scenery. Snow cover is a permanent feature in the highest reaches.

TRANSPORT AND INDUSTRY

ALL FOUR NATIONS concentrate on high-quality manufacturing and services. Austrian iron and steel production is complemented by construction industries; and Slovenia, traditionally the industrial powerhouse of the western Balkans has increasingly diversified industries. Liechtenstein and Switzerland, lacking raw materials, produce pharmaceuticals and precision instruments, such as watches, and act as international banking centres. The spectacular scenery of the region encourages tourism all year round.

THE TRANSPORT NETWORK

119,805 miles (192,923 km)   2044 miles (3292 km)
6227 miles (10,028 km)   984 miles (1584 km)

Tunnels and passes through the Alps are an important feature of this region. The NEAT project, providing two new high-speed rail links between Basel and Milan, was given approval in 1992.

Major industry and infrastructure
- car manufacture
- chemicals
- engineering
- finance
- food processing
- iron & steel
- pharmaceuticals
- textiles
- tourism
- watch making
- winter sports
- capital cities
- major towns
- international airports
- major roads
- major industrial areas

The Schönbrunn Palace in Vienna was the summer residence of the Habsburg monarchy. Today, it is a major tourist attraction.

CENTRAL EUROPE

CZECH REPUBLIC, HUNGARY, POLAND, SLOVAKIA

WHEN SLOVAKIA AND THE CZECH REPUBLIC became separate countries in 1993, they joined Hungary and Poland in a new role as independent nation states, following centuries of shifting boundaries and imperial strife. This turbulent history bequeathed the region a rich cultural heritage, shared through the works of its many great writers and composers, and celebrated in the vibrant historic capitals of Prague, Budapest and Warsaw. Having shaken off Soviet domination in 1989, these states are facing up to the challenge of winning commercial investment to modernize outmoded industry, while bearing the severe environmental impact from forty years of large-scale industrialization.

THE LANDSCAPE

THE FORESTED Carpathian Mountains, uplifted with the Alps, lie southeast of the older Bohemian massif, which contains the Sudeten and Krušné Hory (Erzgebirge) ranges. They divide the fertile plains of the Danube to the south and the Vistula (Wisła), which flows north across vast expanses of glacial deposits into the Baltic Sea.

TRANSPORT AND INDUSTRY

HEAVY INDUSTRY HAS DOMINATED POST-WAR LIFE in Central Europe. Poland has large coal reserves, having inherited the Silesian coalfield from Germany after the Second World War, allowing the export of large quantities of coal, along with other minerals. Hungary specializes in consumer goods and services, while Slovakia's industrial base is still relatively small. The Czech Republic's traditional glassworks and breweries bring some stability to its precarious Soviet-built manufacturing sector.

The huge growth of tourism and business has prompted major investment in the transport infrastructure, with new road-building schemes within and between the main cities of the region.

THE TRANSPORT NETWORK

213,997 miles (344,600 km)	817 miles (1315 km)
27,479 miles (44,249 km)	3784 miles (6094 km)

Major industry and infrastructure

- car manufacture
- chemicals
- engineering
- food processing
- mining
- shipbuilding
- tourism
- capital cities
- major towns
- international airports
- major roads
- major industrial areas

Map callouts

The Biebrza River has left meanders and oxbow lakes as it flows across low-lying ground.

Gerlachovský štít, in the Tatra Mountains, is Slovakia's highest mountain, at 8711ft (2655 m).

Carpathian Mountains

Danube River

Slip-off slope

Bluff

Direction of flow

Meanders form as rivers flow across plains at a low gradient. A steep cliff or bluff, forms on the outside curve, and a gentler slip-off slope on the inside bend.

Pomerania is a sandy coastal region of glacially-formed lakes stretching west from the Vistula (Wisła).

The Great Hungarian Plain formed by the flood plain of the Danube is a mixture of steppe and cultivated land, covering nearly half of Hungary's total area.

Longshore currents moving east along the Baltic coast have built a 40 mile (65 km) spit composed of material from the Vistula (Wisła) River.

Hot mineral springs occur where geothermally heated water wells up through faults and fractures in the rocks of the Sudeten Mountains.

The Slovak Ore Mountains (Slovenské Rudohorie) are noted for their mineral resources, including high-grade iron ore.

Bohemian Massif

Krušné Hory (Erzgebirge)

The Berounka River cuts through the precipitous wooded landscape of the Bohemian massif, banked by a broad flood plain.

Budapest, the capital of Hungary, straddles the Danube. It comprises the historic towns of Buda, on the west bank, and Pest, which contains the Parliament Building, seen here on the far bank.

USING THE LAND

CEREALS, SUGAR BEET AND POTATOES are
Central Europe's main crops, along
with hops for the Czech breweries,
sweet peppers for paprika,
sunflowers and vines in milder
areas. The plains of Poland
and Hungary are well-suited
to livestock-rearing, while
forestry is important in
the mountains of Slovakia.

Land use and
agricultural distribution

- capital cities
- major towns

Land use and agricultural distribution

- cattle
- pigs
- cereals
- potatoes
- root crops
- timber
- vineyards

- pasture
- cropland
- forest

*Hay, used to feed livestock,
is one of the major crops grown
on the fertile foothills of Slovakia's
Tatra Mountains.*

THE URBAN/RURAL POPULATION DIVIDE

urban 65%   rural 35%

POPULATION DENSITY	TOTAL LAND AREA
312 people per sq mile (120 people per sq km)	201,561 sq miles (522,180 sq km)

MAP KEY

POPULATION
- ■ 1 million to 5 million
- ◉ 500,000 to 1 million
- ⊕ 100,000 to 500,000
- ○ 50,000 to 100,000
- ○ 10,000 to 50,000
- ○ below 10,000

ELEVATION
- 2000m / 6562ft
- 1000m / 3281ft
- 500m / 1640ft
- 250m / 820ft
- 100m / 328ft
- sea level

SCALE 1:2,500,000
(projection: Lambert Conformal Conic)

*The upper Dunajec
River of Poland and
eastern Slovakia forms
a gorge through the
Pieniny range of the
Carpathian Mountains.*

SOUTHEAST EUROPE

ALBANIA, BOSNIA & HERZEGOVINA, CROATIA, MACEDONIA, YUGOSLAVIA

FOR 46 YEARS THE FEDERATION of Yugoslavia held together the most diverse ethnic region in Europe, along the picturesque mountain hinterland of the Dalmatian coast. Economic collapse resulted in internal tensions. In the early 1990s, civil war broke out in both Croatia and Bosnia as the ethnic populations struggled to establish their own exclusive territories. Peace was only restored by the UN after NATO launched air strikes in 1995. In the province of Kosovo, attempts to gain autonomy from Yugoslavia in 1998 were crushed by the Serbian government. The slaughter of ethnic Albanians in Kosovo provoked the West to launch NATO air strikes yet again in the region, and Yugoslav forces withdrew. The flood of refugees from Kosovo has strained Albania severely.

THE LANDSCAPE

THE TISZA, SAVA AND DRAVA RIVERS drain the broad northern lowland, meeting the Danube after it crosses the Hungarian border. In the west, the Dinaric Alps divide the Adriatic Sea from the interior. Mainland valleys and elongated islands run parallel to the steep Dalmatian (Dalmacija) coastline, following alternating bands of resistant limestone.

Poljes in the Kosovo region

Sheer limestone walls enclose all sides

Flat polje floor

Underground drainage along joints in the rock

Spring at foot of cliff

Rain and underground water dissolve limestone along massive vertical joints (cracks). This creates poljes: depressions several miles across with steep walls and broad, flat floors.

At Iron Gate (derdap), on the border with Romania, the Danube narrows and cuts through foothills of the Balkan and Carpathian mountains, forming the deepest gorge in Europe.

A major earthquake at Skopje, Macedonia, in 1963 killed 1000 people. The whole region lies on an active crustal plate margin.

Lake Ohrid

Lake Ohrid borders Albania and Macedonia. Ohrid is the deepest lake in the Western Balkans, reaching depths of 938 ft (286 m).

The river flood plains of the Pannonian Basin are flanked by terraces of gravel and wind-blown glacial deposits known as loess.

At least 70% of the fresh water in the Western Balkans drains eastwards into the Black Sea, mostly via the Danube (Dunav).

Tisza River

Drava River

Sava River

The elongated islands, promontories and straits of the Dalmatian (Dalmacija) coast were formed as the Adriatic Sea rose to flood valleys running parallel to the shore.

Dalmatian (Dalmacija) coast

A series of river valleys breaking through the Dinaric Alps from the lowlands of western Albania, give access to the interior.

Limestone cliffs along the Dalmatian (Dalmacija) shoreline are heavily eroded, as salt water dissolves the rock along existing horizontal cracks, or joints. This tends to form a platform of rock at the foot of the cliff.

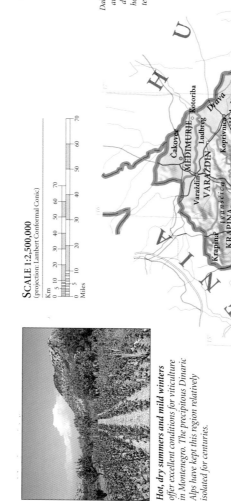

Hot, dry summers and mild winters offer excellent conditions for viticulture in Montenegro. The precipitous Dinaric Alps have kept this region relatively isolated for centuries.

SCALE 1:2,500,000
(projection: Lambert Conformal Conic)

Km
0 5 10 20 30 40 50 60 70

Miles
0 5 10 20 30 40 50 60 70

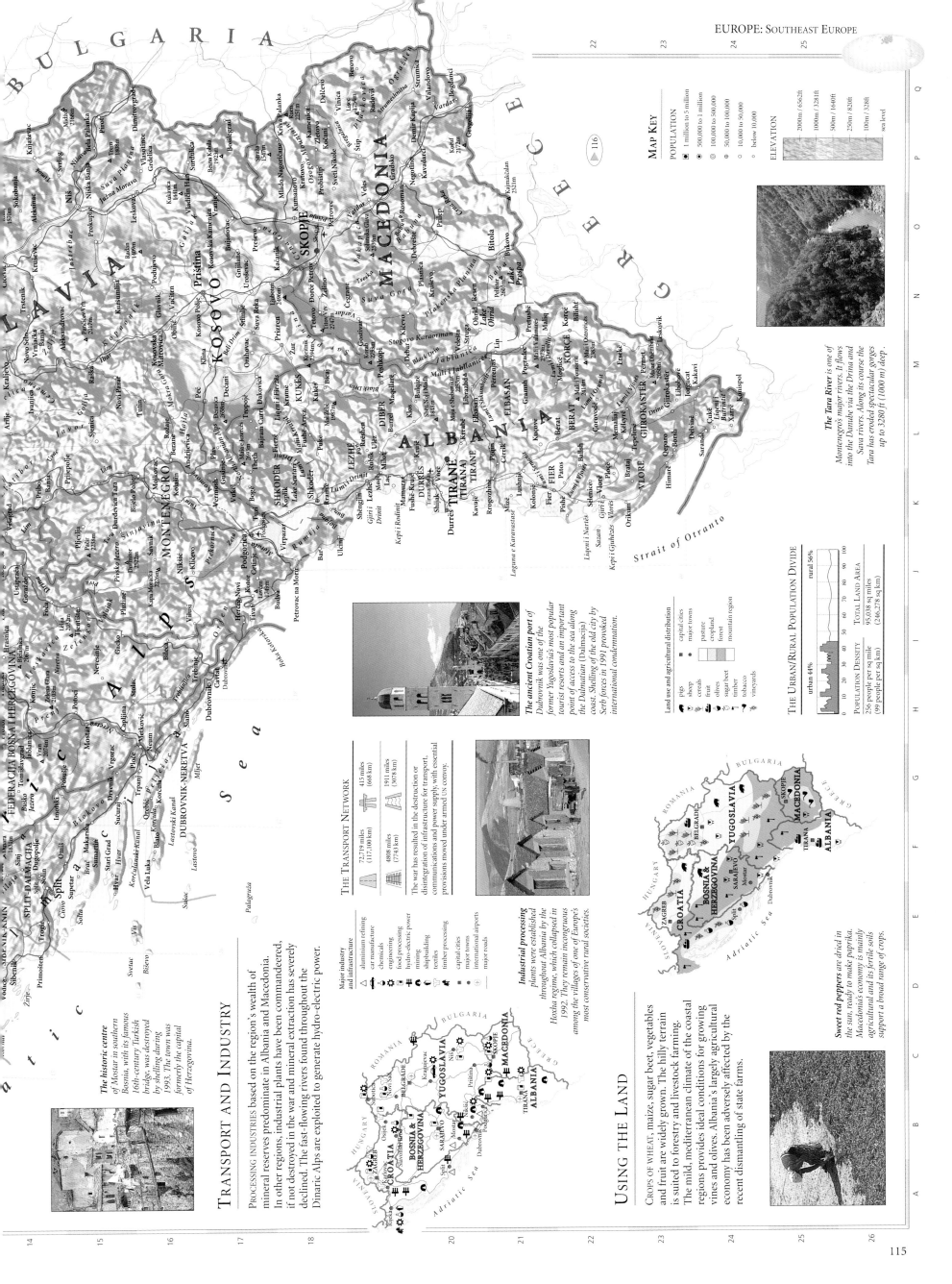

TRANSPORT AND INDUSTRY

PROCESSING INDUSTRIES based on the region's wealth of mineral reserves predominate in Albania and Macedonia. In other regions, industrial plants have been commandeered, if not destroyed in the war and mineral extraction has severely declined. The fast-flowing rivers found throughout the Dinaric Alps are exploited to generate hydro-electric power.

The historic centre of Mostar in southern Bosnia, with its famous 16th-century Turkish bridge, was destroyed by shelling during 1993. The town was formerly the capital of Herzegovina.

THE TRANSPORT NETWORK

72,719 miles (117,100 km)		415 miles (668 km)	
4808 miles (7743 km)		1911 miles (3078 km)	

The war has resulted in the destruction or disintegration of infrastructure for transport, communications and power supply, with essential provisions moved under armed UN convoy.

The ancient Croatian port of Dubrovnik was one of the former Yugoslavia's most popular tourist resorts and an important point of access to the sea along the Dalmatian (Dalmacija) coast. Shelling of the old city by Serb forces in 1991 provoked international condemnation.

Major industry and infrastructure

- aluminium refining
- car manufacture
- chemicals
- engineering
- food processing
- hydro-electric power
- mining
- shipbuilding
- textiles
- timber processing
- capital cities
- major towns
- international airports
- major roads

Industrial processing plants were established throughout Albania by the Hoxha regime, which collapsed in 1992. They remain incongruous among the villages of one of Europe's most conservative rural societies.

USING THE LAND

CROPS OF WHEAT, maize, sugar beet, vegetables and fruit are widely grown. The hilly terrain is suited to forestry and livestock farming. The mild, mediterranean climate of the coastal regions provides ideal conditions for growing vines and olives. Albania's largely agricultural economy has been adversely affected by the recent dismantling of state farms.

Land use and agricultural distribution

- pigs
- sheep
- cereals
- fruit
- olives
- sugar beet
- tobacco
- vineyards
- capital cities
- major towns
- pasture
- cropland
- forest
- mountain region

Sweet red peppers are dried in the sun, ready to make paprika. Macedonia's economy is mainly agricultural and its fertile soils support a broad range of crops.

THE URBAN/RURAL POPULATION DIVIDE

urban 44%   rural 56%

POPULATION DENSITY	TOTAL LAND AREA
256 people per sq mile (99 people per sq km)	95,038 sq miles (246,278 sq km)

The Tara River is one of Montenegro's major rivers. It flows into the Danube via the Drina and Sava rivers. Along its course the Tara has eroded spectacular gorges up to 3280 ft (1000 m) deep.

MAP KEY

POPULATION

- ● 1 million to 5 million
- ● 500,000 to 1 million
- ● 100,000 to 500,000
- ● 50,000 to 100,000
- ○ 10,000 to 50,000
- ○ below 10,000

ELEVATION

2000m / 6562ft	
1000m / 3281ft	
500m / 1640ft	
250m / 820ft	
100m / 328ft	
sea level	

BULGARIA & GREECE

Including EUROPEAN TURKEY

GREECE IS RENOWNED as the original hearth of Western civilization. The rugged terrain and numerous islands have profoundly affected its development, creating a strong agricultural and maritime tradition. In the past 50 years, this formerly rural society has rapidly urbanized, with more than half the population now living in the capital, Athens, and in the northern city of Salonica. Bulgaria, dominated for centuries by the Ottoman Turks, became part of the eastern bloc after the Second World War, only slowly emerging from Soviet influence in 1989. Moves towards democracy have led to some political instability and Bulgaria has been slow to align its economy with the rest of Europe.

TRANSPORT AND INDUSTRY

SOVIET INVESTMENT introduced heavy industry into Bulgaria, and the processing of agricultural produce, such as tobacco, is important throughout the country. Both countries have substantial shipyards and Greece has one of the world's largest merchant fleets. Many small craft workshops, producing textiles and processed foods, are clustered around Greek cities. The service and construction sectors have profited from the successful tourist industry.

Major industry and infrastructure
- chemicals
- engineering
- food processing
- shipbuilding
- textiles
- tourism
- capital cities
- major towns
- international airports
- major roads
- major industrial areas

THE TRANSPORT NETWORK

- 103,930 miles (167,630 km)
- 345 miles (557 km)
- 4346 miles (6995 km)
- 294 miles (474 km)

Bulgaria's railways require investment to revive an outdated infrastructure. In Greece, despite a developing road network, ferry-boats remain the most effective form of transport in many areas.

A towering pinnacle at Metéora in central Greece is home to the monastery of Roussanou. The 24 rock towers which dominate the plain of Thessaly (Thessalia) are remnants of an old plateau. Long-term weathering along fissures in the rock has worn away the plateau.

THE LANDSCAPE

BULGARIA'S BALKAN MOUNTAINS divide the Danubian Plain (*Dunavska Ravnina*) and Maritsa Basin, meeting the Black Sea in the east along sandy beaches. The steep Rhodope Mountains form a natural barrier with Greece, while the younger Pindus form a rugged central spine which descends into the Aegean Sea to give a vast archipelago of over 2000 islands, the largest of which is Crete.

Mount Olympus is the mythical home of the Greek Gods and, at 9570 ft (2917 m), is the highest mountain in Greece.

Mount Olympus is a composite of rocks formed by two major tectonic events. First the older metamorphic rocks were thrust over the limestones, then two million years ago regional warping and subsequent erosion, re-exposed the limestone.

Mount Olympus
- Ancient metamorphic rock, formed miles below the surface
- Limestone rocks exposed by erosion of metamorphic rocks
- Younger limestones created in shallow seas

The Peloponnese consist of several mountainous peninsulas, linked to the mainland by the Isthmus of Corinth. The Corinth Canal (*Dioryga Korinthou*), built in 1893, cuts through the isthmus, linking the Aegean and Ionian seas.

The Danube, Europe's second longest river, forms most of Bulgaria's northern border. The Danubian Plain (*Dunavska Ravnina*), extending from the southern bank, is extremely fertile.

The Arda river cuts through the Rhodope mountains in rugged, rocky gorges.

The islands of Crete, Kythira, Karpathos and Rhodes are part of an arc which bends southeastwards from the Peloponnese, forming the southern boundary of the Aegean.

Layers of black volcanic ash still cover the island of Thira. This volcano last erupted 3500 years ago, but still shows signs of volcanic activity.

Balkan Mountains
Maritsa Basin
Rhodope Mountains
Pindus Mountains
Crete
Kythira
Karpathos
Rhodes
Corinth Canal (*Dioryga Korinthou*)

SCALE 1:2,500,000
(projection: Lambert Conformal Conic)

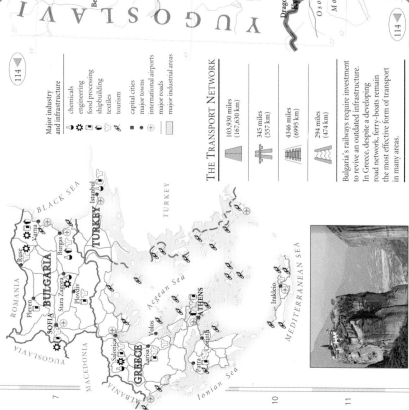

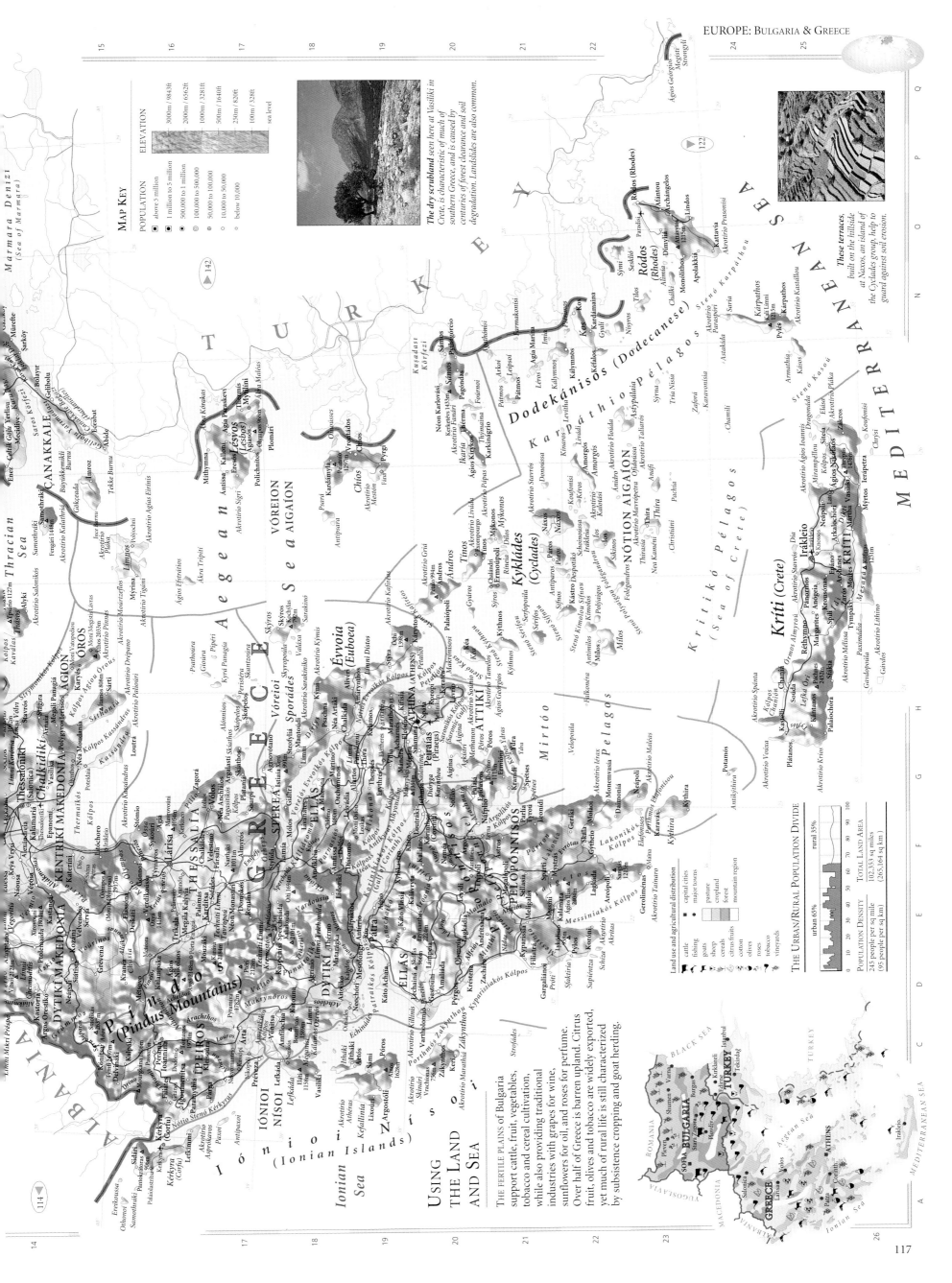

The dry scrubland seen here at Vasiliki in Crete, is characteristic of much of southern Greece, and is caused by centuries of forest clearance and soil degradation. Landslides are also common.

These terraces, built on the hillside at Naxos, an island of the Cyclades group, help to guard against soil erosion.

USING THE LAND AND SEA

THE FERTILE PLAINS of Bulgaria support cattle, fruit, vegetables, tobacco and cereal cultivation, while also providing traditional industries with grapes for wine, sunflowers for oil, and roses for perfume. Citrus fruit, olives and tobacco are widely exported, yet much of rural life is still characterized by subsistence cropping and goat herding.

THE URBAN/RURAL POPULATION DIVIDE

urban 65%	rural 35%

POPULATION DENSITY	TOTAL LAND AREA
245 people per sq mile (95 people per sq km)	102,353 sq miles (265,164 sq km)

Land use and agricultural distribution

capital cities
major towns

pasture
cropland
forest
mountain region

cattle
fishing
goats
sheep
cereals
citrus fruits
cotton
olives
roses
tobacco
vineyards

ROMANIA, MOLDOVA & UKRAINE

THE INDUSTRIAL, SOCIAL AND CULTURAL make-up of Romania and the former Soviet states of Moldova and Ukraine still bear the imprint of their communist past. As part of the USSR, Ukraine was a leading agricultural, industrial and energy producer. These industries, like those in Moldova and Romania, are now being reoriented more firmly towards Western markets. As a result of shifting borders, and Soviet policy actively encouraging Russian immigration into other Soviet states like Ukraine and Moldova, all three countries now contain large numbers of foreign nationals. Moldovans and Romanians are still close in terms of language and culture, although Moldova is striving to remain an independent nation.

USING THE LAND

THE FERTILE BLACK SOILS of Ukraine, often called 'the breadbasket of Europe', have enabled the cultivation of a variety of cereals and vegetables, which are widely exported. Romania and Moldova also grow cereals, sunflowers and vegetables, and are noted for the quality of their wines.

The fertile lands and tolerant climate of Moldova are ideally suited to growing grapes for wine.

Land use and agricultural distribution
- cattle
- pigs
- poultry
- sheep
- cereals
- cotton
- sugar beet
- sunflowers
- vineyards
- capital cities
- major towns
- pasture
- cropland
- forest
- wetland

THE URBAN/RURAL POPULATION DIVIDE

urban 65%   rural 35%

POPULATION DENSITY	TOTAL LAND AREA
232 people per sq mile (89 people per sq km)	334,947 sq miles (867,740 sq km)

Glacial lakes are found throughout the Transylvanian Alps (Carpaţii Meridionali), although the mountains no longer have any permanent snow cover.

TRANSPORT AND INDUSTRY

HEAVY INDUSTRY using local raw materials characterizes much of this region. The industrial heartland of Ukraine, specializing in metal and machine-building industries, is based around its vast mineral reserves in the Donbass region. In Moldova, food processing draws on produce from its agricultural sector. Romanian industry relies both on local raw materials and imported iron, steel and oil.

Major industry and infrastructure
- car manufacture
- chemicals
- coal
- engineering
- food processing
- mining
- oil & gas
- textiles
- tourism
- capital cities
- major towns
- international airports
- major roads
- major industrial areas

THE TRANSPORT NETWORK

151,089 miles (243,300 km)	70 miles (113 km)
21,889 miles (35,248 km)	3803 miles (6124 km)

Increased industrialization has necessitated the upgrading of road and rail networks in all three countries. Modernization has tended to focus only on major cities and industrial areas.

During the 1960s and 1970s, many industries, like this carbon factory, developed using the mineral resources on the flanks of the Transylvanian Alps (Carpaţii Meridionali).

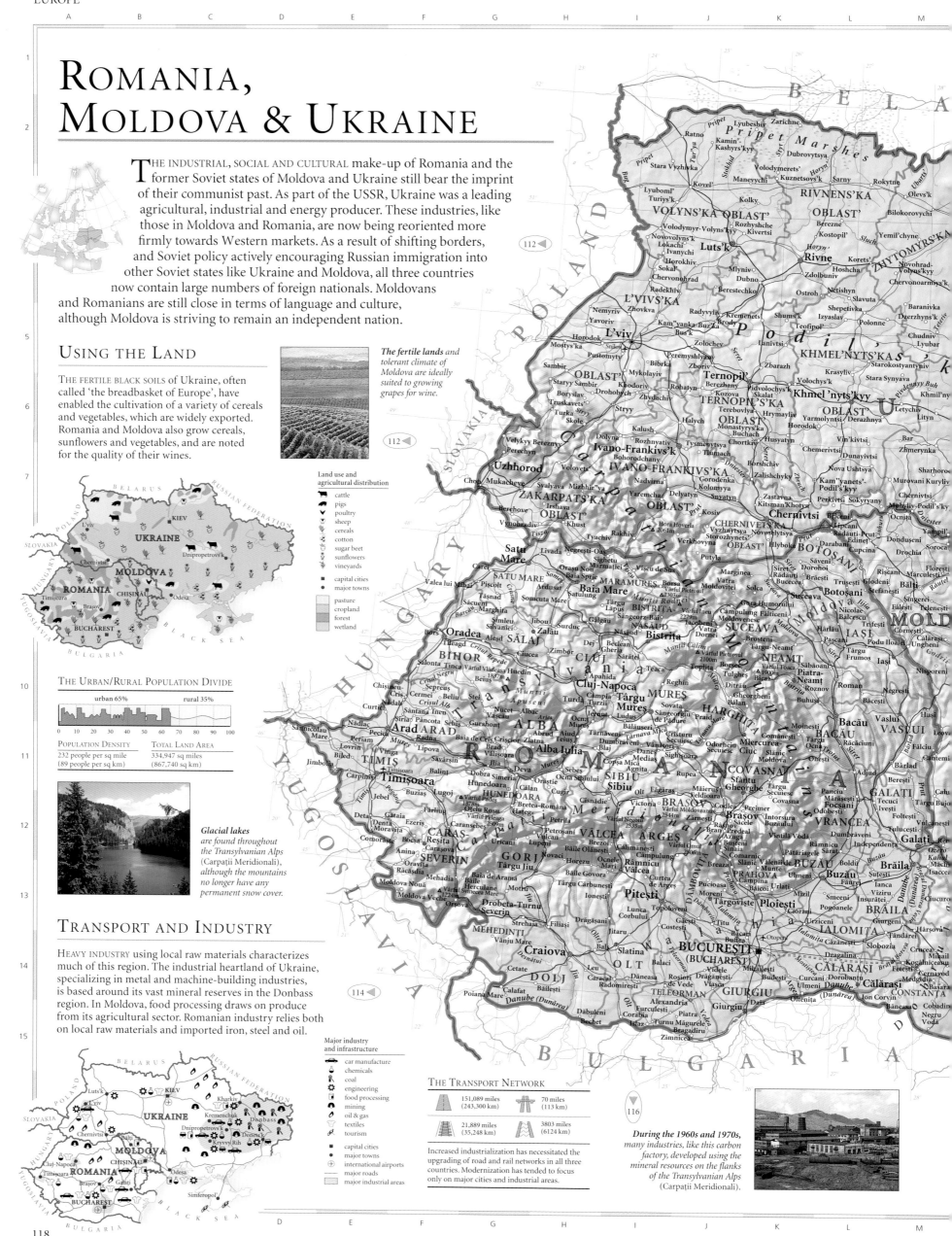

SCALE 1:3,250,000
(projection: Lambert Conformal Conic)

Km
0 10 20 30 40 50 60 70 80 90 100

Miles
0 10 20 30 40 50 60 70 80 90 100

MAP KEY

POPULATION
- 1 million to 5 million
- 500,000 to 1 million
- 100,000 to 500,000
- 50,000 to 100,000
- 10,000 to 50,000
- below 10,000

ELEVATION
- 2000m / 6562ft
- 1000m / 3281ft
- 500m / 1640ft
- 250m / 820ft
- 100m / 328ft
- sea level

The Swallow's Nest castle at Yalta is one of many tourist resorts on the Crimean (Krym) coast, dubbed the 'Russian riviera'.

THE LANDSCAPE

VAST FLAT LOWLANDS and gently rolling hills cover most of southeastern Europe. In the southwest, the Carpathian Mountains form a gentle arc. To the south of the Carpathian Mountains lies the Danube Plain, across which the Danube River flows to the Black Sea. To the north and east, the hills of Moldova level out into low plains, running east to the steppes of Ukraine.

Divided into crystalline massifs, the southern arm of the Carpathian Mountains, the Transylvanian Alps (Carpaţii Meridionali), extend 170 miles (274 km) across southwestern Romania.

Uplifted and folded at the same time as the Alps, some 250 miles (400 km) of the eastern Carpathian Mountains contain ancient volcanic cones and craters.

The Apuseni Mountains (*Munţii Apuşeni*) are rich in mineral deposits, including gold and iron ore.

Transylvanian Alps (*Carpaţii Meridionali*)

The Danube forms a natural border between Romania and Bulgaria.

The Codrii Hills dominate the landscape of central Moldova; they are intersected by deep, flat valleys and ravines.

Steppe landscape covers two-thirds of Ukraine. These flat, treeless grasslands extend from central Europe to central Asia.

Most of the major rivers in southeastern Europe, like the Danube, the Dniester and Dnieper flow south and east to the Black Sea.

The three branches of the Danube Delta (*Delta Dunării*) form a triangle of wetlands covering some 1950 sq miles (5050 sq km).

At Kryms'ki Hory, three flat-topped, parallel limestone ridges run 80 miles (128 km) along the southern coast of the Crimean (*Krym*) Peninsula.

Balkas are common throughout Ukraine. They are large U-shaped valleys, formed during the last Ice Age, which contain narrower, deep valleys. These were incised by a sudden flow of water, following an ice melt.

Anti-clockwise currents have created the sandspits which fringe the Sea of Azov.

Water has eroded a new post-glacial valley

Old glaciated valley

THE BALTIC STATES & BELARUS

BELARUS, ESTONIA, LATVIA, LITHUANIA, KALININGRAD

OCCUPYING EUROPE's main corridor to Russia, the four distinct cultures of Estonia, Latvia, Lithuania and Belarus share a history of struggle for nationhood against the interests of more powerful neighbours. As the first republics to declare their independence from the Soviet Union in 1990–91, the Baltic states of Estonia, Latvia and Lithuania have sought an economic role in the EU, while reaffirming their European cultural roots through the church and a strong musical tradition. Meanwhile, Belarus has shown economic and political allegiance to Russia by joining the Commonwealth of Independent States.

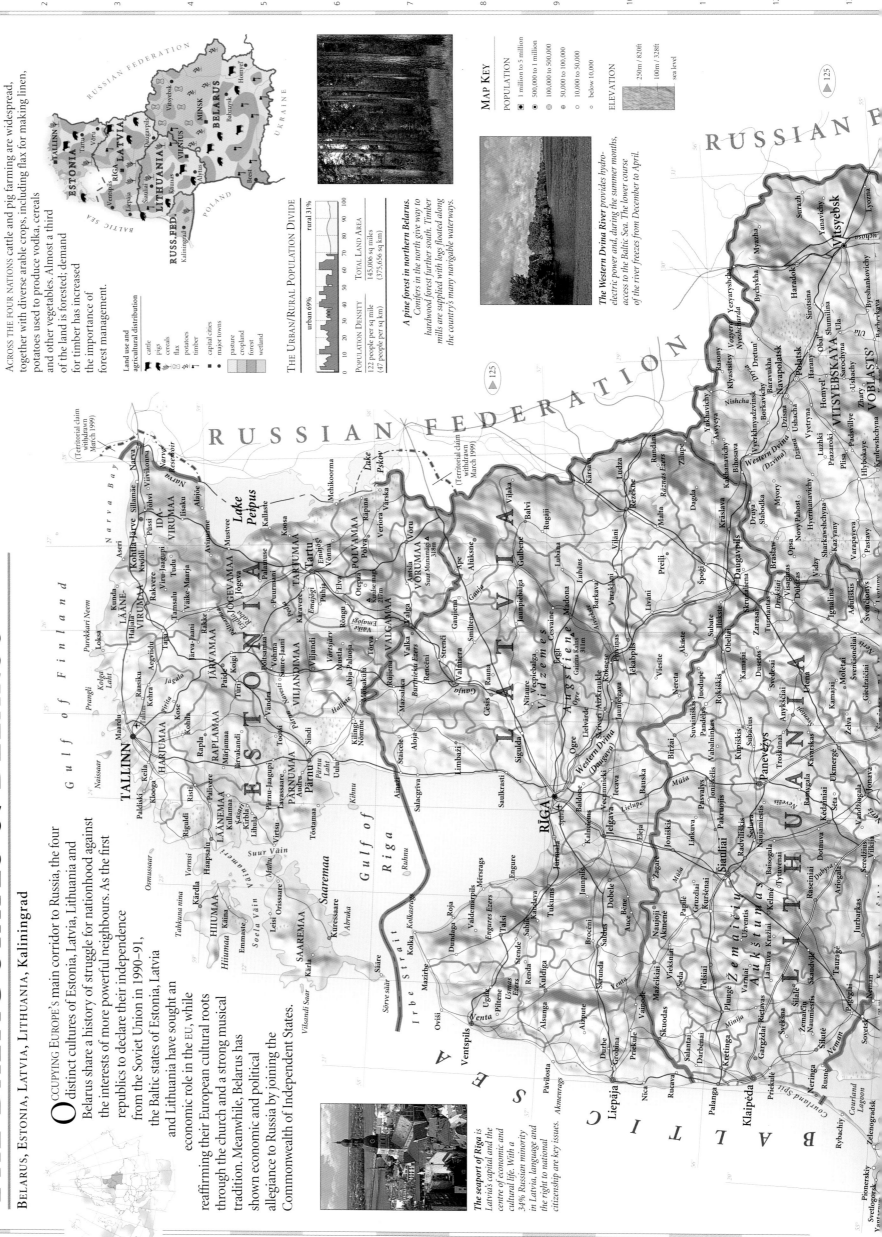

The seaport of Riga is Latvia's capital and the centre of economic and cultural life. With a 34% Russian minority in Latvia, language and the right to national citizenship are key issues.

USING THE LAND

ACROSS THE FOUR NATIONS cattle and pig farming are widespread, together with diverse arable crops, including flax for making linen, potatoes used to produce vodka, cereals and other vegetables. Almost a third of the land is forested; demand for timber has increased the importance of forest management.

Land use and agricultural distribution

- cattle
- pigs
- flax
- timber

- capital cities
- major towns

- pasture
- cropland
- forest
- wetland

THE URBAN/RURAL POPULATION DIVIDE

urban 69%   rural 31%

POPULATION DENSITY
122 people per sq mile
(47 people per sq km)

TOTAL LAND AREA
145,000 sq miles
(375,656 sq km)

A pine forest in northern Belarus. Conifers in the north give way to hardwood forest further south. Timber mills are supplied with logs floated along the country's many navigable waterways.

The Western Dvina River provides hydro-electric power and, during the summer months, access to the Baltic Sea. The lower course of the river freezes from December to April.

MAP KEY

POPULATION
- ◉ 1 million to 5 million
- ◉ 500,000 to 1 million
- ⊕ 100,000 to 500,000
- ⊕ 50,000 to 100,000
- ○ 10,000 to 50,000
- ○ below 10,000

ELEVATION
- 250m/820ft
- 100m/328ft
- sea level

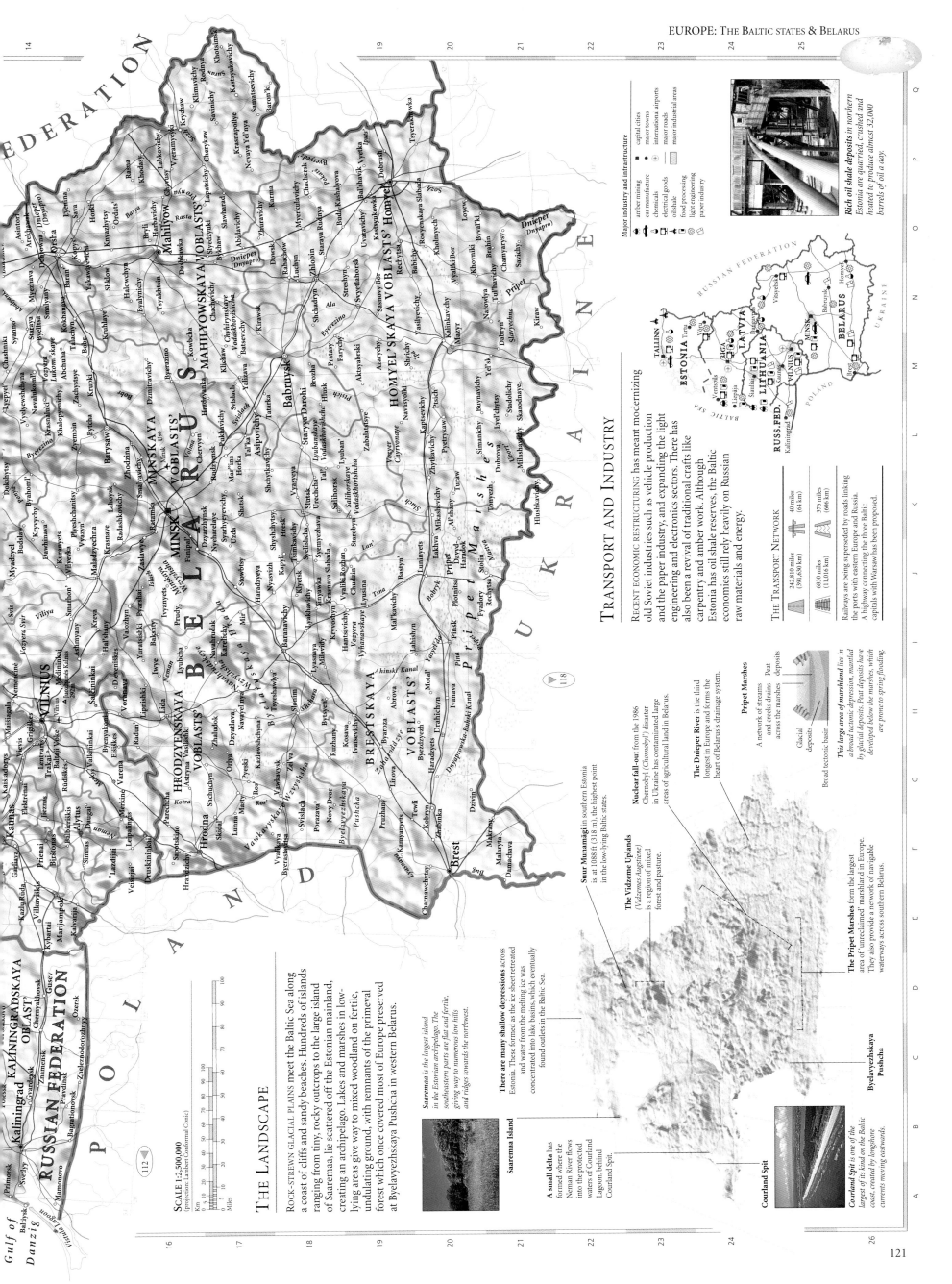

TRANSPORT AND INDUSTRY

RECENT ECONOMIC RESTRUCTURING has meant modernizing old Soviet industries such as vehicle production and the paper industry, and expanding the light engineering and electronics sectors. There has also been a revival of traditional crafts like carpentry and amber work. Although Estonia has oil shale reserves, the Baltic economies still rely heavily on Russian raw materials and energy.

Major industry and infrastructure

- amber mining
- car manufacture
- chemicals
- electrical goods
- oil shale
- food processing
- light engineering
- paper industry

- capital cities
- major towns
- international airports
- major roads
- major industrial areas

Rich oil shale deposits in northern Estonia are quarried, crushed and heated to produce almost 32,000 barrels of oil a day.

THE TRANSPORT NETWORK

242,810 miles (391,630 km)	40 miles (64 km)
6830 miles (11,016 km)	376 miles (606 km)

Railways are being superseded by roads linking the ports with eastern Europe and Russia. A highway connecting the three Baltic capitals with Warsaw has been proposed.

Nuclear fall-out from the 1986 Chernobyl (*Chornobyl'*) disaster in Ukraine has contaminated large areas of agricultural land in Belarus.

The Dnieper River is the third longest in Europe and forms the heart of Belarus's drainage system.

Pripet Marshes

A network of streams and creeks drains across the marshes

Peat deposits

This large area of marshland lies in a broad tectonic depression, marked by glacial deposits. Peat deposits have developed below the marshes, which are prone to spring flooding.

Glacial deposits

Broad tectonic basin

The Pripet Marshes form the largest area of "unreclaimed" marshland in Europe. They also provide a network of navigable waterways across southern Belarus.

Byelavyezhskaya Pushcha

THE LANDSCAPE

ROCK-STREWN GLACIAL PLAINS meet the Baltic Sea along a coast of cliffs and sandy beaches. Hundreds of islands ranging from tiny, rocky outcrops to the large island of Saaremaa, lie scattered off the Estonian mainland, creating an archipelago. Lakes and marshes in low-lying areas give way to mixed woodland on fertile, undulating ground, with remnants of the primeval forest which once covered most of Europe preserved at Byelavyezhskaya Pushcha in western Belarus.

Saaremaa Island

Saaremaa is the largest island in the Estonian archipelago. The southeastern parts are flat and fertile, giving way to numerous low hills and ridges towards the northwest.

There are many shallow depressions across Estonia. These formed as the ice sheet retreated and water from the melting ice was concentrated into lake basins, which eventually found outlets in the Baltic Sea.

A small delta has formed where the Neman River flows into the protected waters of Courland Lagoon, behind Courland Spit.

Suur Munamägi in southern Estonia is, at 1088 ft (318 m), the highest point in the low-lying Baltic states.

The Vidzeme Uplands (*Vidzemes Augstiene*) is a region of mixed forest and pasture.

Courland Spit

Courland Spit is one of the largest of its kind on the Baltic coast, created by longshore currents moving eastwards.

SCALE 1:2,500,000
(projection: Lambert Conformal Conic)

RUSSIAN FEDERATION

ESTONIA · LATVIA · LITHUANIA · BELARUS · RUSS.FED. · Kaliningrad

POLAND · UKRAINE

MAHILYOWSKAYA VOBLASTS'
MINSKAYA VOBLASTS'
HOMYEL'SKAYA VOBLASTS'
HRODZYENSKAYA VOBLASTS'
BRESTSKAYA VOBLASTS'

B E L A R U S

MINSK
VILNIUS
Kaunas
Hrodna
Brest
Babruysk
Baranavichy
Pinsk

U K R A I N E

Pripet Marshes

THE MEDITERRANEAN

THE MEDITERRANEAN SEA stretches over 2500 miles (4000 km) east to west, separating Europe from Africa. At its most westerly point it is connected to the Atlantic Ocean through the Strait of Gibraltar. In the east, the Suez Canal, opened in 1869, gives passage to the Indian Ocean. In the northeast, linked by the Sea of Marmara, lies the Black Sea. The Mediterranean is bordered by 28 states and territories, and more than 100 million people live on its shores and islands. Throughout history, the Mediterranean has been a focal area for many great empires and civilizations, reflected in the variety of cultures found on its shores. Since the 1960s, development along the southern coast of Europe has expanded rapidly to accommodate increasing numbers of tourists and to enable the exploitation of oil and gas reserves. This has resulted in rising levels of pollution, threatening the future of the sea.

USING THE LAND AND SEA

A QUARTER OF THE FISH SPECIES found in the Mediterranean are economically important. Sardines are the main catch in northern and western regions and aquaculture, including oyster farming, is becoming increasingly important in the eastern Mediterranean. Olives, citrus fruit, cork trees and vines thrive in the mediterranean climate, enjoying hot, dry summers and mild, wet winters. Italy and Spain are world leaders in commercial olive production.

The growing of citrus fruit such as lemons, limes, oranges and grapefruit is common along the coasts surrounding the Mediterranean.

Land use and agricultural distribution

- goats
- sheep
- cereals
- citrus fruits
- cork
- fishing
- olives
- sunflowers
- tobacco
- vineyards
- major towns
- pasture
- cropland
- forest
- mountain region
- wetland
- desert

THE LANDSCAPE

THE MEDITERRANEAN SEA IS ALMOST TOTALLY LANDLOCKED, joined to the Atlantic Ocean through the Strait of Gibraltar, which is only 8 miles (13 km) wide. Lying on an active plate margin, sea floor movements have formed a variety of basins, troughs and ridges. A submarine ridge running from Tunisia to the island of Sicily divides the Mediterranean into two distinct basins. The western basin is characterized by broad, smooth abyssal (or ocean) plains. In contrast, the eastern basin is dominated by a large ridge system, running east to west.

The narrow Strait of Gibraltar inhibits water exchange between the Mediterranean Sea and the Atlantic Ocean, producing a high degree of salinity and a low tidal range within the Mediterranean. The lack of tides has encouraged the build-up of pollutants in many semi-enclosed bays.

Main surface current

Denser, more saline currents flow back to Atlantic

Dense currents sink below surface

Because the Mediterranean is almost enclosed by land, its circulation is quite different to the oceans. There is one major current which flows in from the Atlantic and moves east. Currents flowing back to the Atlantic are denser and flow below the main current.

The Dalmatian (Dalmacija) coast has many long, elongated islands running parallel to the mainland. These resulted when rising sea levels drowned valleys running parallel with the coast.

The Atlas Mountains are a range of fold mountains which lie in Morocco and Algeria. They run parallel to the Mediterranean, forming a topographical and climatic divide between the Mediterranean coast and the western Sahara.

The edge of the Eurasian Plate is edged by a continental shelf. In the Mediterranean Sea this is widest at the Ebro Fan where it extends 60 miles (96 km).

Beneath the Strait of Sicily lies a submarine ridge which rises to 1200 ft (360 m) below sea level. It divides the eastern and western basins of the Mediterranean.

An arc of active submarine, island and mainland volcanoes, including Etna and Vesuvius, lie in and around southern Italy. The area is also susceptible to earthquakes and landslides.

The shallow basin of the Aegean contains numerous small islands, many of volcanic origin.

Nutrient flows into the eastern Mediterranean, and sediment flows to the Nile Delta have been severely lowered by the building of the Aswan Dam across the Nile in Egypt. This is causing the delta to shrink.

TRANSPORT AND INDUSTRY

THE OPENING OF THE SUEZ CANAL in 1869 made the Mediterranean a key shipping route to Asia. Oil and gas reserves, although comparatively small on a world scale, are being explored and exploited off the coasts of Libya, Greece, Italy, Spain and Tunisia. The Mediterranean's greatest natural resources are its miles of beaches and warm sea. Over half the world's income from tourism is generated in the Mediterranean.

Benidorm is one of the most popular resorts on Spain's Costa Blanca. Many of the Mediterranean's coastal resorts have grown up since the 1950s, expanding from small fishing villages to large resorts catering almost exclusively for tourists.

The Ionian Basin is the deepest in the Mediterranean, reaching depths of 16,800 ft (5121 m).

Industrial pollution flowing from the Dnieper and Danube rivers has destroyed a large proportion of the fish population that used to inhabit the upper layers of the Black Sea.

The eastern basin of the Mediterranean contains many features which indicate the force of a colliding plate margin, including volcanoes, earthquake zones, ridges and seamounts.

THE RUSSIAN FEDERATION

THE COLD WAR ERA OF GLOBAL RELATIONS was concluded in 1991 with the formal dissolution of the Soviet Union. The Russian Federation declared its separate sovereignty from the foundering communist empire following independence declarations from a number of former Soviet republics. As the leading member of the Commonwealth of Independent States, the Russian Federation has a central role in the development of post-Soviet Eurasia. Crossing 11 time zones, the Russian Federation is almost twice the size of the USA, and with more than 150 ethnic minorities and 21 autonomous republics, regionalist dissent within its own territory remains a danger.

Summer beds of moss and lichen scatter a 90% surface cover of ice across the islands of Franz Josef Land (Zemlya Frantsa-Iosifa), the northernmost land in the eastern hemisphere.

MAP KEY

POPULATION

- ◼ above 5 million
- ◼ 1 million to 5 million
- ◉ 500,000 to 1 million
- ◎ 100,000 to 500,000
- ⊕ 50,000 to 100,000
- ○ 10,000 to 50,000
- ○ below 10,000

ELEVATION

- 4000m / 13,124ft
- 3000m / 9843ft
- 2000m / 6562ft
- 1000m / 3281ft
- 500m / 1640ft
- 250m / 820ft
- 100m / 328ft
- sea level

THE RUSSIAN FEDERATION: ADMINISTRATIVE REGIONS

1. PSKOVSKAYA OBLAST'
2. YAROSLAVSKAYA OBLAST'
3. IVANOVSKAYA OBLAST'
4. SMOLENSKAYA OBLAST'
5. MOSKOVSKAYA OBLAST
6. VLADIMIRSKAYA OBLAST'
7. RESPUBLIKA MARIY EL
8. CHUVASHSKAYA RESPUBLIKA
9. KALUZHSKAYA OBLAST'
10. TUL'SKAYA OBLAST'
11. RYAZANSKAYA OBLAST'
12. RESPUBLIKA MORDOVIYA
13. UL'YANOVSKAYA OBLAST'
14. SAMARSKAYA OBLAST'
15. BRYANSKAYA OBLAST'
16. ORLOVSKAYA OBLAST'
17. LIPETSKAYA OBLAST'
18. TAMBOVSKAYA OBLAST'
19. KURSKAYA OBLAST'
20. BELGORODSKAYA OBLAST'
21. VORONEZHSKAYA OBLAST'
22. KRASNODARSKIY KRAY
23. RESPUBLIKA ADYGEYA
24. KARACHAYEVO-CHERKESSKAYA RESPUBLIKA
25. KABARDINO-BALKARSKAYA RESPUBLIKA
26. RESPUBLIKA SEVERNAYA OSETIYA - ALANIYA
27. INGUSHSKAYA RESPUBLIKA
28. CHECHENSKAYA RESPUBLIKA
29. YEVREYSKAYA AVTONOMNAYA OBLAST'

USING THE LAND

THE MAIN AGRICULTURAL REGIONS follow the belt of rich, black *chernozem* soils between Ukraine and Novosibirsk, producing cereals, fodder, and a broad range of crops for industrial use. Small pockets of pastureland are also found in this region. Large areas of terrain are uncultivable, and the constraints of a severe climate force the Federation to be partly dependent on imported grain. The wilds of Siberia are given over to hunting and reindeer herding, and contain the world's largest timber reserves.

Land use and agricultural distribution

- cattle
- cereals
- root crops
- timber
- capital cities
- major towns
- pasture
- cropland
- forest
- desert
- mountain region
- barren

RUSSIAN FEDERATION

THE URBAN/RURAL POPULATION DIVIDE

0 10 20 30 40 50 60 70 80 90 100

POPULATION DENSITY
22 people per sq mile
(9 people per sq km)

TOTAL LAND AREA
6,592,800 sq miles
(17,075,400 sq km)

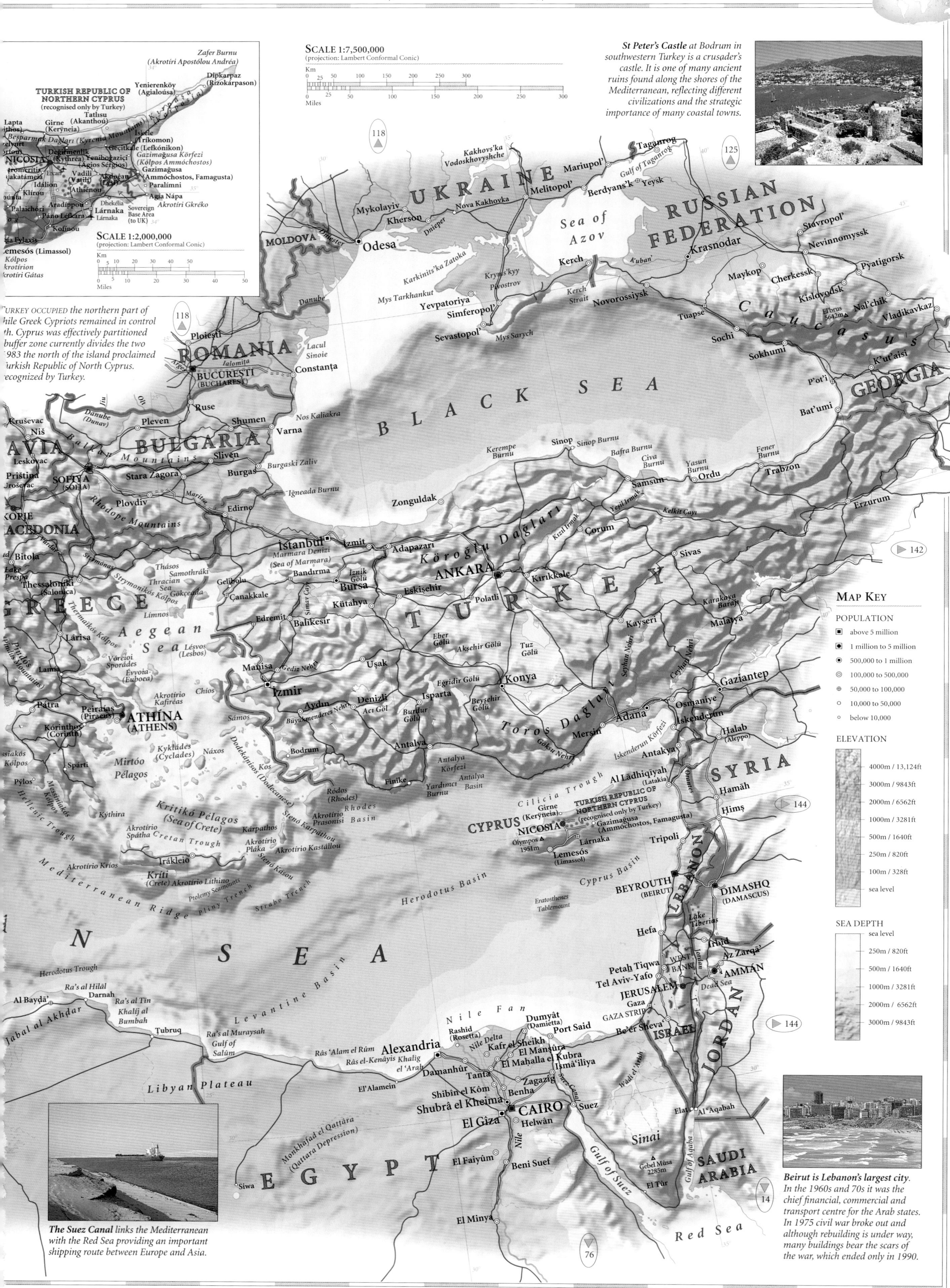

TURKISH REPUBLIC OF
NORTHERN CYPRUS
(recognised only by Turkey)

SCALE 1:2,000,000
(projection: Lambert Conformal Conic)

Km
0 5 10   20   30   40   50
Miles
0   5   10   20   30   40   50

SCALE 1:7,500,000
(projection: Lambert Conformal Conic)

Km
0 25 50   100   150   200   250   300
Miles
0   50   100   150   200   250   300

St Peter's Castle at Bodrum in southwestern Turkey is a crusader's castle. It is one of many ancient ruins found along the shores of the Mediterranean, reflecting different civilizations and the strategic importance of many coastal towns.

TURKEY OCCUPIED the northern part of ... hile Greek Cypriots remained in control ... th. Cyprus was effectively partitioned ... buffer zone currently divides the two ... 1983 the north of the island proclaimed ... urkish Republic of North Cyprus. ... ecognized by Turkey.

MAP KEY

POPULATION
- above 5 million
- 1 million to 5 million
- 500,000 to 1 million
- 100,000 to 500,000
- 50,000 to 100,000
- 10,000 to 50,000
- below 10,000

ELEVATION
- 4000m / 13,124ft
- 3000m / 9843ft
- 2000m / 6562ft
- 1000m / 3281ft
- 500m / 1640ft
- 250m / 820ft
- 100m / 328ft
- sea level

SEA DEPTH
- sea level
- 250m / 820ft
- 500m / 1640ft
- 1000m / 3281ft
- 2000m / 6562ft
- 3000m / 9843ft

The Suez Canal links the Mediterranean with the Red Sea providing an important shipping route between Europe and Asia.

Beirut is Lebanon's largest city. In the 1960s and 70s it was the chief financial, commercial and transport centre for the Arab states. In 1975 civil war broke out and although rebuilding is under way, many buildings bear the scars of the war, which ended only in 1990.

Monaco is just one of the luxurious resorts scattered along the Riviera, which stretches along the coast from Cannes in France to La Spezia in Italy. The region's mild winters and hot summers have attracted wealthy tourists since the early 19th century.

CYPRUS

Major industry and infrastructure
- fishing port
- oil & gas
- tourism
- major towns
- international airports
- major roads
- major industrial areas

Oxygen in the Black Sea is dissolved only in its upper layers; at depths below 230–300 ft (70–100 m) the sea is 'dead' and can support no lifeforms other than specially-adapted bacteria.

The city of Venice is built on an archipelago of islands and mud-flats in the middle of a lagoon at the head of the Adriatic Sea. The city's numerous canals follow water routes between the original 118 islands.

Cyprus is the third largest Mediterranean island after Sardinia and Sicily. The island is mountainous; containing two main ranges, the Troodos and the Kyrenia mountains.

Both the Dead Sea in Jordan and the Gulf of Aqaba are extensions of the Great Rift Valley which runs through eastern Africa.

The Suez Canal, opened in 1869, extends 100 miles (160 km) from Port Said to the Gulf of Suez.

MALTA

Ras San Dimitri
Gozo
Victoria
Ras il-Wardija
Nadur
Mearr
Comino (Kemmuna)
Mellieħa
San Pawl il-Baħar
Mosta
St Julian's
Sliema
Ħamrun
Paola
VALLETTA
Rabat
Birżebbuġa
Marsaxlokk Bay
Il-Kullana
Malta
Mediterranean Sea

SCALE 1:900,000
(projection: Lambert Conformal Conic)

0 5 10 20 Km
0 5 10 20 Miles

Commercial fisheries are found throughout the Mediterranean. Operations have traditionally been small-scale. As elsewhere, high demand has caused a decline in fish stocks.

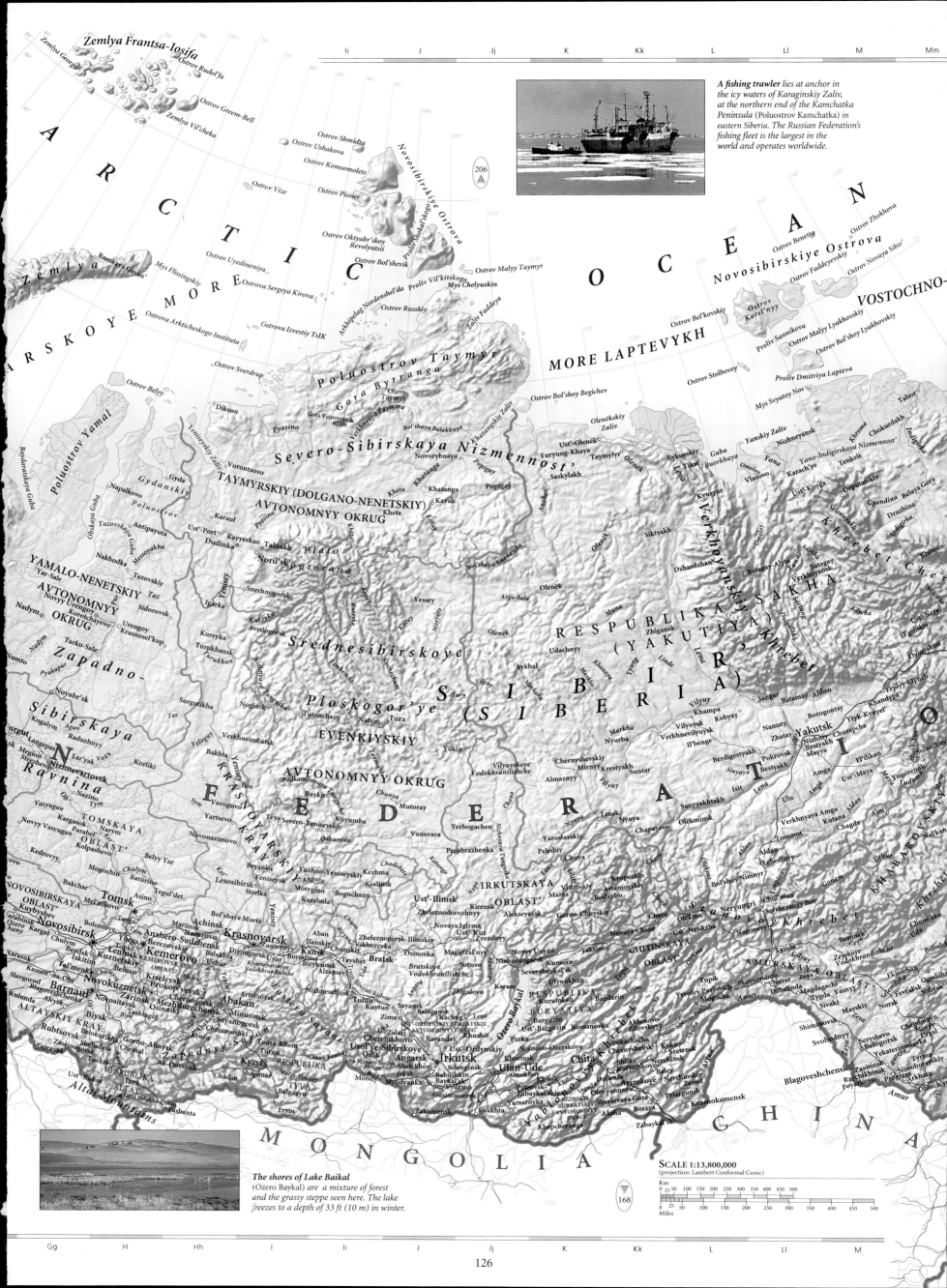

A fishing trawler lies at anchor in the icy waters of Karaginskiy Zaliv, at the northern end of the Kamchatka Peninsula (Poluostrov Kamchatka) in eastern Siberia. The Russian Federation's fishing fleet is the largest in the world and operates worldwide.

The shores of Lake Baikal (Ozero Baykal) are a mixture of forest and the grassy steppe seen here. The lake freezes to a depth of 33 ft (10 m) in winter.

SCALE 1:13,800,000
(projection: Lambert Conformal Conic)

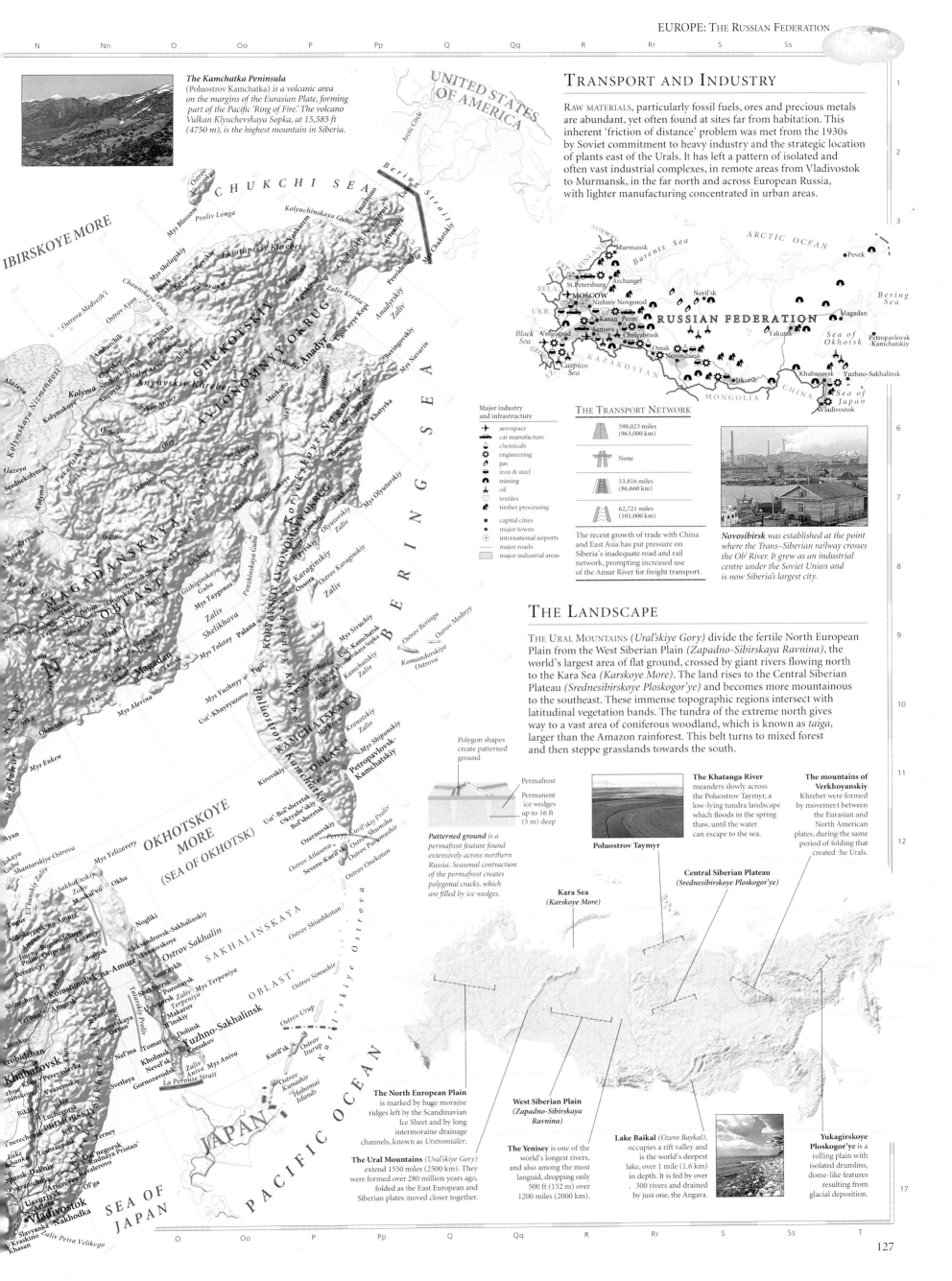

The Kamchatka Peninsula
(Poluostrov Kamchatka) *is a volcanic area on the margins of the Eurasian Plate, forming part of the Pacific 'Ring of Fire'. The volcano Vulkan Klyuchevskaya Sopka, at 15,585 ft (4750 m), is the highest mountain in Siberia.*

TRANSPORT AND INDUSTRY

RAW MATERIALS, particularly fossil fuels, ores and precious metals are abundant, yet often found at sites far from habitation. This inherent 'friction of distance' problem was met from the 1930s by Soviet commitment to heavy industry and the strategic location of plants east of the Urals. It has left a pattern of isolated and often vast industrial complexes, in remote areas from Vladivostok to Murmansk, in the far north and across European Russia, with lighter manufacturing concentrated in urban areas.

Major industry and infrastructure

- ✈ aerospace
- 🚗 car manufacture
- chemicals
- ⚙ engineering
- gas
- iron & steel
- ⛏ mining
- oil
- textiles
- 🌲 timber processing
- ◉ capital cities
- ● major towns
- ⊕ international airports
- — major roads
- ▨ major industrial areas

THE TRANSPORT NETWORK

598,023 miles (963,000 km)	
None	
53,816 miles (86,660 km)	
62,721 miles (101,000 km)	

The recent growth of trade with China and East Asia has put pressure on Siberia's inadequate road and rail network, prompting increased use of the Amur River for freight transport.

Novosibirsk was established at the point where the Trans–Siberian railway crosses the Ob' River. It grew as an industrial centre under the Soviet Union and is now Siberia's largest city.

THE LANDSCAPE

THE URAL MOUNTAINS (Ural'skiye Gory) divide the fertile North European Plain from the West Siberian Plain (Zapadno-Sibirskaya Ravnina), the world's largest area of flat ground, crossed by giant rivers flowing north to the Kara Sea (Karskoye More). The land rises to the Central Siberian Plateau (Srednesibirskoye Ploskogor'ye) and becomes more mountainous to the southeast. These immense topographic regions intersect with latitudinal vegetation bands. The tundra of the extreme north gives way to a vast area of coniferous woodland, which is known as *taiga*, larger than the Amazon rainforest. This belt turns to mixed forest and then steppe grasslands towards the south.

Polygon shapes create patterned ground

Permafrost

Permanent ice wedges up to 16 ft (5 m) deep

Patterned ground is a permafrost feature found extensively across northern Russia. Seasonal contraction of the permafrost creates polygonal cracks, which are filled by ice wedges.

The Khatanga River meanders slowly across the Poluostrov Taymyr, a low-lying tundra landscape which floods in the spring thaw, until the water can escape to the sea.

Poluostrov Taymyr

The mountains of Verkhoyanskiy Khrebet were formed by movement between the Eurasian and North American plates, during the same period of folding that created the Urals.

Kara Sea (Karskoye More)

Central Siberian Plateau (Srednesibirskoye Ploskogor'ye)

The North European Plain is marked by huge moraine ridges left by the Scandinavian Ice Sheet and by long intermoraine drainage channels, known as Urstromtäler.

The Ural Mountains (Ural'skiye Gory) extend 1550 miles (2500 km). They were formed over 280 million years ago, folded as the East European and Siberian plates moved closer together.

West Siberian Plain (Zapadno-Sibirskaya Ravnina)

The Yenisey is one of the world's longest rivers, and also among the most languid, dropping only 500 ft (152 m) over 1200 miles (2000 km).

Lake Baikal (Ozero Baykal), occupies a rift valley and is the world's deepest lake, over 1 mile (1.6 km) in depth. It is fed by over 300 rivers and drained by just one, the Angara.

Yukagirskoye Ploskogor'ye is a rolling plain with isolated drumlins, dome-like features resulting from glacial deposition.

Northern European Russia

Reaching into the Arctic Circle, this region of lakeland, forest and tundra is historically bound to Europe by St Petersburg, the old imperial capital of Tsarist Russia and home to a third of the region's population. Communist rule from Moscow left the north politically marginalized, contributing to the present problems of outmoded industry, poor infrastructure and serious environmental neglect. However, with borders embracing Finland, Norway, the Baltic and the northern sea route to the Atlantic, the region's success in foreign trade is now of prime importance to the Russian economy.

St Peter and Paul Fortress is the oldest building in St Petersburg, founded by Peter the Great in 1703 as a modern, European capital for Russia.

The Landscape

The ancient bedrock of the Scandinavian Shield lies exposed across the glacially scoured Khibiny Mountains of the Kola Peninsula *(Kol'skiy Poluostrov)*, becoming mantled with till towards the North European Plain. The Valdai Hills *(Valdayskaya Vozvyshennost')* form an important watershed for the plain's rivers, while thick forest veils a complicated topography of moraines, lakes and ground disturbed by frost action. The Ural Mountains *(Ural'skiye Gory)* form a border with Asia in the east.

The Khibiny Mountains were formed by volcanic intrusions into the Scandinavian Shield, over 570 million years ago.

Kola Peninsula *(Kol'skiy Poluostrov)*

The Kola Peninsula (Kol'skiy Poluostrov) *is part of the Scandinavian Shield, an area of ancient bedrock underlying Scandinavia. Rocks in excess of 2500 million years old are exposed across the peninsula.*

Karst features, including sinkholes, lakes and caverns, are found in limestone outcrops across the plain of the Severnaya Dvina and Mezen' rivers.

The low-lying plains of the Pechora, Mezen' and Severnaya Dvina rivers were flooded by the sea while the land was still isostatically depressed following the last Ice Age, a process which has hidden the landforms created by glacial deposition.

Retreating glacier
Meltwater channels
Terminal moraine

Terminal moraines are crescent-shaped ridges of glacial deposits, widely found in central Russia. Detritus is carried by the glacier and deposited at its terminus (snout) as it melts, marking the limit of the ice advance.

Lake Onega (Onezhskoye Ozero) *is the remnant of a body of water which, 12,000 years ago, connected the White Sea (Beloye More) with the Gulf of Finland and the Baltic Sea.*

Ural Mountains *(Ural'skiye Gory)*

Two of Europe's biggest rivers, the Volga and Western Dvina, rise in the swampy uplands of the Valdai Hills *(Valdayskaya Vozvyshennost')*.

Using the Land and Sea

The cold climate confines agriculture mainly to southern and western provinces, where dairy farming predominates and arable land is given over to fodder crops as well as flax, potatoes, oats and rye. Areas beyond the northern margins of cultivation are used for forestry, hunting, herding and fishing, with some vegetables grown in hothouses around urban areas.

Land use and agricultural distribution

- cattle
- fishing
- reindeer
- timber
- fodder
- major towns
- pasture
- cropland
- forest
- mountain region
- wetland
- tundra
- barren
- ice

RUSSIAN FEDERATION

The Urban/Rural Population Divide

urban 74%   rural 26%

0 10 20 30 40 50 60 70 80 90 100

POPULATION DENSITY	TOTAL LAND AREA
26 people per sq mile	829,398 sq miles
10 people per sq km	(2,148,700 sq km)

***Many rapids** are found along the 175 mile (280 km) course of the Suna River.*

94 ◀

120 ◀

120 ▼

The Ural Mountains
(Ural'skiye Gory) *form the traditional boundary between Europe and Asia. Elevations rarely exceed 6000 ft (1830 m). The region is extremely barren in the far northern latitudes.*

SCALE 1:5,500,000
(projection: Lambert Conformal Conic)

MAP KEY

POPULATION

- 1 million to 5 million
- 500,000 to 1 million
- 100,000 to 500,000
- 50,000 to 100,000
- 10,000 to 50,000
- below 10,000

ELEVATION

- 1000m / 3281ft
- 500m / 1640ft
- 250m / 820ft
- 100m / 328ft
- sea level

TRANSPORT AND INDUSTRY

THE PORTS OF ST PETERSBURG, Murmansk and Archangel serve a regional economy led by large-scale resource extraction. Nickel, iron ore and apatite are mined in the Kola Peninsula (Kol'skiy Poluostrov), and fossil fuels in the Pechora Basin. Paper production is central to Archangel's vast timber industry, while St Petersburg, drawing on ample labour, has become a major manufacturing centre.

Major industry and infrastructure

- chemicals
- coal
- defence
- engineering
- food processing
- hydro-electric power
- mining
- oil & gas
- textiles
- timber processing
- major towns
- international airports
- major roads
- major industrial areas

THE TRANSPORT NETWORK

- 53,700 miles (85,920 km)
- None
- 10,300 miles (16,572 km)
- 12,500 miles (20,000 km)

Railways linking remote industrial centres with the region's ports are the principal means of supply, although the impressive system of canals, linking natural waterways, is used for freight haulage during the summer.

Ice forces the port at St Petersburg to close in winter, yet Murmansk, on the Barents Sea, remains open, its waters prevented from freezing by warmer ocean currents extending from the North Atlantic Drift.

Kaliningrad has been a Russian enclave since 1945. The port is an important centre for the Russian Federation's Baltic fishing fleet.

St Basil's Cathedral, completed in 1561, stands in Moscow's Red Square next to the Kremlin; the original fortified stronghold of the city.

SOUTHERN EUROPEAN RUSSIA

THIS REGION, DIVIDED FROM ASIA by desert, seas and mountains, has exerted a powerful influence both east and west since the 13th century. Over 70 years of Communist rule produced a highly urbanized, industrial society dominated by Moscow, which was the capital of the Soviet Union until 1991. Almost two-thirds of the Russian Federation's population live in this core area, with a relatively high *per capita* share of its wealth. However, the rapid growth of a market economy has caused great social upheaval, with rising crime and political instability.

THE LANDSCAPE

ANCIENT FOLDS in the deep sedimentary strata of the North European Plain have created a sequence of high and low regions. The Central Russian Upland (*Srednerusskaya Vozvyshennost'*) in the west is deeply incised by rivers draining into the lowland of the Oka and Don rivers. In the east the Volga, Europe's longest river flows south to the Caspian Sea, dividing the Volga Uplands (*Privolzhskaya Vozvyshennost'*) from the foothills of the Ural Mountains (*Ural'skiye Gory*). The Caucasus Mountains and the Black Sea form a natural border to the southwest.

The Smolensk-Moscow Upland (*Smolensko-Moskovskaya Vozvyshennost'*) is a series of terminal moraine ridges marking the southern extent of the last glaciation.

Glacial till covers the bedrock to the north of the North European Plain, giving a gentle surface relief.

A plantation of Scots pine helps consolidate the loose sandy soils of the Meshchera Lowland (Meshcherskaya Nizina), which lies on the bed of an old glacial lake.

The lowland of the Oka and Don rivers lies over a broad trough, between the upfolds of the Volga Uplands (*Privolzhskaya Vozvyshennost'*) to the east, and the Central Russian Upland (*Srednerusskaya Vozvyshennost'*) to the west.

The southern Ural Mountains (*Ural'skiye Gory*) consist of several parallel ranges of ancient fold mountains running from north to south.

Central Russian Upland (*Srednerusskaya Vozvyshennost'*).

The flood plain of the Volga forms a long oasis of verdant vegetation, contrasting with the aridity of the surrounding Caspian hinterland.

The marshlands of the Volga Delta are visited by over 260 species of bird each year, migrating between South Africa and Arctic Siberia.

The Caspian Depression is a large downfold (or syncline) which became flooded, forming the Caspian Sea. The shoreline is 98 ft (30 m) below sea level.

The Caucasus Mountains run from the Black Sea to the Caspian Sea. They include El'brus which, at 18,511 ft (5642 m), is the highest point in Europe. It is still uplifting at a rate of 0.4 inches (10 mm/yr).

Drifting sand occupies large areas of the south, forming dunes up to 50 ft (15 m) high.

Salt dome

Salt dome is forced up and through the rock strata

Sedimentary strata

Salts are forced upwards by denser overlying strata

Salt domes, rounded hills up to 500 ft (150 m) high, are produced as less dense rock salts are displaced under the extreme pressure of denser, overlying strata and forced up towards the surface creating domes. They are widespread in the Caspian Depression.

SCALE 1:5,500,000
(projection: Lambert Conformal Conic)

MAP KEY

POPULATION

◼ above 5 million
◾ 1 million to 5 million
◉ 500,000 to 1 million
◍ 100,000 to 500,000
◦ 50,000 to 100,000
○ 10,000 to 50,000
○ below 10,000

ELEVATION

4000m / 13,124ft
3000m / 9843ft
2000m / 6562ft
1000m / 3281ft
500m / 1640ft
250m / 820ft
100m / 328ft
sea level

USING THE LAND

IN THE COLD, HUMID NORTH and in the southern Urals (*Ural'skiye Gory*), small grains, potatoes and flax are commonly rotated with legumes which support livestock farming. The rich chernozem (or black earth) areas support diverse crops such as sugar beet, hemp, sunflowers, millet and vegetables. Further south, aridity restricts husbandry to extensive grazing, with intensive fruit and rice cultivation along the oasis of the Volga.

THE URBAN/RURAL POPULATION DIVIDE

urban 65%   rural 35%

0 10 20 30 40 50 60 70 80 90 100

POPULATION DENSITY
119 people per sq mile
(46 people per sq km)

TOTAL LAND AREA
705,916 sq miles
(1,828,800 sq km)

Land use and agricultural distribution

- sheep
- flax
- potatoes
- rice
- sunflowers
- sugar beet
- timber
- ◼ capital cities
- major towns
- pasture
- cropland
- forest
- wetland
- mountain region
- tundra

TRANSPORT AND INDUSTRY

MANUFACTURING is largely based around Moscow and the Volga region, which became a major industrial area during the Second World War. Both Moscow and Nizhniy Novgorod are centres of skilled labour for light manufacturing and engineering. Most of Russia's main chemical plants are located along the Volga, and one of the world's largest car factories was recently opened in Tol'yatti. Processing and machine construction plants use oil, gas and hydro-electric power from the Volga Basin and metallic minerals from the Urals (*Ural'skiye Gory*) and Kursk.

Industrial plants are massed along the Volga. Environmental stress from decades of unbridled industrial development has prompted widespread concern about pollution levels.

THE TRANSPORT NETWORK

| 250,000 miles (402,000 km) | None |
| 28,000 miles (44,800 km) | 16,300 miles (26,080 km) |

Seventy private and national flag airlines have been created from the reorganization of the state airline Aeroflot, which maintained the world's largest fleet of aircraft during the Soviet era.

Major industry and infrastructure

- aerospace
- car manufacture
- chemicals
- defence
- electronics
- engineering
- gas
- mining
- oil
- textiles
- ◼ capital cities
- major towns
- international airports
- major roads
- major industrial areas

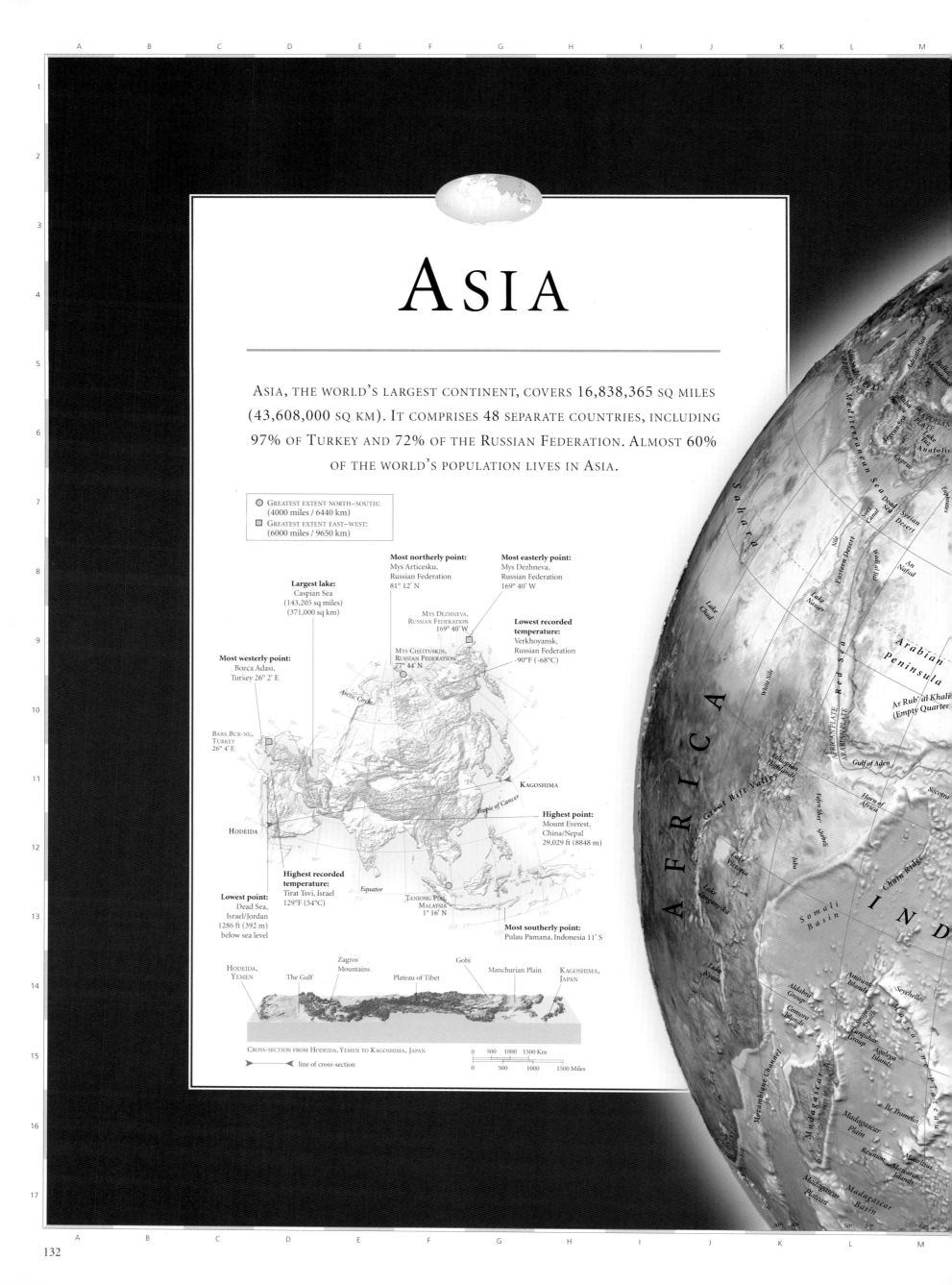

ASIA

ASIA, THE WORLD'S LARGEST CONTINENT, COVERS 16,838,365 SQ MILES (43,608,000 SQ KM). IT COMPRISES 48 SEPARATE COUNTRIES, INCLUDING 97% OF TURKEY AND 72% OF THE RUSSIAN FEDERATION. ALMOST 60% OF THE WORLD'S POPULATION LIVES IN ASIA.

⬤ GREATEST EXTENT NORTH–SOUTH:
(4000 miles / 6440 km)
◼ GREATEST EXTENT EAST–WEST:
(6000 miles / 9650 km)

Largest lake:
Caspian Sea
(143,205 sq miles)
(371,000 sq km)

Most northerly point:
Mys Articesku,
Russian Federation
81° 12' N

Most easterly point:
Mys Dezhneva,
Russian Federation
169° 40' W

MYS DEZHNEVA,
RUSSIAN FEDERATION
169° 40' W

Lowest recorded temperature:
Verkhoyansk,
Russian Federation
-90°F (-68°C)

MYS CHELYUSKIN,
RUSSIAN FEDERATION
77° 44' N

Most westerly point:
Bozca Adası,
Turkey 26° 2' E

Arctic Circle

BABA BUR-NU,
TURKEY
26° 4' E

KAGOSHIMA

Tropic of Cancer

Highest point:
Mount Everest,
China/Nepal
29,029 ft (8848 m)

HODEIDA

Highest recorded temperature:
Tirat Tsvi, Israel
129°F (54°C)

Equator

TANJONG PIAI,
MALAYSIA
1° 16' N

Lowest point:
Dead Sea,
Israel/Jordan
1286 ft (392 m)
below sea level

Most southerly point:
Pulau Pamana, Indonesia 11' S

HODEIDA,
YEMEN

The Gulf

Zagros
Mountains

Plateau of Tibet

Gobi

Manchurian Plain

KAGOSHIMA,
JAPAN

CROSS-SECTION FROM HODEIDA, YEMEN TO KAGOSHIMA, JAPAN

◀ line of cross-section

| 0 | 500 | 1000 | 1500 Km |
| 0 | 500 | 1000 | 1500 Miles |

ARCTIC OCEAN
North Pole
NORTH AMERICAN PLATE
EURASIAN PLATE

EUROPE
ASIA

Norwegian Sea
Scandinavia
North Sea
Baltic Sea
Gulf of Bothnia
Gulf of Finland
Lake Ladoga
Lake Onega
Kola Peninsula
White Sea
Barents Sea
North Cape
Novaya Zemlya
Franz Josef Land
Kara Sea
Severnaya Zemlya
Mys Chelyuskin
Laptev Sea
New Siberian Islands
East Siberian Sea
Long Strait
Bering Strait
Bering Sea

Rhine
Baltic Sea
North European Plain
Central Russian Upland
Dnieper
Dniester
Desna
Volga
Oka
Khoper
Vyatka
Kama
Ural Mountains
West Siberian Plain
Ob
Pur
Taz
Yenisey
Poluostrov Yamal
Poluostrov Gydanskiy
Putorana Mountains
North Siberian Lowland
Olenek
Lena
Central Siberian Plateau
Khatanga
Lower Tunguska
Stony Tunguska
Verkhoyanskiy Khrebet
Khrebet Cherskogo
Kolyma
Indigirka
Koryak Range
Kamchatka

Black Sea
Sea of Azov
Caucasus
Caspian Sea
Caspian Depression
Aral Sea
Ustyurt Plateau
Turan Lowland
Kirghiz Steppe
Lake Tengiz
Sarysu
Lake Balkhash
Lake Zaysan
Altai Mountains
Sayanskiy Khrebet
Lake Baikal
Stanovoy Khrebet
Zeya Reservoir
Amur
Sea of Okhotsk
Kurile Trench

ASIA
Gobi
Plateau of Mongolia
Manchurian Plain
Lake Khanka
Hokkaido
Sea of Japan
PACIFIC OCEAN

Lake Urmia
Lake Van
Zagros Mountains
Elburz Mountains
Great Salt Desert
Iranian Plateau
EURASIAN PLATE
IRANIAN PLATE
Tigris
Tien Shan
Syr Darya
Amu Darya
Naryn
Ozero Issyk-Kul'
Pamirs
Dzungaria
Tarim He
Tarim Basin
Takla Makan Desert
Lop Nur
Shule He
Qilian Shan
Ordos Desert
Yellow River
Wudai Shan
Bo Hai
Korea Bay
Korea Strait
Yellow Sea
Cheju-do
Shikoku
Kyushu
Honshu

The Gulf
Strait of Hormuz
Gulf of Oman
Oman Basin
Hamun
Jaz Murian
Central Makran Range
Rigestan
Hindu Kush
Karakoram Range
Altun Shan
Kunlun Mountains
Plateau of Tibet
Nan Shan
Qinghai Hu
Ningxia Shan
Bayan Har Shan
Han Shui
Yangtze
Great Plain of China
Yangtze
Tai Hu
East China Sea
Ryukyu Islands

Khalij Masirah
ARABIAN PLATE
INDO-AUSTRALIAN PLATE
Gulf of Kachchh
Suleiman Range
Jhelum
Indus
Punjab Plains
Sutlej
Thar Desert
Luni
Himalayas
Annapurna
Mount Everest 8848m
Siling Co
Tangra Yumco
Nam Co
Brahmaputra
Dogai Coring
Ganges
Ghaghara
Ganges
Brahmaputra
Khasi Hills
Arakan Yoma
Pakai Range
Hong Hu
Dongting Hu
Yuan Jiang
Feng Shui
Gui Jiang
Wuyi Shan
Taiwan
Tropic of Cancer
Luzon Strait
PHILIPPINE PLATE
Philippine Sea

Arabian Sea
Arabian Basin
Owen Fracture Zone
Sabarmati
Mahi
Bana
Chambal
Betwa
Son
Narmada
Vindhya Range
Satpura Range
Ajanta Range
Godavari
Wainganga
Mahanadi
Deccan
Bhima
Krishna
Indravati
Godavari
Mouths of the Ganges
Bay of Bengal
Chindwin
Irrawaddy
Salween
Sittang
Mun Ma
Red River
Black River
Gulf of Tongking
Hainan
Hainan Strait
South China Sea
Mindoro
Luzon
Philippine Basin
Philippine
Samar
Panay
Negros

Carlsberg Ridge
Laccadive Islands
Western Ghats
Eastern Ghats
Kaveri
Penneru
Coromandel Coast
Malabar Coast
Turigabhadra
Cape Comorin
Gulf of Mannar
Sri Lanka
Maldives
Laccadive Plateau
INDIAN OCEAN
Andaman Islands
Andaman Sea
Nicobar Islands
Gulf of Martaban
Gulf of Thailand
Isthmus of Kra
Chao Phraya
Tônlé Sap
Mekong
Mun
Chi
Truong Phan
South China Basin
Mouths of the Mekong
South China Basin
Palawan
Sulu Sea
Mindanao
Celebes Sea
Palau
CAROLINE PLATE
PHILIPPINE TRENCH

INDIAN OCEAN
Ceylon Plain
Chagos-Laccadive Plateau
Chagos Bank
Chagos Trench
Mid-Indian Ridge
INDO-AUSTRALIAN PLATE
ARGO PLATE
Nikitin Seamount
Ninetyeast Ridge
EURASIAN PLATE
INDO-AUSTRALIAN PLATE
Malay Peninsula
Strait of Malacca
Tanjong Piai
Sumatra
Danau Toba
Gunung Kerinci 3806m
Mentawai Ridge
Selat Sunda
Pulau Bangka
Anambas Islands
Natuna Islands
Sunda Shelf
Greater Sunda Islands
Borneo
Gunung Kinabalu 4904m
Kapuas Sungai
Celebes
Makassar Strait
Buru
Banda Sea
Seram
New Guinea Trench
BISMARCK PLATE
Equator

Mid-Indian Basin
Cocos Basin
Cocos Islands
Investigator Ridge
Java Trench
Christmas Island
Java
Bali
Java Sea
Flores Sea
Flores
Sunda Trough
Lesser Sunda Islands
Sumba Islands
East Indies
Moluccas Sea
Molucca
Halmahera
Arafura Sea
Torres Strait
Timor Trough
Timor
Tropic of Capricorn
AUSTRALIA

133

ASIAN RESOURCES

ALTHOUGH AGRICULTURE REMAINS THE ECONOMIC MAINSTAY of most Asian countries, the number of people employed in agriculture has steadily declined, as new industries have been developed during the past 30 years. China, Indonesia, Malaysia, Thailand and Turkey have all experienced far-reaching structural change in their economies, while the breakup of the Soviet Union has created a new economic challenge in the Central Asian republics. The countries of The Gulf illustrate the rapid transformation from rural nomadism to modern, urban society which oil wealth has brought to parts of the continent. Asia's most economically dynamic countries, Japan, Singapore, South Korea, and Taiwan, fringe the Pacific Ocean and are known as the Pacific Rim. In contrast, other Southeast Asian countries like Laos and Cambodia remain both economically and industrially underdeveloped.

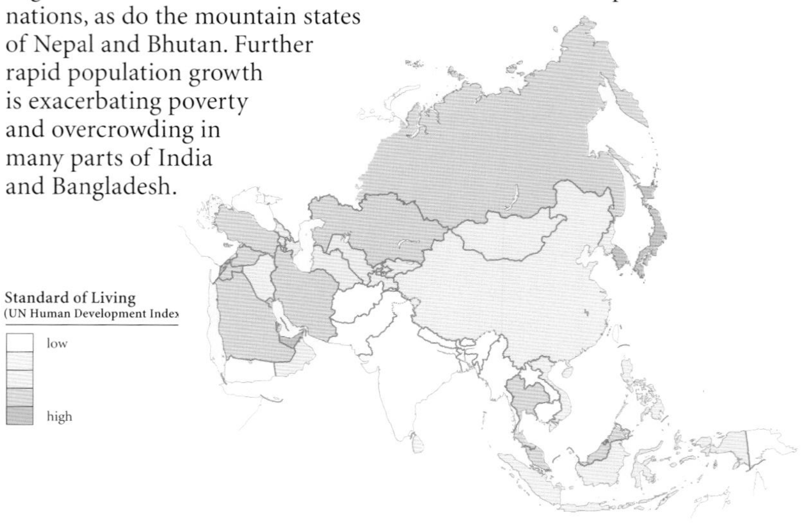

INDUSTRY

JAPANESE INDUSTRY LEADS THE CONTINENT in both productivity and efficiency; electronics, hi-tech industries, car manufacture and shipbuilding are important. In recent years, the so-called economic 'tigers' of the Pacific Rim such as Taiwan and South Korea are now challenging Japan's economic dominance. Heavy industries such as engineering, chemicals, and steel typify the industrial complexes along the corridor created by the Trans-Siberian Railway, the Fergana Valley in Central Asia, and also much of the huge industrial plain of east China. The discovery of oil in The Gulf has brought immense wealth to countries that previously relied on subsistence agriculture on marginal desert land.

Industry

- aerospace
- brewing
- car/vehicle manufacture
- cement
- chemicals
- electronics
- engineering
- finance
- fish processing
- food processing
- hi-tech industry
- iron & steel
- pharmaceuticals
- printing & publishing
- shipbuilding
- sugar processing
- tea processing
- textiles
- timber processing
- tobacco processing
- coal
- oil
- gas
- industrial cities
- major industrial areas

STANDARD OF LIVING

DESPITE JAPAN'S HIGH STANDARDS OF LIVING, and Southwest Asia's oil-derived wealth, immense disparities exist across the continent. Afghanistan remains one of the world's most underdeveloped nations, as do the mountain states of Nepal and Bhutan. Further rapid population growth is exacerbating poverty and overcrowding in many parts of India and Bangladesh.

Standard of Living
(UN Human Development Index)
- low
- high

On a small island at the southern tip of the Malay Peninsula lies Singapore, one of the Pacific Rim's most vibrant economic centres. Multinational banking and finance form the core of the city's wealth.

GNP per capita (US$)
- 0–499
- 500–999
- 1000–4999
- 5000–9999
- 10000–19999
- 20000+

Iron and steel, engineering and shipbuilding typify the heavy industry found in eastern China's industrial cities, especially the nation's leading manufacturing centre, Shanghai.

Traditional industries are still crucial to many rural economies across Asia. Here, on the Vietnamese coast, salt has been extracted from seawater by evaporation and is being loaded into a van to take to market.

ARCTIC OCEAN

PACIFIC OCEAN

Sea of Okhotsk

RUSSIAN FEDERATION

Yakutsk

Trans-Siberian Railway

Khabarovsk

Yekaterinburg
Chelyabinsk
Magnitogorsk
Omsk
Novosibirsk
Kemerovo
Krasnoyarsk
Bratsk
Novokuznetsk
Irkutsk
Karaganda

Vladivostok

Harbin
Shenyang

JAPAN
Tokyo
Nagoya
Kobe

NORTH KOREA
Pyongyang
Seoul
Pusan
SOUTH KOREA
Dalian
Qingdao

Istanbul
Izmir
Ankara
TURKEY
GEORGIA
Tbilisi
ARMENIA
Yerevan
AZERB.
Baku

CYPRUS
LEBANON
Beirut
Tel Aviv-Yafo
ISRAEL
Amman
JORDAN
SYRIA
Damascus

Kirkuk
Baghdad
IRAQ
Basra
Kuwait
KUWAIT
The Gulf
SAUDI ARABIA
Ad Damman
BAHRAIN
QATAR
Abu Dhabi
Dubai
UAE
Jedda
Riyadh

Caspian Sea
Aral Sea

KAZAKHSTAN

UZBEKISTAN
Tashkent
Farghona
KYRGYZSTAN
TURKMENISTAN
Ashgabat
Dushanbe
TAJIKISTAN

Tehran
Isfahan
IRAN

AFGHANISTAN

Rawalpindi
Lahore
PAKISTAN
Karachi

MONGOLIA
Ulan Bator

Urumqi

Alma-Ata

CHINA
Lanzhou
Xi'an
Zhengzhou
Nanjing
Shanghai
Wuhan
Beijing
Tianjin
Jinan
Taiyuan
Chengdu
Chongqing
Kunming
Guangzhou
Hong Kong

TAIWAN
Taipei

Red Sea
YEMEN
OMAN
Gulf of Oman
Gulf of Aden

NEPAL
BHUTAN
Delhi
Kanpur
Ahmadabad
Indore
Jamshedpur
BANGLADESH
Dhaka
Chittagong
Calcutta (Kolkata)
INDIA
Nagpur
Mumbai (Bombay)
Bangalore
Chennai (Madras)

BURMA
Mandalay
Rangoon

LAOS
VIETNAM
Hanoi
Da Nang
THAILAND
Bangkok
CAMBODIA
Ho Chi Minh City

South China Sea

Manila
PHILIPPINES

Arabian Sea

SRI LANKA
INDIAN OCEAN

MALAYSIA
BRUNEI
Kuala Lumpur
Singapore
SINGAPORE

INDONESIA
Jakarta
Surabaya

EAST TIMOR
(under UN Transitional Authority from Feb 2000)

ENVIRONMENTAL ISSUES

THE TRANSFORMATION OF UZBEKISTAN by the former Soviet Union into the world's second largest producer of cotton led to the diversion of several major rivers for irrigation. Starved of this water, the Aral Sea diminished in volume by over 50% in 30 years, irreversibly altering the ecology of the area. Heavy industries in eastern China have polluted coastal waters, rivers and urban air, while in Burma, Malaysia and Indonesia, ancient hardwood rainforests are felled faster than they can regenerate.

Although Siberia remains a quintessentially frozen, inhospitable wasteland, vast untapped mineral reserves – especially the oil and gas of the West Siberian Plain – have lured industrial development to the area since the 1950s and 1960s.

ARCTIC OCEAN

Noril'sk

Chelyabinsk
Omsk   Bratsk   Khabarovsk
Angarsk

Shenyang   Tokyo
Beijing   Osaka
Seoul
Xi'an   Shanghai
Tehran   Yellow River
Kuwait   Lahore
Euphrates   Delhi   Yangtze
Tigris   Amu Darya   Guangzhou
Syr Darya   Vi Jiang   Hong Kong
Indus   Ganges   Calcutta
Mumbai   Manila

PACIFIC OCEAN

INDIAN OCEAN

Bangkok

Kuala Lumpur

Jakarta

Environmental Issues
- tropical forest
- forest destroyed
- desert
- desertification
- acid rain
- polluted rivers
- marine pollution
- heavy marine pollution
- radioactive contamination
- poor urban air quality

The long-term environmental impact of the Gulf War (1991) is still uncertain. As Iraqi troops left Kuwait, equipment was abandoned to rust and thousands of oil wells were set alight, pouring crude oil into The Gulf.

MINERAL RESOURCES

AT LEAST 60% OF THE WORLD'S known oil and gas deposits are found in Asia; notably the vast oil fields of The Gulf, and the less-exploited oil and gas fields of the Ob' Basin in west Siberia. Immense coal reserves in Siberia and China have been utilized to support large steel industries. Southeast Asia has some of the world's largest deposits of tin, found in a belt running down the Malay Peninsula to Indonesia.

ARCTIC OCEAN

Mineral Resources
- oil field
- gas field
- coal field
- chromite
- copper
- gold
- iron
- lead
- nickel
- platinum
- tin
- wolfram

Himalayas

PACIFIC OCEAN

INDIAN OCEAN

USING THE LAND AND SEA

VAST AREAS OF ASIA REMAIN UNCULTIVATED as a result of unsuitable climatic and soil conditions. In favourable areas such as river deltas, farming is intensive. Rice is the staple crop of most Asian countries, grown in paddy fields on waterlogged alluvial plains and terraced hillsides, and often irrigated for higher yields. Across the black earth region of the Eurasian steppe in southern Siberia and Kazakhstan, wheat farming is the dominant activity. Cash crops, like tea in Sri Lanka and dates in the Arabian Peninsula, are grown for export, and provide valuable income. The sovereignty of the rich fishing grounds in the South China Sea is disputed by China, Malaysia, Taiwan, the Philippines and Vietnam, because of potential oil reserves.

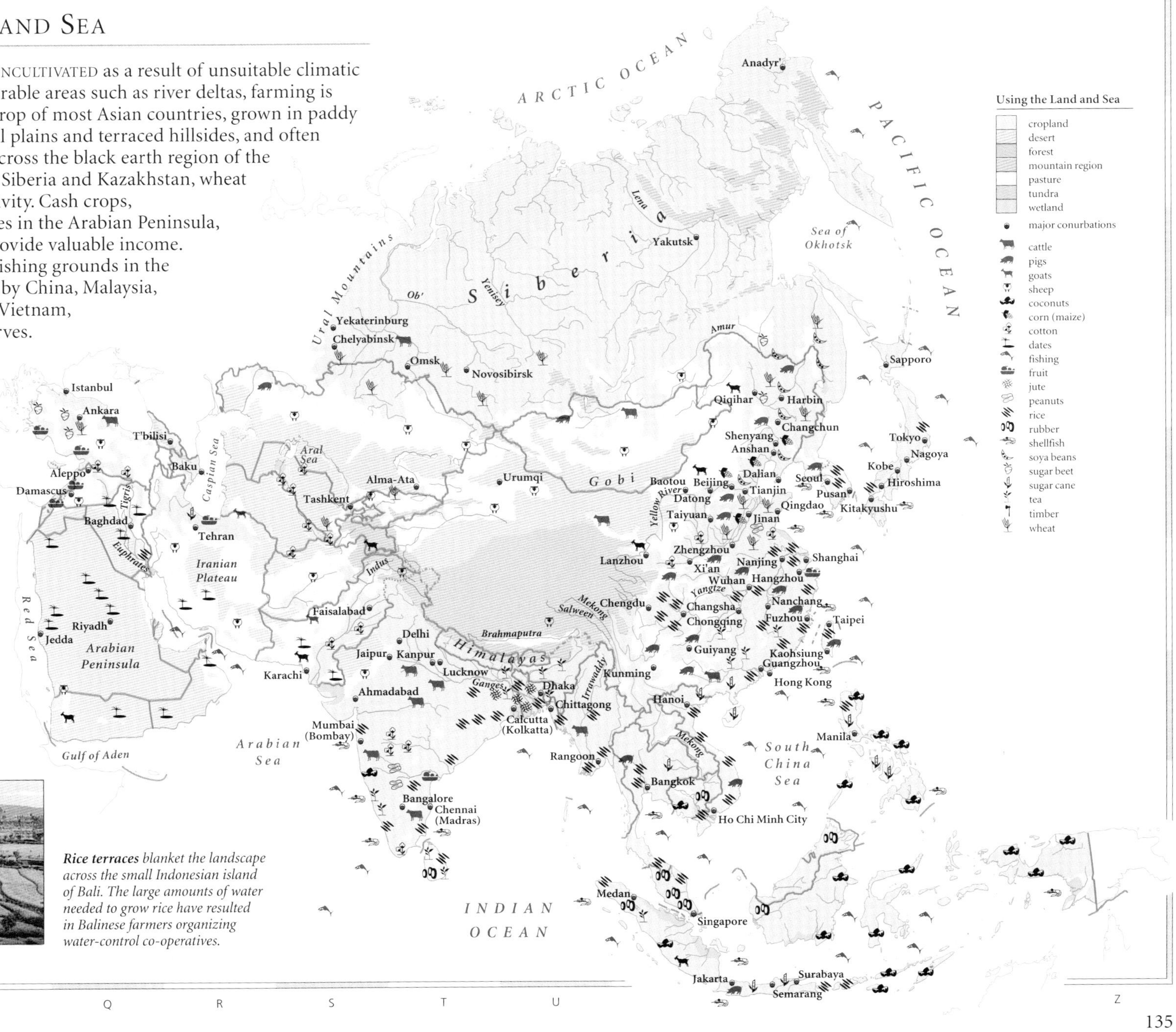

Using the Land and Sea
- cropland
- desert
- forest
- mountain region
- pasture
- tundra
- wetland
- major conurbations
- cattle
- pigs
- goats
- sheep
- coconuts
- corn (maize)
- cotton
- dates
- fishing
- fruit
- jute
- peanuts
- rice
- rubber
- shellfish
- soya beans
- sugar beet
- sugar cane
- tea
- timber
- wheat

ARCTIC OCEAN

PACIFIC OCEAN

Anadyr'

Lena   Sea of Okhotsk

Yakutsk

Ural Mountains   Siberia   Sapporo
Yekaterinburg   Yenisei   Amur
Chelyabinsk   Ob'   Qiqihar   Harbin
Omsk   Novosibirsk   Changchun   Tokyo
Istanbul   Shenyang   Nagoya
Ankara   Aral   Anshan   Kobe
T'bilisi   Sea   Urumqi   Gobi   Baotou Beijing   Dalian   Hiroshima
Aleppo   Baku   Alma-Ata   Yellow river   Datong   Tianjin   Pusan   Kitakyushu
Damascus   Caspian Sea   Tashkent   Taiyuan   Jinan   Qingdao   Seoul
Baghdad   Tigris   Lanzhou   Zhengzhou   Nanjing   Shanghai
Iranian   Euphrates   Xi'an   Wuhan   Hangzhou
Plateau   Tehran   Mekong   Chengdu   Changsha   Nanchang
Faisalabad   Salween   Chongqing   Fuzhou   Taipei
Red Sea   Indus   Brahmaputra   Guiyang   Kaohsiung
Riyadh   Delhi   Himalayas   Kunming   Guangzhou
Jedda   Jaipur Kanpur   Hong Kong
Arabian   Karachi   Lucknow   Ganges   Dhaka
Peninsula   Ahmadabad   Chittagong   Hanoi   South
                Mumbai   Calcutta (Kolkata)   Rangoon   China Sea
                (Bombay)   Mekong   Manila
Gulf of Aden   Arabian Sea   Bangalore   Bangkok
                Chennai (Madras)   Ho Chi Minh City
Arabian Sea

INDIAN OCEAN

Medan

Singapore

Jakarta   Surabaya
Semarang

Date palms have been cultivated in oases throughout the Arabian Peninsula since antiquity. In addition to the fruit, palms are used for timber, fuel, rope, and for making vinegar, syrup and a liquor known as arrack.

Rice terraces blanket the landscape across the small Indonesian island of Bali. The large amounts of water needed to grow rice have resulted in Balinese farmers organizing water-control co-operatives.

SIBERIAN PLATEAU AND PLAIN

THE WEST SIBERIAN PLAIN is one of the largest in the world, and contains a vast system of marshes. The whole area is covered by glacial deposits, underlain by the Angara Shield, a remnant of the ancient continent of Laurasia. The flat relief of the region and thick surface deposits result in poor drainage; this, combined with the freezing and thawing of the extensive permafrost layer leads to the formation of the vast swamps which cover the area. Many of the north-flowing rivers are also frozen for up to half the year.

Section across Siberia showing the Central Siberian Plateau and its drainage.

THE ARABIAN SHIELD AND IRANIAN PLATEAU

APPROXIMATELY FIVE MILLION YEARS AGO, rifting of the continental crust split the Arabian Plate from the African Plate and flooded the Red Sea. As this rift spread, the Arabian Plate collided with the Eurasian Plate, transforming part of the Tethys seabed into the Zagros Mountains which run northwest-southeast across western Iran.

Cross-section through southwestern Asia, showing the Mesopotamian Depression, the folded Zagros Mountains and the Iranian Plateau.

THE TURAN BASIN AND KAZAKH UPLANDS

THE TURAN BASIN AND KAZAKH UPLANDS are a complex mixture of mountain foothills, an arid limestone plateau and deserts including the Kyzl Kum and Kara Kum. In the centre of the Turan Lowland – an area of inland drainage – is the desiccated Aral Sea, reduced to a fraction of its former size because of the diversion of its flow into irrigation channels. The only rivers with sufficient water to cross this arid region are the Syr Dayra and Amu Dayra.

THE INDIAN SHIELD AND HIMALAYAN SYSTEM

THE LARGE SHIELD AREA beneath the Indian subcontinent is between 2.5 and 3.5 billion years old. As the floor of the southern Indian Ocean spread, it pushed the Indian Shield north. This was eventually driven beneath the Plateau of Tibet. This process closed up the ancient Tethys Sea and uplifted the world's highest mountain chain, the Himalayas. Much of the uplifted rock strata was from the seabed of the Tethys Sea, partly accounting for the weakness of the rocks and the high levels of erosion found in the Himalayas.

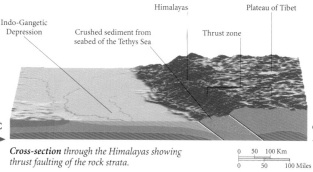

Cross-section through the Himalayas showing thrust faulting of the rock strata.

CENTRAL ASIAN PLATEAUX AND BASINS

THE PLATEAU OF TIBET lies north of the Himalayas and covers 965,250 sq miles (2,500,000 sq km); its average elevation is 16,500 ft (5000 m). The region is noted for its extreme aridity. In the south, the Himalayan mountain belt blocks moisture-bearing winds. The pressure from the Indo-Australian Plate against the plateau is causing both uplift and, when combined with the downward force caused by weight of the plateau, extension east and west of the of the more malleable underlying crust. The brittle upper rock layers are extensively faulted.

Cross-section across the Plateau of Tibet showing uplift and crustal extension caused by the collision of the Indo-Australian and Eurasian plates.

PHYSICAL ASIA

THE STRUCTURE OF ASIA can be divided into two distinct regions. The landscape of northern Asia consists of old mountain chains, shields, plateaux and basins, like the Ural Mountains in the west and the Central Siberian Plateau to the east. To the south of this region, are a series of plateaux and basins, including the vast Plateau of Tibet and the Tarim Basin. In contrast, the landscapes of southern Asia are much younger, formed by tectonic activity beginning about 65 million years ago, leading to an almost continuous mountain chain running from Europe, across much of Asia, and culminating in the mighty Himalayan mountain belt, formed when the Indo-Australian Plate collided with the Eurasian Plate. They are still being uplifted today. North of the mountains lies a belt of deserts, including the Gobi and the Takla Makan. In the far south, tectonic activity has formed narrow island arcs, extending over 4000 miles (7000 km). To the west lies the Arabian Shield, once part of the African Plate. As it was rifted apart from Africa, the Arabian Plate collided with the Eurasian Plate, uplifting the Zagros Mountains.

SHAPING THE LANDSCAPE

IN THE NORTH, melting of extensive permafrost leads to typical periglacial features such as thermokarst. In the arid areas wind action transports sand creating extensive dune systems. An active tectonic margin in the south causes continued uplift, and volcanic and seismic activity, but also high rates of weathering and erosion. Across the continent, huge rivers erode and transport vast quantities of sediment depositing it on the plains or forming large deltas.

PERIGLACIATION

1 Permafrost is widespread across northern Siberia. When ground ice, which makes up a large proportion of the soil layer, melts, it contracts and extensive ground subsidence occurs. Over time this process leads to depressions in the landscape and the gradual movement of soil down slopes. Eventually the accumulation of water in the depressions leads to thermokarstic lakes (left).

PERIGLACIATION: FORMATION OF THERMOKARST

THE EVOLVING LANDSCAPE

Landscape

- ▨ limestone region
- sinking land
- stable land
- uplifting land
- ● ● ● area of tectonic activity
- - - limit of permafrost
- ▲ active volcano
- → ocean current

RIVER SYSTEMS

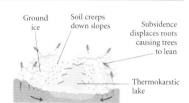

2 Vast river systems flow across Asia, many originating in the Himalayas and the Plateau of Tibet. Seasonal melting of snow and monsoon rains swell the river flow leading to flooding and erosion. The Yellow River (above) gets its colour from the high level of eroded material from the loess plateau.

RIVER SYSTEMS: EROSION OF THE LOESS PLATEAU BY THE YELLOW RIVER

TECTONIC ACTIVITY

7 The Dead Sea (above) lies in a pull-apart basin. The sliding of the African Plate against the Arabian Plate, at unequal rates, led to the sinking of blocks of crust. This depression has been filled by the waters of the Dead Sea and Lake Tiberias (Sea of Galilee). The plates continue to move causing intermittent earthquakes.

TECTONIC ACTIVITY: THE FORMATION OF A PULL-APART BASIN

CHEMICAL WEATHERING

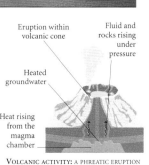

3 Tower karsts are widespread across south China (above) and Vietnam. It is thought the karstic towers were formed under a soil cover, where small depressions in the limestone bedrock began to be weathered by soil water acids, eventually creating larger hollows. This process continued over millions of years, deepening the hollows and leaving steep-sided limestone hills.

SEDIMENTATION

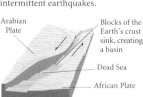

6 The Ganges/Brahmaputra is a tide-dominated delta (above). The two rivers transport huge quantities of mountain sediment, which is deposited on the delta plain. This debris is then redistributed by tidal currents, to form extensions to the bars, beach ridges and deltaic deposits.

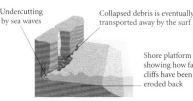

SEDIMENTATION: THE DESTRUCTION OF A DELTA

COASTAL EROSION

5 The erosion of cliffs along the coast of Indonesia (above) and Thailand occurs when waves and currents undermine the base leading to collapse of material. The surf then gradually erodes this material away, exposing the cliff to further undercutting. This process eventually creates shore platforms.

COASTAL EROSION: THE UNDERCUTTING OF A CLIFF

VOLCANIC ACTIVITY

4 Volcanic eruptions occur frequently across Southeast Asia's island arcs (above). Low-level eruptions occur when groundwater, superheated by underlying magma, becomes pressurized, forcing hot fluid and rocks up through cracks in the volcanic cone. This is known as a phreatic eruption.

VOLCANIC ACTIVITY: A PHREATIC ERUPTION

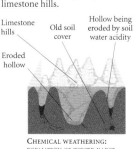

CHEMICAL WEATHERING: FORMATION OF TOWER KARST

POLITICAL ASIA

ASIA IS THE WORLD'S LARGEST CONTINENT, encompassing many different and discrete realms, from the desert Arab lands of the southwest to the subtropical archipelago of Indonesia; from the vast barren wastes of Siberia to the fertile river valleys of China and South Asia, seats of some of the world's most ancient civilizations. The collapse of the Soviet Union has fragmented the north of the continent into the Siberian portion of the Russian Federation, and the new republics of Central Asia. Strong religious traditions heavily influence the politics of South and Southwest Asia. Hindu and Muslim rivalries threaten to upset the political equilibrium in South Asia where India – in terms of population – remains the world's largest democracy. Communist China is the last great world empire; a population giant, but still relatively closed to the western world, while on its doorstep, the economically progressive and dynamic Pacific Rim countries, led by Japan, continue to assert their worldwide economic force.

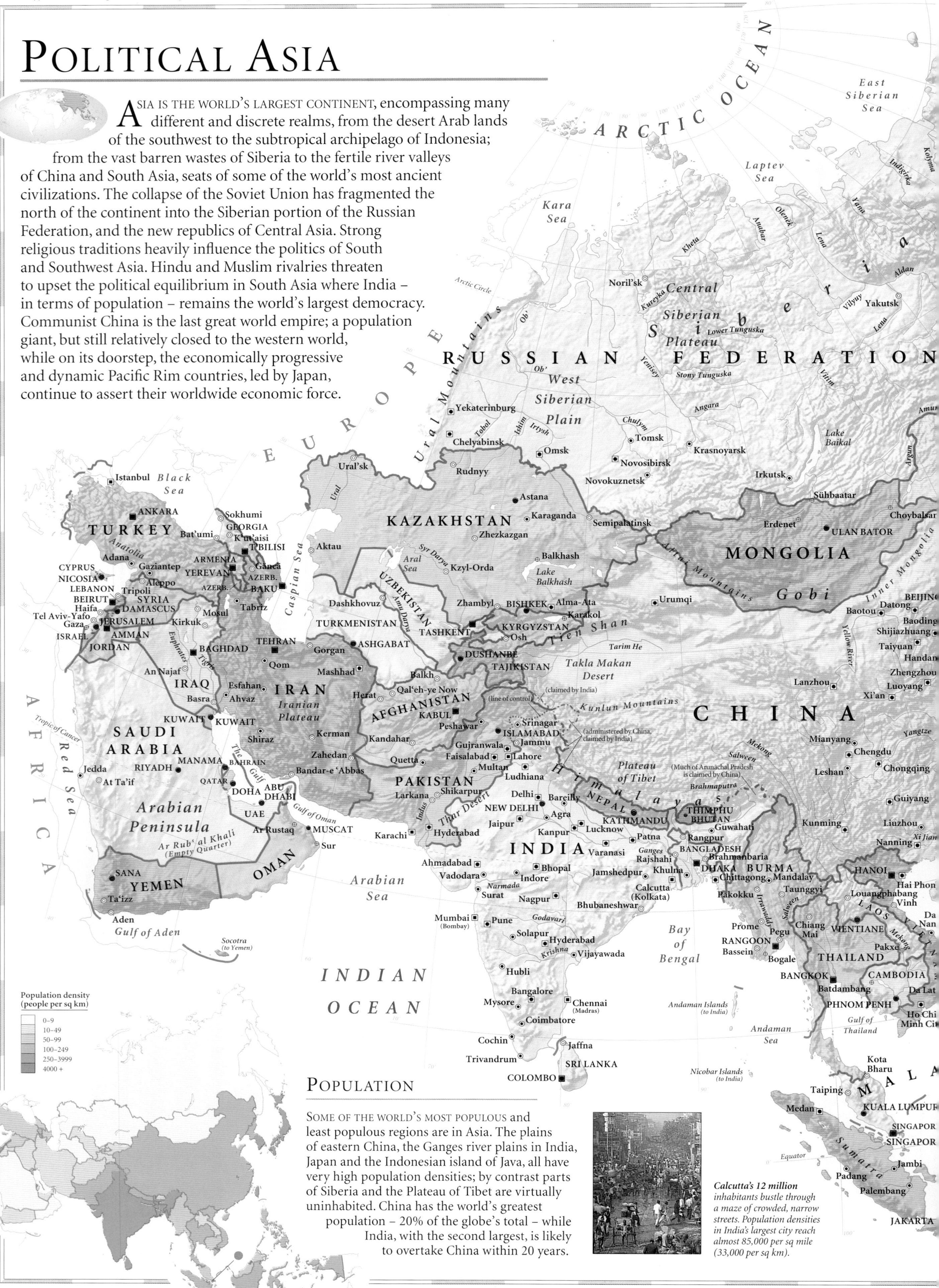

Population density
(people per sq km)
- 0–9
- 10–49
- 50–99
- 100–249
- 250–3999
- 4000 +

POPULATION

SOME OF THE WORLD'S MOST POPULOUS and least populous regions are in Asia. The plains of eastern China, the Ganges river plains in India, Japan and the Indonesian island of Java, all have very high population densities; by contrast parts of Siberia and the Plateau of Tibet are virtually uninhabited. China has the world's greatest population – 20% of the globe's total – while India, with the second largest, is likely to overtake China within 20 years.

Calcutta's 12 million inhabitants bustle through a maze of crowded, narrow streets. Population densities in India's largest city reach almost 85,000 per sq mile (33,000 per sq km).

Map labels

ARCTIC OCEAN
East Siberian Sea
Laptev Sea
Kara Sea
Indigirka
Kolyma
Yana
Olenek
Lena
Kheta
Khatanga
Lower Tunguska
Stony Tunguska
Yenisey
Angara
Ob'
Tobol
Irtysh
Ishim
Ural Mountains
Arctic Circle
Central Siberian Plateau
West Siberian Plain
RUSSIAN FEDERATION
Siberia
Noril'sk
Yakutsk
Vilyuy
Aldan
Yekaterinburg
Chelyabinsk
Omsk
Rudnyy
Tomsk
Chulym
Novosibirsk
Novokuznetsk
Krasnoyarsk
Irkutsk
Lake Baikal
Amur
Argun
Sü'baatar
Choybalsan
Erdenet
ULAN BATOR
MONGOLIA
Gobi
Altai Mountains
Inner Mongolia
EUROPE
Istanbul
Black Sea
ANKARA
Sokhumi
GEORGIA
Bat'umi
K'ut'aisi
T'BILISI
TURKEY
Anatolia
Adana
Gaziantep
Aleppo
ARMENIA
YEREVAN
Ganca
AZERB.
BAKU
CYPRUS
NICOSIA
LEBANON
BEIRUT
Tripoli
SYRIA
DAMASCUS
Haifa
Tel Aviv-Yafo
JERUSALEM
Gaza
ISRAEL
AMMAN
JORDAN
Kirkuk
Mosul
Tabriz
Caspian Sea
Ural'sk
Ural
Aktau
Aral Sea
Syr Darya
KAZAKHSTAN
Astana
Karaganda
Semipalatinsk
Zhezkazgan
Balkhash
Lake Balkhash
Kzyl-Orda
Zhambyl
Alma-Ata
BISHKEK
KYRGYZSTAN
Karakol
Osh
Urumqi
Tien Shan
Dashkhovuz
UZBEKISTAN
Amu Darya
TURKMENISTAN
TASHKENT
ASHGABAT
Gorgan
Mashhad
Balkh
DUSHANBE
TAJIKISTAN
Takla Makan Desert
Tarim He
(claimed by India)
Kunlun Mountains
CHINA
BAGHDAD
An Najaf
Euphrates
Tigris
IRAQ
Basra
Esfahan
Ahvaz
Qom
TEHRAN
IRAN
Iranian Plateau
Herat
Qal'eh-ye Now
AFGHANISTAN
KABUL
(line of control)
(administered by China, claimed by India)
Srinagar
Jammu
ISLAMABAD
Peshawar
Plateau of Tibet
(Much of Arunachal Pradesh is claimed by China)
Brahmaputra
Himalayas
KUWAIT
KUWAIT
SAUDI ARABIA
RIYADH
Shiraz
Kerman
Zahedan
Kandahar
Quetta
Gujranwala
Faisalabad
Lahore
Ludhiana
Multan
PAKISTAN
Larkana
Shikarpur
Delhi
Bareilly
NEW DELHI
Jaipur
Kanpur
Lucknow
Agra
NEPAL
KATHMANDU
THIMPHU
BHUTAN
Guwahati
Rangpur
MANAMA
BAHRAIN
The Gulf
QATAR
DOHA
ABU DHABI
UAE
Bandar-e 'Abbas
Gulf of Oman
Ar Rustaq
MUSCAT
Sur
Jedda
Red Sea
Tropic of Cancer
AFRICA
At Ta'if
Arabian Peninsula
Ar Rub' al Khali
(Empty Quarter)
OMAN
Karachi
Hyderabad
Thar Desert
Indus
Ahmadabad
Vadodara
Indore
Bhopal
Narmada
Jamshedpur
INDIA
Varanasi
Patna
Ganges
Rajshahi
BANGLADESH
DHAKA
Khulna
Brahmanbaria
Chittagong
BURMA
Mandalay
Taunggyi
Irrawaddy
HANOI
SANA
YEMEN
Ta'izz
Aden
Gulf of Aden
Socotra
(to Yemen)
Surat
Nagpur
Bhubaneshwar
Arabian Sea
Mumbai
(Bombay)
Pune
Godavari
Solapur
Hyderabad
Vijayawada
Krishna
Calcutta
(Kolkata)
Pakokku
Bay of Bengal
Prome
Pegu
RANGOON
Bassein
Bogale
Chiang Mai
WIENTIANE
Pakxe
LAOS
Louangphabang
Vinh
Da Nan
THAILAND
Hubli
Bangalore
Mysore
Chennai
(Madras)
Coimbatore
INDIAN OCEAN
Andaman Islands
(to India)
Andaman Sea
BANGKOK
Batdambang
CAMBODIA
Da Lat
PHNOM PENH
Ho Chi Minh Cit
Gulf of Thailand
Cochin
Jaffna
Trivandrum
SRI LANKA
COLOMBO
Nicobar Islands
(to India)
Kota Bharu
Taiping
Medan
MALA
KUALA LUMPUR
SINGAPOR
SINGAPORE
Sumatra
Jambi
Padang
Palembang
Equator
JAKARTA

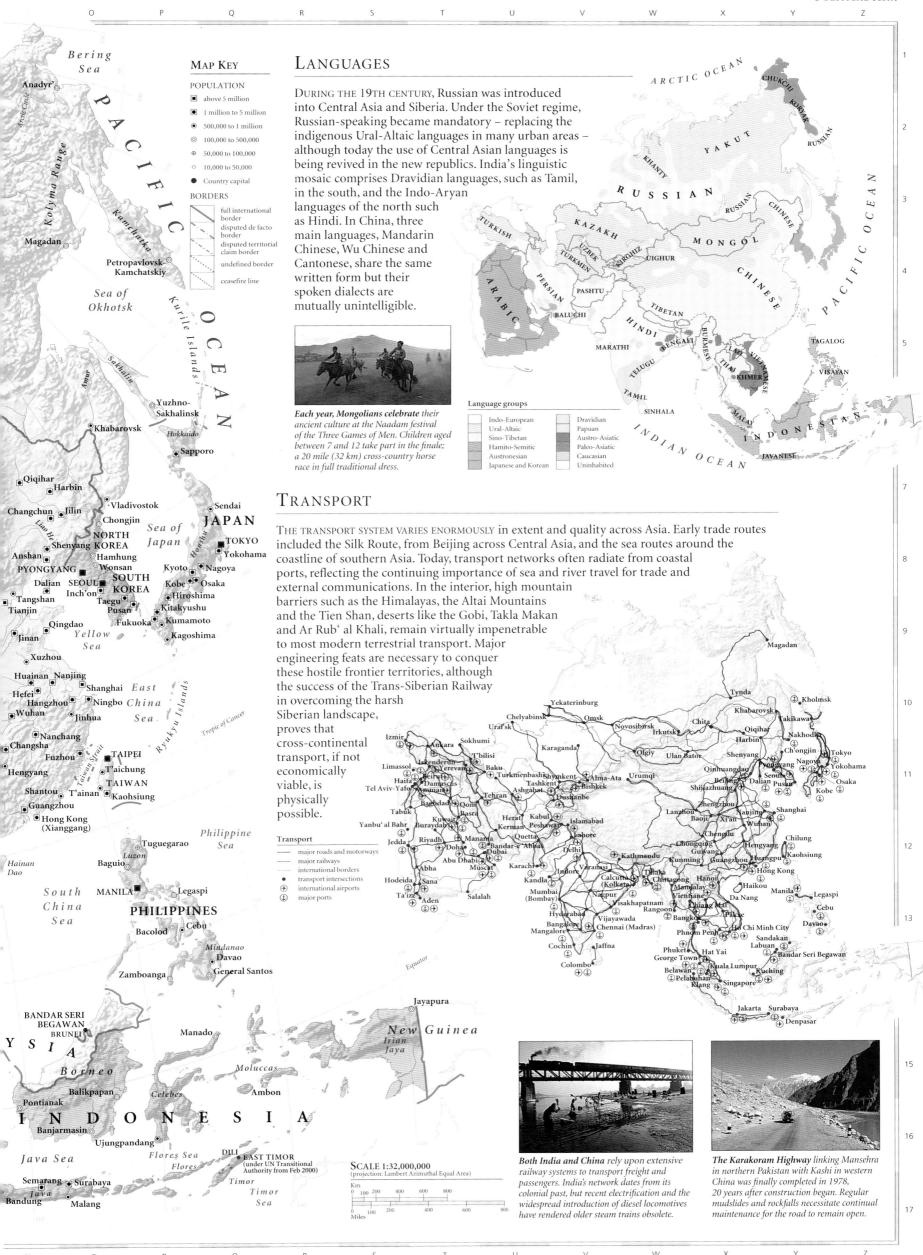

LANGUAGES

DURING THE 19TH CENTURY, Russian was introduced into Central Asia and Siberia. Under the Soviet regime, Russian-speaking became mandatory – replacing the indigenous Ural-Altaic languages in many urban areas – although today the use of Central Asian languages is being revived in the new republics. India's linguistic mosaic comprises Dravidian languages, such as Tamil, in the south, and the Indo-Aryan languages of the north such as Hindi. In China, three main languages, Mandarin Chinese, Wu Chinese and Cantonese, share the same written form but their spoken dialects are mutually unintelligible.

Each year, Mongolians celebrate their ancient culture at the Naadam festival of the Three Games of Men. Children aged between 7 and 12 take part in the finale; a 20 mile (32 km) cross-country horse race in full traditional dress.

Language groups

Indo-European	Dravidian
Ural-Altaic	Papuan
Sino-Tibetan	Austro-Asiatic
Hamito-Semitic	Paleo-Asiatic
Austronesian	Caucasian
Japanese and Korean	Uninhabited

TRANSPORT

THE TRANSPORT SYSTEM VARIES ENORMOUSLY in extent and quality across Asia. Early trade routes included the Silk Route, from Beijing across Central Asia, and the sea routes around the coastline of southern Asia. Today, transport networks often radiate from coastal ports, reflecting the continuing importance of sea and river travel for trade and external communications. In the interior, high mountain barriers such as the Himalayas, the Altai Mountains and the Tien Shan, deserts like the Gobi, Takla Makan and Ar Rub' al Khali, remain virtually impenetrable to most modern terrestrial transport. Major engineering feats are necessary to conquer these hostile frontier territories, although the success of the Trans-Siberian Railway in overcoming the harsh Siberian landscape, proves that cross-continental transport, if not economically viable, is physically possible.

Transport

- major roads and motorways
- major railways
- international borders
- transport intersections
- international airports
- major ports

MAP KEY

POPULATION
- above 5 million
- 1 million to 5 million
- 500,000 to 1 million
- 100,000 to 500,000
- 50,000 to 100,000
- 10,000 to 50,000
- Country capital

BORDERS
- full international border
- disputed de facto border
- disputed territorial claim border
- undefined border
- ceasefire line

Both India and China rely upon extensive railway systems to transport freight and passengers. India's network dates from its colonial past, but recent electrification and the widespread introduction of diesel locomotives have rendered older steam trains obsolete.

The Karakoram Highway linking Mansehra in northern Pakistan with Kashi in western China was finally completed in 1978, 20 years after construction began. Regular mudslides and rockfalls necessitate continual maintenance for the road to remain open.

SCALE 1:32,000,000
(projection: Lambert Azimuthal Equal Area)

Km
0 100 200 400 600 800

Miles
0 100 200 400 600 800

CLIMATE

THE CLIMATE OF ASIA exhibits marked differences from region to region, with freezing polar conditions in the north, hot and cold deserts in central regions and subtropical conditions throughout the south. Much of this variation can be attributed to enormous mountain barriers and internal depressions found across the continent. Monsoon winds, which reverse semi-annually, cause alternate wet and dry seasons across southern Asia. These air masses moving north from the ocean are stripped of their moisture over the Himalayas causing arid conditions across the Plateau of Tibet. Both the south and east are susceptible to tropical cyclones or typhoons.

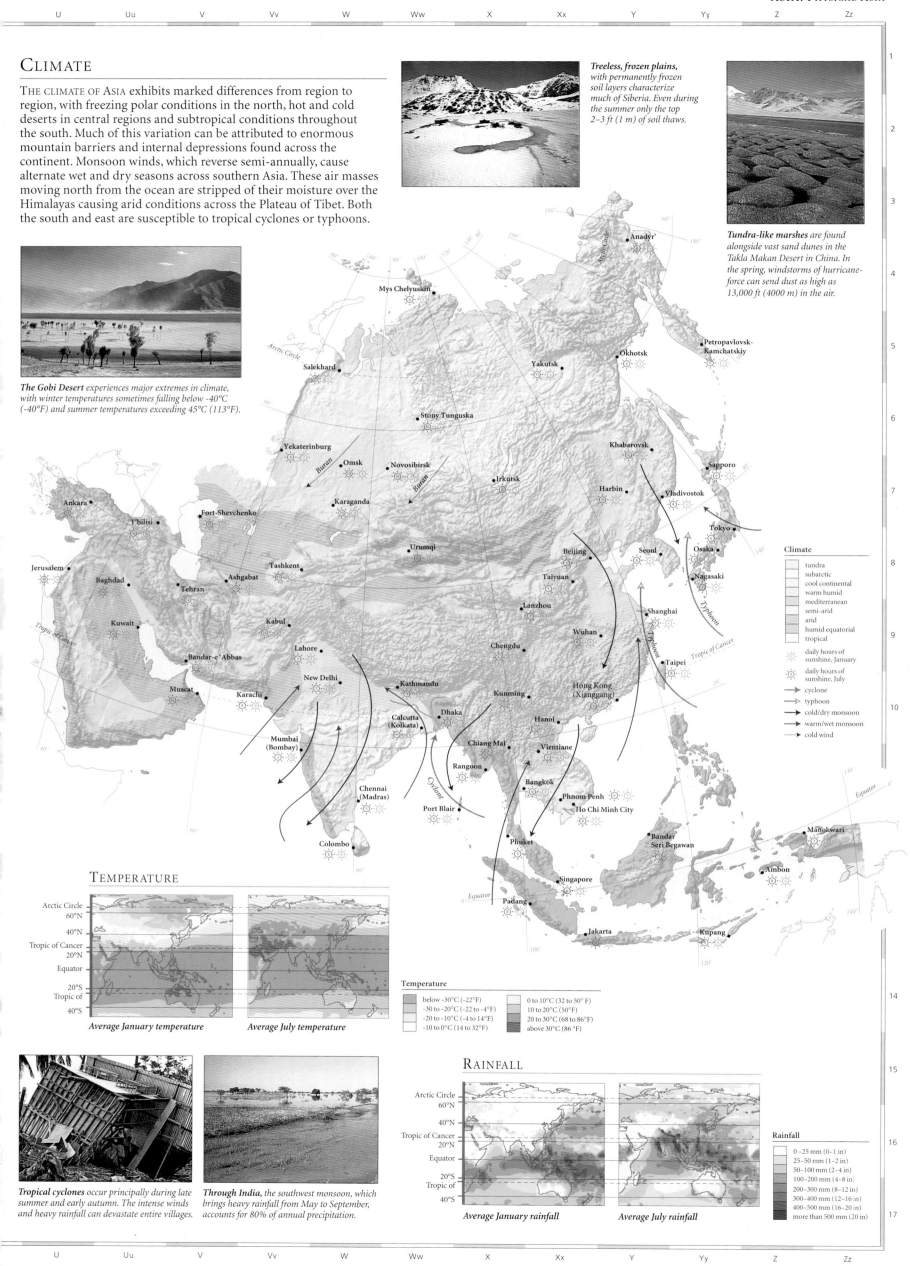

Treeless, frozen plains, with permanently frozen soil layers characterize much of Siberia. Even during the summer only the top 2–3 ft (1 m) of soil thaws.

Tundra-like marshes are found alongside vast sand dunes in the Takla Makan Desert in China. In the spring, windstorms of hurricane-force can send dust as high as 13,000 ft (4000 m) in the air.

The Gobi Desert experiences major extremes in climate, with winter temperatures sometimes falling below -40°C (-40°F) and summer temperatures exceeding 45°C (113°F).

Climate
tundra
subarctic
cool continental
warm humid
mediterranean
semi-arid
arid
humid equatorial
tropical

daily hours of sunshine, January
daily hours of sunshine, July
cyclone
typhoon
cold/dry monsoon
warm/wet monsoon
cold wind

TEMPERATURE

Average January temperature *Average July temperature*

Temperature
below -30°C (-22°F)
-30 to -20°C (-22 to -4°F)
-20 to -10°C (-4 to 14°F)
-10 to 0°C (14 to 32°F)
0 to 10°C (32 to 50°F)
10 to 20°C (50°F)
20 to 30°C (68 to 86°F)
above 30°C (86°F)

Tropical cyclones occur principally during late summer and early autumn. The intense winds and heavy rainfall can devastate entire villages.

Through India, the southwest monsoon, which brings heavy rainfall from May to September, accounts for 80% of annual precipitation.

RAINFALL

Average January rainfall *Average July rainfall*

Rainfall
0–25 mm (0–1 in)
25–50 mm (1–2 in)
50–100 mm (2–4 in)
100–200 mm (4–8 in)
200–300 mm (8–12 in)
300–400 mm (12–16 in)
400–500 mm (16–20 in)
more than 500 mm (20 in)

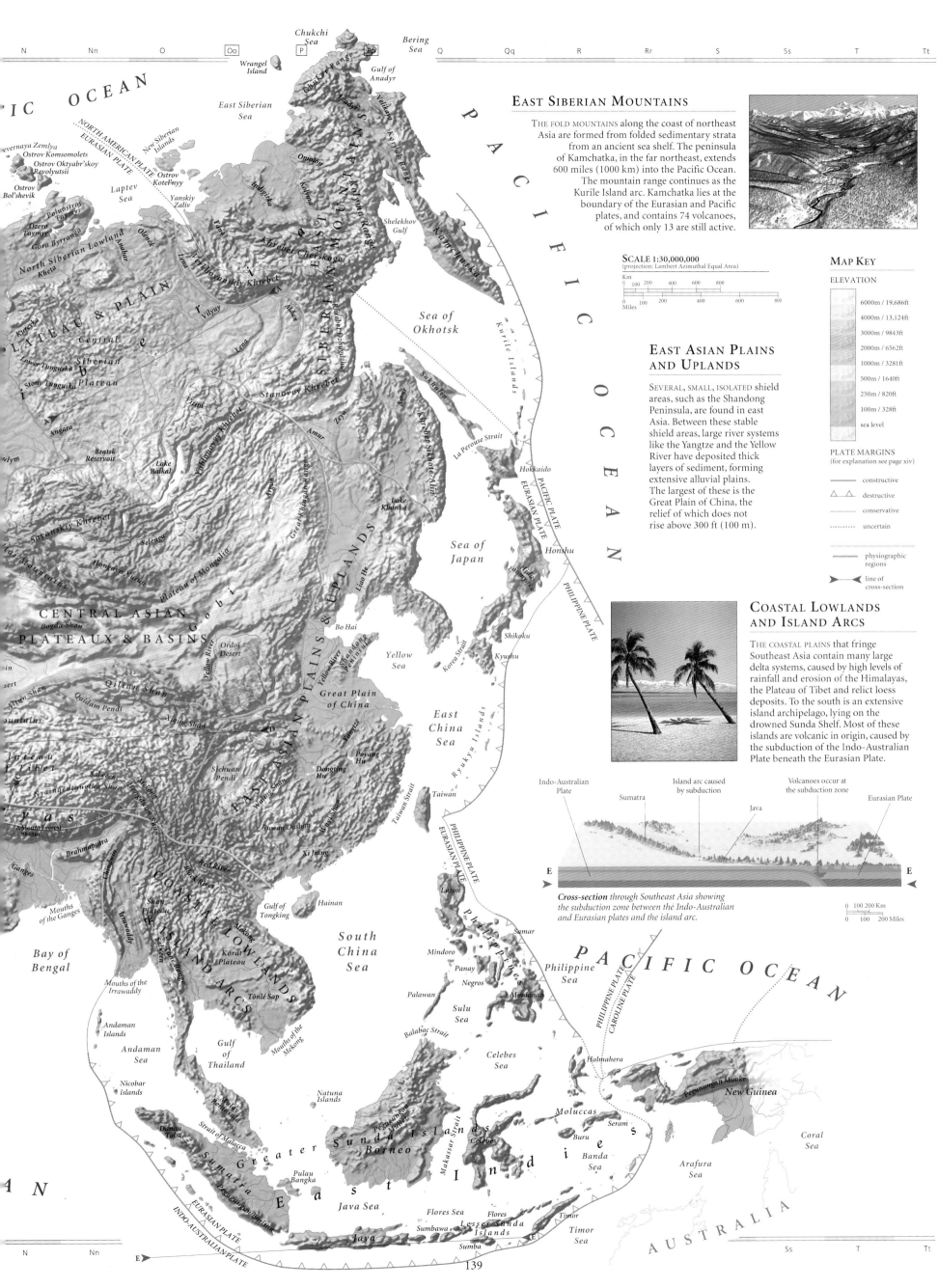

EAST SIBERIAN MOUNTAINS

THE FOLD MOUNTAINS along the coast of northeast Asia are formed from folded sedimentary strata from an ancient sea shelf. The peninsula of Kamchatka, in the far northeast, extends 600 miles (1000 km) into the Pacific Ocean. The mountain range continues as the Kurile Island arc. Kamchatka lies at the boundary of the Eurasian and Pacific plates, and contains 74 volcanoes, of which only 13 are still active.

SCALE 1:30,000,000
(projection: Lambert Azimuthal Equal Area)

MAP KEY

ELEVATION

6000m / 19,686ft
4000m / 13,124ft
3000m / 9843ft
2000m / 6562ft
1000m / 3281ft
500m / 1640ft
250m / 820ft
100m / 328ft
sea level

PLATE MARGINS
(for explanation see page xiv)

△ △ constructive
△ △ destructive
conservative
uncertain
physiographic regions
line of cross-section

EAST ASIAN PLAINS AND UPLANDS

SEVERAL, SMALL, ISOLATED shield areas, such as the Shandong Peninsula, are found in east Asia. Between these stable shield areas, large river systems like the Yangtze and the Yellow River have deposited thick layers of sediment, forming extensive alluvial plains. The largest of these is the Great Plain of China, the relief of which does not rise above 300 ft (100 m).

COASTAL LOWLANDS AND ISLAND ARCS

THE COASTAL PLAINS that fringe Southeast Asia contain many large delta systems, caused by high levels of rainfall and erosion of the Himalayas, the Plateau of Tibet and relict loess deposits. To the south is an extensive island archipelago, lying on the drowned Sunda Shelf. Most of these islands are volcanic in origin, caused by the subduction of the Indo-Australian Plate beneath the Eurasian Plate.

Cross-section through Southeast Asia showing the subduction zone between the Indo-Australian and Eurasian plates and the island arc.

TURKEY & THE CAUCASUS

ARMENIA, AZERBAIJAN, GEORGIA, TURKEY

THIS REGION OCCUPIES THE FRAGMENTED JUNCTION between Europe, Asia and the Russian Federation. Sunni Islam provides a common identity for the secular state of Turkey, which the revered leader Kemal Atatürk established from the remnants of the Ottoman Empire after the First World War. Turkey has a broad resource base and expanding trade links with Europe, but the east is relatively undeveloped and strife between the state and a large Kurdish minority has yet to be resolved. Georgia is similarly challenged by ethnic separatism, while the Christian state of Armenia and the mainly Muslim and oil-rich Azerbaijan are locked in conflict over the territory of Nagornyy Karabakh.

TRANSPORT AND INDUSTRY

TURKEY LEADS THE REGION's well-diversified economy. Petrochemicals, textiles, engineering and food processing are the main industries. Azerbaijan is able to export oil, while the other states rely heavily on hydro-electric power and imported fuel. Georgia produces precision machinery. War and earthquake damage have devastated Armenia's infrastructure.

Azerbaijan has substantial oil reserves, located in and around the Caspian Sea. They were some of the earliest oilfields in the world to be exploited.

USING THE LAND AND SEA

TURKEY IS LARGELY SELF-SUFFICIENT in food. The irrigated Black Sea coastlands have the world's highest yields of hazelnuts. Tobacco, cotton, sultanas, tea and figs are the region's main cash crops and a great range of fruit and vegetables are grown. Wine grapes are among the labour-intensive crops which allow full use of limited agricultural land in the Caucasus. Sturgeon fishing is particularly important in Azerbaijan.

Land use and agricultural distribution

- cattle
- goats
- cotton
- fishing
- fruit
- hazelnuts
- olives
- sugar beet
- tobacco
- vineyards

- capital cities
- major towns

- pasture
- cropland
- forest

THE URBAN/RURAL POPULATION DIVIDE

urban 67%   rural 23%

0 10 20 30 40 50 60 70 80 90 100

POPULATION DENSITY	TOTAL LAND AREA
218 people per sq mile (84 people per sq km)	368,912 sq miles (955,730 sq km)

For many centuries, Istanbul has held tremendous strategic importance as a crucial gateway between Europe and Asia. Founded by the Greeks as Byzantium, the city became the centre of the East Roman Empire and was known as Constantinople to the Romans. From the 15th century onwards the city became the centre of the great Ottoman Empire.

Major industry and infrastructure

- carpet weaving
- cement
- chemicals
- coal
- engineering
- food processing
- oil
- textiles
- tourism
- vehicle manufacture

- capital cities
- major towns
- international airports
- major roads
- major industrial areas

THE TRANSPORT NETWORK

76,289 miles (122,849 km)	
774 miles (1246 km)	
9047 miles (14,569 km)	
745 miles (1200 km)	

Physical and political barriers have severely limited communications between Armenia, Georgia and Azerbaijan. Turkey has a relatively well-developed transport network.

THE LANDSCAPE

THE DEEPLY-ERODED HILLS and salty basins of the Anatolian Plateau are bordered by several mountain ranges along the Black Sea coast, and the limestone Taurus Mountains (Toros Dağlari) in the south. A lowland trough divides the Caucasus and the Lesser Caucasus, which form a formidable barrier of peaks in the north.

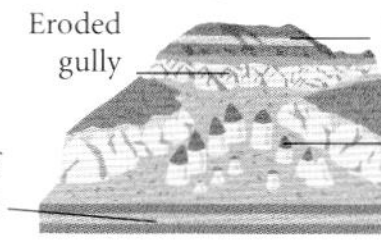

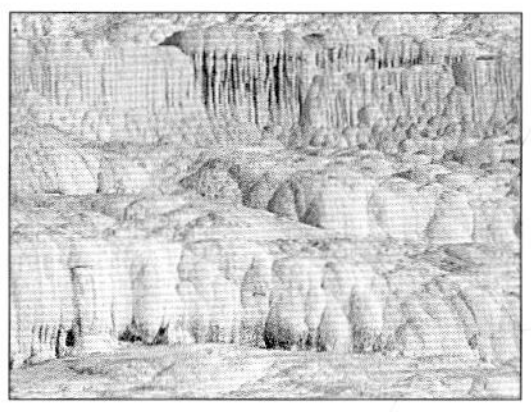

The white rock terraces at Pamukkale in western Turkey were formed when underground water, heated by volcanic activity, dissolved minerals in the rocks. When the water reached the surface and evaporated the minerals were left behind in these extraordinary formations.

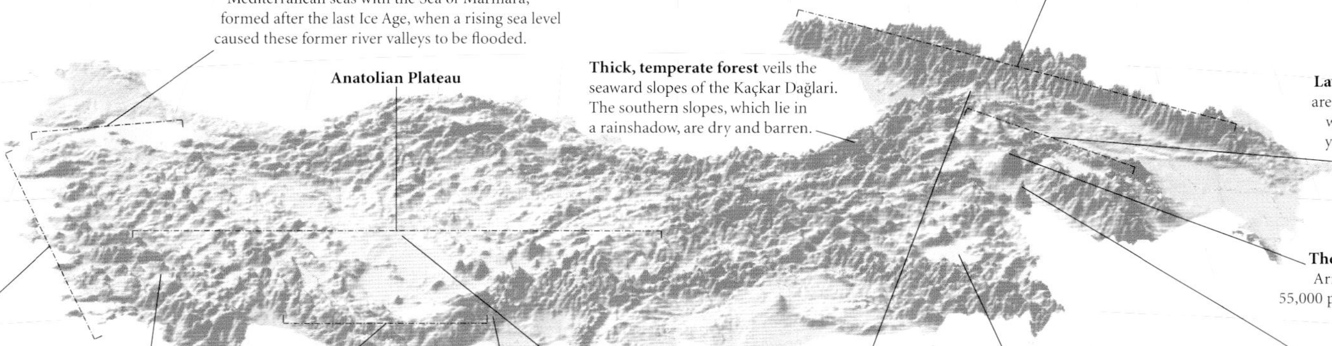

Long, parallel mountain ranges run from east to west into the Aegean Sea, which has risen since the last Ice Age to form a drowned coastline of numerous islands and extended inlets.

MAP KEY

POPULATION

- above 5 million
- 1 million to 5 million
- 500,000 to 1 million
- 100,000 to 500,000
- 50,000 to 100,000
- 10,000 to 50,000
- below 10,000

ELEVATION

- 4000m / 13,124ft
- 3000m / 9843ft
- 2000m / 6562ft
- 1000m / 3281ft
- 500m / 1640ft
- 250m / 820ft
- 100m / 328ft
- sea level

Limestone weathering in the Anatolian Plateau

Eroded gully · High plateau · Remnant landforms · Layers of tephra

In central Turkey, rainwater has chemically weathered away numerous layers of limestone, leaving isolated outcrops and pinnacles and deep eroded gullies.

The straits of the Bosporus and the Dardanelles, respectively linking the Black and Mediterranean seas with the Sea of Marmara, formed after the last Ice Age, when a rising sea level caused these former river valleys to be flooded.

Anatolian Plateau

Pamukkale

Thick, temperate forest veils the seaward slopes of the Kaçkar Dağlari. The southern slopes, which lie in a rainshadow, are dry and barren.

The folded peaks of the Taurus Mountains (Toros Dağlari) were formed 60–65 million years ago, at the same time as the Alps. The rock is mainly limestone, with deep caves, gorges and underground rivers.

The Cilician Gates (Grlek Boğazi), a major pass through the Taurus Mountains (Toros Dağlari), is the point where streams flow from the interior plateau onto the lowland of Adana.

Many of the rivers crossing the Anatolian Plateau never reach the sea, but drain into salt marshes and shallow salt lakes such as Lake Tuz (Tuz Gölü), where much of the water is lost to evaporation.

The granite massif near Suram divides the lowlands of Georgia from the oil-rich basin of Azerbaijan's Kura River, which has built a large delta into the Caspian Sea.

The shallow, saline Lake Van (Van Gölü) is the largest lake in Turkey. Dry terraces mark a previous shoreline 181 ft (55 m) above the present water level.

The Caucasus are fold mountains, which formed around the same time as the Taurus Mountains (Toros Dağlari) around 65 million years ago and have since been modified by volcanic erruptions.

Lava has flowed over large areas of the Lesser Caucasus within the last five million years, producing extensive basalt plateaux.

The earthquake that struck Armenia in 1988 killed over 55,000 people and devastated the country's infrastructure.

The volcanic cone of Mount Ararat is the highest peak in Turkey, with an altitude of 16,853 ft (5137 m).

Since the 6th century BC, the pinnacles and caves of east-central Anatolia have been utilized as dwellings. Many are still inhabited today.

SCALE 1:4,000,000
(projection: Lambert Conformal Conic)

Km 0 10 20 40 60 80 100 120
Miles 0 10 20 40 60 80 100 120

The fisheries of Azerbaijan are noted for their hauls of sturgeon, and the Caspian Sea accounts for 80% of the world's total catch. Sturgeon roe is used to make internationally-famed caviar.

Traditional steam baths are found throughout Turkey, and are used for socializing as well as for bathing.

MAP LABELS:

RUSSIAN FEDERATION · GEORGIA · ARMENIA · AZERBAIJAN · IRAN · IRAQ · SYRIA · Caspian Sea

Sokhumi · Gagra · Bichvint'a · Gudaut'a · ABKHAZIA · Och'amch'ire · Gali · Mestia · Kazbek 5047m · Qazbegi · Tebulosmt'a 4493m · Oni · Rioni · Zugdidi · Khobi · K'ut'aisi · Chiat'ura · Zestap'oni · South Ossetia · Ts'khinvali · Gori · Dushet'i · T'elavi · Lagodekhi · P'ot'i · Samtredia · Surami · Khashuri · Borjomi · Kaspi · T'bilisi · Gurjaani · Zaqatala · Xudat · Xaçmax · Qusar · Quba · Däväçi · Şamur · Ozurget'i · AJARIA · Akhalts'ikhe · T'BILISI · Rust'avi · Marneuli · Bolnisi · Bərdə · Ağsu · Ismailly · Şemakha · Suraxanı · Mastağa · Abşeron Yarımadası · Bat'umi · K'obulet'i · Achkasar 3196m · Tashir · Alaverdi · Ağstafa · Tovuz · Gäncä · Mingäçevir · Göyçay · Yevlax · Ucar · Kürdämir · Ağsu · Şamaxı · Akhsu · Sumqayıt · Baki · BAKI (Baku) · Ostrov Zhiloy

Hopa · Borçka · Pazar · Ardeşen · ARTVİN · Ardanuç · Posof · Ardahan · ARDAHAN · Çıldır · Çıldır Gölü · Akhalk'alak'i · Stepanavan · Spitak · Klaverdi · İjevan · Şämkir · Xanlar · Naftalan · Nagornyy Karabakh · Beyläqan · Mil Düzü · Salyan · Bankä · Bilasuvar · Cälilabad · Masallı · Port-ilic · Länkärän · Astara · Talış Mountains

Trabzon · Tirebolu · Vakfıkebir · Görele · Akçaabat · Sürmene · Of · Rize · RIZE · Kızdere · Kaçkar Dağlari · Yusufeli · Artvin · Şavşat · Göle · Olur · Oltu · Kars · KARS · Senkaya · Sarıkamış · Gyumri · Art'ik · Vanadzor · Sevan · Sevana Lich · Vardenis · Sisian · Goris · Qubadlı · Zängilan · Kapan · Qapıcıq Dağı 3629m · K'ajaran · Meghri · Ordubad · Culfa

Ordu · Bulancak · Giresun · GIRESUN · Doğu Karadeniz Dağlari · Torul · Gümüşhane · GÜMÜŞHANE · Kelkit · Şebinkarahisar · Siran · İspir · Tortum · Erzurum · ERZURUM · Pasinler · Horasan · Ağrı · Taşlıçay · Doğubayazıt · Büyükağrı Dağı (Mount Ararat) 5137m · Aralık · İğdir · İGDIR · Tuzluca · Kağızman · Digor · Iğdir · Artashat · Ararat · Mount Gogi · Şarur · Naxçıvan · AZERBAIJAN

Refahiye · Kelkit Çayı · ERZINCAN · Erzincan · Kemah · Tercan · Aşkale · Çat · Tekman · Karayazı · Tutak · Hınıs · Karlıova · Varto · Malazgirt · Bulanık · Muradiye · Erciş · VAN · Van · Van Gölü · BİTLİS · Bitlis · Tatvan · Gevaş · Başkale

YEREVAN · Ejmiatsin · Aragats Lerr 4090m · Hoktemberyan · Hrazdan · Ch'arents'avan · Martuni · Vayk' · Yeghegnadzor

Hekimhan · Keban Barajı · ELAZIĞ · Elazığ · Karakaya Barajı · Hazar Gölü · Maden · Palu · Kulp · Lice · Muş · MUŞ · Nazik Gölü · Ercek Gölü · Serafettin Dağları · Bingöl · BİNGÖL · Genç · Hani · Ergani · Çermik · Deveçgeçidi Barajı

Doğanşehir · Malatya · ADIYAMAN · Adıyaman · Kâhta · Atatürk Barajı · ŞANLIURFA · Şanlıurfa · Şanlıurfa Yaylası · Bozova · Birecik · Suruç · DIYARBAKIR · Diyarbakır · Silvan · Bismil · Çınar · İlisu Barajı · Batman · BATMAN · Siverek · Tigris · SİİRT · Siirt · Kurtalan · Pervari · Baykan · Eruh · Mardin Dağları · MARDIN · Mardin · Midyat · Derik · Kızıltepe · Nusaybin · Viranşehir · Ceylanpınar · ŞIRNAK · Şırnak · Cizre · Great Zab · Kurdistan · HAKKARİ · Hakkâri · Yüksekova

125 · 148 · 144 · 144

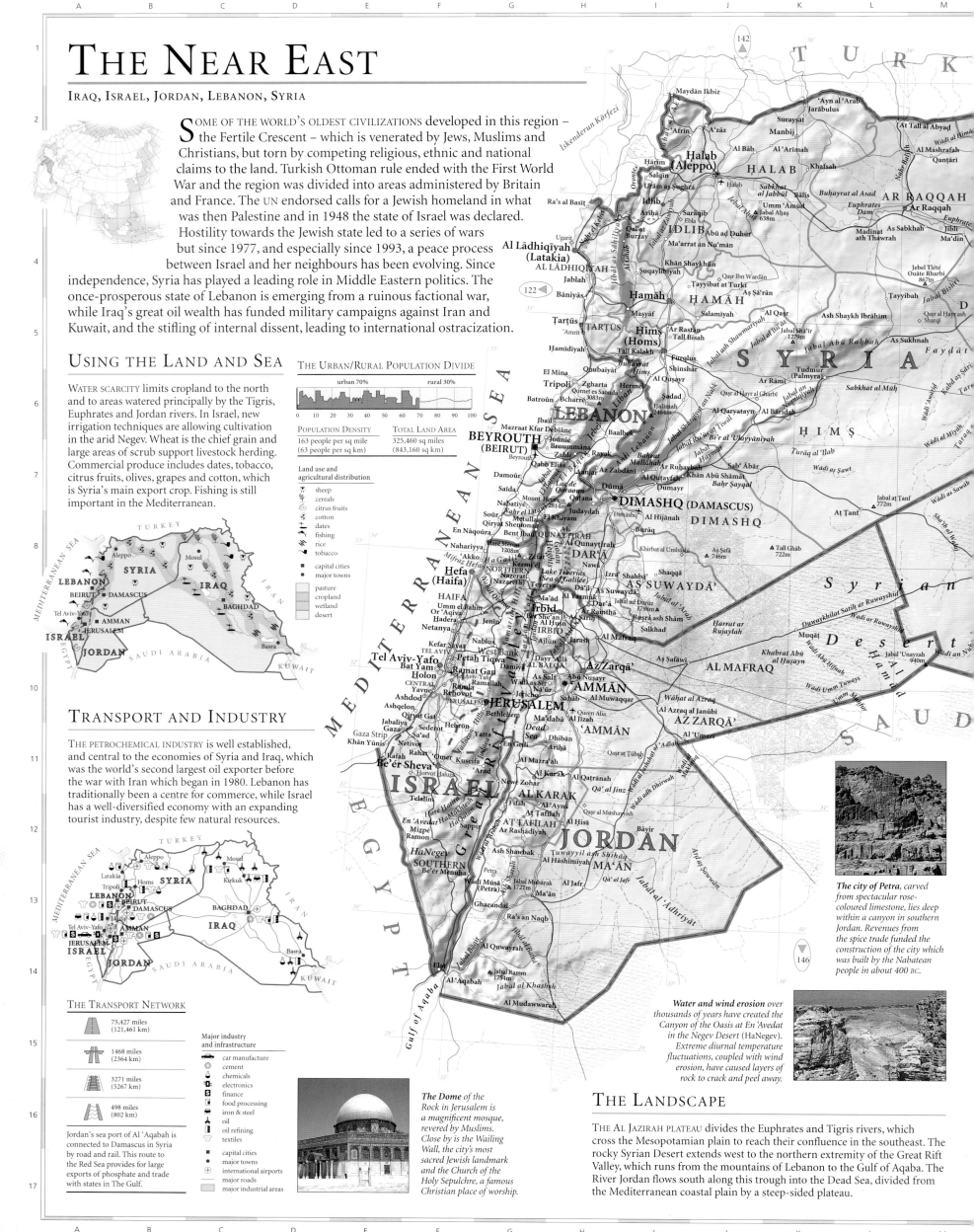

THE NEAR EAST

IRAQ, ISRAEL, JORDAN, LEBANON, SYRIA

SOME OF THE WORLD'S OLDEST CIVILIZATIONS developed in this region – the Fertile Crescent – which is venerated by Jews, Muslims and Christians, but torn by competing religious, ethnic and national claims to the land. Turkish Ottoman rule ended with the First World War and the region was divided into areas administered by Britain and France. The UN endorsed calls for a Jewish homeland in what was then Palestine and in 1948 the state of Israel was declared. Hostility towards the Jewish state led to a series of wars but since 1977, and especially since 1993, a peace process between Israel and her neighbours has been evolving. Since independence, Syria has played a leading role in Middle Eastern politics. The once-prosperous state of Lebanon is emerging from a ruinous factional war, while Iraq's great oil wealth has funded military campaigns against Iran and Kuwait, and the stifling of internal dissent, leading to international ostracization.

USING THE LAND AND SEA

WATER SCARCITY limits cropland to the north and to areas watered principally by the Tigris, Euphrates and Jordan rivers. In Israel, new irrigation techniques are allowing cultivation in the arid Negev. Wheat is the chief grain and large areas of scrub support livestock herding. Commercial produce includes dates, tobacco, citrus fruits, olives, grapes and cotton, which is Syria's main export crop. Fishing is still important in the Mediterranean.

THE URBAN/RURAL POPULATION DIVIDE

urban 70%   rural 30%

POPULATION DENSITY
163 people per sq mile
(63 people per sq km)

TOTAL LAND AREA
325,460 sq miles
(843,160 sq km)

Land use and
agricultural distribution
- sheep
- cereals
- citrus fruits
- cotton
- dates
- fishing
- rice
- tobacco
- capital cities
- major towns

pasture
cropland
wetland
desert

TRANSPORT AND INDUSTRY

THE PETROCHEMICAL INDUSTRY is well established, and central to the economies of Syria and Iraq, which was the world's second largest oil exporter before the war with Iran which began in 1980. Lebanon has traditionally been a centre for commerce, while Israel has a well-diversified economy with an expanding tourist industry, despite few natural resources.

THE TRANSPORT NETWORK

75,427 miles
(121,461 km)

1468 miles
(2364 km)

3271 miles
(5267 km)

498 miles
(802 km)

Jordan's sea port of Al 'Aqabah is connected to Damascus in Syria by road and rail. This route to the Red Sea provides for large exports of phosphate and trade with states in The Gulf.

Major industry
and infrastructure
- car manufacture
- cement
- chemicals
- electronics
- finance
- food processing
- iron & steel
- oil
- oil refining
- textiles
- capital cities
- major towns
- international airports
- major roads
- major industrial areas

The Dome of the Rock in Jerusalem is a magnificent mosque, revered by Muslims. Close by is the Wailing Wall, the city's most sacred Jewish landmark and the Church of the Holy Sepulchre, a famous Christian place of worship.

The city of Petra, carved from spectacular rose-coloured limestone, lies deep within a canyon in southern Jordan. Revenues from the spice trade funded the construction of the city which was built by the Nabatean people in about 400 BC.

Water and wind erosion over thousands of years have created the Canyon of the Oasis at En 'Avedat in the Negev Desert (HaNegev). Extreme diurnal temperature fluctuations, coupled with wind erosion, have caused layers of rock to crack and peel away.

THE LANDSCAPE

THE AL JAZIRAH PLATEAU divides the Euphrates and Tigris rivers, which cross the Mesopotamian plain to reach their confluence in the southeast. The rocky Syrian Desert extends west to the northern extremity of the Great Rift Valley, which runs from the mountains of Lebanon to the Gulf of Aqaba. The River Jordan flows south along this trough into the Dead Sea, divided from the Mediterranean coastal plain by a steep-sided plateau.

The island of El Hlayaye near Saida in southern Lebanon is linked to the mainland by a bridge built as part of the fort in the 12th century.

MAP KEY

POPULATION

- ◉ 1 million to 5 million
- ◉ 500,000 to 1 million
- ◎ 100,000 to 500,000
- ⊕ 50,000 to 100,000
- ○ 10,000 to 50,000
- ○ below 10,000

ELEVATION

- 4000m / 13,124ft
- 3000m / 9843ft
- 2000m / 6562ft
- 1000m / 3281ft
- 500m / 1640ft
- 250m / 820ft
- 100m / 328ft
- sea level

SCALE 1:3,250,000
(projection: Lambert Conformal Conic)

Km
0 10 20 40 60 80 100 120

Miles
0 10 20 40 60 80 100 120

The marshlands of the Tigris/Euphrates Delta have for centuries been home to the Marsh Arabs who maintain a unique lifestyle, living in reed houses, such as this one at Al Qurnah. These marshes are increasingly being threatened by drainage projects.

▶ 148

▶ 146

▶ 148

The shores of the Dead Sea are the lowest land on the Earth's surface – 1286 ft (392 m) below sea level. This highly saline lake is fed by the River Jordan but has no outlet to the sea. The water level has continued to fall in recent years, due to increased use of the River Jordan for irrigation.

Ancient eruptions of lava formed the plateau of Jabal ad Duruz which is deeply weathered and eroded along the edge of the Great Rift Valley. The lava impounded the waters of the River Jordan to form the Sea of Galilee (Lake Tiberias).

Dead Sea

The Nahr el Litani, Lebanon's only permanent river, flows along the fertile El Beqaa Valley, which runs for 110 miles (175 km), between the Jebel Liban and Anti-Lebanon mountains.

The gravel-strewn terrain of the Syrian Desert is interrupted by wadis – river valleys which remain dry for most of the year.

Iraq Marshlands

Great quantities of sediment, deposited by the Tigris and Euphrates rivers, have infilled the head of The Gulf, shifting the coastline south by more than 150 miles (250 km) in the last 5000 years.

Extensive marshlands surround the lake of Hawr al Hammar, which is 70 miles (110 km) long.

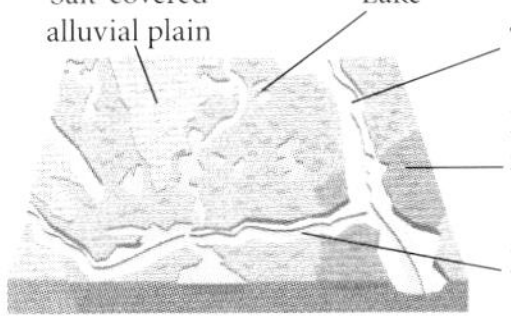

Salt-covered alluvial plain
Lake
Tigris
Dried salt marsh
Euphrates

The flood plains of southern Iraq are crossed by the Tigris and Euphrates rivers. Salt marshes and alluvial plains crusted with salt cover much of the area. The many small lakes are filled with brackish water and the marshes are colonized by reeds.

THE ARABIAN PENINSULA

BAHRAIN, KUWAIT, OMAN, QATAR, SAUDI ARABIA, UNITED ARAB EMIRATES (UAE), YEMEN

HUGE EXPANSES OF DESERT cover much of the Arabian Peninsula, limiting settlement to oases, the mountains along the Red Sea and coastal belts. The most populous area is the fertile highlands of Yemen. The Islamic faith and Arabic language give the region a cultural and religious unity, and the Saudi city of Mecca *(Makkah)* is Islam's most holy place, visited by over two million pilgrims each year. More than half the world's oil reserves are contained in this region, and the exploitation of oil and gas has brought great wealth, particularly to Saudi Arabia. Yemen and Oman are the least developed of the Arabian states, with large rural populations. Within Saudi Arabia over two-thirds of the people live in urban areas.

USING THE LAND

MOST OF THE ARABIAN PENINSULA is unsuited to settled agriculture, making irrigation and land reclamation projects essential. The narrow coastal plain and isolated oases, commonly amounting to less than 1% of the land area, are used to cultivate grains, coffee and exotic fruits. Goats, sheep and camels are widespread throughout the region.

THE URBAN/RURAL POPULATION DIVIDE

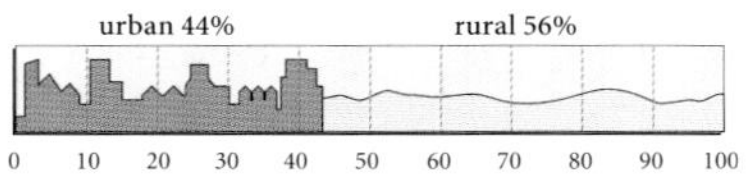

urban 44%   rural 56%

0 10 20 30 40 50 60 70 80 90 100

POPULATION DENSITY
37 people per sq mile
(14 people per sq km)

TOTAL LAND AREA
1,147,856 sq miles
(2,973,720 sq km)

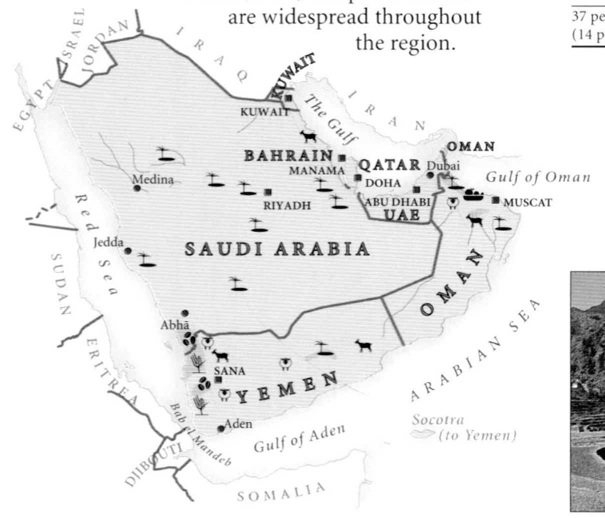

Land use and agricultural distribution

- goats
- sheep
- cereals
- coffee
- dates
- fruit

- capital cities
- major towns

- pasture
- cropland
- desert

The fertile soils of Yemen have encouraged settlement of almost all of the land from sea level up to the mountains at 10,000 ft (3050 m). In the higher reaches elaborate terraces have been constructed to facilitate crop cultivation.

THE LANDSCAPE

A PLATEAU MORE THAN 2500 ft (760 m) high extends across much of the Arabian Peninsula. The plateau slopes eastwards from the massive, rifted escarpment along the coast of the Red Sea, to the shallow waters of The Gulf. The interior is characterized by *cuestas* and valleys, drained by a system of *wadis*. A crescent of sand and gravel deserts lies to the east.

The An Nafud Desert is covered with *barchan* dunes varying between 30–100 ft (10–30 m) high. The 'horns' of the crescent-shaped dunes reflect the direction in which they are being moved by the wind.

Inselbergs are dotted over a wide area of the Najd Plateau. These resistant remnants of the ancient basement rock are left standing when the softer weathered rock has been worn away.

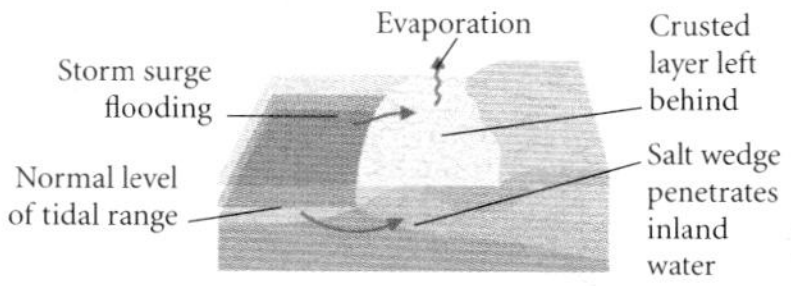

Evaporation
Storm surge flooding
Normal level of tidal range
Crusted layer left behind
Salt wedge penetrates inland water

A sabkha is a flat, salt-encrusted plain which occurs near the coast just above the high water mark. Flooding by sea water leads to saturation of the land with saline-rich groundwater. As this evaporates, a cracked layer of sand, cemented together with salt, gypsum and calcium carbonate is left behind.

Few areas in the Arabian Peninsula have rivers flowing through them. Most are drained by ephemeral watercourses called *wadis*.

The Hejaz *(Al Ḥijāz)* and Asir Mountains form part of the same geological region as the highlands of Sudan and Eritrea, to which they were once joined. They were separated when faulting opened the Red Sea, over 50 million years ago.

Across the Najd Plateau the flat relief is broken by *mesas*; steep-sided rock plateaux and *cuestas*; ridges with one steep and one gentle slope.

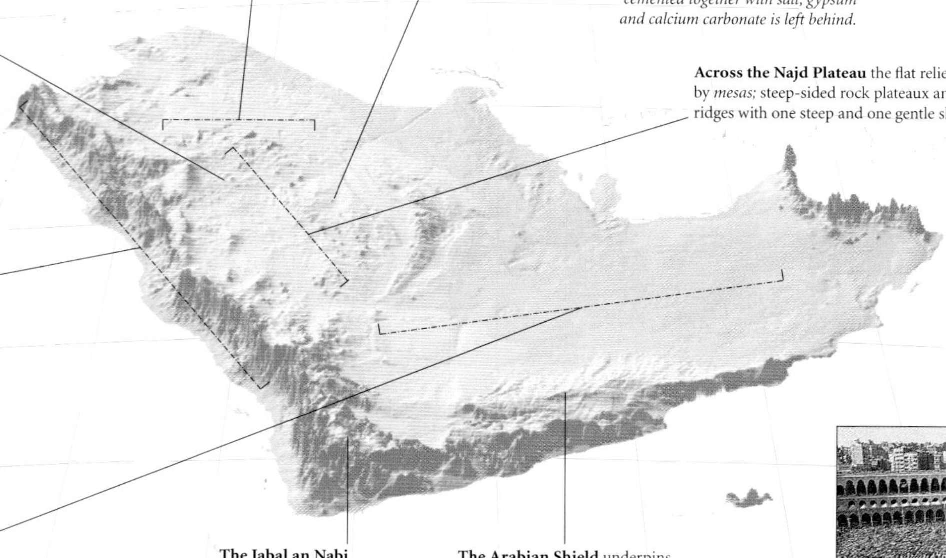

Ar Rub' al Khali, also known as the Empty Quarter, is the most arid part of the Arabian Peninsula. It is the largest uninterrupted sand desert in the world. Ridges of sand up to 25 miles (40 km) long, run northeast–southwest, giving characteristic linear dunes.

The Jabal an Nabi Shu'ayb in Yemen is the highest point on the peninsula, rising to 12,336 ft (3760 m).

The Arabian Shield underpins the west of the peninsula. It is a fragment of the ancient continent, Gondwanaland, which was separated by rifting millions of years ago.

Every Muslim must make at least one pilgrimage or hajj to Mecca (Makkah), in Saudi Arabia, during their lifetime. The cloth-covered shrine is called the Ka'bah, and is regarded by Muslims as the most sacred place on Earth.

TRANSPORT AND INDUSTRY

THE EXTRACTION AND REFINING OF OIL AND GAS are the major industrial activities in the Arabian Peninsula. The region also has an active construction sector, with many Arab cities reflecting the wealth generated by the oil industry. The service sector is dominated by financial and technical institutions, which, like the construction sector, mainly serve the oil industry. Traditional handicrafts such as carpet-weaving are found in rural areas.

Saudi Arabia contains the world's largest oil reserves, lying mainly along The Gulf coast. Each day the region produces 8.3 million barrels of oil. Here, in the desert, excess oil is being burnt off.

THE TRANSPORT NETWORK

65,239 miles (105,054 km)	2071 miles (3333 km)
864 miles (1392 km)	none

Internal surface transport is poorly developed across the peninsula. Along the coast, commercial routes have developed, but connections between bordering states rely on major airports.

Major industry and infrastructure
- cement
- chemicals
- iron & steel
- oil
- oil refining
- food processing
- capital cities
- major towns
- international airports
- major roads
- major industrial areas

Seasonal watercourses or wadis drain much of the interior of the Arabian Peninsula. Although they remain dry for much of the year, they are prone to flash floods after heavy rains.

MAP KEY

POPULATION
- 1 million to 5 million
- 500,000 to 1 million
- 100,000 to 500,000
- 50,000 to 100,000
- 10,000 to 50,000
- below 10,000

ELEVATION
- 3000m / 9843ft
- 2000m / 6562ft
- 1000m / 3281ft
- 500m / 1640ft
- 250m / 820ft
- 100m / 328ft
- sea level

SCALE 1:7,500,000
(projection: Lambert Conformal Conic)

IRAN & THE GULF STATES

BAHRAIN, IRAN, KUWAIT, QATAR, UNITED ARAB EMIRATES (UAE)

THE DISCOVERY OF OIL in The Gulf in the 1930s brought great wealth to the surrounding states. The revenue was largely used to modernize industry and infrastructure, initiating great social change in these formerly agrarian countries. Today, over 80% of the people in the Gulf states live in urban areas, and foreign nationals make up a sizeable proportion of the population in Kuwait, Qatar and the United Arab Emirates. The importance of control of the oil reserves has led to a number of territorial disputes, including most recently the Iran–Iraq War and the Gulf War. Islam is practised almost exclusively throughout the region and two distinct strands are found; Sunni Muslims in Qatar, Kuwait and UAE, and Shi'a Muslims in Iran and Bahrain. In 1979 Iran became the world's largest theocracy.

THE LANDSCAPE

THE LAND RISES STEEPLY from the fragmented coastal lowlands bordering The Gulf, to reach Iran's interior plateau, bounded by heavily-eroded mountain chains. An unstable plate boundary runs northwest to southeast across Iran causing frequent earthquakes. On the sandy west coast of The Gulf, the relief is generally flat, with patches of salt marsh. Bahrain consists of two groups of islands, which are mostly small and rocky.

Pyroclastic layers | Lava flow | Lava flow layers

Qolleh-ye Damavand in the Elburz Mountains is a composite volcano. It comprises layers of lava and pyroclasts fragmentary rocks which accumulate on the slopes of the volcano after being ejected into the air.

Marine sediments from deep beneath the ancient Tethys Sea have been uplifted to form the Elburz Mountains, which stretch along the shores of the Caspian Sea, northern Iran.

Lava and ash from previous volcanic activity covers a 200-mile (320-km) stretch from the border with Azerbaijan to the Caspian Sea.

Iran's two mountain chains, the Zagros and Elburz, were uplifted at the same time as the Alps in Europe, when the African Plate collided with the Eurasian Plate.

Caspian Sea

Qolleh-ye Damavand

Dominated by a vast, semi-arid interior plateau, most of Iran lies above 1640 ft (500 m). The region is poorly drained with many of its basins remaining dry for months at a time.

The fierce Shamal wind affects much of this region. Every summer it blows dust south from the flood plains of the Tigris and Euphrates, reducing visibility to such an extent that Kuwait International Airport is frequently forced to close.

The oilfields of The Gulf are formed from marine shale deposits lying in sedimentary basins at the margins of the Zagros Mountains.

Prolific springs tapping artesian water make cultivation possible across the north of Bahrain's main island. This provides a sharp contrast to the sandy plains in the south and west.

Autumn winds blowing across The Gulf can reach speeds of up to 95 mph (150 kmph) causing severe storms, squalls and waterspouts.

Numerous islands lie along the southern coast of The Gulf. Some of these are salt domes, created when less dense salts were displaced and forced up to the surface by denser, overlying strata.

The Dasht-e Lut

The Dasht-e Lut covers a large portion of eastern Iran with its dry, wind-eroded plain of scattered sandstone pillars and salty depressions. During the summer, temperatures soar, making it one of the world's hottest, driest places.

USING THE LAND AND SEA

ALONG THE COAST of the Caspian Sea, desalinated water allows fruits and vegetables to be produced, although water shortages and desert soils still limit farming. Sheep are the most important livestock raised in Iran and commercial forests cover the northwest of the country. Shrimp stocks were decimated by pollution during the Gulf War, but fishing remains important for domestic and export markets.

All of the Gulf states have commercial fishing fleets. Before the discovery of oil, fishing was the region's leading industry.

Land use and agricultural distribution

- goats
- sheep
- cereals
- citrus fruits
- cotton
- dates
- fishing
- timber
- capital cities
- major towns
- pasture
- cropland
- forest
- desert
- wetland

THE URBAN/RURAL POPULATION DIVIDE

urban 59% | rural 41%

0 10 20 30 40 50 60 70 80 90 100

POPULATION DENSITY
118 people per sq mile
(46 people per sq km)

TOTAL LAND AREA
642,883 sq miles
(1,665,500 sq km)

The Kuwait Towers in the centre of Kuwait are symbols of the vast wealth oil has brought to the country. Before 1960, the city had only one main street and was surrounded by a mud wall.

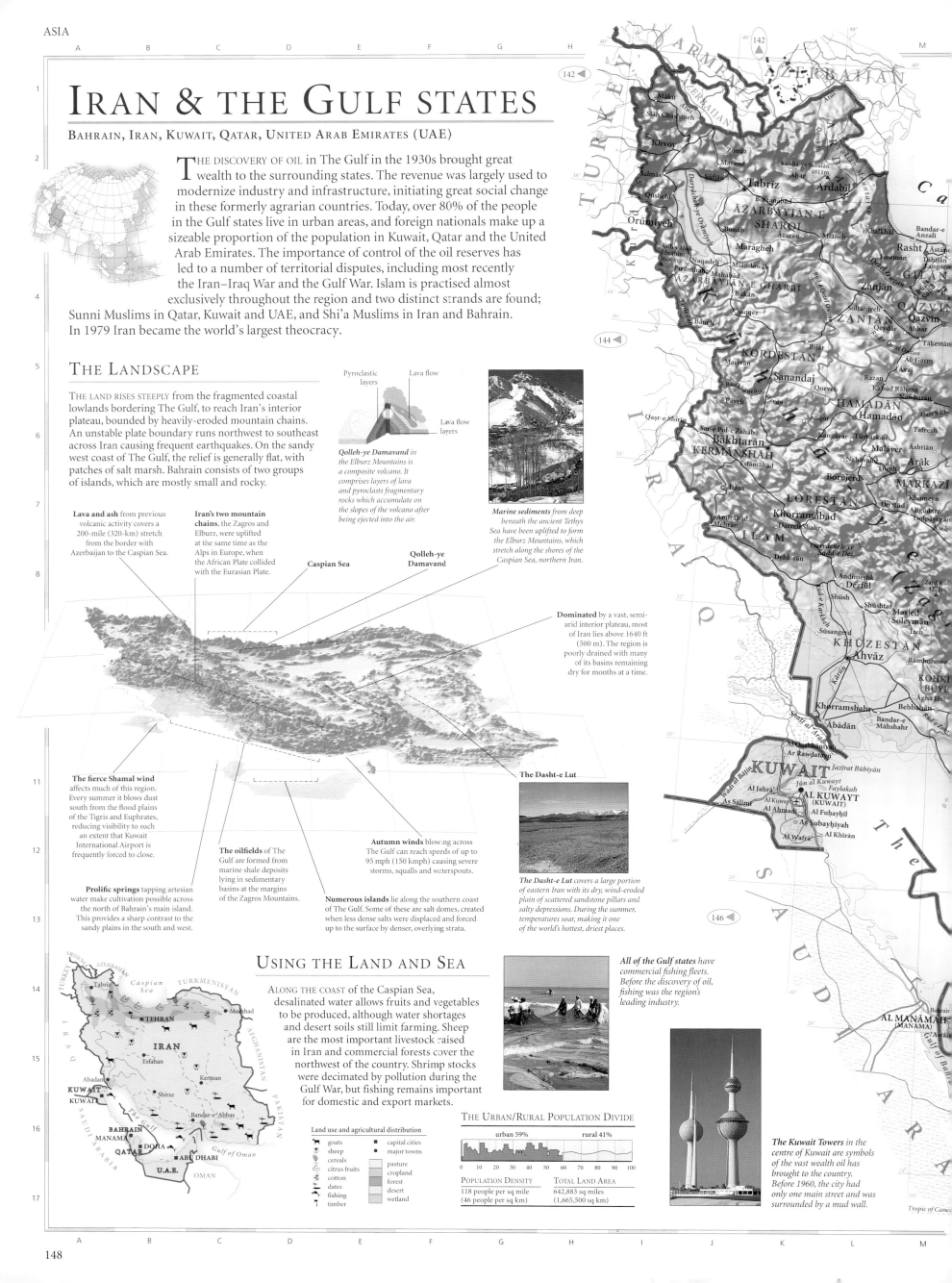

Many volcanoes lie in Iran's 1200 mile (1930 km) volcanic belt, including the country's highest peak, the now-extinct Qolleh-ye Damavand at 18,600 ft (5671 m).

Extensive oil and gas exploitation in the Gulf region has allowed the economic transformation of the Gulf states. Kuwait and the United Arab Emirates today have the highest per capita incomes in the world.

TRANSPORT AND INDUSTRY

BOTH ONSHORE AND OFFSHORE oil reserves are exploited throughout the region. Kuwait not only extracts but also refines 80% of its oil. Bahrain has diversified its economy to become the main commercial and financial centre in The Gulf. Iran produces a wide range of products: textile mills are widespread and carpet-weaving is an important export industry.

Major industry and infrastructure

- carpet manufacture
- chemicals
- finance
- food processing
- oil
- oil refining
- textiles
- capital city
- major towns
- international airports
- major roads
- major industrial areas

THE TRANSPORT NETWORK

50,340 miles (81,063 km)	466 miles (750 km)
3723 miles (5995 km)	81 miles (130 km)

Major towns and neighbouring countries are linked by adequate road networks, although rural areas are less well served. Bahrain is linked to the mainland by a 15 mile (25 km) long causeway.

MAP KEY

POPULATION

- above 5 million
- 1 million to 5 million
- 500,000 to 1 million
- 100,000 to 500,000
- 50,000 to 100,000
- 10,000 to 50,000
- below 10,000

ELEVATION

- 4000m / 13,124ft
- 3000m / 9843ft
- 2000m / 6562ft
- 1000m / 3281ft
- 500m / 1640ft
- 250m / 820ft
- 100m / 328ft
- sea level

SCALE 1:5,500,000
(projection: Lambert Conformal Conic)

Tropic of Cancer

A B C D E F G H I J K L M

KAZAKHSTAN

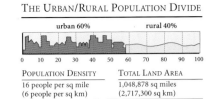

ABUNDANT NATURAL RESOURCES lie in the immense steppe grasslands, deserts and central plateau of the former Soviet republic of Kazakhstan. An intensive programme of industrial and agricultural development to exploit these resources during the Soviet era resulted in catastrophic industrial pollution, including fallout from nuclear testing and the shrinkage of the Aral Sea. Since independence, the government has encouraged foreign investment and liberalized the economy to promote growth. The adoption of Kazakh as the national language is intended to encourage a new sense of national identity in a state where living conditions for the majority remain harsh, both in cramped urban centres and impoverished rural areas.

TRANSPORT AND INDUSTRY

THE SINGLE MOST IMPORTANT INDUSTRY in Kazakhstan is mining, based around extensive oil deposits near the Caspian Sea, the world's largest chromium mine, and vast reserves of iron ore. Recent foreign investment has helped to develop industries including food processing and steel manufacture, and to expand the exploitation of mineral resources. The Russian space programme is still based at Baykonur, near Zhezkazgan in central Kazakhstan.

Major industry and infrastructure

- chemicals
- engineering
- fish processing
- food processing
- iron & steel
- metallurgy
- mining
- oil
- capital cities
- major towns
- international airports
- major roads
- major industrial areas

THE TRANSPORT NETWORK

87,561 miles (141,000 km)

8483 miles (13,660 km)

Industrial areas in the north and east are well-connected to Russia. Air and rail links with Germany and China have been established through foreign investment. Better access to Baltic ports is being sought.

125 ◄

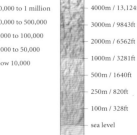

An open-cast coal mine in Kazakhstan. Foreign investment is being actively sought by the Kazakh government in order to fully exploit the potential of the country's rich mineral reserves.

MAP KEY

POPULATION
- ▣ 1 million to 5 million
- ◉ 500,000 to 1 million
- ◎ 100,000 to 500,000
- ⊕ 50,000 to 100,000
- ⊙ 10,000 to 50,000
- ○ below 10,000

ELEVATION
- 4000m / 13,124ft
- 3000m / 9843ft
- 2000m / 6562ft
- 1000m / 3281ft
- 500m / 1640ft
- 250m / 820ft
- 100m / 328ft
- sea level

USING THE LAND AND SEA

THE REARING OF LARGE HERDS of sheep and goats on the steppe grasslands forms the core of Kazakh agriculture. Arable cultivation and cotton-growing in pasture and desert areas was encouraged during the Soviet era, but relative yields are low. The heavy use of fertilizers and the diversion of natural water sources for irrigation has degraded much of the land.

THE URBAN/RURAL POPULATION DIVIDE

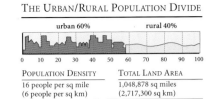

urban 60%   rural 40%

0 10 20 30 40 50 60 70 80 90 100

POPULATION DENSITY	TOTAL LAND AREA
16 people per sq mile (6 people per sq km)	1,048,878 sq miles (2,717,300 sq km)

Land use and agricultural distribution
- cattle
- goats
- sheep
- cotton
- fishing
- wheat
- capital cities
- major towns
- pasture
- cropland
- forest
- mountain region
- desert

The nomadic peoples who moved their herds around the steppe grasslands are now largely settled, although echoes of their traditional lifestyle, in particular their superb riding skills, remain.

SCALE 1:6,250,000
(projection: Lambert Conformal Conic)

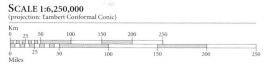

Km
0 25 50 100 150 200 250
Miles

THE LANDSCAPE

STRETCHING MORE THAN 1250 MILES (2000 km) from the Caspian Sea in the west to China in the east, more than 40% of Kazakhstan is covered by steppe grasslands which give way to barren desert in the south. The land rises eastwards towards the mineral-rich central plateau, to form the Altai Mountains.

1960 *1996* *2010*

Since 1960, the Aral Sea has shrunk by 40%, become extremely saline, and lost all but five of its once-abundant fish species. Factors in this ecological disaster include the excessive use of fertilizers, defoliants and the diversion of its main source rivers for the irrigation of desert lands.

The Caspian Sea is the largest body of inland water in the world.

The desert of Peski Bol'shiye Barsuki is mainly sandy, displaying a number of classic dune formations. Groundwater supports a small amount of vegetation.

A large number of salt lakes fill depressions in the rolling uplands of central Kazakhstan.

The Altai Mountains lie on Kazakhstan's eastern borders with China and the Russian Federation. Cold and largely barren, they are the source of many of the rivers which flow across the steppe.

Altai Mountains

Tien Shan

Aral Sea

Khrebet Kanchingiz

Its waters taken for industry and irrigation, the Syr Darya, one of Kazakhstan's major rivers, now barely reaches the Aral Sea which it used to fill. Like many Kazakh rivers it has been heavily polluted with chemicals and its flow has been restricted by up to 60%.

The waters of Lake Balkhash (*Ozero Balkhash*), unlike those of the Aral Sea, are still able to support a fishing industry.

The central Kazakh Uplands (*Kazakhskiy Melkosopochnik*) contain much of the country's mineral riches. The landscape is largely flat with occasional rocky outcrops and hillocks.

Immense stretches of steppe grasslands characterize much of the Kazakh landscape. These lowland areas have been used for arable cultivation in recent years, although problems with irrigation have meant that much of the land is being allowed to revert to its natural vegetation and pastoral usage.

Rows of pine trees edge this valley near Alma-Ata. The snow-covered slopes in the background are used for skiing.

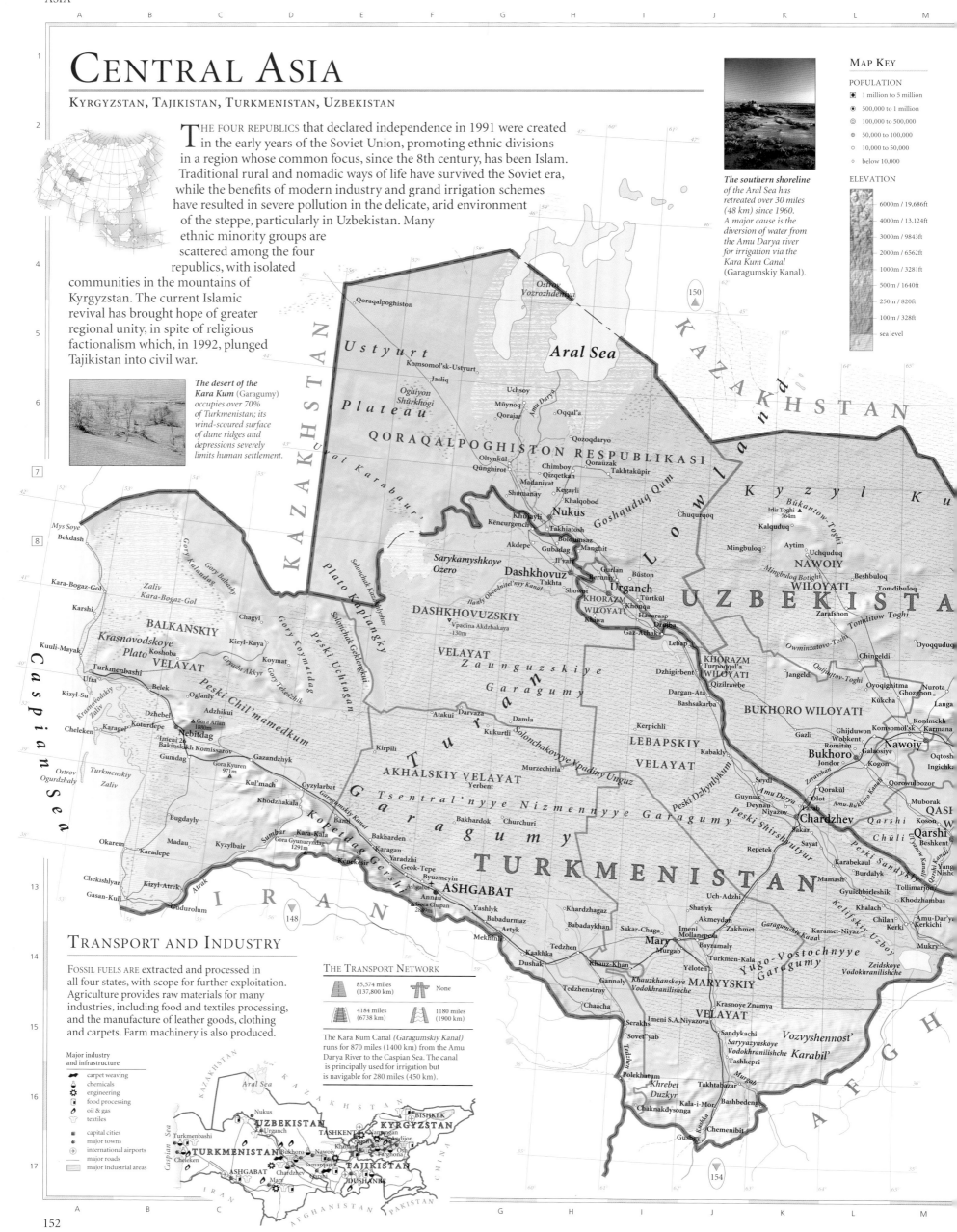

CENTRAL ASIA

KYRGYZSTAN, TAJIKISTAN, TURKMENISTAN, UZBEKISTAN

THE FOUR REPUBLICS that declared independence in 1991 were created in the early years of the Soviet Union, promoting ethnic divisions in a region whose common focus, since the 8th century, has been Islam. Traditional rural and nomadic ways of life have survived the Soviet era, while the benefits of modern industry and grand irrigation schemes have resulted in severe pollution in the delicate, arid environment of the steppe, particularly in Uzbekistan. Many ethnic minority groups are scattered among the four republics, with isolated communities in the mountains of Kyrgyzstan. The current Islamic revival has brought hope of greater regional unity, in spite of religious factionalism which, in 1992, plunged Tajikistan into civil war.

The southern shoreline of the Aral Sea has retreated over 30 miles (48 km) since 1960. A major cause is the diversion of water from the Amu Darya river for irrigation via the Kara Kum Canal (Garagumskiy Kanal).

The desert of the Kara Kum (Garagumy) occupies over 70% of Turkmenistan; its wind-scoured surface of dune ridges and depressions severely limits human settlement.

MAP KEY

POPULATION
- 1 million to 5 million
- 500,000 to 1 million
- 100,000 to 500,000
- 50,000 to 100,000
- 10,000 to 50,000
- below 10,000

ELEVATION
- 6000m / 19,686ft
- 4000m / 13,124ft
- 3000m / 9843ft
- 2000m / 6562ft
- 1000m / 3281ft
- 500m / 1640ft
- 250m / 820ft
- 100m / 328ft
- sea level

TRANSPORT AND INDUSTRY

FOSSIL FUELS ARE extracted and processed in all four states, with scope for further exploitation. Agriculture provides raw materials for many industries, including food and textiles processing, and the manufacture of leather goods, clothing and carpets. Farm machinery is also produced.

THE TRANSPORT NETWORK

85,574 miles (137,800 km)		None
4184 miles (6738 km)		1180 miles (1900 km)

The Kara Kum Canal *(Garagumskiy Kanal)* runs for 870 miles (1400 km) from the Amu Darya River to the Caspian Sea. The canal is principally used for irrigation but is navigable for 280 miles (450 km).

Major industry and infrastructure
- carpet weaving
- chemicals
- engineering
- food processing
- oil & gas
- textiles
- capital cities
- major towns
- international airports
- major roads
- major industrial areas

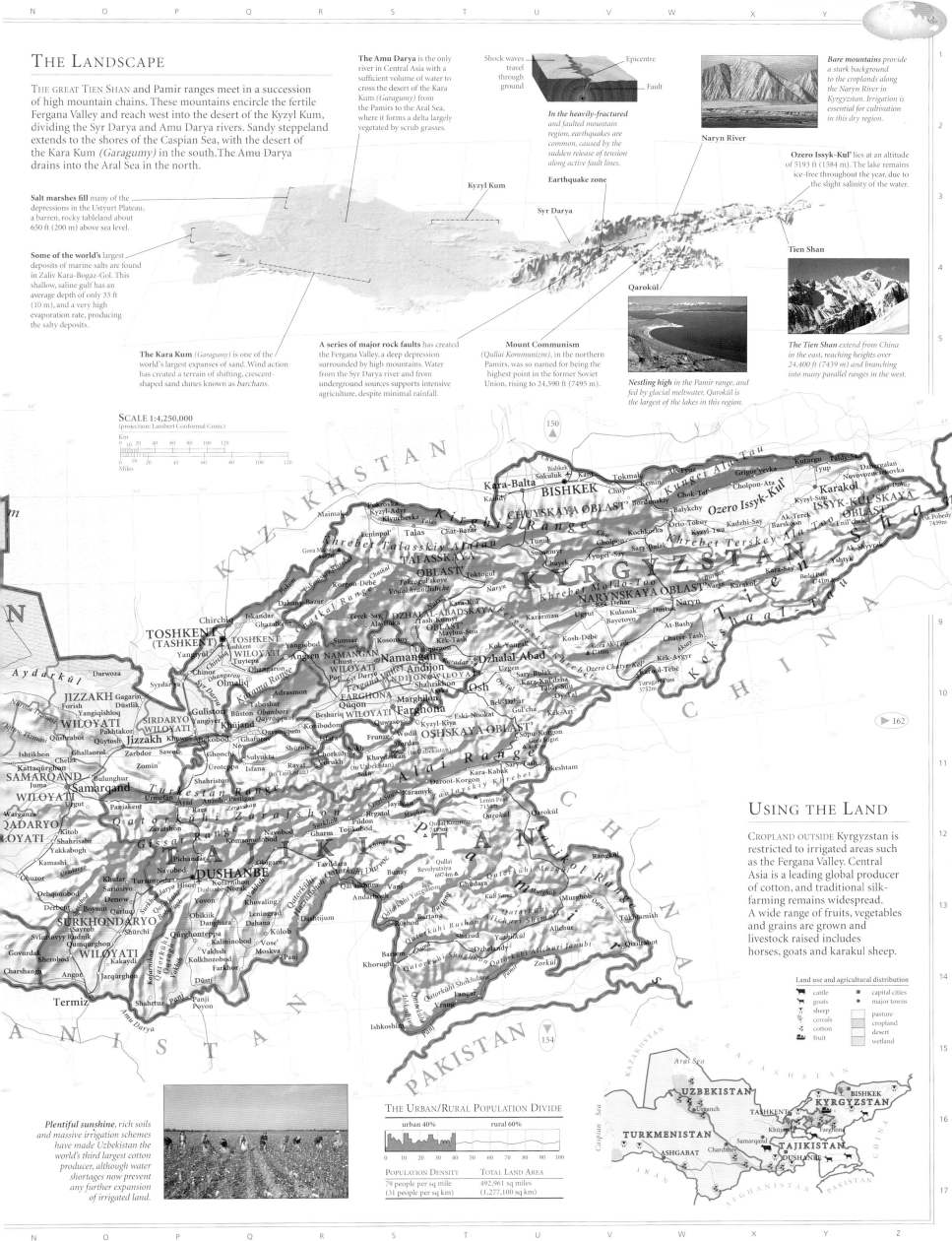

THE LANDSCAPE

THE GREAT TIEN SHAN and Pamir ranges meet in a succession of high mountain chains. These mountains encircle the fertile Fergana Valley and reach west into the desert of the Kyzyl Kum, dividing the Syr Darya and Amu Darya rivers. Sandy steppeland extends to the shores of the Caspian Sea, with the desert of the Kara Kum (Garagumy) in the south. The Amu Darya drains into the Aral Sea in the north.

Salt marshes fill many of the depressions in the Ustyurt Plateau, a barren, rocky tableland about 650 ft (200 m) above sea level.

Some of the world's largest deposits of marine salts are found in Zaliv Kara-Bogaz-Gol. This shallow, saline gulf has an average depth of only 33 ft (10 m), and a very high evaporation rate, producing the salty deposits.

The Kara Kum (Garagumy) is one of the world's largest expanses of sand. Wind action has created a terrain of shifting, crescent-shaped sand dunes known as *barchans*.

A series of major rock faults has created the Fergana Valley, a deep depression surrounded by high mountains. Water from the Syr Darya river and from underground sources supports intensive agriculture, despite minimal rainfall.

The Amu Darya is the only river in Central Asia with a sufficient volume of water to cross the desert of the Kara Kum (Garagumy) from the Pamirs to the Aral Sea, where it forms a delta largely vegetated by scrub grasses.

Shock waves travel through ground
Epicentre
Fault

In the heavily-fractured and faulted mountain region, earthquakes are common, caused by the sudden release of tension along active fault lines.

Kyzyl Kum

Earthquake zone

Mount Communism (Qullai Kommunizm), in the northern Pamirs, was so named for being the highest point in the former Soviet Union, rising to 24,590 ft (7495 m).

Naryn River

Syr Darya

Qarokül

Bare mountains provide a stark background to the croplands along the Naryn River in Kyrgyzstan. Irrigation is essential for cultivation in this dry region.

Ozero Issyk-Kul' lies at an altitude of 5193 ft (1584 m). The lake remains ice-free throughout the year, due to the slight salinity of the water.

Tien Shan

The Tien Shan extend from China in the east, reaching heights over 24,400 ft (7439 m) and branching into many parallel ranges in the west.

Nestling high in the Pamir range, and fed by glacial meltwater, Qarokül is the largest of the lakes in this region.

SCALE 1:4,250,000
(projection: Lambert Conformal Conic)

USING THE LAND

CROPLAND OUTSIDE Kyrgyzstan is restricted to irrigated areas such as the Fergana Valley. Central Asia is a leading global producer of cotton, and traditional silk-farming remains widespread. A wide range of fruits, vegetables and grains are grown and livestock raised includes horses, goats and karakul sheep.

Land use and agricultural distribution

cattle
goats
sheep
cereals
cotton
fruit

capital cities
major towns

pasture
cropland
desert
wetland

Plentiful sunshine, rich soils and massive irrigation schemes have made Uzbekistan the world's third largest cotton producer, although water shortages now prevent any further expansion of irrigated land.

THE URBAN/RURAL POPULATION DIVIDE

urban 40%   rural 60%

POPULATION DENSITY
79 people per sq mile
(31 people per sq km)

TOTAL LAND AREA
492,961 sq miles
(1,277,100 sq km)

AFGHANISTAN & PAKISTAN

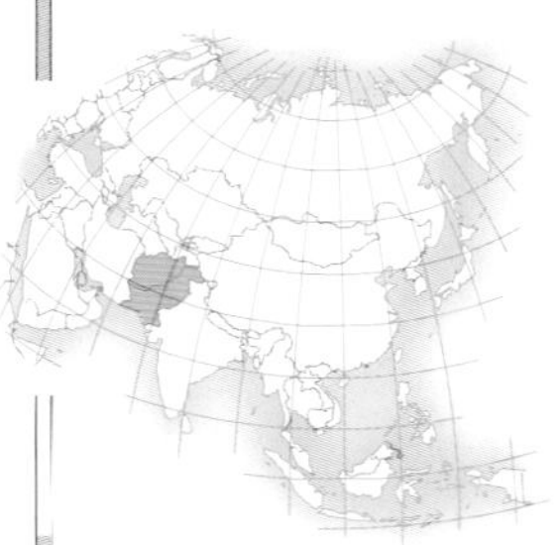

PAKISTAN WAS CREATED by the partition of British India in 1947, becoming the western arm of a new Islamic state for Indian Muslims; the eastern sector, in Bengal, seceded to become the separate country of Bangladesh in 1971. Over half of Pakistan's 147 million people live in the Punjab, at the fertile head of the great Indus Basin. The river sustains a national economy based on irrigated agriculture, including cotton for the vital textiles industry. Afghanistan, a mountainous, landlocked country, with an ancient and independent culture, has been wracked by war since 1979, when calls for help from a beleaguered government led to a Soviet invasion. Despite the Soviet withdrawal, factional strife continues and five million Afghan refugees remain over the border in Pakistan.

The town of Bamian lies high in the Hindu Kush, 250 miles (420 km) west of the Afghan capital, Kabul. It contains two huge statues of Buddha and a number of sanctuaries and cells carved in the rock. In 1222, the ancient city was destroyed by Chinghiz Khan.

TRANSPORT AND INDUSTRY

PAKISTAN IS HIGHLY dependent on the cotton textiles industry, although diversified manufacture is expanding around cities such as Karachi and Lahore. Afghanistan's limited industry is based mainly on the processing of agricultural raw materials and includes traditional crafts such as carpet-making.

Major industry and infrastructure

- carpet weaving
- chemicals
- engineering
- finance
- food processing
- iron & steel
- oil & gas
- textiles
- capital cities
- major towns
- international airports
- major roads
- major industrial areas

THE TRANSPORT NETWORK

141,340 miles (227,600 km)	
211 miles (340 km)	
4852 miles (7814 km)	
745 miles (1200 km)	

The Karakoram Highway was completed after 20 years of construction in 1978. It breaches the Himalayan mountain barrier providing a commercial motor route linking lowland Pakistan and China.

The Karakoram Highway is one of the highest major roads in the world. It took over 24,000 workers almost 20 years to complete.

THE LANDSCAPE

AFGHANISTAN'S TOPOGRAPHY is dominated by the mountains of the Hindu Kush, which spread south and west into numerous mountain spurs. The dry plateau of southwestern Afghanistan extends into Pakistan and the hills which overlook the great Indus Basin. In northern Pakistan the Hindu Kush, Himalayan and Karakoram ranges meet to form one of the world's highest mountain regions.

The arid Hindu Kush makes much of Afghanistan uninhabitable, with over 50% of the land lying above 6500 ft (2000 m).

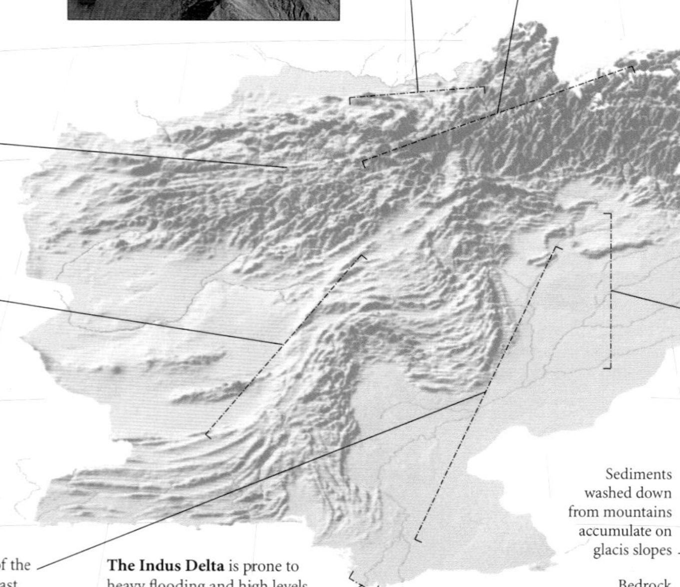

Frequent earthquakes mean that mountain-building processes are continuing in this region, as the Indo-Australian Plate drifts northwards, colliding with the Eurasian Plate.

Mountain chains running southwest from the Hindu Kush into Pakistan form a barrier to the humid winds which blow from the Indian Ocean, creating arid conditions across southern Afghanistan.

The Hunza River rises in the northern Karakoram Range, running for 120 miles (193 km) before joining the Gilgit River.

Hunza River

The plains and foothills which extend from the northern slopes of the Hindu Kush are part of the great grassy steppe lands of Central Asia.

K2 (Mount Godwin Austen), in the Karakoram Range, is the second highest mountain in the world, at an altitude of 28,251 ft (8611 m).

Hindu Kush

Some of the largest glaciers outside the polar regions are found in the Karakoram Range, including Siachen Glacier (Siachen Muztagh), which is 40 miles (72 km) long.

Himalayas

The soils of the Punjab Plain are nourished by enormous quantities of sediment, carried from the Himalayas by the five tributaries of the Indus River.

The Indus Basin is part of the Indus-Ganges lowland, a vast depression which has been filled with layers of sediment over the last 50 million years. These deposits are estimated to be over 16,400 ft (5000 m) deep.

The Indus Delta is prone to heavy flooding and high levels of salinity. It remains a largely uncultivated wilderness area.

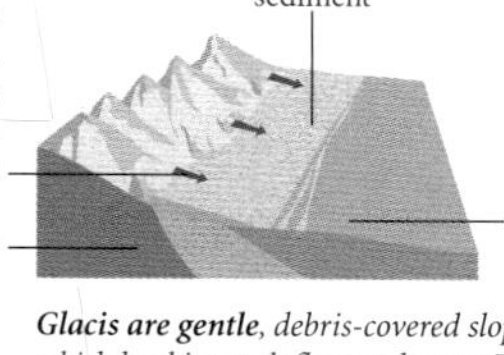

Sediments washed down from mountains accumulate on glacis slopes

Glacis covered by coarse-grained sediment

Bedrock

Fine sediments deposited on salt flats are removed by wind erosion

Glacis are gentle, debris-covered slopes which lead into salt flats or deserts. They typically occur at the base of mountains in arid regions such as Afghanistan.

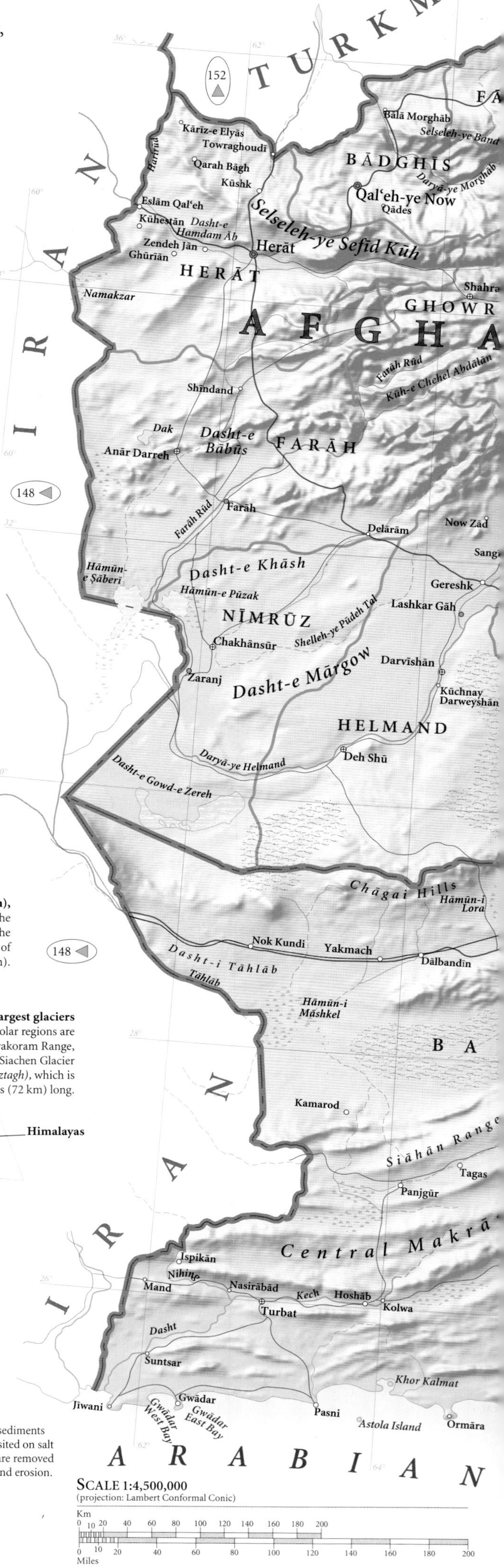

SCALE 1:4,500,000
(projection: Lambert Conformal Conic)

Km
0 10 20 40 60 80 100 120 140 160 180 200

Miles
0 10 20 40 60 80 100 120 140 160 180 200

Map labels:

TURKMEN
IRAN
UZBEKISTAN
TAJIKISTAN
CHINA
TURKMENISTAN
AFGHANISTAN
PAKISTAN
INDIA
ARABIAN SEA

BĀDGHIS
Bālā Morghāb
Selseleh-ye Band
Kāriz-e Elyās
Towraghoudi
Qarah Bāgh
Kūshk
Eslām Qal'eh
Qal'eh-ye Now
Qādes
Kūhestān
Dasht-e Hamdam Āb
Zendeh Jān
Ghūriān
Herāt
HERĀT
Namakzar
Selseleh-ye Sefīd Kūh
GHOWR
Shahra
AFGHA
Shindand
Dak
Dasht-e Bābūs
Farāh Rūd
Kūh-e Chehel Abdālān
Anār Darreh
FARĀH
Farah
Delārām
Now Zād
Sanga
Hāmūn-e Şāberī
Dasht-e Khāsh
Hāmūn-e Pūzak
Gereshk
NĪMRŪZ
Shelleh-ye Pūdeh Tak
Lashkar Gāh
Chakhānsūr
Darvīshān
Zaranj
Dasht-e Mārgow
Kūchnay Darweyshān
HELMAND
Daryā-ye Helmand
Deh Shū
Dasht-e Gowd-e Zereh
Chāgai Hills
Hāmūn-i Lora
Dasht-i Tāhlāb
Nok Kundi
Yakmach
Tāhlāb
Dālbandin
Hāmūn-i Māshkel
BA
Kamarod
Siāhān Range
Tagas
Central Makrā
Panjgūr
Ispikan
Nīhing
Nasīrābād
Kech
Hoshāb
Mand
Dasht
Turbat
Kolwa
Suntsar
Khor Kalmat
Jiwani
Gwādar West Bay
Gwādar
Gwādar East Bay
Pasni
Astola Island
Ormāra
ARABIAN

Inset map labels:
UZBEKISTAN
TAJIKISTAN
TURKMENISTAN
CHINA
Mazar-e Sharif
Herat
KABUL
Peshawar
ISLAMABAD
Rawalpindi
AFGHANISTAN
Kandahar
Lahore
Quetta
Faisalabad
Multan
Bahawalpur
PAKISTAN
Sukkur
INDIA
IRAN
Karachi
Hyderabad
ARABIAN SEA

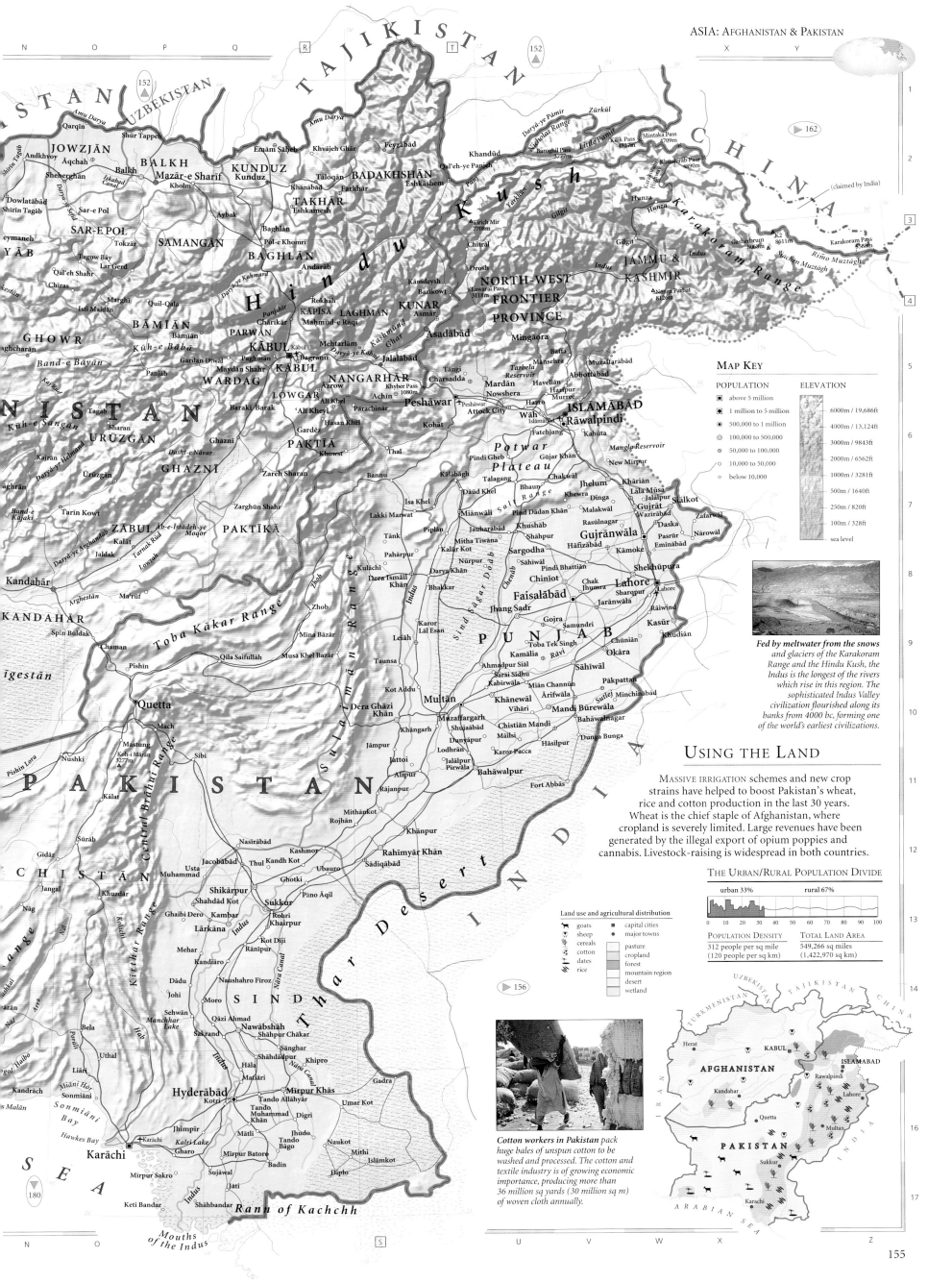

MAP KEY

POPULATION

- ■ above 5 million
- ◙ 1 million to 5 million
- ◉ 500,000 to 1 million
- ⊗ 100,000 to 500,000
- ⊕ 50,000 to 100,000
- ○ 10,000 to 50,000
- ∘ below 10,000

ELEVATION

- 6000m / 19,686ft
- 4000m / 13,124ft
- 3000m / 9843ft
- 2000m / 6562ft
- 1000m / 3281ft
- 500m / 1640ft
- 250m / 820ft
- 100m / 328ft
- sea level

Fed by meltwater from the snows and glaciers of the Karakoram Range and the Hindu Kush, the Indus is the longest of the rivers which rise in this region. The sophisticated Indus Valley civilization flourished along its banks from 4000 bc, forming one of the world's earliest civilizations.

USING THE LAND

MASSIVE IRRIGATION schemes and new crop strains have helped to boost Pakistan's wheat, rice and cotton production in the last 30 years. Wheat is the chief staple of Afghanistan, where cropland is severely limited. Large revenues have been generated by the illegal export of opium poppies and cannabis. Livestock-raising is widespread in both countries.

THE URBAN/RURAL POPULATION DIVIDE

urban 33%   rural 67%

0 10 20 30 40 50 60 70 80 90 100

POPULATION DENSITY
312 people per sq mile
(120 people per sq km)

TOTAL LAND AREA
549,266 sq miles
(1,422,970 sq km)

Land use and agricultural distribution

- goats
- sheep
- cereals
- cotton
- dates
- rice
- ■ capital cities
- ● major towns
- pasture
- cropland
- forest
- mountain region
- desert
- wetland

Cotton workers in Pakistan pack huge bales of unspun cotton to be washed and processed. The cotton and textile industry is of growing economic importance, producing more than 36 million sq yards (30 million sq m) of woven cloth annually.

SOUTH ASIA

BANGLADESH, BHUTAN, INDIA, MALDIVES, NEPAL, PAKISTAN, SRI LANKA

MORE THAN ONE-FIFTH of the world's population lives in the south Asian subcontinent. Great cultural diversity has come from a long succession of foreign invaders, including Hindu Aryans, Islamic Moguls and the British, whose empire incorporated the princely states of the Maharajas and extended to the borders of Nepal and Bhutan in the Himalayas. Half a century after independence, India is the world's largest democracy, and at the current rate of growth, may overtake China as the world's most populous country within the next century. There are points of tension in the region over claims for independence by the Sikhs in the Indian Punjab and the Tamil separatists in Sri Lanka, and the long-standing dispute with Pakistan over Jammu and Kashmir in the north.

THE LANDSCAPE

SOUTH ASIA is effectively isolated from the rest of Asia by desert along the western flank of Pakistan, and a continuous wall of mountains, dominated by the Himalayas, to the north and east. The great basins of the Indus and Ganges separate this mountain fringe from the rolling plateau of the Indian peninsula, which is bordered by a line of coastal hills, the Eastern and Western Ghats.

The Himalayas are the highest and most extensive mountain system in the world. They were formed when the Indo-Australian Plate collided with the Eurasian Plate about 40 million years ago, thrusting up huge masses of land and creating a 'ripple' effect, which formed lesser mountain ranges in Tibet and Southeast Asia. Mount Everest is the world's tallest mountain at 29,028 ft (8848 m).

Almost all of Bangladesh lies in the immense delta formed by the Ganges and the Brahmaputra which merge and flow out into the Bay of Bengal.

The Deccan Plateau covers an area of more than 123,553 sq miles (320,000 sq km). It is formed of deep layers of volcanic basalt, reaching thicknesses of more than 9800 ft (3000 m) towards the coast. Distinctive stepped valleys cut in the basalt plateau by rivers are known as 'traps'.

Coastal deposition has formed many typical features along the western coast of Sri Lanka. These include spits and bars, sometimes enclosing lagoons.

Trivandrum in southern India normally receives the first of the monsoon rains, which are essential to south Asian agriculture and moderate the extreme summer heat. The monsoon then moves northwards over a period of about two months.

The Western Ghats are formed by a fault scarp which runs unbroken for more than 930 miles (1500 km). They reach their highest point at the southern Cardamon Hills.

Rivers flowing from the Himalayas into a broad depression in northern India have formed marshes around Bharatpur. They are now a sanctuary for numerous bird species.

The Indus River flows more than 1970 miles (3180 km) from southwestern Tibet to its mouth on the Arabian Sea. It has an estimated catchment area of 450,000 sq miles (1,165,500 sq km).

The coast of western Pakistan is a staircase of folded rock strata caused by successive periods of rapid uplift.

The Indus Valley near Skardu in northern Pakistan has been partially infilled by great quantities of eroded sediment. Most of this is carried from the region's bare slopes by swollen rivers during the spring thaw and mass movement activity.

The towering Karakoram and Hindu Kush ranges, formed at the same time as the Himalayas, dominate Pakistan's northern borders. K2 on the border of northern Pakistan is the second highest mountain on Earth, at 28,251 ft (8611 m).

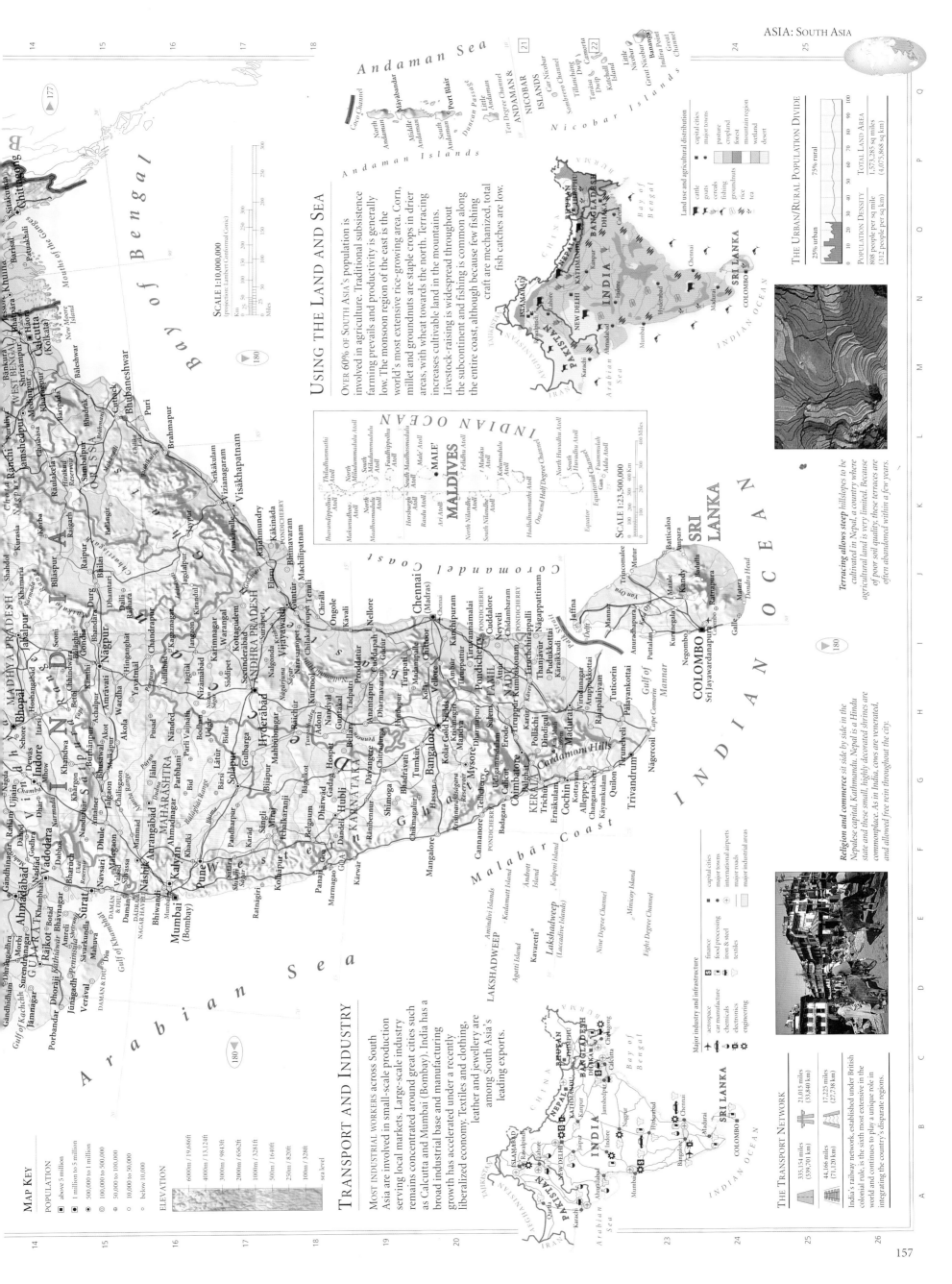

MAP KEY

POPULATION

- above 5 million
- 1 million to 5 million
- 500,000 to 1 million
- 100,000 to 500,000
- 50,000 to 100,000
- 10,000 to 50,000
- below 10,000

ELEVATION

- 6000m / 19,686ft
- 4000m / 13,124ft
- 3000m / 9843ft
- 2000m / 6562ft
- 1000m / 3281ft
- 500m / 1640ft
- 250m / 820ft
- 100m / 328ft
- sea level

USING THE LAND AND SEA

OVER 60% OF SOUTH ASIA'S population is involved in agriculture. Traditional subsistence farming prevails and productivity is generally low. The monsoon region of the east is the world's most extensive rice-growing area. Corn, millet and groundnuts are staple crops in drier areas, with wheat towards the north. Terracing increases cultivable land in the mountains. Livestock-raising is widespread throughout the subcontinent and fishing is common along the entire coast, although because few fishing craft are mechanized, total fish catches are low.

Land use and agricultural distribution

- capital cities
- major towns
- cattle
- goats
- cereals
- fishing
- groundnuts
- rice
- tea
- pasture
- cropland
- forest
- mountain region
- desert

THE URBAN/RURAL POPULATION DIVIDE

- 25% urban
- 75% rural

POPULATION DENSITY
808 people per sq mile
(312 people per sq km)

TOTAL LAND AREA
1,573,285 sq miles
(4,075,868 sq km)

Terracing allows steep hillsides to be cultivated in Nepal, a country where agricultural land is very limited. Because of poor soil quality, these terraces are often abandoned within a few years.

Religion and commerce sit side by side in the Nepalese capital, Kathmandu. Nepal is a Hindu state and these small, highly decorated shrines are commonplace. As in India, cows are venerated, and allowed free rein throughout the city.

TRANSPORT AND INDUSTRY

MOST INDUSTRIAL WORKERS across South Asia are involved in small-scale production serving local markets. Large-scale industry remains concentrated around great cities such as Calcutta and Mumbai (Bombay). India has a broad industrial base and manufacturing growth has accelerated under a recently liberalized economy. Textiles and clothing, leather and jewellery are among South Asia's leading exports.

Major industry and infrastructure

- aerospace
- car manufacture
- chemicals
- electronics
- engineering
- finance
- food processing
- iron & steel
- textiles
- capital cities
- major towns
- international airports
- major roads
- major industrial areas

THE TRANSPORT NETWORK

335,154 miles (539,701 km)	21,015 miles (33,840 km)
44,166 miles (71,120 km)	17,225 miles (27,738 km)

India's railway network, established under British colonial rule, is the sixth most extensive in the world and continues to play a unique role in integrating the country's disparate regions.

SCALE 1:10,000,000
(projection: Lambert Conformal Conic)

SCALE 1:23,500,000

NORTHERN INDIA & THE HIMALAYAN STATES

BANGLADESH, BHUTAN, NEPAL, Arunachal Pradesh,
Assam, Bihar, Chandigarh, Delhi, Haryana,
Himachal Pradesh, Jammu & Kashmir, Manipur,
Meghalaya, Mizoram, Nagaland, Punjab, Rajasthan,
Sikkim, Tripura, Uttar Pradesh, West Bengal

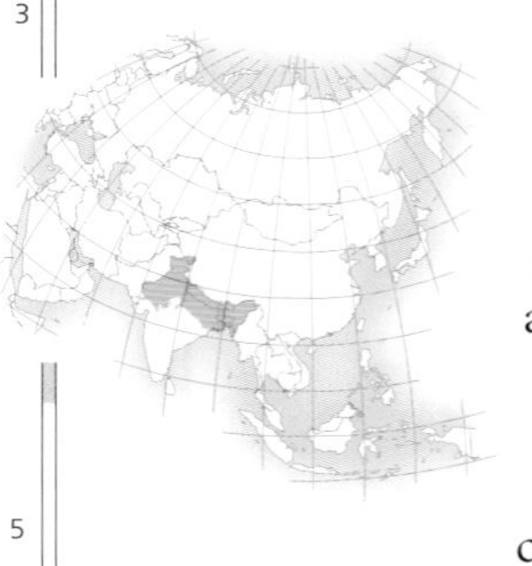

THE GANGES AND BRAHMAPUTRA river basins and the massive mountain barrier of the Himalayas define this region's landscape and have served to reinforce potent cultural and religious differences among its people. Hinduism pervades most aspects of national life and is a growing political force within India, a secular country which also encompasses the centre of Sikhism at Amritsar and the world's largest Muslim minority. Nepal is a crowded mountain state, which faces severe ecological problems from deforestation, while the tiny Himalayan Buddhist kingdom of Bhutan is emerging from long-term isolation, to welcome selected visitors. The Muslim state of Bangladesh, formerly East Pakistan, is one of the world's most densely populated countries and one of the poorest, with more than 120 million people living largely on the massive Ganges/Brahmaputra Delta. Many Bangladeshis live under threat of repeated, catastrophic floods.

The Golden Temple in Amritsar, the most sacred shrine of the Sikh religion, was the scene of violent clashes between Sikh separatists and government forces in 1984.

MAP KEY

POPULATION
- ▣ 1 million to 5 million
- ◉ 500,000 to 1 million
- ⊕ 100,000 to 500,000
- ⊕ 50,000 to 100,000
- ⊙ 10,000 to 50,000
- ○ below 10,000

ELEVATION
- 6000m / 19,686ft
- 4000m / 13,124ft
- 3000m / 9843ft
- 2000m / 6562ft
- 1000m / 3281ft
- 500m / 1640ft
- 250m / 820ft
- 100m / 328ft
- sea level

TRANSPORT AND INDUSTRY

TEXTILES, ENGINEERING, chemicals and electronics are leading industries in north India. The plateau of Chota Nagpur provides ore for iron and steel production in the major industrial region northeast of Calcutta. Bangladesh processes jute and Nepal has a small manufacturing sector based on agricultural produce, while Bhutan's limited industry is concentrated in the southern lowland area.

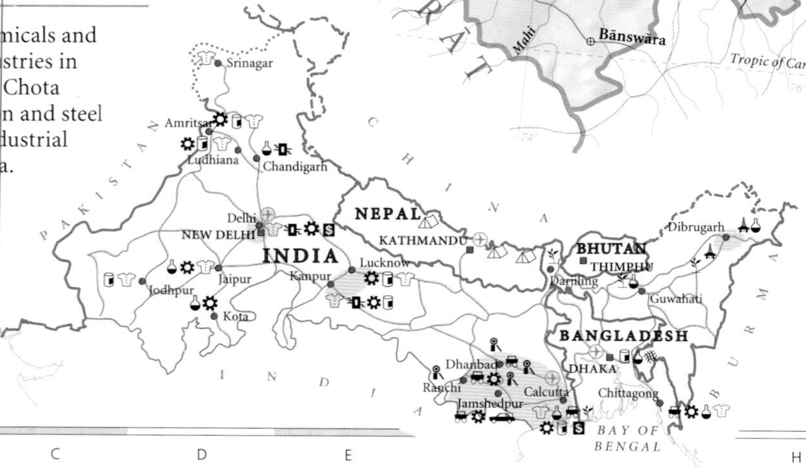

SCALE 1:5,750,000
(projection: Lambert Conformal Conic)

Km
0 10 20 40 60 80 100 120 140 160 180 200
Miles
0 10 20 40 60 80 100 120 140 160 180 200

Major industry and infrastructure
- ⛵ adventure tourism
- 🚗 car manufacture
- chemicals
- coal
- electronics
- engineering
- finance
- food processing
- iron & steel
- jute processing
- oil
- tea processing
- textiles
- ■ capital cities
- ■ major towns
- ✈ international airports
- major roads
- major industrial areas

THE TRANSPORT NETWORK

Over 60% of Bangladesh's internal trade is carried by boat. The country has a very disjointed land transport network, with no bridges over the Brahmaputra and few road crossings on the Ganges River.

Map labels (selected): AFGHANISTAN, CHINA, PAKISTAN, JAMMU AND KASHMIR, HIMACHAL PRADESH, PUNJAB, HARYANA, RAJASTHAN, UTTAR PRADESH, GUJARAT, MADHYA PRADESH, NEPAL, BHUTAN, BANGLADESH, INDIA, Thar Desert, Aravalli Range, Bay of Bengal, Tropic of Cancer

Srinagar, Jammu, Amritsar, Ludhiana, Chandigarh, Shimla, Delhi, NEW DELHI, Jaipur, Jodhpur, Jaisalmer, Bikaner, Udaipur, Kota, Ajmer, Agra, Mathura, Aligarh, Bareilly, Lucknow, Kanpur, Allahabad, Jhansi, KATHMANDU, THIMPHU, DHAKA, Calcutta, Chittagong, Guwahati, Dibrugarh

THE LANDSCAPE

MOST OF THE REGION is drained by the River Ganges, which meets the Brahmaputra in Bangladesh to form an immense delta before flowing into the Bay of Bengal. The Himalayas extend eastwards over 1500 miles (2400 km), from the parallel ranges running through Jammu and Kashmir. The Thar Desert occupies the southwest.

The Indian Punjab lies mainly to the west of the Ganges watershed and its rivers flow into the Indus. Control of this water resource has been a source of great friction with neighbouring Pakistan.

The border between India and Pakistan runs through the Thar Desert, an area of sandy *seif* dunes 50–100 ft (15–30 m) in height. Fossils found in the desert indicate that the dunes, stabilized by vegetation, have been in their current position for about 3000 years.

Sambhar Salt Lake in Rajasthan is India's largest lake. Unlike most of the Himalayan lakes which are glacial in origin – formed in ice-scoured basins or as the result of depositional damming – it is an ephemeral salt lake filled periodically by flash flooding.

The Pir Panjal Range in southwestern Kashmir rises to elevations of 12,500 ft (3810 m). Despite the freezing conditions, settlements and extensive pastures are found above the tree line.

The northern ranges of the Himalayas contain the highest mountains in the world, with average heights of more than 23,000 ft (7000 m) and many peaks higher than 26,000 ft (8000 m).

In the last 40 million years, the course of the Brahmaputra has been diverted hundreds of miles to the east by the rising landmass of the Himalayas.

The Khasi Hills are an example of a *horst*, a fractured block of bedrock which has been thrust upwards.

The summit of Machhapuchhre rises to 22,942 ft (6993 m). It is also known as the 'Fish's Tail' because of its distinctive peak.

Debris slides in the middle Himalayas

Soil blocks
Debris fans at base of slope
Slide plain

Soil loss in the middle Himalayas has largely been attributed to debris slides, where large blocks of soil are mobilized by saturation along a slide plane. Once mobile, the soil slides down the slope, gaining speed and thinning to form a fan at the base of the slope.

The Ganges River, sacred to the Hindu people, drains a vast lowland area at the base of the Himalayas. The northern plains are covered by sandy deposits, broken by mud-banks formed when the river floods.

The rapid deforestation of Himalayan valleys has led to acute soil erosion and increased rates of rainwater run-off, both cited as possible causes of the worsening floods downstream in the Ganges/Brahmaputra Delta, although natural rates are high and may be the real cause.

Over half of the great Ganges/Brahmaputra Delta floods each year during the monsoon as rivers, swollen by meltwater from the Himalayas and by excess rainwater, break their banks and fertilize the land with nutrient-rich sediment.

USING THE LAND

GRAIN PRODUCTION dominates land use. Rice is most widely grown in the east. Irrigation and new crop strains have dramatically increased yields in the Punjab, a major wheat-producing area. River flood plains are intensively farmed and livestock-herding is widespread, particularly in Bhutan. Regional crops include jute in Bangladesh, tea in Assam, cardamom in Sikkim and saffron in Kashmir.

THE URBAN/RURAL POPULATION DIVIDE

urban 23%   rural 77%

0 10 20 30 40 50 60 70 80 90 100

POPULATION DENSITY
782 people per sq mile
(302 people per sq km)

TOTAL LAND AREA
665,104 sq miles
(1,723,068 sq km)

Land use and agricultural distribution

- cattle
- goats
- sheep
- cereals
- jute
- rice
- tea

- capital cities
- major towns

- pasture
- cropland
- forest
- mountain region
- wetland
- desert

An adverse climate, steep slopes and poor soils limit crop cultivation in Bhutan, which is a largely agrarian economy. Rice, corn and wheat are the main staples, although orchards are being established as the soil and climate suit this type of farming.

Flooded streets in Dhaka, Bangladesh are a testament to the region's vulnerability to flooding. In 1988 alone, 75% of the country was flooded, leaving thousands of people dead and over 25 million homeless.

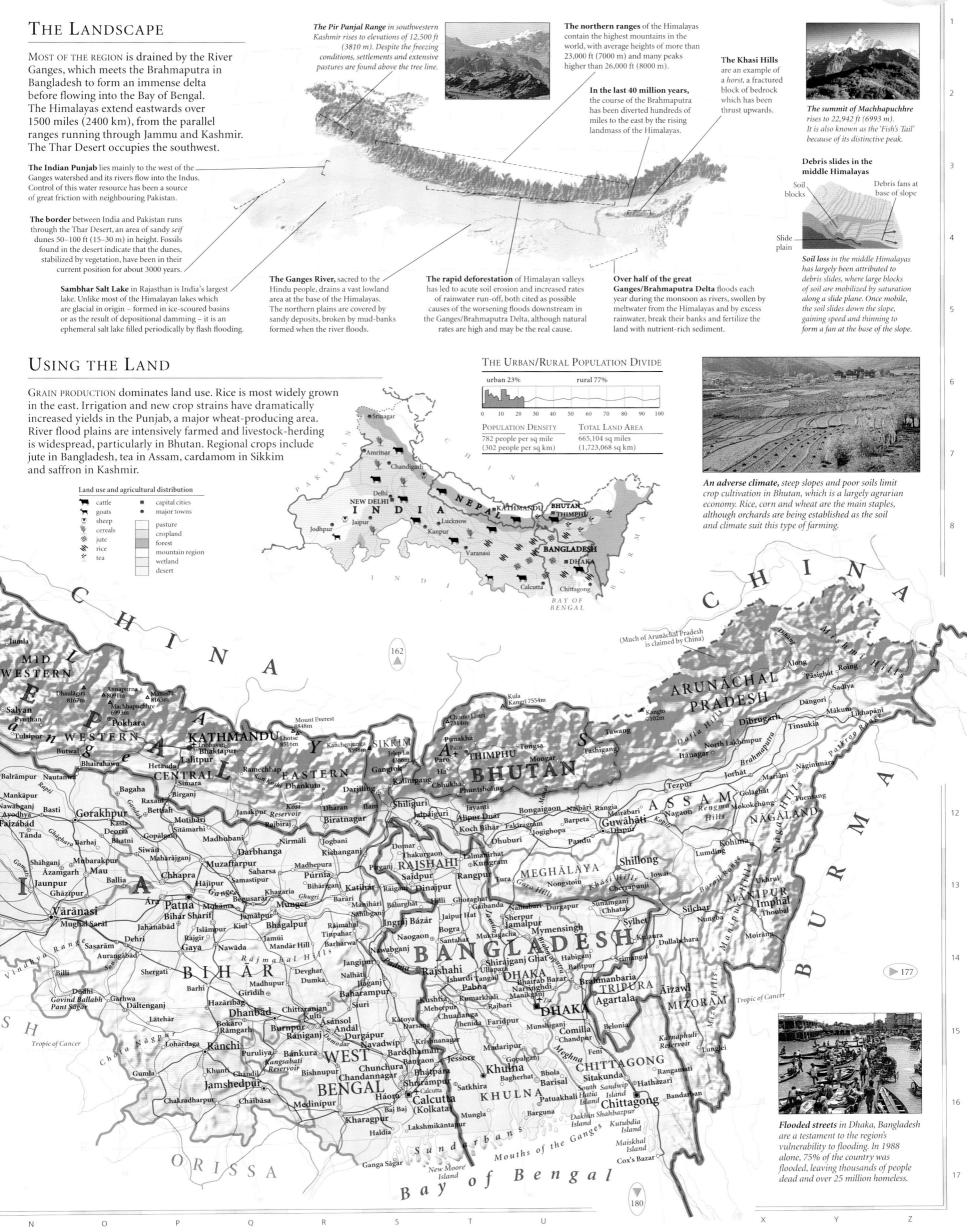

SOUTHERN INDIA & SRI LANKA

Sri Lanka, Andhra Pradesh, Dadra & Nagar Haveli, Daman & Diu, Goa, Gujarat, Karnataka, Kerala, Lakshadweep, Madhya Pradesh, Maharashtra, Orissa, Pondicherry, Tamil Nadu

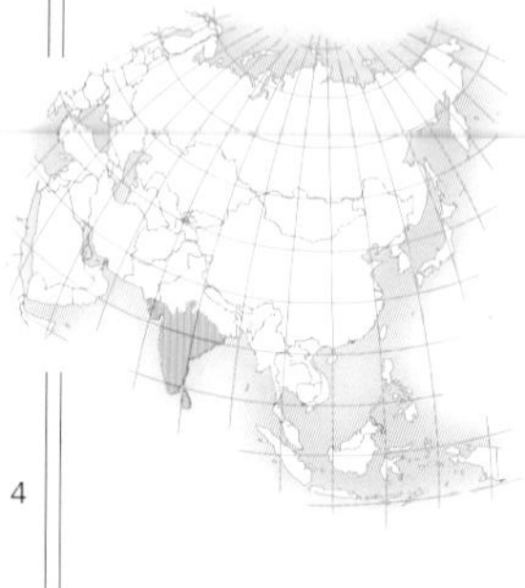

THE UNIQUE AND HIGHLY INDEPENDENT southern states reflect the diverse and decentralized nature of India, which has fourteen official languages. The southern half of the peninsula lay beyond the reach of early invaders from the north and retained the distinct and ancient culture of the Dravidian peoples such as the Tamils, whose language is spoken in preference to Hindi throughout southern India. The interior plateau of southern India is less densely populated than the coastal lowlands, where the European colonial imprint is strongest. Urban and industrial growth is accelerating, but southern India's vast population remains predominantly rural. The island of Sri Lanka has two distinct cultural groups; the mainly Buddhist Sinhalese majority, and the Tamil minority whose struggle for a homeland in the northeast has led to prolonged civil war.

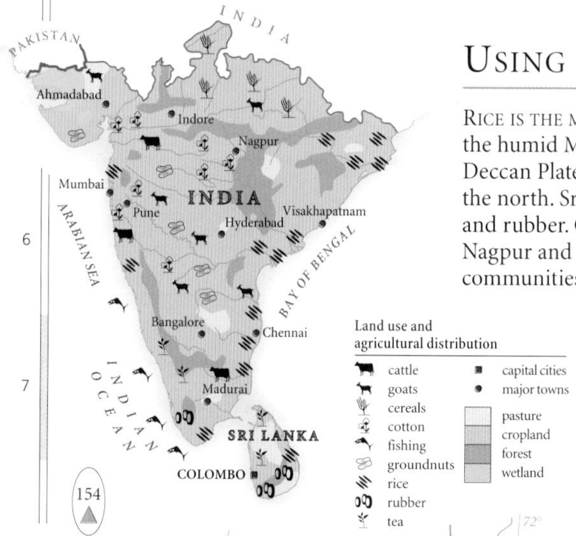

THE LANDSCAPE

THE UNDULATING DECCAN PLATEAU underlies most of southern India; it slopes gently down towards the east and is largely enclosed by the Ghats coastal hill ranges. The Western Ghats run continuously along the Arabian Sea coast, while the Eastern Ghats are interrupted by rivers which follow the slope of the plateau and flow across broad lowlands into the Bay of Bengal. The plateaux and basins of Sri Lanka's central highlands are surrounded by a broad plain.

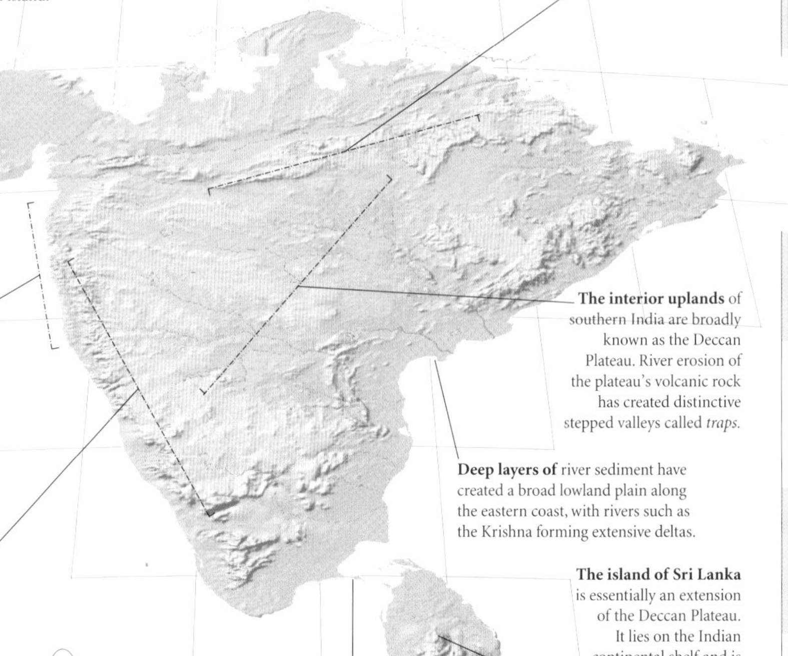

Along the northern boundary of the Deccan Plateau, old basement rocks are interspersed with younger sedimentary strata. This creates spectacular scarplands, cut by numerous waterfalls along the softer sedimentary strata.

The interior uplands of southern India are broadly known as the Deccan Plateau. River erosion of the plateau's volcanic rock has created distinctive stepped valleys called *traps*.

Deep layers of river sediment have created a broad lowland plain along the eastern coast, with rivers such as the Krishna forming extensive deltas.

The island of Sri Lanka is essentially an extension of the Deccan Plateau. It lies on the Indian continental shelf and is composed of the same hard, crystalline rocks.

The Rann of Kachchh tidal marshes encircle the low-lying Kachchh Peninsula. For several months during the rainy season the water level of the marshes rises and Kachchh becomes an island.

The Konkan coast, which runs between Daman and Goa, is characterized by rocky headlands, and bays with crescent-shaped beaches. Flooded river valleys known as *rias* extend inland.

The Western Ghats run north–south marking the western boundary of the Deccan Plateau. Their height rises to the south where their summits reach altitudes of 8000 ft (2500 m).

Adam's Bridge

Ocean currents cause sediment build up

Sri Lanka

Relict of ancient tombolo

Adam's Bridge

Adam's Bridge (Rama's Bridge) is a chain of sandy shoals lying about 4 ft (1.2 m) under the sea between India and Sri Lanka. They once formed the world's longest tombolo, or land bridge, before the sea level began to rise several thousand years ago.

USING THE LAND AND SEA

RICE IS THE MAIN staple in the east, in Sri Lanka and along the humid Malabar Coast. Groundnuts are grown on the Deccan Plateau, with wheat, corn and chickpeas, towards the north. Sri Lanka is a leading exporter of tea, coconuts and rubber. Cotton plantations supply local mills around Nagpur and Mumbai (Bombay). Fishing supports many communities in Kerala and the Laccadive Islands.

Commercial plantations, growing tea, (seen here), cardamom, coffee, coconuts and rubber, occupy about half the agricultural land in Kerala, necessitating food imports for local consumption.

Land use and agricultural distribution

- cattle
- goats
- cotton
- fishing
- groundnuts
- rice
- rubber
- tea

- capital cities
- major towns
- pasture
- cropland
- forest
- wetland

THE URBAN/RURAL POPULATION DIVIDE

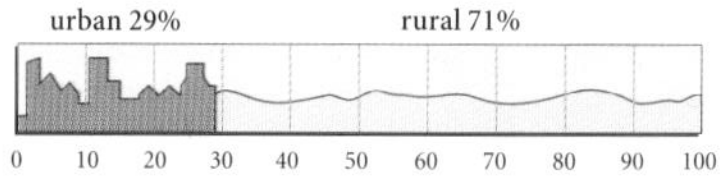

urban 29%   rural 71%

TOTAL LAND AREA
698,295 sq miles
(1,809,054 sq km)

POPULATION DENSITY
715 people per sq mile
(276 people per sq km)

0 10 20 30 40 50 60 70 80 90 100

TRANSPORT AND INDUSTRY

SOUTH INDIA HAS a broad industrial base, with three leading regions. Around Mumbai, Bangalore and Ahmadabad, cotton mills and chemical plants make use of cheap hydro-electric power generated in the Western Ghats. Light engineering and textiles are well established to the south and west of Chennai (Madras). Sri Lanka's industry is based mainly on the processing of agricultural products.

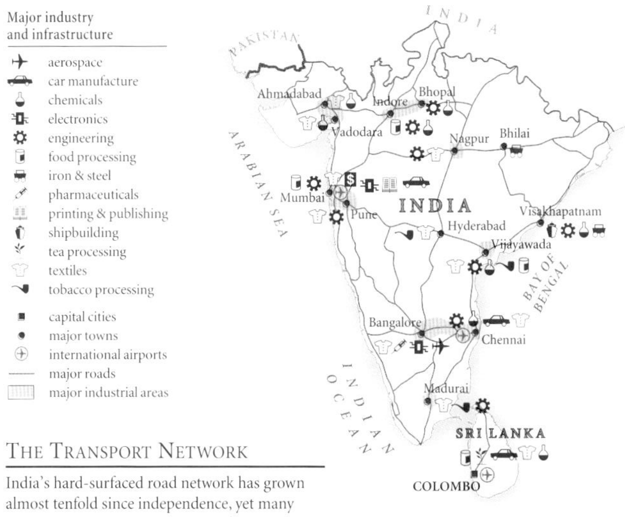

The great triumphal arch of Charminar, built in 1591, epitomizes the fine Islamic architecture which the Moghuls brought from the north to Hyderabad, the capital of Andhra Pradesh.

Major industry and infrastructure

- aerospace
- car manufacture
- chemicals
- electronics
- engineering
- food processing
- pharmaceuticals
- printing & publishing
- shipbuilding
- tea processing
- textiles
- tobacco processing
- capital cities
- major towns
- international airports
- major roads
- major industrial areas

THE TRANSPORT NETWORK

India's hard-surfaced road network has grown almost tenfold since independence, yet many villages are still only accessible on foot, even in densely-populated rural areas.

Mumbai is one of the largest and most densely-populated cities in the world. It is the centre of India's textile trade and has important finance and commerce sectors.

MAP KEY

POPULATION

- ■ above 5 million
- ■ 1 million to 5 million
- ⊙ 500,000 to 1 million
- ⊕ 100,000 to 500,000
- ⊙ 50,000 to 100,000
- ○ 10,000 to 50,000
- ○ below 10,000

ELEVATION

- 2000m / 6562ft
- 1000m / 3281ft
- 500m / 1640ft
- 250m / 820ft
- 100m / 328ft
- sea level

SCALE 1:6,250,000
(projection: Lambert Conformal Conic)

Sea pencils thrive on the coral reefs around the coast of the Laccadive Islands and Sri Lanka. The reefs support an amazing diversity of marine life, but are increasingly under threat from growing coastal populations.

Local fisheries around Sri Lanka afford great potential for exploitation, but development has been hampered by technological constraints. Most fishermen live on the coastal fringes and operate on a small scale.

INDIA

ANDHRA PRADESH

KARNATAKA

KERALA

TAMIL NADU

SRI LANKA

BAY OF BENGAL

ARABIAN SEA

INDIAN OCEAN

Mumbai (Bombay)

Hyderabad

Bangalore

Chennai (Madras)

COLOMBO

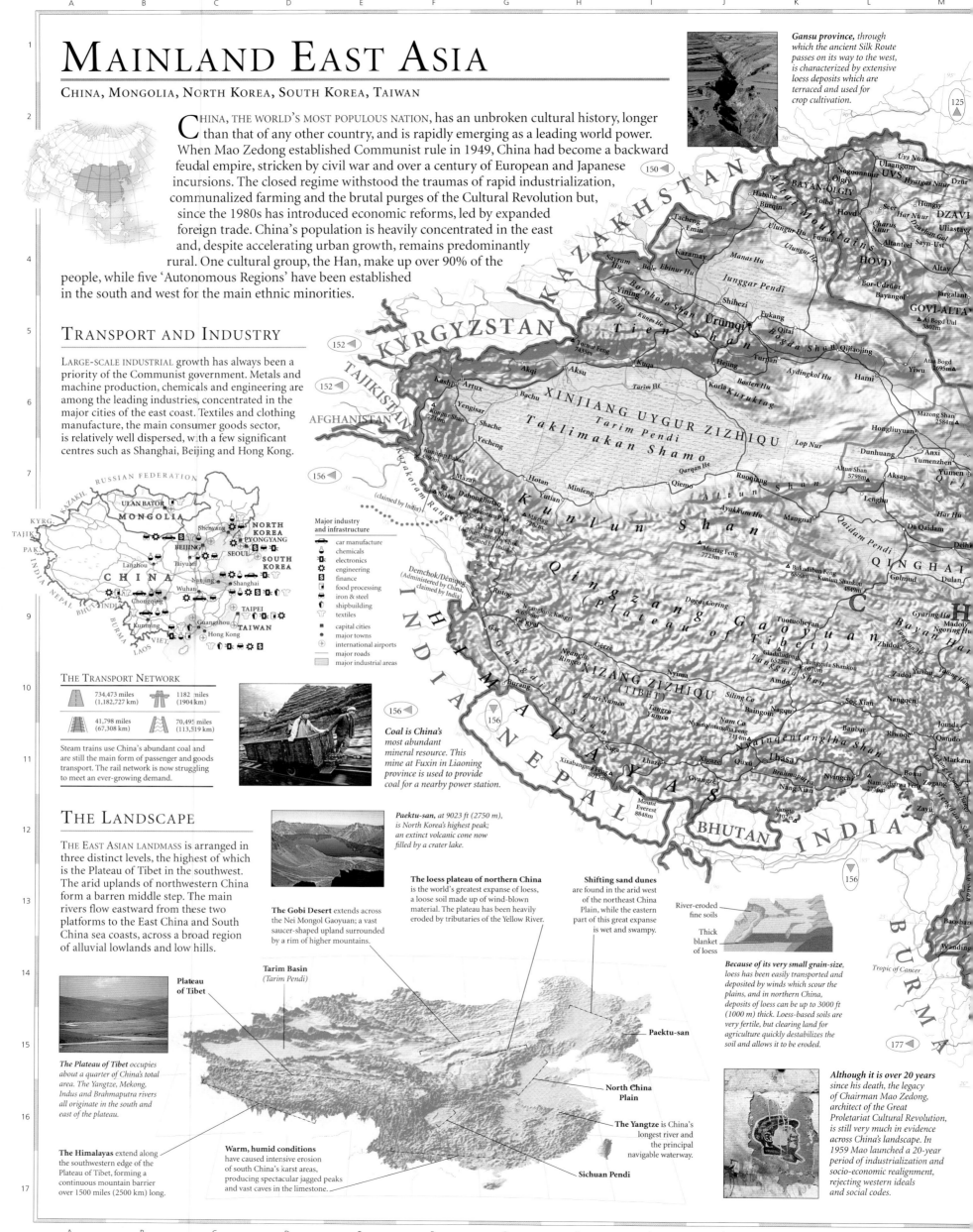

MAINLAND EAST ASIA

CHINA, MONGOLIA, NORTH KOREA, SOUTH KOREA, TAIWAN

CHINA, THE WORLD'S MOST POPULOUS NATION, has an unbroken cultural history, longer than that of any other country, and is rapidly emerging as a leading world power. When Mao Zedong established Communist rule in 1949, China had become a backward feudal empire, stricken by civil war and over a century of European and Japanese incursions. The closed regime withstood the traumas of rapid industrialization, communalized farming and the brutal purges of the Cultural Revolution but, since the 1980s has introduced economic reforms, led by expanded foreign trade. China's population is heavily concentrated in the east and, despite accelerating urban growth, remains predominantly rural. One cultural group, the Han, make up over 90% of the people, while five 'Autonomous Regions' have been established in the south and west for the main ethnic minorities.

TRANSPORT AND INDUSTRY

LARGE-SCALE INDUSTRIAL growth has always been a priority of the Communist government. Metals and machine production, chemicals and engineering are among the leading industries, concentrated in the major cities of the east coast. Textiles and clothing manufacture, the main consumer goods sector, is relatively well dispersed, with a few significant centres such as Shanghai, Beijing and Hong Kong.

Major industry and infrastructure

- car manufacture
- chemicals
- electronics
- engineering
- finance
- food processing
- iron & steel
- shipbuilding
- textiles
- capital cities
- major towns
- international airports
- major roads
- major industrial areas

THE TRANSPORT NETWORK

734,473 miles (1,182,727 km)	1182 miles (1904 km)
41,798 miles (67,308 km)	70,495 miles (113,519 km)

Steam trains use China's abundant coal and are still the main form of passenger and goods transport. The rail network is now struggling to meet an ever-growing demand.

Coal is China's most abundant mineral resource. This mine at Fuxin in Liaoning province is used to provide coal for a nearby power station.

THE LANDSCAPE

THE EAST ASIAN LANDMASS is arranged in three distinct levels, the highest of which is the Plateau of Tibet in the southwest. The arid uplands of northwestern China form a barren middle step. The main rivers flow eastward from these two platforms to the East China and South China sea coasts, across a broad region of alluvial lowlands and low hills.

The Plateau of Tibet occupies about a quarter of China's total area. The Yangtze, Mekong, Indus and Brahmaputra rivers all originate in the south and east of the plateau.

The Himalayas extend along the southwestern edge of the Plateau of Tibet, forming a continuous mountain barrier over 1500 miles (2500 km) long.

The Gobi Desert extends across the Nei Mongol Gaoyuan; a vast saucer-shaped upland surrounded by a rim of higher mountains.

Tarim Basin (Tarim Pendi)

Plateau of Tibet

Warm, humid conditions have caused intensive erosion of south China's karst areas, producing spectacular jagged peaks and vast caves in the limestone.

Sichuan Pendi

North China Plain

The Yangtze is China's longest river and the principal navigable waterway.

The loess plateau of northern China is the world's greatest expanse of loess, a loose soil made up of wind-blown material. The plateau has been heavily eroded by tributaries of the Yellow River.

Shifting sand dunes are found in the arid west of the northeast China Plain, while the eastern part of this great expanse is wet and swampy.

Paektu-san

Gansu province, through which the ancient Silk Route passes on its way to the west, is characterized by extensive loess deposits which are terraced and used for crop cultivation.

Paektu-san, at 9023 ft (2750 m), is North Korea's highest peak; an extinct volcanic cone now filled by a crater lake.

River-eroded fine soils

Thick blanket of loess

Because of its very small grain-size, loess has been easily transported and deposited by winds which scour the plains, and in northern China, deposits of loess can be up to 3000 ft (1000 m) thick. Loess-based soils are very fertile, but clearing land for agriculture quickly destabilizes the soil and allows it to be eroded.

Although it is over 20 years since his death, the legacy of Chairman Mao Zedong, architect of the Great Proletariat Cultural Revolution, is still very much in evidence across China's landscape. In 1959 Mao launched a 20-year period of industrialization and socio-economic realignment, rejecting western ideals and social codes.

The Great Wall of China remains one of the world's largest-ever construction projects, and is so vast that it is visible from space. Finally completed in AD 214, it runs for over 4000 miles (6400 km) from the Yellow Sea, stretching into Central Asia.

SCALE 1:12,500,000
(projection: Lambert Conformal Conic)

Km
0 25 50 100 150 200 250 300 350 400 450 500
Miles
0 25 50 100 150 200 250 300 350 400 450 500

MAP KEY

POPULATION

- ■ above 5 million
- ■ 1 million to 5 million
- ◉ 500,000 to 1 million
- ◉ 100,000 to 500,000
- ⊕ 50,000 to 100,000
- ○ 10,000 to 50,000
- ○ below 10,000

ELEVATION

- 6000m / 19,686ft
- 4000m / 13,124ft
- 3000m / 9843ft
- 2000m / 6562ft
- 1000m / 3281ft
- 500m / 1640ft
- 250m / 820ft
- 100m / 328ft
- sea level

USING THE LAND AND SEA

AROUND 90% OF China is unsuitable for cultivation, being either climatically or topographically adverse, or lacking sufficiently fertile soils. Most of the west is used for nomadic herding, while farmland is concentrated in the eastern monsoon region, with rice grown in the tropical and subtropical south. Cereals and soya beans predominate as rainfall and temperatures decline further north.

Land use and agricultural distribution
- pigs
- sheep
- corn (maize)
- cotton
- fishing
- fruit
- rice
- sugar cane
- soya beans
- ■ capital cities
- ■ major towns
- pasture
- cropland
- forest
- mountain region

Beijing (formerly Peking), is China's capital city and, with Shanghai, one of its leading industrial and cultural centres. The morning and evening rush-hours are dominated by bicycles, which constitute the bulk of traffic.

THE URBAN/RURAL POPULATION DIVIDE

urban 32%   rural 68%

0 10 20 30 40 50 60 70 80 90 100

POPULATION DENSITY
297 people per sq mile
(115 people per sq km)

TOTAL LAND AREA
4,288,672 sq miles
(11,110,550 sq km)

RUSSIAN FEDERATION

MONGOLIA

CHINA

NORTH KOREA
PYONGYANG
SEOUL
SOUTH KOREA

TAIPEI
TAIWAN

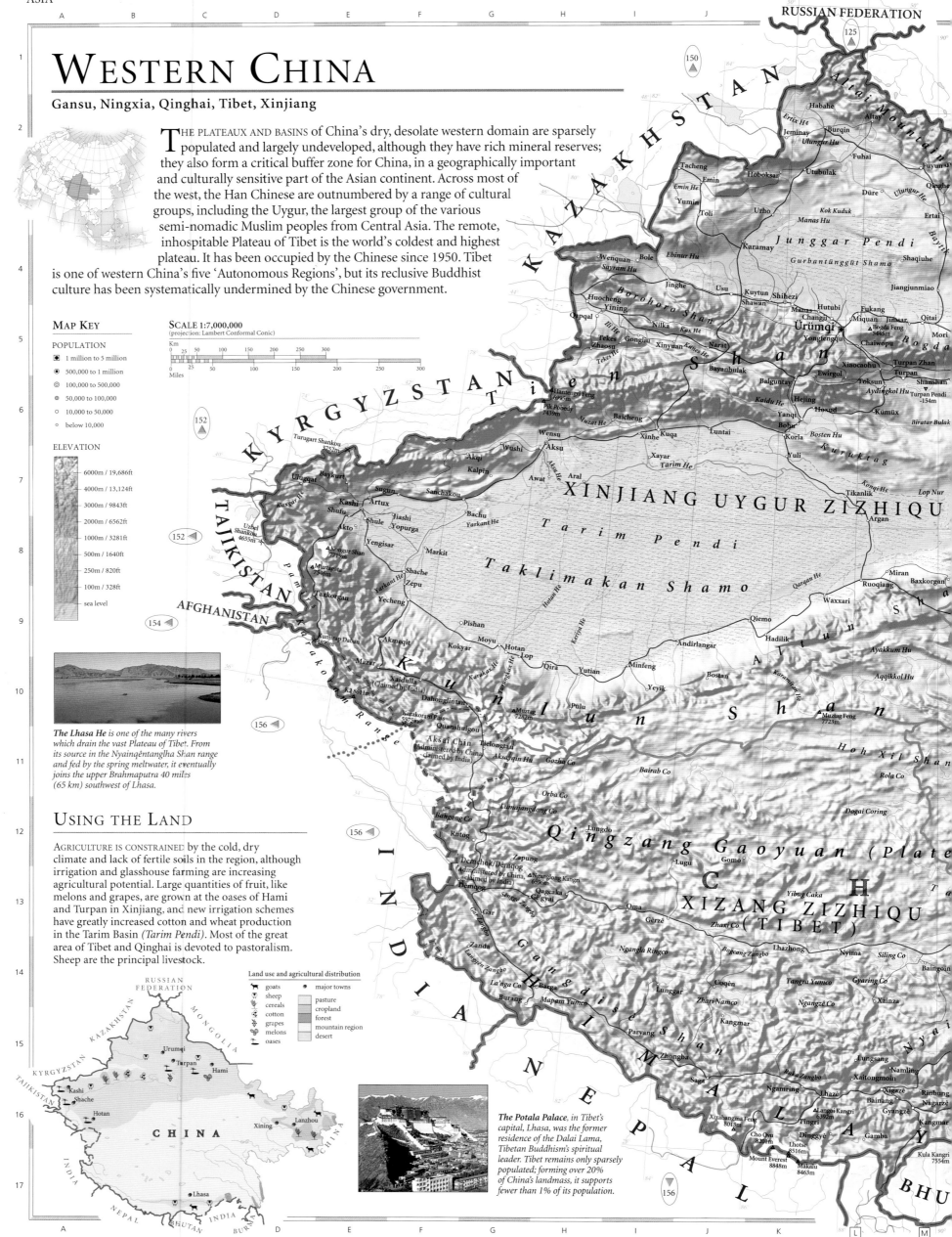

RUSSIAN FEDERATION

WESTERN CHINA

Gansu, Ningxia, Qinghai, Tibet, Xinjiang

THE PLATEAUX AND BASINS of China's dry, desolate western domain are sparsely populated and largely undeveloped, although they have rich mineral reserves; they also form a critical buffer zone for China, in a geographically important and culturally sensitive part of the Asian continent. Across most of the west, the Han Chinese are outnumbered by a range of cultural groups, including the Uygur, the largest group of the various semi-nomadic Muslim peoples from Central Asia. The remote, inhospitable Plateau of Tibet is the world's coldest and highest plateau. It has been occupied by the Chinese since 1950. Tibet is one of western China's five 'Autonomous Regions', but its reclusive Buddhist culture has been systematically undermined by the Chinese government.

MAP KEY

POPULATION

- ◉ 1 million to 5 million
- ◉ 500,000 to 1 million
- ◉ 100,000 to 500,000
- ⊕ 50,000 to 100,000
- ○ 10,000 to 50,000
- ○ below 10,000

ELEVATION

- 6000m / 19,686ft
- 4000m / 13,124ft
- 3000m / 9843ft
- 2000m / 6562ft
- 1000m / 3281ft
- 500m / 1640ft
- 250m / 820ft
- 100m / 328ft
- sea level

SCALE 1:7,000,000
(projection: Lambert Conformal Conic)

Km
0 25 50 100 150 200 250 300

Miles
0 25 50 100 150 200 250 300

The Lhasa He is one of the many rivers which drain the vast Plateau of Tibet. From its source in the Nyainqêntanglha Shan range and fed by the spring meltwater, it eventually joins the upper Brahmaputra 40 miles (65 km) southwest of Lhasa.

USING THE LAND

AGRICULTURE IS CONSTRAINED by the cold, dry climate and lack of fertile soils in the region, although irrigation and glasshouse farming are increasing agricultural potential. Large quantities of fruit, like melons and grapes, are grown at the oases of Hami and Turpan in Xinjiang, and new irrigation schemes have greatly increased cotton and wheat production in the Tarim Basin (*Tarim Pendi*). Most of the great area of Tibet and Qinghai is devoted to pastoralism. Sheep are the principal livestock.

Land use and agricultural distribution

- 🐐 goats
- 🐑 sheep
- 🌾 cereals
- 🌱 cotton
- 🌿 grapes
- 🍈 melons
- oases
- ● major towns

- pasture
- cropland
- forest
- mountain region
- desert

The Potala Palace, in Tibet's capital, Lhasa, was the former residence of the Dalai Lama, Tibetan Buddhism's spiritual leader. Tibet remains only sparsely populated; forming over 20% of China's landmass, it supports fewer than 1% of its population.

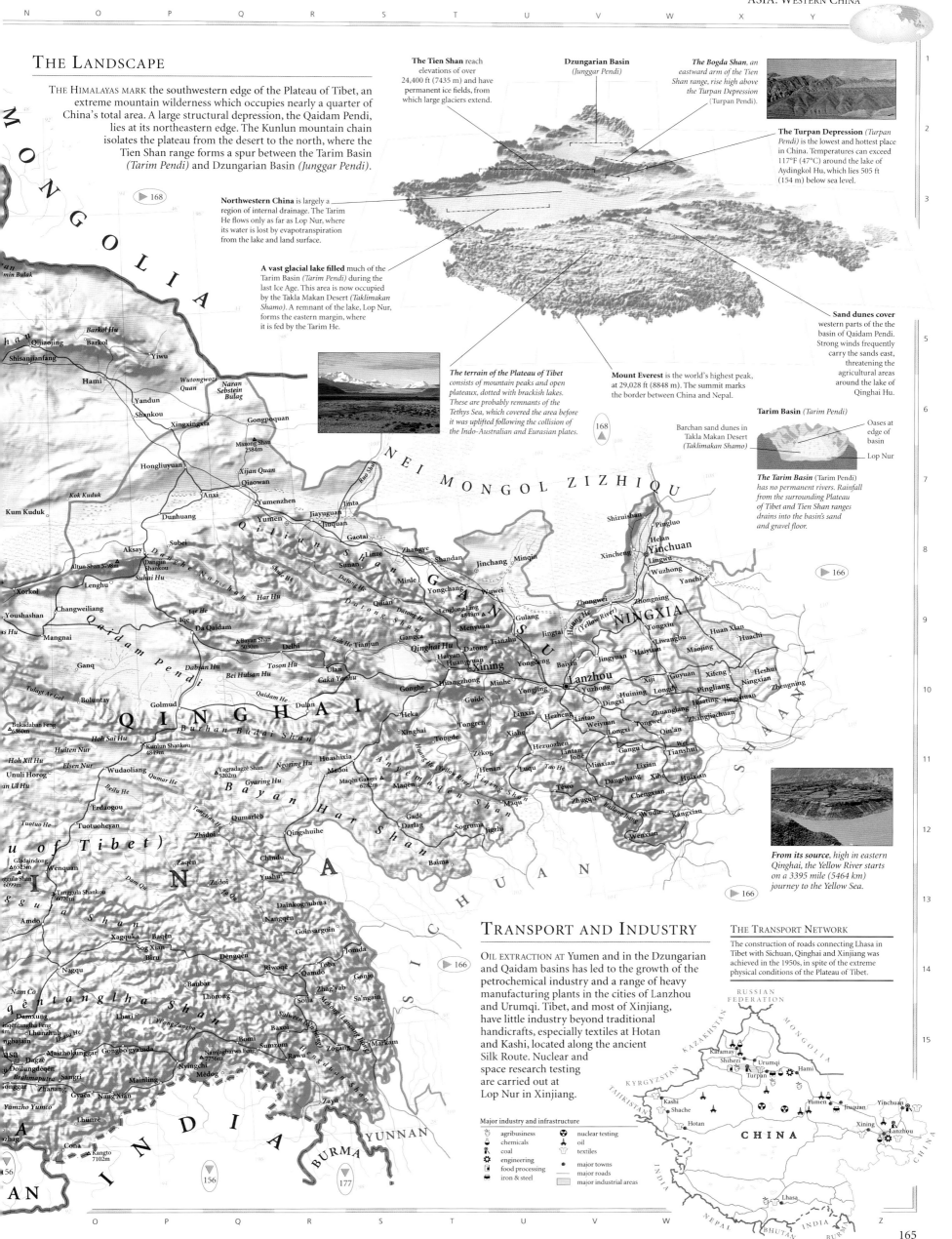

THE LANDSCAPE

THE HIMALAYAS MARK the southwestern edge of the Plateau of Tibet, an extreme mountain wilderness which occupies nearly a quarter of China's total area. A large structural depression, the Qaidam Pendi, lies at its northeastern edge. The Kunlun mountain chain isolates the plateau from the desert to the north, where the Tien Shan range forms a spur between the Tarim Basin (*Tarim Pendi*) and Dzungarian Basin (*Junggar Pendi*).

The Tien Shan reach elevations of over 24,400 ft (7435 m) and have permanent ice fields, from which large glaciers extend.

Dzungarian Basin (*Junggar Pendi*)

The Bogda Shan, an eastward arm of the Tien Shan range, rise high above the Turpan Depression (Turpan Pendi).

The Turpan Depression (*Turpan Pendi*) is the lowest and hottest place in China. Temperatures can exceed 117°F (47°C) around the lake of Aydingkol Hu, which lies 505 ft (154 m) below sea level.

Northwestern China is largely a region of internal drainage. The Tarim He flows only as far as Lop Nur, where its water is lost by evapotranspiration from the lake and land surface.

A vast glacial lake filled much of the Tarim Basin (*Tarim Pendi*) during the last Ice Age. This area is now occupied by the Takla Makan Desert (*Taklimakan Shamo*). A remnant of the lake, Lop Nur, forms the eastern margin, where it is fed by the Tarim He.

Sand dunes cover western parts of the the basin of Qaidam Pendi. Strong winds frequently carry the sands east, threatening the agricultural areas around the lake of Qinghai Hu.

The terrain of the Plateau of Tibet consists of mountain peaks and open plateaux, dotted with brackish lakes. These are probably remnants of the Tethys Sea, which covered the area before it was uplifted following the collision of the Indo-Australian and Eurasian plates.

Mount Everest is the world's highest peak, at 29,028 ft (8848 m). The summit marks the border between China and Nepal.

Barchan sand dunes in Takla Makan Desert (*Taklimakan Shamo*)

Oases at edge of basin
Lop Nur

Tarim Basin (*Tarim Pendi*)

The Tarim Basin (Tarim Pendi) has no permanent rivers. Rainfall from the surrounding Plateau of Tibet and Tien Shan ranges drains into the basin's sand and gravel floor.

From its source, high in eastern Qinghai, the Yellow River starts on a 3395 mile (5464 km) journey to the Yellow Sea.

TRANSPORT AND INDUSTRY

OIL EXTRACTION AT Yumen and in the Dzungarian and Qaidam basins has led to the growth of the petrochemical industry and a range of heavy manufacturing plants in the cities of Lanzhou and Urumqi. Tibet, and most of Xinjiang, have little industry beyond traditional handicrafts, especially textiles at Hotan and Kashi, located along the ancient Silk Route. Nuclear and space research testing are carried out at Lop Nur in Xinjiang.

THE TRANSPORT NETWORK

The construction of roads connecting Lhasa in Tibet with Sichuan, Qinghai and Xinjiang was achieved in the 1950s, in spite of the extreme physical conditions of the Plateau of Tibet.

Major industry and infrastructure

- agribusiness
- chemicals
- coal
- engineering
- food processing
- iron & steel
- nuclear testing
- oil
- textiles
- major towns
- major roads
- major industrial areas

EASTERN CHINA

TAIWAN, Anhui, Beijing, Fujian, Guangdong, Guangxi, Guizhou, Hainan, Hebei, Henan, Hubei, Hunan, Jiangsu, Jiangxi, Shaanxi, Shandong, Shanghai, Shanxi, Sichuan, Tianjin, Yunnan, Zhejiang

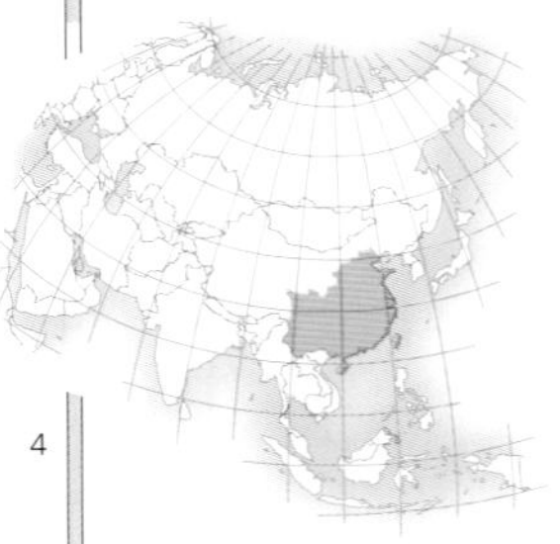

THE EAST IS CHINA'S HEARTLAND. Massive industrial development since 1949 has transformed much of the densely populated rural landscape, in a region still prone to flooding and drought. Over 20 cities have populations of over a million, including the giant metropolis of Shanghai and the capital Beijing, which has been China's cultural and political centre since the 13th century. The ethnically diverse southwest and the oil-rich interior provinces of Sichuan and Shaanxi have largely missed out on the remarkable economic growth occurring in designated free-trade areas along the coasts of the South and East China seas. The republic of Taiwan was established in 1949 by Chinese nationalists ousted from the mainland by the victorious Communist forces. Taiwan now has one of the strongest economies in the world but its sovereignty is not recognized by China. Hong Kong provides a major international trade link for China; a 99-year 'lease' period of British control was concluded in 1997.

North of the Qin Ling range in Shaanxi province, is an agriculturally fertile region covered with fine, wind-blown deposits and known as the loess plateau. The loose sediments are vulnerable to water erosion.

USING THE LAND AND SEA

THIS IS A REGION of intensive cultivation. Wheat, millet, sorghum and cotton are the main crops of the Yellow River basin. South from Sichuan, rice becomes the principal crop, grown with wheat, corn and cotton along the Yangtze River. Tea is produced in the hills and sugar cane along the coast of the southeast, where flat land is limited. Pigs and poultry are raised in great numbers.

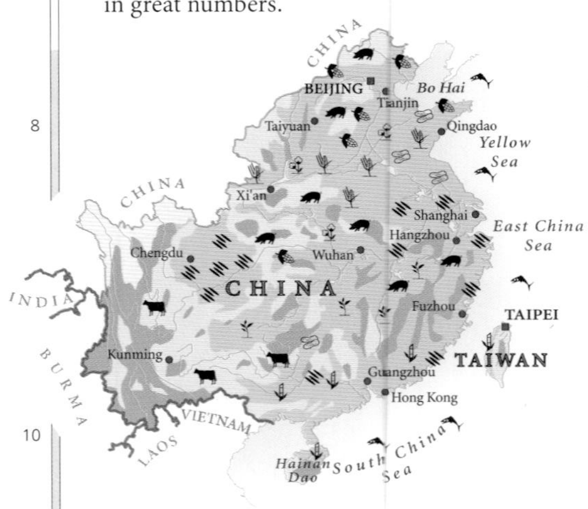

Land use and agricultural distribution

- cattle
- pigs
- cereals
- corn (maize)
- cotton
- fishing
- peanuts
- rice
- sugar cane
- tea
- capital cities
- major towns
- pasture
- cropland
- forest
- mountain region

On the hills above the North China Plain, slopes are terraced to utilize the rich loess soils of the Taihang Shan range.

MAP KEY

POPULATION
- ▣ above 5 million
- ◉ 1 million to 5 million
- ◉ 500,000 to 1 million
- ⊙ 100,000 to 500,000
- ⊕ 50,000 to 100,000
- ○ 10,000 to 50,000
- ○ below 10,000

ELEVATION
- 6000m / 19,686ft
- 4000m / 13,124ft
- 3000m / 9843ft
- 2000m / 6562ft
- 1000m / 3281ft
- 500m / 1640ft
- 250m / 820ft
- 100m / 328ft
- sea level

SCALE 1:7,750,000
(projection: Lambert Conformal Conic)

Km
0 25 50   100   150   200   250   300

Miles
0 25 50   100   150   200   250   300

The former Portuguese territory of Macao, with its colonial architecture, bars and casinos, reverted to Chinese rule in 1999.

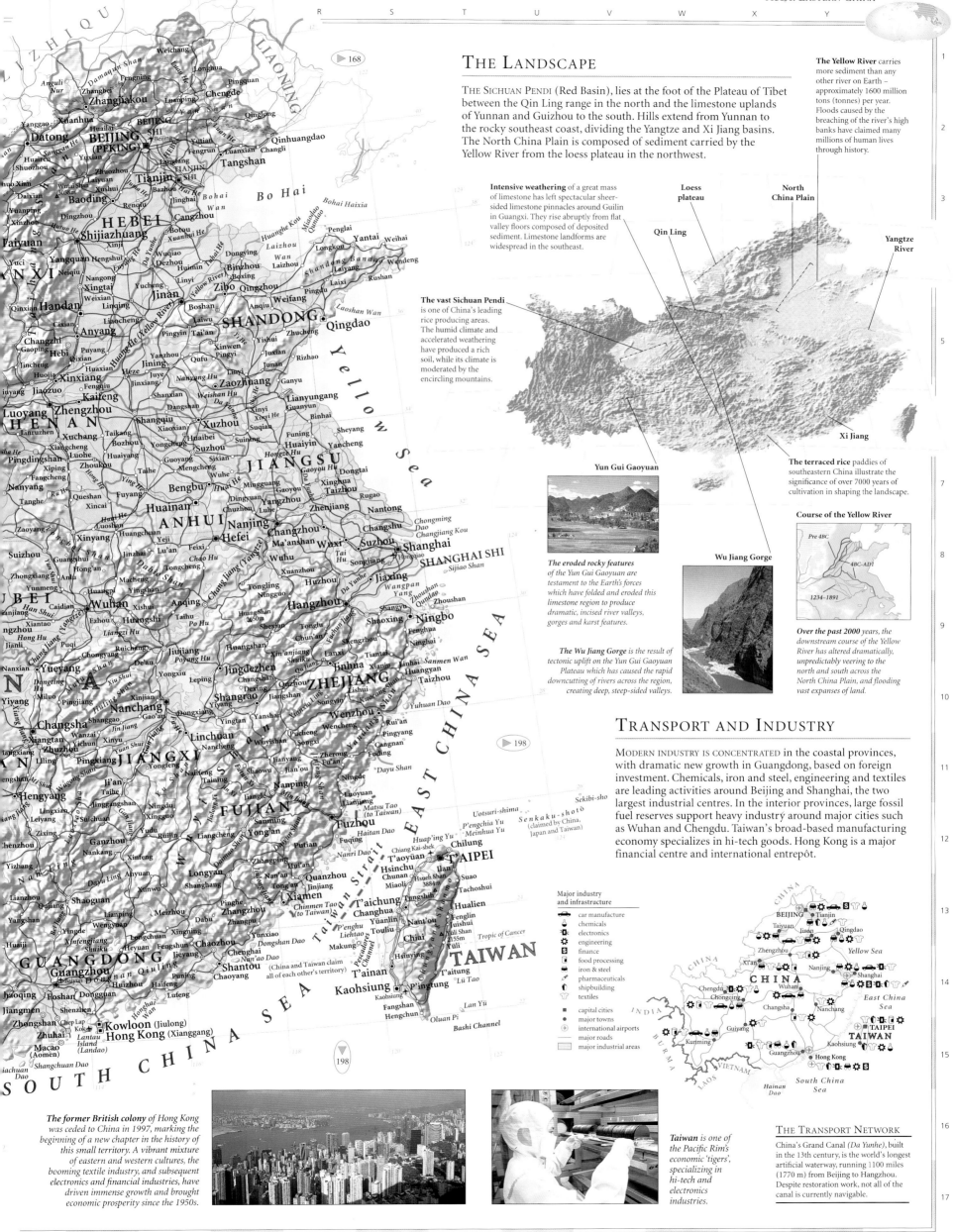

THE LANDSCAPE

THE SICHUAN PENDI (Red Basin), lies at the foot of the Plateau of Tibet between the Qin Ling range in the north and the limestone uplands of Yunnan and Guizhou to the south. Hills extend from Yunnan to the rocky southeast coast, dividing the Yangtze and Xi Jiang basins. The North China Plain is composed of sediment carried by the Yellow River from the loess plateau in the northwest.

The Yellow River carries more sediment than any other river on Earth – approximately 1600 million tons (tonnes) per year. Floods caused by the breaching of the river's high banks have claimed many millions of human lives through history.

Intensive weathering of a great mass of limestone has left spectacular sheer-sided limestone pinnacles around Guilin in Guangxi. They rise abruptly from flat valley floors composed of deposited sediment. Limestone landforms are widespread in the southeast.

Loess plateau

North China Plain

Qin Ling

Yangtze River

Xi Jiang

The vast Sichuan Pendi is one of China's leading rice producing areas. The humid climate and accelerated weathering have produced a rich soil, while its climate is moderated by the encircling mountains.

The terraced rice paddies of southeastern China illustrate the significance of over 7000 years of cultivation in shaping the landscape.

Yun Gui Gaoyuan

The eroded rocky features of the Yun Gui Gaoyuan are testament to the Earth's forces which have folded and eroded this limestone region to produce dramatic, incised river valleys, gorges and karst features.

The Wu Jiang Gorge is the result of tectonic uplift on the Yun Gui Gaoyuan Plateau which has caused the rapid downcutting of rivers across the region, creating deep, steep-sided valleys.

Wu Jiang Gorge

Course of the Yellow River

Pre 4BC

4BC-AD1

1234–1891

Over the past 2000 years, the downstream course of the Yellow River has altered dramatically, unpredictably veering to the north and south across the North China Plain, and flooding vast expanses of land.

TRANSPORT AND INDUSTRY

MODERN INDUSTRY IS CONCENTRATED in the coastal provinces, with dramatic new growth in Guangdong, based on foreign investment. Chemicals, iron and steel, engineering and textiles are leading activities around Beijing and Shanghai, the two largest industrial centres. In the interior provinces, large fossil fuel reserves support heavy industry around major cities such as Wuhan and Chengdu. Taiwan's broad-based manufacturing economy specializes in hi-tech goods. Hong Kong is a major financial centre and international entrepôt.

Major industry and infrastructure

- car manufacture
- chemicals
- electronics
- engineering
- finance
- food processing
- iron & steel
- pharmaceuticals
- shipbuilding
- textiles
- ■ capital cities
- ● major towns
- major roads
- major industrial areas
- international airports

The former British colony of Hong Kong was ceded to China in 1997, marking the beginning of a new chapter in the history of this small territory. A vibrant mixture of eastern and western cultures, the booming textile industry, and subsequent electronics and financial industries, have driven immense growth and brought economic prosperity since the 1950s.

Taiwan is one of the Pacific Rim's economic 'tigers', specializing in hi-tech and electronics industries.

THE TRANSPORT NETWORK

China's Grand Canal (Da Yunhe), built in the 13th century, is the world's longest artificial waterway, running 1100 miles (1770 m) from Beijing to Hangzhou. Despite restoration work, not all of the canal is currently navigable.

NORTHEASTERN CHINA, MONGOLIA & KOREA

MONGOLIA, NORTH KOREA, SOUTH KOREA, Heilongjiang, Inner Mongolia, Jilin, Liaoning

THIS NORTHERLY REGION has for centuries been a domain of shifting borders and competing colonial powers. Mongolia was the heartland of Chinghiz Khan's vast Mongol empire in the 13th century, while northeastern China was home to the Manchus, China's last ruling dynasty (1644–1911). The mineral and forest wealth of the northeast helped make this China's principal region of heavy industry, although the outdated state factories now face decline. South Korea's state-led market economy has grown dramatically and Seoul is now one of the world's largest cities. The austere communist regime of North Korea has isolated itself from the expanding markets of the Pacific Rim and faces continuing economic stagnation.

The Eurasian steppe stretches from the mouth of the Danube in Europe, to Mongolia. In Mongolia, nomadic people have lived in felt huts called yurts or gers, for thousands of years.

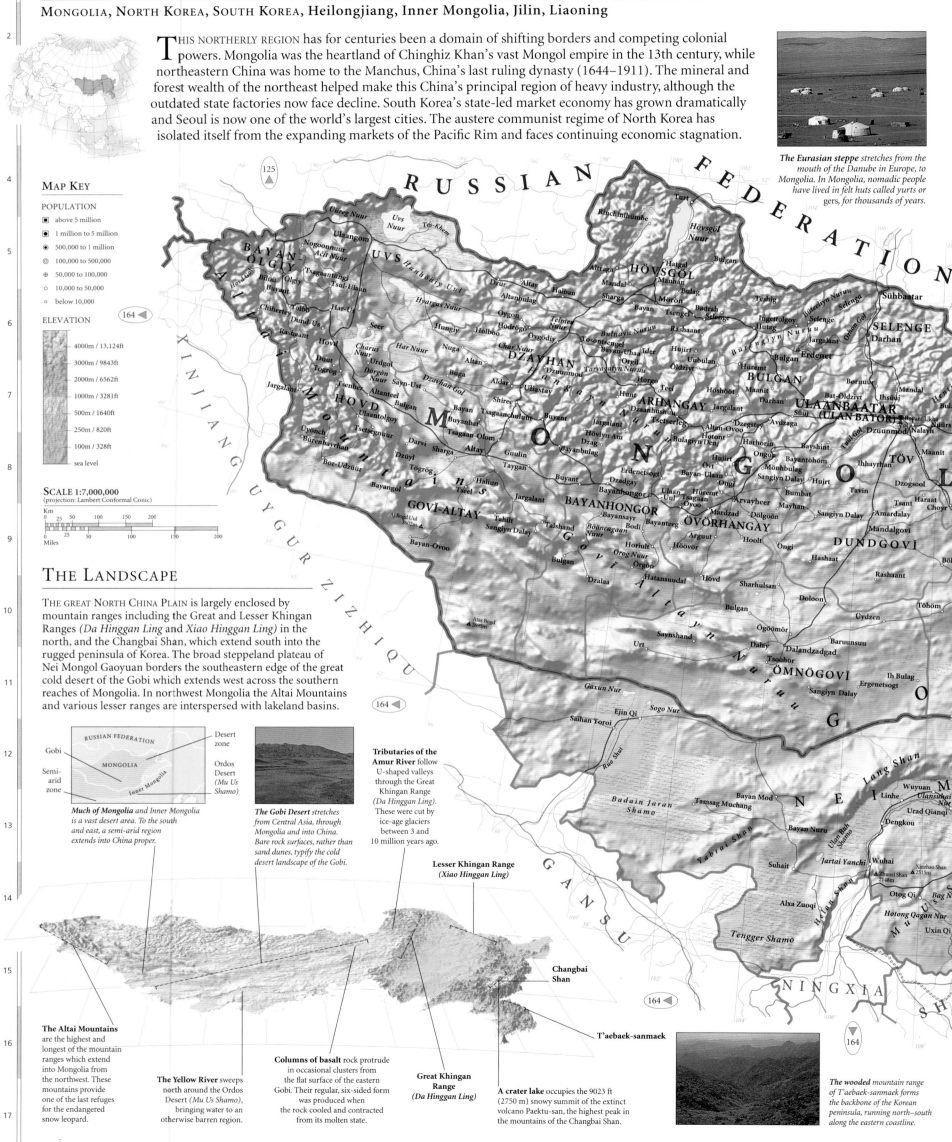

MAP KEY

POPULATION

- ■ above 5 million
- ▣ 1 million to 5 million
- ◉ 500,000 to 1 million
- ⊕ 100,000 to 500,000
- ⊕ 50,000 to 100,000
- ○ 10,000 to 50,000
- ∘ below 10,000

ELEVATION

- 4000m / 13,124ft
- 3000m / 9843ft
- 2000m / 6562ft
- 1000m / 3281ft
- 500m / 1640ft
- 250m / 820ft
- 100m / 328ft
- sea level

SCALE 1:7,000,000
(projection: Lambert Conformal Conic)

THE LANDSCAPE

THE GREAT NORTH CHINA PLAIN is largely enclosed by mountain ranges including the Great and Lesser Khingan Ranges (*Da Hinggan Ling* and *Xiao Hinggan Ling*) in the north, and the Changbai Shan, which extend south into the rugged peninsula of Korea. The broad steppeland plateau of Nei Mongol Gaoyuan borders the southeastern edge of the great cold desert of the Gobi which extends west across the southern reaches of Mongolia. In northwest Mongolia the Altai Mountains and various lesser ranges are interspersed with lakeland basins.

Much of Mongolia and Inner Mongolia is a vast desert area. To the south and east, a semi-arid region extends into China proper.

The Gobi Desert stretches from Central Asia, through Mongolia and into China. Bare rock surfaces, rather than sand dunes, typify the cold desert landscape of the Gobi.

Tributaries of the Amur River follow U-shaped valleys through the Great Khingan Range (*Da Hinggan Ling*). These were cut by ice-age glaciers between 3 and 10 million years ago.

Lesser Khingan Range (*Xiao Hinggan Ling*)

Changbai Shan

T'aebaek-sanmaek

The Altai Mountains are the highest and longest of the mountain ranges which extend into Mongolia from the northwest. These mountains provide one of the last refuges for the endangered snow leopard.

The Yellow River sweeps north around the Ordos Desert (*Mu Us Shamo*), bringing water to an otherwise barren region.

Columns of basalt rock protrude in occasional clusters from the flat surface of the eastern Gobi. Their regular, six-sided form was produced when the rock cooled and contracted from its molten state.

Great Khingan Range (*Da Hinggan Ling*)

A crater lake occupies the 9023 ft (2750 m) snowy summit of the extinct volcano Paektu-san, the highest peak in the mountains of the Changbai Shan.

The wooded mountain range of T'aebaek-sanmaek forms the backbone of the Korean peninsula, running north–south along the eastern coastline.

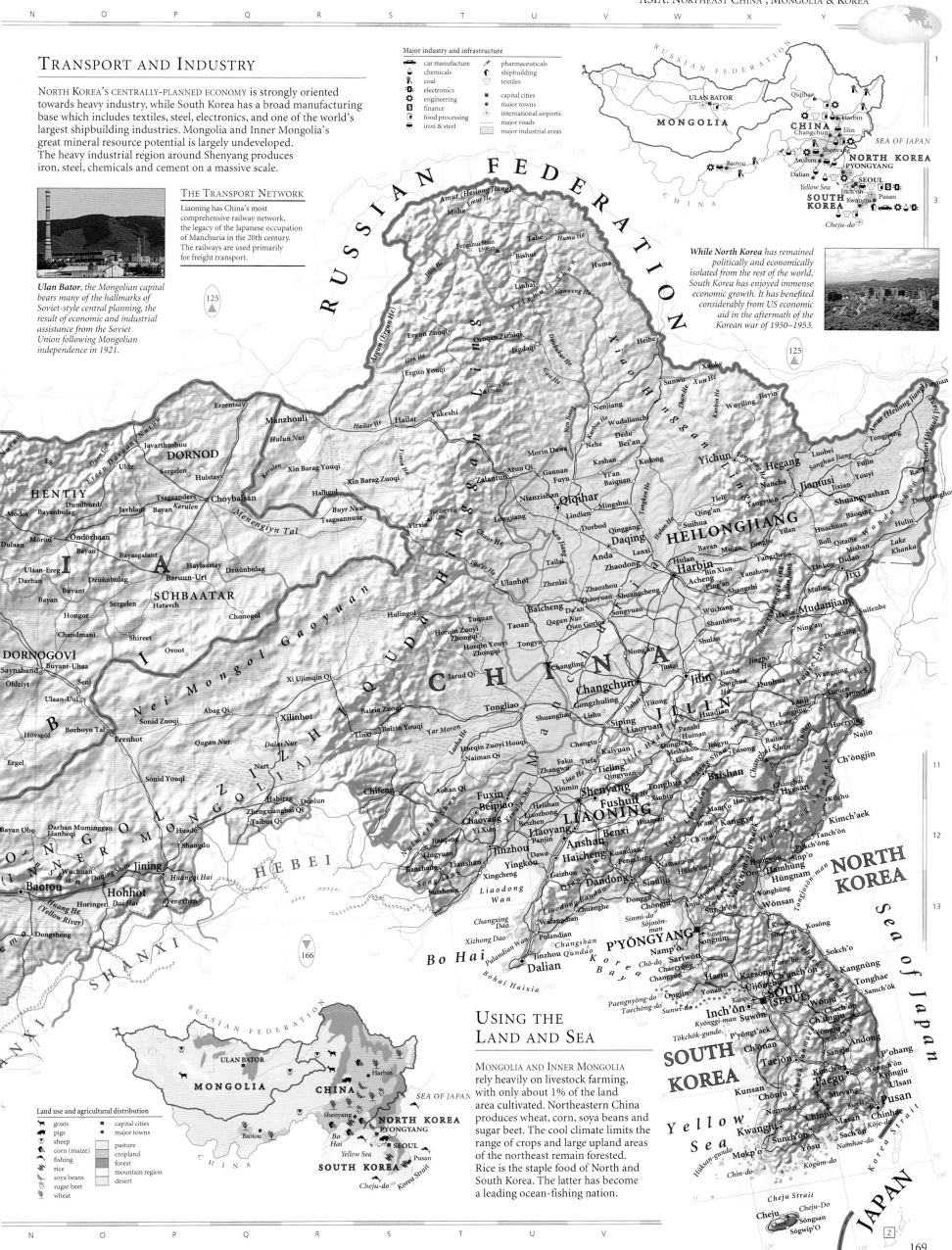

TRANSPORT AND INDUSTRY

NORTH KOREA'S CENTRALLY-PLANNED ECONOMY is strongly oriented towards heavy industry, while South Korea has a broad manufacturing base which includes textiles, steel, electronics, and one of the world's largest shipbuilding industries. Mongolia and Inner Mongolia's great mineral resource potential is largely undeveloped. The heavy industrial region around Shenyang produces iron, steel, chemicals and cement on a massive scale.

THE TRANSPORT NETWORK

Liaoning has China's most comprehensive railway network, the legacy of the Japanese occupation of Manchuria in the 20th century. The railways are used primarily for freight transport.

Ulan Bator, the Mongolian capital bears many of the hallmarks of Soviet-style central planning, the result of economic and industrial assistance from the Soviet Union following Mongolian independence in 1921.

While North Korea has remained politically and economically isolated from the rest of the world, South Korea has enjoyed immense economic growth. It has benefited considerably from US economic aid in the aftermath of the Korean war of 1950–1953.

Major industry and infrastructure

- car manufacture
- chemicals
- coal
- electronics
- engineering
- finance
- food processing
- iron & steel
- pharmaceuticals
- shipbuilding
- textiles
- capital cities
- major towns
- international airports
- major roads
- major industrial areas

USING THE LAND AND SEA

MONGOLIA AND INNER MONGOLIA rely heavily on livestock farming, with only about 1% of the land area cultivated. Northeastern China produces wheat, corn, soya beans and sugar beet. The cool climate limits the range of crops and large upland areas of the northeast remain forested. Rice is the staple food of North and South Korea. The latter has become a leading ocean-fishing nation.

Land use and agricultural distribution

- goats
- pigs
- sheep
- corn (maize)
- fishing
- rice
- soya beans
- sugar beet
- wheat
- capital cities
- major towns
- pasture
- cropland
- forest
- mountain region
- desert

A   Aa   B   Bb   C   Cc   D   Dd   E   Ee   F   Ff   G

Japan

In the years since the end of the Second World War, Japan has become the world's most dynamic industrial nation. The country comprises a string of over 4000 islands which lie in a great northeast to southwest arc in the northwest Pacific. Four major islands: Hokkaido, Honshu, Shikoku and Kyushu are home to the great majority of Japan's population of 125.9 million people, although the mountainous terrain of the central region means that most cities are situated on the coast. A densely populated industrial belt stretches along much of Honshu's southern coast, including Japan's crowded capital, Tokyo. Alongside its spectacular economic growth and the increasing westernization of its cities, Japan still maintains a most singular culture, reflected in its traditional food, formal behavioural codes, unique Shinto religion and the reverence for the emperor, who is officially regarded as a god.

TRANSPORT AND INDUSTRY

Japan is the world's second largest market economy, outranked only by the USA. Technological development, particularly of computers, electronic goods, cars and motorcycles is second to none. Japanese industry invests in its workforce, and in long-term research and development to maintain the high standard of its products, and a reputation for innovation. Japanese businesses are now global both in their manufacturing bases and in the distribution of goods.

THE TRANSPORT NETWORK

720,360 miles (1,160,000 km)		6070 miles (12,529 km)	
12,529 miles (20,175 km)		1099 miles (1770 km)	

Japanese road construction traditionally lagged behind that of its extensive and technologically advanced railway network. The road network's relative lack of development has led to severe urban congestion, although expressways have now been built in some cities.

Major industry and infrastructure

- brewing
- car manufacture
- chemicals
- hi-tech industry
- engineering
- finance
- iron & steel
- research & development
- shipbuilding
- textiles
- winter sports
- ■ capital cities
- ● major towns
- ⊕ international airports
- major roads
- major industrial areas

Known in the west as the 'bullet train', the Shinkansen is the second-fastest train in the world. It speeds past the snow-capped peak of Mount Fuji between the cities of Tokyo and Osaka.

USING THE LAND AND SEA

Although only about 11% of Japan is suitable for cultivation, substantial government support, a favourable climate and intensive farming methods enable the country to be virtually self-sufficient in rice production. Northern Hokkaido, the largest and most productive farming region, has an open terrain and climate similar to that of the US Midwest, and produces over half of Japan's cereal requirements. Farmers are being encouraged to diversify by growing fruit, vegetables and wheat, as well as raising livestock.

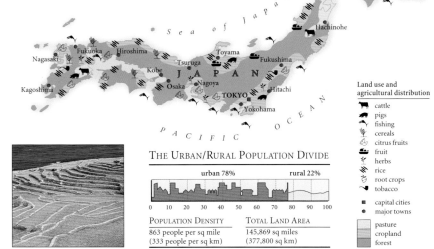

Land use and agricultural distribution
- cattle
- pigs
- fishing
- cereals
- citrus fruits
- fruit
- herbs
- rice
- root crops
- tobacco
- ■ capital cities
- ● major towns
- pasture
- cropland
- forest

THE URBAN/RURAL POPULATION DIVIDE

urban 78%   rural 22%

0 10 20 30 40 50 60 70 80 90 100

POPULATION DENSITY	TOTAL LAND AREA
863 people per sq mile (333 people per sq km)	145,869 sq miles (377,800 sq km)

Cutting terraces maximizes the limited agricultural land, enabling Japan to produce large quantities of rice.

The Kobe earthquake in January 1995 highlighted Japan's vulnerability to earthquakes, despite technological advances. It shattered much of the infrastructure of this important port. More than 5000 people died as buildings and overhead highways collapsed and fires broke out.

A number of new volcanoes emerged in Japan during the 20th century. They exist alongside older cones like this one in Aso-Kuju National Park on Kyushu, now dormant and grass-covered.

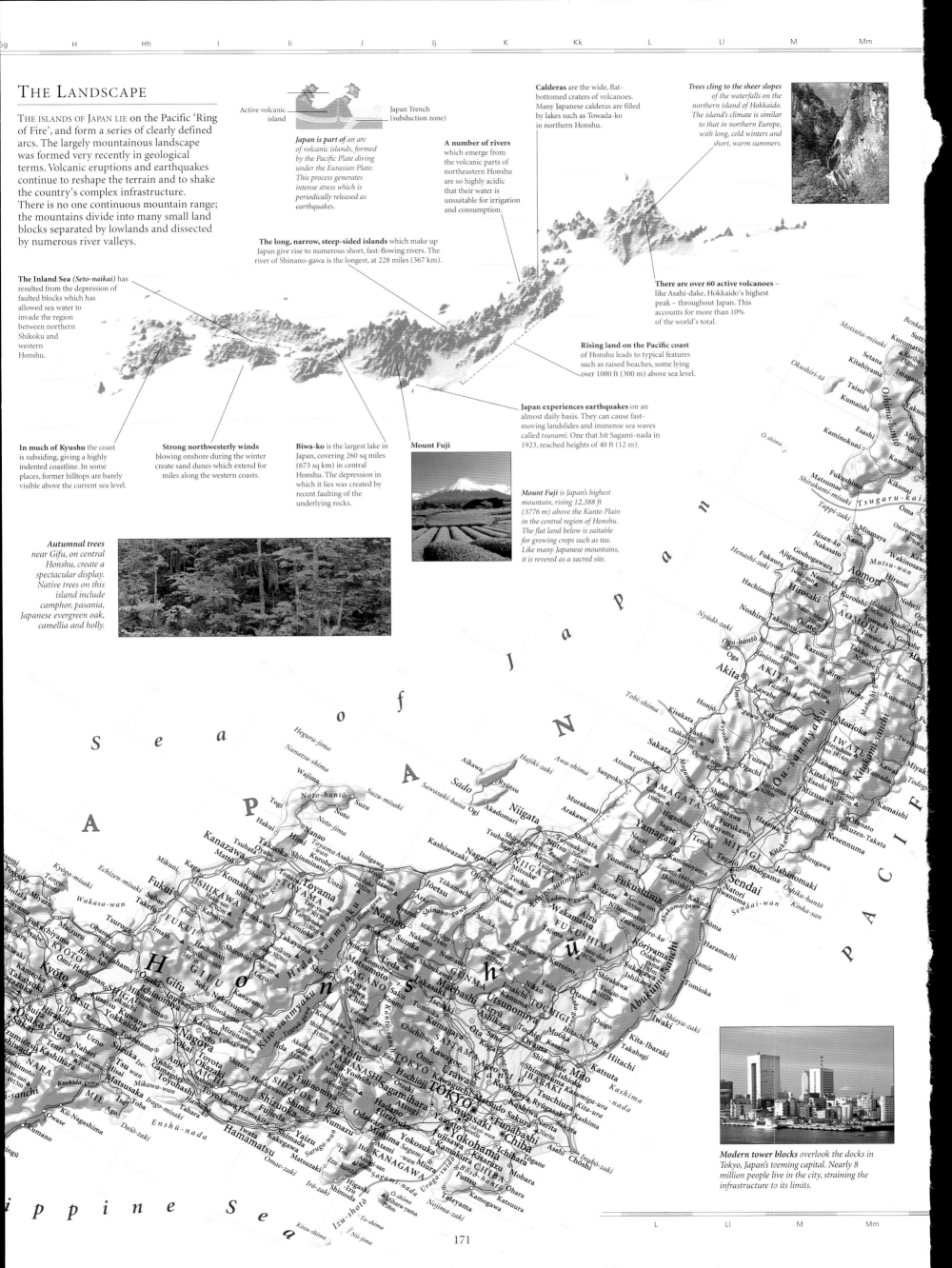

THE LANDSCAPE

THE ISLANDS OF JAPAN LIE on the Pacific 'Ring of Fire', and form a series of clearly defined arcs. The largely mountainous landscape was formed very recently in geological terms. Volcanic eruptions and earthquakes continue to reshape the terrain and to shake the country's complex infrastructure. There is no one continuous mountain range; the mountains divide into many small land blocks separated by lowlands and dissected by numerous river valleys.

Active volcanic island

Japan Trench (subduction zone)

Japan is part of an arc of volcanic islands, formed by the Pacific Plate diving under the Eurasian Plate. This process generates intense stress which is periodically released as earthquakes.

A number of rivers which emerge from the volcanic parts of northeastern Honshu are so highly acidic that their water is unsuitable for irrigation and consumption.

Calderas are the wide, flat-bottomed craters of volcanoes. Many Japanese calderas are filled by lakes such as Towada-ko in northern Honshu.

Trees cling to the sheer slopes of the waterfalls on the northern island of Hokkaido. The island's climate is similar to that in northern Europe, with long, cold winters and short, warm summers.

The long, narrow, steep-sided islands which make up Japan give rise to numerous short, fast-flowing rivers. The river of Shinano-gawa is the longest, at 228 miles (367 km).

There are over 60 active volcanoes – like Asahi-dake, Hokkaido's highest peak – throughout Japan. This accounts for more than 10% of the world's total.

The Inland Sea *(Seto-naikai)* has resulted from the depression of faulted blocks which has allowed sea water to invade the region between northern Shikoku and western Honshu.

Rising land on the Pacific coast of Honshu leads to typical features such as raised beaches, some lying over 1000 ft (300 m) above sea level.

Japan experiences earthquakes on an almost daily basis. They can cause fast-moving landslides and immense sea waves called *tsunami*. One that hit Sagami-nada in 1923, reached heights of 40 ft (12 m).

In much of Kyushu the coast is subsiding, giving a highly indented coastline. In some places, former hilltops are barely visible above the current sea level.

Strong northwesterly winds blowing onshore during the winter create sand dunes which extend for miles along the western coasts.

Biwa-ko is the largest lake in Japan, covering 260 sq miles (673 sq km) in central Honshu. The depression in which it lies was created by recent faulting of the underlying rocks.

Mount Fuji

Mount Fuji is Japan's highest mountain, rising 12,388 ft (3776 m) above the Kanto Plain in the central region of Honshu. The flat land below is suitable for growing crops such as tea. Like many Japanese mountains, it is revered as a sacred site.

Autumnal trees near Gifu, on central Honshu, create a spectacular display. Native trees on this island include camphor, pasania, Japanese evergreen oak, camellia and holly.

Modern tower blocks overlook the docks in Tokyo, Japan's teeming capital. Nearly 8 million people live in the city, straining the infrastructure to its limits.

Malaysia exports a greater tonnage of tropical timber than anywhere else in the world. Much of it comes from Sarawak in Borneo. Although in principle logging is only allowed on a sustainable basis, environmentalists fear that the rainforest in Sarawak will have disappeared by the early 21st century.

This tiny island near Kota Kinabalu, in Sabah, eastern Malaysia, is a part of a designated national park. Thickly forested, it is surrounded by broad, sandy beaches and shallow inland seas.

MALAYSIA

SOUTH CHINA SEA

Natuna Sea

Java Sea

MAP KEY

POPULATION

- ■ above 5 million
- ◼ 1 million to 5 million
- ◉ 500,000 to 1 million
- ◎ 100,000 to 500,000
- ⊕ 50,000 to 100,000
- ⊙ 10,000 to 50,000
- ○ below 10,000

ELEVATION

- 4000m / 13,124ft
- 3000m / 9843ft
- 2000m / 6562ft
- 1000m / 3281ft
- 500m / 1640ft
- 250m / 820ft
- 100m / 328ft
- sea level

SCALE 1:6,250,000
(projection: Mercator)

Km
0 25 50 100 150
0 25 50 100 150
Miles

Throughout Southeast Asia, where agricultural land is at a premium, terraces are cut into the slopes to maximize the area available for cultivation. These terraces on the Indonesian island of Bali are used to support rice paddies.

MARITIME SOUTHEAST ASIA

BRUNEI, EAST TIMOR, INDONESIA, MALAYSIA, SINGAPORE

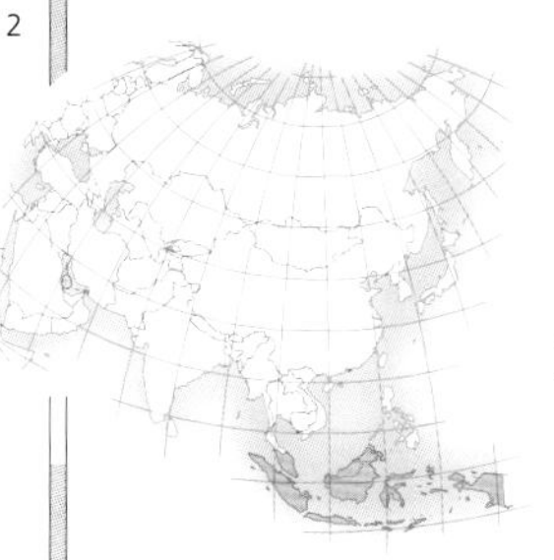

THE INTRICATE ARC OF ISLANDS which runs from peninsular Malaysia east to Irian Jaya in western New Guinea sustains a huge variety of peoples, languages and cultures. Indonesia is by far the largest country in the region, and 87% of its huge, predominantly Muslim, population is crowded onto Java, the most habitable of Indonesia's 13,677 islands. Malaysia, split between the mainland and the east Malaysian states of Sabah and Sarawak on Borneo, has a diverse population, as well as a fast-growing economy, although the pace of its development is still far outstripped by that of Singapore. This small island nation is the financial and commercial capital of Southeast Asia, and an Asian 'tiger' economy. The Sultanate of Brunei in northern Borneo, one of the world's last princely states, also has an extremely high standard of living, based on its oil revenues.

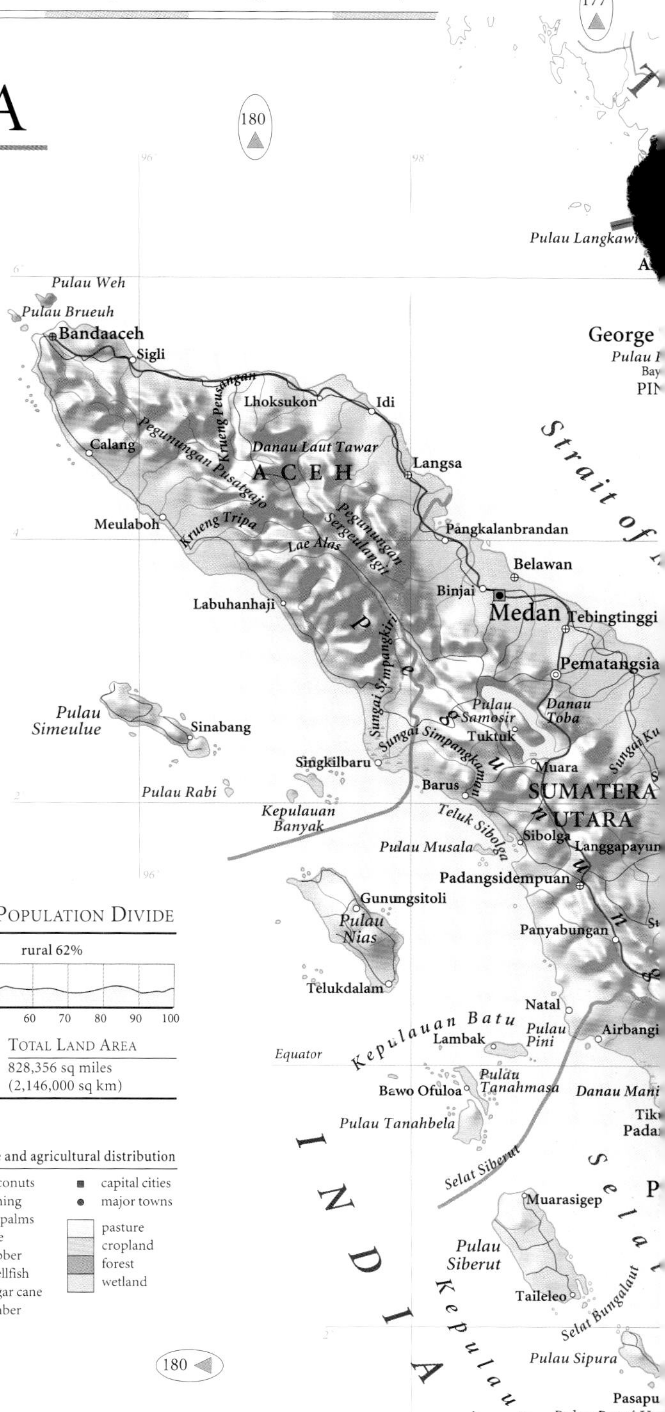

USING THE LAND AND SEA

RICE IS THE MOST IMPORTANT ARABLE CROP in Indonesia and Malaysia, and both countries manage to meet almost all of their domestic demand. Malaysian rubber accounts for 25% of world production and is the main cash crop, grown on plantations and small farms, along with oil palms and copra. Timber is exported from both Malaysia and Indonesia. Modern agricultural techniques enable Singapore to produce fruit and vegetables despite a shortage of suitable land.

Spiral cuts in the bark of this rubber palm show where it has been tapped. Sophisticated 'cloning' techniques mean that trees which produce consistently high quantities of rubber can be easily reproduced.

THE URBAN/RURAL POPULATION DIVIDE

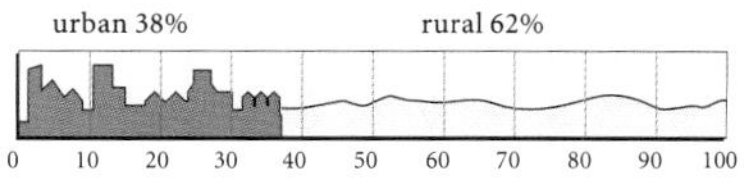

urban 38%   rural 62%

POPULATION DENSITY
262 people per sq mile
(101 people per sq km)

TOTAL LAND AREA
828,356 sq miles
(2,146,000 sq km)

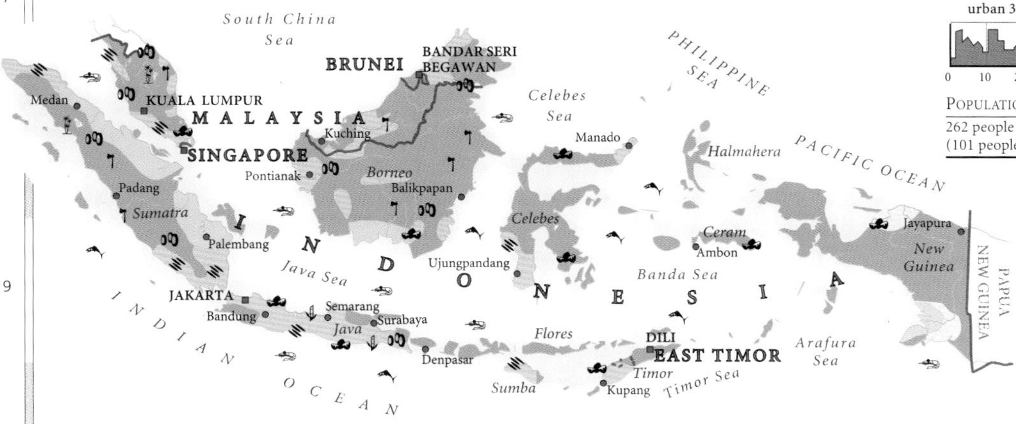

Land use and agricultural distribution

- coconuts
- fishing
- oil palms
- rice
- rubber
- shellfish
- sugar cane
- timber

- capital cities
- major towns

- pasture
- cropland
- forest
- wetland

THE LANDSCAPE

FROM SUMATRA IN THE WEST, the volcanic islands of Indonesia run for nearly 3100 miles (5000 km). The Sunda Shelf, an extension of the Eurasian Plate, lies between Java, Bali, Sumatra, Lombok and Borneo. Their volcanic mountains rise from a base below the sea and they were once joined together by dry land, which has since been submerged by rising sea levels.

Malay Peninsula has a rugged east coast, but the west coast, fronting the Strait of Malacca, has many sheltered beaches and bays. The two coasts are divided by the Banjaran Titiwangsa, which run the length of the peninsula.

The river of Sungai Mahakam cuts through the central highlands of Borneo, the third largest island in the world, with a total area of 290,000 sq miles (757,050 sq km). Although mountainous, Borneo is one of the most stable of the Indonesian islands, with little volcanic activity.

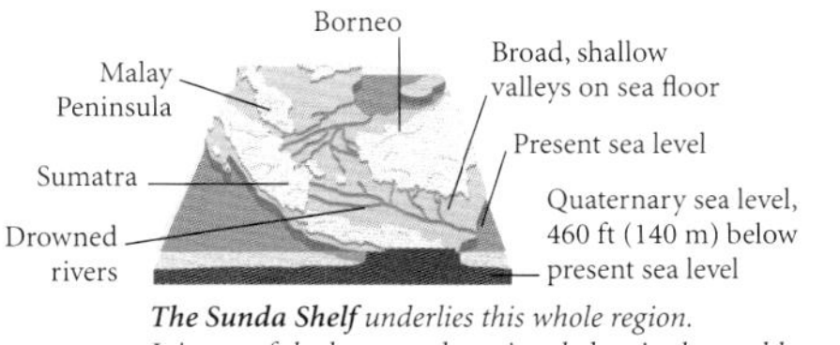

The Sunda Shelf underlies this whole region. It is one of the largest submarine shelves in the world, covering an area of 714,285 sq miles (1,850,000 sq km). During the early Quaternary period, when sea levels were lower, the shelf was exposed.

Broad, shallow valleys on sea floor
Present sea level
Quaternary sea level, 460 ft (140 m) below present sea level
Borneo
Malay Peninsula
Sumatra
Drowned rivers

Gunung Kinabalu is the highest peak in Malaysia, rising 13,455 ft (4101 m).

The four-pronged island of Celebes is the product of complex tectonic activity which ruptured and then reattached small fragments of the Earth's crust to form the island's many peninsulas.

Irian Jaya contains some of the most dense and least explored tropical rainforests in the world, inhabited by many rare species of plants and animals.

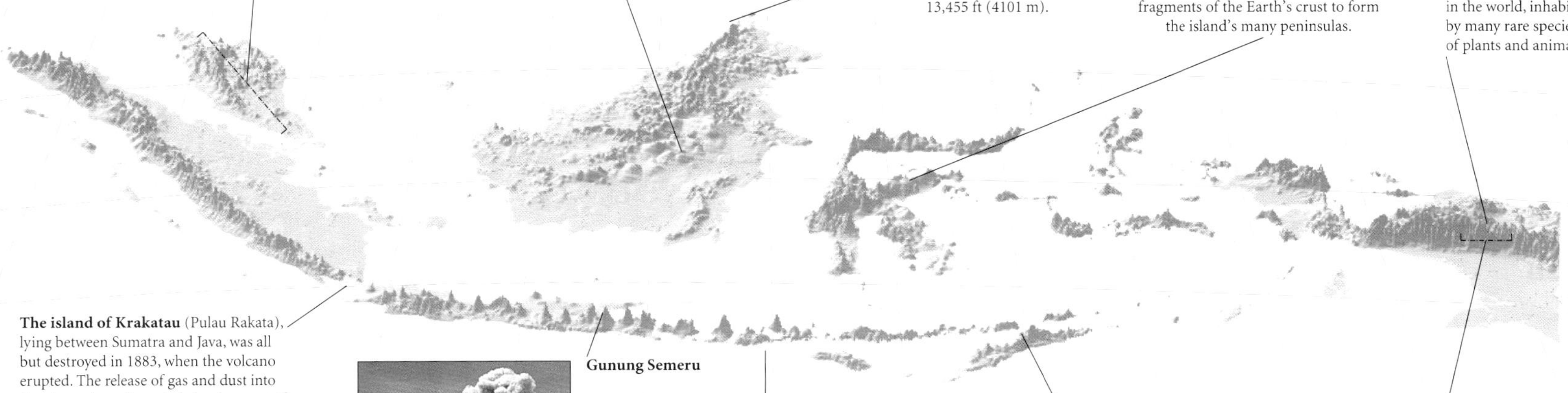

The island of Krakatau (Pulau Rakata), lying between Sumatra and Java, was all but destroyed in 1883, when the volcano erupted. The release of gas and dust into the atmosphere disrupted cloud cover and global weather patterns for several years.

Gunung Semeru

The volcano of Gunung Semeru in eastern Java lies on the Pacific 'Rim of Fire'. It is part of the ancient Tennegger volcano and remains highly active.

Indonesia has more than 220 volcanoes, most of which are still active. They are strung out along the island arc from Sumatra through the Lesser Sunda Islands, into the Moluccas and Celebes.

Coral islands such as Timor in eastern Indonesia show evidence of very recent and dramatic movements of the Earth's plates. Reefs in Timor have risen by as much as 4000 ft (1300 m) in the last million years.

The Pegunungan Jayawijaya range in central Irian Jaya contains the world's highest range of limestone mountains, some with peaks more than 16,400 ft (5000 m) high. Heavy rainfall and high temperatures, which promote rapid weathering, have led to the creation of large underground caves and river systems such as the river of Sungai Baliem.

Map labels

South China Sea
BRUNEI
BANDAR SERI BEGAWAN
Medan
KUALA LUMPUR
MALAYSIA
Kuching
SINGAPORE
Pontianak
Borneo
Balikpapan
Manado
Celebes Sea
PHILIPPINE SEA
Halmahera
PACIFIC OCEAN
Padang
Sumatra
Palembang
INDONESIA
Celebes
Ceram
Ambon
New Guinea
Jayapura
PAPUA NEW GUINEA
JAKARTA
Bandung
Java Sea
Ujungpandang
Banda Sea
Semarang
Surabaya
Java
Flores
DILI
EAST TIMOR
Arafura Sea
INDIAN OCEAN
Denpasar
Sumba
Timor
Kupang
Timor Sea

Pulau Weh
Pulau Brueuh
Bandaaceh
Lhoksukon
Idi
Sigli
Calang
Pegunungan Barisan
Danau Laut Tawar
A C E H
Langsa
Meulaboh
Krueng Tripa
Pangkalanbrandan
Belawan
Labuhanhaji
Binjai
Medan
Tebingtinggi
Pematangsia
George
Strait of
Pulau Simeulue
Sinabang
Pulau Samosir
Danau Toba
Tuktuk
Singkilbaru
Muara
Barus
SUMATERA UTARA
Pulau Rabi
Kepulauan Banyak
Teluk Sibolga
Sibolga
Langgapayun
Pulau Musala
Padangsidempuan
Gunungsitoli
Panyabungan
Pulau Nias
Natal
Telukdalam
Kepulauan Batu
Airbangi
Equator
Lambak
Pulau Pini
Bewo Ofuloa
Pulau Tanahmasa
Danau Mani
Pulau Tanahbela
Selat Siberut
Muarasigep
Pulau Siberut
Taileleo
Selat Bungalaun
Pulau Sipura
Pasapu
Pulau Pagai Ute
Kepulauan Mentawai
INDIAN OCEAN

Pulau Langkawi

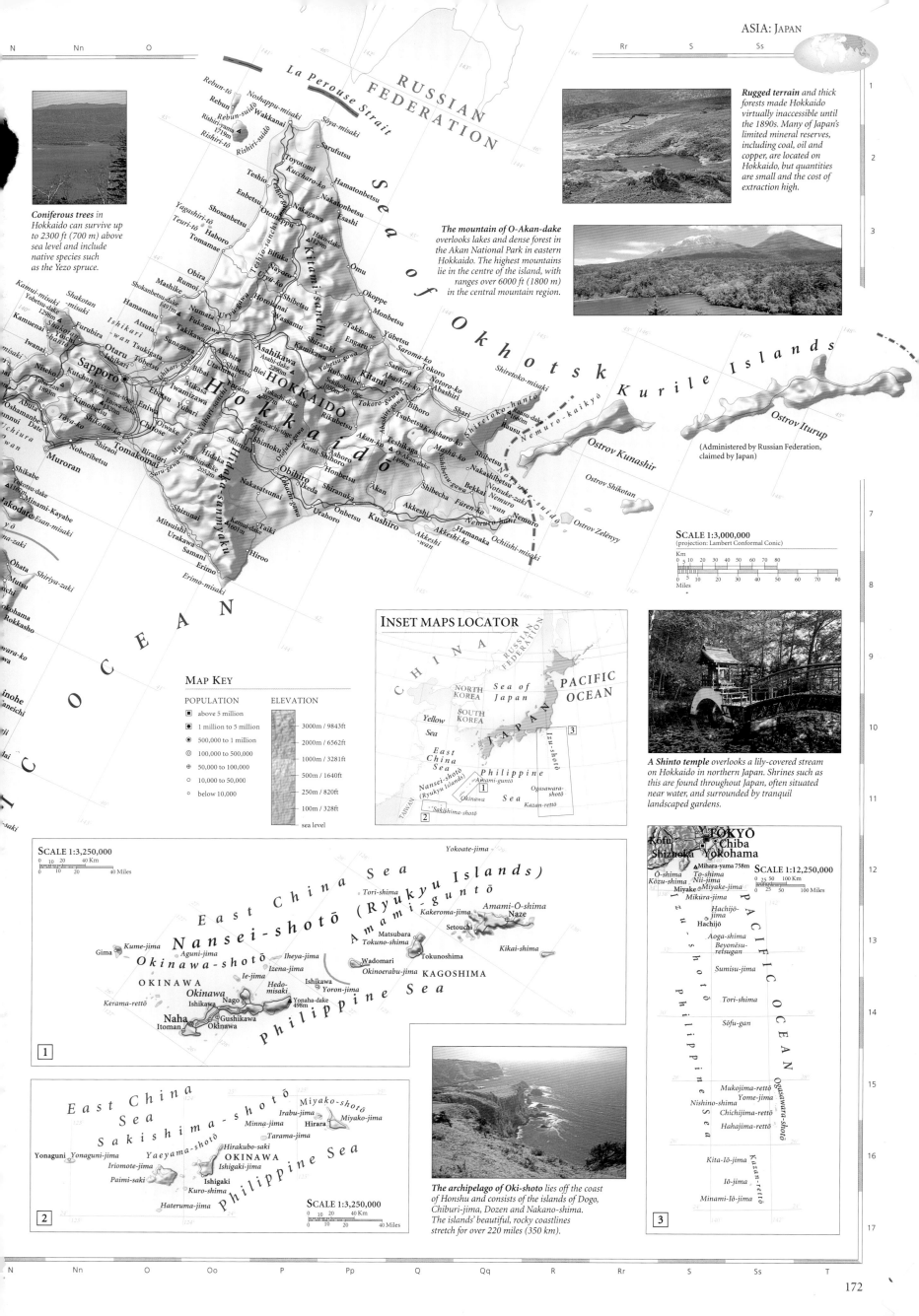

Coniferous trees in Hokkaido can survive up to 2300 ft (700 m) above sea level and include native species such as the Yezo spruce.

Rugged terrain and thick forests made Hokkaido virtually inaccessible until the 1890s. Many of Japan's limited mineral reserves, including coal, oil and copper, are located on Hokkaido, but quantities are small and the cost of extraction high.

The mountain of O-Akan-dake overlooks lakes and dense forest in the Akan National Park in eastern Hokkaido. The highest mountains lie in the centre of the island, with ranges over 6000 ft (1800 m) in the central mountain region.

A Shinto temple overlooks a lily-covered stream on Hokkaido in northern Japan. Shrines such as this are found throughout Japan, often situated near water, and surrounded by tranquil landscaped gardens.

The archipelago of Oki-shoto lies off the coast of Honshu and consists of the islands of Dogo, Chiburi-jima, Dozen and Nakano-shima. The islands' beautiful, rocky coastlines stretch for over 220 miles (350 km).

(Administered by Russian Federation, claimed by Japan)

MAP KEY

POPULATION
- ■ above 5 million
- ■ 1 million to 5 million
- ◉ 500,000 to 1 million
- ◎ 100,000 to 500,000
- ⊕ 50,000 to 100,000
- ○ 10,000 to 50,000
- ○ below 10,000

ELEVATION
- 3000m / 9843ft
- 2000m / 6562ft
- 1000m / 3281ft
- 500m / 1640ft
- 250m / 820ft
- 100m / 328ft
- sea level

INSET MAPS LOCATOR

SCALE 1:3,000,000
(projection: Lambert Conformal Conic)

SCALE 1:3,250,000

SCALE 1:12,250,000

SCALE 1:3,250,000

MAINLAND SOUTHEAST ASIA & THE PHILIPPINES

BURMA, CAMBODIA, LAOS, PHILIPPINES, THAILAND, VIETNAM

THICKLY FORESTED MOUNTAINS, intercut by the broad valleys of five great rivers characterize the landscape of Southeast Asia's mainland countries. Agriculture remains the main activity for much of the population, which is concentrated in the river flood plains and deltas. Linked ethnic and cultural roots give the region a distinct identity. Most people on the mainland are Theravada Buddhists, and the Philippines is the only predominantly Christian country in Southeast Asia. Foreign intervention began in the 16th century with the opening of the spice trade; Cambodia, Laos and Vietnam were French colonies until the end of the Second World War, Burma was under British control; and the Philippines was controlled by Spain and the USA in the 20th century. Only Thailand was never colonized. Today, Thailand and the Philippines are poised to play a leading role in the economic development of the Pacific Rim, and Laos and Vietnam have begun to mend the devastation of the Vietnam War, and to develop their economies. With continuing political instability and a shattered infrastructure, Cambodia faces an uncertain future, while Burma is seeking investment and the ending of its 38-year isolation from the world community.

The Irrawaddy River is Burma's vital central artery, watering the ricefields and providing a rich source of fish, as well as an important transport link, particularly for local traffic.

Commercial logging – still widespread in Burma – has now been stopped in Thailand because of over-exploitation of the tropical rainforest.

THE LANDSCAPE

A SERIES OF MOUNTAIN RANGES runs north–south through the mainland, formed as the result of the collision between the Eurasian Plate and the Indian subcontinent, which created the Himalayas. They are interspersed by the valleys of a number of great rivers. On their passage to the sea these rivers have deposited sediment, forming huge, fertile flood plains and deltas. The Philippines' 7000 islands are mountainous and volcanic, with narrow coastal plains.

Lake Taal on the Philippine island of Luzon lies within the crater of an immense volcano which erupted twice in the 20th century, first in 1911 and again in 1965, causing the deaths of more than 3200 people.

The Irrawaddy River runs virtually north–south, draining the plains of northern Burma. The Irrawaddy Delta is the country's main rice-growing area.

Hkakabo Razi is the highest point in mainland Southeast Asia. It rises 19,300 ft (5885 m) at the border between China and Burma.

Mountains dominate the Laotian landscape with more than 90% of the land lying more than 600 ft (180 m) above sea level. The mountains of the Chaîne Annamitique form the country's eastern border.

The Red River Delta in northern Vietnam is fringed to the north by steep-sided, round-topped limestone hills, typical of karst scenery.

Mindanao has five mountain ranges, many of which have large numbers of active volcanoes. Lying just west of the Philippine Trench, which forms the boundary between the colliding Philippine and Eurasian plates, the entire island chain is subject to earthquakes and volcanic activity.

The fast-flowing waters of the Mekong River cascade over this waterfall in Champasak province in Laos. The force of the water erodes rocks at the base of the fall.

Salween River

The Mekong River flows through southern China and Burma, then for much of its length forms the border between Laos and Thailand, flowing through Cambodia before terminating in a vast delta on the southern Vietnamese coast.

Malay Peninsula

Tonle Sap, a freshwater lake, drains into the Mekong Delta via the Mekong River. It is the largest lake in Southeast Asia.

Thailand

The coastline of the Isthmus of Kra

Longshore drift / Spit / Lagoon / Eroded coastline / Wave attack

The east and west coasts of the Isthmus of Kra differ greatly. The tectonically uplifting west coast is exposed to the harsh south-westerly monsoon and is heavily eroded. On the east coast, longshore currents produce depositional features such as spits and lagoons.

Bohol

Bohol in the southern Philippines is famous for its so-called 'chocolate hills'. There are more than 1000 of these regular mounds on the island. The hills are limestone in origin, the smoothed remains of an earlier cycle of erosion. Their brown appearance in the dry season gives the hills their name.

The coast of the Isthmus of Kra, in southeast Thailand has many small, precipitous islands like these, formed by chemical erosion on limestone, which is weathered along vertical cracks. The humidity of the climate in Southeast Asia increases the rate of weathering.

TRANSPORT AND INDUSTRY

SINGAPORE HAS A THRIVING ECONOMY based on international trade and finance. Annual trade through the port is among the highest of any port in the world. Indonesia still depends on natural resources, particularly wood, petroleum and gas, although the economy is rapidly diversifying, with manufactured exports including garments, consumer electronics and footwear; a high-profile aircraft industry has developed at Bandung. In Malaysia, although oil, gas and timber remain important resource-based industries, it has a fast-growing and varied manufacturing sector.

Major industry and infrastructure

- aerospace
- copra processing
- chemicals
- electronics
- engineering
- finance
- food processing
- iron & steel
- oil
- ship building
- timber processing
- textiles
- capital cities
- major towns
- international airports
- major roads
- major industrial areas

Ranks of gleaming skyscrapers, new motorways and infrastructure construction reflect the investment which is pouring into Southeast Asian cities like the Malaysian capital, Kuala Lumpur. Traditional housing and markets still exist amidst the new developments. Many of the city's inhabitants subsist at a level far removed from the prosperity implied by its outward modernity.

THE TRANSPORT NETWORK

- 160,350 miles (258,213 km)
- 188 miles (302 km)
- 5,482 miles (8,828 km)
- 15,523 miles (32,903km)

Singapore's metro system, completed in 1991, is among the most efficient in the world. Malaysia has several fast, modern highways and most roads are paved. Indonesia's many islands make improvement of the shipping infrastructure a priority.

Although Indonesia is now a mainly Muslim country, relics of other civilizations are found throughout its many islands. These scattered columns are the ruins of a Hindu settlement which flourished on Java more than a thousand years ago.

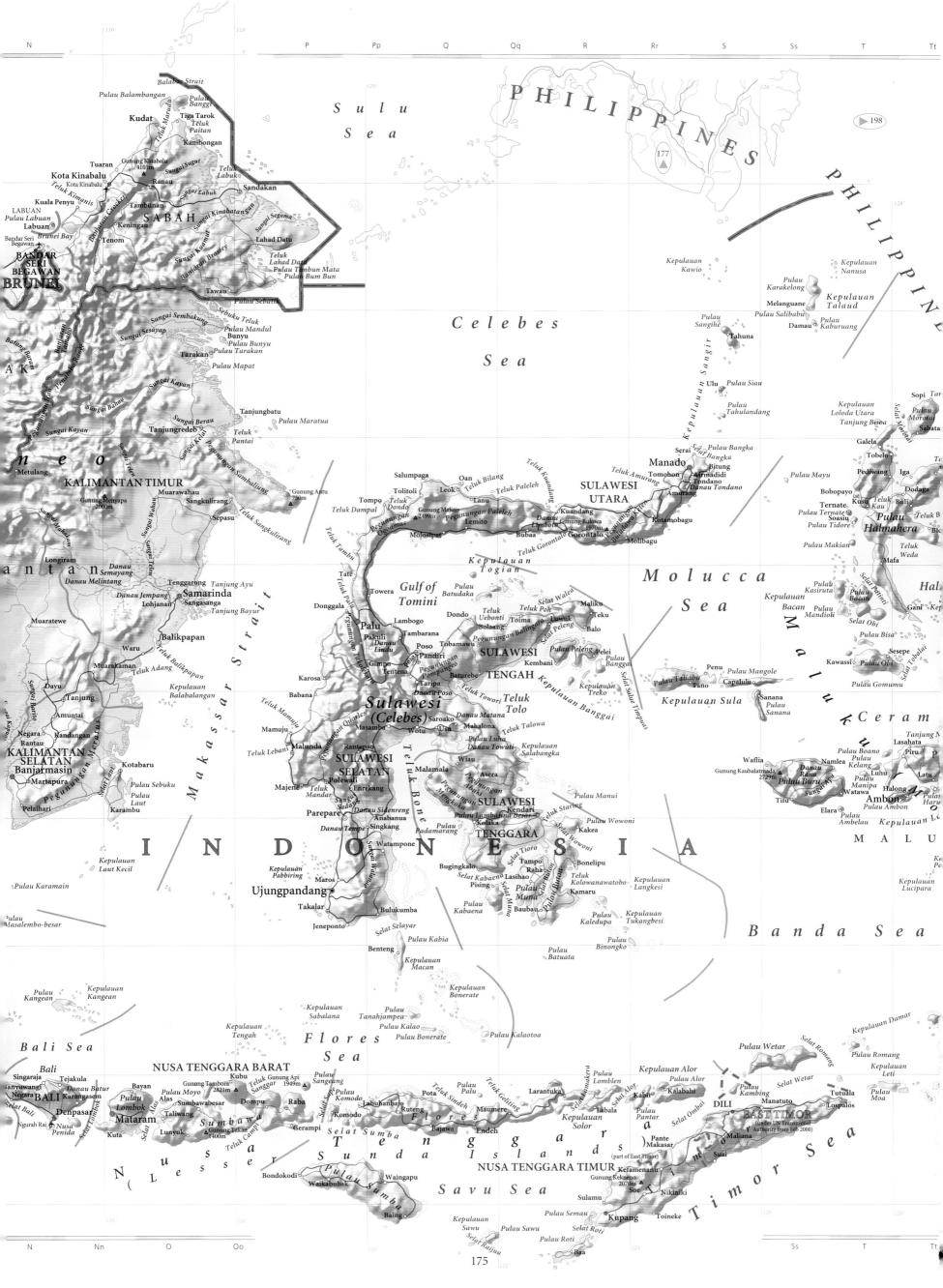

USING THE LAND AND SEA

THE FERTILE FLOOD PLAINS of rivers such as the Mekong and Salween, and the humid climate, enable the production of rice throughout the region. Cambodia, Burma and Laos still have substantial forests, producing hardwoods such as teak and rosewood. Cash crops include tropical fruits such as coconuts, bananas and pineapples, rubber, oil palm, sugar cane and the jute substitute, kenaf. Pigs and cattle are the main livestock raised. Large quantities of marine and freshwater fish are caught throughout the region.

162

Land use and agricultural distribution

- cattle
- pigs
- bananas
- coconuts
- fishing
- oil palms
- rice
- rubber
- sugar cane
- timber

- capital cities
- major towns

- pasture
- cropland
- forest
- wetland

THE URBAN/RURAL POPULATION DIVIDE

urban 30%   rural 70%

0 10 20 30 40 50 60 70 80 90 100

POPULATION DENSITY	TOTAL LAND AREA
322 people per sq mile (124 people per sq km)	733,828 sq miles (1,901,110 sq km)

The Paracel Islands and the Spratly Islands are two strategically sensitive island groups, disputed by several surrounding countries. The Paracels are claimed by China, Taiwan and Vietnam, though only China has actually occupied them. The Spratlys are claimed by China, Taiwan, Vietnam, Malaysia and the Philippines and are particularly important as they lie on oil and gas deposits.

The city of Hue in central Vietnam was the country's capital under the 13 emperors of the Nguyen dynasty from 1802 to 1945. It is the site of a number of religious monuments, including the Thien-Mu Pagoda.

TRANSPORT AND INDUSTRY

INDUSTRIAL MANUFACTURING has become increasingly important in Thailand, Vietnam and the Philippines in recent years. The assembling of component-based electrical and electronic goods is becoming more common throughout this region, with foreign companies benefiting from low labour costs and the upgrading of technology. The economies of Burma and Cambodia are still based on agricultural produce and the processing of raw materials. Tin is the region's most important metal, and nickel, copper and chromite are also mined, although the quantities produced are not significant on a global scale. Thailand's successful tourist industry is the country's highest earner of foreign exchange.

THE TRANSPORT NETWORK

131,566 miles (211,845 km)	267 miles (430 km)
7785 miles (12,536 km)	28,393 miles (45,722 km)

Transport development has concentrated on the building of road networks. Water and sea transport remain important, although air links have improved, particularly in Thailand and the Philippines.

Major industry and infrastructure

- chemicals
- electronics
- engineering
- finance
- food processing
- iron & steel
- oil & gas
- mining
- shipbuilding
- textiles
- timber processing
- capital cities
- major towns
- international airports
- major roads
- major industrial areas

Opium poppies are destroyed under army supervision in Thailand. This action is part of a government-sponsored initiative to reduce the trade in drugs such as heroin, which is derived from these plants. Drug trafficking is a major problem throughout the region; the area is known as the 'Golden Triangle', and Laos is the third-largest producer of opium poppies in the world.

The terracing of land to restrict soil erosion and create flat surfaces for agriculture is a common practice throughout Southeast Asia, particularly where land is scarce. These terraces are on Luzon in the Philippines.

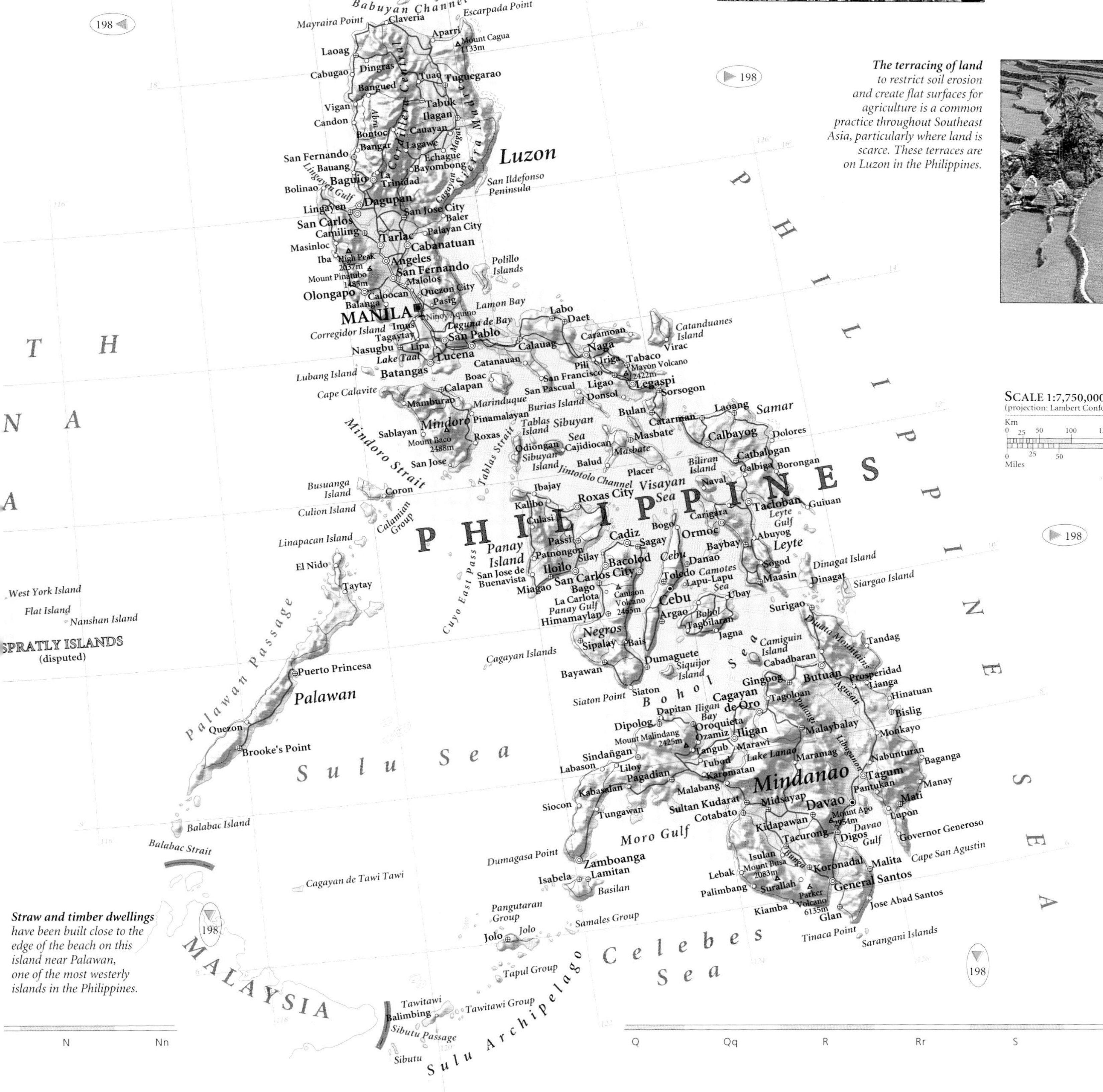

Straw and timber dwellings have been built close to the edge of the beach on this island near Palawan, one of the most westerly islands in the Philippines.

SCALE 1:7,750,000
(projection: Lambert Conformal Conic)

Km
0 25 50 100 150 200

Miles
0 25 50 100 150 200

MAP KEY

POPULATION

- above 5 million
- 1 million to 5 million
- 500,000 to 1 million
- 100,000 to 500,000
- 50,000 to 100,000
- 10,000 to 50,000
- below 10,000

ELEVATION

4000m / 13,124ft	
3000m / 9843ft	
2000m / 6562ft	
1000m / 3281ft	
500m / 1640ft	
250m / 820ft	
100m / 328ft	
sea level	

Map labels (mainland inset)

INDIA · BANGLADESH · CHINA · BURMA · Mandalay · Chiang Mai · Hai Phong · HANOI · Gulf of Tongking · LAOS · VIENTIANE · Hue · Da Nang · Luzon Strait · Luzon · Philippine Sea · MANILA · PHILIPPINES · Cebu · Mindanao · Davao · Zamboanga · Sulu Sea · Celebes Sea · Rangoon · Moulmein · THAILAND · BANGKOK · Andaman Sea · CAMBODIA · PHNOM PENH · Ho Chi Minh City · VIETNAM · South China Sea · Gulf of Thailand · Hat Yai · MALAYSIA · BRUNEI · Bay of Bengal

Map labels (Philippines main map)

Bashi Channel · Batan Islands · Luzon Strait · Balintang Channel · Babuyan Island · Babuyan Channel · Escarpada Point · Mayraira Point · Claveria · Aparri · Mount Cagua 1133m · Laoag · Dingras · Tuao · Tuguegarao · Cabugao · Bangued · Tabuk · Vigan · Ilagan · Candon · Cauayan · Bontoc · Lagawe · San Fernando · Echague · Bauang · Bayombong · Baguio · La Trinidad · San Ildefonso Peninsula · Bolinao · Dagupan · San José City · Lingayen Gulf · Baler · San Carlos · Palayan City · Camiling · Tarlac · Masinloc · Cabanatuan · Iba · High Peak 2037m · Angeles · Polillo Islands · Mount Pinatubo 1485m · San Fernando · Olongapo · Malolos · Quezon City · Caloocan · Pasig · Lamon Bay · Batangas · MANILA · Ninoy Aquino · Labo · Daet · Corregidor Island · Imus · Laguna de Bay · Caramoan · Catanduanes Island · Tagaytay · San Pablo · Calauag · Naga · Virac · Nasugbu · Lipa · Lucena · Catanauan · Tigaon · Tabaco · Lake Taal · Pili · Mayon Volcano 2422m · San Francisco · Legaspi · Lubang Island · Boac · Ligao · Sorsogon · Cape Calavite · Batangas · San Pascual · Donsol · Calapan · Marinduque · Burias Island · Bulan · Laoang · Samar · Mamburao · Pinamalayan · Tablas · Sibuyan · Catarman · Calbayog · Sablayan · Mindoro · Mount Baco 2488m · Sibuyan Sea · Masbate · Dolores · Catbalogan · San José · Romblon · Cajidiocan · Placer · Biliran · Calbiga · Borongan · Busuanga Island · Odiongan · Sibuyan Island · Balud · Naval · Coron · Culion Island · Jintotolo Channel · Roxas City · Visayan Sea · Tacloban · Leyte Gulf · Guiuan · Calamian Group · Kalibo · Carigara · Abuyog · Linapacan Island · Ibajay · Cuiasi · Cadiz · Bogo · Ormoc · Baybay · Leyte · El Nido · Panay Island · Passi · Sagay · Cebu · Sogod · Dinagat Island · West York Island · Cuyo East Pass · Patnongon · Silay · Toledo · Lapu-Lapu · Camotes Sea · Ubay · Dinagat · Siargao Island · Flat Island · Nanshan Island · Iloilo · Bacolod · Danao · Maasin · SPRATLY ISLANDS (disputed) · San José de Buenavista · San Carlos City · Cebu · Surigao · Miagao · Bago · Panay Gulf · Canlaon Volcano 2460m · Argao · Bohol · Camiguin Island · Tandag · La Carlota · Himamaylan · Tagbilaran · Jagna · Cabadbaran · Puerto Princesa · Negros · Bais · Sipalay · Dumaguete · Siquijor Island · Gingoog · Butuan · Prosperidad · Palawan · Cagayan Islands · Bayawan · Siaton · Lianga · Quezon · Siaton Point · Cagayan de Oro · Tagoloan · Hinatuan · Brooke's Point · Dapitan · Iligan · Dipolog · Bohol Sea · Bislig · Balabac Island · Sulu Sea · Oroquieta · Ozamiz · Iligan · Malaybalay · Monkayo · Sindangan · Mount Malindang 2425m · Tubod · Marawi · Lake Lanao · Maramag · Nabunturan · Balabac Strait · Liloy · Pagadian · Tangub · Karomatan · Baganga · Dumagasa Point · Labason · Kabasalan · Malabang · Mindanao · Tagum · Manay · Siocon · Tungawan · Sultan Kudarat · Midsayap · Davao · Pantukan · Cotabato · Mount Apo 2954m · Lupon · Zamboanga · Lamitan · Kidapawan · Davao Gulf · Digos · Governor Generoso · Isabela · Basilan · Lebak · Isulan · Mount Busa 2083m · Koronadal · Malita · Cape San Agustin · Pangutaran Group · Palimbang · Surallah · General Santos · Jolo · Kiamba · Parker Volcano 1824m · Glan · Jose Abad Santos · Samales Group · Tinaca Point · Sarangani Islands · Moro Gulf · Celebes Sea · Tapul Group · Tawitawi · Balimbing · Tawitawi Group · Sibutu Passage · Sibutu · Sulu Archipelago · MALAYSIA · Cagayan de Tawi Tawi

THE INDIAN OCEAN

DESPITE BEING THE SMALLEST of the three major oceans, the evolution of the Indian Ocean was the most complex. The ocean basin was formed during the break up of the supercontinent Gondwanaland, when the Indian subcontinent moved northeast, Africa moved west and Australia separated from Antarctica. Like the Pacific Ocean, the warm waters of the Indian Ocean are punctuated by coral atolls and islands. About one-fifth of the world's population – over 1000 million people – live on its shores. Those people living along the northern coasts are constantly threatened by flooding and typhoons caused by the monsoon winds.

THE LANDSCAPE

THE INDIAN OCEAN BEGAN FORMING about 150 million years ago, but in its present form it is relatively young, only about 36 million years old. Along the three subterranean mountain chains of its mid-ocean ridge the seafloor is still spreading. The Indian Ocean has fewer trenches than other oceans and only a narrow continental shelf around most of its surrounding land.

The mid-oceanic ridge runs from the Arabian Sea. It diverges east of Madagascar, one arm runs southwest to join the Mid-Atlantic Ridge, the other branches southeast, joining the Pacific-Antarctic Ridge, southeast of Tasmania.

The Ninetyeast Ridge takes its name from the line of longitude it follows. It is the world's longest and straightest under-sea ridge.

Indus River

Two of the world's largest rivers flow into the Indian Ocean; the Indus and the Ganges/Brahmaputra. Both have deposited enormous fans of sediment.

Sediments come from Ganges/Brahmaputra river system

Submarine canyons transport sediment to fan – some of these are more than 1500 miles (2500 km) long

Sri Lanka

The Ganges Fan is one of the world's largest submarine accumulations of sediment, extending far beyond Sri Lanka. It is fed by the Ganges/Brahmaputra river system, whose sediment is carried through a network of underwater canyons at the edge of the continental shelf.

A large proportion of the coast of Thailand, on the Isthmus of Kra, is stabilized by mangrove thickets. They act as an important breeding ground for wildlife.

The Java Trench is the world's longest, it runs 1600 miles (2570 km) from the southwest of Java, but is only 50 miles (80 km) wide.

The relief of Madagascar rises from a low-lying coastal strip in the east, to the central plateau. The plateau is also a major watershed separating Madagascar's three main river basins.

The central group of the Seychelles are mountainous, granite islands. They have a narrow coastal belt and lush, tropical vegetation cloaks the highlands.

The Kerguelen Islands in the Southern Ocean were created by a hot spot in the Earth's crust. The islands were formed in succession as the Antarctic Plate moved slowly over the hot spot.

The circulation in the northern Indian Ocean is controlled by the monsoon winds. Biannually these winds reverse their pattern, causing a reversal in the surface currents and alternative high and low pressure conditions over Asia and Australia.

RESOURCES

MANY OF THE SMALL ISLANDS in the Indian Ocean rely exclusively on tuna-fishing and tourism to maintain their economies. Most fisheries are artisanal, although large-scale tuna-fishing does take place in the Seychelles, Mauritius and the western Indian Ocean. Non-living resources include oil in The Gulf, pearls in the Red Sea and tin from deposits off the shores of Burma, Thailand and Indonesia.

The recent use of large drag nets for tuna-fishing has not only threatened the livelihoods of many small-scale fisheries, but also caused widespread environmental concern about the potential impact on other marine species.

Resources (including wildlife)
- fish
- penguins
- shellfish
- whales
- oil & gas
- tin deposits
- tourism
- major towns
- major ports

Coral reefs support an enormous diversity of animal and plant life. Many species of tiny tropical fish, like these squirrel fish, live and feed around the profusion of reefs and atolls in the Indian Ocean.

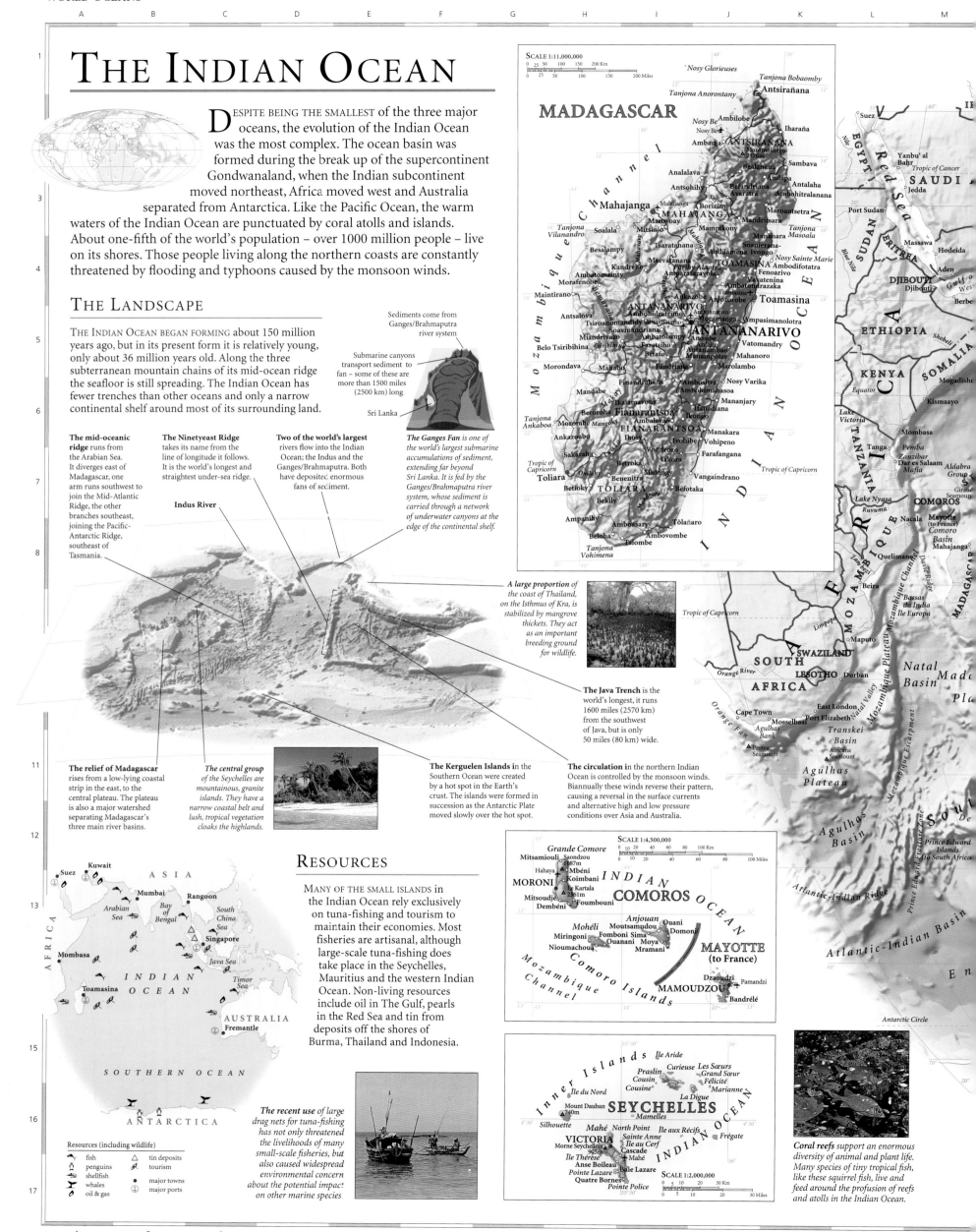

SCALE 1:11,000,000

MADAGASCAR

COMOROS
SCALE 1:4,500,000
Grande Comore
Mitsamiouli Saondzou
1087m
Hahaya Mbéni
Koimbani
MORONI Ile Kartala
2361m
Mitsoudje Foumbouni
Dembéni
Anjouan
Mohéli Moutsamoudou Ouani
Miringoni Fomboni Sima Domoni
Ouanani Moya
Nioumachoua Mramani
Comoro Islands
MAYOTTE
(to France)
Dzaoudzi Pamandzi
MAMOUDZOU
Bandrélé

SEYCHELLES
Inner Islands
Ile Aride
Ile du Nord Curieuse Les Sœurs
Praslin Grand Sœur
Cousin Félicité
Cousine Marianne
La Digue
Mount Dauban
740m
Mamelles
Silhouette Mahé North Point Ile aux Récifs
VICTORIA Sainte Anne Frégate
Morne Seychellois Ile au Cerf
905m Cascade
Ile Thérèse Mahé
Anse Boileau
Pointe Lazare Baie Lazare
Quatre Bornes
Pointe Police
SCALE 1:2,000,000

The steeper eastern side of Madagascar is drained by numerous short, fast-flowing rivers. In contrast, larger, more languid rivers flow across the west. Both erode huge quantities of Madagascar's reddish soil.

There are over 1300 small coral islands in the Maldives, but only about 200 are inhabited. They are based around an ancient submerged volcanic mountain range and all the islands are low-lying, none rising more than 6 ft (1.8 m) above sea level.

SCALE 1:42,000,000
(projection: Mollweide)

The island of Mauritius is volcanic in origin. Its central plateau is bounded by mountains which may once have formed the rim of a volcanic crater.

INSET MAP KEY

POPULATION
- 500,000 to 1 million
- 100,000 to 500,000
- 50,000 to 100,000
- 10,000 to 50,000
- below 10,000

ELEVATION
- 3000m / 9843ft
- 2000m / 6562ft
- 1000m / 3281ft
- 500m / 1640ft
- 250m / 820ft
- 100m / 328ft
- sea level

OCEAN MAP KEY

SEA DEPTH
- sea level
- 250m / 820ft
- 500m / 1640ft
- 1000m / 3281ft
- 2000m / 6562ft
- 3000m / 9843ft

RÉUNION (to France)
SCALE 1:2,000,000

MAURITIUS
SCALE 1:2,000,000

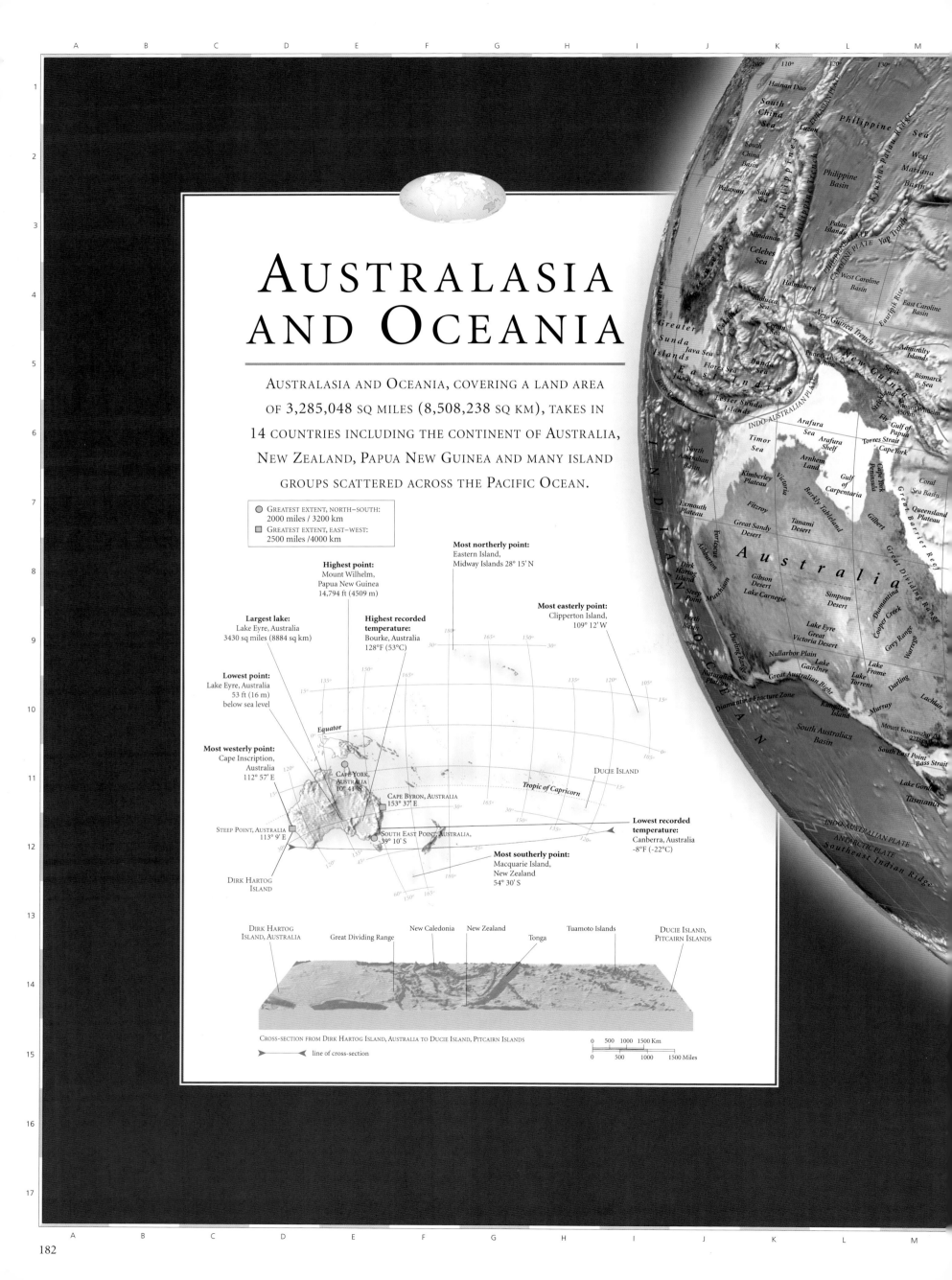

AUSTRALASIA AND OCEANIA

AUSTRALASIA AND OCEANIA, COVERING A LAND AREA
OF 3,285,048 SQ MILES (8,508,238 SQ KM), TAKES IN
14 COUNTRIES INCLUDING THE CONTINENT OF AUSTRALIA,
NEW ZEALAND, PAPUA NEW GUINEA AND MANY ISLAND
GROUPS SCATTERED ACROSS THE PACIFIC OCEAN.

● GREATEST EXTENT, NORTH–SOUTH:
   2000 miles / 3200 km
■ GREATEST EXTENT, EAST–WEST:
   2500 miles /4000 km

Most northerly point:
Eastern Island,
Midway Islands 28° 15' N

Highest point:
Mount Wilhelm,
Papua New Guinea
14,794 ft (4509 m)

Most easterly point:
Clipperton Island,
109° 12' W

Largest lake:
Lake Eyre, Australia
3430 sq miles (8884 sq km)

**Highest recorded
temperature:**
Bourke, Australia
128°F (53°C)

Lowest point:
Lake Eyre, Australia
53 ft (16 m)
below sea level

Most westerly point:
Cape Inscription,
Australia
112° 57' E

CAPE YORK,
AUSTRALIA
10° 41' S

DUCIE ISLAND

Tropic of Capricorn

CAPE BYRON, AUSTRALIA
153° 37' E

**Lowest recorded
temperature:**
Canberra, Australia
-8°F (-22°C)

STEEP POINT, AUSTRALIA
113° 9' E

SOUTH EAST POINT, AUSTRALIA,
39° 10' S

Most southerly point:
Macquarie Island,
New Zealand
54° 30' S

DIRK HARTOG
ISLAND

DIRK HARTOG
ISLAND, AUSTRALIA

Great Dividing Range

New Caledonia

New Zealand

Tonga

Tuamoto Islands

DUCIE ISLAND,
PITCAIRN ISLANDS

CROSS-SECTION FROM DIRK HARTOG ISLAND, AUSTRALIA TO DUCIE ISLAND, PITCAIRN ISLANDS

line of cross-section

| 0 | 500 | 1000 | 1500 Km |
| 0 | 500 | 1000 | 1500 Miles |

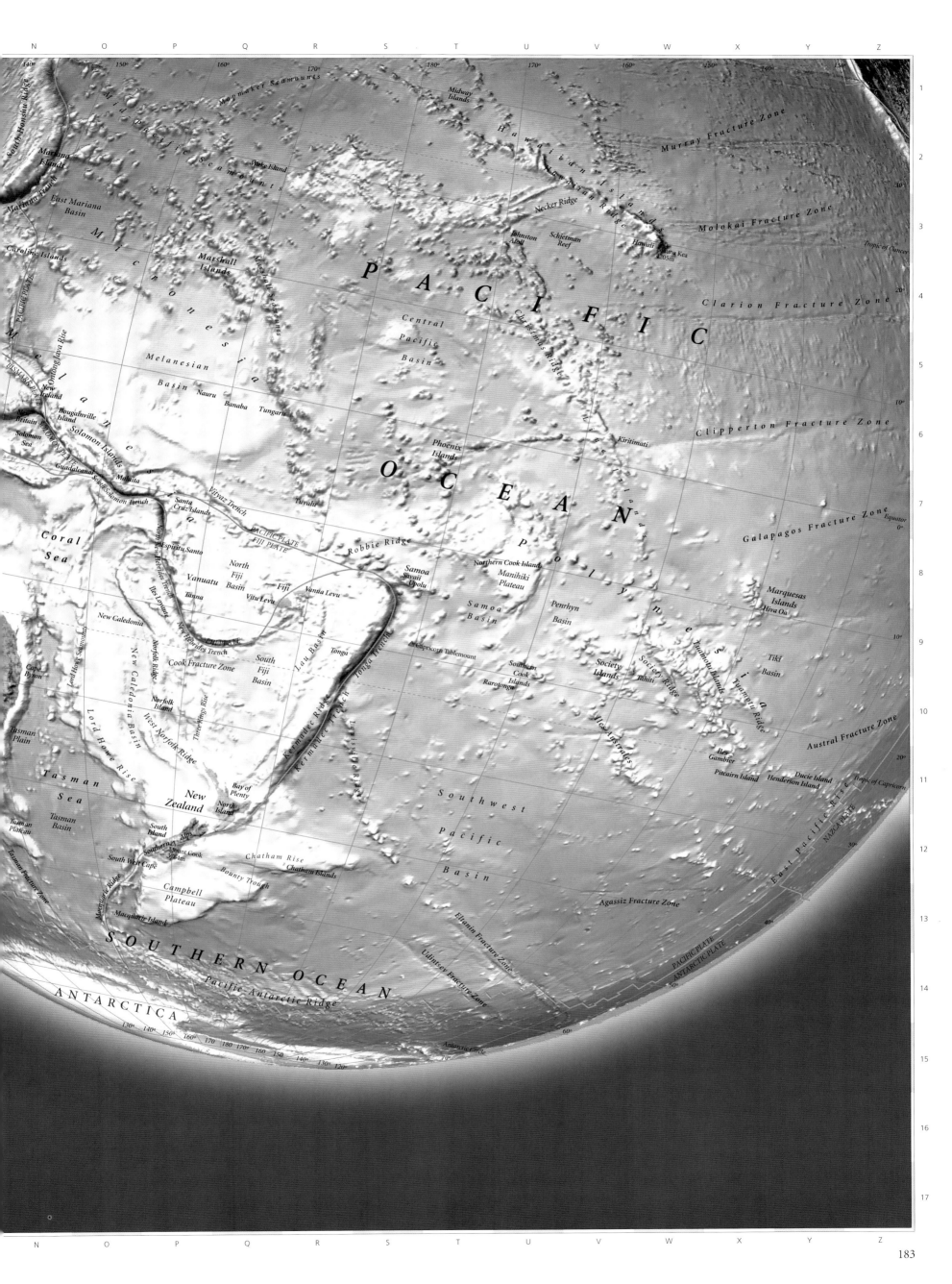

PACIFIC

OCEAN

SOUTHERN OCEAN

ANTARCTICA

South Honshu Ridge

Mid-Pacific Seamounts

Marcus-Necker Seamounts

Mariana
Islands

Mariana Trench

East Mariana
Basin

Wake Island

Micronesia

Marshall
Islands

Magellan Seamounts

Midway
Islands

Hawaiian Islands

Hawaiian Ridge

Necker Ridge

Johnston
Atoll

Schjetman
Reef

Hawaii
Mauna Kea
4205m

Murray Fracture Zone

Molokai Fracture Zone

Tropic of Cancer

Clarion Fracture Zone

Caroline Islands

PACIFIC PLATE

Central
Pacific
Basin

Christmas Ridge

Clipperton Fracture Zone

Melanesian
Basin

Nauru
Banaba
Tungaru

Kiritimati

Line Islands

Polynesia

Melanesia

BISMARCK PLATE

Ontong Java Rise

New
Ireland

Bougainville
Island

Solomon
Sea

Solomon Islands

Guadalcanal
Malaita

New Britain Trench

South Solomon Trench

Vityaz Trench

Santa
Cruz Islands

Tuvalu

Phoenix
Islands

Northern Cook Islands

Manihiki
Plateau

Galapagos Fracture Zone

Equator

Coral
Sea

PACIFIC PLATE
FIJI PLATE

Espíritu Santo

North New Hebrides Trench

North
Fiji
Basin

Robbie Ridge

Samoa
Savaii
Upolu

Marquesas
Islands
Hiva Oa

Vanuatu

Tanna

Iles Loyauté

Fiji

Vitu Levu

Vanua Levu

Samoa
Basin

Penrhyn
Basin

New Caledonia

New Hebrides Trench

INDO PLATE

Capricorn Tablemount

Southern
Cook
Islands
Rarotonga

Society
Islands

Society Ridge

Tuamotu Islands

Tiki
Basin

Tuamotu Ridge

Tahiti

Cape Byron

Lord Howe Seamounts

New Caledonia Basin

Norfolk Ridge

Cook Fracture Zone

South
Fiji
Basin

Lau Basin

Tonga

Kermadec Ridge

Tonga Trench

Iles Australes

Austral Fracture Zone

Tasman
Plain

Norfolk
Island

West Norfolk Ridge

Three Kings Rise

Kermadec Trench

Louisville Ridge

Iles
Gambier

Pitcairn Island

Ducie Island

Henderson Island

Tropic of Capricorn

Lord Howe Rise

Tasman
Sea

Lord Norfolk Ridge

New
Zealand

Bay of
Plenty

North
Island

Southwest

East Pacific Rise

NAZCA PLATE

Tasman
Plateau

Tasman
Basin

South
Island

Southern Alps

Mount Cook
2754m

Chatham Rise

Chatham Islands

Pacific

Basin

South West Cape

Bounty Trough

Campbell
Plateau

Agassiz Fracture Zone

Tasman Fracture Zone

Macquarie Ridge

Macquarie Island

Eltanin Fracture Zone

Udintsev Fracture Zone

PACIFIC PLATE
ANTARCTIC PLATE

Pacific-Antarctic Ridge

130° 140° 150° 160 170 180 170° 160 150 140° 130° 120

60°

Antarctic Circle

70°

POLITICAL AUSTRALASIA AND OCEANIA

Western Australia's mineral wealth has transformed its state capital, Perth, into one of Australia's major cities. Perth is one of the world's most isolated cities – over 2500 miles (4000 km) from the population centres of the eastern seaboard.

Vast expanses of ocean separate this geographically fragmented realm, characterized more by each country's isolation than by any political unity. Australia's and New Zealand's traditional ties with the United Kingdom, as members of the Commonwealth, are now being called into question as Australasian and Oceanian nations are increasingly looking to forge new relationships with neighbouring Asian countries like Japan. External influences have featured strongly in the politics of the Pacific Islands; the various territories of Micronesia were largely under US control until the late 1980s, and France, New Zealand, the USA and the UK still have territories under colonial rule in Polynesia. Nuclear weapons-testing by Western superpowers was widespread during the Cold War period, but has now been discontinued.

POPULATION

Density of settlement in the region is generally low. Australia is one of the least densely populated countries on Earth with over 80% of its population living within 25 miles (40 km) of the coast – mostly in the southeast of the country. New Zealand, and the island groups of Melanesia, Micronesia and Polynesia, are much more densely populated, although many of the smaller islands remain uninhabited.

Population density
(people per sq km)

- 0–4
- 5–24
- 25–49
- 50–99
- 100–199
- 200–299
- 300 +

The myriad of small coral islands which are scattered across the Pacific Ocean are often uninhabited, as they offer little shelter from the weather, often no fresh water, and only limited food supplies.

The planes of the Australian Royal Flying Doctor Service are able to cover large expanses of barren land quickly, bringing medical treatment to the most inaccessible and far-flung places.

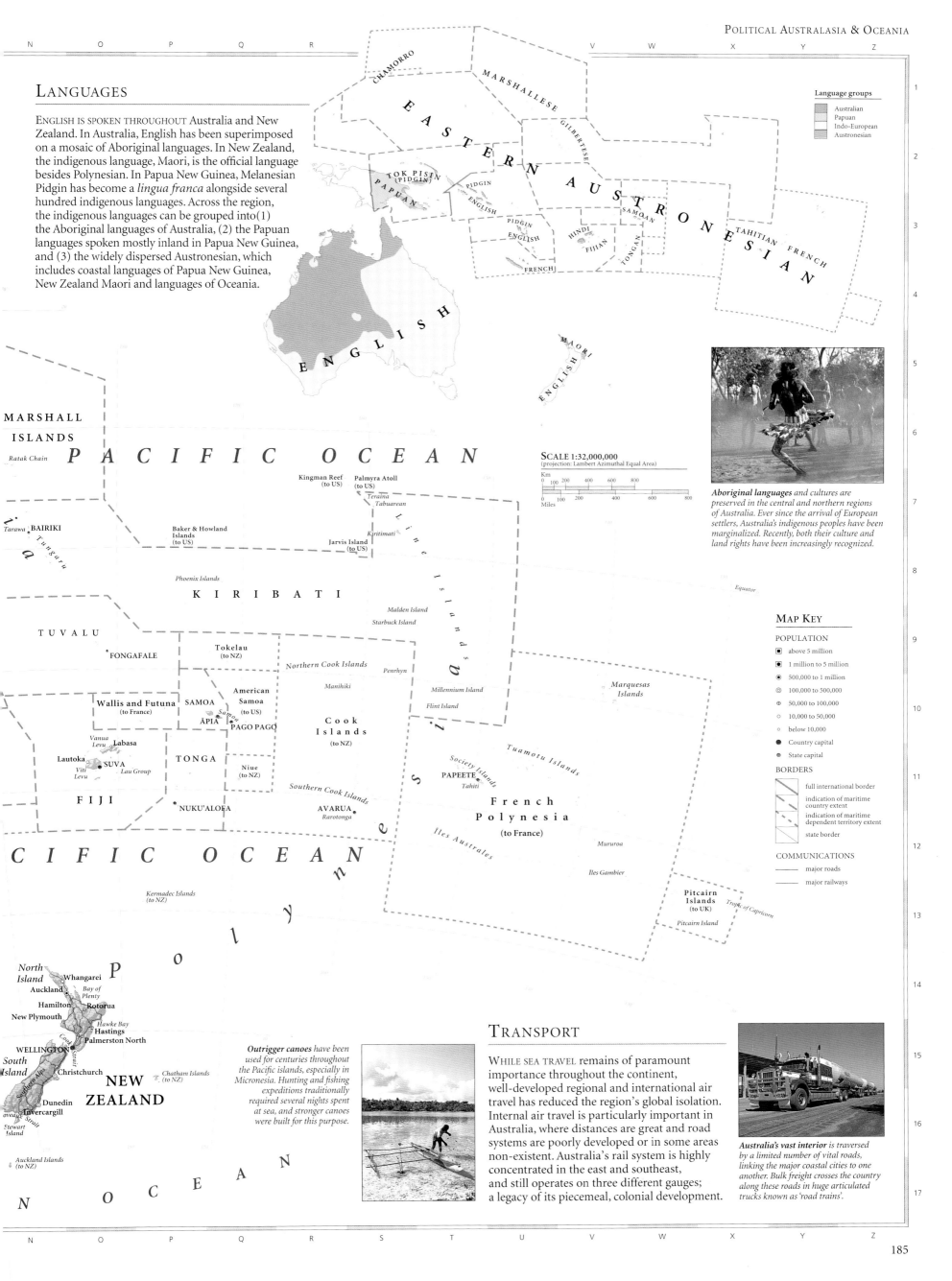

LANGUAGES

ENGLISH IS SPOKEN THROUGHOUT Australia and New Zealand. In Australia, English has been superimposed on a mosaic of Aboriginal languages. In New Zealand, the indigenous language, Maori, is the official language besides Polynesian. In Papua New Guinea, Melanesian Pidgin has become a *lingua franca* alongside several hundred indigenous languages. Across the region, the indigenous languages can be grouped into (1) the Aboriginal languages of Australia, (2) the Papuan languages spoken mostly inland in Papua New Guinea, and (3) the widely dispersed Austronesian, which includes coastal languages of Papua New Guinea, New Zealand Maori and languages of Oceania.

Language groups

- Australian
- Papuan
- Indo-European
- Austronesian

SCALE 1:32,000,000
(projection: Lambert Azimuthal Equal Area)

Km
0 100 200 400 600 800

Miles
0 100 200 400 600 800

Aboriginal languages and cultures are preserved in the central and northern regions of Australia. Ever since the arrival of European settlers, Australia's indigenous peoples have been marginalized. Recently, both their culture and land rights have been increasingly recognized.

MAP KEY

POPULATION

- ▣ above 5 million
- ⊡ 1 million to 5 million
- ⊚ 500,000 to 1 million
- ⊛ 100,000 to 500,000
- ⊕ 50,000 to 100,000
- ○ 10,000 to 50,000
- · below 10,000
- ● Country capital
- ● State capital

BORDERS

- full international border
- indication of maritime country extent
- indication of maritime dependent territory extent
- state border

COMMUNICATIONS

- major roads
- major railways

TRANSPORT

WHILE SEA TRAVEL remains of paramount importance throughout the continent, well-developed regional and international air travel has reduced the region's global isolation. Internal air travel is particularly important in Australia, where distances are great and road systems are poorly developed or in some areas non-existent. Australia's rail system is highly concentrated in the east and southeast, and still operates on three different gauges; a legacy of its piecemeal, colonial development.

Outrigger canoes have been used for centuries throughout the Pacific islands, especially in Micronesia. Hunting and fishing expeditions traditionally required several nights spent at sea, and stronger canoes were built for this purpose.

Australia's vast interior is traversed by a limited number of vital roads, linking the major coastal cities to one another. Bulk freight crosses the country along these roads in huge articulated trucks known as 'road trains'.

AUSTRALASIAN AND OCEANIAN RESOURCES

The largely unpolluted waters of the Pacific Ocean support rich and varied marine life, much of which is farmed commercially. Here, oysters are gathered for market off the coast of New Zealand's South Island.

NATURAL RESOURCES ARE OF MAJOR ECONOMIC IMPORTANCE throughout Australasia and Oceania. Australia in particular is a major world exporter of raw materials such as coal, iron ore and bauxite, while New Zealand's agricultural economy is dominated by sheep-raising. Trade with western Europe has declined significantly in the last 20 years, and the Pacific Rim countries of Southeast Asia are now the main trading partners, as well as a source of new settlers to the region. Australasia and Oceania's greatest resources are its climate and environment; tourism increasingly provides a vital source of income for the whole continent.

Huge flocks of sheep are a common sight in New Zealand, where they outnumber people by 20 to 1. New Zealand is one of the world's largest exporters of wool and frozen lamb.

STANDARD OF LIVING

IN MARKED CONTRAST TO ITS NEIGHBOUR, Australia, with one of the world's highest life expectancies and standards of living, Papua New Guinea is one of the world's least developed countries. In addition, high population growth and urbanization rates throughout the Pacific islands contribute to overcrowding. The Aboriginal and Maori people of Australia and New Zealand have been isolated for many years. Recently, their traditional land ownership rights have begun to be legally recognized in an effort to ease their social and economic isolation, and to improve living standards.

Standard of Living
(UN Human Development Index)

- low
- high
- figures unavailable

ENVIRONMENTAL ISSUES

THE PROSPECT OF RISING SEA LEVELS poses a threat to many low-lying islands in the Pacific. Nuclear weapons-testing, once common throughout the region, was finally discontinued in 1996. Australia's ecological balance has been irreversibly altered by the introduction of alien species. Although it has the world's largest underground water reserve, the Great Artesian Basin, the availability of fresh water in Australia remains critical. Periodic droughts combined with over-grazing lead to desertification and increase the risk of devastating bush fires, and occasional flash floods.

Environmental Issues

- national parks
- tropical forest
- forest destroyed
- desert
- desertification
- polluted rivers
- radioactive contamination
- marine pollution
- heavy marine pollution
- poor urban air quality

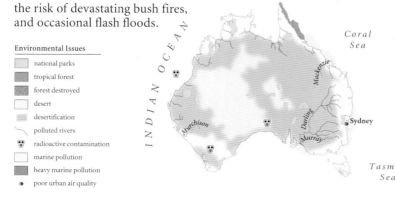

In 1946 Bikini Atoll, in the Marshall Islands, was chosen as the site for Operation Crossroads – investigating the effects of atomic bombs upon naval vessels. Further nuclear tests continued until the early 1990s. The long-term environmental effects are unknown.

MICRO

Northern Mariana Islands
(to US)

Saipan

Guam
(to US)

PALAU

Mel

PAPUA NEW GUINEA

New Guinea

Port Moresby

Arafura Sea

Torres Strait

Timor Sea

Darwin

Gulf of Carpentaria

Great Barrier Reef

Townsville

AUSTRALIA

INDIAN OCEAN

Adelaide

Geelong

Perth

Bikini Atoll

Eniwetak Atoll

SOUTHERN

Malden Island

Fangataufa

PACIFIC OCEAN

INDIAN OCEAN

Coral Sea

Murchison

Darling

Mackenzie

Murray

Sydney

Tasman Sea

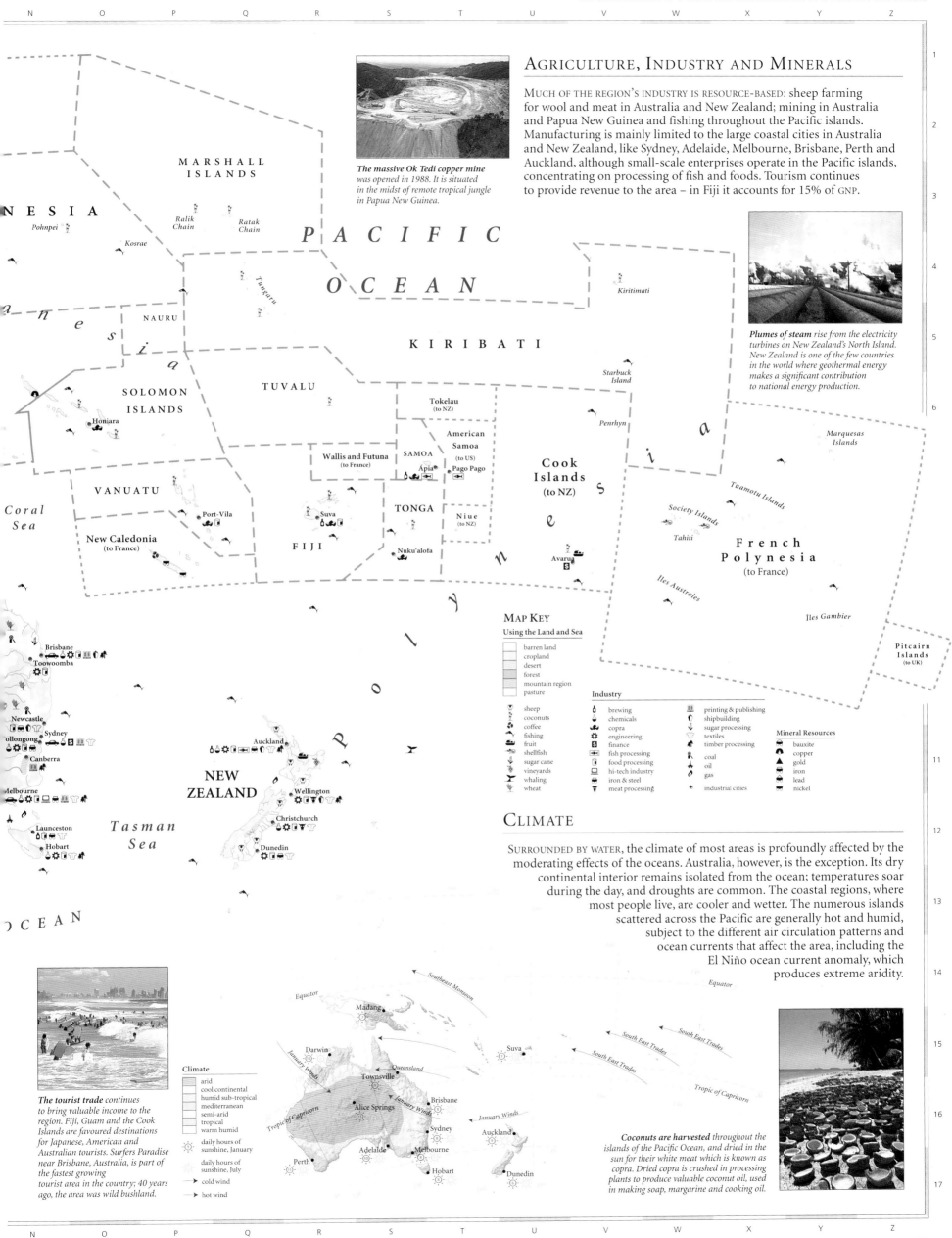

AGRICULTURE, INDUSTRY AND MINERALS

MUCH OF THE REGION'S INDUSTRY IS RESOURCE-BASED: sheep farming for wool and meat in Australia and New Zealand; mining in Australia and Papua New Guinea and fishing throughout the Pacific islands. Manufacturing is mainly limited to the large coastal cities in Australia and New Zealand, like Sydney, Adelaide, Melbourne, Brisbane, Perth and Auckland, although small-scale enterprises operate in the Pacific islands, concentrating on processing of fish and foods. Tourism continues to provide revenue to the area – in Fiji it accounts for 15% of GNP.

The massive Ok Tedi copper mine was opened in 1988. It is situated in the midst of remote tropical jungle in Papua New Guinea.

Plumes of steam rise from the electricity turbines on New Zealand's North Island. New Zealand is one of the few countries in the world where geothermal energy makes a significant contribution to national energy production.

MAP KEY

Using the Land and Sea

- barren land
- cropland
- desert
- forest
- mountain region
- pasture

Industry

- sheep
- coconuts
- coffee
- fishing
- fruit
- shellfish
- sugar cane
- vineyards
- whaling
- wheat

- brewing
- chemicals
- copra
- engineering
- finance
- fish processing
- food processing
- hi-tech industry
- iron & steel
- meat processing

- printing & publishing
- shipbuilding
- sugar processing
- textiles
- timber processing
- coal
- oil
- gas
- industrial cities

Mineral Resources

- bauxite
- copper
- gold
- iron
- lead
- nickel

CLIMATE

SURROUNDED BY WATER, the climate of most areas is profoundly affected by the moderating effects of the oceans. Australia, however, is the exception. Its dry continental interior remains isolated from the ocean; temperatures soar during the day, and droughts are common. The coastal regions, where most people live, are cooler and wetter. The numerous islands scattered across the Pacific are generally hot and humid, subject to the different air circulation patterns and ocean currents that affect the area, including the El Niño ocean current anomaly, which produces extreme aridity.

The tourist trade continues to bring valuable income to the region. Fiji, Guam and the Cook Islands are favoured destinations for Japanese, American and Australian tourists. Surfers Paradise near Brisbane, Australia, is part of the fastest growing tourist area in the country; 40 years ago, the area was wild bushland.

Climate

- arid
- cool continental
- humid sub-tropical
- mediterranean
- semi-arid
- tropical
- warm humid
- daily hours of sunshine, January
- daily hours of sunshine, July
- cold wind
- hot wind

Coconuts are harvested throughout the islands of the Pacific Ocean, and dried in the sun for their white meat which is known as copra. Dried copra is crushed in processing plants to produce valuable coconut oil, used in making soap, margarine and cooking oil.

AUSTRALIA

AUSTRALIA IS THE WORLD's smallest continent, a stable landmass lying between the Indian and Pacific oceans. Previously home only to its aboriginal peoples, since the end of the 18th century immigration has transformed the face of the country. Initially settlers came mainly from western Europe, particularly the UK, and for years Australia remained wedded to its British colonial past. Latterly, more immigrants have come from eastern Europe, and from Asian countries such as Japan, South Korea and Indonesia. Australia is now forging strong trading links with these 'Pacific Rim' countries and its economic future seems to lie with Asia and the Americas, rather than Europe, its traditional partner.

Uluru (Ayers Rock), the world's largest free-standing rock, is a massive outcrop of red sandstone in Australia's desert centre. Wind and sandstorms have ground the rock into the smooth curves seen here. Uluru is revered as a sacred site by many aboriginal peoples.

SCALE 1:10,500,000
(projection: Lambert Conformal Conic)

Km
0 25 50 100 150 200 250 300 350

Miles
0 25 50 100 150 200 250 300 350

MAP KEY

POPULATION

■ 1 million to 5 million
◉ 500,000 to 1 million
◎ 100,000 to 500,000
⊕ 50,000 to 100,000
○ 10,000 to 50,000
○ below 10,000

ELEVATION

2000m / 6562ft
1000m / 3281ft
500m / 1640ft
250m / 820ft
100m / 328ft
sea level

160 ▲

USING THE LAND

OVER 165 MILLION SHEEP are dispersed in vast herds around the country, contributing to a major export industry. Cattle-ranching is important, particularly in the west. Wheat, and grapes for Australia's wine industry, are grown mainly in the south. Much of the country is desert, unsuitable for agriculture unless irrigation is used.

THE URBAN/RURAL POPULATION DIVIDE

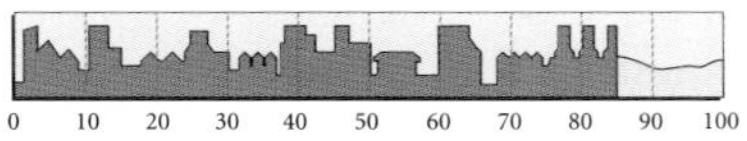

urban 85%   rural 15%

0 10 20 30 40 50 60 70 80 90 100

POPULATION DENSITY
6 people per sq mile
(2 people per sq km)

TOTAL LAND AREA
2,967,893 sq miles
(7,686,850 sq km)

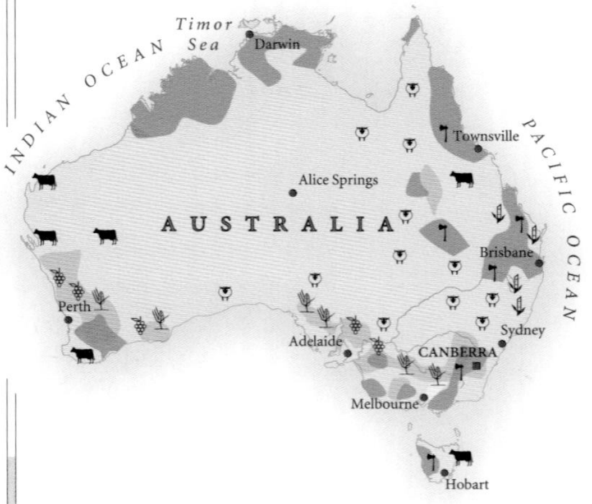

Land use and agricultural distribution

🐄 cattle   ■ capital cities
🐑 sheep   • major towns
🌾 cereals   pasture
🎋 sugar cane cropland
🌲 timber   forest
🍇 vineyards desert
              mountain region

Lines of ripening vines stretch for miles in Barossa Valley, a major wine-growing region near Adelaide.

THE LANDSCAPE

AUSTRALIA CONSISTS OF MANY ERODED PLATEAUX, lying firmly in the middle of the Indo-Australian Plate. It is the world's flattest continent, and the driest, after Antarctica. The coasts tend to be more hilly and fertile, especially in the east. The mountains of the Great Dividing Range form a natural barrier between the eastern coastal areas and the flat, dry plains and desert regions of the Australian 'outback'.

The Great Barrier Reef is the world's largest area of coral islands and reefs. It runs for about 1240 miles (2000 km) along the Queensland coast.

The Pinnacles are a series of rugged sandstone pillars. Their strange shapes have been formed by water and wind erosion.

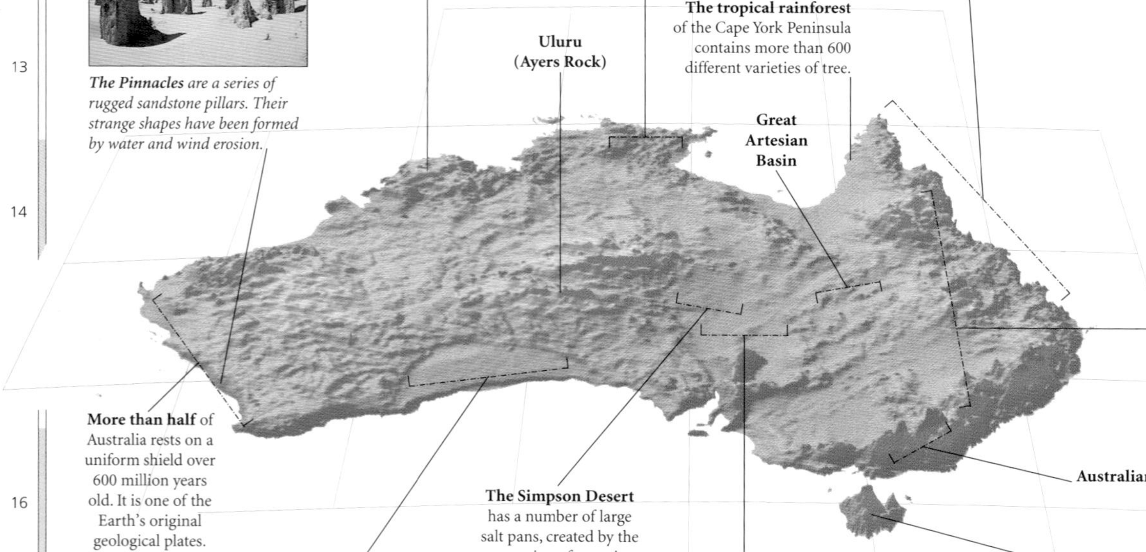

The ancient Kimberley Plateau is the source of some of Australia's richest mineral deposits, including diamonds.

Arnhem Land

Uluru (Ayers Rock)

The tropical rainforest of the Cape York Peninsula contains more than 600 different varieties of tree.

Great Artesian Basin

More than half of Australia rests on a uniform shield over 600 million years old. It is one of the Earth's original geological plates.

The Simpson Desert has a number of large salt pans, created by the evaporation of past rivers and now sourced by seasonal rains. Some are crusted with gypsum, but most are covered with common salt crystals.

The Nullarbor Plain is a low-lying limestone plateau which is so flat that the Trans-Australian Railway runs through it in a straight line for more than 300 miles (483 km).

The Lake Eyre basin, lying 51 ft (16 m) below sea level, is one of the largest inland drainage systems in the world, covering an area of more than 500,000 sq miles (1,300,000 sq km).

Australian Alps

Tasmania has the same geological structure as the Australian Alps. During the last period of glaciation, 18,000 years ago, sea levels were some 300 ft (100 m) lower and it was joined to the mainland.

The Great Dividing Range forms a watershed between east- and west-flowing rivers. Erosion has created deep valleys, gorges and waterfalls where rivers tumble over escarpments on their way to the sea.

Great Artesian Basin

Rainwater replenishes aquifer
Aquifers from which artesian water is obtained
Lake Eyre
Underground water movements

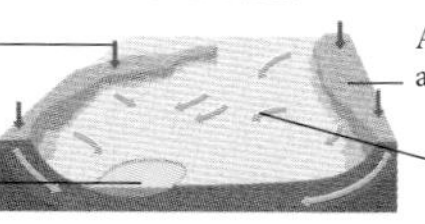

The Great Artesian Basin underlies nearly 20% of the total area of Australia, providing a valuable store of underground water, essential to Australian agriculture. The ephemeral rivers which drain the northern part of the basin have highly braided courses and, in consequence, the area is known as 'channel country'.

Map labels

INDIAN OCEAN

Cape Londonderry
Cape Bougainville
Kalumburu
Bigge Island
Bonaparte Archipelago
Heywood Islands
Adele Island
Mount Hann 779m▲
Kimberley
Collier Bay
King Sound
Kupingarri
King Leopold Ranges
Plateau
Lombadina
Derby
Fitzroy Crossing
Broome
Fitzroy River
Eighty Mile Beach
Great Sandy Desert
De Grey River
Percival Lakes
Tobin Lake
Port Hedland
Wickham
Whim Creek
Marble Bar
Lake Dora
Lake Auld
Dampier Archipelago
Dampier
Karratha
Roebourne
Barrow Island
Fortescue River
Onslow
Wittenoom
Hamersley Range
Lake Disappointment
North West Cape
Exmouth
Learmonth
Exmouth Gulf
Ashburton River
Tom Price
Mount Meharry 1251m▲
Newman
Little Sandy Desert
Gibson Desert
Coral Bay
Barlee Range
Kenneth Range
Paraburdoo
Minilya
Mount Augustus ▲1105m
Kumarina Roadhouse
Carnarvon Range
WESTERN
Lake Macleod
Waldburg Range
Gascoyne River
Robinson Range
Lake Gregory
Lake Carnegie
Bernier Island
Carnarvon
Gascoyne Junction
Wiluna
Dorre Island
Shark Bay
Denham
Murchison River
Lake Way
Lake Wells
Dirk Hartog Island
Lake Annean
Lake Throssell
Lake Yeo
Lake Austin
Meekatharra
AUSTRALIA
Kalbarri
Lake Carey
Mount Magnet
Leonora
Yalgoo
Lake Ballard
Menzies
Lake Rebecca
Geraldton
Mongers Lake
Lake Barlee
Lake Moore
Nu
Rawlinna
Kalgoorlie
Kitchener
Wubin
Coolgardie
Pithara
Kambalda
Lake Lefroy
Moora
Southern Cross
Lake Cowan
The Pinnacles
Merredin
Lake Johnston
Caiguna
Gingin
Northam
Norseman
Balladonia
Wanneroo
York
Lake Dundas
Perth
Brookton
Kondinin
Lake Hope
Fremantle
Rockingham
Narrogin
Lake King
Mandurah
Wagin
Ravensthorpe
Katanning
Esperance
Bunbury
Collie
Busselton
Bridgetown
Manjimup
Margaret River
Pemberton
Mount Barker
Cape Leeuwin
Augusta
Albany
Tower Peak 594m▲

Africa inset map (USING THE LAND)

Timor Sea
Darwin
Townsville
AUSTRALIA
Alice Springs
Brisbane
Perth
Sydney
Adelaide
CANBERRA
Melbourne
Hobart
INDIAN OCEAN
PACIFIC OCEAN

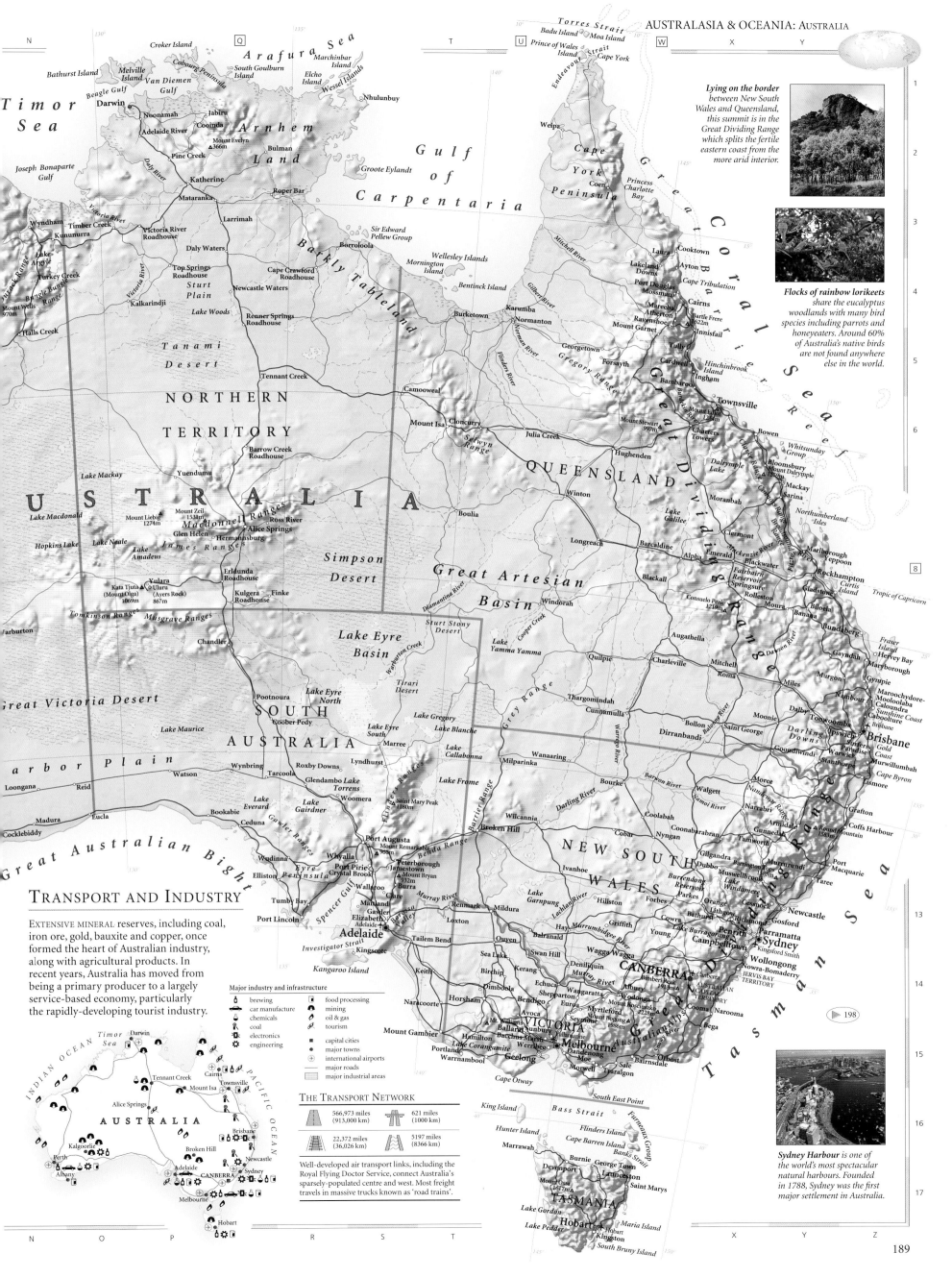

Lying on the border between New South Wales and Queensland, this summit is in the Great Dividing Range which splits the fertile eastern coast from the more arid interior.

Flocks of rainbow lorikeets share the eucalyptus woodlands with many bird species including parrots and honeyeaters. Around 60% of Australia's native birds are not found anywhere else in the world.

TRANSPORT AND INDUSTRY

EXTENSIVE MINERAL reserves, including coal, iron ore, gold, bauxite and copper, once formed the heart of Australian industry, along with agricultural products. In recent years, Australia has moved from being a primary producer to a largely service-based economy, particularly the rapidly-developing tourist industry.

Major industry and infrastructure

- brewing
- car manufacture
- chemicals
- coal
- electronics
- engineering
- food processing
- mining
- oil & gas
- tourism
- capital cities
- major towns
- international airports
- major roads
- major industrial areas

THE TRANSPORT NETWORK

566,973 miles (913,000 km)	621 miles (1000 km)
22,372 miles (36,026 km)	5197 miles (8366 km)

Well-developed air transport links, including the Royal Flying Doctor Service, connect Australia's sparsely-populated centre and west. Most freight travels in massive trucks known as 'road trains'.

Sydney Harbour is one of the world's most spectacular natural harbours. Founded in 1788, Sydney was the first major settlement in Australia.

▶ 198

189

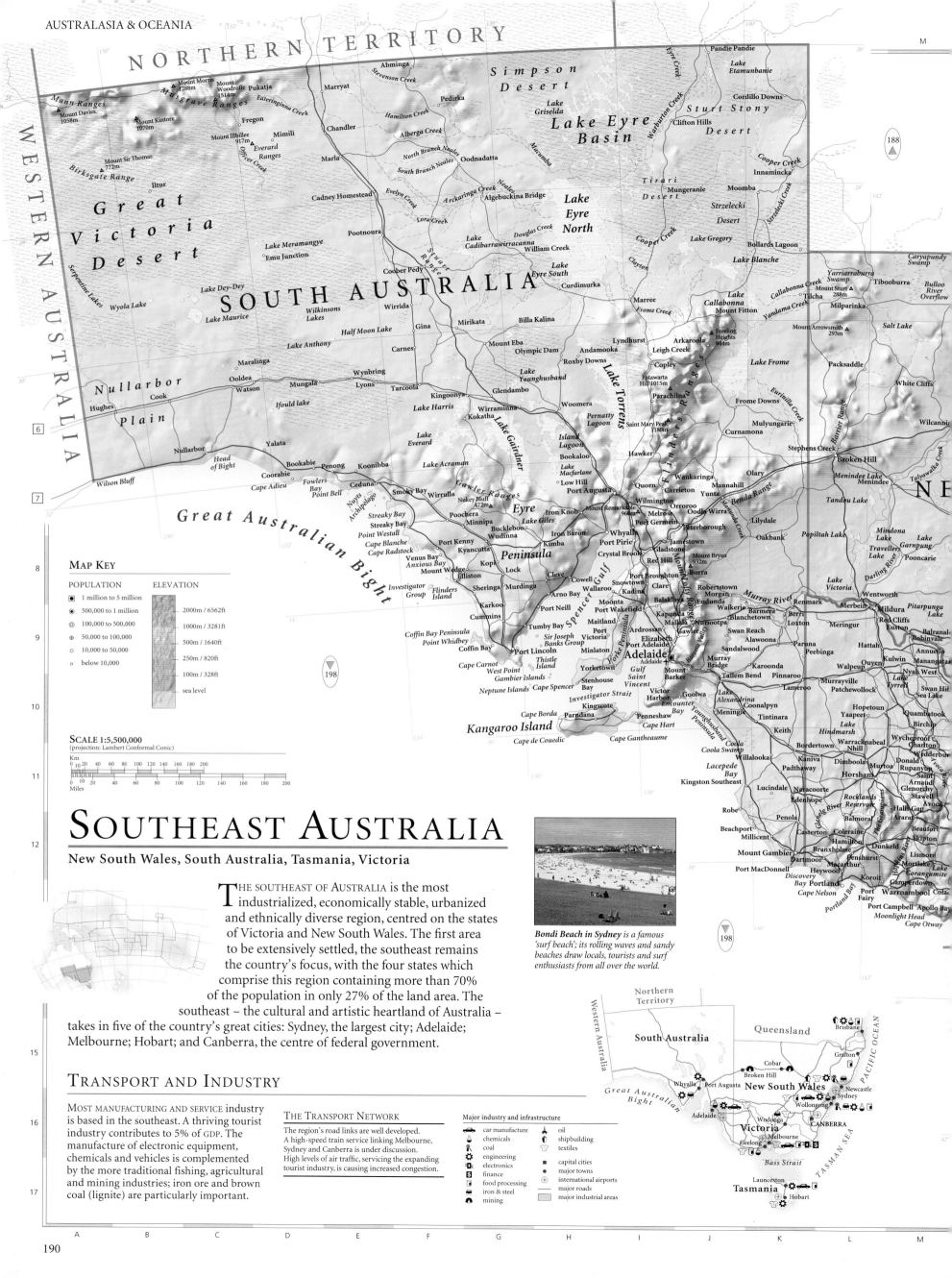

MAP KEY

POPULATION

- ◉ 1 million to 5 million
- ◉ 500,000 to 1 million
- ◉ 100,000 to 500,000
- ⊕ 50,000 to 100,000
- ○ 10,000 to 50,000
- ○ below 10,000

ELEVATION

- 2000m / 6562ft
- 1000m / 3281ft
- 500m / 1640ft
- 250m / 820ft
- 100m / 328ft
- sea level

SCALE 1:5,500,000
(projection: Lambert Conformal Conic)

SOUTHEAST AUSTRALIA

New South Wales, South Australia, Tasmania, Victoria

THE SOUTHEAST OF AUSTRALIA is the most industrialized, economically stable, urbanized and ethnically diverse region, centred on the states of Victoria and New South Wales. The first area to be extensively settled, the southeast remains the country's focus, with the four states which comprise this region containing more than 70% of the population in only 27% of the land area. The southeast – the cultural and artistic heartland of Australia – takes in five of the country's great cities: Sydney, the largest city; Adelaide; Melbourne; Hobart; and Canberra, the centre of federal government.

Bondi Beach in Sydney is a famous 'surf beach'; its rolling waves and sandy beaches draw locals, tourists and surf enthusiasts from all over the world.

TRANSPORT AND INDUSTRY

MOST MANUFACTURING AND SERVICE industry is based in the southeast. A thriving tourist industry contributes to 5% of GDP. The manufacture of electronic equipment, chemicals and vehicles is complemented by the more traditional fishing, agricultural and mining industries; iron ore and brown coal (lignite) are particularly important.

THE TRANSPORT NETWORK

The region's road links are well developed. A high-speed train service linking Melbourne, Sydney and Canberra is under discussion. High levels of air traffic, servicing the expanding tourist industry, is causing increased congestion.

Major industry and infrastructure

- car manufacture
- chemicals
- coal
- engineering
- electronics
- finance
- food processing
- iron & steel
- mining
- oil
- shipbuilding
- textiles
- ■ capital cities
- ● major towns
- ✈ international airports
- — major roads
- major industrial areas

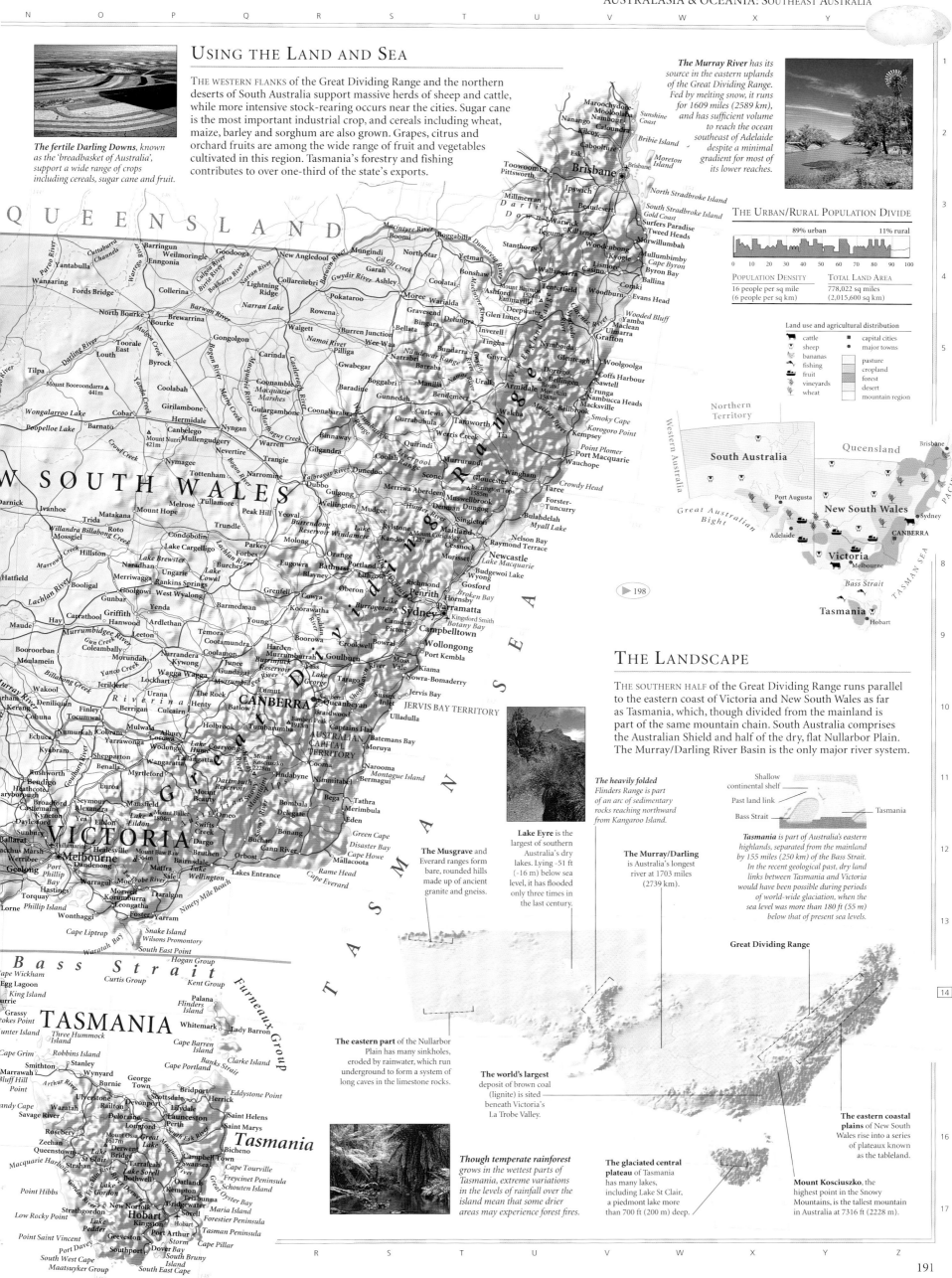

USING THE LAND AND SEA

THE WESTERN FLANKS of the Great Dividing Range and the northern deserts of South Australia support massive herds of sheep and cattle, while more intensive stock-rearing occurs near the cities. Sugar cane is the most important industrial crop, and cereals including wheat, maize, barley and sorghum are also grown. Grapes, citrus and orchard fruits are among the wide range of fruit and vegetables cultivated in this region. Tasmania's forestry and fishing contributes to over one-third of the state's exports.

The fertile Darling Downs, known as the 'breadbasket of Australia', support a wide range of crops including cereals, sugar cane and fruit.

The Murray River has its source in the eastern uplands of the Great Dividing Range. Fed by melting snow, it runs for 1609 miles (2589 km), and has sufficient volume to reach the ocean southeast of Adelaide despite a minimal gradient for most of its lower reaches.

THE URBAN/RURAL POPULATION DIVIDE

89% urban   11% rural

POPULATION DENSITY	TOTAL LAND AREA
16 people per sq mile (6 people per sq km)	778,022 sq miles (2,015,600 sq km)

Land use and agricultural distribution

- cattle
- sheep
- bananas
- fishing
- fruit
- vineyards
- wheat
- capital cities
- major towns
- pasture
- cropland
- forest
- desert
- mountain region

▶ 198

THE LANDSCAPE

THE SOUTHERN HALF of the Great Dividing Range runs parallel to the eastern coast of Victoria and New South Wales as far as Tasmania, which, though divided from the mainland is part of the same mountain chain. South Australia comprises the Australian Shield and half of the dry, flat Nullarbor Plain. The Murray/Darling River Basin is the only major river system.

The heavily folded Flinders Range is part of an arc of sedimentary rocks reaching northward from Kangaroo Island.

The Musgrave and Everard ranges form bare, rounded hills made up of ancient granite and gneiss.

Lake Eyre is the largest of southern Australia's dry lakes. Lying -51 ft (-16 m) below sea level, it has flooded only three times in the last century.

The Murray/Darling is Australia's longest river at 1703 miles (2739 km).

Shallow continental shelf
Past land link
Bass Strait
Tasmania

Tasmania is part of Australia's eastern highlands, separated from the mainland by 155 miles (250 km) of the Bass Strait. In the recent geological past, dry land links between Tasmania and Victoria would have been possible during periods of world-wide glaciation, when the sea level was more than 180 ft (55 m) below that of present sea levels.

Great Dividing Range

The eastern part of the Nullarbor Plain has many sinkholes, eroded by rainwater, which run underground to form a system of long caves in the limestone rocks.

The world's largest deposit of brown coal (lignite) is sited beneath Victoria's La Trobe Valley.

Though temperate rainforest grows in the wettest parts of Tasmania, extreme variations in the levels of rainfall over the island mean that some drier areas may experience forest fires.

The glaciated central plateau of Tasmania has many lakes, including Lake St Clair, a piedmont lake more than 700 ft (200 m) deep.

The eastern coastal plains of New South Wales rise into a series of plateaux known as the tableland.

Mount Kosciuszko, the highest point in the Snowy Mountains, is the tallest mountain in Australia at 7316 ft (2228 m).

NEW ZEALAND

LYING 1500 MILES EAST-SOUTHEAST OF AUSTRALIA, New Zealand was originally settled by the Maori, a people with Polynesian roots. It was one of the last major landmasses to be visited by Europeans. The islands' rugged topography means that most settlement has concentrated in coastal areas. People of European origin make up more than 85% of the population of 3.7 million, following immigration from the 1920s onwards. Many recent settlers have come from Asia, including India and China, and a number of the Pacific islands. Although the Maori now make up a minority of less than half a million, their ancient claims to at least half of national territory are gaining increasing legal credence.

THE LANDSCAPE

NEW ZEALAND comprises two large islands and many scattered smaller islands. On South Island the Alpine Fault marks the boundary between the Pacific and Indo-Australian plates. Tectonic activity has strongly influenced the formation of the Southern Alps, snow-capped mountains with several peaks over 9800 ft (3000 m). North Island has a lower and less extensive mountain region, containing forested hills, a central volcanic plateau and downlands.

Mountain-building in the Southern Alps

North Island
Alpine Fault
Pacific Plate

The Southern Alps have been formed by slip faulting. The Indo-Australian and Pacific plates run in opposite directions along the Alpine Fault. Although they slide past each other, they are also being thrust over one another, causing the continental crust of the Pacific Plate to be uplifted to form the Alps.

South Island
Southern Alps
Indo-Australian Plate

The Southern Alps run for more than 300 miles, (483 km) forming the backbone of South Island. They were uplifted following the collision of the Pacific and Indo-Australian plates.

Probable location of Alpine Fault

Fiordland, in the far south west, contains a large number of flooded glacial valleys.

Sutherland Falls

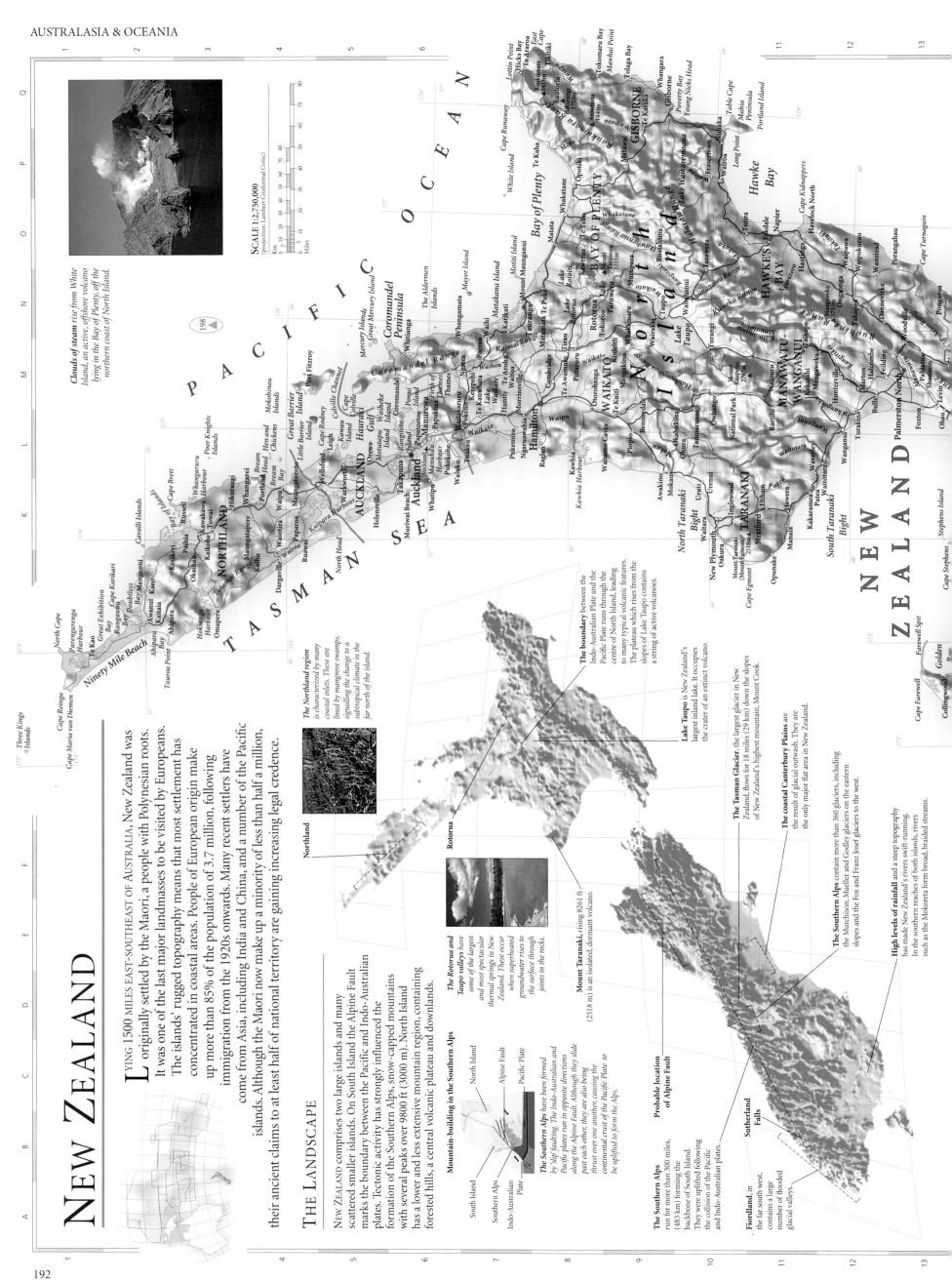

Clouds of steam rise from White Island, an active, offshore volcano lying in the Bay of Plenty, off the northern coast of North Island.

SCALE 1:2,750,000
(projection: Lambert Conformal Conic)

The Northland region is characterized by many coastal inlets. These are lined by mangrove swamps, signalling the change to a subtropical climate in the far north of the island.

Northland

The Rotorua and Taupo valleys have some of the largest and most spectacular thermal springs in New Zealand. These occur when superheated groundwater rises to the surface through joints in the rocks.

Rotorua

Mount Taranaki, rising 8261 ft (2518 m) is an isolated, dormant volcano.

The boundary between the Indo-Australian Plate and the Pacific Plate runs through the centre of North Island, leading to many typical volcanic features. The plateau which rises from the slopes of Lake Taupo contains a string of active volcanoes.

Lake Taupo is New Zealand's largest inland lake. It occupies the crater of an extinct volcano.

The Tasman Glacier, the largest glacier in New Zealand, flows for 18 miles (29 km) down the slopes of New Zealand's highest mountain, Mount Cook.

The coastal Canterbury Plains are the result of glacial outwash. They are the only major flat area in New Zealand.

The Southern Alps contain more than 360 glaciers, including the Murchison, Mueller and Godley glaciers on the eastern slopes and the Fox and Franz Josef glaciers to the west.

High levels of rainfall and a steep topography has made New Zealand's rivers swift-running. In the southern reaches of both islands, rivers such as the Mokoreta form broad, braided streams.

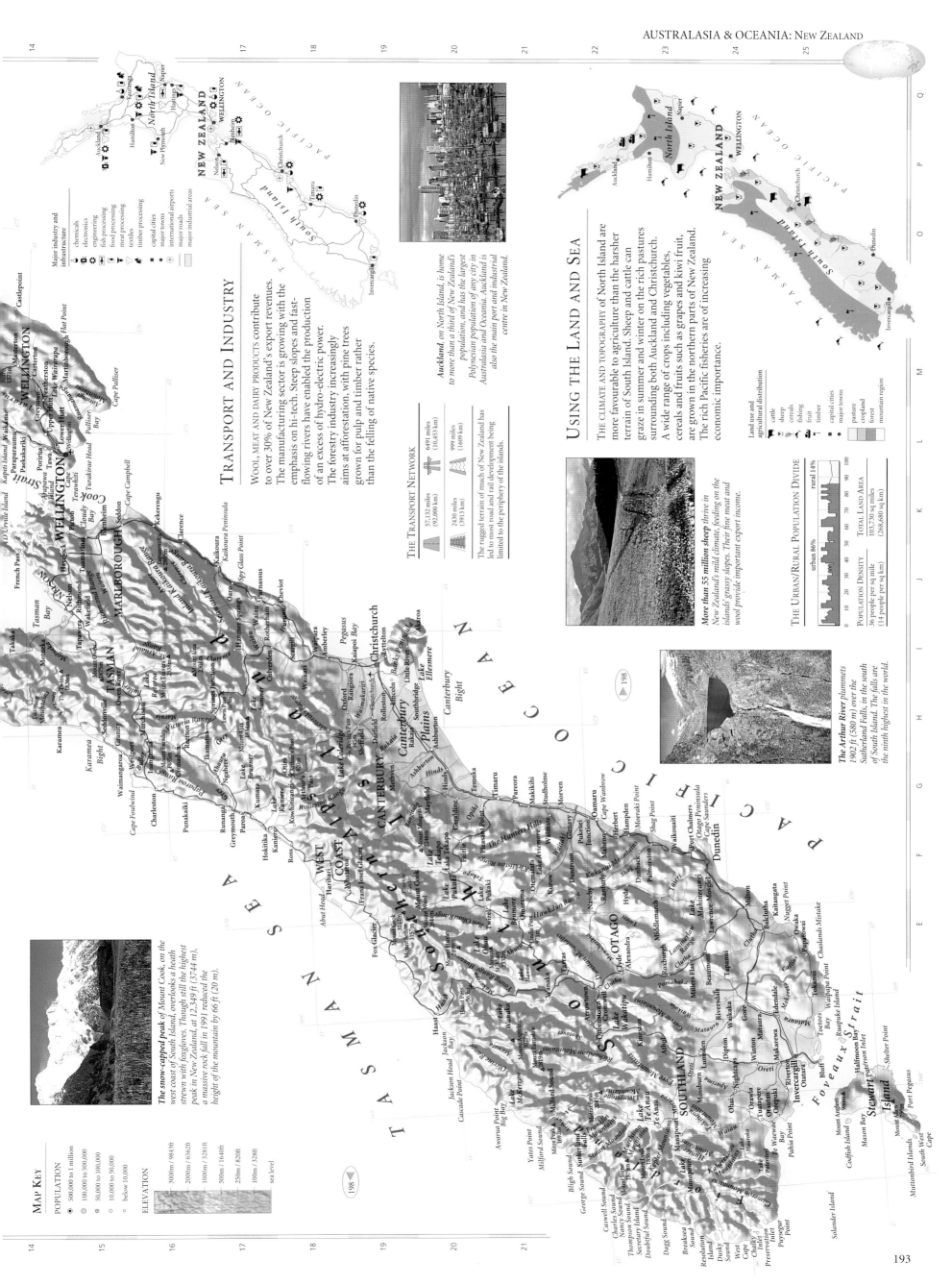

NEW ZEALAND

Major industry and infrastructure

- chemicals
- electronics
- engineering
- fish processing
- food processing
- textiles
- timber processing
- capital cities
- major towns
- international airports
- major roads
- major industrial areas

TRANSPORT AND INDUSTRY

WOOL, MEAT AND DAIRY PRODUCTS contribute to over 30% of New Zealand's export revenues. The manufacturing sector is growing with the emphasis on hi-tech. Steep slopes and fast-flowing rivers have enabled the production of an excess of hydro-electric power. The forestry industry increasingly aims at afforestation, with pine trees grown for pulp and timber rather than the felling of native species.

Auckland on North Island, is home to more than a third of New Zealand's population, and has the largest Polynesian population of any city in Australasia and Oceania. Auckland is also the main port and industrial centre in New Zealand.

THE TRANSPORT NETWORK

57,732 miles (92,000 km)	6491 miles (10,453 km)
2430 miles (3913 km)	999 miles (1609 km)

The rugged terrain of much of New Zealand has led to most road and rail development being limited to the periphery of the islands.

USING THE LAND AND SEA

THE CLIMATE AND TOPOGRAPHY of North Island are more favourable to agriculture than the harsher terrain of South Island. Sheep and cattle can graze in summer and winter on the rich pastures surrounding both Auckland and Christchurch. A wide range of crops including vegetables, cereals and fruits such as grapes and kiwi fruit, are grown in the northern parts of New Zealand. The rich Pacific fisheries are of increasing economic importance.

Land use and agricultural distribution

- cattle
- sheep
- cereals
- fishing
- fruit
- timber
- capital cities
- major towns
- pasture
- cropland
- forest
- mountain region

More than 55 million sheep thrive in New Zealand's mild climate, feeding on the islands' grassy slopes. Their fine meat and wool provide important export income.

The Arthur River plummets 1902 ft (580 m) over the Sutherland Falls, in the south of South Island. The falls are the ninth highest in the world.

THE URBAN/RURAL POPULATION DIVIDE

urban 86% rural 14%

POPULATION DENSITY
36 people per sq mile
(14 people per sq km)

TOTAL LAND AREA
103,730 sq miles
(268,680 sq km)

MAP KEY

POPULATION

- ● 500,000 to 1 million
- ◉ 100,000 to 500,000
- ⊛ 50,000 to 100,000
- ○ 10,000 to 50,000
- ○ below 10,000

ELEVATION

- 3000m / 9843ft
- 2000m / 6562ft
- 1000m / 328ft
- 500m / 1640ft
- 250m / 820ft
- 100m / 328ft
- sea level

The snow-capped peak of Mount Cook, on the west coast of South Island, overlooks a heath strewn with foxgloves. Though still the highest peak in New Zealand, at 12,349 ft (3744 m), a massive rock fall in 1991 reduced the height of the mountain by 66 ft (20 m).

PAPUA NEW GUINEA & THE SOLOMON ISLANDS

CUT OFF BY INACCESSIBLE, largely mountainous terrain, the peoples of Papua New Guinea have maintained a remarkable diversity of language and culture. There are over 750 separate languages, and yet more distinct tribes. Much of the country remains isolated, with many of the indigenous inhabitants of the interior living as hunter-gatherers. To the east of Papua New Guinea, the Solomons form an archipelago of several hundred islands, scattered over an area of 252,897 sq miles (655,000 sq km). The Solomon Islanders, a mainly Melanesian people, live on the six largest islands.

USING THE LAND AND SEA

MOST AGRICULTURE IN Papua New Guinea is at a subsistence level, with more than two-thirds of the land used for rough grazing, particularly for pigs. The tropical rainforest is a rich timber resource. The Solomon Islanders rely heavily on coconuts for export revenue and fishing, mainly for tuna, is a staple industry.

Over 70% of Papua New Guinea is covered by dense, tropical rainforest, sustained by high levels of rainfall. Uncontrolled logging in the formerly inaccessible rainforest has led to species loss and soil erosion on steep slopes.

THE URBAN/RURAL POPULATION DIVIDE

urban 16%   rural 84%

0 10 20 30 40 50 60 70 80 90 100

POPULATION DENSITY	TOTAL LAND AREA
17 people per sq mile (7 people per sq km)	290,210 sq miles (751,840 sq km)

MAP KEY

POPULATION
◉ 100,000 to 500,000
⊕ 50,000 to 100,000
○ 10,000 to 50,000
○ below 10,000

ELEVATION
4000m / 13,124ft
3000m / 9843ft
2000m / 6562ft
1000m / 3281ft
500m / 1640ft
250m / 820ft
100m / 328ft
sea level

Land use and agricultural distribution
bananas
cocoa
coconuts
fishing
oil palms
rubber
timber
■ capital cities
• major towns
cropland
forest
wetland

TRANSPORT AND INDUSTRY

PAPUA NEW GUINEA has substantial mineral resources including the world's largest copper reserves at Panguna on Bougainville Island; gold, and potential oil and natural gas. Political instability on Bougainville and an undeveloped infrastructure deters the investment necessary for exploition of these reserves. The Solomon Islanders rely mainly on copra and timber with some production of palm oil and cocoa. Traditional crafts are made for the tourist market and for export.

THE TRANSPORT NETWORK

🛣	460 miles (740 km)
	None
	None
✈	6794 miles (10,940 km)

Much of Papua New Guinea and the Solomons is inaccessible by road. A network of airstrips serves even remote villages on the islands. The Solomons' airport has been extended to take jumbo jets to improve connections for tourism.

The slopes of this extinct volcano near Talasea on the island of New Britain have been almost entirely colonized by rainforest vegetation.

Major industry and infrastructure
beverages
coffee processing
copra processing
food processing
mining
textiles
timber processing
■ capital cities
• major towns
⊕ international airports
— major roads

Huli tribesmen from Southern Highlands Province in Papua New Guinea parade in ceremonial dress, their powdered wigs decorated with exotic plumage and their faces and bodies painted with coloured pigments.

SCALE 1:5,500,000
(projection: Mercator)

Km
0 10 20 40 60 80 100 120 140 160 180 200

Miles
0 10 20 40 60 80 100 120 140 160 180 200

N O P Q R S T U V W X Y

The Sepik River drains the lowlands north of the Central Range, flowing eastwards into the Bismarck Sea.

The Bismarck Range is precipitous, rugged and covered in dense vegetation, rising to 14,793 ft (4509 m) at Mount Wilhelm in central Papua New Guinea.

Most of Papua New Guinea's outlying islands, including New Britain, Bougainville Island and New Ireland, are precipitous and of volcanic origin.

THE LANDSCAPE

THE PLATE MARGIN between the Pacific and Indo-Australian plates runs through the mainland of Papua New Guinea, which is dominated by steep and forested mountain ranges. The 600 or so outer islands are mainly high, volcanic islands, fringed by coral reefs. The Solomons comprise six large volcanic islands which form two parallel chains, and several hundred small islands and atolls.

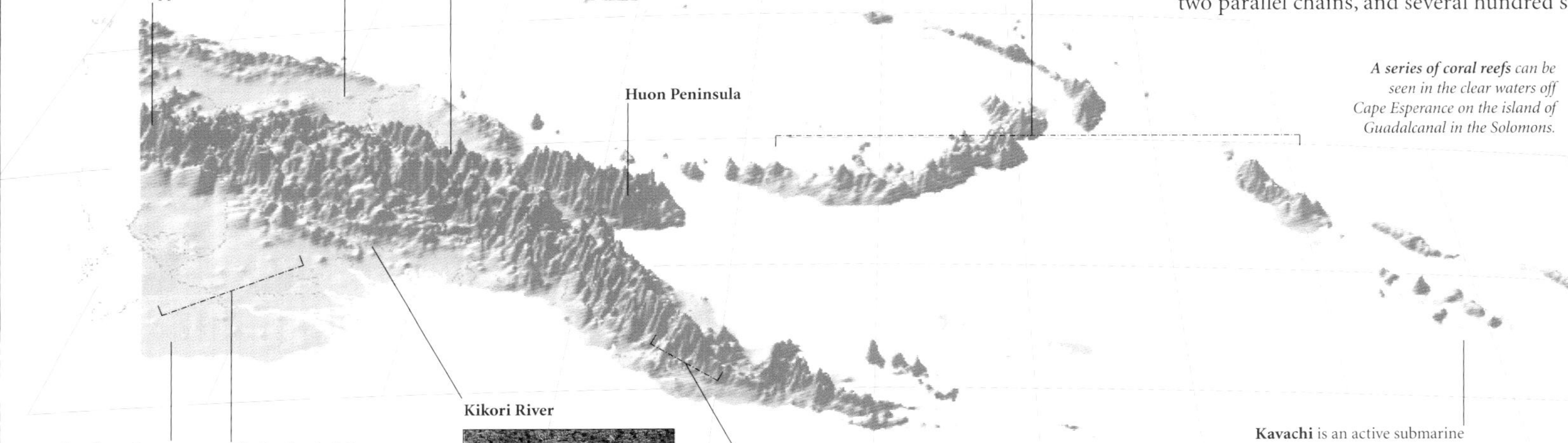

The Star Mountains include some of the most remote terrain on Earth. The area is rich in gold and copper.

A series of coral reefs can be seen in the clear waters off Cape Esperance on the island of Guadalcanal in the Solomons.

Huon Peninsula

Cape Esperance

Kikori River

Southern Papua New Guinea is part of the Indo-Australian Plate. New Guinea only became separated physically from Australia about 8000 years ago following the flooding of the Torres Strait.

The lowland plains in the south and north of the main island are swampy, and contain some fertile alluvial soils. This contrasts with the mountainous islands in the rest of Papua New Guinea where soils are generally thin and nutrients are retained in the existing vegetation.

The Owen Stanley Range contains several of Papua New Guinea's highest peaks, the greatest of which is Mount Victoria at 13,200 ft (4035 m).

Kavachi is an active submarine volcano near New Georgia, which erupts every few years.

The Louisiade Archipelago contains 10 volcanic islands and numerous coral islets. Tagula Island is the largest of the islands, containing the archipelago's highest peak at 2645 ft (806 m).

Papua New Guinea's rivers, though fairly short, carry extremely high sediment loads, largely due to soil erosion. This is caused by a combination of very steep slopes and heavy rainfall, and is made worse by forest clearance, particularly 'slash and burn' techniques and road or mine operations.

Huon Peninsula

Caves and undercut cliffs mark former shoreline

Stream cuts down through recently exposed land

Former level of beach

Current beach

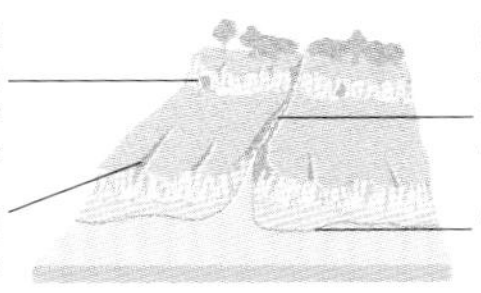

Uplift of the land in tectonically active regions can lead to former coastlines being lifted beyond the reach of the sea. New cliffs and caves are formed at a lower level, and rivers cut down through the lower land to reach sea level once more.

St.Matthias Group

Emirau Island

Isabel Channel

PACIFIC OCEAN

SOLOMON ISLANDS

Duff Islands

Reef Islands

TEMOTU

Tinakula

Santa Cruz Islands

Nendö   Noka
Lata

Utupua

Vanikolo

(same scale as main map)

New Hanover
Taskul
North Cape
Kavieng
Tatau Island
Tabar Islands
Meteran
Simberi Island
Tabar Island
Dyaul Island
Konos
Lihir Group
Lihir Island

Tanga Islands
Boang Island
Malendok Island

Nuguria Islands

NEW IRELAND

Konogogo
Namatanai
New Ireland

Feni Islands

PACIFIC OCEAN

Cape Lambert
Rabaul
Kokopo
Gazelle Peninsula
Toriu

Mount Konogaiang
1860m
Ambitle Island
Babase Island

Green Islands
Pinipel Island
Nissan Island

St. George's Channel

Cape St.George

Taron

Nukumanu Islands

Lolobau Island
Open Bay
Mount Sinewit
1360m
Wide Bay
Sampun

Lemankoa
Buka Island
Hutjena

Tulun Islands

Takuu Islands

Willaumez Peninsula

Jacquinot Bay

EAST NEW BRITAIN

NORTH SOLOMONS

Ontong Java Atoll

Kimbe Bay
Hoskins
Talasea
Kimbe
Ubai
Lau
Pomio

Nakanai Mountains

Mount Balbi
2685m
Wakunai

Gasmata

New Britain

Torokina
Empress Augusta Bay

Arawa
Kieta
Panguna

Roncador Reef

Bougainville Island

Buin
Mauro
Nukiki
Panggoe
Lutti

Lying close to the banks of the Sepik River in northern Papua New Guinea, this building is known as the Spirit House. It is constructed from leaves and twigs, ornately woven and trimmed into geometric patterns. The house is decorated with a mask and topped by a carved statue.

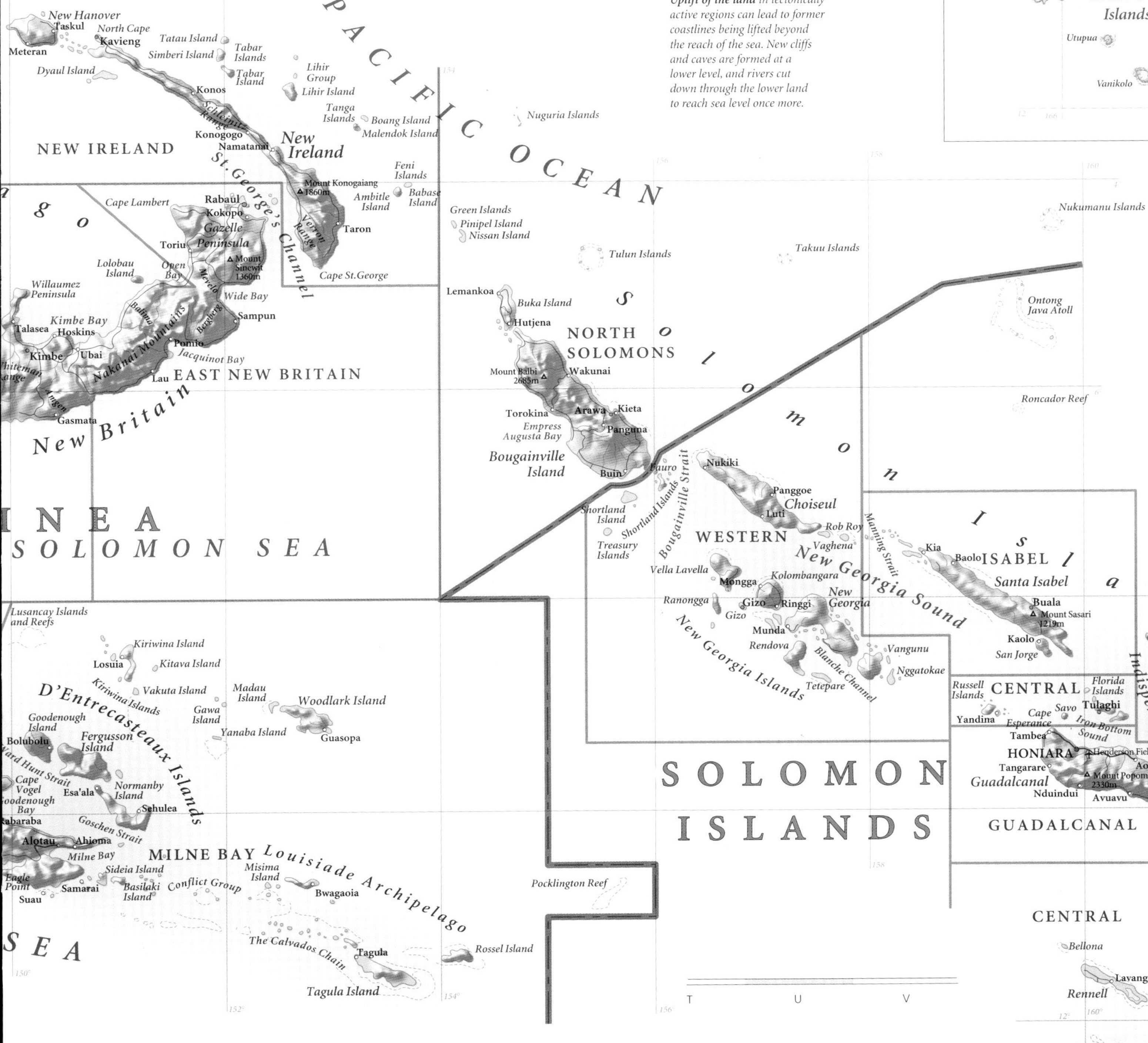

SOLOMON SEA

Shortland Island
Treasury Islands

Shortland Islands Strait

Bougainville Strait

WESTERN

Choiseul

Rob Roy

Manning Strait

Kia
Baolo
ISABEL

Santa Isabel

198

Lusancay Islands and Reefs

Vaghena
Vella Lavella
Kolombangara
Mongga
Ranongga
Gizo
Ringgi
Gizo
Munda
Rendova

New Georgia Sound

New Georgia

Vangunu
Blanche Channel
Tetepare
Nggatokae

Buala
Mount Sasari
1219m
Kaolo
San Jorge

MALAITA

Maluu
Kwailibesi

Sikaiana

Kiriwina Island
Kitava Island
Losuia
Kiriwina Islands
Vakuta Island
Madau Island
Gawa Island
Woodlark Island
Yanaba Island
Guasopa

New Georgia Islands

Russell Islands
CENTRAL
Florida Islands
Yandina
Cape Esperance
Savo
Iron Bottom Sound
Tambea
HONIARA
Tangarare
Guadalcanal
Nduindui
Avuavu

Auki
Malaita
Olomburi
Baunani

Tarapaina
Maramasike
Apio

Ulawa Island

D'Entrecasteaux Islands

Goodenough Island
Bolubolu
Fergusson Island
Cape Vogel
Esa'ala
Normanby Island

Sehulea

GUADALCANAL

Henderson Field
Mount Popomanaseu
2330m
Aola

SOLOMON ISLANDS

Heuru
Three Sisters Islands

Ahioma
Milne Bay
Goschen Strait
Sideia Island
MILNE BAY
Misima Island

Louisiade Archipelago

Kirakira
San Cristobal
Star Harbour

Alotau
Samarai
Basilaki Island
Conflict Group
Bwagaoia

Pocklington Reef

Hauraha

MAKIRA

Eagle Point
Suau

The Calvados Chain

Tagula

Rossel Island

CENTRAL

Bellona
Lavanggu
Rennell

Tagula Island

SEA

195

PACIFIC OCEAN

THE PACIFIC IS THE WORLD'S LARGEST AND DEEPEST OCEAN. It is nearly twice the area of the Atlantic and contains almost three times as much water. The ocean is dotted with islands and surrounded by some of the world's most populous states; over half the world's population lives on its shores. The Pacific is bordered by active plate margins known as the 'Ring of Fire', causing earthquakes and tsunamis, and creating volcanic islands and subterranean mountain chains. The largest underwater mountains break the surface as island arcs. The fisheries of the Pacific are some of the most productive in the world and provide a vital resource for many of the Pacific islands. Since the Second World War there has been a shift in trading patterns, with a considerable growth in trade between the United States and the countries of the Pacific Rim.

AMERICAN SAMOA AND SAMOA

AMERICAN SAMOA AND SAMOA are part of the island archipelago of Polynesia. The two most populous islands are Tutuila in American Samoa and Upolu in Samoa. Although the economies of both these states remain predominantly resource-based, both are expanding their light manufacturing sectors, and the US administration is the primary employer in American Samoa. Tuna fishing is particularly important: 25% of all tuna consumed in the USA is processed and canned in Pago Pago.

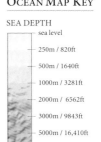
Japan is one of the major trading nations within the Pacific, importing iron and steel from Australia, and grain from the USA. The major exports from the 'Pacific Rim' are electronics, precision equipment and motor cars.

INSET MAP KEY

POPULATION
○ below 10,000

ELEVATION
1000m / 3281ft
500m / 1640ft
250m / 820ft
100m / 328ft
sea level

OCEAN MAP KEY

SEA DEPTH
sea level
250m / 820ft
500m / 1640ft
1000m / 3281ft
2000m / 6562ft
3000m / 9843ft
5000m / 16,410ft

SCALE 1:50,000,000
(projection: Mollweide)

Km 0 200 400 600 800 1000
Miles 0 200 400 600 800 1000

Many of the buildings in Samoa reflect the country's colonial past. Once a colony of New Zealand, Samoa is now an independent state; American Samoa remains an unincorporated territory of the United States.

THE RING OF FIRE

THE ACTIVE PLATE MARGINS surrounding the Pacific have created numerous land and island volcanoes along its border. The actual basin of the Pacific is made up of a number of separate tectonic plates which move away from each other, colliding with other plates. When they collide, the oceanic plates, being thinner, are forced beneath the thicker continental plates, forming deep ocean trenches and high ridges. These collision zones are known as subduction zones and are characterized by intense seismic and volcanic activity.

RESOURCES

MANY OF THE SMALL ISLANDS in the Pacific rely heavily on marine resources to provide valuable export incomes. These fisheries tend to be small-scale and are forced to compete with the large commerical fleets from Japan and the Russian Federation. Although many metallic mineral deposits have been discovered in the Pacific, few are exploited. The major areas of oil and gas extraction are off the coast of Vietnam, along the Kamchatka Peninsula and off the coast of Alaska. The numerous reefs which fringe the islands of the Pacific are harvested for corals.

Farms such as this black pearl oyster farm in Tahiti are widespread throughout the Pacific. The culturing or farming of marine organisms, such as molluscs and crustaceans, has been practised for hundreds of years.

Resources
⌐ fish
⌐ shellfish
Y whales
◊ oil & gas
● major towns
⊕ major ports

Mayon Volcano in the Philippines is one of many active volcanoes on the Pacific 'Ring of Fire'. It is noted for its perfect conical shape; the base of the cone is 80 miles (130 km) in circumference.

Ring of Fire
— plate boundaries
● major volcanoes

The Hawaiian volcanoes lie in the centre of a plate, not on a plate margin, and are known as intraplate volcanoes. They are associated with hot spots, whereby a plume of hot molten rock rises to the surface as the plate moves over it.

A B C D E F G H I J K L

MELANESIA

FIJI, VANUATU, *New Caledonia* (to France)

THREE MAIN ISLAND groups make up the area of southern Melanesia in the southwestern Pacific: the independent countries of Fiji and Vanuatu and the French overseas territory of New Caledonia. The major Melanesian island group, the Solomon Islands, lies to the east of Papua New Guinea (pages 194–95). Most of the larger islands are volcanic in origin; the smaller ones are mainly coral atolls and are largely uninhabited. The economy in all three island groups is increasingly driven by tourism, not necessarily to the benefit of other economic activities.

VANUATU

A STRING OF MOUNTAINOUS VOLCANIC ISLANDS covering more than 4706 sq miles (12,190 sq km) of the south Pacific, Vanuatu achieved independence from France and the UK in 1980. The majority of the population relies on subsistence fishing and agriculture. Once-important copra and cocoa exports are declining as a result of cost-effective substitutes from elsewhere, and alternatives are being explored. There is further resource potential in the forests and fishing grounds, and beef and arable farming are of growing importance. Tourism, accounting for 40% of GDP, is the fastest-growing sector of the economy, and further expansion is planned.

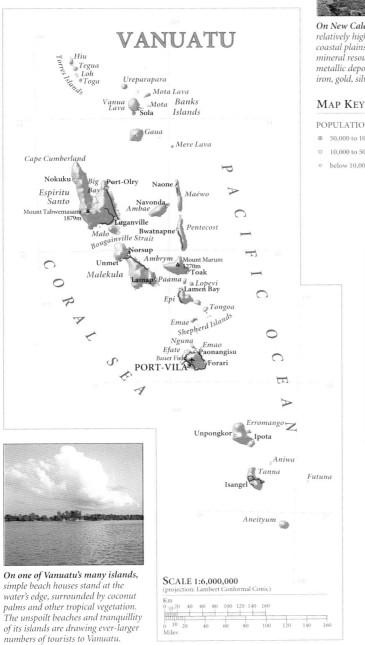

SCALE 1:6,000,000
(projection: Lambert Conformal Conic)

Km
0 10 20 40 60 80 100 120 140 160
Miles
0 10 20 40 60 80 100 120 140 160

On one of Vanuatu's many islands, simple beach houses stand at the water's edge, surrounded by coconut palms and other tropical vegetation. The unspoilt beaches and tranquillity of its islands are drawing ever-larger numbers of tourists to Vanuatu.

SCALE 1:6,000,000
(projection: Lambert Conformal Conic)

Km
0 10 20 40 60 80 100 120 140 160
Miles
0 10 20 40 60 80 100 120 140 160

NEW CALEDONIA (to France)

NEW CALEDONIA, a French overseas territory known as Kanaky by its indigenous peoples, comprises a large main island, 260 miles (418 km) long, and many smaller islands and atolls. Socio-economic inequality, unemployment and the issue of independence have caused tension between the Kanaks and the French-speaking expatriate population. This resulted in a long history of political violence, although the Nouméa accord, signed in 1998, allowed for greater autonomy. New Caledonia produces 25% of the world's nickel, and improved incomes from tourism and agriculture have benefited the economy.

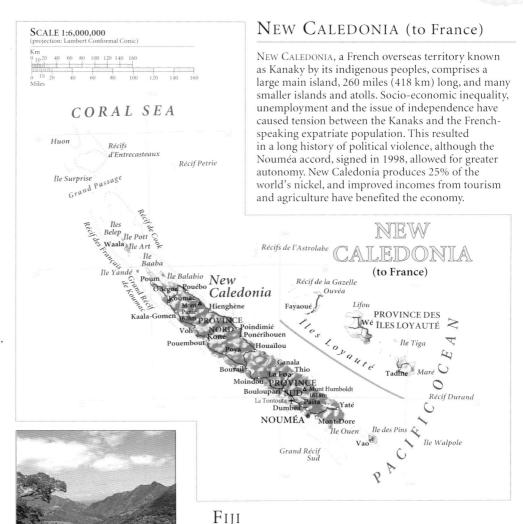

On New Caledonia's main island, relatively high interior plateaus descend to coastal plains. Nickel is the most important mineral resource, but the hills also harbour metallic deposits including chrome, cobalt, iron, gold, silver and copper.

MAP KEY

POPULATION
⊕ 50,000 to 100,000
○ 10,000 to 50,000
○ below 10,000

ELEVATION
1000m / 3281ft
500m / 1640ft
250m / 820ft
100m / 328ft
sea level

FIJI

FIJI IS A VOLCANIC ARCHIPELAGO in the southwestern Pacific consisting of two large islands and 880 smaller islets, and covering a total area of 7054 sq miles (18,270 sq km). The majority of the population lives on the two largest islands. The people are split fairly evenly between Indo-Fijians, who arrived when Fiji was still a British colony, and the indigenous Fijians who have, since 1987, controlled the government. Sugar and copra are the most important crops in a diversified agricultural base and forestry is becoming increasingly important. A relatively varied economy has potential for mineral and hydro-electric exploitation, while Fiji's climate and location on the main Pacific air routes are an impetus to tourism.

SCALE 1:6,000,000
(projection: Mercator)

Km
0 10 20 40 60 80 100 120 140 160 180 200
Miles
0 10 20 40 60 80 100 120 140 160 180 200

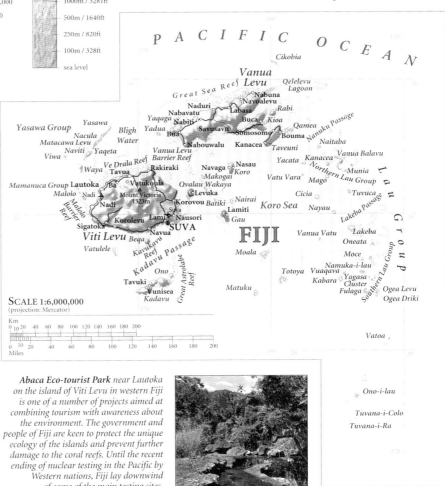

Abaca Eco-tourist Park near Lautoka on the island of Viti Levu in western Fiji is one of a number of projects aimed at combining tourism with awareness about the environment. The government and people of Fiji are keen to protect the unique ecology of the islands and prevent further damage to the coral reefs. Until the recent ending of nuclear testing in the Pacific by Western nations, Fiji lay downwind of some of the main testing sites.

MICRONESIA

MARSHALL ISLANDS, MICRONESIA, NAURU, PALAU, *Guam, Northern Mariana Islands, Wake Island*

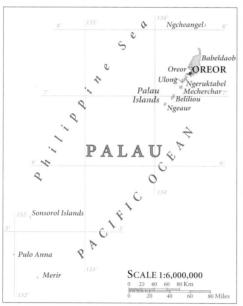

THE MICRONESIAN ISLANDS lie in the western reaches of the Pacific Ocean and are all part of the same volcanic zone. The Federated States of Micronesia is the largest group, with more than 600 atolls and forested volcanic islands in an area of more than 1120 sq miles (2900 sq km). Micronesia is a mixture of former colonies, overseas territories and dependencies. Most of the region still relies on aid and subsidies to sustain economies limited by resources, isolation, and an emigrating population, drawn to New Zealand and Australia by the attractions of a western lifestyle.

PALAU

PALAU IS AN ARCHIPELAGO OF OVER 200 ISLANDS, only eight of which are inhabited. It was the last remaining UN trust territory in the Pacific, controlled by the USA until 1994, when it became independent. The economy operates on a subsistence level, with coconuts and cassava the principal crops. Fishing licences and tourism provide foreign currency.

SCALE 1:750,000

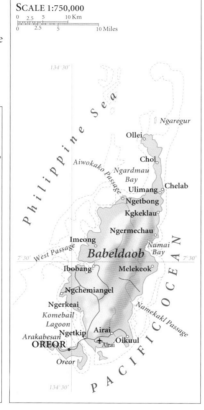

SCALE 1:6,000,000

GUAM (to US)

LYING AT THE SOUTHERN END of the Mariana Islands, Guam is an important US military base and tourist destination. Social and political life is dominated by the indigenous Chamorro, who make up just under half the population, although the increasing prevalence of western culture threatens Guam's traditional social stability.

The tranquillity of these coastal lagoons, at Inarajan in southern Guam, belies the fact that the island lies in a region where typhoons are common.

SCALE 1:825,000

NORTHERN MARIANA ISLANDS (to US)

A US COMMONWEALTH TERRITORY, the Northern Marianas comprise the whole of the Mariana archipelago except for Guam. The islands retain their close links with the United States and continue to receive US aid. Tourism, though bringing in much-needed revenue, has speeded the decline of the traditional subsistence economy. Most of the population lives on Saipan.

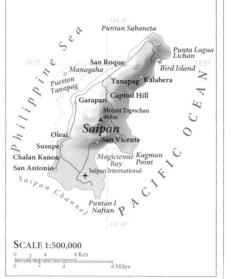

SCALE 1:500,000

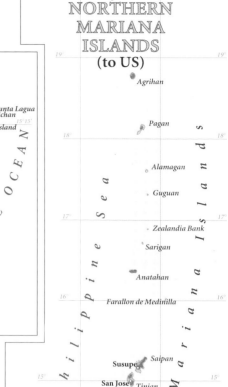

The Palau Islands have numerous hidden lakes and lagoons. These sustain their own ecosystems which have developed in isolation. This has produced adaptations in the animals and plants which are often unique to each lake.

SCALE 1:5,000,000

MICRONESIA

A MIXTURE OF HIGH VOLCANIC ISLANDS and low-lying coral atolls, the Federated States of Micronesia include all the Caroline Islands except Palau. Pohnpei, Kosrae, Chuuk and Yap are the four main island cluster states, each of which has its own language, with English remaining the official language. Nearly half the population is concentrated on Pohnpei, the largest island. Independent since 1986, the islands continue to receive considerable aid from the USA which supplements an economy based primarily on fishing and copra processing.

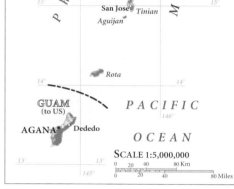

SCALE 1:825,000

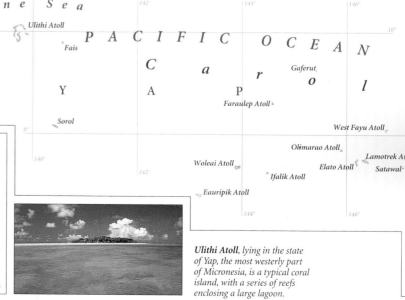

Ulithi Atoll, lying in the state of Yap, the most westerly part of Micronesia, is a typical coral island, with a series of reefs enclosing a large lagoon.

N   O   P   Q   R   S   T   U   V   W   X   Y

MARSHALL ISLANDS

A GROUP OF 34 WIDELY-SCATTERED ATOLLS in the central Pacific Ocean, the Marshall Islands include some of the largest atolls in the world, formed from low coral islands with sandy beaches and enclosing vast lagoons. Formerly under US protection as part of the UN Trust Territory of the Pacific Islands, and including the former US nuclear testing sites of Bikini Atoll and Enewetak Atoll, the Marshall Islands became self-governing in 1979. The economy is reliant on US aid and on the rent paid by the USA for its missile base on Kwajalein Atoll.

SCALE 1:1,000,000

Majuro Atoll

Rongrong
Iroj
Kallalen
Laura
Majuro Lagoon
Enigu
Djarrit
Dalap
Majuro

PACIFIC OCEAN

PACIFIC OCEAN

Sibylla Island
Bokaak Atoll

Bikar Atoll

Enewetak Atoll
Bikini Atoll
Rongelap Atoll
Ailinginae Atoll
Rongrik Atoll
Taka Atoll
Utrik Atoll

MARSHALL ISLANDS

Wotho Atoll
Ailuk Atoll
Mejit Island
Jemo Island
Likiep Atoll
Wotje Atoll
Erikub Atoll
Maloelap Atoll

Ujelang Atoll

Ujae Atoll
Kwajalein Atoll
Lae Atoll
Lib
Namu Atoll

Ralik Chain
Ratak Chain

Aur Atoll

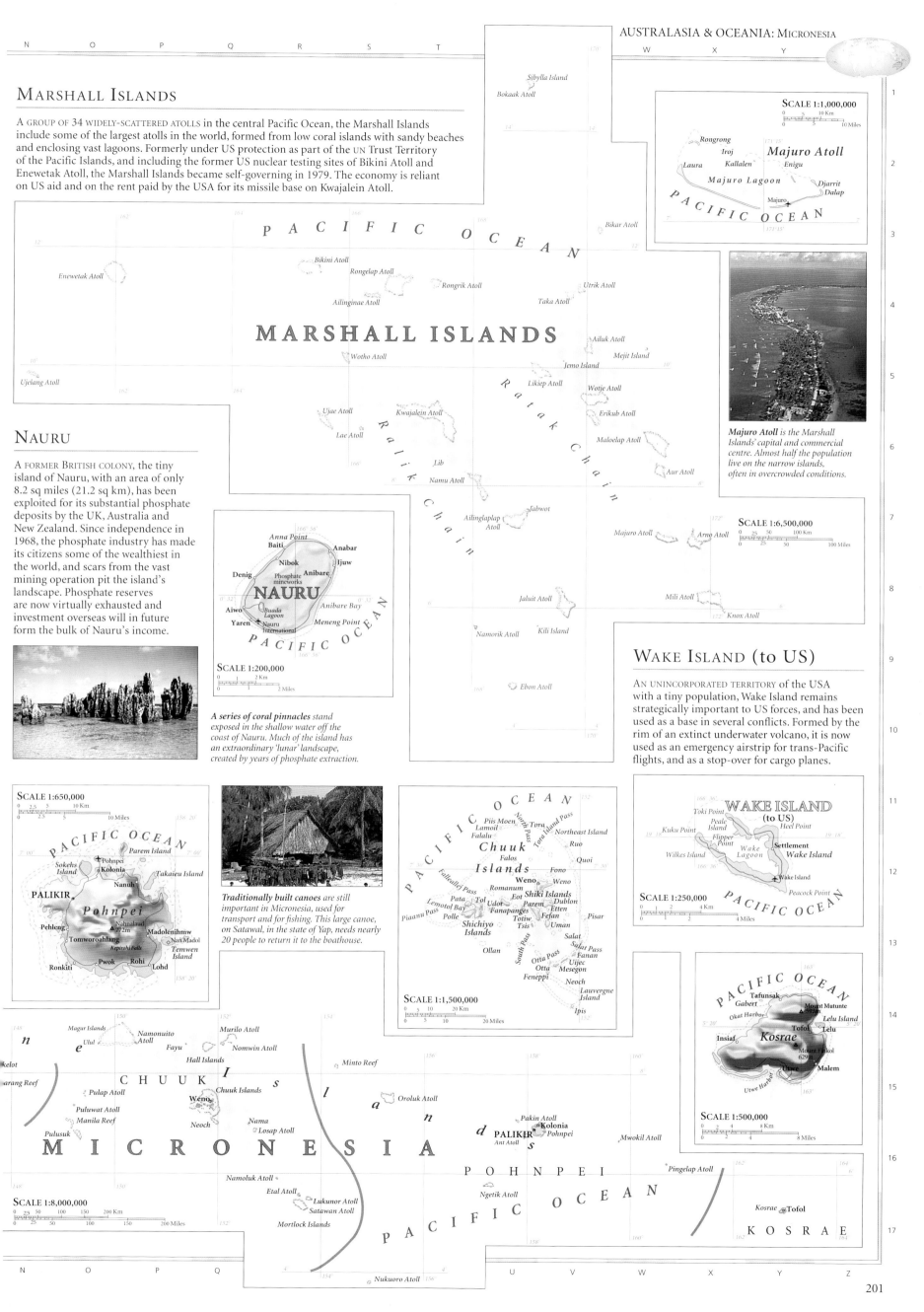

Majuro Atoll is the Marshall Islands' capital and commercial centre. Almost half the population live on the narrow islands, often in overcrowded conditions.

Jabwot

Ailinglaplap Atoll

Majuro Atoll
Arno Atoll

SCALE 1:6,500,000

NAURU

A FORMER BRITISH COLONY, the tiny island of Nauru, with an area of only 8.2 sq miles (21.2 sq km), has been exploited for its substantial phosphate deposits by the UK, Australia and New Zealand. Since independence in 1968, the phosphate industry has made its citizens some of the wealthiest in the world, and scars from the vast mining operation pit the island's landscape. Phosphate reserves are now virtually exhausted and investment overseas will in future form the bulk of Nauru's income.

Anna Point
Baiti
Anabar
Nibok
Ijuw
Denig
Phosphate mineworks
Anibare
NAURU
Aiwo
Buada Lagoon
Anibare Bay
Yaren
Nauru International
Meneng Point

PACIFIC OCEAN

SCALE 1:200,000

Mili Atoll
Knox Atoll

Jaluit Atoll

Namorik Atoll
Kili Island

Ebon Atoll

WAKE ISLAND (to US)

AN UNINCORPORATED TERRITORY of the USA with a tiny population, Wake Island remains strategically important to US forces, and has been used as a base in several conflicts. Formed by the rim of an extinct underwater volcano, it is now used as an emergency airstrip for trans-Pacific flights, and as a stop-over for cargo planes.

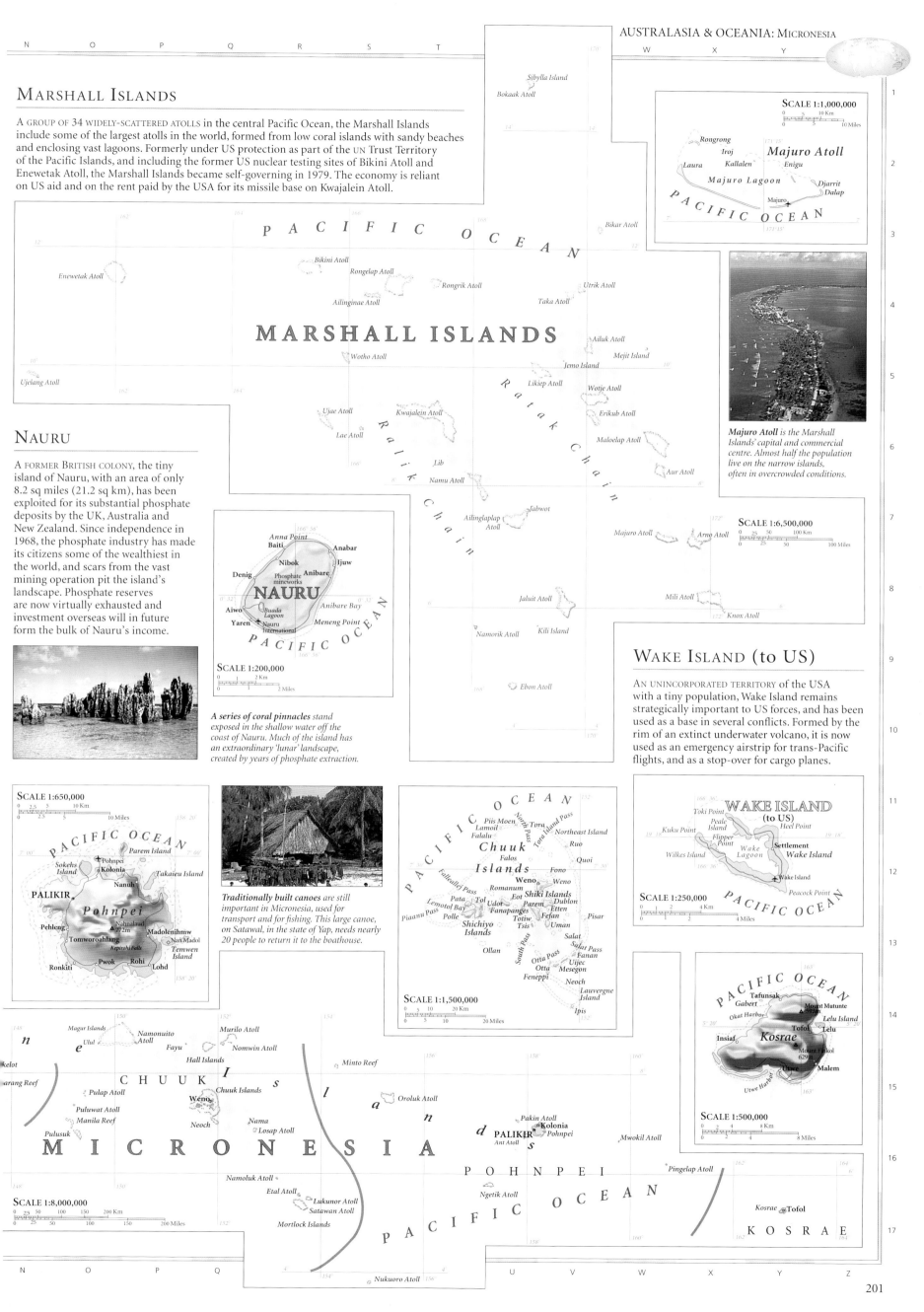

A series of coral pinnacles stand exposed in the shallow water off the coast of Nauru. Much of the island has an extraordinary 'lunar' landscape, created by years of phosphate extraction.

SCALE 1:650,000

PACIFIC OCEAN
Parem Island
Sokehs Island
Pohnpei
Kolonia
Takaieu Island
Nanuh
PALIKIR
Pohnpei
Pehleng
Nahnalaud 772m
Madolenihmw
Tomworoahlang
Kepirohi Falls
Nan Madol
Temwen Island
Ronkiti
Pwok
Rohi
Lohd

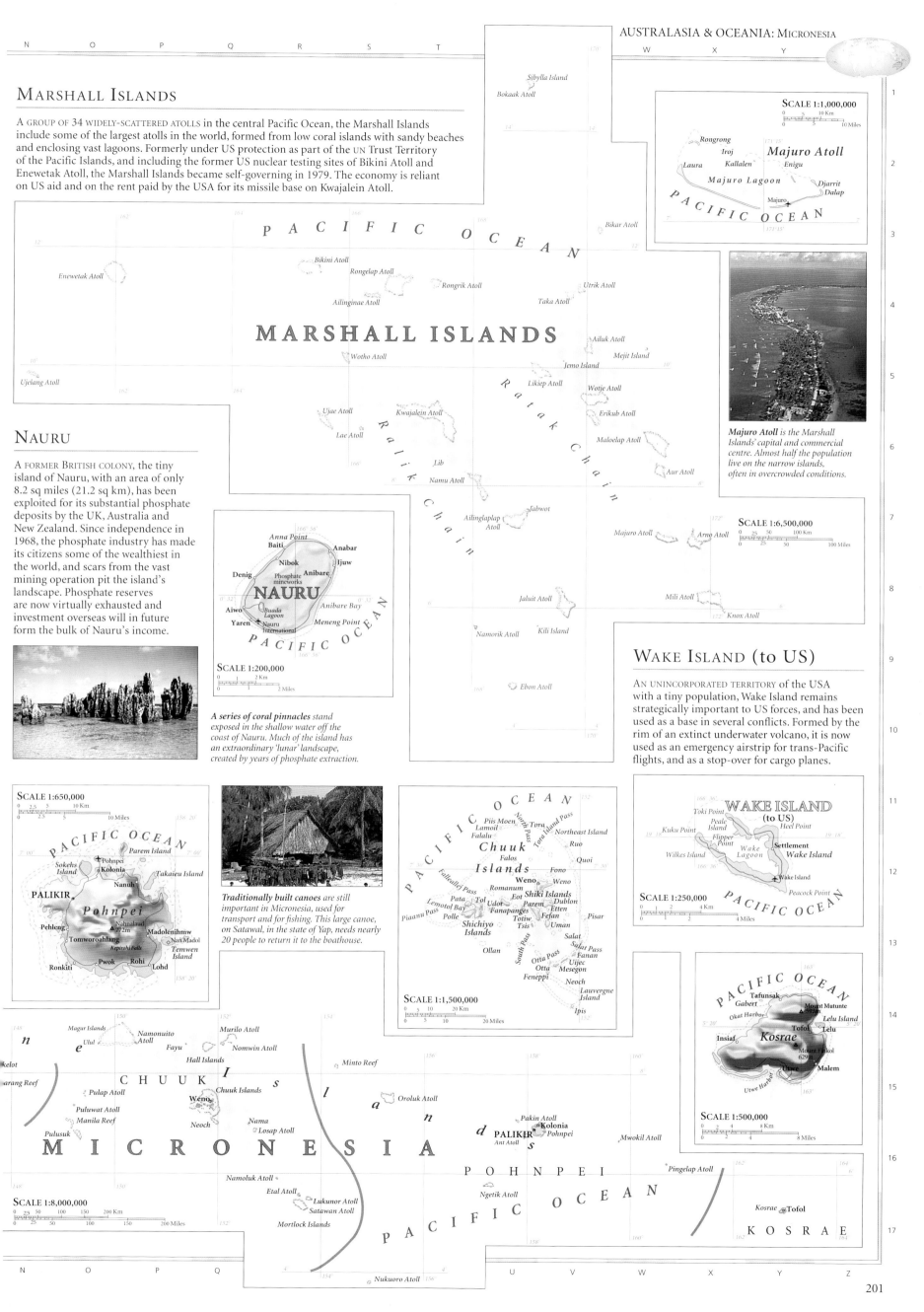

Traditionally built canoes are still important in Micronesia, used for transport and for fishing. This large canoe, on Satawal, in the state of Yap, needs nearly 20 people to return it to the boathouse.

PACIFIC OCEAN

Piis Moen
North Pass
Lamoil
Falalu
Tora
Tora Island Pass
Northeast Island
Ruo
Chuuk Islands
Falos
Fono
Quoi
Fanitcalitej Pass
Weno
Weno
Romanum
Pata
Tol
Udot
Shiki Islands
Lemotol Bay
Fanapanges
Parem
Dublon
Etten
Piaanu Pass
Polle
Totiw
Tsis
Fefan
Uman
Shichiyo Islands
Salat
Pisar
Ollan
Salat Pass
South Pass
Uijec
Fanan
Otta
Mesegon
Otta Pass
Neoch
Feneppi
Lauvergne Island
Ipis

WAKE ISLAND (to US)
Toki Point
Peale Island
Heel Point
Kuku Point
Flipper Point
Wilkes Island
Wake Lagoon
Settlement
Wake Island
Wake Island
Peacock Point

PACIFIC OCEAN

SCALE 1:250,000

SCALE 1:1,500,000

PACIFIC OCEAN
Tafunsak
Gabert
Mount Mutunte 593m
Okat Harbor
Lelu Island
Insiaf
Tofol
Lelu
Kosrae
Mount Finkol 629m
Malem
Utwe

SCALE 1:500,000

n
e
Magur Islands
Ulul
Namonuito Atoll
Fayu
Murilo Atoll
Nomwin Atoll
kelot
arang Reef
Hall Islands
Minto Reef
CHUUK
Pulap Atoll
Chuuk Islands
Oroluk Atoll
Puluwat Atoll
Weno
Manila Reef
Nama
Losap Atoll
Neoch
Pulusuk
I   s   l   a   n   d
Pakin Atoll
Kolonia
PALIKIR
Pohnpei
Ant Atoll
Mwokil Atoll
Oroluk Atoll

MICRONESIA

POHNPEI

PACIFIC OCEAN

Namoluk Atoll
Etal Atoll
Lukunor Atoll
Satawan Atoll
Mortlock Islands
Ngetik Atoll
Pingelap Atoll

Kosrae
Tofol

KOSRAE

SCALE 1:8,000,000

Nukuoro Atoll

N   O   P   Q   R   S   T   U   V   W   X   Y   Z

THE LANDSCAPE

ALTHOUGH IT IS STILL THE LARGEST OCEAN, the basin of the Pacific has been gradually decreasing in size due to the movement of the Indo-Australian Plate. The oldest parts are about 135 million years old. The eastern border of the Pacific is characterized by a continuous mountain chain running the length of the North and South American continents. The eastern basin has a low, uninterrupted relief, at depths averaging 15,000 ft (4570 m). In contrast, the western Pacific is scattered with island arcs and bounded by a series of deep ocean trenches. An almost continuous chain of volcanoes surrounds the ocean and an active mid-ocean ridge runs northeast–southwest.

Micronesia consists of numerous small, oceanic islands in the western Pacific. The Micronesian islands are all oceanic in origin, rising directly up from the ocean floor.

The Emperor Seamounts were formed over 40 million years ago. Like other islands and seamounts of the same era, they trend in a north–south direction. Younger chains run northwest–southeast.

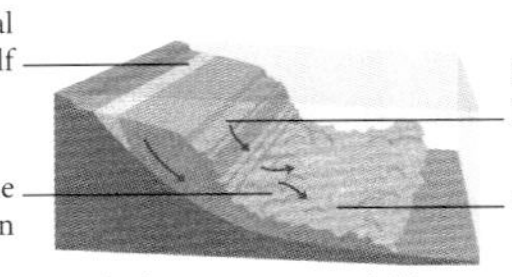

Turbidity currents are sinking masses of sediment-laden water. Their erosive force creates deep, narrow submarine canyons along the continental shelf to the ocean floor, where the sediments are deposited.

Continental shelf
Sediment-laden current
Submarine canyon
Ocean floor

The Mariana Trench marks a subduction zone between the Pacific Plate and the Philippine Plate. It is the world's deepest trench, reaching depths of 36,201 ft (11,034 m).

The Tonga Trench lies north of New Zealand's North Island. The trench reaches average depths of 34,448 ft (10,500 m), which is more than twice the average depth of the ocean.

The Pacific mid-ocean ridge is spreading at a rate of 6.5 inches (15 cm) a year. The northeastern part is no longer apparent, having merged with the strike-slip fault systems of North America.

The Peru–Chile Trench is the longest trench in the Pacific, extending 3660 miles (5900 km), and following the line of the Andes mountain range down the west coast of South America.

Bora-Bora

Bora-Bora's twin mountain peaks are the remnants of an ancient volcano, now surrounded by a large lagoon, fringed with coral.

Northern Chile

The powerful erosive capacity of Pacific waves can be seen along this stretch of coastline in northern Chile. Wave erosion has cut back the bedrock, exposing numerous rock layers.

TONGA

THE KINGDOM OF TONGA lies in the southwest Pacific, about 2000 miles (3000 km) off the east coast of Australia. It comprises 169 islands of which only 36 are permanently inhabited. The majority of the population live on the largest island, Tongatapu. There are only three sizeable towns and the main commercial centre is the capital Nuku'alofa. Tonga's economy is based mainly on agriculture; coconuts, bananas and vanilla are grown as cash crops for export. Although there is some light manufacturing, growing land shortages have forced increased migration to New Zealand and Australia.

The islands of Tonga fall into two belts; those in the east are low, coral islands, while those in the west are high and volcanic. Four of the islands still contain active volcanoes. The mountainous, western islands are covered with verdant tropical vegetation.

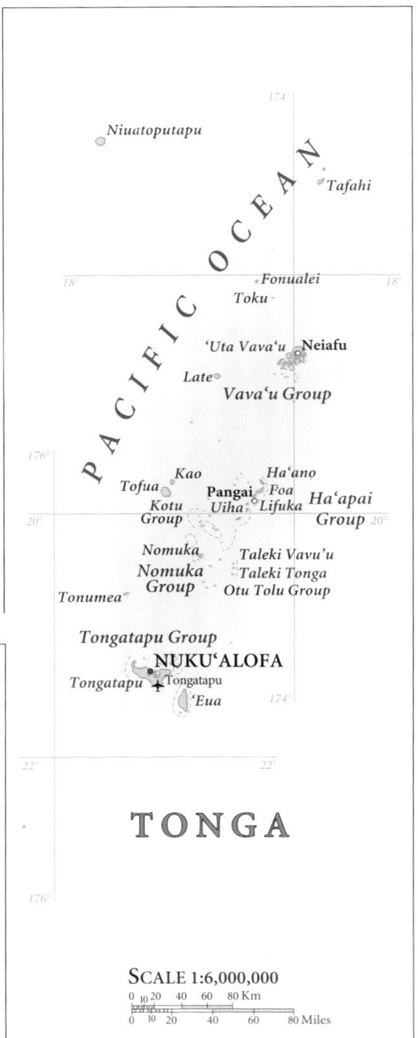

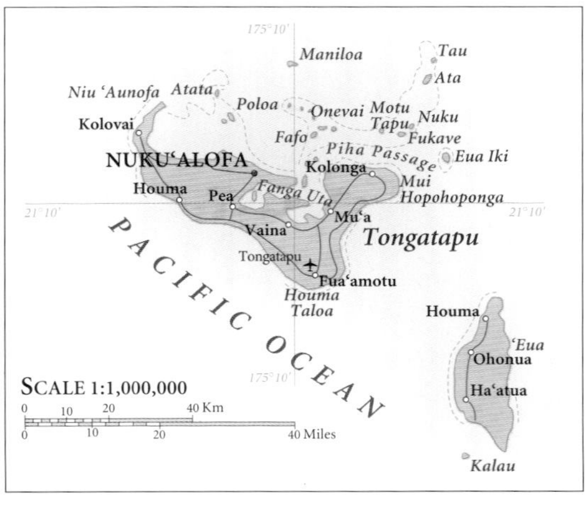

Coral reefs and atolls are found throughout the warm waters of the south Pacific. Reefs build up from the skeletons of millions of coral polyps – tiny sea creatures that cling to the reef and secrete calcium carbonate around their bodies, forming a hard protective skeleton.

SCALE 1:1,000,000

0   10   20   40 Km

0   10   20   40 Miles

SCALE 1:6,000,000

0 20 40 60 80 Km

0 20 40 60 80 Miles

Wave action has eroded this shoreline near Port Campbell in southeastern Australia leaving isolated pinnacles of rock cut off from the main coastline. They are known as the 'Twelve Apostles'.

POLYNESIA

KIRIBATI, TUVALU, Cook Islands, Easter Island, French Polynesia, Niue, Pitcairn Islands, Tokelau, Wallis & Futuna

THE NUMEROUS ISLAND GROUPS OF POLYNESIA lie to the east of Australia, scattered over a vast area in the south Pacific. The islands are a mixture of low-lying coral atolls, some of which enclose lagoons, and the tips of great underwater volcanoes. The populations on the islands are small, and most people are of Polynesian origin, as are the Maori of New Zealand. Local economies remain simple, relying mainly on subsistence crops, mineral deposits – many now exhausted – fishing and tourism.

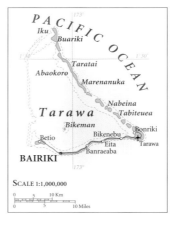

SCALE 1:1,000,000

KIRIBATI

A FORMER BRITISH COLONY, Kiribati became independent in 1979. Banaba's phosphate deposits ran out in 1980, following decades of exploitation by the British. Economic development remains slow and most agriculture is at a subsistence level, though coconuts provide export income, and underwater agriculture is being developed.

With the exception of Banaba all the islands in Kiribati's three groups are low-lying, coral atolls. This aerial view shows the sparsely vegetated islands, intercut by many small lagoons.

TUVALU

A CHAIN of nine coral atolls, 360 miles (579 km) long with a land area of just over 9 sq miles (23 sq km), Tuvalu is one of the world's smallest and most isolated states. As the Ellice Islands, Tuvalu was linked to the Gilbert Islands (now part of Kiribati) as a British colony until independence in 1978. Politically and socially conservative, Tuvaluans live by fishing and subsistence farming.

Funafuti Atoll contains more than 40% of Tuvalu's people, giving it an extremely high population density.

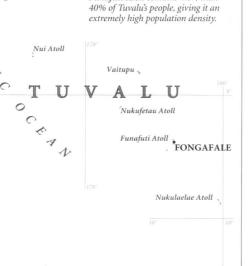

SCALE 1:6,000,000

SCALE 1:500,000

TOKELAU (to New Zealand)

A LOW-LYING CORAL ATOLL, Tokelau is a dependent territory of New Zealand with few natural resources. Although a 1990 cyclone destroyed crops and infrastructure, a tuna cannery and the sale of fishing licences have raised revenue and a catamaran link between the islands has increased their tourism potential. Tokelau's small size and economic weakness makes independence from New Zealand unlikely.

Fishermen cast their nets to catch small fish in the shallow waters off Atafu Atoll, the most westerly island in Tokelau.

SCALE 1:2,000,000

WALLIS & FUTUNA (to France)

IN CONTRAST TO OTHER FRENCH overseas territories in the south Pacific, the inhabitants of Wallis and Futuna have shown little desire for greater autonomy. A subsistence economy produces a variety of tropical crops, while foreign currency remittances come from expatriates and from the sale of licences to Japanese and Korean fishing fleets.

SCALE 1:1,000,000

SCALE 1:1,000,000

COOK ISLANDS (to New Zealand)

A MIXTURE OF CORAL ATOLLS and volcanic peaks, the Cook Islands achieved self-government in 1965 but exist in free association with New Zealand. A diverse economy includes pearl and giant clam farming, plus tourism and banking. A 1991 friendship treaty with France provides for French surveillance of territorial waters.

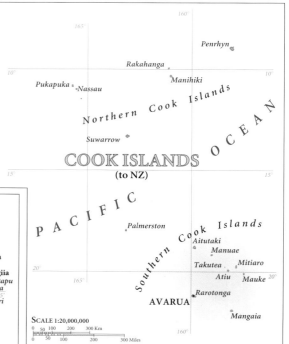

SCALE 1:20,000,000

NIUE (to New Zealand)

NIUE, the world's largest coral island, is self-governing but exists in free association with New Zealand. Tropical fruits are grown for local consumption; tourism and the sale of postage stamps provide foreign currency. The lack of local job prospects has led more than 10,000 Niueans to emigrate to New Zealand, which has now invested heavily in Niue's economy in the hope of reversing this trend.

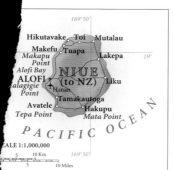

SCALE 1:1,000,000

Waves have cut back the original coastline, exposing a sandy beach, near Mutalau in the northeast corner of Niue.

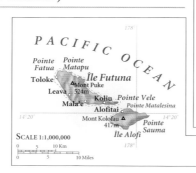

Palm trees fringe the white sands of a beach on Aitutaki in the Southern Cook Islands, where tourism is of increasing economic importance.

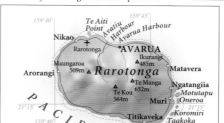

SCALE 1:325,000

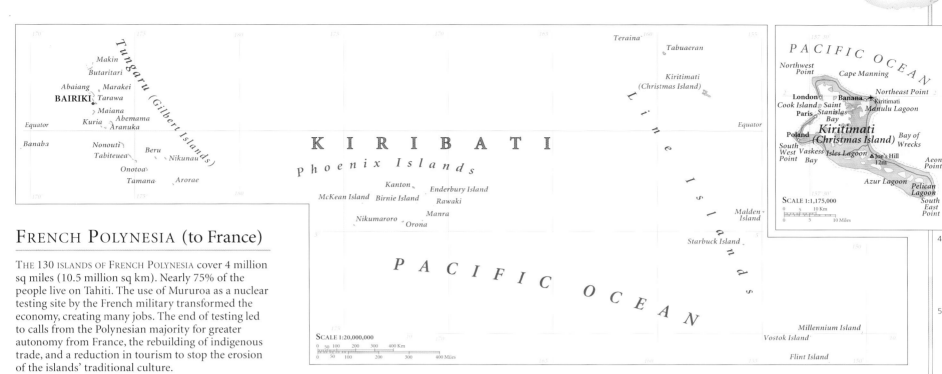

KIRIBATI

Tungaru (Gilbert Islands)

Makin
Butaritari
Abaiang · Marakei
BAIRIKI · Tarawa
Maiana
Kuria · Abemama
Aranuka
Banaba
Nonouti · Beru
Tabiteuea · Nikunau
Onotoa
Tamana · Arorae

Equator

phoenix Islands

Kanton
McKean Island · Birnie Island · Enderbury Island
Rawaki
Nikumaroro · Orona
Manra

Teraina
Tabuaeran

Kiritimati
(Christmas Island)

Line Islands

Malden Island

Starbuck Island

Millennium Island
Vostok Island

Flint Island

SCALE 1:20,000,000

PACIFIC OCEAN

(Kiritimati inset)

PACIFIC OCEAN

Northwest Point · Cape Manning
London · **Banana** · Northeast Point
Cook Island · Saint · Kiritimati
Paris · Stanislas · Manulu Lagoon
Bay
Poland · Vaskess · Isles Lagoon
South · Bay · Joe's Hill · Bay of Wrecks
West · 12m
Point
Azur Lagoon · Aeon Point
Pelican Lagoon
South East Point

SCALE 1:1,175,000

FRENCH POLYNESIA (to France)

THE 130 ISLANDS OF FRENCH POLYNESIA cover 4 million sq miles (10.5 million sq km). Nearly 75% of the people live on Tahiti. The use of Mururoa as a nuclear testing site by the French military transformed the economy, creating many jobs. The end of testing led to calls from the Polynesian majority for greater autonomy from France, the rebuilding of indigenous trade, and a reduction in tourism to stop the erosion of the islands' traditional culture.

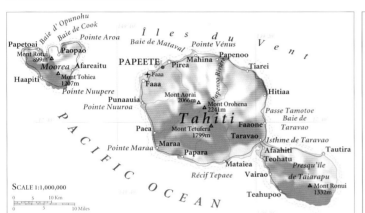

Îles du Vent

Papetoai · Baie d'Opunohu · Baie de Cook
Pointe Aroa · Pointe Vénus
Mont Rotui · Paopao · Baie de Matavai · Pointe Vénus
Moorea · Afareaitu · **PAPEETE** · Papenoo
Mont Tohiea · Mahina · Pirea · Tiarei
Haapiti · Faaa · Faaa
Pointe Nuupere · Hitiaa
Punaauia · Mont Aorai · Mont Orohena
Pointe Nuuroa · 2066m · 2241m
Paea · **Tahiti** · Passe Tamotoe
Mont Tetufera · Faaone · Baie de
Maraa · 1799m · Taravao
Pointe Maraa · Afaahiti · Isthme de Taravao
Papara · Teohatu · Tautira
Mataiea · Vairao · Presqu'île
Récif Tepaee · Teahupoo · de Taiarapu
Mont Ronui · 1332m

SCALE 1:1,000,000

PACIFIC OCEAN

The traditional Tahitian welcome for visitors, who are greeted by parties of canoes, has become a major tourist attraction.

PITCAIRN ISLANDS (to UK)

BRITAIN'S MOST ISOLATED DEPENDENCY, Pitcairn Island was first populated by mutineers from the HMS *Bounty* in 1790. Emigration is further depleting the already limited gene pool of the island's inhabitants, with associated social and health problems. Barter, fishing and subsistence farming form the basis of the economy although postage stamp sales provide foreign currency earnings, and offshore mineral exploitation may boost the economy in future.

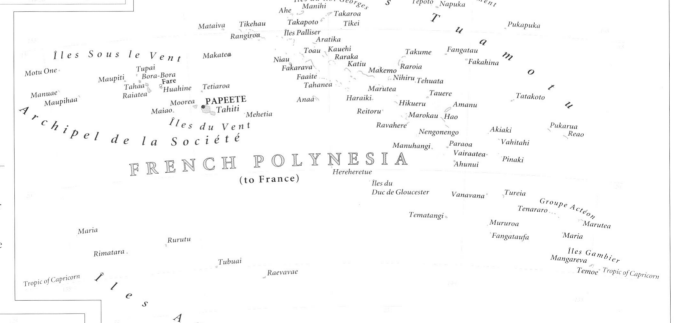

Îles Marquises

Hatutu
Eiao
Nuku Hiva · Ua Huka
Taiohae
Ua Pu · Hiva Oa
Atuona
Tahuata · Motane
Fatu Hiva · Omoa

PACIFIC OCEAN

Îles Sous le Vent

Motu One
Tupai
Maupiti · Bora-Bora
Manuae · Tahaa · **Fare**
Maupihaa · Raiatea · Huahine
Moorea · Tetiaroa
Maiao · **PAPEETE**
Tahiti
Mehetia

Archipel de la Société

Îles du Vent

Îles Tuamotu

Mataiva · Tikehau · Ahe · Manihi
Rangiroa · Takapoto · Takaroa
Iles Palliser · Tikei
Aratika
Makatea · Toau · Kauehi
Niau · Raraka · Takume · Fangatau
Fakarava · Katiu · Fakahina
Faaite · Makemo · Raroia
Tahanea · Marutea · Nihiru · Tehuata
Anaa · Haraiki · Tauere · Amanu
Reitoru · Hikueru · Tatakoto
Ravahere · Marokau · Hao
Nengonengo · Akiaki
Manuhangi · Paraoa · Pukarua
Vairaatea · Vahitahi · Reao
Hereheretue · Ahunui · Pinaki
Iles du Duc de Gloucester · Vanavana · Tureia
Groupe Actéon
Tenararo · Marutea
Tematangi · Mururoa · Maria
Fangataufa · Îles Gambier
Mangareva
Temoe

Îles Australes

Maria
Rimatara · Rurutu
Tubuai
Raevavae
Tropic of Capricorn

Rapa Iti
Marotiri

FRENCH POLYNESIA
(to France)

SCALE 1:14,500,000

PITCAIRN ISLANDS
(to UK)

Oeno Island
Henderson Island
Ducie Island
Pitcairn Island

PACIFIC OCEAN

SCALE 1:10,000,000

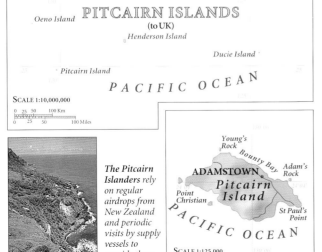

The Pitcairn Islanders rely on regular airdrops from New Zealand and periodic visits by supply vessels to provide them with basic commodities.

Young's Rock
Bounty Bay
ADAMSTOWN · Adam's Rock
Pitcairn Island
Point Christian
St Paul's Point

PACIFIC OCEAN

SCALE 1:125,000

EASTER ISLAND (to Chile)

ONE OF THE MOST EASTERLY ISLANDS in Polynesia, Easter Island *(Isla de Pascua)* – also known as Rapa Nui, is part of Chile. The mainly Polynesian inhabitants support themselves by farming, which is mainly of a subsistence nature, and includes cattle rearing and crops such as sugar cane, bananas, corn, gourds and potatoes. In recent years, tourism has become the most important source of income and the island sustains a small commercial airport.

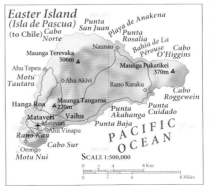

Easter Island
(Isla de Pascua)
(to Chile)

Punta San Juan · Cabo Norte · Playa de Anakena
Naunau · Punta Rosalia
Maunga Terevaka · Bahia de La Pérouse · Cabo O'Higgins
506m
Ahu Tepeu · Maunga Pukatikei
Motu · 370m
Tautara · Ahu Akivi
Maunga Tangaroa · Rano Raraku · Cabo Roggewein
270m · Punta Cuidado
Hanga Roa · Punta Akahanga
Mataveri · Vaihu · Punta Baja
Mataveri
Rano Kau · Ahu Vinapu
Orongo · Cabo Sur
Motu Nui

PACIFIC OCEAN

SCALE 1:500,000

The Naunau, a series of huge stone statues overlook Playa de Anakena, on Easter Island. Carved from a soft volcanic rock, they were erected between 400 and 900 years ago.

ANTARCTICA

The ice-covered continent of Antarctica, which is the Earth's most southerly region, has for over 200 years drawn explorers and entrepreneurs seeking challenge and riches in its wintry lands. The extreme climate has deterred any large-scale settlement of the continent, and though commercial hunters built outposts in the past, habitation is now limited to scientific bases. The Antarctic Treaty, which came into force in 1961, provides for international governance and scientific co-operation in place of potential territorial conflict.

RESOURCES

Many ore minerals, including iron and gold, are found in the Antarctic, and there are also coal reserves in the Transantarctic Mountains. The severe conditions and environmental importance of the region mean that exploitation of potential mineral resources is both uneconomic and undesirable. The unique wildlife and landscape draw a small number of tourists annually.

Resources (including wildlife)

- coal
- fish
- minerals
- oil & gas
- penguins
- seals
- whales
- polar research base

Most settlements in Antarctica are research bases such as this one at Rothera on Adelaide Island, although there is a small Chilean settlement on King George Island.

THE LANDSCAPE

There are two distinct parts to Antarctica: Lesser Antarctica, a series of ice-covered, mountainous islands, joined together by the ice; and the high plateau of Greater Antarctica. The Ross Sea and the Weddell Sea are outliers of the Atlantic and Pacific oceans – deep bays partially covered by thick ice shelves.

Grease ice   Pancake ice   Sea-ice sheet   Ice floe

Pack ice forms out at sea in freezing temperatures. At the outer limits, grease ice congeals on the surface of the ocean. This is then spun around by wind and waves into irregular 'pancakes', freezing and breaking up several times before bonding together again to form sea-ice sheets, which finally cement into enormous ice floes.

On Elephant Island, the coast is edged by glaciers, although the land is not permanently covered by ice.

During the winter the seas surrounding Antarctica freeze, increasing the size of the continent by 100%.

Upper Wright Valley

Limit of summer pack ice

Limit of winter pack ice

Elephant Island

High winds carrying snow form huge snowdrifts. The erosive power of the wind-borne snow can also sculpt the ice sheet to produce landforms known as sastrugi which align with the direction of the wind.

Many volcanoes, some of them still active, can be found in the mountains of the Antarctic Peninsula.

The Lambert Glacier is the largest glacier system in the world, up to 50 miles (80 km) wide at its seaward limit, and reaching 180 miles (300 km) into the interior by way of the Prince Charles Mountains.

Antarctica is the highest continent on Earth, because of the great thickness of ice which overlays the land. In places the ice alone can reach up to 15,700 ft (4800 m) thick. Much of the basement rock of west Antarctica lies below sea level, pushed down by the weight of the ice.

The mountainous Antarctic Peninsula is formed of rocks 65–225 million years old, overlain by more recent rocks and glacial deposits. It is connected to the Andes in South America by a submarine ridge.

Nearly half – 44% – of the Antarctic coastline is bounded by ice shelves, like the Ronne Ice Shelf, which float on the Ocean. These are joined to the inland ice sheet by dome-shaped ice 'rises'.

More than 30% of Antarctic ice is contained in the Ross Ice Shelf.

The barren, flat-bottomed Upper Wright Valley was once filled by a glacier, but is now dry, strewn with boulders and pebbles. In some dry valleys, there has been no rain for over 2 million years.

Large colonies of seabirds live in the extremely harsh Antarctic climate. The Emperor penguins seen here, the smaller Adélie penguin, the Antarctic petrel and the South Polar skua are the only birds which breed exclusively on the continent.

TERRITORIAL CLAIMS

Argentinian claim
Brazilian zone of interest
British claim
Norwegian undefined limit
Australian claim
Chilean claim
French claim
Australian claim
New Zealand claim

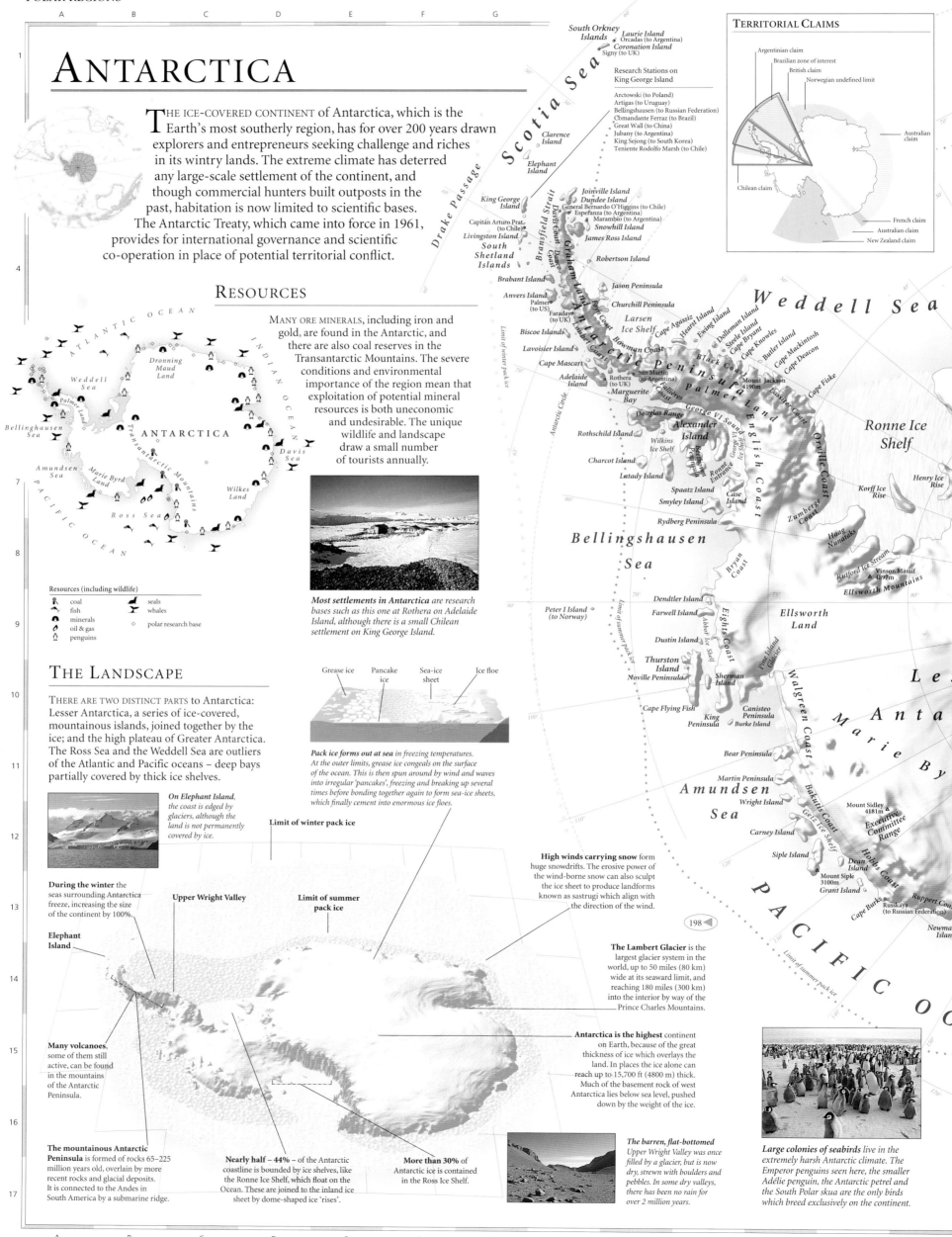

(map labels)

South Orkney Islands — Laurie Island, Orcadas (to Argentina), Coronation Island, Signy (to UK)

Scotia Sea

Research Stations on King George Island
Arctowski (to Poland)
Artigas (to Uruguay)
Bellingshausen (to Russian Federation)
Comandante Ferraz (to Brazil)
Great Wall (to China)
Jubany (to Argentina)
King Sejong (to South Korea)
Teniente Rodolfo Marsh (to Chile)

Clarence Island
Elephant Island
King George Island
Capitán Arturo Prat (to Chile)
Livingston Island
South Shetland Islands
Brabant Island
Anvers Island (to US)
Palmer (to US)
Faraday (to UK)
Biscoe Islands
Lavoisier Island
Cape Mascart
Adelaide Island
Rothera (to UK)
Marguerite Bay
Rothschild Island
Charcot Island
Latady Island
Spaatz Island
Smyley Island
Rydberg Peninsula

Drake Passage

Joinville Island
Dundee Island
General Bernardo O'Higgins (to Chile)
Esperanza (to Argentina)
Marambio (to Argentina)
Snowhill Island
James Ross Island
Robertson Island
Jason Peninsula
Churchill Peninsula
Larsen Ice Shelf
Bowman Coast
San Martin (to Argentina)
Douglas Range
Alexander Island
Wilkins Ice Shelf
Ronne Entrance

Davis Coast
Danco Coast
Graham Land
Oscar II Coast

Bransfield Strait

Weddell Sea

Cape Agassiz
Hearst Island
Ewing Island
Dolleman Island
Steele Island
Cape Bryant
Cape Knowles
Black Coast
Buller Island
Cape Mackintosh
Cape Deacon
Cape Fiske

Palmer Land

English Coast
Orville Coast
Ronne Ice Shelf
Korff Ice Rise
Henry Ice Rise
Haag Nunataks
Rutford Ice Stream
Vinson Massif 4897m
Ellsworth Mountains

Mount Jackson 3190m
Lassiter Coast

Bellingshausen Sea

Peter I Island (to Norway)

Dendtler Island
Farwell Island
Dustin Island
Thurston Island
Noville Peninsula
Sherman Island
Cape Flying Fish
King Peninsula
Canisteo Peninsula
Burke Island
Bear Peninsula
Martin Peninsula
Wright Island

Amundsen Sea

Eights Coast
Abbot Ice Shelf
Pine Island Glacier

Ellsworth Land

Bryan Coast

Zumberge Coast
Case Island

Walgreen Coast
Bakutis Coast
Getz Ice Shelf
Carney Island
Siple Island
Mount Siple 3100m
Grant Island
Cape Burks

Marie Byrd Land

Mount Sidley 4181m
Executive Committee Range
Dean Island
Hobbs Coast
Russkaya (to Russian Federation)
Ruppert Coast
Newman Island

Pacific Ocean

ATLANTIC OCEAN
INDIAN OCEAN
Dronning Maud Land
Weddell Sea
Palmer Land
Bellingshausen Sea
ANTARCTICA
Transantarctic Mountains
Amundsen Sea
Marie Byrd Land
Ross Sea
PACIFIC OCEAN
Davis Sea
Wilkes Land

Antarctic Circle

Limit of winter pack ice
Limit of summer pack ice

198

The sun sets over the Antarctic Peninsula for more than six months during the winter. However, there are more hours of sunshine during the brief Antarctic summer than most equatorial countries experience in a whole year.

Immense, flat-topped icebergs are formed when blocks of ice break away from the main ice sheet. Though the exposed area is enormous, the volume of ice concealed beneath the water may be many times greater.

SCALE 1:14,750,000
(projection: Lambert Azimuthal Equal Area)

MAP KEY

ELEVATION

ice cap

ice shelf

exposed land

THE ARCTIC

THREE CONTINENTS, ASIA, NORTH AMERICA AND EUROPE, reach into the Arctic Circle at their northernmost limits, almost entirely encircling the Arctic Ocean. Despite the region's extraordinarily harsh climate, it has been inhabited for thousands of years by peoples such as the European Lapps, the Russian Nenet, and the North American Inuit, who draw a living from fishing, herding and hunting. More recently, particularly in the Russian Arctic, opportunities to exploit oil and other mineral reserves have encouraged immigration. Pollution of the Arctic's unique ecology and damage to the traditional lifestyles of many native peoples have been the unfortunate results of this activity, and international co-operation is needed to safeguard the future of the region.

MAP KEY

POPULATION

- ■ above 5 million
- ■ 1 million to 5 million
- ◉ 500,000 to 1 million
- ◎ 100,000 to 500,000
- ⊕ 50,000 to 100,000
- ⊙ 10,000 to 50,000
- ○ below 10,000

SEA DEPTH

	sea level
	250m / 820ft
	500m / 1640ft
	1000m / 3281ft
	2000m / 6562ft
	3000m / 9843ft

SCALE 1:21,000,000
(projection: Lambert Azimuthal Equal Area)

198 ◀

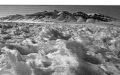

Wind-blown snow etches deep patterns in the ice sheet known as sastrugi. They align with the direction of the wind

14 ◀

RESOURCES

LARGE QUANTITIES of coal, oil and natural gas are to be found in the basins of the Arctic Ocean, and in northern Canada, Alaska and the Russian Federation. The cost and difficulty of extraction and, more recently, awareness of damage to the environment, have limited exploitation to coastal regions. The unfrozen waters have stocks of fish including cod, plaice and haddock. Quotas have now been put in place to restrict the number of fish caught annually. Reindeer are herded in large numbers by many of the native Arctic peoples. Most grain and vegetables are imported from elsewhere.

Icebreakers, ships with specially strengthened hulls, designed to break a path through the ice, are used to keep important routes open during the winter, when falling temperatures cause much of the Arctic Ocean to freeze over.

Resources
- ⛏ coal
- 🐟 fish
- ⛰ mining
- ◖ oil & gas
- ☢ radioactive contamination
- ■ major towns
- ⊕ major ports

14 ◀

THE LANDSCAPE

THE ARCTIC OCEAN comprises two large ocean basins divided by three submarine ridges, the greatest of which, the Lomonosov Ridge, is a huge underwater mountain range which has an average height of more than 10,000 ft (3000 m). The lands which encircle the Arctic Ocean are underlain by great shield areas of ancient rocks, which were heavily glaciated during the last Ice Age.

Icebergs are constantly broken up and re-shaped by wind and the oceans. This flat-topped iceberg has been undercut, leaving a craggy ice cliff.

A complex and ancient mountain system, extending from the Queen Elizabeth Islands to eastern Greenland was formed more than 245 million years ago.

The Canadian Shield underlies almost all of the Canadian Arctic. It is a very stable plateau of ancient rock, now covered by glacial lakes and sediment, which supports tundra vegetation.

The Arctic Ocean is the world's smallest ocean with a total area of 5,440,000 sq miles (15,100,000 sq km).

At a latitude of more than 75° N, the Arctic Ocean is almost permanently covered by pack-ice, though high winds and the movement of the seas may cause the ice to crack and break up.

In the more southerly reaches of the Arctic, like Siberia, much of the land is covered by permafrost. In the summer, higher temperatures warm the frozen ground, causing a number of typical phenomena. These include solifluction, the fast downhill movement of top soil layers; freeze/thaw activity, which patterns the ground into regular polygonal shapes, and the formation of large domes with a frozen ice core, known as pingos.

Lomonosov Ridge

Lomonosov Ridge

Arctic ice shelf

Much of Greenland is covered by a massive ice sheet more than 650,000 sq miles (1,683,400 sq km) in extent. The weight of the ice has depressed the central land area to form a basin lying more than 1000 ft (300 m) below sea level. Only at the edges of the island is bare rock visible.

Iceland has five major glaciers, sustained by heavy snowfall. Parts of the ice cap cover active volcanoes, such as Bárdharbunga, which periodically erupt causing the melted ice to form a great lake at the glacier margins.

Ice sheet

Crevasses occur at the edge of the ice sheet

Iceberg

Sea water melts the edge of the ice sheet

At the boundary of the Arctic ice shelves, sea water flows under the ice causing melting and forming crevasses on the surface. This eventually weakens blocks of ice which break away as icebergs. This process is known as calving.

66 ▽

Map labels

Bering Sea
ASIA
NORTH AMERICA
Inuvik
Tiksi
ARCTIC OCEAN
Noril'sk
Qaanaaq
Murmansk
Reykjavík
ATLANTIC OCEAN
EUROPE

CANADA
NORTH AMERICA
Mackenzie
Great Bear Lake
Great Slave Lake
Coppermine
Bathurst Inlet
Coronation Gulf
Cambridge Bay
Queen Maud Gulf
King William Island
Boothia Peninsula
Nelson
Back
Gulf of
Churchill
Southampton Island
Repulse Bay
Melville Peninsula
Hudson Bay
Coats Island
Mansel Island
Foxe Basin
Prince Charles Island
Ivujivik
Inukjuak
Foxe Peninsula
Baffin Island
Hudson Strait
Lake Harbour
Frobisher Bay
Cumberland Sound
Ungava Bay
Cape Chidley
Davis Strait
Labrador Sea
Maniitsoq
NUUK
Nain
Paamiut
Ivittuut
Labrador Basin
Qaqortoq
Kong
Nanortalik
Narsarsuaq
Nunap Isua (Kap Farvel)
Eirik Ridge
ATLANTIC

N O P Q R S T U V W X Y

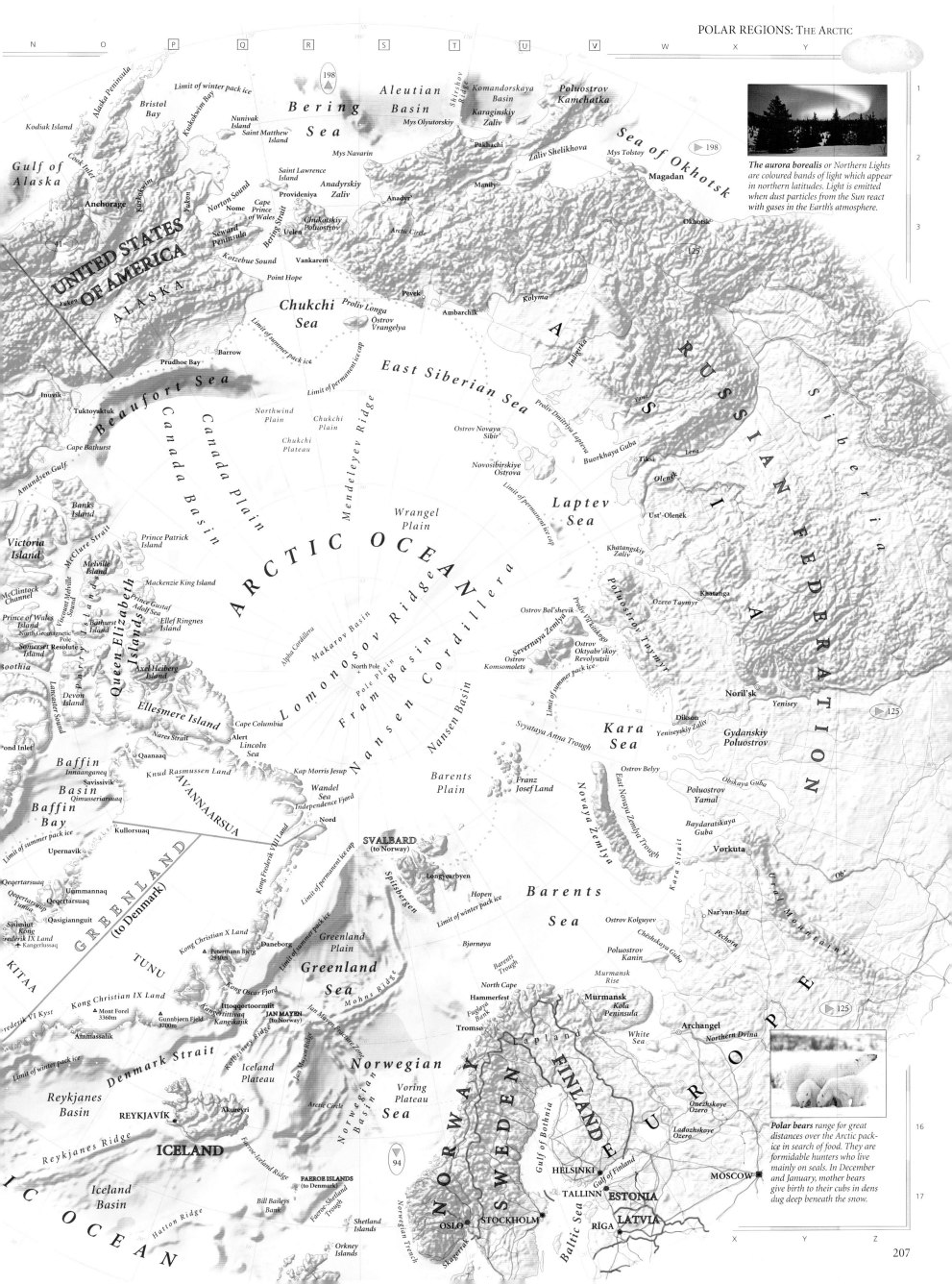

The **aurora borealis** or Northern Lights are coloured bands of light which appear in northern latitudes. Light is emitted when dust particles from the Sun react with gases in the Earth's atmosphere.

Kodiak Island

Gulf of Alaska

Alaska Peninsula

Bristol Bay

Kuskokwim Bay

Nunivak Island

Saint Matthew Island

Limit of winter pack ice

Bering Sea

Aleutian Basin

Shirshov Ridge

Komandorskaya Basin

Poluostrov Kamchatka

Karaginskiy Zaliv

Mys Olyutorskiy

Mys Navarin

Saint Lawrence Island

Anadyrskiy Zaliv

Pakhachi

Zaliv Shelikhova

Manily

Sea of Okhotsk

Mys Tolstoy

Magadan

Okhotsk

Cook Inlet

Anchorage

UNITED STATES OF AMERICA

Nome

Seward Peninsula

Norton Sound

Provideniya

Uelen

Chukotskiy Poluostrov

Cape Prince of Wales

Bering Strait

Kotzebue Sound

Arctic Circle

ALASKA

Yukon

Kuskokwim

Anadyr

Vankarem

Point Hope

Chukchi Sea

Proliv Longa

Ostrov Vrangelya

Pevek

Ambarchik

Kolyma

A

R U S S I A N

Indigirka

Siberia

Barrow

Prudhoe Bay

Limit of summer pack ice

Limit of permanent ice cap

East Siberian Sea

Proliv Dmitriya Lapteva

Yana

Inuvik

Tuktoyaktuk

Beaufort Sea

Northwind Plain

Chukchi Plain

Ostrov Novaya Sibir'

Buorkhaya Guba

Tiksi

Lena

F

Cape Bathurst

Canada Plain

Chukchi Plateau

Mendeleyev Ridge

Novosibirskiye Ostrova

Olenek

Ust'-Olenek

E

Amundsen Gulf

Canada Basin

Limit of permanent ice cap

Laptev Sea

D

Banks Island

ARCTIC OCEAN

Wrangel Plain

Khatangskiy Zaliv

Ozero Taymyr

Khatanga

E

Victoria Island

Prince Patrick Island

McClure Strait

Melville Island

Mackenzie King Island

Makarov Basin

Poluostrov Taymyr

R

McClintock Channel

Prince Gustaf Adolf Sea

Alpha Cordillera

Ostrov Bol'shevik

Proliv Vil'kitskogo

Severnaya Zemlya

A

Prince of Wales Island

Ellef Ringnes Island

Axel Heiberg Island

Lomonosov Ridge

North Pole

Fram Basin

Nansen Cordillera

Ostrov Komsomolets

Ostrov Oktyabr'skoy Revolyutsii

Noril'sk

T

Yenisey

Bathurst Island

North Geomagnetic Pole

Pole Plain

Nansen Basin

Limit of summer pack ice

Dikson

Yeniseyskiy Zaliv

Gydanskiy Poluostrov

Somerset Island

Resolute

Queen Elizabeth Islands

Parry Islands

Viscount Melville Sound

Devon Island

Ellesmere Island

Cape Columbia

Kara Sea

Obskaya Guba

I

Boothia

Lancaster Sound

Nares Strait

Lincoln Sea

Alert

Kap Morris Jesup

Svyataya Anna Trough

Ostrov Belyy

Poluostrov Yamal

Pond Inlet

Qaanaaq

Knud Rasmussen Land

SAVANNAARSUA

Barents Plain

Franz Josef Land

East Novaya Zemlya Trough

Baydaratskaya Guba

Vorkuta

Baffin Basin

Innaanganeq

Savissivik

Qimusseriarsuaq

Wandel Sea

Independence Fjord

Nord

Kong Frederik VIII Land

Novaya Zemlya

Kara Strait

Ob'

O

Baffin Bay

Kullorsuaq

SVALBARD (to Norway)

Longyearbyen

Nar'yan-Mar

Pechora

N

Upernavik

Limit of summer pack ice

GREENLAND (to Denmark)

Spitsbergen

Barents Sea

Ostrov Kolguyev

Chëshskaya Guba

Poluostrov Kanin

Ural Mountains

Qeqertarsuaq

Uummannaq

Qeqertarsuaq

Qeqertarsuup Tunua

Kong Christian X Land

Daneborg

Greenland Plain

Hopen

Bjørnøya

Barents Trough

Murmansk Rise

White Sea

Archangel

E

Sisimiut

Kong Frederik IX Land

Kangerlussuaq

Petermann Bjerg 2940m

Ittoqqortoormiit

Kong Oscar Fjord

Greenland Sea

Mohns Ridge

North Cape

Hammerfest

Fugløya Bank

Murmansk

Kola Peninsula

Northern Dvina

KITAA

TUNU

Kong Christian IX Land

Mont Forel 3360m

Gunnbjørn Fjeld 3700m

Kangertittivaq Kangikajik

JAN MAYEN (to Norway)

Jan Mayen Fracture Zone

Jan Mayen Ridge

Tromsø

Lapland

Onezhskoye Ozero

Frederik VI Kyst

Ammassalik

Kolbeinsey Ridge

Norwegian Basin

Norwegian Sea

Voring Plateau

NORWAY

SWEDEN

FINLAND

Ladozhskoye Ozero

E U R O P E

ARCTIC OCEAN

Limit of winter pack ice

Denmark Strait

Reykjanes Basin

Iceland Plateau

Akureyri

Arctic Circle

REYKJAVÍK

ICELAND

Reykjanes Ridge

Iceland Basin

Faeroe-Iceland Ridge

FAEROE ISLANDS (to Denmark)

Bill Baileys Bank

Faeroe-Shetland Trough

Shetland Islands

Orkney Islands

Hatton Ridge

OSLO

STOCKHOLM

Skagerrak

Gulf of Bothnia

HELSINKI

TALLINN

ESTONIA

Gulf of Finland

MOSCOW

RĪGA

LATVIA

Baltic Sea

Norwegian Trench

Polar bears range for great distances over the Arctic pack-ice in search of food. They are formidable hunters who live mainly on seals. In December and January, mother bears give birth to their cubs in dens dug deep beneath the snow.

198

198

125

125

125

94

41

1
2
3
16
17

X Y Z

207

GEOGRAPHICAL COMPARISONS

LARGEST COUNTRIES

Russian Federation	6,592,800 sq miles	(17,075,400 sq km)
Canada	3,851,788 sq miles	(9,976,140 sq km)
USA	3,681,760 sq miles	(9,372,610 sq km)
China	3,600,292 sq miles	(9,326,410 sq km)
Brazil	3,286,472 sq miles	(8,511,970 sq km)
Australia	2,967,893 sq miles	(7,686,850 sq km)
India	1,269,338 sq miles	(3,287,590 sq km)
Argentina	1,068,296 sq miles	(2,766,890 sq km)
Kazakhstan	1,049,150 sq miles	(2,717,300 sq km)
Sudan	967,493 sq miles	(2,505,815 sq km)

SMALLEST COUNTRIES

Vatican City	0.17 sq miles	(0.44 sq km)
Monaco	0.75 sq miles	(1.95 sq km)
Nauru	8.2 sq miles	(21.2 sq km)
Tuvalu	10 sq miles	(26 sq km)
San Marino	24 sq miles	(61 sq km)
Liechtenstein	62 sq miles	(160 sq km)
Marshall Islands	70 sq miles	(181 sq km)
Seychelles	108 sq miles	(280 sq km)
Maldives	116 sq miles	(300 sq km)
Malta	124 sq miles	(320 sq km)

LARGEST ISLANDS

(TO THE NEAREST 1000 - OR 100,000 FOR THE LARGEST)

Greenland	849,400 sq miles	(2,200,000 sq km)
New Guinea	312,000 sq miles	(808,000 sq km)
Borneo	292,222 sq miles	(757,050 sq km)
Madagascar	229,300 sq miles	(594,000 sq km)
Sumatra	202,300 sq miles	(524,000 sq km)
Baffin Island	183,800 sq miles	(476,000 sq km)
Honshu	88,800 sq miles	(230,000 sq km)
Britain	88,700 sq miles	(229,800 sq km)
Victoria Island	81,900 sq miles	(212,000 sq km)
Ellesmere Island	75,700 sq miles	(196,000 sq km)

RICHEST COUNTRIES

(GNP PER CAPITA, IN US$)

Luxembourg	45,360
Switzerland	44,350
Japan	40,940
Liechtenstein	40,000
Norway	34,510
Denmark	32,100
Singapore	30,550
Germany	28,870
Austria	28,110
USA	28,020

POOREST COUNTRIES

(GNP PER CAPITA, IN US$)

Mozambique	80
Somalia	100
Ethiopia	100
Eritrea	100
Congo (Zaire)	130
Chad	160
Tanzania	170
Burundi	170
Malawi	180
Rwanda	190
Sierra Leone	200
Niger	200

MOST POPULOUS COUNTRIES

China	1,255,100,000
India	935,700,000
USA	263,300,000
Indonesia	197,600,000
Brazil	165,800,000
Russian Federation	147,000,000
Pakistan	140,500,000
Japan	125,100,000
Bangladesh	120,400,000
Nigeria	111,700,000

LEAST POPULOUS COUNTRIES

Vatican City	1000
Tuvalu	9000
Nauru	10,000
Palau	16,200
San Marino	24,000
Liechtenstein	30,630
Monaco	31,000
St Kitts & Nevis	44,000
Marshall Islands	52,000
Andorra	64,000
Dominica	71,000
Seychelles	73,000

MOST DENSELY POPULATED COUNTRIES

Monaco	41,332 people per sq mile	(15,897 per sq km)
Singapore	11,894 people per sq mile	(4590 per sq km)
Vatican City	5890 people per sq mile	(2273 per sq km)
Malta	3239 people per sq mile	(1250 per sq km)
Maldives	2591 people per sq mile	(1000 per sq km)
Bangladesh	2330 people per sq mile	(899 per sq km)
Bahrain	2286 people per sq mile	(882 per sq km)
Barbados	1809 people per sq mile	(698 per sq km)
Taiwan	1682 people per sq mile	(649 per sq km)
Mauritius	1542 people per sq mile	(595 per sq km)

MOST SPARSELY POPULATED COUNTRIES

Australia	5 people per sq mile	(2 per sq km)
Mauritania	5 people per sq mile	(2 per sq km)
Mongolia	5 people per sq mile	(2 per sq km)
Namibia	5 people per sq mile	(2 per sq km)
Surinam	5 people per sq mile	(2 per sq km)
Botswana	8 people per sq mile	(3 per sq km)
Canada	8 people per sq mile	(3 per sq km)
Iceland	8 people per sq mile	(3 per sq km)
Libya	8 people per sq mile	(3 per sq km)
Guyana	10 people per sq mile	(4 per sq km)

MOST WIDELY SPOKEN LANGUAGES

1. Chinese (Mandarin)	6. Arabic
2. English	7. Bengali
3. Hindi	8. Portuguese
4. Spanish	9. Malay-Indonesian
5. Russian	10. French

COUNTRIES WITH THE MOST LAND BORDERS

14: China *(Afghanistan, Bhutan, Burma, India, Kazakhstan, Kyrgyzstan, Laos, Mongolia, Nepal, North Korea, Pakistan, Russian Federation, Tajikistan, Vietnam)*

14: Russian Federation *(Azerbaijan, Belarus, China, Estonia, Finland, Georgia, Kazakhstan, Latvia, Lithuania, Mongolia, North Korea, Norway, Poland, Ukraine)*

10: Brazil *(Argentina, Bolivia, Colombia, French Guiana, Guyana, Paraguay, Peru, Surinam, Uruguay, Venezuela)*

9: Congo (Zaire) *(Angola, Burundi, Central African Republic, Congo, Rwanda, Sudan, Tanzania, Uganda, Zambia)*

9: Germany *(Austria, Belgium, Czech Republic, Denmark, France, Luxembourg, Netherlands, Poland, Switzerland)*

9: Sudan *(Central African Republic, Chad, Congo (Zaire), Egypt, Eritrea, Ethiopia, Kenya, Libya, Uganda)*

8: Austria *(Czech Republic, Germany, Hungary, Italy, Liechtenstein, Slovakia, Slovenia, Switzerland)*
8: France *(Andorra, Belgium, Germany, Italy, Luxembourg, Monaco, Spain, Switzerland)*
8: Tanzania *(Burundi, Congo (Zaire), Kenya, Malawi, Mozambique, Rwanda, Uganda, Zambia)*
8: Turkey *(Armenia, Azerbaijan, Bulgaria, Georgia, Greece, Iran, Iraq, Syria)*
8: Zambia *(Angola, Botswana, Congo (Zaire), Malawi, Mozambique, Namibia, Tanzania, Zimbabwe)*

LONGEST RIVERS

Nile (NE Africa) . . . . 4160 miles . . . . (6695 km)
Amazon (South America) . . . . 4049 miles . . . .(6516 km)
Yangtze (China) . . . . 3915 miles . . . .(6299 km)
Mississippi/Missouri (USA) . . . . 3710 miles . . . .(5969 km)
Ob'-Irtysh (Russian Federation) . . . . 3461 miles . . . .(5570 km)
Yellow River (China) . . . . 3395 miles . . . .(5464 km)
Congo (Central Africa) . . . . 2900 miles . . . .(4667 km)
Mekong (Southeast Asia) . . . . 2749 miles . . . .(4425 km)
Lena (Russian Federation) . . . . 2734 miles . . . .(4400 km)
Mackenzie (Canada) . . . . 2640 miles . . . .(4250 km)
Yenisey (Russian Federation). . . . . 2541 miles . . . .(4090km)

HIGHEST MOUNTAINS
(HEIGHT ABOVE SEA LEVEL)

Everest . . . . .29,030 ft . . . .(8848 m)
K2 . . . . .28,253 ft . . . .(8611 m)
Kanchenjunga I . . . . .28,210 ft . . . .(8598 m)
Makalu I . . . . .27,767 ft . . . .(8463 m)
Cho Oyu . . . . .26,907 ft . . . .(8201 m)
Dhaulagiri I . . . . .26,796 ft . . . .(8167 m)
Manaslu I . . . . .26,783 ft . . . .(8163 m)
Nanga Parbat I . . . . .26,661 ft . . . .(8126 m)
Annapurna I . . . . .26,547 ft . . . .(8091 m)
Gasherbrum I . . . . .26,471 ft . . . .(8068 m)

LARGEST BODIES OF INLAND WATER
(WITH AREA AND DEPTH)

Caspian Sea . . . . .143,243 sq miles (371,000 sq km) . . . . .3215 ft (980 m)
Lake Superior . . . . .31,151 sq miles (83,270 sq km) . . . . .1289 ft (393 m)
Lake Victoria . . . . .26,828 sq miles (69,484 sq km) . . . . .328 ft (100 m)
Lake Huron . . . . . . .23,436 sq miles (60,700 sq km) . . . . .751 ft (229 m)
Lake Michigan . . . .22,402 sq miles (58,020 sq km) . . . . .922 ft (281 m)
Lake Tanganyika . .12,703 sq miles (32,900 sq km) . . . .4700 ft (1435 m)
Great Bear Lake . . .12,274 sq miles (31,790 sq km) . . . .1047 ft (319 m)
Lake Baikal . . . . . . .11,776 sq miles (30,500 sq km) . . . .5712 ft (1741 m)
Great Slave Lake . . .10,981 sq miles (28,440 sq km) . . . . .459 ft (140 m)
Lake Erie . . . . .9,915 sq miles (25,680 sq km) . . . . . .197 ft (60 m)

DEEPEST OCEAN FEATURES

Challenger Deep, Marianas Trench (Pacific). . . . . 36,201 ft . . . . .(11,034 m)
Vityaz III Depth, Tonga Trench (Pacific). . . . . 35,704 ft . . . . .(10,882 m)
Vityaz Depth, Kurile-Kamchatka Trench (Pacific) . . . 34,588 ft . . . . .(10,542 m)
Cape Johnson Deep, Philippine Trench (Pacific) . . . . . 34,441 ft . . . . .(10,497 m)
Kermadec Trench (Pacific) . . . . 32,964 ft . . . . .(10,047 m)
Ramapo Deep, Japan Trench (Pacific) . . . . 32,758 ft . . . . . .(9984 m)
Milwaukee Deep, Puerto Rico Trench (Atlantic) . . . . . 30,185 ft . . . . . .(9200 m)
Argo Deep, Torres Trench (Pacific). . . . . 30,070 ft . . . . . .(9165 m)
Meteor Depth, South Sandwich Trench (Atlantic) . . . . 30,000 ft . . . . . .(9144 m)
Planet Deep, New Britain Trench (Pacific) . . . . 29,988 ft . . . . . .(9140 m)

GREATEST WATERFALLS
(MEAN FLOW OF WATER)

Boyoma (Congo (Zaire)) . . . . .600,400 cu. ft/sec . .(17,000 cu.m/sec)
Khône (Laos/Cambodia) . . . . .410,000 cu. ft/sec . .(11,600 cu.m/sec)
Niagara (USA/Canada) . . . . .195,000 cu. ft/sec . .(5500 cu.m/sec)
Grande (Uruguay) .160,000 cu. ft/sec . .(4500 cu.m/sec)
Paulo Afonso (Brazil) . . . . .100,000 cu. ft/sec . .(2800 cu.m/sec)
Urubupunga (Brazil) . . . . .97,000 cu. ft/sec . .(2750 cu.m/sec)
Iguaçu (Argentina/Brazil) . . . . .62,000 cu. ft/sec . .(1700 cu.m/sec)
Maribondo (Brazil) .53,000 cu. ft/sec . .(1500 cu.m/sec)
Victoria (Zimbabwe) . . . . .39,000 cu. ft/sec . .(1100 cu.m/sec)
Kabalega (Uganda) .42,000 cu. ft/sec . .(1200 cu.m/sec)

Churchill (Canada) .35,000 cu. ft/sec . . . .(1000 cu.m/sec)
Cauvery (India) . . . . .33,000 cu. ft/sec . . . . .(900 cu.m/sec)

HIGHEST WATERFALLS

Angel (Venezuela) .3212 ft . . . .(979 m)
Tugela (South Africa) . . . . .3110 ft . . . .(948 m)
Utigard (Norway) . . . . .2625 ft . . . .(800 m)
Mongefossen (Norway) . . . . .2539 ft . . . .(774 m)
Mtarazi (Zimbabwe) . . . . .2500 ft . . . .(762 m)
Yosemite (USA) . . . . .2425 ft . . . .(739 m)
Ostre Mardola Foss (Norway) . . . . .2156 ft . . . .(657 m)
Tyssestrengane (Norway) . . . . .2119 ft . . . .(646 m)
***Cuquenan** (Venezuela) . . . . .2001 ft . . . .(610 m)
Sutherland (New Zealand) . . . . .1903 ft . . . .(580 m)
***Kjellfossen** (Norway) . . . . .1841 ft . . . .(561 m)

* indicates that the total height is a single leap

LARGEST DESERTS

Sahara . . . . .3,450,000 sq miles . . . . . .(9,065,000 sq km)
Gobi . . . . .500,000 sq miles . . . . .(1,295,000 sq km)
Ar Rub al Khali . . . . .289,600 sq miles . . . .(750,000 sq km)
Great Victorian . . . . .249,800 sq miles . . . .(647,000 sq km)
Sonoran . . . . .120,000 sq miles . . . .(311,000 sq km)
Kalahari . . . . .120,000 sq miles . . . .(310,800 sq km)
Kara Kum . . . . .115,800 sq miles . . . .(300,000 sq km)
Takla Makan . . . . .100,400 sq miles . . . .(260,000 sq km)
Namib . . . . .52,100 sq miles . . . .(135,000 sq km)
Thar . . . . .33,670 sq miles . . . .(130,000 sq km)

NB – Most of Antarctica is a polar desert, with only 50 mm of precipitation annually

HOTTEST INHABITED PLACES

Djibouti (Djibouti)	86° F	(30 °C)
Timbouctou (Mali)	84.7° F	(29.3 °C)
Tirunelveli (India)		
Tuticorin (India)		
Nellore (India)	84.5° F	(29.2 °C)
Santa Marta (Colombia)		
Aden (Yemen)	84° F	(28.9 °C)
Madurai (India)		
Niamey (Niger)		
Hodeida (Yemen)	83.8° F	(28.8 °C)
Ouagadougou (Burkina)		
Thanjavur (India)		
Tiruchchirappalli (India)		

DRIEST INHABITED PLACES

Aswân (Egypt) .0.02 in . . . .(0.5 mm)
Luxor (Egypt) . . . . .0.03 in . . . .(0.7 mm)
Arica (Chile) . . . . .0.04 in . . . .(1.1 mm)
Ica (Peru) . . . . .0.1 in . . . .(2.3 mm)
Antofagasta (Chile) . . . . .0.2 in . . . .(4.9 mm)
El Minya (Egypt) . . . . .0.2 in . . . .(5.1 mm)
Asyût (Egypt) . . . . .0.2 in . . . .(5.2 mm)
Callao (Peru) . . . . .0.5 in . . . .(12.0 mm)
Trujillo (Peru) . . . . .0.55 in . . . .(14.0 mm)
El Faiyûm (Egypt) . . . . .0.8 in . . . .(19.0 mm)

WETTEST INHABITED PLACES

Buenaventura (Colombia) . . . . .265 in . . . .(6743 mm)
Monrovia (Liberia) . . . . .202 in . . . .(5131 mm)
Pago Pago (American Samoa) . . . . .196 in . . . .(4990 mm)
Moulmein (Burma) . . . . .191 in . . . .(4852 mm)
Lae (Papua New Guinea) . . . . .183 in . . . .(4645 mm)
Baguio (Luzon Island, Philippines) . . . . . .180 in . . . .(4573 mm)
Sylhet (Bangladesh) . . . . .176 in . . . .(4457 mm)
Padang (Sumatra, Indonesia) . . . . .166 in . . . .(4225 mm)
Bogor (Java, Indonesia) . . . . .166 in . . . .(4225 mm)
Conakry (Guinea) . . . . .171 in . . . .(4341 mm)

THE TIME ZONES

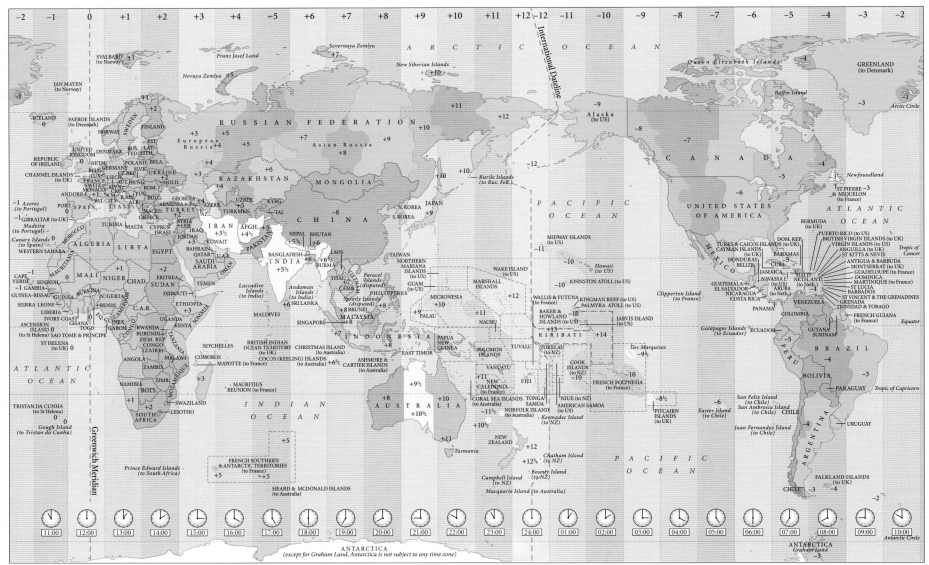

The numbers at the top of the map indicate the number of hours each time zone is ahead or behind Greenwich Mean Time (GMT). The clocks and 24-hour times given at the bottom of the map show the time in each time zone when it is 12:00 hours noon GMT.

TIME ZONES

The present system of international timekeeping divides the world into 24 time zones by means of 24 standard meridians of longitude, each 15° apart. Time is measured in each zone as so many hours ahead or behind the time at the Greenwich Meridian (GMT). Countries, or parts of countries, falling in the vicinity of each zone, adopt its time as shown on the map above. Therefore, using the map, when it is 12:00 noon GMT, it will be 2:00 pm in Zambia; similarly, when it is 4:30 pm. GMT, it will be 11:30 am in Peru.

GREENWICH MEAN TIME (GMT)

Greenwich Mean Time (or Universal Time, as it is more correctly called) has been the internationally accepted basis for calculating solar time – measured in relation to the Earth's rotation around the Sun – since 1884. Greenwich Mean Time is specifically the solar time at the site of the former Royal Observatory in the London Borough of Greenwich, United Kingdom. The Greenwich Meridian is an imaginary line around the world that runs through the North and South poles. It corresponds to 0° of longitude, which lies on this site at Greenwich. Time is measured around the world in relation to the official time along the Meridian.

STANDARD TIME

Standard time is the official time, designated by law, in any specific country or region. Standard

time was initiated in 1884, after it became apparent that the practice of keeping various systems of local time was causing confusion – particularly in the USA and Canada, where several railroad routes passed through scores of areas which calculated local time by different rules. The standard time of a particular region is calculated in reference to the longitudinal time zone in which it falls. In practice, these zones do not always match their longitudinal position; in some places the area of the zone has been altered in shape for the convenience of inhabitants, as can be seen in the map. For example, while Greenland occupies three time zones, the majority of the territory uses a standard time of -3 hours GMT. Similarly China, which spans five time zones, is standardized at -8 hours GMT.

THE INTERNATIONAL DATELINE

The International Dateline is an imaginary line that extends from pole to pole, and roughly corresponds to a line of 180° longitude for much of its length. This line is the arbitrary marker between calendar days. By moving from east to west across the line, a traveller will need to set their calendar back one day, while those travelling in the opposite direction will need to add a day. This is to compensate for the use of standard time around the world, which is based on the time at noon along the Greenwich Meridian, approximately halfway around the world. Wide deviations from 180° longitude occur through the

Bering Strait – to avoid dividing Siberia into two separate calendar days – and in the Pacific Ocean – to allow certain Pacific islands the same calendar day as New Zealand. Changes were made to the International Dateline in 1995 that made Millennium Island (formerly Caroline Island) in Kiribati the first land area to witness the beginning of the year 2000.

DAYLIGHT SAVING TIME

Also known as summer time, daylight saving is a system of advancing clocks in order to extend the waking day during periods of later daylight hours. This normally means advancing clocks by one hour in early spring, and reverting back to standard time in early autumn. The system of daylight saving is used throughout much of Europe, the USA, Australia, and many other countries worldwide, although there are no standardized dates for the changeover to summer time due to the differences in hours of daylight at different latitudes. Daylight saving was first introduced in certain countries during the First World War, to decrease the need for artificial light and heat – the system stayed in place after the war, as it proved practical. During the Second World War, some countries went so far as to keep their clocks an hour ahead of standard time continuously, and the UK temporarily introduced 'double summer time', which advanced clocks two hours ahead of standard time during the summer months.

COUNTRIES OF THE WORLD

THERE ARE CURRENTLY 192 independent countries in the world – more than at any previous time – and 59 dependencies. Antarctica is the only land area on Earth that is not officially part of, and does not belong to, any single country.

In 1950, the world comprised 82 countries. In the decades following, many more states came into being as they achieved independence from their former colonial rulers. Most recently, the breakup of the former Soviet Union in 1991, and the former Yugoslavia in 1992, swelled the ranks of independent states.

COUNTRY FACTFILE KEY

Formation Date of independence / date current borders were established
Population Total population / population density – based on total *land* area / percentage of urban-based population
Languages An asterisk (*) denotes the official language(s)
Calorie consumption Average number of calories consumed daily per person

---

AFGHANISTAN
Central Asia

Official name Islamic State of Afghanistan
Formation 1919 / 1919
Capital Kabul
Population 23.4 million / 93 people per sq mile (36 people per sq km) / 20%
Total area 251,770 sq miles (652,090 sq km)
Languages Persian*, Pashtu*, Dari, Uzbek, Turkmen
Religions Sunni Muslim 84%, Shi'a Muslim 15%, other 1%
Ethnic mix Pashto 38%, Tajik 25%, Hazara 19%, Uzbek 6%, other 12%
Government Islamic regime
Currency Afghani = 100 puls
Literacy rate 31%
Calorie consumption 1523 kilocalories

ALBANIA
Southeast Europe

Official name Republic of Albania
Formation 1912 / 1921
Capital Tiranë
Population 3.4 million / 321 people per sq mile (124 people per sq km) / 37%
Total area 11,100 sq miles (28,750 sq km)
Languages Albanian*, Greek, Macedonian
Religions Muslim 70%, Greek Orthodox 20%, Roman Catholic 10%
Ethnic mix Albanian 96%, Greek 2%, other (including Macedonian) 2%
Government Multiparty republic
Currency Lek = 100 qindars
Literacy rate 85%
Calorie consumption 2605 kilocalories

ALGERIA
North Africa

Official name Democratic and Popular Republic of Algeria
Formation 1962 / 1962
Capital Algiers
Population 27.9 million / 33 people per sq mile (13 people per sq km) / 56%
Total area 919,590 sq miles (2,381,740 sq km)
Languages Arabic*, Berber, French
Religions Muslim 99%, Christian and Jewish 1%
Ethnic mix Arab and Berber 99%, European 1%
Government Multiparty republic
Currency Dinar = 100 centimes
Literacy rate 60%
Calorie consumption 2897 kilocalories

ANDORRA
Southwest Europe

Official name Principality of Andorra
Formation 1278 / 1278
Capital Andorra la Vella
Population 65,000 / 359 people per sq mile (139 people per sq km) / 63%
Total area 181 sq miles (468 sq km)
Languages Catalan*, Spanish, French, Portuguese
Religions Roman Catholic 94%, other 6%
Ethnic mix Catalan 61%, Spanish Castilian 30%, other 9%
Government Parliamentary democracy
Currency French franc, Spanish peseta
Literacy rate 99%
Calorie consumption 3708 kilocalories

ANGOLA
Southern Africa

Official name Republic of Angola
Formation 1975 / 1975
Capital Luanda
Population 12 million / 25 people per sq mile (10 people per sq km) / 32%
Total area 481,551 sq miles (1,246,700 sq km)
Languages Portuguese*, Umbundu, Kimbundu, Kongo
Religions Roman Catholic / Protestant 64%, traditional beliefs 34%, other 2%
Ethnic mix Ovimbundu 37%, Mbundu 25%, Bakongo 13%, other 25%
Government Multiparty republic
Currency Readjusted kwanza = 100 lwei
Literacy rate 45%
Calorie consumption 1839 kilocalories

ANTIGUA & BARBUDA
West Indies

Official name Antigua and Barbuda
Formation 1981 / 1981
Capital St John's
Population 66,000 / 389 people per sq mile (150 people per sq km) / 36%
Total area 170 sq miles (440 sq km)
Languages English*, English patois
Religions Protestant 86%, Roman Catholic 10%, other 4%
Ethnic mix Black 98%, other 2%
Government Parliamentary democracy
Currency E. Caribbean dollar = 100 cents
Literacy rate 95%
Calorie consumption 2458 kilocalories

ARGENTINA
South America

Official name Republic of Argentina
Formation 1816 / 1816
Capital Buenos Aires
Population 36.1 million / 34 people per sq mile (13 people per sq km) / 87%
Total area 1,068,296 sq miles (2,766,890 sq km)
Languages Spanish*, Italian, English, German, French, Amerindian languages
Religions Roman Catholic 90%, Jewish 2%, other 8%
Ethnic mix European 85%, other (including *mestizo* and Indian) 15%
Government Multiparty republic
Currency Peso = 100 centavos
Literacy rate 96%
Calorie consumption 2880 kilocalories

ARMENIA
Southwest Asia

Official name Republic of Armenia
Formation 1991 / 1991
Capital Yerevan
Population 3.6 million / 313 people per sq mile (121 people per sq km) / 69%
Total area 1,505 sq miles (29,000 sq km)
Languages Armenian*, Azerbaijani, Russian, Kurdish
Religions Armenian Apostolic 90%, other Christian and Muslim 10%
Ethnic mix Armenian 93%, Azeri 3%, other 4%
Government Multiparty republic
Currency Dram = 100 louma
Literacy rate 99%
Calorie consumption NOT AVAILABLE

AUSTRALIA
Australasia & Oceania

Official name Commonwealth of Australia
Formation 1901 / 1901
Capital Canberra
Population 18.5 million / 6 people per sq mile (2 people per sq km) / 85%
Total area 2,967,893 sq miles (7,686,850 sq km)
Languages English*, Greek, Italian, Vietnamese, Aboriginal languages
Religions Protestant 38%, Roman Catholic 26%, other 36%
Ethnic mix European 95%, Asian 4%, Aboriginal and other 1%
Government Parliamentary democracy
Currency Australian dollar = 100 cents
Literacy rate 99%
Calorie consumption 3179 kilocalories

AUSTRIA
Central Europe

Official name Republic of Austria
Formation 1918 / 1919
Capital Vienna
Population 8.2 million / 257 people per sq mile (99 people per sq km) / 56%
Total area 32,375 sq miles (83,850 sq km)
Languages German*, Croatian, Slovene
Religions Roman Catholic 78%, Protestant 5%, other (including Jewish and Muslim) 17%
Ethnic mix German 93%, Croat, Slovene, Hungarian 6%, other 1%
Government Multiparty republic
Currency Austrian Schilling = 100 groschen
Literacy rate 99%
Calorie consumption 3497 kilocalories

AZERBAIJAN
Southwestern Asia

Official name Azerbaijani Republic
Formation 1991 / 1991
Capital Baku
Population 7.7 million / 230 people per sq mile (89 people per sq km) / 56%
Total area 33,436 sq miles (86,600 sq km)
Languages Azerbaijani*, Russian, Armenian
Religions Muslim 83%, Armenian Apostolic and Russian Orthodox 17%
Ethnic mix Azeri 83%, Armenian 6%, Russian 5%, Daghestani 3%, other 3%
Government Multiparty republic
Currency Manat = 100 gopik
Literacy rate 96%
Calorie consumption NOT AVAILABLE

BAHAMAS
West Indies

Official name Commonwealth of the Bahamas
Formation 1973 / 1973
Capital Nassau
Population 293,000 / 76 people per sq mile (29 people per sq km) / 87%
Total area 5,359 sq miles (13,880 sq km)
Languages English*, English Creole, Religions Protestant 64%, Roman Catholic 19%, other 17%
Ethnic mix Black 85%, White 15%
Government Parliamentary democracy
Currency Bahamian dollar = 100 cents
Literacy rate 96%
Calorie consumption 2,624 kilocalories

BAHRAIN
Southwestern Asia

Official name State of Bahrain
Formation 1971 / 1971
Capital Manama
Population 594,000 / 2,262 people per sq mile (874 people per sq km) / 90%
Total area 263 sq miles (680 sq km)
Languages Arabic*, English, Urdu
Religions Muslim (Shi'a majority) 85%, Christian 7%, other 8%
Ethnic mix Bahraini 70%, Iranian, Indian, Pakistani 24%, other Arab 4%, European 2%
Government Monarchy with Consultative Council
Currency Bahrain dinar = 1,000 fils
Literacy rate 86%
Calorie consumption NOT AVAILABLE

BANGLADESH
Southern Asia

Official name People's Republic of Bangladesh
Formation 1971 / 1971
Capital Dhaka
Population 124 million / 2,400 people per sq mile (926 people per sq km) / 18%
Total area 55,598 sq miles (143,998 sq km)
Languages Bengali*, Urdu, Chakma, Marma, Garo, Khasi, Santhali, Tripuri, Mro
Religions Muslim 87%, Hindu 12%, other 1%
Ethnic mix Bengali 98%, other 2%
Government Multiparty republic
Currency Taka = 100 paisa
Literacy rate 40%
Calorie consumption 2,019 kilocalories

BARBADOS
West Indies

Official name Barbados
Formation 1966 / 1966
Capital Bridgetown
Population 263,000 / 1,584 people per sq mile (612 people per sq km) / 47%
Total area 166 sq miles (430 sq km)
Languages English*, English Creole
Religions Protestant 55%, Roman Catholic 4%, other 41%
Ethnic mix Black 80%, mixed 15%, White 4%, other 1%
Government Parliamentary democracy
Currency Barbados dollar = 100 cents
Literacy rate 97%
Calorie consumption 3207 kilocalories

BELARUS (BELORUSSIA)
Eastern Europe

Official name Republic of Belarus
Formation 1991 / 1991
Capital Minsk
Population 10.3 million / 129 people per sq mile (50 people per sq km) / 68%
Total area 80,154 sq miles (207,600 sq km)
Languages Belorussian*, Russian*
Religions Russian Orthodox 60%, Roman Catholic 8%, other 32%
Ethnic mix Belorussian 78%, Russian 13%, Polish 4%, other 5%
Government Multiparty republic
Currency Belorussian rouble = 100 kopeks
Literacy rate 99%
Calorie consumption NOT AVAILABLE

BELGIUM
Northwest Europe

Official name Kingdom of Belgium
Formation 1830 / 1919
Capital Brussels
Population 10.2 million / 805 people per sq mile (311 people per sq km) / 97%
Total area 12,780 sq miles (33,100 sq km)
Languages Flemish*, French*, German*
Religions Roman Catholic 88%, other 12%
Ethnic mix Fleming 58%, Walloon 33%, other 9%
Government Constitutional monarchy
Currency Belgian franc = 100 centimes
Literacy rate 99%
Calorie consumption: 3681 kilocalories

BELIZE
Central America

Official name Belize
Formation 1981 / 1981
Capital Belmopan
Population 200,000 / 23 people per sq mile (9 people per sq km) / 47%
Total area 8865 sq miles (22,960 sq km)
Languages English*, English Creole, Spanish
Religions Christian 87%, other 13%
Ethnic mix *Mestizo* 44%, Creole 30%, Maya 11%, Asian 4%, Garifuna 7%, other 4%
Government Parliamentary democracy
Currency Belizean dollar = 100 cents
Literacy rate 75%
Calorie consumption 2662 kilocalories

BENIN
West Africa

Official name Republic of Benin
Formation 1960 / 1960
Capital Porto-Novo
Population 5.9 million / 138 people per sq mile (53 people per sq km) / 31%
Total area 43,480 sq miles (112,620 sq km)
Languages French*, Fon, Bariba, Yoruba, Adja
Religions Traditional beliefs 70%, Muslim 15%, Christian 15%
Ethnic mix Fon 39%, Yoruba 12%, Adja 10%, other 39%
Government Multiparty republic
Currency CFA franc = 100 centimes
Literacy rate 34%
Calorie consumption 2532 kilocalories

BHUTAN
Southeast Asia

Official name Kingdom of Bhutan
Formation 1656 / 1865
Capital Thimphu
Population 1.9 million / 105 people per sq mile (40 people per sq km) / 6%
Total area 18,147 sq miles (47,000 sq km)
Languages Dzongkha*, Nepali, Assamese
Religions Mahayana Buddhist 70%, Hindu 24%, Muslim 5%, other 1%
Ethnic mix Bhutia 61%, Gurung 15%, Assamese 13%, other 11%
Government Constitutional monarchy
Currency Ngultrum = 100 chetrum
Literacy rate 44%
Calorie consumption 2553 kilocalories

BOLIVIA
South America

Official name Republic of Bolivia
Formation 1825 / 1938
Capitals Sucre (official)/La Paz (administrative)
Population 8 million / 19 people per sq mile (7 people per sq km) / 61%
Total area 424,162 sq miles (1,098,580 sq km)
Languages Spanish*, Quechua*, Aymará*
Religions Roman Catholic 93%, other 7%
Ethnic mix Quechua 37%, Aymará 32%, mixed 13%, European 10%, other 8%
Government Multiparty republic
Currency Boliviano = 100 centavos
Literacy rate 84%
Calorie consumption 2094 kilocalories

BOSNIA & HERZEGOVINA
Southeast Europe

Official name Republic of Bosnia and Herzegovina
Formation 1992 / 1992
Capital Sarajevo
Population 4 million / 203 people per sq mile (78 people per sq km) / 49%
Total area 19,741 sq miles (51,130 sq km)
Languages Serbian*, Croatian*
Religions Muslim 40%, Serbian Orthodox 31%, Roman Catholic 15%, other 14%
Ethnic mix Bosnian 44%, Serb 31%, Croat 17%, other 8%
Government Multiparty republic
Currency Maraka = 100 pfenniga
Literacy rate 93%
Calorie consumption NOT AVAILABLE

BOTSWANA
Southern Africa

Official name Republic of Botswana
Formation 1966 / 1966
Capital Gaborone
Population 1.6 million / 7 people per sq mile (3 people per sq km) / 28%
Total area 224,600 sq miles (581,730 sq km)
Languages English*, Tswana, Shona, San
Religions Traditional beliefs 50%, Christian 50%
Ethnic mix Tswana 98%, other 2%
Government Multiparty republic
Currency Pula = 100 thebe
Literacy rate 74%
Calorie consumption 2266 kilocalories

BRAZIL
South America

Official name Federative Republic of Brazil
Formation 1822 / 1889
Capital Brasília
Population 165.2 million / 51 people per sq mile (20 people per sq km) / 78%
Total area 3,286,472 sq miles (8,511,970 sq km)
Languages Portuguese*, German, Italian
Religions Roman Catholic 89%, other 11%
Ethnic mix White (Portuguese, Italian, German, Japanese) 66%, mixed 22%, Black 12%
Government Multiparty republic
Currency Real = 100 centavos
Literacy rate 84%
Calorie consumption 2824 kilocalories

BRUNEI
Southeast Asia

Official name Sultanate of Brunei
Formation 1984 / 1984
Capital Bandar Seri Begawan
Population 313,000 / 154 people per sq mile (57 people per sq km) / 59%
Total area 2228 sq miles (5770 sq km)
Languages Malay*, English, Chinese
Religions Muslim 63%, Buddhist 14%, Christian 10%, other 13%
Ethnic mix Malay 67%, Chinese 16%, other 17%
Government Absolute monarchy
Currency Brunei dollar = 100 cents
Literacy rate 90%
Calorie consumption 2745 kilocalories

BULGARIA
Southeast Europe

Official name Republic of Bulgaria
Formation 1908 / 1947
Capital Sofia
Population 8.4 million / 197 people per sq mile (76 people per sq km) / 71%
Total area 42,822 sq miles (110,910 sq km)
Languages Bulgarian*, Turkish, Macedonian, Romany, Armenian, Russian
Religions Christian 85%, Muslim 13%, Jewish 1%, other 1%
Ethnic mix Bulgarian 85%, Turkish 9%, Macedonian 3%, Romany 3%
Government Multiparty republic
Currency Lev = 100 stoninki
Literacy rate 98%
Calorie consumption 2831 kilocalories

BURKINA
West Africa

Official name Burkina Faso
Formation 1960 / 1960
Capital Ouagadougou
Population 11.4 million / 108 people per sq mile (42 people per sq km) / 27%
Total area 105,870 sq miles (274,200 sq km)
Languages French*, Mossi, Fulani
Religions Traditional beliefs 55%, Muslim 35%, Christian 10%
Ethnic mix Mossi 45%, Mande 10%, Fulani 10%, other 35%
Government Multiparty republic
Currency CFA franc = 100 centimes
Literacy rate 21%
Calorie consumption 2387 kilocalories

BURMA (MYANMAR)
Southeast Asia

Official name Union of Myanmar
Formation 1948 / 1948
Capital Rangoon
Population 47.6 million / 187 people per sq mile (72 people per sq km) / 26%
Total area 261,200 sq miles (676,550 sq km)
Languages Burmese*, Karen, Shan, Mon
Religions Buddhist 87%, Christian 6%, Muslim 4%, other 3%
Ethnic mix Burman 68%, Shan 9%, Karen 6%, Rakhine 4%, other 13%
Government Military regime
Currency Kyat = 100 pyas
Literacy rate 84%
Calorie consumption 2598 kilocalories

BURUNDI
Central Africa

Official name Republic of Burundi
Formation 1962 / 1962
Capital Bujumbura
Population 6.6 million / 666 people per sq mile (257 people per sq km) / 8%
Total area 10,750 sq miles (27,830 sq km)
Languages Kirundi*, French*, Swahili
Religions Christian 68%, Traditional beliefs 32%
Ethnic mix Hutu 85%, Tutsi 14%, Twa 1%
Government Multiparty republic
Currency Burundi franc = 100 centimes
Literacy rate 45%
Calorie consumption 1941 kilocalories

CAMBODIA
Southeast Asia

Official name Kingdom of Cambodia
Formation 1953 / 1953
Capital Phnom Penh
Population 10.8 million / 158 people per sq mile (61 people per sq km) /21%
Total area 69,000 sq miles (181,040 sq km)
Languages Khmer*, French, Chinese, Vietnamese
Religions Theravada Buddhist 88%, Muslim 2%, other 10%
Ethnic mix Khmer 94%, Chinese 4%, other 2%
Government Constitutional monarchy
Currency Riel = 100 sen
Literacy rate 66%
Calorie consumption 2021 kilocalories

CAMEROON
Central Africa

Official name Republic of Cameroon
Formation 1960 / 1961
Capital Yaoundé
Population 14.3 million / 80 people per sq mile (31 people per sq km) / 45%
Total area 183,570 miles (475,440 sq km)
Languages English*, French*, Fang, Bulu, Yaundé, Duala
Religions Traditional beliefs 25%, Christian 53%, Muslim 22%
Ethnic mix Bamileke and Manum 20%, Fang 19%, other 61%
Government Multiparty republic
Currency CFA franc = 100 centimes
Literacy rate 72%
Calorie consumption 1981 kilocalories

CANADA
North America

Official name Canada
Formation 1867 / 1949
Capital Ottawa
Population 30.2 million / 8 people per sq mile (3 people per sq km) / 77%
Total area 3,851,788 sq miles (9,976,140 sq km)
Languages English*, French*, Chinese, Italian, German, Portuguese, Inuit
Religions Roman Catholic 47%, Protestant 41%, other 12%
Ethnic mix British origin 44%, French origin 25%, other European 20%, other 11%
Government Parliamentary democracy
Currency Canadian dollar = 100 cents
Literacy rate 99%
Calorie consumption 3094 kilocalories

CAPE VERDE
Atlantic Ocean

Official Name Republic of Cape Verde
Formation 1975 / 1975
Capital Praia
Population 417,000 / 268 people per sq mile (103 people per sq km) / 54%
Total area 1556 sq miles (4030 sq km)
Languages Portuguese*, Creole
Religions Roman Catholic 98%, Protestant 2%
Ethnic mix Creole 60%, African 30%, other 10%
Government Multiparty republic
Currency Cape Verde escudo = 100 centavos
Literacy rate 71%
Calorie consumption 2805 kilocalories

CENTRAL AFRICAN REPUBLIC
Central Africa

Official name Central African Republic
Formation 1960 / 1960
Capital Bangui
Population 3.5 million / 15 people per sq mile (6 people per sq km) / 39%
Total area 240,530 sq miles (622,980 sq km)
Languages French*, Sango, Banda, Gbaya
Religions Christian 50%, traditional beliefs 27%, Muslim 15%, other 8%
Ethnic mix Baya 34%, Banda 27%, Mandjia 21%, other 18%
Government Multiparty republic
Currency CFA franc = 100 centimes
Literacy rate 42%
Calorie consumption 1690 kilocalories

CHAD
Central Africa

Official name Republic of Chad
Formation 1960 / 1960
Capital N'Djamena
Population 6.9 million / 14 people per sq mile (5 people per sq km) / 21%
Total area 495,752 sq miles (1,284,000 sq km)
Languages French*, Sara, Maba
Religions Muslim 50%, traditional beliefs 43%, Christian 7%
Ethnic mix Bagirmi, Sara and Kreish 31%, Sudanic Arab 26%, Teda 7%, other 36%
Government Multiparty republic
Currency CFA franc = 100 centimes
Literacy rate 50%
Calorie consumption 1989 kilocalories

CHILE
South America

Official name Republic of Chile
Formation 1818 / 1883
Capital Santiago
Population 14.8 million / 51 people per sq mile (20 people per sq km) / 84%
Total area 292,258 sq miles (756,950 sq km)
Languages Spanish*, Amerindian languages
Religions Roman Catholic 80%, Protestant and other 20%
Ethnic mix *Mestizo* and European 90%, Amerindian 10%
Government Multiparty republic
Currency Chilean peso = 100 centavos
Literacy rate 95%
Calorie consumption 2582 kilocalories

CHINA
East Asia

Official name People's Republic of China
Formation 1949 / 1999
Capital Beijing
Population 1.3 billion / 349 people per sq mile (135 people per sq km) / 30%
Total area 3,628,166 sq miles (9,396,960 sq km)
Languages Mandarin*, Wu, Cantonese, Hsiang, Min, Hakka, Kan
Religions Non-religious 59%, traditional beliefs 20%, Buddhist 6%, other 15%
Ethnic mix Han 93%, Zhaung 1%, other 6%
Government Single-party republic
Currency Yuan = 10 jiao
Literacy rate 84%
Calorie consumption 2727 kilocalories

COLOMBIA
South America

Official name Republic of Colombia
Formation 1819 / 1922
Capital Bogotá
Population 37.7 million / 94 people per sq mile (36 people per sq km) / 73%
Total area 439,733 sq miles (1,138,910 sq km)
Languages Spanish*, Amerindian languages, English Creole
Religions Roman Catholic 95%, other 5%
Ethnic mix *Mestizo* 58%, White 20%, European-African 14%, other 8%
Government Multiparty republic
Currency Colombian peso = 100 centavos
Literacy rate 91%
Calorie consumption 2677 kilocalories

COMOROS
Indian Ocean

Official name Federal Islamic Republic of the Comoros
Formation 1975 / 1975
Capital Moroni
Population 672,000 / 780 people per sq mile (301 people per sq km) / 29%
Total area 861 sq miles (2230 sq km)
Languages Arabic*, French*, Comoran
Religions Muslim 98%, Roman Catholic 1%, other 1%
Ethnic mix Comorian 96%, other 4%
Government Islamic republic
Currency Comoros franc = 100 centimes
Literacy rate 55%
Calorie consumption 1897 kilocalories

CONGO
Central Africa

Official name Republic of the Congo
Formation 1960 / 1960
Capital Brazzaville
Population 2.8 million / 21 people per sq km (8 people per sq km) / 59%
Total area 132,040 sq miles (342,000 sq km)
Languages French*, Kongo, Teke, Lingala
Religions Roman Catholic 50%, traditional beliefs 48%, other 2%
Ethnic mix Bakongo 48%, Sangha 20%, Teke 17%, Mbochi 12%, other 3%
Government Multiparty republic
Currency CFA franc = 100 centimes
Literacy rate 77%
Calorie consumption 2296 kilocalories

CONGO, DEM. REP. (ZAIRE)
Central Africa

Official name Democratic Republic of the Congo
Formation 1960 / 1960
Capital Kinshasa
Population 49.2 million / 56 people per sq mile (22 people per sq km) / 29%
Total area 905,563 sq miles (2,345,410 sq km)
Languages French*, Kiswahili, Tshiluba, Lingala
Religions Traditional beliefs 50%, Roman Catholic 37%, Protestant 13%
Ethnic mix Bantu 23%, Hamitic 23%, other 54%
Government Single-party republic
Currency Congolese franc = 100 centimes
Literacy rate 77%
Calorie consumption 2060 kilocalories

COSTA RICA
Central America

Official name Republic of Costa Rica
Formation 1821 / 1838
Capital San José
Population 3.7 million / 188 people per sq mile (72 people per sq km) / 50%
Total area 19,730 miles (51,100 sq km)
Languages Spanish*, English Creole, Bribri, Cabecar
Religions Roman Catholic 76%, other 24%
Ethnic mix White and *mestizo* 96%, Black 2%, Amerindian 2%
Government Multiparty republic
Currency Costa Rica colón = 100 centimos
Literacy rate 95%
Calorie consumption 2883 kilocalories

CROATIA
Southeast Europe

Official name Republic of Croatia
Formation 1991 / 1991
Capital Zagreb
Population 4.5 million / 206 people per sq mile (80 people per sq km) / 64%
Total area 21,830 sq miles (56,540 sq km)
Languages Croatian*, Serbian, Hungarian (Magyar), Slovenian
Religions Roman Catholic 76%, Eastern Orthodox 11%, Protestant 1%, Muslim 1%, other 10%
Ethnic mix Croat 80%, Serb 12%, Hungarian, Slovenian, other 8%
Government Multiparty republic
Currency Kuna = 100 lipa
Literacy rate 98%
Calorie consumption NOT AVAILABLE

CUBA
West Indies

Official name Republic of Cuba
Formation 1902 / 1898
Capital Havana
Population 11.1 million / 259 people per sq mile (100 people per sq km) / 76%
Total area 42,803 sq miles (110,860 sq km)
Languages Spanish*, English, French
Religions Non-religious 55%, Roman Catholic 40%, other 5%
Ethnic mix White 66%, European-African 22%, Black 12%
Government Socialist republic
Currency Cuban peso = 100 centavos
Literacy rate 96%
Calorie consumption 2833 kilocalories

CYPRUS
Southeast Europe

Official name Republic of Cyprus
Formation 1960 / 1983
Capital Nicosia
Population 766,000 / 218 people per sq mile (84 people per sq km) / 54%
Total area 3572 sq miles (9251 sq km)
Languages Greek*, Turkish, English
Religions Greek Orthodox 77%, Muslim 18%, other 5%
Ethnic mix Greek 77%, Turkish 18%, other (mainly British) 5%
Government Multiparty republic
Currency Cyprus pound / Turkish lira
Literacy rate 96%
Calorie consumption 3779 kilocalories

CZECH REPUBLIC
Central Europe

Official name Czech Republic
Formation 1993 / 1993
Capital Prague
Population 10.2 million / 335 people per sq mile (129 people per sq km) / 65%
Total area 30,260 sq miles (78,370 sq km)
Languages Czech*, Slovak, Romany, Hungarian (Magyar)
Religions Non-religious 40%, Roman Catholic 39%, other 21%
Ethnic mix Czech 85%, Moravian 13%, other 2%
Government Multiparty republic
Currency Czech koruna = 100 halura
Literacy rate 99%
Calorie consumption 3156 kilocalories

DENMARK
Northern Europe

Official name Kingdom of Denmark
Formation 950 / 1920
Capital Copenhagen
Population 5.3 million / 324 people per sq mile (125 people per sq km) / 85%
Total area 16,629 sq miles (43,069 sq km)
Languages Danish*, Faeroese, Inuit
Religions Evangelical Lutheran 89% other Christian 11%
Ethnic mix Danish 96%, Faeroese & Inuit 1%, other 3%
Government Constitutional monarchy
Currency Danish krone = 100 øre
Literacy rate 99%
Calorie consumption 3664 kilocalories

DJIBOUTI
East Africa

Official name Republic of Djibouti
Formation 1977 / 1977
Capital Djibouti
Population 652,000 / 73 people per sq mile (28 people per sq km) /83%
Total area 8958 sq miles (23,200 sq km)
Languages Arabic*, French*, Somali, Afar
Religions Christian 87%, other 13%
Ethnic mix Issa 60%, Afar 35%, other 5%
Government Multiparty republic
Currency Djibouti franc = 100 centimes
Literacy rate 48%
Calorie consumption 2338 kilocalories

DOMINICA
West Indies

Official name Commonwealth of Dominica
Formation 1978 / 1978
Capital Roseau
Population 74,000 / 256 people per sq mile (99 people per sq km)/ 69%
Total area 290 sq miles (750 sq km)
Languages English*, French Creole
Religions Roman Catholic 77%, Protestant 15%, other 8%
Ethnic mix Black 98%, Amerindian 2%
Government Multiparty republic
Currency East Caribbean dollar = 100 cents
Literacy rate 94%
Calorie consumption 2778 kilocalories

DOMINICAN REPUBLIC
West Indies

Official name Dominican Republic
Formation 1865 / 1865
Capital Santo Domingo
Population 8.2 million / 439 people per sq mile (169 people per sq km) / 65%
Total area 18,815 sq miles (48,730 sq km)
Languages Spanish*, French Creole
Religions Roman Catholic 92%, other 8%
Ethnic mix European-African 73%, White 16%, Black 11%
Government Multiparty republic
Currency Dom. Republic peso = 100 centavos
Literacy rate 83%
Calorie consumption 2286 kilocalories

ECUADOR
South America

Official name Republic of Ecuador
Formation 1830 / 1941
Capital Quito
Population 12.2 million / 114 people per sq mile (44 people per sq km) / 58%
Total area 109,483 sq miles (283,560 sq km)
Languages Spanish*, Quechua, other Amerindian languages
Religions Roman Catholic 95%, other 5%
Ethnic mix *Mestizo* 55%, Amerindian 25%, Black 10%, White 10%
Government Multiparty republic
Currency Sucre = 100 centavos
Literacy rate 91%
Calorie consumption 2583 kilocalories

EGYPT
North Africa

Official name Arab Republic of Egypt
Formation 1936 / 1982
Capital Cairo
Population 65.7 million / 171 people per sq mile (66 people per sq km) / 45%
Total area 386,660 sq miles (1,001,450 sq km)
Languages Arabic*, French, English, Berber, Greek, Armenian
Religions Muslim 94%, other 6%
Ethnic mix Eastern Hamitic 90%, other (including Greek, Armenian) 10%
Government Multiparty republic
Currency Egyptian pound = 100 piastres
Literacy rate 53%
Calorie consumption 3335 kilocalories

EL SALVADOR
Central America

Official name Republic of El Salvador
Formation 1856 / 1838
Capital San Salvador
Population 6.1 million / 763 people per sq mile (294 people per sq km) /45%
Total area 8124 sq miles (21,040 sq km)
Languages Spanish*, Nahua
Religions Roman Catholic 80%, other 20%
Ethnic mix *Mestizo* 89%, Amerindian 10%, White 1%
Government Multiparty republic
Currency Salvadorean colón = 100 centavos
Literacy rate 73%
Calorie consumption 2663 kilocalories

EQUATORIAL GUINEA
Central Africa

Official name Republic of Equatorial Guinea
Formation 1968 / 1968
Capital Malabo
Population 430,000 / 40 people per sq mile (15 people per sq km) / 42%
Total area 10,830 sq miles (28,050 sq km)
Languages Spanish*, Fang, Bubi
Religions Christian 90%, other 10%
Ethnic mix Fang 72%, Bubi 14%, Duala 3%, other 11%
Government Multiparty republic
Currency CFA franc = 100 centimes
Literacy rate 80%
Calorie consumption NOT AVAILABLE

ERITREA
East Africa

Official name State of Eritrea
Formation 1993 / 1993
Capital Asmara
Population 3.5 million / 97 people per sq mile (37 people per sq km) / 17%
Total area 36,170 sq miles (93,680 sq km)
Languages Tigrinya*, Arabic*, Tigre
Religions Christian 45%, Muslim 45%, other 10%
Ethnic mix Nine main ethnic groups
Government Provisional military government
Currency Nakfa = 100 cents
Literacy rate 25%
Calorie consumption 1610 kilocalories

ESTONIA
Northeast Europe

Official name Republic of Estonia
Formation 1991 / 1991
Capital Tallinn
Population 1.4 million / 80 people per sq mile (31 people per sq km) / 73%
Total area 17,423 sq miles (45,125 sq km)
Languages Estonian*, Russian
Religions Evangelical Lutheran 98%, Eastern Orthodox, Baptist 2%
Ethnic mix Russian 62%, Estonian 30%, Ukrainian 3%, other 5%
Government Multiparty republic
Currency Kroon = 100 cents
Literacy rate 99%
Calorie consumption NOT AVAILABLE

ETHIOPIA
East Africa

Official name Federal Democratic Republic of Ethiopia
Formation 1896 / 1993
Capital Addis Ababa
Population 62.1 million / 146 people per sq mile (56 people per sq km) / 13%
Total area 435,605 sq miles (1,128,221 sq km)
Languages Amharic*, English, Arabic
Religions Muslim 40%, Christian 40%, Traditional beliefs 15%, other 5%
Ethnic mix Oromo 40%, Amhara 25%, Sidamo 9%, Somali 6%, other 20%
Government Multiparty republic
Currency Ethiopian birr = 100 cents
Literacy rate 35%
Calorie consumption 1610 kilocalories

FIJI
Australasia & Oceania

Official name Sovereign Democratic Republic of Fiji
Formation 1970 / 1970
Capital Suva
Population 822,000 / 117 people per sq mile (45 people per sq km) / 40%
Total area 7054 sq miles (18,270 sq km)
Languages English*, Fijian, Hindu, Urdu
Religions Christian 46%, Hindu 38%, Muslim 8%, other 8%
Ethnic mix Native Fijian 49%, Indo-Fijian 46%, other 5%
Government Multiparty republic
Currency Fiji dollar = 100 cents
Literacy rate 92%
Calorie consumption 3089 kilocalories

FINLAND
Northern Europe

Official name Republic of Finland
Formation 1917 / 1947
Capital Helsinki
Population 5.2 million / 44 people per sq mile (17 people per sq km) / 63%
Total area 130,552 sq miles (338,130 sq km)
Languages Finnish*, Swedish*, Lappish
Religions Evangelical Lutheran 89%, Finnish Orthodox 1%, other 10%
Ethnic mix Finnish 93%, Swedish 6%, other (including Sami) 1%
Government Multiparty republic
Currency Markka = 100 pennia
Literacy rate 99%
Calorie consumption 3018 kilocalories

FRANCE
Western Europe

Official name French Republic
Formation 486 / 1919
Capital Paris
Population 58.7 million / 276 people per sq mile (107 people per sq km) / 73%
Total area 212,930 sq miles (551,500 sq km)
Languages French*, Provençal, Breton, Catalan, Basque
Religions Roman Catholic 88%, Muslim 8%, other 4%
Ethnic mix French 90%, North African 6%, German 2%, Breton 1%, other 1%
Government Multiparty republic
Currency Franc = 100 centimes
Literacy rate 99%
Calorie consumption 3633 kilocalories

GABON
Central Africa

Official name Gabonese Republic
Formation 1960 / 1960
Capital Libreville
Population 1.2 million / 12 people per sq mile (5 people per sq km) / 50%
Total area 103,347 sq miles (267,670 sq km)
Languages French*, Fang, Punu, Sira, Nzebi, Mpongwe
Religions Christian 96%, Muslim 2%, other 2%
Ethnic mix Fang 3%, Eshira 25%, other Bantu 25%, European and other African 9%
Government Multiparty republic
Currency CFA franc = 100 centimes
Literacy rate 66%
Calorie consumption 2500 kilocalories

GAMBIA
West Africa

Official name Republic of the Gambia
Formation 1965 / 1965
Capital Banjul
Population 1.9 million / 309 people per sq mile (119 people per sq km) / 26%
Total area 4363 sq miles (11,300 sq km)
Languages English*, Mandinka, Fulani, Wolof, Diola, Soninke
Religions Muslim 85%, Christian 9%, Traditional beliefs 6%
Ethnic mix Mandingo 42%, Fulani 18% Wolof 16%, Jola 10%, Serahull 9%, other 5%
Government Multiparty republic
Currency Dalasi = 100 butut
Literacy rate 33%
Calorie consumption 2360 kilocalories

GEORGIA
Southwest Asia

Official name Republic of Georgia
Formation 1991 / 1991
Capital Tbilisi
Population 5.4 million / 201 people per sq mile (77 people per sq km) / 58%
Total area 26,911 sq miles (69,700 sq km)
Languages Georgian*, Russian
Religions Georgian Orthodox 70%, Russian Orthodox 10%, other 20%
Ethnic mix Georgian 70%, Armenian 8%, Russian 6%, Azeri 6%, other 10%
Government Multiparty republic
Currency Lari = 100 tetri
Literacy rate 99%
Calorie consumption NOT AVAILABLE

GERMANY
Northern Europe

Official name Federal Republic of Germany
Formation 1871 / 1990
Capital Berlin
Population 82.4 million / 611 people per sq mile (236 people per sq km) / 87%
Total area 137,800 sq miles (356,910 sq km)
Languages German*, Sorbian, Turkish
Religions Protestant 36%, Roman Catholic 35%, Muslim 2%, other 27%
Ethnic mix German 92%, other 8%
Government Multiparty republic
Currency Deutsche Mark = 100 pfennigs
Literacy rate 99%
Calorie consumption 3344 kilocalories

GHANA
West Africa

Official name Republic of Ghana
Formation 1957 / 1957
Capital Accra
Population 18.9 million / 213 people per sq mile (82 people per sq km) / 36%
Total area 92,100 sq miles (238,540 sq km)
Languages English*, Akan, Mossi, Ewe
Religions Traditional beliefs 38%, Christian 43%, Muslim 11%, other 8%
Ethnic mix Akan 52%, Mossi 15%, Ewe 12%, Ga 8%, other 13%
Government Multiparty republic
Currency Cedi = 100 pesewas
Literacy rate 66%
Calorie consumption 2199 kilocalories

GREECE
Southeast Europe

Official name Hellenic Republic
Formation 1829 / 1947
Capital Athens
Population 10.6 million / 210 people per sq mile (81 people per sq km) / 65%
Total area 50,961 sq miles (131,990 sq km)
Languages Greek*, Turkish, Albanian, Macedonian
Religions Greek Orthodox 98%, Muslim 1%, other 1%
Ethnic mix Greek 98%, other 2%
Government Multiparty republic
Currency Drachma = 100 lepta
Literacy rate 96%
Calorie consumption 3815 kilocalories

GRENADA
West Indies

Official name Grenada
Formation 1974 / 1974
Capital St George's
Population 98,600 / 751 people per sq mile (290 people per sq km) / 37%
Total area 131 sq miles (340 sq km)
Languages English*, English Creole
Religions Roman Catholic 68%, Anglican 17%, other 15%
Ethnic mix Black 84%, European-African 13%, South Asian 3%
Government Parliamentary democracy
Currency East Caribbean dollar = 100 cents
Literacy rate 98%
Calorie consumption 2402 kilocalories

GUATEMALA
Central America

Official name Republic of Guatemala
Formation 1838 / 1838
Capital Guatemala City
Population 11.6 million / 277 people per sq mile (107 people per sq km) / 41%
Total area 42,043 sq miles (108,890 sq km)
Languages Spanish*, Quiché, Mam, Kekchí
Religions Christian 99%, other 1%
Ethnic mix Amerindian 60%, *mestizo* 30%, other 10%
Government Multiparty republic
Currency Quetzal = 100 centavos
Literacy rate 66%
Calorie consumption 2255 kilocalories

GUINEA
West Africa

Official name Republic of Guinea
Formation 1958 / 1958
Capital Conakry
Population 7.7 million / 81 people per sq mile (31 people per sq km) / 30%
Total area 94,926 sq miles (245,860 sq km)
Languages French*, Fulani, Malinke, Soussou, Kissi
Religions Muslim 85%, Christian 8%, traditional beliefs 7%
Ethnic mix Fila (Fulani) 30%, Malinke 30%, Soussou 15%, Kissi 10% other 20%
Government Multiparty republic
Currency Franc = 100 centimes
Literacy rate 37%
Calorie consumption 2389 kilocalories

GUINEA-BISSAU
West Africa

Official name Republic of Guinea-Bissau
Formation 1974 / 1974
Capital Bissau
Population 1.1 million / 101 people per sq mile (39 people per sq km) / 22%
Total area 13,940 sq miles (36,120 sq km)
Languages Portuguese*, Balante, Fulani, Malinke
Religions Traditional beliefs 52%, Muslim 40%, Christian 8%
Ethnic mix Balante 30%, Fila (Fulani) 22%, Malinke 12%, other 36%
Government Multiparty republic
Currency Guinea peso = 100 centavos
Literacy rate 33%
Calorie consumption 2556 kilocalories

GUYANA
South America

Official name Cooperative Republic of Guyana
Formation 1966 / 1966
Capital Georgetown
Population 856,000 / 11 people per sq mile (4 people per sq km) / 36%
Total area 83,000 sq miles (214,970 sq km)
Languages English*, English Creole, Hindi, Tamil, English
Religions Christian 57%, Hindu 33%, Muslim 9%, other 1%
Ethnic mix East Indian 52%, Black African 38%, Amerindian 4%, other 6%
Government Multiparty republic
Currency Guyana dollar =100 cents
Literacy rate 98%
Calorie consumption 2384 kilocalories

HAITI
West Indies

Official name Republic of Haiti
Formation 1804 / 1844
Capital Port-au-Prince
Population 7.5 million / 705 people per sq mile (272 people per sq km) / 32%
Total area 10,714 sq miles (27,750 sq km)
Languages French*, French Creole*,
Religions Roman Catholic 80%, Protestant 16%, other 4%
Ethnic mix Black 95%, European-African 5%
Government Multiparty republic
Currency Gourde = 100 centimes
Literacy rate 45%
Calorie consumption 1706 kilocalories

HONDURAS
Central America

Official name Republic of Honduras
Formation 1838 / 1838
Capital Tegucigalpa
Population 6.1 million / 141 people per sq mile (55 people per sq km) / 44%
Total area 43,278 sq miles (112,090 sq km)
Languages Spanish*, English Creole, Garifuna, Amerindian languages
Religions Roman Catholic 97%, other 3%
Ethnic mix *Mestizo* 90%, Black African 5%, Amerindian 4%, White 1%
Government Multiparty republic
Currency Lempira = 100 centavos
Literacy rate 70%
Calorie consumption 2305 kilocalories

HUNGARY
Central Europe

Official name Republic of Hungary
Formation 1918 / 1947
Capital Budapest
Population 9.9 million / 278 people per sq mile (107 people per sq km) / 65%
Total area 35,919 sq miles (93,030 sq km)
Languages Hungarian (Magyar)*, German, Slovak
Religions Roman Catholic 64%, Protestant 27%, other 7%
Ethnic mix Hungarian (Magyar) 90%, German 2%, other 8%
Government Multiparty republic
Currency Forint = 100 filler
Literacy rate 99%
Calorie consumption 3503 kilocalories

ICELAND
Northwest Europe

Official name Republic of Iceland
Formation 1944 / 1944
Capital Reykjavík
Population 277,000 / 7 people per sq mile (3 people per sq km) / 92%
Total area 39,770 sq miles (103,000 sq km)
Languages Icelandic*, English
Religions Evangelical Lutheran 93%, non-religious 6%, other Christian 1%
Ethnic mix Icelandic (Norwegian-Celtic descent) 98%, other 2%
Government Constitutional republic
Currency New Icelandic króna = 100 aurar
Literacy rate 99%
Calorie consumption 3058 kilocalories

INDIA
South Asia

Official name Republic of India
Formation 1947 / 1947
Capital New Delhi
Population 976 million / 850 people per sq mile (328 people per sq km) / 27%
Total area 1,269,338 sq miles (3,287,590 sq km)
Languages Hindi*, English*, Urdu, Bengali, Marathi, Telugu, Tamil, Bihari
Religions Hindu 83%, Muslim 11%, Christian 2%, Sikh 2%, other 2%
Ethnic mix Indo-Aryan 72%, Dravidian 25%, Mongoloid and other 3%
Government Multiparty republic
Currency Rupee = 100 paisa
Literacy rate 53%
Calorie consumption 2395 kilocalories

INDONESIA
Southeast Asia

Official name Republic of Indonesia
Formation 1949 / 1963
Capital Jakarta
Population 206.5 million / 295 people per sq mile (114 people per sq km) / 35%
Total area 735,555 sq miles (1,904,570 sq km)
Languages Bahasa Indonesia*, 250 (est.) languages or dialects
Religions Muslim 87%, Christian 9%, Hindu 2%, Buddhist 1%, other 1%
Ethnic mix Javanese 45%, Sundanese 14%, Madurese 8%, Coastal Malays 8%, other 25%
Government Multiparty republic
Currency Rupiah = 100 sen
Literacy rate 82%
Calorie consumption 2752 kilocalories

IRAN
Southwest Asia

Official name Islamic Republic of Iran
Formation 1906 / 1906
Capital Tehran
Population 73.1 million / 116 people per sq mile (45 people per sq km) / 59%
Total area 636,293 sq miles (1,648,000 sq km)
Languages Farsi (Persian)*, Azerbaijani, Gilaki, Mazanderani, Kurdish, Baluchi, Arabic
Religions Shi'a Muslim 95%, Sunni Muslim 4%, other 1%
Ethnic mix Persian 50%, Azeri 20%, Lur and Bakhtiari 10%, Kurd 8%, Arab 2%, other 10%
Government Islamic Republic
Currency Iranian rial = 100 dinars
Literacy rate 73%
Calorie consumption 2860 kilocalories

IRAQ
Southwest Asia

Official name Republic of Iraq
Formation 1932 / 1991
Capital Baghdad
Population 21.8 million / 129 people per sq mile (50 people per sq km) / 73%
Total area 169,235 sq miles (438,320 sq km)
Languages Arabic*, Kurdish, Armenian, Assyrian
Religions Shi'a ithna Muslim 62%, Sunni Muslim 33%, other 5%
Ethnic mix Arab 79%, Kurdish 16%, Persian 3%, Turkoman 2%
Government Single-party republic
Currency Iraqi dinar = 1000 fils
Literacy rate 58%
Calorie consumption 2121 kilocalories

IRELAND
Northwest Europe

Official name Republic of Ireland
Formation 1922 / 1922
Capital Dublin
Population 3.6 million / 135 people per sq mile (52 people per sq km) / 57%
Total area 27,155 sq miles (70,280 sq km)
Languages English*, Irish Gaelic*
Religions Roman Catholic 88%, Protestant 3%, other 9%
Ethnic mix Irish 95%, other 5%
Government Multiparty republic
Currency Punt = 100 pence
Literacy rate 99%
Calorie consumption 3847 kilocalories

ISRAEL
Southwest Asia

Official name State of Israel
Formation 1948 / 1994
Capital Jerusalem
Population 5.9 million / 752 people per sq mile (290 people per sq km) / 91%
Total area 7992 sq miles (20,700 sq km)
Languages Hebrew*, Arabic*, Yiddish
Religions Jewish 82%, Muslim 14%, Christian 2%, Druze and other 2%
Ethnic mix Jewish 82%, Arab 18%
Government Multiparty republic
Currency New Israeli shekel = 100 agorat
Literacy rate 95%
Calorie consumption 3050 kilocalories

ITALY
Southern Europe

Official name Italian Republic
Formation 1871 / 1954
Capital Rome
Population 57.2 million / 504 people per sq mile (195 people per sq km) / 67%
Total area 116,320 sq miles (301,270 sq km)
Languages Italian*, German, French, Rhaeto-Romanic, Sardinian
Religions Roman Catholic 83%, other 17%
Ethnic mix Italian 94%, other 6%
Government Multiparty republic
Currency Lira = 100 centesimi
Literacy rate 98%
Calorie consumption 3561 kilocalories

IVORY COAST
West Africa

Official name Republic of the Ivory Coast
Formation 1960 / 1960
Capital Yamoussoukro
Population 14.6 million / 119 people per sq mile (45 people per sq km) / 42%
Total area 124,503 sq miles (322,463 sq km)
Languages French*, Akran, Kru, Voltaic
Religions Traditional beliefs 63%, Muslim 25%, Christian 12%
Ethnic mix Baoulé 23%, Bété 18%, Kru 17%, Malinke 15%, other 27%
Government Transitional
Currency CFA franc = 100 centimes
Literacy rate 54%
Calorie consumption 2491 kilocalories

JAMAICA
West Indies

Official name Jamaica
Formation 1962 / 1962
Capital Kingston
Population 2.5 million / 598 people per sq mile (231 people per sq km) / 54%
Total area 4243 sq miles (10,990 sq km)
Languages English*, English Creole
Religions Christian 55%, other 45%
Ethnic mix Black 75%, mixed 15%, South Asian 5%, other 5%
Government Parliamentary democracy
Currency Jamaican dollar = 100 cents
Literacy rate 85%
Calorie consumption 2607 kilocalories

JAPAN
East Asia

Official name Japan
Formation 1600 / 1972
Capital Tokyo
Population 125.9 million / 866 people per sq mile (334 people per sq km) / 78%
Total area 145,869 sq miles (377,800 sq km)
Languages Japanese*, Korean, Chinese
Religions Shinto and Buddhist 76%, Buddhist 16%, other 8%
Ethnic mix Japanese 99%, other 1%
Government Constitutional monarchy
Currency Yen = 100 sen
Literacy rate 99%
Calorie consumption 2903 kilocalories

JORDAN
Southwest Asia

Official name Hashemite Kingdom of Jordan
Formation 1946 / 1976
Capital Amman
Population 6 million / 175 people per sq mile (67 people per sq km) / 71%
Total area 34,440 sq miles (89,210 sq km)
Languages Arabic*
Religions Muslim 95%, Christian 5%
Ethnic mix Arab 98%, (40% Palestinian), Armenian 1%, Circassian 1%
Government Constitutional monarchy
Currency Jordanian dinar = 1000 fils
Literacy rate 87%
Calorie consumption 3022 kilocalories

KAZAKHSTAN
Central Asia

Official Name Republic of Kazakhstan
Formation 1991 / 1991
Capital Astana
Population 16.9 million / 16 people per sq mile (6 people per sq km) / 60%
Total area 1,049,150 sq miles (2,717,300 sq km)
Languages Kazakh*, Russian, German
Religions Muslim 47%, other 53% (mostly Russian Orthodox and Lutheran)
Ethnic mix Kazakh 44%, Russian 38%, Ukrainian 6%, German 2%, other 14%
Government Multiparty republic
Currency Tenge = 100 tein
Literacy rate 99%
Calorie consumption NOT AVAILABLE

KENYA
East Africa

Official name Republic of Kenya
Formation 1963 / 1963
Capital Nairobi
Population 29 million / 132 people per sq mile (51 people per sq km) / 28%
Total area 224,081 sq miles (580,370 sq km)
Languages Swahili*, English, Kikuyu, Luo, Kamba
Religions Christian 60%, Traditional beliefs 25%, Muslim 6%, other 9%
Ethnic mix Kikuyu 21%, Luhya 14%, Luo 13%, Kalenjin 11% other 41%
Government Multiparty republic
Currency Kenya shilling = 100 cents
Literacy rate 79%
Calorie consumption 2075 kilocalories

KIRIBATI
Australasia & Oceania

Official Name Republic of Kiribati
Formation 1979 / 1979
Capital Bairiki
Population 78,000 / 284 people per sq mile (110 people per sq km) / 36%
Total area 274 sq miles (710 sq km)
Languages English*, Kiribati
Religions Roman Catholic 53%, Protestant 39%, other 8%
Ethnic mix Micronesian 98%, other 2%
Government Multiparty republic
Currency Australian dollar = 100 cents
Literacy rate 98%
Calorie consumption 2651 kilocalories

KUWAIT
Southwest Asia

Official name State of Kuwait
Formation 1961 / 1961
Capital Kuwait
Population 1.8 million / 262 people per sq mile (101 people per sq km) / 97%
Total area 6880 sq miles (17,820 sq km)
Languages Arabic*, English
Religions Muslim 92%, Christian 6%, other 2%
Ethnic mix Kuwaiti 45%, other Arab 35%, South Asian 9%, Iranian 4%, other 7%
Government Constitutional monarchy
Currency Dinar = 1000 fils
Literacy rate 80%
Calorie consumption 2523 kilocalories

KYRGYZSTAN
Central Asia

Official name Kyrgyz Republic
Formation 1991 / 1991
Capital Bishkek
Population 4.5 million / 59 people per sq mile (23 people per sq km) / 39%
Total area 76,640 sq miles (198,500 sq km)
Languages Kyrgyz*, Russian*, Uzbek
Religions Muslim 65%, other (mostly Russian Orthodox) 35%
Ethnic mix Kyrgyz 57%, Russian 19%, Uzbek 13%, Tatar, Ukrainian, other 11%
Government Multiparty republic
Currency Som =100 teen
Literacy rate 97%
Calorie consumption NOT AVAILABLE

LAOS
Southeast Asia

Official name Lao People's Democratic Republic
Formation 1953 / 1953
Capital Vientiane
Population 5.4 million / 61 people per sq mile (23 people per sq km) / 22%
Total area 91,428 sq miles (236,800 sq km)
Languages Lao*, Miao, Yao
Religions Buddhist 85%, other (including traditional beliefs) 15%
Ethnic mix Lao Loum 56%, Lao Theung 34%, Lao Soung 9%, other 1%
Government Single-party republic
Currency New kip = 100 cents
Literacy rate 58%
Calorie consumption 2259 kilocalories

LATVIA
Northeast Europe

Official name Republic of Latvia
Formation 1991 / 1991
Capital Riga
Population 2.4 million / 96 people per sq mile (37 people per sq km) / 73%
Total area 24,938 sq miles (64,589 sq km)
Languages Latvian*, Russian
Religions Evangelical Lutheran 85%, other Christian 15%
Ethnic mix Latvian 52%, Russian 34%, Belarusian 5%, Ukrainian 4%, other 5%
Government Multiparty republic
Currency Lats = 100 santimi
Literacy rate 99%
Calorie consumption NOT AVAILABLE

LEBANON
Southwest Asia

Official name Republic of Lebanon
Formation 1944 / 1944
Capital Beirut
Population 3.2 million / 810 people per sq mile (313 people per sq km) / 87%
Total area 4015 sq miles (10,400 sq km)
Languages Arabic*, French, Armenian,
Religions Muslim (mainly Shi'a) 70%, Christian (mainly Maronite) 30%
Ethnic mix Arab 93% (Lebanese 83%, Palestinian 10%), other 7%
Government Multiparty republic
Currency Lebanese pound = 100 piastres
Literacy rate 84%
Calorie consumption 3317 kilocalories

LESOTHO
Southern Africa

Official name Kingdom of Lesotho
Formation 1966 / 1966
Capital Maseru
Population 2.2 million / 188 people per sq mile (72 people per sq km) / 23%
Total area 11,718 sq miles (30,350 sq km)
Languages English*, Sesotho*, Zulu
Religions Christian 93%, other 7%
Ethnic mix Basotho 97%, European and Asian 3%
Government Constitutional monarchy
Currency Loti = 100 lisente
Literacy rate 82%
Calorie consumption 2201 kilocalories

LIBERIA
West Africa

Official name Republic of Liberia
Formation 1847 / 1947
Capital Monrovia
Population 2.7 million / 73 people per sq mile (28 people per sq km) / 45%
Total area 43,000 sq miles (111,370 sq km)
Languages English*, Kpelle, Bassa, Vai, Kru, Grebo, Kissi, Gola
Religions Traditional beliefs 70%, Muslim 20%, Christian 10%
Ethnic mix Indigenous tribes (16 main groups) 95%, Americo-Liberians 4%
Government Multiparty republic
Currency Liberian dollar = 100 cents
Literacy rate 38%
Calorie consumption 1640 kilocalories

LIBYA
North Africa

Official name The Great Socialist People's Libyan Arab Jamahiriya
Formation 1951 / 1951
Capital Tripoli
Population 6 million / 9 people per sq mile (3 people per sq km) / 86%
Total area 679,358 sq miles (1,759,540 sq km)
Languages Arabic*, Tuareg
Religions Muslim (mainly Sunni) 97%, other 3%
Ethnic mix Arab and Berber 95%, other 5%
Government Single-party state
Currency Libyan dinar = 1000 dirhams
Literacy rate 76%
Calorie consumption 3308 kilocalories

LIECHTENSTEIN
Southeast Europe

Official name Principality of Liechtenstein
Formation 1719 / 1719
Capital Vaduz
Population 31,000 / 504 people per sq mile (195 people per sq km) / 87%
Total area 62 sq miles (160 sq km)
Languages German*, Alemannish, Italian
Religions Roman Catholic 81%, Protestant 7%, other 12%
Ethnic mix Liechtensteiner 63%, Swiss 15%, German 9%, other 13%
Government Constitutional monarchy
Currency Swiss franc = 100 centimes
Literacy rate 99%
Calorie consumption NOT AVAILABLE

LITHUANIA
Northeast Europe

Official name Republic of Lithuania
Formation 1991 / 1991
Capital Vilnius
Population 3.7 million / 147 people per sq mile (57 people per sq km) / 72%
Total area 25,174 sq miles (65,200 sq km)
Languages Lithuanian*, Russian
Religions Roman Catholic 87%, Russian Orthodox 10%, other 3%
Ethnic mix Lithuanian 80%, Russian 9%, Polish 7%, Belarusian 2%, other 2%
Government Multiparty republic
Currency Litas = 100 centas
Literacy rate 98%
Calorie consumption NOT AVAILABLE

LUXEMBOURG
Northwest Europe

Official name Grand Duchy of Luxembourg
Formation 1867 / 1867
Capital Luxembourg
Population 422,000 / 423 people per sq mile (163 people per sq km) / 89%
Total area 998 sq miles (2586 sq km)
Languages Letzeburgish*, French*, German*
Religions Roman Catholic 97%, other 3%
Ethnic mix Luxembourger 72%, Portuguese 9%, Italian 5%, other 14%
Government Constitutional monarchy
Currency Franc = 100 centimes
Literacy rate 99%
Calorie consumption 3681 kilocalories

MACEDONIA
Southeast Europe

Official name Former Yugoslav Republic of Macedonia
Formation 1991 / 1991
Capital Skopje
Population 2.2 million / 222 people per sq mile (86 people per sq km) / 60%
Total area 9929 sq miles (25,715 sq km)
Languages Macedonian*, Serbian, Croatian
Religions Christian 80%, Muslim 20%
Ethnic mix Macedonian 67%, Albanian 23%, Turkish 4%, Serb 2%, Romany 2%, other 2%
Government Multiparty republic
Currency Macedonian denar = 100 deni
Literacy rate 89%
Calorie consumption NOT AVAILABLE

MADAGASCAR
Indian Ocean

Official name Democratic Republic of Madagascar
Formation 1960 / 1960
Capital Antananarivo
Population 16.3 million / 73 people per sq mile (28 people per sq km) / 27%
Total area 226,660 sq miles (587,040 sq km)
Languages Malagasy*, French*
Religions Traditional beliefs 52%, Christian 41%, Muslim 7%
Ethnic mix Merina 26%, Betsimisaraka 15%, Betsileo 12%, other 47%
Government Multiparty republic
Currency Franc = 100 centimes
Literacy rate 81%
Calorie consumption 2135 kilocalories

MALAWI
Southern Africa

Official name Republic of Malawi
Formation 1964 / 1964
Capital Lilongwe
Population 10.4 million / 286 people per sq mile (111 people per sq km) / 14%
Total area 45,745 sq miles (118,480 sq km)
Languages English*, Chewa, Lomwe, Yao
Religions Christian 75%, Muslim 20% traditional beliefs 5%
Ethnic mix Maravi 55%, Lomwe 17%, Yao 13%, other 15%
Government Multiparty republic
Currency Malawi kwacha = 100 tambala
Literacy rate 57%
Calorie consumption 1825 kilocalories

MALAYSIA
Southeast Asia

Official name Malaysia
Formation 1963 / 1965
Capital Kuala Lumpur
Population 21.5 million / 169 people per sq mile (65 people per sq km) / 54%
Total area 127,317 sq miles (329,750 sq km)
Languages Malay*, English*, Chinese, Tamil
Religions Muslim 53%, Buddhist 19%, Chinese faiths 12%, Christian 7%, other 9%
Ethnic mix Malay 47%, Chinese 32%, Indigenous tribes 12%, Indian 8%, other 1%
Government Federal constitutional monarchy
Currency Ringgit = 100 cents
Literacy rate 85%
Calorie consumption 2888 kilocalories

MALDIVES
Indian Ocean

Official name Republic of Maldives
Formation 1965 / 1965
Capital Male'
Population 282,000 / 2435 people per sq mile (940 people per sq km) / 26%
Total area 116 sq miles (300 sq km)
Languages Dhivehi (Maldivian)*, Sinhala, Tamil
Religions Sunni Muslim 100%
Ethnic mix Maldivian 99%, other 1%
Government Republic
Currency Rufiyaa = 100 laari
Literacy rate 91%
Calorie consumption 2580 kilocalories

MALI
West Africa

Official name Republic of Mali
Formation 1960 / 1960
Capital Bamako
Population 11.8 million / 25 people per sq mile (10 people per sq km) / 27%
Total area 478,837 sq miles (1,240,190 sq km)
Languages French*, Bambara, Fulani, Senufo, Soninké
Religions Muslim 80%, Traditional beliefs 18%, Christian 2%
Ethnic mix Bambara 31%, Fulani 13%, Senufo 12%, other 44%
Government Multiparty republic
Currency CFA franc = 100 centimes
Literacy rate 35%
Calorie consumption 2278 kilocalories

MALTA
Southern Europe

Official name Republic of Malta
Formation 1964 / 1964
Capital Valletta
Population 374,000 / 3027 people per sq mile (1169 people per sq km) / 89%
Total area 124 sq miles (320 sq km)
Languages Maltese*, English*
Religions Roman Catholic 98%, other (mostly Anglican) 2%
Ethnic mix Maltese (mixed Arab, Sicilian, Norman, Spanish, Italian, English) 98%, other 2%
Government Multiparty republic
Currency Maltese lira = 100 cents
Literacy rate 91%
Calorie consumption 3486 kilocalories

MARSHALL ISLANDS
Australasia & Oceania

Official name Republic of the Marshall Islands
Formation 1986 / 1986
Capital Majuro
Population 59,000 / 848 people per sq mile (327 people per sq km) / 69%
Total area 70 sq miles (181 sq km)
Languages English*, Marshallese*
Religions Protestant 80%, Roman Catholic 15%, other 5%
Ethnic mix Micronesian 97%, other 3%
Government Multiparty republic
Currency US dollar = 100 cents
Literacy rate 91%
Calorie consumption NOT AVAILABLE

MAURITANIA
West Africa

Official name Islamic Republic of Mauritania
Formation 1960 / 1960
Capital Nouakchott
Population 2.5 million / 6 people per sq mile (2 people per sq km) / 54%
Total area 395,953 sq miles (1,025,520 sq km)
Languages French*, Arabic*, Wolof
Religions Muslim 100%
Ethnic mix Maure 80%, Wolof 7%, Tukulor 5%, other 8%
Government Multiparty republic
Currency Ouguiya = 5 khoums
Literacy rate 38%
Calorie consumption 2685 kilocalories

MAURITIUS
Indian Ocean

Official name Republic of Mauritius
Formation 1968 / 1968
Capital Port Louis
Population 1.2 million / 1680 people per sq mile (649 people per sq km) / 41%
Total area 718 sq miles (1860 sq km)
Languages English*, French Creole, Hindi, Urdu, Tamil, Chinese
Religions Hindu 52%, Roman Catholic, 26%, Muslim 17%, other 5%
Ethnic mix Creole 55%, South Asian 40%, Chinese 3%, other 2%
Government Multiparty republic
Currency Mauritian rupee = 100 cents
Literacy rate 83%
Calorie consumption 2690 kilocalories

MEXICO
North America

Official name United Mexican States
Formation 1836 / 1848
Capital Mexico City
Population 95.8 million / 130 people per sq mile (50 people per sq km) / 75%
Total area 756,061 sq miles (1,958,200 sq km)
Languages Spanish*, Mayan dialects
Religions Roman Catholic 95%, Protestant 1%, other 4%
Ethnic mix *Mestizo* 55%, Amerindian 20%, European 16%, other 9%
Government Multiparty republic
Currency Mexican peso = 100 centavos
Literacy rate 90%
Calorie consumption 3146 kilocalories

MICRONESIA
Australasia & Oceania

Official name Federated States of Micronesia
Formation 1986 / 1986
Capital Palikir
Population 109,000 / 403 people per sq mile (156 people per sq km) / 28%
Total area 1120 sq miles (2900 sq km)
Languages English*, Trukese, Pohnpeian, Mortlockese, Kosrean
Religions Roman Catholic 50%, Protestant 48%, other 2%
Ethnic mix Micronesian 99%, other 1%
Government Republic
Currency US dollar = 100 cents
Literacy rate 90%
Calorie consumption NOT AVAILABLE

MOLDOVA
Southeast Europe

Official name Republic of Moldova
Formation 1991 / 1991
Capital Chişinău
Population 4.5 million / 346 people per sq mile (134 people per sq km) / 52%
Total area 13,000 sq miles (33,700 sq km)
Languages Romanian*, Moldovan, Russian
Religions Romanian Orthodox 98%, Jewish 1%, other 1%
Ethnic mix Moldovan 65%, Ukrainian 14%, Russian 13%, Gagauz 4%, other 4%
Government Multiparty republic
Currency Moldovan leu = 100 bani
Literacy rate 98%
Calorie consumption NOT AVAILABLE

MONACO
Southern Europe

Official name Principality of Monaco
Formation 1861 / 1861
Capital Monaco
Population 32,000 / 42,503 people per sq mile (16,410 people per sq km) / 100%
Total area 0.75 sq miles (1.95 sq km)
Languages French*, Italian, Monégasque, English
Religions Roman Catholic 89%, other 11%
Ethnic mix French 47%, Monégasque 17%, Italian 16%, other 20%
Government Constitutional monarchy
Currency French franc = 100 centimes
Literacy rate 99%
Calorie consumption NOT AVAILABLE

MONGOLIA
East Asia

Official name Mongolia
Formation 1924 / 1924
Capital Ulan Bator
Population 2.6 million / 4 people per sq mile (2 people per sq km) / 61%
Total area 604,247 sq miles (1,565,000 sq km)
Languages Khalkha Mongol*, Turkic, Russian, Chinese
Religions Predominantly Tibetan Buddhist, with a Muslim minority
Ethnic mix Mongol 90%, Kazakh 4%, Chinese 2%, Russian 2%, other 2%
Government Multiparty republic
Currency Tughrik (togrog) = 100 möngös
Literacy rate 84%
Calorie consumption 1899 kilocalories

MOROCCO
North Africa

Official name Kingdom of Morocco
Formation 1956 / 1956
Capital Rabat
Population 28 million / 162 people per sq mile (63 people per sq km) / 48%
Total area 269,757 sq miles (698,670 sq km)
Religions Muslim 98%, Jewish 1%, Christian 1%
Ethnic mix Arab and Berber 99%, European 1%
Government Constitutional monarchy
Currency Moroccan dirham = 100 centimes
Literacy rate 45%
Calorie consumption 2984 kilocalories

MOZAMBIQUE
Southern Africa

Official name Republic of Mozambique
Formation 1975 / 1975
Capital Maputo
Population 18.7 million / 62 people per sq mile (24 people per sq km) / 34%
Total area 309,493 sq miles (801,590 sq km)
Languages Portuguese*, Makua, Tsonga, Sena
Religions Traditional beliefs 60%, Christian 30%, Muslim 10%
Ethnic mix Makua-Lomwe 47%, Thonga 23%, Malawi 12%, Shona 11%, Yao 4%, other 3%
Government Multiparty republic
Currency Metical = 100 centavos
Literacy rate 40%
Calorie consumption 1680 kilocalories

NAMIBIA
Southern Africa

Official name Republic of Namibia
Formation 1990 / 1994
Capital Windhoek
Population 1.7 million / 5 people per
  sq mile (2 people per sq km) / 37%
Total area 318,260 sq miles (824,290 sq km)
Languages English*, Afrikaans,
  Ovambo, Kavango, Bergdama
Religions Christian 90%, other 10%
Ethnic mix Ovambo 50%, Kavango 9%,
  Herero 8%, Damara 8%, other 25%
Government Multiparty republic
Currency Namibian dollar = 100 cents
Literacy rate 79%
Calorie consumption 2134 kilocalories

NAURU
Australasia & Oceania

Official name Republic of Nauru
Formation 1968 / 1968
Capital No official capital
Population 11,000 / 1332 people per
  sq mile (514 people per sq km) / 100%
Total area 8.2 sq miles (21.2 sq km)
Languages Nauruan*, English, Kiribati,
  Chinese, Tuvaluan
Religions Christian 95%, other 5%
Ethnic mix Nauruan 62%, other Pacific
  islanders 25%, Chinese 8%, European 5%
Government Parliamentary democracy
Currency Australian dollar = 100 cents
Literacy rate 99%
Calorie consumption NOT AVAILABLE

NEPAL
South Asia

Official name Kingdom of Nepal
Formation 1769 / 1769
Capital Kathmandu
Population 23.2 million / 439 people per
  sq mile (170 people per sq km) / 14%
Total area 54,363 sq miles (140,800 sq km)
Languages Nepali*, Maithilli, Bhojpuri
Religions Hindu 90%, Buddhist 4%,
  Muslim 3%, Christian 1%, other 2%
Ethnic mix Nepalese 58%, Bihari 19%,
  Tamang 6%, other 17%
Government Constitutional monarchy
Currency Nepalese rupee = 100 paisa
Literacy rate 38%
Calorie consumption 1957 kilocalories

NETHERLANDS
Northwest Europe

Official name Kingdom of the Netherlands
Formation 1815 / 1839
Capitals Amsterdam, The Hague
Population 15.7 million / 1199 people per
  sq mile (463 people per sq km) / 89%
Total area 14,410 sq miles
  (37,330 sq km)
Languages Dutch*, Frisian
Religions Roman Catholic 36%,
  Protestant 27%, Muslim 3%, other 34%
Ethnic mix Dutch 96%, other 4%
Government Constitutional monarchy
Currency Netherland guilder = 100 cents
Literacy rate 99%
Calorie consumption 3222 kilocalories

NEW ZEALAND
Australasia & Oceania

Official name New Zealand
Formation 1947 / 1947
Capital Wellington
Population 3.7 million / 36 people per
  sq mile (14 people per sq km) / 86%
Total area 103,730 sq miles (268,680 sq km)
Languages English*, Maori
Religions Protestant 47%,
  Roman Catholic 15%, other 38%
Ethnic mix European 82%, Maori 9%,
  Pacific Islanders 3%, other 6%
Government Constitutional monarchy
Currency NZ dollar = 100 cents
Literacy rate 99%
Calorie consumption 3669 kilocalories

NICARAGUA
Central America

Official name Republic of Nicaragua
Formation 1838 / 1838
Capital Managua
Population 4.5 million / 98 people per
  sq mile (38 people per sq km) / 63%
Total area 50,193 sq miles
  (130,000 sq km)
Languages Spanish*, English Creole, Miskito
Religions Roman Catholic 95%, other 5%
Ethnic mix Mestizo 69%, White 14%,
  Black 8%, Amerindian 5%, Zambos 4%
Government Multiparty republic
Currency Córdoba ora = 100 pence
Literacy rate 63%
Calorie consumption 2293 kilocalories

NIGER
West Africa

Official name Republic of Niger
Formation 1960 / 1960
Capital Niamey
Population 10.1 million / 21 people per
  sq mile (8 people per sq km) / 17%
Total area 489,188 sq miles (1,267,000 sq km)
Languages French*, Hausa, Djerma, Fulani,
  Tuareg, Teda
Religions Muslim 85%, traditional
  beliefs 14%, Christian 1%
Ethnic mix Hausa 54%, Djerma and Songhai
  21%, Fulani 10%, Tuareg 9%, other 6%
Government Multiparty republic
Currency CFA franc = 100 centimes
Literacy rate 14%
Calorie consumption 2257 kilocalories

NIGERIA
West Africa

Official name Federal Republic of Nigeria
Formation 1960 / 1961
Capital Abuja
Population 122 million / 346 people per
  sq mile (123 people per sq km) / 34%
Total area 356,668 sq miles (923,770 sq km)
Languages English*, Hausa, Yoruba, Ibo
Religions Muslim 50%, Christian 40%,
  traditional beliefs 10%
Ethnic mix Hausa 21%, Yoruba 21%,
  Ibo 18%, Fulani 11%, other 29%
Government Multiparty republic
Currency Naira = 100 kobo
Literacy rate 59%
Calorie consumption 2124 kilocalories

NORTH KOREA
East Asia

Official name Democratic People's
  Republic of Korea
Formation 1948 / 1953
Capital Pyongyang
Population 23.2 million / 499 people per
  sq mile (193 people per sq km) / 61%
Total area 46,540 sq miles (120,540 sq km)
Languages Korean*, Chinese
Religions Traditional beliefs 16%, Ch'ondogyo
  14%, Buddhist 2%, non-religious 68%
Ethnic mix Korean 99%, other 1%
Government Single-party republic
Currency North Korean Won = 100 chon
Literacy rate 99%
Calorie consumption 2833 kilocalories

NORWAY
Northern Europe

Official name Kingdom of Norway
Formation 1905 / 1905
Capital Oslo
Population 4.4 million / 37 people per
  sq mile (14 people per sq km) / 73%
Total area 125,060 sq miles (323,900 sq km)
Languages Norwegian* (Bokmal and
  Nynorsk), Lappish, Finnish
Religions Evangelical Lutheran 89%, Roman
  Catholic 1%, other and non-religious 10%
Ethnic mix Norwegian 95%, Lapp 1%,
  other 4%
Government Constitutional monarchy
Currency Norwegian krone = 100 øre
Literacy rate 99%
Calorie consumption 3244 kilocalories

OMAN
Southwest Asia

Official name Sultanate of Oman
Formation 1951 / 1951
Capital Muscat
Population 2.5 million / 30 people per
  sq mile (12 people per sq km) / 13%
Total area 82,030 sq miles (212,460 sq km)
Languages Arab*, Baluchi
Religions Ibadi Muslim 75%, other
  Muslim 11%, Hindu 14%
Ethnic mix Arab 75%, Baluchi 15%, other 15%
Government Monarchy with
  Consultative Council
Currency Omani rial = 1000 baizas
Literacy rate 67%
Calorie consumption 3013 kilocalories

PAKISTAN
South Asia

Official name Islamic Republic of Pakistan
Formation 1947 / 1947
Capital Islamabad
Population 147.8 million / 497 people per
  sq mile (192 people per sq km) / 35%
Total area 307,374 sq miles (796,100 sq km)
Main languages Urdu*, Punjabi, Sindhi,
  Pashtu, Baluchi
Religions Sunni Muslim 77%, Shi'a Muslim
  20%, Hindu 2%, Christian 1%
Ethnic mix Punjabi 50%, Sindhi 15%, Pashto
  15%, Mohajir 8%, Baluch 5%, other 7%
Government Multiparty republic
Currency Pakistani rupee = 100 paisa
Literacy rate 40%
Calorie consumption 2315 kilocalories

PALAU
Australasia & Oceania

Official name Palau
Formation 1994 / 1994
Capital Oreor
Population 17,700 /90 people per
  sq mile (35 people per sq km) / 29%
Total area 192 sq miles (497 sq km)
Languages Palauan*, English*,
  Japanese
Religions Roman Catholic 66%,
  Modekngei 34%
Ethnic mix Palauan 99%, other 1%
Government Multiparty republic
Currency US dollar = 100 cents
Literacy rate 92%
Calorie consumption NOT AVAILABLE

PANAMA
Central America

Official name Republic of Panama
Formation 1903 / 1903
Capital Panama City
Population 2.8 million / 95 people per
  sq mile (37 people per sq km) / 53%
Total area 29,761 sq miles (77,080 sq km)
Languages Spanish*, English Creole,
  Amerindian languages
Religions Roman Catholic 93%, other 7%
Ethnic mix Mestizo 60%, White 14%,
  Black 12%, Amerindian 8%, other 6%
Government Multiparty republic
Currency Balboa = 100 centesimos
Literacy rate 91%
Calorie consumption 2242 kilocalories

PAPUA NEW GUINEA
Australasia & Oceania

Official name Independent State of Papua
  New Guinea
Formation 1975 / 1975
Capital Port Moresby
Population 4.6 million / 26 people per
  sq mile (10 people per sq km) / 16%
Total area 178,700 sq miles (462,840 sq km)
Languages English*, Pidgin English, Papuan,
  Motu, 750 (estimated) native languages
Religions Christian 62%, traditional beliefs 38%
Ethnic mix Papuan 85%, other 15%
Government Parliamentary democracy
Currency Kina = 100 toea
Literacy rate 73%
Calorie consumption 2613 kilocalories

PARAGUAY
South America

Official name Paraguay
Formation 1811 / 1938
Capital Asunción
Population 5.2 million / 34 people per
  sq mile (13 people per sq km) / 53%
Total area 157,046 sq miles
  (406,750 sq km)
Languages Spanish*, Guaraní
Religions Roman Catholic 90%,
  other 10%
Ethnic mix Mestizo 90%, Amerindian 2%,
  other 8%
Government Multiparty republic
Literacy rate 92%
Calorie consumption 2670 kilocalories

PERU
South America

Official name Republic of Peru
Formation 1824 / 1941
Capital Lima
Population 24.8 million / 50 people per
  sq mile (19 people per sq km) / 72%
Total area 496,223 sq miles
  (1,285,220 sq km)
Languages Spanish*, Quechua*, Aymará
Religions Roman Catholic 95%, other 5%
Ethnic mix Amerindian 54%,
  mestizo 32%, White 12%, other 2%
Government Multiparty republic
Currency New sol = 100 centimos
Literacy rate 88%
Calorie consumption 1882 kilocalories

PHILIPPINES
Southwest Asia

Official name Republic of the Philippines
Formation 1946 / 1946
Capital Manila
Population 72.2 million / 627 people per
  sq mile (242 people per sq km) / 54%
Total area 115,831 sq miles (300,000 sq km)
Languages Filipino*, English*, Cebuano,
  Hiligaynon, Samaran, Bikol, Ilocano
Religions Roman Catholic 83%,
  Protestant 9%, Muslim 5%, other 3%
Ethnic mix Malay 50%, Indonesian and
  Polynesian 30%, Chinese 10%, other 10%
Government Multiparty republic
Currency Philippine peso = 100 centavos
Literacy rate 94%
Calorie consumption 2257 kilocalories

POLAND
Northern Europe

Official name Republic of Poland
Formation 1918 / 1945
Capital Warsaw
Population 38.7 million / 329 people per
  sq mile (127 people per sq km) / 65%
Total area 120,720 sq miles
  (312,680 sq km)
Languages Polish*, German
Religions Roman Catholic 93%, Eastern
  Orthodox 2%, other and non-religious 5%
Ethnic mix Polish 98%, German 1%, other 1%
Government Multiparty republic
Currency Zloty = 100 groszy
Literacy rate 99%
Calorie consumption 3301 kilocalories

PORTUGAL
Southwest Europe

Official name Republic of Portugal
Formation 1140 / 1640
Capital Lisbon
Population 9.8 million / 276 people per
  sq mile (107 people per sq km) / 36%
Total area 35,670 sq miles
  (92,390 sq km)
Languages Portuguese*
Religions Roman Catholic 97%,
  Protestant 1%, other 2%
Ethnic mix Portuguese 99%, African 1%
Government Multiparty republic
Currency Escudo = 100 centavos
Literacy rate 90%
Calorie consumption 3634 kilocalories

QATAR
Southwest Asia

Official name State of Qatar
Formation 1971 / 1971
Capital Doha
Population 600,000 / 136 people per
  sq mile (53 people per sq km) / 91%
Total area 4247 sq miles (11,000 sq km)
Languages Arabic*, Farsi (Persian),
  Urdu, Hindi, English
Religions Sunni Muslim 86%,
  Hindu 10%, Christian 4%
Ethnic mix Arab 40%, Pakistani 18%,
  Iranian 10% Indian 18%, other 14%
Government Absolute monarchy
Currency Qatar riyal = 100 dirhams
Literacy rate 80%
Calorie consumption NOT AVAILABLE

ROMANIA
Southeast Europe

Official name Romania
Formation 1878 / 1947
Capital Bucharest
Population 22.6 million /254 people
  per sq mile (98 people per sq km) / 55%
Total area 91,700 sq miles (237,500 sq km)
Languages Romanian*, Hungarian,
Religions Romanian Orthodox 70%, Roman
  Catholic 5%, Protestant 4%, other 21%
Ethnic mix Romanian 89%, Magyar 9%,
  Romany 1%, other 1%
Government Multiparty republic
Currency Leu = 100 bani
Literacy rate 97%
Calorie consumption 3051 kilocalories

RUSSIAN FEDERATION
Europe / Asia

Official name Russian Federation
Formation 1991 / 1991
Capital Moscow
Population 147.2 million /22 people per
  sq mile (9 people per sq km) / 76%
Total area 6,592,800 sq miles
  (17,075,400 sq km)
Languages Russian*, Tatar, Ukrainian
Religions Russian Orthodox 75%,
  other (including Jewish, Muslim) 25%
Ethnic mix Russian 82%, Tatar 4%, Ukrainian
  3%, Chuvash 1%, other 10%
Currency Rouble = 100 kopeks
Literacy rate 99%
Calorie consumption NOT AVAILABLE

RWANDA
Central Africa

Official name Rwandese Republic
Formation 1962 / 1962
Capital Kigali
Population 6.5 million / 675 people per
  sq mile (261 people per sq km) / 6%
Total area 10,170 sq miles (26,340 sq km)
Languages Rwandan*, French*,
  Kiswahili, English
Religions Christian 74%, traditional
  beliefs 25%, other 1%
Ethnic mix Hutu 90%, Tutsi 8%, Twa 2%
Government Multiparty republic
Currency Rwanda franc = 100 centimes
Literacy rate 63%
Calorie consumption 1821 kilocalories

SAINT KITTS & NEVIS
West Indies

Official name Federation of Saint
  Christopher and Nevis
Formation 1983 / 1983
Capital Basseterre
Population 41,000 / 295 people per
  sq mile (114 people per sq km) / 42%
Total area 139 sq miles (360 sq km)
Languages English*, English Creole
Religions Protestant 71%, Roman
  Catholic 7%, other 22%
Ethnic mix Black 95%, mixed 5%
Government Parliamentary democracy
Currency E. Caribbean dollar = 100 cents
Literacy rate 90%
Calorie consumption 2419 kilocalories

SAINT LUCIA
West Indies

Official name Saint Lucia
Formation 1979 / 1979
Capital Castries
Population 142,000 / 603 people per
  sq mile (233 people per sq km) / 48%
Total area 239 sq miles (620 sq km)
Languages English*, French Creole,
  Hindi, Urdu
Religions Roman Catholic 90%, other 10%
Ethnic mix Black 90%, African-European 6%,
  South Asian 4%
Government Parliamentary democracy
Currency E. Caribbean dollar = 100 cents
Literacy rate 93%
Calorie consumption 2588 kilocalories

SAINT VINCENT & THE GRENADINES
West Indies

Official name Saint Vincent and the Grenadines
Formation 1979 / 1979
Capital Kingstown
Population 111,000 / 846 people per
  sq mile (327 people per sq km) / 46%
Total area 131 sq miles (340 sq km)
Languages English*, English Creole
Religions Protestant 62%
  Roman Catholic 19%, other 19%
Ethnic mix Black 82%, mixed 14%,
  White 3%, South Asian 1%
Government Parliamentary democracy
Currency E. Caribbean dollar = 100 cents
Literacy rate 82%
Calorie consumption 2347 kilocalories

SAMOA
Australasia & Oceania

Official name Independent State
  of Samoa
Formation 1962 / 1962
Capital Apia
Population 170,000 / 156 people
  per sq mile (60 people per sq km) / 21%
Total area 1027 sq miles (2840 sq km)
Languages Samoan*, English*
Religions Protestant 74%,
  Roman Catholic 26%
Ethnic mix Samoan 90%, other 10%
Government Parliamentary state
Currency Tala = 100 sene
Literacy rate 98%
Calorie consumption 2828 kilocalories

SAN MARINO
Southern Europe

Official name Republic of San Marino
Formation AD 301 / 301
Capital San Marino
Population 25,000 / 1061 people per
  sq mile (410 people per sq km) / 94%
Total area 24 sq miles (61 sq km)
Languages *Italian
Religions Roman Catholic 93%,
  other and non-religious 7%
Ethnic mix Sanmarinesi 95%,
  other 5%
Government Multiparty republic
Currency Lira = 100 centesimi
Literacy rate 96%
Calorie consumption 3561 kilocalories

SAO TOME & PRINCIPE
West Africa

Official name Democratic Republic
  of Sao Tome and Principe
Formation 1975 / 1975
Capital São Tomé
Population 131,000 / 354 people per
  sq mile (137 people per sq km) / 46%
Total area 372 sq miles (964 sq km)
Languages *Portuguese, Portuguese Creole
Religions Roman Catholic 90%,
  other Christian 10%
Ethnic mix Black 90%, Portuguese and
  Creole 10%
Government Multiparty republic
Currency Dobra = 100 centimos
Literacy rate 75%
Calorie consumption 2129 kilocalories

Saudi Arabia
Southwest Asia

Official name Kingdom of Saudi Arabia
Formation 1932 / 1935
Capital Riyadh
Population 20.2 million / 24 people per sq mile (8 people per sq km) / 80%
Total area 829,995 sq miles (2,149,690 sq km)
Languages Arabic*
Religions Sunni Muslim 85%, Shi'a Muslim 15%
Ethnic mix Arab 90%, Afroasian 10%
Government Absolute monarchy
Currency Saudi riyal = 100 malalah
Literacy rate 73%
Calorie consumption 2735 kilocalories

Senegal
West Africa

Official name Republic of Senegal
Formation 1960 / 1960
Capital Dakar
Population 9 million /121 people per sq mile (47 people per sq km) / 42%
Total area 75,950 sq miles (196,720 sq km)
Languages *French, Wolof, Fulani, Serer
Religions Muslim 90%, Traditional beliefs 5%, Christian 5%
Ethnic mix Wolof 46%, Fulani 25%, Serer 16%, other 13%
Government Multiparty republic
Currency CFA franc = 100 centimes
Literacy rate 35%
Calorie consumption 2262 kilocalories

Seychelles
Indian Ocean

Official name Republic of Seychelles
Formation 1976 / 1976
Capital Victoria
Population 75,000 / 722 people per sq mile (279 people per sq km) / 54%
Total area 108 sq miles (280 sq km)
Languages *French Creole, French, English
Religions Roman Catholic 90%, other 10%
Ethnic mix Seychellois (mixed African, South Asian and European) 95%, Chinese and South Asian 5%
Government Multiparty republic
Currency Seychelles rupee = 100 cents
Literacy rate 84%
Calorie consumption 2287 kilocalories

Sierra Leone
West Africa

Official name Republic of Sierra Leone
Formation 1961 / 1961
Capital Freetown
Population 4.6 million / 166 people per sq mile (64 people per sq km) / 36%
Total area 27,699 sq miles (71,740 sq km)
Languages English*, Krio (Creole), Mende, Temne
Religions Traditional beliefs 52%, Muslim 40%, Christian 8%
Ethnic mix Mende 35%, Temne 32%, Limba 8%, Kuranko 4%, other 21%
Government Multiparty republic
Currency Leone = 100 cents
Literacy rate 33%
Calorie consumption 1694 kilocalories

Singapore
Southeast Asia

Official name Republic of Singapore
Formation 1965 / 1965
Capital Singapore
Population 3.5 million / 14,861 people per sq mile (5738 people per sq km) / 100%
Total area 239 sq miles (620 sq km)
Languages Malay*, Chinese*, Tamil*, English*
Religions Buddhist 30%, Christian 20%, Muslim 17%, other 33%
Ethnic mix Chinese 78%, Malay 14%, Indian 6%, other 2%
Government Multiparty republic
Currency Singapore dollar = 100 cents
Literacy rate 91%
Calorie consumption 3128 kilocalories

Slovakia
Central Europe

Official name Slovak Republic
Formation 1993 / 1993
Capital Bratislava
Population 5.4 million / 285 people per sq mile (110 people per sq km) / 59%
Total area 19,100 sq miles (49,500 sq km)
Languages Slovak*, Hungarian (Magyar), Romany, Czech
Religions Roman Catholic 60%, Atheist 10%, Protestant 8%, Orthodox 4%, other 18%
Ethnic mix Slovak 85%, Hungarian 9%, Czech 1%, other 5%
Government Multiparty republic
Currency Koruna = 100 halierov
Literacy rate 99%
Calorie consumption 3156 kilocalories

Slovenia
Central Europe

Official name Republic of Slovenia
Formation 1991 / 1991
Capital Ljubljana
Population 1.9 million / 243 people per sq mile (94 people per sq km) / 64%
Total area 7820 sq miles (20,250 sq km)
Languages Slovene*, Serbian, Croatian
Religions Roman Catholic 96%, Muslim 1%, other 3%
Ethnic mix Slovene 88%, Croat 3%, Serb 2%, Bosniak 1%, other 4%
Government Multiparty republic
Currency Tolar = 100 stotins
Literacy rate 99%
Calorie consumption NOT AVAILABLE

Solomon Islands
Australasia & Oceania

Official name Solomon Islands
Formation 1978 / 1978
Capital Honiara
Population 417,000 / 39 people per sq mile (15 people per sq km) / 17%
Total area 111,583 sq miles (289,000 sq km)
Languages English*, Pidgin English, Melanesian Pidgin
Religions Christian 91%, other 9%
Ethnic mix Melanesian 94%, other 6%
Government Parliamentary democracy
Currency Solomon Islands dollar = 100 cents
Literacy rate 62%
Calorie consumption 2173 kilocalories

Somalia
East Africa

Official name Somali Democratic Republic
Formation 1960 / 1960
Capital Mogadishu
Population 10.7 million / 39 people per sq mile (15 people per sq km) / 25%
Total area 246,200 sq miles (637,660 sq km)
Languages Somali*, Arabic*, English
Religions Sunni Muslim 98%, other (including Christian) 2%
Ethnic mix Somali 98%, Bantu, Arab and other 2%
Government Transitional
Currency Somaili shilling = 100 cents
Literacy rate 24%
Calorie consumption 1499 kilocalories

South Africa
Southern Africa

Official name Republic of South Africa
Formation 1934 / 1994
Capitals Pretoria/Cape Town/Bloemfontein
Population 44.3 million / 94 people per sq mile (36 people per sq km) / 51%
Total area 471,443 sq miles (1,221,040 sq km)
Languages Afrikaans*, English*, 11 African languages
Religions Protestant 55%, Roman Catholic 9%, Hindu 1%, Muslim 1%, other 34%
Ethnic mix Other Black 38%, White 16%, Zulu 23%, mixed 10%, Xhosa 9%, other 4%
Government Multiparty republic
Currency Rand = 100 cents
Literacy rate 82%
Calorie consumption 2695 kilocalories

South Korea
East Asia

Official name Republic of Korea
Formation 1948 / 1953
Capital Seoul
Population 46.1 million / 1209 people per sq mile (467 people per sq km) / 81%
Total area 38,232 sq miles (99,020 sq km)
Languages Korean*, Chinese
Religions Mahayana Buddhist 47%, Protestant 38%, Roman Catholic 11%, Confucianist 3%, other 1%
Ethnic mix Korean 100%
Government Multiparty republic
Currency Won = 100 chon
Literacy rate 97%
Calorie consumption 3285 kilocalories

Spain
Southwest Europe

Official name Kingdom of Spain
Formation 1492 / 1713
Capital Madrid
Population 39.8 million / 206 people per sq mile (80 people per sq km) / 76%
Total area 194,900 sq miles (504,780 sq km)
Languages Castilian Spanish*, Catalan*, Galician*, Basque*
Religions Roman Catholic 96%, other 4%
Ethnic mix Castilian Spanish 72%, Catalan 17%, Galician 6%, other 5%
Government Constitutional monarchy
Currency Spanish Peseta = 100 céntimos
Literacy rate 95%
Calorie consumption 3708 kilocalories

Sri Lanka
South Asia

Official name Democratic Socialist Republic of Sri Lanka
Formation 1948 / 1948
Capital Colombo
Population 18.5 million / 740 people per sq mile (286 people per sq km) / 22%
Total area 25,332 sq miles (65,610 sq km)
Languages Sinhalese*, Tamil, English
Religions Buddhist 70%, Hindu 15%, Christian 8%, Muslim 7%
Ethnic mix Sinhalese 74%, Tamil 18%, other 8%
Government Multiparty republic
Currency Sri Lanka rupee = 100 cents
Literacy rate 90%
Calorie consumption 2273 kilocalories

Sudan
East Africa

Official name Republic of Sudan
Formation 1956 / 1956
Capital Khartoum
Population 28.5 million / 31 people per sq mile (12 people per sq km) / 25%
Total area 967,493 sq miles (2,505,815 sq km)
Languages Arabic*, Dinka, Nuer, Nubian, Beja, Zande, Bari, Fur
Religions Muslim 70%, Traditional beliefs 20%, Christian 9%, other 1%
Ethnic mix Arab 51%, Dinka 13%, Nuba 9%, Beja 7%, other 20%
Government Military regime
Currency Sudanese pound or dinar = 100 piastres
Literacy rate 53%
Calorie consumption 2202 kilocalories

Surinam
South America

Official name Republic of Surinam
Formation 1975 / 1975
Capital Paramaribo
Population 442,000 / 7 people per sq mile (3 people per sq km) / 50%
Total area 63,039 sq miles (163,270 sq km)
Languages Dutch*, Pidgin English (Taki-Taki), Hindi, Javanese, Carib
Religions Christian 48%, Hindu 27%, Muslim 20%, other 5%
Ethnic mix Hindustani 34%, Creole 34%, Javanese 18%, Black 9%, other 5%
Government Multiparty republic
Currency Surinam guilder = 100 cents
Literacy rate 93%
Calorie consumption 2547 kilocalories

Swaziland
Southern Africa

Official name Kingdom of Swaziland
Formation 1968 / 1968
Capital Mbabane
Population 900,000 / 140 people per sq mile (54 people per sq km) / 29%
Total area 6703 sq miles (17,360 sq km)
Languages Siswati*, English*, Zulu
Religions Christian 60%, traditional beliefs 40%
Ethnic mix Swazi 95%, other 5%
Government Executive monarchy
Currency Lilangeni = 100 cents
Literacy rate 77%
Calorie consumption 2706 kilocalories

Sweden
Northern Europe

Official name Kingdom of Sweden
Formation 1809 / 1905
Capital Stockholm
Population 8.9 million / 56 people per sq mile (22 people per sq km) / 83%
Total area 173,730 sq miles (449,960 sq km)
Languages Swedish*, Finnish, Lappish,
Religions Evangelical Lutheran 89%, Roman Catholic 2%, Muslim 1%, other 8%
Ethnic mix Swedish 91%, other European 6%, Finnish and Lapp 3%
Government Constitutional monarchy
Currency Swedish krona = 100 öre
Literacy rate 99%
Calorie consumption 2972 kilocalories

Switzerland
Central Europe

Official name Swiss Confederation
Formation 1291 / 1815
Capital Bern
Population 7.3 million / 475 people per sq mile (184 people per sq km) / 61%
Total area 15,940 sq miles (41,290 sq km)
Languages German*, French*, Italian*, Romansch
Religions Roman Catholic 48%, Protestant 44%, other 8%
Ethnic mix German 65%, French 18%, Italian 10%, other 7%
Government Federal republic
Currency Franc = 100 centimes
Literacy rate 99%
Calorie consumption 3379 kilocalories

Syria
Southwest Asia

Official name Syrian Arab Republic
Formation 1946 / 1967
Capital Damascus
Population 15.3 million / 215 people per sq mile (83 people per sq km) / 52%
Total area 71,500 sq miles (185,180 sq km)
Languages Arabic*, French, Kurdish
Religions Sunni Muslim 74%, other Muslim 16%, Christian 10%
Ethnic mix Arab 89%, Kurdish 6%, Armenian, Turkmen, Circassian 2%, other 3%
Government Single-party republic
Currency Syrian pound = 100 piastres
Literacy rate 71%
Calorie consumption 3175 kilocalories

Taiwan
East Asia

Official name Republic of China
Formation 1949 / 1949
Capital Taipei
Population 21.5 million / 1724 people per sq mile (666 people per sq km) / 69%
Total area 13,969 sq miles (36,179 sq km)
Languages Mandarin Chinese*, Amoy Chinese, Hakka Chinese
Religions Buddhist, Confucianist, Taoist 93%, Christian 5%, other 2%
Ethnic mix Indigenous Chinese, Mainland Chinese 14%, Aborigine 2%
Government Multiparty republic
Currency Taiwan dollar = 100 cents
Literacy rate 94%
Calorie consumption NOT AVAILABLE

Tajikistan
Central Asia

Official name Republic of Tajikistan
Formation 1991 / 1991
Capital Dushanbe
Population 6.2 million / 112 people per sq mile (43 people per sq km) / 32%
Total area 55,251 sq miles (143,100 sq km)
Main languages Tajik*, Uzbek, Russian
Religions Sunni Muslim 80%, Shi'a Muslim 5%, other 15%
Ethnic mix Tajik 62%, Uzbek 24%, Russian 4%, Tatar 2%, other 8%
Government Multiparty republic
Currency Tajik rouble = 100 kopeks
Literacy rate 99%
Calorie consumption NOT AVAILABLE

Tanzania
East Africa

Official name United Republic of Tanzania
Formation 1961 / 1964
Capital Dodoma
Population 32.2 million / 94 people per sq mile (36 people per sq km) / 24%
Total area 364,900 sq miles (945,090 sq km)
Languages English*, Swahili*, Sukuma, Chagga, Nyamwezi, Hehe, Makonde
Religions Muslim 33%, Christian 33%, traditional beliefs 30%, other 4%
Ethnic mix 120 small ethnic Bantu groups 99%, other 1%
Government Multiparty republic
Currency Tanzanian shilling = 100 cents
Literacy rate 71%
Calorie consumption 2018 kilocalories

Thailand
Southeast Asia

Official name Kingdom of Thailand
Formation 1782 / 1907
Capital Bangkok
Population 59.6 million / 302 people per sq mile (117 people per sq km) / 20%
Total area 198,116 sq miles (513,120 sq km)
Languages Thai*, Chinese, Malay, Khmer, Mon, Karen
Religions Buddhist 95%, other 5%
Ethnic mix Thai 80%, Chinese 12%, Malay 4%, Khmer and other 4%
Government Constitutional monarchy
Currency Baht = 100 stangs
Literacy rate 94%
Calorie consumption 2432 kilocalories

Togo
West Africa

Official name Togolese Republic
Formation 1960 / 1960
Capital Lomé
Population 4.4 million /210 people per sq mile (81 people per sq km) / 31%
Total area 21,927 sq miles (56,790 sq km)
Languages French*, Ewe, Kabye, Gurma
Religions Traditional beliefs 50%, Christian 35%, Muslim 15%
Ethnic mix Ewe 43%, Kabye 26%, Gurma 16%, other 15%
Government Multiparty republic
Currency CFA franc = 100 centimes
Literacy rate 53%
Calorie consumption 2242 kilocalories

Tonga
Australasia & Oceania

Official name Kingdom of Tonga
Formation 1970 / 1970
Capital Nuku'alofa
Population 97,000 / 351 people per sq mile (135 people per sq km) / 21%
Total area 290 sq miles (750 sq km)
Languages Tongan*, English*
Religions Protestant 64%, Roman Catholic 15%, other 21%
Ethnic mix Tongan 98%, other 2%
Government Constitutional monarchy
Currency Pa'anga = 100 seniti
Literacy rate 99%
Calorie consumption 2946 kilocalories

Trinidad & Tobago
West Indies

Official name Republic of Trinidad and Tobago
Formation 1962 / 1962
Capital Port-of-Spain
Population 1.3 million / 656 people per sq mile (253 people per sq km) / 72%
Total area 1981 sq miles (5130 sq km)
Languages English*, English Creole, Hindi, French, Spanish
Religions Christian 58%, Hindu 30%, Muslim 8%, other 4%
Ethnic mix Black 43%, Asian 40%, mixed 19%, White and Chinese 1%
Government Multiparty republic
Currency Trinidad & Tobago dollar = 100 cents
Literacy rate 98%
Calorie consumption 2585 kilocalories

Tunisia
North Africa

Official name Republic of Tunisia
Formation 1956 / 1956
Capital Tunis
Population 9.5 million / 158 people per sq mile (61 people per sq km) / 57%
Total area 63,170 sq miles (163,610 sq km)
Languages Arabic*, French
Religions Muslim 98%, Christian 1%, Jewish 1%
Ethnic mix Arab and Berber 98%, European 1%, other 1%
Government Multiparty republic
Currency Tunisian dinar = 1000 millimes
Literacy rate 67%
Calorie consumption 3330 kilocalories

Turkey
Asia / Europe

Official name Republic of Turkey
Formation 1923 / 1939
Capital Ankara
Population 63.8 million / 215 people per sq mile (83 people per sq km) / 69%
Total area 300,950 sq miles (779,450 sq km)
Languages Turkish*, Kurdish, Arabic, Circassian, Armenian
Religions Muslim 99%, other 1%
Ethnic mix Turkish 70%, Kurdish 20%, other 8%, Arab 2%
Government Multiparty republic
Currency Turkish lira = 100 krural
Literacy rate 83%
Calorie consumption 3429 kilocalories

Turkmenistan
Central Asia

Official name Turkmenistan
Formation 1991 / 1991
Capital Ashgabat
Population 4.3 million / 23 people per sq mile (9 people per sq km) / 45%
Total area 188,455 sq miles (488,100 sq km)
Languages Turkmen*, Uzbek, Russian
Religions Muslim 87%, Eastern Orthodox 11%, other 2%
Ethnic mix Turkmen 72%, Russian 9%, Uzbek 9%, other 10%
Government Multiparty republic
Currency Manat = 100 tenge
Literacy rate 98%
Calorie consumption NOT AVAILABLE

Tuvalu
Australasia & Oceania

Official name Tuvalu
Formation 1978 / 1978
Capital Fongafale
Population 9000 / 976 people per sq mile (377 people per sq km) / 46%
Total area 10 sq miles (26 sq km)
Languages Tuvaluan*, Kiribati, English
Religions Protestant 97%, other 3%
Ethnic mix Polynesian 95% other 5%
Government Constitutional monarchy
Currency Australian dollar = 100 cents
Literacy rate 95%
Calorie consumption NOT AVAILABLE

UGANDA
East Africa

Official name Republic of Uganda
Formation 1962 / 1962
Capital Kampala
Population 21.3 million / 276 people per sq mile (107 people per sq km) / 13%
Total area 91,073 sq miles (235,880 sq km)
Languages English*, Luganda, Nkole, Chiga, Lango, Acholi, Teso
Religions Christian 71%, traditional beliefs 13%, Muslim 5%, other (including Hindu) 11%
Ethnic mix Buganda 18%, Banyoro 14%, Teso 9%, other 59%
Government Multiparty republic
Currency New Uganda shilling = 100 cents
Literacy rate 64%
Calorie consumption 2159 kilocalories

UKRAINE
Eastern Europe

Official name Ukraine
Formation 1991 / 1991
Capital Kiev
Population 51.2 million / 220 people per sq mile (85 people per sq km) / 70%
Total area 223,090 sq miles (603,700 sq km)
Languages Ukrainian*, Russian, Tatar
Religions Mostly Ukrainian Orthodox, with Roman Catholic, Protestant and Jewish minorities
Ethnic mix Ukrainian 73%, Russian 22%, other (including Tatar) 5%
Government Multiparty republic
Currency Hryvna = 100 kopiykas
Literacy rate 98%
Calorie consumption NOT AVAILABLE

UNITED ARAB EMIRATES
Southwest Asia

Official name United Arab Emirates
Formation 1971 / 1971
Capital Abu Dhabi
Population 2.4 million / 74 people per sq mile (29 people per sq km) / 84%
Total area 32,278 sq miles (83,600 sq km)
Languages Arabic*, Farsi (Persian), Urdu, Hindi, English
Religions Sunni Muslim 77%, Shi'a Muslim 19%, other 4%
Ethnic mix Asian 50%, Emirian 19%, other Arab 23%, other 8%
Government Federation of monarchs
Currency UAE dirham = 100 fils
Literacy rate 79%
Calorie consumption 3384 kilocalories

UNITED KINGDOM
Northwest Europe

Official name United Kingdom of Great Britain and Northern Ireland
Formation 1707 / 1922
Capital London
Population 58.2 million / 624 people per sq mile (241 people per sq km) / 89%
Total area 94,550 sq miles (244,880 sq km)
Languages English*, Welsh*, Scottish, Gaelic
Religions Protestant 52%, Roman Catholic 9%, Muslim 3%, other 36%
Ethnic mix English 80%, Scottish 10%, Northern Irish 4%, Welsh 2%, West Indian, Asian 4%
Government Constitutional monarchy
Currency Pound sterling = 100 pence
Literacy rate 99%
Calorie consumption 3317 kilocalories

UNITED STATES
North America

Official name United States of America
Formation 1787 / 1959
Capital Washington DC
Population 273.8 million / 77 people per sq mile (30 people per sq km) / 76%
Total area 3,681,760 sq miles (9,372,610 sq km)
Languages English*, Spanish, Italian, German, French, Polish, Chinese, Greek
Religions Protestant 61%, Roman Catholic 25%, Jewish 2%, other 12%
Ethnic mix White (including Hispanic) 84%, Black 12%, Chinese 1%, other 3%
Government Multiparty republic
Currency US dollar = 100 cents
Literacy rate 99%
Calorie consumption 3732 kilocalories

URUGUAY
South America

Official name Oriental Republic of Uruguay
Formation 1828 / 1828
Capital Montevideo
Population 3.2 million / 47 people per sq mile (18 people per sq km) / 90%
Total area 67,494 sq miles (174,810 sq km)
Languages Spanish*
Religions Roman Catholic 66%, Protestant 2%, Jewish 2%, other 30%
Ethnic mix White 90%, *mestizo* 6% Black 4%
Government Multiparty republic
Currency Uruguayan peso = 100 centimes
Literacy rate 97%
Calorie consumption 2750 kilocalories

UZBEKISTAN
Central Asia

Official name Republic of Uzbekistan
Formation 1991 / 1991
Capital Tashkent
Population 24.1 million / 140 people per sq mile (54 people per sq km) / 41%
Total area 172,741 sq miles (447,400 sq km)
Languages Uzbek*, Russian
Religions Muslim 88%, other (mostly Eastern Orthodox) 9%, other 3%
Ethnic mix Uzbek 71%, Russian 8%, Tajik 5%, Kazakh 4%, other 12%
Government Multiparty republic
Currency Sum = 100 teen
Literacy rate 99%
Calorie consumption NOT AVAILABLE

VANUATU
Australasia & Oceania

Official name Republic of Vanuatu
Formation 1980 / 1980
Capital Port-Vila
Population 200,000 / 42 people per sq mile (16 people per sq km) / 19%
Total area 4706 sq miles (12,190 sq km)
Languages Bislama*, English*, French*
Religions Protestant 77%, Roman Catholic 15%, traditional beliefs 8%
Ethnic mix ni-Vanuatu 94%, other 6%
Government Multiparty republic
Currency Vatu = 100 centimes
Literacy rate 64%
Calorie consumption 2739 kilocalories

VATICAN CITY
Southern Europe

Official name Vatican City State
Formation 1929 / 1929
Capital Not applicable
Population 1000 / 5886 people per sq mile (2273 people per sq km) / 100%
Total area 0.17 sq miles (0.44 sq km)
Languages Italian*, Latin*
Religions Roman Catholic 100%
Ethnic mix Italian 90%, Swiss 10% (including the Swiss Guard, which is responsible for papal security)
Government Papal Commission
Currency Italian lira = 100 centesimi
Literacy rate 99%
Calorie consumption 3561 kilocalories

VENEZUELA
South America

Official name Republic of Venezuela
Formation 1830 / 1930
Capital Caracas
Population 23.2 million / 68 people per sq mile (26 people per sq km) / 93%
Total area 352,143 sq miles (912,050 sq km)
Languages Spanish*, Amerindian languages *
Religions Roman Catholic 89%, Protestant and other 11%
Ethnic mix *Mestizo* 69%, White 20%, Black 9%, Amerindian 2%
Government Multiparty republic
Currency Bolívar = 100 centimos
Literacy rate 92%
Calorie consumption 2618 kilocalories

VIETNAM
Southeast Asia

Official name Socialist Republic of Vietnam
Formation 1976 / 1976
Capital Hanoi
Population 77.9 million / 620 people per sq mile (239 people per sq km) / 21%
Total area 127,243 sq miles (329,560 sq km)
Languages Vietnamese*, Chinese, Thai, Khmer, Muong
Religions Buddhist 55%, Christian 7%, other and non-religious 38%
Ethnic mix Vietnamese 88%, Chinese 4%, Thai 2%, other 6%
Government Single-party republic
Currency Dong = 10 hao = 100 xu
Literacy rate 91%
Calorie consumption 2250 kilocalories

YEMEN
Southwest Asia

Official name Republic of Yemen
Formation 1990 / 1990
Capital Sana
Population 16.9 million / 82 people per sq mile (32 people per sq km) / 34%
Total area 203,849 sq miles (527,970 sq km)
Languages Arabic*, Hindi, Tamil, Urdu
Religions Shi'a Muslim 55%, Sunni Muslim 42%, Christian, Hindu, Jewish 3%
Ethnic mix Arab 95%, Afro-Arab 3%, Indian, Somali, European 2%
Government Multiparty republic
Currency Rial (North), Dinar (South) – both are legal currency
Literacy rate 42%
Calorie consumption 2203 kilocalories

YUGOSLAVIA (SERBIA & MONTENEGRO) *Europe*

Official name Federal Republic of Yugoslavia
Formation 1992 / 1992
Capital Belgrade
Population 10.4 million / 264 people per sq mile (102 people per sq km) / 57%
Total area 39,449 sq miles (102,173 sq km)
Languages Serbo-croat*, Albanian
Religions Eastern Orthodox 69%, Muslim 19%, Protestant 1%, other 11%
Ethnic mix Serb 62%, Albanian 17%, Montenegrin 5%, Magyar 3%, other 13%
Government Multiparty republic
Currency Dinar = 100 para
Literacy rate 93%
Calorie consumption NOT AVAILABLE

ZAMBIA
Southern Africa

Official name Republic of Zambia
Formation 1964 / 1964
Capital Lusaka
Population 8.7 million / 30 people per sq mile (12 people per sq km) / 43%
Total area 285,992 sq miles (740,720 sq km)
Languages English*, Bemba, Nyanja, Tonga, Kaonde, Lunda
Religions Christian 63%, Traditional beliefs 36%, other 1%
Ethnic mix Bemba 36%, Maravi 18%, Tonga 15%, other 31%
Government Multiparty republic
Currency Kwacha = 100 ngwee
Literacy rate 75%
Calorie consumption 1931 kilocalories

ZIMBABWE
Southern Africa

Official name Republic of Zimbabwe
Formation 1980 / 1980
Capital Harare
Population 11.9 million / 80 people per sq mile (21 people per sq km) / 32%
Total area 150,800 sq miles (390,580 sq km)
Languages English*, Shona, Ndebele
Religions Syncretic (Christian and traditional beliefs) 50%, Christian 26%, traditional beliefs 24%
Ethnic mix Shona 71%, Ndebele 16%, other African 11%, White, Asian 2%
Government Multiparty republic
Currency Zimbabwe dollar = 100 cents
Literacy rate 90%
Calorie consumption 1985 kilocalories

GEOGRAPHICAL NAMES

THE FOLLOWING GLOSSARY lists all geographical terms occurring on the maps and in main-entry names in the Index-Gazetteer. These terms may precede, follow or be run together with the proper element of the name; where they precede it the term is reversed for indexing purposes – thus Poluostrov Yamal is indexed as Yamal, Poluostrov.

KEY
Geographical term Language, Term

A

Å Danish, Norwegian, River
Āb Persian, River
Adrar Berber, Mountains
Agía, Ágios Greek, Saint
Air Indonesian, River
Ákra Greek, Cape, point
Alpen German, Alps
Alt- German, Old
Altiplanicie Spanish, Plateau
Älve(en) Swedish, River
-ån Swedish, River
Anse French, Bay
'Aqabat Arabic, Pass
Archipiélago Spanish, Archipelago
Arcipelago Italian, Archipelago
Arquipélago Portuguese, Archipelago
Arrecife(s) Spanish, Reef(s)
Aru Tamil, River
Augstiene Latvian, Upland
Aukštuma Lithuanian, Upland
Aust- Norwegian, Eastern
Avtonomnyy Okrug Russian, Autonomous district
Āw Kurdish, River
'Ayn Arabic, Spring, well
'Ayoûn Arabic, Wells

B

Baelt Danish, Strait
Bahía Spanish, Bay
Baḥr Arabic, River
Baía Portuguese, Bay
Baie French, Bay
Bañado Spanish, Marshy land
Bandao Chinese, Peninsula
Banjaran Malay, Mountain range
Barajı Turkish, Dam
Barragem Portuguese, Reservoir
Bassin French, Basin
Batang Malay, Stream
Beinn, Ben Gaelic, Mountain
-berg Afrikaans, Norwegian, Mountain
Besar Indonesian, Malay, Big
Birkat, Birket Arabic, Lake, well, Cistern
Boğazi Turkish, Lake
Boka Serbian, Croatian, Bay
Bol'sh-aya, -iye, -oy, -oye *Russian*, Big
Botigh(i) Uzbek, Depression basin
-bre(en) Norwegian, Glacier
Bredning Danish, Bay
Bucht German, Bay
Bugt(en) Danish, Bay
Buḥayrat Arabic, Lake, reservoir
Buḥeirat Arabic, Lake
Bukit Malay, Mountain
-bukta Norwegian, Bay
bukten Swedish, Bay
Bulag Mongolian, Spring
Bulak Uighur, Spring
Burnu Turkish, Cape, point
Buuraha Somali, Mountains

C

Cabo Portuguese, Cape
Caka Tibetan, Salt lake
Canal Spanish, Channel
Cap French, Cape
Capo Italian, Cape, headland
Cascada Portuguese, Waterfall
Cayo(s) Spanish, Islet(s), rock(s)
Cerro Spanish, Mountain
Chaîne French, Mountain range
Chapada Portuguese, Hills, upland
Chau Cantonese, Island
Chāy Turkish, River
Chhâk Cambodian, Bay
Chhu Tibetan, River
-chŏsuji Korean, Reservoir
Chott Arabic, Depression, salt lake
Chŭli Uzbek, Grassland, steppe
Ch'ün-tao Chinese, Island group
Chuŏr Phnum Cambodian, Mountains
Ciudad Spanish, City, town
Co Tibetan, Lake
Colline(s) French, Hill(s)
Cordillera Spanish, Mountain range
Costa Spanish, Coast
Côte French, Coast
Coxilha Portuguese, Mountains
Cuchilla Spanish, Mountains

D

Daban Mongolian, Uighur, Pass
Daği Azerbaijani, Turkish, Mountain
Dağlari Azerbaijani, Turkish, Mountains
-dake Japanese, Peak
-dal(en) Norwegian, Valley
Danau Indonesian, Lake
Dao Chinese, Island
Đao Vietnamese, Island
Daryā Persian, River
Daryācheh Persian, Lake
Dasht Persian, Desert, plain
Dawḥat Arabic, Bay
Denizi Turkish, Sea
Dere Turkish, Stream
Desierto Spanish, Desert
Dili Azerbaijani, Spit
-do Korean, Island
Dooxo Somali, Valley
Düzü Azerbaijani, Steppe
-dwīp Bengali, Island

E

-eilanden Dutch, Islands
Embalse Spanish, Reservoir
Ensenada Spanish, Bay
Erg Arabic, Dunes
Estany Catalan, Lake
Estero Spanish, Inlet
Estrecho Spanish, Strait
Étang French, Lagoon, lake
-ey Icelandic, Island
Ezero Bulgarian, Macedonian, Lake
Ezers Latvian, Lake

F

Feng Chinese, Peak
Fjord Danish, Fjord
-fjord(en) Danish, Norwegian, Swedish, fjord
-fjørdhur Faeroese, Fjord
Fleuve French, River
Fliegu Maltese, Channel
-fljór Icelandic, River
-flói Icelandic, Bay
Forêt French, Forest

G

-gan Japanese, Rock
-gang Korean, River
Ganga Hindi, Nepali, Sinhala, River
Gaoyuan Chinese, Plateau
Garagumy Turkmen, Sands
-gawa Japanese, River
Gebel Arabic, Mountain
-gebirge German, Mountain range
Ghadir Arabic, Well
Ghubbat Arabic, Bay
Gjiri Albanian, Bay
Gol Mongolian, River
Golfe French, Gulf
Golfo Italian, Spanish, Gulf
Göl(ü) Turkish, Lake
Golyam, -a Bulgarian, Big
Gora Russian, Serbian, Croatian, Mountain
Góra Polish, Mountain
Gory Russian, Mountain
Gryada Russian, Ridge
Guba *Russian*, Bay
-gundo Korean, Island group
Gunung Malay, Mountain

H

Ḥadd Arabic, Spit
-haehyŏp Korean, Strait
Haff German, Lagoon
Hai Chinese, Bay, lake, sea
Haixia Chinese, Strait
Hamada Arabic, Plateau
Ḥammādat Arabic, Plateau
Hāmūn Persian, Lake
-hantō Japanese, Peninsula
Har, Haré Hebrew, Mountain
Ḥarrat Arabic, Lava-field
Hav(et) Danish, Swedish, Sea
Hawr Arabic, Lake
Hāyk' Amharic, Lake
He Chinese, River
-hegység Hungarian, Mountain range
Heide German, Heath, moorland
Helodrano Malagasy, Bay
Higashi- Japanese, East(ern)
Ḥiṣā' Arabic, Well
Hka Burmese, River
-ho Korean, Lake
Hô Korean, Reservoir
Ḥolot Hebrew, Dunes
Hora Belarussian, Czech, Mountain
Hrada Belorussian, Mountain, ridge
Hsi Chinese, River
Hu Chinese, Lake
Huk Danish, Point

I

Île(s) French, Island(s)
Ilha(s) Portuguese, Island(s)
Ilhéu(s) Portuguese, Islet(s)
Imeni Russian, In the name of
Inish- Gaelic, Island
Insel(n) German, Island(s)
Irmağı, Irmak Turkish, River
Isla(s) Spanish, Island(s)
Isola (Isole) Italian, Island(s)

J

Jabal Arabic, Mountain
Jāl Arabic, Ridge
-järv Estonian, Lake
-järvi Finnish, Lake
Jazā'ir Arabic, Islands
Jazīrat Arabic, Island
Jazīreh Persian, Island
Jebel Arabic, Mountain
Jezero Serbian, Croatian, Lake
Jezioro Polish, Lake
Jiang Chinese, River
-jima Japanese, Island
Jižní Czech, Southern
-jõgi Estonian, River
-joki Finnish, River
-jökull Icelandic, Glacier
Jūn Arabic, Bay
Juzur Arabic, Islands

K

Kaikyō Japanese, Strait
-kaise Lappish, Mountain
Kali Nepali, River
Kalnas Lithuanian, Mountain
Kalns Latvian, Mountain
Kang Chinese, Harbour
Kangri Tibetan, Mountain(s)
Kaôh Cambodian, Island
Kapp Norwegian, Cape
Káto Greek, Lower
Kavīr Persian, Desert
K'edi Georgian, Mountain range
Kediet Arabic, Mountain
Kepi Albanian, Cape, point
Kepulauan Indonesian, Malay, Island group
Khalīg, Khalīj Arabic, Gulf
Khawr Arabic, Inlet
Khola Nepali, River
Khrebet Russian, Mountain range
Ko Thai, Island
-ko Japanese, Inlet, lake
Kólpos Greek, Bay
-kopf German, Peak
Körfäzi Azerbaijani, Bay
Körfezi Turkish, Bay
Kõrgustik Estonian, Upland
Kosa Russian, Ukrainian, Spit
Koshi Nepali, River
Kou Chinese, River-mouth
Kowtal Persian, Pass
Kray Russian, Region, territory
Kryazh Russian, Ridge
Kuduk Uighur, Well
Kūh(hā) Persian, Mountain(s)
-kul' Russian, Lake
Kŭl(i) Tajik, Uzbek, Lake
-kundo Korean, Island group
-kysten Norwegian, Coast
Kyun Burmese, Island

L

Laaq Somali, Watercourse
Lac French, Lake
Lacul Romanian, Lake
Lagh Somali, Stream
Lago Italian, *Portuguese, Spanish*, Lake
Lagoa Portuguese, Lagoon
Laguna Italian, Spanish, Lagoon, lake
Laht Estonian, Bay
Laut Indonesian, Bay
Lembalemba Malagasy, Plateau
Lerr Armenian, Mountain
Lerrnashght'a Armenian, Mountain range
Les Czech, Forest
Lich Armenian, Lake
Liehtao Chinese, Island group
Liqeni Albanian, Lake
Límni Greek, Lake
Ling Chinese, Mountain range
Llano Spanish, Plain, prairie
Lumi Albanian, River
Lyman Ukrainian, Estuary

M

Madīnat Arabic, City, town
Mae Nam Thai, River
-mägi Estonian, Hill
Maja Albanian, Mountain
Mal Albanian, Mountains
Mal-aya, -oye, -yy, Russian, Small
-man Korean, Bay
Mar Spanish, Lake
Marios Lithuanian, Lake
Massif French, Mountains
Meer German, Lake
-meer Dutch, Lake
Melkosopochnik Russian, Plain
-meri Estonian, Sea
Mifraz Hebrew, Bay
Minami- Japanese, South(ern)
-misaki Japanese, Cape, point
Monkhafad Arabic, Depression
Montagne(s) French, Mountain(s)
Montañas Spanish, Mountains
Mont(s) French, Mountain(s)
Monte Italian, Portuguese, Mountain
More Russian, Sea
Mörön Mongolian, River
Mys Russian, Cape, point

N

-nada Japanese, Open stretch of water
Nagor'ye Russian, Upland
Naḥal Hebrew, River
Nahr Arabic, River
Nam Laotian, River
Namakzār Persian, Salt desert
Né-a, -on, -os Greek, New
Nedre- Norwegian, Lower
-neem Estonian, Cape, point
Nehri Turkish, River
-nes Norwegian, Cape, point
Nevado Spanish, Mountain (snow-capped)
Nieder- German, Lower
Nishi- Japanese, West(ern)
-nísi Greek, Island
Nisoi Greek, Islands
Nizhn-eye, -iy, -iye, -yaya Russian, Lower
Nizmennost' Russian, Lowland, plain
Nord Danish, French, German, North
Norte Portuguese, Spanish, North
Nos Bulgarian, Point, spit
Nosy Malagasy, Island
Nov-a, -i, Bulgarian, Serbian, Croatian, New
Nov-aya, -o, -oye, -yy, -yye Russian, New
Now-a, -e, -y Polish, New
Nur Mongolian, Lake
Nuruu Mongolian, Mountains
Nuur Mongolian, Lake
Nyzovyna Ukrainian, Lowland, plain

O

-ø Danish, Island
Ober- German, Upper
Oblast' Russian, Province
Órmos Greek, Bay
Orol(i) Uzbek, Island
Øster- Norwegian, Eastern
Ostrov(a) Russian, Island(s)
Otok Serbian, Croatian, Island
Oued Arabic, Watercourse
-oy Faeroese, Island
-øy(a) Norwegian, Island
Oya Sinhala, River
Ozero Russian, Ukrainian, Lake

P

Passo Italian, Pass
Pegunungan Indonesian, Malay, Mountain range
Pélagos Greek, Sea
Pendi Chinese, Basin
Penisola Italian, Peninsula
Pertuis French, Strait
Peski Russian, Sands
Phanom Thai, Mountain
Phou Laotian, Mountain
Pi Chinese, Point
Pic Catalan, French, Peak
Pico Portuguese, Spanish, Peak
-piggen Danish, Peak
Pik Russian, Peak
Pivostriv Ukrainian, Peninsula
Planalto Portuguese, Plateau
Planina, Planini Bulgarian, Macedonian, Serbian, Croatian, Mountain range
Plato Russian, Plateau
Ploskogor'ye Russian, Upland
Poluostrov Russian, Peninsula
Ponta Portuguese, Point
Porthmós Greek, Strait
Pótamos Greek, River
Presa Spanish, Dam
Prokhod Bulgarian, Pass
Proliv Russian, Strait
Pulau Indonesian, Malay, Island
Pulu Malay, Island
Punta Spanish, Point
Pushcha Belorussian, Forest
Puszcza Polish, Forest

Q

Qā' Arabic, Depression
Qalamat Arabic, Well
Qatorkŭh(i) Tajik, Mountain
Qiuling Chinese, Hills
Qolleh Persian, Mountain
Qu Tibetan, Stream
Quan Chinese, Well
Qulla(i) Tajik, Peak
Qundao Chinese, Island group

R

Raas Somali, Cape
-rags Latvian, Cape
Ramlat Arabic, Sands
Ra's Arabic, Cape, headland, point
Ravnina Bulgarian, Russian, Plain
Récif French, Reef
Recife Portuguese, Reef
Reka Bulgarian, River
Represa (Rep.) Portuguese, Spanish, Reservoir
Reshteh Persian, Mountain range
Respublika Russian, Republic, first-order administrative division
Respublika(si) Uzbek, Republic, first-order administrative division
-retsugan Japanese, Chain of rocks
-rettō Japanese, Island chain
Riacho Spanish, Stream
Riban' Malagasy, Mountains
Rio Portuguese, River
Río Spanish, River
Riu Catalan, River
Rivier Dutch, River
Rivière French, River
Rowd Pashtu, River
Rt Serbian, Croatian, Point
Rūd Persian, River
Rūdkhāneh Persian, River
Rudohorie Slovak, Mountains
Ruisseau French, Stream

S

-saar Estonian, Island
-saari Finnish, Island
Sabkhat Arabic, Salt marsh
Sāgar(a) Hindi, Lake, reservoir
Ṣaḥrā' Arabic, Desert
Saint, Sainte French, Saint
Salar Spanish, Salt-pan
Salto Portuguese, Spanish, Waterfall
Samudra Sinhala, Reservoir
-san Japanese, Korean, Mountain
-sanchi Japanese, Mountains
-sandur Icelandic, Beach
Sankt German, Swedish, Saint
-sanmaek Korean, Mountain range
-sanmyaku Japanese, Mountain range
San, Santa, Santo Italian, Portuguese, Spanish, Saint
São Portuguese, Saint
Sarīr Arabic, Desert
Sebkha, Sebkhet Arabic, Depression, salt marsh
Sedlo Czech, Pass
See German, Lake
Selat Indonesian, Strait
Selatan Indonesian, Southern
-selkä Finnish, Lake, ridge
Selseleh Persian, Mountain range
Serra Portuguese, Mountain
Serranía Spanish, Mountain
-seto Japanese, Channel, strait
Sever-naya, -noye, -nyy, -o Russian, Northern
Sha'īb Arabic, Watercourse
Shākh Kurdish, Mountain
Shamo Chinese, Desert
Shan Chinese, Mountain(s)
Shankou Chinese, Pass
Shanmo Chinese, Mountain range
Shaṭṭ Arabic, Distributary
Shet' Amharic, River
Shi Chinese, Municipality
-shima Japanese, Island
Shiqqat Arabic, Depression
-shotō Japanese, Group of islands
Shuiku Chinese, Reservoir
Shŭrkhog(i) Uzbek, Salt marsh
Sierra Spanish, Mountains
Sint Dutch, Saint
-sjø(en) Norwegian, Lake
-sjön Swedish, Lake
Solonchak Russian, Salt lake
Solonchakovyye Vpadiny Russian, Salt basin, wetlands
Sơn Vietnamese, Mountain
Sông Vietnamese, River
Sør- Norwegian, Southern
-spitze German, Peak
Star-á, -é Czech, Old
Star-aya, -oye, -yy, -yye Russian, Old
Stenó Greek, Strait
Step' Russian, Steppe
Štít Slovak, Peak
Stœng Cambodian, River
Stolovaya Strana Russian, Plateau
Stredné Slovak, Middle
Střední Czech, Middle
Stretto Italian, Strait
Su Anbari Azerbaijani, Reservoir
-suidō Japanese, Channel, strait
Sund Swedish, Sound, strait
Sungai Indonesian, Malay, River
Suu Turkish, River

T

Tal Mongolian, Plain
Tandavan' Malagasy, Mountain range
Tangorombohitr' Malagasy, Mountain massif
Tanjung Indonesian, Malay, Cape, point
Tao Chinese, Island
Ṭaraq Arabic, Hills
Tassili Berber, Mountain, plateau
Tau Russian, Mountain(s)
Taungdan Burmese, Mountain range
Techníti Límni Greek, Reservoir
Tekojärvi Finnish, Reservoir
Teluk Indonesian, Malay, Bay
Tengah Indonesian, Middle
Terara Amharic, Mountain
Timur Indonesian, Eastern
-tind(an) Norwegian, Peak
Tizma(si) Uzbek, Mountain range, ridge
-tō Japanese, Island
Tog Somali, Valley
-tōge Japanese, Pass
Togh(i) Uzbek, Mountain
Tônlé Cambodian, Lake
Top Dutch, Peak
-tunturi Finnish, Mountain
Ṭurāq Arabic, Hills
Tur'at Arabic, Channel

U

Udde(n) Swedish, Cape, point
'Uqlat Arabic, Well
Utara Indonesian, Northern
Uul Mongolian, Mountains

V

Väin Estonian, Strait
Vallée French, Valley
-vatn Icelandic, Lake
-vatnet Norwegian, Lake
Velayat Turkmen, Province
-vesi Finnish, Lake
Vestre- Norwegian, Western
-vidda Norwegian, Plateau
-vík Icelandic, Bay
-viken Swedish, Bay, inlet
Vinh Vietnamese, Bay
Víztárloló Hungarian, Reservoir
Vodaskhovishcha Belorussian, Reservoir
Vodokhranilishche (Vdkhr.) Russian, Reservoir
Vodoskhovyshche (Vdskh.) Ukrainian, Reservoir
Volcán Spanish, Volcano
Vostochn-o, yy Russian, Eastern
Vozvyshennost' Russian, Upland, plateau
Vozyera Belorussian, Lake
Vpadina Russian, Depression
Vrchovina Czech, Mountains
Vrha Macedonian, Peak
Vychodné Slovak, Eastern
Vysochyna Ukrainian, Upland
Vysočina Czech, Upland

W

Waadi Somali, Watercourse
Wādī Arabic Watercourse
Wāḥat, Wâhat Arabic, Oasis
Wald German, Forest
Wan Chinese, Bay
Way Indonesian, River
Webi Somali, River
Wenz Amharic, River
Wiloyat(i) Uzbek, Province
Wyżyna Polish, Upland
Wzgórza Polish, Upland
Wzvyshsha Belarussian, Upland

X

Xé Laotian, River
Xi Chinese, Stream

Y

-yama Japanese, Mountain
Yanchi Chinese, Salt lake
Yang Chinese, Bay
Yanhu Chinese, Salt lake
Yarımadası Azerbaijani, Turkish, Peninsula
Yaylası Turkish, Plateau
Yazovir Bulgarian, Reservoir
Yoma Burmese, Mountains
Ytre- Norwegian, Outer
Yü Chinese, Island
Yunhe Chinese, Canal
Yuzhn-o, -yy Russian, Southern

Z

-zaki Japanese, Cape, point
Zaliv Bulgarian, Russian, Bay
-zan Japanese, Mountain
Zangbo Tibetan, River
Zapadn-aya, -o, -yy Russian, Western
Západné Slovak, Western
Západní Czech, Western
Zatoka Polish, Ukrainian, Bay
-zee Dutch, Sea
Zemlya Russian, Earth, land
Zizhiqu Chinese, Autonomous region

25 DE MAYO – ABUYOG

INDEX

GLOSSARY OF ABBREVIATIONS

This glossary provides a comprehensive guide to the abbreviations used in this Atlas, and in the Index.

A

abbrev. abbreviated
AD Anno Domini
Afr. Afrikaans
Alb. Albanian
Amh. Amharic
anc. ancient
approx. approximately
Ar. Arabic
Arm. Armenian
ASEAN Association of South East Asian Nations
ASSR Autonomous Soviet Socialist Republic
Aust. Australian
Az. Azerbaijani
Azerb. Azerbaijan

B

Basq. Basque
BC before Christ
Bel. Belorussian
Ben. Bengali
Ber. Berber
B-H Bosnia-Herzegovina
bn billion (one thousand million)
BP British Petroleum
Bret. Breton
Brit. British
Bul. Bulgarian
Bur. Burmese

C

C central
C. Cape
°C degrees Centigrade
CACM Central America Common Market
Cam. Cambodian
Cant. Cantonese
CAR Central African Republic
Cast. Castilian
Cat. Catalan
CEEAC Central America Common Market
Chin. Chinese
CIS Commonwealth of Independent States
cm centimetre(s)
Cro. Croat
Cz. Czech
Czech Rep. Czech Republic

D

Dan. Danish
Div. Divehi
Dom. Rep. Dominican Republic
Dut. Dutch

E

E east
EC *see* EU
EEC *see* EU
ECOWAS Economic Community of West African States
ECU European Currency Unit
EMS European Monetary System
Eng. English
est estimated
Est. Estonian
EU European Union (previously European Community [EC], European Economic Community [EEC])

F

°F degrees Fahrenheit
Faer. Faeroese
Fij. Fijian
Fin. Finnish
Fr. French
Fris. Frisian
ft foot/feet
FYROM Former Yugoslav Republic of Macedonia

G

g gram(s)
Gael. Gaelic
Gal. Galician
GDP Gross Domestic Product (the total value of goods and services produced by a country excluding income from foreign countries)
Geor. Georgian
Ger. German
Gk Greek
GNP Gross National Product (the total value of goods and services produced by a country)

H

Heb. Hebrew
HEP hydro-electric power
Hind. Hindi
hist. historical
Hung. Hungarian

I

I. Island
Icel. Icelandic
in inch(es)
In. Inuit (Eskimo)
Ind. Indonesian
Intl International
Ir. Irish
Is Islands
It. Italian

J

Jap. Japanese

K

Kaz. Kazakh
kg kilogram(s)
Kir. Kirghiz
km kilometre(s)
km² square kilometre (singular)
Kor. Korean
Kurd. Kurdish

L

L. Lake
LAIA Latin American Integration Association
Lao. Laotian
Lapp. Lappish
Lat. Latin
Latv. Latvian
Liech. Liechtenstein
Lith. Lithuanian
Lux. Luxembourg

M

m million/metre(s)
Mac. Macedonian
Maced. Macedonia
Mal. Malay
Malg. Malagasy
Malt. Maltese
mi. mile(s)
Mong. Mongolian
Mt. Mountain
Mts Mountains

N

N north
NAFTA North American Free Trade Agreement
Nep. Nepali
Neth. Netherlands
Nic. Nicaraguan
Nor. Norwegian
NZ New Zealand

P

Pash. Pashtu
PNG Papua New Guinea
Pol. Polish
Poly. Polynesian
Port. Portuguese
prev. previously

R

Rep. Republic
Res. Reservoir
Rmsch Romansch
Rom. Romanian
Rus. Russian
Russ. Fed. Russian Federation

S

S south
SADC Southern Africa Development Community
SCr. Serbian, Croatian
Sinh. Sinhala
Slvk Slovak
Slvn. Slovene
Som. Somali
Sp. Spanish
St., St Saint
Strs Straits
Swa. Swahili
Swe. Swedish
Switz. Switzerland

T

Taj. Tajik
Th. Thai
Thai. Thailand
Tib. Tibetan
Turk. Turkish
Turkm. Turkmenistan

U

UAE United Arab Emirates
Uigh. Uighur
UK United Kingdom
Ukr. Ukrainian
UN United Nations
Urd. Urdu
US/USA United States of America
USSR Union of Soviet Socialist Republics
Uzb. Uzbek

V

var. variant
Vdkhr. Vodokhranilishche (Russian for reservoir)
Vdskh. Vodoskhovyshche (Ukrainian for reservoir)
Vtn. Vietnamese

W

W west
Wel. Welsh

Y

Yugo. Yugoslavia

THIS INDEX LISTS all the placenames and features shown on the regional and continental maps in this Atlas. Placenames are referenced to the largest scale map on which they appear. The policy followed throughout the Atlas is to use the local spelling or local name at regional level; commonly-used English language names may occasionally be added (in parentheses) where this is an aid to identification e.g. Firenze (Florence). English names, where they exist, have been used for all international features e.g. oceans and country names; they are also used on the continental maps and in the introductory World Today section; these are then fully cross-referenced to the local names found on the regional maps. The index also contains commonly-found alternative names and variant spellings, which are also fully cross-referenced.

All main entry names are those of settlements unless otherwise indicated by the use of italicized definitions or representative symbols, which are keyed at the foot of each page.

1

25 de Mayo *see* Veinticinco de Mayo
143 *Y13* **26 Bakı Komissarı** ***Rus.*** Imeni 26 Bakinskikh Komissarov. SE Azerbaijan *39.18N 49.13E*
26 Baku Komissarlary Adyndaky *see* Imeni 26 Bakinskikh Komissarov
8 *M16* **100 Mile House** ***var.*** Hundred Mile House. British Columbia, SW Canada *51.39N 121.19W*

A

Aa *see* Gauja
Aabenraa *see* Åbenrå
Aabybro *see* Åbybro
103 *C16* **Aachen** ***Dut.*** Aken, ***Fr.*** Aix-la-Chapelle; ***anc.*** Aquae Grani, Aquisgranum. Nordrhein-Westfalen, W Germany *50.47N 6.06E*
Aaiún *see* Laâyoune
Aakirkeby *see* Åkirkeby
Aalborg *see* Ålborg
Aalborg Bugt *see* Ålborg Bugt
103 *J21* **Aalen** Baden-Württemberg, S Germany *48.49N 10.06E*
Aalestrup *see* Ålestrup
100 *I11* **Aalsmeer** Noord-Holland, C Netherlands *52.16N 4.43E*
101 *F18* **Aalst** ***Fr.*** Alost. Oost-Vlaanderen, C Belgium *50.57N 4.03E*
101 *K18* **Aalst** Noord-Brabant, S Netherlands *51.46N 5.07E*
100 *O12* **Aalten** Gelderland, E Netherlands *51.55N 6.34E*
101 *D17* **Aalter** Oost-Vlaanderen, NW Belgium *51.04N 3.28E*
Aanaar *see* Inari
Aanaarjävri *see* Inarijärvi
95 *M17* **Äänekoski** Länsi-Suomi, W Finland *62.33N 25.44E*
144 *H7* **Aanjar** ***var.*** 'Anjar. C Lebanon *33.45N 35.56E*
85 *G21* **Aansluit** Northern Cape, N South Africa *26.41S 22.24E*
Aar *see* Aare
110 *F7* **Aarau** Aargau, N Switzerland *47.22N 8.00E*
110 *D8* **Aarberg** Bern, W Switzerland *47.02N 7.15E*
101 *D16* **Aardenburg** Zeeland, SW Netherlands *51.16N 3.27E*
110 *D8* **Aare** ***var.*** Aar. ≈ W Switzerland
110 *F7* **Aargau** ***Fr.*** Argovie. ◈ *canton* N Switzerland
Aarhus *see* Århus
Aarlen *see* Arlon
Aars *see* Års
101 *I17* **Aarschot** Vlaams Brabant, C Belgium *50.58N 4.49E*
Aassi, Nahr el *see* Orontes
Aat *see* Ath
166 *G7* **Aba** ***prev.*** Ngawa. Sichuan, C China *32.51N 101.46E*
79 *V17* **Aba** Abia, S Nigeria *5.06N 7.22E*
81 *P16* **Aba** Orientale, NE Dem. Rep. Congo (Zaire) *3.52N 30.13E*
146 *J6* **Abā al Qazāz, Bi'r** *well* NW Saudi Arabia *26.37N 36.50E*
Abā as Su'ūd *see* Najrān
61 *G14* **Abacaxis, Rio** ≈ NW Brazil
Abaco Island *see* Great Abaco/Little Abaco
Abaco Island *see* Great Abaco, N Bahamas
148 *K10* **Ābādān** Khūzestān, SW Iran *30.24N 48.18E*
149 *O10* **Ābādeh** Fārs, C Iran *31.10N 52.39E*
76 *H8* **Abadla** W Algeria *31.04N 2.39W*
61 *M20* **Abaeté** Minas Gerais, SE Brazil *19.10S 45.24W*
169 *Q10* **Abag Qi** ***var.*** Xin Hot. Nei Mongol Zizhiqu, N China *43.58N 114.59E*
64 *P7* **Abaí** Caazapá, S Paraguay *25.58S 55.54W*
203 *O2* **Abaiang** ***var.*** Apia; ***prev.*** Charlotte Island. *atoll* Tungaru, W Kiribati
Abaj *see* Abay
79 *U15* **Abaji** Federal Capital District, C Nigeria *8.35N 6.54E*
39 *O7* **Abajo Peak** ▲ Utah, W USA *37.51N 109.28W*
79 *V16* **Abakaliki** Ebonyi, SE Nigeria *6.18N 8.07E*
126 *Hh15* **Abakan** Respublika Khakasiya, S Russian Federation *53.43N 91.25E*
126 *Hh15* **Abakan** ≈ S Russian Federation
79 *S11* **Abala** Tillabéri, SW Niger *14.55N 3.27E*
79 *U11* **Abalak** Tahoua, C Niger *15.28N 6.18E*
121 *N14* **Abalyanka** ***Rus.*** Obolyanka. ≈ N Belarus
126 *Ii14* **Aban** Krasnoyarskiy Kray, S Russian Federation *56.41N 96.04E*
149 *P9* **Āb Anbār-e Kān Sorkh** Yazd, C Iran *31.22N 53.37E*
59 *G16* **Abancay** Apurímac, SE Peru *13.37S 72.52W*
202 *H2* **Abaokoro** *atoll* Tungaru, W Kiribati
Abariringa *see* Kanton
149 *P10* **Abarkū** Yazd, C Iran
172 *Qq5* **Abashiri** ***var.*** Abasiri. Hokkaidō, NE Japan *44.00N 144.15E*
172 *Q6* **Abashiri-gawa** ≈ Hokkaidō, NE Japan
172 *Q5* **Abashiri-ko** ◎ Hokkaidō, NE Japan
Abasiri *see* Abashiri
43 *P10* **Abasolo** Tamaulipas, C Mexico *24.02N 98.18W*
194 *L16* **Abau** Central, S PNG *10.09S 148.40E*
151 *R10* **Abay** ***var.*** Abaj. Karaganda, C Kazakhstan *49.34N 72.54E*
83 *I15* **Ābaya Hāyk'** ***Eng.*** Lake Margherita, ***It.*** Abbaia. ◎ SW Ethiopia
Ābay Wenz *see* Blue Nile
126 *Hh15* **Abaza** Respublika Khakasiya, S Russian Federation *52.40N 89.58E*
Abbaia *see* Ābaya Hāyk'
149 *Q13* **Āb Bārīk** Fārs, S Iran
109 *C18* **Abbasanta** Sardegna, Italy, C Mediterranean Sea *40.08N 8.49E*
Abbatis Villa *see* Abbeville
32 *M3* **Abbaye, Point** *headland* Michigan, N USA *46.58N 88.08W*
Abbazia *see* Opatija
Abbé, Lake *see* Abhe, Lake
105 *N2* **Abbeville** ***anc.*** Abbatis Villa. Somme, N France *50.06N 1.50E*
25 *R7* **Abbeville** Alabama, S USA *31.34N 85.16W*
25 *U6* **Abbeville** Georgia, SE USA *31.58N 83.18W*
24 *I9* **Abbeville** Louisiana, S USA *29.58N 92.08W*
23 *P12* **Abbeville** South Carolina, SE USA *34.10N 82.22W*
99 *B20* **Abbeyfeale** ***Ir.*** Mainistir na Féile. SW Ireland *52.24N 9.21W*
108 *D8* **Abbiategrasso** Lombardia, NW Italy *45.24N 9.04E*
95 *I14* **Abborrträsk** Norrbotten, N Sweden *65.24N 19.33E*
204 *J9* **Abbot Ice Shelf** *ice shelf* Antarctica
8 *M17* **Abbotsford** British Columbia, SW Canada *49.01N 122.18W*
32 *K6* **Abbotsford** Wisconsin, N USA *44.57N 90.19W*
155 *U5* **Abbottābād** North-West Frontier Province, NW Pakistan *34.08N 73.10E*
121 *M14* **Abchuha** ***Rus.*** Obchuga. Minskaya Voblasts', NW Belarus *54.30N 29.23E*
100 *I10* **Abcoude** Utrecht, C Netherlands *52.16N 4.58E*
145 *N2* **'Abd al 'Azīz, Jabal** ▲▲ NE Syria
147 *U17* **'Abd al Kūrī** *island* SE Yemen
145 *Z13* **'Abd Allāh, Khawr** *bay* Iraq/Kuwait
131 *U6* **Abdulino** Orenburgskaya Oblast', W Russian Federation *53.37N 53.39E*
80 *J10* **Abéché** ***var.*** Abécher, Abeshr. Ouaddaï, SE Chad *13.49N 20.49E*
Abécher *see* Abéché
149 *S8* **Āb-e Garm va Sard** Khorāsān, E Iran
79 *R8* **Abeïbara** Kidal, NE Mali *19.07N 1.52E*
107 *P5* **Abejar** Castilla-León, N Spain *41.48N 2.46W*
56 *E9* **Abejorral** Antioquia, W Colombia *5.52N 75.34W*
Abela *see* Ávila
Abellinum *see* Avellino
94 *Q2* **Abeløya** *island* Kong Karls Land, E Svalbard
82 *I13* **Ābeltī** Oromo, C Ethiopia *8.09N 37.31E*
203 *O2* **Abemama** ***var.*** Apamama; ***prev.*** Roger Simpson Island. *atoll* Tungaru, W Kiribati
176 *Yy14* **Abemaree** ***var.*** Abemarre. Irian Jaya, E Indonesia *7.03S 140.10E*
79 *O16* **Abengourou** E Ivory Coast *6.42N 3.27W*
97 *G24* **Åbenrå** ***var.*** Aabenraa, ***Ger.*** Apenrade. Sønderjylland, SW Denmark *55.03N 9.25E*
103 *L22* **Abens** ≈ SE Germany
79 *S16* **Abeokuta** Ogun, SW Nigeria *7.07N 3.21E*
99 *I20* **Aberaeron** SW Wales, UK *52.15N 4.15W*
Aberbrothock *see* Arbroath
Abercorn *see* Mbala
31 *R6* **Abercrombie** North Dakota, N USA *46.25N 96.42W*
191 *T7* **Aberdeen** New South Wales, SE Australia *32.09S 150.55E*
9 *T15* **Aberdeen** Saskatchewan, S Canada *52.15N 106.19W*
85 *H25* **Aberdeen** Eastern Cape, S South Africa *32.30S 24.00E*
98 *L9* **Aberdeen** ***anc.*** Devana. NE Scotland, UK *57.10N 2.04W*
23 *X2* **Aberdeen** Maryland, NE USA *39.28N 76.09W*
25 *N3* **Aberdeen** Mississippi, S USA *33.49N 88.32W*
23 *T10* **Aberdeen** North Carolina, SE USA *35.07N 79.25W*
31 *P8* **Aberdeen** South Dakota, N USA *45.27N 98.29W*
34 *F8* **Aberdeen** Washington, NW USA *46.57N 123.48W*
98 *K9* **Aberdeen** *cultural region* NE Scotland, UK
15 *K6* **Aberdeen Lake** ◎ Nunavut, NE Canada
98 *J10* **Aberfeldy** C Scotland, UK *56.38N 3.48W*
99 *K21* **Abergavenny** ***anc.*** Gobannium. SE Wales, UK *51.50N 3.00W*
Abergwaun *see* Fishguard
Abermarre *see* Abemaree
27 *N5* **Abernathy** Texas, SW USA *33.49N 101.50W*
Abersee *see* Wolfgangsee
Abertawe *see* Swansea
Aberteifi *see* Cardigan
34 *I15* **Abert, Lake** ◎ Oregon, NW USA
99 *I20* **Aberystwyth** W Wales, UK *52.25N 4.04W*
Abeshr *see* Abéché
108 *F10* **Abetone** Toscana, C Italy *44.09N 10.42E*
129 *V5* **Abez'** Respublika Komi, NW Russian Federation *66.32N 61.41E*
148 *M5* **Āb Garm** Qazvin, N Iran
147 *N12* **Abhā** 'Asīr, SW Saudi Arabia *18.16N 42.31E*
148 *M5* **Abhar** Zanjān, NW Iran *36.07N 49.19E*
Abhé Bad/Ābhē Bid Hāyk' *see* Abhe, Lake
82 *K12* **Abhe, Lake** ***var.*** Lake Abbé, ***Amh.*** Ābhē Bid Hāyk', ***Som.*** Abhé Bad. ◎ Djibouti/Ethiopia
79 *V17* **Abia** ◈ *state* SE Nigeria
145 *V9* **'Abīd 'Alī** E Iraq *32.20N 45.58E*
121 *O17* **Abidavichy** ***Rus.*** Obidovichi. Mahilyowskaya Voblasts', E Belarus *53.21N 30.24E*
117 *L15* **Abide** Çanakkale, NW Turkey *40.04N 26.13E*
79 *N17* **Abidjan** S Ivory Coast *5.19N 4.01W*
Āb-i-Istāda *see* Īstādeh-ye Moqor, Āb-e-
29 *N4* **Abilene** Kansas, C USA *38.55N 97.12W*
27 *Q7* **Abilene** Texas, SW USA *32.27N 99.43W*
Abindonia *see* Abingdon
99 *M21* **Abingdon** ***anc.*** Abindonia. S England, UK *51.40N 1.16W*
32 *K12* **Abingdon** Illinois, N USA *40.48N 90.24W*
23 *P8* **Abingdon** Virginia, NE USA *36.42N 81.58W*
Abingdon *see* Pinta, Isla
20 *J15* **Abington** Pennsylvania, NE USA *40.06N 75.05W*
130 *K14* **Abinsk** Krasnodarskiy Kray, SW Russian Federation *44.51N 38.12E*
39 *R9* **Abiquiu Reservoir** ▣ New Mexico, SW USA
94 *I10* **Abisko** Norrbotten, N Sweden *68.21N 18.49E*
10 *G12* **Abitibi** ≈ Ontario, S Canada
10 *H12* **Abitibi, Lac** ◎ Ontario/Quebec, S Canada
82 *J10* **Ābīy Ādī** Tigray, N Ethiopia *13.40N 38.57E*
120 *H6* **Abja-Paluoja** Viljandimaa, S Estonia *58.07N 25.19E*
143 *Q8* **Abkhazia** ◈ *autonomous republic* NW Georgia
190 *F1* **Abminga** South Australia *26.07S 134.49E*
77 *W9* **Abnûb** C Egypt *27.18N 31.09E*
Åbo *see* Turku
158 *G9* **Abohar** Punjab, N India *30.10N 74.12E*
79 *O17* **Aboisso** SE Ivory Coast *5.27N 3.06W*
80 *H5* **Abo, Massif d'** ▲▲ NW Chad
79 *R16* **Abomey** S Benin *7.14N 2.00E*
81 *F16* **Abong Mbang** Est, SE Cameroon *3.58N 13.10E*
113 *L23* **Abony** Pest, C Hungary *47.10N 20.00E*
80 *J11* **Abou-Déïa** Salamat, SE Chad *11.30N 19.18E*
Aboudouhour *see* Abū aḍ Ḍuhūr
Abou Kémal *see* Abū Kamāl
Abou Simbel *see* Abu Simbel
143 *T12* **Abovyan** C Armenia *40.16N 44.33E*
179 *P8* **Abra** ≈ Luzon, N Philippines
147 *P15* **Abrād, Wādī** *seasonal river* W Yemen
Abraham Bay *see* The Carlton
106 *G10* **Abrantes** ***var.*** Abrántes. Santarém, C Portugal *39.28N 8.12W*
64 *J4* **Abra Pampa** Jujuy, N Argentina *22.46S 65.40W*
Abrashlare *see* Brezovo
56 *G7* **Abrego** Norte de Santander, N Colombia *8.07N 73.15W*
Abrene *see* Pytalovo
42 *C7* **Abreojos, Punta** *headland* W Mexico *26.43N 113.36W*
67 *J16* **Abrolhos Bank** *undersea feature* W Atlantic Ocean
121 *H19* **Abrova** ***Rus.*** Obrovo. Brestskaya Voblasts', SW Belarus *52.30N 25.31E*
118 *G11* **Abrud** ***Ger.*** Gross-Schlatten, ***Hung.*** Abrudbánya. Alba, SW Romania *46.15N 23.07E*
Abrudbánya *see* Abrud
120 *E6* **Abruka** *island* SW Estonia
109 *J15* **Abruzzese, Appennino** ▲▲ C Italy
109 *J14* **Abruzzo** ◈ *region* C Italy
147 *N14* **'Abs** ***var.*** Sūq 'Abs. W Yemen *16.42N 42.55E*
35 *T12* **Absaroka Range** ▲▲ Montana/Wyoming, NW USA
143 *Z11* **Abşeron Yarımadası** ***Rus.*** Apsheronskiy Poluostrov. *peninsula* E Azerbaijan
149 *N6* **Āb Shīrīn** Eşfahān, C Iran
145 *X10* **Abtān** SE Iraq *31.37N 47.06E*
111 *R6* **Abtenau** Salzburg, NW Austria *47.33N 13.21E*
170 *Dd12* **Abu** Yamaguchi, Honshū, SW Japan *34.30N 131.26E*
158 *E14* **Ābu** Rājasthān, N India *24.40N 72.49E*
144 *I4* **Abū aḍ Ḍuhūr** ***Fr.*** Aboudouhour. Idlib, NW Syria *35.30N 37.00E*
149 *P17* **Abū al Abyaḍ** *island* C UAE
144 *K10* **Abū al Ḥuşayn, Khabrat** ◎ N Jordan
145 *R8* **Abū al Jīr** C Iraq *33.16N 42.55E*
145 *Y12* **Abū al Khaşīb** ***var.*** Abul Khasib. SE Iraq *30.26N 48.00E*
145 *U12* **Abū at Tubrah, Thaqb** *well* S Iraq *30.54N 45.02E*
77 *V11* **Abu Balâs** ▲ SW Egypt *24.28N 27.36E*
Abu Dhabi *see* Abū Ẓaby
145 *R8* **Abū Farūkh** C Iraq *33.06N 43.18E*
82 *C12* **Abu Gabra** Southern Darfur, W Sudan *11.01N 26.49E*
145 *P10* **Abū Ghār, Sha'īb** *dry watercourse* S Iraq
82 *G7* **Abu Hamed** River Nile, N Sudan *19.31N 33.19E*
145 *O5* **Abū Ḥardān** ***var.*** Hajîne. Dayr az Zawr, E Syria *34.45N 40.49E*
145 *T7* **Abū Ḥāssawīyah** E Iraq *33.52N 44.47E*
144 *K10* **Abū Ḥifnah, Wādī** *dry watercourse* N Jordan
79 *V15* **Abuja** ● (Nigeria) Federal Capital District, C Nigeria *9.04N 7.28E*
145 *R9* **Abū Jahaf, Wādī** *dry watercourse* C Iraq
58 *F12* **Abujao, Río** ≈ E Peru
145 *U12* **Abū Jasrah** S Iraq *30.43N 44.50E*
145 *O6* **Abū Kamāl** ***Fr.*** Abou Kémal. Dayr az Zawr, E Syria *34.28N 40.55E*
175 *Q11* **Abuki, Pegunungan** ▲▲ Sulawesi, C Indonesia
171 *Ll14* **Abukuma-gawa** ≈ Honshū, C Japan
171 *Ll15* **Abukuma-sanchi** ▲▲ Honshū, C Japan
Abula *see* Ávila
Abul Khasib *see* Abū al Khaşīb
81 *K16* **Abumombazi** ***var.*** Abumonbazi. Equateur, N Dem. Rep. Congo (Zaire) *3.43N 22.06E*
Abumonbazi *see* Abumombazi
61 *D15* **Abunã** Rondônia, W Brazil *9.40S 65.19W*
58 *K13* **Abunã, Rio** ***var.*** Río Abuná. ≈ Bolivia/Brazil
144 *G10* **Abū Nuşayr** ***var.*** Abu Nuseir. 'Ammān, W Jordan *32.03N 35.58E*
Abu Nuseir *see* Abū Nuşayr
145 *T12* **Abū Qabr** S Iraq *31.03N 44.34E*
144 *K5* **Abū Raḩbah, Jabal** ▲▲ C Syria
145 *S5* **Abū Rajāsh** N Iraq *34.47N 43.36E*
145 *W13* **Abū Raqrāq, Ghadīr** *well* S Iraq *30.15N 45.57E*
158 *E14* **Ābu Road** Rājasthān, N India *24.28N 72.46E*
82 *I6* **Abu Shagara, Ras** *headland* NE Sudan *18.04N 38.31E*
77 *W12* **Abu Simbel** ***var.*** Abou Simbel, Abū Sunbul. *ancient monument* S Egypt *22.25N 31.37E*
145 *U12* **Abū Sudayrah** S Iraq *30.55N 44.58E*
145 *T10* **Abū Şukhayr** S Iraq *31.54N 44.27E*
Abū Sunbul *see* Abu Simbel
172 *Nn6* **Abuta** Hokkaidō, NE Japan *42.34N 140.44E*
193 *E18* **Abut Head** *headland* South Island, NZ *43.06S 170.16E*
82 *E9* **Abu 'Urug** Northern Kordofan, C Sudan *15.52N 30.25E*
82 *K12* **Ābuyē Mēda** ▲ C Ethiopia *10.23N 39.46E*
179 *R13* **Abuyog** Leyte, C Philippines *10.45N 124.58E*

◆ COUNTRY
● COUNTRY CAPITAL
◇ DEPENDENT TERRITORY
○ DEPENDENT TERRITORY CAPITAL
◈ ADMINISTRATIVE REGION
✕ INTERNATIONAL AIRPORT
▲ MOUNTAIN
▲▲ MOUNTAIN RANGE
VOLCANO
≈ RIVER
◎ LAKE
▣ RESERVOIR

ABU ZABAD – AIRBANGIS

82 D11 **Abu Zabad** Western Kordofan, C Sudan 12.21N 29.16E
Abū Ẓabī *see* Abū Ẓaby
149 P16 **Abū Ẓaby** *var.* Abū Ẓabī, *Eng.* Abu Dhabi. ● (UAE) Abū Ẓaby, C UAE 24.30N 54.20E
77 X8 **Abu Zenîma** E Egypt 29.01N 33.08E
97 N17 **Åby** Östergötland, S Sweden 58.40N 16.19E
Abyaḍ, Al Baḥr al *see* White Nile
97 G20 **Åbybro** *var.* Aabybro. Nordjylland, N Denmark 57.09N 9.45E
82 D13 **Abyei** Western Kordofan, S Sudan 9.34N 28.28E
Abyla *see* Ávila
Abymes *see* les Abymes
Abyssinia *see* Ethiopia
Açâba *see* Assaba
56 F11 **Acacias** Meta, C Colombia 3.58N 73.46W
60 L13 **Açailandia** Maranhão, E Brazil 4.51S 47.25W
Acaill *see* Achill Island
44 E8 **Acajutla** Sonsonate, W El Salvador 13.35N 89.48W
81 D17 **Acalayong** SW Equatorial Guinea 1.05N 9.34E
43 N13 **Acámbaro** Guanajuato, C Mexico 20.01N 100.45W
56 C6 **Acandí** Chocó, NW Colombia 8.28N 77.18W
106 H4 **A Cañiza** *var.* La Cañiza. Galicia, NW Spain 42.13N 8.16W
42 J11 **Acaponeta** Nayarit, C Mexico 22.30N 105.21W
42 J11 **Acaponeta, Río de** ≈ C Mexico
43 O16 **Acapulco** *var.* Acapulco de Juárez. Guerrero, S Mexico 16.51N 99.53W
Acapulco de Juárez *see* Acapulco
57 T13 **Acarai Mountains** *Sp.* Serra Acaraí. ▲▲ Brazil/Guyana
Acaraí, Serra *see* Acarai Mountains
60 O13 **Acaraú** Ceará, NE Brazil 4.35S 37.37W
56 J6 **Acarigua** Portuguesa, N Venezuela 9.34N 69.12W
44 C6 **Acatenango, Volcán de** ⛰ S Guatemala 14.30N 90.52W
43 Q15 **Acatlán** *var.* Acatlán de Osorio. Puebla, S Mexico 18.12N 98.01W
Acatlán de Osorio *see* Acatlán
43 S15 **Acayucan** *var.* Acayucán. Veracruz-Llave, E Mexico 17.58N 94.58W
Accho *see* 'Akko
23 Y5 **Accomac** Virginia, NE USA 37.43N 75.39W
79 Q17 **Accra** ● (Ghana) SE Ghana 5.33N 0.15W
99 L17 **Accrington** NW England, UK 53.46N 2.21W
63 B19 **Acebal** Santa Fe, C Argentina 33.13S 60.49W
173 Ee4 **Aceh** *off.* Daerah Istimewa Aceh, *var.* Acheen, Achin, Atchin, Atjeh. ◈ *autonomous district* NW Indonesia
109 M18 **Acerenza** Basilicata, S Italy 40.46N 15.51E
109 K17 **Acerra** *anc.* Acerrae. Campania, S Italy 40.55N 14.22E
Acerrae *see* Acerra
Ach'asar Lerr *see* Achkasar
59 J17 **Achacachi** La Paz, W Bolivia 16.04S 68.39W
56 K7 **Achaguas** Apure, C Venezuela 7.46N 68.13W
160 H12 **Achalpur** *prev.* Elichpur, Ellichpur. Mahārāshtra, C India 21.19N 77.30E
63 F18 **Achar** Tacuarembó, C Uruguay 32.26S 56.10W
117 H19 **Acharnés** *var.* Aharnes; *prev.* Akharnaí. Attikí, C Greece 38.09N 23.58E
Acheen *see* Aceh
101 K16 **Achel** Limburg, NE Belgium 51.15N 5.31E
117 D16 **Achelóos** *var.* Akhelóös, Aspropótamos; *anc.* Achelous. ≈ W Greece
Achelous *see* Achelóos
169 W8 **Acheng** Heilongjiang, NE China 45.31N 126.55E
111 N6 **Achenkirch** Tirol, W Austria 47.31N 11.42E
103 L24 **Achenpass** *pass* Austria/Germany 47.35N 11.39E
111 N7 **Achensee** ◎ W Austria
103 F22 **Achern** Baden-Württemberg, SW Germany 48.37N 8.04E
117 C16 **Acherón** ≈ W Greece
79 W11 **Achétinamou** ≈ S Niger
158 J12 **Achhnera** Uttar Pradesh, N India 27.10N 77.45E
44 C7 **Achiguate, Río** ≈ S Guatemala
99 A16 **Achill Head** *Ir.* Ceann Acla. *headland* W Ireland 53.58N 10.14W
99 A16 **Achill Island** *Ir.* Acaill. *island* W Ireland
102 H11 **Achim** Niedersachsen, NW Germany 53.01N 9.01E
155 S5 **Achīn** Nangarhār, E Afghanistan 34.04N 70.40E
Achin *see* Aceh
126 Hh14 **Achinsk** Krasnoyarskiy Kray, S Russian Federation 56.21N 90.25E
168 E5 **Achit Nuur** ◎ NW Mongolia
143 T11 **Achkasar** *Arm.* Ach'asar Lerr. ▲ Armenia/Georgia 41.09N 43.55E
130 K13 **Achuyevo** Krasnodarskiy Kray, SW Russian Federation 46.00N 38.01E
83 F16 **Achwa** *var.* Aswa. ≈ N Uganda
142 E15 **Acıgöl** *salt lake* SW Turkey
109 L24 **Acireale** Sicilia, Italy, C Mediterranean Sea 37.36N 15.10E
Aciris *see* Agri
27 N7 **Ackerly** Texas, SW USA 32.31N 101.43W
24 M4 **Ackerman** Mississippi, S USA 33.18N 89.10W
31 W13 **Ackley** Iowa, C USA 42.33N 93.03W
46 J5 **Acklins Island** *island* SE Bahamas
Acla, Ceann *see* Achill Head
64 H11 **Aconcagua, Cerro** ▲ W Argentina 32.36S 69.53W
Açores/Açores, Arquipélago dos/Açores, Ilhas dos *see* Azores
106 G2 **A Coruña** *Cast.* La Coruña ◈ *province* Galicia, NW Spain
106 H2 **A Coruña** *Cast.* La Coruña, *Eng.* Corunna; *anc.* Caronium. Galicia, NW Spain 43.22N 8.24W
44 L10 **Acoyapa** Chontales, S Nicaragua 12.01N 85.08W
108 H13 **Acquapendente** Lazio, C Italy 42.44N 11.52E
108 J13 **Acquasanta Terme** Marche, C Italy 42.46N 13.24E
108 I13 **Acquasparta** Lazio, C Italy 42.41N 12.31E
108 C9 **Acqui Terme** Piemonte, NW Italy 44.40N 8.28E
Acrae *see* Palazzola Acreide
190 F7 **Acraman, Lake** *salt lake* South Australia
61 A15 **Acre** *off.* Estado do Acre. ◈ *state* W Brazil
Acre *see* 'Akko
61 C16 **Acre, Rio** ≈ W Brazil
109 N20 **Acri** Calabria, SW Italy 39.30N 16.22E
Acte *see* Ágion Óros
203 Y12 **Actéon, Groupe** *island group* Îles Tuamotu, SE French Polynesia
13 P12 **Acton-Vale** Quebec, SE Canada 45.39N 72.31W
43 P13 **Actopan** *var.* Actopán. Hidalgo, C Mexico 20.16N 98.57W
61 P14 **Açu** *var.* Assu. Rio Grande do Norte, E Brazil 5.33S 36.55W
Acunum Acusio *see* Montélimar
79 Q17 **Ada** SE Ghana 5.46N 0.37E
31 R5 **Ada** Minnesota, N USA 47.18N 96.31W
33 R12 **Ada** Ohio, N USA 40.46N 83.49W
29 O12 **Ada** Oklahoma, C USA 34.48N 96.38W
114 L8 **Ada** Serbia, N Yugoslavia 45.48N 20.08E
Ada Bazar *see* Adapazarı
42 D3 **Adair, Bahía de** *bay* NW Mexico
106 M7 **Adaja** ≈ N Spain
40 H17 **Adak Island** *island* Aleutian Islands, Alaska, USA
Adalia *see* Antalya
Adalia, Gulf of *see* Antalya Körfezi
147 X9 **Adam** N Oman 22.22N 57.30E
Adama *see* Nazrēt
62 I8 **Adamantina** São Paulo, S Brazil 21.40S 51.04W
81 E14 **Adamaoua** *Eng.* Adamawa. ◈ *province* N Cameroon
70 F11 **Adamaoua, Massif d'** *Eng.* Adamawa Highlands. *plateau* NW Cameroon
79 Y14 **Adamawa** ◈ *state* E Nigeria
Adamawa *see* Adamaoua
Adamawa Highlands *see* Adamaoua, Massif d'
108 F6 **Adamello** ▲ N Italy 46.09N 10.33E
83 J14 **Ādamī Tulu** Oromo, C Ethiopia 7.52N 38.39E
65 M23 **Adam, Mount** *var.* Monte Independencia. ▲ West Falkland, Falkland Islands 51.36S 60.00W
31 R16 **Adams** Nebraska, C USA 40.25N 96.30W
20 H8 **Adams** New York, NE USA 43.48N 75.57W
31 Q3 **Adams** North Dakota, N USA 48.23N 98.01W
161 I23 **Adam's Bridge** *chain of shoals* NW Sri Lanka
34 H10 **Adams, Mount** ▲ Washington, NW USA 46.12N 121.29W
Adam's Peak *see* Sri Pada
203 R16 **Adam's Rock** *island* Pitcairn Island, Pitcairn Islands
203 P16 **Adamstown** ○ (Pitcairn Islands) Pitcairn Island, Pitcairn Islands 25.04S 130.04W
22 G10 **Adamsville** Tennessee, S USA 35.14N 88.23W
27 S9 **Adamsville** Texas, SW USA 31.15N 98.09W
147 O17 **'Adan** *Eng.* Aden. SW Yemen 12.51N 45.04E
142 K16 **Adana** *var.* Seyhan. Adana, S Turkey 37.00N 35.19E
142 K16 **Adana** *var.* Seyhan. ◈ *province* S Turkey
Adâncata *see* Horlivka
175 Nn10 **Adang, Teluk** *bay* Borneo, C Indonesia
142 F11 **Adapazarı** *prev.* Ada Bazar. Sakarya, NW Turkey 40.48N 30.24E
82 H8 **Adarama** River Nile, NE Sudan 17.04N 34.57E
205 Q16 **Adare, Cape** *headland* Antarctica 71.24S 170.27E
108 E6 **Adda** *anc.* Addua. ≈ N Italy
82 A13 **Adda** ≈ W Sudan
149 Q17 **Aḍ Ḍab'īyah** Abū Ẓaby, C UAE 24.16N 54.07E
149 O18 **Aḍ Ḍafrah** *desert* S UAE
147 Q6 **Ad Dahnā'** *desert* E Saudi Arabia
76 A11 **Ad Dakhla** *var.* Dakhla. SW Western Sahara 23.46N 15.56W
Ad Dalanj *see* Dilling
Ad Damar *see* Ed Damer
Ad Damazīn *see* Ed Damazin
Ad Dāmir *see* Ed Damer
181 N2 **Ad Dammām** *desert* NE Saudi Arabia
147 R6 **Ad Dammān** *var.* Dammām. Ash Sharqīyah, NE Saudi Arabia 26.23N 50.04E
Ad Dāmūr *see* Damoûr
146 K5 **Ad Dār al Ḥamrā'** Tabūk, NW Saudi Arabia 27.21N 37.45E
146 M13 **Ad Darb** Jīzān, SW Saudi Arabia 17.45N 42.15E
147 O8 **Ad Dawādimī** Ar Riyāḍ, C Saudi Arabia 24.31N 44.21E
149 N16 **Ad Dawḥah** *Eng.* Doha. ● (Qatar) C Qatar 25.15N 51.36E
149 N16 **Ad Dawḥah** *Eng.* Doha. ✈ C Qatar 25.11N 51.37E
145 S6 **Ad Dawr** N Iraq 34.30N 43.49E
145 Y12 **Ad Dayr** *var.* Dayr, Shahbān. E Iraq 30.45N 47.36E
Addi Arkay *see* Ādī Ārk'ay
145 X15 **Ad Dibdibah** *physical region* Iraq/Kuwait
Aḍ Ḍiffah *see* Libyan Plateau
Addis Ababa *see* Ādīs Ābeba
Addison *see* Webster Springs
145 U10 **Ad Dīwānīyah** *var.* Diwaniyah. C Iraq 32.00N 44.57E
Addua *see* Adda
157 K22 **Addu Atoll** *atoll* S Maldives
Ad Dujail *see* Ad Dujayl
145 T7 **Ad Dujayl** *var.* Ad Dujail. N Iraq 33.49N 44.16E
Ad Duwaym/Ad Duwēm *see* Ed Dueim
101 D16 **Adegem** Oost-Vlaanderen, NW Belgium 51.12N 3.31E
25 U7 **Adel** Georgia, SE USA 31.08N 83.25W
31 U14 **Adel** Iowa, C USA 41.36N 94.01W
190 I9 **Adelaide** *state capital* South Australia 34.55S 138.36E
46 H2 **Adelaide** New Providence, N Bahamas 24.59N 77.30W
190 I9 **Adelaide** ✈ South Australia 34.55S 138.31E
204 H6 **Adelaide Island** *island* Antarctica
15 K4 **Adelaide Peninsula** *peninsula* Nunavut, N Canada
189 P2 **Adelaide River** Northern Territory, N Australia 13.12S 131.06E
78 M10 **'Adel Bagrou** Hodh ech Chargui, SE Mauritania 15.33N 7.04W
194 I11 **Adelbert Range** ▲▲ N PNG
188 K3 **Adele Island** *island* Western Australia
109 O17 **Adelfia** Puglia, SE Italy 41.01N 16.52E
205 V16 **Adélie Coast** *physical region* Antarctica
205 V14 **Adélie, Terre** *physical region* Antarctica
Adelnau *see* Odolanów
Adelsberg *see* Postojna
Aden *see* 'Adan
147 Q17 **Aden, Gulf of** *gulf* SW Arabian Sea
79 V10 **Aderbissinat** Agadez, C Niger 15.30N 7.57E
Adhaim *see* Al 'Uẓaym
149 R16 **Adh Dhayd** *var.* Al Dhaid. Ash Shāriqah, NE UAE 25.19N 55.51E
146 M4 **'Adhfā'** *spring/well* NW Saudi Arabia 29.15N 41.24E
144 I13 **'Ādhriyāt, Jabāl al** ▲▲ S Jordan
194 L12 **Adi** ≈ New Britain, C PNG
82 I10 **Ādī Ārk'ay** *var.* Addi Arkay. Amhara, N Ethiopia 13.18N 37.56E
190 C7 **Adieu, Cape** *headland* South Australia 32.01S 132.12E
108 H8 **Adige** *Ger.* Etsch. ≈ N Italy
82 J10 **Ādīgrat** Tigray, N Ethiopia 14.17N 39.27E
160 I13 **Ādilabād** *var.* Ādilābād. Andhra Pradesh, C India 19.40N 78.31E
37 P2 **Adin** California, W USA 41.10N 120.57W
176 Vv12 **Adi, Pulau** *island* E Indonesia
20 K8 **Adirondack Mountains** ▲▲ New York, NE USA
82 J13 **Ādīs Ābeba** *Eng.* Addis Ababa. ● (Ethiopia) Ādīs Ābeba, C Ethiopia 8.59N 38.43E
82 J13 **Ādīs Ābeba** ✈ Ādīs Ābeba, C Ethiopia 8.58N 38.53E
82 I11 **Ādīs Zemen** Amhara, N Ethiopia 12.00N 37.43E
Adi Ugri *see* Mendefera
143 N15 **Adıyaman** Adıyaman, SE Turkey 37.46N 38.15E
143 N15 **Adıyaman** ◈ *province* S Turkey
118 L11 **Adjud** Vrancea, E Romania 46.06N 27.11E
47 T6 **Adjuntas** C Puerto Rico 18.10N 66.44W
Adjuntas, Presa de las *see* Vicente Guerrero, Presa
Ādkup *see* Erikub Atoll
130 L15 **Adler** Krasnodarskiy Kray, SW Russian Federation 43.25N 39.58E
Adler *see* Orlice
110 G7 **Adliswil** Zürich, NW Switzerland 47.20N 8.30E
15 L1 **Admiralty Inlet** *fjord* Baffin Island, Nunavut, NE Canada
34 G7 **Admiralty Inlet** *inlet* Washington, NW USA
41 X13 **Admiralty Island** *island* Alexander Archipelago, Alaska, USA
194 K8 **Admiralty Islands** *island group* N PNG
142 B14 **Adnan Menderes** ✈ (İzmir) İzmir, W Turkey 38.16N 27.09E
39 V6 **Adobe Creek Reservoir** ▣ Colorado, C USA
79 T16 **Ado-Ekiti** Ekiti, SW Nigeria 7.42N 5.13E
Adola *see* Kibre Mengist
63 C23 **Adolfo González Chaues** Buenos Aires, E Argentina
161 H17 **Ādoni** Andhra Pradesh, C India 15.37N 77.16E
104 K15 **Adour** *anc.* Aturus. ≈ SW France
Adowa *see* Ādwa
107 O15 **Adra** Andalucía, S Spain 36.45N 3.01W
109 L24 **Adrano** Sicilia, Italy, C Mediterranean Sea 37.39N 14.49E
76 I9 **Adrar** C Algeria 27.55N 0.12W
78 K7 **Adrar** ◈ *region* C Mauritania
76 L11 **Adrar** ▲▲ SE Algeria
76 A12 **Adrar Souttouf** ▲▲ SW Western Sahara
Adrasman *see* Adrasmon
153 Q10 **Adrasmon** *Rus.* Adrasman. NW Tajikistan 40.38N 69.56E
80 K10 **Adré** Ouaddaï, E Chad 13.39N 22.09E
108 H9 **Adria** *anc.* Atria, Hadria, Hatria. Veneto, NE Italy 45.03N 12.04E
33 R10 **Adrian** Michigan, N USA 41.54N 84.02W
31 S11 **Adrian** Minnesota, N USA 43.38N 95.55W
29 R5 **Adrian** Missouri, C USA 38.24N 94.21W
26 M2 **Adrian** Texas, SW USA 35.16N 102.39W
23 S4 **Adrian** West Virginia, NE USA 38.53N 80.14W
Adrianople/Adrianopolis *see* Edirne
123 Mm8 **Adriatic Basin** *undersea feature* Adriatic Sea, N Mediterranean Sea
Adriatico, Mare *see* Adriatic Sea
108 L13 **Adriatic Sea** *Alb.* Deti Adriatik, *It.* Mare Adriatico, *SCr.* Jadransko More, *Slvn.* Jadransko Morje. *sea* N Mediterranean Sea
Adriatik, Deti *see* Adriatic Sea
Adua *see* Ādwa
Aduana del Sásabe *see* El Sásabe
81 O17 **Adusa** Orientale, NE Dem. Rep. Congo (Zaire) 1.25N 28.04E
120 J13 **Adutiškis** Švenčionys, E Lithuania 55.09N 26.34E
29 Y7 **Advance** Missouri, C USA 37.06N 89.54W
67 D25 **Adventure Sound** *bay* East Falkland, Falkland Islands
82 J10 **Ādwa** *var.* Adowa, *It.* Adua. Tigray, N Ethiopia 14.08N 38.51E
126 M8 **Adycha** ≈ NE Russian Federation
130 L14 **Adygeya, Respublika** ◈ *autonomous republic* SW Russian Federation
152 C11 **Adzhikui** *Turkm.* Ajyguyy. Balkanskiy Velayat, W Turkmenistan 39.46N 53.57E
79 N17 **Adzopé** SE Ivory Coast 6.07N 3.54W
129 U4 **Adz'va** ≈ NW Russian Federation
129 U5 **Adz'vavom** Respublika Komi, NW Russian Federation 66.35N 59.13E
Ædua *see* Autun
117 K19 **Aegean Islands** *island group* Greece/Turkey
Aegean North *see* Vóreion Aigaíon
117 I17 **Aegean Sea** *Gk.* Aigaíon Pélagos, Aigaío Pélagos, *Turk.* Ege Denizi. *sea* NE Mediterranean Sea
Aegean South *see* Nótion Aigaíon
120 H3 **Aegviidu** *Ger.* Charlottenhof. Harjumaa, NW Estonia 59.16N 25.37E
Aegyptus *see* Egypt
Aelana *see* Al 'Aqabah
Aelok *see* Ailuk Atoll
Aelōninae *see* Ailinginae Atoll
Aeļōnļapļap *see* Ailinglaplap Atoll
Æmilia *see* Emilia-Romagna
Æmilianum *see* Millau
Aemona *see* Ljubljana
Aenaria *see* Ischia
Aeolian Islands *see* Eolie, Isole
203 Z3 **Aeon Point** *headland* Kiritimati, NE Kiribati 1.46N 157.10W
97 G24 **Ærø** *Ger.* Arrö. *island* C Denmark
97 H24 **Ærøskøbing** Fyn, C Denmark 54.52N 10.24E
Æsernia *see* Isernia
106 G3 **A Estrada** Galicia, NW Spain 42.40N 8.28W
117 C18 **Aetós** Itháki, Iónioi Nísoi, Greece, C Mediterranean Sea 38.21N 20.40E
203 Q8 **Afaahiti** Tahiti, W French Polynesia 17.43S 149.18W
145 U10 **'Afak** C Iraq 32.04N 45.16E
Afanasjevo *see* Afanas'yevo
129 T14 **Afanas'yevo** *var.* Afanasjevo. Kirovskaya Oblast', NW Russian Federation 58.55N 53.13E
Afándou *see* Afántou
117 O23 **Afántou** *var.* Afándou. Ródos, Dodekánisos, Greece, Aegean Sea 36.16N 28.10E
Afar Depression *see* Danakil Desert
82 K11 **Afar** ◈ *region* NE Ethiopia
203 O7 **Afareaitu** Moorea, W French Polynesia 17.33S 149.46W
146 L7 **'Afariyah, Bi'r al** *well* NW Saudi Arabia 25.28N 39.21E
Afars et des Issas, Territoire Français des *see* Djibouti
85 D22 **Affenrücken** Karas, SW Namibia 28.05S 15.49E
Afghānestān, Dowlat-e Eslāmī-ye *see* Afghanistan
154 M6 **Afghanistan** *off.* Islamic State of Afghanistan, *Per.* Dowlat-e Eslāmī-ye Afghānestān; *prev.* Republic of Afghanistan. ◆ *Islamic state* C Asia
Afgoi *see* Afgooye
83 N17 **Afgooye** *It.* Afgoi. Shabeellaha Hoose, S Somalia 2.09N 45.07E
147 N8 **'Afīf** Ar Riyāḍ, C Saudi Arabia 23.57N 42.57E
79 V17 **Afikpo** Ebonyi, SE Nigeria 5.52N 7.58E
Afiun Karahissar *see* Afyon
96 H7 **Åfjord** Sør-Trøndelag, C Norway 63.57N 10.12E
111 V6 **Aflenz Kurort** Steiermark, E Austria 47.33N 15.14E
76 J6 **Aflou** N Algeria 34.09N 2.06E
83 L18 **Afmadow** Jubbada Hoose, S Somalia 0.24N 42.03E
41 Q14 **Afognak Island** *island* Alaska, USA
106 J2 **A Fonsagrada** Galicia, NW Spain 43.09N 7.03W
194 L15 **Afore** Northern, S PNG 9.01S 148.22E
61 O15 **Afrânio** Pernambuco, E Brazil 8.31S 40.54W
68-69 **Africa** *continent*
70 L11 **Africa, Horn of** *physical region* Ethiopia/Somalia
180 K11 **Africana Seamount** *undersea feature* SW Indian Ocean 37.10S 29.10E
88 A14 **African Plate** *tectonic feature*
144 I2 **'Afrīn** Ḥalab, N Syria 36.31N 36.51E
142 M15 **Afşin** Kahramanmaraş, C Turkey 38.13N 36.54E
100 J7 **Afsluitdijk** *dam* N Netherlands 53.00N 5.10E
31 U15 **Afton** Iowa, C USA 41.01N 94.12W
31 W9 **Afton** Minnesota, N USA 44.54N 92.46W
29 R8 **Afton** Oklahoma, C USA 36.41N 94.57W
142 F14 **Afyon** *prev.* Afyonkarahisar. Afyon, W Turkey 38.46N 30.31E
142 F14 **Afyon** *var.* Afiun Karahissar, Afyonkarahisar. ◈ *province* W Turkey
Afyonkarahisar *see* Afyon
Agadès *see* Agadez
79 V10 **Agadez** *prev.* Agadès. Agadez, C Niger 16.57N 7.55E
79 W8 **Agadez** ◈ *department* N Niger
76 E8 **Agadir** SW Morocco 30.30N 9.36W
66 M9 **Agadir Canyon** *undersea feature* SE Atlantic Ocean
151 R12 **Agadyr'** Zhezkazgan, C Kazakhstan 48.15N 72.54E
181 O7 **Agalega Islands** *island group* N Mauritius
44 K6 **Agalta, Sierra de** ▲▲ E Honduras
126 Gg10 **Agan** ≈ C Russian Federation
Agana/Agaña *see* Hagåtña
196 B15 **Agana Bay** *bay* NW Guam
196 C16 **Agana Field** ✈ (Agana) C Guam 13.28N 144.48E
171 Kk13 **Agano-gawa** ≈ Honshū, C Japan
196 B17 **Aga Point** *headland* S Guam
160 G9 **Agar** Madhya Pradesh, C India 23.43N 76.01E
83 I14 **Āgaro** Oromo, C Ethiopia 7.52N 36.36E
159 V15 **Agartala** Tripura, NE India 23.49N 91.15E
204 I5 **Agassiz, Cape** *headland* Antarctica 68.28S 62.58W
183 V13 **Agassiz Fracture Zone** *tectonic feature* S Pacific Ocean
196 B16 **Agat** W Guam 13.20N 144.38E
196 B16 **Agat Bay** *bay* W Guam
151 P13 **Agat, Gory** *hill* C Kazakhstan 46.55N 69.13E
Agatha *see* Agde
117 M20 **Agathónisi** *island* Dodekánisos, Greece, Aegean Sea
176 Y13 **Agats** Irian Jaya, E Indonesia 5.33S 138.07E
161 C21 **Agatti Island** *island* Lakshadweep, India, N Indian Ocean
40 D16 **Agattu Island** *island* Aleutian Islands, Alaska, USA
40 D16 **Agattu Strait** *strait* Aleutian Islands, Alaska, USA
12 B8 **Agawa** ≈ Ontario, S Canada
12 B8 **Agawa Bay** *lake bay* Ontario, S Canada
79 N17 **Agboville** SE Ivory Coast 5.56N 4.13W
143 V12 **Ağdam** *Rus.* Agdam. SW Azerbaijan 40.04N 46.00E
105 P16 **Agde** *anc.* Agatha. Hérault, S France 43.19N 3.28E
105 P16 **Agde, Cap d'** *headland* S France 43.17N 3.30E
Agedabia *see* Ajdābiyā
104 L14 **Agen** *anc.* Aginnum. Lot-et-Garonne, SW France 44.12N 0.37E
Agendicum *see* Sens
171 K16 **Ageo** Saitama, Honshū, S Japan 35.58N 139.36E
111 R5 **Ager** ≈ N Austria
Agere Hiywet *see* Hāgere Hiywet
110 G8 **Ägerisee** ◎ W Switzerland
148 M10 **Āghā Jārī** Khūzestān, SW Iran 30.48N 49.45E
41 P15 **Aghiyuk Island** *island* Alaska, USA
76 B12 **Aghouinit** SE Western Sahara 22.14N 13.10W
Aghri Dagh *see* Büyükağrı Dağı
76 B10 **Aghzoumal, Sebkhet** *var.* Sebjet Agsumal. *salt lake* E Western Sahara
117 F15 **Agiá** *var.* Ayiá. Thessalía, C Greece 39.43N 22.45E
42 G7 **Agiabampo, Estero de** *estuary* NW Mexico
124 Nn4 **Agía Fýlaxis** *var.* Ayia Phyla. S Cyprus 34.43N 33.02E
Agialoúsa *see* Yenierenköy
117 M21 **Agía Marína** Léros, Dodekánisos, Greece, Aegean Sea 37.09N 26.51E
124 Oo3 **Agía Nápa** *var.* Ayia Napa. E Cyprus 34.59N 34.00E
117 L16 **Agía Paraskeví** Lésvos, E Greece 39.13N 26.19E
117 J15 **Agías Eirínis, Akrotírio** *headland* Límnos, E Greece 39.47N 25.21E
117 L17 **Agiasós** *var.* Ayiásos, Ayiássos. Lésvos, E Greece 39.04N 26.22E
Aginnum *see* Agen
126 K16 **Aginskiy Buryatskiy Avtonomnyy Okrug** ◈ *autonomous district* S Russian Federation
126 Kk16 **Aginskoye** Aginskiy Buryatskiy Avtonomnyy Okrug, S Russian Federation 51.10N 114.31E
117 I14 **Ágion Óros** *Eng.* Mount Athos. ◈ *monastic republic* NE Greece
117 H14 **Ágion Óros** *var.* Akte, Aktí; *anc.* Acte. *peninsula* NE Greece
116 D13 **Ágios Achílleios** *religious building* Dytikí Makedonía, N Greece 40.46N 21.04E
117 J16 **Ágios Efstrátios** *var.* Áyios Evstrátios, Hagios Evstrátios. *island* E Greece
117 H20 **Ágios Geórgios** *island* Kykládes, Greece, Aegean Sea
117 Q23 **Ágios Geórgios** *island* SE Greece
117 E21 **Ágios Ilías** ▲ S Greece 36.57N 22.19E
117 K25 **Ágios Ioannis, Akrotírio** *headland* Kríti, Greece, E Mediterranean Sea 35.19N 25.46E
117 L20 **Ágios Kírykos** *var.* Áyios Kírikos. Ikaría, Dodekánisos, Greece, Aegean Sea 37.04N 26.16E
117 D16 **Ágios Nikolaos** Thessalía, C Greece 39.33N 21.21E
117 K25 **Ágios Nikólaos** *var.* Áyios Nikólaos. Kríti, Greece, E Mediterranean Sea 35.12N 25.43E
Ágios Sérgios *see* Yeniboğaziçi
117 H14 **Agíou Órous, Kólpos** *gulf* N Greece
109 K24 **Agira** *anc.* Agyrium. Sicilia, Italy, C Mediterranean Sea 37.39N 14.31E
117 G20 **Agkístri** *island* S Greece
116 G12 **Ágkistro** *var.* Angistro. ▲ NE Greece 41.21N 23.29E
105 O17 **Agly** ≈ S France
Agnetheln *see* Agnita
12 E10 **Agnew Lake** ◎ Ontario, S Canada
79 O16 **Agnibilékrou** E Ivory Coast 7.10N 3.10W
118 I11 **Agnita** *Ger.* Agnetheln, *Hung.* Szentágota. Sibiu, SW Romania 45.59N 24.39E
109 K15 **Agnone** Molise, C Italy 41.49N 14.21E
171 Hh17 **Ago** Mie, Honshū, SW Japan 34.18N 136.50E
108 C8 **Agogna** ≈ N Italy
Agoitz *see* Aoiz-Agoitz
79 P17 **Agona Swedru** *var.* Swedru. SE Ghana 5.31N 0.42W
Agordat *see* Akurdet
Agosta *see* Augusta
105 N15 **Agout** ≈ S France
158 J12 **Āgra** Uttar Pradesh, N India 27.09N 78.00E
Agra and Oudh, United Provinces of *see* Uttar Pradesh
Agram *see* Zagreb
107 U5 **Agramunt** Cataluña, NE Spain 41.48N 1.07E
107 Q5 **Agreda** Castilla-León, N Spain 41.51N 1.55W
143 S13 **Ağrı** *var.* Karaköse; *prev.* Karakılısse. Ağrı, NE Turkey 39.43N 43.04E
143 S13 **Ağrı** ◈ *province* NE Turkey
109 N19 **Agri** *anc.* Aciris. ≈ S Italy
Agri Dagi *see* Büyükağrı Dağı
109 J24 **Agrigento** *Gk.* Akragas; *prev.* Girgenti. Sicilia, Italy, C Mediterranean Sea 37.19N 13.33E
196 K4 **Agrihan** *island* N Northern Mariana Islands
117 D18 **Agrínio** *prev.* Agrinion. Dytikí Ellás, W Greece 38.37N 21.25E
Agrinion *see* Agrínio
117 G17 **Agriovótano** Évvoia, C Greece 39.00N 23.18E
109 L18 **Agropoli** Campania, S Italy 40.21N 14.58E
131 T3 **Agryz** Udmurtskaya Respublika, NW Russian Federation 56.27N 52.58E
143 U11 **Ağstafa** *Rus.* Akstafa. NW Azerbaijan 41.06N 45.28E
Agsumal, Sebjet *see* Aghzoumal, Sebkhet
42 J11 **Agua Brava, Laguna** *lagoon* W Mexico
56 F7 **Aguachica** Cesar, N Colombia 8.16N 73.35W
61 J20 **Água Clara** Mato Grosso do Sul, SW Brazil 20.21S 52.58W
46 D5 **Aguada de Pasajeros** Cienfuegos, C Cuba 22.22N 80.50W
56 J5 **Aguada Grande** Lara, N Venezuela 10.34N 69.30W
47 S5 **Aguadilla** W Puerto Rico 18.24N 67.09W
45 S16 **Aguadulce** Coclé, S Panama 8.16N 80.31W
106 L14 **Aguadulce** Andalucía, S Spain 37.15N 4.58W
43 O8 **Agualeguas** Nuevo León, NE Mexico 26.17N 99.30W
42 L9 **Aguanaval, Río** ≈ C Mexico
44 J5 **Aguán, Río** ≈ N Honduras
27 R16 **Agua Nueva** Texas, SW USA 26.57N 98.34W
62 J8 **Aguapeí, Rio** ≈ S Brazil
63 E14 **Aguapey, Río** ≈ NE Argentina
42 G3 **Agua Prieta** Sonora, NW Mexico 31.16N 109.33W
106 G5 **A Guardia** *var.* Laguardia, La Guardia. Galicia, NW Spain 41.54N 8.52W
58 E6 **Aguarico, Río** ≈ Ecuador/Peru
57 O6 **Aguasay** Monagas, NE Venezuela 9.25N 63.43W
42 M12 **Aguascalientes** Aguascalientes, C Mexico 21.53N 102.17W
42 L12 **Aguascalientes** ◈ *state* C Mexico
59 I18 **Aguas Calientes, Río** ≈ S Peru
107 R7 **Aguasvivas** ≈ NE Spain
62 J7 **Água Vermelha, Represa de** ▣ S Brazil
58 E12 **Aguaytía** Ucayali, C Peru 9.04S 75.32W
106 I5 **A Gudiña** *var.* La Gudiña. Galicia, NW Spain 42.04N 7.07W
106 G7 **Águeda** Aveiro, N Portugal 40.34N 8.28W
106 J8 **Águeda** ≈ Portugal/Spain
79 Q8 **Aguelhok** Kidal, NE Mali 19.18N 0.50E
79 V12 **Aguié** Maradi, S Niger 13.28N 7.43E
196 K8 **Aguijan** *island* S Northern Mariana Islands
106 M14 **Aguilar** *var.* Aguilar de la Frontera. Andalucía, S Spain 37.31N 4.40W
106 M3 **Aguilar de Campóo** Castilla-León, N Spain 42.46N 4.15W
Aguilar de la Frontera *see* Aguilar
44 F7 **Aguilares** San Salvador, C El Salvador 13.56N 89.09W
107 Q14 **Aguilas** Murcia, SE Spain 37.24N 1.36W
42 L15 **Aguililla** Michoacán de Ocampo, SW Mexico 18.43N 102.45W
Agulhas *see* L'Agulhas
180 J11 **Agulhas Bank** *undersea feature* SW Indian Ocean
180 K11 **Agulhas Basin** *undersea feature* SW Indian Ocean
85 F26 **Agulhas, Cape** *Afr.* Kaap Agulhas. *headland* SW South Africa 34.51S 19.59E
Agulhas, Kaap *see* Agulhas, Cape
62 O9 **Agulhas Negras, Pico das** ▲ SE Brazil 22.21S 44.39W
180 K11 **Agulhas Plateau** *undersea feature* SW Indian Ocean
172 Oo14 **Aguni-jima** *island* Nansei-shotō, SW Japan
Agurain *see* Salvatierra
179 Rr15 **Agusan** ≈ Mindanao, S Philippines
56 G5 **Agustín Codazzi** *var.* Codazzi. Cesar, N Colombia 10.01N 73.15W
Agyrium *see* Agira
76 L12 **Ahaggar** *high plateau region* SE Algeria
Ahal Welayaty *see* Akhalskiy Velayat
148 K2 **Ahar** Āẕarbāyjān-e Khāvarī, NW Iran 38.25N 47.07E
Aharnes *see* Acharnés
144 J3 **Aḥaṣ, Jabal** ▲ NW Syria
144 J3 **Aḥaṣ, Jebal** ▲▲ W Syria
193 G16 **Ahaura** ≈ South Island, NZ
102 E13 **Ahaus** Nordrhein-Westfalen, NW Germany 52.04N 7.01E
203 U9 **Ahe** *atoll* Îles Tuamotu, C French Polynesia
192 N10 **Ahimanawa Range** ▲▲ North Island, NZ
121 I19 **Ahinski Kanal** *Rus.* Oginskiy Kanal. *canal* SW Belarus
195 N16 **Ahioma** SE PNG 10.18S 150.33E
192 I2 **Ahipara** Northland, North Island, NZ 35.11S 173.07E
192 I2 **Ahipara Bay** *bay* SE Tasman Sea
41 N13 **Ahklun Mountains** ▲▲ Alaska, USA
143 R14 **Ahlat** Bitlis, E Turkey 38.45N 42.30E
103 F14 **Ahlen** Nordrhein-Westfalen, W Germany 51.46N 7.52E
160 D10 **Ahmadābād** *var.* Ahmedabad. Gujarāt, W India 23.03N 72.40E
149 R10 **Ahmadābād** Kermān, C Iran 35.51N 59.36E
Ahmadi *see* Al Aḥmadī
Ahmad Khel *see* Ḥasan Khēl
161 F14 **Ahmadnagar** *var.* Ahmednagar. Mahārāshtra, W India 19.07N 74.48E
155 T9 **Ahmadpur Siāl** Punjab, E Pakistan 30.40N 71.47E
79 N5 **Aḥmar, 'Erg el** *desert* N Mali
82 K13 **Ahmar Mountains** ▲▲ C Ethiopia
Ahmedabad *see* Ahmadābād
Ahmednagar *see* Ahmadnagar
116 N12 **Ahmetbey** Kırklareli, NW Turkey 41.26N 27.35E
12 H12 **Ahmic Lake** ◎ Ontario, S Canada
202 G12 **Ahoa** Île Uvea, E Wallis and Futuna 13.16S 176.12W
42 G8 **Ahomé** Sinaloa, C Mexico 25.55N 109.10W
23 X8 **Ahoskie** North Carolina, SE USA 36.17N 76.59W
103 D17 **Ahr** ≈ W Germany
149 N12 **Ahram** *var.* Ahrom. Būshehr, S Iran 28.52N 51.18E
102 J9 **Ahrensburg** Schleswig-Holstein, N Germany 53.40N 10.13E
Ahrom *see* Ahram
95 L17 **Ähtäri** Länsi-Suomi, W Finland 62.31N 24.11E
42 K12 **Ahuacatlán** Nayarit, C Mexico 21.04N 104.32W
44 E7 **Ahuachapán** Ahuachapán, W El Salvador 13.55N 89.49W
44 A9 **Ahuachapán** ◈ *department* W El Salvador
203 V16 **Ahu Akivi** *var.* Siete Moai. *ancient monument* Easter Island, Chile, E Pacific Ocean
203 W11 **Ahunui** *atoll* Îles Tuamotu, C French Polynesia
193 E20 **Ahuriri** ≈ South Island, NZ
97 L22 **Åhus** Skåne, S Sweden 55.55N 14.18E
Ahu Tahira *see* Ahu Vinapu
203 V16 **Ahu Tepeu** *ancient monument* Easter Island, Chile, E Pacific Ocean
203 V17 **Ahu Vinapu** *var.* Ahu Tahira. *ancient monument* Easter Island, Chile, E Pacific Ocean
148 L9 **Ahvāz** *var.* Ahwāz; *prev.* Nāsiri. Khūzestān, SW Iran 31.19N 48.37E
Ahvenanmaa *see* Åland
147 Q16 **Aḥwar** SW Yemen 13.34N 46.41E
Ahwāz *see* Ahvāz
Aibak *see* Āybak
103 K22 **Aichach** Bayern, SE Germany 48.26N 11.06E
171 I16 **Aichi** *off.* Aichi-ken, *var.* Aiti. ◈ *prefecture* Honshū, SW Japan
Aïdin *see* Aydın
176 Ww12 **Aiduna** Irian Jaya, E Indonesia 4.20S 135.15E
Aidussina *see* Ajdovščina
194 F13 **Aiema** ≈ W PNG
Aifir, Clochán an *see* Giant's Causeway
Aigaíon Pélagos/Aigaío Pélagos *see* Aegean Sea
111 S3 **Aigen im Mülkreis** Oberösterreich, N Austria 48.39N 13.57E
117 G20 **Aígina** *var.* Aíyina, Egina. Aígina, C Greece 37.45N 23.25E
117 G20 **Aígina** *island* S Greece
117 E18 **Aígio** *var.* Egio; *prev.* Aíyion. Dytikí Ellás, S Greece 38.15N 22.04E
110 C10 **Aigle** Vaud, SW Switzerland 46.19N 6.58E
105 P14 **Aigoual, Mont** ▲ S France 44.09N 3.34E
181 O16 **Aigrettes, Pointe des** *headland* W Réunion 21.01S 55.13E
63 G19 **Aiguá** *var.* Aigua. Maldonado, S Uruguay 34.13S 54.46W
105 S13 **Aigues** ≈ SE France
105 N10 **Aigurande** Indre, C France 46.26N 1.49E
Ai-hun *see* Heihe
171 K11 **Aikawa** Niigata, Sado, C Japan 38.04N 138.15E
23 Q13 **Aiken** South Carolina, SE USA 33.33N 81.43W
27 N4 **Aiken** Texas, SW USA 34.06N 101.31W
166 F13 **Ailao Shan** ▲▲ SW China
45 W14 **Ailigandí** San Blas, NE Panama 9.13N 78.04W
201 R4 **Ailinginae Atoll** *var.* Aelōninae. *atoll* Ralik Chain, SW Marshall Islands
201 T7 **Ailinglaplap Atoll** *var.* Aelōnlaplap. *atoll* Ralik Chain, S Marshall Islands
Aillionn, Loch *see* Allen, Lough
98 H13 **Ailsa Craig** *island* SW Scotland, UK
201 V5 **Ailuk Atoll** *var.* Aelok. *atoll* Ratak Chain, NE Marshall Islands
126 Mm12 **Aim** Khabarovskiy Kray, E Russian Federation 58.45N 134.08E
105 R11 **Ain** ◈ *department* E France
105 S10 **Ain** ≈ E France
120 G7 **Ainaži** *Est.* Heinaste, *Ger.* Hainasch. Limbaži, N Latvia 57.51N 24.24E
76 L6 **Aïn Beida** NE Algeria 35.52N 7.25E
78 K4 **'Aïn Ben Tili** Tiris Zemmour, N Mauritania 25.58N 9.30W
76 J5 **Aïn Defla** *var.* Aïn Eddefla. N Algeria 36.16N 1.58E
Aïn Eddefla *see* Aïn Defla
76 L5 **Ain El Bey** ✈ (Constantine) NE Algeria 36.15N 6.36E
117 C19 **Aínos** ▲ Kefallinía, Iónioi Nísoi, Greece, C Mediterranean Sea 38.08N 20.39E
107 T4 **Ainsa** Aragón, NE Spain 42.25N 0.07E
76 I7 **Aïn Sefra** NW Algeria 32.45N 0.32W
31 N13 **Ainsworth** Nebraska, C USA 42.33N 99.51W
Aintab *see* Gaziantep
76 H5 **Aïn Témouchent** N Algeria 35.18N 1.09W
194 H11 **Aiome** Madang, N PNG 5.04S 144.43E
Aïoun el Atrous/Aïoun el Atroûss *see* 'Ayoûn el 'Atroûs
56 E11 **Aipe** Huila, C Colombia 3.15N 75.16W
58 D9 **Aipena, Río** ≈ N Peru
59 L19 **Aiquile** Cochabamba, C Bolivia 18.10S 65.10W
Aïr *see* Aïr, Massif de l'
196 E10 **Airai** Babeldaob, C Palau
196 E10 **Airai** ✈ (Oreor) Babeldaob, N Palau 7.22N 134.34E
173 Ff8 **Airbangis** Sumatera, NW Indonesia 0.12N 99.22E

◆ Country
● Country Capital
◇ Dependent Territory
○ Dependent Territory Capital
◈ Administrative Region
✈ International Airport
▲ Mountain
▲▲ Mountain Range
⛰ Volcano
≈ River
◎ Lake
▣ Reservoir

AIRDRIE – AL DAR AL BAIDA

9 Q16 **Airdrie** Alberta, SW Canada 51.20N 114.00W
98 I12 **Airdrie** S Scotland, UK 55.52N 3.58W
Air du Azbine see Aïr, Massif de l'
99 M17 **Aire** ≈ N England, UK
104 K15 **Aire-sur-l'Adour** Landes, SW France 43.43N 0.16W
105 O1 **Aire-sur-la-Lys** Pas-de-Calais, N France 50.39N 2.24E
16 N2 **Air Force Island** island Baffin Island, Nunavut, NE Canada
174 L11 **Airhitam, Teluk** bay Borneo, C Indonesia
175 Rr7 **Airmadidi** Sulawesi, N Indonesia 1.25N 124.58E
79 V8 **Aïr, Massif de l'** var. Aïr, Air du Azbine, Asben. ▲▲ NC Niger
110 G10 **Airolo** Ticino, S Switzerland 46.32N 8.38E
104 K9 **Airvault** Deux-Sèvres, W France 46.51N 0.07W
103 K19 **Aisch** ≈ S Germany
65 G20 **Aisén** off. Región Aisén del General Carlos Ibañez del Campo, var. Aysen. ◐ region S Chile
8 H7 **Aishihik Lake** ◎ Yukon Territory, W Canada
105 P3 **Aisne** ◐ department N France
105 R4 **Aisne** ≈ NE France
111 Y4 **Aist** ≈ N Austria
116 K13 **Aisými** Anatolikí Makedonía kai Thráki, NE Greece 41.00N 25.55E
107 S11 **Aitana** ▲ E Spain 38.39N 0.15W
194 F9 **Aitape** var. Eitape. Sandaun, NW PNG 3.07S 142.22E
Aiti see Aichi
31 V6 **Aitkin** Minnesota, N USA 46.31N 93.42W
117 D18 **Aitolikó** var. Etoliko; prev. Aitolikón. Dytikí Ellás, C Greece 38.25N 21.21E
Aitolikón see Aitolikó
202 L15 **Aitutaki** island S Cook Islands
118 H11 **Aiud** Ger. Strassburg, Hung. Nagyenyed; prev. Engeten. Alba, SW Romania 46.16N 23.42E
120 I9 **Aiviekste** ≈ C Latvia
201 Q8 **Aiwo** SW Nauru 0.32S 166.54E
196 E8 **Aiwokako Passage** passage Babeldaob, N Palau
Aix see Aix-en-Provence
105 S15 **Aix-en-Provence** var. Aix; anc. Aquae Sextiae. Bouches-du-Rhône, SE France 43.31N 5.27E
Aix-la-Chapelle see Aachen
105 T11 **Aix-les-Bains** Savoie, E France 45.40N 5.55E
194 E11 **Aiyang, Mount** ▲ NW PNG 5.03S 141.15E
Aíyina see Aígina
Aíyion see Aígio
159 W15 **Āīzawl** Mizoram, NE India 23.40N 92.45E
120 H9 **Aizkraukle** Aizkraukle, S Latvia 56.39N 25.07E
120 C9 **Aizpute** Liepāja, W Latvia 56.43N 21.32E
171 L14 **Aizu-Wakamatsu** var. Aizuwakamatu. Fukushima, Honshū, C Japan 37.27N 139.55E
Aizuwakamatu see Aizu-Wakamatsu
105 X15 **Ajaccio** Corse, France, C Mediterranean Sea 41.54N 8.43E
105 X15 **Ajaccio, Golfe d'** gulf Corse, France, C Mediterranean Sea
43 Q15 **Ajalpán** Puebla, S Mexico 18.25N 97.19W
160 F13 **Ajanta Range** ▲▲ C India
143 R10 **Ajaria** ◐ autonomous republic SW Georgia
Ajastan see Armenia
95 G14 **Ajaureforsen** Västerbotten, N Sweden 65.31N 15.43E
193 H17 **Ajax, Mount** ▲ South Island, NZ 42.34S 172.06E
168 F9 **Aj Bogd Uul** ▲ SW Mongolia 44.49N 95.01E
77 R8 **Ajdābiyā** var. Agedabia, Ajdābiyah. NE Libya 30.46N 20.13E
Ajdābiyah see Ajdābiyā
111 S12 **Ajdovščina** Ger. Haidenschaft, It. Aidussina. W Slovenia 45.52N 13.55E
171 Mm8 **Ajigasawa** Aomori, Honshū, C Japan 40.45N 140.11E
Ajjinena see El Geneina
113 H23 **Ajka** Veszprém, W Hungary 47.07N 17.31E
144 G9 **'Ajlūn** Irbid, N Jordan 32.19N 35.45E
144 H9 **'Ajlūn, Jabal** ▲▲ W Jordan
149 R15 **'Ajmān** var. Ajman, 'Ujmān. 'Ajmān, NE UAE 25.36N 55.42E
158 G12 **Ajmer** var. Ajmere. Rājasthān, N India 26.28N 74.40E
38 J15 **Ajo** Arizona, SW USA 32.22N 112.51W
107 N2 **Ajo, Cabo de** headland N Spain 43.31N 3.36W
38 J16 **Ajo Range** ▲▲ Arizona, SW USA
Ajyguyy see Adzhikui
Akaba see Al 'Aqabah
172 P5 **Akabira** Hokkaidō, NE Japan 43.31N 142.03E
171 K12 **Akadomari** Niigata, Sado, C Japan 37.54N 138.24E
83 E20 **Akagera** var. Kagera. ≈ Rwanda/Tanzania see also Kagera
203 W16 **Akahanga, Punta** headland Easter Island, Chile, E Pacific Ocean
171 Ii16 **Akaishi-dake** ▲ Honshū, S Japan 35.26N 138.09E
171 J16 **Akaishi-sanmyaku** ▲▲ Honshū, S Japan
82 J13 **Āk'ak'i** Oromo, C Ethiopia 8.50N 38.51E
161 G15 **Akalkot** Mahārāshtra, W India 17.36N 76.10E
Akamagaseki see Shimonoseki
172 Q7 **Akan** Hokkaidō, NE Japan 43.09N 144.08E
172 Q6 **Akan-ko** ◎ Hokkaidō, NE Japan
Akanthoú see Tatlısu
193 I19 **Akaroa** Canterbury, South Island, NZ 43.48S 172.58E
82 E6 **Akasha** Northern, N Sudan 21.03N 30.45E
170 G14 **Akashi** var. Akasi. Hyōgo, Honshū, SW Japan 34.37N 134.59E
145 N7 **'Akāsh, Wādī** var. Wādī 'Ukash. dry watercourse W Iraq
Akasi see Akashi
94 K11 **Äkäsjokisuu** Lappi, N Finland 67.28N 23.44E
143 S11 **Akbaba Dağı** ▲ Armenia/Turkey 41.04N 43.28E
142 B15 **Akbük Limanı** bay W Turkey
131 V8 **Akbulak** Orenburgskaya Oblast', W Russian Federation 51.01N 55.35E
143 O11 **Akçaabat** Trabzon, NE Turkey 41.00N 39.36E
143 N15 **Akçadağ** Malatya, C Turkey 38.21N 37.58E
142 G11 **Akçakoca** Bolu, NW Turkey 41.04N 31.07E
Akchakaya, Vpadina see Akdzhakaya, Vpadina
78 H7 **Akchâr** desert W Mauritania
151 S12 **Akchatau** Kaz. Aqshataū. Zhezkazgan, C Kazakhstan 47.58N 74.01E
142 L13 **Akdağlar** ▲▲ C Turkey
142 E17 **Ak Dağları** ▲▲ SW Turkey
142 K13 **Akdağmadeni** Yozgat, C Turkey 39.39N 35.48E
152 G8 **Akdepe** prev. Ak-Tepe, Leninsk, Turkm. Lenin. Dashkhovuzskiy Velayat, N Turkmenistan 42.10N 59.17E
Ak-Dere see Byala
124 O3 **Akdoğan** Gk. Lýsi. C Cyprus 35.06N 33.42E
126 Hh16 **Ak-Dovurak** Respublika Tyva, S Russian Federation 51.09N 90.36E
152 F9 **Akdzhakaya, Vpadina** var. Vpadina Akchakaya. depression N Turkmenistan
175 Tt7 **Akelamo** Pulau Halmahera, E Indonesia 1.27N 128.39E
Aken see Aachen
Akermanceaster see Bath
97 P15 **Åkersberga** Stockholm, C Sweden 59.28N 18.19E
97 H15 **Akershus** ◐ county S Norway
81 L16 **Aketi** Orientale, N Dem. Rep. Congo (Zaire) 2.46N 23.42E
Akgyr Erezi see Gryada Akkyr
152 E12 **Akhalskiy Velayat** Turkm. Ahal Welaýaty. ◐ province C Turkmenistan
143 S10 **Akhalts'ikhe** SW Georgia 41.38N 43.03E
Akhangaran see Ohangaron
Akharnaí see Acharnés
77 R7 **Akhḑar, Al Jabal al** hill range NE Libya
Akhelóös see Achelóos
41 Q15 **Akhiok** Kodiak Island, Alaska, USA 56.57N 154.12W
142 C13 **Akhisar** Manisa, W Turkey 38.54N 27.49E
77 X10 **Akhmīm** anc. Panopolis. C Egypt 26.24N 31.50E
158 H6 **Akhnūr** Jammu and Kashmir, NW India 32.57N 74.43E
131 P11 **Akhtuba** ≈ SW Russian Federation
131 P11 **Akhtubinsk** Astrakhanskaya Oblast', SW Russian Federation 48.16N 46.13E
Akhtyrka see Okhtyrka
170 F15 **Aki** Kōchi, Shikoku, SW Japan 33.30N 133.54E
41 N12 **Akiachak** Alaska, USA 60.54N 161.25W
41 N12 **Akiak** Alaska, USA 60.54N 161.12W
203 X11 **Akiaki** atoll Îles Tuamotu, E French Polynesia
10 H9 **Akimiski Island** island Nunavut, C Canada
142 K17 **Akıncı Burnu** headland S Turkey 36.21N 35.47E
Akıncılar see Selçuk
119 U10 **Akinovka** Zaporiz'ka Oblast', S Ukraine
97 M24 **Åkirkeby** var. Aakirkeby. Bornholm, E Denmark 55.04N 14.55E
171 M10 **Akita** Akita, Honshū, C Japan 39.44N 140.06E
171 M10 **Akita** off. Akita-ken. ◐ prefecture Honshū, C Japan
78 H8 **Akjoujt** prev. Fort-Repoux. Inchiri, W Mauritania 19.42N 14.28W
94 H11 **Akkajaure** ◎ N Sweden
Akkala see Oqqal'a
161 L25 **Akkaraipattu** Eastern Province, E Sri Lanka 7.13N 81.51E
94 H11 **Akkavare** ▲ N Sweden 67.33N 17.27E
151 P13 **Akkense** Zhezkazgan, C Kazakhstan 46.39N 68.06E
Akkerman see Bilhorod-Dnistrovs'kyy
131 W8 **Akkermanovka** Orenburgskaya Oblast', W Russian Federation 51.11N 58.03E
172 Qq7 **Akkeshi** Hokkaidō, NE Japan 43.03N 144.48E
172 Qq7 **Akkeshi-ko** ◎ Hokkaidō, NE Japan
172 Qq8 **Akkeshi-wan** bay NW Pacific Ocean
144 F8 **'Akko** Eng. Acre, Fr. Saint-Jean-d'Acre; Bibl. Accho, Ptolemaïs. Northern, N Israel 32.55N 35.04E
151 Q8 **Akkol'** Kaz. Aqköl; prev. Alekseyevka, Kaz. Alekseevka. Akmola, C Kazakhstan 51.58N 70.58E
151 T14 **Akkol'** Kaz. Aqköl. Almaty, SE Kazakhstan 45.01N 75.38E
151 Q16 **Akkol'** Kaz. Aqköl. Zhambyl, S Kazakhstan 43.25N 70.46E
150 M11 **Akkol', Ozero** prev. Ozero Zhaman-Akkol'. ◎ C Kazakhstan
100 L6 **Akkrum** Friesland, N Netherlands 53.01N 5.52E
151 U8 **Akku** prev. Lebyazh'ye. Pavlodar, NE Kazakhstan 51.29N 77.48E
150 F12 **Akkystau** Kaz. Aqqystaū. Atyrau, SW Kazakhstan 47.13N 51.01E
14 Ff3 **Aklavik** Northwest Territories, NW Canada 68.15N 135.01W
120 B9 **Akmenrags** headland W Latvia 56.49N 21.03E
164 E9 **Akmeqit** Xinjiang Uygur Zizhiqu, NW China 37.10N 76.59E
152 J14 **Akmeydan** Maryyskiy Velayat, C Turkmenistan 37.50N 62.08E
Akmola see Astana
151 P9 **Akmola** off. Akmolinskaya Oblast', Kaz. Aqmola Oblysy; prev. Tselinogradskaya Oblast. ◐ province C Kazakhstan
Akmolinsk see Astana
Akmolinskaya Oblast' see Akmola
Aknavásár see Târgu Ocna
120 I11 **Aknīste** Jēkabpils, S Latvia 56.09N 25.43E
170 G14 **Akō** Hyōgo, Honshū, SW Japan 34.44N 134.22E
83 G14 **Akobo** Jonglei, SE Sudan 7.49N 33.04E
83 G14 **Akobo** var. Åkobowenz. ≈ Ethiopia/Sudan
Åkobowenz see Akobo
160 H12 **Akola** Mahārāshtra, C India 20.44N 77.00E
Akordat see Akurdet
79 Q16 **Akosombo Dam** dam SE Ghana 6.23N 0.06E
160 H12 **Akot** Mahārāshtra, C India 20.45N 77.00E
79 N16 **Akoupé** SE Ivory Coast 6.19N 3.54W
10 M3 **Akpatok Island** island Nunavut, E Canada
164 G7 **Akqi** Xinjiang Uygur Zizhiqu, NW China 40.51N 78.20E
144 I2 **Akrad, Jabal al** ▲▲ N Syria
Akragas see Agrigento
94 H3 **Akranes** Vesturland, W Iceland 64.19N 22.01W
145 S2 **Ākrē** Ar. 'Aqrah. N Iraq 36.46N 43.52E
97 C16 **Åkrehamn** Rogaland, S Norway 59.15N 5.12E
79 V9 **Akréréb** Agadez, C Niger 17.45N 9.01E
117 D22 **Akrítas, Akrotírio** headland S Greece 36.43N 21.52E
39 V3 **Akron** Colorado, C USA 40.09N 103.12W
31 R12 **Akron** Iowa, C USA 42.49N 96.33W
33 U12 **Akron** Ohio, N USA 41.04N 81.31W
Akrotiri see Akrotírion
Akrotiri Bay see Akrotírion, Kólpos
124 N4 **Akrotírion** var. Akrotiri. UK air base S Cyprus 34.36N 32.57E
124 Nn4 **Akrotírion, Kólpos** var. Akrotiri Bay. bay S Cyprus
123 Mm4 **Akrotiri Sovereign Base Area** UK military installation S Cyprus 34.34N 32.58E
164 F11 **Aksai Chin** Chin. Aksayqin. disputed region China/India
Aksaj see Aksay
142 I15 **Aksaray** Aksaray, C Turkey 38.23N 33.50E
142 I15 **Aksaray** ◐ province C Turkey
165 P8 **Aksay** var. Aksay Kazakzu Zizhixian. Gansu, N China 39.25N 94.09E
150 G8 **Aksay** var. Aksaj, Kaz. Aqsay. Zapadnyy Kazakhstan, NW Kazakhstan 51.10N 53.03E
131 O11 **Aksay** Volgogradskaya Oblast', SW Russian Federation 47.59N 43.54E
153 W10 **Aksay** var. Toxkan He. ≈ China/Kyrgyzstan
Aksay Kazakzu Zizhixian see Aksay
Aksayqin see Aksai Chin
164 G11 **Aksayqin Hu** ◎ NW China
142 G14 **Akşehir** Konya, W Turkey 38.22N 31.24E
142 G14 **Akşehir Gölü** ◎ C Turkey
142 G16 **Akseki** Antalya, SW Turkey 37.03N 31.46E
126 L15 **Aksenovo-Zilovskoye** Chitinskaya Oblast', S Russian Federation 53.01N 117.26E
126 Kk16 **Aksha** Chitinskaya Oblast', S Russian Federation 50.16N 113.22E
151 V11 **Akshatau, Khrebet** ▲▲ E Kazakhstan
153 Y8 **Ak-Shyyrak** Issyk-Kul'skaya Oblast', E Kyrgyzstan 41.46N 78.34E
Akstafa see Ağstafa
164 H7 **Aksu** Xinjiang Uygur Zizhiqu, NW China 41.16N 80.15E
151 R8 **Aksu** Kaz. Aqsū. Akmola, N Kazakhstan 52.31N 72.00E
151 T8 **Aksu** var. Jermak, Kaz. Ermak; prev. Yermak. Pavlodar, NE Kazakhstan 52.03N 76.55E
151 W13 **Aksu** Kaz. Aqsū. Almaty, SE Kazakhstan 45.31N 79.28E
151 V13 **Aksu** Kaz. Aqsū. ≈ SE Kazakhstan
151 X11 **Aksuat** Kaz. Aqsūat. Vostochnyy Kazakhstan, E Kazakhstan 47.46N 82.49E
151 Y11 **Aksuat** Kaz. Aqsūat. Vostochnyy Kazakhstan, SE Kazakhstan 48.16N 83.39E
131 S4 **Aksubayevo** Respublika Tatarstan, W Russian Federation 54.52N 50.50E
164 H7 **Aksu He** Rus. Sary-Dzhaz. ≈ China/Kyrgyzstan see also Sary-Dzhaz
82 J10 **Āksum** Tigray, N Ethiopia 14.06N 38.42E
151 O12 **Aktas** Kaz. Aqtas. Zhezkazgan, C Kazakhstan 48.03N 66.21E
Aktash see Oqtosh
153 V9 **Ak-Tash, Gora** ▲ C Kyrgyzstan 40.53N 74.39E
151 R10 **Aktau** Kaz. Aqtaū. Karaganda, C Kazakhstan 50.13N 73.06E
150 E11 **Aktau** Kaz. Aqtaū; prev. Shevchenko. Mangistau, W Kazakhstan 43.37N 51.13E
Aktau, Khrebet see Oqtogh, SW Tajikistan
Aktau, Khrebet see Oqtow Tizmasi, C Uzbekistan
Akte see Ágion Óros
Ak-Tepe see Akdepe
153 X7 **Ak-Terek** Issyk-Kul'skaya Oblast', E Kyrgyzstan 42.14N 77.46E
Akti see Ágion Óros
164 E8 **Akto** Xinjiang Uygur Zizhiqu, NW China 39.07N 75.43E
151 V12 **Aktogay** Kaz. Aqtoghay. Vostochnyy Kazakhstan, E Kazakhstan 46.56N 79.40E
151 T12 **Aktogay** Kaz. Aqtoghay. Zhezkazgan, C Kazakhstan 47.46N 74.06E
121 M18 **Aktsyabrski** Rus. Oktyabr'skiy; prev. Karpilovka. Homyel'skaya Voblasts', SE Belarus 52.37N 28.52E
150 I10 **Aktyubinsk** Kaz. Aqtöbe. Aktyubinsk, NW Kazakhstan 50.18N 57.09E
150 H11 **Aktyubinsk** off. Aktyubinskaya Oblast', Kaz. Aqtöbe Oblysy. ◐ province W Kazakhstan
153 W7 **Ak-Tyuz** var. Aktyuz. Chuyskaya Oblast', N Kyrgyzstan 42.50N 76.05E
81 J17 **Akula** Equateur, NW Dem. Rep. Congo (Zaire) 2.21N 20.13E
170 Bb15 **Akune** Kagoshima, Kyūshū, SW Japan 31.59N 130.11E
40 L16 **Akun Island** island Aleutian Islands, Alaska, USA
82 J9 **Akurdet** var. Agordat, Akordat. C Eritrea 15.33N 38.01E
79 T16 **Akure** Ondo, SW Nigeria 7.18N 5.12E
94 J2 **Akureyri** Nordhurland Eystra, N Iceland 65.40N 18.06W
40 L17 **Akutan** Akutan Island, Alaska, USA 54.08N 165.47W
40 K17 **Akutan Island** island Aleutian Islands, Alaska, USA
79 V17 **Akwa Ibom** ◐ state SE Nigeria
Akyab see Sittwe
131 W7 **Ak"yar** Respublika Bashkortostan, W Russian Federation 51.51N 58.13E
151 Y11 **Akzhar** Kaz. Aqzhar. Vostochnyy Kazakhstan, E Kazakhstan 47.36N 83.37E
96 F13 **Ål** Buskerud, S Norway 60.37N 8.33E
121 N18 **Ala** Rus. Ola. ≈ SE Belarus
22 H11 **Alabama** off. State of Alabama; also known as Camellia State, Heart of Dixie, The Cotton State, Yellowhammer State. ◐ state S USA
25 P6 **Alabama River** ≈ Alabama, S USA
25 P4 **Alabaster** Alabama, S USA 33.14N 86.49W
145 U10 **Al 'Abd Allāh** var. Al Abdullah. S Iraq 32.06N 45.08E
Al Abdullah see Al 'Abd Allāh
145 W14 **Al Abṭīyah** well S Iraq 29.27N 45.56E
153 S9 **Ala-Buka** Dzhalal-Abadskaya Oblast', W Kyrgyzstan 41.22N 71.27E
194 K15 **Alabule** ≈ C PNG
142 J12 **Alaca** Çorum, N Turkey 40.10N 34.52E
142 K10 **Alaçam** Samsun, N Turkey 41.35N 35.37E
Alacant see Alicante
25 V9 **Alachua** Florida, SE USA 29.48N 82.29W
143 S13 **Aladağlar** ▲▲ W Turkey
142 K15 **Ala Dağları** ▲▲ C Turkey
131 O16 **Alagir** Respublika Severnaya Osetiya, SW Russian Federation 43.02N 44.10E
108 B6 **Alagna Valsesia** Valle d'Aosta, NW Italy 45.51N 7.50E
105 P12 **Alagnon** ≈ C France
61 P16 **Alagoas** off. Estado de Alagoas. ◐ state E Brazil
61 P17 **Alagoinhas** Bahia, E Brazil 12.09S 38.21W
107 R5 **Alagón** Aragón, NE Spain 41.46N 1.07W
106 J9 **Alagón** ≈ W Spain
95 K16 **Alahärmä** Länsi-Suomi, W Finland 63.15N 22.49E
al Ahdar see Al Akhḑar
148 K12 **Al Aḥmadī** var. Ahmadi. E Kuwait 29.02N 48.01E
Al Ain see Al 'Ayn
107 Z8 **Alaior** prev. Alayor. Menorca, Spain, W Mediterranean Sea 39.55N 4.07E
153 T11 **Alai Range** Rus. Alayskiy Khrebet. ▲▲ Kyrgyzstan/Tajikistan
Alais see Alès
147 X11 **Al 'Ajā'iz** E Oman 19.33N 57.12E
147 X11 **Al 'Ajā'iz** oasis SE Oman
95 L16 **Alajärvi** Länsi-Suomi, W Finland 63.00N 23.50E
120 K4 **Alajõe** Ida-Virumaa, NE Estonia 59.00N 27.26E
44 M13 **Alajuela** Alajuela, C Costa Rica 10.00N 84.12W
44 L12 **Alajuela** off. Provincia de Alajuela. ◐ province N Costa Rica
45 T14 **Alajuela, Lago** ◎ C Panama
40 M11 **Alakanuk** Alaska, USA 62.41N 164.37W
146 K5 **Al Akhḑar** var. al Ahdar. Tabūk, NW Saudi Arabia 28.04N 37.13E
Alaköl see Alakol', Ozero
151 X13 **Alakol', Ozero** Kaz. Alaköl. ◎ SE Kazakhstan
128 I5 **Alakurtti** Murmanskaya Oblast', NW Russian Federation 66.57N 30.27E
40 F10 **Alalakeiki Channel** channel Hawaii, USA, C Pacific Ocean
Al 'Alamayn see El 'Alamein
145 R1 **Al 'Amādīyah** N Iraq 37.09N 43.27E
196 K5 **Alamagan** island C Northern Mariana Islands
145 X10 **Al 'Amārah** var. Amara. E Iraq 31.51N 47.10E
82 J11 **Ālamat'ā** Tigray, N Ethiopia 12.22N 39.32E
39 R11 **Alameda** New Mexico, SW USA 35.09N 106.37W
124 Pp15 **'Alam el Rûm, Râs** headland N Egypt 31.21N 27.23E
Alamícamba see Alamikamba
44 M8 **Alamikamba** var. Alamícamba. Región Autónoma Atlántico Norte, NE Nicaragua 13.29N 84.17W
26 K11 **Alamito Creek** ≈ Texas, SW USA
42 M8 **Alamitos, Sierra de los** ▲ NE Mexico 26.15N 102.14W
37 X9 **Alamo** Nevada, W USA 37.21N 115.07W
22 F9 **Alamo** Tennessee, S USA 35.46N 89.07W
43 Q12 **Álamo** Veracruz-Llave, C Mexico 20.55N 97.40W
39 S14 **Alamogordo** New Mexico, SW USA 32.52N 105.57W
38 J12 **Alamo Lake** ⊡ Arizona, SW USA
42 H7 **Alamos** Sonora, NW Mexico 26.59N 108.53W
39 S7 **Alamosa** Colorado, C USA 37.25N 105.51W
95 J20 **Åland** var. Aland Islands, Fin. Ahvenanmaa. ◐ province SW Finland
95 J19 **Åland** Fin. Ahvenanmaa. island SW Finland
90 K9 **Åland** var. Aland Islands, Fin. Ahvenanmaa. island group SW Finland
Aland Islands see Åland
Aland Sea see Ålands Hav
97 Q14 **Ålands Hav** var. Aland Sea. strait Baltic Sea/Gulf of Bothnia
45 P16 **Alanje** Chiriquí, SW Panama 8.22N 82.36W
27 O2 **Alanreed** Texas, SW USA 35.12N 100.45W
142 G17 **Alanya** Antalya, S Turkey 36.31N 32.01E
25 U7 **Alapaha River** ≈ Florida/Georgia, SE USA
125 Ee11 **Alapayevsk** Sverdlovskaya Oblast', C Russian Federation 57.48N 61.50E
Alappuzha see Alleppey
144 F14 **Al 'Aqabah** var. Akaba, Aqaba, 'Aqaba; anc. Aelana, Elath. Ma'ān, SW Jordan 29.32N 35.00E
Al 'Arabīyah as Su'ūdīyah see Saudi Arabia
al Araïch see Larache
107 Q10 **Alarcón** Castilla-La Mancha, C Spain 39.33N 2.04W
107 Q9 **Alarcón, Embalse de** ⊡ C Spain
144 J2 **Al 'Arīmah** Fr. Arime. Ḩalab, N Syria 36.27N 37.41E
Al 'Arīsh see El 'Arîsh
147 P6 **Al Arṭāwīyah** Ar Riyāḑ, N Saudi Arabia 26.33N 45.19E
175 O16 **Alas** Sumbawa, S Indonesia 8.27S 117.04E
Alasca, Golfo de see Alaska, Gulf of
142 D14 **Alaşehir** Manisa, W Turkey 38.19N 28.30E
145 N5 **Al 'Ashārah** var. Ashara. Dayr az Zawr, E Syria 34.51N 40.36E
Al Ashkhara see Al Ashkharah
147 Z9 **Al Ashkharah** var. Al Ashkhara. NE Oman 21.46N 59.30E
41 P8 **Alaska** off. State of Alaska; also known as Land of the Midnight Sun, The Last Frontier, Seward's Folly; prev. Russian America. ◐ state NW USA
41 T13 **Alaska, Gulf of** var. Golfo de Alasca. gulf Canada/USA
41 O15 **Alaska Peninsula** peninsula Alaska, USA
41 Q11 **Alaska Range** ▲▲ Alaska, USA
173 Ee4 **Alas, Lae** ≈ Sumatera, NW Indonesia
Al-Asnam see Chlef
175 O16 **Alas, Selat** strait Nusa Tenggara, C Indonesia
108 B10 **Alassio** Liguria, NW Italy 44.01N 8.12E
Alat see Olot
143 Y12 **Älät** Rus. Alyat; prev. Alyaty-Pristan'. SE Azerbaijan 39.57N 49.24E
145 S13 **Al 'Athāmīn** S Iraq 30.27N 43.40E
41 P7 **Alatna River** ≈ Alaska, USA
109 J15 **Alatri** Lazio, C Italy 41.43N 13.21E
Alattio see Alta
131 P5 **Alatyr'** Chuvashskaya Respublika, W Russian Federation 54.50N 46.28E
58 C7 **Alausí** Chimborazo, C Ecuador 2.07S 78.44W
107 O3 **Álava** Basq. Araba. ◐ province País Vasco, N Spain
143 T11 **Alaverdi** N Armenia 41.06N 44.37E
Alavo see Alavus
95 N14 **Ala-Vuokki** Oulu, E Finland 64.46N 29.29E
95 K17 **Alavus** Swe. Alavo. Länsi-Suomi, W Finland 62.33N 23.37E
Al 'Awābī see Awābī
145 P6 **Al 'Awānī** W Iraq 34.28N 41.43E
77 U12 **Al Awaynāt** SE Libya 21.46N 24.51E
Al Awaynāt see Al 'Uwaynāt
190 K9 **Alawoona** South Australia 34.45S 140.28E
Alaykel'/Alay-Kuu see Këk-Art
149 R17 **Al 'Ayn** var. Al Ain. Abū Ẓaby, E UAE 24.13N 55.44E
149 R17 **Al 'Ayn** var. Al Ain. ✈ Abū Ẓaby, E UAE 24.16N 55.31E
144 G12 **Al 'Aynā** Al Karak, W Jordan 30.59N 35.43E
Alayor see Alaior
Alayskiy Khrebet see Alai Range
127 N7 **Alazeya** ≈ NE Russian Federation
145 U8 **Al 'Azīzīyah** var. Aziziya. E Iraq 32.54N 45.05E
123 L14 **Al 'Azīzīyah** NW Libya 32.31N 13.01E
144 I10 **Al Azraq al Janūbī** Az Zarqā', N Jordan 31.49N 36.48E
108 B9 **Alba** anc. Alba Pompeia. Piemonte, NW Italy 44.40N 8.01E
27 V6 **Alba** Texas, SW USA 32.47N 95.37W
118 G11 **Alba** ◐ county W Romania
145 P3 **Al Ba'āj** N Iraq 36.02N 41.43E
144 J2 **Al Bāb** Ḩalab, N Syria 36.24N 37.31E
118 G10 **Albac** Hung. Fehérvölgy; prev. Álbák. Alba, SW Romania 46.25N 22.58E
107 Q11 **Albacete** Castilla-La Mancha, C Spain 39.00N 1.52W
107 P11 **Albacete** ◐ province Castilla-La Mancha, C Spain
146 I4 **Al Bad'** Tabūk, NW Saudi Arabia 28.28N 35.00E
106 L7 **Alba de Tormes** Castilla-León, N Spain 40.49N 5.30W
145 P3 **Al Bādī** N Iraq 35.57N 41.37E
147 V8 **Al Badī'ah** ✈ (Abū Ẓaby) Abū Ẓaby, C UAE 24.27N 54.39E
149 P17 **Al Badī'ah** var. Al Bedei'ah. spring/well C UAE 23.44N 53.50E
145 Q7 **Al Baghdādī** var. Khān al Baghdādī. SW Iraq 33.19N 44.22E
Al Bāha see Al Bāḩah
146 M11 **Al Bāḩah** var. Al Bāha. Al Bāḩah, SW Saudi Arabia 20.00N 41.29E
146 M11 **Al Bāḩah** off. Minṭaqat al Bāḩah. ◐ province W Saudi Arabia
Al Baḩrayn see Bahrain
107 S11 **Albaida** País Valenciano, E Spain 38.51N 0.31W
118 H11 **Alba Iulia** Ger. Weissenburg, Hung. Gyulafehérvár; prev. Bălgrad, Karlsburg, Károly-Fehérvár. Alba, W Romania 46.06N 23.33E
Álbák see Albac
144 G10 **Al Balqā'** off. Muḩāfaẓat al Balqā', var. Balqā'. ◐ governorate NW Jordan
12 F11 **Alban** Ontario, S Canada 46.07N 80.37W
105 O15 **Alban** Tarn, S France 43.52N 2.30E
10 K11 **Albanel, Lac** ◎ Quebec, SE Canada
115 L20 **Albania** off. Republic of Albania, Alb. Republika e Shqipërisë, Shqipëria; prev. People's Socialist Republic of Albania. ◆ republic SE Europe
Albania see Aubagne
109 H15 **Albano Laziale** Lazio, C Italy 41.43N 12.40E
188 J14 **Albany** Western Australia 35.03S 117.54E
25 S7 **Albany** Georgia, SE USA 31.34N 84.09W
33 P13 **Albany** Indiana, N USA 40.18N 85.14W
22 L8 **Albany** Kentucky, S USA 36.41N 85.07W
31 U7 **Albany** Minnesota, N USA 45.39N 94.33W
29 R2 **Albany** Missouri, C USA 40.15N 94.15W
20 L10 **Albany** state capital New York, NE USA 42.39N 73.45W
34 G12 **Albany** Oregon, NW USA 44.38N 123.06W
27 Q6 **Albany** Texas, SW USA 32.43N 99.18W
10 F10 **Albany** ≈ Ontario, S Canada
Alba Pompeia see Alba
Alba Regia see Székesfehérvár
144 I6 **Al Bārdah** var. Bāridah. Ḩimş, C Syria 34.15N 37.39E
145 Q11 **Al Barīt** S Iraq 31.16N 42.28E
107 R8 **Albarracín** Aragón, NE Spain 40.24N 1.25W
145 Y12 **Al Baṣrah** Eng. Basra; hist. Busra, Bussora. SE Iraq 30.30N 47.49E
145 V11 **Al Baṭḥā'** SE Iraq 31.06N 45.49E
147 X8 **Al Bāṭinah** var. Batinah. coastal region N Oman
(0) H16 **Albatross Plateau** undersea feature E Pacific Ocean
Al Batrūn see Batroûn
124 Nn14 **Al Bayḑā'** var. Beida. NE Libya 32.46N 21.43E
147 P16 **Al Bayḑā'** var. Al Beida. SW Yemen 13.58N 45.38E
Al Bedei'ah see Al Badī'ah
Al Beida see Al Bayḑā'
23 S10 **Albemarle** var. Albermarle. North Carolina, SE USA 35.21N 80.12W
Albemarle Island see Isabela, Isla
23 N8 **Albemarle Sound** inlet W Atlantic Ocean
108 B10 **Albenga** Liguria, NW Italy 44.04N 8.13E
106 L8 **Alberche** ≈ C Spain
105 O17 **Albères, Chaîne des** var. les Albères, Montes Albères. ▲▲ France/Spain
Albères, Montes see Albères, Chaîne des
190 F2 **Alberga Creek** seasonal river South Australia
106 G7 **Albergaria-a-Velha** Aveiro, N Portugal 40.42N 8.28W
107 S10 **Alberic** País Valenciano, E Spain 39.07N 0.31W
Albermarle see Albemarle
109 P18 **Alberobello** Puglia, SE Italy 40.47N 17.14E
110 J7 **Alberschwende** Vorarlberg, W Austria 47.28N 9.49E
105 O3 **Albert** Somme, N France 50.00N 2.37E
9 O12 **Alberta** ◐ province SW Canada
194 K14 **Albert Edward, Mount** ▲ S PNG 8.23S 147.23E
Albert Edward Nyanza see Edward, Lake
63 C20 **Alberti** Buenos Aires, E Argentina 35.03S 60.15W
113 K23 **Albertirsa** Pest, C Hungary 47.15N 19.36E
101 I16 **Albertkanaal** canal N Belgium
81 P17 **Albert, Lake** var. Albert Nyanza, Lac Mobutu Sese Seko. ◎ Uganda/Dem. Rep. Congo (Zaire)
31 V11 **Albert Lea** Minnesota, N USA 43.39N 93.22W
83 F16 **Albert Nile** ≈ NW Uganda
Albert Nyanza see Albert, Lake
105 T11 **Albertville** Savoie, E France 45.41N 6.24E
25 Q2 **Albertville** Alabama, S USA 34.16N 86.12W
Albertville see Kalemie
105 N15 **Albi** anc. Albiga. Tarn, S France 43.55N 2.09E
31 W15 **Albia** Iowa, C USA 41.01N 92.48W
Albiga see Albi
57 X9 **Albina** Marowijne, NE Surinam 5.31N 54.04W
85 A15 **Albina, Ponta** headland SW Angola 15.52S 11.45E
32 M16 **Albion** Illinois, N USA 38.22N 88.03W
33 P11 **Albion** Indiana, N USA 41.22N 85.23W
31 P14 **Albion** Nebraska, C USA 41.41N 98.00W
20 E9 **Albion** New York, NE USA 43.13N 78.09W
20 B12 **Albion** Pennsylvania, NE USA 41.52N 80.18W
Al Biqā' see El Beqaa
146 J4 **Al Bi'r** var. Bi'r Ibn Hirmās. Tabūk, NW Saudi Arabia 28.52N 36.16E
146 M12 **Al Birk** Makkah, SW Saudi Arabia 18.12N 41.36E
147 Q9 **Al Biyāḑ** desert C Saudi Arabia
100 H13 **Alblasserdam** Zuid-Holland, SW Netherlands 51.52N 4.40E
107 T8 **Albocácer** var. Albocasser. País Valenciano, E Spain 40.21N 0.01E
Albocasser see Albocácer
97 H19 **Ålbæk** Nordjylland, N Denmark 57.33N 10.24E
Albona see Labin
107 O17 **Alborán, Isla de** island S Spain
Alborán, Mar de see Alboran Sea
107 N17 **Alboran Sea** Sp. Mar de Alborán. sea SW Mediterranean Sea
97 G20 **Ålborg** var. Aalborg, Ålborg-Nørresundby; anc. Alburgum. Nordjylland, N Denmark 57.03N 9.55E
97 H21 **Ålborg Bugt** var. Aalborg Bugt. bay N Denmark
Ålborg-Nørresundby see Ålborg
149 O5 **Alborz, Reshteh-ye Kūhhā-ye** Eng. Elburz Mountains. ▲▲ N Iran
107 Q14 **Albox** Andalucía, S Spain 37.22N 2.08W
103 H23 **Albstadt** Baden-Württemberg, SW Germany 48.13N 9.01E
106 G14 **Albufeira** Beja, S Portugal 37.04N 8.15W
145 P5 **Ālbū Gharz, Sabkhat** ◎ W Iraq
107 O15 **Albuñol** Andalucía, S Spain 36.48N 3.10W
39 Q11 **Albuquerque** New Mexico, SW USA 35.04N 106.37W
147 W8 **Al Buraymī** var. Buraimi. N Oman 24.16N 55.48E
149 R17 **Al Buraymī** var. Buraimi. spring/well Oman/UAE 24.27N 55.33E
Al Burayqah see Marsá al Burayqah
Alburgum see Ålborg
106 I10 **Alburquerque** Extremadura, W Spain 39.12N 7.00W
189 V14 **Albury** New South Wales, SE Australia 36.03S 146.52E
147 T14 **Al Buzūn** SE Yemen 15.40N 50.53E
95 G17 **Alby** Västernorrland, C Sweden 62.30N 15.25E
Albyn, Glen see Mor, Glen
106 G12 **Alcácer do Sal** Setúbal, W Portugal 38.21N 8.29W
Alcalá de Chisvert see Alcalá de Chivert
107 T8 **Alcalá de Chivert** var. Alcalá de Chisvert. País Valenciano, E Spain 40.19N 0.13E
106 K14 **Alcalá de Guadaira** Andalucía, S Spain 37.19N 5.49W
107 O8 **Alcalá de Henares** Ar. Alkal'a; anc. Complutum. Madrid, C Spain 40.28N 3.22W
106 K16 **Alcalá de los Gazules** Andalucía, S Spain 36.28N 5.43W
107 N14 **Alcalá La Real** Andalucía, S Spain 37.28N 3.55W
109 I23 **Alcamo** Sicilia, Italy, C Mediterranean Sea 37.58N 12.58E
107 T4 **Alcanadre** ≈ NE Spain
107 T8 **Alcanar** Cataluña, NE Spain 40.33N 0.28E
106 J5 **Alcañices** Castilla-León, N Spain 41.40N 6.21W
107 T7 **Alcañiz** Aragón, NE Spain 41.03N 0.09W
106 I9 **Alcántara** Extremadura, W Spain 39.42N 6.54W
106 J9 **Alcántara, Embalse de** ⊡ W Spain
107 R13 **Alcantarilla** Murcia, SE Spain 37.58N 1.12W
107 P11 **Alcaraz** Castilla-La Mancha, C Spain 38.40N 2.28W
107 P12 **Alcaraz, Sierra de** ▲▲ C Spain
106 I12 **Álcarrache** ≈ SW Spain
107 T6 **Alcarràs** Cataluña, NE Spain 41.34N 0.31E
107 N14 **Alcaudete** Andalucía, S Spain 37.34N 4.04W
Alcázar see Ksar-el-Kebir
107 O10 **Alcázar de San Juan** anc. Alce. Castilla-La Mancha, C Spain 39.24N 3.12W
Alcazarquivir see Ksar-el-Kebir
Alce see Alcázar de San Juan
59 B17 **Alcebo, Volcán** ⛰ Galapagos Islands, Ecuador, E Pacific Ocean 0.25S 91.06W
145 X12 **Al Chabā'ish** var. Al Kaba'ish. SE Iraq 30.58N 47.01E
119 Y7 **Alchevs'k** prev. Kommunarsk, Voroshilovsk. Luhans'ka Oblast', E Ukraine 48.29N 38.52E
Alcira see Alzira
23 N9 **Alcoa** Tennessee, S USA 35.47N 83.58W
106 F9 **Alcobaça** Leiria, C Portugal 39.31N 8.58W
107 N8 **Alcobendas** Madrid, C Spain 40.31N 3.37W
Alcoi see Alcoy
107 P7 **Alcolea del Pinar** Castilla-La Mancha, C Spain 41.01N 2.28W
106 I11 **Alconchel** Extremadura, W Spain 38.31N 7.04W
107 S9 **Alcora** País Valenciano, E Spain 40.04N 0.13W
107 N8 **Alcorcón** Madrid, C Spain 40.20N 3.52W
107 S7 **Alcorisa** Aragón, NE Spain 40.52N 0.22W
63 B19 **Alcorta** Santa Fe, C Argentina 33.31S 61.07W
106 H14 **Alcoutim** Faro, S Portugal 37.28N 7.28W
35 W15 **Alcova** Wyoming, C USA 42.33N 106.40W
107 S11 **Alcoy** var. Alcoi. País Valenciano, E Spain 38.42N 0.28W
107 Y9 **Alcúdia, Badia d'** bay Mallorca, Spain, W Mediterranean Sea
180 M7 **Aldabra Group** island group SW Seychelles
145 U10 **Al Daghghārah** C Iraq 32.10N 44.57E
42 J5 **Aldama** Chihuahua, N Mexico 28.49N 105.52W
43 P11 **Aldama** Tamaulipas, C Mexico 22.55N 98.03W
126 Ll12 **Aldan** Respublika Sakha (Yakutiya), NE Russian Federation 58.31N 125.15E
126 Mm12 **Aldan** ≈ NE Russian Federation
168 G7 **Aldar** Dzavhan, W Mongolia 47.43N 96.36E
al Dar al Baida see Rabat

◆ Country ● Country Capital ◇ Dependent Territory ○ Dependent Territory Capital ◐ Administrative Region ✈ International Airport ▲ Mountain ▲▲ Mountain Range ⛰ Volcano ≈ River ◎ Lake ⊡ Reservoir
221

99 Q20 **Aldeburgh** E England, UK 52.12N 1.35E
107 P5 **Aldehuela de Calatañazor** Castilla-León, N Spain 41.42N 2.46W
Aldeia Nova *see* Aldeia Nova de São Bento
106 H13 **Aldeia Nova de São Bento** *var.* Alde.a Nova. Beja, S Portugal 37.55N 7.24W
31 V11 **Alden** Minnesota, N USA 43.46N 93.34W
192 N6 **Aldermen Islands, The** *island group:* N NZ
99 L25 **Alderney** *island* Channel Islands
99 N22 **Aldershot** S England, UK 51.15N 0.46W
23 R6 **Alderson** West Virginia, NE USA 37.43N 80.38W
Al Dhaid *see* Adh Dhayd
32 J11 **Aledo** Illinois, N USA 41.12N 90.45W
78 H9 **Aleg** Brakna, SW Mauritania 17.03N 13.52W
66 Q10 **Alegranza** *island* Islas Canarias, Spain, NE Atlantic Ocean
39 P12 **Alegres Mountain** ▲ New Mexico, SW USA 34.09N 108.11W
63 F15 **Alegrete** Rio Grande do Sul, S Brazil 29.46S 55.46W
63 C16 **Alejandra** Santa Fe, C Argentina 29.54S 59.49W
200 Oo12 **Alejandro Selkirk, Isla** *island* Islas Juan Fernández, Chile, E Pacific Ocean
128 I12 **Alekhovshchina** Leningradskaya Oblast', NW Russian Federation 60.22N 33.57E
41 O13 **Aleknagik** Alaska, USA 59.16N 158.37W
Aleksandriya *see* Oleksandriya
Aleksandropol' *see* Gyumri
130 L3 **Aleksandrov** Vladimirskaya Oblast', W Russian Federation 56.24N 38.42E
115 N14 **Aleksandrovac** Serbia, C Yugoslavia 43.28N 21.05E
131 R9 **Aleksandrov Gay** Saratovskaya Oblast', W Russian Federation 50.08N 48.34E
131 U6 **Aleksandrovka** Orenburgskaya Oblast', W Russian Federation 52.47N 54.14E
Aleksandrovka *see* Oleksandrivka
116 J8 **Aleksandrovo** Lovech, N Bu.garia 43.16N 24.53E
129 V13 **Aleksandrovsk** Permskaya Oblast', W Russian Federation 59.12N 57.27E
Aleksandrovsk *see* Zaporizhzhya
131 N14 **Aleksandrovskoye** Stavropol'skiy Kray, SW Russian Federation 44.43N 42.56E
127 O14 **Aleksandrovsk-Sakhalinskiy** Ostrcv Sakhalin, Sakhalinskaya Oblast', SE Russian Federation 50.55N 142.12E
112 J10 **Aleksandrów Kujawski** Kujawsko-pomorskie, C Poland 52.51N 18.42E
112 K12 **Aleksandrów Łódzki** Łódzkie, C Poland 51.48N 19.18E
Alekseevka *see* Akko'/Alekseyevka
130 L9 **Alekseevka** Belgorodskaya Oblast', W Russian Federation 50.35N 38.41E
151 P7 **Alekseyevka** *Kaz.* Alekseevka. Severnyy Kazakhstan, N Kazakhstan 53.31N 69.50E
151 Z10 **Alekseyevka** *Kaz.* Alekseevka. Vostochnyy Kazakhstan, E Kazakhstan 48.25N 85.38E
131 S7 **Alekseyevka** Samarskaya Oblast', W Russian Federation 52.37N 51.20E
Alekseyevka *see* Akkol'
126 Jj13 **Alekseyevka** Irkutskaya Oblast', C Russian Federation 57.46M 108.07E
131 R4 **Alekseyevskoye** Respublika Tatarstan, W Russian Federation 55.18N 50.11E
130 K5 **Aleksin** Tul'skaya Oblast', W Russian Federation 54.30N 37.07E
115 O14 **Aleksinac** Serbia, SE Yugoslavia 43.33N 21.43E
202 G11 **Alele** Île Uvea, E Wallis and Futuna 13.13S 176.09W
97 N20 **Älem** Kalmar, S Sweden 56.57N 16.25E
104 L6 **Alençon** Orne, N France 48.25N 0.04E
60 I12 **Alenquer** Pará, NE Brazil 1.58S 54.45W
40 **Alenuihaha Channel** *channel* Hawai'i, USA, C Pacific Ocean
Alep/Aleppo *see* Ḥalab
105 Y15 **Aléria** Corse, France, C Mediterranean Sea 42.06N 9.29E
207 Q11 **Alert** Ellesmere Island, Nunavut, N Canada 82.28N 62.13W
105 Q14 **Alès** *prev.* Alais. Gard, S France 44.07N 4.04E
118 G9 **Aleşd** *Hung.* Élesd. Bihor, SW Romania 47.03N 22.22E
108 C9 **Alessandria** *Fr.* Alexandrie. Piemonte, N Italy 44.54N 8.37E
97 C21 **Ålesund** Møre og Romsdal, S Norway 62.28N 6.10E
110 F10 **Aletschhorn** ▲ SW Switzerland 46.33N 8.01E
207 S1 **Aleutian Basin** *undersea feature* Bering Sea
40 H17 **Aleutian Islands** *island group* Alaska, USA
41 P14 **Aleutian Range** ▲▲ Alaska, USA
(0) B5 **Aleutian Trench** *undersea feature* S Bering Ocean
127 O10 **Alevina, Mys** *headland* E Russian Federation 58.52N 151.21E
13 Q6 **Alex** Québec, SE Canada
30 J3 **Alexander** North Dakota, N USA 47.48N 103.38W
41 W14 **Alexander Archipelago** *island group* Alaska, USA
Alexanderbaai *see* Alexander Bay
85 D21 **Alexander Bay** *Afr.* Alexanderbaai. Northern Cape, W South Africa 28.35S 16.30E
25 Q5 **Alexander City** Alabama, S USA 32.56N 85.57W

204 J6 **Alexander Island** *island* Antarctica
Alexander Range *see* Kirghiz Range
191 O12 **Alexandra** Victoria, SE Australia 37.12S 145.43E
193 D22 **Alexandra** Otago, South Island, NZ 45.15S 169.24E
117 F14 **Alexándreia** *var.* Alexándria. Kentrikí Makedonía, N Greece 40.38N 22.27E
Alexandretta *see* Iskenderun
Alexandretta, Gulf of *see* Iskenderun Körfezi
13 N13 **Alexandria** Ontario, SE Canada 45.19N 74.37W
124 Q15 **Alexandria** *Ar.* Al Iskandarīyah. N Egypt 31.07N 29.51E
46 J12 **Alexandria** C Jamaica 18.18N 77.21W
118 J15 **Alexandria** Teleorman, S Romania 43.58N 25.18E
33 O13 **Alexandria** Indiana, N USA 40.15N 85.40W
22 M4 **Alexandria** Kentucky, S USA 38.56N 84.21W
24 H7 **Alexandria** Louisiana, S USA 31.18N 92.27W
31 T4 **Alexandria** Minnesota, N USA 45.54N 95.22W
31 Q11 **Alexandria** South Dakota, N USA 43.39N 97.46W
23 W4 **Alexandria** Virginia, NE USA 38.48N 77.03W
20 I7 **Alexandria Bay** New York, NE USA 44.20N 75.54W
Alexandrie *see* Alessandria
190 J10 **Alexandrina, Lake** ◎ South Australia
116 K13 **Alexandroúpoli** *var.* Alexandroúpolis, *Turk.* Dedeagaç, Dedeagach. Anatolikí Makedonía kai Thráki, NE Greece 40.51N 25.52E
Alexandroúpolis *see* Alexandroúpoli
8 **Alexis Creek** British Columbia, SW Canada 52.06N 123.25W
126 Gg15 **Aleysk** Altayskiy Kray, S Russian Federation 52.32N 82.46E
145 S8 **Al Fallūjah** *var.* Falluja. C Iraq 33.21N 43.46E
107 R8 **Alfambra** ≈ E Spain
147 R15 **Al Farḍah** C Yemen 14.51N 48.33E
107 Q4 **Alfaro** La Rioja, N Spain 42.09N 1.46W
107 U15 **Alfarràs** Cataluña, NE Spain 41.49N 0.34E
Al Fāshir *see* El Fasher
Al Fashn *see* El Fashn
147 M7 **Alfatar** Silistra, NE Bulgaria 43.56N 27.17E
145 T7 **Al Fatḥah** C Iraq 35.06N 43.34E
145 Q3 **Al Fatsi** N Iraq 36.04N 42.39E
145 Z13 **Al Fāw** *var.* Fao. SE Iraq 29.55N 48.25E
Al Fayyūm *see* El Faiyûm
117 D20 **Alfeiós** *prev.* Alfiós, *anc.* Alpheius, Alpheus. ≈ S Greece
102 I13 **Alfeld** Niedersachsen, C Germany 51.58N 9.49E
Alfiós *see* Alfeiós
96 C11 **Ålfotbreen** *glacier* S Norway
21 P9 **Alfred** Maine, NE USA 43.28N 70.43W
20 F11 **Alfred** New York, NE USA 42.15N 77.47W
63 K14 **Alfredo Vagner** Santa Catarina, S Brazil 27.40S 49.22W
95 M12 **Alfta** Gävleborg, C Sweden 61.19N 16.04E
146 K12 **Al Fuḥayhīl** *var.* Fahaheel. SE Kuwait 29.01N 48.04E
145 Q6 **Al Fuḥaymi** C Iraq 34.17N 42.09E
149 S16 **Al Fujayrah** *Eng.* Fujairah. NE UAE 25.09N 56.18E
149 S16 **Al Fujayrah** *Eng.* Fujairah. ✈ NE UAE 25.04N 56.12E
Al Furāt *see* Euphrates
150 D13 **Alga** *Kaz.* Algha. Aktyubinsk, NW Kazakhstan 49.55N 57.19E
150 G9 **Algabas** Zapadnyy Kazakhstan, NW Kazakhstan 50.45N 52.07E
97 C17 **Ålgård** Rogaland, S Norway 58.45N 5.52E
106 G14 **Algarve** *cultural region* S Portugal
190 G3 **Algebuckina Bridge** South Australia 28.03S 135.48E
106 H16 **Algeciras** Andalucía, SW Spain 36.07N 5.27W
107 S10 **Algemesí** País Valenciano, E Spain 39.10N 0.27E
Al-Genain *see* El Geneina
123 I11 **Alger** *var.* Algiers, El Djazâir, Al Jazâir. ● (Algeria) N Algeria 36.47N 2.58E
76 H9 **Algeria** *off.* Democratic and Popular Republic of Algeria. ◆ *republic* N Africa
123 J9 **Algerian Basin** *var.* Balearic Plain *undersea feature* W Mediterranean Sea
Algha *see* Alga
144 I4 **Al Ghāb** ◎ NW Syria
147 X10 **Al Ghaydah** *var.* Ghaba. E Oman 21.21N 57.13E
147 T13 **Al Ghaydah** S Yemen 16.15N 52.13E
146 M6 **Al Ghazālah** Ḥā'il, NW Saudi Arabia 26.55N 41.23E
109 B17 **Alghero** Sardegna, Italy, C Mediterranean Sea 40.34N 8.19E
97 N16 **Älghult** Kronoberg, S Sweden 57.00N 15.34E
Al Ghurdaqah *see* Hurghada
Algiers *see* Alger
85 I24 **Algoa Bay** *bay* S South Africa
32 **Algodonales** Andalucía, S Spain 36.54N 5.24W
107 N9 **Algodor** ≈ C Spain
33 S6 **Algoma** Wisconsin, N USA 44.41N 87.24W
31 **Algona** Iowa, C USA 43.04N 94.13W
22 L8 **Algood** Tennessee, S USA 36.11N 85.27W

107 O2 **Algorta** País Vasco, N Spain 43.20N 3.00W
63 E18 **Algorta** Río Negro, W Uruguay 32.21S 57.12W
145 X10 **Al Habbārīyah** S Iraq 32.16N 42.12E
Al Hadhar *see* Al Ḥaḍr
145 Q4 **Al Ḥaḍr** *var.* Al Fladhar; *anc.* Hatra. NW Iraq 35.33N 42.43E
145 T13 **Al Hajarah** *desert* S Iraq
147 W8 **Al Hajar al Gharbī** ▲▲ N Oman
147 Y8 **Al Hajar ash Sharqī** ▲▲ NE Oman
147 R15 **Al Hajarayn** C Yemen 15.29N 48.24E
145 L10 **Al Ḥamād** *desert* Jordan/Saudi Arabia
Al Hamad *see* Syrian Desert
77 N9 **Al Ḥamādah al Ḥamrā'** *var.* Al Hamra. *desert* NW Libya
107 N15 **Alhama de Granada** Andalucía, S Spain 37.00N 3.58W
107 R13 **Alhama de Murcia** Murcia, SE Spain 37.51N 1.25W
37 T15 **Alhambra** California, W USA 34.07N 118.06W
145 T12 **Al Ḥammām** S Iraq 31.09N 44.04E
147 X8 **Al Ḥamrā'** NE Oman 23.07N 57.22E
Al Ḥamrā' *var.* Al Ḥamādah al Ḥamrā
147 O6 **Al Ḥamūdīyah** *spring/well* N Saudi Arabia 27.05N 44.24E
146 M7 **Al Ḥanākīyah** Al Madīnah, W Saudi Arabia 24.54N 40.31E
145 W14 **Al Ḥanīyah** *escarpment* Iraq/Saudi Arabia
145 Y12 **Al Hārithah** SE Iraq 30.43N 47.43E
146 L3 **Al Ḥarrah** *desert* NW Saudi Arabia
77 Q10 **Al Harūj al Aswad** *desert* C Libya
Al Hasaifin *see* Al Ḥusayfin
145 N2 **Al Ḥasakah** *var.* Al Hasijah, El Haseke, *Fr.* Hassetché. Al Hasakah, NE Syria 36.22N 40.43E
145 O2 **Al Ḥasakah** *off.* Muḥāfaẓat al Ḥasakah, *var.* Al Hasakah, Āl Hasakah, Hasakah, Hassakeh. ◆ *governorate* NE Syria
145 T9 **Al Hāshimīyah** C Iraq 32.24N 44.39E
144 G13 **Al Hāshimīyah** Maʿān, S Jordan 30.31N 35.46E
Al Hasijah *see* Al Ḥasakah
106 M15 **Alhaurín el Grande** Andalucía, S Spain 36.39N 4.40W
147 Q16 **Al Ḥawrā** S Yemen 13.54N 47.36E
145 V10 **Al Ḥayy** *var.* Kut al Hai, Kūt al Ḥayy. E Iraq 32.11N 46.03E
147 U11 **Al Ḥibāk** *desert* E Saudi Arabia
144 H8 **Al Ḥijānah** *var.* Hejanah, Hijanah. Dimashq, W Syria 33.22N 36.34E
146 K7 **Al Ḥijāz** *Eng.* Hejaz. *physical region* NW Saudi Arabia
Al Hilbeh *see* 'Ulayyāniyah, Bi'r al
145 T9 **Al Ḥillah** *var.* Hilla. C Iraq 32.28N 44.28E
145 T9 **Al Hindīyah** *var.* Hindiya. C Iraq 32.31N 44.13E
144 G12 **Al Ḥisā** Aṭ Ṭafīlah, W Jordan 30.49N 35.58E
76 G5 **Al-Hoceïma** *var.* al Hoceima, Al-Hoceima, Alhucemas; *prev.* Villa Sanjurjo. N Morocco 35.13N 3.55W
Alhucemas *see* Al-Hoceïma
107 N17 **Alhucemas, Peñón de** *island group* S Spain
147 N15 **Al Ḥudaydah** *Eng.* Hodeida. W Yemen 15.00N 42.50E
147 N15 **Al Ḥudaydah** *Eng.* Hodeida. ✈ W Yemen 15.00N 42.50E
146 M4 **Al Ḥudūd ash Shamālīyah** *var.* Minṭaqat al Ḥudūd ash Shamālīyah, *Eng.* Northern Border Region. ◆ *province* N Saudi Arabia
147 S7 **Al Ḥufūf** *var.* Hofuf. Ash Sharqīyah, NE Saudi Arabia 25.21N 49.33E
al-Hurma *see* Al Khurmah
147 X7 **Al Ḥusayfīn** *var.* Al Hasaifin. N Oman 24.33N 56.33E
145 U9 **'Alī** E Iraq 32.43N 45.21E
144 G11 **'Ali al Gharbī** *var.* Jīza. N Jordan 31.42N 35.57E
'Ali Jizah *see* El Gîza
147 P9 **'Aliābad** Yazd, C Iran 36.55N 54.33E
142 B13 **Aliağa** İzmir, W Turkey 38.49N 26.58E
117 F14 **Aliákmon** *prev.* Aliákmonas. ≈ N Greece
117 F14 **Aliákmonas** *prev.* Haliacmon. ≈ N Greece
145 W9 **'Ali al Gharbī** E Iraq 32.28N 46.42E
145 U11 **'Ali al Ḥassūnī** S Iraq 31.25N 44.50E
117 G18 **Aliártos** Stereá Ellás, C Greece 38.22N 23.06E
143 Y12 **Äli-Bayramlı** *Rus.* Ali-Bayramly. SE Azerbaijan 39.57N 48.54E
Ali-Bayramly *see* Äli-Bayramlı
116 P22 **Alibey Barajı** ▨ NW Turkey
79 S13 **Alibori** ≈ N Benin
114 M10 **Alibunar** Serbia, N Yugoslavia 45.06N 20.59E
152 T3 **Alicante** *Cat.* Alacant; *Lat.* Lucentum. País Valenciano, SE Spain 38.21N 0.28W
107 S13 **Alicante** ◆ *province* País Valenciano, SE Spain
107 S13 **Alicante** ✈ Murcia, E Spain 38.21N 0.28W
85 I25 **Alice** Eastern Cape, S South Africa 32.49S 26.49E
27 S14 **Alice** Texas, SW USA 27.45N 98.04W
85 I25 **Alicedale** Eastern Cape, S South Africa 33.19S 26.04E
87 R25 **Alice, Mount** *hill* West Falkland, Falkland Islands
189 P20 **Alice, Punta** *headland* S Italy 39.24N 17.09E
189 Q7 **Alice Springs** Northern Territory, C Australia 23.42S 133.52E
25 N4 **Aliceville** Alabama, S USA 33.07N 88.09W

153 U13 **Alichur** SE Tajikistan 37.49N 73.45E
153 U14 **Alichuri Janūbī, Qatorkūhi** *Rus.* Yuzhno-Alichurskiy Khrebet. ▲▲ SE Tajikistan
153 U13 **Alichuri Shimolī, Qatorkūhi** *Rus.* Severo-Alichurskiy Khrebet. ▲▲ SE Tajikistan
109 K22 **Alicudi, Isola** *island* Isole Eolie, S Italy
153 J11 **Aligarh** Uttar Pradesh, N India 27.54N 78.04E
148 M7 **Aligūdarz** Lorestān, W Iran 33.27N 49.33E
(0) F12 **Alijos, Islas** *island group* California, SW USA
155 R6 **'Ali Kbel** *Pash.* 'Ali Khēl. Paktīkā, E Afghanistan 33.55N 69.49E
Ali Khel *see* 'Ali Kheyl, Paktiā, Afghanistan
'Ali Khēl *see* 'Ali Kbel, Paktīkā, Afghanistan
155 R6 **'Ali Kheyl** *var.* Jaji. Paktīā, SE Afghanistan 33.55N 69.46E
147 V17 **Al Ikhwān** *island group* SE Yemen
81 N19 **Aliki** *see* Alykí
81 N19 **Alima** ≈ C Congo
Al Imārāt al 'Arabīyah al Muttaḥidah *see* United Arab Emirates
194 M12 **Alimbit** ≈ New Britain, C PNG
117 N23 **Alimía** *island* Dodekánisos, Greece, Aegean Sea
57 V12 **Alimimuni Piek** ▲ S Surinam 2.25N 55.46W
81 K15 **Alindao** Basse-Kotto, S Central African Republic 4.58N 21.16E
97 J18 **Alingsås** Västra Götaland, S Sweden 57.55N 12.30E
81 K18 **Alinjugul** *spring/well* E Kenya 0.03S 40.31E
155 S11 **Alipur** Punjab, E Pakistan 29.22N 70.58E
153 T12 **Alipur Duār** West Bengal, NE India 26.28N 89.25E
20 B14 **Aliquippa** Pennsylvania, NE USA 40.36N 80.15W
82 L12 **'Ali Sabieh** *var.* 'Ali Sabīh. S Djibouti 11.07N 42.44E
'Ali Sabih *see* 'Ali Sabieh
146 K3 **Al 'Īsāwiyah** N Al Jawf, NW Saudi Arabia 30.41N 37.58E
145 T8 **Aliseda** Extremadura, W Spain 39.25N 6.42W
145 T8 **Al Iskandarīyah** C Iraq 32.52N 44.22E
Al Iskandarīyah *see* Alexandria
122 Oo5 **Aliskerovo** Chukotskiy Avtonomnyy Okrug, NE Russian Federation 67.40N 167.37E
116 H13 **Alistráti** Kentrikí Makedonía, NE Greece 41.03N 23.58E
41 P15 **Alitak Bay** *bay* Kodiak Island, Alaska, USA
117 H18 **Aliveri** *var.* Alivérion. Évvoia, C Greece 38.25N 24.02E
Alivérion *see* Aliveri
Aliwal-Noord *see* Aliwal North
85 I24 **Aliwal North** *Afr.* Aliwal-Noord. Eastern Cape, SE South Africa 30.39S 26.43E
124 Nn15 **Al Jabal al Akhḍar** ▲▲ NE Libya
144 H13 **Al Jafr** Maʿān, S Jordan 30.18N 36.13E
77 T8 **Al Jaghbūb** NE Libya 29.45N 24.31E
148 K11 **Al Jahrā'** *var.* Al Jahrah, Jahra. C Kuwait 29.17N 47.46E
Al Jahrah *see* Al Jahrā'
Al Jamāhīrīyah al 'Arabīyah al Lībīyah ash Sha'bīyah al Ishtirāk *see* Libya
146 K3 **Al Jarāwī** *spring/well* NW Saudi Arabia 30.12N 38.48E
147 X11 **Al Jawārah** *oasis* SE Oman 18.59N 57.16E
146 L3 **Al Jawf** *var.* Jauf, NW Saudi Arabia 29.51N 39.49E
146 L4 **Al Jawf** *off.* Minṭaqat al Jawf. ◆ *province* N Saudi Arabia
Al Jawlān *see* Golan Heights
145 N4 **Al Jazīrah** *physical region* Iraq/Syria
106 F14 **Aljezur** Faro, S Portugal 37.18N 8.49W
145 S13 **Al Jil** S Iraq 30.28N 43.57E
144 G11 **Al Jīzah** *var.* Jīza. 'Ammān, N Jordan 31.42N 35.57E
147 S6 **Al Jubayl** *var.* Al Jubayl. Ash Sharqīyah, NE Saudi Arabia 27.01N 49.40E
Al Jubayl *see* Al Jubayl
147 T10 **Äl Juḥaysh, Qalamat** *well* N Saudi Arabia 20.35N 51.00E
147 N15 **Al Jumaylīyah** N Qatar 25.37N 51.04E
146 G13 **Al Jumūm** Makkah, W Saudi Arabia 21.37N 39.42E
Al Kaba'ish *see* Al Chabā'ish
Al-Kadhimain *see* Al Kāẓimīyah
Al Kāf *see* El Kef
Alkal'a *see* Alcalá de Henares
37 W4 **Alkali Flat** *salt flat* Nevada, W USA
35 W7 **Alkali Lake** ◎ Nevada, W USA
147 Z9 **Al Kāmil** NE Oman 22.15N 59.12E
144 G11 **Al Karak** *var.* El Karak, Kerak; *anc.* Kir Moab, Kir of Moab. Al Karak, W Jordan 31.11N 35.42E
144 G12 **Al Karak** *off.* Muḥāfaẓat al Karak. ◆ *governorate* W Jordan
144 G12 **Al Karmashīyah** E Iraq
Al-Kashaniya *see* Al Qash'ānīyah
Al Kasr al-Kebir *see* Ksar-el-Kebir
148 K8 **Al Kāẓimīyah** *var.* Al-Kadhimain, Kadhimain. C Iraq 33.25N 44.50E
147 X8 **Al Khābūrah** *var.* Khabura. N Oman 23.56N 57.10E
Al Khalīl *see* Hebron
147 S7 **Al Khāliṣ** C Iraq 33.51N 44.33E
Al Khārijah *see* El Khârga
147 Q8 **Al Kharj** *var.* Al Riyāḍ, C Saudi Arabia 24.12N 47.12E
147 W6 **Al Khaṣab** *var.* Khasab. N Oman 26.10N 56.18E

149 N15 **Al Khawr** *var.* Al Khaur, Al Khor. N Qatar 25.40N 51.33E
148 K12 **Al Khīrān** *var.* Al Khiran. SE Kuwait 28.34N 48.21E
147 W9 **Al Khīrān** *spring/well* NW Oman 22.31N 55.42E
Al-Khobar *see* Al Khubar
Al Khor *var.* Al Khawr
147 S6 **Al Khubar** *var.* Al-Khobar. Ash Sharqīyah, NE Saudi Arabia 26.15N 50.10E
77 T11 **Al Khufrah** SE Libya 24.10N 23.19E
145 R12 **Al Khums** *var.* Homs, Khoms, Khums. NW Libya 32.39N 14.16E
147 R15 **Al Khuraybah** C Yemen 15.05N 48.16E
146 M9 **Al Khurmah** *var.* al-Hurma. Makkah, W Saudi Arabia 21.58N 42.00E
147 V9 **Al Kidan** *desert* NE Saudi Arabia
100 H9 **Alkmaar** Noord-Holland, NW Netherlands 52.37N 4.45E
145 T10 **Al Kūfah** *var.* Kufa. S Iraq 32.01N 44.25E
145 V9 **Al Kūt** *var.* Kūt al 'Amārah, Kut al-Imara. E Iraq 32.30N 45.51E
Al-Kuwait *see* Al Kuwayt
146 K11 **Al Kuwayt** *var.* Al-Kuwait, *Eng.* Kuwait, Kuwait City; *prev.* Qurein. ● (Kuwait) E Kuwait 29.23N 48.00E
148 K11 **Al Kuwayt** ✈ C Kuwait 29.13N 47.57E
117 G19 **Alkyonídon, Kólpos** *gulf* C Greece
147 N4 **Al Labbah** *physical region* N Saudi Arabia
144 G4 **Al Lādhiqīyah** *Eng.* Latakia, *Fr.* Lattaquié; *anc.* Laodicea, Laodicea ad Mare. Al Lādhiqīyah, W Syria 35.31N 35.46E
144 H4 **Al Lādhiqīyah** *off.* Muḥāfaẓat al Lādhiqīyah, *var.* Al Lādhiqīyah, Latakia, Lattakia. ◆ *governorate* W Syria
21 R2 **Allagash River** ≈ Maine, NE USA
158 M13 **Allahābād** Uttar Pradesh, N India 25.27N 81.49E
149 S3 **Allāh Dāgh, Reshteh-ye** ▲▲ NE Iran
41 Q8 **Allakaket** Alaska, USA 66.33N 152.40W
Al-Lallyk *see* Olmaliq
85 J19 **Alldays** Northern, NE South Africa 22.39S 29.04E
20 E12 **Allegheny Mountains** ▲▲ NE USA
20 D11 **Allegheny Plateau** ▲▲ New York/Pennsylvania, NE USA
20 D11 **Allegheny Reservoir** ▨ New York/Pennsylvania, NE USA
20 D11 **Allegheny River** ≈ New York/Pennsylvania, NE USA
24 K9 **Allemands, Lac des** ◎ Louisiana, S USA
27 U6 **Allen** Texas, SW USA 33.06N 96.40W
99 D16 **Allen, Lough** *Ir.* Loch Aillionn. ◎ NW Ireland
193 B26 **Allen, Mount** ▲ Stewart Island, Southland, SW NZ 47.05S 167.49E
43 N6 **Allende** Coahuila de Zaragoza, NE Mexico 28.22N 100.47W
43 O9 **Allende** Nuevo León, NE Mexico 25.19N 100.01W
111 V2 **Allensteig** Niederösterreich, N Austria 48.40N 15.24E
Allenstein *see* Olsztyn
20 I14 **Allentown** Pennsylvania, NE USA 40.37N 75.30W
161 G23 **Alleppey** *var.* Alappuzha; *prev.* Alleppi. Kerala, SW India 9.30N 76.22E
Alleppi *see* Alleppey
102 J12 **Aller** ≈ NW Germany
101 K19 **Alleur** Liège, E Belgium 50.40N 5.33E
29 N14 **Alliance** Nebraska, C USA 42.05N 102.52W
31 V16 **Alliance** Ohio, N USA 40.55N 81.06W
105 O11 **Allier** ◆ *department* C France
46 J13 **Alligator Pond** C Jamaica 17.52N 77.34W
21 Y9 **Alligator River** ≈ North Carolina, SE USA
31 W12 **Allison** Iowa, C USA 42.45N 92.48W
12 G14 **Alliston** Ontario, S Canada 44.09N 79.51W
158 L11 **Al Līth** Makkah, SW Saudi Arabia 21.00N 41.00E
98 J12 **Alloa** C Scotland, UK 56.07N 3.49W
105 S13 **Allos** Alpes-de-Haute-Provence, SE France 44.16N 6.37E
110 D6 **Allschwil** Basel-Land, NW Switzerland 47.34N 7.32E
Al Lubnān *see* Lebanon
147 N14 **Al Luḥayyah** W Yemen 15.43N 42.45E
13 N12 **Allumettes, Île des** *island* Québec, SE Canada
145 S7 **Al Lussuf** *well* S Iraq 30.42N 43.37E
111 S5 **Alm** ≈ N Austria
13 Q7 **Alma** Québec, SE Canada 48.32N 71.41W

29 S10 **Alma** Arkansas, C USA 35.28N 94.13W
25 V7 **Alma** Georgia, SE USA 31.32N 82.27W
29 P4 **Alma** Kansas, C USA 39.01N 96.17W
33 Q8 **Alma** Michigan, N USA 43.22N 84.39W
29 O17 **Alma** Nebraska, C USA 40.06N 99.21W
32 I7 **Alma** Wisconsin, N USA 44.21N 91.54W
145 R12 **Al Ma'āniyah** S Iraq 30.45N 42.57E
Alma-Ata *see* Almaty
Alma-Atinskaya Oblast' *see* Almaty
Almacellas *see* Almacelles
107 T5 **Almacelles** *var.* Almacellas. Cataluña, NE Spain 41.43N 0.25E
106 F11 **Almada** Setúbal, W Portugal 38.40N 9.09W
106 L11 **Almadén** Castilla-La Mancha, C Spain 38.46N 4.49W
68 L6 **Almadies, Pointe des** *headland* W Senegal 14.43N 17.31W
147 L7 **Al Madīnah** *Eng.* Medina. Al Madīnah, W Saudi Arabia 24.25N 39.29E
147 L7 **Al Madīnah** *off.* Minṭaqat al Madīnah. ◆ *province* W Saudi Arabia
144 H9 **Al Mafraq** *var.* Mafraq. Al Mafraq, N Jordan 32.19N 36.12E
144 J10 **Al Mafraq** *off.* governorate of Mafraq. ◆ *governorate* N Jordan
147 R15 **Al Maghārim** C Yemen 15.00N 47.49E
147 N11 **Almagro** Castilla-La Mancha, C Spain 38.54N 3.43W
Al Maḥallah al Kubrā *see* El Maḥalla el Kubra
145 T9 **Al Maḥāwīl** *var.* Khān Maḥāwīl. C Iraq 32.39N 44.28E
145 T8 **Al Maḥmūdīyah** *var.* Mahmudiya. C Iraq 33.04N 44.22E
147 T14 **Al Mahrah** ▲▲ E Yemen
147 P7 **Al Majma'ah** Ar Riyāḍ, C Saudi Arabia 25.55N 45.18E
145 Q11 **Al Makmin** *well* S Iraq 31.38N 42.10E
145 P7 **Al Malikīyah** *var.* Malkiye. N Syria 37.12N 42.13E
Almalyk *see* Olmaliq
Al Mamlakah al Urduniyah al Hāshimiyah *see* Jordan
Al Mamlakah *see* Morocco
149 Q18 **Al Manādir** *var.* Al Manadir. *desert* Oman/UAE
148 L15 **Al Manāmah** *var.* Manama. ● (Bahrain) N Bahrain 26.13N 50.33E
145 O5 **Al Manāşif** ▲▲ E Syria
37 O4 **Almanor, Lake** ◎ California, W USA
107 R11 **Almansa** Castilla-La Mancha, C Spain 38.52N 1.06W
Al Manşūrah *see* El Manşûra
106 L3 **Almanza** Castilla-León, N Spain 42.40N 5.01W
106 L8 **Almanzor** ▲ W Spain 40.13N 5.18W
107 P14 **Almanzora** ≈ SE Spain
145 S9 **Al-Mardah** C Iraq 32.35N 43.30E
Al-Mariyya *see* Almería
77 R7 **Al Marj** *var.* Barka, *It.* Barce. NE Libya 32.30N 20.54E
144 L2 **Al Mashrafah** Ar Raqqah, N Syria 36.25N 39.07E
147 X8 **Al Maşna'ah** *var.* Al Masana'a. N Oman 23.45N 57.37E
107 T9 **Almassora** País Valenciano, E Spain 39.55N 0.02W
147 N5 **Al Mayyāh** Ḥā'il, N Saudi Arabia 27.56N 42.53E
144 H10 **Al Ma'zam** *var.* Al Ma'zim
126 Kk11 **Almaznyy** Respublika Sakha (Yakutiya), NE Russian Federation 62.19N 114.14E
30 J13 **Al Mazra'ah** *var.* Al Mazra'at
Al Mazra'a *see* Al Mazra'ah
152 I7 **Almeida** Guarda, N Portugal 40.43N 6.52W
106 G10 **Almeirim** Santarém, C Portugal 39.12N 8.37W
100 O10 **Almelo** Overijssel, E Netherlands 52.21N 6.40E
107 P12 **Almenar de Soria** Castilla-León, N Spain 41.40N 2.12W
107 P5 **Almenara** País Valenciano, E Spain 39.46N 0.13W
107 P12 **Almenaras** ▲ S Spain 38.33N 2.26W
106 J6 **Almendra, Embalse de** ▨ C Spain
106 K10 **Almendralejo** Extremadura, W Spain 38.41N 6.24E
100 L10 **Almere** *var.* Almere-stad. Flevoland, C Netherlands 52.21N 5.12E
100 L10 **Almere-Buiten** Flevoland, C Netherlands 52.24N 5.15E
100 L10 **Almere-Haven** Flevoland, C Netherlands 52.19N 5.13E
Almere-stad *see* Almere
107 P15 **Almería** *Ar.* Al-Mariyya; *anc.* Unci, *Lat.* Portus Magnus. Andalucía, S Spain 36.49N 2.25W

107 P14 **Almería** ◆ *province* Andalucía, S Spain
107 P15 **Almería, Golfo de** *gulf* S Spain
131 S5 **Al'met'yevsk** Respublika Tatarstan, W Russian Federation 54.52N 52.19E
97 L21 **Älmhult** Kronoberg, S Sweden 56.31N 14.10E
147 U9 **Al Miḥrāḍ** *desert* NE Saudi Arabia
Al Minā' *see* El Mina
106 L17 **Almina, Punta** *headland* Ceuta, Spain, N Africa 35.54N 5.16W
Al Minyā *see* El Minya
Al Miqdādīyah *see* Al Muqdādīyah
45 P14 **Almirante** Bocas del Toro, NW Panama 9.16N 82.24W
Almirós *see* Almyrós
146 M9 **Al Mislāḥ** *spring/well* W Saudi Arabia 22.46N 40.47E
Almissa *see* Omiš
106 G13 **Almodôvar** Beja, S Portugal 37.31N 8.03W
106 M11 **Almodóvar del Campo** Castilla-La Mancha, C Spain 38.43N 4.10W
107 Q9 **Almodóvar del Pinar** Castilla-La Mancha, C Spain 39.43N 1.55W
33 S9 **Almont** Michigan, N USA 42.53N 83.02W
12 L13 **Almonte** Ontario, SE Canada 45.13N 76.12W
106 K9 **Almonte** ≈ SW Spain
158 K9 **Almora** Uttar Pradesh, N India 29.36N 79.40E
106 M8 **Almorox** Castilla-La Mancha, C Spain 40.13N 4.22W
147 S7 **Al Mubarraz** Ash Sharqīyah, E Saudi Arabia 25.28N 49.34E
144 G15 **Al Mudawwarah** Maʿān, SW Jordan 29.20N 36.00E
147 Y9 **Al Muḍaybī** *var.* Al Muḍaibī. NE Oman 22.34N 58.07E
Almudébar *see* Almudévar
107 S5 **Almudévar** Aragón, NE Spain 42.03N 0.34W
147 S15 **Al Mukallā** *var.* Mukalla. SE Yemen 14.36N 49.07E
147 N16 **Al Mukhā** *Eng.* Mocha. SW Yemen 13.18N 43.16E
107 N15 **Almuñécar** Andalucía, S Spain 36.43N 3.40W
145 U7 **Al Muqdādīyah** *var.* Al Miqdādīyah. C Iraq 33.58N 44.58E
146 L3 **Al Murayr** *spring/well* NW Saudi Arabia 30.06N 39.54E
142 M12 **Almus** Tokat, N Turkey 40.23N 36.54E
Al Muşana'a *see* Al Maşna'ah
145 V9 **Al Muwaffaqīyah** S Iraq 32.19N 45.22E
144 H10 **Al Muwaqqar** *var.* El Muwaqqar. 'Ammān, N Jordan 31.49N 36.06E
146 J5 **Al Muwaylīḥ** *var.* Al Muwailih. Tabūk, NW Saudi Arabia 27.39N 35.33E
117 F17 **Almyrós** *var.* Almirós. Thessalía, C Greece 39.10N 22.45E
171 I24 **Almyroú, Órmos** *bay* Krití, Greece, E Mediterranean Sea
98 L13 **Alnwick** N England, UK 55.26N 1.44W
Al Obeid *see* El Obeid
Al Odaid *see* Al 'Udayd
202 B16 **Alofi** ○ (Niue) W Niue 19.01S 169.55E
202 A16 **Alofi Bay** *bay* W Niue, C Pacific Ocean
202 E13 **Alofi, Île** *island* S Wallis and Futuna
202 E13 **Alofi, Île** *island* S Wallis and Futuna 14.21S 178.03W
Aloha State *see* Hawaii
120 G7 **Aloja** Limbaži, N Latvia 57.47N 24.53E
159 X10 **Along** Arunāchal Pradesh, NE India 28.15N 94.56E
117 H16 **Alónnisos** *island* Vóreioi Sporádes, Greece, Aegean Sea
175 Rr15 **Alor, Kepulauan** *island group* E Indonesia
175 Rr16 **Alor, Pulau** *prev.* Ombai. *island* Kepulauan Alor, E Indonesia
175 R16 **Alor, Selat** *strait* Flores Sea/Savu Sea
173 G2 **Alor Setar** *var.* Alor Star, Alur Setar. Kedah, Peninsular Malaysia 6.06N 100.22E
Alost *see* Aalst
160 F9 **Älöt** Madhya Pradesh, C India 23.78S 75.40E
195 N16 **Alotau** Milne Bay, SE PNG 10.18S 150.39E
176 Yy15 **Alor Island** Irian Jaya, E Indonesia 8.07S 140.06E
37 R12 **Al Oued** *see* El Oued
37 R12 **Alpaugh** California, W USA 35.52N 119.29W
Alpen *see* Alps
33 R6 **Alpena** Michigan, N USA 45.04N 83.27W
105 S14 **Alpes-de-Haute-Provence** ◆ *department* SE France
105 U14 **Alpes-Maritimes** ◆ *department* SE France
189 A13 **Alpha** Queensland, E Australia 23.40S 146.38E
207 R9 **Alpha Cordillera** *var.* Alpha Ridge. *undersea feature* Arctic Ocean
Alpha Ridge *see* Alpha Cordillera
Alpheius/Alpheus *see* Alfeiós
100 H12 **Alphen** Noord-Brabant, S Netherlands 51.29N 4.57E
100 I12 **Alphen aan den Rijn** *var.* Alphen. Zuid-Holland, C Netherlands 52.07N 4.40E
Alpheus *see* Alfeiós
Alpi *see* Alps
106 G10 **Alpiarça** Santarém, C Portugal 39.15N 8.34W
26 K10 **Alpine** Texas, SW USA 30.22N 103.40W
110 F8 **Alpnach** Unterwalden, SW Switzerland 46.56N 8.17E
110 D11 **Alps** *Fr.* Alpes, *Ger.* Alpen, *It.* Alpi. ▲▲ C Europe

◆ COUNTRY ◇ DEPENDENT TERRITORY ◆ ADMINISTRATIVE REGION ▲ MOUNTAIN ▲ VOLCANO ◎ LAKE
● COUNTRY CAPITAL ○ DEPENDENT TERRITORY CAPITAL ✈ INTERNATIONAL AIRPORT ▲▲ MOUNTAIN RANGE ≈ RIVER ▨ RESERVOIR

Al Qābil – Anantapur

147 W8 **Al Qābil** *var.* Qabil. N Oman 23.55N 55.49E
Al Qaḑārif *see* Gedaref
77 P8 **Al Qaddāḩīyah** N Libya 31.21N 15.16E
Al Qāhirah *see* Cairo
146 K4 **Al Qalībah** Tabūk, NW Saudi Arabia 28.28N 37.40E
145 O1 **Al Qāmishlī** *var.* Kamishli, Qamishly. Al Ḩasakah, NE Syria 37.00N 41.00E
144 I6 **Al Qaryatayn** *var.* Qaryatayn, *Fr.* Qariateïne. Ḩimş, C Syria 34.13N 37.13E
148 K11 **Al Qash'ānīyah** *var.* Al-Kashaniya. NE Kuwait 29.59N 47.42E
147 N7 **Al Qaşīm** *off.* Minţaqat Qaşīm, Qassim. ⬖ *province* C Saudi Arabia
144 J5 **Al Qaşr** Ḩimş, C Syria 35.06N 37.39E
Al Qaşr *see* El Qaşr
Al Qaşrayn *see* Kasserine
147 S6 **Al Qaţīf** Ash Sharqīyah, NE Saudi Arabia 26.27N 50.01E
144 G11 **Al Qaţrānah** *var.* El Qatrani, Qatrana. Al Karak, W Jordan 31.13N 36.03E
77 P11 **Al Qaţrūn** SW Libya 24.57N 14.40E
Al Qayrawān *see* Kairouan
Al-Qsar al-Kbir *see* Ksar-el-Kebir
Al Qubayyāt *see* Qoubaïyât
Al Quds/Al Quds ash Sharīf *see* Jerusalem
144 G8 **Al Qunayţirah** *var.* El Kuneitra, El Quneitra, Kuneitra, Qunaytra. Al Qunayţirah, SW Syria 33.07N 35.49E
144 G8 **Al Qunayţirah** *off.* Muḩāfaẓat al Qunayţirah, *var.* El Q'unayţirah, Qunaytirah, *Fr.* Kuneitra. ⬖ *governorate* SW Syria
146 M11 **Al Qunfudhah** Makkah, SW Saudi Arabia 19.19N 41.02E
146 K2 **Al Qurayyāt** Al Jawf, NW Saudi Arabia 31.24N 37.25E
145 Y11 **Al Qurnah** *var.* Kurna. SE Iraq 31.01N 47.27E
145 V12 **Al Quşayr** S Iraq 30.36N 45.52E
144 I6 **Al Quşayr** *var.* El Quseir, Quşayr, *Fr.* Kousseir. Ḩimş, W Syria 34.36N 36.36E
Al Quşayr *see* Quseir
144 H7 **Al Quţayfah** *var.* Quţayfah, Qutayfe, Quteife, *Fr.* Kouteifé. Dimashq, W Syria 33.44N 36.33E
147 P8 **Al Quwayīyah** Ar Riyāḑ, C Saudi Arabia 24.06N 45.18E
Al Quwayr *see* Guwēr
144 F14 **Al Quwayrah** *var.* El Quweira. Ma'ān, SW Jordan 29.49N 35.19E
Al Rayyan *see* Ar Rayyān
Al Ruweis *see* Ar Ruways
97 G24 **Als** *Ger.* Alsen. *island* SW Denmark
105 U5 **Alsace** *Ger.* Elsass; *anc.* Alsatia. ⬖ *region* NE France
9 R16 **Alsask** Saskatchewan, S Canada 51.24N 109.55W
Alsasua *see* Altsasu
Alsatia *see* Alsace
103 C16 **Alsdorf** Nordrhein-Westfalen, W Germany 50.52N 6.09E
8 G8 **Alsek** ≈ Canada/USA
Alsen *see* Als
103 F19 **Alsenz** ≈ W Germany
103 H17 **Alsfeld** Hessen, C Germany 50.45N 9.14E
121 K20 **Al'shany** *Rus.* Ol'shany. Brestskaya Voblasts', SW Belarus 52.04N 27.19E
Alsókubin *see* Dolný Kubín
120 C9 **Alsunga** Kuldīga, W Latvia 56.59N 21.31E
Alt *see* Olt
94 K9 **Alta** *Fin.* Alattio. Finnmark, N Norway 69.58N 23.16E
31 T12 **Alta** Iowa, C USA 42.40N 95.17W
110 I7 **Altach** Vorarlberg, W Austria 47.22N 9.39E
94 K9 **Altaelva** ≈ N Norway
94 J8 **Altafjorden** *fjord* NE Norwegian Sea
64 K10 **Alta Gracia** Córdoba, C Argentina 31.42S 64.25W
44 K11 **Alta Gracia** Rivas, SW Nicaragua 11.33N 85.35W
56 H4 **Altagracia** Zulia, NW Venezuela 10.43N 71.30W
56 M5 **Altagracia de Orituco** Guárico, N Venezuela 9.49N 66.22W
Altai *see* Altai Mountains
133 T7 **Altai Mountains** *var.* Altai, *Chin.* Altay Shan, *Rus.* Altay. ▲▲ Asia/Europe
25 V6 **Altamaha River** ≈ Georgia, SE USA
60 J13 **Altamira** Pará, NE Brazil 3.13S 52.15W
56 D12 **Altamira** Huila, S Colombia 2.02N 75.51W
44 M13 **Altamira** Alajuela, N Costa Rica 10.25N 84.21W
43 Q11 **Altamira** Tamaulipas, C Mexico 22.24N 97.57W
32 L15 **Altamont** Illinois, N USA 39.03N 88.45W
29 Q7 **Altamont** Kansas, C USA 37.11N 95.18W
34 H16 **Altamont** Oregon, NW USA 42.12N 121.44W
22 K10 **Altamont** Tennessee, S USA 35.25N 85.42W
25 X11 **Altamonte Springs** Florida, SE USA 28.39N 81.22W
109 O17 **Altamura** *anc.* Lupatia. Puglia, SE Italy 40.50N 16.33E
42 H9 **Altamura, Isla** *island* C Mexico
168 G7 **Altan** Dzavhan, W Mongolia 48.05N 95.48E
168 G6 **Altanbulag** Dzavhan, N Mongolia 49.16N 96.22E
Altan Emel *see* Xin Barag Youqi
168 J8 **Altan-Ovoo** Arhangay, C Mongolia 47.24N 101.51E
168 E7 **Altanteel** Hovd, W Mongolia 47.05N 92.57E
42 F3 **Altar** Sonora, NW Mexico 30.44N 111.49W
42 D2 **Altar, Desierto de** *var.* Sonoran Desert. *desert* Mexico/USA *see also* Sonoran Desert
107 Q8 **Alta, Sierra** ▲ N Spain 40.29N 1.36W
42 H9 **Altata** Sinaloa, C Mexico 24.39N 107.55W
44 D4 **Alta Verapaz** *off.* Departamento de Alta Verapaz. ⬖ *department* C Guatemala
109 L18 **Altavilla Silentia** Campania, S Italy 40.32N 15.06E
23 T7 **Altavista** Virginia, NE USA 37.06N 79.17W
164 L2 **Altay** Xinjiang Uygur Zizhiqu, NW China 47.51N 88.06E
168 G5 **Altay** Dzavhan, N Mongolia 49.40N 96.21E
168 G8 **Altay** Govĭ-Altay, W Mongolia 46.23N 96.16E
Altay *see* Altai Mountains
126 H16 **Altay, Respublika** *var.* Gornyy Altay; *prev.* Gorno-Altayskaya Respublika. ⬖ *autonomous republic* S Russian Federation
Altay Shan *see* Altai Mountains
125 G15 **Altayskiy Kray** ⬖ *territory* S Russian Federation
Altbetsche *see* Bečej
103 L20 **Altdorf** Bayern, SE Germany 49.23N 11.22E
110 G8 **Altdorf** *var.* Altorf. Uri, C Switzerland 46.52N 8.37E
107 T11 **Altea** País Valenciano, E Spain 38.37N 0.03W
102 L10 **Alte Elde** ≈ N Germany
103 M16 **Altenburg** Thüringen, E Germany 50.58N 12.27E
Altenburg *see* București, Romania
Altenburg *see* Baia de Criș, Romania
102 P12 **Alte Oder** ≈ NE Germany
106 H10 **Alter do Chão** Portalegre, C Portugal 39.12N 7.40W
94 I10 **Altevatnet** ⊚ N Norway
29 V12 **Altheimer** Arkansas, C USA 34.19N 91.51W
111 T9 **Althofen** Kärnten, S Austria 46.52N 14.27E
116 H7 **Altimir** Vratsa, NW Bulgaria 43.33N 23.48E
142 K11 **Altınkaya Barajı** ⊡ N Turkey
145 S3 **Altin Köprü** *var.* Altun Kupri. N Iraq 35.45N 44.08E
142 E13 **Altıntaş** Kütahya, W Turkey 39.04N 30.07E
59 K18 **Altiplano** *physical region* W South America
Altkanischa *see* Kanjiža
105 U7 **Altkirch** Haut-Rhin, NE France 47.37N 7.14E
Altlublau *see* Stará L'ubovňa
102 L12 **Altmark** *cultural region* N Germany
Altmoldowa *see* Moldova Veche
27 W8 **Alto** Texas, SW USA 31.39N 95.04W
106 H11 **Alto Alentejo** *physical region* S Portugal
61 I19 **Alto Araguaia** Mato Grosso, C Brazil 17.19S 53.10W
60 L12 **Alto Bonito** Pará, NE Brazil 1.48S 46.18W
85 O15 **Alto Molócuè** Zambézia, NE Mozambique 15.41S 37.42E
32 K15 **Alton** Illinois, N USA 38.53N 90.10W
29 W8 **Alton** Missouri, C USA 36.41N 91.24W
9 X17 **Altona** Manitoba, S Canada 49.12N 97.38W
20 E14 **Altoona** Pennsylvania, NE USA 40.31N 78.22W
32 J6 **Altoona** Wisconsin, N USA 44.49N 91.22W
64 N3 **Alto Paraguay** *off.* Departamento del Alto Paraguay. ⬖ *department* N Paraguay
61 L17 **Alto Paraíso de Goiás** Goiás, S Brazil 14.04S 47.15W
64 P6 **Alto Paraná** *off.* Departamento del Alto Paraná. ⬖ *department* E Paraguay
Alto Paraná *see* Paraná
61 L15 **Alto Parnaíba** Maranhão, E Brazil 9.07S 45.55W
58 H13 **Alto Purús, Río** ≈ E Peru
Altorf *see* Altdorf
65 H19 **Alto Río Senguer** *var.* Alto Río Senguerr. Chubut, S Argentina 45.03S 70.48W
43 Q13 **Altotonga** Veracruz-Llave, E Mexico 19.43N 97.12W
103 N23 **Altötting** Bayern, SE Germany 48.12N 12.37E
Altpasua *see* Stara Pazova
168 I5 **Altraga** Hövsgöl, N Mongolia 50.08N 98.54E
Alt-Schwanenburg *see* Gulbene
107 P3 **Altsasu** *Cast.* Alsasua. Navarra, N Spain 42.54N 2.10W
Altsohl *see* Zvolen
110 I7 **Altstätten** Sankt Gallen, NE Switzerland 47.22N 9.33E
44 G1 **Altun Ha** *ruins* Belize, N Belize 17.46N 88.20W
Altun Kupri *see* Altin Köprü
164 D8 **Altun Shan** ▲ C China 39.19N 93.37E
164 L9 **Altun Shan** *var.* Altyn Tagh. ▲▲ NW China
37 P2 **Alturas** California, W USA 41.28N 120.32W
28 K12 **Altus** Oklahoma, C USA 34.38N 99.19W
28 K11 **Altus Lake** ⊡ Oklahoma, C USA
Altvater *see* Praděd
Altyn Tagh *see* Altun Shan
Alu *see* Shortland Island
al-'Ubaila *see* Al 'Ubaylah
145 O6 **Al 'Ubaydī** W Iraq 34.22N 41.15E
147 T9 **Al 'Ubaylah** *var.* al-'Ubaila. Ash Sharqīyah, E Saudi Arabia 22.01N 50.57E
147 T9 **Al 'Ubaylah** *spring/well* E Saudi Arabia 22.02N 50.56E
Al Ubayyiḑ *see* El Obeid
147 T7 **Al 'Udayd** *var.* Al Odaid. Abū Ẓaby, W UAE 24.34N 51.27E
120 J8 **Alūksne** *Ger.* Marienburg. Alūksne, NE Latvia 57.26N 27.02E
146 K6 **Al 'Ulā** Al Madīnah, NW Saudi Arabia 26.39N 37.55E
181 N4 **Alula-Fartak Trench** *var.* Illaue Fartak Trench. *undersea feature* W Indian Ocean
144 I11 **Al 'Umarī** 'Ammān, E Jordan 37.30N 31.30E
33 S13 **Alum Creek Lake** ⊡ Ohio, N USA
65 H15 **Aluminé** Neuquén, C Argentina 39.15S 71.00W
97 O14 **Alunda** Uppsala, C Sweden 60.04N 18.04E
119 T14 **Alupka** Respublika Krym, S Ukraine 44.24N 34.01E
77 P8 **Al 'Uqaylah** N Libya 30.13N 16.10E
Al Uqşur *see* Luxor
Al Urdunn *see* Jordan
173 G6 **Alur Panal** *bay* Sumatera, W Indonesia
147 V10 **Al 'Urūq al Mu'tariḑah** *salt lake* SE Saudi Arabia
145 Q7 **Ālūs** C Iraq 34.04N 42.27E
119 T13 **Alushta** Respublika Krym, S Ukraine 44.40N 34.24E
77 N11 **Al 'Uwaynāt** *var.* Al Awaynāt. SW Libya 25.47N 10.34E
145 T6 **Al 'Uẓaym** *var.* Adhaim. E Iraq 34.12N 44.31E
28 L8 **Alva** Oklahoma, C USA 36.48N 98.40W
106 H8 **Alva** ≈ N Portugal
97 J18 **Älvängen** Västra Götaland, S Sweden 57.55N 12.09E
12 F14 **Alvanley** Ontario, S Canada 44.33N 81.05W
43 S14 **Alvarado** Veracruz-Llave, E Mexico 18.46N 95.45W
27 T7 **Alvarado** Texas, SW USA 32.24N 97.12W
60 D13 **Alvarães** Amazonas, NW Brazil 3.13S 64.53W
42 G6 **Alvaro Obregón, Presa** ⊡ W Mexico
96 H10 **Alvdal** Hedmark, S Norway 62.07N 10.39E
96 K12 **Älvdalen** Dalarna, C Sweden 61.13N 14.04E
63 E15 **Alvear** Corrientes, NE Argentina 29.03S 56.30W
106 F10 **Alverca do Ribatejo** Lisboa, C Portugal 38.55N 9.01W
97 L20 **Alvesta** Kronoberg, S Sweden 56.52N 14.34E
96 D13 **Ålvik** Hordaland, S Norway 60.26N 6.27E
27 W12 **Alvin** Texas, SW USA 29.25N 95.14W
96 O13 **Älvkarleby** Uppsala, C Sweden 60.34N 17.30E
27 S5 **Alvord** Texas, SW USA 33.22N 97.39W
95 G18 **Älvros** Jämtland, C Sweden 62.04N 14.30E
94 J13 **Älvsbyn** Norrbotten, N Sweden 65.41N 21.00E
148 K12 **Al Wafrā'** SE Kuwait 28.37N 47.56E
146 J6 **Al Wajh** Tabūk, NW Saudi Arabia 26.15N 36.29E
149 N16 **Al Wakrah** *var.* Wakra. C Qatar 25.09N 51.36E
144 M8 **al Walaj, Sha'īb** *dry watercourse* W Iraq
158 I11 **Alwar** Rājasthān, N India 27.31N 76.34E
147 Q5 **Al Wari'ah** Ash Sharqīyah, N Saudi Arabia 27.54N 47.22E
161 G22 **Alwaye** Kerala, SW India 10.06N 76.22E
168 K14 **Alxa Zuoqi** *var.* Ehen Hudag. Nei Mongol Zizhiqu, N China 38.49N 105.40E
Al Yaman *see* Yemen
144 G9 **Al Yarmūk** Irbid, N Jordan 32.41N 35.55E
Alyat/Alyaty-Pristan' *see* Älät
117 I14 **Alykí** *var.* Aliki. Thásos, N Greece 40.36N 24.45E
121 F14 **Alytus** *Pol.* Olita. Alytus, S Lithuania 54.24N 24.02E
103 N23 **Alz** ≈ SE Germany
35 Y11 **Alzada** Montana, NW USA 45.00N 104.24W
126 Ii14 **Alzamay** Irkutskaya Oblast', S Russian Federation 55.33N 98.36E
101 M25 **Alzette** ≈ S Luxembourg
107 S10 **Alzira** *var.* Alcira ; *anc.* Saetabicula, Suero. País Valenciano, E Spain 39.10N 0.27W
Al Zubair *see* Az Zubayr
189 O8 **Amadeus, Lake** *seasonal lake* Northern Territory, C Australia
83 E15 **Amadi** Western Equatoria, SW Sudan 5.31N 30.19E
16 Nn3 **Amadjuak Lake** ⊚ Baffin Island, Nunavut, N Canada
97 J23 **Amager** *island* E Denmark
170 Cc13 **Amagi** Fukuoka, Kyūshū, SW Japan 33.24N 130.37E
171 J17 **Amagi-san** ▲ Honshū, S Japan 34.51N 138.57E
175 Tt11 **Amahai** *var.* Masohi. Pulau Seram, E Indonesia 3.19S 128.55E
40 M16 **Amak Island** *island* Alaska, USA
170 Bb14 **Amakusa-nada** *gulf* Kyūshū, SW Japan
97 J16 **Åmål** Västra Götaland, S Sweden 59.04N 12.40E
56 E8 **Amalfi** Antioquia, N Colombia 6.54N 75.04W
109 L18 **Amalfi** Campania, S Italy 40.37N 14.35E
117 D19 **Amaliáda** *var.* Amaliás. Dytikí Ellás, S Greece 37.48N 21.21E
Amaliás *see* Amaliáda
160 F12 **Amalner** Mahārāshtra, C India 21.03N 75.04E
176 X12 **Amamapare** Irian Jaya, E Indonesia 4.51S 136.43E
61 H21 **Amambaí, Serra de** *var.* Cordillera de Amambay, Serra de Amambay. ▲▲ Brazil/Paraguay *see also* Amambay, Cordillera de
64 P4 **Amambay** *off.* Departamento del Amambay. ⬖ *department* E Paraguay
64 P5 **Amambay, Cordillera de** *var.* Serra de Amambaí, Serra de Amambay. ▲▲ Brazil/Paraguay *see also* Amambaí, Serra de
Amambay, Serra de *see* Amambaí, Serra de/Amambay, Cordillera de
172 Q13 **Amami-guntō** *island group* SW Japan
172 Qq13 **Amami-Ō-shima** *island* S Japan
194 E10 **Amanab** Sandaun, NW PNG 3.34S 141.10E
108 J13 **Amandola** Marche, C Italy 42.58N 13.22E
109 N21 **Amantea** Calabria, SW Italy 39.06N 16.05E
203 W10 **Amanu** *island* Îles Tuamotu, C French Polynesia
60 J10 **Amapá** Amapá, NE Brazil 02.00N 50.50W
60 J11 **Amapá** *off.* Estado de Amapá; *prev.* Território de Amapá. ⬖ *state* NE Brazil
44 H8 **Amapala** Valle, S Honduras 13.18N 87.37W
Amara *see* Al 'Amārah
106 H6 **Amarante** Porto, N Portugal 41.16N 8.04W
177 G5 **Amarapura** Mandalay, C Burma 21.54N 96.01E
168 L9 **Amardalay** Dundgovĭ, C Mongolia 46.09N 106.24E
106 I12 **Amareleja** Beja, S Portugal 38.12N 7.13W
37 V11 **Amargosa Range** ▲▲ California, W USA
27 N2 **Amarillo** Texas, SW USA 35.13N 101.49W
Amarinthos *see* Amárynthos
109 K15 **Amaro, Monte** ▲ C Italy 42.03N 14.06E
117 H18 **Amárynthos** *var.* Amarinthos. Évvoia, C Greece 38.24N 23.53E
Amasia *see* Amasya
142 K12 **Amasya** *anc.* Amasia. Amasya, N Turkey 40.40N 35.49E
142 K11 **Amasya** ⬖ *province* N Turkey
44 F4 **Amatique, Bahía de** *bay* Gulf of Honduras, W Caribbean Sea
44 D6 **Amatitlán, Lago de** ⊚ S Guatemala
109 J14 **Amatrice** Lazio, C Italy 42.38N 13.19E
202 C8 **Amatuku** *atoll* C Tuvalu
101 J20 **Amay** Liège, E Belgium 50.33N 5.19E
50 F7 **Amazon** *Sp.* Amazonas. ≈ Brazil/Peru
61 C14 **Amazonas** *off.* Estado do Amazonas. ⬖ *state* N Brazil
56 G15 **Amazonas** *off.* Comisaria del Amazonas. ⬖ *province* SE Colombia
58 C10 **Amazonas** *off.* Departamento de Amazonas. ⬖ *department* N Peru
56 M12 **Amazonas** *off.* Territorio Amazonas. ⬖ *federal territory* S Venezuela
Amazonas *see* Amazon
50 F7 **Amazon Basin** *basin* N South America
49 V5 **Amazon Fan** *undersea feature* W Atlantic Ocean
60 K11 **Amazon, Mouths of the** *delta* NE Brazil
197 C12 **Ambae** *var.* Aoba, Omba. *island* C Vanuatu
158 I9 **Ambāla** Haryāna, NW India 30.22N 76.49E
161 J26 **Ambalangoda** Southern Province, SW Sri Lanka 6.13N 80.03E
161 K26 **Ambalantota** Southern Province, S Sri Lanka 6.07N 81.01E
180 I6 **Ambalavao** Fianarantsoa, C Madagascar 21.49S 46.55E
56 E10 **Ambalema** Tolima, C Colombia 4.49N 74.48W
81 E17 **Ambam** Sud, S Cameroon 2.22N 11.16E
180 J2 **Ambanja** Antsirañana, N Madagascar 13.40S 48.27E
127 O5 **Ambarchik** Respublika Sakha (Yakutiya), NE Russian Federation 69.33N 162.08E
64 K9 **Ambargasta, Salinas de** *salt lake* C Argentina
128 J6 **Ambarnyy** Respublika Kareliya, NW Russian Federation 65.53N 33.44E
58 C7 **Ambato** Tungurahua, C Ecuador 1.18S 78.39W
180 I5 **Ambatolampy** Antananarivo, C Madagascar 19.21S 47.27E
180 H4 **Ambatomainty** Mahajanga, W Madagascar 17.40S 45.39E
180 J4 **Ambatondrazaka** Toamasina, C Madagascar 17.49S 48.28E
175 Ss12 **Ambelau, Pulau** *see* Ambelau, Pulau
103 L20 **Amberg** *var.* Amberg in der Oberpfalz. Bayern, SE Germany 49.27N 11.51E
Amberg in der Oberpfalz *see* Amberg
44 H1 **Ambergris Cay** *island* NE Belize
105 S11 **Ambérieu-en-Bugey** Ain, E France 45.57N 5.21E
193 I18 **Amberley** Canterbury, South Island, NZ 43.09S 172.43E
105 P11 **Ambert** Puy-de-Dôme, C France 45.34N 3.42E
Ambianum *see* Amiens
78 J11 **Ambidédi** Kayes, SW Mali 14.37N 11.49W
160 M10 **Ambikāpur** Madhya Pradesh, C India 23.09N 83.12E
180 J2 **Ambilobe** Antsirañana, N Madagascar 13.10S 49.03E
195 Q10 **Ambitle Island** *island* Feni Islands, NE PNG
41 O7 **Ambler** Alaska, USA 67.05N 157.51W
Amblève *see* Amel
Ambo *see* Hāgere Hiywet
180 I8 **Amboasary** Toliara, S Madagascar 25.01S 46.22E
180 J4 **Ambodifotatra** *var.* Ambodifototra. Toamasina, E Madagascar 16.58S 49.51E
Amboenten *see* Ambunten
180 I5 **Ambohidratrimo** Antananarivo, C Madagascar 18.48S 47.25E
180 I6 **Ambohimahasoa** Fianarantsoa, SE Madagascar 21.07S 47.13E
180 K3 **Ambohitralanana** Antsirañana, NE Madagascar 15.13S 50.28E
176 X10 **Amboi, Kepulauan** *island group* E Indonesia
Amboina *see* Ambon
104 M8 **Amboise** Indre-et-Loire, C France 47.25N 1.00E
175 T11 **Ambon** *prev.* Amboina, Amboyna. Pulau Ambon, E Indonesia 3.40S 128.10E
175 T12 **Ambon, Pulau** *island* E Indonesia
83 I20 **Amboseli, Lake** ⊚ Kenya/Tanzania
180 I6 **Ambositra** Fianarantsoa, SE Madagascar 20.31S 47.15E
180 I8 **Ambovombe** Toliara, S Madagascar 25.10S 46.06E
37 W14 **Amboy** California, W USA 34.33N 115.44W
32 L11 **Amboy** Illinois, N USA 41.42N 89.19W
Amboyna *see* Ambon
Ambracia *see* Árta
20 B14 **Ambridge** Pennsylvania, NE USA 40.33N 80.11W
Ambrim *see* Ambrym
84 A11 **Ambriz** Bengo, NW Angola 7.55S 13.11E
Ambrizete *see* N'Zeto
197 C13 **Ambrym** *var.* Ambrim. *island* C Vanuatu
174 Mm14 **Ambunten** *prev.* Amboenten. Pulau Madura, E Indonesia 6.55S 113.45E
194 G10 **Ambunti** East Sepik, NW PNG 4.06S 142.49E
161 I20 **Āmbūr** Tamil Nādu, SE India 12.48N 78.43E
40 E17 **Amchitka Island** *island* Aleutian Islands, Alaska, USA
40 F17 **Amchitka Pass** *strait* Aleutian Islands, Alaska, USA
147 R15 **'Amd** C Yemen 15.09N 47.58E
80 J10 **Am Dam** Ouaddaï, E Chad 12.46N 20.28E
176 Uu15 **Amdassa** Pulau Yamdena, E Indonesia 7.40S 131.24E
129 U1 **Amderma** Nenetskiy Avtonomnyy Okrug, NW Russian Federation 69.45N 61.36E
165 N14 **Amdo** Xizang Zizhiqu, W China 32.15N 91.43E
42 K13 **Ameca** Jalisco, SW Mexico 20.31N 104.02W
43 P14 **Amecameca** *var.* Amecameca de Juárez. México, C Mexico 19.07N 98.45W
Amecameca de Juárez *see* Amecameca
63 A20 **Ameghino** Buenos Aires, E Argentina 34.51S 62.28W
101 M21 **Amel** *Fr.* Amblève. Liège, E Belgium 50.20N 6.13E
100 K4 **Ameland** *Fris.* It Amelân. *island* Waddeneilanden, N Netherlands
Amelân, It *see* Ameland
109 H14 **Amelia** Umbria, C Italy 42.33N 12.26E
23 V6 **Amelia Court House** Virginia, NE USA 37.19N 77.57W
25 W8 **Amelia Island** *island* Florida, SE USA
20 L12 **Amenia** New York, NE USA 41.51N 73.31W
America *see* United States of America
67 M21 **America-Antarctica Ridge** *undersea feature* S Atlantic Ocean
America in Miniature *see* Maryland
62 L9 **Americana** São Paulo, S Brazil 22.43S 47.19W
35 Q15 **American Falls** Idaho, NW USA 42.47N 112.51W
35 Q15 **American Falls Reservoir** ⊡ Idaho, NW USA
38 L3 **American Fork** Utah, W USA 40.24N 111.47W
198 D8 **American Samoa** ◇ *US unincorporated territory* W Polynesia
25 S6 **Americus** Georgia, SE USA 32.04N 84.13W
100 K12 **Amerongen** Utrecht, C Netherlands 52.00N 5.30E
100 K11 **Amersfoort** Utrecht, C Netherlands 52.09N 5.22E
99 N21 **Amersham** SE England, UK 51.39N 0.37W
32 I5 **Amery** Wisconsin, N USA 45.18N 92.20W
205 W6 **Amery Ice Shelf** *ice shelf* Antarctica
31 V13 **Ames** Iowa, C USA 42.01N 93.37W
21 P10 **Amesbury** Massachusetts, NE USA 42.51N 70.55W
Amestratus *see* Mistretta
117 F18 **Amfíkleia** *var.* Amfíklia. Stereá Ellás, C Greece 38.37N 22.34E
Amfíklia *see* Amfíkleia
117 D17 **Amfilochía** *var.* Amfilokhía. Dytikí Ellás, C Greece 38.52N 21.09E
Amfilokhía *see* Amfilochía
116 H13 **Amfípoli** *anc.* Amphipolis. *site of ancient city* Kentrikí Makedonía, NE Greece 40.49N 23.51E
117 F18 **Ámfissa** Stereá Ellás, C Greece 38.31N 22.22E
126 M11 **Amga** Respublika Sakha (Yakutiya), NE Russian Federation 60.55N 131.45E
126 M11 **Amga** ≈ NE Russian Federation
Amgalang *see* Xin Barag Zuoqi
195 N12 **Amgen** ≈ New Britain, C PNG
127 P4 **Amguema** ≈ NE Russian Federation
127 Nn14 **Amgun'** ≈ SE Russian Federation
82 J12 **Amhara** ⬖ *region* N Ethiopia
11 P15 **Amherst** Nova Scotia, SE Canada 45.49N 64.13W
20 M11 **Amherst** Massachusetts, NE USA 42.22N 72.31W
20 D10 **Amherst** New York, NE USA 42.57N 78.47W
26 M4 **Amherst** Texas, SW USA 33.59N 102.24W
23 U6 **Amherst** Virginia, NE USA 37.35N 79.03W
Amherst *see* Kyaikkami
12 C18 **Amherstburg** Ontario, S Canada 42.05N 83.06W
23 Q6 **Amherstdale** West Virginia, NE USA 37.46N 81.46W
12 K15 **Amherst Island** *island* Ontario, SE Canada
Amida *see* Diyarbakır
30 J6 **Amidon** North Dakota, N USA 46.26N 103.18W
105 O3 **Amiens** *anc.* Ambianum, Samarobriva. Somme, N France 49.54N 2.18E
145 P8 **'Āmij, Wādī** *var.* Wadi 'Amīq. *dry watercourse* W Iraq
142 L17 **Amik Ovası** ⊚ S Turkey
78 E9 **Amilcar Cabral** ✕ Sal, NE Cape Verde 16.45N 22.56E
Amilḩayt, Wādī *see* Umm al Ḩayt, Wādī
Amíndaion/Amindeo *see* Amýntaio
161 C21 **Amīndīvi Islands** *island group* Lakshadweep, India, N Indian Ocean
145 U6 **Amīn Ḩabīb** E Iraq 34.17N 45.10E
85 E20 **Aminuis** Omaheke, E Namibia 23.37S 19.21E
'Amīq, Wadi *see* 'Āmij, Wādī
148 J7 **Amīrābād** Īlām, NW Iran 33.19N 46.16E
Amirante Bank *see* Amirante Ridge
181 N6 **Amirante Basin** *undersea feature* W Indian Ocean
181 N6 **Amirante Islands** *var.* Amirantes Group. *island group* C Seychelles
181 N7 **Amirante Ridge** *var.* Amirante Bank. *undersea feature* W Indian Ocean
Amirantes Group *see* Amirante Islands
181 N7 **Amirante Trench** *undersea feature* W Indian Ocean
176 Z12 **Amisibil** Irian Jaya, E Indonesia 3.59S 140.35E
9 U13 **Amisk Lake** ⊚ Saskatchewan, C Canada
Amistad, Presa de la *see* Amistad Reservoir
27 O12 **Amistad Reservoir** *var.* Presa de la Amistad. ⊡ Mexico/USA
Amisus *see* Samsun
24 K8 **Amite** *var.* Amite City. Louisiana, S USA 30.40N 90.30W
Amite City *see* Amite
29 T12 **Amity** Arkansas, C USA 34.15N 93.27W
160 H11 **Amla** *prev.* Amulla. Madhya Pradesh, C India 21.57N 78.06E
40 I17 **Amlia Island** *island* Aleutian Islands, Alaska, USA
99 I18 **Amlwch** NW Wales, UK 53.25N 4.22W
Ammaia *see* Portalegre
144 H10 **'Ammān** *var.* Amman; *anc.* Philadelphia, *Bibl.* Rabbah Ammon, Rabbath Ammon. ● (Jordan) 'Ammān, NW Jordan 31.57N 35.55E
144 H10 **'Ammān** *off.* Muḩāfaẓat 'Ammān. ⬖ *governorate* NW Jordan
95 N14 **Ämmänsaari** Oulu, E Finland 64.51N 28.58E
94 H13 **Ammarnäs** Västerbotten, N Sweden 65.58N 16.10E
207 O15 **Ammassalik** *var.* Angmagssalik. Tunu, S Greenland 65.51N 37.30W
103 K24 **Ammer** ≈ SE Germany
103 K24 **Ammersee** ⊚ SE Germany
100 J13 **Ammerzoden** Gelderland, C Netherlands 51.46N 5.07E
Ammóchostos *see* Gazimağusa
Ammóchostos, Kólpos *see* Gazimağusa Körfezi
Amnok-kang *see* Yalu
Amoea *see* Portalegre
Amoentai *see* Amuntai
Amoerang *see* Amurang
149 O4 **Āmol** *var.* Amul. Māzandarān, N Iran 36.30N 52.24E
117 K21 **Amorgós** Amorgós, Kykládes, Greece, Aegean Sea 36.49N 25.54E
117 K22 **Amorgós** *island* Kykládes, Greece, Aegean Sea
25 N3 **Amory** Mississippi, S USA 33.58N 88.29W
10 I13 **Amos** Quebec, SE Canada 48.34N 78.07W
97 G15 **Åmot** Buskerud, S Norway 59.52N 9.55E
97 E15 **Åmot** Telemark, S Norway 59.34N 7.59E
97 J15 **Åmotfors** Värmland, C Sweden 59.46N 12.24E
78 L10 **Amourj** Hodh ech Chargui, SE Mauritania 16.04N 7.12W
Amoy *see* Xiamen
180 H7 **Ampanihy** Toliara, SW Madagascar 24.40S 44.45E
161 L25 **Ampara** *var.* Amparai. Eastern Province, E Sri Lanka 7.16N 81.40E
180 J4 **Amparafaravola** Toamasina, E Madagascar 17.33S 48.13E
Amparai *see* Ampara
62 M9 **Amparo** São Paulo, S Brazil 22.40S 46.49W
180 J5 **Ampasimanolotra** Toamasina, E Madagascar 18.49S 49.04E
59 H17 **Ampato, Nevado** ▲ S Peru 15.52S 71.51W
103 L23 **Amper** ≈ SE Germany
66 M9 **Ampère Seamount** *undersea feature* E Atlantic Ocean 35.05N 13.00W
Amphipolis *see* Amfípoli
178 M10 **Amphitrite Group** *island group* N Paracel Islands
176 U15 **Amplawas** *var.* Emplawas. Pulau Babar, E Indonesia 8.01S 129.42E
107 U7 **Amposta** Cataluña, NE Spain 40.43N 0.34E
13 V7 **Amqui** Quebec, SE Canada 48.28N 67.27W
147 O14 **'Amrān** W Yemen 15.39N 43.59E
Amraoti *see* Amrāvati
160 H12 **Amrāvati** *prev.* Amraoti. Mahārāshtra, C India 20.55N 77.45E
160 C11 **Amreli** Gujarāt, W India 21.36N 71.19E
110 H6 **Amriswil** Thurgau, NE Switzerland 47.33N 9.18E
144 H5 **'Amrīt** *ruins* Tarţūs, W Syria 34.48N 35.54E
158 H7 **Amritsar** Punjab, N India 31.38N 74.54E
158 J10 **Amroha** Uttar Pradesh, N India 28.54N 78.28E
102 G7 **Amrum** *island* NW Germany
95 I15 **Åmsele** Västerbotten, N Sweden 64.31N 19.24E
100 I10 **Amstelveen** Noord-Holland, C Netherlands 52.18N 4.49E
100 I10 **Amsterdam** ● (Netherlands) Noord-Holland, C Netherlands 52.22N 4.54E
20 K10 **Amsterdam** New York, NE USA 42.56N 74.11W
181 Q11 **Amsterdam Fracture Zone** *tectonic feature* S Indian Ocean
181 R11 **Amsterdam Island** *island* NE French Southern and Antarctic Territories
111 U4 **Amstetten** Niederösterreich, N Austria 48.07N 14.52E
80 J11 **Am Timan** Salamat, SE Chad 11.01N 20.16E
152 L12 **Amu-Bukhoro Kanali** *var.* Aral-Bukhorskiy Kanal. *canal* C Uzbekistan
145 O1 **'Āmūdah** *var.* Amude. Al Ḩasakah, N Syria 37.06N 40.56E
152 M14 **Amu-Dar'ya** Lebapskiy Velayat, NE Turkmenistan 37.58N 65.14E
153 O15 **Amu Darya** *Rus.* Amudar'ya, *Taj.* Dar"yoi Amu, *Turkm.* Amyderya, *Uzb.* Amudaryo; *anc.* Oxus. ≈ C Asia
Amudar'ya/Amudaryo/Amu, Dar"yoi *see* Amu Darya
Amude *see* 'Āmūdah
146 L3 **'Amūd, Jabal al** ▲ NW Saudi Arabia 30.59N 39.17E
40 J17 **Amukta Island** *island* Aleutian Islands, Alaska, USA
40 I17 **Amukta Pass** *strait* Aleutian Islands, Alaska, USA
Amul *see* Āmol
Amulla *see* Amla
Amundsen Basin *see* Fram Basin
205 X3 **Amundsen Bay** *bay* Antarctica
205 P10 **Amundsen Coast** *physical region* Antarctica
15 H2 **Amundsen Gulf** *gulf* Northwest Territories, N Canada
199 Ll16 **Amundsen Plain** *undersea feature* S Pacific Ocean
205 Q9 **Amundsen-Scott** *US research station* Antarctica 89.59S 10.00E
204 J11 **Amundsen Sea** *sea* S Pacific Ocean
96 M12 **Amungen** ⊚ C Sweden
175 N10 **Amuntai** *prev.* Amoentai. Borneo, C Indonesia 2.24S 115.13E
133 W6 **Amur** *Chin.* Heilong Jiang. ≈ China/Russian Federation
175 Rr7 **Amurang** *prev.* Amoerang. Sulawesi, C Indonesia 1.12N 124.37E
175 Rr7 **Amurang, Teluk** *bay* Sulawesi, C Indonesia
107 O3 **Amurrio** País Vasco, N Spain 43.03N 3.00W
127 Nn15 **Amursk** Khabarovskiy Kray, SE Russian Federation 50.13N 136.34E
126 M14 **Amurskaya Oblast'** ⬖ *province* SE Russian Federation
82 G7 **'Amur, Wadi** ≈ NE Sudan
117 C17 **Amvrakikós Kólpos** *gulf* W Greece
Amvrosiyevka *see* Amvrosiyivka
119 X8 **Amvrosiyivka** *Rus.* Amvrosiyevka. Donets'ka Oblast', SE Ukraine 47.46N 38.31E
Amyderya *see* Amu Darya
116 E13 **Amýntaio** *var.* Amindeo; *prev.* Amíndaion. Dytikí Makedonía, N Greece 40.42N 21.42E
12 B6 **Amyot** Ontario, S Canada 48.28N 84.58W
203 U10 **Anaa** *atoll* Îles Tuamotu, C French Polynesia
Anabanoea *see* Anabanua
175 Pp12 **Anabanua** *prev.* Anabanoea. Sulawesi, C Indonesia 3.58S 120.07E
201 R8 **Anabar** NE Nauru 0.30S 166.56E
126 K7 **Anabar** ≈ NE Russian Federation
An Abhainn Mhór *see* Blackwater
57 O6 **Anaco** Anzoátegui, NE Venezuela 9.30N 64.28W
35 Q10 **Anaconda** Montana, NW USA 46.09N 112.55W
34 H7 **Anacortes** Washington, NW USA 48.30N 122.36W
28 M11 **Anadarko** Oklahoma, C USA 35.04N 98.14W
116 N12 **Ana Dere** ≈ NW Turkey
106 G8 **Anadia** Aveiro, N Portugal 40.25N 8.27W
Anadolu Dağları *see* Doğu Karadeniz Dağları
127 Pp5 **Anadyr'** Chukotskiy Avtonomnyy Okrug, NE Russian Federation 64.40N 177.22E
127 P5 **Anadyr'** ≈ NE Russian Federation
Anadyr, Gulf of *see* Anadyrskiy Zaliv
133 X4 **Anadyrskiy Khrebet** *var.* Chukot Range. ▲▲ NE Russian Federation
127 Q4 **Anadyrskiy Zaliv** *Eng.* Gulf of Anadyr. *gulf* NE Russian Federation
117 K22 **Anáfi** *anc.* Anaphe. *island* Kykládes, Greece, Aegean Sea
109 J15 **Anagni** Lazio, C Italy 41.43N 13.12E
'Ānah *see* 'Annah
37 T15 **Anaheim** California, W USA 33.50N 117.54W
8 L15 **Anahim Lake** British Columbia, SW Canada 52.26N 125.13W
40 B8 **Anahola** Kauai, Hawaii, USA, C Pacific Ocean 22.09N 159.19W
27 X11 **Anahuac** Texas, SW USA 29.46N 94.40W
43 O7 **Anáhuac** Nuevo León, NE Mexico 27.13N 100.09W
161 G22 **Anai Mudi** ▲ S India 10.16N 77.08E
Anaiza *see* 'Unayzah
161 M15 **Anakāpalle** Andhra Pradesh, E India 17.42N 83.06E
203 W15 **Anakena, Playa de** *beach* Easter Island, Chile, E Pacific Ocean
41 Q7 **Anaktuvuk Pass** Alaska, USA 68.08N 151.44W
41 Q6 **Anaktuvuk River** ≈ Alaska, USA
180 J3 **Analalava** Mahajanga, NW Madagascar 14.37S 47.46E
46 F6 **Ana Maria, Golfo de** *gulf* C Cuba
Anambas Islands *see* Anambas, Kepulauan
174 Ii5 **Anambas, Kepulauan** *var.* Anambas Islands *island group* W Indonesia
79 U17 **Anambra** ⬖ *state* SE Nigeria
31 N4 **Anamoose** North Dakota, N USA 47.50N 100.14W
31 Y13 **Anamosa** Iowa, C USA 42.06N 91.17W
142 H17 **Anamur** İçel, S Turkey 36.06N 32.49E
142 H17 **Anamur Burnu** *headland* S Turkey 36.03N 32.49E
170 Ff16 **Anan** Tokushima, Shikoku, SW Japan 33.54N 134.40E
160 O12 **Ānandadur** Orissa, E India 21.13N 86.08E
161 H18 **Anantapur** Andhra Pradesh, S India 14.40N 77.36E

◆ Country ● Country Capital ◇ Dependent Territory ○ Dependent Territory Capital ⬖ Administrative Region ✕ International Airport ▲ Mountain ▲▲ Mountain Range Volcano ≈ River ⊚ Lake ⊡ Reservoir

ANANTNĀG – APEX

158 H5 Anantnāg var. Islamabad. Jammu and Kashmir, NW India 33.43N 75.10E
Ananyev see Anan'yiv
119 O9 Anan'yiv Rus. Ananyev. Odes'ka Oblast', SW Ukraine 47.43N 29.51E
130 J14 Anapa Krasnodarskiy Kray, SW Russian Federation 44.55N 37.20E
Anaphe see Anáfi
61 K18 Anápolis Goiás, C Brazil 16.19S 48.58W
149 R10 Anār Kermān, C Iran 30.48N 55.17E
Anár see Inari
149 P7 Anārak Eşfahān, C Iran 33.21N 53.43E
Anar Dara see Anār Darreh
154 J7 Anār Darreh var. Anar Dara. Farāh, W Afghanistan 32.45N 61.37E
Anárjohka see Inarijoki
25 X9 Anastasia Island island Florida, SE USA
196 K7 Anatahan island C Northern Mariana Islands
132 M6 Anatolia plateau C Turkey
88 F14 Anatolian Plate tectonic feature Asia/Europe
116 H13 Anatolikí Makedonía kai Thráki Eng. Macedonia East and Thrace. ◆ region NE Greece
Anatom see Aneityum
64 L8 Añatuya Santiago del Estero, N Argentina 28.27S 62.52W
An Baile Meánach see Ballymena
An Bhearú see Barrow
An Bhóinn see Boyne
An Blascaod Mór see Great Blasket Island
An Cabhán see Cavan
An Caisleán Nua see Newcastle
An Caisleán Riabhach see Castlereagh, Northern Ireland, UK
An Caisleán Riabhach see Castlerea, Ireland
58 C13 Ancash off. Departamento de Ancash. ◆ department W Peru
An Cathair see Caher
104 J8 Ancenis Loire-Atlantique, NW France 47.22N 1.10W
An Chanáil Ríoga see Royal Canal
An Cheacha see Caha Mountains
41 R11 Anchorage Alaska, USA 61.12N 149.52W
41 R12 Anchorage ✕ Alaska, USA 61.08N 150.00W
41 Q13 Anchor Point Alaska, USA 59.46N 151.49W
An Chorr Chríochach see Cookstown
67 M24 Anchorstack Point headland W Tristan da Cunha 37.07S 12.21W
An Clár see Clare
An Clochán see Clifden
An Clochán Liath see Dunglow
25 U12 Anclote Keys island group Florida, SE USA
An Cóbh see Cobh
59 J17 Ancohuma, Nevado de ▲ W Bolivia 15.51S 68.33W
An Comar see Comber
59 D14 Ancón Lima, W Peru 11.47S 77.09W
108 J12 Ancona Marche, C Italy 43.37N 13.30E
Ancuabe see Ancuabi
84 Q13 Ancuabi var. Ancuabe. Cabo Delgado, NE Mozambique 12.57S 39.54E
65 F17 Ancud prev. San Carlos de Ancud. Los Lagos, S Chile 41.52S 73.49W
65 G17 Ancud, Golfo de gulf S Chile
Ancyra see Ankara
169 V8 Anda Heilongjiang, NE China 46.22N 125.15E
59 G16 Andahuaylas Apurímac, S Peru 13.38S 73.20W
An Daingean see Dingle
159 R15 Andāl West Bengal, NE India 23.34N 87.13E
96 E9 Åndalsnes Møre og Romsdal, S Norway 62.33N 7.42E
106 K13 Andalucía Eng. Andalusia. ◆ autonomous community S Spain
25 P7 Andalusia Alabama, S USA 31.18N 86.29W
Andalusia see Andalucía
157 Q21 Andaman and Nicobar Islands var. Andamans and Nicobars. ◆ union territory India, NE Indian Ocean
181 T4 Andaman Basin undersea feature NE Indian Ocean
157 P19 Andaman Islands island group India, NE Indian Ocean
181 T4 Andaman Sea sea NE Indian Ocean
59 K19 Andamarca Oruro, C Bolivia 18.50S 67.24W
176 V10 Andamata Irian Jaya, E Indonesia 2.40S 132.30E
190 H5 Andamooka South Australia 30.26S 137.12E
147 Y9 'Andām, Wādī seasonal river NE Oman
180 J3 Andapa Antsirañana, NE Madagascar 14.39S 49.40E
155 R4 Andarāb var. Banow. Baghlān, NE Afghanistan 35.36N 69.18E
Andarbag see Andarbogh
153 S13 Andarbogh Rus. Andarbag, Anderbak. S Tajikistan 37.51N 71.45E
111 Z5 Andau Burgenland, E Austria 47.46N 17.03E
110 I10 Andeer Graubünden, S Switzerland 46.36N 9.24E
94 H9 Andenes Nordland, C Norway 69.18N 16.06E
101 J20 Andenne Namur, SE Belgium 50.28N 5.06E
79 S11 Andéramboukane Gao, E Mali 15.24N 3.03E
Anderbak see Andarbogh
101 G18 Anderlecht Brussels, C Belgium 50.50N 4.18E
101 G21 Anderlues Hainaut, S Belgium 50.24N 4.16E
110 G9 Andermatt Uri, C Switzerland 46.39N 8.36E
103 E17 Andernach anc. Antunnacum. Rheinland-Pfalz, SW Germany 50.25N 7.25E
196 D15 Andersen Air Force Base air base NE Guam 13.34N 144.55E
41 R9 Anderson Alaska, USA 64.20N 149.11W
37 N4 Anderson California, W USA 40.26N 122.21W
33 P13 Anderson Indiana, N USA 40.06N 85.40W
29 R8 Anderson Missouri, C USA 36.39N 94.26W
23 P11 Anderson South Carolina, SE USA 34.30N 82.39W
27 V10 Anderson Texas, SW USA 30.29N 96.00W
15 Gg3 Anderson ⁓ Northwest Territories, NW Canada
97 K20 Anderstorp Jönköping, S Sweden 57.16N 13.46E
56 D9 Andes Antioquia, W Colombia 5.40N 75.55W
49 P7 Andes ▲▲ W South America
31 P12 Andes, Lake ◎ South Dakota, N USA
94 H9 Andfjorden fjord E Norwegian Sea
161 H16 Andhra Pradesh ◆ state E India
100 J8 Andijk Noord-Holland, NW Netherlands 52.38N 5.00E
153 S10 Andijon Rus. Andizhan. Andijon Wiloyati, E Uzbekistan 40.46N 72.19E
153 S10 Andijon Wiloyati Rus. Andizhanskaya Oblast'. ◆ province E Uzbekistan
Andikíthira see Antikýthira
180 J4 Andilamena Toamasina, C Madagascar 17.00S 48.35E
148 L8 Andīmeshk var. Andimishk; prev. Salehābād. Khūzestān, SW Iran 32.28N 48.21E
Andimishk see Andīmeshk
Andipáros see Antíparos
Andipaxi see Antípaxoi
Andípsara see Antípsara
142 L16 Andırın Kahramanmaraş, S Turkey 37.33N 36.18E
164 J8 Andirlangar Xinjiang Uygur Zizhiqu, NW China 37.38N 83.40E
Andírrion see Antírrio
Ándissa see Ántissa
Andizhan see Andijon
Andizhanskaya Oblast' see Andijon Wiloyati
155 N2 Andkhvoy Fāryāb, N Afghanistan 36.55N 65.07E
107 Q2 Andoain País Vasco, N Spain 43.13N 2.01W
176 W9 Andoi Irian Jaya, E Indonesia 0.53S 133.59E
169 Y15 Andong Jap. Antō. E South Korea 36.34N 128.43E
111 R4 Andorf Oberösterreich, N Austria 48.22N 13.33E
107 S7 Andorra Aragón, NE Spain 40.58N 0.27W
107 V4 Andorra off. Principality of Andorra, Cat. Valls d'Andorra, Fr. Vallée d'Andorre. ◆ monarchy SW Europe
Andorra see Andorra la Vella
107 V4 Andorra la Vella var. Andorra, Fr. Andorre la Vielle, Sp. Andorra la Vieja. ● (Andorra) C Andorra 42.30N 1.30E
Andorra la Vieja see Andorra la Vella
Andorra, Valls d'/Andorre, Vallée d' see Andorra
Andorre la Vielle see Andorra la Vella
99 M22 Andover S England, UK 51.13N 1.28W
29 N6 Andover Kansas, C USA 37.42N 97.08W
94 G10 Andøya island C Norway
62 I8 Andradina São Paulo, S Brazil 20.54S 51.25W
41 N10 Andreafsky River ⁓ Alaska, USA
40 H17 Andreanof Islands island group Aleutian Islands, Alaska, USA
128 H16 Andreapol' Tverskaya Oblast', W Russian Federation 56.38N 32.17E
Andreas, Cape see Zafer Burnu
Andreevka see Kabanbay
23 N10 Andrews North Carolina, SE USA 35.19N 84.01W
23 T13 Andrews South Carolina, SE USA 33.27N 79.33W
26 M7 Andrews Texas, SW USA 32.19N 102.33W
181 N5 Andrew Tablemount var. Gora Andryu. undersea feature W Indian Ocean 6.45N 50.30E
Andreyevka see Kabanbay
109 N17 Andria Puglia, SE Italy 41.13N 16.16E
115 K16 Andrijevica Montenegro, SW Yugoslavia 42.45N 19.45E
117 E20 Andrítsaina Pelopónnisos, S Greece 37.29N 21.52E
An Droichead Nua see Newbridge
Andropov see Rybinsk
117 J19 Ándros Ándros, Kykládes, Greece, Aegean Sea 37.49N 24.55E
117 J20 Ándros island Kykládes, Greece, Aegean Sea
21 O7 Androscoggin River ⁓ Maine/New Hampshire, NE USA
46 F3 Andros Island island NW Bahamas
131 R7 Androsovka Samarskaya Oblast', W Russian Federation 52.41N 49.34E
46 G3 Andros Town Andros Island, NW Bahamas 24.40N 77.47W
161 D21 Āndrott Island island Lakshadweep, India, N Indian Ocean
119 N5 Andrushivka Zhytomyrs'ka Oblast', N Ukraine 50.01N 29.02E
113 K17 Andrychów Małopolskie, S Poland 49.51N 19.23E
Andryu, Gora see Andrew Tablemount
94 I10 Andselv Troms, N Norway 69.05N 18.30E
81 O17 Andudu Orientale, NE Dem. Rep. Congo (Zaire) 2.25N 28.39E
107 N13 Andújar anc. Illiturgis. Andalucía, SW Spain 38.01N 4.03W
84 C12 Andulo Bié, W Angola 11.28S 16.43E
105 Q14 Anduze Gard, S France 44.03N 3.59E
An Earagail see Errigal Mountain
97 L19 Aneby Jönköping, S Sweden 57.49N 14.45E
Anécho see Aného
79 Q9 Anéfis Kidal, NE Mali 18.05N 0.38E
47 U8 Anegada island NE British Virgin Islands
63 B25 Anegada, Bahía bay E Argentina
47 U9 Anegada Passage passage Anguilla/British Virgin Islands
79 R17 Aného var. Anécho; prev. Petit-Popo. S Togo 6.13N 1.36E
197 D17 Aneityum var. Anatom; prev. Kéamu. island S Vanuatu
119 N10 Anenii Noi Rus. Novyye Aneny. C Moldova 46.52N 29.10E
194 L12 Anepmete New Britain, E PNG 5.47S 148.37E
107 U4 Aneto ▲ NE Spain 42.36N 0.37E
Änew see Annau
Ānewetak see Enewetak Atoll
79 Y8 Aney Agadez, NE Niger 19.22N 13.00E
An Fheoir see Nore
126 Ii13 Angara ⁓ C Russian Federation
126 Ii15 Angarsk Irkutskaya Oblast', S Russian Federation 52.31N 103.55E
95 G17 Ånge Västernorrland, C Sweden 62.31N 15.40E
Angel see Úhlava
42 D4 Ángel de la Guarda, Isla island NW Mexico
179 Pl6 Angeles off. Angeles City. Luzon, N Philippines 15.16N 120.37E
Angeles City see Angeles
Angel Falls see Ángel, Salto
97 J22 Ängelholm Skåne, S Sweden 56.14N 12.52E
63 A17 Angélica Santa Fe, C Argentina 31.33S 61.33W
27 W8 Angelina River ⁓ Texas, SW USA
57 Q9 Ángel, Salto Eng. Angel Falls. waterfall E Venezuela 5.52N 62.19W
97 M15 Ängelsberg Västmanland, C Sweden 59.57N 16.01E
37 P8 Angels Camp California, W USA 38.03N 120.31W
111 W7 Anger Steiermark, SE Austria 47.16N 15.41E
Angerapp see Ozersk
Angerburg see Węgorzewo
95 H15 Ångermanälven ⁓ N Sweden
102 P11 Angermünde Brandenburg, NE Germany 53.01N 13.59E
104 K7 Angers anc. Juliomagus. Maine-et-Loire, NW France 47.30N 0.33W
13 W7 Angers ⁓ Quebec, SE Canada
95 J16 Ängesön island N Sweden
Angistro see Ágkistro
116 H13 Angítis ⁓ NE Greece
178 J14 Ângk Tasaôm prev. Angtassom. Takêv, S Cambodia 10.59N 104.39E
193 C25 Anglem, Mount ▲ Stewart Island, Southland, SW NZ 46.44S 167.56E
99 I18 Anglesey cultural region NW Wales, UK
99 I18 Anglesey island NW Wales, UK
104 I15 Anglet Pyrénées-Atlantiques, SW France 43.28N 1.30W
27 W12 Angleton Texas, SW USA 29.10N 95.25W
Anglia see England
12 H9 Angliers Quebec, SE Canada 47.33N 79.17W
Anglo-Egyptian Sudan see Sudan
Angmagssalik see Ammassalik
178 I8 Ang Nam Ngum ◎ C Laos
81 N16 Ango Orientale, N Dem. Rep. Congo (Zaire) 4.02N 25.49E
85 Q15 Angoche Nampula, E Mozambique 16.12S 39.55E
65 G14 Angol Araucanía, C Chile 37.48S 72.40W
33 Q11 Angola Indiana, N USA 41.37N 85.00W
84 A9 Angola off. Republic of Angola; prev. People's Republic of Angola, Portuguese West Africa. ◆ republic SW Africa
67 P15 Angola Basin undersea feature E Atlantic Ocean
41 X13 Angoon Admiralty Island, Alaska, USA 57.33N 134.30W
153 O14 Angor Surkhondaryo Wiloyati, S Uzbekistan 37.30N 67.06E
Angora see Ankara
194 H10 Angoram East Sepik, NW PNG 4.01S 144.03E
42 H8 Angostura Sinaloa, C Mexico 25.18N 108.10W
Angostura see Ciudad Bolívar
43 U17 Angostura, Presa de la ⊟ SE Mexico
30 J11 Angostura Reservoir ⊟ South Dakota, N USA
104 L11 Angoulême anc. Iculisma. Charente, W France 45.39N 0.10E
104 K11 Angoumois cultural region W France
66 O2 Angra do Heroísmo Terceira, Azores, Portugal, NE Atlantic Ocean 38.40N 27.13W
62 O10 Angra dos Reis Rio de Janeiro, SE Brazil 22.58S 44.16W
Angra Pequena see Lüderitz
153 Q10 Angren Toshkent Wiloyati, E Uzbekistan 41.04N 70.17E
Angtassom see Ângk Tasaôm
178 Hh11 Ang Thong var. Angthong. Ang Thong, C Thailand 14.34N 100.25E
81 M16 Angu Orientale, N Dem. Rep. Congo (Zaire) 3.38N 24.14E
107 S5 Angüés Aragón, NE Spain 42.07N 0.10W
47 U9 Anguilla ◇ UK dependent territory E West Indies
47 V9 Anguilla island E West Indies
46 F4 Anguilla Cays islets SW Bahamas
Angul see Anugul
167 N1 Anguli Nur ◎ E China
81 O18 Angumu Orientale, E Dem. Rep. Congo (Zaire) 0.10S 27.42E
12 G14 Angus Ontario, S Canada 44.19N 79.52W
98 J10 Angus cultural region E Scotland, UK
61 K19 Anhangüera Goiás, S Brazil 18.12S 48.19W
101 I21 Anhée Namur, S Belgium 50.18N 4.52E
97 I21 Anholt island C Denmark
166 M11 Anhua prev. Dongping. Hunan, S China 28.25N 111.10E
167 P8 Anhui var. Anhui Sheng, Anhwei, Wan. ◆ province E China
Anhui Sheng/Anhwei see Anhui
41 O11 Aniak Alaska, USA 61.34N 159.31W
41 O12 Aniak River ⁓ Alaska, USA
An Iarmhí see Westmeath
201 R8 Anibare E Nauru 0.31S 166.56E
201 R8 Anibare Bay bay E Nauru, W Pacific Ocean
Anicium see le Puy
117 K22 Ánidro island Kykládes, Greece, Aegean Sea
79 R15 Anié C Togo 7.48N 1.12E
79 Q15 Anié ⁓ C Togo
104 J16 Anie, Pic d' ▲ SW France 42.56N 0.44W
131 Y7 Anikhovka Orenburgskaya Oblast', W Russian Federation 51.27N 60.17E
12 G9 Anima Nipissing Lake ◎ Ontario, S Canada
39 O16 Animas New Mexico, SW USA 31.55N 108.49W
39 P16 Animas Peak ▲ New Mexico, SW USA 31.34N 108.46W
39 P16 Animas Valley valley New Mexico, SW USA
118 F13 Anina Ger. Steierdorf, Hung. Stájerlakanina; prev. Ştaierdorf-Anina, Steierdorf-Anina, Steyerlak-Anina. Caraş-Severin, SW Romania 45.04N 21.51E
31 U14 Anita Iowa, C USA 41.27N 94.45W
127 Oo16 Aniva, Mys headland Ostrov Sakhalin, SE Russian Federation 46.02N 143.25E
127 Oo16 Aniva, Zaliv bay SE Russian Federation
197 E16 Aniwa island S Vanuatu
95 M19 Anjalankoski Etelä-Suomi, S Finland 60.39N 26.54E
'Anjar see Aanjar
Anjiangying see Luanping
12 B8 Anjigami Lake ◎ Ontario, S Canada
171 Hh16 Anjō var. Anzyô. Aichi, Honshū, SW Japan 34.58N 137.07E
104 J8 Anjou cultural region NW France
180 I13 Anjouan var. Nzwani, Johanna Island. island SE Comoros
180 J4 Anjozorobe Antananarivo, C Madagascar 18.22S 47.52E
169 W13 Anju W North Korea 39.36N 125.44E
100 M5 Anjum Fris. Eanjum. Friesland, N Netherlands 53.22N 6.09E
180 G6 Ankaboa, Tanjona headland W Madagascar 21.57S 43.16E
166 L7 Ankang prev. Xing'an. Shaanxi, C China 32.45N 109.00E
142 I12 Ankara prev. Angora, anc. Ancyra. ● (Turkey) Ankara, C Turkey 39.55N 32.49E
142 H12 Ankara ◆ province C Turkey
97 N19 Ankarsrum Kalmar, S Sweden 57.40N 16.19E
180 H6 Ankazoabo Toliara, SW Madagascar 22.18S 44.30E
180 I4 Ankazobe Antananarivo, C Madagascar 18.19S 47.07E
31 V14 Ankeny Iowa, C USA 41.43N 93.37W
178 Kk11 An Khê Gia Lai, C Vietnam 13.57N 108.39E
102 O9 Anklam Mecklenburg-Vorpommern, NE Germany 53.51N 13.42E
82 K13 Ānkober Amhara, N Ethiopia 9.36N 39.44E
79 O17 Ankobra ⁓ S Ghana
81 N22 Ankoro Katanga, SE Dem. Rep. Congo (Zaire) 6.45S 26.58E
101 L24 Anlier, Forêt d' forest SE Belgium
166 I13 Anlong Guizhou, S China 25.05N 105.29E
An Longfort see Longford
178 Ii11 Ânlong Vêng Siĕmréab, NW Cambodia 14.16N 104.07E
An Lorgain see Lurgan
167 N8 Anlu Hubei, C China 31.15N 113.41E
An Mhí see Meath
An Mhuir Cheilteach see Celtic Sea
An Muileann gCearr see Mullingar
95 F16 Ånn Jämtland, C Sweden 63.19N 12.34E
130 M8 Anna Voronezhskaya Oblast', W Russian Federation 51.31N 40.23E
32 L17 Anna Illinois, N USA 37.27N 89.15W
27 U5 Anna Texas, SW USA 33.21N 96.33W
76 L5 Annaba prev. Bône. NE Algeria 36.55N 7.46E
An Nabatīyah at Taḥtā see Nabatîyé
103 N17 Annaberg-Buchholz Sachsen, E Germany 50.34N 13.01E
111 T9 Annabichl ✕ (Klagenfurt) Kärnten, S Austria 46.39N 14.21E
146 M5 An Nafūd desert NW Saudi Arabia
145 P6 'Annah var. 'Ānah. NW Iraq 33.27N 43.19E
145 P6 An Nāḥiyah W Iraq 34.24N 41.33E
145 T10 An Najaf var. Najaf. S Iraq 31.58N 44.19E
23 V5 Anna, Lake ⊟ Virginia, NE USA
99 F16 Annalee ⁓ N Ireland
178 Jj9 Annamitique, Chaîne ▲▲ C Laos
99 J14 Annan S Scotland, UK 55.00N 3.19W
31 U8 Annandale Minnesota, N USA 45.15N 94.07W
23 W4 Annandale Virginia, NE USA 38.48N 77.10W
201 Q7 Anna Point headland N Nauru 0.30S 166.55E
23 X3 Annapolis state capital Maryland, NE USA 38.58N 76.29W
196 A10 Anna, Pulo island S Palau
159 O10 Annapurna ▲ C Nepal 28.30N 83.49E
An Nāqūrah see En Nâqoûra
33 R10 Ann Arbor Michigan, N USA 42.16N 83.45W
An Nás see Naas
145 W12 An Nāşirīyah var. Nasiriya. SE Iraq 31.04N 46.16E
145 W11 An Naşr E Iraq 31.34N 46.08E
152 F13 Annau Turkm. Änew. Akhalskiy Velayat, C Turkmenistan 37.51N 58.22E
123 Mm16 An Nawfalīyah var. Al Nūwfalīyah. N Libya 30.46N 17.48E
21 P10 Ann, Cape headland Massachusetts, NE USA 42.39N 70.35W
188 I10 Annean, Lake ◎ Western Australia
Anneciacum see Annecy
105 T11 Annecy anc. Anneciacum. Haute-Savoie, E France 45.53N 6.09E
105 T11 Annecy, Lac d' ◎ E France
105 T10 Annemasse Haute-Savoie, E France 46.10N 6.13E
41 Z14 Annette Island island Alexander Archipelago, Alaska, USA
An Nhon see Binh Dinh
An Nīl al Abyaḍ see White Nile
An Nīl al Azraq see Blue Nile
25 Q3 Anniston Alabama, S USA 33.39N 85.49W
81 A19 Annobón island W Equatorial Guinea
105 R12 Annonay Ardèche, E France 45.15N 4.40E
46 K12 Annotto Bay C Jamaica 18.16N 76.45W
147 R5 An Nu'ayrīyah var. Narıya. Ash Sharqīyah, NE Saudi Arabia 27.30N 48.30E
190 M9 Annuello Victoria, SE Australia 34.54S 142.50E
145 Q10 An Nukhayb S Iraq 32.01N 42.15E
145 U9 An Nu'mānīyah E Iraq 32.34N 45.22E
Áno Arkhánai see Epáno Archánes
117 J25 Anógeia var. Anogia, Anóyia. Kriti, Greece, E Mediterranean Sea 35.17N 24.55E
Anogia see Anógeia
31 V8 Anoka Minnesota, N USA 45.15N 93.26W
An Ómaigh see Omagh
180 I1 Anorontany, Tanjona headland N Madagascar
180 J5 Anosibe An'Ala Toamasina, E Madagascar 19.24S 48.10E
Anóyia see Anógeia
An Pointe see Warrenpoint
167 P9 Anqing Anhui, E China 30.31N 116.58E
167 Q5 Anqiu Shandong, E China 36.25N 119.10E
An Ráth see Ráth Luirc
An Ribhéar see Kenmare River
An Ros see Rush
101 K19 Ans Liège, E Belgium 50.39N 5.31E
Ansāb see Nişāb
176 Ww10 Ansas Irian Jaya, E Indonesia 1.44S 135.52E
103 J20 Ansbach Bayern, SE Germany 49.15N 10.34E
An Sciobairín see Skibbereen
An Scoil see Skull
An Seancheann see Old Head of Kinsale
47 Y5 Anse-Bertrand Grande Terre, N Guadeloupe 16.28N 61.30W
180 H17 Anse Boileau Mahé, NE Seychelles 4.43S 55.28E
47 S11 Anse La Raye NW Saint Lucia 13.57N 61.01W
56 D9 Anserma Caldas, W Colombia 5.15N 75.46W
111 T4 Ansfelden Oberösterreich, N Austria 48.12N 14.17E
169 U12 Anshan Liaoning, NE China 41.06N 122.55E
166 J12 Anshun Guizhou, S China 26.15N 105.58E
63 F17 Ansina Tacuarembó, C Uruguay 31.58S 55.28W
31 O15 Ansley Nebraska, C USA 41.16N 99.22W
27 P6 Anson Texas, SW USA 32.45N 99.54W
79 Q10 Ansongo Gao, E Mali 15.39N 0.33E
An Srath Bán see Strabane
23 R5 Ansted West Virginia, NE USA 38.08N 81.06W
176 Yy10 Ansudu Irian Jaya, E Indonesia 2.09S 139.19E
59 G15 Anta Cusco, S Peru 13.31S 72.12W
59 G16 Antabamba Apurímac, C Peru 14.26S 72.51W
Antafalva see Kovačica
142 L17 Antakya anc. Antioch, Antiochia. Hatay, S Turkey 36.12N 36.10E
180 K3 Antalaha Antsirañana, NE Madagascar 14.52S 50.16E
142 F17 Antalya prev. Adalia, anc. Attaleia, Bibl. Attalia. Antalya, SW Turkey 36.52N 30.42E
142 F17 Antalya ◆ province SW Turkey
142 F16 Antalya ✕ Antalya, SW Turkey 36.53N 30.45E
124 Qq11 Antalya Basin undersea feature E Mediterranean Sea
Antalya, Gulf of see Antalya Körfezi
142 F16 Antalya Körfezi var. Gulf of Adalia, Eng. Gulf of Antalya. gulf SW Turkey
180 J5 Antanambao Manampotsy Toamasina, E Madagascar 19.30S 48.36E
180 I5 Antananarivo prev. Tananarive. ● (Madagascar) Antananarivo, C Madagascar 18.52S 47.30E
180 I4 Antananarivo ◆ province C Madagascar
180 J5 Antananarivo ✕ Antananarivo, C Madagascar 18.52S 47.30E
An tAonach see Nenagh
204-205 Antarctica continent
204 I5 Antarctic Peninsula peninsula Antarctica
59 E15 Antas, Río das ⁓ S Brazil
201 U16 Ant Atoll atoll Caroline Islands, E Micronesia
An Teampall Mór see Templemore
Antep see Gaziantep
106 M15 Antequera anc. Anticaria, Antiquaria. Andalucía, S Spain 37.01N 4.34W
Antequera see Oaxaca
39 S5 Antero Reservoir ⊟ Colorado, C USA
28 M7 Anthony Kansas, C USA 37.09N 98.01W
39 R16 Anthony New Mexico, SW USA 32.00N 106.36W
190 D5 Anthony, Lake salt lake South Australia
76 E8 Anti-Atlas ▲▲ SW Morocco
105 U15 Antibes anc. Antipolis. Alpes-Maritimes, SE France 43.34N 7.07E
105 U15 Antibes, Cap d' headland SE France 43.33N 7.08E
Anticaria see Antequera
11 Q11 Anticosti, Île d' Eng. Anticosti Island. island Quebec, E Canada
Anticosti Island see Anticosti, Île d'
104 K3 Antifer, Cap d' headland N France 49.43N 0.10E
32 L6 Antigo Wisconsin, N USA 45.10N 89.10W
11 Q15 Antigonish Nova Scotia, SE Canada 45.39N 62.00W
66 P11 Antigua Fuerteventura, Islas Canarias, NE Atlantic Ocean
47 X10 Antigua island S Antigua and Barbuda, Leeward Islands
Antigua see Antigua Guatemala
47 W9 Antigua and Barbuda ◆ commonwealth republic E West Indies
44 C6 Antigua Guatemala var. Antigua. Sacatepéquez, SW Guatemala 14.33N 90.39W
43 P11 Antiguo Morelos var. Antiguo-Morelos. Tamaulipas, C Mexico 22.34N 99.06W
117 F19 Antíkyras, Kólpos gulf C Greece
117 G24 Antikýthira var. Andikíthira. island S Greece
144 I7 Anti-Lebanon var. Jebel esh Sharqi, Ar. Al Jabal ash Sharqī, Fr. Anti-Liban. ▲▲ Lebanon/Syria
Anti-Liban see Anti-Lebanon
117 I22 Antímilos island Kykládes, Greece, Aegean Sea
38 L6 Antimony Utah, W USA 38.07N 112.00W
An tInbhear Mór see Arklow
32 M10 Antioch Illinois, N USA 42.28N 88.06W
Antioch see Antakya
104 I10 Antioche, Pertuis d' inlet W France
Antiochia see Antakya
56 D8 Antioquia Antioquia, C Colombia 6.24N 75.52W
56 E8 Antioquia off. Departamento de Antioquia. ◆ province C Colombia
117 J21 Antíparos var. Andipáros. island Kykládes, Greece, Aegean Sea
117 B17 Antípaxoi var. Andipaxi. island Iónioi Nísoi, Greece, C Mediterranean Sea
126 H7 Antipayuta Yamalo-Nenetskiy Avtonomnyy Okrug, N Russian Federation 69.08N 76.43E
199 J14 Antipodes Islands island group S NZ
Antipolis see Antibes
117 J18 Antípsara var. Andípsara. island E Greece
Antiquaria see Antequera
13 N10 Antique, Lac ◎ Quebec, SE Canada
117 E18 Antírrio var. Andírrion. Dytikí Ellás, C Greece 38.20N 21.46E
117 K16 Ántissa var. Ándissa. Lésvos, E Greece 39.15N 25.59E
An tIúr see Newry
Antivari see Bar
58 C6 Antizana ▲ N Ecuador 0.29S 78.08W
29 Q13 Antlers Oklahoma, C USA 34.13N 95.37W
95 J14 Antnäs Norrbotten, N Sweden 65.32N 21.53E
Antō see Andong
64 G5 Antofagasta Antofagasta, N Chile 23.40S 70.22W
64 G6 Antofagasta off. Región de Antofagasta. ◆ region N Chile
64 I7 Antofalla, Salar de salt lake NW Argentina
101 D20 Antoing Hainaut, SW Belgium 50.34N 3.26E
26 M5 Anton Texas, SW USA 33.48N 102.09W
45 S16 Antón Coclé, C Panama 8.22N 80.15W
39 T11 Anton Chico New Mexico, SW USA 35.12N 105.09W
62 K12 Antonina Paraná, S Brazil 25.28S 48.43W
105 O5 Antony Hauts-de-Seine, N France 48.45N 2.16E
Antratsit see Antratsyt
119 Y8 Antratsyt Rus. Antratsit. Luhans'ka Oblast', E Ukraine 48.07N 39.04E
99 G15 Antrim Ir. Aontroim. NE Northern Ireland, UK 54.43N 6.13W
99 G14 Antrim Ir. Aontroim. cultural region NE Northern Ireland, UK
99 G14 Antrim Mountains ▲▲ NE Northern Ireland, UK
180 H5 Antsalova Mahajanga, W Madagascar 18.40S 44.37E
Antserana see Antsirañana
An tSionainn see Shannon
180 J2 Antsirañana var. Antserana; prev. Antsirane, Diégo-Suarez. Antsirañana, N Madagascar 12.19S 49.16E
180 J2 Antsirañana ◆ province N Madagascar
Antsirane see Antsirañana
An tSiúir see Suir
120 I7 Antsla Ger. Anzen. Võrumaa, SE Estonia 57.49N 26.34E
An tSláine see Slaney
180 J3 Antsohihy Mahajanga, NW Madagascar 14.49S 47.58E
65 G14 Antuco, Volcán ▲ C Chile 37.29S 71.25W
175 P7 Antu, Gunung ▲ Borneo, N Indonesia 0.57N 118.51E
An Tullach see Tullow
An-tung see Dandong
Antunnacum see Andernach
Antwerp see Antwerpen
101 G16 Antwerpen Eng. Antwerp, Fr. Anvers. Antwerpen, N Belgium 51.13N 4.25E
101 H16 Antwerpen Eng. Antwerp. ◆ province N Belgium
An Uaimh see Navan
160 N12 Anugul var. Angul. Orissa, E India 20.51N 84.59E
158 F9 Anūpgarh Rājasthān, NW India 29.10N 73.13E
160 K10 Anūppur Madhya Pradesh, C India 23.06N 81.45E
161 K24 Anuradhapura North Central Province, C Sri Lanka 8.19N 80.25E
Anvers see Antwerpen
204 G4 Anvers Island island Antarctica
41 N11 Anvik Alaska, USA 62.39N 160.12W
41 N10 Anvik River ⁓ Alaska, USA
40 F17 Anvil Peak ⩕ Semisopochnoi Island, Alaska, USA 51.59N 179.36E
165 P7 Anxi Gansu, N China 40.31N 95.45E
190 F8 Anxious Bay bay South Australia
167 O5 Anyang Henan, C China 36.10N 114.18E
165 S11 A'nyêmaqên Shan ▲▲ C China
120 H12 Anykščiai Anykščiai, E Lithuania 55.30N 25.34E
167 P13 Anyuan Jiangxi, S China 25.10N 115.25E
127 O6 Anyuysk Chukotskiy Avtonomnyy Okrug, NE Russian Federation 68.22N 161.33E
127 Oo5 Anyuyskiy Khrebet ▲▲ NE Russian Federation
56 D8 Anza Antioquia, C Colombia 6.18N 75.54W
Anzen see Antsla
126 H13 Anzhero-Sudzhensk Kemerovskaya Oblast', S Russian Federation 56.00N 85.42E
109 I16 Anzio Lazio, C Italy 41.27N 12.37E
57 O6 Anzoátegui off. Estado Anzoátegui. ◆ state NE Venezuela
153 P12 Anzob W Tajikistan 39.24N 68.55E
Anzyô see Anjō
Aoba see Ambae
172 Ss13 Aoga-shima island Izu-shotō, SE Japan
169 T12 Aohan Qi Nei Mongol Zizhiqu, N China 42.12N 119.57E
Aoiz see Aoiz-Agoitz
107 R3 Aoiz-Agoitz var. Agoitz, Aoiz. Navarra, N Spain 42.47N 1.23W
195 X16 Aola var. Tenaghau. Guadalcanal, C Solomon Islands 9.32S 160.28E
178 Gg15 Ao Luk Nua Krabi, SW Thailand 8.21N 98.43E
Aomen see Macao
172 N8 Aomori Aomori, Honshū, C Japan 40.49N 140.43E
171 Mm9 Aomori off. Aomori-ken. ◆ prefecture Honshū, C Japan
Aontroim see Antrim
117 C15 Aóos var. Vijosa, Vijosë, Alb. Lumi i Vjosës,. ⁓ Albania/Greece see also Vjosës, Lumi i
203 Q7 Aorai, Mont ⩕ Tahiti, W French Polynesia 17.36S 149.28W
Aoraki see Cook, Mount
178 Ii13 Aôral, Phnum prev. Phnom Aural. ▲ W Cambodia 12.01N 104.10E
Aorangi see Cook, Mount
193 L15 Aorangi Mountains ▲▲ North Island, NZ
192 H13 Aorere ⁓ South Island, NZ
108 A7 Aosta anc. Augusta Praetoria. Valle d'Aosta, NW Italy 45.43N 7.19E
79 O11 Aougoundou, Lac ◎ S Mali
78 K9 Aoukâr var. Aouker. plateau C Mauritania
80 J13 Aouk, Bahr ⁓ Central African Republic/Chad
Aouker see Aoukâr
76 B11 Aousard SE Western Sahara 22.42N 14.22W
170 G12 Aoya Tottori, Honshū, SW Japan 35.31N 134.01E
80 H5 Aozou Borkou-Ennedi-Tibesti, N Chad 22.00N 17.11E
28 M11 Apache Oklahoma, C USA 34.57N 98.21W
38 L14 Apache Junction Arizona, SW USA 33.25N 111.33W
26 J9 Apache Mountains ▲▲ Texas, SW USA
38 M16 Apache Peak ▲ Arizona, SW USA 31.50N 110.25W
118 H10 Apahida Cluj, NW Romania 46.49N 23.45E
25 T9 Apalachee Bay bay Florida, SE USA
25 T3 Apalachee River ⁓ Georgia, SE USA
25 S10 Apalachicola Florida, SE USA 29.43N 84.58W
25 S10 Apalachicola Bay bay Florida, SE USA
25 R9 Apalachicola River ⁓ Florida, SE USA
Apam see Apan
Apamama see Abemama
43 P14 Apan var. Apam. Hidalgo, C Mexico 19.41N 98.24W
44 J8 Apanás, Lago de ◎ NW Nicaragua
56 H14 Apaporis, Río ⁓ Brazil/Colombia
193 C23 Aparima ⁓ South Island, NZ
179 P7 Aparri Luzon, N Philippines 18.16N 121.42E
114 J9 Apatin Serbia, NW Yugoslavia 45.40N 19.01E
128 J4 Apatity Murmanskaya Oblast', NW Russian Federation 67.33N 33.26E
57 X9 Apatou NW French Guiana 5.07N 54.20W
42 M14 Apatzingán var. Apatzingán de la Constitución. Michoacán de Ocampo, SW Mexico 19.04N 102.19W
176 Y9 Apauwar Irian Jaya, E Indonesia 1.36S 138.10E
Apaxtla see Apaxtla de Castrejón
43 O15 Apaxtla de Castrejón var. Apaxtla. Guerrero, S Mexico 18.06N 99.55W
120 J7 Ape Alūksne, NE Latvia 57.32N 26.42E
100 L11 Apeldoorn Gelderland, E Netherlands 52.13N 5.57E
Apennines see Appennino
Apenrade see Åbenrå
59 L17 Apere, Río ⁓ C Bolivia
57 W11 Apetina Sipaliwini, SE Surinam 3.30N 55.03W
23 U9 Apex North Carolina, SE USA 35.43N 78.51W

◆ Country ● Country Capital ◇ Dependent Territory ○ Dependent Territory Capital ◆ Administrative Region ✕ International Airport ▲ Mountain ▲▲ Mountain Range ⩕ Volcano ⁓ River ◎ Lake ⊟ Reservoir

81 M16 **Api Orientale,** N Dem. Rep. Congo (Zaire) *3.42N 25.22E*
158 M9 **Api** ▲ NW Nepal *30.07N 80.57E*
Apia *see* Abaiang
198 Bb8 **Āpia** ● (Samoa) Upolu, SE Samoa *13.49S 171.46W*
62 K11 **Apiaí** São Paulo, S Brazil *24.28S 48.51W*
175 P16 **Api, Gunung** ▲ Pulau Sangeang, S Indonesia *8.09S 119.03E*
195 Y16 **Apio** Maramasike Island, N Solomon Islands *9.36S 161.25E*
43 O15 **Apipilulco** Guerrero, S Mexico *18.10N 99.40W*
43 P14 **Apizaco** Tlaxcala, S Mexico *19.24N 98.10W*
106 I4 **A Pobla de Trives** *Cast.* Puebla de Trives. Galicia, NW Spain *42.21N 7.16W*
57 U9 **Apoera** Sipaliwini, NW Surinam *5.10N 57.08W*
117 O23 **Apolakkiá** Ródos, Dodekánisos, Greece, Aegean Sea *36.02N 27.48E*
103 L16 **Apolda** Thüringen, C Germany *51.01N 11.31E*
198 B8 **Apolima Strait** *strait* C Pacific Ocean
190 M13 **Apollo Bay** Victoria, SE Australia *38.40S 143.44E*
Apollonia *see* Sozopol
59 J16 **Apolo** La Paz, W Bolivia *14.40S 68.33W*
59 J16 **Apolobamba, Cordillera** ▲▲ Bolivia/Peru
179 Rr16 **Apo, Mount** ⛰ Mindanao, S Philippines *6.54N 125.16E*
25 W11 **Apopka** Florida, SE USA *28.40N 81.30W*
25 W11 **Apopka, Lake** ◎ Florida, SE USA
61 J19 **Aporé, Rio** ≈ SW Brazil
32 K2 **Apostle Islands** *island group* Wisconsin, N USA
Apostolas Andreas, Cape *see* Zafer Burnu
63 F14 **Apóstoles** Misiones, NE Argentina *27.54S 55.45W*
Apostólou Andréa, Akrotíri *see* Zafer Burnu
119 S9 **Apostolove** *Rus.* Apostolovo. Dnipropetrovs'ka Oblast', E Ukraine *47.40N 33.45E*
Apostolovo *see* Apostolove
19 Qq9 **Appalachian Mountains** ▲▲ E USA
97 K14 **Äppelbo** Dalarna, C Sweden *60.30N 14.00E*
100 N7 **Appelscha** *Fris.* Appelskea. Friesland, N Netherlands *52.57N 6.19E*
Appelskea *see* Appelscha
108 G11 **Appennino** *Eng.* Apennines. ▲▲ Italy/San Marino
109 L17 **Appennino Campano** ▲▲ C Italy
110 I7 **Appenzell** Appenzell, NW Switzerland *47.19N 9.25E*
110 H7 **Appenzell** ◐ *canton* NE Switzerland
57 V12 **Appikalo** Sipaliwini, S Surinam *2.07N 56.16W*
100 O5 **Appingedam** Groningen, NE Netherlands *53.18N 6.52E*
27 X8 **Appleby** Texas, SW USA *31.43N 94.36W*
99 L15 **Appleby-in-Westmorland** NW England, UK *54.34N 2.26W*
32 K10 **Apple River** ≈ Illinois, N USA
32 I5 **Apple River** ≈ Wisconsin, N USA
27 W9 **Apple Springs** Texas, SW USA *31.13N 94.57W*
31 S8 **Appleton** Minnesota, N USA *45.12N 96.01W*
32 M7 **Appleton** Wisconsin, N USA *44.16N 88.24W*
29 S5 **Appleton City** Missouri, C USA *38.11N 94.01W*
37 U14 **Apple Valley** California, W USA *34.30N 117.11W*
31 V9 **Apple Valley** Minnesota, N USA *44.43N 93.13W*
23 U6 **Appomattox** Virginia, NE USA *37.21N 78.49W*
196 B16 **Apra Harbour** *harbor* W Guam
196 B16 **Apra Heights** W Guam
108 F6 **Aprica, Passo dell'** *pass* N Italy *46.10N 10.08E*
109 M15 **Apricena** *anc.* Hadria Picena. Puglia, SE Italy *41.46N 15.27E*
130 L14 **Apsheronsk** Krasnodarskiy Kray, SW Russian Federation *44.27N 39.45E*
Apsheronskiy Poluostrov *see* Abşeron Yarımadası
105 S15 **Apt** *anc.* Apta Julia. Vaucluse, SE France *43.54N 5.24E*
Apta Julia *see* Apt
40 H12 **Apua Point** *headland* Hawaii, USA, C Pacific Ocean *19.15N 155.13W*
62 I10 **Apucarana** Paraná, S Brazil *23.34S 51.28W*
Apulia *see* Puglia
56 K8 **Apure** *off.* Estado Apure. ◐ *state* C Venezuela
56 J7 **Apure, Río** ≈ W Venezuela
59 F16 **Apurímac** *off.* Departamento de Apurímac. ◐ *department* C Peru
59 F15 **Apurímac, Río** ≈ S Peru
118 G10 **Apuseni, Munții** ▲▲ W Romania
Aqaba/'Aqaba *see* Al 'Aqabah
144 F15 **Aqaba, Gulf of** *var.* Gulf of Elat, *Ar.* Khalīj al 'Aqabah; *anc.* Sinus Aelaniticus. *gulf* NE Red Sea
145 R7 **'Aqabah** C Iraq *33.33N 42.55E*
'Aqabah, Khalīj al *see* Aqaba, Gulf of
155 O2 **Āqchah** *var.* Āqcheh. Jowzjān, N Afghanistan *36.59N 66.07E*
Āqcheh *see* Āqchah
Aqköl *see* Akkol'
Aqmola *see* Astana
Aqmola Oblysy *see* Akmola
164 L10 **Aqqikkol Hu** ◎ NW China
Aqqystaū *see* Akkystau
'Aqrah *see* Ākrē
Aqsay *see* Aksay
Aqshataū *see* Akchatau
Aqsū *see* Aksu
Aqsūat *see* Aksuat
Aqtas *see* Aktas
Aqtaū *see* Aktau
Aqtöbe/Aqtöbe Oblysy *see* Aktyubinsk
Aqtoghay *see* Aktogay
Aquae Augustae *see* Dax
Aquae Calidae *see* Bath
Aquae Flaviae *see* Chaves
Aquae Grani *see* Aachen
Aquae Panoniae *see* Baden
Aquae Sextiae *see* Aix-en-Provence
Aquae Solis *see* Bath
Aquae Tarbelicae *see* Dax
38 J11 **Aquarius Mountains** ▲▲ Arizona, SW USA
64 O5 **Aquidabán, Río** ≈ E Paraguay
61 H20 **Aquidauana** Mato Grosso do Sul, S Brazil *20.27S 55.45W*
42 L15 **Aquila** Michoacán de Ocampo, S Mexico *18.36N 103.32W*
Aquila/Aquila degli Abruzzi *see* L'Aquila
27 T8 **Aquilla** Texas, SW USA *31.51N 97.13W*
46 L9 **Aquin** S Haiti *18.16N 73.24W*
Aquisgranum *see* Aachen
104 J13 **Aquitaine** ◐ *region* SW France
Aqzhar *see* Akzhar
159 P13 **Āra** *prev.* Arrah. Bihār, N India *25.34N 84.40E*
107 S4 **Ara** ≈ NE Spain
25 P2 **Arab** Alabama, S USA *34.19N 86.30W*
Araba *see* Álava
144 G12 **'Arabah, Wādī al** *Heb.* Ha'Arava. *dry watercourse* Israel/Jordan
119 U12 **Arabats'ka Strilka, Kosa** *spit* S Ukraine
119 U12 **Arabats'ka Zatoka** *gulf* S Ukraine
'Arab, Baḥr al *see* Arab, Bahr el
82 C12 **Arab, Bahr el** *var.* Baḥr al 'Arab. ≈ S Sudan
58 E7 **Arabela, Río** ≈ N Peru
181 O4 **Arabian Basin** *undersea feature* N Arabian Sea
Arabian Desert *see* Sahara el Sharqîya
147 N9 **Arabian Peninsula** *peninsula* SW Asia
87 P15 **Arabian Plate** *tectonic feature* Africa/Asia/Europe
147 W14 **Arabian Sea** *sea* NW Indian Ocean
Arabicus, Sinus *see* Red Sea
'Arabī, Khalīj al *see* the Gulf
Arabistan *see* Khūzestān
'Arabīyah as Su'ūdīyah, Al Mamlakah al *see* Saudi Arabia
'Arabīyah Jumhūrīyah, Miṣr al *see* Egypt
144 I9 **'Arab, Jabal al** ▲▲ S Syria
124 Pp14 **'Arab, Khalîg el** *Eng.* Arabs Gulf. *gulf* N Egypt
Arab Republic of Egypt *see* Egypt
Arabs Gulf *see* 'Arab, Khalîg el
145 Y12 **'Arab, Shaṭṭ al** *Eng.* Shatt al Arab, *Per.* Arvand Rūd. ≈ Iran/Iraq
142 I11 **Araç** Kastamonu, N Turkey *41.13N 33.19E*
61 P16 **Aracaju** *state capital* Sergipe, E Brazil *10.45S 37.07W*
56 F5 **Aracataca** Magdalena, N Colombia *10.36N 74.13W*
60 P13 **Aracati** Ceará, E Brazil *4.31S 37.45W*
62 J8 **Araçatuba** São Paulo, S Brazil *21.12S 50.24W*
106 J13 **Aracena** Andalucía, S Spain *37.54N 6.33W*
117 F20 **Arachnaío** ▲▲ S Greece
117 D16 **Árachthos** *var.* Arta; *prev.* Árakhthos, *anc.* Arachthus. ≈ W Greece
Arachthus *see* Árachthos
61 N19 **Araçuai** Minas Gerais, SE Brazil *16.52S 42.03W*
142 I11 **Araç Çayı** ≈ N Turkey
144 F11 **'Arad** Southern, S Israel *31.16N 35.09E*
118 F11 **Arad** Arad, W Romania *46.12N 21.20E*
118 F11 **Arad** ◐ *county* W Romania
80 J9 **Arada** Biltine, NE Chad *15.00N 20.38E*
149 P18 **'Arādah** Abū Ẓaby, S UAE *22.57N 53.24E*
Aradhippou *see* Aradíppou
124 O3 **Aradíppou** *var.* Aradhippou. SE Cyprus *34.57N 33.37E*
182 K6 **Arafura Sea** *Ind.* Laut Arafuru. *sea* W Pacific Ocean
182 L6 **Arafura Shelf** *undersea feature* C Arafura Sea
Arafuru, Laut *see* Arafura Sea
61 J18 **Aragarças** Goiás, C Brazil *15.55S 52.12W*
Aragats, Gora *see* Aragats Lerr
143 T12 **Aragats Lerr** *Rus.* Gora Aragats. ▲ W Armenia *40.31N 44.06E*
34 E14 **Arago, Cape** *headland* Oregon, NW USA *43.17N 124.25W*
107 R6 **Aragón** ◐ *autonomous community* E Spain
107 Q4 **Aragón** ≈ NE Spain
109 I24 **Aragona** Sicilia, Italy, C Mediterranean Sea *37.25N 13.37E*
107 Q7 **Aragoncillo** ▲ C Spain *40.59N 2.01W*
56 L5 **Aragua** *off.* Estado Aragua. ◐ *state* N Venezuela
57 N6 **Aragua de Barcelona** Anzoátegui, NE Venezuela *9.30N 64.45W*
57 O5 **Aragua de Maturín** Monagas, NE Venezuela *9.58N 63.30W*
61 K15 **Araguaia, Río** *var.* Araguaya. ≈ C Brazil
61 K19 **Araguari** Minas Gerais, SE Brazil *18.37S 48.13W*
60 J11 **Araguari, Rio** ≈ SW Brazil
Araguaya *see* Araguaia, Río
106 K14 **Arahal** Andalucía, S Spain *37.15N 5.33W*
171 Jj13 **Arai** Niigata, Honshū, C Japan *36.58N 138.14E*
Árainn *see* Inishmore
Árainn Mhór *see* Aran Island
Ara Jovis *see* Aranjuez
76 J11 **Arak** C Algeria *25.17N 3.45E*
176 Yy15 **Arak** Irian Jaya, E Indonesia *7.14S 139.40E*
148 M7 **Arāk** *prev.* Sultānābād. Markazī, W Iran *34.07N 49.39E*
196 D10 **Arakabesan** *island* Palau Islands, N Palau
57 S7 **Arakaka** NW Guyana *7.37N 59.58W*
177 Ff6 **Arakan State** *var.* Rakhine State. ◐ *state* W Burma
177 Ff5 **Arakan Yoma** ▲▲ W Burma
171 Kk12 **Arakawa** Niigata, Honshū, C Japan *38.06N 139.25E*
Árakhthos *see* Árachthos
Araks/Arak's *see* Aras
164 H7 **Aral** Xinjiang Uygur Zizhiqu, NW China *40.40N 81.19E*
Aral *see* Aral'sk, Kazakhstan
Aral *see* Vose', Tajikistan
Aral-Bukhorskiy Kanal *see* Amu-Bukhoro Kanali
143 T12 **Aralik** Iğdır, E Turkey *39.54N 44.28E*
152 H5 **Aral Sea** *Kaz.* Aral Tengizi, *Rus.* Aral'skoye More, *Uzb.* Orol Dengizi. *inland sea* Kazakhstan/Uzbekistan
150 L13 **Aral'sk** *Kaz.* Aral. Kzylorda, SW Kazakhstan *46.48N 61.40E*
Aral'skoye More/Aral Tengizi *see* Aral Sea
43 O10 **Aramberri** Nuevo León, NE Mexico *24.05N 99.52W*
194 F14 **Aramia** ≈ SW PNG
149 N6 **Ārān** *var.* Golārā. Eşfahān, C Iran *34.03N 51.30E*
107 N5 **Aranda de Duero** Castilla-León, N Spain *41.40N 3.40W*
114 M12 **Aranđelovac** *prev.* Arandjelovac. Serbia, C Yugoslavia *44.18N 20.32E*
Arandjelovac *see* Aranđelovac
99 J19 **Aran Fawddwy** ▲ NW Wales, UK *52.48N 3.42W*
99 C14 **Aran Island** *Ir.* Árainn Mhór. *island* NW Ireland
99 A18 **Aran Islands** *island group* W Ireland
107 N9 **Aranjuez** *anc.* Ara Jovis. Madrid, C Spain *40.01N 3.37W*
85 E20 **Aranos** Hardap, SE Namibia *24.11S 19.07E*
27 U14 **Aransas Bay** *inlet* Texas, SW USA
27 T14 **Aransas Pass** Texas, SW USA *27.54N 97.09W*
203 O3 **Aranuka** *prev.* Nanouki. *atoll* Tungaru, W Kiribati
178 I11 **Aranyaprathet** Prachin Buri, S Thailand *13.42N 102.32E*
Aranyosasztal *see* Zlatý Stôl
Aranyosgyéres *see* Câmpia Turzii
Aranyosmarót *see* Zlaté Moravce
170 Cc14 **Arao** Kumamoto, Kyūshū, SW Japan *33.16N 130.25E*
79 O8 **Araouane** Tombouctou, N Mali *18.58N 3.39W*
28 L10 **Arapaho** Oklahoma, C USA *35.34N 98.57W*
31 N16 **Arapahoe** Nebraska, C USA *40.18N 99.54W*
59 I16 **Arapa, Laguna** ◎ SE Peru
193 K14 **Arapawa Island** *island* C NZ
63 E17 **Arapey Grande, Río** ≈ N Uruguay
61 P16 **Arapiraca** Alagoas, E Brazil *9.45S 36.40W*
146 M3 **'Ar'ar** Al Ḥudūd ash Shamālīyah, NW Saudi Arabia *31.00N 41.00E*
56 G15 **Araracuara** Caquetá, S Colombia *0.36S 72.24W*
63 K15 **Araranguá** Santa Catarina, S Brazil *28.55S 49.30W*
62 L8 **Araraquara** São Paulo, S Brazil *21.46S 48.07W*
61 O13 **Araras** Ceará, E Brazil *4.08S 40.30W*
60 I14 **Araras** Pará, N Brazil *6.03S 54.34W*
62 L9 **Araras** São Paulo, S Brazil *22.21S 47.21W*
62 H11 **Araras, Serra das** ▲▲ S Brazil
143 U12 **Ararat** S Armenia *39.49N 44.45E*
190 M12 **Ararat** Victoria, SE Australia *37.18S 142.57E*
Ararat, Mount *see* Büyükağrı Dağı
146 M3 **'Ar'ar, Wādī** *dry watercourse* Iraq/Saudi Arabia
133 N7 **Aras** *Arm.* Arak's, *Az.* Araz Nehri, *Per.* Rūd-e Aras, *Rus.* Araks; *prev.* Araxes. ≈ SW Asia
107 R9 **Aras de Alpuente** País Valenciano, E Spain *39.55N 1.09W*
143 S13 **Aras Güneyi Dağları** ▲▲ NE Turkey
Aras, Rūd-e *see* Aras
203 U9 **Aratika** *atoll* Îles Tuamotu, C French Polynesia
Aratürük *see* Yiwu
56 I8 **Arauca** Arauca, NE Colombia *7.03N 70.46W*
56 I8 **Arauca** *off.* Intendencia de Arauca. ◐ *province* NE Colombia
65 G15 **Araucanía** *off.* Región de la Araucanía. ◐ *region* C Chile
56 L7 **Arauca, Río** ≈ Colombia/Venezuela
65 F14 **Arauco** Bío Bío, C Chile *37.16S 73.15W*
65 F14 **Arauco, Golfo de** *gulf* S Chile
56 H8 **Arauquita** Arauca, C Colombia *7.01N 71.20W*
Arausio *see* Orange
158 F13 **Arāvali Range** ▲▲ N India
195 S12 **Arawa** Bougainville Island, NE PNG *6.13S 155.37E*
193 C20 **Arawata** ≈ South Island, NZ
194 L12 **Arawe Islands** *island group* E PNG
61 L20 **Araxá** Minas Gerais, SE Brazil *19.37S 46.49W*
Araxes *see* Aras
57 O5 **Araya** Sucre, N Venezuela *10.34N 64.15W*
107 R4 **Arba** ≈ N Spain
83 I15 **Ārba Minch'** Southern, S Ethiopia *6.02N 37.34E*
145 U4 **Arbat** NE Iraq *35.26N 45.34E*
109 D19 **Arbatax** Sardegna, Italy, C Mediterranean Sea *39.57N 9.42E*
Arbe *see* Rab
Arbela *see* Arbīl
145 S3 **Arbīl** *var.* Erbil, Irbīl, *Kurd.* Hawlēr; *anc.* Arbela. N Iraq *36.12N 44.01E*
97 M16 **Arboga** Västmanland, C Sweden *59.24N 15.49E*
97 M16 **Arbogaån** ≈ C Sweden
105 S9 **Arbois** Jura, E France *46.54N 5.45E*
56 D6 **Arboletes** Antioquia, NW Colombia *8.52N 76.25W*
9 X15 **Arborg** Manitoba, S Canada *50.52N 97.20W*
96 N12 **Arbrå** Gävleborg, C Sweden *61.27N 16.21E*
98 K10 **Arbroath** *anc.* Aberbrothock. E Scotland, UK *56.34N 2.34W*
37 N6 **Arbuckle** California, W USA *39.00N 122.05W*
29 N12 **Arbuckle Mountains** ▲▲ Oklahoma, C USA
Arbuzinka *see* Arbyzynka
119 Q8 **Arbyzynka** *Rus.* Arbuzinka. Mykolayivs'ka Oblast', S Ukraine *47.54N 31.19E*
105 U12 **Arc** ≈ E France
104 J13 **Arcachon** Gironde, SW France *44.40N 1.10W*
104 J13 **Arcachon, Bassin d'** *inlet* SW France
20 E10 **Arcade** New York, NE USA *42.32N 78.19W*
25 W14 **Arcadia** Florida, SE USA *27.13N 81.51W*
24 H5 **Arcadia** Louisiana, S USA *32.33N 92.55W*
32 J7 **Arcadia** Wisconsin, N USA *44.15N 91.30W*
Arcae Remorum *see* Châlons-en-Champagne
46 L9 **Arcahaie** C Haiti *18.46N 72.32W*
36 K3 **Arcata** California, W USA *40.51N 124.06W*
37 U6 **Arc Dome** ▲ Nevada, W USA *38.52N 117.20W*
109 J16 **Arce** Lazio, C Italy *41.35N 13.34E*
43 O15 **Arcelia** Guerrero, S Mexico *18.19N 100.16W*
101 M15 **Arcen** Limburg, SE Netherlands *51.28N 6.10E*
Archangel *see* Arkhangel'sk
Archangel Bay *see* Chëshskaya Guba
117 O23 **Archángelos** *var.* Arhangelos, Arkhángelos. Ródos, Dodekánisos, Greece, Aegean Sea *36.13N 28.07E*
116 F7 **Archar** ≈ NW Bulgaria
33 R11 **Archbold** Ohio, N USA *41.31N 84.18W*
107 R12 **Archena** Murcia, SE Spain *38.07N 1.16W*
27 R5 **Archer City** Texas, SW USA *33.36N 98.37W*
106 M14 **Archidona** Andalucía, S Spain *37.06N 4.22W*
67 B25 **Arch Islands** *island group* SW Falkland Islands
108 G13 **Arcidosso** Toscana, C Italy *42.52N 11.30E*
105 Q5 **Arcis-sur-Aube** Aube, N France *48.32N 4.09E*
190 F3 **Arckaringa Creek** *seasonal river* South Australia
108 G7 **Arco** Trentino-Alto Adige, N Italy *45.53N 10.51E*
35 Q14 **Arco** Idaho, NW USA *43.38N 113.18W*
32 M14 **Arcola** Illinois, N USA *39.39N 88.19W*
107 P6 **Arcos de Jalón** Castilla-León, N Spain *41.12N 2.13W*
106 K15 **Arcos de la Frontera** Andalucía, S Spain *36.45N 5.49W*
106 G5 **Arcos de Valdevez** Viana do Castelo, N Portugal *41.51N 8.25W*
61 P15 **Arcoverde** Pernambuco, E Brazil *08.23S 37.00W*
104 H5 **Arcovest, Pointe de l'** *headland* NW France *48.49N 2.58W*
Arctic-Mid Oceanic Ridge *see* Nansen Cordillera
207 R8 **Arctic Ocean** *ocean*
14 G4 **Arctic Red River** ≈ Northwest Territories/Yukon Territory, NW Canada
Arctic Red River *see* Tsiigehtchic
41 S6 **Arctic Village** Alaska, USA *68.07N 145.32W*
204 H1 **Arctowski** *Polish research station* South Shetland Islands, Antarctica *61.57S 58.23W*
116 I12 **Arda** *var.* Ardhas, *Gk.* Ardas. ≈ Bulgaria/Greece *see also* Ardas
148 L2 **Ardabīl** *var.* Ardebil. Ardabīl, NW Iran *38.15N 48.18E*
148 L2 **Ardabīl** *off.* Ostān-e Ardabīl. ◐ *province* NW Iran
143 R11 **Ardahan** Ardahan, NE Turkey *41.07N 42.40E*
143 S11 **Ardahan** ◐ *province* NE Turkey
149 P8 **Ardakān** Yazd, C Iran *32.20N 54.02E*
96 E12 **Årdalstangen** Sogn og Fjordane, S Norway *61.13N 7.43E*
143 R11 **Ardanuç** Artvin, NE Turkey *41.07N 42.04E*
116 L12 **Ardas** *var.* Ardhas, *Bul.* Arda. ≈ Bulgaria/Greece *see also* Arda
144 I13 **Arḍ aş Şawwān** *var.* Ardh es Suwwān. *plain* S Jordan
131 P5 **Ardatov** Respublika Mordoviya, W Russian Federation *54.49N 46.13E*
12 G12 **Ardbeg** Ontario, S Canada *45.38N 80.05W*
Ardeal *see* Transylvania
Ardebil *see* Ardabīl
105 Q13 **Ardèche** ≈ C France
105 Q13 **Ardèche** ◐ *department* E France
99 F17 **Ardee** *Ir.* Baile Átha Fhirdhia. NE Ireland *53.52N 6.33W*
105 Q3 **Ardennes** ◐ *department* NE France
101 J23 **Ardennes** *physical region* Belgium/France
143 Q11 **Ardeşen** Rize, NE Turkey *41.12N 41.02E*
149 O7 **Ardestān** *var.* Ardistan. Eşfahān, C Iran *33.29N 52.16E*
110 J9 **Ardez** Graubünden, SE Switzerland *46.47N 10.09E*
Ardhas *see* Arda/Ardas
Ardh es Suwwān *see* Arḍ aş Şawwān
106 I12 **Ardila, Ribeira de** *Sp.* Ardilla. ≈ Portugal/Spain *see also* Ardilla
9 T17 **Ardill** Saskatchewan, S Canada *49.56N 105.49W*
106 I12 **Ardilla** *Port.* Ribeira de Ardila. ≈ Portugal/Spain *see also* Ardila, Ribeira de
42 M11 **Ardilla, Cerro la** ▲ C Mexico *22.15N 102.33W*
116 J12 **Ardino** Kŭrdzhali, S Bulgaria *41.38N 25.22E*
Ardistan *see* Ardestān
191 P9 **Ardlethan** New South Wales, SE Australia *34.24S 146.52E*
Ard Mhacha *see* Armagh
25 P1 **Ardmore** Alabama, S USA *34.59N 86.51W*
29 N13 **Ardmore** Oklahoma, C USA *34.10N 97.08W*
22 J10 **Ardmore** Tennessee, S USA *35.00N 86.48W*
98 G10 **Ardnamurchan, Point of** *headland* N Scotland, UK *56.42N 6.15W*
101 C17 **Ardooie** West-Vlaanderen, W Belgium *50.59N 3.10E*
190 I9 **Ardrossan** South Australia *34.27S 137.54E*
118 H9 **Ardusat** *Hung.* Erdőszáda. Maramureș, N Romania *47.36N 23.25E*
95 F16 **Åre** Jämtland, C Sweden *63.25N 13.04E*
81 P16 **Arebi** Orientale, NE Dem. Rep. Congo (Zaire) *2.46N 29.34E*
47 T5 **Arecibo** C Puerto Rico *18.28N 66.43W*
176 W10 **Aredo** Irian Jaya, E Indonesia *2.27S 133.59E*
61 P14 **Areia Branca** Rio Grande do Norte, E Brazil *4.53S 37.03W*
121 O14 **Arekhawsk** *Rus.* Orekhovsk. Vitsyebskaya Voblasts', N Belarus *54.42N 30.30E*
Arel *see* Arlon
Arelas/Arelate *see* Arles
Arenal, Embalse de *see* Arenal Laguna
44 L12 **Arenal Laguna** *var.* Embalse de Arenal. ◎ NW Costa Rica
44 L13 **Arenal, Volcán** ⛰ NW Costa Rica *10.21N 84.42W*
36 K6 **Arena, Point** *headland* California, W USA *38.57N 123.44W*
61 H17 **Arenápolis** Mato Grosso, W Brazil *14.25S 56.52W*
42 G10 **Arena, Punta** *headland* W Mexico *23.28N 109.24W*
106 L8 **Arenas de San Pedro** Castilla-León, N Spain *40.12N 5.04W*
65 I24 **Arenas, Punta de** *headland* S Argentina *53.10S 68.15W*
63 B20 **Arenaza** Buenos Aires, E Argentina *34.55S 61.45W*
97 F17 **Arendal** Aust-Agder, S Norway *58.27N 8.45E*
101 J16 **Arendonk** Antwerpen, N Belgium *51.18N 5.06E*
45 T15 **Arenosa** Panamá, N Panama *9.02N 79.57W*
Arensburg *see* Kuressaare
107 W5 **Arenys de Mar** Cataluña, NE Spain *41.34N 2.33E*
108 C9 **Arenzano** Liguria, NW Italy *44.25N 8.43E*
117 F22 **Areópoli** *prev.* Areópolis. Pelopónnisos, S Greece *36.39N 22.24E*
Areópolis *see* Areópoli
59 H18 **Arequipa** Arequipa, SE Peru *16.24S 71.33W*
59 G17 **Arequipa** *off.* Departamento de Arequipa. ◐ *department* SW Peru
63 B19 **Arequito** Santa Fe, C Argentina *33.09S 61.28W*
106 M7 **Arévalo** Castilla-León, N Spain *41.04N 4.43W*
108 H12 **Arezzo** *anc.* Arretium. Toscana, C Italy *43.28N 11.49E*
107 Q4 **Arga** ≈ N Spain
Argaeus *see* Erciyes Dağı
117 G17 **Argalastí** Thessalía, C Greece *39.13N 23.14E*
107 O10 **Argamasilla de Alba** Castilla-La Mancha, C Spain *39.07N 3.04W*
164 L8 **Argan** Xinjiang Uygur Zizhiqu, NW China *40.09N 88.16E*
107 O8 **Arganda** Madrid, C Spain *40.19N 3.25W*
106 H8 **Arganil** Coimbra, N Portugal *40.13N 8.03W*
179 Qq14 **Argao** Cebu, C Philippines *9.52N 123.33E*
159 V15 **Argartala** Tripura, NE India
126 K9 **Arga-Sala** ≈ NE Russian Federation
105 P17 **Argelès-sur-Mer** Pyrénées-Orientales, S France *42.33N 3.01E*
105 T15 **Argens** ≈ SE France
108 H9 **Argenta** Emilia-Romagna, N Italy *44.37N 11.49E*
104 K5 **Argentan** Orne, N France *48.45N 0.01W*
105 N12 **Argentat** Corrèze, C France *45.06N 1.57E*
108 A9 **Argentera** Piemonte, NE Italy *44.25N 6.57E*
105 N5 **Argenteuil** Val-d'Oise, N France *48.57N 2.13E*
64 K13 **Argentina** *off.* Republic of Argentina. ◆ *republic* S South America
Argentina Basin *see* Argentine Basin
Argentine Abyssal Plain *see* Argentine Plain
67 I19 **Argentine Basin** *var.* Argentina Basin. *undersea feature* SW Atlantic Ocean
67 I20 **Argentine Plain** *var.* Argentine Abyssal Plain. *undersea feature* SW Atlantic Ocean
Argentine Rise *see* Falkland Plateau
65 H22 **Argentino, Lago** ◎ S Argentina
104 K8 **Argenton-Château** Deux-Sèvres, W France *46.59N 0.22W*
104 M9 **Argenton-sur-Creuse** Indre, C France *46.34N 1.32E*
Argentoratum *see* Strasbourg
118 I12 **Argeș** ◐ *county* S Romania
118 K14 **Argeș** ≈ S Romania
155 O8 **Arghandāb, Daryā-ye** ≈ SE Afghanistan
Arghastān *see* Arghestān
155 O8 **Arghestān** *Pash.* Arghastān. ≈ SE Afghanistan
Argirocastro *see* Gjirokastër
82 E7 **Argo** Northern, N Sudan *19.31N 30.25E*
181 P7 **Argo Fracture Zone** *tectonic feature* C Indian Ocean
117 F20 **Argolikós Kólpos** *gulf* S Greece
105 R4 **Argonne** *physical region* NE France
174 Mm15 **Argopuro, Gunung** ▲ Jawa, S Indonesia *7.57S 113.32E*
117 F20 **Árgos** Pelopónnisos, S Greece *37.38N 22.42E*
145 S1 **Argōsh** N Iraq *37.07N 44.13E*
117 D14 **Árgos Orestikó** Dytikí Makedonía, N Greece *40.27N 21.15E*
117 B19 **Argostóli** *var.* Argostólion. Kefallinía, Iónioi Nísoi, Greece, C Mediterranean Sea *38.10N 20.29E*
Argostólion *see* Argostóli
Argovie *see* Aargau
37 O14 **Arguello, Point** *headland* California, W USA *34.34N 120.39W*
131 P16 **Argun** Chechenskaya Respublika, SW Russian Federation *43.16N 45.53E*
163 T2 **Argun** *Chin.* Ergun He, *Rus.* Argun'. ≈ China/Russian Federation
79 T12 **Argungu** Kebbi, NW Nigeria *12.45N 4.24E*
168 J9 **Arguut** Övörhangay, C Mongolia *45.27N 102.25E*
189 N3 **Argyle, Lake** *salt lake* Western Australia
98 G12 **Argyll** *cultural region* W Scotland, UK
Argyrokastron *see* Gjirokastër
168 I7 **Arhangay** ◐ *province* C Mongolia
Arhangelos *see* Archángelos
97 P14 **Arholma** Stockholm, C Sweden *59.51N 19.01E*
97 G22 **Århus** *var.* Aarhus. Århus, C Denmark *56.09N 10.10E*
97 G22 **Århus** ◐ *county* C Denmark
145 T1 **Ārī** E Iraq *37.07N 44.34E*
194 M12 **Aria** ≈ New Britain, E PNG
Aria *see* Herāt
170 C13 **Ariake-kai** *bay* NE East China Sea
85 F22 **Ariamsvlei** Karas, SE Namibia *28.07S 19.49E*
109 L17 **Ariano Irpino** Campania, S Italy *41.08N 15.00E*
56 F11 **Ariari, Río** ≈ C Colombia
157 K19 **Ari Atoll** *atoll* C Maldives
79 P11 **Aribinda** N Burkina *14.12N 0.50W*
64 G2 **Arica** *hist.* San Marcos de Arica. Tarapacá, N Chile *18.30S 70.18W*
56 H16 **Arica** Amazonas, S Colombia *2.09S 71.48W*
64 G2 **Arica** ✈ Tarapacá, N Chile *18.30S 70.19W*
170 G16 **Arida** Wakayama, Honshū, SW Japan *34.05N 135.07E*
116 E13 **Aridaía** *var.* Aridea, Aridhaía. Dytikí Makedonía, N Greece *40.58N 22.04E*
Aridea *see* Aridaía
180 I15 **Aride, Île** *island* Inner Islands, NE Seychelles
Aridhaía *see* Aridaía
105 N17 **Ariège** ◐ *department* S France
104 M16 **Ariège** *var.* la Riege. ≈ Andorra/France
118 H11 **Arieș** ≈ W Romania
155 U10 **Ārifwāla** Punjab, E Pakistan *30.14N 73.04E*
Ariguaní *see* El Difícil
144 G11 **Arīhā** Al Karak, W Jordan *31.25N 35.46E*
144 I3 **Arīḥā** *var.* Arīhā. Idlib, W Syria *35.49N 36.36E*
Arīḥā *see* Jericho
39 W4 **Arikaree River** ≈ Colorado/Nebraska, C USA
170 Bb12 **Arikawa** Nagasaki, Nakadōri-jima, SW Japan *32.58N 129.06E*
114 L13 **Arilje** Serbia, W Yugoslavia *43.45N 20.06E*
47 U14 **Arima** Trinidad, Trinidad and Tobago *10.38N 61.16W*
Arime *see* Al 'Arīmah
Ariminum *see* Rimini
61 H16 **Arinos, Rio** ≈ W Brazil
42 M14 **Ario de Rosales** *var.* Ario de Rosáles. Michoacán de Ocampo, SW Mexico *19.12N 101.43W*
120 F12 **Ariogala** Raseiniai, C Lithuania *55.16N 23.30E*
49 T7 **Aripuanã** ≈ W Brazil
61 E15 **Ariquemes** Rondônia, W Brazil *9.55S 63.06W*
124 Rr15 **'Arîsh, Wâdi el** ≈ NE Egypt
56 K6 **Arismendi** Barinas, C Venezuela *8.28N 68.22W*
8 J14 **Aristazabal Island** *island* SW Canada
62 F13 **Aristóbulo del Valle** Misiones, NE Argentina *27.09S 54.54W*
180 I5 **Arivonimamo** ✈ (Antananarivo) Antananarivo, C Madagascar *19.00S 47.11E*
Arixang *see* Wenquan
107 Q6 **Ariza** Aragón, NE Spain *41.19N 2.03W*
64 I6 **Arizaro, Salar de** *salt lake* NW Argentina
64 K13 **Arizona** San Luis, C Argentina *35.43S 65.16W*
38 J12 **Arizona** *off.* State of Arizona; also known as Copper State, Grand Canyon State. ◐ *state* SW USA
42 G4 **Arizpe** Sonora, NW Mexico *30.19N 110.11W*
97 J16 **Årjäng** Värmland, C Sweden *59.24N 12.09E*
149 P8 **Arjenān** Yazd, C Iran *32.19N 53.48E*
94 I13 **Arjeplog** Norrbotten, N Sweden *66.04N 18.00E*
56 E5 **Arjona** Bolívar, N Colombia *10.13N 75.22W*
107 N13 **Arjona** Andalucía, S Spain *37.55N 4.04W*
127 N11 **Arka** Khabarovskiy Kray, E Russian Federation *60.04N 142.17E*
24 L2 **Arkabutla Lake** ⊡ Mississippi, S USA
131 O7 **Arkadak** Saratovskaya Oblast', W Russian Federation *51.55N 43.29E*
29 T13 **Arkadelphia** Arkansas, C USA *34.07N 93.03W*
117 J25 **Arkalochóri** *prev.* Arkalohori, Arkalokhórion. Kríti, Greece, E Mediterranean Sea *35.09N 25.15E*
Arkalohori/Arkalokhórion *see* Arkalochóri
151 O10 **Arkalyk** *Kaz.* Arqalyq. Kostanay, N Kazakhstan *50.15N 66.52E*
29 U10 **Arkansas** *off.* State of Arkansas; also known as The Land of Opportunity. ◐ *state* S USA
29 W14 **Arkansas City** Arkansas, C USA *33.36N 91.12W*
29 O7 **Arkansas City** Kansas, C USA *37.03N 97.02W*
18 Kk10 **Arkansas River** ≈ C USA
190 J5 **Arkaroola** South Australia *30.21S 139.20E*
Arkhángelos *see* Archángelos
128 L8 **Arkhangel'sk** *Eng.* Archangel. Arkhangel'skaya Oblast', NW Russian Federation *64.31N 40.40E*
128 L9 **Arkhangel'skaya Oblast'** ◐ *province* NW Russian Federation
131 O14 **Arkhangel'skoye** Stavropol'skiy Kray, SW Russian Federation *44.37N 44.03E*
127 N16 **Arkhara** Amurskaya Oblast', S Russian Federation *49.20N 130.04E*
99 G19 **Arklow** *Ir.* An tInbhear Mór. SE Ireland *52.48N 6.09W*
117 M20 **Arkoí** *island* Dodekánisos, Greece, Aegean Sea
29 R11 **Arkoma** Oklahoma, C USA *35.19N 94.27W*
102 O7 **Arkona, Kap** *headland* NE Germany *54.40N 13.24E*
97 N17 **Arkösund** Östergötland, S Sweden *58.28N 16.55E*
126 H4 **Arkticheskogo Instituta, Ostrova** *island* N Russian Federation
97 O15 **Arlanda** ✈ (Stockholm) Stockholm, C Sweden *59.40N 17.58E*
152 C11 **Arlan, Gora** ▲ W Turkmenistan *39.39N 54.28E*
107 O5 **Arlanza** ≈ N Spain
107 N5 **Arlanzón** ≈ N Spain
105 R15 **Arles** *var.* Arles-sur-Rhône; *anc.* Arelas, Arelate. Bouches-du-Rhône, SE France *43.40N 4.37E*
Arles-sur-Rhône *see* Arles
105 O17 **Arles-sur-Tech** Pyrénées-Orientales, S France *42.27N 2.37E*
31 U9 **Arlington** Minnesota, N USA *44.36N 94.04W*
31 R15 **Arlington** Nebraska, C USA *41.27N 96.21W*
34 J11 **Arlington** Oregon, NW USA *45.43N 120.10W*
31 R10 **Arlington** South Dakota, N USA *44.21N 97.07W*
22 E10 **Arlington** Tennessee, S USA *35.17N 89.40W*
27 T6 **Arlington** Texas, SW USA *32.43N 97.04W*
23 W4 **Arlington** Virginia, NE USA *38.54N 77.09W*
34 H7 **Arlington** Washington, NW USA *48.12N 122.07W*
32 M10 **Arlington Heights** Illinois, N USA *42.08N 88.03W*
79 U8 **Arlit** Agadez, C Niger *18.54N 7.25E*
101 L24 **Arlon** *Dut.* Aarlen, *Ger.* Arel; *Lat.* Orolaunum. Luxembourg, SE Belgium *49.40N 5.49E*
29 R7 **Arma** Kansas, C USA *37.32N 94.42W*
99 F16 **Armagh** *Ir.* Ard Mhacha. S Northern Ireland, UK *54.15N 6.33W*
99 F16 **Armagh** *cultural region* S Northern Ireland, UK
104 K15 **Armagnac** *cultural region* S France
105 Q7 **Armançon** ≈ C France
62 K10 **Armando Laydner, Represa** ⊡ S Brazil
117 M24 **Armathía** *island* SE Greece
130 M14 **Armavir** Krasnodarskiy Kray, SW Russian Federation *44.59N 41.07E*
56 E10 **Armenia** Quindío, W Colombia *4.31N 75.40W*
143 T12 **Armenia** *off.* Republic of Armenia, *var.* Ajastan, *Arm.* Hayastani Hanrapetut'yun; *prev.* Armenian Soviet Socialist Republic. ◆ *republic* SW Asia
Armenierstadt *see* Gherla
105 O1 **Armentières** Nord, N France *50.40N 2.52E*
42 K14 **Armería** Colima, SW Mexico *18.55N 103.55W*
191 T5 **Armidale** New South Wales, SE Australia *30.31S 151.40E*
31 P11 **Armour** South Dakota, N USA *43.19N 98.21W*
63 B18 **Armstrong** Santa Fe, C Argentina *32.46S 61.39W*
9 N16 **Armstrong** British Columbia, SW Canada *50.27N 119.13W*
10 D11 **Armstrong** Ontario, S Canada *50.19N 89.01W*
31 U11 **Armstrong** Iowa, C USA *43.24N 94.28W*
27 S16 **Armstrong** Texas, SW USA *26.55N 97.47W*
119 S11 **Armyans'k** *Rus.* Armyansk. Respublika Krym, S Ukraine *46.05N 33.43E*
117 H14 **Arnaía** *var.* Arnea. Kentrikí Makedonía, N Greece *40.30N 23.36E*
123 Mm3 **Arnaoúti, Akrotíri** *var.* Arnaoútis, Cape Arnaouti. *headland* W Cyprus *35.06N 32.16E*
Arnaouti, Cape/Arnaoútis *see* Arnaoúti, Akrotíri
10 L4 **Arnaud** ≈ Quebec, E Canada
105 Q8 **Arnay-le-Duc** Côte d'Or, C France *47.08N 4.27E*
Arnea *see* Arnaía
107 Q4 **Arnedo** La Rioja, N Spain *42.13N 2.04W*
97 I14 **Årnes** Akershus, S Norway *60.07N 11.28E*
95 E15 **Årnes** Sør-Trøndelag, S Norway *63.58N 10.12E*
28 K9 **Arnett** Oklahoma, C USA *36.07N 99.46W*
100 L12 **Arnhem** Gelderland, SE Netherlands *51.58N 5.54E*
189 Q2 **Arnhem Land** *physical region* Northern Territory, N Australia
108 F11 **Arno** ≈ C Italy
Arņo *see* Arno Atoll
201 W7 **Arno Atoll** *var.* Arņo. *atoll* Ratak Chain, NE Marshall Islands
190 H8 **Arno Bay** South Australia *33.55S 136.31E*
37 Q8 **Arnold** California, W USA *38.15N 120.19W*
29 X5 **Arnold** Missouri, C USA *38.25N 90.22W*
31 N15 **Arnold** Nebraska, C USA *41.25N 100.11W*
111 R10 **Arnoldstein** *Slvn.* Pod Klošter. Kärnten, S Austria *46.34N 13.43E*
105 N9 **Arnon** ≈ C France
47 P14 **Arnos Vale** ✈ (Kingstown) Saint Vincent, SE Saint Vincent and the Grenadines *13.08N 61.13W*
94 I8 **Arnøy** *island* N Norway
12 L12 **Arnprior** Ontario, SE Canada *45.31N 76.11W*
103 G15 **Arnsberg** Nordrhein-Westfalen, W Germany *51.24N 8.04E*

◆ Country
● Country Capital
◇ Dependent Territory
○ Dependent Territory Capital
◐ Administrative Region
✈ International Airport
▲ Mountain
▲▲ Mountain Range
⛰ Volcano
≈ River
◎ Lake
⊡ Reservoir

ARNSTADT – ATIKOKAN

103 K16 **Arnstadt** Thüringen, C Germany 50.49N 10.57E
Arnswalde *see* Choszczno
56 K5 **Aroa** Yaracuy, N Venezuela 10.25N 68.54W
85 E21 **Aroab** Karas, SE Namibia 26.47S 19.37E
117 E19 **Ároania** ▲ S Greece
203 O6 **Aroa, Pointe** *headland* Moorea, W French Polynesia 17.27S 149.45W
Aroe Islands *see* Aru, Kepulauan
103 H15 **Arolsen** Niedersachsen, C Germany 51.23N 9.00E
108 C7 **Arona** Piemonte, NE Italy 45.45N 8.33E
21 R3 **Aroostook River** ↝ Canada/USA
Arop Island *see* Long Island
40 M12 **Aropuk Lake** ◎ Alaska, USA
203 P4 **Arorae** *atoll* Tungaru, W Kiribati
202 G16 **Arorangi** Rarotonga, S Cook Islands 21.13S 159.49W
110 I9 **Arosa** Graubünden, S Switzerland 46.48N 9.42E
106 F4 **Arousa, Ría de** *estuary* E Atlantic Ocean
176 Uu16 **Aro Usu, Tanjung** *headland* Pulau Selaru, SE Indonesia 8.19S 130.45E
192 P8 **Arowhana** ▲ North Island, NZ 38.07S 177.52E
143 V12 **Arp'a Az.** Arpaçay. ↝ Armenia/Azerbaijan
143 S11 **Arpaçay** Kars, NE Turkey 40.51N 43.19E
Arpaçay *see* Arp'a
Arqalyq *see* Arkalyk
155 N14 **Arra** ↝ SW Pakistan
Arrabona *see* Győr
Arrah *see* Āra
Ar Rahad *see* Er Rahad
145 R9 **Ar Raḥḥālīyah** C Iraq 32.53N 43.21E
62 Q10 **Arraial do Cabo** Rio de Janeiro, SE Brazil 22.57S 42.00W
106 H11 **Arraiolos** Évora, S Portugal 38.43N 7.58W
145 R8 **Ar Ramādī** *var.* Ramadi, Rumadiya. SW Iraq 33.27N 43.19E
144 J6 **Ar Rāmī** Ḥimṣ, C Syria 34.32N 37.54E
Ar Rams *see* Rams
144 H9 **Ar Ramthā** *var.* Ramtha. Irbid, N Jordan 32.34N 36.00E
98 H13 **Arran, Isle of** *island* SW Scotland, UK
144 L3 **Ar Raqqah** *var.* Rakka; *anc.* Nicephorium. Ar Raqqah, N Syria 35.57N 39.03E
144 L3 **Ar Raqqah** *off.* Muḥāfaẓat al Raqqah, *var.* Raqqah, *Fr.* Rakka. ◆ *governorate* N Syria
105 O2 **Arras** *anc.* Nemetocenna. Pas-de-Calais, N France 50.16N 2.46E
Arrasate *see* Mondragón
144 G12 **Ar Rashādīyah** Aṭ Ṭafīlah, W Jordan 30.42N 35.37E
144 I5 **Ar Rastān** *var.* Rastâne. Ḥimṣ, W Syria 34.57N 36.43E
145 X12 **Ar Raṭāwī** E Iraq 30.37N 47.12E
104 L15 **Arrats** ↝ S France
147 N10 **Ar Rawḍah** Makkah, S Saudi Arabia 21.19N 42.48E
147 Q15 **Ar Rawḍah** S Yemen 14.26N 47.13E
148 K11 **Ar Rawḍatayn** *var.* Raudhatain. N Kuwait 29.52N 47.42E
149 N16 **Ar Rayyān** *var.* Al Rayyan. C Qatar 25.18N 51.24E
104 L17 **Arreau** Hautes-Pyrénées, S France 42.55N 0.21E
66 Q11 **Arrecife** *var.* Arrecife de Lanzarote, Puerto Arrecife. Lanzarote, Islas Canarias, NE Atlantic Ocean 28.57N 13.33W
Arrecife de Lanzarote *see* Arrecife
45 P6 **Arrecife Edinburgh** *reef* NE Nicaragua
63 C19 **Arrecifes** Buenos Aires, E Argentina 34.06S 60.09W
104 F6 **Arrée, Monts d'** ▲ NW France
Ar Refa'i *see* Ar Rifā'ī
Arretium *see* Arezzo
Arriaca *see* Guadalajara
111 S9 **Arriach** Kärnten, S Austria 46.43N 13.52E
43 T16 **Arriaga** Chiapas, SE Mexico 16.13N 93.54W
43 N12 **Arriaga** San Luis Potosí, C Mexico 21.55N 101.22W
145 W10 **Ar Rifā'ī** *var.* Ar Refā'ī. SE Iraq 31.46N 46.07E
145 V12 **Ar Riḥāb** *salt flat* S Iraq
106 L2 **Arriondas** Asturias, N Spain 43.22N 5.10W
147 Q7 **Ar Riyāḍ** *Eng.* Riyadh. ● (Saudi Arabia) Ar Riyāḍ, C Saudi Arabia 24.49N 46.49E
147 O8 **Ar Riyāḍ** *off.* Minṭaqat ar Riyāḍ. ◆ *province* C Saudi Arabia
147 S15 **Ar Riyān** S Yemen 14.43N 49.18E
Arrö *see* Ærø
63 H18 **Arroio Grande** Rio Grande do Sul, S Brazil 32.15S 53.02W
104 K15 **Arros** ↝ S France
105 Q9 **Arroux** ↝ C France
27 R5 **Arrowhead, Lake** ⊠ Texas, SW USA
190 L5 **Arrowsmith, Mount** *hill* New South Wales, SE Australia 30.07S 141.37E
193 D21 **Arrowtown** Otago, South Island, NZ 44.57S 168.51E
63 D17 **Arroyo Barú** Entre Ríos, E Argentina 31.52S 58.25W
106 J10 **Arroyo de la Luz** Extremadura, W Spain 39.28N 6.36W
65 J16 **Arroyo de la Ventana** Río Negro, SE Argentina 41.41S 66.03W
37 P13 **Arroyo Grande** California, W USA 35.07N 120.35W
Ar Ru'ays *see* Ar Ruways
147 R11 **Ar Rub' al Khālī** *Eng.* Empty Quarter, Great Sandy Desert. *desert* SW Asia
145 V13 **Ar Ruḍaymah** S Iraq 30.19N 45.25E
63 A16 **Arrufó** Santa Fe, C Argentina 30.15S 61.45W
144 I7 **Ar Ruḥaybah** *var.* Ruhaybeh, *Fr.* Rouhaibé. Dimashq, W Syria 33.45N 36.40E
145 V15 **Ar Rukhaymīyah** *well* S Iraq 29.22N 45.43E
145 U11 **Ar Rumaythah** *var.* Rumaitha. S Iraq 31.31N 45.15E
147 X8 **Ar Rustāq** *var.* Rostak, Rustaq. N Oman 23.34N 57.25E
145 N8 **Ar Ruṭbah** *var.* Rutba. SW Iraq 33.03N 40.16E
146 M3 **Ar Rūthīyah** *spring/well* NW Saudi Arabia 31.18N 41.23E
ar-Ruwaida *see* Ar Ruwayḍah
147 O8 **Ar Ruwayḍah** *var.* ar-Ruwaida. Jīzān, C Saudi Arabia 23.48N 44.44E
149 N15 **Ar Ruways** *var.* Al Ruweis, Ar Ru'ays, Ruwais. N Qatar 26.07N 51.13E
149 O17 **Ar Ruways** *var.* Ar Ru'ays, Ruwaisv. Abū Ẓaby, W UAE 24.09N 52.57E
97 G21 **Års** *var.* Aars. Nordjylland, N Denmark 56.49N 9.31E
Arsanias *see* Murat Nehri
127 Nn18 **Arsen'yev** Primorskiy Kray, SE Russian Federation 44.09N 133.28E
161 G19 **Arsikere** Karnātaka, W India 13.18N 76.15E
131 R3 **Arsk** Respublika Tatarstan, W Russian Federation 56.07N 49.54E
96 N10 **Årskogen** Gävleborg, C Sweden 62.07N 17.19E
124 N3 **Ársos** C Cyprus 34.51N 32.46E
96 N13 **Årsunda** Gävleborg, C Sweden 60.31N 16.45E
Arta *see* Árachthos
117 C17 **Árta** *anc.* Ambracia. Ípeiros, W Greece 39.07N 20.59E
143 T12 **Artashat** S Armenia 39.57N 44.34E
42 M15 **Arteaga** Michoacán de Ocampo, SW Mexico 18.20N 102.18W
127 Nn18 **Artem** Primorskiy Kray, SE Russian Federation 43.24N 132.20E
46 C4 **Artemisa** La Habana, W Cuba 22.49N 82.46W
119 W7 **Artemivs'k** Donets'ka Oblast', E Ukraine 48.35N 37.58E
126 I14 **Artemovsk** Krasnoyarskiy Kray, S Russian Federation 54.22N 93.24E
126 Kk13 **Artemovskiy** Irkutskaya Oblast', C Russian Federation 58.15N 114.51E
125 Ee13 **Artemovskiy** Sverdlovskaya Oblast', C Russian Federation 57.22N 61.55E
107 U5 **Artesa de Segre** Cataluña, NE Spain 41.54N 1.03E
39 U14 **Artesia** New Mexico, SW USA 32.50N 104.24W
27 Q14 **Artesia Wells** Texas, SW USA 28.13N 99.18W
110 G8 **Arth** Schwyz, C Switzerland 47.05N 8.39E
12 F15 **Arthur** Ontario, S Canada 43.49N 80.31W
32 M14 **Arthur** Illinois, N USA 39.42N 88.28W
30 L14 **Arthur** Nebraska, C USA 41.32N 101.42W
31 Q5 **Arthur** North Dakota, N USA 47.03N 97.12W
193 B21 **Arthur** ↝ South Island, NZ
20 B13 **Arthur, Lake** ⊠ Pennsylvania, NE USA
191 N15 **Arthur River** ↝ Tasmania, SE Australia
193 G18 **Arthur's Pass** Canterbury, South Island, NZ 42.59S 171.33E
193 G17 **Arthur's Pass** *pass* South Island, NZ 42.57S 171.36E
46 I3 **Arthur's Town** Cat Island, C Bahamas 24.34N 75.39W
46 M9 **Artibonite, Rivière de l'** ↝ C Haiti
63 E16 **Artigas** *prev.* San Eugenio, San Eugenio del Cuareim. Artigas, N Uruguay 30.25S 56.28W
63 E16 **Artigas** ◆ *department* N Uruguay
204 H1 **Artigas** *Uruguayan research station* Antarctica 61.57S 58.23W
143 T11 **Art'ik** W Armenia 40.38N 43.57E
197 G4 **Art, Île** *island* Îles Belep, W New Caledonia
105 O2 **Artois** *cultural region* N France
142 L12 **Artova** Tokat, N Turkey 40.06N 36.18E
107 Y9 **Artrutx, Cap d'** *var.* Cabo Dartuch. *headland* Menorca, Spain, W Mediterranean Sea 39.55N 3.49E
Artsiz *see* Artsyz
119 N11 **Artsyz** *Rus.* Artsiz. Odes'ka Oblast', SW Ukraine 45.58N 29.25E
164 E7 **Artux** Xinjiang Uygur Zizhiqu, NW China 39.45N 76.09E
143 R11 **Artvin** Artvin, NE Turkey 41.12N 41.48E
143 R11 **Artvin** ◆ *province* NE Turkey
152 G14 **Artyk** Akhalskiy Velayat, C Turkmenistan 37.32N 59.16E
81 Q16 **Aru** Orientale, NE Dem. Rep. Congo (Zaire) 2.52N 30.49E
106 I4 **A Rúa** *var.* La Rúa. Galicia, NW Spain 42.22N 7.12W
83 E17 **Arua** NW Uganda 3.01N 30.55E
Aruângua *see* Luangwa
47 O15 **Aruba** *var.* Oruba. ◇ *Dutch autonomous region* S West Indies
49 Q4 **Aruba** *island* Aruba, Lesser Antilles
Aru Islands *see* Aru, Kepulauan
176 Ww14 **Aru, Kepulauan** *Eng.* Aru Islands; *prev.* Aroe Islands. *island group* E Indonesia
159 W10 **Arunāchal Pradesh** *prev.* North East Frontier Agency, North East Frontier Agency of Assam. ◆ *state* NE India
169 U7 **Arun Qi** Nei Mongol Zizhiqu, N China 48.05N 123.28E
161 H23 **Aruppukkottai** Tamil Nādu, SE India 9.31N 78.03E
176 Ww9 **Aruri, Selat** *strait* Irian Jaya, E Indonesia
83 I20 **Arusha** Arusha, N Tanzania 3.22S 36.40E
83 I21 **Arusha** ◆ *region* E Tanzania
83 I20 **Arusha** ✕ Arusha, N Tanzania 3.26S 37.07E
56 C9 **Arusí, Punta** *headland* NW Colombia 5.36N 77.30W
174 Ll10 **Arut, Sungai** ↝ Borneo, C Indonesia
161 J23 **Aruvi Aru** ↝ NW Sri Lanka
81 M17 **Aruwimi** *var.* Ituri (upper course). ↝ NE Dem. Rep. Congo (Zaire)
Árva *see* Orava
39 T4 **Arvada** Colorado, C USA 39.48N 105.06W
Arvand Rūd *see* 'Arab, Shaṭṭ al
168 J8 **Arvayheer** Övörhangay, C Mongolia 46.13N 102.47E
15 L8 **Arviat** *prev.* Eskimo Point. Nunavut, C Canada 61.10N 94.15W
95 I14 **Arvidsjaur** Norrbotten, N Sweden 65.34N 19.12E
97 J15 **Arvika** Värmland, C Sweden 59.40N 12.37E
94 J8 **Årviksand** Troms, N Norway 70.10N 20.30E
37 S13 **Arvin** California, W USA 35.12N 118.52W
151 P7 **Arykbalyk** *Kaz.* Aryqbalyq. Severnyy Kazakhstan, N Kazakhstan 53.00N 68.11E
Aryqbalyq *see* Arykbalyk
151 P17 **Arys'** *Kaz.* Arys. Yuzhnyy Kazakhstan, S Kazakhstan 42.25N 68.49E
Arys *see* Orzysz
Arys Köli *see* Arys, Ozero
151 O14 **Arys, Ozero** *Kaz.* Arys Köli. ◎ C Kazakhstan
109 D16 **Arzachena** Sardegna, Italy, C Mediterranean Sea 41.05N 9.21E
131 O4 **Arzamas** Nizhegorodskaya Oblast', W Russian Federation 55.25N 43.51E
147 V13 **Arzāt** S Oman 17.03N 54.19E
106 H3 **Arzúa** Galicia, NW Spain 42.55N 8.10W
113 A16 **Aš** *Ger.* Asch. Karlovarský Kraj, W Czech Republic 50.12N 12.12E
97 H15 **Ås** Akershus, S Norway 59.39N 10.48E
97 H20 **Aså** Nordjylland, N Denmark 57.07N 10.24E
85 E21 **Asab** Karas, S Namibia 25.28S 17.58E
79 U16 **Asaba** Delta, S Nigeria 6.10N 6.44E
155 S4 **Asadābād** *var.* Asaḍābād; *prev.* Chaghasarāy. Kunar, E Afghanistan 34.52N 71.09E
144 K3 **Asad, Buḥayrat al** ◎ N Syria
65 H20 **Asador, Pampa del** *plain* S Argentina
171 Kk17 **Asahi** Chiba, Honshū, S Japan 36.08N 140.37E
171 J13 **Asahi** Toyama, Honshū, SW Japan 36.56N 137.34E
172 Pp5 **Asahi-dake** ▲ Hokkaidō, N Japan 43.42N 142.50E
170 Ff13 **Asahi-gawa** ↝ Honshū, SW Japan
172 P5 **Asahikawa** Hokkaidō, N Japan 43.46N 142.22E
153 S10 **Asaka** *Rus.* Assake; *prev.* Leninsk. Andijon Wiloyati, E Uzbekistan 40.39N 72.16E
79 P17 **Asamankese** SE Ghana 5.46N 0.41W
171 Jj15 **Asama-yama** ▲ Honshū, S Japan 36.25N 138.34E
196 B15 **Asan** W Guam 13.28N 144.43E
196 B15 **Asan Point** *headland* W Guam
159 R15 **Āsānsol** West Bengal, NE India 23.40N 86.58E
82 K12 **Āsayita** Afar, NE Ethiopia 11.35N 41.23E
176 V9 **Asbakin** Irian Jaya, E Indonesia 0.45S 131.40E
Asben *see* Aïr, Massif de l'
125 Ee11 **Asbest** Sverdlovskaya Oblast', C Russian Federation 57.12N 61.18E
13 Q12 **Asbestos** Quebec, SE Canada 45.46N 71.55W
31 Y13 **Asbury** Iowa, C USA 42.30N 90.45W
20 K15 **Asbury Park** New Jersey, NE USA 40.13N 74.00W
43 Z12 **Ascención, Bahiá de la** *bay* NW Caribbean Sea
42 I3 **Ascensión** Chihuahua, N Mexico 31.07N 107.58W
67 M14 **Ascension Fracture Zone** *tectonic feature* C Atlantic Ocean
67 G14 **Ascension Island** ◇ *dependency of St. Helena* C Atlantic Ocean
67 N16 **Ascension Island** *island* C Atlantic Ocean
Asch *see* Aš
111 S3 **Aschach an der Donau** Oberösterreich, N Austria 48.22N 14.00E
103 H18 **Aschaffenburg** Bayern, SW Germany 49.58N 9.09E
103 F14 **Ascheberg** Nordrhein-Westfalen, W Germany 51.46N 7.36E
103 L14 **Aschersleben** Sachsen-Anhalt, C Germany 51.46N 11.28E
108 G12 **Asciano** Toscana, C Italy 43.15N 11.32E
108 J13 **Ascoli Piceno** *anc.* Asculum Picenum. Marche, C Italy 42.51N 13.34E
109 M17 **Ascoli Satriano** *anc.* Asculub, Ausculum Apulum. Puglia, SE Italy 41.13N 15.31E
110 G11 **Ascona** Ticino, S Switzerland 46.10N 8.45E
Asculub *see* Ascoli Satriano
Asculum Picenum *see* Ascoli Piceno
82 L11 **Aseb** *var.* Assab, *Amh.* Āseb. SE Eritrea 13.03N 42.36E
97 M20 **Åseda** Kronoberg, S Sweden 57.10N 15.19E
131 T6 **Asekeyevo** Orenburgskaya Oblast', W Russian Federation 53.36N 52.53E
194 J13 **Aseki** Morobe, C PNG 7.18S 146.10E
83 J14 **Āsela** *var.* Asella, Aselle, Asselle. Oromo, C Ethiopia 7.55N 39.08E
95 H15 **Åsele** Västerbotten, N Sweden 64.10N 17.19E
Asella/Aselle *see* Āsela
96 K12 **Åsen** Dalarna, C Sweden 61.18N 13.49E
116 J11 **Asenovgrad** *prev.* Stanimaka. Plovdiv, C Bulgaria 42.01N 24.54E
175 Q11 **Asera** Sulawesi, C Indonesia 3.24S 121.42E
97 E17 **Åseral** Vest-Agder, S Norway 58.37N 7.27E
120 J3 **Aseri** *var.* Asserien, *Ger.* Asserin. Ida-Virumaa, NE Estonia 59.28N 26.50E
42 J10 **Aserradero** Durango, W Mexico
97 H16 **Åsgårdstrand** Vestfold, S Norway 59.19N 10.28E
125 E11 **Asha** Chelyabinskaya Oblast', C Russian Federation 55.01N 57.11E
Ashara *see* Al 'Ashārah
25 T6 **Ashburn** Georgia, SE USA 31.42N 83.39W
193 G19 **Ashburton** Canterbury, South Island, NZ 43.55S 171.46E
193 G19 **Ashburton** ↝ South Island, NZ
188 H8 **Ashburton River** ↝ Western Australia
151 V10 **Ashchysu** ↝ E Kazakhstan
8 M16 **Ashcroft** British Columbia, SW Canada 50.40N 121.16W
144 E10 **Ashdod** *anc.* Azotos, *Lat.* Azotus. Central, W Israel 31.48N 34.37E
29 S14 **Ashdown** Arkansas, C USA 33.40N 94.07W
23 T9 **Asheboro** North Carolina, SE USA 35.42N 79.48W
9 X15 **Ashern** Manitoba, S Canada 51.10N 98.22W
23 P10 **Asheville** North Carolina, SE USA 35.36N 82.33W
10 E8 **Asheweig** ↝ Ontario, C Canada
29 V9 **Ash Flat** Arkansas, C USA 36.13N 91.36W
191 T4 **Ashford** New South Wales, SE Australia 29.18S 151.09E
99 P22 **Ashford** SE England, UK 51.09N 0.52E
38 K11 **Ash Fork** Arizona, SW USA 35.12N 112.31W
152 F13 **Ashgabat** *prev.* Ashkhabad, Poltoratsk. ● (Turkmenistan) Akhalskiy Velayat, C Turkmenistan 37.58N 58.22E
152 F13 **Ashgabat** ✕ Akhalskiy Velayat, C Turkmenistan 38.06N 58.10E
29 T7 **Ash Grove** Missouri, C USA 37.19N 93.35W
171 K15 **Ashikaga** *var.* Asikaga. Tochigi, Honshū, S Japan 36.19N 139.26E
171 Mm10 **Ashiro** Iwate, Honshū, C Japan 40.04N 141.00E
170 E16 **Ashizuri-misaki** *headland* Shikoku, SW Japan 32.43N 132.59E
Ashkelon *see* Ashqelon
Ashkhabad *see* Ashgabat
25 Q4 **Ashland** Alabama, S USA 33.16N 85.50W
28 K7 **Ashland** Kansas, C USA 37.11N 99.46W
23 P5 **Ashland** Kentucky, S USA 38.28N 82.39W
21 S2 **Ashland** Maine, NE USA 46.36N 68.24W
24 M1 **Ashland** Mississippi, S USA 34.51N 89.10W
29 U4 **Ashland** Missouri, C USA 38.46N 92.15W
31 S15 **Ashland** Nebraska, C USA 41.01N 96.21W
33 T12 **Ashland** Ohio, N USA 40.52N 82.19W
34 G15 **Ashland** Oregon, NW USA 42.11N 122.42W
23 W6 **Ashland** Virginia, NE USA 37.45N 77.28W
32 K3 **Ashland** Wisconsin, N USA 46.34N 90.54W
22 I8 **Ashland City** Tennessee, S USA 36.16N 87.03W
191 S4 **Ashley** New South Wales, SE Australia 29.21S 149.49E
31 O7 **Ashley** North Dakota, N USA 46.00N 99.22W
181 W7 **Ashmore and Cartier Islands** ◇ *Australian external territory* E Indian Ocean
121 I14 **Ashmyany** *Rus.* Oshmyany. Hrodzyenskaya Voblasts', W Belarus 54.24N 25.57E
20 K12 **Ashokan Reservoir** ⊠ New York, NE USA
172 Pp6 **Ashoro** Hokkaidō, NE Japan 43.16N 143.33E
144 E10 **Ashqelon** *var.* Ashkelon. Southern, C Israel 31.40N 34.34E
Ashraf *see* Behshahr
145 O3 **Ash Shadādah** *var.* Ash Shaddādah, Jisr ash Shadadi, Shaddādī, Shedadi, Tell Shedadi. Al Ḥasakah, NE Syria 36.00N 40.42E
Ash Shaddādah *see* Ash Shadādah
145 Y12 **Ash Shāfī** E Iraq 30.49N 47.30E
145 R4 **Ash Shakk** *var.* Shaykh. C Iraq 35.15N 43.27E
Ash Sham/Ash Shām *see* Dimashq
145 T10 **Ash Shāmīyah** *var.* Shamiya. C Iraq 31.55N 44.37E
145 Y13 **Ash Shāmīyah** *var.* Al Bādiyah al Janūbīyah. *desert* S Iraq
145 T11 **Ash Shanāfīyah** *var.* Ash Shināfīyah. S Iraq 31.34N 44.38E
144 G13 **Ash Sharāh** *var.* Esh Sharā. ▲ W Jordan
149 R16 **Ash Shāriqah** *Eng.* Sharjah. Ash Shāriqah, NE UAE 25.22N 55.28E
149 R16 **Ash Shāriqah** *var.* Sharjah. ✕ Ash Shāriqah, NE UAE 25.19N 55.37E
146 I4 **Ash Sharmah** *var.* Šarma. Tabūk, NW Saudi Arabia 28.01N 35.16E
145 R4 **Ash Sharqāṭ** NW Iraq 35.30N 43.15E
147 S10 **Ash Sharqīyah** *off.* Al Minṭaqah ash Sharqīyah, *Eng.* Eastern Region. ◆ *province* E Saudi Arabia
145 W11 **Ash Shaṭrah** *var.* Shatra. SE Iraq 31.25N 46.10E
144 G13 **Ash Shawbak** Ma'ān, W Jordan 30.31N 35.34E
144 L5 **Ash Shaykh Ibrāhīm** Ḥimṣ, C Syria 35.03N 38.50E
147 O17 **Ash Shaykh 'Uthmān** SW Yemen 12.53N 45.00E
147 S15 **Ash Shiḥr** SE Yemen 14.45N 49.24E
Ash Shināfīyah *see* Ash Shanāfīyah
147 V12 **Ash Shiṣar** *var.* Shisur. SW Oman 18.13N 53.34E
145 S13 **Ash Shubrūm** *well* S Iraq 30.09N 43.59E
147 R10 **Ash Shuqqān** *desert* E Saudi Arabia
77 O9 **Ash Shuwayrif** *var.* Ash Shwayrif. N Libya 29.54N 14.16E
Ash Shwayrif *see* Ash Shuwayrif
33 U10 **Ashtabula** Ohio, N USA 41.54N 80.46W
31 Q5 **Ashtabula, Lake** ⊠ North Dakota, N USA
143 T12 **Ashtarak** W Armenia 40.18N 44.22E
148 M6 **Āshtiān** *var.* Āshtiyān. Markazī, W Iran 34.24N 49.55E
Āshtiyān *see* Āshtiān
35 R13 **Ashton** Idaho, NW USA 44.04N 111.27W
11 O10 **Ashuanipi Lake** ◎ Newfoundland, E Canada
13 P6 **Ashuapmushuan** ↝ Quebec, SE Canada
25 Q3 **Ashville** Alabama, S USA 33.50N 86.15W
33 S14 **Ashville** Ohio, N USA 39.43N 82.57W
32 K3 **Ashwabay, Mount** *hill* Wisconsin, N USA 46.49N 90.57W
176 Uu7 **Asia, Kepulauan** *island group* E Indonesia
160 N13 **Āsika** Orissa, E India 19.37N 84.40E
Asikaga *see* Ashikaga
95 M18 **Asikkala** *var.* Vääksy. Etelä-Suomi, S Finland 61.09N 25.36E
76 G5 **Asilah** N Morocco 35.18N 6.04W
'Aṣī, Nahr al *see* Orontes
109 B16 **Asinara, Isola** *island* W Italy
126 H13 **Asino** Tomskaya Oblast', C Russian Federation 56.56N 86.02E
121 O14 **Asintorf** *Rus.* Osintorf. Vitsyebskaya Voblasts', N Belarus 54.43N 30.35E
121 L17 **Asipovichy** *Rus.* Osipovichi. Mahilyowskaya Voblasts', C Belarus 53.18N 28.40E
147 N12 **'Asīr** *off.* Minṭaqat 'Asīr. ◆ *province* SW Saudi Arabia
146 M11 **'Asīr** *Eng.* Asir. ▲ SW Saudi Arabia
145 X10 **Askal** E Iraq 31.45N 47.07E
143 P13 **Aşkale** Erzurum, NE Turkey 39.56N 40.39E
119 T11 **Askaniya-Nova** Khersons'ka Oblast', S Ukraine 46.27N 33.54E
97 H15 **Asker** Akershus, S Norway 59.49N 10.29E
97 L17 **Askersund** Örebro, C Sweden 58.55N 14.55E
Askī Kalak *see* Eski Kaļak
97 I15 **Askim** Østfold, S Norway 59.34N 11.10E
131 V3 **Askino** Respublika Bashkortostan, W Russian Federation 56.07N 56.39E
117 D14 **Áskio** ▲ N Greece
158 L9 **Askot** Uttar Pradesh, N India 29.43N 80.19E
96 C12 **Askvoll** Sogn og Fjordane, S Norway 61.21N 5.04E
142 A13 **Aslan Burnu** *headland* W Turkey 38.44N 26.43E
142 L16 **Aslantaş Barajı** ⊠ S Turkey
155 S4 **Asmār** *var.* Bar Kunar. Kunar, E Afghanistan 34.58N 71.28E
82 I9 **Asmara** *Amh.* Āsmera. ● (Eritrea) C Eritrea 15.15N 38.57E
Āsmera *see* Asmara
97 L21 **Åsnen** ◎ S Sweden
117 F19 **Asopós** ↝ S Greece
176 X10 **Asori** Irian Jaya, E Indonesia 2.37S 136.06E
82 G12 **Āsosa** Benishangul, W Ethiopia 10.06N 34.27E
34 M10 **Asotin** Washington, NW USA 46.18N 117.03W
Aspadana *see* Eşfahān
Aspang *see* Aspang Markt
111 X6 **Aspang Markt** *var.* Aspang. Niederösterreich, E Austria 47.34N 16.07E
107 S12 **Aspe** País Valenciano, E Spain 38.21N 0.43W
39 R5 **Aspen** Colorado, C USA 39.12N 106.49W
27 P6 **Aspermont** Texas, SW USA 33.07N 100.13W
Asphaltites, Lacus *see* Dead Sea
Aspinwall *see* Colón
193 C20 **Aspiring, Mount** ▲ South Island, NZ 44.21S 168.47E
117 B16 **Asprókavos, Akrotírio** *headland* Kérkyra, Iónioi Nísoi, Greece, C Mediterranean Sea 39.22N 20.07E
Aspropótamos *see* Achelóos
Assab *see* Aseb
78 J10 **Assaba** *var.* Açâba. ◆ *region* S Mauritania
144 L4 **As Sabkhah** *var.* Sabkha. Ar Raqqah, NE Syria 35.30N 35.54E
145 U6 **As Sa'dīyah** E Iraq 34.11N 45.09E
Assad, Lake *see* Asad, Buḥayrat al
144 I8 **Aş Şafā** ▲ S Syria 33.03N 37.07E
144 I10 **Aş Şafāwī** Al Mafraq, N Jordan 37.12N 32.30E
Aş Şaff *see* El Şaff
145 N2 **Aş Şafīḥ** Al Ḥasakah, N Syria 36.42N 40.12E
Aş Şaḥrā' al Gharbīyah *see* Sahara el Gharbîya
Aş Şaḥrā' ash Sharqīyah *see* Sahara el Sharqîya
Assake *see* Asaka
As Salamīyah *see* Salamīyah
147 Q4 **As Sālimī** *var.* Salemy. SW Kuwait 29.07N 46.41E
69 W7 **'Assal, Lac** ◎ C Djibouti
As Sallūm *see* Salûm
145 T13 **As Salmān** S Iraq 30.28N 44.34E
144 G10 **As Salṭ** *var.* Salt. Al Balqā', NW Jordan 32.03N 35.43E
148 M16 **As Salwā** *var.* Salwa, Salwah. S Qatar 24.43N 50.52E
159 V12 **Assam** ◆ *state* NE India
Assamaka *see* Assamakka
79 T8 **Assamakka** *var.* Assamaka. Agadez, NW Niger 19.24N 5.52E
145 U11 **As Samāwah** *var.* Samawa. S Iraq 31.17N 45.06E
As Saqia al Hamra *see* Saguia al Hamra
144 J4 **Aş Şā'rān** Ḥamāh, C Syria 35.15N 37.28E
144 G9 **Aş Şarīḥ** Irbid, N Jordan 32.31N 35.54E
23 Z5 **Assateague Island** *island* Maryland, NE USA
145 O6 **As Sayyāl** *var.* Sayyāl. Dayr az Zawr, E Syria 34.37N 40.52E
101 G18 **Asse** Vlaams Brabant, C Belgium 50.55N 4.12E
101 D16 **Assebroek** West-Vlaanderen, NW Belgium 51.12N 3.16E
Asselle *see* Āsela
109 C20 **Assemini** Sardegna, Italy, C Mediterranean Sea 39.16N 8.58E
100 N7 **Assen** Drenthe, NE Netherlands 53.00N 6.34E
101 E16 **Assenede** Oost-Vlaanderen, NW Belgium 51.15N 3.43E
97 G24 **Assens** Fyn, C Denmark 55.16N 9.54E
Asserien/Asserin *see* Aseri
101 I21 **Assesse** Namur, SE Belgium 50.22N 5.01E
147 Y8 **As Sib** *var.* Seeb. NE Oman 23.40N 58.03E
145 Z13 **As Sibah** *var.* Sibah. SE Iraq 30.13N 47.24E
9 T17 **Assiniboia** Saskatchewan, S Canada 49.39N 105.58W
9 V15 **Assiniboine** ↝ Manitoba, S Canada
9 P16 **Assiniboine, Mount** ▲ Alberta/British Columbia, SW Canada 50.54N 115.43W
Assiout *see* Asyûṭ
62 J9 **Assis** São Paulo, S Brazil 22.37S 50.25W
108 I13 **Assisi** Umbria, C Italy 43.04N 12.36E
Assiut *see* Asyûṭ
Assling *see* Jesenice
Assouan *see* Aswân
Assu *see* Açu
Assuan *see* Aswân
148 K12 **Aş Şubayḥīyah** *var.* Subiyah. S Kuwait 28.55N 47.57E
147 R16 **As Sufāl** S Yemen 14.06N 48.42E
144 L5 **As Sukhnah** *var.* Sukhne, *Fr.* Soukhné. Ḥimṣ, C Syria 34.55N 38.52E
145 U4 **As Sulaymānīyah** *var.* Sulaimaniya, *Kurd.* Slēmānī. NE Iraq 35.31N 45.27E
147 P11 **As Sulayyil** Ar Riyāḍ, S Saudi Arabia 20.28N 45.33E
123 M16 **As Sulṭān** N Libya 31.01N 17.21E
147 Q5 **Aş Şummān** *desert* N Saudi Arabia
147 Q16 **Aş Şurrah** SW Yemen 13.56N 46.23E
145 N4 **Aş Şuwār** *var.* Şuwār. Dayr az Zawr, E Syria 35.31N 40.37E
144 H9 **As Suwaydā'** *var.* El Suweida, Es Suweida, Suweida, *Fr.* Soueida. As Suwaydā', SW Syria 32.43N 36.33E
144 H9 **As Suwaydā'** *off.* Muḥāfaẓat as Suwaydā', *var.* As Suwaydā, Suwaydā, Suweida, *Fr.* Soueida. ◆ *governorate* S Syria
147 Z9 **As Suwayḥ** NE Oman 22.07N 59.42E
147 X8 **As Suwayq** *var.* Suwaik. N Oman 23.51N 57.20E
145 T8 **Aş Şuwayrah** *var.* Suwaira. E Iraq 32.57N 44.46E
As Suways *see* Suez
Asta Colonia *see* Asti
Astacus *see* İzmit
117 M23 **Astakída** *island* SE Greece
151 Q9 **Astana** *prev.* Akmola, Akmolinsk, Tselinograd, Aqmola. ● (Kazakhstan) Akmola, N Kazakhstan 51.12N 71.25E
148 M3 **Āstāneh** Gīlān, NW Iran 37.16N 49.58E
Asta Pompeia *see* Asti
143 Y14 **Astara** S Azerbaijan 38.28N 48.51E
Astarabad *see* Gorgān
101 L15 **Asten** Noord-Brabant, SE Netherlands 51.24N 5.45E
Asterābād *see* Gorgān
108 C8 **Asti** *anc.* Asta Colonia, Asta Pompeia, Hasta Colonia, Hasta Pompeia. Piemonte, NW Italy 44.54N 8.10E
Astigi *see* Ecija
Astipálaia *see* Astypálaia
154 L16 **Astola Island** *island* SW Pakistan
158 H4 **Astor** Jammu and Kashmir, NW India 35.21N 74.52E
106 K4 **Astorga** *anc.* Asturica Augusta. Castilla-León, N Spain 42.27N 6.04W
34 F10 **Astoria** Oregon, NW USA 46.12N 123.49W
(0) F8 **Astoria Fan** *undersea feature* E Pacific Ocean
97 J22 **Åstorp** Skåne, S Sweden 56.09N 12.57E
Astrabad *see* Gorgān
131 Q13 **Astrakhan'** Astrakhanskaya Oblast', SW Russian Federation 46.20N 48.00E
Astrakhan-Bazar *see* Cälilabad
131 Q11 **Astrakhanskaya Oblast'** ◆ *province* SW Russian Federation
95 J15 **Åsträsk** Västerbotten, N Sweden 64.38N 20.00E
Astrida *see* Butare
67 O22 **Astrid Ridge** *undersea feature* S Atlantic Ocean
194 J11 **Astrolabe Bay** *inlet* N PNG
197 I4 **Astrolabe, Récifs de l'** *reef* C New Caledonia
124 Nn3 **Astromerítis** N Cyprus 35.09N 33.02E
117 F20 **Ástros** Pelopónnisos, S Greece 37.24N 22.43E
121 G16 **Astryna** *Rus.* Ostryna. Hrodzyenskaya Voblasts', W Belarus 53.44N 24.33E
106 J2 **Asturias** ◆ *autonomous community* NW Spain
Asturias *see* Oviedo
Asturica Augusta *see* Astorga
117 L22 **Astypálaia** *var.* Astipálaia, *It.* Stampalia. *island* Kykládes, Greece, Aegean Sea
198 Aa8 **Āsuisui, Cape** *headland* Savai'i, W Samoa 13.43S 172.28W
205 S2 **Asuka** *Japanese research station* Antarctica 71.49S 23.52E
64 O6 **Asunción** ● (Paraguay) Central, S Paraguay 25.16S 57.36W
64 O6 **Asunción** ✕ Central, S Paraguay 25.15S 57.40W
196 K3 **Asunción Island** *island* N Northern Mariana Islands
44 E6 **Asunción Mita** Jutiapa, SE Guatemala 14.19N 89.42W
Asunción Nochixtlán *see* Nochixtlán
42 E3 **Asunción, Río** ↝ NW Mexico
97 M18 **Åsunden** ◎ S Sweden
120 K11 **Asveyskaye Vozyera** *Rus.* Osveya. Vitsyebskaya Voblasts', N Belarus 56.00N 28.05E
Aswa *see* Achwa
77 X11 **Aswân** *var.* Assouan, Assuan; *anc.* Syene. SE Egypt 24.03N 32.58E
77 X11 **Aswân High Dam** *dam* SE Egypt 23.54N 32.51E
77 W9 **Asyûṭ** *var.* Assiout, Assiut, Siut; *anc.* Lycopolis. C Egypt 27.05N 31.10E
200 R15 **Ata** *island* Tongatapu Group, SW Tonga
64 G8 **Atacama** *off.* Región de Atacama. ◆ *region* C Chile
Atacama Desert *see* Atacama, Desierto de
64 H4 **Atacama, Desierto de** *Eng.* Atacama Desert. *desert* N Chile
64 I6 **Atacama, Puna de** ▲ NW Argentina
64 I5 **Atacama, Salar de** *salt lake* N Chile
56 E11 **Ataco** Tolima, C Colombia 3.33N 75.25W
202 H8 **Atafu Atoll** *island* NW Tokelau
202 H8 **Atafu Village** Atafu Atoll, NW Tokelau 8.40S 172.40W
76 K12 **Atakor** ▲ SE Algeria
79 R14 **Atakora, Chaîne de l'** *var.* Atakora Mountains. ▲ N Benin
Atakora Mountains *see* Atakora, Chaîne de l'
79 R16 **Atakpamé** C Togo 7.31N 1.07E
152 F11 **Atakui** Akhalskiy Velayat, C Turkmenistan 40.04N 58.03E
60 B13 **Atalaia do Norte** Amazonas, N Brazil 4.22S 70.10W
171 J17 **Atami** Shizuoka, Honshū, S Japan 35.04N 139.03E
78 I7 **Atâr** Adrar, W Mauritania 20.30N 13.03W
168 G10 **Atas Bogd** ▲ SW Mongolia 43.17N 96.47E
37 P12 **Atascadero** California, W USA 35.28N 120.40W
27 S13 **Atascosa River** ↝ Texas, SW USA
151 R11 **Atasu** Zhezkazgan, C Kazakhstan 48.42N 71.37E
151 R12 **Atasu** ↝ C Kazakhstan
200 Qq15 **Atata** *island* Tongatapu Group, S Tonga
142 H10 **Atatürk** ✕ (İstanbul) İstanbul, NW Turkey 40.58N 28.50E
143 N16 **Atatürk Barajı** ⊠ S Turkey
Atax *see* Aude
82 G8 **Atbara** *var.* 'Aṭbārah. River Nile, NE Sudan 17.42N 34.00E
82 H8 **Atbara** *var.* Nahr 'Aṭbarah. ↝ Eritrea/Sudan
'Aṭbārah/'Aṭbarah, Nahr *see* Atbara
151 P9 **Atbasar** Akmola, N Kazakhstan 51.49N 68.18E
At-Bashi *see* At-Bashy
153 W9 **At-Bashy** *var.* At-Bashi. Narynskaya Oblast', C Kyrgyzstan 41.07N 75.48E
24 I10 **Atchafalaya Bay** *bay* Louisiana, S USA
24 I8 **Atchafalaya River** ↝ Louisiana, S USA
Atchin *see* Aceh
29 Q3 **Atchison** Kansas, C USA 39.31N 95.07W
79 P16 **Atebubu** C Ghana 7.47N 1.00W
107 Q6 **Ateca** Aragón, NE Spain 41.19N 1.49W
42 K11 **Atengo, Río** ↝ C Mexico
Aternum *see* Pescara
109 K15 **Atessa** Abruzzo, C Italy 42.03N 14.25E
Ateste *see* Este
101 E19 **Ath** *var.* Aat. Hainaut, SW Belgium 50.37N 3.46E
9 Q13 **Athabasca** Alberta, SW Canada 54.43N 113.15W
9 Q12 **Athabasca** *var.* Athabaska. ↝ Alberta, SW Canada
9 R10 **Athabasca, Lake** ◎ Alberta/Saskatchewan, SW Canada
Athabaska *see* Athabasca
117 C16 **Athamánon** ▲ C Greece
99 F17 **Athboy** *Ir.* Baile Átha Buí. E Ireland 53.37N 6.54W
Athenae *see* Athína
99 C18 **Athenry** *Ir.* Baile Átha an Rí. W Ireland 53.19N 8.49W
25 P2 **Athens** Alabama, S USA 34.48N 86.58W
25 T3 **Athens** Georgia, SE USA 33.57N 83.24W
33 T14 **Athens** Ohio, N USA 39.19N 82.06W
22 M10 **Athens** Tennessee, S USA 35.26N 84.35W
27 V7 **Athens** Texas, SW USA 32.12N 95.51W
Athens *see* Athína
117 B18 **Athéras, Akrotírio** *headland* Kefallinía, Iónioi Nísoi, Greece, C Mediterranean Sea 38.20N 20.24E
189 W4 **Atherton** Queensland, NE Australia 17.18S 145.29E
83 I19 **Athi** ↝ S Kenya
124 O3 **Athiénou** SE Cyprus 35.01N 33.31E
117 H19 **Athína** *Eng.* Athens; *prev.* Athínai, *anc.* Athenae. ● (Greece) Attikí, C Greece 37.58N 23.44E
Athínai *see* Athína
145 S10 **Athiyah** C Iraq 32.01N 44.04E
99 D18 **Athlone** *Ir.* Baile Átha Luain. C Ireland 53.25N 7.55W
161 F16 **Athni** Karnātaka, W India 16.43N 75.04E
193 C23 **Athol** Southland, South Island, NZ 45.30S 168.35E
21 N11 **Athol** Massachusetts, NE USA 42.35N 72.11W
117 I15 **Áthos** ▲ NE Greece 40.10N 24.21E
Athos, Mount *see* Ágion Óros
Ath Thawrah *see* Madīnat ath Thawrah
147 P5 **Ath Thumāmī** *spring/well* N Saudi Arabia 27.56N 45.06E
101 L25 **Athus** Luxembourg, SE Belgium 49.34N 5.49E
99 E19 **Athy** *Ir.* Baile Átha Í. C Ireland 52.58N 6.58W
80 I10 **Ati** Batha, C Chad 13.10N 18.19E
83 F16 **Atiak** NW Uganda 3.13N 32.04E
59 G17 **Atico** Arequipa, SW Peru 16.13S 73.13W
107 O6 **Atienza** Castilla-La Mancha, C Spain 41.12N 2.52W
41 Q6 **Atigun Pass** *pass* Alaska, USA 68.01N 149.36W
10 B12 **Atikokan** Ontario, S Canada 48.45N 91.37W

◆ Country ● Country Capital ◇ Dependent Territory ○ Dependent Territory Capital ◆ Administrative Region ✕ International Airport ▲ Mountain ▲ Mountain Range ⅄ Volcano ↝ River ◎ Lake ⊠ Reservoir

Atikonak Lac – Baa

11 O9 **Atikonak Lac** ⊚ Newfoundland, E Canada
44 C6 **Atitlán, Lago de** ⊚ W Guatemala
202 L16 **Atiu** island S Cook Islands
Atjeh see Aceh
127 O9 **Atka** Magadanskaya Oblast', E Russian Federation 60.45N 151.34E
40 H17 **Atka** Atka Island, Alaska, USA 52.12N 174.13W
40 H17 **Atka Island** island Aleutian Islands, Alaska, USA
131 O7 **Atkarsk** Saratovskaya Oblast', W Russian Federation 52.15N 43.48E
29 U11 **Atkins** Arkansas, C USA 35.15N 92.56W
31 O13 **Atkinson** Nebraska, C USA 42.31N 98.57W
176 U10 **Atkri** Irian Jaya, E Indonesia 1.45S 130.04E
43 O13 **Atlacomulco** var. Atlacomulco de Fabela. México, C Mexico 19.48N 99.52W
Atlacomulco de Fabela see Atlacomulco
25 S3 **Atlanta** state capital Georgia, SE USA 33.45N 84.22W
33 R6 **Atlanta** Michigan, N USA 45.01N 84.07W
27 X6 **Atlanta** Texas, SW USA 33.06N 94.09W
31 T15 **Atlantic** Iowa, C USA 41.24N 95.00W
23 Y10 **Atlantic** North Carolina, SE USA 34.52N 76.20W
25 W8 **Atlantic Beach** Florida, SE USA 30.19N 81.24W
20 J17 **Atlantic City** New Jersey, NE USA 39.22N 74.27W
180 L14 **Atlantic-Indian Basin** undersea feature SW Indian Ocean
180 K13 **Atlantic-Indian Ridge** undersea feature SW Indian Ocean
56 E4 **Atlántico** off. Departamento del Atlántico. ◐ province NW Colombia
66-67 **Atlantic Ocean** ocean
44 K7 **Atlántico Norte, Región Autónoma** prev. Zelaya Norte. ◐ autonomous region NE Nicaragua
44 L10 **Atlántico Sur, Región Autónoma** prev. Zelaya Sur. ◐ autonomous region SE Nicaragua
44 I5 **Atlántida** ◐ department N Honduras
79 Y15 **Atlantika Mountains** ▲▲ E Nigeria
66 J10 **Atlantis Fracture Zone** tectonic feature NW Atlantic Ocean
76 H7 **Atlas Mountains** ▲▲ NW Africa
127 Pp13 **Atlasova, Ostrov** island SE Russian Federation
127 Pp16 **Atlasovo** Kamchatskaya Oblast', E Russian Federation 55.42N 159.34E
123 H13 **Atlas Saharien** var. Saharan Atlas. ▲▲ Algeria/Morocco
Atlas, Tell see Atlas Tellien
123 Gg10 **Atlas Tellien** Eng. Tell Atlas. ▲▲ N Algeria
8 I9 **Atlin** British Columbia, W Canada 59.31N 133.40W
8 I9 **Atlin Lake** ⊚ British Columbia, W Canada
43 P14 **Atlixco** Puebla, S Mexico 18.55N 98.25W
96 B11 **Atløyna** island S Norway
161 I17 **Ātmakūr** Andhra Pradesh, C India 15.52N 78.42E
25 O8 **Atmore** Alabama, S USA 31.01N 87.29W
103 J20 **Atmühl** ≈ S Germany
96 H11 **Atna** ≈ S Norway
170 E12 **Atō** Yamaguchi, Honshū, SW Japan 34.24N 131.42E
59 L21 **Atocha** Potosí, S Bolivia 20.55S 66.13W
29 P12 **Atoka** Oklahoma, C USA 34.23N 96.07W
29 O12 **Atoka Lake** var. Atoka Reservoir. ⊡ Oklahoma, C USA
Atoka Reservoir see Atoka Lake
35 Q14 **Atomic City** Idaho, NW USA 43.26N 112.48W
42 L10 **Atotonilco** Zacatecas, C Mexico 24.12N 102.46W
42 M13 **Atotonilco el Alto** var. Atotonilco. Jalisco, SW Mexico 20.32N 102.27W
79 N7 **Atouila, 'Erg** desert N Mali
43 N16 **Atoyac** var. Atoyac de Alvarez. Guerrero, S Mexico 17.10N 100.27W
Atoyac de Alvarez see Atoyac
43 P15 **Atoyac, Río** ≈ S Mexico
41 O5 **Atqasuk** Alaska, USA 70.28N 157.24W
152 C13 **Atrak** Per. Rūd-e Atrak, Rus. Atrek, Turkm. Etrek. ≈ Iran/Turkmenistan
Atrak, Rūd-e see Atrak
97 J20 **Ätran** ≈ S Sweden
56 C7 **Atrato, Río** ≈ NW Colombia
Atrek see Atrak
109 K14 **Atri** Abruzzo, C Italy 42.34N 13.58E
Atria see Adria
171 Jj16 **Atsugi** var. Atugi. Kanagawa, Honshū, S Japan 35.27N 139.21E
171 L12 **Atsumi** Yamagata, Honshū, C Japan 38.38N 139.36E
172 Oo4 **Atsuta** Hokkaidō, NE Japan 43.28N 141.24E
176 Y13 **Atsy** Irian Jaya, E Indonesia 5.40S 138.19E
149 Q17 **Aṭ Ṭaff** desert C UAE
144 G12 **Aṭ Ṭafīlah** var. Et Tafila, Tafila. Aṭ Ṭafīlah, W Jordan 30.52N 35.36E
144 G12 **Aṭ Ṭafīlah** off. Muḥāfaẓat aṭ Ṭafīlah. ◐ governorate W Jordan
146 L10 **Aṭ Ṭā'if** Makkah, W Saudi Arabia 21.49N 40.49E
Attaleia/Attalia see Antalya
25 Q3 **Attalla** Alabama, S USA 34.01N 86.05W
144 L2 **At Tall al Abyaḍ** var. Tall al Abyaḍ, Tell Abyad, Fr. Tell Abiad. Ar Raqqah, N Syria 36.36N 34.00E
144 L7 **Aṭ Ṭanf** Ḥimṣ, S Syria 33.29N 38.39E
Attapu see Samakhixai
145 S10 **At Ṭaqṭaqānah** C Iraq 32.03N 43.54E
117 O23 **Attávytos** ▲ Ródos, Dodekánisos, Greece, Aegean Sea 36.10N 27.50E
145 V15 **At Tawal** desert Iraq/Saudi Arabia
10 G9 **Attawapiskat** Ontario, C Canada 52.55N 82.25W
10 F9 **Attawapiskat** ≈ Ontario, S Canada
10 D9 **Attawapiskat Lake** ⊚ Ontario, C Canada
At Taybé see Ṭayyibah
103 F16 **Attendorn** Nordrhein-Westfalen, W Germany 51.07N 7.54E
111 R5 **Attersee** Salzburg, NW Austria 47.55N 13.31E
111 R5 **Attersee** ⊚ N Austria
101 L24 **Attert** Luxembourg, SE Belgium 49.45N 5.47E
144 M4 **At Tibnī** var. Tibnī. Dayr az Zawr, NE Syria 35.30N 39.48E
33 N13 **Attica** Indiana, N USA 40.17N 87.15W
20 E10 **Attica** New York, NE USA 42.51N 78.13W
Attica see Attikí
11 N7 **Attikamagen Lake** ⊚ Newfoundland, E Canada
117 H20 **Attikí** Eng. Attica. ◐ region C Greece
21 O12 **Attleboro** Massachusetts, NE USA 41.55N 71.15W
111 R5 **Attnang** Oberösterreich, N Austria 48.01N 13.43E
155 U6 **Attock City** Punjab, E Pakistan 33.52N 72.19E
Attopeu see Samakhixai
27 X8 **Attoyac River** ≈ Texas, SW USA
40 D16 **Attu** Attu Island, Alaska, USA 52.53N 173.18E
145 Y12 **Aṭ Ṭūbah** E Iraq 30.29N 47.28E
146 K4 **Aṭ Ṭubayq** plain Jordan/Saudi Arabia
40 C16 **Attu Island** island Aleutian Islands, Alaska, USA
Aṭ Ṭūr see El Ṭûr
161 I21 **Āttūr** Tamil Nādu, SE India 11.34N 78.39E
147 N17 **At Turbah** SW Yemen 12.42N 43.31E
64 I12 **Atuel, Río** ≈ C Argentina
Atugi see Atsugi
203 X7 **Atuona** Hiva Oa, NE French Polynesia 9.46S 139.03W
Aturus see Adour
97 M18 **Åtvidaberg** Östergötland, S Sweden 58.12N 16.00E
37 P9 **Atwater** California, W USA 37.19N 120.33W
31 T8 **Atwater** Minnesota, N USA 45.08N 94.48W
28 I2 **Atwood** Kansas, C USA 39.48N 101.02W
33 U12 **Atwood Lake** ⊡ Ohio, N USA
131 P5 **Atyashevo** Respublika Mordoviya, W Russian Federation 54.36N 46.04E
150 F12 **Atyrau** prev. Gur'yev. Atyrau, W Kazakhstan 47.07N 51.55E
150 E11 **Atyrau** off. Atyrauskaya Oblast', var. Kaz. Atyraū Oblysy; prev. Gur'yevskaya Oblast'. ◐ province W Kazakhstan
Atyraū Oblysy/Atyrauskaya Oblast' see Atyrau
110 J7 **Au** Vorarlberg, NW Austria 47.19N 10.01E
194 G8 **Aua Island** island NW PNG
105 S16 **Aubagne** anc. Albania. Bouches-du-Rhône, SE France 43.16N 5.34E
101 L25 **Aubange** Luxembourg, SE Belgium 49.34N 5.48E
105 Q6 **Aube** ◐ department N France
105 R6 **Aube** ≈ N France
101 L19 **Aubel** Liège, E Belgium 50.45N 5.49E
105 Q13 **Aubenas** Ardèche, E France 44.37N 4.24E
105 O8 **Aubigny-sur-Nère** Cher, C France 47.30N 2.27E
105 O13 **Aubin** Aveyron, S France 44.30N 2.18E
105 O13 **Aubrac, Monts d'** ▲▲ S France
38 J10 **Aubrey Cliffs** cliff Arizona, SW USA
25 R5 **Auburn** Alabama, S USA 32.37N 85.30W
37 P6 **Auburn** California, W USA 38.53N 121.03W
32 K14 **Auburn** Illinois, N USA 39.35N 89.45W
33 Q11 **Auburn** Indiana, N USA 41.22N 85.03W
22 J7 **Auburn** Kentucky, S USA 36.52N 86.42W
21 P8 **Auburn** Maine, NE USA 44.05N 70.15W
21 N11 **Auburn** Massachusetts, NE USA 42.11N 71.47W
31 S16 **Auburn** Nebraska, C USA 40.23N 95.50W
20 H10 **Auburn** New York, NE USA 42.55N 76.31W
34 H8 **Auburn** Washington, NW USA 47.18N 122.13W
105 N11 **Aubusson** Creuse, C France 45.58N 2.10E
120 E10 **Auce** Ger. Autz. Dobele, SW Latvia 56.28N 22.54E
104 L15 **Auch** Lat. Augusta Auscorum, Elimberrum. Gers, S France 43.39N 0.37E
79 U16 **Auchi** Edo, S Nigeria 7.01N 6.17E
25 T9 **Aucilla River** ≈ Florida/Georgia, SE USA
192 L6 **Auckland** Auckland, North Island, NZ 36.53S 174.46E
192 K5 **Auckland** off. Auckland Region. ◐ region North Island, NZ
192 L6 **Auckland** ✕ Auckland, North Island, NZ 37.01S 174.49E
199 Ii15 **Auckland Islands** island group S NZ
105 O16 **Aude** ◐ department S France
105 N16 **Aude** anc. Atax. ≈ S France
Audenarde see Oudenaarde
Audern see Audru
104 E6 **Audierne** Finistère, NW France 48.01N 4.30W
104 E6 **Audierne, Baie d'** bay NW France
105 U7 **Audincourt** Doubs, E France 47.28N 6.49E
120 G5 **Audru** Ger. Audern. Pärnumaa, SW Estonia 58.25N 24.21E
31 T14 **Audubon** Iowa, C USA 41.44N 94.56W
103 N17 **Aue** Sachsen, E Germany 50.34N 12.42E
102 H12 **Aue** ≈ NW Germany
102 L9 **Auerbach** Bayern, SE Germany 49.41N 11.41E
103 M17 **Auerbach** Sachsen, E Germany 50.30N 12.24E
110 I10 **Auererrhein** ≈ SW Switzerland
103 N17 **Auersberg** ▲ E Germany 50.30N 12.42E
189 W9 **Augathella** Queensland, E Australia 25.54S 146.38E
33 Q12 **Auglaize River** ≈ Ohio, N USA
85 F22 **Augrabies Falls** waterfall W South Africa 28.37S 20.24E
33 R7 **Au Gres River** ≈ Michigan, N USA
Augsbourg see Augsburg
103 K22 **Augsburg** Fr. Augsbourg; anc. Augusta Vindelicorum. Bayern, S Germany 48.22N 10.54E
188 I14 **Augusta** Western Australia 34.18S 115.10E
109 L25 **Augusta** It. Agosta. Sicilia, Italy, C Mediterranean Sea 37.19N 15.13E
29 W11 **Augusta** Arkansas, C USA 35.16N 91.22W
25 V3 **Augusta** Georgia, SE USA 33.29N 81.58W
29 O6 **Augusta** Kansas, C USA 37.40N 96.59W
21 Q7 **Augusta** state capital Maine, NE USA 44.19N 69.44W
35 Q8 **Augusta** Montana, NW USA 47.28N 112.23W
Augusta see London
Augusta Auscorum see Auch
Augusta Emerita see Mérida
Augusta Praetoria see Aosta
Augusta Suessionum see Soissons
Augusta Trajana see Stara Zagora
Augusta Treverorum see Trier
Augusta Vangionum see Worms
Augusta Vindelicorum see Augsburg
97 G24 **Augustenborg** Ger. Augustenburg. Sønderjylland, SW Denmark 54.57N 9.52E
Augustenburg see Augustenborg
41 Q13 **Augustine Island** island Alaska, USA
12 L9 **Augustines, Lac des** ⊚ Quebec, SE Canada
Augustobona Tricassium see Troyes
Augustodunum see Autun
Augustodurum see Bayeux
Augustoritum Lemovicensium see Limoges
112 O8 **Augustów** Rus. Avgustov. Podlaskie, NE Poland 53.51N 22.58E
Augustow Canal see Augustowski, Kanał
112 O8 **Augustowski, Kanał** Eng. Augustow Canal, Rus. Avgustovskiy Kanal. canal NE Poland
188 I9 **Augustus, Mount** ▲ Western Australia 24.42S 117.42E
195 X15 **Auki** Malaita, N Solomon Islands 8.48S 160.45E
23 W8 **Aulander** North Carolina, SE USA 36.15N 77.16W
188 L7 **Auld, Lake** salt lake Western Australia
Aulie Ata/Auliye-Ata see Taraz
108 E10 **Aulla** Toscana, C Italy 44.15N 10.00E
104 F6 **Aulne** ≈ NW France
Aulong see Ulong
39 T3 **Ault** Colorado, C USA 40.34N 104.43W
105 N3 **Aumale** Seine-Maritime, N France 49.45N 1.43E
Auminzatau, Gory see Owminzatovo-Toshi
79 T14 **Auna** Niger, W Nigeria 10.13N 4.43E
97 H21 **Auning** Århus, C Denmark 56.25N 10.22E
198 Cc9 **Aunu'u Island** island W American Samoa
85 E20 **Auob** var. Oup. ≈ Namibia/South Africa
95 K19 **Aura** Länsi-Suomi, W Finland 60.37N 22.34E
111 R5 **Aurach** ≈ N Austria
Aural, Phnom see Aôral, Phnum
159 O14 **Aurangābād** Bihār, N India 24.48N 84.22E
160 F13 **Aurangābād** Mahārāshtra, C India 19.52N 75.22E
201 V7 **Aur Atoll** atoll E Marshall Islands
104 G7 **Auray** Morbihan, NW France 47.40N 2.58W
96 G13 **Aurdal** Oppland, S Norway 60.51N 9.25E
96 F8 **Aure** Møre og Romsdal, S Norway 63.16N 8.31E
31 T12 **Aurelia** Iowa, C USA 42.42N 95.26W
Aurelia Aquensis see Baden-Baden
Aurelianum see Orléans
123 J12 **Aurès, Massif de l'** ▲▲ NE Algeria
102 F10 **Aurich** Niedersachsen, NW Germany 53.28N 7.28E
105 O13 **Aurillac** Cantal, C France 44.55N 2.25E
Aurine, Alpi see Zillertaler Alpen
Aurium see Ourense
12 H15 **Aurora** Ontario, S Canada 44.00N 79.26W
57 S8 **Aurora** NW Guyana 6.46N 59.45W
39 T4 **Aurora** Colorado, C USA 39.42N 104.51W
32 M11 **Aurora** Illinois, N USA 41.45N 88.19W
33 Q15 **Aurora** Indiana, N USA 39.01N 84.55W
31 W4 **Aurora** Minnesota, N USA 47.31N 92.14W
29 S8 **Aurora** Missouri, C USA 36.58N 93.43W
31 P16 **Aurora** Nebraska, C USA 40.52N 98.00W
38 J5 **Aurora** Utah, W USA 38.55N 111.55W
Aurora see Maéwo, Vanuatu
Aurora see San Francisco, Philippines
96 F10 **Aursjøen** ⊚ S Norway
96 I9 **Aursunden** ⊚ S Norway
85 D21 **Aus** Karas, SW Namibia 26.37S 16.18E
Ausa see Vic
12 E16 **Ausable** ≈ Ontario, S Canada
33 O3 **Au Sable Point** headland Michigan, N USA 46.40N 86.08W
33 S7 **Au Sable Point** headland Michigan, N USA 44.19N 83.20W
33 R6 **Au Sable River** ≈ Michigan, N USA
59 H16 **Ausangate, Nevado** ▲ C Peru 13.46S 71.13W
Auschwitz see Oświęcim
Ausculum Apulum see Ascoli Satriano
107 Q4 **Ausejo** La Rioja, N Spain 42.21N 2.10W
Aussig see Ústí nad Labem
97 F17 **Aust-Agder** ◐ county S Norway
94 P2 **Austfonna** glacier NE Svalbard
33 P15 **Austin** Indiana, N USA 38.45N 85.48W
31 W11 **Austin** Minnesota, N USA 43.40N 92.58W
37 U5 **Austin** Nevada, W USA 39.28N 117.04W
27 S10 **Austin** state capital Texas, S USA 30.16N 97.44W
188 J10 **Austin, Lake** salt lake Western Australia
33 V11 **Austintown** Ohio, N USA 41.06N 80.45W
27 V9 **Austonio** Texas, SW USA 31.09N 95.39W
Australes, Archipel des see Australes, Îles
Australes et Antarctiques Françaises, Terres see French Southern and Antarctic Territories
203 T14 **Australes, Îles** var. Archipel des Australes, Îles Tubuai, Tubuai Islands, Eng. Austral Islands. island group SW French Polynesia
183 Y11 **Austral Fracture Zone** tectonic feature S Pacific Ocean
189 O7 **Australia** off. Commonwealth of Australia. ◆ commonwealth republic
182 M8 **Australia** continent
191 Q12 **Australian Alps** ▲▲ SE Australia
191 R11 **Australian Capital Territory** prev. Federal Capital Territory. ◐ territory SE Australia
Australie, Bassin Nord de l' see North Australian Basin
Austral Islands see Australes, Îles
Austrava see Ostrov
111 T6 **Austria** off. Republic of Austria, Ger. Österreich. ◆ republic C Europe
94 K3 **Austurland** ◐ region SE Iceland
94 G10 **Austvågøya** island C Norway
60 G13 **Autazes** Amazonas, N Brazil 3.37S 59.07W
104 M16 **Auterive** Haute-Garonne, S France 43.22N 1.28E
Autesiodorum see Auxerre
105 N2 **Authie** ≈ N France
Autissiodorum see Auxerre
42 K14 **Autlán** var. Autlán de Navarro. Jalisco, SW Mexico 19.46N 104.22W
Autlán de Navarro see Autlán
Autricum see Chartres
105 Q9 **Autun** anc. Ædua, Augustodunum. Saône-et-Loire, C France 46.57N 4.18E
Autz see Auce
101 H20 **Auvelais** Namur, S Belgium 50.27N 4.37E
105 P11 **Auvergne** ◐ region C France
104 M12 **Auvézère** ≈ W France
105 P7 **Auxerre** anc. Autesiodorum, Autissiodorum. Yonne, C France 47.48N 3.34E
105 N2 **Auxi-le-Château** Pas-de-Calais, N France 50.14N 2.06E
105 S8 **Auxonne** Côte d'Or, C France 47.12N 5.22E
57 P9 **Auyan Tebuy** ▲ SE Venezuela 5.48N 62.27W
105 O10 **Auzances** Creuse, C France 46.01N 2.29E
29 U8 **Ava** Missouri, C USA 36.57N 92.39W
148 M5 **Āvaj** Qazvin, N Iran
97 C15 **Avaldsnes** Rogaland, S Norway 59.21N 5.16E
105 Q8 **Avallon** Yonne, C France 47.30N 3.54E
104 K6 **Avaloirs, Mont des** ▲ NW France 48.27N 0.11W
37 S16 **Avalon** Santa Catalina Island, California, W USA 33.20N 118.19W
20 J17 **Avalon** New Jersey, NE USA 39.04N 74.42W
11 V13 **Avalon Peninsula** peninsula Newfoundland, E Canada
207 Q11 **Avannaarsua** ◐ province N Greenland
62 K10 **Avaré** São Paulo, S Brazil 23.06S 48.57W
Avaricum see Bourges
202 H16 **Avarua** ○ (Cook Islands) Rarotonga, S Cook Islands 21.12S 159.46W
202 H16 **Avarua Harbour** harbor Rarotonga, S Cook Islands
Avasfelsőfalu see Negreşti-Oaş
40 L17 **Avatanak Island** island Aleutian Islands, Alaska, USA
202 B16 **Avatele** S Niue 19.06S 169.55E
202 H16 **Avatiu** Rarotonga, S Cook Islands 21.12S 159.46W
202 H15 **Avatiu Harbour** harbor Rarotonga, S Cook Islands
Avdeyevka see Avdiyivka
116 J13 **Ávdira** Anatolikí Makedonía kai Thráki, NE Greece 40.58N 24.58E
119 X8 **Avdiyivka** Rus. Avdeyevka. Donets'ka Oblast', SE Ukraine 48.06N 37.46E
168 K7 **Avdzaga** C Mongolia 47.43N 103.30E
106 G6 **Ave** ≈ N Portugal
106 G7 **Aveiro** anc. Talabriga. Aveiro, W Portugal 40.37N 8.40W
106 G7 **Aveiro** ◐ district N Portugal
Avela see Ávila
101 D18 **Avelgem** West-Vlaanderen, W Belgium 50.46N 3.25E
63 D20 **Avellaneda** Buenos Aires, E Argentina 34.43S 58.23W
109 L17 **Avellino** anc. Abellinum. Campania, S Italy 40.54N 14.46E
37 Q12 **Avenal** California, W USA 36.00N 120.07W
Avenio see Avignon
96 E8 **Averøya** island S Norway
109 K17 **Aversa** Campania, S Italy 40.58N 14.10E
35 N9 **Avery** Idaho, NW USA 47.14N 115.48W
27 W5 **Avery** Texas, SW USA 33.33N 94.46W
Aves, Islas de see Las Aves, Islas
Avesnes see Avesnes-sur-Helpe
105 Q2 **Avesnes-sur-Helpe** var. Avesnes. Nord, N France 50.07N 3.57E
66 G12 **Aves Ridge** undersea feature SE Caribbean Sea
97 M14 **Avesta** Dalarna, C Sweden 60.09N 16.10E
105 O14 **Aveyron** ◐ department S France
105 N14 **Aveyron** ≈ S France
109 J15 **Avezzano** Abruzzo, C Italy 42.01N 13.25E
117 D16 **Avgó** ▲ C Greece 39.31N 21.24E
Avgustov see Augustów
Avgustovskiy Kanal see Augustowski, Kanał
98 J9 **Aviemore** N Scotland, UK 57.06N 4.01W
193 F21 **Aviemore, Lake** ⊚ South Island, NZ
105 R15 **Avignon** anc. Avenio. Vaucluse, SE France 43.57N 4.49E
106 M7 **Ávila** var. Avila; anc. Abela, Abula, Abyla, Avela. Castilla-León, C Spain 40.39N 4.42W
106 L8 **Ávila** ◐ province Castilla-León, C Spain
106 K2 **Avilés** Asturias, NW Spain 43.33N 5.55W
120 J4 **Avinurme** Ger. Awwinorm. Ida-Virumaa, NE Estonia 58.58N 26.52E
106 H10 **Avis** Portalegre, C Portugal 39.03N 7.52W
97 F22 **Avlum** Ringkøbing, C Denmark 56.16N 8.48E
190 M11 **Avoca** Victoria, SE Australia 37.09S 143.34E
31 T14 **Avoca** Iowa, C USA 41.27N 95.20W
190 M11 **Avoca River** ≈ Victoria, SE Australia
109 L25 **Avola** Sicilia, Italy, C Mediterranean Sea 36.54N 15.07E
20 F10 **Avon** New York, NE USA 42.53N 77.41W
31 P12 **Avon** South Dakota, N USA 43.00N 98.03W
99 M23 **Avon** ≈ S England, UK
99 L20 **Avon** ≈ C England, UK
38 K13 **Avondale** Arizona, SW USA 33.25N 112.20W
25 X13 **Avon Park** Florida, SE USA 27.36N 81.30W
104 J5 **Avranches** Manche, N France 48.42N 1.21W
105 O3 **Avre** ≈ N France
195 X16 **Avuavu** var. Kolotambu. Guadalcanal, C Solomon Islands 9.52S 160.25E
Avveel see Ivalo, Finland
Avveel see Ivalojoki, Finland
Avvil see Ivalo
79 O17 **Awaaso** var. Awaso. SW Ghana 6.10N 2.18W
147 X8 **Awābī** var. Al 'Awābī. NE Oman 23.19N 57.34E
170 G15 **Awaji-shima** island SW Japan
192 L9 **Awakino** Waikato, North Island, NZ 38.40S 174.37E
148 M15 **'Awālī** C Bahrain 26.06N 50.33E
101 K19 **Awans** Liège, E Belgium 50.39N 5.30E
192 I2 **Awanui** Northland, North Island, NZ 35.01S 173.16E
154 M14 **Awārān** Baluchistān, SW Pakistan 26.31N 65.10E
83 K16 **Awara Plain** plain NE Kenya
82 M13 **Āwarē** Somali, E Ethiopia 8.12N 44.09E
144 M6 **'Awāriḍ, Wādī** dry watercourse E Syria
193 B20 **Awarua Point** headland South Island, NZ 44.15S 168.03E
83 J14 **Āwasa** Southern, S Ethiopia 6.54N 38.26E
82 K13 **Āwash** Afar, NE Ethiopia 8.59N 40.15E
82 K12 **Āwash** var. Hawash. ≈ C Ethiopia
171 Kk11 **Awa-shima** island C Japan
Awaso see Awaaso
164 H7 **Awat** Xinjiang Uygur Zizhiqu, NW China 40.36N 80.22E
193 J15 **Awatere** ≈ South Island, NZ
77 O10 **Awbārī** SW Libya 26.34N 12.46E
77 N9 **Awbārī, Idhān** var. Edeyen d'Oubari. desert Algeria/Libya
82 C13 **Aweil** Northern Bahr el Ghazal, SW Sudan 8.44N 27.25E
98 H11 **Awe, Loch** ⊚ W Scotland, UK
79 U16 **Awka** Anambra, SW Nigeria 6.12N 7.04E
41 O6 **Awuna River** ≈ Alaska, USA
Awwinorm see Avinurme
Ax see Dax
Axarfjördhur see Öxarfjördhur
105 N17 **Axat** Aude, S France 42.46N 2.13E
101 F16 **Axel** Zeeland, SW Netherlands 51.16N 3.55E
207 P9 **Axel Heiberg Island** var. Axel Heiburg. island Nunavut, N Canada
Axel Heiburg see Axel Heiberg Island
79 O17 **Axim** S Ghana 4.52N 2.13W
116 F13 **Axiós** var. Vardar. ≈ Greece/FYR Macedonia see also Vardar
105 N17 **Ax-les-Thermes** Ariège, S France 42.43N 1.49E
171 Gg14 **Ayabe** Kyōto, Honshū, SW Japan 35.16N 135.15E
122 F13 **Ayachi, Jbel** ▲ C Morocco 32.30N 5.00W
63 D22 **Ayacucho** Buenos Aires, E Argentina 37.09S 58.30W
59 F15 **Ayacucho** Ayacucho, S Peru 13.10S 74.15W
59 E16 **Ayacucho** off. Departamento de Ayacucho. ◐ department SW Peru
151 W11 **Ayagoz** var. Ayaguz, Kaz. Ayaköz; prev. Sergiopol. Vostochnyy Kazakhstan, E Kazakhstan 47.54N 80.25E
151 V12 **Ayagoz** var. Ayaguz, Kaz. Ayaköz. ≈ E Kazakhstan
Ayaguz see Ayagoz
Ayakagytma see Oyoqighitma
Ayakkuduk see Oyoqquduq
164 L10 **Ayakkum Hu** ⊚ NW China
Ayaköz see Ayagoz
106 H14 **Ayamonte** Andalucía, S Spain 37.13N 7.24W
127 N12 **Ayan** Khabarovskiy Kray, E Russian Federation 56.27N 138.09E
142 J10 **Ayancık** Sinop, N Turkey 41.55N 34.34E
57 S9 **Ayanganna Mountain** ▲ C Guyana 5.21N 59.54W
79 U16 **Ayangba** Kogi, C Nigeria 7.36N 7.10E
127 P6 **Ayanka** Koryakskiy Avtonomnyy Okrug, E Russian Federation 63.42N 167.31E
56 E7 **Ayapel** Córdoba, NW Colombia 8.17N 75.13W
142 H12 **Ayaş** Ankara, N Turkey 40.01N 32.21E
59 I16 **Ayaviri** Puno, S Peru 14.52S 70.34W
155 P3 **Āybak** var. Aibak, Haibak; prev. Samangān. Samangān, NE Afghanistan 36.16N 68.04E
153 N10 **Aydarkŭl** Rus. Ozero Aydarkul'. ⊚ C Uzbekistan
Aydarkul', Ozero see Aydarkŭl
23 W10 **Ayden** North Carolina, SE USA 35.28N 77.25W
142 C15 **Aydın** var. Aïdin; anc. Tralles. Aydın, SW Turkey 37.51N 27.51E
142 C15 **Aydın** var. Aïdin. ◐ province SW Turkey
142 I17 **Aydıncık** İçel, S Turkey 36.10N 33.16E
142 C15 **Aydın Dağları** ▲▲ W Turkey
164 L6 **Aydingkol Hu** ⊚ NW China
131 X7 **Aydyrlinskiy** Orenburgskaya Oblast', W Russian Federation 52.03N 59.54E
107 S4 **Ayerbe** Aragón, NE Spain 42.16N 0.40W
Ayers Rock see Uluru
Ayeyarwady see Irrawaddy
Ayiá see Agiá
Ayia Napa see Agía Nápa
Ayia Phyla see Agía Fýlaxis
Ayiásos/Ayiássos see Agiasós
Áyios Evstrátios see Ágios Efstrátios
Áyios Kírikos see Ágios Kírykos
Áyios Nikólaos see Ágios Nikólaos
Ayios Seryios see Yeniboğaziçi
82 I11 **Āykel** Amhara, N Ethiopia 12.33N 37.01E
126 K10 **Aykhal** Respublika Sakha (Yakutiya), NE Russian Federation 66.07N 110.25E
12 J12 **Aylen Lake** ⊚ Ontario, SE Canada
99 N21 **Aylesbury** SE England, UK 51.49N 0.49W
107 O6 **Ayllón** Castilla-León, N Spain 41.25N 3.22W
12 F17 **Aylmer** Ontario, S Canada 42.46N 80.57W
12 L12 **Aylmer** Quebec, SE Canada 45.22N 75.51W
13 R12 **Aylmer, Lac** ⊚ Quebec, SE Canada
15 J6 **Aylmer Lake** ⊚ Northwest Territories, NW Canada
151 V14 **Aynabulak** Almaty, SE Kazakhstan 44.37N 77.58E
144 K2 **'Ayn al 'Arab** Ḥalab, N Syria 36.55N 38.21E
Aynayn see 'Aynīn
145 V12 **'Ayn Ḥamūd** S Iraq 30.51N 45.37E
153 P12 **Ayní** prev. Rus. Varzimanor Ayni. W Tajikistan 39.24N 68.30E
146 M10 **'Aynīn** var. Aynayn. spring/well SW Saudi Arabia 20.52N 41.41E
23 U12 **Aynor** South Carolina, SE USA 33.59N 79.11W
145 Q7 **'Ayn Zāzūh** C Iraq 33.29N 42.34E
159 N12 **Ayodhya** Uttar Pradesh, N India 26.46N 82.12E
127 O5 **Ayon, Ostrov** island NE Russian Federation
107 R11 **Ayora** País Valenciano, E Spain 39.04N 1.04W
79 Q11 **Ayorou** Tillabéri, W Niger 14.44N 0.54E
81 E16 **Ayos** Centre, S Cameroon 3.52N 12.31E
78 L5 **'Ayoûn 'Abd el Mâlek** well N Mauritania 24.51N 7.38W
78 K10 **'Ayoûn el 'Atroûs** var. Aïoun el Atrous, Aïoun el Atroûss. Hodh el Gharbi, SE Mauritania 16.37N 9.36W
98 I13 **Ayr** W Scotland, UK 55.28N 4.37W
98 I13 **Ayr** ≈ W Scotland, UK
98 I13 **Ayrshire** cultural region SW Scotland, UK
Aysen see Aisén
82 L12 **Āysha** Somali, E Ethiopia 10.36N 42.31E
150 L14 **Ayteke Bi** Kaz. Zhangaqazaly; prev. Novokazalinsk. Kyzylorda, SW Kazakhstan 45.52N 62.09E
152 K8 **Aytim** Nawoiy Wiloyati, N Uzbekistan 42.15N 63.25E
189 W4 **Ayton** Queensland, NE Australia 15.54S 145.19E
116 M9 **Aytos** Burgas, E Bulgaria 42.43N 27.13E
176 Uu7 **Ayu, Kepulauan** island group E Indonesia
A Yun Pa see Cheo Reo
175 O8 **Ayu, Tanjung** headland Borneo, N Indonesia 0.25N 117.34E
42 K13 **Ayutla** Jalisco, C Mexico 20.07N 104.18W
43 P16 **Ayutlá** var. Ayutla de los Libres. Guerrero, S Mexico 16.56N 99.22W
Ayutla de los Libres see Ayutlá
178 H11 **Ayutthaya** var. Phra Nakhon Si Ayutthaya. Phra Nakhon Si Ayutthaya, C Thailand 14.19N 100.34E
142 B13 **Ayvalık** Balıkesir, W Turkey 39.18N 26.42E
101 L20 **Aywaille** Liège, E Belgium 50.28N 5.40E
147 R13 **'Aywat aş Şay'ar, Wādī** seasonal river N Yemen
Azaffal see Azeffâl
107 T9 **Azahar, Costa del** coastal region E Spain
107 S6 **Azaila** Aragón, NE Spain 41.16N 0.30W
106 F10 **Azambuja** Lisboa, C Portugal 39.04N 8.52W
159 N13 **Āzamgarh** Uttar Pradesh, N India 26.03N 83.10E
79 O9 **Azaouâd** desert C Mali
79 S10 **Azaouagh, Vallée de l'** var. Azaouak. ≈ W Niger
Azaouak see Azaouagh, Vallée de l'
63 F14 **Azara** Misiones, NE Argentina 28.03S 55.42W
148 K3 **Āzarān** Āżarbāyjān-e Khāvarī, N Iran 37.34N 47.10E
Azärbaycan/Azärbaycan Respublikası see Azerbaijan
Āżarbāyjān-e Bākhtarī see Āżarbāyjān-e Gharbī
148 I4 **Āżarbāyjān-e Gharbī** off. Ostān-e Āżarbāyjān-e Gharbī Eng. West Azerbaijan prev. Āżarbāyjān-e Bākhtarī. ◐ province NW Iran
Āżarbāyjān-e Khāvarī see Āżarbāyjān-e Sharqī
148 J3 **Āżarbāyjān-e Sharqī** off. Ostān-e Āżarbāyjān-e Sharqī, Eng. East Azerbaijan; prev. Āżarbāyjān-e Sharqī. ◐ province NW Iran
79 W13 **Azare** Bauchi, N Nigeria 11.41N 10.09E
121 M19 **Azarychy** Rus. Ozarichi. Homyel'skaya Voblasts', SE Belarus 52.31N 29.19E
104 L8 **Azay-le-Rideau** Indre-et-Loire, C France 47.16N 0.25E
144 I2 **A'zāz** Ḥalab, NW Syria 36.34N 37.03E
78 H7 **Azeffâl** var. Azaffal. desert Mauritania/Western Sahara
143 V12 **Azerbaijan** off. Azerbaijani Republic, Az. Azärbaycan, Azärbaycan Respublikası; prev. Azerbaijan SSR. ◆ republic SE Asia
151 T7 **Azhbulat, Ozero** ⊚ NE Kazakhstan
76 F7 **Azilal** C Morocco 31.58N 6.53W
Azimabad see Patna
21 O6 **Aziscohos Lake** ⊡ Maine, NE USA
Azizbekov see Vayk'
Azizie see Telish
Aziziya see Al 'Azīzīyah
131 T4 **Aznakayevo** Respublika Tatarstan, W Russian Federation 54.55N 53.15E
58 C8 **Azogues** Cañar, S Ecuador 2.41S 78.54W
66 N2 **Azores** var. Açores, Ilhas dos Açores, Port. Arquipélago dos Açores. island group Portugal, NE Atlantic Ocean
66 L8 **Azores-Biscay Rise** undersea feature E Atlantic Ocean
Azotos/Azotus see Ashdod
80 K11 **Azoum, Bahr** seasonal river SE Chad
130 L12 **Azov** Rostovskaya Oblast', SW Russian Federation 47.06N 39.26E
130 J13 **Azov, Sea of** Rus. Azovskoye More, Ukr. Azovs'ke More. sea NE Black Sea
Azovs'ke More/Azovskoye More see Azov, Sea of
144 I10 **Azraq, Wāḥat al** oasis N Jordan 31.51N 36.51E
Āzro see Āzrow
76 G6 **Azrou** C Morocco 33.30N 5.12W
155 R5 **Āzrow** var. Āzro. Lowgar, E Afghanistan 34.10N 69.39E
39 P8 **Aztec** New Mexico, SW USA 36.49N 107.59W
38 M13 **Aztec Peak** ▲ Arizona, SW USA 33.48N 110.54W
47 N9 **Azua** var. Azua de Compostela. S Dominican Republic 18.25N 70.44W
Azua de Compostela see Azua
106 K12 **Azuaga** Extremadura, W Spain 38.16N 5.40W
58 B8 **Azuay** ◐ province W Ecuador
170 Bb11 **Azuchi-Ō-shima** island SW Japan
107 O11 **Azuer** ≈ C Spain
45 S17 **Azuero, Península de** peninsula S Panama
64 I6 **Azufre, Volcán** var. Volcán Lastarria. ▲ N Chile 25.16S 68.35W
118 J12 **Azuga** Prahova, SE Romania 45.27N 25.34E
63 C22 **Azul** Buenos Aires, E Argentina 36.46S 59.49W
64 I8 **Azul, Cerro** ▲ NW Argentina 28.28S 68.43W
58 E12 **Azul, Cordillera** ▲▲ C Peru
171 Ll14 **Azuma-san** ▲ Honshū, C Japan 37.44N 140.05E
105 V15 **Azur, Côte d'** coastal region SE France
203 Z3 **Azur Lagoon** ⊚ Kiritimati, E Kiribati
'Azza see Gaza
Az Zāb al Kabīr see Great Zab
144 H7 **Az Zabdānī** var. Zabadani. Dimashq, W Syria 33.45N 36.07E
147 W8 **Aẓ Ẓāhirah** desert NW Oman
147 S6 **Aẓ Ẓahrān** Eng. Dhahran. Ash Sharqīyah, NE Saudi Arabia 26.18N 50.01E
147 R6 **Aẓ Ẓahrān al Khubar** var. Dhahran Al Khobar. ✕ Ash Sharqīyah, NE Saudi Arabia 26.28N 49.42E
Az Zaqāzīq see Zagazig
144 H10 **Az Zarqā'** var. Zarqa. Az Zarqā', NW Jordan 32.04N 36.06E
144 I11 **Az Zarqā'** off. Muḥāfaẓat az Zarqā', var. Zarqa. ◐ governorate N Jordan
77 O7 **Az Zāwiyah** var. Zawia. NW Libya 32.45N 12.43E
147 N15 **Az Zaydīyah** W Yemen 15.19N 43.03E
76 I11 **Azzel Matti, Sebkha** var. Sebkra Azz el Matti. salt flat C Algeria
147 P6 **Az Zilfī** Ar Riyāḍ, N Saudi Arabia 26.16N 44.48E
145 Y13 **Az Zubayr** var. Al Zubair. SE Iraq 30.24N 47.45E
Az Zuqur see Jabal Zuuqar, Jazīrat

B

197 H14 **Ba** prev. Mba. Viti Levu, W Fiji 17.34S 177.40E
Ba see Đa Răng
175 R18 **Baa** Pulau Rote, C Indonesia 10.43S 123.06E

◆ Country ● Country Capital ◇ Dependent Territory ○ Dependent Territory Capital ◐ Administrative Region ✕ International Airport ▲ Mountain ▲▲ Mountain Range Volcano ≈ River ⊚ Lake ⊡ Reservoir
227

Baaba, Île – Baldy Mountain

197 G5 **Baaba, Île** *island* Îles Belep, W New Caledonia
144 H7 **Baalbek** *var.* Baʻlabakk; *anc.* Heliopolis. E Lebanon 34.00N 36.15E
110 G8 **Baar** Zug, N Switzerland 47.12N 8.31E
83 L17 **Baardheere** *var.* Bardere, *It.* Bardera. Gedo, SW Somalia 2.13N 42.19E
82 Q12 **Baargaal** Bari, NE Somalia 11.12N 51.04E
101 I15 **Baarle-Hertog** Antwerpen, N Belgium 51.26N 4.56E
101 I15 **Baarle-Nassau** Noord-Brabant, S Netherlands 51.27N 4.56E
100 J11 **Baarn** Utrecht, C Netherlands 52.13N 5.16E
116 D13 **Baba** *var.* Buševa, *Gk.* Varnoús. ▲▲ FYR Macedonia/Greece
78 H10 **Bababé** Brakna, W Mauritania 16.22N 13.57W
142 G10 **Baba Burnu** *headland* NW Turkey 41.18N 31.24E
119 N13 **Babadag** Tulcea, SE Romania 44.53N 28.46E
143 X10 **Babadağ Dağı** ▲ NE Azerbaijan 41.02N 48.04E
Babadayhan *see* Babadaykhan
152 H14 **Babadaykhan** *Turkm.* Babadayhan; *prev.* Kirovsk. Akhalskiy Velayat, C Turkmenistan 37.39N 60.17E
152 G14 **Babadurmaz** Akhalskiy Velayat, C Turkmenistan 37.39N 59.03E
116 M12 **Babaeski** Kırklareli, NW Turkey 41.26N 27.06E
145 T4 **Bāba Gurgur** N Iraq 35.34N 44.18E
58 B7 **Babahoyo** *prev.* Bodegas. Los Ríos, C Ecuador 1.49S 79.33W
155 P5 **Bābā, Kūh-e** ▲▲ C Afghanistan
175 P10 **Babana** Sulawesi, C Indonesia 2.03S 119.13E
176 U16 **Babar, Kepulauan** *island group* E Indonesia
176 U15 **Babar, Pulau** *island* Kepulauan Babar, E Indonesia
158 G4 **Bābāsar Pass** *pass* India/Pakistan
195 Q10 **Babase Island** *island* Feni Islands, NE PNG
152 C9 **Babashy** ▲▲ W Turkmenistan
174 Ll15 **Babat** Jawa, S Indonesia 7.07S 112.07E
174 I10 **Babat** Sumatera, W Indonesia 2.45S 104.01E
Babatag, Khrebet *see* Bobotogh, Qatorkŭhi
83 H21 **Babati** Arusha, NE Tanzania 4.12S 35.45E
128 J13 **Babayevo** Vologodskaya Oblast', NW Russian Federation 59.22N 35.51E
131 Q15 **Babayurt** Respublika Dagestan, SW Russian Federation 43.38N 46.49E
35 P6 **Babb** Montana, NW USA 48.51N 113.26W
31 X4 **Babbitt** Minnesota, N USA 47.42N 91.56W
196 E9 **Babeldaob** *var.* Babeldaop, Babelthuap. *island* N Palau
Babeldaop *see* Babeldaob
147 N17 **Bab el Mandeb** *strait* Gulf of Aden/Red Sea
Babelthuap *see* Babeldaob
113 K17 **Babia Góra** *var.* Babia Hora. ▲ Poland/Slovakia 49.33N 19.32E
Babia Hora *see* Babia Góra
Babian Jiang *see* Black River
Babichi *see* Babichy
121 N19 **Babichy** *Rus.* Babichi. Homyel'skaya Voblasts', SE Belarus 52.17N 30.00E
114 I10 **Babina Greda** Vukovar-Srijem, E Croatia 45.09N 18.33E
8 K13 **Babine Lake** ◎ British Columbia, SW Canada
176 Vv10 **Babo** Irian Jaya, E Indonesia 2.29S 133.30E
149 O4 **Bābol** *var.* Babul, Balfrush, Barfrush; *prev.* Barfurush. Māzandarān, N Iran 36.34N 52.39E
149 O4 **Bābolsar** *var.* Babulsar; *prev.* Meshed-i-Sar. Māzandarān, N Iran 36.42N 52.37E
38 L16 **Baboquivari Peak** ▲ Arizona, SW USA 31.46N 111.36W
81 G15 **Baboua** Nana-Mambéré, W Central African Republic 5.46N 14.47E
121 M17 **Babruysk** *Rus.* Bobruysk. Mahilyowskaya Voblasts', E Belarus 53.07N 29.13E
Babu *see* Hexian
Babul *see* Bābol
Babulsar *see* Bābolsar
115 O19 **Babuna** ≈ C FYR Macedonia
115 O19 **Babuna** ▲▲ C FYR Macedonia
154 K7 **Bābūs, Dasht-e** *Pash.* Bebas, Dasht-i. ▲▲ W Afghanistan
126 Jj16 **Babushkin** Respublika Buryatiya, S Russian Federation 51.35N 105.49E
179 P7 **Babuyan Channel** *channel* N Philippines
179 Pp7 **Babuyan Island** *island* N Philippines
145 T9 **Babylon** *site of ancient city* C Iraq 32.33N 44.25E
114 J9 **Bač** *Ger.* Batsch. Serbia, NW Yugoslavia 45.24N 19.17E
60 M13 **Bacabal** Maranhão, E Brazil 4.15S 44.45W
43 Y14 **Bacalar** Quintana Roo, SE Mexico 18.38N 88.17W
43 Y14 **Bacalar Chico, Boca** *strait* SE Mexico
175 Ss8 **Bacan, Kepulauan** *island group* E Indonesia
175 T8 **Bacan, Pulau** *prev.* Batjan. *island* Maluku, E Indonesia
118 L10 **Bacău** *Hung.* Bákó. Bacău, NE Romania 46.36N 26.55E
118 K11 **Bacău** ◐ *county* E Romania
Băc Bô, Vinh *see* Tongking, Gulf of
178 Jj5 **Băc Can** Băc Thai, N Vietnam 22.07N 105.50E
105 T5 **Baccarat** Meurthe-et-Moselle, NE France 48.27N 6.46E
191 N12 **Bacchus Marsh** Victoria, SE Australia 37.46S 144.27E
42 H4 **Bacerac** Sonora, NW Mexico 30.27N 108.55W
118 L10 **Băceşti** Vaslui, E Romania 46.49N 27.13E
178 Jj6 **Băc Giang** Ha Băc, N Vietnam 21.17N 106.12E
56 I5 **Bachaquero** Zulia, NW Venezuela 9.57N 71.09W
Bacher *see* Pohorje
120 M13 **Bacheykava** *Rus.* Bocheykovo. Vitsyebskaya Voblasts', N Belarus 55.01N 29.09E
42 I5 **Bachíniva** Chihuahua, N Mexico 28.41N 107.13W
164 G8 **Bachu** Xinjiang Uygur Zizhiqu, NW China 39.46N 78.30E
15 J6 **Back** ≈ Nunavut, N Canada
114 K10 **Bačka Palanka** *prev.* Palanka. Serbia, NW Yugoslavia 44.22N 20.57E
114 K8 **Bačka Topola** *Hung.* Topolya; *prev. Hung.* Bácstopolya. Serbia, N Yugoslavia 45.48N 19.39E
97 J17 **Bäckefors** Västra Götaland, S Sweden 58.49N 12.07E
Bäckermühle Schulzenmühle *see* Żywiec
97 L16 **Bäckhammar** Värmland, C Sweden 59.09N 14.13E
114 K9 **Bački Petrovac** *Hung.* Petrőcz; *prev.* Petrovac, Petrovácz. Serbia, NW Yugoslavia 45.22N 19.34E
103 I21 **Backnang** Baden-Württemberg, SW Germany 48.46N 9.25E
178 J15 **Bac Liêu** *var.* Vinh Loi. Minh Hai, S Vietnam 9.19N 105.42E
178 Jj6 **Băc Ninh** Ha Băc, N Vietnam 21.10N 106.04E
42 G4 **Bacoachi** Sonora, NW Mexico 30.37N 109.57W
179 Q13 **Bacolod** *off.* Bacolod City. Negros, C Philippines 10.43N 122.58E
179 P12 **Baco, Mount** ▲ Mindoro, N Philippines 12.50N 121.08E
113 K25 **Bácsalmás** Bács-Kiskun, S Hungary 46.09N 19.17E
Bácsjózseffalva *see* Žednik
113 J24 **Bács-Kiskun** *off.* Bács-Kiskun Megye. ◐ *county* S Hungary
Bácsszenttamás *see* Srbobran
Bácstopolya *see* Bačka Topola
Bactra *see* Balkh
161 F21 **Badagara** Kerala, SW India 11.24N 75.45E
103 M24 **Bad Aibling** Bayern, SE Germany 47.52N 12.00E
168 I13 **Badain Jaran Shamo** *desert* N China
106 I11 **Badajoz** *anc.* Pax Augusta. Extremadura, W Spain 38.52N 6.58W
106 J11 **Badajoz** ◐ *province* Extremadura, W Spain
155 S2 **Badakhshān** ◐ *province* NE Afghanistan
107 W6 **Badalona** *anc.* Baetulo. Cataluña, E Spain 41.27N 2.15E
160 O11 **Bādāmapāhārh** Orissa, E India 22.04N 86.06E
158 K8 **Badarīnāth** ▲ N India 30.43N 79.28E
174 Jj8 **Badas, Kepulauan** *island group* W Indonesia
111 S6 **Bad Aussee** Salzburg, E Austria 47.35N 13.44E
33 S8 **Bad Axe** Michigan, N USA 43.48N 83.00W
103 G16 **Bad Berleburg** Nordrhein-Westfalen, W Germany 51.03N 8.24E
103 L17 **Bad Blankenburg** Thüringen, C Germany 50.43N 11.19E
Bad Borseck *see* Borsec
103 G18 **Bad Camberg** Hessen, W Germany 50.18N 8.15E
102 L8 **Bad Doberan** Mecklenburg-Vorpommern, N Germany 54.06N 11.55E
103 N14 **Bad Düben** Sachsen, E Germany 51.35N 12.34E
111 X4 **Baden** *var.* Baden bei Wien; *anc.* Aquae Panoniae, Thermae Pannonicae. Niederösterreich, NE Austria 48.01N 16.13E
110 F9 **Baden** Aargau, N Switzerland 47.28N 8.19E
103 G21 **Baden-Baden** *anc.* Aurelia Aquensis. Baden-Württemberg, SW Germany 48.46N 8.13E
Baden bei Wien *see* Baden
103 G22 **Baden-Württemberg** *Fr.* Bade-Wurtemberg. ◐ *state* SW Germany
114 A10 **Baderna** Istra, NW Croatia 45.12N 13.45E
Bade-Wurtemberg *see* Baden-Württemberg
103 H20 **Bad Fredrichshall** Baden-Württemberg, S Germany 49.13N 9.15E
102 P11 **Bad Freienwalde** Brandenburg, NE Germany 52.46N 14.03E
111 Q8 **Badgastein** *var.* Gastein. Salzburg, NW Austria 47.07N 13.09E
Badger State *see* Wisconsin
154 L4 **Bādghīs** ◐ *province* NW Afghanistan
111 T5 **Bad Hall** Oberösterreich, N Austria 48.03N 14.13E
103 J14 **Bad Harzburg** Niedersachsen, C Germany 51.52N 10.34E
103 I16 **Bad Hersfeld** Hessen, C Germany 50.52N 9.41E
100 I10 **Badhoevedorp** Noord-Holland, C Netherlands 52.21N 4.46E
111 Q8 **Bad Hofgastein** Salzburg, NW Austria 47.10N 13.07E
Bad Homburg *see* Bad Homburg vor der Höhe
103 G18 **Bad Homburg vor der Höhe** *var.* Bad Homburg. Hessen, W Germany 50.13N 8.37E
103 E17 **Bad Honnef** Nordrhein-Westfalen, W Germany 50.39N 7.13E
155 Q17 **Badīn** Sind, SE Pakistan 24.40N 68.49E
23 S10 **Badin Lake** ⊠ North Carolina, SE USA
42 I8 **Badiraguato** Sinaloa, C Mexico 25.26N 107.33W
111 R6 **Bad Ischl** Oberösterreich, N Austria 47.43N 13.35E
Badjawa *see* Bajawa
103 J18 **Bad Kissingen** Bayern, SE Germany 50.12N 10.04E
Bad Königswart *see* Lázně Kynžvart
103 F19 **Bad Kreuznach** Rheinland-Pfalz, SW Germany 49.49N 7.52E
103 F24 **Bad Krozingen** Baden-Württemberg, SW Germany 47.55N 7.43E
103 G16 **Bad Laasphe** Nordrhein-Westfalen, W Germany 50.57N 8.24E
30 J6 **Badlands** *physical region* North Dakota, N USA
103 K16 **Bad Langensalza** Thüringen, C Germany 51.05N 10.40E
111 T3 **Bad Leonfelden** Oberösterreich, N Austria 48.31N 14.17E
103 I20 **Bad Mergentheim** Baden-Württemberg, SW Germany 49.30N 9.46E
103 H17 **Bad Nauheim** Hessen, W Germany 50.22N 8.45E
103 E17 **Bad Neuenahr-Arhweiler** Rheinland-Pfalz, W Germany 50.33N 7.07E
Bad Neustadt *see* Bad Neustadt an der Saale
103 J18 **Bad Neustadt an der Saale** *var.* Bad Neustadt. Berlin, C Germany 50.21N 10.13E
Badnur *see* Betūl
176 Yy15 **Bado** Irian Jaya, E Indonesia 7.06S 139.33E
102 H13 **Bad Oeynhausen** Nordrhein-Westfalen, NW Germany 52.12N 8.48E
102 J9 **Bad Oldesloe** Schleswig-Holstein, N Germany 53.49N 10.22E
79 Q16 **Badou** C Togo 7.37N 0.37E
Bad Polzin *see* Połczyn-Zdrój
102 H13 **Bad Pyrmont** Niedersachsen, C Germany 51.58N 9.16E
111 X9 **Bad Radkersburg** Steiermark, SE Austria 46.40N 16.02E
145 V8 **Badrah** E Iraq 33.06N 45.58E
168 J6 **Badrah** Hövsgöl, N Mongolia 49.33N 101.58E
103 N24 **Bad Reichenhall** Bayern, SE Germany 47.43N 12.52E
146 K8 **Badr Ḩunayn** Al Madīnah, W Saudi Arabia 23.46N 38.45E
30 M10 **Bad River** ≈ South Dakota, N USA
32 K4 **Bad River** ≈ Wisconsin, N USA
102 H13 **Bad Salzuflen** Nordrhein-Westfalen, NW Germany 52.04N 8.45E
103 J16 **Bad Salzungen** Thüringen, C Germany 50.48N 10.15E
111 V8 **Bad Sankt Leonhard im Lavanttal** Kärnten, S Austria 46.55N 14.51E
102 K9 **Bad Schwartau** Schleswig-Holstein, N Germany 53.55N 10.42E
103 L24 **Bad Tölz** Bayern, SE Germany 47.44N 11.34E
189 U1 **Badu Island** *island* Queensland, NE Australia
161 K25 **Badulla** Uva Province, C Sri Lanka 6.58N 81.03E
111 X5 **Bad Vöslau** Niederösterreich, NE Austria 47.58N 16.12E
103 I24 **Bad Waldsee** Baden-Württemberg, S Germany 47.54N 9.44E
37 U11 **Badwater Basin** *depression* California, W USA
103 J20 **Bad Windsheim** Bayern, C Germany 49.30N 10.25E
103 J23 **Bad Wörishofen** Bayern, S Germany 48.00N 10.36E
102 G10 **Bad Zwischenahn** Niedersachsen, NW Germany 53.10N 8.01E
106 M13 **Baena** Andalucía, S Spain 37.37N 4.22W
Baeterrae/Baeterrae Septimanorum *see* Béziers
Baetic Cordillera/Baetic Mountains *see* Béticos, Sistemas
Baetulo *see* Badalona
59 K18 **Baeza** Napo, NE Ecuador 0.30S 77.52W
107 N13 **Baeza** Andalucía, S Spain 38.00N 3.28W
81 D15 **Bafang** Ouest, W Cameroon 5.10N 10.10E
78 H12 **Bafatá** C Guinea-Bissau 12.09N 14.37W
155 U5 **Baffa** North-West Frontier Province, NW Pakistan 34.28N 73.14E
207 O11 **Baffin Basin** *undersea feature* N Labrador Sea
207 N12 **Baffin Bay** *bay* Canada/Greenland
27 T15 **Baffin Bay** *inlet* Texas, SW USA
206 M12 **Baffin Island** *island* Nunavut, NE Canada
81 E15 **Bafia** Centre, C Cameroon 4.49N 11.13E
79 R14 **Bafilo** NE Togo 9.22N 1.19E
78 J12 **Bafing** ≈ W Africa
78 J12 **Bafoulabé** Kayes, W Mali 13.43N 10.49W
81 D15 **Bafoussam** Ouest, W Cameroon 5.31N 10.25E
149 R9 **Bāfq** Yazd, C Iran 31.34N 55.21E
142 L10 **Bafra** Samsun, N Turkey 41.34N 35.55E
142 L10 **Bafra Burnu** *headland* N Turkey 41.42N 36.02E
149 S12 **Bāft** Kermān, S Iran 29.12N 56.36E
81 N18 **Bafwabalinga** Orientale, NE Dem. Rep. Congo (Zaire) 0.52N 26.55E
81 N18 **Bafwaboli** Orientale, NE Dem. Rep. Congo (Zaire) 0.42N 26.06E
81 N17 **Bafwasende** Orientale, NE Dem. Rep. Congo (Zaire) 1.00N 27.09E
194 J11 **Bagabag Island** *island* N PNG
44 K13 **Bagaces** Guanacaste, NW Costa Rica 10.29N 85.13W
159 O12 **Bagaha** Bihār, N India 27.07N 84.04E
161 F16 **Bāgalkot** Karnātaka, W India 16.10N 75.42E
83 J22 **Bagamoyo** Pwani, E Tanzania 6.25S 38.55E
174 Gg4 **Bagan Datuk** *var.* Bagan Datok. Perak, Peninsular Malaysia 3.58N 100.46E
179 Rr15 **Baganga** Mindanao, S Philippines 7.31N 126.34E
174 Gg6 **Bagansiapiapi** *var.* Pasirpangarayan. Sumatera, W Indonesia 2.09N 100.50E
Bagaria *see* Bagheria
79 T11 **Bagaroua** Tahoua, W Niger 14.34N 4.24E
81 I20 **Bagata** Bandundu, W Dem. Rep. Congo (Zaire) 3.46S 17.57E
Bagdad *see* Baghdād
126 Kk15 **Bagdarin** Respublika Buryatiya, S Russian Federation 54.27N 113.34E
63 G17 **Bagé** Rio Grande do Sul, S Brazil 31.22S 54.06W
Bagenalstown *see* Muine Bheag
Bagerhat *see* Bagherhat
105 P16 **Bages et de Sigean, Étang de** ◎ S France
35 W17 **Baggs** Wyoming, C USA 41.02N 107.39W
160 F11 **Bāgh** Madhya Pradesh, C India 22.22N 74.49E
145 T8 **Baghdād** *var.* Bagdad, *Eng.* Baghdad. ● (Iraq) C Iraq 33.19N 44.25E
145 T8 **Baghdād** ✕ C Iraq 33.19N 44.25E
159 T16 **Bagherhat** *var.* Bagerhat. Khulna, S Bangladesh 22.40N 89.48E
109 J23 **Bagheria** *var.* Bagaria. Sicilia, Italy, C Mediterranean Sea 38.04N 13.31E
149 S10 **Bāghīn** Kermān, C Iran 30.50N 57.00E
155 Q3 **Baghlān** Baghlān, NE Afghanistan 36.10N 68.43E
155 Q3 **Baghlān** *var.* Bāghlān. ◐ *province* NE Afghanistan
154 M7 **Bāghrān** Helmand, S Afghanistan 32.55N 64.57E
31 T4 **Bagley** Minnesota, N USA 47.31N 95.24W
108 H10 **Bagnacavallo** Emilia-Romagna, C Italy 44.00N 12.59E
104 K16 **Bagnères-de-Bigorre** Hautes-Pyrénées, S France 43.04N 0.09E
104 L17 **Bagnères-de-Luchon** Hautes-Pyrénées, S France 42.46N 0.34E
108 F11 **Bagni di Lucca** Toscana, C Italy 44.01N 10.38E
108 H11 **Bagno di Romagna** Emilia-Romagna, C Italy 43.51N 11.57E
105 R14 **Bagnols-sur-Cèze** Gard, S France 44.10N 4.37E
168 M14 **Bag Nur** ◎ N China
179 Q13 **Bago** *off.* Bago City. Negros, C Philippines 10.30N 122.49E
Bago *see* Pegu
78 M13 **Bagoé** ≈ Ivory Coast/Mali
Bagrāmē *see* Bagrāmī
155 R5 **Bagrāmī** *var.* Bagrāmē. Kābul, E Afghanistan 34.28N 69.16E
121 B14 **Bagrationovsk** *Ger.* Preussisch Eylau. Kaliningradskaya Oblast', W Russian Federation 54.24N 20.39E
Bagrax *see* Bohu
Bagrax Hu *see* Bosten Hu
58 C10 **Bagua** Amazonas, NE Peru 5.34S 78.24W
179 P9 **Baguio** *off.* Baguio City. Luzon, N Philippines 16.25N 120.36E
79 V9 **Bagzane, Monts** ▲ N Niger 17.48N 8.43E
Bāḩah, Minţaqat al *see* Al Bāḩah
Bahama Islands *see* Bahamas
46 H3 **Bahamas** *off.* Commonwealth of the Bahamas. ◆ *commonwealth republic* N West Indies
(0) L13 **Bahamas** *var.* Bahama Islands. *island group* N West Indies
159 S15 **Baharampur** *prev.* Berhampore. West Bengal, NE India 24.03N 88.16E
175 Nn6 **Bahau, Sungai** ≈ Borneo, N Indonesia
155 U10 **Bahāwalnagar** Punjab, E Pakistan 30.00N 73.03E
155 T11 **Bahāwalpur** Punjab, E Pakistan 29.24N 71.39E
142 L16 **Bahçe** Osmaniye, S Turkey 37.11N 36.32E
166 J8 **Ba He** ≈ C China
Bäherden *see* Bakharden
61 N16 **Bahia** *off.* Estado da Bahia. ◐ *state* E Brazil
63 B24 **Bahía Blanca** Buenos Aires, E Argentina 38.43S 62.19W
42 L15 **Bahía Bufadero** Michoacán de Ocampo, SW Mexico
65 J19 **Bahía Bustamante** Chubut, SE Argentina 45.06S 66.30W
42 D5 **Bahía de los Ángeles** Baja California, NW Mexico
42 C6 **Bahía de Tortugas** Baja California Sur, W Mexico 27.42N 114.54W
44 J4 **Bahía, Islas de la** *Eng.* Bay Islands. *island group* N Honduras
42 E5 **Bahía Kino** Sonora, NW Mexico 28.48N 111.55W
42 E9 **Bahía Magdalena** *var.* Puerto Magdalena. Baja California Sur, W Mexico 24.34N 112.07W
56 C8 **Bahía Solano** *var.* Ciudad Mutis, Solano. Chocó, W Colombia 6.13N 77.27W
82 I11 **Bahir Dar** *var.* Bahr Dar, Bahrdar Giyorgis. Amhara, N Ethiopia 11.33N 37.22E
147 X8 **Bahlā'** *var.* Bahlah, Bahlat. NW Oman 22.55N 57.16E
Bāhla *see* Bālān
Bahlah/Bahlat *see* Bahlā'
158 M11 **Bahraich** Uttar Pradesh, N India 27.34N 81.36E
149 M14 **Bahrain** *off.* State of Bahrain, Dawlat al Bahrayn, *Ar.* Al Baḩrayn; *prev.* Bahrein, *anc.* Tylos or Tyros. ◆ *monarchy* SW Asia
148 M14 **Bahrain** ✕ C Bahrain 26.15N 50.39E
148 M15 **Bahrain, Gulf of** *gulf* Persian Gulf, NW Arabian Sea
144 I7 **Baḩrat Mallāḩah** ◎ W Syria
Bahrayn, Dawlat al *see* Bahrain
Bahr Dar/Bahrdar Giyorgis *see* Bahir Dar
Bahrein *see* Bahrain
83 E16 **Bahr el Gabel** ◐ *state* S Sudan
82 E13 **Bahr ez Zaref** ≈ C Sudan
69 R8 **Bahr Kameur** ≈ N Central African Republic
Bahr Tabariya, Sea of *see* Tiberias, Lake
149 W15 **Bāhū Kalāt** Sīstān va Balūchestān, SE Iran 25.42N 61.28E
120 N13 **Bahushewsk** *Rus.* Bogushëvsk. Vitsyebskaya Voblasts', NE Belarus 54.51N 30.13E
Bai *see* Tagow Bāy
118 G13 **Baia de Aramă** Mehedinţi, SW Romania 45.00N 22.43E
118 G11 **Baia de Criş** *Ger.* Altenburg, *Hung.* Körösbánya. Hunedoara, SW Romania 46.10N 22.40E
85 A16 **Baia dos Tigres** Namibe, SW Angola 16.36S 11.44E
84 A13 **Baia Farta** Benguela, W Angola 12.38S 13.12E
118 H9 **Baia Mare** *Ger.* Frauenbach, *Hung.* Nagybánya; *prev.* Neustadt. Maramureş, NW Romania 47.39N 23.35E
118 H8 **Baia Sprie** *Ger.* Mittelstadt, *Hung.* Felsőbánya. Maramureş, NW Romania 47.40N 23.42E
80 G13 **Baïbokoum** Logone-Oriental, SW Chad 7.46N 15.43E
166 F12 **Baicao Ling** ▲▲ SW China
169 U9 **Baicheng** *var.* Pai-ch'eng; *prev.* T'aon-an. Jilin, NE China 45.31N 122.50E
164 I6 **Baicheng** *var.* Bay. Xinjiang Uygur Zizhiqu, NW China 41.49N 81.45E
118 J13 **Băicoi** Prahova, SE Romania 45.01N 25.52E
Baidoa *see* Baydhabo
13 U6 **Baie-Comeau** Quebec, SE Canada 49.12N 68.10W
13 T7 **Baie-des-Bacon** Quebec, SE Canada 48.31N 69.17W
13 S8 **Baie-des-Rochers** Quebec, SE Canada 47.57N 69.50W
13 U6 **Baie-des-Sables** Quebec, SE Canada 48.41N 67.55W
10 K11 **Baie-du-Poste** Quebec, SE Canada 50.19N 73.49W
180 H17 **Baie Lazare** Mahé, NE Seychelles 4.45S 55.28E
47 Y5 **Baie-Mahault** Basse Terre, C Guadeloupe 16.17N 61.34W
13 R9 **Baie-St-Paul** Quebec, SE Canada 47.27N 70.30W
13 V5 **Baie-Trinité** Quebec, SE Canada 49.25N 67.19W
11 T11 **Baie Verte** Newfoundland, SE Canada 49.58N 56.06W
169 X11 **Baihe** *prev.* Erdaobaihe. Jilin, NE China 42.24N 128.09E
Baiguan *see* Shangyu
145 U11 **Bā'ij al Mahdī** S Iraq 31.21N 44.57E
Baiji *see* Bayjī
Baikal, Lake *see* Baykal, Ozero
Bailādila *see* Kirandul
Baile an Chaistil *see* Ballycastle
Baile an Róba *see* Ballinrobe
Baile an tSratha *see* Ballintra
Baile Átha an Rí *see* Athenry
Baile Átha Buí *see* Athboy
Baile Átha Cliath *see* Dublin
Baile Átha Fhirdhia *see* Ardee
Baile Átha Í *see* Athy
Baile Átha Luain *see* Athlone
Baile Átha Troim *see* Trim
Baile Brigín *see* Balbriggan
Baile Easa Dara *see* Ballysadare
118 I13 **Băile Govora** Vâlcea, SW Romania 45.00N 24.08E
118 F13 **Băile Herculane** *Ger.* Herkulesbad, *Hung.* Herkulesfürdő. Caraş-Severin, SW Romania 44.50N 22.23E
Baile Locha Riach *see* Loughrea
Baile Mhistéala *see* Mitchelstown
Baile Monaidh *see* Ballymoney
107 N12 **Bailén** Andalucía, S Spain 38.06N 3.46W
Baile na hInse *see* Ballynahinch
Baile na Lorgan *see* Castleblayney
Baile na Mainistreach *see* Newtownabbey
Baile Nua na hArda *see* Newtownards
118 I12 **Băile Olăneşti** Vâlcea, SW Romania 45.16N 24.13E
118 H14 **Băileşti** Dolj, SW Romania 44.01N 23.20E
Bailingmiao *see* Darhan Muminggan Lianheqi
60 K11 **Bailique, Ilha** *island* NE Brazil
105 O1 **Bailleul** Nord, N France 50.43N 2.43E
80 H12 **Ba Illi** Chari-Baguirmi, SW Chad 10.31N 16.28E
165 V12 **Bailong Jiang** ≈ C China
84 C13 **Bailundo** *Port.* Vila Teixeira da Silva. Huambo, C Angola 12.12S 15.52E
165 T13 **Baima** *var.* Sêraitang. Qinghai, C China 32.55N 100.44E
176 W14 **Baimun** Pulau Workai, E Indonesia 6.41S 134.40E
194 H14 **Baimuru** Gulf, S PNG 7.31S 144.44E
164 M16 **Bainang** Xizang Zizhiqu, W China 28.57N 89.31E
25 S8 **Bainbridge** Georgia, SE USA 30.54N 84.33W
175 Pp17 **Baing** Pulau Sumba, SE Indonesia 10.09S 120.34E
164 M14 **Baingoin** Xizang Zizhiqu, W China 31.25N 90.01E
106 G2 **Baio Grande** Galicia, NW Spain 43.08N 8.58W
106 G4 **Baiona** Galicia, NW Spain 42.06N 8.49W
169 V7 **Baiquan** Heilongjiang, NE China 47.37N 126.04E
Bā'ir *see* Bāyir
164 I11 **Bairab Co** ◎ W China
27 Q7 **Baird** Texas, SW USA 32.23N 99.23W
41 N7 **Baird Mountains** ▲▲ Alaska, USA
15 Mm2 **Baird Peninsula** *peninsula* Baffin Island, Nunavut, NE Canada
Baireuth *see* Bayreuth
202 H3 **Bairiki** ● (Kiribati) Tarawa, NW Kiribati 1.19N 173.01E
169 S11 **Bairin Youqi** *var.* Daban. Nei Mongol Zizhiqu, N China 43.33N 118.40E
169 S10 **Bairin Zuoqi** *var.* Lindong. Nei Mongol Zizhiqu, N China 43.59N 119.24E
151 P17 **Bairkum** *Kaz.* Bayyrqum. Yuzhnyy Kazakhstan, S Kazakhstan 41.57N 68.05E
191 P12 **Bairnsdale** Victoria, SE Australia 37.51S 147.37E
179 Q14 **Bais** Negros, S Philippines 9.36N 123.07E
104 L15 **Baïse** *var.* Baise. ≈ S France
169 W11 **Baishan** *prev.* Hunjiang. Jilin, NE China 41.57N 126.31E
120 F12 **Baisogala** Radviliškis, C Lithuania 55.38N 23.44E
201 Q7 **Baiti** N Nauru 0.30S 166.55E
106 G13 **Baixo Alentejo** *physical region* S Portugal
66 P5 **Baixo, Ilhéu de** *island* Madeira, Portugal, NE Atlantic Ocean
85 E15 **Baixo Longa** Cuando Cubango, SE Angola 15.39S 18.39E
165 V10 **Baiyin** Gansu, C China 36.33N 104.11E
166 E8 **Baiyü** Sichuan, C China 30.37N 97.15E
167 N14 **Baiyun** ✕ (Guangzhou) Guangdong, S China 23.12N 113.19E
166 K4 **Baiyu Shan** ▲▲ C China
113 J25 **Baja** Bács-Kiskun, S Hungary 46.12N 18.56E
42 C4 **Baja California** ◐ *state* NW Mexico
42 C4 **Baja California** *Eng.* Lower California. *peninsula* NW Mexico
42 E9 **Baja California Sur** ◐ *state* W Mexico
Bājah *see* Béja
Bajan *see* Bayan
203 V16 **Baja, Punta** *headland* Easter Island, Chile, E Pacific Ocean 27.10S 109.21W
42 B4 **Baja, Punta** *headland* NW Mexico 29.57N 115.48W
57 R5 **Baja, Punta** *headland* NE Venezuela
44 D5 **Baja Verapaz** *off.* Departamento de Baja Verapaz. ◐ *department* C Guatemala
175 Q16 **Bajawa** *prev.* Badjawa. Flores, S Indonesia 8.46S 120.58E
159 S16 **Baj Baj** *prev.* Budge-Budge. West Bengal, E India 22.28N 88.10E
147 N15 **Bājil** W Yemen 15.05N 43.16E
191 U4 **Bajimba, Mount** ▲ New South Wales, SE Australia 29.19S 152.04E
114 K13 **Bajina Bašta** Serbia, W Yugoslavia 43.58N 19.33E
159 U14 **Bajitpur** Dhaka, E Bangladesh 24.12N 90.57E
114 K8 **Bajmok** Serbia, NW Yugoslavia 45.59N 19.25E
Bajo Boquete *see* Boquete
115 L17 **Bajram Curri** Kukës, N Albania 42.22N 20.06E
81 J14 **Bakala** Ouaka, C Central African Republic 6.03N 20.31E
131 T4 **Bakaly** Respublika Bashkortostan, W Russian Federation 55.10N 53.46E
Bakan *see* Shimonoseki
151 U14 **Bakanas** *Kaz.* Baqanas. Almaty, SE Kazakhstan 44.50N 76.13E
151 V12 **Bakanas** *Kaz.* Baqanas. ≈ E Kazakhstan
151 U14 **Bakbakty** *Kaz.* Baqbaqty. Almaty, SE Kazakhstan 44.36N 76.41E
126 Gg13 **Bakchar** Tomskaya Oblast', C Russian Federation 56.58N 81.59E
78 I11 **Bakel** E Senegal 13.43N 13.40W
37 W13 **Baker** California, W USA 35.15N 116.04W
24 J8 **Baker** Louisiana, S USA 30.35N 91.10W
35 Y9 **Baker** Montana, NW USA 46.22N 104.16W
34 L12 **Baker** Oregon, NW USA 44.46N 117.49W
199 Jj8 **Baker and Howland Islands** ◇ *US unincorporated territory* W Polynesia
38 L12 **Baker Butte** ▲ Arizona, SW USA 34.24N 111.22W
41 X15 **Baker Island** *island* Alexander Archipelago, Alaska, USA
15 Kk6 **Baker Lake** Nunavut, N Canada 64.19N 96.10W
15 Kk6 **Baker Lake** ◎ Nunavut, N Canada
34 H6 **Baker, Mount** ▲ Washington, NW USA 48.46N 121.48W
37 R13 **Bakersfield** California, W USA 35.22N 119.01W
26 M9 **Bakersfield** Texas, SW USA 30.54N 102.21W
23 P9 **Bakersville** North Carolina, SE USA 36.03N 82.10W
Bakhābī *see* Bū Khābī
152 E12 **Bakharden** *Turkm.* Bäherden; *prev.* Bakherden. Akhalskiy Velayat, C Turkmenistan 38.30N 57.18E
152 F12 **Bakhardok** *Turkm.* Bokurdak. Akhalskiy Velayat, C Turkmenistan 38.51N 58.34E
149 U5 **Bākharz, Kuhhā-ye** ▲▲ NE Iran
158 D13 **Bākhāsar** Rājasthān, NW India 24.43N 71.09E
Bakhchisaray *see* Bakhchysaray
119 T13 **Bakhchysaray** *Rus.* Bakhchisaray. Respublika Krym, S Ukraine 44.43N 33.53E
Bakherden *see* Bakharden
119 R3 **Bakhmach** Chernihivs'ka Oblast', N Ukraine 51.10N 32.48E
126 Hh11 **Bakhta** Krasnoyarskiy Kray, C Russian Federation 62.25N 88.56E
148 K6 **Bākhtarān** *prev.* Kermānshāh, Qahremānshahr. Kermānshāh, W Iran 34.19N 47.04E
Bākhtarān *see* Kermānshāh
149 Q11 **Bakhtegān, Daryācheh-ye** ◎ C Iran
151 X12 **Bakhty** Vostochnyy Kazakhstan, E Kazakhstan 46.41N 82.45E
143 Z11 **Bakı** *Eng.* Baku. ● (Azerbaijan) E Azerbaijan 40.23N 49.51E
143 Z11 **Bakı** ✕ E Azerbaijan 40.26N 49.55E
142 C13 **Bakır Çayı** ≈ W Turkey
94 L1 **Bakkafjördhur** Austurland, NE Iceland 66.01N 14.49W
94 L1 **Bakkaflói** *sea area* W Norwegian Sea
83 I15 **Bako** Southern, S Ethiopia 5.45N 36.39E
78 L15 **Bako** NW Ivory Coast 9.06N 7.34W
Bákó *see* Bacău
113 H23 **Bakony** *Eng.* Bakony Mountains, *Ger.* Bakonywald. ▲▲ W Hungary
Bakony Mountains/Bakonywald *see* Bakony
83 M16 **Bakool** *off.* Gobolka Bakool. ◐ *region* W Somalia
81 L15 **Bakouma** Mbomou, SE Central African Republic 5.42N 22.43E
131 N15 **Baksan** Kabardino-Balkarskaya Respublika, SW Russian Federation 43.43N 43.31E
121 I16 **Bakshty** Hrodzyenskaya Voblasts', W Belarus 53.56N 26.13E
Baku *see* Bakı
204 K12 **Bakutis Coast** *physical region* Antarctica
Bakwanga *see* Mbuji-Mayi
151 O15 **Bakyrly** Yuzhnyy Kazakhstan, S Kazakhstan 44.30N 67.41E
12 H13 **Bala** Ontario, S Canada 45.01N 79.37W
99 J19 **Bala** NW Wales, UK 52.54N 3.31W
142 I13 **Balâ** Ankara, C Turkey 39.34N 33.07E
179 O16 **Balabac Island** *island* W Philippines
Balabac, Selat *see* Balabac Strait
175 O1 **Balabac Strait** *var.* Selat Balabac. *strait* Malaysia/Philippines
Baʻlabakk *see* Baalbek
175 O10 **Balabalangan, Kepulauan** *island group* N Indonesia
197 H4 **Balabio, Île** *island* Province Nord, W New Caledonia
118 I14 **Balaci** Teleorman, S Romania 44.21N 24.55E
145 S7 **Balad** N Iraq 34.00N 44.07E
145 U7 **Balad Rūz** E Iraq 33.42N 45.04E
126 J15 **Balagansk** Irkutskaya Oblast', S Russian Federation 54.02N 102.48E
160 J11 **Bālāghāt** Madhya Pradesh, C India 21.48N 80.10E
161 F14 **Bālāghāt Range** ▲▲ W India
105 X14 **Balagne** *physical region* Corse, France, C Mediterranean Sea
107 U5 **Balaguer** Cataluña, NE Spain 41.48N 0.48E
107 S3 **Balaïtous** *var.* Pic de Balaitous, Pic de Balaïtous. ▲ France/Spain 42.51N 0.17W
Balaitous, Pic de *see* Balaïtous
131 O3 **Balakhna** Nizhegorodskaya Oblast', W Russian Federation 56.26N 43.43E
126 I14 **Balakhta** Krasnoyarskiy Kray, S Russian Federation 55.22N 91.24E
190 I9 **Balaklava** South Australia 34.10S 138.22E
Balakleya *see* Balakliya
119 V6 **Balakliya** *Rus.* Balakleya. Kharkivs'ka Oblast', E Ukraine 49.26N 36.51E
131 Q7 **Balakovo** Saratovskaya Oblast', W Russian Federation 52.03N 47.47E
85 P14 **Balama** Cabo Delgado, N Mozambique 13.18S 38.39E
175 Nn1 **Balambangan, Pulau** *island* East Malaysia
154 L3 **Bālā Morghāb** Laghmān, NW Afghanistan 35.37N 63.21E
158 E11 **Bālān** *prev.* Bāhla. Rājasthān, NW India 27.45N 71.31E
118 J10 **Bălan** *Hung.* Balánbánya. Harghita, C Romania 46.39N 25.45E
Balánbánya *see* Bălan
179 P10 **Balanga** Luzon, N Philippines 14.40N 120.32E
160 M12 **Balāngīr** *prev.* Bolangir. Orissa, E India 20.46N 83.31E
131 N8 **Balashov** Saratovskaya Oblast', W Russian Federation 51.31N 43.14E
Balasore *see* Bāleshwar
113 K21 **Balassagyarmat** Nógrád, N Hungary 48.04N 19.16E
31 S10 **Balaton** Minnesota, N USA 44.13N 95.52W
113 H24 **Balaton** *var.* Lake Balaton, *Ger.* Plattensee. ◎ W Hungary
113 I23 **Balatonfüred** *var.* Füred. Veszprém, W Hungary 46.56N 17.51E
Balaton, Lake *see* Balaton
118 I11 **Bălăuşeri** *Ger.* Bladenmarkt, *Hung.* Balavásár. Mureş, C Romania 46.24N 24.41E
Balavásár *see* Bălăuşeri
107 Q11 **Balazote** Castilla-La Mancha, C Spain 38.54N 2.09W
Balázsfalva *see* Blaj
121 F14 **Balbieriškis** Prienai, S Lithuania 54.29N 23.52E
195 S12 **Balbi, Mount** ▲ Bougainville Island, NE PNG 5.51S 154.58E
60 F11 **Balbina, Represa** ⊠ NW Brazil
45 T15 **Balboa** Panamá, C Panama 8.55N 79.36W
99 G17 **Balbriggan** *Ir.* Baile Brigín. E Ireland 53.37N 6.10W
Balbunar *see* Kubrat
83 N17 **Balcad** Shabeellaha Dhexe, C Somalia 2.19N 45.19E
63 D23 **Balcarce** Buenos Aires, E Argentina 37.51S 58.16W
9 U16 **Balcarres** Saskatchewan, S Canada 50.49N 103.31W
116 O8 **Balchik** Dobrich, NE Bulgaria 43.25N 28.11E
193 E24 **Balclutha** Otago, South Island, NZ 46.15S 169.44E
27 Q12 **Balcones Escarpment** *escarpment* Texas, SW USA
20 F14 **Bald Eagle Creek** ≈ Pennsylvania, NE USA
Baldenburg *see* Biały Bór
23 V12 **Bald Head Island** *island* North Carolina, SE USA
29 W10 **Bald Knob** Arkansas, C USA 35.18N 91.34W
32 K17 **Bald Knob** *hill* Illinois, N USA 37.33N 89.21W
Baldohn *see* Baldone
120 G9 **Baldone** *Ger.* Baldohn. Rīga, W Latvia 56.46N 24.18E
24 I9 **Baldwin** Louisiana, S USA 29.50N 91.32W
33 P7 **Baldwin** Michigan, N USA 43.54N 85.49W
29 Q4 **Baldwin City** Kansas, C USA 38.43N 95.12W
41 N8 **Baldwin Peninsula** *headland* Alaska, USA 66.45N 162.19W
20 H9 **Baldwinsville** New York, NE USA 43.09N 76.19W
25 N2 **Baldwyn** Mississippi, S USA 34.30N 88.38W
9 W15 **Baldy Mountain** ▲ Manitoba, S Canada 51.29N 100.46W
35 T7 **Baldy Mountain** ▲ Montana, NW USA 48.09N 109.39W

228

◆ Country ● Country Capital ◇ Dependent Territory ○ Dependent Territory Capital ◐ Administrative Region ✕ International Airport ▲ Mountain ▲▲ Mountain Range Volcano ≈ River ◎ Lake ⊠ Reservoir

BALDY PEAK – BARCOO

39 O13 **Baldy Peak** ▲ Arizona, SW USA 33.56N 109.37W
Bâle *see* Basel
107 X9 **Baleares** ⬖ *autonomous community* E Spain
107 X11 **Baleares, Islas** *Eng.* Balearic Islands. *island group* Spain, W Mediterranean Sea
Baleares Major *see* Mallorca
Balearic Islands *see* Baleares, Islas
Balearic Plain *see* Algerian Basin
Balearis Minor *see* Menorca
174 M6 **Baleh, Batang** ≈ East Malaysia
10 J8 **Baleine, Grande Rivière de la** ≈ Quebec, E Canada
10 K7 **Baleine, Petite Rivière de la** ≈ Quebec, SE Canada
11 N6 **Baleine, Rivière à la** ≈ Quebec, E Canada
101 J16 **Balen** Antwerpen, N Belgium 51.11N 5.12E
179 P9 **Baler** Luzon, N Philippines 15.47N 121.30E
160 P11 **Bāleshwar** *prev.* Balasore. Orissa, E India 21.31N 86.58E
126 L16 **Baley** Chitinskaya Oblast', S Russian Federation 51.30N 116.16E
79 S12 **Baléyara** Tillabéri, W Niger 13.48N 2.57E
131 T1 **Balezino** Udmurtskaya Respublika, NW Russian Federation 57.57N 53.03E
44 J4 **Balfate** Colón, N Honduras 15.47N 86.24W
9 O17 **Balfour** British Columbia, SW Canada 49.39N 116.57W
31 N3 **Balfour** North Dakota, N USA 47.55N 100.34W
Balfrush *see* Bābol
126 I16 **Balgazyn** Respublika Tyva, S Russian Federation 50.53N 95.12E
9 U16 **Balgonie** Saskatchewan, S Canada 50.30N 104.12W
Bălgrad *see* Alba Iulia
83 J19 **Balguda** *spring/well* S Kenya 1.28S 39.50E
164 K6 **Balguntay** Xinjiang Uygur Zizhiqu, NW China 42.51N 86.19E
147 R16 **Balḥāf** S Yemen 14.02N 48.15E
158 F13 **Bāli** Rājasthān, N India 25.17N 73.16E
175 N15 **Bali** ⬖ *province* S Indonesia
175 N16 **Bali** *island* C Indonesia
113 K16 **Balice** ✈ (Kraków) Małopolskie, S Poland 49.57N 19.49E
176 Yy13 **Baliem, Sungai** ≈ Irian Jaya, E Indonesia
142 C12 **Balıkesir** Balıkesir, W Turkey 39.38N 27.52E
142 C12 **Balıkesir** ⬖ *province* NW Turkey
144 L3 **Balīkh, Nahr** ≈ N Syria
175 O9 **Balikpapan** Borneo, C Indonesia 1.15S 116.49E
175 O9 **Balikpapan, Teluk** *bay* Borneo, C Indonesia
Bali, Laut *see* Bali Sea
195 O11 **Balima** ≈ New Britain, C PNG
179 P17 **Balimbing** Tawitawi, SW Philippines 5.10N 120.00E
194 G14 **Balimo** Western, SW PNG 8.01S 142.52E
Bálinc *see* Balinț
175 Qq9 **Balingara, Pegunungan** ▲▲ Sulawesi, N Indonesia
103 H23 **Balingen** Baden-Württemberg, SW Germany 48.16N 8.51E
118 F11 **Balinț** *Hung.* Bálinc. Timiș, W Romania 45.52N 21.54E
179 Pp6 **Balintang Channel** *channel* N Philippines
144 K3 **Bālis** Ḥalab, N Syria 36.01N 38.03E
175 N15 **Bali Sea** *Ind.* Laut Bali. *sea* C Indonesia
175 N16 **Bali, Selat** *strait* C Indonesia
100 K7 **Balk** Friesland, N Netherlands 52.54N 5.34E
124 O7 **Balkan Mountains** *Bul./SCr.* Stara Planina. ▲▲ Bulgaria/Yugoslavia
152 B9 **Balkanskiy Velayat** *Turkm.* Balkan Welayaty. ⬖ *province* W Turkmenistan
Balkan Welayaty *see* Balkanskiy Velayat
151 P8 **Balkashino** Akmola, N Kazakhstan 52.32N 68.43E
155 O2 **Balkh** *anc.* Bactra. Balkh, N Afghanistan 36.46N 66.54E
155 P2 **Balkh** ⬖ *province* N Afghanistan
151 T13 **Balkhash** *Kaz.* Balqash. Zhezkazgan, SE Kazakhstan 46.52N 74.54E
Balkhash, Lake *see* Balkhash, Ozero
151 T13 **Balkhash, Ozero** *Eng.* Lake Balkhash, *Kaz.* Balqash. ◎ SE Kazakhstan
Balla Balla *see* Mbalabala
98 H10 **Ballachulish** N Scotland, UK 56.40N 5.10W
188 M12 **Balladonia** Western Australia 32.21S 123.31E
99 C16 **Ballaghaderreen** *Ir.* Bealach an Doirín. C Ireland 53.51N 8.29W
94 H10 **Ballangen** Nordland, NW Norway 68.18N 16.48E
99 H14 **Ballantrae** W Scotland, UK 55.04N 5.00W
191 N12 **Ballarat** Victoria, SE Australia 37.36S 143.51E
188 K11 **Ballard, Lake** *salt lake* Western Australia
Ballari *see* Bellary
78 L11 **Ballé** Koulikoro, W Mali 15.18N 8.31W
42 D7 **Ballenas, Bahía de** *bay* W Mexico
42 D5 **Ballenas, Canal de** *channel* NW Mexico
205 R17 **Balleny Islands** *island group* Antarctica
42 J7 **Balleza** *var.* San Pablo Balleza. Chihuahua, N Mexico 26.55N 106.21W
116 M13 **Ballı** Tekirdağ, NW Turkey 40.48N 27.03E
159 O13 **Ballia** Uttar Pradesh, N India 25.45N 84.09E
191 V4 **Ballina** New South Wales, SE Australia 28.49S 153.33E
99 C16 **Ballina** *Ir.* Béal an Átha. W Ireland 54.07N 9.09W
99 D16 **Ballinamore** *Ir.* Béal an Átha Móir. NW Ireland 54.03N 7.46W
99 D18 **Ballinasloe** *Ir.* Béal Átha na Sluaighe. W Ireland 53.19N 8.13W
27 P8 **Ballinger** Texas, SW USA 31.44N 99.57W
99 C17 **Ballinrobe** *Ir.* Baile an Róba. W Ireland 53.37N 9.14W
99 A21 **Ballinskelligs Bay** *Ir.* Bá na Scealg. *inlet* SW Ireland
99 D15 **Ballintra** *Ir.* Baile an tSratha. NW Ireland 54.34N 8.07W
105 T7 **Ballon d'Alsace** ▲ NE France 47.50N 6.54E
Ballon de Guebwiller *see* Grand Ballon
115 K21 **Ballsh** *var.* Ballshi. Fier, SW Albania 40.35N 19.45E
Ballshi *see* Ballsh
100 K4 **Ballum** Friesland, N Netherlands 53.27N 5.40E
99 F16 **Ballybay** *Ir.* Béal Átha Beithe. N Ireland 54.07N 6.54W
99 E14 **Ballybofey** *Ir.* Bealach Féich. NW Ireland 54.48N 7.46W
99 G14 **Ballycastle** *Ir.* Baile an Chaistil. N Northern Ireland, UK 55.12N 6.13W
99 G15 **Ballyclare** *Ir.* Bealach Cláir. E Northern Ireland, UK 54.45N 6.00W
99 E16 **Ballyconnell** *Ir.* Béal Átha Conaill. N Ireland 54.07N 7.34W
99 C17 **Ballyhaunis** *Ir.* Beál Átha hAmhnais. W Ireland 53.45N 8.45W
99 G14 **Ballymena** *Ir.* An Baile Meánach. NE Northern Ireland, UK 54.52N 6.16W
99 F14 **Ballymoney** *Ir.* Baile Monaidh. NE Northern Ireland, UK 55.10N 6.30W
99 G15 **Ballynahinch** *Ir.* Baile na hInse. SE Northern Ireland, UK 54.24N 5.54W
99 D16 **Ballysadare** *Ir.* Baile Easa Dara. NW Ireland 54.13N 8.30W
99 D15 **Ballyshannon** *Ir.* Béal Átha Seanaidh. NW Ireland 54.30N 8.10W
65 H19 **Balmaceda** Aisén, S Chile 45.54S 71.47W
65 G23 **Balmaceda, Cerro** ▲ S Chile 51.27S 73.26W
113 N22 **Balmazújváros** Hajdú-Bihar, E Hungary 47.36N 21.18E
110 E10 **Balmhorn** ▲ SW Switzerland 46.27N 7.41E
190 L12 **Balmoral** Victoria, SE Australia 37.16S 141.38E
26 K9 **Balmorhea** Texas, SW USA 30.58N 103.44W
Balneario Claromecó *see* Claromecó
175 R9 **Balo** Sulawesi, N Indonesia 0.58S 123.19E
Balochistān *see* Baluchistān
84 B13 **Balombo** *Port.* Norton de Matos, Vila Norton de Matos. Benguela, W Angola 12.21S 14.46E
84 B13 **Balombo** ≈ W Angola
189 X10 **Balonne River** ≈ Queensland, E Australia
158 E13 **Bālotra** Rājasthān, N India 25.51N 72.18E
151 V14 **Balpyk Bi** *prev.* Kirovskiy *Kaz.* Kīrov. Almaty, SE Kazakhstan 44.52N 78.10E
Balqā'/Balqā', Muḥāfaẓat al *see* Al Balqā'
Balqash *see* Balkhash/Balkhash, Ozero
158 M12 **Balrāmpur** Uttar Pradesh, N India 27.25N 82.10E
190 M9 **Balranald** New South Wales, SE Australia 34.39S 143.33E
118 H14 **Balș** Olt, S Romania 44.19N 24.06E
12 H11 **Balsam Creek** Ontario, S Canada 46.26N 79.10W
32 I5 **Balsam Lake** Wisconsin, N USA 45.27N 92.28W
12 I14 **Balsam Lake** ◎ Ontario, SE Canada
61 M14 **Balsas** Maranhão, E Brazil 07.30S 46.00W
42 M15 **Balsas, Río** *var.* Río Mexcala. ≈ S Mexico
45 W16 **Balsas, Río** ≈ SE Panama
121 O18 **Bal'shavik** *Rus.* Bol'shevik. Homyel'skaya Voblasts', SE Belarus 52.34N 30.49E
97 O15 **Bålsta** Uppsala, C Sweden 59.33N 17.35E
110 E7 **Balsthal** Solothurn, NW Switzerland 47.20N 7.50E
119 O8 **Balta** Odes'ka Oblast', SW Ukraine 47.58N 29.39E
121 H14 **Baltaji Voke** Vilnius, SE Lithuania 54.35N 25.13E
107 N5 **Baltanás** Castilla-León, N Spain 41.56N 4.12W
63 E16 **Baltasar Brum** Artigas, N Uruguay 30.43S 57.19W
118 M9 **Bălți** *Rus.* Bel'tsy. N Moldova 47.45N 27.57E
Baltic Port *see* Paldiski
120 B10 **Baltic Sea** *Ger.* Ostee, *Rus.* Baltiskoye More. *sea* N Europe
23 X3 **Baltimore** Maryland, NE USA 39.17N 76.36W
33 T13 **Baltimore** Ohio, N USA 39.48N 82.33W
23 X3 **Baltimore-Washington** ✈ Maryland, E USA 39.10N 76.40W
Baltischport/Baltiski *see* Paldiski
Baltiskoye More *see* Baltic Sea
121 A14 **Baltiysk** *Ger.* Pillau. Kaliningradskaya Oblast', W Russian Federation 54.39N 19.54E
Baltkrievija *see* Belarus
194 K9 **Baluan Island** *island* N PNG
Balūchestān va Sīstān *see* Sīstān va Balūchestān
154 M12 **Baluchistān** *var.* Balochistān, Beluchistan. ⬖ *province* SW Pakistan
179 Q12 **Balud** Masbate, N Philippines 12.03N 123.12E
174 Mm6 **Balui, Batang** ≈ East Malaysia
159 S13 **Bālurghat** West Bengal, NE India 25.14N 88.43E
120 J8 **Balvi** Balvi, NE Latvia 57.07N 27.14E
194 H12 **Balyer River** Western Highlands, C PNG
153 W7 **Balykchy** *Kir.* Ysyk-Köl; *prev.* Issyk-Kul', Rybach'ye. Issyk-Kul'skaya Oblast', NE Kyrgyzstan 42.28N 76.08E
58 B7 **Balzar** Guayas, W Ecuador 1.25S 79.54W
110 I8 **Balzers** S Liechtenstein 47.04N 9.31E
149 T12 **Bam** Kermān, SE Iran 29.08N 58.27E
79 Y13 **Bama** Borno, NE Nigeria 11.28N 13.46E
78 L12 **Bamako** ● (Mali) Capital District, SW Mali 12.39N 8.01W
79 P10 **Bamba** Gao, C Mali 17.03N 1.19W
44 M8 **Bambana, Río** ≈ NE Nicaragua
81 J15 **Bambari** Ouaka, C Central African Republic 5.45N 20.37E
189 W5 **Bambaroo** Queensland, NE Australia 19.00S 146.16E
103 K19 **Bamberg** Bayern, SE Germany 49.54N 10.52E
23 R14 **Bamberg** South Carolina, SE USA 33.18N 81.02W
81 M16 **Bambesa** Orientale, N Dem. Rep. Congo (Zaire) 3.25N 25.43E
78 G11 **Bambey** W Senegal 14.43N 16.26W
81 H16 **Bambio** Sangha-Mbaéré, SW Central African Republic 3.57N 16.54E
85 I24 **Bamboesberge** ▲ S South Africa 31.24S 26.10E
81 D14 **Bamenda** Nord-Ouest, W Cameroon 5.55N 10.09E
8 K17 **Bamfield** Vancouver Island, British Columbia, SW Canada 48.48N 125.05W
152 E12 **Bami** *Turkm.* Bamy. Akhalskiy Velayat, C Turkmenistan 38.42N 56.47E
155 P4 **Bāmīān** *var.* Bāmiān. Bāmīān, NE Afghanistan 34.50N 67.51E
155 O4 **Bāmīān** ⬖ *province* C Afghanistan
81 J14 **Bamingui** Bamingui-Bangoran, C Central African Republic 7.38N 20.06E
80 J13 **Bamingui** ≈ N Central African Republic
80 J13 **Bamingui-Bangoran** ⬖ *prefecture* N Central African Republic
149 V13 **Bampūr** Sīstān va Balūchestān, SE Iran 27.13N 60.28E
194 G14 **Bamu** ≈ SW PNG
Bamy *see* Bami
Bán *see* Bánovce nad Bebravou
83 N17 **Banaadir** *off.* Gobolka Banaadir. ⬖ *region* S Somalia
203 N3 **Banaba** *var.* Ocean Island. *island* Tungaru, W Kiribati
61 O14 **Banabuiú, Açude** ⊠ NE Brazil
59 O19 **Bañados del Izozog** *salt lake* SE Bolivia
99 D18 **Banagher** *Ir.* Beannchar. C Ireland 53.12N 7.56W
81 M17 **Banalia** Orientale, N Dem. Rep. Congo (Zaire) 1.39N 25.19E
78 L12 **Banamba** Koulikoro, W Mali 13.33N 7.25W
42 G4 **Banámichi** Sonora, NW Mexico 30.01N 110.13W
189 Y9 **Banana** Queensland, E Australia 24.33S 150.07E
203 Z2 **Banana** *prev.* Main Camp. Kiritimati, E Kiribati 02.00N 157.25W
61 K16 **Bananal, Ilha do** *island* C Brazil
25 Y12 **Banana River** *lagoon* Florida, SE USA
157 Q22 **Bananga** Andaman and Nicobar Islands, India, NE Indian Ocean 6.57N 93.54E
Banaras *see* Vārānasi
116 N13 **Banarlı** Tekirdağ, NW Turkey 41.04N 27.21E
158 H12 **Banās** ≈ N India
77 Z11 **Banâs, Râs** *headland* E Egypt 23.55N 35.47E
114 N10 **Banatski Karlovac** Serbia, NE Yugoslavia 45.03N 21.02E
147 P16 **Banā, Wādī** *dry watercourse* SW Yemen
142 E14 **Banaz** Uşak, W Turkey 38.46N 29.46E
142 E14 **Banaz Çayı** ≈ W Turkey
165 P14 **Banbar** Xizang Zizhiqu, W China 31.01N 94.43E
99 G15 **Banbridge** *Ir.* Droichead na Banna. SE Northern Ireland, UK 54.21N 6.16W
Ban Bua Yai *see* Bua Yai
99 M21 **Banbury** S England, UK 52.04N 1.19W
178 H7 **Ban Chiang Dao** Chiang Mai, NW Thailand 19.22N 98.59E
98 K9 **Banchory** NE Scotland, UK 58.04N 0.35W
12 J13 **Bancroft** Ontario, SE Canada 45.04N 77.49W
35 R15 **Bancroft** Idaho, NW USA 42.43N 111.54W
31 U11 **Bancroft** Iowa, C USA 43.17N 94.13W
160 I9 **Banda** Madhya Pradesh, C India 24.04N 78.57E
158 L13 **Bānda** Uttar Pradesh, N India 25.28N 80.19E
173 E3 **Bandaaceh** *var.* Banda Atjeh; *prev.* Koetaradja, Kutaradja, Kutaraja. Sumatera, W Indonesia 5.30N 95.19E
Banda Atjeh *see* Bandaaceh
176 U12 **Banda, Kepulauan** *island group* E Indonesia
Banda, Laut *see* Banda Sea
79 N17 **Bandama** *var.* Bandama Fleuve. ≈ S Ivory Coast
79 N15 **Bandama Blanc** ≈ C Ivory Coast
Bandama Fleuve *see* Bandama
Bandar 'Abbās *see* Bandar-e 'Abbās
159 W16 **Bandarban** Chittagong, SE Bangladesh 22.13N 92.13E
82 Q13 **Bandarbeyla** *var.* Bender Beila, Bender Beyla. Bari, NE Somalia 9.28N 50.48E
149 R14 **Bandar-e 'Abbās** *var.* Bandar 'Abbās; *prev.* Gombroon. Hormozgān, S Iran 27.10N 56.10E
148 M3 **Bandar-e Anzalī** Gīlān, NW Iran 37.25N 49.28E
149 N12 **Bandar-e Būshehr** *var.* Būshehr, *Eng.* Bushire. Būshehr, S Iran 28.58N 50.49E
148 M11 **Bandar-e Gonāveh** *var.* Ganāveh; *prev.* Gonāveh. Būshehr, SW Iran 29.33N 50.39E
149 R14 **Bandar-e Khamīr** Hormozgān, S Iran 26.59N 55.30E
149 Q14 **Bandar-e Langeh** *var.* Bandar-e Lengeh, Lingeh. Hormozgān, S Iran 26.34N 54.52E
Bandar-e Lengeh *see* Bandar-e Langeh
148 L10 **Bandar-e Māhshahr** *var.* Māh-Shahr; *prev.* Bandar-e Ma'shūr. Khūzestān, SW Iran 30.33N 49.10E
Bandar-e Ma'shūr *see* Bandar-e Māhshahr
149 O14 **Bandar-e Nakhīlū** Hormozgān, S Iran
Bandar-e Shāh *see* Bandar-e Torkaman
149 P4 **Bandar-e Torkaman** *var.* Bandar-e Torkeman, Bandar-e Torkman; *prev.* Bandar-e Shāh. Golestān, N Iran 36.55N 54.04E
Bandar-e Torkeman/Bandar-e Torkman *see* Bandar-e Torkaman
Bandar Kassim *see* Boosaaso
174 Ii13 **Bandarlampung** *prev.* Tanjungkarang, Teloekbetoeng, Telukbetung. Sumatera, W Indonesia 5.28N 105.16E
Bandar Maharani *see* Muar
Bandar Masulipatnam *see* Machilīpatnam
Bandar Penggaram *see* Batu Pahat
175 N3 **Bandar Seri Begawan** *prev.* Brunei Town. ● (Brunei) N Brunei 4.55N 114.58E
174 Mm3 **Bandar Seri Begawan** ✈ N Brunei 4.55N 114.58E
175 Ss13 **Banda Sea** *var.* Laut Banda. *sea* E Indonesia
106 H5 **Bande** Galicia, NW Spain 42.01N 7.58W
61 G15 **Bandeirantes** Mato Grosso, W Brazil 9.04S 57.53W
61 N20 **Bandeira, Pico da** ▲ SE Brazil 20.25S 41.45W
85 K19 **Bandelierkop** Northern, NE South Africa 23.21S 29.46E
64 L8 **Bandera** Santiago del Estero, N Argentina 28.52S 62.15W
27 Q11 **Bandera** Texas, SW USA 29.43N 99.07W
42 J13 **Banderas, Bahía de** *bay* W Mexico
79 O11 **Bandiagara** Mopti, C Mali 14.22N 3.42W
158 I12 **Bāndīkūi** Rājasthān, N India 27.07N 76.34E
142 C11 **Bandırma** *var.* Penderma. Balıkesir, NW Turkey 40.21N 27.58E
Bandjarmasin *see* Banjarmasin
Bandoeng *see* Bandung
99 C21 **Bandon** *Ir.* Droicheadna Bandan. SW Ireland 51.43N 8.43W
34 E14 **Bandon** Oregon, NW USA 43.07N 124.24W
178 J8 **Ban Dong Bang** Nong Khai, E Thailand 18.00N 104.08E
178 I6 **Ban Donkon** Oudômxai, N Laos 20.20N 101.37E
180 J14 **Bandrélé** SE Mayotte
81 H20 **Bandundu** *prev.* Banningville. Bandundu, W Dem. Rep. Congo (Zaire) 3.18S 17.24E
81 I21 **Bandundu** *off.* Région de Bandundu. ⬖ *region* W Dem. Rep. Congo (Zaire)
174 Jj14 **Bandung** *prev.* Bandoeng. Jawa, C Indonesia 6.47S 107.28E
118 L15 **Băneasa** Constanța, SW Romania 44.03N 27.42E
148 J4 **Bāneh** Kordestān, N Iran 35.58N 45.54E
46 I7 **Banes** Holguín, E Cuba 20.58N 75.43W
9 P16 **Banff** Alberta, SW Canada 51.10N 115.34W
98 K8 **Banff** NE Scotland, UK 57.39N 2.33W
98 K8 **Banff** *cultural region* NE Scotland, UK
Bánffyhunyad *see* Huedin
79 N14 **Banfora** SW Burkina 10.36N 4.45W
161 H19 **Bangalore** Karnātaka, S India 12.58N 77.34E
159 S16 **Bangaon** West Bengal, NE India 23.01N 88.49E
179 P9 **Bangar** Luzon, N Philippines 16.51N 120.25E
81 L15 **Bangassou** Mbomou, SE Central African Republic 4.51N 22.55E
194 K12 **Bangeta, Mount** ▲ C PNG 6.11S 147.02E
175 Qq10 **Banggai, Kepulauan** *island group* C Indonesia
175 R9 **Banggai, Pulau** *island* Kepulauan Banggai, N Indonesia
176 X11 **Banggelapa** Irian Jaya, E Indonesia 3.47S 136.53E
Banggi *see* Banggi, Pulau
175 O1 **Banggi, Pulau** *var.* Banggi. *island* East Malaysia
124 N15 **Banghāzī** *Eng.* Bengazi, Benghazi, *It.* Bengasi. NE Libya 32.07N 20.04E
Bang Hieng *see* Xé Banghiang
174 K8 **Bangkai, Tanjung** *var.* Bankai. *headland* Borneo, N Indonesia 0.21N 108.53E
174 M14 **Bangkalan** Pulau Madura, C Indonesia 7.04S 112.43E
175 S6 **Bangka, Pulau** *island* N Indonesia
174 J10 **Bangka, Pulau** *island* W Indonesia
174 Ii10 **Bangka, Selat** *strait* Sumatera, W Indonesia
175 Rr6 **Bangka, Selat** *var.* Selat Likupang. *strait* Sulawesi, N Indonesia
174 Gg8 **Bangkinang** Sumatera, W Indonesia 0.21N 100.56E
174 H10 **Bangko** Sumatera, W Indonesia 2.03S 102.15E
Bangkok *see* Krung Thep
Bangkok, Bight of *see* Krung Thep, Ao
159 T14 **Bangladesh** *off.* People's Republic of Bangladesh; *prev.* East Pakistan. ◆ *republic* S Asia
178 Kk13 **Ba Ngoi** Khanh Hoa, S Vietnam 11.55N 109.07E
158 K5 **Bangong Co** *var.* Pangong Tso. ◎ China/India *see also* Pangong Tso
99 G15 **Bangor** *Ir.* Beannchar. E Northern Ireland, UK 54.40N 5.40W
99 I18 **Bangor** NW Wales, UK 53.13N 4.07W
21 R6 **Bangor** Maine, NE USA 44.48N 68.46W
20 I14 **Bangor** Pennsylvania, NE USA 40.52N 75.12W
69 R8 **Bangoran** ≈ S Central African Republic
Bang Phra *see* Trat
Bang Pla Soi *see* Chon Buri
27 Q8 **Bangs** Texas, SW USA 31.43N 99.07W
178 H13 **Bang Saphan** *var.* Bang Saphan Yai. Prachuap Khiri Khan, SW Thailand 11.10N 99.27E
Bang Saphan Yai *see* Bang Saphan
38 I8 **Bangs, Mount** ▲ Arizona, SW USA 36.47N 113.51W
95 E15 **Bangsund** Nord-Trøndelag, C Norway 64.22N 11.22E
179 P8 **Bangued** Luzon, N Philippines 17.36N 120.40E
81 I15 **Bangui** ● (Central African Republic) Ombella-Mpoko, SW Central African Republic 4.21N 18.31E
81 I15 **Bangui** ✈ Ombella-Mpoko, SW Central African Republic 4.19N 18.34E
85 N16 **Bangula** Southern, S Malawi 16.38S 35.04E
Bangwaketse *see* Southern
84 K12 **Bangweulu, Lake** *var.* Lake Bengweulu. ◎ N Zambia
Banhā *see* Benha
Ban Hat Yai *see* Hat Yai
178 I8 **Ban Hin Heup** Viangchan, C Laos 18.37N 102.19E
Ban Houayxay/Ban Houei Sai *see* Houayxay
178 H12 **Ban Hua Hin** *var.* Hua Hin. Prachuap Khiri Khan, SW Thailand 12.29N 99.55E
81 L14 **Bani** Haute-Kotto, E Central African Republic 7.06N 22.51E
79 N12 **Bani** ≈ S Mali
47 O9 **Baní** S Dominican Republic 18.14N 70.18W
Banias *see* Bāniyās
79 S11 **Bani Bangou** Tillabéri, SW Niger 15.04N 2.40E
78 M12 **Banifing** *var.* Ngorolaka. ≈ Burkina/Mali
79 R13 **Banikoara** N Benin 11.18N 2.25E
Banī Mazār *see* Beni Mazâr
116 K8 **Baniski Lom** ≈ N Bulgaria
23 U7 **Banister River** ≈ Virginia, NE USA
Banī Suwayf *see* Beni Suef
77 O8 **Banī Walīd** NW Libya 31.46N 13.58E
144 H5 **Bāniyās** *var.* Banias, Baniyas, Paneas. Tarṭūs, W Syria 35.12N 35.57E
115 K14 **Banja** Serbia, W Yugoslavia 43.33N 19.35E
Banjak, Kepulauan *see* Banyak, Kepulauan
114 J12 **Banja Koviljača** Serbia, W Yugoslavia 44.31N 19.11E
114 G11 **Banja Luka** Republika Srpska, NW Bosnia and Herzegovina 44.46N 17.10E
175 N11 **Banjarmasin** *prev.* Bandjarmasin. Borneo, C Indonesia 3.22S 114.33E
Banjoewangi *see* Banyuwangi
78 F11 **Banjul** *prev.* Bathurst. ● (Gambia) W Gambia 13.25N 16.43W
78 F11 **Banjul** ✈ W Gambia 13.18N 16.39W
Banjuwangi *see* Banyuwangi
Bank *see* Bankä
143 Y13 **Bankä** *Rus.* Bank. SE Azerbaijan 39.25N 49.13E
178 Jj11 **Ban Kadian** *var.* Ban Kadiene. Champasak, S Laos 14.25N 105.42E
Ban Kadiene *see* Ban Kadian
Bankai *see* Bangkai, Tanjung
178 Gg15 **Ban Kam Phuam** Phangnga, SW Thailand 9.16N 98.24E
Ban Kantang *see* Kantang
79 O11 **Bankass** Mopti, S Mali 14.05N 3.30W
97 L19 **Bankeryd** Jönköping, S Sweden 57.51N 14.07E
85 K16 **Banket** Mashonaland West, N Zimbabwe 17.25S 30.25E
178 Jj11 **Ban Khamphô** Attapu, S Laos 14.35N 106.18E
25 O4 **Bankhead Lake** ⊠ Alabama, S USA
79 Q11 **Bankilaré** Tillabéri, SW Niger 14.34N 0.41E
Banks, Îles *see* Banks Islands
8 I14 **Banks Island** *island* British Columbia, SW Canada
15 Hh1 **Banks Island** *island* Banks Island, Northwest Territories, NW Canada
197 C10 **Banks Islands** *Fr.* Îles Banks. *island group* N Vanuatu
25 U8 **Banks Lake** ◎ Georgia, SE USA
34 K8 **Banks Lake** ⊠ Washington, NW USA
193 I19 **Banks Peninsula** *peninsula* South Island, NZ
191 Q15 **Banks Strait** *strait* SW Tasman Sea
Ban Kui Nua *see* Kui Buri
159 R16 **Bānkura** West Bengal, NE India 23.13N 87.04E
178 J8 **Ban Lakxao** *var.* Lak Sao. Bolikhamxai, C Laos 18.10N 104.58E
178 H17 **Ban Lam Phai** Songkhla, SW Thailand 6.43N 100.57E
Ban Mae Sot *see* Mae Sot
Ban Mae Suai *see* Mae Suai
Ban Mak Khaeng *see* Udon Thani
177 G3 **Banmauk** Sagaing, N Burma 24.25N 95.54E
Banmo *see* Bhamo
178 Jj10 **Ban Mun-Houamuang** S Laos 15.11N 106.44E
99 F14 **Bann** *var.* Lower Bann, Upper Bann. ≈ N Northern Ireland, UK
178 Jj10 **Ban Nadou** Salavan, S Laos 15.51N 105.37E
178 J10 **Ban Nakala** Savannakhét, S Laos 16.14N 105.09E
178 I8 **Ban Nakha** Viangchan, C Laos 18.13N 102.29E
178 Jj9 **Ban Nakham** Khammouan, S Laos 17.10N 105.25E
178 I8 **Ban Namoun** Xaignabouli, N Laos 18.40N 101.34E
178 Hh17 **Ban Nang Sata** Yala, SW Thailand 6.15N 101.13E
178 Gg15 **Ban Na San** Surat Thani, SW Thailand 8.52N 99.21E
178 Ii7 **Ban Nasi** Xiangkhoang, N Laos 19.37N 103.33E
46 I3 **Bannerman Town** Eleuthera Island, C Bahamas 24.38N 76.09W
37 V15 **Banning** California, W USA 33.55N 116.52W
Banningville *see* Bandundu
178 Jj11 **Ban Nongsim** Champasak, S Laos 14.45N 106.00E
155 S7 **Bannu** *prev.* Edwardesabad. North-West Frontier Province, NW Pakistan 32.00N 70.36E
Bañolas *see* Banyoles
58 C7 **Baños** Tungurahua, C Ecuador 1.20S 78.24W
Bánovce *see* Bánovce nad Bebravou
113 I19 **Bánovce nad Bebravou** *var.* Bánovce, *Hung.* Bán. Trenčiansky Kraj, W Slovakia 48.43N 18.15E
114 I12 **Banovići** Federacija Bosna I Hercegovina, E Bosnia and Herzegovina 44.25N 18.31E
Banow *see* Andarāb
Ban Pak Phanang *see* Pak Phanang
178 Hh7 **Ban Pan Nua** Lampang, NW Thailand 18.51N 99.57E
178 I10 **Ban Phai** Khon Kaen, E Thailand 16.00N 102.42E
178 Jj9 **Ban Phou A Douk** Khammouan, C Laos 17.12N 106.07E
178 I8 **Ban Phu** Uthai Thani, W Thailand
178 H11 **Ban Pong** Ratchaburi, W Thailand 13.49N 99.52E
202 I3 **Banraeaba** Tarawa, W Kiribati 1.19N 173.01E
178 Gg11 **Ban Sai Yok** Kanchanaburi, W Thailand 14.24N 98.54E
Ban Sattahip/Ban Sattahipp *see* Sattahip
Ban Sichon *see* Sichon
Ban Si Racha *see* Siracha
113 J19 **Banská Bystrica** *Ger.* Neusohl, *Hung.* Besztercebánya. Banskobystrický Kraj, C Slovakia 48.45N 19.08E
113 K20 **Banskobystrický Kraj** ⬖ *region* C Slovakia
178 J8 **Ban Sôppheung** Bolikhamxai, C Laos 18.33N 104.18E
Ban Sop Prap *see* Sop Prap
158 G15 **Bānswāra** Rājasthān, N India 23.31N 74.28E
178 Gg15 **Ban Ta Khun** Surat Thani, SW Thailand 8.53N 98.52E
Ban Takua Pa *see* Takua Pa
178 Jj9 **Ban Talak** Khammouan, C Laos 17.33N 105.40E
79 R15 **Bantè** W Benin 8.21N 1.55E
178 Ii8 **Ban Thabôk** Bolikhamxai, C Laos 18.21N 103.12E
178 Jj10 **Ban Tôp** Savannakhét, S Laos 16.07N 106.07E
99 B21 **Bantry** *Ir.* Beanntraí. SW Ireland 51.40N 9.27W
99 A21 **Bantry Bay** *Ir.* Bá Bheanntraí. *bay* SW Ireland
174 L15 **Bantul** *prev.* Bantoel. Jawa, C Indonesia 7.55S 110.21E
161 F19 **Bantvāl** *var.* Bantwāl. Karnātaka, E India 12.57N 75.04E
Bantwāl *see* Bantvāl
116 N9 **Banya** Burgas, E Bulgaria 42.46N 27.49E
173 Ee6 **Banyak, Kepulauan** *prev.* Kepulauan Banjak. *island group* NW Indonesia
107 U8 **Banya, La** *headland* E Spain 40.34N 0.37E
81 E14 **Banyo** Adamaoua, NW Cameroon 6.46N 11.49E
107 X4 **Banyoles** *var.* Bañolas. Cataluña, NE Spain 42.07N 2.46E
178 H16 **Ban Yong Sata** Trang, SW Thailand 7.09N 99.42E
174 Mm16 **Banyuwangi** *var.* Banjuwangi; *prev.* Banjoewangi. Jawa, S Indonesia 8.12S 114.22E
205 X14 **Banzare Coast** *physical region* Antarctica
181 Q14 **Banzare Seamounts** *undersea feature* S Indian Ocean
Banzart *see* Bizerte
Baochang *see* Taibus Qi
167 O3 **Baoding** *var.* Pao-ting; *prev.* Tsingyuan. Hebei, E China 38.52N 115.28E
Baoebaoe *see* Baubau
Baoi, Oileán *see* Dursey Island
166 J6 **Baoji** *var.* Pao-chi, Paoki. Shaanxi, C China 34.22N 107.16E
195 V14 **Baolo** Santa Isabel, N Solomon Islands 7.41S 158.47E
178 K13 **Bao Lôc** Lâm Đông, S Vietnam 11.33N 107.48E
169 Z7 **Baoqing** Heilongjiang, NE China 46.15N 132.12E
Baoqing *see* Shaoyang
81 H15 **Baoro** Nana-Mambéré, W Central African Republic 5.40N 16.00E
166 E12 **Baoshan** *var.* Pao-shan. Yunnan, SW China 25.04N 99.07E
169 N13 **Baotou** *var.* Pao-t'ou, Paotow. Nei Mongol Zizhiqu, N China 40.37N 109.58E
78 L14 **Baoulé** ≈ S Mali
78 K12 **Baoulé** ≈ W Mali
105 O2 **Bapaume** Pas-de-Calais, N France 50.06N 2.50E
12 J13 **Baptiste Lake** ◎ Ontario, SE Canada
Baqanas *see* Bakanas
Baqbaqty *see* Bakbakty
165 P14 **Baqên** *var.* Dartang. Xizang Zizhiqu, W China 31.50N 94.08E
144 F14 **Bāqir, Jabal** ▲▲ S Jordan
145 T7 **Ba'qūbah** *var.* Qubba. C Iraq 33.45N 44.40E
64 H5 **Baquedano** Antofagasta, N Chile 23.19S 69.49W
118 M6 **Bar** Vinnyts'ka Oblast', C Ukraine 49.04N 27.39E
115 J18 **Bar** *It.* Antivari. Montenegro, SW Yugoslavia 42.02N 19.09E
82 E10 **Bara** Northern Kordofan, C Sudan 13.42N 30.21E
83 M18 **Baraawe** *It.* Brava. Shabeellaha Hoose, S Somalia 1.09N 43.59E
158 M12 **Bāra Banki** Uttar Pradesh, N India 26.55N 81.10E
125 G13 **Barabinsk** Novosibirskaya Oblast', C Russian Federation 55.19N 78.01E
32 L8 **Baraboo** Wisconsin, N USA 43.27N 89.45W
32 K8 **Baraboo Range** *hill range* Wisconsin, N USA
Baracaldo *see* San Vicente de Barakaldo
13 Y6 **Barachois** Quebec, SE Canada 48.37N 64.14W
46 J7 **Baracoa** Guantánamo, E Cuba 20.19N 74.31W
63 C19 **Baradero** Buenos Aires, E Argentina 33.47S 59.29W
191 R6 **Baradine** New South Wales, SE Australia 30.55S 149.03E
Baraf Daja Islands *see* Damar, Kepulauan
160 M12 **Baragarh** Orissa, E India 21.20N 83.36E
83 I17 **Baragoi** Rift Valley, W Kenya 1.39N 36.46E
47 N9 **Barahona** SW Dominican Republic 18.13N 71.07W
159 W13 **Barail Range** ▲▲ NE India
82 I9 **Baraka** *var.* Barka, *Ar.* Khawr Barakah. *seasonal river* Eritrea/Sudan
82 G10 **Barakat** Gezira, C Sudan 14.18N 33.31E
Barakī *see* Barakī Barak
155 Q6 **Barakī Barak** *var.* Barakī, Baraki Rajan. Lowgar, E Afghanistan 33.58N 68.58E
Baraki Rajan *see* Barakī Barak
160 N11 **Bārākot** Orissa, E India 21.35N 85.00E
Baram *see* Baram, Batang
57 S7 **Barama River** ≈ N Guyana
161 E14 **Bārāmati** Mahārāshtra, W India 18.12N 74.39E
174 Mm4 **Baram, Batang** *var.* Baram, Barram. ≈ East Malaysia
158 H5 **Bāramūla** Jammu and Kashmir, NW India 34.15N 74.24E
121 N14 **Baran'** Vitsyebskaya Voblasts', NE Belarus 54.28N 30.18E
158 I14 **Bārān** Rājasthān, N India 25.07N 76.31E
145 U4 **Barānān, Shākh-i** ▲▲ E Iraq
121 I17 **Baranavichy** *Pol.* Baranowicze, *Rus.* Baranovichi. Brestskaya Voblasts', SW Belarus 53.07N 26.01E
127 Oo5 **Baranikha** Chukotskiy Avtonomnyy Okrug, NE Russian Federation 68.29N 168.13E
118 M4 **Baranivka** Zhytomyrs'ka Oblast', N Ukraine 50.16N 27.40E
41 W14 **Baranof Island** *island* Alexander Archipelago, Alaska, USA
Baranovichi/Baranowicze *see* Baranavichy
113 N15 **Baranów Sandomierski** Podkarpackie, SE Poland 50.28N 21.31E
113 I26 **Baranya** *off.* Baranya Megye. ⬖ *county* S Hungary
159 R13 **Barāri** Bihār, NE India 25.31N 87.22E
24 L10 **Barataria Bay** *bay* Louisiana, S USA
Barat Daya, Kepulauan *see* Damar, Kepulauan
120 L12 **Baravukha** *Rus.* Borovukha. Vitsyebskaya Voblasts', N Belarus 55.36N 28.33E
56 E11 **Baraya** Huila, C Colombia 3.10N 75.04W
61 M21 **Barbacena** Minas Gerais, SE Brazil 21.13S 43.46W
56 B13 **Barbacoas** Nariño, SW Colombia 1.37N 78.07W
56 L6 **Barbacoas** Aragua, N Venezuela 9.28N 66.58W
47 Z13 **Barbados** ◆ *commonwealth republic* SE West Indies
49 S3 **Barbados** *island* Barbados
107 U11 **Barbaria, Cap de** *var.* Cabo de Berberia. *headland* Formentera, E Spain 38.39N 1.24E
116 N13 **Barbaros** Tekirdağ, NW Turkey 40.55N 27.28E
76 A11 **Barbas, Cap** *headland* S Western Sahara 22.14N 16.45W
107 T5 **Barbastro** Aragón, NE Spain 42.01N 0.07E
106 K16 **Barbate** ≈ SW Spain
106 K16 **Barbate de Franco** Andalucía, S Spain 36.11N 5.55W
85 K21 **Barberton** Mpumalanga, NE South Africa 25.45S 31.01E
33 U12 **Barberton** Ohio, N USA 41.02N 81.37W
104 K12 **Barbezieux-St-Hilaire** Charente, W France 45.28N 0.09W
56 G9 **Barbosa** Santander, C Colombia 5.57N 73.37W
23 N7 **Barbourville** Kentucky, S USA 36.52N 83.53W
47 W9 **Barbuda** *island* N Antigua and Barbuda
189 W8 **Barcaldine** Queensland, E Australia 23.33S 145.20E
Barcarozsnyó *see* Râșnov
106 I11 **Barcarrota** Extremadura, W Spain 38.31N 6.51W
Barcău *see* Berettyó
Barce *see* Al Marj
109 L23 **Barcellona** *var.* Barcellona Pozzo di Gotto. Sicilia, Italy, C Mediterranean Sea 38.09N 15.15E
Barcellona Pozzo di Gotto *see* Barcellona
107 W6 **Barcelona** *anc.* Barcino, Barcinona. Cataluña, E Spain 41.25N 2.10E
57 N5 **Barcelona** Anzoátegui, NE Venezuela 10.07N 64.43W
107 S5 **Barcelona** ⬖ *province* Cataluña, NE Spain
107 W6 **Barcelona** ✈ Cataluña, E Spain 41.25N 2.10E
105 U14 **Barcelonnette** Alpes-de-Haute-Provence, SE France 44.24N 6.37E
60 E12 **Barcelos** Amazonas, N Brazil 0.58S 62.58W
106 G5 **Barcelos** Braga, N Portugal 41.31N 8.37W
112 I10 **Barcin** *Ger.* Bartschin. Kujawski-pomorskie, C Poland 52.51N 17.55E
Barcino/Barcinona *see* Barcelona
Barcoo *see* Cooper Creek

◆ Country
● Country Capital
◇ Dependent Territory
○ Dependent Territory Capital
⬖ Administrative Region
✈ International Airport
▲ Mountain
▲▲ Mountain Range
Volcano
≈ River
◎ Lake
⊠ Reservoir

◆ COUNTRY   ◇ DEPENDENT TERRITORY   ◆ ADMINISTRATIVE REGION   ▲ MOUNTAIN   ▲ VOLCANO   ◉ LAKE
● COUNTRY CAPITAL   ○ DEPENDENT TERRITORY CAPITAL   ✈ INTERNATIONAL AIRPORT   ▲ MOUNTAIN RANGE   ≈ RIVER   ▣ RESERVOIR

BAYOU D'ARBONNE LAKE – BÉNÉNA

24 H4 **Bayou D'Arbonne Lake** ⊠ Louisiana, S USA
25 N9 **Bayou La Batre** Alabama, S USA 30.24N 88.15W
Bayou State see Mississippi
Bayqadam see Saudakent
Bayqongyr see Baykonyr
Bayram-Ali see Bayramaly
152 J14 **Bayramaly** prev. Bayram-Ali. Maryyskiy Velayat, S Turkmenistan 37.33N 62.08E
103 L19 **Bayreuth** var. Baireuth. Bayern, SE Germany 49.57N 11.34E
Bayrische Alpen see Bavarian Alps
Bayrūt see Beyrouth
24 L9 **Bay Saint Louis** Mississippi, S USA 30.18N 89.19W
Baysān see Bet She'an
168 L8 **Bayshint** Töv, C Mongolia 47.22N 105.04E
12 H13 **Bays, Lake of** ◎ Ontario, S Canada
24 M6 **Bay Springs** Mississippi, S USA 31.58N 89.17W
Bay State see Massachusetts
Baysun see Boysun
12 H13 **Baysville** Ontario, S Canada 45.10N 79.03W
147 N15 **Bayt al Faqīh** W Yemen 14.30N 43.20E
164 M4 **Baytik Shan** ▲▲ China/Mongolia
Bayt Laḥm see Bethlehem
27 W11 **Baytown** Texas, SW USA 29.44N 94.58W
175 O9 **Bayur, Tanjung** headland Borneo, N Indonesia 0.43S 117.32E
123 U16 **Bayy al Kabīr, Wādī** dry watercourse NW Libya
Bayyrqum see Bairkum
107 P14 **Baza** Andalucía, S Spain 37.30N 2.45W
143 X10 **Bazardüzü Dağı** Rus. Gora Bazardyuzyu. ▲ N Azerbaijan 41.13N 47.50E
Bazardyuzyu, Gora see Bazardüzü Dağı
Bazargic see Dobrich
85 N18 **Bazaruto, Ilha do** island SE Mozambique
104 K14 **Bazas** Gironde, SW France 44.27N 0.11W
107 O14 **Baza, Sierra de** ▲▲ S Spain
166 J8 **Bazhong** Sichuan, C China 31.55N 106.44E
167 P3 **Bazhou** prev. Baxian, Ba Xian. Hebei, E China 39.04N 116.24E
12 M9 **Bazin** ≈ Quebec, SE Canada
Bazin see Pezinok
145 Q7 **Bāzīyah** C Iraq 33.49N 42.41E
144 H6 **Bcharré** var. Bcharreh, Bsharrī, Bsherri. NE Lebanon 34.16N 36.01E
Bcharreh see Bcharré
30 J5 **Beach** North Dakota, N USA 46.55N 104.00W
190 K12 **Beachport** South Australia 37.29S 140.03E
99 O23 **Beachy Head** headland SE England, UK 50.44N 0.16E
20 K13 **Beacon** New York, NE USA 41.30N 73.54W
65 J25 **Beagle Channel** channel Argentina/Chile
189 O1 **Beagle Gulf** gulf Northern Territory, N Australia
Bealach an Doirín see Ballaghaderreen
Bealach Cláir see Ballyclare
Bealach Féich see Ballybofey
180 J3 **Bealanana** Mahajanga, NE Madagascar 14.33S 48.43E
Béal an Átha see Ballina
Béal an Átha Móir see Ballinamore
Béal an Mhuirhead see Belmullet
Béal Átha Beithe see Ballybay
Béal Átha Conaill see Ballyconnell
Beál Átha hAmhnais see Ballyhaunis
Béal Átha na Sluaighe see Ballinasloe
Béal Átha Seanaidh see Ballyshannon
Bealdovuopmi see Peltovuoma
Béal Feirste see Belfast
Béal Tairbirt see Belturbet
Beanna Boirche see Mourne Mountains
Beannchar see Banagher, Ireland
Beannchar see Bangor, Northern Ireland, UK
Beanntraí see Bantry
25 N2 **Bear Creek** ≈ Alabama/Mississippi, S USA
32 J13 **Bear Creek** ≈ Illinois, N USA
29 U13 **Bearden** Arkansas, C USA 33.43N 92.37W
205 Q10 **Beardmore Glacier** glacier Antarctica
32 K13 **Beardstown** Illinois, N USA 40.01N 90.25W
30 L14 **Bear Hill** ▲ Nebraska, C USA 41.24N 101.49W
Bear Island see Bjørnøya
12 H12 **Bear Lake** Ontario, S Canada 45.28N 79.31W
38 M1 **Bear Lake** ◎ Idaho/Utah, NW USA
41 U11 **Bear, Mount** ▲ Alaska, USA 61.16N 141.09W
104 J16 **Béarn** cultural region SW France
204 J11 **Bear Peninsula** peninsula Antarctica
158 I7 **Beās** ≈ India/Pakistan
107 P3 **Beasain** País Vasco, N Spain 43.03N 2.10W
107 O12 **Beas de Segura** Andalucía, S Spain 38.16N 2.53W
47 N10 **Beata, Cabo** headland SW Dominican Republic 17.34N 71.25W
47 N10 **Beata, Isla** island SW Dominican Republic
66 F11 **Beata Ridge** undersea feature N Caribbean Sea
31 R17 **Beatrice** Nebraska, C USA 40.14N 96.43W
85 L16 **Beatrice** Mashonaland East, NE Zimbabwe 18.13S 30.52E
9 N11 **Beatton** ≈ British Columbia, W Canada
9 N11 **Beatton River** British Columbia, W Canada 57.35N 121.10W
37 V10 **Beatty** Nevada, W USA 36.53N 116.44W
23 N6 **Beattyville** Kentucky, S USA 37.34N 83.39W
181 X16 **Beau Bassin** W Mauritius 20.13S 57.27E
105 R15 **Beaucaire** Gard, S France 43.49N 4.37E
12 I8 **Beauchastel, Lac** ◎ Quebec, SE Canada
12 I10 **Beauchêne, Lac** ◎ Quebec, SE Canada
191 V3 **Beaudesert** Queensland, E Australia 28.00S 152.27E
190 M12 **Beaufort** Victoria, SE Australia 37.27S 143.24E
23 X11 **Beaufort** North Carolina, SE USA 34.45N 76.50W
23 R15 **Beaufort** South Carolina, SE USA 32.25N 80.40W
40 M11 **Beaufort Sea** sea Arctic Ocean
Beaufort-Wes see Beaufort West
85 G25 **Beaufort West** Afr. Beaufort-Wes. Western Cape, SW South Africa 32.21S 22.34E
105 N7 **Beaugency** Loiret, C France 47.46N 1.38E
21 R1 **Beau Lake** ⊠ Maine, NE USA
98 I8 **Beauly** N Scotland, UK 57.28N 4.28W
101 G21 **Beaumont** Hainaut, S Belgium 50.12N 4.13E
193 E23 **Beaumont** Otago, South Island, NZ 45.48S 169.32E
24 M7 **Beaumont** Mississippi, S USA 31.10N 88.55W
27 X10 **Beaumont** Texas, SW USA 30.05N 94.06W
104 M15 **Beaumont-de-Lomagne** Tarn-et-Garonne, S France 43.54N 1.00E
104 L6 **Beaumont-sur-Sarthe** Sarthe, NW France 48.15N 0.07E
105 R8 **Beaune** Côte d'Or, C France 47.01N 4.49E
13 R9 **Beaupré** Quebec, SE Canada 47.03N 70.52W
104 J8 **Beaupréau** Maine-et-Loire, NW France 47.13N 0.57W
101 I22 **Beauraing** Namur, SE Belgium 50.07N 4.57E
105 R12 **Beaurepaire** Isère, E France 45.20N 5.03E
9 Y16 **Beausejour** Manitoba, S Canada 50.04N 96.30W
105 N4 **Beauvais** anc. Bellovacum, Caesaromagus. Oise, N France 49.27N 2.04E
9 S13 **Beauval** Saskatchewan, C Canada 55.10N 107.37W
104 I9 **Beauvoir-sur-Mer** Vendée, NW France 46.54N 2.03W
41 R8 **Beaver** Alaska, USA 66.22N 147.31W
28 J8 **Beaver** Oklahoma, C USA 36.49N 100.31W
20 B14 **Beaver** Pennsylvania, NE USA 40.39N 80.19W
38 K6 **Beaver** Utah, W USA 38.16N 112.38W
8 L9 **Beaver** ≈ British Columbia/Yukon Territory, W Canada
9 S13 **Beaver** ≈ Saskatchewan, C Canada
31 N17 **Beaver City** Nebraska, C USA 40.08N 99.49W
8 G6 **Beaver Creek** Yukon Territory, W Canada 62.19N 140.45W
33 R14 **Beavercreek** Ohio, N USA 39.42N 83.58W
41 S8 **Beaver Creek** ≈ Alaska, USA
28 H3 **Beaver Creek** ≈ Kansas/Nebraska, C USA
30 J5 **Beaver Creek** ≈ Montana/North Dakota, N USA
31 Q14 **Beaver Creek** ≈ Nebraska, C USA
27 Q4 **Beaver Creek** ≈ Texas, SW USA
32 M8 **Beaver Dam** Wisconsin, N USA 43.28N 88.49W
32 M8 **Beaver Dam Lake** ◎ Wisconsin, N USA
20 B14 **Beaver Falls** Pennsylvania, NE USA 40.45N 80.20W
35 P12 **Beaverhead Mountains** ▲▲ Idaho/Montana, NW USA
35 Q12 **Beaverhead River** ≈ Montana, NW USA
67 A25 **Beaver Island** island W Falkland Islands
33 P5 **Beaver Island** island Michigan, N USA
29 S9 **Beaver Lake** ⊠ Arkansas, C USA
9 N13 **Beaverlodge** Alberta, W Canada 55.10N 119.28W
20 I8 **Beaver River** ≈ New York, NE USA
28 J8 **Beaver River** ≈ Oklahoma, C USA
20 B13 **Beaver River** ≈ Pennsylvania, NE USA
67 A25 **Beaver Settlement** Beaver Island, W Falkland Islands 51.30S 61.15W
Beaver State see Oregon
12 H14 **Beaverton** Ontario, S Canada 44.24N 79.07W
34 G11 **Beaverton** Oregon, NW USA 45.29N 122.48W
158 G12 **Beāwar** Rājasthān, N India 26.07N 74.21E
Bebas, Dasht-i see Bābūs, Dasht-e
62 L8 **Bebedouro** São Paulo, S Brazil 20.58S 48.28W
103 I16 **Bebra** Hessen, C Germany 50.59N 9.46E
43 W12 **Becal** Campeche, SE Mexico 19.49N 90.28W
13 Q11 **Bécancour** ≈ Quebec, SE Canada
99 Q19 **Beccles** E England, UK 52.27N 1.32E
114 L9 **Bečej** Ger. Altbetsche, Hung. Óbecse, Rácz-Becse; prev. Magyar-Becse, Stari Bečej. Serbia, N Yugoslavia 45.36N 20.02E
106 I3 **Becerreá** Galicia, NW Spain 42.51N 7.10W
76 H7 **Béchar** prev. Colomb-Béchar. W Algeria 31.38N 2.10W
41 O14 **Becharof Lake** ◎ Alaska, USA
118 H15 **Bechet** var. Bechetu. Dolj, SW Romania 43.45N 23.57E
Bechetu see Bechet
23 R6 **Beckley** West Virginia, NE USA 37.46N 81.11W
103 G14 **Beckum** Nordrhein-Westfalen, W Germany 51.45N 8.03E
27 X7 **Beckville** Texas, SW USA 32.14N 94.27W
37 X4 **Becky Peak** ▲ Nevada, W USA 39.59N 114.33W
118 I9 **Beclean** Hung. Bethlen; prev. Betlen. Bistrița-Năsăud, N Romania 47.10N 24.10E
Bécs see Wien
113 H18 **Bečva** Ger. Betschau, Pol. Beczwa. ≈ E Czech Republic
Beczwa see Bečva
105 P15 **Bédarieux** Hérault, S France 43.37N 3.10E
122 D12 **Beddouza, Cap** headland W Morocco 32.35N 9.16W
82 I13 **Bedelē** Oromo, C Ethiopia 8.25N 36.21E
153 Y8 **Bedel Pass** Rus. Pereval Bedel. pass China/Kyrgyzstan 41.22N 78.19E
Bedel, Pereval see Bedel Pass
97 H22 **Beder** Århus, C Denmark 56.03N 10.13E
99 N20 **Bedford** E England, UK 52.07N 0.28W
33 O15 **Bedford** Indiana, N USA 38.51N 86.29W
31 U16 **Bedford** Iowa, C USA 40.40N 94.43W
22 L4 **Bedford** Kentucky, S USA 38.34N 85.18W
20 D15 **Bedford** Pennsylvania, NE USA 40.00N 78.29W
23 T6 **Bedford** Virginia, NE USA 37.19N 79.31W
99 N20 **Bedfordshire** cultural region E England, UK
131 N5 **Bednodem'yanovsk** Penzenskaya Oblast', W Russian Federation 53.55N 43.14E
100 N5 **Bedum** Groningen, NE Netherlands 53.18N 6.36E
29 V11 **Beebe** Arkansas, C USA 35.04N 91.52W
47 T9 **Beef Island** ✕ (Road Town) Tortola, E British Virgin Islands 18.25N 64.31W
Beehive State see Utah
101 L18 **Beek** Limburg, SE Netherlands 50.55N 5.46E
101 L18 **Beek** ✕ (Maastricht) Limburg, SE Netherlands 50.55N 5.47E
101 K14 **Beek-en-Donk** Noord-Brabant, S Netherlands 51.31N 5.37E
144 F13 **Be'ér Menuḥa** var. Be'er Menukha. Southern, S Israel 30.21N 35.09E
Be'er Menukha see Be'ér Menuḥa
101 D16 **Beernem** West-Vlaanderen, NW Belgium 51.09N 3.18E
101 I16 **Beerse** Antwerpen, N Belgium 51.20N 4.52E
Beersheba see Be'ér Sheva'
144 E11 **Be'ér Sheva'** var. Beersheba, Ar. Bir es Saba. Southern, S Israel 31.15N 34.46E
100 J13 **Beesd** Gelderland, C Netherlands 51.52N 5.12E
101 M16 **Beesel** Limburg, SE Netherlands 51.16N 6.01E
85 J21 **Beestekraal** North-West, N South Africa 25.21S 27.40E
204 J7 **Beethoven Peninsula** peninsula Alexander Island, Antarctica
Beetstersweach see Beetsterzwaag
100 M6 **Beetsterzwaag** Fris. Beetstersweach. Friesland, N Netherlands 53.03N 6.04E
27 S13 **Beeville** Texas, SW USA 28.25N 97.46W
81 J18 **Befale** Equateur, NW Dem. Rep. Congo (Zaire) 0.25N 20.48E
Befandriana see Befandriana Avaratra
180 J3 **Befandriana Avaratra** var. Befandriana, Befandriana Nord. Mahajanga, NW Madagascar 15.13S 48.33E
Befandriana Nord see Befandriana Avaratra
81 K18 **Befori** Equateur, N Dem. Rep. Congo (Zaire) 0.09N 22.18E
180 I7 **Befotaka** Fianarantsoa, S Madagascar 23.49S 47.00E
191 R11 **Bega** New South Wales, SE Australia 36.43S 149.49E
104 G5 **Bégard** Côtes d'Armor, NW France 48.37N 3.18W
114 M9 **Begejski Kanal** canal NE Yugoslavia
151 V9 **Begen'** Vostochnyy Kazakhstan, E Kazakhstan 51.11N 79.03E
96 G13 **Begna** ≈ S Norway
Begoml' see Byahoml'
Begovat see Bekobod
159 Q13 **Begusarāi** Bihār, NE India 25.25N 86.07E
149 R9 **Behābād** Yazd, C Iran 32.22N 59.49E
Behagle see Laï
57 Z10 **Béhague, Pointe** headland E French Guiana 4.37N 51.52W
Behar see Bihār
148 M10 **Behbahān** var. Behbehān. Khūzestān, SW Iran 30.37N 50.07E
Behbehān see Behbahān
46 G3 **Behring Point** Andros Island, W Bahamas 24.28N 77.44W
149 P4 **Behshahr** prev. Ashraf. Māzandarān, N Iran 36.42N 53.36E
169 V6 **Bei'an** Heilongjiang, NE China 48.16N 126.28E
Beibunar see Sredishte
Beibu Wan see Tongking, Gulf of
Beida see Al Bayḍā'
82 H13 **Beigi** Oromo, C Ethiopia 9.13N 34.48E
166 L16 **Beihai** Guangxi Zhuangzu Zizhiqu, S China 21.28N 109.10E
165 Q10 **Bei Hulsan Hu** ◎ C China
167 N13 **Bei Jiang** ≈ S China
167 O2 **Beijing** var. Pei-ching, Eng. Peking; prev. Pei-p'ing. country/municipality capital (China) Beijing Shi, E China 39.58N 116.22E
167 P2 **Beijing** ✕ Beijing Shi, E China 39.54N 116.22E
Beijing see Beijing Shi
167 O2 **Beijing Shi** var. Beijing, Jing, Pei-ching, Eng. Peking; prev. Pei-p'ing. ◐ municipality E China
78 G8 **Beïla** Trarza, W Mauritania 18.07N 15.55W
100 N7 **Beilen** Drenthe, NE Netherlands 52.52N 6.27E
166 L15 **Beiliu** Guangxi Zhuangzu Zizhiqu, S China 22.43N 110.21E
165 O12 **Beilu He** ≈ W China
Beilul see Beylul
98 H8 **Beinn Dearg** ▲ N Scotland, UK 57.47N 4.52W
Beinn MacDuibh see Ben Macdui
166 I12 **Beipan Jiang** ≈ S China
169 T12 **Beipiao** Liaoning, NE China 41.46N 120.51E
85 N17 **Beira** Sofala, C Mozambique 19.45S 34.55E
85 N17 **Beira** ✕ Sofala, C Mozambique 19.39S 35.05E
106 I7 **Beira Alta** former province N Portugal
106 H9 **Beira Baixa** former province C Portugal
106 G8 **Beira Litoral** former province N Portugal
Beirut see Beyrouth
Beisān see Bet She'an
9 Q16 **Beiseker** Alberta, SW Canada 51.20N 113.34W
85 K19 **Beitbridge** Matabeleland South, S Zimbabwe 22.10S 30.02E
118 G10 **Beiuș** Hung. Belényes. Bihor, NW Romania 46.40N 22.18E
169 U12 **Beizhen** Liaoning, NE China 41.34N 121.51E
106 H12 **Beja** anc. Pax Julia. Beja, SE Portugal 38.01N 7.52W
106 G13 **Beja** ◐ district S Portugal
76 M5 **Béja** var. Bājah. N Tunisia 36.45N 9.04E
123 Ii11 **Béjaïa** var. Bejaïa, Fr. Bougie; anc. Saldae. NE Algeria 36.45N 5.02E
106 K8 **Béjar** Castilla-León, N Spain 40.24N 5.45W
Bejraburi see Phetchaburi
Bekaa Valley see El Beqaa
Bekabad see Bekobod
Békás see Bicaz
174 J14 **Bekasi** Jawa, C Indonesia 6.13S 106.59E
Bek-Budi see Qarshi
152 A8 **Bekdash** Balkanskiy Velayat, NW Turkmenistan 41.33N 52.33E
153 T10 **Bek-Dzhar** Oshskaya Oblast', SW Kyrgyzstan 40.22N 73.08E
113 N24 **Békés** Rom. Bichiș. Békés, SE Hungary 46.47N 21.09E
113 M24 **Békés** off. Békés Megye. ◐ county SE Hungary
113 M24 **Békéscsaba** Rom. Bichiș-Ciaba. Békés, SE Hungary 46.40N 21.04E
145 S2 **Bēkhma** E Iraq 36.40N 44.15E
180 H7 **Bekily** Toliara, S Madagascar 24.12S 45.19E
172 Qq7 **Bekkai** Hokkaidō, NE Japan 43.23N 145.07E
153 Q11 **Bekobod** Rus. Bekabad; prev. Begovat. Toshkent Wiloyati, E Uzbekistan 40.17N 69.10E
131 O7 **Bekovo** Penzenskaya Oblast', W Russian Federation 52.27N 43.41E
Bél see Beliu
158 M13 **Bela** Uttar Pradesh, N India 25.55N 82.00E
155 N15 **Bela** Baluchistān, SW Pakistan 26.12N 66.22E
81 F15 **Bélabo** Est, C Cameroon 4.54N 13.10E
114 N10 **Bela Crkva** Ger. Weisskirchen, Hung. Fehértemplom. Serbia, W Yugoslavia 44.55N 21.28E
181 Y16 **Bel Air** var. Rivière Sèche. E Mauritius
106 L12 **Belalcázar** Andalucía, S Spain 38.33N 5.07W
115 P15 **Bela Palanka** Serbia, SE Yugoslavia 43.13N 22.19E
121 H16 **Belarus** off. Republic of Belarus, var. Belorussia, Latv. Baltkrievija; prev. Belorussian SSR, Rus. Belorusskaya SSR. ◆ republic E Europe
Belau see Palau
61 H21 **Bela Vista** Mato Grosso do Sul, SW Brazil 22.04S 56.25W
85 L21 **Bela Vista** Maputo, S Mozambique 26.19S 32.40E
173 Ff4 **Belawan** Sumatera, W Indonesia 3.44N 98.39E
Bèla Woda see Weisswasser
131 U4 **Belaya** ≈ W Russian Federation
127 P7 **Belaya Gora** Respublika Sakha (Yakutiya), NE Russian Federation 68.25N 146.12E
130 M11 **Belaya Kalitiva** Rostovskaya Oblast', SW Russian Federation 48.09N 40.43E
129 R14 **Belaya Kholunitsa** Kirovskaya Oblast', NW Russian Federation 58.54N 50.52E
Belaya Tserkov' see Bila Tserkva
79 V11 **Belbédji** Zinder, S Niger 14.35N 8.00E
112 K13 **Bełchatów** var. Belchatow. Łodzkie, C Poland 51.22N 19.19E
Belcher, Îles see Belcher Islands
10 H7 **Belcher Islands** Fr. Îles Belcher. island group Nunavut, SE Canada
107 S6 **Belchite** Aragón, NE Spain 41.18N 0.45W
31 O2 **Belcourt** North Dakota, N USA 48.50N 99.44W
33 P9 **Belding** Michigan, N USA 43.06N 85.13W
131 U5 **Belebey** Respublika Bashkortostan, W Russian Federation 54.04N 54.13E
83 N16 **Beledweyne** var. Belet Huen, It. Belet Uen. Hiiraan, C Somalia 4.39N 45.12E
152 B10 **Belek** Balkanskiy Velayat, W Turkmenistan 39.57N 53.51E
60 L12 **Belém** var. Pará. state capital Pará, N Brazil 1.27S 48.28W
67 I14 **Belém Ridge** undersea feature C Atlantic Ocean
39 R12 **Belen** New Mexico, SW USA 34.37N 106.46W
64 I7 **Belén** Catamarca, NW Argentina 27.40S 67.01W
56 G9 **Belén** Boyacá, C Colombia 5.59N 72.55W
44 J11 **Belén** Rivas, SW Nicaragua 11.30N 85.55W
64 O5 **Belén** Concepción, C Paraguay 23.25S 57.13W
63 D16 **Belén** Salto, N Uruguay 30.36S 57.46W
63 D20 **Belén de Escobar** Buenos Aires, E Argentina 34.21S 58.46W
116 J7 **Belene** Pleven, N Bulgaria 43.39N 25.09E
116 J7 **Belene, Ostrov** island N Bulgaria
45 R15 **Belén, Río** ≈ C Panama
Belényes see Beiuș
197 G4 **Belep, Îles** island group W New Caledonia
106 H3 **Belesar, Embalse de** ⊠ NW Spain
Belet Huen/Belet Uen see Beledweyne
130 J5 **Belëv** Tul'skaya Oblast', W Russian Federation 53.48N 36.07E
99 G15 **Belfast** Ir. Béal Feirste. ◐ E Northern Ireland, UK 54.34N 5.55W
21 R7 **Belfast** Maine, NE USA 44.25N 69.02W
99 G15 **Belfast** ✕ E Northern Ireland, UK 54.37N 6.11W
99 G15 **Belfast Lough** Ir. Loch Lao inlet E Northern Ireland, UK
30 K5 **Belfield** North Dakota, N USA 46.53N 103.12W
105 U7 **Belfort** Territoire-de-Belfort, E France 47.37N 6.52E
Belgard see Białogard
161 E17 **Belgaum** Karnātaka, W India 15.52N 74.30E
Belgian Congo see Congo (Democratic Republic of)
205 T3 **Belgica Mountains** ▲▲ Antarctica
België/Belgique see Belgium
101 F20 **Belgium** off. Kingdom of Belgium, Dut. België, Fr. Belgique. ◆ monarchy NW Europe
130 J8 **Belgorod** Belgorodskaya Oblast', W Russian Federation 50.37N 36.37E
Belgorod-Dnestrovskiy see Bilhorod-Dnistrovs'kyy
130 J8 **Belgorodskaya Oblast'** ◐ province W Russian Federation
Belgrad see Beograd
31 T8 **Belgrade** Minnesota, N USA 45.27N 94.59W
35 S11 **Belgrade** Montana, NW USA 45.46N 111.10W
Belgrade see Beograd
205 N5 **Belgrano II** Argentinian research station Antarctica 77.50S 35.25W
Belgrano, Cabo see Meredith, Cape
23 X9 **Belhaven** North Carolina, SE USA 35.36N 76.50W
109 I23 **Belice** anc. Hypsas. ≈ Sicilia, Italy, C Mediterranean Sea
Belice see Belize/Belize City
115 M16 **Beli Drim** Alb. Drini i Bardhë. ≈ Albania/Yugoslavia
Beligrad see Berat
196 C8 **Beliliou** prev. Peleliu. island S Palau
116 L8 **Beli Lom, Yazovir** ⊠ NE Bulgaria
114 I8 **Beli Manastir** Hung. Pélmonostor; prev. Monostor. Osijek-Baranja, NE Croatia 45.46N 16.38E
104 J13 **Bélin-Béliet** Gironde, SW France 44.30N 0.48W
81 F17 **Bélinga** Ogooué-Ivindo, NE Gabon 1.05N 13.12E
23 S4 **Belington** West Virginia, NE USA 39.01N 79.57W
131 O6 **Belinskiy** Penzenskaya Oblast', W Russian Federation 52.58N 43.25E
174 Ii9 **Belinyu** Pulau Bangka, W Indonesia 1.34S 105.45E
174 Jj11 **Belitung, Pulau** island W Indonesia
118 F10 **Beliu** Hung. Bel. Arad, W Romania 46.31N 21.57E
116 I9 **Beli Vit** ≈ NW Bulgaria
44 G2 **Belize** Sp. Belice; prev. British Honduras, Colony of Belize. ◆ commonwealth republic Central America
44 F2 **Belize** Sp. Belice. ◐ district NE Belize
44 G2 **Belize** ≈ Belize/Guatemala
Belize see Belize City
44 G2 **Belize City** var. Belize, Sp. Belice. Belize, NE Belize 17.28N 88.10W
44 G2 **Belize City** ✕ Belize, NE Belize 17.31N 88.15W
Beljak see Villach
41 N16 **Belkofski** Alaska, USA 55.06N 162.03W
126 L4 **Bel'kovskiy, Ostrov** island Novosibirskiye Ostrova, NE Russian Federation
12 J8 **Bell** ≈ Quebec, SE Canada
8 J15 **Bella Bella** British Columbia, SW Canada 52.04N 128.07W
104 M10 **Bellac** Haute-Vienne, C France 46.07N 1.04E
8 K15 **Bella Coola** British Columbia, SW Canada 52.22N 126.46W
108 D6 **Bellagio** Lombardia, N Italy 45.58N 9.15E
33 P6 **Bellaire** Michigan, N USA 44.58N 85.12W
108 D6 **Bellano** Lombardia, N Italy 46.06N 9.21E
161 G17 **Bellary** var. Ballari. Karnātaka, S India 15.10N 76.54E
191 S5 **Bellata** New South Wales, SE Australia 29.58S 149.49E
63 D16 **Bella Unión** Artigas, N Uruguay 30.18S 57.34W
63 C14 **Bella Vista** Corrientes, NE Argentina 28.34S 58.58W
64 J7 **Bella Vista** Tucumán, N Argentina 27.04S 65.19W
64 P4 **Bella Vista** Amambay, C Paraguay 22.12S 56.30W
58 B10 **Bellavista** Cajamarca, N Peru 5.43S 78.46W
58 D11 **Bellavista** San Martín, N Peru 7.02S 76.36W
191 U6 **Bellbrook** New South Wales, SE Australia 30.48S 152.32E
29 V5 **Belle** Missouri, C USA 38.17N 91.43W
23 Q5 **Belle** West Virginia, NE USA 38.13N 81.32W
33 R13 **Bellefontaine** Ohio, N USA 40.21N 83.45W
20 F14 **Bellefonte** Pennsylvania, NE USA 40.54N 77.43W
30 J9 **Belle Fourche** South Dakota, N USA 44.40N 103.49W
30 J9 **Belle Fourche Reservoir** ⊠ South Dakota, N USA
30 K9 **Belle Fourche River** ≈ South Dakota/Wyoming, N USA
105 S10 **Bellegarde-sur-Valserine** Ain, E France 46.06N 5.49E
25 Y14 **Belle Glade** Florida, SE USA 26.40N 80.40W
104 G8 **Belle Île** island NW France
11 T9 **Belle Isle** island Belle Isle, Newfoundland, E Canada
11 S10 **Belle Isle, Strait of** strait Newfoundland, E Canada
Bellenz see Bellinzona
31 W14 **Belle Plaine** Iowa, C USA 41.54N 92.16W
31 V9 **Belle Plaine** Minnesota, N USA 44.39N 93.47W
12 I9 **Belleterre** Quebec, SE Canada 47.24N 78.40W
12 J15 **Belleville** Ontario, SE Canada 44.10N 77.22W
105 R10 **Belleville** Rhône, E France 46.09N 4.42E
32 K15 **Belleville** Illinois, N USA 38.31N 89.58W
29 N3 **Belleville** Kansas, C USA 39.46N 97.37W
31 Z13 **Bellevue** Iowa, C USA 42.15N 90.25W
31 S15 **Bellevue** Nebraska, C USA 41.08N 95.53W
33 S11 **Bellevue** Ohio, N USA 41.16N 82.50W
27 S5 **Bellevue** Texas, SW USA 33.38N 98.00W
34 H8 **Bellevue** Washington, NW USA 47.36N 122.12W
57 Y11 **Bellevue de l'Inini, Montagnes** ▲▲ S French Guiana
105 S11 **Belley** Ain, E France 45.46N 5.40E
191 V6 **Bellingen** New South Wales, SE Australia 30.27S 152.53E
99 L14 **Bellingham** N England, UK 55.09N 2.16W
34 H6 **Bellingham** Washington, NW USA 48.45N 122.29W
Belling Hausen Mulde see Southeast Pacific Basin
204 H2 **Bellingshausen** Russian research station South Shetland Islands, Antarctica 61.57S 58.23W
Bellingshausen see Motu One
Bellingshausen Abyssal Plain see Bellingshausen Plain
200 N16 **Bellingshausen Plain** var. Bellingshausen Abyssal Plain. undersea feature SE Pacific Ocean
204 I8 **Bellingshausen Sea** sea Antarctica
100 P6 **Bellingwolde** Groningen, NE Netherlands 53.07N 7.10E
110 H11 **Bellinzona** Ger. Bellenz. Ticino, S Switzerland 46.12N 9.01E
27 T8 **Bellmead** Texas, SW USA 31.36N 97.02W
56 E8 **Bello** Antioquia, W Colombia 6.19N 75.34W
63 B21 **Bellocq** Buenos Aires, E Argentina 35.55S 61.31W
Bello Horizonte see Belo Horizonte
195 W17 **Bellona** var. Mungiki. island S Solomon Islands
Bellovacum see Beauvais
190 D7 **Bell, Point** headland South Australia 32.13S 133.08E
22 F9 **Bells** Tennessee, S USA 35.42N 89.05W
27 U5 **Bells** Texas, SW USA 33.36N 96.24W
94 N3 **Bellsund** inlet SW Svalbard
108 H6 **Belluno** Veneto, NE Italy 46.07N 12.06E
64 L11 **Bell Ville** Córdoba, C Argentina 32.42S 62.42W
85 E26 **Bellville** Western Cape, SW South Africa 33.49S 18.43E
27 U11 **Bellville** Texas, SW USA 29.57N 96.15W
106 L12 **Belmez** Andalucía, S Spain 38.16N 5.12W
31 V12 **Belmond** Iowa, C USA 42.51N 93.36W
20 E11 **Belmont** New York, NE USA 42.13N 78.01W
23 R10 **Belmont** North Carolina, SE USA 35.13N 81.01W
61 O18 **Belmonte** Bahia, E Brazil 15.52S 38.54W
106 I8 **Belmonte** Castelo Branco, C Portugal 40.21N 7.19W
107 P10 **Belmonte** Castilla-La Mancha, C Spain 39.34N 2.43W
44 G2 **Belmopan** ● (Belize) Cayo, C Belize 17.13N 88.48W
99 B16 **Belmullet** Ir. Béal an Mhuirhead. W Ireland 54.13N 9.58W
126 Mm15 **Belogorsk** Amurskaya Oblast', SE Russian Federation 50.53N 128.24E
Belogorsk see Bilohirs'k
116 F7 **Belogradchik** Vidin, NW Bulgaria 43.37N 22.42E
180 H8 **Beloha** Toliara, S Madagascar 25.09S 45.04E
61 M20 **Belo Horizonte** prev. Bello Horizonte. state capital Minas Gerais, SE Brazil 19.54S 43.54W
28 M3 **Beloit** Kansas, C USA 39.27N 98.06W
32 L9 **Beloit** Wisconsin, N USA 42.31N 89.01W
Belokorovichi see Bilokorovychi
126 H15 **Belokurikha** Altayskiy Kray, S Russian Federation 51.57N 84.56E
128 J8 **Belomorsk** Respublika Kareliya, NW Russian Federation 64.30N 34.43E
128 J8 **Belomorsko-Baltiyskiy Kanal** Eng. White Sea-Baltic Canal, White Sea Canal. canal NW Russian Federation
159 V15 **Belonia** Tripura, NE India 23.15N 91.25E
Belopol'ye see Bilopillya
107 O4 **Belorado** Castilla-León, N Spain 42.25N 3.10W
130 L14 **Belorechensk** Krasnodarskiy Kray, SW Russian Federation 44.46N 39.53E
131 W5 **Beloretsk** Respublika Bashkortostan, W Russian
Belorussia/Belorussian SSR see Belarus
Belorusskaya Gryada see Byelaruskaya Hrada
Belorusskaya SSR see Belarus
Beloshchel'ye see Nar'yan-Mar
116 N8 **Beloslav** Varna, E Bulgaria 43.13N 27.42E
Belostok see Białystok
180 H5 **Belo Tsiribihina** var. Belo-sur-Tsiribihina. Toliara, W Madagascar 19.40S 44.30E
Belovár see Bjelovar
Belovezhskaya Pushcha see Białowieska, Puszcza/Byelavyezhskaya Pushcha
116 H10 **Belovo** Pazardzhik, C Bulgaria 42.12N 24.02E
126 H14 **Belovo** Kemerovskaya Oblast', S Russian Federation 54.25N 86.13E
Belovodsk see Bilovods'k
125 Ff9 **Beloyarskiy** Khanty-Mansiyskiy Avtonomnyy Okrug, N Russian Federation 63.40N 66.31E
128 K7 **Beloye More** Eng. White Sea. sea NW Russian Federation
128 K13 **Beloye, Ozero** ◎ NW Russian Federation
116 J10 **Belozem** Plovdiv, C Bulgaria 42.11N 25.00E
128 K13 **Belozërsk** Vologodskaya Oblast', NW Russian Federation 59.58N 37.49E
101 E20 **Belœil** Hainaut, SW Belgium 50.33N 3.45E
110 D8 **Belp** Bern, W Switzerland 46.54N 7.31E
110 D8 **Belp** ✕ (Bern) Bern, C Switzerland 46.55N 7.29E
109 L24 **Belpasso** Sicilia, Italy, C Mediterranean Sea 37.34N 14.58E
33 U14 **Belpre** Ohio, N USA 39.14N 81.34W
100 M8 **Belterwijde** ◎ N Netherlands
29 R4 **Belton** Missouri, C USA 38.48N 94.31W
23 P11 **Belton** South Carolina, SE USA 34.31N 82.29W
27 T9 **Belton** Texas, SW USA 31.03N 97.27W
27 S9 **Belton Lake** ⊠ Texas, SW USA
Bel'tsy see Bălţi
99 E16 **Belturbet** Ir. Béal Tairbirt. N Ireland 54.06N 7.25W
Beluchistan see Baluchistān
151 Z9 **Belukha, Gora** ▲ Kazakhstan/Russian Federation 49.42N 86.33E
109 M20 **Belvedere Marittimo** Calabria, SW Italy 39.37N 15.52E
32 L10 **Belvidere** Illinois, N USA 42.15N 88.50W
20 J14 **Belvidere** New Jersey, NE USA 40.49N 75.03W
Bely see Belyy
131 V8 **Belyayevka** Orenburgskaya Oblast', W Russian Federation 51.25N 56.26E
Belynichi see Byalynichy
128 H17 **Belyy** var. Bely, Beyj. Tverskaya Oblast', W Russian Federation 55.51N 32.57E
130 I6 **Belyye Berega** Bryanskaya Oblast', W Russian Federation 53.11N 34.42E
126 H5 **Belyy, Ostrov** island N Russian Federation
126 H12 **Belyy Yar** Tomskaya Oblast', C Russian Federation 58.26N 84.57E
102 N13 **Belzig** Brandenburg, NE Germany 52.09N 12.37E
24 K4 **Belzoni** Mississippi, S USA 33.10N 90.29W
180 H4 **Bemaraha** var. Plateau du Bemaraha. ▲ W Madagascar
84 B10 **Bembe** Uíge, NW Angola 7.01S 14.18E
79 S14 **Bembèrèkè** var. Bimbéréké. N Benin 10.10N 2.40E
106 K12 **Bembézar** ≈ SW Spain
106 J3 **Bembibre** Castilla-León, N Spain 42.37N 6.25W
31 T4 **Bemidji** Minnesota, N USA 47.27N 94.53W
100 L12 **Bemmel** Gelderland, SE Netherlands 51.52N 5.54E
176 U11 **Bemu** Pulau Seram, E Indonesia 3.21S 129.58E
Benāb see Bonāb
107 T5 **Benabarre** var. Benavarn. Aragón, NE Spain 42.06N 0.28E
Benaco see Garda, Lago di
81 L20 **Bena-Dibele** Kasai Oriental, C Dem. Rep. Congo (Zaire) 4.01S 22.50E
107 R9 **Benageber, Embalse de** ⊠ E Spain
191 O11 **Benalla** Victoria, SE Australia 36.33S 146.00E
106 M14 **Benamejí** Andalucía, S Spain 37.16N 4.33W
Benares see Vārānasi
Benavarn see Benabarre
106 F10 **Benavente** Santarém, C Portugal 38.58N 8.49W
106 K5 **Benavente** Castilla-León, N Spain 42.00N 5.40W
27 S15 **Benavides** Texas, SW USA 27.36N 98.24W
98 F8 **Benbecula** island NW Scotland, UK
Bencovazzo see Benkovac
34 H13 **Bend** Oregon, NW USA 44.03N 121.18W
190 K7 **Benda Range** ▲▲ South Australia
191 T6 **Bendemeer** New South Wales, SE Australia 30.54S 151.12E
Bender see Tighina
Bender Beila/Bender Beyla see Bandarbeyla
Bender Cassim/Bender Qaasim see Boosaaso
Bendery see Tighina
191 N11 **Bendigo** Victoria, SE Australia 36.46S 144.18E
120 E10 **Bēne** Dobele, SW Latvia 56.30N 23.04E
100 K13 **Beneden-Leeuwen** Gelderland, C Netherlands 51.52N 5.32E
103 L24 **Benediktenwand** ▲ S Germany 47.39N 11.28E
Benemérita de San Cristóbal see San Cristóbal
79 N12 **Bénéna** Ségou, S Mali 13.04N 4.20W

◆ Country ● Country Capital ◇ Dependent Territory ○ Dependent Territory Capital ◐ Administrative Region ✕ International Airport ▲ Mountain ▲▲ Mountain Range Volcano ≈ River ◎ Lake ⊠ Reservoir

BENENITRA – BIDBID

180 I7 **Benenitra** Toliara, S Madagascar *23.25S 45.06E*
Beneschau *see* Benešov
Beneški Zaliv *see* Venice, Gulf of
113 D17 **Benešov** *Ger.* Beneschau. Středočeský Kraj, W Czech Republic *49.48N 14.40E*
126 Ll3 **Benetta, Ostrov** *island* Novosibirskiye Ostrova, NE Russian Federation
109 L17 **Benevento** *anc.* Beneventum, Malventum. Campania, S Italy *41.07N 14.45E*
Beneventum *see* Benevento
181 S3 **Bengal, Bay of** *bay* N Indian Ocean
81 M17 **Bengamisa** Orientale, N Dem. Rep. Congo (Zaire) *0.58N 25.10E*
Bengasi *see* Banghāzī
174 Ll15 **Bengawan, Sungai** ∼ Jawa, S Indonesia
Bengazi *see* Banghāzī
167 P7 **Bengbu** *var.* Peng-pu. Anhui, E China *32.57N 117.17E*
34 L9 **Benge** Washington, NW USA *46.55N 118.01W*
Benghazi *see* Banghāzī
174 H7 **Bengkalis** Pulau Bengkalis, W Indonesia *1.29N 102.07E*
174 H6 **Bengkalis, Pulau** *island* W Indonesia
174 Kk7 **Bengkayang** Borneo, C Indonesia *0.45N 109.28E*
Bengkoelen/Bengkoeloe *see* Bengkulu
174 H12 **Bengkulu** *prev.* Bengkoeloe, Benkoelen, Benkulen. Sumatera, W Indonesia *3.46S 102.16E*
174 H11 **Bengkulu** *off.* Propinsi Bengkulu; *prev.* Bengkoelen, Benkoelen, Benkulen. ◈ *province* W Indonesia
84 A11 **Bengo** ◈ *province* W Angola
97 J16 **Bengtsfors** Västra Götaland, S Sweden *59.03N 12.13E*
84 B13 **Benguela** *var.* Benguella. Benguela, W Angola *12.34S 13.30E*
85 A14 **Benguela** ◈ *province* W Angola
Benguella *see* Benguela
Bengweulu, Lake *see* Bangweulu, Lake
124 Qq15 **Benha** *var.* Banhā. N Egypt *30.22N 31.16E*
198 G6 **Benham Seamount** *undersea feature* W Philippine Sea *15.48N 124.15E*
98 H6 **Ben Hope** ▲ N Scotland, UK *58.25N 4.36W*
81 P18 **Beni** Nord Kivu, NE Dem. Rep. Congo (Zaire) *0.31N 29.29E*
59 L15 **Beni** *var.* El Beni. ◈ *department* N Bolivia
76 H8 **Beni Abbès** W Algeria *30.07N 2.09W*
107 T8 **Benicarló** País Valenciano, E Spain *40.25N 0.25E*
107 T9 **Benicasim** País Valenciano, E Spain *40.03N 0.03E*
107 T12 **Benidorm** País Valenciano, SE Spain *38.33N 0.09W*
77 W9 **Beni Mazâr** *var.* Banī Mazār. C Egypt *28.24N 30.38E*
122 F12 **Beni-Mellal** C Morocco *32.20N 6.21W*
79 R14 **Benin** *off.* Republic of Benin; *prev.* Dahomey. ◆ *republic* W Africa
79 S17 **Benin, Bight of** *gulf* W Africa
79 U16 **Benin City** Edo, SW Nigeria *6.22N 5.39E*
59 K16 **Beni, Río** ∼ N Bolivia
123 Gg11 **Beni Saf** *var.* Beni-Saf. NW Algeria *35.16N 1.33W*
82 H12 **Benishangul** ◈ *region* W Ethiopia
107 T11 **Benissa** País Valenciano, E Spain *38.43N 0.03E*
124 Qq17 **Beni Suef** *var.* Banī Suwayf. N Egypt *29.09N 31.03E*
9 V15 **Benito** Manitoba, S Canada *51.57N 101.24W*
Benito *see* Uolo, Río
63 C23 **Benito Juárez** Buenos Aires, E Argentina *37.43S 59.48W*
43 P14 **Benito Juaréz Internacional** ✕ (México) México, S Mexico *19.24N 99.02W*
27 P5 **Benjamin** Texas, SW USA *33.34N 99.47W*
60 B13 **Benjamin Constant** Amazonas, N Brazil *4.22S 70.01W*
42 F4 **Benjamín Hill** Sonora, NW Mexico *30.13N 111.07W*
65 F19 **Benjamín, Isla** *island* Archipiélago de los Chonos, S Chile
172 N5 **Benkei-misaki** *headland* Hokkaidō, NE Japan *42.49N 140.10E*
30 L17 **Benkelman** Nebraska, C USA *40.04N 101.30W*
98 I7 **Ben Klibreck** ▲ N Scotland, UK *58.15N 4.23W*
Benkoelen *see* Bengkulu
114 D13 **Benkovac** *It.* Bencovazzo. Zadar, SW Croatia *44.02N 15.36E*
Benkulen *see* Bengkulu
98 I11 **Ben Lawers** ▲ C Scotland, UK *56.33N 4.13W*
98 J9 **Ben Macdui** *var.* Beinn MacDuibh. ▲ C Scotland, UK *57.02N 3.42W*
98 G11 **Ben More** ▲ W Scotland, UK *56.26N 6.00W*
98 I11 **Ben More** ▲ C Scotland, UK *56.22N 4.31W*
98 H7 **Ben More Assynt** ▲ N Scotland, UK *58.09N 4.51W*
193 E20 **Benmore, Lake** ◎ South Island, NZ
100 L12 **Bennekom** Gelderland, SE Netherlands *52.00N 5.40E*
23 T11 **Bennettsville** South Carolina, SE USA *34.37N 79.41W*
98 H10 **Ben Nevis** ▲ N Scotland, UK *56.46N 5.01W*
192 M9 **Benneydale** Waikato, North Island, NZ *38.31S 175.22E*
Bennichab *see* Bennichchāb
78 H8 **Bennichchâb** *var.* Bennichab. Inchiri, W Mauritania *19.25N 15.21W*
20 L10 **Bennington** Vermont, NE USA *42.51N 73.09W*
193 E20 **Ben Ohau Range** ▲▲ South Island, NZ
85 J21 **Benoni** Gauteng, NE South Africa *26.04S 28.18E*
180 J2 **Be, Nosy** *var.* Nossi-Bé. *island* NW Madagascar
Bénoué *see* Benue
44 F2 **Benque Viejo del Carmen** Cayo, W Belize *17.04N 89.08W*
103 G19 **Bensheim** Hessen, W Germany *49.40N 8.37E*
39 N16 **Benson** Arizona, SW USA *31.55N 110.16W*
31 S8 **Benson** Minnesota, N USA *45.19N 95.36W*
23 U10 **Benson** North Carolina, SE USA *35.22N 78.33W*
175 Pp14 **Benteng** Pulau Selayar, C Indonesia *6.07S 120.28E*
85 A14 **Bentiaba** Namibe, SW Angola *14.18S 12.27E*
189 T4 **Bentinck Island** *island* Wellesley Islands, Queensland, N Australia
82 E13 **Bentiu** Wahda, S Sudan *9.13N 29.49E*
144 G8 **Bent Jbaïl** *var.* Bint Jubayl. S Lebanon *33.07N 35.25E*
9 Q15 **Bentley** Alberta, SW Canada *52.27N 114.02W*
63 I15 **Bento Gonçalves** Rio Grande do Sul, S Brazil *29.06S 51.29W*
29 U12 **Benton** Arkansas, C USA *34.33N 92.35W*
32 L16 **Benton** Illinois, N USA *38.00N 88.55W*
22 H7 **Benton** Kentucky, S USA *36.51N 88.21W*
24 G5 **Benton** Louisiana, S USA *32.41N 93.44W*
29 Y7 **Benton** Missouri, C USA *37.05N 89.34W*
22 M10 **Benton** Tennessee, S USA *35.10N 84.39W*
33 O10 **Benton Harbor** Michigan, N USA *42.07N 86.27W*
29 S9 **Bentonville** Arkansas, C USA *36.22N 94.12W*
79 V16 **Benue** ◈ *state* SE Nigeria
80 F13 **Benue** *Fr.* Bénoué. ∼ Cameroon/Nigeria
174 Hh6 **Benut** Johor, Peninsular Malaysia *1.37N 103.15E*
169 V12 **Benxi** *prev.* Pen-ch'i, Penhsihu, Penki. Liaoning, NE China *41.11N 123.46E*
Benyakoni *see* Byenyakoni
114 K10 **Beočin** Serbia, N Yugoslavia *45.13N 19.43E*
Beodericsworth *see* Bury St Edmunds
114 M11 **Beograd** *Eng.* Belgrade, *Ger.* Belgrad; *anc.* Singidunum. ● (Yugoslavia) Serbia, N Yugoslavia *44.48N 20.27E*
114 L11 **Beograd** *Eng.* Belgrade. ✕ Serbia, N Yugoslavia *44.45N 20.21E*
78 M16 **Béoumi** C Ivory Coast *7.40N 5.34W*
37 V3 **Beowawe** Nevada, W USA *40.33N 116.31W*
176 Ww8 **Bepondi, Pulau** *see* Bepondi, Pulau
170 D13 **Beppu** Ōita, Kyūshū, SW Japan *33.16N 131.28E*
170 Dd14 **Beppu-wan** *bay* SW Japan
197 H15 **Beqa** *prev.* Mbengga. *island* W Fiji
Beqa Barrier Reef *see* Kavukavu Reef
47 Y14 **Bequia** *island* C Saint Vincent and the Grenadines
115 L16 **Berane** *prev.* Ivangrad. Montenegro, SW Yugoslavia *42.51N 19.51E*
115 L21 **Berat** *var.* Berati, *SCr.* Beligrad. Berat, C Albania *40.42N 19.57E*
115 L21 **Berat** ◈ *district* C Albania
Berătău *see* Berettyó
Berati *see* Berat
Beraun *see* Berounka, Czech Republic
Beraun *see* Beroun, Czech Republic
175 O6 **Berau, Sungai** ∼ Borneo, N Indonesia
176 V10 **Berau, Teluk** *var.* MacCluer Gulf. *bay* Irian Jaya, E Indonesia
82 G8 **Berber** River Nile, NE Sudan *18.01N 34.00E*
82 N12 **Berbera** Woqooyi Galbeed, NW Somalia *10.24N 45.01E*
81 H16 **Berbérati** Mambéré-Kadéï, SW Central African Republic *4.13N 15.49E*
Berberia, Cabo de *see* Barbaria, Cap de
57 T9 **Berbice River** ∼ NE Guyana
Berchid *see* Berrechid
105 N2 **Berck-Plage** Pas-de-Calais, N France *50.24N 1.34E*
27 T13 **Berclair** Texas, SW USA *28.33N 97.32W*
119 W10 **Berda** ∼ SE Ukraine
Berdichev *see* Berdychiv
126 Ll11 **Berdigestyakh** Respublika Sakha (Yakutiya), NE Russian Federation *62.02N 127.03E*
126 H14 **Berdsk** Novosibirskaya Oblast', C Russian Federation *54.42N 82.56E*
119 W10 **Berdyans'k** *Rus.* Berdyansk; *prev.* Osipenko. Zaporiz'ka Oblast', SE Ukraine *46.46N 36.48E*
119 W10 **Berdyans'ka Kosa** *spit* SE Ukraine
119 V10 **Berdyans'ka Zatoka** *gulf* S Ukraine
119 N5 **Berdychiv** *Rus.* Berdichev. Zhytomyrs'ka Oblast', N Ukraine *49.52N 28.39E*
22 M6 **Berea** Kentucky, S USA *37.34N 84.18W*
Beregovo/Beregszász *see* Berehove
118 G8 **Berehove** *Cz.* Berehovo, *Hung.* Beregszász, *Rus.* Beregovo. Zakarpats'ka Oblast', W Ukraine *48.13N 22.39E*
Berehovo *see* Berehove
194 J15 **Bereina** Central, S PNG *8.39S 146.25E*
47 O12 **Berekua** S Dominica *15.14N 61.19W*
79 O16 **Berekum** W Ghana *7.27N 2.34W*
77 Y11 **Berenice** *var.* Mînâ Baranîs. SE Egypt *23.58N 35.29E*
15 L14 **Berens** ∼ Manitoba/Ontario, C Canada
9 X14 **Berens River** Manitoba, C Canada *52.22N 97.00W*
31 R12 **Beresford** South Dakota, N USA *43.02N 96.45W*
118 J4 **Berestechko** Volyns'ka Oblast', NW Ukraine *50.21N 25.06E*
118 M11 **Bereşti** Galaţi, E Romania *46.04N 27.54E*
119 U6 **Berestova** ∼ E Ukraine
Beretău *see* Berettyó
113 N23 **Berettyó** *Rom.* Barcău; *prev.* Berătău, Beretău. ∼ Hungary/Romania
113 N23 **Berettyóújfalu** Hajdú-Bihar, E Hungary *47.15N 21.33E*
Berëza/Bereza Kartuska *see* Byaroza
119 Q4 **Berezan'** Kyyivs'ka Oblast', N Ukraine *50.18N 31.30E*
119 Q10 **Berezanka** Mykolayivs'ka Oblast', S Ukraine *46.51N 31.24E*
118 J6 **Berezhany** *Pol.* Brzeżany. Ternopil's'ka Oblast', W Ukraine *49.29N 25.00E*
Berezina *see* Byerezino
Berezino *see* Byerazino
119 P10 **Berezivka** *Rus.* Berezovka. Odes'ka Oblast', SW Ukraine *47.12N 30.55E*
119 Q2 **Berezna** Chernihivs'ka Oblast', NE Ukraine *51.35N 31.50E*
118 L3 **Berezne** Rivnens'ka Oblast', NW Ukraine *51.00N 26.46E*
119 R9 **Bereznehuvate** Mykolayivs'ka Oblast', S Ukraine *47.18N 32.52E*
129 N10 **Bereznik** Arkhangel'skaya Oblast', NW Russian Federation *62.50N 42.40E*
129 U13 **Berezniki** Permskaya Oblast', NW Russian Federation *59.25N 56.49E*
Berezovka *see* Berezivka
125 Ff9 **Berezovo** Khanty-Mansiyskiy Avtonomnyy Okrug, N Russian Federation *63.48N 64.38E*
131 O9 **Berezovskaya** Volgogradskaya Oblast', SW Russian Federation *50.17N 43.58E*
126 H14 **Berezovskiy** Kemerovskaya Oblast', S Russian Federation *55.40N 86.06E*
127 N14 **Berezovyy** Khabarovskiy Kray, E Russian Federation *51.42N 135.39E*
85 E25 **Berg** ∼ W South Africa
Berg *see* Berg bei Rohrbach
107 V4 **Berga** Cataluña, NE Spain *42.06N 1.40E*
97 N20 **Berga** Kalmar, S Sweden *57.13N 16.03E*
142 B13 **Bergama** İzmir, W Turkey *39.07N 27.10E*
108 E7 **Bergamo** *anc.* Bergomum. Lombardia, N Italy *45.42N 9.40E*
107 P3 **Bergara** País Vasco, N Spain *43.05N 2.25W*
111 S3 **Berg bei Rohrbach** *var.* Berg. Oberösterreich, N Austria *48.34N 14.02E*
195 O11 **Bergberg** ∼ New Britain, C Papau New Guinea
102 O6 **Bergen** Mecklenburg-Vorpommern, NE Germany *54.25N 13.24E*
103 I11 **Bergen** Niedersachsen, NW Germany *52.49N 9.57E*
100 H8 **Bergen** Noord-Holland, NW Netherlands *52.40N 4.42E*
96 C13 **Bergen** Hordaland, S Norway *60.24N 5.19E*
Bergen *see* Mons
57 W9 **Bergen en Dal** Brokopondo, C Surinam *5.15N 55.20W*
101 G15 **Bergen op Zoom** Noord-Brabant, S Netherlands *51.30N 4.18E*
104 L13 **Bergerac** Dordogne, SW France *44.51N 0.30E*
101 J16 **Bergeyk** Noord-Brabant, S Netherlands *51.19N 5.21E*
103 D16 **Bergheim** Nordrhein-Westfalen, W Germany *50.57N 6.39E*
57 X10 **Bergi** Sipaliwini, E Surinam *4.36N 54.24W*
103 E16 **Bergisch Gladbach** Nordrhein-Westfalen, W Germany *50.59N 7.07E*
103 F14 **Bergkamen** Nordrhein-Westfalen, W Germany *51.36N 7.39E*
97 N21 **Bergkvara** Kalmar, S Sweden *56.22N 16.04E*
Bergomum *see* Bergamo
100 K13 **Bergse Maas** ∼ S Netherlands
97 P15 **Bergshamra** Stockholm, C Sweden *59.37N 18.40E*
96 N10 **Bergsjö** Gävleborg, C Sweden *62.00N 17.10E*
95 J14 **Bergsviken** Norrbotten, N Sweden *65.16N 21.24E*
100 L6 **Bergum** *Fris.* Burgum. Friesland, N Netherlands *53.12N 5.58E*
100 M6 **Bergumer Meer** ◎ N Netherlands
96 N12 **Bergviken** ◎ C Sweden
174 I9 **Berhala, Selat** *strait* Sumatera, W Indonesia
Berhampore *see* Baharampur
127 Q9 **Beringa, Ostrov** *island* E Russian Federation
101 J17 **Beringen** Limburg, NE Belgium *51.04N 5.13E*
41 T12 **Bering Glacier** *glacier* Alaska, USA
Beringov Proliv *see* Bering Strait
127 Q5 **Beringovskiy** Chukotskiy Avtonomnyy Okrug, NE Russian Federation *63.04N 179.09E*
199 K2 **Bering Sea** *sea* N Pacific Ocean
40 L9 **Bering Strait** *Rus.* Beringov Proliv. *strait* Bering Sea/ Chukchi Sea
Berislav *see* Beryslav
107 O15 **Berja** Andalucía, S Spain *36.51N 2.55W*
96 H9 **Berkåk** Sør-Trøndelag, S Norway *62.50N 10.01E*
100 N11 **Berkel** ∼ Germany/Netherlands
37 N8 **Berkeley** California, W USA *37.52N 122.16W*
67 E24 **Berkeley Sound** *sound* NE Falkland Islands
23 V2 **Berkeley Springs** *var.* Bath. West Virginia, NE USA *39.36N 78.12W*
205 N6 **Berkner Island** *island* Antarctica
116 G8 **Berkovitsa** Montana, NW Bulgaria *43.16N 23.07E*
99 M22 **Berkshire** *cultural region* S England, UK
101 H17 **Berlaar** Antwerpen, N Belgium *51.08N 4.39E*
Berlanga *see* Berlanga de Duero
107 P6 **Berlanga de Duero** *var.* Berlanga. Castilla-León, N Spain *41.28N 2.51W*
(0) I16 **Berlanga Rise** *undersea feature* E Pacific Ocean
101 F17 **Berlare** Oost-Vlaanderen, NW Belgium *51.01N 4.01E*
106 E9 **Berlenga, Ilha da** *island* C Portugal
94 M7 **Berlevåg** Finnmark, N Norway *70.51N 29.04E*
102 O12 **Berlin** ● (Germany) Berlin, NE Germany *52.31N 13.26E*
23 Z4 **Berlin** Maryland, NE USA *38.19N 75.13W*
21 O7 **Berlin** New Hampshire, NE USA *44.27N 71.13W*
20 D16 **Berlin** Pennsylvania, NE USA *39.54N 78.57W*
32 L7 **Berlin** Wisconsin, N USA *43.57N 88.59W*
102 O12 **Berlin** ◈ *state* NE Germany
Berlinchen *see* Barlinek
33 U12 **Berlin Lake** ⊠ Ohio, N USA
191 R11 **Bermagui** New South Wales, SE Australia *36.26S 150.01E*
42 L8 **Bermejillo** Durango, C Mexico *25.55N 103.39W*
64 M6 **Bermejo (viejo), Río** ∼ N Argentina
64 L5 **Bermejo, Río** ∼ N Argentina
64 I10 **Bermejo, Río** ∼ W Argentina
107 P2 **Bermeo** País Vasco, N Spain *43.25N 2.43W*
106 K6 **Bermillo de Sayago** Castilla-León, N Spain *41.22N 6.07W*
108 E6 **Bermina, Pizzo** *Rmsch.* Piz Bernina. ▲ Italy/Switzerland *see also* Bernina, Piz *46.22N 9.52E*
66 A12 **Bermuda** *var.* Bermuda Islands, Bermudas; *prev.* Somers Islands. ◇ *UK crown colony* NW Atlantic Ocean
1 N11 **Bermuda** *var.* Great Bermuda, Long Island, Main Island. *island* Bermuda
Bermuda Islands *see* Bermuda
Bermuda-New England Seamount Arc *see* New England Seamounts
1 N11 **Bermuda Rise** *undersea feature* C Sargasso Sea
Bermudas *see* Bermuda
110 D8 **Bern** *Fr.* Berne. ● (Switzerland) Bern, W Switzerland *46.57N 7.25E*
110 D9 **Bern** *Fr.* Berne. ◈ *canton* W Switzerland
39 R11 **Bernalillo** New Mexico, SW USA *35.18N 106.33W*
12 H12 **Bernard Lake** ◎ Ontario, S Canada
63 B18 **Bernardo de Irigoyen** Santa Fe, NE Argentina *32.09S 61.06W*
20 J14 **Bernardsville** New Jersey, NE USA *40.43N 74.34W*
65 K14 **Bernasconi** La Pampa, C Argentina *37.55S 63.43W*
102 O12 **Bernau** Brandenburg, NE Germany *52.40N 13.36E*
104 L4 **Bernay** Eure, N France *49.04N 0.36E*
103 L14 **Bernburg** Sachsen-Anhalt, C Germany *51.46N 11.45E*
111 X5 **Berndorf** Niederösterreich, NE Austria *47.55N 16.10E*
33 Q12 **Berne** Indiana, N USA *40.39N 84.57W*
Berne *see* Bern
110 D10 **Berner Alpen** *var.* Berner Oberland, *Eng.* Bernese Oberland. ▲▲ SW Switzerland
Berner Oberland/Bernese Oberland *see* Berner Alpen
111 Y2 **Bernhardsthal** Niederösterreich, N Austria *48.40N 16.51E*
24 H4 **Bernice** Louisiana, S USA *32.49N 92.39W*
29 Y8 **Bernie** Missouri, C USA *36.40N 89.58W*
188 G9 **Bernier Island** *island* Western Australia
Bernina Pass *see* Bernina, Passo del
110 J10 **Bernina, Passo del** *Eng.* Bernina Pass. *pass* SE Switzerland *46.23N 10.00E*
110 J10 **Bernina, Piz** *It.* Pizzo Bermina. ▲ Italy/Switzerland *see also* Bermina, Pizzo *46.22N 9.55E*
101 E20 **Bernissart** Hainaut, SW Belgium *50.29N 3.37E*
103 E18 **Bernkastel-Kues** Rheinland-Pfalz, W Germany *49.55N 7.04E*
Beroea *see* Ḩalab
180 H6 **Beroroha** Toliara, SW Madagascar *21.40S 45.10E*
Béroubouay *see* Gbéroubouè
113 C17 **Beroun** *Ger.* Beraun. Středočeský Kraj, W Czech Republic *49.58N 14.04E*
113 C16 **Berounka** *Ger.* Beraun. ∼ W Czech Republic
115 Q18 **Berovo** E FYR Macedonia *41.45N 22.50E*
76 F6 **Berrechid** *var.* Berchid. W Morocco *33.16N 7.32W*
105 R15 **Berre, Étang de** ◎ SE France
105 S15 **Berre-l'Étang** Bouches-du-Rhône, SE France *43.28N 5.10E*
190 K9 **Berri** South Australia *34.16S 140.35E*
33 O10 **Berrien Springs** Michigan, N USA *41.57N 86.20W*
191 O10 **Berrigan** New South Wales, SE Australia *35.41S 145.50E*
105 N9 **Berry** *cultural region* C France
37 N7 **Berryessa, Lake** ◎ California, W USA
46 G2 **Berry Islands** *island group* N Bahamas
29 T9 **Berryville** Arkansas, C USA *36.21N 93.30W*
23 V3 **Berryville** Virginia, NE USA *39.09N 77.58W*
85 D21 **Berseba** Karas, S Namibia *26.00S 17.46E*
119 O8 **Bershad'** Vinnyts'ka Oblast', C Ukraine *48.19N 29.28E*
30 L3 **Berthold** North Dakota, N USA *48.16N 101.48W*
39 T3 **Berthoud** Colorado, C USA *40.18N 105.04W*
39 S4 **Berthoud Pass** *pass* Colorado, C USA *39.48N 105.46W*
81 F15 **Bertoua** Est, E Cameroon *4.34N 13.42E*
27 S10 **Bertram** Texas, SW USA *30.44N 98.03W*
65 G22 **Bertrand, Cerro** ▲ S Argentina *50.00S 73.27W*
101 J23 **Bertrix** Luxembourg, SE Belgium *49.52N 5.15E*
203 P3 **Beru** *var.* Peru. *atoll* Tungaru, W Kiribati
Beruni *see* Beruniy
152 I9 **Beruniy** *var.* Biruni, *Rus.* Beruni. Qoraqalpoghiston Respublikasi, W Uzbekistan *41.48N 60.39E*
60 F13 **Beruri** Amazonas, NW Brazil *3.44S 61.13W*
20 H14 **Berwick** Pennsylvania, NE USA *41.03N 76.13W*
98 K12 **Berwick** *cultural region* SE Scotland, UK
98 L12 **Berwick-upon-Tweed** N England, UK *55.46N 2.00W*
119 S10 **Beryslav** *Rus.* Berislav. Khersons'ka Oblast', S Ukraine *46.51N 33.27E*
Berytus *see* Beyrouth
180 H4 **Besalampy** Mahajanga, W Madagascar *16.43S 44.28E*
105 T8 **Besançon** *anc.* Besontium, Vesontio. Doubs, E France *47.13N 6.01E*
105 P10 **Besbre** ∼ C France
Bescanuova *see* Baška
Besdan *see* Bezdan
Besed' *see* Byesyedz'
153 R10 **Besharyq** *Rus.* Besharyk; *prev.* Kirovo. Farghona Wiloyati, E Uzbekistan *40.26N 70.33E*
Besharyk *see* Besharyq
152 L9 **Beshbuloq** *Rus.* Beshulak. Nawoiy Wiloyati, N Uzbekistan *41.55N 64.13E*
Beshenkovichi *see* Byeshankovichy
152 M13 **Beshkent** Qashqadaryo Wiloyati, S Uzbekistan *38.47N 65.42E*
Beshulak *see* Beshbuloq
176 Uu8 **Besir** Irian Jaya, E Indonesia *0.25S 130.38E*
114 L10 **Beška** Serbia, N Yugoslavia *45.09N 20.04E*
Beskra *see* Biskra
131 O16 **Beslan** Respublika Severnaya Osetiya, SW Russian Federation *43.12N 44.33E*
115 P16 **Besna Kobila** ▲ SE Yugoslavia *42.30N 22.16E*
143 N16 **Besni** Adıyaman, S Turkey *37.42N 37.52E*
Besontium *see* Besançon
124 Nn2 **Beşparmak Dağları** *Eng.* Kyrenia Mountains. ▲▲ N Cyprus
Bessarabka *see* Basarabeasca
94 O2 **Bessels, Kapp** *headland* C Svalbard *78.36N 21.43E*
25 P4 **Bessemer** Alabama, S USA *33.24N 86.57W*
32 K3 **Bessemer** Michigan, N USA *46.28N 90.03W*
23 Q10 **Bessemer City** North Carolina, SE USA *35.16N 81.16W*
104 M10 **Bessines-sur-Gartempe** Haute-Vienne, C France *46.06N 1.22E*
101 K15 **Best** Noord-Brabant, S Netherlands *51.31N 5.24E*
27 N9 **Best** Texas, SW USA *31.13N 101.34W*
129 O11 **Bestuzhevo** Arkhangel'skaya Oblast', NW Russian Federation *61.36N 43.54E*
126 M11 **Bestyakh** Respublika Sakha (Yakutiya), NE Russian Federation *61.25N 129.05E*
Beszterce *see* Bistriţa
Besztercebánya *see* Banská Bystrica
180 I5 **Betafo** Antananarivo, C Madagascar *19.49S 46.49E*
106 H2 **Betanzos** Galicia, NW Spain *43.16N 8.16W*
106 G2 **Betanzos, Ría de** *estuary* NW Spain
81 G15 **Bétaré Oya** Est, E Cameroon *5.34N 14.09E*
107 S9 **Bétera** País Valenciano, E Spain *39.34N 0.28W*
79 R15 **Bétérou** C Benin *9.13N 2.18E*
85 K21 **Bethal** Mpumalanga, NE South Africa *26.27S 29.28E*
32 K15 **Bethalto** Illinois, N USA *38.54N 90.02W*
85 D21 **Bethanie** *var.* Bethanien, Bethany. Karas, S Namibia *26.26S 17.06E*
Bethanien *see* Bethanie
29 S2 **Bethany** Missouri, C USA *40.15N 94.03W*
29 N10 **Bethany** Oklahoma, C USA *35.31N 97.37W*
Bethany *see* Bethanie
41 N12 **Bethel** Alaska, USA *60.47N 161.45W*
21 P7 **Bethel** Maine, NE USA *44.24N 70.47W*
23 W9 **Bethel** North Carolina, SE USA *35.46N 77.21W*
20 B15 **Bethel Park** Pennsylvania, NE USA *40.21N 80.03W*
23 W3 **Bethesda** Maryland, NE USA *38.58N 77.06W*
85 J22 **Bethlehem** Free State, C South Africa *28.11S 28.16E*
20 I14 **Bethlehem** Pennsylvania, NE USA *40.36N 75.22W*
144 F10 **Bethlehem** *Ar.* Bayt Laḩm, *Heb.* Bet Leḥem. C West Bank *31.43N 35.12E*
Bethlen *see* Beclean
85 I24 **Bethulie** Free State, C South Africa *30.29S 25.54E*
105 O1 **Béthune** Pas-de-Calais, N France *50.31N 2.37E*
104 M3 **Béthune** ∼ N France
106 M14 **Béticos, Sistemas** *var.* Sistema Penibético, *Eng.* Baetic Cordillera, Baetic Mountains. ▲▲ S Spain
56 I6 **Betijoque** Trujillo, NW Venezuela *9.27N 70.47W*
61 M20 **Betim** Minas Gerais, SE Brazil *19.55S 44.10W*
202 H3 **Betio** Tarawa, W Kiribati *1.21N 172.55E*
180 H7 **Betioky** Toliara, S Madagascar *23.42S 44.22E*
Bet Leḥem *see* Bethlehem
Betlen *see* Beclean
178 H17 **Betong** Yala, SW Thailand *5.47N 101.04E*
81 I16 **Bétou** La Likouala, N Congo *3.07N 18.30E*
151 P14 **Betpak-Dala** *Kaz.* Betpaqdala. *plateau* S Kazakhstan
Betpaqdala *see* Betpak-Dala
180 H7 **Betroka** Toliara, S Madagascar *23.15S 46.07E*
Betschau *see* Bečva
144 G9 **Bet She'an** *Ar.* Baysān, Beisān; *anc.* Scythopolis. Northern, N Israel *32.29N 35.25E*
13 T6 **Betsiamites** Quebec, SE Canada *48.55N 68.40W*
13 T6 **Betsiamites** ∼ Quebec, SE Canada
180 I4 **Betsiboka** ∼ N Madagascar
101 M25 **Bettembourg** Luxembourg, S Luxembourg *49.31N 6.06E*
101 M23 **Bettendorf** Diekirch, NE Luxembourg *49.52N 6.13E*
31 Z14 **Bettendorf** Iowa, C USA *41.31N 90.31W*
77 R13 **Bette, Pic** *var.* Bikkū Bittī, *It.* Picco Bette. ▲ S Libya *22.02N 19.07E*
Bette, Picco *see* Bette, Pic
159 P12 **Bettiah** Bihār, N India *26.49N 84.30E*
41 Q7 **Bettles** Alaska, USA *66.54N 151.40W*
97 N17 **Bettna** Södermanland, C Sweden *58.52N 16.40E*
160 H11 **Betūl** *prev.* Badnur. Madhya Pradesh, C India *21.55N 77.54E*
160 H9 **Betwa** ∼ C India
103 F16 **Betzdorf** Rheinland-Pfalz, W Germany *50.47N 7.50E*
84 C9 **Béu** Uíge, NW Angola *6.16S 15.28E*
33 P6 **Beulah** Michigan, N USA *44.37N 86.04W*
30 L5 **Beulah** North Dakota, N USA *47.16N 101.48W*
100 M8 **Beulakerwijde** ◎ N Netherlands
100 L13 **Beuningen** Gelderland, SE Netherlands *51.52N 5.47E*
Beuthen *see* Bytom
105 N7 **Beuvron** ∼ C France
101 F16 **Beveren** Oost-Vlaanderen, N Belgium *51.13N 4.15E*
23 T9 **B.Everett Jordan Reservoir** *var.* Jordan Lake. ⊠ North Carolina, SE USA
99 N17 **Beverley** E England, UK *53.51N 0.25W*
Beverley *see* Beverly
101 J17 **Beverlo** Limburg, NE Belgium *51.06N 5.14E*
21 P11 **Beverly** Massachusetts, NE USA *42.33N 70.49W*
34 J9 **Beverly** *var.* Beverley. Washington, NW USA *46.50N 119.57W*
37 S15 **Beverly Hills** California, W USA *34.02N 118.25W*
103 I14 **Beverungen** Nordrhein-Westfalen, C Germany *51.39N 9.22E*
100 H9 **Beverwijk** Noord-Holland, W Netherlands *52.28N 4.37E*
110 C10 **Bex** Vaud, W Switzerland *46.15N 7.00E*
99 P23 **Bexhill** *var.* Bexhill-on-Sea. SE England, UK *50.49N 0.28E*
Bexhill-on-Sea *see* Bexhill
142 E17 **Bey Dağları** ▲▲ SW Turkey
Beyj *see* Belyy
142 E10 **Beykoz** İstanbul, NW Turkey *41.09N 29.06E*
78 K15 **Beyla** Guinée-Forestière, SE Guinea *8.43N 8.41W*
143 X12 **Beyläqan** *prev.* Zhdanov. SW Azerbaijan *39.43N 47.38E*
82 L10 **Beylul** *var.* Beilul. SE Eritrea *13.10N 42.27E*
150 H14 **Beyneu** *Kaz.* Beyneū. Mangistau, SW Kazakhstan *45.19N 55.11E*
Beyneū *see* Beyneu
172 Ss14 **Beyonēsu-retsugan** *Eng.* Bayonnaise Rocks. *island group* SE Japan
142 G12 **Beypazarı** Ankara, NW Turkey *40.10N 31.55E*
161 F21 **Beypore** Kerala, SW India *11.10N 75.49E*
144 G7 **Beyrouth** *var.* Bayrūt, *Eng.* Beirut; *anc.* Berytus. ● (Lebanon) W Lebanon *33.54N 35.31E*
144 G7 **Beyrouth** ✕ W Lebanon *33.52N 35.30E*
142 G15 **Beyşehir** Konya, SW Turkey *37.39N 31.42E*
142 G15 **Beyşehir Gölü** ◎ C Turkey
110 J7 **Bezau** Vorarlberg, NW Austria *47.24N 9.55E*
114 J8 **Bezdan** *Ger.* Besdan, *Hung.* Bezdán. Serbia, NW Yugoslavia *45.51N 19.00E*
Bezdezh *see* Byezdzyezh
128 G15 **Bezhanitsy** Pskovskaya Oblast', W Russian Federation *56.57N 29.53E*
128 K15 **Bezhetsk** Tverskaya Oblast', W Russian Federation *57.47N 36.42E*
105 P16 **Béziers** *anc.* Baeterrae, Baeterrae Septimanorum, Julia Beterrae. Hérault, S France *43.21N 3.13E*
Bezmein *see* Byuzmeyin
Bezwada *see* Vijayawāda
160 P12 **Bhadrak** *var.* Bhadrakh. Orissa, E India *21.06N 86.31E*
Bhadrakh *see* Bhadrak
161 F19 **Bhadra Reservoir** ⊠ SW India
161 F18 **Bhadrāvati** Karnātaka, SW India *13.52N 75.43E*
159 R14 **Bhāgalpur** Bihār, NE India *25.13N 86.58E*
Bhairab *see* Bhairab Bazar
159 U14 **Bhairab Bazar** *var.* Bhairab. Dhaka, C Bangladesh *24.04N 91.00E*
159 O11 **Bhairahawa** Western, S Nepal *27.31N 83.27E*
155 S8 **Bhakkar** Punjab, E Pakistan *31.41N 71.04E*
159 P11 **Bhaktapur** Central, C Nepal *27.47N 85.21E*
178 Gg3 **Bhamo** *var.* Banmo. Kachin State, N Burma *24.15N 97.15E*
Bhamragad *see* Bhāmragarh
160 K13 **Bhāmragarh** *var.* Bhamragad. Mahārāshtra, C India *19.28N 80.39E*
160 J12 **Bhandāra** Mahārāshtra, C India *21.10N 79.40E*
Bhārat *see* India
158 J12 **Bharatpur** *prev.* Bhurtpore. Rājasthān, N India *27.13N 77.28E*
160 D11 **Bharūch** Gujarāt, W India *21.48N 72.54E*
161 E18 **Bhatkal** Karnātaka, W India *13.59N 74.34E*
159 O13 **Bhatni** *var.* Bhatni Junction. Uttar Pradesh, N India *26.22N 83.55E*
Bhatni Junction *see* Bhatni
159 S16 **Bhātpāra** West Bengal, NE India *22.55N 88.30E*
155 U7 **Bhaun** Punjab, E Pakistan *32.53N 72.45E*
Bhaunagar *see* Bhāvnagar
160 M13 **Bhavānīpātna** Orissa, E India *19.56N 83.09E*
161 H21 **Bhavānīsāgar Reservoir** ⊠ S India
160 D11 **Bhāvnagar** *prev.* Bhaunagar. Gujarāt, W India *21.46N 72.13E*
Bheanntraí, Bá *see* Bantry Bay
Bheara, Béal an *see* Gweebarra Bay
160 K12 **Bhilai** Madhya Pradesh, C India *21.13N 81.26E*
158 G13 **Bhīlwāra** Rājasthān, N India *25.22N 74.39E*
161 E14 **Bhīma** ∼ S India
161 K16 **Bhimavaram** Andhra Pradesh, E India *16.34N 81.34E*
160 I7 **Bhind** Madhya Pradesh, C India *26.33N 78.46E*
158 E13 **Bhīnmāl** Rājasthān, N India *25.01N 72.22E*
Bhir *see* Bīd
160 D13 **Bhiwandi** Mahārāshtra, W India *19.21N 73.07E*
158 H10 **Bhiwāni** Haryāna, N India *28.49N 76.07E*
158 L13 **Bhognīpur** Uttar Pradesh, N India *26.12N 79.48E*
159 U16 **Bhola** Khulna, S Bangladesh *22.42N 90.43E*
160 H10 **Bhopāl** Madhya Pradesh, C India *23.16N 77.24E*
161 J14 **Bhopālpatnam** Madhya Pradesh, C India *18.51N 80.22E*
161 E14 **Bhor** Mahārāshtra, W India *18.10N 73.55E*
160 O12 **Bhubaneshwar** *prev.* Bhubaneswar, Bhuvaneshwar. Orissa, E India *20.16N 85.51E*
Bhubaneswar *see* Bhubaneshwar
160 B9 **Bhuj** Gujarāt, W India *23.16N 69.40E*
Bhuket *see* Phuket
Bhurtpore *see* Bharatpur
Bhusaval *see* Bhusāwal
160 G12 **Bhusāwal** *prev.* Bhusaval. Mahārāshtra, C India *21.01N 75.49E*
159 T12 **Bhutan** *off.* Kingdom of Bhutan, *var.* Druk-yul. ◆ *monarchy* S Asia
Bhuvaneshwar *see* Bhubaneshwar
149 T15 **Biābān, Kūh-e** ▲▲ S Iran
79 V18 **Biafra, Bight of** *var.* Bight of Bonny. *bay* W Africa
176 X9 **Biak** Irian Jaya, E Indonesia *1.10S 136.04E*
176 Ww9 **Biak, Pulau** *island* E Indonesia
112 P12 **Biała Podlaska** Lubelskie, E Poland *52.03N 23.08E*
112 F7 **Białogard** *Ger.* Belgard. Zachodniopomorskie, NW Poland *54.00N 15.58E*
112 P10 **Białowieska, Puszcza** *Bel.* Byelavyezhskaya Pushcha, *Rus.* Belovezhskaya Pushcha. *physical region* Belarus/Poland *see also* Byelavyezhskaya Pushcha
112 G8 **Biały Bór** *Ger.* Baldenburg. Zachodniopomorskie, NW Poland *53.53N 16.49E*
112 P9 **Białystok** *Rus.* Belostok, Bielostok. Podlaskie, NE Poland *53.08N 23.09E*
109 L24 **Biancavilla** *prev.* Inessa. Sicilia, Italy, C Mediterranean Sea *37.37N 14.52E*
Bianco, Monte *see* Blanc, Mont
78 L15 **Biankouma** W Ivory Coast *7.43N 7.37W*
178 Ii7 **Bia, Phou** *var.* Pou Bia. ▲ C Laos *18.59N 103.09E*
Bia, Pou *see* Bia, Phou
149 R5 **Biārjmand** Semnān, N Iran *36.04N 55.49E*
107 P4 **Biarra** ∼ NE Spain
104 I15 **Biarritz** Pyrénées-Atlantiques, SW France *43.24N 1.39W*
110 H10 **Biasca** Ticino, S Switzerland *46.22N 8.59E*
63 E17 **Biassini** Salto, N Uruguay *31.18S 57.05W*
172 Oo5 **Bibai** Hokkaidō, NE Japan *43.22N 141.52E*
85 B15 **Bibala** *Port.* Vila Arriaga. Namibe, SW Angola *14.45S 13.18E*
106 I4 **Bibéi** ∼ NW Spain
Biberach *see* Biberach an der Riss
103 I23 **Biberach an der Riss** *var.* Biberach, *Ger.* Biberach an der Riß. Baden-Württemberg, S Germany *48.06N 9.46E*
110 E7 **Biberist** Solothurn, NW Switzerland *47.10N 7.34E*
79 O16 **Bibiani** SW Ghana *6.28N 2.19W*
114 C13 **Bibinje** Zadar, SW Croatia *44.04N 15.17E*
Biblical Gebal *see* Jbail
118 I5 **Bibrka** *Pol.* Bóbrka, *Rus.* Bobrka. L'vivs'ka Oblast', NW Ukraine *49.39N 24.16E*
119 N10 **Bic** ∼ S Moldova
115 M18 **Bicaj** Kukës, NE Albania *42.00N 20.24E*
118 K10 **Bicaz** *Hung.* Békás. Neamţ, NE Romania *46.53N 26.04E*
191 Q16 **Bicheno** Tasmania, SE Australia *41.56S 148.15E*
Bichiş *see* Békés
Bichiş-Ciaba *see* Békéscsaba
Bichitra *see* Phichit
143 P8 **Bichvint'a** *Rus.* Pitsunda. NW Georgia *43.12N 40.21E*
13 T7 **Bic, Île du** *island* Quebec, SE Canada
34 J10 **Bickleton** Washington, NW USA *46.00N 120.16W*
38 L6 **Bicknell** Utah, W USA *38.20N 111.32W*
175 Tt7 **Bicoli** Pulau Halmahera, E Indonesia *0.34N 128.33E*
113 J22 **Bicske** Fejér, C Hungary *47.28N 18.38E*
161 F14 **Bīd** *prev.* Bhir. Mahārāshtra, W India *19.17N 75.22E*
79 U15 **Bida** Niger, C Nigeria *9.06N 6.02E*
161 H15 **Bīdar** Karnātaka, C India *17.55N 77.34E*
147 Y8 **Bidbid** NE Oman *23.25N 58.07E*

◆ Country ● Country Capital ◇ Dependent Territory ○ Dependent Territory Capital ◈ Administrative Region ✕ International Airport ▲ Mountain ▲▲ Mountain Range Volcano ∼ River ◎ Lake ⊠ Reservoir

BIDDEFORD – BLANDING

21 P9 Biddeford Maine, NE USA 43.28N 70.27W
100 L9 Biddinghuizen Flevoland, C Netherlands 52.28N 5.41E
35 X11 Biddle Montana, NW USA 45.04N 105.21W
99 J23 Bideford SW England, UK 51.01N 4.12W
84 D13 Bié ◐ province C Angola
37 O2 Bieber California, W USA 41.07N 121.09W
112 O9 Biebrza ~ NE Poland
172 P5 Biei Hokkaidō, NE Japan 43.33N 142.28E
110 D8 Biel Fr. Bienne. Bern, W Switzerland 47.09N 7.16E
102 G13 Bielefeld Nordrhein-Westfalen, NW Germany 52.01N 8.31E
110 D8 Bieler See Fr. Lac de Bienne. ◎ W Switzerland
Bielitz/Bielitz-Biala see Bielsko-Biała
108 C7 Biella Piemonte, N Italy 45.33N 8.03E
Bielostok see Białystok
113 J17 Bielsko-Biała Ger. Bielitz, Bielitz-Biala. Śląskie, S Poland 49.48N 19.01E
112 P10 Bielsk Podlaski Białystok, E Poland 52.45N 23.11E
Biên Bien see Điên Biên
Biên Đông see South China Sea
9 V17 Bienfait Saskatchewan, S Canada 49.06N 102.47W
178 Jj14 Biên Hoa Đông Nai, S Vietnam 10.58N 106.49E
Bienne see Biel
Bienne, Lac de see Bieler See
10 K8 Bienville, Lac ◎ Quebec, C Canada
84 D13 Bié, Planalto do var. Bié Plateau. plateau C Angola
Bié Plateau see Bié, Planalto do
110 B9 Bière Vaud, W Switzerland 46.32N 6.19E
100 O4 Bierum Groningen, NE Netherlands 53.25N 6.51E
100 I13 Biesbos var. Biesbosch. wetland S Netherlands
Biesbosch see Biesbos
101 H21 Biesme Namur, S Belgium 50.19N 4.43E
103 H21 Bietigheim-Bissingen Baden-Württemberg, SW Germany 48.57N 9.07E
101 J23 Bièvre Namur, SE Belgium 49.56N 5.01E
81 D18 Bifoun Moyen-Ogooué, NW Gabon 0.15S 10.24E
172 Pp3 Bifuka Hokkaidō, NE Japan 44.28N 142.20E
142 C11 Biga Çanakkale, NW Turkey 40.13N 27.13E
142 C13 Bigadiç Balıkesir, W Turkey 39.24N 28.07E
28 J7 Big Basin basin Kansas, C USA
193 B20 Big Bay bay South Island, NZ
197 B12 Big Bay bay C Vanuatu
33 O5 Big Bay de Noc ◎ Michigan, N USA
33 N3 Big Bay Point headland Michigan, N USA 46.51N 87.40W
35 R10 Big Belt Mountains ▲▲ Montana, NW USA
31 N10 Big Bend Dam dam South Dakota, N USA 44.03N 99.27W
26 K12 Big Bend National Park national park Texas, S USA
24 K5 Big Black River ~ Mississippi, S USA
29 O3 Big Blue River ~ Kansas/Nebraska, C USA
26 M10 Big Canyon ~ Texas, SW USA
35 N12 Big Creek Idaho, NW USA 45.05N 115.20W
25 N8 Big Creek Lake ▣ Alabama, S USA
25 X15 Big Cypress Swamp wetland Florida, SE USA
41 S9 Big Delta Alaska, USA 64.09N 145.50W
32 K6 Big Eau Pleine Reservoir ▣ Wisconsin, N USA
21 P5 Bigelow Mountain ▲ Maine, NE USA 45.09N 70.17W
31 U3 Big Falls Minnesota, N USA 48.13N 93.48W
35 P8 Bigfork Montana, NW USA 48.03N 114.04W
31 U3 Big Fork River ~ Minnesota, N USA
9 S15 Biggar Saskatchewan, S Canada 52.03N 107.58W
188 L3 Bigge Island island Western Australia
37 O5 Biggs California, W USA 39.24N 121.44W
34 I11 Biggs Oregon, NW USA 45.39N 120.49W
12 K13 Big Gull Lake ◎ Ontario, SE Canada
39 P16 Big Hachet Peak ▲ New Mexico, SW USA 31.38N 108.24W
35 P11 Big Hole River ~ Montana, NW USA
35 V13 Bighorn Basin basin Wyoming, C USA
35 U11 Bighorn Lake ◎ Montana/Wyoming, N USA
35 W13 Bighorn Mountains ▲▲ Wyoming, C USA
38 J13 Big Horn Peak ▲ Arizona, SW USA 33.40N 113.01W
35 V11 Bighorn River ~ Montana/Wyoming, NW USA
16 O5 Big Island island Nunavut, NE Canada
41 O16 Big Koniuji Island island Shumagin Islands, Alaska, USA
27 N9 Big Lake Texas, SW USA 31.11N 101.27W
21 T3 Big Lake ◎ Maine, NE USA
32 I3 Big Manitou Falls waterfall Wisconsin, N USA 46.32N 92.07W
37 R2 Big Mountain ▲ Nevada, W USA 41.18N 119.03W
110 G10 Bignasco Ticino, S Switzerland 46.21N 8.37E
31 R16 Big Nemaha River ~ Nebraska, C USA
78 G12 Bignona SW Senegal 12.49N 16.16W
Bigorra see Tarbes
Bigosovo see Bihosava
37 S10 Big Pine California, W USA 37.09N 118.18W
37 Q14 Big Pine Mountain ▲ California, W USA 34.41N 119.37W
29 V6 Big Piney Creek ~ Missouri, C USA
67 M24 Big Point headland N Tristan da Cunha
33 P8 Big Rapids Michigan, N USA 43.42N 85.28W
32 K6 Big Rib River ~ Wisconsin, N USA
12 L14 Big Rideau Lake ◎ Ontario, SE Canada
9 T14 Big River Saskatchewan, C Canada 53.48N 106.55W
29 X5 Big River ~ Missouri, C USA
33 N7 Big Sable Point headland Michigan, N USA 44.03N 86.30W
35 S7 Big Sandy Montana, NW USA 48.08N 110.09W
27 W6 Big Sandy Texas, SW USA 32.34N 95.06W
39 V5 Big Sandy Creek ~ Colorado, C USA
31 Q16 Big Sandy Creek ~ Nebraska, C USA
31 V5 Big Sandy Lake ◎ Minnesota, N USA
38 J11 Big Sandy River ~ Arizona, SW USA
23 P5 Big Sandy River ~ S USA
25 V6 Big Satilla Creek ~ Georgia, SE USA
31 R12 Big Sioux River ~ Iowa/South Dakota, N USA
37 U7 Big Smoky Valley valley Nevada, W USA
27 N7 Big Spring Texas, SW USA 32.15N 101.30W
21 Q5 Big Squaw Mountain ▲ Maine, NE USA 45.28N 69.42W
23 O7 Big Stone Gap Virginia, NE USA 36.52N 82.45W
31 Q8 Big Stone Lake ◎ Minnesota/South Dakota, N USA
24 K4 Big Sunflower River ~ Mississippi, S USA
35 T11 Big Timber Montana, NW USA 45.50N 109.57W
10 D8 Big Trout Lake Ontario, C Canada 53.40N 90.00W
12 I12 Big Trout Lake ◎ Ontario, SE Canada
37 O2 Big Valley Mountains ▲▲ California, W USA
27 Q13 Big Wells Texas, SW USA 28.34N 99.34W
12 F11 Bigwood Ontario, S Canada 46.03N 80.37W
114 D11 Bihać Federacija Bosna I Hercegovina, NW Bosnia and Herzegovina 44.49N 15.53E
159 P14 Bihār prev. Behar. ◐ state N India
Bihār see Bihār Sharīf
83 F20 Biharamulo Kagera, NW Tanzania 2.37S 31.19E
159 R13 Bihārīganj Bihār, NE India 25.43N 86.58E
159 P14 Bihār Sharīf var. Bihār. Bihār, N India 25.13N 85.31E
118 F10 Bihor ◐ county NW Romania
172 Q6 Bihoro Hokkaidō, NE Japan 43.50N 144.05E
120 K11 Bihosava Rus. Bigosovo. Vitsyebskaya Voblasts', NW Belarus 55.50N 27.45E
Bijagos Archipelago see Bijagós, Arquipélago dos
78 G13 Bijagós, Arquipélago dos var. Bijagos Archipelago. island group W Guinea-Bissau
161 F16 Bījāpur Karnātaka, C India 16.49N 75.42E
148 K5 Bījār Kordestān, W Iran 35.54N 47.36E
114 J11 Bijeljina Republika Srpska, NE Bosnia and Herzegovina 44.46N 19.13E
115 K15 Bijelo Polje Montenegro, SW Yugoslavia 43.03N 19.44E
166 I11 Bijie Guizhou, S China 27.18N 105.16E
158 J10 Bijnor Uttar Pradesh, N India 29.22N 78.09E
158 F11 Bīkāner Rājasthān, NW India 28.01N 73.22E
201 V3 Bikar Atoll var. Pikaar. atoll Ratak Chain, N Marshall Islands
202 H3 Bikeman atoll Tungaru, W Kiribati
202 I3 Bikenebu Tarawa, W Kiribati
127 Nn16 Bikin Khabarovskiy Kray, SE Russian Federation 46.45N 134.06E
127 Nn16 Bikin ~ SE Russian Federation
201 R3 Bikini Atoll var. Pikinni. atoll Ralik Chain, NW Marshall Islands
85 L17 Bikita Masvingo, E Zimbabwe 20.04S 31.38E
Bikkū Bitti see Bette, Pic
81 I19 Bikoro Equateur, W Dem. Rep. Congo (Zaire) 0.45S 18.09E
147 Z9 Bilād Banī Bū 'Alī NE Oman 22.01N 59.18E
147 Z9 Bilād Banī Bū Ḩasan NE Oman 22.09N 59.13E
147 X9 Bilād Manaḩ var. Manaḩ. NE Oman 22.37N 57.27E
79 Q12 Bilanga C Burkina 12.35N 0.08W
175 Q7 Bilang, Teluk bay Sulawesi, N Indonesia
158 F12 Bilāra Rājasthān, N India 26.14N 73.48E
158 K10 Bilāri Uttar Pradesh, N India 28.37N 78.48E
144 J5 Bil'ās, Jabal al ▲ C Syria
158 I8 Bilāspur Himāchal Pradesh, N India 31.19N 76.46E
160 L11 Bilāspur Madhya Pradesh, C India 22.06N 82.08E
173 G6 Bila, Sungai ~ Sumatera, W Indonesia
143 Y13 Biläsuvar Rus. Bilyasuvar; prev. Pushkino. SE Azerbaijan 39.26N 48.33E
119 O5 Bila Tserkva Rus. Belaya Tserkov'. Kyyivs'ka Oblast', N Ukraine 49.48N 30.07E
178 H11 Bilauktaung Range var. Thanintari Taungdan. ▲▲ Burma/Thailand
107 O2 Bilbao Basq. Bilbo. País Vasco, N Spain 43.15N 2.55W
Bilbo see Bilbao
94 H2 Bíldudalur Vestfirdhir, NW Iceland 65.40N 23.35W
115 I16 Bileća Republika Srpska, S Bosnia and Herzegovina 42.53N 18.27E
142 E12 Bilecik Bilecik, NW Turkey 39.59N 29.54E
142 F12 Bilecik ◐ province NW Turkey
118 E11 Biled Ger. Billed, Hung. Billéd. Timiş, W Romania 45.55N 20.55E
113 O15 Biłgoraj Lubelskie, E Poland 50.32N 22.42E
119 P11 Bilhorod-Dnistrovs'kyy Rus. Belgorod-Dnestrovskiy, Rom. Cetatea Albă; prev. Akkerman, anc. Tyras. Odes'ka Oblast', SW Ukraine 46.10N 30.18E
81 M16 Bili Orientale, N Dem. Rep. Congo (Zaire) 4.07N 25.09E
127 Oo5 Bilibino Chukotskiy Avtonomnyy Okrug, NE Russian Federation 67.56N 166.45E
178 Gg8 Bilin Mon State, S Burma 17.13N 97.12E
179 Qq12 Biliran Island island C Philippines
115 N21 Bilisht var. Bilishti. Korçë, SE Albania 40.36N 21.00E
Bilishti see Bilisht
191 N10 Billabong Creek var. Moulamein Creek. seasonal river New South Wales, SE Australia
190 G4 Billa Kalina South Australia 29.57S 136.13E
207 Q17 Bill Baileys Bank undersea feature N Atlantic Ocean 60.34N 10.15W
Billed/Billéd see Biled
159 N14 Billi Uttar Pradesh, N India 24.30N 82.58E
99 M15 Billingham N England, UK 54.36N 1.16W
35 U11 Billings Montana, NW USA 45.47N 108.32W
97 J16 Billingsfors Västra Götaland, S Sweden 58.57N 12.14E
Bill of Cape Clear, The see Clear, Cape
30 L9 Billsburg South Dakota, N USA 44.22N 101.40W
97 F23 Billund Ribe, W Denmark 55.43N 9.07E
38 L11 Bill Williams Mountain ▲ Arizona, SW USA 35.12N 112.12W
38 I12 Bill Williams River ~ Arizona, SW USA
79 Y8 Bilma Agadez, NE Niger 18.22N 13.01E
79 Y8 Bilma, Grand Erg de desert NE Niger
189 Y9 Biloela Queensland, E Australia 24.27S 150.31E
114 G8 Bilo Gora ▲▲ N Croatia
119 U13 Bilohirs'k Rus. Belogorsk; prev. Karasubazar. Respublika Krym, S Ukraine 45.01N 34.45E
118 M3 Bilokorovychi Rus. Belokorovichi. Zhytomyrs'ka Oblast', N Ukraine 51.07N 28.02E
119 X5 Bilokurakine Luhans'ka Oblast', E Ukraine 49.32N 38.44E
119 T3 Bilopillya Rus. Belopol'ye. Sums'ka Oblast', NE Ukraine 51.09N 34.16E
119 Y6 Bilovods'k Rus. Belovodsk. Luhans'ka Oblast', E Ukraine 49.10N 39.34E
24 M9 Biloxi Mississippi, S USA 30.24N 88.53W
119 R10 Bilozerka Khersons'ka Oblast', S Ukraine 46.36N 32.23E
119 W7 Bilozers'ke Donets'ka Oblast', E Ukraine 48.29N 37.03E
100 J11 Bilthoven Utrecht, C Netherlands 52.07N 5.12E
80 K9 Biltine Biltine, E Chad 14.30N 20.52E
80 J9 Biltine off. Préfecture de Biltine. ◐ prefecture E Chad
168 D5 Bilüü Bayan-Ölgiy, W Mongolia 48.54N 89.40E
Bilwi see Puerto Cabezas
Bilyasuvar see Biläsuvar
119 O11 Bilyayivka Odes'ka Oblast', SW Ukraine 46.28N 30.11E
101 K18 Bilzen Limburg, NE Belgium 50.52N 5.31E
Bimbéréké see Bembèrèkè
191 R10 Bimberi Peak ▲ New South Wales, SE Australia 35.42S 148.46E
79 Q15 Bimbila E Ghana 8.54N 0.04E
81 I15 Bimbo Ombella-Mpoko, SW Central African Republic 4.19N 18.27E
46 F2 Bimini Islands island group W Bahamas
160 I9 Bīna Madhya Pradesh, C India 24.09N 78.10E
149 T4 Bīnālūd, Kūh-e ▲▲ NE Iran
101 F20 Binche Hainaut, S Belgium 50.25N 4.10E
Bindloe Island see Marchena, Isla
85 L16 Bindura Mashonaland Central, NE Zimbabwe 17.18S 31.13E
107 T5 Binefar Aragón, NE Spain 41.51N 0.16E
85 J16 Binga Matabeleland North, W Zimbabwe 17.42S 27.21E
191 T5 Bingara New South Wales, SE Australia 29.54S 150.36E
103 F18 Bingen am Rhein Rheinland-Pfalz, SW Germany 49.58N 7.54E
28 M11 Binger Oklahoma, C USA 35.19N 98.19W
Bingerau see Węgrów
Bin Ghalfān, Jazā'ir see Ḩalāniyāt, Juzur al
21 Q6 Bingham Maine, NE USA 45.01N 69.51W
20 H11 Binghamton New York, NE USA 42.06N 75.55W
Bin Ghanīmah, Jabal see Bin Ghunaymah, Jabal
77 P11 Bin Ghunaymah, Jabal var. Jabal Bin Ghanīmah. ▲ C Libya
145 U3 Bingird NE Iraq 36.03N 45.03E
143 P14 Bingöl Bingöl, E Turkey 38.54N 40.28E
143 P14 Bingöl ◐ province E Turkey
167 R6 Binhai var. Binhai Xian. Jiangsu, E China 34.03N 119.46E
Binhai Xian see Binhai
178 Kk12 Binh Đinh var. An Nhon. Binh Đinh, C Vietnam 13.52N 109.07E
178 Kk10 Binh Sơn var. Châu Ổ. Quang Ngai, C Vietnam 15.18N 108.45E
Binimani see Bintimani
173 Ff5 Binjai Sumatera, W Indonesia 3.37N 98.30E
191 R6 Binnaway New South Wales, SE Australia 31.34S 149.24E
110 E6 Binningen Basel-Land, NW Switzerland 47.31N 7.34E
175 R13 Binongko, Pulau island Kepulauan Tukangbesi, C Indonesia
174 Gg3 Bintan, Banjaran ▲▲ Peninsular Malaysia
174 I7 Bintan, Pulau island Kepulauan Riau, W Indonesia
78 J14 Bintimani var. Binimani. ▲ NE Sierra Leone 9.21N 11.09W
Bint Jubayl see Bent Jbaïl
174 M5 Bintulu Sarawak, East Malaysia 3.12N 113.01E
176 Vv10 Bintuni prev. Steenkool. Irian Jaya, E Indonesia 2.03S 133.45E
176 Vv10 Bintuni, Teluk bay Irian Jaya, E Indonesia
169 W8 Bin Xian Heilongjiang, NE China 45.43N 127.24E
166 K14 Binyang Guangxi Zhuangzu Zizhiqu, S China 23.15N 108.47E
167 Q4 Binzhou Shandong, E China 37.22N 118.03E
65 G14 Bío Bío off. Región del Bío Bío. ◐ region C Chile
65 G14 Bío Bío, Río ~ C Chile
81 C16 Bioco, Isla de var. Bioko, Eng. Fernando Po, Sp. Fernando Póo; prev. Macías Nguema Biyogo. island NW Equatorial Guinea
114 D13 Biograd na Moru It. Zaravecchia. Zadar, SW Croatia 43.57N 15.27E
Bioko see Bioco, Isla de
115 F14 Biokovo ▲▲ S Croatia
Biorra see Birr
Bipontium see Zweibrücken
149 W13 Birag, Kūh-e ▲ SE Iran
77 O10 Birāk var. Brak. C Libya 27.31N 14.16E
145 S10 Bi'r al Islām C Iraq 32.15N 43.40E
160 N11 Biramitrapur Orissa, E India 22.24N 84.42E
145 T11 Bi'r an Nişf S Iraq 31.22N 44.07E
80 L12 Birao Vakaga, NE Central African Republic 10.14N 22.49E
164 M6 Biratar Bulak well NW China 42.00N 90.26E
159 R12 Birātnagar Eastern, SE Nepal 26.28N 87.16E
172 Oo6 Biratori Hokkaidō, NE Japan 42.35N 142.07E
41 S8 Birch Creek Alaska, USA 66.17N 145.54W
40 M11 Birch Creek ~ Alaska, USA
9 T14 Birch Hills Saskatchewan, S Canada 52.58N 105.22W
190 M10 Birchip Victoria, SE Australia 36.01S 142.55E
31 X4 Birch Lake ◎ Minnesota, N USA
9 Q11 Birch Mountains ▲▲ Alberta, W Canada
9 V15 Birch River Manitoba, S Canada 52.22N 101.03W
46 H12 Birchs Hill hill W Jamaica 18.22N 78.05W
41 R11 Birchwood Alaska, USA 61.24N 149.28W
196 I5 Bird Island island S Northern Mariana Islands
143 N16 Birecik Şanlıurfa, S Turkey 37.02N 38.01E
158 M10 Birendranagar var. Surkhet. Mid Western, W Nepal 28.35N 81.36E
Bir es Saba see Be'ér Sheva'
76 A12 Bir-Gandouz SW Western Sahara 21.35N 16.27W
159 P12 Birganj Central, C Nepal 27.03N 84.53E
83 B14 Biri ~ W Sudan
Bi'r Ibn Hirmās see Al Bi'r
176 Yy10 Biri, Sungai ~ Irian Jaya, E Indonesia
149 U8 Bīrjand Khorāsān, E Iran 32.54N 59.13E
145 T11 Birkat Ḩāmid well S Iraq 31.16N 44.04E
97 F18 Birkeland Aust-Agder, S Norway 58.18N 8.13E
103 E19 Birkenfeld Rheinland-Pfalz, SW Germany 49.39N 7.09E
99 K18 Birkenhead NW England, UK 53.24N 3.01W
111 W7 Birkfeld Steiermark, SE Austria 47.21N 15.40E
190 A2 Birksgate Range ▲▲ South Australia
Bîrlad see Bârlad
99 K20 Birmingham C England, UK 52.30N 1.49W
25 P4 Birmingham Alabama, S USA 33.30N 86.47W
99 M20 Birmingham ✕ C England, UK 52.27N 1.46W
Bir Moghrein see Bîr Mogreïn
78 J4 Bîr Mogreïn var. Bir Moghrein; prev. Fort-Trinquet. Tiris Zemmour, N Mauritania 25.10N 11.34W
203 S4 Birnie Island atoll Phoenix Islands, C Kiribati
Birni-Ngaouré see Birnin Gaouré
79 S12 Birnin Gaouré var. Birni-Ngaouré. Dosso, SW Niger 12.59N 3.02E
79 S12 Birnin Kebbi Kebbi, NW Nigeria 12.28N 4.08E
Birni-Nkonni see Birnin Konni
79 T12 Birnin Konni var. Birni-Nkonni. Tahoua, SW Niger 13.50N 5.14E
79 W13 Birnin Kudu Jigawa, N Nigeria 11.28N 9.29E
127 N16 Birobidzhan Yevreyskaya Avtonomnaya Oblast', SE Russian Federation 48.41N 132.55E
99 D18 Birr var. Parsonstown, Ir. Biorra. C Ireland 53.06N 7.54W
191 P4 Birrie River ~ New South Wales/Queensland, SE Australia
110 D7 Birse ~ NW Switzerland
Birsen see Biržai
110 E6 Birsfelden Basel-Land, NW Switzerland 47.33N 7.37E
131 U4 Birsk Respublika Bashkortostan, W Russian Federation 55.24N 55.33E
121 F14 Birštonas Prienai, C Lithuania 54.37N 24.00E
165 P14 Biru Xinjiang Uygur Zizhiqu, W China 31.30N 93.55E
Biruni see Beruniy
126 Ii14 Biryusa ~ C Russian Federation
126 Ii14 Biryusinsk Irkutskaya Oblast', C Russian Federation 55.52N 97.48E
120 G10 Biržai Ger. Birsen. Biržai, NE Lithuania 56.12N 24.47E
123 Jj17 Birżebbuġa SE Malta 35.50N 14.32E
Bisanthe see Tekirdağ
175 T9 Bisa, Pulau island Maluku, E Indonesia
39 N17 Bisbee Arizona, SW USA 31.27N 109.55W
31 O2 Bisbee North Dakota, N USA 48.36N 99.21W
Biscaia, Baía de see Biscay, Bay of
104 I13 Biscarrosse et de Parentis, Étang de ◎ SW France
106 M1 Biscay, Bay of Sp. Golfo de Vizcaya, Port. Baía de Biscaia. bay France/Spain
25 Z16 Biscayne Bay bay Florida, SE USA
66 M7 Biscay Plain undersea feature SE Bay of Biscay
109 N17 Bisceglie Puglia, SE Italy 41.13N 16.31E
Bischoflack see Škofja Loka
Bischofsburg see Biskupiec
111 Q7 Bischofshofen Salzburg, NW Austria 47.25N 13.13E
103 P15 Bischofswerda Sachsen, E Germany 51.07N 14.13E
105 V5 Bischwiller Bas-Rhin, NE France 48.46N 7.52E
23 T10 Biscoe North Carolina, SE USA 35.20N 79.46W
204 G5 Biscoe Islands island group Antarctica
12 E9 Biscotasi Lake ◎ Ontario, S Canada
12 E9 Biscotasing Ontario, S Canada 47.16N 82.04W
56 J6 Biscucuy Portuguesa, NW Venezuela 9.22N 69.58W
116 K11 Biser Khaskovo, S Bulgaria 41.52N 25.58E
115 D15 Biševo It. Busi. island SW Croatia
147 N12 Bishah, Wādī dry watercourse C Saudi Arabia
153 U7 Bishkek var. Pishpek; prev. Frunze. ● (Kyrgyzstan) Chuyskaya Oblast', N Kyrgyzstan 42.53N 74.46E
153 U7 Bishkek ✕ Chuyskaya Oblast', N Kyrgyzstan 42.55N 74.37E
159 R16 Bishnupur West Bengal, NE India 23.04N 87.19E
85 J25 Bisho Eastern Cape, S South Africa 32.46S 27.21E
37 S9 Bishop California, W USA 37.22N 118.24W
27 S15 Bishop Texas, SW USA 27.36N 97.49W
99 L15 Bishop Auckland N England, UK 54.40N 1.40W
Bishop's Lynn see King's Lynn
99 O21 Bishop's Stortford E England, UK 51.45N 0.12E
23 S12 Bishopville South Carolina, SE USA 34.13N 80.15W
144 M5 Bishrī, Jabal ▲ E Syria
169 U4 Bishui Heilongjiang, NE China 52.06N 123.42E
83 G17 Bisina, Lake prev. Lake Salisbury. ◎ E Uganda
Biskara see Biskra
76 L6 Biskra var. Beskra, Biskara. NE Algeria 34.51N 5.44E
112 M8 Biskupiec Ger. Bischofsburg. Warmińsko-Mazurskie, NE Poland 53.51N 20.56E
179 Rr15 Bislig Mindanao, S Philippines 8.10N 126.18E
29 X6 Bismarck Missouri, C USA 37.46N 90.37W
30 M5 Bismarck state capital North Dakota, N USA 46.48N 100.46W
194 K9 Bismarck Archipelago island group NE PNG
133 Z16 Bismarck Plate tectonic feature W Pacific Ocean
194 I12 Bismarck Range ▲▲ N PNG
194 J10 Bismarck Sea sea W Pacific Ocean
143 P15 Bismil Diyarbakır, SE Turkey 37.52N 40.37E
45 N6 Bismuna, Laguna lagoon NE Nicaragua
Bisnulok see Phitsanulok
175 T6 Bisoa, Tanjung headland Pulau Halmahera, N Indonesia 2.15N 127.57E
30 K7 Bison South Dakota, N USA 45.30N 102.25W
95 H17 Bispfors Jämtland, C Sweden 63.00N 16.40E
78 G13 Bissau ● (Guinea-Bissau) W Guinea-Bissau 11.52N 15.39W
78 G13 Bissau ✕ W Guinea-Bissau 11.53N 15.41W
101 M24 Bissen Luxembourg, C Luxembourg 49.46N 6.04E
78 G12 Bissorā W Guinea-Bissau 12.16N 15.34W
9 O10 Bistcho Lake ◎ Alberta, W Canada
24 G5 Bistineau, Lake ▣ Louisiana, S USA
Bistrica see Ilirska Bistrica
118 I9 Bistrița Ger. Bistritz, Hung. Beszterce; prev. Nösen. Bistrița-Năsăud, N Romania 47.10N 24.30E
118 K10 Bistrița Ger. Bistritz. ~ NE Romania
118 I9 Bistrița-Năsăud ◐ county N Romania
Bistritz see Bistrița
Bistritz ober Pernstein see Bystřice nad Pernštejnem
158 L11 Biswān Uttar Pradesh, N India 27.30N 81.00E
112 M7 Bisztynek Warmińsko-Mazurskie, NE Poland 54.05N 20.53E
81 E17 Bitam Woleu-Ntem, N Gabon 2.04N 11.30E
103 D18 Bitburg Rheinland-Pfalz, SW Germany 49.57N 6.31E
105 U4 Bitche Moselle, NE France 49.01N 7.27E
80 I11 Bitkine Guéra, C Chad 11.58N 18.13E
143 R15 Bitlis Bitlis, SE Turkey 38.22N 42.04E
143 R14 Bitlis ◐ province E Turkey
Bitoeng see Bitung
115 N20 Bitola Turk. Monastir; prev. Bitolj. S FYR Macedonia 41.01N 21.21E
Bitolj see Bitola
109 O17 Bitonto anc. Butuntum. Puglia, SE Italy 41.07N 16.40E
79 Q13 Bitou var. Bittou. SE Burkina 11.19N 0.16W
161 C20 Bitra Island island Lakshadweep, India, N Indian Ocean
103 M14 Bitterfeld Sachsen-Anhalt, E Germany 51.36N 12.18E
34 O9 Bitterroot Range ▲▲ Idaho/Montana, NW USA
35 P10 Bitterroot River ~ Montana, NW USA
109 D18 Bitti Sardegna, Italy, C Mediterranean Sea 40.30N 9.31E
Bittou see Bitou
175 S7 Bitung prev. Bitoeng. Sulawesi, C Indonesia 1.28N 125.13E
62 I12 Bituruna Paraná, S Brazil 26.11S 51.34W
79 Y13 Biu Borno, E Nigeria 10.35N 12.13E
Biumba see Byumba
171 H14 Biwa-ko ◎ Honshū, SW Japan
176 Y13 Biwarlaut Irian Jaya, E Indonesia 5.44S 138.14E
29 P10 Bixby Oklahoma, C USA 35.56N 95.52W
126 H15 Biya ~ S Russian Federation
Biy-Khem see Bol'shoy Yenisey
126 H15 Biysk Altayskiy Kray, S Russian Federation 52.34N 85.09E
170 Ff14 Bizen Okayama, Honshū, SW Japan 34.43N 134.10E
Bizerta see Bizerte
123 K11 Bizerte Ar. Banzart, Eng. Bizerta. N Tunisia 37.18N 9.48E
Bizkaia see Vizcaya
94 G2 Bjargtangar headland W Iceland 63.30N 24.28W
Bjärnå see Perniö
97 K22 Bjärnum Skåne, S Sweden 56.15N 13.45E
95 I16 Bjästa Västernorrland, C Sweden 63.12N 18.30E
115 I14 Bjelašnica ▲ SE Bosnia and Herzegovina 43.13N 18.18E
114 C10 Bjelolasica ▲ NW Croatia 45.13N 14.56E
114 F8 Bjelovar Hung. Belovár. Bjelovar-Bilogora, N Croatia 45.54N 16.49E
114 F8 Bjelovar-Bilogora off. Bjelovarsko-Bilogorska Županija. ◐ province NE Croatia
Bjelovarsko-Bilogorska Županija see Bjelovar-Bilogora
94 H10 Bjerkvik Nordland, C Norway 68.31N 16.08E
97 G21 Bjerringbro Viborg, NW Denmark 56.22N 9.40E
Bjeshkët e Namuna see North Albanian Alps
97 L14 Björbo Dalarna, C Sweden 60.28N 14.44E
97 I15 Bjørkelangen Akershus, S Norway 59.52N 11.34E
97 O14 Björklinge Uppsala, C Sweden 60.03N 17.33E
95 I14 Björksele Västerbotten, N Sweden 64.58N 18.30E
95 I16 Björna Västernorrland, C Sweden 63.34N 18.38E
97 C14 Bjørnafjorden fjord S Norway
97 L16 Björneborg Värmland, C Sweden 59.13N 14.15E
Björneborg see Pori
97 E14 Bjornesfjorden ◎ S Norway
94 M9 Bjørnevatn Finnmark, N Norway 69.40N 29.57E
207 T13 Bjørnøya Eng. Bear Island. island N Norway
95 I15 Bjurholm Västerbotten, N Sweden 63.57N 19.16E
97 J22 Bjuv Skåne, S Sweden 56.04N 12.57E
78 M12 Bla Ségou, W Mali 12.58N 5.45W
189 W8 Blackall Queensland, E Australia 24.25S 145.31E
31 V2 Black Bay lake bay Minnesota, N USA
29 N9 Black Bear Creek ~ Oklahoma, C USA
99 K17 Blackburn NW England, UK 53.45N 2.28W
47 W10 Blackburne ✕ (Plymouth) E Montserrat 16.45N 62.09W
41 T11 Blackburn, Mount ▲ Alaska, USA 61.43N 143.25W
37 N5 Black Butte Lake ▣ California, W USA
204 J5 Black Coast physical region Antarctica
9 Q16 Black Diamond Alberta, SW Canada 50.42N 114.09W
20 K11 Black Dome ▲ New York, NE USA 42.16N 74.07W
115 L18 Black Drin Alb. Lumi i Drinit të Zi, SCr. Crni Drim. ~ Albania/FYR Macedonia
10 D6 Black Duck ~ Ontario, C Canada
31 U4 Blackduck Minnesota, N USA 47.45N 94.33W
35 R14 Blackfoot Idaho, NW USA 43.11N 112.20W
35 P9 Blackfoot River ~ Montana, NW USA
Black Forest see Schwarzwald
30 J10 Blackhawk South Dakota, N USA 44.09N 103.18W
30 I10 Black Hills ▲▲ South Dakota/Wyoming, N USA
9 T10 Black Lake ◎ Saskatchewan, C Canada
33 Q5 Black Lake ◎ Michigan, N USA
20 I7 Black Lake ◎ New York, NE USA
24 G6 Black Lake ▣ Louisiana, S USA
28 F7 Black Mesa ▲ Oklahoma, C USA 37.00N 103.07W
23 P10 Black Mountain North Carolina, SE USA 35.37N 82.19W
37 P13 Black Mountain ▲ California, W USA 35.22N 120.21W
39 Q2 Black Mountain ▲ Colorado, C USA 40.47N 107.23W
23 O7 Black Mountain ▲ Kentucky, E USA 36.54N 82.53W
98 K1 Black Mountains ▲▲ SE Wales, UK
38 H10 Black Mountains ▲▲ Arizona, SW USA
35 Q16 Black Pine Peak ▲ Idaho, NW USA 42.07N 113.07W
99 K17 Blackpool NW England, UK 53.49N 3.03W
39 Q14 Black Range ▲▲ New Mexico, SW USA
46 I12 Black River W Jamaica 18.01N 77.52W
12 J14 Black River ~ Ontario, SE Canada
133 U12 Black River Chin. Babian Jiang, Lixian Jiang, Fr. Rivière Noire, Vtn. Sông Đa. ~ China/Vietnam
46 I12 Black River ~ W Jamaica
41 T7 Black River ~ Alaska, USA
39 N13 Black River ~ Arizona, SW USA
29 X7 Black River ~ Arkansas/Missouri, C USA
24 I7 Black River ~ Louisiana, S USA
33 S8 Black River ~ Michigan, N USA
33 Q5 Black River ~ Michigan, N USA
20 I8 Black River ~ New York, NE USA
23 T13 Black River ~ South Carolina, SE USA
32 J7 Black River ~ Wisconsin, N USA
32 J7 Black River Falls Wisconsin, N USA 44.18N 90.51W
37 R3 Black Rock Desert desert Nevada, W USA
Black Sand Desert see Garagumy
23 S7 Blacksburg Virginia, NE USA 37.16N 80.25W
142 H10 Black Sea var. Euxine Sea, Bul. Cherno More, Rom. Marea Neagră, Rus. Chernoye More, Turk. Karadeniz, Ukr. Chorne More. sea Asia/Europe
119 Q10 Black Sea Lowland Ukr. Prychornomors'ka Nyzovyna. depression SE Europe
35 S17 Blacks Fork ~ Wyoming, C USA
25 V7 Blackshear Georgia, SE USA 31.18N 82.14W
25 S6 Blackshear, Lake ▣ Georgia, SE USA
99 A16 Blacksod Bay Ir. Cuan an Fhóid Duibh. inlet W Ireland
23 V7 Blackstone Virginia, NE USA 37.04N 78.00W
79 O14 Black Volta var. Borongo, Mouhoun, Moun Hou, Fr. Volta Noire. ~ W Africa
25 O5 Black Warrior River ~ Alabama, S USA
189 X8 Blackwater Queensland, E Australia 23.34S 148.51E
99 D20 Blackwater Ir. An Abhainn Mhór. ~ S Ireland
29 T4 Blackwater River ~ Missouri, C USA
23 W7 Blackwater River ~ Virginia, NE USA
Blackwater State see Nebraska
29 N8 Blackwell Oklahoma, C USA 36.48N 97.16W
27 P7 Blackwell Texas, SW USA 32.05N 100.19W
101 J15 Bladel Noord-Brabant, S Netherlands 51.22N 5.13E
Bladenmarkt see Bălăuşeri
116 G11 Blagoevgrad prev. Gorna Dzhumaya. Blagoevgrad, SW Bulgaria 42.01N 23.04E
116 G11 Blagoevgrad ◐ province SW Bulgaria
126 Gg14 Blagoveshchenka Altayskiy Kray, S Russian Federation 52.49N 79.54E
126 M16 Blagoveshchensk Amurskaya Oblast', SE Russian Federation 50.19N 127.30E
131 V4 Blagoveshchensk Respublika Bashkortostan, W Russian Federation 55.03N 56.01E
104 I7 Blain Loire-Atlantique, NW France 47.26N 1.47W
31 V8 Blaine Minnesota, N USA 45.09N 93.13W
34 H6 Blaine Washington, NW USA 48.59N 122.45W
9 T15 Blaine Lake Saskatchewan, S Canada 52.49N 106.48W
31 S14 Blair Nebraska, C USA 41.32N 96.07W
98 J10 Blairgowrie C Scotland, UK 56.18N 3.24W
20 C15 Blairsville Pennsylvania, NE USA 40.25N 79.12W
118 H11 Blaj Ger. Blasendorf, Hung. Balázsfalva. Alba, SW Romania 46.10N 23.56E
66 F9 Blake-Bahama Ridge undersea feature W Atlantic Ocean
25 S7 Blakely Georgia, SE USA 31.22N 84.55W
66 E10 Blake Plateau var. Blake Terrace. undersea feature W Atlantic Ocean
32 M1 Blake Point headland Michigan, N USA 48.11N 88.25W
Blake Terrace see Blake Plateau
63 B24 Blanca, Bahía bay E Argentina
58 C12 Blanca, Cordillera ▲▲ W Peru
107 T12 Blanca, Costa physical region SE Spain
39 S7 Blanca Peak ▲ Colorado, C USA 37.34N 105.29W
26 I9 Blanca, Sierra ▲ Texas, SW USA 31.15N 105.26W
123 K11 Blanc, Cap headland N Tunisia 37.20N 9.41E
Blanc, Cap see Nouâdhibou, Râs
33 R12 Blanchard River ~ Ohio, N USA
190 E8 Blanche, Cape headland South Australia 33.03S 134.10E
195 U15 Blanche Channel channel NW Solomon Islands
190 J4 Blanche, Lake ◎ South Australia
33 R14 Blanchester Ohio, N USA 39.17N 83.59W
190 J9 Blanchetown South Australia 34.21S 139.36E
47 U13 Blanchisseuse Trinidad, Trinidad and Tobago 10.47N 61.18W
105 T11 Blanc, Mont It. Monte Bianco. ▲ France/Italy 45.45N 6.51E
27 R11 Blanco Texas, SW USA 30.06N 98.25W
44 K14 Blanco, Cabo headland NW Costa Rica 9.34N 85.06W
34 D14 Blanco, Cape headland Oregon, NW USA 42.49N 124.33W
64 H10 Blanco, Río ~ W Argentina
58 F10 Blanco, Río ~ NE Peru
13 O9 Blanc, Réservoir ▣ Quebec, SE Canada
23 R7 Bland Virginia, NE USA 37.06N 81.07W
94 I2 Blanda ~ N Iceland
39 O7 Blanding Utah, W USA 37.37N 109.28W

◆ Country ● Country Capital ◇ Dependent Territory ○ Dependent Territory Capital ◐ Administrative Region ✕ International Airport ▲ Mountain ▲▲ Mountain Range Volcano ~ River ◎ Lake ▣ Reservoir
233

BLANES – BONNE TERRE

107 X5 **Blanes** Cataluña, NE Spain *41.40N 2.48E*
105 N3 **Blangy-sur-Bresle** Seine-Maritime, N France *49.55N 1.37E*
113 C18 **Blanice** *Ger.* Blanitz. ≈ SE Czech Republic
Blanitz *see* Blanice
101 C16 **Blankenberge** West-Vlaanderen, NW Belgium *51.19N 3.07E*
103 D17 **Blankenheim** Nordrhein-Westfalen, W Germany *50.25N 6.41E*
27 R8 **Blanket** Texas, SW USA *31.49N 98.47W*
57 O3 **Blanquilla, Isla** *var.* La Blanquilla. *island* N Venezuela
Blanquilla, La *see* Blanquilla, Isla
63 F18 **Blanquillo** Durazno, C Uruguay *32.52S 55.37W*
113 G18 **Blansko** *Ger.* Blanz. Brněnský Kraj, SE Czech Republic *49.22N 16.39E*
85 N15 **Blantyre** *var.* Blantyre-Limbe. Southern, S Malawi *15.45S 35.03E*
85 N15 **Blantyre** ✈ Southern, S Malawi *15.34S 35.03E*
Blantyre-Limbe *see* Blantyre
Blanz *see* Blansko
100 J10 **Blaricum** Noord-Holland, C Netherlands *52.16N 5.15E*
Blasendorf *see* Blaj
Blatnitsa *see* Durankulak
115 F15 **Blato** *It.* Blatta. Dubrovnik-Neretva, S Croatia *42.57N 16.47E*
Blatta *see* Blato
110 E10 **Blatten** Valais, SW Switzerland *46.22N 8.00E*
103 J20 **Blaufelden** Baden-Württemberg, SW Germany *49.21N 10.01E*
97 E23 **Blåvands Huk** *headland* W Denmark *55.33N 8.04E*
104 G6 **Blavet** ≈ NW France
104 J12 **Blaye** Gironde, SW France *45.07N 0.36W*
191 R8 **Blayney** New South Wales, SE Australia *33.33S 149.13E*
67 D25 **Bleaker Island** *island* SE Falkland Islands
111 T10 **Bled** *Ger.* Veldes. NW Slovenia *46.23N 14.06E*
101 D20 **Bléharies** Hainaut, SW Belgium *50.31N 3.25E*
111 U9 **Bleiburg** *Slvn.* Pliberk. Kärnten, S Austria *46.36N 14.49E*
103 L17 **Bleiloch-Stausee** ⊠ C Germany
100 H12 **Bleiswijk** Zuid-Holland, W Netherlands *52.01N 4.31E*
97 L22 **Blekinge** ◈ *county* S Sweden
12 D17 **Blenheim** Ontario, S Canada *42.19N 81.58W*
193 K15 **Blenheim** Marlborough, South Island, NZ *41.31S 174.00E*
101 M15 **Blerick** Limburg, SE Netherlands *51.22N 6.10E*
Blesae *see* Blois
27 V13 **Blessing** Texas, SW USA *28.52N 96.12W*
12 I10 **Bleu, Lac** ◎ Quebec, SE Canada
Blibba *see* Blitta
123 I11 **Blida** *var.* El Boulaida, El Boulaïda. N Algeria *36.32N 2.49E*
97 P15 **Blidö** Stockholm, C Sweden *59.37N 18.55E*
97 K18 **Blidsberg** Västra Götaland, S Sweden *57.55N 13.30E*
193 A21 **Bligh Sound** *sound* South Island, NZ
197 H13 **Bligh Water** *strait* NW Fiji
12 D11 **Blind River** Ontario, S Canada *46.11N 82.55W*
33 R11 **Blissfield** Michigan, N USA *41.49N 83.51W*
174 Ll16 **Blitar** Jawa, C Indonesia *8.06S 112.12E*
79 R15 **Blitta** *prev.* Blibba. C Togo *8.19N 0.58E*
21 O13 **Block Island** *island* Rhode Island, NE USA
21 O13 **Block Island Sound** *sound* Rhode Island, NE USA
100 H10 **Bloemendaal** Noord-Holland, W Netherlands *52.23N 4.39E*
85 H23 **Bloemfontein** *var.* Mangaung. ● (South Africa-judicial capital) Free State, C South Africa *29.07S 26.13E*
85 I22 **Bloemhof** North-West, NW South Africa *27.38S 25.33E*
104 M7 **Blois** *anc.* Blesae. Loir-et-Cher, C France *47.36N 1.19E*
100 L8 **Blokzijl** Overijssel, N Netherlands *52.46N 5.58E*
97 N20 **Blomstermåla** Kalmar, S Sweden *56.58N 16.19E*
94 I2 **Blönduós** Nordhurland Vestra, N Iceland *65.39N 20.15W*
112 L11 **Błonie** Mazowieckie, C Poland *52.13N 20.36E*
99 C14 **Bloody Foreland** *Ir.* Cnoc Fola. *headland* NW Ireland *55.09N 8.18W*
33 N15 **Bloomfield** Indiana, N USA *39.01N 86.58W*
31 X16 **Bloomfield** Iowa, C USA *40.45N 92.24W*
29 Y8 **Bloomfield** Missouri, C USA *36.53N 89.55W*
39 P9 **Bloomfield** New Mexico, SW USA *36.42N 108.00W*
27 U7 **Blooming Grove** Texas, SW USA *32.05N 96.43W*
31 W10 **Blooming Prairie** Minnesota, N USA *43.52N 93.03W*
32 L13 **Bloomington** Illinois, N USA *40.28N 88.59W*
33 O15 **Bloomington** Indiana, N USA *39.10N 86.31W*
31 V9 **Bloomington** Minnesota, N USA *44.50N 93.18W*
27 U13 **Bloomington** Texas, SW USA *28.39N 96.53W*
20 H14 **Bloomsburg** Pennsylvania, NE USA *40.58N 76.27W*
189 X7 **Bloomsbury** Queensland, NE Australia *20.46S 148.34E*
174 Ll14 **Blora** Jawa, C Indonesia *6.55S 111.28E*
20 G12 **Blossburg** Pennsylvania, NE USA *41.38N 77.00W*
27 V5 **Blossom** Texas, SW USA *33.39N 95.23W*
127 Oo3 **Blossom, Mys** *headland* Ostrov Vrangelya, NE Russian Federation *70.49N 178.49E*
25 R8 **Blountstown** Florida, SE USA *30.26N 85.03W*
23 P8 **Blountville** Tennessee, S USA *36.31N 82.19W*
23 Q9 **Blowing Rock** North Carolina, SE USA *36.15N 81.53W*
110 J8 **Bludenz** Vorarlberg, W Austria *47.10N 9.49E*
38 L6 **Blue Bell Knoll** ▲ Utah, W USA *38.11N 111.31W*
25 Y12 **Blue Cypress Lake** ◎ Florida, SE USA
31 U11 **Blue Earth** Minnesota, N USA *43.38N 94.06W*
23 Q7 **Bluefield** Virginia, NE USA *37.15N 81.16W*
23 R7 **Bluefield** West Virginia, NE USA *37.16N 81.13W*
45 N10 **Bluefields** Región Autónoma Atlántico Sur, SE Nicaragua *12.01N 83.47W*
45 N10 **Bluefields, Bahía de** *bay* W Caribbean Sea
31 Z14 **Blue Grass** Iowa, C USA *41.30N 90.46W*
Bluegrass State *see* Kentucky
Blue Hen State *see* Delaware
21 S7 **Blue Hill** Maine, NE USA *44.25N 68.36W*
31 P16 **Blue Hill** Nebraska, C USA *40.19N 98.27W*
32 J5 **Blue Hills** *hill range* Wisconsin, N USA
36 L3 **Blue Lake** California, W USA *40.52N 124.00W*
Blue Law State *see* Connecticut
39 Q6 **Blue Mesa Reservoir** ⊠ Colorado, C USA
29 S12 **Blue Mountain** ▲ Arkansas, C USA *34.42N 94.04W*
21 O6 **Blue Mountain** ▲ New Hampshire, NE USA *44.48N 71.26W*
20 K8 **Blue Mountain** ▲ New York, NE USA *43.52N 74.24W*
20 H15 **Blue Mountain** *ridge* Pennsylvania, NE USA
46 H10 **Blue Mountain Peak** ▲ E Jamaica *18.02N 76.34W*
191 S8 **Blue Mountains** ▲▲ New South Wales, SE Australia
34 L11 **Blue Mountains** ▲▲ Oregon/Washington, NW USA
82 G12 **Blue Nile** ◈ *state* E Sudan
82 H12 **Blue Nile** *var.* Abai, Bahr el Azraq, *Amh.* Ābay Wenz, *Ar.* An Nīl al Azraq. ≈ Ethiopia/Sudan
15 Hh4 **Bluenose Lake** ◎ Nunavut, NW Canada
29 O3 **Blue Rapids** Kansas, C USA *39.39N 96.38W*
25 S1 **Blue Ridge** Georgia, SE USA *34.51N 84.19W*
19 Q10 **Blue Ridge** *var.* Blue Ridge Mountains. ▲▲ North Carolina/Virginia, E USA
25 S1 **Blue Ridge Lake** ⊠ Georgia, SE USA
Blue Ridge Mountains *see* Blue Ridge
9 N15 **Blue River** British Columbia, SW Canada *52.03N 119.21W*
29 O12 **Blue River** ≈ Oklahoma, C USA
29 R4 **Blue Springs** Missouri, C USA *39.01N 94.16W*
23 R6 **Bluestone Lake** ⊠ West Virginia, NE USA
193 C25 **Bluff** Southland, South Island, NZ *46.36S 168.22E*
39 O8 **Bluff** Utah, W USA *37.15N 109.36W*
23 P8 **Bluff City** Tennessee, S USA *36.28N 82.15W*
67 E24 **Bluff Cove** East Falkland, Falkland Islands *51.45S 58.10W*
27 S7 **Bluff Dale** Texas, SW USA *32.18N 98.01W*
191 N15 **Bluff Hill Point** *headland* Tasmania, SE Australia *41.03S 144.35E*
33 Q12 **Bluffton** Indiana, N USA *40.44N 85.10W*
33 R12 **Bluffton** Ohio, N USA *40.54N 83.53W*
27 T7 **Blum** Texas, SW USA *32.08N 97.24W*
103 G24 **Blumberg** Baden-Württemberg, SW Germany *47.48N 8.31E*
62 K13 **Blumenau** Santa Catarina, S Brazil *26.55S 49.07W*
31 N9 **Blunt** South Dakota, N USA *44.30N 99.58E*
34 H15 **Bly** Oregon, NW USA *42.22N 121.04W*
41 R13 **Blying Sound** *sound* Alaska, USA
99 M14 **Blyth** N England, UK *55.07N 1.30W*
37 Y16 **Blythe** California, W USA *33.35N 114.36W*
29 Y9 **Blytheville** Arkansas, C USA *35.55N 89.55W*
119 V7 **Blyznyuky** Kharkivs'ka Oblast', E Ukraine *48.51N 36.32E*
78 I15 **Bo** S Sierra Leone *7.58N 11.45W*
97 G16 **Bø** Telemark, S Norway *59.24N 9.04E*
179 Pp11 **Boac** Marinduque, N Philippines *13.26N 121.50E*
44 K10 **Boaco** Boaco, S Nicaragua *12.27N 85.45W*
44 J10 **Boaco** ◈ *department* C Nicaragua
81 I15 **Boali** Ombella-Mpoko, SW Central African Republic *4.52N 18.00E*
Boalsert *see* Bolsward
194 K13 **Boana** Morobe, C PNG *6.30S 146.54E*
195 Q10 **Boang Island** *island* Tanga Islands, NE PNG
33 V12 **Boardman** Ohio, N USA *41.01N 80.39W*
34 J11 **Boardman** Oregon, NW USA *45.50N 119.42W*
12 F13 **Boat Lake** ◎ Ontario, S Canada
60 F10 **Boa Vista** *state capital* Roraima, NW Brazil *2.51N 60.43W*
78 D9 **Boa Vista** *island* Ilhas de Barlavento, E Cape Verde
25 Q2 **Boaz** Alabama, S USA *34.12N 86.10W*
166 L15 **Bobai** Guangxi Zhuangzu Zizhiqu, S China *22.09N 109.57E*
180 J1 **Bobaomby, Tanjona** *Fr.* Cap d'Ambre. *headland* N Madagascar *11.58S 49.13E*
161 M14 **Bobbili** Andhra Pradesh, E India *18.31N 83.28E*
108 D9 **Bobbio** Emilia-Romagna, C Italy *44.48N 9.27E*
12 I14 **Bobcaygeon** Ontario, SE Canada *44.31N 78.33W*
Bober *see* Bóbr
105 O5 **Bobigny** Seine-St-Denis, N France *48.55N 2.27E*
79 N13 **Bobo-Dioulasso** SW Burkina *11.12N 4.21W*
112 G8 **Bobolice** *Ger.* Bublitz. Zachodniopomorskie, NW Poland *53.56N 16.37E*
175 T7 **Bobopayo** Pulau Halmahera, E Indonesia *1.07N 127.26E*
153 P13 **Bobotogh, Qatorkŭhi** *Rus.* Khrebet Babatag. ▲▲ Tajikistan/Uzbekistan
116 G10 **Bobovdol** Kyustendil, W Bulgaria *42.21N 22.58E*
121 M15 **Bobr** Minskaya Voblasts', NW Belarus *54.20N 29.18E*
121 M15 **Bobr** ≈ C Belarus
113 E14 **Bóbr** *Eng.* Bobrawa, *Ger.* Bober. ≈ SW Poland
Bobrawa *see* Bóbr
Bobrik *see* Bobryk
Bobrinets *see* Bobrynets'
Bobrka/Bóbrka *see* Bibrka
130 L8 **Bobrov** Voronezhskaya Oblast', W Russian Federation *51.10N 40.03E*
119 Q4 **Bobrovytsya** Chernihivs'ka Oblast', N Ukraine *50.43N 31.24E*
Bobruysk *see* Babruysk
121 J19 **Bobryk** *Rus.* Bobrik. ≈ SW Belarus
119 Q8 **Bobrynets'** *Rus.* Bobrinets. Kirovohrads'ka Oblast', C Ukraine *48.01N 32.09E*
12 K14 **Bobs Lake** ◎ Ontario, SE Canada
56 I6 **Bobures** Zulia, NW Venezuela *9.15N 71.10W*
44 H1 **Boca Bacalar Chico** *headland* N Belize *15.05N 82.12W*
114 G11 **Bočac** Republika Srpska, NW Bosnia and Herzegovina *44.32N 17.09E*
43 R14 **Boca del Río** Veracruz-Llave, S Mexico *19.07N 96.07W*
57 O4 **Boca de Pozo** Nueva Esparta, NE Venezuela *11.01N 64.21W*
61 C15 **Boca do Acre** Amazonas, N Brazil *8.45S 67.22W*
57 N12 **Boca Mavaca** Amazonas, S Venezuela *2.30N 65.10W*
81 G14 **Bocaranga** Ouham-Pendé, W Central African Republic *7.07N 15.40E*
25 Z15 **Boca Raton** Florida, SE USA *26.22N 80.04W*
45 P14 **Bocas del Toro** Bocas del Toro, NW Panama *9.21N 82.14W*
45 P15 **Bocas del Toro** *off.* Provincia de Bocas del Toro. ◈ *province* NW Panama
45 P15 **Bocas del Toro, Archipiélago de** *island group* NW Panama
44 L7 **Bocay** Jinotega, N Nicaragua *14.19N 85.07W*
107 N6 **Boceguillas** Castilla-León, N Spain *41.23N 3.37W*
Bocheykovo *see* Bacheykava
113 L17 **Bochnia** Małopolskie, SE Poland *49.58N 20.27E*
101 K16 **Bocholt** Limburg, NE Belgium *51.10N 5.37E*
103 D14 **Bocholt** Nordrhein-Westfalen, W Germany *51.49N 6.37E*
103 E15 **Bochum** Nordrhein-Westfalen, W Germany *51.28N 7.13E*
105 Y15 **Bocognano** Corse, France, C Mediterranean Sea *42.04N 9.03E*
56 I6 **Boconó** Trujillo, NW Venezuela *9.12N 70.16W*
118 F12 **Bocşa** *Ger.* Bokschen, *Hung.* Boksánbánya. Caraş-Severin, SW Romania *45.24N 21.46E*
81 H15 **Boda** Lobaye, SW Central African Republic *4.17N 17.25E*
96 L12 **Boda** Dalarna, C Sweden *61.00N 15.15E*
97 O20 **Böda** Kalmar, S Sweden *57.16N 17.04E*
97 L19 **Bodafors** Jönköping, S Sweden *57.30N 14.40E*
126 Kk13 **Bodaybo** Irkutskaya Oblast', E Russian Federation *57.52N 114.04E*
24 G5 **Bodcau, Bayou** *var.* Bodcau Creek. ≈ Louisiana, S USA
Bodcau Creek *see* Bodcau, Bayou
46 D8 **Bodden Town** *var.* Boddentown. Grand Cayman, SW Cayman Islands *19.17N 81.10W*
103 K14 **Bode** ≈ C Germany
36 L7 **Bodega Head** *headland* California, W USA *38.16N 123.04W*
Bodegas *see* Babahoyo
100 H11 **Bodegraven** Zuid-Holland, C Netherlands *52.04N 4.45E*
80 H8 **Bodélé** *depression* W Chad
94 J13 **Boden** Norrbotten, N Sweden *65.49N 21.43E*
Bodensee *see* Constance, Lake, C Europe
67 M15 **Bode Verde Fracture Zone** *tectonic feature* E Atlantic Ocean
161 H14 **Bodhan** Andhra Pradesh, C India *18.40N 77.51E*
168 I9 **Bodĭ** Bayanhongor, C Mongolia *45.25N 100.33E*
161 H22 **Bodināyakkanūr** Tamil Nādu, SE India *10.01N 77.18E*
110 H10 **Bodio** Ticino, S Switzerland *46.23N 8.55E*
99 I24 **Bodmin** SW England, UK *50.28N 4.43W*
99 I24 **Bodmin Moor** *moorland* SW England, UK
94 G12 **Bodø** Nordland, C Norway *67.16N 14.22E*
61 H20 **Bodoquena, Serra da** ▲▲ SW Brazil
142 B16 **Bodrum** Muğla, SW Turkey *37.03N 27.28E*
Bodzafordulő *see* Întorsura Buzăului
101 L14 **Boekel** Noord-Brabant, SE Netherlands *51.35N 5.42E*
Boeloekoemba *see* Bulukumba
105 Q11 **Boën** Loire, E France *45.45N 4.01E*
81 K18 **Boende** Equateur, C Dem. Rep. Congo (Zaire) *0.12S 20.54E*
27 R11 **Boerne** Texas, SW USA *29.47N 98.43W*
Boeroe *see* Buru, Pulau
Boetoeng *see* Buton, Pulau
24 I5 **Boeuf River** ≈ Arkansas/Louisiana, S USA
78 H14 **Boffa** Guinée-Maritime, W Guinea *10.12N 14.01W*
Bó Finne, Inis *see* Inishbofin
Boga *see* Bogë
177 Ff9 **Bogale** Irrawaddy, SW Burma *16.16N 95.21E*
24 L8 **Bogalusa** Louisiana, S USA *30.47N 89.51W*
79 Q12 **Bogandé** C Burkina *13.01N 0.07W*
81 I15 **Bogangolo** Ombella-Mpoko, C Central African Republic *5.36N 18.17E*
191 Q7 **Bogan River** ≈ New South Wales, SE Australia
27 W5 **Bogata** Texas, SW USA *33.28N 95.12W*
113 D14 **Bogatynia** *Ger.* Reichenau. Dolnośląskie, SW Poland *50.52N 14.54E*
142 K13 **Boğazlıyan** Yozgat, C Turkey *39.13N 35.16E*
81 J17 **Bogbonga** Equateur, NW Dem. Rep. Congo (Zaire) *1.36N 19.24E*
164 J14 **Bogcang Zangbo** ≈ W China
164 L5 **Bogda Feng** ▲ NW China *43.51N 88.14E*
116 I9 **Bogdan** ▲ C Bulgaria *42.37N 24.28E*
115 Q20 **Bogdanci** SE FYR Macedonia *41.12N 22.34E*
164 M5 **Bogda Shan** *var.* Po-ko-to Shan. ▲▲ NW China
115 K17 **Bogë** *var.* Boga. Shkodër, N Albania *42.25N 19.38E*
Bogendorf *see* Łuków
97 G23 **Bogense** Fyn, C Denmark *55.34N 10.06E*
191 T3 **Boggabilla** New South Wales, SE Australia *28.37S 150.21E*
191 S6 **Boggabri** New South Wales, SE Australia *30.44S 150.00E*
194 I10 **Bogia** Madang, N PNG *4.12S 144.55E*
99 N23 **Bognor Regis** SE England, UK *50.46N 0.40W*
179 Qq13 **Bogo** Cebu, C Philippines *11.04N 123.59E*
Bogodukhov *see* Bohodukhiv
189 V15 **Bogong, Mount** ▲ Victoria, SE Australia *36.43S 147.19E*
174 J14 **Bogor** *Dut.* Buitenzorg. Jawa, C Indonesia *6.34S 106.45E*
130 L5 **Bogoroditsk** Tul'skaya Oblast', W Russian Federation *53.46N 38.09E*
131 O3 **Bogorodsk** Nizhegorodskaya Oblast', W Russian Federation *56.06N 43.29E*
Bogorodskoje *see* Bogorodskoye
127 Nn14 **Bogorodskoye** Khabarovskiy Kray, SE Russian Federation *52.22N 140.33E*
129 R15 **Bogorodskoye** *var.* Bogorodskoje. Kirovskaya Oblast', NW Russian Federation *57.50N 50.41E*
56 F10 **Bogotá** *prev.* Santa Fe, Santa Fe de Bogotá. ● (Colombia) Cundinamarca, C Colombia *4.37N 74.04W*
159 T14 **Bogra** Rajshahi, N Bangladesh *24.52N 89.28E*
Bogschan *see* Boldu
126 Ii13 **Boguchany** Krasnoyarskiy Kray, C Russian Federation *58.20N 97.20E*
130 M9 **Boguchar** Voronezhskaya Oblast', W Russian Federation *49.57N 40.34E*
78 H10 **Bogué** Brakna, SW Mauritania *16.36N 14.15W*
24 K8 **Bogue Chitto** ≈ Louisiana/Mississippi, S USA
Bogushëvsk *see* Bahushewsk
Boguslav *see* Bohuslav
46 K12 **Bog Walk** C Jamaica *18.06N 77.01W*
167 Q3 **Bo Hai** *var.* Gulf of Chihli. *gulf* NE China
167 R3 **Bohai Haixia** *strait* NE China
167 Q3 **Bohai Wan** *bay* NE China
113 C17 **Bohemia** *Cz.* Čechy, *Ger.* Böhmen. *cultural and historical region* W Czech Republic
113 B18 **Bohemian Forest** *Cz.* Ceský Les, Šumava, *Ger.* Böhmerwald. ▲▲ C Europe
Bohemian-Moravian Highlands *see* Českomoravská Vrchovina
79 R16 **Bohicon** S Benin *7.08N 2.07E*
111 S11 **Bohinjska Bistrica** *Ger.* Wocheiner Feistritz. NW Slovenia *46.16N 13.55E*
Bohkká *see* Pokka
Böhmen *see* Bohemia
Böhmerwald *see* Bohemian Forest
Böhmisch-Krumau *see* Český Krumlov
Böhmisch-Leipa *see* Česká Lípa
Böhmisch-Mährische Höhe *see* Českomoravská Vrchovina
Böhmisch-Trübau *see* Česká Třebová
119 U5 **Bohodukhiv** *Rus.* Bogodukhov. Kharkivs'ka Oblast', E Ukraine *50.09N 35.31E*
179 Qq14 **Bohol** *island* C Philippines
179 Qq15 **Bohol Sea** *var.* Mindanao Sea. *sea* S Philippines
118 I7 **Bohorodchany** Ivano-Frankivs'ka Oblast', W Ukraine *48.46N 24.31E*
168 M9 **Böhöt** Dundgovĭ, C Mongolia *45.13N 108.12E*
164 K6 **Bohu** *var.* Bagrax. Xinjiang Uygur Zizhiqu, NW China *42.00N 86.28E*
113 I17 **Bohumín** *Ger.* Oderberg; *prev.* Neuoderberg, Nový Bohumín. Ostravský Kray, E Czech Republic *49.55N 18.19E*
119 P6 **Bohuslav** *Rus.* Boguslav. Kyyivs'ka Oblast', N Ukraine *49.33N 30.53E*
60 F11 **Boiaçu** Roraima, N Brazil *0.27S 61.46W*
109 K16 **Boiano** Molise, C Italy *41.28N 14.28E*
13 R8 **Boilleau** Quebec, SE Canada *48.06N 70.49W*
61 O17 **Boipeba, Ilha de** *island* SE Brazil
106 G3 **Boiro** Galicia, NW Spain *42.39N 8.53W*
33 Q5 **Bois Blanc Island** *island* Michigan, N USA
31 R7 **Bois de Sioux River** ≈ Minnesota, N USA
35 N14 **Boise** *var.* Boise City. *state capital* Idaho, NW USA *43.38N 116.14W*
28 G8 **Boise City** Oklahoma, C USA *36.43N 102.30W*
35 N14 **Boise River, Middle Fork** ≈ Idaho, NW USA
Bois, Lac des *see* Woods, Lake of the
Bois-le-Duc *see* 's-Hertogenbosch
9 W17 **Boissevain** Manitoba, S Canada *49.13N 100.01W*
13 T7 **Boisvert, Pointe au** *headland* Quebec, SE Canada *48.34N 69.07W*
102 K10 **Boizenburg** Mecklenburg-Vorpommern, N Germany *53.23N 10.43E*
Bojador *see* Boujdour
115 K18 **Bojana** *Alb.* Bunë. ≈ Albania/Yugoslavia *see also* Bunë
149 S3 **Bojnūrd** *var.* Bujnurd. Khorāsān, N Iran *37.30N 57.24E*
174 Ll15 **Bojonegoro** *prev.* Bodjonegoro. Jawa, C Indonesia *7.06S 111.49E*
201 T1 **Bokaak Atoll** *var.* Bokak, Taongi. *atoll* Ratak Chain, NE Marshall Islands
Bokak *see* Bokaak Atoll
159 Q15 **Bokāro** Bihār, N India *23.46N 85.55E*
81 I18 **Bokatola** Equateur, NW Dem. Rep. Congo (Zaire) *0.37S 18.45E*
78 H13 **Boké** Guinée-Maritime, W Guinea *10.55N 14.18W*
Bokhara *see* Bukhoro
191 Q4 **Bokharra River** ≈ New South Wales/Queensland, SE Australia
97 C16 **Boknafjorden** *fjord* S Norway
80 H11 **Bokoro** Chari-Baguirmi, W Chad *12.22N 17.03E*
81 K19 **Bokota** Equateur, NW Dem. Rep. Congo (Zaire) *0.56S 22.20E*
178 Gg13 **Bokpyin** Tenasserim, S Burma *11.16N 98.47E*
Boksánbánya/Bokschen *see* Bocşa
85 F21 **Bokspits** Kgalagadi, SW Botswana *26.50S 20.41E*
81 K18 **Bokungu** Equateur, C Dem. Rep. Congo (Zaire) *0.39S 22.13E*
Bokurdak *see* Bakhardok
80 G10 **Bol** Lac, W Chad *13.27N 14.40E*
175 Qq9 **Bolaang** Sulawesi, N Indonesia *0.58S 122.10E*
78 G13 **Bolama** SW Guinea-Bissau *11.34N 15.32W*
Bolangir *see* Balāngīr
Bolanos *see* Bolanos, Mount, Guam
Bolaños *see* Bolaños de Calatrava, Spain
107 N11 **Bolaños de Calatrava** *var.* Bolaños. Castilla-La Mancha, C Spain *38.55N 3.39W*
196 B17 **Bolanos, Mount** *var.* Bolanos. ▲ S Guam *13.18N 144.41E*
42 L12 **Bolaños, Río** ≈ C Mexico
117 M14 **Bolayır** Çanakkale, NW Turkey *40.31N 26.46E*
104 L3 **Bolbec** Seine-Maritime, N France *49.34N 0.31E*
118 L13 **Boldu** *var.* Bogschan. Buzău, SE Romania *45.18N 27.15E*
152 H8 **Boldumsaz** *prev.* Kalinin, Kalininsk, Porsy. Dashkhovuzskiy Velayat, N Turkmenistan *42.12N 59.33E*
164 I4 **Bole** *var.* Bortala. Xinjiang Uygur Zizhiqu, NW China *44.52N 82.06E*
79 O15 **Bole** NW Ghana *9.01N 2.28W*
81 J19 **Boleko** Equateur, W Dem. Rep. Congo (Zaire) *1.27S 19.52E*
113 E14 **Bolesławiec** *Ger.* Bunzlau. Dolnośląskie, SW Poland *51.16N 15.34E*
131 R4 **Bolgar** *prev.* Kuybyshev. Respublika Tatarstan, W Russian Federation *54.58N 49.03E*
79 P14 **Bolgatanga** N Ghana *10.45N 0.52W*
Bolgrad *see* Bolhrad
119 N12 **Bolhrad** *Rus.* Bolgrad. Odes'ka Oblast', SW Ukraine *45.42N 28.34E*
169 Y8 **Boli** Heilongjiang, NE China *45.45N 130.32E*
81 I19 **Bolia** Bandundu, W Dem. Rep. Congo (Zaire) *1.34S 18.24E*
95 J14 **Boliden** Västerbotten, N Sweden *64.52N 20.19E*
176 Uu11 **Bolifar** Pulau Seram, E Indonesia *3.08S 130.34E*
179 Oo9 **Bolinao** Luzon, N Philippines *16.22N 119.52E*
29 T6 **Bolivar** Missouri, C USA *37.36N 93.24W*
22 F10 **Bolivar** Tennessee, S USA *35.15N 88.59W*
56 C12 **Bolívar** Cauca, SW Colombia *1.49N 76.58W*
56 F7 **Bolívar** *off.* Departmento de Bolívar. ◈ *province* N Colombia
58 A13 **Bolívar** ◈ *province* C Ecuador
57 N9 **Bolívar** *off.* Estado Bolívar. ◈ *state* SE Venezuela
27 X12 **Bolivar Peninsula** *headland* Texas, SW USA *29.26N 94.41W*
56 I6 **Bolívar, Pico** ▲ W Venezuela *8.33N 71.05W*
59 K17 **Bolivia** *off.* Republic of Bolivia. ◆ *republic* W South America
114 O13 **Boljevac** Serbia, E Yugoslavia *43.50N 21.57E*
Bolkenhain *see* Bolków
130 J5 **Bolkhov** Orlovskaya Oblast', W Russian Federation *53.28N 36.00E*
113 F14 **Bolków** *Ger.* Bolkenhain. Dolnośląskie, SW Poland *50.55N 15.49E*
190 K3 **Bollards Lagoon** South Australia *28.58S 140.52E*
105 R14 **Bollène** Vaucluse, SE France *44.16N 4.45E*
96 N12 **Bollnäs** Gävleborg, C Sweden *61.18N 16.27E*
189 W10 **Bollon** Queensland, C Australia *28.07S 147.28E*
199 Jj14 **Bollons Tablemount** *undersea feature* S Pacific Ocean *49.40S 176.10W*
95 H17 **Bollstabruk** Västernorrland, C Sweden *63.00N 17.41E*
Bolluilos de Par del Condado *see* Bollulos Par del Condado
106 J14 **Bollulos Par del Condado** *var.* Bolluilos de Par del Condado. Andalucía, S Spain *37.19N 6.31W*
97 K21 **Bolmen** ◎ S Sweden
143 T10 **Bolnisi** S Georgia *41.28N 44.34E*
81 H19 **Bolobo** Bandundu, W Dem. Rep. Congo (Zaire) *2.10S 16.16E*
127 N14 **Bolodek** Khabarovskiy Kray, SE Russian Federation *53.45N 133.22E*
108 G10 **Bologna** Emilia-Romagna, N Italy *44.30N 11.19E*
128 I15 **Bologoye** Tverskaya Oblast', W Russian Federation *57.54N 34.04E*
81 J18 **Bolomba** Equateur, NW Dem. Rep. Congo (Zaire) *0.24N 19.10E*
43 X13 **Bolónchén de Rejón** *var.* Bolonchén de Rejón. Campeche, SE Mexico *20.00N 89.34W*
126 H14 **Bolotnoye** Novosibirskaya Oblast', C Russian Federation *55.39N 84.19E*
116 J13 **Boloústra, Akrotírio** *headland* NE Greece *40.56N 24.58E*
178 Jj10 **Bolovens, Plateau des** *plateau* S Laos
108 H13 **Bolsena** Lazio, C Italy *42.39N 11.59E*
109 G14 **Bolsena, Lago di** ◎ C Italy
130 B3 **Bol'shakovo** *Ger.* Kreuzingen; *prev.* Gross-Skaisgirren. Kaliningradskaya Oblast', W Russian Federation *54.53N 21.38E*
126 J6 **Bol'shaya Balakhnya** ≈ N Russian Federation
Bol'shaya Berëstovitsa *see* Vyalikaya Byerastavitsa
131 S7 **Bol'shaya Chernigovka** Samarskaya Oblast', W Russian Federation *52.07N 50.49E*
131 S7 **Bol'shaya Glushitsa** Samarskaya Oblast', W Russian Federation *52.22N 50.29E*
150 H9 **Bol'shaya Khobda** *Kaz.* Ülkenqobda. ≈ Kazakhstan/Russian Federation
126 Jj8 **Bol'shaya Kuonamka** ≈ NE Russian Federation
130 M12 **Bol'shaya Martynovka** Rostovskaya Oblast', SW Russian Federation *47.19N 41.40E*
126 I13 **Bol'shaya Murta** Krasnoyarskiy Kray, C Russian Federation *56.51N 93.10E*
129 V4 **Bol'shaya Rogovaya** ≈ NW Russian Federation
129 U7 **Bol'shaya Synya** ≈ NW Russian Federation
151 V9 **Bol'shaya Vladimirovka** Vostochnyy Kazakhstan, E Kazakhstan *50.52N 79.28E*
125 G13 **Bol'sherech'ye** Omskaya Oblast', C Russian Federation *56.03N 74.37E*
127 Pp12 **Bol'sheretsk** Kamchatskaya Oblast', E Russian Federation *52.20N 156.24E*
131 W3 **Bol'sheust'ikinskoye** Respublika Bashkortostan, W Russian Federation *56.00N 58.13E*
Bol'shevik *see* Bal'shavik
126 Ii3 **Bol'shevik, Ostrov** *island* Severnaya Zemlya, N Russian Federation
129 U4 **Bol'shezemel'skaya Tundra** *physical region* NW Russian Federation
150 J13 **Bol'shiye Barsuki, Peski** *desert* SW Kazakhstan
125 Ff12 **Bol'shiye Uki** Omskaya Oblast', C Russian Federation *56.57N 72.26E*
127 O6 **Bol'shoy Anyuy** ≈ NE Russian Federation
126 K6 **Bol'shoy Begichev, Ostrov** *island* NE Russian Federation
131 O4 **Bol'shoye Murashkino** Nizhegorodskaya Oblast', W Russian Federation *55.46N 44.48E*
131 W4 **Bol'shoy Iremel'** ▲ W Russian Federation *54.31N 58.47E*
131 R7 **Bol'shoy Irgiz** ≈ W Russian Federation
126 M5 **Bol'shoy Lyakhovskiy, Ostrov** *island* NE Russian Federation
126 Ll13 **Bol'shoy Nimnyr** Respublika Sakha (Yakutiya), NE Russian Federation *57.55N 125.34E*
Bol'shoy Rozhan *see* Vyaliki Rozhan
150 E10 **Bol'shoy Uzen'** *Kaz.* Ülkenözen. ≈ Kazakhstan/Russian Federation
126 Ii15 **Bol'shoy Yenisey** *var.* Biy-Khem. ≈ S Russian Federation
42 K6 **Bolson de Mapimi** ▲▲ NW Mexico
100 K6 **Bolsward** *Fris.* Boalsert. Friesland, N Netherlands *53.04N 5.31E*
107 T4 **Boltaña** Aragón, NE Spain *42.28N 0.02E*
12 G15 **Bolton** Ontario, S Canada *43.52N 79.45W*
99 K17 **Bolton** *prev.* Bolton-le-Moors. NW England, UK *53.34N 2.25W*
23 V12 **Bolton** North Carolina, SE USA *34.22N 78.26W*
Bolton-le-Moors *see* Bolton
142 G11 **Bolu** Bolu, NW Turkey *40.45N 31.37E*
142 G11 **Bolu** ◈ *province* NW Turkey
195 N15 **Bolubolu** Goodenough Island, S PNG *9.22S 150.22E*
94 H1 **Bolungarvík** Vestfirdhir, NW Iceland *66.09N 23.16W*
165 O10 **Boluntay** Qinghai, W China *36.30N 92.10E*
142 F14 **Bolvadin** Afyon, W Turkey *38.43N 31.01E*
116 M10 **Bolyarovo** *prev.* Pashkeni. Yambol, E Bulgaria *42.09N 26.49E*
108 G6 **Bolzano** *Ger.* Bozen; *anc.* Bauzanum. Trentino-Alto Adige, N Italy *46.30N 11.22E*
81 F22 **Boma** Bas-Congo, W Dem. Rep. Congo (Zaire) *5.42S 13.05E*
191 R12 **Bombala** New South Wales, SE Australia *36.54S 149.15E*
106 F10 **Bombarral** Leiria, C Portugal *39.15N 9.09W*
Bombay *see* Mumbai
176 Vv11 **Bomberai** ≈ Irian Jaya, E Indonesia
176 Vv11 **Bomberai, Jazirah** *peninsula* Irian Jaya, E Indonesia
176 Vv11 **Bomberai, Semenanjung** *headland* Irian Jaya, E Indonesia *3.01S 133.25E*
83 F18 **Bombo** S Uganda *0.38N 32.31E*
81 I17 **Bomboma** Equateur, NW Dem. Rep. Congo (Zaire) *2.22N 19.03E*
61 I14 **Bom Futuro** Pará, N Brazil *6.27S 54.44W*
165 Q15 **Bomi** *var.* Bowo, Zhamo. Xizang Zizhiqu, W China *29.43N 96.12E*
81 N17 **Bomili** Orientale, NE Dem. Rep. Congo (Zaire) *1.45N 27.01E*
61 N17 **Bom Jesus da Lapa** Bahia, E Brazil *13.16S 43.22W*
62 Q8 **Bom Jesus do Itabapoana** Rio de Janeiro, SE Brazil *21.07S 41.43W*
97 C15 **Bømlafjorden** *fjord* S Norway
97 B15 **Bømlo** *island* S Norway
126 M14 **Bomnak** Amurskaya Oblast', SE Russian Federation *54.43N 128.50E*
81 I17 **Bomongo** Equateur, NW Dem. Rep. Congo (Zaire) *1.22N 18.21E*
63 K14 **Bom Retiro** Santa Catarina, S Brazil *27.52S 49.33W*
81 L15 **Bomu** *var.* Mbomou, Mbomu, M'Bomu. ≈ Central African Republic/Dem. Rep. Congo (Zaire)
148 J3 **Bonāb** *var.* Benāb, Bunab. Āžarbāyjān-e Khāvarī, N Iran *37.24N 45.59E*
47 Q16 **Bonaire** *island* E Netherlands Antilles
41 U11 **Bona, Mount** ▲ Alaska, USA *61.22N 141.45W*
194 M16 **Bonando** ≈ SE Papau New Guinea
191 Q12 **Bonang** Victoria, SE Australia *37.13S 148.43E*
44 L7 **Bonanza** Región Autónoma Atlántico Norte, NE Nicaragua *13.58N 84.37W*
39 O4 **Bonanza** Utah, W USA *40.01N 109.12W*
47 O9 **Bonao** C Dominican Republic *18.55N 70.25W*
188 L3 **Bonaparte Archipelago** *island group* Western Australia
34 K6 **Bonaparte, Mount** ▲ Washington, NW USA *48.47N 119.07W*
41 N11 **Bonasila Dome** ▲ Alaska, USA *62.24N 160.28W*
94 H11 **Bonåsjøen** Nordland, C Norway *67.35N 15.39E*
47 T15 **Bonasse** Trinidad, Trinidad and Tobago *10.02N 61.48W*
13 X7 **Bonaventure** Quebec, SE Canada *48.03N 65.30W*
13 X7 **Bonaventure** ≈ Quebec, SE Canada
11 V11 **Bonavista** Newfoundland, SE Canada *48.36N 53.07W*
11 U11 **Bonavista Bay** *inlet* NW Atlantic Ocean
123 Kk11 **Bon, Cap** *headland* N Tunisia *37.05N 11.04E*
81 E19 **Bonda** Ogooué-Lolo, C Gabon *0.50S 12.28E*
131 N6 **Bondari** Tambovskaya Oblast', W Russian Federation *52.58N 42.02E*
108 G9 **Bondeno** Emilia-Romagna, C Italy *44.53N 11.24E*
32 L4 **Bond Falls Flowage** ◎ Michigan, N USA
81 L16 **Bondo** Orientale, N Dem. Rep. Congo (Zaire) *3.51N 23.41E*
175 P17 **Bondokodi** Pulau Sumba, S Indonesia *9.36S 119.01E*
79 O15 **Bondoukou** E Ivory Coast *8.03N 2.45W*
Bondoukui/Bondoukuy *see* Boundoukui
174 Mm15 **Bondowoso** Jawa, C Indonesia *7.54S 113.49E*
35 S14 **Bondurant** Wyoming, C USA *43.14N 110.26W*
Bone *see* Watampone, Indonesia
Bône *see* Annaba, Algeria
32 I5 **Bone Lake** ◎ Wisconsin, N USA
175 R12 **Bonelipu** Pulau Buton, C Indonesia *4.42S 123.09E*
175 Q14 **Bonerate, Kepulauan** *var.* Macan. *island group* C Indonesia
175 Pp15 **Bonerate, Pulau** *island* Kepulauan Bonerate, C Indonesia
31 O12 **Bonesteel** South Dakota, N USA *43.01N 98.55W*
64 I8 **Bonete, Cerro** ▲ N Argentina *27.58S 68.22W*
175 Pp11 **Bone, Teluk** *bay* Sulawesi, C Indonesia
110 D6 **Bonfol** Jura, NW Switzerland *47.28N 7.08E*
159 U12 **Bongaigaon** Assam, NE India *26.30N 90.30E*
81 K17 **Bongandanga** Equateur, NW Dem. Rep. Congo (Zaire) *1.30N 21.03E*
80 L13 **Bongo, Massif des** *var.* Chaîne des Mongos. ▲▲ NE Central African Republic
80 G12 **Bongor** Mayo-Kébbi, SW Chad *10.18N 15.19E*
79 N16 **Bongouanou** E Ivory Coast *6.39N 4.12W*
178 Kk11 **Bông Sơn** *var.* Hoai Nhơn. Binh Đinh, C Vietnam *14.28N 109.00E*
27 U5 **Bonham** Texas, SW USA *33.34N 96.10W*
Bonhard *see* Bonyhád
105 U6 **Bonhomme, Col du** *pass* NE France *48.10N 7.07E*
105 Y16 **Bonifacio** Corse, France, C Mediterranean Sea *41.23N 9.09E*
Bonifacio, Bocche de/Bonifacio, Bouches de *see* Bonifacio, Strait of
105 Y16 **Bonifacio, Strait of** *Fr.* Bouches de Bonifacio, *It.* Bocche de Bonifacio. *strait* C Mediterranean Sea
25 Q8 **Bonifay** Florida, SE USA *30.49N 85.42W*
Bonin Islands *see* Ogasawara-shotō
199 H6 **Bonin Trench** *undersea feature* NW Pacific Ocean
25 W15 **Bonita Springs** Florida, SE USA *26.19N 81.48W*
44 I5 **Bonito, Pico** ▲ N Honduras *15.33N 86.55W*
103 E17 **Bonn** Nordrhein-Westfalen, W Germany *50.43N 7.06E*
12 J12 **Bonnechere** Ontario, SE Canada *45.39N 77.36W*
12 J12 **Bonnechere** ≈ Ontario, SE Canada
35 N7 **Bonners Ferry** Idaho, NW USA *48.41N 116.19W*
29 R4 **Bonner Springs** Kansas, C USA *39.03N 94.52W*
104 L6 **Bonnétable** Sarthe, NW France *48.09N 0.24E*
29 X6 **Bonne Terre** Missouri, C USA *37.55N 90.33W*

◆ Country
● Country Capital
◇ Dependent Territory
○ Dependent Territory Capital
◈ Administrative Region
✈ International Airport
▲ Mountain
▲▲ Mountain Range
⛰ Volcano
≈ River
◎ Lake
⊠ Reservoir

Bonnet Plume – Bras, Pulau

8 J5 **Bonnet Plume** ≈ Yukon Territory, NW Canada
104 M6 **Bonneval** Eure-et-Loir, C France 48.12N 1.23E
105 T10 **Bonneville** Haute-Savoie, E France 46.04N 6.25E
38 J3 **Bonneville Salt Flats** *salt flat* Utah, W USA
79 U18 **Bonny** Rivers, S Nigeria 4.25N 7.13E
Bonny, Bight of *see* Biafra, Bight of
39 W4 **Bonny Reservoir** ⊠ Colorado, C USA
9 R14 **Bonnyville** Alberta, SW Canada 54.16N 110.46W
109 C18 **Bono** Sardegna, Italy, C Mediterranean Sea 40.24N 9.01E
176 Xx10 **Bonoi** Irian Jaya, E Indonesia 1.46S 137.45E
Bononia *see* Vidin, Bulgaria
Bononia *see* Boulogne-sur-Mer, France
109 B18 **Bonorva** Sardegna, Italy, C Mediterranean Sea 40.27N 8.46E
32 M15 **Bonpas Creek** ≈ Illinois, N USA
202 I3 **Bonriki** Tarawa, W Kiribati 1.22N 173.09E
191 T4 **Bonshaw** New South Wales, SE Australia 29.06S 151.15E
78 I16 **Bonthe** SW Sierra Leone 7.26N 12.32W
179 P8 **Bontoc** Luzon, N Philippines 17.04N 120.58E
194 M16 **Bonua** ≈ S PNG
27 Y9 **Bon Wier** Texas, SW USA 30.43N 93.40W
113 J25 **Bonyhád** *Ger.* Bonhard. Tolna, S Hungary 46.17N 18.31E
Bonzabaai *see* Bonza Bay
85 J25 **Bonza Bay** *Afr.* Bonzabaai. Eastern Cape, S South Africa 32.58S 27.58E
190 D7 **Bookabie** South Australia 31.49S 132.41E
190 H6 **Bookaloo** South Australia 31.56S 137.21E
39 P5 **Book Cliffs** *cliff* Colorado/Utah, W USA
175 Tt9 **Boo, Kepulauan** *island group* E Indonesia
27 P1 **Booker** Texas, SW USA 36.27N 100.32W
78 K15 **Boola** Guinée-Forestière, SE Guinea 8.22N 8.40W
191 O8 **Booligal** New South Wales, SE Australia 33.56S 144.54E
101 G17 **Boom** Antwerpen, N Belgium 51.05N 4.24E
45 N6 **Boom** *var.* Boon. Región Autónoma Atlántico Norte, NE Nicaragua 14.52N 83.36W
191 S3 **Boomi** New South Wales, SE Australia 28.43S 149.35E
Boon *see* Boom
31 V13 **Boone** Iowa, C USA 42.04N 93.52W
23 Q8 **Boone** North Carolina, SE USA 36.13N 81.40W
29 S11 **Booneville** Arkansas, C USA 35.08N 93.55W
23 N6 **Booneville** Kentucky, S USA 37.27N 83.41W
25 N2 **Booneville** Mississippi, S USA 34.39N 88.34W
23 V3 **Boonsboro** Maryland, NE USA 39.30N 77.39W
168 H9 **Böön Tsagaan Nuur** ◎ S Mongolia
36 L6 **Boonville** California, W USA 38.58N 123.21W
33 N16 **Boonville** Indiana, N USA 38.03N 87.16W
29 U4 **Boonville** Missouri, C USA 38.58N 92.44W
20 I9 **Boonville** New York, NE USA 43.28N 75.17W
82 M12 **Boorama** Woqooyi Galbeed, NW Somalia 9.58N 43.15E
191 O6 **Booroondarra, Mount** *hill* New South Wales, SE Australia 31.07S 145.20E
191 N9 **Booroorban** New South Wales, SE Australia 34.55S 144.45E
191 R9 **Boorowa** New South Wales, SE Australia 34.26S 148.42E
101 H17 **Boortmeerbeek** Vlaams Brabant, C Belgium 50.58N 4.27E
82 P11 **Boosaaso** *var.* Bandar Kassim, Bender Qaasim, Bosaso, *It.* Bender Cassim. Bari, N Somalia 11.26N 49.37E
21 Q8 **Boothbay Harbor** Maine, NE USA 43.52N 69.35W
Boothia Felix *see* Boothia Peninsula
15 Kk2 **Boothia, Gulf of** *gulf* Nunavut, NE Canada
15 K2 **Boothia Peninsula** *prev.* Boothia Felix. *peninsula* Nunavut, NE Canada
81 E18 **Booué** Ogooué-Ivindo, NE Gabon 0.03S 11.58E
103 J21 **Bopfingen** Baden-Württemberg, S Germany 48.51N 10.21E
103 F18 **Boppard** Rheinland-Pfalz, W Germany 50.13N 7.35E
64 M4 **Boquerón** *off.* Departamento de Boquerón. ⬖ *department* W Paraguay
45 P15 **Boquete** *var.* Bajo Boquete. Chiriquí, W Panama 8.45N 82.26W
42 J6 **Boquilla, Presa de la** ⊠ N Mexico
42 L5 **Boquillas** *var.* Boquillas del Carmen. Coahuila de Zaragoza, NE Mexico 29.10N 102.55W
Boquillas del Carmen *see* Boquillas
126 I11 **Bor** Krasnoyarskiy Kray, C Russian Federation 61.28N 90.09E
83 F15 **Bor** Jonglei, S Sudan 6.12N 31.33E
97 L20 **Bor** Jönköping, S Sweden 57.04N 14.10E
142 J15 **Bor** Niğde, S Turkey 37.48N 34.30E
114 P12 **Bor** Serbia, E Yugoslavia 44.05N 22.06E
203 S10 **Bora-Bora** *island* Îles Sous le Vent, W French Polynesia
178 Ii10 **Borabu** Maha Sarakham, E Thailand 16.01N 103.06E
35 P13 **Borah Peak** ▲ Idaho, NW USA 44.21N 113.53W
Boralday *see* Burunday
97 J19 **Borås** Västra Götaland, S Sweden 57.43N 12.55E
149 N11 **Borāzjān** *var.* Borazjān. Būshehr, S Iran 29.19N 51.12E
Borazjān *see* Borāzjān
60 G13 **Borba** Amazonas, N Brazil 4.39S 59.34W
106 H11 **Borba** Évora, S Portugal 38.48N 7.28W
Borbetomagus *see* Worms
57 O7 **Borbón** Bolívar, E Venezuela 7.55N 64.03W
61 Q15 **Borborema, Planalto da** *plateau* NE Brazil
118 M14 **Borcea, Braţul** ≈ S Romania
Borchalo *see* Marneuli
205 R15 **Borchgrevink Coast** *physical region* Antarctica
143 Q11 **Borçka** Artvin, NE Turkey 41.24N 41.37E
100 N11 **Borculo** Gelderland, E Netherlands 52.07N 6.31E
190 G10 **Borda, Cape** *headland* South Australia 35.45S 136.34E
104 K13 **Bordeaux** *anc.* Burdigala. Gironde, SW France 44.49N 0.33W
9 T15 **Borden** Saskatchewan, S Canada 52.23N 107.10W
12 D8 **Borden Lake** ◎ Ontario, S Canada
15 L1 **Borden Peninsula** *peninsula* Baffin Island, Nunavut, NE Canada
190 K11 **Bordertown** South Australia 36.21S 140.48E
94 H2 **Bordheyri** Vestfirdhir, NW Iceland 65.12N 21.09W
97 B18 **Bordhoy** *Dan.* Bordø *Island* Faeroe Islands 62.17N 6.30W
108 B11 **Bordighera** Liguria, NW Italy 43.48N 7.40E
76 K5 **Bordj-Bou-Arreridj** *var.* Bordj Bou Arreridj, Bordj Bou Arréridj. N Algeria 36.04N 4.45E
123 I10 **Bordj El Bahri, Cap de** *headland* N Algeria 36.52N 3.13E
76 L10 **Bordj Omar Driss** E Algeria 28.09N 6.52E
149 N13 **Bord Khūn** Hormozgān, S Iran
153 V7 **Bordunskiy** Chuyskaya Oblast', N Kyrgyzstan 42.37N 75.31E
97 M17 **Borensberg** Östergötland, S Sweden 58.33N 15.15E
Borgå *see* Porvoo
94 L2 **Borgarfjördhur** Austurland, NE Iceland 65.32N 13.46W
94 H3 **Borgarnes** Vesturland, W Iceland 64.33N 21.54W
95 G14 **Børgefjellet** ▲▲ C Norway
100 O7 **Borger** Drenthe, NE Netherlands 52.54N 6.48E
27 N2 **Borger** Texas, SW USA 35.40N 101.24W
97 N20 **Borgholm** Kalmar, S Sweden 56.50N 16.40E
109 N22 **Borgia** Calabria, SW Italy 38.48N 16.28E
101 J18 **Borgloon** Limburg, NE Belgium 50.48N 5.21E
205 P2 **Borg Massif** ▲▲ Antarctica
24 L9 **Borgne, Lake** ◎ Louisiana, S USA
108 C7 **Borgomanero** Piemonte, NE Italy 45.42N 8.33E
108 G10 **Borgo Panigale** ✈ (Bologna) Emilia-Romagna, N Italy 44.33N 11.16E
109 J15 **Borgorose** Lazio, C Italy 42.10N 13.15E
108 A9 **Borgo San Dalmazzo** Piemonte, N Italy 44.19N 7.28E
108 G11 **Borgo San Lorenzo** Toscana, C Italy 43.58N 11.22E
108 C7 **Borgosesia** Piemonte, NE Italy 45.41N 8.21E
108 E9 **Borgo Val di Taro** Emilia-Romagna, C Italy 44.29N 9.48E
108 G6 **Borgo Valsugana** Trentino-Alto Adige, N Italy 46.04N 11.31E
169 O11 **Borhoyn Tal** Dornogovĭ, SE Mongolia 43.43N 111.53E
178 Ii8 **Borikhan** *var.* Borikhane. Bolikhamxai, C Laos 18.36N 103.43E
Borikhane *see* Borikhan
Borislav *see* Boryslav
131 N8 **Borisoglebsk** Voronezhskaya Oblast', W Russian Federation 51.23N 42.00E
Borisov *see* Barysaw
Borisovgrad *see* Pŭrvomay
Borispol' *see* Boryspil'
180 I3 **Boriziny** Mahajanga, NW Madagascar 15.31S 47.40E
107 Q5 **Borja** Aragón, NE Spain 41.49N 1.31W
Borjas Blancas *see* Les Borges Blanques
143 S10 **Borjomi** *Rus.* Borzhomi. C Georgia 41.50N 43.24E
120 L12 **Borkavichy** *Rus.* Borkovichi. Vitsyebskaya Voblasts', N Belarus 55.40N 28.18E
103 H16 **Borken** Hessen, C Germany 51.01N 9.16E
103 E14 **Borken** Nordrhein-Westfalen, W Germany 51.51N 6.51E
94 H10 **Borkenes** Troms, N Norway 68.46N 16.10E
80 H7 **Borkou-Ennedi-Tibesti** *off.* Préfecture du Borkou-Ennedi-Tibesti. ⬖ *prefecture* N Chad
Borkovichi *see* Borkavichy
102 E9 **Borkum** *island* NW Germany
83 K17 **Bor, Lagh** *var.* Lak Bor. *dry watercourse* NE Kenya
Bor, Lak *see* Bor, Lagh
97 M14 **Borlänge** Dalarna, C Sweden 60.28N 15.25E
108 C9 **Bormida** ≈ NW Italy
108 F6 **Bormio** Lombardia, N Italy 46.27N 10.24E
103 M16 **Borna** Sachsen, E Germany 51.07N 12.30E
100 O10 **Borne** Overijssel, E Netherlands 52.18N 6.45E
101 F17 **Bornem** Antwerpen, N Belgium 51.06N 4.13E
174 M6 **Borneo** *island* Brunei/Indonesia/Malaysia
103 E16 **Bornheim** Nordrhein-Westfalen, W Germany 50.46N 6.58E
97 L24 **Bornholm** ⬖ *county* E Denmark
97 L24 **Bornholm** *island* E Denmark
79 Y13 **Borno** ⬖ *state* NE Nigeria
106 K15 **Bornos** Andalucía, S Spain 36.49N 5.42W
168 L7 **Bornuur** Töv, C Mongolia 48.28N 106.15E
126 I14 **Borodino** Krasnoyarskiy Kray, S Russian Federation 55.54N 94.45E
119 O4 **Borodyanka** Kyyivs'ka Oblast', N Ukraine 50.40N 29.54E
126 M10 **Borogontsy** Respublika Sakha (Yakutiya), NE Russian Federation 62.42N 131.01E
164 I5 **Borohoro Shan** ▲▲ NW China
79 O13 **Boromo** SW Burkina 11.46N 2.54W
37 T13 **Boron** California, W USA 35.00N 117.42W
179 R12 **Borongan** Samar, C Philippines 11.26N 125.30E
Borongo *see* Black Volta
Boron'ki *see* Baron'ki
Borosjenő *see* Ineu
Borossebes *see* Sebiş
78 L15 **Borotou** NW Ivory Coast 8.46N 7.30W
119 W6 **Borova** Kharkivs'ka Oblast', E Ukraine 49.22N 37.39E
116 H8 **Borovan** Vratsa, NW Bulgaria 43.25N 23.45E
128 I14 **Borovichi** Novgorodskaya Oblast', W Russian Federation 58.23N 33.56E
Borovlje *see* Ferlach
114 J9 **Borovo** Vukovar-Srijem, NE Croatia 45.22N 18.57E
151 Q7 **Borovoye** *Kaz.* Būrabay. Severnyy Kazakhstan, N Kazakhstan 53.07N 70.19E
130 K4 **Borovsk** Kaluzhskaya Oblast', W Russian Federation 55.12N 36.22E
125 F12 **Borovskiy** Tyumenskaya Oblast', C Russian Federation 57.04N 65.37E
151 N7 **Borovskoy** Kostanay, N Kazakhstan 53.49N 64.12E
Borovukha *see* Baravukha
97 L23 **Borrby** Skåne, S Sweden 55.27N 14.10E
189 R3 **Borroloola** Northern Territory, N Australia 16.09S 136.18E
118 F9 **Bors** Bihor, NW Romania 47.06N 21.47E
118 I9 **Borşa** *Hung.* Borsa. Maramureş, N Romania 47.40N 24.37E
118 J10 **Borsec** *Ger.* Bad Borseck, *Hung.* Borszék. Harghita, C Romania 46.57N 25.32E
94 K8 **Børselv** Finnmark, N Norway 70.18N 25.35E
115 L23 **Borsh** *var.* Borshi. Vlorë, S Albania 40.04N 19.51E
Borshchev *see* Borshchiv
118 K7 **Borshchiv** *Pol.* Borszczów, *Rus.* Borshchev. Ternopil's'ka Oblast', W Ukraine 48.48N 26.00E
Borshi *see* Borsh
113 L20 **Borsod-Abaúj-Zemplén** *off.* Borsod-Abaúj-Zemplén Megye. ⬖ *county* NE Hungary
101 E15 **Borssele** Zeeland, SW Netherlands 51.26N 3.45E
Borszczów *see* Borshchiv
Borszék *see* Borsec
Bortala *see* Bole
105 O12 **Bort-les-Orgues** Corrèze, C France 45.28N 2.31E
Bor u České Lípy *see* Nový Bor
168 E8 **Bor-Udzüür** Hovd, W Mongolia 45.46N 92.13E
149 N9 **Borūjen** Chahār Maḩall va Bakhtīārī, C Iran 32.00N 51.08E
148 L7 **Borūjerd** *var.* Burujird. Lorestān, W Iran 33.55N 48.45E
118 H6 **Boryslav** *Pol.* Borysław, *Rus.* Borislav. L'vivs'ka Oblast', NW Ukraine 49.18N 23.28E
Borysław *see* Boryslav
119 P4 **Boryspil'** *Rus.* Borispol'. Kyyivs'ka Oblast', N Ukraine 50.20N 30.58E
119 P4 **Boryspil'** *Rus.* Borispol'. ✈ (Kyyiv) Kyyivs'ka Oblast', N Ukraine 50.21N 30.46E
Borzhomi *see* Borjomi
119 R3 **Borzna** Chernihivs'ka Oblast', NE Ukraine 51.15N 32.25E
126 L16 **Borzya** Chitinskaya Oblast', S Russian Federation 50.18N 116.24E
109 B18 **Bosa** Sardegna, Italy, C Mediterranean Sea 40.18N 8.28E
114 F10 **Bosanska Dubica** *var.* Kozarska Dubica. Republika Srpska, NW Bosnia and Herzegovina 45.09N 16.47E
114 G10 **Bosanska Gradiška** *var.* Gradiška. Republika Srpska, N Bosnia and Herzegovina 45.09N 17.14E
114 F10 **Bosanska Kostajnica** *var.* Srpska Kostajnica. Republika Srpska, NW Bosnia and Herzegovina 45.12N 16.33E
114 E11 **Bosanska Krupa** *var.* Krupa, Krupa na Uni. Federacija Bosna I Hercegovina, NW Bosnia and Herzegovina 44.52N 16.09E
114 H10 **Bosanski Brod** *var.* Srpski Brod. Republika Srpska, N Bosnia and Herzegovina 45.07N 17.59E
114 E10 **Bosanski Novi** *var.* Novi Grad. Republika Srpska, NW Bosnia and Herzegovina 45.03N 16.22E
114 E11 **Bosanski Petrovac** *var.* Petrovac. Federacija Bosna I Hercegovina, NW Bosnia and Herzegovina 44.34N 16.21E
114 N12 **Bosanski Petrovac** Serbia, E Yugoslavia 44.22N 21.25E
114 I10 **Bosanski Šamac** *var.* Šamac. Republika Srpska, N Bosnia and Herzegovina 45.03N 18.27E
114 E12 **Bosansko Grahovo** *var.* Grahovo, Hrvatsko Grahovo. Federacija Bosna I Hercegovina, W Bosnia and Herzegovina 44.10N 16.22E
Bosaso *see* Boosaaso
194 G13 **Bosavi, Mount** Ѫ W PNG 6.33S 142.50E
166 J14 **Bose** Guangxi Zhuangzu Zizhiqu, S China 23.55N 106.31E
167 Q5 **Boshan** Shandong, E China 36.31N 117.46E
115 P16 **Bosilegrad** *prev.* Bosiljgrad. Serbia, SE Yugoslavia 42.30N 22.30E
Bosiljgrad *see* Bosilegrad
Bösing *see* Pezinok
100 H12 **Boskoop** Zuid-Holland, C Netherlands 52.04N 4.40E
113 G18 **Boskovice** *Ger.* Boskowitz. Brněnský Kraj, SE Czech Republic 49.30N 16.39E
Boskowitz *see* Boskovice
114 I10 **Bosna** ≈ N Bosnia and Herzegovina
176 X9 **Bosnabraidi** Irian Jaya, E Indonesia 0.49S 136.00E
115 G14 **Bosna I Hercegovina, Federacija** ⬖ *republic* Bosnia and Herzegovina
114 H12 **Bosnia and Herzegovina** *off.* Republic of Bosnia and Herzegovina. ◆ *republic* SE Europe
81 J16 **Bosobolo** Equateur, NW Dem. Rep. Congo (Zaire) 4.10N 19.55E
171 K17 **Bōsō-hantō** *peninsula* Honshū, S Japan
Bosora *see* Buşrá ash Shām
Bosphorus/Bosporus *see* İstanbul Boğazı
Bosporus Cimmerius *see* Kerch Strait
Bosporus Thracius *see* İstanbul Boğazı
Bosra *see* Buşrá ash Shām
81 H14 **Bossangoa** Ouham, C Central African Republic 6.31N 17.24E
Bossé Bangou *see* Bossey Bangou
81 I15 **Bossembélé** Ombella-Mpoko, C Central African Republic 5.13N 17.39E
81 H15 **Bossentélé** Ouham-Pendé, W Central African Republic 5.36N 16.37E
79 R12 **Bossey Bangou** *var.* Bossé Bangou. Tillabéri, SW Niger 13.22N 1.18E
24 G5 **Bossier City** Louisiana, S USA 32.31N 93.43W
85 D20 **Bossiesvlei** Hardap, S Namibia 25.01S 16.45E
79 Y11 **Bosso** Diffa, SE Niger 13.42N 13.18E
63 F15 **Bossoroca** Rio Grande do Sul, S Brazil 28.45S 54.54W
164 J10 **Bostan** Xinjiang Uygur Zizhiqu, W China 41.19N 83.15E
148 K3 **Bostānābād** Āžarbāyjān-e Khāvarī, N Iran 37.52N 46.51E
164 K6 **Bosten Hu** *var.* Bagrax Hu. ◎ NW China
99 O18 **Boston** *prev.* St.Botolph's Town. E England, UK 52.58N 0.01W
21 O11 **Boston** *state capital* Massachusetts, NE USA 42.21N 71.03W
8 M17 **Boston Bar** British Columbia, SW Canada 49.54N 121.22W
29 T10 **Boston Mountains** ▲▲ Arkansas, C USA
13 P8 **Bostonnais** ≈ Quebec, SE Canada
Bostyn' *see* Bastyn'
114 J10 **Bosut** ≈ E Croatia
160 C11 **Botād** Gujarāt, W India 22.12N 71.43E
191 T9 **Botany Bay** *inlet* New South Wales, SE Australia
85 G18 **Boteti** *var.* Botletle. ≈ N Botswana
116 J9 **Botev** ▲ C Bulgaria 42.45N 24.57E
116 H9 **Botevgrad** *prev.* Orkhaniye. Sofiya, W Bulgaria 42.55N 23.46E
95 J16 **Bothnia, Gulf of** *Fin.* Pohjanlahti, *Swe.* Bottniska Viken. *gulf* N Baltic Sea
191 P17 **Bothwell** Tasmania, SE Australia 42.24S 147.01E
106 H5 **Boticas** Vila Real, N Portugal 41.40N 7.40W
57 W10 **Boti-Pasi** Sipaliwini, C Surinam 4.08N 55.27W
Botletle *see* Boteti
131 P16 **Botlikh** Chechenskaya Respublika, SW Russian Federation 42.39N 46.12E
119 N10 **Botna** ≈ E Moldova
118 I9 **Botoşani** *Hung.* Botosány. Botoşani, NE Romania 47.43N 26.40E
118 K8 **Botoşani** ⬖ *county* NE Romania
Botosány *see* Botoşani
167 P4 **Botou** *prev.* Bozhen. Hebei, E China 38.09N 116.37E
101 M20 **Botrange** ▲ E Belgium 50.30N 6.03E
109 O21 **Botricello** Calabria, SW Italy 38.56N 16.51E
85 I23 **Botshabelo** Free State, C South Africa 29.15S 26.51E
95 J15 **Botsmark** Västerbotten, N Sweden 64.15N 20.15E
85 G19 **Botswana** *off.* Republic of Botswana. ◆ *republic* S Africa
31 N2 **Bottineau** North Dakota, N USA 48.49N 100.28W
Bottniska Viken *see* Bothnia, Gulf of
62 L9 **Botucatu** São Paulo, S Brazil 22.52S 48.30W
78 M16 **Bouaflé** C Ivory Coast 6.58N 5.45W
79 N16 **Bouaké** *var.* Bwake. C Ivory Coast 7.39N 5.01W
81 G14 **Bouar** Nana-Mambéré, W Central African Republic 5.58N 15.38E
76 H7 **Bouarfa** NE Morocco 32.33N 1.54W
113 B19 **Boubín** ▲ SW Czech Republic 49.00N 13.51E
81 I14 **Bouca** Ouham, W Central African Republic 6.57N 18.18E
13 T5 **Boucher** ≈ Quebec, SE Canada
105 R15 **Bouches-du-Rhône** ⬖ *department* SE France
76 C9 **Bou Craa** *var.* Bu Craa. NW Western Sahara 26.31N 12.52W
79 O9 **Boû Djébéha** *oasis* C Mali 18.39N 3.45W
110 C8 **Boudry** Neuchâtel, W Switzerland 46.57N 6.46E
188 L2 **Bougainville, Cape** *headland* Western Australia 13.53S 126.01E
67 E24 **Bougainville, Cape** *headland* East Falkland, Falkland Islands 51.18S 58.28W
Bougainville, Détroit de *see* Bougainville Strait, Vanuatu
195 S13 **Bougainville Island** *island* NE PNG
195 T13 **Bougainville Strait** *strait* N Solomon Islands
197 B12 **Bougainville Strait** *Fr.* Détroit de Bougainville. *strait* C Vanuatu
176 U8 **Bouganville, Selat** *strait* Irian Jaya, E Indonesia
123 J11 **Bougaroun, Cap** *headland* NE Algeria 37.07N 6.18E
79 R8 **Boughessa** Kidal, NE Mali 20.05N 2.13E
Bougie *see* Béjaïa
78 L13 **Bougouni** Sikasso, SW Mali 11.22N 7.24W
101 J24 **Bouillon** Luxembourg, SE Belgium 49.46N 5.04E
76 K5 **Bouira** *var.* Bouïra. N Algeria 36.22N 3.55E
76 D8 **Bou-Izakarn** SW Morocco 29.12N 9.43W
76 B9 **Boujdour** *var.* Bojador. W Western Sahara 26.06N 14.28W
76 G5 **Boukhalef** ✈ (Tanger) N Morocco 35.45N 5.53W
Boukombé *see* Boukoumbé
79 R14 **Boukoumbé** *var.* Boukombé. C Benin 10.13N 1.09E
78 G6 **Boû Lanouâr** Dakhlet Nouâdhibou, W Mauritania 21.16N 16.28W
39 T4 **Boulder** Colorado, C USA 40.01N 105.18W
35 R10 **Boulder** Montana, NW USA 46.14N 112.07W
37 X12 **Boulder City** Nevada, W USA 35.58N 114.49W
189 T7 **Boulia** Queensland, C Australia 23.02S 139.58E
13 N10 **Boullé** ≈ Quebec, SE Canada
104 J9 **Boulogne** ≈ NW France
Boulogne *see* Boulogne-sur-Mer
104 L16 **Boulogne-sur-Gesse** Haute-Garonne, S France 43.18N 0.39E
105 N1 **Boulogne-sur-Mer** *var.* Boulogne; *anc.* Bononia, Gesoriacum, Gessoriacum. Pas-de-Calais, N France 50.43N 1.36E
197 I7 **Bouloupari** Province Sud, S New Caledonia 21.54S 166.04E
79 Q12 **Boulsa** C Burkina 12.40N 0.28W
79 W11 **Boultoum** Zinder, C Niger 14.43N 10.22E
197 K13 **Bouma** Taveuni, N Fiji 16.49S 179.50W
81 G16 **Boumba** ≈ SE Cameroon
78 J9 **Boûmdeïd** *var.* Boumdeït. Assaba, S Mauritania 17.25N 11.21W
Boumdeït *see* Boûmdeïd
117 C17 **Boumistós** ▲ W Greece 38.48N 20.59E
79 O15 **Bouna** NE Ivory Coast 9.16N 3.00W
21 P4 **Boundary Bald Mountain** ▲ Maine, NE USA 45.45N 70.10W
37 S8 **Boundary Peak** ▲ Nevada, W USA 37.50N 118.21W
78 M14 **Boundiali** N Ivory Coast 9.31N 6.28W
81 G19 **Boundji** Cuvette, C Congo 1.04S 15.18E
79 O13 **Boundoukui** *var.* Bondoukui, Bondoukuy. W Burkina 11.51N 3.47W
38 L2 **Bountiful** Utah, W USA 40.53N 111.52W
Bounty Basin *see* Bounty Trough
203 Q16 **Bounty Bay** *bay* Pitcairn Island, C Pacific Ocean
199 Jj14 **Bounty Islands** *island group* S NZ
183 Q13 **Bounty Trough** *var.* Bounty Basin. *undersea feature* S Pacific Ocean
197 I6 **Bourail** Province Sud, C New Caledonia 21.35S 165.29E
29 V5 **Bourbeuse River** ≈ Missouri, C USA
105 Q9 **Bourbon-Lancy** Saône-et-Loire, C France 46.39N 3.48E
33 N11 **Bourbonnais** Illinois, N USA 41.08N 87.52W
105 O10 **Bourbonnais** *cultural region* C France
105 S7 **Bourbonne-les-Bains** Haute-Marne, N France 48.00N 5.43E
Bourbon Vendée *see* la Roche-sur-Yon
76 M8 **Bourdj Messaouda** E Algeria 30.18N 9.19E
79 Q10 **Bourem** Gao, C Mali 16.56N 0.21W
Bourg *see* Bourg-en-Bresse
105 N11 **Bourganeuf** Creuse, C France 45.57N 1.47E
Bourgas *see* Burgas
Bourge-en-Bresse *see* Bourg-en-Bresse
105 S10 **Bourg-en-Bresse** *var.* Bourg, Bourge-en-Bresse. Ain, E France 46.12N 5.13E
105 O8 **Bourges** *anc.* Avaricum. Cher, C France 47.06N 2.24E
105 T11 **Bourget, Lac du** ◎ E France
105 P8 **Bourgogne** *Eng.* Burgundy. ⬖ *region* E France
105 S11 **Bourgoin-Jallieu** Isère, E France 45.34N 5.16E
105 R14 **Bourg-St-Andéol** Ardèche, E France 44.24N 4.36E
105 U11 **Bourg-St-Maurice** Savoie, E France 45.37N 6.49E
110 C11 **Bourg St.Pierre** Valais, SW Switzerland 45.54N 7.10E
78 H8 **Boû Rjeimât** *well* W Mauritania 19.06N 15.16W
191 P5 **Bourke** New South Wales, SE Australia 30.07S 145.57E
99 M24 **Bournemouth** S England, UK 50.43N 1.54W
101 M23 **Bourscheid** Diekirch, NE Luxembourg 49.55N 6.04E
76 K6 **Bou Saâda** *var.* Bou Saada. N Algeria 35.13N 4.09E
38 I13 **Bouse Wash** ≈ Arizona, SW USA
105 N10 **Boussac** Creuse, C France 46.20N 2.12E
104 M16 **Boussens** Haute-Garonne, S France 43.10N 0.58E
80 H12 **Bousso** *prev.* Fort-Bretonnet. Chari-Baguirmi, S Chad 10.31N 16.45E
78 H9 **Boutilimit** Trarza, SW Mauritania 17.33N 14.42W
67 D21 **Bouvet Island** ◇ *Norwegian dependency* S Atlantic Ocean
79 U11 **Bouza** Tahoua, SW Niger 14.25N 6.09E
111 R10 **Bovec** *Ger.* Flitsch, *It.* Plezzo. NW Slovenia 46.21N 13.33E
100 J8 **Bovenkarspel** Noord-Holland, NW Netherlands 52.33N 5.03E
31 V5 **Bovey** Minnesota, N USA 47.18N 93.25W
34 M9 **Bovill** Idaho, NW USA 46.50N 116.24W
26 L4 **Bovina** Texas, SW USA 34.30N 102.52W
109 M17 **Bovino** Puglia, SE Italy 41.14N 15.19E
63 C17 **Bovril** Entre Ríos, E Argentina 31.24S 59.25W
30 L2 **Bowbells** North Dakota, N USA 48.48N 102.15W
9 Q16 **Bow City** Alberta, SW Canada 50.27N 112.16W
31 O8 **Bowdle** South Dakota, N USA 45.27N 99.39W
189 X6 **Bowen** Queensland, NE Australia 20.00S 148.10E
198 B4 **Bowers Ridge** *undersea feature* S Bering Sea
15 Jj4 **Bowes Point** *headland* Nunavut, N Canada 67.46N 101.51W
27 S5 **Bowie** Texas, SW USA 33.33N 97.51W
9 R17 **Bow Island** Alberta, SW Canada 49.52N 111.24W
Bowkān *see* Būkān
22 J7 **Bowling Green** Kentucky, S USA 36.59N 86.26W
29 V3 **Bowling Green** Missouri, C USA 39.20N 91.12W
33 R11 **Bowling Green** Ohio, N USA 41.22N 83.40W
23 W5 **Bowling Green** Virginia, NE USA 38.01N 77.20W
30 J6 **Bowman** North Dakota, N USA 46.10N 103.25W
16 N3 **Bowman Bay** *bay* NW Atlantic Ocean
204 I5 **Bowman Coast** *physical region* Antarctica
30 J7 **Bowman-Haley Lake** ⊠ North Dakota, N USA
205 Z11 **Bowman Island** *island* Antarctica
Bowo *see* Bomi
191 S9 **Bowral** New South Wales, SE Australia 34.29S 150.28E
194 K14 **Bowutu Mountains** ▲▲ C PNG
85 I16 **Bowwood** Southern, S Zambia 17.09S 26.16E
30 I12 **Box Butte Reservoir** ⊠ Nebraska, C USA
30 J10 **Box Elder** South Dakota, N USA 44.06N 103.04W
97 M18 **Boxholm** Östergötland, S Sweden 58.12N 15.04E
Bo Xian/Boxian *see* Bozhou
167 Q4 **Boxing** Shandong, E China 37.06N 118.05E
101 L14 **Boxmeer** Noord-Brabant, SE Netherlands 51.39N 5.57E
101 J14 **Boxtel** Noord-Brabant, S Netherlands 51.36N 5.19E
142 J10 **Boyabat** Sinop, N Turkey 41.27N 34.45E
56 F9 **Boyacá** *off.* Departamento de Boyacá. ⬖ *province* C Colombia
119 O4 **Boyarka** Kyyivs'ka Oblast', N Ukraine 50.19N 30.19E
24 H7 **Boyce** Louisiana, S USA 31.23N 92.40W
35 U11 **Boyd** Montana, NW USA 45.27N 109.03W
27 S6 **Boyd** Texas, SW USA 33.01N 97.33W
23 V8 **Boydton** Virginia, NE USA 36.40N 78.24W
Boyer Ahmadī va Kohkīlūyeh *see* Kohkīlūyeh va Būyer Aḩmadī
31 T13 **Boyer River** ≈ Iowa, C USA
23 W8 **Boykins** Virginia, NE USA 36.35N 77.11W
9 Q13 **Boyle** Alberta, SW Canada 54.38N 112.45W
99 D16 **Boyle** *Ir.* Mainistirna Búille. C Ireland 53.58N 8.18W
99 F17 **Boyne** *Ir.* An Bhóinn. ≈ E Ireland
33 Q5 **Boyne City** Michigan, N USA 45.13N 85.00W
25 Z14 **Boynton Beach** Florida, SE USA 26.31N 80.04W
153 O13 **Boysun** *Rus.* Baysun. Surkhondaryo Wiloyati, S Uzbekistan 38.13N 67.07E
Bozau *see* Întorsura Buzăului
142 B12 **Bozcaada** *island* Çanakkale, NW Turkey
142 C14 **Boz Dağları** ▲▲ W Turkey
35 S11 **Bozeman** Montana, NW USA 45.40N 111.02W
Bozen *see* Bolzano
81 J16 **Bozene** Equateur, NW Dem. Rep. Congo (Zaire) 2.55N 19.15E
167 P7 **Bozhou** *var.* Boxian, Bo Xian. Anhui, E China 33.49N 115.49E
142 H16 **Bozkır** Konya, S Turkey 37.10N 32.15E
142 K13 **Bozok Yaylası** *plateau* C Turkey
81 H14 **Bozoum** Ouham-Pendé, W Central African Republic 6.17N 16.26E
143 N16 **Bozova** Sanlıurfa, S Turkey 37.22N 38.33E
Bozrah *see* Buşrá ash Shām
142 E12 **Bozüyük** Bilecik, NW Turkey 39.55N 30.01E
108 B9 **Bra** Piemonte, NW Italy 44.42N 7.51E
204 G4 **Brabant Island** *island* Antarctica
101 I20 **Brabant Wallon** ⬖ *province* C Belgium
115 F15 **Brač** *var.* Brach, *It.* Brazza; *anc.* Brattia. *island* S Croatia
Bracara Augusta *see* Braga
109 H15 **Bracciano** Lazio, C Italy 42.04N 12.12E
109 H14 **Bracciano, Lago di** ◎ C Italy
12 H13 **Bracebridge** Ontario, S Canada 45.01N 79.19W
Brach *see* Brač
95 G17 **Bräcke** Jämtland, C Sweden 62.42N 15.30E
27 P12 **Brackettville** Texas, SW USA 29.18N 100.25W
99 N22 **Bracknell** S England, UK 51.25N 0.46W
63 K14 **Braço do Norte** Santa Catarina, S Brazil 28.16S 49.11W
118 G11 **Brad** *Hung.* Brád. Hunedoara, SW Romania 45.52N 23.00E
109 N18 **Bradano** ≈ S Italy
25 V13 **Bradenton** Florida, SE USA 27.30N 82.34W
12 H14 **Bradford** Ontario, S Canada 44.09N 79.34W
99 L17 **Bradford** N England, UK 53.48N 1.45W
29 W10 **Bradford** Arkansas, C USA 35.25N 91.27W
20 D12 **Bradford** Pennsylvania, NE USA 41.57N 78.38W
29 T15 **Bradley** Arkansas, C USA 33.06N 93.39W
27 P7 **Bradshaw** Texas, SW USA 32.06N 99.52W
27 Q9 **Brady** Texas, SW USA 31.07N 99.22W
27 Q9 **Brady Creek** ≈ Texas, SW USA
98 J10 **Braemar** NE Scotland, UK 57.12N 2.52W
118 K8 **Brăeşti** Botoşani, NW Romania 47.50N 26.26E
106 G5 **Braga** *anc.* Bracara Augusta. Braga, NW Portugal 41.31N 8.25W
106 G5 **Braga** ⬖ *district* N Portugal
118 J15 **Bragadiru** Teleorman, S Romania 43.43N 25.32E
63 C20 **Bragado** Buenos Aires, E Argentina 35.10S 60.28W
106 J5 **Bragança** *Eng.* Braganza; *anc.* Julio Briga. Bragança, NE Portugal 41.46N 6.46W
106 I5 **Bragança** ⬖ *district* N Portugal
62 N9 **Bragança Paulista** São Paulo, S Brazil 22.55S 46.30W
Braganza *see* Bragança
Bragin *see* Brahin
31 V7 **Braham** Minnesota, N USA 45.43N 93.10W
Brahe *see* Brda
Brahestad *see* Raahe
121 O20 **Brahin** *Rus.* Bragin. Homyel'skaya Voblasts', SE Belarus 51.46N 30.16E
159 U15 **Brahmanbaria** Chittagong, E Bangladesh 23.58N 91.04E
160 O12 **Brāhmani** ≈ E India
160 N13 **Brahmapur** Orissa, E India 19.21N 84.51E
133 S10 **Brahmaputra** *var.* Padma, Tsangpo, *Ben.* Jamuna, *Chin.* Yarlung Zangbo Jiang, *Ind.* Bramaputra, Dihang, Siang. ≈ S Asia
99 H19 **Braich y Pwll** *headland* NW Wales, UK 52.47N 4.46W
191 R10 **Braidwood** New South Wales, SE Australia 35.26S 149.48E
32 M11 **Braidwood** Illinois, N USA 41.16N 88.12W
118 M13 **Brăila** Brăila, E Romania 45.17N 27.57E
118 L13 **Brăila** ⬖ *county* SE Romania
101 G19 **Braine-l'Alleud** Brabant Wallon, C Belgium 50.40N 4.22E
101 F19 **Braine-le-Comte** Hainaut, SW Belgium 50.37N 4.07E
31 U6 **Brainerd** Minnesota, N USA 46.22N 94.10W
101 J19 **Braives** Liège, E Belgium 50.37N 5.09E
85 H23 **Brak** ≈ C South Africa
Brak *see* Birāk
101 E18 **Brakel** Oost-Vlaanderen, SW Belgium 50.50N 3.48E
100 J13 **Brakel** Gelderland, C Netherlands 51.49N 5.05E
78 H9 **Brakna** ⬖ *region* S Mauritania
97 J17 **Brålanda** Västra Götaland, S Sweden 58.32N 12.18E
Bramaputra *see* Brahmaputra
97 F23 **Bramming** Ribe, W Denmark 55.28N 8.42E
12 G15 **Brampton** Ontario, S Canada 43.42N 79.46W
102 F12 **Bramsche** Niedersachsen, NW Germany 52.25N 7.58E
118 J12 **Bran** *Ger.* Törzburg, *Hung.* Törcsvár. Braşov, S Romania 45.31N 25.23E
31 W8 **Branch** Minnesota, N USA 45.29N 92.57W
23 R14 **Branchville** South Carolina, SE USA 33.15N 80.49W
49 Y6 **Branco, Cabo** *headland* E Brazil 7.07S 34.45W
60 F11 **Branco, Rio** ≈ N Brazil
110 J8 **Brand** Vorarlberg, W Austria 47.07N 9.45E
85 B18 **Brandberg** ▲ NW Namibia 21.20S 14.22E
97 H14 **Brandbu** Oppland, S Norway 60.24N 10.30E
97 F22 **Brande** Ringkøbing, W Denmark 55.57N 9.07E
Brandebourg *see* Brandenburg
102 M12 **Brandenburg** *var.* Brandenburg an der Havel. Brandenburg, NE Germany 52.25N 12.34E
22 K5 **Brandenburg** Kentucky, S USA 37.58N 86.11W
102 N12 **Brandenburg** *off.* Freie und Hansestadt Hamburg, *Fr.* Brandebourg. ⬖ *state* NE Germany
Brandenburg an der Havel *see* Brandenburg
85 I23 **Brandfort** Free State, C South Africa 28.42S 26.28E
9 W16 **Brandon** Manitoba, S Canada 49.49N 99.57W
25 V12 **Brandon** Florida, SE USA 27.56N 82.17W
24 L6 **Brandon** Mississippi, S USA 32.16N 90.01W
99 A20 **Brandon Mountain** *Ir.* Cnoc Bréanainn. ▲ SW Ireland 52.13N 10.16W
Brandsen *see* Coronel Brandsen
97 I14 **Brandval** Hedmark, S Norway 60.18N 12.01E
85 F24 **Brandvlei** Northern Cape, W South Africa 30.19S 20.31E
25 U9 **Branford** Florida, SE USA 29.57N 82.54W
112 K7 **Braniewo** *Ger.* Braunsberg. Warmińsko-Mazurskie, NE Poland 54.24N 19.49E
204 H3 **Bransfield Strait** *strait* Antarctica
39 U8 **Branson** Colorado, C USA 37.01N 103.52W
29 T8 **Branson** Missouri, C USA 36.38N 93.13W
12 G16 **Brantford** Ontario, S Canada 43.04N 80.21W
104 L12 **Brantôme** Dordogne, SW France 45.21N 0.37E
190 L12 **Branxholme** Victoria, SE Australia 37.51S 141.48E
Brasil *see* Brazil
61 C16 **Brasiléia** Acre, W Brazil 10.58S 48.45W
61 K18 **Brasília** ● (Brazil) Distrito Federal, C Brazil 15.45S 47.57W
Braslav *see* Braslaw
120 J12 **Braslaw** *Pol.* Brasław, *Rus.* Braslav. Vitsyebskaya Voblasts', N Belarus 55.37N 27.01E
118 J12 **Braşov** *Ger.* Kronstadt, *Hung.* Brassó; *prev.* Oraşul Stalin. Braşov, C Romania 45.40N 25.34E
118 I12 **Braşov** ⬖ *county* C Romania
176 W7 **Bras, Pulau** *island* Kepulauan Mapia, E Indonesia

◆ Country
● Country Capital
◇ Dependent Territory
○ Dependent Territory Capital
⬖ Administrative Region
✈ International Airport
▲ Mountain
▲▲ Mountain Range
Ѫ Volcano
≈ River
◎ Lake
⊠ Reservoir

BRASS – BUDRIO

79 U18 **Brass** Bayelsa, S Nigeria 4.19N 6.21E
101 H16 **Brasschaat** *var.* Brasschaet. Antwerpen, N Belgium 51.16N 4.30E
Brasschaet *see* Brasschaat
175 O4 **Brassey, Banjaran** *var.* Brassey Range. ▲▲ East Malaysia
Brassey Range *see* Brassey, Banjaran
Brassó *see* Braşov
25 T1 **Brasstown Bald** ▲ Georgia, SE USA 34.52N 83.48W
115 K22 **Brataj** Vlorë, SW Albania 40.18N 19.37E
116 J10 **Bratan** *var.* Morozov. ▲ C Bulgaria 42.31N 25.08E
113 F21 **Bratislava** *Ger.* Pressburg, *Hung.* Pozsony. ● (Slovakia) Bratislavský Kraj, W Slovakia 48.10N 17.10E
113 H21 **Bratislavský Kraj** ◈ *region* W Slovakia
116 H10 **Bratiya** ▲ C Bulgaria 42.36N 24.08E
126 J14 **Bratsk** Irkutskaya Oblast', C Russian Federation 56.19N 101.49E
119 Q8 **Brats'ke** Mykolayivs'ka Oblast', S Ukraine 47.52N 31.34E
126 J14 **Bratskoye Vodokhranilishche** *Eng.* Bratsk Reservoir. ▣ S Russian Federation
Bratsk Reservoir *see* Bratskoye Vodokhranilishche
Brattia *see* Brač
96 D9 **Brattvåg** Møre og Romsdal, S Norway 62.36N 6.21E
114 K12 **Bratunac** Republika Srpska, E Bosnia and Herzegovina 44.10N 19.21E
116 J10 **Bratya Daskalovi** *prev.* Grozdovo. Stara Zagora, C Bulgaria 42.13N 25.21E
111 U2 **Braunau** ≈ N Austria
Braunau *see* Braunau am Inn
111 Q4 **Braunau am Inn** *var.* Braunau. Oberösterreich, N Austria 48.16N 13.03E
Braunsberg *see* Braniewo
102 J13 **Braunschweig** *Eng./Fr.* Brunswick. Niedersachsen, N Germany 52.16N 10.31E
Brava *see* Baraawe
107 Y6 **Brava, Costa** *coastal region* NE Spain
45 V16 **Brava, Punta** *headland* E Panama 8.21N 78.22W
97 N17 **Bråviken** *inlet* S Sweden
58 B10 **Bravo, Cerro** ▲ N Peru 5.33S 79.10W
Bravo del Norte, Río/Bravo, Río *see* Grande, Rio
37 X17 **Brawley** California, W USA 32.58N 115.31W
99 G18 **Bray** *Ir.* Bré. E Ireland 53.12N 6.06W
61 G16 **Brazil** *off.* Federative Republic of Brazil, *Port.* Repùblica Federativa do Brasil, *Sp.* Brasil; *prev.* United States of Brazil. ◆ *federal republic* South America
67 K15 **Brazil Basin** *var.* Brazilian Basin, Brazil'skaya Kotlovina. *undersea feature* W Atlantic Ocean
Brazilian Basin *see* Brazil Basin
Brazilian Highlands *see* Central, Planalto
Brazil'skaya Kotlovina *see* Brazil Basin
27 U10 **Brazos River** ≈ Texas, SW USA
176 Yy13 **Brazza** ≈ Irian Jaya, E Indonesia
Brazza *see* Brač
81 G21 **Brazzaville** ● (Congo) Capital District, S Congo 4.13S 15.13E
81 G21 **Brazzaville** ✕ Le Pool, S Congo 4.15S 15.15E
114 J11 **Brčko** Republika Srpska, NE Bosnia and Herzegovina 44.52N 18.49E
112 H8 **Brda** *Ger.* Brahe. ≈ N Poland
Bré *see* Bray
193 A23 **Breaksea Sound** *sound* South Island, NZ
192 L4 **Bream Bay** *bay* North Island, NZ
192 L4 **Bream Head** *headland* North Island, NZ 35.51S 174.35E
Bréanainn, Cnoc *see* Brandon Mountain
47 S6 **Brea, Punta** *headland* W Puerto Rico 17.56N 66.55W
24 I9 **Breaux Bridge** Louisiana, S USA 30.16N 91.54W
118 J13 **Breaza** Prahova, SE Romania 45.06N 25.44E
174 K14 **Brebes** Jawa, C Indonesia 6.54S 109.00E
98 K10 **Brechin** E Scotland, UK 56.44N 2.38W
101 H15 **Brecht** Antwerpen, N Belgium 51.21N 4.32E
39 S4 **Breckenridge** Colorado, C USA 39.28N 106.02W
31 R6 **Breckenridge** Minnesota, N USA 46.15N 96.35W
27 R6 **Breckenridge** Texas, SW USA 32.45N 98.54W
99 J21 **Brecknock** *cultural region* SE Wales, UK
65 G25 **Brecknock, Península** *headland* S Chile 54.39S 71.48W
113 G19 **Břeclav** *Ger.* Lundenburg. Brněnský Kraj, SE Czech Republic 49.04N 16.51E
99 J21 **Brecon** E Wales, UK 51.57N 3.26W
99 J21 **Brecon Beacons** ▲▲ S Wales, UK
101 I14 **Breda** Noord-Brabant, S Netherlands 51.34N 4.46E
97 K20 **Bredaryd** Jönköping, S Sweden 57.10N 13.45E
85 F26 **Bredasdorp** Western Cape, SW South Africa 34.28S 20.03E
95 H16 **Bredbyn** Västernorrland, N Sweden 63.28N 18.04E
125 E13 **Bredy** Chelyabinskaya Oblast', C Russian Federation 52.23N 60.24E
101 K17 **Bree** Limburg, NE Belgium 51.07N 5.36E
69 T15 **Breede** ≈ S South Africa
100 I7 **Breezand** Noord-Holland, NW Netherlands 52.52N 4.47E
115 P18 **Bregalnica** ≈ E FYR Macedonia
110 I6 **Bregenz** *anc.* Brigantium. Vorarlberg, W Austria 47.31N 9.44E
110 J7 **Bregenzer Wald** ▲▲ W Austria
116 F6 **Bregovo** Vidin, NW Bulgaria 44.07N 22.40E
104 H5 **Bréhat, Île de** *island* NW France
94 H2 **Breidhafjördhur** *bay* W Iceland
94 L3 **Breidhdalsvík** Austurland, E Iceland 64.48N 14.02W
110 H9 **Breil** *Ger.* Brigels. Graubünden, S Switzerland 46.46N 9.04E
94 J8 **Breivikbotn** Finnmark, N Norway 70.36N 22.19E
96 I9 **Brekken** Sør-Trøndelag, S Norway 62.39N 11.49E
96 G7 **Brekstad** Sør-Trøndelag, S Norway 63.42N 9.40E
96 B10 **Bremangerlandet** *island* S Norway
Brême *see* Bremen
102 H11 **Bremen** *Fr.* Brême. Bremen, NW Germany 53.05N 8.48E
25 R3 **Bremen** Georgia, SE USA 33.43N 85.09W
33 O11 **Bremen** Indiana, N USA 41.24N 86.07W
102 H10 **Bremen** *off.* Freie Hansestadt Bremen, *Fr.* Brême. ◈ *state* N Germany
102 G9 **Bremerhaven** Bremen, NW Germany 53.33N 8.34E
Bremersdorp *see* Manzini
34 G8 **Bremerton** Washington, NW USA 47.34N 122.37W
102 H10 **Bremervörde** Niedersachsen, NW Germany 53.29N 9.06E
27 U9 **Bremond** Texas, SW USA 31.10N 96.40W
27 U10 **Brenham** Texas, SW USA 30.10N 96.24W
110 M8 **Brenner** Tirol, W Austria 47.10N 11.51E
Brenner, Col du/Brennero, Passo del *see* Brenner Pass
110 M8 **Brenner Pass** *var.* Brenner Sattel, *Fr.* Col du Brenner, *Ger.* Brennerpass, *It.* Passo del Brennero. *pass* Austria/Italy 47.00N 11.29E
Brenner Sattel *see* Brenner Pass
110 G10 **Brenno** ≈ SW Switzerland
108 F7 **Breno** Lombardia, N Italy 45.58N 10.18E
25 O5 **Brent** Alabama, S USA 32.54N 87.10W
108 H7 **Brenta** ≈ NE Italy
99 P21 **Brentwood** E England, UK 51.38N 0.21E
20 L14 **Brentwood** Long Island, New York, NE USA 40.46N 73.12W
108 F7 **Brescia** *anc.* Brixia. Lombardia, N Italy 45.33N 10.13E
101 D15 **Breskens** Zeeland, SW Netherlands 51.24N 3.33E
Breslau *see* Dolnośląskie
108 H5 **Bressanone** *Ger.* Brixen. Trentino-Alto Adige, N Italy 46.43N 11.41E
98 M2 **Bressay** *island* NE Scotland, UK
104 K9 **Bressuire** Deux-Sèvres, W France 46.50N 0.29W
121 F20 **Brest** *Pol.* Brześć nad Bugiem, *Rus.* Brest-Litovsk; *prev.* Brześć Litewski. Brestskaya Voblasts', SW Belarus 52.06N 23.42E
104 F5 **Brest** Finistère, NW France 48.24N 4.30W
Brest-Litovsk *see* Brest
114 A10 **Brestova** Istra, NW Croatia 45.09N 14.13E
Brestskaya Oblast' *see* Brestskaya Voblasts'
121 G19 **Brestskaya Voblasts'** *prev. Rus.* Brestskaya Oblast'. ◈ *province* SW Belarus
104 G6 **Bretagne** *Eng.* Brittany; *Lat.* Britannia Minor. ◈ *region* NW France
118 G12 **Bretea-Română** *Hung.* Oláhbrettye; *prev.* Bretea-Romînă. Hunedoara, W Romania 45.39N 23.00E
Bretea-Romînă *see* Bretea-Română
105 O3 **Breteuil** Oise, N France 49.37N 2.18E
104 I10 **Breton, Pertuis** *inlet* W France
24 L10 **Breton Sound** *sound* Louisiana, S USA
192 K2 **Brett, Cape** *headland* North Island, NZ 35.11S 174.21E
103 G21 **Bretten** Baden-Württemberg, SW Germany 49.01N 8.42E
101 K15 **Breugel** Noord-Brabant, S Netherlands 51.30N 5.30E
108 B6 **Breuil-Cervinia** *It.* Cervinia. Valle d'Aosta, NW Italy 45.57N 7.37E
100 I11 **Breukelen** Utrecht, C Netherlands 52.11N 5.01E
23 P10 **Brevard** North Carolina, SE USA 35.13N 82.43W
40 L9 **Brevig Mission** Alaska, USA 65.19N 166.29W
97 G16 **Brevik** Telemark, S Norway 59.03N 9.40E
191 P5 **Brewarrina** New South Wales, SE Australia 30.01S 146.50E
21 R6 **Brewer** Maine, NE USA 44.46N 68.44W
31 T11 **Brewster** Minnesota, N USA 43.43N 95.28W
31 N14 **Brewster** Nebraska, C USA 41.54N 99.52W
33 U12 **Brewster** Ohio, N USA 40.42N 81.36W
191 O8 **Brewster, Lake** ◎ New South Wales, SE Australia
25 P7 **Brewton** Alabama, S USA 31.06N 87.04W
Brezhnev *see* Naberezhnyye Chelny
111 W12 **Brežice** *Ger.* Rann. E Slovenia 45.54N 15.35E
116 G9 **Breznik** Pernik, W Bulgaria 42.45N 22.54E
113 K19 **Brezno** *Ger.* Bries, Briesen, *Hung.* Breznóbánya; *prev.* Brezno nad Hronom. Banskobystrický Kraj, C Slovakia 48.49N 19.40E
Breznóbánya/Brezno nad Hronom *see* Brezno
118 I12 **Brezoi** Vâlcea, SW Romania 45.18N 24.15E
116 J10 **Brezovo** *prev.* Abrashlare. Plovdiv, C Bulgaria 42.19N 25.05E
81 K14 **Bria** Haute-Kotto, C Central African Republic 6.30N 22.00E
105 U13 **Briançon** *anc.* Brigantio. Hautes-Alpes, SE France 44.55N 6.37E
38 K7 **Brian Head** ▲ Utah, W USA 37.40N 112.49W
105 O7 **Briare** Loiret, C France 47.35N 2.46E
191 V2 **Bribie Island** *island* Queensland, E Australia
45 O14 **Bribrí** Limón, E Costa Rica 9.37N 82.51W
118 L8 **Briceni** *var.* Brinceni, *Rus.* Brichany. N Moldova 48.21N 27.02E
Bricgstow *see* Bristol
Brichany *see* Briceni
101 M24 **Bridel** Luxembourg, C Luxembourg 49.40N 6.03E
99 J22 **Bridgend** S Wales, UK 51.30N 3.37W
12 I14 **Bridgenorth** Ontario, SE Canada 44.21N 78.22W
25 Q1 **Bridgeport** Alabama, S USA 34.57N 85.42W
37 R8 **Bridgeport** California, W USA 38.14N 119.13W
20 L13 **Bridgeport** Connecticut, NE USA 41.10N 73.12W
33 N15 **Bridgeport** Illinois, N USA 38.42N 87.45W
30 J14 **Bridgeport** Nebraska, C USA 41.37N 103.07W
27 S6 **Bridgeport** Texas, SW USA 33.12N 97.45W
23 S3 **Bridgeport** West Virginia, NE USA 39.17N 80.15W
27 S5 **Bridgeport, Lake** ▣ Texas, SW USA
35 U11 **Bridger** Montana, NW USA 45.16N 108.55W
20 I17 **Bridgeton** New Jersey, NE USA 39.24N 75.10W
188 J14 **Bridgetown** Western Australia 34.01S 116.07E
47 Y14 **Bridgetown** ● (Barbados) SW Barbados 13.05N 59.36W
191 P17 **Bridgewater** Tasmania, SE Australia 42.47S 147.15E
11 P16 **Bridgewater** Nova Scotia, SE Canada 44.19N 64.30W
21 P12 **Bridgewater** Massachusetts, NE USA 41.59N 70.58W
31 Q11 **Bridgewater** South Dakota, N USA 43.33N 97.30W
23 U5 **Bridgewater** Virginia, NE USA 38.22N 78.58W
21 P8 **Bridgton** Maine, NE USA 44.04N 70.43W
99 K23 **Bridgwater** SW England, UK 51.08N 3.00W
99 K22 **Bridgwater Bay** *bay* SW England, UK
99 O16 **Bridlington** E England, UK 54.04N 0.12W
99 O16 **Bridlington Bay** *bay* E England, UK
191 P15 **Bridport** Tasmania, SE Australia 41.03S 147.26E
99 K24 **Bridport** S England, UK 50.43N 2.43W
105 O5 **Brie** *cultural region* N France
Brieg *see* Brzeg
Briel *see* Brielle
100 G12 **Brielle** *var.* Briel, Bril, *Eng.* The Brill. Zuid-Holland, SW Netherlands 51.54N 4.10E
110 E9 **Brienz** Bern, C Switzerland 46.45N 8.00E
110 E9 **Brienzer See** ◎ SW Switzerland
Bries/Briesen *see* Brezno
Brietzig *see* Brzesko
105 S4 **Briey** Meurthe-et-Moselle, NE France 49.15N 5.57E
110 E10 **Brig** *Fr.* Brigue, *It.* Briga. Valais, SW Switzerland 46.19N 8.00E
Briga *see* Brig
103 G24 **Brigach** ≈ S Germany
20 K17 **Brigantine** New Jersey, NE USA 39.23N 74.21W
Brigantio *see* Briançon
Brigantium *see* Bregenz
Brigels *see* Breil
27 S9 **Briggs** Texas, SW USA 30.52N 97.55W
38 L1 **Brigham City** Utah, W USA 41.30N 112.00W
12 J15 **Brighton** Ontario, SE Canada 44.01N 77.44W
99 O23 **Brighton** SE England, UK 50.49N 0.10W
39 T4 **Brighton** Colorado, C USA 39.58N 104.46W
32 K15 **Brighton** Illinois, N USA 39.01N 90.09W
105 T16 **Brignoles** Var, W France 43.25N 6.03E
Brigue *see* Brig
107 O7 **Brihuega** Castilla-La Mancha, C Spain 40.45N 2.52W
114 A10 **Brijuni** *It.* Brioni. *island group* NW Croatia
78 G12 **Brikama** W Gambia 13.13N 16.37W
Bril *see* Brielle
Brill, The *see* Brielle
103 G15 **Brilon** Nordrhein-Westfalen, W Germany 51.24N 8.34E
Brinceni *see* Briceni
109 Q18 **Brindisi** *anc.* Brundisium, Brundusium. Puglia, SE Italy 40.39N 17.55E
29 W11 **Brinkley** Arkansas, C USA 34.53N 91.11W
Brioni *see* Brijuni
105 P12 **Brioude** *anc.* Brivas. Haute-Loire, C France 45.18N 3.22E
Briovera *see* St-Lô
191 U2 **Brisbane** *state capital* Queensland, E Australia 27.30S 153.00E
191 V2 **Brisbane** ✕ Queensland, E Australia 27.30S 153.00E
27 P2 **Briscoe** Texas, SW USA 35.34N 100.17W
108 H10 **Brisighella** Emilia-Romagna, C Italy 44.12N 11.45E
110 G11 **Brissago** Ticino, S Switzerland 46.07N 8.40E
99 K22 **Bristol** *anc.* Bricgstow. SW England, UK 51.27N 2.34W
20 M12 **Bristol** Connecticut, NE USA 41.40N 72.56W
25 R9 **Bristol** Florida, SE USA 30.25N 84.58W
21 N9 **Bristol** New Hampshire, NE USA 43.34N 71.42W
31 Q8 **Bristol** South Dakota, N USA 45.18N 97.45W
23 P8 **Bristol** Tennessee, S USA 36.36N 82.11W
20 M8 **Bristol** Vermont, NE USA 44.07N 73.00W
41 N14 **Bristol Bay** *bay* Alaska, USA
99 I22 **Bristol Channel** *inlet* England/Wales, UK
37 W14 **Bristol Lake** ◎ California, W USA
29 P10 **Bristow** Oklahoma, C USA 35.49N 96.23W
88 C10 **Britain** *var.* Great Britain. *island* UK
Britannia Minor *see* Bretagne
8 L12 **British Columbia** *Fr.* Colombie-Britannique. ◈ *province* SW Canada
British Guiana *see* Guyana
British Honduras *see* Belize
181 Q7 **British Indian Ocean Territory** ◇ *UK dependent territory* C Indian Ocean
88 B9 **British Isles** *island group* NW Europe
8 I1 **British Mountains** ▲▲ Yukon Territory, NW Canada
British North Borneo *see* Sabah
British Solomon Islands Protectorate *see* Solomon Islands
47 S8 **British Virgin Islands** *var.* Virgin Islands. ◇ *UK dependent territory* E West Indies
85 J21 **Brits** North-West, N South Africa 25.39S 27.46E
85 H24 **Britstown** Northern Cape, W South Africa 30.36S 23.30E
12 F12 **Britt** Ontario, S Canada 45.46N 80.34W
31 V12 **Britt** Iowa, C USA 43.06N 93.48W
Brittany *see* Bretagne
31 Q7 **Britton** South Dakota, N USA 45.47N 97.45W
Briva Curretia *see* Brive-la-Gaillarde
Briva Isarae *see* Pontoise
Brivas *see* Brioude
Brive *see* Brive-la-Gaillarde
104 M12 **Brive-la-Gaillarde** *prev.* Brive, *anc.* Briva Curretia. Corrèze, C France 45.09N 1.31E
107 O4 **Briviesca** Castilla-León, N Spain 42.33N 3.19W
Brixen *see* Bressanone
Brixia *see* Brescia
151 S15 **Brlik** *prev.* Novotroickoje, Novotroitskoye. Zhambyl, SE Kazakhstan 43.39N 73.45E
113 G19 **Brněnský Kraj** ◈ *region* SE Czech republic
113 G18 **Brno** *Ger.* Brünn. Brněnský Kraj, SE Czech Republic 49.10N 16.35E
98 G7 **Broad Bay** *bay* NW Scotland, UK
27 X8 **Broaddus** Texas, SW USA 31.18N 94.16W
191 O12 **Broadford** Victoria, SE Australia 37.07S 145.04E
98 G9 **Broadford** N Scotland, UK 57.14N 5.54W
98 J13 **Broad Law** ▲ S Scotland, UK 55.30N 3.22W
25 U3 **Broad River** ≈ Georgia, SE USA
23 N8 **Broad River** ≈ North Carolina/South Carolina, SE USA
189 Y8 **Broadsound Range** ▲▲ Queensland, E Australia
35 X11 **Broadus** Montana, NW USA 45.28N 105.22W
23 U4 **Broadway** Virginia, NE USA 38.36N 78.48W
120 E9 **Brocēni** Saldus, SW Latvia 56.41N 22.31E
9 U11 **Brochet** Manitoba, C Canada 57.55N 101.40W
9 U10 **Brochet, Lac** ◎ Manitoba, C Canada
13 S5 **Brochet, Lac au** ◎ Quebec, SE Canada
103 K14 **Brocken** ▲ C Germany 51.48N 10.38E
21 O12 **Brockton** Massachusetts, NE USA 42.04N 71.01W
12 L14 **Brockville** Ontario, SE Canada 44.36N 75.42W
20 D13 **Brockway** Pennsylvania, NE USA 41.14N 78.45W
Brod/Bród *see* Slavonski Brod
15 Kk1 **Brodeur Peninsula** *peninsula* Baffin Island, Nunavut, NE Canada
98 H13 **Brodick** W Scotland, UK 55.34N 5.09W
Brod na Savi *see* Slavonski Brod
112 K9 **Brodnica** *Ger.* Buddenbrock. Kujawski-pomorskie, C Poland 53.15N 19.22E
114 G10 **Brod-Posavina** *off.* Brodsko-Posavska Županija. ◈ *province* NE Croatia
118 J5 **Brody** L'vivs'ka Oblast', NW Ukraine 50.04N 25.07E
97 G22 **Brædstrup** Vejle, C Denmark 55.58N 9.37E
100 I10 **Broek-in-Waterland** Noord-Holland, C Netherlands 52.27N 4.58E
34 L13 **Brogan** Oregon, NW USA 44.15N 117.34W
112 N10 **Brok** Mazowieckie, C Poland 52.42N 21.53E
29 P9 **Broken Arrow** Oklahoma, C USA 36.03N 95.47W
191 T9 **Broken Bay** *bay* New South Wales, SE Australia
31 N15 **Broken Bow** Nebraska, C USA 41.24N 99.38W
29 R13 **Broken Bow** Oklahoma, C USA 34.01N 94.44W
29 R12 **Broken Bow Lake** ▣ Oklahoma, C USA
190 L6 **Broken Hill** New South Wales, SE Australia 31.58S 141.27E
181 S10 **Broken Ridge** *undersea feature* S Indian Ocean
194 H10 **Broken Water Bay** *bay* W Bismarck Sea
57 W10 **Brokopondo** Brokopondo, NE Surinam 05.04N 55.00W
57 W10 **Brokopondo** ◈ *district* C Surinam
Bromberg *see* Bydgoszcz
97 L22 **Bromölla** Skåne, S Sweden 56.04N 14.28E
99 L20 **Bromsgrove** W England, UK 52.19N 2.03W
97 G20 **Brønderslev** Nordjylland, N Denmark 57.16N 9.58E
108 D8 **Broni** Lombardia, N Italy 45.04N 9.18E
8 K11 **Bronlund Peak** ▲ British Columbia, W Canada 57.27N 126.43W
95 F14 **Brønnøysund** Nordland, C Norway 65.28N 12.13E
25 V10 **Bronson** Florida, SE USA 29.25N 82.38W
33 Q11 **Bronson** Michigan, N USA 41.52N 85.11W
27 X8 **Bronson** Texas, SW USA 31.20N 94.00W
109 L24 **Bronte** Sicilia, Italy, C Mediterranean Sea 37.46N 14.49E
27 P8 **Bronte** Texas, SW USA 31.53N 100.17W
27 Y9 **Brookeland** Texas, SW USA 31.05N 93.57W
179 O15 **Brooke's Point** Palawan, W Philippines 8.54N 117.54E
29 T3 **Brookfield** Missouri, C USA 39.46N 93.04W
24 K7 **Brookhaven** Mississippi, S USA 31.34N 90.26W
34 E16 **Brookings** Oregon, NW USA 42.03N 124.16W
31 R10 **Brookings** South Dakota, N USA 44.15N 96.46W
31 W14 **Brooklyn** Iowa, C USA 41.43N 92.27W
31 U8 **Brooklyn Park** Minnesota, N USA 45.06N 93.18W
23 U7 **Brookneal** Virginia, NE USA 37.03N 78.56W
9 R16 **Brooks** Alberta, SW Canada 50.34N 111.54W
27 V11 **Brookshire** Texas, SW USA 29.47N 95.57W
40 L8 **Brooks Mountain** ▲ Alaska, USA 65.31N 167.24W
40 M11 **Brooks Range** ▲▲ Alaska, USA
33 O12 **Brookston** Indiana, N USA 40.34N 86.53W
25 V11 **Brooksville** Florida, SE USA 28.33N 82.23W
25 N4 **Brooksville** Mississippi, S USA 33.13N 88.34W
188 J13 **Brookton** Western Australia 32.24S 117.04E
33 Q14 **Brookville** Indiana, N USA 39.25N 85.00W
20 D13 **Brookville** Pennsylvania, NE USA 41.07N 79.05W
33 Q14 **Brookville Lake** ▣ Indiana, N USA
188 K5 **Broome** Western Australia 17.58S 122.15E
39 S4 **Broomfield** Colorado, C USA 39.55N 105.05W
Broos *see* Orăştie
98 J7 **Brora** N Scotland, UK 57.58N 4.00W
98 I7 **Brora** ≈ N Scotland, UK
97 F23 **Brørup** Ribe, W Denmark 55.28N 9.01E
97 L23 **Brösarp** Skåne, S Sweden 55.43N 14.10E
118 J9 **Broşteni** Suceava, NE Romania 47.13N 25.43E
104 M6 **Brou** Eure-et-Loir, C France 48.12N 1.10E
Broucsella *see* Brussel/Bruxelles
Broughton Bay *see* Tongjosŏn-man
16 O1 **Broughton Island** Nunavut, NE Canada 67.34N 63.55W
144 G7 **Broummâna** C Lebanon 33.53N 35.39E
24 I9 **Broussard** Louisiana, S USA 30.09N 91.57W
100 E13 **Brouwersdam** *dam* SW Netherlands 51.46N 3.51E
100 E13 **Brouwershaven** Zeeland, SW Netherlands 51.44N 3.50E
119 P4 **Brovary** Kyyivs'ka Oblast', N Ukraine 50.30N 30.43E
97 G20 **Brovst** Nordjylland, N Denmark 57.06N 9.31E
33 S8 **Brown City** Michigan, N USA 43.12N 82.50W
26 M6 **Brownfield** Texas, SW USA 33.10N 102.16W
35 Q7 **Browning** Montana, NW USA 48.33N 113.00W
35 R6 **Brown, Mount** ▲ Montana, NW USA 48.52N 111.08W
194 K15 **Brown River** ≈ S PNG
(0) M9 **Browns Bank** *undersea feature* NW Atlantic Ocean
33 O14 **Brownsburg** Indiana, N USA 39.50N 86.24W
20 J16 **Browns Mills** New Jersey, NE USA 39.58N 74.33W
46 J12 **Browns Town** C Jamaica 18.28N 77.22W
33 P15 **Brownstown** Indiana, N USA 38.52N 86.02W
31 R8 **Browns Valley** Minnesota, N USA 45.36N 96.49W
22 K7 **Brownsville** Kentucky, S USA 37.09N 86.13W
22 F9 **Brownsville** Tennessee, S USA 35.34N 89.15W
27 T17 **Brownsville** Texas, SW USA 25.55N 97.28W
57 W10 **Brownsweg** Brokopondo, C Surinam
31 U9 **Brownton** Minnesota, N USA 44.43N 94.21W
21 R5 **Brownville Junction** Maine, NE USA 45.20N 69.04W
27 R8 **Brownwood** Texas, SW USA 31.41N 98.59W
27 R8 **Brownwood Lake** ▣ Texas, SW USA
106 I9 **Brozas** Extremadura, W Spain 39.37N 6.48W
121 M18 **Brozha** Mahilyowskaya Voblasts', E Belarus 52.57N 29.07E
105 O2 **Bruay-en-Artois** Pas-de-Calais, N France 50.31N 2.30E
105 P2 **Bruay-sur-l'Escaut** Nord, N France 50.24N 3.33E
12 F13 **Bruce Peninsula** *peninsula* Ontario, S Canada
22 H9 **Bruceton** Tennessee, S USA 36.02N 88.14W
27 T9 **Bruceville** Texas, SW USA 31.17N 97.15W
103 G21 **Bruchsal** Baden-Württemberg, SW Germany 49.07N 8.34E
111 Q7 **Bruck** Salzburg, NW Austria 47.18N 12.51E
Bruck *see* Bruck an der Mur
111 Y4 **Bruck an der Leitha** Niederösterreich, NE Austria 48.02N 16.47E
111 V7 **Bruck an der Mur** *var.* Bruck. Steiermark, C Austria 47.26N 15.13E
103 M24 **Bruckmühl** Bayern, SE Germany 47.52N 11.54E
173 Dd3 **Brueuh, Pulau** *island* NW Indonesia
Bruges *see* Brugge
110 F6 **Brugg** Aargau, NW Switzerland 47.28N 8.13E
101 C16 **Brugge** *Fr.* Bruges. West-Vlaanderen, NW Belgium 51.13N 3.13E
111 R9 **Bruggen** Kärnten, S Austria 46.46N 13.13E
103 E16 **Brühl** Nordrhein-Westfalen, W Germany 50.49N 6.54E
101 F14 **Bruinisse** Zeeland, SW Netherlands 51.40N 4.04E
174 L5 **Bruit, Pulau** *island* East Malaysia
12 K10 **Brûlé, Lac** ◎ Quebec, SE Canada
32 M4 **Brule River** ≈ Michigan/Wisconsin, N USA
101 H23 **Brûly** Namur, S Belgium 49.55N 4.31E
61 N17 **Brumado** Bahia, E Brazil 14.13S 41.37W
100 M11 **Brummen** Gelderland, E Netherlands 52.04N 6.10E
96 H13 **Brumunddal** Hedmark, S Norway 60.52N 10.55E
25 Q6 **Brundidge** Alabama, S USA 31.43N 85.49W
Brundisium/Brundusium *see* Brindisi
35 N15 **Bruneau River** ≈ Idaho, NW USA
Bruneck *see* Brunico
174 Mm4 **Brunei** *off.* Sultanate of Brunei, *Mal.* Negara Brunei Darussalam. ◆ *monarchy* SE Asia
175 N3 **Brunei Bay** *var.* Teluk Brunei. *bay* N Brunei
Brunei, Teluk *see* Brunei Bay
Brunei Town *see* Bandar Seri Begawan
108 H5 **Brunico** *Ger.* Bruneck. Trentino-Alto Adige, N Italy 46.49N 11.57E
Brünn *see* Brno
193 G17 **Brunner, Lake** ◎ South Island, NZ
101 M18 **Brunssum** Limburg, SE Netherlands 50.57N 5.58E
25 W7 **Brunswick** Georgia, SE USA 31.09N 81.30W
21 Q8 **Brunswick** Maine, NE USA 43.54N 69.58W
23 V3 **Brunswick** Maryland, NE USA 39.18N 77.37W
29 T3 **Brunswick** Missouri, C USA 39.25N 93.07W
33 T11 **Brunswick** Ohio, N USA 41.14N 81.50W
Brunswick *see* Braunschweig
65 H24 **Brunswick, Península** *headland* S Chile 53.30S 71.27W
113 H17 **Bruntál** *Ger.* Freudenthal. Ostravský Kraj, E Czech Republic 50.00N 17.27E
205 N3 **Brunt Ice Shelf** *ice shelf* Antarctica
Brusa *see* Bursa
39 U3 **Brush** Colorado, C USA 40.15N 103.37W
44 M5 **Brus Laguna** Gracias a Dios, E Honduras 15.46N 84.31W
62 K13 **Brusque** Santa Catarina, S Brazil 27.07S 48.54W
Brussa *see* Bursa
101 E18 **Brussel** *var.* Brussels, *Fr.* Bruxelles, *Ger.* Brüssel; *anc.* Broucsella. ● (Belgium) Brussels, C Belgium *see also* Bruxelles 50.52N 4.21E
Brüssel/Brussels *see* Brussel/Bruxelles
119 O5 **Brusyliv** Zhytomyrs'ka Oblast', N Ukraine 50.16N 29.31E
191 Q12 **Bruthen** Victoria, SE Australia 37.43S 147.49E
Bruttium *see* Calabria
Brüx *see* Most
101 E18 **Bruxelles** *var.* Brussels, *Dut.* Brussel, *Ger.* Brüssel; *anc.* Broucsella. ● (Belgium) Brussels, C Belgium *see also* Brussel 50.52N 4.21E
56 J7 **Bruzual** Apure, W Venezuela 7.59N 69.18W
33 Q11 **Bryan** Ohio, N USA 41.28N 84.33W
27 U10 **Bryan** Texas, SW USA 30.40N 96.22W
204 J4 **Bryan Coast** *physical region* Antarctica
126 I13 **Bryanka** Krasnoyarskiy Kray, C Russian Federation 59.01N 93.13E
119 Y7 **Bryanka** Luhans'ka Oblast', E Ukraine 48.30N 38.45E
190 J8 **Bryan, Mount** ▲ South Australia 33.25S 138.59E
130 I6 **Bryansk** Bryanskaya Oblast', W Russian Federation 53.15N 34.06E
130 H6 **Bryanskaya Oblast'** ◈ *province* W Russian Federation
204 J5 **Bryant, Cape** *headland* Antarctica
29 U8 **Bryant Creek** ≈ Missouri, C USA
38 K8 **Bryce Canyon** *canyon* Utah, W USA
121 O15 **Bryli** *Rus.* Bryli. Mahilyowskaya Voblasts', E Belarus 53.55N 30.31E
97 C17 **Bryne** Rogaland, S Norway 58.43N 5.37E
27 R6 **Bryson** Texas, SW USA 33.09N 98.23W
23 N10 **Bryson City** North Carolina, SE USA 35.33N 83.39W
12 K11 **Bryson, Lac** ◎ Quebec, SE Canada
130 K13 **Bryukhovetskaya** Krasnodarskiy Kray, SW Russian Federation 45.49N 38.01E
113 H15 **Brzeg** *Ger.* Brieg; *anc.* Civitas Altae Ripae. Opolskie, S Poland 50.52N 17.27E
113 G14 **Brzeg Dolny** *Ger.* Dyhernfurth. Dolnośląskie, SW Poland 51.15N 16.42E
Brześć Litewski/Brześć nad Bugiem *see* Brest
113 L17 **Brzesko** *Ger.* Brietzig. Małopolskie, S Poland 49.57N 20.35E
Brzeżany *see* Berezhany
112 K12 **Brzeziny** Łódzkie, C Poland 51.48N 19.42E
Brzostowica Wielka *see* Vyalikaya Byerastavitsa
113 O17 **Brzozów** Podkarpackie, SE Poland 49.38N 22.00E
Bsharrī/Bsherri *see* Bcharré
197 I13 **Bua** Vanua Levu, N Fiji 16.48S 178.36E
97 J20 **Bua** Halland, S Sweden 57.13N 12.07E
84 M13 **Bua** ≈ C Malawi
Bua *see* Čiovo
83 L18 **Bu'aale** *It.* Buale. Jubbada Dhexe, SW Somalia 0.52N 42.37E
201 Q8 **Buada Lagoon** *lagoon* Nauru, C Pacific Ocean
195 W14 **Buala** Santa Isabel, E Solomon Islands 8.06S 159.31E
Buale *see* Bu'aale
202 H1 **Buariki** *atoll* Tungaru, W Kiribati
178 I10 **Bua Yai** *var.* Ban Bua Yai. Nakhon Ratchasima, E Thailand 15.34N 102.25E
77 P8 **Bu'ayrāt al Ḩasūn** *var.* Buwayrāt al Hasūn. C Libya 31.22N 15.41E
78 H13 **Buba** S Guinea-Bissau 11.36N 14.55W
175 Qq7 **Bubaa** Sulawesi, N Indonesia 0.32N 122.27E
83 D20 **Bubanza** NW Burundi 3.04S 29.22E
85 K18 **Bubi** *prev.* Bubye. ≈ S Zimbabwe
148 L11 **Būbīyan, Jazīrat** *island* E Kuwait
Bublitz *see* Bobolice
Bubye *see* Bubi
197 J13 **Buca** *prev.* Mbutha. Vanua Levu, N Fiji 16.39S 179.51E
142 F16 **Bucak** Burdur, SW Turkey 37.26N 30.32E
56 G8 **Bucaramanga** Santander, N Colombia 7.07N 73.10W
109 M18 **Buccino** Campania, S Italy 40.37N 15.25E
118 K9 **Bucecea** Botoşani, NE Romania 47.43N 26.24E
118 J6 **Buchach** *Pol.* Buczacz. Ternopil's'ka Oblast', W Ukraine 49.04N 25.22E
191 Q12 **Buchan** Victoria, SE Australia 37.26S 148.11E
78 J17 **Buchanan** *prev.* Grand Bassa. SW Liberia 5.52N 10.03W
25 R3 **Buchanan** Georgia, SE USA 33.48N 85.11W
33 O11 **Buchanan** Michigan, N USA 41.49N 86.21W
23 T6 **Buchanan** Virginia, NE USA 37.31N 79.40W
27 R10 **Buchanan Dam** Texas, SW USA 30.42N 98.24W
27 R10 **Buchanan, Lake** ▣ Texas, SW USA
98 L8 **Buchan Ness** *headland* NE Scotland, UK 57.28N 1.46W
11 T12 **Buchans** Newfoundland, SE Canada 48.49N 56.44W
Bucharest *see* Bucureşti
103 H20 **Buchen** Baden-Württemberg, SW Germany 49.31N 9.18E
102 I10 **Buchholz in der Nordheide** Niedersachsen, NW Germany 53.19N 9.52E
110 F7 **Buchs** Aargau, N Switzerland 47.24N 8.03E
110 I8 **Buchs** Sankt Gallen, NE Switzerland 47.10N 9.26E
102 H13 **Bückeburg** Niedersachsen, NW Germany 52.16N 9.03E
38 K14 **Buckeye** Arizona, SW USA 33.22N 112.34W
Buckeye State *see* Ohio
23 S4 **Buckhannon** West Virginia, NE USA 38.59N 80.13W
27 T9 **Buckholts** Texas, SW USA 30.52N 97.07W
98 K8 **Buckie** NE Scotland, UK 57.39N 2.55W
12 M12 **Buckingham** Quebec, SE Canada 45.34N 75.25W
23 U6 **Buckingham** Virginia, NE USA 37.33N 78.33W
99 N21 **Buckinghamshire** *cultural region* SE England, UK
41 N8 **Buckland** Alaska, USA 65.58N 161.07W
190 G7 **Buckleboo** South Australia 32.55S 136.11E
28 K7 **Bucklin** Kansas, C USA 37.33N 99.37W
29 T3 **Bucklin** Missouri, C USA 39.46N 92.53W
38 I12 **Buckskin Mountains** ▲▲ Arizona, SW USA
21 R7 **Bucksport** Maine, NE USA 44.34N 68.46W
84 A9 **Buco Zau** Cabinda, NW Angola 4.47S 12.32E
Bu Craa *see* Bou Craa
118 K14 **Bucureşti** *Eng.* Bucharest, *Ger.* Bukarest; *prev.* Altenburg, *anc.* Cetatea Damboviţei. ● (Romania) Bucureşti, S Romania 44.27N 26.06E
33 S12 **Bucyrus** Ohio, N USA 40.48N 82.58W
Buczacz *see* Buchach
96 E9 **Bud** Møre og Romsdal, S Norway 62.55N 6.55E
27 S11 **Buda** Texas, SW USA 30.05N 97.50W
121 O18 **Buda-Kashalyova** *Rus.* Buda-Koshelëvo. Homyel'skaya Voblasts', SE Belarus 52.43N 30.34E
Buda-Koshelëvo *see* Buda-Kashalyova
177 G4 **Budalin** Sagaing, C Burma 22.24N 95.07E
113 J22 **Budapest** *off.* Budapest Főváros, *SCr.* Budimpešta. ● (Hungary) Pest, N Hungary 47.30N 19.03E
158 K11 **Budaun** Uttar Pradesh, N India 28.01N 79.07E
147 O9 **Budayyi'ah** *oasis* C Saudi Arabia 23.04N 43.29E
205 Y12 **Budd Coast** *physical region* Antarctica
Buddenbrock *see* Brodnica
109 C17 **Budduso** Sardegna, Italy, C Mediterranean Sea 40.37N 9.19E
99 I23 **Bude** SW England, UK 50.49N 4.33W
24 J7 **Bude** Mississippi, S USA 31.27N 90.51W
113 C18 **Budějovický Kraj** ◈ *region* S Czech Republic
101 K16 **Budel** Noord-Brabant, SE Netherlands 51.16N 5.34E
102 I8 **Büdelsdorf** Schleswig-Holstein, N Germany 54.20N 9.40E
131 O14 **Budënnovsk** Stavropol'skiy Kray, SW Russian Federation 44.46N 44.07E
118 K14 **Budeşti** Călăraşi, SE Romania 44.13N 26.31E
Budgewoi *see* Budgewoi Lake
191 T8 **Budgewoi Lake** *var.* Budgewoi. New South Wales, SE Australia 33.13S 151.34E
94 I2 **Búdhardalur** Vesturland, W Iceland 65.07N 21.45W
Budimpešta *see* Budapest
81 J16 **Budjala** Equateur, NW Dem. Rep. Congo (Zaire) 2.39N 19.42E
108 G10 **Budrio** Emilia-Romagna, C Italy 44.33N 11.34E

◆ Country
● Country Capital
◇ Dependent Territory
○ Dependent Territory Capital
◈ Administrative Region
✕ International Airport
▲ Mountain
▲▲ Mountain Range
Volcano
≈ River
◎ Lake
▣ Reservoir

BUDSLAV – BYTOM

Budslav *see* Budslaw
121 K14 **Budslaw** *Rus.* Budslav. Minskaya Voblasts', N Belarus 54.46N 27.26E
Budua *see* Budva
174 Ll5 **Budu, Tanjung** *headland* East Malaysia 2.51N 111.42E
115 J17 **Budva** *It.* Budua. Montenegro, SW Yugoslavia 42.17N 18.49E
Budweis *see* České Budějovice
Budyšin *see* Bautzen
81 D16 **Buea** Sud-Ouest, SW Cameroon 4.09N 9.13E
105 S13 **Buëch** ≈ SE France
20 J17 **Buena** New Jersey, NE USA 39.30N 74.55W
64 K12 **Buena Esperanza** San Luis, C Argentina 34.45S 65.15W
56 C11 **Buenaventura** Valle del Cauca, W Colombia 3.54N 77.01W
42 I4 **Buenaventura** Chihuahua, N Mexico 29.52N 107.25W
59 M18 **Buena Vista** Santa Cruz, C Bolivia 17.27S 63.40W
42 G10 **Buenavista** Baja California Sur, W Mexico 23.39N 109.40W
39 S5 **Buena Vista** Colorado, C USA 38.50N 106.07W
25 S5 **Buena Vista** Georgia, SE USA 32.19N 84.31W
23 T6 **Buena Vista** Virginia, NE USA 37.43N 79.21W
46 F5 **Buena Vista, Bahia de** *bay* N Cuba
37 R13 **Buena Vista Lake Bed** ◎ California, W USA
107 P8 **Buendía, Embalse de** ▣ C Spain
65 F16 **Bueno, Río** ≈ S Chile
64 N12 **Buenos Aires** *hist.* Santa Maria del Buen Aire. ● (Argentina) Buenos Aires, E Argentina 34.40S 58.30W
45 O15 **Buenos Aires** Puntarenas, SE Costa Rica 9.09N 83.15W
63 C20 **Buenos Aires** *off.* Provincia de Buenos Aires. ◐ *province* E Argentina
65 H19 **Buenos Aires, Lago** *var.* Lago General Carrera. ◎ Argentina/Chile
56 C13 **Buesaco** Nariño, SW Colombia 1.22N 77.07W
31 U8 **Buffalo** Minnesota, N USA 45.10N 93.49W
28 T6 **Buffalo** Missouri, C USA 37.38N 93.05W
20 D10 **Buffalo** New York, NE USA 42.53N 78.52W
29 K8 **Buffalo** Oklahoma, C USA 36.50N 99.37W
30 J7 **Buffalo** South Dakota, N USA 45.35N 103.32W
27 V8 **Buffalo** Texas, SW USA 31.25N 96.04W
35 W12 **Buffalo** Wyoming, C USA 44.21N 106.40W
31 U11 **Buffalo Center** Iowa, C USA 43.23N 93.57W
26 M3 **Buffalo Lake** ▣ Texas, SW USA
32 K7 **Buffalo Lake** ▣ Wisconsin, N USA
9 S12 **Buffalo Narrows** Saskatchewan, C Canada 55.52N 108.28W
29 U9 **Buffalo River** ≈ Arkansas, C USA
31 R5 **Buffalo River** ≈ Minnesota, N USA
22 I10 **Buffalo River** ≈ Tennessee, S USA
32 J6 **Buffalo River** ≈ Wisconsin, N USA
46 L12 **Buff Bay** E Jamaica 18.18N 76.40W
25 T3 **Buford** Georgia, SE USA 34.07N 84.00W
30 J3 **Buford** North Dakota, N USA 48.00N 103.58W
35 Y17 **Buford** Wyoming, C USA 41.05N 105.17W
118 J14 **Buftea** București, S Romania 44.34N 25.57E
86 I9 **Bug** *Bel.* Zakhodni Buh, *Eng.* Western Bug, *Rus.* Zapadnyy Bug, *Ukr.* Zakhidnyy Buh. ≈ E Europe
56 D11 **Buga** Valle del Cauca, W Colombia 3.52N 76.16W
168 F7 **Buga** Dzavhan, W Mongolia 47.42N 94.53E
105 O17 **Bugarach, Pic du** ▲ S France 42.52N 2.23E
152 B12 **Bugdayly** Balkanskiy Velayat, W Turkmenistan 38.42N 54.14E
Buggs Island Lake *see* John H.Kerr Reservoir
Bughotu *see* Santa Isabel
175 Q12 **Bugingkalo** Sulawesi, C Indonesia 4.49S 121.42E
66 P6 **Bugio** *island* Madeira, Portugal, NE Atlantic Ocean
94 M8 **Bugøynes** Finnmark, N Norway 69.57N 29.34E
129 Q3 **Bugrino** Nenetskiy Avtonomnyy Okrug, NW Russian Federation 68.48N 49.12E
131 T5 **Bugul'ma** Respublika Tatarstan, W Russian Federation 54.31N 52.45E
Bügür *see* Luntai
131 T6 **Buguruslan** Orenburgskaya Oblast', W Russian Federation 53.37N 52.30E
165 R9 **Buh He** ≈ C China
35 O15 **Buhl** Idaho, NW USA 42.36N 114.45W
103 F22 **Bühl** Baden-Württemberg, SW Germany 48.42N 8.07E
118 K10 **Buhuși** Bacău, E Romania 46.34N 26.55E
Buie d'Istria *see* Buje
99 J20 **Builth Wells** E Wales, UK 52.07N 3.27W
195 S13 **Buin** Bougainville Island, NE PNG 6.50S 155.42E
110 J9 **Buin, Piz** ▲ Austria/Switzerland 46.51N 10.07E
131 Q4 **Buinsk** Chuvashskaya Respublika, W Russian Federation 55.09N 47.00E
131 Q4 **Buinsk** Respublika Tatarstan, W Russian Federation 54.58N 48.16E
169 R8 **Buir Nur** *Mong.* Buyr Nuur. ◎ China/Mongolia *see also* Buyr Nuur
100 M5 **Buitenpost** *Fris.* Bûtenpost. Friesland, N Netherlands 53.15N 6.09E
Buitenzorg *see* Bogor
85 F19 **Buitepos** Omaheke, E Namibia 22.17S 19.59E
107 N7 **Buitrago del Lozoya** Madrid, C Spain 41.00N 3.38W
Buj *see* Buy
106 M13 **Bujalance** Andalucía, S Spain 37.54N 4.22W
115 O17 **Bujanovac** Serbia, SE Yugoslavia 42.29N 21.43E
107 S6 **Bujaraloz** Aragón, NE Spain 41.28N 0.10W
114 A9 **Buje** *It.* Buie d'Istria. Istra, NW Croatia 45.23N 13.40E
Bujnurd *see* Bojnūrd
83 D21 **Bujumbura** *prev.* Usumbura. ● (Burundi) W Burundi 3.25S 29.23E
83 D20 **Bujumbura** ✈ W Burundi 3.21S 29.19E
126 L15 **Bukachacha** Chitinskaya Oblast', S Russian Federation 52.49N 116.39E
165 N11 **Bukadaban Feng** ▲ C China 36.09N 90.52E
195 R11 **Buka Island** *island* NE PNG
83 F18 **Bukakata** S Uganda 0.18S 31.57E
81 N24 **Bukama** Katanga, SE Dem. Rep. Congo (Zaire) 9.13S 25.52E
148 J4 **Būkān** *var.* Bowkān. Āzarbāyjān-e Bākhtarī, NW Iran 36.31N 46.14E
Bukantau, Gory *see* Bŭkantow-Toghi
152 K8 **Bŭkantow-Toghi** *Rus.* Gory Bukantau. ▲▲ N Uzbekistan
Bukarest *see* București
81 O19 **Bukavu** *prev.* Costermansville. Sud Kivu, E Dem. Rep. Congo (Zaire) 2.18S 28.49E
83 F21 **Bukene** Tabora, NW Tanzania 4.15S 32.51E
147 W8 **Bū Khābī** *var.* Bakhābī. NW Oman 23.28N 56.06E
Bukhara *see* Bukhoro
Bukharskaya Oblast' *see* Bukhoro Wiloyati
152 L11 **Bukhoro** *var.* Bokhara, *Rus.* Bukhara. Bukhoro Wiloyati, C Uzbekistan 39.50N 64.22E
152 J11 **Bukhoro Wiloyati** *Rus.* Bukharskaya Oblast'. ◐ *province* C Uzbekistan
174 I12 **Bukitkemuning** Sumatera, W Indonesia 4.43S 104.27E
173 G8 **Bukittinggi** *prev.* Fort de Kock. Sumatera, W Indonesia 0.18S 100.19E
113 L21 **Bükk** ▲▲ NE Hungary
83 F19 **Bukoba** Kagera, NW Tanzania 1.19S 31.49E
115 N20 **Bukovo** S FYR Macedonia 40.59N 21.20E
110 G6 **Bülach** Zürich, NW Switzerland 47.31N 8.30E
Būlaevo *see* Bulayevo
168 I6 **Bulag** Hövsgöl, N Mongolia 49.51N 100.41E
168 M7 **Bulag** Töv, C Mongolia 48.09N 108.33E
168 I8 **Bulagiyn Denj** Arhangay, C Mongolia 47.14N 100.56E
191 U7 **Bulahdelah** New South Wales, SE Australia 32.24S 152.13E
176 Yy15 **Bulaka, Sungai** ≈ Irian Jaya, E Indonesia
179 Qq12 **Bulan** Luzon, N Philippines 12.40N 123.55E
143 N11 **Bulancak** Giresun, N Turkey 40.57N 38.13E
158 J10 **Bulandshahr** Uttar Pradesh, N India 28.30N 77.49E
143 R14 **Bulanık** Muş, E Turkey 39.04N 42.16E
131 V7 **Bulanovo** Orenburgskaya Oblast', W Russian Federation 52.27N 55.08E
85 J17 **Bulawayo** *var.* Buluwayo. Matabeleland North, SW Zimbabwe 20.08S 28.36E
85 J17 **Bulawayo** ✈ Matabeleland North, SW Zimbabwe 20.00S 28.36E
151 Q6 **Bulayevo** *Kaz.* Būlaevo. Severnyy Kazakhstan, N Kazakhstan 54.55N 70.28E
142 D15 **Buldan** Denizli, SW Turkey 38.03N 28.49E
160 G12 **Buldāna** Mahārāshtra, C India 20.31N 76.18E
40 E16 **Buldir Island** *island* Aleutian Islands, Alaska, USA
Buldur *see* Burdur
168 H9 **Bulgan** Bayanhongor, C Mongolia 44.48N 98.39E
168 K6 **Bulgan** Bulgan, N Mongolia 50.31N 101.30E
168 F7 **Bulgan** Hovd, W Mongolia 46.57N 93.40E
168 J5 **Bulgan** Hövsgöl, N Mongolia 50.30N 101.28E
168 J10 **Bulgan** Ömnögovĭ, S Mongolia 44.07N 103.28E
168 J7 **Bulgan** ◐ *province* N Mongolia
116 H10 **Bulgaria** *off.* Republic of Bulgaria, *Bul.* Bŭlgariya; *prev.* People's Republic of Bulgaria. ◆ *republic* SE Europe
Bŭlgariya *see* Bulgaria
116 L9 **Bŭlgarka** ▲ E Bulgaria 42.43N 26.19E
175 T7 **Buli** Pulau Halmahera, E Indonesia 0.56N 128.17E
175 Tt7 **Buli, Teluk** *bay* Pulau Halmahera, E Indonesia
166 J13 **Buliu He** ≈ S China
Bullange *see* Büllingen
106 M11 **Bullaque** ≈ C Spain
107 Q13 **Bullas** Murcia, SE Spain 38.01N 1.40W
82 M12 **Bullaxaar** Woqooyi Galbeed, NW Somalia 10.28N 44.15E
110 C9 **Bulle** Fribourg, SW Switzerland 46.37N 7.04E
193 G15 **Buller** ≈ South Island, NZ
191 P12 **Buller, Mount** ▲ Victoria, SE Australia 37.10S 146.31E
38 H11 **Bullhead City** Arizona, SW USA 35.07N 114.32W
101 N21 **Büllingen** *Fr.* Bullange. Liège, E Belgium 50.23N 6.15E
Bullion State *see* Missouri
23 T14 **Bull Island** *island* South Carolina, SE USA
190 M4 **Bulloo River Overflow** *wetland* New South Wales, SE Australia
192 M12 **Bulls** Manawatu-Wanganui, North Island, NZ 40.10S 175.22E
23 T14 **Bulls Bay** *bay* South Carolina, SE USA
29 U9 **Bull Shoals Lake** ▣ Arkansas/Missouri, C USA
189 Q2 **Bulman** Northern Territory, N Australia 13.39S 134.21E
168 I6 **Bulnayn Nuruu** ▲▲ N Mongolia
194 J13 **Bulolo** Morobe, C PNG 7.11S 146.34E
175 Qq7 **Bulowa, Gunung** ▲ Sulawesi, N Indonesia 0.33N 123.39E
Bulqiza *see* Bulqizë
115 L19 **Bulqizë** *var.* Bulqiza. Dibër, C Albania 41.30N 20.16E
Bulsar *see* Valsād
175 R7 **Buludawa Keten, Pegunungan** ▲▲ Sulawesi, N Indonesia
175 Pp13 **Bulukumba** *prev.* Boeloekoemba. Sulawesi, C Indonesia 5.34S 120.13E
153 O11 **Bulunghur** *Rus.* Bulungur; *prev.* Krasnogvardeysk. Samarqand Wiloyati, C Uzbekistan 39.46N 67.18E
81 I21 **Bulungu** Bandundu, SW Dem. Rep. Congo (Zaire) 4.34S 18.33E
Bulungur *see* Bulunghur
Buluwayo *see* Bulawayo
81 K17 **Bumba** Equateur, N Dem. Rep. Congo (Zaire) 2.14N 22.25E
124 O15 **Bumbah, Khalīj al** *gulf* N Libya
168 K8 **Bumbat** Övörhangay, C Mongolia 46.30N 104.08E
83 F19 **Bumbire Island** *island* N Tanzania
175 Oo4 **Bum Bun, Pulau** *island* East Malaysia
83 J17 **Buna** North Eastern, NE Kenya 2.40N 39.34E
27 Y10 **Buna** Texas, SW USA 30.25N 94.00W
Bunab *see* Bonāb
Bunai *see* M'bunai
153 S13 **Bunay** S Tajikistan 38.29N 71.41E
188 I13 **Bunbury** Western Australia 33.24S 115.43E
99 E14 **Buncrana** *Ir.* Bun Cranncha. NW Ireland 55.07N 7.27W
Bun Cranncha *see* Buncrana
189 Z9 **Bundaberg** Queensland, E Australia 24.49S 152.16E
191 T5 **Bundarra** New South Wales, SE Australia 30.12S 151.06E
102 G13 **Bünde** Nordrhein-Westfalen, NW Germany 52.12N 8.34E
158 H13 **Būndi** Rājasthān, N India 25.28N 75.42E
194 I12 **Bundi** Madang, N PNG 5.40S 145.10E
Bun Dobhráin *see* Bundoran
99 D15 **Bundoran** *Ir.* Bun Dobhráin. NW Ireland 54.28N 8.16W
115 K18 **Bunë** *SCr.* Bojana. ≈ Albania/Yugoslavia *see also* Bojana
179 R16 **Bunga** ≈ Mindanao, S Philippines
173 Ff10 **Bungalaut, Selat** *strait* W Indonesia
178 Ii8 **Bung Kan** Nong Khai, E Thailand 18.19N 103.39E
189 N4 **Bungle Bungle Range** ▲▲ Western Australia
84 C10 **Bungo** Uíge, NW Angola 7.30S 15.24E
83 G18 **Bungoma** Western, W Kenya 0.34N 34.34E
170 Dd15 **Bungo-suidō** *strait* SW Japan
170 Dd13 **Bungo-Takada** Ōita, Kyūshū, SW Japan 33.36N 131.28E
102 K8 **Bungsberg** *hill* N Germany 54.12N 10.45E
Bungur *see* Bunyu
81 P17 **Bunia** Orientale, NE Dem. Rep. Congo (Zaire) 1.33N 30.16E
37 U6 **Bunker Hill** ▲ Nevada, W USA 39.16N 117.06W
24 I7 **Bunkie** Louisiana, S USA 30.58N 92.12W
25 X10 **Bunnell** Florida, SE USA 29.28N 81.15W
107 S10 **Buñol** País Valenciano, E Spain 39.25N 0.46W
100 K11 **Bunschoten** Utrecht, C Netherlands 52.15N 5.22E
142 K14 **Bünyan** Kayseri, C Turkey 38.51N 35.49E
175 Oo5 **Bunyu** *var.* Bungur. Borneo, N Indonesia 3.33N 117.50E
175 Oo5 **Bunyu, Pulau** *island* N Indonesia
Bunzlau *see* Bolesławiec
Buoddobohki *see* Patoniva
126 Ll6 **Buorkhaya Guba** *bay* N Russian Federation
176 Z15 **Bupul** Irian Jaya, E Indonesia 7.24S 140.57E
83 K19 **Bura** Coast, SE Kenya 1.06S 40.01E
82 P12 **Buraan** Sanaag, N Somalia 10.03N 49.08E
Būrabay *see* Borovoye
Buraida *see* Buraydah
Buraimi *see* Al Buraymī
151 Y11 **Buran** Vostochnyy Kazakhstan, E Kazakhstan 48.00N 85.09E
164 G15 **Burang** Xizang Zizhiqu, W China 30.28N 81.13E
Burao *see* Burco
144 H8 **Burāq** Dar'ā, S Syria 33.10N 36.28E
147 O6 **Buraydah** *var.* Buraida. Al Qaşīm, N Saudi Arabia 26.50N 44.00E
37 S15 **Burbank** California, W USA 34.10N 118.19W
33 N11 **Burbank** Illinois, N USA 41.45N 87.48W
191 Q8 **Burcher** New South Wales, SE Australia 33.29S 147.16E
82 N13 **Burco** *var.* Burao, Bur'o. Togdheer, NW Somalia 9.29N 45.30E
152 L13 **Burdalyk** Lebapskiy Velayat, E Turkmenistan 38.31N 64.21E
189 W6 **Burdekin River** ≈ Queensland, NE Australia
29 O7 **Burden** Kansas, C USA 37.18N 96.45W
Burdigala *see* Bordeaux
142 E15 **Burdur** *var.* Buldur. Burdur, SW Turkey 37.43N 30.16E
142 E15 **Burdur** *var.* Buldur. ◐ *province* SW Turkey
142 E15 **Burdur Gölü** *salt lake* SW Turkey
67 H21 **Burdwood Bank** *undersea feature* SW Atlantic Ocean
82 I12 **Burē** Amhara, N Ethiopia 10.43N 37.09E
82 H13 **Burē** Oromo, C Ethiopia 8.13N 35.09E
95 J15 **Bureå** Västerbotten, N Sweden 64.36N 21.15E
103 G14 **Büren** Nordrhein-Westfalen, W Germany 51.34N 8.34E
168 K6 **Bürengiyn Nuruu** ▲▲ N Mongolia
168 E8 **Bürenhayrhan** Hovd, W Mongolia 46.04N 91.34E
Būrewāla *see* Mandi Būrewāla
127 N17 **Bureya** ≈ SE Russian Federation
94 J9 **Burfjord** Troms, N Norway 69.55N 21.54E
102 L13 **Burg** *var.* Burg an der Ihle, Burg bei Magdeburg. Sachsen-Anhalt, C Germany 52.16N 11.51E
Burg an der Ihle *see* Burg
116 N10 **Burgas** *var.* Bourgas. Burgas, E Bulgaria 42.31N 27.30E
116 N9 **Burgas** ✈ Burgas, E Bulgaria 42.35N 27.33E
116 M10 **Burgas** ◐ *province* E Bulgaria
116 N10 **Burgaski Zaliv** *gulf* E Bulgaria
116 M10 **Burgasko Ezero** *lagoon* E Bulgaria
23 V11 **Burgaw** North Carolina, SE USA 34.33N 77.54W
Burg bei Magdeburg *see* Burg
110 E8 **Burgdorf** Bern, NW Switzerland 47.03N 7.37E
111 Y7 **Burgenland** *off.* Land Burgenland. ◐ *state* SE Austria
11 S13 **Burgeo** Newfoundland, SE Canada 47.42N 57.29W
85 I24 **Burgersdorp** Eastern Cape, SE South Africa 31.00S 26.20E
85 K20 **Burgersfort** Mpumalanga, NE South Africa 24.39S 30.18E
103 N23 **Burghausen** Bayern, SE Germany 48.10N 12.48E
145 O5 **Burghūth, Sabkhat al** ◎ E Syria
103 M20 **Burglengenfeld** Bayern, SE Germany 49.11N 12.01E
43 P9 **Burgos** Tamaulipas, C Mexico 24.55N 98.46W
107 N4 **Burgos** Castilla-León, N Spain 42.21N 3.40W
107 N4 **Burgos** ◐ *province* Castilla-León, N Spain
Burgstadlberg *see* Hradiště
97 P20 **Burgsvik** Gotland, SE Sweden 57.01N 18.18E
Burgum *see* Bergum
Burgundy *see* Bourgogne
165 Q11 **Burhan Budai Shan** ▲▲ C China
142 B12 **Burhaniye** Balıkesir, W Turkey 39.28N 26.58E
160 G12 **Burhānpur** Madhya Pradesh, C India 21.18N 76.13E
179 Q11 **Burias Island** *island* C Philippines
131 W7 **Buribay** Respublika Bashkortostan, W Russian Federation 51.57N 58.11E
45 O17 **Burica, Punta** *headland* Costa Rica/Panama 8.02N 82.53W
178 Ii10 **Buriram** *var.* Buri Ram, Puriramya. Buri Ram, E Thailand 15.01N 103.06E
107 S10 **Burjassot** País Valenciano, E Spain 39.33N 0.25W
83 N16 **Burka Giibi** Hiiraan, C Somalia 3.52N 45.07E
153 X8 **Burkan** ≈ E Kyrgyzstan
27 R4 **Burkburnett** Texas, SW USA 34.06N 98.34W
31 O12 **Burke** South Dakota, N USA 43.09N 99.18W
8 K15 **Burke Channel** *channel* British Columbia, W Canada
204 J10 **Burke Island** *island* Antarctica
22 L7 **Burkesville** Kentucky, S USA 36.47N 85.22W
189 T4 **Burketown** Queensland, NE Australia 17.48S 139.28E
27 Q8 **Burkett** Texas, SW USA 32.01N 99.17W
27 Y9 **Burkeville** Texas, SW USA 30.58N 93.41W
23 V7 **Burkeville** Virginia, NE USA 37.11N 78.12W
79 O12 **Burkina** *off.* Burkina Faso; *prev.* Upper Volta. ◆ *republic* W Africa
Burkina Faso *see* Burkina
204 L13 **Burks, Cape** *headland* Antarctica
12 H12 **Burk's Falls** Ontario, S Canada 45.38N 79.25W
103 H23 **Burladingen** Baden-Württemberg, S Germany 48.18N 9.05E
27 T7 **Burleson** Texas, SW USA 32.32N 97.19W
35 P15 **Burley** Idaho, NW USA 42.32N 113.47W
150 G8 **Burlin** Zapadnyy Kazakhstan, NW Kazakhstan 51.25N 52.42E
12 G16 **Burlington** Ontario, S Canada 43.21N 79.45W
39 W4 **Burlington** Colorado, C USA 39.16N 102.16W
31 Y15 **Burlington** Iowa, C USA 40.48N 91.05W
29 P5 **Burlington** Kansas, C USA 38.11N 95.44W
23 T9 **Burlington** North Carolina, SE USA 36.06N 79.26W
30 M3 **Burlington** North Dakota, N USA 48.16N 101.25W
20 L7 **Burlington** Vermont, NE USA 44.28N 73.13W
32 M9 **Burlington** Wisconsin, N USA 42.38N 88.12W
29 Q1 **Burlington Junction** Missouri, C USA 40.27N 95.04W
178 Gg4 **Burma** *off.* Union of Myanmar, ◆ *military dictatorship* SE Asia
8 L17 **Burnaby** British Columbia, SW Canada 49.16N 122.58W
119 O12 **Burnas, Ozero** ◎ SW Ukraine
27 S10 **Burnet** Texas, SW USA 30.45N 98.13W
37 O3 **Burney** California, W USA 40.52N 121.42W
191 O16 **Burnie** Tasmania, SE Australia 41.06S 145.52E
99 L17 **Burnley** NW England, UK 53.48N 2.13W
Burnoye *see* Bauyrzhan Momysh-Uly
159 R15 **Burnpur** West Bengal, NE India 23.39N 86.55E
34 K14 **Burns** Oregon, NW USA 43.35N 119.03W
28 K11 **Burns Flat** Oklahoma, C USA 35.21N 99.10W
22 M7 **Burnside** Kentucky, S USA 36.55N 84.34W
15 Ii5 **Burnside** ≈ Nunavut, NW Canada
34 L15 **Burns Junction** Oregon, NW USA 42.46N 117.51W
8 L13 **Burns Lake** British Columbia, SW Canada 54.13N 125.45W
31 V9 **Burnsville** Minnesota, N USA 44.49N 93.14W
23 P9 **Burnsville** North Carolina, SE USA 35.55N 82.18W
23 R4 **Burnsville** West Virginia, NE USA 38.50N 80.39W
12 I13 **Burnt River** ≈ Ontario, SE Canada
12 I11 **Burntroot Lake** ◎ Ontario, SE Canada
9 W12 **Burntwood** ≈ Manitoba, C Canada
Bur'o *see* Burco
164 L2 **Burqin** Xinjiang Uygur Zizhiqu, NW China 47.42N 86.49E
190 J8 **Burra** South Australia 33.41S 138.54E
191 S9 **Burragorang, Lake** ▣ New South Wales, SE Australia
98 K5 **Burray** *island* NE Scotland, UK
115 L19 **Burrel** *var.* Burreli. Dibër, C Albania 41.36N 20.00E
Burreli *see* Burrel
191 R8 **Burrendong Reservoir** ▣ New South Wales, SE Australia
191 R5 **Burren Junction** New South Wales, SE Australia 30.06S 149.01E
107 T9 **Burriana** País Valenciano, E Spain 39.54N 0.04W
191 R10 **Burrinjuck Reservoir** ▣ New South Wales, SE Australia
38 J12 **Burro Creek** ≈ Arizona, SW USA
42 M5 **Burro, Serranías del** ▲▲ NW Mexico
64 K7 **Burruyacú** Tucumán, N Argentina 26.28S 64.30W
142 E12 **Bursa** *var.* Brussa; *prev.* Brusa, *anc.* Prusa. Bursa, NW Turkey 40.12N 29.04E
142 D12 **Bursa** *var.* Brusa, Brussa. ◐ *province* NW Turkey
77 Y9 **Bûr Safâga** *var.* Būr Safājah. E Egypt 26.41N 33.58E
Būr Safājah *see* Bûr Safâga
Būr Sa'īd *see* Port Said
83 O14 **Bur Tinle** Mudug, C Somalia 7.50N 48.01E
33 Q5 **Burt Lake** ◎ Michigan, N USA
Burtnieks *see* Burtnieku Ezers
120 H7 **Burtnieku Ezers** *var.* Burtnieks. ◎ N Latvia
33 Q9 **Burton** Michigan, N USA 43.00N 84.16W
Burton on Trent *see* Burton upon Trent
99 M19 **Burton upon Trent** *var.* Burton on Trent, Burton-upon-Trent. C England, UK 52.48N 1.36W
95 J15 **Burträsk** Västerbotten, N Sweden 64.31N 20.40E
151 S14 **Burubaytal** *prev.* Burylbaytal. Zhambyl, SE Kazakhstan 45.01N 73.58E
Burujird *see* Borūjerd
Burultokay *see* Fuhai
147 R15 **Burūm** SE Yemen 14.22N 48.53E
151 U16 **Burunday** *Kaz.* Boralday. Almaty, SE Kazakhstan 43.21N 76.48E
83 D21 **Burundi** *off.* Republic of Burundi; *prev.* Kingdom of Burundi, Urundi. ◆ *republic* C Africa
175 S11 **Buru, Pulau** *prev.* Boeroe. *island* E Indonesia
79 T17 **Burutu** Delta, S Nigeria 5.18N 5.32E
8 G7 **Burwash Landing** Yukon Territory, W Canada 61.26N 139.12W
31 O14 **Burwell** Nebraska, C USA 41.46N 99.04W
99 L17 **Bury** NW England, UK 53.36N 2.16W
126 K15 **Buryatiya, Respublika** *prev.* Buryatskaya ASSR. ◐ *autonomous republic* S Russian Federation
Buryatskaya ASSR *see* Buryatiya, Respublika
Burylbaytal *see* Burubaytal
119 S3 **Buryn'** Sums'ka Oblast', NE Ukraine 51.12N 33.49E
99 P20 **Bury St Edmunds** *hist.* Beodericsworth. E England, UK 52.15N 0.43E
116 G8 **Bŭrziya** ≈ NW Bulgaria
108 D9 **Busalla** Liguria, NW Italy 44.35N 8.55E
179 R17 **Busa, Mount** ▲ Mindanao, S Philippines 6.19N 124.29E
Busan *see* Pusan
145 N5 **Buşayrah** Dayr az Zawr, E Syria 35.03N 40.28E
Buševa *see* Baba
149 N12 **Būshehr** *off.* Ostān-e Būshehr. ◐ *province* SW Iran
Būshehr/Bushire *see* Bandar-e Būshehr
27 N2 **Bushland** Texas, SW USA 35.11N 102.04W
32 J12 **Bushnell** Illinois, N USA 40.33N 90.30W
Busi *see* Biševo
83 G18 **Busia** SE Uganda 1.20N 34.48E
Busiasch *see* Buziaş
81 K16 **Businga** Equateur, NW Dem. Rep. Congo (Zaire) 3.19N 20.52E
81 J18 **Busira** ≈ NW Dem. Rep. Congo (Zaire)
118 I5 **Bus'k** *Rus.* Busk. L'vivs'ka Oblast', W Ukraine 49.59N 24.34E
97 E14 **Buskerud** ◐ *county* S Norway
115 F14 **Buško Jezero** ▣ SW Bosnia and Herzegovina
113 M15 **Busko-Zdrój** Świętokrzyskie, C Poland 50.28N 20.43E
Busra *see* Al Başrah, Iraq
Buşrá *see* Buşrá ash Shām, Syria
144 H9 **Buşrá ash Shām** *var.* Bosora, Bosra, Bozrah, Buşrá. Dar'ā, S Syria 32.31N 36.31E
188 I13 **Busselton** Western Australia 33.43S 115.15E
83 C14 **Busseri** ≈ W Sudan
108 E9 **Busseto** Emilia-Romagna, C Italy 45.00N 10.06E
108 A8 **Bussoleno** Piemonte, NE Italy 45.11N 7.07E
Bussora *see* Al Başrah
100 J10 **Bussum** Noord-Holland, C Netherlands 52.16N 5.10E
43 N7 **Bustamante** Nuevo León, NE Mexico 26.29N 100.30W
65 I23 **Bustamante, Punta** *headland* S Argentina 51.34S 68.58W
Bustan *see* Bŭston
118 J12 **Buşteni** Prahova, SE Romania 45.23N 25.31E
108 D7 **Busto Arsizio** Lombardia, N Italy 45.37N 8.49E
153 Q10 **Bŭston** *Rus.* Buston. NW Tajikistan 40.31N 69.21E
152 I9 **Bŭston** *Rus.* Bustan. Qoraqalpoghiston Respublikasi, W Uzbekistan 41.49N 60.51E
179 P12 **Busuanga Island** *island* Calamian Group, W Philippines
102 H8 **Büsum** Schleswig-Holstein, N Germany 54.08N 8.52E
81 M16 **Buta** Orientale, N Dem. Rep. Congo (Zaire) 2.50N 24.41E
83 E20 **Butare** *prev.* Astrida. S Rwanda 2.39S 29.44E
203 O2 **Butaritari** *atoll* Tungaru, W Kiribati
Butawal *see* Butwal
98 H13 **Bute** *cultural region* SW Scotland, UK
168 K6 **Büteeliyn Nuruu** ▲▲ N Mongolia
8 L16 **Bute Inlet** *fjord* British Columbia, W Canada
98 H12 **Bute, Island of** *island* SW Scotland, UK
81 P18 **Butembo** Nord Kivu, NE Dem. Rep. Congo (Zaire) 0.09N 29.16E
Bûtenpost *see* Buitenpost
109 K25 **Butera** Sicilia, Italy, C Mediterranean Sea 37.12N 14.12E
101 M20 **Bütgenbach** Liège, E Belgium 50.25N 6.12E
Butha Qi *see* Zalantun
177 F5 **Buthidaung** Arakan State, W Burma 20.52N 92.32E
63 I16 **Butiá** Rio Grande do Sul, S Brazil 30.09S 51.55W
83 F17 **Butiaba** NW Uganda 1.48N 31.21E
25 N6 **Butler** Alabama, S USA 32.05N 88.13W
25 S5 **Butler** Georgia, SE USA 32.33N 84.14W
33 Q11 **Butler** Indiana, N USA 41.25N 84.52W
29 R5 **Butler** Missouri, C USA 38.15N 94.19W
20 B14 **Butler** Pennsylvania, NE USA 40.51N 79.52W
204 K5 **Butler Island** *island* Antarctica
23 U8 **Butner** North Carolina, SE USA 36.07N 78.45W
175 Qq13 **Buton, Pulau** *var.* Pulau Butung; *prev.* Boetoeng. *island* C Indonesia
175 Qq13 **Buton, Selat** *strait* C Indonesia
Bütow *see* Bytów
115 L23 **Butrintit, Liqeni i** ◎ S Albania
25 N3 **Buttahatchee River** ≈ Alabama/Mississippi, S USA
35 Q10 **Butte** Montana, NW USA 46.01N 112.33W
31 O12 **Butte** Nebraska, C USA 42.54N 98.51W
173 G3 **Butterworth** Pinang, Peninsular Malaysia 5.24N 100.22E
85 J25 **Butterworth** *var.* Gcuwa. Eastern Cape, SE South Africa 32.19S 28.09E
11 O3 **Button Islands** *island group* Nunavut, NE Canada
37 R13 **Buttonwillow** California, W USA 35.24N 119.26W
179 R14 **Butuan** *off.* Butuan City. Mindanao, S Philippines 8.56N 125.32E
Butung, Pulau *see* Buton, Pulau
Butuntum *see* Bitonto
130 M8 **Buturlinovka** Voronezhskaya Oblast', W Russian Federation 50.48N 40.33E
159 O11 **Butwal** *var.* Butawal. Western, C Nepal 27.41N 83.28E
103 G17 **Butzbach** Hessen, W Germany 50.26N 8.40E
102 L9 **Bützow** Mecklenburg-Vorpommern, N Germany 53.49N 11.58E
82 N13 **Buuhoodle** Togdheer, N Somalia 8.18N 46.15E
83 N16 **Buulobarde** *var.* Buulo Berde. Hiiraan, C Somalia Africa 3.52N 45.36E
Buulo Berde *see* Buulobarde
82 P12 **Buuraha Cal Miskaat** ▲▲ NE Somalia
83 L19 **Buur Gaabo** Jubbada Hoose, S Somalia 1.14S 41.48E
101 M22 **Buurgplaatz** ▲ N Luxembourg 50.09N 6.02E
Buwayrāt al Hasūn *see* Bu'ayrāt al Ḩasūn
102 I10 **Buxtehude** Niedersachsen, NW Germany 53.28N 9.42E
99 L18 **Buxton** C England, UK 53.18N 1.52W
128 M14 **Buy** *var.* Buj. Kostromskaya Oblast', NW Russian Federation 58.27N 41.31E
168 G7 **Buyanbat** Govĭ-Altay, W Mongolia 47.00N 95.57E
168 H8 **Buyant** Bayanhongor, C Mongolia 46.07N 98.45E
168 D6 **Buyant** Bayan-Ölgiy, W Mongolia 48.31N 89.36E
168 H7 **Buyant** Dzavhan, C Mongolia 47.14N 97.14E
169 N9 **Buyant** Hentiy, C Mongolia 46.15N 110.50E
169 N10 **Buyant-Uhaa** Dornogovĭ, SE Mongolia 44.52N 110.12E
168 M7 **Buyant Ukha** ✈ (Ulaanbaatar) Töv, N Mongolia
131 Q16 **Buynaksk** Respublika Dagestan, SW Russian Federation 42.52N 47.03E
121 L20 **Buynavichy** *Rus.* Buynovichi. Homyel'skaya Voblasts', SE Belarus 51.53N 28.31E
Buynovichi *see* Buynavichy
78 L16 **Buyo** SW Ivory Coast 6.23N 7.04W
78 L16 **Buyo, Lac de** ▣ W Ivory Coast
169 R7 **Buyr Nuur** *var.* Buir Nur. ◎ China/Mongolia *see also* Buir Nur
143 T13 **Büyükağrı Dağı** *var.* Aghri Dagh, Agri Dagi, Koh I Noh, Masis, *Eng.* Great Ararat, Mount Ararat. ▲ E Turkey 39.43N 44.19E
143 R15 **Büyük Çayı** ≈ NE Turkey
116 O13 **Büyük Çekmece** İstanbul, NW Turkey 41.02N 28.36E
116 N12 **Büyükkarıştıran** Kırklareli, NW Turkey 41.17N 27.33E
117 L14 **Büyükkemikli Burnu** *headland* NW Turkey 40.19N 26.14E
142 E15 **Büyükmenderes Nehri** ≈ SW Turkey
Büyükzap Suyu *see* Great Zab
104 M9 **Buzançais** Indre, C France 46.53N 1.25E
118 K13 **Buzău** Buzău, SE Romania 45.08N 26.51E
118 K13 **Buzău** ◐ *county* SE Romania
118 L12 **Buzău** ≈ E Romania
77 S11 **Buzaymah** *var.* Bzīmah. SE Libya 24.53N 22.01E
170 D13 **Buzen** Fukuoka, Kyūshū, SW Japan 33.30N 131.26E
118 F12 **Buziaş** *Ger.* Busiasch, *Hung.* Buziásfürdő; *prev.* Buziás. Timiş, W Romania 45.38N 21.37E
Buziásfürdő *see* Buziaş
85 M18 **Búzi, Rio** ≈ C Mozambique
119 Q10 **Buz'kyy Lyman** *bay* S Ukraine
Büzmeyin *see* Byuzmeyin
151 O8 **Buzuluk** Akmola, C Kazakhstan 51.52N 66.09E
131 T6 **Buzuluk** Orenburgskaya Oblast', W Russian Federation 52.47N 52.15E
131 N8 **Buzuluk** ≈ SW Russian Federation
21 P12 **Buzzards Bay** Massachusetts, NE USA 41.45N 70.37W
21 P13 **Buzzards Bay** *bay* Massachusetts, NE USA
85 G16 **Bwabata** Caprivi, NE Namibia 17.52S 22.39E
195 P17 **Bwagaoia** Misima Island, SE PNG 10.39S 152.48E
Bwake *see* Bouaké
197 C12 **Bwatnapne** Pentecost, C Vanuatu 15.42S 168.07E
121 K14 **Byahoml'** *Rus.* Begoml'. Vitsyebskaya Voblasts', N Belarus 54.44N 28.03E
116 J8 **Byala** Ruse, N Bulgaria 43.32N 27.51E
116 N9 **Byala** *prev.* Ak-Dere. Varna, E Bulgaria 42.52N 27.53E
Byala Reka *see* Erydropótamos
116 H8 **Byala Slatina** Vratsa, NW Bulgaria 43.28N 23.57E
121 N15 **Byalynichy** *Rus.* Belynichi. Mahilyowskaya Voblasts', E Belarus 53.58N 29.44E
121 G19 **Byaroza** *Pol.* Bereza Kartuska, *Rus.* Berëza. Brestskaya Voblasts', SW Belarus 52.33N 24.58E
Bybles *see* Jbaïl
113 O14 **Bychawa** Lubelskie, SE Poland 51.06N 22.34E
Bychikha *see* Bychykha
120 N11 **Bychykha** *Rus.* Bychikha. Vitsyebskaya Voblasts', NE Belarus 55.40N 29.58E
113 I14 **Byczyna** *Ger.* Pitschen. Opolskie, S Poland 51.06N 18.13E
112 I10 **Bydgoszcz** *Ger.* Bromberg. Kujawski-pomorskie, C Poland 53.16N 18.00E
121 I17 **Byelaruskaya Hrada** *Rus.* Belorusskaya Gryada. *ridge* N Belarus
121 G18 **Byelavyezhskaya Pushcha** *Pol.* Puszcza Białowieska, *Rus.* Belovezhskaya Pushcha. *forest* Belarus/Poland *see also* Białowieska, Puszcza
121 H15 **Byenyakoni** *Rus.* Benyakoni. Hrodzyenskaya Voblasts', W Belarus 54.15N 25.22E
121 M16 **Byerazino** *Rus.* Berezino. Minskaya Voblasts', C Belarus 53.49N 28.58E
120 L13 **Byerazino** *Rus.* Berezino. Vitsyebskaya Voblasts', N Belarus 54.54N 28.12E
121 L14 **Byerezino** *Rus.* Berezina. ≈ C Belarus
120 M13 **Byeshankovichy** *Rus.* Beshenkovichi. Vitsyebskaya Voblasts', N Belarus 55.03N 29.28E
33 U13 **Byesville** Ohio, N USA 39.58N 81.32W
121 P18 **Byesyedz'** *Rus.* Besed'. ≈ SE Belarus
121 H19 **Byezdzyezh** *Rus.* Bezdezh. Brestskaya Voblasts', SW Belarus 52.18N 25.16E
95 J15 **Bygdeå** Västerbotten, N Sweden 64.03N 20.49E
96 F12 **Bygdin** ◎ S Norway
95 J15 **Bygdsiljum** Västerbotten, N Sweden 64.20N 20.31E
97 E17 **Bygland** Aust-Agder, S Norway 58.46N 7.50E
97 E17 **Byglandsfjord** Aust-Agder, S Norway 58.42N 7.51E
121 N16 **Bykhaw** *Rus.* Bykhov. Mahilyowskaya Voblasts', E Belarus 53.31N 30.15E
Bykhov *see* Bykhaw
131 P9 **Bykovo** Volgogradskaya Oblast', SW Russian Federation 49.52N 45.24E
126 L6 **Bykovskiy** Respublika Sakha (Yakutiya), NE Russian Federation 71.57N 129.07E
205 R12 **Byrd Glacier** *glacier* Antarctica
12 K10 **Byrd, Lac** ◎ Quebec, SE Canada
191 P5 **Byrock** New South Wales, SE Australia 30.40S 146.24E
32 L10 **Byron** Illinois, N USA 42.06N 89.15W
191 V4 **Byron Bay** New South Wales, SE Australia 28.39S 153.34E
191 V4 **Byron, Cape** *headland* New South Wales, E Australia 28.37S 153.40E
65 F21 **Byron, Isla** *island* S Chile
Byron Island *see* Nikunau
67 B24 **Byron Sound** *sound* NW Falkland Islands
126 J5 **Byrranga, Gora** ▲▲ N Russian Federation
95 J14 **Byske** Västerbotten, N Sweden 64.58N 21.10E
113 K18 **Bystrá** ▲ N Slovakia 49.10N 19.49E
113 F18 **Bystřice nad Pernštejnem** *Ger.* Bistritz ober Pernstein. Jihlavský Kraj, C Czech Republic 49.30N 16.16E
Bystrovka *see* Kemin
113 G16 **Bystrzyca Kłodzka** *Ger.* Habelschwerdt. Wałbrzych, SW Poland 50.19N 16.39E
113 I18 **Bytča** Žilinský Kraj, N Slovakia 49.15N 18.31E
121 L15 **Bytcha** *Rus.* Bytcha. Minskaya Voblasts', NE Belarus 54.19N 28.24E
Byteń/Byten' *see* Bytsyen'
113 J16 **Bytom** *Ger.* Beuthen. Śląskie, S Poland 50.21N 18.51E

◆ Country
● Country Capital
◇ Dependent Territory
○ Dependent Territory Capital
◐ Administrative Region
✈ International Airport
▲ Mountain
▲▲ Mountain Range
⛰ Volcano
≈ River
◎ Lake
▣ Reservoir

BYTÓW – CÃNADÓN GRANDE, SIERRA

112 H7 **Bytów** *Ger.* Bütow. Pomorskie, N Poland *54.09N 17.30E*
121 H18 **Bytsyen'** *Pol.* Byteń, *Rus.* Byten'. Brestskaya Voblasts', SW Belarus *52.53N 25.32E*
83 E19 **Byumba** *var.* Biumba. N Rwanda *1.37S 30.05E*
152 F13 **Byuzmeyin** *Turkm.* Büzmeyin; *prev.* Bezmein. Akhalskiy Velayat, C Turkmenistan *38.07N 57.52E*
121 O20 **Byval'ki** Homyel'skaya Voblasts', SE Belarus *51.51N 30.37E*
97 O20 **Byxelkrok** Kalmar, S Sweden *57.18N 17.01E*
Byzantium *see* Istanbul
Bzīmah *see* Buzaymah

C

64 O6 **Caacupé** Cordillera, S Paraguay *25.22S 57.04W*
64 P6 **Caaguazú** *off.* Departamento de Caaguazú. ◆ *department* C Paraguay
84 C13 **Caála** *var.* Kaala, Robert Williams, *Port.* Vila Robert Williams. Huambo, C Angola *12.51S 15.33E*
64 P7 **Caazapá** Caazapá, S Paraguay *26.09S 56.21W*
64 P7 **Caazapá** *off.* Departamento de Caazapá. ◆ *department* SE Paraguay
83 P15 **Cabaad, Raas** *headland* C Somalia *6.13N 49.01E*
179 R14 **Cabadbaran** Mindanao, S Philippines *9.07N 125.34E*
57 N10 **Cabadisocaña** Amazonas, S Venezuela *4.28N 64.45W*
46 F5 **Cabaiguán** Sancti Spíritus, C Cuba *22.04N 79.31W*
Caballeria, Cabo *see* Cavalleria, Cap de
39 Q14 **Caballo Reservoir** ⊠ New Mexico, SW USA
42 L6 **Caballos Mesteños, Llano de los** *plain* N Mexico
106 L2 **Cabañaquinta** Asturias, N Spain *43.10N 5.37W*
44 B9 **Cabañas** ◆ *department* E El Salvador
179 P10 **Cabanatuan** *off.* Cabanatuan City. Luzon, N Philippines *15.27N 120.57E*
13 T8 **Cabano** Quebec, SE Canada *47.40N 68.55W*
106 L11 **Cabeza del Buey** Extremadura, W Spain *38.43N 5.13W*
47 V5 **Cabezas de San Juan** *headland* E Puerto Rico *18.23N 65.37W*
107 N2 **Cabezón de la Sal** Cantabria, N Spain *43.19N 4.13W*
Cabhán *see* Cavan
63 B23 **Cabildo** Buenos Aires, E Argentina *38.28S 61.49W*
Cabillonum *see* Chalon-sur-Saône
56 H5 **Cabimas** Zulia, NW Venezuela *10.25N 71.27W*
84 A9 **Cabinda** *var.* Kabinda. Cabinda, NW Angola *5.34S 12.12E*
84 A9 **Cabinda** *var.* Kabinda. ◆ *province* NW Angola
35 N7 **Cabinet Mountains** ▲ Idaho/Montana, NW USA
84 B11 **Cabiri** Bengo, NW Angola *8.50S 13.42E*
65 J20 **Cabo Blanco** Santa Cruz, SE Argentina *47.13S 65.43W*
84 P13 **Cabo Delgado** *off.* Província de Capo Delgado. ◆ *province* NE Mozambique
12 L9 **Cabonga, Réservoir** ⊠ Quebec, SE Canada
29 V7 **Cabool** Missouri, C USA *37.07N 92.06W*
191 V2 **Caboolture** Queensland, E Australia *27.05S 152.56E*
Cabora Bassa, Lake *see* Cahora Bassa, Albufeira de
42 F3 **Caborca** Sonora, NW Mexico *30.44N 112.06W*
Cabo San Lucas *see* San Lucas
29 V11 **Cabot** Arkansas, C USA *34.58N 92.01W*
12 F12 **Cabot Head** *headland* Ontario, S Canada *45.13N 81.17W*
16 Ss10 **Cabot Strait** *strait* E Canada
Cabo Verde, Ilhas do *see* Cape Verde
106 M14 **Cabra** Andalucía, S Spain *37.28N 4.28W*
109 B19 **Cabras** Sardegna, Italy, C Mediterranean Sea *39.55N 8.30E*
196 A15 **Cabras Island** *island* W Guam
47 O8 **Cabrera** N Dominican Republic *19.34N 69.55W*
107 X10 **Cabrera** *anc.* Capraria. *island* Islas Baleares, Spain, W Mediterranean Sea
106 J4 **Cabrera** ⚘ NW Spain
107 Q15 **Cabrera, Sierra** ▲ S Spain
9 S16 **Cabri** Saskatchewan, S Canada *50.37N 108.28W*
107 R10 **Cabriel** ⚘ E Spain
56 M7 **Cabruta** Guárico, C Venezuela *7.39N 66.19W*
179 Oo8 **Cabugao** Luzon, N Philippines *17.55N 120.29E*
56 G10 **Cabuyaro** Meta, C Colombia *4.16N 72.47W*
62 I13 **Caçador** Santa Catarina, S Brazil *26.47S 51.00W*
44 G8 **Cacaguatique, Cordillera** *var.* Cordillera. ▲ NE El Salvador
114 L13 **Čačak** Serbia, C Yugoslavia *43.52N 20.23E*
57 Y10 **Cacao** NE French Guiana *4.37N 52.28W*
63 H16 **Caçapava do Sul** Rio Grande do Sul, S Brazil *30.28S 53.28W*
23 U3 **Cacapon River** ⚘ West Virginia, NE USA
109 J23 **Caccamo** Sicilia, Italy, C Mediterranean Sea *37.55N 13.40E*
109 A17 **Caccia, Capo** *headland* Sardegna, Italy, C Mediterranean Sea *40.34N 8.09E*
61 G18 **Cáceres** Mato Grosso, W Brazil *16.04S 57.40W*
106 J10 **Cáceres** *Ar.* Qazris. Extremadura, W Spain *39.28N 6.22W*
106 J9 **Cáceres** ◆ *province* Extremadura, W Spain
Cachacrou *see* Scotts Head Village
63 C21 **Cacharí** Buenos Aires, E Argentina *36.24S 59.31W*
28 L12 **Cache** Oklahoma, C USA *34.37N 98.37W*
8 M16 **Cache Creek** British Columbia, SW Canada *50.49N 121.19W*
37 N6 **Cache Creek** ⚘ California, W USA
39 S3 **Cache La Poudre River** ⚘ Colorado, C USA
Cacheo *see* Cacheu
29 W11 **Cache River** ⚘ Arkansas, C USA
32 L17 **Cache River** ⚘ Illinois, N USA
78 G12 **Cacheu** *var.* Cacheo. W Guinea-Bissau *12.12N 16.10W*
61 I15 **Cachimbo** Pará, NE Brazil *9.21S 54.58W*
61 H15 **Cachimbo, Serra do** ▲ C Brazil
84 D13 **Cachingues** Bié, C Angola *13.05S 16.48E*
56 G7 **Cáchira** Norte de Santander, N Colombia *7.46N 73.03W*
63 H16 **Cachoeira do Sul** Rio Grande do Sul, S Brazil *29.58S 52.54W*
61 O20 **Cachoeiro de Itapemirim** Espírito Santo, SE Brazil *20.51S 41.07W*
84 E12 **Cacolo** Lunda Sul, NE Angola *10.09S 19.17E*
85 C14 **Caconda** Huíla, C Angola *13.43S 15.03E*
84 A9 **Cacongo** Cabinda, NW Angola *5.16S 12.10E*
37 U9 **Cactus Peak** ▲ Nevada, W USA *37.42N 116.51W*
84 A11 **Cacuaco** Luanda, NW Angola *8.49S 13.24E*
85 B14 **Cacula** Huíla, SW Angola *14.31S 14.07E*
69 R12 **Caculuvar** ⚘ SW Angola
61 O19 **Caçumba, Ilha** *island* SE Brazil
57 N10 **Cacuri** Amazonas, S Venezuela
83 N17 **Cadale** Shabeellaha Dhexe, E Somalia *2.48N 46.19E*
107 X4 **Cadaqués** Cataluña, NE Spain *42.16N 3.16E*
113 J18 **Čadca** *Hung.* Csaca. Žilinský Kraj, N Slovakia *49.27N 18.46E*
29 P13 **Caddo** Oklahoma, C USA *34.07N 96.15W*
27 R6 **Caddo** Texas, SW USA *32.42N 98.40W*
27 X6 **Caddo Lake** ◎ Louisiana/Texas, SW USA
29 S12 **Caddo Mountains** ▲ Arkansas, C USA
43 O8 **Cadereyta** Nuevo León, NE Mexico *25.35N 99.54W*
99 J19 **Cader Idris** ▲ NW Wales, United Kingdom *52.43N 3.57W*
190 F3 **Cadibarrawirracanna, Lake** *salt lake* South Australia
12 I7 **Cadillac** Quebec, SE Canada *48.12N 78.23W*
9 T17 **Cadillac** Saskatchewan, S Canada *49.43N 107.41W*
104 K13 **Cadillac** Gironde, SW France *44.37N 0.16W*
33 P7 **Cadillac** Michigan, N USA *44.16N 85.22W*
107 V4 **Cadí, Torre de** ▲ NE Spain *42.16N 1.38E*
179 Q13 **Cadiz** *off.* Cadiz City. Negros, C Philippines *10.58N 123.18E*
22 H7 **Cadiz** Kentucky, S USA *36.53N 87.49W*
33 U13 **Cadiz** Ohio, N USA *40.16N 81.00W*
106 J15 **Cádiz** *anc.* Gades, Gadier, Gadir, Gadire. Andalucía, SW Spain *36.31N 6.18W*
106 K15 **Cádiz** ◆ *province* Andalucía, SW Spain
106 I15 **Cádiz, Bahía de** *bay* SW Spain
Cadiz City *see* Cadiz
106 H15 **Cádiz, Golfo de** *Eng.* Gulf of Cadiz. *gulf* Portugal/Spain
Cadiz, Gulf of *see* Cádiz, Golfo de
37 X14 **Cadiz Lake** ◎ California, W USA
190 E2 **Cadney Homestead** South Australia *27.52S 134.03E*
Cadurcum *see* Cahors
85 F17 **Caecae** Ngamiland, NW Botswana *19.52S 21.04E*
104 K4 **Caen** Calvados, N France *49.10N 0.19W*
Caene/Caenepolis *see* Qena
Caerdydd *see* Cardiff
Caer Glou *see* Gloucester
Caer Gybi *see* Holyhead
Caerleon *see* Chester
Caer Luel *see* Carlisle
99 I18 **Caernarfon** *var.* Caernarvon, Carnarvon. NW Wales, UK *53.07N 4.16W*
99 H18 **Caernarfon Bay** *bay* NW Wales, UK
99 I19 **Caernarvon** *cultural region* NW Wales, UK
Caernarvon *see* Caernarfon
Caesaraugusta *see* Zaragoza
Caesarea Mazaca *see* Kayseri
Caesarobriga *see* Talavera de la Reina
Caesarodunum *see* Tours
Caesaromagus *see* Beauvais
Caesena *see* Cesena
61 N17 **Caetité** Bahia, E Brazil *14.04S 42.28W*
64 J6 **Cafayate** Salta, N Argentina *26.02S 66.00W*
179 Pp9 **Cagayan** ⚘ Luzon, N Philippines
179 R15 **Cagayan de Oro** *off.* Cagayan de Oro City. Mindanao, S Philippines *8.28N 124.38E*
179 Oo17 **Cagayan de Tawi Tawi** *island* S Philippines
179 Pp14 **Cagayan Islands** *island group* C Philippines
33 O14 **Cagles Mill Lake** ◎ Indiana, N USA
108 I12 **Cagli** Marche, C Italy *43.33N 12.39E*
109 C20 **Cagliari** *anc.* Caralis. Sardegna, Italy, C Mediterranean Sea *39.15N 9.06E*
109 C20 **Cagliari, Golfo di** *gulf* Sardegna, Italy, C Mediterranean Sea
105 U15 **Cagnes-sur-Mer** Alpes-Maritimes, SE France *43.40N 7.09E*
56 L5 **Cagua** Aragua, N Venezuela *10.09N 67.27W*
179 Pp8 **Cagua, Mount** ▲ Luzon, N Philippines *18.10N 122.03E*
56 F13 **Caguán, Río** ⚘ SW Colombia
47 U6 **Caguas** E Puerto Rico *18.13N 66.02W*
25 P5 **Cahaba River** ⚘ Alabama, S USA
44 E5 **Cahabón, Río** ⚘ C Guatemala
85 B15 **Cahama** Cunene, SW Angola *16.16S 14.19E*
99 B21 **Caha Mountains** *Ir.* An Cheacha. ▲ SW Ireland
99 D20 **Caher** *Ir.* An Cathair. S Ireland *52.21N 7.58W*
99 A21 **Cahersiveen** *Ir.* Cathair Saidhbhín. SW Ireland *51.56N 10.12W*
32 K15 **Cahokia** Illinois, N USA *38.34N 90.11W*
85 L15 **Cahora Bassa, Albufeira de** *var.* Lake Cabora Bassa. ⊠ NW Mozambique
99 G20 **Cahore Point** *Ir.* Rinn Chathóir. *headland* SE Ireland *52.33N 6.11W*
104 M14 **Cahors** *anc.* Cadurcum. Lot, S France *44.26N 1.27E*
58 D9 **Cahuapanas, Río** ⚘ N Peru
118 M12 **Cahul** *Rus.* Kagul. S Moldova *45.52N 28.13E*
Cahul, Lacul *see* Kahul, Ozero
85 N16 **Caia** Sofala, C Mozambique *17.51S 35.22E*
61 J19 **Caiapó, Serra do** ▲ C Brazil
46 F5 **Caibarién** Villa Clara, C Cuba *22.31N 79.28W*
57 O5 **Caicara** Monagas, NE Venezuela *9.49N 63.37W*
56 L5 **Caicara del Orinoco** Bolívar, C Venezuela *7.38N 66.10W*
61 P14 **Caicó** Rio Grande do Norte, E Brazil *6.25S 37.04W*
46 M6 **Caicos Islands** *island group* W Turks and Caicos Islands
46 L5 **Caicos Passage** *strait* Bahamas/Turks and Caicos Islands
167 O9 **Caidian** *prev.* Hanyang. Hubei, C China *30.33N 114.03E*
Caiffa *see* Hefa
188 M12 **Caiguna** Western Australia *32.14S 125.33E*
Caillí, Ceann *see* Hag's Head
42 J11 **Caimanero, Laguna del** *var.* Laguna del Camaronero. *lagoon* E Pacific Ocean
119 N10 **Căinari** *Rus.* Kaynary. C Moldova *46.43N 29.00E*
59 L19 **Caine, Río** ⚘ C Bolivia
Caiphas *see* Hefa
205 N4 **Caird Coast** *physical region* Antarctica
98 J9 **Cairn Gorm** ▲ C Scotland, UK *57.07N 3.38W*
98 J9 **Cairngorm Mountains** ▲ C Scotland, UK
41 P12 **Cairn Mountain** ▲ Alaska, USA *61.07N 155.23W*
189 W4 **Cairns** Queensland, NE Australia *16.51S 145.43E*
124 Qq16 **Cairo** *Ar.* Al Qāhirah, *var.* El Qâhira. ● (Egypt) N Egypt *30.01N 31.18E*
25 T8 **Cairo** Georgia, SE USA *30.52N 84.12W*
32 L17 **Cairo** Illinois, N USA *37.00N 89.10W*
77 V8 **Cairo** ✈ C Egypt *30.06N 31.36E*
Caiseal *see* Cashel
Caisleán an Bharraigh *see* Castlebar
Caisleán na Finne *see* Castlefinn
98 J6 **Caithness** *cultural region* N Scotland, UK
85 D15 **Caiundo** Cuando Cubango, S Angola *15.41S 17.28E*
58 C11 **Cajamarca** *prev.* Caxamarca. Cajamarca, NW Peru *7.09S 78.31W*
58 B11 **Cajamarca** *off.* Departamento de Cajamarca. ◆ *department* N Peru
105 N14 **Cajarc** Lot, S France *44.28N 1.51E*
179 Q12 **Cajidiocan** Sibuyan Island, C Philippines *12.20N 122.39E*
44 G6 **Cajón, Represa El** ⊠ NW Honduras
60 N12 **Caju, Ilha do** *island* NE Brazil
Cakaubalavu Reef *see* Kavukavu Reef
165 R10 **Caka Yanhu** ◎ C China
114 E7 **Čakovec** *Ger.* Csakathurn, *Hung.* Csáktornya; *prev. Ger.* Tschakathurn. Medimurje, N Croatia *46.24N 16.29E*
79 V17 **Calabar** Cross River, S Nigeria *4.55N 8.25E*
12 K13 **Calabogie** Ontario, SE Canada *45.18N 76.43W*
56 L6 **Calabozo** Guárico, C Venezuela *8.53N 67.28W*
109 N20 **Calabria** *anc.* Bruttium. ◆ *region* SW Italy
106 M16 **Calaburra, Punta de** *headland* S Spain *36.30N 4.38W*
118 G14 **Calafat** Dolj, SW Romania *43.55N 23.01E*
Calafate *see* El Calafate
107 Q4 **Calahorra** La Rioja, N Spain *42.19N 1.58W*
105 N1 **Calais** Pas-de-Calais, N France *51.00N 1.53E*
21 T5 **Calais** Maine, NE USA *45.09N 67.15W*
Calais, Pas de *see* Dover, Strait of
Calalen *see* Kallalen
64 H4 **Calama** Antofagasta, N Chile *22.25S 68.52W*
Calamianes *see* Calamian Group
179 P13 **Calamian Group** *var.* Calamianes. *island group* W Philippines
107 R7 **Calamocha** Aragón, NE Spain *40.54N 1.18W*
31 N14 **Calamus River** ⚘ Nebraska, C USA
118 G12 **Călan** *Ger.* Kalan, *Hung.* Pusztakalán. Hunedoara, SW Romania *45.45N 22.59E*
107 S7 **Calanda** Aragón, NE Spain *40.55N 0.15W*
173 E4 **Calang** Sumatera, W Indonesia *4.37N 95.37E*
179 P11 **Calapan** Mindoro, N Philippines *13.23N 121.08E*
Călăraşi *see* Călăraşi
118 M9 **Călăraşi** *var.* Călăras, *Rus.* Kalarash. C Moldova *47.19N 28.13E*
118 L14 **Călăraşi** Călăraşi, SE Romania *44.18N 26.52E*
118 K14 **Călăraşi** ◆ *county* SE Romania
56 E10 **Calarca** Quindío, W Colombia *4.31N 75.37W*
107 Q12 **Calasparra** Murcia, SE Spain *38.13N 1.40W*
109 I23 **Calatafimi** Sicilia, Italy, C Mediterranean Sea *37.54N 12.52E*
107 Q6 **Calatayud** Aragón, NE Spain *41.21N 1.39W*
179 Pp11 **Calauag** Luzon, N Philippines *13.57N 122.18E*
37 P8 **Calaveras River** ⚘ California, W USA
179 Oo11 **Calavite, Cape** *headland* Mindoro, N Philippines *13.25N 120.16E*
179 Qq12 **Calbayog** *off.* Calbayog City. Samar, C Philippines *12.07N 124.35E*
179 R12 **Calbiga** Samar, C Philippines *11.37N 125.00E*
24 G9 **Calcasieu Lake** ◎ Louisiana, S USA
24 H8 **Calcasieu River** ⚘ Louisiana, S USA
58 B6 **Calceta** Manabí, W Ecuador *0.51S 80.09W*
63 B16 **Calchaquí** Santa Fe, C Argentina *29.55S 60.13W*
64 J6 **Calchaquí, Río** ⚘ NW Argentina
60 J10 **Calçoene** Amapá, NE Brazil *2.29N 51.01W*
159 S16 **Calcutta** *var.* Kolkata. West Bengal, NE India *22.30N 88.19E*
159 S16 **Calcutta** ✈ West Bengal, N India *22.30N 88.20E*
56 E9 **Caldas** *off.* Departamento de Caldas. ◆ *province* W Colombia
106 F10 **Caldas da Rainha** Leiria, W Portugal *39.24N 9.07W*
106 G3 **Caldas de Reis** *var.* Caldas de Reyes. Galicia, NW Spain *42.36N 8.39W*
Caldas de Reyes *see* Caldas de Reis
60 F13 **Caldeirão** Amazonas, NW Brazil *3.18S 60.22W*
64 G7 **Caldera** Atacama, N Chile *27.04S 70.48W*
44 L14 **Caldera** Puntarenas, W Costa Rica *9.55N 84.42W*
107 N10 **Calderina** ▲ C Spain *39.18N 3.49W*
143 T13 **Çaldıran** Van, E Turkey *39.10N 43.52E*
34 M14 **Caldwell** Idaho, NW USA *43.39N 116.41W*
29 N8 **Caldwell** Kansas, C USA *37.01N 97.36W*
12 G15 **Caledon** Ontario, S Canada *43.51N 79.58W*
85 I23 **Caledon** *var.* Mohokare. ⚘ Lesotho/South Africa
44 G1 **Caledonia** Corozal, N Belize *18.13N 88.27W*
12 G16 **Caledonia** Ontario, S Canada *43.04N 79.57W*
31 X11 **Caledonia** Minnesota, N USA *43.37N 91.30W*
107 X5 **Calella** *var.* Calella de la Costa. Cataluña, NE Spain *41.37N 2.40E*
Calella de la Costa *see* Calella
25 P4 **Calera** Alabama, S USA *33.06N 86.45W*
65 I19 **Caleta Olivia** Santa Cruz, SE Argentina *46.21S 67.37W*
37 X17 **Calexico** California, W USA *32.39N 115.28W*
99 H16 **Calf of Man** *island* SW Isle of Man
9 Q16 **Calgary** Alberta, SW Canada *51.04N 114.04W*
9 Q16 **Calgary** ✈ Alberta, SW Canada *51.15N 114.03W*
39 U5 **Calhan** Colorado, C USA *39.00N 104.18W*
66 O5 **Calheta** Madeira, Portugal, NE Atlantic Ocean *32.42N 17.12W*
25 R2 **Calhoun** Georgia, SE USA *34.30N 84.57W*
22 I6 **Calhoun** Kentucky, S USA *37.32N 87.10W*
24 M3 **Calhoun City** Mississippi, S USA *33.51N 89.18W*
23 P12 **Calhoun Falls** South Carolina, SE USA *34.05N 82.36W*
56 D11 **Cali** Valle del Cauca, W Colombia *3.24N 76.30W*
29 V9 **Calico Rock** Arkansas, C USA *36.07N 92.08W*
161 F21 **Calicut** *var.* Kozhikode. Kerala, SW India *11.17N 75.49E*
37 Y9 **Caliente** Nevada, W USA *37.37N 114.30W*
29 U5 **California** Missouri, C USA *38.38N 92.33W*
20 B15 **California** Pennsylvania, NE USA *40.02N 79.52W*
37 Q12 **California** *off.* State of California; also known as El Dorado, The Golden State. ◆ *state* W USA
37 P11 **California Aqueduct** *aqueduct* California, W USA
37 T13 **California City** California, W USA *35.06N 117.55W*
42 F6 **California, Golfo de** *Eng.* Gulf of California; *prev.* Sea of Cortez. *gulf* W Mexico
California, Gulf of *see* California, Golfo de
143 Y13 **Cälilabad** *Rus.* Dzhalilabad; *prev.* Astrakhan-Bazar. S Azerbaijan *39.15N 48.30E*
118 I12 **Călimăneşti** Vâlcea, SW Romania *45.13N 24.19E*
118 J9 **Călimani, Munţii** ▲ N Romania
Calinisc *see* Cupcina
37 X17 **Calipatria** California, W USA *33.07N 115.30W*
Calisia *see* Kalisz
36 M7 **Calistoga** California, W USA *38.34N 122.37W*
85 G25 **Calitzdorp** Western Cape, SW South Africa *33.33S 21.40E*
43 W12 **Calkiní** Campeche, E Mexico *20.21N 90.03W*
190 K4 **Callabonna Creek** *var.* Tilcha Creek. *seasonal river* New South Wales/South Australia
190 J4 **Callabonna, Lake** ◎ South Australia
104 G5 **Callac** Côtes d'Armor, NW France *48.28N 3.22W*
37 U5 **Callaghan, Mount** ▲ Nevada, W USA *39.38N 116.57W*
Callain *see* Callan
99 E19 **Callan** *Ir.* Callain. S Ireland *52.33N 7.22W*
12 H11 **Callander** Ontario, S Canada *46.12N 79.20W*
98 I11 **Callander** C Scotland, UK *56.14N 4.16W*
100 H7 **Callantsoog** Noord-Holland, NW Netherlands *52.51N 4.41E*
59 D14 **Callao** Callao, W Peru *12.03S 77.09W*
59 D15 **Callao** *off.* Departamento del Callao. ◆ *constitutional province* W Peru
58 F11 **Callaria, Río** ⚘ E Peru
Callatis *see* Mangalia
9 Q13 **Calling Lake** Alberta, W Canada *55.12N 113.07W*
Callosa de Ensarriá *see* Callosa d'En Sarrià
107 T11 **Callosa d'En Sarrià** *var.* Callosa de Ensarriá. País Valenciano, E Spain *38.40N 0.07W*
107 S12 **Callosa de Segura** País Valenciano, E Spain *38.07N 0.52W*
31 X11 **Calmar** Iowa, C USA *43.10N 91.51W*
Calmar *see* Kalmar
45 R16 **Calobre** Veraguas, C Panama *8.18N 80.49W*
179 P10 **Caloocan** *municipality* Luzon, N Philippines *14.37N 120.58E*
25 X14 **Caloosahatchee River** ⚘ Florida, SE USA
191 V2 **Caloundra** Queensland, E Australia *26.48S 153.07E*
107 T11 **Calpe** País Valenciano, E Spain *38.39N 0.03E*
43 P14 **Calpulalpan** Tlaxcala, S Mexico *19.36N 98.30W*
109 K25 **Caltagirone** Sicilia, Italy, C Mediterranean Sea *37.13N 14.31E*
109 J24 **Caltanissetta** Sicilia, Italy, C Mediterranean Sea *37.30N 14.00E*
84 E11 **Caluango** Lunda Norte, NE Angola *8.16S 19.36E*
84 C12 **Calucinga** Bié, W Angola *11.18S 16.10E*
84 B12 **Calulo** Cuanza Sul, NW Angola *9.58S 14.56E*
85 B14 **Caluquembe** Huíla, W Angola *13.46S 14.40E*
82 Q11 **Caluula** Bari, NE Somalia *11.55N 50.51E*
104 K4 **Calvados** ◆ *department* N France
195 P17 **Calvados Chain, The** *island group* SE PNG
27 U9 **Calvert** Texas, SW USA *30.58N 96.40W*
22 H7 **Calvert City** Kentucky, S USA *37.01N 88.21W*
105 X14 **Calvi** Corse, France, C Mediterranean Sea *42.34N 8.44E*
42 L12 **Calvillo** Aguascalientes, C Mexico *21.51N 102.42W*
85 F24 **Calvinia** Northern Cape, W South Africa *31.26S 19.45E*
106 K8 **Calvitero** ▲ W Spain *40.16N 5.48W*
103 G22 **Calw** Baden-Württemberg, SW Germany *48.43N 8.43E*
Calydon *see* Kalydón
107 N11 **Calzada de Calatrava** Castilla-La Mancha, C Spain *38.42N 3.46W*
Cama *see* Kama
84 C11 **Camabatela** Cuanza Norte, NW Angola *8.13S 15.22E*
66 Q5 **Camacha** Porto Santo, Madeira, Portugal, NE Atlantic Ocean *32.40N 16.52W*
12 L8 **Camachigama, Lac** ◎ Quebec, SE Canada
42 M9 **Camacho** Zacatecas, C Mexico *24.23N 102.20W*
84 D13 **Camacupa** *var.* General Machado, *Port.* Vila General Machado. Bié, C Angola *11.59S 17.30E*
56 L7 **Camaguán** Guárico, C Venezuela *8.05N 67.34W*
46 G6 **Camagüey** *prev.* Puerto Príncipe. Camagüey, C Cuba *21.24N 77.54W*
46 G5 **Camagüey, Archipiélago de** *island group* C Cuba
42 D5 **Camalli, Sierra de** ▲ NW Mexico *28.21N 113.26W*
59 G18 **Camana** *var.* Camaná. Arequipa, SW Peru *16.37S 72.42W*
31 Z14 **Camanche** Iowa, C USA *41.47N 90.15W*
37 P8 **Camanche Reservoir** ⊠ California, W USA
63 I16 **Camaquã** Rio Grande do Sul, S Brazil *30.49S 51.49W*
63 H16 **Camaquã, Rio** ⚘ S Brazil
66 P6 **Câmara de Lobos** Madeira, Portugal, NE Atlantic Ocean *32.37N 16.58W*
105 U16 **Camarat, Cap** *headland* SE France *43.12N 6.42E*
43 O8 **Camargo** Tamaulipas, C Mexico *26.16N 98.49W*
105 R15 **Camargue** *physical region* SE France
106 F2 **Camariñas** Galicia, NW Spain *43.07N 9.10W*
Camaronero, Laguna del *see* Caimanero, Laguna del
65 J18 **Camarones** Chaco, S Argentina *44.48S 65.42W*
65 J18 **Camarones, Bahía** *bay* S Argentina
106 J14 **Camas** Andalucía, S Spain *37.24N 6.01W*
178 J15 **Ca Mau** *prev.* Quan Long. Minh Hai, S Vietnam *9.11N 105.09E*
84 E11 **Camaxilo** Lunda Norte, NE Angola *8.19S 18.52E*
106 G3 **Cambados** Galicia, NW Spain *42.31N 8.49W*
Cambay, Gulf of *see* Khambhāt, Gulf of
Camberia *see* Chambéry
99 N22 **Camberley** SE England, UK *51.21N 0.45W*
178 Ii12 **Cambodia** *off.* Kingdom of Cambodia, *var.* Democratic Kampuchea, Roat Kampuchea, *Cam.* Kampuchea; *prev.* People's Democratic Republic of Kampuchea. ◆ *republic* SE Asia
104 I16 **Cambo-les-Bains** Pyrénées-Atlantiques, SW France *43.22N 1.24W*
105 P2 **Cambrai** *Flem.* Kambryk; *prev.* Cambray, *anc.* Cameracum. Nord, N France *50.10N 3.13E*
Cambray *see* Cambrai
106 H2 **Cambre** Galicia, NW Spain *43.18N 8.21W*
37 O12 **Cambria** California, W USA *35.33N 121.04W*
99 J20 **Cambrian Mountains** ▲ C Wales, UK
12 G16 **Cambridge** Ontario, S Canada *43.22N 80.16W*
46 I12 **Cambridge** W Jamaica *18.19N 77.54W*
192 M8 **Cambridge** Waikato, North Island, NZ *37.53S 175.28E*
99 O20 **Cambridge** *Lat.* Cantabrigia. E England, UK *52.12N 0.07E*
34 M12 **Cambridge** Idaho, NW USA *44.34N 116.42W*
32 K11 **Cambridge** Illinois, N USA *41.18N 90.11W*
23 Y4 **Cambridge** Maryland, NE USA *38.33N 76.04W*
21 O11 **Cambridge** Massachusetts, NE USA *42.21N 71.05W*
31 V7 **Cambridge** Minnesota, N USA *45.34N 93.13W*
31 N16 **Cambridge** Nebraska, C USA *40.18N 100.10W*
33 U13 **Cambridge** Ohio, NE USA *40.00N 81.34W*
15 J3 **Cambridge Bay** Victoria Island, Nunavut, NW Canada *68.55N 105.08W*
99 O20 **Cambridgeshire** *cultural region* E England, UK
107 U6 **Cambrils de Mar** Cataluña, NE Spain *41.06N 1.02E*
Cambundi-Catembo *see* Nova Gaia
143 N11 **Çam Burnu** *headland* N Turkey *41.07N 37.48E*
191 S9 **Camden** New South Wales, SE Australia *34.04S 150.40E*
25 O6 **Camden** Alabama, S USA *31.59N 87.17W*
29 U14 **Camden** Arkansas, C USA *33.34N 92.49W*
23 Y3 **Camden** Delaware, NE USA *39.06N 75.30W*
21 R7 **Camden** Maine, NE USA *44.12N 69.04W*
20 I16 **Camden** New Jersey, NE USA *39.55N 75.07W*
20 I9 **Camden** New York, NE USA *43.21N 75.45W*
23 R12 **Camden** South Carolina, SE USA *34.15N 80.36W*
22 H8 **Camden** Tennessee, S USA *36.03N 88.06W*
27 X9 **Camden** Texas, SW USA *30.55N 94.43W*
41 S5 **Camden Bay** *bay* S Beaufort Sea
29 U6 **Camdenton** Missouri, C USA *38.01N 92.44W*
Camellia State *see* Alabama
20 M7 **Camels Hump** ▲ Vermont, NE USA *44.18N 72.50W*
119 N8 **Camenca** *Rus.* Kamenka. N Moldova *48.01N 28.43E*
Cameracum *see* Cambrai
24 G9 **Cameron** Louisiana, S USA *29.48N 93.19W*
27 T9 **Cameron** Texas, SW USA *30.51N 96.58W*
32 J5 **Cameron** Wisconsin, N USA *45.25N 91.42W*
8 M12 **Cameron** ⚘ British Columbia, W Canada
193 A24 **Cameron Mountains** ▲ South Island, NZ
81 D15 **Cameroon** *off.* Republic of Cameroon, *Fr.* Cameroun. ◆ *republic* W Africa
81 D15 **Cameroon Mountain** ▲ SW Cameroon *4.12N 9.00E*
Cameroon Ridge *see* Camerounaise, Dorsale
Cameroun *see* Cameroon
81 E14 **Camerounaise, Dorsale** *Eng.* Cameroon Ridge. *ridge* NW Cameroon
179 R14 **Camiguin Island** *island* S Philippines
179 P10 **Camiling** Luzon, N Philippines *15.41N 120.22E*
25 T7 **Camilla** Georgia, SE USA *31.13N 84.12W*
106 G5 **Caminha** Viana do Castelo, N Portugal *41.52N 8.49W*
37 P7 **Camino** California, W USA *38.43N 120.39W*
142 B15 **Çamiçi Gölü** ◎ SW Turkey
109 J24 **Cammarata** Sicilia, Italy, C Mediterranean Sea *37.36N 13.39E*
44 K10 **Camoapa** Boaco, S Nicaragua *12.24N 85.32W*
60 O13 **Camocim** Ceará, E Brazil *2.55S 40.49W*
108 D10 **Camogli** Liguria, NW Italy *44.21N 9.10E*
189 S5 **Camooweal** Queensland, C Australia *19.57S 138.14E*
57 Y11 **Camopi** E French Guiana *3.12N 52.19W*
157 Q22 **Camorta** *island* Nicobar Islands, India, NE Indian Ocean
179 R13 **Camotes Sea** *sea* C Philippines
44 I6 **Campamento** Olancho, C Honduras *14.33N 86.37W*
63 D19 **Campana** Buenos Aires, E Argentina *34.06S 59.04W*
65 F21 **Campana, Isla** *island* S Chile
106 K11 **Campanario** Extremadura, W Spain *38.52N 5.36W*
109 L17 **Campania** *Eng.* Champagne. ◆ *region* S Italy
29 Y8 **Campbell** Missouri, C USA *36.29N 90.04W*
193 K15 **Campbell, Cape** *headland* South Island, NZ *41.44S 174.16E*
12 J14 **Campbellford** Ontario, SE Canada *44.18N 77.48W*
33 R13 **Campbell Hill** *hill* Ohio, N USA *40.22N 83.43W*
199 J14 **Campbell Island** *island* S NZ
183 P13 **Campbell Plateau** *undersea feature* SW Pacific Ocean
8 K17 **Campbell River** Vancouver Island, British Columbia, SW Canada *49.58N 125.18W*
22 L6 **Campbellsville** Kentucky, S USA *37.20N 85.20W*
11 O13 **Campbellton** New Brunswick, SE Canada *48.00N 66.41W*
191 P16 **Campbell Town** Tasmania, SE Australia *41.57S 147.30E*
191 S9 **Campbelltown** New South Wales, SE Australia *34.04S 150.46E*
98 G13 **Campbeltown** W Scotland, UK *55.25N 5.37W*
43 W13 **Campeche** Campeche, SE Mexico *19.46N 90.28W*
43 W14 **Campeche** ◆ *state* SE Mexico
43 T14 **Campeche, Bahía de** *Eng.* Bay of Campeche. *bay* E Mexico
Campeche, Banco de *see* Campeche Bank
66 C11 **Campeche Bank** *Sp.* Banco de Campeche, Sonda de Campeche. *undersea feature* S Gulf of Mexico
Campeche, Bay of *see* Campeche, Bahía de
Campeche, Sonda de *see* Campeche Bank
46 H7 **Campechuela** Granma, E Cuba *20.11N 77.14W*
190 M13 **Camperdown** Victoria, SE Australia *38.16S 143.10E*
178 K6 **Câm Pha** Quang Ninh, N Vietnam *21.04N 107.20E*
118 H10 **Câmpia Turzii** *Ger.* Jerischmarkt, *Hung.* Aranyosgyéres; *prev.* Cîmpia Turzii, Ghiriş, Gyéres. Cluj, NW Romania *46.33N 23.53E*
106 K12 **Campillo de Llerena** Extremadura, W Spain *38.30N 5.48W*
106 L15 **Campillos** Andalucía, S Spain *37.04N 4.51W*
118 J13 **Câmpina** *prev.* Cîmpina. Prahova, SE Romania *45.08N 25.44E*
61 Q15 **Campina Grande** Paraíba, E Brazil *7.15S 35.49W*
62 L9 **Campinas** São Paulo, S Brazil *22.54S 47.06W*
40 L10 **Camp Kulowiye** Saint Lawrence Island, Alaska, USA *63.15N 168.45W*
81 D17 **Campo** *var.* Kampo. Sud, SW Cameroon *2.22N 9.49E*
Campo *see* Ntem
61 N15 **Campo Alegre de Lourdes** Bahia, E Brazil *9.28S 43.01W*
109 L16 **Campobasso** Molise, C Italy *41.34N 14.40E*
109 H24 **Campobello di Mazara** Sicilia, Italy, C Mediterranean Sea *37.37N 12.45E*
Campo Criptana *see* Campo de Criptana
107 O10 **Campo de Criptana** *var.* Campo Criptana. Castilla-La Mancha, C Spain *39.25N 3.07W*
61 I16 **Campo de Diauarum** *var.* Pôsto Diuarum. Mato Grosso, W Brazil *11.08S 53.16W*
56 E5 **Campo de la Cruz** Atlántico, N Colombia *10.22N 74.52W*
107 P11 **Campo de Montiel** *physical region* C Spain
Campo dos Goitacazes *see* Campos
62 H12 **Campo Erê** Santa Catarina, S Brazil *26.24S 53.04W*
64 L7 **Campo Gallo** Santiago del Estero, N Argentina *26.36S 62.50W*
61 I20 **Campo Grande** *state capital* Mato Grosso do Sul, SW Brazil *20.24S 54.34W*
62 K12 **Campo Largo** Paraná, S Brazil *25.27S 49.29W*
60 N13 **Campo Maior** Piauí, E Brazil *4.49S 42.12W*
106 I10 **Campo Maior** Portalegre, C Portugal *39.01N 7.04W*
62 H10 **Campo Mourão** Paraná, S Brazil *24.01S 52.24W*
62 Q9 **Campos** *var.* Campo dos Goitacazes. Rio de Janeiro, SE Brazil *21.46S 41.21W*
61 L17 **Campos Belos** Goiás, S Brazil *13.11S 46.46W*
62 N9 **Campos do Jordão** São Paulo, S Brazil *22.45S 45.36W*
62 I13 **Campos Novos** Santa Catarina, S Brazil *27.22S 51.11W*
61 O14 **Campos Sales** Ceará, E Brazil *7.01S 40.21W*
27 Q9 **Camp San Saba** Texas, SW USA *30.57N 99.16W*
23 N6 **Campton** Kentucky, S USA *37.43N 83.28W*
118 I13 **Câmpulung** *prev.* Câmpulung-Muşcel, Cîmpulung. Argeş, S Romania *45.16N 25.03E*
118 J9 **Câmpulung Moldovenesc** *var.* Cîmpulung Moldovenesc, *Ger.* Kimpolung, *Hung.* Hosszúmezjő. Suceava, NE Romania *47.31N 25.34E*
Câmpulung-Muşcel *see* Câmpulung
Campus Stellae *see* Santiago
38 L12 **Camp Verde** Arizona, SW USA *34.33N 111.52W*
27 P11 **Camp Wood** Texas, SW USA *29.40N 100.00W*
178 Kk13 **Cam Ranh** Khanh Hoa, S Vietnam *11.54N 109.13E*
9 Q15 **Camrose** Alberta, SW Canada *53.01N 112.48W*
Camulodunum *see* Colchester
142 B12 **Çan** Çanakkale, NW Turkey *40.01N 26.59E*
20 L12 **Canaan** Connecticut, NE USA *42.00N 73.17W*
15 Kk13 **Canada** ◆ *commonwealth republic* N North America
207 P6 **Canada Basin** *undersea feature* Arctic Ocean
63 B18 **Cañada de Gómez** Santa Fe, C Argentina *32.49S 61.22W*
207 P6 **Canada Plain** *undersea feature* Arctic Ocean
63 A18 **Cañada Rosquín** Santa Fe, C Argentina *32.04S 61.35W*
27 P1 **Canadian** Texas, SW USA *35.54N 100.22W*
18 Kk11 **Canadian River** ⚘ SW USA
15 K12 **Canadian Shield** *physical region* Canada
65 I18 **Cañadón Grande, Sierra** ▲ S Argentina

◆ Country ● Country Capital ◇ Dependent Territory ○ Dependent Territory Capital ◆ Administrative Region ✈ International Airport ▲ Mountain ▲ Mountain Range ⚠ Volcano ⚘ River ◎ Lake ⊠ Reservoir

Canaima – Carthage

57 P9 **Canaima** Bolívar, SE Venezuela *9.40N 72.33W*
142 B11 **Çanakkale** *var.* Dardanelli; *prev.* Chanak, Kale Sultanie. Çanakkale, W Turkey *40.09N 26.25E*
142 B12 **Çanakkale** ◐ *province* NW Turkey
142 B11 **Çanakkale Boğazı** *Eng.* Dardanelles. *strait* NW Turkey
197 I6 **Canala** Province Nord, C New Caledonia *21.31S 165.57E*
61 A15 **Canamari** Amazonas, W Brazil *7.37S 72.33W*
20 G10 **Canandaigua** New York, NE USA *42.52N 77.14W*
20 F10 **Canandaigua Lake** ◎ New York, NE USA
42 G3 **Cananea** Sonora, NW Mexico *30.58N 110.19W*
58 B8 **Cañar** ◐ *province* C Ecuador
66 N10 **Canarias, Islas** *Eng.* Canary Islands. ◐ *autonomous community* Spain, NE Atlantic Ocean
Canaries Basin *see* Canary Basin
46 C6 **Canarreos, Archipiélago de los** *island group* W Cuba
68 K3 **Canary Basin** *var.* Canaries Basin, Monaco Basin. *undersea feature* E Atlantic Ocean
Canary Islands *see* Canarias, Islas
44 L13 **Cañas** Guanacaste, NW Costa Rica *10.25N 85.07W*
20 I10 **Canastota** New York, NE USA *43.04N 75.45W*
42 K9 **Canatlán** Durango, C Mexico *24.33N 104.45W*
106 J9 **Cañaveral** Extremadura, W Spain *39.46N 6.24W*
25 Y11 **Canaveral, Cape** *headland* Florida, SE USA *28.27N 80.31W*
61 O18 **Canavieiras** Bahia, E Brazil *15.43S 38.58W*
45 R16 **Cañazas** Veraguas, W Panama *8.19N 81.09W*
108 H6 **Canazei** Trentino-Alto Adige, N Italy *46.29N 11.50E*
191 P6 **Canbelego** New South Wales, SE Australia *31.36S 146.20E*
191 R10 **Canberra** ● (Australia) Australian Capital Territory, SE Australia *35.21S 149.08E*
191 R10 **Canberra** ✕ Australian Capital Territory, SE Australia *35.19S 149.12E*
37 P2 **Canby** California, W USA *41.27N 120.51W*
31 S9 **Canby** Minnesota, N USA *44.42N 96.17W*
105 N2 **Canche** ⁓ N France
104 L13 **Cancon** Lot-et-Garonne, SW France *44.33N 0.37E*
43 Z11 **Cancún** Quintana Roo, SE Mexico *21.05N 86.48W*
106 K2 **Candás** Asturias, N Spain *43.35N 5.45W*
104 J7 **Cande** Maine-et-Loire, NW France *47.33N 1.03W*
43 W14 **Candelaria** Campeche, SE Mexico *18.10N 91.00W*
26 J11 **Candelaria** Texas, SW USA *30.05N 104.40W*
43 W15 **Candelaria, Río** ⁓ Guatemala/Mexico
106 L8 **Candeleda** Castilla-León, N Spain *40.10N 5.13W*
Candia *see* Irákleio
43 P8 **Cándido Aguilar** Tamaulipas, C Mexico *25.30N 97.57W*
41 N8 **Candle** Alaska, USA *65.54N 161.55W*
9 T14 **Candle Lake** Saskatchewan, C Canada *53.43N 105.09W*
20 L13 **Candlewood, Lake** ⊡ Connecticut, NE USA
31 O3 **Cando** North Dakota, N USA *48.29N 99.12W*
179 P8 **Candon** Luzon, N Philippines *17.15N 120.25E*
Canea *see* Chaniá
47 O12 **Canefield** ✕ (Roseau) SW Dominica *15.20N 61.24W*
63 F20 **Canelones** *prev.* Guadalupe. Canelones, S Uruguay *34.31S 56.16W*
63 E20 **Canelones** ◐ *department* S Uruguay
Canendiyú *see* Canindeyú
65 F14 **Cañete** Bío Bío, C Chile *37.48S 73.21W*
107 Q9 **Cañete** Castilla-La Mancha, C Spain *40.03N 1.39W*
Cañete *see* San Vicente de Cañete
29 P8 **Caney** Kansas, C USA *37.00N 95.56W*
29 P8 **Caney River** ⁓ Kansas/Oklahoma, C USA
107 S3 **Canfranc-Estación** Aragón, NE Spain *42.42N 0.31W*
85 E14 **Cangamba** *Port.* Vila de Aljustrel. Moxico, E Angola *13.39S 19.57E*
84 C12 **Cangandala** Malanje, NW Angola *9.46S 16.27E*
106 G4 **Cangas** Galicia, NW Spain *42.16N 8.46W*
106 J2 **Cangas del Narcea** Asturias, N Spain *43.10N 6.31W*
106 L2 **Cangas de Onís** Asturias, N Spain *43.21N 5.07W*
167 S11 **Cangnan** *prev.* Lingxi. Zhejiang, SE China *27.29N 120.23E*
84 C10 **Cangola** Uíge, NW Angola *7.54S 15.57E*
85 E14 **Cangombe** Moxico, E Angola *14.27S 20.05E*
65 H21 **Cangrejo, Cerro** ▲ S Argentina *49.19S 72.18W*
63 H17 **Canguçu** Rio Grande do Sul, S Brazil *31.25S 52.37W*
167 P3 **Cangzhou** Hebei, E China *38.19N 116.54E*
10 M7 **Caniapiscau** ⁓ Quebec, E Canada
10 M8 **Caniapiscau, Réservoir de** ⊡ Quebec, C Canada
109 J24 **Canicattì** Sicilia, Italy, C Mediterranean Sea *37.22N 13.51E*
142 L11 **Canik Dağları** ▲▲ N Turkey
107 P14 **Caniles** Andalucía, S Spain *37.24N 2.41W*
61 B16 **Canindé** Acre, W Brazil *10.55S 69.45W*
64 P6 **Canindeyú** *var.* Canendiyú, Canindiyú. ◐ *department* E Paraguay
Canindiyú *see* Canindeyú
204 J10 **Canisteo Peninsula** *peninsula* Antarctica
20 F11 **Canisteo River** ⁓ New York, NE USA
42 M10 **Cañitas** *var.* Cañitas de Felipe Pescador. Zacatecas, C Mexico *23.35N 102.39W*
Cañitas de Felipe Pescador *see* Cañitas
107 P15 **Canjáyar** Andalucía, S Spain *37.00N 2.45W*
142 I12 **Çankırı** *var.* Chankiri; *anc.* Gangra, Germanicopolis. Çankırı, N Turkey *40.36N 33.35E*
142 I11 **Çankırı** *var.* Chankiri. ◐ *province* N Turkey
179 Qq13 **Canlaon Volcano** ※ Negros, C Philippines *10.24N 123.05E*
9 P16 **Canmore** Alberta, SW Canada *51.07N 115.18W*
98 F9 **Canna** *island* NW Scotland, UK
161 F20 **Cannanore** *var.* Kananur, Kannur. Kerala, SW India *11.52N 75.22E*
33 O17 **Cannelton** Indiana, N USA *37.54N 86.44W*
105 U15 **Cannes** Alpes-Maritimes, SE France *43.33N 6.58E*
41 R5 **Canning River** ⁓ Alaska, USA
108 C6 **Cannobio** Piemonte, NE Italy *46.04N 8.39E*
99 L19 **Cannock** C England, UK *52.40N 2.03W*
30 M6 **Cannonball River** ⁓ North Dakota, N USA
31 W9 **Cannon Falls** Minnesota, N USA *44.30N 92.54W*
20 I11 **Cannonsville Reservoir** ⊡ New York, NE USA
191 R12 **Cann River** Victoria, SE Australia *37.34S 149.11E*
63 I16 **Canoas** Rio Grande do Sul, S Brazil *29.42S 51.07W*
63 I14 **Canoas, Rio** ⁓ S Brazil
12 I12 **Canoe Lake** ◎ Ontario, SE Canada
62 J12 **Canoinhas** Santa Catarina, S Brazil *26.12S 50.24W*
39 T6 **Canon City** Colorado, C USA *38.25N 105.14W*
57 P8 **Caño Negro** Bolívar, SE Venezuela
181 X15 **Canonniers Point** *headland* N Mauritius
25 W6 **Canoochee River** ⁓ Georgia, SE USA
9 V15 **Canora** Saskatchewan, S Canada *51.37N 102.28W*
47 Y14 **Canouan** *island* S Saint Vincent and the Grenadines
11 R15 **Canso** Nova Scotia, SE Canada *45.20N 61.00W*
106 M3 **Cantabria** ◐ *autonomous community* N Spain
106 K3 **Cantábrica, Cordillera** ▲▲ N Spain
Cantabrigia *see* Cambridge
105 O12 **Cantal** ◐ *department* C France
107 N6 **Cantalejo** Castilla-León, N Spain *41.15N 3.57W*
105 O12 **Cantal, Monts du** ▲▲ C France
106 G8 **Cantanhede** Coimbra, C Portugal *40.21N 8.37W*
Canton *see* Cataño
57 O6 **Cantaura** Anzoátegui, NE Venezuela *9.18N 64.21W*
118 M11 **Cantemir** *Rus.* Kantemir. S Moldova *46.17N 28.12E*
99 Q22 **Canterbury** *hist.* Cantwaraburh, *anc.* Durovernum, *Lat.* Cantuaria. SE England, UK *51.16N 1.04E*
193 F19 **Canterbury** *off.* Canterbury Region. ◐ *region* South Island, NZ
193 H20 **Canterbury Bight** *bight* South Island, NZ
193 H19 **Canterbury Plains** *plain* South Island, NZ
178 Jj15 **Cần Thơ** Cần Thơ, S Vietnam *10.03N 105.46E*
106 K13 **Cantillana** Andalucía, S Spain *37.34N 5.48W*
61 N15 **Canto do Buriti** Piauí, NE Brazil *8.07S 43.00W*
25 S2 **Canton** Georgia, SE USA *34.14N 84.29W*
32 K12 **Canton** Illinois, N USA *40.33N 90.02W*
24 L5 **Canton** Mississippi, S USA *32.36N 90.02W*
29 V2 **Canton** Missouri, C USA *40.07N 91.31W*
20 J7 **Canton** New York, NE USA *44.36N 75.10W*
23 O10 **Canton** North Carolina, SE USA *35.31N 82.50W*
33 U12 **Canton** Ohio, N USA *40.48N 81.22W*
28 L9 **Canton** Oklahoma, C USA *36.03N 98.35W*
20 G12 **Canton** Pennsylvania, NE USA *41.38N 76.49W*
31 R11 **Canton** South Dakota, N USA *43.19N 96.33W*
27 V7 **Canton** Texas, SW USA *32.34N 95.50W*
Canton *see* Guangzhou
Canton Island *see* Kanton
28 L9 **Canton Lake** ◎ Oklahoma, C USA
108 D7 **Cantù** Lombardia, N Italy *45.43N 9.07E*
Cantuaria/Cantwaraburh *see* Canterbury
41 R10 **Cantwell** Alaska, USA *63.23N 148.57W*
61 O16 **Canudos** Bahia, E Brazil *9.51S 39.07W*
49 T7 **Canumã, Rio** ⁓ N Brazil
Canusium *see* Puglia, Canosa di
26 G7 **Canutillo** Texas, SW USA *31.53N 106.34W*
27 N3 **Canyon** Texas, SW USA *34.58N 101.55W*
35 S12 **Canyon** Wyoming, C USA *44.44N 110.30W*
34 K13 **Canyon City** Oregon, NW USA *44.22N 118.58W*
35 R10 **Canyon Ferry Lake** ◎ Montana, NW USA
27 S11 **Canyon Lake** ⊡ Texas, SW USA
178 Jj5 **Cao Bằng** *var.* Caobang. Cao Bằng, N Vietnam *22.40N 106.16E*
166 J12 **Caodu He** ⁓ S China
178 Jj14 **Cao Lanh** Đồng Tháp, S Vietnam *10.35N 105.25E*
84 C11 **Caombo** Malanje, NW Angola *8.42S 16.33E*
Caorach, Cuan na g *see* Sheep Haven
Caozhou *see* Heze
175 S10 **Capalulu** Pulau Mangole, E Indonesia *1.51S 125.53E*
56 K8 **Capanaparo, Río** ⁓ Colombia/Venezuela
60 L12 **Capanema** Pará, NE Brazil *1.07S 47.07W*
62 L10 **Capão Bonito** São Paulo, S Brazil *24.01S 48.22W*
62 I13 **Capão Doce, Morro do** ▲ S Brazil *26.37S 51.28W*
56 I4 **Capatárida** Falcón, N Venezuela *11.10N 70.38W*
104 I15 **Capbreton** Landes, SW France *43.40N 1.25W*
Cap-Breton, Île du *see* Cape Breton Island
13 W6 **Cap-Chat** Quebec, SE Canada *49.04N 66.43W*
13 P11 **Cap-de-la-Madeleine** Quebec, SE Canada *46.22N 72.31W*
105 N13 **Capdenac** Aveyron, S France *44.35N 2.06E*
191 Q15 **Cape Barren Island** *island* Furneaux Group, Tasmania, SE Australia
67 O18 **Cape Basin** *undersea feature* S Atlantic Ocean
11 R14 **Cape Breton Island** *Fr.* Île du Cap-Breton. *island* Nova Scotia, SE Canada
25 Y11 **Cape Canaveral** Florida, SE USA *28.24N 80.36W*
23 Y6 **Cape Charles** Virginia, NE USA *37.16N 76.01W*
79 P17 **Cape Coast** *prev.* Cape Coast Castle. S Ghana *5.10N 1.13W*
Cape Coast Castle *see* Cape Coast
21 Q12 **Cape Cod Bay** *bay* Massachusetts, NE USA
25 W15 **Cape Coral** Florida, SE USA *26.33N 81.57W*
189 R4 **Cape Crawford Roadhouse** Northern Territory, N Australia *16.39S 135.44E*
16 N4 **Cape Dorset** Baffin Island, Nunavut, NE Canada *64.12N 76.31W*
23 N8 **Cape Fear River** ⁓ North Carolina, SE USA
29 Y7 **Cape Girardeau** Missouri, C USA *37.17N 89.31W*
23 T14 **Cape Island** *island* South Carolina, SE USA
194 E11 **Capella** ▲ NW PNG *5.00S 141.09E*
100 H12 **Capelle aan den IJssel** Zuid-Holland, SW Netherlands *51.55N 4.36E*
85 C15 **Capelongo** Huíla, C Angola *14.45S 15.02E*
20 J17 **Cape May** New Jersey, NE USA *38.54N 74.54W*
20 J17 **Cape May Court House** New Jersey, NE USA *39.03N 74.46W*
Cape Palmas *see* Harper
15 H2 **Cape Parry** Northwest Territories, N Canada *70.10N 124.33W*
67 P19 **Cape Rise** *undersea feature* SW Indian Ocean
Cape Saint Jacques *see* Vung Tau
Capesterre *see* Capesterre-Belle-Eau
47 Y6 **Capesterre-Belle-Eau** *var.* Capesterre. Basse Terre, S Guadeloupe *16.03N 61.33W*
85 D26 **Cape Town** *var.* Ekapa, *Afr.* Kaapstad, Kapstad. ● (South Africa-legislative capital) Western Cape, SW South Africa *33.55S 18.28E*
85 E26 **Cape Town** ✕ Western Cape, SW South Africa *31.51S 21.06E*
78 D9 **Cape Verde** *off.* Republic of Cape Verde, *Port.* Cabo Verde, Ilhas do Cabo Verde. ◆ *republic* E Atlantic Ocean
66 L11 **Cape Verde Basin** *undersea feature* E Atlantic Ocean
68 K5 **Cape Verde Islands** *island group* E Atlantic Ocean
66 L10 **Cape Verde Plain** *undersea feature* E Atlantic Ocean
Cape Verde Plateau/Cape Verde Rise *see* Cape Verde Terrace
66 L11 **Cape Verde Terrace** *var.* Cape Verde Plateau, Cape Verde Rise. *undersea feature* E Atlantic Ocean
189 V2 **Cape York Peninsula** *peninsula* Queensland, N Australia
46 M8 **Cap-Haïtien** *var.* Le Cap. N Haiti *19.43N 72.12W*
45 T15 **Capira** Panamá, C Panama *8.45N 79.52W*
12 K8 **Capitachouane** ⁓ Quebec, SE Canada
12 L8 **Capitachouane, Lac** ◎ Quebec, SE Canada
39 T13 **Capitan** New Mexico, SW USA *33.33N 105.34W*
204 G3 **Capitán Arturo Prat** *Chilean research station* South Shetland Islands, Antarctica *62.24S 59.42W*
39 S13 **Capitan Mountains** ▲▲ New Mexico, SW USA
64 M3 **Capitán Pablo Lagerenza** *var.* Mayor Pablo Lagerenza. Chaco, N Paraguay *19.55S 60.46W*
39 T13 **Capitan Peak** ▲ New Mexico, SW USA *33.35N 105.15W*
196 H5 **Capitol Hill** Saipan, S Northern Mariana Islands
62 I9 **Capivara, Represa** ⊡ S Brazil
63 J16 **Capivari** Rio Grande do Sul, S Brazil *30.08S 50.32W*
115 H15 **Čapljina** Federacija Bosna I Hercegovina, S Bosnia and Herzegovina *43.07N 17.42E*
85 M15 **Capoche** *var.* Kapoche. ⁓ Mozambique/Zambia
Capo Delgado, Província de *see* Cabo Delgado
109 K17 **Capodichino** ✕ (Napoli) Campania, S Italy *40.53N 14.15E*
Capodistria *see* Koper
108 E12 **Capraia, Isola** *island* Archipelago Toscano, C Italy
109 B16 **Caprara, Punta** *var.* Punta dello Scorno. *headland* Isola Asinara, W Italy *41.07N 8.19E*
Capraria, Isola di to Capraia, Isola *see* Cabrera
12 F10 **Capreol** Ontario, S Canada *46.43N 80.55W*
109 K18 **Capri** Campania, S Italy *40.33N 14.14E*
183 S9 **Capricorn Tablemount** *undersea feature* W Pacific Ocean *18.34S 172.12W*
109 J18 **Capri, Isola di** *island* S Italy
85 G16 **Caprivi** ◐ *district* NE Namibia
Caprivi Concession *see* Caprivi Strip
85 F16 **Caprivi Strip** *Ger.* Caprivizipfel; *prev.* Caprivi Concession. *cultural region* NE Namibia
Caprivizipfel *see* Caprivi Strip
27 O5 **Cap Rock Escarpment** *cliffs* Texas, SW USA
13 R10 **Cap-Rouge** Quebec, SE Canada *46.45N 71.18W*
Cap Saint-Jacques *see* Vung Tau
40 F12 **Captain Cook** Hawaii, USA, C Pacific Ocean *19.30N 155.55W*
191 R10 **Captains Flat** New South Wales, SE Australia *35.37S 149.28E*
104 K14 **Captieux** Gironde, SW France *44.16N 0.15W*
109 K17 **Capua** Campania, S Italy *41.06N 14.13E*
56 F14 **Caquetá** *off.* Departamento del Caquetá. ◐ *province* S Colombia
56 E13 **Caquetá, Río** *var.* Rio Japurá, Yapurá. ⁓ Brazil/Colombia *see also* Japurá, Rio
CAR *see* Central African Republic
Cara *see* Kara
59 I16 **Carabaya, Cordillera** ▲▲ E Peru
56 K5 **Carabobo** *off.* Estado Carabobo. ◐ *state* N Venezuela
118 I14 **Caracal** Olt, S Romania *44.07N 24.18E*
60 F10 **Caracaraí** Rondônia, W Brazil *1.46N 61.10W*
56 L5 **Caracas** ● (Venezuela) Distrito Federal, N Venezuela *10.28N 66.53W*
56 I5 **Carache** Trujillo, N Venezuela *9.40N 70.15W*
62 N10 **Caraguatatuba** São Paulo, S Brazil *23.37S 45.24W*
50 I7 **Carajás, Serra dos** ▲▲ N Brazil
Caralis *see* Cagliari
56 E9 **Caramanta** Antioquia, W Colombia *5.36N 75.37W*
179 Q11 **Caramoan** Catanduanes Island, N Philippines *13.47N 123.49E*
Caramurat *see* Mihail Kogălniceanu
118 F12 **Caransebeş** *Ger.* Karansebesch, *Hung.* Karánsebes. Caraş-Severin, SW Romania *45.23N 22.13E*
Carapella *see* Carapelle
109 M16 **Carapelle** *var.* Carapella. ⁓ SE Italy
57 O9 **Carapo** Bolívar, SE Venezuela
11 P13 **Caraquet** New Brunswick, SE Canada *47.48N 64.58W*
Caras *see* Caraz
118 F12 **Caraşova** *Hung.* Krassóvár. Caraş-Severin, SW Romania *45.10N 21.51E*
118 F12 **Caraş-Severin** ◐ *county* SW Romania
44 M5 **Caratasca, Laguna de** *lagoon* NE Honduras
60 C13 **Carauari** Amazonas, NW Brazil *4.55S 66.57W*
Caravaca *see* Caravaca de la Cruz
107 Q12 **Caravaca de la Cruz** *var.* Caravaca. Murcia, SE Spain *38.06N 1.51W*
108 E7 **Caravaggio** Lombardia, N Italy *45.31N 9.39E*
109 C18 **Caravai, Passo di** *pass* Sardegna, Italy, C Mediterranean Sea *40.06N 9.19E*
61 O19 **Caravelas** Bahia, E Brazil *17.45S 39.15W*
58 C12 **Caraz** *var.* Caras. Ancash, W Peru *9.01S 77.48W*
63 H14 **Carazinho** Rio Grande do Sul, S Brazil *28.16S 52.46W*
44 J11 **Carazo** ◐ *department* SW Nicaragua
Carballiño *see* O Carballiño
106 G2 **Carballo** Galicia, NW Spain *43.12N 8.42W*
9 W16 **Carberry** Manitoba, S Canada *49.52N 99.19W*
42 F4 **Carbó** Sonora, NW Mexico *29.40N 110.54W*
109 C20 **Carbonara, Capo** *headland* Sardegna, Italy, C Mediterranean Sea *39.06N 9.31E*
39 Q5 **Carbondale** Colorado, C USA *39.24N 107.12W*
32 L17 **Carbondale** Illinois, N USA *37.43N 89.13W*
29 Q4 **Carbondale** Kansas, C USA *38.49N 95.41W*
20 I13 **Carbondale** Pennsylvania, NE USA *41.34N 75.30W*
11 V12 **Carbonear** Newfoundland, SE Canada *47.45N 53.16W*
107 Q9 **Carboneras de Guadazaón** *var.* Carboneras de Guadazón. Castilla-La Mancha, C Spain *39.54N 1.49W*
Carboneras de Guadazón *see* Carboneras de Guadazaón
25 O3 **Carbon Hill** Alabama, S USA *33.53N 87.31W*
109 B20 **Carbonia** *var.* Carbonia Centro. Sardegna, Italy, C Mediterranean Sea *39.10N 8.31E*
Carbonia Centro *see* Carbonia
107 S10 **Carcaixent** País Valenciano, E Spain *39.07N 0.28W*
Carcaso *see* Carcassonne
67 B24 **Carcass Island** *island* NW Falkland Islands
105 O16 **Carcassonne** *anc.* Carcaso. Aude, S France *43.13N 2.21E*
107 R12 **Carche** ▲ S Spain *38.24N 1.11W*
58 A13 **Carchi** ◐ *province* N Ecuador
8 I8 **Carcross** Yukon Territory, W Canada *60.10N 134.40W*
Cardamomes, Chaîne des *see* Krâvanh, Chuŏr Phnum
161 G22 **Cardamom Hills** ▲▲ SW India
Cardamom Mountains *see* Krâvanh, Chuŏr Phnum
106 M12 **Cardeña** Andalucía, S Spain *38.16N 4.19W*
46 D4 **Cárdenas** Matanzas, W Cuba *23.01N 81.12W*
43 O11 **Cárdenas** San Luis Potosí, C Mexico *22.03N 99.30W*
43 U15 **Cárdenas** Tabasco, SE Mexico *18.00N 93.21W*
65 H21 **Cardiel, Lago** ◎ S Argentina
99 K22 **Cardiff** *Wel.* Caerdydd. ◐ S Wales, UK *51.30N 3.13W*
99 J22 **Cardiff-Wales** ✕ S Wales, UK *51.24N 3.22W*
99 I21 **Cardigan** *Wel.* Aberteifi. SW Wales, UK *52.06N 4.40W*
99 I20 **Cardigan** *cultural region* W Wales, UK
99 I20 **Cardigan Bay** *bay* W Wales, UK
21 N8 **Cardigan, Mount** ▲ New Hampshire, NE USA *43.39N 71.52W*
12 M13 **Cardinal** Ontario, SE Canada *44.48N 75.22W*
107 V5 **Cardona** Cataluña, NE Spain *41.55N 1.40E*
63 E19 **Cardona** Soriano, SW Uruguay *33.52S 57.18W*
107 V4 **Cardoner** ⁓ NE Spain
9 Q17 **Cardston** Alberta, SW Canada *49.13N 113.19W*
189 W5 **Cardwell** Queensland, NE Australia *18.24S 146.06E*
118 G8 **Carei** *Ger.* Gross-Karol, Karol, *Hung.* Nagykároly; *prev.* Careii-Mari. Satu Mare, NW Romania *47.40N 22.27E*
Careii-Mari *see* Carei
60 F13 **Careiro** Amazonas, NW Brazil *3.39S 60.22W*
104 J4 **Carentan** Manche, N France *49.18N 1.15W*
106 M2 **Cares** ⁓ N Spain
35 P14 **Carey** Idaho, NW USA *43.17N 113.58W*
33 S12 **Carey** Ohio, N USA *40.57N 83.22W*
27 P4 **Carey** Texas, SW USA *34.28N 100.18W*
188 L11 **Carey, Lake** ◎ Western Australia
181 O8 **Cargados Carajos Bank** *undersea feature* C Indian Ocean
104 G6 **Carhaix-Plouguer** Finistère, NW France *48.16N 3.34W*
63 A22 **Carhué** Buenos Aires, E Argentina *37.10S 62.45W*
57 O5 **Cariaco** Sucre, NE Venezuela *10.28N 63.33W*
109 O20 **Cariati** Calabria, SW Italy *39.30N 16.57E*
2 H17 **Caribbean Plate** *tectonic feature*
46 I11 **Caribbean Sea** *sea* W Atlantic Ocean
9 N15 **Cariboo Mountains** ▲▲ British Columbia, SW Canada
9 W9 **Caribou** Manitoba, C Canada *59.27N 97.43W*
21 S2 **Caribou** Maine, NE USA *46.51N 68.00W*
9 P10 **Caribou Mountains** ▲▲ Alberta, SW Canada
Caribrod *see* Dimitrovgrad
42 I6 **Carichic** Chihuahua, N Mexico *27.57N 107.01W*
179 Qq13 **Carigara** Leyte, C Philippines *11.15N 124.43E*
105 R3 **Carignan** Ardennes, N France *49.38N 5.08E*
191 Q5 **Carinda** New South Wales, SE Australia *30.26S 147.45E*
107 R6 **Cariñena** Aragón, NE Spain *41.19N 1.13W*
109 I23 **Carini** Sicilia, Italy, C Mediterranean Sea *38.06N 13.09E*
109 K17 **Carinola** Campania, S Italy *41.14N 14.03E*
Carinthi *see* Kärnten
57 O5 **Caripe** Monagas, NE Venezuela *10.06N 63.30W*
57 P5 **Caripito** Monagas, NE Venezuela *10.03N 63.05W*
13 W7 **Carleton** Quebec, SE Canada *48.07N 66.07W*
33 S10 **Carleton** Michigan, N USA *42.03N 83.23W*
11 O14 **Carleton, Mount** ▲ New Brunswick, SE Canada *47.10N 66.54W*
12 L13 **Carleton Place** Ontario, SE Canada *45.09N 76.07W*
37 V3 **Carlin** Nevada, W USA *40.40N 116.09W*
32 K14 **Carlinville** Illinois, N USA *39.16N 89.52W*
99 K14 **Carlisle** *anc.* Caer Luel, Luguvallium, Luguvallum. NW England, UK *54.54N 2.55W*
29 V11 **Carlisle** Arkansas, C USA *34.46N 91.45W*
33 N15 **Carlisle** Indiana, N USA *38.57N 87.23W*
31 V14 **Carlisle** Iowa, C USA *41.30N 93.29W*
23 N5 **Carlisle** Kentucky, S USA *38.19N 83.59W*
20 F15 **Carlisle** Pennsylvania, NE USA *40.10N 77.10W*
23 Q11 **Carlisle** South Carolina, SE USA *34.35N 81.27W*
40 J17 **Carlisle Island** *island* Aleutian Islands, Alaska, USA
29 R7 **Carl Junction** Missouri, C USA *37.10N 94.34W*
109 A20 **Carloforte** Sardegna, Italy, C Mediterranean Sea *39.10N 8.17E*
Carlopago *see* Karlobag
63 B21 **Carlos Casares** Buenos Aires, E Argentina *35.39S 61.28W*
63 E18 **Carlos Reyles** Durazno, C Uruguay *33.04S 56.28W*
63 A21 **Carlos Tejedor** Buenos Aires, E Argentina *35.23S 62.31W*
99 F19 **Carlow** *Ir.* Ceatharlach. SE Ireland *52.49N 6.55W*
99 F19 **Carlow** *Ir.* Cheatharlach. *cultural region* SE Ireland
98 F7 **Carloway** NW Scotland, UK *58.16N 6.48W*
Carlsbad *see* Karlovy Vary
37 U17 **Carlsbad** California, W USA *33.09N 117.21W*
39 U15 **Carlsbad** New Mexico, SW USA *32.24N 104.14W*
133 N13 **Carlsberg Ridge** *undersea feature* S Arabian Sea
Carlsruhe *see* Karlsruhe
31 W6 **Carlton** Minnesota, N USA *46.39N 92.25W*
9 V17 **Carlyle** Saskatchewan, S Canada *49.39N 102.18W*
32 L15 **Carlyle** Illinois, N USA *38.36N 89.22W*
32 L15 **Carlyle Lake** ⊡ Illinois, N USA
8 H7 **Carmacks** Yukon Territory, W Canada *62.04N 136.21W*
108 B9 **Carmagnola** Piemonte, NW Italy *44.50N 7.43E*
9 X16 **Carman** Manitoba, S Canada *49.31N 97.58W*
Carmana/Carmania *see* Kermān
99 I21 **Carmarthen** SW Wales, UK *51.52N 4.19W*
99 I21 **Carmarthen** *cultural region* SW Wales, UK
99 I22 **Carmarthen Bay** *inlet* SW Wales, UK
105 N14 **Carmaux** Tarn, S France *44.03N 2.09E*
37 N11 **Carmel** California, W USA *36.32N 121.54W*
33 O13 **Carmel** Indiana, N USA *39.58N 86.07W*
20 L13 **Carmel** New York, NE USA *41.25N 73.40W*
99 H18 **Carmel Head** *headland* NW Wales, UK *53.24N 4.35W*
44 E2 **Carmelita** Petén, N Guatemala *17.33N 90.10W*
63 D19 **Carmelo** Colonia, SW Uruguay *34.00S 58.20W*
43 V14 **Carmen** *var.* Ciudad del Carmen. Campeche, SE Mexico *18.37N 91.49W*
63 A25 **Carmen de Patagones** Buenos Aires, E Argentina *40.45S 63.00W*
42 F8 **Carmen, Isla** *island* W Mexico
42 M5 **Carmen, Sierra del** ▲▲ NW Mexico
32 M16 **Carmi** Illinois, N USA *38.05N 88.09W*
37 O7 **Carmichael** California, W USA *38.36N 121.21W*
Carmiel *see* Karmi'él
27 U11 **Carmine** Texas, SW USA *30.07N 96.40W*
106 K14 **Carmona** Andalucía, S Spain *37.28N 5.37W*
Carmona *see* Uíge
Carnaro *see* Kvarner
12 I13 **Carnarvon** Ontario, SE Canada *45.03N 78.41W*
85 G24 **Carnarvon** Northern Cape, W South Africa *30.58S 22.07E*
Carnarvon *see* Caernarfon
188 K9 **Carnarvon Range** ▲▲ Western Australia
188 G9 **Carnarvon** Western Australia *24.57S 113.37E*
Carn Domhnach *see* Carndonagh
98 E13 **Carndonagh** *Ir.* Carn Domhnach. NW Ireland *55.15N 7.15W*
9 V17 **Carnduff** Saskatchewan, S Canada *49.10N 101.49W*
28 L11 **Carnegie** Oklahoma, C USA *35.06N 98.36W*
188 L9 **Carnegie, Lake** *salt lake* Western Australia
200 Oo8 **Carnegie Ridge** *undersea feature* E Pacific Ocean
98 H9 **Carn Eige** ▲ N Scotland, UK *57.18N 5.04W*
190 F5 **Carnes** South Australia *30.12S 134.31E*
204 J12 **Carney Island** *island* Antarctica
20 H16 **Carneys Point** New Jersey, NE USA *39.38N 75.29W*
Carniche, Alpi *see* Karnische Alpen
157 Q21 **Car Nicobar** *island* Nicobar Islands, India, NE Indian Ocean
81 H15 **Carnot** Mambéré-Kadéï, W Central African Republic *4.58N 15.55E*
190 F10 **Carnot, Cape** *headland* South Australia *34.57S 135.39E*
98 K11 **Carnoustie** E Scotland, UK *56.29N 2.42W*
99 F20 **Carnsore Point** *Ir.* Ceann an Chairn. *headland* SE Ireland *52.10N 6.22W*
15 Gg4 **Carnwath** ⁓ Northwest Territories, NW Canada
33 R8 **Caro** Michigan, N USA *43.29N 83.24W*
25 Z15 **Carol City** Florida, SE USA *25.56N 80.15W*
61 L14 **Carolina** Maranhão, E Brazil *7.19S 47.25W*
47 U5 **Carolina** E Puerto Rico *18.22N 65.57W*
23 V12 **Carolina Beach** North Carolina, SE USA *34.02N 77.53W*
Caroline Island *see* Millennium Island
201 N15 **Caroline Islands** *island group* C Micronesia
133 Z14 **Caroline Plate** *tectonic feature*
199 H7 **Caroline Ridge** *undersea feature* E Philippine Sea
Carolopois *see* Châlons-en-Champagne
47 V14 **Caroni Arena Dam** ⊡ Trinidad, Trinidad and Tobago
Caronie, Monti *see* Nebrodi, Monti
57 P7 **Caroní, Río** ⁓ E Venezuela
47 U14 **Caroni River** ⁓ Trinidad, Trinidad and Tobago
Caronium *see* A Coruña
56 J5 **Carora** Lara, N Venezuela *10.09N 70.06W*
88 F12 **Carpathian Mountains** *var.* Carpathians, *Cz./Pol.* Karpaty, *Ger.* Karpaten. ▲▲ Europe
Carpathians *see* Carpathian Mountains
Carpathos/Carpathus *see* Kárpathos
118 H12 **Carpaţii Meridionali** *var.* Alpi Transilvaniei, Carpaţii Sudici, *Eng.* South Carpathians, Transylvanian Alps, *Ger.* Südkarpaten, Transsylvanische Alpen, *Hung.* Déli-Kárpátok, Erdélyi-Havasok. ▲▲ C Romania
Carpaţii Sudici *see* Carpaţii Meridionali
182 L7 **Carpentaria, Gulf of** *gulf* N Australia
Carpentoracte *see* Carpentras
105 R14 **Carpentras** *anc.* Carpentoracte. Vaucluse, SE France *44.03N 5.03E*
108 F9 **Carpi** Emilia-Romagna, N Italy *44.46N 10.52E*
118 E11 **Cărpiniş** *Hung.* Gyertyámos. Timiş, W Romania *45.46N 20.51E*
37 R14 **Carpinteria** California, W USA *34.24N 119.30W*
25 S9 **Carrabelle** Florida, SE USA *29.51N 84.39W*
Carraig Aonair *see* Fastnet Rock
Carraig Fhearghais *see* Carrickfergus
Carraig Mhachaire Rois *see* Carrickmacross
Carraig na Siúire *see* Carrick-on-Suir
Carrantual *see* Carrauntoohil
108 E10 **Carrara** Toscana, C Italy *44.04N 10.07E*
63 F20 **Carrasco** ✕ (Montevideo) Canelones, S Uruguay *34.51S 56.00W*
107 P9 **Carrascosa del Campo** Castilla-La Mancha, C Spain *40.01N 2.34W*
56 H4 **Carrasquero** Zulia, NW Venezuela *11.00N 72.01W*
191 O9 **Carrathool** New South Wales, SE Australia *34.25S 145.30E*
Carrauntohil *see* Carrauntoohil
99 B21 **Carrauntoohil** *Ir.* Carrantual, Carrauntohil, Corrán Tuathail. ▲ SW Ireland *51.59N 9.45W*
47 Y15 **Carriacou** *island* N Grenada
99 G15 **Carrickfergus** *Ir.* Carraig Fhearghais. NE Northern Ireland, UK *54.43N 5.49W*
99 F16 **Carrickmacross** *Ir.* Carraig Mhachaire Rois. N Ireland *53.58N 6.43W*
99 D16 **Carrick-on-Shannon** *Ir.* Cora Droma Rúisc. NW Ireland *53.57N 8.04W*
99 E20 **Carrick-on-Suir** *Ir.* Carraig na Siúire. S Ireland *52.21N 7.25W*
190 I7 **Carrieton** South Australia *32.27S 138.33E*
42 L7 **Carrillo** Chihuahua, N Mexico *25.53N 103.54W*
31 O4 **Carrington** North Dakota, N USA *47.27N 99.07W*
106 M4 **Carrión** ⁓ N Spain
106 M4 **Carrión de los Condes** Castilla-León, N Spain *42.19N 4.37W*
27 P13 **Carrizo Springs** Texas, SW USA *28.31N 99.51W*
39 S13 **Carrizozo** New Mexico, SW USA *33.38N 105.52W*
31 T13 **Carroll** Iowa, C USA *42.04N 94.52W*
25 N4 **Carrollton** Alabama, S USA *33.13N 88.05W*
25 R3 **Carrollton** Georgia, SE USA *33.33N 85.04W*
32 K14 **Carrollton** Illinois, N USA *39.18N 90.24W*
22 L4 **Carrollton** Kentucky, S USA *38.40N 85.10W*
33 R8 **Carrollton** Michigan, N USA *43.27N 83.55W*
29 T3 **Carrollton** Missouri, C USA *39.21N 93.30W*
33 U12 **Carrollton** Ohio, N USA *40.34N 81.05W*
27 T6 **Carrollton** Texas, SW USA *32.57N 96.53W*
9 U14 **Carrot** ⁓ Saskatchewan, S Canada
9 U14 **Carrot River** Saskatchewan, C Canada *53.18N 103.31W*
20 J7 **Carry Falls Reservoir** ⊡ New York, NE USA
142 L11 **Çarşamba** Samsun, N Turkey *41.13N 36.43E*
30 L6 **Carson** North Dakota, N USA *46.21N 101.33W*
37 Q6 **Carson City** *state capital* Nevada, W USA *39.10N 119.46W*
37 R6 **Carson River** ⁓ Nevada, W USA
37 S5 **Carson Sink** *salt flat* Nevada, W USA
9 Q16 **Carstairs** Alberta, SW Canada *51.34N 114.01W*
Carstensz, Puntjak *see* Jaya, Puncak
56 E5 **Cartagena** *var.* Cartagena de los Indes. Bolívar, NW Colombia *10.24N 75.33W*
107 R13 **Cartagena** *anc.* Carthago Nova. Murcia, SE Spain *37.36N 0.58W*
Cartagena de los Indes *see* Cartagena
56 D10 **Cartago** Valle del Cauca, W Colombia *4.45N 75.55W*
45 N14 **Cartago** Cartago, C Costa Rica *9.49N 83.53W*
44 M14 **Cartago** *off.* Provincia de Cartago. ◐ *province* C Costa Rica
27 O11 **Carta Valley** Texas, SW USA *29.46N 100.37W*
106 F10 **Cartaxo** Santarém, C Portugal *39.10N 8.46W*
106 I14 **Cartaya** Andalucía, S Spain *37.16N 7.09W*
Carteret Islands *see* Tulun Islands
31 S15 **Carter Lake** Iowa, C USA *41.17N 95.55W*
25 S3 **Cartersville** Georgia, SE USA *34.10N 84.48W*
193 M14 **Carterton** Wellington, North Island, NZ *41.01S 175.32E*
32 J13 **Carthage** Illinois, N USA *40.25N 91.09W*
24 L5 **Carthage** Mississippi, S USA *32.43N 89.31W*
29 R7 **Carthage** Missouri, C USA *37.10N 94.18W*
20 I8 **Carthage** New York, NE USA *43.58N 75.36W*
23 T10 **Carthage** North Carolina, SE USA *35.19N 79.24W*
22 K8 **Carthage** Tennessee, S USA *36.16N 85.57W*
27 X7 **Carthage** Texas, SW USA *32.09N 94.20W*
76 M5 **Carthage** ✕ (Tunis) N Tunisia *36.51N 10.12E*

◆ Country ● Country Capital ◇ Dependent Territory ○ Dependent Territory Capital ◐ Administrative Region ✕ International Airport ▲ Mountain ▲▲ Mountain Range ※ Volcano ⁓ River ◎ Lake ⊡ Reservoir
239

CARTHAGO NOVA – CERRETO SANNITA

Carthago Nova see Cartagena
12 E10 Cartier Ontario, S Canada 46.40N 81.31W
56 E13 Cartogena de Chaira Caquetá, S Colombia 1.19N 74.52W
11 S8 Cartwright Newfoundland, E Canada 53.40N 57.00W
57 P9 Caruana de Montaña Bolívar, SE Venezuela 5.16N 63.12W
61 Q15 Caruaru Pernambuco, E Brazil 8.15S 35.55W
57 P5 Carúpano Sucre, NE Venezuela 10.39N 63.13W
Carusbur see Cherbourg
60 M12 Carutapera Maranhão, E Brazil 1.12S 45.57W
29 Y9 Caruthersville Missouri, C USA 36.07N 89.38W
105 O1 Carvin Pas-de-Calais, N France 50.31N 3.00E
60 E12 Carvoeiro Amazonas, NW Brazil 1.24S 61.59W
106 E10 Carvoeiro, Cabo headland C Portugal 39.19N 9.27W
23 U9 Cary North Carolina, SE USA 35.47N 78.46W
190 M3 Caryapundy Swamp wetland New South Wales/Queensland, SE Australia
67 E24 Carysfort, Cape headland East Falkland, Falkland Islands 51.25S 57.49W
76 F6 Casablanca Ar. Dar-el-Beida. NW Morocco 33.39N 7.30W
62 M8 Casa Branca São Paulo, S Brazil 21.47S 47.05W
38 L14 Casa Grande Arizona, SW USA 32.52N 111.45W
108 C8 Casale Monferrato Piemonte, NW Italy 45.07N 8.28E
108 E8 Casalpusterlengo Lombardia, N Italy 45.10N 9.37E
56 H10 Casanare off. Intendencia de Casanare. ◈ province C Colombia
57 P5 Casanay Sucre, NE Venezuela 10.30N 63.25W
26 K11 Casa Piedra Texas, SW USA 29.43N 104.03W
109 Q19 Casarano Puglia, SE Italy 40.01N 18.10E
44 J11 Casares Carazo, W Nicaragua 11.37N 86.19W
107 R10 Casas Ibáñez Castilla-La Mancha, C Spain 39.16N 1.28W
63 I14 Casca Rio Grande do Sul, S Brazil 28.39S 51.55W
180 I17 Cascade Mahé, NE Seychelles 4.39S 55.28E
35 N13 Cascade Idaho, NW USA 44.31N 116.02W
31 Y13 Cascade Iowa, C USA 42.18N 91.00W
35 R9 Cascade Montana, NW USA 47.15N 111.46W
193 B20 Cascade Point headland South Island, NZ 44.00S 168.23E
34 G13 Cascade Range ▲ Oregon/Washington, NW USA
35 N12 Cascade Reservoir ⊠ Idaho, NW USA
(0) E8 Cascadia Basin undersea feature NE Pacific Ocean
106 E11 Cascais Lisboa, C Portugal 38.40N 9.25W
13 W7 Cascapédia ≈ Quebec, SE Canada
61 I22 Cascavel Ceará, E Brazil 4.10S 38.15W
62 G11 Cascavel Paraná, S Brazil 24.55S 53.28W
108 I13 Cascia Umbria, C Italy 42.45N 13.01E
108 F11 Cascina Toscana, C Italy 43.40N 10.33E
21 Q8 Casco Bay bay Maine, NE USA
204 J7 Case Island island Antarctica
108 B8 Caselle ✕ (Torino) Piemonte, NW Italy 45.06N 7.41E
109 K17 Caserta Campania, S Italy 41.04N 14.19E
13 N8 Casey Quebec, SE Canada 47.50N 74.09W
32 M14 Casey Illinois, N USA 39.18N 87.59W
205 Y12 Casey Australian research station Antarctica 65.58S 111.04E
205 W3 Casey Bay bay Antarctica
82 Q11 Caseyr, Raas headland NE Somalia 11.51N 51.16E
99 D20 Cashel Ir. Caiseal. S Ireland 52.31N 7.52W
56 G6 Casigua Zulia, W Venezuela 8.46N 72.30W
63 B19 Casilda Santa Fe, C Argentina 33.04S 61.10W
Casim see General Toshevo
191 V4 Casino New South Wales, SE Australia 28.49S 153.01E
Casinum see Cassino
113 E17 Čáslav Ger. Tschaslau. Střední Čechy, C Czech Republic 49.54N 15.22E
58 C13 Casma Ancash, C Peru 9.27S 78.21W
178 J7 Ca, Sông ≈ N Vietnam
109 K17 Casoria Campania, S Italy 40.54N 14.28E
107 T6 Caspe Aragón, NE Spain 41.13N 0.03W
35 X15 Casper Wyoming, C USA 42.48N 106.22W
86 M10 Caspian Depression Kaz. Kaspiy Mangy Oypaty, Rus. Prikaspiyskaya Nizmennost'. depression Kazakhstan/Russian Federation
138 Kk9 Caspian Sea Az. Xäzär Dänizi, Kaz. Kaspiy Tengizi, Per. Bahr-e Khazar, Daryā-ye Khazar, Rus. Kaspiyskoye More. inland sea Asia/Europe
85 L14 Cassacatiza Tete, NW Mozambique 14.20S 32.24E
Cassai see Kasai
84 F13 Cassamba Moxico, E Angola 13.07S 20.22E
109 N20 Cassano allo Ionio Calabria, SE Italy 39.46N 16.16E
33 S8 Cass City Michigan, N USA 43.36N 83.10W
Cassel see Kassel
12 M13 Casselman Ontario, SE Canada 45.19N 75.04W
31 R5 Casselton North Dakota, N USA 46.53N 97.10W
61 M16 Cássia var. Santa Rita de Cassia. Bahia, E Brazil 11.03S 44.16W
8 J9 Cassiar British Columbia, W Canada 59.16N 129.45W
8 K10 Cassiar Mountains ▲ British Columbia, W Canada
85 C15 Cassinga Huíla, SW Angola 15.06S 16.05E
109 J16 Cassino prev. San Germano; anc. Casinum. Lazio, C Italy 41.29N 13.49E
31 T4 Cass Lake Minnesota, N USA 47.22N 94.36W
31 T4 Cass Lake ◎ Minnesota, N USA
33 P10 Cassopolis Michigan, N USA 41.56N 86.00W
33 S8 Cass River ≈ Michigan, N USA
29 S8 Cassville Missouri, C USA 36.40N 93.52W
Castamoni see Kastamonu
60 L12 Castanhal Pará, NE Brazil 1.16S 47.55W
106 G8 Castanheira de Pêra Leiria, C Portugal 40.01N 8.12W
43 N7 Castaños Coahuila de Zaragoza, NE Mexico 26.48N 101.25W
110 I10 Castasegna Graubünden, SE Switzerland 46.21N 9.30E
108 D8 Casteggio Lombardia, N Italy 45.01N 9.10E
109 K23 Castelbuono Sicilia, Italy, C Mediterranean Sea 37.55N 14.04E
109 K15 Castel di Sangro Abruzzo, C Italy 41.46N 14.03E
108 H7 Castelfranco Veneto Veneto, NE Italy 45.40N 11.55E
104 K14 Casteljaloux Lot-et-Garonne, SW France 44.19N 0.03E
109 L18 Castellabate var. Santa Maria di Castellabate. Campania, S Italy 40.16N 14.57E
109 I23 Castellammare del Golfo Sicilia, Italy, C Mediterranean Sea 38.01N 12.52E
109 H22 Castellammare, Golfo di gulf Sicilia, Italy, C Mediterranean Sea
105 U15 Castellane Alpes-de-Haute-Provence, SE France 43.49N 6.34E
109 O18 Castellaneta Puglia, SE Italy 40.37N 16.57E
108 E9 Castel l'Arquato Emilia-Romagna, C Italy 44.52N 9.51E
63 E21 Castelli Buenos Aires, E Argentina 36.07S 57.46W
107 T9 Castelló de la Plana var. Castellón. País Valenciano, E Spain 39.58N 0.03W
107 S8 Castellón ◈ province País Valenciano, E Spain
Castellón see Castelló de la Plana
107 S7 Castellote Aragón, NE Spain 40.46N 0.18W
105 N16 Castelnaudary Aude, S France 43.18N 1.57E
104 L16 Castelnau-Magnoac Hautes-Pyrénées, S France 43.18N 0.30E
108 F10 Castelnovo ne' Monti Emilia-Romagna, C Italy 44.26N 10.24E
Castelnuovo see Herceg-Novi
106 H9 Castelo Branco Castelo Branco, C Portugal 39.49N 7.30W
106 H8 Castelo Branco ◈ district C Portugal
106 I10 Castelo de Vide Portalegre, C Portugal 39.25N 7.27W
106 G9 Castelo do Bode, Barragem do ⊠ C Portugal
108 G10 Castel San Pietro Terme Emilia-Romagna, C Italy 44.22N 11.34E
109 B17 Castelsardo Sardegna, Italy, C Mediterranean Sea 40.54N 8.42E
104 M14 Castelsarrasin Tarn-et-Garonne, S France 44.01N 1.06E
109 I24 Casteltermini Sicilia, Italy, C Mediterranean Sea 37.33N 13.37E
109 H24 Castelvetrano Sicilia, Italy, C Mediterranean Sea 37.40N 12.46E
190 L12 Casterton Victoria, SE Australia 37.37S 141.22E
104 J15 Castets Landes, SW France 43.55N 1.08W
108 H12 Castiglione del Lago Umbria, C Italy 43.07N 12.02E
108 F13 Castiglione della Pescaia Toscana, C Italy 42.46N 10.53E
108 F8 Castiglione delle Stiviere Lombardia, N Italy 45.24N 10.31E
106 M9 Castilla-La Mancha ◈ autonomous community NE Spain
106 L5 Castilla-León var. Castilla y Leon. ◈ autonomous community NW Spain
107 N10 Castilla Nueva cultural region C Spain
107 N6 Castilla Vieja cultural region N Spain
Castilla y Leon see Castilla-León
Castillo de Locubim see Castillo de Locubín
107 N14 Castillo de Locubín var. Castillo de Locubim. Andalucía, S Spain 37.31N 3.55W
104 K13 Castillon-la-Bataille Gironde, SW France 44.51N 0.01W
65 I19 Castillo, Pampa del plain S Argentina
63 G19 Castillos Rocha, SE Uruguay 34.12S 53.52W
99 B16 Castlebar Ir. Caisleán an Bharraigh. W Ireland 53.52N 9.16W
99 F16 Castleblayney Ir. Baile na Lorgan. N Ireland 54.07N 6.43W
47 O11 Castle Bruce E Dominica 15.25N 61.15W
38 M5 Castle Dale Utah, W USA 39.10N 111.02W
38 I14 Castle Dome Peak ▲ Arizona, SW USA 33.04N 114.08W
99 J14 Castle Douglas S Scotland, UK 54.56N 3.55W
99 E14 Castlefinn Ir. Caisleán na Finne. NW Ireland 54.48N 7.36W
99 M17 Castleford N England, UK 53.43N 1.21W
9 O17 Castlegar British Columbia, SW Canada 49.18N 117.48W
66 B12 Castle Harbour inlet Bermuda, NW Atlantic Ocean
23 V12 Castle Hayne North Carolina, SE USA 34.23N 78.07W
99 B20 Castleisland Ir. Oileán Ciarral. SW Ireland 52.12N 9.30W
191 N12 Castlemaine Victoria, SE Australia 37.06S 144.13E
39 R5 Castle Peak ▲ Colorado, C USA 39.00N 106.51W
35 O13 Castle Peak ▲ Idaho, NW USA 44.02N 114.42W
192 N13 Castlepoint Wellington, North Island, NZ 40.54S 176.13E
99 D17 Castlerea Ir. An Caisleán Riabhach. W Ireland 53.45N 8.31W
99 G15 Castlereagh Ir. An Caisleán Riabhach. N Northern Ireland, UK 54.33N 5.53W
191 R6 Castlereagh River ≈ New South Wales, SE Australia
39 T5 Castle Rock Colorado, C USA 39.22N 104.51W
32 K7 Castle Rock Lake ⊠ Wisconsin, N USA
67 G25 Castle Rock Point headland S Saint Helena 16.01S 5.45W
99 I16 Castletown SE Isle of Man 54.04N 4.39W
31 R9 Castlewood South Dakota, N USA 44.43N 97.01W
9 R15 Castor Alberta, SW Canada 52.13N 111.54W
12 M13 Castor ≈ Ontario, SE Canada
29 X7 Castor River ≈ Missouri, C USA
Castra Albiensium see Castres
Castra Regina see Regensburg
105 N15 Castres anc. Castra Albiensium. Tarn, S France 43.36N 2.15E
100 H9 Castricum Noord-Holland, W Netherlands 52.33N 4.40E
47 S11 Castries ● (Saint Lucia) N Saint Lucia 14.01N 60.59W
62 J11 Castro Paraná, S Brazil 24.45S 50.58W
65 F17 Castro Los Lagos, W Chile 42.27S 73.48W
106 H7 Castro Daire Viseu, N Portugal 40.54N 7.55W
106 M13 Castro del Río Andalucía, S Spain 37.40N 4.28W
Castrogiovanni see Enna
106 H14 Castro Marim Faro, S Portugal 37.13N 7.25W
106 J2 Castropol Asturias, N Spain 43.30N 7.01W
107 O2 Castro-Urdiales var. Castro Urdiales. Cantabria, N Spain 43.22N 3.10W
106 G13 Castro Verde Beja, S Portugal 37.42N 8.04W
109 N19 Castrovillari Calabria, SW Italy 39.48N 16.12E
37 N10 Castroville California, W USA 36.46N 121.46W
27 R12 Castroville Texas, SW USA 29.21N 98.52W
106 K11 Castuera Extremadura, W Spain 38.43N 5.33W
63 F19 Casupá Florida, S Uruguay 34.04S 55.39W
193 A22 Caswell Sound sound South Island, NZ
143 Q13 Çat Erzurum, NE Turkey 39.40N 41.03E
44 K6 Catacamas Olancho, C Honduras 14.50N 85.54W
58 A10 Catacaos Piura, NW Peru 5.22S 80.40W
24 I7 Catahoula Lake ◎ Louisiana, S USA
143 S15 Çatak Van, SE Turkey 38.01N 43.04E
143 S15 Çatak Çayi ≈ SE Turkey
116 O12 Çatalca İstanbul, NW Turkey 41.09N 28.28E
116 O12 Çatalca Yarımadası physical region NW Turkey
64 H6 Catalina Antofagasta, N Chile 25.19S 69.37W
Catalonia see Cataluña
107 U5 Cataluña Cat. Catalunya; Eng. Catalonia. ◈ autonomous community N Spain
Catalunya see Cataluña
64 I7 Catamarca off. Provincia de Catamarca. ◈ province NW Argentina
Catamarca see San Fernando del Valle de Catamarca
179 Pp11 Catanauan Luzon, N Philippines 13.36N 122.19E
85 M16 Catandica Manica, C Mozambique 18.04S 33.10E
179 Qq11 Catanduanes Island island N Philippines
62 K8 Catanduva São Paulo, S Brazil 21.06S 48.57W
109 L24 Catania Sicilia, Italy, C Mediterranean Sea 37.31N 15.04E
109 M24 Catania, Golfo di gulf Sicilia, Italy, C Mediterranean Sea
47 U5 Cataño var. Cantaño. E Puerto Rico 18.26N 66.06W
109 O21 Catanzaro Calabria, SW Italy 38.53N 16.36E
109 O22 Catanzaro Marina var. Marina di Catanzaro. Calabria, S Italy 38.48N 16.33E
27 Q14 Catarina Texas, SW USA 28.19N 99.36W
179 Qq12 Catarman Samar, C Philippines 12.29N 124.34E
107 S10 Catarroja País Valenciano, E Spain 39.24N 0.24W
23 R11 Catawba River ≈ North Carolina/South Carolina, SE USA
179 R12 Catbalogan Samar, C Philippines 11.49N 124.55E
12 I14 Catchacoma Ontario, SE Canada 44.43N 78.19W
43 S15 Catemaco Veracruz-Llave, SE Mexico 18.28N 95.10W
Cathair na Mart see Westport
Cathair Saidhbhín see Cahersiveen
33 P5 Cat Head Point headland Michigan, N USA 45.11N 85.37W
25 Q2 Cathedral Caverns cave Alabama, S USA 34.36N 86.11W
37 V16 Cathedral City California, W USA 33.45N 116.27W
26 K10 Cathedral Mountain ▲ Texas, SW USA 30.10N 103.39W
34 G10 Cathlamet Washington, NW USA 46.12N 123.24W
78 G13 Catió S Guinea-Bissau 11.17N 15.16W
57 O10 Catisimiña Bolívar, SE Venezuela 4.07N 63.40W
44 J3 Cat Island island C Bahamas
10 B9 Cat Lake Ontario, S Canada 51.47N 91.52W
23 P5 Catlettsburg Kentucky, S USA 38.24N 82.37W
193 D24 Catlins ≈ South Island, NZ
37 R1 Catnip Mountain ▲ Nevada, W USA 41.53N 119.19W
43 Z11 Catoche, Cabo headland SE Mexico 21.36N 87.04W
29 P9 Catoosa Oklahoma, C USA 36.11N 95.45W
43 N10 Catorce San Luis Potosí, C Mexico 23.42N 100.49W
65 I14 Catriel Río Negro, C Argentina 37.54S 67.52W
64 K13 Catriló La Pampa, C Argentina 36.24S 63.25W
60 F11 Catrimani Roraima, N Brazil 0.24N 61.30W
60 E10 Catrimani, Rio ≈ N Brazil
20 K11 Catskill New York, NE USA 42.13N 73.52W
20 K11 Catskill Creek ≈ New York, NE USA
20 J11 Catskill Mountains ▲ New York, NE USA
20 D11 Cattaraugus Creek ≈ New York, NE USA
Cattaro see Kotor
Cattaro, Bocche di see Kotorska, Boka
109 I24 Cattolica Eraclea Sicilia, Italy, C Mediterranean Sea 37.27N 13.24E
85 B14 Catumbela ≈ W Angola
85 N14 Catur Niassa, N Mozambique 13.50S 35.43E
84 C10 Cauale ≈ NE Angola
179 Pp9 Cauayan Luzon, N Philippines 16.55N 121.46E
56 C12 Cauca off. Departamento del Cauca. ◈ province SW Colombia
49 P5 Cauca ≈ SE Venezuela
60 P13 Caucaia Ceará, E Brazil 3.43S 38.45W
56 E7 Cauca, Río ≈ N Colombia
56 E7 Caucasia Antioquia, NW Colombia 7.58N 75.13W
143 Q8 Caucasus Rus. Kavkaz. ▲ Georgia/Russian Federation
64 I10 Caucete San Juan, W Argentina 31.37S 68.16W
107 R11 Caudete Castilla-La Mancha, C Spain 38.42N 1.00W
105 P2 Caudry Nord, N France 50.07N 3.24E
84 D11 Caungula Lunda Norte, NE Angola 8.22S 18.37E
64 G13 Cauquenes Maule, C Chile 35.58S 72.22W
57 N8 Caura, Río ≈ C Venezuela
13 V7 Causapscal Quebec, SE Canada 48.22N 67.13W
119 N10 Căuşeni Rus. Kaushany. E Moldova 46.37N 29.21E
104 M14 Caussade Tarn-et-Garonne, S France 44.10N 1.31E
104 K17 Cauterets Hautes-Pyrénées, S France 42.53N 0.08W
8 J15 Caution, Cape headland British Columbia, SW Canada 51.10N 127.43W
46 H7 Cauto ≈ E Cuba
Cauvery see Kāveri
104 L3 Caux, Pays de physical region N France
109 L18 Cava dei Tirreni Campania, S Italy 40.42N 14.42E
106 G6 Cávado ≈ N Portugal
Cavaia see Kavajë
105 R15 Cavaillon Vaucluse, SE France 43.51N 5.01E
105 U16 Cavalaire-sur-Mer Var, SE France 43.10N 6.31E
108 G6 Cavalese Ger. Gablös. Trentino-Alto Adige, N Italy 46.18N 11.29E
31 Q2 Cavalier North Dakota, N USA 48.47N 97.37W
78 L17 Cavalla var. Cavally, Cavally Fleuve. ≈ Ivory Coast/Liberia
107 Y8 Cavalleria, Cap de var. Cabo Caballeria. headland Menorca, Spain, W Mediterranean Sea 40.04N 4.06E
192 K2 Cavalli Islands island group N NZ
Cavally/Cavally Fleuve see Cavalla
99 E16 Cavan Ir. Cabhán. N Ireland 54.00N 7.21W
99 E16 Cavan Ir. An Cabhán. cultural region N Ireland
108 H8 Cavarzere Veneto, NE Italy 45.07N 12.04E
29 W9 Cave City Arkansas, C USA 35.56N 91.33W
22 K7 Cave City Kentucky, S USA 37.08N 85.57W
67 M25 Cave Point headland S Tristan da Cunha
23 N5 Cave Run Lake ⊠ Kentucky, S USA
60 K11 Caviana de Fora, Ilha var. Ilha Caviana. island N Brazil
Caviana, Ilha see Caviana de Fora, Ilha
115 I16 Cavtat It. Ragusavecchia. Dubrovnik-Neretva, SE Croatia 42.36N 18.13E
Cawnpore see Kānpur
Caxamarca see Cajamarca
60 A13 Caxias Amazonas, W Brazil 4.27S 71.27W
60 N13 Caxias Maranhão, E Brazil 4.52S 43.19W
63 I15 Caxias do Sul Rio Grande do Sul, S Brazil 29.13S 51.10W
44 J4 Caxinas, Punta headland N Honduras 16.01N 86.02W
84 B11 Caxito Bengo, NW Angola 8.34S 13.37E
142 F14 Çay Afyon, W Turkey 38.34N 31.01E
42 L15 Cayacal, Punta var. Punta Mongrove. headland S Mexico 17.55N 102.09W
58 C6 Cayambe Pichincha, N Ecuador 0.01N 78.10W
58 C6 Cayambe ▲ N Ecuador 0.00N 77.58W
23 R12 Cayce South Carolina, SE USA 33.58N 81.04W
57 Y10 Cayenne ○ (French Guiana) NE French Guiana 4.55N 52.18W
57 Y10 Cayenne ✕ NE French Guiana 4.55N 52.18W
46 K10 Cayes var. Les Cayes. SW Haiti 18.10N 73.48W
47 U6 Cayey C Puerto Rico 18.06N 66.09W
47 U6 Cayey, Sierra de ▲ E Puerto Rico
105 N14 Caylus Tarn-et-Garonne, S France 44.13N 1.42E
46 E8 Cayman Brac island E Cayman Islands
46 D8 Cayman Islands ◇ UK dependent territory W West Indies
66 D11 Cayman Trench undersea feature NW Caribbean Sea
49 O3 Cayman Trough undersea feature NW Caribbean Sea
82 O13 Caynabo Togdheer, N Somalia 8.55N 46.28E
44 F3 Cayo ◈ district SW Belize
Cayo see San Ignacio
45 N9 Cayos Guerrero reef E Nicaragua
45 O9 Cayos King reef E Nicaragua
46 E4 Cay Sal islet SW Bahamas
12 G16 Cayuga Ontario, S Canada 42.57N 79.49W
27 V8 Cayuga Texas, SW USA 31.55N 95.57W
20 G10 Cayuga Lake ◎ New York, NE USA
106 K13 Cazalla de la Sierra Andalucía, S Spain 37.56N 5.46W
118 L14 Căzănești Ialomița, SE Romania 44.36N 27.02E
104 M16 Cazères Haute-Garonne, S France 43.15N 1.11E
114 E10 Cazin Federacija Bosna I Hercegovina, NW Bosnia and Herzegovina 44.58N 15.58E
84 G13 Cazombo Moxico, E Angola 11.53S 22.52E
107 O13 Cazorla Andalucía, S Spain 37.55N 3.00W
Cazza see Sušac
106 L4 Cea ≈ NW Spain
Ceadâr-Lunga see Ciadîr-Lunga
Ceanannas see Kells
Ceann Toirc see Kanturk
60 O13 Ceará off. Estado do Ceará. ◈ state C Brazil
Ceará see Fortaleza
Ceara Abyssal Plain see Ceará Plain
61 Q14 Ceará Mirim Rio Grande do Norte, E Brazil 5.30S 35.50W
66 J13 Ceará Plain var. Ceara Abyssal Plain. undersea feature W Atlantic Ocean
66 I13 Ceará Ridge undersea feature C Atlantic Ocean
Ceatharlach see Carlow
45 Q17 Cébaco, Isla island SW Panama
42 K7 Ceballos Durango, C Mexico 26.33N 104.07W
63 G19 Cebollatí Rocha, E Uruguay 33.15S 53.49W
63 G19 Cebollatí, Río ≈ E Uruguay
107 P5 Cebollera ▲ N Spain 42.01N 2.40W
106 M8 Cebreros Castilla-León, N Spain 40.27N 4.28W
179 Qq14 Cebu off. Cebu City. Cebu, C Philippines 10.16N 123.45E
179 Qq13 Cebu island C Philippines
109 J16 Ceccano Lazio, C Italy 41.34N 13.19E
Čechy see Bohemia
108 F12 Cecina Toscana, C Italy 43.18N 10.31E
28 K4 Cedar Bluff Reservoir ⊠ Kansas, C USA
32 M8 Cedarburg Wisconsin, N USA 43.18N 87.58W
38 J7 Cedar City Utah, W USA 37.40N 113.03W
27 T11 Cedar Creek Texas, SW USA 30.04N 97.30W
30 L7 Cedar Creek ≈ North Dakota, N USA
27 U7 Cedar Creek Reservoir ⊠ Texas, SW USA
31 W13 Cedar Falls Iowa, C USA 42.31N 92.27W
33 N8 Cedar Grove Wisconsin, N USA 43.31N 87.48W
23 Y6 Cedar Island island Virginia, NE USA
25 U11 Cedar Key Cedar Keys, Florida, SE USA 29.08N 83.03W
25 U11 Cedar Keys island group Florida, SE USA
9 V14 Cedar Lake ◎ Manitoba, C Canada
12 I11 Cedar Lake ◎ Ontario, SE Canada
26 M6 Cedar Lake ◎ Texas, SW USA
31 X13 Cedar Rapids Iowa, C USA 41.58N 91.39W
31 X14 Cedar River ≈ Iowa/Minnesota, C USA
31 O14 Cedar River ≈ Nebraska, C USA
33 P8 Cedar Springs Michigan, N USA 43.13N 85.33W
25 R3 Cedartown Georgia, SE USA 34.00N 85.16W
29 O7 Cedar Vale Kansas, C USA 37.06N 96.30W
37 Q2 Cedarville California, W USA 41.30N 120.10W
106 H1 Cedeira Galicia, NW Spain 43.40N 8.03W
44 H8 Cedeño Choluteca, S Honduras 13.10N 87.25W
43 N10 Cedral San Luis Potosí, C Mexico 23.47N 100.40W
44 I6 Cedros Francisco Morazán, C Honduras 14.38N 87.09W
42 M9 Cedros Zacatecas, C Mexico 24.39N 101.47W
42 B5 Cedros, Isla island W Mexico
199 Mm6 Cedros Trench undersea feature E Pacific Ocean
190 E7 Ceduna South Australia 32.09S 133.43E
112 D10 Cedynia Ger. Zehden. Zachodniopomorskie, W Poland 52.54N 14.15E
82 P12 Ceelaayo Sanaag, N Somalia 11.18N 49.20E
83 O16 Ceel Buur It. El Bur; Galguduud, C Somalia 4.36N 46.33E
83 N15 Ceel Dheere var. Ceel Dher, It. El Dere. Galguduud, C Somalia 5.18N 46.07E
Ceel Dher see Ceel Dheere
83 P14 Ceel Xamure Mudug, E Somalia 7.15N 48.55E
82 O12 Ceerigaabo var. Erigabo, Erigavo. Sanaag, N Somalia 10.34N 47.22E
109 J23 Cefalu anc. Cephaloedium. Sicilia, Italy, C Mediterranean Sea 38.01N 14.01E
107 N6 Cega ≈ N Spain
113 K23 Cegléd prev. Czegléd. Pest, C Hungary 47.08N 19.45E
115 N18 Čegrane W FYR Macedonia 41.50N 20.59E
107 Q13 Cehegín Murcia, SE Spain 38.04N 1.48W
142 K12 Çekerek Yozgat, N Turkey 40.04N 35.30E
109 J15 Celano Abruzzo, C Italy 42.06N 13.33E
106 H4 Celanova Galicia, NW Spain 42.09N 7.58W
44 F6 Celaque, Cordillera de ▲ W Honduras
43 N13 Celaya Guanajuato, C Mexico 20.31N 100.48W
Celebes see Sulawesi
198 Ff8 Celebes Basin undersea feature SE South China Sea
175 Qq4 Celebes Sea Ind. Laut Sulawesi. sea Indonesia/Philippines
43 W12 Celestún Yucatán, E Mexico 20.49N 90.22W
33 Q12 Celina Ohio, N USA 40.33N 84.34W
22 L8 Celina Tennessee, S USA 36.30N 85.30W
27 U5 Celina Texas, SW USA 33.19N 96.46W
114 G11 Čelinac Donji Republika Srpska, N Bosnia and Herzegovina 44.43N 17.19E
111 V10 Celje Ger. Cilli. C Slovenia 46.16N 15.14E
113 G23 Celldömölk Vas, W Hungary 47.16N 17.10E
102 J12 Celle var. Zelle. Niedersachsen, N Germany 52.37N 10.04E
101 D19 Celles Hainaut, SW Belgium 50.42N 3.25E
106 I7 Celorico da Beira Guarda, N Portugal 40.37N 7.24W
Celovec see Klagenfurt
66 M7 Celtic Sea Ir. An Mhuir Cheilteach. sea SW British Isles
66 N7 Celtic Shelf undersea feature E Atlantic Ocean
116 L13 Çeltik Gölu ◎ NW Turkey
115 M14 Čemerno ≈ C Yugoslavia
175 Oo16 Cempi, Teluk bay Nusa Tenggara, S Indonesia
107 Q12 Cenajo, Embalse del ⊠ S Spain
176 Ww10 Cenderawasih, Teluk var. Teluk Irian, Teluk Sarera. bay W Pacific Ocean
107 P4 Cenicero La Rioja, N Spain 42.28N 2.37W
108 E9 Ceno ≈ NW Italy
104 K13 Cenon Gironde, SW France 44.51N 0.33W
12 K13 Centennial Lake ◎ Ontario, SE Canada
Centennial State see Colorado
39 S7 Center Colorado, C USA 37.45N 106.06W
31 Q13 Center Nebraska, C USA 42.33N 97.51W
30 M5 Center North Dakota, N USA 47.07N 101.18W
27 X8 Center Texas, SW USA 31.46N 94.10W
31 W8 Center City Minnesota, N USA 45.22N 92.46W
38 L5 Centerfield Utah, W USA 39.07N 111.49W
22 K9 Center Hill Lake ⊠ Tennessee, S USA
31 X13 Center Point Iowa, C USA 42.11N 91.47W
27 R11 Center Point Texas, SW USA 29.56N 99.01W
31 W16 Centerville Iowa, C USA 40.42N 92.49W
29 W7 Centerville Missouri, C USA 37.27N 91.01W
31 R12 Centerville South Dakota, N USA 43.07N 96.57W
22 I9 Centerville Tennessee, S USA 35.43N 87.27W
27 V9 Centerville Texas, SW USA 31.15N 95.58W
42 M5 Centinela, Picacho del ▲ NE Mexico 29.07N 102.40W
108 G9 Cento Emilia-Romagna, N Italy 44.43N 11.16E
Centrafricaine, République see Central African Republic
41 S8 Central Alaska, USA 65.34N 144.48W
39 P15 Central New Mexico, SW USA 32.46N 108.09W
85 H18 Central ◈ district E Botswana
144 E10 Central ◈ district C Israel
83 I19 Central ◈ province C Kenya
84 M13 Central ◈ region C Malawi
159 P12 Central ◈ zone C Nepal
194 J15 Central ◈ province S PNG
65 I21 Central ◈ department C Paraguay
195 W15 Central off. Central Province. ◈ province S Solomon Islands
85 J14 Central ◈ province C Zambia
119 P11 Central ✕ (Odesa) Odes'ka Oblast', SW Ukraine 46.26N 30.41E
Central see Centre
81 H14 Central African Republic var. République Centrafricaine, abbrev. CAR; prev. Ubangi-Shari, Oubangui-Chari, Territoire de l'Oubangui-Chari. ◆ republic C Africa
198 G6 Central Basin Trough undersea feature W Pacific Ocean
Central Borneo see Kalimantan Tengah
155 P12 Central Brāhui Range ▲ W Pakistan
Central Celebes see Sulawesi Tengah
31 Y13 Central City Iowa, C USA 42.12N 91.31W
22 I6 Central City Kentucky, S USA 37.17N 87.07W
31 P15 Central City Nebraska, C USA 41.04N 97.59W
50 D6 Central, Cordillera ▲ W Bolivia
56 D11 Central, Cordillera ▲ W Colombia
44 M13 Central, Cordillera ▲ C Costa Rica
47 N9 Central, Cordillera ▲ C Dominican Republic
45 R16 Central, Cordillera ▲ C Panama
179 P8 Central, Cordillera ▲ Luzon, N Philippines
47 S6 Central, Cordillera ▲ Puerto Rico
44 H7 Central District var. Tegucigalpa. ◈ district C Honduras
32 L15 Centralia Illinois, N USA 38.31N 89.07W
29 U4 Centralia Missouri, C USA 39.12N 92.08W
34 G9 Centralia Washington, NW USA 46.43N 122.57W
Central Indian Ridge see Mid-Indian Ridge
Central Java see Jawa Tengah
Central Kalimantan see Kalimantan Tengah
154 L14 Central Makrān Range ▲ W Pakistan
199 J8 Central Pacific Basin undersea feature C Pacific Ocean
61 M19 Central, Planalto var. Brazilian Highlands. ▲ E Brazil
34 F15 Central Point Oregon, NW USA 42.22N 122.55W
161 K25 Central Province ◈ province C Sri Lanka
Central Provinces and Berar see Madhya Pradesh
194 G11 Central Range ▲ NW PNG
Central Russian Upland see Srednerusskaya Vozvyshennost'
Central Siberian Plateau/Central Siberian Uplands see Srednesibirskoye Ploskogor'ye
106 K8 Central, Sistema ▲ C Spain
Central Sulawesi see Sulawesi Tengah
37 N3 Central Valley California, W USA 40.39N 122.21W
37 P8 Central Valley valley California, W USA
25 Q3 Centre Alabama, S USA 34.09N 85.40W
81 E15 Centre Eng. Central. ◈ province C Cameroon
104 M8 Centre ◈ region N France
181 Y16 Centre de Flacq E Mauritius 20.12S 57.43E
57 Y9 Centre Spatial Guyanais space station N French Guiana 5.11N 52.42W
25 O5 Centreville Alabama, S USA 32.58N 87.08W
23 X3 Centreville Maryland, NE USA 39.02N 76.04W
24 J7 Centreville Mississippi, S USA 31.05N 91.04W
Centum Cellae see Civitavecchia
166 M14 Cenxi Guangxi Zhuangzu Zizhiqu, S China 22.58N 111.00E
Ceos see Kéa
Cephaloedium see Cefalu
114 I9 Čepin Hung. Csepén. Osijek-Baranja, E Croatia 45.32N 18.33E
174 Ll15 Cepu prev. Tjepoe, Tjepu. Jawa, C Indonesia 7.07S 111.34E
Ceram see Seram, Pulau
175 T10 Ceram Sea Ind. Laut Seram. sea E Indonesia
198 G9 Ceram Trough undersea feature W Pacific Ocean
Cerasus see Giresun
38 I10 Cerbat Mountains ▲ Arizona, SW USA
105 P17 Cerbère, Cap headland S France 42.28N 3.15E
106 F13 Cercal do Alentejo Setúbal, S Portugal 37.48N 8.40W
113 A18 Čerchov Ger. Czerkow. ▲ W Czech Republic 49.24N 12.47E
105 O13 Cère ≈ C France
63 A16 Ceres Santa Fe, C Argentina 29.55S 61.55W
61 K18 Ceres Goiás, C Brazil 15.21S 49.34W
Ceresio see Lugano, Lago di
105 O17 Céret Pyrénées-Orientales, S France 42.30N 2.43E
56 E6 Cereté Córdoba, NW Colombia 8.51N 75.48W
180 I17 Cerf, Île au island Inner Islands, NE Seychelles
101 G22 Cerfontaine Namur, S Belgium 50.08N 4.25E
Cergy-Pontoise see Pontoise
109 N16 Cerignola Puglia, SE Italy 41.16N 15.52E
Cerigo see Kýthira
105 O9 Cérilly Allier, C France 46.38N 2.51E
142 I11 Çerkeş Çankırı, N Turkey 40.51N 32.52E
142 D10 Çerkezköy Tekirdağ, NW Turkey 41.18N 27.58E
111 T12 Cerknica Ger. Zirknitz. SW Slovenia 45.48N 14.21E
111 S11 Cerkno W Slovenia 46.07N 13.58E
118 F10 Cermei Hung. Csermő. Arad, W Romania 46.33N 21.51E
143 O15 Çermik Diyarbakır, SE Turkey 38.09N 39.27E
114 I10 Cerna Vukovar-Srijem, E Croatia 45.10N 18.36E
Cernăuți see Chernivtsi
118 M14 Cernavodă Constanța, SW Romania 44.19N 28.01E
105 U7 Cernay Haut-Rhin, NE France 47.49N 7.10E
Černice see Schwarzach
43 O8 Cerralvo Nuevo León, NE Mexico 26.01N 99.37W
42 G9 Cerralvo, Isla island W Mexico
109 L16 Cerreto Sannita Campania, S Italy 41.17N 14.39E

◆ Country ● Country Capital ◇ Dependent Territory ○ Dependent Territory Capital ◈ Administrative Region ✕ International Airport ▲ Mountain ▲ Mountain Range Volcano ≈ River ◎ Lake ⊠ Reservoir

CĒRRIK – CHAVANTES, REPRESA DE

115 *L20* **Cërrik** *var.* Cerriku. Elbasan, C Albania *41.01N 19.55E*
Cerriku *see* Cërrik
43 *O11* **Cerritos** San Luis Potosí, C Mexico *22.25N 100.16W*
62 *K11* **Cerro Azul** Paraná, S Brazil *24 48S 49.13W*
63 *F18* **Cerro Chato** Treinta y Tres, E Uruguay *33.08S 55.07W*
63 *F19* **Cerro Colorado** Florida, S Uruguay *33.52S 55.33W*
58 *E13* **Cerro de Pasco** Pasco, C Peru *10 43S 76.15W*
63 *G18* **Cerro Largo** ◐ *department* NE Uruguay
63 *G14* **Cêrro Largo** Rio Grande do Sul, S Brazil *28.10S 54.43W*
44 *E7* **Cerrón Grande, Embalse** ⊠ N El Salvador
65 *I14* **Cerros Colorados, Embalse** ⊚ W Argentina
107 *V5* **Cervera** Cataluña, NE Spain *41.40N 1.16E*
106 *M3* **Cervera del Pisuerga** Castilla-León, N Spain *42.51N 4.30W*
107 *Q5* **Cervera del Río Alhama** La Rioja, N Spain *42.01N 1.58W*
109 *H15* **Cerveteri** Lazio, C Italy *42.00N 12.06E*
108 *H10* **Cervia** Emilia-Romagna, N Italy *44.14N 12.22E*
108 *J7* **Cervignano del Friuli** Friuli-Venezia Giulia, NE Italy *45.49N 13.18E*
109 *L17* **Cervinara** Campania, S Italy *41.01N 14.36E*
Cervinia *see* Breuil-Cervinia
108 *B6* **Cervino, Monte** *var.* Matterhorn. ▲ Italy/Switzerland *see also* Matterhorn *46.00N 7.39E*
105 *Y14* **Cervione** Corse, France, C Mediterranean Sea *42.22N 9.28E*
106 *I1* **Cervo** Galicia, NW Spain *43.39N 7.25W*
56 *F5* **Cesar** *off.* Departamento del Cesar. ◐ *province* N Colombia
108 *H10* **Cesena** *anc.* Caesena. Emilia-Romagna, N Italy *44.09N 12.13E*
108 *I10* **Cesenatico** Emilia-Romagna, N Italy *44.12N 12.24E*
120 *H8* **Cēsis** *Ger.* Wenden. Cēsis, C Latvia *57.19N 25.17E*
113 *D15* **Česká Lípa** *Ger.* Böhmisch-Leipa. Liberecký Kraj, N Czech Republic *50.40N 14.32E*
Česká Republika *see* Czech Republic
113 *F17* **Česká Třebová** *Ger.* Böhmisch-Trübau. Pardubický Kraj, C Czech Republic *49.54N 16.27E*
113 *D19* **České Budějovice** *Ger.* Budweis. Budějovický Kraj, S Czech Republic *48.58N 14.28E*
113 *D19* **České Velenice** Budějovický Kraj, S Czech Republic *48.49N 14.57E*
113 *E18* **Českomoravská Vrchovina** *var.* Českomoravská Vysočina, *Eng.* Bohemian-Moravian Highlands, *Ger.* Böhmisch-Mährische Höhe. ▲ S Czech Republic
Českomoravská Vysočina *see* Českomoravská Vrchovina
113 *C19* **Český Krumlov** *var.* Böhmisch-Krumau, *Ger.* Krummau. Budějovický Kraj, S Czech Republic *48.48N 14.18E*
Ceský Les *see* Bohemian Forest
114 *F8* **Česma** ⩫ N Croatia
142 *A14* **Çeşme** Izmir, W Turkey *38.19N 26.19E*
Cess *see* Cestos
191 *T8* **Cessnock** New South Wales, SE Australia *32.51S 151.21E*
78 *K17* **Cestos** *var.* Cess. ⩫ S Liberia
120 *I9* **Cesvaine** Madona, E Latvia *56.58N 26.15E*
118 *G14* **Cetate** Dolj, SW Romania *44.06N 23.03E*
Cetatea Albă *see* Bilhorod-Dnistrovs'kyy
115 *J17* **Cetinje** *It.* Cettigne. Montenegro, SW Yugoslavia *42.23N 18.55E*
109 *N20* **Cetraro** Calabria, S Italy *39.30N 15.59E*
Cette *see* Sète
196 *A17* **Cetti Bay** *bay* SW Guam
Cettigne *see* Cetinje
106 *L17* **Ceuta** *var.* Sebta. Ceuta, Spain, N Africa *35.52N 5.19W*
90 *C15* **Ceuta** *enclave* Spain, N Africa
108 *B9* **Ceva** Piemonte, NE Italy *44.24N 8.01E*
105 *P14* **Cévennes** ▲ S France
110 *G10* **Cevio** Ticino, S Switzerland *46.18N 8.36E*
142 *K16* **Ceyhan** Adana, S Turkey *37.01N 35.48E*
142 *K17* **Ceyhan Nehri** ⩫ S Turkey
143 *P17* **Ceylanpınar** Şanlıurfa, SE Turkey *36.53N 40.01E*
Ceylon *see* Sri Lanka
181 *R6* **Ceylon Plain** *undersea feature* N Indian Ocean
Ceyre to the Caribs *see* Marie-Galante
105 *Q14* **Cèze** ⩫ S France
152 *H15* **Chaacha** *Turkm.* Chäche. Akhalskiy Velayat, S Turkmenistan *36.49N 60.33E*
131 *P6* **Chaadayevka** Penzenskaya Oblast', W Russian Federation *53.07N 45.55E*
178 *H12* **Cha-Am** Phetchaburi, SW Thailand *12.48N 99.58E*
149 *W15* **Chābahār** *var.* Chāh Bahār, Chahbar. Sīstān va Balūchestān, SE Iran *25.21N 60.38E*
63 *B19* **Chabas** Santa Fe, C Argentina *33.16S 61.22W*
105 *T10* **Chablais** *physical region* E France
63 *B20* **Chacabuco** Buenos Aires, E Argentina *34.38S 60.31W*
44 *K8* **Chachagón, Cerro** ▲ N Nicaragua *13.18N 85.39W*
58 *C10* **Chachapoyas** Amazonas, NW Peru *6.13S 77.54W*
Châche *see* Chaacha
121 *O18* **Chachersk** *Rus.* Chechersk. Homyel'skaya Voblasts', SE Belarus *52.54N 30.54E*
121 *N16* **Chachevichy** *Rus.* Chechevichi. Mahilyowskaya Voblasts', E Belarus *53.31N 29.49E*
63 *B14* **Chaco** *off.* Provincia de Chaco. ◐ *province* NE Argentina
Chaco *see* Gran Chaco
64 *M6* **Chaco Austral** *physical region* N Argentina
64 *M3* **Chaco Boreal** *physical region* N Paraguay
64 *M6* **Chaco Central** *physical region* N Argentina
41 *Y15* **Chacon, Cape** *headland* Prince of Wales Island, Alaska, USA *54.41N 132.00W*
80 *H9* **Chad** *off.* Republic of Chad, *Fr.* Tchad. ◆ *republic* C Africa
126 *Hh16* **Chadan** Respublika Tyva, S Russian Federation *51.16N 91.25E*
23 *U12* **Chadbourn** North Carolina, SE USA *34.19N 78.49W*
85 *L14* **Chadiza** Eastern, E Zambia *14.04S 32.27E*
69 *Q7* **Chad, Lake** *Fr.* Lac Tchad. ⊚ C Africa
126 *J13* **Chadobets** ⩫ C Russian Federation
30 *J12* **Chadron** Nebraska, C USA *42.48N 102.57W*
Chadyr-Lunga *see* Ciadîr-Lunga
169 *W14* **Chaeryŏng** SW North Korea *38.22N 125.35E*
107 *P17* **Chafarinas, Islas** *island group* S Spain
29 *Y7* **Chaffee** Missouri, C USA *37.10N 89.39W*
154 *L12* **Chāgai Hills** *var.* Chāh Gay. ▲ Afghanistan/Pakistan
126 *M12* **Chagda** Respublika Sakha (Yakutiya), NE Russian Federation *58.43N 130.38E*
Chaghasarāy *see* Asadābād
155 *N5* **Chaghcharān** *var.* Chakhcharan, Cheghcheran, Qala Āhangarān. Ghowr, C Afghanistan *34.28N 65.18E*
105 *R9* **Chagny** Saône-et-Loire, C France *46.54N 4.45E*
181 *Q7* **Chagos Archipelago** *var.* Oil Islands. *island group* British Indian Ocean Territory
133 *O15* **Chagos Bank** *undersea feature* C Indian Ocean
133 *O14* **Chagos-Laccadive Plateau** *undersea feature* N Indian Ocean
181 *Q7* **Chagos Trench** *undersea feature* N Indian Ocean
45 *T14* **Chagres, Río** ⩫ C Panama
47 *U14* **Chaguanas** Trinidad, Trinidad and Tobago *10.29N 61.24W*
56 *M6* **Chaguaramas** Guárico, N Venezuela *9.21N 66.15W*
152 *C9* **Chagyl** Balkanskiy Velayat, NW Turkmenistan *40.48N 55.21E*
Chahārmahāl and Bakhtiārī *see* Chahār Maḩall va Bakhtiārī
148 *M9* **Chahār Maḩall va Bakhtiārī** *off.* Ostān-e Chahār Maḩall va Bakhtiārī, *var.* Chahārmahāl and Bakhtiārī. ◐ *province* SW Iran
Chāh Bahār/Chahbar *see* Chābahār
149 *V13* **Chāh Derāz** Sīstān va Balūchestān, SE Iran
Chāh Gay *see* Chāgai Hills
178 *Hh10* **Chai Badan** Lop Buri, C Thailand *15.07N 101.03E*
159 *Q16* **Chāībāsa** Bihār, N India *22.34N 85.48E*
81 *E19* **Chaillu, Massif du** ▲ C Gabon
178 *Hh10* **Chai Nat** *var.* Chainat, Jainat, Jayanath. Chai Nat, C Thailand *15.12N 100.12E*
67 *M14* **Chain Fracture Zone** *tectonic feature* E Atlantic Ocean
181 *N5* **Chain Ridge** *undersea feature* W Indian Ocean
Chairn, Ceann an *see* Carnsore Point
164 *L5* **Chaiwopu** Xinjiang Uygur Zizhiqu, W China *43.31N 87.55E*
178 *I10* **Chaiyaphum** *var.* Jayabum. Chaiyaphum, C Thailand *15.49N 102.03E*
64 *N10* **Chajarí** Entre Ríos, E Argentina *30.45S 57.57W*
44 *C5* **Chajul** Quiché, W Guatemala *15.28N 91.02W*
85 *K16* **Chakari** Mashonaland West, N Zimbabwe *18.04S 29.49E*
154 *J9* **Chakhānsūr** Nīmrūz, SW Afghanistan *31.11N 62.06E*
Chakhānsūr *see* Nīmrūz
Chakhcharan *see* Chaghcharān
155 *V8* **Chak Jhumra** *var.* Jhumra. Punjab, E Pakistan *31.33N 73.13E*
152 *I16* **Chaknakdysonga** Akhalskiy Velayat, S Turkmenistan *35.39N 61.24E*
159 *P16* **Chakradharpur** Bihār, N India *22.37N 85.28E*
158 *J8* **Chakrāta** Uttar Pradesh, N India *30.42N 77.52E*
155 *U7* **Chakwāl** Punjab, NE Pakistan *32.56N 72.49E*
59 *F17* **Chala** Arequipa, SW Peru *15.52S 74.13W*
104 *K12* **Chalais** Charente, W France *45.16N 0.02E*
110 *D10* **Chalais** Valais, SW Switzerland *46.18N 7.37E*
117 *J20* **Chalándri** *var.* Halandri; *prev.* Khalándrion. *prehistoric site* Sýros, Kykládes, Greece, Aegean Sea *37.28N 24.56E*
196 *H6* **Chalan Kanoa** Saipan, S Northern Mariana Islands *15.07S 145.43E*
196 *C16* **Chalan Pago** C Guam
Chalap Dalam/Chalap Dalan *see* Chehel Abdālān, Kūh-e
44 *F7* **Chalatenango** Chalatenango, N El Salvador *14.03N 88.54W*
44 *A9* **Chalatenango** ◐ *department* NW El Salvador
85 *P15* **Chalaua** Nampula, NE Mozambique *16.04S 39.08E*
83 *I16* **Chalbi Desert** *desert* N Kenya
44 *D7* **Chalchuapa** Santa Ana, W El Salvador *13.58N 89.39W*
Chalcidice *see* Chalkidikí
Chalcis *see* Chalkída
105 *N6* **Châlette-sur-Loing** Loiret, C France *48.01N 2.45E*
13 *X8* **Chaleur Bay** *Fr.* Baie des Chaleurs. *bay* New Brunswick/Quebec, E Canada
Chaleurs, Baie des *see* Chaleur Bay
59 *G16* **Chalhuanca** Apurímac, S Peru *14.21S 73.16W*
160 *F12* **Chālisgaon** Mahārāshtra, C India *20.28N 75.10E*
117 *N23* **Chálki** *island* Dodekánisos, Greece, Aegean Sea
117 *F16* **Chalkiádes** Thessalía, C Greece *39.24N 22.25E*
117 *H18* **Chalkída** *var.* Halkida; *prev.* Khalkís, *anc.* Chalcis. Evvoia, E Greece *38.27N 23.38E*
117 *G14* **Chalkidikí** *var.* Khalkidhikí; *anc.* Chalcidice. *peninsula* NE Greece
193 *A24* **Chalky Inlet** *inlet* South Island, NZ
41 *S7* **Chalkyitsik** Alaska, USA *66.39N 143.43W*
104 *I9* **Challans** Vendée, NW France *46.51N 1.52W*
59 *K19* **Challapata** Oruro, SW Bolivia *19.02S 66.46W*
199 *H7* **Challenger Deep** *undersea feature* W Pacific Ocean
200 *Nn12* **Challenger Fracture Zone** *tectonic feature* SE Pacific Ocean
199 *Ii13* **Challenger Plateau** *undersea feature* E Tasman Sea
35 *P13* **Challis** Idaho, NW USA *44.31N 114.14W*
24 *L9* **Chalmette** Louisiana, S USA *29.56N 89.57W*
128 *J11* **Chalna** Respublika Kareliya, NW Russian Federation *61.53N 33.59E*
105 *Q5* **Châlons-en-Champagne** *prev.* Châlons-sur-Marne, *hist.* Arcae Remorum, *anc.* Carolopois. Marne, NE France *48.58N 4.22E*
Châlons-sur-Marne *see* Châlons-en-Champagne
105 *R9* **Chalon-sur-Saône** *anc.* Cabillonum. Saône-et-Loire, C France *46.46N 4.51E*
Chaltel, Cerro *see* Fitzroy, Monte
149 *N4* **Chālūs** Māzandarān, N Iran *36.40N 51.25E*
104 *M11* **Châlus** Haute-Vienne, C France *45.38N 1.00E*
103 *N20* **Cham** Bayern, SE Germany *49.13N 12.40E*
110 *F7* **Cham** Zug, N Switzerland *47.10N 8.28E*
39 *R8* **Chama** New Mexico, SW USA *36.54N 106.34W*
Cha Mai *see* Thung Song
85 *E22* **Chamaites** Karas, S Namibia *27.13S 17.55E*
155 *O9* **Chaman** Baluchistān, SW Pakistan *30.55N 66.27E*
39 *R9* **Chama, Rio** ⩫ New Mexico, SW USA
158 *I6* **Chamba** Himāchal Pradesh, N India *32.33N 76.10E*
83 *I25* **Chamba** Ruvuma, S Tanzania *11.33S 37.01E*
156 *H12* **Chambal** ⩫ C India
9 *U16* **Chamberlain** Saskatchewan, S Canada *50.49N 105.29W*
31 *O11* **Chamberlain** South Dakota, N USA *43.48N 99.19W*
21 *R3* **Chamberlain Lake** ⊚ Maine, NE USA
41 *S5* **Chamberlin, Mount** ▲ Alaska, USA *69.16N 144.54W*
39 *O11* **Chambers** Arizona, SW USA *35.11N 109.25W*
20 *F16* **Chambersburg** Pennsylvania, NE USA *39.54N 77.39W*
33 *N5* **Chambers Island** *island* Wisconsin, N USA
105 *T11* **Chambéry** *anc.* Camberia. Savoie, E France *45.34N 5.55E*
84 *L12* **Chambeshi** Northern, NE Zambia *10.55S 31.07E*
84 *L12* **Chambeshi** ⩫ NE Zambia
76 *M6* **Chambi, Jebel** *var.* Jabal ash Sha'nabī. ▲ W Tunisia *35.16N 8.39E*
13 *Q7* **Chambord** Quebec, SE Canada *48.25N 72.02W*
194 *G10* **Chambri Lake** ⊚ W PNG
145 *U11* **Chamcham** S Iraq *31.17N 45.05E*
145 *T4* **Chamchamāl** N Iraq *35.31N 44.49E*
42 *J14* **Chamela** Jalisco, SW Mexico *19.33N 105.04W*
44 *G5* **Chamelecón, Río** ⩫ NW Honduras
64 *J9* **Chamical** La Rioja, C Argentina *30.21S 66.19W*
117 *L23* **Chamilí** *island* Kykládes, Greece, Aegean Sea
178 *Ii13* **Chāmnar** Kaôh Kông, SW Cambodia *11.45N 103.32E*
158 *K9* **Chamoli** Uttar Pradesh, N India *30.22N 79.19E*
105 *U11* **Chamonix-Mont-Blanc** Haute-Savoie, E France *45.55N 6.52E*
160 *L11* **Chāmpa** Madhya Pradesh, C India *22.01N 82.42E*
8 *H8* **Champagne** Yukon Territory, W Canada *60.48N 136.22W*
105 *Q5* **Champagne** *cultural region* N France
Champagne *see* Campania
105 *Q5* **Champagne-Ardenne** ◐ *region* N France
105 *S9* **Champagnole** Jura, E France *46.43N 5.55E*
32 *M13* **Champaign** Illinois, N USA *40.07N 88.14W*
178 *Jj11* **Champasak** Champasak, S Laos *14.50N 105.51E*
105 *U6* **Champ de Feu** ▲ NE France *48.24N 7.15E*
11 *O7* **Champdoré, Lac** ⊚ Quebec, NE Canada
44 *B6* **Champerico** Retalhuleu, SW Guatemala *14.18N 91.54W*
110 *C11* **Champéry** Valais, SW Switzerland *46.12N 6.52E*
20 *L6* **Champlain** New York, NE USA *44.58N 73.25W*
20 *L9* **Champlain Canal** *canal* New York, NE USA
13 *P13* **Champlain, Lac** ⊚ Quebec, SE Canada
20 *L7* **Champlain, Lake** ⊚ Canada/USA
105 *S7* **Champlitte** Haute-Saône, E France *47.36N 5.31E*
43 *W13* **Champotón** Campeche, SE Mexico *19.18N 90.43W*
106 *G10* **Chamusca** Santarém, C Portugal *39.21N 8.28W*
121 *O20* **Chamyarysy** *Rus.* Chemerisy. Homyel'skaya Voblasts', SE Belarus *51.42N 30.26E*
131 *P5* **Chamzinka** Respublika Mordoviya, W Russian Federation *54.22N 45.22E*
Chanáil Mhór, An *see* Grand Canal
Chanak *see* Çanakkale
64 *G7* **Chañaral** Atacama, N Chile *26.19S 70.34W*
106 *H13* **Chança, Rio** *var.* Chanza. ⩫ Portugal/Spain
59 *D14* **Chancay** Lima, W Peru *11.33S 77.16W*
Chan-chiang/Chanchiang *see* Zhanjiang
64 *G13* **Chanco** Maule, Chile *35.43S 72.35W*
41 *R7* **Chandalar** Alaska, USA *67.30N 148.29W*
41 *R6* **Chandalar River** ⩫ Alaska, USA
158 *L10* **Chandan Chauki** Uttar Pradesh, N India *28.31N 80.43E*
159 *S16* **Chandannagar** *prev.* Chandernagore. West Bengal, E India *22.52N 88.21E*
158 *K10* **Chandausi** Uttar Pradesh, N India *28.27N 78.43E*
24 *M10* **Chandeleur Islands** *island group* Louisiana, S USA
24 *M9* **Chandeleur Sound** *sound* N Gulf of Mexico
158 *I8* **Chandīgarh** Punjab, N India *30.41N 76.51E*
159 *Q16* **Chāndil** Bihār, NE India *22.58N 86.04E*
190 *D2* **Chandler** South Australia *26.59S 133.22E*
13 *Y7* **Chandler** Quebec, SE Canada *48.21N 64.40W*
38 *L14* **Chandler** Arizona, SW USA *33.18N 111.50W*
29 *O10* **Chandler** Oklahoma, C USA *35.42N 96.52W*
27 *V7* **Chandler** Texas, SW USA *32.18N 95.28W*
41 *Q6* **Chandler River** ⩫ Alaska, USA
58 *H13* **Chandless, Río** ⩫ E Peru
169 *N9* **Chandmanī** Dornogovĭ, SE Mongolia *45.36N 110.30E*
12 *J13* **Chandos Lake** ⊚ Ontario, SE Canada
159 *U15* **Chandpur** Chittagong, C Bangladesh *23.13N 90.43E*
160 *I13* **Chandrapur** Mahārāshtra, C India *19.58N 79.21E*
85 *J15* **Changa** Southern, S Zambia *16.24S 28.27E*
Changan *see* Xi'an, Shaanxi, China
Chang'an *see* Rong'an, Guangxi Zhuangzu Zizhiqu, China
161 *G23* **Changanācheri** Kerala, SW India *9.27N 76.34E*
85 *M19* **Changane** ⩫ S Mozambique
85 *M16* **Changara** Tete, NW Mozambique *16.54S 33.15E*
169 *X11* **Changbai** *var.* Changbai Chaoxianzu Zizhixian. Jilin, NE China *41.25N 128.08E*
Changbai Chaoxianzu Zizhixian *see* Changbai
169 *X11* **Changbai Shan** ▲ NE China
169 *V10* **Changchun** *var.* Ch'angch'un, Ch'ang-ch'un; *prev.* Hsinking. Jilin, NE China *43.52N 125.18E*
166 *M10* **Changde** Hunan, S China *29.04N 111.42E*
167 *S13* **Changhua** *Jap.* Shōka. C Taiwan *24.06N 120.31E*
174 *I7* **Changi** ✕ (Singapore) E Singapore *1.22N 103.58E*
164 *L5* **Changji** Xinjiang Uygur Zizhiqu, NW China *44.02N 87.12E*
163 *O13* **Chang Jiang** *var.* Yangtze Kiang, *Eng.* Yangtze. ⩫ C China
166 *L17* **Changjiang** *prev.* Shiliu. Hainan, S China *19.16N 109.09E*
167 *S8* **Changjiang Kou** *delta* E China
178 *I13* **Chang, Ko** *island* S Thailand
167 *Q2* **Changli** Hebei, E China *39.43N 119.13E*
169 *V10* **Changling** Jilin, NE China *44.15N 124.03E*
167 *N11* **Changsha** *var.* Ch'angsha, Ch'ang-sha. Hunan, S China *28.10N 113.00E*
167 *Q10* **Changshan** Zhejiang, SE China *28.54N 118.26E*
169 *V14* **Changshan Qundao** *island group* NE China
167 *S8* **Changshu** *var.* Ch'ang-shu. Jiangsu, E China *31.36N 120.42E*
169 *V11* **Changtu** Liaoning, NE China *42.49N 123.58E*
45 *P14* **Changuinola** Bocas del Toro, NW Panama *9.25N 82.31W*
165 *N9* **Changweiliang** Qinghai, W China *38.24N 92.07E*
166 *K6* **Changwu** Shaanxi, C China *35.12N 107.45E*
169 *U13* **Changxing Dao** *island* N China
166 *M9* **Changyang** Hubei, C China *30.45N 111.13E*
169 *W14* **Changyŏn** SW North Korea *38.19N 125.14E*
167 *N5* **Changzhi** Shanxi, C China *36.09N 113.01E*
167 *R8* **Changzhou** Jiangsu, E China *31.53N 119.58E*
117 *H24* **Chaniá** *var.* Hania, Khaniá, *Eng.* Canea; *anc.* Cydonia. Kriti, Greece, E Mediterranean Sea *35.31N 24.01E*
64 *J5* **Chañi, Nevado de** ▲ NW Argentina *24.09S 65.44W*
117 *H24* **Chanión, Kólpos** *gulf* Kriti, Greece, E Mediterranean Sea
Chankiri *see* Çankırı
32 *M11* **Channahon** Illinois, N USA *41.25N 88.13W*
161 *H20* **Channapatna** Karnātaka, E India *12.43N 77.13E*
99 *K26* **Channel Islands** *Fr.* Îles Normandes. *island group* S English Channel
37 *R16* **Channel Islands** *island group* California, W USA
11 *S13* **Channel-Port aux Basques** Newfoundland, SE Canada *47.35N 59.02W*
Channel, The *see* English Channel
99 *Q23* **Channel Tunnel** *tunnel* France/UK
26 *M2* **Channing** Texas, SW USA *35.40N 102.19W*
Chantabun/Chantaburi *see* Chanthaburi
106 *H3* **Chantada** Galicia, NW Spain *42.36N 7.46W*
178 *I12* **Chanthaburi** *var.* Chantabun, Chantaburi. Chantaburi, S Thailand *12.34N 102.07E*
105 *O4* **Chantilly** Oise, N France *49.12N 2.28E*
15 *Kk4* **Chantrey Inlet** *inlet* Nunavut, N Canada
145 *V12* **Chanūn as Sa'ūdī** S Iraq *31.04N 46.00E*
29 *Q6* **Chanute** Kansas, C USA *37.40N 95.27W*
125 *G13* **Chany, Ozero** ⊚ C Russian Federation
Chanza *see* Chança, Rio
Ch'ao-an/Chaochow *see* Chaozhou
167 *P8* **Chao Hu** ⊚ E China
178 *Hh11* **Chao Phraya, Mae Nam** ⩫ C Thailand
169 *T8* **Chaor He** ⩫ NE China
Chaouèn *see* Chefchaouen
167 *P14* **Chaoyang** Guangdong, S China *23.16N 116.30E*
169 *T12* **Chaoyang** Liaoning, NE China *41.33N 120.28E*
Chaoyang *see* Huinan, Jilin, China
Chaoyang *see* Jiayin, Heilongjiang, China
167 *Q14* **Chaozhou** *var.* Chaoan, Chao'an, Ch'ao-an; *prev.* Chaochow. Guangdong, SE China *23.39N 116.34E*
60 *N13* **Chapadinha** Maranhão, E Brazil *3.45S 43.22W*
10 *K12* **Chapais** Quebec, SE Canada *49.46N 74.54W*
42 *L13* **Chapala** Jalisco, SW Mexico *20.17N 103.13W*
42 *L13* **Chapala, Lago de** ⊚ C Mexico
152 *F13* **Chapan, Gora** ▲ C Turkmenistan *37.48N 58.03E*
59 *M18* **Chapare, Río** ⩫ C Bolivia
56 *E11* **Chaparral** Tolima, C Colombia *3.44N 75.33W*
150 *F9* **Chapayevo** Zapadnyy Kazakhstan, NW Kazakhstan *50.13N 51.05E*
126 *Kk12* **Chapayevo** Respublika Sakha (Yakutiya), NE Russian Federation *60.03N 117.19E*
131 *R6* **Chapayevsk** Samarskaya Oblast', W Russian Federation *52.57N 49.41E*
62 *H13* **Chapecó** Santa Catarina, S Brazil *27.06S 52.39W*
62 *I13* **Chapecó, Rio** ⩫ S Brazil
22 *J9* **Chapel Hill** Tennessee, S USA *35.38N 86.40W*
46 *J12* **Chapelton** C Jamaica *18.04N 77.16W*
12 *C8* **Chapleau** Ontario, SE Canada *47.49N 83.24W*
12 *D7* **Chapleau** ⩫ Ontario, S Canada
9 *T16* **Chaplin** Saskatchewan, S Canada *50.27N 106.37W*
130 *M6* **Chaplygin** Lipetskaya Oblast', W Russian Federation *53.13N 39.58E*
119 *S11* **Chaplynka** Khersons'ka Oblast', S Ukraine *46.20N 33.34E*
15 *L3* **Chapman, Cape** *headland* Nunavut, NE Canada *69.15N 89.09W*
27 *T15* **Chapman Ranch** Texas, SW USA *27.32N 97.25W*
Chapman's *see* Okwa
23 *P5* **Chapmanville** West Virginia, NE USA *37.58N 82.01W*
30 *K15* **Chappell** Nebraska, C USA *41.05N 102.28W*
Chapra *see* Chhapra
58 *D9* **Chapuli, Río** ⩫ N Peru
78 *I6* **Châr** *well* N Mauritania *21.31N 12.55W*
126 *Kk13* **Chara** Chitinskaya Oblast', S Russian Federation *56.57N 118.05E*
126 *Kk13* **Chara** ⩫ C Russian Federation
56 *G8* **Charala** Santander, C Colombia *6.16N 73.09W*
43 *N10* **Charcas** San Luis Potosí, C Mexico *23.09N 101.04W*
27 *T13* **Charco** Texas, SW USA *28.42N 97.35E*
204 *H7* **Charcot Island** *island* Antarctica
66 *M8* **Charcot Seamounts** *undersea feature* E Atlantic Ocean
Chardara *see* Shardara
151 *P17* **Chardarinskoye Vodokhranilishche** ⊠ S Kazakhstan
33 *U11* **Chardon** Ohio, N USA *41.33N 81.10W*
46 *K9* **Chardonnières** SW Haiti *18.17N 74.09W*
152 *K12* **Chardzhev** *prev.* Chardzhou, Chardzhui, Leninsk-Turkmenski, *Turkm.* Chärjew. Lebapskiy Velayat, E Turkmenistan *39.07N 63.30E*
Chardzhevskaya Oblast' *see* Lebapskiy Velayat
Chardzhou/Chardzhui *see* Chardzhev
104 *L11* **Charente** ◐ *department* W France
104 *J11* **Charente** ⩫ W France
104 *J10* **Charente-Maritime** ◐ *department* W France
143 *U12* **Ch'arents'avan** C Armenia *40.23N 44.41E*
80 *I12* **Chari** *var.* Shari. ⩫ Central African Republic/Chad
80 *G11* **Chari-Baguirmi** *off.* Préfecture du Chari-Baguirmi. ◐ *prefecture* SW Chad
155 *Q4* **Chārīkār** Parwān, NE Afghanistan *35.01N 69.10E*
31 *V15* **Chariton** Iowa, C USA *41.00N 93.18W*
29 *U3* **Chariton River** ⩫ Missouri, C USA
57 *T7* **Charity** NW Guyana *7.22N 58.34W*
33 *R7* **Charity Island** *island* Michigan, N USA
Chärjew *see* Chardzhev
Chärjew Oblasty *see* Lebapskiy Velayat
Charkhlik/Charkhliq *see* Ruoqiang
101 *G20* **Charleroi** Hainaut, S Belgium *50.25N 4.27E*
9 *V12* **Charles** Manitoba, C Canada *55.27N 100.58W*
13 *R10* **Charlesbourg** Quebec, SE Canada *46.49N 71.14W*
23 *Y7* **Charles, Cape** *headland* Virginia, NE USA *37.09N 75.57W*
31 *W12* **Charles City** Iowa, C USA *43.04N 92.40W*
23 *W6* **Charles City** Virginia, NE USA *37.19N 77.01W*
105 *O5* **Charles de Gaulle** ✕ (Paris) Seine-et-Marne, N France *49.04N 2.36E*
10 *K1* **Charles Island** *island* Nunavut, NE Canada
Charles Island *see* Santa María, Isla
18 *Mm5* **Charles-Lindbergh** ✕ (Minneapolis/Saint Paul) Minnesota, N USA *44.47N 93.12W*
32 *K9* **Charles Mound** *hill* Illinois, N USA *42.30N 90.14W*
193 *A22* **Charles Sound** *sound* South Island, NZ
193 *G15* **Charleston** West Coast, South Island, NZ *41.54S 171.25E*
29 *S11* **Charleston** Arkansas, C USA *35.18N 94.02W*
32 *M14* **Charleston** Illinois, N USA *39.30N 88.10W*
24 *L3* **Charleston** Mississippi, S USA *34.00N 90.03W*
29 *Z7* **Charleston** Missouri, C USA *36.55N 89.21W*
23 *T15* **Charleston** South Carolina, SE USA *32.48N 79.57W*
23 *Q5* **Charleston** *state capital* West Virginia, NE USA *38.21N 81.37W*
12 *L14* **Charleston Lake** ⊚ Ontario, SE Canada
37 *W11* **Charleston Peak** ▲ Nevada, W USA *36.16N 115.40W*
47 *W10* **Charlestown** Nevis, Saint Kitts and Nevis *17.05N 62.35W*
33 *P16* **Charlestown** Indiana, N USA *38.27N 85.40W*
20 *M9* **Charlestown** New Hampshire, NE USA *43.14N 72.23W*
23 *V3* **Charles Town** West Virginia, NE USA *39.17N 77.51W*
189 *W9* **Charleville** Queensland, E Australia *26.24S 146.18E*
105 *R3* **Charleville-Mézières** Ardennes, N France *49.45N 4.43E*
33 *P5* **Charlevoix** Michigan, N USA *45.19N 85.15W*
33 *Q6* **Charlevoix, Lake** ⊚ Michigan, N USA
41 *T9* **Charley River** ⩫ Alaska, USA
66 *J6* **Charlie-Gibbs Fracture Zone** *tectonic feature* N Atlantic Ocean
105 *Q10* **Charlieu** Loire, E France *46.11N 4.10E*
33 *Q9* **Charlotte** Michigan, N USA *42.33N 84.50W*
23 *R10* **Charlotte** North Carolina, SE USA *35.13N 80.50W*
22 *I8* **Charlotte** Tennessee, S USA *36.11N 87.18W*
27 *R13* **Charlotte** Texas, SW USA *28.51N 98.42W*
23 *R10* **Charlotte** ✕ North Carolina, SE USA *35.12N 80.54W*
47 *T9* **Charlotte Amalie** *prev.* Saint Thomas. ○ (Virgin Islands (US)) Saint Thomas, N Virgin Islands (US) *18.22N 64.55W*
23 *U7* **Charlotte Court House** Virginia, NE USA *37.04N 78.37W*
25 *W14* **Charlotte Harbor** *inlet* Florida, SE USA
Charlotte Island *see* Abaiang
97 *J15* **Charlottenberg** Värmland, C Sweden *59.52N 12.16E*
Charlottenhof *see* Aegviidu
23 *U5* **Charlottesville** Virginia, NE USA *38.01N 78.28W*
Charlotte Town *see* Roseau, Dominica
Charlotte Town *see* Gouyave, Grenada
11 *Q14* **Charlottetown** Prince Edward Island, Prince Edward Island, SE Canada *46.13N 63.09W*
47 *Z16* **Charlotteville** Tobago, Trinidad and Tobago *11.16N 60.33W*
190 *M11* **Charlton** Victoria, SE Australia *36.18S 143.19E*
10 *H10* **Charlton Island** *island* Nunavut, C Canada
105 *T6* **Charmes** Vosges, NE France *48.19N 6.19E*
121 *F19* **Charnawchytsy** *Rus.* Chernavchitsy. Brestskaya Voblasts', SW Belarus *52.13N 23.43E*
13 *R10* **Charny** Quebec, SE Canada *46.43N 71.14W*
155 *T5* **Chārsadda** North-West Frontier Province, NW Pakistan *34.12N 71.46E*
152 *M14* **Charshanga** *prev.* Charshangy, *Turkm.* Charshangngy. Lebapskiy Velayat, E Turkmenistan *37.31N 65.58E*
Charshangngy/Charshangy *see* Charshanga
Charsk *see* Shar
189 *W6* **Charters Towers** Queensland, NE Australia *20.01S 146.19E*
13 *R12* **Chartierville** Quebec, SE Canada *45.19N 71.13W*
104 *M6* **Chartres** *anc.* Autricum, Civitas Carnutum. Eure-et-Loir, C France *48.27N 1.27E*
151 *W15* **Charyn** *Kaz.* Sharyn. Almaty, SE Kazakhstan *43.48N 79.22E*
63 *D21* **Chascomús** Buenos Aires, E Argentina *35.34S 58.01W*
9 *N16* **Chase** British Columbia, SW Canada *50.49N 119.40W*
23 *U7* **Chase City** Virginia, NE USA *36.48N 78.27W*
21 *S4* **Chase, Mount** ▲ Maine, NE USA *46.06N 68.30W*
120 *M13* **Chashniki** *Rus.* Chashniki. Vitsyebskaya Voblasts', N Belarus *54.51N 29.09E*
117 *D15* **Chásia** ▲ C Greece
31 *V9* **Chaska** Minnesota, N USA *44.47N 93.36W*
193 *D25* **Chaslands Mistake** *headland* South Island, NZ *46.37S 169.21E*
129 *R11* **Chasovo** Respublika Komi, NW Russian Federation *61.58N 50.34E*
Chasovo *see* Vazhgort
128 *H14* **Chastova** Novgorodskaya Oblast', NW Russian Federation *58.37N 32.04E*
149 *R3* **Chāt** Golestān, N Iran *37.52N 55.27E*
Chatak *see* Chhatak
41 *R9* **Chatanika** Alaska, USA *65.06N 147.28W*
41 *R9* **Chatanika River** ⩫ Alaska, USA
153 *T8* **Chat-Bazar** Talasskaya Oblast', NW Kyrgyzstan *42.29N 72.37E*
47 *Y14* **Chateaubelair** Saint Vincent, W Saint Vincent and the Grenadines *13.16N 61.14W*
104 *J7* **Châteaubriant** Loire-Atlantique, NW France *47.43N 1.22W*
105 *Q8* **Château-Chinon** Nièvre, C France *47.04N 3.50E*
110 *C10* **Château d'Oex** Vaud, W Switzerland *46.28N 7.09E*
104 *L7* **Château-du-Loir** Sarthe, NW France *47.40N 0.25E*
104 *M6* **Châteaudun** Eure-et-Loir, C France *48.04N 1.19E*
104 *K7* **Château-Gontier** Mayenne, NW France *47.49N 0.42W*
13 *O13* **Châteauguay** Quebec, SE Canada *45.21N 73.46W*
104 *F6* **Châteaulin** Finistère, NW France *48.12N 4.07W*
105 *N9* **Châteaumeillant** Cher, C France *46.33N 2.10E*
104 *K11* **Châteauneuf-sur-Charente** Charente, W France *45.34N 0.33W*
104 *M7* **Château-Renault** Indre-et-Loire, C France *47.34N 0.52E*
105 *N9* **Châteauroux** *prev.* Indreville. Indre, C France *46.50N 1.42E*
105 *T5* **Château-Salins** Moselle, NE France *48.50N 6.29E*
105 *P4* **Château-Thierry** Aisne, N France *49.03N 3.24E*
101 *H21* **Châtelet** Hainaut, S Belgium *50.24N 4.31E*
Châtelherault *see* Châtellerault
104 *L9* **Châtellerault** *var.* Châtelherault. Vienne, W France *46.49N 0.33E*
31 *X10* **Chatfield** Minnesota, N USA *43.51N 92.11W*
11 *O14* **Chatham** New Brunswick, SE Canada *47.01N 65.30W*
12 *D17* **Chatham** Ontario, S Canada *42.24N 82.10W*
99 *P22* **Chatham** SE England, UK *51.22N 0.31E*
32 *K14* **Chatham** Illinois, N USA *39.40N 89.42W*
23 *T7* **Chatham** Virginia, NE USA *36.49N 79.24W*
65 *F22* **Chatham, Isla** *island* S Chile
183 *R12* **Chatham Island** *island* Chatham Islands, NZ
Chatham Island *see* San Cristóbal, Isla
Chatham Island Rise *see* Chatham Rise
199 *Jj14* **Chatham Islands** *island group* NZ, SW Pacific Ocean
183 *Q12* **Chatham Rise** *var.* Chatham Island Rise. *undersea feature* S Pacific Ocean
41 *X13* **Chatham Strait** *strait* Alaska, USA
Chathóir, Rinn *see* Cahore Point
104 *M9* **Châtillon-sur-Indre** Indre, C France *46.58N 1.10E*
105 *Q7* **Châtillon-sur-Seine** Côte d'Or, C France *47.51N 4.30E*
153 *S8* **Chatkal** *Uzb.* Chotqol. ⩫ Kyrgyzstan/Uzbekistan
153 *R9* **Chatkal Range** *Rus.* Chatkal'skiy Khrebet. ▲ Kyrgyzstan/Uzbekistan
Chatkal'skiy Khrebet *see* Chatkal Range
25 *N7* **Chatom** Alabama, S USA *31.28N 88.15W*
Chatrapur *see* Chhatrapur
149 *S10* **Chatrūd** Kermān, C Iran *30.39N 56.57E*
25 *S2* **Chatsworth** Georgia, SE USA *34.46N 84.46W*
Chāttagām *see* Chittagong
25 *S8* **Chattahoochee** Florida, SE USA *30.40N 84.51W*
25 *R8* **Chattahoochee River** ⩫ SE USA
22 *L10* **Chattanooga** Tennessee, S USA *35.05N 85.16W*
153 *V10* **Chatyr-Kël', Ozero** ⊚ C Kyrgyzstan
153 *W9* **Chatyr-Tash** Narynskaya Oblast', C Kyrgyzstan *40.54N 76.22E*
13 *R12* **Chaudière** ⩫ Quebec, SE Canada
178 *J14* **Châu Đốc** *var.* Chauphu, Chau Phu. An Giang, S Vietnam *10.52N 105.07E*
158 *D13* **Chauhtan** *prev.* Chohtan. Rājasthān, NW India *25.27N 71.07E*
117 *Ff5* **Chauk** Magwe, W Burma *20.52N 94.49E*
105 *R6* **Chaumont** *prev.* Chaumont-en-Bassigny. Haute-Marne, N France *48.07N 5.07E*
Chaumont-en-Bassigny *see* Chaumont
127 *O4* **Chaunskaya Guba** *bay* NE Russian Federation
105 *P3* **Chauny** Aisne, N France *49.37N 3.13E*
Châu Ô *see* Binh Sơn
Chau Phu *see* Châu Đốc
104 *I5* **Chausey, Îles** *island group* N France
Chausy *see* Chavusy
20 *C11* **Chautauqua Lake** ⊚ New York, NE USA
104 *L9* **Chauvigny** Vienne, W France *46.35N 0.37E*
128 *L6* **Chavan'ga** Murmanskaya Oblast', NW Russian Federation *66.07N 37.44E*
12 *K10* **Chavannes, Lac** ⊚ Quebec, SE Canada
Chavantes, Represa de *see* Xavantes, Represa de

◆ Country ● Country Capital ◇ Dependent Territory ○ Dependent Territory Capital ◐ Administrative Region ✕ International Airport ▲ Mountain ▲ Mountain Range ⛰ Volcano ⩫ River ⊚ Lake ⊠ Reservoir

CHAVARRÍA – CHIPPEWA RIVER

63 D15 **Chavarría** Corrientes, NE Argentina *28.57S 58.34W*
Chavash Respubliki *see* Chuvashskaya Respublika
106 I5 **Chaves** *anc.* Aquae Flaviae. Vila Real, N Portugal *41.43N 7.28W*
Chávez, Isla *see* Santa Cruz, Isla
84 G13 **Chavuma** North Western, NW Zambia *13.04S 22.43E*
121 O16 **Chavusy** *Rus.* Chausy. Mahilyowskaya Voblasts', E Belarus *53.49N 30.59E*
151 Q16 **Chayan** Yuzhnyy Kazakhstan, S Kazakhstan *42.55N 69.32E*
153 U8 **Chayek** Narynskaya Oblast', C Kyrgyzstan *41.54N 74.28E*
145 T6 **Chāy Khānah** E Iraq *34.19N 44.33E*
129 T16 **Chaykovskiy** Permskaya Oblast', NW Russian Federation *56.45N 54.09E*
178 K12 **Chbar** Môndól Kiri, E Cambodia *12.46N 107.10E*
25 Q4 **Cheaha Mountain** ▲ Alabama, S USA *33.29N 85.48W*
Cheatharlach *see* Carlow
23 S2 **Cheat River** ≈ NE USA
113 A16 **Cheb** *Ger.* Eger. Karlovarský Kraj, W Czech Republic *50.04N 12.23E*
131 Q3 **Cheboksary** Chuvashskaya Respublika, W Russian Federation *56.06N 47.14E*
33 Q5 **Cheboygan** Michigan, N USA *45.40N 84.28W*
Chechaouèn *see* Chefchaouen
Chechenia *see* Chechenskaya Respublika
131 O15 **Chechenskaya Respublika** *Eng.* Chechenia, Chechnia, *Rus.* Chechnya. ◈ *autonomous republic* SW Russian Federation
69 N4 **Chech, Erg** *desert* Algeria/Mali
Chechersk *see* Chachersk
Chechevichi *see* Chachevichy
Che-chiang *see* Zhejiang
Chechnia/Chechnya *see* Chechenskaya Respublika
169 Y15 **Chech'ŏn** *Jap.* Teisen. N South Korea *37.06N 128.15E*
113 L15 **Chęciny** Świętokrzyskie, S Poland *50.51N 20.31E*
29 Q10 **Checotah** Oklahoma, C USA *35.28N 95.31W*
11 R15 **Chedabucto Bay** *inlet* Nova Scotia, E Canada
177 F7 **Cheduba Island** *island* W Burma
39 T5 **Cheesman Lake** ⊠ Colorado, C USA
205 S16 **Cheetham, Cape** *headland* Antarctica *70.25S 162.40E*
76 G5 **Chefchaouen** *var.* Chaouèn, Chechaouèn, *Sp.* Xauen. N Morocco *35.09N 5.16W*
Chefoo *see* Yantai
40 M12 **Chefornak** Alaska, USA *60.09N 164.09W*
126 Mm15 **Chegdomyn** Khabarovskiy Kray, SE Russian Federation *51.09N 132.58E*
78 M4 **Chegga** Tiris Zemmour, NE Mauritania *25.27N 5.49W*
Cheghcheran *see* Chaghcharān
34 G9 **Chehalis** Washington, NW USA *46.39N 122.57W*
34 G9 **Chehalis River** ≈ Washington, NW USA
154 M6 **Chehel Abdālān, Kūh-e** *var.* Chalap Dalam, *Pash.* Chalap Dalan. ▲▲ C Afghanistan
117 D14 **Cheimadítis, Límni** ◎ N Greece
105 U15 **Cheiron, Mont** ▲ SE France *43.49N 7.00E*
169 X17 **Cheju** *Jap.* Saishū. S South Korea *33.31N 126.34E*
169 Y17 **Cheju** ✕ S South Korea *33.31N 126.28E*
169 Y17 **Cheju-do** *Jap.* Saishū; *prev.* Quelpart. *island* S South Korea
169 X17 **Cheju-haehyŏp** *strait* S South Korea
Chekiang *see* Zhejiang
Chekichler *see* Chekishlyar
152 B13 **Chekishlyar** *Turkm.* Chekichler. Balkanskiy Velayat, W Turkmenistan *37.35N 53.52E*
196 F8 **Chelab** Babeldaob, N Palau
153 N11 **Chelak** *Rus.* Chelek. Samarqand Wiloyati, C Uzbekistan *39.55N 66.45E*
34 J7 **Chelan, Lake** ⊠ Washington, NW USA
Chelek *see* Chelak
152 A11 **Cheleken** Balkanskiy Velayat, W Turkmenistan *39.25N 53.07E*
Chélif/Chéliff *see* Chelif, Oued
76 J5 **Chelif, Oued** *var.* Chélif, Chéliff, Chellif, Shellif. ≈ N Algeria
150 K12 **Chelkar** Aktyubinsk, W Kazakhstan *47.49N 59.28E*
Chelkar, Ozero *see* Shalkar, Ozero
Chellif *see* Chelif, Oued
113 P14 **Chełm** *Rus.* Kholm. Lubelskie, SE Poland *51.07N 23.28E*
112 I9 **Chełmno** *Ger.* Culm, Kulm. Kujawski-pomorskie, C Poland *53.21N 18.27E*
12 F10 **Chelmsford** Ontario, S Canada *46.33N 81.16W*
99 P21 **Chelmsford** E England, UK *51.43N 0.28E*
112 J9 **Chełmża** *Ger.* Culmsee, Kulmsee. Kujawski-pomorskie, C Poland *53.12N 18.36E*
29 Q8 **Chelsea** Oklahoma, C USA *36.32N 95.25W*
20 M8 **Chelsea** Vermont, NE USA *43.57N 72.24W*
99 L21 **Cheltenham** C England, UK *51.54N 2.04W*
107 R9 **Chelva** País Valenciano, E Spain *39.45N 1.00W*
125 Ee12 **Chelyabinsk** Chelyabinskaya Oblast', C Russian Federation *55.12N 61.25E*
125 E12 **Chelyabinskaya Oblast'** ◈ *province* C Russian Federation
126 Jj4 **Chelyuskin, Mys** *headland* N Russian Federation *77.42N 104.13E*
126 H15 **Chemal** Altayskiy Kray, S Russian Federation *51.22N 85.08E*
43 Y12 **Chemax** Yucatán, SE Mexico *20.41N 87.54W*
85 N16 **Chemba** Sofala, C Mozambique *17.10S 34.52E*
84 J13 **Chembe** Luapula, NE Zambia *11.58S 28.45E*
152 J17 **Chemenibit** Maryyskiy Velayat, S Turkmenistan *35.27N 62.19E*
Chemerisy *see* Chamyarysy
118 K7 **Chemerivtsi** Khmel'nyts'ka Oblast', W Ukraine *49.00N 26.21E*
104 J8 **Chemillé** Maine-et-Loire, NW France *47.15N 0.42W*
181 X17 **Chemin Grenier** S Mauritius *20.28S 57.28E*
103 N16 **Chemnitz** *prev.* Karl-Marx-Stadt. Sachsen, E Germany *50.49N 12.55E*
Chemulpo *see* Inch'ŏn
34 H14 **Chemult** Oregon, NW USA *43.14N 121.48W*
20 G12 **Chemung River** ≈ New York/Pennsylvania, NE USA
155 U8 **Chenāb** ≈ India/Pakistan
41 S9 **Chena Hot Springs** Alaska, USA *65.06N 146.02W*
20 I11 **Chenango River** ≈ New York, NE USA
174 Gg3 **Chenderoh, Tasik** ◎ Peninsular Malaysia
13 Q11 **Chêne, Rivière du** ≈ Quebec, SE Canada
34 L8 **Cheney** Washington, NW USA *47.29N 117.34W*
28 M6 **Cheney Reservoir** ⊠ Kansas, C USA
Chengchiatun *see* Liaoyuan
Ch'eng-chou/Chengchow *see* Zhengzhou
167 P1 **Chengde** *var.* Jehol. Hebei, E China *41.00N 117.57E*
166 I9 **Chengdu** *var.* Chengtu, Ch'eng-tu. Sichuan, C China *30.40N 104.03E*
167 Q14 **Chenghai** Guangdong, S China *23.33N 116.42E*
Chenghsien *see* Zhengzhou
166 L17 **Chengmai** Hainan, S China *19.45N 109.56E*
Chengtu/Ch'eng-tu *see* Chengdu
165 W12 **Chengxian** *var.* Cheng Xian. Gansu, C China *33.42N 105.45E*
Chenkiang *see* Zhenjiang
161 J19 **Chennai** *prev.* Madras. Tamil Nādu, S India *13.04N 80.18E*
161 J19 **Chennai** ✕ Tamil Nādu, S India *13.07N 80.13E*
105 R8 **Chenôve** Côte d'Or, C France *47.16N 5.00E*
Chenstokhov *see* Częstochowa
166 L11 **Chenxi** Hunan, S China *28.01N 110.15E*
Chen Xian/Chenxian/Chen Xiang *see* Chenzhou
167 N12 **Chenzhou** *var.* Chenxian, Chen Xian, Chen Xiang. Hunan, S China *25.51N 113.01E*
178 Kk12 **Cheo Reo** *var.* A Yun Pa. Gia Lai, S Vietnam *13.19N 108.27E*
116 I11 **Chepelare** Smolyan, S Bulgaria *41.43N 24.40E*
116 I11 **Chepelarska Reka** ≈ S Bulgaria
58 B11 **Chepén** La Libertad, C Peru *7.12S 79.24W*
64 J10 **Chepes** La Rioja, C Argentina *31.23S 66.34W*
167 O15 **Chep Lap Kok** ✕ (Hong Kong) S China *22.23N 114.11E*
45 U14 **Chepo** Panamá, C Panama *9.10N 79.05W*
Chepping Wycombe *see* High Wycombe
129 R14 **Cheptsa** ≈ NW Russian Federation
32 K3 **Chequamegon Point** *headland* Wisconsin, N USA *46.42N 90.45W*
105 O8 **Cher** ◈ *department* C France
104 M8 **Cher** ≈ C France
Cherangani Hills *see* Cherangany Hills
83 H17 **Cherangany Hills** *var.* Cherangani Hills. ▲▲ W Kenya
23 S11 **Cheraw** South Carolina, SE USA *34.42N 79.52W*
104 I3 **Cherbourg** *anc.* Carusbur. Manche, N France *49.39N 1.36W*
131 R5 **Cherdakly** Ul'yanovskaya Oblast', W Russian Federation *54.21N 48.54E*
129 U12 **Cherdyn'** Permskaya Oblast', NW Russian Federation *60.21N 56.39E*
128 J14 **Cherekha** ≈ W Russian Federation
126 J15 **Cheremkhovo** Irkutskaya Oblast', S Russian Federation *53.16N 102.44E*
126 Hh15 **Cheremushki** Respublika Khakastya, S Russian Federation *52.48N 91.20E*
Cheren *see* Keren
128 K14 **Cherepovets** Vologodskaya Oblast', NW Russian Federation *59.09N 37.49E*
129 O11 **Cherevkovo** Arkhangel'skaya Oblast', NW Russian Federation *61.45N 45.16E*
76 I6 **Chergui, Chott ech** *salt lake* NW Algeria
Cherikov *see* Cherykaw
119 P6 **Cherkas'ka Oblast'** *var.* Cherkasy, *Rus.* Cherkasskaya Oblast'. ◈ *province* C Ukraine
Cherkasskaya Oblast' *see* Cherkas'ka Oblast'
Cherkassy *see* Cherkasy
119 Q6 **Cherkasy** *Rus.* Cherkassy. Cherkas'ka Oblast', C Ukraine *49.25N 32.04E*
Cherkasy *see* Cherkas'ka Oblast'
130 M15 **Cherkessk** Karachayevo-Cherkesskaya Respublika, SW Russian Federation *44.12N 42.06E*
125 G13 **Cherlak** Omskaya Oblast', C Russian Federation *54.06N 74.59E*
125 Ff14 **Cherlakskiy** Omskaya Oblast', C Russian Federation *53.42N 74.23E*
129 U13 **Chermoz** Permskaya Oblast', NW Russian Federation *58.49N 56.07E*
Chernavchitsy *see* Charnawchytsy
129 T3 **Chernaya** Nenetskiy Avtonomnyy Okrug, NW Russian Federation *68.36N 56.34E*
129 T4 **Chernaya** ≈ NW Russian Federation
Chernigov *see* Chernihiv
Chernigovskaya Oblast' *see* Chernihivs'ka Oblast'
119 Q2 **Chernihiv** *Rus.* Chernigov. Chernihivs'ka Oblast', NE Ukraine *48.18N 25.59E*
Chernihiv *see* Chernihivs'ka Oblast'
119 V9 **Chernihivka** Zaporiz'ka Oblast', SE Ukraine *47.11N 36.10E*
119 P2 **Chernihivs'ka Oblast'** *var.* Chernihiv, *Rus.* Chernigovskaya Oblast'. ◈ *province* NE Ukraine
116 I9 **Cherni Osŭm** ≈ N Bulgaria
118 J8 **Chernivets'ka Oblast'** *var.* Chernivtsi, *Rus.* Chernovitskaya Oblast'. ◈ *province* W Ukraine
116 I9 **Cherni Vit** ≈ NW Bulgaria
116 G10 **Cherni Vrŭkh** ▲ W Bulgaria *42.33N 23.18E*
118 K8 **Chernivtsi** *Ger.* Czernowitz, *Rom.* Cernăuţi, *Rus.* Chernovtsy. Chernivets'ka Oblast', W Ukraine *48.18N 25.55E*
118 M7 **Chernivtsi** Vinnyts'ka Oblast', C Ukraine *48.33N 28.06E*
Chernivtsi *see* Chernivets'ka Oblast'
Chernobyl' *see* Chornobyl'
126 Hh15 **Chernogorsk** Respublika Khakasiya, S Russian Federation *53.48N 91.03E*
Cherno More *see* Black Sea
Chernomorskoye *see* Chornomors'ke
151 T7 **Chernoretskoye** Pavlodar, NE Kazakhstan *52.51N 76.37E*
Chernovitskaya Oblast' *see* Chernivets'ka Oblast'
Chernovtsy *see* Chernivtsi
151 U8 **Chernoye** Pavlodar, NE Kazakhstan *51.40N 77.33E*
Chernoye More *see* Black Sea
129 U16 **Chernushka** Permskaya Oblast', NW Russian Federation *56.30N 56.07E*
119 N4 **Chernyakhiv** *Rus.* Chernyakhov. Zhytomyrs'ka Oblast', N Ukraine *50.31N 28.38E*
Chernyakhov *see* Chernyakhiv
121 C14 **Chernyakhovsk** *Ger.* Insterburg. Kaliningradskaya Oblast', W Russian Federation *54.36N 21.49E*
130 K8 **Chernyanka** Belgorodskaya Oblast', W Russian Federation *50.59N 37.54E*
129 V5 **Chernyshëva, Gryada** ▲▲ NW Russian Federation
150 J14 **Chernyshëva, Zaliv** *gulf* SW Kazakhstan
126 L15 **Chernyshevsk** Chitinskaya Oblast', S Russian Federation *52.28N 116.52E*
126 K11 **Chernyshevskiy** Respublika Sakha (Yakutiya), NE Russian Federation *62.57N 112.29E*
131 P13 **Chërnyye Zemli** *plain* SW Russian Federation
Chërnyy Irtysh *see* Ertix He
131 V7 **Chernyy Otrog** Orenburgskaya Oblast', W Russian Federation *52.03N 56.09E*
31 T12 **Cherokee** Iowa, C USA *42.45N 95.33W*
28 M8 **Cherokee** Oklahoma, C USA *36.45N 98.22W*
27 R9 **Cherokee** Texas, SW USA *30.56N 98.42W*
23 O8 **Cherokee Lake** ⊠ Tennessee, S USA
Cherokees, Lake O' The *see* Grand Lake O' The Cherokees
46 H1 **Cherokee Sound** Great Abaco, N Bahamas *26.16N 77.03W*
159 V13 **Cherrapunji** Meghālaya, NE India *25.16N 91.42E*
30 L9 **Cherry Creek** ≈ South Dakota, N USA
20 J16 **Cherry Hill** New Jersey, NE USA *39.55N 75.01W*
29 Q7 **Cherryvale** Kansas, C USA *37.16N 95.33W*
23 Q10 **Cherryville** North Carolina, SE USA *35.22N 81.22W*
Cherski Range *see* Cherskogo, Khrebet
127 O5 **Cherskiy** Respublika Sakha (Yakutiya), NE Russian Federation *68.45N 161.15E*
126 Mm8 **Cherskogo, Khrebet** *var.* Cherski Range. ▲▲ NE Russian Federation
Cherso *see* Cres
130 L10 **Chertkovo** Rostovskaya Oblast', SW Russian Federation *49.22N 40.10E*
Cherven' *see* Chervyen'
116 H8 **Cherven Bryag** Pleven, N Bulgaria *43.17N 24.06E*
118 M4 **Chervonoarmiys'k** Zhytomyrs'ka Oblast', N Ukraine *50.27N 28.15E*
Chervonograd *see* Chervonohrad
118 I4 **Chervonohrad** *Rus.* Chervonograd. L'vivs'ka Oblast', NW Ukraine *50.27N 24.11E*
119 W6 **Chervonooskil's'ke Vodoskhovyshche** *Rus.* Krasnoosol'skoye Vodokhranilishche. ⊠ NE Ukraine
Chervonoye, Ozero *see* Chyrvonaye, Vozyera
119 S4 **Chervonozavods'ke** Poltavs'ka Oblast', C Ukraine *50.24N 33.22E*
121 L16 **Chervyen'** *Rus.* Cherven'. Minskaya Voblasts', C Belarus *53.42N 28.23E*
121 P16 **Cherykaw** *Rus.* Cherikov. Mahilyowskaya Voblasts', E Belarus *53.34N 31.19E*
33 R9 **Chesaning** Michigan, N USA *43.10N 84.07W*
23 X5 **Chesapeake Bay** *inlet* NE USA
Cheshevlya *see* Tsyeshawlya
99 K18 **Cheshire** *cultural region* C England, UK
129 P5 **Chëshskaya Guba** *var.* Archangel Bay, Chesha Bay, Dvina Bay. *bay* NW Russian Federation
12 F14 **Chesley** Ontario, S Canada *44.17N 81.06W*
23 Q10 **Chesnee** South Carolina, SE USA *35.09N 81.51W*
99 K18 **Chester** *Wel.* Caerleon; *hist.* Legaceaster, *Lat.* Deva, Devana Castra. C England, UK *53.12N 2.54W*
37 O4 **Chester** California, W USA *40.18N 121.14W*
32 K16 **Chester** Illinois, N USA *37.54N 89.49W*
35 S7 **Chester** Montana, NW USA *48.30N 110.59W*
20 I16 **Chester** Pennsylvania, NE USA *39.51N 75.21W*
23 R1 **Chester** South Carolina, SE USA *34.42N 81.12W*
27 X9 **Chester** Texas, SW USA *30.55N 94.36W*
23 W6 **Chester** Virginia, NE USA *37.22N 77.27W*
23 R11 **Chester** West Virginia, NE USA *40.34N 80.33W*
99 M18 **Chesterfield** C England, UK *53.15N 1.25W*
23 S11 **Chesterfield** South Carolina, SE USA *34.44N 80.05W*
23 W6 **Chesterfield** Virginia, NE USA *37.22N 77.31W*
199 I10 **Chesterfield, Îles** *island group* NW New Caledonia
15 Ll6 **Chesterfield Inlet** Nunavut, NW Canada *63.19N 90.57W*
15 L6 **Chesterfield Inlet** *inlet* Nunavut, N Canada
23 Y3 **Chester River** ≈ Delaware/Maryland, NE USA
23 X3 **Chestertown** Maryland, NE USA *39.12N 76.04W*
21 R4 **Chesuncook Lake** ◎ Maine, NE USA
32 J5 **Chetek** Wisconsin, N USA *45.19N 91.37W*
11 R14 **Chéticamp** Nova Scotia, SE Canada *46.13N 61.19W*
29 Q8 **Chetopa** Kansas, C USA *37.02N 95.05W*
43 Y14 **Chetumal** *var.* Payo Obispo. Quintana Roo, SE Mexico *18.32N 88.15W*
Chetumal, Bahia/Chetumal, Bahía de *see* Chetumal Bay
44 G1 **Chetumal Bay** *var.* Bahia Chetumal, Bahía de Chetumal. *bay* Belize/Mexico
8 M13 **Chetwynd** British Columbia, W Canada *55.42N 121.36W*
40 M11 **Chevak** Alaska, USA *61.31N 165.35W*
38 M12 **Chevelon Creek** ≈ Arizona, SW USA
193 J17 **Cheviot** Canterbury, South Island, NZ *42.48S 173.17E*
98 L13 **Cheviot Hills** *hill range* England/Scotland, UK
98 L13 **Cheviot, The** ▲ NE England, UK *55.28N 2.10W*
12 M11 **Chevreuil, Lac du** ◎ Quebec, SE Canada
83 I16 **Ch'ew Bahir** *var.* Lake Stefanie. ◎ Ethiopia/Kenya
34 L7 **Chewelah** Washington, NW USA *48.16N 117.42W*
28 K10 **Cheyenne** Oklahoma, C USA *35.38N 99.40W*
35 Z17 **Cheyenne** *state capital* Wyoming, C USA *41.08N 104.45W*
28 L5 **Cheyenne Bottoms** ◎ Kansas, C USA
18 Kk6 **Cheyenne River** ≈ South Dakota/Wyoming, N USA
39 W5 **Cheyenne Wells** Colorado, C USA *38.49N 102.21W*
110 C9 **Cheyres** Vaud, W Switzerland *46.48N 6.48E*
Chezdi-Oşorheiu *see* Târgu Secuiesc
159 P13 **Chhapra** *prev.* Chapra. Bihār, N India *25.49N 84.42E*
159 V13 **Chhatak** *var.* Chatak. Chittagong, NE Bangladesh *25.02N 91.33E*
160 J9 **Chhatarpur** Madhya Pradesh, C India *24.54N 79.34E*
160 N13 **Chhatrapur** *prev.* Chatrapur; Orissa, E India *19.25N 85.01E*
160 L12 **Chhattīsgarh** *plain* C India
160 I11 **Chhindwāra** Madhya Pradesh, C India *22.04N 78.58E*
159 T12 **Chhukha** SW Bhutan *27.01N 89.36E*
167 S14 **Chiai** *var.* Chia-i, Chiayi, Kiayi, Jiayi, *Jap.* Kagi. C Taiwan *23.28N 120.27E*
Chia-mu-ssu *see* Jiamusi
85 B15 **Chiange** *Port.* Vila de Almoster. Huíla, SW Angola *15.49S 13.52E*
Chiang-hsi *see* Jiangxi
167 S12 **Chiang Kai-shek** ✕ (T'aipei) N Taiwan *25.09N 121.20E*
178 I8 **Chiang Khan** Loei, E Thailand *17.51N 101.43E*
178 H7 **Chiang Mai** *var.* Chiangmai, Chiengmai, Kiangmai. Chiang Mai, NW Thailand *18.48N 98.58E*
178 H7 **Chiang Mai** ✕ Chiang Mai, NW Thailand *18.44N 98.53E*
178 Hh6 **Chiang Rai** *var.* Chianpai, Chienrai, Muang Chiang Rai. Chiang Rai, NW Thailand *19.55N 99.51E*
Chiang-su *see* Jiangsu
Chianning/Chian-ning *see* Nanjing
Chianpai *see* Chiang Rai
108 G12 **Chianti** *cultural region* C Italy
Chiapa *see* Chiapa de Corzo
43 U16 **Chiapa de Corzo** *var.* Chiapa. Chiapas, SE Mexico *16.42N 92.58W*
43 V16 **Chiapas** ◈ *state* SE Mexico
108 J12 **Chiaravalle** Marche, C Italy *43.36N 13.19E*
109 N22 **Chiaravalle Centrale** Calabria, SW Italy *38.40N 16.25E*
108 E7 **Chiari** Lombardia, N Italy *45.33N 10.00E*
110 H12 **Chiasso** Ticino, S Switzerland *45.51N 9.01E*
143 S9 **Chiat'ura** C Georgia *42.13N 43.11E*
43 P15 **Chiautla** *var.* Chiautla de Tapia. Puebla, S Mexico *18.16N 98.31W*
Chiautla de Tapia *see* Chiautla
108 D10 **Chiavari** Liguria, NW Italy *44.19N 9.19E*
108 E6 **Chiavenna** Lombardia, N Italy *46.19N 9.22E*
Chiayi *see* Chiai
Chiazza *see* Piazza Armerina
172 Ss12 **Chiba** *var.* Tiba. Chiba, Honshū, S Japan *35.37N 140.05E*
171 K17 **Chiba** *off.* Chiba-ken, *var.* Tiba. ◈ *prefecture* Honshū, S Japan
85 M18 **Chibabava** Sofala, C Mozambique *20.16S 33.39E*
85 B15 **Chibia** *Port.* João de Almeida, Vila João de Almeida. Huíla, SW Angola *15.09S 13.45E*
85 M18 **Chiboma** Sofala, C Mozambique *20.06S 33.54E*
84 J12 **Chibondo** Luapula, N Zambia *10.42S 28.42E*
84 K11 **Chibote** Luapula, NE Zambia *9.52S 29.33E*
10 K12 **Chibougamau** Quebec, SE Canada *49.55N 74.24W*
170 Ff11 **Chiburi-jima** *island* Oki-shotō, SW Japan
85 M20 **Chibuto** Gaza, S Mozambique *24.40S 33.33E*
33 N11 **Chicago** Illinois, N USA *41.51N 87.39W*
33 N11 **Chicago Heights** Illinois, N USA *41.30N 87.38W*
13 W6 **Chic-Chocs, Monts** *Eng.* Shickshock Mountains. ▲▲ Quebec, SE Canada
41 W13 **Chichagof Island** *island* Alexander Archipelago, Alaska, USA
59 K20 **Chichas, Cordillera de** ▲▲ SW Bolivia
43 X12 **Chichén-Itzá, Ruinas** *ruins* Yucatán, SE Mexico *20.35N 88.34W*
99 N23 **Chichester** SE England, UK *50.49N 0.48W*
171 Jj16 **Chichibu** *var.* Titibu. Saitama, Honshū, S Japan *35.58N 139.06E*
44 C5 **Chichicastenango** Quiché, W Guatemala *14.55N 91.06W*
44 I9 **Chichigalpa** Chinandega, NW Nicaragua *12.34N 87.04W*
Ch'i-ch'i-ha-erh *see* Qiqihar
172 T16 **Chichijima-rettō** *Eng.* Beechy Group. *island group* SE Japan
56 K4 **Chichiriviche** Falcón, N Venezuela *10.58N 68.16W*
41 R11 **Chickaloon** Alaska, USA *61.48N 148.27W*
22 L10 **Chickamauga Lake** ⊠ Tennessee, S USA
25 N7 **Chickasawhay River** ≈ Mississippi, S USA
28 M11 **Chickasha** Oklahoma, C USA *35.03N 97.56W*
41 T9 **Chicken** Alaska, USA *64.04N 141.56W*
106 J16 **Chiclana de la Frontera** Andalucía, S Spain *36.25N 6.09W*
58 B11 **Chiclayo** Lambayeque, NW Peru *6.46S 79.46W*
37 N5 **Chico** California, W USA *39.42N 121.51W*
85 L15 **Chicoa** Tete, NW Mozambique *15.45S 32.25E*
85 M20 **Chicomo** Gaza, S Mozambique *24.29S 34.15E*
20 M11 **Chicopee** Massachusetts, NE USA *42.08N 72.34W*
65 I19 **Chico, Río** ≈ SE Argentina
65 I21 **Chico, Río** ≈ S Argentina
29 W14 **Chicot, Lake** ◎ Arkansas, C USA
13 R7 **Chicoutimi** Quebec, SE Canada *48.24N 71.04W*
13 Q8 **Chicoutimi** ≈ Quebec, SE Canada
85 L19 **Chicualacuala** Gaza, SW Mozambique *22.06S 31.42E*
85 B14 **Chicuma** Benguela, C Angola *13.33S 14.41E*
161 J21 **Chidambaram** Tamil Nādu, SE India *11.25N 79.42E*
206 K13 **Chidley, Cape** *headland* Newfoundland, E Canada *60.25N 64.39W*
103 N24 **Chiemsee** ◎ SE Germany
Chiengmai *see* Chiang Mai
Chienrai *see* Chiang Rai
108 B8 **Chieri** Piemonte, NW Italy *45.01N 7.49E*
108 F8 **Chiese** ≈ N Italy
109 K14 **Chieti** *var.* Teate. Abruzzo, C Italy *42.22N 14.10E*
101 E19 **Chièvres** Hainaut, SW Belgium *50.34N 3.49E*
169 S12 **Chifeng** *var.* Ulanhad. Nei Mongol Zizhiqu, N China *42.16N 118.55E*
84 F13 **Chifumage** ≈ E Angola
84 M13 **Chifunda** Eastern, NE Zambia *11.57S 32.36E*
151 S14 **Chiganak** *var.* Čiganak. Zhambyl, SE Kazakhstan *45.10N 73.55E*
41 P15 **Chiginagak, Mount** ▲ Alaska, USA *57.10N 157.00W*
Chigirin *see* Chyhyryn
43 P13 **Chignahuapan** Puebla, S Mexico *19.52N 98.03W*
41 O15 **Chignik** Alaska, USA *56.18N 158.24W*
85 M19 **Chigombe** ≈ S Mozambique
56 D7 **Chigorodó** Antioquia, NW Colombia *7.42N 76.45W*
85 M19 **Chigubo** Gaza, S Mozambique *22.50S 33.30E*
168 D6 **Chihertey** Bayan-Ölgiy, W Mongolia *48.10N 89.35E*
Chih-fu *see* Yantai
Chihli *see* Hebei
Chihli, Gulf of *see* Bo Hai
42 J6 **Chihuahua** Chihuahua, NW Mexico *28.40N 106.06W*
42 I6 **Chihuahua** ◈ *state* N Mexico
151 O15 **Chiili** Kzylorda, S Kazakhstan *44.09N 66.44E*
28 M7 **Chikaskia River** ≈ Kansas/Oklahoma, C USA
161 H19 **Chik Ballāpur** Karnātaka, W India *13.28N 77.42E*
128 G15 **Chikhachevo** Pskovskaya Oblast', W Russian Federation *57.17N 29.51E*
161 F19 **Chikmagalūr** Karnātaka, W India *13.19N 75.46E*
133 V7 **Chikoy** ≈ C Russian Federation
85 J15 **Chikumbi** Lusaka, C Zambia *15.16S 28.18E*
84 M13 **Chikwa** Eastern, NE Zambia *11.39S 32.45E*
Chikwana *see* Chikwawa
85 N15 **Chikwawa** *var.* Chikwana. Southern, S Malawi *16.01S 34.51E*
161 J16 **Chilakalūrupet** Andhra Pradesh, E India *16.09N 80.13E*
152 L14 **Chilan** Lebapskiy Velayat, E Turkmenistan *37.57N 64.58E*
Chilapa *see* Chilapa de Alvarez
43 P16 **Chilapa de Alvarez** *var.* Chilapa. Guerrero, S Mexico *17.36N 99.09W*
161 J25 **Chilaw** North Western Province, W Sri Lanka *7.34N 79.49E*
59 D15 **Chilca** Lima, W Peru *12.33S 76.44W*
25 Q4 **Childersburg** Alabama, S USA *33.16N 86.21W*
27 P4 **Childress** Texas, SW USA *34.25N 100.13W*
65 G14 **Chile** *off.* Republic of Chile. ◆ *republic* SW South America
49 R10 **Chile Basin** *undersea feature* E Pacific Ocean
65 H20 **Chile Chico** Aisén, W Chile *46.34S 71.43W*
64 I9 **Chilecito** La Rioja, NW Argentina *29.10S 67.30W*
64 H12 **Chilecito** Mendoza, W Argentina *33.52S 69.03W*
85 L14 **Chilembwe** Eastern, E Zambia *13.54S 31.38E*
200 O13 **Chile Rise** *undersea feature* SE Pacific Ocean
119 N13 **Chilia Braţul** ≈ SE Romania
Chilia-Nouă *see* Kiliya
151 V15 **Chilik** Almaty, SE Kazakhstan *43.35N 78.17E*
151 V15 **Chilik** ≈ SE Kazakhstan
160 O13 **Chilika Lake** *var.* Chilka Lake. ◎ E India
84 J13 **Chililabombwe** Copperbelt, C Zambia *12.19S 27.52E*
Chi-lin *see* Jilin
Chilka Lake *see* Chilika Lake
8 H9 **Chilkoot Pass** *pass* British Columbia, W Canada *59.41N 135.13W*
Chill Ala, Cuan *see* Killala Bay
64 G13 **Chillán** Bío Bío, C Chile *36.37S 72.10W*
63 C22 **Chillar** Buenos Aires, E Argentina *37.16S 59.58W*
Chill Chiaráin, Cuan *see* Kilkieran Bay
32 K12 **Chillicothe** Illinois, N USA *40.55N 89.29W*
29 S3 **Chillicothe** Missouri, C USA *39.48N 93.33W*
33 S14 **Chillicothe** Ohio, N USA *39.19N 82.58W*
27 Q4 **Chillicothe** Texas, SW USA *34.15N 99.31W*
8 M17 **Chilliwack** British Columbia, SW Canada *49.09N 121.54W*
Chill Mhantáin, Ceann *see* Wicklow Head
Chill Mhantáin, Sléibhte *see* Wicklow Mountains
110 C10 **Chillon** Vaud, W Switzerland *46.24N 6.56E*
152 C11 **Chil'mamedkum, Peski** *Turkm.* Chilmämetgum. *desert* W Turkmenistan
Chilmämetgum *see* Chil'mamedkum, Peski
65 F17 **Chiloé, Isla de** *var.* Isla Grande de Chiloé. *island* W Chile
34 H15 **Chiloquin** Oregon, NW USA *42.33N 121.33W*
43 O16 **Chilpancingo** *var.* Chilpancingo de los Bravos. Guerrero, S Mexico *17.33N 99.30W*
Chilpancingo de los Bravos *see* Chilpancingo
99 N21 **Chiltern Hills** *hill range* S England, UK
32 M7 **Chilton** Wisconsin, N USA *44.04N 88.10W*
84 F11 **Chiluage** Lunda Sul, NE Angola *9.32S 21.48E*
84 N12 **Chilumba** *prev.* Deep Bay. Northern, N Malawi *10.27S 34.12E*
167 T12 **Chilung** *var.* Keelung, *Jap.* Kirun, Kirun'; *prev. Sp.* Santissima Trinidad. N Taiwan *25.10N 121.43E*
85 N15 **Chilwa, Lake** *var.* Lago Chirua, Lake Shirwa. ◎ SE Malawi
178 J10 **Chi, Mae Nam** ≈ E Thailand
44 C6 **Chimaltenango** Chimaltenango, C Guatemala *14.37N 90.48W*
44 A2 **Chimaltenango** *off.* Departamento de Chimaltenango. ◈ *department* S Guatemala
45 V15 **Chimán** Panamá, E Panama *8.41N 78.37W*
85 M17 **Chimanimani** *prev.* Mandidzudzure, Melsetter. Manicaland, E Zimbabwe *19.48S 32.52E*
101 G22 **Chimay** Hainaut, S Belgium *50.03N 4.19E*
39 S10 **Chimayo** New Mexico, SW USA *36.00N 105.55W*
Chimbay *see* Chimboy
58 A13 **Chimborazo** ◈ *province* C Ecuador
58 C7 **Chimborazo** ⛰ C Ecuador *1.29S 78.50W*
58 C12 **Chimbote** Ancash, W Peru *9.04S 78.34W*
152 H7 **Chimboy** *Rus.* Chimbay. Qoraqalpoghiston Respublikasi, NW Uzbekistan *43.03N 59.52E*
194 H12 **Chimbu** ◈ *province* C PNG
56 F6 **Chimichagua** Cesar, N Colombia *9.19N 73.51W*
Chimishliya *see* Cimişlia
Chimkent *see* Shymkent
Chimkentskaya Oblast' *see* Yuzhnyy Kazakhstan
30 I14 **Chimney Rock** *rock* Nebraska, C USA *41.40N 103.21W*
85 M17 **Chimoio** Manica, C Mozambique *19.07S 33.28E*
84 K11 **Chimpembe** Northern, NE Zambia *9.33S 29.30E*
43 O8 **China** Nuevo León, NE Mexico *25.44N 99.09W*
162 M9 **China** *off.* People's Republic of China, *Chin.* Chung-hua Jen-min Kung-ho-kuo, Zhonghua Renmin Gongheguo; *prev.* Chinese Empire. ◆ *republic* E Asia
21 Q7 **China Lake** ◎ Maine, NE USA
44 F8 **Chinameca** San Miguel, E El Salvador *13.28N 88.21W*
Chi-nan/Chinan *see* Jinan
44 H9 **Chinandega** Chinandega, NW Nicaragua *12.37N 87.07W*
44 H9 **Chinandega** ◈ *department* NW Nicaragua
China, People's Republic of *see* China
China, Republic of *see* Taiwan
26 J11 **Chinati Mountains** ▲▲ Texas, SW USA
Chinaz *see* Chinoz
59 E15 **Chincha Alta** Ica, SW Peru *13.25S 76.08W*
9 N11 **Chinchaga** ≈ Alberta, SW Canada
Chin-chiang *see* Quanzhou
Chinchilla *see* Chinchilla de Monte Aragón
107 Q11 **Chinchilla de Monte Aragón** *var.* Chinchilla. Castilla-La Mancha, C Spain *38.55N 1.43W*
56 D10 **Chinchiná** Caldas, W Colombia *4.58N 75.37W*
107 O8 **Chinchón** Madrid, C Spain *40.07N 3.25W*
43 Z14 **Chinchorro, Banco** *island* SE Mexico
Chin-chou/Chinchow *see* Jinzhou
23 Z5 **Chincoteague** Assateague Island, Virginia, NE USA *37.55N 75.22W*
85 O17 **Chinde** Zambézia, NE Mozambique *18.34S 36.25E*
169 X17 **Chin-do** *Jap.* Chin-tō. *island* SW South Korea
165 R13 **Chindu** Qinghai, C China *33.19N 97.08E*
177 G2 **Chindwin** ≈ N Burma
Chinese Empire *see* China
152 L10 **Chingeldi** *Rus.* Chingildi. Nawoiy Wiloyati, N Uzbekistan *40.59N 64.13E*
Ch'ing Hai *see* Qinghai Hu
Chinghai *see* Qinghai
Chingildi *see* Chingeldi
150 H9 **Chingirlau** *Kaz.* Shyngghyrlaū. Zapadnyy Kazakhstan, W Kazakhstan *51.10N 53.44E*
84 J13 **Chingola** Copperbelt, C Zambia *12.31S 27.52E*
Ching-Tao/Ch'ing-tao *see* Qingdao
84 C13 **Chinguar** Huambo, C Angola *12.33S 16.22E*
78 I7 **Chinguețți** *var.* Chinguetti. Adrar, C Mauritania *20.25N 12.24W*
169 Z16 **Chinhae** *Jap.* Chinkai. S South Korea *35.06N 128.48E*
177 Ff4 **Chin Hills** ▲▲ W Burma
85 K16 **Chinhoyi** *prev.* Sinoia. Mashonaland West, N Zimbabwe *17.19S 30.06E*
Chinhsien *see* Jinzhou
41 Q14 **Chiniak, Cape** *headland* Kodiak Island, Alaska, USA *57.37N 152.10W*
12 G10 **Chiniguchi Lake** ◎ Ontario, S Canada
155 U8 **Chinīot** Punjab, NE Pakistan *31.40N 73.00E*
169 Y16 **Chinju** *Jap.* Shinshū. S South Korea *35.11N 128.06E*
Chinkai *see* Chinhae
80 M13 **Chinko** ≈ E Central African Republic
39 O9 **Chinle** Arizona, SW USA *36.09N 109.33W*
167 R13 **Chinmen Tao** *var.* Jinmen Dao, Quemoy. *island* W Taiwan
Chinnchâr *see* Shinshār
Chinnereth *see* Tiberias, Lake
171 J15 **Chino** *var.* Tino. Nagano, Honshū, S Japan *36.00N 138.10E*
104 L8 **Chinon** Indre-et-Loire, C France *47.10N 0.15E*
35 T7 **Chinook** Montana, NW USA *48.35N 109.13W*
Chinook State *see* Washington
199 Jj3 **Chinook Trough** *undersea feature* N Pacific Ocean
38 K11 **Chino Valley** Arizona, SW USA *34.45N 112.27W*
153 P10 **Chinoz** *Rus.* Chinaz. Toshkent Wiloyati, E Uzbekistan *40.58N 68.46E*
84 L12 **Chinsali** Northern, NE Zambia *10.33S 32.04E*
177 F4 **Chin State** ◈ *state* W Burma
Chinsura *see* Chunchura
Chin-tō *see* Chin-do
56 E6 **Chinú** Córdoba, NW Colombia *9.07N 75.25W*
101 K24 **Chiny, Forêt de** *forest* SE Belgium
85 M15 **Chioco** Tete, NW Mozambique *16.22S 32.50E*
108 H8 **Chioggia** *anc.* Fossa Claudia. Veneto, NE Italy *45.13N 12.16E*
116 H12 **Chionótrypa** ▲ NE Greece *41.16N 24.06E*
117 L18 **Chíos** *var.* Hios, Khíos, *It.* Scio, *Turk.* Sakiz-Adasi. Chíos, E Greece *38.22N 26.07E*
117 K18 **Chíos** *var.* Khíos. *island* E Greece
85 M14 **Chipata** *prev.* Fort Jameson. Eastern, E Zambia *13.40S 32.42E*
85 C14 **Chipindo** Huíla, C Angola *13.53S 15.47E*
25 R8 **Chipley** Florida, SE USA *30.46N 85.32W*
161 D15 **Chiplūn** Mahārāshtra, W India *17.31N 73.31E*
83 H22 **Chipogolo** Dodoma, C Tanzania *6.52S 36.03E*
25 R8 **Chipola River** ≈ Florida, SE USA
99 L22 **Chippenham** S England, UK *51.28N 2.07W*
32 J6 **Chippewa Falls** Wisconsin, N USA *44.55N 91.25W*
32 J4 **Chippewa, Lake** ⊠ Wisconsin, N USA
33 Q8 **Chippewa River** ≈ Michigan, N USA
32 I6 **Chippewa River** ≈ Wisconsin, N USA

◆ COUNTRY
● COUNTRY CAPITAL
◇ DEPENDENT TERRITORY
○ DEPENDENT TERRITORY CAPITAL
◈ ADMINISTRATIVE REGION
✕ INTERNATIONAL AIRPORT
▲ MOUNTAIN
▲▲ MOUNTAIN RANGE
⛰ VOLCANO
≈ RIVER
◎ LAKE
⊠ RESERVOIR

Chipping Wycombe – Ciudad Trujillo

Chipping Wycombe *see* High Wycombe
116 G8 **Chiprovtsi** Montana, NW Bulgaria 43.23N 22.53E
21 T4 **Chiputneticook Lakes** *lakes* Canada/USA
58 D13 **Chiquián** Ancash, W Peru 10.03S 77.11W
43 Y11 **Chiquilá** Quintana Roo, SE Mexico 21.25N 87.20W
44 E6 **Chiquimula** Chiquimula, SE Guatemala 14.45N 89.31W
44 A3 **Chiquimula** *off.* Departamento de Chiquimula. ◐ *department* SE Guatemala
44 D7 **Chiquimulilla** Santa Rosa, S Guatemala 14.06N 90.22W
56 F9 **Chiquinquirá** Boyacá, C Colombia 5.37N 73.51W
161 J17 **Chirāla** Andhra Pradesh, E India 15.49N 80.21E
155 N4 **Chiras** Ghowr, N Afghanistan 35.15N 65.39E
158 H11 **Chirāwa** Rājasthān, N India 28.15N 75.42E
Chirchik *see* Chirchiq
153 Q9 **Chirchiq** *Rus.* Chirchik. Toshkent Wiloyati, E Uzbekistan 41.30N 69.31E
153 P10 **Chirchiq** ≈ E Uzbekistan
Chire *see* Shire
85 L18 **Chiredzi** Masvingo, SE Zimbabwe 21.03S 31.40E
27 X8 **Chireno** Texas, SW USA 31.30N 94.21W
79 X7 **Chirfa** Agadez, NE Niger 21.01N 12.41E
39 O16 **Chiricahua Mountains** ▲ Arizona, SW USA
39 O16 **Chiricahua Peak** ▲ Arizona, SW USA 31.51N 109.17W
56 F6 **Chiriguaná** Cesar, N Colombia 9.24N 73.37W
41 P15 **Chirikof Island** *island* Alaska, USA
45 P16 **Chiriquí** *off.* Provincia de Chiriquí. ◐ *province* SW Panama
45 P17 **Chiriquí, Golfo de** *Eng.* Chiriqui Gulf. *gulf* SW Panama
45 P15 **Chiriquí Grande** Bocas del Toro, W Panama 8.55N 82.08W
Chiriqui Gulf *see* Chiriquí, Golfo de
45 P15 **Chiriquí, Laguna de** *lagoon* NW Panama
45 O16 **Chiriquí Viejo, Río** ≈ W Panama
Chiriquí, Volcán de *see* Barú, Volcán
85 N15 **Chiromo** Southern, S Malawi 16.32S 35.07E
116 J10 **Chirpan** Stara Zagora, C Bulgaria 42.13N 25.22E
45 N14 **Chirripó Atlántico, Río** ≈ E Costa Rica
Chirripó, Cerro *see* Chirripó Grande, Cerro
45 N14 **Chirripó Grande, Cerro** *var.* Cerro Chirripó. ▲ SE Costa Rica 9.31N 83.28W
45 N13 **Chirripó, Río** *var.* Río Chirripó del Pacífico. ≈ NE Costa Rica
Chirua, Lago *see* Chilwa, Lake
85 J15 **Chirundu** Southern, S Zambia 16.01S 28.52E
31 W8 **Chisago City** Minnesota, N USA 45.22N 92.53W
85 J14 **Chisamba** Central, C Zambia 14.58S 28.21E
41 T10 **Chisana** Alaska, USA 62.09N 142.07W
84 I13 **Chisasa** North Western, NW Zambia 12.09S 25.30E
10 I9 **Chisasibi** Quebec, C Canada 53.45N 79.01W
44 D4 **Chisec** Alta Verapaz, C Guatemala 15.47N 90.13W
131 U5 **Chishmy** Respublika Bashkortostan, W Russian Federation 54.33N 55.21E
31 V4 **Chisholm** Minnesota, N USA 47.29N 92.52W
166 I11 **Chishui He** ≈ C China
Chisimaio/Chisimayu *see* Kismaayo
119 N10 **Chişinău** *Rus.* Kishinev. ● (Moldova) C Moldova 47.00N 28.50E
119 N10 **Chişinău** ✈ S Moldova 46.54N 28.56E
Chişinău-Criş *see* Chişineu-Criş
118 F10 **Chişineu-Criş** *Hung.* Kisjenő; *prev.* Chişinău-Criş. Arad, W Romania 46.33N 21.29E
85 K14 **Chisomo** Central, C Zambia 13.30S 30.37E
108 A8 **Chisone** ≈ NW Italy
26 K12 **Chisos Mountains** ▲ Texas, SW USA
155 U10 **Chistiān Mandi** Punjab, E Pakistan 29.52N 72.46E
41 T10 **Chistochina** Alaska, USA 62.34N 144.39W
131 R4 **Chistopol'** Respublika Tatarstan, W Russian Federation 55.20N 50.39E
151 O8 **Chistopol'ye** Severnyy Kazakhstan, N Kazakhstan 52.37N 67.13E
126 Kk16 **Chita** Chitinskaya Oblast', S Russian Federation 52.03N 113.34E
85 B16 **Chitado** Cunene, SW Angola 17.16S 13.54E
Chitaldroog/Chitaldrug *see* Chitradurga
85 C15 **Chitanda** ≈ S Angola
Chitangwiza *see* Chitungwiza
84 F10 **Chitato** Lunda Norte, NE Angola 7.23S 20.45E
85 C14 **Chitembo** Bié, C Angola 13.31S 16.44E
41 T11 **Chitina** Alaska, USA 61.31N 144.26W
41 T11 **Chitina River** ≈ Alaska, USA
126 Kk14 **Chitinskaya Oblast'** ◐ *province* S Russian Federation
84 M11 **Chitipa** Northern, NW Malawi 9.40S 33.19E
172 Oo6 **Chitose** *var.* Titose. Hokkaidō, NE Japan 42.50N 141.39E
161 G18 **Chitradurga** *prev.* Chitaldroog, Chitaldrug. Karnātaka, W India 14.15N 76.24E
155 T3 **Chitrāl** North-West Frontier Province, NW Pakistan 35.51N 71.46E
45 S16 **Chitré** Herrera, S Panama 7.57N 80.25W
159 V16 **Chittagong** *Ben.* Chāttagām. Chittagong, SE Bangladesh 22.19N 91.48E
159 U16 **Chittagong** ◐ *division* E Bangladesh
159 Q15 **Chittaranjan** West Bengal, NE India 23.52N 86.40E
158 G14 **Chittaurgarh** Rājasthān, N India 24.54N 74.42E
161 I19 **Chittoor** Andhra Pradesh, E India 13.13N 79.06E
161 G21 **Chittūr** Kerala, SW India 10.42N 76.46E
85 K16 **Chitungwiza** *prev.* Chitangwiza. Mashonaland East, NE Zimbabwe 18.00S 31.06E
64 H4 **Chiuchiu** Antofagasta, N Chile 22.13S 68.34W
84 F12 **Chiumbe** *var.* Tshiumbe. ≈ Angola/Dem. Rep. Congo (Zaire)
85 F15 **Chiume** Moxico, E Angola 15.08S 21.09E
84 K13 **Chiundaponde** Northern, NE Zambia 12.14S 30.40E
108 H13 **Chiusi** Toscana, C Italy 43.00N 11.56E
56 J5 **Chivacoa** Yaracuy, N Venezuela 10.10N 68.54W
108 B8 **Chivasso** Piemonte, NW Italy 45.13N 7.54E
85 L17 **Chivhu** *prev.* Enkeldoorn. Midlands, C Zimbabwe 19.01S 30.54E
63 C20 **Chivilcoy** Buenos Aires, E Argentina 34.55S 60.00W
84 N12 **Chiweta** Northern, N Malawi 10.36S 34.09E
44 D4 **Chixoy, Río** *var.* Río Negro, Río Salinas. ≈ Guatemala/Mexico
84 H13 **Chizela** North Western, NW Zambia 13.11S 24.59E
129 O5 **Chizha** Nenetskiy Avtonomnyy Okrug, NW Russian Federation 67.04N 44.19E
170 G13 **Chizu** Tottori, Honshū, SW Japan 35.15N 134.14E
Chkalov *see* Orenburg
76 J5 **Chlef** *var.* Ech Cheliff, Ech Chleff; *prev.* Al-Asnam, El Asnam, Orléansville. NW Algeria 36.10N 1.21E
117 G18 **Chlómo** ▲ C Greece 38.36N 22.57E
113 M15 **Chmielnik** Świętokrzyskie, C Poland 50.37N 20.43E
178 J11 **Chŏâm Khsant** Preăh Vihéar, N Cambodia 14.13N 104.55E
64 G10 **Choapa, Río** *var.* Choapo. ≈ C Chile
Choapas *see* Las Choapas
Choarta *see* Chwārtā
85 H17 **Chobe** ◐ *district* NE Botswana
69 T13 **Chobe** ≈ N Botswana
12 K8 **Chochocouane** ≈ Quebec, SE Canada
112 E13 **Chocianów** *Ger.* Kotzenan. Dolnośląskie, SW Poland 51.23N 15.55E
56 C9 **Chocó** *off.* Departamento del Chocó. ◐ *province* W Colombia
37 X16 **Chocolate Mountains** ▲ California, W USA
23 W9 **Chocowinity** North Carolina, SE USA 35.33N 77.03W
29 N10 **Choctaw** Oklahoma, C USA 35.30N 97.16W
25 Q8 **Choctawhatchee Bay** *bay* Florida, SE USA
25 Q8 **Choctawhatchee River** ≈ Florida, SE USA
Chodau *see* Chodov
169 V14 **Chŏ-do** *island* SW North Korea
Chodorów *see* Khodoriv
113 A16 **Chodov** *Ger.* Chodau. Karlovarský Kraj, W Czech Republic 50.15N 12.45E
112 G10 **Chodzież** Wielkopolskie, C Poland 53.00N 16.55E
65 J15 **Choele Choel** Río Negro, C Argentina 39.18S 65.42W
85 L14 **Chofombo** Tete, NW Mozambique 14.43S 31.48E
Chohtan *see* Chauhtan
9 U14 **Choiceland** Saskatchewan, C Canada 53.28N 104.26W
195 U13 **Choiseul** *var.* Lauru. *island* NW Solomon Islands
65 M23 **Choiseul Sound** *sound* East Falkland, Falkland Islands
42 H7 **Choix** Sinaloa, C Mexico 26.43N 108.20W
112 D10 **Chojna** Zachodniopomorskie, W Poland 52.56N 14.25E
112 H8 **Chojnice** *Ger.* Konitz. Pomorskie, N Poland 53.41N 17.34E
113 F14 **Chojnów** *Ger.* Hainau, Haynau. Dolnośląskie, SW Poland 51.16N 15.55E
171 Ll11 **Chōkai-san** ▲ Honshū, C Japan 39.06N 140.02E
178 I11 **Chok Chai** Nakhon Ratchasima, C Thailand 14.45N 102.10E
82 I12 **Ch'ok'ē** *var.* Choke Mountains. ▲ NW Ethiopia
27 R13 **Choke Canyon Lake** ⊠ Texas, SW USA
Choke Mountains *see* Ch'ok'ē
151 T15 **Chokpar** *Kaz.* Shoqpar. Zhambyl, S Kazakhstan 43.49N 74.25E
153 W7 **Chok-Tal** *var.* Choktal. Issyk-Kul'skaya Oblast', E Kyrgyzstan 42.37N 76.45E
Chókué *see* Chokwé
126 Mm6 **Chokurdakh** Respublika Sakha (Yakutiya), NE Russian Federation 70.38N 148.18E
85 L20 **Chokwé** *var.* Chókué. Gaza, S Mozambique 24.36S 33.06E
196 F8 **Chol** Babeldaob, N Palau
166 E8 **Chola Shan** ▲ C China
104 J8 **Cholet** Maine-et-Loire, NW France 47.03N 0.52W
65 H17 **Cholila** Chubut, W Argentina 42.33S 71.28W
Cholo *see* Thyolo
153 V8 **Cholpon** Narynskaya Oblast', C Kyrgyzstan 42.07N 75.25E
153 X7 **Cholpon-Ata** Issyk-Kul'skaya Oblast', E Kyrgyzstan 42.39N 77.05E
43 P14 **Cholula** Puebla, S Mexico 19.03N 98.19W
44 I8 **Choluteca** Choluteca, S Honduras 13.16N 87.11W
44 H8 **Choluteca** ◐ *department* S Honduras
44 G6 **Choluteca, Río** ≈ SW Honduras
85 I15 **Choma** Southern, S Zambia 16.47S 26.58E
159 T11 **Chomo Lhari** ▲ NW Bhutan 27.59N 89.24E
178 H7 **Chom Thong** Chiang Mai, NW Thailand 18.28N 98.41E
113 B15 **Chomutov** *Ger.* Komotau. Ústecký Kraj, NW Czech Republic 50.28N 13.24E
126 K12 **Chona** ≈ C Russian Federation
169 X15 **Ch'ŏnan** *Jap.* Tenan. W South Korea 36.51N 127.10E
178 Hh12 **Chon Buri** *prev.* Bang Pla Soi. Chon Buri, S Thailand 13.17N 100.58E
58 B6 **Chone** Manabí, W Ecuador 0.41S 80.06W
169 W13 **Ch'ŏngch'ŏn-gang** ≈ W North Korea
169 Y11 **Ch'ŏngjin** NE North Korea 41.48N 129.43E
169 W13 **Chŏngju** W North Korea 39.43N 125.13E
167 S8 **Chongming Dao** *island* E China
166 J10 **Chongqing** *var.* Ch'ung-ching, Ch'ung-ch'ing, Chungking, Pahsien, Tchongking, Yuzhou. Chongqing Shi, C China 29.34N 106.27E
Chŏngup *see* Chŏnju
167 O10 **Chongyang** Hubei, C China 29.34N 114.03E
169 Y16 **Chŏnju** *prev.* Chŏngup, *Jap.* Seiyu. SW South Korea 35.51N 127.08E
169 Y15 **Chŏnju** *Jap.* Zenshū. SW South Korea 35.51N 127.08E
Chonnacht *see* Connaught
169 Q9 **Chonogol** Sühbaatar, E Mongolia 45.55N 115.19E
65 F19 **Chonos, Archipiélago de los** *island group* S Chile
44 K10 **Chontales** ◐ *department* S Nicaragua
178 Jj14 **Chơn Thanh** Sông Be, S Vietnam 11.25N 106.37E
164 K17 **Cho Oyu** *var.* Qowowuyag. ▲ China/Nepal 28.07N 86.37E
118 G7 **Chop** *Cz.* Cop, *Hung.* Csap. Zakarpats'ka Oblast', W Ukraine 48.25N 22.13E
23 Y3 **Choptank River** ≈ Maryland, NE USA
Chorcaí, Cuan *see* Cork Harbour
45 P15 **Chorcha, Cerro** ▲ W Panama 8.39N 82.07W
Chorku *see* Chorkūh
153 R11 **Chorkūh** *Rus.* Chorku. N Tajikistan 40.04N 70.30E
99 K17 **Chorley** NW England, UK 53.40N 2.37W
Chorne More *see* Black Sea
119 R5 **Chornobay** Cherkas'ka Oblast', C Ukraine 49.40N 32.20E
Chornobyl' *Rus.* Chernobyl'. Kyyivs'ka Oblast', N Ukraine 51.16N 30.15E
119 R12 **Chornomors'ke** *Rus.* Chernomorskoye. Respublika Krym, S Ukraine 45.29N 32.45E
119 R4 **Chornukhy** Poltavs'ka Oblast', C Ukraine 50.15N 32.57E
Chorokh/Chorokhi *see* Çoruh Nehri
112 O9 **Choroszcz** Podlaskie, NE Poland 53.09N 22.59E
118 K6 **Chortkiv** *Rus.* Chortkov. Ternopil's'ka Oblast', W Ukraine 49.01N 25.45E
Chortkov *see* Chortkiv
Chorum *see* Çorum
112 M9 **Chorzele** Mazowieckie, C Poland 53.16N 20.53E
113 J16 **Chorzów** *Ger.* Königshütte; *prev.* Królewska Huta. Śląskie, S Poland 50.17N 18.57E
169 W12 **Ch'osan** N North Korea 40.45N 125.52E
Chōsen-kaikyō *see* Korea Strait
171 Kk17 **Chōshi** *var.* Tyôsi. Chiba, Honshū, S Japan 35.43N 140.48E
65 H14 **Chos Malal** Neuquén, W Argentina 37.22S 70.16W
Chosŏn-minjujuŭi-inmin-kanghwaguk *see* North Korea
112 E9 **Choszczno** *Ger.* Arnswalde. Zachodniopomorskie, NW Poland 53.10N 15.24E
159 O15 **Chota Nāgpur** *plateau* N India
35 R8 **Choteau** Montana, NW USA 47.48N 112.40W
Chotqol *see* Chatkal
12 M8 **Chouart** ≈ Quebec, SE Canada
78 I7 **Choûm** Adrar, C Mauritania 21.18N 12.58W
29 Q9 **Chouteau** Oklahoma, C USA 36.11N 95.20W
23 X8 **Chowan River** ≈ North Carolina, SE USA
37 Q10 **Chowchilla** California, W USA 37.06N 120.15W
169 P7 **Choybalsan** Dornod, E Mongolia 48.02N 114.31E
168 M9 **Choyr** Dornogovĭ, C Mongolia 46.20N 108.21E
193 I19 **Christchurch** Canterbury, South Island, NZ 43.31S 172.39E
99 M24 **Christchurch** S England, UK 50.43N 1.45W
193 I18 **Christchurch** ✈ Canterbury, South Island, NZ 43.28S 172.33E
46 J12 **Christiana** C Jamaica 18.13N 77.28W
85 H22 **Christiana** Free State, C South Africa 27.55S 25.10E
117 J23 **Christiáni** *island* Kykládes, Greece, Aegean Sea
Christiania *see* Oslo
12 G13 **Christian Island** *island* Ontario, S Canada
203 P16 **Christian, Point** *headland* Pitcairn Island, Pitcairn Islands 25.04S 130.07E
40 M11 **Christian River** ≈ Alaska, USA
Christiansand *see* Kristiansand
23 S7 **Christiansburg** Virginia, NE USA 37.07N 80.24W
97 G23 **Christiansfeld** Sønderjylland, SW Denmark 55.21N 9.30E
Christianshåb *see* Qasigiannguit
41 X14 **Christian Sound** *inlet* Alaska, USA
47 T9 **Christiansted** Saint Croix, S Virgin Islands (US) 17.43N 64.42W
Christiansund *see* Kristiansund
27 R13 **Christine** Texas, SW USA 28.47N 98.30W
181 U7 **Christmas Island** ◇ *Australian external territory* E Indian Ocean
133 T17 **Christmas Island** *island* E Indian Ocean
Christmas Island *see* Kiritimati
199 K8 **Christmas Ridge** *undersea feature* C Pacific Ocean
32 L16 **Christopher** Illinois, N USA 37.58N 89.03W
27 P9 **Christoval** Texas, SW USA 31.09N 100.30W
113 F17 **Chrudim** Pardubický Kraj, C Czech Republic 49.58N 15.49E
117 K25 **Chrýsi** *island* SE Greece
123 Mm3 **Chrysochoú, Kólpos** *var.* Khrysokhou Bay. *bay* E Mediterranean Sea
116 I13 **Chrysoúpoli** *var.* Hrisoupoli; *prev.* Khrisoúpolis. Anatolikí Makedonía kai Thráki, NE Greece 40.58N 24.42E
113 K16 **Chrzanów** *var.* Chrzanow, *Ger.* Zaumgarten. Śląskie, S Poland 50.09N 19.18E
133 Q7 **Chu** *Kaz.* Shū. ≈ Kazakhstan/Kyrgyzstan
44 C5 **Chucaús, Sierra de** ▲ W Guatemala
159 S15 **Chuadanga** Khulna, W Bangladesh 23.37N 88.52E
Chuan *see* Sichuan
Ch'uan-chou *see* Quanzhou
41 O11 **Chuathbaluk** Alaska, USA 61.36N 159.14W
194 I12 **Chuave** Chimbu, W PNG 6.06S 145.06E
Chubek *see* Moskva
65 I17 **Chubut** *off.* Provincia de Chubut. ◐ *province* S Argentina
65 I17 **Chubut, Río** ≈ SE Argentina
45 V15 **Chucanti, Cerro** ▲ E Panama 8.48N 78.27W
Ch'u-chiang *see* Shaoguan
45 W15 **Chucunaque, Río** ≈ E Panama
Chudin *see* Chudzin
118 M5 **Chudniv** Zhytomyrs'ka Oblast', N Ukraine 50.02N 28.06E
128 H13 **Chudovo** Novgorodskaya Oblast', W Russian Federation 59.07N 31.42E
Chudskoye Ozero *see* Peipus, Lake
121 J18 **Chudzin** *Rus.* Chudin. Brestskaya Voblasts', SW Belarus 52.43N 26.56E
41 Q13 **Chugach Islands** *island group* Alaska, USA
41 S11 **Chugach Mountains** ▲ Alaska, USA
170 Ee12 **Chūgoku-sanchi** ▲ Honshū, SW Japan
Chuguyev *see* Chuhuyiv
119 V5 **Chuhuyiv** *var.* Chuguyev. Kharkivs'ka Oblast', E Ukraine 49.51N 36.44E
63 H19 **Chuí** Rio Grande do Sul, S Brazil 33.40S 53.24W
Chuí *see* Chuy
151 S15 **Chu-Iliyskiye Gory** *Kaz.* Shū-Ile Taūlary. ▲ S Kazakhstan
Chukai *see* Cukai
Chukchi Avtonomnyy Okrug *see* Chukotskiy Avtonomnyy Okrug
Chukchi Peninsula *see* Chukotskiy Poluostrov
207 R6 **Chukchi Plain** *undersea feature* Arctic Ocean
207 R6 **Chukchi Plateau** *undersea feature* Arctic Ocean
207 R4 **Chukchi Sea** *Rus.* Chukotskoye More. *sea* Arctic Ocean
129 N14 **Chukhloma** Kostromskaya Oblast', NW Russian Federation 58.42N 42.39E
Chukotka *see* Chukotskiy Avtonomnyy Okrug
Chukot Range *see* Anadyrskiy Khrebet
127 Oo5 **Chukotskiy Avtonomnyy Okrug** *var.* Chukchi Avtonomnyy Okrug, Chukotka. ◐ *autonomous district* NE Russian Federation
127 Q4 **Chukotskiy, Mys** *headland* NE Russian Federation 64.15N 173.03W
127 Pp4 **Chukotskiy Poluostrov** *Eng.* Chukchi Peninsula. *peninsula* NE Russian Federation
Chukotskoye More *see* Chukchi Sea
Chukurkak *see* Chuqurqoq
Chulakkurgan *see* Shollakorgan
37 U17 **Chula Vista** California, W USA 32.38N 117.04W
126 Ll13 **Chul'man** Respublika Sakha (Yakutiya), NE Russian Federation 56.50N 124.47E
58 B9 **Chulucanas** Piura, NW Peru 5.07S 80.10W
126 Gg14 **Chulym** Novosibirskaya Oblast', C Russian Federation 55.03N 80.53E
126 H13 **Chulym** ≈ C Russian Federation
158 K6 **Chumar** Jammu and Kashmir, N India 32.37N 78.36E
116 K9 **Chumerna** ▲ C Bulgaria 42.45N 25.58E
127 N13 **Chumikan** Khabarovskiy Kray, E Russian Federation 54.41N 135.12E
178 I9 **Chum Phae** Khon Kaen, C Thailand 16.31N 102.09E
178 Gg14 **Chumphon** *var.* Jumporn. Chumphon, SW Thailand 10.30N 99.10E
178 Hh10 **Chumsaeng** *var.* Chum Saeng. Nakhon Sawan, C Thailand 15.52N 100.20E
126 H14 **Chumysh** ≈ S Russian Federation
126 Ii13 **Chuna** ≈ C Russian Federation
167 R9 **Chun'an** *var.* Pailing. Zhejiang, SE China 29.37N 118.59E
167 S13 **Chunan** N Taiwan 24.44N 120.51E
169 Y14 **Ch'unch'ŏn** *Jap.* Shunsen. N South Korea 37.52N 127.48E
159 S16 **Chunchura** *prev.* Chinsura. West Bengal, NE India 22.54N 88.19E
151 W15 **Chundzha** Almaty, SE Kazakhstan 43.31N 79.28E
Ch'ung-ch'ing/Ch'ung-ching *see* Chongqing
Chung-hua Jen-min Kung-ho-kuo *see* China
169 Y15 **Ch'ungju** *Jap.* Chūshū. C South Korea 36.57N 127.49E
Chungking *see* Chongqing
167 T14 **Chungyang Shanmo** *Chin.* Taiwan Shan. ▲ C Taiwan
155 V9 **Chūniān** Punjab, E Pakistan 30.57N 74.01E
126 Ii14 **Chunskiy** Irkutskaya Oblast', S Russian Federation 56.10N 99.15E
126 J11 **Chunya** ≈ C Russian Federation
128 I6 **Chupa** Respublika Kareliya, NW Russian Federation 66.15N 33.02E
129 P8 **Chuprovo** Respublika Komi, NW Russian Federation 64.16N 46.27E
59 G17 **Chuquibamba** Arequipa, SW Peru 15.54S 72.37W
64 H4 **Chuquicamata** Antofagasta, N Chile 22.19S 68.55W
59 L21 **Chuquisaca** ◐ *department* S Bolivia
Chuquisaca *see* Sucre
152 I8 **Chuqurqoq** *Rus.* Chukurkak. Qoraqalpoghiston Respublikasi, NW Uzbekistan 42.44N 61.33E
131 T2 **Chur** Udmurtskaya Respublika, NW Russian Federation 57.06N 52.57E
110 I9 **Chur** *Fr.* Coire, *It.* Coira, *Rmsch.* Cuera, Quera; *anc.* Curia Rhaetorum. Graubünden, E Switzerland 46.52N 9.31E
126 M11 **Churapcha** Respublika Sakha (Yakutiya), NE Russian Federation 61.59N 132.06E
9 V16 **Churchbridge** Saskatchewan, S Canada 50.55N 101.53W
23 O8 **Church Hill** Tennessee, S USA 36.31N 82.42W
9 X9 **Churchill** Manitoba, C Canada 58.46N 94.10W
9 X10 **Churchill** ≈ Manitoba/Saskatchewan, C Canada
11 P9 **Churchill** ≈ Newfoundland, E Canada
9 Y9 **Churchill, Cape** *headland* Manitoba, C Canada 58.42N 93.12W
11 P9 **Churchill Falls** Newfoundland, E Canada 53.38N 64.00W
9 S12 **Churchill Lake** ◎ Saskatchewan, C Canada
21 Q3 **Churchill Lake** ⊠ Maine, NE USA
204 I5 **Churchill Peninsula** *peninsula* Antarctica
24 H8 **Church Point** Louisiana, S USA 30.24N 92.13W
31 O3 **Churchs Ferry** North Dakota, N USA 48.15N 99.12W
152 G12 **Churchuri** Akhalskiy Velayat, C Turkmenistan 38.55N 59.13E
23 T5 **Churchville** Virginia, NE USA 38.13N 79.10W
158 G10 **Chūru** Rājasthān, NW India 28.18N 75.00E
56 J4 **Churuguara** Falcón, N Venezuela 10.48N 69.30W
150 J12 **Chushkakul, Gory** ▲ SW Kazakhstan
Chūshū *see* Ch'ungju
39 O9 **Chuska Mountains** ▲ Arizona/New Mexico, SW USA
Chu, Sông *see* Sam, Nam
125 Ee11 **Chusovaya** ≈ W Russian Federation
129 V14 **Chusovoy** Permskaya Oblast', NW Russian Federation 58.17N 57.54E
153 R10 **Chust** Namangan Wiloyati, E Uzbekistan 40.58N 71.12E
Chust *see* Khust
13 U6 **Chute-aux-Outardes** Quebec, SE Canada 49.07N 68.25W
119 U5 **Chutove** Poltavs'ka Oblast', C Ukraine 49.45N 35.11E
201 O15 **Chuuk** *var.* Truk. ◐ *state* C Micronesia
201 P15 **Chuuk Islands** *var.* Hogoley Islands; *prev.* Truk Islands. *island group* Caroline Islands, C Micronesia
Chuvashia *see* Chuvashskaya Respublika
131 P4 **Chuvashskaya Respublika** *var.* Chavash Respubliki, *Eng.* Chuvashia. ◐ *autonomous republic* W Russian Federation
Chuwārtah *see* Chwārtā
Chu Xian/Chuxian *see* Chuzhou
166 G13 **Chuxiong** Yunnan, SW China 25.01N 101.31E
153 V7 **Chuy** Chuyskaya Oblast', N Kyrgyzstan 42.45N 75.11E
63 H19 **Chuy** *var.* Chuí. Rocha, E Uruguay 33.42S 53.27W
126 K12 **Chuya** Respublika Sakha (Yakutiya), NE Russian Federation 59.30N 112.26E
Chüy Oblasty *see* Chuyskaya Oblast'
153 U8 **Chuyskaya Oblast'** *Kir.* Chüy Oblasty. ◐ *province* N Kyrgyzstan
167 Q7 **Chuzhou** *var.* Chuxian, Chu Xian. Anhui, E China 32.21N 118.15E
145 U3 **Chwārtā** *var.* Choarta, Chuwārtah. NE Iraq 35.10N 45.58E
121 N16 **Chyhirynskaye Vodaskhovishcha** ⊠ E Belarus
119 R6 **Chyhyryn** *Rus.* Chigirin. Cherkas'ka Oblast', N Ukraine 49.03N 32.40E
Chyrvonaya Slabada *see* Krasnaya Slabada
121 L19 **Chyrvonaye, Vozyera** *Rus.* Ozero Chervonoye. ◎ SE Belarus
178 K12 **Chư Sê** Gia Lai, C Vietnam 13.38N 108.06E
119 N11 **Ciadîr-Lunga** *var.* Ceadâr-Lunga, *Rus.* Chadyr-Lunga. S Moldova 46.03N 28.50E
174 K15 **Ciamis** *prev.* Tjiamis. Jawa, C Indonesia 7.19S 108.21E
109 I16 **Ciampino** ✈ Lazio, C Italy 41.48N 12.36W
174 J14 **Cianjur** *prev.* Tjiandjoer. Jawa, C Indonesia 6.49S 107.09E
62 H10 **Cianorte** Paraná, S Brazil 23.37S 52.38W
Ciarraí *see* Kerry
114 N13 **Čičevac** Serbia, E Yugoslavia 43.44N 21.25E
197 K14 **Cicia** *prev.* Thithia. *island* Lau Group, E Fiji
107 P4 **Cidacos** ≈ N Spain
142 I10 **Cide** Kastamonu, N Turkey 41.52N 33.01E
112 L10 **Ciechanów** *prev.* Zichenau. Mazowieckie, C Poland 52.53N 20.36E
112 O10 **Ciechanowiec** *Ger.* Rudelstadt. Podlaskie, E Poland 52.43N 22.30E
112 J10 **Ciechocinek** Kujawsko-pomorskie, C Poland 52.53N 18.48E
46 F6 **Ciego de Ávila** Ciego de Ávila, C Cuba 21.50N 78.44W
56 F4 **Ciénaga** Magdalena, N Colombia 10.58N 74.15W
56 E6 **Ciénaga de Oro** Córdoba, NW Colombia 8.52N 75.37W
46 E5 **Cienfuegos** Cienfuegos, C Cuba 22.10N 80.27W
106 F4 **Cíes, Illas** *island group* NW Spain
113 P16 **Cieszanów** Podkarpackie, SE Poland 50.15N 23.09E
113 J17 **Cieszyn** *Cz.* Těšín, *Ger.* Teschen. Śląskie, S Poland 49.45N 18.37E
107 R12 **Cieza** Murcia, SE Spain 38.13N 1.25W
142 F13 **Çifteler** Eskişehir, W Turkey 39.25N 31.00E
107 P7 **Cifuentes** Castilla-La Mancha, C Spain 40.46N 2.37W
Čiganak *see* Chiganak
107 P9 **Cigüela** ≈ C Spain
142 H14 **Cihanbeyli** Konya, C Turkey 38.40N 32.55E
142 H14 **Cihanbeyli Yaylası** *plateau* C Turkey
106 L10 **Cijara, Embalse de** ⊠ C Spain
174 K15 **Cikalong** Jawa, S Indonesia 7.46S 108.13E
174 Ii14 **Cikawung** Jawa, S Indonesia 6.49S 105.29E
197 K12 **Cikobia** *prev.* Thikombia. *island* N Fiji
174 K15 **Cilacap** *prev.* Tjilatjap. Jawa, C Indonesia 07.44S 109.00E
181 O16 **Cilaos** C Réunion 21.07S 55.28E
143 S11 **Çıldır** Ardahan, NE Turkey 41.07N 43.07E
143 S11 **Çıldır Gölü** ◎ NE Turkey
174 K14 **Ciledug** *prev.* Tjiledoeg. Jawa, SW Indonesia 6.55S 108.43E
166 M10 **Cili** Hunan, S China 29.27N 111.03E
124 R12 **Cilicia Trough** *undersea feature* E Mediterranean Sea
Cill Airne *see* Killarney
Cill Chainnigh *see* Kilkenny
Cill Chaoi *see* Kilkee
Cill Choca *see* Kilcock
Cill Dara *see* Kildare
107 N3 **Cilleruelo de Bezana** Castilla-León, N Spain 42.58N 3.50W
Cilli *see* Celje
Cill Mhantáin *see* Wicklow
Cill Rois *see* Kilrush
28 J6 **Cimarron** Kansas, C USA 37.49N 100.20W
39 T9 **Cimarron** New Mexico, SW USA 36.30N 104.55W
28 M9 **Cimarron River** ≈ Kansas/Oklahoma, C USA
119 N11 **Cimişlia** *Rus.* Chimishliya. S Moldova 46.31N 28.45E
Cîmpia Turzii *see* Câmpia Turzii
Cîmpina *see* Câmpina
Cîmpulung *see* Câmpulung
Cîmpulung Moldovenesc *see* Câmpulung Moldovenesc
143 P15 **Çınar** Diyarbakır, SE Turkey 37.45N 40.22E
56 I8 **Cinaruco, Río** ≈ Colombia/Venezuela
Cina Selatan, Laut *see* South China Sea
107 T5 **Cinca** ≈ NE Spain
114 G13 **Cincar** ▲ SW Bosnia and Herzegovina 43.55N 17.05E
33 Q15 **Cincinnati** Ohio, N USA 39.04N 84.33W
23 M4 **Cincinnati** ✈ Kentucky, S USA 39.03N 84.39W
Cinco de Outubro *see* Xá-Muteba
142 C15 **Çine** Aydın, SW Turkey 37.37N 28.03E
101 J21 **Ciney** Namur, SE Belgium 50.16N 5.06E
106 H6 **Cinfães** Viseu, N Portugal 41.04N 8.06W
108 J12 **Cingoli** Marche, C Italy 43.25N 13.09E
43 U16 **Cintalapa** *var.* Cintalapa de Figueroa. Chiapas, SE Mexico 16.42N 93.40W
Cintalapa de Figueroa *see* Cintalapa
105 X14 **Cinto, Monte** ▲ Corse, France, C Mediterranean Sea 42.22N 8.57E
Cintra *see* Sintra
107 Q5 **Cintruénigo** Navarra, N Spain 42.04N 1.49W
Cionn tSáile *see* Kinsale
118 K13 **Ciorani** Prahova, SE Romania 44.49N 26.25E
115 E14 **Čiovo** *It.* Bua. *island* S Croatia
174 J14 **Cipanas** Jawa, S Indonesia
Cipiúr *see* Kippure
65 I15 **Cipolletti** Río Negro, C Argentina 38.55S 68.00W
123 L8 **Circeo, Capo** *headland* C Italy 41.15N 13.03E
41 S8 **Circle** *var.* Circle City. Alaska, USA 65.51N 144.04W
35 X8 **Circle** Montana, NW USA 47.25N 105.32W
Circle City *see* Circle
33 S14 **Circleville** Ohio, N USA 39.36N 82.57W
38 K6 **Circleville** Utah, W USA 38.10N 112.16W
174 K14 **Cirebon** *prev.* Tjirebon. Jawa, S Indonesia 6.46S 108.33E
99 L21 **Cirencester** *anc.* Corinium, Corinium Dobunorum. C England, UK 51.43N 1.58W
Cirkvenica *see* Crikvenica
109 O20 **Ciro** Calabria, SW Italy 39.22N 17.02E
109 O20 **Ciro Marina** Calabria, S Italy 39.21N 17.07E
104 K14 **Ciron** ≈ SW France
Cirquenizza *see* Crikvenica
27 R7 **Cisco** Texas, SW USA 32.23N 98.58W
118 I12 **Cisnădie** *Ger.* Heltau, *Hung.* Nagydisznód. Sibiu, SW Romania 45.42N 24.08E
65 G18 **Cisnes, Río** ≈ S Chile
27 T11 **Cistern** Texas, SW USA 29.46N 97.12W
106 L3 **Cistierna** Castilla-León, N Spain 42.46N 5.07W
174 Ii14 **Citeureup** Jawa, S Indonesia 6.34S 105.41E
Citharista *see* la Ciotat
Citlaltépetl *see* Orizaba, Volcán Pico de
57 X10 **Citron** NW French Guiana 4.49N 53.56W
25 N7 **Citronelle** Alabama, S USA 31.05N 88.13W
37 O7 **Citrus Heights** California, W USA 38.42N 121.18W
108 H7 **Cittadella** Veneto, NE Italy 45.37N 11.46E
108 H13 **Città della Pieve** Umbria, C Italy 42.57N 12.01E
108 H12 **Città di Castello** Umbria, C Italy 43.27N 12.13E
109 I14 **Cittaducale** Lazio, C Italy 42.24N 12.55E
109 N22 **Cittanova** Calabria, SW Italy 38.21N 16.04E
Cittavecchia *see* Starigrad
118 G10 **Ciucea** *Hung.* Csucsa. Cluj, NW Romania 46.57N 22.51E
118 M13 **Ciucurova** Tulcea, SE Romania 44.57N 28.24E
Ciudad Acuña *see* Villa Acuña
43 N15 **Ciudad Altamirano** Guerrero, S Mexico 18.22N 100.39W
44 G7 **Ciudad Barrios** San Miguel, NE El Salvador 13.46N 88.13W
56 I7 **Ciudad Bolívar** Barinas, NW Venezuela 8.23N 70.34W
57 N7 **Ciudad Bolívar** *prev.* Angostura. Bolívar, E Venezuela 8.07N 63.31W
42 K6 **Ciudad Camargo** Chihuahua, N Mexico 27.42N 105.10W
42 E8 **Ciudad Constitución** Baja California Sur, W Mexico 25.06N 111.42W
Ciudad Cortés *see* Cortés
43 V17 **Ciudad Cuauhtémoc** Chiapas, SE Mexico 15.23N 91.11W
44 J9 **Ciudad Darío** *var.* Dario. Matagalpa, W Nicaragua 12.42N 86.06W
Ciudad de Dolores Hidalgo *see* Dolores Hidalgo
44 C6 **Ciudad de Guatemala** *Eng.* Guatemala City; *prev.* Santiago de los Caballeros. ● (Guatemala) Guatemala, C Guatemala 14.37N 90.29W
Ciudad del Carmen *see* Carmen
64 Q6 **Ciudad del Este** *prev.* Cuidad Presidente Stroessner, Presidente Stroessner, Puerto Presidente Stroessner. Alto Paraná, SE Paraguay 25.34S 54.40W
64 K5 **Ciudad de Libertador General San Martín** *var.* Libertador General San Martín. Jujuy, C Argentina 23.49S 64.45W
Ciudad Delicias *see* Delicias
43 O11 **Ciudad del Maíz** San Luis Potosí, C Mexico 22.25N 99.36W
Ciudad de México *see* México
56 J7 **Ciudad de Nutrias** Barinas, NW Venezuela 8.03N 69.17W
Ciudad de Panamá *see* Panamá
57 P7 **Ciudad Guayana** *prev.* San Tomé de Guayana, Santo Tomé de Guayana. Bolívar, NE Venezuela 8.22N 62.37W
42 K14 **Ciudad Guzmán** Jalisco, SW Mexico 19.40N 103.30W
43 V17 **Ciudad Hidalgo** Chiapas, SE Mexico 14.45N 92.13W
43 N14 **Ciudad Hidalgo** Michoacán de Ocampo, SW Mexico 19.40N 100.34W
42 J3 **Ciudad Juárez** Chihuahua, N Mexico 31.39N 106.25W
42 L8 **Ciudad Lerdo** Durango, C Mexico 25.34N 103.30W
43 Q11 **Ciudad Madero** *var.* Villa Cecilia. Tamaulipas, C Mexico 22.18N 97.55W
43 P11 **Ciudad Mante** Tamaulipas, C Mexico 22.43N 99.01W
44 F2 **Ciudad Melchor de Mencos** *var.* Melchor de Mencos. Petén, NE Guatemala 17.03N 89.12W
43 P8 **Ciudad Miguel Alemán** Tamaulipas, C Mexico 26.19N 98.55W
Ciudad Mutis *see* Bahía Solano
42 G6 **Ciudad Obregón** Sonora, NW Mexico 27.32N 109.52W
56 I5 **Ciudad Ojeda** Zulia, NW Venezuela 10.09N 71.15W
57 P7 **Ciudad Piar** Bolívar, E Venezuela 7.25N 63.19W
Ciudad Porfirio Díaz *see* Piedras Negras
Ciudad Quesada *see* Quesada
107 N11 **Ciudad Real** Castilla-La Mancha, C Spain 38.58N 3.55W
107 N11 **Ciudad Real** ◐ *province* Castilla-La Mancha, C Spain
106 J7 **Ciudad-Rodrigo** Castilla-León, N Spain 40.36N 6.33W
44 A6 **Ciudad Tecún Umán** San Marcos, SW Guatemala 14.40N 92.06W
Ciudad Trujillo *see* Santo Domingo

◆ Country ● Country Capital ◇ Dependent Territory ○ Dependent Territory Capital ◐ Administrative Region ✈ International Airport ▲ Mountain ▲ Mountain Range ⩓ Volcano ≈ River ◎ Lake ⊠ Reservoir

243

◆ COUNTRY   ◇ DEPENDENT TERRITORY   ◎ ADMINISTRATIVE REGION   ▲ MOUNTAIN   🌋 VOLCANO   ☐ LAKE
● COUNTRY CAPITAL   ○ DEPENDENT TERRITORY CAPITAL   ✈ INTERNATIONAL AIRPORT   ▲ MOUNTAIN RANGE   ✍ RIVER   ☐ RESERVOIR

COLUMBIA – COSAMALOAPAN DE CARPIO

23 Y9 **Columbia** North Carolina, SE USA 35.53N 76.16W
20 G16 **Columbia** Pennsylvania, NE USA 40.01N 76.30W
23 Q12 **Columbia** state capital South Carolina, SE USA 34.00N 81.00W
22 I9 **Columbia** Tennessee, S USA 35.37N 87.02W
(0) F9 **Columbia** ≈ Canada/USA
34 K9 **Columbia Basin** basin Washington, NW USA
207 Q10 **Columbia, Cape** headland Ellesmere Island, Nunavut, NE Canada
33 Q12 **Columbia City** Indiana, N USA 41.09N 85.29W
23 W3 **Columbia, District of** ◈ federal district NE USA
35 P7 **Columbia Falls** Montana, NW USA 48.22N 114.10W
9 O15 **Columbia Icefield** icefield Alberta/British Columbia, S Canada
9 O15 **Columbia, Mount** ▲ Alberta/British Columbia, SW Canada 52.07N 117.30W
9 N15 **Columbia Mountains** ▲▲ British Columbia, SW Canada
25 P4 **Columbiana** Alabama, S USA 33.10N 86.36W
33 V12 **Columbiana** Ohio, N USA 40.53N 80.41W
34 M14 **Columbia Plateau** plateau Idaho/Oregon, NW USA
31 P7 **Columbia Road Reservoir** ☒ South Dakota, N USA
67 K16 **Columbia Seamount** undersea feature C Atlantic Ocean 20.30S 32.00W
85 D25 **Columbine, Cape** headland SW South Africa 32.50S 17.39E
107 U9 **Columbretes, Islas** island group E Spain
25 R5 **Columbus** Georgia, SE USA 32.28N 84.58W
33 P14 **Columbus** Indiana, N USA 39.12N 85.55W
29 R7 **Columbus** Kansas, C USA 37.10N 94.50W
25 N4 **Columbus** Mississippi, S USA 33.30N 88.25W
35 U11 **Columbus** Montana, NW USA 45.38N 109.15W
31 Q15 **Columbus** Nebraska, C USA 41.25N 97.22W
39 Q16 **Columbus** New Mexico, SW USA 31.49N 107.38W
23 P10 **Columbus** North Carolina, SE USA 35.15N 82.09W
30 K2 **Columbus** North Dakota, N USA 48.52N 102.47W
33 S13 **Columbus** state capital Ohio, N USA 39.57N 83.00W
27 U11 **Columbus** Texas, SW USA 29.42N 96.32W
32 L8 **Columbus** Wisconsin, N USA 43.21N 89.00W
33 R12 **Columbus Grove** Ohio, N USA 40.55N 84.03W
31 Y15 **Columbus Junction** Iowa, C USA 41.16N 91.21W
46 J3 **Columbus Point** headland Cat Island, C Bahamas 24.07N 75.19W
37 T8 **Columbus Salt Marsh** salt marsh Nevada, W USA
37 N6 **Colusa** California, W USA 39.10N 122.03W
34 L7 **Colville** Washington, NW USA 48.33N 117.54W
192 M5 **Colville, Cape** headland North Island, NZ 36.28S 175.20E
192 M5 **Colville Channel** channel North Island, NZ
41 P6 **Colville River** ≈ Alaska, USA
99 J18 **Colwyn Bay** N Wales, UK 53.18N 3.43W
108 H9 **Comacchio** var. Commachio; anc. Comactium. Emilia-Romagna, N Italy 44.40N 12.10E
108 H9 **Comacchio, Valli di** lagoon Adriatic Sea, N Mediterranean Sea
Comactium see Comacchio
43 V17 **Comalapa** Chiapas, SE Mexico 15.42N 92.06W
43 U15 **Comalcalco** Tabasco, SE Mexico 18.16N 93.05W
65 H16 **Comallo** Río Negro, SW Argentina 40.58S 70.13W
28 M12 **Comanche** Oklahoma, C USA 34.22N 97.57W
27 R8 **Comanche** Texas, SW USA 31.54N 98.36W
204 H2 **Comandante Ferraz** Brazilian research station Antarctica 61.57S 58.23W
64 N6 **Comandante Fontana** Formosa, N Argentina 25.19S 59.42W
65 I22 **Comandante Luis Peidra Buena** Santa Cruz, S Argentina 50.04S 68.55W
61 O18 **Comandatuba** Bahia, SE Brazil 15.13S 39.00W
118 K11 **Comănești** Hung. Kománfalva. Bacău, SW Romania 46.24N 26.27E
59 M19 **Comarapa** Santa Cruz, C Bolivia 17.52S 64.34W
118 J13 **Comarnic** Prahova, SE Romania 45.13N 25.36E
44 H6 **Comayagua** Comayagua, W Honduras 14.33N 87.37W
44 H6 **Comayagua** ◈ department W Honduras
44 I6 **Comayagua, Montañas de** ▲▲ C Honduras
23 R15 **Combahee River** ≈ South Carolina, SE USA
64 G10 **Combarbalá** Coquimbo, C Chile 31.15S 71.03W
105 S7 **Combeaufontaine** Haute-Saône, E France 47.43N 5.52E
99 G15 **Comber** Ir. An Comar. E Northern Ireland, UK 54.33N 5.45W
101 K20 **Comblain-au-Pont** Liège, E Belgium 50.29N 5.36E
104 I6 **Combourg** Ille-et-Vilaine, NW France 48.21N 1.44W
46 M9 **Comendador** prev. Elías Piña. W Dominican Republic 18.51N 71.40W
Comer See see Como, Lago di
27 R11 **Comfort** Texas, SW USA 29.58N 98.54W
159 V15 **Comilla** Ben. Kumillā. Chittagong, E Bangladesh 23.28N 91.10E
101 B18 **Comines** Hainaut, W Belgium 50.46N 2.58E
123 J16 **Comino** Malt. Kemmuna. island C Malta
109 D18 **Comino, Capo** headland Sardegna, Italy, C Mediterranean Sea 40.32N 9.49E
109 K25 **Comiso** Sicilia, Italy, C Mediterranean Sea 36.57N 14.37E
43 V16 **Comitán** var. Comitán de Domínguez. Chiapas, SE Mexico 16.14N 92.06W
Comitán de Domínguez see Comitán
Commachio see Comacchio
Commander Islands see Komandorskiye Ostrova
105 O10 **Commentry** Allier, C France 46.18N 2.46E
25 T2 **Commerce** Georgia, SE USA 34.12N 83.27W
29 R8 **Commerce** Oklahoma, C USA 36.55N 94.52W
27 V5 **Commerce** Texas, SW USA 33.16N 95.52W
39 T4 **Commerce City** Colorado, C USA 39.45N 104.54W
105 S5 **Commercy** Meuse, NE France 48.46N 5.36E
57 W9 **Commewijne** var. Commewyne. ◈ district NE Surinam
Commewyne see Commewijne
13 P8 **Commissaires, Lac des** ◎ Quebec, SE Canada
66 A12 **Commissioner's Point** headland W Bermuda
15 I3 **Committee Bay** bay Nunavut, N Canada
108 D7 **Como** anc. Comum. Lombardia, N Italy 45.48N 9.04E
65 J19 **Comodoro Rivadavia** Chubut, SE Argentina 45.49S 67.30W
108 D6 **Como, Lago di** var. Lario, Eng. Lake Como, Ger. Comer See. ◎ N Italy
Como, Lake see Como, Lago di
42 E7 **Comondú** Baja California Sur, W Mexico 26.01N 111.50W
118 F12 **Comorâşte** Hung. Komornok. Caraş-Severin, SW Romania 45.13N 21.34E
Comores, République Fédérale Islamique des see Comoros
161 G24 **Comorin, Cape** headland SE India 8.00N 77.10E
180 M8 **Comoro Basin** undersea feature SW Indian Ocean
180 K14 **Comoro Islands** island group W Indian Ocean
180 H13 **Comoros** off. Federal Islamic Republic of the Comoros, Fr. République Fédérale Islamique des Comores. ◆ republic W Indian Ocean
8 L17 **Comox** Vancouver Island, British Columbia, SW Canada 49.40N 124.55W
105 O4 **Compiègne** Oise, N France 49.25N 2.49E
Complutum see Alcalá de Henares
Compniacum see Cognac
42 K12 **Compostela** Nayarit, C Mexico 21.14N 104.52W
Compostella see Santiago
62 L11 **Comprida, Ilha** island S Brazil
119 N11 **Comrat** Rus. Komrat. S Moldova 46.18N 28.40E
27 O11 **Comstock** Texas, SW USA 29.39N 101.10W
33 P9 **Comstock Park** Michigan, N USA 43.00N 85.40W
199 Kk3 **Comstock Seamount** undersea feature N Pacific Ocean 48.15N 156.55W
Comum see Como
165 N17 **Cona** Xizang Zizhiqu, W China 27.58N 91.54E
78 H14 **Conakry** ● (Guinea) Conakry, SW Guinea 9.31N 13.43W
78 H14 **Conakry** ✈ Conakry, SW Guinea 9.37N 13.32W
Conamara see Connemara
Conca see Cuenca
27 Q12 **Concan** Texas, SW USA 29.27N 99.43W
104 F6 **Concarneau** Finistère, NW France 47.52N 3.55W
85 O17 **Conceição** Sofala, C Mozambique 18.47S 36.18E
61 K15 **Conceição do Araguaia** Pará, NE Brazil 8.15S 49.15W
60 F10 **Conceição do Maú** Roraima, W Brazil 3.34N 59.52W
63 D14 **Concepción** var. Concepcion. Corrientes, NE Argentina 28.25S 57.54W
64 J8 **Concepción** Tucumán, N Argentina 27.19S 65.34W
59 O17 **Concepción** Santa Cruz, E Bolivia 16.15S 62.07W
64 G13 **Concepción** Bío Bío, C Chile 36.47S 73.01W
56 E14 **Concepción** Putumayo, S Colombia 0.03N 75.39W
64 O5 **Concepción** var. Villa Concepción. Concepción, C Paraguay 23.26S 57.23W
64 O5 **Concepción** off. Departamento de Concepción. ◈ department E Paraguay
Concepción see La Concepción
Concepción de la Vega see La Vega
43 N9 **Concepción del Oro** Zacatecas, C Mexico 24.37N 101.25W
63 D18 **Concepción del Uruguay** Entre Ríos, E Argentina 32.30S 58.15W
44 K11 **Concepción, Volcán** Ѫ SW Nicaragua 11.31N 85.37W
46 J4 **Conception Island** island C Bahamas
37 P14 **Conception, Point** headland California, W USA 34.27N 120.28W
56 H6 **Concha** Zulia, W Venezuela 9.01N 71.45W
62 L9 **Conchas** São Paulo, S Brazil 23.00S 47.58W
39 U11 **Conchas Dam** New Mexico, SW USA 35.21N 104.11W
39 U10 **Conchas Lake** ☒ New Mexico, SW USA
104 M5 **Conches-en-Ouche** Eure, N France 49.00N 1.00E
39 N12 **Concho** Arizona, SW USA 34.28N 109.33W
42 J5 **Conchos, Río** ≈ NW Mexico
43 O8 **Conchos, Río** ≈ C Mexico
110 C8 **Concise** Vaud, W Switzerland 46.52N 6.40E
37 N8 **Concord** California, W USA 37.58N 122.01W
21 O9 **Concord** state capital New Hampshire, NE USA 43.10N 71.31W
23 R10 **Concord** North Carolina, SE USA 35.30N 80.34W
63 D17 **Concordia** Entre Ríos, E Argentina 31.25S 58.00W
56 D9 **Concordia** Antioquia, W Colombia 6.03N 75.57W
42 J10 **Concordia** Sinaloa, C Mexico 23.18N 106.03W
59 I19 **Concordia** Tacna, SW Peru 18.12S 70.19W
29 N3 **Concordia** Kansas, C USA 39.34N 97.39W
29 S4 **Concordia** Missouri, C USA 38.58N 93.34W
62 I13 **Concórdia** Santa Catarina, S Brazil 27.13S 52.01W
178 J7 **Con Cuông** Nghê An, N Vietnam 19.02N 104.54E
178 Jj16 **Côn Đao** var. Con Son. island S Vietnam
Condate see St-Claude, Jura, France
Condate see Rennes, Ille-et-Vilaine, France
Condate see Montereau-Faut-Yonne, Seine-St-Denis, France
31 P8 **Conde** South Dakota, N USA 45.08N 98.07W
44 J8 **Condega** Estelí, NW Nicaragua 13.21N 86.23W
105 P2 **Condé-sur-l'Escaut** Nord, N France 50.27N 3.36E
104 K5 **Condé-sur-Noireau** Calvados, N France 48.52N 0.31W
Condivincum see Nantes
191 P8 **Condobolin** New South Wales, SE Australia 33.04S 147.08E
104 L15 **Condom** Gers, S France 43.56N 0.23E
34 J11 **Condon** Oregon, NW USA 45.13N 120.11W
56 D9 **Condoto** Chocó, W Colombia 5.06N 76.37W
25 P7 **Conecuh River** ≈ Alabama/Florida, SE USA
108 H7 **Conegliano** Veneto, NE Italy 45.52N 12.18E
63 C19 **Conesa** Buenos Aires, E Argentina 33.36S 60.21W
12 F15 **Conestogo** ≈ Ontario, S Canada
195 O17 **Conflict Group** island group SE PNG
Confluentes see Koblenz
104 L10 **Confolens** Charente, W France 46.00N 0.40E
38 J4 **Confusion Range** ▲▲ Utah, W USA
64 N6 **Confuso, Río** ≈ C Paraguay
23 R12 **Congaree River** ≈ South Carolina, SE USA
Công Hoa Xa Hôi Chu Nghia Viêt Nam see Vietnam
166 K12 **Congjiang** prev. Bingmei. Guizhou, S China 25.48N 108.55E
81 K19 **Congo** off. Democratic Republic of Congo; prev. Zaire, Belgian Congo, Congo (Kinshasa). ◆ republic C Africa
81 G18 **Congo** off. Republic of the Congo, Fr. Moyen-Congo; prev. Middle Congo. ◆ republic C Africa
69 T11 **Congo** var. Kongo, Fr. Zaire. ≈ C Africa
Congo see Zaire (province, Angola)
Congo/Congo (Kinshasa) see Congo (Democratic Republic of)
70 G12 **Congo Basin** drainage basin W Dem. Rep. Congo (Zaire)
69 Q11 **Congo Canyon** var. Congo Seavalley, Congo Submarine Canyon. undersea feature E Atlantic Ocean
Congo Cone see Congo Fan
67 P15 **Congo Fan** var. Congo Cone. undersea feature E Atlantic Ocean
Coni see Cuneo
65 H18 **Cónico, Cerro** ▲ SW Argentina 43.12S 71.42W
Conimbria/Conimbriga see Coimbra
Conjeeveram see Kānchipuram
9 R13 **Conklin** Alberta, C Canada 55.36N 111.06W
26 M1 **Conlen** Texas, SW USA 36.16N 102.10W
Con, Loch see Conn, Lough
Connacht see Connaught
99 B17 **Connaught** var. Connacht, Ir. Chonnacht, Cúige. cultural region W Ireland
33 V10 **Conneaut** Ohio, N USA 41.56N 80.32W
20 L13 **Connecticut** off. State of Connecticut; also known as Blue Law State, Constitution State, Land of Steady Habits, Nutmeg State. ◈ state NE USA
21 N8 **Connecticut** ≈ Canada/USA
21 O6 **Connecticut Lakes** lakes New Hampshire, NE USA
34 K9 **Connell** Washington, NW USA 46.39N 118.51W
99 B17 **Connemara** Ir. Conamara. region W Ireland
33 Q14 **Connersville** Indiana, N USA 39.38N 85.15W
99 B16 **Conn, Lough** Ir. Loch Con. ◎ W Ireland
37 X6 **Connors Pass** pass Nevada, W USA 39.01N 114.37W
189 X7 **Connors Range** ▲▲ Queensland, E Australia
58 E7 **Cononaco, Río** ≈ E Ecuador
31 W13 **Conrad** Iowa, C USA 42.13N 92.52W
35 R7 **Conrad** Montana, NW USA 48.10N 111.58W
27 W10 **Conroe** Texas, SW USA 30.18N 95.27W
27 V10 **Conroe, Lake** ☒ Texas, SW USA
63 C17 **Conscripto Bernardi** Entre Ríos, E Argentina 31.03S 59.04W
61 M20 **Conselheiro Lafaiete** Minas Gerais, SE Brazil 20.40S 43.48W
Consentia see Cosenza
99 L14 **Consett** N England, UK 54.49N 1.52W
46 B5 **Consolación del Sur** Pinar del Río, W Cuba 22.29N 83.31W
Con Son see Côn Đao
9 R15 **Consort** Alberta, SW Canada 51.58N 110.44W
Constance see Konstanz
110 I6 **Constance, Lake** Ger. Bodensee. ◎ C Europe
106 G9 **Constância** Santarém, C Portugal 39.28N 8.22W
119 N14 **Constanța** var. Küstendje, Eng. Constanza, Ger. Konstanza, Turk. Küstence. Constanța, SE Romania 44.09N 28.36E
118 L14 **Constanța** ◈ county SE Romania
Constantia see Coutances, France
Constantia see Konstanz, Germany
106 K13 **Constantina** Andalucía, S Spain 37.54N 5.36W
76 L5 **Constantine** var. Qacentina, Ar. Qoussantina. NE Algeria 36.22N 6.43E
41 O14 **Constantine, Cape** headland Alaska, USA 58.23N 158.53W
Constantinople see İstanbul
Constantiola see Oltenișa
Constanz see Konstanz
Constanza see Constanța
64 G13 **Constitución** Maule, C Chile 35.25S 72.19W
63 D17 **Constitución** Salto, N Uruguay 31.04S 57.51W
Constitution State see Connecticut
107 N10 **Consuegra** Castilla-La Mancha, C Spain 39.28N 3.36W
189 X9 **Consuelo Peak** ▲ Queensland, E Australia 24.45S 148.01E
58 E11 **Contamana** Loreto, N Peru 7.19S 75.04W
Contrasto, Colle del see Contrasto, Portella del
109 K23 **Contrasto, Portella del** var. Colle del Contrasto. pass Sicilia, Italy, C Mediterranean Sea 37.51N 14.22E
56 G8 **Contratación** Santander, C Colombia 6.18N 73.27W
104 M8 **Contres** Loir-et-Cher, C France 47.24N 1.30E
109 O17 **Conversano** Puglia, SE Italy 40.58N 17.07E
29 U11 **Conway** Arkansas, C USA 35.05N 92.26W
21 O8 **Conway** New Hampshire, NE USA 43.58N 71.05W
23 U13 **Conway** South Carolina, SE USA 33.50N 79.03W
27 N2 **Conway** Texas, SW USA 35.10N 101.23W
29 U11 **Conway, Lake** ☒ Arkansas, C USA
29 N7 **Conway Springs** Kansas, C USA 37.23N 97.38W
99 J18 **Conwy** N Wales, UK 53.16N 3.51W
25 T3 **Conyers** Georgia, SE USA 33.40N 84.01W
Coo see Kos
190 F4 **Coober Pedy** South Australia 29.01S 134.46E
189 P2 **Cooinda** Northern Territory, N Australia 12.54S 132.31E
190 B6 **Cook** South Australia 30.37S 130.26E
31 W4 **Cook** Minnesota, N USA 47.51N 92.41W
203 N6 **Cook, Baie de** bay Moorea, W French Polynesia
8 J16 **Cook, Cape** headland Vancouver Island, British Columbia, SW Canada 50.04N 127.52W
39 Q15 **Cookes Peak** ▲ New Mexico, SW USA 32.32N 107.43W
22 L8 **Cookeville** Tennessee, S USA 36.09N 85.30W
183 P9 **Cook Fracture Zone** tectonic feature S Pacific Ocean
Cook, Grand Récif de see Cook, Récif de
41 Q12 **Cook Inlet** inlet Alaska, USA
203 X2 **Cook Island** island Line Islands, E Kiribati
202 J14 **Cook Islands** ◇ territory in free association with NZ S Pacific Ocean
193 E19 **Cook, Mount** prev. Aoraki, Aorangi. ▲ South Island, NZ 43.38S 170.05E
197 G4 **Cook, Récif de** var. Grand Récif de Cook. reef S New Caledonia
12 G14 **Cookstown** Ontario, S Canada 44.12N 79.39W
99 F15 **Cookstown** Ir. An Chorr Chríochach. C Northern Ireland, UK 54.39N 6.45W
193 K14 **Cook Strait** var. Raukawa. strait NZ
189 W3 **Cooktown** Queensland, NE Australia 15.28S 145.15E
191 P6 **Coolabah** New South Wales, SE Australia 31.03S 146.42E
190 J11 **Coola Coola Swamp** wetland South Australia
191 S7 **Coolah** New South Wales, SE Australia 31.49S 149.43E
191 P9 **Coolamon** New South Wales, SE Australia 34.49S 147.13E
191 T4 **Coolatai** New South Wales, SE Australia 29.16S 150.45E
188 K12 **Coolgardie** Western Australia 31.00S 121.12E
38 L14 **Coolidge** Arizona, SW USA 32.58N 111.29W
27 U8 **Coolidge** Texas, SW USA 31.45N 96.39W
191 Q11 **Cooma** New South Wales, SE Australia 36.16S 149.09E
Coomassie see Kumasi
191 R6 **Coonabarabran** New South Wales, SE Australia 31.19S 149.18E
190 J10 **Coonalpyn** South Australia 35.43S 139.50E
191 R6 **Coonamble** New South Wales, SE Australia 30.56S 148.22E
Coondapoor see Kundāpura
161 G21 **Coonoor** Tamil Nādu, SE India 11.21N 76.46E
31 U14 **Coon Rapids** Iowa, C USA 41.52N 94.40W
31 V8 **Coon Rapids** Minnesota, N USA 45.12N 93.18W
27 V5 **Cooper** Texas, SW USA 33.23N 95.41W
189 U9 **Cooper Creek** var. Barcoo, Cooper's Creek. seasonal river Queensland/South Australia
41 R12 **Cooper Landing** Alaska, USA 60.27N 149.59W
23 T14 **Cooper River** ≈ South Carolina, SE USA
Cooper's Creek see Cooper Creek
46 H1 **Coopers Town** Great Abaco, N Bahamas 26.46N 77.27W
20 J10 **Cooperstown** New York, NE USA 42.43N 74.55W
31 P4 **Cooperstown** North Dakota, N USA 47.26N 98.07W
33 P9 **Coopersville** Michigan, N USA 43.03N 85.55W
190 D7 **Coorabie** South Australia 31.57S 132.18E
25 Q3 **Coosa River** ≈ Alabama/Georgia, S USA
34 E14 **Coos Bay** Oregon, NW USA 43.22N 124.13W
191 Q9 **Cootamundra** New South Wales, SE Australia 34.40S 148.03E
99 E16 **Cootehill** Ir. Muinchille. N Ireland 54.04N 7.04W
Çop see Chop
59 J17 **Copacabana** La Paz, W Bolivia 16.11S 69.02W
65 H14 **Copahué, Volcán** ▲ C Chile 37.56S 71.04W
43 U16 **Copainalá** Chiapas, SE Mexico 17.04N 93.13W
34 F8 **Copalis Beach** Washington, NW USA 47.05N 124.11W
44 F6 **Copán** ◈ department W Honduras
Copán see Copán Ruinas
27 T14 **Copano Bay** bay NW Gulf of Mexico
44 F6 **Copán Ruinas** var. Copán. Copán, W Honduras 14.51N 89.07W
Copenhagen see København
109 Q19 **Copertino** Puglia, SE Italy 40.16N 18.03E
64 H7 **Copiapó** Atacama, N Chile 27.17S 70.25W
64 G8 **Copiapó, Bahía** bay N Chile
64 G7 **Copiapó, Río** ≈ N Chile
116 M12 **Çöpköy** Edirne, NW Turkey 41.14N 26.51E
190 I5 **Copley** South Australia 30.36S 138.26E
108 H9 **Copparo** Emilia-Romagna, C Italy 44.53N 11.53E
57 V10 **Coppename Rivier** var. Koppename. ≈ C Surinam
27 S9 **Copperas Cove** Texas, SW USA 31.07N 97.54W
84 J13 **Copperbelt** ◈ province C Zambia
41 S11 **Copper Center** Alaska, USA 61.57N 145.21W
Coppermine see Kugluktuk
15 I5 **Coppermine** ≈ Northwest Territories/Nunavut, N Canada
41 T11 **Copper River** ≈ Alaska, USA
Copper State see Arizona
118 I11 **Copşa Mică** Ger. Kleinkopisch, Hung. Kiskapus. Sibiu, C Romania 46.48N 24.08E
164 J14 **Coqên** Xizang Zizhiqu, W China 31.13N 85.12E
Coquilhatville see Mbandaka
34 E14 **Coquille** Oregon, NW USA 43.10N 124.11W
64 G9 **Coquimbo** Coquimbo, N Chile 29.59S 71.18W
64 G9 **Coquimbo** off. Región de Coquimbo. ◈ region C Chile
118 I15 **Corabia** Olt, S Romania 43.46N 24.31E
59 F17 **Coracora** Ayacucho, SW Peru 15.07S 73.45W
Cora Droma Rúisc see Carrick-on-Shannon
46 K9 **Corail** SW Haiti 18.32N 73.54W
191 V4 **Coraki** New South Wales, SE Australia 29.01S 153.15E
188 G8 **Coral Bay** Western Australia 23.02S 113.51E
25 Y16 **Coral Gables** Florida, SE USA 25.43N 80.16W
15 M5 **Coral Harbour** Southampton Island, Northwest Territories, NE Canada 64.10N 83.15W
199 I10 **Coral Sea** sea SW Pacific Ocean
182 M7 **Coral Sea Basin** undersea feature N Coral Sea
199 Hh10 **Coral Sea Islands** ◇ Australian external territory SW Pacific Ocean
190 M12 **Corangamite, Lake** ◎ Victoria, SE Australia
Corantijn Rivier see Courantyne River
20 B14 **Coraopolis** Pennsylvania, NE USA 40.28N 80.08W
109 N17 **Corato** Puglia, SE Italy 41.09N 16.25E
105 O17 **Corbières** ▲▲ S France
105 P8 **Corbigny** Nièvre, C France 47.15N 3.42E
23 N7 **Corbin** Kentucky, S USA 36.57N 84.06W
106 L14 **Corbones** ≈ SW Spain
Corcaigh see Cork
37 R11 **Corcoran** California, W USA 36.06N 119.33W
49 T14 **Corcovado, Golfo** gulf S Chile
65 G18 **Corcovado, Volcán** ▲ S Chile 43.13S 72.45W
106 F3 **Corcubión** Galicia, NW Spain 42.55N 9.12W
Corcyra Nigra see Korčula
62 Q9 **Cordeiro** Rio de Janeiro, SE Brazil 22.01S 42.20W
25 T6 **Cordele** Georgia, SE USA 31.58N 83.49W
28 L11 **Cordell** Oklahoma, C USA 35.18N 98.58W
105 N14 **Cordes** Tarn, S France 44.03N 1.57E
64 O6 **Cordillera** off. Departamento de la Cordillera. ◈ department C Paraguay
190 K1 **Cordillo Downs** South Australia 26.44S 140.37E
64 K10 **Córdoba** Córdoba, C Argentina 31.25S 64.10W
43 R14 **Córdoba** Veracruz-Llave, E Mexico 18.52N 96.48W
106 M13 **Córdoba** var. Cordoba, Eng. Cordova; anc. Corduba. Andalucía, SW Spain 37.52N 4.46W
64 K11 **Córdoba** off. Provincia de Córdoba. ◈ province C Argentina
56 D7 **Córdoba** off. Departamento de Córdoba. ◈ province NW Colombia
106 L13 **Córdoba** ◈ province Andalucía, S Spain
64 K10 **Córdoba, Sierras de** ▲▲ C Argentina
25 O3 **Cordova** Alabama, S USA 33.45N 87.10W
41 S12 **Cordova** Alaska, USA 60.32N 145.45W
Cordova/Corduba see Córdoba
Corentyne River see Courantyne River
Corfu see Kérkyra
106 J9 **Coria** Extremadura, W Spain 39.58N 6.31W
106 J14 **Coria del Río** Andalucía, S Spain 37.18N 6.04W
191 S8 **Coricudgy, Mount** ▲ New South Wales, SE Australia 32.49S 150.28E
109 N20 **Corigliano Calabro** Calabria, SW Italy 39.35N 16.30E
Corinium/Corinium Dobunorum see Cirencester
25 N1 **Corinth** Mississippi, S USA 34.56N 88.29W
Corinth see Kórinthos
Corinth Canal see Dióryga Korinthou
Corinth, Gulf of/Corinthiacus Sinus see Korinthiakós Kólpos
Corinthus see Kórinthos
44 I9 **Corinto** Chinandega, NW Nicaragua 12.28N 87.10W
99 C21 **Cork** Ir. Corcaigh. S Ireland 51.54N 7.06W
99 C21 **Cork** Ir. Corcaigh. cultural region SW Ireland
99 C21 **Cork** ✈ SW Ireland 51.52N 8.25W
99 D21 **Cork Harbour** Ir. Cuan Chorcaí. inlet SW Ireland
109 I23 **Corleone** Sicilia, Italy, C Mediterranean Sea 37.49N 13.18E
116 N13 **Çorlu** Tekirdağ, NW Turkey 41.10N 27.48E
116 N12 **Çorlu Çayı** ≈ NW Turkey
Cormaiore see Courmayeur
9 V13 **Cormorant** Manitoba, C Canada 54.12N 100.33W
25 T2 **Cornelia** Georgia, SE USA 34.30N 83.31W
62 J10 **Cornélio Procópio** Paraná, S Brazil 23.07S 50.40W
57 V9 **Corneliskondre** Sipaliwini, N Surinam 5.21N 56.10W
32 J5 **Cornell** Wisconsin, N USA 45.09N 91.10W
11 S12 **Corner Brook** Newfoundland, E Canada 48.58N 57.58W
Corner Rise Seamounts see Corner Seamounts
66 I9 **Corner Seamounts** var. Corner Rise Seamounts. undersea feature NW Atlantic Ocean
118 M9 **Cornești** Rus. Korneshty. C Moldova 47.23N 28.00E
Corneto see Tarquinia
Cornhusker State see Nebraska
29 X8 **Corning** Arkansas, C USA 36.26N 90.35W
37 N5 **Corning** California, W USA 39.54N 122.12W
31 U15 **Corning** Iowa, C USA 40.58N 94.46W
20 G11 **Corning** New York, NE USA 42.08N 77.03W
Corn Islands see Maíz, Islas del
109 J14 **Corno Grande** ▲ C Italy 42.26N 13.29E
13 N13 **Cornwall** Ontario, SE Canada 45.01N 74.45W
99 H25 **Cornwall** cultural region SW England, UK
99 G25 **Cornwall, Cape** headland SW England, UK 50.11N 5.39W
56 J4 **Coro** prev. Santa Ana de Coro. Falcón, NW Venezuela 11.27N 69.40W
59 J18 **Corocoro** La Paz, W Bolivia 17.10S 68.28W
59 K17 **Coroico** La Paz, W Bolivia 16.09S 67.41W
192 M5 **Coromandel** Waikato, North Island, NZ 36.47S 175.30E
161 K20 **Coromandel Coast** coast E India
192 M5 **Coromandel Peninsula** peninsula North Island, NZ
192 M6 **Coromandel Range** ▲▲ North Island, NZ
179 P12 **Coron** Busuanga Island, W Philippines 12.02N 120.10E
37 T15 **Corona** California, W USA 33.52N 117.34W
39 T12 **Corona** New Mexico, SW USA 34.15N 105.36W
9 U17 **Coronach** Saskatchewan, S Canada 49.07N 105.33W
37 U17 **Coronado** California, W USA 32.41N 117.10W
45 N15 **Coronado, Bahía de** bay S Costa Rica
9 R15 **Coronation** Alberta, SW Canada 52.06N 111.25W
15 I4 **Coronation Gulf** gulf Nunavut, N Canada
204 I1 **Coronation Island** island Antarctica
41 X14 **Coronation Island** island Alexander Archipelago, Alaska, USA
63 B18 **Coronda** Santa Fe, C Argentina 31.58S 60.55W
65 F14 **Coronel** Bío Bío, C Chile 37.01S 73.07W
63 D20 **Coronel Brandsen** var. Brandsen. Buenos Aires, E Argentina 35.07S 58.15W
64 K4 **Coronel Cornejo** Salta, N Argentina 22.46S 63.49W
63 B24 **Coronel Dorrego** Buenos Aires, E Argentina 38.38S 61.15W
64 P6 **Coronel Oviedo** Caaguazú, SE Paraguay 25.30S 56.27W
63 B23 **Coronel Pringles** Buenos Aires, E Argentina 37.58S 61.26W
63 B23 **Coronel Suárez** Buenos Aires, E Argentina 37.27S 61.57W
63 E22 **Coronel Vidal** Buenos Aires, E Argentina 37.28S 57.45W
57 V9 **Coronie** ◈ district NW Surinam
59 G17 **Coropuna, Nevado** ▲ S Peru 15.31S 72.31W
Çorovoda see Çorovodë
115 L22 **Çorovodë** var. Çorovoda. Berat, S Albania 40.29N 20.15E
191 P11 **Corowa** New South Wales, SE Australia 36.01S 146.22E
44 G1 **Corozal** Corozal, N Belize 18.22N 88.22W
56 E6 **Corozal** Sucre, NW Colombia 9.18N 75.19W
44 G1 **Corozal** ◈ district N Belize
27 T14 **Corpus Christi** Texas, SW USA 27.48N 97.24W
27 T14 **Corpus Christi Bay** inlet Texas, SW USA
27 R14 **Corpus Christi, Lake** ☒ Texas, SW USA
65 F16 **Corral** Los Lagos, C Chile 39.55S 73.30W
107 O9 **Corral de Almaguer** Castilla-La Mancha, C Spain 39.45N 3.10W
106 K6 **Corrales** Castilla-León, N Spain 41.22N 5.43W
39 R11 **Corrales** New Mexico, SW USA 35.11N 106.37W
Corrán Tuathail see Carrauntoohil
108 F9 **Correggio** Emilia-Romagna, C Italy 44.47N 10.46E
179 P11 **Corregidor Island** island NW Philippines
61 M16 **Corrente** Piauí, E Brazil 10.28S 45.10W
61 I19 **Correntes, Rio** ≈ SW Brazil
105 N12 **Corrèze** ◈ department C France
99 C17 **Corrib, Lough** Ir. Loch Coirib. ◎ W Ireland
63 C14 **Corrientes** Corrientes, NE Argentina 27.28S 58.42W
63 D15 **Corrientes** off. Provincia de Corrientes. ◈ province NE Argentina
46 A5 **Corrientes, Cabo** headland W Cuba 21.48N 84.30W
42 I13 **Corrientes, Cabo** headland SW Mexico 20.25N 105.42W
Corrientes, Provincia de see Corrientes
63 C16 **Corrientes, Río** ≈ NE Argentina
58 E8 **Corrientes, Río** ≈ Ecuador/Peru
27 W9 **Corrigan** Texas, SW USA 31.00N 94.49W
57 U9 **Corriverton** E Guyana 5.55N 57.09W
Corriza see Korçë
191 Q11 **Corryong** Victoria, SE Australia 36.14S 147.54E
105 Y12 **Corse** Eng. Corsica. ◈ region France, C Mediterranean Sea
105 X13 **Corse** Eng. Corsica. island France, C Mediterranean Sea
105 Y13 **Corse, Cap** headland Corse, France, C Mediterranean Sea 43.01N 9.25E
105 X15 **Corse-du-Sud** ◈ department Corse, France, C Mediterranean Sea
31 P11 **Corsica** South Dakota, N USA 43.25N 98.24W
Corsica see Corse
27 U7 **Corsicana** Texas, SW USA 32.04N 96.27W
105 Y15 **Corte** Corse, France, C Mediterranean Sea 42.19N 9.09E
65 G16 **Corte Alto** Los Lagos, S Chile 40.58S 73.04W
106 I13 **Cortegana** Andalucía, S Spain 37.55N 6.49W
45 N15 **Cortés** var. Ciudad Cortés. Puntarenas, SE Costa Rica 8.59N 83.32W
44 G5 **Cortés** ◈ department NW Honduras
39 P8 **Cortez** Colorado, C USA 37.22N 108.36W
Cortez, Sea of see California, Golfo de
108 H6 **Cortina d'Ampezzo** Veneto, NE Italy 46.33N 12.09E
20 H11 **Cortland** New York, NE USA 42.34N 76.09W
33 V11 **Cortland** Ohio, N USA 41.19N 80.43W
108 H12 **Cortona** Toscana, C Italy 43.15N 12.01E
78 H13 **Corubal, Rio** ≈ E Guinea-Bissau
106 G10 **Coruche** Santarém, C Portugal 38.58N 8.31W
Çoruh see Rize
143 R11 **Çoruh Nehri** Geor. Chorokhi, Rus. Chorokh. ≈ Georgia/Turkey
142 K12 **Çorum** var. Chorum. Çorum, N Turkey 40.31N 34.57E
142 J12 **Çorum** var. Chorum. ◈ province N Turkey
61 H19 **Corumbá** Mato Grosso do Sul, S Brazil 19.00S 57.35W
12 D16 **Corunna** Ontario, S Canada 42.49N 82.25W
Corunna see A Coruña
34 F12 **Corvallis** Oregon, NW USA 44.34N 122.36W
66 M1 **Corvo** var. Ilha do Corvo. island Azores, Portugal, NE Atlantic Ocean
Corvo, Ilha do see Corvo
33 O16 **Corydon** Indiana, N USA 38.12N 86.07W
31 V16 **Corydon** Iowa, C USA 40.45N 93.19W
Cos see Kos
42 I9 **Cosalá** Sinaloa, C Mexico 24.25N 106.39W
43 R15 **Cosamaloapan** var. Cosamaloapan de Carpio. Veracruz-Llave, E Mexico 18.21N 95.50W
Cosamaloapan de Carpio see Cosamaloapan

◆ Country ● Country Capital ◇ Dependent Territory ○ Dependent Territory Capital ◈ Administrative Region ✈ International Airport ▲ Mountain ▲▲ Mountain Range Ѫ Volcano ≈ River ◎ Lake ☒ Reservoir

Curnamona – Darya Khān

190 J6 **Curnamona** South Australia 31.39S 139.35E
85 A15 **Curoca** ≈ SW Angola
191 T6 **Currabubula** New South Wales, SE Australia 31.17S 150.43E
61 Q14 **Currais Novos** Rio Grande do Norte, E Brazil 6.12S 36.30W
37 W7 **Currant** Nevada, W USA 38.43N 115.27W
37 W6 **Currant Mountain** ▲ Nevada, W USA 38.56N 115.19W
46 H2 **Current** Eleuthera Island, C Bahamas 25.24N 76.44W
29 W8 **Current River** ≈ Arkansas/Missouri, C USA
190 M14 **Currie** Tasmania, SE Australia 39.59S 143.51E
23 Y8 **Currituck** North Carolina, SE USA 36.27N 76.02W
23 Y8 **Currituck Sound** *sound* North Carolina, SE USA
41 R11 **Curry** Alaska, USA 62.36N 150.00W
Curtbunar *see* Tervel
118 I13 **Curtea de Argeş** *var.* Curtea-de-Arges. Argeş, S Romania 45.06N 24.40E
118 E10 **Curtici** *Ger.* Kurtitsch, *Hung.* Kürtös. Arad, W Romania 46.21N 21.17E
30 M16 **Curtis** Nebraska, C USA 40.36N 100.27W
106 H2 **Curtis-Estación** Galicia, NW Spain 43.09N 8.10W
191 O14 **Curtis Group** *island group* Tasmania, SE Australia
189 Y8 **Curtis Island** *island* Queensland, SE Australia
60 K11 **Curuá, Ilha do** *island* NE Brazil
49 U7 **Curuá, Rio** ≈ N Brazil
61 A14 **Curuçá, Rio** ≈ NW Brazil
114 L9 **Čurug** *Hung.* Csurog. Serbia, N Yugoslavia 45.30N 20.02E
63 D16 **Curuzú Cuatiá** Corrientes, NE Argentina 29.45S 58.01W
61 M19 **Curvelo** Minas Gerais, SE Brazil 18.45S 44.27W
20 E14 **Curwensville** Pennsylvania, NE USA 40.57N 78.29W
32 M3 **Curwood, Mount** ▲ Michigan, N USA 46.42N 88.14W
Curytiba *see* Curitiba
Curzola *see* Korčula
44 A10 **Cuscatlán** ◐ *department* C El Salvador
59 H15 **Cusco** *var.* Cuzco. Cusco, C Peru 13.34S 72.01W
59 H15 **Cusco** *off.* Departamento de Cusco; *var.* Cuzco. ◐ *department* C Peru
29 O9 **Cushing** Oklahoma, C USA 36.01N 96.46W
27 W8 **Cushing** Texas, SW USA 31.48N 94.50W
42 J6 **Cusihuiriachic** Chihuahua, N Mexico 28.16N 106.46W
105 P10 **Cusset** Allier, C France 46.07N 3.27E
25 S6 **Cusseta** Georgia, SE USA 32.18N 84.46W
30 J10 **Custer** South Dakota, N USA 43.46N 103.36W
Cüstrin *see* Kostrzyn
35 Q7 **Cut Bank** Montana, NW USA 48.37N 112.19W
Cutch, Gulf of *see* Kachchh, Gulf of
25 S6 **Cuthbert** Georgia, SE USA 31.46N 84.47W
9 S15 **Cut Knife** Saskatchewan, S Canada 52.40N 108.54W
25 Y16 **Cutler Ridge** Florida, SE USA 25.34N 80.21W
24 K10 **Cut Off** Louisiana, S USA 29.32N 90.20W
65 I15 **Cutral-Có** Neuquén, C Argentina 38.55S 69.13W
109 O21 **Cutro** Calabria, SW Italy 39.01N 16.59E
191 O4 **Cuttaburra Channels** *seasonal river* New South Wales, SE Australia
160 O12 **Cuttack** Orissa, E India 20.28N 85.52E
85 C15 **Cuvelai** Cunene, SW Angola 15.40S 15.48E
81 G18 **Cuvette** *var.* Région de la Cuvette. ◐ *province* C Congo
181 V9 **Cuvier Basin** *undersea feature* E Indian Ocean
181 U9 **Cuvier Plateau** *undersea feature* E Indian Ocean
84 B12 **Cuvo** ≈ W Angola
102 H9 **Cuxhaven** Niedersachsen, NW Germany 53.51N 8.42E
Cuyabá *see* Cuiabá
179 Pp13 **Cuyo East Pass** *passage* C Philippines
179 P13 **Cuyo West Pass** *passage* C Philippines
Cuyuni, Río *see* Cuyuni River
57 S8 **Cuyuni River** *var.* Río Cuyuni. ≈ Guyana/Venezuela
Cuzco *see* Cusco
99 K22 **Cwmbran** *Wel.* Cwmbrân. SW Wales, UK 51.39N 3.00W
30 K15 **C.W.McConaughy, Lake** ⊟ Nebraska, C USA
83 D20 **Cyangugu** SW Rwanda 2.27S 29.00E
112 D11 **Cybinka** *Ger.* Ziebingen. Lubuskie, W Poland 52.11N 14.46E
Cyclades *see* Kykládes
Cydonia *see* Chaniá
Cymru *see* Wales
22 M5 **Cynthiana** Kentucky, S USA 38.23N 84.17W
9 S17 **Cypress Hills** ▲▲ Alberta/Saskatchewan, SW Canada
Cypro-Syrian Basin *see* Cyprus Basin
123 Mm1 **Cyprus** *off.* Republic of Cyprus, *Gk.* Kypros, *Turk.* Kıbrıs, Kıbrıs Cumhuriyeti. ◆ *republic* E Mediterranean Sea
86 L14 **Cyprus** *Gk.* Kypros, *Turk.* Kıbrıs. *island* E Mediterranean Sea
123 Gg10 **Cyprus Basin** *var.* Cypro-Syrian Basin. *undersea feature* E Mediterranean Sea
Cythera *see* Kýthira
Cythnos *see* Kýthnos
112 F9 **Czaplinek** *Ger.* Tempelburg. Zachodniopomorskie, NW Poland 53.33N 16.14E
Czarna Woda *see* Wda
112 G8 **Czarne** Pomorskie, N Poland 53.40N 17.00E
112 G10 **Czarnków** Wielkopolskie, C Poland 52.52N 16.31E
113 E17 **Czech Republic** *Cz.* Česká Republika. ◆ *republic* C Europe
Czegléd *see* Cegléd
112 G12 **Czempiń** Wielkolpolskie, C Poland 52.10N 16.46E
Czenstochau *see* Częstochowa
Czerkow *see* Čerchov
Czernowitz *see* Chernivtsi
112 I8 **Czersk** Pomorskie, N Poland 53.48N 17.58E
113 J15 **Częstochowa** *Ger.* Czenstochau, Tschenstochau, *Rus.* Chenstokhov. Śląskie, S Poland 50.51N 19.09E
112 F10 **Człopa** *Ger.* Schloppe. Zachodniopomorskie, NW Poland 53.04N 16.04E
112 H8 **Człuchów** *Ger.* Schlochau. Pomorskie, NW Poland 53.40N 17.19E

D

169 V9 **Da'an** *var.* Dalai. Jilin, NE China 45.28N 124.18E
13 S10 **Daaquam** Quebec, SE Canada 46.36N 70.03W
Daawo, Webi *see* Dawa Wenz
56 I4 **Dabajuro** Falcón, NW Venezuela 11.00N 70.41W
79 N15 **Dabakala** NE Ivory Coast 8.19N 4.24W
Daban *see* Bairin Youqi
113 K23 **Dabas** Pest, C Hungary 47.13N 19.18E
166 L8 **Daba Shan** ▲▲ C China
146 J5 **Dabbāgh, Jabal** ▲ NW Saudi Arabia 27.52N 35.48E
56 D8 **Dabeiba** Antioquia, NW Colombia 6.57N 76.13W
160 E11 **Dabhoi** Gujarāt, W India 22.07N 73.28E
167 P8 **Dabie Shan** ▲▲ C China
78 J13 **Dabola** Haute-Guinée, C Guinea 10.48N 11.01W
79 N17 **Dabou** S Ivory Coast 5.19N 4.22W
112 P8 **Dąbrowa Białostocka** Podlaskie, NE Poland 53.38N 23.18E
113 M16 **Dąbrowa Tarnowska** Małopolskie, S Poland 50.10N 21.00E
121 M20 **Dabryn'** *Rus.* Dobryn'. Homyel'skaya Voblasts', SE Belarus 51.46N 29.12E
165 P10 **Dabsan Hu** ◎ C China
167 Q13 **Dabu** *prev.* Huliao. Guangdong, S China 24.19N 116.07E
118 H15 **Dăbuleni** Dolj, SW Romania 43.47N 24.05E
Dacca *see* Dhaka
103 L23 **Dachau** Bayern, SE Germany 48.16N 11.25E
166 K8 **Dachuan** *prev.* Daxian, Da Xian. Sichuan, C China 31.16N 107.31E
Dacia Bank *see* Dacia Seamount
66 M10 **Dacia Seamount** *var.* Dacia Bank. *undersea feature* E Atlantic Ocean 31.10N 13.42W
39 T3 **Dacono** Colorado, C USA 40.04N 104.56W
Đắc Tô *see* Đak Tô
Dacura *see* Dákura
25 W12 **Dade City** Florida, SE USA 28.21N 82.12W
158 L10 **Dadeldhura** *var.* Dandeldhura. Far Western, W Nepal 29.12N 80.31E
25 Q5 **Dadeville** Alabama, S USA 32.49N 85.45W
105 N15 **Dadou** ≈ S France
160 D12 **Dādra and Nagar Havelī** ◐ *union territory* W India
155 P14 **Dādu** Sind, SE Pakistan 26.42N 67.48E
178 K11 **Da Du Boloc** Kon Tum, C Vietnam 14.06N 107.40E
166 G9 **Dadu He** ≈ C China
Daegu *see* Taegu
Daerah Istimewa Aceh *see* Aceh
179 Q11 **Daet** Luzon, N Philippines 14.06N 122.57E
166 I11 **Dafang** Guizhou, S China 27.07N 105.40E
159 W11 **Dafla Hills** ▲▲ NE India
9 U15 **Dafoe** Saskatchewan, S Canada 51.46N 104.11W
78 G10 **Dagana** N Senegal 16.28N 15.35W
Dagana *see* Dahana, Tajikistan
Dagana *see* Massakory, Chad
120 K11 **Dagda** Krāslava, SE Latvia 56.06N 27.36E
Dagden *see* Hiiumaa
Dagden-Sund *see* Soela Väin
131 P16 **Dagestan, Respublika** *prev.* Dagestanskaya ASSR, *Eng.* Daghestan. ◐ *autonomous republic* SW Russian Federation
Dagestanskaya ASSR *see* Dagestan, Respublika
131 R17 **Dagestanskiye Ogni** Respublika Dagestan, SW Russian Federation 42.09N 48.08E
193 A23 **Dagg Sound** *sound* South Island, NZ
Daghestan *see* Dagestan, Respublika
147 Y8 **Daghmar** NE Oman 23.09N 59.01E
Dağlıq Qarabağ *see* Nagornyy Karabakh
Dagö *see* Hiiumaa
56 D11 **Dagua** Valle del Cauca, W Colombia 3.37N 76.42W
166 H11 **Daguan** Yunnan, SW China 27.42N 103.51E
179 P9 **Dagupan** *off.* Dagupan City. Luzon, N Philippines 16.04N 120.21E
165 N16 **Dagzê** Xizang Zizhiqu, W China 29.38N 91.15E
153 Q13 **Dahana** *Rus.* Dagana, Dakhana. SW Tajikistan 38.03N 69.51E
169 V10 **Dahei Shan** ▲ N China
169 T7 **Da Hinggan Ling** *Eng.* Great Khingan Range. ▲▲ NE China
Dahlac Archipelago *see* Dahlak Archipelago
82 K9 **Dahlak Archipelago** *var.* Dahlac Archipelago. *island group* E Eritrea
25 T2 **Dahlonega** Georgia, SE USA 34.31N 83.59W
103 O14 **Dahme** Brandenburg, E Germany 52.10N 13.47E
102 O13 **Dahme** ≈ E Germany
147 O14 **Dahm, Ramlat** *desert* NW Yemen
160 E10 **Dāhod** *prev.* Dohad. Gujarāt, W India 22.48N 74.18E
Dahomey *see* Benin
164 G10 **Dahongliutan** Xinjiang Uygur Zizhiqu, NW China 35.59N 79.12E
Dahra *see* Dara
145 R2 **Dahūk** *var.* Dohuk, *Kurd.* Dihōk. N Iraq 36.52N 43.01E
118 J15 **Daia** Giurgiu, S Romania 44.00N 25.59E
171 L15 **Daigo** Ibaraki, Honshū, S Japan 36.43N 140.22E
169 O13 **Dai Hai** ◎ N China
Daihoku *see* T'aipei
195 X14 **Dai Island** *island* N Solomon Islands
177 G8 **Daik-u** Pegu, SW Burma 17.46N 96.40E
144 H9 **Dā'īl** Dar'ā, S Syria 32.45N 36.07E
178 Kk12 **Dai Lanh** Khanh Hoa, S Vietnam 12.49N 109.20E
167 Q13 **Daimao Shan** ▲▲ SE China
107 N11 **Daimiel** Castilla-La Mancha, C Spain 39.04N 3.37W
117 F22 **Daimoniá** Pelopónnisos, S Greece 36.38N 22.54E
Dainan *see* T'ainan
27 W6 **Daingerfield** Texas, SW USA 33.01N 94.43W
Daingin, Bá an *see* Dingle Bay
165 R13 **Dainkognubma** Xizang Zizhiqu, W China 32.25N 97.58E
171 Hh17 **Daiō-zaki** *headland* Honshū, SW Japan 34.15N 136.50E
Dairbhre *see* Valencia Island
63 B22 **Daireaux** Buenos Aires, E Argentina 36.36S 61.42W
Dairen *see* Dalian
77 W9 **Dairūṭ** *var.* Dairûṭ. C Egypt 27.31N 30.46E
170 Ff12 **Dai-sen** ▲ Kyūshū, SW Japan 35.22N 133.33E
27 X10 **Daisetta** Texas, SW USA 30.06N 94.38W
199 Gg5 **Daitō-jima** *island group* SW Japan
199 Gg5 **Daitō Ridge** *undersea feature* N Philippine Sea
167 N3 **Daixian** *var.* Dai Xian. Shanxi, C China 39.07N 112.54E
167 Q12 **Daiyun Shan** ▲▲ SE China
46 M8 **Dajabón** NW Dominican Republic 19.29N 71.40W
166 G8 **Dajin Chuan** ≈ C China
154 J6 **Dak** ◎ W Afghanistan
78 F11 **Dakar** ● (Senegal) W Senegal 14.43N 17.27W
78 F11 **Dakar** ✕ W Senegal 14.42N 17.27W
178 K11 **Đak Glây** Kon Tum, C Vietnam 15.05N 107.42E
Dakhana *see* Dahana
159 U16 **Dakhin Shahbazpur Island** *island* S Bangladesh
Dakhla *see* Ad Dakhla
78 F7 **Dakhlet Nouâdhibou** ◐ *region* NW Mauritania
Đak Lap *see* Kiên Đưc
178 K13 **Đak Nông** Đăc Lăc, S Vietnam 11.58N 107.42E
79 U11 **Dakoro** Maradi, S Niger 14.28N 6.45E
31 U12 **Dakota City** Iowa, C USA 42.42N 94.13W
31 R13 **Dakota City** Nebraska, C USA 42.25N 96.25W
115 M17 **Đakovica** *var.* Djakovica, *Alb.* Gjakovë. Serbia, S Yugoslavia 42.22N 20.30E
114 I10 **Đakovo** *var.* Djakovo, *Hung.* Diakovár. Osijek-Baranja, E Croatia 45.18N 18.24E
Dakshin *see* Deccan
178 K11 **Đak Tô** *var.* Đăc Tô. Kon Tum, C Vietnam 14.35N 107.55E
45 N7 **Dákura** *var.* Dacura. Región Autónoma Atlántico Norte, NE Nicaragua 14.22N 83.13W
97 I14 **Dal** Akershus, S Norway 60.19N 11.16E
84 E12 **Dala** Lunda Sul, E Angola 11.03S 20.12E
110 J8 **Dalaas** Vorarlberg, W Austria 47.08N 10.03E
78 I13 **Dalaba** Moyenne-Guinée, W Guinea 10.46N 12.12W
Dalai *see* Da'an
Dalain Hob *see* Ejin Qi
Dalai Nor *see* Hulun Nur
169 Q11 **Dalai Nur** *salt lake* N China
Dala-Jarna *see* Järna
97 M14 **Dalälven** ≈ C Sweden
142 C16 **Dalaman** Muğla, SW Turkey 36.46N 28.46E
142 C16 **Dalaman** ✕ Muğla, SW Turkey 36.37N 28.51E
142 D16 **Dalaman Çayı** ≈ SW Turkey
168 K11 **Dalandzadgad** Ömnögovĭ, S Mongolia 43.35N 104.23E
97 D17 **Dalane** *physical region* S Norway
201 Z2 **Dalap-Uliga-Djarrit** *var.* Delap-Uliga-Darrit, D-U-D. *island group* Ratak Chain, SE Marshall Islands
96 J12 **Dalarna** *prev.* Kopparberg ◐ *county* C Sweden
96 L13 **Dalarna** *prev. Eng.* Dalecarlia. *cultural region* C Sweden
97 P16 **Dalarö** Stockholm, C Sweden 59.07N 18.25E
178 Kk13 **Đa Lat** Lâm Đông, S Vietnam 11.55N 108.25E
168 J11 **Dalay** Ömnögovĭ, S Mongolia 43.27N 103.30E
154 L12 **Dālbandīn** *var.* Dāl Bandin. Baluchistān, SW Pakistan 28.48N 64.08E
97 J17 **Dalbosjön** *lake bay* S Sweden
189 Y10 **Dalby** Queensland, E Australia 27.14S 151.16E
96 D13 **Dale** Hordaland, S Norway 60.34N 5.48E
96 C12 **Dale** Sogn og Fjordane, S Norway 61.22N 5.24E
34 K12 **Dale** Oregon, NW USA 44.58N 118.56W
27 T11 **Dale** Texas, SW USA 29.56N 97.34W
Dalecarlia *see* Dalarna
23 W4 **Dale City** Virginia, NE USA 38.38N 77.18W
22 L8 **Dale Hollow Lake** ⊟ Kentucky/Tennessee, S USA
100 O8 **Dalen** Drenthe, NE Netherlands 52.42N 6.45E
97 E15 **Dalen** Telemark, S Norway 59.25N 7.58E
177 F4 **Daletme** Chin State, W Burma 21.44N 92.48E
25 Q7 **Daleville** Alabama, S USA 31.18N 85.42W
100 M9 **Dalfsen** Overijssel, E Netherlands 52.31N 6.16E
26 M1 **Dalhart** Texas, SW USA 36.04N 102.31W
11 O13 **Dalhousie** New Brunswick, SE Canada 48.03N 66.22W
158 I6 **Dalhousie** Himāchal Pradesh, N India 32.31N 76.01E
166 F12 **Dali** *var.* Xiaguan. Yunnan, SW China 25.33N 100.10E
Dali *see* Idálion
169 U14 **Dalian** *var.* Dairen, Dalien, Lüda, Ta-lien, *Rus.* Dalny. Liaoning, NE China 38.53N 121.36E
107 O15 **Dalías** Andalucía, S Spain 36.49N 2.50W
Dalien *see* Dalian
Dalijan *see* Delījān
114 J9 **Dalj** *Hung.* Dalja. Osijek-Baranja, E Croatia 45.29N 19.00E
Dalja *see* Dalj
34 F12 **Dallas** Oregon, NW USA 44.55N 123.19W
27 U6 **Dallas** Texas, SW USA 32.46N 96.48W
27 T7 **Dallas-Fort Worth** ✕ Texas, SW USA 32.37N 97.16W
160 K12 **Dalli Rājhara** Madhya Pradesh, C India 20.33N 81.06E
41 X15 **Dall Island** *island* Alexander Archipelago, Alaska, USA
40 M12 **Dall Lake** ◎ Alaska, USA
79 S12 **Dallol Bosso** *seasonal river* W Niger
147 U7 **Dalmā** *island* W UAE
115 E14 **Dalmacija** *Eng.* Dalmatia, *Ger.* Dalmatien, *It.* Dalmazia. *cultural region* S Croatia
Dalmatia/Dalmatien/Dalmazia *see* Dalmacija
127 Nn17 **Dal'negorsk** Primorskiy Kray, SE Russian Federation 44.27N 135.30E
127 Nn17 **Dal'nerechensk** Primorskiy Kray, SE Russian Federation 45.57N 133.42E
Dalny *see* Dalian
78 M16 **Daloa** C Ivory Coast 6.52N 6.28W
166 J11 **Dalou Shan** ▲▲ S China
189 X7 **Dalrymple Lake** ◎ Queensland, E Australia
12 H14 **Dalrymple Lake** ◎ Ontario, S Canada
189 X7 **Dalrymple, Mount** ▲ Queensland, E Australia 21.01S 148.34E
95 K20 **Dalsbruk** *Fin.* Taalintehdas. Länsi-Suomi, W Finland 60.01N 22.33E
97 K19 **Dalsjöfors** Västra Götaland, S Sweden 57.43N 13.04E
97 J17 **Dals Långed** *var.* Långed. Västra Götaland, S Sweden 58.54N 12.20E
159 O15 **Dāltenganj** *prev.* Daltonganj. Bihār, N India 23.59N 84.07E
25 R2 **Dalton** Georgia, SE USA 34.46N 84.58W
Daltonganj *see* Dāltenganj
205 X14 **Dalton Iceberg Tongue** *ice feature* Antarctica
94 J1 **Dalvík** Nordhurland Eystra, N Iceland 65.58N 18.31W
37 N8 **Daly City** California, W USA 37.44N 122.27W
189 P2 **Daly River** ≈ Northern Territory, N Australia
189 Q3 **Daly Waters** Northern Territory, N Australia 16.21S 133.22E
121 F20 **Damachava** *var.* Damachova, *Pol.* Domaczewo, *Rus.* Domachëvo. Brestskaya Voblasts', SW Belarus 51.45N 23.36E
Damachova *see* Damachava
79 W11 **Damagaram Takaya** Zinder, S Niger 14.02N 9.28E
160 D12 **Damān** Damān and Diu, W India 20.25N 72.58E
160 B12 **Damān and Diu** ◐ *union territory* W India
77 V7 **Damanhûr** *anc.* Hermopolis Parva. N Egypt 31.02N 30.30E
Damāo *see* Damān
167 O1 **Damaqun Shan** ▲▲ E China
81 I15 **Damara** Ombella-Mpoko, S Central African Republic 5.00N 18.45E
85 D18 **Damaraland** *physical region* C Namibia
175 T15 **Damar, Kepulauan** *var.* Baraf Daja Islands, Kepulauan Barat Daya. *island group* C Indonesia
174 Gg4 **Damar Laut** Perak, Peninsular Malaysia 4.13N 100.36E
175 Tt15 **Damar, Pulau** *island* Maluku, E Indonesia
Damas *see* Dimashq
79 Y12 **Damasak** Borno, NE Nigeria 13.10N 12.40E
Damasco *see* Dimashq
23 Q8 **Damascus** Virginia, NE USA 36.37N 81.46W
Damascus *see* Dimashq
79 X13 **Damaturu** Yobe, NE Nigeria 11.44N 11.58E
175 Ss4 **Damau** Pulau Kaburuang, N Indonesia 3.46N 126.49E
149 O5 **Damāvand, Qolleh-ye** ▲ N Iran 35.59N 52.06E
84 B10 **Damba** Uíge, NW Angola 6.42S 15.07E
116 M12 **Dambaslar** Tekirdağ, NW Turkey 41.13N 27.13E
118 J13 **Dâmboviţa** *prev.* Dîmboviţa. ◐ *county* SE Romania
118 J13 **Dâmboviţa** *prev.* Dîmboviţa. ≈ S Romania
181 Y15 **D'Ambre, Île** *island* NE Mauritius
161 K24 **Dambulla** Central Province, C Sri Lanka 7.51N 80.40E
46 K9 **Dame-Marie** SW Haiti 18.31N 74.24W
46 J9 **Dame Marie, Cap** *headland* SW Haiti 18.37N 74.24W
149 Q4 **Dāmghān** Semnān, N Iran 36.13N 54.22E
Damietta *see* Dumyāt
144 G10 **Dāmiyā** Al Balqā', NW Jordan 32.07N 35.33E
152 G11 **Damla** Dashkhovuzskiy Velayat, N Turkmenistan 40.05N 59.15E
Dammām *see* Ad Dammān
102 G12 **Damme** Niedersachsen, NW Germany 52.31N 8.12E
159 R15 **Dāmodar** ≈ NE India
160 J9 **Damoh** Madhya Pradesh, C India 23.52N 79.24E
79 P15 **Damongo** NW Ghana 9.06N 1.46W
144 G7 **Damoûr** *var.* Ad Dāmūr. W Lebanon 33.36N 35.30E
175 Pp7 **Dampal, Teluk** *bay* Sulawesi, C Indonesia
188 H7 **Dampier** Western Australia 20.40S 116.40E
188 H6 **Dampier Archipelago** *island group* Western Australia
176 Uu9 **Dampier, Selat** *strait* Irian Jaya, E Indonesia
194 L12 **Dampier Strait** *strait* NE PNG
147 U14 **Damqawt** *var.* Damqut. E Yemen 16.35N 52.39E
165 O13 **Dam Qu** ≈ C China
Damqut *see* Damqawt
178 Ii13 **Dâmrei, Chuŏr Phnum** *Fr.* Chaîne de l'Éléphant. ▲▲ SW Cambodia
110 C7 **Damvant** Jura, NW Switzerland 47.22N 6.55E
Damwâld *see* Damwoude
100 L5 **Damwoude** *Fris.* Damwâld. Friesland, N Netherlands 53.18N 5.59E
165 N15 **Damxung** Xizang Zizhiqu, W China 30.28N 91.01E
82 K11 **Danakil Desert** *var.* Afar Depression, Danakil Plain. *desert* E Africa
Danakil Plain *see* Danakil Desert
37 R8 **Dana, Mount** ▲ California, W USA 37.54N 119.13W
78 L16 **Danané** W Ivory Coast 7.16N 8.09W
178 Kk10 **Đà Nẵng** *prev.* Tourane. Quang Nam-Đa Nẵng, C Vietnam 16.04N 108.13E
179 Qq13 **Danao** *var.* Danao City. Cebu, C Philippines 10.34N 124.00E
166 G9 **Danba** Sichuan, C China 30.54N 101.49E
Danborg *see* Daneborg
20 L13 **Danbury** Connecticut, NE USA 41.21N 73.27W
27 W12 **Danbury** Texas, SW USA 29.13N 95.20W
37 X15 **Danby Lake** ◎ California, W USA
204 H4 **Danco Coast** *physical region* Antarctica
84 B11 **Dande** ≈ NW Angola
Dandeldhura *see* Dadeldhura
161 E17 **Dandeli** Karnātaka, W India 15.18N 74.42E
191 O12 **Dandenong** Victoria, SE Australia 38.01S 145.13E
169 V13 **Dandong** *var.* Tan-tung; *prev.* An-tung. Liaoning, NE China 40.09N 124.23E
207 Q14 **Daneborg** *var.* Danborg. Tunu, N Greenland 74.34N 19.51W
27 V12 **Danevang** Texas, SW USA 29.03N 96.11W
Dānew *see* Deynau
12 L12 **Danford Lake** Quebec, SE Canada 45.55N 76.12W
21 T4 **Danforth** Maine, NE USA 45.39N 67.54W
39 P3 **Danforth Hills** ▲▲ Colorado, C USA
Dangara *see* Danghara
165 V12 **Dangchang** Gansu, C China 34.01N 104.19E
Dangchengwan *see* Subei
84 B10 **Dange** Uíge, NW Angola 7.55S 15.01E
Dangerous Archipelago *see* Tuamotu, Îles
85 E26 **Danger Point** *headland* SW South Africa 34.37S 19.20E
153 Q13 **Danghara** *Rus.* Dangara. SW Tajikistan 38.04N 69.14E
165 P8 **Danghe Nanshan** ▲▲ W China
82 I12 **Dangila** *var.* Dānglā. Amhara, NW Ethiopia 11.08N 36.51E
165 P8 **Dangjin Shankou** *pass* N China 39.22N 94.19E
Dangla *see* Tanggula Shan
Dānglā *see* Dangila, NW Ethiopia
Dangme Chu *see* Manās
159 Y11 **Dāngori** Assam, NE India 27.40N 95.34E
Dang Raek, Phanom/Dangrek, Chaîne des *see* Dângrêk, Chuŏr Phnum
178 Ii11 **Dângrêk, Chuŏr Phnum** *var.* Phanom Dang Raek, Phanom Dong Rak, *Fr.* Chaîne des Dangrek. ▲▲ Cambodia/Thailand
44 G3 **Dangriga** *prev.* Stann Creek. Stann Creek, E Belize 16.58N 88.13W
167 P6 **Dangshan** Anhui, E China 34.28N 116.24E
35 T15 **Daniel** Wyoming, C USA 42.49N 110.04W
85 H22 **Daniëlskuil** Northern Cape, N South Africa 28.07S 23.35E
21 N12 **Danielson** Connecticut, NE USA 41.48N 71.53W
128 M15 **Danilov** Yaroslavskaya Oblast', W Russian Federation 58.11N 40.11E
131 O9 **Danilovka** Volgogradskaya Oblast', SW Russian Federation 50.21N 44.03E
Danish West Indies *see* Virgin Islands (US)
166 L7 **Dan Jiang** ≈ C China
166 M7 **Danjiangkou Shuiku** ⊟ C China
147 W8 **Ḑank** *var.* Dhank. NW Oman 23.34N 56.16E
158 I7 **Dankhar** Himāchal Pradesh, N India 32.07N 78.12E
130 L6 **Dankov** Lipetskaya Oblast', W Russian Federation 53.17N 39.07E
44 J7 **Danlí** El Paraíso, S Honduras 14.02N 86.34W
Danmark *see* Denmark
Danmarksstraedet *see* Denmark Strait
97 O14 **Dannemora** Uppsala, C Sweden 60.13N 17.49E
20 L6 **Dannemora** New York, NE USA 44.42N 73.42W
102 K11 **Dannenberg** Niedersachsen, N Germany 53.05N 11.06E
192 N12 **Dannevirke** Manawatu-Wanganui, North Island, NZ 40.13S 176.04E
23 U8 **Dan River** ≈ Virginia, NE USA
178 Hh9 **Dan Sai** Loei, C Thailand 17.15N 101.04E
20 F10 **Dansville** New York, NE USA 42.34N 77.40W
Dantzig *see* Gdańsk
88 E12 **Danube** *Bul.* Dunav, *Cz.* Dunaj, *Ger.* Donau, *Hung.* Duna, *Rom.* Dunărea. ≈ C Europe
Danubian Plain *see* Dunavska Ravnina
177 Ff8 **Danubyu** Irrawaddy, SW Burma 17.15N 95.34E
Danum *see* Doncaster
21 P11 **Danvers** Massachusetts, NE USA 42.34N 70.54W
29 T11 **Danville** Arkansas, C USA 35.03N 93.23W
33 N13 **Danville** Illinois, N USA 40.10N 87.37W
33 O14 **Danville** Indiana, N USA 39.45N 86.31W
31 Y15 **Danville** Iowa, C USA 40.52N 91.18W
22 M6 **Danville** Kentucky, S USA 37.39N 84.46W
20 G14 **Danville** Pennsylvania, NE USA 40.57N 76.36W
23 T6 **Danville** Virginia, NE USA 36.35N 79.24W
Danxian/Dan Xian *see* Danzhou
166 L17 **Danzhou** *prev.* Danxian, Dan Xian, Nada. Hainan, S China 19.31N 109.31E
Danzig *see* Gdańsk
Danziger Bucht *see* Danzig, Gulf of
112 J6 **Danzig, Gulf of** *var.* Gulf of Gdańsk, *Ger.* Danziger Bucht, *Pol.* Zakota Gdańska, *Rus.* Gdan'skaya Bukhta. *gulf* N Poland
166 F10 **Daocheng** Sichuan, C China 29.05N 100.14E
Daokou *see* Huaxian
106 H7 **Dão, Rio** ≈ N Portugal
Daosa *see* Dausa
79 Y7 **Dao Timmi** Agadez, NE Niger 20.31N 13.34E
166 M13 **Daoxian** *var.* Dao Xian. Hunan, S China 25.30N 111.37E
79 Q14 **Dapaong** N Togo 10.52N 0.12E
25 N8 **Daphne** Alabama, S USA 30.36N 87.54W
179 Qq15 **Dapitan** Mindanao, S Philippines 8.39N 123.25E
165 P9 **Da Qaidam** Qinghai, C China 37.49N 95.18E
169 V8 **Daqing** Heilongjiang, NE China 46.29N 125.07E
169 O13 **Daqing Shan** ▲▲ N China
Daqm *see* Duqm
145 T5 **Dāqūq** *var.* Tāwūq. N Iraq 35.07N 44.27E
78 G10 **Dara** *var.* Dahra. NW Senegal 15.20N 15.28W
144 H9 **Dar'ā** *var.* Der'a, *Fr.* Déraa. Dar'ā, SW Syria 32.37N 36.06E
144 H8 **Dar'ā** *off.* Muḩāfaẓat Dar'ā, *var.* Darā, Derá, Derrá. ◐ *governorate* S Syria
149 Q12 **Dārāb** Fārs, S Iran 28.52N 54.25E
118 K8 **Darabani** Botoşani, NW Romania 48.10N 26.40E
Daraj *see* Dirj
148 M8 **Dārān** Eşfahān, W Iran 33.02N 50.27E
178 Kk12 **Đa Răng, Sông** *var.* Ba. ≈ S Vietnam
126 Kk16 **Darasun** Chitinskaya Oblast', S Russian Federation 51.36N 113.58E
Daraut-Kurgan *see* Daroot-Korgon
79 W13 **Darazo** Bauchi, E Nigeria 11.01N 10.27E
145 S3 **Darband** N Iraq 36.15N 44.17E
145 V4 **Darband-i Khān, Sadd** *dam* NE Iraq 35.07N 45.42E
145 N1 **Darbāsīyah** *var.* Derbisîye. Al Ḩasakah, N Syria 37.06N 40.42E
120 C11 **Darbėnai** Kretinga, NW Lithuania 56.02N 21.16E
159 Q13 **Darbhanga** Bihār, N India 26.10N 85.54E
40 M9 **Darby, Cape** *headland* Alaska, USA 64.19N 162.46W
114 I9 **Darda** *Hung.* Dárda. Osijek-Baranja, E Croatia 45.37N 18.41E
29 T11 **Dardanelle** Arkansas, C USA 35.13N 93.09W
29 S11 **Dardanelle, Lake** ⊟ Arkansas, C USA
Dardanelles *see* Çanakkale Boğazı
Dardanelli *see* Çanakkale
Dar-el-Beida *see* Casablanca
142 M14 **Darende** Malatya, C Turkey 38.33N 37.31E
83 J22 **Dar es Salaam** Dar es Salaam, E Tanzania 6.51S 39.18E
83 J22 **Dar es Salaam** ✕ Pwani, E Tanzania 6.57S 39.17E
193 H18 **Darfield** Canterbury, South Island, NZ 43.28S 172.07E
108 F7 **Darfo** Lombardia, N Italy 45.54N 10.12E
82 B10 **Darfur** *var.* Darfur Massif. *cultural region* W Sudan
Darfur Massif *see* Darfur
152 J10 **Dargan-Ata** *var.* Darganata. Lebapskiy Velayat, NE Turkmenistan 40.30N 62.09E
Darganata *see* Dargan-Ata
149 T3 **Dargaz** *var.* Darreh Gaz; *prev.* Moḩammadābād. Khorāsān, NE Iran 37.28N 59.08E
145 U4 **Dargazayn** NE Iraq 35.39N 45.00E
191 P12 **Dargo** Victoria, SE Australia 37.29S 147.15E
168 K7 **Darhan** Bulgan, C Mongolia 48.07N 103.54E
169 N8 **Darhan** Hentiy, C Mongolia 46.38N 109.25E
168 L6 **Darhan** Selenge, N Mongolia 49.24N 105.57E
169 N12 **Darhan Muminggan Lianheqi** *var.* Bailingmiao. Nei Mongol Zizhiqu, N China 41.41N 110.25E
25 W7 **Darien** Georgia, SE USA 31.22N 81.25W
45 W16 **Darién** *off.* Provincia del Darién. ◐ *province* SE Panama
Darién, Golfo del *see* Darien, Gulf of
45 X14 **Darien, Gulf of** *Sp.* Golfo del Darién. *gulf* S Caribbean Sea
Darien, Isthmus of *see* Panamá, Istmo de
44 K9 **Dariense, Cordillera** ▲▲ C Nicaragua
45 W15 **Darién, Serranía del** ▲▲ Colombia/Panama
Dario *see* Ciudad Darío
Dariorigum *see* Vannes
Dariv *see* Darvi
Darj *see* Dirj
Darjeeling *see* Darjiling
159 S12 **Darjiling** *prev.* Darjeeling. West Bengal, NE India 27.00N 88.13E
Darkehnen *see* Ozersk
165 S12 **Darlag** Qinghai, C China 33.43N 99.42E
191 T3 **Darling Downs** *hill range* Queensland, E Australia
30 M2 **Darling, Lake** ⊟ North Dakota, N USA
188 I12 **Darling Range** ▲▲ Western Australia
190 L8 **Darling River** ≈ New South Wales, SE Australia
99 M15 **Darlington** N England, UK 54.31N 1.34W
23 T12 **Darlington** South Carolina, SE USA 34.18N 79.52W
32 K9 **Darlington** Wisconsin, N USA 42.40N 90.07W
112 G7 **Darłowo** Zachodniopomorskie, NW Poland 54.24N 16.21E
103 G19 **Darmstadt** Hessen, SW Germany 49.52N 8.39E
77 S7 **Darnah** *var.* Dérna. NE Libya 32.46N 22.39E
105 S6 **Darney** Vosges, NE France 48.06N 5.58E
190 M7 **Darnick** New South Wales, SE Australia 32.52S 143.38E
205 Y6 **Darnley, Cape** *headland* Antarctica 67.36S 70.04E
107 R7 **Daroca** Aragón, NE Spain 41.07N 1.25W
153 U11 **Daroot-Korgon** *var.* Daraut-Kurgan. Oshskaya Oblast', SW Kyrgyzstan 39.34N 72.13E
63 A23 **Darragueira** *var.* Darregueira. Buenos Aires, E Argentina 37.40S 63.12W
Darregueira *see* Darragueira
Darreh Gaz *see* Dargaz
148 K7 **Darreh Shahr** *var.* Darreh-ye Shahr. Īlām, W Iran 33.10N 47.18E
Darreh-ye Shahr *see* Darreh Shahr
34 J7 **Darrington** Washington, NW USA 48.15N 121.36W
27 P1 **Darrouzett** Texas, SW USA 36.27N 100.19W
159 S15 **Darsana** *var.* Darshana. Khulna, N Bangladesh 23.31N 88.49E
Darshana *see* Darsana
102 M7 **Darss** *peninsula* NE Germany
102 M7 **Darsser Ort** *headland* NE Germany 54.28N 12.31E
99 J24 **Dart** ≈ SW England, UK
Dartang *see* Baqên
99 P22 **Dartford** SE England, UK 51.27N 0.13E
190 L12 **Dartmoor** Victoria, SE Australia 37.56S 141.18E
99 I24 **Dartmoor** *moorland* SW England, UK
11 Q15 **Dartmouth** Nova Scotia, SE Canada 44.40N 63.34W
99 J24 **Dartmouth** SW England, UK 50.20N 3.34W
13 Y6 **Dartmouth** ≈ Quebec, SE Canada
191 Q11 **Dartmouth Reservoir** ⊟ Victoria, SE Australia
Dartuch, Cabo *see* Artrutx, Cap d'
194 G15 **Daru** Western, SW PNG 9.04S 143.12E
114 G9 **Daruvar** *Hung.* Daruvár. Bjelovar-Bilogora, NE Croatia 45.34N 17.12E
152 F10 **Darvaza** *Turkm.* Derweze. Akhalskiy Velayat, C Turkmenistan 40.10N 58.27E
Darvaza *see* Darwoza
Darvazskiy Khrebet *see* Darvoz, Qatorkŭhi
168 F8 **Darvi** *var.* Dariv. Govĭ-Altay, W Mongolia 46.20N 94.11E
154 L9 **Darvīshān** *var.* Darweshan, Garmser. Helmand, S Afghanistan 31.01N 64.12E
153 R13 **Darvoz, Qatorkŭhi** *Rus.* Darvazskiy Khrebet. ▲▲ C Tajikistan
Darweshan *see* Darvīshān
65 J15 **Darwin** Río Negro, S Argentina 39.13S 65.41W
189 O1 **Darwin** *prev.* Palmerston, Port Darwin. *territory capital* Northern Territory, N Australia 12.27S 130.52E
67 D24 **Darwin** *var.* Darwin Settlement. East Falkland, Falkland Islands 51.51S 58.55W
64 H8 **Darwin, Cordillera** ▲▲ N Chile
59 B17 **Darwin, Volcán** ▲ Galapagos Islands, Ecuador, E Pacific Ocean 0.12S 91.17W
153 O10 **Darwoza** *Rus.* Darvaza. Jizzakh Wiloyati, C Uzbekistan 40.59N 67.19E
155 S8 **Darya Khān** Punjab, E Pakistan 31.48N 71.05E

◆ Country ● Country Capital ◇ Dependent Territory ○ Dependent Territory Capital ◐ Administrative Region ✕ International Airport ▲ Mountain ▲▲ Mountain Range ▲ Volcano ≈ River ◎ Lake ⊟ Reservoir

DAR'YALYKTAKYR, RAVNINA – DESLOGE

151 O15 Dar'yalyktakyr, Ravnina plain S Kazakhstan
149 T11 Dārzīn Kermān, S Iran 29.10N 58.09E
166 L8 Dashennongjia ▲ C China 31.24N 110.16E
Dashhowuz see Dashkhovuz
Dashhowuz Welayaty see Dashkhovuzskiy Velayat
121 O16 Dashkawka Rus. Dashkovka. Mahilyowskaya Voblasts', E Belarus 53.42N 30.17E
152 H8 Dashkhovuz Turkm. Dashhowuz; prev. Tashauz. Dashkhovuzskiy Velayat, N Turkmenistan 41.51N 59.52E
Dashkhovuz see Dashkhovuzskiy Velayat
152 E9 Dashkhovuzskiy Velayat var. Dashkhovuz, Turkm. Dashhowuz Welayaty. ◈ province N Turkmenistan
Dashköpri see Tashkepri
Dashkovka see Dashkawka
154 J15 Dasht ↝ SW Pakistan
Dashtidzhum see Dashtijum
153 R13 Dashtijum Rus. Dashtidzhum. SW Tajikistan 38.06N 70.11E
155 W7 Daska Punjab, NE Pakistan 32.21N 74.20E
Đa, Sông see Black River
79 R15 Dassa var. Dassa-Zoumé. S Benin 7.46N 2.15E
Dassa-Zoumé see Dassa
31 U8 Dassel Minnesota, N USA 45.06N 94.18W
158 H3 Dastegil Sar var. Disteghil Sār. ▲ N India
142 C16 Datça Muğla, SW Turkey 36.46N 27.40E
172 Nn6 Date Hokkaidō, NE Japan 42.28N 140.51E
160 I8 Datia prev. Duttia. Madhya Pradesh, C India 25.40N 78.28E
165 T10 Datong Qinghai, C China 37.01N 101.33E
167 N2 Datong var. Tatung, Ta-t'ung. Shanxi, C China 40.09N 113.16E
165 S9 Datong He ↝ C China
165 S9 Datong Shan ▲ C China
174 Kk6 Datu, Tanjung headland Indonesia/Malaysia 2.01N 109.37E
Daua see Dawa Wenz
180 H16 Dauban, Mount ▲ Silhouette, NE Seychelles
155 T7 Dāūd Khel Punjab, E Pakistan 32.52N 71.34E
121 G15 Daugai Alytus, S Lithuania 54.22N 24.20E
Daugava see Western Dvina
120 J11 Daugavpils Ger. Dünaburg; prev. Rus. Dvinsk. municipality Daugvapils, SE Latvia 55.53N 26.33E
Dauka see Dawkah
Daulatabad see Malāyer
103 D18 Daun Rheinland-Pfalz, W Germany 50.13N 6.50E
161 E14 Daund prev. Dhond. Mahārāshtra, W India 18.28N 74.37E
178 Gg12 Daung Kyun island S Burma
9 W15 Dauphin Manitoba, S Canada 51.09N 100.04W
105 S13 Dauphiné cultural region E France
25 N9 Dauphin Island island Alabama, S USA
9 X15 Dauphin River Manitoba, S Canada 51.55N 98.03W
79 V12 Daura Katsina, N Nigeria 13.03N 8.18E
158 H12 Dausa prev. Daosa. Rājasthān, N India 26.54N 76.18E
Dauwa see Dawwah
143 Y10 Däväçi Rus. Divichi. NE Azerbaijan 41.15N 48.58E
161 F18 Dāvangere Karnātaka, W India 14.30N 75.52E
179 Rr16 Davao off. Davao City. Mindanao, S Philippines 7.06N 125.35E
179 Rr16 Davao Gulf gulf Mindanao, S Philippines
13 Q11 Daveluyville Quebec, SE Canada 46.12N 72.07W
31 Z14 Davenport Iowa, C USA 41.31N 90.34W
34 L8 Davenport Washington, NW USA 47.39N 118.09W
45 P16 David Chiriquí, W Panama 8.25N 82.25W
13 O11 David ↝ Quebec, SE Canada
31 R15 David City Nebraska, C USA 41.15N 97.07W
David-Gorodok see Davyd-Haradok
9 T16 Davidson Saskatchewan, S Canada 51.15N 105.58W
23 R10 Davidson North Carolina, SE USA 35.29N 80.49W
28 K12 Davidson Oklahoma, C USA 34.15N 99.06W
41 S6 Davidson Mountains ▲ Alaska, USA
180 M8 Davie Ridge undersea feature W Indian Ocean
190 A1 Davies, Mount ▲ South Australia 26.14S 129.14E
37 O7 Davis California, W USA 38.31N 121.46W
29 N12 Davis Oklahoma, C USA 34.30N 97.07W
205 Y7 Davis Australian research station Antarctica 68.30S 78.15E
204 H3 Davis Coast physical region Antarctica
20 C16 Davis, Mount ▲ Pennsylvania, NE USA 39.47N 79.10W
26 K9 Davis Mountains ▲ Texas, SW USA
205 Z9 Davis Sea sea Antarctica
67 O20 Davis Seamounts undersea feature S Atlantic Ocean
206 M13 Davis Strait strait Baffin Bay/Labrador Sea
131 U5 Davlekanovo Respublika Bashkortostan, W Russian Federation 54.13N 55.06E
110 J9 Davos Rmsch. Tavau. Graubünden, E Switzerland 46.48N 9.50E
121 J20 Davyd-Haradok Pol. Dawidgródek, Rus. David-Gorodok. Brestskaya Voblasts', SW Belarus 52.03N 27.13E
169 U12 Dawa Liaoning, NE China 40.55N 122.02E
147 O11 Dawāsir, Wādī ad dry watercourse S Saudi Arabia
83 K15 Dawa Wenz var. Daua, Webi Daawo. ↝ E Africa
Dawaymah, Birkat ad see Umm al Baqar, Hawr
Dawei see Tavoy
121 K14 Dawhinava Rus. Dolginovo. Minskaya Voblasts', N Belarus 54.39N 27.28E
Dawidgródek see Davyd-Haradok
147 V12 Dawkah var. Dauka. SW Oman 18.32N 54.03E
Dawlat Qaṭar see Qatar
26 M3 Dawn Texas, SW USA 34.54N 102.10W
146 M11 Daws Al Bāḩah, SW Saudi Arabia 20.19N 41.12E
8 H5 Dawson var. Dawson City. Yukon Territory, NW Canada 64.04N 139.24W
25 S6 Dawson Georgia, SE USA 31.46N 84.27W
31 S9 Dawson Minnesota, N USA 44.55N 96.03W
Dawson City see Dawson
9 N13 Dawson Creek British Columbia, W Canada 55.48N 120.18W
8 H7 Dawson Range ▲ Yukon Territory, W Canada
189 Y9 Dawson River ↝ Queensland, E Australia
8 J15 Dawsons Landing British Columbia, SW Canada 51.33N 127.38W
22 I7 Dawson Springs Kentucky, S USA 37.10N 87.41W
25 S2 Dawsonville Georgia, SE USA 34.28N 84.07W
166 G8 Dawu Sichuan, C China 30.55N 101.08E
Dawu see Maqên
Dawukou see Shizuishan
147 Y10 Dawwah var. Dauwa. W Oman 20.36N 58.52E
104 J15 Dax var. Ax; anc. Aquae Augustae, Aquae Tarbelicae. Landes, SW France 43.43N 1.03W
Da Xian/Daxian see Dachuan
166 G9 Daxue Shan ▲ C China
166 G12 Dayao Yunnan, SW China 25.41N 101.23E
Dayishan see Gaoyou
191 N12 Daylesford Victoria, SE Australia 37.24S 144.07E
37 U10 Daylight Pass pass California, W USA 36.44N 116.55W
63 D17 Daymán, Río ↝ N Uruguay
Dayr see Ad Dayr
144 G10 Dayr 'Allā var. Deir 'Alla. Al Balqā', N Jordan 32.39N 36.06E
145 N4 Dayr az Zawr var. Deir ez Zor. Dayr az Zawr, E Syria 35.12N 40.12E
144 M5 Dayr az Zawr off. Muḩāfaẓat Dayr az Zawr, var. Dayr Az-Zor. ◈ governorate E Syria
Dayr Az-Zor see Dayr az Zawr
Dayrūṭ see Dairût
9 Q15 Daysland Alberta, SW Canada 52.53N 112.19W
33 R14 Dayton Ohio, N USA 39.45N 84.11W
22 L10 Dayton Tennessee, S USA 35.30N 85.01W
27 W11 Dayton Texas, SW USA 30.03N 94.53W
34 L10 Dayton Washington, NW USA 46.19N 117.58W
25 X10 Daytona Beach Florida, SE USA 29.12N 81.03W
175 N10 Dayu Borneo, C Indonesia 1.58S 115.04E
167 O13 Dayu Ling ▲ S China
167 R7 Da Yunhe Eng. Grand Canal. canal E China
167 S11 Dayu Shan island SE China
166 J9 Dazhu Sichuan, C China 30.45N 107.10E
166 J9 Dazu Chongqing Shi, C China 29.48N 105.46E
85 H24 De Aar Northern Cape, C South Africa 30.40S 24.01E
204 K5 Deacon, Cape headland Antarctica
41 R5 Deadhorse Alaska, USA 70.15N 148.28W
35 T12 Dead Indian Peak ▲ Wyoming, C USA 44.36N 109.45W
25 R9 Dead Lake ◎ Florida, SE USA
46 J4 Deadman's Cay Long Island, C Bahamas 23.09N 75.06W
144 G11 Dead Sea var. Bahret Lut, Lacus Asphaltites, Ar. Al Baḩr al Mayyit, Baḩrat Lūt, Heb. Yam HaMelaḩ. salt lake Israel/Jordan
30 J9 Deadwood South Dakota, N USA 44.22N 103.43W
99 Q22 Deal SE England, UK 51.14N 1.22E
85 I22 Dealesville Free State, C South Africa 28.40S 25.46E
Dealnu see Tana/Teno
167 P10 De'an Jiangxi, S China 29.24N 115.46E
64 K9 Deán Funes Córdoba, C Argentina 30.25S 64.22W
204 L12 Dean Island island Antarctica
33 S10 Dearborn Michigan, N USA 42.16N 83.13W
29 R3 Dearborn Missouri, C USA 39.31N 94.46W
34 K9 Deary Idaho, NW USA 46.46N 116.33W
34 M9 Deary Washington, NW USA 46.42N 116.36W
8 J10 Dease ↝ British Columbia, W Canada
8 J10 Dease Lake British Columbia, W Canada 58.28N 130.04W
37 U11 Death Valley California, W USA 36.25N 116.50W
37 U11 Death Valley valley California, W USA
104 L4 Deauville Calvados, N France 49.21N 0.06E
119 X7 Debal'tseve Rus. Debal'tsevo. Donets'ka Oblast', E Ukraine 48.21N 38.25E
Debal'tsevo see Debal'tseve
115 M19 Debar Ger. Dibra, Turk. Debre. W FYR Macedonia 41.32N 20.33E
41 O9 Debauch Mountain ▲ Alaska, USA 64.31N 159.52W
De Behagle see Laï
27 X7 De Berry Texas, SW USA 32.18N 94.09W
131 T2 Debesy Udmurtskaya Respublika, NW Russian Federation 57.41N 53.56E
113 N16 Dębica Podkarpackie, SE Poland 50.03N 21.24E
De Bildt see De Bilt
100 J11 De Bilt var. De Bildt. Utrecht, C Netherlands 52.06N 5.10E
127 O9 Debin Magadanskaya Oblast', E Russian Federation 62.18N 150.42E
112 N13 Dęblin Rus. Ivangorod. Lubelskie, E Poland 51.34N 21.49E
112 D10 Dębno Zachodniopomorskie, NW Poland 52.44N 14.42E
41 S10 Deborah, Mount ▲ Alaska, USA 63.38N 147.13W
35 N8 De Borgia Montana, NW USA 47.23N 115.24W
Debra Birhan see Debre Birhan
Debra Marcos see Debre Mark'os
Debra Tabor see Debre Tabor
Debre see Debar
82 J13 Debre Birhan var. Debra Birhan. Amhara, N Ethiopia 9.45N 39.40E
113 N22 Debrecen Ger. Debreczin, Rom. Debreţin; prev. Debreczen. Hajdú-Bihar, E Hungary 47.31N 21.37E
Debreczen/Debreczin see Debrecen
82 I12 Debre Mark'os var. Debra Marcos. Amhara, N Ethiopia 10.18N 37.48E
115 N19 Debrešte SW FYR Macedonia 41.29N 21.20E
82 J11 Debre Tabor var. Debra Tabor. Amhara, N Ethiopia 11.46N 38.06E
Debreţin see Debrecen
82 J13 Debre Zeyt Oromo, C Ethiopia 8.41N 39.00E
115 L16 Dečani Serbia, S Yugoslavia 42.33N 20.18E
25 P2 Decatur Alabama, S USA 34.36N 86.58W
25 S3 Decatur Georgia, SE USA 33.46N 84.18W
32 L13 Decatur Illinois, N USA 39.50N 88.57W
33 Q12 Decatur Indiana, N USA 40.48N 84.55W
24 M5 Decatur Mississippi, S USA 32.26N 89.06W
31 S14 Decatur Nebraska, C USA 42.00N 96.19W
27 S6 Decatur Texas, SW USA 33.14N 97.32W
22 H9 Decaturville Tennessee, S USA 35.34N 88.07W
105 O13 Decazeville Aveyron, S France 44.34N 2.18E
161 H17 Deccan Hind. Dakshin. plateau C India
12 J8 Decelles, Réservoir ⊡ Quebec, SE Canada
10 K2 Déception Quebec, NE Canada 62.06N 74.36W
166 G11 Dechang Sichuan, C China 27.24N 102.09E
113 C15 Děčín Ger. Tetschen. Ústecký Kraj, NW Czech Republic 50.48N 14.15E
105 P9 Decize Nièvre, C France 46.51N 3.25E
100 I6 De Cocksdorp Noord-Holland, NW Netherlands 53.09N 4.52E
31 X11 Decorah Iowa, C USA 43.18N 91.47W
Dedeagaç/Dedeagach see Alexandroúpoli
196 C15 Dededo N Guam 13.30N 144.51E
100 N9 Dedemsvaart Overijssel, E Netherlands 52.36N 6.28E
21 O11 Dedham Massachusetts, NE USA 42.14N 71.10W
65 H19 Dedo, Cerro ▲ SW Argentina 44.46S 71.48W
79 O13 Dédougou W Burkina 12.25N 3.27W
128 G15 Dedovichi Pskovskaya Oblast', W Russian Federation 57.31N 29.53E
169 V6 Dedu var. Qingshan. Heilongjiang, NE China 48.30N 126.17E
161 J24 Deduru Oya ↝ W Sri Lanka
85 N14 Dedza Central, S Malawi 14.24S 34.15E
85 N14 Dedza Mountain ▲ C Malawi 14.22S 34.16E
99 J19 Dee Wel. Afon Dyfrdwy. ↝ England/Wales, UK
98 K9 Dee ↝ NE Scotland, UK
Deep Bay see Chilumba
23 T3 Deep Creek Lake ⊡ Maryland, NE USA
38 J4 Deep Creek Range ▲ Utah, W USA
29 P10 Deep Fork ↝ Oklahoma, C USA
12 J11 Deep River Ontario, SE Canada 46.05N 77.28W
23 T10 Deep River ↝ North Carolina, SE USA
191 U4 Deepwater New South Wales, SE Australia 29.27S 151.52E
33 S14 Deer Creek Lake ◎ Ohio, N USA
25 Z15 Deerfield Beach Florida, SE USA 26.19N 80.06W
41 N8 Deering Alaska, USA 66.04N 162.43W
40 M16 Deer Island island Alaska, USA
21 S7 Deer Isle island Maine, NE USA
11 S11 Deer Lake Newfoundland, SE Canada 49.10N 57.18W
101 D18 Deerlijk West-Vlaanderen, W Belgium 50.52N 3.21E
35 Q10 Deer Lodge Montana, NW USA 46.24N 112.43W
34 L8 Deer Park Washington, NW USA 47.55N 117.28W
31 U5 Deer River Minnesota, N USA 47.19N 93.47W
Deés see Dej
33 R11 Defiance Ohio, N USA 41.16N 84.21W
25 Q8 De Funiak Springs Florida, SE USA 30.43N 86.07W
97 L23 Degeberga Skåne, S Sweden 55.48N 14.06E
106 H12 Degebe, Ribeira ↝ S Portugal
82 M13 Degeh Bur Somali, E Ethiopia 8.08N 43.35E
13 U9 Dégelis Quebec, SE Canada 47.30N 68.38W
79 U17 Degema Rivers, S Nigeria 4.46N 6.47E
97 L16 Degerfors Örebro, C Sweden 59.13N 14.25E
200 N16 De Gerlache Seamounts undersea feature SE Pacific Ocean
103 N21 Deggendorf Bayern, SE Germany 48.49N 12.58E
124 Nn2 Değirmenlik Gk. Kythréa. N Cyprus 35.14N 33.28E
82 I11 Degoma Amhara, N Ethiopia 12.22N 37.36E
De Gordyk see Gorredijk
29 T12 De Gray Lake ⊡ Arkansas, C USA
188 J6 De Grey River ↝ Western Australia
130 M10 Degtevo Rostovskaya Oblast', SW Russian Federation 49.12N 40.39E
149 X13 Dehak Sīstān va Balūchestān, SE Iran 27.10N 62.34E
149 R9 Deh 'Alī Kermān, C Iran 31.40N 56.10E
149 S13 Dehbārez var. Rūdān. Hormozgān, S Iran 27.30N 57.10E
149 P10 Deh Bīd Fārs, C Iran 30.37N 53.11E
148 M10 Deh Dasht Kohkīlūyeh va Būyer Aḩmadī, SW Iran 30.49N 50.36E
77 N8 Dehibat SE Tunisia 31.58N 10.43E
Dehli see Delhi
148 K8 Dehlorān Īlām, W Iran 32.40N 47.18E
153 N13 Dehqonobod Rus. Dekhkanabad. Qashqadaryo Wiloyati, S Uzbekistan 38.24N 66.31E
158 J9 Dehra Dūn Uttar Pradesh, N India 30.18N 78.03E
159 O14 Dehri Bihār, N India 24.55N 84.10E
154 K10 Deh Shū var. Deshu. Helmand, S Afghanistan 30.28N 63.21E
101 D17 Deinze Oost-Vlaanderen, NW Belgium 50.58N 3.31E
Deir 'Alla see Dayr 'Allā
Deir ez Zor see Dayr az Zawr
Deirgeirt, Loch see Derg, Lough
118 H9 Dej Hung. Dés; prev. Deés. Cluj, NW Romania 47.08N 23.55E
97 K15 Deje Värmland, C Sweden 59.34N 13.28E
176 Y14 De Jongs, Tanjung headland Irian Jaya, SE Indonesia 6.55S 138.31E
De Jouwer see Joure
32 M10 De Kalb Illinois, N USA 41.55N 88.45W
24 M5 De Kalb Mississippi, S USA 32.46N 88.39W
27 W5 De Kalb Texas, SW USA 33.30N 94.34W
Dekéleia see Dhekélia
81 K20 Dekese Kasai Occidental, C Dem. Rep. Congo (Zaire) 3.28S 21.24E
Dekhkanabad see Dehqonobod
81 I14 Dékoa Kémo, C Central African Republic 6.17N 19.07E
100 H6 De Koog Noord-Holland, NW Netherlands 53.06N 4.43E
32 M9 Delafield Wisconsin, N USA 43.03N 88.22W
63 C23 De La Garma Buenos Aires, E Argentina 37.58S 60.25W
12 K10 Delahey, Lac ◎ Quebec, SE Canada
82 E11 Delami Southern Kordofan, C Sudan 11.51N 30.30E
25 X11 De Land Florida, SE USA 29.01N 81.18W
37 R12 Delano California, W USA 35.46N 119.15W
31 V8 Delano Minnesota, N USA 45.03N 93.46W
38 K6 Delano Peak ▲ Utah, W USA 38.22N 112.21W
Delap-Uliga-Darrit see Dalap-Uliga-Djarrit
154 L7 Delārām Farāh, SW Afghanistan 32.10N 63.27E
40 F17 Delarof Islands island group Aleutian Islands, Alaska, USA
32 M9 Delavan Wisconsin, N USA 42.37N 88.37W
33 S13 Delaware Ohio, N USA 40.18N 83.04W
20 I17 Delaware off. State of Delaware; also known as Blue Hen State, Diamond State, First State. ◈ state NE USA
20 I17 Delaware Bay bay NE USA
26 J8 Delaware Mountains ▲ Texas, SW USA
20 I12 Delaware River ↝ NE USA
29 Q3 Delaware River ↝ Kansas, C USA
20 J14 Delaware Water Gap valley New Jersey/Pennsylvania, NE USA
103 G14 Delbrück Nordrhein-Westfalen, W Germany 51.46N 8.34E
9 Q15 Delburne Alberta, SW Canada 52.09N 113.11W
180 M12 Del Cano Rise undersea feature SW Indian Ocean
115 Q18 Delčevo NE FYR Macedonia 41.57N 22.45E
Delcommune, Lac see Nzilo, Lac
100 O10 Delden Overijssel, E Netherlands 52.16N 6.40E
191 R12 Delegate New South Wales, SE Australia 37.04S 148.57E
De Lemmer see Lemmer
110 D7 Delémont Ger. Delsberg. Jura, NW Switzerland 47.22N 7.21E
27 R7 De Leon Texas, SW USA 32.06N 98.33W
117 F18 Delfoí Stereá Ellás, C Greece 38.28N 22.31E
100 G12 Delft Zuid-Holland, W Netherlands 52.01N 4.22E
161 J23 Delft island NW Sri Lanka
100 O5 Delfzijl Groningen, NE Netherlands 53.19N 6.55E
(0) E9 Delgada Fan undersea feature NE Pacific Ocean
44 F7 Delgado San Salvador, SW El Salvador 13.44N 89.07W
84 Q12 Delgado, Cabo headland N Mozambique 10.41S 40.40E
82 E6 Delgo Northern, N Sudan 20.07N 30.34E
165 R10 Delhi var. Delingha. Qinghai, C China 37.19N 97.22E
158 I10 Delhi var. Dehli, Hind. Dilli; hist. Shahjahanabad. Delhi, N India 28.40N 77.11E
24 J5 Delhi Louisiana, S USA 32.28N 91.29W
20 J11 Delhi New York, NE USA 42.16N 74.55W
158 I10 Delhi ◈ union territory NW India
142 J17 Deli Burnu headland S Turkey 36.43N 34.55E
57 X10 Délices C French Guiana 4.46N 53.42W
142 J12 Delice Çayı ↝ C Turkey
42 J6 Delicias var. Ciudad Delicias. Chihuahua, N Mexico 28.09N 105.22W
149 N7 Delījān var. Dalijan, Dilijan. Markazī, W Iran 34.01N 50.39E
114 P12 Deli Jovan ▲ E Yugoslavia
Déli-Kárpátok see Carpaţii Meridionali
15 H6 Déline prev. Fort Franklin. Northwest Territories, NW Canada 65.10N 123.30W
Delingha see Delhi
13 Q7 Delisle Quebec, SE Canada 48.39N 71.42W
9 T15 Delisle Saskatchewan, S Canada 51.54N 107.01W
103 M15 Delitzsch Sachsen, E Germany 51.31N 12.19E
35 Q12 Dell Montana, NW USA 44.41N 112.42W
26 I7 Dell City Texas, SW USA 31.56N 105.12W
105 U7 Delle Territoire-de-Belfort, E France 47.30N 7.00E
38 J9 Dellenbaugh, Mount ▲ Arizona, SW USA 36.06N 113.32W
31 R11 Dell Rapids South Dakota, N USA 43.50N 96.42W
23 Y4 Delmar Maryland, NE USA 38.26N 75.32W
20 K11 Delmar New York, NE USA 42.37N 73.49W
102 G11 Delmenhorst Niedersachsen, NW Germany 53.03N 8.37E
114 C9 Delnice Primorje-Gorski Kotar, NW Croatia 45.24N 14.49E
39 R7 Del Norte Colorado, C USA 37.40N 106.21W
41 N6 De Long Mountains ▲ Alaska, USA
191 P16 Deloraine Tasmania, SE Australia 41.34S 146.43E
9 W17 Deloraine Manitoba, S Canada 49.12N 100.28W
33 O12 Delphi Indiana, N USA 40.35N 86.40W
33 Q12 Delphos Ohio, N USA 40.49N 84.20W
25 Z15 Delray Beach Florida, SE USA 26.27N 80.04W
27 O12 Del Rio Texas, SW USA 29.22N 100.55W
Delsberg see Delémont
96 N11 Delsbo Gävleborg, C Sweden 61.49N 16.34E
39 P6 Delta Colorado, C USA 38.44N 108.04W
38 K5 Delta Utah, W USA 39.21N 112.34W
79 T17 Delta ◈ state S Nigeria
57 Q6 Delta Amacuro off. Territorio Delta Amacuro. ◈ federal district NE Venezuela
41 S9 Delta Junction Alaska, USA 64.02N 145.43W
25 X11 Deltona Florida, SE USA 28.54N 81.15W
191 T5 Delungra New South Wales, SE Australia 29.40S 150.49E
160 C12 Delvāda Gujarāt, W India 20.46N 71.01E
63 B21 Del Valle Buenos Aires, E Argentina 35.55S 60.42W
Delvina see Delvinë
117 C15 Delvináki var. Dhelvinákion; prev. Pogónion. Ípeiros, W Greece 39.56N 20.27E
115 L23 Delvinë var. Delvina, It. Delvino. Vlorë, S Albania 39.56N 20.07E
Delvino see Delvinë
118 I7 Delyatyn Ivano-Frankivs'ka Oblast', W Ukraine 48.32N 24.38E
131 U5 Dëma ↝ W Russian Federation
107 O5 Demanda, Sierra de la ▲ W Spain
41 T5 Demarcation Point headland Alaska, USA 69.40N 141.19W
81 K21 Demba Kasai Occidental, C Dem. Rep. Congo (Zaire) 5.24S 22.16E
180 H13 Dembéni Grande Comore, NW Comoros 11.49S 43.25E
81 M15 Dembia Mbomou, SE Central African Republic 5.08N 24.25E
Dembidollo see Dembī Dolo
82 H13 Dembī Dolo var. Dembidollo. Oromo, C Ethiopia 8.33N 34.49E
158 K6 Demchok var. Dēmqog. China/India see also Dēmqog 32.30N 79.42E
158 L6 Demchok var. Dēmqog. disputed region China/India see also Dēmqog
100 I12 De Meern Utrecht, C Netherlands 52.06N 5.00E
101 I17 Demer ↝ C Belgium
66 H12 Demerara Plain undersea feature W Atlantic Ocean
66 H12 Demerara Plateau undersea feature W Atlantic Ocean
57 T9 Demerara River ↝ NE Guyana
130 H3 Demidov Smolenskaya Oblast', W Russian Federation 55.15N 31.30E
39 Q15 Deming New Mexico, SW USA 32.13N 107.46W
34 H6 Deming Washington, NW USA 48.49N 122.13W
60 E10 Demini, Rio ↝ NW Brazil
142 D13 Demirci Manisa, W Turkey 39.03N 28.40E
115 P19 Demir Kapija prev. Železna Vrata. SE FYR Macedonia 41.25N 22.15E
116 N11 Demirköy Kırklareli, NW Turkey 41.49N 27.47E
102 N9 Demmin Mecklenburg-Vorpommern, NE Germany 53.53N 13.03E
25 O5 Demopolis Alabama, S USA 32.31N 87.50W
33 N11 Demotte Indiana, N USA 41.13N 87.07W
164 F13 Dēmqog var. Demchok. China/India see also Demchok 32.36N 79.28E
158 L6 Dēmqog var. Demchok. disputed region China/India see also Demchok
176 Yy10 Demta Irian Jaya, E Indonesia 2.19S 140.06E
125 G11 Dem'yanka ↝ C Russian Federation
128 H15 Demyansk Novgorodskaya Oblast', W Russian Federation 57.39N 32.31E
125 Ff11 Dem'yanskoye Tyumenskaya Oblast', C Russian Federation 59.39N 69.15E
105 P2 Denain Nord, N France 50.19N 3.24E
41 S10 Denali Alaska, USA 63.08N 147.33W
Denali see McKinley, Mount
83 M14 Denan Somali, E Ethiopia 6.40N 43.31E
Denau see Denow
99 J18 Denbigh Wel. Dinbych. NE Wales, UK 53.10N 3.25W
99 J18 Denbigh cultural region N Wales, UK
100 I6 Den Burg Noord-Holland, NW Netherlands 53.03N 4.46E
101 F18 Dender Fr. Dendre. ↝ W Belgium
101 F18 Denderleeuw Oost-Vlaanderen, NW Belgium 50.52N 4.04E
101 F17 Dendermonde Fr. Termonde. Oost-Vlaanderen, NW Belgium 51.01N 4.07E
Dendre see Dender
204 I9 Dendtler Island island Antarctica
100 P10 Denekamp Overijssel, E Netherlands 52.23N 7.00E
79 W12 Dengas Zinder, S Niger 13.15N 9.43E
Dêngkagoin see Têwo
168 L13 Dengkou var. Bayan Gol. Nei Mongol Zizhiqu, N China 40.15N 106.58E
165 Q14 Dêngqên Xizang Zizhiqu, W China 31.28N 95.28E
Deng Xian see Dengzhou
166 M7 Dengzhou prev. Deng Xian. Henan, C China 32.43N 112.02E
Dengzhou see Penglai
Den Haag see 's-Gravenhage
100 N9 Den Ham Overijssel, E Netherlands 52.30N 6.30E
188 H10 Denham Western Australia 25.56S 113.35E
46 J12 Denham, Mount ▲ C Jamaica 18.13N 77.33W
24 J8 Denham Springs Louisiana, S USA 30.29N 90.57W
100 I7 Den Helder Noord-Holland, NW Netherlands 52.54N 4.45E
107 T11 Denia País Valenciano, E Spain 38.51N 0.07E
201 Q8 Denig W Nauru
191 N10 Deniliquin New South Wales, SE Australia 35.33S 144.58E
31 T14 Denison Iowa, C USA 42.00N 95.22W
27 U5 Denison Texas, SW USA 33.45N 96.32W
142 D15 Denizli Denizli, SW Turkey 37.46N 29.04E
142 D15 Denizli ◈ province SW Turkey
Denjong see Sikkim
191 S7 Denman New South Wales, SE Australia 32.24S 150.43E
205 Y10 Denman Glacier glacier Antarctica
23 R14 Denmark South Carolina, SE USA 33.19N 81.08W
97 G23 Denmark off. Kingdom of Denmark, Dan. Danmark; anc. Hafnia. ◆ monarchy N Europe
94 H1 Denmark Strait var. Danmarksstraedet. strait Greenland/Iceland
47 T11 Dennery E Saint Lucia 13.55N 60.53W
100 I7 Den Oever Noord-Holland, NW Netherlands 52.56N 5.01E
153 O13 Denow Rus. Denau. Surkhondaryo Wiloyati, S Uzbekistan 38.19N 67.48E
175 N16 Denpasar prev. Paloe. Bali, C Indonesia 8.40S 115.13E
118 E12 Denta Timiş, W Romania 45.18N 21.14E
23 Y3 Denton Maryland, NE USA 38.52N 75.49W
27 T6 Denton Texas, SW USA 33.10N 97.08W
195 O15 D'Entrecasteaux Islands island group SE PNG
39 T4 Denver state capital Colorado, C USA 39.44N 105.00W
18 K8 Denver ✈ Colorado, C USA 39.57N 104.38W
26 L6 Denver City Texas, SW USA 32.57N 102.49W
158 J9 Deoband Uttar Pradesh, N India 29.40N 77.40E
Deoghar see Devghar
160 E13 Deolāli Mahārāshtra, W India 19.55N 73.49E
160 I10 Deori Madhya Pradesh, C India 23.09N 78.39E
159 O12 Deoria Uttar Pradesh, N India 26.31N 83.48E
101 A17 De Panne West-Vlaanderen, W Belgium 51.06N 2.34E
56 M5 Dependencia Federal off. Territorio Dependencia Federal. ◈ federal dependency N Venezuela
Dependencia Federal, Territorio see Dependencia Federal
32 M7 De Pere Wisconsin, N USA 44.26N 88.03W
20 D10 Depew New York, NE USA 42.54N 78.41W
101 E17 De Pinte Oost-Vlaanderen, NW Belgium 51.00N 3.37E
27 V5 Deport Texas, SW USA 33.31N 95.19W
126 M7 Deputatskiy Respublika Sakha (Yakutiya), NE Russian Federation 69.18N 139.48E
29 S13 De Queen Arkansas, C USA 34.02N 94.20W
24 G8 De Quincy Louisiana, S USA 30.27N 93.25W
83 J20 Dera spring/well S Kenya 2.39S 39.52E
Der'a/Derá/Déraa see Dar'ā
155 S10 Dera Ghāzi Khān var. Dera Ghāzikhān. Punjab, C Pakistan 30.01N 70.37E
155 S8 Dera Ismāīl Khān North-West Frontier Province, C Pakistan 31.51N 70.55E
115 L16 Đeravica ▲ S Yugoslavia 42.33N 20.08E
118 L6 Derazhnya Khmel'nyts'ka Oblast', W Ukraine 49.16N 27.24E
131 R17 Derbent Respublika Dagestan, SW Russian Federation 42.01N 48.16E
153 N13 Derbent Surkhondaryo Wiloyati, S Uzbekistan 38.15N 66.59E
Derbisiye see Darbāsīyah
81 M15 Derbissaka Mbomou, SE Central African Republic 5.43N 24.48E
188 L4 Derby Western Australia 17.18S 123.36E
99 M19 Derby C England, UK 52.55N 1.30W
29 N7 Derby Kansas, C USA 37.33N 97.16W
99 L18 Derbyshire cultural region C England, UK
114 O11 Đerdap physical region E Yugoslavia
Dereli see Gönoi
176 X11 Derew ↝ Irian Jaya, E Indonesia
131 R8 Dergachi Saratovskaya Oblast', W Russian Federation 51.15N 48.58E
Dergachi see Derhachi
99 C19 Derg, Lough Ir. Loch Deirgeirt. ◎ W Ireland
119 V5 Derhachi Rus. Dergachi. Kharkivs'ka Oblast', E Ukraine 50.08N 36.10E
24 G8 De Ridder Louisiana, S USA 30.51N 93.18W
143 P16 Derik Mardin, SE Turkey 37.22N 40.16E
85 E20 Derm Hardap, C Namibia 23.38S 18.12E
150 M14 Dermentobe prev. Dyurmen'tyube. Kzylorda, S Kazakhstan 45.46N 63.42E
29 W14 Dermott Arkansas, C USA 33.31N 91.26W
Dérna see Darnah
Dernberg, Cape see Dolphin Head
24 J11 Dernieres, Isles island group Louisiana, S USA
Dernis see Drniš
104 I4 Déroute, Passage de la strait Channel Islands/France
Derrá see Dar'ā
Derry see Londonderry
Dertona see Tortona
Dertosa see Tortosa
82 H8 Derudeb Red Sea, NE Sudan 17.28N 36.04E
114 H10 Derventa Republika Srpska, N Bosnia and Herzegovina 44.57N 17.55E
191 O16 Derwent Bridge Tasmania, SE Australia 42.10S 146.13E
191 O17 Derwent, River ↝ Tasmania, SE Australia
Derweze see Darvaza
Deržavinsk see Derzhavinsk
151 O9 Derzhavinsk var. Deržavinsk. Akmola, C Kazakhstan 51.04N 66.19E
Dés see Dej
59 J18 Desaguadero Puno, S Peru 16.31S 69.01W
59 J18 Desaguadero, Río ↝ Bolivia/Peru
203 W9 Désappointement, Îles du island group Îles Tuamotu, C French Polynesia
29 W11 Des Arc Arkansas, C USA 34.58N 91.30W
12 C10 Desbarats Ontario, S Canada 46.20N 83.52W
64 H13 Descabezado Grande, Volcán ▲ C Chile 35.34S 70.40W
42 B2 Descanso Baja California, NW Mexico 32.08N 116.51W
104 L9 Descartes Indre-et-Loire, C France 46.58N 0.40E
9 T13 Deschambault Lake ◎ Saskatchewan, C Canada
Deschnaer Koppe see Velká Deštná
34 I11 Deschutes River ↝ Oregon, NW USA
82 J12 Desē var. Desse, It. Dessie. Amhara, N Ethiopia 11.01N 39.39E
65 J20 Deseado, Río ↝ S Argentina
108 F8 Desenzano del Garda Lombardia, N Italy 45.28N 10.31E
38 K3 Deseret Peak ▲ Utah, W USA 40.27N 112.37W
66 P6 Deserta Grande island Madeira, Portugal, NE Atlantic Ocean
66 P6 Desertas, Ilhas island group Madeira, Portugal, NE Atlantic Ocean
37 X16 Desert Center California, W USA 33.42N 115.22W
37 V15 Desert Hot Springs California, W USA 33.57N 116.33W
12 K10 Désert, Lac ◎ Quebec, SE Canada
38 J2 Desert Peak ▲ Utah, W USA 41.03N 113.22W
33 R11 Deshler Ohio, N USA 41.12N 83.55W
Deshu see Deh Shū
Desiderii Fanum see St-Dizier
108 D7 Desio Lombardia, N Italy 45.37N 9.12E
117 E15 Deskáti var. Dheskáti. Dytikí Makedonía, N Greece 39.55N 21.49E
30 L2 Des Lacs River ↝ North Dakota, N USA
29 X6 Desloge Missouri, C USA 37.52N 90.31W

◆ Country ● Country Capital ◇ Dependent Territory ○ Dependent Territory Capital ◈ Administrative Region ✈ International Airport ▲ Mountain ▲ Mountain Range ☒ Volcano ↝ River ◎ Lake ⊡ Reservoir

Desmarais – Dobruja

9 Q12 **Desmarais** Alberta, W Canada 55.58N 113.55W
31 Q10 **De Smet** South Dakota, N USA 44.23N 97.33W
31 V14 **Des Moines** *state capital* Iowa, C USA 41.36N 93.36W
19 N8 **Des Moines River** ≈ C USA
119 P4 **Desna** ≈ Russian Federation/Ukraine
118 G14 **Desnățui** ≈ S Romania
65 F24 **Desolación, Isla** *island* S Chile
31 V14 **De Soto** Iowa, C USA 41.31N 94.00W
25 Q4 **De Soto Falls** *waterfall* Alabama, S USA 33.22N 86.12W
85 I25 **Despatch** Eastern Cape, S South Africa 33.48S 25.28E
107 N12 **Despeñaperros, Desfiladero de** *pass* S Spain 38.25N 3.26W
33 N10 **Des Plaines** Illinois, N USA 42.01N 87.52W
117 J21 **Despotikó** *island* Kykládes, Greece, Aegean Sea
114 N12 **Despotovac** Serbia, E Yugoslavia 44.06N 21.25E
103 M14 **Dessau** Sachsen-Anhalt, E Germany 51.51N 12.15E
Desse *see* Desē
101 J16 **Dessel** Antwerpen, N Belgium 51.15N 5.07E
Dessie *see* Desē
Destêrro *see* Florianópolis
25 P9 **Destin** Florida, SE USA 30.23N 86.30W
Deštná *see* Velká Deštná
200 Oo11 **Desventurados, Islas de los** *island group* W Chile
105 N1 **Desvres** Pas-de-Calais, N France 50.41N 1.48E
118 E12 **Deta** *Ger.* Detta. Timiș, W Romania 45.22N 21.13E
103 H14 **Detmold** Nordrhein-Westfalen, W Germany 51.55N 8.52E
33 S10 **Detroit** Michigan, N USA 42.19N 83.03W
27 W5 **Detroit** Texas, SW USA 33.39N 95.16W
33 S10 **Detroit** ≈ Canada/USA
31 S6 **Detroit Lakes** Minnesota, N USA 46.49N 95.49W
33 S10 **Detroit Metropolitan** ✈ Michigan, N USA 42.12N 83.16W
Detta *see* Deta
178 J11 **Det Udom** Ubon Ratchathani, E Thailand 14.54N 105.03E
113 K20 **Detva** *Hung.* Gyeva. Banskobystrický Kraj, C Slovakia 48.34N 19.25E
160 G13 **Deūlgaon Rāja** Mahārāshtra, C India 20.04N 76.08E
101 L15 **Deurne** Noord-Brabant, SE Netherlands 51.28N 5.46E
101 H16 **Deurne** ✈ (Antwerpen) Antwerpen, N Belgium 51.10N 4.28E
Deutsch-Brod *see* Havlíčkův Brod
Deutschendorf *see* Poprad
Deutsch-Eylau *see* Iława
111 Y6 **Deutschkreutz** Burgenland, E Austria 47.36N 16.38E
Deutsch Krone *see* Wałcz
Deutschland/Deutschland, Bundesrepublik *see* Germany
111 V9 **Deutschlandsberg** Steiermark, SE Austria 46.52N 15.13E
Deutsch-Südwestafrika *see* Namibia
111 Y3 **Deutsch-Wagram** Niederösterreich, E Austria 48.19N 16.33E
Deux-Ponts *see* Zweibrücken
12 I11 **Deux Rivieres** Ontario, SE Canada 46.13N 78.16W
104 K9 **Deux-Sèvres** ◈ *department* W France
118 G11 **Deva** *Ger.* Diemrich, *Hung.* Déva. Hunedoara, W Romania 45.55N 22.54E
Deva *see* Chester
Devana *see* Aberdeen
Devana Castra *see* Chester
Đevđelija *see* Gevgelija
142 L12 **Deveci Dağları** ▲▲ N Turkey
143 P15 **Devegeçidi Barajı** ⊠ SE Turkey
142 K15 **Develi** Kayseri, C Turkey 38.22N 35.28E
100 M11 **Deventer** Overijssel, E Netherlands 52.15N 6.10E
13 O10 **Devenyns, Lac** ◎ Quebec, SE Canada
98 K8 **Deveron** ≈ NE Scotland, UK
159 R14 **Devghar** *prev.* Deoghar. Bihār, NE India
29 R10 **Devil's Den** *plateau* Arkansas, C USA
37 R7 **Devils Gate** *pass* California, W USA 38.20N 119.23W
32 J2 **Devils Island** *island* Apostle Islands, Wisconsin, N USA
Devil's Island *see* Diable, Île du
31 P3 **Devils Lake** North Dakota, N USA 48.07N 98.49W
33 R10 **Devils Lake** ◎ Michigan, N USA
31 O3 **Devils Lake** ◎ North Dakota, N USA
37 W13 **Devils Playground** *desert* California, W USA
27 O11 **Devils River** ≈ Texas, SW USA
35 Y12 **Devils Tower** ▲ Wyoming, C USA 44.33N 104.45W
116 I11 **Devin** *prev.* Dovlen. Smolyan, SW Bulgaria 41.45N 24.24E
27 R12 **Devine** Texas, SW USA 29.08N 98.54W
158 H13 **Devli** Rājasthān, N India 25.46N 75.22E
Devne *see* Devnya
116 N8 **Devnya** *prev.* Devne. Varna, E Bulgaria 43.13N 27.36E
33 U14 **Devola** Ohio, N USA 39.28N 81.28W
Devoll *see* Devollit, Lumi i
115 M21 **Devollit, Lumi i** *var.* Devoll. ≈ SE Albania
9 Q14 **Devon** Alberta, SW Canada 53.21N 113.47W
99 I23 **Devon** *cultural region* SW England, UK
207 N10 **Devon Island** *prev.* North Devon Island. *island* Parry Islands, Nunavut, NE Canada
191 O16 **Devonport** Tasmania, SE Australia 41.14S 146.20E
142 H11 **Devrek** Zonguldak, N Turkey 41.13N 31.57E
160 G10 **Dewās** Madhya Pradesh, C India 22.58N 76.03E
De Westerein *see* Zwaagwesteinde
29 P8 **Dewey** Oklahoma, C USA 36.48N 95.56W
Dewey *see* Culebra
100 M8 **De Wijk** Drenthe, NE Netherlands 52.41N 6.13E
29 W12 **De Witt** Arkansas, C USA 34.17N 91.20W
31 Z14 **De Witt** Iowa, C USA 41.49N 90.32W
31 R16 **De Witt** Nebraska, C USA 40.23N 96.55W
99 M17 **Dewsbury** N England, UK 53.42N 1.37W
167 Q10 **Dexing** Jiangxi, S China 28.49N 117.37E
29 Y8 **Dexter** Missouri, C USA 36.48N 89.57W
39 U14 **Dexter** New Mexico, SW USA 33.12N 104.25W
166 I8 **Deyang** Sichuan, C China 31.07N 104.22E
190 C4 **Dey-Dey, Lake** *salt lake* South Australia
149 S7 **Deyhūk** Khorāsān, E Iran 33.18N 57.30E
152 K12 **Deynau** *var.* Dyanev, *Turkm.* Dänew. Lebapskiy Velayat, NE Turkmenistan 39.16N 63.09E
148 L8 **Dezfūl** *var.* Dizful. Khūzestān, SW Iran 32.22N 48.28E
133 X4 **Dezhneva, Mys** *headland* NE Russian Federation 66.07N 69.40W
167 P4 **Dezhou** Shandong, E China 37.28N 116.18E
Dezh Shāhpūr *see* Marīvān
Dhahran *see* Aẓ Ẓahrān
Dhahran Al Khobar *see* Aẓ Ẓahrān al Khubar
159 U14 **Dhaka** *prev.* Dacca. ● (Bangladesh) Dhaka, C Bangladesh 23.42N 90.22E
159 T15 **Dhaka** ◈ *division* C Bangladesh
Dhali *see* Idálion
147 O15 **Dhamār** W Yemen 14.31N 44.25E
Dhambul *see* Taraz
160 K12 **Dhamtari** Madhya Pradesh, C India 20.43N 81.36E
159 Q15 **Dhanbād** Bihār, NE India 23.48N 86.27E
158 L10 **Dhangadhi** *var.* Dhangarhi. Far Western, W Nepal 28.45N 80.38E
Dhangarhi *see* Dhangadhi
Dhank *see* Ḍank
159 R12 **Dhankuta** Eastern, E Nepal 27.06N 87.21E
158 I6 **Dhaola Dhār** ▲▲ NE India
160 F10 **Dhār** Madhya Pradesh, C India 22.36N 75.23E
159 R12 **Dharan** *var.* Dharan Bazar. Eastern, E Nepal 26.51N 87.18E
161 H21 **Dhārāpuram** Tamil Nādu, SE India 10.45N 77.33E
161 H20 **Dharmapuri** Tamil Nādu, SE India 12.10N 78.07E
161 H18 **Dharmavaram** Andhra Pradesh, E India 14.27N 77.43E
160 M11 **Dharmjaygarh** Madhya Pradesh, C India 22.27N 83.16E
Dharmsāla *see* Dharmshāla
158 I7 **Dharmshāla** *prev.* Dharmsāla. Himāchal Pradesh, N India 32.13N 76.24E
161 F17 **Dhārwād** *prev.* Dharwar. Karnātaka, SW India 15.30N 75.04E
Dharwar *see* Dhārwād
159 O10 **Dhaulāgiri** ▲ C Nepal 28.45N 83.27E
83 L18 **Dheere Laaq** *var.* Lak Dera, *It.* Lach Dera. *seasonal river* Kenya/Somalia
124 O3 **Dhekéleia Sovereign Base Area** *UK military installation* E Cyprus 34.59N 33.45E
124 O3 **Dhekélia** *Eng.* Dhekelia. *Gk.* Dekéleia. *UK air base* SE Cyprus 35.00N 33.45E
Dhelvinákion *see* Delvináki
115 M22 **Dhëmbelit, Majae** ▲ S Albania 40.10N 20.22E
160 O12 **Dhenkānāl** Orissa, E India 20.40N 85.36E
Dheskáti *see* Deskáti
144 G11 **Dhībān** ʻAmmān, NW Jordan 31.30N 35.46E
Dhidhimótikhon *see* Didymóteicho
Dhíkti Ori *see* Díkti
144 I12 **Dhirwah, Wādī adh** *dry watercourse* C Jordan
Dhístomon *see* Dístomo
Dhodhekánisos *see* Dodekánisos
Dhodhóni *see* Dodóni
Dhofar *see* Ẓufār
Dhomokós *see* Domokós
Dhond *see* Daund
161 H17 **Dhone** Andhra Pradesh, C India 15.25N 77.52E
160 B11 **Dhorāji** Gujarāt, W India 21.43N 70.27E
Dhráma *see* Dráma
160 C10 **Dhrāngadhra** Gujarāt, W India 22.58N 71.31E
Dhrepanon, Akrotírio *see* Drépano, Akrotírio
159 T13 **Dhuburi** Assam, NE India 26.06N 89.55E
160 F12 **Dhule** *prev.* Dhulia. Mahārāshtra, C India 20.54N 74.46E
Dhulia *see* Dhule
Dhún Dealgan, Cuan *see* Dundalk Bay
Dhún Droma, Cuan *see* Dundrum Bay
Dhún na nGall, Bá *see* Donegal Bay
Dhū Shaykh *see* Qazānīyah
82 Q13 **Dhuudo** Bari, NE Somalia 9.21N 50.19E
83 N15 **Dhuusa Marreeb** *var.* Dusa Marreb, *It.* Dusa Mareb. Galguduud, C Somalia 5.33N 46.24E
117 J24 **Día** *island* SE Greece
57 Y9 **Diable, Île du** *var.* Devil's Island. *island* N French Guiana
13 N12 **Diable, Rivière du** ≈ Quebec, SE Canada
37 N8 **Diablo, Mount** ▲ California, W USA 37.52N 121.57W
37 O9 **Diablo Range** ▲▲ California, W USA
26 I8 **Diablo, Sierra** ▲▲ Texas, SW USA
47 O11 **Diablotins, Morne** ▲ N Dominica 15.30N 61.23W
79 N11 **Diafarabé** Mopti, C Mali 14.12N 5.01W
79 N11 **Diaka** ≈ SW Mali
Diakovár *see* Đakovo
78 I12 **Dialakoto** S Senegal 13.21N 13.19W
63 B18 **Diamante** Entre Ríos, E Argentina 32.04S 60.40W
64 I12 **Diamante, Río** ≈ C Argentina
61 M19 **Diamantina** Minas Gerais, SE Brazil 18.16S 43.37W
61 N17 **Diamantina, Chapada** ▲▲ E Brazil
181 U11 **Diamantina Fracture Zone** *tectonic feature* E Indian Ocean
189 T8 **Diamantina River** ≈ Queensland/South Australia
40 D9 **Diamond Head** *headland* Oahu, Hawaii, USA, C Pacific Ocean 21.15N 157.48W
39 P2 **Diamond Peak** ▲ Colorado, C USA 40.56N 108.56W
37 W5 **Diamond Peak** ▲ Nevada, W USA 39.34N 115.46W
Diamond State *see* Delaware
78 J11 **Diamou** Kayes, SW Mali 14.04N 11.16W
97 I23 **Dianalund** Vestsjælland, C Denmark 55.31N 11.30E
67 G25 **Diana's Peak** ▲ C Saint Helena
166 M16 **Dianbai** Guangdong, S China 21.33N 110.58E
166 G13 **Dian Chi** ⊠ SW China
108 B10 **Diano Marina** Liguria, NW Italy 43.55N 8.06E
79 R13 **Diapaga** E Burkina 12.04N 1.47E
Diarbekr *see* Diyarbakır
109 J15 **Diavolo, Passo del** *pass* C Italy 41.55N 13.42E
63 B18 **Díaz** Santa Fe, C Argentina 32.22S 61.04W
147 W6 **Dibā al Ḩiṣn** *var.* Dibāh, Dibba. Ash Shāriqah, NE UAE 25.34N 56.16E
145 S3 **Dībaga** N Iraq 35.51N 43.49E
Dibāh *see* Dibā al Ḩiṣn
81 L22 **Dibaya** Kasai Occidental, S Dem. Rep. Congo (Zaire) 6.31S 22.57E
Dibba *see* Dibā al Ḩiṣn
205 W15 **Dibble Iceberg Tongue** *ice feature* Antarctica
115 L19 **Dibër** ◈ *district* E Albania
85 I20 **Dibete** Central, SE Botswana 23.45S 26.29E
27 W9 **Diboll** Texas, SW USA 31.11N 94.46W
Dibra *see* Debar
159 X11 **Dibrugarh** Assam, NE India 27.29N 94.49E
56 G4 **Dibulla** La Guajira, N Colombia 11.14N 73.22W
27 O5 **Dickens** Texas, SW USA 33.37N 100.50W
21 R2 **Dickey** Maine, NE USA 47.04N 69.05W
32 K9 **Dickeyville** Wisconsin, N USA 42.37N 90.36W
30 K5 **Dickinson** North Dakota, N USA 46.54N 102.48W
(0) E6 **Dickins Seamount** *undersea feature* NE Pacific Ocean
29 O13 **Dickson** Oklahoma, C USA 34.11N 96.58W
22 I9 **Dickson** Tennessee, S USA 36.04N 87.23W
Dicle *see* Tigris
Dicsőszentmárton *see* Târnăveni
100 M12 **Didam** Gelderland, E Netherlands 51.55N 6.07E
169 Y8 **Didao** Heilongjiang, NE China 45.20N 130.54E
78 L12 **Didiéni** Koulikoro, W Mali 13.48N 8.01W
Didimo *see* Dídymo
Didimotiho *see* Didymóteicho
83 K17 **Didimtu** *spring/well* NE Kenya 2.58N 40.07E
69 U9 **Didinga Hills** ▲▲ S Sudan
9 Q16 **Didsbury** Alberta, SW Canada 51.39N 114.09W
158 G11 **Dīdwāna** Rājasthān, N India 27.22N 74.36E
117 G20 **Dídymo** *var.* Didimo. ▲ S Greece 37.28N 23.12E
116 L12 **Didymóteicho** *var.* Dhidhimótikhon, Didimotiho. Anatolikí Makedonía kai Thráki, NE Greece 41.22N 26.28E
105 S13 **Die** Drôme, E France 44.46N 5.21E
79 O13 **Diébougou** SW Burkina 11.00N 3.12W
Diedenhofen *see* Thionville
9 S16 **Diefenbaker, Lake** ⊠ Saskatchewan, S Canada
64 H7 **Diego de Almagro** Atacama, N Chile 26.24S 70.10W
65 F23 **Diego de Almagro, Isla** *island* S Chile
63 A20 **Diego de Alvear** Santa Fe, C Argentina 34.24S 62.04W
181 Q7 **Diego Garcia** *island* S British Indian Ocean Territory
Diégo-Suarez *see* Antsirañana
101 M23 **Diekirch** Diekirch, C Luxembourg 49.52N 6.10E
101 L23 **Diekirch** ◈ *district* N Luxembourg
78 K11 **Diéma** Kayes, W Mali 14.28N 9.10W
103 H15 **Diemel** ≈ W Germany
100 I10 **Diemen** Noord-Holland, C Netherlands 52.21N 4.58E
Diemrich *see* Deva
178 Ii6 **Điên Biên** *var.* Bien Bien, Dien Bien Phu. Lai Châu, N Vietnam 21.22N 103.01E
Dien Bien Phu *see* Điên Biên
178 Jj8 **Diên Châu** Nghê An, N Vietnam 18.54N 105.35E
101 K18 **Diepenbeek** Limburg, NE Belgium 50.54N 5.25E
100 N11 **Diepenheim** Overijssel, E Netherlands 52.10N 6.37E
100 M10 **Diepenveen** Overijssel, E Netherlands 52.18N 6.09E
102 G12 **Diepholz** Niedersachsen, NW Germany 52.36N 8.22E
104 M3 **Dieppe** Seine-Maritime, N France 49.55N 1.04E
100 M12 **Dieren** Gelderland, E Netherlands 52.03N 6.06E
29 S13 **Dierks** Arkansas, C USA 34.07N 94.01W
101 J17 **Diest** Vlaams Brabant, C Belgium 50.58N 5.03E
110 F7 **Dietikon** Zürich, NW Switzerland 47.24N 8.25E
105 R13 **Dieulefit** Drôme, E France 44.30N 5.01E
105 T5 **Dieuze** Moselle, NE France 48.49N 6.41E
121 H15 **Dieveniškės** Šalčininkai, SE Lithuania 54.12N 25.38E
100 N7 **Diever** Drenthe, NE Netherlands 52.49N 6.19E
103 F17 **Diez** Rheinland-Pfalz, W Germany 50.22N 8.01E
79 Y12 **Diffa** Diffa, SE Niger 13.20N 12.39E
79 Y10 **Diffa** ◈ *department* SE Niger
101 L25 **Differdange** Luxembourg, SW Luxembourg 49.31N 5.52E
11 O16 **Digby** Nova Scotia, SE Canada 44.37N 65.46W
28 J5 **Dighton** Kansas, C USA 38.28N 100.28W
Dignano d'Istria *see* Vodnjan
105 T14 **Digne** *var.* Digne-les-Bains. Alpes-de-Haute-Provence, SE France 44.04N 6.13E
Digne-les-Bains *see* Digne
Digoel *see* Digul, Sungai
105 Q10 **Digoin** Saône-et-Loire, C France 46.30N 3.59E
179 Rr16 **Digos** Mindanao, S Philippines 6.46N 125.21E
155 Q16 **Digri** Sind, SE Pakistan 25.10N 69.10E
176 Z13 **Digul Barat, Sungai** ≈ Irian Jaya, E Indonesia
176 Z14 **Digul, Sungai** *prev.* Digoel. ≈ Irian Jaya, E Indonesia
176 Z13 **Digul Timur, Sungai** ≈ Irian Jaya, E Indonesia
Dihang *see* Brahmaputra
159 X10 **Dihāng** ≈ NE India
Dihōk *see* Dahūk
83 L17 **Diinsoor** Bay, S Somalia 2.28N 43.00E
Dijlah *see* Tigris
101 H17 **Dijle** ≈ C Belgium
105 R8 **Dijon** *anc.* Dibio. Côte d'Or, C France 47.21N 5.03E
95 H14 **Dikanäs** Västerbotten, N Sweden 65.15N 16.00E
82 L12 **Dikhil** SW Djibouti 11.07N 42.18E
142 B13 **Dikili** İzmir, W Turkey 39.04N 26.52E
101 B17 **Diksmuide** *var.* Dixmuide, *Fr.* Dixmude. West-Vlaanderen, W Belgium 51.01N 2.52E
126 Hh6 **Dikson** Taymyrskiy (Dolgano-Nenetskiy) Avtonomnyy Okrug, N Russian Federation 73.30N 80.35E
117 K25 **Díkti** *var.* Dhíkti Ori. ▲▲ Kríti, Greece, E Mediterranean Sea
79 Z13 **Dikwa** Borno, NE Nigeria 12.00N 13.57E
83 J15 **Dīla** Southern, S Ethiopia 6.19N 38.16E
101 G18 **Dilbeek** Vlaams Brabant, C Belgium 50.51N 4.16E
175 S16 **Dili** *var.* Dilli, Dilly. ○ (East Timor) N East Timor 8.33S 125.34E
79 Y11 **Dilia** *var.* Dillia. ≈ SE Niger
Dilijan *see* Delījān
178 K13 **Di Linh** Lâm Đông, S Vietnam 11.34N 108.04E
103 G16 **Dillenburg** Hessen, W Germany 50.45N 8.16E
27 Q13 **Dilley** Texas, SW USA 28.40N 99.10W
Dilli *see* Delhi, India
Dilli *see* Dili, East Timor
Dillia *see* Dilia
82 E11 **Dilling** *var.* Ad Dalanj. Southern Kordofan, C Sudan 12.01N 29.40E
103 D20 **Dillingen** Saarland, SW Germany 49.20N 6.43E
Dillingen *see* Dillingen an der Donau
103 J22 **Dillingen an der Donau** *var.* Dillingen. Bayern, S Germany 48.34N 10.29E
41 O13 **Dillingham** Alaska, USA 59.03N 158.30W
35 Q12 **Dillon** Montana, NW USA 45.13N 112.37W
23 T12 **Dillon** South Carolina, SE USA 34.25N 79.22W
33 T13 **Dillon Lake** ⊠ Ohio, N USA
Dilly *see* Dili
Dilman *see* Salmās
81 K24 **Dilolo** Katanga, S Dem. Rep. Congo (Zaire) 10.42S 22.21E
117 J20 **Dílos** *island* Kykládes, Greece, Aegean Sea
147 Y11 **Ḑil', Ra's aḑ** *headland* E Oman 19.12N 57.53E
31 R5 **Dilworth** Minnesota, N USA 46.53N 96.38W
144 H7 **Dimashq** *var.* Ash Shām, Esh Sham, *Eng.* Damascus, *Fr.* Damas, *It.* Damasco. ● (Syria) Dimashq, SW Syria 33.30N 36.19E
144 I8 **Dimashq** *off.* Muḩāfaẓat Dimashq, *var.* Damascus, *Ar.* Ash Sham, Ash Shām, Damasco, Esh Sham, *Fr.* Damas. ◈ *governorate* S Syria
144 I7 **Dimashq** ✈ Dimashq, S Syria 33.30N 36.19E
81 L21 **Dimbelenge** Kasai Occidental, C Dem. Rep. Congo (Zaire) 5.36S 23.04E
79 N16 **Dimbokro** E Ivory Coast 6.39N 4.43W
190 L11 **Dimboola** Victoria, SE Australia 36.29S 142.03E
Dîmbovița *see* Dâmbovița
Dimitrov *see* Dymytrov
116 K11 **Dimitrovgrad** Khaskovo, S Bulgaria 42.03N 25.36E
131 R5 **Dimitrovgrad** Ul'yanovskaya Oblast', W Russian Federation 54.14N 49.37E
115 Q15 **Dimitrovgrad** *prev.* Caribrod. Serbia, SE Yugoslavia 43.01N 22.46E
Dimitrovo *see* Pernik
Dimlang *see* Vogel Peak
26 M3 **Dimmitt** Texas, SW USA 34.33N 102.18W
116 F7 **Dimovo** Vidin, NW Bulgaria 43.46N 22.46E
61 A16 **Dimpolis** Acre, W Brazil 9.52S 71.51W
117 O23 **Dimyliá** Ródos, Dodekánisos, Greece, Aegean Sea 36.17N 27.59E
179 R13 **Dinagat** Dinagat Island, S Philippines 10.00N 125.36E
179 Rr13 **Dinagat Island** *island* S Philippines
159 S13 **Dinajpur** Rajshahi, NW Bangladesh 25.37N 88.39E
104 I6 **Dinan** Côtes d'Armor, NW France 48.27N 2.01W
101 I21 **Dinant** Namur, S Belgium 50.16N 4.55E
142 E15 **Dinar** Afyon, SW Turkey 38.04N 30.09E
114 F13 **Dinara** ▲ W Croatia 43.49N 16.42E
Dinara *see* Dinaric Alps
104 I5 **Dinard** Ille-et-Vilaine, NW France 48.38N 2.04W
114 F13 **Dinaric Alps** *var.* Dinara. ▲▲ Bosnia and Herzegovina/Croatia
149 N10 **Dīnār, Kūh-e** ▲ C Iran 30.51N 51.36E
Dinbych *see* Denbigh
161 H22 **Dindigul** Tamil Nādu, SE India 10.23N 78.00E
85 M19 **Dindiza** Gaza, S Mozambique 23.22S 33.28E
155 V7 **Dinga** Punjab, E Pakistan 32.37N 73.45E
81 H21 **Dinga** Bandundu, SW Dem. Rep. Congo (Zaire) 5.00S 16.29E
164 L16 **Dinggyê** Xizang Zizhiqu, W China 28.18N 88.06E
99 A20 **Dingle** *Ir.* An Daingean. SW Ireland 52.08N 10.16W
99 A20 **Dingle Bay** *Ir.* Bá an Daingin. *bay* SW Ireland
20 I13 **Dingmans Ferry** Pennsylvania, NE USA 41.12N 74.51W
103 N22 **Dingofling** Bayern, SE Germany 48.37N 12.28E
179 P8 **Dingras** Luzon, N Philippines 18.06N 120.43E
78 J13 **Dinguiraye** Haute-Guinée, N Guinea 11.19N 10.49W
98 I8 **Dingwall** N Scotland, UK 57.36N 4.25W
165 V10 **Dingxi** Gansu, C China 35.36N 104.33E
167 Q7 **Dingyuan** Anhui, E China 32.30N 117.40E
167 O3 **Dingzhou** *prev.* Ding Xian. Hebei, E China 38.31N 114.52E
178 K6 **Đinh Lâp** Lang Sơn, N Vietnam 21.33N 107.03E
178 K14 **Đinh Quan** Đông Nai, S Vietnam 11.11N 107.20E
102 E13 **Dinkel** ≈ Germany/Netherlands
103 J21 **Dinkelsbühl** Bayern, S Germany 49.06N 10.18E
103 D14 **Dinslaken** Nordrhein-Westfalen, W Germany 51.34N 6.43E
37 R11 **Dinuba** California, W USA 36.32N 119.23W
23 W7 **Dinwiddie** Virginia, NE USA 37.04N 77.34W
100 N13 **Dinxperlo** Gelderland, E Netherlands 51.51N 6.30E
117 F14 **Dió** *anc.* Dium. *site of ancient city* Kentrikí Makedonía, N Greece 40.13N 22.30E
Diófás *see* Nucet
78 M12 **Dioïla** Koulikoro, W Mali 12.28N 6.43W
117 G19 **Dióryga Korinthou** *Eng.* Corinth Canal. *canal* S Greece
78 G12 **Diouloulou** SW Senegal 13.00N 16.34W
79 N11 **Dioura** Mopti, W Mali 14.48N 5.20W
78 G11 **Diourbel** W Senegal 14.38N 16.12W
158 L10 **Dipayal** Far Western, W Nepal 29.09N 80.46E
124 Oo2 **Dipkarpaz** *Gk.* Rizokarpaso, Rizokárpason. NE Cyprus 35.36N 34.23E
155 R17 **Diplo** Sind, SE Pakistan 24.29N 69.36E
179 Qq15 **Dipolog** *var.* Dipolog City. Mindanao, S Philippines 8.31N 123.20E
193 C23 **Dipton** Southland, South Island, NZ 45.55S 168.21E
79 O10 **Diré** Tombouctou, C Mali 16.12N 3.31W
82 L13 **Dirē Dawa** Dirē Dawa, E Ethiopia 9.34N 41.53E
Dirfis *see* Dírfys
117 H18 **Dírfys** *var.* Dirfis. ▲▲ Évvioa, C Greece
77 N9 **Dirj** *var.* Daraj, Darj. W Libya 30.09N 10.25E
188 G10 **Dirk Hartog Island** *island* Western Australia
79 Y8 **Dirkou** Agadez, NE Niger 18.45N 13.00E
189 X11 **Dirranbandi** Queensland, E Australia 28.37S 148.13E
83 O16 **Dirri** Galguduud, C Somalia 4.15N 46.31E
Dirschau *see* Tczew
39 N6 **Dirty Devil River** ≈ Utah, W USA
34 E10 **Disappointment, Cape** *headland* Washington, NW USA 46.16N 124.06W
188 L8 **Disappointment, Lake** *salt lake* Western Australia
191 R12 **Disaster Bay** *bay* New South Wales, SE Australia
46 J11 **Discovery Bay** C Jamaica 18.27N 77.23W
190 K13 **Discovery Bay** *inlet* SE Australia
69 Y15 **Discovery II Fracture Zone** *tectonic feature* SW Indian Ocean
Discovery Seamount/Discovery Seamounts *see* Discovery Tablemount
67 O19 **Discovery Tablemount** *var.* Discovery Seamount, Discovery Seamounts. *undersea feature* SW Indian Ocean 42.00S 0.10E
110 G9 **Disentis** *Rmsch.* Mustér. Graubünden, S Switzerland 46.43N 8.52E
41 O10 **Dishna River** ≈ Alaska, USA
205 X4 **Dismal Mountains** ▲▲ Antarctica
30 M14 **Dismal River** ≈ Nebraska, C USA
Disna *see* Dzisna
101 L19 **Dison** Liège, E Belgium 50.37N 5.52E
159 V12 **Dispur** Assam, NE India 26.03N 91.52E
13 R11 **Disraeli** Quebec, SE Canada 45.58N 71.21W
117 F18 **Dístomo** *prev.* Dhístomon. Stereá Ellás, C Greece 38.25N 22.40E
117 H18 **Dístos, Límni** ◎ Évvoia, C Greece
61 L18 **Distrito Federal** *Eng.* Federal District. ◈ *federal district* C Brazil
43 P14 **Distrito Federal** ◈ *federal district* S Mexico
56 L4 **Distrito Federal** *off.* Territorio Distrito Federal. ◈ *federal district* N Venezuela
Distrito Federal, Territorio *see* Distrito Federal
118 J10 **Ditrău** *Hung.* Ditró. Harghita, C Romania 46.47N 25.30E
Ditró *see* Ditrău
160 B12 **Diu** Damān and Diu, W India 20.42N 70.58E
179 Rr14 **Diuata Mountains** ▲▲ Mindanao, S Philippines
Dium *see* Dió
111 S13 **Divača** SW Slovenia 45.40N 13.58E
104 K5 **Dives** ≈ N France
Divichi *see* Däväçi
35 Q11 **Divide** Montana, NW USA 45.44N 112.47W
Divin *see* Dzivin
85 N18 **Divinhe** Sofala, E Mozambique 20.41S 34.46E
61 L20 **Divinópolis** Minas Gerais, SE Brazil 20.07S 44.55W
126 I14 **Divnogorsk** Krasnoyarskiy Kray, S Russian Federation 55.53N 92.15E
131 N13 **Divnoye** Stavropol'skiy Kray, SW Russian Federation 45.54N 43.18E
78 M17 **Divo** S Ivory Coast 5.49N 5.22W
Divodurum Mediomatricum *see* Metz
143 N13 **Divriği** Sivas, C Turkey 39.22N 38.06E
Diwaniyah *see* Ad Dīwānīyah
12 J10 **Dix Milles, Lac** ◎ Quebec, SE Canada
12 M8 **Dix Milles, Lac des** ◎ Quebec, SE Canada
Dixmude/Dixmuide *see* Diksmuide
37 N7 **Dixon** California, W USA 38.19N 121.49W
32 L10 **Dixon** Illinois, N USA 41.51N 89.26W
22 I6 **Dixon** Kentucky, S USA 37.30N 87.39W
29 V6 **Dixon** Missouri, C USA 37.59N 92.05W
39 S9 **Dixon** New Mexico, SW USA 36.10N 105.49W
41 Y15 **Dixon Entrance** *strait* Canada/USA
20 D14 **Dixonville** Pennsylvania, NE USA 40.43N 79.01W
143 T13 **Diyadin** Ağrı, E Turkey 39.33N 43.40E
145 V5 **Diyālá, Nahr** *var.* Rudkhaneh-ye Sīrvān, Sirwan. ≈ Iran/Iraq *see also* Sīrvān, Rudkhaneh-ye
143 P15 **Diyarbakır** *var.* Diarbekr; *anc.* Amida. Dıyarbakır, SE Turkey 37.55N 40.13E
143 P15 **Diyarbakır** *var.* Diarbekr. ◈ *province* SE Turkey
Dizful *see* Dezfūl
81 F16 **Dja** ≈ SE Cameroon
Djadié *see* Zadié
79 X7 **Djado** Agadez, NE Niger 21.00N 12.11E
79 X6 **Djado, Plateau du** ▲▲ NE Niger
Djailolo *see* Halmahera, Pulau
Djajapura *see* Jayapura
Djakarta *see* Jakarta
Djakovica *see* Đakovica
Djakovo *see* Đakovo
81 G20 **Djambala** Plateaux, C Congo 2.31S 14.43E
Djambi *see* Jambi
Djambi *see* Hari, Batang, Sumatera, W Indonesia
76 M9 **Djanet** E Algeria 28.43N 8.57E
76 M11 **Djanet** *prev.* Fort Charlet. SE Algeria 24.34N 9.33E
Djatiwangi *see* Jatiwangi
Djaul *see* Dyaul Island
Djawa *see* Jawa
Djéblé *see* Jablah
80 I10 **Djédaa** Batha, C Chad 13.31N 18.34E
76 J6 **Djelfa** *var.* El Djelfa. N Algeria 34.42N 3.16E
81 M14 **Djéma** Haut-Mbomou, E Central African Republic 6.03N 25.19E
Djeneponto *see* Jeneponto
79 N12 **Djenné** *var.* Jenné. Mopti, C Mali 13.55N 4.34W
Djérablous *see* Jarābulus
Djerba *see* Jerba, Île de
81 F15 **Djérem** ≈ C Cameroon
Djevdjelija *see* Gevgelija
79 P11 **Djibo** N Burkina 14.09N 1.37W
82 L12 **Djibouti** *var.* Jibuti. ● (Djibouti) E Djibouti 11.32N 42.55E
82 L12 **Djibouti** *off.* Republic of Djibouti, *var.* Jibuti; *prev.* French Somaliland, French Territory of the Afars and Issas, *Fr.* Côte Française des Somalis, Territoire Français des Afars et des Issas. ◆ *republic* E Africa
82 L12 **Djibouti** ✈ C Djibouti 11.29N 42.54E
Djidjel/Djidjelli *see* Jijel
57 W10 **Djoemoe** Sipaliwini, C Surinam 4.00N 55.27W
Djokjakarta *see* Yogyakarta
81 K21 **Djoku-Punda** Kasai Occidental, S Dem. Rep. Congo (Zaire) 5.27S 20.58E
81 K18 **Djolu** Equateur, N Dem. Rep. Congo (Zaire) 0.42N 22.23E
Djorče Petrov *see* Đorče Petrov
81 F17 **Djoua** ≈ Congo/Gabon
79 R14 **Djougou** W Benin 9.42N 1.38E
81 F16 **Djoum** Sud, S Cameroon 2.38N 12.51E
80 I8 **Djourab, Erg du** *dunes* N Chad
81 P17 **Djugu** Orientale, NE Dem. Rep. Congo (Zaire) 1.55N 30.31E
Djumbir *see* Ďumbier
94 L3 **Djúpivogur** Austurland, SE Iceland 64.39N 14.18W
96 L13 **Djura** Dalarna, C Sweden 60.37N 15.00E
Djurdjevac *see* Đurđevac
85 G18 **D'Kar** Ghanzi, NW Botswana 21.31S 21.55E
207 U6 **Dmitriya Lapteva, Proliv** *strait* N Russian Federation
130 J7 **Dmitriyev-L'govskiy** Kurskaya Oblast', W Russian Federation 52.08N 35.09E
Dmitriyevsk *see* Makiyivka
130 K3 **Dmitrov** Moskovskaya Oblast', W Russian Federation 56.23N 37.30E
Dmitrovichi *see* Dzmitravichy
130 J6 **Dmitrovsk-Orlovskiy** Orlovskaya Oblast', W Russian Federation 52.28N 35.01E
119 R3 **Dmytrivka** Chernihivs'ka Oblast', N Ukraine 50.56N 32.57E
Dnepr *see* Dnieper
Dneprodzerzhinsk *see* Dniprodzerzhyns'k
Dneprodzerzhinskoye Vodokhranilishche *see* Dniprodzerzhyns'ke Vodoskhovyshche
Dnepropetrovsk *see* Dnipropetrovs'k
Dnepropetrovskaya Oblast' *see* Dnipropetrovs'ka Oblast'
Dneprorudnoye *see* Dniprorudne
Dneprovskiy Liman *see* Dniprovs'kyy Lyman
Dneprovsko-Bugskiy Kanal *see* Dnyaprowska-Buhski, Kanal
Dnestr *see* Dniester
Dnestrovskiy Liman *see* Dnistrovs'kyy Lyman
88 H11 **Dnieper** *Bel.* Dnyapro, *Rus.* Dnepr, *Ukr.* Dnipro. ≈ E Europe
119 P3 **Dnieper Lowland** *Bel.* Prydnyaprowskaya Nizina, *Ukr.* Prydniprovs'ka Nyzovyna. *lowlands* Belarus/Ukraine
118 M8 **Dniester** *Rom.* Nistru, *Rus.* Dnestr, *Ukr.* Dnister; *anc.* Tyras. ≈ Moldova/Ukraine
Dnipro *see* Dnieper
119 T7 **Dniprodzerzhyns'k** *Rus.* Dneprodzerzhinsk; *prev.* Kamenskoye. Dnipropetrovs'ka Oblast', E Ukraine 48.30N 34.35E
119 T7 **Dniprodzerzhyns'ke Vodoskhovyshche** *Rus.* Dneprodzerzhinskoye Vodokhranilishche. ⊠ C Ukraine
119 U7 **Dnipropetrovs'k** *Rus.* Dnepropetrovsk; *prev.* Yekaterinoslav. Dnipropetrovs'ka Oblast', E Ukraine 48.28N 34.59E
119 U8 **Dnipropetrovs'k** ✈ Dnipropetrovs'ka Oblast', S Ukraine 48.20N 35.04E
Dnipropetrovs'k *see* Dnipropetrovs'ka Oblast'
119 T7 **Dnipropetrovs'ka Oblast'** *var.* Dnipropetrovs'k, *Rus.* Dnepropetrovskaya Oblast'. ◈ *province* E Ukraine
119 U9 **Dniprorudne** *Rus.* Dneprorudnoye. Zaporiz'ka Oblast', SE Ukraine 47.21N 35.00E
119 Q11 **Dniprovs'kyy Lyman** *Rus.* Dneprovskiy Liman. *bay* S Ukraine
Dnister *see* Dniester
119 O11 **Dnistrovs'kyy Lyman** *Rus.* Dnestrovskiy Liman. *inlet* S Ukraine
128 G14 **Dno** Pskovskaya Oblast', W Russian Federation 57.48N 29.58E
Dnyapro *see* Dnieper
121 H20 **Dnyaprowska-Buhski, Kanal** *Rus.* Dneprovsko-Bugskiy Kanal. *canal* SW Belarus
11 O14 **Doaktown** New Brunswick, SE Canada 46.34N 66.06W
80 H13 **Doba** Logone-Oriental, S Chad 8.40N 16.49E
120 E9 **Dobele** *Ger.* Doblen. Dobele, W Latvia 56.36N 23.14E
103 N16 **Döbeln** Sachsen, E Germany 51.07N 13.07E
176 Vv9 **Doberai, Jazirah** *Dut.* Vogelkop. *peninsula* Irian Jaya, E Indonesia
112 F10 **Dobiegniew** *Ger.* Lubuskie, W Poland 52.58N 15.43E
Doblen *see* Dobele
83 K18 **Dobli** *spring/well* SW Somalia 0.24N 41.18E
176 W13 **Dobo** Pulau Wamar, E Indonesia 5.45S 134.12E
114 H11 **Doboj** Republika Srpska, N Bosnia and Herzegovina 44.45N 18.03E
112 L8 **Dobre Miasto** *Ger.* Guttstadt. Warmińsko-Mazurskie, NE Poland 53.59N 20.25E
116 N7 **Dobrich** *Rom.* Bazargic; *prev.* Tolbukhin. Dobrich, NE Bulgaria 43.34N 27.49E
116 N7 **Dobrich** ◈ *province* NE Bulgaria
130 M8 **Dobrinka** Lipetskaya Oblast', W Russian Federation 52.10N 40.30E
130 M7 **Dobrinka** Volgogradskaya Oblast', SW Russian Federation 50.52N 41.48E
Dobrla Vas *see* Eberndorf
113 I15 **Dobrodzień** *Ger.* Guttentag. Opolskie, S Poland 50.43N 18.24E
Dobrogea *see* Dobruja
119 W7 **Dobropillya** *Rus.* Dobropol'ye. Donets'ka Oblast', SE Ukraine 48.29N 37.06E
Dobropol'ye *see* Dobropillya
119 P8 **Dobrovelychkivka** Kirovohrads'ka Oblast', C Ukraine 48.22N 31.12E
Dobrudja/Dobrudzha *see* Dobruja
116 O7 **Dobruja** *var.* Dobrudja, *Bul.* Dobrudzha, *Rom.* Dobrogea. *physical region* Bulgaria/Romania

◆ Country ● Country Capital ◇ Dependent Territory ○ Dependent Territory Capital ◈ Administrative Region ✈ International Airport ▲ Mountain ▲▲ Mountain Range Volcano ≈ River ◎ Lake ⊠ Reservoir
249

DOBRUSH – DUBAYY

121 P19 **Dobrush** Homyel'skaya Voblasts', SE Belarus *52.25N 31.21E*
129 U14 **Dobryanka** Permskaya Oblast', NW Russian Federation *58.28N 56.27E*
119 P2 **Dobryanka** Chernihivs'ka Oblast', N Ukraine *52.03N 31.09E*
Dobryn' *see* Dabryn'
23 R8 **Dobson** North Carolina, SE USA *36.30N 80.54W*
61 N20 **Doce, Rio** SE Brazil
95 I16 **Docksta** Västernorrland, C Sweden *63.06N 18.22E*
43 N10 **Doctor Arroyo** Nuevo León, NE Mexico *23.40N 100.09W*
64 L4 **Doctor Pedro P. Peña** Boquerón, W Paraguay *22.22S 62.22W*
175 T7 **Dodaga** Pulau Halmahera, E Indonesia *1.06N 128.10E*
161 G21 **Dodda Betta** ▲ S India *11.28N 76.44E*
Dodecanese *see* Dodekánisos
117 M22 **Dodekánisos** *var.* Nóties Sporádes, *Eng.* Dodecanese; *prev.* Dhodhekánisos. *island group* SE Greece
28 J6 **Dodge City** Kansas, C USA *37.45N 100.01W*
32 K9 **Dodgeville** Wisconsin, N USA *42.57N 90.07W*
99 H25 **Dodman Point** *headland* SW England, UK *50.13N 4.47W*
83 J14 **Dodola** Oromo, C Ethiopia *7.00N 39.15E*
83 H22 **Dodoma** ● (Tanzania) Dodoma, C Tanzania *6.10S 35.45E*
83 H22 **Dodoma** ◐ *region* C Tanzania
117 C16 **Dodóni** *var.* Dhodhóni. *site of ancient city* Ípeiros, W Greece *39.33N 20.47E*
35 U7 **Dodson** Montana, NW USA *48.25N 108.18W*
27 P3 **Dodson** Texas, SW USA *34.46N 100.01W*
100 M12 **Doesburg** Gelderland, E Netherlands *52.01N 6.07E*
100 N12 **Doetinchem** Gelderland, E Netherlands *51.58N 6.16E*
164 L12 **Dogai Coring** *var.* Lake Montcalm. ◎ W China
143 N15 **Doğanşehir** Malatya, C Turkey *38.06N 37.52E*
86 E9 **Dogger Bank** *undersea feature* C North Sea
25 S10 **Dog Island** *island* Florida, SE USA
12 C7 **Dog Lake** ◎ Ontario, S Canada
108 B9 **Dogliani** Piemonte, NE Italy *44.33N 7.55E*
170 G11 **Dōgo** *island* Oki-shotō, SW Japan
Do Gonbadān *see* Dow Gonbadān
79 S12 **Dogondoutchi** Dosso, SW Niger *13.37N 4.03E*
Dōgo-san *see* Dōgo-yama
170 F13 **Dōgo-yama** *var.* Dōgo-san. ▲ Kyūshū, SW Japan *35.03N 133.12E*
Dogrular *see* Pravda
143 T13 **Doğubayazıt** Ağrı, E Turkey *39.33N 44.07E*
143 P12 **Doğu Karadeniz Dağları** *var.* Anadolu Dağları. ▲ NE Turkey
Doha *see* Ad Dawḥah
Dohad *see* Dāhod
Dohuk *see* Dahūk
165 N16 **Doilungdêqên** Xizang Zizhiqu, W China *29.41N 90.58E*
116 F12 **Doïranis, Límnis** *Bul.* Ezero Doyransko. ◎ N Greece
Doire *see* Londonderry
101 H22 **Doische** Namur, S Belgium *50.09N 4.43E*
61 P17 **Dois de Julho** ✕ (Salvador) Bahia, NE Brazil *12.04S 38.58W*
62 H12 **Dois Vizinhos** Paraná, S Brazil *25.47S 53.03W*
82 H10 **Doka** Gedaref, E Sudan *13.30N 35.46E*
Doka *see* Kéita, Bahr
145 T3 **Dokan** *var.* Dūkān. E Iraq *35.55N 44.58E*
96 H13 **Dokka** Oppland, S Norway *60.49N 10.04E*
100 L5 **Dokkum** Friesland, N Netherlands *53.20N 6.00E*
100 L5 **Dokkumer Ee** N Netherlands
78 K13 **Doko** Haute-Guinée, NE Guinea *11.46N 8.58W*
Dokshitsy *see* Dokshytsy
120 K13 **Dokshytsy** *Rus.* Dokshitsy. Vitsyebskaya Voblasts', N Belarus *54.54N 27.46E*
119 X8 **Dokuchayevs'k** *var.* Dokuchayevsk. Donets'ka Oblast', SE Ukraine *47.43N 37.40E*
Dolak, Pulau *see* Yos Sudarso, Pulau
31 P9 **Doland** South Dakota, N USA *44.51N 98.06W*
65 J18 **Dolavón** Chaco, S Argentina *43.20S 65.42W*
13 P6 **Dolbeau** Québec, SE Canada *48.52N 72.15W*
104 I5 **Dol-de-Bretagne** Ille-et-Vilaine, NW France *48.33N 1.45W*
66 J13 **Doldrums Fracture Zone** *tectonic feature* W Atlantic Ocean
105 S8 **Dôle** Jura, E France *47.04N 5.30E*
99 J19 **Dolgellau** NW Wales, UK *52.44N 3.54W*
Dolginovo *see* Dawhinava
Dolgi, Ostrov *see* Dolgiy, Ostrov
129 U2 **Dolgiy, Ostrov** *var.* Ostrov Dolgi. *island* NW Russian Federation
168 J9 **Dölgöön** Övörhangay, C Mongolia *45.57N 103.14E*
109 C20 **Dolianova** Sardegna, Italy, C Mediterranean Sea *39.23N 9.08E*
Dolina *see* Dolyna
127 Oo15 **Dolinsk** Ostrov Sakhalin, Sakhalinskaya Oblast', SE Russian Federation *47.20N 142.52E*
Dolinskaya *see* Dolyns'ka
81 F21 **Dolisie** *prev.* Loubomo. Le Niari, S Congo *4.12S 12.40E*
118 G14 **Dolj** ◐ *county* SW Romania
100 P5 **Dollard** *bay* NW Germany
204 J5 **Dolleman Island** *island* Antarctica
116 I8 **Dolni Dŭbnik** Pleven, N Bulgaria *43.24N 24.25E*
116 F8 **Dolni Lom** Vidin, NW Bulgaria *43.31N 22.46E*
Dolnja Lendava *see* Lendava
116 K9 **Dolno Panicherevo** *var.* Panicherevo. Sliven, C Bulgaria *42.36N 25.51E*
113 F14 **Dolnośląskie** ◐ *province* SW Poland
113 K18 **Dolný Kubín** *Hung.* Alsókubin. Žilinský Kraj, N Slovakia *49.13N 19.16E*
108 H8 **Dolo** Veneto, NE Italy *45.25N 12.06E*
Dolomites/Dolomiti *see* Dolomitiche, Alpi
108 H6 **Dolomitiche, Alpi** *var.* Dolomiti, *Eng.* Dolomites. ▲ NE Italy
Dolonnur *see* Duolun
168 K10 **Doloon** Ömnögovĭ, S Mongolia *44.28N 105.22E*
63 E21 **Dolores** Buenos Aires, E Argentina *36.21S 57.39W*
44 E3 **Dolores** Petén, N Guatemala *16.33N 89.25W*
179 R12 **Dolores** Samar, C Philippines *12.01N 125.27E*
107 S12 **Dolores** País Valenciano, E Spain *38.09N 0.45W*
63 D19 **Dolores** Soriano, SW Uruguay *33.34S 58.15W*
43 N12 **Dolores Hidalgo** *var.* Ciudad de Dolores Hidalgo. Guanajuato, C Mexico *21.10N 100.55W*
15 Hh3 **Dolphin and Union Strait** *strait* Northwest Territories / Nunavut, N Canada
67 D23 **Dolphin, Cape** *headland* East Falkland, Falkland Islands *51.15S 58.57W*
46 H12 **Dolphin Head** *hill* W Jamaica *18.21N 78.08W*
85 B21 **Dolphin Head** *var.* Cape Dernberg. *headland* SW Namibia *25.33S 14.36E*
112 G12 **Dolsk** *Ger.* Dolzig. Wielkolpolskie, C Poland *51.59N 17.03E*
178 J8 **Đô Lương** Nghê An, N Vietnam *18.51N 105.19E*
118 I6 **Dolyna** *Rus.* Dolina. Ivano-Frankivs'ka Oblast', W Ukraine *48.58N 24.01E*
119 R8 **Dolyns'ka** *Rus.* Dolinskaya. Kirovohrads'ka Oblast', S Ukraine *48.06N 32.46E*
Dolzig *see* Dolsk
Domachëvo/Domaczewo *see* Damachava
119 P9 **Domanivka** Mykolayivs'ka Oblast', S Ukraine *47.40N 30.56E*
159 S13 **Domar** Rajshahi, N Bangladesh *26.09N 88.49E*
110 I9 **Domat/Ems** Graubünden, SE Switzerland *46.49N 9.28E*
113 A18 **Domažlice** *Ger.* Taus. Plzeňský Kraj, W Czech Republic *49.25N 12.55E*
131 X8 **Dombarovskiy** Orenburgskaya Oblast', W Russian Federation *50.53N 59.18E*
96 G10 **Dombås** Oppland, S Norway *62.04N 9.07E*
85 M17 **Dombe** Manica, C Mozambique *19.59S 33.24E*
84 A13 **Dombe Grande** Benguela, C Angola *12.57S 13.07E*
105 R10 **Dombes** *physical region* E France
176 Xx10 **Dombo** Irian Jaya, E Indonesia *1.52S 137.09E*
113 I25 **Dombóvár** Tolna, S Hungary *46.24N 18.09E*
101 D14 **Domburg** Zeeland, SW Netherlands *51.34N 3.30E*
60 L13 **Dom Eliseu** Pará, NE Brazil *4.02S 47.31W*
Domel Island *see* Letsôk-aw Kyun
105 O11 **Dôme, Puy de** ▲ C France *45.46N 3.00E*
38 H13 **Dome Rock Mountains** ▲ Arizona, SW USA
Domesnes, Cape *see* Kolkasrags
64 G8 **Domeyko** Atacama, N Chile *28.57S 70.54W*
64 H5 **Domeyko, Cordillera** ▲ N Chile
104 K5 **Domfront** Orne, N France *48.35N 0.39W*
176 Xx10 **Dom, Gunung** ▲ Irian Jaya, E Indonesia *2.41S 137.00E*
47 X11 **Dominica** *off.* Commonwealth of Dominica. ◆ *republic* E West Indies
49 S3 **Dominica** *island* Dominica
Dominica Channel *see* Martinique Passage
45 N15 **Dominical** Puntarenas, SE Costa Rica *9.16N 83.52W*
47 Q8 **Dominican Republic** ◆ *republic* C West Indies
47 X11 **Dominica Passage** *passage* E Caribbean Sea
101 K14 **Dommel** S Netherlands
83 O14 **Domo** Somali, E Ethiopia *7.53N 46.55E*
130 L4 **Domodedovo** ✕ (Moskva) Moskovskaya Oblast', W Russian Federation *55.19N 37.55E*
108 C6 **Domodossola** Piemonte, NE Italy *46.07N 8.20E*
117 F17 **Domokós** *var.* Dhomokós. Stereá Ellás, C Greece *39.07N 22.18E*
180 I14 **Domoni** Anjouan, SE Comoros *12.15S 44.39E*
63 G16 **Dom Pedrito** Rio Grande do Sul, S Brazil *30.55S 54.39W*
Dompoe *see* Dompu
175 Oo16 **Dompu** *prev.* Dompoe. Sumbawa, C Indonesia *8.30S 118.28E*
Domschale *see* Domžale
64 H13 **Domuyo, Volcán** W Argentina *36.36S 70.22W*
111 U11 **Domžale** *Ger.* Domschale. C Slovenia *46.09N 14.33E*
131 O10 **Don** *var.* Duna, Tanais. SW Russian Federation
98 K9 **Don** NE Scotland, UK
190 M11 **Donald** Victoria, SE Australia *36.27S 143.03E*
24 J9 **Donaldsonville** Louisiana, S USA *30.06N 90.59W*
25 S8 **Donalsonville** Georgia, SE USA *31.02N 84.52W*
Donau *see* Danube
103 G23 **Donaueschingen** Baden-Württemberg, SW Germany *47.57N 8.30E*
103 K22 **Donaumoos** *wetland* S Germany
103 K22 **Donauwörth** Bayern, S Germany *48.43N 10.46E*
111 U7 **Donawitz** Steiermark, SE Austria *47.23N 15.00E*
119 X7 **Donbass** *industrial region* Russian Federation/Ukraine
106 K11 **Don Benito** Extremadura, W Spain *38.57N 5.52W*
99 M17 **Doncaster** *anc.* Danum. N England, UK *53.31N 1.07W*
46 K12 **Don Christophers Point** *headland* C Jamaica *18.19N 76.48W*
57 V9 **Donderkamp** Sipaliwini, NW Surinam *5.18N 56.22W*
84 B12 **Dondo** Cuanza Norte, NW Angola *9.40S 14.24E*
175 Q9 **Dondo** Sulawesi, N Indonesia *0.54S 121.33E*
85 N17 **Dondo** Sofala, C Mozambique *19.36S 34.46E*
175 Pp7 **Dondo, Teluk** *bay* Sulawesi, N Indonesia
161 K26 **Dondra Head** *headland* S Sri Lanka *5.57N 80.33E*
Donduşani *see* Donduşeni
118 M8 **Donduşeni** *var.* Donduşani, *Rus.* Dondyushany. N Moldova *48.13N 27.38E*
Dondyushany *see* Donduşeni
99 D15 **Donegal** *Ir.* Dún na nGall. NW Ireland *54.39N 8.06W*
99 D14 **Donegal** *Ir.* Dún na nGall. *cultural region* NW Ireland
99 C15 **Donegal Bay** *Ir.* Bá Dhún na nGall. *bay* NW Ireland
86 K10 **Donets** Russian Federation/Ukraine
119 X8 **Donets'k** *Rus.* Donetsk; *prev.* Stalino. Donets'ka Oblast', E Ukraine *47.58N 37.49E*
119 W8 **Donets'k** ✕ Donets'ka Oblast', E Ukraine *48.03N 37.44E*
Donets'k *see* Donets'ka Oblast'
119 W8 **Donets'ka Oblast'** *var.* Donets'k, *Rus.* Donetskaya Oblast'; *prev. Rus.* Stalinskaya Oblast'. ◐ *province* SE Ukraine
Donetskaya Oblast' *see* Donets'ka Oblast'
69 P8 **Donga** Cameroon/Nigeria
163 O13 **Dongchuan** Yunnan, SW China *26.09N 103.10E*
101 I14 **Dongen** Noord-Brabant, S Netherlands *51.37N 4.55E*
166 K17 **Dongfang** *var.* Basuo. Hainan, S China *19.05N 108.40E*
169 Z7 **Dongfanghong** Heilongjiang, NE China *46.13N 133.13E*
169 W11 **Dongfeng** Jilin, NE China *42.39N 125.33E*
175 P9 **Donggala** Sulawesi, C Indonesia *0.40S 119.43E*
169 V13 **Donggou** Liaoning, NE China *39.52N 124.07E*
167 O14 **Dongguan** Guangdong, S China *23.03N 113.43E*
178 K9 **Đông Hà** Quang Tri, C Vietnam *16.45N 107.10E*
Dong Hai *see* East China Sea
166 M16 **Donghai Dao** *island* S China
178 Jj9 **Đông Hơi** Quang Binh, C Vietnam *17.30N 106.34E*
110 H10 **Dongio** Ticino, S Switzerland *46.27N 8.58E*
Dongkan *see* Binhai
166 L11 **Dongkou** Hunan, S China *27.06N 110.34E*
Dongliao *see* Liaoyuan
Dong-nai *see* Đông Nai, Sông
178 K13 **Đông Nai, Sông** *var.* Dong-nai, Dong Noi, Donnai. S Vietnam
167 O14 **Dongnan Qiuling** *plateau* SE China
169 Y9 **Dongning** Heilongjiang, NE China *44.01N 131.03E*
Dong Noi *see* Đông Nai, Sông
85 C14 **Dongo** Huíla, C Angola *14.35S 15.51E*
82 E7 **Dongola** *var.* Donqola, Dunqulah. Northern, N Sudan *19.10N 30.27E*
81 I17 **Dongou** La Likouala, NE Congo *2.04N 18.00E*
178 Jj13 **Đông Phu** Sông Be, S Vietnam *11.31N 106.55E*
Dong Rak, Phanom *see* Dângrêk, Chuŏr Phnum
167 Q14 **Dongshan Dao** *island* SE China
169 N14 **Dongsheng** Nei Mongol Zizhiqu, N China *39.51N 110.00E*
167 R7 **Dongtai** Jiangsu, E China *32.52N 120.13E*
167 N10 **Dongting Hu** *var.* Tung-t'ing Hu. ◎ S China
167 P10 **Dongxiang** Jiangxi, S China *28.17N 116.36E*
167 Q4 **Dongying** Shandong, E China *37.27N 118.01E*
29 X8 **Doniphan** Missouri, C USA *36.37N 90.49W*
8 G7 **Donjek** Yukon Territory, W Canada
114 E11 **Donji Lapac** Lika-Senj, W Croatia *44.33N 15.58E*
114 H8 **Donji Miholjac** Osijek-Baranja, NE Croatia *45.45N 18.10E*
114 P12 **Donji Milanovac** Serbia, E Yugoslavia *44.27N 22.06E*
114 G12 **Donji Vakuf** *var.* Srbobran. Federacija Bosna I Hercegovina, C Bosnia & Herzegovina *44.08N 17.23E*
100 M6 **Donkerbroek** Friesland, N Netherlands *52.58N 5.15E*
178 Hh11 **Don Muang** ✕ (Krung Thep) Nonthaburi, C Thailand *13.51N 100.40E*
27 S17 **Donna** Texas, SW USA *26.10N 98.03W*
13 Q10 **Donnacona** Quebec, SE Canada *46.41N 71.46W*
Donnai *see* Đông Nai, Sông
31 Y16 **Donnellson** Iowa, C USA *40.38N 91.33W*
9 O13 **Donnelly** Alberta, W Canada *55.42N 117.06W*
37 P6 **Donner Pass** *pass* California, W USA *39.19N 120.19W*
103 F19 **Donnersberg** ▲ W Germany *49.37N 7.54E*
Donoso *see* Miguel de la Borda
107 P2 **Donostia-San Sebastián** País Vasco, N Spain *43.19N 1.58W*
117 K21 **Donoússa** *island* Kykládes, Greece, Aegean Sea
37 P8 **Don Pedro Reservoir** ▣ California, W USA
Donqola *see* Dongola
130 L5 **Donskoy** Tul'skaya Oblast', W Russian Federation *54.02N 38.27E*
179 Q11 **Donsol** Luzon, N Philippines *12.56N 123.34E*
83 L16 **Doolow** Somali, E Ethiopia *4.10N 42.04E*
41 Q7 **Doonerak, Mount** ▲ Alaska, USA *67.54N 150.33W*
100 J12 **Doorn** Utrecht, C Netherlands *52.01N 5.21E*
Doornik *see* Tournai
33 N6 **Door Peninsula** *peninsula* Wisconsin, N USA
82 P13 **Dooxo Nugaaleed** *var.* Nogal Valley. *valley* E Somalia
166 G8 **Do Qu** C China
108 B7 **Dora Baltea** *anc.* Duria Major. NW Italy
188 K7 **Dora, Lake** *salt lake* Western Australia
108 A8 **Dora Riparia** *anc.* Duria Minor. NW Italy
Dorbiljin *see* Emin
169 V8 **Dorbod** *var.* Dorbod Mongolzu Zizhixian, Talkang. Heilongjiang, NE China *46.50N 124.25E*
Dorbod Mongolzu Zizhixian *see* Dorbod
115 N18 **Đorče Petrov** *var.* Djorče Petrov, Gorče Petrov. N FYR Macedonia *42.01N 21.21E*
12 F16 **Dorchester** Ontario, S Canada *43.00N 81.04W*
99 L24 **Dorchester** *anc.* Durnovaria. S England, UK *50.43N 2.25W*
15 Mm4 **Dorchester, Cape** *headland* Baffin Island, Nunavut, NE Canada *65.25N 77.25W*
85 D19 **Dordabis** Khomas, C Namibia *22.57S 17.39E*
104 L12 **Dordogne** ◐ *department* SW France
105 N12 **Dordogne** W France
100 H13 **Dordrecht** *var.* Dordt, Dort. Zuid-Holland, SW Netherlands *51.48N 4.40E*
Dordt *see* Dordrecht
105 P11 **Dore** C France
9 S13 **Doré Lake** Saskatchewan, C Canada *54.37N 107.36W*
105 O12 **Dore, Monts** ▲ C France
103 M23 **Dorfen** Bayern, SE Germany *48.16N 12.06E*
109 D18 **Dorgali** Sardegna, Italy, C Mediterranean Sea *40.18N 9.34E*
168 F7 **Döröö Nuur** ◎ NW Mongolia
79 Q12 **Dori** N Burkina *14.03N 0.01W*
85 E24 **Doring** S South Africa
103 E16 **Dormagen** Nordrhein-Westfalen, W Germany *51.06N 6.49E*
105 P4 **Dormans** Marne, N France *49.03N 3.44E*
110 E6 **Dornach** Solothurn, NW Switzerland *47.28N 7.37E*
Dorna Watra *see* Vatra Dornei
110 J7 **Dornbirn** Vorarlberg, W Austria *47.25N 9.46E*
98 I7 **Dornoch** N Scotland, UK *57.52N 4.00W*
98 J7 **Dornoch Firth** *inlet* N Scotland, UK
169 P7 **Dornod** ◐ *province* E Mongolia
169 N10 **Dornogovĭ** ◐ *province* SE Mongolia
79 P10 **Doro** Tombouctou, S Mali *16.07N 0.57W*
118 L14 **Dorobanţu** Călăraşi, S Romania *44.15N 26.55E*
113 J22 **Dorog** Komárom-Esztergom, N Hungary *47.42N 18.44E*
130 I4 **Dorogobuzh** Smolenskaya Oblast', W Russian Federation *54.56N 33.16E*
118 K8 **Dorohoi** Botoşani, NE Romania *47.57N 26.24E*
95 H15 **Dorotea** Västerbotten, N Sweden *64.16N 16.30E*
Dorpat *see* Tartu
188 G10 **Dorre Island** *island* Western Australia
191 U5 **Dorrigo** New South Wales, SE Australia *30.22S 152.43E*
37 N1 **Dorris** California, W USA *41.58N 121.54W*
12 H13 **Dorset** Ontario, SE Canada *45.12N 78.52W*
99 K23 **Dorset** *cultural region* S England, UK
103 E14 **Dorsten** Nordrhein-Westfalen, W Germany *51.40N 6.58E*
Dort *see* Dordrecht
103 F15 **Dortmund** Nordrhein-Westfalen, W Germany *51.31N 7.28E*
102 F12 **Dortmund-Ems-Kanal** *canal* W Germany
142 L17 **Dörtyol** Hatay, S Turkey *36.51N 36.10E*
148 L7 **Do Rūd** *var.* Dow Rūd, Durud. Lorestān, W Iran *33.31N 49.03E*
81 O15 **Doruma** Orientale, N Dem. Rep. Congo (Zaire) *4.35N 27.43E*
13 O12 **Dorval** ✕ (Montréal) Quebec, SE Canada *45.27N 73.46W*
47 T5 **Dos Bocas, Lago** ◎ C Puerto Rico
106 K14 **Dos Hermanas** Andalucía, S Spain *37.16N 5.55W*
Dospad Dagh *see* Rhodope Mountains
37 P10 **Dos Palos** California, W USA *37.00N 120.39W*
116 I11 **Dospat** Smolyan, S Bulgaria *41.39N 24.10E*
116 H11 **Dospat, Yazovir** ▣ SW Bulgaria
102 M11 **Dosse** NE Germany
79 S12 **Dosso** Dosso, SW Niger *13.03N 3.13E*
79 S12 **Dosso** ◐ *department* SW Niger
150 G12 **Dossor** Atyrau, SW Kazakhstan *47.32N 52.58E*
153 V9 **Dostuk** Narynskaya Oblast', C Kyrgyzstan *41.19N 75.40E*
151 X13 **Dostyk** *prev.* Druzhba. Almaty, SE Kazakhstan *45.15N 82.28E*
25 R7 **Dothan** Alabama, S USA *31.13N 85.23W*
41 T9 **Dot Lake** Alaska, USA *63.39N 144.10W*
120 F12 **Dotnuva** Kėdainiai, C Lithuania *55.22N 23.52E*
101 D19 **Dottignies** Hainaut, W Belgium *50.43N 3.16E*
105 P2 **Douai** *prev.* Douay, *anc.* Duacum. Nord, N France *50.22N 3.04E*
12 L9 **Douaire, Lac** ◎ Quebec, SE Canada
81 D16 **Douala** *var.* Duala. Littoral, W Cameroon *4.04N 9.43E*
81 D16 **Douala** ✕ Littoral, W Cameroon *3.57N 9.48E*
104 F6 **Douarnenez** Finistère, NW France *48.04N 4.19W*
104 E6 **Douarnenez, Baie de** *bay* NW France
Douay *see* Douai
27 O6 **Double Mountain Fork Brazos River** Texas, SW USA
25 O3 **Double Springs** Alabama, S USA *34.09N 87.24W*
105 T8 **Doubs** ◐ *department* E France
110 C8 **Doubs** France/Switzerland
193 A22 **Doubtful Sound** *sound* South Island, NZ
192 J2 **Doubtless Bay** *bay* North Island, NZ
27 X9 **Doucette** Texas, SW USA *30.48N 94.25W*
104 K8 **Doué-la-Fontaine** Maine-et-Loire, NW France *47.12N 0.16W*
79 O11 **Douentza** Mopti, S Mali *14.59N 2.57W*
40 L9 **Douglas** East Falkland, Falkland Islands
99 I16 **Douglas** ○ (Isle of Man) E Isle of Man *54.09N 4.28W*
85 H23 **Douglas** Northern Cape, C South Africa *29.03S 23.46E*
41 X13 **Douglas** Alexander Archipelago, Alaska, USA *58.12N 134.18W*
39 O17 **Douglas** Arizona, SW USA *31.20N 109.32W*
25 U7 **Douglas** Georgia, SE USA *31.30N 82.51W*
35 Y15 **Douglas** Wyoming, C USA *42.48N 105.22W*
23 O7 **Douglas, Cape** *headland* Alaska USA *64.59N 166.41W*
8 J14 **Douglas Channel** *channel* British Columbia, W Canada
190 G3 **Douglas Creek** *seasonal river* South Australia
33 P5 **Douglas Lake** ◎ Michigan, N USA
23 O9 **Douglas Lake** ▣ Tennessee, S USA
41 Q13 **Douglas, Mount** ▲ Alaska, USA *58.51N 153.31W*
204 I6 **Douglas Range** ▲ Alexander Island, Antarctica
124 N10 **Doukáto, Akrotírio** *headland* Lefkáda, W Greece *38.35N 20.33E*
105 O2 **Doullens** Somme, N France *50.09N 2.21E*
Douma *see* Dūmā
81 F15 **Doumé** Est, E Cameroon *4.13N 13.27E*
101 E21 **Dour** Hainaut, S Belgium *50.24N 3.46E*
61 K18 **Dourada, Serra** ▲ S Brazil
61 I21 **Dourados** Mato Grosso do Sul, S Brazil *22.09S 54.52W*
105 N5 **Dourdan** Essonne, N France *48.33N 1.58E*
106 I6 **Douro** *Sp.* Duero. Portugal/Spain ***see also*** Duero
106 G6 **Douro Litoral** *former province* N Portugal
Douvres *see* Dover
104 K15 **Douze** SW France
191 P17 **Dover** Tasmania, SE Australia *43.19S 147.01E*
99 Q22 **Dover** *Fr.* Douvres; *Lat.* Dubris Portus. SE England, UK *51.08N 3.00W*
19 Rr8 **Dover** *state capital* Delaware, NE USA *39.09N 75.31W*
21 P9 **Dover** New Hampshire, NE USA *43.10N 70.50W*
20 J14 **Dover** New Jersey, NE USA *40.51N 74.33W*
33 U12 **Dover** Ohio, N USA *40.31N 81.28W*
22 H8 **Dover** Tennessee, S USA *36.29N 87.50W*
99 Q23 **Dover, Strait of** *var.* Straits of Dover, *Fr.* Pas de Calais. *strait* England, UK/France
Dover, Straits of *see* Dover, Strait of
Dovlen *see* Devin
96 G11 **Dovre** Oppland, S Norway *61.59N 9.16E*
96 G10 **Dovrefjell** *plateau* S Norway
Dovsk *see* Dowsk
85 M14 **Dowa** Central, C Malawi *13.42S 33.55E*
33 O10 **Dowagiac** Michigan, N USA *41.58N 86.06W*
149 N10 **Dow Gonbadān** *var.* Do Gonbadān, Gonbadān. Kohkīlūyeh va Būyer Aḥmadī, SW Iran *30.24N 50.45E*
154 M2 **Dowlatābād** Fāryāb, N Afghanistan *36.30N 64.51E*
99 G16 **Down** *cultural region* SE Northern Ireland, UK
35 R16 **Downey** Idaho, NW USA *42.25N 112.06W*
37 P5 **Downieville** California, W USA *39.33N 120.49W*
99 G16 **Downpatrick** *Ir.* Dún Pádraig. SE Northern Ireland, UK *54.19N 5.43W*
28 M3 **Downs** Kansas, C USA *39.30N 98.33W*
20 J12 **Downsville** New York, NE USA *42.03N 74.59W*
Dow Rūd *see* Do Rūd
31 V12 **Dows** Iowa, C USA *42.39N 93.30W*
121 O17 **Dowsk** *Rus.* Dovsk. Homyel'skaya Voblasts', SE Belarus *53.09N 30.27E*
37 Q4 **Doyle** California, W USA *40.00N 120.06W*
20 I15 **Doylestown** Pennsylvania, NE USA *40.18N 75.07W*
Doyransko, Ezero *see* Doïranis, Límnis
116 I8 **Doyrentsi** Lovech, N Bulgaria *43.13N 24.46E*
170 Ff11 **Dōzen** *island* Oki-shotō, SW Japan
12 K9 **Dozois, Réservoir** ▣ Quebec, SE Canada
76 D9 **Drâa** *seasonal river* S Morocco
Drâa, Hammada du *see* Dra, Hamada du
Drabble *see* José Enrique Rodó
119 Q5 **Drabiv** Cherkas'ka Oblast', C Ukraine *49.57N 32.10E*
Drabble *see* José Enrique Rodó
105 S13 **Drac** E France
Drač/Draç *see* Durrës
62 I8 **Dracena** São Paulo, S Brazil *21.27S 51.30W*
100 M6 **Drachten** Friesland, N Netherlands *53.07N 6.06E*
94 H11 **Drag** Nordland, C Norway *68.02N 16.00E*
118 L14 **Dragalina** Călăraşi, SE Romania *44.25N 27.17E*
118 J14 **Drăgăneşti-Vlaşca** Teleorman, S Romania *44.05N 25.39E*
118 I13 **Drăgăşani** Vâlcea, SW Romania *44.40N 24.16E*
116 G9 **Dragoman** Sofiya, W Bulgaria *42.57N 22.53E*
117 L25 **Dragonáda** *island* SE Greece
Dragonera, Isla *see* Sa Dragonera
47 T14 **Dragon's Mouths, The** *strait* Trinidad and Tobago/Venezuela
97 J23 **Dragør** København, E Denmark *55.36N 12.42E*
116 F10 **Dragovishtitsa** Kyustendil, W Bulgaria *42.22N 22.39E*
105 U15 **Draguignan** Var, SE France *43.31N 6.31E*
76 E9 **Dra, Hamada du** *var.* Hammada du Drâa, Haut Plateau du Dra. *plateau* W Algeria
Dra, Haut Plateau du *see* Dra, Hamada du
121 H19 **Drahichyn** *Pol.* Drohiczyn Poleski, *Rus.* Drogichin. Brestskaya Voblasts', SW Belarus *52.10N 25.10E*
31 N4 **Drake** North Dakota, N USA *47.54N 100.23W*
85 K23 **Drakensberg** ▲ Lesotho/South Africa
204 F3 **Drake Passage** *passage* Atlantic Ocean/Pacific Ocean
116 L8 **Dralfa** Tŭrgovishte, N Bulgaria *43.17N 26.25E*
116 I12 **Dráma** *var.* Dhráma. Anatolikí Makedonía kai Thráki, NE Greece *41.09N 24.10E*
Dramburg *see* Drawsko Pomorskie
97 H15 **Drammen** Buskerud, S Norway *59.43N 10.12E*
97 H15 **Drammensfjorden** *fjord* S Norway
94 H1 **Drangajökull** ▲ NW Iceland *66.13N 22.18W*
97 F16 **Drangedal** Telemark, S Norway *59.04N 9.01E*
94 I2 **Drangsnes** Vestfirdhir, NW Iceland *65.42N 21.27W*
Drann *see* Dravinja
111 T10 **Drau** *var.* Drava, *Eng.* Drave, *Hung.* Dráva. C Europe ***see also*** Drava
86 I11 **Drava** *var.* Drau, *Eng.* Drave, *Hung.* Dráva. C Europe ***see also*** Drau
Dráva *see* Drau/Drava
Drave *see* Drau/Drava
111 W10 **Dravinja** *Ger.* Drann. NE Slovenia
111 V9 **Dravograd** *Ger.* Unterdrauburg; *prev.* Spodnji Dravograd. N Slovenia *46.36N 15.00E*
112 F10 **Drawa** NW Poland
112 F9 **Drawno** Zachodniopomorskie, NW Poland *53.12N 15.44E*
112 F9 **Drawsko Pomorskie** *Ger.* Dramburg. Zachodniopomorskie, NW Poland *53.31N 15.48E*
31 R3 **Drayton** North Dakota, N USA *48.34N 97.10W*
9 P14 **Drayton Valley** Alberta, SW Canada *53.15N 115.00W*
194 F10 **Dreikikir** East Sepik, NW PNG *3.34S 142.44E*
Dreikirchen *see* Teiuş
100 N7 **Drenthe** ◐ *province* NE Netherlands
117 H15 **Drépano, Akrotírio** *var.* Akra Dhrepanon. *headland* N Greece *39.56N 23.57E*
Drepanum *see* Trapani
12 D17 **Dresden** Ontario, S Canada *42.34N 82.09W*
103 O16 **Dresden** Sachsen, E Germany *51.02N 13.43E*
22 G8 **Dresden** Tennessee, S USA *36.17N 88.42W*
120 M11 **Dretun'** *Rus.* Dretun'. Vitsyebskaya Voblasts', N Belarus *55.42N 29.12E*
104 M5 **Dreux** *anc.* Drocae, Durocasses. Eure-et-Loir, C France *48.43N 1.22E*
96 I11 **Drevsjø** Hedmark, S Norway *61.52N 12.01E*
24 K3 **Drew** Mississippi, S USA *33.48N 90.31W*
112 F10 **Drezdenko** *Ger.* Driesen. Lubuskie, W Poland *52.51N 15.49E*
100 J12 **Driebergen** *var.* Driebergen-Rijsenburg. Utrecht, C Netherlands *52.03N 5.16E*
Driebergen-Rijsenburg *see* Driebergen
Driesen *see* Drezdenko
99 N16 **Driffield** E England, UK *54.00N 0.28W*
67 D25 **Driftwood Point** *headland* East Falkland, Falkland Islands *52.15S 59.00W*
35 S14 **Driggs** Idaho, NW USA *43.44N 111.06W*
Drin *see* Drinit, Lumi i
114 K12 **Drina** Bosnia and Herzegovina/Yugoslavia
Drin, Gulf of *see* Drinit, Gjiri i
115 K18 **Drinit, Gjiri i** *var.* Pellg i Drinit, *Eng.* Gulf of Drin. *gulf* NW Albania
115 L17 **Drinit, Lumi i** *var.* Drin. NW Albania
Drinit, Pellg i *see* Drinit, Gjiri i
Drinit të Zi, Lumi i *see* Black Drin
115 L22 **Dríno** *var.* Drino, Drínos Pótamos, *Alb.* Lumi i Drinos. Albania/Greece
Drinos, Lumi i/Drínos Pótamos *see* Dríno
27 S11 **Dripping Springs** Texas, SW USA *30.11N 98.04W*
27 S15 **Driscoll** Texas, SW USA *27.40N 97.45W*
24 H5 **Driskill Mountain** ▲ Louisiana, S USA *32.25N 92.54W*
Drissa *see* Drysa
96 G10 **Driva** S Norway
114 E13 **Drniš** *It.* Šibenik-Knin, S Croatia *43.51N 16.10E*
97 H15 **Drøbak** Akershus, S Norway *59.40N 10.37E*
118 G13 **Drobeta-Turnu Severin** *prev.* Turnu Severin. Mehedinţi, SW Romania *44.39N 22.39E*
Drocae *see* Dreux
118 M8 **Drochia** *Rus.* Drokiya. N Moldova *48.02N 27.46E*
99 F17 **Drogheda** *Ir.* Droichead Átha. NE Ireland *53.43N 6.21W*
Drogichin *see* Drahichyn
Drogobych *see* Drohobych
Drohiczyn Poleski *see* Drahichyn
118 H6 **Drohobych** *Pol.* Drohobycz, *Rus.* Drogobych. L'vivs'ka Oblast', NW Ukraine *49.22N 23.34E*
Drohobycz *see* Drohobych
Droichead Átha *see* Drogheda
Droicheadna Bandan *see* Bandon
Droichead na Banna *see* Banbridge
Droim Mór *see* Dromore
Drokiya *see* Drochia
105 R13 **Drôme** ◐ *department* E France
105 S13 **Drôme** E France
99 G15 **Dromore** *Ir.* Droim Mór. SE Northern Ireland, UK *54.25N 6.09W*
108 A9 **Dronero** Piemonte, NE Italy *44.28N 7.25E*
104 L12 **Dronne** SW France
205 Q3 **Dronning Maud Land** *physical region* Antarctica
100 K6 **Dronrijp** *Fris.* Dronryp. Friesland, N Netherlands *53.12N 5.37E*
Dronryp *see* Dronrijp
100 L9 **Dronten** Flevoland, C Netherlands *52.31N 5.40E*
Drontheim *see* Trondheim
104 L13 **Dropt** SW France
155 T4 **Drosh** North-West Frontier Province, NW Pakistan *35.33N 71.48E*
Drossen *see* Ośno Lubuskie
Drug *see* Durg
152 I9 **Drujba** *Rus.* Druzhba. Khorazm Wiloyati, W Uzbekistan *41.14N 61.13E*
120 I12 **Drūkšiai** ◎ NE Lithuania
Druk-yul *see* Bhutan
9 Q16 **Drumheller** Alberta, SW Canada *51.28N 112.42W*
35 Q10 **Drummond** Montana, NW USA *46.39N 113.12W*
33 R4 **Drummond Island** *island* Michigan, N USA
Drummond Island *see* Tabiteuea
23 X7 **Drummond, Lake** ◎ Virginia, NE USA
13 P12 **Drummondville** Quebec, SE Canada *45.52N 72.28W*
41 T11 **Drum, Mount** ▲ Alaska, USA *62.11N 144.37W*
29 O9 **Drumright** Oklahoma, C USA *35.59N 96.36W*
101 J14 **Drunen** Noord-Brabant, S Netherlands *51.40N 5.07E*
Druskieniki *see* Druskininkai
121 F15 **Druskininkai** *Pol.* Druskienniki. Druskininkai, S Lithuania *54.00N 24.00E*
100 K13 **Druten** Gelderland, SE Netherlands *51.52N 5.37E*
120 K11 **Druya** Vitsyebskaya Voblasts', NW Belarus *55.48N 27.27E*
119 S2 **Druzhba** Sums'ka Oblast', NE Ukraine *52.01N 33.56E*
Druzhba *see* Dostyk, Kazakhstan
Druzhba *see* Drujba, Uzbekistan
126 Mm7 **Druzhina** Respublika Sakha (Yakutiya), NE Russian Federation *68.01N 144.58E*
119 X7 **Druzhkivka** Donets'ka Oblast', E Ukraine *48.38N 37.31E*
114 E12 **Drvar** Federacija Bosna I Hercegovina, Bosnia and Herzegovina *44.21N 16.24E*
115 G15 **Drvenik** Split-Dalmacija, SE Croatia *43.10N 17.13E*
116 K9 **Dryanovo** Gabrovo, N Bulgaria *42.58N 25.28E*
28 G7 **Dry Cimarron River** Kansas/Oklahoma, C USA
10 B11 **Dryden** Ontario, C Canada *49.48N 92.48W*
26 M11 **Dryden** Texas, SW USA *30.01N 102.06W*
205 Q14 **Drygalski Ice Tongue** *ice feature* Antarctica
120 L11 **Drysa** *Rus.* Drissa. N Belarus
25 V17 **Dry Tortugas** *island* Florida, SE USA
81 D15 **Dschang** Ouest, W Cameroon *5.28N 10.01E*
56 J5 **Duaca** Lara, N Venezuela *10.16N 69.12W*
Duacum *see* Douai
Duala *see* Douala
47 N9 **Duarte, Pico** ▲ C Dominican Republic *19.02N 70.57W*
146 J5 **Ḍubā** Tabūk, NW Saudi Arabia *27.25N 35.42E*
Dubai *see* Dubayy
119 N9 **Dubăsari** *Rus.* Dubossary. NE Moldova *47.16N 29.07E*
119 N9 **Dubăsari Reservoir** ▣ NE Moldova
15 Jj8 **Dubawnt** Nunavut, NW Canada
15 K7 **Dubawnt Lake** ◎ Northwest Territories/Nunavut, N Canada
32 L6 **Du Bay, Lake** ▣ Wisconsin, N USA
147 U7 **Dubayy** *Eng.* Dubai. Dubayy, NE UAE *25.10N 55.18E*

◆ Country
● Country Capital
◇ Dependent Territory
○ Dependent Territory Capital
◐ Administrative Region
✕ International Airport
▲ Mountain
▲ Mountain Range
Volcano
River
◎ Lake
▣ Reservoir

Dubayy – East Cape

147 W7 **Dubayy** *Eng.* Dubai. ✈ Dubayy, NE UAE 25.15N 55.22E
191 R7 **Dubbo** New South Wales, SE Australia 32.16S 148.40E
110 G7 **Dübendorf** Zürich, NW Switzerland 47.24N 8.36E
99 F18 **Dublin** *Ir.* Baile Átha Cliath; *anc.* Eblana. ● (Ireland), E Ireland 53.19N 6.15W
25 U5 **Dublin** Georgia, SE USA 32.32N 82.54W
27 R7 **Dublin** Texas, SW USA 32.05N 98.20W
99 G18 **Dublin** *Ir.* Baile Átha Cliath; *anc.* Eblana. *cultural region* E Ireland
99 G18 **Dublin Airport** ✈ E Ireland 53.25N 6.18W
201 V12 **Dublon** *var.* Tonoas. *island* Chuuk Islands, C Micronesia
130 K2 **Dubna** Moskovskaya Oblast', W Russian Federation 56.45N 37.09E
113 G19 **Dubňany** *Ger.* Dubnian. Brněnský Kraj, SE Czech Republic 48.54N 17.00E
Dubnian *see* Dubňany
113 I19 **Dubnica nad Váhom** *Hung.* Máriatölgyes; *prev.* Dubnicz. Trenčiansky Kraj, W Slovakia 48.58N 18.10E
Dubnicz *see* Dubnica nad Váhom
118 K4 **Dubno** Rivnens'ka Oblast', NW Ukraine 50.27N 25.39E
20 D13 **Du Bois** Pennsylvania, NE USA 41.07N 78.45W
35 R13 **Dubois** Idaho, NW USA 44.10N 112.13W
35 T14 **Dubois** Wyoming, C USA 43.31N 109.37W
Dubossary *see* Dubăsari
131 O10 **Dubovka** Volgogradskaya Oblast', SW Russian Federation 49.10N 48.49E
78 H14 **Dubréka** Guinée-Maritime, SW Guinea 9.48N 13.31W
12 B7 **Dubreuilville** Ontario, S Canada 48.21N 84.31W
Dubris Portus *see* Dover
121 L20 **Dubrova** *Rus.* Dubrova. Homyel'skaya Voblasts', SE Belarus 51.46N 28.13E
130 I5 **Dubrovka** Bryanskaya Oblast', W Russian Federation 53.44N 33.27E
115 H16 **Dubrovnik** *It.* Ragusa. Dubrovnik-Neretva, SE Croatia 42.39N 18.06E
115 I16 **Dubrovnik** ✈ Dubrovnik-Neretva, SE Croatia 42.34N 18.17E
115 F16 **Dubrovnik-Neretva** *off.* Dubrovačko-Neretvanska Županija. ◐ *province* SE Croatia
Dubrovno *see* Dubrowna
118 L2 **Dubrovytsya** Rivnens'ka Oblast', NW Ukraine 51.34N 26.37E
121 O14 **Dubrowna** *Rus.* Dubrovno. Vitsyebskaya Voblasts', N Belarus 54.34N 30.40E
31 Z13 **Dubuque** Iowa, C USA 42.30N 90.39W
120 E12 **Dubysa** ≈ C Lithuania
178 K12 **Đưc Cơ** Gia Lai, C Vietnam 13.48N 107.41E
203 V12 **Duc de Gloucester, Îles du** *Eng.* Duke of Gloucester Islands. *island group* C French Polynesia
113 C15 **Duchcov** *Ger.* Dux. Ústecký Kraj, NW Czech Republic 50.37N 13.40E
39 N3 **Duchesne** Utah, W USA 40.09N 110.24W
203 P17 **Ducie Island** *atoll* E Pitcairn Islands
9 W15 **Duck Bay** Manitoba, S Canada 52.11N 100.08W
25 X17 **Duck Key** *island* Florida Keys, Florida, SE USA
9 T14 **Duck Lake** Saskatchewan, S Canada 52.52N 106.12W
9 V15 **Duck Mountain** ▲▲ Manitoba, S Canada
22 I9 **Duck River** ≈ Tennessee, S USA
22 M10 **Ducktown** Tennessee, S USA 35.01N 84.24W
178 Kk11 **Đưc Phô** Quang Ngai, C Vietnam 14.55N 108.55E
178 Jj8 **Đưc Tho** Ha Tinh, N Vietnam 18.30N 105.36E
178 Kk13 **Đưc Trong** *var.* Liên Nghia. Lâm Đông, S Vietnam 11.45N 108.24E
D-U-D *see* Dalap-Uliga-Djarrit
101 M25 **Dudelange** *var.* Forge du Sud, *Ger.* Dudelingen. Luxembourg, S Luxembourg 49.28N 6.04E
Dudelingen *see* Dudelange
103 J15 **Duderstadt** Niedersachsen, C Germany 51.31N 10.16E
159 N15 **Dūdhi** Uttar Pradesh, N India 24.13N 83.18E
126 I8 **Dudinka** Taymyrskiy (Dolgano-Nenetskiy) Avtonomnyy Okrug, N Russian Federation 69.27N 86.13E
99 L20 **Dudley** C England, UK 52.30N 2.04W
160 G13 **Dudna** ≈ C India
78 L16 **Duékoué** W Ivory Coast 6.45N 7.21W
106 M5 **Dueñas** Castilla-León, N Spain 41.52N 4.33W
106 K4 **Duerna** ≈ NW Spain
107 O6 **Duero** *Port.* Douro. ≈ Portugal/Spain *see also* Douro
Duesseldorf *see* Düsseldorf
23 P12 **Due West** South Carolina, SE USA 34.19N 82.23W
205 P11 **Dufek Coast** *physical region* Antarctica
101 H17 **Duffel** Antwerpen, C Belgium 51.06N 4.30E
37 S2 **Duffer Peak** ▲ Nevada, W USA 41.40N 118.45W
195 X7 **Duff Islands** *island group* E Solomon Islands
Dufour, Pizzo/Dufour, Punta *see* Dufour Spitze
110 E12 **Dufour Spitze** *It.* Pizzo Dufour, Punta Dufour. ▲ Italy/Switzerland 45.54N 7.50E
114 D9 **Duga Resa** Karlovac, C Croatia 45.25N 15.30E
24 H5 **Dugdemona River** ≈ Louisiana, S USA
160 J12 **Duggīpar** Mahārāshtra, C India 21.06N 80.10E
114 B13 **Dugi Otok** *var.* Isola Grossa, *It.* Isola Lunga. *island* W Croatia
115 F14 **Dugopolje** Split-Dalmacija, S Croatia 43.35N 16.35E
166 L8 **Du He** ≈ C China
56 M11 **Duida, Cerro** ▲ S Venezuela 3.21N 65.45W
Duinekerke *see* Dunkerque
103 E15 **Duisburg** *prev.* Duisburg-Hamborn. Nordrhein-Westfalen, W Germany 51.25N 6.47E
Duisburg-Hamborn *see* Duisburg
101 F14 **Duiveland** *island* SW Netherlands
100 M12 **Duiven** Gelderland, E Netherlands 51.57N 6.02E
145 W10 **Dujaylah, Hawr ad** ◎ S Iraq
83 L18 **Dujuuma** Shabeellaha Hoose, S Somalia 1.04N 42.37E
Dūkān *see* Dokan
41 Z14 **Duke Island** *island* Alexander Archipelago, Alaska, USA
Dukelský Priesmy/Dukelský Průsmyk *see* Dukla Pass
Duke of Gloucester Islands *see* Duc de Gloucester, Îles du
83 F14 **Duk Faiwil** Jonglei, SE Sudan 7.30N 31.27E
147 T7 **Dukhān** C Qatar 25.29N 50.48E
Dukhan Heights *see* Dukhān, Jabal
149 N16 **Dukhān, Jabal** *var.* Dukhan Heights. *hill range* S Qatar
131 Q7 **Dukhovnitskoye** Saratovskaya Oblast', W Russian Federation 52.31N 48.32E
130 H4 **Dukhovshchina** Smolenskaya Oblast', W Russian Federation 55.15N 32.22E
Dukielska, Przełęcz *see* Dukla Pass
113 N17 **Dukla** Podkarpackie, SE Poland 49.33N 21.40E
Duklai Hág *see* Dukla Pass
113 N18 **Dukla Pass** *Cz.* Dukelský Průsmyk, *Ger.* Dukla-Pass, *Hung.* Duklai Hág, *Pol.* Przełęcz Dukielska, *Slvk.* Dukelský Priesmy. *pass* Poland/Slovakia 49.25N 21.42E
Dukou *see* Panzhihua
120 I12 **Dūkštas** Ignalina, E Lithuania 55.32N 26.21E
168 M8 **Dulaan** Hentiy, C Mongolia 47.09N 108.48E
165 R10 **Dulan** *var.* Qagan Us. Qinghai, C China 36.11N 97.51E
39 R8 **Dulce** New Mexico, SW USA 36.55N 107.00W
45 N16 **Dulce, Golfo** *gulf* S Costa Rica
Dulce, Golfo *see* Izabal, Lago de
44 K6 **Dulce Nombre de Culmí** Olancho, C Honduras 15.04N 85.35W
64 L9 **Dulce, Río** ≈ C Argentina
126 M9 **Dulgalakh** ≈ NE Russian Federation
116 M8 **Dŭlgopol** Varna, E Bulgaria 43.05N 27.24E
159 V14 **Dullabchara** Assam, NE India 24.25N 92.22E
22 D3 **Dulles** ✈ (Washington DC) Virginia, NE USA 39.00N 77.27W
103 E14 **Dülmen** Nordrhein-Westfalen, W Germany 51.51N 7.17E
116 M7 **Dulovo** Silistra, NE Bulgaria 43.50N 27.10E
31 W5 **Duluth** Minnesota, N USA 46.46N 92.06W
144 H7 **Dūmā** *Fr.* Douma. Dimashq, SW Syria 33.33N 36.24E
179 Pp16 **Dumagasa Point** *headland* Mindanao, S Philippines 7.01N 121.54E
179 Qq14 **Dumaguete** *var.* Dumaguete City. Negros, C Philippines 9.16N 123.17E
174 Gg6 **Dumai** Sumatera, W Indonesia 1.40N 101.27E
191 T4 **Dumaresq River** ≈ New South Wales/Queensland, SE Australia
29 W13 **Dumas** Arkansas, C USA 33.53N 91.29W
27 N1 **Dumas** Texas, SW USA 35.51N 101.57W
144 I7 **Ḑumayr** Dimashq, W Syria 33.36N 36.28E
98 I12 **Dumbarton** W Scotland, UK 55.57N 4.34W
98 I12 **Dumbarton** *cultural region* C Scotland, UK
197 J7 **Dumbéa** Province Sud, S New Caledonia 22.11S 166.27E
113 K19 **Ďumbier** *Ger.* Djumbir, *Hung.* Gyömbér. ▲ C Slovakia 48.54N 19.36E
118 I11 **Dumbrăveni** *Ger.* Elisabethstedt, *Hung.* Erzsébetváros; *prev.* Ebesfalva, Eppeschdorf, Ibaşfalău. Sibiu, C Romania 45.48N 24.08E
118 L12 **Dumbrăveni** Vrancea, E Romania 45.30N 27.08E
99 J14 **Dumfries** S Scotland, UK 55.04N 3.37W
99 J14 **Dumfries** *cultural region* SW Scotland, UK
159 R15 **Dumka** Bihār, NE India 24.16N 87.15E
Dümmer *see* Dümmersee
102 G12 **Dümmersee** *var.* Dümmer. ◎ NW Germany
12 J11 **Dumoine** ≈ Quebec, SE Canada
12 J10 **Dumoine, Lac** ◎ Quebec, SE Canada
205 V16 **Dumont d'Urville** *French research station* Antarctica 66.24S 139.38E
205 W15 **Dumont d'Urville Sea** S Pacific Ocean
12 K11 **Dumont, Lac** ◎ Quebec, SE Canada
77 W7 **Dumyāṭ** *Eng.* Damietta. N Egypt 31.25N 31.48E
Duna *see* Don, Russian Federation
Duna *see* Danube, C Europe
Dūna *see* Western Dvina
Dünaburg *see* Daugavpils
113 J24 **Dunaföldvár** Tolna, C Hungary 46.16N 18.54E
Dunaj *see* Wien, Austria
Dunaj *see* Danube, C Europe
113 L18 **Dunajec** ≈ S Poland
113 H21 **Dunajská Streda** *Hung.* Dunaszerdahely. Trnavský Kraj, W Slovakia 48.00N 17.27E
Dunapentele *see* Dunaújváros
Dunărea *see* Danube
118 M13 **Dunărea Veche, Braţul** ≈ SE Romania
119 N13 **Dunării, Delta** *delta* SE Romania
Dunaszerdahely *see* Dunajská Streda
113 J23 **Dunaújváros** *prev.* Dunapentele, Sztálinváros. Fejér, C Hungary 47.00N 18.55E
Dunav *see* Danube
116 J8 **Dunavska Ravnina** *Eng.* Danubian Plain. *plain* N Bulgaria
116 G7 **Dunavtsi** Vidin, NW Bulgaria 43.56N 22.49E
Dunayevtsy *see* Dunayivtsi
118 L7 **Dunayivtsi** *Rus.* Dunayevtsy. Khmel'nyts'ka Oblast', NW Ukraine 48.54N 26.51E
193 F22 **Dunback** Otago, South Island, NZ 45.22S 170.37E
8 L17 **Duncan** Vancouver Island, British Columbia, SW Canada 48.46N 123.10W
39 O15 **Duncan** Arizona, SW USA 32.43N 109.06W
28 M12 **Duncan** Oklahoma, C USA 34.30N 97.57W
Duncan Island *see* Pinzón, Isla
157 Q20 **Duncan Passage** *strait* Andaman Sea/Bay of Bengal
98 K6 **Duncansby Head** *headland* N Scotland, UK 58.37N 3.01W
12 G12 **Dunchurch** Ontario, S Canada 45.36N 79.54W
120 D7 **Dundaga** Talsi, NW Latvia 57.29N 22.19E
12 G14 **Dundalk** Ontario, S Canada 44.11N 80.22W
99 F16 **Dundalk** *Ir.* Dún Dealgan. NE Ireland 54.01N 6.25W
23 X3 **Dundalk** Maryland, NE USA 39.15N 76.31W
99 F16 **Dundalk Bay** *Ir.* Cuan Dhún Dealgan. *bay* NE Ireland
12 G16 **Dundas** Ontario, S Canada 43.16N 79.55W
188 L12 **Dundas, Lake** *salt lake* Western Australia
169 O7 **Dundbürd** Hentiy, E Mongolia 47.55N 111.37E
Dún Dealgan *see* Dundalk
13 N13 **Dundee** Quebec, SE Canada 45.01N 74.27W
85 K22 **Dundee** KwaZulu/Natal, E South Africa 28.08S 30.12E
98 K11 **Dundee** E Scotland, UK 56.28N 3.00W
33 R10 **Dundee** Michigan, N USA 41.57N 83.39W
27 R5 **Dundee** Texas, SW USA 33.43N 98.52W
204 H3 **Dundee Island** *island* Antarctica
168 L9 **Dundgovĭ** ◐ *province* C Mongolia
99 G16 **Dundrum Bay** *Ir.* Cuan Dhún Droma. *inlet* NW Irish Sea
176 Y11 **Dundu** ≈ Irian Jaya, E Indonesia
9 T15 **Dundurn** Saskatchewan, S Canada 51.43N 106.27W
168 E6 **Dund-Us** Hovd, W Mongolia 48.06N 91.22E
193 F23 **Dunedin** Otago, South Island, NZ 45.51S 170.31E
191 R7 **Dunedoo** New South Wales, SE Australia 32.04S 149.23E
99 D14 **Dunfanaghy** *Ir.* Dún Fionnachaidh. NW Ireland 55.10N 7.58W
98 J12 **Dunfermline** C Scotland, UK 56.04N 3.28W
Dún Fionnachaidh *see* Dunfanaghy
155 V10 **Dunga Bunga** Punjab, E Pakistan 29.51N 73.19E
99 F15 **Dungannon** *Ir.* Dún Geanainn. C Northern Ireland, UK 54.31N 6.46W
Dun Garbháin *see* Dungarvan
158 F15 **Dūngarpur** Rājasthān, N India 23.53N 73.39E
99 E21 **Dungarvan** *Ir.* Dun Garbháin. S Ireland 52.04N 7.37W
103 N21 **Dungau** *cultural region* SE Germany
Dún Geanainn *see* Dungannon
99 P23 **Dungeness** *headland* SE England, UK 50.55N 0.58E
65 I23 **Dungeness, Punta** *headland* S Argentina 52.25S 68.25W
Dungloe *see* Dunglow
99 D14 **Dunglow** *var.* Dungloe, *Ir.* An Clochán Liath. NW Ireland 54.57N 8.22W
191 T7 **Dungog** New South Wales, SE Australia 32.24S 151.45E
81 O16 **Dungu** Orientale, NE Dem. Rep. Congo (Zaire) 3.40N 28.31E
174 Hh3 **Dungun** *var.* Kuala Dungun. Terengganu, Peninsular Malaysia 4.46N 103.25E
82 I6 **Dungûnab** Red Sea, NE Sudan 21.06N 37.06E
13 P13 **Dunham** Quebec, SE Canada 45.08N 72.48W
Dunheved *see* Launceston
Dunholme *see* Durham
169 X10 **Dunhua** Jilin, NE China 43.22N 128.12E
165 P8 **Dunhuang** Gansu, N China 40.10N 94.43E
190 L12 **Dunkeld** Victoria, SE Australia 37.41S 142.19E
105 O1 **Dunkerque** *Eng.* Dunkirk, *Flem.* Duinekerke; *prev.* Dunquerque. Nord, N France 51.06N 2.34E
99 K23 **Dunkery Beacon** ▲ SW England, UK 51.10N 3.36W
20 C11 **Dunkirk** New York, NE USA 42.28N 79.19W
Dunkirk *see* Dunkerque
79 P17 **Dunkwa** SW Ghana 5.58N 1.45W
99 G18 **Dún Laoghaire** *Eng.* Dunleary; *prev.* Kingstown. E Ireland 53.16N 6.07W
31 S14 **Dunlap** Iowa, C USA 41.51N 95.36W
22 L10 **Dunlap** Tennessee, S USA 35.22N 85.23W
Dunleary *see* Dún Laoghaire
Dún Mánmhaí *see* Dunmanway
99 B21 **Dunmanway** *Ir.* Dún Mánmhaí. SW Ireland 51.43N 9.07W
20 I13 **Dunmore** Pennsylvania, NE USA 41.25N 75.37W
23 U10 **Dunn** North Carolina, SE USA 35.18N 78.36W
Dún na nGall *see* Donegal
25 V11 **Dunnellon** Florida, SE USA 29.03N 82.27W
98 J6 **Dunnet Head** *headland* N Scotland, UK 58.40N 3.27W
31 N14 **Dunning** Nebraska, C USA 41.49N 100.04W
67 B24 **Dunnose Head Settlement** West Falkland, Falkland Islands 51.24S 60.28W
12 G17 **Dunnville** Ontario, S Canada 42.54N 79.36W
Dún Pádraig *see* Downpatrick
Dunquerque *see* Dunkerque
Dunqulah *see* Dongola
98 L12 **Duns** SE Scotland, UK 55.46N 2.13W
31 N2 **Dunseith** North Dakota, N USA 48.48N 100.03W
37 N2 **Dunsmuir** California, W USA 41.12N 122.19W
99 N21 **Dunstable** *Lat.* Durocobrivae. E England, UK 51.52N 0.31W
193 D21 **Dunstan Mountains** ▲▲ South Island, NZ
105 O9 **Dun-sur-Auron** Cher, C France 46.52N 2.40E
193 F21 **Duntroon** Canterbury, South Island, NZ 44.52S 170.40E
155 T10 **Dunyāpur** Punjab, E Pakistan 29.48N 71.48E
169 U5 **Duobukur He** ≈ NE China
169 R12 **Duolun** *var.* Dolonnur. Nei Mongol Zizhiqu, N China 42.11N 116.30E
178 Ii14 **Dương Đông** Kiên Giang, S Vietnam 10.15N 103.58E
116 G10 **Dupnitsa** *prev.* Marek, Stanke Dimitrov. Kyustendil, W Bulgaria 42.15N 23.09E
30 L8 **Dupree** South Dakota, N USA 45.03N 101.36W
35 Q7 **Dupuyer** Montana, NW USA 48.13N 112.34W
147 Y11 **Duqm** *var.* Daqm. E Oman 19.42N 57.39E
65 F23 **Duque de York, Isla** *island* S Chile
189 N4 **Durack Range** ▲▲ Western Australia
142 K10 **Durağan** Sinop, N Turkey 41.25N 35.03E
105 S15 **Durance** ≈ SE France
33 R9 **Durand** Michigan, N USA 42.54N 83.58W
32 I6 **Durand** Wisconsin, N USA 44.37N 91.55W
197 L7 **Durand, Récif** *reef* SE New Caledonia
42 K10 **Durango** *var.* Victoria de Durango. Durango, W Mexico 24.03N 104.37W
107 P3 **Durango** País Vasco, N Spain 43.10N 2.37W
39 Q8 **Durango** Colorado, C USA 37.13N 107.51W
42 J9 **Durango** ◐ *state* C Mexico
116 O7 **Durankulak** *Rom.* Răcari; *prev.* Blatnitsa, Duranulac. Dobrich, NE Bulgaria 43.41N 28.31E
24 L4 **Durant** Mississippi, S USA 33.04N 89.51W
29 P13 **Durant** Oklahoma, C USA 33.59N 96.22W
Duranulac *see* Durankulak
107 N6 **Duratón** ≈ N Spain
63 E19 **Durazno** *var.* San Pedro de Durazno. Durazno, C Uruguay 33.24S 56.28W
63 E19 **Durazno** ◐ *department* C Uruguay
Durazzo *see* Durrës
85 K23 **Durban** *var.* Port Natal. KwaZulu/Natal, E South Africa 29.51S 31.00E
85 K23 **Durban** ✈ KwaZulu/Natal, E South Africa 29.55S 31.01E
120 C9 **Durbe** *Ger.* Durben. Liepāja, W Latvia 56.34N 21.22E
Durben *see* Durbe
101 K21 **Durbuy** Luxembourg, SE Belgium 50.21N 5.27E
107 N15 **Dúrcal** Andalucía, S Spain 37.00N 3.24W
114 F8 **Đurđevac** *Ger.* Sankt Georgen, *Hung.* Szentgyörgy; *prev.* Djurdjevac, Gjurgjevac. Koprivnica-Križevci, N Croatia 46.02N 17.03E
115 K15 **Đurđevica Tara** Montenegro, SW Yugoslavia 43.09N 19.18E
99 L24 **Durdle Door** *natural arch* S England, UK
164 L3 **Düre** Xinjiang Uygur Zizhiqu, W China 46.30N 88.25E
103 D16 **Düren** *anc.* Marcodurum. Nordrhein-Westfalen, W Germany 50.48N 6.28E
160 K12 **Durg** *prev.* Drug. Madhya Pradesh, C India 21.12N 81.19E
159 U13 **Durgapur** Dhaka, N Bangladesh 25.10N 90.41E
159 R15 **Durgāpur** West Bengal, NE India 23.30N 87.19E
12 F14 **Durham** Ontario, S Canada 44.10N 80.48W
99 M14 **Durham** *hist.* Dunholme. N England, UK 54.46N 1.34W
23 U9 **Durham** North Carolina, SE USA 35.59N 78.54W
99 L15 **Durham** *cultural region* N England, UK
174 Gg7 **Duri** Sumatera, W Indonesia 1.13N 101.13E
Duria Major *see* Dora Baltea
Duria Minor *see* Dora Riparia
Durlas *see* Thurles
147 P8 **Ḑurmā** Ar Riyāḑ, C Saudi Arabia 24.37N 46.06E
115 J15 **Durmitor** ▲ N Yugoslavia 43.06N 19.00E
98 H6 **Durness** N Scotland, UK 58.34N 4.45W
111 Y3 **Dürnkrut** Niederösterreich, E Austria 48.28N 16.50E
Durnovaria *see* Dorchester
Durobrivae *see* Rochester
Durocasses *see* Dreux
Durocobrivae *see* Dunstable
Durocortorum *see* Reims
Durostorum *see* Silistra
Durovernum *see* Canterbury
115 K20 **Durrës** *var.* Durrësi, Dursi, *It.* Durazzo, *SCr.* Drač, *Turk.* Draç. Durrës, W Albania 41.19N 19.25E
115 K19 **Durrës** ◐ *district* W Albania
Durrësi *see* Durrës
99 A21 **Dursey Island** *Ir.* Oileán Baoi. *island* SW Ireland
Dursi *see* Durrës
Durud *see* Do Rūd
116 P12 **Durusu** İstanbul, NW Turkey 41.18N 28.41E
116 O12 **Durusu Gölü** ◎ NW Turkey
144 I9 **Durūz, Jabal ad** ▲ SW Syria 37.00N 32.30E
192 K13 **D'Urville Island** *island* C NZ
176 Xx9 **D'Urville, Tanjung** *headland* Irian Jaya, E Indonesia 1.26S 137.52E
Dusa Mareb/Dusa Marreb *see* Dhuusa Marreeb
120 I11 **Dusetos** Zarasai, NE Lithuania 55.44N 25.49E
152 H14 **Dushak** Akhalskiy Velayat, S Turkmenistan 37.15N 59.57E
166 K12 **Dushan** Guizhou, S China 25.45N 107.33E
153 P13 **Dushanbe** *var.* Dyushambe; *prev.* Stalinabad, *Taj.* Stalinobod. ● (Tajikistan) W Tajikistan 38.35N 68.43E
153 P13 **Dushanbe** ✈ W Tajikistan 38.31N 68.49E
143 T9 **Dushet'i** E Georgia 42.07N 44.44E
20 H13 **Dushore** Pennsylvania, NE USA 41.30N 76.23W
193 A23 **Dusky Sound** *sound* South Island, NZ
103 E15 **Düsseldorf** *var.* Duesseldorf. Nordrhein-Westfalen, W Germany 51.13N 6.49E
153 P14 **Dŭstí** *Rus.* Dusti. SW Tajikistan 37.22N 68.41E
204 I9 **Dustin Island** *island* Antarctica
153 O10 **Dŭstlik** Jizzakh Wiloyati, C Uzbekistan 40.37N 67.59E
Dutch East Indies *see* Indonesia
Dutch Guiana *see* Surinam
40 L17 **Dutch Harbor** Unalaska Island, Alaska, USA 53.50N 166.33W
38 J3 **Dutch Mount** ▲ Utah, W USA 40.16N 113.56W
Dutch New Guinea *see* Irian Jaya
Dutch West Indies *see* Netherlands Antilles
85 H20 **Dutlwe** Kweneng, S Botswana 23.56S 23.53E
69 V16 **Du Toit Fracture Zone** *tectonic feature* SW Indian Ocean
129 U8 **Dutovo** Respublika Komi, NW Russian Federation 63.45N 56.38E
79 V13 **Dutsan Wai** *var.* Dutsen Wai. Kaduna, C Nigeria 10.49N 8.15E
79 W13 **Dutse** Jigawa, N Nigeria 11.43N 9.25E
Dutsen Wai *see* Dutsan Wai
Duttia *see* Datia
12 E17 **Dutton** Ontario, S Canada 42.40N 81.28W
38 L7 **Dutton, Mount** ▲ Utah, W USA 38.00N 112.10W
168 E7 **Duut** Hovd, W Mongolia 47.28N 91.52E
12 K11 **Duval, Lac** ◎ Quebec, SE Canada
131 W3 **Duvan** Respublika Bashkortostan, W Russian Federation 55.42N 57.56E
144 L9 **Duwaykhilat Satīḩ ar Ruwayshid** *seasonal river* SE Jordan
Dux *see* Duchcov
166 J13 **Duyang Shan** ▲▲ S China
178 Jj15 **Duyên Hai** Tra Vinh, S Vietnam 9.39N 106.28E
166 K12 **Duyun** Guizhou, S China 26.16N 107.28E
142 G11 **Düzce** Bolu, NW Turkey 40.51N 31.09E
Duzdab *see* Zāhedān
Duzenkyr, Khrebet *see* Duzkyr, Khrebet
152 I16 **Duzkyr, Khrebet** *prev.* Khrebet Duzenkyr. ▲▲ S Turkmenistan
Dvina Bay *see* Chëshskaya Guba
Dvinsk *see* Daugavpils
128 L7 **Dvinskaya Guba** *bay* NW Russian Federation
114 E10 **Dvor** Sisak-Moslavina, C Croatia 45.05N 16.22E
119 W5 **Dvorichna** Kharkivs'ka Oblast', E Ukraine 49.52N 37.43E
113 F16 **Dvůr Králové nad Labem** *Ger.* Königinhof an der Elbe. Hradecký Kraj, NE Czech Republic 50.25N 15.48E
160 A10 **Dwārka** Gujarāt, W India 22.13N 68.58E
32 M12 **Dwight** Illinois, N USA 41.05N 88.25W
100 N8 **Dwingeloo** Drenthe, NE Netherlands 52.49N 6.20E
35 N10 **Dworshak Reservoir** ⊡ Idaho, NW USA
Dyal *see* Dyaul Island
Dyanev *see* Deynau
Dyatlovo *see* Dzyatlava
195 N9 **Dyaul Island** *var.* Djaul, Dyal. *island* NE PNG
22 G8 **Dyer** Tennessee, S USA 36.04N 88.59W
16 O1 **Dyer, Cape** *headland* Baffin Island, Nunavut, NE Canada 66.37N 61.13W
22 F8 **Dyersburg** Tennessee, S USA 36.01N 89.23W
31 Y13 **Dyersville** Iowa, C USA 42.29N 91.07W
99 I21 **Dyfed** *cultural region* SW Wales, UK
Dyfrdwy, Afon *see* Dee
Dyhernfurth *see* Brzeg Dolny
113 E19 **Dyje** *var.* Thaya. ≈ Austria/Czech Republic *see also* Thaya
119 T5 **Dykanska** Poltavs'ka Oblast', C Ukraine 49.48N 34.33E
194 L15 **Dyke Ackland Bay** *inlet* E PNG
131 N16 **Dykhtau** ▲ SW Russian Federation 43.01N 42.56E
113 A16 **Dyleń** *Ger.* Tillenberg. ▲ NW Czech Republic 49.58N 12.31E
112 K9 **Dylewska Góra** ▲ N Poland 53.33N 19.57E
119 O4 **Dymer** Kyyivs'ka Oblast', N Ukraine 50.50N 30.21E
119 W7 **Dymytrov** *Rus.* Dimitrov. Donets'ka Oblast', SE Ukraine 48.18N 37.19E
113 O17 **Dynów** Podkarpackie, SE Poland 49.49N 22.14E
31 X13 **Dysart** Iowa, C USA 42.10N 92.18W
Dysna *see* Dzisna
117 D18 **Dytikí Ellás** *Eng.* Greece West. ◐ *region* C Greece
117 C14 **Dytikí Makedonía** *Eng.* Macedonia West. ◐ *region* N Greece
Dyurmen'tyube *see* Dermentobe
131 U4 **Dyurtyuli** Respublika Bashkortostan, W Russian Federation 55.31N 54.49E
Dyushambe *see* Dushanbe
168 I7 **Dzaanhushuu** Arhangay, C Mongolia 47.36N 101.06E
Dza Chu *see* Mekong
168 I8 **Dzadgay** Bayanhongor, C Mongolia 46.12N 99.29E
168 H8 **Dzag** Bayanhongor, C Mongolia 46.54N 99.11E
168 H10 **Dzalaa** Bayanhongor, C Mongolia 44.29N 99.19E
180 J14 **Dzaoudzi** E Mayotte 12.48S 45.18E
Dzaudzhikau *see* Vladikavkaz
168 G7 **Dzavhan** ◐ *province* NW Mongolia
168 G7 **Dzavhan Gol** ≈ NW Mongolia
168 J7 **Dzegstey** Arhangay, C Mongolia 47.38N 102.31E
131 O3 **Dzerzhinsk** Nizhegorodskaya Oblast', W Russian Federation 56.20N 43.22E
Dzerzhinsk *see* Dzyarzhynsk, Belarus
Dzerzhinsk *see* Dzerzhyns'k, Ukraine
Dzerzhinskiy *see* Nar'yan-Mar
151 W13 **Dzerzhinskoye** Almaty, SE Kazakhstan 45.49N 81.04E
119 X7 **Dzerzhyns'k** *Rus.* Dzerzhinsk. Donets'ka Oblast', SE Ukraine 48.21N 37.50E
118 M5 **Dzerzhyns'k** Zhytomyrs'ka Oblast', N Ukraine 50.07N 27.56E
Dzhailgan *see* Jayilgan
151 N14 **Dzhalagash** *Kaz.* Zhalashash. Kzylorda, S Kazakhstan 45.06N 64.40E
153 T10 **Dzhalal-Abad** *Kir.* Jalal-Abad. Dzhalal-Abadskaya Oblast', W Kyrgyzstan 40.55N 73.00E
153 S9 **Dzhalal-Abadskaya Oblast'** *Kir.* Jalal-Abad Oblasty. ◐ *province* W Kyrgyzstan
Dzhalilabad *see* Cälilabad
126 Ll15 **Dzhalinda** Amurskaya Oblast', SE Russian Federation 53.29N 123.53E
150 G9 **Dzhambeyty** *Kaz.* Zhympīty. Zapadnyy Kazakhstan, W Kazakhstan 50.16N 52.34E
Dzhambulskaya Oblast' *see* Zhambyl
Dzhankel'dy *see* Jangeldi
119 T12 **Dzhankoy** Respublika Krym, S Ukraine 45.42N 34.24E
151 V14 **Dzhansugurov** *Kaz.* Zhansūgirov. Almaty, SE Kazakhstan 45.25N 79.23E
153 R9 **Dzhany-Bazar** *var.* Yangibazar. Dzhalal-Abadskaya Oblast', W Kyrgyzstan 41.40N 70.49E
150 D9 **Dzhanybek** *Kaz.* Zhänibek. Zapadnyy Kazakhstan, W Kazakhstan 49.27N 46.51E
126 L8 **Dzhardzhan** Respublika Sakha (Yakutiya), NE Russian Federation 68.47N 123.51E
Dzharkurgan *see* Jarqŭrghon
119 S11 **Dzharylhats'ka Zatoka** *gulf* S Ukraine
Dzhayilgan *see* Jayilgan
152 B11 **Dzhebel** *Turkm.* Jebel. Balkanskiy Velayat, W Turkmenistan 39.42N 54.10E
153 T14 **Dzhelandy** SE Tajikistan 37.34N 72.34E
153 Y7 **Dzhergalan** *Kir.* Jyrgalan. Issyk-Kul'skaya Oblast', NE Kyrgyzstan 42.37N 78.55E
150 L8 **Dzhetygara** *Kaz.* Zhetiqara. Kostanay, NW Kazakhstan 52.10N 61.12E
Dzhetysay *see* Zhetysay.
Dzhezkazgan *see* Zhezkazgan
152 J10 **Dzhigirbent** *Turkm.* Jigerbent. Lebapskiy Velayat, NE Turkmenistan 40.44N 61.56E
Dzhirgatal' *see* Jirgatol
Dzhizak *see* Jizzakh
Dzhizakskaya Oblast' *see* Jizzakh Wiloyati
127 N12 **Dzhugdzhur, Khrebet** ▲▲ E Russian Federation
Dzhul'fa *see* Culfa
Dzhuma *see* Juma
151 W14 **Dzhungarskiy Alatau** ▲▲ China/Kazakhstan
150 M14 **Dzhusaly** *Kaz.* Zholsaly. Kzylorda, SW Kazakhstan 45.28N 64.04E
152 J12 **Dzhynlykum, Peski** *desert* E Turkmenistan
112 L9 **Działdowo** Warmińsko-Mazurskie, C Poland 53.13N 20.11E
113 L16 **Działoszyce** Świętokrzyskie, C Poland 50.21N 20.19E
43 X11 **Dzidzantún** Yucatán, E Mexico
113 G15 **Dzierżoniów** *Ger.* Reichenbach. Dolnośląskie, SW Poland 50.43N 16.40E
43 X11 **Dzilam de Bravo** Yucatán, E Mexico 21.24N 88.52W
120 K12 **Dzisna** *Rus.* Disna. Vitsyebskaya Voblasts', N Belarus 55.33N 28.13E
120 K12 **Dzisna** *Lith.* Dysna, *Rus.* Disna. ≈ Belarus/Lithuania
121 G20 **Dzivin** *Rus.* Divin. Brestskaya Voblasts', SW Belarus 51.58N 24.33E
121 M15 **Dzmitravichy** *Rus.* Dmitrovichi. Minskaya Voblasts', C Belarus 53.58N 29.14E
168 M8 **Dzogsool** Töv, C Mongolia 46.46N 107.18E
133 S8 **Dzungaria** *var.* Sungaria, Zungaria. *physical region* W China
Dzungarian Basin *see* Junggar Pendi
168 G5 **Dzür** Dzavhan, W Mongolia 49.36N 95.46E
169 Q8 **Dzüünbulag** Dornod, E Mongolia 46.48N 115.21E
169 O8 **Dzüünbulag** Sühbaatar, E Mongolia 46.30N 112.22E
168 H7 **Dzuunmod** Dzavhan, C Mongolia 48.09N 97.22E
168 L8 **Dzuunmod** Töv, C Mongolia 47.45N 107.00E
Dzüün Soyonĭ Nuruu *see* Eastern Sayans
168 F8 **Dzüyl** Govĭ-Altay, SW Mongolia 46.09N 93.55E
Dzvina *see* Western Dvina
121 J16 **Dzyarzhynsk** *Rus.* Dzerzhinsk; *prev.* Kaydanovo. Minskaya Voblasts', C Belarus 53.41N 27.09E
121 H17 **Dzyatlava** *Pol.* Zdzięcioł, *Rus.* Dyatlovo. Hrodzyenskaya Voblasts', W Belarus 53.27N 25.23E

E

E *see* Hubei
Éadan Doire *see* Edenderry
39 W6 **Eads** Colorado, C USA 38.28N 102.46W
39 O13 **Eagar** Arizona, SW USA 34.05N 109.17W
41 T8 **Eagle** Alaska, USA 64.47N 141.12W
11 S8 **Eagle** ≈ Newfoundland, E Canada
8 I3 **Eagle** ≈ Yukon Territory, NW Canada
31 T7 **Eagle Bend** Minnesota, N USA 46.10N 95.02W
30 M8 **Eagle Butte** South Dakota, N USA 44.58N 101.13W
31 V12 **Eagle Grove** Iowa, C USA 42.39N 93.54W
21 R2 **Eagle Lake** Maine, NE USA 47.01N 68.35W
27 U11 **Eagle Lake** Texas, SW USA 29.35N 96.19W
10 A11 **Eagle Lake** ◎ Ontario, S Canada
37 P3 **Eagle Lake** ◎ California, W USA
21 R3 **Eagle Lake** ◎ Maine, NE USA
31 Y3 **Eagle Mountain** ▲ Minnesota, N USA 47.54N 90.33W
27 T6 **Eagle Mountain Lake** ⊡ Texas, SW USA
39 S9 **Eagle Nest Lake** ⊡ New Mexico, SW USA
27 P13 **Eagle Pass** Texas, SW USA 28.43N 100.31W
67 C25 **Eagle Passage** *passage* SW Atlantic Ocean
37 R8 **Eagle Peak** ▲ California, W USA 38.11N 119.22W
37 Q2 **Eagle Peak** ▲ California, W USA 41.16N 120.12W
39 P13 **Eagle Peak** ▲ New Mexico, SW USA 33.39N 109.36W
8 I4 **Eagle Plain** Yukon Territory, NW Canada 66.23N 136.42W
34 G15 **Eagle Point** Oregon, NW USA 42.28N 122.48W
195 N17 **Eagle Point** *headland* SE PNG 10.31S 149.53E
41 R11 **Eagle River** Alaska, USA 61.18N 149.38W
32 M2 **Eagle River** Michigan, N USA 47.24N 88.18W
32 L4 **Eagle River** Wisconsin, N USA 45.55N 89.15W
23 S6 **Eagle Rock** Virginia, NE USA 37.40N 79.46W
38 J13 **Eagletail Mountains** ▲▲ Arizona, SW USA
178 Kk12 **Ea Hleo** Đắc Lắc, S Vietnam 13.09N 108.14E
178 Kk12 **Ea Kar** Đắc Lắc, S Vietnam 12.47N 108.26E
Eanjum *see* Anjum
Eanodat *see* Enontekiö
10 B10 **Ear Falls** Ontario, C Canada 50.37N 93.13W
29 X10 **Earle** Arkansas, C USA 35.16N 90.28W
37 R12 **Earlimart** California, W USA 35.52N 119.17W
22 I6 **Earlington** Kentucky, S USA 37.16N 87.30W
12 H8 **Earlton** Ontario, S Canada 47.41N 79.46W
31 T13 **Early** Iowa, C USA 42.27N 95.09W
98 J11 **Earn** ≈ N Scotland, UK
193 C21 **Earnslaw, Mount** ▲ South Island, NZ 44.34S 168.26E
26 M4 **Earth** Texas, SW USA 34.13N 102.24W
23 P11 **Easley** South Carolina, SE USA 34.49N 82.36W
East *see* Est
East Açores Fracture Zone *see* East Azores Fracture Zone
99 P19 **East Anglia** *physical region* E England, UK
13 Q12 **East Angus** Quebec, SE Canada 45.29N 71.39W
East Antarctica *see* Greater Antarctica
20 E10 **East Aurora** New York, NE USA 42.44N 78.36W
East Australian Basin *see* Tasman Basin
East Azerbaijan *see* Āzarbāyjān-e Sharqī
66 L9 **East Azores Fracture Zone** *var.* East Açores Fracture Zone. *tectonic feature* E Atlantic Ocean
24 M11 **East Bay** *bay* Louisiana, S USA
27 V11 **East Bernard** Texas, SW USA 29.31N 96.04W
31 V8 **East Bethel** Minnesota, N USA 45.24N 93.14W
East Borneo *see* Kalimantan Timur
99 P23 **Eastbourne** SE England, UK 50.46N 0.16E
13 R11 **East-Broughton** Quebec, SE Canada 46.13N 71.03W
46 M6 **East Caicos** *island* E Turks and Caicos Islands
192 R7 **East Cape** *headland* North Island, NZ 37.40S 178.31E

◆ Country ● Country Capital ◇ Dependent Territory ○ Dependent Territory Capital ◐ Administrative Region ✈ International Airport ▲ Mountain ▲▲ Mountain Range ⛰ Volcano ≈ River ◎ Lake ⊡ Reservoir

El Escorial – Epe

El Escorial see San Lorenzo de El Escorial
Élesd see Aleşd
116 F11 Eleshnitsa ≈ W Bulgaria
143 S13 Eleşkirt Ağrı, E Turkey 39.22N 42.48E
44 F5 El Estor Izabal, E Guatemala 15.31N 89.19W
Eleutherae see Eléftheres
46 I2 Eleuthera Island island N Bahamas
39 S5 Elevenmile Canyon Reservoir ⊡ Colorado, C USA
29 W8 Eleven Point River ≈ Arkansas/Missouri, C USA
Elevsis see Elefsína
Elevtheroúpolis see Eleftheroúpoli
77 W8 El Faiyûm var. Al Fayyūm. N Egypt 29.24N 30.52E
82 B10 El Fasher var. Al Fāshir. Northern Darfur, W Sudan 13.37N 25.22E
77 W8 El Fashn var. Al Fashn. C Egypt 28.49N 30.54E
El Ferrol/El Ferrol del Caudillo see Ferrol
41 W13 Elfin Cove Chichagof Island, Alaska, USA 58.09N 136.16W
107 W4 El Fluvià ≈ NE Spain
42 H7 El Fuerte Sinaloa, W Mexico 26.28N 108.34W
82 D11 El Fula Western Kordofan, C Sudan 11.43N 28.19E
El Gedaref see Gedaref
82 A10 El Geneina var. Ajjinena, Al-Genain, Al Junaynah. Western Darfur, W Sudan 13.27N 22.30E
98 J8 Elgin NE Scotland, UK 57.39N 3.19W
32 M10 Elgin Illinois, N USA 42.02N 88.16W
31 P14 Elgin Nebraska, C USA 41.58N 98.04W
37 Y9 Elgin Nevada, W USA 37.19N 114.30W
30 L6 Elgin North Dakota, N USA 46.24N 101.51W
28 M12 Elgin Oklahoma, C USA 34.46N 98.17W
27 T10 Elgin Texas, SW USA 30.21N 97.22W
127 N9 El'ginskiy Respublika Sakha (Yakutiya), NE Russian Federation 64.27N 141.57E
77 W8 El Gîza var. Al Jīzah, Gīza, Gizeh. N Egypt 30.01N 31.13E
76 J8 El Goléa var. Al Golea. C Algeria 30.35N 2.58E
42 D2 El Golfo de Santa Clara Sonora, NW Mexico 31.44N 114.34W
83 G18 Elgon, Mount ▲ E Uganda 1.07N 34.29E
96 I10 Elgpiggen ▲ S Norway 62.13N 11.18E
107 T4 El Grado Aragón, NE Spain 42.09N 0.13E
42 L6 El Guaje, Laguna ⊡ NE Mexico
56 H6 El Guayabo Zulia, W Venezuela 8.37N 72.19W
79 O6 El Guețțâra oasis N Mali 22.01N 3.00W
78 J6 El Ḥammâmi desert N Mauritania
78 M5 El Ḥank cliff N Mauritania
El Haseke see Al Ḥasakah
82 H10 El Hawata Gedaref, E Sudan 13.25N 34.42E
El Higo see Higos
176 Uu16 Eliase Pulau Selaru, E Indonesia 8.16S 130.49E
Elías Piña see Comendador
27 R6 Eliasville Texas, SW USA 32.55N 98.46W
Elichpur see Achalpur
39 V13 Elida New Mexico, SW USA 33.57N 103.39W
117 F18 Elikónas ▲ C Greece
69 T10 Elila ≈ W Dem. Rep. Congo (Zaire)
41 N9 Elim Alaska, USA 64.37N 162.15W
Elimberrum see Auch
Eliocroca see Lorca
63 B16 Elisa Santa Fe, C Argentina 30.42S 61.04W
Elisabethstedt see Dumbrăveni
Élisabethville see Lubumbashi
131 O13 Elista Respublika Kalmykiya, SW Russian Federation 46.17N 44.09E
190 I9 Elizabeth South Australia 34.44S 138.39E
23 Q3 Elizabeth West Virginia, NE USA 39.03N 81.22W
21 Q9 Elizabeth, Cape headland Maine, NE USA 43.34N 70.12W
23 Y8 Elizabeth City North Carolina, SE USA 36.18N 76.13W
23 P8 Elizabethton Tennessee, S USA 36.21N 82.12W
32 M17 Elizabethtown Illinois, N USA 37.24N 88.21W
22 K6 Elizabethtown Kentucky, S USA 37.41N 85.51W
20 L7 Elizabethtown New York, NE USA 44.13N 73.37W
23 U11 Elizabethtown North Carolina, SE USA 34.37N 78.36W
20 G15 Elizabethtown Pennsylvania, NE USA 40.08N 76.36W
76 E6 El-Jadida prev. Mazagan. W Morocco 33.15N 8.27W
El Jafr see Jafr, Qā' al
82 F11 El Jebelein White Nile, E Sudan 12.37N 32.51E
112 N8 Ełk Ger. Lyck. Warmińsko-Mazurskie, NE Poland 53.51N 22.19E
112 O8 Ełk ≈ NE Poland
31 Y12 Elkader Iowa, C USA 42.51N 91.24W
82 G9 El Kamlin Gezira, C Sudan 15.01N 33.02E
35 N11 Elk City Idaho, NW USA 45.50N 115.28W
28 K10 Elk City Oklahoma, C USA 35.24N 99.24W
29 P7 Elk City Lake ⊡ Kansas, C USA
36 M5 Elk Creek California, W USA 39.34N 122.34W
30 J10 Elk Creek ≈ South Dakota, N USA
76 M5 El Kef var. Al Kāf, Le Kef. NW Tunisia 36.13N 8.44E
76 F7 El Kelâa Srarhna var. Kal al Sraghna. C Morocco 32.05N 7.20W
El Kerak see Al Karak
9 P17 Elkford British Columbia, SW Canada 49.58N 114.57W
El Khalil see Hebron
82 E7 El Khandaq Northern, N Sudan 18.34N 30.34E
77 W10 El Khârga var. Al Khārijah. C Egypt 25.31N 30.36E
33 P11 Elkhart Indiana, N USA 41.40N 85.58W
28 H7 Elkhart Kansas, C USA 37.00N 101.51W
27 V8 Elkhart Texas, SW USA 31.37N 95.34W
32 M7 Elkhart Lake ◎ Wisconsin, N USA
El Khartûm see Khartoum
39 Q3 Elkhead Mountains ▲▲ Colorado, C USA
20 I12 Elk Hill ▲ Pennsylvania, NE USA 41.42N 75.33W
144 G8 El Khiyam var. Al Khiyām, Khiam. S Lebanon 33.12N 35.42E
31 S15 Elkhorn Nebraska, C USA 41.17N 96.13W
32 M9 Elkhorn Wisconsin, N USA 42.40N 88.34W
31 R14 Elkhorn River ≈ Nebraska, C USA
131 O16 El'khotovo Respublika Severnaya Osetiya, SW Russian Federation 43.18N 44.17E
116 L10 Elkhovo prev. Kizilagach. Yambol, E Bulgaria 42.12N 26.36E
23 R8 Elkin North Carolina, SE USA 36.14N 80.51W
23 S4 Elkins West Virginia, NE USA 38.55N 79.51W
205 X3 Elkins, Mount ▲ Antarctica 66.25S 53.54E
12 G8 Elk Lake Ontario, S Canada 47.44N 80.19W
33 P6 Elk Lake ◎ Michigan, N USA
20 F12 Elkland Pennsylvania, NE USA 41.59N 77.16W
37 W3 Elko Nevada, W USA 40.48N 115.46W
9 R14 Elk Point Alberta, SW Canada 53.52N 110.49W
31 R12 Elk Point South Dakota, N USA 42.42N 96.37W
31 V8 Elk River Minnesota, N USA 45.18N 93.34W
22 J10 Elk River ≈ Alabama/Tennessee, S USA
23 R4 Elk River ≈ West Virginia, NE USA
22 I7 Elkton Kentucky, S USA 36.48N 87.07W
23 Y2 Elkton Maryland, NE USA 39.36N 75.49W
31 R10 Elkton South Dakota, N USA 44.14N 96.28W
22 I10 Elkton Tennessee, S USA 35.01N 86.51W
23 U5 Elkton Virginia, NE USA 38.22N 78.35W
El Kuneitra see Al Qunayţirah
83 L15 El Kure Somali, E Ethiopia 5.37N 42.05E
82 D12 El Lagowa Western Kordofan, C Sudan 11.22N 29.10E
41 S12 Ellamar Alaska, USA 60.54N 146.37W
Ellás see Greece
25 S6 Ellaville Georgia, SE USA 32.14N 84.18W
207 P9 Ellef Ringnes Island island Nunavut, N Canada
31 V10 Ellendale Minnesota, N USA 43.53N 93.19W
31 P7 Ellendale North Dakota, N USA 45.57N 98.33W
38 M6 Ellen, Mount ▲ Utah, W USA 38.06N 110.48W
34 I9 Ellensburg Washington, NW USA 47.00N 120.34W
20 K12 Ellenville New York, NE USA 41.43N 74.24W
Ellep see Lib
23 T10 Ellerbe North Carolina, SE USA 35.04N 79.45W
207 P10 Ellesmere Island island Queen Elizabeth Islands, Nunavut, N Canada
193 H19 Ellesmere, Lake ◎ South Island, NZ
99 K18 Ellesmere Port C England, UK 53.16N 2.54W
33 O14 Ellettsville Indiana, N USA 39.13N 86.37W
101 E19 Ellezelles Hainaut, SW Belgium 50.44N 3.40E
15 Jj4 Ellice ≈ Nunavut, NE Canada
Ellice Islands see Tuvalu
Ellichpur see Achalpur
23 W3 Ellicott City Maryland, NE USA 39.16N 76.48W
25 S2 Ellijay Georgia, SE USA 34.42N 84.28W
29 W7 Ellington Missouri, C USA 37.14N 90.58W
28 L5 Ellinwood Kansas, C USA 38.21N 98.34W
85 J24 Elliot Eastern Cape, SE South Africa 31.19S 27.51E
12 D10 Elliot Lake Ontario, S Canada 46.24N 82.37W
189 X6 Elliot, Mount ▲ Queensland, E Australia 19.36S 147.02E
23 T5 Elliott Knob ▲ Virginia, NE USA 38.10N 79.18W
28 K4 Ellis Kansas, C USA 38.56N 99.33W
190 F8 Elliston South Australia 33.39S 134.56E
24 M7 Ellisville Mississippi, S USA 31.36N 89.12W
107 V5 El Llobregat ≈ NE Spain
98 L9 Ellon NE Scotland, UK 57.22N 2.06W
Ellore see Elūru
23 S13 Elloree South Carolina, SE USA 33.34N 80.37W
28 M4 Ellsworth Kansas, C USA 38.43N 98.13W
21 S7 Ellsworth Maine, NE USA 44.32N 68.25W
32 I6 Ellsworth Wisconsin, N USA 44.43N 92.28W
28 M11 Ellsworth, Lake ⊡ Oklahoma, C USA
204 K9 Ellsworth Land physical region Antarctica
204 L9 Ellsworth Mountains ▲▲ Antarctica
103 J21 Ellwangen Baden-Württemberg, S Germany 48.58N 10.07E
20 B14 Ellwood City Pennsylvania, NE USA 40.49N 80.15W
110 H8 Elm Glarus, NE Switzerland 46.55N 9.09E
34 G9 Elma Washington, NW USA 47.00N 123.24W
124 Qq15 El Maḥalla el Kubra var. Al Maḥallah al Kubrā, Mahalla el Kubra. N Egypt 30.58N 31.10E
76 E9 El Mahbas var. Mahbés. SW Western Sahara 27.25N 9.09W
65 H17 El Maitén Chubut, W Argentina 42.03S 71.10W
142 E16 Elmalı Antalya, SW Turkey 36.40N 29.54E
82 G10 El Manaqil Gezira, C Sudan 14.12N 33.01E
56 M12 El Mango Amazonas, S Venezuela 1.55N 66.34W
77 W7 El Manṣûra var. Al Manṣūrah, Manṣūra. N Egypt 31.02N 31.30E
57 P8 El Manteco Bolívar, E Venezuela 7.17N 62.31W
31 O16 Elm Creek Nebraska, C USA 40.43N 99.22W
El Mediyya see Médéa
79 V9 Elméki Agadez, C Niger 17.52N 8.07E
110 K7 Elmen Tirol, W Austria 47.22N 10.34E
20 I16 Elmer New Jersey, NE USA 39.34N 75.09W
144 G6 El Mina var. Al Mīnā'. N Lebanon 34.28N 35.49E
77 W9 El Minya var. Al Minyā, Minya. C Egypt 28.06N 30.40E
12 F15 Elmira Ontario, S Canada 43.35N 80.34W
20 G11 Elmira New York, NE USA 42.06N 76.49W
38 K13 El Mirage Arizona, SW USA 33.36N 112.19W
31 O7 Elm Lake ⊡ South Dakota, N USA
El Moján see San Rafael
107 N7 El Molar Madrid, C Spain 40.43N 3.34W
78 L7 El Mrâyer well C Mauritania 21.40N 7.50W
78 L5 El Mreiti well N Mauritania 23.40N 7.23W
78 L8 El Mreyyé desert E Mauritania
31 P8 Elm River ≈ North Dakota/South Dakota, N USA
102 I9 Elmshorn Schleswig-Holstein, N Germany 53.45N 9.39E
82 D12 El Muglad Western Kordofan, C Sudan 11.01N 27.43E
El Muwaqqar see Al Muwaqqar
12 G14 Elmvale Ontario, S Canada 44.34N 79.53W
32 K12 Elmwood Illinois, N USA 40.46N 89.58W
28 J8 Elmwood Oklahoma, C USA 36.37N 100.31W
105 P17 Elne anc. Illiberis. Pyrénées-Orientales, S France 42.36N 2.58E
56 F11 El Nevado, Cerro elevation C Colombia 3.56N 74.20W
179 Oo13 El Nido Palawan, W Philippines 11.10N 119.25E
64 I12 El Nihuil Mendoza, W Argentina 35.07S 68.38W
77 W7 El Nouzha ✕ (Alexandria) N Egypt 31.06N 29.58E
82 E10 El Obeid var. Al Obayyid, Al Ubayyiḍ. Northern Kordofan, C Sudan 13.10N 30.10E
43 O13 El Oro México, S Mexico 19.51N 100.07W
58 B8 El Oro ◐ province SW Ecuador
63 B19 Elortondo Santa Fe, C Argentina 33.42S 61.37W
56 J8 Elorza Apure, C Venezuela 7.01N 69.30W
El Ouâdi see El Oued
76 L7 El Oued var. Al Oued, El Ouâdi, El Wad. NE Algeria 33.19N 6.52E
38 L15 Eloy Arizona, SW USA 32.47N 111.33W
57 Q7 El Palmar Bolívar, E Venezuela 8.03N 61.51W
42 K8 El Palmito Durango, W Mexico 25.40N 104.58W
57 P7 El Pao Bolívar, E Venezuela 8.02N 62.38W
56 K5 El Pao Cojedes, N Venezuela 9.42N 68.12W
44 J7 El Paraíso El Paraíso, S Honduras 13.52N 86.32W
44 I7 El Paraíso ◐ department SE Honduras
32 L12 El Paso Illinois, N USA 40.44N 89.01W
26 G8 El Paso Texas, SW USA 31.45N 106.30W
26 G8 El Paso ✕ Texas, SW USA 31.48N 106.24W
107 U7 El Perelló Cataluña, NE Spain 40.52N 0.43E
57 P5 El Pilar Sucre, NE Venezuela 10.33N 63.13W
44 F7 El Pital, Cerro ▲ El Salvador/Honduras 14.19N 89.06W
37 Q9 El Portal California, W USA 37.40N 119.46W
42 J3 El Porvenir Chihuahua, N Mexico 31.13N 105.51W
45 U14 El Porvenir San Blas, N Panama 9.33N 78.55W
107 W6 El Prat de Llobregat Cataluña, NE Spain 41.19N 2.04E
44 H5 El Progreso Yoro, NW Honduras 15.25N 87.49W
44 A2 El Progreso off. Departamento de El Progreso. ◐ department C Guatemala
El Progreso see Guastatoya
106 L9 El Puente del Arzobispo Castilla-La Mancha, C Spain 39.48N 5.10W
106 J15 El Puerto de Santa María Andalucía, S Spain 36.36N 6.13W
64 I8 El Puesto Catamarca, NW Argentina 27.57S 67.37W
El Qâhira see Cairo
77 V10 El Qaṣr var. Al Qaṣr. C Egypt 25.39N 28.54E
El Qatrani see Al Qaṭrānah
42 I10 El Quelite Sinaloa, C Mexico 23.37N 106.26W
64 G9 Elqui, Río ≈ N Chile
El Quneitra see Al Qunayţirah
El Quseir see Al Quşayr
El Quweira see Al Quwayrah
147 O15 El-Rahaba ✕ (Şan'ā') W Yemen 15.28N 44.12E
44 M10 El Rama Región Autónoma Atlántico Sur, SE Nicaragua 12.12N 84.13W
45 W16 El Real var. El Real de Santa María. Darién, SE Panama 8.07N 77.42W
El Real de Santa María see El Real
28 M10 El Reno Oklahoma, C USA 35.31N 97.57W
42 K9 El Rodeo Durango, C Mexico 25.08N 104.34W
106 J13 El Ronquillo Andalucía, S Spain 37.43N 6.09W
9 S16 Elrose Saskatchewan, S Canada 51.07N 107.59W
32 K8 Elroy Wisconsin, N USA 43.43N 90.16W
27 S17 Elsa Texas, SW USA 26.17N 97.59W
77 W8 El Ṣaff var. Aş Şaff. N Egypt 29.26N 31.19E
42 J10 El Salto Durango, C Mexico 23.46N 105.22W
44 D8 El Salvador off. Republica de El Salvador. ◆ republic Central America
56 K7 El Samán de Apure Apure, C Venezuela 7.51N 68.47W
12 D7 Elsas Ontario, S Canada 48.31N 82.53W
42 F3 El Sásabe var. Aduana del Sásabe. Sonora, NW Mexico 31.27N 111.31W
Elsass see Alsace
42 J5 El Sáuz Chihuahua, N Mexico 29.03N 106.15W
29 W4 Elsberry Missouri, C USA 39.10N 90.46W
47 P9 El Seibo var. Santa Cruz de El Seibo, Santa Cruz del Seibo. E Dominican Republic 18.45N 69.04W
44 B7 El Semillero Barra Nahualate Escuintla, SW Guatemala 14.01N 91.28W
Elsene see Ixelles
165 N11 Elsen Nur ◎ C China
38 L6 Elsinore Utah, W USA 38.40N 112.09W
Elsinore see Helsingør
101 L18 Elsloo Limburg, SE Netherlands 50.57N 5.46E
62 G13 El Soberbio Misiones, NE Argentina 27.15S 54.04W
57 N6 El Socorro Guárico, C Venezuela 9.00N 65.42W
56 L6 El Sombrero Guárico, N Venezuela 9.25N 67.06W
100 L10 Elspeet Gelderland, E Netherlands 52.19N 5.47E
100 L12 Elst Gelderland, E Netherlands 51.55N 5.51E
103 O15 Elsterwerda Brandenburg, E Germany 51.27N 13.32E
42 J4 El Sueco Chihuahua, N Mexico 29.52N 106.23W
El Suweida see As Suwaydā'
El Suweis see Suez
56 D12 El Tambo Cauca, SW Colombia 2.25N 76.49W
183 T13 Eltanin Fracture Zone tectonic feature SE Pacific Ocean
107 X5 El Ter ≈ NE Spain
192 K11 Eltham Taranaki, North Island, NZ 39.25S 174.17E
57 O6 El Tigre Anzoátegui, NE Venezuela 8.55N 64.15W
El Tigrito see San José de Guanipa
56 J5 El Tocuyo Lara, N Venezuela 9.47N 69.48W
131 Q10 El'ton Volgogradskaya Oblast', SW Russian Federation 49.07N 46.50E
34 K10 Eltopia Washington, NW USA 46.33N 118.59W
63 A18 El Trébol Santa Fe, C Argentina 32.12S 61.40W
42 J13 El Tuito Jalisco, SW Mexico 20.20N 105.19W
77 X8 El Ṭûr var. Aṭ Ṭūr. NE Egypt 28.18N 33.37E
161 K16 Elūru prev. Ellore. Andhra Pradesh, E India 16.45N 81.10E
120 H13 Elva Ger. Elwa. Tartumaa, SE Estonia 58.13N 26.27E
39 R9 El Vado Reservoir ⊡ New Mexico, SW USA
45 S15 El Valle Coclé, C Panama 8.39N 80.07W
106 I11 Elvas Portalegre, C Portugal 38.52N 7.10W
56 K7 El Venado Apure, C Venezuela 7.25N 68.46W
107 V6 El Vendrell Cataluña, NE Spain 41.13N 1.31E
96 I13 Elverum Hedmark, S Norway 60.52N 11.34E
44 I9 El Viejo Chinandega, NW Nicaragua 12.37N 87.09W
56 G7 El Viejo, Cerro ▲ C Colombia 7.31N 72.56W
56 H6 El Vigía Mérida, NW Venezuela 8.37N 71.39W
107 Q4 El Villar de Arnedo La Rioja, N Spain 42.19N 2.05W
61 A14 Elvira Amazonas, W Brazil 7.12S 69.56W
Elwa see Elva
El Wad see El Oued
83 K17 El Wak North Eastern, NE Kenya 2.46N 40.57E
35 R7 Elwell, Lake ⊡ Montana, NW USA
33 P13 Elwood Indiana, N USA 40.16N 85.50W
29 R3 Elwood Kansas, C USA 39.43N 94.52W
31 N16 Elwood Nebraska, C USA 40.35N 99.51W
Elx-Elche see Elche
99 O20 Ely E England, UK 52.24N 0.15E
31 X4 Ely Minnesota, N USA 47.54N 91.52W
37 X6 Ely Nevada, W USA 39.15N 114.53W
El Yopal see Yopal
33 T11 Elyria Ohio, N USA 41.22N 82.06W
47 S9 El Yunque ▲ E Puerto Rico 18.15N 65.46W
103 F23 Elz ≈ SW Germany
197 C14 Emae island Shepherd Islands, C Vanuatu
120 I5 Emajõgi Ger. Embach. ≈ SE Estonia
Emāmrūd see Shāhrūd
155 Q2 Emām Şāḥeb var. Emam Saheb, Hazarat Imam. Kunduz, NE Afghanistan 37.10N 68.55E
Emāmshahr see Shāhrūd
97 M20 Emån ≈ S Sweden
197 D14 Emao island C Vanuatu
150 J11 Emba Kaz. Embi. Aktyubinsk, W Kazakhstan 48.49N 58.10E
150 H12 Emba Kaz. Zhem. ≈ W Kazakhstan
Embach see Emajõgi
64 K5 Embarcación Salta, N Argentina 23.15S 64.04W
32 M15 Embarras River ≈ Illinois, N USA
Embi see Emba
83 I19 Embu Eastern, C Kenya 0.30N 37.30E
102 E10 Emden Niedersachsen, NW Germany 53.22N 7.12E
31 Q4 Emerado North Dakota, N USA 47.55N 97.21W
189 X8 Emerald Queensland, E Australia 23.33S 148.10E
Emerald Isle see Montserrat
59 J15 Emero, Río ≈ W Bolivia
9 Y17 Emerson Manitoba, S Canada 49.01N 97.07W
31 T15 Emerson Iowa, C USA 41.00N 95.22W
31 R13 Emerson Nebraska, C USA 42.16N 96.43W
38 M5 Emery Utah, W USA 38.54N 111.16W
Emesa see Ḥimş
142 E13 Emet Kütahya, W Turkey 39.21N 29.15E
194 G14 Emeti Western, SW PNG 7.51S 143.14E
37 V3 Emigrant Pass pass Nevada, W USA 40.39N 116.15W
80 I6 Emi Koussi ▲ N Chad 19.52N 18.34E
Emilia see Emilia-Romagna
43 V15 Emiliano Zapata Chiapas, SE Mexico 17.45N 91.45W
108 E9 Emilia-Romagna prev. Emilia, anc. Æmilia. ◐ region N Italy
164 J3 Emin var. Dorbiljin. Xinjiang Uygur Zizhiqu, NW China 46.31N 83.35E
155 W8 Eminābād Punjab, E Pakistan 32.01N 73.51E
23 L5 Eminence Kentucky, S USA 38.22N 85.10W
29 W7 Eminence Missouri, C USA 37.09N 91.21W
116 N9 Emine, Nos headland E Bulgaria 42.43N 27.53E
164 I3 Emin He ≈ NW China
195 N8 Emirau Island island N PNG
142 F13 Emirdağ Afyon, W Turkey 39.01N 31.09E
97 M21 Emmaboda Kalmar, S Sweden 56.36N 15.30E
120 E5 Emmaste Hiiumaa, W Estonia 58.43N 22.36E
20 I15 Emmaus Pennsylvania, NE USA 40.32N 75.28W
191 U4 Emmaville New South Wales, SE Australia 29.26S 151.38E
110 E9 Emme ≈ W Switzerland
100 L8 Emmeloord Flevoland, N Netherlands 52.43N 5.46E
100 O8 Emmen Drenthe, NE Netherlands 52.48N 6.57E
110 F8 Emmen Luzern, C Switzerland 47.03N 8.14E
103 F23 Emmendingen Baden-Württemberg, SW Germany 48.07N 7.51E
100 P8 Emmer-Compascuum Drenthe, NE Netherlands 52.47N 7.03E
103 D14 Emmerich Nordrhein-Westfalen, W Germany 51.49N 6.16E
31 U12 Emmetsburg Iowa, C USA 43.06N 94.40W
34 M14 Emmett Idaho, NW USA 43.52N 116.30W
40 M10 Emmonak Alaska, USA 62.46N 164.31W
Emona see Ljubljana
Emonti see East London
26 L12 Emory Peak ▲ Texas, SW USA 29.15N 103.18W
42 F6 Empalme Sonora, NW Mexico 27.57N 110.49W
85 L23 Empangeni KwaZulu/Natal, E South Africa 28.40S 31.57E
63 C14 Empedrado Corrientes, NE Argentina 27.57S 58.46W
199 Ii3 Emperor Seamounts undersea feature NW Pacific Ocean
199 J3 Emperor Trough undersea feature N Pacific Ocean
37 R4 Empire Nevada, W USA 40.26N 119.21W
Empire State of the South see Georgia
Emplawas see Amplawas
108 F11 Empoli Toscana, C Italy 43.43N 10.57E
29 P5 Emporia Kansas, C USA 38.24N 96.10W
23 W7 Emporia Virginia, NE USA 36.41N 77.32W
20 E13 Emporium Pennsylvania, NE USA 41.31N 78.13W
195 S12 Empress Augusta Bay inlet Bougainville Island, PNG
Empty Quarter see Ar Rub' al Khālī
102 E10 Ems Dut. Eems. ≈ NW Germany
102 F13 Emsdetten Nordrhein-Westfalen, NW Germany 52.10N 7.31E
Ems-Hunte Canal see Küstenkanal
102 F10 Ems-Jade-Kanal canal NW Germany
102 F11 Emsland cultural region NW Germany
190 D3 Emu Junction South Australia 28.39S 132.13E
169 T3 Emur He ≈ NE China
57 R8 Enachu Landing NW Guyana 6.09N 60.01W
95 F16 Enafors Jämtland, C Sweden 63.16N 12.24E
96 N11 Enånger Gävleborg, C Sweden 61.30N 17.10E
98 G7 Enard Bay bay NW Scotland, UK
Enareträsk see Inarijärvi
176 X12 Enarotali Irian Jaya, E Indonesia 3.55S 136.21E
171 I15 Ena-san ▲ Honshū, S Japan 35.27N 137.36E
144 E12 En 'Avedat var. Ein 'Avedat, well S Israel
172 P2 Enbetsu Hokkaidō, NE Japan 44.44N 141.47E
63 H16 Encantadas, Serra das ▲ S Brazil
42 E7 Encantado, Cerro ▲ NW Mexico 26.46N 112.33W
64 P7 Encarnación Itapúa, S Paraguay 27.19S 55.49W
42 M12 Encarnación de Díaz Jalisco, SW Mexico 21.33N 102.13W
79 O17 Enchi SW Ghana 5.52N 2.48W
27 Q14 Encinal Texas, SW USA 28.02N 99.21W
37 U17 Encinitas California, W USA 33.02N 117.17W
27 S16 Encino Texas, SW USA 26.58N 98.06W
56 H6 Encontrados Zulia, NW Venezuela 9.01N 72.16W
190 I10 Encounter Bay inlet South Australia
63 F15 Encruzilhada Rio Grande do Sul, S Brazil 28.58S 55.31W
63 H16 Encruzilhada do Sul Rio Grande do Sul, S Brazil 30.30S 52.31W
113 M20 Encs Borsod-Abaúj-Zemplén, NE Hungary 48.21N 21.09E
199 M3 Endeavour Seamount undersea feature N Pacific Ocean 48.15N 129.04W
189 V1 Endeavour Strait strait Queensland, NE Australia
175 Q16 Endeh Flores, S Indonesia 8.48S 121.37E
97 G23 Endelave island C Denmark
203 T4 Enderbury Island atoll Phoenix Islands, C Kiribati
9 N16 Enderby British Columbia, SW Canada 50.34N 119.09W
205 W4 Enderby Land physical region Antarctica
181 N14 Enderby Plain undersea feature S Indian Ocean
31 Q6 Enderlin North Dakota, N USA 46.37N 97.36W
Endersdorf see Jędrzejów
30 K16 Enders Reservoir ⊡ Nebraska, C USA
20 H11 Endicott New York, NE USA 42.06N 76.03W
41 P7 Endicott Mountains ▲▲ Alaska, USA
120 I5 Endla Raba wetland C Estonia
119 T9 Enerhodar Zaporiz'ka Oblast', SE Ukraine 47.30N 34.40E
59 F14 Ene, Río ≈ C Peru
201 N4 Enewetak Atoll var. Ānewetak, Eniwetok. atoll Ralik Chain, W Marshall Islands
116 L13 Enez Edirne, NW Turkey 40.43N 26.04E
23 W8 Enfield North Carolina, SE USA 36.10N 77.40W
194 G12 Enga ◐ province W PNG
47 Q9 Engaño, Cabo headland E Dominican Republic 18.36N 68.19W
172 Q5 Engaru Hokkaidō, NE Japan 44.06N 143.30E
144 F11 'En Gedi Southern, E Israel 31.23N 35.21E
110 F9 Engelberg Unterwalden, C Switzerland 46.51N 8.25E
23 Y9 Engelhard North Carolina, SE USA 35.30N 76.00W
131 P8 Engel's Saratovskaya Oblast', W Russian Federation 51.27N 46.09E
103 G24 Engen Baden-Württemberg, SW Germany 47.52N 8.46E
Engeten see Aiud
174 H13 Enggano, Pulau island W Indonesia
82 J8 Enghershatu ▲ N Eritrea 16.41N 38.21E
101 F19 Enghien Dut. Edingen. Hainaut, SW Belgium 50.42N 4.03E
29 V12 England Arkansas, C USA 34.32N 91.58W
99 M20 England Lat. Anglia. national region UK
15 L2 Englefield, Cape headland Nunavut, NE Canada 69.51N 85.31W
12 H8 Englehart Ontario, S Canada 47.49N 79.52W
39 T4 Englewood Colorado, C USA 39.39N 104.59W
33 O16 English Indiana, N USA 38.19N 86.28W
41 Q13 English Bay Alaska, USA 59.21N 151.55W
English Bazar see Ingrāj Bāzār
99 N25 English Channel var. The Channel, Fr. la Manche. channel NW Europe
204 J7 English Coast physical region Antarctica
107 S11 Enguera País Valenciano, E Spain 38.58N 0.42W
120 E8 Engure Tukums, W Latvia 57.09N 23.13E
120 E8 Engures Ezers ◎ NW Latvia
143 R9 Enguri Rus. Inguri. ≈ NW Georgia
Engyum see Gangi
28 M9 Enid Oklahoma, C USA 36.24N 97.52W
24 L3 Enid Lake ⊡ Mississippi, S USA
201 Y2 Enigu island Ratak Chain, SE Marshall Islands
Enikale Strait see Kerch Strait
153 Z8 Enil'chek Issyk-Kul'skaya Oblast', E Kyrgyzstan 42.04N 79.01E
117 F17 Enipéfs ≈ C Greece
172 O6 Eniwa Hokkaidō, NE Japan 42.54N 141.33E
172 O6 Eniwa-dake ⊼ Hokkaidō, NE Japan 42.48N 141.15E
Eniwetok see Enewetak Atoll
Enkeldoorn see Chivhu
127 Nn11 Enken, Mys headland NE Russian Federation 58.29N 141.27E
100 J8 Enkhuizen Noord-Holland, NW Netherlands 52.34N 5.03E
111 Q4 Enknach ≈ N Austria
97 N15 Enköping Uppsala, C Sweden 59.39N 17.07E
109 K24 Enna var. Castrogiovanni, Henna. Sicilia, Italy, C Mediterranean Sea 37.34N 14.18E
82 D11 En Nahud Western Kordofan, C Sudan 12.40N 28.28E
144 F8 En Nâqoûra var. An Nāqūrah. SW Lebanon 33.06N 33.30E
En Nazira see Nazerat
80 K8 Ennedi plateau E Chad
103 E15 Ennepetal Nordrhein-Westfalen, W Germany 51.18N 7.22E
191 P4 Enngonia New South Wales, SE Australia 29.19S 145.52E
99 C19 Ennis Ir. Inis. W Ireland 52.49N 8.58W
35 R11 Ennis Montana, NW USA 45.21N 111.45W
27 U7 Ennis Texas, SW USA 32.19N 96.37W
99 F20 Enniscorthy Ir. Inis Córthaidh. SE Ireland 52.30N 6.34W
99 E15 Enniskillen var. Inniskilling, Ir. Inis Ceithleann. SW Northern Ireland, UK 54.21N 7.37W
99 B19 Ennistimon Ir. Inis Díomáin. W Ireland 52.56N 9.17W
111 T4 Enns Oberösterreich, N Austria 48.12N 14.29E
111 T4 Enns ≈ C Austria
95 O16 Eno Itä-Suomi, E Finland 62.45N 30.15E
26 M5 Enochs Texas, SW USA 33.51N 102.46W
95 N17 Enonkoski Isä-Suomi, E Finland 62.04N 28.53E
94 K10 Enontekiö Lapp. Eanodat. Lappi, N Finland 68.25N 23.40E
23 Q11 Enoree South Carolina, SE USA 34.39N 81.58W
23 P11 Enoree River ≈ South Carolina, SE USA
20 M6 Enosburg Falls Vermont, NE USA 44.54N 72.50W
175 P11 Enrekang Sulawesi, C Indonesia 3.33S 119.46E
47 N10 Enriquillo SW Dominican Republic 17.53N 71.13W
47 N9 Enriquillo, Lago ◎ SW Dominican Republic
100 L9 Ens Flevoland, N Netherlands 52.39N 5.49E
100 P11 Enschede Overijssel, E Netherlands 52.13N 6.55E
42 B2 Ensenada Baja California, NW Mexico 31.52N 116.31W
103 E20 Ensheim ✕ (Saarbrücken) Saarland, W Germany 49.13N 7.09E
166 L9 Enshi Hubei, C China 30.16N 109.25E
171 Hh17 Enshū-nada gulf SW Japan
25 O8 Ensley Florida, SE USA 30.31N 87.16W
Enso see Svetogorsk
83 F18 Entebbe S Uganda 0.07N 32.29E
83 F18 Entebbe ✕ C Uganda 0.04N 32.29E
103 M18 Entenbühl ▲ Czech Republic/Germany 50.09N 12.10E
100 N10 Enter Overijssel, E Netherlands 52.19N 6.34E
25 Q7 Enterprise Alabama, S USA 31.19N 85.50W
34 L11 Enterprise Oregon, NW USA 45.25N 117.16W
38 J7 Enterprise Utah, W USA 37.33N 113.42W
34 J8 Entiat Washington, NW USA 47.39N 120.15W
107 P15 Entinas, Punta de las headland S Spain 36.40N 2.44W
110 F8 Entlebuch Luzern, W Switzerland 47.02N 8.04E
110 F8 Entlebuch valley C Switzerland
65 I22 Entrada, Punta headland S Argentina
105 O13 Entraygues-sur-Truyère Aveyron, S France 44.39N 2.36E
197 G3 Entrecasteaux, Récifs d' reef N New Caledonia
63 C17 Entre Ríos off. Provincia de Entre Ríos. ◐ province NE Argentina
44 K7 Entre Ríos, Cordillera ▲▲ Honduras/Nicaragua
106 G9 Entroncamento Santarém, C Portugal 39.28N 8.28W
176 Z10 Entrop Irian Jaya, E Indonesia 2.37S 140.43E
79 V16 Enugu Enugu, S Nigeria 6.24N 7.24E
79 U16 Enugu ◐ state SE Nigeria
127 Pp3 Enurmino Chukotskiy Avtonomnyy Okrug, NE Russian Federation 66.46N 171.40W
56 E9 Envigado Antioquia, W Colombia 6.09N 75.37W
61 B15 Envira Amazonas, W Brazil 7.12S 69.58W
Enyélé see Enyellé
81 I16 Enyellé var. Enyélé. La Likouala, NE Congo 2.48N 18.01E
103 H21 Enz ≈ SW Germany
171 J16 Enzan Yamanashi, Honshū, S Japan 35.42N 138.43E
106 I2 Eo ≈ NW Spain
Eochaill see Youghal
Eochaille, Cuan see Youghal Bay
109 K22 Eolie, Isole var. Isole Lipari, Eng. Aeolian Islands, Lipari Islands. island group S Italy
201 U12 Eot island Chuuk, C Micronesia
117 J25 Epáno Archánes var. Áno Arkhánai; prev. Epáno Arkhánai. Kríti, Greece, E Mediterranean Sea 35.12N 25.10E
Epáno Arkhánai see Epáno Archánes
117 G14 Epanomí Kentrikí Makedonía, N Greece 40.25N 22.55E
100 M10 Epe Gelderland, E Netherlands 52.21N 5.58E

◆ Country
● Country Capital
◇ Dependent Territory
○ Dependent Territory Capital
◐ Administrative Region
✕ International Airport
▲ Mountain
▲▲ Mountain Range
⊼ Volcano
≈ River
◎ Lake
⊡ Reservoir

Epe – Ezeriş

79 S16 **Epe** Lagos, S Nigeria 6.37N 4.01E
81 I17 **Epéna** La Likouala, NE Congo 1.27N 17.28E
Eperies/Eperjes see Prešov
105 Q4 **Épernay** anc. Sparnacum. Marne, N France 49.01N 3.58E
38 L5 **Ephraim** Utah, W USA 39.21N 111.35W
20 H15 **Ephrata** Pennsylvania, NE USA 40.09N 76.08W
34 J8 **Ephrata** Washington, NW USA 47.19N 119.33W
197 C13 **Epi** var. Épi island C Vanuatu
107 R6 **Épila** Aragón, NE Spain 41.34N 1.19W
105 T6 **Épinal** Vosges, NE France 48.10N 6.28E
Epiphania see Ḩamāh
Epirus see Ípeiros
124 N4 **Episkopí** SW Cyprus 34.37N 32.53E
Episkopi Bay see Episkopí, Kólpos
124 N4 **Episkopí, Kólpos** var. Episkopi Bay. bay SE Cyprus
Epitoli see Pretoria
Epoon see Ebon Atoll
Eporedia see Ivrea
Eppeschdorf see Dumbrăveni
103 H21 **Eppingen** Baden-Württemberg, SW Germany 49.09N 8.54E
85 E18 **Epukiro** Omaheke, E Namibia 21.40S 19.09E
31 Y13 **Epworth** Iowa, C USA 42.27N 90.55W
149 O10 **Eqlīd** var. Iqlid. Fārs, C Iran 30.54N 52.43E
Equality State see Wyoming
81 J18 **Equateur** off. Région de l' Equateur. ◆ region N Dem. Rep. Congo (Zaire)
157 K22 **Equatorial Channel** channel S Maldives
81 B17 **Equatorial Guinea** off. Republic of Equatorial Guinea. ◆ republic C Africa
194 H14 **Era** ≈ S PNG
124 R13 **Eratosthenes Tablemount** undersea feature E Mediterranean Sea 33.48N 32.53E
Erautini see Johannesburg
194 H13 **Erave** Southern Highlands, W PNG 6.36S 143.55E
142 L12 **Erbaa** Tokat, N Turkey 40.39N 36.37E
103 E19 **Erbeskopf** ▲ W Germany 49.43N 7.04E
Erbil see Arbīl
124 Nn3 **Ercan** ✕ (Nicosia) N Cyprus 35.07N 33.30E
Ercegnovi see Herceg-Novi
143 T14 **Erçek Gölü** ◎ E Turkey
143 S14 **Erciş** Van, E Turkey 39.02N 43.21E
142 K14 **Erciyes Dağı** anc. Argaeus. ▲ C Turkey 38.35N 35.27E
113 J22 **Érd** Ger. Hanselbeck. Pest, C Hungary 47.22N 18.55E
Erdaobaihe see Baihe
165 O12 **Erdaogou** Qinghai, W China 34.30N 92.49E
169 X11 **Erdao Jiang** ▲▲ NE China
Erdăt-Sângeorz see Sângeorgiu de Pădure
142 C11 **Erdek** Balıkesir, NW Turkey 40.25N 27.49E
Erdély see Transylvania
Erdélyi-Havasok see Carpaţii Meridionali
142 J17 **Erdemli** İçel, S Turkey 36.39N 34.18E
168 K6 **Erdenet** Bulgan, N Mongolia 49.01N 104.06E
168 I8 **Erdenetsogt** Bayanhongor, C Mongolia 46.27N 100.53E
80 K7 **Erdi** plateau NE Chad
80 L7 **Erdi Ma** desert NE Chad
103 M23 **Erding** Bayern, SE Germany 48.18N 11.54E
Erdőszáda see Ardusat
Erdőszentgyörgy see Sângeorgiu de Pădure
104 I7 **Erdre** ≈ NW France
205 R13 **Erebus, Mount** ▲ Ross Island, Antarctica 78.11S 165.09E
63 H14 **Erechim** Rio Grande do Sul, S Brazil 27.34S 52.15W
169 O7 **Ereen Davaanï Nuruu** ▲▲ NE Mongolia
169 Q6 **Ereentsav** Dornod, NE Mongolia 49.51N 115.41E
142 I16 **Ereğli** Konya, S Turkey 37.30N 34.01E
142 I15 **Ereğli Gölü** ◎ W Turkey
117 A15 **Ereíkoussa** island Iónioi Nísoi, Greece, C Mediterranean Sea
169 O11 **Erenhot** var. Erlian. Nei Mongol Zizhiqu, NE China 43.35N 112.00E
106 M6 **Eresma** ≈ N Spain
117 K17 **Eresós** var. Eressós. Lésvos, E Greece 39.10N 25.57E
Eressós see Eresós
Erevan see Yerevan
Ereymentaū see Yereymentau
101 K21 **Érezée** Luxembourg, SE Belgium 50.16N 5.34E
76 G7 **Erfoud** SE Morocco 31.29N 4.18W
103 D16 **Erft** ≈ W Germany
103 K16 **Erfurt** Thüringen, C Germany 50.59N 11.02E
143 P15 **Ergani** Dıyarbakır, SE Turkey 38.16N 39.43E
169 N11 **Ergel** Dornogovĭ, SE Mongolia 43.10N 109.13E
Ergene Irmağı see Ergene Çayı
168 L11 **Ergenetsogt** Ömnögovĭ, S Mongolia 42.54N 106.16E
142 C10 **Ergene Çayı** var. Ergene Irmağı. ≈ NW Turkey
120 I9 **Ērgļi** Madona, C Latvia 56.54N 25.37E
80 H11 **Erguig, Bahr** ≈ SW Chad
Ergun He see Argun
169 S5 **Ergun Youqi** Nei Mongol Zizhiqu, N China 50.13N 120.09E
169 T5 **Ergun Zuoqi** Nei Mongol Zizhiqu, N China 50.48N 121.30E
166 F12 **Er Hai** ⊠ SW China
104 G4 **Er, Îles d'** island group NW France
106 K4 **Ería** ≈ NW Spain
82 H8 **Eriba** Kassala, NE Sudan 16.37N 36.04E
98 I6 **Eriboll, Loch** inlet NW Scotland, UK
67 Q18 **Erica Seamount** undersea feature SW Indian Ocean 38.15S 14.30E
109 H23 **Erice** Sicilia, Italy, C Mediterranean Sea 38.02N 12.35E
106 E10 **Ericeira** Lisboa, C Portugal 38.58N 9.25W
98 H10 **Ericht, Loch** ◎ C Scotland, UK
28 J11 **Erick** Oklahoma, C USA 35.13N 99.52W
20 B11 **Erie** Pennsylvania, NE USA 42.06N 80.03W
20 E9 **Erie Canal** canal New York, NE USA
Érié, Lac see Erie, Lake
33 T10 **Erie, Lake** Fr. Lac Érié. ◎ Canada/USA
Erigabo see Ceerigaabo
79 N8 **'Erîgât** desert N Mali
Erigavo see Ceerigaabo
94 P2 **Erik Eriksenstretet** strait E Svalbard
9 X15 **Eriksdale** Manitoba, S Canada 50.52N 98.07W
201 V6 **Erikub Atoll** var. Ādkup. atoll Ratak Chain, C Marshall Islands
Erimanthos see Erýmanthos
172 P8 **Erimo** Hokkaidō, NE Japan 42.01N 143.07E
172 Oo8 **Erimo-misaki** headland Hokkaidō, NE Japan 41.57N 143.12E
22 H8 **Erin** Tennessee, S USA 36.19N 87.41W
98 E9 **Eriskay** island NW Scotland, UK
Erithraí see Erythrés
82 I9 **Eritrea** off. State of Eritrea, Tig. Ērtra. ◆ transitional government E Africa
Erivan see Yerevan
103 D16 **Erkelenz** Nordrhein-Westfalen, W Germany 51.04N 6.19E
97 P15 **Erken** ◎ C Sweden
103 K19 **Erlangen** Bayern, S Germany 49.35N 11.00E
166 G9 **Erlang Shan** ▲ C China 29.56N 102.24E
Erlau see Eger
111 V5 **Erlauf** ≈ NE Austria
189 Q8 **Erldunda Roadhouse** Northern Territory, N Australia 25.13S 133.13E
Erlian see Erenhot
29 T15 **Erling, Lake** ⊠ Arkansas, USA
111 O8 **Erlsbach** Tirol, W Austria 46.54N 12.15E
Ermak see Aksu
100 K10 **Ermelo** Gelderland, C Netherlands 52.18N 5.37E
85 K21 **Ermelo** Mpumalanga, NE South Africa 26.31S 29.58E
142 H17 **Ermenek** Karaman, S Turkey 36.37N 32.55E
Érmihályfalva see Valea lui Mihai
117 G20 **Ermióni** Pelopónnisos, S Greece 37.24N 23.15E
117 J20 **Ermoúpoli** var. Hermoupolis; prev. Ermoúpolis. Sýros, Kykládes, Greece, Aegean Sea 37.26N 24.55E
Ermoúpolis see Ermoúpoli
Ernabella see Pukatja
161 G22 **Ernākulam** Kerala, SW India 10.04N 76.18E
104 J6 **Ernée** Mayenne, NW France 48.18N 0.54W
63 H14 **Ernestina, Barragem** ⊠ S Brazil
56 E4 **Ernesto Cortissoz** ✕ (Barranquilla) Atlántico, N Colombia
161 H21 **Erode** Tamil Nādu, SE India 11.21N 77.43E
Eroj see Iroj
85 C19 **Erongo** ⬖ district W Namibia
101 F21 **Erquelinnes** Hainaut, S Belgium 50.18N 4.07E
76 G7 **Er-Rachidia** var. Ksar al Soule. E Morocco 31.58N 4.22W
82 E11 **Er Rahad** var. Ar Rahad. Northern Kordofan, C Sudan 12.42N 30.33E
Er Ramle see Ramla
85 O15 **Errego** Zambézia, NE Mozambique 16.02S 37.12E
Errenteria see Rentería
Er Rif/Er Riff see Rif
99 D14 **Errigal Mountain** Ir. An Earagail. ▲ N Ireland 55.03N 8.09W
99 A15 **Erris Head** Ir. Ceann Iorrais. headland W Ireland 54.18N 10.01W
197 D15 **Erromango** island S Vanuatu
Error Guyot see Error Tablemount
181 O4 **Error Tablemount** var. Error Guyot. undersea feature W Indian Ocean 10.19N 56.04E
82 G11 **Er Roseires** Blue Nile, E Sudan 11.52N 34.22E
Erseka see Ersekë
115 M22 **Ersekë** var. Erseka, Kolonjë. Korçë, SE Albania 40.19N 20.39E
Érsekújvár see Nové Zámky
31 S4 **Erskine** Minnesota, N USA 47.42N 96.00W
105 V6 **Erstein** Bas-Rhin, NE France 48.24N 7.39E
110 G9 **Erstfeld** Uri, C Switzerland 46.49N 8.41E
164 M3 **Ertai** Xinjiang Uygur Zizhiqu, NW China 46.04N 90.06E
130 M7 **Ertil'** Voronezhskaya Oblast', W Russian Federation 51.51N 40.46E
Ertis see Irtysh, C Asia
Ertis see Irtyshsk, Kazakhstan
164 K2 **Ertix He** Rus. Chërnyy Irtysh. ≈ China/Kazakhstan
Ērtra see Eritrea
23 P9 **Erwin** North Carolina, SE USA 35.19N 78.40W
116 L12 **Erydropótamos** Bul. Byala Reka. ≈ Bulgaria/Greece
117 E19 **Erýmanthos** var. Erimanthos. ▲ S Greece 37.57N 21.51E
117 G19 **Erythrés** prev. Erithraí. Stereá Ellás, C Greece 38.19N 23.20E
166 F12 **Eryuan** Yunnan, SW China 26.09N 100.01E
111 U6 **Erzbach** ≈ W Austria
Erzerum see Erzurum
103 N17 **Erzgebirge** Cz. Krušné Hory, Eng. Ore Mountains. ▲▲ Czech Republic/Germany see also Krušné Hory
126 I16 **Erzin** Respublika Tyva, S Russian Federation 50.17N 95.03E
143 O13 **Erzincan** var. Erzinjan. Erzincan, E Turkey 39.43N 39.30E
143 N13 **Erzincan** var. Erzinjan. ⬖ province NE Turkey
Erzinjan see Erzincan
Erzsébetváros see Dumbrăveni
143 Q13 **Erzurum** prev. Erzerum. Erzurum, NE Turkey 39.57N 41.16E
143 Q12 **Erzurum** prev. Erzerum. ⬖ province NE Turkey
195 N16 **Esa'ala** Normanby Island, SE PNG 9.45S 150.47E
172 Nn7 **Esan-misaki** headland Hokkaidō, N Japan 41.49N 141.12E
172 Pp3 **Esashi** Hokkaidō, NE Japan 44.57N 142.32E
171 M11 **Esashi** var. Esasi. Iwate, Honshū, C Japan 39.13N 141.08E
171 Mm6 **Esasho** Hokkaidō, N Japan
Esasi see Esashi
97 F23 **Esbjerg** Ribe, W Denmark 55.28N 8.28E
Esbo see Espoo
38 L7 **Escalante** Utah, W USA 37.46N 111.36W
38 M7 **Escalante River** ≈ Utah, W USA
12 L12 **Escalier, Réservoir l'** ⊠ Quebec, SE Canada
42 K7 **Escalón** Chihuahua, N Mexico 26.43N 104.20W
106 M8 **Escalona** Castilla-La Mancha, C Spain 40.10N 4.24W
25 O8 **Escambia River** ≈ Florida, SE USA
33 N5 **Escanaba** Michigan, N USA 45.45N 87.03W
33 N4 **Escanaba River** ≈ Michigan, N USA
107 R8 **Escandón, Puerto de** pass E Spain 40.17N 0.57W
43 W14 **Escárcega** Campeche, SE Mexico 18.33N 90.41W
179 Pp7 **Escarpada Point** headland Luzon, N Philippines 18.28N 122.10E
25 N8 **Escatawpa River** ≈ Alabama/Mississippi, S USA
105 P2 **Escaut** ≈ N France
Escaut see Scheldt
101 M25 **Esch-sur-Alzette** Luxembourg, S Luxembourg 49.30N 5.58E
103 J15 **Eschwege** Hessen, C Germany 51.10N 10.03E
103 D16 **Eschweiler** Nordrhein-Westfalen, W Germany 50.48N 6.15E
Esclaves, Grand Lac des see Great Slave Lake
47 O8 **Escocesa, Bahía** bay N Dominican Republic
45 W15 **Escocés, Punta** headland NE Panama 8.50N 77.37W
37 U17 **Escondido** California, W USA 33.07N 117.05W
44 M10 **Escondido, Río** ≈ SE Nicaragua
13 S7 **Escoumins, Rivière des** ≈ Quebec, SE Canada
39 O13 **Escudilla Mountain** ▲ Arizona, SW USA 33.57N 109.07W
42 J11 **Escuinapa** var. Escuinapa de Hidalgo. Sinaloa, C Mexico 22.49N 105.46W
Escuinapa de Hidalgo see Escuinapa
44 C6 **Escuintla** Escuintla, S Guatemala 14.16N 90.46W
43 V17 **Escuintla** Chiapas, SE Mexico 15.15N 92.39W
44 A2 **Escuintla** off. Departamento de Escuintla. ⬖ department S Guatemala
13 W7 **Escuminac** ≈ Quebec, SE Canada
81 D16 **Eséka** Centre, SW Cameroon 3.40N 10.48E
142 I12 **Esenboğa** ✕ (Ankara) Ankara, C Turkey 40.05N 33.01E
Esenguly see Gasan-Kuli
142 D17 **Eşen Çayı** ≈ SW Turkey
107 T4 **Ésera** ≈ NE Spain
149 N8 **Eşfahān** Eng. Isfahan; anc. Aspadana. Eşfahān, C Iran 32.40N 51.40E
149 O7 **Eşfahān** off. Ostān-e Eşfahān. ⬖ province C Iran
107 N5 **Esgueva** ≈ N Spain
155 Q3 **Eshkamesh** Takhār, NE Afghanistan 36.25N 69.10E
155 T2 **Eshkāshem** Badakhshān, NE Afghanistan 36.43N 71.34E
85 L23 **Eshowe** KwaZulu/Natal, E South Africa 28.49S 31.29E
149 T5 **'Eshqābād** Khorāsān, NE Iran 36.00N 59.01E
Esh Sham see Dimashq
Esh Sharā see Ash Sharāh
Esik see Yesik
Esil see Ishim, Kazakhstan/Russian Federation
Esil see Yesil', Kazakhstan
191 V2 **Esk** Queensland, E Australia 27.15S 152.22E
192 O11 **Eskdale** Hawke's Bay, North Island, NZ 39.24S 176.51E
Eski Dzhumaya see Tŭrgovishte
94 L2 **Eskifjördhur** Austurland, E Iceland 65.04N 14.01W
145 S3 **Eski Kaļak** var. Askī Kalak, Kalak. N Iraq 36.16N 43.40E
97 N16 **Eskilstuna** Södermanland, C Sweden 59.22N 16.31E
14 G2 **Eskimo Lakes** lakes Northwest Territories, NW Canada
15 L8 **Eskimo Point** headland Nunavut, E Canada 61.19N 93.49W
Eskimo Point see Arviat
145 Q2 **Eski Mosul** N Iraq 36.31N 42.45E
153 T10 **Eski-Nookat** var. Iski-Nauket. Oshskaya Oblast', SW Kyrgyzstan 40.18N 72.29E
142 F12 **Eskişehir** var. Eskishehr. Eskişehir, W Turkey 39.46N 30.30E
142 F13 **Eskişehir** var. Eski shehr. ⬖ province NW Turkey
Eskishehr see Eskişehir
106 K5 **Esla** ≈ NW Spain
148 J6 **Eslāmābād** var. Eslāmābād-e Gharb; prev. Harunabad, Shāhābād. Kermānshāhān, W Iran 34.07N 46.34E
Eslāmābād-e Gharb see Eslāmābād
154 J4 **Eslām Qal'eh** Pash. Islam Qala. Herāt, W Afghanistan 34.41N 61.03E
97 K23 **Eslöv** Skåne, S Sweden 55.49N 13.19E
149 S12 **Esmā'īlābād** Kermān, S Iran 28.48N 56.39E
149 U8 **Esmā'īlābād** Khorāsān, E Iran 35.19N 60.30E
142 D14 **Eşme** Uşak, W Turkey 38.25N 28.58E
46 G6 **Esmeralda** Camagüey, E Cuba 21.51N 78.10W
65 F21 **Esmeralda, Isla** island S Chile
58 B5 **Esmeraldas** Esmeraldas, N Ecuador 0.55N 79.40W
58 B5 **Esmeraldas** ⬖ province NW Ecuador
Esna see Isna
12 B6 **Esnagi Lake** ◎ Ontario, S Canada
149 V14 **Espakeh** Sīstān va Balūchestān, SE Iran 26.54N 60.09E
105 O13 **Espalion** Aveyron, S France 44.31N 2.45E
España see Spain
12 E11 **Espanola** Ontario, S Canada 46.15N 81.46W
39 S10 **Espanola** New Mexico, SW USA 35.59N 106.04W
59 C18 **Española, Isla** var. Hood Island. island Galapagos Islands, Ecuador, E Pacific Ocean
106 M13 **Espejo** Andalucía, S Spain 37.40N 4.34W
96 C13 **Espeland** Hordaland, S Norway 60.22N 5.27E
102 G12 **Espelkamp** Nordrhein-Westfalen, NW Germany 52.22N 8.37E
40 M8 **Espenberg, Cape** headland Alaska, USA 66.33N 163.36W
188 L13 **Esperance** Western Australia 33.49S 121.52E
195 W15 **Esperance, Cape** headland Guadacanal, C Solomon Islands 9.09S 159.38E
59 P18 **Esperancita** Santa Cruz, E Bolivia
63 B17 **Esperanza** Santa Fe, C Argentina 31.25S 60.59W
42 G6 **Esperanza** Sonora, NW Mexico 27.37N 109.51W
26 H9 **Esperanza** Texas, SW USA 31.09N 105.40W
204 H3 **Esperanza** Argentinian research station Antarctica 63.29S 56.53W
106 E12 **Espichel, Cabo** headland S Portugal 38.25N 9.15W
56 E10 **Espinal** Tolima, C Colombia 4.09N 74.54W
50 K10 **Espinhaço, Serra do** ▲▲ SE Brazil
106 G6 **Espinho** Aveiro, N Portugal 41.01N 8.37W
61 N18 **Espinosa** Minas Gerais, SE Brazil 14.58S 42.49W
105 O15 **Espinouse** ▲▲ S France
62 Q8 **Espírito Santo** off. Estado do Espírito Santo. ⬖ state E Brazil
197 B12 **Espiritu Santo** var. Santo. island W Vanuatu
43 Z13 **Espíritu Santo, Bahía del** bay SE Mexico
42 F9 **Espíritu Santo, Isla del** island W Mexico
43 Y12 **Espita** Yucatán, SE Mexico 21.00N 88.17W
13 Y7 **Espoir, Cap d'** headland Quebec, SE Canada 48.24N 64.21W
Esponsede/Esponsende see Esposende
95 L20 **Espoo** Swe. Esbo. Etelä-Suomi, S Finland 60.10N 24.42E
106 G5 **Esposende** var. Esponsede, Esponsende. Braga, N Portugal 41.30N 8.46W
85 M18 **Espungabera** Manica, SW Mozambique 20.27S 32.48E
65 H17 **Esquel** Chubut, SW Argentina 42.55S 71.19W
8 L17 **Esquimalt** Vancouver Island, British Columbia, SW Canada 48.25N 123.27W
63 C16 **Esquina** Corrientes, NE Argentina 30.00S 59.30W
44 E6 **Esquipulas** Chiquimula, SE Guatemala 14.34N 89.20W
44 K9 **Esquipulas** Matagalpa, C Nicaragua 12.39N 85.48W
96 I8 **Essandjøen** ◎ S Norway
76 E7 **Essaouira** prev. Mogador. W Morocco 31.33N 9.40W
Esseg see Osijek
Es Semara see Smara
101 G15 **Essen** Antwerpen, N Belgium 51.28N 4.28E
103 E15 **Essen** var. Essen an der Ruhr. Nordrhein-Westfalen, W Germany 51.28N 7.01E
Essen an der Ruhr see Essen
76 I5 **Es Senia** ✕ (Oran) NW Algeria 35.34N 0.42W
57 T8 **Essequibo Islands** island group N Guyana
57 T11 **Essequibo River** ≈ C Guyana
12 C18 **Essex** Ontario, S Canada 42.06N 82.52W
31 T16 **Essex** Iowa, C USA 40.49N 95.18W
99 P21 **Essex** cultural region E England, UK
33 R8 **Essexville** Michigan, N USA 43.37N 83.50W
103 H22 **Esslingen** var. Esslingen am Neckar. Baden-Württemberg, SW Germany 48.45N 9.18E
Esslingen am Neckar see Esslingen
105 N6 **Essonne** ⬖ department N France
Es Suweida see As Suwaydā'
81 F16 **Est** Eng. East. ⬖ province SE Cameroon
106 I1 **Estaca de Bares, Punta da** point NW Spain 43.46N 7.40W
26 M5 **Estacado, Llano** plain New Mexico/Texas, SW USA
65 K25 **Estados, Isla de los** prev. Eng. Staten Island. island S Argentina
149 P12 **Eşţahbān** Fārs, S Iran
12 F11 **Estaire** Ontario, S Canada 46.19N 80.47W
39 S12 **Estancia** New Mexico, SW USA 34.45N 106.03W
61 P16 **Estância** Sergipe, E Brazil 11.15S 37.28W
106 G7 **Estarreja** Aveiro, N Portugal 40.45N 8.34W
104 M17 **Estats, Pic d'** Sp. Pico d'Estats. ▲ France/Spain 42.39N 1.24E
Estats, Pico d' see Estats, Pic d'
85 K23 **Estcourt** KwaZulu/Natal, E South Africa 28.58S 29.54E
108 H8 **Este** anc. Ateste. Veneto, NE Italy 45.14N 11.40E
44 J9 **Estelí** Estelí, NW Nicaragua 13.04N 86.21W
44 J9 **Estelí** ⬖ department NW Nicaragua
Estella see Estella-Lizarra
107 Q4 **Estella-Lizarra** Bas. Lizarra var Estella Navarra, N Spain 42.40N 2.01W
31 R9 **Estelline** South Dakota, N USA 44.34N 96.54W
27 P4 **Estelline** Texas, SW USA 34.33N 100.26W
106 L14 **Estepa** Andalucía, S Spain 37.16N 4.52W
106 L16 **Estepona** Andalucía, S Spain 36.25N 5.09W
41 R9 **Ester** Alaska, USA 64.49N 148.03W
9 V16 **Esterhazy** Saskatchewan, S Canada 50.40N 102.01W
39 S3 **Estes Park** Colorado, C USA 40.22N 105.31W
9 V17 **Estevan** Saskatchewan, S Canada 49.07N 103.04W
31 T11 **Estherville** Iowa, C USA 43.24N 94.49W
23 R15 **Estill** South Carolina, SE USA 32.45N 81.14W
105 Q6 **Estissac** Aube, N France 48.17N 3.51E
13 T9 **Est, Lac de l'** ◎ Quebec, SE Canada
Estland see Estonia
9 S16 **Eston** Saskatchewan, S Canada 51.09N 108.41W
120 G5 **Estonia** off. Republic of Estonia, Est. Eesti Vabariik, Ger. Estland, Latv. Igaunija; prev. Estonian SSR, Rus. Estonskaya SSR. ◆ republic NE Europe
Estonskaya SSR see Estonia
106 E11 **Estoril** Lisboa, W Portugal 38.42N 9.22W
61 L14 **Estreito** Maranhão, E Brazil 6.34S 47.22W
106 I8 **Estrela, Serra da** ▲▲ C Portugal
42 D3 **Estrella, Punta** headland NW Mexico 30.53N 114.45W
Estremadura see Extremadura
106 F10 **Estremadura** cultural and historical region W Portugal
106 H11 **Estremoz** Évora, S Portugal 38.49N 7.34W
81 D18 **Estuaire** off. Province de l'Estuaire, var. L'Estuaire. ⬖ province NW Gabon
Eszék see Osijek
113 I22 **Esztergom** Ger. Gran; anc. Strigonium. Komárom-Esztergom, N Hungary 47.46N 18.44E
158 K11 **Etah** Uttar Pradesh, N India 27.33N 78.39E
201 R17 **Etal Atoll** atoll Mortlock Islands, C Micronesia
101 K24 **Étalle** Luxembourg, SE Belgium 49.40N 5.36E
105 N6 **Étampes** Essonne, N France 48.25N 2.10E
190 J1 **Etamunbanie, Lake** salt lake South Australia
105 N1 **Étaples** Pas-de-Calais, N France 50.31N 1.37E
158 K12 **Etāwah** Uttar Pradesh, N India 26.46N 79.01E
13 R10 **Etchemin** ≈ Quebec, SE Canada
Etchmiadzin see Ejmiatsin
42 G7 **Etchojoa** Sonora, NW Mexico 26.54N 109.37W
95 L19 **Etelä-Suomi** ⬖ province S Finland
85 B16 **Etengua** Kunene, NW Namibia 17.24S 13.05E
101 K25 **Éthe** Luxembourg, SE Belgium 49.34N 5.32E
9 W15 **Ethelbert** Manitoba, S Canada 51.30N 100.22W
82 H12 **Ethiopia** off. Federal Democratic Republic of Ethiopia; prev. Abyssinia, People's Democratic Republic of Ethiopia. ◆ republic E Africa
82 I13 **Ethiopian Highlands** var. Ethiopian Plateau. plateau N Ethiopia
Ethiopian Plateau see Ethiopian Highlands
36 M2 **Etna** California, W USA 41.25N 122.53W
20 B14 **Etna** Pennsylvania, NE USA 40.29N 79.55W
96 G12 **Etna** ≈ S Norway
109 L24 **Etna, Monte** Eng. Mount Etna. ▲ Sicilia, Italy, C Mediterranean Sea 37.46N 15.00E
Etna, Mount see Etna, Monte
97 C15 **Etne** Hordaland, S Norway 59.40N 5.55E
Etoliko see Aitolikó
41 Y14 **Etolin Island** island Alexander Archipelago, Alaska, USA
40 L12 **Etolin Strait** strait Alaska, USA
85 C17 **Etosha Pan** salt lake N Namibia
81 G18 **Etoumbi** Cuvette, NW Congo 0.01N 14.57E
22 M10 **Etowah** Tennessee, S USA 35.19N 84.31W
25 S2 **Etowah River** ≈ Georgia, SE USA
Etrek see Atrak
104 L3 **Étretat** Seine-Maritime, N France 49.46N 0.23E
116 H9 **Etropole** Sofiya, W Bulgaria 42.50N 24.00E
Etsch see Adige
Et Tafila see Aţ Ţafīlah
101 M23 **Ettelbrück** Diekirch, C Luxembourg 49.51N 6.06E
201 V12 **Etten** atoll Chuuk Islands, C Micronesia
101 H14 **Etten-Leur** Noord-Brabant, S Netherlands 51.34N 4.37E
78 G7 **Et Tîdra** var. Ile Tîdra. island Dakhlet Nouâdhibou, NW Mauritania
103 G21 **Ettlingen** Baden-Württemberg, SW Germany 48.57N 8.25E
104 M2 **Eu** Seine-Maritime, N France 50.01N 1.24E
200 Rr16 **'Eua** prev. Middleburg Island. island Tongatapu Group, SE Tonga
200 R15 **Eua Iki** island Tongatapu Group, S Tonga
Euboea see Évvoia
189 O12 **Eucla** Western Australia 31.40S 128.50E
33 U11 **Euclid** Ohio, N USA 41.35N 81.31W
29 W14 **Eudora** Arkansas, C USA 33.06N 91.15W
29 Q4 **Eudora** Kansas, C USA 38.56N 95.06W
190 J9 **Eudunda** South Australia 34.11S 139.03E
25 R6 **Eufaula** Alabama, S USA 31.53N 85.09W
29 Q11 **Eufaula** Oklahoma, C USA 35.17N 95.34W
29 Q11 **Eufaula Lake** var. Eufaula Reservoir. ⊠ Oklahoma, C USA
Eufaula Reservoir see Eufaula Lake
34 F13 **Eugene** Oregon, NW USA 44.03N 123.05W
42 B6 **Eugenia, Punta** headland W Mexico 27.48N 115.03W
191 Q8 **Eugowra** New South Wales, SE Australia 33.28S 148.21E
106 I2 **Eume** ≈ NW Spain
106 H2 **Eume, Embalse do** ⊠ NW Spain
Eumolpias see Plovdiv
61 O18 **Eunápolis** Bahia, SE Brazil 16.19S 39.36W
24 H8 **Eunice** Louisiana, S USA 30.29N 92.25W
39 W15 **Eunice** New Mexico, SW USA 32.26N 103.09W
101 M19 **Eupen** Liège, E Belgium 50.37N 6.01E
138 Jj9 **Euphrates** Ar. Al Furāt, Turk. Firat Nehri. ≈ SW Asia
144 L3 **Euphrates Dam** dam N Syria 35.52N 38.34E
24 M4 **Eupora** Mississippi, S USA 33.32N 89.16W
95 K19 **Eura** Länsi-Suomi, W Finland 61.06N 22.12E
95 K19 **Eurajoki** Länsi-Suomi, W Finland 61.13N 21.44E
0-1 **Eurasian Plate** tectonic feature
104 L4 **Eure** ⬖ department N France
104 M4 **Eure** ≈ N France
104 M6 **Eure-et-Loir** ⬖ department C France
36 K3 **Eureka** California, W USA 40.47N 124.12W
29 P6 **Eureka** Kansas, C USA 37.47N 96.15W
35 O6 **Eureka** Montana, NW USA 48.52N 115.03W
37 V5 **Eureka** Nevada, W USA 39.30N 115.58W
31 O7 **Eureka** South Dakota, N USA 45.46N 99.37W
38 L4 **Eureka** Utah, W USA 39.57N 112.07W
34 K10 **Eureka** Washington, NW USA 46.21N 118.41W
29 S9 **Eureka Springs** Arkansas, C USA 36.25N 93.43W
190 K6 **Eurinilla Creek** seasonal river South Australia
191 O11 **Euroa** Victoria, SE Australia 36.46S 145.35E
180 M9 **Europa** island W Madagascar
106 L3 **Europa, Picos de** ▲▲ N Spain
106 L16 **Europa Point** headland S Gibraltar 36.07N 5.20W
86-87 **Europe** continent
100 F12 **Europoort** Zuid-Holland, W Netherlands 51.59N 4.08E
Euskadi see País Vasco
103 D17 **Euskirchen** Nordrhein-Westfalen, W Germany 50.40N 6.47E
25 W11 **Eustis** Florida, SE USA 28.51N 81.41W
190 M9 **Euston** New South Wales, SE Australia 34.34S 142.45E
25 N5 **Eutaw** Alabama, S USA 32.50N 87.53W
102 K8 **Eutin** Schleswig-Holstein, N Germany 54.07N 10.37E
8 K14 **Eutsuk Lake** ⊠ British Columbia, SW Canada
Euxine Sea see Black Sea
85 C16 **Evale** Cunene, SW Angola 16.36S 15.46E
39 T3 **Evans** Colorado, C USA 40.22N 104.41W
9 P14 **Evansburg** Alberta, SW Canada 53.34N 114.57W
31 X13 **Evansdale** Iowa, C USA 42.28N 92.16W
191 V4 **Evans Head** New South Wales, SE Australia 29.07S 153.27E
10 J11 **Evans, Lac** ◎ Quebec, SE Canada
39 S5 **Evans, Mount** ▲ Colorado, C USA 39.15N 106.10W
15 Mm6 **Evans Strait** strait Nunavut, N Canada
33 N10 **Evanston** Illinois, N USA 42.02N 87.41W
35 S17 **Evanston** Wyoming, C USA 41.16N 110.57W
12 D11 **Evansville** Manitoulin Island, Ontario, S Canada 45.48N 82.34W
33 N16 **Evansville** Indiana, N USA 37.58N 87.33W
32 L9 **Evansville** Wisconsin, N USA 42.46N 89.16W
27 S8 **Evant** Texas, SW USA 31.28N 98.09W
149 P13 **Evaz** Fārs, S Iran 27.48N 53.58E
31 W4 **Eveleth** Minnesota, N USA 47.27N 92.32W
190 E3 **Evelyn Creek** seasonal river South Australia
189 Q2 **Evelyn, Mount** ▲ Northern Territory, N Australia 13.28S 132.50E
126 I11 **Evenkiyskiy Avtonomnyy Okrug** ⬖ autonomous district N Russian Federation
191 R13 **Everard, Cape** headland Victoria, SE Australia 37.48S 149.21E
190 F6 **Everard, Lake** salt lake South Australia
190 C2 **Everard Ranges** ▲▲ South Australia
159 R11 **Everest, Mount** Chin. Qomolangma Feng, Nep. Sagarmatha. ▲ China/Nepal 27.58N 86.57E
20 E15 **Everett** Pennsylvania, NE USA 40.00N 78.22W
34 H7 **Everett** Washington, NW USA 47.58N 122.12W
101 E17 **Evergem** Oost-Vlaanderen, NW Belgium 51.07N 3.43E
25 X16 **Everglades City** Florida, SE USA 25.51N 81.22W
25 Y16 **Everglades, The** wetland Florida, SE USA
25 P7 **Evergreen** Alabama, S USA 31.25N 86.55W
39 T4 **Evergreen** Colorado, C USA 39.37N 105.19W
Evergreen State see Washington
99 L21 **Evesham** C England, UK 52.06N 1.57W
105 T10 **Évian-les-Bains** Haute-Savoie, E France 46.22N 6.34E
95 K16 **Evijärvi** Länsi-Suomi, W Finland 63.22N 23.30E
81 D17 **Evinayong** var. Ebinayon, Evinayoung. C Equatorial Guinea 1.28N 10.17E
Evinayoung see Evinayong
117 E18 **Évinos** ≈ C Greece
97 E17 **Evje** Aust-Agder, S Norway 58.34N 7.49E
Evmolpia see Plovdiv
106 H11 **Évora** anc. Ebora, Lat. Liberalitas Julia. Évora, C Portugal 38.34N 7.54W
106 G11 **Évora** ⬖ district S Portugal
104 M4 **Évreux** anc. Civitas Eburovicum. Eure, N France 49.01N 1.09E
104 K6 **Évron** Mayenne, NW France 48.10N 0.24W
116 L13 **Évros** Bul. Maritsa, Turk. Meriç; anc. Hebrus. ≈ SE Europe see also Maritsa/Meriç
117 F21 **Evrótas** ≈ S Greece
105 O5 **Évry** Essonne, N France 48.38N 2.27E
27 O8 **E.V.Spence Reservoir** ⊠ Texas, SW USA
117 I18 **Évvoia** Lat. Euboea. island C Greece
40 D9 **Ewa Beach** Oahu, Hawaii, USA, C Pacific Ocean 21.19N 158.00W
34 L9 **Ewan** Washington, NW USA 47.06N 117.46W
46 K12 **Ewarton** C Jamaica 18.10N 77.04W
83 J18 **Ewaso Ng'iro** var. Nyiro. ≈ C Kenya
194 E13 **Ewe** ≈ W PNG
31 P13 **Ewing** Nebraska, C USA 42.13N 98.20W
204 J5 **Ewing Island** island Antarctica
67 P17 **Ewing Seamount** undersea feature E Atlantic Ocean 23.19S 8.45E
164 L6 **Ewirgol** Xinjiang Uygur Zizhiqu, W China 42.55N 87.39E
81 G19 **Ewo** Cuvette, W Congo 0.55S 14.49E
29 S3 **Excelsior Springs** Missouri, C USA 39.20N 94.13W
99 J23 **Exe** ≈ SW England, UK
204 L12 **Executive Committee Range** ▲▲ Antarctica
12 E16 **Exeter** Ontario, S Canada 43.19N 81.26W
99 J24 **Exeter** anc. Isca Damnoniorum. SW England, UK 50.43N 3.31W
37 R11 **Exeter** California, W USA 36.17N 119.08W
21 P10 **Exeter** New Hampshire, NE USA 42.57N 70.55W
Exin see Kcynia
31 T14 **Exira** Iowa, C USA 41.36N 94.55W
99 J23 **Exmoor** moorland SW England, UK
23 Y6 **Exmore** Virginia, NE USA 37.31N 75.48W
188 G8 **Exmouth** Western Australia 22.00S 114.06E
99 J24 **Exmouth** SW England, UK 50.36N 3.24W
188 G8 **Exmouth Gulf** gulf Western Australia
181 V8 **Exmouth Plateau** undersea feature E Indian Ocean
117 J20 **Exompourgo** ancient monument Tínos, Kykládes, Greece, Aegean Sea 37.34N 25.12E
106 I10 **Extremadura** var. Estremadura. ⬖ autonomous community W Spain
80 F12 **Extrême-Nord** Eng. Extreme North. ⬖ province N Cameroon
Extreme North see Extrême-Nord
46 I3 **Exuma Cays** islets C Bahamas
46 I3 **Exuma Sound** sound C Bahamas
83 H20 **Eyasi, Lake** ◎ N Tanzania
97 F17 **Eydehavn** Aust-Agder, S Norway 58.31N 8.52E
98 L12 **Eyemouth** SE Scotland, UK 55.51N 2.06W
98 G7 **Eye Peninsula** peninsula NW Scotland, UK
82 Q13 **Eyl** It. Eil. Nugaal, E Somalia 8.03N 49.49E
105 N11 **Eymoutiers** Haute-Vienne, C France 45.45N 1.43E
Eyo (lower course) see Uolo, Río
31 X10 **Eyota** Minnesota, N USA 44.00N 92.13W
190 H2 **Eyre Basin, Lake** salt lake South Australia
190 I1 **Eyre Creek** seasonal river Northern Territory/South Australia
182 L9 **Eyre, Lake** salt lake South Australia
193 C22 **Eyre Mountains** ▲▲ South Island, NZ
190 H3 **Eyre North, Lake** salt lake South Australia
190 G7 **Eyre Peninsula** peninsula South Australia
190 H4 **Eyre South, Lake** salt lake South Australia
97 B18 **Eysturoy** Dan. Østerø Island Faeroe Islands 62.15N 6.55W
63 D20 **Ezeiza** ✕ (Buenos Aires) Buenos Aires, E Argentina 34.49S 58.30W
Ezeres see Ezeriş
118 F12 **Ezeriş** Hung. Ezeres. Caraş-Severin, W Romania 45.21N 21.55E

◆ Country ● Country Capital ◇ Dependent Territory ○ Dependent Territory Capital ⬖ Administrative Region ✕ International Airport ▲ Mountain ▲▲ Mountain Range ▲ Volcano ≈ River ◎ Lake ⊠ Reservoir

◆ COUNTRY ◇ DEPENDENT TERRITORY ◈ ADMINISTRATIVE REGION ▲ MOUNTAIN ▲ VOLCANO ◎ LAKE
● COUNTRY CAPITAL ○ DEPENDENT TERRITORY CAPITAL ✕ INTERNATIONAL AIRPORT ▲ MOUNTAIN RANGE ⌁ RIVER ◙ RESERVOIR

255

FFESTINIOG – FOSSANO

99 J19 **Ffestiniog** NW Wales, UK 52.55N 3.54W
Fhóid Duibh, Cuan an *see* Blacksod Bay
64 I8 **Fiambalá** Catamarca, NW Argentina 27.45S 67.37W
180 I6 **Fianarantsoa** Fianarantsoa, C Madagascar 21.27S 47.04E
180 H6 **Fianarantsoa** ◈ *province* SE Madagascar
80 G12 **Fianga** Mayo-Kébbi, SW Chad 9.57N 15.09E
Ficce *see* Fichē
82 J12 **Fichē** *It.* Ficce. Oromo, C Ethiopia 9.48N 38.43E
103 N17 **Fichtelberg** ▲ Czech Republic/Germany 50.26N 12.57E
103 M18 **Fichtelgebirge** ▲▲ SE Germany
103 M19 **Fichtelnaab** ≈ SE Germany
108 E9 **Fidenza** Emilia-Romagna, N Italy 44.52N 10.04E
115 K21 **Fier** *var.* Fieri. Fier, SW Albania 40.44N 19.34E
115 K21 **Fier** ◈ *district* W Albania
Fieri *see* Fier
Fierza *see* Fierzë
115 L17 **Fierzë** *var.* Fierza. Shkodër, N Albania 42.15N 20.02E
115 L17 **Fierzës, Liqeni i** ◎ N Albania
110 F10 **Fiesch** Valais, SW Switzerland 46.25N 8.09E
108 G11 **Fiesole** Toscana, C Italy 43.50N 11.18E
144 G12 **Fīfah** Aţ Ţafīlah, W Jordan 30.55N 35.25E
98 K11 **Fife** *var.* Kingdom of Fife. *cultural region* E Scotland, UK
98 K11 **Fife Ness** *headland* E Scotland, UK 56.16N 2.35W
Fifteen Twenty Fracture Zone *see* Barracuda Fracture Zone
105 N13 **Figeac** Lot, S France 44.37N 2.01E
97 N19 **Figeholm** Kalmar, SE Sweden 57.12N 16.34E
Figig *see* Figuig
85 J18 **Figtree** Matabeleland South, SW Zimbabwe 20.20S 28.20E
106 F8 **Figueira da Foz** Coimbra, W Portugal 40.09N 8.51W
107 X4 **Figueres** Cataluña, E Spain 42.16N 2.57E
76 H7 **Figuig** *var.* Figig. E Morocco 32.09N 1.13W
Fijāj, Shaţţ al *see* Fedjaj, Chott el
197 J14 **Fiji** *off.* Sovereign Democratic Republic of Fiji, *Fij.* Viti. ◆ *republic* SW Pacific Ocean
197 J13 **Fiji** *island group* SW Pacific Ocean
183 Q8 **Fiji Plate** *tectonic feature*
107 P14 **Filabres, Sierra de los** ▲▲ SE Spain
85 K18 **Filabusi** Matabeleland South, S Zimbabwe 20.31S 29.16E
44 K13 **Filadelfia** Guanacaste, W Costa Rica 10.24N 85.33W
113 K20 **Fil'akovo** *Hung.* Fülek. Banskobystrický Kraj, C Slovakia 48.15N 19.53E
205 N5 **Filchner Ice Shelf** *ice shelf* Antarctica
12 J11 **Fildegrand** ≈ Quebec, SE Canada
35 O15 **Filer** Idaho, NW USA 42.34N 114.36W
Filevo *see* Vŭrbitsa
118 H14 **Filiaşi** Dolj, SW Romania 44.32N 23.30E
117 B16 **Filiátes** Ípeiros, W Greece 39.36N 20.19E
117 D21 **Filiatrá** Pelopónnisos, S Greece 37.10N 21.35E
109 K22 **Filicudi, Isola** *island* Isole Eolie, S Italy
147 Y10 **Filim** E Oman 20.37N 58.11E
Filimon Sîrbu *see* Făurei
79 S11 **Filingué** Tillabéri, W Niger 14.12N 3.16E
116 K13 **Filiourí** ≈ NE Greece
116 I13 **Fílippoi** *anc.* Philippi. *site of ancient city* Anatolikí Makedonía kai Thráki, NE Greece 41.01N 24.15E
97 L15 **Filipstad** Värmland, C Sweden 59.43N 14.10E
110 I9 **Filisur** Graubünden, S Switzerland 46.40N 9.43E
96 E12 **Fillefjell** ▲▲ S Norway
37 R14 **Fillmore** California, W USA 34.23N 118.56W
38 K5 **Fillmore** Utah, W USA 38.57N 112.19W
12 J10 **Fils, Lac du** ◎ Quebec, SE Canada
142 H11 **Filyos Çayı** ≈ N Turkey
205 Q2 **Fimbulheimen** *physical region* Antarctica
205 Q1 **Fimbul Ice Shelf** *ice shelf* Antarctica
108 G9 **Finale Emilia** Emilia-Romagna, C Italy 44.50N 11.17E
108 C10 **Finale Ligure** Liguria, NW Italy 44.11N 8.21E
107 P14 **Fiñana** Andalucía, S Spain 37.09N 2.47W
180 I6 **Finandrahana** Fianarantsoa, SE Madagascar
23 S6 **Fincastle** Virginia, NE USA 37.29N 79.51W
101 M25 **Findel** ✕ (Luxembourg) Luxembourg, C Luxembourg 49.39N 6.16E
98 J9 **Findhorn** ≈ N Scotland, UK
33 R12 **Findlay** Ohio, N USA 41.02N 83.39W
20 G11 **Finger Lakes** *lakes* New York, NE USA
85 L14 **Fingoè** Tete, NW Mozambique 15.01S 31.52E
142 E17 **Finike** Antalya, SW Turkey 36.18N 30.07E
104 F6 **Finistère** ◈ *department* NW France
194 J12 **Finisterre, Mount** ▲ C PNG 5.58S 146.30E
194 J12 **Finisterre Range** ▲▲ N PNG
189 Q8 **Finke** Northern Territory, N Australia 25.37S 134.35E
111 S10 **Finkenstein** Kärnten, S Austria 46.34N 13.53E
201 Y15 **Finkol, Mount** *var.* Mount Crozer. ▲ Kosrae, E Micronesia 5.18N 163.00E
95 L17 **Finland** *off.* Republic of Finland, *Fin.* Suomen Tasavalta, Suomi. ◆ *republic* N Europe
128 F12 **Finland, Gulf of** *Est.* Soome Laht, *Fin.* Suomenlahti, *Ger.* Finnischer Meerbusen, *Rus.* Finskiy Zaliv, *Swe.* Finska Viken. *gulf* E Baltic Sea
8 L11 **Finlay** ≈ British Columbia, W Canada
191 O10 **Finley** New South Wales, SE Australia 35.41S 145.33E
31 Q4 **Finley** North Dakota, N USA 47.30N 97.50W
Finnischer Meerbusen *see* Finland, Gulf of
94 K9 **Finnmark** ◈ *county* N Norway
94 K9 **Finnmarksvidda** *physical region* N Norway
94 I9 **Finnsnes** Troms, N Norway 69.13N 17.58E
194 K13 **Finschhafen** Morobe, C PNG 6.38S 147.49E
96 E13 **Finse** Hordaland, S Norway 60.35N 7.33E
Finska Viken/Finskiy Zaliv *see* Finland, Gulf of
97 M17 **Finspång** Östergötland, S Sweden 58.42N 15.45E
110 F10 **Finsteraarhorn** ▲ Swtizerland 46.33N 8.07E
103 O14 **Finsterwalde** Brandenburg, E Germany 51.37N 13.43E
193 A23 **Fiordland** *physical region* South Island, NZ
108 E9 **Fiorenzuola d'Arda** Emilia-Romagna, C Italy 44.57N 9.53E
Firat Nehri *see* Euphrates
Firdaus *see* Ferdows
20 M14 **Fire Island** *island* New York, NE USA
108 G11 **Firenze** *Eng.* Florence; *anc.* Florentia. Toscana, C Italy 43.46N 11.15E
108 G10 **Firenzuola** Toscana, C Italy 44.07N 11.22E
12 C6 **Fire River** Ontario, S Canada 48.46N 83.34W
Fîrliug *see* Fârliug
63 B19 **Firmat** Santa Fe, C Argentina 33.28S 61.28W
105 Q12 **Firminy** Loire, E France 45.22N 4.18E
Firmum Picenum *see* Fermo
158 J12 **Fīrozābād** Uttar Pradesh, N India 27.09N 78.24E
158 G8 **Fīrozpur** *var.* Ferozepore. Punjab, NW India 30.55N 74.37E
First State *see* Delaware
149 O12 **Fīrūzābād** Fārs, S Iran 28.51N 52.34E
Fischamend *see* Fischamend Markt
111 Y4 **Fischamend Markt** *var.* Fischamend. Niederösterreich, NE Austria 48.06N 16.37E
111 W6 **Fischbacher Alpen** ▲▲ E Austria
Fischhausen *see* Primorsk
85 D21 **Fish** *var.* Vis. ≈ S Namibia
85 F24 **Fish** *Afr.* Vis. ≈ SW South Africa
9 X15 **Fisher Branch** Manitoba, S Canada 51.09N 97.34W
9 X15 **Fisher River** Manitoba, S Canada 51.25N 97.23W
21 N13 **Fishers Island** *island* New York, NE USA
39 U8 **Fishers Peak** ▲ Colorado, C USA 37.06N 104.27W
15 M6 **Fisher Strait** *strait* Nunavut, N Canada
99 H21 **Fishguard** *Wel.* Abergwaun. SW Wales, UK 51.58N 4.49W
21 R2 **Fish River Lake** ◎ Maine, NE USA
204 K6 **Fiske, Cape** *headland* Antarctica 74.27S 60.28W
105 P4 **Fismes** Marne, N France 49.19N 3.41E
106 F3 **Fisterra, Cabo** *headland* NW Spain 42.53N 9.16W
21 N11 **Fitchburg** Massachusetts, NE USA 42.34N 71.48W
98 L3 **Fitful Head** *headland* NE Scotland, UK 59.57N 1.24W
97 C14 **Fitjar** Hordaland, S Norway 59.55N 5.19E
198 Bb8 **Fito** ▲ Upolu, C Samoa 13.57S 171.42W
25 U6 **Fitzgerald** Georgia, SE USA 31.42N 83.15W
188 M5 **Fitzroy Crossing** Western Australia 18.10S 125.40E
65 G21 **Fitzroy, Monte** *var.* Cerro Chaltel. ▲ S Argentina 49.18S 73.06W
189 Y8 **Fitzroy River** ≈ Queensland, E Australia
188 L5 **Fitzroy River** ≈ Western Australia
12 E12 **Fitzwilliam Island** *island* Ontario, S Canada
109 J15 **Fiuggi** Lazio, C Italy 41.47N 13.16E
Fiume *see* Rijeka
109 H15 **Fiumicino** Lazio, C Italy 41.46N 12.13E
Fiumicino *see* Leonardo da Vinci
108 E10 **Fivizzano** Toscana, C Italy 44.13N 10.06E
81 O21 **Fizi** Sud Kivu, E Dem. Rep. Congo (Zaire) 4.15S 28.57E
Fizuli *see* Füzuli
94 I11 **Fjällåsen** Norrbotten, N Sweden 67.31N 20.07E
97 G20 **Fjerritslev** Nordjylland, N Denmark 57.06N 9.16E
F.J.S. *see* Franz Josef Strauss
97 L16 **Fjugesta** Örebro, C Sweden 59.10N 14.50E
Fladstrand *see* Frederikshavn
39 V5 **Flagler** Colorado, C USA 39.17N 103.04W
25 X10 **Flagler Beach** Florida, SE USA 29.28N 81.07W
38 L11 **Flagstaff** Arizona, SW USA 35.12N 111.39W
67 H24 **Flagstaff Bay** *bay* Saint Helena, C Atlantic Ocean
21 P5 **Flagstaff Lake** ◎ Maine, NE USA
96 E13 **Flåm** Sogn og Fjordane, S Norway 60.51N 7.06E
13 O8 **Flamand** ≈ Quebec, SE Canada
32 J5 **Flambeau River** ≈ Wisconsin, N USA
99 O16 **Flamborough Head** *headland* E England, UK 54.06N 0.03W
102 N13 **Fläming** *hill range* NE Germany
18 Ii7 **Flaming Gorge Reservoir** ⊡ Utah/Wyoming, NW USA
176 Xx13 **Flamingo, Teluk** *bay* N Arafura Sea
101 B18 **Flanders** *Dut.* Vlaanderen, *Fr.* Flandre. *cultural region* Belgium/France
Flandre *see* Flanders
31 R10 **Flandreau** South Dakota, N USA 44.03N 96.36W
98 D6 **Flannan Isles** *island group* NW Scotland, UK
30 M6 **Flasher** North Dakota, N USA 46.25N 101.12W
95 G15 **Flåsjön** ◎ N Sweden
41 O11 **Flat** Alaska, USA 62.27N 158.00W
14 G7 **Flat** ≈ Northwest Territories, NW Canada
94 H1 **Flateyri** Vestfirdhir, Nw Iceland 66.03N 23.28W
35 P8 **Flathead Lake** ◎ Montana, NW USA
181 Y15 **Flat Island** *Fr.* Île Plate. *island* N Mauritius
179 N14 **Flat Island** *island* NE Spratly Islands
27 T11 **Flatonia** Texas, SW USA 29.41N 97.06W
193 M14 **Flat Point** *headland* North Island, NZ 41.12S 176.03E
29 X6 **Flat River** Missouri, C USA 37.51N 90.31W
33 P8 **Flat River** ≈ Michigan, N USA
33 P14 **Flatrock River** ≈ Indiana, N USA
34 E6 **Flattery, Cape** *headland* Washington, NW USA 48.22N 124.43W
66 B12 **Flatts Village** *var.* The Flatts Village. C Bermuda 32.19N 64.43W
110 H7 **Flawil** Sankt Gallen, NE Switzerland 47.25N 9.12E
99 N22 **Fleet** S England, UK 51.16N 0.49W
99 K16 **Fleetwood** NW England, UK 53.55N 3.01W
20 H15 **Fleetwood** Pennsylvania, NE USA 40.27N 75.49W
97 D18 **Flekkefjord** Vest-Agder, S Norway 58.16N 6.40E
23 N5 **Flemingsburg** Kentucky, S USA 38.25N 83.43W
20 J15 **Flemington** New Jersey, NE USA 40.30N 74.51W
66 I7 **Flemish Cap** *undersea feature* NW Atlantic Ocean
97 N16 **Flen** Södermanland, C Sweden 59.03N 16.37E
102 I6 **Flensburg** Schleswig-Holstein, N Germany 54.46N 9.25E
102 J6 **Flensburger Förde** *inlet* Denmark/Germany
104 K5 **Flers** Orne, N France 48.45N 0.34W
97 C14 **Flesland** ✕ (Bergen) Hordaland, S Norway 60.18N 5.15E
Flessingue *see* Vlissingen
23 P10 **Fletcher** North Carolina, SE USA 35.24N 82.29W
33 R6 **Fletcher Pond** ◎ Michigan, N USA
104 L15 **Fleurance** Gers, S France 43.50N 0.39E
110 B8 **Fleurier** Neuchâtel, W Switzerland 46.55N 6.37E
101 H20 **Fleurus** Hainaut, S Belgium 50.28N 4.33E
105 N7 **Fleury-les-Aubrais** Loiret, C France 47.55N 1.55E
100 K10 **Flevoland** ◈ *province* C Netherlands
Flickertail State *see* North Dakota
110 H9 **Flims** Glarus, NE Switzerland 46.50N 9.16E
190 F8 **Flinders Island** *island* Investigator Group, South Australia
191 P14 **Flinders Island** *island* Furneaux Group, Tasmania, SE Australia
190 I6 **Flinders Ranges** ▲▲ South Australia
189 U5 **Flinders River** ≈ Queensland, NE Australia
9 V13 **Flin Flon** Manitoba, C Canada 54.46N 101.51W
99 K18 **Flint** NE Wales, UK 53.15N 3.09W
33 R9 **Flint** Michigan, N USA 43.00N 83.41W
99 J18 **Flint** *cultural region* NE Wales, UK
29 O7 **Flint Hills** *hill range* Kansas, C USA
203 Y6 **Flint Island** *island* Line Islands, E Kiribati
25 S4 **Flint River** ≈ Georgia, SE USA
33 R9 **Flint River** ≈ Michigan, N USA
201 X12 **Flipper Point** *headland* C Wake Island 19.18N 166.37E
96 I13 **Flisa** Hedmark, S Norway 60.36N 12.01E
96 J13 **Flisa** ≈ S Norway
126 Hh4 **Flissingskiy, Mys** *headland* Novaya Zemlya, NW Russian Federation 76.43N 69.01E
Flitsch *see* Bovec
107 U6 **Flix** Cataluña, NE Spain 41.13N 0.32E
97 J19 **Floda** Västra Götaland, S Sweden 57.46N 12.19E
103 O16 **Flöha** ≈ E Germany
27 O4 **Flomot** Texas, SW USA 34.13N 100.58W
31 V5 **Floodwood** Minnesota, N USA 46.55N 92.55W
32 M15 **Flora** Illinois, N USA 38.40N 88.29W
105 P14 **Florac** Lozère, S France 44.18N 3.35E
25 Q8 **Florala** Alabama, S USA 31.00N 86.19W
105 S4 **Florange** Moselle, NE France 49.21N 6.06E
Floreana, Isla *see* Santa María, Isla
25 O2 **Florence** Alabama, S USA 34.48N 87.40W
38 L14 **Florence** Arizona, SW USA 33.01N 111.23W
39 T6 **Florence** Colorado, C USA 38.20N 105.06W
29 O5 **Florence** Kansas, C USA 38.13N 96.56W
22 M4 **Florence** Kentucky, S USA 39.00N 84.37W
34 E13 **Florence** Oregon, NW USA 43.58N 124.06W
23 T12 **Florence** South Carolina, SE USA 34.12N 79.45W
27 S9 **Florence** Texas, SW USA 30.50N 97.47W
Florence *see* Firenze
56 E13 **Florencia** Caquetá, S Colombia 1.37N 75.37W
101 H21 **Florennes** Namur, S Belgium 50.15N 4.36E
Florentia *see* Firenze
65 J18 **Florentino Ameghino, Embalse** ◎ S Argentina
101 J24 **Florenville** Luxembourg, SE Belgium 49.42N 5.19E
44 E3 **Flores** Petén, N Guatemala 16.54N 89.55W
63 E19 **Flores** ◈ *department* S Uruguay
175 Pp16 **Flores** *island* Nusa Tenggara, C Indonesia
66 M1 **Flores** *island* Azores, Portugal, NE Atlantic Ocean
Floreshty *see* Floreşti
Flores, Lago de *see* Petén Itzá, Lago
Flores, Laut *see* Flores Sea
175 P15 **Flores Sea** *Ind.* Laut Flores. *sea* C Indonesia
118 M8 **Floreşti** *Rus.* Floreshty. N Moldova 47.52N 28.19E
27 S12 **Floresville** Texas, SW USA 29.07N 98.09W
61 N14 **Floriano** Piauí, E Brazil 06.45S 43.00W
63 K14 **Florianópolis** *prev.* Destêrro. *state capital* Santa Catarina, S Brazil 27.34S 48.31W
46 G6 **Florida** Camagüey, C Cuba 21.31N 78.13W
63 F19 **Florida** Florida, S Uruguay 34.04S 56.13W
63 F19 **Florida** ◈ *department* S Uruguay
25 U9 **Florida** *off.* State of Florida; also known as Peninsular State, Sunshine State. ◈ *state* SE USA
25 Y17 **Florida Bay** *bay* Florida, SE USA
56 G8 **Floridablanca** Santander, N Colombia 7.04N 73.06W
195 X15 **Florida Islands** *island group* C Solomon Islands
25 Y17 **Florida Keys** *island group* Florida, SE USA
39 Q16 **Florida Mountains** ▲▲ New Mexico, SW USA
66 D10 **Florida, Straits of** *strait* Atlantic Ocean/Gulf of Mexico
116 D13 **Flórina** *var.* Phlórina. Dytikí Makedonía, N Greece 40.48N 21.25E
29 X4 **Florissant** Missouri, C USA 38.47N 90.19W
96 C11 **Florø** Sogn og Fjordane, S Norway 61.34N 5.01E
117 L22 **Floúda, Akrotírio** *headland* Astypálaia, Kykládes, Greece, Aegean Sea 36.38N 26.23E
23 S7 **Floyd** Virginia, NE USA 36.53N 80.21W
27 N4 **Floydada** Texas, SW USA 33.58N 101.20W
Flüela Wisshorn *see* Weisshorn
100 K7 **Fluessen** ◎ N Netherlands
107 S5 **Flúmen** ≈ NE Spain
109 C20 **Flumendosa** ≈ Sardegna, Italy, C Mediterranean Sea
33 R9 **Flushing** Michigan, N USA 43.03N 83.51W
Flushing *see* Vlissingen
27 O6 **Fluvanna** Texas, SW USA 32.54N 101.06W
194 F14 **Fly** ≈ Indonesia/PNG
204 I10 **Flying Fish, Cape** *headland* Thurston Island, Antarctica 72.00S 102.25W
Flylân *see* Vlieland
200 Ss13 **Foa** *island* Ha'apai Group, C Tonga
9 U15 **Foam Lake** Saskatchewan, S Canada 51.37N 103.31W
115 J14 **Foča** *var* Srbinje, Republika Srpska, Bosnia and Herzegovina 43.32N 18.45E
118 L12 **Focşani** Vrancea, E Romania 45.45N 27.13E
Fogaras/Fogarasch *see* Făgăraş
109 M16 **Foggia** Puglia, SE Italy 41.28N 15.31E
Foggo *see* Faggo
78 D10 **Fogo** *island* Ilhas de Sotavento, SW Cape Verde
11 U11 **Fogo Island** *island* Newfoundland, E Canada
111 U7 **Fohnsdorf** Steiermark, SE Austria 47.13N 14.40E
102 G7 **Föhr** *island* NW Germany
106 F14 **Fóia** ▲ S Portugal 37.19N 8.39W
12 I10 **Foins, Lac aux** ◎ Quebec, SE Canada
105 N17 **Foix** Ariège, S France 42.58N 1.39E
130 I5 **Fokino** Bryanskaya Oblast', W Russian Federation 53.22N 34.22E
Fola, Cnoc *see* Bloody Foreland
96 E13 **Folarskardnuten** ▲ S Norway 60.34N 7.18E
94 G11 **Folda** *fjord* C Norway
95 E14 **Foldafjorden** *fjord* C Norway
Földvár *see* Feldioara
95 F14 **Foldereid** Nord-Trøndelag, C Norway 64.58N 12.09E
117 J22 **Folégandros** *island* Kykládes, Greece, Aegean Sea
25 O9 **Foley** Alabama, S USA 30.24N 87.40W
31 U7 **Foley** Minnesota, N USA 45.39N 93.54W
12 E7 **Foleyet** Ontario, S Canada 48.15N 82.25W
97 D14 **Folgefonni** *glacier* S Norway
108 I13 **Foligno** Umbria, C Italy 42.58N 12.40E
99 Q23 **Folkestone** SE England, UK 51.04N 1.10E
25 W8 **Folkston** Georgia, SE USA 30.49N 82.00W
96 H10 **Folldal** Hedmark, S Norway 62.08N 10.00E
27 P1 **Follett** Texas, SW USA 36.25N 100.08W
108 F13 **Follonica** Toscana, C Italy 42.55N 10.45E
23 T15 **Folly Beach** South Carolina, SE USA 32.39N 79.56W
37 O7 **Folsom** California, W USA 38.40N 121.11W
118 M12 **Folteşti** Galaţi, E Romania 45.45N 28.00E
180 H14 **Fomboni** Mohéli, S Comoros 12.18S 43.46E
20 K10 **Fonda** New York, NE USA 42.57N 74.24W
9 S10 **Fond-du-Lac** Saskatchewan, C Canada 59.19N 107.09W
32 M8 **Fond du Lac** Wisconsin, N USA 43.48N 88.27W
9 T10 **Fond-du-Lac** ≈ Saskatchewan, C Canada
202 C9 **Fongafale** *var.* Funafuti. ● (Tuvalu) Funafuti Atoll, SE Tuvalu 8.31N 179.11E
202 G8 **Fongafale** *atoll* C Tuvalu
109 C18 **Fonni** Sardegna, Italy, C Mediterranean Sea 40.07N 9.17E
201 V12 **Fono** *island* Chuuk, C Micronesia
56 G4 **Fonseca** La Guajira, N Colombia 10.54N 72.54W
Fonseca, Golfo de *see* Fonseca, Gulf of
44 H8 **Fonseca, Gulf of** *Sp.* Golfo de Fonseca. *gulf* Central America
105 O6 **Fontainebleau** Seine-et-Marne, N France 48.24N 2.42E
65 G19 **Fontana, Lago** ◎ W Argentina
23 N10 **Fontana Lake** ⊡ North Carolina, SE USA
109 L24 **Fontanarossa** ✕ (Catania) Sicilia, Italy, C Mediterranean Sea 37.28N 15.04E
9 N11 **Fontas** ≈ British Columbia, W Canada
60 D12 **Fonte Boa** Amazonas, N Brazil 2.31S 66.01W
104 J10 **Fontenay-le-Comte** Vendée, NW France 46.28N 0.48W
35 T16 **Fontenelle Reservoir** ⊡ Wyoming, C USA
200 Ss12 **Fonualei** *island* Vava'u Group, N Tonga
113 H24 **Fonyód** Somogy, W Hungary 46.43N 17.31E
Foochow *see* Fuzhou
41 Q10 **Foraker, Mount** ▲ Alaska, USA 62.57N 151.24W
197 D14 **Forari** Éfaté, C Vanuatu 17.42S 168.33E
105 U4 **Forbach** Moselle, NE France 49.10N 6.54E
191 Q8 **Forbes** New South Wales, SE Australia 33.24S 148.00E
79 T17 **Forcados** Delta, S Nigeria 5.16N 5.25E
105 S14 **Forcalquier** Alpes-de-Haute-Provence, SE France 43.57N 5.46E
103 K19 **Forchheim** Bayern, SE Germany 49.43N 11.07E
176 V14 **Fordate, Pulau** *island* Kepulauan Tanimbar, E Indonesia
37 R13 **Ford City** California, W USA 35.09N 119.27W
96 D11 **Førde** Sogn og Fjordane, S Norway 61.27N 5.49E
33 N4 **Ford River** ≈ Michigan, N USA
191 O4 **Fords Bridge** New South Wales, SE Australia 29.44S 145.25E
22 J6 **Fordsville** Kentucky, S USA 37.36N 86.39W
29 U13 **Fordyce** Arkansas, C USA 33.49N 92.24W
78 I14 **Forécariah** Guinée-Maritime, SW Guinea 9.28N 13.06W
207 O14 **Forel, Mont** ▲ SE Greenland 66.55N 36.45W
9 R17 **Foremost** Alberta, SW Canada 49.30N 111.34W
12 D16 **Forest** Ontario, S Canada 43.05N 82.00W
24 L5 **Forest** Mississippi, S USA 32.22N 89.30W
33 S12 **Forest** Ohio, N USA 40.47N 83.26W
31 V11 **Forest City** Iowa, C USA 43.15N 93.38W
23 Q10 **Forest City** North Carolina, SE USA 35.19N 81.52W
34 G11 **Forest Grove** Oregon, NW USA 45.31N 123.06W
191 P17 **Forestier Peninsula** *peninsula* Tasmania, SE Australia
31 V8 **Forest Lake** Minnesota, N USA 45.16N 92.59W
25 S3 **Forest Park** Georgia, SE USA 33.37N 84.22W
31 Q3 **Forest River** ≈ North Dakota, N USA
13 T6 **Forestville** Quebec, SE Canada 48.45N 69.04W
105 Q11 **Forez, Monts du** ▲▲ C France
98 K10 **Forfar** E Scotland, UK 56.37N 2.54W
28 J8 **Forgan** Oklahoma, C USA 36.54N 100.32W
Forge du Sud *see* Dudelange
103 J24 **Forggensee** ◎ S Germany
153 N10 **Forish** *Rus.* Farish. Jizzakh Wiloyati, C Uzbekistan 40.33N 66.52E
22 F9 **Forked Deer River** ≈ Tennessee, S USA
34 F7 **Forks** Washington, NW USA 47.57N 124.22W
94 N2 **Forlandsundet** *sound* W Svalbard
108 H10 **Forlì** *anc.* Forum Livii. Emilia-Romagna, N Italy 44.13N 12.01E
31 Q7 **Forman** North Dakota, N USA 46.07N 97.39W
99 K17 **Formby** NW England, UK 53.34N 3.04W
107 V11 **Formentera** *anc.* Ophiusa, *Lat.* Frumentum. *island* Islas Baleares, Spain, W Mediterranean Sea
Formentor, Cabo de *see* Formentor, Cap de
107 Y9 **Formentor, Cap de** *var.* Cabo de Formentor, Cape Formentor. *headland* Mallorca, Spain, W Mediterranean Sea 39.57N 3.12E
Formentor, Cape *see* Formentor, Cap de
109 J16 **Formia** Lazio, C Italy 41.16N 13.37E
64 O7 **Formosa** Formosa, NE Argentina 26.07S 58.13W
64 M6 **Formosa** *off.* Provincia de Formosa. ◈ *province* NE Argentina
Formosa/Formo'sa *see* Taiwan
61 I17 **Formosa, Serra** ▲▲ C Brazil
Formosa Strait *see* Taiwan Strait
97 H15 **Fornebu** ✕ (Oslo) Akershus, S Norway 59.54N 10.37E
27 U6 **Forney** Texas, SW USA 32.45N 96.28W
97 H21 **Fornæs** *headland* C Denmark 56.26N 10.57E
108 E9 **Fornovo di Taro** Emilia-Romagna, C Italy 44.42N 10.07E
119 T14 **Foros** Respublika Krym, S Ukraine 44.24N 33.47E
Føroyar *see* Faeroe Islands
98 J8 **Forres** NE Scotland, UK 57.32N 3.37W
29 X11 **Forrest City** Arkansas, C USA 35.01N 90.48W
41 Y15 **Forrester Island** *island* Alexander Archipelago, Alaska, USA
27 N7 **Forsan** Texas, SW USA 32.06N 101.22W
189 V5 **Forsayth** Queensland, NE Australia 18.31S 143.37E
97 L19 **Forserum** Jönköping, S Sweden 57.42N 14.28E
97 K15 **Forshaga** Värmland, C Sweden 59.33N 13.28E
95 L19 **Forssa** Etelä-Suomi, S Finland 60.49N 23.40E
103 Q14 **Forst** *Lus.* Baršć Łužyca. Brandenburg, E Germany 51.43N 14.38E
191 U7 **Forster-Tuncurry** New South Wales, SE Australia 32.13S 152.31E
25 T4 **Forsyth** Georgia, SE USA 33.00N 83.57W
29 T8 **Forsyth** Missouri, C USA 36.41N 93.07W
35 W10 **Forsyth** Montana, NW USA 46.16N 106.40W
155 U11 **Fort Abbās** Punjab, E Pakistan 29.11N 72.54E
10 G10 **Fort Albany** Ontario, C Canada 52.15N 81.34W
58 L13 **Fortaleza** Pando, N Bolivia 9.48S 65.28W
60 P13 **Fortaleza** *prev.* Ceará. *state capital* Ceará, NE Brazil 3.45S 38.34W
61 D16 **Fortaleza** Rondônia, W Brazil 8.45S 64.06W
58 C13 **Fortaleza, Río** ≈ W Peru
Fort-Archambault *see* Sarh
23 U3 **Fort Ashby** West Virginia, NE USA 39.30N 78.46W
98 I9 **Fort Augustus** N Scotland, UK 57.13N 4.37W
Fort-Bayard *see* Zhanjiang
35 S8 **Fort Benton** Montana, NW USA 47.49N 110.40W
37 Q1 **Fort Bidwell** California, W USA 41.50N 120.07W
36 L5 **Fort Bragg** California, W USA 39.25N 123.48W
33 N16 **Fort Branch** Indiana, N USA 38.15N 87.34W
Fort-Bretonnet *see* Bousso
35 T17 **Fort Bridger** Wyoming, C USA 41.18N 110.19W
Fort-Cappolani *see* Tidjikja
Fort Charlet *see* Djanet
Fort-Chimo *see* Kuujjuaq
9 R10 **Fort Chipewyan** Alberta, C Canada 58.42N 111.07W
Fort Cobb Lake *see* Fort Cobb Reservoir
28 L11 **Fort Cobb Reservoir** *var.* Fort Cobb Lake. ⊡ Oklahoma, C USA
39 T3 **Fort Collins** Colorado, C USA 40.35N 105.04W
12 K12 **Fort-Coulonge** Quebec, SE Canada 45.51N 76.43W
Fort-Crampel *see* Kaga Bandoro
Fort-Dauphin *see* Tôlañaro
26 K10 **Fort Davis** Texas, SW USA 30.34N 103.55W
39 O10 **Fort Defiance** Arizona, SW USA 35.44N 109.04W
47 Q12 **Fort-de-France** *prev.* Fort-Royal. ○ (Martinique) W Martinique 14.36N 61.04W
47 P12 **Fort-de-France, Baie de** *bay* W Martinique
Fort de Kock *see* Bukittinggi
25 P6 **Fort Deposit** Alabama, S USA 31.58N 86.34W
31 U13 **Fort Dodge** Iowa, C USA 42.30N 94.10W
11 S10 **Forteau** Quebec, E Canada 51.30N 56.55W
108 E11 **Forte dei Marmi** Toscana, C Italy 43.59N 10.10E
12 H17 **Fort Erie** Ontario, S Canada 42.55N 78.55W
188 H7 **Fortescue River** ≈ Western Australia
21 S2 **Fort Fairfield** Maine, NE USA 46.45N 67.51W
Fort-Foureau *see* Kousséri
10 A11 **Fort Frances** Ontario, S Canada 48.37N 93.22W
Fort Franklin *see* Déline
25 R7 **Fort Gaines** Georgia, SE USA 31.36N 85.03W
39 T8 **Fort Garland** Colorado, C USA 37.22N 105.24W
23 P5 **Fort Gay** West Virginia, NE USA 38.06N 82.35W
Fort George *see* La Grande Rivière
29 Q10 **Fort Gibson** Oklahoma, C USA 35.48N 95.15W
29 Q9 **Fort Gibson Lake** ⊡ Oklahoma, C USA
15 Gg5 **Fort Good Hope** *var.* Good Hope. Northwest Territories, NW Canada 66.16N 128.37W
25 V4 **Fort Gordon** Georgia, SE USA 33.25N 82.09W
Fort Gouraud *see* Fdérik
98 I11 **Forth** ≈ C Scotland, UK
Fort Hall *see* Murang'a
26 H8 **Fort Hancock** Texas, SW USA 31.18N 105.49W
Fort Hertz *see* Putao
98 K12 **Forth, Firth of** *estuary* E Scotland, UK
12 L14 **Forthton** Ontario, SE Canada 44.43N 75.31W
12 M8 **Fortier** ≈ Quebec, SE Canada
Fortín General Eugenio Garay *see* General Eugenio A. Garay
Fort Jameson *see* Chipata
Fort Johnston *see* Mangochi
21 R1 **Fort Kent** Maine, NE USA 47.15N 68.33W
Fort-Lamy *see* Ndjamena
25 Z15 **Fort Lauderdale** Florida, SE USA 26.07N 80.08W
23 R11 **Fort Lawn** South Carolina, SE USA 34.43N 80.46W
15 Gg9 **Fort Liard** *var.* Liard. Northwest Territories, W Canada 60.13N 123.28W
46 M8 **Fort-Liberté** NE Haiti 19.37N 71.51W
23 N9 **Fort Loudoun Lake** ⊡ Tennessee, S USA
39 T3 **Fort Lupton** Colorado, C USA 40.04N 104.48W
9 R12 **Fort MacKay** Alberta, C Canada 57.12N 111.40W
9 Q17 **Fort Macleod** *var.* MacLeod. Alberta, SW Canada 49.43N 113.24W
31 Y16 **Fort Madison** Iowa, C USA 40.37N 91.15W
Fort Manning *see* Mchinji
27 P9 **Fort McKavett** Texas, SW USA 30.50N 100.07W
9 R12 **Fort McMurray** Alberta, C Canada 56.43N 111.22W
14 Ff3 **Fort McPherson** *var.* McPherson. Northwest Territories, NW Canada 67.28N 134.49W
23 R11 **Fort Mill** South Carolina, SE USA 35.00N 80.57W
Fort-Millot *see* Ngouri
39 U3 **Fort Morgan** Colorado, C USA 40.13N 103.48W
25 W14 **Fort Myers** Florida, SE USA 26.39N 81.52W
25 W15 **Fort Myers Beach** Florida, SE USA 26.27N 81.57W
8 M10 **Fort Nelson** British Columbia, W Canada 58.48N 122.43W
8 M10 **Fort Nelson** ≈ British Columbia, W Canada
Fort Norman *see* Tulita.
25 Q2 **Fort Payne** Alabama, S USA 34.23N 85.43W
35 W7 **Fort Peck** Montana, NW USA 48.00N 106.28W
35 V8 **Fort Peck Lake** ⊡ Montana, NW USA
25 Y13 **Fort Pierce** Florida, SE USA 27.28N 80.19W
31 N10 **Fort Pierre** South Dakota, N USA 44.21N 100.22W
83 E18 **Fort Portal** SW Uganda 0.39N 30.16E
15 Hh8 **Fort Providence** *var.* Providence. Northwest Territories, W Canada 61.21N 117.39W
9 U16 **Fort Qu'Appelle** Saskatchewan, S Canada 50.49N 103.52W
Fort-Repoux *see* Akjoujt
15 I8 **Fort Resolution** *var.* Resolution. Northwest Territories, W Canada 61.10N 113.39W
35 T13 **Fortress Mountain** ▲ Wyoming, C USA 44.20N 109.51W
Fort Rosebery *see* Mansa
Fort-Rousset *see* Owando
Fort-Royal *see* Fort-de-France
10 I10 **Fort Rupert** *prev.* Rupert House. Quebec, SE Canada 51.30N 79.45W
14 G12 **Fort St.James** British Columbia, SW Canada 54.25N 124.15W
9 N12 **Fort St.John** British Columbia, W Canada 56.16N 120.51W
Fort Sandeman *see* Zhob
9 Q14 **Fort Saskatchewan** Alberta, SW Canada 53.42N 113.12W
29 R6 **Fort Scott** Kansas, C USA 37.49N 94.42W
10 E6 **Fort Severn** Ontario, C Canada 56.00N 87.40W
33 R12 **Fort Shawnee** Ohio, N USA 40.41N 84.08W
150 E14 **Fort-Shevchenko** Mangistau, W Kazakhstan 44.28N 50.16E
Fort-Sibut *see* Sibut
15 H8 **Fort Simpson** *var.* Simpson. Northwest Territories, W Canada 61.52N 121.22W
15 Ii9 **Fort Smith** *district capital* Northwest Territories, W Canada 60.01N 111.55W
29 R10 **Fort Smith** Arkansas, C USA 35.23N 94.24W
39 T13 **Fort Stanton** New Mexico, SW USA 33.28N 105.31W
26 L9 **Fort Stockton** Texas, SW USA 30.54N 102.54W
39 U12 **Fort Sumner** New Mexico, SW USA 34.28N 104.15W
28 K8 **Fort Supply** Oklahoma, C USA 36.34N 99.34W
28 K8 **Fort Supply Lake** ⊡ Oklahoma, C USA
31 O10 **Fort Thompson** South Dakota, N USA 44.01N 99.22W
Fort-Trinquet *see* Bîr Mogreïn
107 R12 **Fortuna** Murcia, SE Spain 38.10N 1.07W
36 K3 **Fortuna** California, W USA 40.35N 124.07W
30 J2 **Fortuna** North Dakota, N USA 48.53N 103.46W
25 T5 **Fort Valley** Georgia, SE USA 32.33N 83.53W
9 P11 **Fort Vermilion** Alberta, W Canada 58.22N 115.58W
Fort Victoria *see* Masvingo
33 P13 **Fortville** Indiana, N USA 39.55N 85.51W
25 P9 **Fort Walton Beach** Florida, SE USA 30.24N 86.37W
33 P12 **Fort Wayne** Indiana, N USA 41.07N 85.07W
98 H10 **Fort William** N Scotland, UK 56.49N 5.07W
27 T6 **Fort Worth** Texas, SW USA 32.43N 97.19W
30 M7 **Fort Yates** North Dakota, N USA 46.05N 100.37W
41 S7 **Fort Yukon** Alaska, USA 66.35N 145.05W
Forum Alieni *see* Ferrara
Forum Julii *see* Fréjus
Forum Livii *see* Forlì
149 Q15 **Forūr, Jazīreh-ye** *island* S Iran
96 H7 **Fosen** *physical region* S Norway
167 N14 **Foshan** *var.* Fatshan, Fo-shan, Namhoi. Guangdong, S China 23.03N 113.05E
Fossa Claudia *see* Chioggia
108 B9 **Fossano** Piemonte, NW Italy 44.33N 7.43E

◆ Country
● Country Capital
◇ Dependent Territory
○ Dependent Territory Capital
◈ Administrative Region
✕ International Airport
▲ Mountain
▲▲ Mountain Range
Volcano
≈ River
◎ Lake
⊡ Reservoir

FOSSES-LA-VILLE – FYN

101 H21 **Fosses-la-Ville** Namur, S Belgium *50.24N 4.42E*
34 J12 **Fossil** Oregon, NW USA *44.58N 120.15W*
Foss Lake *see* Foss Reservoir
108 I11 **Fossombrone** Marche, C Italy *43.42N 12.48E*
28 K10 **Foss Reservoir** *var.* Foss Lake. ⊠ Oklahoma, C USA
31 S4 **Fosston** Minnesota, N USA *47.34N 95.45W*
191 O13 **Foster** Victoria, SE Australia *38.40S 146.15E*
9 T12 **Foster Lakes** ◎ Saskatchewan, C Canada
33 S12 **Fostoria** Ohio, N USA *41.09N 83.25W*
81 D19 **Fougamou** Ngounié, C Gabon *1.15S 10.37E*
104 J6 **Fougères** Ille-et-Vilaine, NW France *48.21N 1.12W*
Fou-hsin *see* Fuxin
29 S14 **Fouke** Arkansas, C USA *33.15N 93.53W*
98 K2 **Foula** *island* NE Scotland, UK
67 D24 **Foul Bay** *bay* East Falkland, Falkland Islands
99 P21 **Foulness Island** *island* SE England, UK
193 F15 **Foulwind, Cape** *headland* South Island, NZ *41.45S 171.28E*
81 E15 **Foumban** Ouest, NW Cameroon *5.43N 10.49E*
180 H13 **Foumbouni** Grande Comore, NW Comoros *11.49S 43.30E*
205 N8 **Foundation Ice Stream** *glacier* Antarctica
39 T6 **Fountain** Colorado, C USA *38.40N 104.42W*
38 L4 **Fountain Green** Utah, W USA *39.37N 111.37W*
23 P11 **Fountain Inn** South Carolina, SE USA *34.41N 82.12W*
29 S11 **Fourche LaFave River** ≈ Arkansas, C USA
35 Z13 **Four Corners** Wyoming, C USA *44.04N 104.08W*
105 Q2 **Fourmies** Nord, N France *50.01N 4.03E*
40 J17 **Four Mountains, Islands of** *island group* Aleutian Islands, Alaska, USA
181 P17 **Fournaise, Piton de la** ▲ SE Réunion *21.13S 55.43E*
12 J8 **Fournière, Lac** ◎ Quebec, SE Canada
117 L20 **Foúrnoi** *island* Dodekánisos, Greece, Aegean Sea
66 K13 **Four North Fracture Zone** *tectonic feature* W Atlantic Ocean
Fouron-Saint-Martin *see* Sint-Martens-Voeren
32 L3 **Fourteen Mile Point** *headland* Michigan, N USA *46.59N 89.07W*
78 I13 **Fouta Djallon** *var.* Futa Jallon. ▲▲ W Guinea
193 C25 **Foveaux Strait** *strait* S NZ
37 Q11 **Fowler** California, W USA *36.35N 119.40W*
39 U6 **Fowler** Colorado, C USA *38.07N 104.01W*
33 N12 **Fowler** Indiana, N USA *40.36N 87.20W*
190 D7 **Fowlers Bay** *bay* South Australia
27 R13 **Fowlerton** Texas, SW USA *28.27N 98.48W*
148 M3 **Fowman** *var.* Fuman, Fumen. Gīlān, NW Iran *37.15N 49.19E*
67 C25 **Fox Bay East** West Falkland, Falkland Islands
67 C25 **Fox Bay West** West Falkland, Falkland Islands
12 J14 **Foxboro** Ontario, SE Canada *44.16N 77.23W*
9 O14 **Fox Creek** Alberta, W Canada *54.25N 116.57W*
66 G5 **Foxe Basin** *sea* Nunavut, N Canada
66 G5 **Foxe Channel** *channel* Nunavut, N Canada
97 I16 **Foxen** ◎ C Sweden
16 N4 **Foxe Peninsula** *peninsula* Baffin Island, Nunavut, NE Canada
193 E19 **Fox Glacier** West Coast, South Island, NZ *43.28S 170.00E*
40 L17 **Fox Islands** *island* Aleutian Islands, Alaska, USA
32 M10 **Fox Lake** Illinois, N USA *42.24N 88.10W*
9 V12 **Fox Mine** Manitoba, C Canada *56.36N 101.48W*
37 R3 **Fox Mountain** ▲ Nevada, W USA *41.01N 119.30W*
67 E25 **Fox Point** *headland* East Falkland, Falkland Islands *51.55S 58.24W*
32 M11 **Fox River** ≈ Illinois/Wisconsin, N USA
32 L7 **Fox River** ≈ Wisconsin, N USA
192 L13 **Foxton** Manawatu-Wanganui, North Island, NZ *40.30S 175.17E*
9 S16 **Fox Valley** Saskatchewan, S Canada *50.28N 109.28W*
9 W16 **Foxwarren** Manitoba, S Canada *50.30N 101.09W*
99 E14 **Foyle, Lough** *Ir.* Loch Feabhail. *inlet* N Ireland
204 H5 **Foyn Coast** *physical region* Antarctica
106 I2 **Foz** Galicia, NW Spain *43.33N 7.16W*
62 I12 **Foz do Areia, Represa de** ⊠ S Brazil
61 A16 **Foz do Breu** Acre, W Brazil *9.21S 72.40W*
85 A16 **Foz do Cunene** Namibe, SW Angola *17.11S 11.52E*
62 G12 **Foz do Iguaçu** Paraná, S Brazil *25.33S 54.31W*
60 C12 **Foz do Mamoriá** Amazonas, NW Brazil *2.28S 66.06W*
107 T6 **Fraga** Aragón, NE Spain *41.31N 0.21E*
46 F5 **Fragoso, Cayo** *island* C Cuba
63 G18 **Fraile Muerto** Cerro Largo, NE Uruguay *32.30S 54.30W*
101 H21 **Fraire** Namur, S Belgium *50.16N 4.30E*
101 L21 **Fraiture, Baraque de** *hill* SE Belgium *50.22N 5.50E*
Frakštát *see* Hlohovec
207 S10 **Fram Basin** *var.* Amundsen Basin. *undersea feature* Arctic Ocean
101 F20 **Frameries** Hainaut, S Belgium *50.25N 3.40E*
21 O11 **Framingham** Massachusetts, NE USA *42.15N 71.24W*
62 L7 **Franca** São Paulo, S Brazil *20.33S 47.27W*
197 G4 **Français, Récif des** *reef* W New Caledonia
109 K14 **Francavilla al Mare** Abruzzo, C Italy *42.25N 14.16E*
109 P18 **Francavilla Fontana** Puglia, SE Italy *40.31N 17.34E*
104 M8 **France** *off.* French Republic, *It./Sp.* Francia; *prev.* Gaul, Gaule, *Lat.* Gallia. ◆ *republic* W Europe
47 O8 **Francés Viejo, Cabo** *headland* NE Dominican Republic *19.39N 69.57W*
81 F19 **Franceville** *var.* Massoukou, Masuku. Haut-Ogooué, E Gabon *1.40S 13.31E*
81 F19 **Franceville** ✕ Haut-Ogooué, E Gabon *1.38S 13.24E*
Francfort *see* Frankfurt am Main
105 T8 **Franche-Comté** ◐ *region* E France
Francia *see* France
31 O11 **Francis Case, Lake** ⊠ South Dakota, N USA
62 H12 **Francisco Beltrão** Paraná, S Brazil *26.04S 53.04W*
Francisco I. Madero *see* Villa Madero
63 A21 **Francisco Madero** Buenos Aires, E Argentina *35.52S 62.03W*
44 H6 **Francisco Morazán** *prev.* Tegucigalpa. ◐ *department* C Honduras
85 J18 **Francistown** North East, NE Botswana *21.08S 27.31E*
Franconian Forest *see* Frankenwald
Franconian Jura *see* Fränkische Alb
100 K6 **Franeker** *Fris.* Frjentsjer. Friesland, N Netherlands *53.10N 5.33E*
Frankenalb *see* Fränkische Alb
103 H16 **Frankenberg** Hessen, C Germany *51.04N 8.49E*
103 J20 **Frankenhöhe** *hill range* C Germany
33 R8 **Frankenmuth** Michigan, N USA *43.19N 83.44W*
103 F20 **Frankenstein** *hill* W Germany *49.24N 8.04E*
Frankenstein/Frankenstein in Schlesien *see* Ząbkowice Śląskie
103 G20 **Frankenthal** Rheinland-Pfalz, W Germany *49.33N 8.21E*
103 L18 **Frankenwald** *Eng.* Franconian Forest. ▲▲ C Germany
46 J12 **Frankfield** C Jamaica *18.07N 77.22W*
12 J14 **Frankford** Ontario, SE Canada *44.12N 77.36W*
33 O13 **Frankfort** Indiana, N USA *40.16N 86.30W*
29 O3 **Frankfort** Kansas, C USA *39.42N 96.25W*
22 L5 **Frankfort** *state capital* Kentucky, S USA *38.12N 84.52W*
Frankfort on the Main *see* Frankfurt am Main
Frankfurt *see* Słubice, Poland
Frankfurt *see* Frankfurt am Main, Germany
103 G18 **Frankfurt am Main** *var.* Frankfurt, *Fr.* Francfort; *prev. Eng.* Frankfort on the Main. Hessen, SW Germany *50.07N 8.40E*
102 Q12 **Frankfurt an der Oder** Brandenburg, E Germany *52.19N 14.31E*
103 L21 **Fränkische Alb** *var.* Frankenalb, *Eng.* Franconian Jura. ▲▲ S Germany
103 I18 **Fränkische Saale** ≈ C Germany
103 L19 **Fränkische Schweiz** *hill range* C Germany
25 R4 **Franklin** Georgia, SE USA *33.15N 85.06W*
33 P14 **Franklin** Indiana, N USA *39.28N 86.01W*
22 J7 **Franklin** Kentucky, S USA *36.43N 86.34W*
24 I9 **Franklin** Louisiana, S USA *29.48N 91.30W*
31 O17 **Franklin** Nebraska, C USA *40.06N 98.57W*
23 N10 **Franklin** North Carolina, SE USA *35.07N 83.22W*
20 C13 **Franklin** Pennsylvania, NE USA *41.24N 79.49W*
22 J9 **Franklin** Tennessee, S USA *35.55N 86.52W*
27 U9 **Franklin** Texas, SW USA *31.01N 96.29W*
23 X7 **Franklin** Virginia, NE USA *36.40N 76.55W*
23 T4 **Franklin** West Virginia, NE USA *38.39N 79.19W*
32 M9 **Franklin** Wisconsin, N USA *42.53N 88.00W*
15 H2 **Franklin Bay** *inlet* Northwest Territories, N Canada
34 K7 **Franklin D.Roosevelt Lake** ⊠ Washington, NW USA
37 W4 **Franklin Lake** ◎ Nevada, W USA
193 B22 **Franklin Mountains** ▲▲ South Island, NZ
41 R5 **Franklin Mountains** ▲▲ Alaska, USA
41 N4 **Franklin, Point** *headland* Alaska, USA *70.54N 158.48W*
191 O17 **Franklin River** ≈ Tasmania, SE Australia
15 K2 **Franklin Strait** *strait* Nunavut, N Canada
24 K8 **Franklinton** Louisiana, S USA *30.51N 90.09W*
23 U9 **Franklinton** North Carolina, SE USA *36.06N 78.27W*
Frankstadt *see* Frenštát pod Radhoštěm
27 V7 **Frankston** Texas, SW USA *32.03N 95.30W*
35 U12 **Frannie** Wyoming, C USA *44.57N 108.37W*
13 U5 **Franquelin** Quebec, SE Canada *49.17N 67.52W*
13 U5 **Franquelin** ≈ Quebec, SE Canada
85 C18 **Fransfontein** Kunene, NW Namibia *20.10S 15.03E*
95 H17 **Fränsta** Västernorrland, C Sweden *62.30N 16.06E*
126 H1 **Frantsa-Iosifa, Zemlya** *Eng.* Franz Josef Land. *island group* N Russian Federation
193 E18 **Franz Josef Glacier** West Coast, South Island, NZ *43.22S 170.11E*
Franz Josef Land *see* Frantsa-Iosifa, Zemlya
Franz-Josef Spitze *see* Gerlachovský stít
103 L23 **Franz Josef Strauss** *abbrev.* F.J.S. ✕ (München) Bayern, SE Germany *48.07N 11.43E*
109 A19 **Frasca, Capo della** *headland* Sardegna, Italy, C Mediterranean Sea *39.46N 8.27E*
109 I15 **Frascati** Lazio, C Italy *41.48N 12.40E*
9 N14 **Fraser** ≈ British Columbia, SW Canada
85 G24 **Fraserburg** Western Cape, SW South Africa *31.49S 21.29E*
98 L8 **Fraserburgh** NE Scotland, UK *57.41N 2.19W*
189 Z9 **Fraser Island** *var.* Great Sandy Island. *island* Queensland, E Australia
8 L14 **Fraser Lake** British Columbia, SW Canada *54.00N 124.45W*
8 L15 **Fraser Plateau** *plateau* British Columbia, SW Canada
192 P10 **Frasertown** Hawke's Bay, North Island, NZ *38.58S 177.25E*
101 E19 **Frasnes-lez-Buissenal** Hainaut, SW Belgium *50.40N 3.37E*
110 I7 **Frastanz** Vorarlberg, NW Austria *47.13N 9.37E*
12 B8 **Frater** Ontario, S Canada *47.19N 84.28W*
Frauenbach *see* Baia Mare
Frauenburg *see* Saldus, Latvia
Frauenburg *see* Frombork, Poland
110 H6 **Frauenfeld** Thurgau, NE Switzerland *47.34N 8.54E*
111 Z5 **Frauenkirchen** Burgenland, E Austria *47.49N 16.57E*
63 D19 **Fray Bentos** Río Negro, W Uruguay *33.09S 58.14W*
63 F19 **Fray Marcos** Florida, S Uruguay *34.13S 55.43W*
31 S6 **Frazee** Minnesota, N USA *46.42N 95.40W*
106 M5 **Frechilla** Castilla-León, N Spain *42.07N 4.49W*
32 I4 **Frederic** Wisconsin, N USA *45.42N 92.30W*
97 G23 **Fredericia** Vejle, C Denmark *55.34N 9.46E*
23 W3 **Frederick** Maryland, NE USA *39.24N 77.24W*
28 L12 **Frederick** Oklahoma, C USA *34.23N 99.01W*
31 P7 **Frederick** South Dakota, N USA *45.49N 98.31W*
31 X12 **Fredericksburg** Iowa, C USA *42.58N 92.12W*
27 R10 **Fredericksburg** Texas, SW USA *30.16N 98.52W*
23 W5 **Fredericksburg** Virginia, NE USA *38.16N 77.27W*
41 X13 **Frederick Sound** *sound* Alaska, USA
29 X6 **Fredericktown** Missouri, C USA *37.33N 90.17W*
62 H13 **Frederico Westphalen** Rio Grande do Sul, S Brazil *27.22S 53.20W*
11 O15 **Fredericton** New Brunswick, SE Canada *45.57N 66.40W*
97 I22 **Frederiksborg** *off.* Frederiksborgs Amt. ◐ *county* E Denmark
Frederikshåb *see* Paamiut
97 H19 **Frederikshavn** *prev.* Fladstrand. Nordjylland, N Denmark *57.28N 10.33E*
97 J22 **Frederikssund** Frederiksborg, E Denmark *55.51N 12.04E*
47 T9 **Frederiksted** Saint Croix, S Virgin Islands (US) *17.41N 64.51W*
97 I22 **Frederiksværk** *var.* Frederiksværk og Hanehoved. Frederiksborg, E Denmark *55.58N 12.01E*
Frederiksværk og Hanehoved *see* Frederiksværk
56 E9 **Fredonia** Antioquia, W Colombia *5.57N 75.42W*
38 K8 **Fredonia** Arizona, SW USA *36.57N 112.31W*
29 P7 **Fredonia** Kansas, C USA *37.31N 95.49W*
20 C11 **Fredonia** New York, NE USA *42.26N 79.19W*
37 P4 **Fredonyer Pass** *pass* California, W USA *40.21N 120.52W*
95 I15 **Fredrika** Västerbotten, N Sweden *64.03N 18.25E*
97 L14 **Fredriksberg** Dalarna, C Sweden *60.07N 14.22E*
Fredrikshald *see* Halden
Fredrikshamn *see* Hamina
97 H16 **Fredrikstad** Østfold, S Norway *59.12N 10.57E*
32 K16 **Freeburg** Illinois, N USA *38.25N 89.54W*
20 K15 **Freehold** New Jersey, NE USA *40.14N 74.14W*
20 H14 **Freeland** Pennsylvania, NE USA *41.01N 75.54W*
190 J5 **Freeling Heights** ▲ South Australia *30.09S 139.24E*
37 Q7 **Freel Peak** ▲ California, W USA *38.52N 119.52W*
16 T7 **Freels, Cape** *headland* Newfoundland, E Canada *49.16N 53.30W*
31 Q11 **Freeman** South Dakota, N USA *43.21N 97.26W*
46 G1 **Freeport** Grand Bahama Island, N Bahamas *26.28N 78.43W*
32 L10 **Freeport** Illinois, N USA *42.18N 89.37W*
27 W12 **Freeport** Texas, SW USA *28.57N 95.21W*
46 G1 **Freeport** ✕ Grand Bahama Island, N Bahamas *26.31N 78.48W*
27 R14 **Freer** Texas, SW USA *27.52N 98.37W*
85 I22 **Free State** *off.* Free State Province; *prev.* Orange Free State, *Afr.* Oranje Vrystaat. ◐ *province* C South Africa
Freetown *see* Maryland
78 G15 **Freetown** ● (Sierra Leone) W Sierra Leone *8.27N 13.16W*
180 J16 **Frégate** *island* Inner Islands, NE Seychelles
106 J12 **Fregenal de la Sierra** Extremadura, W Spain *38.10N 6.39W*
190 C2 **Fregon** South Australia *26.44S 132.03E*
104 H5 **Fréhel, Cap** *headland* NW France *48.41N 2.21W*
96 F8 **Frei** Møre og Romsdal, S Norway *63.02N 7.47E*
103 O16 **Freiberg** Sachsen, E Germany *50.55N 13.21E*
103 O16 **Freiberger Mulde** ≈ E Germany
Freiburg *see* Fribourg, Switzerland
Freiburg *see* Freiburg im Breisgau, Germany
103 F23 **Freiburg im Breisgau** *var.* Freiburg, *Fr.* Fribourg-en-Brisgau. Baden-Württemberg, SW Germany *48.00N 7.52E*
Freiburg in Schlesien *see* Świebodzice
Freie Hansestadt Bremen *see* Bremen
Freie und Hansestadt Hamburg *see* Brandenburg
103 L22 **Freising** Bayern, SE Germany *48.24N 11.45E*
111 T3 **Freistadt** Oberösterreich, N Austria *48.30N 14.27E*
Freistadtl *see* Hlohovec
103 O16 **Freital** Sachsen, E Germany *51.00N 13.40E*
Freiwaldau *see* Jeseník
106 J6 **Freixo de Espada à Cinta** Bragança, N Portugal *41.04N 6.49W*
105 U15 **Fréjus** *anc.* Forum Julii. Var, SE France *43.25N 6.43E*
188 I13 **Fremantle** Western Australia *32.07S 115.43E*
37 N9 **Fremont** California, W USA *37.32N 121.56W*
33 Q11 **Fremont** Indiana, N USA *41.43N 84.54W*
31 W15 **Fremont** Iowa, C USA *41.12N 92.26W*
33 P8 **Fremont** Michigan, N USA *43.28N 85.56W*
31 R15 **Fremont** Nebraska, C USA *41.25N 96.30W*
33 S11 **Fremont** Ohio, N USA *41.21N 83.07W*
35 T14 **Fremont Peak** ▲ Wyoming, C USA *43.07N 109.37W*
38 M6 **Fremont River** ≈ Utah, W USA
23 O9 **French Broad River** ≈ Tennessee, S USA
23 N5 **Frenchburg** Kentucky, S USA *37.57N 83.41W*
20 C12 **French Creek** ≈ Pennsylvania, NE USA
34 K15 **Frenchglen** Oregon, NW USA *42.49N 118.55W*
57 Y10 **French Guiana** *var.* Guiana, Guyane. ◇ *French overseas department* N South America
French Guinea *see* Guinea
33 O15 **French Lick** Indiana, N USA *38.33N 86.37W*
193 J14 **French Pass** Marlborough, South Island, NZ *40.57S 173.49E*
203 T11 **French Polynesia** ◇ *French overseas territory* C Polynesia
French Republic *see* France
12 F11 **French River** ≈ Ontario, S Canada
French Somaliland *see* Djibouti
181 P12 **French Southern and Antarctic Territories** *Fr.* Terres Australes et Antarctiques Françaises. ◇ *French overseas territory* S Indian Ocean
French Sudan *see* Mali
French Territory of the Afars and Issas *see* Djibouti
French Togoland *see* Togo
76 J6 **Frenda** NW Algeria *35.06N 1.03E*
113 I18 **Frenštát pod Radhoštěm** *Ger.* Frankstadt. Ostravský Kraj E Czech Republic *49.33N 18.10E*
78 M17 **Fresco** S Ivory Coast *5.05N 5.34W*
205 U16 **Freshfield, Cape** *headland* Antarctica
42 L10 **Fresnillo** *var.* Fresnillo de González Echeverría. Zacatecas, C Mexico *23.10N 102.52W*
Fresnillo de González Echeverría *see* Fresnillo
37 Q10 **Fresno** California, W USA *36.44N 119.48W*
Freu, Cabo del *see* Freu, Cap des
107 Y9 **Freu, Cap des** *var.* Cabo del Freu. *headland* Mallorca, Spain, W Mediterranean Sea *39.44N 3.28E*
103 G22 **Freudenstadt** Baden-Württemberg, SW Germany *48.28N 8.25E*
Freudenthal *see* Bruntál
191 Q17 **Freycinet Peninsula** *peninsula* Tasmania, SE Australia
78 H14 **Fria** Guinée-Maritime, W Guinea *10.27N 13.37W*
85 A17 **Fria, Cape** *headland* NW Namibia *18.32S 12.00E*
37 Q10 **Friant** California, W USA *36.56N 119.44W*
64 K8 **Frías** Catamarca , N Argentina *28.40S 65.00W*
110 D9 **Fribourg** *Ger.* Freiburg. Fribourg, W Switzerland *46.49N 7.10E*
110 C9 **Fribourg** *Ger.* Freiburg. ◐ *canton* W Switzerland
Fribourg-en-Brisgau *see* Freiburg im Breisgau
34 G7 **Friday Harbor** San Juan Islands, Washington, NW USA *48.31N 123.01W*
194 F11 **Frieda** ≈ NW PNG
Friedau *see* Ormož
103 K23 **Friedberg** Bayern, S Germany *48.21N 10.58E*
103 H18 **Friedberg** Hessen, W Germany *50.19N 8.46E*
Friedeberg Neumark *see* Strzelce Krajeńskie
Friedek-Mistek *see* Frýdek-Místek
Friedland *see* Pravdinsk
103 I24 **Friedrichshafen** Baden-Württemberg, S Germany *47.39N 9.28E*
Friedrichstadt *see* Jaunjelgava
31 Q16 **Friend** Nebraska, C USA *40.37N 97.16W*
Friendly Islands *see* Tonga
57 V9 **Friendship** Coronie, N Surinam *5.49N 56.16W*
32 L7 **Friendship** Wisconsin, N USA *43.58N 89.48W*
111 T8 **Friesach** Kärnten, S Austria *46.58N 14.24E*
Friesche Eilanden *see* Frisian Islands
103 F22 **Friesenheim** Baden-Württemberg, SW Germany *48.27N 7.56E*
Friesische Inseln *see* Frisian Islands
100 K6 **Friesland** ◐ *province* N Netherlands
62 Q10 **Frio, Cabo** *headland* SE Brazil *23.01S 41.59W*
26 M3 **Friona** Texas, SW USA *34.38N 102.43W*
44 L12 **Frío, Río** ≈ N Costa Rica
27 R13 **Frio River** ≈ Texas, SW USA
101 M25 **Frisange** Luxembourg, S Luxembourg *49.31N 6.12E*
Frisches Haff *see* Vistula Lagoon
38 J6 **Frisco Peak** ▲ Utah, W USA *38.31N 113.17W*
86 F9 **Frisian Islands** *Dut.* Friesche Eilanden, *Ger.* Friesische Inseln. *island group* N Europe
20 L12 **Frissell, Mount** ▲ Connecticut, NE USA *42.01N 73.25W*
97 J19 **Fristad** Västra Götaland, S Sweden *57.49N 13.01E*
27 N2 **Fritch** Texas, SW USA *35.38N 101.36W*
97 J19 **Fritsla** Västra Götaland, S Sweden *57.33N 12.46E*
103 H16 **Fritzlar** Hessen, C Germany *51.09N 9.16E*
108 H6 **Friuli-Venezia Giulia** ◐ *region* NE Italy
Frjentsjer *see* Franeker
206 L13 **Frobisher Bay** *inlet* Baffin Island, Nunavut, NE Canada
Frobisher Bay *see* Iqaluit
9 S12 **Frobisher Lake** ◎ Saskatchewan, C Canada
96 G7 **Frohavet** *sound* C Norway
Frohenbruck *see* Veselí nad Lužnicí
111 V7 **Frohnleiten** Steiermark, SE Austria *47.16N 15.19E*
101 G22 **Froidchapelle** Hainaut, S Belgium *50.10N 4.18E*
131 O9 **Frolovo** Volgogradskaya Oblast', SW Russian Federation *49.46N 43.38E*
112 K7 **Frombork** *Ger.* Frauenburg. Warmińsko-Mazurskie, NE Poland *54.21N 19.40E*
99 L22 **Frome** SW England, UK *51.15N 2.21W*
190 I4 **Frome Creek** *seasonal river* South Australia
190 J6 **Frome Downs** South Australia *31.17S 139.48E*
190 J5 **Frome, Lake** *salt lake* South Australia
Fronicken *see* Wronki
106 H10 **Fronteira** Portalegre, C Portugal *39.03N 7.39W*
42 M7 **Frontera** Coahuila de Zaragoza, NE Mexico *26.55N 101.27W*
43 U14 **Frontera** Tabasco, SE Mexico *18.32N 92.35W*
42 G3 **Fronteras** Sonora, NW Mexico *30.51N 109.36W*
105 Q16 **Frontignan** Hérault, S France *43.27N 3.45E*
56 D8 **Frontino** Antioquia, NW Colombia *6.46N 76.10W*
23 V4 **Front Royal** Virginia, NE USA *38.52N 78.09W*
109 J16 **Frosinone** *anc.* Frusino. Lazio, C Italy *41.37N 13.19E*
109 K16 **Frosolone** Molise, C Italy *41.34N 14.25E*
27 U7 **Frost** Texas, SW USA *32.04N 96.48W*
23 U2 **Frostburg** Maryland, NE USA *39.39N 78.55W*
25 X13 **Frostproof** Florida, SE USA *27.45N 81.31W*
Frostviken *see* Kvarnbergsvattnet
97 M15 **Frövi** Örebro, C Sweden *59.28N 15.24E*
96 F7 **Frøya** *island* W Norway
39 P5 **Fruita** Colorado, C USA *39.10N 108.42W*
30 J9 **Fruitdale** South Dakota, N USA *44.39N 103.38W*
25 W11 **Fruitland Park** Florida, SE USA *28.51N 81.54W*
Frumentum *see* Formentera
153 S11 **Frunze** Oshskaya Oblast', SW Kyrgyzstan *40.07N 71.40E*
Frunze *see* Bishkek
119 O9 **Frunzivka** Odes'ka Oblast', SW Ukraine *47.19N 29.46E*
Frusino *see* Frosinone
110 E9 **Frutigen** Bern, W Switzerland *46.35N 7.38E*
113 I17 **Frýdek-Místek** *Ger.* Friedek-Mistek. Ostravský Kraj, E Czech Republic *49.40N 18.22E*
200 Qq16 **Fua'amotu** Tongatapu, S Tonga *21.15S 175.08W*
202 A9 **Fuafatu** *island* Funafuti Atoll, C Tuvalu
202 A9 **Fuagea** *island* Funafuti Atoll, C Tuvalu
202 B8 **Fualifeke** *atoll* C Tuvalu
202 A8 **Fualopa** *island* Funafuti Atoll, C Tuvalu
157 K22 **Fuammulah** *var.* Gnaviyani Atoll. *atoll* S Maldives
167 R11 **Fu'an** Fujian, SE China *27.11N 119.42E*
Fu-chien *see* Fujian
Fu-chou *see* Fuzhou
170 F13 **Fuchū** *var.* Hutyû. Hiroshima, Honshū, SW Japan *34.33N 133.16E*
166 M13 **Fuchuan** Guangxi Zhuangzu Zizhiqu, S China *24.56N 111.15E*
172 N11 **Fudai** Iwate, Honshū, C Japan *39.59N 141.50E*
167 S11 **Fuding** Fujian, SE China *27.21N 120.10E*
83 J20 **Fudua** *spring/well* S Kenya *2.13S 39.43E*
106 M16 **Fuengirola** Andalucía, S Spain *36.31N 4.37W*
106 J12 **Fuente de Cantos** Extremadura, W Spain *38.15N 6.18W*
106 J11 **Fuente del Maestre** Extremadura, W Spain *38.31N 6.26W*
106 L12 **Fuente Obejuna** Andalucía, S Spain *38.15N 5.25W*
106 L6 **Fuentesaúco** Castilla-León, N Spain *41.13N 5.30W*
64 O3 **Fuerte Olimpo** *var.* Olimpo. Alto Paraguay, NE Paraguay *21.01S 57.51W*
42 H8 **Fuerte, Río** ≈ C Mexico
66 Q11 **Fuerteventura** *island* Islas Canarias, Spain, NE Atlantic Ocean
147 S14 **Fughmah** *var.* Faghman, Fugma. C Yemen *16.07N 49.22E*
94 M2 **Fuglehuken** *headland* W Svalbard *78.54N 10.30E*
97 B18 **Fugloy** *Dan.* Fugló *Island* Faeroe Islands *62.21N 6.16W*
207 T15 **Fugløya Bank** *undersea feature* E Norwegian Sea
166 E11 **Fugong** Yunnan, SW China *27.00N 98.48E*
Fugma *see* Fughmah
83 K16 **Fugugo** *spring/well* NE Kenya *3.19N 39.39E*
164 L2 **Fuhai** *var.* Burultokay. Xinjiang Uygur Zizhiqu, NW China *47.15N 87.39E*
167 P10 **Fu He** ≈ S China
Fuhkien *see* Fujian
102 J9 **Fuhlsbüttel** ✕ (Hamburg) Hamburg, N Germany *53.37N 9.57E*
103 L14 **Fuhne** ≈ C Germany
Fu-hsin *see* Fuxin
Fujairah *see* Al Fujayrah
171 J17 **Fuji** *var.* Huzi. Shizuoka, Honshū, S Japan *35.08N 138.39E*
167 Q12 **Fujian** *var.* Fu-chien, Fuhkien, Fujian Sheng, Fukien, Min. ◐ *province* SE China
166 I9 **Fu Jiang** ≈ C China
Fujian Sheng *see* Fujian
171 Ii17 **Fujieda** *var.* Huzieda. Shizuoka, Honshū, S Japan *34.54N 138.15E*
Fuji, Mount/Fujiyama *see* Fuji-san
169 Y7 **Fujin** Heilongjiang, NE China *47.12N 132.01E*
171 J16 **Fujinomiya** *var.* Huzinomiya. Shizuoka, Honshū, S Japan *35.19N 138.34E*
171 J16 **Fuji-san** *var.* Fujiyama, *Eng.* Mount Fuji. ▲ Honshū, SE Japan *35.23N 138.44E*
171 Jj17 **Fujisawa** *var.* Huzisawa. Kanagawa, Honshū, S Japan *35.22N 139.28E*
171 J16 **Fuji-Yoshida** *var.* Huziyosida. Yamanashi, Honshū, S Japan *35.30N 138.48E*
172 Oo4 **Fukagawa** *var.* Hukagawa. Hokkaidō, NE Japan *43.44N 142.01E*
164 L5 **Fukang** Xinjiang Uygur Zizhiqu, W China *44.07N 87.55E*
171 M8 **Fukaura** Aomori, Honshū, C Japan *40.38N 139.55E*
200 R15 **Fukave** *island* Tongatapu Group, S Tonga
Fukien *see* Fujian
171 Gg14 **Fukuchiyama** *var.* Hukutiyama. Kyōto, Honshū, SW Japan *35.16N 135.07E*
170 B12 **Fukue** *var.* Hukue. Nagasaki, Fukue-jima, SW Japan *32.40N 128.46E*
170 B12 **Fukue-jima** *island* Gotō-rettō, SW Japan
171 Hh13 **Fukui** *var.* Hukui. Fukui, Honshū, SW Japan *36.03N 136.12E*
171 Hh14 **Fukui** *off.* Fukui-ken, *var.* Hukui. ◐ *prefecture* Honshū, SW Japan
170 C12 **Fukuoka** *var.* Hukuoka; *hist.* Najima. Fukuoka, Kyūshū, SW Japan *33.36N 130.24E*
170 Cc13 **Fukuoka** *off.* Fukuoka-ken, *var.* Hukuoka. ◐ *prefecture* Kyūshū, SW Japan
171 L13 **Fukushima** *var.* Hukusima. Fukushima, Honshū, C Japan *37.46N 140.27E*
171 Mm7 **Fukushima** Hokkaidō, NE Japan *41.27N 140.14E*
171 Kk14 **Fukushima** *off.* Fukushima-ken, *var.* Hukusima. ◐ *prefecture* Honshū, C Japan
170 F14 **Fukuyama** *var.* Hukuyama. Hiroshima, Honshū, SW Japan *34.28N 133.23E*
78 G13 **Fulacunda** C Guinea-Bissau *11.46N 15.09W*
133 P8 **Fūlādī, Kūh-e** ▲ E Afghanistan *34.37N 67.31E*
197 K16 **Fulaga** *island* Lau Group, E Fiji
103 I17 **Fulda** Hessen, C Germany *50.33N 9.40E*
31 S10 **Fulda** Minnesota, N USA *43.52N 95.36W*
103 I16 **Fulda** ≈ C Germany
Fülek *see* Fil'akovo
Fulin *see* Hanyuan
166 K10 **Fuling** Chongqing Shi, C China *29.45N 107.23E*
37 T15 **Fullerton** California, SE USA *33.52N 117.55W*
31 P15 **Fullerton** Nebraska, C USA *41.21N 97.58W*
110 M8 **Fulpmes** Tirol, W Austria *47.11N 11.22E*
22 G8 **Fulton** Kentucky, S USA *36.31N 88.52W*
25 N2 **Fulton** Mississippi, S USA *34.16N 88.24W*
29 V4 **Fulton** Missouri, C USA *38.51N 91.57W*
20 H9 **Fulton** New York, NE USA *43.18N 76.22W*
Fuman/Fumen *see* Fowman
105 R3 **Fumay** Ardennes, N France *49.58N 4.42E*
104 M13 **Fumel** Lot-et-Garonne, SW France *44.31N 0.58E*
171 K17 **Funabashi** *var.* Hunabasi. Chiba, Honshū, S Japan *35.40N 139.57E*
202 B10 **Funafara** *atoll* C Tuvalu
202 C9 **Funafuti** ✕ Funafuti Atoll, C Tuvalu *8.30S 179.12E*
Funafuti *see* Fongafale
202 F8 **Funafuti Atoll** *atoll* C Tuvalu
202 B9 **Funangongo** *atoll* C Tuvalu
95 F17 **Funäsdalen** Jämtland, C Sweden *62.33N 12.33E*
66 O6 **Funchal** Madeira, Portugal, NE Atlantic Ocean *32.40N 16.55W*
66 P5 **Funchal** ✕ Madeira, Portugal, NE Atlantic Ocean *32.37N 16.52W*
56 F5 **Fundación** Magdalena, N Colombia *10.28N 74.10W*
106 I8 **Fundão** *var.* Fundáo. Castelo Branco, C Portugal *40.07N 7.30W*
11 O16 **Fundy, Bay of** *bay* Canada/USA
Fünen *see* Fyn
56 C13 **Fúnes** Nariño, SW Colombia *0.58N 77.27W*
Fünfkirchen *see* Pécs
85 M19 **Funhalouro** Inhambane, S Mozambique *23.04S 34.24E*
167 R6 **Funing** Jiangsu, E China *33.43N 119.47E*
166 I14 **Funing** Yunnan, SW China *23.39N 105.41E*
166 M7 **Funiu Shan** ▲▲ C China
79 U13 **Funtua** Katsina, N Nigeria *11.31N 7.19E*
167 R12 **Fuqing** Fujian, SE China *25.40N 119.23E*
85 M14 **Furancungo** Tete, NW Mozambique *14.49S 33.32E*
172 P5 **Furano** *var.* Hurano. Hokkaidō, NE Japan *43.22N 142.25E*
118 I15 **Furculești** Teleorman, S Romania *43.51N 25.07E*
Füred *see* Balatonfüred
172 Qq7 **Füren-ko** ◎ Hokkaidō, NE Japan
149 R12 **Fürg** Fārs, S Iran *28.16N 55.13E*
Furluk *see* Fârliug
Fürmanov/Furmanovka *see* Moyynkum
Furmanovo *see* Zhalpaktal
61 L20 **Furnas, Represa de** ⊠ SE Brazil
191 Q14 **Furneaux Group** *island group* Tasmania, SE Australia
Furnes *see* Veurne
166 J10 **Furong Jiang** ≈ S China
144 I5 **Furqlus** Ḥimṣ, W Syria *34.40N 37.02E*
102 F12 **Fürstenau** Niedersachsen, NW Germany *52.30N 7.40E*
111 X8 **Fürstenfeld** Steiermark, SE Austria *47.03N 16.01E*
103 L23 **Fürstenfeldbruck** Bayern, S Germany *48.10N 11.16E*
102 P12 **Fürstenwalde** Brandenburg, NE Germany *52.22N 14.04E*
103 K20 **Fürth** Bayern, S Germany *49.28N 10.58E*
111 W3 **Furth bei Göttweig** Niederösterreich, NE Austria *48.22N 15.33E*
172 O4 **Furubira** Hokkaidō, NE Japan *43.14N 140.38E*
96 L12 **Furudal** Dalarna, C Sweden *61.10N 15.07E*
171 Ii14 **Furukawa** Gifu, Honshū, SW Japan *36.13N 137.11E*
171 M12 **Furukawa** *var.* Hurukawa. Miyagi, Honshū, C Japan *38.36N 140.56E*
56 F10 **Fusagasugá** Cundinamarca, C Colombia *4.22N 74.21W*
Fusan *see* Pusan
Fushë-Arëzi/Fushë-Arrësi *see* Fushë-Arrëz
115 L18 **Fushë-Arrëz** *var.* Fushë-Arëzi, Fushë-Arrësi. Shkodër, N Albania *42.05N 20.01E*
Fushë-Kruja *see* Fushë-Krujë
115 K19 **Fushë-Krujë** *var.* Fushë-Kruja. Durrës, C Albania *41.30N 19.43E*
169 V12 **Fushun** *var.* Fou-shan, Fu-shun. Liaoning, NE China *41.49N 123.54E*
Fusin *see* Fuxin
110 G10 **Fusio** Ticino, S Switzerland *46.27N 8.39E*
169 X11 **Fusong** Jilin, NE China *42.19N 127.16E*
103 K24 **Füssen** Bayern, S Germany *47.34N 10.42E*
166 K15 **Fusui** *prev.* Funan. Guangxi Zhuangzu Zizhiqu, S China *22.39N 107.49E*
Futa Jallon *see* Fouta Djallon
65 G18 **Futaleufú** Los Lagos, S Chile *43.12S 71.53W*
114 K10 **Futog** Serbia, NW Yugoslavia *45.15N 19.43E*
171 K17 **Futtsu** *var.* Huttu. Chiba, Honshū, S Japan *35.11N 139.52E*
197 E16 **Futuna** *island* S Vanuatu
202 D12 **Futuna, Île** *island* S Wallis and Futuna
167 Q11 **Futun Xi** ≈ SE China
166 L5 **Fuxian** *var.* Fu Xian. Shaanxi, C China *36.03N 109.19E*
Fuxian *see* Wafangdian
166 G13 **Fuxian Hu** ◎ SW China
169 U12 **Fuxin** *var.* Fou-hsin, Fu-hsin, Fusin. Liaoning, NE China *41.59N 121.39E*
Fuxing *see* Wangmo
167 P7 **Fuyang** Anhui, E China *32.54N 115.47E*
167 O4 **Fuyang He** ≈ E China
169 U7 **Fuyu** Heilongjiang, NE China *47.48N 124.25E*
Fuyu/Fu-yü *see* Songyuan
169 Z6 **Fuyuan** Heilongjiang, NE China *48.20N 134.22E*
164 M3 **Fuyun** *var.* Koktokay. Xinjiang Uygur Zizhiqu, NW China *46.57N 89.29E*
113 L22 **Füzesabony** Heves, E Hungary *47.44N 20.23E*
167 R12 **Fuzhou** *var.* Foochow, Fu-chou. Fujian, SE China *26.09N 119.16E*
Fuzhou *see* Linchuan
143 W13 **Füzuli** *Rus.* Fizuli. SW Azerbaijan *39.33N 47.09E*
121 I20 **Fyadory** *Rus.* Fëdory. Brestskaya Voblasts', SW Belarus *51.56N 26.24E*
97 G24 **Fyn** *off.* Fyns Amt, *var.* Fünen. ◐ *county* C Denmark
97 G23 **Fyn** *Ger.* Fünen. *island* C Denmark

◆ Country ● Country Capital ◇ Dependent Territory ○ Dependent Territory Capital ◐ Administrative Region ✕ International Airport ▲ Mountain ▲▲ Mountain Range ⛰ Volcano ≈ River ◎ Lake ⊠ Reservoir
257

FYNE, LOCH – GEDID RAS EL FIL

98 H12 Fyne, Loch inlet W Scotland, UK
97 E16 Fyresvatnet ◎ S Norway
FYR Macedonia/FYROM see Macedonia, FYR
Fyzabad see Feyẓābād

G

83 O14 Gaalkacyo var. Galka'yo, It. Galcaio. Mudug, C Somalia 6.42N 47.24E
Gabakly see Kabakly
116 H8 Gabare Vratsa, NW Bulgaria 43.20N 23.57E
104 K15 Gabas ~ SW France
37 T7 Gabbs Nevada, W USA 38.51N 117.55W
84 B12 Gabela Cuanza Sul, W Angola 10.49S 14.21E
Gaberones see Gaborone
201 X14 Gabert island Caroline Islands, E Micronesia
76 M7 Gabès var. Qābis. E Tunisia 33.53N 10.03E
76 M6 Gabès, Golfe de Ar. Khalīj Qābis. gulf E Tunisia
Gablonz an der Neisse see Jablonec nad Nisou
Gablös see Cavalese
81 E18 Gabon off. Gabonese Republic. ◆ republic C Africa
85 I20 Gaborone prev. Gaberones. ● (Botswana) South East, SE Botswana 24.42S 25.49E
85 I20 Gaborone ✕ South East, SE Botswana 24.45S 25.49E
106 K8 Gabriel y Galán, Embalse de ⊠ W Spain
149 U15 Gābrīk, Rūd-e ~ SE Iran
116 J9 Gabrovo Gabrovo, N Bulgaria 42.54N 25.19E
116 J9 Gabrovo ◐ province N Bulgaria
78 H12 Gabú prev. Nova Lamego. E Guinea-Bissau 12.16N 14.09W
31 O6 Gackle North Dakota, N USA 46.34N 99.07W
115 I15 Gacko Republika Srpska, Bosnia and Herzegovina 43.08N 18.29E
161 F17 Gadag Karnātaka, W India 15.25N 75.37E
95 G15 Gäddede Jämtland, C Sweden 64.30N 14.15E
165 S12 Gadê Qinghai, C China 33.56N 99.49E
Gades/Gadier/Gadir/Gadire see Cádiz
107 P15 Gádor, Sierra de ▲ S Spain
155 S15 Gadra Sind, SE Pakistan 25.39N 70.28E
25 Q3 Gadsden Alabama, S USA 34.00N 86.00W
38 H15 Gadsden Arizona, SW USA 32.33N 114.45W
Gadyach see Hadyach
81 H15 Gadzi Mambéré-Kadéï, SW Central African Republic 4.46N 16.42E
118 J13 Găeşti Dâmboviţa, S Romania 44.41N 25.18E
109 J17 Gaeta Lazio, C Italy 41.12N 13.34E
109 J17 Gaeta, Golfo di var. Gulf of Gaeta. gulf C Italy
196 L14 Gaferut atoll Caroline Islands, W Micronesia
23 Q10 Gaffney South Carolina, SE USA 35.04N 81.39W
Gäfle see Gävle
Gäfleborg see Gävleborg
76 M6 Gafsa var. Qafşah. W Tunisia 34.24N 8.51E
Gafurov see Ghafurov
130 J3 Gagarin Smolenskaya Oblast', W Russian Federation 55.33N 35.00E
153 O10 Gagarin Jizzakh Wiloyati, C Uzbekistan 40.40N 68.04E
103 G21 Gaggenau Baden-Württemberg, SW Germany 48.48N 8.19E
196 F16 Gagil Tamil var. Gagil-Tomil. island Caroline Islands, W Micronesia
Gagil-Tomil see Gagil Tamil
131 O4 Gagino Nizhegorodskaya Oblast', W Russian Federation 55.18N 45.01E
109 Q19 Gagliano del Capo Puglia, SE Italy 39.49N 18.22E
96 L13 Gagnef Dalarna, C Sweden 60.34N 15.04E
78 M17 Gagnoa C Ivory Coast 6.10N 5.56W
11 N10 Gagnon Quebec, E Canada 51.55N 68.16W
Gago Coutinho see Lumbala N'Guimbo
175 Tt8 Gag, Pulau island E Indonesia
143 P8 Gagra NW Georgia 43.17N 40.17E
33 S13 Gahanna Ohio, N USA 40.01N 82.52W
149 R13 Gahkom Hormozgān, S Iran 28.14N 55.48E
Gahnpa see Ganta
59 Q19 Gaíba, Laguna ◎ E Bolivia
159 T13 Gaibanda var. Gaibandah. Rajshahi, NW Bangladesh 25.15N 89.32E
Gaibandah see Gaibanda
Gaibhlte, Cnoc Mór na n see Galtymore Mountain
111 R9 Gail ~ S Austria
103 I21 Gaildorf Baden-Württemberg, S Germany 48.41N 10.08E
105 N15 Gaillac var. Gaillac-sur-Tarn. Tarn, S France 43.54N 1.54E
Gaillac-sur-Tarn see Gaillac
Gaillimh see Galway
Gaillimhe, Cuan na see Galway Bay
111 Q9 Gailtaler Alpen ▲ S Austria
65 J17 Gaimán Chaco, S Argentina 43.15S 65.30W
22 K8 Gainesboro Tennessee, S USA 36.21N 85.39W
25 V10 Gainesville Florida, SE USA 29.39N 82.19W
25 T2 Gainesville Georgia, SE USA 34.18N 83.49W
29 U8 Gainesville Missouri, C USA 36.36N 92.25W
27 T5 Gainesville Texas, SW USA 33.37N 97.09W
111 X5 Gainfarn Niederösterreich, NE Austria 47.59N 16.11E
99 N18 Gainsborough E England, UK 53.24N 0.48W
190 G6 Gairdner, Lake salt lake South Australia
Gaissane see Gáissát
94 L8 Gáissát var. Gaissane ▲ N Norway
45 T15 Gaital, Cerro ▲ C Panama 8.37N 80.04W
23 W3 Gaithersburg Maryland, NE USA 39.07N 77.07W
169 U13 Gaizhou Liaoning, NE China 40.24N 122.16E
Gaiziņ see Gaizina Kalns
120 I9 Gaiziņa Kalns var. Gaiziņ. ▲ E Latvia 56.51N 25.58E
Gajac see Villeneuve-sur-Lot
174 L15 Gajahmungkur, Danau ◎ Jawa, S Indonesia
41 S10 Gakona Alaska, USA 62.21N 145.16W
Galaassiya see Galaosiye
Galāġil see Jalājil
Galam, Pulau see Gelam, Pulau
64 J6 Galán, Cerro ▲ NW Argentina 25.54S 66.45W
113 H21 Galanta Hung. Galánta. Trnavský Kraj, W Slovakia 48.11N 17.45E
152 L11 Galaosiye Rus. Galaassiya. Bukhoro Wiloyati, C Uzbekistan 39.53N 64.25E
59 B17 Galápagos off. Provincia de Galápagos. ◐ province Ecuador, E Pacific Ocean
199 M9 Galapagos Fracture Zone tectonic feature E Pacific Ocean
200 O10 Galapagos Rise undersea feature E Pacific Ocean
98 K13 Galashiels SE Scotland, UK 55.37N 2.49W
118 M12 Galaţi Ger. Galatz. Galaţi, E Romania 45.27N 28.00E
118 L12 Galaţi ◐ county E Romania
109 Q19 Galatina Puglia, SE Italy 40.10N 18.10E
109 Q19 Galatone Puglia, SE Italy 40.09N 18.04E
Galatz see Galaţi
23 R8 Galax Virginia, NE USA 36.39N 80.55W
Galaymor see Kala-i-Mor
Galcaio see Gaalkacyo
66 P11 Gáldar Gran Canaria, Islas Canarias, NE Atlantic Ocean 28.09N 15.40W
96 F11 Galdhøpiggen ▲ S Norway 61.30N 8.08E
42 I4 Galeana Chihuahua, N Mexico 30.07N 107.35W
43 O9 Galeana Nuevo León, NE Mexico 24.45N 99.59W
62 P9 Galeão ✕ (Rio de Janeiro) Rio de Janeiro, SE Brazil 22.48S 43.16W
175 T6 Galela Pulau Halmahera, E Indonesia 1.52N 127.48E
41 O9 Galena Alaska, USA 64.43N 156.55W
32 K10 Galena Illinois, N USA 42.25N 90.25W
29 R7 Galena Kansas, C USA 37.04N 94.38W
29 T8 Galena Missouri, C USA 36.45N 93.30W
47 V15 Galeota Point headland Trinidad, Trinidad and Tobago 10.07N 60.59W
107 P13 Galera Andalucía, S Spain 37.45N 2.33W
47 Y16 Galera Point headland Trinidad, Trinidad and Tobago 10.49N 60.54W
58 A5 Galera, Punta headland NW Ecuador 0.49N 80.03W
32 K12 Galesburg Illinois, N USA 40.57N 90.22W
32 J7 Galesville Wisconsin, N USA 44.04N 91.21W
20 F12 Galeton Pennsylvania, NE USA 41.43N 77.38W
118 H9 Gâlgău Hung. Galgó; prev. Gîlgău. Sălaj, NW Romania 47.15N 23.44E
Galgó see Gâlgău
Galgóc see Hlohovec
83 N15 Galguduud off. Gobolka Galguduud. ◐ region E Somalia
143 Q9 Gali W Georgia 42.40N 41.39E
129 N14 Galich Kostromskaya Oblast', NW Russian Federation 58.21N 42.21E
116 H7 Galiche Vratsa, NW Bulgaria 43.36N 23.53E
106 H3 Galicia anc. Gallaecia. ◐ autonomous community NW Spain
66 M8 Galicia Bank undersea feature E Atlantic Ocean
Galilee see HaGalil
189 W7 Galilee, Lake ◎ Queensland, NE Australia
Galilee, Sea of see Tiberias, Lake
108 E11 Galileo Galilei ✕ (Pisa) Toscana, C Italy 43.40N 10.22E
33 S12 Galion Ohio, N USA 40.43N 82.47W
Galka'yo see Gaalkacyo
82 H11 Gallabat Gedaref, E Sudan 12.56N 36.08E
Gallaecia see Galicia
108 C7 Gallarate Lombardia, NW Italy 45.39N 8.46E
29 S2 Gallatin Missouri, C USA 39.54N 93.57W
22 J8 Gallatin Tennessee, S USA 36.23N 86.27W
35 R11 Gallatin Peak ▲ Montana, NW USA 45.22N 111.21W
35 R12 Gallatin River ~ Montana/Wyoming, NW USA
161 J26 Galle prev. Point de Galle. Southern Province, SW Sri Lanka 6.04N 80.11E
107 S5 Gállego ~ NE Spain
200 N9 Gallego Rise undersea feature E Pacific Ocean
Gallegos see Río Gallegos
65 H23 Gallegos, Río ~ Argentina/Chile
Gallia see France
24 K10 Galliano Louisiana, S USA 29.26N 90.18W
116 G13 Gallikós ~ N Greece
39 S12 Gallinas Peak ▲ New Mexico, SW USA 34.14N 105.47W
56 H3 Gallinas, Punta headland NE Colombia 12.27N 71.43W
39 T11 Gallinas River ~ New Mexico, SW USA
109 Q19 Gallipoli Puglia, SE Italy 40.07N 18.00E
Gallipoli see Gelibolu
Gallipoli Peninsula see Gelibolu Yarımadası
33 T15 Gallipolis Ohio, N USA 38.45N 82.13W
94 J12 Gällivare Norrbotten, N Sweden 67.08N 20.39E
111 T4 Gallneukirchen Oberösterreich, N Austria 48.21N 14.22E
107 Q7 Gallo ~ C Spain
95 G17 Gällö Jämtland, C Sweden 62.57N 15.15E
109 I23 Gallo, Capo headland Sicilia, Italy, C Mediterranean Sea 38.13N 13.18E
39 P13 Gallo Mountains ▲ New Mexico, SW USA
20 G8 Galloo Island island New York, NE USA
99 H15 Galloway, Mull of headland S Scotland, UK 54.37N 4.54W
39 P10 Gallup New Mexico, SW USA 35.31N 108.45W
107 R5 Gallur Aragón, NE Spain 41.51N 1.21W
Gâlma see Guelma
37 O8 Galt California, W USA 38.13N 121.19W
76 C10 Galtat-Zemmour C Western Sahara 25.07N 12.21W
97 G22 Galten Århus, C Denmark 56.09N 9.54E
99 D20 Galtymore Mountain Ir. Cnoc Mór na nGaibhlte. ▲ S Ireland 52.21N 8.09W
99 D20 Galty Mountains Ir. Na Gaibhlte. ▲ S Ireland
32 K11 Galva Illinois, N USA 41.10N 90.02W
27 X12 Galveston Texas, SW USA 29.16N 94.48W
27 W11 Galveston Bay inlet Texas, SW USA
27 W12 Galveston Island island Texas, SW USA
63 B18 Gálvez Santa Fe, C Argentina 31.57S 61.13W
99 C18 Galway Ir. Gaillimh. W Ireland 53.16N 9.03W
99 B18 Galway Ir. Gaillimh. cultural region W Ireland
99 B18 Galway Bay Ir. Cuan na Gaillimhe. bay W Ireland
85 F18 Gam Otjozondjupa, NE Namibia 20.10S 20.51E
194 G14 Gama ~ SW PNG
171 Hh16 Gamagōri Aichi, Honshū, SW Japan 34.49N 137.12E
56 F7 Gamarra Cesar, N Colombia 8.21N 73.46W
Gámas see Kaamanen
164 L17 Gamba Xizang Zizhiqu, W China 28.13N 88.31E
79 P14 Gambaga NE Ghana 10.32N 0.28W
82 G13 Gambēla Gambēla, W Ethiopia 8.09N 34.15E
83 H14 Gambēla ◐ region , W Ethiopia 8.09N 34.15E
40 K10 Gambell Saint Lawrence Island, Alaska, USA 63.43N 171.40W
78 E12 Gambia off. Republic of The Gambia, The Gambia. ◆ republic W Africa
78 I12 Gambia Fr. Gambie. ~ W Africa
66 K12 Gambia Plain undersea feature E Atlantic Ocean
Gambie see Gambia
33 T13 Gambier Ohio, N USA 40.22N 82.24W
203 Y13 Gambier, Îles island group E French Polynesia
190 G10 Gambier Islands island group South Australia
81 H19 Gamboma Plateaux, E Congo 1.52S 15.51E
81 G16 Gamboula Mambéré-Kadéï, SW Central African Republic 4.09N 15.12E
39 P10 Gamerco New Mexico, SW USA 35.34N 108.45W
143 V12 Gamış Dağı ▲ W Azerbaijan 40.18N 46.15E
Gamlakarleby see Kokkola
97 N18 Gamleby Kalmar, S Sweden 57.54N 16.25E
Gammelstad see Gammelstaden
95 J14 Gammelstaden var. Gammelstad. Norrbotten, N Sweden 65.37N 22.04E
Gammouda see Sidi Bouzid
161 J25 Gampaha Western Province, W Sri Lanka 07.05N 80.00E
161 K25 Gampola Central Province, C Sri Lanka 7.10N 80.34E
176 Uu8 Gam, Pulau island E Indonesia
178 Jj5 Gâm, Sông ~ N Vietnam
94 L7 Gamvik Finnmark, N Norway 71.04N 28.08E
156 H13 Gan Addu Atoll, C Maldives
Gan see Gansu, China
Gan see Jiangxi, China
Ganaane see Juba
39 O10 Ganado Arizona, SW USA 35.42N 109.31W
27 U12 Ganado Texas, SW USA 29.02N 96.30W
12 L14 Gananoque Ontario, SE Canada 44.19N 76.10W
Ganāveh see Bandar-e Gonāveh
143 V11 Gäncä Rus. Gyandzha; prev. Kirovabad, Yelisavetpol. W Azerbaijan 40.41N 46.22E
Ganchi see Ghonchí
Gand see Gent
84 B13 Ganda var. Mariano Machado, Port. Vila Mariano Machado. Benguela, W Angola 12.59S 14.37E
81 L22 Gandajika Kasai Oriental, S Dem. Rep. Congo (Zaire) 6.42S 24.00E
159 O12 Gandak Nep. Nārāyāni. ~ India/Nepal
11 U11 Gander Newfoundland, SE Canada 48.55N 54.33W
11 U11 Gander ✕ Newfoundland, E Canada 49.03N 54.49W
102 G11 Ganderkesee Niedersachsen, NW Germany 53.01N 8.33E
107 T7 Gandesa Cataluña, NE Spain 41.03N 0.25E
160 B10 Gāndhīdhām Gujarāt, W India 23.07N 70.05E
160 D10 Gāndhīnagar Gujarāt, W India 23.12N 72.37E
160 F9 Gāndhi Sāgar ◎ C India
107 T11 Gandía País Valenciano, E Spain 38.58N 0.10W
165 O10 Gang Qinghai, W China
158 G9 Gangānagar Rājasthān, NW India 29.54N 73.55E
158 I12 Gangāpur Rājasthān, N India 26.30N 76.49E
159 S17 Ganga Sāgar West Bengal, NE India 21.39N 88.04E
Gangavathi see Gangāwati
161 G17 Gangāwati var. Gangavathi. Karnātaka, C India 15.26N 76.35E
165 S9 Gangca var. Shaliuhe. Qinghai, C China 37.21N 100.09E
164 H14 Gangdisê Shan Eng. Kailas Range. ▲ W China
105 Q15 Ganges Hérault, S France 43.57N 3.42E
159 P13 Ganges Ben. Padma. ~ Bangladesh/India see also Padma
Ganges Cone see Ganges Fan
181 S3 Ganges Fan var. Ganges Cone. undersea feature N Bay of Bengal
159 U17 Ganges, Mouths of the delta Bangladesh/India
109 K23 Gangi anc. Engyum. Sicilia, Italy, C Mediterranean Sea 37.48N 14.13E
158 K8 Gangotri Uttar Pradesh, N India 30.55N 79.01E
Gangra see Çankırı
159 S11 Gangtok Sikkim, N India 27.19N 88.39E
165 W11 Gangu Gansu, C China 34.46N 105.21E
169 U5 Gan He ~ NE China
175 T9 Gani Pulau Halmahera, E Indonesia 0.45S 128.13E
167 O12 Gan Jiang ~ S China
152 H15 Gannaly Akhalskiy Velayat, S Turkmenistan 37.02N 60.43E
169 U7 Gannan Heilongjiang, NE China 47.58N 123.36E
105 P10 Gannat Allier, C France 46.06N 3.12E
35 T14 Gannett Peak ▲ Wyoming, C USA 43.10N 109.39W
31 O10 Gannvalley South Dakota, N USA 44.01N 98.59W
111 Y3 Gänserndorf Niederösterreich, NE Austria 48.22N 16.43E
Gansos, Lago dos see Goose Lake
165 T9 Gansu var. Gan, Gansu Sheng, Kansu. ◐ province N China
Gansu Sheng see Gansu
78 K16 Ganta var. Gahnpa. NE Liberia 7.15N 8.58W
190 H11 Gantheaume, Cape headland South Australia 36.04S 137.28E
Gantsevichi see Hantsavichy
167 Q6 Ganyu var. Qingkou. Jiangsu, E China 34.52N 119.06E
150 D12 Ganyushkino Atyrau, SW Kazakhstan 46.35N 49.15E
167 O12 Ganzhou Jiangxi, S China 25.51N 114.58E
79 Q10 Gao Gao, E Mali 16.15N 0.03E
79 R10 Gao ◐ region SE Mali
167 O10 Gao'an Jiangxi, S China 28.24N 115.27E
167 N5 Gaoping Shanxi, C China 35.51N 112.55E
165 S8 Gaotai Gansu, N China 39.22N 99.44E
Gaoth Dobhair see Gweedore
79 O14 Gaoua SW Burkina 10.18N 3.12W
78 I13 Gaoual Moyenne-Guinée, N Guinea 11.43N 13.13W
Gaoxiong see Kaohsiung
167 R7 Gaoyou var. Dayishan. Jiangsu, E China 32.45N 119.30E
167 R7 Gaoyou Hu ◎ E China
166 M15 Gaozhou Guangdong, S China 21.56N 110.49E
105 T13 Gap anc. Vapincum. Hautes-Alpes, SE France 44.33N 6.04E
164 G13 Gar var. Gar Xincun. Xizang Zizhiqu, W China 32.04N 80.01E
Garabekevyul/Garabekewül see Karabekaul
Garabogazköl see Kara-Bogaz-Gol
45 V16 Garachiné Darién, SE Panama 8.03N 78.22W
45 V16 Garachiné, Punta headland SE Panama 8.05N 78.23W
Garagan see Karagan
56 G10 Garagoa Boyacá, C Colombia 5.04N 73.19W
Garagöl see Karagel'
Garagum see Garagumy
Garagum Kanaly see Garagumskiy Kanal
152 E12 Garagumskiy Kanal var. Kara Kum Canal, Karakumskiy Kanal, Turkm. Garagum Kanaly. canal C Turkmenistan
152 F12 Garagumy var. Qara Qum, Eng. Black Sand Desert, Kara Kum, Turkm. Garagum; prev. Peski Karakumy. desert C Turkmenistan
191 S4 Garah New South Wales, SE Australia 29.07S 149.37E
66 O11 Garajonay ▲ Gomera, Islas Canarias, NE Atlantic Ocean 28.07N 17.13W
116 M8 Gara Khitrino Shumen, NE Bulgaria 43.26N 26.55E
78 L13 Garalo Sikasso, SW Mali 10.58N 7.26W
Garam see Hron
Garamätnyyaz see Karamet-Niyaz
Garamszentkereszt see Žiar nad Hronom
79 Q13 Garango S Burkina 11.45N 0.30W
61 Q15 Garanhuns Pernambuco, E Brazil 8.52S 36.28W
196 H5 Garapan Saipan, S Northern Mariana Islands 15.12S 145.43E
Gárassavon see Kaaresuvanto
80 J13 Garba Bamingui-Bangoran, N Central African Republic 9.09N 20.24E
83 L16 Garbahaarrey It. Garba Harre. Gedo, SW Somalia 3.14N 42.18E
Garba Harre see Garbahaarrey
83 J18 Garba Tula Eastern, C Kenya 0.31N 38.35E
29 N9 Garber Oklahoma, C USA 36.26N 97.35W
36 L4 Garberville California, W USA 40.07N 123.48W
102 I12 Garbsen Niedersachsen, N Germany 52.24N 9.36E
62 K9 Garça São Paulo, S Brazil 22.13S 49.36W
106 L10 García de Solá, Embalse de ⊠ C Spain
105 Q14 Gard ◐ department S France
105 Q14 Gard ~ S France
108 F7 Garda, Lago di var. Benaco, Eng. Lake Garda, Ger. Gardasee. ◎ NE Italy
Garda, Lake see Garda, Lago di
Gardan Dīwāl see Gardan Dīwāl
155 Q5 Gardan Dīwāl var. Gardan Diwal. Wardag, C Afghanistan 34.30N 68.15E
105 S15 Gardanne Bouches-du-Rhône, SE France 43.27N 5.28E
Gardasee see Garda, Lago di
102 L12 Gardelegen Sachsen-Anhalt, C Germany 52.31N 11.25E
12 B10 Garden ◎ Ontario, S Canada
25 X6 Garden City Georgia, SE USA 32.06N 81.09W
28 I6 Garden City Kansas, C USA 37.58N 100.52W
29 S5 Garden City Missouri, C USA 38.34N 94.12W
27 N8 Garden City Texas, SW USA 31.50N 101.29W
25 P3 Gardendale Alabama, S USA 33.39N 86.48W
33 P5 Garden Island island Michigan, N USA
24 M11 Garden Island Bay bay Louisiana, S USA
33 O5 Garden Peninsula peninsula Michigan, N USA
Garden State see New Jersey
97 I14 Gardermoen Akershus, S Norway 60.10N 11.04E
Gardeyz see Gardēz
155 Q6 Gardēz var. Gardeyz, Gordiaz. Paktīā, E Afghanistan 33.34N 69.14E
95 G14 Gardiken ◎ N Sweden
21 Q7 Gardiner Maine, NE USA 44.13N 69.46W
35 S12 Gardiner Montana, NW USA 45.02N 110.42W
21 N13 Gardiners Island island New York, NE USA
Gardner Island see Nikumaroro
21 T6 Gardner Lake ◎ Maine, NE USA
37 Q6 Gardnerville Nevada, W USA 38.55N 119.44W
Gardo see Qardho
108 F7 Gardone Val Trompia Lombardia, N Italy 45.40N 10.11E
Garegegasnjárga see Karigasniemi
40 F17 Gareloi Island island Aleutian Islands, Alaska, USA
108 B10 Garessio Piemonte, NE Italy 44.14N 8.01E
34 M9 Garfield Washington, NW USA 47.00N 117.07W
33 U11 Garfield Heights Ohio, N USA 41.25N 81.36W
Gargaliani see Gargaliánoi
117 D21 Gargaliánoi var. Gargaliani. Pelopónnisos, S Greece 37.04N 21.37E
109 N15 Gargano, Promontorio del headland SE Italy 41.51N 16.11E
110 J8 Gargellen Graubünden, W Switzerland 46.57N 9.55E
95 I14 Gargnäs Västerbotten, N Sweden 65.19N 18.00E
120 C11 Gargždai Gargždai, W Lithuania 55.42N 21.24E
160 J13 Garhchiroli Mahārāshtra, C India 20.14N 79.58E
159 O15 Garhwa Bihār, N India 24.07N 83.52E
176 Ww11 Gariau Irian Jaya, E Indonesia 3.43S 134.54E
85 E24 Garies Northern Cape, W South Africa 30.25S 17.55E
109 K17 Garigliano ~ C Italy
83 K19 Garissa Coast, E Kenya 0.27S 39.39E
23 V11 Garland North Carolina, SE USA 34.45N 78.25W
27 T6 Garland Texas, SW USA 32.54N 96.36W
38 L1 Garland Utah, W USA 41.43N 112.07W
108 D8 Garlasco Lombardia, N Italy 45.12N 8.59E
121 F14 Garliava Kaunas, S Lithuania 54.49N 23.52E
Garm see Gharm
148 M9 Garm, Āb-e var. Rūd-e Khersān. ~ SW Iran
103 K25 Garmisch-Partenkirchen Bayern, S Germany 47.30N 11.06E
149 O5 Garmsār prev. Qishlaq. Semnān, N Iran 35.18N 52.21E
Garmser see Darvishān
31 V12 Garner Iowa, C USA 43.06N 93.36W
23 U9 Garner North Carolina, SE USA 35.42N 78.36W
29 Q5 Garnett Kansas, C USA 38.16N 95.14W
101 M25 Garnich Luxembourg, SW Luxembourg 49.37N 5.57E
190 M8 Garnpung, Lake salt lake New South Wales, SE Australia
Garoe see Garoowe
Garoet see Garut
159 U13 Gāro Hills hill range NE India
104 K13 Garonne anc. Garumna. ~ S France
82 P13 Garoowe var. Garoe. Nugaal, N Somalia 8.24N 48.29E
80 F12 Garoua var. Garua. Nord, N Cameroon 9.16N 13.22E
81 G14 Garoua Boulaï Est, E Cameroon 5.54N 14.33E
79 O10 Garou, Lac ◎ C Mali
194 M11 Garove Island island Witu Islands, C PNG
97 L16 Garphyttan Örebro, C Sweden 59.18N 14.54E
31 R11 Garretson South Dakota, N USA 43.43N 96.30W
33 Q11 Garrett Indiana, N USA 41.21N 85.08W
35 Q10 Garrison Montana, NW USA 46.32N 112.46W
30 M4 Garrison North Dakota, N USA 47.36N 101.25W
27 X8 Garrison Texas, SW USA 31.49N 94.29W
30 L4 Garrison Dam dam North Dakota, N USA 47.29N 101.24W
106 J9 Garrovillas Extremadura, W Spain 39.43N 6.33W
Garrygala see Kara-Kala
15 Jj6 Garry Lake ◎ Nunavut, N Canada
Gars see Gars am Kamp
111 W3 Gars am Kamp var. Gars. Niederösterreich, NE Austria 48.35N 15.40E
83 K20 Garsen Coast, S Kenya 2.16S 40.07E
Garshy see Karshi
12 F10 Garson Ontario, S Canada 46.33N 80.51W
111 T5 Garsten Oberösterreich, N Austria 48.00N 14.24E
Gartar see Qianning
104 M10 Gartempe ~ C France
Gartog see Markam
Garua see Garoua
85 D21 Garub Karas, SW Namibia 26.33S 16.00E
Garumna see Garonne
174 Jj15 Garut prev. Garoet. Jawa, C Indonesia 7.15S 107.55E
193 C20 Garvie Mountains ▲ South Island, NZ
112 N12 Garwolin Mazowieckie, E Poland 51.53N 21.36E
27 U12 Garwood Texas, SW USA 29.25N 96.25W
Gar Xincun see Gar
33 N11 Gary Indiana, N USA 41.35N 87.21W
27 X7 Gary Texas, SW USA 32.00N 94.21W
170 E12 Garyū-san ▲ Kyūshū, SW Japan 34.40N 132.12E
164 G13 Gar Zangbo ~ W China
166 F8 Garzê Sichuan, C China 31.40N 99.58E
56 E12 Garzón Huila, S Colombia 2.13N 75.37W
152 B13 Gasan-Kuli var. Esenguly. Balkanskiy Velayat, W Turkmenistan 37.29N 53.56E
33 P13 Gas City Indiana, N USA 40.29N 85.36W
104 K15 Gascogne Eng. Gascony. cultural region S France
Gascogne, Golfe de see Gascony, Gulf of
28 V5 Gasconade River ~ Missouri, C USA
Gascony see Gascogne
188 H9 Gascoyne Junction Western Australia 25.06S 115.10E
181 V8 Gascoyne Plain undersea feature E Indian Ocean
188 H9 Gascoyne River ~ Western Australia
199 I12 Gascoyne Tablemount undersea feature N Tasman Sea 36.30S 156.30E
69 U6 Gash var. Nahr al Qāsh. ~ W Sudan
155 X3 Gasherbrum ▲ NE Pakistan 35.39N 76.34E
165 N9 Gas Hu ◎ C China
79 X12 Gashua Yobe, NE Nigeria 12.55N 11.10E
176 Uu9 Gasim Irian Jaya, E Indonesia 1.21S 131.27E
195 N12 Gasmata New Britain, E PNG 6.12S 150.25E
25 V14 Gasparilla Island island Florida, SE USA
174 Jj11 Gaspar, Selat strait W Indonesia
13 Y6 Gaspé Quebec, SE Canada 48.50N 64.33W
13 Z6 Gaspé, Cap de headland Quebec, SE Canada 48.45N 64.10W
13 X6 Gaspé, Péninsule de var. Péninsule de la Gaspésie. peninsula Quebec, SE Canada
Gaspésie, Péninsule de la see Gaspé, Péninsule de
171 Ll12 Gas-san ▲ Honshū, C Japan 38.33N 140.02E
79 W15 Gassol Taraba, E Nigeria 8.28N 10.24E
Gastein see Badgastein
23 R10 Gastonia North Carolina, SE USA 35.15N 81.11W
23 V8 Gaston, Lake ⊠ North Carolina/Virginia, SE USA
117 D19 Gastoúni Dytikí Ellás, S Greece 37.51N 21.15E
65 I17 Gastre Chubut, S Argentina 42.20S 69.10W
Gat see Ghāt
107 P15 Gata, Cabo de headland S Spain 36.43N 2.11W
Gata, Cape see Gátas, Akrotíri
107 T11 Gata de Gorgos País Valenciano, E Spain 38.45N 0.06E
118 E12 Gătaia Ger. Gataja, Hung. Gátalja; prev. Gáttája. Timiş, W Romania 45.24N 21.25E
Gataja/Gátalja see Gătaia
124 Nn4 Gátas, Akrotíri var. Cape Gata. headland S Cyprus 34.34N 33.03E
106 J8 Gata, Sierra de ▲ W Spain
128 G13 Gatchina Leningradskaya Oblast', NW Russian Federation 59.33N 30.06E
23 P8 Gate City Virginia, NE USA 36.38N 82.34W
99 M14 Gateshead NE England, UK 54.57N 1.35W
15 Jj2 Gateshead Island island Nunavut, N Canada
23 X8 Gatesville North Carolina, SE USA 36.23N 76.43W
27 S8 Gatesville Texas, SW USA 31.26N 97.44W
12 L12 Gatineau Quebec, SE Canada 45.28N 75.40W
12 L11 Gatineau ~ Ontario/Quebec, SE Canada
23 N9 Gatlinburg Tennessee, S USA 35.42N 83.30W
Gatooma see Kadoma
Gáttája see Gătaia
45 T14 Gatún, Lago ⊠ C Panama
61 N14 Gaturiano Piauí, NE Brazil 6.53S 41.45W
99 O22 Gatwick ✕ (London) SE England, UK 51.10N 0.12W
197 J15 Gau prev. Ngau. island C Fiji
197 C11 Gaua var Santa Maria, island Banks Islands, N Vanuatu
106 L16 Gaucín Andalucía, S Spain 36.31N 5.19W
Gauhāti see Guwāhāti
120 I8 Gauja Ger. Aa. ~ Estonia/Latvia
120 I7 Gaujiena Alūksne, NE Latvia 57.31N 26.24E
Gaul/Gaule see France
96 H9 Gauldalen valley S Norway
23 R5 Gauley River ~ West Virginia, NE USA
101 D19 Gaurain-Ramecroix Hainaut, SW Belgium 50.35N 3.31E
97 F15 Gausta ▲ S Norway 59.50N 8.39E
85 J21 Gauteng off. Gauteng Province; prev. Pretoria-Witwatersrand-Vereeniging. ◐ province NE South Africa
Gauteng see Germiston, South Africa
Gauteng see Johannesburg, South Africa
176 Y10 Gauttier, Pegunungan ▲ Irian Jaya, E Indonesia
149 P14 Gāvbandī Hormozgān, S Iran 27.07N 53.21E
117 H25 Gavdopoúla island SE Greece
117 H26 Gávdos island SE Greece
104 K16 Gave de Pau var. Gave-de-Pay. ~ SW France
Gave-de-Pay see Gave de Pau
104 J16 Gave d'Oloron ~ SW France
101 E18 Gavere Oost-Vlaanderen, NW Belgium 50.56N 3.40E
96 N13 Gävle var. Gäfle; prev. Gefle. Gävleborg, C Sweden 60.40N 17.09E
96 M11 Gävleborg var. Gäfleborg, Gefleborg. ◐ county C Sweden
96 O13 Gävlebukten bay C Sweden
128 L16 Gavrilov-Yam Yaroslavskaya Oblast', W Russian Federation 57.19N 39.52E
195 P15 Gawa Island island SE Papau New Guinea
190 I9 Gawler South Australia 34.37S 138.43E
190 G7 Gawler Ranges hill range South Australia
Gawso see Goaso
168 H11 Gaxun Nur ◎ N China
159 P14 Gaya Bihār, N India 24.48N 85.00E
79 S13 Gaya Dosso, SW Niger 11.54N 3.25E
Gaya see Kyjov
33 Q6 Gaylord Michigan, N USA 45.01N 84.40W
31 U9 Gaylord Minnesota, N USA 44.33N 94.13W
189 Y9 Gayndah Queensland, E Australia 25.37S 151.30E
129 T12 Gayny Komi-Permyatskiy Avtonomnyy Okrug, NW Russian Federation 60.19N 54.15E
Gaysin see Haysyn
Gayvorno see Hayvoron
144 E11 Gaza Ar. Ghazzah, Heb. 'Azza. NE Gaza Strip 31.30N 34.00E
85 L20 Gaza off. Província de Gaza. ◐ province SW Mozambique
152 I9 Gaz-Achak Turkm. Gazojak. Lebapskiy Velayat, NE Turkmenistan 41.12N 61.24E
Gazalkent see Ghazalkent
152 C11 Gazandzhyk Turkm. Gazanjyk; prev. Kazandzhik. Balkanskiy Velayat, W Turkmenistan 39.16N 55.27E
Gazanjyk see Gazandzhyk
79 V12 Gazaoua Maradi, S Niger 13.28N 7.54E
144 E11 Gaza Strip Ar. Qiṭā' Ghazzah. disputed region SW Asia
195 P11 Gazelle Peninsula headland New Britain, E PNG 4.32S 151.56E
197 J5 Gazelle, Récif de la reef C New Caledonia
Gazgan see Ghozghon
Gazi Antep see Gaziantep
142 M16 Gaziantep var. Gazi Antep; prev. Aintab, Antep. Gaziantep, S Turkey 37.04N 37.21E
142 M17 Gaziantep var. Gazi Antep. ◐ province S Turkey
116 M13 Gaziköy Tekirdağ, NW Turkey 40.45N 27.18E
124 O3 Gazimağusa var. Famagusta, Gk. Ammóchostos. E Cyprus 35.06N 33.57E
124 Nn2 Gazimağusa Körfezi var. Famagusta Bay, Gk. Kólpos Ammóchostos. bay E Cyprus
152 K11 Gazli Bukhoro Wiloyati, C Uzbekistan 40.09N 63.28E
Gazojak see Gaz-Achak
81 K15 Gbadolite Equateur, NW Dem. Rep. Congo (Zaire) 4.18N 20.55E
78 K16 Gbanga var. Gbarnga. N Liberia 7.01N 9.30W
Gbarnga see Gbanga
79 S14 Gbéroubouè var. Béroubouay. N Benin 10.35N 2.47E
79 W16 Gboko Benue, S Nigeria 7.21N 8.57E
Gcuwa see Butterworth
112 J7 Gdańsk Fr. Dantzig, Ger. Danzig. Pomorskie, N Poland 54.21N 18.35E
Gdan'skaya Bukhta/Gdańsk, Gulf of see Danzig, Gulf of
Gdańska, Zatoka see Danzig, Gulf of
Gdingen see Gdynia
128 F13 Gdov Pskovskaya Oblast', W Russian Federation 58.43N 27.51E
112 I6 Gdynia Ger. Gdingen. Pomorskie, N Poland 54.31N 18.30E
28 M10 Geary Oklahoma, C USA 35.37N 98.19W
Geavvú see Kevo
78 H12 Gêba, Rio ~ C Guinea-Bissau
175 T8 Gebe, Pulau island E Indonesia
142 E11 Gebze Kocaeli, NW Turkey 40.48N 29.25E
124 O2 Geçitkale Gk. Lefkonico, Lefkónikon. NE Cyprus 35.16N 33.44E
82 H10 Gedaref var. Al Qaḍārif, El Gedaref. Gedaref, E Sudan 14.03N 35.24E
82 H10 Gedaref ◐ state E Sudan
82 B11 Gedid Ras el Fil Southern Darfur, W Sudan 12.48N 25.42E

◆ Country ● Country Capital ◇ Dependent Territory ○ Dependent Territory Capital ◐ Administrative Region ✕ International Airport ▲ Mountain ▲ Mountain Range ☒ Volcano ~ River ◎ Lake ⊠ Reservoir

Gedinne – Glamsbjerg

101 I23 **Gedinne** Namur, SE Belgium 49.57N 4.55E
142 E13 **Gediz** Kütahya, W Turkey 39.04N 29.25E
142 C14 **Gediz Nehri** ≈ W Turkey
83 N14 **Gedlegubē** Somali, E Ethiopia 6.53N 45.08E
83 L17 **Gedo** *off.* Gobolka Gedo. ◐ *region* SW Somalia
97 I25 **Gedser** Storstrøm, SE Denmark 54.34N 11.57E
101 I16 **Geel** *var.* Gheel. Antwerpen, N Belgium 51.10N 4.58E
191 N13 **Geelong** Victoria, SE Australia 38.09S 144.20E
Ge'e'mu *see* Golmud
101 I14 **Geertruidenberg** Noord-Brabant, S Netherlands 51.43N 4.52E
102 H10 **Geeste** ≈ NW Germany
102 J10 **Geesthacht** Schleswig-Holstein, N Germany 53.25N 10.22E
191 P17 **Geeveston** Tasmania, SE Australia 43.12S 146.54E
Gefle *see* Gävle
Gefleborg *see* Gävleborg
164 G13 **Gê'gyai** Xizang Zizhiqu, W China 32.28N 81.03E
79 X12 **Geidam** Yobe, NE Nigeria 12.52N 11.55E
9 T11 **Geikie** ≈ Saskatchewan, C Canada
96 F13 **Geilo** Buskerud, S Norway 60.31N 8.13E
96 E10 **Geiranger** Møre og Romsdal, S Norway 62.07N 7.12E
103 I22 **Geislingen** *var.* Geislingen an der Steige. Baden-Württemberg, SW Germany 48.35N 9.52E
Geislingen an der Steige *see* Geislingen
83 F20 **Geita** Mwanza, NW Tanzania 2.52S 32.12E
97 G15 **Geithus** Buskerud, S Norway 59.55N 9.57E
166 H14 **Gejiu** *var.* Kochiu. Yunnan, S China 23.21N 103.07E
Gëkdepe *see* Geok-Tepe
152 E9 **Geklengkui, Solonchak** *var.* Solonchak Goklenkuy. *salt marsh* NW Turkmenistan
83 D14 **Gel** ≈ W Sudan
109 K25 **Gela** *prev.* Terranova di Sicilia. Sicilia, Italy, C Mediterranean Sea 37.04N 14.15E
Gêladaindong *see* Gladaindong
83 N14 **Geladī** Somali, E Ethiopia 6.58N 46.24E
174 Kk11 **Gelam, Pulau** *var.* Pulau Galam. *island* N Indonesia
100 L11 **Gelderland** *prev. Eng.* Guelders. ◐ *province* E Netherlands
100 J13 **Geldermalsen** Gelderland, C Netherlands 51.52N 5.16E
103 D14 **Geldern** Nordrhein-Westfalen, W Germany 51.31N 6.19E
101 K15 **Geldrop** Noord-Brabant, SE Netherlands 51.25N 5.31E
101 L17 **Geleen** Limburg, SE Netherlands 50.57N 5.49E
130 K14 **Gelendzhik** Krasnodarskiy Kray, SW Russian Federation 44.34N 38.06E
Gelib *see* Jilib
142 B11 **Gelibolu** *Eng.* Gallipoli. Çanakkale, NW Turkey 40.25N 26.40E
117 L14 **Gelibolu Yarımadası** *Eng.* Gallipoli Peninsula. *peninsula* NW Turkey
Gelinting, Teluk *see* Geliting, Teluk
175 Qq16 **Geliting, Teluk** *var.* Teluk Gelinting. *bay* Nusa Tenggara, S Indonesia
83 O14 **Gellinsor** Mudug, C Somalia 6.25N 46.44E
103 H18 **Gelnhausen** Hessen, C Germany 50.12N 9.12E
103 E14 **Gelsenkirchen** Nordrhein-Westfalen, W Germany 51.33N 7.06E
85 C20 **Geluk** Hardap, SW Namibia 24.35S 15.48E
101 H20 **Gembloux** Namur, Belgium 50.34N 4.42E
194 I12 **Gembogl** Chimbu, C PNG 5.52S 145.06E
81 J16 **Gemena** Equateur, NW Dem. Rep. Congo (Zaire) 3.13N 19.49E
101 L14 **Gemert** Noord-Brabant, SE Netherlands 51.33N 5.40E
142 E11 **Gemlik** Bursa, NW Turkey 40.25N 29.10E
Gem of the Mountains *see* Idaho
108 J6 **Gemona del Friuli** Friuli-Venezia Giulia, NE Italy 46.18N 13.11E
Gem State *see* Idaho
Genalē Wenz *see* Juba
174 Ll7 **Genali, Danau** ◎ Borneo, N Indonesia
101 G19 **Genappe** Wallon Brabant, C Belgium 50.39N 4.27E
143 P14 **Genç** Bingöl, E Turkey 38.45N 40.31E
Genck *see* Genk
100 M9 **Genemuiden** Overijssel, E Netherlands 52.38N 6.03E
65 K14 **General Acha** La Pampa, C Argentina 37.24S 64.34W
63 C21 **General Alvear** Buenos Aires, E Argentina 36.03S 60.01W
64 I12 **General Alvear** Mendoza, W Argentina 34.58S 67.40W
63 B20 **General Arenales** Buenos Aires, E Argentina 34.21S 61.19W
63 D21 **General Belgrano** Buenos Aires, E Argentina 35.46S 58.30W
204 H3 **General Bernardo O'Higgins** *Chilean research station* Antarctica 63.09S 57.13W
43 O8 **General Bravo** Nuevo León, NE Mexico 25.47N 99.04W
64 M7 **General Capdevila** Chaco, N Argentina 27.25S 61.30W
General Carrera, Lago *see* Buenos Aires, Lago
43 N9 **General Cepeda** Coahuila de Zaragoza, NE Mexico 25.18N 101.24W
65 K15 **General Conesa** Río Negro, E Argentina 40.07S 64.32W
63 G18 **General Enrique Martínez** Treinta y Tres, E Uruguay 33.13S 53.46W
64 L3 **General Eugenio A. Garay** *var.* Fortín General Eugenio Garay; *prev.* Yrendagüé. Nueva Asunción, NW Paraguay 20.31S 62.09W
63 C18 **General Galarza** Entre Ríos, E Argentina 32.43S 59.24W
63 E22 **General Guido** Buenos Aires, E Argentina 36.36S 57.45W
General José F.Uriburu *see* Zárate
63 E22 **General Juan Madariaga** Buenos Aires, E Argentina 37.02S 57.06W
43 O16 **General Juan N Alvarez** ✈ (Acapulco) Guerrero, S Mexico 16.47N 99.47W
63 B22 **General La Madrid** Buenos Aires, E Argentina 37.13S 61.10W
63 E21 **General Lavalle** Buenos Aires, E Argentina 36.25S 56.55W
General Machado *see* Camacupa
64 I8 **General Manuel Belgrano, Cerro** ▲ W Argentina 29.05S 67.05W
43 O8 **General Mariano Escobero** ✈ (Monterrey) Nuevo León, NE Mexico 25.47N 100.00W
63 B20 **General O'Brien** Buenos Aires, E Argentina 34.54S 60.45W
64 K13 **General Pico** La Pampa, C Argentina 35.40S 63.44W
64 M7 **General Pinedo** Chaco, N Argentina 27.16S 61.19W
63 B20 **General Pinto** Buenos Aires, E Argentina 34.45S 61.49W
63 E22 **General Pirán** Buenos Aires, E Argentina 37.16S 57.46W
45 N15 **General, Río** ≈ S Costa Rica
65 I15 **General Roca** Río Negro, C Argentina 39.00S 67.35W
179 Rr17 **General Santos** *off.* General Santos City. Mindanao, S Philippines 6.09N 125.10E
43 O9 **General Terán** Nuevo León, NE Mexico 25.17N 99.37W
116 N7 **General Toshevo** *Rom.* I.G.Duca, *prev.* Casim, Kasimköj. Dobrich, NE Bulgaria 43.43N 28.04E
63 B20 **General Viamonte** Buenos Aires, E Argentina 35.01S 61.00W
63 A20 **General Villegas** Buenos Aires, E Argentina 35.01S 63.01W
Gênes *see* Genova
20 E11 **Genesee River** ≈ New York/Pennsylvania, NE USA
32 K11 **Geneseo** Illinois, N USA 41.27N 90.08W
20 F10 **Geneseo** New York, NE USA 42.48N 77.46W
59 L14 **Geneshuaya, Río** ≈ N Bolivia
25 Q8 **Geneva** Alabama, S USA 31.01N 85.51W
32 M10 **Geneva** Illinois, N USA 41.53N 88.18W
31 Q16 **Geneva** Nebraska, C USA 40.31N 97.36W
20 G10 **Geneva** New York, NE USA 42.52N 76.58W
33 U10 **Geneva** Ohio, NE USA 41.48N 80.53W
Geneva *see* Genève
110 B10 **Geneva, Lake** *Fr.* Lac de Genève, Lac Léman, le Léman, *Ger.* Genfer See. ◎ France/Switzerland
110 A10 **Genève** *Eng.* Geneva, *Ger.* Genf, *It.* Ginevra. Genève, SW Switzerland 46.13N 6.09E
110 A11 **Genève** *Eng.* Geneva, *Ger.* Genf, *It.* Ginevra. ◐ *canton* SW Switzerland
110 A10 **Genève** *var.* Geneva. ✈ Vaud, SW Switzerland 46.13N 6.06E
Genève, Lac de *see* Geneva, Lake
Genf *see* Genève
Genfer See *see* Geneva, Lake
169 S5 **Gen He** ≈ NE China
Genichesk *see* Heniches'k
106 L14 **Genil** ≈ S Spain
101 K18 **Genk** *var.* Genck. Limburg, NE Belgium 50.58N 5.30E
170 Cc12 **Genkai-nada** *gulf* Kyūshū, SW Japan
109 C19 **Gennargentu, Monti del** ▲ Sardegna, Italy, C Mediterranean Sea 40.01N 9.14E
101 M14 **Gennep** Limburg, SE Netherlands 51.43N 5.58E
32 M10 **Genoa** Illinois, N USA 42.06N 88.41W
31 Q15 **Genoa** Nebraska, C USA 41.27N 97.43W
Genoa *see* Genova
Genoa, Gulf of *see* Genova, Golfo di
108 D10 **Genova** *Eng.* Genoa, *Fr.* Gênes; *anc.* Genua. Liguria, NW Italy 44.28N 9.00E
108 D10 **Genova, Golfo di** *Eng.* Gulf of Genoa. *gulf* NW Italy
59 C17 **Genovesa, Isla** *var.* Tower Island. *island* Galapagos Islands, Ecuador, E Pacific Ocean
Genshū *see* Wŏnju
101 E17 **Gent** *Eng.* Ghent, *Fr.* Gand. Oost-Vlaanderen, NW Belgium 51.01N 3.42E
174 J15 **Genteng** Jawa, C Indonesia 7.21S 106.19E
102 M12 **Genthin** Sachsen-Anhalt, E Germany 52.24N 12.10E
29 R9 **Gentry** Arkansas, C USA 36.16N 94.28W
Genua *see* Genova
109 I15 **Genzano di Roma** Lazio, C Italy 41.42N 12.42E
Geokchay *see* Göyçay
152 F13 **Geok-Tepe** *var.* Gëkdepe, *Turkm.* Gökdepe. Akhalskiy Velayat, C Turkmenistan 38.05N 58.07E
126 Gg1 **Georga, Zemlya** *Eng.* George Land. *island* Zemlya Frantsa-Iosifa, N Russian Federation
85 G26 **George** Western Cape, S South Africa 33.51S 22.28E
31 S11 **George** Iowa, C USA 43.20N 96.00W
11 O5 **George** ≈ Newfoundland/Quebec, E Canada
67 C25 **George Island** *island* S Falkland Islands
191 R10 **George, Lake** ◎ New South Wales, SE Australia
83 E18 **George, Lake** ◎ SW Uganda
25 W10 **George, Lake** ◎ Florida, SE USA
20 L8 **George, Lake** ⊠ New York, NE USA
George Land *see* Georga, Zemlya
Georgenburg *see* Jurbarkas
George River *see* Kangiqsualujjuaq
66 G8 **Georges Bank** *undersea feature* W Atlantic Ocean
193 A21 **George Sound** *sound* South Island, NZ
67 F15 **Georgetown** ○ (Ascension Island) NW Ascension Island 17.55S 14.25W
189 V5 **Georgetown** Queensland, NE Australia 18.17S 143.37E
191 P15 **George Town** Tasmania, SE Australia 41.07S 146.50E
46 I4 **George Town** Great Exuma Island, C Bahamas 23.28N 75.47W
46 D8 **George Town** *var.* Georgetown. ○ (Cayman Islands) Grand Cayman, SW Cayman Islands 19.15N 81.22W
78 H12 **Georgetown** E Gambia 13.33N 14.49W
57 T8 **Georgetown** ● (Guyana) N Guyana 6.46N 58.10W
173 Ff3 **George Town** *var.* Penang, Pinang. Pinang, Peninsular Malaysia 5.28N 100.19E
47 Y14 **Georgetown** Saint Vincent, Saint Vincent and the Grenadines 13.14N 61.07W
23 Y4 **Georgetown** Delaware, NE USA 38.39N 75.22W
25 R6 **Georgetown** Georgia, SE USA 31.52N 85.04W
22 M5 **Georgetown** Kentucky, S USA 38.13N 84.33W
23 T13 **Georgetown** South Carolina, SE USA 33.22N 79.17W
27 S10 **Georgetown** Texas, SW USA 30.37N 97.40W
57 T8 **Georgetown** ✈ N Guyana 6.46N 58.10W
205 U16 **George V Coast** *physical region* Antarctica
205 T15 **George V Land** *physical region* Antarctica
204 J7 **George VI Ice Shelf** *ice shelf* Antarctica
204 J6 **George VI Sound** *sound* Antarctica
27 S14 **George West** Texas, SW USA 28.19N 98.07W
143 R9 **Georgia** *off.* Republic of Georgia, *Geor.* Sak'art'velo, *Rus.* Gruzinskaya SSR, Gruziya; *prev.* Georgian SSR. ◆ *republic* SW Asia
25 S5 **Georgia** *off.* State of Georgia; also known as Empire State of the South, Peach State. ◐ *state* SE USA
12 F12 **Georgian Bay** *lake bay* Ontario, S Canada
8 L17 **Georgia, Strait of** *strait* British Columbia, W Canada
Georgi Dimitrov *see* Kostenets
Georgi Dimitrov, Yazovir *see* Koprinka, Yazovir
116 M9 **Georgi Traykov, Yazovir** ⊠ NE Bulgaria
Georgiu-Dezh *see* Liski
151 W10 **Georgiyevka** Vostochnyy Kazakhstan, E Kazakhstan 49.19N 81.34E
Georgiyevka *see* Korday,
131 N15 **Georgiyevsk** Stavropol'skiy Kray, SW Russian Federation 44.07N 43.22E
102 G13 **Georgsmarienhütte** Niedersachsen, NW Germany 52.12N 8.04E
205 O1 **Georg von Neumayer** *German research station* Antarctica 70.41S 8.18W
103 M16 **Gera** Thüringen, E Germany 50.51N 12.13E
103 K16 **Gera** ≈ C Germany
101 E19 **Geraardsbergen** Oost-Vlaanderen, SW Belgium 50.46N 3.52E
117 F21 **Geráki** Pelopónnisos, S Greece 36.56N 22.46E
29 W5 **Gerald** Missouri, C USA 38.24N 91.20W
49 V8 **Geral de Goiás, Serra** ▲▲ E Brazil
193 G20 **Geraldine** Canterbury, South Island, NZ 44.06S 171.13E
188 H11 **Geraldton** Western Australia 28.47S 114.39E
10 E11 **Geraldton** Ontario, S Canada 49.43N 86.58W
62 J12 **Geral, Serra** ▲▲ S Brazil
175 P16 **Gerampi** Sumbawa, S Indonesia 8.47S 118.51E
105 U6 **Gérardmer** Vosges, NE France 48.05N 6.54E
Gerasa *see* Jarash
Gerdauen *see* Zheleznodorozhnyy
41 Q11 **Gerdine, Mount** ▲ Alaska, USA 61.40N 152.21W
142 H11 **Gerede** Bolu, N Turkey 40.48N 32.13E
142 H11 **Gerede Çayı** ≈ N Turkey
154 M8 **Gereshk** Helmand, SW Afghanistan 31.49N 64.31E
103 L24 **Geretsried** Bayern, S Germany 47.51N 11.28E
107 P14 **Gérgal** Andalucía, S Spain 37.07N 2.34W
194 K13 **Gerhards, Cape** *headland* C PNG 6.43S 147.31E
30 I14 **Gering** Nebraska, C USA 41.49N 103.39W
37 R3 **Gerlach** Nevada, W USA 40.38N 119.21W
Gerlachfalvi Csúcs/Gerlachovka *see* Gerlachovský štít
113 L18 **Gerlachovský štít** *var.* Gerlachovka, *Ger.* Gerlsdorfer Spitze, *Hung.* Gerlachfalvi Csúcs; *prev.* Stalinov Štít, *Ger.* Franz-Josef Spitze, *Hung.* Ferencz-József Csúcs. ▲ N Slovakia 49.12N 20.09E
110 E8 **Gerlafingen** Solothurn, NW Switzerland 47.10N 7.34E
Gerlsdorfer Spitze *see* Gerlachovský štít
145 V3 **Germak** E Iraq 35.49N 46.09E
German East Africa *see* Tanzania
Germanicopolis *see* Çankırı
Germanicum, Mare/German Ocean *see* North Sea
Germanovichi *see* Hyermanavichy
German Southwest Africa *see* Namibia
22 E10 **Germantown** Tennessee, S USA 35.06N 89.51W
103 I15 **Germany** *off.* Federal Republic of Germany, *Ger.* Bundesrepublik Deutschland, Deutschland. ◆ *federal republic* N Europe
103 L23 **Germering** Bayern, SE Germany 48.07N 11.22E
85 J21 **Germiston** *var.* Gauteng. Gauteng, NE South Africa 26.15S 28.10E
Gernika *see* Gernika-Lumo
107 P2 **Gernika-Lumo** *var.* Gernika, Guernica, Guernica y Lumo. País Vasco, N Spain 43.19N 2.40W
171 Ii15 **Gero** Gifu, Honshū, SW Japan 35.48N 137.15E
117 F22 **Geroliménas** Pelopónnisos, S Greece 36.28N 22.25E
Gerona *see* Girona
101 H21 **Gerpinnes** Hainaut, S Belgium 50.20N 4.37E
104 L15 **Gers** ◐ *department* S France
104 L14 **Gers** ≈ S France
Gerunda *see* Girona
142 K10 **Gerze** Sinop, N Turkey 41.48N 35.13E
164 I13 **Gêrzê** Xizang Zizhiqu, W China 32.19N 84.05E
Gesoriacum/Gessoriacum *see* Boulogne-sur-Mer
101 J21 **Gesves** Namur, SE Belgium 50.24N 5.04E
95 J20 **Geta** Åland, SW Finland 60.22N 19.49E
107 N8 **Getafe** Madrid, C Spain 40.18N 3.43W
97 J21 **Getinge** Halland, S Sweden 56.46N 12.42E
20 F16 **Gettysburg** Pennsylvania, NE USA 39.49N 77.13W
31 N8 **Gettysburg** South Dakota, N USA 45.00N 99.57W
204 K12 **Getz Ice Shelf** *ice shelf* Antarctica
143 S15 **Gevaş** Van, SE Turkey 38.16N 43.04E
Gevgeli *see* Gevgelija
115 Q20 **Gevgelija** *var.* Đevđelija, Djevdjelija, *Turk.* Gevgeli. SE FYR Macedonia 41.09N 22.30E
105 T10 **Gex** Ain, E France 46.21N 6.02E
94 I3 **Geysir** *physical region* SW Iceland
142 F11 **Geyve** Sakarya, NW Turkey 40.31N 30.18E
82 G10 **Gezira** ◐ *state* E Sudan
111 V3 **Gföhl** Niederösterreich, N Austria 48.30N 15.27E
85 H22 **Ghaap Plateau** *Afr.* Ghaapplato. *plateau* C South Africa
Ghaapplato *see* Ghaap Plateau
Ghaba *see* Al Ghābah
144 J8 **Ghāb, Tall** ▲ SE Syria 33.09N 37.48E
145 Q9 **Ghadaf, Wādī al** *dry watercourse* C Iraq
Ghadamès *see* Ghadāmis
76 M9 **Ghadāmis** *var.* Ghadamès, Rhadames. W Libya 30.07N 9.30E
147 Y10 **Ghadan** E Oman 20.20N 57.58E
77 O10 **Ghaddūwah** C Libya 26.36N 14.26E
153 Q11 **Ghafurov** *Rus.* Gafurov; *prev.* Sovetabad. NW Tajikistan 40.13N 69.42E
159 N12 **Ghāghara** ≈ S Asia
155 P13 **Ghaibi Dero** Sind, SE Pakistan 27.34N 67.42E
147 Y10 **Ghalat** E Oman 21.06N 58.51E
153 O11 **Ghallaorol** Jizzakh Wiloyati, C Uzbekistan 40.01N 67.30E
145 W11 **Ghamūkah, Hawr** ◎ S Iraq
79 P15 **Ghana** *off.* Republic of Ghana. ◆ *republic* W Africa
147 X12 **Ghānah** *spring/well* S Oman 18.35N 56.34E
Ghanongga *see* Ranongga
Ghansi/Ghansiland *see* Ghanzi
85 F18 **Ghanzi** *var.* Khanzi. Ghanzi, W Botswana 21.39S 21.38E
85 G19 **Ghanzi** *var.* Ghansi, Ghansiland, Khanzi. ◐ *district* C Botswana
69 T14 **Ghanzi** *var.* Knanzi. ≈ Botswana/South Africa
Ghap'an *see* Kapan
144 F13 **Gharandal** Ma'ān, SW Jordan 30.12N 35.18E
Gharbt, Jabal al *see* Liban, Jebel
76 K7 **Ghardaïa** N Algeria 32.29N 3.44E
145 U14 **Gharibīyah, Sha'īb al** ≈ S Iraq
153 R12 **Gharm** *Rus.* Garm. C Tajikistan 39.03N 70.25E
155 P17 **Gharo** Sind, SE Pakistan 24.43N 67.34E
145 W10 **Gharrāf, Shaṭṭ al** ≈ S Iraq
Gharvān *see* Gharyān
77 O7 **Gharyān** *var.* Gharvān. NW Libya 32.10N 13.01E
76 M11 **Ghāt** *var.* Gat. SW Libya 24.58N 10.10E
Ghawdex *see* Gozo
147 U8 **Ghayathi** Abū Ẓaby, W UAE 23.51N 53.01E
Ghazāl, Baḥr al *see* Ghazal, Bahr el
80 H9 **Ghazal, Bahr el** *var.* Soro. *seasonal river* C Chad
82 E13 **Ghazal, Bahr el** *var.* Baḥr al Ghazāl. ≈ S Sudan
153 Q9 **Ghazalkent** *Rus.* Gazalkent. Toshkent Wiloyati, E Uzbekistan 41.30N 69.46E
76 H6 **Ghazaouet** NW Algeria 35.05N 1.52W
158 J10 **Ghāziābād** Uttar Pradesh, N India 28.42N 77.28E
159 O13 **Ghāzīpur** Uttar Pradesh, N India 25.38N 83.33E
155 Q6 **Ghaznī** *var.* Ghazni. Ghaznī, E Afghanistan 33.31N 68.24E
155 P7 **Ghaznī** ◐ *province* SE Afghanistan
Ghazzah *see* Gaza
Gheel *see* Geel
Ghelîzâne *see* Relizane
Ghent *see* Gent
Gheorghe Braţul *see* Sfântu Gheorghe, Braţul
Gheorghe Gheorghiu-Dej *see* Oneşti
118 J10 **Gheorgheni** *prev.* Gheorghieni, Sînt-Miclăuş, *Ger.* Niklasmarkt, *Hung.* Gyergyószentmiklós. Harghita, C Romania 46.43N 25.34E
Gheorghieni *see* Gheorgheni
118 H10 **Gherla** *Ger.* Neuschliss, *Hung.* Szamosújvár; *prev.* Armenierstadt. Cluj, NW Romania 47.02N 23.55E
Gheweifat *see* Ghuwayfāt
152 L11 **Ghijduwon** *Rus.* Gizhduvan. Bukhoro Wiloyati, C Uzbekistan 40.06N 64.38E
Ghilan *see* Gīlān
109 C18 **Ghilarza** Sardegna, Italy, C Mediterranean Sea 40.09N 8.50E
Ghilizane *see* Relizane
Ghimbi *see* Gīmbī
Ghiriş *see* Câmpia Turzii
105 Y15 **Ghisonaccia** Corse, France, C Mediterranean Sea 42.00N 9.25E
Ghizo *see* Gizo
153 Q11 **Ghonchí** *Rus.* Ganchi. NW Tajikistan 39.57N 69.10E
Ghor *see* Ghowr
159 T13 **Ghoraghat** Rajshahi, NW Bangladesh 25.17N 89.16E
155 R13 **Ghotki** Sind, SE Pakistan 28.00N 69.21E
154 M5 **Ghowr** *var.* Ghor. ◐ *province* C Afghanistan
152 M10 **Ghozghon** *Rus.* Gazgan. Nawoiy Wiloyati, C Uzbekistan 40.36N 65.29E
153 T13 **Ghŭdara** *var.* Gudara, *Rus.* Kudara. SE Tajikistan 38.28N 72.39E
159 R13 **Ghugri** ≈ N India
153 S14 **Ghund** *Rus.* Gunt. ≈ SE Tajikistan
Ghurdaqah *see* Hurghada
154 J5 **Ghūrīān** Herāt, W Afghanistan 34.19N 61.25E
147 T8 **Ghuwayfāt** *var.* Gheweifat. Abū Ẓaby, W UAE 24.06N 51.40E
123 Mm17 **Ghuzayyil, Sabkhat** *salt lake* N Libya
153 N13 **Ghuzor** *Rus.* Guzar. Qashqadaryo Wiloyati, S Uzbekistan 38.41N 66.12E
117 G17 **Giáltra** Évvoia, C Greece 38.21N 22.58E
Giamame *see* Jamaame
116 F13 **Giannitsá** *var.* Yiannitsá. Kentrikí Makedonía, N Greece 40.48N 22.24E
109 F14 **Giannutri, Isola di** *island* Archipelago Toscano, C Italy
98 F13 **Giant's Causeway** *Ir.* Clochán an Aifir. *lava flow* N Northern Ireland, UK
178 J15 **Gia Rai** Minh Hai, S Vietnam 9.16N 105.25E
109 L24 **Giarre** Sicilia, Italy, C Mediterranean Sea 37.43N 15.12E
46 I7 **Gibara** Holguín, E Cuba 21.05N 76.08W
31 O16 **Gibbon** Nebraska, C USA 40.45N 98.50W
34 K11 **Gibbon** Oregon, NW USA 45.40N 118.22W
35 P11 **Gibbonsville** Idaho, NW USA 45.33N 113.55W
66 A13 **Gibb's Hill** *hill* S Bermuda 32.15N 64.51W
94 I9 **Gibostad** Troms, N Norway 69.21N 18.01E
106 I14 **Gibraleón** Andalucía, S Spain 37.22N 6.58W
106 L16 **Gibraltar** ○ (Gibraltar) S Gibraltar 36.08N 5.21W
106 L16 **Gibraltar** ◇ *UK dependent territory* SW Europe
Gibraltar, Détroit de/Gibraltar, Estrecho de *see* Gibraltar, Strait of
106 J17 **Gibraltar, Strait of** *Fr.* Détroit de Gibraltar, *Sp.* Estrecho de Gibraltar. *strait* Atlantic Ocean/Mediterranean Sea
33 S11 **Gibsonburg** Ohio, N USA 41.22N 83.19W
32 M13 **Gibson City** Illinois, N USA 40.27N 88.24W
188 L8 **Gibson Desert** *desert* Western Australia
8 L17 **Gibsons** British Columbia, SW Canada 49.24N 123.31W
155 N12 **Gīdār** Baluchistān, SW Pakistan 28.16N 66.00E
161 I17 **Giddalūr** Andhra Pradesh, E India 15.24N 78.54E
27 U10 **Giddings** Texas, SW USA 30.10N 96.56W
29 Y8 **Gideon** Missouri, C USA 36.27N 89.55W
83 I15 **Gīdolē** Southern, S Ethiopia 5.31N 37.26E
120 H13 **Giedraičiai** Molėtai, E Lithuania 55.05N 25.16E
105 O7 **Gien** Loiret, C France 47.40N 2.37E
103 G17 **Giessen** Hessen, W Germany 50.34N 8.40E
100 O6 **Gieten** Drenthe, NE Netherlands 53.00N 6.43E
25 Y13 **Gifford** Florida, SE USA 27.40N 80.24W
15 Ll1 **Gifford** ≈ Baffin Island, Nunavut, NE Canada
102 J12 **Gifhorn** Niedersachsen, N Germany 52.28N 10.33E
9 P13 **Gift Lake** Alberta, W Canada 55.49N 115.57W
171 Hh15 **Gifu** *var.* Gihu. Gifu, Honshū, SW Japan 35.23N 136.46E
171 I14 **Gifu** *off.* Gifu-ken, *var.* Gihu. ◐ *prefecture* Honshū, SW Japan
130 M13 **Gigant** Rostovskaya Oblast', SW Russian Federation 46.29N 41.18E
42 E8 **Giganta, Sierra de la** ▲▲ W Mexico
56 E12 **Gigante** Huila, S Colombia 2.24N 75.34W
116 I7 **Gigen** Pleven, N Bulgaria 43.40N 24.31E
Giggiga *see* Jijiga
98 G12 **Gigha Island** *island* SW Scotland, UK
109 E14 **Giglio, Isola del** *island* Archipelago Toscano, C Italy
Gihu *see* Gifu
106 L2 **Gijón** *var.* Xixón. Asturias, NW Spain 43.31N 5.40W
83 D20 **Gikongoro** SW Rwanda 2.30S 29.32E
38 K14 **Gila Bend** Arizona, SW USA 32.57N 112.43W
38 J14 **Gila Bend Mountains** ▲▲ Arizona, SW USA
39 N14 **Gila Mountains** ▲▲ Arizona, SW USA
38 I15 **Gila Mountains** ▲▲ Arizona, SW USA
148 M4 **Gīlān** *off.* Ostān-e Gīlān; *var.* Ghilan, Guilan. ◐ *province* NW Iran
Gilani *see* Gnjilane
38 L14 **Gila River** ≈ Arizona, SW USA
31 W4 **Gilbert** Minnesota, N USA 47.29N 92.27W
Gilbert Islands *see* Tungaru
8 L16 **Gilbert, Mount** ▲ British Columbia, SW Canada 50.49N 124.03W
189 U4 **Gilbert River** ≈ Queensland, NE Australia
(0) C6 **Gilbert Seamounts** *undersea feature* NE Pacific Ocean
35 S7 **Gildford** Montana, NW USA 48.34N 110.21W
85 P15 **Gilé** Zambézia, NE Mozambique 16.04S 38.16E
32 K4 **Gile Flowage** ◎ Wisconsin, N USA
190 G7 **Giles, Lake** *salt lake* South Australia
77 U12 **Gilf Kebir Plateau** *Ar.* Haḍabat al Jilf al Kabīr. *plateau* SW Egypt
191 R6 **Gilgandra** New South Wales, SE Australia 31.43S 148.39E
Gîlgău *see* Gâlgău
83 I19 **Gilgil** Rift Valley, SW Kenya 0.33S 36.18E
191 S4 **Gil Gil Creek** ≈ New South Wales, SE Australia
155 V3 **Gilgit** Jammu and Kashmir, NE Pakistan 35.54N 74.19E
155 V3 **Gilgit** ≈ N Pakistan
9 X11 **Gillam** Manitoba, C Canada 56.25N 94.45W
97 J22 **Gilleleje** Frederiksborg, E Denmark 56.05N 12.17E
32 K14 **Gillespie** Illinois, N USA 39.07N 89.49W
29 W13 **Gillett** Arkansas, C USA 34.07N 91.22W
35 X12 **Gillette** Wyoming, C USA 44.17N 105.30W
99 P22 **Gillingham** SE England, UK 51.24N 0.33E
205 X6 **Gillock Island** *island* Antarctica
181 O16 **Gillot** ✈ (St-Denis) N Réunion 20.52S 55.31E
67 H25 **Gill Point** *headland* E Saint Helena 15.58S 5.37W
32 M12 **Gilman** Illinois, N USA 40.44N 87.58W
27 W6 **Gilmer** Texas, SW USA 32.43N 94.56W
Gilolo *see* Halmahera, Pulau
83 G14 **Gīlo Wenz** ≈ SW Ethiopia
37 O10 **Gilroy** California, W USA 37.00N 121.34W
194 H12 **Giluwe, Mount** ▲ W PNG 6.03S 143.52E
126 M14 **Gilyuy** ≈ SE Russian Federation
101 I14 **Gilze** Noord-Brabant, S Netherlands 51.33N 4.55E
172 O14 **Gima** Okinawa, Kume-jima, SW Japan
82 H13 **Gīmbī** *It.* Oromo, C Ethiopia 9.13N 35.39E
47 T12 **Gimie, Mount** ▲ C Saint Lucia 13.51N 61.00W
9 X16 **Gimli** Manitoba, S Canada 50.39N 97.00W
Gimma *see* Jīma
97 O14 **Gimo** Uppsala, C Sweden 60.10N 18.12E
104 L15 **Gimone** ≈ S France
Gimpoe *see* Gimpu
175 Pp9 **Gimpu** *prev.* Gimpoe. Sulawesi, C Indonesia 1.38S 120.00E
190 F5 **Gina** South Australia 29.56S 134.33E
Ginevra *see* Genève
101 J19 **Gingelom** Limburg, NE Belgium 50.46N 5.09E
188 I12 **Gingin** Western Australia 31.22S 115.51E
179 R14 **Gingoog** Mindanao, S Philippines 8.47N 125.05E
83 K14 **Gīnīr** Oromo, C Ethiopia 7.12N 40.43E
Giohar *see* Jawhar
109 O17 **Gioia del Colle** Puglia, SE Italy 40.46N 16.55E
109 M22 **Gioia, Golfo di** *gulf* S Italy
Giona *see* Gkióna
117 I16 **Gioúra** *island* Vóreioi Sporádes, Greece, Aegean Sea
109 O17 **Giovinazzo** Puglia, SE Italy 41.10N 16.40E
Gipeswic *see* Ipswich
Gipuzkoa *see* Guipúzcoa
Giran *see* Ilan
32 K14 **Girard** Illinois, N USA 39.27N 89.46W
29 R7 **Girard** Kansas, C USA 37.30N 94.50W
27 O6 **Girard** Texas, SW USA 33.18N 100.38W
56 E10 **Girardot** Cundinamarca, C Colombia 4.19N 74.46W
180 M7 **Giraud Seamount** *undersea feature* SW Indian Ocean 9.57S 46.55E
85 A15 **Giraul** ≈ SW Angola
98 L9 **Girdle Ness** *headland* NE Scotland, UK 57.09N 2.04W
143 N11 **Giresun** *var.* Kerasunt; *anc.* Cerasus, Pharnacia. Giresun, NE Turkey 40.55N 38.34E
143 N12 **Giresun** *var.* Kerasunt. ◐ *province* NE Turkey
143 N12 **Giresun Dağları** ▲▲ N Turkey
77 X10 **Girga** *var.* Girgeh, Jirjā. C Egypt 26.19N 31.49E
Girgeh *see* Girga
Girgenti *see* Agrigento
194 H10 **Girgir, Cape** *headland* NW PNG 3.48S 144.29E
159 Q15 **Girīdīh** Bihār, NE India 24.10N 86.19E
191 P6 **Girilambone** New South Wales, SE Australia 31.19S 146.57E
Girin *see* Jilin
124 R12 **Girne** *Gk.* Kerýneia, Kyrenia. N Cyprus 35.19N 33.19E
107 X5 **Girona** *var.* Gerona; *anc.* Gerunda. Cataluña, NE Spain 41.58N 2.49E
107 W5 **Girona** *var.* Gerona ◐ *province* Cataluña, NE Spain
104 J12 **Gironde** ◐ *department* SW France
104 J11 **Gironde** *estuary* SW France
107 V5 **Gironella** Cataluña, NE Spain 42.01N 1.52E
105 N15 **Girou** ≈ S France
99 H14 **Girvan** W Scotland, UK 55.14N 4.53W
26 M9 **Girvin** Texas, SW USA 31.05N 102.24W
192 Q9 **Gisborne** Gisborne, North Island, NZ 38.41S 178.01E
192 P9 **Gisborne** *off.* Gisborne District. ◐ *unitary authority* North Island, NZ
Giseifu *see* Ŭijŏngbu
Gisenye *see* Gisenyi
83 D19 **Gisenyi** *var.* Gisenye. NW Rwanda 1.42S 29.18E
97 K20 **Gislaved** Jönköping, S Sweden 57.19N 13.30E
105 N4 **Gisors** Eure, N France 49.18N 1.46E
Gissar *see* Hisor
153 P12 **Gissar Range** *Rus.* Gissarskiy Khrebet. ▲▲ Tajikistan/Uzbekistan
Gissarskiy Khrebet *see* Gissar Range
101 B16 **Gistel** West-Vlaanderen, W Belgium 51.09N 2.58E
110 F9 **Giswil** Unterwalden, C Switzerland 46.49N 8.11E
117 B16 **Gitánes** *ancient monument* Ípeiros, W Greece 39.34N 20.19E
83 E20 **Gitarama** C Rwanda 2.05S 29.45E
83 E20 **Gitega** C Burundi 3.20S 29.56E
Githio *see* Gýtheio
110 H11 **Giubiasco** Ticino, S Switzerland 46.10N 9.01E
108 K13 **Giulianova** Abruzzo, C Italy 42.45N 13.58E
Giulie, Alpi *see* Julian Alps
Giumri *see* Gyumri
118 M13 **Giurgeni** Ialomiţa, SE Romania 44.46N 27.51E
118 J15 **Giurgiu** Giurgiu, S Romania 43.54N 25.58E
118 J14 **Giurgiu** ◐ *county* SE Romania
97 F22 **Give** Vejle, C Denmark 55.51N 9.15E
105 R2 **Givet** Ardennes, N France 50.08N 4.50E
105 R11 **Givors** Rhône, E France 45.36N 4.46E
85 K19 **Giyani** Northern, NE South Africa 23.19S 30.37E
82 I13 **Giyon** Oromo, C Ethiopia 8.31N 37.56E
Gîza/Gizeh *see* El Gîza
77 V8 **Giza, Pyramids of** *ancient monument* N Egypt 29.46N 31.03E
Gizhduvan *see* Ghijduwon
127 Oo8 **Gizhiga** Magadanskaya Oblast', E Russian Federation 61.57N 160.16E
127 Oo8 **Gizhiginskaya Guba** *bay* E Russian Federation
195 T14 **Gizo** Gizo, NW Solomon Islands 8.03S 156.49E
195 T14 **Gizo** *var.* Ghizo. *island* NW Solomon Islands
112 N7 **Giżycko** *Ger.* Warmińsko-Mazurskie, NE Poland 54.03N 21.48E
Gízymałów *see* Hrymayliv
Gjakovë *see* Đakovica
96 F12 **Gjende** ◎ S Norway
97 F17 **Gjerstad** Aust-Agder, S Norway 58.54N 9.03E
Gjilan *see* Gnjilane
Gjinokastër *see* Gjirokastër
115 L23 **Gjirokastër** *var.* Gjirokastra; *prev.* Gjinokastër, *Gk.* Argyrokastron, *It.* Argirocastro. Gjirokastër, S Albania 40.04N 20.09E
115 L22 **Gjirokastër** ◐ *district* S Albania
15 K3 **Gjoa Haven** King William Island, Nunavut, NW Canada 68.37N 95.57W
96 H13 **Gjøvik** Oppland, S Norway 60.46N 10.40E
115 J22 **Gjuhëzës, Kepi i** *headland* SW Albania 40.25N 19.19E
Gjurgjevac *see* Đurđevac
117 E18 **Gkióna** *var.* Giona. ▲▲ C Greece
124 Oo3 **Gkréko, Akrotíri** *var.* Cape Greco, Pidálion. *headland* E Cyprus 34.57N 34.06E
101 I18 **Glabbeek-Zuurbemde** Vlaams Brabant, C Belgium 50.54N 4.58E
11 R14 **Glace Bay** Cape Breton Island, Nova Scotia, SE Canada 46.12N 59.57W
9 O16 **Glacier** British Columbia, SW Canada 51.12N 117.33W
41 W12 **Glacier Bay** *inlet* Alaska, USA
34 I7 **Glacier Peak** ▲ Washington, NW USA 48.06N 121.06W
165 N13 **Gladaindong** *var.* Gêladaindong. ▲ C China 33.24N 91.00E
23 Q7 **Glade Spring** Virginia, NE USA 36.47N 81.46W
45 W7 **Gladewater** Texas, SW USA 32.32N 94.57W
189 Y8 **Gladstone** Queensland, E Australia 23.52S 151.16E
190 I8 **Gladstone** South Australia 33.16S 138.21E
9 X16 **Gladstone** Manitoba, S Canada 50.12N 98.56W
33 O5 **Gladstone** Michigan, N USA 45.51N 87.01W
29 R4 **Gladstone** Missouri, C USA 39.12N 94.33W
33 Q7 **Gladwin** Michigan, N USA 43.58N 84.29W
97 J15 **Glafsfjorden** ◎ C Sweden
94 H2 **Gláma** *physical region* NW Iceland
96 I12 **Glåma** *var.* Glommen, Glomma. ≈ S Norway
114 F13 **Glamoč** Federacija Bosna I Hercegovina, NE Bosnia and Herzegovina 44.01N 16.51E
99 J22 **Glamorgan** *cultural region* S Wales, UK
97 G24 **Glamsbjerg** Fyn, C Denmark 55.16N 10.07E

◆ Country
● Country Capital
◇ Dependent Territory
○ Dependent Territory Capital
◐ Administrative Region
✈ International Airport
▲ Mountain
▲▲ Mountain Range
Volcano
≈ River
◎ Lake
⊠ Reservoir

179 Rr17 **Glan** Mindanao, S Philippines 5.49N 125.11E
97 M17 **Glan** ◎ S Sweden
111 T9 **Glan** ≈ SE Austria
103 F19 **Glan** ≈ W Germany
Glaris *see* Glarus
110 H9 **Glarner Alpen** ***Eng.*** Glarus Alps. ▲▲ E Switzerland
110 H8 **Glarus** Glarus, E Switzerland 47.03N 9.04E
110 H9 **Glarus** ***Fr.*** Glaris. ◈ *canton* C Switzerland
Glarus Alps *see* Glarner Alpen
29 N3 **Glasco** Kansas, C USA 39.21N 97.50W
98 I12 **Glasgow** S Scotland, UK 55.52N 4.15W
22 K7 **Glasgow** Kentucky, S USA 37.00N 85.54W
29 T4 **Glasgow** Missouri, C USA 39.13N 92.51W
35 W7 **Glasgow** Montana, NW USA 48.12N 106.37W
23 T6 **Glasgow** Virginia, NE USA 37.37N 79.27W
98 I12 **Glasgow** ✕ W Scotland, UK 55.52N 4.27W
9 S14 **Glaslyn** Saskatchewan, S Canada 53.20N 108.18W
20 I16 **Glassboro** New Jersey, NE USA 39.40N 75.05W
26 L10 **Glass Mountains** ▲▲ Texas, SW USA
99 K23 **Glastonbury** SW England, UK 51.09N 2.43W
Glatz *see* Kłodzko
103 N16 **Glauchau** Sachsen, E Germany 50.48N 12.31E
Glavn'a Morava *see* Velika Morava
115 N16 **Glavnik** Serbia, S Yugoslavia 42.53N 21.10E
131 T1 **Glazov** Udmurtskaya Respublika, NW Russian Federation 58.05N 52.38E
Głda *see* Gwda
111 U8 **Gleinalpe** ▲▲ SE Austria
111 W8 **Gleisdorf** Steiermark, SE Austria 47.07N 15.43E
Gleiwitz *see* Gliwice
41 S11 **Glenallen** Alaska, USA 62.06N 145.33W
104 F7 **Glénan, Îles** *island group* NW France
193 G21 **Glenavy** Canterbury, South Island, NZ 44.53S 171.04E
8 H5 **Glenboyle** Yukon Territory, NW Canada 63.55N 138.43W
23 X3 **Glen Burnie** Maryland, NE USA 39.09N 76.37W
38 L8 **Glen Canyon** *canyon* Utah, W USA
38 L8 **Glen Canyon Dam** *dam* Arizona, SW USA 36.56N 111.28W
32 K15 **Glen Carbon** Illinois, N USA 38.45N 89.58W
12 E17 **Glencoe** Ontario, S Canada 42.44N 81.42W
85 K22 **Glencoe** KwaZulu/Natal, E South Africa 28.09S 30.12E
31 U9 **Glencoe** Minnesota, N USA 44.46N 94.09W
98 H10 **Glen Coe** *valley* N Scotland, UK
38 K13 **Glendale** Arizona, SW USA 33.32N 112.11W
37 S15 **Glendale** California, W USA 34.09N 118.17W
190 G5 **Glendambo** South Australia 30.59S 135.45E
35 Y8 **Glendive** Montana, NW USA 47.07N 104.42W
35 Y15 **Glendo** Wyoming, C USA 42.27N 105.01W
57 S10 **Glendor Mountians** ▲▲ C Guyana
190 K12 **Glenelg River** ≈ South Australia/Victoria, SE Australia
31 P4 **Glenfield** North Dakota, N USA 47.25N 98.33W
27 V12 **Glen Flora** Texas, SW USA 29.22N 96.12W
189 P7 **Glen Helen** Northern Territory, N Australia 23.45S 132.46E
191 U5 **Glen Innes** New South Wales, SE Australia 29.42S 151.45E
33 P6 **Glen Lake** ◎ Michigan, N USA
8 I7 **Glenlyon Peak** ▲ Yukon Territory, W Canada 62.32N 134.51W
39 N16 **Glenn, Mount** ▲ Arizona, SW USA 31.55N 110.00W
35 N15 **Glenns Ferry** Idaho, NW USA 42.57N 115.18W
25 W6 **Glennville** Georgia, SE USA 31.56N 81.55W
8 J10 **Glenora** British Columbia, W Canada 57.52N 131.16W
190 M11 **Glenorchy** Victoria, SE Australia 36.56S 142.39E
191 V5 **Glenreagh** New South Wales, SE Australia 30.04S 153.00E
35 X15 **Glenrock** Wyoming, C USA 42.51N 105.52W
98 K11 **Glenrothes** E Scotland, UK 56.11N 3.09W
20 L9 **Glens Falls** New York, NE USA 43.18N 73.38W
99 D14 **Glenties** ***Ir.*** Na Gleannta. NW Ireland 54.46N 8.16W
30 L5 **Glen Ullin** North Dakota, N USA 46.49N 101.49W
23 R4 **Glenville** West Virginia, NE USA 38.55N 80.50W
29 T12 **Glenwood** Arkansas, C USA 34.19N 93.33W
31 S15 **Glenwood** Iowa, C USA 41.03N 95.44W
31 T7 **Glenwood** Minnesota, N USA 45.39N 95.23W
38 L5 **Glenwood** Utah, W USA 38.45N 111.59W
32 I5 **Glenwood City** Wisconsin, N USA 45.04N 92.11W
39 Q4 **Glenwood Springs** Colorado, C USA 39.33N 107.21W
110 F10 **Gletsch** Valais, S Switzerland 46.34N 8.21E
Glevum *see* Gloucester
31 U14 **Glidden** Iowa, C USA 42.03N 94.43W
114 E9 **Glina** Sisak-Moslavina, NE Croatia 45.19N 16.07E
96 F11 **Glittertind** ▲ S Norway 61.24N 8.19E
113 J16 **Gliwice** ***Ger.*** Gleiwitz. Śląskie, S Poland 50.19N 18.49E
38 M14 **Globe** Arizona, SW USA 33.24N 110.47W
Globino *see* Hlobyne
110 L9 **Glockturm** ▲ SW Austria 46.54N 10.42E
118 L9 **Glodeni** ***Rus.*** Glodyany. N Moldova 47.47N 27.33E
111 S9 **Glödnitz** Kärnten, S Austria 46.57N 14.03E
Glodyany *see* Glodeni
Glogau *see* Głogów
111 W6 **Gloggnitz** Niederösterreich, E Austria 47.41N 15.57E
112 F13 **Głogów** ***Ger.*** Glogau, Glogow. Dolnośląskie, SW Poland 51.39N 16.04E
113 I16 **Głogówek** ***Ger.*** Oberglogau. Opolskie, S Poland 50.21N 17.51E
94 G12 **Glomfjord** Nordland, C Norway 66.48N 13.57E
Glommen *see* Glåma
95 I14 **Glommersträsk** Norrbotten, N Sweden 65.16N 19.40E
180 I1 **Glorieuses, Nosy** *island group* N Madagascar
67 C25 **Glorious Hill** *hill* East Falkland, Falkland Islands
40 J12 **Glory of Russia Cape** *headland* Saint Matthew Island, Alaska, USA 60.36N 172.57W
24 J7 **Gloster** Mississippi, S USA 31.12N 91.01W
191 U7 **Gloucester** New South Wales, SE Australia 32.01S 152.00E
194 L12 **Gloucester** New Britain, E PNG 5.28S 148.28E
99 L21 **Gloucester** ***hist.*** Caer Glou, ***Lat.*** Glevum. C England, UK 51.52N 2.13W
21 P10 **Gloucester** Massachusetts, NE USA 42.36N 70.36W
23 X6 **Gloucester** Virginia, NE USA 37.23N 76.30W
99 K21 **Gloucestershire** *cultural region* C England, UK
33 T14 **Glouster** Ohio, N USA 39.30N 82.04W
44 H3 **Glovers Reef** *reef* E Belize
20 K10 **Gloversville** New York, NE USA 43.03N 74.20W
112 K12 **Głowno** Łódź, C Poland 51.58N 19.43E
113 H16 **Głubczyce** ***Ger.*** Leobschütz. Opolskie, S Poland 50.11N 17.49E
130 L11 **Glubokiy** Rostovskaya Oblast', SW Russian Federation 48.34N 40.16E
151 W9 **Glubokoye** Vostochnyy Kazakhstan, E Kazakhstan 50.10N 82.16E
Glubokoye *see* Hlybokaye
113 H16 **Głuchołazy** ***Ger.*** Ziegenhais. Opolskie, S Poland 50.18N 17.22E
102 I9 **Glückstadt** Schleswig-Holstein, N Germany 53.47N 9.25E
Glukhov *see* Hlukhiv
Glushkevichi *see* Hlushkavichy
Glusk/Glussk *see* Hlusk
Glybokaya *see* Hlyboka
97 F21 **Glyngøre** Viborg, NW Denmark 56.45N 8.55E
131 Q9 **Gmelinka** Volgogradskaya Oblast', SW Russian Federation 50.50N 46.51E
111 R8 **Gmünd** Kärnten, S Austria 46.56N 13.32E
111 U2 **Gmünd** Niederösterreich, N Austria 48.45N 14.57E
Gmünd *see* Schwäbisch Gmünd
111 S5 **Gmunden** Oberösterreich, N Austria 47.54N 13.46E
Gmundner See *see* Traunsee
96 N10 **Gnarp** Gävleborg, C Sweden 62.03N 17.19E
111 W8 **Gnas** Steiermark, SE Austria 46.53N 15.48E
Gnesen *see* Gniezno
97 O16 **Gnesta** Södermanland, C Sweden 59.02N 17.19E
112 H11 **Gniezno** ***Ger.*** Gnesen. Wielkolpolskie, C Poland 52.33N 17.35E
115 O17 **Gnjilane** ***var.*** Gilani, ***Alb.*** Gjilan. Serbia, S Yugoslavia 42.27N 21.28E
97 K20 **Gnosjö** Jönköping, S Sweden 57.22N 13.43E
161 E17 **Goa** ***prev.*** Old Goa, Vela Goa, Velha Goa. Goa, W India 15.31N 73.55E
161 E17 **Goa** ***var.*** Old Goa. ◈ *state* W India
44 H7 **Goascorán, Río** ≈ El Salvador/Honduras
79 O16 **Goaso** ***var.*** Gawso. W Ghana 6.49N 2.27W
83 K14 **Goba** ***It.*** Oromo, S Ethiopia 7.02N 39.58E
85 C20 **Gobabed** Erongo, W Namibia 23.36S 15.03E
85 E19 **Gobabis** Omaheke, E Namibia 22.24S 18.58E
Gobannium *see* Abergavenny
66 M7 **Goban Spur** *undersea feature* NW Atlantic Ocean
Gobbà *see* Goba
65 H21 **Gobernador Gregores** Santa Cruz, S Argentina 48.43S 70.21W
63 F14 **Gobernador Ingeniero Virasoro** Corrientes, NE Argentina
168 L12 **Gobi** *desert* China/Mongolia
170 G16 **Gobō** Wakayama, Honshū, SW Japan 33.52N 135.09E
103 D14 **Goch** Nordrhein-Westfalen, W Germany 51.41N 6.10E
85 E20 **Gochas** Hardap, S Namibia 24.54S 18.43E
161 I14 **Godāvari** ***var.*** Godavari. ≈ C India
161 L16 **Godāvari, Mouths of the** *delta* E India
13 V5 **Godbout** Quebec, SE Canada 49.19N 67.37W
13 U5 **Godbout** ≈ Quebec, SE Canada
13 U5 **Godbout Est** ≈ Quebec, SE Canada
29 N6 **Goddard** Kansas, C USA 37.39N 97.34W
12 E15 **Goderich** Ontario, S Canada 43.45N 81.42W
Godhavn *see* Qeqertarsuaq
160 E10 **Godhra** Gujarāt, W India 22.49N 73.40E
Göding *see* Hodonín
113 K22 **Gödöllő** Pest, N Hungary 47.36N 19.19E
64 H11 **Godoy Cruz** Mendoza, W Argentina 32.58S 68.49W
9 Y11 **Gods** ≈ Manitoba, C Canada
9 Y13 **Gods Lake** Manitoba, C Canada 54.29N 94.21W
9 X13 **Gods Lake** ◎ Manitoba, C Canada
Godthaab/Godthåb *see* Nuuk
Godwin Austen, Mount *see* K2
Goede Hoop, Kaap de *see* Good Hope, Cape of
Goedgegun *see* Nhlangano
Goeie Hoop, Kaap die *see* Good Hope, Cape of
11 O7 **Goélands, Lac aux** ◎ Quebec, SE Canada
100 E13 **Goeree** *island* SW Netherlands
101 F15 **Goes** Zeeland, SW Netherlands 51.30N 3.55E
Goettingen *see* Göttingen
21 O10 **Goffstown** New Hampshire, NE USA 43.01N 71.34W
12 E8 **Gogama** Ontario, S Canada 47.42N 81.43W
170 Ee12 **Gō-gawa** ≈ Honshū, SW Japan
32 L3 **Gogebic, Lake** ◎ Michigan, N USA
32 K3 **Gogebic Range** *hill range* Michigan/Wisconsin, N USA
143 V13 **Gogi, Mount** ***Arm.*** Gogi Lerr, ***Az.*** Küküdağ. ▲ Armenia/Azerbaijan 39.33N 45.35E
128 F12 **Gogland, Ostrov** *island* NW Russian Federation
113 I15 **Gogolin** Opolskie, S Poland 50.28N 18.04E
Gogonou *see* Gogounou
79 S14 **Gogounou** ***var.*** Gogonou. N Benin 10.49N 2.49E
158 I10 **Gohāna** Haryāna, N India 29.06N 76.43E
61 K18 **Goianésia** Goiás, C Brazil 15.21S 49.01W
61 K18 **Goiânia** ***prev.*** Goyania. *state capital* Goiás, C Brazil 16.43S 49.18W
61 K18 **Goiás** Goiás, C Brazil 15.57S 50.07W
61 J18 **Goiás** ***off.*** Estado de Goiás; ***prev.*** Goiaz, Goyaz. ◈ *state* C Brazil
Goiaz *see* Goiás
165 R14 **Goinsargoin** Xizang Zizhiqu, W China 31.55N 98.04E
62 H10 **Goio-Erê** Paraná, SW Brazil 24.08S 53.07W
101 I15 **Goirle** Noord-Brabant, S Netherlands 51.31N 5.04E
106 H8 **Góis** Coimbra, N Portugal 40.10N 8.06W
171 Gg16 **Gojō** ***var.*** Gozyô. Nara, Honshū, SW Japan 34.21N 135.42E
171 M10 **Gojōme** Akita, Honshū, NW Japan 39.55N 140.07E
155 U9 **Gojra** Punjab, E Pakistan 31.09N 72.39E
170 D15 **Gokase-gawa** ≈ Kyūshū, SW Japan
142 A11 **Gökçeada** ***var.*** Imroz Adası, ***Gk.*** Imbros. *island* NW Turkey
Gökçeada *see* İmroz
Gökdepe *see* Geok-Tepe
142 I10 **Gökırmak** ≈ N Turkey
Goklenkuy, Solonchak *see* Geklengkui, Solonchak
142 C16 **Gökova Körfezi** *gulf* SW Turkey
142 K15 **Göksu** ≈ S Turkey
142 L15 **Göksun** Kahramanmaraş, C Turkey 38.03N 36.30E
142 I17 **Göksu Nehri** ≈ S Turkey
85 J16 **Gokwe** Midlands, NW Zimbabwe 18.10S 28.54E
96 F13 **Gol** Buskerud, S Norway 60.42N 8.57E
159 X12 **Golāghāt** Assam, NE India 26.31N 93.54E
112 H10 **Gołańcz** Wielkopolskie, C Poland 52.57N 17.17E
144 G8 **Golan Heights** ***Ar.*** Al Jawlān, ***Heb.*** HaGolan. ▲▲ SW Syria
Golārā *see* Ārān
Golaya Pristan *see* Hola Prystan'
149 T11 **Golbāf** Kermān, C Iran 29.51N 57.43E
142 M15 **Gölbaşı** Adıyaman, S Turkey 37.46N 37.40E
111 P9 **Gölbner** ▲ SW Austria 46.51N 12.31E
32 M17 **Golconda** Illinois, N USA 37.18N 88.30W
37 T3 **Golconda** Nevada, W USA 40.56N 117.29W
142 E11 **Gölcük** Kocaeli, NW Turkey 40.42N 29.50E
110 I7 **Goldach** Sankt Gallen, NE Switzerland 47.28N 9.28E
112 N7 **Gołdap** ***Ger.*** Goldap. Warmińsko-Mazurskie, NE Poland 54.18N 22.23E
34 E15 **Gold Beach** Oregon, NW USA 42.24N 124.25W
Goldberg *see* Złotoryja
70 D11 **Gold Coast** *coastal region* S Ghana
191 V3 **Gold Coast** *cultural region* Queensland, E Australia
41 R10 **Gold Creek** Alaska, USA 62.48N 149.40W
9 O16 **Golden** British Columbia, SW Canada 51.19N 116.58W
39 T4 **Golden** Colorado, C USA 39.40N 105.12W
192 I13 **Golden Bay** *bay* South Island, NZ
29 R7 **Golden City** Missouri, C USA 37.23N 94.05W
34 I11 **Goldendale** Washington, NW USA 45.49N 120.49W
Goldener Tisch *see* Zlatý Stôl
46 L13 **Golden Grove** E Jamaica 17.55N 76.16W
12 J12 **Golden Lake** ◎ Ontario, SE Canada
24 K10 **Golden Meadow** Louisiana, S USA 29.22N 90.15W
47 V10 **Golden Rock** ✕ (Basseterre) Saint Kitts, Saint Kitts and Nevis 17.16N 62.43W
Golden State, The *see* California
85 K16 **Golden Valley** Mashonaland West, N Zimbabwe 18.15S 29.46E
37 U9 **Goldfield** Nevada, W USA 37.40N 117.13W
Goldingen *see* Kuldīga
Goldmarkt *see* Zlatna
8 K17 **Gold River** Vancouver Island, British Columbia, SW Canada 49.48N 126.01W
23 V10 **Goldsboro** North Carolina, SE USA 35.22N 77.59W
26 M8 **Goldsmith** Texas, SW USA 31.58N 102.36W
27 R8 **Goldthwaite** Texas, SW USA 31.27N 98.34W
143 R11 **Göle** Ardahan, NE Turkey 40.46N 42.36E
Golema Ada *see* Ostrovo
116 H9 **Golema Planina** ▲▲ W Bulgaria
116 F9 **Golemi Vrŭkh** ▲ W Bulgaria 42.41N 22.38E
112 D8 **Goleniów** ***Ger.*** Gollnow. Zachodniopomorskie, NW Poland 53.33N 14.48E
149 R3 **Golestān** ◈ *province* N Iran
37 Q14 **Goleta** California, W USA 34.25N 119.51W
45 O16 **Golfito** Puntarenas, SE Costa Rica 8.37N 83.07W
27 T13 **Goliad** Texas, SW USA 28.40N 97.23W
115 L14 **Golija** ▲▲ SW Yugoslavia
115 O16 **Goljak** ▲▲ SE Yugoslavia
142 M12 **Gölköy** Ordu, N Turkey 40.42N 37.37E
Gollel *see* Lavumisa
111 X3 **Göllersbach** ≈ NE Austria
Gollnow *see* Goleniów
Golmo *see* Golmud
165 P10 **Golmud** ***var.*** Ge'e'mu, Golmo, ***Chin.*** Ko-erh-mu. Qinghai, C China 36.22N 94.56E
105 Y14 **Golo** ≈ Corse, France, C Mediterranean Sea
Golovanevsk *see* Holovanivs'k
Golovchin *see* Halowchyn
41 N9 **Golovin** Alaska, USA 64.33N 162.54W
148 M7 **Golpāyegān** ***var.*** Gulpaigan. Eşfahān, W Iran 33.22N 50.18E
Golshan *see* Ţabas
Gol'shany *see* Hal'shany
98 J7 **Golspie** N Scotland, UK 57.58N 3.55W
114 O11 **Golubac** Serbia, NE Yugoslavia 44.38N 21.36E
112 J9 **Golub-Dobrzyń** Kujawski-pomorskie, C Poland 53.06N 19.03E
151 S7 **Golubovka** Pavlodar, N Kazakhstan 53.07N 74.11E
84 B11 **Golungo Alto** Cuanza Norte, NW Angola 9.10S 14.45E
116 M8 **Golyama Kamchiya** ≈ E Bulgaria
116 L8 **Golyama Reka** ≈ N Bulgaria
116 H11 **Golyama Syutkya** ▲ SW Bulgaria 41.55N 24.03E
116 I12 **Golyam Perelik** ▲ S Bulgaria 41.37N 24.34E
116 I11 **Golyam Persenk** ▲ S Bulgaria 41.50N 24.33E
125 F12 **Golyshmanovo** Tyumenskaya Oblast', C Russian Federation 56.22N 68.25E
81 P19 **Goma** Nord Kivu, NE Dem. Rep. Congo (Zaire) 1.36S 29.07E
171 Gg16 **Gomadan-zan** ▲ Honshū, SW Japan 34.03N 135.34E
Gomati *see* Gumti
79 X14 **Gombe** Gombe, E Nigeria 10.19N 11.02E
69 U10 **Gombe** ***var.*** Igombe. ≈ E Tanzania
79 Y14 **Gombi** Adamawa, E Nigeria 10.07N 12.45E
Gombroon *see* Bandar-e 'Abbās
Gomel' *see* Homyel'
Gomel'skaya Oblast' *see* Homyel'skaya Voblasts'
66 N11 **Gomera** *island* Islas Canarias, Spain, NE Atlantic Ocean
42 I5 **Gómez Farias** Chihuahua, N Mexico 29.25N 107.46W
42 L8 **Gómez Palacio** Durango, C Mexico 25.39N 103.30W
164 J13 **Gomo** Xizang Zizhiqu, W China 33.37N 86.40E
175 T11 **Gomumu, Pulau** *see* Gomumu, Pulau
149 T6 **Gonābād** ***var.*** Gunabad. Khorāsān, NE Iran 36.21N 58.38E
46 L8 **Gonaïves** ***var.*** Les Gonaïves. N Haiti 19.26N 72.40W
126 M13 **Gonam** ≈ NE Russian Federation
46 L9 **Gonâve, Canal de la** ***var.*** Canal de Sud. *channel* N Caribbean Sea
46 K9 **Gonâve, Golfe de la** *gulf* N Caribbean Sea
Gonāveh *see* Bandar-e Gonāveh
46 K9 **Gonâve, Île de la** *island* C Haiti
Gonbadān *see* Dow Gonbadān
149 Q3 **Gonbad-e Kāvūs** ***var.*** Gunbad-i-Qawus. Golestān, N Iran 37.15N 55.10E
158 M12 **Gonda** Uttar Pradesh, N India 27.07N 81.58E
Gondar *see* Gonder
82 I11 **Gonder** ***var.*** Gondar. Amhara, N Ethiopia 12.35N 37.27E
80 J13 **Gondey** Moyen-Chari, S Chad 9.07N 19.10E
160 J12 **Gondia** Mahārāshtra, C India 21.27N 80.12E
106 G6 **Gondomar** Porto, NW Portugal 41.10N 8.34W
142 C12 **Gönen** Balıkesir, W Turkey 40.06N 27.39E
142 C12 **Gönen Çayı** ≈ NW Turkey
165 O15 **Gongbo'gyamda** Xizang Zizhiqu, W China 30.03N 93.10E
165 N16 **Gonggar** Xizang Zizhiqu, W China 29.18N 90.56E
166 G9 **Gongga Shan** ▲ C China 29.49N 101.55E
165 T10 **Gonghe** Qinghai, C China 36.22N 100.44E
164 I5 **Gongliu** ***var.*** Tokkuztara. Xinjiang Uygur Zizhiqu, NW China 43.29N 82.16E
79 W14 **Gongola** ≈ E Nigeria
Gongoleh State *see* Jonglei
191 P5 **Gongolgon** New South Wales, SE Australia 30.19S 146.57E
165 Q6 **Gongpoquan** Gansu, N China 41.45N 100.27E
166 I10 **Gongxian** ***var.*** Gong Xian. Sichuan, C China 28.25N 104.51E
163 V10 **Gongzhuling** *prev.* Huaide. Jilin, NE China 43.30N 124.48E
165 S14 **Gonjo** Xizang Zizhiqu, W China 30.51N 98.16E
109 B20 **Gonnesa** Sardegna, Italy, C Mediterranean Sea 39.15N 8.27E
Gonni/Gónnos *see* Gónnoi
117 F15 **Gónnoi** ***var.*** Gonni, Gónnos; ***prev.*** Derelí. Thessalía, C Greece 39.52N 22.27E
172 N9 **Gonohe** Aomori, Honshū, C Japan 40.34N 141.18E
170 Cc11 **Gōnoura** Nagasaki, Iki, SW Japan 33.44N 129.41E
37 O11 **Gonzales** California, W USA 36.30N 121.26W
24 J9 **Gonzales** Louisiana, S USA 30.14N 90.55W
27 T12 **Gonzales** Texas, SW USA 29.30N 97.27W
43 P11 **González** Tamaulipas, C Mexico 22.52N 98.25W
23 V6 **Goochland** Virginia, NE USA 37.40N 77.53W
195 N16 **Goodenough Bay** *inlet* SE PNG
205 X14 **Goodenough, Cape** *headland* Antarctica 66.15S 126.34E
195 N15 **Goodenough Island** ***var.*** Morata. *island* SE PNG
Good Hope *see* Fort Good Hope
41 N8 **Goodhope Bay** *bay* Alaska, USA
85 D26 **Good Hope, Cape of** ***Afr.*** Kaap de Goede Hoop, Kaap die Goeie Hoop. *headland* SW South Africa 34.19S 18.25E
8 K10 **Good Hope Lake** British Columbia, W Canada 59.15N 129.18W
85 E23 **Goodhouse** Northern Cape, W South Africa 28.54S 18.13E
35 O15 **Gooding** Idaho, NW USA 42.56N 114.42W
28 H3 **Goodland** Kansas, C USA 39.21N 101.42W
181 Y15 **Goodlands** NW Mauritius 20.01S 57.39E
22 J8 **Goodlettsville** Tennessee, S USA 36.19N 86.42W
41 N13 **Goodnews** Alaska, USA 59.07N 161.35W
27 O3 **Goodnight** Texas, SW USA 35.00N 101.07W
191 Q4 **Goodooga** New South Wales, SE Australia 29.09S 147.30E
31 N4 **Goodrich** North Dakota, N USA 47.24N 100.07W
27 W10 **Goodrich** Texas, SW USA 30.36N 94.57W
31 X10 **Goodview** Minnesota, N USA 44.04N 91.42W
28 H8 **Goodwell** Oklahoma, C USA 36.36N 101.38W
99 N17 **Goole** E England, UK 53.43N 0.46W
191 O8 **Goolgowi** New South Wales, SE Australia 34.00S 145.43E
190 I10 **Goolwa** South Australia 35.31S 138.43E
189 Y11 **Goondiwindi** Queensland, E Australia 28.33S 150.22E
100 O11 **Goor** Overijssel, E Netherlands 52.13N 6.33E
Goose Bay *see* Happy Valley-Goose Bay
35 V13 **Gooseberry Creek** ≈ Wyoming, C USA
23 S14 **Goose Creek** South Carolina, SE USA 32.58N 80.01W
65 M23 **Goose Green** ***var.*** Prado del Ganso. East Falkland, Falkland Islands 51.52S 59.00W
17 G6 **Goose Lake** ***var.*** Lago dos Gansos. ◎ California/Oregon, W USA
31 Q4 **Goose River** ≈ North Dakota, N USA
159 T16 **Gopalganj** Dhaka, S Bangladesh 23.03N 89.52E
159 O12 **Gopālganj** Bihār, N India 26.28N 84.25E
Gopher State *see* Minnesota
103 I22 **Göppingen** Baden-Württemberg, SW Germany 48.42N 9.39E
112 G13 **Góra** ***Ger.*** Guhrau. Dolnośląskie, SW Poland 51.40N 16.30E
112 M12 **Góra Kalwaria** Mazowieckie, C Poland 52.00N 21.14E
159 O12 **Gorakhpur** Uttar Pradesh, N India 26.45N 83.22E
Gorany *see* Harany
115 J14 **Goražde** Federacija Bosna I Hercegovina, Bosnia and Herzegovina 43.39N 18.58E
Gorbovichi *see* Harbavichy
Gorče Petrov *see* Đorče Petrov
(0) E9 **Gorda Ridges** *undersea feature* NE Pacific Ocean
Gordiaz *see* Gardēz
80 K12 **Gordil** Vakaga, N Central African Republic 9.37N 21.42E
25 U5 **Gordon** Georgia, SE USA 32.52N 83.19W
30 K12 **Gordon** Nebraska, C USA 42.48N 102.12W
27 R7 **Gordon** Texas, SW USA 32.32N 98.21W
30 L13 **Gordon Creek** ≈ Nebraska, C USA
65 I25 **Gordon, Isla** *island* S Chile
191 O17 **Gordon, Lake** ◎ Tasmania, SE Australia
191 O17 **Gordon River** ≈ Tasmania, SE Australia
23 V5 **Gordonsville** Virginia, NE USA 38.08N 78.11W
82 H13 **Gorē** Oromo, C Ethiopia 8.08N 35.33E
193 D24 **Gore** Southland, South Island, NZ 46.06S 168.58E
80 H13 **Goré** Logone-Oriental, S Chad 7.55N 16.37E
12 D11 **Gore Bay** Manitoulin Island, Ontario, S Canada 45.54N 82.28W
27 Q5 **Goree** Texas, SW USA 33.28N 99.31W
143 O11 **Görele** Giresun, NE Turkey 41.00N 39.00E
21 N6 **Gore Mountain** ▲ Vermont, NE USA 44.55N 71.47W
41 R13 **Gore Point** *headland* Alaska, USA 59.12N 150.57W
39 R4 **Gore Range** ▲▲ Colorado, C USA
99 F19 **Gorey** ***Ir.*** Guaire. SE Ireland 52.40N 6.18W
149 R12 **Gorgāb** Kermān, S Iran
149 Q4 **Gorgān** ***var.*** Astarabad, Astrabad, Gurgan; ***prev.*** Asterābād, ***anc.*** Hyrcania. Golestān, N Iran 36.53N 54.28E
149 Q4 **Gorgān, Rūd-e** ≈ N Iran
78 I10 **Gorgol** ◈ *region* S Mauritania
108 D12 **Gorgona, Isola di** *island* Archipelago Toscano, C Italy
21 P8 **Gorham** Maine, NE USA 43.41N 70.27W
143 T10 **Gori** C Georgia 42.00N 44.07E
100 I13 **Gorinchem** ***var.*** Gorkum. Zuid-Holland, C Netherlands 51.49N 4.58E
143 V13 **Goris** SE Armenia 39.31N 46.20E
128 K16 **Goritsy** Tverskaya Oblast', W Russian Federation 57.09N 36.44E
108 J7 **Gorizia** ***Ger.*** Görz. Friuli-Venezia Giulia, NE Italy 45.55N 13.37E
118 G13 **Gorj** ◈ *county* SW Romania
111 W12 **Gorjanci** ***var.*** Uskočke Planine, Žumberak, Žumberačko Gorje, ***Ger.*** Uskokengebirge; ***prev.*** Sichelburger Gerbirge. ▲▲ Croatia/Slovenia *see also* Žumberačko Gorje
Görkau *see* Jirkov
Gorki *see* Horki
Gor'kiy *see* Nizhniy Novgorod
Gor'kiy Reservoir *see* Gor'kovskoye Vodokhranilishche
125 D9 **Gor'kovskoye Vodokhranilishche** ***Eng.*** Gor'kiy Reservoir. ⊠ W Russian Federation
Gorkum *see* Gorinchem
97 I23 **Gørlev** Vestsjælland, E Denmark 55.33N 11.13E
113 M17 **Gorlice** Małopolskie, S Poland 49.37N 21.08E
103 Q15 **Görlitz** Sachsen, E Germany 51.09N 14.57E
Görlitz *see* Zgorzelec
Gorlovka *see* Horlivka
27 R7 **Gorman** Texas, SW USA 32.12N 98.40W
23 T3 **Gormania** West Virginia, NE USA 39.16N 79.18W
Gorna Dzhumaya *see* Blagoevgrad
116 K8 **Gorna Oryakhovitsa** Veliko Tŭrnovo, N Bulgaria 43.12N 25.38E
116 J8 **Gorna Studena** Veliko Tŭrnovo, N Bulgaria 43.26N 25.21E
Gornja Mužlja *see* Mužlja
111 X9 **Gornja Radgona** ***Ger.*** Oberradkersburg. NE Slovenia 46.39N 16.00E
114 M13 **Gornji Milanovac** Serbia, C Yugoslavia 44.01N 20.26E
114 G13 **Gornji Vakuf** ***var.*** Uskoplje. Federacija Bosna I Hercegovina, W Bosnia and Herzegovina 43.55N 17.34E
126 H15 **Gorno-Altaysk** Respublika Altay, S Russian Federation 51.58N 85.55E
Gorno-Altayskaya Respublika *see* Altay, Respublika
126 K13 **Gorno-Chuyskiy** Irkutskaya Oblast', C Russian Federation 57.33N 111.38E
129 V14 **Gornozavodsk** Permskaya Oblast', NW Russian Federation 58.21N 58.24E
127 O16 **Gornozavodsk** Ostrov Sakhalin, Sakhalinskaya Oblast', SE Russian Federation 46.34N 141.52E
126 Gg15 **Gornyak** Altayskiy Kray, S Russian Federation 50.58N 81.24E
131 R8 **Gornyy** Saratovskaya Oblast', W Russian Federation 51.42N 48.26E
Gornyy Altay *see* Altay, Respublika
131 O10 **Gornyy Balykley** Volgogradskaya Oblast', SW Russian Federation 49.37N 45.03E
82 I13 **Goroch'an** ▲ W Ethiopia 9.09N 37.16E
Gorodenka *see* Horodenka
131 O3 **Gorodets** Nizhegorodskaya Oblast', W Russian Federation 56.36N 43.27E
Gorodets *see* Haradzyets
Gorodeya *see* Haradzyeya
131 P6 **Gorodishche** Penzenskaya Oblast', W Russian Federation 53.17N 45.39E
Gorodishche *see* Horodyshche
Gorodnya *see* Horodnya
Gorodok *see* Haradok
Gorodok/Gorodok Yagellonski *see* Horodok
130 M13 **Gorodovikovsk** Respublika Kalmykiya, SW Russian Federation 46.07N 41.56E
194 I12 **Goroka** Eastern Highlands, C PNG 6.03S 145.22E
Gorokhov *see* Horokhiv
131 N3 **Gorokhovets** Vladimirskaya Oblast', W Russian Federation 56.12N 42.40E
79 Q11 **Gorom-Gorom** NE Burkina 14.27N 0.13W
176 V12 **Gorong, Kepulauan** *island group* E Indonesia
85 M17 **Gorongosa** Sofala, C Mozambique 18.40S 34.03E
176 Uu12 **Gorong, Pulau** *island* Kepulauan Gorong, E Indonesia
175 R8 **Gorontalo** Sulawesi, C Indonesia 0.33N 123.04E
175 Qq8 **Gorontalo, Teluk** *bay* Sulawesi, C Indonesia
Gorontalo, Teluk *see* Tomini, Gulf of
112 L7 **Górowo Iławeckie** ***Ger.*** Landsberg. Warmińsko-Mazurskie, NE Poland, 54.18N 20.30E
100 M7 **Gorredijk** ***Fris.*** De Gordyk. Friesland, N Netherlands 53.00N 6.04E
86 C14 **Gorringe Ridge** *undersea feature* E Atlantic Ocean
100 M11 **Gorssel** Gelderland, E Netherlands 52.12N 6.13E
111 T8 **Görtschitz** ≈ S Austria
Goryn *see* Horyn'
Görz *see* Gorizia
112 E10 **Gorzów Wielkopolski** ***Ger.*** Landsberg, Landsberg an der Warthe. Lubuskie, W Poland 52.43N 15.12E
110 G9 **Göschenen** Uri, C Switzerland 46.40N 8.36E
195 N16 **Goschen Strait** *strait* SE PNG
171 Kk13 **Gosen** Niigata, Honshū, C Japan 37.43N 139.11E
191 T8 **Gosford** New South Wales, SE Australia 33.25S 151.22E
33 P11 **Goshen** Indiana, N USA 41.34N 85.49W
20 K13 **Goshen** New York, NE USA 41.24N 74.17W
Goshoba *see* Koshoba
171 Mm8 **Goshogawara** ***var.*** Gosyogawara. Aomori, Honshū, C Japan 40.46N 140.24E
152 I8 **Goshquduq Qum** ***var.*** Tosquduq Qumlari, ***Rus.*** Peski Taskuduk. *desert* W Uzbekistan
103 J14 **Goslar** Niedersachsen, C Germany 51.55N 10.25E
29 Y9 **Gosnell** Arkansas, C USA 35.57N 89.58W
114 C11 **Gospić** Lika-Senj, C Croatia 44.32N 15.21E
99 N23 **Gosport** S England, UK 50.48N 1.07W
96 D9 **Gossa** *island* S Norway
110 H7 **Gossau** Sankt Gallen, NE Switzerland 47.25N 9.16E
101 G20 **Gosselies** ***var.*** Goss'lies. Hainaut, S Belgium 50.28N 4.25E
79 P10 **Gossi** Tombouctou, C Mali 15.44N 1.19W
Goss'lies *see* Gosselies
115 N18 **Gostivar** W FYR Macedonia 41.48N 20.55E
Gostomel' *see* Hostomel'
112 G12 **Gostyń** ***var.*** Gostyn. Wielkopolskie, C Poland 51.53N 16.59E
112 K11 **Gostynin** Mazowieckie, C Poland 52.25N 19.27E
Gosyogawara *see* Goshogawara
97 J18 **Göta Älv** ≈ S Sweden
97 N17 **Göta kanal** *canal* S Sweden
97 K18 **Götaland** *cultural region* S Sweden
97 H17 **Göteborg** ***Eng.*** Gothenburg. Västra Götaland, S Sweden 57.43N 11.58E
79 X16 **Gotel Mountains** ▲▲ E Nigeria
97 K17 **Götene** Västra Götaland, S Sweden 58.31N 13.28E
Gotera *see* San Francisco
103 K16 **Gotha** Thüringen, C Germany 50.57N 10.43E
31 N15 **Gothenburg** Nebraska, C USA 40.57N 100.09W
Gothenburg *see* Göteborg
79 R12 **Gothèye** Tillabéri, SW Niger 13.52N 1.27E
Gothland *see* Gotland
97 P19 **Gotland** ***var.*** Gothland, Gottland. ◈ *county* SE Sweden
97 O18 **Gotland** *island* SE Sweden
170 B12 **Gotō-rettō** *island group* SW Japan
116 H12 **Gotse Delchev** ***prev.*** Nevrokop. Blagoevgrad, SW Bulgaria 41.35N 23.43E
97 P17 **Gotska Sandön** *island* SE Sweden
170 Ee12 **Gōtsu** ***var.*** Gôtu. Shimane, Honshū, SW Japan 35.00N 132.13E
103 I15 **Göttingen** ***var.*** Goettingen. Niedersachsen, C Germany 51.33N 9.55E
Gottland *see* Gotland
95 I16 **Gottne** Västernorrland, C Sweden 63.27N 18.25E
Gottschee *see* Kočevje
Gottwaldov *see* Zlín
Gôtu *see* Gōtsu
Goturdepe *see* Koturdepe
110 I7 **Götzis** Vorarlberg, NW Austria 47.21N 9.40E
100 H12 **Gouda** Zuid-Holland, C Netherlands 52.01N 4.42E
78 I11 **Goudiri** ***var.*** Goudiry. E Senegal 14.12N 12.40W
Goudiry *see* Goudiri
79 X12 **Goudoumaria** Diffa, S Niger 13.28N 11.15E
13 R9 **Gouffre, Rivière du** ≈ Quebec, SE Canada
67 M19 **Gough Fracture Zone** *tectonic feature* S Atlantic Ocean
67 M19 **Gough Island** *island* Tristan da Cunha, S Atlantic Ocean
13 N8 **Gouin, Réservoir** ⊠ Quebec, SE Canada
12 B10 **Goulais River** Ontario, S Canada 46.41N 84.22W
191 R9 **Goulburn** New South Wales, SE Australia 34.45S 149.43E
191 O11 **Goulburn River** ≈ Victoria, SE Australia
205 O10 **Gould Coast** *physical region* Antarctica
Goulimime *see* Guelmime
116 F13 **Gouménissa** Kentrikí Makedonía, N Greece 40.55N 22.27E
79 O10 **Goundam** Tombouctou, NW Mali 16.25N 3.41W
80 H12 **Goundi** Moyen-Chari, S Chad 9.18N 17.21E
80 G12 **Gounou-Gaya** Mayo-Kébbi, SW Chad 9.37N 15.30E
79 O12 **Gourci** ***var.*** Gourcy. NW Burkina 13.14N 2.22W
Gourcy *see* Gourci
104 M13 **Gourdon** Lot, S France 44.45N 1.22E
79 W11 **Gouré** Zinder, SE Niger 13.58N 10.16E
104 G6 **Gourin** Morbihan, NW France 48.07N 3.37W
79 P10 **Gourma-Rharous** Tombouctou, C Mali 16.54N 1.55W
105 N4 **Gournay-en-Bray** Seine-Maritime, N France 49.29N 1.42E
80 J6 **Gouro** Borkou-Ennedi-Tibesti, N Chad 19.26N 19.36E
106 H8 **Gouveia** Guarda, N Portugal 40.28N 7.34W
20 I7 **Gouverneur** New York, NE USA 44.20N 75.27W
101 L21 **Gouvy** Luxembourg, E Belgium 50.10N 5.55E
47 R14 **Gouyave** ***var.*** Charlotte Town. NW Grenada 12.10N 61.43W
Goverla, Gora *see* Hoverla, Hora

◆ Country
● Country Capital
◇ Dependent Territory
○ Dependent Territory Capital
◈ Administrative Region
✕ International Airport
▲ Mountain
▲▲ Mountain Range
Volcano
≈ River
◎ Lake
⊠ Reservoir

Governador Valadares – Grenada Basin

61 N20 **Governador Valadares** Minas Gerais, SE Brazil 18.51S 41.57W
179 Rr16 **Governor Generoso** Mindanao, S Philippines 6.36N 126.06E
46 I2 **Governor's Harbour** Eleuthera Island, C Bahamas 25.11N 76.15W
168 F9 **Govĭ-Altay** ◐ province SW Mongolia
168 I10 **Govĭ Altayn Nuruu** ▲▲ S Mongolia
160 L9 **Govind Ballabh Pant Sāgar** ⊡ C India
158 I7 **Govind Sāgar** ⊡ NE India
153 N14 **Govurdak** *Turkm.* Gowurdak; *prev.* Guardak. Lebapskiy Velayat, E Turkmenistan 37.50N 66.06E
20 D11 **Gowanda** New York, NE USA 42.25N 78.55W
154 J10 **Gowd-e Zereh, Dasht-e** *var.* Guad-i-Zirreh. *marsh* SW Afghanistan
12 F8 **Gowganda** Ontario, S Canada 47.39N 80.43W
12 G8 **Gowganda Lake** ◎ Ontario, S Canada
31 U13 **Gowrie** Iowa, C USA 42.16N 94.17W
Gowurdak *see* Govurdak
63 C15 **Goya** Corrientes, NE Argentina 29.10S 59.15W
Goyania *see* Goiânia
143 X11 **Göyçay** *Rus.* Geokchay. C Azerbaijan 40.38N 47.44E
Goymat *see* Koymat
Goymatdag *see* Koymatdag, Gory
142 F12 **Göynük** Bolu, NW Turkey 40.24N 30.45E
172 N12 **Goyō-san** ▲ Honshū, C Japan 39.12N 141.40E
80 K11 **Goz Beïda** Ouaddaï, SE Chad 12.06N 21.22E
164 H11 **Gozha Co** ◎ W China
123 J15 **Gozo** *Malt.* Ghawdex. *island* N Malta
82 H9 **Göz Regeb** Kassala, NE Sudan 16.03N 35.33E
Gozyô *see* Gojō
85 H25 **Graaff-Reinet** Eastern Cape, S South Africa 32.16S 24.31E
Graasten *see* Gråsten
78 L17 **Grabo** SW Ivory Coast 4.57N 7.30W
114 P11 **Grabovica** Serbia, E Yugoslavia 44.30N 22.29E
112 I13 **Grabów nad Prosną** Wielkopolskie, C Poland 51.30N 18.06E
110 I8 **Grabs** Sankt Gallen, NE Switzerland 47.10N 9.27E
114 D12 **Gračac** Zadar, C Croatia 44.18N 15.52E
114 I11 **Gračanica** Federacija Bosna I Hercegovina, NE Bosnia and Herzegovina 44.41N 18.20E
12 L11 **Gracefield** Quebec, SE Canada 46.06N 76.03W
101 K19 **Grâce-Hollogne** Liège, E Belgium 50.38N 5.30E
25 R8 **Graceville** Florida, SE USA 30.57N 85.31W
31 R8 **Graceville** Minnesota, N USA 45.34N 96.25W
44 G6 **Gracias** Lempira, W Honduras 14.34N 88.34W
Gracias *see* Lempira
44 L5 **Gracias a Dios** ◐ *department* E Honduras
45 O6 **Gracias a Dios, Cabo de** *headland* Honduras/Nicaragua 15.00N 83.10W
66 O2 **Graciosa** *var.* Ilha Graciosa. *island* Azores, Portugal, NE Atlantic Ocean
66 Q11 **Graciosa** *island* Islas Canarias, Spain, NE Atlantic Ocean
Graciosa, Ilha *see* Graciosa
114 I11 **Gradačac** Federacija Bosna I Hercegovina, N Bosnia and Herzegovina 44.51N 18.24E
61 J15 **Gradaús, Serra dos** ▲▲ C Brazil
106 L3 **Gradefes** Castilla-León, N Spain 42.37N 5.13W
Gradiška *see* Bosanska Gradiška
Gradizhsk *see* Hradyz'k
108 J7 **Grado** Friuli-Venezia Giulia, NE Italy 45.41N 13.24E
106 K2 **Grado** Asturias, N Spain 43.22N 6.04W
115 P19 **Gradsko** C FYR Macedonia 41.34N 21.56E
39 V11 **Grady** New Mexico, SW USA 34.49N 103.19W
31 T12 **Graettinger** Iowa, C USA 43.14N 94.45W
103 M23 **Grafing** Bayern, SE Germany 48.01N 11.57E
27 S6 **Graford** Texas, SW USA 32.56N 98.15W
191 V5 **Grafton** New South Wales, SE Australia 29.41S 152.55E
31 Q3 **Grafton** North Dakota, N USA 48.24N 97.24W
23 S3 **Grafton** West Virginia, NE USA 39.20N 80.01W
23 T9 **Graham** North Carolina, SE USA 36.04N 79.24W
27 R6 **Graham** Texas, SW USA 33.06N 98.34W
Graham Bell Island *see* Greem-Bell, Ostrov
8 I13 **Graham Island** *island* Queen Charlotte Islands, British Columbia, SW Canada
21 S6 **Graham Lake** ◎ Maine, NE USA
204 H4 **Graham Land** *physical region* Antarctica
39 N15 **Graham, Mount** ▲ Arizona, SW USA 32.42N 109.52W
Grahamstad *see* Grahamstown
85 I25 **Grahamstown** *Afr.* Grahamstad. Eastern Cape, S South Africa 33.18S 26.31E
Grahovo *see* Bosansko Grahovo
70 C11 **Grain Coast** *coastal region* S Liberia
174 Mm16 **Grajagan** Jawa, S Indonesia 8.33S 114.13E
174 Mm16 **Grajagan, Teluk** *bay* Jawa, S Indonesia
61 L14 **Grajaú** Maranhão, E Brazil 5.49S 45.12W
60 M13 **Grajaú, Rio** ~ NE Brazil
112 O8 **Grajewo** Podlaskie, NE Poland 53.38N 22.25E
97 F24 **Gram** Sønderjylland, SW Denmark 55.18N 9.03E
105 N13 **Gramat** Lot, S France 44.45N 1.45E
24 H5 **Grambling** Louisiana, S USA 32.31N 92.43W
117 C14 **Grámmos** ▲▲ Albania/Greece
98 I9 **Grampian Mountains** ▲▲ C Scotland, UK
190 L12 **Grampians, The** ▲▲ Victoria, SE Australia
100 O9 **Gramsbergen** Overijssel, E Netherlands 52.37N 6.39E
115 L21 **Gramsh** *var.* Gramshi. Elbasan, C Albania 40.52N 20.12E
Gramshi *see* Gramsh
Gran *see* Hron, Slovakia
Gran *see* Esztergom, N Hungary
56 F11 **Granada** Meta, C Colombia 3.36N 73.44W
44 J10 **Granada** Granada, SW Nicaragua 11.55N 85.58W
107 N14 **Granada** Andalucía, S Spain 37.13N 3.40W
39 W6 **Granada** Colorado, C USA 38.00N 102.18W
44 J11 **Granada** ◐ *department* SW Nicaragua
107 N14 **Granada** ◐ *province* Andalucía, S Spain
65 I21 **Gran Altiplanicie Central** *plain* S Argentina
99 E17 **Granard** *Ir.* Gránard. C Ireland 53.46N 7.30W
65 J20 **Gran Bajo** *basin* S Argentina
65 J15 **Gran Bajo del Gualicho** *basin* E Argentina
65 I21 **Gran Bajo de San Julián** *basin* SE Argentina
27 S7 **Granbury** Texas, SW USA 32.26N 97.47W
13 P12 **Granby** Quebec, SE Canada 45.24N 72.40W
29 S8 **Granby** Missouri, C USA 36.55N 94.14W
39 S3 **Granby, Lake** ⊡ Colorado, C USA
66 O12 **Gran Canaria** *var.* Grand Canary. *island* Islas Canarias, Spain, NE Atlantic Ocean
49 T11 **Gran Chaco** *var.* Chaco. *lowland plain* South America
47 R14 **Grand Anse** SW Grenada 12.01N 61.45W
Grand-Anse *see* Portsmouth
46 G1 **Grand Bahama Island** *island* N Bahamas
Grand Balé *see* Tui
105 U7 **Grand Ballon** *Ger.* Ballon de Guebwiller. ▲ NE France 47.53N 7.06E
11 T13 **Grand Bank** Newfoundland, SE Canada 47.04N 55.46W
66 I7 **Grand Banks of Newfoundland** *undersea feature* NW Atlantic Ocean
Grand Bassa *see* Buchanan
79 N17 **Grand-Bassam** *var.* Bassam. SE Ivory Coast 5.13N 3.46W
12 E16 **Grand Bend** Ontario, S Canada 43.17N 81.46W
78 L17 **Grand-Bérébi** *var.* Grand-Béréby. SW Ivory Coast 4.37N 6.55W
Grand-Béréby *see* Grand-Bérébi
47 X11 **Grand-Bourg** Marie-Galante, SE Guadeloupe 15.53N 61.18W
46 M6 **Grand Caicos** *var.* Middle Caicos. *island* C Turks and Caicos Islands
12 K12 **Grand Calumet, Île du** *island* Quebec, SE Canada
99 E18 **Grand Canal** *Ir.* An Chanáil Mhór. *canal* C Ireland
Grand Canary *see* Gran Canaria
38 K10 **Grand Canyon** Arizona, SW USA 36.01N 112.10W
38 J9 **Grand Canyon** *canyon* Arizona, SW USA
Grand Canyon State *see* Arizona
46 D8 **Grand Cayman** *island* SW Cayman Islands
9 R14 **Grand Centre** Alberta, SW Canada 54.25N 110.13W
78 L17 **Grand Cess** SE Liberia 4.36N 8.12W
110 D12 **Grand Combin** ▲ S Switzerland 45.58N 7.27E
34 K8 **Grand Coulee** Washington, NW USA 47.56N 119.00W
34 J8 **Grand Coulee** *valley* Washington, NW USA
47 X5 **Grand Cul-de-Sac Marin** *bay* N Guadeloupe
Grand Duchy of Luxembourg *see* Luxembourg
65 I22 **Grande, Bahía** *bay* S Argentina
9 N14 **Grande Cache** Alberta, W Canada 53.52N 119.07W
105 U12 **Grande Casse** ▲ E France 45.22N 6.50E
180 G12 **Grande Comore** *var.* Njazidja, Great Comoro. *island* NW Comoros
63 G18 **Grande, Cuchilla** *hill range* E Uruguay
47 S5 **Grande de Añasco, Río** ~ W Puerto Rico
Grande de Chiloé, Isla *see* Chiloé, Isla de
60 J12 **Grande de Gurupá, Ilha** *river island* NE Brazil
59 K21 **Grande de Lipez, Río** ~ SW Bolivia
47 U6 **Grande de Loíza, Río** ~ E Puerto Rico
47 T5 **Grande de Manatí, Río** ~ C Puerto Rico
44 L9 **Grande de Matagalpa, Río** ~ C Nicaragua
42 K12 **Grande de Santiago, Río** *var.* Santiago. ~ C Mexico
45 O15 **Grande de Térraba, Río** *var.* Río Térraba. ~ SE Costa Rica
10 J9 **Grande Deux, Réservoir la** ⊡ Quebec, E Canada
62 O10 **Grande, Ilha** *island* SE Brazil
9 O13 **Grande Prairie** Alberta, W Canada 55.10N 118.52W
76 I8 **Grand Erg Occidental** *desert* W Algeria
76 L9 **Grand Erg Oriental** *desert* Algeria/Tunisia
61 J20 **Grande, Rio** ~ S Brazil
2 F15 **Grande, Rio** *var.* Río Bravo, *Sp.* Río Bravo del Norte, Bravo del Norte. ~ Mexico/USA
59 M18 **Grande, Río** ~ C Bolivia
13 Y7 **Grande-Rivière** Quebec, SE Canada 48.27N 64.37W
13 Y6 **Grande Rivière** ~ Quebec, SE Canada
46 M8 **Grande-Rivière-du-Nord** N Haiti 19.28N 72.07W
64 K9 **Grande, Salina** *var.* Gran Salitral. *salt lake* C Argentina
13 S7 **Grandes-Bergeronnes** Quebec, SE Canada 48.16N 69.32W
49 W6 **Grande, Serra** ▲▲ W Brazil
42 K4 **Grande, Sierra** ▲▲ N Mexico
105 S12 **Grandes Rousses** ▲▲ E France
65 K17 **Grandes, Salinas** *salt lake* E Argentina
47 Y5 **Grande Terre** *island* E West Indies
13 X5 **Grande-Vallée** Quebec, SE Canada 49.12N 65.08W
47 Y5 **Grande Vigie, Pointe de la** *headland* Grande Terre, N Guadeloupe 16.31N 61.27W
11 N14 **Grand Falls** New Brunswick, SE Canada 47.01N 67.46W
11 T11 **Grand Falls** Newfoundland, SE Canada 48.57N 55.48W
26 L9 **Grandfalls** Texas, SW USA 31.20N 102.51W
23 P9 **Grandfather Mountain** ▲ North Carolina, SE USA 36.06N 81.48W
28 L13 **Grandfield** Oklahoma, C USA 34.15N 98.40W
9 N17 **Grand Forks** British Columbia, SW Canada 49.01N 118.30W
31 R4 **Grand Forks** North Dakota, N USA 47.54N 97.02W
33 O9 **Grand Haven** Michigan, N USA 43.03N 86.13W
Grandichi *see* Hrandzichy
31 P15 **Grand Island** Nebraska, C USA 40.55N 98.20W
33 O3 **Grand Island** *island* Michigan, N USA
24 K10 **Grand Isle** Louisiana, S USA 29.12N 90.00W
67 A23 **Grand Jason** *island* Jason Islands, NW Falkland Islands
39 P5 **Grand Junction** Colorado, C USA 39.03N 108.33W
22 F10 **Grand Junction** Tennessee, S USA 35.03N 89.11W
12 J9 **Grand-Lac-Victoria** Quebec, SE Canada 47.33N 77.28W
12 J9 **Grand lac Victoria** ◎ Quebec, SE Canada
79 N17 **Grand-Lahou** *var.* Grand Lahu. S Ivory Coast 5.09N 5.01W
Grand Lahu *see* Grand-Lahou
39 S3 **Grand Lake** Colorado, C USA 40.15N 105.49W
11 S11 **Grand Lake** ◎ Newfoundland, E Canada
24 G9 **Grand Lake** ◎ Louisiana, S USA
33 R5 **Grand Lake** ◎ Michigan, N USA
33 Q13 **Grand Lake** ⊡ Ohio, N USA
29 R9 **Grand Lake O' The Cherokees** *var.* Lake O' The Cherokees. ⊡ Oklahoma, C USA
33 Q9 **Grand Ledge** Michigan, N USA 42.45N 84.45W
104 I8 **Grand-Lieu, Lac de** ◎ NW France
21 U6 **Grand Manan Channel** *channel* Canada/USA
11 O15 **Grand Manan Island** *island* New Brunswick, SE Canada
31 Y4 **Grand Marais** Minnesota, N USA 47.45N 90.19W
13 P10 **Grand-Mère** Quebec, SE Canada 46.36N 72.41W
39 P5 **Grand Mesa** ▲▲ Colorado, C USA
110 C10 **Grand Muveran** ▲ W Switzerland 46.16N 7.12E
106 G12 **Grândola** Setúbal, S Portugal 38.10N 8.34W
Grand Paradis *see* Gran Paradiso
197 G4 **Grand Passage** *passage* N New Caledonia
79 R16 **Grand-Popo** S Benin 6.19N 1.49E
31 Z3 **Grand Portage** Minnesota, N USA 48.00N 89.36W
27 T6 **Grand Prairie** Texas, SW USA 32.45N 97.00W
9 W14 **Grand Rapids** Manitoba, C Canada 53.12N 99.19W
33 P9 **Grand Rapids** Michigan, N USA 42.57N 86.40W
31 V5 **Grand Rapids** Minnesota, N USA 47.14N 93.31W
197 G5 **Grand Récif de Koumac** *reef* W New Caledonia
197 J8 **Grand Récif Sud** *reef* S New Caledonia
12 L10 **Grand-Remous** Quebec, SE Canada 46.36N 75.53W
12 F15 **Grand River** ~ Ontario, S Canada
33 P9 **Grand River** ~ Michigan, N USA
29 T3 **Grand River** ~ Missouri, C USA
30 M7 **Grand River** ~ South Dakota, N USA
47 Q11 **Grand' Rivière** N Martinique 14.51N 61.12W
34 F11 **Grand Ronde** Oregon, NW USA 45.03N 123.43W
34 L11 **Grand Ronde River** ~ Oregon/Washington, NW USA
Grand-Saint-Bernard, Col du *see* Great Saint Bernard Pass
27 V6 **Grand Saline** Texas, SW USA 32.40N 95.42W
57 X10 **Grand-Santi** W French Guiana 4.19N 54.24W
Grandsee *see* Grandson
110 B9 **Grandson** *prev.* Grandsee. Vaud, W Switzerland 46.49N 6.39E
180 J16 **Grand Sœur** *island* Les Sœurs, NE Seychelles
35 S14 **Grand Teton** ▲ Wyoming, C USA 43.44N 110.48W
33 P5 **Grand Traverse Bay** *lake bay* Michigan, N USA
47 N6 **Grand Turk** ○ (Turks and Caicos Islands) Grand Turk Island, S Turks and Caicos Islands 21.24N 71.08W
47 N6 **Grand Turk Island** *island* SE Turks and Caicos Islands
105 S13 **Grand Veymont** ▲ E France 44.51N 5.32E
9 W15 **Grandview** Manitoba, S Canada 51.10N 100.40W
29 R4 **Grandview** Missouri, C USA 38.53N 94.31W
38 I10 **Grand Wash Cliffs** *cliff* Arizona, SW USA
12 J8 **Granet, Lac** ◎ Quebec, SE Canada
97 L14 **Grangärde** Dalarna, C Sweden 60.15N 15.00E
46 H12 **Grange Hill** W Jamaica 18.18N 78.10W
98 J12 **Grangemouth** C Scotland, UK 56.01N 3.43W
27 T10 **Granger** Texas, SW USA 30.43N 97.26W
34 J10 **Granger** Washington, NW USA 46.20N 120.11W
35 T17 **Granger** Wyoming, C USA 41.37N 109.58W
Granges *see* Grenchen
97 L14 **Grängesberg** Dalarna, C Sweden 60.06N 15.00E
35 N11 **Grangeville** Idaho, NW USA 45.55N 116.07W
8 K13 **Granisle** British Columbia, SW Canada 54.55N 126.13W
32 K15 **Granite City** Illinois, N USA 38.42N 90.09W
31 S9 **Granite Falls** Minnesota, N USA 44.48N 95.33W
23 Q9 **Granite Falls** North Carolina, SE USA 35.48N 81.25W
38 K12 **Granite Mountain** ▲ Arizona, SW USA 34.38N 112.34W
35 T12 **Granite Peak** ▲ Montana, NW USA 45.09N 109.48W
37 T2 **Granite Peak** ▲ Nevada, W USA 41.40N 117.35W
38 J3 **Granite Peak** ▲ Utah, W USA 40.09N 113.18W
Granite State *see* New Hampshire
109 H24 **Granitola, Capo** *headland* Sicilia, Italy, C Mediterranean Sea 37.33N 12.39E
193 H15 **Granity** West Coast, South Island, NZ 41.37S 171.53E
Gran Lago *see* Nicaragua, Lago de
65 J18 **Gran Laguna Salada** ◎ S Argentina
Gran Malvina, Isla *see* West Falkland
97 L18 **Gränna** Jönköping, S Sweden 58.01N 14.30E
107 W5 **Granollers** *var.* Granollérs. Cataluña, NE Spain 41.37N 2.18E
108 A7 **Gran Paradiso** *Fr.* Grand Paradis. ▲ NW Italy 45.31N 7.13E
Gran Pilastro *see* Hochfeiler
Gran Salitral *see* Grande, Salina
Gran San Bernardo, Passo di *see* Great Saint Bernard Pass
Gran Santiago *see* Santiago
109 J14 **Gran Sasso d'Italia** ▲▲ C Italy
102 N11 **Gransee** Brandenburg, NE Germany 53.00N 13.10E
30 L15 **Grant** Nebraska, C USA 40.50N 101.43W
29 R1 **Grant City** Missouri, C USA 40.29N 94.24W
99 N19 **Grantham** E England, UK 52.55N 0.39W
67 D24 **Grantham Sound** *sound* East Falkland, Falkland Islands
204 K13 **Grant Island** *island* Antarctica
47 Z14 **Grantley Adams** ✕ (Bridgetown) SE Barbados 13.04N 59.29W
37 S7 **Grant, Mount** ▲ Nevada, W USA 38.34N 118.47W
98 J9 **Grantown-on-Spey** N Scotland, UK 57.11N 3.52W
37 W8 **Grant Range** ▲▲ Nevada, W USA
39 Q11 **Grants** New Mexico, SW USA 35.09N 107.50W
32 I4 **Grantsburg** Wisconsin, N USA 45.46N 92.40W
34 F15 **Grants Pass** Oregon, NW USA 42.26N 123.19W
38 K3 **Grantsville** Utah, W USA 40.36N 112.27W
23 R4 **Grantsville** West Virginia, NE USA 38.54N 81.04W
104 I5 **Granville** Manche, N France 48.49N 1.34W
9 V12 **Granville Lake** ◎ Manitoba, C Canada
27 V8 **Grapeland** Texas, SW USA 31.29N 95.28W
27 T6 **Grapevine** Texas, SW USA 32.55N 97.04W
85 K20 **Graskop** Mpumalanga, NE South Africa 24.58S 30.49E
97 P14 **Gräsö** Uppsala, C Sweden 60.22N 18.30E
95 I19 **Gräsö** *island* C Sweden
105 U15 **Grasse** Alpes-Maritimes, SE France 43.42N 6.52E
20 E14 **Grassflat** Pennsylvania, NE USA 41.00N 78.04W
35 U9 **Grassrange** Montana, NW USA 47.02N 108.48W
20 J6 **Grass River** ~ New York, NE USA
37 P6 **Grass Valley** California, W USA 39.12N 121.04W
191 N14 **Grassy** Tasmania, SE Australia 40.03S 144.04E
30 K4 **Grassy Butte** North Dakota, N USA 47.20N 103.13W
23 R5 **Grassy Knob** ▲ West Virginia, NE USA 38.04N 80.31W
97 G24 **Gråsten** *var.* Graasten. Sønderjylland, SW Denmark 54.55N 9.37E
97 J18 **Grästorp** Västra Götaland, S Sweden 58.19N 12.45E
Gratianopolis *see* Grenoble
111 V8 **Gratwein** Steiermark, SE Austria 47.06N 15.18E
Gratz *see* Graz
110 I9 **Graubünden** *Fr.* Grisons, *It.* Grigioni. ◐ *canton* SE Switzerland
Graudenz *see* Grudziądz
105 N15 **Graulhet** Tarn, S France 43.45N 1.58E
107 T4 **Graus** Aragón, NE Spain 42.11N 0.21E
63 I16 **Gravataí** Rio Grande do Sul, S Brazil 29.55S 51.00W
100 L13 **Grave** Noord-Brabant, SE Netherlands 51.45N 5.45E
9 T17 **Gravelbourg** Saskatchewan, S Canada 49.52N 106.33W
105 N1 **Gravelines** Nord, N France 51.00N 2.07E
Graven *see* Grez-Doiceau
12 H13 **Gravenhurst** Ontario, S Canada 44.55N 79.22W
35 O10 **Grave Peak** ▲ Idaho, NW USA 46.24N 114.43W
104 I11 **Grave, Pointe de** *headland* W France 45.33N 1.24W
191 S4 **Gravesend** New South Wales, SE Australia 29.37S 150.15E
99 P22 **Gravesend** SE England, UK 51.27N 0.24E
109 N17 **Gravina di Puglia** *Eng.* Gravina in Puglia. Puglia, SE Italy 40.48N 16.25E
Gravina in Puglia *see* Gravina di Puglia
105 S8 **Gray** Haute-Saône, E France 47.28N 5.34E
25 T4 **Gray** Georgia, SE USA 33.00N 83.31W
205 V16 **Gray, Cape** *headland* Antarctica, 67.30S 143.30E
34 F9 **Grayland** Washington, NW USA 46.46N 124.07W
41 N10 **Grayling** Alaska, USA 62.55N 160.07W
33 Q6 **Grayling** Michigan, N USA 44.40N 84.43W
34 F9 **Grays Harbor** *inlet* Washington, NW USA
23 O5 **Grayson** Kentucky, S USA 38.19N 82.57W
39 S4 **Grays Peak** ▲ Colorado, C USA 39.37N 105.49W
32 M16 **Grayville** Illinois, N USA 38.15N 87.59W
111 V8 **Graz** *prev.* Gratz. Steiermark, SE Austria 47.04N 15.23E
106 L15 **Grazalema** Andalucía, S Spain 36.46N 5.22W
115 P15 **Grdelica** Serbia, SE Yugoslavia 42.54N 22.05E
46 H1 **Great Abaco** *var.* Abaco Island. *island* N Bahamas
Great Admiralty Island *see* Manus Island
Great Alfold *see* Great Hungarian Plain
Great Ararat *see* Büyükağrı Dağı
189 U8 **Great Artesian Basin** *lowlands* Queensland, C Australia
197 I15 **Great Astrolabe Reef** *reef* Kadavu, SW Fiji
189 O12 **Great Australian Bight** *bight* S Australia
66 E11 **Great Bahama Bank** *undersea feature* E Gulf of Mexico
192 M4 **Great Barrier Island** *island* N NZ
189 X4 **Great Barrier Reef** *reef* Queensland, NE Australia
20 L11 **Great Barrington** Massachusetts, NE USA 42.11N 73.20W
(0) F10 **Great Basin** *basin* W USA
15 H5 **Great Bear Lake** *Fr.* Grand Lac de l'Ours. ◎ Northwest Territories, NW Canada
Great Belt *see* Storebælt
28 L5 **Great Bend** Kansas, C USA 38.21N 98.45W
Great Bermuda *see* Bermuda
99 A20 **Great Blasket Island** *Ir.* An Blascaod Mór. *island* SW Ireland
Great Britain *see* Britain
157 Q23 **Great Channel** *channel* Andaman Sea/Indian Ocean
177 F10 **Great Coco Island** *island* SW Burma
Great Crosby *see* Crosby
23 X7 **Great Dismal Swamp** *wetland* North Carolina/Virginia, SE USA
35 V16 **Great Divide Basin** *basin* Wyoming, C USA
189 W7 **Great Dividing Range** ▲▲ NE Australia
12 D12 **Great Duck Island** *island* Ontario, S Canada
Great Elder Reservoir *see* Waconda Lake
205 V8 **Greater Antarctica** *var.* East Antarctica. *physical region* Antarctica
46 G8 **Greater Antilles** *island group* West Indies
133 V16 **Greater Sunda Islands** *var.* Sunda Islands. *island group* Indonesia
192 I1 **Great Exhibition Bay** *inlet* North Island, NZ
46 H4 **Great Exuma Island** *island* C Bahamas
35 R8 **Great Falls** Montana, NW USA 47.30N 111.18W
23 R11 **Great Falls** South Carolina, SE USA 34.34N 80.54W
86 F9 **Great Fisher Bank** *undersea feature* C North Sea
Great Glen *see* Mor, Glen
Great Grimsby *see* Grimsby
46 I4 **Great Guana Cay** *island* C Bahamas
66 I5 **Great Hellefiske Bank** *undersea feature* N Atlantic Ocean
113 L24 **Great Hungarian Plain** *var.* Great Alfold, Plain of Hungary, *Hung.* Alföld. *plain* SE Europe
46 L7 **Great Inagua** *var.* Inagua Islands. *island* S Bahamas
Great Indian Desert *see* Thar Desert
85 G25 **Great Karoo** *var.* Great Karroo, High Veld, *Afr.* Groot Karoo, Hoë Karoo. *plateau region* S South Africa
Great Karroo *see* Great Karoo
Great Kei *see* Groot-Kei
Great Khingan Range *see* Da Hinggan Ling
12 E11 **Great La Cloche Island** *island* Ontario, S Canada
191 P16 **Great Lake** ◎ Tasmania, SE Australia
Great Lake *see* Tônlé Sap
16 O16 **Great Lakes** *lakes* Ontario, Canada/USA
Great Lakes State *see* Michigan
99 L20 **Great Malvern** W England, UK 52.07N 2.19W
192 M5 **Great Mercury Island** *island* N NZ
Great Meteor Seamount *see* Great Meteor Tablemount
66 K10 **Great Meteor Tablemount** *var.* Great Meteor Seamount. *undersea feature* E Atlantic Ocean 30.00N 28.30W
33 Q14 **Great Miami River** ~ Ohio, N USA
157 Q24 **Great Nicobar** *island* Nicobar Islands, India, NE Indian Ocean
99 O19 **Great Ouse** *var.* Ouse. ~ E England, UK
191 Q17 **Great Oyster Bay** *bay* Tasmania, SE Australia
46 I13 **Great Pedro Bluff** *headland* W Jamaica 17.51N 77.44W
23 T12 **Great Pee Dee River** ~ North Carolina/South Carolina, SE USA
133 W9 **Great Plain of China** *plain* E China
(0) F12 **Great Plains** *var.* High Plains. *plains* Canada/USA
39 W6 **Great Plains Reservoirs** ⊡ Colorado, C USA
21 Q13 **Great Point** *headland* Nantucket Island, Massachusetts, NE USA 41.23N 70.03W
70 I13 **Great Rift Valley** *var.* Rift Valley. *depression* Asia/Africa
83 I23 **Great Ruaha** ~ S Tanzania
20 K10 **Great Sacandaga Lake** ⊡ New York, NE USA
110 C12 **Great Saint Bernard Pass** *Fr.* Col du Grand-Saint-Bernard, *It.* Passo di Gran San Bernardo. *pass* Italy/Switzerland 45.52N 7.10E
46 F1 **Great Sale Cay** *island* N Bahamas
Great Salt Desert *see* Kavīr, Dasht-e
38 K1 **Great Salt Lake** *salt lake* Utah, W USA
38 J3 **Great Salt Lake Desert** *plain* Utah, W USA
28 M8 **Great Salt Plains Lake** ⊡ Oklahoma, C USA
77 T9 **Great Sand Sea** *desert* Egypt/Libya
188 L6 **Great Sandy Desert** *desert* Western Australia
Great Sandy Desert *see* Ar Rub' al Khālī
Great Sandy Island *see* Fraser Island
197 I13 **Great Sea Reef** *reef* Vanua Levu, N Fiji
40 H17 **Great Sitkin Island** *island* Aleutian Islands, Alaska, USA
15 I8 **Great Slave Lake** *Fr.* Grand Lac des Esclaves. ◎ Northwest Territories, NW Canada
23 O10 **Great Smoky Mountains** ▲▲ North Carolina/Tennessee, SE USA
8 L11 **Great Snow Mountain** ▲ British Columbia, W Canada 57.22N 124.08W
66 A12 **Great Sound** *bay* Bermuda, NW Atlantic Ocean
188 M10 **Great Victoria Desert** *desert* South Australia/Western Australia
204 H2 **Great Wall** *Chinese research station* South Shetland Islands, Antarctica 61.57S 58.23W
21 T7 **Great Wass Island** *island* Maine, NE USA
99 Q19 **Great Yarmouth** *var.* Yarmouth. E England, UK 52.37N 1.43E
145 S1 **Great Zab** *Ar.* Az Zāb al Kabīr, *Kurd.* Zê-i Bādinān, *Turk.* Büyükzap Suyu. ~ Iraq/Turkey
97 I17 **Grebbestad** Västra Götaland, S Sweden 58.42N 11.15E
Grebenka *see* Hrebinka
44 M13 **Grecia** Alajuela, C Costa Rica 10.04N 84.19W
63 E18 **Greco** Río Negro, W Uruguay 32.49S 57.03W
Greco, Cape *see* Gkréko, Akrotíri
106 L8 **Gredos, Sierra de** ▲▲ W Spain
20 F9 **Greece** New York, NE USA 43.12N 77.41W
117 E17 **Greece** *off.* Hellenic Republic, *Gk.* Elláѕ; *anc.* Hellas. ◆ *republic* SE Europe
Greece Central *see* Stereá Elláѕ
Greece West *see* Dytikí Elláѕ
39 T3 **Greeley** Colorado, C USA 40.21N 104.41W
31 P14 **Greeley** Nebraska, C USA 41.33N 98.31W
126 Hh1 **Greem-Bell, Ostrov** *Eng.* Graham Bell Island. *island* Zemlya Frantsa-Iosifa, N Russian Federation
32 M6 **Green Bay** Wisconsin, N USA 44.32N 88.00W
33 N6 **Green Bay** *lake bay* Michigan/Wisconsin, N USA
23 S5 **Greenbrier River** ~ West Virginia, NE USA
31 S2 **Greenbush** Minnesota, N USA 48.42N 96.10W
191 R12 **Green Cape** *headland* New South Wales, SE Australia 37.15S 150.03E
33 O14 **Greencastle** Indiana, N USA 39.38N 86.51W
20 F16 **Greencastle** Pennsylvania, NE USA 39.47N 77.43W
29 T2 **Green City** Missouri, C USA 40.16N 92.57W
23 O9 **Greeneville** Tennessee, S USA 36.09N 82.49W
37 O11 **Greenfield** California, W USA 36.19N 121.15W
33 P14 **Greenfield** Indiana, N USA 39.47N 85.46W
31 U15 **Greenfield** Iowa, C USA 41.18N 94.27W
20 M11 **Greenfield** Massachusetts, NE USA 42.33N 72.34W
29 S7 **Greenfield** Missouri, C USA 37.25N 93.50W
33 S14 **Greenfield** Ohio, N USA 39.21N 83.22W
22 G8 **Greenfield** Tennessee, S USA 36.09N 88.48W
32 M9 **Greenfield** Wisconsin, N USA 42.55N 87.59W
29 T9 **Green Forest** Arkansas, C USA 36.19N 93.24W
39 T7 **Greenhorn Mountain** ▲ Colorado, C USA 37.50N 104.59W
Green Island *see* Lü Tao
195 R10 **Green Islands** *var.* Nissan Islands. *island group* NE PNG
9 S14 **Green Lake** Saskatchewan, C Canada 54.15N 107.51W
32 L8 **Green Lake** ◎ Wisconsin, N USA
207 O14 **Greenland** *Dan.* Grønland, *Inuit* Kalaallit Nunaat. ◇ Danish external territory NE North America
86 D4 **Greenland** *island* NE North America
207 R13 **Greenland Plain** *undersea feature* N Greenland Sea
207 R14 **Greenland Sea** *sea* Arctic Ocean
39 R4 **Green Mountain Reservoir** ⊡ Colorado, C USA
20 M8 **Green Mountains** ▲▲ Vermont, NE USA
Green Mountain State *see* Vermont
98 H12 **Greenock** W Scotland, UK 55.57N 4.45W
41 T5 **Greenough, Mount** ▲ Alaska, USA 69.15N 141.37W
194 E10 **Green River** Sandaun, NW PNG 3.46S 141.10E
39 N5 **Green River** Utah, W USA 39.00N 110.07W
35 U17 **Green River** Wyoming, C USA 41.33N 109.27W
18 Ii7 **Green River** ~ W USA
32 K11 **Green River** ~ Illinois, N USA
22 J7 **Green River** ~ Kentucky, S USA
30 K5 **Green River** ~ North Dakota, N USA
39 N6 **Green River** ~ Utah, W USA
35 T16 **Green River** ~ Wyoming, C USA
22 L7 **Green River Lake** ⊡ Kentucky, S USA
25 O5 **Greensboro** Alabama, S USA 32.42N 87.36W
25 U3 **Greensboro** Georgia, SE USA 33.34N 83.10W
23 T9 **Greensboro** North Carolina, SE USA 36.04N 79.47W
33 P14 **Greensburg** Indiana, N USA 39.20N 85.28W
28 K6 **Greensburg** Kansas, C USA 37.36N 99.17W
22 L7 **Greensburg** Kentucky, S USA 37.15N 85.28W
20 C15 **Greensburg** Pennsylvania, NE USA 40.18N 79.32W
39 O13 **Greens Peak** ▲ Arizona, SW USA 34.06N 109.34W
23 V12 **Green Swamp** *wetland* North Carolina, SE USA
23 O4 **Greenup** Kentucky, S USA 38.34N 82.49W
38 M16 **Green Valley** Arizona, SW USA 31.49N 111.00W
78 K17 **Greenville** *var.* Sino, Sinoe. SE Liberia 5.01N 9.03W
25 P6 **Greenville** Alabama, S USA 31.49N 86.37W
25 T8 **Greenville** Florida, SE USA 30.28N 83.37W
25 S4 **Greenville** Georgia, SE USA 33.03N 84.42W
32 L15 **Greenville** Illinois, N USA 38.53N 89.24W
22 I7 **Greenville** Kentucky, S USA 37.12N 87.10W
21 Q5 **Greenville** Maine, NE USA 45.26N 69.36W
33 P9 **Greenville** Michigan, N USA 43.10N 85.15W
24 J4 **Greenville** Mississippi, S USA 33.24N 91.03W
23 W9 **Greenville** North Carolina, SE USA 35.36N 77.22W
33 Q13 **Greenville** Ohio, N USA 40.06N 84.37W
21 O12 **Greenville** Rhode Island, NE USA 41.52N 71.33W
23 P11 **Greenville** South Carolina, SE USA 34.51N 82.23W
27 U6 **Greenville** Texas, SW USA 33.08N 96.06W
33 T12 **Greenwich** Ohio, N USA 41.01N 82.31W
29 S11 **Greenwood** Arkansas, C USA 35.13N 94.15W
33 O14 **Greenwood** Indiana, N USA 39.38N 86.06W
24 K4 **Greenwood** Mississippi, S USA 33.30N 90.11W
23 P12 **Greenwood** South Carolina, SE USA 34.12N 82.09W
23 Q12 **Greenwood, Lake** ⊡ South Carolina, SE USA
23 P11 **Greer** South Carolina, SE USA 34.56N 82.13W
29 V10 **Greers Ferry Lake** ⊡ Arkansas, C USA
29 S13 **Greeson, Lake** ⊡ Arkansas, C USA
31 O12 **Gregory** South Dakota, N USA 43.11N 99.26W
190 J3 **Gregory, Lake** *salt lake* South Australia
188 J9 **Gregory Lake** ◎ Western Australia
189 V5 **Gregory Range** ▲▲ Queensland, E Australia
Greifenberg/Greifenberg in Pommern *see* Gryfice
Greifenhagen *see* Gryfino
102 O8 **Greifswald** Mecklenburg-Vorpommern, NE Germany 54.04N 13.24E
102 O8 **Greifswalder Bodden** *bay* NE Germany
111 U4 **Grein** Oberösterreich, N Austria 48.14N 14.50E
103 M17 **Greiz** Thüringen, C Germany 50.40N 12.10E
Gremicha/Gremiha *see* Gremikha
128 M4 **Gremikha** *var.* Gremicha, Gremiha. Murmanskaya Oblast', NW Russian Federation 68.01N 39.31E
129 V14 **Gremyachinsk** Permskaya Oblast', NW Russian Federation 58.33N 57.52E
97 H21 **Grenå** *var.* Grenaa. Århus, C Denmark 56.25N 10.52E
Grenaa *see* Grenå
24 L3 **Grenada** Mississippi, S USA 33.46N 89.48W
47 W15 **Grenada** ◆ *commonwealth republic* SE West Indies
49 S4 **Grenada** *island* Grenada
49 R4 **Grenada Basin** *undersea feature* W Atlantic Ocean

◆ Country ● Country Capital ◇ Dependent Territory ○ Dependent Territory Capital ◐ Administrative Region ✕ International Airport ▲ Mountain ▲▲ Mountain Range Volcano ~ River ◎ Lake ⊡ Reservoir

GRENADA LAKE – GUMA

24 L3 **Grenada Lake** ⊠ Mississippi, S USA
47 Y14 **Grenadines, The** *island group* Grenada/St Vincent and the Grenadines
110 D7 **Grenchen** *Fr.* Granges. Solothurn, NW Switzerland *47.12N 7.30E*
191 Q9 **Grenfell** New South Wales, SE Australia *33.54S 148.09E*
9 V16 **Grenfell** Saskatchewan, S Canada *50.24N 102.55W*
94 J1 **Grenivík** Nordhurland Eystra, N Iceland *65.57N 18.10W*
105 S12 **Grenoble** *anc.* Cularo, Gratianopolis. Isère, E France *45.10N 5.41E*
30 J2 **Grenora** North Dakota, N USA *48.36N 103.57W*
94 N8 **Grense-Jakobselv** Finnmark, N Norway *69.46N 30.39E*
47 S14 **Grenville** E Grenada *12.07N 61.37W*
34 G11 **Gresham** Oregon, NW USA *45.30N 122.25W*
Gresk *see* Hresk
108 B7 **Gressoney-St-Jean** Valle d'Aosta, NW Italy *45.48N 7.49E*
24 K9 **Gretna** Louisiana, S USA *29.54N 90.03W*
23 T7 **Gretna** Virginia, NE USA *36.57N 79.21W*
100 F13 **Grevelingen** *inlet* S North Sea
102 F13 **Greven** Nordrhein-Westfalen, NW Germany *52.06N 7.37E*
117 D15 **Grevená** Dytikí Makedonía, N Greece *40.06N 21.26E*
103 D16 **Grevenbroich** Nordrhein-Westfalen, W Germany *51.06N 6.34E*
101 N24 **Grevenmacher** Grevenmacher, E Luxembourg *49.40N 6.27E*
101 M24 **Grevenmacher** ◈ *district* E Luxembourg
102 K9 **Grevesmühlen** Mecklenburg-Vorpommern, N Germany *53.52N 11.12E*
193 H16 **Grey** ∼ South Island, NZ
35 V12 **Greybull** Wyoming, C USA *44.29N 108.03W*
35 U13 **Greybull River** ∼ Wyoming, C USA
67 A24 **Grey Channel** *sound* Falkland Islands
Greyerzer See *see* Gruyère, Lac de la
11 T10 **Grey Islands** *island group* Newfoundland, E Canada
20 L10 **Greylock, Mount** ▲ Massachusetts, NE USA *42.38N 73.09W*
193 G17 **Greymouth** West Coast, South Island, NZ *42.28S 171.13E*
189 U10 **Grey Range** ▲▲ New South Wales/Queensland, E Australia
99 G18 **Greystones** *Ir.* Na Clocha Liatha. E Ireland *53.07N 6.04W*
193 M14 **Greytown** Wellington, North Island, NZ *41.05S 175.25E*
85 K23 **Greytown** KwaZulu/Natal, E South Africa *29.04S 30.34E*
Greytown *see* San Juan del Norte
101 H19 **Grez-Doiceau** *Dut.* Graven. Wallon Brabant, C Belgium *50.43N 4.41E*
117 J19 **Griá, Akrotírio** *headland* Ándros, Kykládes, Greece, Aegean Sea *37.54N 24.57E*
131 N8 **Gribanovskiy** Voronezhskaya Oblast', W Russian Federation *51.27N 41.53E*
80 I13 **Gribingui** ∼ N Central African Republic
37 O6 **Gridley** California, W USA *39.21N 121.41W*
85 G23 **Griekwastad** Northern Cape, C South Africa *28.50S 23.16E*
25 S4 **Griffin** Georgia, SE USA *33.15N 84.16W*
191 O9 **Griffith** New South Wales, SE Australia *34.16S 146.01E*
12 F13 **Griffith Island** *island* Ontario, S Canada
23 W10 **Grifton** North Carolina, SE USA *35.22N 77.26W*
Grigioni *see* Graubünden
121 H14 **Grigiškes** Trakai, SE Lithuania *54.42N 25.00E*
119 N10 **Grigoriopol** C Moldova *47.09N 29.18E*
153 X7 **Grigor'yevka** Issyk-Kul'skaya Oblast', E Kyrgyzstan *42.43N 77.27E*
200 Oo9 **Grijalva Ridge** *undersea feature* E Pacific Ocean
43 U15 **Grijalva, Río** *var.* Tabasco. ∼ Guatemala/Mexico
100 N5 **Grijpskerk** Groningen, NE Netherlands *53.15N 6.18E*
85 C22 **Grillenthal** Karas, SW Namibia *26.55S 15.24E*
81 J15 **Grimari** Ouaka, C Central African Republic *5.44N 20.02E*
Grimaylov *see* Hrymayliv
101 G18 **Grimbergen** Vlaams Brabant, C Belgium *50.55N 4.22E*
191 N15 **Grim, Cape** *headland* Tasmania, SE Australia *40.42S 144.42E*
102 N8 **Grimmen** Mecklenburg-Vorpommern, NE Germany *54.06N 13.03E*
12 G16 **Grimsby** Ontario, S Canada *43.10N 79.34W*
99 O17 **Grimsby** *prev.* Great Grimsby. E England, UK *53.34N 0.04W*
94 J1 **Grímsey** *var.* Grimsey. *island* N Iceland
9 O12 **Grimshaw** Alberta, W Canada *56.12N 117.37W*
97 F18 **Grimstad** Aust-Agder, S Norway *58.19N 8.34E*
94 H4 **Grindavík** Reykjanes, W Iceland *65.57N 18.10W*
110 F9 **Grindelwald** Bern, S Switzerland *46.37N 8.04E*
97 F23 **Grindsted** Ribe, W Denmark *55.46N 8.55E*
31 W14 **Grinnell** Iowa, C USA *41.44N 92.43W*
111 U10 **Grintovec** ▲ N Slovenia *46.21N 14.31E*
190 H1 **Griselda, Lake** *salt lake* South Australia
Grisons *see* Graubünden
97 P14 **Grisslehamn** Stockholm, C Sweden *60.04N 18.49E*
31 T15 **Griswold** Iowa, C USA *41.14N 95.08W*
104 M1 **Griz Nez, Cap** *headland* N France *50.51N 1.34E*
114 P13 **Grljan** Serbia, E Yugoslavia *43.52N 22.18E*
114 E11 **Grmeč** ▲▲ NW Bosnia and Herzegovina
101 H16 **Grobbendonk** Antwerpen, N Belgium *51.12N 4.41E*
Grobin *see* Grobiņa
120 C10 **Grobiņa** *Ger.* Grobin. Liepāja, W Latvia *56.32N 21.12E*
85 K20 **Groblersdal** Mpumalanga, NE South Africa *25.15S 29.25E*
85 G23 **Groblershoop** Northern Cape, W South Africa *28.51S 22.01E*
Gródek Jagielloński *see* Horodok
111 Q6 **Grödig** Salzburg, W Austria *47.42N 13.06E*
113 H15 **Grodków** Opolskie, S Poland *50.42N 17.23E*
Grodnenskaya Oblast' *see* Hrodzyenskaya Voblasts'
Grodno *see* Hrodna
112 L12 **Grodzisk Mazowiecki** Mazowieckie, C Poland *52.07N 20.40E*
112 F12 **Grodzisk Wielkopolski** Wielkolpolskie, C Poland *52.13N 16.21E*
Grodzyanka *see* Hradzyanka
100 O12 **Groenlo** Gelderland, E Netherlands *52.01N 6.36E*
85 E22 **Groenrivier** Karas, SE Namibia *27.27S 18.52E*
27 U8 **Groesbeck** Texas, SW USA *31.31N 96.34W*
100 L13 **Groesbeek** Gelderland, SE Netherlands *51.46N 5.55E*
104 G7 **Groix, Îles de** *island group* NW France
112 M12 **Grójec** Mazowieckie, C Poland *51.51N 20.52E*
67 K15 **Gröll Seamount** *undersea feature* C Atlantic Ocean *12.54S 33.24W*
102 E13 **Gronau** *var.* Gronau in Westfalen. Nordrhein-Westfalen, NW Germany *52.12N 7.01E*
Gronau in Westfalen *see* Gronau
95 F15 **Grong** Nord-Trøndelag, C Norway *64.29N 12.19E*
97 N22 **Grönhögen** Kalmar, S Sweden *56.16N 16.09E*
100 N5 **Groningen** Groningen, NE Netherlands *53.13N 6.34E*
57 W9 **Groningen** Saramacca, N Surinam *5.45N 55.31W*
100 N5 **Groningen** ◈ *province* NE Netherlands
Grønland *see* Greenland
110 H11 **Grono** Graubünden, S Switzerland *46.15N 9.07E*
97 M20 **Grönskåra** Kalmar, S Sweden *57.04N 15.45E*
27 O2 **Groom** Texas, SW USA *35.12N 101.06W*
37 W9 **Groom Lake** ◎ Nevada, W USA
85 H25 **Groot** ∼ S South Africa
189 S2 **Groote Eylandt** *island* Northern Territory, N Australia
100 M6 **Grootegast** Groningen, NE Netherlands *53.11N 6.12E*
85 D17 **Grootfontein** Otjozondjupa, N Namibia *19.31S 18.04E*
85 E22 **Groot Karasberge** ▲▲ S Namibia
Groot Karoo *see* Great Karoo
85 J25 **Groot-Kei** *Eng.* Great Kei. ∼ S South Africa
47 T10 **Gros Islet** N Saint Lucia *14.04N 60.57W*
46 L8 **Gros-Morne** NW Haiti *19.37N 72.39W*
11 S11 **Gros Morne** ▲ Newfoundland, E Canada *49.38N 57.45W*
105 R9 **Grosne** ∼ C France
47 S12 **Gros Piton** ▲ SW Saint Lucia *13.48N 61.04W*
Grossa, Isola *see* Dugi Otok
Grossbetschkerek *see* Zrenjanin
Grosse Isper *see* Grosse Ysper
Grosse Kokel *see* Târnava Mare
103 M21 **Grosse Laaber** *var.* Grosse Laber. ∼ SE Germany
Grosse Laber *see* Grosse Laaber
Grosse Morava *see* Velika Morava
103 O15 **Grossenhain** Sachsen, E Germany *51.18N 13.31E*
111 Y4 **Grossenzersdorf** Niederösterreich, NE Austria *48.11N 16.34E*
103 O21 **Grosser Arber** ▲ SE Germany *49.07N 13.10E*
103 K17 **Grosser Beerberg** ▲ C Germany *50.39N 10.45E*
103 G18 **Grosser Feldberg** ▲ W Germany *50.13N 8.28E*
111 O8 **Grosser Löffler** *It.* Monte Lovello. ▲ Austria/Italy *47.02N 11.56E*
111 N8 **Grosser Möseler** *var.* Mesule. ▲ Austria/Italy *47.01N 11.52E*
102 J8 **Grosser Plöner See** ◎ N Germany
103 O21 **Grosser Rachel** ▲ SE Germany *48.59N 13.23E*
Grosser Sund *see* Suur Väin
13 V6 **Grosses-Roches** Quebec, SE Canada *48.55N 67.06W*
111 P8 **Grosses Weiesbachhorn** *var.* Wiesbachhorn. ▲ W Austria *47.09N 12.44E*
108 F13 **Grosseto** Toscana, C Italy *42.45N 11.07E*
103 M22 **Grosse Vils** ∼ SE Germany
111 U4 **Grosse Ysper** *var.* Grosse Isper. ∼ N Austria
103 G19 **Gross-Gerau** Hessen, W Germany *49.55N 8.28E*
111 U3 **Gross Gerungs** Niederösterreich, N Austria *48.33N 14.58E*
111 P8 **Grossglockner** ▲ W Austria *47.05N 12.39E*
Grosskanizsa *see* Nagykanizsa
Gross-Karol *see* Carei
Grosskikinda *see* Kikinda
111 W9 **Grossklein** Steiermark, SE Austria *46.43N 15.24E*
Grosskoppe *see* Velká Deštná
Grossmeseritsch *see* Velké Meziříčí
Grossmichel *see* Michalovce
103 H19 **Grossostheim** Bayern, C Germany *49.54N 9.03E*
111 X7 **Grosspetersdorf** Burgenland, SE Austria *47.15N 16.19E*
111 T5 **Grossraming** Oberösterreich, C Austria *47.54N 14.34E*
103 P14 **Grossräschen** Brandenburg, E Germany *51.34N 14.00E*
Grossrauschenbach *see* Revúca
Gross-Sankt-Johannis *see* Suure-Jaani
Gross-Schlatten *see* Abrud
111 V2 **Gross-Siegharts** Niederösterreich, N Austria *48.48N 15.25E*
Gross-Skaisgirren *see* Bol'shakovo
Gross-Steffelsdorf *see* Rimavská Sobota
Gross Strehlitz *see* Strzelce Opolskie
111 O8 **Grossvenediger** ▲ W Austria *47.07N 12.19E*
Grosswardein *see* Oradea
Gross Wartenberg *see* Syców
111 U11 **Grosuplje** C Slovenia *46.00N 14.36E*
101 H17 **Grote Nete** ∼ N Belgium
96 E10 **Grotli** Oppland, S Norway *62.02N 7.36E*
21 N13 **Groton** Connecticut, NE USA *41.20N 72.03W*
31 P8 **Groton** South Dakota, N USA *45.27N 98.06W*
109 P18 **Grottaglie** Puglia, SE Italy *40.31N 17.25E*
109 L17 **Grottaminarda** Campania, S Italy *41.04N 15.02E*
108 K13 **Grottammare** Marche, C Italy *43.00N 13.52E*
23 U5 **Grottoes** Virginia, NE USA *38.16N 78.49W*
Grou *see* Grouw
11 N10 **Groulx, Monts** ▲▲ Quebec, E Canada
12 E7 **Groundhog** ∼ Ontario, S Canada
38 J1 **Grouse Creek** Utah, W USA *41.41N 113.52W*
38 J1 **Grouse Creek Mountains** ▲▲ Utah, W USA
100 L6 **Grouw** *Fris.* Grou. Friesland, N Netherlands *53.07N 5.51E*
29 R8 **Grove** Oklahoma, C USA *36.35N 94.46W*
33 S13 **Grove City** Ohio, N USA *39.52N 83.05W*
20 B13 **Grove City** Pennsylvania, NE USA *41.09N 80.02W*
25 O6 **Grove Hill** Alabama, S USA *31.42N 87.46W*
35 S15 **Grover** Wyoming, C USA *42.48N 110.57W*
37 P13 **Grover City** California, W USA *35.08N 120.37W*
27 Y11 **Groves** Texas, SW USA *29.57N 93.55W*
21 O7 **Groveton** New Hampshire, NE USA *44.35N 71.28W*
27 W9 **Groveton** Texas, SW USA *31.03N 95.07W*
38 J15 **Growler Mountains** ▲▲ Arizona, SW USA
Grozdovo *see* Bratya Daskalovi
131 P16 **Groznyy** Chechenskaya Respublika, SW Russian Federation *43.20N 45.42E*
Grubeshov *see* Hrubieszów
114 G9 **Grubišno Polje** Bjelovar-Bilogora, NE Croatia *45.42N 17.09E*
Grudovo *see* Sredets
112 J9 **Grudziądz** *Ger.* Graudenz. Kujawsko-pomorskie, C Poland *53.28N 18.45E*
27 R17 **Grulla** *var.* La Grulla. Texas, SW USA *26.15N 98.37W*
42 K14 **Grullo** Jalisco, SW Mexico *19.45N 104.15W*
69 V10 **Grumeti** ∼ N Tanzania
97 K16 **Grums** Värmland, C Sweden *59.22N 13.10E*
111 S5 **Grünau im Almtal** Oberösterreich, N Austria *47.51N 13.56E*
103 H17 **Grünberg** Hessen, W Germany *50.36N 8.57E*
Grünberg/Grünberg in Schlesien *see* Zielona Góra
Grünberg in Schlesien *see* Zielona Góra
94 H3 **Grundarfjördhur** Vestfirdhir, W Iceland *64.55N 23.15W*
23 P7 **Grundy** Virginia, NE USA *37.16N 82.06W*
31 W13 **Grundy Center** Iowa, C USA *42.21N 92.46W*
Grüneberg *see* Zielona Góra
27 N1 **Gruver** Texas, SW USA *36.16N 101.24W*
110 C9 **Gruyère, Lac de la** *Ger.* Greyerzer See. ◎ SW Switzerland
110 C9 **Gruyères** Fribourg, W Switzerland *46.34N 7.04E*
120 E11 **Gruzdiai** Šiauliai, N Lithuania *56.06N 23.15E*
Gruzinskaya SSR/Gruziya *see* Georgia
152 C10 **Gryada Akkyr** *Turkm.* Akgyr Erezi. *hill range* NW Turkmenistan
130 L7 **Gryazi** Lipetskaya Oblast', W Russian Federation *52.27N 39.56E*
128 M14 **Gryazovets** Vologodskaya Oblast', NW Russian Federation *58.52N 40.12E*
113 M17 **Grybów** Małopolskie, SE Poland *49.35N 20.54E*
96 M13 **Grycksbo** Dalarna, C Sweden *60.40N 15.30E*
112 E8 **Gryfice** *Ger.* Greifenberg, Greifenberg in Pommern. Zachodniopomorskie, NW Poland *53.55N 15.10E*
112 D9 **Gryfino** *Ger.* Greifenhagen. Zachodniopomorskie, NW Poland *53.15N 14.30E*
94 H9 **Gryllefjord** Troms, N Norway *69.21N 17.07E*
97 L15 **Grythyttan** Örebro, C Sweden *59.52N 14.31E*
110 D10 **Gstaad** Bern, W Switzerland *46.30N 7.16E*
45 P14 **Guabito** Bocas del Toro, NW Panama *9.30N 82.35W*
46 G7 **Guacanayabo, Golfo de** *gulf* S Cuba
42 I7 **Guachochi** Chihuahua, N Mexico
106 J11 **Guadajira** ∼ SW Spain
106 M13 **Guadajoz** ∼ S Spain
42 L13 **Guadalajara** Jalisco, C Mexico *20.43N 103.23W*
107 O8 **Guadalajara** *Ar.* Wad Al-Hajarah; *anc.* Arriaca. Castilla-La Mancha, C Spain *40.37N 3.10W*
107 O7 **Guadalajara** ◈ *province* Castilla-La Mancha, C Spain
106 K12 **Guadalcanal** Andalucía, S Spain *38.06N 5.49W*
195 W16 **Guadalcanal** *off.* Guadalcanal Province. ◈ *province* C Solomon Islands
195 W16 **Guadalcanal** *island* C Solomon Islands
107 O12 **Guadalén** ∼ S Spain
107 R13 **Guadalentín** ∼ SE Spain
106 K15 **Guadalete** ∼ SW Spain
107 O13 **Guadalimar** ∼ S Spain
107 P12 **Guadalmena** ∼ S Spain
106 L11 **Guadalmez** ∼ W Spain
107 S7 **Guadalope** ∼ E Spain
106 K13 **Guadalquivir** ∼ W Spain
106 J14 **Guadalquivir, Marismas del** *var.* Las Marismas. *wetland* SW Spain
42 M11 **Guadalupe** Zacatecas, C Mexico *22.44N 102.27W*
59 E16 **Guadalupe** Ica, W Peru *13.59S 75.49W*
106 L10 **Guadalupe** Extremadura, W Spain *39.26N 5.18W*
38 L14 **Guadalupe** Arizona, SW USA *33.20N 111.57W*
37 P13 **Guadalupe** California, W USA *34.55N 120.34W*
199 Mm5 **Guadalupe** *island* NW Mexico
Guadalupe *see* Canelones
42 J3 **Guadalupe Bravos** Chihuahua, N Mexico *31.22N 106.04W*
42 A4 **Guadalupe, Isla** *island* NW Mexico
39 U15 **Guadalupe Mountains** ▲▲ New Mexico/Texas, SW USA
26 J8 **Guadalupe Peak** ▲ Texas, SW USA *31.53N 104.51W*
27 R11 **Guadalupe River** ∼ SW USA
106 K10 **Guadalupe, Sierra de** ▲▲ W Spain
42 K9 **Guadalupe Victoria** Durango, C Mexico *24.30N 104.03W*
42 I8 **Guadalupe y Calvo** Chihuahua, N Mexico *26.04N 106.58W*
107 N7 **Guadarrama** Madrid, C Spain *40.40N 4.06W*
107 N7 **Guadarrama** ∼ C Spain
106 M7 **Guadarrama, Puerto de** *pass* C Spain *40.41N 4.14W*
107 N9 **Guadarrama, Sierra de** ▲▲ C Spain
107 Q9 **Guadazaón** ∼ C Spain
47 X10 **Guadeloupe** ◇ *French overseas department* E West Indies
49 S3 **Guadeloupe** *island group* E West Indies
47 W10 **Guadeloupe Passage** *passage* E Caribbean Sea
106 H13 **Guadiana** ∼ Portugal/Spain
107 O13 **Guadiana Menor** ∼ S Spain
107 Q8 **Guadiela** ∼ C Spain
107 O14 **Guadix** Andalucía, S Spain *37.19N 3.07W*
Guad-i-Zirreh *see* Gowd-e Zereh, Dasht-e
200 O13 **Guafo Fracture Zone** *tectonic feature* SE Pacific Ocean
65 F18 **Guafo, Isla** *island* S Chile
44 I6 **Guaimaca** Francisco Morazán, C Honduras *14.33N 86.49W*
56 J12 **Guainía** *off.* Comisaría del Guainía. ◈ *province* E Colombia
56 K12 **Guainía, Río** ∼ Colombia/Venezuela
57 O9 **Guaiquinima, Cerro** *elevation* SE Venezuela *5.45N 63.46W*
64 O7 **Guairá** *off.* Departamento del Guairá. ◈ *department* S Paraguay
62 G10 **Guaíra** Paraná, S Brazil *24.04S 54.15W*
62 L7 **Guaíra** São Paulo, S Brazil *20.17S 48.21W*
Guaire *see* Gorey
65 F18 **Guaiteca, Isla** *island* S Chile
46 G6 **Guajaba, Cayo** *headland* C Cuba *21.50N 77.33W*
61 D16 **Guajará-Mirim** Rondônia, W Brazil *10.49S 65.21W*
Guajira *see* La Guajira
56 H3 **Guajira, Península de la** *peninsula* N Colombia
44 J6 **Gualaco** Olancho, C Honduras *15.00N 86.03W*
36 L7 **Gualala** California, W USA *38.45N 123.33W*
44 E5 **Gualán** Zacapa, C Guatemala *15.06N 89.20W*
63 C19 **Gualeguay** Entre Ríos, E Argentina *33.09S 59.19W*
63 D18 **Gualeguaychú** Entre Ríos, E Argentina *32.58S 58.30W*
63 C18 **Gualeguay, Río** ∼ E Argentina
65 K16 **Gualicho, Salina del** *salt lake* E Argentina
196 B15 **Guam** ◇ *US unincorporated territory* W Pacific Ocean
65 F19 **Guamblin, Isla** *island* Archipiélago de los Chonos, S Chile
63 A22 **Guaminí** Buenos Aires, E Argentina *37.04S 62.22W*
42 H8 **Guamúchil** Sinaloa, C Mexico *25.23N 108.00W*
56 H4 **Guana** *var.* Misión de Guana. Zulia, NW Venezuela *11.07N 72.17W*
46 C4 **Guanabacoa** La Habana, W Cuba *23.01N 82.12W*
44 K13 **Guanacaste** *off.* Provincia de Guanacaste. ◈ *province* NW Costa Rica
44 K12 **Guanacaste, Cordillera de** ▲▲ NW Costa Rica
42 J8 **Guanaceví** Durango, C Mexico *25.55N 105.51W*
46 A5 **Guanahacabibes, Golfo de** *gulf* W Cuba
44 K4 **Guanaja, Isla de** *island* Islas de la Bahía, N Honduras
46 C4 **Guanajay** La Habana, W Cuba *22.52N 82.39W*
43 N12 **Guanajuato** Guanajuato, C Mexico *21.00N 101.16W*
42 M12 **Guanajuato** ◈ *state* C Mexico
56 J6 **Guanare** Portuguesa, N Venezuela *9.04N 69.45W*
56 K7 **Guanare, Río** ∼ W Venezuela
56 J6 **Guanarito** Portuguesa, NW Venezuela *8.39N 69.12W*
166 M3 **Guancen Shan** ▲▲ C China
64 I9 **Guandacol** La Rioja, W Argentina *29.31S 68.30W*
46 A5 **Guane** Pinar del Río, W Cuba *22.12N 84.05W*
167 N14 **Guangdong** *var.* Guangdong Sheng, Kuang-tung, Kwangtung, Yue. ◈ *province* S China
Guangdong Sheng *see* Guangdong
Guanghua *see* Laohekou
Guangju *see* Kwangju
166 I13 **Guangnan** Yunnan, SW China *24.07N 104.54E*
167 N8 **Guangshui** *prev.* Yingshan. Hubei, C China *31.41N 113.53E*
Guangxi *see* Guangxi Zhuangzu Zizhiqu
166 K14 **Guangxi Zhuangzu Zizhiqu** *var.* Guangxi, Gui, Kuang-hsi, Kwangsi, *Eng.* Kwangsi Chuang Autonomous Region. ◈ *autonomous region* S China
166 J8 **Guangyuan** *var.* Kuang-yuan, Kwangyuan. Sichuan, C China *32.27N 105.49E*
167 N14 **Guangzhou** *var.* Kuang-chou, Kwangchow, *Eng.* Canton. Guangdong, S China *23.10N 113.19E*
61 N19 **Guanhães** Minas Gerais, SE Brazil *18.46S 42.58W*
166 I12 **Guanling** *var.* Guanling Bouyeizu Miaozu Zizhixian. Guizhou, S China *25.56N 105.36E*
Guanling Bouyeizu Miaozu Zizhixian *see* Guanling
57 N5 **Guanta** Anzoátegui, NE Venezuela *10.15N 64.37W*
46 J8 **Guantánamo** Guantánamo, SE Cuba *20.06N 75.16W*
166 H9 **Guanxian** *var.* Guan Xian. Sichuan, C China *31.01N 103.40E*
167 Q6 **Guanyun** Jiangsu, E China *34.19N 119.16E*
56 C12 **Guapí** Cauca, SW Colombia *2.36N 77.54W*
45 N13 **Guápiles** Limón, NE Costa Rica *10.11N 83.45W*
63 I15 **Guaporé** Rio Grande do Sul, S Brazil *28.55S 51.53W*
49 S8 **Guaporé, Rio** *var.* Río Iténez. ∼ Bolivia/Brazil *see also* Iténez, Río
58 B7 **Guaranda** Bolívar, C Ecuador *1.34S 78.58W*
62 H11 **Guaraniaçu** Paraná, S Brazil *25.05S 52.52W*
61 O20 **Guarapari** Espírito Santo, SE Brazil *20.39S 40.31W*
62 I12 **Guarapuava** Paraná, S Brazil *25.22S 51.28W*
62 J8 **Guararapes** São Paulo, S Brazil *21.16S 50.37W*
107 S4 **Guara, Sierra de** ▲▲ NE Spain
62 N10 **Guaratinguetá** São Paulo, S Brazil *22.44S 45.16W*
106 I7 **Guarda** Guarda, N Portugal *40.31N 7.16W*
106 I7 **Guarda** ◈ *district* N Portugal
Guardak *see* Govurdak
106 M3 **Guardo** Castilla-León, N Spain *42.48N 4.49W*
106 K11 **Guareña** Extremadura, W Spain *38.51N 6.06W*
62 J11 **Guaricana, Pico** ▲ S Brazil *25.13S 48.50W*
56 L6 **Guárico** *off.* Estado Guárico. ◈ *state* N Venezuela
46 J7 **Guarico, Punta** *headland* E Cuba *20.36N 74.43W*
56 L7 **Guárico, Río** ∼ C Venezuela
62 M10 **Guarujá** São Paulo, SE Brazil *23.50S 46.27W*
63 L22 **Guarulhos** ✕ (São Paulo) São Paulo, S Brazil *23.23S 46.32W*
45 R17 **Guarumal** Veraguas, S Panama *7.48N 81.15W*
Guasapa *see* Guasopa
42 H8 **Guasave** Sinaloa, C Mexico *25.33N 108.28W*
56 I8 **Guasdualito** Apure, C Venezuela *7.13N 70.45W*
57 Q7 **Guasipati** Bolívar, E Venezuela *7.29N 61.54W*
195 Q15 **Guasopa** *var.* Guasapa. Woodlark Island, SE PNG *9.12S 152.55E*
108 F9 **Guastalla** Emilia-Romagna, C Italy *44.54N 10.38E*
44 D6 **Guastatoya** *var.* El Progreso. El Progreso, C Guatemala *14.51N 90.02W*
44 D5 **Guatemala** *off.* Republic of Guatemala. ◆ *republic* Central America
44 A2 **Guatemala** *off.* Departamento de Guatemala. ◈ *department* S Guatemala
200 O7 **Guatemala Basin** *undersea feature* E Pacific Ocean
Guatemala City *see* Ciudad de Guatemala
47 V14 **Guatuaro Point** *headland* Trinidad, Trinidad and Tobago *10.19N 60.58W*
194 G14 **Guavi** ∼ SW PNG
56 G13 **Guaviare** *off.* Comisaría Guaviare. ◈ *province* S Colombia
56 J11 **Guaviare, Río** ∼ E Colombia
63 E15 **Guaviravi** Corrientes, NE Argentina *29.19S 56.49W*
56 G12 **Guayabero, Río** ∼ SW Colombia
47 U6 **Guayama** E Puerto Rico *17.58N 66.07W*
44 J7 **Guayambre, Río** ∼ S Honduras
Guayanas, Macizo de las *see* Guiana Highlands
47 V6 **Guayanés, Punta** *headland* E Puerto Rico *18.03N 65.48W*
44 J6 **Guayape, Río** ∼ C Honduras
58 B7 **Guayaquil** *var.* Santiago de Guayaquil. Guayas, SW Ecuador *2.13S 79.54W*
Guayaquil *see* Simon Bolivar
58 A8 **Guayaquil, Golfo de** *var.* Gulf of Guayaquil. *gulf* SW Ecuador
Guayaquil, Gulf of *see* Guayaquil, Golfo de
58 A7 **Guayas** ◈ *province* W Ecuador
64 N7 **Guaycurú, Río** ∼ NE Argentina
42 F6 **Guaymas** Sonora, NW Mexico *27.56N 110.54W*
47 U5 **Guaynabo** E Puerto Rico *18.19N 66.05W*
82 H12 **Guba** Benishangul, W Ethiopia *11.11N 35.21E*
152 H8 **Gubadag** *Turkm.* Tel'man; *prev.* Tel'mansk. Dashkhovuzskiy Velayat, N Turkmenistan *42.07N 59.55E*
129 T1 **Guba Dolgaya** Nenetskiy Avtonomnyy Okrug, NW Russian Federation *70.16N 58.45E*
129 V13 **Gubakha** Permskaya Oblast', NW Russian Federation *58.52N 57.35E*
108 I12 **Gubbio** Umbria, C Italy *43.27N 12.34E*
102 Q13 **Guben** *var.* Wilhelm-Pieck-Stadt. Brandenburg, E Germany *51.58N 14.42E*
Guben *see* Gubin
112 D12 **Gubin** *Ger.* Guben. Lubuskie, W Poland *51.58N 14.42E*
130 K8 **Gubkin** Belgorodskaya Oblast', W Russian Federation *51.16N 37.32E*
Gudara *see* Ghŭdara
107 S8 **Gúdar, Sierra de** ▲▲ E Spain
143 P8 **Gudaut'a** NW Georgia *43.06N 40.35E*
96 G12 **Gudbrandsdalen** *valley* S Norway
97 G21 **Gudenå** *var.* Gudenaa. ∼ C Denmark
Gudenaa *see* Gudenå
131 P16 **Gudermes** Chechenskaya Respublika, SW Russian Federation *43.23N 46.06E*
161 J18 **Gūdūr** Andhra Pradesh, E India *14.10N 79.51E*
152 B13 **Gudurolum** Balkanskiy Velayat, W Turkmenistan *37.28N 54.30E*
96 D13 **Gudvangen** Sogn og Fjordane, S Norway *60.54N 6.49E*
105 U7 **Guebwiller** Haut-Rhin, NE France *47.55N 7.13E*
Guéckédou *see* Guékédou
12 K8 **Guéguen, Lac** ◎ Quebec, SE Canada
78 J15 **Guékédou** *var.* Guéckédou. Guinée-Forestière, S Guinea *8.33N 10.08W*
43 R16 **Guelatao** Oaxaca, SE Mexico
Guelders *see* Gelderland
80 G11 **Guélengdeng** Mayo-Kébbi, W Chad *10.55N 15.31E*
76 L5 **Guelma** *var.* Gâlma. NE Algeria *36.28N 7.25E*
76 D8 **Guelmime** *var.* Goulimime. SW Morocco *28.59N 10.10W*
12 G15 **Guelph** Ontario, S Canada *43.33N 80.12W*
104 I7 **Gueméné-Penfao** Loire-Atlantique, NW France *47.37N 1.49W*
104 I7 **Guer** Morbihan, NW France *47.54N 2.07W*
80 I11 **Guéra** *off.* Préfecture du Guéra. ◈ *prefecture* S Chad
104 H8 **Guérande** Loire-Atlantique, NW France *47.19N 2.25W*
80 K9 **Guéréda** Biltine, E Chad *14.30N 22.04E*
105 N10 **Guéret** Creuse, C France *46.10N 1.52E*
Guernica/Guernica y Lumo *see* Gernika-Lumo
35 Z15 **Guernsey** Wyoming, C USA *42.16N 104.44W*
99 K25 **Guernsey** *island* Channel Islands, NW Europe
78 J10 **Guérou** Assaba, S Mauritania *16.48N 11.40W*
27 R16 **Guerra** Texas, SW USA *26.54N 98.53W*
43 O15 **Guerrero** ◈ *state* S Mexico
42 D6 **Guerrero Negro** Baja California Sur, NW Mexico *27.55N 114.04W*
105 P9 **Gueugnon** Saône-et-Loire, C France *46.36N 4.03E*
78 M17 **Guéyo** S Ivory Coast *5.25N 6.04W*
109 L15 **Guglionesi** Molise, C Italy *41.54N 14.54E*
196 K5 **Guguan** *island* C Northern Mariana Islands
Guhrau *see* Góra
Gui *see* Guangxi Zhuangzu Zizhiqu
Guiana *see* French Guiana
49 V4 **Guiana Basin** *undersea feature* W Atlantic Ocean
50 G6 **Guiana Highlands** *var.* Macizo de las Guayanas. ▲▲ N South America
Guiba *see* Juba
104 I7 **Guichen** Ille-et-Vilaine, NW France *47.57N 1.47W*
63 E18 **Guichón** Paysandú, W Uruguay *32.21S 57.12W*
79 U12 **Guidan-Roumji** Maradi, S Niger *13.40N 6.41E*
Guidder *see* Guider
165 T10 **Guide** Qinghai, C China *36.06N 101.25E*
80 F12 **Guider** *var.* Guidder. Nord, N Cameroon *9.55N 13.58E*
78 I11 **Guidimaka** ◈ *region* S Mauritania
79 W12 **Guidimouni** Zinder, S Niger *13.40N 9.31E*
78 G10 **Guier, Lac de** *var.* Lac de Guiers. ◎ N Senegal
166 L14 **Guigang** *prev.* Guixian, Gui Xian. Guangxi Zhuangzu Zizhiqu, S China *23.06N 109.36E*
78 L16 **Guiglo** W Ivory Coast *6.33N 7.28W*
56 L5 **Güigüe** Carabobo, N Venezuela *10.04N 67.48W*
85 M20 **Guijá** Gaza, S Mozambique *24.30S 33.07E*
44 E7 **Güija, Lago de** ◎ El Salvador/Guatemala
106 K8 **Guijuelo** Castilla-León, N Spain *40.34N 5.40W*
Guilan *see* Gīlān
99 N22 **Guildford** SE England, UK *51.13N 0.34W*
21 R5 **Guildford** Maine, NE USA *45.10N 69.22W*
21 O7 **Guildhall** Vermont, NE USA *44.34N 71.36W*
105 R13 **Guilherand** Ardèche, E France *44.57N 4.49E*
166 L13 **Guilin** *var.* Kuei-lin, Kweilin. Guangxi Zhuangzu Zizhiqu, S China *25.15N 110.16E*
10 J6 **Guillaume-Delisle, Lac** ◎ Quebec, NE Canada
105 U13 **Guillestre** Hautes-Alpes, SE France *44.41N 6.39E*
106 H6 **Guimarães** *var.* Guimaráes. Braga, N Portugal *41.25N 8.19W*
60 D11 **Guimarães Rosas, Pico** ▲ NW Brazil
25 N3 **Guin** Alabama, S USA *33.58N 87.54W*
Güina *see* Wina
78 I14 **Guinea** *off.* Republic of Guinea, *var.* Guinée; *prev.* French Guinea, People's Revolutionary Republic of Guinea. ◆ *republic* W Africa
66 N13 **Guinea Basin** *undersea feature* E Atlantic Ocean
78 E12 **Guinea-Bissau** *off.* Republic of Guinea-Bissau, *Fr.* Guinée-Bissau, *Port.* Guiné-Bissau; *prev.* Portuguese Guinea. ◆ *republic* W Africa
68 K7 **Guinea Fracture Zone** *tectonic feature* E Atlantic Ocean
66 O13 **Guinea, Gulf of** *Fr.* Golfe de Guinée. *gulf* E Atlantic Ocean
Guiné-Bissau *see* Guinea-Bissau
Guinée *see* Guinea
Guinée-Bissau *see* Guinea-Bissau
78 K15 **Guinée-Forestière** ◈ *state* SE Guinea
Guinée, Golfe de *see* Guinea, Gulf of
78 H13 **Guinée-Maritime** ◈ *state* W Guinea
46 C4 **Güines** La Habana, W Cuba *22.50N 82.02W*
104 G5 **Guingamp** Côtes d'Armor, NW France *48.34N 3.09W*
107 P3 **Guipúzcoa** *Basq.* Gipuzkoa. ◈ *province* País Vasco, N Spain
46 C5 **Güira de Melena** La Habana, W Cuba *22.43N 82.31W*
76 G8 **Guir, Hamada du** *desert* Algeria/Morocco
57 P5 **Güiria** Sucre, NE Venezuela *10.37N 62.21W*
166 L14 **Gui Shui** ∼ S China
106 H2 **Guitiriz** Galicia, NW Spain *43.10N 7.52W*
79 N17 **Guitri** S Ivory Coast *5.31N 5.13W*
179 R13 **Guiuan** Samar, C Philippines *11.02N 125.45E*
Gui Xian/Guixian *see* Guigang
166 J12 **Guiyang** *var.* Kuei-Yang, Kuei-yang, Kueyang, Kweiyang; *prev.* Kweichu. Guizhou, S China *26.33N 106.44E*
166 J12 **Guizhou** *var.* Guizhou Sheng, Kuei-chou, Kweichow, Qian. ◈ *province* S China
Guizhou Sheng *see* Guizhou
104 J13 **Gujan-Mestras** Gironde, SW France *44.39N 1.04W*
160 B10 **Gujarāt** *var.* Gujerat. ◈ *state* W India
155 V6 **Gūjar Khān** Punjab, E Pakistan *33.15N 73.18E*
Gujerat *see* Gujarāt
155 V7 **Gujrānwāla** Punjab, NE Pakistan *32.11N 74.08E*
155 V7 **Gujrāt** Punjab, E Pakistan *32.33N 74.03E*
165 U9 **Gulang** Gansu, C China *37.31N 102.55E*
191 R6 **Gulargambone** New South Wales, SE Australia *31.19S 148.31E*
161 G15 **Gulbarga** Karnātaka, C India *17.22N 76.46E*
120 J8 **Gulbene** *Ger.* Alt-Schwanenburg. Gulbene, NE Latvia *57.10N 26.44E*
153 U10 **Gul'cha** *Kir.* Gülchö. Oshskaya Oblast', SW Kyrgyzstan *40.16N 73.27E*
Gülchö *see* Gul'cha
181 T10 **Gulden Draak Seamount** *undersea feature* E Indian Ocean *33.45S 101.00E*
142 J16 **Gülek Boğazı** *var.* Cilician Gates. *pass* S Turkey *37.19N 34.49E*
194 I14 **Gulf** ◈ *province* S PNG
25 O9 **Gulf Breeze** Florida, SE USA *30.21N 87.09W*
25 V13 **Gulfport** Florida, SE USA *27.45N 82.42W*
24 M9 **Gulfport** Mississippi, S USA *30.22N 89.05W*
25 O9 **Gulf Shores** Alabama, S USA *30.15N 87.40W*
147 T5 **Gulf, The** *var.* Persian Gulf, Ar. Khalīj al ʿArabī, Per. Khalīj-e Fars. gulf SW Asia
191 R7 **Gulgong** New South Wales, SE Australia *32.22S 149.31E*
166 I11 **Gulin** Sichuan, C China *28.06N 105.47E*
176 V12 **Gulir** Pulau Kasiui, E Indonesia *4.27S 131.41E*
Gulistan *see* Guliston
153 P10 **Guliston** *Rus.* Gulistan. Sirdaryo Wiloyati, E Uzbekistan *40.28N 68.45E*
169 T6 **Guliya Shan** ▲ NE China *49.42N 122.22E*
Gulja *see* Yining
41 S11 **Gulkana** Alaska, USA *62.17N 145.25W*
9 S17 **Gull Lake** Saskatchewan, S Canada *50.04N 108.30W*
33 P10 **Gull Lake** ◎ Michigan, N USA
31 T6 **Gull Lake** ◎ Minnesota, N USA
97 L16 **Gullspång** Västra Götaland, S Sweden *58.58N 14.04E*
158 H5 **Gulmarg** Jammu and Kashmir, NW India *34.04N 74.25E*
Gulpaigan *see* Golpāyegān
101 L18 **Gulpen** Limburg, SE Netherlands *50.48N 5.53E*
151 S13 **Gul'shad** *Kaz.* Gulshat. Zhezkazgan, E Kazakhstan *46.37N 74.21E*
Gulshat *see* Gul'shad
83 F17 **Gulu** N Uganda *2.46N 32.21E*
116 K10 **Gŭlŭbovo** Stara Zagora, C Bulgaria *42.10N 25.52E*
116 I7 **Gulyantsi** Pleven, N Bulgaria *43.37N 24.40E*
Gulyaypole *see* Hulyaypole
Guma *see* Pishan

◆ Country
● Country Capital
◇ Dependent Territory
○ Dependent Territory Capital
◈ Administrative Region
✕ International Airport
▲ Mountain
▲▲ Mountain Range
Volcano
∼ River
◎ Lake
⊠ Reservoir

GUMBA – ḤAMĪDĪYAH

81 K16 **Gumba** Equateur, NW Dem. Rep. Congo (Zaire) 2.58N 21.23E
Gumbinnen see Gusev
83 H24 **Gumbiro** Ruvuma, S Tanzania 10.19S 35.40E
152 B11 **Gumdag** prev. Kum-Dag. Balkanskiy Velayat, W Turkmenistan 39.13N 54.35E
79 W12 **Gumel** Jigawa, N Nigeria 12.37N 9.23E
107 N5 **Gumiel de Hizán** Castilla-León, N Spain 41.46N 3.42W
194 I12 **Gumine** var. Gumire. Chimbu, C PNG 6.12S 144.53E
Gumire see Gumine
159 P16 **Gumla** Bihār, N India 23.03N 84.36E
Gumma see Gunma
103 F16 **Gummersbach** Nordrhein-Westfalen, W Germany 51.01N 7.34E
79 T13 **Gummi** Zamfara, NW Nigeria 12.07N 5.07E
Gumpolds see Humpolec
159 N13 **Gumti** var. Gomati. ≈ N India
Gümülcine/Gümüljina see Komotini
Gümüşane see Gümüşhane
143 O12 **Gümüşhane** var. Gümüşane, Gumushkhane. Gümüşhane, NE Turkey 40.30N 39.27E
143 O12 **Gümüşhane** var. Gümüşane, Gumushkhane. ◐ province NE Turkey
Gumushkhane see Gümüşhane
176 W13 **Gumzai** Pulau Kola, E Indonesia 5.27S 134.38E
160 H9 **Guna** Madhya Pradesh, C India 24.39N 77.21E
Gunabad see Gonābād
Gunbad-i-Qawus see Gonbad-e Kāvūs
191 O9 **Gunbar** New South Wales, SE Australia 34.03S 145.32E
191 O9 **Gun Creek** seasonal river New South Wales, SE Australia
191 Q10 **Gundagai** New South Wales, SE Australia 35.06S 148.03E
81 K17 **Gundji** Equateur, N Dem. Rep. Congo (Zaire) 2.13N 21.31E
161 G20 **Gundlupet** Karnātaka, W India 11.48N 76.42E
142 G16 **Gündoğmuş** Antalya, S Turkey 36.52N 32.01E
143 O14 **Güney Doğu Toroslar** ▲▲ SE Turkey
81 J21 **Gungu** Bandundu, SW Dem. Rep. Congo (Zaire) 5.43S 19.19E
131 P17 **Gunib** Respublika Dagestan, SW Russian Federation 42.24N 46.55E
114 J11 **Gunja** Vukovar-Srijem, E Croatia 44.53N 18.51E
33 P9 **Gun Lake** ◎ Michigan, N USA
171 Jj15 **Gunma** off. Gunma-ken, var. Gumma. ◐ prefecture Honshū, S Japan
207 P15 **Gunnbjørn Fjeld** var. Gunnbjörns Bjerge. ▲ C Greenland 69.03N 29.36W
191 S6 **Gunnedah** New South Wales, SE Australia 30.58S 150.15E
181 Y15 **Gunner's Quoin** var. Coin de Mire. island N Mauritius
39 R6 **Gunnison** Colorado, C USA 38.33N 106.55W
38 L5 **Gunnison** Utah, W USA 39.09N 111.49W
39 P5 **Gunnison River** ≈ Colorado, C USA
23 X2 **Gunpowder River** ≈ Maryland, NE USA
Güns see Kőszeg
Gunsan see Kunsan
111 S4 **Gunskirchen** Oberösterreich, N Austria 48.07N 13.54E
Gunt see Ghund
161 H17 **Guntakal** Andhra Pradesh, C India 15.10N 77.24E
25 Q2 **Guntersville** Alabama, S USA 34.21N 86.17W
25 Q2 **Guntersville Lake** ⊡ Alabama, S USA
111 X4 **Guntramsdorf** Niederösterreich, E Austria 48.03N 16.19E
161 J16 **Guntūr** var. Guntur. Andhra Pradesh, SE India 16.19N 80.27E
173 F7 **Gunungsitoli** Pulau Nias, W Indonesia 1.11N 97.35E
161 M14 **Gunupur** Orissa, E India 19.04N 83.52E
103 J23 **Günz** ≈ S Germany
Gunzan see Kunsan
103 J22 **Günzburg** Bayern, S Germany 48.26N 10.18E
103 K21 **Gunzenhausen** Bayern, S Germany 49.07N 10.45E
167 P7 **Guoyang** Anhui, E China 33.29N 116.14E
118 G11 **Gurahonţ** Hung. Honctő. Arad, W Romania 46.16N 22.20E
Gurahumora see Gura Humorului
118 K9 **Gura Humorului** Ger. Gurahumora. Suceava, NE Romania 47.31N 26.00E
164 K4 **Gurbantünggüt Shamo** desert W China
158 H7 **Gurdāspur** Punjab, N India 32.02N 75.23E
29 T13 **Gurdon** Arkansas, C USA 33.55N 93.09W
Gurdzhaani see Gurjaani
Gurgan see Gorgān
158 I10 **Gurgaon** Haryāna, N India 28.24N 76.59E
61 M15 **Gurguéia, Rio** ≈ NE Brazil
57 Q7 **Guri, Embalse de** ⊡ E Venezuela
143 V10 **Gurjaani** Rus. Gurdzhaani. E Georgia 41.42N 45.47E
111 T8 **Gurk** Kärnten, S Austria 46.52N 14.17E
111 T9 **Gurk** Slvn. Krka. ≈ S Austria
Gurkfeld see Krško
116 K9 **Gurkovo** prev. Kolupchii. Stara Zagora, C Bulgaria 42.42N 25.46E
111 S9 **Gurktaler Alpen** ▲▲ S Austria
152 H8 **Gurlan** Rus. Gurlen. Khorazm Wiloyati, W Uzbekistan 41.54N 60.18E
Gurlen see Gurlan
85 M16 **Guro** Manica, C Mozambique 17.25S 33.23E
142 M14 **Gürün** Sivas, C Turkey 38.43N 37.15E
61 K16 **Gurupi** Tocantins, C Brazil 11.43S 49.01W
60 L12 **Gurupi, Rio** ≈ NE Brazil
158 E14 **Guru Sikhar** ▲ NW India 24.45N 72.51E
Gur'yev/Gur'yevskaya Oblast' see Atyrau
79 U13 **Gusau** Zamfara, NW Nigeria 12.18N 6.27E
130 C3 **Gusev** Ger. Gumbinnen. Kaliningradskaya Oblast', W Russian Federation 54.36N 22.13E
152 J17 **Gushgy** prev. Kushka. Maryyskiy Velayat, S Turkmenistan 35.18N 62.17E
Gushiago see Gushiegu
79 Q14 **Gushiegu** var. Gushiago. NE Ghana 9.54N 0.12W
172 P15 **Gushikawa** Okinawa, Okinawa, SW Japan 26.21N 127.49E
115 L16 **Gusinje** Montenegro, SW Yugoslavia 42.34N 19.51E
126 Jj16 **Gusinoozersk** Respublika Buryatiya, S Russian Federation 51.18N 106.28E
130 M4 **Gus'-Khrustal'nyy** Vladimirskaya Oblast', W Russian Federation 55.39N 40.42E
109 B19 **Guspini** Sardegna, Italy, C Mediterranean Sea 39.33N 8.39E
111 X8 **Güssing** Burgenland, SE Austria 47.04N 16.18E
111 V6 **Gusswerk** Steiermark, E Austria 47.43N 15.18E
94 O2 **Gustav Adolf Land** physical region NE Svalbard
205 X5 **Gustav Bull Mountains** ▲▲ Antarctica
41 W13 **Gustavus** Alaska, USA 58.24N 135.44W
94 O1 **Gustav V Land** physical region NE Svalbard
37 P9 **Gustine** California, W USA 37.14N 121.00W
27 R8 **Gustine** Texas, SW USA 31.51N 98.24W
102 M9 **Güstrow** Mecklenburg-Vorpommern, NE Germany 53.48N 12.11E
97 N18 **Gusum** Östergötland, S Sweden 58.15N 16.30E
Guta/Gúta see Kolárovo
Gutenstein see Ravne na Koroškem
103 G14 **Gütersloh** Nordrhein-Westfalen, W Germany 51.54N 8.22E
29 N10 **Guthrie** Oklahoma, C USA 35.52N 97.25W
27 P5 **Guthrie** Texas, SW USA 33.37N 100.21W
31 U14 **Guthrie Center** Iowa, C USA 41.40N 94.30W
43 Q13 **Gutiérrez Zamora** Veracruz-Llave, E Mexico 20.29N 97.07W
Gutta see Kolárovo
31 Y12 **Guttenberg** Iowa, C USA 42.47N 91.06W
Guttentag see Dobrodzień
Guttstadt see Dobre Miasto
168 G8 **Guulin** Govĭ-Altay, C Mongolia 46.33N 97.21E
159 V12 **Guwāhāti** prev. Gauhāti. Assam, NE India 26.09N 91.42E
145 R3 **Guwēr** var. Al Kuwayr, Al Quwayr, Quwair. N Iraq 36.03N 43.30E
Guwlumayak see Kuuli-Mayak
57 R9 **Guyana** off. Cooperative Republic of Guyana; prev. British Guiana. ◆ republic N South America
23 P5 **Guyandotte River** ≈ West Virginia, NE USA
Guyane see French Guiana
Guyi see Sanjiang
28 H8 **Guymon** Oklahoma, C USA 36.40N 101.28W
152 K12 **Guynuk** Lebapskiy Velayat, NE Turkmenistan 39.18N 63.00E
23 O9 **Guyot, Mount** ▲ North Carolina/Tennessee, SE USA 35.42N 83.15W
191 U5 **Guyra** New South Wales, SE Australia 30.13S 151.42E
165 W10 **Guyuan** Ningxia, N China 35.57N 106.13E
Guzar see Ghuzor
124 N3 **Güzelyurt** Gk. Mórfou, Morphou. W Cyprus 35.11N 33.00E
124 N2 **Güzelyurt Körfezi** var. Morfou Bay, Morphou Bay, Gk. Kólpos Mórfou. bay W Cyprus
42 I3 **Guzmán** Chihuahua, N Mexico 31.13N 107.27W
121 B14 **Gvardeysk** Ger. Tapaiu. Kaliningradskaya Oblast', W Russian Federation 54.39N 21.02E
Gvardeyskoye see Hvardiys'ke
191 R5 **Gwabegar** New South Wales, SE Australia 30.34S 148.58E
154 J16 **Gwādar** var. Gwadur. Baluchistān, SW Pakistan 25.09N 62.21E
154 J16 **Gwādar East Bay** bay SW Pakistan
154 J16 **Gwādar West Bay** bay SW Pakistan
Gwadur see Gwādar
85 J17 **Gwai** Matabeleland North, W Zimbabwe 19.17S 27.37E
160 I7 **Gwalior** Madhya Pradesh, C India 26.15N 78.12E
85 J18 **Gwanda** Matabeleland South, SW Zimbabwe 20.56S 29.00E
81 N15 **Gwane** Orientale, N Dem. Rep. Congo (Zaire) 4.40N 25.51E
85 I17 **Gwayi** ≈ W Zimbabwe
112 G8 **Gwda** var. Głda, Ger. Küddow. ≈ NW Poland
99 C14 **Gweebarra Bay** Ir. Béal an Bheara. inlet W Ireland
99 D14 **Gweedore** Ir. Gaoth Dobhair. NW Ireland 55.03N 8.13W
Gwelo see Gweru
99 K21 **Gwent** cultural region S Wales, UK
85 K17 **Gweru** prev. Gwelo. Midlands, C Zimbabwe 19.27S 29.49E
31 Q7 **Gwinner** North Dakota, N USA 46.10N 97.42W
79 Y13 **Gwoza** Borno, NE Nigeria 11.07N 13.40E
Gwy see Wye
191 R4 **Gwydir River** ≈ New South Wales, SE Australia
99 I19 **Gwynedd** var. Gwyneth. cultural region NW Wales, UK
Gwyneth see Gwynedd
165 O16 **Gyaca** Xizang Zizhiqu, W China 29.06N 92.37E
Gya'gya see Saga
117 M22 **Gyalí** var. Yialí. island Dodekánisos, Greece, Aegean Sea
Gyandzha see Gäncä
164 M16 **Gyangzê** Xizang Zizhiqu, W China 28.49N 89.32E
164 L14 **Gyaring Co** ◎ W China
165 Q12 **Gyaring Hu** ◎ C China
117 I20 **Gyáros** var. Yioúra. island Kykládes, Greece, Aegean Sea
126 Hh7 **Gyda** Yamalo-Nenetskiy Avtonomnyy Okrug, N Russian Federation 70.55N 78.34E
126 H7 **Gydanskiy Poluostrov** Eng. Gyda Peninsula. peninsula N Russian Federation
Gyda Peninsula see Gydanskiy Poluostrov
Gyéres see Câmpia Turzii
Gyergyószentmiklós see Gheorgheni
Gyergyótölgyes see Tulgheş
Gyertyámos see Cărpiniş
Gyeva see Detva
Gyigang see Zayü
97 I23 **Gyldenløves Høy** hill range C Denmark
189 Z10 **Gympie** Queensland, E Australia 26.04S 152.40E
177 Ff7 **Gyobingauk** Pegu, SW Burma 18.13N 95.39E
113 M23 **Gyomaendrőd** Békés, SE Hungary 46.55N 20.49E
Gyömbér see Ďumbier
113 L22 **Gyöngyös** Heves, NE Hungary 47.43N 19.48E
113 H22 **Győr** Ger. Raab; Lat. Arrabona. Győr-Moson-Sopron, NW Hungary 47.40N 17.40E
113 G22 **Győr-Moson-Sopron** off. Győr-Moson-Sopron Megye. ◐ county NW Hungary
9 X15 **Gypsumville** Manitoba, S Canada 51.46N 98.37W
10 M4 **Gyrfalcon Islands** island group Nunavut, NE Canada
97 N14 **Gysinge** Gävleborg, C Sweden 60.16N 16.55E
117 F22 **Gýtheio** var. Githio; prev. Yíthion. Pelopónnisos, S Greece 36.46N 22.34E
152 L13 **Gyuichbirleshik** Lebapskiy Velayat, E Turkmenistan 38.10N 64.33E
113 N24 **Gyula** Rom. Jula. Békés, SE Hungary 46.37N 21.19E
Gyulafehérvár see Alba Iulia
Gyulovo see Roza
145 T11 **Gyumri** var. Giumri, Rus. Kumayri; prev. Aleksandropol', Leninakan. W Armenia 40.48N 43.51E
152 D13 **Gyunuzyndag, Gora** ▲ W Turkmenistan 38.15N 56.25E
152 D12 **Gyzylarbat** prev. Kizyl-Arvat. Balkanskiy Velayat, W Turkmenistan 39.01N 56.14E
Gyzylbaydak see Krasnoye Znamya
Gyzyletrek see Kizyl-Atrek
Gyzylgaya see Kizyl-Kaya
Gyzylsu see Kizyl-Su

H

159 T12 **Ha** W Bhutan 27.16N 89.22E
Haabai see Ha'apai Group
101 H17 **Haacht** Vlaams Brabant, C Belgium 50.58N 4.37E
111 T4 **Haag** Niederösterreich, NE Austria 48.07N 14.32E
204 L8 **Haag Nunataks** ▲▲ Antarctica
94 N2 **Haakon VII Land** physical region NW Svalbard
100 O11 **Haaksbergen** Overijssel, E Netherlands 52.09N 6.45E
101 E14 **Haamstede** Zeeland, SW Netherlands 51.43N 3.45E
200 Ss13 **Ha'ano** island Ha'apai Group, C Tonga
200 Ss13 **Ha'apai Group** var. Haabai. island group C Tonga
95 L15 **Haapajärvi** Oulu, C Finland 63.45N 25.19E
95 L17 **Haapamäki** Länsi-Suomi, W Finland 62.11N 24.32E
95 L15 **Haapavesi** Oulu, C Finland 64.09N 25.25E
203 N7 **Haapiti** Moorea, W French Polynesia 17.33S 149.52W
120 F4 **Haapsalu** Ger. Hapsal. Läänemaa, W Estonia 58.57N 23.32E
Ha'Arava see 'Arabah, Wādī al
Haarby see Hårby
100 H10 **Haarlem** prev. Harlem. Noord-Holland, W Netherlands 52.22N 4.39E
193 D19 **Haast** West Coast, South Island, NZ 43.53S 169.01E
193 C20 **Haast** ≈ South Island, NZ
193 D20 **Haast Pass** pass South Island, NZ 44.07S 169.18E
200 R16 **Ha'atua** 'Eau, E Tonga 21.23S 174.57W
155 P15 **Hab** ≈ SW Pakistan
147 W7 **Haba** var. Al Haba. Dubayy, NE UAE 25.01N 55.37E
164 K2 **Habahe** var. Kaba. Xinjiang Uygur Zizhiqu, NW China 48.04N 86.20E
147 U13 **Ḥabarūt** var. Habrut. SW Oman 17.19N 52.45E
83 J18 **Habaswein** North Eastern, NE Kenya 1.01N 39.27E
101 L24 **Habay-la-Neuve** Luxembourg, SE Belgium 49.43N 5.38E
145 S8 **Ḥabbānīyah, Buḥayrat** ◎ C Iraq
Habelschwerdt see Bystrzyca Kłodzka
159 V14 **Habiganj** Chittagong, NE Bangladesh 24.22N 91.25E
169 Q12 **Habirag** Nei Mongol Zizhiqu, N China 42.18N 115.40E
97 L19 **Habo** Västra Götaland, S Sweden 57.55N 14.04E
127 P16 **Habomai Islands** island group Kuril'skiye Ostrova, SE Russian Federation
172 P3 **Haboro** Hokkaidō, NE Japan 44.19N 141.42E
159 S16 **Habra** West Bengal, NE India 22.39N 88.17E
Habrut see Ḥabarūt
149 P17 **Ḥabshān** Abū Ẓaby, C UAE 23.51N 53.34E
56 E14 **Hacha** Putumayo, S Colombia 00.02S 75.30W
172 Ss13 **Hachijō** Tōkyō, Hachijō-jima, SE Japan 33.04N 139.19E
172 Ss13 **Hachijō-jima** var. Hatizyô Zima. island Izu-shotō, SE Japan
171 I14 **Hachiman** Gifu, Honshū, SW Japan 35.46N 136.57E
171 M9 **Hachimori** Akita, Honshū, C Japan 40.22N 139.59E
172 N10 **Hachinohe** Aomori, Honshū, C Japan 40.30N 141.28E
171 Jj16 **Hachiōji** var. Hatiôzi. Tōkyō, Honshū, S Japan 35.39N 139.17E
95 G17 **Hackås** Jämtland, C Sweden 62.55N 14.31E
20 K14 **Hackensack** New Jersey, NE USA 40.51N 73.57W
Hadama see Nazrēt
171 J16 **Hadano** Kanagawa, Honshū, S Japan 35.23N 139.13E
147 W13 **Ḥaḍbaram** S Oman 17.27N 55.13E
145 U13 **Ḥaddānīyah** well S Iraq 30.27N 44.40E
98 K12 **Haddington** SE Scotland, UK 55.59N 2.45W
147 Z8 **Ḥadd, Ra's al** headland NE Oman 22.28N 59.58E
Haded see Xadeed
79 W12 **Hadejia** Jigawa, N Nigeria 12.22N 10.02E
79 W12 **Hadejia** ≈ N Nigeria
144 F9 **Ḥadera** var. Khadera. Haifa, C Israel 32.25N 34.55E
Hadersleben see Haderslev
97 G24 **Haderslev** Ger. Hadersleben. Sønderjylland, SW Denmark 55.15N 9.30E
157 J21 **Hadhdhunmathi Atoll** var. Haddummati Atoll, Laamu Atoll. atoll S Maldives
Hadhramaut see Ḥaḍramawt
147 W17 **Ḥadīboh** Suquṭrā, SE Yemen 12.37N 54.04E
164 K9 **Hadilik** Xinjiang Uygur Zizhiqu, W China 37.51N 86.10E
142 H16 **Hadım** Konya, S Turkey 36.58N 32.27E
146 K7 **Hadīyah** Al Madīnah, W Saudi Arabia 25.36N 38.31E
15 J1 **Hadley Bay** bay Victoria Island, Nunavut, N Canada
178 Jj6 **Ha Đông** var. Hadong. Ha Tây, N Vietnam 20.58N 105.46E
147 R15 **Ḥaḍramawt** Eng. Hadhramaut. ▲▲ S Yemen
Hadria see Adria
Hadrianopolis see Edirne
Hadria Picena see Apricena
97 G22 **Hadsten** Århus, C Denmark 56.19N 10.03E
97 G21 **Hadsund** Nordjylland, N Denmark 56.43N 10.07E
119 S4 **Hadyach** Rus. Gadyach. Poltavs'ka Oblast', NE Ukraine 50.21N 34.00E
114 I13 **Hadžići** Federacija Bosna I Hercegovina, SE Bosnia and Herzegovina 43.49N 18.12E
169 W14 **Haeju** S North Korea 38.04N 125.40E
Haerbin/Haerhpin/Ha-erh-pin see Harbin
147 P5 **Ḥafar al Bāṭin** Ash Sharqīyah, N Saudi Arabia 28.25N 45.58E
9 T15 **Hafford** Saskatchewan, S Canada 52.43N 107.19W
142 M13 **Hafik** Sivas, N Turkey 39.52N 37.24E
155 V8 **Ḥāfizābād** Punjab, E Pakistan 32.05N 73.37E
94 H4 **Hafnarfjördhur** Reykjanes, W Iceland 64.03N 21.57W
Hafnia see København, Denmark
Hafnia see Denmark
Hafren see Severn
Hafun see Xaafuun
Hafun, Ras see Xaafuun, Raas
82 G10 **Hag 'Abdullah** Sinnar, E Sudan 13.58N 33.34E
83 K18 **Hagadera** North Eastern, E Kenya 0.06N 40.23E
144 G8 **HaGalil** Eng. Galilee. ▲▲ N Israel
12 G10 **Hagar** Ontario, S Canada 46.27N 80.22W
161 G18 **Hagari** var. Vedāvati. ≈ W India
196 B16 **Hagåtña** var. Agana, Agaña. ○ (Guam) NW Guam 13.27N 144.45E
102 M13 **Hagelberg** hill NE Germany 52.03N 12.33E
41 N14 **Hagemeister Island** island Alaska, USA
103 F15 **Hagen** Nordrhein-Westfalen, W Germany 51.21N 7.27E
102 K10 **Hagenow** Mecklenburg-Vorpommern, N Germany 53.27N 11.10E
8 K15 **Hagensborg** British Columbia, SW Canada 52.24N 126.24W
82 I13 **Hägere Hiywet** var. Agere Hiywet, Ambo. Oromo, C Ethiopia 9.00N 37.55E
35 O15 **Hagerman** Idaho, NW USA 42.48N 114.53W
39 U14 **Hagerman** New Mexico, SW USA 33.07N 104.19W
23 V2 **Hagerstown** Maryland, NE USA 39.38N 77.43W
12 G16 **Hagersville** Ontario, S Canada 42.58N 80.03W
104 J15 **Hagetmau** Landes, SW France 43.40N 0.36W
97 K14 **Hagfors** Värmland, C Sweden 60.03N 13.45E
95 G16 **Häggenås** Jämtland, C Sweden 63.24N 14.53E
170 Dd12 **Hagi** Yamaguchi, Honshū, SW Japan 34.24N 131.22E
178 J5 **Ha Giang** Ha Giang, N Vietnam 22.49N 104.58E
Hagios Evstrátios see Ágios Efstrátios
HaGolan see Golan Heights
105 T4 **Hagondange** Moselle, NE France 49.15N 6.06E
99 B18 **Hag's Head** Ir. Ceann Caillí. headland W Ireland 52.56N 9.29W
104 I3 **Hague, Cap de la** headland N France 49.43N 1.56W
105 V5 **Haguenau** Bas-Rhin, NE France 48.49N 7.46E
172 T16 **Hahajima-rettō** island group SE Japan
13 R8 **Há Há, Lac** ◎ Quebec, SE Canada
180 H13 **Hahaya** ✈ (Moroni) Grande Comore, NW Comoros
24 K9 **Hahnville** Louisiana, S USA 29.58N 90.24W
85 E22 **Haib** Karas, S Namibia 28.12S 18.19E
Haibak see Āybak
155 N15 **Haibo** ≈ SW Pakistan
169 U12 **Haicheng** Liaoning, NE China 40.52N 122.45E
Haida see Nový Bor
Haidarabad see Hyderābād
Haidenschaft see Ajdovščina
178 Jj6 **Hai Dương** Hai Hưng, N Vietnam 20.55N 106.21E
144 F9 **Haifa** ◐ district NW Israel
Haifa see Ḥefa
Haifa, Bay of see Ḥefa, Mifraẓ
167 P14 **Haifeng** Guangdong, S China 22.58N 115.16E
Haifong see Hai Phong
167 P3 **Hai He** ≈ E China
Haikang see Leizhou
166 L17 **Haikou** var. Hai-k'ou, Hoihow, Fr. Hoï-Hao. Hainan, S China 20.00N 110.16E
Hai-k'ou see Haikou
146 M6 **Ḥā'il** Ḥā'il, NW Saudi Arabia 27.00N 42.50E
147 N5 **Ḥā'il** off. Minṭaqah Ḥā'il. ◐ province N Saudi Arabia
Hai-la-erh see Hailar
169 S6 **Hailar** var. Hai-la-erh; prev. Hulun. Nei Mongol Zizhiqu, N China 49.15N 119.40E
169 S6 **Hailar He** ≈ NE China
35 P14 **Hailey** Idaho, NW USA 43.31N 114.18W
12 H9 **Haileybury** Ontario, S Canada 47.27N 79.39W
169 X9 **Hailin** Heilongjiang, NE China 44.37N 129.24E
Ḥā'il, Minṭaqah see Ḥā'il
Hailong see Meihekou
95 K14 **Hailuoto** Swe. Karlö. island W Finland
Haima see Haymā'
Haimen see Taizhou
166 M17 **Hainan** var. Hainan Sheng, Qiong. ◐ province S China
166 K17 **Hainan Dao** island S China
Hainan Sheng see Hainan
Hainan Strait see Qiongzhou Haixia
Hainasch see Ainaži
Hainau see Chojnów
101 E20 **Hainaut** ◐ province SW Belgium
Hainburg see Hainburg an der Donau
111 Z4 **Hainburg an der Donau** var. Hainburg. Niederösterreich, NE Austria 48.08N 16.57E
41 W12 **Haines** Alaska, USA 59.13N 135.27W
34 L12 **Haines** Oregon, NW USA 44.53N 117.56W
25 W12 **Haines City** Florida, SE USA 28.06N 81.37W
8 H8 **Haines Junction** Yukon Territory, W Canada 60.45N 137.30W
111 W4 **Hainfeld** Niederösterreich, NE Austria 48.01N 15.45E
103 N16 **Hainichen** Sachsen, E Germany 50.58N 13.07E
178 K6 **Hai Phong** var. Haifong, Haiphong. N Vietnam 20.49N 106.40E
167 S12 **Haitan Dao** island SE China
46 K8 **Haiti** off. Republic of Haiti. ◆ republic C West Indies
37 T11 **Haiwee Reservoir** ⊡ California, W USA
82 I7 **Haiya** Red Sea, NE Sudan 18.16N 36.21E
165 T10 **Haiyan** Qinghai, W China 36.55N 100.54E
166 M13 **Haiyang Shan** ▲▲ S China
165 V10 **Haiyuan** Ningxia, N China 36.32N 105.31E
Hajda see Nový Bor
113 M22 **Hajdú-Bihar** off. Hajdú-Bihar Megye. ◐ county E Hungary
113 N22 **Hajdúböszörmény** Hajdú-Bihar, E Hungary 47.39N 21.32E
113 N22 **Hajdúhadház** Hajdú-Bihar, E Hungary 47.40N 21.40E
113 N21 **Hajdúnánás** Hajdú-Bihar, E Hungary 47.49N 21.25E
113 N22 **Hajdúszoboszló** Hajdú-Bihar, E Hungary 47.27N 21.24E
148 I3 **Ḥājī Ebrāhīm, Kūh-e** ▲ Iran/Iraq 36.53N 44.56E
171 Kk11 **Hajiki-zaki** headland Sado, C Japan 38.19N 138.28E
Hajine see Abū Ḥardān
159 P13 **Hājīpur** Bihār, N India 25.40N 85.13E
147 N14 **Ḥajjah** W Yemen 15.43N 43.33E
145 U11 **Ḥajjama** S Iraq 31.24N 45.20E
149 R12 **Ḥājjīābād** Hormozgān, C Iran 28.19N 55.55E
145 U14 **Ḥājj, Thaqb al** well S Iraq 29.58N 44.32E
115 L16 **Hajla** ▲ SW Yugoslavia
112 P10 **Hajnówka** Ger. Hermhausen. Podlaskie, NE Poland 52.43N 23.37E
177 Ff4 **Haka** Chin State, W Burma 22.42N 93.40E
Hakapehi see Punaauia
Hakâri see Hakkâri
143 T16 **Hakkâri** var. Çölemerik, Hakâri. Hakkâri, SE Turkey 37.36N 43.45E
143 T16 **Hakkâri** var. Hakkari. ◐ province SE Turkey
94 J12 **Hakkas** Norrbotten, N Sweden 66.52N 21.36E
171 Gg16 **Hakken-zan** ▲ Honshū, SW Japan 34.11N 135.57E
172 N9 **Hakkōda-san** ▲ Honshū, C Japan 40.40N 140.49E
172 Pp3 **Hako-dake** ▲ Hokkaidō, NE Japan 44.40N 142.22E
172 N7 **Hakodate** Hokkaidō, NE Japan 41.46N 140.42E
171 Ii12 **Hakui** Ishikawa, Honshū, SW Japan 36.52N 136.45E
202 B16 **Hakupu** SE Niue 19.06S 169.49E
171 I14 **Haku-san** ▲ Honshū, SW Japan 36.07N 136.45E
Hal see Halle
155 Q15 **Hāla** Sind, SE Pakistan 25.46N 68.28E
144 I3 **Ḥalab** Eng. Aleppo, Fr. Alep; anc. Beroea. Ḥalab, NW Syria 36.13N 37.10E
144 I3 **Ḥalab** off. Muḥāfaẓat Ḥalab, var. Aleppo, Halab. ◐ governorate NW Syria
144 I3 **Ḥalab** ✈ Ḥalab, NW Syria 36.12N 37.10E
147 O8 **Ḥalabān** var. Halībān. Ar Riyāḍ, C Saudi Arabia 23.28N 44.19E
145 V4 **Ḥalabja** NE Iraq 35.10N 45.58E
202 A16 **Halagigie Point** headland W Niue
77 Z11 **Halaib** SE Egypt 22.10N 36.33E
202 G12 **Halalo** Île Uvea, N Wallis and Futuna 13.21S 176.10W
Halandri see Chalándri
147 X13 **Ḥalānīyāt, Juzur al** var. Jazā'ir Bin Ghalfān, Eng. Kuria Muria Islands. island group S Oman
147 W13 **Ḥalānīyāt, Khalīj al** Eng. Kuria Muria Bay. bay S Oman
Halas see Kiskunhalas
40 G11 **Halawa** Haw. Hālawa. Hawaii, USA, C Pacific Ocean 20.13N 155.46W
40 F9 **Halawa, Cape** headland Molokai, Hawaii, USA, C Pacific Ocean 21.09N 156.43W
168 H6 **Halban** Hövsgöl, N Mongolia 49.30N 97.33E
103 K14 **Halberstadt** Sachsen-Anhalt, C Germany 51.54N 11.04E
192 M12 **Halcombe** Manawatu-Wanganui, North Island, NZ 40.09S 175.30E
97 I16 **Halden** prev. Fredrikshald. Østfold, S Norway 59.07N 11.19E
102 L13 **Haldensleben** Sachsen-Anhalt, C Germany 52.18N 11.25E
Háldi see Halti
159 S17 **Haldia** West Bengal, NE India 22.07N 88.06E
158 K10 **Haldwāni** Uttar Pradesh, N India 29.13N 79.31E
40 F10 **Haleakala** crater Maui, Hawaii, USA, C Pacific Ocean 20.45N 156.12W
27 N4 **Hale Center** Texas, SW USA 34.03N 101.50W
101 J18 **Halen** Limburg, NE Belgium 50.35N 5.08E
25 O2 **Haleyville** Alabama, S USA 34.13N 87.37W
79 O17 **Half Assini** SW Ghana 5.03N 2.57W
37 R8 **Half Dome** ▲ California, W USA 37.46N 119.27W
193 C25 **Halfmoon Bay** var. Oban. Stewart Island, Southland, NZ 46.52S 168.08E
190 E5 **Half Moon Lake** salt lake South Australia
169 R7 **Halhgol** Dornod, E Mongolia 47.57N 118.07E
Haliacmon see Aliákmonas
Halībān see Ḥalabān
12 I13 **Haliburton** Ontario, SE Canada 45.03N 78.32W
12 I12 **Haliburton Highlands** var. Madawaska Highlands. hill range Ontario, SE Canada
11 Q15 **Halifax** Nova Scotia, SE Canada 44.37N 63.34W
99 L17 **Halifax** N England, UK 53.43N 1.52W
23 W8 **Halifax** North Carolina, SE USA 36.18N 77.35W
23 U7 **Halifax** Virginia, NE USA 36.46N 78.55W
11 Q15 **Halifax** ✈ Nova Scotia, SE Canada 44.33N 63.48W
149 T13 **Halīl Rūd** seasonal river SE Iran
144 I6 **Ḥalīmah** ▲ Lebanon/Syria 34.12N 36.37E
168 G8 **Haliun** Govĭ-Altay, W Mongolia 45.55N 96.06E
120 I3 **Haljala** Ger. Halljal. Lääne-Virumaa, N Estonia 59.25N 26.18E
41 Q4 **Halkett, Cape** headland Alaska, USA 70.48N 152.11W
Halkida see Chalkída
98 J6 **Halkirk** N Scotland, UK 58.30N 3.29W
13 X7 **Hall** ≈ Quebec, SE Canada
Hall see Schwäbisch Hall
95 H15 **Hälla** Västerbotten, N Sweden 63.55N 17.19E
98 J6 **Halladale** ≈ N Scotland, UK
97 J21 **Halland** ◐ county S Sweden
25 Z15 **Hallandale** Florida, SE USA 25.58N 80.09W
97 K22 **Hallandsås** physical region S Sweden
15 M2 **Hall Beach** Nunavut, N Canada 68.10N 81.55W
101 G19 **Halle** Fr. Hal. Vlaams Brabant, C Belgium 50.43N 4.13E
103 M15 **Halle** var. Halle an der Saale. Sachsen-Anhalt, C Germany 51.28N 11.58E
Halle an der Saale see Halle
37 W3 **Halleck** Nevada, W USA 40.57N 115.27W
97 L15 **Hällefors** Örebro, C Sweden 59.48N 14.27E
97 N16 **Hälleforsnäs** Södermanland, C Sweden 59.10N 16.30E
111 Q6 **Hallein** Salzburg, N Austria 47.40N 13.06E
103 L15 **Halle-Neustadt** Sachsen-Anhalt, C Germany 51.28N 11.54E
27 U12 **Hallettsville** Texas, SW USA 29.27N 96.57W
205 N4 **Halley** UK research station Antarctica 75.42S 26.30W
30 L4 **Halliday** North Dakota, N USA 47.19N 102.19W
39 S2 **Halligan Reservoir** ⊡ Colorado, C USA
102 G7 **Halligen** island group N Germany
96 G13 **Hallingdal** valley S Norway
40 J12 **Hall Island** island Alaska, USA
Hall Island see Maiana
201 P15 **Hall Islands** island group C Micronesia
120 H6 **Halliste** ≈ S Estonia
Halljal see Haljala
95 I15 **Hällnäs** Västerbotten, N Sweden 64.19N 19.41E
31 R2 **Hallock** Minnesota, N USA 48.47N 96.56W
16 Oo3 **Hall Peninsula** peninsula Baffin Island, Nunavut, NE Canada
22 F9 **Halls** Tennessee, S USA 35.52N 89.24W
97 M16 **Hallsberg** Örebro, C Sweden 59.04N 15.07E
189 N5 **Halls Creek** Western Australia 18.17S 127.39E
190 L12 **Halls Gap** Victoria, SE Australia 37.09S 142.30E
97 N15 **Hallstahammar** Västmanland, C Sweden 59.25N 16.16E
111 R6 **Hallstatt** Salzburg, W Austria 47.32N 13.39E
111 R6 **Hallstatter See** ◎ C Austria
97 P14 **Hallstavik** Stockholm, C Sweden 60.12N 18.45E
27 X7 **Hallsville** Texas, SW USA 32.31N 94.30W
105 P1 **Halluin** Nord, N France 50.46N 3.07E
Halmahera, Laut see Halmahera Sea
175 T7 **Halmahera, Pulau** prev. Djailolo, Gilolo, Jailolo. island E Indonesia
175 T18 **Halmahera Sea** Ind. Laut Halmahera. sea E Indonesia
97 J21 **Halmstad** Halland, S Sweden 56.41N 12.48E
175 T11 **Halong** Pulau Ambon, E Indonesia 3.39S 128.13E
121 N15 **Halowchyn** Rus. Golovchin. Mahilyowskaya Voblasts', E Belarus 54.03N 29.52E
97 H20 **Hals** Nordjylland, N Denmark 57.00N 10.19E
96 F8 **Halsa** Møre og Romsdal, S Norway 63.04N 8.13E
121 I15 **Hal'shany** Rus. Gol'shany. Hrodzyenskaya Voblasts', W Belarus 54.15N 26.01E
Hälsingborg see Helsingborg
31 R5 **Halstad** Minnesota, N USA 47.21N 96.49W
29 N6 **Halstead** Kansas, C USA 38.00N 97.30W
101 G15 **Halsteren** Noord-Brabant, S Netherlands 51.31N 4.16E
95 L16 **Halsua** Länsi-Suomi, W Finland 63.28N 24.10E
103 E14 **Haltern** Nordrhein-Westfalen, W Germany 51.45N 7.10E
94 J9 **Halti** var. Haltiatunturi, Lapp. Háldi. ▲ Finland/Norway 69.18N 21.19E
Haltiatunturi see Halti
118 J6 **Halych** Ivano-Frankivs'ka Oblast', W Ukraine 49.08N 24.44E
Halycus see Platani
105 P3 **Ham** Somme, N France 49.46N 3.03E
Hama see Ḥamāh
170 Ee12 **Hamada** Shimane, Honshū, SW Japan 34.54N 132.07E
148 L6 **Hamadān** anc. Ecbatana. Hamadān, W Iran 34.50N 48.31E
148 L6 **Hamadān** off. Ostān-e Hamadān. ◐ province W Iran
144 I5 **Ḥamāh** var. Hama; anc. Epiphania, Bibl. Hamath. Ḥamāh, W Syria 35.09N 36.43E
144 I5 **Ḥamāh** off. Muḥāfaẓat Ḥamāh, var. Hama. ◐ governorate C Syria
171 I17 **Hamakita** Shizuoka, Honshū, S Japan 34.46N 137.46E
172 O4 **Hamamasu** Hokkaidō, NE Japan 43.37N 141.24E
171 I17 **Hamamatsu** var. Hamamatu. Shizuoka, Honshū, S Japan 34.43N 137.45E
Hamamatu see Hamamatsu
172 Qq7 **Hamanaka** Hokkaidō, NE Japan 43.05N 145.05E
171 I17 **Hamana-ko** ◎ Honshū, S Japan
96 I13 **Hamar** prev. Storhammer. Hedmark, S Norway 60.48N 11.04E
147 U10 **Ḥamārir al Kidan, Qalamat** well E Saudi Arabia 21.40N 53.13E
170 G12 **Hamasaka** Hyōgo, Honshū, SW Japan 35.37N 134.27E
Hamath see Ḥamāh
172 Pp2 **Hamatonbetsu** Hokkaidō, NE Japan 45.07N 142.21E
161 K26 **Hambantota** Southern Province, SE Sri Lanka 6.11N 81.10E
194 G10 **Hambili** ≈ NW PNG
Hambourg see Hamburg
102 J9 **Hamburg** Hamburg, N Germany 53.33N 10.02E
29 V14 **Hamburg** Arkansas, C USA 33.13N 91.48W
31 S16 **Hamburg** Iowa, C USA 40.36N 95.39W
20 D10 **Hamburg** New York, NE USA 42.40N 78.49W
102 I10 **Hamburg** Fr. Hambourg. ◐ state N Germany
154 K5 **Hamdam Āb, Dasht-e** Pash. Dasht-i Hamdamab. ▲▲ W Afghanistan
Hamdamab, Dasht-i see Hamdam Āb, Dasht-e
20 M13 **Hamden** Connecticut, NE USA 41.22N 72.55W
146 K6 **Ḥamḍ, Wādī al** dry watercourse W Saudi Arabia
95 K18 **Hämeenkyrö** Länsi-Suomi, W Finland 61.39N 23.10E
95 L19 **Hämeenlinna** Swe. Tavastehus. Etelä-Suomi, S Finland 61.00N 24.25E
HaMelaḥ, Yam see Dead Sea
Hamelin see Hameln
102 I13 **Hameln** Eng. Hamelin. Niedersachsen, N Germany 52.05N 9.21E
188 I8 **Hamersley Range** ▲▲ Western Australia
169 Y12 **Hamgyŏng-sanmaek** ▲▲ N North Korea
169 X13 **Hamhŭng** C North Korea 39.53N 127.31E
165 O6 **Hami** var. Ha-mi, Uigh. Kumul, Qomul. Xinjiang Uygur Zizhiqu, NW China 42.48N 93.27E
145 X10 **Ḥāmid Amīn** E Iraq 32.06N 46.53E
147 W11 **Hamīdān, Khawr** oasis SE Saudi Arabia 20.25N 54.43E
144 H5 **Ḥamīdīyah** var. Hamīdīyé. Tarṭūs, W Syria 34.43N 35.58E

◆ Country ● Country Capital ◇ Dependent Territory ○ Dependent Territory Capital ◐ Administrative Region ✈ International Airport ▲ Mountain ▲▲ Mountain Range ⛰ Volcano ≈ River ◎ Lake ⊡ Reservoir
263

HAMIDIYE – HAWK JUNCTION

116 L12 **Hamidiye** Edirne, NW Turkey 41.09N 26.40E
Hamîdîyé see Ḩamīdīyah
190 L12 **Hamilton** Victoria, SE Australia 37.45S 142.04E
66 B12 **Hamilton** ○ (Bermuda) C Bermuda 32.18N 64.48W
12 G16 **Hamilton** Ontario, S Canada 43.15N 79.49W
192 M7 **Hamilton** Waikato, North Island, NZ 37.48S 175.15E
98 I12 **Hamilton** S Scotland, UK 55.46N 4.03W
25 N3 **Hamilton** Alabama, S USA 34.08N 87.59W
40 M10 **Hamilton** Alaska, USA 62.54N 163.53W
32 J13 **Hamilton** Illinois, N USA 40.24N 91.20W
29 S3 **Hamilton** Missouri, C USA 39.44N 94.00W
35 P10 **Hamilton** Montana, NW USA 46.15N 114.09W
27 S8 **Hamilton** Texas, SW USA 31.42N 98.07W
12 G16 **Hamilton** ✕ Ontario, SE Canada 43.12N 79.54W
66 I6 **Hamilton Bank** undersea feature SE Labrador Sea
190 E1 **Hamilton Creek** seasonal river South Australia
11 R8 **Hamilton Inlet** inlet Newfoundland, E Canada
29 T12 **Hamilton, Lake** ▣ Arkansas, C USA
37 W6 **Hamilton, Mount** ▲ Nevada, W USA 39.15N 115.30W
77 S8 **Ḩamīm, Wādī al** ≈ NE Libya
95 N19 **Hamina** Swe. Fredrikshamn. Etelä-Suomi, S Finland 60.33N 27.15E
9 W16 **Hamiota** Manitoba, S Canada 50.13N 100.37W
158 L13 **Hamīrpur** Uttar Pradesh, N India 25.57N 80.07E
Hamīs Musait see Khamīs Mushayt
23 T11 **Hamlet** North Carolina, SE USA 34.52N 79.41W
27 P6 **Hamlin** Texas, SW USA 32.52N 100.07W
23 P5 **Hamlin** West Virginia, NE USA 38.16N 82.06W
33 O7 **Hamlin Lake** ◎ Michigan, N USA
103 F14 **Hamm** var. Hamm in Westfalen. Nordrhein-Westfalen, W Germany 51.39N 7.49E
Ḩammāmāt, Khalīj al see Hammamet, Golfe de
77 N5 **Hammamet, Golfe de** Ar. Khalīj al Ḩammāmāt. gulf NE Tunisia
145 R3 **Ḩammān al 'Alīl** N Iraq 36.07N 43.15E
145 X12 **Ḩammār, Hawr al** ◎ SE Iraq
95 J20 **Hammarland** Åland, SW Finland 60.13N 19.45E
95 H16 **Hammarstrand** Jämtland, C Sweden 63.07N 16.27E
95 O17 **Hammaslahti** Itä-Suomi, E Finland 62.26N 29.58E
101 F17 **Hamme** Oost-Vlaanderen, NW Belgium 51.06N 4.07E
102 H10 **Hamme** ≈ NW Germany
97 G22 **Hammel** Århus, C Denmark 56.15N 9.52E
103 I18 **Hammelburg** Bayern, C Germany 50.06N 9.50E
101 H18 **Hamme-Mille** Wallon Brabant, C Belgium 50.48N 4.42E
102 H10 **Hamme-Oste-Kanal** canal NW Germany
95 G16 **Hammerdal** Jämtland, C Sweden 63.34N 15.19E
94 K8 **Hammerfest** Finnmark, N Norway 70.40N 23.40E
103 D14 **Hamminkeln** Nordrhein-Westfalen, W Germany 51.43N 6.36E
Hamm in Westfalen see Hamm
28 K10 **Hammon** Oklahoma, C USA 35.37N 99.22W
33 N11 **Hammond** Indiana, N USA 41.35N 87.30W
24 K8 **Hammond** Louisiana, S USA 30.30N 90.27W
101 K20 **Hamoir** Liège, E Belgium 50.28N 5.35E
101 J21 **Hamois** Namur, SE Belgium 50.21N 5.09E
101 K16 **Hamont** Limburg, NE Belgium 51.15N 5.33E
193 F22 **Hampden** Otago, South Island, NZ 45.18S 170.49E
21 R6 **Hampden** Maine, NE USA 44.44N 68.51W
99 M23 **Hampshire** cultural region S England, UK
11 O15 **Hampton** New Brunswick, SE Canada 45.30N 65.49W
29 U14 **Hampton** Arkansas, C USA 33.33N 92.28W
31 V12 **Hampton** Iowa, C USA 42.44N 93.12W
21 P10 **Hampton** New Hampshire, NE USA 42.55N 70.48W
23 R14 **Hampton** South Carolina, SE USA 32.52N 81.06W
23 P8 **Hampton** Tennessee, S USA 36.16N 82.10W
23 X7 **Hampton** Virginia, NE USA 37.01N 76.21W
96 L11 **Hamra** Gävleborg, C Sweden 61.40N 15.00E
82 D10 **Hamrat esh Sheikh** Northern Kordofan, C Sudan 14.37N 27.55E
145 S5 **Ḩamrīn, Jabal** ▲▲ N Iraq
123 Jj16 **Hamrun** C Malta 35.53N 14.28E
178 K14 **Ham Thuân Nam** Binh Thuân, S Vietnam 10.49N 107.49E
176 Ww11 **Hamuku** Irian Jaya, E Indonesia 3.18S 135.00E
Hāmūn, Daryācheh-ye see Şāberī, Hāmūn-e/Sīstān, Daryācheh-ye
Hamwih see Southampton
40 G10 **Hana** Haw. Hāna. Maui, Hawaii, USA, C Pacific Ocean 20.45N 155.59W
23 S14 **Hanahan** South Carolina, SE USA 32.55N 80.01W
40 B8 **Hanalei** Kauai, Hawaii, USA, C Pacific Ocean 22.12N 159.30W
178 Kk10 **Ha Nam** Quang Nam-Đa Năng, C Vietnam 15.42N 108.24E
171 Mm11 **Hanamaki** Iwate, Honshū, C Japan 39.25N 141.04E
40 F10 **Hanamanioa, Cape** headland Maui, Hawaii, USA, C Pacific Ocean 20.34N 156.22W
202 B16 **Hanan** ✕ (Alofi) SW Niue
103 H18 **Hanau** Hessen, W Germany 50.06N 8.56E
15 J7 **Hanbury** ≈ Northwest Territories, NW Canada
Hânceşti see Hînceşti
8 M15 **Hanceville** British Columbia, SW Canada 51.54N 122.56W
25 P3 **Hanceville** Alabama, S USA 34.03N 86.46W
Hancewicze see Hantsavichy
166 L6 **Hancheng** Shaanxi, C China 35.22N 110.27E
23 V2 **Hancock** Maryland, NE USA 39.42N 78.10W
32 M3 **Hancock** Michigan, N USA 47.07N 88.34W
31 S8 **Hancock** Minnesota, N USA 45.30N 95.47W
20 I12 **Hancock** New York, NE USA 41.57N 75.15W
82 Q12 **Handa** Bari, NE Somalia 10.35N 51.09E
167 O5 **Handan** var. Han-tan. Hebei, E China 36.34N 114.28E
97 P16 **Handen** Stockholm, C Sweden 59.12N 18.09E
83 J22 **Handeni** Tanga, E Tanzania 5.25S 38.04E
39 Q7 **Handies Peak** ▲ Colorado, C USA 37.54N 107.30W
113 J19 **Handlová** Ger. Krickerhäu, Hung. Nyitrabánya; prev. Ger. Kriegerhaj. Trenčiansky Kraj, W Slovakia 48.45N 18.45E
171 K17 **Haneda** ✕ (Tōkyō) Tōkyō, Honshū, S Japan 35.33N 139.45E
144 F13 **HaNegev** Eng. Negev. desert S Israel
37 Q11 **Hanford** California, W USA 36.19N 119.39W
203 V16 **Hanga Roa** Easter Island, Chile, E Pacific Ocean 27.09S 109.25W
168 H7 **Hangayn Nuruu** ▲▲ C Mongolia
Hang-chou/Hangchow see Hangzhou
97 K20 **Hånger** Jönköping, S Sweden 57.06N 13.58E
Hangö see Hanko
167 R9 **Hangzhou** var. Hang-chou, Hangchow. Zhejiang, SE China 30.18N 120.07E
168 F5 **Hanhöhiy Uul** ▲▲ NW Mongolia
Hanhowuz see Khauz-Khan
143 P15 **Hani** Diyarbakır, SE Turkey 38.25N 40.22E
Hania see Chaniá
147 R11 **Ḩanīsh al Kabīr, Jazīrat al** island SW Yemen
Hanka, Lake see Khanka, Lake
95 M17 **Hankasalmi** Länsi-Suomi, W Finland 62.25N 26.27E
31 R7 **Hankinson** North Dakota, N USA 46.04N 96.54W
95 K20 **Hanko** Swe. Hangö. Etelä-Suomi, SW Finland 59.50N 23.00E
Han-kou/Han-k'ou/Hankow see Wuhan
38 M6 **Hanksville** Utah, W USA 38.21N 110.43W
158 K6 **Hanle** Jammu and Kashmir, NW India 32.46N 79.01E
193 I17 **Hanmer Springs** Canterbury, South Island, NZ 42.30S 172.48E
9 R16 **Hanna** Alberta, SW Canada 51.37N 111.55W
29 V3 **Hannibal** Missouri, C USA 39.42N 91.23W
188 M3 **Hann, Mount** ▲ Western Australia 15.53S 125.46E
102 I12 **Hannover** Eng. Hanover. Niedersachsen, NW Germany 52.23N 9.43E
101 J19 **Hannut** Liège, C Belgium 50.40N 5.04E
97 L22 **Hanöbukten** bay S Sweden
178 Jj6 **Ha Nôi** Eng. Hanoi, Fr. Ha noï. ● (Vietnam) N Vietnam 21.01N 105.52E
12 F14 **Hanover** Ontario, S Canada 44.22N 81.01W
33 P15 **Hanover** Indiana, N USA 38.42N 85.28W
20 G16 **Hanover** Pennsylvania, NE USA 39.46N 76.57W
23 W6 **Hanover** Virginia, NE USA 37.44N 77.21W
Hanover see Hannover
65 G23 **Hanover, Isla** island S Chile
Hanselbeck see Érd
205 X5 **Hansen Mountains** ▲▲ Antarctica
166 M8 **Han Shui** ≈ C China
158 H10 **Hānsi** Haryāna, NW India 29.07N 75.58E
97 F20 **Hanstholm** Viborg, NW Denmark 57.05N 8.39E
Han-tan see Handan
164 H6 **Hantengri Feng** var. Pik Khan-Tengri. ▲ China/Kazakhstan see also Khan-Tengri, Pik 42.17N 80.11E
121 I18 **Hantsavichy** Pol. Hancewicze, Rus. Gantsevichi. Brestskaya Voblasts', SW Belarus 52.45N 26.27E
16 N2 **Hantzsch** ≈ Baffin Island, Nunavut, NE Canada
158 G9 **Hanumāngarh** Rājasthān, NW India 29.33N 74.21E
191 O9 **Hanwood** New South Wales, SE Australia 34.19S 146.03E
Hanyang see Caidian
Hanyang see Wuhan
166 H10 **Hanyuan** var. Fulin. Sichuan, C China 29.22N 102.39E
166 J7 **Hanzhong** Shaanxi, C China 33.12N 106.59E
203 W11 **Hao** atoll Îles Tuamotu, C French Polynesia
159 S16 **Hāora** prev. Howrah. West Bengal, NE India 22.34N 88.19E
80 K8 **Haouach, Ouadi** dry watercourse E Chad
94 K13 **Haparanda** Norrbotten, N Sweden 65.49N 24.04E
27 N3 **Happy** Texas, SW USA 34.44N 101.51W
36 M1 **Happy Camp** California, W USA 41.48N 123.24W
11 Q9 **Happy Valley-Goose Bay** prev. Goose Bay. Newfoundland, E Canada 53.19N 60.24W
Hapsal see Haapsalu
158 J10 **Hāpur** Uttar Pradesh, N India 28.43N 77.46E
144 F12 **HaQatan, HaMakhtesh** ▲▲ S Israel
146 I4 **Ḩaql** Tabūk, NW Saudi Arabia 29.18N 34.58E
176 Vv13 **Har** Pulau Kai Besar, E Indonesia 5.21S 133.09E
168 M8 **Haraat** Dundgovĭ, C Mongolia 46.30N 107.39E
147 R8 **Ḩaraḑ** var. Haradh. Ash Sharqīyah, E Saudi Arabia 24.08N 49.01E
Haradh see Ḩaraḑ
120 N12 **Haradok** Rus. Gorodok. Vitsyebskaya Voblasts', N Belarus 55.27N 30.00E
94 J13 **Harads** Norrbotten, N Sweden 66.04N 21.04E
121 G19 **Haradzyets** Rus. Gorodets. Brestskaya Voblasts', SW Belarus 52.11N 24.41E
121 J17 **Haradzyeya** Rus. Gorodeya. Minskaya Voblasts', C Belarus 53.18N 26.33E
203 V10 **Haraiki** atoll Îles Tuamotu, C French Polynesia
171 L14 **Haramachi** Fukushima, Honshū, E Japan 37.39N 140.55E
120 M12 **Harany** Rus. Gorany. Vitsyebskaya Voblasts', N Belarus 55.25N 29.03E
85 L16 **Harare** prev. Salisbury. ● (Zimbabwe) Mashonaland East, NE Zimbabwe 17.47S 31.03E
85 L16 **Harare** ✕ Mashonaland East, NE Zimbabwe 17.51S 31.06E
80 I10 **Haraz-Djombo** Batha, C Chad 14.10N 19.35E
121 O16 **Harbavichy** Rus. Gorbovichi. Mahilyowskaya Voblasts', E Belarus 53.51N 30.42E
78 J16 **Harbel** W Liberia 6.19N 10.19W
169 W8 **Harbin** var. Haerbin, Ha-erh-pin, Kharbin; prev. Haerhpin, Pingkiang, Pinkiang. Heilongjiang, NE China 45.45N 126.40E
33 S7 **Harbor Beach** Michigan, N USA 43.50N 82.39W
11 T13 **Harbour Breton** Newfoundland, E Canada 47.28N 55.49W
67 D25 **Harbours, Bay of** bay East Falkland, Falkland Islands
97 G24 **Hårby** var. Haarby. Fyn, C Denmark 55.13N 10.07E
38 I13 **Harcuvar Mountains** ▲▲ Arizona, SW USA
110 I7 **Hard** Vorarlberg, NW Austria 47.28N 9.42E
160 H11 **Harda Khās** Madhya Pradesh, C India 22.22N 77.06E
97 D14 **Hardanger** physical region S Norway
97 D14 **Hardangerfjorden** fjord S Norway
96 E13 **Hardangerjøkulen** glacier S Norway
97 E14 **Hardangervidda** plateau S Norway
85 D20 **Hardap** ⬖ district S Namibia
23 R15 **Hardeeville** South Carolina, SE USA 32.18N 81.04W
100 L5 **Hardegarijp** Fris. Hurdegaryp. Friesland, N Netherlands 53.13N 5.57E
100 O9 **Hardenberg** Overijssel, E Netherlands 52.34N 6.37E
191 Q9 **Harden-Murrumburrah** New South Wales, SE Australia 34.33S 148.22E
100 K10 **Harderwijk** Gelderland, C Netherlands 52.21N 5.36E
32 J14 **Hardin** Illinois, N USA 39.10N 90.37W
35 V11 **Hardin** Montana, NW USA 45.43N 107.34W
25 R5 **Harding, Lake** ▣ Alabama/Georgia, SE USA
22 J6 **Hardinsburg** Kentucky, S USA 37.46N 86.27W
100 I13 **Hardinxveld-Giessendam** Zuid-Holland, C Netherlands 51.52N 4.49E
9 R15 **Hardisty** Alberta, SW Canada 52.42N 111.22W
158 L12 **Hardoi** Uttar Pradesh, N India 27.22N 80.06E
25 U4 **Hardwick** Georgia, SE USA 33.03N 83.13W
29 W9 **Hardy** Arkansas, C USA 36.19N 91.28W
96 D10 **Hareid** Møre og Romsdal, S Norway 62.22N 6.01E
15 Gg5 **Hare Indian** ≈ Northwest Territories, NW Canada
101 D18 **Harelbeke** var. Harlebeke. West-Vlaanderen, W Belgium 50.51N 3.19E
Harem see Ḩārim
102 E11 **Haren** Niedersachsen, NW Germany 52.47N 7.16E
100 N6 **Haren** Groningen, NE Netherlands 53.09N 6.36E
82 L13 **Hārer** Hārer, E Ethiopia 9.17N 42.18E
97 P14 **Harg** Uppsala, C Sweden 60.13N 18.25E
Hargeisa see Hargeysa
82 M13 **Hargeysa** var. Hargeisa. Woqooyi Galbeed, NW Somalia 9.31N 44.06E
118 J10 **Harghita** ⬖ county NE Romania
27 S17 **Hargill** Texas, SW USA 26.26N 98.00W
168 J8 **Harhorin** Övörhangay, C Mongolia 47.13N 102.48E
165 Q9 **Har Hu** ◎ C China
Hariana see Haryāna
147 P15 **Ḩarīb** W Yemen 15.08N 45.35E
174 I9 **Hari, Batang** prev. Djambi. ≈ Sumatera, W Indonesia
158 J9 **Haridwār** prev. Hardwar. Uttar Pradesh, N India 29.58N 78.09E
161 F18 **Harihar** Karnātaka, W India 14.33N 75.43E
193 F18 **Harihari** West Coast, South Island, NZ 43.09S 170.35E
144 I3 **Ḩārim** var. Harem. Idlib, W Syria 36.30N 36.30E
170 G14 **Harima-nada** sea S Japan
100 F13 **Haringvliet** channel SW Netherlands
100 F13 **Haringvlietdam** dam SW Netherlands 51.49N 4.04E
155 U5 **Harīpur** North-West Frontier Province, NW Pakistan 34.00N 73.01E
154 J4 **Harīrūd** var. Tedzhen, Turkm. Tejen. ≈ Afghanistan/Iran see also Tedzhen
96 J11 **Härjåhågnen** Swe. Härjahågnen, Härjehågna. ▲ Norway/Sweden 61.43N 12.07E
95 K18 **Harjavalta** Länsi-Suomi, W Finland 61.17N 22.04E
Härjehågna see Härjåhågnen
120 G4 **Harjumaa** off. Harju Maakond. ⬖ province NW Estonia
23 X11 **Harkers Island** North Carolina, SE USA 34.42N 76.33W
145 S1 **Harki** N Iraq 37.03N 43.39E
31 T14 **Harlan** Iowa, C USA 41.40N 95.19W
23 O7 **Harlan** Kentucky, S USA 36.50N 83.19W
31 N17 **Harlan County Lake** ▣ Nebraska, C USA
118 L9 **Hârlău** var. Hîrlău. Iaşi, NE Romania 47.24N 26.56E
Harlebeke see Harelbeke
35 U7 **Harlem** Montana, NW USA 48.31N 108.46W
Harlem see Haarlem
97 G22 **Harlev** Århus, C Denmark 56.08N 10.00E
100 K6 **Harlingen** Fris. Harns. Friesland, N Netherlands 53.10N 5.25E
27 T17 **Harlingen** Texas, SW USA 26.12N 97.43W
99 O21 **Harlow** E England, UK 51.46N 0.07E
35 T10 **Harlowton** Montana, NW USA 46.26N 109.49W
96 N11 **Harmånger** Gävleborg, C Sweden 61.55N 17.19E
100 I11 **Harmelen** Utrecht, C Netherlands 52.06N 4.58E
31 X11 **Harmony** Minnesota, N USA 43.33N 92.00W
34 J14 **Harney Basin** basin Oregon, NW USA
(0) F9 **Harney Basin** ▲▲ Oregon, NW USA
34 J14 **Harney Lake** ◎ Oregon, NW USA
30 J10 **Harney Peak** ▲ South Dakota, N USA 43.52N 103.31W
95 H17 **Härnösand** var. Hernösand. Västernorrland, C Sweden 62.37N 17.55E
Harns see Harlingen
168 F6 **Har Nuur** ◎ NW Mongolia
107 P4 **Haro** La Rioja, N Spain 42.34N 2.52W
42 F6 **Haro, Cabo** headland NW Mexico 27.50N 110.55W
96 D9 **Harøy** island S Norway
99 N21 **Harpenden** E England, UK 51.49N 0.22W
78 L18 **Harper** var. Cape Palmas. NE Liberia 4.25N 7.43W
28 M7 **Harper** Kansas, C USA 37.17N 98.01W
34 L13 **Harper** Oregon, NW USA 43.51N 117.37W
27 Q10 **Harper** Texas, SW USA 30.18N 99.18W
37 U13 **Harper Lake** salt flat California, W USA
41 T9 **Harper, Mount** ▲ Alaska, USA 64.18N 143.54W
97 J21 **Harplinge** Halland, S Sweden 56.45N 12.45E
38 J13 **Harquahala Mountains** ▲▲ Arizona, SW USA
147 T15 **Ḩarrah** SE Yemen 15.02N 50.22E
10 H11 **Harricana** ≈ Quebec, SE Canada
22 M9 **Harriman** Tennessee, S USA 35.57N 84.33W
11 R11 **Harrington Harbour** Quebec, E Canada 50.34N 59.29W
66 B12 **Harrington Sound** bay Bermuda, NW Atlantic Ocean
98 F8 **Harris** physical region NW Scotland, UK
29 X10 **Harrisburg** Arkansas, C USA 35.33N 90.43W
32 M17 **Harrisburg** Illinois, N USA 37.44N 88.32W
30 I14 **Harrisburg** Nebraska, C USA 41.31N 103.43W
34 F12 **Harrisburg** Oregon, NW USA 44.16N 123.10W
20 G15 **Harrisburg** state capital Pennsylvania, NE USA 40.16N 76.52W
190 F6 **Harris, Lake** ◎ South Australia
25 W11 **Harris, Lake** ◎ Florida, SE USA
85 J22 **Harrismith** Free State, E South Africa 28.16S 29.06E
29 T9 **Harrison** Arkansas, C USA 36.13N 93.06W
33 Q7 **Harrison** Michigan, N USA 44.01N 84.49W
30 I12 **Harrison** Nebraska, C USA 42.39N 103.53W
41 Q5 **Harrison Bay** inlet Alaska, USA
24 I6 **Harrisonburg** Louisiana, S USA 31.44N 91.51W
23 U4 **Harrisonburg** Virginia, NE USA 38.27N 78.52W
11 R7 **Harrison, Cape** headland Newfoundland, E Canada 54.55N 57.48W
29 R5 **Harrisonville** Missouri, C USA 38.39N 94.21W
Harris Ridge see Lomonosov Ridge
199 K3 **Harris Seamount** undersea feature N Pacific Ocean 46.09N 161.25W
98 F8 **Harris, Sound of** strait NW Scotland, UK
33 R6 **Harrisville** Michigan, N USA 44.39N 83.19W
23 R3 **Harrisville** West Virginia, NE USA 39.12N 81.03W
22 M6 **Harrodsburg** Kentucky, S USA 37.45N 84.50W
99 M16 **Harrogate** N England, UK 54.00N 1.33W
27 Q4 **Harrold** Texas, SW USA 34.05N 99.02W
29 S5 **Harry S.Truman Reservoir** ▣ Missouri, C USA
102 G13 **Harsewinkel** Nordrhein-Westfalen, W Germany 51.58N 8.13E
118 M14 **Hârşova** prev. Hîrşova. Constanţa, SE Romania 44.40N 27.58E
94 H10 **Harstad** Troms, N Norway 68.48N 16.31E
33 O8 **Hart** Michigan, N USA 43.43N 86.22W
26 M4 **Hart** Texas, SW USA 34.23N 102.07W
8 I5 **Hart** ≈ Yukon Territory, NW Canada
85 F23 **Hartbees** ≈ C South Africa
111 X7 **Hartberg** Steiermark, SE Austria 47.15N 15.55E
190 I10 **Hart, Cape** headland South Australia 35.54S 138.01E
97 E14 **Hårteigen** ▲ S Norway 60.11N 7.01E
25 Q7 **Hartford** Alabama, S USA 31.06N 85.42W
29 R11 **Hartford** Arkansas, C USA 35.01N 94.22W
20 M12 **Hartford** state capital Connecticut, NE USA 41.45N 72.41W
22 J6 **Hartford** Kentucky, S USA 37.24N 86.52W
33 P10 **Hartford** Michigan, N USA 42.12N 85.54W
31 R11 **Hartford** South Dakota, N USA 43.37N 96.56W
32 M8 **Hartford** Wisconsin, N USA 43.19N 88.25W
33 P13 **Hartford City** Indiana, N USA 40.27N 85.22W
31 Q13 **Hartington** Nebraska, C USA 42.37N 97.15W
11 N14 **Hartland** New Brunswick, SE Canada 46.18N 67.31W
99 H23 **Hartland Point** headland SW England, UK 51.01N 4.33W
99 M15 **Hartlepool** N England, UK 54.40N 1.13W
31 T12 **Hartley** Iowa, C USA 43.10N 95.28W
26 M1 **Hartley** Texas, SW USA 35.52N 102.24W
34 J15 **Hart Mountain** ▲ Oregon, NW USA 42.24N 119.46W
181 U10 **Hartog Ridge** undersea feature W Indian Ocean
95 M18 **Hartola** Etelä-Suomi, S Finland 61.34N 26.04E
69 U14 **Harts** var. Hartz. ≈ N South Africa
25 P2 **Hartselle** Alabama, S USA 34.26N 86.56W
25 S3 **Hartsfield Atlanta** ✕ Georgia, SE USA 33.38N 84.24W
29 Q11 **Hartshorne** Oklahoma, C USA 34.51N 95.33W
23 S12 **Hartsville** South Carolina, SE USA 34.22N 80.04W
22 K8 **Hartsville** Tennessee, S USA 36.23N 86.10W
29 U7 **Hartville** Missouri, C USA 37.15N 92.30W
25 U2 **Hartwell** Georgia, SE USA 34.21N 82.55W
23 O11 **Hartwell Lake** ▣ Georgia/South Carolina, SE USA
Hartz see Harts
Harunabad see Eslāmābād
168 E6 **Har-Us** Hovd, W Mongolia 48.30N 91.25E
168 E6 **Har Us Nuur** ◎ NW Mongolia
32 M10 **Harvard** Illinois, N USA 42.25N 88.36W
31 P16 **Harvard** Nebraska, C USA 40.37N 98.06W
39 R5 **Harvard, Mount** ▲ Colorado, C USA 38.55N 106.19W
33 N11 **Harvey** Illinois, N USA 41.36N 87.39W
31 N4 **Harvey** North Dakota, N USA 47.43N 99.55W
99 Q21 **Harwich** E England, UK 51.55N 1.16E
158 H10 **Haryāna** var. Hariana. ⬖ state N India
147 Y9 **Ḩaryān, Ţawī al** spring/well NE Oman 21.56N 58.33E
103 J14 **Harz** ▲▲ C Germany
Hasakah see Al Ḩasakah
171 M12 **Hasama** Miyagi, Honshū, C Japan 38.42N 141.09E
142 J15 **Hasan Dağı** ▲ C Turkey 38.09N 34.15E
145 T9 **Ḩasan Ibn Ḩassūn** C Iraq 32.24N 44.13E
155 R6 **Ḩasan Khēl** var. Ahmad Khel. Paktīā, SE Afghanistan 33.46N 69.37E
102 F12 **Hase** ≈ NW Germany
Haselberg see Krasnoznamensk
102 F12 **Haselünne** Niedersachsen, NW Germany 52.40N 7.28E
168 K9 **Hashaat** Dundgovĭ, C Mongolia 45.09N 104.51E
Hashemite Kingdom of Jordan see Jordan
145 V8 **Hāshimah** E Iraq 33.22N 45.56E
171 Gg16 **Hashimoto** var. Hasimoto. Wakayama, Honshū, SW Japan 34.18N 135.34E
147 W13 **Ḩāsik** S Oman 17.22N 55.18E
155 U10 **Hāsilpur** Punjab, E Pakistan 29.44N 72.33E
Hasimoto see Hashimoto
29 Q10 **Haskell** Oklahoma, C USA 35.49N 95.40W
27 Q6 **Haskell** Texas, SW USA 33.09N 99.43W
116 M11 **Hasköy** Edirne, NW Turkey 41.37N 26.51E
97 L24 **Hasle** Bornholm, E Denmark 55.12N 14.43E
99 N23 **Haslemere** SE England, UK 51.06N 0.45W
104 I16 **Hasparren** Pyrénées-Atlantiques, SW France 43.22N 1.18W
Hassakeh see Al Ḩasakah
161 G19 **Hassan** Karnātaka, W India 13.01N 76.03E
38 J13 **Hassayampa River** ≈ Arizona, SW USA
103 J18 **Hassberge** hill range C Germany
96 N10 **Hassela** Gävleborg, C Sweden 62.06N 16.45E
101 J18 **Hasselt** Limburg, NE Belgium 50.55N 5.19E
100 M9 **Hasselt** Overijssel, E Netherlands 52.36N 6.06E
Hassetché see Al Ḩasakah
103 J18 **Hassfurt** Bayern, C Germany 50.02N 10.32E
76 L9 **Hassi Bel Guebbour** E Algeria 28.41N 6.29E
76 L8 **Hassi Messaoud** E Algeria 31.41N 6.10E
97 K22 **Hässleholm** Skåne, S Sweden 56.09N 13.45E
Hasta Colonia/Hasta Pompeia see Asti
191 O13 **Hastings** Victoria, SE Australia 38.18S 145.12E
192 O11 **Hastings** Hawke's Bay, North Island, NZ 39.39S 176.51E
99 P23 **Hastings** SE England, UK 50.51N 0.36E
33 P9 **Hastings** Michigan, N USA 42.37N 85.16W
31 W9 **Hastings** Minnesota, N USA 44.44N 92.51W
31 P16 **Hastings** Nebraska, C USA 40.35N 98.23W
97 K22 **Hästveda** Skåne, S Sweden 56.16N 13.55E
94 J8 **Hasvik** Finnmark, N Norway 70.29N 22.08E
39 V6 **Haswell** Colorado, C USA 38.27N 103.09W
168 I10 **Hatansuudal** Bayanhongor, C Mongolia 44.34N 100.41E
169 P9 **Hatavch** Sühbaatar, E Mongolia 46.10N 112.57E
142 K17 **Hatay** ⬖ province S Turkey
39 R15 **Hatch** New Mexico, SW USA 32.40N 107.10W
38 K7 **Hatch** Utah, W USA 37.39N 112.25W
22 F9 **Hatchie River** ≈ Tennessee, S USA
118 G12 **Haţeg** Ger. Wallenthal, Hung. Hátszeg; prev. Hatzeg, Hötzing. Hunedoara, SW Romania 45.35N 22.57E
172 Oo17 **Hateruma-jima** island Yaeyama-shotō, SW Japan
191 N8 **Hatfield** New South Wales, SE Australia 33.54S 143.43E
168 I5 **Hatgal** Hövsgöl, N Mongolia 50.24N 100.12E
159 V16 **Hathazari** Chittagong, SE Bangladesh 22.30N 91.46E
147 T13 **Hathūt, Hiṣā'** oasis NE Yemen 17.46N 51.14E
178 Ii14 **Ha Tiên** Kiên Giang, S Vietnam 10.24N 104.30E
178 Jj8 **Ha Tinh** Ha Tinh, N Vietnam 18.21N 105.55E
Hatiôzi see Hachiōji
144 F12 **Ḩatira, Haré** hill range S Israel
178 J6 **Hat Lot** Sơn La, N Vietnam 21.07N 104.10E
47 P16 **Hato Airport** ✕ (Willemstad) Curaçao, SW Netherlands Antilles 12.10N 68.56W
56 H9 **Hato Corozal** Casanare, C Colombia 6.07N 71.45W
Hato del Volcán see Volcán
47 P9 **Hato Mayor** E Dominican Republic 18.44N 69.16W
Hatra see Al Ḩaḑr
Hatria see Adria
Hátszeg see Haţeg
149 R16 **Ḩattá** Dubayy, NE UAE 24.50N 56.06E
190 L9 **Hattah** Victoria, SE Australia 34.49S 142.18E
100 M9 **Hattem** Gelderland, E Netherlands 52.28N 6.04E
23 Z10 **Hatteras** Hatteras Island, North Carolina, SE USA 35.13N 75.39W
23 Rr10 **Hatteras, Cape** headland North Carolina, SE USA 35.29N 75.33W
23 Z9 **Hatteras Island** island North Carolina, SE USA
66 F10 **Hatteras Plain** undersea feature W Atlantic Ocean
95 G14 **Hattfjelldal** Troms, N Norway 65.37N 13.58E
24 M7 **Hattiesburg** Mississippi, S USA 31.19N 89.17W
31 Q4 **Hatton** North Dakota, N USA 47.38N 97.27W
Hatton Bank see Hatton Ridge
66 L6 **Hatton Ridge** var. Hatton Bank. undersea feature N Atlantic Ocean
203 W6 **Hatutu** island Îles Marquises, NE French Polynesia
113 K22 **Hatvan** Heves, NE Hungary 47.40N 19.38E
178 H17 **Hat Yai** var. Ban Hat Yai. Songkhla, SW Thailand 7.01N 100.27E
Hatzeg see Haţeg
Hatzfeld see Jimbolia
82 N13 **Haud** plateau Ethiopia/Somalia
97 D18 **Hauge** Rogaland, S Norway 58.19N 6.16E
97 C15 **Haugesund** Rogaland, S Norway 59.24N 5.16E
111 X2 **Haugsdorf** Niederösterreich, NE Austria 48.41N 16.04E
192 M9 **Hauhungaroa Range** ▲▲ North Island, NZ
97 E15 **Haukeligrend** Telemark, S Norway 59.45N 7.33E
95 L14 **Haukipudas** Oulu, C Finland 65.11N 25.21E
95 M17 **Haukivesi** ◎ SE Finland
95 M17 **Haukivuori** Isä-Suomi, E Finland 62.02N 27.11E
Hauptkanal see Havelländ Grosse
195 Z17 **Hauraha** San Cristobal, SE Solomon Islands 10.47S 162.00E
192 L5 **Hauraki Gulf** gulf North Island, NZ
193 B24 **Hauroko, Lake** ◎ South Island, NZ
178 Jj15 **Hâu, Sông** ≈ S Vietnam
94 N12 **Hautajärvi** Lappi, NE Finland 66.30N 29.01E
76 F7 **Haut Atlas** Eng. High Atlas. ▲▲ C Morocco
81 M17 **Haut-Congo** off. Région du Haut-Congo; prev. Haut-Zaïre. ⬖ region NE Dem. Rep. Congo (Zaire)
105 Y14 **Haute-Corse** ⬖ department Corse, France, C Mediterranean Sea
104 L16 **Haute-Garonne** ⬖ department S France
78 J13 **Haute-Guinée** ⬖ state NE Guinea
81 K14 **Haute-Kotto** ⬖ prefecture E Central African Republic
105 P12 **Haute-Loire** ⬖ department C France
105 R6 **Haute-Marne** ⬖ department N France
104 M3 **Haute-Normandie** ⬖ region N France
13 U6 **Hauterive** Quebec, SE Canada 49.10N 68.16W
105 T13 **Hautes-Alpes** ⬖ department SE France
105 S7 **Haute-Saône** ⬖ department E France
105 T10 **Haute-Savoie** ⬖ department E France
101 M20 **Hautes Fagnes** Ger. Hohes Venn. ▲▲ E Belgium
104 K16 **Hautes-Pyrénées** ⬖ department S France
101 L23 **Haute Sûre, Lac de la** ▣ NW Luxembourg
104 M11 **Haute-Vienne** ⬖ department C France
21 S8 **Haut, Isle au** island Maine, NE USA
81 M14 **Haut-Mbomou** ⬖ préfecture SE Central African Republic
105 Q2 **Hautmont** Nord, N France 50.15N 3.55E
81 F19 **Haut-Ogooué** off. Province du Haut-Ogooué, var. Le Haut-Ogooué. ⬖ province SE Gabon
Haut-Ogooué, Le see Haut-Ogooué
105 U7 **Haut-Rhin** ⬖ department NE France
76 I6 **Hauts Plateaux** plateau Algeria/Morocco
40 D9 **Hauula** Haw. Hau'ula. Oahu, Hawaii, USA, C Pacific Ocean 21.36N 157.54W
103 O22 **Hauzenberg** Bayern, SE Germany 48.39N 13.37E
32 K13 **Havana** Illinois, N USA 40.18N 90.03W
Havana see La Habana
99 N23 **Havant** S England, UK 50.51N 0.58W
37 Y14 **Havasu, Lake** ▣ Arizona/California, W USA
97 J23 **Havdrup** Roskilde, E Denmark 55.33N 12.07E
102 N10 **Havel** ≈ NE Germany
101 J21 **Havelange** Namur, SE Belgium 50.23N 5.14E
102 M11 **Havelberg** Sachsen-Anhalt, NE Germany 52.49N 12.05E
155 U5 **Haveliān** North-West Frontier Province, NW Pakistan 34.07N 73.12E
102 N12 **Havelländ Grosse** var. Hauptkanal. canal NE Germany
12 J14 **Havelock** Ontario, SE Canada 44.22N 77.57W
193 J14 **Havelock** Marlborough, South Island, NZ 41.17S 173.46E
23 X11 **Havelock** North Carolina, SE USA 34.52N 76.54W
192 O11 **Havelock North** Hawke's Bay, North Island, NZ 39.40S 176.53E
100 M8 **Havelte** Drenthe, NE Netherlands 52.46N 6.14E
29 N6 **Haven** Kansas, C USA 37.54N 97.46W
99 H21 **Haverfordwest** SW Wales, UK 51.49N 4.57W
99 P20 **Haverhill** E England, UK 52.04N 0.26E
21 O10 **Haverhill** Massachusetts, NE USA 42.46N 71.02W
95 G17 **Haverö** Västernorrland, C Sweden 62.25N 15.04E
113 I17 **Havířov** Ostravský Kraj, E Czech Republic 49.47N 18.30E
113 E17 **Havlíčkův Brod** Ger. Deutsch-Brod; prev. Německý Brod. Jihlavský Kraj, C Czech Republic 49.41N 15.47E
94 K7 **Havøysund** Finnmark, N Norway 70.59N 24.39E
35 T7 **Havre** Montana, NW USA 48.33N 109.40W
Havre see le Havre
101 F20 **Havré** Hainaut, S Belgium 50.28N 4.03E
11 P11 **Havre-St-Pierre** Quebec, E Canada 50.16N 63.36W
142 B10 **Havsa** Edirne, NW Turkey 41.33N 26.49E
40 D8 **Hawaii** off. State of Hawaii; also known as Aloha State, Paradise of the Pacific. ⬖ state USA, C Pacific Ocean
40 G12 **Hawaii** Haw. Hawai'i. island Hawaiian Islands, USA, C Pacific Ocean
199 K5 **Hawaiian Islands** prev. Sandwich Islands. island group Hawaii, USA, C Pacific Ocean
199 Jj6 **Hawaiian Ridge** undersea feature N Pacific Ocean
199 Kk6 **Hawaiian Trough** undersea feature N Pacific Ocean
31 R12 **Hawarden** Iowa, C USA 43.00N 96.29W
Hawash see Āwash
145 P6 **Hawbayn al Gharbīyah** C Iraq 34.24N 42.06E
193 D21 **Hawea, Lake** ◎ South Island, NZ
192 K11 **Hawera** Taranaki, North Island, NZ 39.36S 174.16E
22 J5 **Hawesville** Kentucky, S USA 37.53N 86.44W
40 G11 **Hawi** Haw. Hāwī. Hawaii, USA, C Pacific Ocean 20.13N 155.49W
98 K13 **Hawick** SE Scotland, UK 55.24N 2.49W
145 S4 **Ḩawījah** C Iraq 35.15N 43.54E
145 Y10 **Ḩawīzah, Hawr al** ◎ S Iraq
193 E21 **Hawkdun Range** ▲▲ South Island, NZ
192 P10 **Hawke Bay** bay North Island, NZ
190 I6 **Hawker** South Australia 31.54S 138.25E
192 N11 **Hawke's Bay** off. Hawkes Bay Region. ⬖ region North Island, NZ
155 O16 **Hawkes Bay** bay SE Pakistan
13 N12 **Hawkesbury** Ontario, SE Canada 45.35N 74.37W
Hawkeye State see Iowa
25 T5 **Hawkinsville** Georgia, SE USA 32.16N 83.28W
12 B7 **Hawk Junction** Ontario, S Canada 48.05N 84.34W

◆ Country
● Country Capital
◇ Dependent Territory
○ Dependent Territory Capital
⬖ Administrative Region
✕ International Airport
▲ Mountain
▲▲ Mountain Range
Volcano
≈ River
◎ Lake
▣ Reservoir

HAW KNOB – HIKURANGI TRENCH

23 N10 **Haw Knob** ▲ North Carolina/Tennessee, SE USA *35.18N 84.01W*
23 Q9 **Hawksbill Mountain** ▲ North Carolina, SE USA *35.54N 81.53W*
35 Z16 **Hawk Springs** Wyoming, C USA *41.48N 104.17W*
Hawlēr *see* Arbīl
31 S5 **Hawley** Minnesota, N USA *46.53N 96.18W*
27 P7 **Hawley** Texas, SW USA *32.36N 99.47W*
147 R14 **Ḥawrā'** C Yemen *15.39N 48.20E*
145 P7 **Ḥawrān, Wadi** *dry watercourse* W Iraq
23 T9 **Haw River** ≈ North Carolina, SE USA
145 U5 **Hawshqūrah** E Iraq *34.34N 45.33E*
37 S7 **Hawthorne** Nevada, W USA *38.30N 118.38W*
39 W3 **Haxtun** Colorado, C USA *40.36N 102.38W*
191 N9 **Hay** New South Wales, SE Australia *34.31S 144.50E*
9 O10 **Hay** ≈ W Canada
176 U11 **Haya** Pulau Seram, E Indonesia *3.22S 129.31E*
172 N11 **Hayachine-san** ▲ Honshū, C Japan *39.31N 141.28E*
105 S4 **Hayange** Moselle, NE France *49.19N 6.04E*
HaYarden *see* Jordan
Hayastani Hanrapetut'yun *see* Armenia
Hayasui-seto *see* Hōyo-kaikyō
41 N9 **Haycock** Alaska, USA *65.12N 161.10W*
38 M14 **Hayden** Arizona, SW USA *33.00N 110.46W*
39 Q3 **Hayden** Colorado, C USA *40.29N 107.15W*
30 M10 **Hayes** South Dakota, N USA *44.20N 101.01W*
9 X13 **Hayes** ≈ Manitoba, C Canada
15 Kk11 **Hayes** ≈ Nunavut, NE Canada
30 M16 **Hayes Center** Nebraska, C USA *40.28N 101.01W*
41 S10 **Hayes, Mount** ▲ Alaska, USA *63.37N 146.43W*
23 N11 **Hayesville** North Carolina, SE USA *35.15N 84.15W*
37 X10 **Hayford Peak** ▲ Nevada, W USA *36.40N 115.10W*
36 M3 **Hayfork** California, W USA *40.33N 123.10W*
Hayir, Qasr al *see* Ḥayr al Gharbī, Qaṣr al
169 P8 **Haylaastay** Sühbaatar, E Mongolia *46.44N 113.51E*
12 I12 **Hay Lake** ⊚ Ontario, SE Canada
147 X11 **Haymā'** *var.* Haima. C Oman *19.58N 56.20E*
142 H13 **Haymana** Ankara, C Turkey *39.25N 32.30E*
144 J7 **Ḥaymūr, Jabal** ▲ W Syria
Haynau *see* Chojnów
24 G4 **Haynesville** Louisiana, S USA *32.57N 93.08W*
25 P6 **Hayneville** Alabama, S USA *32.13N 86.34W*
116 M12 **Hayrabolu** Tekirdağ, NW Turkey *41.12N 27.08E*
142 C10 **Hayrabolu Deresi** ≈ NW Turkey
144 J6 **Ḥayr al Gharbī, Qaṣr al** *var.* Qasr al Hayir, Qasr al Hir al Gharbi. *ruins* Ḥimṣ, C Syria *34.23N 37.40E*
144 L5 **Ḥayr ash Sharqī, Qaṣr al** *var.* Qasr al Hir Ash Sharqī. *ruins* Ḥimṣ, C Syria *35.07N 39.06E*
15 Hh9 **Hay River** Northwest Territories, W Canada *60.51N 115.42W*
28 K4 **Hays** Kansas, C USA *38.52N 99.19W*
30 K12 **Hay Springs** Nebraska, C USA *42.40N 102.41W*
67 H25 **Haystack, The** ▲ NE Saint Helena *15.55S 5.40W*
29 N7 **Haysville** Kansas, C USA *37.34N 97.21W*
119 O7 **Haysyn** *Rus.* Gaysin. Vinnyts'ka Oblast', C Ukraine *48.49N 29.29E*
29 Y9 **Hayti** Missouri, C USA *36.13N 89.45W*
31 Q9 **Hayti** South Dakota, N USA *44.39N 97.11W*
119 O8 **Hayvoron** *Rus.* Gayvorno. Kirovohrads'ka Oblast', C Ukraine *48.19N 29.54E*
37 N9 **Hayward** California, W USA *37.40N 122.07W*
32 J4 **Hayward** Wisconsin, N USA *46.01N 91.25W*
99 O23 **Haywards Heath** SE England, UK *51.00N 0.06W*
149 S11 **Hazārān, Kūh-e** *var.* Kūh-e ā Hazr. ▲ SE Iran *29.26N 57.15E*
Hazarat Imam *see* Emām Ṣāḥeb
23 O7 **Hazard** Kentucky, S USA *37.15N 83.11W*
143 O15 **Hazar Gölü** ⊚ C Turkey
159 P15 **Hazārībāg** *var.* Hazārībāgh. Bihār, N India *24.00N 85.23E*
Hazārībāgh *see* Hazārībāg
105 O1 **Hazebrouck** Nord, N France *50.43N 2.33E*
32 K9 **Hazel Green** Wisconsin, N USA *42.33N 90.26W*
199 Ii10 **Hazel Holme Bank** *undersea feature* S Pacific Ocean *12.49S 174.30E*
8 K13 **Hazelton** British Columbia, SW Canada *55.15N 127.37W*
31 N6 **Hazelton** North Dakota, N USA *46.27N 100.17W*
37 R5 **Hazen** Nevada, W USA *39.33N 119.02W*
30 L5 **Hazen** North Dakota, N USA *47.18N 101.37W*
40 L12 **Hazen Bay** *bay* E Bering Sea
145 S5 **Hazim, Bi'r** *well* C Iraq *34.50N 43.25E*
25 V6 **Hazlehurst** Georgia, SE USA *31.51N 82.35W*
24 K6 **Hazlehurst** Mississippi, S USA *31.51N 90.24W*
20 K15 **Hazlet** New Jersey, NE USA *40.24N 74.10W*
152 I9 **Hazorasp** *Rus.* Khazarosp. Khorazm Wiloyati, W Uzbekistan *41.21N 61.01E*
153 R13 **Hazratishoh, Qatorkŭhi** *var.* Khrebet Khazretishi, *Rus.* Khrebet Khozretishi. ▲▲ S Tajikistan
Hazr, Kūh-e ā *see* Hazārān, Kūh-e
155 U6 **Hazro** Punjab, E Pakistan *33.55N 72.33E*
25 R7 **Headland** Alabama, S USA *31.21N 85.20W*
190 C6 **Head of Bight** *headland* South Australia *31.33S 131.05E*
35 N10 **Headquarters** Idaho, NW USA *46.38N 115.52W*
36 M7 **Healdsburg** California, W USA *38.36N 122.52W*
29 N13 **Healdton** Oklahoma, C USA *34.13N 97.29W*
191 O12 **Healesville** Victoria, SE Australia *37.41S 145.31E*
41 R10 **Healy** Alaska, USA *63.51N 148.58W*
181 R13 **Heard and McDonald Islands** ◇ *Australian external territory* S Indian Ocean
181 R13 **Heard Island** *island* Heard and McDonald Islands, S Indian Ocean
27 U9 **Hearne** Texas, SW USA *30.52N 96.35W*
10 F12 **Hearst** Ontario, S Canada *49.42N 83.40W*
204 J5 **Hearst Island** *island* Antarctica
Heart of Dixie *see* Alabama
30 L5 **Heart River** ≈ North Dakota, N USA
33 T13 **Heath** Ohio, N USA *40.01N 82.26W*
191 N11 **Heathcote** Victoria, SE Australia *36.57S 144.43E*
99 N22 **Heathrow** ✈ (London)SE England, UK *51.28N 0.27W*
23 X5 **Heathsville** Virginia, NE USA *37.54N 76.25W*
29 R11 **Heavener** Oklahoma, C USA *34.53N 94.36W*
27 R15 **Hebbronville** Texas, SW USA *27.18N 98.40W*
169 Q13 **Hebei** *var.* Hebei Sheng, Hopeh, Hopei, Ji; *prev.* Chihli. ◆ *province* E China
Hebei Sheng *see* Hebei
176 U9 **Hebera** Irian Jaya, E Indonesia *1.08S 129.54E*
38 M3 **Heber City** Utah, W USA *40.29N 111.24W*
29 V10 **Heber Springs** Arkansas, C USA *35.30N 91.58W*
167 N5 **Hebi** Henan, C China *35.57N 114.07E*
34 F11 **Hebo** Oregon, NW USA *45.10N 123.55W*
98 F9 **Hebrides, Sea of the** *sea* NW Scotland, UK
11 P5 **Hebron** Newfoundland, E Canada *58.15N 62.45W*
33 N11 **Hebron** Indiana, N USA *41.19N 87.12W*
31 Q17 **Hebron** Nebraska, C USA *40.10N 97.35W*
30 L5 **Hebron** North Dakota, N USA *46.54N 102.03W*
144 F11 **Hebron** *var.* Al Khalil, El Khalil, *Heb.* Hevron; *anc.* Kiriath-Arba. S West Bank *31.30N 35.00E*
Hebrus *see* Évros/Maritsa/Meriç
97 N14 **Heby** Västmanland, C Sweden *59.55N 16.52E*
8 I14 **Hecate Strait** *strait* British Columbia, W Canada
43 W12 **Hecelchakán** Campeche, SE Mexico *20.09N 90.04W*
166 K13 **Hechi** *var.* Jinchengjiang. Guangxi Zhuangzu Zizhiqu, S China *24.40N 108.05E*
103 H23 **Hechingen** Baden-Württemberg, S Germany *48.20N 8.58E*
101 K17 **Hechtel** Limburg, NE Belgium *51.07N 5.24E*
166 J9 **Hechuan** Chongqing Shi, C China *30.01N 106.15E*
31 P7 **Hecla** South Dakota, N USA *45.52N 98.09W*
31 T9 **Hector** Minnesota, N USA *44.44N 94.43W*
95 F17 **Hede** Jämtland, C Sweden *62.25N 13.33E*
97 M14 **Hedemora** Dalarna, C Sweden *60.18N 15.58E*
94 K13 **Hedenäset** Norrbotten, N Sweden *66.12N 23.40E*
97 G23 **Hedensted** Vejle, C Denmark *55.46N 9.43E*
97 N14 **Hedesunda** Gävleborg, C Sweden *60.25N 17.00E*
97 N14 **Hedesundafjord** ⊚ C Sweden
27 O3 **Hedley** Texas, SW USA *34.52N 100.39W*
96 I12 **Hedmark** ◆ *county* S Norway
172 Pp14 **Hedo-misaki** *headland* Okinawa, SW Japan *26.55N 128.15E*
31 X15 **Hedrick** Iowa, C USA *41.10N 92.18W*
101 L16 **Heel** Limburg, SE Netherlands *51.12N 6.01E*
201 Y12 **Heel Point** *point* Wake Island *19.18N 166.39E*
100 H9 **Heemskerk** Noord-Holland, W Netherlands *52.31N 4.40E*
100 M10 **Heerde** Gelderland, E Netherlands *52.24N 6.01E*
100 L7 **Heerenveen** *Fris.* It Hearrenfean. Friesland, N Netherlands *52.57N 5.55E*
100 I8 **Heerhugowaard** Noord-Holland, NW Netherlands *52.40N 4.49E*
94 O3 **Heer Land** *physical region* C Svalbard
101 M18 **Heerlen** Limburg, SE Netherlands *50.55N 6.00E*
101 J19 **Heers** Limburg, NE Belgium *50.46N 5.17E*
Heerwegen *see* Polkowice
100 K13 **Heesch** Noord-Brabant, S Netherlands *51.43N 5.31E*
101 K15 **Heeze** Noord-Brabant, SE Netherlands *51.22N 5.34E*
144 F8 **Ḥefa** *var.* Haifa; *hist.* Caiffa, Caiphas, *anc.* Sycaminum. Haifa, N Israel *32.49N 34.58E*
144 F8 **Ḥefa, Mifraz** *Eng.* Bay of Haifa. *bay* N Israel
167 Q8 **Hefei** *var.* Hofei; *hist.* Luchow. Anhui, E China *31.51N 117.20E*
25 R3 **Heflin** Alabama, S USA *33.39N 85.35W*
169 X7 **Hegang** Heilongjiang, NE China *47.18N 130.15E*
171 Ii11 **Hegura-jima** *island* SW Japan
Heguri-jima *see* Heigun-tō
Hei *see* Heilongjiang
102 H8 **Heide** Schleswig-Holstein, N Germany *54.12N 9.06E*
103 G20 **Heidelberg** Baden-Württemberg, SW Germany *49.24N 8.40E*
85 J21 **Heidelberg** Gauteng, NE South Africa *26.27S 28.21E*
24 M6 **Heidelberg** Mississippi, S USA *31.53N 88.58W*
Heidenheim *see* Heidenheim an der Brenz
103 J22 **Heidenheim an der Brenz** *var.* Heidenheim. Baden-Württemberg, S Germany *48.40N 10.09E*
111 U2 **Heidenreichstein** Niederösterreich, N Austria *48.53N 15.07E*
170 E14 **Heigun-tō** *var.* Heguri-jima. *island* SW Japan
169 W5 **Heihe** *prev.* Ai-hun. Heilongjiang, NE China *50.13N 127.29E*
Hei-ho *see* Nagqu
85 J22 **Heilbron** Free State, N South Africa *27.16S 27.58E*
103 H21 **Heilbronn** Baden-Württemberg, SW Germany *49.09N 9.13E*
Heiligenbeil *see* Mamonovo
111 Q8 **Heiligenblut** Tirol, W Austria *47.04N 12.50E*
102 K7 **Heiligenhafen** Schleswig-Holstein, N Germany *54.22N 10.57E*
Heiligenkreuz *see* Žiar nad Hronom
103 J15 **Heiligenstadt** Thüringen, C Germany *51.22N 10.09E*
Heilong Jiang *see* Amur
169 W8 **Heilongjiang** *var.* Hei, Heilongjiang Sheng, Hei-lung-chiang, Heilungkiang. ◆ *province* NE China
Heilongjiang Sheng *see* Heilongjiang
100 H9 **Heiloo** Noord-Holland, NW Netherlands *52.36N 4.43E*
Heilsberg *see* Lidzbark Warmiński
Hei-lung-chiang/Heilungkiang *see* Heilongjiang
94 I4 **Heimaey** *var.* Heimaæy. *island* S Iceland
96 H8 **Heimdal** Sør-Trøndelag, S Norway *63.21N 10.22E*
Heinaste *see* Ainaži
95 N17 **Heinävesi** Itä-Suomi, E Finland *62.22N 28.42E*
101 M22 **Heinerscheid** Diekirch, N Luxembourg *50.06N 6.04E*
100 M10 **Heino** Overijssel, E Netherlands *52.26N 6.13E*
95 M18 **Heinola** Etelä-Suomi, S Finland *61.13N 26.04E*
103 C16 **Heinsberg** Nordrhein-Westfalen, W Germany *51.02N 6.01E*
169 U12 **Heishan** Liaoning, NE China *41.43N 122.12E*
166 H8 **Heishui** Sichuan, C China *32.08N 102.54E*
101 H17 **Heist-op-den-Berg** Antwerpen, C Belgium *51.04N 4.43E*
Heitō *see* P'ingtung
176 Y14 **Heitske** Irian Jaya, E Indonesia *7.02S 138.45E*
Hejanah *see* Al Hījānah
Hejaz *see* Al Ḥijāz
166 M14 **He Jiang** ≈ S China
164 K6 **Hejing** Xinjiang Uygur Zizhiqu, NW China *42.21N 86.19E*
Héjjasfalva *see* Vânători
165 S11 **Heka** Qinghai, W China *35.49N 99.49E*
143 N14 **Hekimhan** Malatya, C Turkey *38.49N 37.55E*
94 J4 **Hekla** ▲ S Iceland *63.56N 19.42W*
112 J6 **Hel** *Ger.* Hela. Pomorskie, N Poland *54.35N 18.48E*
Hela *see* Hel
95 F17 **Helagsfjället** ▲ C Sweden *62.57N 12.31E*
165 W8 **Helan** *var.* Xigang. Ningxia, N China *38.33N 106.21E*
168 K14 **Helan Shan** ▲▲ N China
101 M16 **Helden** Limburg, SE Netherlands *51.20N 6.00E*
29 X12 **Helena** Arkansas, C USA *34.32N 90.34W*
35 R10 **Helena** *state capital* Montana. NW USA *46.35N 112.02W*
98 H12 **Helensburgh** W Scotland, UK *56.00N 4.45W*
192 K5 **Helensville** Auckland, North Island, NZ *36.42S 174.25E*
97 L20 **Helgasjön** ⊚ S Sweden
102 G8 **Helgoland** *Eng.* Heligoland. *island* NW Germany
Helgoland Bay *see* Helgoländer Bucht
102 G8 **Helgoländer Bucht** *var.* Helgoland Bay, Heligoland Bight. *bay* NW Germany
Heligoland *see* Helgoland
Heligoland Bight *see* Helgoländer Bucht
Heliopolis *see* Baalbek
94 I4 **Hella** Sudhurland, SW Iceland *63.51N 20.24W*
Hellas *see* Greece
149 N11 **Ḥelleh, Rūd-e** ≈ S Iran
100 N10 **Hellendoorn** Overijssel, E Netherlands *52.22N 6.27E*
Hellenic Republic *see* Greece
123 Gg10 **Hellenic Trough** *undersea feature* Aegean Sea, C Mediterranean Sea
96 E10 **Hellesylt** Møre og Romsdal, S Norway *62.06N 6.51E*
100 F13 **Hellevoetsluis** Zuid-Holland, SW Netherlands *51.49N 4.07E*
107 Q12 **Hellín** Castilla-La Mancha, C Spain *38.31N 1.43W*
117 H19 **Hellinikon** ✈ (Athína) Attikí, C Greece *37.53N 23.43E*
34 M12 **Hells Canyon** *valley* Idaho/Oregon, NW USA
154 L9 **Helmand** ◆ *province* S Afghanistan
154 K10 **Helmand, Daryā-ye** *var.* Rūd-e Hirmand. ≈ Afghanistan/Iran *see also* Hirmand, Rūd-e
Helmantica *see* Salamanca
103 K15 **Helme** ≈ C Germany
101 L15 **Helmond** Noord-Brabant, S Netherlands *51.28N 5.40E*
98 J7 **Helmsdale** N Scotland, UK *58.06N 3.36W*
102 K13 **Helmstedt** Niedersachsen, N Germany *52.13N 11.01E*
169 Y10 **Helong** Jilin, NE China *42.38N 129.01E*
38 M4 **Helper** Utah, W USA *39.40N 110.52W*
102 O10 **Helpter Berge** *hill* NE Germany *53.29N 13.37E*
97 J22 **Helsingborg** *prev.* Hälsingborg. Skåne, S Sweden *55.59N 12.48E*
Helsingfors *see* Helsinki
97 J22 **Helsingør** *Eng.* Elsinore. Frederiksborg, E Denmark *56.03N 12.37E*
95 M20 **Helsinki** *Swe.* Helsingfors. ● (Finland) Etelä-Suomi, S Finland *60.18N 24.58E*
99 H25 **Helston** SW England, UK *50.04N 5.16W*
Heltau *see* Cisnădie
63 C17 **Helvecia** Santa Fe, C Argentina *31.09S 60.09W*
99 K15 **Helvellyn** ▲ NW England, UK *54.31N 3.00W*
Helvetia *see* Switzerland
77 W8 **Helwān** *var.* Hilwān, Hulwan, Hulwān. N Egypt *29.51N 31.19E*
99 N21 **Hemel Hempstead** E England, UK *51.46N 0.28W*
37 U16 **Hemet** California, W USA *33.45N 116.58W*
30 J13 **Hemingford** Nebraska, C USA *42.18N 103.02W*
23 T13 **Hemingway** South Carolina, SE USA *33.45N 79.25W*
94 G13 **Hemnesberget** Nordland, C Norway *66.13N 13.33E*
27 Y8 **Hemphill** Texas, SW USA *31.20N 93.51W*
27 V11 **Hempstead** Texas, SW USA *30.06N 96.04W*
97 P20 **Hemse** Gotland, SE Sweden *57.12N 18.22E*
96 F13 **Hemsedal** *valley* S Norway
165 T11 **Henan** *var.* Henan Mongolzu Zizhixian, Yêgainnyin. Qinghai, C China *34.42N 101.36E*
167 N6 **Henan** *var.* Henan Sheng, Honan, Yu. ◆ *province* C China
192 L4 **Hen and Chickens** *island group* N NZ
Henan Mongolzu Zizhixian/Henan Sheng *see* Henan
107 O7 **Henares** ≈ C Spain
171 M8 **Henashi-zaki** *headland* Honshū, C Japan *40.37N 139.51E*
104 I16 **Hendaye** Pyrénées-Atlantiques, SW France *43.22N 1.46W*
142 F11 **Hendek** Sakarya, NW Turkey *40.49N 30.40E*
63 B21 **Henderson** Buenos Aires, E Argentina *36.18S 61.43W*
22 I5 **Henderson** Kentucky, S USA *37.50N 87.35W*
37 X11 **Henderson** Nevada, W USA *36.02N 114.58W*
23 V8 **Henderson** North Carolina, SE USA *36.19N 78.24W*
22 G10 **Henderson** Tennessee, S USA *35.25N 88.37W*
27 W7 **Henderson** Texas, SW USA *32.09N 94.48W*
32 J12 **Henderson Creek** ≈ Illinois, N USA
195 X16 **Henderson Field** ✈ (Honiara) Guadalcanal, C Solomon Islands *9.28S 160.02E*
203 O17 **Henderson Island** *atoll* N Pitcairn Islands
23 O10 **Hendersonville** North Carolina, SE USA *35.19N 82.27W*
22 J8 **Hendersonville** Tennessee, S USA *36.18N 86.37W*
149 O14 **Hendorābī, Jazīreh-ye** *island* S Iran
57 V10 **Hendrik Top** *var.* Hendriktop. *elevation* C Surinam *4.14N 56.07W*
Hendū Kosh *see* Hindu Kush
12 L12 **Heney, Lac** ⊚ Quebec, SE Canada
194 I12 **Henganofi** Eastern Highlands, C PNG *6.13S 145.31E*
Hengchow *see* Hengyang
167 S15 **Hengchun** S Taiwan *22.09N 120.43E*
165 R16 **Hengduan Shan** ▲▲ SW China
100 N12 **Hengelo** Gelderland, E Netherlands *52.02N 6.18E*
100 O10 **Hengelo** Overijssel, E Netherlands *52.15N 6.48E*
Hengnan *see* Hengyang
167 N11 **Hengshan** Hunan, S China *27.17N 112.51E*
166 L4 **Hengshan** Shaanxi, C China *37.57N 109.17E*
167 O4 **Hengshui** Hebei, E China *37.42N 115.39E*
167 N12 **Hengyang** *var.* Hengnan, Heng-yang; *prev.* Hengchow. Hunan, S China *26.54N 112.33E*
119 U11 **Heniches'k** *Rus.* Genichesk. Khersons'ka Oblast', S Ukraine *46.10N 34.49E*
23 Z4 **Henlopen, Cape** *headland* Delaware, NE USA *38.48N 75.06W*
Henna *see* Enna
96 M10 **Hennan** Gävleborg, C Sweden *62.01N 15.55E*
104 G7 **Hennebont** Morbihan, NW France *47.48N 3.16W*
32 L11 **Hennepin** Illinois, N USA *41.13N 89.21W*
28 M9 **Hennessey** Oklahoma, C USA *36.06N 97.54W*
102 N12 **Hennigsdorf** *var.* Hennigsdorf bei Berlin. Brandenburg, NE Germany *52.37N 13.13E*
Hennigsdorf bei Berlin *see* Hennigsdorf
21 N9 **Henniker** New Hampshire, NE USA *43.10N 71.47W*
27 S5 **Henrietta** Texas, SW USA *33.49N 98.12W*
Henrique de Carvalho *see* Saurimo
32 L12 **Henry** Illinois, N USA *41.06N 89.21W*
23 Y7 **Henry, Cape** *headland* Virginia, NE USA *36.55N 76.01W*
29 P10 **Henryetta** Oklahoma, C USA *35.26N 95.58W*
204 M7 **Henry Ice Rise** *ice cap* Antarctica
16 N1 **Henry Kater, Cape** *headland* Baffin Island, Nunavut, NE Canada *69.09N 66.45W*
35 R13 **Henrys Fork** ≈ Idaho, NW USA
12 E15 **Hensall** Ontario, S Canada *43.25N 81.28W*
102 J9 **Henstedt-Ulzburg** Schleswig-Holstein, N Germany *53.45N 9.59E*
169 N7 **Hentiy** ◆ *province* N Mongolia
168 M7 **Hentiyn Nuruu** ▲▲ N Mongolia
191 P10 **Henty** New South Wales, SE Australia *35.33S 147.03E*
177 Ff8 **Henzada** Irrawaddy, SW Burma *17.36N 95.25E*
103 G19 **Heppenheim** Hessen, W Germany *49.39N 8.38E*
34 J11 **Heppner** Oregon, NW USA *45.21N 119.33W*
166 L15 **Hepu** *prev.* Lianzhou. Guangxi Zhuangzu Zizhiqu, S China *21.40N 109.12E*
94 J2 **Heradhsvötn** ≈ C Iceland
Herakleion *see* Irákleio
154 K5 **Herāt** *var.* Herat; *anc.* Aria. Herāt, W Afghanistan *34.22N 62.11E*
154 J5 **Herāt** ◆ *province* W Afghanistan
105 P14 **Hérault** ◆ *department* S France
105 P15 **Hérault** ≈ S France
9 T16 **Herbert** Saskatchewan, S Canada *50.27N 107.09W*
193 F22 **Herbert** Otago, South Island, NZ *45.14S 170.48E*
40 J17 **Herbert Island** *island* Aleutian Islands, Alaska, USA
194 I12 **Herbert, Mount** ▲ C PNG *5.44S 145.00E*
Herbertshöhe *see* Kokopo
13 Q7 **Hérbertville** Quebec, SE Canada *48.22N 71.42W*
103 G17 **Herborn** Hessen, W Germany *50.40N 8.18E*
115 I17 **Herceg-Novi** *It.* Castelnuovo; *prev.* Ercegnovi. Montenegro, SW Yugoslavia *42.28N 18.35E*
9 X10 **Herchmer** Manitoba, C Canada *57.25N 94.12W*
194 K14 **Hercules Bay** *bay* E PNG
94 K2 **Herdhubreidh** ▲ C Iceland *65.12N 16.26W*
44 M13 **Heredia** Heredia, C Costa Rica *10.00N 84.06W*
44 M12 **Heredia** *off.* Provincia de Heredia. ◆ *province* N Costa Rica
99 K21 **Hereford** W England, UK *52.04N 2.43W*
26 M3 **Hereford** Texas, SW USA *34.49N 102.25W*
13 Q13 **Hereford, Mont** ▲ Quebec, SE Canada *45.04N 71.38W*
99 K21 **Herefordshire** *cultural region* W England, UK
203 U11 **Hereheretue** *atoll* Îles Tuamotu, C French Polynesia
107 N10 **Herencia** Castilla-La Mancha, C Spain *39.19N 3.19W*
101 H18 **Herent** Vlaams Brabant, C Belgium *50.54N 4.40E*
101 I16 **Herentals** *var.* Herenthals. Antwerpen, N Belgium *51.10N 4.49E*
Herenthals *see* Herentals
101 H17 **Herenthout** Antwerpen, N Belgium *51.09N 4.45E*
97 J23 **Herfølge** Roskilde, E Denmark *55.25N 12.09E*
102 G13 **Herford** Nordrhein-Westfalen, NW Germany *52.07N 8.40E*
29 O5 **Herington** Kansas, C USA *38.37N 96.55W*
110 H7 **Herisau** *Fr.* Hérisau. Appenzell Ausser Rhoden, NE Switzerland *47.22N 9.16E*
Héristal *see* Herstal
101 J18 **Herk-de-Stad** Limburg, NE Belgium *50.57N 5.12E*
Herkulesbad/Herkulesfürdő *see* Băile Herculane
Herlen Gol/Herlen He *see* Kerulen
37 Q4 **Herlong** California, W USA *40.07N 120.06W*
99 L26 **Herm** *island* Channel Islands
111 R9 **Hermagor** *Slvn.* Šmohor. Kärnten, S Austria *46.37N 13.24E*
31 S7 **Herman** Minnesota, N USA *45.49N 96.08W*
98 L1 **Herma Ness** *headland* NE Scotland, UK *60.51N 0.55W*
29 V4 **Hermann** Missouri, C USA *38.40N 91.25W*
189 Q8 **Hermannsburg** Northern Territory, N Australia *23.59S 132.55E*
Hermannstadt *see* Sibiu
96 E12 **Hermansverk** Sogn og Fjordane, S Norway *61.10N 6.52E*
144 H6 **Hermel** *var.* Hirmil. NE Lebanon *34.23N 36.19E*
Hermhausen *see* Hajnówka
191 P6 **Hermidale** New South Wales, SE Australia *31.36S 146.42E*
57 X9 **Herminadorp** Sipaliwini, NE Surinam *5.05N 54.22W*
34 K11 **Hermiston** Oregon, NW USA *45.50N 119.17W*
29 T6 **Hermitage** Missouri, C USA *37.57N 93.21W*
194 I8 **Hermit Islands** *island group* N PNG
27 O7 **Hermleigh** Texas, SW USA *32.37N 100.44W*
144 G7 **Hermon, Mount** *Ar.* Jabal ash Shaykh. ▲ S Syria *35.30N 33.30E*
Hermopolis Parva *see* Damanhûr
30 J10 **Hermosa** South Dakota, N USA *43.49N 103.12W*
42 F5 **Hermosillo** Sonora, NW Mexico *28.58N 110.53W*
Hermoupolis *see* Ermoúpoli
113 N20 **Hernád** *var.* Hornád, *Ger.* Kundert. ≈ Hungary/Slovakia
63 C18 **Hernández** Entre Ríos, E Argentina *32.21S 60.01W*
25 V11 **Hernando** Florida, SE USA *28.54N 82.22W*
24 L1 **Hernando** Mississippi, S USA *34.49N 89.59W*
107 Q2 **Hernani** País Vasco, N Spain *43.16N 1.58W*
101 F19 **Herne** Vlaams Brabant, C Belgium *50.45N 4.03E*
103 E14 **Herne** Nordrhein-Westfalen, W Germany *51.33N 7.13E*
97 F22 **Herning** Ringkøbing, W Denmark *56.07N 8.58E*
Hernösand *see* Härnösand
124 Q13 **Herodotus Basin** *undersea feature* E Mediterranean Sea
124 Nn14 **Herodotus Trough** *undersea feature* C Mediterranean Sea
31 T11 **Heron Lake** Minnesota, N USA *43.48N 95.18W*
Herowābād *see* Khalkhāl
97 G16 **Herre** Telemark, S Norway *59.06N 9.34E*
31 N7 **Herreid** South Dakota, N USA *45.49N 100.04W*
103 H22 **Herrenberg** Baden-Württemberg, S Germany *48.36N 8.52E*
106 L14 **Herrera** Andalucía, S Spain *37.22N 4.49W*
45 R17 **Herrera** *off.* Provincia de Herrera. ◆ *province* S Panama
106 L10 **Herrera del Duque** Extremadura, W Spain *39.10N 5.03W*
106 M4 **Herrera de Pisuerga** Castilla-León, N Spain *42.34N 4.19W*
43 Z13 **Herrero, Punta** *headland* SE Mexico *19.15N 87.28W*
191 P16 **Herrick** Tasmania, SE Australia *41.07S 147.53E*
32 L17 **Herrin** Illinois, N USA *37.48N 89.01W*
22 M6 **Herrington Lake** ⊠ Kentucky, S USA
97 K18 **Herrljunga** Västra Götaland, S Sweden *58.04N 13.01E*
105 N16 **Hers** ≈ S France
8 I1 **Herschel Island** *island* Yukon Territory, NW Canada
101 I17 **Herselt** Antwerpen, C Belgium *51.03N 4.52E*
20 G15 **Hershey** Pennsylvania, NE USA *40.17N 76.39W*
101 K19 **Herstal** *Fr.* Héristal. Liège, E Belgium *50.40N 5.37E*
99 O21 **Hertford** E England, UK *51.48N 0.04W*
23 X8 **Hertford** North Carolina, SE USA *36.11N 76.28W*
99 O21 **Hertfordshire** *cultural region* E England, UK
189 Z9 **Hervey Bay** Queensland, E Australia *25.17S 152.48E*
103 O14 **Herzberg** Brandenburg, E Germany *51.42N 13.15E*
101 E18 **Herzele** Oost-Vlaanderen, NW Belgium *50.52N 3.52E*
103 K20 **Herzogenaurach** Bayern, SE Germany *49.34N 10.52E*
111 W4 **Herzogenburg** Niederösterreich, NE Austria *48.18N 15.43E*
Herzogenbusch *see* 's-Hertogenbosch
105 N2 **Hesdin** Pas-de-Calais, N France *50.21N 2.00E*
166 K14 **Heshan** Guangxi Zhuangzu Zizhiqu, S China *23.45N 108.58E*
165 X10 **Heshui** *var.* Xihuachi. Gansu, C China *35.42N 108.06E*
101 M25 **Hespérange** Luxembourg, SE Luxembourg *49.34N 6.10E*
37 U14 **Hesperia** California, W USA *34.25N 117.17W*
39 P7 **Hesperus Mountain** ▲ Colorado, C USA *37.27N 108.05W*
8 J6 **Hess** ≈ Yukon Territory, NW Canada
Hesse *see* Hessen
103 J21 **Hesselberg** ▲ S Germany *49.04N 10.32E*
97 I22 **Hesselo** *island* E Denmark
103 H17 **Hessen** *Eng./Fr.* Hesse. ◆ *state* C Germany
199 Jj6 **Hess Tablemount** *undersea feature* C Pacific Ocean *17.49N 174.15W*
29 N6 **Hesston** Kansas, C USA *38.08N 97.25W*
95 G15 **Hestskjølen** ▲ C Norway *64.21N 13.57E*
99 K18 **Heswall** NW England, UK *53.19N 3.06W*
159 P12 **Hetauda** Central, C Nepal
Hétfalu *see* Săcele
30 K7 **Hettinger** North Dakota, N USA *46.00N 102.38W*
103 L14 **Hettstedt** Sachsen-Anhalt, C Germany *51.39N 11.31E*
94 P3 **Heuglin, Kapp** *headland* SE Svalbard *78.15N 22.49E*
195 Y16 **Heuru** San Cristobal, SE Solomon Islands *10.13S 161.25E*
101 J17 **Heusden** Limburg, NE Belgium *51.01N 5.16E*
100 J13 **Heusden** Noord-Brabant, S Netherlands *51.43N 5.05E*
104 K3 **Hève, Cap de la** *headland* N France *49.28N 0.13W*
101 H18 **Heverlee** Vlaams Brabant, C Belgium *50.52N 4.41E*
113 L22 **Heves** Heves, NE Hungary *47.37N 20.17E*
113 L22 **Heves** *off.* Heves Megye. ◆ *county* NE Hungary
Hevron *see* Hebron
47 Y13 **Hewanorra** ✈ (Saint Lucia) S Saint Lucia *13.44N 60.57W*
166 M13 **Hexian** *var.* Babu, He Xian. Guangxi Zhuangzu Zizhiqu, S China *24.25N 111.31E*
166 L6 **Heyang** Shaanxi, C China *35.03N 109.55E*
Heydebrech *see* Kędzierzyn-Kozle
Heydekrug *see* Šilutė
99 K16 **Heysham** NW England, UK *54.02N 2.54W*
167 O14 **Heyuan** Guangdong, S China *23.50N 114.43E*
190 L12 **Heywood** Victoria, SE Australia *38.09S 141.38E*
188 K3 **Heywood Islands** *island group* Western Australia
167 O6 **Heze** *var.* Caozhou. Shandong, E China *35.16N 115.27E*
165 U11 **Hezheng** Gansu, C China *35.24N 103.21E*
165 U11 **Hezuozhen** Gansu, C China *34.55N 102.49E*
25 Z16 **Hialeah** Florida, SE USA *25.51N 80.16W*
29 Q3 **Hiawatha** Kansas, C USA *39.48N 95.31W*
38 M4 **Hiawatha** Utah, W USA *39.28N 111.00W*
31 V4 **Hibbing** Minnesota, N USA *47.24N 92.55W*
191 N17 **Hibbs, Point** *headland* Tasmania, SE Australia *42.37S 145.15E*
Hibernia *see* Ireland
170 D12 **Hibiki-nada** *inlet* SW Japan
22 F8 **Hickman** Kentucky, S USA *36.34N 89.11W*
23 Q9 **Hickory** North Carolina, SE USA *35.44N 81.20W*
23 Q9 **Hickory, Lake** ⊚ North Carolina, SE USA
192 Q7 **Hicks Bay** Gisborne, North Island, NZ *37.36S 178.18E*
27 S8 **Hico** Texas, SW USA *31.58N 98.01W*
172 Oo6 **Hidaka** Hokkaidō, NE Japan *42.53N 142.24E*
171 Gg13 **Hidaka** Hyōgo, Honshū, SW Japan *35.27N 134.43E*
172 P7 **Hidaka-sanmyaku** ▲▲ Hokkaidō, NE Japan
43 O6 **Hidalgo** *var.* Villa Hidalgo. Coahuila de Zaragoza, NE Mexico *27.46N 99.54W*
43 N8 **Hidalgo** Nuevo León, NE Mexico *29.58N 100.27W*
43 O10 **Hidalgo** Tamaulipas, C Mexico *24.17N 99.21W*
43 O13 **Hidalgo** ◆ *state* C Mexico
42 J7 **Hidalgo del Parral** *var.* Parral. Chihuahua, N Mexico *26.58N 105.40W*
171 J14 **Hida-sanmyaku** ▲▲ Honshū, S Japan
102 N7 **Hiddensee** *island* NE Germany
82 G6 **Hidiglib, Wadi** ≈ NE Sudan
111 U6 **Hieflau** Salzburg, E Austria *47.36N 14.34E*
197 H5 **Hienghène** Province Nord, C New Caledonia *20.43S 164.54E*
Hierosolyma *see* Jerusalem
66 N12 **Hierro** *var.* Ferro. *island* Islas Canarias, Spain, NE Atlantic Ocean
170 Ee13 **Higashi-Hiroshima** *var.* Higasihirosima. Hiroshima, Honshū, SW Japan *34.25N 132.45E*
171 J18 **Higashi-Izu** Shizuoka, Honshū, S Japan *34.43N 138.58E*
171 Ll12 **Higashine** *var.* Higasine. Yamagata, Honshū, C Japan *38.26N 140.23E*
170 C11 **Higashi-suidō** *strait* SW Japan
Higasihirosima *see* Higashi-Hiroshima
Higasine *see* Higashine
27 P1 **Higgins** Texas, SW USA *36.06N 100.01W*
33 P7 **Higgins Lake** ⊚ Michigan, N USA
29 S4 **Higginsville** Missouri, C USA *39.04N 93.43W*
High Atlas *see* Haut Atlas
32 M5 **High Falls Reservoir** ⊠ Wisconsin, N USA
46 K12 **Highgate** C Jamaica *18.15N 76.53W*
27 X11 **High Island** Texas, SW USA *29.35N 94.24W*
33 O5 **High Island** *island* Michigan, N USA
32 K15 **Highland** Illinois, N USA *38.44N 89.40W*
33 N10 **Highland Park** Illinois, N USA *42.10N 87.48W*
23 O10 **Highlands** North Carolina, SE USA *35.04N 83.10W*
9 O11 **High Level** Alberta, W Canada *58.31N 117.07W*
31 O9 **Highmore** South Dakota, N USA *44.29N 99.26W*
179 Oo10 **High Peak** ▲ Luzon, N Philippines *15.28N 120.07E*
High Plains *see* Great Plains
23 S9 **High Point** North Carolina, SE USA *35.58N 80.00W*
20 J13 **High Point** *hill* New Jersey, NE USA *41.19N 74.38W*
9 P13 **High Prairie** Alberta, W Canada *55.27N 116.28W*
9 Q16 **High River** Alberta, SW Canada *50.34N 113.49W*
23 S9 **High Rock Lake** ⊠ North Carolina, SE USA
25 V9 **High Springs** Florida, SE USA *29.49N 82.36W*
High Veld *see* Great Karoo
99 J24 **High Willhays** ▲ SW England, UK *50.39N 3.58W*
99 N22 **High Wycombe** *prev.* Chepping Wycombe, Chipping Wycombe. SE England, UK *51.37N 0.46W*
43 P12 **Higos** *var.* El Higo. Veracruz-Llave, E Mexico *21.47N 98.28W*
104 I16 **Higuer, Cap** *headland* NE Spain *43.23N 1.46W*
47 R5 **Higüero, Punta** *headland* W Puerto Rico *18.21N 67.15W*
47 P9 **Higüey** *var.* Salvaleón de Higüey. E Dominican Republic *18.34N 68.43W*
202 G11 **Hihifo** ✈ (Matā'utu) Île Uvea, N Wallis and Futuna
83 N16 **Hiiraan** *off.* Gobolka Hiiraan. ◆ *region* C Somalia
120 E4 **Hiiumaa** *off.* Hiiumaa Maakond. ◆ *province* W Estonia
120 D4 **Hiiumaa** *Ger.* Dagden, *Swe.* Dagö. *island* W Estonia
Hijanah *see* Al Hījānah
107 S6 **Híjar** Aragón, NE Spain *41.10N 0.27W*
170 E13 **Hikari** Yamaguchi, Honshū, SW Japan *33.55N 131.58E*
170 Ff15 **Hiketa** Kagawa, Shikoku, SW Japan *34.15N 134.20E*
171 Hh15 **Hikone** Shiga, Honshū, SW Japan *35.15N 136.14E*
170 D13 **Hiko-san** ▲ Kyūshū, SW Japan *33.29N 130.55E*
203 V10 **Hikueru** *atoll* Îles Tuamotu, C French Polynesia
192 K3 **Hikurangi** Northland, North Island, NZ *35.37S 174.16E*
192 Q8 **Hikurangi** ▲ North Island, NZ *37.55S 177.59E*
199 J13 **Hikurangi Trench** *var.* Hikurangi Trough. *undersea feature* SW Pacific Ocean

◆ Country ● Country Capital ◇ Dependent Territory ○ Dependent Territory Capital ◆ Administrative Region ✈ International Airport ▲ Mountain ▲▲ Mountain Range Volcano ≈ River ⊚ Lake ⊠ Reservoir

265

HIKURANGI TROUGH – HORLICK MOUNTAINS

Hikurangi Trough see Hikurangi Trench
202 B15 **Hikutavake** NW Niue
124 Nn14 **Hilāl, Ra's al** headland N Libya 32.55N 22.09E
63 A24 **Hilario Ascasubi** Buenos Aires, E Argentina 39.22S 62.39W
103 K17 **Hildburghausen** Thüringen, C Germany 50.26N 10.44E
103 E15 **Hilden** Nordrhein-Westfalen, W Germany 51.10N 6.55E
102 I13 **Hildesheim** Niedersachsen, N Germany 52.09N 9.57E
35 T9 **Hilger** Montana, NW USA 47.15N 109.18W
Hili see Hilli
Hilla see Al Ḩillah
47 O14 **Hillaby, Mount** ▲ N Barbados 13.12N 59.34W
97 K19 **Hillared** Västra Götaland, S Sweden 57.37N 13.10E
205 R12 **Hillary Coast** physical region Antarctica
44 G2 **Hill Bank** Orange Walk, N Belize 17.36N 88.43W
35 O14 **Hill City** Idaho, NW USA 43.18N 115.03W
28 K3 **Hill City** Kansas, C USA 39.21N 99.51W
31 V5 **Hill City** Minnesota, N USA 46.59N 93.36W
30 J10 **Hill City** South Dakota, N USA 43.54N 103.33W
67 C24 **Hill Cove Settlement** West Falkland, Falkland Islands
100 H10 **Hillegom** Zuid-Holland, W Netherlands 52.18N 4.34E
97 J22 **Hillerød** Frederiksborg, E Denmark 55.55N 12.19E
38 M7 **Hillers, Mount** ▲ Utah, W USA 37.53N 110.42W
159 S13 **Hilli** var. Hili. Rajshahi, NW Bangladesh 25.17N 89.02E
31 R11 **Hills** Minnesota, N USA 43.31N 96.21W
32 L14 **Hillsboro** Illinois, N USA 39.09N 89.29W
29 N5 **Hillsboro** Kansas, C USA 38.21N 97.12W
29 X5 **Hillsboro** Missouri, C USA 38.13N 90.33W
21 N10 **Hillsboro** New Hampshire, NE USA 43.06N 71.52W
39 Q14 **Hillsboro** New Mexico, SW USA 32.55N 107.33W
31 R4 **Hillsboro** North Dakota, N USA 47.25N 97.03W
33 R14 **Hillsboro** Ohio, N USA 39.12N 83.36W
34 G11 **Hillsboro** Oregon, NW USA 45.31N 122.59W
27 T8 **Hillsboro** Texas, SW USA 32.01N 97.08W
32 K8 **Hillsboro** Wisconsin, N USA 43.40N 90.21W
25 Y14 **Hillsboro Canal** canal Florida, SE USA
47 Y15 **Hillsborough** Carriacou, N Grenada 12.28N 61.28W
99 G15 **Hillsborough** E Northern Ireland, UK 54.27N 6.06W
23 U9 **Hillsborough** North Carolina, SE USA 36.04N 79.06W
33 Q10 **Hillsdale** Michigan, N USA 41.55N 84.37W
191 O8 **Hillston** New South Wales, SE Australia 33.30S 145.33E
23 R7 **Hillsville** Virginia, NE USA 36.45N 80.44W
98 L2 **Hillswick** NE Scotland, UK 60.28N 1.37W
Hill Tippera see Tripura
40 H11 **Hilo** Hawaii, USA, C Pacific Ocean 19.42N 155.04W
20 F9 **Hilton** New York, NE USA 43.17N 77.47W
12 C10 **Hilton Beach** Ontario, S Canada 46.14N 83.51W
23 R16 **Hilton Head Island** South Carolina, SE USA 32.13N 80.45W
23 R16 **Hilton Head Island** island South Carolina, SE USA
101 J15 **Hilvarenbeek** Noord-Brabant, S Netherlands 51.28N 5.07E
100 J11 **Hilversum** Noord-Holland, C Netherlands 52.13N 5.10E
Hilwān see Helwān
158 J7 **Himāchal Pradesh** ◐ state NW India
Himalaya/Himalaya Shan see Himalayas
158 M9 **Himalayas** var. Himalaya, Chin. Himalaya Shan. ▲▲ S Asia
179 Q14 **Himamaylan** Negros, C Philippines 10.04N 122.52E
95 K15 **Himanka** Länsi-Suomi, W Finland 64.03N 24.40E
Himara see Himarë
115 L23 **Himarë** var. Himara. Vlorë, S Albania 40.06N 19.45E
144 M2 **Ḩimār, Wādī al** dry watercourse N Syria
160 D9 **Himatnagar** Gujarāt, W India 23.37N 73.01E
111 Y4 **Himberg** Niederösterreich, E Austria 48.03N 16.27E
171 J14 **Hime-gawa** ≈ Honshū, S Japan
170 G14 **Himeji** var. Himezi. Hyōgo, Honshū, SW Japan 34.47N 134.32E
170 Dd13 **Hime-jima** island SW Japan
Himezi see Himeji
171 Ii13 **Himi** Toyama, Honshū, SW Japan 36.52N 136.59E
111 S9 **Himmelberg** Kärnten, S Austria 46.45N 14.01E
144 I5 **Ḩimş** var. Homs; anc. Emesa. Ḩimş, C Syria 34.43N 36.43E
144 K6 **Ḩimş** off. Muḩāfaẓat Ḩimş, var. Homs. ◐ governorate C Syria
144 I5 **Ḩimş, Buḩayrat** var. Buḩayrat Qaţţīnah. ◎ W Syria
179 Rr15 **Hinatuan** Mindanao, S Philippines 8.21N 126.19E
119 N10 **Hinceşti** var. Hânceşti; prev. Kotovsk. C Moldova 46.48N 28.33E
46 M9 **Hinche** C Haiti 19.07N 72.00W
189 X5 **Hinchinbrook Island** island Queensland, NE Australia
41 S12 **Hinchinbrook Island** island Alaska, USA
99 M19 **Hinckley** C England, UK 52.33N 1.21W
31 V7 **Hinckley** Minnesota, N USA 46.01N 92.57W
38 K5 **Hinckley** Utah, W USA 39.21N 112.39W
20 J9 **Hinckley Reservoir** ⊡ New York, NE USA
158 I12 **Hindaun** Rājasthān, N India 26.43N 77.01E
Hindenburg/Hindenburg in Oberschlesien see Zabrze
Hindiya see Al Hindīyah
23 O6 **Hindman** Kentucky, S USA 37.20N 82.58W
190 L10 **Hindmarsh, Lake** ◎ Victoria, SE Australia
193 G19 **Hinds** Canterbury, South Island, NZ 44.00S 171.33E
193 G19 **Hinds** ≈ South Island, NZ
97 H23 **Hindsholm** island C Denmark
155 S4 **Hindu Kush** Per. Hendū Kosh. ▲▲ Afghanistan/Pakistan
161 H19 **Hindupur** Andhra Pradesh, E India 13.46N 77.33E
9 O12 **Hines Creek** Alberta, W Canada 56.14N 118.36W
25 W6 **Hinesville** Georgia, SE USA 31.51N 81.36W
160 I12 **Hinganghāt** Mahārāshtra, C India 20.31N 78.52E
155 N15 **Hingol** ≈ SW Pakistan
160 H13 **Hingoli** Mahārāshtra, C India 19.45N 77.08E
143 R13 **Hınıs** Erzurum, E Turkey 39.22N 41.43E
94 O2 **Hinlopenstretet** strait N Svalbard
94 G10 **Hinnøya** island C Norway
170 D15 **Hinokage** Miyazaki, Kyūshū, SW Japan 32.39N 131.20E
170 F11 **Hino-misaki** headland Honshū, SW Japan 35.25N 132.37E
110 H10 **Hinterrhein** ≈ SW Switzerland
9 O14 **Hinton** Alberta, SW Canada 53.24N 117.34W
28 M10 **Hinton** Oklahoma, C USA 35.28N 98.21W
23 R6 **Hinton** West Virginia, NE USA 37.40N 80.53W
Hios see Chíos
43 N8 **Hipolito** Coahuila de Zaragoza, NE Mexico 25.42N 101.22W
Hipponium see Vibo Valentia
170 C12 **Hirado** Nagasaki, Hirado-shima, SW Japan 33.22N 129.32E
170 C12 **Hirado-shima** island SW Japan
171 Gg15 **Hirakata** Ōsaka, Honshū, SW Japan 34.48N 135.37E
172 P17 **Hirakubo-saki** headland Ishigaki-jima, SW Japan 24.36N 124.19E
160 M11 **Hīrākud Reservoir** ⊡ E India
Hir al Gharbi, Qasr al see Ḩayr al Gharbi, Qaşr al
172 N9 **Hiranai** Aomori, Honshū, N Japan 40.56N 140.55E
172 Pp16 **Hirara** Okinawa, Miyako-jima, SW Japan 24.48N 125.16E
Qasr al Hir Ash Sharqī see Ḩayr ash Sharqī, Qaşr al
170 F12 **Hirata** Shimane, Honshū, SW Japan 35.26N 132.50E
171 Jj17 **Hiratsuka** var. Hiratuka. Kanagawa, Honshū, S Japan 35.20N 139.20E
Hiratuka see Hiratsuka
142 I13 **Hirfanlı Barajı** ⊡ C Turkey
161 G18 **Hiriyūr** Karnātaka, W India 13.58N 76.33E
Hîrlău see Hârlău
154 K10 **Hirmand, Rūd-e** var. Daryā-ye Helmand. ≈ Afghanistan/Iran see also Helmand, Daryā-ye
Hirmil see Hermel
172 P8 **Hiroo** Hokkaidō, NE Japan 42.16N 143.16E
171 Mm9 **Hirosaki** Aomori, Honshū, C Japan 40.34N 140.28E
170 E13 **Hiroshima** var. Hirosima. Hiroshima, Honshū, SW Japan 34.22N 132.25E
170 Ee13 **Hiroshima** off. Hiroshima-ken, var. Hirosima. ◐ prefecture Honshū, SW Japan
Hirosima see Hiroshima
Hirschberg/Hirschberg im Riesengebirge/Hirschberg in Schlesien see Jelenia Góra
105 Q3 **Hirson** Aisne, N France 49.55N 4.04E
Hîrşova see Hârşova
97 G19 **Hirtshals** Nordjylland, N Denmark 57.34N 9.58E
171 H16 **Hisai** Mie, Honshū, SW Japan 34.38N 136.27E
158 H10 **Hisār** Haryāna, NW India 29.10N 75.45E
194 J15 **Hisiu** Central, SW PNG 9.01S 146.49E
153 P13 **Hisor** Rus. Gissar. W Tajikistan 38.34N 68.29E
Hispalis see Sevilla
Hispana/Hispania see Spain
46 M7 **Hispaniola** island Dominion Republic/Haiti
66 F11 **Hispaniola Basin** var. Hispaniola Trough. undersea feature SW Atlantic Ocean
Hispaniola Trough see Hispaniola Basin
Histonium see Vasto
145 R7 **Hīt** SW Iraq 33.38N 42.50E
170 D14 **Hita** Ōita, Kyūshū, SW Japan 33.20N 130.55E
171 L16 **Hitachi** var. Hitati. Ibaraki, Honshū, S Japan 36.40N 140.42E
171 L15 **Hitachi-Ōta** var. Hitatiôta. Ibaraki, Honshū, S Japan 36.31N 140.31E
Hitati see Hitachi
Hitatiôta see Hitachi-Ōta
99 O21 **Hitchin** E England, UK 51.57N 0.16W
203 Q7 **Hitiaa** Tahiti, W French Polynesia 17.34S 149.16W
170 Cc15 **Hitoyoshi** var. Hitoyosi. Kumamoto, Kyūshū, SW Japan 32.12N 130.45E
Hitoyosi see Hitoyoshi
96 F7 **Hitra** prev. Hitteren. island S Norway
Hitteren see Hitra
197 B10 **Hiu** island Torres Islands, N Vanuatu
171 K14 **Hiuchi-take** ▲ Honshū, C Japan 36.57N 139.18E
170 Ee14 **Hiuchi-nada** gulf S Japan
203 X7 **Hiva Oa** island Îles Marquises, N French Polynesia
22 M10 **Hiwassee Lake** ⊡ North Carolina, SE USA
22 M10 **Hiwassee River** ≈ SE USA
97 H20 **Hjallerup** Nordjylland, N Denmark 57.10N 10.10E
97 M16 **Hjälmaren** Eng. Lake Hjalmar. ◎ C Sweden
Hjalmar, Lake see Hjälmaren
97 C14 **Hjellestad** Hordaland, S Norway 60.15N 5.13E
97 D16 **Hjelmeland** Rogaland, S Norway 59.12N 6.07E
96 G10 **Hjerkinn** Oppland, S Norway 62.13N 9.37E
97 L18 **Hjo** Västra Götaland, S Sweden 58.16N 14.07E
97 G19 **Hjørring** Nordjylland, N Denmark 57.28N 9.58E
178 H1 **Hkakabo Razi** ▲ Burma/China 28.17N 97.28E
178 H1 **Hkring Bum** ▲ N Burma 27.05N 97.16E
85 L21 **Hlathikulu** var. Hlatikulu. S Swaziland 26.57S 31.19E
Hlatikulu see Hlathikulu
Hliboka see Hlyboka
113 F17 **Hlinsko** var. Hlinsko v Čechách. Pardubický Kraj, C Czech Republic 49.46N 15.54E
Hlinsko v Čechách see Hlinsko
119 S6 **Hlobyne** Rus. Globino. Poltavs'ka Oblast', NE Ukraine 49.24N 33.16E
113 H20 **Hlohovec** Ger. Freistadtl, Hung. Galgóc; prev. Frakštát. Trnavský Kraj, W Slovakia 48.27N 17.47E
85 J23 **Hlotse** var. Leribe. NW Lesotho 28.55S 28.01E
113 I17 **Hlučín** Ger. Hultschin, Pol. Hulczyn. Ostravský Kraj, E Czech Republic 49.54N 18.10E
119 S2 **Hlukhiv** Rus. Glukhov. Sums'ka Oblast', NE Ukraine 51.39N 33.52E
121 K21 **Hlushkavichy** Rus. Glushkevichi. Homyel'skaya Voblasts', SE Belarus 51.33N 27.48E
121 L18 **Hlusk** Rus. Glusk, Glussk. Mahilyowskaya Voblasts', E Belarus 52.54N 28.40E
118 K8 **Hlyboka** Ger. Hliboka, Rus. Glybokaya. Chernivets'ka Oblast', W Ukraine 48.04N 25.55E
120 K13 **Hlybokaye** Rus. Glubokoye. Vitsyebskaya Voblasts', N Belarus 55.08N 27.40E
79 Q16 **Ho** SE Ghana 6.36N 0.28E
178 Jj6 **Hoa Binh** Hoa Binh, N Vietnam 20.49N 105.19E
85 E20 **Hoachanas** Hardap, C Namibia 23.52S 18.02E
Hoai Nhơn see Bông Sơn
178 Jj8 **Hoa Lac** Quang Binh, C Vietnam 17.54N 106.24E
178 J5 **Hoang Liên Sơn** ▲▲ N Vietnam
85 B17 **Hoanib** ≈ NW Namibia
35 S15 **Hoback Peak** ▲ Wyoming, C USA 43.04N 110.34W
191 P17 **Hobart** prev. Hobarton, Hobart Town. state capital Tasmania, SE Australia 42.54S 147.18E
28 L11 **Hobart** Oklahoma, C USA 35.01N 99.05W
191 P17 **Hobart** ✕ Tasmania, SE Australia 42.52S 147.28E
Hobarton/Hobart Town see Hobart
39 W14 **Hobbs** New Mexico, SW USA 32.42N 103.08W
204 L12 **Hobbs Coast** physical region Antarctica
25 Z14 **Hobe Sound** Florida, SE USA 27.03N 80.08W
Hobicaurikány see Uricani
56 E12 **Hobo** Huila, S Colombia 2.34N 75.28W
101 G16 **Hoboken** Antwerpen, N Belgium 51.12N 4.22E
164 K3 **Hoboksar** var. Hoboksar Mongol Zizhixian. Xinjiang Uygur Zizhiqu, NW China 46.48N 85.42E
Hoboksar Mongol Zizhixian see Hoboksar
97 G21 **Hobro** Nordjylland, N Denmark 56.39N 9.51E
23 X10 **Hobucken** North Carolina, SE USA 35.15N 76.31W
97 O20 **Hoburgen** headland SE Sweden 56.54N 18.07E
83 P15 **Hobyo** It. Obbia. Mudug, E Somalia 5.16N 48.24E
111 R8 **Hochalmspitze** ▲ SW Austria 47.00N 13.19E
111 Q4 **Hochburg** Oberösterreich, N Austria 48.10N 12.57E
110 F8 **Hochdorf** Luzern, N Switzerland 47.10N 8.16E
111 N8 **Hochfeiler** It. Gran Pilastro. ▲ Austria/Italy 46.59N 11.42E
178 Jj14 **Hô Chi Minh** var. Ho Chi Minh City; prev. Saigon. S Vietnam 10.46N 106.43E
Ho Chi Minh City see Hô Chi Minh
110 I7 **Höchst** Vorarlberg, NW Austria 47.28N 9.40E
Höchstadt see Höchstadt an der Aisch
103 K19 **Höchstadt an der Aisch** var. Höchstadt. Bayern, C Germany 49.43N 10.48E
110 L9 **Hochwilde** It. L'Altissima. ▲ Austria/Italy 46.45N 11.00E
111 S7 **Hochwildstelle** ▲ C Austria 47.21N 13.53E
33 T14 **Hocking River** ≈ Ohio, N USA
Hoctúm see Hoctún
43 X12 **Hoctún** var. Hoctúm. Yucatán, E Mexico 20.48N 89.13W
Hodeida see Al Ḩudaydah
22 K6 **Hodgenville** Kentucky, S USA 37.34N 85.44W
9 T17 **Hodgeville** Saskatchewan, S Canada 50.06N 106.55W
78 L9 **Hodh ech Chargui** ◐ region E Mauritania
Hodh el Garbi see Hodh el Gharbi
78 I10 **Hodh el Gharbi** var. Hodh el Garbi. ◐ region S Mauritania
113 L25 **Hódmezővásárhely** Csongrád, SE Hungary 46.27N 20.17E
76 J6 **Hodna, Chott El** var. Chott el-Hodna, Ar. Shatt al-Hodna. salt lake N Algeria
Hodna, Shatt al- see Hodna, Chott El
113 G19 **Hodonín** Ger. Göding. Brněnský Kraj, SE Czech Republic 48.51N 17.07E
168 G6 **Hödrögö** Dzavhan, N Mongolia 48.51N 96.48E
Hodság/Hodschag see Odžaci
41 R7 **Hodzana River** ≈ Alaska, USA
Hoei see Huy
101 H19 **Hoeilaart** Vlaams Brabant, C Belgium 50.46N 4.28E
Hoë Karoo see Great Karoo
100 F12 **Hoek van Holland** Eng. Hook of Holland. Zuid-Holland, W Netherlands 52.00N 4.07E
100 L11 **Hoenderloo** Gelderland, E Netherlands 52.08N 5.46E
101 L18 **Hoensbroek** Limburg, SE Netherlands 50.55N 5.55E
169 Y11 **Hoeryŏng** NE North Korea 42.23N 129.46E
101 K18 **Hoeselt** Limburg, NE Belgium 50.49N 5.30E
100 K11 **Hoevelaken** Gelderland, C Netherlands 52.10N 5.27E
Hoey see Huy
103 M18 **Hof** Bayern, SE Germany 50.19N 11.55E
Höfdhakaupstadhur see Skagaströnd
Hofei see Hefei
103 G18 **Hofheim am Taunus** Hessen, W Germany 50.04N 8.27E
Hofmarkt see Odorheiu Secuiesc
94 L3 **Höfn** Austurland, SE Iceland 64.14N 15.17W
96 N13 **Hofors** Gävleborg, C Sweden 60.33N 16.21E
94 J6 **Hofsjökull** glacier C Iceland
94 J1 **Hofsós** Nordhurland Vestra, N Iceland 65.54N 19.25W
170 Dd13 **Hōfu** Yamaguchi, Honshū, SW Japan 34.01N 131.34E
Hofuf see Al Hufūf
97 J22 **Höganäs** Skåne, S Sweden 56.11N 12.39E
191 P14 **Hogan Group** island group Tasmania, SE Australia
25 R4 **Hogansville** Georgia, SE USA 33.10N 84.55W
41 P8 **Hogatza River** ≈ Alaska, USA
30 I14 **Hogback Mountain** ▲ Nebraska, C USA 41.40N 103.44W
97 G14 **Høgevarde** ▲ S Norway 60.19N 9.27E
Högfors see Karkkila
33 P5 **Hog Island** island Michigan, N USA
23 Y6 **Hog Island** island Virginia, NE USA
Hogoley Islands see Chuuk Islands
97 N20 **Högsby** Kalmar, S Sweden 57.10N 16.03E
38 K1 **Hogup Mountains** ▲▲ Utah, W USA
103 E17 **Hohe Acht** ▲ W Germany 50.23N 7.00E
Hohenelbe see Vrchlabí
110 I7 **Hohenems** Vorarlberg, W Austria 47.22N 9.43E
Hohenmauth see Vysoké Mýto
Hohensalza see Inowrocław
Hohenstadt see Zábřeh
Hohenstein in Ostpreussen see Olsztynek
22 I9 **Hohenwald** Tennessee, S USA 35.33N 87.33W
103 L17 **Hohenwarte-Stausee** ⊡ C Germany
Hohes Venn see Hautes Fagnes
111 Q8 **Hohe Tauern** ▲▲ W Austria
169 O13 **Hohhot** var. Huhehot, Huhuohaote, Mong. Kukukhoto; prev. Kweisui, Kwesui. Nei Mongol Zizhiqu, N China 40.49N 111.37E
105 U6 **Hohneck** ▲ NE France 48.04N 7.01E
79 Q16 **Hohoe** E Ghana 7.07N 0.31E
170 D12 **Hōhoku** Yamaguchi, Honshū, SW Japan 34.15N 130.56E
165 O11 **Hoh Sai Hu** ◎ C China
165 N11 **Hoh Xil Hu** ◎ C China
164 L11 **Hoh Xil Shan** ▲▲ W China
178 Kk10 **Hôi An** prev. Faifo. Quang Nam-Đa Nang, C Vietnam 15.54N 108.19E
Hoï-Hao/Hoihow see Haikou
83 F17 **Hoima** W Uganda 1.25N 31.22E
28 L5 **Hoisington** Kansas, C USA 38.31N 98.46W
Hojagala see Khodzhakala
Hojambaz see Khodzhambas
97 H23 **Højby** Fyn, C Denmark 55.19N 10.27E
97 F24 **Højer** Sønderjylland, SW Denmark 54.57N 8.43E
170 Ee14 **Hōjō** var. Hôzyô. Ehime, Shikoku, SW Japan 33.58N 132.47E
192 J3 **Hokianga Harbour** inlet SE Tasman Sea
193 F17 **Hokitika** West Coast, South Island, NZ 42.43S 170.58E
172 P5 **Hokkai-dō** ◐ territory Hokkaidō, NE Japan
172 Oo5 **Hokkaidō** prev. Ezo, Yeso, Yezo. island NE Japan
97 G15 **Hokksund** Buskerud, S Norway 59.46N 9.54E
149 S4 **Hokmābād** Khorāsān, N Iran 36.37N 57.34E
Hokō see P'ohang
Hoko-guntō/Hoko-shotō see P'enghu Liehtao
143 T12 **Hoktemberyan** Rus. Oktemberyan. SW Armenia 40.09N 43.58E
96 F13 **Hol** Buskerud, S Norway 60.36N 8.18E
119 R11 **Hola Prystan'** Rus. Golaya Pristan. Khersons'ka Oblast', S Ukraine 46.31N 32.31E
97 I23 **Holbæk** Vestsjælland, E Denmark 55.42N 11.42E
168 G6 **Holboo** Dzavhan, W Mongolia 48.35N 95.25E
191 P10 **Holbrook** New South Wales, SE Australia 35.45S 147.18E
39 N11 **Holbrook** Arizona, SW USA 34.54N 110.09W
29 S5 **Holden** Missouri, C USA 38.42N 93.59W
38 K5 **Holden** Utah, W USA 39.06N 112.16W
29 O11 **Holdenville** Oklahoma, C USA 35.04N 96.24W
31 O16 **Holdrege** Nebraska, C USA 40.28N 99.28W
37 X3 **Hole in the Mountain Peak** ▲ Nevada, W USA 40.54N 115.06W
161 G20 **Hole Narsipur** Karnātaka, W India 12.46N 76.13E
113 H18 **Holešov** Ger. Holleschau. Zlínský Kraj, E Czech Republic 49.19N 17.34E
47 N14 **Holetown** prev. Jamestown. W Barbados 13.09N 59.37W
33 Q12 **Holgate** Ohio, N USA 41.12N 84.06W
46 I7 **Holguín** Holguín, SE Cuba 20.51N 76.16W
25 V12 **Holiday** Florida, SE USA 28.11N 82.44W
41 O12 **Holitna River** ≈ Alaska, USA
96 J13 **Höljes** Värmland, C Sweden 60.54N 12.34E
111 X3 **Hollabrunn** Niederösterreich, NE Austria 48.33N 16.06E
38 L3 **Holladay** Utah, W USA 40.39N 111.49W
9 X16 **Holland** Manitoba, S Canada 49.36N 98.52W
33 O9 **Holland** Michigan, N USA 42.47N 86.06W
27 T9 **Holland** Texas, SW USA 30.52N 97.24W
Holland see Netherlands
24 K4 **Hollandale** Mississippi, S USA 33.10N 90.51W
Hollandia see Jayapura
Hollandsch Diep see Hollands Diep
101 H14 **Hollands Diep** var. Hollandsch Diep. channel SW Netherlands
Holleschau see Holešov
27 R5 **Holliday** Texas, SW USA 33.49N 98.41W
20 E15 **Hollidaysburg** Pennsylvania, NE USA 40.24N 78.22W
23 S6 **Hollins** Virginia, NE USA 37.20N 79.56W
28 J12 **Hollis** Oklahoma, C USA 34.42N 99.54W
37 O10 **Hollister** California, W USA 36.51N 121.25W
29 T8 **Hollister** Missouri, C USA 36.37N 93.13W
95 M19 **Hollola** Etelä-Suomi, S Finland 60.59N 25.31E
100 K4 **Hollum** Friesland, N Netherlands 53.27N 5.38E
97 J23 **Höllviksnäs** Skåne, S Sweden 55.25N 12.57E
39 W6 **Holly** Colorado, C USA 38.03N 102.07W
33 R9 **Holly** Michigan, N USA 42.47N 83.37W
23 S14 **Holly Hill** South Carolina, SE USA 33.19N 80.24W
23 W11 **Holly Ridge** North Carolina, SE USA 34.31N 77.31W
24 L1 **Holly Springs** Mississippi, S USA 34.46N 89.25W
25 Z15 **Hollywood** Florida, SE USA 26.00N 80.09W
15 I2 **Holman** Victoria Island, Northwest Territories, N Canada 70.42N 117.45W
94 I2 **Hólmavík** Vestfirdhir, NW Iceland 65.42N 21.43W
32 J7 **Holmen** Wisconsin, N USA 43.57N 91.14W
25 R8 **Holmes Creek** ≈ Alabama/Florida, SE USA
97 H16 **Holmestrand** Vestfold, S Norway 59.28N 10.19E
95 J16 **Holmön** island N Sweden
97 E22 **Holmsland Klit** beach W Denmark
95 J16 **Holmsund** Västerbotten, N Sweden 63.42N 20.25E
97 Q18 **Holmudden** headland SE Sweden 57.59N 19.14E
194 L15 **Holnicote Bay** headland SW PNG 8.30S 148.18E
144 F10 **Holon** var. Kholon. Tel Aviv, C Israel 32.01N 34.46E
119 P8 **Holovanivs'k** Rus. Golovanevsk. Kirovohrads'ka Oblast', C Ukraine 48.21N 30.26E
97 F21 **Holstebro** Ringkøbing, W Denmark 56.22N 8.37E
97 F23 **Holsted** Ribe, W Denmark 55.30N 8.54E
31 T13 **Holstein** Iowa, C USA 42.29N 95.32W
Holsteinborg/Holsteinsborg/Holstenborg/Holstensborg see Sisimiut
23 O8 **Holston River** ≈ Tennessee, S USA
33 Q9 **Holt** Michigan, N USA 42.38N 84.31W
100 N10 **Holten** Overijssel, E Netherlands 52.16N 6.25E
29 P3 **Holton** Kansas, C USA 39.28N 95.44W
29 U5 **Holts Summit** Missouri, C USA 38.38N 92.07W
37 X17 **Holtville** California, W USA 32.48N 115.22W
100 L5 **Holwerd** Fris. Holwert. Friesland, N Netherlands 53.22N 5.51E
Holwert see Holwerd
41 O11 **Holy Cross** Alaska, USA 62.12N 159.46W
39 R4 **Holy Cross, Mount Of The** ▲ Colorado, C USA 39.28N 106.28W
99 I18 **Holyhead** Wel. Caer Gybi. NW Wales, UK 53.19N 4.37W
99 H18 **Holy Island** island NW Wales, UK
98 L12 **Holy Island** island NE England, UK
39 W3 **Holyoke** Colorado, C USA 40.31N 102.18W
20 M11 **Holyoke** Massachusetts, NE USA 42.12N 72.37W
103 I14 **Holzminden** Niedersachsen, C Germany 51.49N 9.27E
83 G19 **Homa Bay** Nyanza, W Kenya 0.31S 34.30E
Homāyūnshahr see Khomeynīshahr
79 P11 **Hombori** Mopti, S Mali 15.13N 1.39W
103 E20 **Homburg** Saarland, SW Germany 49.19N 7.19E
16 Nn1 **Home Bay** bay Baffin Bay, Nunavut, NE Canada
Homenau see Humenné
41 Q13 **Homer** Alaska, USA 59.38N 151.33W
24 H4 **Homer** Louisiana, S USA 32.47N 93.03W
20 H10 **Homer** New York, NE USA 42.38N 76.10W
25 V7 **Homerville** Georgia, SE USA 31.02N 82.45W
25 Y16 **Homestead** Florida, SE USA 25.28N 80.28W
29 O9 **Hominy** Oklahoma, C USA 36.24N 96.24W
96 H8 **Hommelvik** Sør-Trøndelag, S Norway 63.24N 10.46E
97 C16 **Hommersåk** Rogaland, S Norway 58.55N 5.51E
161 H15 **Homnābād** Karnātaka, C India 17.46N 77.08E
24 J7 **Homochitto River** ≈ Mississippi, S USA
85 N20 **Homoine** Inhambane, SE Mozambique 23.51S 35.04E
114 O12 **Homoljske Planine** ▲ E Yugoslavia
Homonna see Humenné
Homs see Al Khums, Libya
Homs see Ḩimş, Syria
121 P19 **Homyel'** Rus. Gomel'. Homyel'skaya Voblasts', SE Belarus 52.24N 31.00E
120 L12 **Homyel'** Vitsyebskaya Voblasts', N Belarus 55.20N 28.52E
121 L19 **Homyel'skaya Voblasts'** prev. Rus. Gomel'skaya Oblast'. ◐ province SE Belarus
Honan see Henan, China
Honan see Luoyang, China
172 Pp6 **Honbetsu** Hokkaidō, NE Japan 43.09N 143.46E
Honctő see Gurahonţ
56 E9 **Honda** Tolima, C Colombia 5.12N 74.45W
85 D24 **Hondeklip** Afr. Hondeklipbaai. Northern Cape, W South Africa 30.15S 17.17E
Hondeklipbaai see Hondeklip
9 Q13 **Hondo** Alberta, W Canada 54.43N 113.14W
170 C14 **Hondo** Kumamoto, Shimo-jima, SW Japan 32.27N 130.10E
27 Q12 **Hondo** Texas, SW USA 29.21N 99.08W
44 G1 **Hondo** ≈ Central America
Hondo see Honshū
44 G6 **Honduras** off. Republic of Honduras. ◆ republic Central America
Honduras, Golfo de see Honduras, Gulf of
44 H4 **Honduras, Gulf of** Sp. Golfo de Honduras. gulf W Caribbean Sea
9 V12 **Hone** Manitoba, C Canada 56.13N 101.12W
23 P12 **Honea Path** South Carolina, SE USA 34.27N 82.23W
97 H14 **Hønefoss** Buskerud, S Norway 60.10N 10.15E
33 S12 **Honey Creek** ≈ Ohio, N USA
27 V5 **Honey Grove** Texas, SW USA 33.34N 95.54W
37 Q4 **Honey Lake** ◎ California, W USA
104 L4 **Honfleur** Calvados, N France 49.25N 0.13E
Hon Gai see Hông Gai
167 O8 **Hong'an** prev. Huang'an. Hubei, C China 31.20N 114.43E
Hongay see Hông Gai
178 K6 **Hông Gai** var. Hon Gai, Hongay. Quang Ninh, N Vietnam 20.57N 107.06E
167 O15 **Honghai Wan** bay N South China Sea
Hông Hà, Sông see Red River
167 O7 **Hong He** ≈ C China
167 N9 **Hong Hu** ◎ C China
166 L11 **Hongjiang** Hunan, S China 27.09N 109.58E
167 O15 **Hong Kong** Chin. Xianggang. S China 22.16N 114.09E
165 P7 **Hongliuyuan** Gansu, N China 41.01N 95.24E
169 O9 **Hongor** Dornogovĭ, SE Mongolia 45.49N 111.20E
167 S8 **Hongqiao** ✕ (Shanghai) Shanghai Shi, E China 31.28N 121.08E
166 K14 **Hongshui He** ≈ S China
166 M5 **Hongtong** Shanxi, C China 36.30N 111.42E
170 G16 **Hongū** Wakayama, Honshū, SW Japan 33.50N 135.42E
Honguedo, Détroit d' see Honguedo Passage
13 Y5 **Honguedo Passage** var. Honguedo Strait, Fr. Détroit d'Honguedo. strait Quebec, E Canada
Honguedo Strait see Honguedo Passage
Hongwan see Sunan
169 X13 **Hongwŏn** E North Korea 40.03N 127.54E
166 H7 **Hongyuan** prev. Hurama. Sichuan, C China 32.49N 102.40E
167 Q7 **Hongze Hu** var. Hung-tse Hu. ◎ E China
195 W16 **Honiara** ● (Solomon Islands) Guadalcanal, C Solomon Islands 9.27S 159.55E
171 Ll11 **Honjō** var. Honzyô. Akita, Honshū, C Japan 39.22N 140.03E
95 K18 **Honkajoki** Länsi-Suomi, W Finland 62.00N 22.15E
171 Ii16 **Honkawane** Shizuoka, Honshū, S Japan 35.07N 138.07E
94 K7 **Honningsvåg** Finnmark, N Norway 70.58N 25.58E
97 I19 **Hönö** Västra Götaland, S Sweden 57.42N 11.39E
40 G11 **Honokaa** Haw. Honoka'a. Hawaii, USA, C Pacific Ocean 20.04N 155.27W
40 G11 **Honokohau** Haw. Honokōhau. Hawaii, USA, C Pacific Ocean 19.40N 156.01W
40 D9 **Honolulu** ◐ Oahu, Hawaii, USA, C Pacific Ocean 21.18N 157.51W
40 H11 **Honomu** Haw. Honomū. Hawaii, USA, C Pacific Ocean 19.51N 155.06W
107 P10 **Honrubia** Castilla-La Mancha, C Spain 39.36N 2.16W
171 I15 **Honshū** var. Hondo, Honsyû. island SW Japan
Honsyû see Honshū
Honte see Westerschelde
Honzyô see Honjō
15 I5 **Hood** ≈ Nunavut, NW Canada
Hood Island see Española, Isla
34 H11 **Hood, Mount** ▲ Oregon, NW USA 45.22N 121.41W
194 K16 **Hood Point** headland S PNG 10.04S 147.42E
34 H11 **Hood River** Oregon, NW USA 45.42N 121.31W
100 H10 **Hoofddorp** Noord-Holland, W Netherlands 52.18N 4.40E
101 G15 **Hoogerheide** Noord-Brabant, S Netherlands 51.25N 4.19E
100 N8 **Hoogeveen** Drenthe, NE Netherlands 52.43N 6.30E
100 O6 **Hoogezand-Sappemeer** Groningen, NE Netherlands 53.10N 6.46E
100 J8 **Hoogkarspel** Noord-Holland, NW Netherlands 52.42N 4.59E
100 N5 **Hoogkerk** Groningen, NE Netherlands 53.13N 6.30E
100 G13 **Hoogvliet** Zuid-Holland, SW Netherlands 51.51N 4.23E
28 I8 **Hooker** Oklahoma, C USA 36.51N 101.12W
99 E21 **Hook Head** Ir. Rinn Duáin. headland SE Ireland 52.07N 6.55W
Hook of Holland see Hoek van Holland
168 J9 **Hoolt** Övörhangay, C Mongolia 45.31N 103.06E
41 W13 **Hoonah** Chichagof Island, Alaska, USA 58.05N 135.21W
40 L11 **Hooper Bay** Alaska, USA 61.31N 166.06W
33 N13 **Hoopeston** Illinois, N USA 40.28N 87.40W
97 K22 **Höör** Skåne, S Sweden 55.55N 13.33E
100 I9 **Hoorn** Noord-Holland, NW Netherlands 52.37N 5.04E
20 L10 **Hoosic River** ≈ New York, NE USA
Hoosier State see Indiana
37 Y11 **Hoover Dam** dam Arizona/Nevada, W USA 36.01N 114.44W
168 I9 **Höövör** Övörhangay, C Mongolia 45.10N 101.19E
143 Q11 **Hopa** Artvin, NE Turkey 41.23N 41.27E
20 J14 **Hopatcong** New Jersey, NE USA 40.55N 74.39W
8 M17 **Hope** British Columbia, SW Canada 49.21N 121.28W
41 R12 **Hope** Alaska, USA 60.55N 149.38W
29 T14 **Hope** Arkansas, C USA 33.40N 93.35W
33 P14 **Hope** Indiana, N USA 39.18N 85.46W
31 Q5 **Hope** North Dakota, N USA 47.18N 97.42W
11 Q7 **Hopedale** Newfoundland, NE Canada 55.25N 60.14W
Hopeh/Hopei see Hebei
188 K13 **Hope, Lake** salt lake Western Australia
43 X13 **Hopelchén** Campeche, SE Mexico 19.44N 89.52W
23 U11 **Hope Mills** North Carolina, SE USA 34.58N 78.57W
191 O7 **Hope, Mount** New South Wales, SE Australia 32.49S 145.55E
94 P4 **Hopen** island SE Svalbard
207 Q4 **Hope, Point** headland Alaska, USA
10 M3 **Hopes Advance, Cap** headland Quebec, NE Canada 61.07N 69.30W
190 L10 **Hopetoun** Victoria, SE Australia 35.46S 142.23E
85 H23 **Hopetown** Northern Cape, W South Africa 29.38S 24.06E
23 W6 **Hopewell** Virginia, NE USA 37.16N 77.15W
111 O7 **Hopfgarten-im-Brixental** Tirol, W Austria 47.28N 12.14E
189 N8 **Hopkins Lake** salt lake Western Australia
190 M12 **Hopkins River** ≈ Victoria, SE Australia
22 I7 **Hopkinsville** Kentucky, S USA 36.52N 87.29W
36 M6 **Hopland** California, W USA 38.58N 123.09W
97 G24 **Hoptrup** Sønderjylland, SW Denmark 55.09N 9.27E
34 F9 **Hoquiam** Washington, NW USA 46.58N 123.53W
31 R6 **Horace** North Dakota, N USA 46.44N 96.54W
143 R12 **Horasan** Erzurum, NE Turkey 40.03N 42.10E
103 G22 **Horb am Neckar** Baden-Württemberg, S Germany 48.27N 8.42E
97 K23 **Hörby** Skåne, S Sweden 55.50N 13.42E
45 P16 **Horconcitos** Chiriquí, W Panama 8.17N 82.10W
97 C14 **Hordaland** ◐ county S Norway
118 H13 **Horezu** Vâlcea, SW Romania 45.06N 24.00E
110 G7 **Horgen** Zürich, N Switzerland 47.16N 8.36E
168 I7 **Horgo** Arhangay, C Mongolia 48.06N 99.52E
Hörin see Fenglin
169 O13 **Horinger** Nei Mongol Zizhiqu, N China 40.23N 111.48E
168 I9 **Horiult** Bayanhongor, C Mongolia 45.09N 100.50E
9 U17 **Horizon** Saskatchewan, S Canada 49.33N 105.05W
199 J10 **Horizon Bank** undersea feature S Pacific Ocean
199 Jj11 **Horizon Deep** undersea feature W Pacific Ocean
97 L14 **Horken** Örebro, S Sweden 60.03N 14.55E
121 O15 **Horki** Rus. Gorki. Mahilyowskaya Voblasts', E Belarus 54.17N 30.59E
205 O10 **Horlick Mountains** ▲▲ Antarctica

◆ Country ● Country Capital ◇ Dependent Territory ○ Dependent Territory Capital ◐ Administrative Region ✕ International Airport ▲ Mountain ▲▲ Mountain Range Volcano ≈ River ◎ Lake ⊡ Reservoir

Horlivka – Huntington Creek

119 X7 **Horlivka** Rom. Adâncata, Rus. Gorlovka. Donets'ka Oblast', E Ukraine 48.19N 38.04E
149 V11 **Ḩormak** Sīstān va Balūchestān, SE Iran 30.00N 60.50E
149 R13 **Hormozgān** off. Ostān-e Hormozgān. ◐ province S Iran
Hormoz, Tangeh-ye see Hormuz, Strait of
147 W6 **Hormuz, Strait of** var. Strait of Ormuz, Per. Tangeh-ye Hormoz. strait Iran/Oman
111 W2 **Horn** Niederösterreich, NE Austria 48.39N 15.37E
97 M18 **Horn** Östergötland, S Sweden 57.54N 15.49E
15 Hh8 **Horn** ≈ Northwest Territories, NW Canada
Hornád see Hernád
15 H3 **Hornaday** ≈ Northwest Territories, NW Canada
94 H13 **Hornavan** ◎ N Sweden
67 C24 **Hornby Mountains** hill range West Falkland, Falkland Islands
Horn, Cape see Hornos, Cabo de
99 O18 **Horncastle** E England, UK 53.12N 0.07W
97 N14 **Horndal** Dalarna, C Sweden 60.16N 16.25E
95 I16 **Hörnefors** Västerbotten, N Sweden 63.37N 19.54E
20 F11 **Hornell** New York, NE USA 42.19N 77.38W
Horné Nové Mesto see Kysucké Nové Mesto
10 F12 **Hornepayne** Ontario, S Canada 49.13N 84.48W
96 D10 **Hornindalsvatnet** ◎ S Norway
103 G22 **Hornisgrinde** ▲ SW Germany 48.37N 8.13E
24 M9 **Horn Island** island Mississippi, S USA
65 J26 **Hornos, Cabo de** Eng. Cape Horn. headland S Chile 55.52S 67.00W
119 S10 **Hornostayivka** Khersons'ka Oblast', S Ukraine 47.00N 33.42E
191 T9 **Hornsby** New South Wales, SE Australia 33.44S 151.08E
99 O16 **Hornsea** E England, UK 53.54N 0.09W
96 O11 **Hornslandet** peninsula C Sweden
97 H22 **Hornslet** Århus, C Denmark 56.19N 10.19E
94 O4 **Hornsundtind** ▲ S Svalbard 76.54N 16.07E
Horochów see Horokhiv
118 J7 **Horodenka** Rus. Gorodenka. Ivano-Frankivs'ka Oblast', W Ukraine 48.41N 25.28E
119 Q2 **Horodnya** Rus. Gorodnya. Chernihivs'ka Oblast', NE Ukraine 51.54N 31.30E
118 K6 **Horodok** Khmel'nyts'ka Oblast', W Ukraine 49.10N 26.34E
118 H5 **Horodok** Pol. Gródek Jagielloński, Rus. Gorodok, Gorodok Yagellonski. L'vivs'ka Oblast', NW Ukraine 49.48N 23.39E
119 Q6 **Horodyshche** Rus. Gorodishche. Cherkas'ka Oblast', C Ukraine 49.18N 31.27E
172 P4 **Horokanai** Hokkaidō, NE Japan 44.02N 142.08E
118 J4 **Horokhiv** Pol. Horochów, Rus. Gorokhov. Volyns'ka Oblast', NW Ukraine 50.31N 24.50E
172 P7 **Horoshiri-dake** var. Horosiri Dake. ▲ Hokkaidō, N Japan 42.43N 142.41E
Horosiri Dake see Horoshiri-dake
113 C17 **Hořovice** Ger. Horowitz. Středočeský Kraj, W Czech Republic 49.49N 13.53E
Horowitz see Hořovice
169 T9 **Horqin Youyi Zhongqi** Nei Mongol Zizhiqu, NE China 45.02N 121.33E
169 U11 **Horqin Zuoyi Houqi** Nei Mongol Zizhiqu, N China 42.53N 122.22E
169 T9 **Horqin Zuoyi Zhongqi** Nei Mongol Zizhiqu, N China 45.02N 121.28E
64 O5 **Horqueta** Concepción, C Paraguay 23.23S 57.04W
57 O12 **Horqueta Minas** Amazonas, S Venezuela 2.19N 63.31W
97 J20 **Horred** Västra Götaland, S Sweden 57.22N 12.25E
157 J19 **Horsburgh Atoll** atoll N Maldives
22 K7 **Horse Cave** Kentucky, S USA 37.10N 85.54W
39 V6 **Horse Creek** ≈ Colorado, C USA
29 S6 **Horse Creek** ≈ Missouri, C USA
20 G11 **Horseheads** New York, NE USA 42.10N 76.49W
39 P13 **Horse Mount** ▲ New Mexico, SW USA 33.58N 108.10W
97 G22 **Horsens** Vejle, C Denmark 55.52N 9.52E
67 F25 **Horse Pasture Point** headland W Saint Helena 15.57S 5.46W
35 N13 **Horseshoe Bend** Idaho, NW USA 43.55N 116.11W
38 L13 **Horseshoe Reservoir** ⊠ Arizona, SW USA
66 M9 **Horseshoe Seamounts** undersea feature E Atlantic Ocean
190 L11 **Horsham** Victoria, SE Australia 36.44S 142.13E
99 O23 **Horsham** SE England, UK 51.01N 0.21W
101 M15 **Horst** Limburg, SE Netherlands 51.29N 6.04E
66 N2 **Horta** Faial, Azores, Portugal, NE Atlantic Ocean 38.31N 28.39W
97 H16 **Horten** Vestfold, S Norway 59.25N 10.24E
113 M23 **Hortobágy-Berettyó** ≈ E Hungary
29 Q3 **Horton** Kansas, C USA 39.39N 95.31W
15 H3 **Horton** ≈ Northwest Territories, NW Canada
97 I23 **Hørve** Vestsjælland, E Denmark 55.46N 11.28E
97 L22 **Hörvik** Blekinge, S Sweden 56.01N 14.45E
144 E11 **Horvot Haluza** var. Khorvot Khalutsa. ruins Southern, S Israel 30.49N 34.50E
12 E7 **Horwood Lake** ◎ Ontario, S Canada
118 K4 **Horyn'** Rus. Goryn. ≈ NW Ukraine
83 I14 **Hosa'ina** var. Hosseina, It. Hosanna. Southern, S Ethiopia 7.38N 37.58E
Hosanna see Hosa'ina
103 H18 **Hösbach** Bayern, C Germany 50.00N 9.12E
Hose Mountains see Hose, Pegunungan
174 Mm6 **Hose, Pegunungan** var. Hose Mountains. ▲▲ East Malaysia
154 L15 **Hoshāb** Baluchistān, SW Pakistan 26.01N 63.51E
160 H10 **Hoshangābād** Madhya Pradesh, C India 22.43N 77.45E
118 L4 **Hoshcha** Rivnens'ka Oblast', NW Ukraine 50.37N 26.38E
158 I7 **Hoshiārpur** Punjab, NW India 31.35N 75.57E
168 J7 **Höshööt** Arhangay, C Mongolia 48.06N 102.34E
101 M23 **Hosingen** Diekirch, NE Luxembourg 50.01N 6.04E
195 N12 **Hoskins** New Britain, E PNG 5.28S 150.25E
161 G17 **Hospet** Karnātaka, C India 15.16N 76.19E
106 K4 **Hospital de Orbigo** Castilla-León, N Spain 42.27N 5.52W
Hospitalet see L'Hospitalet de Llobregat
94 N13 **Hossa** Oulu, E Finland 65.28N 29.36E
Hosseina see Hosa'ina
Hosszúmezjő see Câmpulung Moldovenesc
65 I25 **Hoste, Isla** island S Chile
119 O4 **Hostomel'** Rus. Gostomel'. Kyyivs'ka Oblast', N Ukraine 50.40N 30.15E
161 H20 **Hosūr** Tamil Nādu, SE India 12.45N 77.51E
178 H8 **Hot** Chiang Mai, NW Thailand 18.14N 98.35E
164 G10 **Hotan** var. Khotan, Chin. Ho-t'ien. Xinjiang Uygur Zizhiqu, NW China 37.10N 79.51E
164 H9 **Hotan He** ≈ NW China
85 G22 **Hotazel** Northern Cape, N South Africa 27.12S 22.58E
39 Q5 **Hotchkiss** Colorado, C USA 38.47N 107.43W
37 V7 **Hot Creek Range** ▲▲ Nevada, W USA
Hote see Hoti
176 U11 **Hoti** var. Hote. Pulau Seram, E Indonesia 2.58S 130.19E
Ho-t'ien see Hotan
Hotin see Khotyn
95 H15 **Hoting** Jämtland, C Sweden 64.07N 16.14E
168 L14 **Hotong Qagan Nur** ◎ N China
168 J8 **Hotont** Arhangay, C Mongolia 47.21N 102.27E
29 T12 **Hot Springs** Arkansas, C USA 34.30N 93.03W
30 J11 **Hot Springs** South Dakota, N USA 43.25N 103.28W
23 S5 **Hot Springs** Virginia, NE USA 38.00N 79.50W
37 Q4 **Hot Springs Peak** ▲ California, W USA 40.23N 120.06W
29 T12 **Hot Springs Village** Arkansas, C USA 34.39N 93.03W
Hotspur Bank see Hotspur Seamount
67 J16 **Hotspur Seamount** var. Hotspur Bank. undersea feature C Atlantic Ocean 18.00S 35.00W
15 Hh6 **Hottah Lake** ◎ Northwest Territories, NW Canada
46 K9 **Hotte, Massif de la** ▲▲ SW Haiti
101 K21 **Hotton** Luxembourg, SE Belgium 50.18N 5.25E
Hötzing see Hațeg
197 I6 **Houaïlou** Province Nord, C New Caledonia 21.17S 165.37E
76 K5 **Houari Boumediène** ✈ (Alger) N Algeria 36.38N 3.15E
178 Hh6 **Houayxay** var. Ban Houayxay, Ban Houei Sai. Bokèo, N Laos 20.16N 100.27E
105 N5 **Houdan** Yvelines, N France 48.48N 1.36E
101 F20 **Houdeng-Goegnies** var. Houdeng-Gœgnies. Hainaut, S Belgium 50.28N 4.10E
104 K14 **Houeillès** Lot-et-Garonne, SW France 44.15N 0.02E
101 L22 **Houffalize** Luxembourg, SE Belgium 50.08N 5.47E
32 M3 **Houghton** Michigan, N USA 41.55N 84.37W
33 Q7 **Houghton Lake** Michigan, N USA 44.18N 84.45W
33 Q7 **Houghton Lake** ◎ Michigan, N USA
21 T3 **Houlton** Maine, NE USA 46.09N 67.49W
166 M5 **Houma** Shanxi, C China 35.33N 111.19E
200 Q15 **Houma** 'Eua, C Tonga 21.10S 175.17W
200 R16 **Houma** Tongatapu, S Tonga 21.18S 174.55W
24 J10 **Houma** Louisiana, S USA 29.34N 90.43W
200 Qq16 **Houma Taloa** headland Tongatapu, S Tonga 21.16S 175.07W
79 O13 **Houndé** SW Burkina 11.34N 3.31W
104 J12 **Hourtin-Carcans, Lac d'** ◎ SW France
38 J5 **House Range** ▲▲ Utah, W USA
8 K13 **Houston** British Columbia, SW Canada 54.24N 126.39W
41 R11 **Houston** Alaska, USA 61.37N 149.50W
31 X10 **Houston** Minnesota, N USA 43.45N 91.34W
24 M3 **Houston** Mississippi, S USA 33.54N 89.00W
29 V7 **Houston** Missouri, C USA 37.19N 91.57W
27 W11 **Houston** Texas, SW USA 29.45N 95.21W
27 W11 **Houston** ✈ Texas, SW USA 30.03N 95.18W
100 J12 **Houten** Utrecht, C Netherlands 52.01N 5.10E
101 K17 **Houthalen** Limburg, NE Belgium 51.01N 5.22E
101 I22 **Houyet** Namur, SE Belgium 50.10N 5.00E
97 H22 **Hov** Århus, C Denmark 55.54N 10.13E
97 L17 **Hova** Västra Götaland, S Sweden 58.52N 14.13E
168 E6 **Hovd** var. Khovd. Hovd, W Mongolia 47.58N 91.40E
168 J10 **Hovd** Övörhangay, C Mongolia 44.43N 102.08E
168 E7 **Hovd** ◐ province W Mongolia
168 C5 **Hovd Gol** ≈ NW Mongolia
99 O23 **Hove** SE England, UK 50.49N 0.10W
31 N8 **Hoven** South Dakota, N USA 45.12N 99.47W
118 I8 **Hoverla, Hora** Rus. Gora Goverla. ▲ W Ukraine 48.09N 24.30E
168 H8 **Höviyn Am** Bayanhongor, C Mongolia 47.08N 98.41E
97 M21 **Hovmantorp** Kronoberg, S Sweden 56.46N 15.07E
169 N11 **Hövsgöl** Dornogovĭ, SE Mongolia 43.35N 109.40E
168 I5 **Hövsgöl** ◐ province N Mongolia
Hovsgol, Lake see Hövsgöl Nuur
168 J5 **Hövsgöl Nuur** var. Lake Hovsgol. ◎ N Mongolia
80 L9 **Howa, Ouadi** var. Wādi Howar. ≈ Chad/Sudan see also Howar, Wādi
29 P7 **Howard** Kansas, C USA 37.28N 96.15W
31 Q10 **Howard** South Dakota, N USA 43.58N 97.31W
27 N10 **Howard Draw** valley Texas, SW USA
31 U8 **Howard Lake** Minnesota, N USA 45.03N 94.03W
82 B8 **Howar, Wādi** var. Ouadi Howa. ≈ Chad/Sudan see also Howa, Ouadi
27 U5 **Howe** Texas, SW USA 33.29N 96.38W
191 R12 **Howe, Cape** headland New South Wales/Victoria, SE Australia 37.30S 149.58E
33 R9 **Howell** Michigan, N USA 42.36N 83.55W
30 L9 **Howes** South Dakota, N USA 44.34N 102.03W
85 K23 **Howick** KwaZulu/Natal, E South Africa 29.29S 30.13E
Howrah see Hāora
29 W9 **Hoxie** Arkansas, C USA 36.03N 90.58W
28 J3 **Hoxie** Kansas, C USA 39.21N 100.26W
103 I14 **Höxter** Nordrhein-Westfalen, W Germany 51.46N 9.22E
164 K6 **Hoxud** Xinjiang Uygur Zizhiqu, NW China 42.18N 86.51E
98 J5 **Hoy** island N Scotland, UK
45 S17 **Hoya, Cerro** ▲ S Panama 7.22N 80.38W
96 D12 **Høyanger** Sogn og Fjordane, S Norway 61.13N 6.04E
103 P15 **Hoyerswerda** Sachsen, E Germany 51.27N 14.17E
170 Dd15 **Hōyo-kaikyō** var. Hayasui-seto. strait SW Japan
106 J8 **Hoyos** Extremadura, W Spain 40.10N 6.43W
31 W4 **Hoyt Lakes** Minnesota, N USA 47.31N 92.08W
89 V2 **Hoyvík** Streymoy, N Faeroe Islands
143 O14 **Hozat** Tunceli, E Turkey 39.09N 39.13E
Hôzyô see Hōjō
113 F16 **Hradec Králové** Ger. Königgrätz. Hradecký Kraj, N Czech Republic 50.13N 15.49E
113 E16 **Hradecký Kraj** ◐ region N Czech Republic
113 B16 **Hradiště** Ger. Burgstadlberg. ▲ NW Czech Republic 50.12N 13.04E
119 R6 **Hradyz'k** Rus. Gradizhsk. Poltavs'ka Oblast', NE Ukraine 49.12N 33.08E
121 M16 **Hradzyanka** Rus. Grodzyanka. Mahilyowskaya Voblasts', E Belarus 53.36N 28.47E
121 F16 **Hrandzichy** Rus. Grandichi. Hrodzyenskaya Voblasts', W Belarus 53.43N 23.50E
113 H18 **Hranice** Ger. Mährisch-Weisskirchen. Olomoucký Kraj, E Czech Republic 49.34N 17.45E
114 I13 **Hrasnica** Federacija Bosna I Hercegovina, SE Bosnia and Herzegovina 43.48N 18.19E
111 V11 **Hrastnik** C Slovenia 46.09N 15.08E
143 U12 **Hrazdan** Rus. Razdan. C Armenia 40.30N 44.50E
143 T12 **Hrazdan** var. Zanga, Rus. Razdan. ≈ C Armenia
119 R5 **Hrebinka** Rus. Grebenka. Poltavs'ka Oblast', NE Ukraine 50.08N 32.27E
121 K17 **Hresk** Rus. Gresk. Minskaya Voblasts', C Belarus 53.10N 27.28E
Hrisoupoli see Chrysoúpoli
121 F16 **Hrodna** Pol. Grodno. Hrodzyenskaya Voblasts', W Belarus 53.40N 23.50E
121 F16 **Hrodzyenskaya Voblasts'** prev. Rus. Grodnenskaya Oblast'. ◐ province W Belarus
113 J21 **Hron** Ger. Gran, Hung. Garam. ≈ C Slovakia
113 Q14 **Hrubieszów** Rus. Grubeshov. Lubelskie, E Poland 50.48N 23.54E
114 F13 **Hrvace** Split-Dalmacija, SE Croatia 43.46N 16.35E
Hrvatska see Croatia
114 F10 **Hrvatska Kostajnica** var. Kostajnica. Sisak-Moslavina, C Croatia 45.14N 16.35E
Hrvatsko Grahovo see Bosansko Grahovo
118 K6 **Hrymayliv** Pol. Gízymałów, Rus. Grimaylov. Ternopil's'ka Oblast', W Ukraine 49.18N 26.02E
178 H4 **Hsenwi** Shan State, E Burma 23.20N 97.59E
Hsia-men see Xiamen
Hsiang-t'an see Xiangtan
Hsi Chiang see Xi Jiang
178 Gg6 **Hsihseng** Shan State, C Burma 20.07N 97.16E
167 S13 **Hsinchu** municipality N Taiwan 24.51N 121.01E
Hsing-k'ai Hu see Khanka, Lake
Hsi-ning/Hsining see Xining
Hsinking see Changchun
Hsin-yang see Xinyang
167 S14 **Hsinying** var. Sinying, Jap. Shinei. C Taiwan 23.12N 120.15E
178 Gg4 **Hsipaw** Shan State, C Burma 22.36N 97.16E
Hsu-chou see Xuzhou
167 S13 **Hsüeh Shan** ▲ N Taiwan
Hu see Shanghai Shi
85 B18 **Huab** ≈ W Namibia
59 M21 **Huacaya** Chuquisaca, S Bolivia 20.55S 63.24W
59 J19 **Huachacalla** Oruro, SW Bolivia 19.01S 68.22W
165 X9 **Huachi** var. Rouyuanchengzi. Gansu, C China 36.24N 107.58E
59 N16 **Huachi, Laguna** ◎ N Bolivia
59 D14 **Huacho** Lima, W Peru 11.09S 77.37W
169 Y8 **Huachuan** Heilongjiang, NE China 46.21N 130.43E
169 P12 **Huade** Nei Mongol Zizhiqu, N China 41.52N 113.58E
169 W10 **Huadian** Jilin, NE China 42.58N 126.37E
58 E13 **Huagaruncho, Cordillera** ▲▲ C Peru
Hua Hin see Ban Hua Hin
203 S10 **Huahine** island Îles Sous le Vent, W French Polynesia
Huahua, Rio see Wawa, Río
178 Ii9 **Huai** ≈ E Thailand
167 P6 **Huaibei** Anhui, E China 34.00N 116.48E
Huaide see Gongzhuling
163 T10 **Huai He** ≈ C China
166 L11 **Huaihua** Hunan, S China 27.36N 109.56E
167 N14 **Huaiji** Guangdong, S China 23.54N 112.12E
167 O2 **Huailai** prev. Shacheng. Hebei, E China 40.22N 115.34E
167 P7 **Huainan** var. Huai-nan, Hwainan. Anhui, E China 32.36N 116.56E
167 N2 **Huairen** Shanxi, C China 35.28N 110.29E
167 O7 **Huaiyang** Henan, C China 33.39N 114.34E
167 Q7 **Huaiyin** var. Qingjiang. Jiangsu, E China 33.33N 119.03E
178 Gg16 **Huai Yot** Trang, SW Thailand 7.45N 99.36E
43 Q15 **Huajuapan** var. Huajuapan de León. Oaxaca, SE Mexico 17.49N 97.48W
Huajuapan de León see Huajuapan
43 O9 **Hualahuises** Nuevo León, NE Mexico 24.55N 99.44W
38 I11 **Hualapai Mountains** ▲▲ Arizona, SW USA
38 I11 **Hualapai Peak** ▲ Arizona, SW USA 35.04N 113.54W
64 J7 **Hualfin** Catamarca, N Argentina 27.15S 66.52W
167 T13 **Hualien** var. Hwalien, Jap. Karen. C Taiwan 23.58N 121.34E
58 E10 **Huallaga, Río** ≈ N Peru
58 C11 **Huamachuco** La Libertad, C Peru 7.50S 78.03W
43 Q14 **Huamantla** Tlaxcala, S Mexico 19.18N 97.57W
84 C13 **Huambo** Port. Nova Lisboa. Huambo, C Angola 12.48S 15.45E
84 B13 **Huambo** ◐ province C Angola
43 P15 **Huamuxtitlán** Guerrero, S Mexico 17.49N 98.34W
65 H17 **Huancache, Sierra** ▲▲ SW Argentina
59 I17 **Huancané** Puno, SE Peru 15.15S 69.47W
59 F16 **Huancapi** Ayacucho, C Peru 13.36S 74.09W
59 E15 **Huancavelica** Huancavelica, SW Peru 12.45S 75.03W
59 E15 **Huancavelica** off. Departamento de Huancavelica. ◐ department W Peru
59 E14 **Huancayo** Junín, C Peru 12.03S 75.13W
59 K20 **Huanchaca, Cerro** ▲ S Bolivia 20.12S 66.35W
58 C12 **Huandoy, Nevado** ▲ W Peru 8.48S 77.33W
167 O8 **Huangchuan** Henan, C China 32.08N 115.03E
Huang Hai see Yellow Sea
163 Q8 **Huang He** var. Yellow River. ≈ C China
167 Q4 **Huanghe Kou** delta E China
166 L5 **Huangling** Shaanxi, C China 35.34N 109.12E
167 O9 **Huangpi** Hubei, C China 30.53N 114.16E
169 P13 **Huangqi Hai** ◎ N China
167 Q9 **Huang Shan** ▲ Anhui, E China 29.43N 118.19E
167 Q9 **Huangshan** var. Tunxi. Anhui, E China 29.48N 118.17E
167 O9 **Huangshi** var. Huang-shih, Hwangshih. Hubei, C China 30.14N 115.00E
Huang-shih see Huangshi
166 L5 **Huangtu Gaoyuan** plateau C China
63 B22 **Huanguelén** Buenos Aires, E Argentina 37.01S 61.57W
167 S10 **Huangyan** Zhejiang, SE China 28.42N 121.13E
165 T10 **Huangyuan** Qinghai, C China 36.40N 101.12E
165 T10 **Huangzhong** Qinghai, C China 36.31N 101.32E
169 W12 **Huanren** Liaoning, NE China 41.16N 125.25E
59 F15 **Huanta** Ayacucho, C Peru 12.54S 74.13W
58 E13 **Huánuco** Huánuco, C Peru 9.57S 76.15W
58 D13 **Huánuco** off. Departamento de Huánuco. ◐ department C Peru
59 K19 **Huanuni** Oruro, W Bolivia 18.15S 66.54W
165 X9 **Huan Xian** Gansu, C China 36.30N 107.20E
167 S12 **Huap'ing Yu** island N Taiwan
64 H3 **Huara** Tarapacá, N Chile 19.59S 69.42W
59 D14 **Huaral** Lima, W Peru 11.28S 77.12W
Huarás see Huaraz
58 D13 **Huaraz** var. Huarás. Ancash, W Peru 9.30S 77.31W
59 I16 **Huari Huari, Río** ≈ S Peru
58 C13 **Huarmey** Ancash, W Peru 10.03S 78.09W
42 H4 **Huásabas** Sonora, NW Mexico 29.46N 109.18W
58 D8 **Huasaga, Río** ≈ Ecuador/Peru
178 H16 **Hua Sai** Nakhon Si Thammarat, SW Thailand 8.01N 100.18E
58 D12 **Huascarán, Nevado** ▲ W Peru 9.01S 77.27W
64 G8 **Huasco** Atacama, N Chile 28.28S 71.12W
64 G8 **Huasco, Río** ≈ C Chile
165 S11 **Huashikia** Qinghai, W China
42 G7 **Huatabampo** Sonora, NW Mexico 26.49N 109.40W
165 W10 **Huating** Gansu, C China 35.13N 106.39E
178 Jj7 **Huatt, Phou** ▲ N Vietnam 19.45N 104.48E
43 Q14 **Huatusco** var. Huatusco de Chicuellar. Veracruz-Llave, C Mexico 19.13N 96.57W
Huatusco de Chicuellar see Huatusco
43 P13 **Huauchinango** Puebla, S Mexico 20.12N 98.03W
Huaunta see Wounta
43 R15 **Huautla** var. Huautla de Jiménez. Oaxaca, SE Mexico 18.10N 96.51W
Huautla de Jiménez see Huautla
167 O5 **Huaxian** var. Daokou, Hua Xian. Henan, C China 35.33N 114.30E
31 V13 **Hubbard** Iowa, C USA 42.18N 93.18W
27 U8 **Hubbard** Texas, SW USA 31.52N 96.43W
27 Q6 **Hubbard Creek Lake** ◎ Texas, SW USA
33 R6 **Hubbard Lake** ◎ Michigan, N USA
166 M9 **Hubei** var. E, Hubei Sheng, Hupeh, Hupei. ◐ province C China
Hubei Sheng see Hubei
111 P8 **Huben** Tirol, W Austria 46.55N 12.35E
33 R13 **Huber Heights** Ohio, N USA 39.50N 84.07W
161 F17 **Hubli** Karnātaka, SW India 15.19N 75.13E
169 X12 **Huch'ang** N North Korea 41.24N 127.04E
99 M18 **Hucknall** C England, UK 53.01N 1.10W
99 L17 **Huddersfield** N England, UK 53.39N 1.46W
97 O16 **Huddinge** Stockholm, C Sweden 59.15N 17.57E
96 N11 **Hudiksvall** Gävleborg, C Sweden 61.45N 17.12E
31 W13 **Hudson** Iowa, C USA 42.24N 92.27W
21 O11 **Hudson** Massachusetts, NE USA 42.24N 71.34W
33 Q11 **Hudson** Michigan, N USA 41.51N 84.21W
32 H6 **Hudson** Wisconsin, N USA 44.58N 92.43W
9 V14 **Hudson Bay** Saskatchewan, S Canada 58.13N 90.48W
10 G6 **Hudson Bay** bay NE Canada
205 T16 **Hudson, Cape** headland Antarctica 68.15S 154.00E
Hudson, Détroit d' see Hudson Strait
29 Q9 **Hudson, Lake** ⊠ Oklahoma, C USA
20 K9 **Hudson River** ≈ New Jersey/New York, NE USA
8 M12 **Hudson's Hope** British Columbia, W Canada 56.03N 121.58W
10 L2 **Hudson Strait** Fr. Détroit d'Hudson. strait Nunavut/Quebec, NE Canada
Hudūd ash Shamālīyah, Minţaqat al see Al Ḩudūd ash Shamālīyah
Hudur see Xuddur
178 K9 **Huê** Thưa Thiên-Huê, C Vietnam 16.28N 107.34E
106 J7 **Huebra** ≈ W Spain
26 H8 **Hueco Mountains** ▲▲ Texas, SW USA
118 G10 **Huedin** Hung. Bánffyhunyad. Cluj, NW Romania 46.51N 23.01E
42 J10 **Huehuento, Cerro** ▲ C Mexico 24.04N 105.42W
44 B5 **Huehuetenango** Huehuetenango, W Guatemala 15.19N 91.25W
44 B4 **Huehuetenango** off. Departamento de Huehuetenango. ◐ department W Guatemala
42 L11 **Huejuquilla** Jalisco, SW Mexico 22.40N 103.52W
43 P12 **Huejutla** var. Huejutla de Reyes. Hidalgo, C Mexico 21.08N 98.16W
Huejutla de Reyes see Huejutla
104 G6 **Huelgoat** Finistère, NW France 48.22N 3.45W
107 O13 **Huelma** Andalucía, S Spain 37.39N 3.28W
106 I14 **Huelva** anc. Onuba. Andalucía, SW Spain 37.15N 6.55W
106 I13 **Huelva** ◐ province Andalucía, SW Spain
106 J13 **Huelva** ≈ SW Spain
107 Q14 **Huercal-Overa** Andalucía, S Spain 37.22N 1.55W
39 Q9 **Huerfano Mountain** ▲ New Mexico, SW USA 36.25N 107.50W
39 T7 **Huerfano River** ≈ Colorado, C USA
107 S12 **Huertas, Cabo** headland SE Spain 38.21N 0.25W
107 R6 **Huerva** ≈ N Spain
107 S4 **Huesca** anc. Osca. Aragón, NE Spain 42.07N 0.25W
107 T4 **Huesca** ◐ province Aragón, NE Spain
107 P13 **Huéscar** Andalucía, S Spain 37.39N 2.31W
43 N15 **Huetamo** var. Huetamo de Núñez. Michoacán de Ocampo, SW Mexico 18.37N 100.53W
Huetamo de Núñez see Huetamo
107 P8 **Huete** Castilla-La Mancha, C Spain 40.07N 2.40W
25 P4 **Hueytown** Alabama, S USA 33.27N 87.00W
30 L16 **Hugh Butler Lake** ⊠ Nebraska, C USA
189 V6 **Hughenden** Queensland, NE Australia 20.56S 144.15E
190 A6 **Hughes** South Australia 30.41S 129.31E
41 P8 **Hughes** Alaska, USA 66.03N 154.15W
29 X11 **Hughes** Arkansas, C USA 34.57N 90.28W
27 W6 **Hughes Springs** Texas, SW USA 33.00N 94.37W
39 V5 **Hugo** Colorado, C USA 39.08N 103.28W
29 Q13 **Hugo** Oklahoma, C USA 34.01N 95.31W
29 Q13 **Hugo Lake** ⊠ Oklahoma, C USA
28 H7 **Hugoton** Kansas, C USA 37.10N 101.21W
Huhehot/Huhuohaote see Hohhot
167 R13 **Hui'an** Fujian, SE China 25.06N 118.45E
192 O9 **Huiarau Range** ▲▲ North Island, NZ
85 D22 **Huib-Hoch Plateau** plateau S Namibia
43 O13 **Huichapán** Hidalgo, C Mexico 20.22N 99.42W
Huicheng see Shexian
169 W13 **Hŭich'ŏn** C North Korea 40.09N 126.17E
56 E12 **Huila** off. Departamento del Huila. ◐ province S Colombia
85 B15 **Huíla** ◐ province SW Angola
56 D11 **Huila, Nevado del** elevation C Colombia 2.56N 75.59W
85 B15 **Huíla Plateau** plateau S Angola
166 G12 **Huili** Sichuan, C China 26.39N 102.13E
167 P4 **Huimin** Shandong, E China 37.28N 117.30E
169 W11 **Huinan** var. Chaoyang. Jilin, NE China 42.40N 126.03E
64 K12 **Huinca Renancó** Córdoba, C Argentina 34.51S 64.22W
165 V10 **Huining** Gansu, C China 35.42N 105.01E
166 J12 **Huishui** Guizhou, S China 26.07N 106.39E
104 L6 **Huisne** ≈ NW France
100 L12 **Huissen** Gelderland, SE Netherlands 51.57N 5.57E
165 N11 **Huiten Nur** ◎ C China
95 K19 **Huittinen** Länsi-Suomi, W Finland 61.10N 22.40E
43 O15 **Huitzuco** var. Huitzuco de los Figueroa. Guerrero, S Mexico 18.18N 99.22W
Huitzuco de los Figueroa see Huitzuco
165 W11 **Huixian** var. Hui Xian. Gansu, C China 33.48N 106.02E
43 V17 **Huixtla** Chiapas, SE Mexico 15.07N 92.29W
166 H12 **Huize** Yunnan, SW China 26.28N 103.18E
100 J10 **Huizen** Noord-Holland, C Netherlands 52.16N 5.15E
167 O14 **Huizhou** Guangdong, S China 23.05N 114.22E
168 J6 **Hujirt** Arhangay, C Mongolia 48.49N 101.20E
168 J8 **Hujirt** Övörhangay, C Mongolia 46.50N 102.38E
168 K8 **Hujrt** Töv, C Mongolia 46.41N 104.40E
Hukagawa see Fukagawa
Hŭksan-chedo see Hŭksan-gundo
169 W17 **Hŭksan-gundo** var. Hŭksan-chedo. island group SW South Korea
Hukue see Fukue
Hukui see Fukui
85 G20 **Hukuntsi** Kgalagadi, SW Botswana 23.58S 21.43E
Hukuoka see Fukuoka
Hukusima see Fukushima
Hukutiyama see Fukuchiyama
Hukuyama see Fukuyama
169 W8 **Hulan** Heilongjiang, NE China 45.58N 126.37E
169 W8 **Hulan He** ≈ NE China
33 Q4 **Hulbert Lake** ◎ Michigan, N USA
Hulczyn see Hlučín
169 Z8 **Hulin** Heilongjiang, NE China 45.48N 133.06E
169 S9 **Hulingol** prev. Huolin Gol. Nei Mongol Zizhiqu, N China 45.35N 119.53E
12 L12 **Hull** Quebec, SE Canada 45.25N 75.45W
31 S12 **Hull** Iowa, C USA 43.11N 96.07W
Hull see Kingston upon Hull
Hull Island see Orona
101 F16 **Hulst** Zeeland, SW Netherlands 51.16N 4.03E
169 Q7 **Hulstay** Dornod, NE Mongolia 48.25N 114.56E
Hultschin see Hlučín
97 M19 **Hultsfred** Kalmar, S Sweden 57.30N 15.49E
Hulun see Hailar
Hu-lun Ch'ih see Hulun Nur
169 Q6 **Hulun Nur** var. Hu-lun Ch'ih; prev. Dalai Nor. ◎ NE China
Hulwan/Hulwân see Helwân
119 V8 **Hulyaypole** Rus. Gulyaypole. Zaporiz'ka Oblast', SE Ukraine 47.41N 36.10E
169 V4 **Huma** Heilongjiang, NE China 51.40N 126.38E
47 V6 **Humacao** E Puerto Rico 18.09N 65.49W
169 U4 **Huma He** ≈ NE China
64 J5 **Humahuaca** Jujuy, N Argentina 23.13S 65.19W
61 E14 **Humaitá** Amazonas, N Brazil 7.33S 63.01W
64 N7 **Humaitá** Ñeembucú, S Paraguay 27.06S 58.28W
85 H26 **Humansdorp** Eastern Cape, S South Africa 34.01S 24.45E
29 S6 **Humansville** Missouri, C USA 37.47N 93.34W
42 I8 **Humaya, Río** ≈ C Mexico
85 C16 **Humbe** Cunene, SW Angola 16.37S 14.52E
99 N17 **Humber** estuary E England, UK
99 N17 **Humberside** cultural region E England, UK
Humberto see Umberto
27 W11 **Humble** Texas, SW USA 29.58N 95.15W
9 U15 **Humboldt** Saskatchewan, S Canada 52.13N 105.09W
31 U12 **Humboldt** Iowa, C USA 42.42N 94.13W
29 Q6 **Humboldt** Kansas, C USA 37.48N 95.26W
31 S17 **Humboldt** Nebraska, C USA 40.09N 95.56W
37 S3 **Humboldt** Nevada, W USA 40.36N 118.15W
22 G9 **Humboldt** Tennessee, S USA 35.49N 88.55W
36 K3 **Humboldt Bay** bay California, W USA
37 S4 **Humboldt Lake** ◎ Nevada, W USA
197 J7 **Humboldt, Mont** ▲ S New Caledonia 21.57S 166.24E
37 S4 **Humboldt River** ≈ Nevada, W USA
37 T5 **Humboldt Salt Marsh** wetland Nevada, W USA
191 P11 **Hume, Lake** ◎ New South Wales/Victoria, SE Australia
113 N19 **Humenné** Ger. Homenau, Hung. Homonna. Prešovský Kraj, E Slovakia 48.57N 21.54E
31 V15 **Humeston** Iowa, C USA 40.51N 93.30W
56 J5 **Humocaro Bajo** Lara, N Venezuela 9.42N 70.02W
31 Q14 **Humphrey** Nebraska, C USA 41.38N 97.29W
37 S9 **Humphreys, Mount** ▲ California, W USA 37.11N 118.39W
38 L11 **Humphreys Peak** ▲ Arizona, SW USA 35.18N 111.40W
113 E17 **Humpolec** Ger. Gumpolds, Humpoletz. Jihlavský Kraj, C Czech Republic 49.33N 15.22E
Humpoletz see Humpolec
95 K19 **Humppila** Etelä-Suomi, S Finland 60.54N 23.21E
34 F8 **Humptulips** Washington, NW USA 47.13N 123.57W
44 H7 **Humuya, Río** ≈ W Honduras
77 P9 **Hūn** N Libya 29.06N 15.56E
Hunabasi see Funabashi
94 I1 **Húnaflói** bay NW Iceland
166 M11 **Hunan** var. Hunan Sheng, Xiang. ◐ province S China
Hunan Sheng see Hunan
169 Y10 **Hunchun** Jilin, NE China 42.51N 130.21E
97 I22 **Hundested** Frederiksborg, E Denmark 55.58N 11.52E
Hundred Mile House see 100 Mile House
118 G12 **Hunedoara** Ger. Eisenmarkt, Hung. Vajdahunyad. Hunedoara, SW Romania 45.45N 22.54E
118 G12 **Hunedoara** ◐ county W Romania
103 I17 **Hünfeld** Hessen, C Germany 50.40N 9.46E
113 H23 **Hungary** off. Republic of Hungary, Ger. Ungarn, Hung. Magyarország, Rom. Ungaria, SCr. Mađarska, Ukr. Uhorshchyna; prev. Hungarian People's Republic. ◆ republic C Europe
Hungary, Plain of see Great Hungarian Plain
168 F6 **Hungiy** Dzavhan, W Mongolia 48.31N 94.15E
169 X13 **Hŭngnam** E North Korea 39.50N 127.36E
35 P8 **Hungry Horse Reservoir** ⊠ Montana, NW USA
Hungt'ou see Lan Yü
Hung-tse Hu see Hongze Hu
178 Jj6 **Hưng Yên** Hai Hưng, N Vietnam 20.37N 106.04E
Hunjiang see Baishan
97 I18 **Hunnebostrand** Västra Götaland, S Sweden 58.26N 11.19E
103 E19 **Hunsrück** ▲▲ W Germany
99 P18 **Hunstanton** E England, UK 52.57N 0.28E
161 G20 **Hunsūr** Karnātaka, E India 12.18N 76.15E
168 I7 **Hunt** Arhangay, C Mongolia 47.49N 99.24E
102 G12 **Hunte** ≈ NW Germany
31 Q5 **Hunter** North Dakota, N USA 47.10N 97.11W
27 S11 **Hunter** Texas, SW USA 29.47N 98.01W
193 D20 **Hunter** ≈ South Island, NZ
191 N15 **Hunter Island** island Tasmania, SE Australia
20 K11 **Hunter Mountain** ▲ New York, NE USA 42.10N 74.13W
193 B23 **Hunter Mountains** ▲▲ South Island, NZ
191 S7 **Hunter River** ≈ New South Wales, SE Australia
34 L7 **Hunters** Washington, NW USA 48.07N 118.13W
193 F20 **Hunters Hills, The** hill range South Island, NZ
192 M12 **Hunterville** Manawatu-Wanganui, North Island, NZ 39.55S 175.34E
33 N16 **Huntingburg** Indiana, N USA 38.18N 86.57W
99 O20 **Huntingdon** E England, UK 52.19N 0.12W
20 E15 **Huntingdon** Pennsylvania, NE USA 40.28N 78.00W
22 G9 **Huntingdon** Tennessee, S USA 36.00N 88.25W
99 O20 **Huntingdonshire** cultural region C England, UK
33 P12 **Huntington** Indiana, N USA 40.52N 85.30W
34 L13 **Huntington** Oregon, NW USA 44.22N 117.18W
27 X9 **Huntington** Texas, SW USA 31.16N 94.34W
38 M5 **Huntington** Utah, W USA 39.19N 110.57W
23 P5 **Huntington** West Virginia, NE USA 38.24N 82.27W
37 T16 **Huntington Beach** California, W USA 33.39N 118.00W
37 W4 **Huntington Creek** ≈ Nevada, W USA

◆ Country
● Country Capital
◇ Dependent Territory
○ Dependent Territory Capital
◐ Administrative Region
✈ International Airport
▲ Mountain
▲▲ Mountain Range
Volcano
≈ River
◎ Lake
⊠ Reservoir

HUNTLY – INDAIATUBA

192 L7 **Huntly** Waikato, North Island, NZ *37.33S 175.09E*
98 K8 **Huntly** NE Scotland, UK *57.25N 2.48W*
8 K8 **Hunt, Mount** ▲ Yukon Territory, NW Canada *61.29N 129.10W*
12 H12 **Huntsville** Ontario, S Canada *45.18N 79.12W*
25 P2 **Huntsville** Alabama, S USA *34.43N 86.35W*
29 S9 **Huntsville** Arkansas, C USA *36.05N 93.43W*
29 U3 **Huntsville** Missouri, C USA *39.26N 92.33W*
22 M8 **Huntsville** Tennessee, S USA *36.25N 84.30W*
27 V10 **Huntsville** Texas, SW USA *30.43N 95.34W*
38 L2 **Huntsville** Utah, W USA *41.16N 111.47W*
43 W12 **Hunucmá** Yucatán, SE Mexico *20.59N 89.55W*
155 W3 **Hunza** *var.* Karīmābād. Jammu and Kashmir, NE Pakistan *36.22N 74.43E*
155 W3 **Hunza** ≈ NE Pakistan
Hunze *see* Oostermoers Vaart
164 H4 **Huocheng** *var.* Shuiding. Xinjiang Uygur Zizhiqu, NW China *44.03N 80.49E*
167 N6 **Huojia** Henan, C China *35.13N 113.37E*
Huolin Gol *see* Hulingol
197 F3 **Huon** *reef* N New Caledonia
194 K13 **Huon Gulf** *gulf* E PNG
194 K13 **Huon Peninsula** *headland* C PNG *6.24S 147.50E*
Huoshao Dao *see* Lü Tao
Huoshao Tao *see* Lan Yü
Hupeh/Hupei *see* Hubei
Hurano *see* Furano
97 H14 **Hurdalssjøen** ◎ S Norway
12 E13 **Hurd, Cape** *headland* Ontario, S Canada *45.12N 81.43W*
Hurdegaryp *see* Hardegarijp
31 N4 **Hurdsfield** North Dakota, N USA *47.24N 99.55W*
168 J7 **Hüremt** Bulgan, C Mongolia *48.40N 102.33E*
168 J8 **Hüremt** Övörhangay, C Mongolia *46.18N 102.27E*
77 X9 **Hurghada** *var.* Al Ghurdaqah, Ghurdaqah. E Egypt *27.16N 33.46E*
69 V9 **Huri Hills** ▲▲ NW Kenya
39 P15 **Hurley** New Mexico, SW USA *32.42N 108.07W*
32 K4 **Hurley** Wisconsin, N USA *46.25N 90.15W*
23 Y4 **Hurlock** Maryland, NE USA *38.37N 75.51W*
31 P10 **Huron** South Dakota, N USA *44.19N 98.13W*
33 S6 **Huron, Lake** ◎ Canada/USA
33 N3 **Huron Mountains** *hill range* Michigan, N USA
38 J8 **Hurricane** Utah, W USA *37.10N 113.18W*
23 P5 **Hurricane** West Virginia, NE USA *38.25N 82.01W*
38 J8 **Hurricane Cliffs** *cliff* Arizona, SW USA
25 V6 **Hurricane Creek** ≈ Georgia, SE USA
96 E12 **Hurrungane** ▲ S Norway *61.25N 7.48E*
103 E16 **Hürth** Nordrhein-Westfalen, W Germany *50.52N 6.52E*
Hurukawa *see* Furukawa
193 I17 **Hurunui** ≈ South Island, NZ
97 F21 **Hurup** Viborg, NW Denmark *56.46N 8.25E*
119 T14 **Hurzuf** Respublika Krym, S Ukraine *44.33N 34.18E*
Huş *see* Huşi
97 B19 **Húsavík** *Dan.* Husevig Faeroe Islands *61.19N 6.41W*
94 K1 **Húsavík** Nordhurland Eystra, NE Iceland *66.03N 17.19W*
118 M10 **Huşi** *var.* Huş. Vaslui, E Romania *46.40N 28.05E*
97 L19 **Huskvarna** Jönköping, S Sweden *57.46N 14.15E*
41 P8 **Huslia** Alaska, USA *65.42N 156.24W*
Husn *see* Al Ḥuṣn
97 C15 **Husnes** Hordaland, S Norway *59.52N 5.46E*
96 D8 **Hustadvika** *sea area* S Norway
Husté *see* Khust
102 H7 **Husum** Schleswig-Holstein, N Germany *54.28N 9.04E*
95 I16 **Husum** Västernorrland, C Sweden *63.21N 19.12E*
118 K6 **Husyatyn** Ternopil's'ka Oblast', W Ukraine *49.04N 26.10E*
Huszt *see* Khust
168 K6 **Hutag** Bulgan, N Mongolia *49.22N 102.50E*
28 M6 **Hutchinson** Kansas, C USA *38.03N 97.55W*
31 U9 **Hutchinson** Minnesota, N USA *44.53N 94.22W*
25 Y13 **Hutchinson Island** *island* Florida, SE USA
38 L11 **Hutch Mountain** ▲ Arizona, SW USA *34.49N 111.22W*
147 O14 **Ḥūth** NW Yemen *16.13N 44.00E*
195 R11 **Hutjena** Buka Island, NE PNG *5.19S 154.40E*
111 T8 **Hüttenberg** Kärnten, S Austria *46.58N 14.33E*
27 T10 **Hutto** Texas, SW USA *30.32N 97.33W*
Huttu *see* Futtsu
110 E8 **Huttwil** Bern, W Switzerland *47.06N 7.48E*
164 K5 **Hutubi** Xinjiang Uygur Zizhiqu, NW China *44.10N 86.51E*
167 N4 **Hutuo He** ≈ C China
Hutyû *see* Fuchū
193 E20 **Huxley, Mount** ▲ South Island, NZ *44.02S 169.42E*
101 J20 **Huy** *Dut.* Hoei, Hoey. Liège, E Belgium *50.31N 5.13E*
167 R8 **Huzhou** *var.* Wuxing. Zhejiang, SE China *30.54N 120.04E*
Huzi *see* Fuji
Huzieda *see* Fujieda
Huzinomiya *see* Fujinomiya
Huzisawa *see* Fujisawa
Huziyosida *see* Fuji-Yoshida
94 I2 **Hvammstangi** Nordhurland Vestra, N Iceland *65.22N 20.54W*
94 K4 **Hvannadalshnúkur** ▲ S Iceland *64.01N 16.39W*
115 E15 **Hvar** *It.* Lesina. Split-Dalmacija, S Croatia *43.10N 16.27E*
115 F15 **Hvar** *It.* Lesina; *anc.* Pharus. *island* S Croatia
119 T13 **Hvardiys'ke** *Rus.* Gvardeyskoye. Respublika Krym, S Ukraine *45.07N 34.01E*
94 I4 **Hveragerdhi** Sudhurland, SW Iceland *64.00N 21.13W*
97 E22 **Hvide Sande** Ringkøbing, W Denmark *56.00N 8.08E*
94 I3 **Hvitá** ≈ C Iceland
97 G15 **Hvittingfoss** Buskerud, S Norway *59.28N 10.00E*
94 I4 **Hvolsvöllur** Sudhurland, SW Iceland *63.44N 20.12W*
Hwach'ŏn-chŏsuji *see* P'aro-ho
Hwainan *see* Huainan
Hwalien *see* Hualien
85 I16 **Hwange** *prev.* Wankie. Matabeleland North, W Zimbabwe *18.18S 26.30E*
Hwang-Hae *see* Yellow Sea
Hwangshih *see* Huangshi
85 L17 **Hwedza** Mashonaland East, E Zimbabwe *18.15S 29.48E*
65 G20 **Hyades, Cerro** ▲ S Chile *46.57S 73.09W*
21 Q12 **Hyannis** Massachusetts, NE USA *41.38N 70.15W*
30 L13 **Hyannis** Nebraska, C USA *41.58N 101.45W*
168 F6 **Hyargas Nuur** ◎ NW Mongolia
Hybla/Hybla Major *see* Paternò
41 Y14 **Hydaburg** Prince of Wales Island, Alaska, USA *55.10N 132.44W*
193 F22 **Hyde** Otago, South Island, NZ *45.17S 170.17E*
23 O7 **Hyden** Kentucky, S USA *37.07N 83.22W*
20 K12 **Hyde Park** New York, NE USA *41.46N 73.52W*
41 Z14 **Hyder** Alaska, USA *55.55N 130.01W*
161 I15 **Hyderābād** *var.* Haidarabad. Andhra Pradesh, C India *17.22N 78.25E*
155 Q16 **Hyderābād** *var.* Haidarabad. Sind, SE Pakistan *25.25N 68.21E*
105 T16 **Hyères** Var, SE France *43.07N 6.07E*
105 T16 **Hyères, Îles d'** *island group* S France
120 K12 **Hyermanavichy** *Rus.* Germanovichi. Vitsyebskaya Voblasts', N Belarus *55.25N 27.43E*
169 X12 **Hyesan** NE North Korea *41.17N 128.13E*
8 K8 **Hyland** ≈ Yukon Territory, NW Canada
97 K20 **Hyltebruk** Halland, S Sweden *57.00N 13.14E*
20 D16 **Hyndman** Pennsylvania, NE USA *39.49N 78.42W*
35 P14 **Hyndman Peak** ▲ Idaho, NW USA *43.45N 114.07W*
170 G13 **Hyōgo** *off.* Hyōgo-ken. ◈ *prefecture* Honshū, SW Japan
170 G13 **Hyōno-sen** ▲ Kyūshū, SW Japan *35.21N 134.30E*
Hypanis *see* Kuban'
Hypsas *see* Belice
Hyrcania *see* Gorgān
38 L1 **Hyrum** Utah, W USA *41.37N 111.51W*
95 N14 **Hyrynsalmi** Oulu, C Finland *64.40N 28.30E*
35 V10 **Hysham** Montana, NW USA *46.16N 107.14W*
9 N13 **Hythe** Alberta, W Canada *55.18N 119.44W*
99 Q23 **Hythe** SE England, UK *51.04N 1.04E*
170 D15 **Hyūga** Miyazaki, Kyūshū, SW Japan *32.24N 131.34E*
Hyvinge *see* Hyvinkää
95 L19 **Hyvinkää** *Swe.* Hyvinge. Etelä-Suomi, S Finland *60.37N 24.49E*

I

118 J9 **Iacobeni** *Ger.* Jakobeny. Suceava, NE Romania *47.24N 25.19E*
Iader *see* Zadar
180 I7 **Iakora** Fianarantsoa, SE Madagascar *23.04S 46.40E*
194 H12 **Ialibu** Southern Highlands, W PNG *6.15S 143.55E*
118 K14 **Ialomiţa** *var.* Jalomitsa. ◈ *county* SE Romania
118 K14 **Ialomiţa** ≈ SE Romania
119 N10 **Ialoveni** *Rus.* Yaloveny. C Moldova *46.57N 28.47E*
119 N11 **Ialpug** *var.* Ialpugul Mare, *Rus.* Yalpug. ≈ Moldova/Ukraine
Ialpugul Mare *see* Ialpug
25 T8 **Iamonia, Lake** ◎ Florida, SE USA
118 L13 **Ianca** Brăila, SE Romania *45.06N 27.29E*
118 M10 **Iaşi** *Ger.* Jassy. Iaşi, NE Romania *47.08N 27.38E*
118 L9 **Iaşi** *Ger.* Jassy, Yassy. ◈ *county* NE Romania
116 J13 **Íasmos** Anatolikí Makedonía kai Thráki, NE Greece *41.07N 25.12E*
24 H6 **Iatt, Lake** ⊠ Louisiana, S USA
60 B11 **Iauaretê** Amazonas, NW Brazil *0.37N 69.10W*
179 Oo10 **Iba** Luzon, N Philippines *15.25N 119.55E*
79 S16 **Ibadan** Oyo, SW Nigeria *7.21N 4.01E*
56 E10 **Ibagué** Tolima, C Colombia *4.27N 75.13W*
62 J10 **Ibaiti** Paraná, S Brazil *23.52S 50.09W*
179 Pp12 **Ibajay** Panay Island, C Philippines *11.42N 122.17E*
38 J4 **Ibapah Peak** ▲ Utah, W USA *39.51N 113.55W*
115 M15 **Ibar** *Alb.* Ibër. ≈ C Yugoslavia
170 F14 **Ibara** Okayama, Honshū, SW Japan *34.36N 133.27E*
171 Kk16 **Ibaraki** *off.* Ibaraki-ken. ◈ *prefecture* Honshū, S Japan
58 C5 **Ibarra** *var.* San Miguel de Ibarra. Imbabura, N Ecuador *0.22S 78.07W*
Ibaşfalău *see* Dumbrăveni
147 O16 **Ibb** W Yemen *13.55N 44.10E*
102 F13 **Ibbenbüren** Nordrhein-Westfalen, NW Germany *52.17N 7.43E*
81 H16 **Ibenga** ≈ N Congo
Ibër *see* Ibar
59 I14 **Iberia** Madre de Dios, E Peru *11.21S 69.36W*
Iberia *see* Spain
68 M1 **Iberian Basin** *undersea feature* E Atlantic Ocean
Iberian Mountains *see* Ibérico, Sistema
86 D12 **Iberian Peninsula** *physical region* Portugal/Spain
66 M8 **Iberian Plain** *undersea feature* E Atlantic Ocean
Ibérica, Cordillera *see* Ibérico, Sistema
107 P6 **Ibérico, Sistema** *var.* Cordillera Ibérica, *Eng.* Iberian Mountains. ▲▲ NE Spain
10 K7 **Iberville Lac d'** ◎ Quebec, NE Canada
79 T14 **Ibeto** Niger, W Nigeria *10.30N 5.07E*
79 W15 **Ibi** Taraba, C Nigeria *8.13N 9.46E*
107 S11 **Ibi** País Valenciano, E Spain *38.37N 0.34W*
61 L20 **Ibiá** Minas Gerais, SE Brazil *19.30S 46.31W*
63 F15 **Ibicuí, Rio** ≈ S Brazil
63 C19 **Ibicuy** Entre Ríos, E Argentina *33.46S 59.07W*
63 F16 **Ibirapuitã** ≈ S Brazil
Ibiza *see* Eivissa
144 J4 **Ibn Wardān, Qaṣr** *ruins* Ḥamāh, C Syria *35.19N 37.13E*
Ibo *see* Sassandra
196 E9 **Ibobang** Babeldaob, N Palau
176 Vv11 **Ibonma** Irian Jaya, E Indonesia *3.27S 133.30E*
61 N17 **Ibotirama** Bahia, E Brazil *12.13S 43.12W*
147 Y8 **Ibrā** NE Oman *22.45N 58.30E*
131 Q4 **Ibresi** Chuvashskaya Respublika, W Russian Federation *55.22N 47.04E*
147 X8 **'Ibrī** NW Oman *23.12N 56.28E*
170 Bb16 **Ibusuki** Kagoshima, Kyūshū, SW Japan *31.13N 130.37E*
59 E16 **Ica** Ica, SW Peru *14.01S 75.48W*
59 E16 **Ica** *off.* Departamento de Ica. ◈ *department* SW Peru
60 C11 **Içana** Amazonas, NW Brazil *0.22N 67.25W*
Icaria *see* Ikaría
60 B13 **Içá, Rio** *var.* Río Putumayo. ≈ NW South America *see also* Putumayo, Río
142 I17 **İçel** *var.* Ichili. ◈ *province* S Turkey
94 I3 **Iceland** *off.* Republic of Iceland, *Dan.* Island, *Icel.* Ísland. ◆ *republic* N Atlantic Ocean
88 B7 **Iceland** *island* N Atlantic Ocean
66 L5 **Iceland Basin** *undersea feature* N Atlantic Ocean
Icelandic Plateau *see* Iceland Plateau
207 Q15 **Iceland Plateau** *var.* Icelandic Plateau. *undersea feature* S Greenland Sea
161 E16 **Ichalkaranji** Mahārāshtra, W India *16.42N 74.28E*
170 Cc15 **Ichifusa-yama** ▲ Kyūshū, SW Japan *32.18N 131.05E*
171 K17 **Ichihara** *var.* Itihara. Chiba, Honshū, S Japan *35.30N 140.08E*
Ichili *see* İçel
171 I15 **Ichinomiya** *var.* Itinomiya. Aichi, Honshū, SW Japan *35.19N 136.47E*
171 Mm12 **Ichinoseki** *var.* Itinoseki. Iwate, Honshū, C Japan *38.25N 141.16E*
119 R3 **Ichnya** Chernihivs'ka Oblast', NE Ukraine *50.52N 32.24E*
59 L17 **Ichoa, Río** ≈ C Bolivia
I-ch'un *see* Yichun
Iconium *see* Konya
Iculisma *see* Angoulême
41 U12 **Icy Bay** *inlet* Alaska, USA
41 N5 **Icy Cape** *headland* Alaska, USA *70.19N 161.52W*
41 W13 **Icy Strait** *strait* Alaska, USA
29 R13 **Idabel** Oklahoma, C USA *33.54N 94.49W*
31 T13 **Ida Grove** Iowa, C USA *42.21N 95.28W*
79 U16 **Idah** Kogi, S Nigeria *7.06N 6.45E*
35 N13 **Idaho** *off.* State of Idaho; also known as Gem of the Mountains, Gem State. ◈ *state* NW USA
35 N14 **Idaho City** Idaho, NW USA *43.48N 115.51W*
35 R14 **Idaho Falls** Idaho, NW USA *43.28N 112.01W*
124 Nn3 **Idálion** *var.* Dali, Dhali. C Cyprus *35.00N 33.25E*
27 N5 **Idalou** Texas, SW USA *33.40N 101.40W*
106 I9 **Idanha-a-Nova** Castelo Branco, C Portugal *39.55N 7.15W*
103 E19 **Idar-Oberstein** Rheinland-Pfalz, SW Germany *49.43N 7.19E*
120 J3 **Ida-Virumaa** *off.* Ida-Viru Maakond. ◈ *province* NE Estonia
128 J8 **Idel'** Respublika Kareliya, NW Russian Federation *64.08N 34.12E*
81 C15 **Idenao** Sud-Ouest, SW Cameroon *4.04N 9.01E*
Idenburg-rivier *see* Taritatu, Sungai
Idensalmi *see* Iisalmi
168 I6 **Ider** Hövsgöl, C Mongolia *48.45N 99.52E*
77 X10 **Idfu** *var.* Edfu. SE Egypt *24.57N 32.51E*
Ídhi Óros *see* Ídi
Ídhra *see* Ýdra
173 F3 **Idi** Sumatera, W Indonesia *5.00N 98.00E*
117 I25 **Ídi** *var.* Ídhi Óros. ▲▲ Kríti, Greece, E Mediterranean Sea
Idi Amin, Lac *see* Edward, Lake
108 G10 **Idice** ≈ N Italy
78 G9 **Idîni** Trarza, W Mauritania *17.58N 15.40W*
81 J21 **Idiofa** Bandundu, SW Dem. Rep. Congo (Zaire) *5.00S 19.38E*
41 O10 **Iditarod River** ≈ Alaska, USA
97 M14 **Idkerberget** Dalarna, C Sweden *60.22N 15.15E*
144 I3 **Idlib** Idlib, NW Syria *35.57N 36.37E*
144 I4 **Idlib** *off.* Muḥāfaẓat Idlib. ◈ *governorate* NW Syria
Idra *see* Ýdra
96 J11 **Idre** Dalarna, C Sweden *61.52N 12.45E*
Idria *see* Idrija
111 S11 **Idrija** *It.* Idria. W Slovenia *46.00N 14.59E*
103 G18 **Idstein** Hessen, W Germany *50.10N 8.16E*
85 J25 **Idutywa** Eastern Cape, SE South Africa *32.06S 28.19E*
Idzhevan *see* Ijevan
120 G9 **Iecava** Bauska, S Latvia *56.36N 24.10E*
172 P14 **Ie-jima** *var.* Ii-shima. *island* Nansei-shotō, SW Japan
101 B18 **Ieper** *Fr.* Ypres. West-Vlaanderen, W Belgium *50.51N 2.52E*
117 K25 **Ierápetra** Kríti, Greece, E Mediterranean Sea *35.00N 25.45E*
117 G22 **Iérax, Akrotírio** *headland* S Greece *36.45N 23.06E*
Ierisós *see* Ierissós
117 H14 **Ierissós** *var.* Ierisós. Kentrikí Makedonía, N Greece *40.24N 23.52E*
118 I11 **Iernut** *Hung.* Radnót. Mureş, C Romania *46.27N 24.18E*
108 J12 **Iesi** *var.* Jesi. Marche, C Italy *43.33N 13.16E*
94 K9 **Iešjávri** *var.* Jiesjavrre. ◎ N Norway
Iesolo *see* Jesolo
196 K16 **Ifalik Atoll** *atoll* Caroline Islands, C Micronesia
180 I6 **Ifanadiana** Fianarantsoa, SE Madagascar *21.19S 47.39E*
79 T16 **Ife** Osun, SW Nigeria *7.25N 4.31E*
79 V8 **Iferouâne** Agadez, N Niger *19.08N 8.21E*
Iferten *see* Yverdon
94 L8 **Ifjord** Finnmark, N Norway *70.27N 27.06E*
79 R8 **Ifôghas, Adrar des** *var.* Adrar des Iforas. ▲▲ NE Mali
Iforas, Adrar des *see* Ifôghas, Adrar des
190 D6 **Ifould lake** *salt lake* South Australia
76 G6 **Ifrane** C Morocco *33.31N 5.09W*
175 T7 **Iga** Pulau Halmahera, E Indonesia *1.23N 128.17E*
83 G18 **Iganga** SE Uganda *0.34N 33.27E*
62 L7 **Igarapava** São Paulo, S Brazil *20.01S 47.46W*
126 Hh9 **Igarka** Krasnoyarskiy Kray, N Russian Federation *67.31N 86.33E*
Igaunija *see* Estonia
I.G.Duca *see* General Toshevo
Igel *see* Jihlava
143 T12 **Iğdır** ◈ *province* E Turkey
96 N11 **Iggesund** Gävleborg, C Sweden *61.37N 17.15E*
41 P7 **Igikpak, Mount** ▲ Alaska, USA *67.28N 154.55W*
41 P13 **Igiugig** Alaska, USA *59.19N 155.53W*
Iglau/Iglawa/Igława *see* Jihlava
109 B20 **Iglesias** Sardegna, Italy, C Mediterranean Sea *39.19N 8.33E*
131 V4 **Iglino** Respublika Bashkortostan, W Russian Federation *54.51N 56.29E*
Igló *see* Spišská Nová Ves
15 Ll2 **Igloolik** Nunavut, N Canada *69.24N 81.55W*
10 B11 **Ignace** Ontario, S Canada *49.25N 91.40W*
120 I12 **Ignalina** Ignalina, E Lithuania *55.20N 26.10E*
131 Q5 **Ignatovka** Ul'yanovskaya Oblast', W Russian Federation *53.56N 47.40E*
128 K12 **Ignatovo** Vologodskaya Oblast', NW Russian Federation *60.47N 37.51E*
116 N11 **İğneada** Kırklareli, NW Turkey *41.54N 27.58E*
124 P7 **İğneada Burnu** *headland* NW Turkey *41.54N 28.03E*
Igombe *see* Gombe
117 B16 **Igoumenítsa** Ípeiros, W Greece *39.30N 20.16E*
131 T2 **Igra** Udmurtskaya Respublika, NW Russian Federation *57.30N 53.01E*
125 Ff9 **Igrim** Khanty-Mansiyskiy Avtonomnyy Okrug, N Russian Federation *63.09N 64.33E*
62 G12 **Iguaçu, Rio** *Sp.* Río Iguazú. ≈ Argentina/Brazil *see also* Iguazú, Río
61 I22 **Iguaçu, Salto do** *Sp.* Cataratas del Iguazú; *prev.* Victoria Falls. *waterfall* Argentina/Brazil *see also* Iguazú, Cataratas del *25.37S 54.28W*
43 O15 **Iguala** *var.* Iguala de la Independencia. Guerrero, S Mexico *18.21N 99.33W*
107 V5 **Igualada** Cataluña, NE Spain *41.34N 1.37E*
Iguala de la Independencia *see* Iguala
62 G12 **Iguazú, Cataratas del** *Port.* Salto do Iguaçu, *prev.* Victoria Falls. *waterfall* Argentina/Brazil *see also* Iguaçu, Salto do *25.40S 54.25W*
64 Q6 **Iguazú, Río** *Port.* Rio Iguaçu. ≈ Argentina/Brazil *see also* Iguaçu, Rio
81 D19 **Iguéla** Ogooué-Maritime, SW Gabon *2.00S 9.23E*
Iguid, Erg *see* Iguîdi, 'Erg
69 M5 **Iguîdi, 'Erg** *var.* Erg Iguid. *desert* Algeria/Mauritania
180 K2 **Iharaña** *prev.* Vohémar. Antsirañana, NE Madagascar *13.22S 50.00E*
157 K18 **Ihavandippolhu Atoll** *var.* Ihavandiffulu Atoll. *atoll* N Maldives
168 M11 **Ih Bulag** Ömnögovĭ, S Mongolia *43.04N 107.43E*
172 Pp14 **Iheya-jima** *island* Nansei-shotō, SW Japan
168 L8 **Ihhayrhan** Töv, C Mongolia *46.57N 105.51E*
180 I6 **Ihosy** Fianarantsoa, S Madagascar *22.22S 46.09E*
168 L7 **Ihsüüj** Töv, C Mongolia *48.12N 106.23E*
95 L14 **Ii** Oulu, C Finland *65.18N 25.23E*
171 Ii16 **Iida** Nagano, Honshū, S Japan *35.30N 137.48E*
171 L13 **Iide-san** ▲ Honshū, C Japan *38.03N 139.39E*
95 M14 **Iijoki** ≈ C Finland
120 J4 **Iisaku** *Ger.* Isaak. Ida-Virumaa, NE Estonia *59.07N 27.18E*
95 M16 **Iisalmi** *var.* Idensalmi. Itä-Suomi, C Finland *63.31N 27.10E*
171 Jj14 **Iiyama** Nagano, Honshū, S Japan *36.52N 138.22E*
170 D13 **Iizuka** Fukuoka, Kyūshū, SW Japan *33.37N 130.40E*
79 S16 **Ijebu-Ode** Ogun, SW Nigeria *6.46N 3.57E*
143 U11 **Ijevan** *Rus.* Idzhevan. N Armenia *40.53N 45.07E*
100 H9 **IJmuiden** Noord-Holland, W Netherlands *52.28N 4.34E*
100 M12 **IJssel** *var.* Yssel. ≈ Netherlands/Germany
100 J8 **IJsselmeer** *prev.* Zuider Zee. ◎ N Netherlands
100 L9 **IJsselmuiden** Overijssel, E Netherlands *52.34N 5.55E*
100 I12 **IJsselstein** Utrecht, C Netherlands *52.01N 5.01E*
63 G14 **Ijuí** Rio Grande do Sul, S Brazil *28.22S 53.55W*
63 G14 **Ijuí, Rio** ≈ S Brazil
201 R8 **Ijuw** NE Nauru *0.30S 166.57E*
101 E16 **IJzendijke** Zeeland, SW Netherlands *51.20N 3.36E*
101 A18 **Ijzer** ≈ W Belgium
95 K18 **Ikaalinen** Länsi-Suomi, W Finland *61.46N 23.04E*
180 I6 **Ikalamavony** Fianarantsoa, SE Madagascar *21.10S 46.34E*
193 G16 **Ikamatua** West Coast, South Island, NZ *42.16S 171.42E*
79 U16 **Ikare** Ondo, SW Nigeria *7.36N 5.52E*
117 L20 **Ikaría** *var.* Kariot, Nicaria, Nikaria; *anc.* Icaria. *island* Dodekánisos, Greece, Aegean Sea
97 F22 **Ikast** Ringkøbing, W Denmark *56.09N 9.10E*
192 O9 **Ikawhenua Range** ▲▲ North Island, NZ
172 Pp7 **Ikeda** Hokkaidō, NE Japan *42.54N 143.25E*
170 F15 **Ikeda** Tokushima, Shikoku, SW Japan *34.00N 133.47E*
79 S16 **Ikeja** Lagos, SW Nigeria *6.36N 3.16E*
81 L19 **Ikela** Equateur, C Dem. Rep. Congo (Zaire) *1.10S 23.16E*
116 H10 **Ikhtiman** Sofiya, W Bulgaria *42.25N 23.49E*
170 Cc12 **Iki** *island* SW Japan
131 O13 **Iki Burul** Respublika Kalmykiya, SW Russian Federation *45.48N 44.44E*
170 C12 **Iki-suidō** *strait* SW Japan
170 Bb12 **Ikitsuki-shima** *island* SW Japan
143 P11 **İkizdere** Rize, NE Turkey *40.46N 40.34E*
41 P14 **Ikolik, Cape** *headland* Kodiak Island, Alaska, USA *57.12N 154.46W*
79 V17 **Ikom** Cross River, SE Nigeria *5.57N 8.43E*
180 I6 **Ikongo** *prev.* Fort-Carnot. Fianarantsoa, SE Madagascar *21.52S 47.27E*
41 P5 **Ikpikpuk River** ≈ Alaska, USA
202 H1 **Iku** *prev.* Lone Tree Islet. *atoll* Tungaru, W Kiribati
171 Gg14 **Ikuno** Hyōgo, Honshū, SW Japan *35.13N 134.48E*
202 H16 **Ikurangi** ▲ Rarotonga, S Cook Islands *21.12S 159.45W*
176 Xx12 **Ilaga** Irian Jaya, E Indonesia *3.54S 137.30E*
179 Pp8 **Ilagan** Luzon, N Philippines *17.07N 121.54E*
159 R12 **Ilam** Eastern, E Nepal *26.52N 87.58E*
148 J7 **Īlām** *var.* Elam. Īlām, W Iran *33.40N 46.24E*
148 J8 **Īlām** *off.* Ostān-e Īlām. ◈ *province* W Iran
167 T13 **Ilan** *Jap.* Giran. N Taiwan *24.46N 121.46E*
152 G9 **Ilanly Obvodnitel'nyy Kanal** *canal* N Turkmenistan
126 Ii14 **Ilanskiy** Krasnoyarskiy Kray, S Russian Federation *56.16N 95.59E*
110 H9 **Ilanz** Graubünden, S Switzerland *46.46N 9.10E*
79 S16 **Ilaro** Ogun, SW Nigeria *6.52N 3.01E*
59 I17 **Ilave** Puno, S Peru *16.07S 69.37W*
112 K8 **Iława** *Ger.* Deutsch-Eylau. Warmińsko-Mazurskie, NE Poland, *53.36N 19.34E*
126 Ll11 **Il'benge** Respublika Sakha (Yakutiya), NE Russian Federation *62.52N 124.13E*
Ile *see* Ili
9 S13 **Ile-à-la-Crosse** Saskatchewan, C Canada *55.29N 108.00W*
81 J21 **Ilebo** *prev.* Port-Francqui. Kasai Occidental, W Dem. Rep. Congo (Zaire) *4.19S 20.31E*
105 N5 **Île-de-France** ◈ *region* N France
150 I9 **Ilek** *Kaz.* Elek. ≈ Kazakhstan/Russian Federation
Ilerda *see* Lleida
79 T16 **Ilesha** Osun, SW Nigeria *7.35N 4.49E*
197 J5 **Îles Loyauté, Province des** ◈ *province* E New Caledonia
9 X12 **Ilford** Manitoba, C Canada *56.02N 95.48W*
99 I23 **Ilfracombe** SW England, UK *51.12N 4.09W*
142 I11 **Ilgaz Dağları** ▲▲ N Turkey
142 G15 **Ilgın** Konya, W Turkey *38.16N 31.57E*
62 I7 **Ilha Solteira** São Paulo, S Brazil *20.28S 51.19W*
106 G7 **Ílhavo** Aveiro, N Portugal *40.36N 8.40W*
61 O18 **Ilhéus** Bahia, E Brazil *14.49S 39.06W*
133 R7 **Ili** *Kaz.* Ile, *Rus.* Reka Ili. ≈ China/Kazakhstan
Ili *see* Ili He
118 G11 **Ilia** *Hung.* Marosillye. Hunedoara, SW Romania *45.57N 22.39E*
41 P13 **Iliamna** Alaska, USA *59.42N 154.49W*
41 P13 **Iliamna Lake** ◎ Alaska, USA
143 N13 **Iliç** Erzincan, C Turkey *39.27N 38.34E*
Il'ichevsk *see* Şärur, Azerbaijan
Il'ichevsk *see* Illichivs'k, Ukraine
Ilici *see* Elche
39 V2 **Iliff** Colorado, C USA *40.46N 103.04W*
179 R15 **Iligan** *off.* Iligan City. Mindanao, S Philippines *8.12N 124.15E*
179 R15 **Iligan Bay** *bay* S Philippines
164 I5 **Ili He** *Rus.* Ili. ≈ China/Kazakhstan
58 C6 **Iliniza** ▲ N Ecuador *0.37S 78.41W*
Ilinski *see* Il'inskiy
129 U14 **Il'inskiy** *var.* Ilinski. Permskaya Oblast', NW Russian Federation *58.33N 55.31E*
127 Oo15 **Il'inskiy** Ostrov Sakhalin, Sakhalinskaya Oblast', SE Russian Federation *47.59N 142.14E*
20 I10 **Ilion** New York, NE USA *43.01N 75.02W*
40 E9 **Ilio Point** *headland* Molokai, Hawaii, USA, C Pacific Ocean *21.13N 157.15W*
111 T13 **Ilirska Bistrica** *prev.* Bistrica, *Ger.* Feistritz, Illyrisch-Feistritz, *It.* Villa del Nevoso. SW Slovenia *45.34N 14.12E*
143 Q16 **Ilisu Barajı** ⊠ SE Turkey
161 G17 **Ilkal** Karnātaka, C India *15.59N 76.08E*
99 M19 **Ilkeston** C England, UK *52.58N 1.18W*
123 Jj17 **Il-Kullana** *headland* SW Malta *35.49N 14.26E*
110 J8 **Ill** ≈ W Austria
105 U6 **Ill** ≈ NE France
64 G10 **Illapel** Coquimbo, C Chile *31.40S 71.13W*
Illaue Fartak Trench *see* Alula-Fartak Trench
190 C2 **Illbillee, Mount** ▲ South Australia *27.01S 132.13E*
104 I6 **Ille-et-Vilaine** ◈ *department* NW France
79 T11 **Illéla** Tahoua, SW Niger *14.25N 5.10E*
103 J24 **Iller** ≈ S Germany
103 J23 **Illertissen** Bayern, S Germany *48.13N 10.08E*
107 N8 **Illescas** Castilla-La Mancha, C Spain *40.07N 3.51W*
Ille-sur-la-Têt *see* Ille-sur-Têt
105 O17 **Ille-sur-Têt** *var.* Ille-sur-la-Têt. Pyrénées-Orientales, S France *42.40N 2.37E*
Illiberis *see* Elne
119 P11 **Illichivs'k** *Rus.* Il'ichevsk. Odes'ka Oblast', SW Ukraine *46.18N 30.36E*
Illicis *see* Elche
104 M6 **Illiers-Combray** Eure-et-Loir, C France *48.19N 1.14E*
32 K12 **Illinois** *off.* State of Illinois; also known as Prairie State, Sucker State. ◈ *state* C USA
32 J13 **Illinois River** ≈ Illinois, N USA
119 N6 **Illintsi** Vinnyts'ka Oblast', C Ukraine *49.07N 29.13E*
Illiturgis *see* Andújar
76 M10 **Illizi** SE Algeria *26.30N 8.28E*
29 Y7 **Illmo** Missouri, C USA *37.13N 89.30W*
Illur co *see* Lorca
Illuro *see* Mataró
Illyrisch-Feistritz *see* Ilirska Bistrica
103 K16 **Ilm** ≈ C Germany
103 K17 **Ilmenau** Thüringen, C Germany *50.40N 10.55E*
128 H14 **Il'men', Ozero** ◎ NW Russian Federation
59 H18 **Ilo** Moquegua, SW Peru *17.39S 71.22W*
179 Q13 **Iloilo** *off.* Iloilo City. Panay Island, C Philippines *10.42N 122.34E*
114 K10 **Ilok** *Hung.* Újlak. Serbia, NW Yugoslavia *45.12N 19.22E*
95 O16 **Ilomantsi** Itä-Suomi, E Finland *62.40N 30.55E*
44 F8 **Ilopango, Lago de** *volcanic lake* C El Salvador
79 T15 **Ilorin** Kwara, W Nigeria *8.32N 4.34E*
119 X8 **Ilovays'k** *Rus.* Ilovaysk. Donets'ka Oblast', SE Ukraine *47.54N 38.13E*
131 O10 **Ilovlya** Volgogradskaya Oblast', SW Russian Federation *49.45N 44.18E*
131 O10 **Ilovlya** ≈ SW Russian Federation
127 P8 **Il'pyrskiy** Koryakskiy Avtonomnyy Okrug, E Russian Federation *60.00N 164.16E*
130 K14 **Il'skiy** Krasnodarskiy Kray, SW Russian Federation *44.52N 38.26E*
190 B2 **Iltur** South Australia *27.33S 130.31E*
176 Y11 **Ilugwa** Irian Jaya, E Indonesia *3.42S 139.09E*
İluh *see* Batman
120 I11 **Ilūkste** Daugvapils, SE Latvia *55.58N 26.21E*
176 Uu12 **Ilur** Pulau Gorong, E Indonesia *4.00S 131.25E*
34 F10 **Ilwaco** Washington, NW USA *46.19N 124.03W*
152 H8 **Il'yaly** *var.* Yylanly. Dashkhovuzskiy Velayat, N Turkmenistan *41.56N 59.42E*
İlyasbaba Burnu *see* Tekke Burnu
129 U9 **Ilych** ≈ NW Russian Federation
103 O21 **Ilz** ≈ SE Germany
113 M14 **Iłża** Radom, SE Poland *51.09N 21.15E*
170 Ee14 **Imabari** *var.* Imaharu. Ehime, Shikoku, SW Japan *34.04N 132.58E*
172 N5 **Imagane** Hokkaidō, NE Japan *42.26N 140.00E*
Imaharu *see* Imabari
171 K15 **Imaichi** *var.* Imaiti. Tochigi, Honshū, S Japan *36.43N 139.40E*
Imaiti *see* Imaichi
171 Hh14 **Imajō** Fukui, Honshū, SW Japan *35.45N 136.10E*
145 R9 **Imām Ibn Hāshim** C Iraq *32.46N 43.21E*
145 T11 **Imān 'Abd Allāh** S Iraq *31.36N 44.34E*
128 J4 **Imandra, Ozero** ◎ NW Russian Federation
170 E16 **Imano-yama** ▲ Shikoku, SW Japan *32.51N 132.48E*
170 C13 **Imari** Saga, Kyūshū, SW Japan *33.16N 129.51E*
Imarssuak Mid-Ocean Seachannel *see* Imarssuak Seachannel
66 J6 **Imarssuak Seachannel** *var.* Imarssuak Mid-Ocean Seachannel. *channel* N Atlantic Ocean
95 N18 **Imatra** Etelä-Suomi, S Finland *61.13N 28.49E*
171 H14 **Imazu** Shiga, Honshū, SW Japan *35.25N 136.00E*
58 C6 **Imbabura** ◈ *province* N Ecuador
57 R9 **Imbaimadai** W Guyana *5.44N 60.23W*
63 K14 **Imbituba** Santa Catarina, S Brazil *28.15S 48.43W*
29 W9 **Imboden** Arkansas, C USA *36.12N 91.10W*
Imbros *see* Gökçeada
152 B11 **Imeni 26 Bakinskikh Komissarov** *Turkm.* 26 Baku Komissarlary Adyndaky. Balkanskiy Velayat, W Turkmenistan *39.24N 54.04E*
Imeni 26 Bakinskikh Komissarov *see* 26 Bakı Komissarı
129 N13 **Imeni Babushkina** Vologodskaya Oblast', NW Russian Federation *59.40N 43.04E*
130 J7 **Imeni Karla Libknekhta** Kurskaya Oblast', W Russian Federation *51.36N 35.28E*
152 I14 **Imeni Mollanepesa** Maryyskiy Velayat, S Turkmenistan *37.36N 61.54E*
127 N14 **Imeni Poliny Osipenko** Khabarovskiy Kray, SE Russian Federation *52.21N 136.17E*
152 J15 **Imeni S.A.Niyazova** Maryyskiy Velayat, S Turkmenistan *36.44N 62.23E*
Imeni Sverdlova Rudnik *see* Sverdlovs'k
196 E9 **Imeong** Babeldaob, N Palau
83 L14 **Īmī** Somali, E Ethiopia *6.27N 42.10E*
117 M21 **Imia** *Turk.* Kardak. *island* Dodekánisos, Greece, Aegean Sea
Imishli *see* İmişli
143 X12 **İmişli** *Rus.* Imishli. C Azerbaijan *39.54N 48.04E*
169 X14 **Imjin-gang** ≈ North Korea/South Korea
37 S3 **Imlay** Nevada, W USA *40.39N 118.10W*
33 S9 **Imlay City** Michigan, N USA *43.01N 83.04W*
25 X15 **Immokalee** Florida, SE USA *26.24N 81.25W*
79 U17 **Imo** ◈ *state* SE Nigeria
108 G10 **Imola** Emilia-Romagna, N Italy *44.22N 11.43E*
194 E9 **Imonda** Sandaun, NW PNG *3.19S 141.10E*
Imoschi *see* Imotski
115 G14 **Imotski** *It.* Imoschi. Split-Dalmacija, SE Croatia *43.28N 17.13E*
61 L14 **Imperatriz** Maranhão, NE Brazil *5.31S 47.28W*
108 B10 **Imperia** Liguria, NW Italy *43.52N 8.03E*
59 E15 **Imperial** Lima, W Peru *13.04S 76.20W*
37 X17 **Imperial** California, W USA *32.51N 115.34W*
30 L16 **Imperial** Nebraska, C USA *40.30N 101.37W*
26 M9 **Imperial** Texas, SW USA *31.15N 102.40W*
37 Y17 **Imperial Dam** *dam* California, W USA *32.52N 114.27W*
81 I17 **Impfondo** La Likouala, NE Congo *1.40N 18.02E*
159 X14 **Imphāl** Manipur, NE India *24.46N 93.55E*
105 P9 **Imphy** Nièvre, C France *46.55N 3.16E*
108 G11 **Impruneta** Toscana, C Italy *43.42N 11.16E*
117 K15 **İmroz** *var.* Gökçeada. Çanakkale, NW Turkey *40.11N 25.53E*
Imroz Adası *see* Gökçeada
110 L7 **Imst** Tirol, W Austria *47.13N 10.40E*
42 F3 **Imuris** Sonora, NW Mexico *30.48N 110.52W*
179 P11 **Imus** Luzon, N Philippines *14.27N 120.55E*
171 J15 **Ina** Nagano, Honshū, S Japan *35.55N 137.59E*
67 M18 **Inaccessible Island** *island* W Tristan da Cunha
117 F20 **Ínachos** ≈ S Greece
196 H6 **I Naftan, Puntan** *headland* Saipan, S Northern Mariana Islands
Inagua Islands *see* Great Inagua/Little Inagua
193 H15 **Inangahua** West Coast, South Island, NZ *41.51S 171.58E*
176 V10 **Inanwatan** Irian Jaya, E Indonesia *2.06S 132.07E*
59 I14 **Iñapari** Madre de Dios, E Peru *11.00S 69.34W*
196 B17 **Inarajan** SE Guam *13.16N 144.45E*
94 L10 **Inari** *Lapp.* Anár, Aanaar. Lappi, N Finland *68.54N 27.06E*
94 L10 **Inarijärvi** *Lapp.* Aanaarjävri, *Swe.* Enareträsk. ◎ N Finland
94 L9 **Inarijoki** *Lapp.* Anárjohka. ≈ Finland/Norway
Inău *see* Ineu
171 L14 **Inawashiro-ko** *var.* Inawasiro Ko. ◎ Honshū, C Japan
Inawasiro Ko *see* Inawashiro-ko
64 H7 **Inca de Oro** Atacama, N Chile *26.45S 69.54W*
117 J15 **İnce Burnu** *headland* NW Turkey *40.08N 25.39E*
142 K9 **İnce Burnu** *headland* N Turkey *42.06N 34.57E*
142 I17 **İncekum Burnu** *headland* S Turkey *36.13N 33.57E*
78 G7 **Inchiri** ◈ *region* NW Mauritania
169 X15 **Inch'ŏn** *off.* Inch'ŏn-gwangyŏksi, *Jap.* Jinsen; *prev.* Chemulpo. NW South Korea *37.27N 126.40E*
85 M17 **Inchope** Manica, C Mozambique *19.09S 33.54E*
Incoronata *see* Kornat
105 Y15 **Incudine, Monte** ▲ Corse, France, C Mediterranean Sea *41.52N 9.13E*
62 M10 **Indaiatuba** São Paulo, S Brazil *23.03S 47.14W*

◆ Country ● Country Capital ◇ Dependent Territory ○ Dependent Territory Capital ◈ Administrative Region ✕ International Airport ▲ Mountain ▲▲ Mountain Range Volcano ≈ River ◎ Lake ⊠ Reservoir

INDAL – ISSYK-KUL', OZERO

95 H17 Indal Västernorrland, C Sweden 62.36N 17.06E
95 H17 Indalsälven ≈ C Sweden
42 K8 Inde Durango, C Mexico 25.55N 105.10W
Indefatigable Island see Santa Cruz, Isla
37 S10 Independence California, W USA 36.48N 118.12W
31 X13 Independence Iowa, C USA 42.28N 91.42W
29 P7 Independence Kansas, C USA 37.13N 95.42W
22 M4 Independence Kentucky, S USA 38.56N 84.32W
29 R4 Independence Missouri, C USA 39.05N 94.25W
23 R8 Independence Virginia, NE USA 36.37N 81.09W
32 J7 Independence Wisconsin, N USA 44.21N 91.25W
207 R12 Independence Fjord fjord N Greenland
Independence Island see Malden Island
37 W2 Independence Mountains ▲▲ Nevada, W USA
59 K18 Independencia Cochabamba, C Bolivia 17.07S 66.52W
59 E16 Independencia, Bahía de la bay W Peru
Independencia, Monte see Adam, Mount
118 M12 Independenţa Galaţi, SE Romania 45.27N 27.45E
Inderagiri see Indragiri, Sungai
Inderbor see Inderborskiy
150 F11 Inderborskiy Kaz. Inderbor. Atyrau, W Kazakhstan 48.35N 51.45E
157 I14 India off. Republic of India, var. Indian Union, Union of India, Hind. Bhārat. ◆ republic S Asia
India see Indija
20 D14 Indiana Pennsylvania, NE USA 40.37N 79.09W
33 N13 Indiana off. State of Indiana; also known as The Hoosier State. ◐ state N USA
33 O14 Indianapolis state capital Indiana, N USA 39.46N 86.09W
9 O10 Indian Cabins Alberta, W Canada 59.51N 117.06W
44 G1 Indian Church Orange Walk, N Belize 17.47N 88.39W
Indian Desert see Thar Desert
9 U16 Indian Head Saskatchewan, S Canada 50.31N 103.40W
33 O4 Indian Lake ⊚ Michigan, N USA
20 K9 Indian Lake ⊚ New York, NE USA
33 R13 Indian Lake ⊠ Ohio, N USA
180-181 Indian Ocean ocean
31 V15 Indianola Iowa, C USA 41.21N 93.33W
24 K4 Indianola Mississippi, S USA 33.27N 90.39W
38 J6 Indian Peak ▲ Utah, W USA 38.18N 113.52W
25 Y13 Indian River lagoon Florida, SE USA
37 W10 Indian Springs Nevada, W USA 36.33N 115.40W
25 Y14 Indiantown Florida, SE USA 27.01N 80.29W
61 K19 Indiara Goiás, S Brazil 17.12S 50.09W
129 Q4 Indiga Nenetskiy Avtonomnyy Okrug, NW Russian Federation 67.40N 49.01E
126 Mm6 Indigirka ≈ NE Russian Federation
114 L10 Inđija Hung. India; prev. Indjija. Serbia, N Yugoslavia 45.03N 20.04E
37 V16 Indio California, W USA 33.42N 116.13W
44 M12 Indio, Río ≈ SE Nicaragua
158 I10 Indira Gandhi International ✕ (Delhi) Delhi, N India
157 Q23 Indira Point headland Andaman and Nicobar Islands, India, NE Indian Ocean 6.54N 93.54E
195 X15 Indispensable Strait strait C Solomon Islands
Indjija see Inđija
133 Q13 Indo-Australian Plate tectonic feature
181 N11 Indomed Fracture Zone tectonic feature SW Indian Ocean
175 Nn12 Indonesia off. Republic of Indonesia, Ind. Republik Indonesia; prev. Dutch East Indies, Netherlands East Indies, United States of Indonesia. ◆ republic SE Asia
Indonesian Borneo see Kalimantan
160 G10 Indore Madhya Pradesh, C India 22.42N 75.50E
174 Hh8 Indragiri, Sungai var. Batang Kuantan, Inderagiri. ≈ Sumatera, W Indonesia
Indramajoe/Indramaju see Indramayu
174 K14 Indramayu prev. Indramajoe, Indramaju. Jawa, C Indonesia 6.22S 108.19E
161 K14 Indrāvati ≈ S India
105 N9 Indre ◐ department C France
104 M8 Indre ≈ C France
104 L8 Indre-et-Loire ◐ department C France
Indreville see Châteauroux
158 G3 Indus Chin. Yindu He; prev. Yin-tu Ho. ≈ S Asia
Indus Cone see Indus Fan
181 P3 Indus Fan var. Indus Cone. undersea feature N Arabian Sea
155 P17 Indus, Mouths of the delta S Pakistan
85 I24 Indwe Eastern Cape, SE South Africa 31.28S 27.19E
142 I10 İnebolu Kastamonu, N Turkey 41.57N 33.45E
79 P8 I-n-Échaï oasis C Mali 20.04N 2.00W
116 M13 İnecik Tekirdağ, NW Turkey 40.55N 27.16E
142 E12 İnegöl Bursa, NW Turkey 40.06N 29.31E
Inessa see Biancavilla
118 F10 Ineu Hung. Borosjenő; prev. Ináu. Arad, W Romania 46.25N 21.50E
Ineul/Ineu, Vîrful see Ineu, Vârful
118 J9 Ineu, Vârful var. Ineul; prev. Vîrful Ineu. ▲ N Romania 47.31N 24.52E
23 P6 Inez Kentucky, S USA 37.53N 82.33W
76 E8 Inezgane ✕ (Agadir) W Morocco 30.35N 9.27W
43 T17 Inferior, Laguna lagoon S Mexico
42 M15 Infiernillo, Presa del ⊠ S Mexico
106 L2 Infiesto Asturias, N Spain 43.21N 5.21W
95 L20 Ingå Fin. Inkoo. Etelä-Suomi, S Finland 60.01N 24.05E
79 U10 Ingal var. I-n-Gall. Agadez, C Niger 16.52N 6.57E
I-n-Gall see Ingal
101 C18 Ingelmunster West-Vlaanderen, W Belgium 50.12N 3.15E
81 I18 Ingende Equateur, W Dem. Rep. Congo (Zaire) 0.15S 18.58E
64 L5 Ingeniero Guillermo Nueva Juárez Formosa, N Argentina 23.55S 61.49W
65 H16 Ingeniero Jacobacci Río Negro, C Argentina 41.21S 69.46W
12 F16 Ingersoll Ontario, S Canada 43.03N 80.52W
168 K6 Ingettolgoy Bulgan, N Mongolia 49.27N 103.59E
189 W5 Ingham Queensland, NE Australia 18.34S 146.12E
152 M11 Ingichka Samarqand Wiloyati, C Uzbekistan 39.46N 65.56E
99 L16 Ingleborough ▲ N England, UK 54.07N 2.22W
27 T14 Ingleside Texas, SW USA 27.52N 97.12W
192 K10 Inglewood Taranaki, North Island, NZ 39.10S 174.12E
37 S15 Inglewood California, W USA 33.57N 118.21W
126 Kk16 Ingoda ≈ S Russian Federation
103 L21 Ingolstadt Bayern, S Germany 48.46N 11.25E
35 V9 Ingomar Montana, NW USA 46.34N 107.21W
11 R14 Ingonish Beach Cape Breton Island, Nova Scotia, SE Canada 46.42N 60.22W
159 S14 Ingrāj Bāzār prev. English Bazar. West Bengal, NE India 25.00N 88.10E
27 Q11 Ingram Texas, SW USA 30.04N 99.14W
205 X7 Ingrid Christensen Coast physical region Antarctica
76 K14 I-n-Guezzam S Algeria 19.35N 5.49E
Ingulets see Inhulets'
Inguri see Enguri
Ingushetia/Ingushetiya, Respublika see Ingushskaya Respublika
131 O15 Ingushskaya Respublika var. Respublika Ingushetiya, Eng. Ingushetia. ◐ autonomous republic SW Russian Federation
85 N20 Inhambane Inhambane, SE Mozambique 23.52S 35.31E
85 M20 Inhambane off. Província de Inhambane. ◐ province S Mozambique
85 N17 Inhaminga Sofala, C Mozambique 18.22S 35.02E
85 N20 Inharrime Inhambane, SE Mozambique 24.28S 35.01E
85 M18 Inhassoro Inhambane, E Mozambique 21.31S 35.13E
119 S9 Inhulets' Rus. Ingulets. Dnipropetrovs'ka Oblast', E Ukraine 47.40N 33.15E
119 R10 Inhulets' Rus. Ingulets. ≈ S Ukraine
107 Q10 Iniesta Castilla-La Mancha, C Spain 39.27N 1.45W
I-ning see Yining
56 K11 Inírida, Río ≈ E Colombia
Inis see Ennis
Inis Ceithleann see Enniskillen
Inis Córthaidh see Enniscorthy
Inis Díomáin see Ennistimon
99 A17 Inishbofin Ir. Inis Bó Finne. island W Ireland
99 B18 Inisheer var. Inishere, Ir. Inis Oírr. island W Ireland
Inishere see Inisheer
99 B18 Inishmaan Ir. Inis Meáin. island W Ireland
99 A18 Inishmore Ir. Árainn. island W Ireland
98 E13 Inishtrahull Ir. Inis Trá Tholl. island NW Ireland
99 A17 Inishturk Ir. Inis Toirc. island W Ireland
Inkoo see Ingå
193 J16 Inland Kaikoura Range ▲▲ South Island, NZ
Inland Sea see Seto-naikai
23 P11 Inman South Carolina, SE USA 35.03N 82.05W
110 L7 Inn ≈ C Europe
207 O11 Innaanganeq var. Kap York. headland NW Greenland 75.54N 66.27W
190 K2 Innamincka South Australia 27.47S 140.45E
96 J12 Innbygda ≈ Hedmark, S Norway 61.18N 12.16E
94 G12 Inndyr Nordland, C Norway 67.01N 14.00E
44 G3 Inner Channel inlet SE Belize
98 F11 Inner Hebrides island group W Scotland, UK
180 H15 Inner Islands var. Central Group. island group NE Seychelles
Inner Mongolia/Inner Mongolian Autonomous Region see Nei Mongol Zizhiqu
98 G8 Inner Sound strait NW Scotland, UK
102 J13 Innerste ≈ C Germany
189 W5 Innisfail Queensland, NE Australia 17.29S 146.03E
9 Q15 Innisfail Alberta, SW Canada 52.01N 113.58W
Inniskilling see Enniskillen
41 O11 Innoko River ≈ Alaska, USA
170 F14 Innoshima var. Innosima. Hiroshima, SW Japan 34.18N 133.09E
Innosima see Innoshima
Innsbruch see Innsbruck
110 M7 Innsbruck var. Innsbruch. Tirol, W Austria 47.16N 11.25E
81 I19 Inongo Bandundu, W Dem. Rep. Congo (Zaire) 1.55S 18.19E
Inoucdjouac see Inukjuak
Inowrazlaw see Inowrocław
112 I10 Inowrocław Ger. Hohensalza; prev. Inowrazlaw. Kujawski-pomorskie, C Poland 52.47N 18.15E
59 K18 Inquisivi La Paz, W Bolivia 17.01S 67.03W
Inrin see Yüanlin
79 O8 I-n-Sâkâne, 'Erg desert N Mali
76 J10 I-n-Salah var. In Salah. C Algeria 27.10N 2.31E
131 O5 Insar Respublika Mordoviya, W Russian Federation 53.52N 44.26E
201 X15 Insiaf Kosrae, E Micronesia
96 L13 Insjön Dalarna, C Sweden 60.40N 15.05E
Insterburg see Chernyakhovsk
Insula see Lille
118 L13 Însurăţei Brăila, SE Romania 44.55N 27.40E
129 V6 Inta Respublika Komi, NW Russian Federation 66.00N 60.09E
79 R9 I-n-Tebezas Kidal, E Mali 17.58N 1.51E
Interamna see Teramo
Interamna Nahars see Terni
30 L11 Interior South Dakota, N USA 43.42N 101.57W
110 E9 Interlaken Bern, SW Switzerland 46.40N 7.51E
31 V2 International Falls Minnesota, N USA 48.37N 93.25W
178 Gg7 Inthanon, Doi ▲ NW Thailand 18.33N 98.29E
44 G7 Intibucá ◐ department SW Honduras
44 G8 Intipucá La Unión, SE El Salvador 13.10N 88.03W
63 B15 Intiyaco Santa Fe, C Argentina 28.43S 60.04W
118 K12 Întorsura Buzăului Ger. Bozau, Hung. Bodzafordulő. Covasna, E Romania 45.49N 26.10E
24 H9 Intracoastal Waterway inland waterway system Louisiana, S USA
27 V13 Intracoastal Waterway inland waterway system Texas, SW USA
110 G11 Intragna Ticino, S Switzerland 46.12N 8.42E
171 Kk17 Inubō-zaki headland Honshū, S Japan 35.42N 140.51E
170 D14 Inukai Ōita, Kyūshū, SW Japan 33.05N 131.37E
10 I5 Inukjuak var. Inoucdjouac; prev. Port Harrison. Quebec, NE Canada 58.28N 77.58W
65 I24 Inútil, Bahía bay S Chile
Inuuvik see Inuvik
14 G3 Inuvik var. Inuuvik. Northwest Territories, NW Canada 68.25N 133.34W
171 I15 Inuyama Aichi, Honshū, SW Japan 35.22N 136.55E
58 G13 Inuya, Río ≈ E Peru
129 U13 In'va ≈ NW Russian Federation
98 H11 Inveraray W Scotland, UK 56.13N 5.04W
193 C24 Invercargill Southland, South Island, NZ 46.25S 168.22E
191 T5 Inverell New South Wales, SE Australia 29.49S 151.07E
98 I8 Invergordon N Scotland, UK 57.42N 4.01W
9 P16 Invermere British Columbia, SW Canada 50.30N 116.00W
11 R14 Inverness Cape Breton Island, Nova Scotia, SE Canada 46.13N 61.19W
98 I8 Inverness N Scotland, UK 57.27N 4.15W
25 V11 Inverness Florida, SE USA 28.50N 82.19W
98 I9 Inverness cultural region NW Scotland, UK
98 K9 Inverurie NE Scotland, UK 57.13N 2.13W
190 F8 Investigator Group island group South Australia
181 T7 Investigator Ridge undersea feature E Indian Ocean
190 H10 Investigator Strait strait South Australia
31 R11 Inwood Iowa, C USA 43.16N 96.25W
126 H16 Inya Respublika Altay, S Russian Federation 50.27N 86.45E
127 Nn10 Inya ≈ E Russian Federation
Inyanga see Nyanga
85 M16 Inyangani ▲ NE Zimbabwe 18.22S 32.57E
85 J17 Inyathi Matabeleland North, SW Zimbabwe 19.36S 28.52E
37 T12 Inyokern California, W USA 35.37N 117.48W
37 T10 Inyo Mountains ▲▲ California, W USA
131 P6 Inza Ul'yanovskaya Oblast', W Russian Federation 53.51N 46.21E
131 W5 Inzer Respublika Bashkortostan, W Russian Federation 54.11N 57.37E
131 N7 Inzhavino Tambovskaya Oblast', W Russian Federation 52.18N 42.28E
117 C16 Ioánnina var. Janina, Yannina. Ípeiros, W Greece 39.39N 20.52E
170 B17 Iō-jima var. Iwojima. island Nansei-shotō, SW Japan
128 L4 Iokan'ga ≈ NW Russian Federation
29 Q6 Iola Kansas, C USA 37.55N 95.24W
Iolcus see Iolkós
117 G16 Iolkós anc. Iolcus. site of ancient city Thessalía, C Greece 39.24N 22.56E
Iolotan' see Yëloten
85 A16 Iona Namibe, SW Angola 16.54S 12.39E
98 F11 Iona island W Scotland, UK
118 M15 Ion Corvin Constanţa, SE Romania 44.06N 27.49E
37 P7 Ione California, W USA 38.21N 120.55W
118 I13 Ioneşti Vâlcea, SW Romania 44.51N 24.12E
33 Q9 Ionia Michigan, N USA 42.59N 85.04W
Ionia Basin see Ionian Basin
123 Mm12 Ionian Basin var. Ionia Basin. undersea feature Ionian Sea, C Mediterranean Sea
Ionian Islands see Iónioi Nísoi
123 Mm11 Ionian Sea Gk. Iónio Pélagos, It. Mar Ionio. sea C Mediterranean Sea
117 B17 Iónioi Nísoi Eng. Ionian Islands. ◐ region W Greece
117 B17 Iónioi Nísoi Eng. Ionian Islands. island group W Greece
Iónio, Mar/Iónio Pélagos see Ionian Sea
Iordan see Jordan
143 U10 Iori var. Qabırrı. ≈ Azerbaijan/Georgia
Iorrais, Ceann see Erris Head
117 J22 Íos Íos, Kykládes, Greece, Aegean Sea 36.42N 25.16E
117 J22 Íos var. Nio. island Kykládes, Greece, Aegean Sea
24 G9 Iowa Louisiana, S USA 30.12N 93.00W
31 V13 Iowa off. State of Iowa; also known as The Hawkeye State. ◐ state C USA
31 Y14 Iowa City Iowa, C USA 41.39N 91.31W
31 V13 Iowa Falls Iowa, C USA 42.31N 93.15W
27 R4 Iowa Park Texas, SW USA 33.57N 98.40W
31 Y14 Iowa River ≈ Iowa, C USA
121 M19 Ipa Rus. Ipa. ≈ SE Belarus
61 N20 Ipatinga Minas Gerais, SE Brazil 19.31S 42.30W
131 N13 Ipatovo Stavropol'skiy Kray, SW Russian Federation 45.40N 42.51E
117 C16 Ípeiros Eng. Epirus. ◐ region W Greece
Ipek see Peć
113 J21 Ipel' var. Ipoly, Ger. Eipel. ≈ Hungary/Slovakia
56 C13 Ipiales Nariño, SW Colombia 0.50N 77.42W
201 V14 Ipis atoll Chuuk Islands, C Micronesia
61 A14 Ipixuna Amazonas, W Brazil 6.57S 71.42W
174 Gg4 Ipoh Perak, Peninsular Malaysia 4.36N 101.01E
Ipoly see Ipel'
197 D15 Ipota Erromango, S Vanuatu 18.54S 169.19E
81 K14 Ippy Ouaka, C Central African Republic 6.17N 21.13E
116 L13 İpsala Edirne, NW Turkey 40.55N 26.24E
Ipsario see Ypsário
191 V3 Ipswich Queensland, E Australia 27.36S 152.49E
99 Q20 Ipswich hist. Gipeswic. E England, UK 52.05N 1.08E
31 O8 Ipswich South Dakota, N USA 45.24N 99.00W
Iput' see Iputs'
121 P18 Iputs' Rus. Iput'. ≈ Belarus/Russian Federation
16 O3 Iqaluit prev. Frobisher Bay. Baffin Island, Nunavut, NE Canada 63.43N 68.28W
165 P9 Iqe Qinghai, W China 38.03N 94.45E
165 P9 Iqe He ≈ C China
Iqlid see Eqlīd
64 G3 Iquique Tarapacá, N Chile 20.15S 70.07W
58 G8 Iquitos Loreto, N Peru 3.51S 73.13W
27 N9 Iraan Texas, SW USA 30.52N 101.52W
81 K14 Ira Banda Haute-Kotto, E Central African Republic 5.57N 22.05E
172 Pp16 Irabu-jima island Miyako-shotō, SW Japan
57 Y9 Iracoubo N French Guiana 5.28N 53.15W
171 Hh17 Irago-misaki headland Honshū, SW Japan 34.35N 137.00E
62 H13 Iraí Rio Grande do Sul, S Brazil 27.15S 53.16W
116 G12 Irákleia Kentrikí Makedonía, N Greece 41.09N 23.16E
117 J21 Iráklia island Kykládes, Greece, Aegean Sea
117 J25 Irákleio var. Herakleion, Eng. Candia; prev. Iráklion. Kríti, Greece, E Mediterranean Sea 35.19N 25.07E
117 J25 Irákleio ✕ Kríti, Greece, E Mediterranean Sea 35.20N 25.10E
117 F15 Irákleio anc. Heracleum. castle Kentrikí Makedonía, N Greece 40.02N 22.34E
Iráklion see Irákleio
149 O7 Iran off. Islamic Republic of Iran; prev. Persia. ◆ republic SW Asia
60 F13 Iranduba Amazonas, NW Brazil 3.19S 60.09W
87 P13 Iranian Plate tectonic feature
149 Q9 Iranian Plateau var. Plateau of Iran. plateau N Iran
175 N6 Iran, Pegunungan var. Iran Mountains. ▲▲ Indonesia/Malaysia
Iran, Plateau of see Iranian Plateau
149 W13 Īrānshahr Sīstān va Balūchestān, SE Iran 27.14N 60.40E
57 P5 Irapa Sucre, NE Venezuela 10.33N 62.37W
43 N13 Irapuato Guanajuato, C Mexico 20.40N 101.22W
145 R7 Iraq off. Republic of Iraq, Ar. 'Irāq. ◆ republic SW Asia
62 J12 Irati Paraná, S Brazil 25.25S 50.37W
107 R3 Irati ≈ N Spain
129 T8 Irayël' Respublika Komi, NW Russian Federation 64.28N 55.20E
45 N13 Irazú, Volcán ⨳ C Costa Rica 9.57N 83.52W
Irbenskiy Zaliv/Irbes Šaurums see Irbe Strait
120 D7 Irbe Strait Est. Kura Kurk, Latv. Irbes Šaurums, Rus. Irbenskiy Zaliv; prev. Est. Irbe Väin. strait Estonia/Latvia
Irbe Väin see Irbe Strait
144 G9 Irbid Irbid, N Jordan 32.33N 35.51E
144 G9 Irbid off. Muḥāfaẓat Irbid. ◐ governorate N Jordan
Irbil see Arbīl
125 F11 Irbit Sverdlovskaya Oblast', C Russian Federation 57.37N 63.10E
111 S6 Irdning Steiermark, SE Austria 47.29N 14.04E
81 I18 Irebu Equateur, W Dem. Rep. Congo (Zaire) 0.32S 17.44E
86 C9 Ireland Lat. Hibernia. island Ireland/UK
Ireland see Ireland, Republic of
66 A12 Ireland Island North island W Bermuda
66 A12 Ireland Island South island W Bermuda
99 D17 Ireland, Republic of off. Republic of Ireland, var. Ireland, Ir. Éire. ◆ republic NW Europe
129 V15 Iren' ≈ NW Russian Federation
193 A22 Irene, Mount ▲ South Island, NZ 45.04S 167.24E
Irgalem see Yirga 'Alem
150 L11 Irgiz Aktyubinsk, C Kazakhstan 48.37N 61.12E
Irian see New Guinea
Irian Barat see Irian Jaya
176 Y13 Irian Jaya var. Irian Barat, West Irian, West New Guinea, West Papua; prev. Dutch New Guinea, Netherlands New Guinea. ◐ province E Indonesia
Irian, Teluk see Cenderawasih, Teluk
80 K9 Iriba Biltine, NE Chad 15.10N 22.10E
179 Q11 Iriga Luzon, N Philippines 13.25N 123.24E
131 X7 Iriklinskoye Vodokhranilishche ⊠ W Russian Federation
83 H23 Iringa Iringa, C Tanzania 7.49S 35.39E
83 H23 Iringa ◐ region S Tanzania
172 O17 Iriomote-jima island Sakishima-shotō, SW Japan
44 L4 Iriona Colón, NE Honduras 15.53N 85.08W
49 U7 Iriri ≈ N Brazil
60 I13 Iriri, Rio ≈ C Brazil
Iris see Yeşilırmak
37 W9 Irish, Mount ▲ Nevada, W USA 37.39N 115.22W
99 H17 Irish Sea Ir. Muir Éireann. sea C British Isles
145 U12 Irjal ash Shaykhīyah S Iraq 30.49N 44.58E
153 U11 Irkeshtam Oshskaya Oblast', SW Kyrgyzstan 39.39N 73.49E
126 J16 Irkut ≈ S Russian Federation
126 Jj16 Irkutsk Irkutskaya Oblast', S Russian Federation 52.18N 104.15E
126 Jj13 Irkutskaya Oblast' ◐ province S Russian Federation
Irlir, Gora see Irlir Toghi
152 K8 Irlir Toghi var. Gora Irlir. ▲ N Uzbekistan 42.43N 63.24E
Irminger Basin see Reykjanes Basin
23 R12 Irmo South Carolina, SE USA 34.05N 81.10W
104 E6 Iroise sea NW France
201 X2 Iroj var. Eroj. island Ratak Chain, SE Marshall Islands
190 H7 Iron Baron South Australia 33.01S 137.13E
195 X15 Iron Bottom Sound sound C Solomon Islands
12 C10 Iron Bridge Ontario, S Canada 46.16N 83.12W
22 H10 Iron City Tennessee, S USA 35.01N 87.34W
12 I13 Irondale ≈ Ontario, SE Canada
190 H7 Iron Knob South Australia 32.46S 137.08E
32 M5 Iron Mountain Michigan, N USA 45.51N 88.03W
32 M4 Iron River Michigan, N USA 46.05N 88.38W
32 J3 Iron River Wisconsin, N USA 46.34N 91.22W
29 X6 Ironton Missouri, C USA 37.36N 90.37W
33 S15 Ironton Ohio, N USA 38.32N 82.40W
32 K4 Ironwood Michigan, N USA 46.27N 90.10W
10 H12 Iroquois Falls Ontario, S Canada 48.46N 80.40W
33 N12 Iroquois River ≈ Illinois/Indiana, N USA
171 I18 Irō-zaki headland Honshū, S Japan 34.36N 138.49E
Irpen' see Irpin'
119 O4 Irpin' Rus. Irpen'. Kyyivs'ka Oblast', N Ukraine 50.31N 30.15E
119 O4 Irpin' Rus. Irpen'. ≈ N Ukraine
147 Q16 'Irqah SW Yemen 13.42N 47.21E
177 Ff8 Irrawaddy var. Ayeyarwady. ◐ division SW Burma
177 G6 Irrawaddy var. Ayeyarwady. ≈ W Burma
177 Ff9 Irrawaddy, Mouths of the delta SW Burma
119 N4 Irsha ≈ N Ukraine
118 H7 Irshava Zakarpats'ka Oblast', W Ukraine 48.19N 23.03E
109 N18 Irsina Basilicata, S Italy 40.42N 16.18E
Irtish see Irtysh
133 R5 Irtysh var. Irtish, Kaz. Ertis. ≈ C Asia
151 S7 Irtyshsk Kaz. Ertis. Pavlodar, NE Kazakhstan 53.21N 75.27E
81 P17 Irumu Orientale, E Dem. Rep. Congo (Zaire) 1.27N 29.52E
107 Q2 Irún País Vasco, N Spain 43.19N 1.48W
Iruña see Pamplona
107 Q3 Irurtzun Navarra, N Spain 42.55N 1.49W
98 I13 Irvine W Scotland, UK 55.37N 4.40W
23 N6 Irvine Kentucky, S USA 37.42N 83.58W
27 T6 Irving Texas, SW USA 32.48N 96.57W
22 K5 Irvington Kentucky, S USA 37.52N 86.16W
Isaak see Iisaku
30 L8 Isabel South Dakota, N USA 45.21N 101.25W
195 W14 Isabel off. Isabel Province. ◐ province N Solomon Islands
179 Q17 Isabela Basilan Island, SW Philippines 6.41N 122.00E
47 S5 Isabela W Puerto Rico 18.30N 67.01W
47 N8 Isabela, Cabo headland NW Dominican Republic 19.54N 71.03W
59 A18 Isabela, Isla var. Albemarle Island. island Galapagos Islands, Ecuador, E Pacific Ocean
42 I12 Isabela, Isla island C Mexico
44 K9 Isabella, Cordillera ▲▲ NW Nicaragua
37 S12 Isabella Lake ⊠ California, W USA
33 N2 Isabelle, Point headland Michigan, N USA 47.20N 87.56W
Isabel Segunda see Vieques
118 M13 Isaccea Tulcea, E Romania 45.16N 28.28E
94 H1 Ísafjarðardjúp inlet NW Iceland
94 H1 Ísafjörður Vestfirdhir, NW Iceland 66.04N 23.09W
170 C13 Isahaya Nagasaki, Kyūshū, SW Japan 32.51N 130.04E
155 S7 Īsa Khel Punjab, E Pakistan 32.39N 71.12E
180 H7 Isalo var. Massif de L'Isalo. ▲▲ SW Madagascar
Isalo, Massif de L' see Isalo
81 K20 Isandja Kasai Occidental, C Dem. Rep. Congo (Zaire) 3.03S 21.57E
197 D16 Isangel Tanna, S Vanuatu 19.34S 169.17E
81 M18 Isangi Orientale, C Dem. Rep. Congo (Zaire) 0.46N 24.15E
103 L24 Isar ≈ Austria/Germany
103 M23 Isar-Kanal canal SE Germany
Isbarta see Isparta
Isca Damnoniorum see Exeter
109 K18 Ischia var. Isola d'Ischia; anc. Aenaria. Campania, S Italy 40.43N 13.57E
109 J18 Ischia, Isola d' island S Italy
56 B12 Iscuandé var. Santa Bárbara. Nariño, SW Colombia 2.31N 78.04W
171 Hh16 Ise Mie, Honshū, SW Japan 34.28N 136.42E
102 J12 Ise ≈ N Germany
97 I23 Isefjord fjord E Denmark
Iseghem see Izegem
199 Jj17 Iselin Seamount undersea feature S Pacific Ocean 72.30S 179.00W
Isenhof see Püssi
108 E7 Iseo Lombardia, N Italy 45.40N 10.03E
105 U12 Iseran, Col de l' pass E France 45.26N 7.00E
105 S11 Isère ◐ department E France
105 S12 Isère ≈ E France
103 F15 Iserlohn Nordrhein-Westfalen, W Germany 51.22N 7.42E
109 K16 Isernia var. Æsernia. Molise, C Italy 41.34N 14.13E
171 Jj15 Isesaki Gunma, Honshū, S Japan 36.19N 139.10E
133 Q5 Iset' ≈ C Russian Federation
171 Hh16 Ise-wan bay S Japan
79 S15 Iseyin Oyo, W Nigeria 7.56N 3.33E
Isfahan see Eşfahān
153 Q11 Isfana Oshskaya Oblast', SW Kyrgyzstan 39.51N 69.31E
153 R11 Isfara N Tajikistan 40.06N 70.34E
155 O4 Isfi Maidān Ghowr, N Afghanistan 35.09N 66.16E
94 O3 Isfjorden fjord W Svalbard
Isha Baydhabo see Baydhabo
129 V11 Isherim, Gora ▲ NW Russian Federation 61.06N 59.09E
131 Q5 Isheyevka Ul'yanovskaya Oblast', W Russian Federation 54.27N 48.18E
172 Oo17 Ishigaki Okinawa, Ishigaki-jima, SW Japan 24.19N 124.09E
172 P17 Ishigaki-jima var. Isigaki Zima. island Sakishima-shotō, SW Japan
172 O5 Ishikari Hokkaidō, NE Japan 43.12N 141.21E
172 Oo5 Ishikari-gawa var. Isikari Gawa. ≈ Hokkaidō, NE Japan
172 O4 Ishikari-wan bay Hokkaidō, NE Japan
171 L14 Ishikawa Fukushima, Honshū, C Japan 37.08N 140.26E
172 Oo14 Ishikawa var. Isikawa. Okinawa, Okinawa, SW Japan 26.25N 127.46E
171 I13 Ishikawa off. Ishikawa-ken, var. Isikawa. ◐ prefecture Honshū, SW Japan
125 Ff12 Ishim Tyumenskaya Oblast', C Russian Federation 56.12N 69.25E
133 R6 Ishim Kaz. Esil. ≈ Kazakhstan/Russian Federation
131 V6 Ishimbay Respublika Bashkortostan, W Russian Federation 53.21N 56.03E
151 O9 Ishimskoye Akmola, C Kazakhstan 51.22N 67.07E
171 M13 Ishinomaki var. Isinomaki. Miyagi, Honshū, C Japan 38.25N 141.16E
171 Kk16 Ishioka var. Isioka. Ibaraki, Honshū, S Japan 36.12N 140.18E
170 Ee15 Ishizuchi-san ▲ Shikoku, SW Japan 33.44N 133.07E
Ishkashim see Ishkoshim
Ishkashimskiy Khrebet see Ishkoshim, Qatorkŭhi
153 S15 Ishkoshim Rus. Ishkashim. S Tajikistan 36.46N 71.35E
153 S15 Ishkoshim, Qatorkŭhi Rus. Ishkashimskiy Khrebet. ▲▲ SE Tajikistan
33 N4 Ishpeming Michigan, N USA 46.29N 87.40W
153 N11 Ishtikhon Rus. Ishtykhan. Samarqand Wiloyati, C Uzbekistan 39.59N 66.28E
Ishtykhan see Ishtikhon
159 T15 Ishurdi var. Iswardi. Rajshahi, W Bangladesh 24.10N 89.04E
63 G17 Isidoro Noblia Cerro Largo, NE Uruguay 31.58S 54.09W
104 J4 Isigny-sur-Mer Calvados, N France 49.20N 1.06W
Isikari Gawa see Ishikari-gawa
Isikawa see Ishikawa
142 C11 Işıklar Dağı ▲ NW Turkey
109 C19 Isili Sardegna, Italy, C Mediterranean Sea 39.46N 9.06E
125 Ff13 Isil'kul' Omskaya Oblast', C Russian Federation 54.52N 71.07E
Isinomaki see Ishinomaki
Isioka see Ishioka
83 I18 Isiolo Eastern, C Kenya 0.21N 37.33E
81 O16 Isiro Orientale, NE Dem. Rep. Congo (Zaire) 2.51N 27.46E
94 P2 Isispynten headland NE Svalbard 79.51N 26.44E
126 Ll11 Isit Respublika Sakha (Yakutiya), NE Russian Federation 60.53N 125.32E
155 O2 Iskabad Canal canal N Afghanistan
153 Q9 Iskandar Rus. Iskander. Toshkent Wiloyati, E Uzbekistan 41.32N 69.46E
Iskander see Iskandar
Iskăr see Iskŭr
124 O2 İskele var. Trikomo, Gk. Tríkomon. E Cyprus 35.16N 33.54E
142 K17 İskenderun Eng. Alexandretta. Hatay, S Turkey 36.34N 36.10E
144 H2 İskenderun Körfezi Eng. Gulf of Alexandretta. gulf S Turkey
142 J11 İskilip Çorum, N Turkey 40.45N 34.28E
Iski-Nauket see Eski-Nookat
126 Gg14 Iskitim Novosibirskaya Oblast', C Russian Federation 54.36N 83.05E
116 J11 Iskra prev. Popovo. Kŭrdzhali, S Bulgaria 41.55N 25.12E
116 G10 Iskŭr var. Iskăr. ≈ NW Bulgaria
116 H10 Iskŭr, Yazovir prev. Yazovir Stalin. ⊠ W Bulgaria
43 S15 Isla Veracruz-Llave, SE Mexico 18.01N 95.30W
121 J15 Islach Rus. Isloch'. ≈ C Belarus
106 H14 Isla Cristina Andalucía, S Spain 37.12N 7.19W
Isla de León see San Fernando
155 U6 Islāmābād ● (Pakistan) Federal Capital Territory Islāmābād, NE Pakistan 33.40N 73.07E
155 V6 Islāmābād ✕ Federal Capital Territory Islāmābād, NE Pakistan 33.40N 73.07E
Islamabad see Anantnāg
155 R17 Islāmkot Sind, SE Pakistan 24.37N 70.04E
25 Y17 Islamorada Florida Keys, Florida, SE USA 24.55N 80.37W
159 P14 Islāmpur Bihār, N India 25.09N 85.13E
Islam Qala see Eslām Qal'eh
Island/Ísland see Iceland
20 K16 Island Beach spit New Jersey, NE USA
21 S4 Island Falls Maine, NE USA 45.59N 68.16W
190 H6 Island Lagoon ⊚ South Australia
9 Y13 Island Lake ⊚ Manitoba, C Canada
31 W5 Island Lake Reservoir ⊠ Minnesota, N USA
35 R13 Island Park Idaho, NW USA 44.27N 111.21W
21 N6 Island Pond Vermont, NE USA 44.48N 71.51W
192 K2 Islands, Bay of inlet North Island, NZ
105 R7 Is-sur-Tille Côte d'Or, C France 47.34N 5.03E
44 J3 Islas de la Bahía ◐ department N Honduras
67 L20 Islas Orcadas Rise undersea feature S Atlantic Ocean
98 F12 Islay island SW Scotland, UK
118 I15 Islaz Teleorman, S Romania 43.43N 24.52E
31 V7 Isle Minnesota, N USA 46.08N 93.28W
104 M12 Isle ≈ W France
99 I16 Isle of Man ◇ UK crown dependency NW Europe
23 X7 Isle of Wight Virginia, NE USA 36.54N 76.41W
99 M24 Isle of Wight cultural region S England, UK
203 Y3 Isles Lagoon ⊚ Kiritimati, E Kiribati
39 R11 Isleta Pueblo New Mexico, SW USA 34.54N 106.40W
Isloch' see Islach
63 E19 Ismael Cortinas Flores, S Uruguay 33.57S 57.04W
Ismailia see Ismâ'iliya
77 W7 Ismâ'iliya var. Ismailia. N Egypt 30.31N 32.13E
Ismid see İzmit
77 X10 Isna var. Esna. SE Egypt 25.16N 32.24E
95 K18 Isojoki Länsi-Suomi, W Finland 62.07N 22.00E
84 M12 Isoka Northern, NE Zambia 10.07S 32.42E
Isola d'Ischia see Ischia
Isola d'Istria see Izola
Isonzo see Soča
13 U4 Isoukustouc ≈ Quebec, SE Canada
142 F15 Isparta var. Isbarta. Isparta, SW Turkey 37.46N 30.31E
142 F15 Isparta var. Isbarta. ◐ province SW Turkey
116 M7 Isperikh prev. Kemanlar. Razgrad, N Bulgaria 43.43N 26.49E
109 L26 Ispica Sicilia, Italy, C Mediterranean Sea 36.46N 14.55E
154 J14 Ispikān Baluchistān, SW Pakistan 26.21N 62.15E
143 Q12 İspir Erzurum, NE Turkey 40.28N 41.01E
144 E12 Israel off. State of Israel, var. Medinat Israel, Heb. Yisrael, Yisra'el. ◆ republic SW Asia
Issa see Vis
57 S9 Issano C Guyana 5.49N 59.28W
78 M16 Issia SW Ivory Coast 6.33N 6.33W
Issiq Köl see Issyk-Kul', Ozero
105 P11 Issoire Puy-de-Dôme, C France 45.33N 3.15E
105 N9 Issoudun anc. Uxellodunum. Indre, C France 46.57N 1.58E
83 H22 Issuna Singida, C Tanzania 5.24S 34.48E
Issyk see Yesik
Issyk-Kul' see Balykchy
153 X7 Issyk-Kul', Ozero var. Issiq Köl, Kir. Ysyk-Köl. ⊚ E Kyrgyzstan

◆ Country ● Country Capital ◇ Dependent Territory ○ Dependent Territory Capital ◐ Administrative Region ✕ International Airport ▲ Mountain ▲▲ Mountain Range ⨳ Volcano ≈ River ⊚ Lake ⊠ Reservoir

Issyk-Kul'skaya Oblast' – Järva-Jaani

153 X7 **Issyk-Kul'skaya Oblast'** *Kir.* Ysyk-Köl Oblasty. ◈ *province* E Kyrgyzstan
155 Q7 **Īstādeh-ye Moqor, Āb-e-** *var.* Āb-i-Istāda. ◎ SE Afghanistan
142 D11 **İstanbul** *Bul.* Tsarigrad, *Eng.* Istanbul; *prev.* Constantinople, *anc.* Byzantium. İstanbul, NW Turkey *41.01N 28.57E*
116 P12 **İstanbul** ◈ *province* NW Turkey
116 P12 **İstanbul Boğazı** *var.* Bosporus Thracius, *Eng.* Bosphorus, Bosporus, *Turk.* Karadeniz Boğazı. *strait* NW Turkey
Istarska Županija *see* Istra
117 G19 **Isthmía** Pelopónnisos, S Greece *37.55N 23.02E*
117 G17 **Istiaía** Évvoia, C Greece *38.57N 23.09E*
56 D9 **Istmina** Chocó, W Colombia *5.09N 76.42W*
25 W13 **Istokpoga, Lake** ◎ Florida, SE USA
114 A9 **Istra** *off.* Istarska županija. ◈ *province* NW Croatia
114 I10 **Istra** *Eng.* Istria, *Ger.* Istrien. *cultural region* NW Croatia
105 R15 **Istres** Bouches-du-Rhône, SE France *43.30N 4.58E*
Istria/Istrien *see* Istra
179 R16 **Isulan** Mindanao, S Philippines *6.36N 124.36E*
194 I11 **Isumrud Strait** *strait* NE PNG
Iswardi *see* Ishurdi
131 V7 **Isyangulovo** Respublika Bashkortostan, W Russian Federation *52.10N 56.38E*
64 O6 **Itá** Central, S Paraguay *25.28S 57.21W*
61 O17 **Itaberaba** Bahia, E Brazil *12.34S 40.21W*
61 M20 **Itabira** *prev.* Presidente Vargas. Minas Gerais, SE Brazil *19.39S 43.13W*
61 O18 **Itabuna** Bahia, E Brazil *14.48S 39.18W*
61 J18 **Itacaiu** Mato Grosso, S Brazil *14.49S 51.21W*
60 G12 **Itacoatiara** Amazonas, N Brazil *3.06S 58.22W*
56 D9 **Itagüí** Antioquia, W Colombia *6.12N 75.40W*
62 D13 **Itá Ibaté** Corrientes, NE Argentina *27.27S 57.24W*
62 G11 **Itaipú, Represa de** ⊠ Brazil/Paraguay
60 H13 **Itaituba** Pará, NE Brazil *4.15S 55.55W*
62 K13 **Itajaí** Santa Catarina, S Brazil *26.49S 48.39W*
Italia/Italiana, Republica/Italian Republic, The *see* Italy
Italian Somaliland *see* Somalia
27 T7 **Italy** Texas, SW USA *32.10N 96.52W*
108 G12 **Italy** *off.* The Italian Republic, *It.* Italia, Republica Italiana. ◆ *republic* S Europe
61 O19 **Itamaraju** Bahia, E Brazil *16.58S 39.31W*
61 C14 **Itamarati** Amazonas, W Brazil *6.12S 68.16W*
61 M19 **Itambé, Pico de** ▲ SE Brazil *18.22S 43.21W*
171 Gg15 **Itami** ✈ (Ōsaka) Ōsaka, Honshū, SW Japan *34.47N 135.24E*
117 H15 **Ítamos** ▲ N Greece *40.06N 23.51E*
159 W11 **Itānagar** Arunāchal Pradesh, NE India *27.09N 93.35E*
Itany *see* Litani
61 N19 **Itaobim** Minas Gerais, SE Brazil *16.34S 41.27W*
61 P15 **Itaparica, Represa de** ⊠ E Brazil
60 M13 **Itapecuru-Mirim** Maranhão, E Brazil *3.24S 44.19W*
62 Q8 **Itaperuna** Rio de Janeiro, SE Brazil *21.13S 41.51W*
61 O18 **Itapetinga** Bahia, E Brazil *15.16S 40.16W*
62 L10 **Itapetininga** São Paulo, S Brazil *23.33S 48.03W*
62 K10 **Itapeva** São Paulo, S Brazil *23.58S 48.54W*
49 W6 **Itapicuru, Rio** ≈ NE Brazil
60 O13 **Itapipoca** Ceará, E Brazil *3.28S 39.34W*
62 M9 **Itapira** São Paulo, S Brazil *22.25S 46.46W*
62 K8 **Itápolis** São Paulo, S Brazil *21.36S 48.43W*
62 K10 **Itaporanga** São Paulo, S Brazil *23.43S 49.28W*
64 P7 **Itapúa** *off.* Departamento de Itapúa. ◈ *department* SE Paraguay
61 E15 **Itapuã do Oeste** Rondônia, W Brazil *9.21S 63.07W*
63 E15 **Itaqui** Rio Grande do Sul, S Brazil *29.10S 56.28W*
62 K10 **Itararé** São Paulo, S Brazil *24.07S 49.16W*
62 K10 **Itararé, Rio** ≈ S Brazil
160 H11 **Itārsi** Madhya Pradesh, C India *22.42N 77.55E*
27 T7 **Itasca** Texas, SW USA *32.09N 97.09W*
Itassi *see* Vieille Case
95 N17 **Itä-Suomi** ◈ *province* E Finland
62 D13 **Itatí** Corrientes, NE Argentina *27.16S 58.15W*
62 K10 **Itatinga** São Paulo, S Brazil *23.08S 48.36W*
117 F18 **Itéas, Kólpos** *gulf* C Greece
59 N15 **Iténez, Río** *var.* Rio Guaporé. ≈ Bolivia/Brazil *see also* Guaporé, Rio
56 H11 **Iteviate, Río** ≈ C Colombia
102 I13 **Ith** *hill range* C Germany
33 Q8 **Ithaca** Michigan, N USA *43.17N 84.36W*
20 H11 **Ithaca** New York, NE USA *42.25N 76.30W*
117 C18 **Itháki** Itháki, Iónioi Nísoi, Greece, C Mediterranean Sea *38.22N 20.43E*
117 C18 **Itháki** *island* Iónioi Nísoi, Greece, C Mediterranean Sea
It Hearrenfean *see* Heerenveen
Itihara *see* Ichihara
81 L17 **Itimbiri** ≈ N Dem. Rep. Congo (Zaire)
Itinomiya *see* Ichinomiya
Itinoseki *see* Ichinoseki
41 Q5 **Itkilik River** ≈ Alaska, USA
171 J17 **Itō** Shizuoka, Honshū, S Japan *34.59N 139.03E*
171 J13 **Itoigawa** Niigata, Honshū, C Japan *37.01N 137.52E*
13 R6 **Itomamo, Lac** ◎ Quebec, SE Canada
172 Oo15 **Itoman** Okinawa, SW Japan *26.04N 127.40E*
104 M5 **Iton** ≈ N France
59 M16 **Itonamas Río** ≈ NE Bolivia
Itoupé, Mont *see* Sommet Tabulaire
Itseqqortoormiit *see* Ittoqqortoormiit
24 K4 **Itta Bena** Mississippi, S USA *33.30N 90.19W*
109 B17 **Ittiri** Sardegna, Italy, C Mediterranean Sea *40.36N 8.34E*
207 Q14 **Ittoqqortoormiit** *var.* Itseqqortoormiit, *Dan.* Scoresbysund, *Eng.* Scoresby Sound. Tunu, C Greenland *70.33N 21.52W*
62 M10 **Itu** São Paulo, S Brazil *23.17S 47.16W*
178 Mm14 **Itu Aba Island** *island* W Spratly Islands
56 D8 **Ituango** Antioquia, NW Colombia *7.06N 75.51W*
61 A14 **Ituí, Rio** ≈ NW Brazil
81 O20 **Itula** Sud Kivu, E Dem. Rep. Congo (Zaire) *3.30S 27.49E*
61 K19 **Itumbiara** Goiás, C Brazil *18.25S 49.15W*
57 T9 **Ituni** E Guyana *5.24N 58.18W*
43 X13 **Iturbide** Campeche, SE Mexico *19.41N 89.29W*
Ituri *see* Aruwimi
127 Pp16 **Iturup, Ostrov** *island* Kuril'skiye Ostrova, SE Russian Federation
62 L7 **Ituverava** São Paulo, S Brazil *20.22S 47.48W*
61 C15 **Ituxi, Rio** ≈ W Brazil
63 E14 **Ituzaingó** Corrientes, NE Argentina *27.34S 56.43W*
103 K18 **Itz** ≈ C Germany
102 I9 **Itzehoe** Schleswig-Holstein, N Germany *53.55N 9.31E*
25 N2 **Iuka** Mississippi, S USA *34.48N 88.11W*
62 I11 **Ivaiporã** Paraná, S Brazil *24.16S 51.46W*
62 I11 **Ivaí, Rio** ≈ S Brazil
94 L10 **Ivalo** *Lapp.* Avveel, Avvil. Lappi, N Finland *68.34N 27.29E*
94 L10 **Ivalojoki** *Lapp.* Avreel. ≈ N Finland
121 H20 **Ivanava** *Pol.* Janów, Janów Poleski, *Rus.* Ivanovo. Brestskaya Voblasts', SW Belarus *52.07N 25.31E*
Ivangorod *see* Dęblin
Ivangrad *see* Berane
191 N7 **Ivanhoe** New South Wales, SE Australia *32.54S 144.20E*
31 S9 **Ivanhoe** Minnesota, N USA *44.27N 96.15W*
12 D8 **Ivanhoe** ≈ Ontario, S Canada
114 E8 **Ivanić-Grad** Sisak-Moslavina, N Croatia *45.43N 16.23E*
119 T10 **Ivanivka** Khersons'ka Oblast', S Ukraine *46.43N 34.28E*
119 P10 **Ivanivka** Odes'ka Oblast', SW Ukraine *46.57N 30.26E*
115 L14 **Ivanjica** Serbia, C Yugoslavia *43.36N 20.14E*
114 G11 **Ivanjska** *var.* Potkozarje. Republika Srpska, NW Bosnia & Herzegovina *44.54N 17.04E*
113 H21 **Ivanka** ✈ (Bratislava) Bratislavský Kraj, W Slovakia *48.10N 17.13E*
119 O3 **Ivankiv** *Rus.* Ivankov. Kyyivs'ka Oblast', N Ukraine *50.55N 29.53E*
Ivankov *see* Ivankiv
41 O15 **Ivanof Bay** Alaska, USA *55.55N 159.28W*
118 J7 **Ivano-Frankivs'k** *Ger.* Stanislau, *Pol.* Stanisławów, *Rus.* Ivano-Frankovsk; *prev.* Stanislav. Ivano-Frankivs'ka Oblast', W Ukraine *48.55N 24.45E*
Ivano-Frankivs'k *see* Ivano-Frankivs'ka Oblast'
118 I7 **Ivano-Frankivs'ka Oblast'** *var.* Ivano-Frankivs'k, *Rus.* Ivano-Frankovskaya Oblast'; *prev.* Stanislavskaya Oblast'. ◈ *province* W Ukraine
Ivano-Frankovsk *see* Ivano-Frankivs'k
Ivano-Frankovskaya Oblast' *see* Ivano-Frankivs'ka Oblast'
128 M16 **Ivanovo** Ivanovskaya Oblast', W Russian Federation *57.01N 40.58E*
Ivanovo *see* Ivanava
125 A16 **Ivanovskaya Oblast'** ◈ *province* W Russian Federation
37 X12 **Ivanpah Lake** ◎ California, W USA
114 E7 **Ivanščica** ▲▲ NE Croatia
116 M8 **Ivanski** Shumen, NE Bulgaria *43.09N 27.02E*
131 R7 **Ivanteyevka** Saratovskaya Oblast', W Russian Federation *52.13N 49.06E*
Ivantsevichi/Ivatsevichi *see* Ivatsevichy
118 I4 **Ivanychi** Volyns'ka Oblast', NW Ukraine *50.37N 24.22E*
121 H18 **Ivatsevichy** *Pol.* Iwacewicze, *Rus.* Ivantsevichi, Ivatsevichi. Brestskaya Voblasts', SW Belarus *52.43N 25.21E*
116 L12 **Ivaylovgrad** Khaskovo, S Bulgaria *41.32N 26.06E*
116 K11 **Ivaylovgrad, Yazovir** ⊠ S Bulgaria
125 F10 **Ivdel'** Sverdlovskaya Oblast', C Russian Federation *60.42N 60.07E*
Ivenets *see* Ivyanyets
118 L12 **Iveşti** Galaţi, E Romania *45.27N 28.00E*
Ivigtut *see* Ivittuut
81 F18 **Ivindo** ≈ Congo/Gabon
61 I21 **Ivinheima** Mato Grosso do Sul, SW Brazil *22.16S 53.52W*
206 M15 **Ivittuut** *var.* Ivigtut. Kitaa, S Greenland *61.28N 48.33W*
Iviza *see* Eivissa
180 I6 **Ivohibe** Fianarantsoa, SE Madagascar *22.28S 46.52E*
Ivoire, Côte d' *see* Ivory Coast
194 I14 **Ivori** ≈ S PNG
78 L15 **Ivory Coast** *off.* Republic of the Ivory Coast, *Fr.* Côte d'Ivoire, République de la Côte d'Ivoire. ◆ *republic* W Africa
70 C11 **Ivory Coast** *Fr.* Côte d'Ivoire. *coastal region* S Ivory Coast
97 L22 **Ivösjön** ◎ S Sweden
108 B7 **Ivrea** *anc.* Eporedia. Piemonte, NW Italy *45.28N 7.52E*
10 J2 **Ivujivik** Quebec, NE Canada *62.25N 77.49W*
121 J16 **Ivyanyets** *Rus.* Ivenets. Minskaya Voblasts', C Belarus *53.52N 26.45E*
Iv'ye *see* Iwye
Iwacewicze *see* Ivatsevichy
172 N11 **Iwaizumi** Iwate, Honshū, NE Japan *39.48N 141.46E*
171 Ll15 **Iwaki** Fukushima, Honshū, N Japan *37.01N 140.52E*
171 Mm9 **Iwaki-san** ▲ Honshū, C Japan *40.39N 140.20E*
170 E13 **Iwakuni** Yamaguchi, Honshū, SW Japan *34.07N 132.06E*
172 Oo5 **Iwamizawa** Hokkaidō, NE Japan *43.11N 141.43E*
172 Nn5 **Iwanai** Hokkaidō, NE Japan *42.51N 140.21E*
171 Ll13 **Iwanuma** Miyagi, Honshū, C Japan *38.07N 140.49E*
171 I17 **Iwata** Shizuoka, Honshū, S Japan *34.42N 137.49E*
172 N10 **Iwate** Iwate, Honshū, N Japan *40.02N 141.12E*
171 Mm11 **Iwate** *off.* Iwate-ken. ◈ *prefecture* Honshū, C Japan
171 Mm10 **Iwate-san** ▲ Honshū, C Japan *39.52N 140.59E*
Iwje *see* Iwye
79 S15 **Iwo** Oyo, SW Nigeria *7.21N 3.58E*
Iwojima *see* Iō-jima
121 I16 **Iwye** *Pol.* Iwje, *Rus.* Iv'ye. Hrodzyenskaya Voblasts', W Belarus *53.55N 25.46E*
44 C4 **Ixcán, Río** ≈ Guatemala/Mexico
101 G18 **Ixelles** *Dut.* Elsene. Brussels, C Belgium *50.49N 4.21E*
59 J16 **Ixiamas** La Paz, NW Bolivia *13.43S 68.10W*
43 O13 **Ixmiquilpan** *var.* Ixmiquilpán. Hidalgo, C Mexico *20.28N 99.11W*
85 K23 **Ixopo** KwaZulu/Natal, E South Africa *30.07S 30.03E*
Ixtaccíhuatal, Volcán *see* Iztaccíhuati, Volcán
42 M16 **Ixtapa** Guerrero, S Mexico *17.37N 101.29W*
43 S16 **Ixtepec** Oaxaca, SE Mexico *16.32N 95.03W*
42 K12 **Ixtlán** *var.* Ixtlán del Río. Nayarit, C Mexico *21.03N 104.23W*
Ixtlán del Río *see* Ixtlán
125 F12 **Iyevlevo** Tyumenskaya Oblast', C Russian Federation *57.36N 67.20E*
170 E14 **Iyo** Ehime, Shikoku, SW Japan *33.44N 132.42E*
170 F15 **Iyomishima** *var.* Iyomisima. Ehime, Shikoku, SW Japan *33.58N 133.31E*
Iyomisima *see* Iyomishima
170 Dd14 **Iyo-nada** *sea* S Japan
44 E4 **Izabal** *off.* Departamento de Izabal. ◈ *department* E Guatemala
44 F5 **Izabal, Lago de** *prev.* Golfo Dulce. ◎ E Guatemala
149 O9 **Īzad Khvāst** Fārs, C Iran *31.31N 52.08E*
43 X12 **Izamal** Yucatán, SE Mexico *20.58N 89.00W*
131 Q16 **Izberbash** Respublika Dagestan, SW Russian Federation *42.32N 47.51E*
101 C18 **Izegem** *prev.* Iseghem. West-Vlaanderen, W Belgium *50.55N 3.13E*
148 M9 **Īzeh** Khūzestān, SW Iran *31.48N 49.52E*
172 P14 **Izena-jima** *island* Nansei-shotō, SW Japan
116 N10 **Izgrev** Burgas, E Bulgaria *42.09N 27.49E*
131 T2 **Izhevsk** *prev.* Ustinov. Udmurtskaya Respublika, NW Russian Federation *56.48N 53.12E*
129 S7 **Izhma** Respublika Komi, NW Russian Federation *64.56N 53.52E*
129 S7 **Izhma** ≈ NW Russian Federation
147 X8 **Izkī** NE Oman *22.45N 57.35E*
Izmail *see* Izmayil
119 N13 **Izmayil** *Rus.* Izmail. Odes'ka Oblast', SW Ukraine *45.19N 28.48E*
142 E14 **İzmir** *prev.* Smyrna. İzmir, W Turkey *38.25N 27.10E*
142 C14 **İzmir** *prev.* Smyrna. ◈ *province* W Turkey
142 E11 **İzmit** *var.* Ismid; *anc.* Astacus. Kocaeli, NW Turkey *40.46N 29.55E*
106 M14 **Iznájar** Andalucía, S Spain *37.17N 4.16W*
106 M14 **Iznajar, Embalse de** ⊠ S Spain
107 N14 **Iznalloz** Andalucía, S Spain *37.23N 3.31W*
142 E11 **İznik** Bursa, NW Turkey *40.27N 29.43E*
142 E12 **İznik Gölü** ◎ NW Turkey
130 M14 **Izobil'nyy** Stavropol'skiy Kray, SW Russian Federation *45.22N 41.40E*
111 S13 **Izola** *It.* Isola d'Istria. SW Slovenia *45.31N 13.40E*
144 H9 **Izra'** *var.* Ezra, Ezraa. Dar'ā, S Syria *32.52N 36.15E*
43 P14 **Iztaccíhuati, Volcán** *var.* Volcán Ixtaccíhuatal. ⛰ S Mexico *19.07N 98.37W*
44 C7 **Iztapa** Escuintla, SE Guatemala *13.55N 90.45W*
Izúcar de Matamoros *see* Matamoros
171 J17 **Izu-hantō** *peninsula* Honshū, S Japan
170 C11 **Izuhara** Nagasaki, Tsushima, SW Japan *34.11N 129.16E*
170 C15 **Izumi** Kagoshima, Kyūshū, SW Japan *32.05N 130.22E*
171 Gg15 **Izumiōtsu** Ōsaka, Honshū, SW Japan *34.29N 135.25E*
171 Gg15 **Izumi-Sano** Ōsaka, Honshū, SW Japan *34.24N 135.19E*
170 F12 **Izumo** Shimane, Honshū, SW Japan *35.22N 132.45E*
Izu Shichito *see* Izu-shotō
172 Ss13 **Izu-shotō** *var.* Izu Shichito. *island group* S Japan
199 H4 **Izu Trench** *undersea feature* NW Pacific Ocean
126 I4 **Izvestiy TsIK, Ostrova** *island* N Russian Federation
116 G10 **Izvor** Pernik, W Bulgaria *42.27N 22.53E*
118 L5 **Izyaslav** Khmel'nyts'ka Oblast', W Ukraine *50.08N 26.53E*
119 W6 **Izyum** Kharkivs'ka Oblast', E Ukraine *49.12N 37.18E*

J

95 M18 **Jaala** Etelä-Suomi, S Finland *61.04N 26.30E*
146 J5 **Jabal ash Shifā** *desert* NW Saudi Arabia
147 U8 **Jabal az Ẓannah** *var.* Jebel Dhanna. Abū Ẓaby, W UAE *24.10N 52.36E*
144 E11 **Jabalīya** *var.* Jabāliyah. NE Gaza Strip *31.30N 34.25E*
Jabāliyah *see* Jabalīya
107 N11 **Jabalón** ≈ C Spain
160 J10 **Jabalpur** *prev.* Jubbulpore. Madhya Pradesh, C India *23.10N 79.58E*
147 N15 **Jabal Zuuqar, Jazīrat** *var.* Az Zuqur. *island* SW Yemen
Jabat *see* Jabwot
144 J3 **Jabbūl, Sabkhat al** *salt flat* NW Syria
189 P1 **Jabiru** Northern Territory, N Australia *12.44S 132.48E*
144 H4 **Jablah** *var.* Jeble, *Fr.* Djéblé. Al Lādhiqīyah, W Syria *35.00N 36.00E*
114 C11 **Jablanac** Lika-Senj, W Croatia *44.43N 14.54E*
115 H14 **Jablanica** Federacija Bosna I Hercegovina, SW Bosnia and Herzegovina *43.39N 17.43E*
115 M20 **Jablanica** *Alb.* Mali i Jabllanicës, *var.* Malet e Jabllanicës. ▲▲ Albania/FYR Macedonia *see also* Jabllanicës, Mali i
Jabllanicës, Malet e *see* Jablanica/Jabllanicës, Mali i
115 M20 **Jabllanicës, Mali i** *var.* Malet e Jabllanicës, *Mac.* Jablanica. ▲▲ Albania/FYR Macedonia *see also* Jablanica
113 E15 **Jablonec nad Nisou** *Ger.* Gablonz an der Neisse. Liberecký Kraj, N Czech Republic *50.43N 15.10E*
Jabłonków/Jablunkau *see* Jablunkov
112 J9 **Jabłonowo Pomorskie** Kujawski-pomorskie, C Poland *53.24N 19.08E*
113 J17 **Jablunkov** *Ger.* Jablunkau, *Pol.* Jabłonków. Ostravský Kraj, E Czech Republic *49.34N 18.45E*
61 Q15 **Jaboatão** Pernambuco, E Brazil *08.05S 35.00W*
62 L8 **Jaboticabal** São Paulo, S Brazil *21.15S 48.16W*
201 U7 **Jabwot** *var.* Jabat, Jebat, Jōwat. *island* Ralik Chain, S Marshall Islands
107 S4 **Jaca** Aragón, NE Spain *42.34N 0.33W*
44 B4 **Jacaltenango** Huehuetenango, W Guatemala *15.39N 91.46W*
61 G14 **Jacaré-a-Canga** Pará, NE Brazil *5.58S 57.31W*
62 N10 **Jacareí** São Paulo, S Brazil *23.18S 45.55W*
61 I18 **Jaciara** Mato Grosso, W Brazil *15.58S 54.57W*
61 E15 **Jaciparaná** Rondônia, W Brazil *9.20S 64.27W*
21 P5 **Jackman** Maine, NE USA *45.35N 70.14W*
37 X1 **Jackpot** Nevada, W USA *41.57N 114.41W*
22 M8 **Jacksboro** Tennessee, S USA *36.19N 84.10W*
27 S6 **Jacksboro** Texas, SW USA *33.13N 98.10W*
25 N7 **Jackson** Alabama, S USA *31.30N 87.53W*
37 P7 **Jackson** California, W USA *38.19N 120.46W*
25 T4 **Jackson** Georgia, SE USA *33.17N 83.58W*
23 O6 **Jackson** Kentucky, S USA *37.30N 83.22W*
24 J8 **Jackson** Louisiana, S USA *30.50N 91.13W*
33 Q10 **Jackson** Michigan, N USA *42.15N 84.24W*
31 T11 **Jackson** Minnesota, N USA *43.38N 95.00W*
24 K5 **Jackson** *state capital* Mississippi, S USA *32.19N 90.12W*
29 Y7 **Jackson** Missouri, C USA *37.22N 89.40W*
23 W8 **Jackson** North Carolina, SE USA *36.24N 77.22W*
33 T15 **Jackson** Ohio, NE USA *39.03N 82.40W*
22 G9 **Jackson** Tennessee, S USA *35.37N 88.46W*
35 S14 **Jackson** Wyoming, C USA *43.28N 110.45W*
193 C19 **Jackson Bay** *bay* South Island, NZ
194 K16 **Jackson Field** ✈ (Port Moresby) Central/National Capital District, S PNG *9.28S 147.12E*
193 C20 **Jackson Head** *headland* South Island, NZ *43.57S 168.38E*
25 S8 **Jackson, Lake** ◎ Florida, SE USA
35 S13 **Jackson Lake** ◎ Wyoming, C USA
204 J6 **Jackson, Mount** ▲ Antarctica *71.43S 63.45W*
39 U3 **Jackson Reservoir** ◎ Colorado, C USA
25 Q3 **Jacksonville** Alabama, S USA *33.48N 85.45W*
29 V11 **Jacksonville** Arkansas, C USA *34.52N 92.06W*
25 W8 **Jacksonville** Florida, SE USA *30.19N 81.39W*
32 K14 **Jacksonville** Illinois, N USA *39.43N 90.13W*
23 W11 **Jacksonville** North Carolina, SE USA *34.45N 77.25W*
27 W7 **Jacksonville** Texas, SW USA *31.57N 95.16W*
25 X9 **Jacksonville Beach** Florida, SE USA *30.17N 81.23W*
46 L9 **Jacmel** *var.* Jaquemel. S Haiti *18.13N 72.33W*
Jacob *see* Nkayi
155 Q12 **Jacobābād** Sind, SE Pakistan *28.16N 68.30E*
57 T11 **Jacobs Ladder Falls** *waterfall* S Guyana *2.57N 58.06W*
47 O11 **Jaco, Pointe** *headland* N Dominica *15.38N 61.25W*
13 Q9 **Jacques-Cartier** ≈ Quebec, SE Canada
11 P11 **Jacques-Cartier, Détroit de** *var.* Jacques-Cartier Passage. *strait* Gulf of St. Lawrence/St. Lawrence River
13 W6 **Jacques-Cartier, Mont** ▲ Quebec, SE Canada *48.58N 66.00W*
Jacques-Cartier Passage *see* Jacques-Cartier, Détroit de
195 O12 **Jacquinot Bay** *inlet* New Britain, PNG
63 H16 **Jacuí, Rio** ≈ S Brazil
62 L11 **Jacupiranga** São Paulo, S Brazil *24.42S 48.00W*
102 G10 **Jade** ≈ NW Germany
102 G10 **Jadebusen** *bay* NW Germany
Jadotville *see* Likasi
Jadransko More/Jadransko Morje *see* Adriatic Sea
107 O7 **Jadraque** Castilla-La Mancha, C Spain *40.55N 2.55W*
58 C10 **Jaén** Cajamarca, N Peru *5.43S 78.46W*
107 N13 **Jaén** Andalucía, SW Spain *37.46N 3.48W*
107 N13 **Jaén** ◈ *province* Andalucía, S Spain
161 J23 **Jaffna** Northern Province, N Sri Lanka *9.42N 80.03E*
161 K23 **Jaffna Lagoon** *lagoon* N Sri Lanka
21 N10 **Jaffrey** New Hampshire, NE USA *42.46N 72.00W*
144 H13 **Jafr, Qā' al** *var.* El Jafr. *salt pan* S Jordan
158 J9 **Jagādhri** Haryāna, N India *30.10N 77.18E*
120 H4 **Jägala** *var.* Jägala Jõgi, *Ger.* Jaggowal. ≈ NW Estonia
Jägala Jõgi *see* Jägala
Jagannath *see* Puri
161 L14 **Jagdalpur** Madhya Pradesh, C India *19.07N 82.04E*
169 U5 **Jagdaqi** Nei Mongol Zizhiqu, N China *50.25N 124.02E*
Jägerndorf *see* Krnov
Jaggowal *see* Jägala
145 O2 **Jaghjaghah, Nahr** ≈ N Syria
179 Qq14 **Jagna** Bohol, C Philippines *9.37N 124.16E*
114 N13 **Jagodina** *prev.* Svetozarevo. Serbia, C Yugoslavia *43.59N 21.15E*
114 K12 **Jagodnja** ▲▲ W Yugoslavia
103 I20 **Jagst** ≈ SW Germany
161 I14 **Jagtiāl** Andhra Pradesh, C India *18.49N 78.53E*
63 H18 **Jaguarão** Rio Grande do Sul, S Brazil *32.32S 53.20W*
63 H18 **Jaguarão, Rio** *var.* Río Yaguarón. ≈ Brazil/Uruguay
62 K11 **Jaguariaíva** Paraná, S Brazil *24.15S 49.43W*
46 D5 **Jagüey Grande** Matanzas, W Cuba *22.31N 81.09W*
159 P14 **Jahānābād** Bihār, N India *25.13N 84.58E*
Jahra *see* Al Jahrā'
149 P12 **Jahrom** *var.* Jahrum. Fārs, S Iran *28.34N 53.32E*
Jahrum *see* Jahrom
Jailolo *see* Halmahera, Pulau
175 Tt8 **Jailolo, Selat** *strait* E Indonesia
Jainat *see* Chai Nat
Jainti *see* Jayanti
158 H12 **Jaipur** *prev.* Jeypore. Rājasthān, N India *26.54N 75.46E*
159 T14 **Jaipur Hat** Rajshahi, NW Bangladesh *25.04N 89.03E*
158 D11 **Jaisalmer** Rājasthān, NW India *26.55N 70.56E*
160 O12 **Jājapur** Orissa, E India *18.54N 82.36E*
149 R4 **Jājarm** Khorāsān, NE Iran *36.58N 56.25E*
114 G12 **Jajce** Federacija Bosna I Hercegovina, W Bosnia and Herzegovina *44.20N 17.16E*
Jajı *see* 'Alī Kheyl
85 D17 **Jakalsberg** Otjozondjupa, N Namibia *19.22S 17.28E*
174 J14 **Jakarta** *prev.* Djakarta, *Dut.* Batavia. ● (Indonesia) Jawa, C Indonesia *6.07S 106.45E*
8 I8 **Jakes Corner** Yukon Territory, W Canada *60.18N 134.00W*
158 H9 **Jākhal** Haryāna, NW India *29.46N 75.51E*
Jakobeny *see* Iacobeni
95 K16 **Jakobstad** *Fin.* Pietarsaari. Länsi-Suomi, W Finland *63.40N 22.40E*
Jakobstadt *see* Jēkabpils
115 O18 **Jakupica** ▲▲ C FYR Macedonia
39 W15 **Jal** New Mexico, SW USA *32.07N 103.10W*
147 P7 **Jalājil** *var.* Ğalāğıl. Ar Riyāḑ, C Saudi Arabia *25.42N 45.22E*
Jalal-Abad *see* Dzhalal-Abad, Dzhalal-Abadskaya Oblast', W Kyrgyzstan
155 S5 **Jalālābād** *var.* Jalalabad, Jelalabad. Nangarhār, E Afghanistan *34.25N 70.28E*
Jalal-Abad Oblasty *see* Dzhalal-Abadskaya Oblast'
155 V7 **Jalālpur** Punjab, E Pakistan *32.39N 74.10E*
155 T11 **Jalālpur Pīrwāla** Punjab, E Pakistan *29.30N 71.19E*
158 H8 **Jalandhar** *prev.* Jullundur. Punjab, N India *31.19N 75.36E*
44 J7 **Jalán, Río** ≈ S Honduras
44 E6 **Jalapa** Jalapa, C Guatemala *14.39N 89.58W*
44 J7 **Jalapa** Nueva Segovia, NW Nicaragua *13.57N 86.09W*
44 A3 **Jalapa** *off.* Departamento de Jalapa. ◈ *department* SE Guatemala
44 E6 **Jalapa, Río** ≈ SE Guatemala
149 X13 **Jālaq** Sīstān va Balūchestān, SE Iran
95 K17 **Jalasjärvi** Länsi-Suomi, W Finland *62.30N 22.49E*
155 O8 **Jaldak** Zābul, SE Afghanistan *32.00N 66.45E*
62 J7 **Jales** São Paulo, S Brazil *20.15S 50.34W*
160 P11 **Jaleshwar** *var.* Jaleswar. Orissa, NE India *21.51N 87.15E*
Jaleswar *see* Jaleshwar
160 F12 **Jalgaon** Mahārāshtra, C India *21.01N 75.34E*
145 W12 **Jalībah** S Iraq *30.37N 46.31E*
145 W13 **Jalīb Shahāb** S Iraq *30.25N 46.08E*
79 X15 **Jalingo** Taraba, E Nigeria *8.54N 11.22E*
42 K13 **Jalisco** ◈ *state* SW Mexico
160 G13 **Jālna** Mahārāshtra, W India *19.52N 75.55E*
Jalomitsa *see* Ialomiţa
107 R5 **Jalón** ≈ N Spain
158 E13 **Jālor** Rājasthān, N India *25.21N 72.43E*
114 K11 **Jalovik** Serbia, W Yugoslavia *44.37N 19.48E*
42 L12 **Jalpa** Zacatecas, C Mexico *21.40N 103.00W*
159 S12 **Jalpāiguri** West Bengal, NE India *26.43N 88.24E*
43 O12 **Jalpán** *var.* Jalpan. Querétaro de Arteaga, C Mexico *21.13N 99.28W*
69 P2 **Jalta** *island* N Tunisia
77 S9 **Jālū** *var.* Jūlā. NE Libya *29.01N 21.33E*
201 U8 **Jaluit Atoll** *var.* Jālwōj. *atoll* Ralik Chain, S Marshall Islands
Jālwōj *see* Jaluit Atoll
83 L18 **Jamaame** *It.* Giamame; *prev.* Margherita. Jubbada Hoose, S Somalia *0.00N 42.43E*
79 W13 **Jamaare** ≈ NE Nigeria
46 G9 **Jamaica** ◆ *commonwealth republic* W West Indies
49 P3 **Jamaica** *island* W West Indies
46 I9 **Jamaica Channel** *channel* Haiti/Jamaica
159 T14 **Jamalpur** Dhaka, N Bangladesh *24.54N 89.57E*
159 Q14 **Jamālpur** Bihār, NE India *25.19N 86.30E*
174 I6 **Jamaluang** *var.* Jemaluang. Johor, Peninsular Malaysia *2.13N 103.48E*
61 I14 **Jamanxim, Rio** ≈ C Brazil
58 B8 **Jambeli, Canal de** *channel* S Ecuador
101 I20 **Jambes** Namur, SE Belgium *50.26N 4.51E*
174 Hh9 **Jambi** *var.* Telanaipura; *prev.* Djambi. Sumatera, W Indonesia *1.34S 103.37E*
174 H9 **Jambi** *off.* Propinsi Jambi, *var.* Djambi. ◈ *province* W Indonesia
Jamdena *see* Yamdena, Pulau
10 H8 **James Bay** *bay* Ontario/Quebec, E Canada
65 F19 **James, Isla** *island* Archipiélago de los Chonos, S Chile
189 Q8 **James Ranges** ▲▲ Northern Territory, C Australia
31 P8 **James River** ≈ North Dakota/South Dakota, N USA
23 X7 **James River** ≈ Virginia, NE USA
204 H4 **James Ross Island** *island* Antarctica
190 I8 **Jamestown** South Australia *33.13S 138.36E*
67 G25 **Jamestown** ○ (Saint Helena) NW Saint Helena *15.55S 5.43W*
37 P8 **Jamestown** California, W USA *37.57N 120.25W*
22 L7 **Jamestown** Kentucky, S USA *36.58N 85.03W*
20 D11 **Jamestown** New York, NE USA *42.04N 79.15W*
31 P5 **Jamestown** North Dakota, N USA *46.54N 98.42W*
22 L8 **Jamestown** Tennessee, S USA *36.25N 84.57W*
Jamestown *see* Holetown
13 N10 **Jamet** ≈ Quebec, SE Canada
43 Q17 **Jamiltepec** *var.* Santiago Jamiltepec. Oaxaca, SE Mexico *16.16N 97.50W*
97 F20 **Jammerbugten** *bay* Skagerrak, E North Sea
158 H6 **Jammu** *prev.* Jummoo. Jammu and Kashmir, NW India *32.43N 74.54E*
158 I5 **Jammu and Kashmir** *var.* Jammu-Kashmir, Kashmir. ◈ *state* NW India
155 V4 **Jammu and Kashmir** *disputed region* India/Pakistan
160 B10 **Jāmnagar** *prev.* Navanagar. Gujarāt, W India *22.28N 70.06E*
155 S11 **Jāmpur** Punjab, E Pakistan *29.39N 70.34E*
95 L18 **Jämsä** Länsi-Suomi, W Finland *61.51N 25.10E*
95 L18 **Jämsänkoski** Länsi-Suomi, W Finland *61.54N 25.10E*
159 Q16 **Jamshedpur** Bihār, NE India *22.46N 86.12E*
96 K9 **Jämtland** ◈ *county* C Sweden
159 Q14 **Jamūi** Bihār, NE India *24.57N 86.13E*
159 T14 **Jamuna** ≈ N Bangladesh
Jamuna *see* Brahmaputra
Jamundá *see* Nhamundá, Rio
56 D11 **Jamundí** Valle del Cauca, SW Colombia *3.16N 76.31W*
159 Q12 **Janakpur** Central, C Nepal *26.45N 85.55E*
61 N18 **Janaúba** Minas Gerais, SE Brazil *15.46S 43.16W*
60 K11 **Janaucu, Ilha** *island* NE Brazil
149 Q7 **Jandaq** Eşfahān, C Iran *34.04N 54.25E*
66 Q11 **Jandia, Punta de** *headland* Fuerteventura, Islas Canarias, Spain, NE Atlantic Ocean *28.03N 14.31W*
61 B14 **Jandiatuba, Rio** ≈ NW Brazil
107 N12 **Jándula** ≈ S Spain
31 V10 **Janesville** Minnesota, N USA *44.07N 93.43W*
32 L9 **Janesville** Wisconsin, N USA *42.42N 89.01W*
155 N13 **Jangal** Baluchistān, SW Pakistan *28.00N 65.48E*
85 N20 **Jangamo** Inhambane, SE Mozambique *24.04S 35.25E*
161 J14 **Jangaon** Andhra Pradesh, C India *18.47N 79.25E*
152 K10 **Jangeldi** *Rus.* Dzhankel'dy. Bukhoro Wiloyati, C Uzbekistan *40.50N 63.16E*
159 S14 **Jangīpur** West Bengal, NE India *24.31N 88.03E*
Janina *see* Ioánnina
Janischken *see* Joniškis
114 J11 **Janja** Republika Srpska, NE Bosnia and Herzegovina *44.40N 19.15E*
Jankovac *see* Jánoshalma
207 Q15 **Jan Mayen** ◇ *Norwegian dependency* N Atlantic Ocean
86 D5 **Jan Mayen** *island* N Atlantic Ocean
207 R15 **Jan Mayen Fracture Zone** *tectonic feature* Greenland Sea/Norwegian Sea
207 R15 **Jan Mayen Ridge** *undersea feature* Greenland Sea/ Norwegian Sea
42 H3 **Janos** Chihuahua, N Mexico *30.45N 108.21W*
113 K25 **Jánoshalma** *SCr.* Jankovac. Bács-Kiskun, S Hungary *46.18N 19.16E*
Janow/Janów *see* Jonava, Lithuania
Janów *see* Ivanava, Belarus
112 H10 **Janowiec Wielkopolski** *Ger.* Janowitz. Kujawski-pomorskie, C Poland *52.47N 17.30E*
Janowitz *see* Janowiec Wielkopolski
113 O15 **Janów Lubelski** Lubelskie, E Poland *50.43N 22.24E*
Janów Poleski *see* Ivanava
85 H25 **Jansenville** Eastern Cape, S South Africa *32.55S 24.40E*
176 W12 **Jantan** Irian Jaya, E Indonesia *3.53S 134.20E*
61 M18 **Januária** Minas Gerais, SE Brazil *15.28S 44.22W*
Janūbīyah, Al Bādiyah al *see* Ash Shāmīyah
104 I7 **Janzé** Ille-et-Vilaine, NW France *47.55N 1.28W*
160 F10 **Jaora** Madhya Pradesh, C India *23.40N 75.10E*
171 H12 **Japan** *var.* Nippon, *Jap.* Nihon. ◆ *monarchy* E Asia
133 Y9 **Japan** *island group* E Asia
199 H3 **Japan Basin** *undersea feature* N Sea of Japan
133 Y8 **Japan, Sea of** *var.* East Sea, *Rus.* Yapanskoye More. *sea* NW Pacific Ocean
199 H4 **Japan Trench** *undersea feature* NW Pacific Ocean
Japen *see* Yapen, Pulau
61 A15 **Japiim** *var.* Máncio Lima. Acre, W Brazil *8.00S 73.39W*
60 D12 **Japurá** Amazonas, N Brazil *1.43S 66.14W*
60 C12 **Japurá, Rio** *var.* Río Caquetá, Yapurá. ≈ Brazil/Colombia *see also* Caquetá, Río
45 W17 **Jaqué** Darién, SE Panama *7.30N 78.09W*
Jaquemel *see* Jacmel
Jarablos *see* Jarābulus
144 K2 **Jarābulus** *var.* Jarablos, Jerablus, *Fr.* Djérablous. Ḩalab, N Syria *36.51N 38.02E*
62 K13 **Jaraguá do Sul** Santa Catarina, S Brazil *26.28S 49.07W*
106 K9 **Jaraicejo** Extremadura, W Spain *39.40N 5.49W*
106 K9 **Jaráiz de la Vera** Extremadura, W Spain *40.04N 5.45W*
107 O7 **Jarama** ≈ C Spain
65 J20 **Jaramillo** Santa Cruz, SE Argentina *47.10S 67.07W*
Jarandilla de la Vega *see* Jarandilla de la Vera
106 K8 **Jarandilla de la Vera** *var.* Jarandilla de la Vega. Extremadura, W Spain *40.07N 5.39W*
155 V9 **Jarānwāla** Punjab, E Pakistan *31.19N 73.25E*
144 G9 **Jarash** *var.* Jerash; *anc.* Gerasa. Irbid, NW Jordan *32.16N 35.54E*
Jarbah, Jazīrat *see* Jerba, Île de
96 N13 **Järbo** Gävleborg, C Sweden *60.43N 16.40E*
Jardan *see* Jordan
46 F7 **Jardines de la Reina, Archipiélago de los** *island group* C Cuba
168 J7 **Jargalant** Arhangay, C Mongolia *47.46N 101.56E*
168 I8 **Jargalant** Bayanhongor, C Mongolia *47.14N 99.43E*
168 D7 **Jargalant** Bayan-Ölgiy, W Mongolia *46.56N 91.07E*
168 K6 **Jargalant** Bulgan, N Mongolia *49.09N 104.19E*
168 G9 **Jargalant** Govĭ-Altay, W Mongolia *45.39N 97.10E*
Jarīd, Shaṭṭ al *see* Jerid, Chott el
60 I11 **Jari, Rio** *var.* Jary. ≈ N Brazil
147 N7 **Jarīr, Wādī al** *dry watercourse* C Saudi Arabia
Jarja *see* Yur'ya
96 L13 **Järna** *var.* Dala-Jarna. Dalarna, C Sweden *60.31N 14.22E*
97 O16 **Järna** Stockholm, C Sweden *59.04N 17.34E*
104 K11 **Jarnac** Charente, W France *45.41N 0.10W*
112 H12 **Jarocin** Wielkopolskie, C Poland *51.58N 17.30E*
113 F16 **Jaroměř** *Ger.* Jermer. Hradecký Kraj, N Czech Republic *50.22N 15.55E*
Jaroslau *see* Jarosław
113 O16 **Jarosław** *Ger.* Jaroslau, *Rus.* Yaroslav. Podkarpackie, SE Poland *50.01N 22.41E*
95 F16 **Järpen** Jämtland, C Sweden *63.21N 13.30E*
153 O14 **Jarqŭrghon** *Rus.* Dzharkurgan. Surkhondaryo Wiloyati, S Uzbekistan *37.31N 67.20E*
145 P2 **Jarrāh, Wadi** *dry watercourse* NE Syria
Jars, Plain of *see* Xiangkhoang, Plateau de
168 K14 **Jartai Yanchi** ◎ N China
61 E16 **Jaru** Rondônia, W Brazil *10.24S 62.45W*
169 T10 **Jarud Qi** Nei Mongol Zizhiqu, N China *44.25N 121.12E*
120 I4 **Järva-Jaani** *Ger.* Sankt-Johannis. Järvamaa, N Estonia *59.02N 25.52E*

◆ Country
● Country Capital
◇ Dependent Territory
○ Dependent Territory Capital
◈ Administrative Region
✈ International Airport
▲ Mountain
▲▲ Mountain Range
⛰ Volcano
≈ River
◎ Lake
⊠ Reservoir

◆ COUNTRY ◇ DEPENDENT TERRITORY ◆ ADMINISTRATIVE REGION ▲ MOUNTAIN ☒ VOLCANO ☺ LAKE
● COUNTRY CAPITAL ○ DEPENDENT TERRITORY CAPITAL ✕ INTERNATIONAL AIRPORT ▲ MOUNTAIN RANGE ♒ RIVER ◙ RESERVOIR

271

José Pedro Varela – Kalimantan

63 F19 **José Pedro Varela** var. José P.Varela. Lavalleja, S Uruguay 33.30S 54.28W
189 N2 **Joseph Bonaparte Gulf** gulf N Australia
39 N11 **Joseph City** Arizona, SW USA 34.56N 110.18W
11 O9 **Joseph, Lake** ◎ Newfoundland, E Canada
12 G13 **Joseph, Lake** ◎ Ontario, S Canada
194 I11 **Josephstaal** Madang, N PNG 4.42S 144.59E
José P.Varela see José Pedro Varela
61 J14 **José Rodrigues** Pará, N Brazil 5.45S 51.19W
158 K9 **Joshīmath** Uttar Pradesh, N India 30.33N 79.34E
27 T7 **Joshua** Texas, SW USA 32.27N 97.23W
37 V15 **Joshua Tree** California, W USA 34.07N 116.18W
79 V14 **Jos Plateau** plateau C Nigeria
104 H6 **Josselin** Morbihan, NW France 47.57N 2.35W
Jos Sudarso see Yos Sudarso, Pulau
96 E11 **Jostedalsbreen** glacier S Norway
96 F12 **Jotunheimen** ▲▲ S Norway
144 G7 **Joûnié** var. Juniyah. W Lebanon 33.54N 33.36E
27 R13 **Jourdanton** Texas, SW USA 28.55N 98.33W
100 L7 **Joure** Fris. De Jouwer. Friesland, N Netherlands 52.58N 5.48E
95 M18 **Joutsa** Länsi-Suomi, W Finland 61.46N 26.09E
95 N18 **Joutseno** Etelä-Suomi, S Finland 61.06N 28.30E
94 M12 **Joutsijärvi** Lappi, NE Finland 66.40N 28.00E
110 A9 **Joux, Lac de** ◎ W Switzerland
46 D5 **Jovellanos** Matanzas, W Cuba 22.49N 81.14W
159 V13 **Jowai** Meghālaya, NE India 25.25N 92.21E
Jōwat see Jabwot
Jowhar see Jawhar
149 O12 **Jowkān** Fārs, S Iran
149 Q10 **Jowzam** Kermān, C Iran
155 N2 **Jowzjān** ◐ province N Afghanistan
Józseffalva see Žabalj
J.Storm Thurmond Reservoir see Clark Hill Lake
47 T6 **Juana Díaz** C Puerto Rico 18.03N 66.30W
42 L9 **Juan Aldama** Zacatecas, C Mexico 24.18N 103.23W
(0) E9 **Juan de Fuca Plate** tectonic feature
34 F7 **Juan de Fuca, Strait of** strait Canada/USA
Juan Fernandez Islands see Juan Fernández, Islas
200 Oo12 **Juan Fernández, Islas** Eng. Juan Fernandez Islands. island group W Chile
57 O4 **Juangriego** Nueva Esparta, NE Venezuela 11.03N 63.58W
58 D11 **Juanjuí** var. Juanjuy. San Martín, N Peru 7.12S 76.45W
Juanjuy see Juanjuí
95 N16 **Juankoski** Itä-Suomi, C Finland 63.01N 28.24E
Juan Lacaze see Juan L.Lacaze
63 E20 **Juan L.Lacaze** var. Juan Lacaze, Puerto Sauce; prev. Sauce. Colonia, SW Uruguay 34.25S 57.25W
64 L5 **Juan Solá** Salta, N Argentina 23.30S 62.42W
65 F21 **Juan Stuven, Isla** island S Chile
61 H16 **Juará** Mato Grosso, W Brazil 11.10S 57.28W
43 N7 **Juárez** var. Villa Juárez. Coahuila de Zaragoza, NE Mexico 27.39N 100.43W
42 C2 **Juárez, Sierra de** ▲▲ NW Mexico
61 O15 **Juazeiro** prev. Joazeiro. Bahia, E Brazil 9.25S 40.30W
61 P14 **Juazeiro do Norte** Ceará, E Brazil 7.10S 39.18W
83 F15 **Juba** var. Jūbā. Bahr el Gabel, S Sudan 4.49N 31.34E
83 L17 **Juba** Amh. Genalē Wenz, It. Guiba, Som. Ganaane, Webi Jubba. ~ Ethiopia/Somalia
204 H2 **Jubany** Argentinian research station Antarctica 61.57S 58.23W
Jubayl see Jbail
83 L18 **Jubbada Dhexe** off. Gobolka Jubbada Dhexe. ◐ region SW Somalia
83 K18 **Jubbada Hoose** ◐ region SW Somalia
Jubba, Webi see Juba
Jubbulpore see Jabalpur
Jubeil see Jbail
76 B9 **Juby, Cap** headland SW Morocco 27.58N 12.56W
107 R10 **Júcar** var. Jucar. ~ C Spain
42 L12 **Juchipila** Zacatecas, C Mexico 21.25N 103.06W
43 S16 **Juchitán** var. Juchitán de Zaragosa. Oaxaca, SE Mexico 16.27N 95.00W
Juchitán de Zaragosa see Juchitán
144 G11 **Judaea** cultural region Israel/West Bank
144 F11 **Judaean Hills** Heb. Haré Yehuda. hill range E Israel
144 H8 **Judaydah** Fr. Jdaïdé. Dimashq, W Syria 33.17N 36.15E
145 P11 **Judayyidat Hāmir** S Iraq 31.29N 41.25E
111 U8 **Judenburg** Steiermark, C Austria 47.09N 14.42E
35 T8 **Judith River** ~ Montana, NW USA
29 V11 **Judsonia** Arkansas, C USA 35.16N 91.38W
147 P14 **Jufrah, Wādī al** dry watercourse NW Yemen
Jugoslavija/Jugoslavija, Savezna Republika see Yugoslavia
44 K10 **Juigalpa** Chontales, S Nicaragua 12.04N 85.21W
167 T13 **Juishui** C Taiwan 23.43N 121.28E
102 E9 **Juist** island NW Germany
61 M21 **Juiz de Fora** Minas Gerais, SE Brazil 21.46S 43.22W
64 J5 **Jujuy** off. Provincia de Jujuy. ◐ province N Argentina
Jujuy see San Salvador de Jujuy
94 J11 **Jukkasjärvi** Norrbotten, N Sweden 67.52N 20.39E
Jula see Gyula, Hungary
Jūlā see Jālū, Libya
39 W2 **Julesburg** Colorado, C USA 40.59N 102.15W
Julia Beterrae see Béziers
59 I17 **Juliaca** Puno, SE Peru 15.32S 70.10W
189 U6 **Julia Creek** Queensland, C Australia 20.40S 141.49E
37 V17 **Julian** California, W USA 33.04N 116.36W
100 H7 **Julianadorp** Noord-Holland, NW Netherlands 52.53N 4.43E
111 S11 **Julian Alps** Ger. Julische Alpen, It. Alpi Giulie, Slvn. Julijske Alpe. ▲▲ Italy/Slovenia
57 V11 **Juliana Top** ▲ C Surinam 3.39N 56.36W
Julianehåb see Qaqortoq
Julijske Alpe see Julian Alps
42 J6 **Julimes** Chihuahua, N Mexico 28.29N 105.21W
Julio Briga see Bragança, Portugal
Juliobriga see Logroño, Spain
63 G15 **Júlio de Castilhos** Rio Grande do Sul, S Brazil 29.14S 53.42W
Juliomagus see Angers
Julische Alpen see Julian Alps
Jullundur see Jalandhar
153 N11 **Juma** Rus. Dzhuma. Samarqand Wiloyati, C Uzbekistan 39.43N 66.37E
167 O3 **Juma He** ~ E China
83 L18 **Jumboo** Jubbada Hoose, S Somalia 0.12S 42.34E
37 Y11 **Jumbo Peak** ▲ Nevada, W USA 36.12N 114.09W
107 R12 **Jumilla** Murcia, SE Spain 38.28N 1.19W
159 N10 **Jumla** Mid Western, NW Nepal 29.22N 82.13E
Jummoo see Jammu
Jumna see Yamuna
Jumporn see Chumphon
32 K5 **Jump River** ~ Wisconsin, N USA
160 B11 **Jūnāgadh** var. Junagarh. Gujarāt, W India 21.31N 70.31E
Junagarh see Jūnāgadh
167 Q6 **Junan** prev. Shizilu. Shandong, E China 35.11N 118.47E
64 G11 **Juncal, Cerro** ▲ C Chile 33.03S 70.02W
27 Q10 **Junction** Texas, SW USA 30.29N 99.46W
38 K6 **Junction** Utah, W USA 38.14N 112.13W
29 O4 **Junction City** Kansas, C USA 39.01N 96.49W
34 F13 **Junction City** Oregon, NW USA 44.13N 123.12W
62 M10 **Jundiaí** São Paulo, S Brazil 23.10S 46.54W
194 E13 **June** ~ W PNG
41 X12 **Juneau** state capital Alaska, USA 58.13N 134.11W
32 M8 **Juneau** Wisconsin, N USA 43.22N 88.42W
107 U6 **Juneda** Cataluña, NE Spain 41.33N 0.49E
191 Q9 **Junee** New South Wales, SE Australia 34.51S 147.33E
37 R8 **June Lake** California, W USA 37.46N 119.04W
Jungbunzlau see Mladá Boleslav
164 L4 **Junggar Pendi** Eng. Dzungarian Basin. basin NW China
101 N24 **Junglinster** Grevenmacher, C Luxembourg 49.43N 6.15E
20 F14 **Juniata River** ~ Pennsylvania, NE USA
63 B20 **Junín** Buenos Aires, E Argentina 34.36S 61.01W
59 E14 **Junín** Junín, C Peru 11.13S 76.01W
59 F14 **Junín** off. Departamento de Junín. ◐ department C Peru
65 H15 **Junín de los Andes** Neuquén, W Argentina 39.57S 71.04W
59 D14 **Junín, Lago de** ◎ C Peru
Juniyah see Joûnié
Junkseylon see Phuket
166 I11 **Junlian** Sichuan, C China 28.11N 104.31E
27 O11 **Juno** Texas, SW USA 30.09N 101.07W
94 J11 **Junosuando** Norrbotten, N Sweden 67.25N 22.28E
95 H16 **Junsele** Västernorrland, C Sweden 63.42N 16.54E
Junten see Sunch'ŏn
34 L14 **Juntura** Oregon, NW USA 43.43N 118.05W
95 N14 **Juntusranta** Oulu, E Finland 65.12N 29.30E
120 H11 **Juodupė** Rokiškis, NE Lithuania 56.07N 25.37E
121 H14 **Juozapinės Kalnas** ▲ SE Lithuania 54.29N 25.27E
101 K19 **Juprelle** Liège, E Belgium 50.43N 5.31E
82 D13 **Jur** ~ C Sudan
105 S9 **Jura** ◐ department E France
110 C7 **Jura** ◐ canton NW Switzerland
110 B8 **Jura** var. Jura Mountains. ▲▲ France/Switzerland
98 G12 **Jura** island SW Scotland, UK
Juraciszki see Yuratsishki
56 C8 **Juradó** Chocó, NW Colombia 7.07N 77.45W
Jura Mountains see Jura
98 G12 **Jura, Sound of** strait W Scotland, UK
145 V15 **Juraybīyāt, Bi'r** well S Iraq 29.13N 45.28E
120 E13 **Jurbarkas** Ger. Georgenburg, Jurburg. Jurbarkas, W Lithuania 55.04N 22.45E
101 F20 **Jurbise** Hainaut, SW Belgium 50.33N 3.54E
Jurburg see Jurbarkas
120 F9 **Jūrmala** Rīga, C Latvia 56.56N 23.42E
176 Ww13 **Jursian, Pulau** island E Indonesia
60 D13 **Juruá** Amazonas, NW Brazil 3.08S 65.59W
50 F7 **Juruá, Rio** var. Río Yuruá. ~ Brazil/Peru
61 G16 **Juruena** Mato Grosso, W Brazil 10.32S 58.38W
61 G16 **Juruena** ~ W Brazil
171 Mm8 **Jūsan-ko** ◎ Honshū, C Japan
27 O6 **Justiceburg** Texas, SW USA 32.57N 101.07W
Justinianopolis see Kirşehir
64 K11 **Justo Daract** San Luis, C Argentina 33.52S 65.12W
61 C14 **Jutaí** Amazonas, W Brazil 5.10S 68.45W
60 C13 **Jutaí, Rio** ~ NW Brazil
102 N13 **Jüterbog** Brandenburg, E Germany 51.58N 13.06E
44 E6 **Jutiapa** Jutiapa, S Guatemala 14.18N 89.52W
44 A3 **Jutiapa** off. Departamento de Jutiapa. ◐ department SE Guatemala
44 J6 **Juticalpa** Olancho, C Honduras 14.39N 86.12W
84 I13 **Jutila** North Western, NW Zambia 12.33S 26.09E
Jutland see Jylland
86 F8 **Jutland Bank** undersea feature SE North Sea
95 N16 **Juuka** Itä-Suomi, E Finland 63.12N 29.16E
95 N17 **Juva** Isä-Suomi, SE Finland 61.55N 27.54E
Juvavum see Salzburg
46 A6 **Juventud, Isla de la** var. Isla de Pinos, Eng. Isle of Youth; prev. The Isle of the Pines. island W Cuba
Ju Xian see Juxian
167 Q5 **Juxian** var. Ju Xian. Shandong, E China 35.33N 118.45E
167 P6 **Juye** Shandong, E China 35.25N 116.04E
115 O15 **Južna Morava** Ger. Südliche Morava. ~ SE Yugoslavia
97 I23 **Jyderup** Vestsjælland, E Denmark 55.40N 11.25E
97 F22 **Jylland** Eng. Jutland. peninsula W Denmark
Jyrgalan see Dzhergalan
95 M17 **Jyväskylä** Länsi-Suomi, W Finland 62.07N 25.47E

K

155 X2 **K2** Chin. Qogir Feng, Eng. Mount Godwin Austen. ▲ China/Pakistan 35.55N 76.30E
40 D9 **Kaaawa** Haw. Ka'a'awa. Oahu, Hawaii, USA, C Pacific Ocean 21.33N 157.51W
83 G16 **Kaabong** NE Uganda 3.30N 34.07E
Kaaden see Kadaň
57 V9 **Kaaimanston** Sipaliwini, N Surinam 5.06N 56.04W
152 G14 **Kaakhka** var. Kaka. Akhalskiy Velayat, S Turkmenistan 37.19N 59.36E
Kaala see Caála
197 H5 **Kaala-Gomen** Province Nord, W New Caledonia 20.40S 164.24E
94 L9 **Kaamanen** Lapp. Gámas. Lappi, N Finland 69.04N 27.16E
Kaapstad see Cape Town
Kaarasjoki see Karasjok
Kaaresuanto see Karesuando
94 J10 **Kaaresuvanto** Lapp. Gárassavon. Lappi, N Finland 68.28N 22.29E
95 K19 **Kaarina** Länsi-Suomi, W Finland 60.24N 22.25E
101 I14 **Kaatsheuvel** Noord-Brabant, S Netherlands 51.39N 5.01E
95 N16 **Kaavi** Itä-Suomi, C Finland 62.58N 28.30E
Ka'a'awa see Kaaawa
176 Y15 **Kaba** Irian Jaya, E Indonesia 7.34S 138.27E
Kaba see Habahe
175 Q13 **Kabaena, Pulau** island C Indonesia
175 Q13 **Kabaena, Selat** strait Sulawesi, C Indonesia
152 J11 **Kabakly** Turkm. Gabakly. Lebapskiy Velayat, NE Turkmenistan 39.45N 62.30E
78 J14 **Kabala** N Sierra Leone 9.40N 11.36W
83 E19 **Kabale** SW Uganda 1.15S 29.58E
57 U10 **Kabalebo Rivier** ~ W Surinam
81 N22 **Kabalo** Katanga, SE Dem. Rep. Congo (Zaire) 6.01S 26.55E
151 W13 **Kabanbay** Kaz. Qabanbay prev. Andreyevka, Kaz. Andreevka. Almaty, SE Kazakhstan 45.49N 80.34E
81 O21 **Kabambare** Maniema, E Dem. Rep. Congo (Zaire) 4.40S 27.40E
197 K15 **Kabara** prev. Kambara. island Lau Group, E Fiji
Kabardino-Balkaria see Kabardino-Balkarskaya Respublika
130 M15 **Kabardino-Balkarskaya Respublika** Eng. Kabardino-Balkaria. ◐ autonomous republic SW Russian Federation
81 O19 **Kabare** Sud Kivu, E Dem. Rep. Congo (Zaire) 2.13S 28.40E
176 Uu8 **Kabarei** Irian Jaya, E Indonesia 0.01S 130.58E
179 Q16 **Kabasalan** Mindanao, S Philippines 7.46N 122.49E
79 U15 **Kabba** Kogi, S Nigeria 7.48N 6.07E
94 I13 **Kåbdalis** Norrbotten, N Sweden 66.08N 20.03E
144 M6 **Kabd aş Şārim** hill range E Syria
12 B7 **Kabenung Lake** ◎ Ontario, S Canada
31 W3 **Kabetogama Lake** ◎ Minnesota, N USA
Kabia, Pulau see Kabin, Pulau
81 M22 **Kabinda** Kasai Oriental, SE Dem. Rep. Congo (Zaire) 6.09S 24.28E
Kabinda see Cabinda
175 P13 **Kabin, Pulau** var. Pulau Kabia. island W Indonesia
175 Rr16 **Kabir** Pulau Pantar, S Indonesia 8.15S 124.12E
155 T10 **Kabīrwāla** Punjab, E Pakistan 30.24N 71.51E
176 U8 **Kable Bet** Irian Jaya, E Indonesia 0.24S 129.54E
80 I13 **Kabo** Ouham, NW Central African Republic 7.43N 18.38E
Kābol see Kābul
85 H14 **Kabompo** North Western, W Zambia 13.36S 24.10E
85 H14 **Kabompo** ~ W Zambia
81 M22 **Kabongo** Katanga, SE Dem. Rep. Congo (Zaire) 7.19S 25.34E
123 Kk12 **Kaboudia, Rass** headland E Tunisia 35.13N 11.09E
128 J14 **Kabozha** Novgorodskaya Oblast', W Russian Federation 58.48N 35.00E
149 U4 **Kabūd Gonbad** Khorāsān, NE Iran 37.01N 59.46E
148 L5 **Kabūd Rāhang** Hamadān, W Iran 35.12N 48.43E
84 L12 **Kabuko** Northern, NE Zambia 11.31S 31.16E
155 Q5 **Kābul** var. Kabul, Per. Kābol. ● (Afghanistan) Kābul, E Afghanistan 34.34N 69.07E
155 Q5 **Kābul** Eng. Kabul, Per. Kābol. ◐ province E Afghanistan
155 Q5 **Kābul** ✈ Kābul, E Afghanistan 34.31N 69.10E
155 R5 **Kābul** var. Daryā-ye Kābul. ~ Afghanistan/Pakistan see also Kābul, Daryā-ye
155 S5 **Kābul, Daryā-ye** var. Kabul. ~ Afghanistan/Pakistan see also Kabul
81 O25 **Kabunda** Katanga, SE Dem. Rep. Congo (Zaire) 12.21S 29.14E
175 Ss4 **Kaburuang, Pulau** island Kepulauan Talaud, N Indonesia
82 G8 **Kabushiya** River Nile, NE Sudan 16.54N 33.40E
85 J14 **Kabwe** Central, C Zambia 14.28S 28.25E
194 K12 **Kabwum** Morobe, C PNG 6.07S 147.11E
115 N17 **Kačanik** Serbia, S Yugoslavia 42.13N 21.16E
176 U8 **Kacepi** Pulau Gebe, E Indonesia 0.05S 129.30E
120 F13 **Kačerginė** Kaunas, C Lithuania 54.55N 23.40E
119 S13 **Kacha** Respublika Krym, S Ukraine 44.46N 33.33E
160 A10 **Kachchh, Gulf of** var. Gulf of Cutch, Gulf of Kutch. gulf W India
160 I11 **Kachchhīdhāna** Madhya Pradesh, C India 21.33N 78.54E
155 Q11 **Kachchh, Rann of** var. Rann of Kachh, Rann of Kutch. salt marsh India/Pakistan
41 Q13 **Kachemak Bay** bay Alaska, USA
Kachh, Rann of see Kachchh, Rann of
79 V14 **Kachia** Kaduna, C Nigeria 9.52N 8.00E
178 Gg2 **Kachin State** ◐ state N Burma
151 T7 **Kachiry** Pavlodar, NE Kazakhstan 53.04N 76.05E
126 Jj15 **Kachug** Irkutskaya Oblast', S Russian Federation 53.52N 105.54E
143 Q11 **Kaçkar Dağları** ▲▲ NE Turkey
161 C21 **Kadamatt Island** island Lakshadweep, India, N Indian Ocean
113 B15 **Kadaň** Ger. Kaaden.Ústecký Kraj, NW Czech Republic 50.22N 13.14E
178 Gg12 **Kadan Kyun** prev. King Island. island Mergui Archipelago, S Burma
197 I16 **Kadavu** prev. Kandavu. island S Fiji
197 I15 **Kadavu Passage** channel S Fiji
81 G16 **Kadéï** ~ Cameroon/Central African Republic
Kadhimain see Al Kāẓimīyah
Kadijica see Kadiytsa
116 M13 **Kadıköy Barajı** ⊠ NW Turkey
190 I8 **Kadina** South Australia 33.59S 137.43E
142 H15 **Kadınhanı** Konya, C Turkey 38.15N 32.13E
78 M14 **Kadiolo** Sikasso, S Mali 10.30N 5.43W
142 L16 **Kadirli** Osmaniye, S Turkey 37.22N 36.04E
116 G11 **Kadiytsa** Mac. Kadijica. ▲ Bulgaria/FYR Macedonia 41.48N 22.58E
30 L10 **Kadoka** South Dakota, N USA 43.49N 101.30W
131 N5 **Kadom** Ryazanskaya Oblast', W Russian Federation 54.35N 42.27E
85 K16 **Kadoma** prev. Gatooma. Mashonaland West, C Zimbabwe 18.18S 29.55E
82 E12 **Kadugli** Southern Kordofan, S Sudan 11.00N 29.44E
79 V14 **Kaduna** Kaduna, C Nigeria 10.32N 7.25E
79 V14 **Kaduna** ◐ state C Nigeria
79 V15 **Kaduna** ~ N Nigeria
128 K14 **Kaduy** Vologodskaya Oblast', NW Russian Federation 59.10N 37.11E
160 E13 **Kadwa** ~ W India
127 Nn9 **Kadykchan** Magadanskaya Oblast', E Russian Federation 62.54N 146.53E
Kadzharan see K'ajaran
129 T7 **Kadzherom** Respublika Komi, NW Russian Federation 64.42N 55.51E
153 X8 **Kadzhi-Say** Kir. Kajisay. Issyk-Kul'skaya Oblast', NE Kyrgyzstan 42.07N 77.10E
78 I10 **Kaédi** Gorgol, S Mauritania 16.12N 13.31W
80 G12 **Kaélé** Extrême-Nord, N Cameroon 10.09N 14.25E
40 C9 **Kaena Point** headland Oahu, Hawaii, USA, C Pacific Ocean 21.34N 158.16W
192 J2 **Kaeo** Northland, North Island, NZ 35.03S 173.40E
169 X14 **Kaesŏng** var. Kaesŏng-si. S North Korea 37.57N 126.30E
Kaesŏng-si see Kaesŏng
Kaewieng see Kavieng
81 L24 **Kafakumba** Katanga, S Dem. Rep. Congo (Zaire) 9.39S 23.43E
Kafan see Kapan
79 V14 **Kafanchan** Kaduna, C Nigeria 9.32N 8.18E
Kaffa see Feodosiya
78 G11 **Kaffrine** C Senegal 14.07N 15.27W
Kafiau see Kofiau, Pulau
117 I19 **Kafiréas, Akrotírio** headland Évvoia, C Greece 38.10N 24.35E
117 I19 **Kafiréos, Stenó** strait Évvoia/Kykládes, Greece, Aegean Sea
Kafirnigan see Kofarnihon
Kafo see Kafu
Kafr ash Shaykh/Kafrel Sheik see Kafr el Sheikh
77 W7 **Kafr el Sheikh** var. Kafr ash Shaykh, Kafrel Sheik. N Egypt 31.08N 30.58E
83 F17 **Kafu** var. Kafo. ~ W Uganda
85 J15 **Kafue** Lusaka, SE Zambia 15.43S 28.10E
85 I14 **Kafue** ~ C Zambia
69 T13 **Kafue Flats** plain C Zambia
171 I13 **Kaga** Ishikawa, Honshū, SW Japan 36.18N 136.19E
81 J14 **Kaga Bandoro** prev. Fort-Crampel. Nana-Grébizi, C Central African Republic 6.54N 19.09E
83 E18 **Kagadi** W Uganda 0.57N 30.52E
40 H17 **Kagalaska Island** island Aleutian Islands, Alaska, USA
Kagan see Kogon
Kaganovichabad see Kolkhozobod
Kagarlyk see Kaharlyk
170 F15 **Kagawa** off. Kagawa-ken. ◐ prefecture Shikoku, SW Japan
160 J13 **Kagaznagar** Andhra Pradesh, C India 19.25N 79.30E
95 J14 **Kåge** Västerbotten, N Sweden 64.49N 21.00E
83 E19 **Kagera** var. Ziwa Magharibi, Eng. West Lake. ◐ region NW Tanzania
83 E19 **Kagera** var. Akagera. ~ Rwanda/Tanzania see also Akagera
78 L5 **Kâgheț** var. Karet. physical region N Mauritania
Kagi see Chiai
143 S12 **Kağızman** Kars, NE Turkey 40.08N 43.10E
196 I6 **Kagman Point** headland Saipan, S Northern Mariana Islands
170 Bb15 **Kagoshima** var. Kagosima. Kagoshima, Kyūshū, SW Japan 31.36N 130.33E
172 Qq14 **Kagoshima** off. Kagoshima-ken, var. Kagosima. ◐ prefecture Kyūshū, SW Japan
170 Bb16 **Kagoshima-wan** bay SW Japan
Kagosima see Kagoshima
194 H12 **Kagua** Southern Highlands, W PNG 6.25S 143.48E
Kagul see Cahul
Kagul, Ozero see Kahul, Ozero
40 B8 **Kahala Point** headland Kauai, Hawaii, USA, C Pacific Ocean 22.08N 159.17W
40 G12 **Kahaluu** Haw. Kahalu'u. Hawaii, USA, C Pacific Ocean 19.34N 155.58W
83 F21 **Kahama** Shinyanga, NW Tanzania 3.48S 32.36E
119 P5 **Kaharlyk** Rus. Kagarlyk. Kyyivs'ka Oblast', N Ukraine 49.49N 30.49E
174 Mm10 **Kahayan, Sungai** ~ Borneo, C Indonesia
81 I22 **Kahemba** Bandundu, SW Dem. Rep. Congo (Zaire) 7.20S 19.00E
193 A23 **Kaherekoau Mountains** ▲▲ South Island, NZ
149 W14 **Kahīrī** var. Kūhīrī. Sīstān va Balūchestān, SE Iran 26.55N 61.04E
103 L16 **Kahla** Thüringen, C Germany 50.49N 11.33E
103 G15 **Kahler Asten** ▲ W Germany 51.11N 8.32E
155 Q4 **Kahmard, Daryā-ye** prev. Darya-i-Surkhab. ~ NE Afghanistan
149 T13 **Kahnūj** Kermān, SE Iran 27.59N 57.40E
29 V1 **Kahoka** Missouri, C USA 40.25N 91.43W
40 E10 **Kahoolawe** island Hawaii, USA, C Pacific Ocean
142 M16 **Kahramanmaraş** var. Kahraman Maraş, Maraş, Marash. Kahramanmaraş, S Turkey 37.34N 36.54E
142 L15 **Kahramanmaraş** var. Kahraman Maraş, Maraş, Marash. ◐ province C Turkey
Kahror/Kahror Pakka see Karor Pacca
143 N15 **Kâhta** Adıyaman, S Turkey 37.48N 38.34E
40 D8 **Kahuku** Oahu, Hawaii, USA, C Pacific Ocean 21.40N 157.57W
40 D8 **Kahuku Point** headland Oahu, Hawaii, USA, C Pacific Ocean 21.42N 157.59W
118 M12 **Kahul, Ozero** var. Lacul Cahul, Rus. Ozero Kagul. ◎ Moldova/Ukraine
149 V11 **Kahūrak** Sīstān va Balūchestān, SE Iran 29.25N 59.32E
192 G13 **Kahurangi Point** headland South Island, NZ 40.41S 171.57E
155 V6 **Kahūta** Punjab, E Pakistan 33.34N 73.22E
79 S14 **Kaiama** Kwara, W Nigeria 9.37N 3.58E
194 J12 **Kaiapit** Morobe, C PNG 6.16S 146.13E
193 I18 **Kaiapoi** Canterbury, South Island, NZ 43.22S 172.40E
38 K9 **Kaibab Plateau** plain Arizona, SW USA
171 Gg14 **Kaibara** Hyōgo, Honshū, SW Japan 35.06N 135.03E
176 Vv13 **Kai Besar, Pulau** island Kepulauan Kai, E Indonesia
38 L9 **Kaibito Plateau** plain Arizona, SW USA
164 K6 **Kaidu He** var. Karaxahar. ~ NW China
57 S10 **Kaieteur Falls** waterfall C Guyana 5.04N 59.32W
167 O6 **Kaifeng** Henan, C China 34.46N 114.19E
192 J3 **Kaihu** Northland, North Island, NZ 35.47S 173.39E
176 V13 **Kai Kecil, Pulau** island Kepulauan Kai, E Indonesia
176 V14 **Kai, Kepulauan** prev. Kei Islands. island group Maluku, SE Indonesia
192 J3 **Kaikohe** Northland, North Island, NZ 35.25S 173.48E
193 J16 **Kaikoura** Canterbury, South Island, NZ 42.21S 173.40E
193 J16 **Kaikoura Peninsula** peninsula South Island, NZ
Kailas Range see Gangdisê Shan
166 K12 **Kaili** Guizhou, S China 26.34N 107.58E
40 F10 **Kailua** Maui, Hawaii, USA, C Pacific Ocean 20.53N 156.13W
40 G11 **Kailua** var. Kailua-Kona, Kona. Hawaii, USA, C Pacific Ocean 19.43N 155.58W
Kailua-Kona see Kailua
194 E13 **Kaim** ~ W PNG
176 Y13 **Kaima** Irian Jaya, E Indonesia 5.36S 138.39E
192 M7 **Kaimai Range** ▲ North Island, NZ
116 E13 **Kaïmaktsalán** ▲ Greece/FYR Macedonia 40.57N 21.48E
193 C20 **Kaimanawa Mountains** ▲▲ North Island, NZ
120 E4 **Käina** Ger. Keinis; prev. Keina. Hiiumaa, W Estonia 58.49N 22.45E
111 V7 **Kainach** ~ SE Austria
170 G16 **Kainan** Tokushima, Shikoku, SW Japan 33.36N 134.20E
170 Ff16 **Kainan** Wakayama, Honshū, SW Japan 34.10N 135.11E
194 I12 **Kainantu** Eastern Highlands, C PNG 6.16S 145.49E
153 U7 **Kaindy** Kir. Kayyngdy. Chuyskaya Oblast', N Kyrgyzstan 42.48N 73.39E
79 T14 **Kainji Dam** dam W Nigeria 9.52N 4.36E
Kainji Lake see Kainji Reservoir
79 T14 **Kainji Reservoir** var. Kainji Lake. ⊠ W Nigeria
194 J14 **Kaintiba** var. Kamina. Gulf, S PNG 7.29S 146.04E
94 K12 **Kainulaisjärvi** Norrbotten, N Sweden 67.00N 22.31E
192 K5 **Kaipara Harbour** harbor North Island, NZ
158 I10 **Kairāna** Uttar Pradesh, N India 29.24N 77.10E
194 G9 **Kairiru Island** island NW PNG
76 M6 **Kairouan** var. Al Qayrawān. E Tunisia 35.45N 10.11E
Kaisaria see Kayseri
103 F20 **Kaiserslautern** Rheinland-Pfalz, SW Germany 49.27N 7.46E
120 G13 **Kaišiadorys** Kaišiadorys, S Lithuania 54.51N 24.27E
192 I2 **Kaitaia** Northland, North Island, NZ 35.07S 173.13E
193 E24 **Kaitangata** Otago, South Island, NZ 46.15S 169.49E
158 I9 **Kaithal** Haryāna, NW India 29.46N 76.20E
174 J11 **Kait, Tanjung** headland Sumatera, W Indonesia 3.13S 106.03E
40 E9 **Kaiwi Channel** channel Hawaii, USA, C Pacific Ocean
166 K9 **Kaixian** var. Kai Xian. Sichuan, C China 31.13N 108.25E
169 V11 **Kaiyuan** var. K'ai-yüan. Liaoning, NE China 42.36N 124.03E
166 H14 **Kaiyuan** Yunnan, SW China 23.42N 103.13E
41 O9 **Kaiyuh Mountains** ▲▲ Alaska, USA
95 M15 **Kajaani** Swe. Kajana. Oulu, C Finland 64.16N 27.46E
155 N7 **Kajaki, Band-e** ◎ C Afghanistan
Kajan see Kayan, Sungai
Kajana see Kajaani
143 V13 **K'ajaran** Rus. Kadzharan. SE Armenia 39.10N 46.09E
Kajisay see Kadzhi-Say
115 O20 **Kajmakčalan** ▲ S FYR Macedonia 40.57N 21.48E
Kajnar see Kaynar
155 N6 **Kajrān** Urūzgān, C Afghanistan 33.12N 65.28E
155 N5 **Kaj Rūd** ~ C Afghanistan
Kaka see Kaakhka
10 C12 **Kakabeka Falls** Ontario, S Canada 48.24N 89.40W
85 F23 **Kakamas** Northern Cape, W South Africa 28.45S 20.33E
83 H18 **Kakamega** Western, W Kenya 0.13N 34.45E
114 H13 **Kakanj** Federacija Bosna I Hercegovina, Bosnia and Herzegovina 44.06N 18.07E
193 F22 **Kakanui Mountains** ▲ South Island, NZ
192 K11 **Kakaramea** Taranaki, North Island, NZ 39.42S 174.27E
78 J16 **Kakata** C Liberia 6.34N 10.19W
192 M11 **Kakatahi** Manawatu-Wanganui, North Island, NZ 39.40S 175.20E
115 M23 **Kakavi** Gjirokastër, S Albania 39.55N 20.19E
153 O14 **Kakaydi** Surkhondaryo Wiloyati, S Uzbekistan 37.37N 67.30E
170 Ee13 **Kake** Hiroshima, Honshū, SW Japan 34.37N 132.17E
41 X13 **Kake** Kupreanof Island, Alaska, USA 56.58N 133.57W
175 R12 **Kakea** Pulau Wowoni, C Indonesia 4.09S 123.06E
171 Ii17 **Kakegawa** Shizuoka, Honshū, S Japan 34.58N 138.21E
172 Qq13 **Kakeromajima** Kagoshima, SW Japan
149 T6 **Kākhak** var. Kākhk. Khorāsān, E Iran
120 L11 **Kakhanavichy** Rus. Kokhanovichi. Vitsyebskaya Voblasts', N Belarus 55.57N 28.06E
41 P13 **Kakhonak** Alaska, USA 59.26N 154.48W
119 S10 **Kakhovka** Khersons'ka Oblast', S Ukraine 46.48N 33.30E
119 U9 **Kakhovs'ka Vodoskhovyshche** Rus. Kakhovskoye Vodokhranilishche. ⊠ SE Ukraine
Kakhovskoye Vodokhranilishche see Kakhovs'ka Vodoskhovyshche
119 T11 **Kakhovs'kyy Kanal** canal S Ukraine
Kakia see Khakhea
161 L16 **Kākināda** prev. Cocanada. Andhra Pradesh, E India 16.55N 82.13E
Käkisalmi see Priozersk
170 G14 **Kakogawa** Hyōgo, Honshū, SW Japan 34.49N 134.52E
83 F18 **Kakoge** C Uganda 1.03N 32.30E
151 O7 **Kak, Ozero** ◎ N Kazakhstan
Ka-Krem see Malyy Yenisey
Kakshaal-Too, Khrebet see Kokshaal-Tau
41 S5 **Kaktovik** Alaska, USA 70.07N 143.37W
171 Ll13 **Kakuda** Miyagi, Honshū, C Japan 37.59N 140.47E
171 M11 **Kakunodate** Akita, Honshū, C Japan 39.36N 140.38E
Kalaallit Nunaat see Greenland
155 T7 **Kālābāgh** Punjab, E Pakistan 32.58N 71.30E
175 Rr16 **Kalabahi** Pulau Alor, S Indonesia 8.13S 124.31E
196 I5 **Kalabera** Saipan, S Northern Mariana Islands
85 G14 **Kalabo** Western, W Zambia 14.52S 22.33E
130 M9 **Kalach** Voronezhskaya Oblast', W Russian Federation 50.24N 41.00E
125 G13 **Kalachinsk** Omskaya Oblast', C Russian Federation 55.03N 74.30E
131 N10 **Kalach-na-Donu** Volgogradskaya Oblast', SW Russian Federation 48.45N 43.29E
177 F5 **Kaladan** ~ W Burma
12 K14 **Kaladar** Ontario, SE Canada 44.38N 77.06W
40 G13 **Ka Lae** var. South Cape, South Point. headland Hawaii, USA, C Pacific Ocean 18.54N 155.40W
85 G19 **Kalahari Desert** desert Southern Africa
40 B8 **Kalaheo** Haw. Kalāheo. Kauai, Hawaii, USA, C Pacific Ocean 21.55N 159.31W
Kalaikhum see Qal'aikhum
152 I16 **Kala-i-Mor** Turkm. Galaymor. Maryyskiy Velayat, S Turkmenistan 35.40N 62.28E
95 K15 **Kalajoki** Oulu, W Finland 64.15N 24.00E
Kalak see Eski Kaļak
Kal al Sraghna see El Kelâa Srarhna
34 G10 **Kalama** Washington, NW USA 46.00N 122.50W
Kalámai see Kalámata
117 G14 **Kalamariá** Kentrikí Makedonía, N Greece 40.36N 22.58E
117 E21 **Kalámata** prev. Kalámai. Pelopónnisos, S Greece 37.01N 22.07E
33 P10 **Kalamazoo** Michigan, N USA 42.17N 85.35W
33 P9 **Kalamazoo River** ~ Michigan, N USA
Kalambaka see Kalampáka
119 S13 **Kalamits'ka Zatoka** Rus. Kalamitskiy Zaliv. gulf S Ukraine
Kalamitskiy Zaliv see Kalamits'ka Zatoka
117 H18 **Kálamos** Attikí, C Greece 38.16N 23.51E
117 C18 **Kálamos** island Iónioi Nísoi, Greece, C Mediterranean Sea
117 D15 **Kalampáka** var. Kalambaka. Thessalía, C Greece 39.43N 21.36E
Kalan see Călan, Romania
Kalan see Tunceli, Turkey
119 S11 **Kalanchak** Khersons'ka Oblast', S Ukraine 46.14N 33.19E
175 Pp15 **Kalao, Pulau** island Kepulauan Bonerate, W Indonesia
175 Q15 **Kalaotoa, Pulau** island W Indonesia
161 J24 **Kala Oya** ~ NW Sri Lanka
Kalarash see Călărași
95 H17 **Kälarne** Jämtland, C Sweden 63.00N 16.10E
149 V15 **Kalar Rūd** ~ SE Iran
178 Ii9 **Kalasin** var. Muang Kalasin. Kalasin, E Thailand 16.28N 103.31E
155 O8 **Kalāt** Per. Qalāt. Zābul, S Afghanistan 32.10N 66.54E
155 O11 **Kālat** var. Kelat, Khelat. Baluchistān, SW Pakistan 29.02N 66.34E
117 J14 **Kalathriá, Akrotírio** headland Samothráki, NE Greece 40.24N 25.34E
200 R17 **Kalau** island Tongatapu Group, SE Tonga
40 E9 **Kalaupapa** Molokai, Hawaii, USA, C Pacific Ocean 21.11N 156.59W
131 N13 **Kalaus** ~ SW Russian Federation
Kalávrita see Kalávryta
117 E19 **Kalávryta** var. Kalávrita. Dytikí Ellás, S Greece 38.01N 22.06E
147 Y10 **Kalbān** W Oman 20.19N 58.40E
188 H11 **Kalbarri** Western Australia 27.43S 114.08E
151 X10 **Kalbinskiy Khrebet** Kaz. Qalba Zhotasy. ▲▲ E Kazakhstan
150 G10 **Kaldygayty** ~ W Kazakhstan
142 I12 **Kalecik** Ankara, N Turkey 40.08N 33.27E
175 R13 **Kaledupa, Pulau** island Kepulauan Tukangbesi, C Indonesia
81 O19 **Kalehe** Sud Kivu, E Dem. Rep. Congo (Zaire) 2.04S 28.52E
81 P22 **Kalemie** prev. Albertville. Katanga, SE Dem. Rep. Congo (Zaire) 5.55S 29.09E
177 Ff3 **Kalemyo** Sagaing, W Burma 23.11N 94.03E
84 H12 **Kalene Hill** North Western, NW Zambia 11.10S 24.12E
Kale Sultanie see Çanakkale
128 I7 **Kalevala** Respublika Kareliya, NW Russian Federation 65.12N 31.16E
177 Ff3 **Kalewa** Sagaing, C Burma 23.15N 94.19E
Kalgan see Zhangjiakou
41 Q12 **Kalgin Island** island Alaska, USA
188 L12 **Kalgoorlie** Western Australia 30.51S 121.27E
Kali see Sārda
117 E17 **Kaliakoúda** ▲ C Greece 38.47N 21.42E
116 O8 **Kaliakra, Nos** headland NE Bulgaria 43.22N 28.28E
117 F19 **Kaliánoi** Pelopónnisos, S Greece 37.55N 22.28E
179 Q13 **Kalibo** Panay Island, C Philippines 11.40N 122.21E
117 N24 **Kalí Límni** ▲ Kárpathos, SE Greece 35.34N 27.08E
81 N20 **Kalima** Maniema, E Dem. Rep. Congo (Zaire) 2.33S 26.27E
174 M8 **Kalimantan** Eng. Indonesian Borneo. geopolitical region Borneo, C Indonesia

◆ Country ● Country Capital ◇ Dependent Territory ○ Dependent Territory Capital ◐ Administrative Region ✈ International Airport ▲ Mountain ▲▲ Mountain Range Volcano ~ River ◎ Lake ⊠ Reservoir

KALIMANTAN BARAT – KARABULAK

174 L8 **Kalimantan Barat** *off.* Propinsi Kalimantan Barat, *Eng.* West Borneo, West Kalimantan. ◐ *province* N Indonesia
174 Mm11 **Kalimantan Selatan** *off.* Propinsi Kalimantan Selatan, *Eng.* South Borneo, South Kalimantan. ◐ *province* N Indonesia
174 M9 **Kalimantan Tengah** *off.* Propinsi Kalimantan Tengah, *Eng.* Central Borneo, Central Kalimantan. ◐ *province* N Indonesia
175 N7 **Kalimantan Timur** *off.* Propinsi Kalimantan Timur, *Eng.* East Borneo, East Kalimantan. ◐ *province* N Indonesia
Kálimnos *see* Kálymnos
159 S12 **Kālimpang** West Bengal, NE India 27.05N 88.25E
Kalinin *see* Tver', Russian Federation
Kalinin *see* Boldumsaz, Turkmenistan
Kalininabad *see* Kalininobod
130 B3 **Kaliningrad** Kaliningradskaya Oblast', W Russian Federation 54.48N 21.33E
Kaliningrad *see* Kaliningradskaya Oblast'
130 A3 **Kaliningradskaya Oblast'** *var.* Kaliningrad. ◐ *province and enclave* W Russian Federation
Kalinino *see* Tashir
153 P14 **Kalininobod** *Rus.* Kalininabad. SW Tajikistan 37.49N 68.55E
131 O8 **Kalininsk** Saratovskaya Oblast', W Russian Federation 51.31N 44.25E
Kalininsk *see* Boldumsaz
Kalinisk *see* Cupcina
121 M19 **Kalinkavichy** *Rus.* Kalinkovichi. Homyel'skaya Voblasts', SE Belarus 52.07N 29.19E
Kalinkovichi *see* Kalinkavichy
83 G18 **Kaliro** SE Uganda 0.54N 33.30E
Kalisch/Kalish *see* Kalisz
35 O7 **Kalispell** Montana, NW USA 48.12N 114.18W
112 I13 **Kalisz** *Ger.* Kalisch, *Rus.* Kalish; *anc.* Calisia. Wielkopolskie, C Poland 51.46N 18.04E
112 F9 **Kalisz Pomorski** *Ger.* Kallies. Zachodniopomorskie, NW Poland 53.55N 15.55E
130 M10 **Kalitva** ∾ SW Russian Federation
83 F21 **Kaliua** Tabora, C Tanzania 5.03S 31.48E
94 K13 **Kalix** Norrbotten, N Sweden 65.51N 23.13E
94 K12 **Kalixälven** ∾ N Sweden
94 J11 **Kalixfors** Norrbotten, N Sweden 67.45N 20.20E
151 T8 **Kalkaman** Pavlodar, NE Kazakhstan 51.57N 75.58E
Kalkandelen *see* Tetovo
189 O4 **Kalkarindji** Northern Territory, N Australia 17.31S 130.40E
33 P6 **Kalkaska** Michigan, N USA 44.43N 85.12W
95 F16 **Kall** Jämtland, C Sweden 63.30N 13.15E
201 X2 **Kallalen** *var.* Calalen. *island* Ratak Chain, SE Marshall Islands
120 J5 **Kallaste** *Ger.* Krasnogor. Tartumaa, SE Estonia 58.37N 27.12E
95 N16 **Kallavesi** ◎ SE Finland
117 F17 **Kallídromo** ▲▲ C Greece
Kallies *see* Kalisz Pomorski
97 M22 **Kallinge** Blekinge, S Sweden 56.13N 15.16E
117 L16 **Kalloní** Lésvos, E Greece 39.14N 26.15E
95 F16 **Kallsjön** ◎ C Sweden
97 N21 **Kalmar** *var.* Calmar. Kalmar, S Sweden 56.40N 16.22E
97 M19 **Kalmar** *var.* Calmar. ◐ *county* S Sweden
97 N20 **Kalmarsund** *strait* S Sweden
154 L16 **Kalmat, Khor** *Eng.* Kalmat Lagoon. *lagoon* SW Pakistan
Kalmat Lagoon *see* Kalmat, Khor
119 X9 **Kal'mius** ∾ E Ukraine
101 H15 **Kalmthout** Antwerpen, N Belgium 51.24N 4.27E
Kalmykia/Kalmykiya-Khal'mg Tangch, Respublika *see* Kalmykiya, Respublika
131 O12 **Kalmykiya, Respublika** *var.* Respublika Kalmykiya-Khal'mg Tangch, *Eng.* Kalmykia; *prev.* Kalmytskaya ASSR. ◐ *autonomous republic* SW Russian Federation
Kalmytskaya ASSR *see* Kalmykiya, Respublika
120 F9 **Kalnciems** Jelgava, C Latvia 56.46N 23.37E
116 L10 **Kalnitsa** ∾ SE Bulgaria
113 J24 **Kalocsa** Bács-Kiskun, S Hungary 46.31N 19.00E
116 J9 **Kalofer** Plovdiv, C Bulgaria 42.36N 25.00E
40 E10 **Kalohi Channel** *channel* C Pacific Ocean
85 I16 **Kalomo** Southern, S Zambia 17.04S 26.27E
31 X14 **Kalona** Iowa, C USA 41.28N 91.42W
117 K22 **Kalotási, Akrotírio** *headland* Amorgós, Kykládes, Greece, Aegean Sea 36.47N 25.45E
158 J8 **Kalpa** Himāchal Pradesh, N India 31.33N 78.16E
117 C15 **Kalpáki** Ípeiros, W Greece 39.53N 20.38E
161 C22 **Kalpeni Island** *island* Lakshadweep, India, N Indian Ocean
158 K13 **Kālpi** Uttar Pradesh, N India 26.07N 79.43E
164 G7 **Kalpin** Xinjiang Uygur Zizhiqu, NW China 40.35N 78.52E
152 K8 **Kalquduq** *Rus.* Kulkuduk. Nawoiy Wiloyati, N Uzbekistan 42.36N 63.24E
155 P16 **Kalri Lake** ◎ SE Pakistan
149 R5 **Kāl Shūr** ∾ N Iran
41 N11 **Kalskag** Alaska, USA 61.32N 160.15W
97 B18 **Kalsoy** *Dan.* Kalsø *Island* Faeroe Islands 62.20N 6.46W
41 O9 **Kaltag** Alaska, USA 64.19N 158.43W
110 H7 **Kaltbrunn** Sankt Gallen, NE Switzerland 47.11N 9.00E
Kaltdorf *see* Pruszków
79 X14 **Kaltungo** Gombe, E Nigeria 9.49N 11.22E
130 K4 **Kaluga** Kaluzhskaya Oblast', W Russian Federation 54.31N 36.16E
161 J26 **Kalu Ganga** ∾ S Sri Lanka
84 J13 **Kalulushi** Copperbelt, C Zambia 12.52S 28.06E
188 M2 **Kalumburu** Western Australia 14.11S 126.40E
97 H23 **Kalundborg** Vestsjælland, E Denmark 55.42N 11.06E
84 K11 **Kalungwishi** ∾ N Zambia
155 T8 **Kalūr Kot** Punjab, E Pakistan 32.07N 71.19E
118 I6 **Kalush** *Pol.* Kałusz. Ivano-Frankivs'ka Oblast', W Ukraine 49.01N 24.21E
Kałusz *see* Kalush
112 N11 **Kałuszyn** Mazowieckie, C Poland 52.12N 21.43E
161 J26 **Kalutara** Western Province, SW Sri Lanka 6.34N 79.58E
Kaluwawa *see* Fergusson Island
130 I5 **Kaluzhskaya Oblast'** ◐ *province* W Russian Federation
121 E14 **Kalvarija** *Pol.* Kalwaria. Marijampolė, S Lithuania 54.25N 23.13E
95 K15 **Kälviä** Länsi-Suomi, W Finland 63.50N 23.31E
111 U6 **Kalwang** Steiermark, E Austria 47.25N 14.48E
Kalwaria *see* Kalvarija
160 D13 **Kalyān** Mahārāshtra, W India 19.16N 73.10E
128 K16 **Kalyazin** Tverskaya Oblast', W Russian Federation 57.15N 37.53E
117 D18 **Kalydón** *anc.* Calydon. *site of ancient city* Dytikí Ellás, C Greece 38.24N 21.31E
117 M21 **Kálymnos** *var.* Kálimnos. Kálymnos, Dodekánisos, Greece, Aegean Sea 36.57N 26.58E
117 M21 **Kálymnos** *var.* Kálimnos. *island* Dodekánisos, Greece, Aegean Sea
119 O5 **Kalynivka** Kyyivs'ka Oblast', N Ukraine 50.14N 30.16E
119 N6 **Kalynivka** Vinnyts'ka Oblast', C Ukraine 49.27N 28.32E
44 M10 **Kama** *var.* Cama. Región Autónoma Atlántico Sur, SE Nicaragua 12.06N 83.55W
125 E9 **Kama** ∾ NW Russian Federation
172 N12 **Kamaishi** *var.* Kamaisi. Iwate, Honshū, C Japan 39.17N 141.51E
Kamaisi *see* Kamaishi
120 H13 **Kamajai** Molėtai, E Lithuania 55.49N 25.30E
120 H11 **Kamajai** Rokiškis, NE Lithuania 55.16N 25.30E
171 Jj17 **Kamakura** Kanagawa, Honshū, S Japan 35.17N 139.31E
155 U9 **Kamālia** Punjab, NE Pakistan 30.43N 72.39E
85 I14 **Kamalondo** North Western, NW Zambia 13.42S 25.38E
142 I13 **Kaman** Kirşehir, C Turkey 39.22N 33.43E
81 O20 **Kamanyola** Sud Kivu, E Dem. Rep. Congo (Zaire) 2.54S 29.04E
147 N14 **Kamarān** *island* W Yemen
57 R9 **Kamarang** W Guyana 5.49N 60.38W
Kāmāreddi/Kamareddy *see* Rāmāreddi
Kama Reservoir *see* Kamskoye Vodokhranilishche
154 K13 **Kamarod** Baluchistān, SW Pakistan 27.34N 63.36E
175 R13 **Kamaru** Pulau Buton, C Indonesia 5.10S 123.03E
153 N12 **Kamashi** Qashqadaryo Wiloyati, S Uzbekistan 38.52N 66.30E
79 S13 **Kamba** Kebbi, NW Nigeria 11.50N 3.44E
Kambaeng Petch *see* Kamphaeng Phet
188 L12 **Kambalda** Western Australia 31.15S 121.33E
155 P13 **Kambar** *var.* Qambar. Sind, SE Pakistan 27.34N 68.03E
Kambara *see* Kabara
78 I14 **Kambia** W Sierra Leone 9.09N 12.52W
175 S16 **Kambing, Pulau** *island* W East Timor
Kambos *see* Kámpos
81 N25 **Kambove** Katanga, SE Dem. Rep. Congo (Zaire) 10.49S 26.39E
Kambryk *see* Cambrai
127 Pp10 **Kamchatka** ∾ E Russian Federation
Kamchatka *see* Kamchatka, Poluostrov
Kamchatka Basin *see* Komandorskaya Basin
127 P11 **Kamchatka, Poluostrov** *Eng.* Kamchatka. *peninsula* E Russian Federation
127 Pp11 **Kamchatskaya Oblast'** ◐ *province* E Russian Federation
127 Pp10 **Kamchatskiy Zaliv** *gulf* E Russian Federation
116 N9 **Kamchiya** ∾ E Bulgaria
116 L9 **Kamchiya, Yazovir** ⊠ E Bulgaria
Kamdesh *see* Kāmdeysh
155 T4 **Kāmdeysh** *var.* Kamdesh. Kunar, E Afghanistan 35.25N 71.25E
170 Ee14 **Kamega-mori** ▲ Shikoku, SW Japan 33.45N 133.12E
120 M13 **Kamen'** *Rus.* Kamen'. Vitsyebskaya Voblasts', N Belarus 55.01N 28.52E
Kamenets *see* Kamyanyets
Kamenets-Podol'skaya Oblast' *see* Khmel'nyts'ka Oblast'
Kamenets-Podol'skiy *see* Kam"yanets'-Podil's'kyy
115 Q18 **Kamenica** NE FYR Macedonia 42.03N 22.34E
114 A11 **Kamenjak, Rt** *headland* NW Croatia
150 F8 **Kamenka** Zapadnyy Kazakhstan, NW Kazakhstan 51.06N 51.16E
129 O6 **Kamenka** Arkhangel'skaya Oblast', NW Russian Federation 65.55N 44.01E
130 O6 **Kamenka** Penzenskaya Oblast', W Russian Federation 53.12N 44.00E
131 L8 **Kamenka** Voronezhskaya Oblast', W Russian Federation 50.44N 39.31E
Kamenka *see* Camenca, Moldova
Kamenka *see* Kam"yanka, Ukraine
Kamenka-Bugskaya *see* Kam"yanka-Buz'ka
Kamenka Dneprovskaya *see* Kam"yanka-Dniprovs'ka
Kamen Kashirskiy *see* Kamin'-Kashyrs'kyy
126 Gg14 **Kamen'-na-Obi** Altayskiy Kray, S Russian Federation 53.42N 81.04E
130 L15 **Kamennomostskiy** Respublika Adygeya, SW Russian Federation 44.13N 40.12E
130 L11 **Kamenolomni** Rostovskaya Oblast', SW Russian Federation 47.36N 40.18E
131 P8 **Kamenskiy** Saratovskaya Oblast', W Russian Federation 50.56N 45.32E
127 P7 **Kamenskoye** Koryakskiy Avtonomnyy Okrug, E Russian Federation 62.29N 166.16E
Kamenskoye *see* Dniprodzerzhyns'k
130 L11 **Kamensk-Shakhtinskiy** Rostovskaya Oblast', SW Russian Federation 48.18N 40.16E
125 Ee11 **Kamensk-Ural'skiy** Sverdlovskaya Oblast', C Russian Federation 56.30N 61.45E
103 P15 **Kamenz** Sachsen, E Germany 51.15N 14.06E
171 Gg14 **Kameoka** Kyōto, Honshū, SW Japan 35.02N 135.35E
130 M3 **Kameshkovo** Vladimirskaya Oblast', W Russian Federation 56.21N 41.01E
171 H15 **Kameyama** Mie, Honshū, SW Japan 34.52N 136.25E
170 Cc10 **Kami-Agata** Nagasaki, Tsushima, SW Japan 34.40N 129.27E
35 N10 **Kamiah** Idaho, NW USA 46.13N 116.01W
Kamień Koszyrski *see* Kamin'-Kashyrs'kyy
112 H9 **Kamień Krajeński** *Ger.* Kamin in Westpreussen. Kujawsko-pomorskie, C Poland 53.31N 17.31E
113 F15 **Kamienna Góra** *Ger.* Landeshut, Landeshut in Schlesien. Dolnośląskie, SW Poland 50.48N 16.00E
112 D8 **Kamień Pomorski** *Ger.* Cammin in Pommern. Zachodniopomorskie, NW Poland 53.57N 14.44E
172 N7 **Kamiiso** Hokkaidō, NE Japan 41.50N 140.38E
81 L22 **Kamiji** Kasai Oriental, S Dem. Rep. Congo (Zaire) 6.35S 23.18E
172 Pp5 **Kamikawa** Hokkaidō, NE Japan 43.51N 142.47E
170 Bb15 **Kami-Koshiki-jima** *island* SW Japan
81 M23 **Kamina** Katanga, S Dem. Rep. Congo (Zaire) 8.42S 25.01E
Kamina *see* Kaintiba
44 C6 **Kaminaljuyú** *ruins* Guatemala, C Guatemala 14.34N 90.36W
Kamin in Westpreussen *see* Kamień Krajeński
118 J2 **Kamin'-Kashyrs'kyy** *Pol.* Kamień Koszyrski, *Rus.* Kamen Kashirskiy. Volyns'ka Oblast', NW Ukraine 51.39N 24.59E
172 N6 **Kaminokuni** Hokkaidō, NE Japan 41.48N 140.05E
171 Ll13 **Kaminoyama** Yamagata, Honshū, C Japan 38.09N 140.15E
171 Ii14 **Kamioka** Gifu, Honshū, SW Japan 36.20N 137.18E
41 Q13 **Kamishak Bay** *bay* Alaska, USA
172 Pp6 **Kami-Shihoro** Hokkaidō, NE Japan 43.14N 143.18E
Kamishli *see* Al Qāmishlī
Kamissar *see* Kamsar
170 Cc10 **Kami-Tsushima** Nagasaki, Tsushima, SW Japan 34.40N 129.27E
81 O20 **Kamituga** Sud Kivu, E Dem. Rep. Congo (Zaire) 3.07S 28.10E
170 B17 **Kamiyaku** Kagoshima, Yaku-shima, SW Japan 30.24N 130.32E
9 N16 **Kamloops** British Columbia, SW Canada 50.39N 120.24W
109 G25 **Kamma** Sicilia, Italy, C Mediterranean Sea 36.46N 12.03E
199 I14 **Kammu Seamount** *undersea feature* N Pacific Ocean 32.09N 173.00E
111 U11 **Kamnik** *Ger.* Stein. C Slovenia 46.13N 14.34E
Kamniške Alpe *see* Kamniško-Savinjske Alpe
111 T10 **Kamniško-Savinjske Alpe** *var.* Kamniške Alpe, Sanntaler Alpen, *Ger.* Steiner Alpen. ▲▲ N Slovenia
171 Kk13 **Kamo** Niigata, Honshū, C Japan 37.42N 139.03E
171 K17 **Kamogawa** Chiba, Honshū, S Japan 35.05N 140.04E
155 W8 **Kāmoke** Punjab, E Pakistan 31.58N 74.13E
84 L13 **Kamoto** Eastern, E Zambia 13.16S 32.04E
111 V3 **Kamp** ∾ N Austria
83 F18 **Kampala** ● (Uganda) S Uganda 0.21N 32.28E
174 H8 **Kampar, Sungai** ∾ Sumatera, W Indonesia
174 Ii10 **Kampa, Teluk** *bay* Pulau Bangka, W Indonesia
100 L9 **Kampen** Overijssel, E Netherlands 52.33N 5.55E
81 N20 **Kampene** Maniema, E Dem. Rep. Congo (Zaire) 3.34S 26.40E
31 Q9 **Kampeska, Lake** ◎ South Dakota, N USA
178 Gg9 **Kamphaeng Phet** *var.* Kambaeng Petch. Kamphaeng Phet, W Thailand 16.28N 99.31E
Kampo *see* Campo, Cameroon
Kampo *see* Ntem, Cameroon/Equatorial Guinea
178 J13 **Kâmpóng Cham** *prev.* Kompong Cham. Kâmpóng Cham, C Cambodia 12.00N 105.27E
178 J13 **Kâmpóng Chhnăng** *prev.* Kompong. Kâmpóng Chhnăng, C Cambodia 12.15N 104.40E
178 Ii12 **Kâmpóng Khleăng** *prev.* Kompong Kleang. Siĕmréab, NW Cambodia 13.04N 104.07E
178 I14 **Kâmpóng Saôm** *prev.* Kompong Som, Sihanoukville. Kâmpóng Saôm, SW Cambodia 10.37N 103.30E
178 J13 **Kâmpóng Spoe** *prev.* Kompong Speu. Kâmpóng Spœ, S Cambodia 11.28N 104.29E
124 N3 **Kámpos** *var.* Kambos. NW Cyprus 35.03N 32.44E
178 Ii14 **Kâmpôt** Kâmpôt, SW Cambodia 10.37N 104.10E
Kamptee *see* Kāmthi
79 O14 **Kampti** SW Burkina 10.07N 3.22W
Kampuchea *see* Cambodia
174 Ll5 **Kampung Sirik** Sarawak, East Malaysia 2.42N 111.28E
176 Y13 **Kampung, Sungai** ∾ Irian Jaya, E Indonesia
176 Vv12 **Kamrau, Teluk** *bay* Irian Jaya, E Indonesia
9 V15 **Kamsack** Saskatchewan, S Canada 51.34N 101.51W
78 H13 **Kamsar** *var.* Kamissar. Guinée-Maritime, W Guinea 10.36N 14.34W
131 R4 **Kamskoye Ust'ye** Respublika Tatarstan, W Russian Federation 55.13N 49.11E
129 U14 **Kamskoye Vodokhranilishche** *var.* Kama Reservoir. ⊠ NW Russian Federation
160 I12 **Kāmthi** *prev.* Kamptee. Mahārāshtra, C India 21.19N 79.11E
Kamuela *see* Waimea
172 Nn5 **Kamuenai** Hokkaidō, NE Japan 43.07N 140.25E
172 P7 **Kamui-dake** ▲ Hokkaidō, NE Japan 42.24N 142.57E
172 Nn4 **Kamui-misaki** *headland* Hokkaidō, NE Japan 43.20N 140.20E
45 O15 **Kámuk, Cerro** ▲ SE Costa Rica 9.15N 83.01W
176 Vv9 **Kamundan, Sungai** ∾ Irian Jaya, E Indonesia
176 X12 **Kamura, Sungai** ∾ Irian Jaya, E Indonesia
118 K7 **Kam"yanets'-Podil's'kyy** *Rus.* Kamenets-Podol'skiy. Khmel'nyts'ka Oblast', W Ukraine 48.42N 26.36E
119 Q6 **Kam"yanka** *Rus.* Kamenka. Cherkas'ka Oblast', C Ukraine 49.03N 32.06E
118 I5 **Kam"yanka-Buz'ka** *Rus.* Kamenka-Bugskaya. L'vivs'ka Oblast', NW Ukraine 50.03N 24.20E
119 T9 **Kam"yanka-Dniprovs'ka** *Rus.* Kamenka Dneprovskaya. Zaporiz'ka Oblast', SE Ukraine 47.28N 34.24E
121 F19 **Kamyanyets** *Rus.* Kamenets. Brestskaya Voblasts', SW Belarus 52.24N 23.50E
131 P9 **Kamyshin** Volgogradskaya Oblast', SW Russian Federation 50.06N 45.20E
125 Ee11 **Kamyshlov** Sverdlovskaya Oblast', C Russian Federation 56.55N 62.37E
131 Q13 **Kamyzyak** Astrakhanskaya Oblast', SW Russian Federation 46.07N 48.03E
10 K8 **Kanaaupscow** ∾ Québec, C Canada
38 K8 **Kanab** Utah, W USA 37.03N 112.31W
38 K9 **Kanab Creek** ∾ Arizona/Utah, SW USA
197 J13 **Kanacea** *prev.* Kanathea. Taveuni, N Fiji 16.59S 179.54E
197 K14 **Kanacea** *island* Lau Group, E Fiji
40 G17 **Kanaga Island** *island* Aleutian Islands, Alaska, USA
40 G17 **Kanaga Volcano** ▲ Kanaga Island, Alaska, USA 51.55N 177.09W
171 J17 **Kanagawa** *off.* Kanagawa-ken. ◐ *prefecture* Honshū, S Japan
11 Q8 **Kanairiktok** ∾ Newfoundland, E Canada
Kanaky *see* New Caledonia
81 K22 **Kananga** *prev.* Luluabourg. Kasai Occidental, S Dem. Rep. Congo (Zaire) 5.51S 22.22E
Kananur *see* Cannanore
Kanara *see* Karnātaka
38 J7 **Kanarraville** Utah, W USA 37.32N 113.10W
131 Q4 **Kanash** Chuvashskaya Respublika, W Russian Federation 55.30N 47.27E
Kanathea *see* Kanacea
23 Q4 **Kanawha River** ∾ West Virginia, NE USA
171 I15 **Kanayama** Gifu, Honshū, SW Japan 35.46N 137.15E
171 I12 **Kanazawa** Ishikawa, Honshū, SW Japan 36.34N 136.40E
177 G4 **Kanbalu** Sagaing, C Burma 23.10N 95.31E
177 Ff8 **Kanbe** Yangon, SW Burma 16.40N 96.01E
178 H11 **Kanchanaburi** Kanchanaburi, W Thailand 14.01N 99.31E
Kānchenjunga *see* Kangchenjunga
151 V11 **Kanchingiz, Khrebet** ▲▲ E Kazakhstan
161 J19 **Kānchīpuram** *prev.* Conjeeveram. Tamil Nādu, SE India 12.49N 79.43E
155 N8 **Kandahār** *Per.* Qandahār. Kandahār, S Afghanistan 31.36N 65.48E
155 N9 **Kandahār** *Per.* Qandahār. ◐ *province* SE Afghanistan
Kandalakša *see* Kandalaksha
128 I5 **Kandalaksha** *var.* Kandalakša, *Fin.* Kantalahti. Murmanskaya Oblast', NW Russian Federation 67.09N 32.13E
Kandalaksha Gulf/Kandalakshskaya Guba *see* Kandalakshskiy Zaliv
128 K6 **Kandalakshskiy Zaliv** *var.* Kandalakshskaya Guba, *Eng.* Kandalaksha Gulf. *bay* NW Russian Federation
Kandalangodi *see* Kandalengoti
85 G17 **Kandalengoti** *var.* Kandalangodi. Ngamiland, NW Botswana 19.25S 22.12E
175 N10 **Kandangan** Borneo, C Indonesia 2.49S 115.15E
Kandau *see* Kandava
120 E8 **Kandava** *Ger.* Kandau. Tukums, W Latvia 57.02N 22.48E
Kandavu *see* Kadavu
79 R14 **Kandé** *var.* Kanté. NE Togo 9.55N 1.01E
103 F23 **Kandel** ▲ SW Germany 48.03N 8.00E
194 G12 **Kandep** Enga, W PNG 5.50S 143.26E
155 R12 **Kandh Kot** Sind, SE Pakistan 28.15N 69.18E
79 S13 **Kandi** N Benin 11.04N 2.58E
155 P14 **Kandiāro** Sind, SE Pakistan 27.01N 68.16E
142 F11 **Kandıra** Kocaeli, NW Turkey 41.04N 30.07E
191 S8 **Kandos** New South Wales, SE Australia 32.52S 149.58E
154 M16 **Kandrāch** *var.* Kanrach. Baluchistān, SW Pakistan 25.26N 65.28E
180 I4 **Kandreho** Mahajanga, C Madagascar 17.27S 46.06E
194 M12 **Kandrian** New Britain, E PNG 6.10S 149.33E
Kandukur *see* Kondukūr
161 K25 **Kandy** Central Province, C Sri Lanka 7.16N 80.40E
150 I10 **Kandyagash** *Kaz.* Qandyaghash; *prev.* Oktyabr'sk. Aktyubinsk, W Kazakhstan 49.25N 57.24E
20 D12 **Kane** Pennsylvania, NE USA 41.39N 78.47W
66 I11 **Kane Fracture Zone** *tectonic feature* NW Atlantic Ocean
Kanëka *see* Kanëvka
80 G9 **Kanem** *off.* Préfecture du Kanem. ◐ *prefecture* W Chad
40 D9 **Kaneohe** *Haw.* Kāne'ohe. Oahu, Hawaii, USA, C Pacific Ocean 21.25N 157.48W
Kanestron, Akrotírio *see* Palioúri, Akrotírio
Kanëv *see* Kaniv
128 M5 **Kanëvka** *var.* Kanëka. Murmanskaya Oblast', NW Russian Federation 67.07N 39.43E
130 K13 **Kanevskaya** Krasnodarskiy Kray, SW Russian Federation 46.07N 38.57E
Kanevskoye Vodokhranilishche *see* Kanivs'ke Vodoskhovyshche
171 Ll12 **Kaneyama** Yamagata, Honshū, C Japan 38.54N 140.20E
85 G20 **Kang** Kgalagadi, C Botswana 23.40S 22.49E
78 L13 **Kangaba** Koulikoro, SW Mali 11.57N 8.24W
142 M13 **Kangal** Sivas, C Turkey 39.15N 37.22E
149 O13 **Kangān** Būshehr, S Iran 25.50N 57.30E
149 S15 **Kangān** Hormozgān, SE Iran 27.49N 52.04E
173 G2 **Kangar** Perlis, Peninsular Malaysia 6.28N 100.10E
78 L13 **Kangaré** Sikasso, S Mali 11.39N 8.10W
190 F10 **Kangaroo Island** *island* South Australia
95 M17 **Kangasniemi** Itä-Suomi, E Finland 61.58N 26.36E
148 K6 **Kangāvar** *var.* Kangāwar. Kermānshāh, W Iran 34.30N 47.53E
Kangāwar *see* Kangāvar
159 S11 **Kangchenjunga** *var.* Kānchenjunga. ▲ NE India 27.36N 88.06E
166 G9 **Kangding** Sichuan, C China 30.03N 101.56E
175 Nn14 **Kangean, Kepulauan** *island group* S Indonesia
175 N14 **Kangean, Pulau** *island* Kepulauan Kangean, S Indonesia
69 U8 **Kangen** *var.* Kengen. ∾ SE Sudan
207 N14 **Kangerlussuaq** *Dan.* Søndre Strømfjord ✈ Kitaa, W Greenland 66.59N 50.28W
207 Q15 **Kangertittivaq** *Dan.* Scoresby Sund. *fjord* E Greenland
178 H2 **Kangfang** Kachin State, N Burma 26.09N 98.36E
176 Z13 **Kanggup** Irian Jaya, E Indonesia 5.56S 140.49E
169 X12 **Kanggye** N North Korea 40.57N 126.37E
207 P15 **Kangikajik** *var.* Kap Brewster. *headland* E Greenland 70.10N 22.00W
11 N5 **Kangiqsualujjuaq** *prev.* George River, Port-Nouveau-Québec. Quebec, E Canada 58.34N 65.58W
10 L2 **Kangiqsujuaq** *prev.* Maricourt, Wakeham Bay. Quebec, NE Canada 61.35N 72.00W
10 M4 **Kangirsuk** *prev.* Bellin, Payne. Quebec, E Canada 60.00N 70.01W
164 J15 **Kangmar** Xizang Zizhiqu, W China 30.45N 85.43E
164 M16 **Kangmar** Xizang Zizhiqu, W China 28.34N 89.40E
169 Y14 **Kangnŭng** *Jap.* Kōryō. NE South Korea 37.47N 128.51E
81 D18 **Kango** Estuaire, NW Gabon 0.17N 10.00E
158 I7 **Kāngra** Himāchal Pradesh, NW India 32.04N 76.16E
159 Q16 **Kangsabati Reservoir** ⊠ N India
165 O17 **Kangto** ▲ China/India 27.54N 92.33E
165 W12 **Kangxian** *var.* Kang Xian, Zuitaizi. Gansu, C China 33.21N 105.40E
177 Ff4 **Kani** Sagaing, C Burma 22.24N 94.55E
78 M15 **Kani** NW Ivory Coast 8.24N 6.38W
81 M23 **Kaniama** Katanga, S Dem. Rep. Congo (Zaire) 7.31S 24.10E
Kanibadam *see* Konibodom
175 O2 **Kanibongan** Sabah, East Malaysia 6.40N 117.12E
193 F17 **Kaniere** West Coast, South Island, NZ 42.45S 171.00E
193 G17 **Kaniere, Lake** ◎ South Island, NZ
196 E17 **Kanifaay** Yap, W Micronesia
129 O4 **Kanin Kamen'** ▲▲ NW Russian Federation
129 N3 **Kanin Nos** Nenetskiy Avtonomnyy Okrug, NW Russian Federation 68.38N 43.19E
129 N3 **Kanin Nos, Mys** *headland* NW Russian Federation 68.39N 43.14E
129 O5 **Kanin, Poluostrov** *peninsula* NW Russian Federation
145 V8 **Kāni Sakht** E Iraq 33.19N 46.04E
145 T3 **Kāni Sulaymān** N Iraq 35.54N 44.35E
172 N8 **Kanita** Aomori, Honshū, C Japan 41.04N 140.36E
119 Q5 **Kaniv** *Rus.* Kanëv. Cherkas'ka Oblast', C Ukraine 49.46N 31.28E
190 K11 **Kaniva** Victoria, SE Australia 36.25S 141.13E
119 Q5 **Kanivs'ke Vodoskhovyshche** *Rus.* Kanevskoye Vodokhranilishche. ⊠ C Ukraine
114 L8 **Kanjiža** *Ger.* Altkanischa, *Hung.* Magyarkanizsa, Ókanizsa; *prev.* Stara Kanjiža. Serbia, N Yugoslavia 46.03N 20.03E
95 K18 **Kankaanpää** Länsi-Suomi, W Finland 61.46N 22.25E
32 M12 **Kankakee** Illinois, N USA 41.07N 87.51W
33 O11 **Kankakee River** ∾ Illinois/Indiana, N USA
78 K14 **Kankan** Haute-Guinée, E Guinea 10.25N 9.19W
160 K13 **Kānker** Madhya Pradesh, C India 20.19N 81.29E
78 J10 **Kankossa** Assaba, S Mauritania 15.54N 11.31W
178 Gg13 **Kanmaw Kyun** *var.* Kisseraing, Kithareng. *island* Mergui Archipelago, S Burma
170 E13 **Kanmuri-yama** ▲ Kyūshū, SW Japan 34.28N 132.03E
23 R10 **Kannapolis** North Carolina, SE USA 35.29N 80.37W
95 L16 **Kannonkoski** Länsi-Suomi, W Finland 62.58N 25.19E
Kannur *see* Cannanore
95 K15 **Kannus** Länsi-Suomi, W Finland 63.51N 23.55E
79 V13 **Kano** Kano, N Nigeria 11.56N 8.30E
79 V13 **Kano** ◐ *state* N Nigeria
79 V13 **Kano** ✈ Kano, N Nigeria 11.56N 8.26E
170 F14 **Kan'onji** *var.* Kanonzi. Kagawa, Shikoku, SW Japan 34.10N 133.38E
Kanonzi *see* Kan'onji
28 M5 **Kanopolis Lake** ⊠ Kansas, C USA
38 K5 **Kanosh** Utah, W USA 38.48N 112.26W
174 Ll6 **Kanowit** Sarawak, East Malaysia 2.03N 112.15E
170 Bb17 **Kanoya** Kagoshima, Kyūshū, SW Japan 31.21N 130.49E
158 L13 **Kānpur** *Eng.* Cawnpore. Uttar Pradesh, N India 26.28N 80.21E
Kanrach *see* Kandrāch
171 Gg15 **Kansai** ✈ (Ōsaka) Ōsaka, Honshū, SW Japan 34.25N 135.13E
29 R9 **Kansas** Oklahoma, C USA 36.14N 94.46W
28 L5 **Kansas** *off.* State of Kansas; *also known as* Jayhawker State, Sunflower State. ◐ *state* C USA
29 R4 **Kansas City** Kansas, C USA 39.06N 94.37W
29 R4 **Kansas City** Missouri, C USA 39.06N 94.34W
29 R3 **Kansas City** ✈ Missouri, C USA 39.18N 94.45W
29 P4 **Kansas River** ∾ Kansas, C USA
126 I14 **Kansk** Krasnoyarskiy Kray, S Russian Federation 56.11N 95.32E
Kansu *see* Gansu
153 V7 **Kant** Chuyskaya Oblast', N Kyrgyzstan 42.54N 74.47E
Kantalahti *see* Kandalaksha
178 Gg16 **Kantang** *var.* Ban Kantang. Trang, SW Thailand 7.25N 99.30E
117 H25 **Kántanos** Kríti, Greece, E Mediterranean Sea 35.20N 23.42E
79 R12 **Kantchari** E Burkina 12.28N 1.31E
Kanté *see* Kandé
Kantemir *see* Cantemir
130 L9 **Kantemirovka** Voronezhskaya Oblast', W Russian Federation 49.43N 39.53E
178 J11 **Kantharalak** Si Sa Ket, E Thailand 14.32N 104.37E
Kantipur *see* Kathmandu
41 Q9 **Kantishna River** ∾ Alaska, USA
171 K16 **Kantō** *physical region* Honshū, SW Japan
203 S3 **Kanton** *var.* Abariringa, Canton Island; *prev.* Mary Island. *atoll* Phoenix Islands, C Kiribati
171 Jj15 **Kantō-sanchi** ▲▲ Honshū, S Japan
99 C20 **Kanturk** *Ir.* Ceann Toirc. SW Ireland 52.12N 8.54W
57 T11 **Kanuku Mountains** ▲▲ S Guyana
171 Kk15 **Kanuma** Tochigi, Honshū, S Japan 36.36N 139.46E
85 H20 **Kanye** Southern, SE Botswana 24.54S 25.14E
85 H17 **Kanyu** Ngamiland, C Botswana 20.07S 24.36E
177 G7 **Kanyutkwin** Pegu, C Burma 18.19N 96.30E
81 M24 **Kanzenze** Katanga, SE Dem. Rep. Congo (Zaire) 10.33S 25.28E
200 Ss13 **Kao** *island* Kotu Group, W Tonga
167 S14 **Kaohsiung** *var.* Gaoxiong, *Jap.* Takao, Takow. S Taiwan 22.36N 120.16E
167 S14 **Kaohsiung** ✈ S Taiwan 22.26N 120.32E
Kaokaona *see* Kirakira
85 B17 **Kaoko Veld** ▲▲ N Namibia
78 G11 **Kaolack** *var.* Kaolak. W Senegal 14.09N 16.07W
Kaolak *see* Kaolack
Kaolan *see* Lanzhou
195 W15 **Kaolo** San Jorge, N Solomon Islands 8.24S 159.35E
85 H14 **Kaoma** Western, W Zambia 14.43S 24.46E
40 B8 **Kapaa** *Haw.* Kapa'a. Kauai, Hawaii, USA, C Pacific Ocean 22.04N 159.19W
115 J16 **Kapa Moračka** ▲ SW Yugoslavia 42.53N 19.01E
143 V13 **Kapan** *Rus.* Kafan; *prev.* Ghap'an. SE Armenia 39.13N 46.25E
84 L13 **Kapandashila** Northern, NE Zambia 12.43S 31.00E
81 L23 **Kapanga** Katanga, S Dem. Rep. Congo (Zaire) 8.22S 22.37E
151 U15 **Kapchagay** *Kaz.* Kapshagay. Almaty, SE Kazakhstan 43.52N 77.05E
151 V15 **Kapchagayskoye Vodokhranilishche** *Kaz.* Qapshagay Böyeni. ⊠ SE Kazakhstan
101 F15 **Kapelle** Zeeland, SW Netherlands 51.28N 3.58E
101 G16 **Kapellen** Antwerpen, N Belgium 51.19N 4.25E
97 P15 **Kapellskär** Stockholm, C Sweden 59.43N 19.03E
83 H18 **Kapenguria** Rift Valley, W Kenya 1.13N 35.07E
111 V6 **Kapfenberg** Steiermark, C Austria 47.27N 15.15E
85 J14 **Kapiri Mposhi** Central, C Zambia 13.54S 28.40E
155 R4 **Kāpīsā** ◐ *province* E Afghanistan
10 G10 **Kapiskau** ∾ Ontario, C Canada
192 K13 **Kapiti Island** *island* C NZ
80 K9 **Kapka, Massif du** ▲▲ E Chad
Kaplamada *see* Kaubalatmada, Gunung
24 H9 **Kaplan** Louisiana, S USA 30.00N 92.16W
152 E9 **Kaplangky, Plato** *ridge* Turkmenistan/Uzbekistan
113 D19 **Kaplice** *Ger.* Kaplitz. Budějovický Kraj, S Czech Republic 48.42N 14.27E
Kaplitz *see* Kaplice
Kapoche *see* Capoche
176 U10 **Kapocol** Irian Jaya, E Indonesia 1.59S 130.11E
178 Gg14 **Kapoe** Ranong, SW Thailand 9.33N 98.37E
Kapoeas *see* Kapuas, Sungai
83 G15 **Kapoeta** Eastern Equatoria, SE Sudan 4.49N 33.34E
113 I25 **Kapos** ∾ S Hungary
113 H25 **Kaposvár** Somogy, SW Hungary 46.22N 17.54E
96 H13 **Kapp** Oppland, S Norway 60.42N 10.49E
102 I7 **Kappeln** Schleswig-Holstein, N Germany 54.40N 9.56E
Kaproncza *see* Koprivnica
111 P7 **Kaprun** Salzburg, C Austria 47.15N 12.48E
Kapshagay *see* Kapchagay
Kapstad *see* Cape Town
Kapsukas *see* Marijampolė
176 Yy10 **Kaptiau** Irian Jaya, E Indonesia 2.23S 139.51E
121 L19 **Kaptsevichy** *Rus.* Koptsevichi. Homyel'skaya Voblasts', SE Belarus 52.13N 28.19E
Kapuas Hulu, Banjaran/Kapuas Hulu, Pegunungan *see* Kapuas Mountains
174 M7 **Kapuas Mountains** *Ind.* Banjaran Kapuas Hulu, Pegunungan Kapuas Hulu. ▲▲ Indonesia/Malaysia
174 Kk8 **Kapuas, Sungai** ∾ Borneo, N Indonesia
175 N10 **Kapuas, Sungai** *prev.* Kapoeas. ∾ Borneo, C Indonesia
190 J9 **Kapunda** South Australia 34.23S 138.51E
158 H8 **Kapūrthala** Punjab, N India 31.22N 75.15E
174 L14 **Kapur Utara, Pegunungan** ▲▲ Jawa, S Indonesia
10 G12 **Kapuskasing** Ontario, S Canada 49.25N 82.25W
12 D6 **Kapuskasing** ∾ Ontario, S Canada
131 P11 **Kapustin Yar** Astrakhanskaya Oblast', SW Russian Federation 48.36N 45.49E
84 K11 **Kaputa** Northern, NE Zambia 8.27S 29.35E
113 G22 **Kapuvár** Győr-Moson-Sopron, NW Hungary 47.35N 17.01E
Kapydzhik, Gora *see* Qapiciğ Daği
121 J17 **Kapyl'** *Rus.* Kopyl'. Minskaya Voblasts', C Belarus 53.09N 27.04E
45 N9 **Kara** *var.* Cara. Región Autónoma Atlántico Sur, E Nicaragua 12.52N 83.35W
79 R14 **Kara** *var.* Lama-Kara. NE Togo 9.36N 1.12E
79 Q14 **Kara** ∾ N Togo
153 U7 **Kara-Balta** Chuyskaya Oblast', N Kyrgyzstan 42.50N 73.51E
150 G11 **Karabau** Atyrau, W Kazakhstan 48.29N 53.05E
152 E7 **Karabaur', Uval** *Kaz.* Korabavur Pastligi, *Uzb.* Qorabowur Kirlari. *physical region* Kazakhstan/Uzbekistan
152 L13 **Karabekaul** *var.* Garabekevyul, *Turkm.* Garabekewül. Lebapskiy Velayat, E Turkmenistan 38.31N 64.04E
152 K15 **Karabil', Vozvyshennost'** ▲▲ S Turkmenistan
152 A9 **Kara-Bogaz-Gol** *Turkm.* Garabogazköl. Balkanskiy Velayat, NW Turkmenistan 41.03N 52.52E
152 B9 **Kara-Bogaz-Gol, Zaliv** *bay* NW Turkmenistan
151 R15 **Karaboget** *Kaz.* Qaraböget. Zhambyl, S Kazakhstan 44.36N 72.03E
142 H11 **Karabük** Karabük, NW Turkey 41.12N 32.36E
142 H11 **Karabük** ◐ *province* NW Turkey
126 Ii13 **Karabula** Krasnoyarskiy Kray, C Russian Federation 58.01N 97.17E
151 V14 **Karabulak** *Kaz.* Qarabulaq. Almaty, SE Kazakhstan 44.54N 78.29E

◆ Country ● Country Capital ◇ Dependent Territory ○ Dependent Territory Capital ◐ Administrative Region ✈ International Airport ▲ Mountain ▲▲ Mountain Range Volcano ∾ River ◎ Lake ⊠ Reservoir

KARABULAK – KAVKAZ

151 Y11 **Karabulak** *Kaz.* Qarabulaq. Vostochnyy Kazakhstan, E Kazakhstan 47.33N 84.38E
151 Q17 **Karabulak** *Kaz.* Qarabulaq. Yuzhnyy Kazakhstan, S Kazakhstan 42.31N 69.46E
142 C17 **Kara Burnu** *headland* SW Turkey 36.34N 28.00E
150 K10 **Karabutak** *Kaz.* Qarabutaq. Aktyubinsk, W Kazakhstan 49.58N 60.06E
142 D12 **Karacabey** Bursa, NW Turkey 40.13N 28.22E
116 O12 **Karacaköy** İstanbul, NW Turkey 41.24N 28.21E
116 M12 **Karacaoğlan** Kırklareli, NW Turkey 41.30N 27.06E
Karachay-Cherkessia *see* Karachayevo-Cherkesskaya Respublika
130 L15 **Karachayevo-Cherkesskaya Respublika** *Eng.* Karachay-Cherkessia. ◆ *autonomous republic* SW Russian Federation
130 M15 **Karachayevsk** Karachayevo-Cherkesskaya Respublika, SW Russian Federation 43.43N 41.53E
130 J6 **Karachev** Bryanskaya Oblast', W Russian Federation 53.07N 35.56E
155 O16 **Karāchi** Sind, SE Pakistan 24.51N 67.01E
155 O16 **Karāchi** ✈ Sind, S Pakistan 24.51N 67.01E
Karácsonkő *see* Piatra-Neamţ
161 E15 **Karād** Mahārāshtra, W India 17.19N 74.15E
142 H16 **Karadağ** ▲ S Turkey 37.00N 33.00E
153 T10 **Karadar'ya** *Uzb.* Qoradaryo. ≈ Kyrgyzstan/Uzbekistan
Karadeniz *see* Black Sea
Karadeniz Boğazı *see* İstanbul Boğazı
152 B13 **Karadepe** Balkanskiy Velayat, W Turkmenistan 38.04N 54.01E
Karadzhar *see* Qorajar
Karaferiye *see* Véroia
152 E13 **Karagan** *Turkm.* Garagan. Akhalskiy Velayat, C Turkmenistan 38.16N 57.34E
151 R10 **Karaganda** *Kaz.* Qaraghandy. Karaganda, C Kazakhstan 49.52N 73.07E
151 R10 **Karaganda** *off.* Karagandinskaya Oblast', *Kaz.* Qaraghandy Oblysy. ◆ *province* C Kazakhstan
Karagandinskaya Oblast' *see* Karaganda
151 T10 **Karagayly** *Kaz.* Qaraghayly. Karaganda, C Kazakhstan 49.25N 75.31E
152 A11 **Karagel'** *Turkm.* Garagöl. Balkanskiy Velayat, W Turkmenistan 39.24N 53.13E
127 Pp8 **Karaginskiy, Ostrov** *island* E Russian Federation
207 T1 **Karaginskiy Zaliv** *bay* E Russian Federation
143 P13 **Karagöl Dağları** ▲▲ NE Turkey
116 L13 **Karahisar** Edirne, NW Turkey 40.47N 26.34E
131 V3 **Karaidel'** Respublika Bashkortostan, W Russian Federation 55.50N 56.55E
131 V3 **Karaidel'skiy** Respublika Bashkortostan, W Russian Federation 55.51N 57.09E
116 L13 **Karaidemir Barajı** ▣ NW Turkey
161 J21 **Kāraikāl** Pondicherry, SE India 10.58N 79.49E
161 I22 **Kāraikkudi** Tamil Nādu, SE India 10.04N 78.46E
151 Y11 **Kara Irtysh** *Rus.* Chërnyy Irtysh. ≈ NE Kazakhstan
149 N5 **Karaj** Tehrān, N Iran 35.43N 51.25E
174 H5 **Karak** Pahang, Peninsular Malaysia 3.24N 101.58E
Karak *see* Al Karak
153 T11 **Kara-Kabak** Oshskaya Oblast', SW Kyrgyzstan 39.40N 72.45E
152 D12 **Kara-Kala** *var.* Garrygala. Balkanskiy Velayat, W Turkmenistan 38.27N 56.15E
Karakala *see* Oqqal'a
Karakalpakstan, Respublika *see* Qoraqalpoghiston Respublikasi
Karakalpakya *see* Qoraqalpoghiston
Karakax *see* Moyu
164 G10 **Karakax He** ≈ NW China
124 S9 **Karakaya Barajı** ▣ C Turkey
175 Ss4 **Karakelang, Pulau** *island* N Indonesia
Karakılısse *see* Ağrı
Karak, Muḩāfaẓat al *see* Al Karak
Kara-Köl *see* Kara-Kul'
153 Y7 **Karakol** *prev.* Przheval'sk. Issyk-Kul'skaya Oblast', NE Kyrgyzstan 42.31N 78.20E
153 X8 **Karakol** *var.* Karakolka. Issyk-Kul'skaya Oblast', NE Kyrgyzstan 41.30N 77.18E
Karakolka *see* Karakol
155 W2 **Karakoram Highway** *road* China/Pakistan
155 Z3 **Karakoram Pass** *Chin.* Karakoram Shankou. *pass* C Asia 35.23N 77.45E
158 I3 **Karakoram Range** ▲▲ C Asia
Karakoram Shankou *see* Karakoram Pass
Karaköse *see* Ağrı
151 P14 **Karakoyyn, Ozero** *Kaz.* Qaraqoyyn. ◎ C Kazakhstan
85 F19 **Karakubis** Ghanzi, W Botswana 22.03S 20.36E
153 T9 **Kara-Kul'** *Kir.* Kara-Köl. Dzhalal-Abadskaya Oblast', W Kyrgyzstan 40.35N 73.36E
Karakul' *see* Qarokŭl, Tajikistan
Karakul' *see* Qorakŭl, Uzbekistan
153 U10 **Kara-Kul'dzha** Oshskaya Oblast', SW Kyrgyzstan 40.32N 73.50E
131 T3 **Karakulino** Udmurtskaya Respublika, NW Russian Federation 56.02N 53.45E
Karakul', Ozero *see* Qarokŭl
Kara Kum *see* Garagumy
Kara Kum Canal/Karakumskiy Kanal *see* Garagumskiy Kanal
Karakumy, Peski *see* Garagumy
85 E17 **Karakuwisa** Okavango, NE Namibia 18.55S 19.40E
126 Jj14 **Karam** Irkutskaya Oblast', S Russian Federation 55.07N 107.21E
Karamai *see* Karamay
175 N13 **Karamain, Pulau** *island* N Indonesia
142 I16 **Karaman** Karaman, S Turkey 37.10N 33.13E
142 H16 **Karaman** ◆ *province* S Turkey
116 M8 **Karamandere** ≈ NE Bulgaria
164 J4 **Karamay** *var.* Karamai, Kelamayi, *prev. Chin.* K'o-la-ma-i. Xinjiang Uygur Zizhiqu, NW China 45.33N 84.45E
175 Nn11 **Karambu** Borneo, N Indonesia 3.48S 116.06E
193 H14 **Karamea** West Coast, South Island, NZ 41.15S 172.07E
193 H14 **Karamea** ≈ South Island, NZ
193 G15 **Karamea Bight** *gulf* South Island, NZ
152 L14 **Karamet-Niyaz** *Turkm.* Garamäbnyyaz. Lebapskiy Velayat, E Turkmenistan 37.45N 64.28E
164 K10 **Karamiran He** ≈ NW China
176 Yy11 **Karamor, Pegunungan** ▲▲ Irian Jaya, E Indonesia
153 S11 **Karamyk** Oshskaya Oblast', SW Kyrgyzstan 39.28N 71.45E
175 Nn16 **Karangasem** Bali, S Indonesia 8.24S 115.40E
160 H12 **Kāranja** Mahārāshtra, C India 20.30N 77.26E
Karanpur *see* Karanpura
158 F9 **Karanpura** *var.* Karanpur. Rājasthān, NW India 29.46N 73.30E
Karánsebes/Karansebesch *see* Caransebeş
151 T14 **Karaoy** *Kaz.* Qaraoy. Almaty, SE Kazakhstan 45.52N 74.44E
116 N7 **Karapelit** *Rom.* Stejarul. Dobrich, NE Bulgaria 43.40N 27.33E
142 I15 **Karapınar** Konya, C Turkey 37.43N 33.34E
85 D22 **Karas** ◆ *district* S Namibia
153 Y8 **Kara-Say** Issyk-Kul'skaya Oblast', NE Kyrgyzstan 41.34N 77.55E
85 E22 **Karasburg** Karas, S Namibia 27.59S 18.45E
Kara Sea *see* Karskoye More
94 K9 **Kárášjohka** *var.* Karašjokka. ≈ N Norway
94 L9 **Karasjok** *Fin.* Kaarasjoki. Finnmark, N Norway 69.27N 25.28S
Karašjokka *see* Kárášjohka
Kara Strait *see* Karskiye Vorota, Proliv
Kara Su *see* Mesta/Néstos
151 N8 **Karasu** *Kaz.* Qarasū. Kostanay, N Kazakhstan 52.43N 65.28E
142 F11 **Karasu** Sakarya, NW Turkey 41.03N 30.39E
Karasubazar *see* Bilohirs'k
125 G14 **Karasuk** Novosibirskaya Oblast', C Russian Federation 53.41N 78.04E
151 U13 **Karatal** *Kaz.* Qaratal. ≈ SE Kazakhstan
142 K17 **Karataş** Adana, S Turkey 36.37N 35.24E
151 Q16 **Karatau** *Kaz.* Qarataū. Zhambyl, S Kazakhstan 43.09N 70.28E
Karatau *see* Karatau, Khrebet
151 P16 **Karatau, Khrebet** *var.* Karatau, *Kaz.* Qarataū. ▲▲ S Kazakhstan
150 G13 **Karaton** *Kaz.* Qaraton. Atyrau, W Kazakhstan 46.33N 53.31E
170 C12 **Karatsu** *var.* Karatu. Saga, Kyūshū, SW Japan 33.27N 129.55E
Karatu *see* Karatsu
126 Hh7 **Karaul** Taymyrskiy (Dolgano-Nenetskiy) Avtonomnyy Okrug, N Russian Federation 70.07N 83.12E
Karaulbazar *see* Qorowulbozor
Karauzyak *see* Qoraūzak
117 D16 **Karáva** ▲ C Greece 39.19N 21.33E
Karavanke *see* Karawanken
117 F22 **Karavás** Kýthira, S Greece 36.21N 22.57E
115 J20 **Karavastasë, Laguna e** *var.* Kënet' e Karavastas, Kravasta Lagoon. *lagoon* W Albania
Karavastas, Kënet' e *see* Karavastasë, Laguna e
120 I5 **Karavere** Tartumaa, E Estonia 58.25N 26.29E
117 L23 **Karavonísia** *island* Kykládes, Greece, Aegean Sea
174 Jj14 **Karawang** *prev.* Krawang. Jawa, C Indonesia 6.13S 107.16E
111 T10 **Karawanken** *Slvn.* Karavanke. ▲▲ Austria/Yugoslavia
Karaxahar *see* Kaidu He
143 R13 **Karayazı** Erzurum, NE Turkey 39.40N 42.09E
151 Q12 **Karazhal** Zhezkazgan, C Kazakhstan 48.02N 70.52E
145 S9 **Karbalā'** *var.* Kerbala, Kerbela. S Iraq 32.37N 44.03E
96 L11 **Kårböle** Gävleborg, C Sweden 61.59N 15.16E
113 M23 **Karcag** Jász-Nagykun-Szolnok, E Hungary 47.21N 20.51E
Kardak *see* Imia
116 N7 **Kardam** Dobrich, NE Bulgaria 43.45N 28.06E
117 M22 **Kardámaina** Kos, Dodekánisos, Greece, Aegean Sea 36.46N 27.08E
Kardamila *see* Kardámyla
117 L18 **Kardámyla** *var.* Kardamila, Kardhámila. Chíos, E Greece 38.33N 26.04E
Kardeljevo *see* Ploče
Kardh *see* Qardho
Kardhámila *see* Kardámyla
Kardhítsa *see* Karditsa
117 E16 **Kardítsa** *var.* Kardhítsa. Thessalía, C Greece 39.22N 21.55E
120 E4 **Kärdla** *Ger.* Kertel. Hiiumaa, W Estonia 59.00N 22.42E
Karelia *see* Kareliya, Respublika
121 I16 **Karelichy** *Pol.* Korelicze, *Rus.* Korelichi. Hrodzyenskaya Voblasts', W Belarus 53.34N 26.07E
128 I10 **Kareliya, Respublika** *prev.* Karel'skaya ASSR, *Eng.* Karelia. ◆ *autonomous republic* NW Russian Federation
Karel'skaya ASSR *see* Kareliya, Respublika
83 E22 **Karema** Rukwa, W Tanzania 6.49S 30.25E
Karen *see* Hualien
85 I14 **Karenda** Central, C Zambia 14.42S 26.52E
178 Gg8 **Karen State** *var.* Kawthule State, Kayin State. ◆ *state* S Burma
94 J10 **Karesuando** *Lapp.* Kaaresuanto. Norrbotten, N Sweden 68.25N 22.28E
Karet *see* Kâgheţ
Kareyz-e-Elyās/Kārez Iliās *see* Kārīz-e Elyās
126 Gg12 **Kargasok** Tomskaya Oblast', C Russian Federation 59.01N 80.34E
126 Gg14 **Kargat** Novosibirskaya Oblast', C Russian Federation 55.07N 80.19E
142 J11 **Kargı** Çorum, N Turkey 41.09N 34.31E
158 I5 **Kargil** Jammu and Kashmir, NW India 34.34N 76.06E
Kargilik *see* Yecheng
128 L11 **Kargopol'** Arkhangel'skaya Oblast', NW Russian Federation 61.30N 38.53E
112 F12 **Kargowa** *Ger.* Unruhstadt. Lubuskie, W Poland 52.05N 15.50E
79 X13 **Kari** Bauchi, E Nigeria 11.13N 10.34E
85 J15 **Kariba** Mashonaland West, N Zimbabwe 16.28S 28.47E
85 J16 **Kariba, Lake** ▣ Zambia/Zimbabwe
172 Nn5 **Kariba-yama** ▲ Hokkaidō, NE Japan 42.36N 139.55E
85 C19 **Karibib** Erongo, C Namibia 21.56S 15.51E
Karies *see* Karyés
94 L9 **Karigasniemi** *Lapp.* Garegegasnjárga. Lappi, N Finland 69.24N 25.52E
172 P6 **Karikachi-tōge** *pass* Hokkaidō, NE Japan 43.08N 142.46E
192 J2 **Karikari, Cape** *headland* North Island, NZ 34.47S 173.24E
Karīmābād *see* Hunza
174 K10 **Karimata, Kepulauan** *island group* N Indonesia
174 K9 **Karimata, Pulau** *island* Kepulauan Karimata, N Indonesia
174 K10 **Karimata, Selat** *strait* W Indonesia
161 I14 **Karīmnagar** Andhra Pradesh, C India 18.28N 79.09E
194 I13 **Karimui** Chimbu, C PNG 6.19S 144.48E
174 L13 **Karimunjawa, Pulau** *island* S Indonesia
82 N12 **Karin** Woqooyi Galbeed, N Somalia 10.48N 45.46E
Kariot *see* Ikaría
95 L20 **Karis** *Fin.* Karjaa. Etelä-Suomi, SW Finland 60.05N 23.39E
Káristos *see* Kárystos
154 J4 **Kārīz-e Elyās** *var.* Kareyz-e-Elyās, Kārez Iliās. Herāt, NW Afghanistan 35.26N 61.24E
Karjaa *see* Karis
151 T10 **Karkaralinsk** *Kaz.* Qarqaraly. Karaganda, E Kazakhstan 49.31N 75.53E
194 J11 **Karkar Island** *island* N PNG
149 N7 **Karkas, Kūh-e** ▲▲ C Iran
148 K8 **Karkheh, Rūd-e** ≈ SW Iran
117 L20 **Karkinágrio** Ikaría, Dodekánisos, Greece, Aegean Sea 37.31N 26.01E
119 R12 **Karkinits'ka Zatoka** *Rus.* Karkinitskiy Zaliv. *gulf* S Ukraine
Karkinitskiy Zaliv *see* Karkinits'ka Zatoka
95 L19 **Karkkila** *Swe.* Högfors. Etelä-Suomi, S Finland 60.31N 24.10E
95 M19 **Kärkölä** Etelä-Suomi, S Finland 60.52N 25.17E
190 G9 **Karkoo** South Australia 34.03S 135.45E
Karkūk *see* Kirkūk
120 D5 **Kärla** *Ger.* Kergel. Saaremaa, W Estonia 58.19N 22.15E
Karleby *see* Kokkola
112 F7 **Karlino** *Ger.* Körlin an der Persante. Zachodniopomorskie, NW Poland 54.02N 15.52E
143 Q13 **Karlıova** Bingöl, E Turkey 39.16N 41.01E
119 U6 **Karlivka** Poltavs'ka Oblast', C Ukraine 49.27N 35.08E
Karl-Marx-Stadt *see* Chemnitz
Karlö *see* Hailuoto
114 C11 **Karlobag** *It.* Carlopago. Lika-Senj, W Croatia 44.31N 15.06E
114 D9 **Karlovac** *Ger.* Karlstadt, *Hung.* Károlyváros. Karlovac, C Croatia 45.28N 15.31E
114 C10 **Karlovac** *off.* Karlovačka Županija. ◆ *province* C Croatia
Karlovačka Županija *see* Karlovac
113 A16 **Karlovarský Kraj** ◆ W Czech Republic
116 J9 **Karlovo** *prev.* Levskigrad. Plovdiv, C Bulgaria 42.39N 24.49E
113 A16 **Karlovy Vary** *Ger.* Karlsbad; *prev. Eng.* Carlsbad. Karlovarský Kraj, W Czech Republic 50.13N 12.51E
Karlsbad *see* Karlovy Vary
97 L17 **Karlsborg** Västra Götaland, S Sweden 58.31N 14.31E
Karlsburg *see* Alba Iulia
97 L22 **Karlshamn** Blekinge, S Sweden 56.10N 14.49E
97 L16 **Karlskoga** Örebro, C Sweden 59.19N 14.33E
97 M22 **Karlskrona** Blekinge, S Sweden 56.11N 15.38E
103 G21 **Karlsruhe** *var.* Carlsruhe. Baden-Württemberg, SW Germany 49.01N 8.24E
97 K16 **Karlstad** Värmland, C Sweden 59.22N 13.36E
31 R3 **Karlstad** Minnesota, N USA 48.34N 96.31W
103 I18 **Karlstadt** Bayern, C Germany 49.58N 9.46E
Karlstadt *see* Karlovac
41 Q14 **Karluk** Kodiak Island, Alaska, USA 57.34N 154.27W
Karluk *see* Qarluq
121 O17 **Karma** *Rus.* Korma. Homyel'skaya Voblasts', SE Belarus 53.07N 30.48E
161 F14 **Karmāla** Mahārāshtra, W India 18.26N 75.08E
152 M11 **Karmana** Nawoiy Wiloyati, C Uzbekistan 40.09N 65.18E
144 G8 **Karmi'él** *var.* Carmiel. Northern, N Israel 32.55N 35.21E
97 B16 **Karmøy** *island* S Norway
158 I9 **Karnāl** Haryāna, N India 29.40N 76.58E
159 W15 **Karnaphuli Reservoir** ▣ NE India
161 F17 **Karnātaka** *var.* Kanara; *prev.* Maisur, Mysore. ◆ *state* W India
27 S13 **Karnes City** Texas, SW USA 28.52N 97.54W
111 P9 **Karnische Alpen** *It.* Alpi Carniche. ▲▲ Austria/Italy
116 M9 **Karnobat** Burgas, E Bulgaria 42.39N 26.58E
111 Q9 **Kärnten** *off.* Land Kärnten, *Eng.* Carinthi, *Slvn.* Koroška. ◆ *state* S Austria
Karnul *see* Kurnool
85 K16 **Karoi** Mashonaland West, N Zimbabwe 16.49S 29.40E
Karol *see* Carei
Károly-Fehérvár *see* Alba Iulia
Károlyváros *see* Karlovac
179 Qq15 **Karomatan** Mindanao, S Philippines 7.47N 123.48E
84 M12 **Karonga** Northern, N Malawi 9.56S 33.54E
153 W10 **Karool-Tëbë** Narynskaya Oblast', C Kyrgyzstan 40.33N 75.52E
190 J9 **Karoonda** South Australia 35.04S 139.58E
155 S9 **Karor Lāl Esan** Punjab, E Pakistan 31.15N 70.54E
155 T11 **Karor Pacca** *var.* Kahror, Kahror Pakka. Punjab, E Pakistan 29.37N 71.58E
175 P10 **Karosa** Sulawesi, C Indonesia 1.38S 119.21E
Karpasía/Karpas Peninsula *see* Kırpaşa
Karpaten *see* Carpathian Mountains
117 L22 **Karpáthio Pélagos** *sea* Dodekánisos, Greece, Aegean Sea
117 N24 **Kárpathos** Kárpathos, SE Greece 35.30N 27.13E
117 N24 **Kárpathos** *It.* Scarpanto; *anc.* Carpathos, Carpathus. *island* SE Greece
Karpathos Strait *see* Karpathou, Stenó
117 N24 **Karpathou, Stenó** *var.* Karpathos Strait, Scarpanto Strait. *strait* Dodekánisos, Greece, Aegean Sea
Karpaty *see* Carpathian Mountains
117 E17 **Karpenísi** *prev.* Karpenísion. Stereá Ellás, C Greece 38.55N 21.45E
Karpenísion *see* Karpenísi
Karpilovka *see* Aktsyabrski
129 O8 **Karpogory** Arkhangel'skaya Oblast', NW Russian Federation 64.01N 44.22E
188 I7 **Karratha** Western Australia 20.43S 116.52E
143 S12 **Kars** *var.* Qars. Kars, NE Turkey 40.34N 43.04E
143 S12 **Kars** *var.* Qars. ◆ *province* NE Turkey
151 O12 **Karsakpay** *Kaz.* Qarsaqbay. Zhezkazgan, C Kazakhstan 47.51N 66.42E
95 L15 **Kärsämäki** Oulu, C Finland 63.58N 25.49E
Karsau *see* Kārsava
120 K9 **Kārsava** *Ger.* Karsau; *prev. Rus.* Korsovka. Ludza, E Latvia 56.46N 27.39E
152 A9 **Karshi** *Turkm.* Garshy. Balkanskiy Velayat, NW Turkmenistan 40.45N 52.50E
Karshi *see* Qarshi
Karshinskaya Step *see* Qarshi Chŭli
Karshinskiy Kanal *see* Qarshi Kanali
86 I5 **Karskiye Vorota, Proliv** *Eng.* Kara Strait. *strait* N Russian Federation
126 Gg5 **Karskoye More** *Eng.* Kara Sea. *sea* Arctic Ocean
95 L17 **Karstula** Länsi-Suomi, W Finland 62.52N 24.48E
131 Q5 **Karsun** Ul'yanovskaya Oblast', W Russian Federation 54.12N 47.00E
125 E12 **Kartaly** Chelyabinskaya Oblast', C Russian Federation 53.02N 60.42E
20 E13 **Karthaus** Pennsylvania, NE USA 41.06N 78.03W
112 I7 **Kartuzy** Pomorskie, NW Poland 54.21N 18.10E
172 N10 **Karumai** Iwate, Honshū, C Japan 40.19N 141.27E
189 U4 **Karumba** Queensland, NE Australia 17.31S 140.51E
148 L10 **Kārūn** *var.* Rūd-e Kārūn. ≈ SW Iran
94 K13 **Karungi** Norrbotten, N Sweden 66.03N 23.55E
94 K13 **Karunki** Lappi, N Finland 66.01N 24.06E
Kārūn, Rūd-e *see* Kārūn
161 H21 **Karūr** Tamil Nādu, SE India 10.58N 78.03E
95 K17 **Karvia** Länsi-Suomi, W Finland 62.07N 22.34E
113 J17 **Karviná** *Ger.* Karwin, *Pol.* Karwina; *prev.* Nová Karvinná. Ostravský Kraj, E Czech Republic 49.51N 18.33E
161 E17 **Kārwār** Karnātaka, W India 14.49N 74.09E
110 M7 **Karwendelgebirge** ▲▲ Austria/Germany
Karwin/Karwina *see* Karviná
117 I14 **Karyés** *var.* Karies. Ágion Óros, N Greece 40.15N 24.15E
126 Kk16 **Karymskoye** Chitinskaya Oblast', S Russian Federation 51.36N 114.02E
117 I19 **Kárystos** *var.* Káristos. Évvoia, C Greece 38.01N 24.25E
142 E17 **Kaş** Antalya, SW Turkey 36.12N 29.37E
41 Y14 **Kasaan** Prince of Wales Island, Alaska, USA 55.32N 132.24W
170 G14 **Kasai** Hyōgo, Honshū, SW Japan 34.56N 134.49E
81 K21 **Kasai** *var.* Cassai, Kassai. ≈ Angola/Dem. Rep. Congo (Zaire)
81 K22 **Kasai Occidental** *off.* Région Kasai Occidental. ◆ *region* S Dem. Rep. Congo (Zaire)
81 L21 **Kasai Oriental** *off.* Région Kasai Oriental. ◆ *region* C Dem. Rep. Congo (Zaire)
81 L24 **Kasaji** Katanga, S Dem. Rep. Congo (Zaire) 10.22S 23.29E
171 Kk16 **Kasama** Ibaraki, Honshū, S Japan 36.21N 140.15E
84 L12 **Kasama** Northern, N Zambia 10.13S 31.12E
Kasan *see* Koson
85 H16 **Kasane** Chobe, NE Botswana 17.48S 25.06E
83 E23 **Kasanga** Rukwa, W Tanzania 8.27S 31.10E
81 G21 **Kasangulu** Bas-Congo, W Dem. Rep. Congo (Zaire) 4.33S 15.12E
Kasansay *see* Kosonsoy
Kasargen *see* Kasari
161 E20 **Kāsaragod** Kerala, SW India 12.30N 75.01E
120 P13 **Kasari** *var.* Kasari Jōgi, *Ger.* Kasargen. ≈ W Estonia
Kasari Jōgi *see* Kasari
15 K9 **Kasba Lake** ◎ Northwest Territories/Nunavut, N Canada
Kaschau *see* Košice
170 Bb16 **Kaseda** Kagoshima, Kyūshū, SW Japan 31.23N 130.18E
85 I14 **Kasempa** North Western, NW Zambia 13.27S 25.49E
81 O24 **Kasenga** Katanga, SE Dem. Rep. Congo (Zaire) 10.22S 28.37E
81 P17 **Kasenye** *var.* Kasenyi. Orientale, NE Dem. Rep. Congo (Zaire) 1.22N 30.25E
Kasenyi *see* Kasenye
83 E18 **Kasese** SW Uganda 0.10N 30.06E
81 O19 **Kasese** Maniema, E Dem. Rep. Congo (Zaire) 1.36S 27.31E
158 J11 **Kāsganj** Uttar Pradesh, N India 27.48N 78.36E
149 U4 **Kashaf Rūd** ≈ NE Iran
149 N7 **Kāshān** Eşfahān, C Iran 33.57N 51.30E
130 M10 **Kashary** Rostovskaya Oblast', SW Russian Federation 49.02N 40.58E
41 O12 **Kashegelok** Alaska, USA 60.57N 157.46W
Kashgar *see* Kashi
164 E7 **Kashi** *Chin.* Kaxgar, K'o-shih, *Uigh.* Kashgar. Xinjiang Uygur Zizhiqu, NW China 39.32N 75.58E
171 Gg16 **Kashihara** *var.* Kasihara. Nara, Honshū, SW Japan 34.31N 135.49E
171 Kk17 **Kashima** Ibaraki, Honshū, S Japan 35.59N 140.37E
170 C13 **Kashima** *var.* Kasima. Saga, Kyūshū, SW Japan 33.09N 130.07E
171 L16 **Kashima-nada** *gulf* S Japan
128 K15 **Kashin** Tverskaya Oblast', W Russian Federation 57.20N 37.34E
158 K10 **Kāshīpur** Uttar Pradesh, N India 29.13N 78.58E
130 L4 **Kashira** Moskovskaya Oblast', W Russian Federation 54.53N 38.13E
171 K17 **Kashiwa** *var.* Kasiwa. Chiba, Honshū, S Japan 35.50N 139.59E
171 Jj13 **Kashiwazaki** *var.* Kasiwazaki. Niigata, Honshū, C Japan 37.22N 138.33E
Kashkadar'inskaya Oblast' *see* Qashqadaryo Wiloyati
149 T5 **Kāshmar** *var.* Turshiz; *prev.* Solţānābād, Torshiz. Khorāsān, NE Iran 35.15N 58.28E
Kashmir *see* Jammu and Kashmir
155 R12 **Kashmor** Sind, SE Pakistan 28.23N 69.43E
155 S5 **Kashmūnd Ghar** *Eng.* Kashmund Range. ▲▲ E Afghanistan
Kashmund Range *see* Kashmūnd Ghar
Kasi *see* Vārānasi
159 O12 **Kasia** Uttar Pradesh, N India 26.45N 83.55E
41 N12 **Kasigluk** Alaska, USA 60.54N 162.31W
Kasihara *see* Kashihara
41 R12 **Kasilof** Alaska, USA 60.20N 151.16W
Kasima *see* Kashima
Kasimköj *see* General Toshevo
130 M4 **Kasimov** Ryazanskaya Oblast', W Russian Federation 54.59N 41.22E
81 P18 **Kasindi** Nord Kivu, E Dem. Rep. Congo (Zaire) 0.07N 29.41E
175 Ss8 **Kasiruta, Pulau** *island* Kepulauan Bacan, E Indonesia
84 M12 **Kasitu** ≈ N Malawi
176 V12 **Kasiui, Pulau** *island* Kepulauan Watubela, E Indonesia
Kasiwa *see* Kashiwa
Kasiwazaki *see* Kashiwazaki
32 L14 **Kaskaskia River** ≈ Illinois, N USA
95 J17 **Kaskinen** *Swe.* Kaskö. Länsi-Suomi, W Finland 62.19N 21.15E
Kaskö *see* Kaskinen
Kas Kong *see* Kŏng, Kaôh
9 O17 **Kaslo** British Columbia, SW Canada 49.54N 116.57W
Käsmark *see* Kežmarok
174 M10 **Kasongan** Borneo, C Indonesia 2.01S 113.21E
81 N21 **Kasongo** Maniema, E Dem. Rep. Congo (Zaire) 4.22S 26.42E
81 H22 **Kasongo-Lunda** Bandundu, SW Dem. Rep. Congo (Zaire) 6.30S 16.51E
117 M24 **Kásos** *island* S Greece
Kasos Strait *see* Kasou, Stenó
117 M25 **Kasou, Stenó** *var.* Kasos Strait. *strait* Dodekánisos/Kríti, Greece, Aegean Sea
143 T10 **Kaspi** C Georgia 41.54N 44.25E
116 M8 **Kaspichan** Shumen, NE Bulgaria 43.18N 27.09E
Kaspīy Mangy Oypaty *see* Caspian Depression
131 Q16 **Kaspiysk** Respublika Dagestan, SW Russian Federation 42.52N 47.40E
Kaspiyskiy *see* Lagan'
Kaspiyskoye More/Kaspiy Tengizi *see* Caspian Sea
Kassa *see* Košice
Kassai *see* Kasai
82 I9 **Kassala** Kassala, E Sudan 15.24N 36.25E
82 H9 **Kassala** ◆ *state* NE Sudan
117 G15 **Kassándra** *prev.* Pallíni; *anc.* Pallene. *peninsula* NE Greece
117 G15 **Kassándras, Akrotírio** *headland* N Greece 39.58N 23.22E
117 H15 **Kassándras, Kólpos** *var.* Kólpos Toronaíos. *gulf* N Greece
145 Y11 **Kassārah** E Iraq 31.21N 47.25E
103 I15 **Kassel** *prev.* Cassel. Hessen, C Germany 51.19N 9.30E
76 M6 **Kasserine** *var.* Al Qaşrayn. W Tunisia 35.15N 8.52E
12 J14 **Kasshabog Lake** ◎ Ontario, SE Canada
145 O5 **Kassīr, Sabkhat al** ◎ E Syria
31 W10 **Kasson** Minnesota, N USA 44.00N 92.42W
117 C17 **Kassópi** *site of ancient city* Ípeiros, W Greece 39.08N 20.38E
117 N24 **Kastállou, Akrotírio** *headland* Kárpathos, SE Greece 35.24N 27.08E
142 I11 **Kastamonu** *var.* Castamoni, Kastamuni. Kastamonu, N Turkey 41.22N 33.46E
142 I10 **Kastamonu** *var.* Kastamuni. ◆ *province* N Turkey
Kastamuni *see* Kastamonu
117 E14 **Kastaneá** Kentrikí Makedonía, N Greece 40.25N 22.09E
117 H24 **Kastélli** Kríti, Greece, E Mediterranean Sea 35.30N 23.39E
Kastellórizon *see* Megísti
97 N21 **Kastlösa** Kalmar, S Sweden 56.25N 16.25E
117 D14 **Kastoría** Dytikí Makedonía, N Greece 40.30N 21.16E
130 K7 **Kastornoye** Kurskaya Oblast', W Russian Federation 51.49N 38.07E
117 I21 **Kástro** Sífnos, Kykládes, Greece, Aegean Sea 36.58N 24.45E
97 J23 **Kastrup** ✈ (København) København, E Denmark 55.36N 12.39E
121 Q17 **Kastsyukovichy** *Rus.* Kostyukovichi. Mahilyowskaya Voblasts', E Belarus 53.19N 32.03E
121 O18 **Kastsyukowka** *Rus.* Kostyukovka. Homyel'skaya Voblasts', SE Belarus 52.32N 30.54E
170 Cc12 **Kasuga** Fukuoka, Kyūshū, SW Japan 33.31N 130.27E
171 I15 **Kasugai** Aichi, Honshū, SW Japan 35.15N 136.57E
83 E21 **Kasulu** Kigoma, W Tanzania 4.33S 30.06E
171 Gg13 **Kasumi** Hyōgo, Honshū, SW Japan 35.36N 134.37E
171 Kk16 **Kasumiga-ura** ◎ Honshū, S Japan
131 R17 **Kasumkent** Respublika Dagestan, SW Russian Federation 41.39N 48.09E
84 M13 **Kasungu** Central, C Malawi 13.01S 33.30E
155 W9 **Kasūr** Punjab, E Pakistan 31.07N 74.30E
85 G15 **Kataba** Western, W Zambia 15.28S 23.25E
21 R4 **Katahdin, Mount** ▲ Maine, NE USA 45.55N 68.52W
81 M20 **Katako-Kombe** Kasai Oriental, C Dem. Rep. Congo (Zaire) 3.24S 24.25E
41 T12 **Katalla** Alaska, USA 60.12N 144.31W
Katana *see* Qaţanā
81 L24 **Katanga** *off.* Région du Katanga; *prev.* Shaba. ◆ *region* SE Dem. Rep. Congo (Zaire)
126 J12 **Katanga** ≈ C Russian Federation
160 J11 **Katangi** Madhya Pradesh, C India 21.46N 79.49E
188 J13 **Katanning** Western Australia 33.44S 117.33E
189 P8 **Kata Tjuta** *var.* Mount Olga ▲ Northern Territory, C Australia 25.20S 130.47E
Katawaz *see* Zarghūn Shahr
157 Q22 **Katchall Island** *island* Nicobar Islands, India, NE Indian Ocean
117 F14 **Kateríni** Kentrikí Makedonía, N Greece 40.17N 22.30E
119 P7 **Katerynopil'** Cherkas'ka Oblast', C Ukraine 49.00N 30.59E
178 Gg3 **Katha** Sagaing, N Burma 24.10N 96.19E
189 P2 **Katherine** Northern Territory, N Australia 14.28S 132.19E
160 B11 **Kāthiāwār Peninsula** *peninsula* W India
159 P11 **Kathmandu** *prev.* Kantipur. ● (Nepal) Central, C Nepal 27.46N 85.16E
158 H7 **Kathua** Jammu and Kashmir, NW India 32.24N 75.33E
78 L12 **Kati** Koulikoro, SW Mali 12.45N 8.06W
159 R13 **Katihār** Bihār, NE India 25.33N 87.34E
192 N7 **Katikati** Bay of Plenty, North Island, NZ 37.33S 175.55E
85 H16 **Katima Mulilo** Caprivi, NE Namibia 17.31S 24.19E
79 N15 **Katiola** C Ivory Coast 8.12N 5.04W
203 V10 **Katiu** *atoll* Îles Tuamotu, C French Polynesia
119 N12 **Katlabukh, Ozero** ◎ SW Ukraine
41 P14 **Katmai, Mount** ▲ Alaska, USA 58.16N 154.57W
160 J9 **Katni** Madhya Pradesh, C India 23.46N 80.28E
117 D19 **Káto Achaïa** *var.* Kato Ahaia, Káto Akhaía. Dytikí Ellás, S Greece 38.08N 21.35E
Kato Ahaia/Káto Akhaía *see* Káto Achaïa
124 Nn3 **Kato Lakatámeia** *var.* Kato Lakatamia. C Cyprus 35.07N 33.20E
Kato Lakatamia *see* Kato Lakatámeia
81 N22 **Katompi** Katanga, SE Dem. Rep. Congo (Zaire) 6.10S 26.19E
85 K14 **Katondwe** Lusaka, C Zambia 15.08S 30.10E
116 H12 **Káto Nevrokópi** *prev.* Káto Nevrokópion. Anatolikí Makedonía kai Thráki, NE Greece 41.21N 23.52E
Káto Nevrokópion *see* Káto Nevrokópi
83 E18 **Katonga** ≈ S Uganda
117 F15 **Káto Ólympos** ▲▲ C Greece
117 D17 **Katoúna** Dytikí Ellás, C Greece 38.46N 21.07E
117 E19 **Káto Vlasiá** Dytikí Makedonía, S Greece 38.02N 21.54E
113 J16 **Katowice** *Ger.* Kattowitz. Śląskie, S Poland 50.14N 19.00E
159 S15 **Kātoya** West Bengal, NE India 23.39N 88.10E
142 E16 **Katrançik Dağı** ▲▲ SW Turkey
97 N16 **Katrineholm** Södermanland, C Sweden 58.58N 16.15E
98 I11 **Katrine, Loch** ◎ C Scotland, UK
79 V12 **Katsina** Katsina, N Nigeria 12.58N 7.33E
79 U12 **Katsina** ◆ *state* N Nigeria
69 P8 **Katsina Ala** ≈ S Nigeria
170 C11 **Katsumoto** Nagasaki, Iki, SW Japan 33.49N 129.42E
171 L16 **Katsuta** *var.* Katuta. Ibaraki, Honshū, S Japan 36.24N 140.31E
171 K17 **Katsuura** *var.* Katuura. Chiba, Honshū, S Japan 35.09N 140.16E
171 I14 **Katsuyama** *var.* Katuyama. Fukui, Honshū, SW Japan 36.03N 136.28E
170 Ff13 **Katsuyama** Okayama, Honshū, SW Japan 35.06N 133.43E
Kattakurgan *see* Kattaqŭrghon
153 N11 **Kattaqŭrghon** *Rus.* Kattakurgan. Samarqand Wiloyati, C Uzbekistan 39.55N 66.11E
117 O23 **Kattavía** Ródos, Dodekánisos, Greece, Aegean Sea 35.56N 27.47E
97 I21 **Kattegat** *Dan.* Kattegatt. *strait* N Europe
Kattegatt *see* Kattegat
97 P19 **Katthammarsvik** Gotland, SE Sweden 57.27N 18.54E
Kattowitz *see* Katowice
127 N17 **Katun'** ≈ S Russian Federation
Katuta *see* Katsuta
Katuura *see* Katsuura
Katuyama *see* Katsuyama
Katwijk *see* Katwijk aan Zee
100 G11 **Katwijk aan Zee** *var.* Katwijk. Zuid-Holland, W Netherlands 52.12N 4.24E
40 B8 **Kauai** *Haw.* Kaua'i. *island* Hawaiian Islands, Hawaii, USA, C Pacific Ocean
40 C8 **Kauai Channel** *channel* Hawaii, USA, C Pacific Ocean
175 Ss11 **Kaubalatmada, Gunung** *var.* Kaplamada. ▲ Pulau Buru, E Indonesia 3.16S 126.17E
203 U10 **Kauehi** *atoll* Îles Tuamotu, C French Polynesia
Kauen *see* Kaunas
103 K24 **Kaufbeuren** Bayern, S Germany 47.52N 10.37E
27 U7 **Kaufman** Texas, SW USA 32.35N 96.18W
103 I15 **Kaufungen** Hessen, C Germany 51.16N 9.39E
95 K17 **Kauhajoki** Länsi-Suomi, W Finland 62.24N 22.12E
95 K16 **Kauhava** Länsi-Suomi, W Finland 63.06N 23.07E
32 M7 **Kaukauna** Wisconsin, N USA 44.18N 88.18W
94 L11 **Kaukonen** Lappi, N Finland 67.28N 24.49E
40 A8 **Kaulakahi Channel** *channel* Hawaii, USA, C Pacific Ocean
40 E9 **Kaunakakai** Molokai, Hawaii, USA, C Pacific Ocean 21.05N 157.01W
40 F12 **Kauna Point** *headland* Hawaii, USA, C Pacific Ocean 19.02N 155.52W
120 F13 **Kaunas** *Ger.* Kauen, *Pol.* Kowno; *prev. Rus.* Kovno. Kaunas, C Lithuania 54.54N 23.57E
194 H10 **Kaup** East Sepik, NW PNG 3.48S 143.56E
79 U12 **Kaura Namoda** Zamfara, NW Nigeria 12.43N 6.17E
Kaushany *see* Căuşeni
95 K16 **Kaustinen** Länsi-Suomi, W Finland 63.33N 23.40E
175 T7 **Kau, Teluk** *bay* Pulau Halmahera, E Indonesia
101 M23 **Kautenbach** Diekirch, NE Luxembourg 49.57N 6.01E
94 K10 **Kautokeino** Finnmark, N Norway 69.00N 23.01E
Kavadar *see* Kavadarci
115 P19 **Kavadarci** *Turk.* Kavadar. C FYR Macedonia 41.25N 22.00E
Kavaja *see* Kavajë
115 K20 **Kavajë** *It.* Cavaia, Kavaja. Tiranë, W Albania 41.11N 19.33E
116 M13 **Kavak Çayı** ≈ NW Turkey
Kavakli *see* Topolovgrad
116 I13 **Kavála** *prev.* Kaválla. Anatolikí Makedonía kai Thráki, NE Greece 40.57N 24.25E
116 I13 **Kaválas, Kólpos** *gulf* Aegean Sea, NE Mediterranean Sea
127 Nn17 **Kavalerovo** Primorskiy Kray, SE Russian Federation 44.17N 135.06E
161 J17 **Kāvali** Andhra Pradesh, E India 15.04N 80.02E
Kaválla *see* Kavála
Kavango *see* Cubango/Okavango
161 C21 **Kavaratti** Lakshadweep, SW India 10.33N 72.37E
116 O8 **Kavarna** Dobrich, NE Bulgaria 43.26N 28.21E
120 G12 **Kavarskas** Anykščiai, E Lithuania 55.27N 24.55E
78 I13 **Kavendou** ▲ C Guinea 10.49N 12.14W
Kavengo *see* Cubango/Okavango
161 F20 **Kāveri** *var.* Cauvery. ≈ S India
195 N9 **Kavieng** *var.* Kaewieng. NE PNG 2.34S 150.48E
85 H16 **Kavimba** Chobe, NE Botswana 18.03S 24.30E
85 I15 **Kavingu** Southern, S Zambia 15.39S 26.03E
149 Q6 **Kavīr, Dasht-e** *var.* Great Salt Desert. *salt pan* N Iran
Kavirondo Gulf *see* Winam Gulf
Kavkaz *see* Caucasus

◆ Country
● Country Capital
◇ Dependent Territory
○ Dependent Territory Capital
◆ Administrative Region
✈ International Airport
▲ Mountain
▲▲ Mountain Range
Volcano
≈ River
◎ Lake
▣ Reservoir

KÄVLINGE – KHALKÍS

97 K23 **Kävlinge** Skåne, S Sweden 55.46N 13.04E
197 I15 **Kavukavu Reef** var. Beqa Barrier Reef, Cakaubalavu Reef. reef Viti Levu, SW Fiji
84 G12 **Kavungo** Moxico, E Angola 11.31S 22.59E
171 M10 **Kawabe** Akita, Honshū, C Japan 39.39N 140.14E
171 K15 **Kawagoe** Saitama, Honshū, S Japan 35.55N 139.30E
171 K16 **Kawaguchi** var. Kawaguti. Saitama, Honshū, S Japan 35.49N 139.40E
Kawaguti see Kawaguchi
172 N11 **Kawai** Iwate, Honshū, C Japan 39.36N 141.40E
40 A8 **Kawaihoa Point** headland Niihau, Hawaii, USA, C Pacific Ocean 21.47N 160.12W
192 K3 **Kawakawa** Northland, North Island, NZ 35.23S 174.03E
84 I13 **Kawama** North Western, NW Zambia 13.04S 25.59E
84 K11 **Kawambwa** Luapula, N Zambia 9.48S 29.04E
170 F14 **Kawanoe** Ehime, Shikoku, SW Japan 34.01N 133.32E
160 K11 **Kawardha** Madhya Pradesh, C India 21.59N 81.12E
12 I14 **Kawartha Lakes** ◎ Ontario, SE Canada
171 K17 **Kawasaki** Kanagawa, Honshū, S Japan 35.33N 139.40E
175 T9 **Kawassi** Pulau Obi, E Indonesia 1.32S 127.25E
172 N8 **Kawauchi** Aomori, Honshū, C Japan 41.11N 141.00E
192 L5 **Kawau Island** island N NZ
192 N10 **Kaweka Range** ▲▲ North Island, NZ
Kawelecht see Puhja
176 Z13 **Kawentinkim** Irian Jaya, E Indonesia 5.04S 140.55E
192 O8 **Kawerau** Bay of Plenty, North Island, NZ 38.06S 176.42E
192 L8 **Kawhia** Waikato, North Island, NZ 38.04S 174.49E
192 K8 **Kawhia Harbour** inlet North Island, NZ
37 V8 **Kawich Peak** ▲ Nevada, W USA 38.00N 116.27W
37 V9 **Kawich Range** ▲▲ Nevada, W USA
12 G12 **Kawigamog Lake** ◎ Ontario, S Canada
175 Rr3 **Kawio, Kepulauan** island group N Indonesia
178 Gg9 **Kawkareik** Karen State, S Burma 16.34N 98.14E
29 O8 **Kaw Lake** ⊠ Oklahoma, C USA
177 G3 **Kawlin** Sagaing, N Burma 23.48N 95.40E
Kawm Umbū see Kôm Ombo
Kawthule State see Karen State
Kaxgar see Kashi
164 D7 **Kaxgar He** ≈ NW China
164 J5 **Kax He** ≈ NW China
79 P12 **Kaya** C Burkina 13.04N 1.09W
178 Gg7 **Kayah State** ◐ state C Burma
126 J7 **Kayak** Taymyrskiy (Dolgano-Nenetskiy) Avtonomnyy Okrug, N Russian Federation 71.27N 103.21E
41 T12 **Kayak Island** island Alaska, USA
116 M11 **Kayalıköy Barajı** ⊠ NW Turkey
161 G23 **Kāyamkulam** Kerala, SW India 9.10N 76.31E
177 G8 **Kayan** Yangon, SW Burma 16.54N 96.34E
175 N6 **Kayan, Sungai** prev. Kajan. ≈ Borneo, C Indonesia
150 F14 **Kaydak, Sor** salt flat SW Kazakhstan
Kaydanovo see Dzyarzhynsk
39 N9 **Kayenta** Arizona, SW USA 36.43N 110.15W
78 J11 **Kayes** Kayes, W Mali 14.25N 11.21W
78 J11 **Kayes** ◐ region SW Mali
Kayin State see Karen State
151 U10 **Kaynar** var. Kajnar. Vostochnyy Kazakhstan, E Kazakhstan 49.13N 77.27E
Kaynary see Căinari
85 H15 **Kayoya** Western, W Zambia 16.13S 24.09E
Kayrakkum see Qayroqqum
Kayrakkumskoye Vodokhranilishche see Qayroqqum, Obanbori
142 K14 **Kayseri** var. Kaisaria; anc. Caesarea Mazaca, Mazaca. Kayseri, C Turkey 38.42N 35.28E
142 K14 **Kayseri** var. Kaisaria. ◐ province C Turkey
38 L2 **Kaysville** Utah, W USA 41.10N 111.55W
126 Hh8 **Kayyerkan** Taymyrskiy (Dolgano-Nenetskiy) Avtonomnyy Okrug, N Russian Federation 69.26N 87.31E
Kayyngdy see Kaindy
12 L11 **Kazabazua** Quebec, SE Canada 45.58N 76.00W
12 L12 **Kazabazua** ≈ Quebec, SE Canada
126 M7 **Kazach'ye** Respublika Sakha (Yakutiya), NE Russian Federation 70.38N 135.54E
Kazakdar'ya see Qozoqdaryo
152 E9 **Kazakhlyshor, Solonchak** var. Solonchak Shorkazakhly. salt marsh NW Turkmenistan
Kazakhskaya SSR/Kazakh Soviet Socialist Republic see Kazakhstan
151 R9 **Kazakhskiy Melkosopochnik** Eng. Kazakh Uplands, Kirghiz Steppe, Kaz. Saryarqa. uplands C Kazakhstan
150 L12 **Kazakhstan** off. Republic of Kazakhstan, var. Kazakstan, Kaz. Qazaqstan, Qazaqstan Respublikasy; prev. Kazakh Soviet Socialist Republic, Rus. Kazakhskaya SSR. ◆ republic C Asia
Kazakh Uplands see Kazakhskiy Melkosopochnik
Kazakstan see Kazakhstan
150 L14 **Kazalinsk** Kzylorda, S Kazakhstan 45.51N 62.08E
131 R4 **Kazan'** Respublika Tatarstan, W Russian Federation 55.43N 49.07E
131 R4 **Kazan'** ✕ Respublika Tatarstan, W Russian Federation 55.46N 49.21E
15 K8 **Kazan** ≈ Nunavut, NW Canada
Kazandzhik see Gazandzhyk
119 R8 **Kazanka** Mykolayivs'ka Oblast', S Ukraine 47.49N 32.50E
Kazanketken see Qizqetkan
Kazanlik see Kazanlŭk
116 J9 **Kazanlŭk** prev. Kazanlik. Stara Zagora, C Bulgaria 42.38N 25.24E
172 T17 **Kazan-rettō** Eng. Volcano Islands. island group SE Japan
125 F12 **Kazanskoye** Tyumenskaya Oblast', C Russian Federation 55.39N 69.06E
119 V12 **Kazantip, Mys** headland S Ukraine 45.27N 35.50E
153 U9 **Kazarman** Narynskaya Oblast', C Kyrgyzstan 41.21N 74.03E
Kazatin see Kozyatyn
Kazbegi see Kazbek
Kazbegi see Qazbegi
143 T9 **Kazbek** var. Kazbegi, Geor. Mqinvartsveri. ▲ N Georgia 42.43N 44.28E
84 M13 **Kazembe** Eastern, NE Zambia 12.06S 32.45E
149 N11 **Kāzerūn** Fārs, S Iran 29.40N 51.38E
129 R12 **Kazhym** Respublika Komi, NW Russian Federation 60.19N 51.26E
Kazi Ahmad see Qāzi Ahmad
Kazi Magomed see Qazimämmäd
142 H16 **Kazımkarabekir** Karaman, S Turkey 37.13N 32.58E
113 M20 **Kazincbarcika** Borsod-Abaúj-Zemplén, NE Hungary 48.15N 20.40E
121 H17 **Kazlowshchyna** Pol. Kozlowszczyzna, Rus. Kozlovshchina. Hrodzyenskaya Voblasts', W Belarus 53.19N 25.18E
121 E14 **Kazlų Rūda** Marijampolė, S Lithuania 54.45N 23.28E
150 E9 **Kaztalovka** Zapadnyy Kazakhstan, W Kazakhstan 49.47N 48.40E
81 K22 **Kazumba** Kasai Occidental, S Dem. Rep. Congo (Zaire) 6.19S 21.57E
171 Mm10 **Kazuno** Akita, Honshū, C Japan 40.08N 140.47E
Kazvin see Qazvīn
120 J12 **Kaz'yany** Rus. Koz'yany. Vitsyebskaya Voblasts', NW Belarus 55.19N 26.52E
125 Ff9 **Kazym** ≈ N Russian Federation
112 H10 **Kcynia** Ger. Exin. Kujawsko-pomorskie, C Poland 53.00N 17.29E
117 I20 **Kéa** Kéa, Kykládes, Greece, Aegean Sea 37.22N 24.21E
117 I20 **Kéa** prev. Kéos, anc. Ceos. island Kykládes, Greece, Aegean Sea
40 H11 **Keaau** Haw. Kea'au. Hawaii, USA, C Pacific Ocean 19.36N 155.01W
40 F11 **Keahole Point** headland Hawaii, USA, C Pacific Ocean 19.43N 156.03W
40 G12 **Kealakekua** Hawaii, USA, C Pacific Ocean 19.31N 155.55W
40 H11 **Kea, Mauna** ▲ Hawaii, USA, C Pacific Ocean 19.50N 155.30W
39 N10 **Keams** Arizona, SW USA 35.47N 110.09W
Kéamu see Aneityum
31 O16 **Kearney** Nebraska, C USA 40.42N 99.06W
38 L3 **Kearns** Utah, W USA 40.39N 112.00W
117 H20 **Kéas, Stenó** strait SE Greece
143 O14 **Keban Barajı** dam C Turkey 38.49N 38.46E
143 O14 **Keban Barajı** ⊠ C Turkey
79 S13 **Kebbi** ◐ state NW Nigeria
78 G10 **Kébémèr** NW Senegal 15.24N 16.25W
76 M7 **Kebili** var. Qibilī. C Tunisia 33.42N 9.06E
144 H4 **Kebir, Nahr el** ≈ NW Syria
82 A10 **Kebkabiya** Northern Darfur, W Sudan 13.39N 24.04E
94 I11 **Kebnekaise** ▲ N Sweden 68.01N 18.24E
83 M14 **K'ebrī Dehar** Somali, E Ethiopia 6.43N 44.15E
154 K15 **Kech** ≈ SW Pakistan
8 K10 **Kechika** ≈ British Columbia, W Canada
113 K23 **Kecskemét** Bács-Kiskun, C Hungary 46.54N 19.41E
174 Gg2 **Kedah** ◐ state Peninsular Malaysia
120 F12 **Kėdainiai** Kėdainiai, C Lithuania 55.19N 24.00E
Kedder see Kehra
11 N13 **Kedgwick** New Brunswick, SE Canada 47.37N 67.21W
174 Ll15 **Kediri** Jawa, C Indonesia 7.45S 112.01E
176 Y10 **Kedir Sarmi** Irian Jaya, E Indonesia 2.00S 139.01E
169 V7 **Kedong** Heilongjiang, NE China 48.00N 126.15E
78 I12 **Kédougou** SE Senegal 12.34N 12.09W
126 Gg13 **Kedrovyy** Tomskaya Oblast', C Russian Federation 57.31N 79.45E
113 H16 **Kędzierzyn-Kozle** Ger. Heydebrech. Opolskie, S Poland 50.20N 18.12E
14 G6 **Keele** ≈ Northwest Territories, NW Canada
8 K6 **Keele Peak** ▲ Yukon Territory, NW Canada 63.31N 130.21W
Keelung see Chilung
21 N10 **Keene** New Hampshire, NE USA 42.56N 72.14W
101 H17 **Keerbergen** Vlaams Brabant, C Belgium 51.01N 4.39E
85 E21 **Keetmanshoop** Karas, S Namibia 26.36S 18.07E
10 A11 **Keewatin** Ontario, S Canada 49.46N 94.30W
31 V4 **Keewatin** Minnesota, N USA 47.24N 93.04W
117 B18 **Kefallinía** var. Kefallonía. island Iónioi Nísoi, Greece, C Mediterranean Sea
Kefallonía see Kefallinía
117 M22 **Kéfalos** Kos, Dodekánisos, Greece, Aegean Sea 36.44N 26.58E
175 Rr17 **Kefamenanu** Timor, C Indonesia 9.31S 124.28E
144 F10 **Kefar Sava** var. Kfar Saba. Central, C Israel 32.12N 34.58E
Kefe see Feodosiya
79 V15 **Keffi** Nassarawa, C Nigeria 8.52N 7.54E
94 H4 **Keflavík** ✕ (Reykjavík) Reykjanes, W Iceland 63.58N 22.37W
94 H4 **Keflavík** Reykjanes, W Iceland 64.01N 22.35W
Kegalee see Kegalla
161 J25 **Kegalla** var. Kegalee, Kegalle. Sabaragamuwa Province, C Sri Lanka 7.13N 80.21E
Kegalle see Kegalla
152 H7 **Kegayli** Rus. Kegeyli. Qoraqalpoghiston Respublikasi, W Uzbekistan 42.46N 59.49E
Kegel see Keila
151 W16 **Kegen** Almaty, SE Kazakhstan 42.57N 79.15E
Kegeyli see Kegayli
103 F22 **Kehl** Baden-Württemberg, SW Germany 48.34N 7.49E
120 H3 **Kehra** Ger. Kedder. Harjumaa, NW Estonia 59.19N 25.22E
119 U6 **Kehychivka** Kharkivs'ka Oblast', E Ukraine 49.18N 35.46E
99 L17 **Keighley** N England, UK 53.51N 1.53W
Kei Islands see Kai, Kepulauan
Keijō see Sŏul
120 G3 **Keila** Ger. Kegel. Harjumaa, NW Estonia 59.19N 24.28E
Keilberg see Klínovec
85 F23 **Keimoes** Northern Cape, W South Africa 28.41S 20.57E
Keina/Keinis see Käina
176 Yy14 **Keisak** Irian Jaya, E Indonesia 7.01S 140.02E
Keishū see Kyŏngju
79 T11 **Keïta** Tahoua, C Niger 14.43N 5.45E
80 J12 **Kéita, Bahr** var. Doka. ≈ S Chad
95 M16 **Keitele** ◎ C Finland
190 K10 **Keith** South Australia 36.01S 140.22E
98 K8 **Keith** NE Scotland, UK 57.33N 2.57W
28 K3 **Keith Sebelius Lake** ⊠ Kansas, C USA
34 G11 **Keizer** Oregon, NW USA 44.59N 123.01W
40 A8 **Kekaha** Kauai, Hawaii, USA, C Pacific Ocean 21.58N 159.43W
153 U10 **Këk-Art** prev. Alaykel', Alay-Kuu. Oshskaya Oblast', SW Kyrgyzstan 40.15N 74.21E
153 W10 **Këk-Aygyr** var. Keyaygyr. Narynskaya Oblast', C Kyrgyzstan 40.42N 75.37E
153 V9 **Këk-Dzhar** Narynskaya Oblast', C Kyrgyzstan 41.28N 74.48E
12 L8 **Kekek** ≈ Quebec, SE Canada
193 K15 **Kekerengu** Canterbury, South Island, NZ 41.55S 174.05E
113 L21 **Kékes** ▲ N Hungary 47.53N 19.59E
175 Rr17 **Kekneno, Gunung** ▲ Timor, S Indonesia
153 S9 **Këk-Tash** Kir. Kök-Tash. Dzhalal-Abadskaya Oblast', W Kyrgyzstan 41.08N 72.25E
83 M15 **K'elafo** Somali, E Ethiopia 5.36N 44.12E
175 O6 **Kelai, Sungai** ≈ Borneo, N Indonesia
Kelamayi see Karamay
Kelang see Klang
174 H3 **Kelantan** ◐ state Peninsular Malaysia
Kelantan see Kelantan, Sungai
174 H3 **Kelantan, Sungai** var. Kelantan. ≈ Peninsular Malaysia
Kelat see Kālat
Këlcyra see Këlcyrë
115 L22 **Këlcyrë** var. Këlcyra. Gjirokastër, S Albania 40.19N 20.10E
152 L14 **Kelifskiy Uzboy** salt marsh E Turkmenistan
143 O12 **Kelkit** Gümüşhane, NE Turkey 40.05N 39.25E
142 M12 **Kelkit Çayı** ≈ N Turkey
79 W11 **Kellé** Zinder, S Niger 14.10N 10.10E
81 G18 **Kéllé** Cuvette, W Congo 0.04S 14.33E
151 P7 **Kellerovka** Severnyy Kazakhstan, N Kazakhstan 53.51N 69.15E
15 H1 **Kellett, Cape** headland Banks Island, Northwest Territories, NW Canada 71.57N 125.55W
33 S11 **Kelleys Island** island Ohio, N USA
35 N8 **Kellogg** Idaho, NW USA 47.30N 116.07W
94 M12 **Kelloselkä** Lappi, N Finland 66.55N 28.52E
99 F17 **Kells** Ir. Ceanannas. E Ireland 53.43N 6.52W
120 E12 **Kelmė** Kelmė, C Lithuania 55.39N 22.57E
101 M19 **Kelmis** var. La Calamine. Liège, E Belgium 50.43N 6.01E
80 H12 **Kélo** Tandjilé, SW Chad 9.21N 15.49E
85 I14 **Kelongwa** North Western, NW Zambia 13.41S 26.19E
9 N17 **Kelowna** British Columbia, SW Canada 49.49N 119.28W
9 X12 **Kelsey** Manitoba, C Canada 56.02N 96.31W
36 M6 **Kelseyville** California, W USA 38.58N 122.51W
98 K13 **Kelso** SE Scotland, UK 55.36N 2.27W
34 G10 **Kelso** Washington, NW USA 46.09N 122.54W
205 W15 **Keltie, Cape** headland Antarctica
Keltsy see Kielce
174 Hh6 **Keluang** var. Kluang. Johor, Peninsular Malaysia 2.01N 103.18E
174 I8 **Kelume** Pulau Lingga, W Indonesia 0.12S 104.27E
9 U15 **Kelvington** Saskatchewan, S Canada 52.10N 103.30W
128 J7 **Kem'** Respublika Kareliya, NW Russian Federation 64.55N 34.17E
128 I7 **Kem'** ≈ NW Russian Federation
143 O13 **Kemah** Erzincan, E Turkey 39.34N 39.01E
143 N13 **Kemaliye** Erzincan, C Turkey 39.17N 38.30E
Kemaman see Cukai
Kemanlar see Isperikh
8 K14 **Kemano** British Columbia, SW Canada 53.39N 127.58W
Kemarat see Khemmarat
175 Qq9 **Kembani** Pulau Peleng, N Indonesia 1.32S 122.57E
142 F17 **Kemer** Antalya, SW Turkey 36.39N 30.33E
126 H14 **Kemerovo** prev. Shcheglovsk. Kemerovskaya Oblast', C Russian Federation 55.25N 86.04E
126 H14 **Kemerovskaya Oblast'** ◐ province S Russian Federation
94 L13 **Kemi** Lappi, NW Finland 65.46N 24.34E
94 M12 **Kemijärvi** Swe. Kemiträsk. Lappi, N Finland 66.41N 27.24E
94 M12 **Kemijärvi** ◎ N Finland
94 L13 **Kemijoki** ≈ NW Finland
153 V7 **Kemin** prev. Bystrovka. Chuyskaya Oblast', N Kyrgyzstan 42.49N 75.37E
94 L13 **Keminmaa** Lappi, NW Finland 65.49N 24.34E
Kemins Island see Nikumaroro
Kemiö see Kimito
Kemiträsk see Kemijärvi
131 P5 **Kemlya** Respublika Mordoviya, W Russian Federation 54.42N 45.16E
101 B18 **Kemmel** West-Vlaanderen, W Belgium 50.42N 2.51E
35 S16 **Kemmerer** Wyoming, C USA 41.47N 110.32W
Kemmuna see Comino
81 I14 **Kémo** ◐ prefecture S Central African Republic
27 U7 **Kemp** Texas, SW USA 32.26N 96.13W
95 L14 **Kempele** Oulu, C Finland 64.55N 25.25E
103 D15 **Kempen** Nordrhein-Westfalen, W Germany 51.22N 6.25E
27 Q5 **Kemp, Lake** ◎ Texas, SW USA
205 W5 **Kemp Land** physical region Antarctica
27 S9 **Kempner** Texas, SW USA 31.03N 98.01W
46 H3 **Kemp's Bay** Andros Island, W Bahamas 24.02N 77.32W
191 U6 **Kempsey** New South Wales, SE Australia 31.04S 152.49E
103 J24 **Kempten** Bayern, S Germany 47.43N 10.19E
13 N9 **Kempt, Lac** ◎ Quebec, SE Canada
191 P17 **Kempton** Tasmania, SE Australia 42.34S 147.13E
160 J9 **Ken** ≈ C India
41 R12 **Kenai** Alaska, USA 60.33N 151.15W
(0) D5 **Kenai Mountains** ▲▲ Alaska, USA
41 R12 **Kenai Peninsula** peninsula Alaska, USA
23 V11 **Kenansville** North Carolina, SE USA 34.57N 77.54W
124 Pp15 **Kenâyis, Râs el-** headland N Egypt 31.13N 27.53E
99 K16 **Kendal** NW England, UK 54.19N 2.45W
25 Y16 **Kendall** Florida, SE USA 25.39N 80.18W
15 L6 **Kendall, Cape** headland Nunavut, E Canada 63.31N 87.09W
20 J15 **Kendall Park** New Jersey, NE USA 40.25N 74.33W
33 Q11 **Kendallville** Indiana, N USA 41.24N 85.10W
175 Qq12 **Kendari** Sulawesi, C Indonesia 3.57S 122.36E
174 L10 **Kendawangan** Borneo, C Indonesia 2.31S 110.13E
174 Ll15 **Kendeng, Pegunungan** ▲▲ Jawa, S Indonesia
160 O12 **Kendrāpāra** var. Kendrāparha. Orissa, E India 20.29N 86.25E
Kendrāparha see Kendrāpāra
160 O11 **Kendujhargarh** prev. Keonjihargarh. Orissa, E India 21.42N 85.36E
27 S13 **Kenedy** Texas, SW USA 28.49N 97.51W
152 E13 **Kënekesir** Turkm. Könekesir. Balkanskiy Velayat, W Turkmenistan 38.16N 56.51E
78 J15 **Kenema** SE Sierra Leone 7.55N 11.12W
31 P16 **Kenesaw** Nebraska, C USA 40.37N 98.39W
152 G8 **Këneurgench** Turkm. Köneürgench; prev. Kunya-Urgench. Dashkhovuzskiy Velayat, N Turkmenistan 42.20N 59.09E
81 H21 **Kenge** Bandundu, SW Dem. Rep. Congo (Zaire) 4.52S 16.58E
Kengen see Kangen
178 Hh5 **Keng Tung** var. Kentung. Shan State, E Burma 21.18N 99.36E
85 F23 **Kenhardt** Northern Cape, W South Africa 29.20S 21.10E
78 J12 **Kéniéba** Kayes, W Mali 12.47N 11.16W
Kenimekh see Konimekh
175 Nn3 **Keningau** Sabah, East Malaysia 5.21N 116.10E
76 F6 **Kénitra** prev. Port-Lyautey. NW Morocco 34.19N 6.29W
23 V9 **Kenly** North Carolina, SE USA 35.39N 78.16W
99 B21 **Kenmare** Ir. Neidín. S Ireland 51.52N 9.34W
30 L2 **Kenmare** North Dakota, N USA 48.40N 102.04W
99 A21 **Kenmare River** Ir. An Ribhéar. inlet NE Atlantic Ocean
20 D10 **Kenmore** New York, NE USA 42.58N 78.52W
27 W8 **Kennard** Texas, SW USA 31.21N 95.10W
31 N10 **Kennebec** South Dakota, N USA 43.53N 99.52W
21 Q7 **Kennebec River** ≈ Maine, NE USA
21 P9 **Kennebunk** Maine, NE USA 43.22N 70.33W
41 R13 **Kennedy Entrance** strait Alaska, USA
177 Ff3 **Kennedy Peak** ▲ W Burma 23.18N 93.52E
24 K9 **Kenner** Louisiana, S USA 29.57N 90.15W
188 I8 **Kenneth Range** ▲▲ Western Australia
29 Y9 **Kennett** Missouri, C USA 36.14N 90.03W
20 I16 **Kennett Square** Pennsylvania, NE USA 39.50N 75.40W
34 K10 **Kennewick** Washington, NW USA 46.12N 119.08W
10 E11 **Kenogami** ≈ Ontario, S Canada
13 Q7 **Kénogami, Lac** ◎ Quebec, SE Canada
12 G8 **Kenogami Lake** Ontario, S Canada 48.04N 80.10W
12 F7 **Kenogamissi Lake** ◎ Ontario, S Canada
8 I6 **Keno Hill** Yukon Territory, NW Canada 63.54N 135.18W
10 A11 **Kenora** Ontario, S Canada 49.46N 94.25W
33 N9 **Kenosha** Wisconsin, N USA 42.34N 87.49W
11 P14 **Kensington** Prince Edward Island, SE Canada 46.25N 63.39W
28 L3 **Kensington** Kansas, C USA 39.46N 99.01W
34 I11 **Kent** Oregon, NW USA 45.14N 120.43W
26 J9 **Kent** Texas, SW USA 31.03N 104.13W
34 H8 **Kent** Washington, NW USA 47.22N 122.13W
99 P22 **Kent** cultural region SE England, UK
151 P16 **Kentau** Yuzhnyy Kazakhstan, S Kazakhstan 43.28N 68.46E
191 P14 **Kent Group** island group Tasmania, SE Australia
33 N12 **Kentland** Indiana, N USA 40.46N 87.25W
33 R12 **Kenton** Ohio, N USA 40.39N 83.36W
15 J4 **Kent Peninsula** peninsula Nunavut, N Canada
117 F14 **Kentrikí Makedonía** Eng. Macedonia Central. ◐ region N Greece
22 J6 **Kentucky** off. Commonwealth of Kentucky; also known as The Bluegrass State. ◐ state C USA
22 H8 **Kentucky Lake** ⊠ Kentucky/Tennessee, S USA
Kentung see Keng Tung
11 P15 **Kentville** Nova Scotia, SE Canada 45.04N 64.30W
24 K8 **Kentwood** Louisiana, S USA 30.56N 90.30W
33 P9 **Kentwood** Michigan, N USA 42.52N 85.33W
83 H17 **Kenya** off. Republic of Kenya. ◆ republic E Africa
Kenya, Mount see Kirinyaga
174 Hh3 **Kenyir, Tasik** var. Tasek Kenyir. ◎ Peninsular Malaysia
31 W10 **Kenyon** Minnesota, N USA 44.16N 92.59W
31 Y16 **Keokuk** Iowa, C USA 40.24N 91.22W
Keonjihargarh see Kendujhargarh
Kéos see Kéa
31 X16 **Keosauqua** Iowa, C USA 40.43N 91.58W
31 X15 **Keota** Iowa, C USA 41.21N 91.57W
23 O11 **Keowee, Lake** ⊠ South Carolina, SE USA
128 I7 **Kepa** var. Kepe. Respublika Kareliya, NW Russian Federation 65.09N 32.15E
Kepe see Kepa
201 O13 **Kepirohi Falls** waterfall Pohnpei, E Micronesia
193 B22 **Kepler Mountains** ▲▲ South Island, NZ
113 I14 **Kępno** Wielkopolskie, C Poland 51.17N 17.56E
67 C24 **Keppel Island** island N Falkland Islands
Keppel Island see Niuatoputapu
67 C23 **Keppel Sound** sound N Falkland Islands
142 D12 **Kepsut** Balıkesir, NW Turkey 39.40N 28.09E
176 W12 **Kerai** Irian Jaya, E Indonesia 3.53S 134.30E
Kerak see Al Karak
161 F22 **Kerala** ◐ state S India
194 H10 **Keram** ≈ N PNG
172 O14 **Kerama-rettō** island group SW Japan
191 N10 **Kerang** Victoria, SE Australia 35.46S 144.01E
Kerasunt see Giresun
117 H19 **Keratéa** var. Keratea. Attikí, C Greece 37.48N 23.58E
95 M19 **Kerava** Swe. Kervo. Etelä-Suomi, S Finland 60.22N 25.01E
Kerbala/Kerbela see Karbalā'
34 F15 **Kerby** Oregon, NW USA 42.10N 123.39W
119 W12 **Kerch** Rus. Kerch'. Respublika Krym, SE Ukraine 45.22N 36.30E
Kerchens'ka Protska/Kerchenskiy Proliv see Kerch Strait
119 V13 **Kerchens'kyy Pivostriv** peninsula S Ukraine
124 R4 **Kerch Strait** var. Bosporus Cimmerius, Enikale Strait, Rus. Kerchenskiy Proliv, Ukr. Kerchens'ka Protska. strait Black Sea/Sea of Azov
158 K8 **Kerdārnāth** Uttar Pradesh, N India 30.43N 79.03E
Kerdilio see Kerdýlio
116 H13 **Kerdýlio** var. Kerdilio. ▲ N Greece 40.46N 23.37E
194 J14 **Kerema** Gulf, S PNG 7.58S 145.46E
Keremitlik see Lyulyakovo
142 I9 **Kerempe Burnu** headland N Turkey 42.01N 33.20E
82 J9 **Keren** var. Cheren. C Eritrea 15.45N 38.22E
27 U7 **Kerens** Texas, SW USA 32.07N 96.13W
192 M6 **Kerepehi** Waikato, North Island, NZ 37.18S 175.33E
151 P10 **Kerey, Ozero** ◎ C Kazakhstan
Kergel see Kärla
181 Q12 **Kerguelen** island C French Southern and Antarctic Territories
181 Q13 **Kerguelen Plateau** undersea feature S Indian Ocean
117 C20 **Kerí** Zákynthos, Iónioi Nísoi, Greece, C Mediterranean Sea 37.40N 20.48E
83 H19 **Kericho** Rift Valley, W Kenya 0.21S 35.16E
192 K2 **Kerikeri** Northland, North Island, NZ 35.13S 173.57E
95 O17 **Kerimäki** Isä-Suomi, E Finland 61.55N 29.18E
174 Gg10 **Kerinci, Danau** ◎ Sumatera, W Indonesia
174 Gg9 **Kerinci, Gunung** ▲ Sumatera, W Indonesia 2.00S 101.40E
Keriya see Yutian
164 H9 **Keriya He** ≈ NW China
100 J9 **Kerkbuurt** Noord-Holland, C Netherlands 52.29N 5.08E
100 J13 **Kerkdriel** Gelderland, C Netherlands 51.46N 5.21E
77 N6 **Kerkenah, Îles de** var. Kerkenna Islands, Ar. Juzur Qarqannah. island group E Tunisia
Kerkenna Islands see Kerkenah, Îles de
117 M20 **Kerketévs** ▲ Sámos, Dodekánisos, Greece, Aegean Sea 37.44N 26.39E
31 T8 **Kerkhoven** Minnesota, N USA 45.12N 95.18W
152 M14 **Kerki** Lebapskiy Velayat, E Turkmenistan 37.51N 65.06E
152 M14 **Kerkichi** Lebapskiy Velayat, E Turkmenistan 37.46N 65.18E
117 F16 **Kerkíneo** prehistoric site Thessalía, C Greece 39.32N 22.42E
116 G12 **Kerkinitis, Límni** ◎ N Greece
Kérkira see Kérkyra
101 M18 **Kerkrade** Limburg, SE Netherlands 50.52N 6.04E
Kerkuk see Kirkūk
117 B16 **Kérkyra** ✕ Kérkyra, Iónioi Nísoi, Greece, C Mediterranean Sea 39.36N 19.55E
117 B16 **Kérkyra** var. Kérkira, Eng. Corfu. Kérkyra, Iónioi Nísoi, Greece, C Mediterranean Sea 39.36N 19.55E
117 A16 **Kérkyra** var. Kérkira, Eng. Corfu. island Iónioi Nísoi, Greece, C Mediterranean Sea
199 Jj12 **Kermadec Islands** island group NZ, SW Pacific Ocean
183 R10 **Kermadec Ridge** undersea feature SW Pacific Ocean
183 R11 **Kermadec Trench** undersea feature SW Pacific Ocean
149 S10 **Kermān** var. Kirman; anc. Carmana. Kermān, C Iran 30.18N 57.04E
149 R11 **Kermān** off. Ostān-e Kermān, var. Kirman; anc. Carmania. ◐ province SE Iran
149 U12 **Kermān, Bīābān-e** var. Kerman Desert. desert SE Iran
149 Q9 **Kermānshāh** Yazd, C Iran 34.19N 47.04E
148 J6 **Kermānshāh** off. Ostān-e Kermānshāh; prev. Bākhtarān, Kermānshāhān. ◐ province W Iran
Kermānshāhān see Kermānshāh
116 L10 **Kermen** Sliven, C Bulgaria 42.30N 26.12E
26 L8 **Kermit** Texas, SW USA 31.51N 103.05W
23 P6 **Kermit** West Virginia, NE USA 37.51N 82.24W
23 S9 **Kernersville** North Carolina, SE USA 36.12N 80.13W
37 S12 **Kern River** ≈ California, W USA
37 S12 **Kernville** California, W USA 35.44N 118.25W
117 K21 **Kéros** island Kykládes, Greece, Aegean Sea
78 K14 **Kérouané** Haute-Guinée, SE Guinea 9.16N 9.00W
103 D16 **Kerpen** Nordrhein-Westfalen, W Germany 50.51N 6.40E
152 I11 **Kerpichli** Lebapskiy Velayat, NE Turkmenistan 40.12N 61.09E
26 M1 **Kerrick** Texas, SW USA 36.29N 102.14W
Kerr Lake see John H.Kerr Reservoir
9 S15 **Kerrobert** Saskatchewan, S Canada 51.55N 109.09W
27 Q11 **Kerrville** Texas, SW USA 30.03N 99.06W
99 B20 **Kerry** Ir. Ciarraí. cultural region SW Ireland
23 S11 **Kershaw** South Carolina, SE USA 34.33N 80.34W
Kertel see Kärdla
97 H23 **Kerteminde** Fyn, C Denmark 55.27N 10.40E
169 Q7 **Kerulen** Chin. Herlen He, Mong. Herlen Gol. ≈ China/Mongolia
Kervo see Kerava
Kerýneia see Girne
10 H11 **Kesagami Lake** ◎ Ontario, SE Canada
95 O17 **Kesälahti** Itä-Suomi, E Finland 61.54N 29.49E
142 B11 **Keşan** Edirne, NW Turkey 40.52N 26.38E
171 Mm12 **Kesennuma** Miyagi, Honshū, C Japan 38.54N 141.34E
169 V7 **Keshan** Heilongjiang, NE China 48.00N 125.46E
32 M6 **Keshena** Wisconsin, N USA 44.54N 88.37W
142 I13 **Keskin** Kırıkkale, C Turkey 39.40N 33.36E
Késmárk see Kežmarok
128 I6 **Kesten'ga** var. Kest Enga. Respublika Kareliya, NW Russian Federation 65.53N 31.47E
100 K12 **Kesteren** Gelderland, C Netherlands 51.55N 5.34E
12 H14 **Keswick** Ontario, S Canada 44.15N 79.26W
99 K15 **Keswick** NW England, UK 54.30N 3.03W
113 H24 **Keszthely** Zala, SW Hungary 46.46N 17.16E
126 Hh13 **Ket'** ≈ C Russian Federation
79 R17 **Keta** SE Ghana 5.54N 1.01E
174 Kk10 **Ketapang** Borneo, C Indonesia 1.49S 109.58E
131 O12 **Ketchenery** prev. Sovetskoye. Respublika Kalmykiya, SW Russian Federation 47.18N 44.31E
41 Y14 **Ketchikan** Revillagigedo Island, Alaska, USA 55.20N 131.39W
35 O14 **Ketchum** Idaho, NW USA 43.40N 114.24W
Kete/Kete Krakye see Kete-Krachi
79 Q15 **Kete-Krachi** var. Kete, Kete Krakye. E Ghana 7.49N 0.03W
100 L9 **Ketelmeer** channel E Netherlands
155 P17 **Keti Bandar** Sind, SE Pakistan 23.55N 67.31E
151 W16 **Ketmen', Khrebet** ▲▲ SE Kazakhstan
79 S16 **Kétou** SE Benin 7.25N 2.36E
112 M7 **Kętrzyn** Ger. Rastenburg. Warmińsko-Mazurskie, NE Poland, 54.03N 21.22E
99 N20 **Kettering** C England, UK 52.24N 0.43W
33 R14 **Kettering** Ohio, N USA 39.41N 84.10W
20 F13 **Kettle Creek** ≈ Pennsylvania, NE USA
34 L7 **Kettle Falls** Washington, NW USA 48.36N 118.03W
12 D16 **Kettle Point** headland Ontario, S Canada 43.12N 82.01W
31 V6 **Kettle River** ≈ Minnesota, N USA
194 E12 **Ketu** ≈ W PNG
20 G10 **Keuka Lake** ◎ New York, NE USA
Keupriya see Primorsko
95 L17 **Keuruu** Länsi-Suomi, W Finland 62.15N 24.34E
Kevevára see Kovin
94 L9 **Kevo** Lapp. Geavvú. Lappi, N Finland 69.42N 27.08E
46 M6 **Kew** North Caicos, N Turks and Caicos Islands 21.52N 71.57W
32 K11 **Kewanee** Illinois, N USA 41.15N 89.55W
33 N7 **Kewaunee** Wisconsin, N USA 44.27N 87.31W
32 M3 **Keweenaw Bay** ◎ Michigan, N USA
33 N2 **Keweenaw Peninsula** peninsula Michigan, N USA 47.15N 88.19W
33 N2 **Keweenaw Point** headland Michigan, N USA 47.24N 87.42W
31 N12 **Keya Paha River** ≈ Nebraska/South Dakota, N USA
Keyaygyr see Këk-Aygyr
25 Z16 **Key Biscayne** Florida, SE USA 25.41N 80.09W
28 G8 **Keyes** Oklahoma, C USA 36.48N 102.15W
25 Y17 **Key Largo** Key Largo, Florida, SE USA 25.06N 80.24W
23 U3 **Keyser** West Virginia, NE USA 39.26N 78.58W
29 O9 **Keystone Lake** ⊠ Oklahoma, C USA
38 L16 **Keystone Peak** ▲ Arizona, SW USA 31.52N 111.12W
Keystone State see Pennsylvania
23 U7 **Keysville** Virginia, NE USA 37.02N 78.28W
29 T3 **Keytesville** Missouri, C USA 39.25N 92.56W
25 W17 **Key West** Florida Keys, Florida, SE USA 24.34N 81.48W
131 T1 **Kez** Udmurtskaya Respublika, NW Russian Federation 57.55N 53.42E
Kezdivásárhely see Târgu Secuiesc
126 J13 **Kezhma** Krasnoyarskiy Kray, C Russian Federation 58.57N 101.00E
113 L18 **Kežmarok** Ger. Käsmark, Hung. Késmárk. Prešovský Kraj, E Slovakia 49.09N 20.25E
Kfar Saba see Kefar Sava
85 F20 **Kgalagadi** ◐ district SW Botswana
85 I20 **Kgatleng** ◐ district SE Botswana
196 F8 **Kgkeklau** Babeldaob, N Palau
129 R6 **Khabarikha** var. Chabaricha. Respublika Komi, NW Russian Federation 65.52N 52.19E
127 N16 **Khabarovsk** Khabarovskiy Kray, SE Russian Federation 48.31N 135.07E
126 Mm12 **Khabarovskiy Kray** ◐ territory E Russian Federation
147 W7 **Khabb** Abū Ẓaby, E UAE 24.39N 55.43E
Khabour, Nahr al see Khābūr, Nahr al
Khabura see Al Khābūrah
145 N2 **Khābūr, Nahr al** var. Nahr al Khabour. ≈ Syria/Turkey
Khachmas see Xaçmaz
82 B12 **Khadari** ≈ W Sudan
Khadera see Ḥadera
147 X12 **Khādhil** var. Khudal. SE Oman 18.48N 56.48E
161 E14 **Khadki** prev. Kirkee. Mahārāshtra, W India 18.34N 73.52E
130 L14 **Khadyzhensk** Krasnodarskiy Kray, SW Russian Federation 44.26N 39.31E
116 N9 **Khadzhiyska Reka** ≈ E Bulgaria
119 P10 **Khadzhybeys'kyy Lyman** ◎ SW Ukraine
144 K3 **Khafsah** Ḥalab, N Syria 36.16N 38.03E
158 M13 **Khāga** Uttar Pradesh, N India 25.46N 81.04E
159 Q13 **Khagaria** Bihār, NE India 25.31N 86.27E
155 Q13 **Khairpur** Sind, SE Pakistan 27.30N 68.49E
126 Hh15 **Khakasiya, Respublika** prev. Khakasskaya Avtonomnaya Oblast', Eng. Khakassia. ◐ autonomous republic C Russian Federation
Khakassia/Khakasskaya Avtonomnaya Oblast' see Khakasiya, Respublika
178 H9 **Kha Khaeng, Khao** ▲ W Thailand 16.13N 99.03E
85 G20 **Khakhea** var. Kakia. Southern, S Botswana 24.40S 23.28E
152 L13 **Khalach** Lebapskiy Velayat, E Turkmenistan 38.05N 64.46E
Khalándrion see Chalándri
131 W7 **Khalilovo** Orenburgskaya Oblast', W Russian Federation 51.25N 58.13E
Khalkabad see Khalqobod
148 L3 **Khalkhāl** prev. Herowābād. Ardabīl, NW Iran 37.40N 48.34E
Khalkidhikí see Chalkidikí
Khalkís see Chalkída

◆ Country ● Country Capital ◇ Dependent Territory ○ Dependent Territory Capital ◐ Administrative Region ✕ International Airport ▲ Mountain ▲▲ Mountain Range Volcano ≈ River ◎ Lake ⊠ Reservoir

KHAL'MER-YU – KINGSTON

129 W3 Khal'mer-Yu Respublika Komi, NW Russian Federation 68.00N 64.45E
121 M14 Khalopyenichy Rus. Kholopenichi. Minskaya Voblasts', NE Belarus 54.31N 28.58E
152 H7 Khalqobod Rus. Khalkabad. Qoraqalpogʻiston Respublikasi, W Uzbekistan 42.42N 59.46E
Khalturin see Orlov
147 Y10 Khalūf var. Al Khaluf. E Oman 20.27N 57.58E
160 K10 Khamaria Madhya Pradesh, C India 23.07N 80.54E
160 D11 Khambhāt Gujarāt, W India 22.19N 72.39E
160 C12 Khambhāt, Gulf of Eng. Gulf of Cambay. gulf W India
178 K10 Khâm Đức Quang Nam-Đa Nâng, C Vietnam 15.28N 107.49E
160 G12 Khāmgaon Mahārāshtra, C India 20.40N 76.34E
147 O14 Khamir var. Khamr. W Yemen 16.00N 43.56E
147 N12 Khamīs Mushayt var. Hamīs Musait. 'Asīr, SW Saudi Arabia 18.19N 42.41E
126 L10 Khampa Respublika Sakha (Yakutiya), NE Russian Federation 63.43N 123.02E
Khamr see Khamir
85 C19 Khan ≈ W Namibia
155 Q2 Khānābād Kunduz, NE Afghanistan 36.42N 69.07E
Khân Abou Châmâte/Khan Abou Ech Cham see Khān Abū Shāmāt
144 I7 Khān Abū Shāmāt var. Khân Abou Châmâte, Khan Abou Ech Cham. Dimashq, W Syria 33.43N 36.56E
Khān al Baghdādī see Al Baghdādī
Khān al Maḥāwīl see Al Maḥāwīl
145 T7 Khān al Mashāhidah C Iraq 33.40N 44.15E
145 T10 Khān al Muṣallā S Iraq 32.09N 44.19E
145 U6 Khānaqīn E Iraq 34.22N 45.22E
145 T11 Khān ar Ruḥbah S Iraq 31.42N 44.18E
145 P2 Khān as Sūr N Iraq 36.28N 41.36E
145 T8 Khān Āzād C Iraq 33.07N 44.21E
160 N13 Khandaparha prev. Khandpara. Orissa, E India 20.15N 85.10E
Khandpara see Khandaparha
155 T2 Khandūd var. Khandud, Wakhan. Badakhshān, NE Afghanistan 36.57N 72.19E
160 G11 Khandwa Madhya Pradesh, C India 21.49N 76.22E
126 Mm10 Khandyga Respublika Sakha (Yakutiya), NE Russian Federation 62.39N 135.30E
155 T10 Khānewāl Punjab, NE Pakistan 30.18N 71.55E
155 S10 Khāngarh Punjab, E Pakistan 29.56N 71.10E
Khanh Hung see Soc Trăng
Khaniá see Chaniá
Khanka see Khonqa
169 Z8 Khanka, Lake var. Hsing-k'ai Hu, Lake Hanka, Chin. Xingkai Hu, Rus. Ozero Khanka. ◎ China/Russian Federation
Khanka, Ozero see Khanka, Lake
Khankendi see Xankändi
Khanlar see Xanlar
126 Kk10 Khannya ≈ NE Russian Federation
155 S12 Khānpur Punjab, SE Pakistan 23.37N 70.40E
155 S12 Khānpur Punjab, E Pakistan 28.31N 70.30E
144 I4 Khān Shaykhūn var. Khan Sheikhun. Idlib, NW Syria 35.27N 36.37E
Khan Sheikhun see Khān Shaykhūn
151 S15 Khantau Zhambyl, S Kazakhstan 44.13N 73.47E
151 W16 Khan Tengri, Pik ▲ SE Kazakhstan 42.13N 80.13E
178 I9 Khanthabouli prev. Savannakhét. Savannakhét, S Laos 16.37N 104.48E
125 Ff10 Khanty-Mansiysk prev. Ostyako-Voguls'k. Khanty-Mansiyskiy Avtonomnyy Okrug, C Russian Federation 61.01N 69.00E
129 V8 Khanty-Mansiyskiy Avtonomnyy Okrug ◈ autonomous district C Russian Federation
145 R4 Khānūqah C Iraq 35.25N 43.15E
144 E11 Khān Yūnis var. Khān Yūnus. S Gaza Strip 31.23N 34.19E
Khān Yūnus see Khān Yūnis
Khanzi see Ghanzi
145 U5 Khān Zūr E Iraq 35.03N 45.08E
178 H10 Khao Laem Reservoir ⊡ W Thailand
126 Kk17 Khapcheranga Chitinskaya Oblast', S Russian Federation 49.46N 112.21E
131 Q12 Kharabali Astrakhanskaya Oblast', SW Russian Federation 47.28N 47.14E
159 R16 Kharagpur West Bengal, NE India 22.30N 87.19E
145 V11 Khara'ib 'Abd al Karim S Iraq 31.07N 45.33E
149 Q8 Kharānaq Yazd, C Iran 31.54N 54.21E
Kharbin see Harbin
152 H13 Khardzhagaz Akhalskiy Velayat, C Turkmenistan 37.54N 60.10E
Khārga Oasis see Great Oasis, The
160 F11 Khargon Madhya Pradesh, C India 21.49N 75.39E
155 V7 Khāriān Punjab, NE Pakistan 32.52N 73.52E
119 X8 Kharisyz'k Donets'ka Oblast', E Ukraine 48.01N 38.10E
119 V5 Kharkiv Rus. Khar'kov. Kharkivs'ka Oblast', NE Ukraine 50.00N 36.14E
119 V5 Kharkiv ✈ Kharkivs'ka Oblast', E Ukraine 49.54N 36.20E
Kharkiv see Kharkivs'ka Oblast'
119 U5 Kharkivs'ka Oblast' var. Kharkiv, Rus. Khar'kovskaya Oblast'. ◈ province E Ukraine
Khar'kov see Kharkiv
Khar'kovskaya Oblast' see Kharkivs'ka Oblast'
128 L3 Kharlovka Murmanskaya Oblast', NW Russian Federation 68.47N 37.09E
116 K11 Kharmanli Khaskovo, S Bulgaria 41.55N 25.54E
116 K11 Kharmanliyska Reka ≈ S Bulgaria
128 M13 Kharovsk Vologodskaya Oblast', NW Russian Federation 59.57N 40.05E
82 F9 Khartoum var. El Khartûm, Khartum. ● (Sudan) Khartoum, C Sudan 15.33N 32.31E
82 F9 Khartoum ◈ state NE Sudan
82 F9 Khartoum ✈ Khartoum, C Sudan 15.36N 32.37E
82 F9 Khartoum North Khartoum, C Sudan 15.37N 32.33E
119 X8 Khartsyz'k Rus. Khartsyzsk. Donets'ka Oblast', SE Ukraine 48.01N 38.10E
Khartsyzsk see Khartsyz'k
Khartum see Khartoum
Khasab see Al Khaṣab
127 N18 Khasan Primorskiy Kray, SE Russian Federation 42.24N 130.45E
131 P16 Khasavyurt Respublika Dagestan, SW Russian Federation 43.16N 46.33E
149 W12 Khāsh prev. Vāsht. Sīstān va Balūchestān, SE Iran 28.15N 61.11E
154 K8 Khāsh, Dasht-e Eng. Khash Desert. desert SW Afghanistan
Khash Desert see Khāsh, Dasht-e
Khashim Al Qirba/Khashm al Qirbah see Khashm el Girba
82 H9 Khashm el Girba var. Khashim Al Qirba, Khashm al Qirbah. Kassala, E Sudan 15.00N 35.59E
144 G14 Khashsh, Jabal al ▲ S Jordan
143 S10 Khashuri C Georgia 41.59N 43.36E
159 V13 Khāsi Hills hill range NE India
116 K11 Khaskovo Khaskovo, S Bulgaria 41.56N 25.34E
116 K11 Khaskovo ◈ province S Bulgaria
126 J7 Khatanga Taymyrskiy (Dolgano-Nenetskiy) Avtonomnyy Okrug, N Russian Federation 71.55N 102.17E
126 J7 Khatanga ≈ N Russian Federation
Khatanga, Gulf of see Khatangskiy Zaliv
126 Jj6 Khatangskiy Zaliv var. Gulf of Khatanga. bay N Russian Federation
147 W7 Khatmat al Malāḥah N Oman 24.56N 56.22E
149 S16 Khaṭmat al Malāḥah Ash Shāriqah, E UAE
127 Q6 Khatyrka Chukotskiy Avtonomnyy Okrug, NE Russian Federation 62.03N 175.09E
152 I14 Khauz-Khan Turkm. Hanhowuz. Akhalskiy Velayat, S Turkmenistan 37.15N 61.12E
152 I14 Khauzkhanskoye Vodokhranilishche ⊡ S Turkmenistan
Khavaling see Khovaling
Khavast see Khowos
145 W10 Khawrah, Nahr al ≈ S Iraq
Khawr Barakah see Baraka
147 W7 Khawr Fakkān var. Khor Fakkan. Ash Shāriqah, NE UAE 25.21N 56.19E
146 L6 Khaybar Al Madīnah, NW Saudi Arabia 25.52N 39.15E
Khaybar, Kowtal-e see Khyber Pass
153 S11 Khaydarkan var. Khaydarken. Oshskaya Oblast', SW Kyrgyzstan 39.56N 71.16E
Khaydarken see Khaydarkan
129 U2 Khaypudyrskaya Guba bay NW Russian Federation
145 S1 Khayrūzuk E Iraq 36.58N 44.19E
Khazar, Baḥr-e/Khazar, Daryā-ye see Caspian Sea
Khazarosp see Hazorasp
Khazretishi, Khrebet see Hazratishoh, Qatorkŭhi
Khelat see Kālat
76 F6 Khemisset NW Morocco 33.52N 6.04W
178 J10 Khemmarat var. Kemarat. Ubon Ratchathani, E Thailand 16.03N 105.10E
76 L6 Khenchela var. Khenchla. NE Algeria 35.22N 7.09E
Khenchla see Khenchela
76 G7 Khénifra C Morocco 32.59N 5.37W
Khersān, Rūd-e see Garm, Āb-e
119 R10 Kherson Khersons'ka Oblast', S Ukraine 46.39N 32.37E
Kherson see Khersons'ka Oblast'
119 S14 Khersones, Mys Rus. Mys Khersonesskiy. headland S Ukraine 44.34N 33.24E
Khersonesskiy, Mys see Khersones, Mys
119 R10 Khersons'ka Oblast' var. Kherson, Rus. Khersonskaya Oblast'. ◈ province S Ukraine
Khersonskaya Oblast' see Khersons'ka Oblast'
126 J7 Kheta Taymyrskiy (Dolgano-Nenetskiy) Avtonomnyy Okrug, N Russian Federation 71.33N 99.40E
126 J7 Kheta ≈ N Russian Federation
178 Jj8 Khe Ve Quang Binh, C Vietnam 17.52N 105.49E
155 U7 Khewra Punjab, E Pakistan 32.40N 73.04E
Khiam see El Khiyam
128 J4 Khibiny ▲ NW Russian Federation
126 K16 Khilok Chitinskaya Oblast', S Russian Federation 51.26N 110.25E
126 K16 Khilok ≈ S Russian Federation
130 K3 Khimki Moskovskaya Oblast', W Russian Federation 55.57N 37.48E
153 S12 Khingov Rus. Obi-Khingou. ≈ C Tajikistan
Khíos see Chíos
155 R15 Khipro Sind, SE Pakistan 25.50N 69.18E
145 S10 Khirr, Wādī al dry watercourse S Iraq
116 I10 Khisarya Plovdiv, C Bulgaria 42.33N 24.43E
Khiva see Khiwa
152 H9 Khiwa Rus. Khiva. Khorazm Wiloyati, W Uzbekistan 41.22N 60.21E
178 H9 Khlong Khlung Kamphaeng Phet, W Thailand 16.15N 99.41E
178 Gg16 Khlong Thom Krabi, SW Thailand 7.55N 99.09E
178 I12 Khlung Chantaburi, S Thailand 12.25N 102.12E
Khmel'nik see Khmil'nyk
Khmel'nitskaya Oblast' see Khmel'nyts'ka Oblast'
Khmel'nitskiy see Khmel'nyts'kyy
118 K5 Khmel'nyts'ka Oblast' var. Khmel'nyts'kyy, Rus. Khmel'nitskaya Oblast'; prev. Kamenets-Podol'skaya Oblast'. ◈ province NW Ukraine
118 L6 Khmel'nyts'kyy Rus. Khmel'nitskiy; prev. Proskurov. Khmel'nyts'ka Oblast', W Ukraine 49.24N 26.59E
Khmel'nyts'kyy see Khmel'nyts'ka Oblast'
118 M6 Khmil'nyk Rus. Khmel'nik. Vinnyts'ka Oblast', C Ukraine 49.36N 27.59E
143 R9 Khobi W Georgia 42.20N 41.54E
121 P15 Khodasy Rus. Khodosy. Mahilyowskaya Voblasts', E Belarus 53.56N 31.28E
118 I6 Khodoriv Pol. Chodorów, Rus. Khodorov. L'vivs'ka Oblast', NW Ukraine 49.19N 24.19E
Khodorov see Khodoriv
Khodosy see Khodasy
152 D12 Khodzhakala Turkm. Hojagala. Balkanskiy Velayat, W Turkmenistan 38.46N 56.14E
152 M13 Khodzhambas Turkm. Hojambaz. Lebapskiy Velayat, E Turkmenistan 38.11N 64.33E
Khodzhent see Khŭjand
Khodzheyli see Khŭjayli
Khoi see Khvoy
Khojend see Khŭjand
Khokand see Qŭqon
130 L8 Khokhol'skiy Voronezhskaya Oblast', W Russian Federation 51.33N 38.43E
178 Hh10 Khok Samrong Lop Buri, C Thailand 15.03N 100.43E
155 P2 Kholm var. Tashqurghan, Pash. Khulm. Balkh, N Afghanistan 36.42N 67.40E
128 H15 Kholm Novgorodskaya Oblast', W Russian Federation 57.10N 31.06E
Kholm see Chełm
Kholmech' see Kholmyech
127 Oo16 Kholmsk Ostrov Sakhalin, Sakhalinskaya Oblast', SE Russian Federation 46.57N 142.10E
121 O19 Kholmyech Rus. Kholmech'. Homyel'skaya Voblasts', SE Belarus 52.09N 30.37E
Kholon see Ḥolon
Kholopenichi see Khalopyenichy
85 D19 Khomas ◈ district C Namibia
85 D19 Khomas Hochland var. Khomasplato. plateau C Namibia
Khomasplato see Khomas Hochland
Khomein see Khomeyn
148 M7 Khomeyn var. Khomein, Khumain. Markazī, W Iran 33.37N 50.03E
149 N8 Khomeynīshahr prev. Homāyūnshahr. Eşfahān, C Iran 32.39N 51.34E
Khoms see Al Khums
Khong Sedone see Muang Khôngxédôn
178 Ii9 Khon Kaen var. Muang Khon Kaen. Khon Kaen, E Thailand 16.25N 102.49E
152 I9 Khonqa Rus. Khanka. Khorazm Wiloyati, W Uzbekistan 41.31N 60.39E
178 I9 Khon San Khon Kaen, E Thailand 16.40N 101.51E
127 N8 Khonuu Respublika Sakha (Yakutiya), NE Russian Federation 66.24N 143.15E
131 N8 Khopër var. Khoper. ≈ SW Russian Federation
127 Nn16 Khor Khabarovskiy Kray, SE Russian Federation 47.43N 134.48E
127 Nn16 Khor ≈ SE Russian Federation
149 S6 Khorāsān off. Ostān-e Khorāsān, var. Khorassan, Khurasan. ◈ province NE Iran
Khorassan see Khorāsān
Khorat see Nakhon Ratchasima
152 H9 Khorazm Wiloyati Rus. Khorezmskaya Oblast'. ◈ province W Uzbekistan
160 O13 Khordha prev. Khurda. Orissa, E India 20.13N 85.39E
129 U4 Khorey-Ver Nenetskiy Avtonomnyy Okrug, NW Russian Federation 67.25N 58.05E
Khorezmskaya Oblast' see Khorazm Wiloyati
Khor Fakkan see Khawr Fakkān
151 W15 Khorgos Almaty, SE Kazakhstan 44.13N 80.22E
126 K16 Khorinsk Respublika Buryatiya, S Russian Federation 52.13N 109.52E
85 C18 Khorixas Kunene, NW Namibia 20.22S 14.55E
147 O17 Khormaksar var. Aden. ✈ ('Aden) SW Yemen 12.56N 45.00E
Khormal see Khurmāl
Khormuj see Khvormūj
Khorog see Khorugh
119 S5 Khorol Poltavs'ka Oblast', NE Ukraine 49.49N 33.16E
148 L7 Khorramābād var. Khurramabad. Lorestān, W Iran 33.28N 48.21E
148 K10 Khorramshahr var. Khurramshahr, Muhammerah; prev. Mohammerah. Khūzestān, SW Iran 30.29N 48.09E
153 S14 Khorugh Rus. Khorog. S Tajikistan 37.29N 71.31E
131 Q12 Khosheutovo Astrakhanskaya Oblast', SW Russian Federation 47.04N 47.49E
Khotan see Hotan
Khorvot Khalutsa see Ḥorvot Ḥaluẓa
Khotimsk see Khotsimsk
Khotin see Khotyn
121 R16 Khotsimsk Rus. Khotimsk. Mahilyowskaya Voblasts', E Belarus 53.24N 32.34E
118 K7 Khotyn Rom. Hotin, Rus. Khotin. Chernivets'ka Oblast', W Ukraine 48.29N 26.30E
76 F7 Khouribga C Morocco 32.54N 6.51W
153 Q13 Khovaling Rus. Khavaling. SW Tajikistan 38.22N 69.54E
Khovd see Hovd
153 P11 Khowos var. Ursat'yevskaya, Rus. Khavast. Sirdaryo Wiloyati, E Uzbekistan 40.14N 68.46E
155 R6 Khowst Paktīā, E Afghanistan 33.22N 69.57E
Khoy see Khvoy
121 N20 Khoyniki Rus. Khoyniki. Homyel'skaya Voblasts', SE Belarus 51.53N 29.58E
Khozretishi, Khrebet see Hazratishoh, Qatorkŭhi
Khrisoúpolis see Chrysoúpoli
126 Mm6 Khroma ≈ NE Russian Federation
150 J10 Khromtau Kaz. Khromtaū. Aktyubinsk, W Kazakhstan 50.14N 58.22E
Khrysokhou Bay see Chrysochoú, Kólpos
119 O7 Khrystynivka Cherkas'ka Oblast', C Ukraine 48.49N 29.55E
178 J10 Khuang Nai Ubon Ratchathani, E Thailand 15.22N 104.33E
Khudal see Khādhil
Khudat see Xudat
155 W9 Khudiān Punjab, E Pakistan 30.58N 74.19E
Khudzhand see Khŭjand
153 O13 Khufar Surkhondaryo Wiloyati, S Uzbekistan 38.31N 67.45E
85 G21 Khuis Kgalagadi, SW Botswana 26.37S 21.50E
153 Q11 Khŭjand var. Khodzhent, Khojend, Rus. Khudzhand; prev. Leninabad, Taj. Leninobod. N Tajikistan 40.16N 69.37E
152 H8 Khŭjayli Rus. Khodzheyli. Qoraqalpogʻiston Respublikasi, W Uzbekistan 42.23N 59.27E
178 Ii11 Khukhan Si Sa Ket, E Thailand 14.38N 104.12E
Khulm see Kholm
159 T16 Khulna Khulna, SW Bangladesh 22.48N 89.31E
159 T16 Khulna ◈ division SW Bangladesh
Khumain see Khomeyn
Khums see Al Khums
155 W2 Khunjerāb Pass Chin. Kunjirap Daban. pass China/Pakistan see also Kunjirap Daban 36.46N 75.16E
159 P16 Khunti Bihār, N India 23.01N 85.19E
178 Gg7 Khun Yuam Mae Hong Son, NW Thailand 18.54N 97.54E
Khurais see Khurayş
Khurasan see Khorāsān
147 R7 Khurayş var. Khurais. Ash Sharqīyah, C Saudi Arabia 25.06N 48.02E
Khurda see Khordha
158 J11 Khurja Uttar Pradesh, N India 28.15N 77.51E
145 V4 Khurmāl var. Khormal. NE Iraq 35.19N 46.06E
Khurramabad see Khorramābād
Khurramshahr see Khorramshahr
155 U7 Khushāb Punjab, NE Pakistan 32.16N 72.18E
118 H8 Khust Cz. Chust, Husté, Hung. Huszt. Zakarpats'ka Oblast', W Ukraine 48.10N 23.19E
82 D11 Khuwei Western Kordofan, C Sudan 13.01N 29.13E
155 O13 Khuzdār Baluchistān, SW Pakistan 27.49N 66.33E
148 L9 Khūzestān off. Ostān-e Khūzestān, var. Khuzistan; prev. Arabistan, anc. Susiana. ◈ province SW Iran
126 Jj15 Khuzhir Respublika Buryatiya, S Russian Federation 53.10N 107.18E
Khuzistan see Khūzestān
155 R2 Khvājeh Ghār var. Khwajaghar, Khwaja-i-Ghar. Takhār, NE Afghanistan 37.05N 69.28E
131 Q7 Khvalynsk Saratovskaya Oblast', W Russian Federation 52.30N 48.06E
149 N12 Khvormūj var. Khormuj. Būshehr, S Iran 28.32N 51.22E
148 I2 Khvoy var. Khoi, Khoy. Āżarbāyjān-e Bākhtarī, NW Iran 38.36N 45.03E
Khwajaghar/Khwaja-i-Ghar see Khvājeh Ghār
155 S5 Khyber Pass var. Kowtal-e Khaybar. pass Afghanistan/Pakistan 34.07N 71.05E
195 V14 Kia Santa Isabel, N Solomon Islands 7.34S 158.31E
191 S10 Kiama New South Wales, SE Australia 34.40S 150.49E
179 R17 Kiamba Mindanao, S Philippines 5.59N 124.36E
81 O22 Kiambi Katanga, SE Dem. Rep. Congo (Zaire) 7.15S 28.01E
29 Q12 Kiamichi Mountains ▲ Oklahoma, C USA
29 Q12 Kiamichi River ≈ Oklahoma, C USA
12 M10 Kiamika, Réservoir ⊡ Quebec, SE Canada
Kiamusze see Jiamusi
41 N7 Kiana Alaska, USA 66.58N 160.25W
Kiangmai see Chiang Mai
Kiang-ning see Nanjing
Kiangsi see Jiangxi
Kiangsu see Jiangsu
95 M14 Kiantajärvi ◎ E Finland
117 F19 Kiáto prev. Kiáton. Pelopónnisos, S Greece 38.01N 22.45E
Kiáton see Kiáto
Kiayi see Chiai
69 T9 Kibali var. Uele (upper course). ≈ NE Dem. Rep. Congo (Zaire)
81 E20 Kibangou Le Niari, SW Congo 3.27S 12.21E
Kibarty see Kybartai
94 M8 Kiberg Finnmark, N Norway 70.17N 30.47E
97 F22 Kibæk Ringkøbing, W Denmark 56.03N 8.52E
81 N20 Kibombo Maniema, E Dem. Rep. Congo (Zaire) 3.52S 25.59E
83 E20 Kibondo Kigoma, NW Tanzania 3.34S 30.40E
83 J15 Kibre Mengist var. Adola. Oromo, C Ethiopia 5.50N 39.06E
Kıbrıs/Kıbrıs Cumhuriyeti see Cyprus
83 E20 Kibungo var. Kibungu. SE Rwanda 2.09S 30.30E
Kibungu see Kibungo
115 N19 Kičevo SW FYR Macedonia 41.31N 20.57E
129 P13 Kichmengskiy Gorodok Vologodskaya Oblast', NW Russian Federation 60.00N 45.52E
32 J8 Kickapoo River ≈ Wisconsin, N USA
9 P16 Kicking Horse Pass pass Alberta/British Columbia, SW Canada 51.27N 116.13W
79 R9 Kidal Kidal, C Mali 18.22N 1.21E
79 Q8 Kidal ◈ region NE Mali
179 R16 Kidapawan Mindanao, S Philippines 7.02N 125.04E
99 L20 Kidderminster C England, UK 52.22N 2.13W
78 I11 Kidira E Senegal 14.27N 12.18W
192 O11 Kidnappers, Cape headland North Island, NZ 41.13S 175.15E
102 J8 Kiel Schleswig-Holstein, N Germany 54.21N 10.04E
113 L15 Kielce Rus. Keltsy. Świętokrzyskie, C Poland 50.52N 20.39E
102 K7 Kieler Bucht bay N Germany
102 J7 Kieler Förde inlet N Germany
178 K13 Kiên Đưc var. Đak Lap. Đăc Lăc, S Vietnam 11.59N 107.30E
81 N24 Kienge Katanga, SE Dem. Rep. Congo (Zaire) 10.33S 27.33E
195 S12 Kieta Bougainville Island, NE PNG 6.13S 155.39E
102 Q12 Kietz Brandenburg, NE Germany 52.33N 14.36E
Kiev see Kyyiv
Kiev Reservoir see Kyyivs'ke Vodoskhovyshche
78 J10 Kiffa Assaba, S Mauritania 16.37N 11.22W
117 H19 Kifisiá Attikí, C Greece 38.04N 23.49E
117 F18 Kifisós ≈ C Greece
145 U5 Kifri N Iraq 34.43N 44.58E
83 D20 Kigali ● (Rwanda) C Rwanda 1.58S 30.02E
83 E20 Kigali ✈ C Rwanda 1.43S 30.01E
143 P13 Kiğı Bingöl, E Turkey 39.19N 40.19E
83 E21 Kigoma Kigoma, W Tanzania 4.52S 29.36E
83 E21 Kigoma ◈ region W Tanzania
40 F10 Kihei Haw. Kīhei. Maui, Hawaii, USA, C Pacific Ocean 20.47N 156.28W
95 K17 Kihniö Länsi-Suomi, W Finland 62.10N 23.10E
120 F6 Kihnu var. Kihnu Saar, Ger. Kühnö. island SW Estonia
Kihnu Saar see Kihnu
40 A8 Kii Landing Niihau, Hawaii, USA, C Pacific Ocean 21.58N 160.03W
95 L14 Kiiminki Oulu, C Finland 65.05N 25.46E
171 H16 Kii-Nagashima var. Nagashima. Mie, Honshū, SW Japan 34.10N 136.18E
171 Gg16 Kii-sanchi ▲ Honshū, SW Japan
94 L11 Kiistala Lappi, N Finland 67.52N 25.19E
170 Ff16 Kii-suidō strait S Japan
172 R14 Kikai-shima var. Kikaiga-shima. island Nansei-shotō, SW Japan
114 M8 Kikinda Ger. Grosskikinda, Hung. Nagykikinda; prev. Velika Kikinda. Serbia, N Yugoslavia 45.48N 20.29E
Kikládhes see Kykládes
172 N7 Kikonai Hokkaidō, NE Japan 41.40N 140.25E
194 H14 Kikori Gulf, S PNG 7.31S 144.16E
194 G13 Kikori ≈ W PNG
170 Cc14 Kikuchi var. Kikuti. Kumamoto, Kyūshū, SW Japan 33.00N 130.49E
Kikuti see Kikuchi
131 N8 Kikvidze Volgogradskaya Oblast', SW Russian Federation 50.47N 42.58E
12 I10 Kikwissi, Lac ◎ Quebec, SE Canada
81 I21 Kikwit Bandundu, W Dem. Rep. Congo (Zaire) 4.59S 18.53E
97 K15 Kil Värmland, C Sweden 59.30N 13.19E
96 N12 Kilafors Gävleborg, C Sweden 61.13N 16.34E
40 B8 Kilauea Haw. Kīlauea. Kauai, Hawaii, USA, C Pacific Ocean 22.12N 159.24W
40 H12 Kilauea Caldera crater Hawaii, USA, C Pacific Ocean 19.25N 155.16W
111 V4 Kilb Niederösterreich, C Austria 48.06N 15.21E
41 O12 Kilbuck Mountains ▲ Alaska, USA
169 Y12 Kilchu NE North Korea 40.57N 129.22E
99 F18 Kilcock Ir. Cill Choca. E Ireland 53.25N 6.40W
191 V2 Kilcoy Queensland, E Australia 26.58S 152.30E
99 F18 Kildare Ir. Cill Dara. E Ireland 53.10N 6.55W
99 F18 Kildare Ir. Cill Dara. cultural region E Ireland
128 K2 Kil'din, Ostrov island NW Russian Federation
27 W7 Kilgore Texas, SW USA 32.23N 94.52W
Kilien Mountains see Qilian Shan
116 K9 Kilifarevo Veliko Tŭrnovo, N Bulgaria 43.00N 25.36E
83 K20 Kilifi Coast, SE Kenya 3.37S 39.49E
201 U9 Kili Island var. Kōle. island Ralik Chain, S Marshall Islands
155 V2 Kilik Pass pass Afghanistan/China 37.03N 74.31E
Kilimane see Quelimane
83 I21 Kilimanjaro ◈ region E Tanzania
83 I20 Kilimanjaro var. Uhuru Peak. ▲ NE Tanzania 3.01S 37.14E
Kilimbangara see Kolombangara
Kilinailau Islands see Tulun Islands
83 K23 Kilindoni Pwani, E Tanzania 7.55S 39.40E
120 H6 Kilingi-Nõmme Ger. Kurkund. Pärnumaa, SW Estonia 58.07N 24.00E
142 M17 Kilis Kilis, S Turkey 36.43N 37.07E
142 M16 Kilis ◈ province S Turkey
119 N12 Kiliya Rom. Chilia-Nouă. Odes'ka Oblast', SW Ukraine 45.29N 29.16E
99 B19 Kilkee Ir. Cill Chaoi. W Ireland 52.40N 9.37W
99 E19 Kilkenny Ir. Cill Chainnigh. S Ireland 52.39N 7.15W
99 E19 Kilkenny Ir. Cill Chainnigh. cultural region S Ireland
99 B18 Kilkieran Bay Ir. Cuan Chill Chiaráin. bay W Ireland
116 G13 Kilkís Kentrikí Makedonía, N Greece 40.59N 22.54E
99 C15 Killala Bay Ir. Cuan Chill Ala. inlet NW Ireland
9 R15 Killam Alberta, SW Canada 52.45N 111.46W
191 U3 Killarney Queensland, E Australia 28.18S 152.15E
9 W17 Killarney Manitoba, S Canada 49.12N 99.40W
12 E11 Killarney Ontario, S Canada 45.58N 81.27W
99 B20 Killarney Ir. Cill Airne. SW Ireland 52.03N 9.30W
30 K4 Killdeer North Dakota, N USA 47.21N 102.45W
30 J4 Killdeer Mountains ▲ North Dakota, N USA
47 V15 Killdeer River ≈ Trinidad, Trinidad and Tobago
27 S9 Killeen Texas, SW USA 31.07N 97.43W
41 P6 Killik River ≈ Alaska, USA
16 P4 Killinek Island island Nunavut, NE Canada
Killini see Kyllíni
117 C19 Killinis, Akrotírio headland S Greece 37.55N 21.07E
99 D15 Killybegs Ir. Na Cealla Beaga. NW Ireland 54.37N 8.27W
Kilmain see Quelimane
98 I13 Kilmarnock W Scotland, UK 55.37N 4.30W
23 X6 Kilmarnock Virginia, NE USA 37.42N 76.22W
129 S16 Kil'mez' Kirovskaya Oblast', NW Russian Federation 56.55N 51.03E
131 S2 Kil'mez' Udmurtskaya Respublika, NW Russian Federation 57.04N 51.22E
129 R16 Kil'mez' ≈ NW Russian Federation
69 V11 Kilombero ≈ S Tanzania
94 J10 Kilpisjarvi Lappi, N Finland 69.03N 20.49E
99 B19 Kilrush Ir. Cill Rois. W Ireland 52.39N 9.28W
81 O24 Kilwa Katanga, SE Dem. Rep. Congo (Zaire) 9.22S 28.19E
Kilwa see Kilwa Kivinje
83 J24 Kilwa Kivinje var. Kilwa. Lindi, SE Tanzania 8.45S 39.21E
83 J24 Kilwa Masoko Lindi, SE Tanzania 8.55S 39.31E
176 Uu11 Kilwo Pulau Seram, E Indonesia 3.36S 130.48E
116 P12 Kilyos İstanbul, NW Turkey 41.15N 29.01E
39 V8 Kim Colorado, C USA 37.12N 103.22W
175 N3 Kimanis, Teluk bay Sabah, East Malaysia
190 H8 Kimba South Australia 33.09S 136.26E
30 I15 Kimball Nebraska, C USA 41.16N 103.40W
31 O11 Kimball South Dakota, N USA 43.45N 98.57W
81 I21 Kimbao Bandundu, SW Dem. Rep. Congo (Zaire) 5.27S 17.40E
195 N12 Kimbe New Britain, E PNG 5.36S 150.10E
195 N11 Kimbe Bay inlet New Britain, E PNG
9 P17 Kimberley British Columbia, SW Canada 49.40N 115.58W
85 H23 Kimberley Northern Cape, C South Africa 28.45S 24.46E
188 M4 Kimberley Plateau plateau Western Australia
35 P15 Kimberly Idaho, NW USA 42.31N 114.21W
169 Y12 Kimch'aek prev. Sŏngjin. E North Korea 40.42N 129.12E
169 Y15 Kimch'ŏn C South Korea 36.08N 128.06E
169 Z16 Kim Hae var. Pusan. ✈ (Pusan) SE South Korea 35.10N 128.57E
Kími see Kými
95 K20 Kimito Swe. Kemiö. Länsi-Suomi, W Finland 60.10N 22.45E
172 O6 Kimobetsu Hokkaidō, NE Japan 42.47N 140.55E
117 I21 Kímolos island Kykládes, Greece, Aegean Sea
117 I21 Kimolou Sifnou, Stenó strait Kykládes, Greece, Aegean Sea
130 L5 Kimovsk Tul'skaya Oblast', W Russian Federation 53.59N 38.34E
169 X15 Kimpo ✈ (Sŏul) NW South Korea 37.37N 126.42E
Kimpolung see Câmpulung Moldovenesc
128 K16 Kimry Tverskaya Oblast', W Russian Federation 56.52N 37.21E
81 H21 Kimvula Bas-Congo, SW Dem. Rep. Congo (Zaire) 5.38S 15.51E
175 Nn2 Kinabalu, Gunung ▲ East Malaysia 5.52N 116.08E
Kinabatangan see Kinabatangan, Sungai
175 Oo3 Kinabatangan, Sungai var. Kinabatangan. ≈ East Malaysia
117 L21 Kínaros island Kykládes, Greece, Aegean Sea
9 O15 Kinbasket Lake ⊡ British Columbia, SW Canada
98 I7 Kinbrace N Scotland, UK 58.16N 2.59W
12 E14 Kincardine Ontario, S Canada 44.10N 81.35W
98 K10 Kincardine cultural region E Scotland, UK
81 K21 Kinda Kasai Occidental, SE Dem. Rep. Congo (Zaire) 4.48S 21.49E
81 M24 Kinda Katanga, SE Dem. Rep. Congo (Zaire) 9.19S 25.06E
177 Ff3 Kindat Sagaing, N Burma 23.42N 94.28E
111 V6 Kindberg Steiermark, C Austria 47.31N 15.27E
24 H8 Kinder Louisiana, S USA 30.29N 92.51W
100 H13 Kinderdijk Zuid-Holland, SW Netherlands 51.52N 4.37E
99 M17 Kinder Scout ▲ C England, UK 53.25N 1.52W
9 S16 Kindersley Saskatchewan, S Canada 51.28N 109.08W
78 I14 Kindia Guinée-Maritime, SW Guinea 10.12N 12.26W
66 B11 Kindley Field air base E Bermuda
31 R6 Kindred North Dakota, N USA 46.39N 97.01W
81 N20 Kindu prev. Kindu-Port-Empain. Maniema, C Dem. Rep. Congo (Zaire) 2.57S 25.54E
Kindu-Port-Empain see Kindu
131 S6 Kinel' Samarskaya Oblast', W Russian Federation 53.14N 50.40E
129 N15 Kineshma Ivanovskaya Oblast', W Russian Federation 57.28N 42.07E
King see King William's Town
146 K10 King Abdul Aziz ✈ (Makkah) Makkah, W Saudi Arabia 21.44N 39.08E
23 X6 King and Queen Court House Virginia, NE USA 37.40N 76.49W
King Charles Islands see Kong Karls Land
King Christian IX Land see Kong Christian IX Land
King Christian X Land see Kong Christian X Land
37 O11 King City California, W USA 36.12N 121.09W
29 R2 King City Missouri, C USA 40.03N 94.31W
40 M16 King Cove Alaska, USA 55.03N 162.19W
28 M10 Kingfisher Oklahoma, C USA 35.49N 97.56W
King Frederik VI Coast see Kong Frederik VI Kyst
King Frederik VIII Land see Kong Frederik VIII Land
67 B24 King George Bay bay West Falkland, Falkland Islands
204 G3 King George Island var. King George Land. island South Shetland Islands, Antarctica
10 I6 King George Islands island group Nunavut, C Canada
King George Land see King George Island
128 G13 Kingisepp Leningradskaya Oblast', NW Russian Federation 59.23N 28.37E
191 N14 King Island island Tasmania, SE Australia
8 J15 King Island island British Columbia, SW Canada
King Island see Kadan Kyun
Kingissepp see Kuressaare
147 Q7 King Khalid ✈ (Ar Riyāḍ) Ar Riyāḍ, C Saudi Arabia 25.00N 46.40E
37 S2 King Lear Peak ▲ Nevada, W USA 41.13N 118.30W
205 Y8 King Leopold and Queen Astrid Land physical region Antarctica
188 M4 King Leopold Ranges ▲ Western Australia
38 I11 Kingman Arizona, SW USA 35.12N 114.02W
28 M6 Kingman Kansas, C USA 37.39N 98.06W
199 K7 Kingman Reef ◇ US territory C Pacific Ocean
81 N20 Kingombe Maniema, E Dem. Rep. Congo (Zaire) 2.37S 26.39E
190 F5 Kingoonya South Australia 30.56S 135.20E
204 J10 King Peninsula peninsula Antarctica
41 P13 King Salmon Alaska, USA 58.41N 156.39W
37 Q6 Kings Beach California, W USA 39.13N 120.02W
37 R11 Kingsburg California, W USA 36.30N 119.33W
190 I10 Kingscote South Australia 35.41S 137.36E
King's County see Offaly
204 H2 King Sejong South Korean research station Antarctica 61.57S 58.23W
191 T9 Kingsford Smith ✈ (Sydney) New South Wales, SE Australia 33.58S 151.09E
9 P17 Kingsgate British Columbia, SW Canada 48.58N 116.09W
25 W8 Kingsland Georgia, SE USA 30.48N 81.41W
31 S13 Kingsley Iowa, C USA 42.35N 95.58W
99 O19 King's Lynn var. Bishop's Lynn, Kings Lynn, Lynn, Lynn Regis. E England, UK 52.45N 0.24E
23 Q10 Kings Mountain North Carolina, SE USA 35.15N 81.20W
188 K4 King Sound sound Western Australia
39 N2 Kings Peak ▲ Utah, W USA 40.43N 110.27W
23 O8 Kingsport Tennessee, S USA 36.32N 82.31W
37 R11 Kings River ≈ California, W USA
191 P17 Kingston Tasmania, SE Australia 42.58S 147.18E
12 K14 Kingston Ontario, SE Canada 44.13N 76.30W

◆ Country ● Country Capital ◇ Dependent Territory ○ Dependent Territory Capital ◈ Administrative Region ✈ International Airport ▲ Mountain ▲ Mountain Range Volcano ≈ River ◎ Lake ⊡ Reservoir

KINGSTON – KOGALYM

46 K13 **Kingston** ● (Jamaica) E Jamaica 17.58N 76.48W
193 C22 **Kingston** Otago, South Island, NZ 45.20S 168.45E
21 P12 **Kingston** Massachusetts, NE USA 41.59N 70.43W
29 S3 **Kingston** Missouri, C USA 39.36N 94.02W
20 K12 **Kingston** New York, NE USA 41.55N 74.00W
33 S14 **Kingston** Ohio, N USA 39.28N 82.54W
21 O13 **Kingston** Rhode Island, NE USA 41.28N 71.31W
22 M9 **Kingston** Tennessee, S USA 35.52N 84.30W
37 W12 **Kingston Peak** ▲ California, W USA 35.43N 115.54W
190 J11 **Kingston Southeast** South Australia 36.51S 139.53E
99 N17 **Kingston upon Hull** *var.* Hull. E England, UK 53.45N 0.19W
99 N22 **Kingston upon Thames** SE England, UK 51.25N 0.18W
47 P14 **Kingstown** ● (Saint Vincent and the Grenadines) Saint Vincent, Saint Vincent and the Grenadines 13.09N 61.13W
Kingstown *see* Dún Laoghaire
23 T13 **Kingstree** South Carolina, SE USA 33.40N 79.49W
66 L8 **Kings Trough** *undersea feature* E Atlantic Ocean
12 C18 **Kingsville** Ontario, S Canada 42.03N 82.43W
27 S15 **Kingsville** Texas, SW USA 27.31N 97.52W
23 W6 **King William** Virginia, NE USA 37.42N 77.03W
15 K3 **King William Island** *island* Nunavut, N Canada Arctic Ocean
85 I25 **King William's Town** *var.* King, Kingwilliamstown. Eastern Cape, S South Africa 32.51S 27.20E
23 T3 **Kingwood** West Virginia, NE USA 39.28N 79.40W
142 C13 **Kınık** İzmir, W Turkey 39.04N 27.25E
81 G21 **Kinkala** Le Pool, S Congo 4.18S 14.49E
171 Mm14 **Kinka-san** *headland* Honshū, C Japan 38.17N 141.34E
192 M8 **Kinleith** Waikato, North Island, NZ 38.16S 175.53E
97 J19 **Kinna** Västra Götaland, S Sweden 57.31N 12.42E
98 L8 **Kinnaird Head** *var.* Kinnairds Head. *headland* NE Scotland, UK 58.39N 3.22W
97 K20 **Kinnared** Halland, S Sweden 57.01N 13.04E
Kinneret, Yam *see* Tiberias, Lake
161 K24 **Kinniyai** Eastern Province, NE Sri Lanka 8.30N 81.10E
95 L16 **Kinnula** Länsi-Suomi, W Finland 63.24N 25.00E
12 I8 **Kinojévis** ≈ Quebec, SE Canada
170 G16 **Kino-kawa** ≈ Honshū, SW Japan
9 U11 **Kinoosao** Saskatchewan, C Canada 57.06N 101.01W
101 L17 **Kinrooi** Limburg, NE Belgium 51.09N 5.47E
98 J11 **Kinross** C Scotland, UK 56.13N 3.26W
98 J11 **Kinross** *cultural region* C Scotland, UK
99 C21 **Kinsale** *Ir.* Cionn tSáile. SW Ireland 51.42N 8.31W
97 D14 **Kinsarvik** Hordaland, S Norway 60.22N 6.43E
81 G21 **Kinshasa** *prev.* Léopoldville. ● (Zaire) Kinshasa, W Dem. Rep. Congo (Zaire) 4.21S 15.16E
81 G21 **Kinshasa** *off.* Ville de Kinshasa, *var.* Kinshasa City. ◈ *region* SW Dem. Rep. Congo (Zaire)
81 G21 **Kinshasa** ✈ Kinshasa, SW Dem. Rep. Congo (Zaire) 4.23S 15.30E
Kinshasa City *see* Kinshasa
119 U9 **Kins'ka** ≈ SE Ukraine
28 K6 **Kinsley** Kansas, C USA 37.52N 99.25W
23 W10 **Kinston** North Carolina, SE USA 35.15N 77.34W
79 P15 **Kintampo** W Ghana 6.36N 0.28E
190 B1 **Kintore, Mount** ▲ South Australia 26.30S 130.24E
98 G13 **Kintyre** *peninsula* W Scotland, UK
98 G13 **Kintyre, Mull of** *headland* W Scotland, UK 55.16N 5.46W
177 G4 **Kin-u** Sagaing, C Burma 22.46N 95.36E
10 G8 **Kinushseo** ≈ Ontario, C Canada
9 P13 **Kinuso** Alberta, W Canada 55.19N 115.23W
160 I13 **Kinwat** Mahārāshtra, C India 19.37N 78.12E
83 F16 **Kinyeti** ▲ S Sudan 3.56N 32.52E
103 I17 **Kinzig** ≈ SW Germany
197 J13 **Kioa** *island* N Fiji
Kioga, Lake *see* Kyoga, Lake
28 M8 **Kiowa** Kansas, C USA 37.01N 98.29W
29 P12 **Kiowa** Oklahoma, C USA 34.43N 95.54W
Kiparissía *see* Kyparissía
12 H10 **Kipawa, Lac** ◎ Quebec, SE Canada
83 G24 **Kipengere Range** ▲▲ SW Tanzania
83 E23 **Kipili** Rukwa, W Tanzania 7.30S 30.39E
83 K20 **Kipini** Coast, SE Kenya 2.30S 40.30E
9 V16 **Kipling** Saskatchewan, S Canada 50.04N 102.45W
40 M13 **Kipnuk** Alaska, USA 59.56N 164.02W
99 F18 **Kippure** *Ir.* Cipiúr. ▲ E Ireland 53.10N 6.22W
81 N25 **Kipushi** Katanga, SE Dem. Rep. Congo (Zaire) 11.45S 27.19E
195 Y17 **Kirakira** *var.* Kaokaona. San Cristobal, SE Solomon Islands 10.28S 161.54E
161 K14 **Kirandul** *var.* Bailādila. Madhya Pradesh, C India 18.46N 81.18E
161 I21 **Kīranūr** Tamil Nādu, SE India 11.37N 79.10E
121 N21 **Kiraw** *Rus.* Kirovo. Homyel'skaya Voblasts', SE Belarus 51.30N 29.25E
121 M17 **Kirawsk** *Rus.* Kirovsk; *prev.* Startsy. Mahilyowskaya Voblasts', E Belarus 53.16N 29.28E
120 F5 **Kirbla** Läänemaa, W Estonia 58.45N 23.57E
27 Y9 **Kirbyville** Texas, SW USA 30.39N 93.53W
116 M12 **Kırcasalih** Edirne, NW Turkey 41.24N 26.48E
111 W8 **Kirchbach** *var.* Kirchbach in Steiermark. Steiermark, SE Austria 46.55N 15.40E
Kirchbach in Steiermark *see* Kirchbach
110 H7 **Kirchberg** Sankt Gallen, NE Switzerland 47.24N 9.03E
111 S5 **Kirchdorf an der Krems** Oberösterreich, N Austria 47.54N 14.06E
Kirchheim *see* Kirchheim unter Teck
103 I22 **Kirchheim unter Teck** *var.* Kirchheim. Baden-Württemberg, SW Germany 48.39N 9.27E
Kirdzhali *see* Kŭrdzhali
126 Jj14 **Kirenga** ≈ S Russian Federation
126 Jj13 **Kirensk** Irkutskaya Oblast', C Russian Federation 57.37N 107.54E
Kirghizia *see* Kyrgyzstan
151 S16 **Kirghiz Range** *Rus.* Kirgizskiy Khrebet; *prev.* Alexander Range. ▲▲ Kazakhstan/Kyrgyzstan
Kirghiz SSR *see* Kyrgyzstan
Kirghiz Steppe *see* Kazakhskiy Melkosopochnik
Kirgizskaya SSR *see* Kyrgyzstan
Kirgizskiy Khrebet *see* Kirghiz Range
81 I19 **Kiri** Bandundu, W Dem. Rep. Congo (Zaire) 1.29S 19.00E
Kiriath-Arba *see* Hebron
203 R3 **Kiribati** *off.* Republic of Kiribati. ◆ *republic* C Pacific Ocean
142 L17 **Kırıkhan** Hatay, S Turkey 36.30N 36.19E
142 I13 **Kırıkkale** Kırıkkale, C Turkey 39.50N 33.31E
142 C10 **Kırıkkale** ◈ *province* C Turkey
128 L13 **Kirillov** Vologodskaya Oblast', NW Russian Federation 59.52N 38.24E
Kirin *see* Jilin
83 I18 **Kirinyaga** *prev.* Mount Kenya. 🌋 C Kenya 0.02S 37.19E
128 H13 **Kirishi** *var.* Kirisi. Leningradskaya Oblast', NW Russian Federation 59.28N 32.02E
170 C16 **Kirishima-yama** ▲ Kyūshū, SW Japan 31.58N 130.51E
Kirisi *see* Kirishi
203 Y2 **Kiritimati** ✈ Kiritimati, E Kiribati 2.00N 157.30W
203 Y2 **Kiritimati** *prev.* Christmas Island. *atoll* Line Islands, E Kiribati
195 O15 **Kiriwina Island** *Eng.* Trobriand Island. *island* SE PNG
195 O15 **Kiriwina Islands** *var.* Trobriand Islands. *island group* S PNG
98 K12 **Kirkcaldy** E Scotland, UK 56.07N 3.10W
99 I14 **Kirkcudbright** S Scotland, UK 54.49N 4.03W
99 I14 **Kirkcudbright** *cultural region* S Scotland, UK
Kirkee *see* Khadki
94 M8 **Kirkenes** *var.* Kirkkoniemi. Finnmark, N Norway 69.43N 30.01E
97 I14 **Kirkenær** Hedmark, S Norway 60.27N 12.04E
94 J4 **Kirkjubæjarklaustur** Sudhurland, S Iceland 63.46N 18.03W
Kirk-Kilissa *see* Kırklareli
Kirkkoniemi *see* Kirkenes
95 L20 **Kirkkonummi** *Swe.* Kyrkslätt. Etelä-Suomi, S Finland 60.06N 24.25E
12 G7 **Kirkland Lake** Ontario, S Canada 48.10N 80.01W
142 C9 **Kırklareli** *prev.* Kirk-Kilissa. Kırklareli, NW Turkey 41.45N 27.12E
142 I13 **Kırklareli** ◈ *province* NW Turkey
193 F20 **Kirkliston Range** ▲▲ South Island, NZ
12 D10 **Kirkpatrick Lake** ◎ Ontario, S Canada
205 Q11 **Kirkpatrick, Mount** ▲ Antarctica 84.37S 164.36E
29 U2 **Kirksville** Missouri, C USA 40.11N 92.34W
145 T4 **Kirkūk** *var.* Karkūk, Kerkuk. N Iraq 35.28N 44.25E
145 U7 **Kir Kush** E Iraq 33.42N 45.15E
98 K5 **Kirkwall** NE Scotland, UK
85 H25 **Kirkwood** Eastern Cape, S South Africa 33.23S 25.19E
29 X5 **Kirkwood** Missouri, C USA 38.34N 90.24W
Kirman *see* Kermān
Kir Moab/Kir of Moab *see* Al Karak
130 I5 **Kirov** Kaluzhskaya Oblast', W Russian Federation 54.01N 34.16E
129 R14 **Kirov** *prev.* Vyatka. Kirovskaya Oblast', NW Russian Federation 58.34N 49.38E
Kīrov *see* Balpyk Bi, Kazakhstan
Kīrov *see* Kirova, Almaty, Kazakhstan
151 U13 **Kirova** *Kaz.* Kīrov. Almaty, SE Kazakhstan 46.24N 77.16E
Kirovabad *see* Gäncä, Azerbaijan
Kirovabad *see* Panj, Tajikistan
Kirovakan *see* Vanadzor
Kirovo *see* Kiraw, Belarus
Kirovo/Kirovograd *see* Kirovohrad, Ukraine
Kirovo *see* Beshariq, Uzbekistan
129 R14 **Kirovo-Chepetsk** Kirovskaya Oblast', NW Russian Federation 58.33N 50.06E
Kirovogradskaya Oblast'/Kirovohrad *see* Kirovohrads'ka Oblast'
119 R7 **Kirovohrad** *Rus.* Kirovograd; *prev.* Kirovo, Yelizavetgrad, Zinov'yevsk. Kirovohrads'ka Oblast', C Ukraine 48.30N 31.17E
119 P7 **Kirovohrads'ka Oblast'** *var.* Kirovohrad, *Rus.* Kirovogradskaya Oblast'. ◈ *province* C Ukraine
128 J4 **Kirovsk** Murmanskaya Oblast', NW Russian Federation 67.37N 33.38E
Kirovsk *see* Babadaykhan, Turkmenistan
Kirovsk *see* Kirawsk, Belarus
119 X7 **Kirovs'k** Luhans'ka Oblast', E Ukraine 48.40N 38.39E
125 Dd9 **Kirovskaya Oblast'** ◈ *province* NW Russian Federation
119 X8 **Kirov'ske** Donets'ka Oblast', E Ukraine 48.12N 38.19E
119 U13 **Kirovs'ke** *Rus.* Kirovskoye. Respublika Krym, S Ukraine 45.13N 35.12E
127 P12 **Kirovskiy** Kamchatskaya Oblast', E Russian Federation 54.06N 155.48E
Kirovskiy *see* Balpyk Bi
Kirovskoye *see* Kyzyl-Adyr
Kirovskoye *see* Kirovs'ke
124 Oo2 **Kırpaşa** *var.* Karpas Peninsula, *Gk.* Karpasía. *peninsula* NE Cyprus
152 E11 **Kirpili** Akhalskiy Velayat, C Turkmenistan 39.31N 57.13E
98 K10 **Kirriemuir** E Scotland, UK 56.37N 3.00W
129 S13 **Kirs** Kirovskaya Oblast', NW Russian Federation 59.22N 52.20E
131 N7 **Kirsanov** Tambovskaya Oblast', W Russian Federation 52.40N 42.48E
142 J14 **Kırşehir** *anc.* Justinianopolis. Kırşehir, C Turkey 39.09N 34.07E
142 I13 **Kırşehir** ◈ *province* C Turkey
155 P4 **Kīrthar Range** ▲▲ S Pakistan
39 P9 **Kirtland** New Mexico, SW USA 36.43N 108.21W
Kirun/Kirun' *see* Chilung
94 J11 **Kiruna** Norrbotten, N Sweden 67.50N 20.16E
81 M18 **Kirundu** Orientale, NE Dem. Rep. Congo (Zaire) 0.45S 25.28E
28 L3 **Kirwin Reservoir** ⊠ Kansas, C USA
131 Q4 **Kirya** Chuvashskaya Respublika, W Russian Federation 55.04N 46.50E
Kiryat Gat *see* Qiryat Gat
171 K15 **Kiryū** Gunma, Honshū, S Japan 36.24N 139.19E
97 M18 **Kisa** Östergötland, S Sweden 58.00N 15.39E
171 Ll11 **Kisakata** Akita, Honshū, C Japan 39.12N 139.55E
Kisalföld *see* Little Alföld
81 L18 **Kisangani** *prev.* Stanleyville. Orientale, NE Dem. Rep. Congo (Zaire) 0.30N 25.13E
41 N12 **Kisaralik River** ≈ Alaska, USA
171 K17 **Kisarazu** Chiba, Honshū, S Japan 35.19N 139.51E
113 I22 **Kisbér** Komárom-Esztergom, NW Hungary 47.30N 18.00E
9 V17 **Kisbey** Saskatchewan, S Canada 49.41N 102.39W
126 H14 **Kiselevsk** Kemerovskaya Oblast', S Russian Federation 54.00N 86.38E
159 R13 **Kishanganj** Bihār, NE India 26.06N 87.57E
158 G12 **Kishangarh** Rājasthān, N India 26.33N 74.52E
Kishegyes *see* Mali Iđoš
79 S15 **Kishi** Oyo, W Nigeria 9.01N 3.53E
Kishinev *see* Chişinău
Kishiözen *see* Malyy Uzen'
171 Gg15 **Kishiwada** *var.* Kisiwada. Ōsaka, Honshū, SW Japan 34.28N 135.22E
149 P14 **Kīsh, Jazīreh-ye** *var.* Qeys. *island* S Iran
151 R7 **Kishkenekol'** *prev.* Kzyltu. *Kaz.* Qyzyltu; Severnyy Kazakhstan, N Kazakhstan 53.39N 72.22E
158 I6 **Kishtwār** Jammu and Kashmir, NW India 33.19N 75.49E
83 H19 **Kisii** Nyanza, SW Kenya 0.40S 34.46E
83 J23 **Kisiju** Pwani, E Tanzania 7.25S 39.19E
Kisiwada *see* Kishiwada
Kisjenő *see* Chişineu-Criş
40 E17 **Kiska Island** *island* Aleutian Islands, Alaska, USA
Kiskapus *see* Copşa Mică
113 M22 **Kiskörei-víztároló** ⊠ E Hungary
Kis-Küküllo *see* Târnava Mică
113 L24 **Kiskunfélegyháza** *var.* Félegyháza. Bács-Kiskun, C Hungary 46.42N 19.52E
113 K25 **Kiskunhalas** *var.* Halas. Bács-Kiskun, S Hungary 46.25N 19.28E
113 K24 **Kiskunmajsa** Bács-Kiskun, S Hungary 46.31N 19.45E
131 N15 **Kislovodsk** Stavropol'skiy Kray, SW Russian Federation 43.55N 42.44E
83 L18 **Kismaayo** *var.* Chisimayu, Kismayu, *It.* Chisimaio. Jubbada Hoose, S Somalia 0.04S 42.34E
Kismayu *see* Kismaayo
171 Ii15 **Kiso-sanmyaku** ▲▲ Honshū, S Japan
Kisseraing *see* Kanmaw Kyun
78 K14 **Kissidougou** Guinée-Forestière, S Guinea 9.15N 10.07W
25 X12 **Kissimmee** Florida, SE USA 28.17N 81.24W
25 X12 **Kissimmee, Lake** ◎ Florida, SE USA
25 X13 **Kissimmee River** ≈ Florida, SE USA
9 V13 **Kississing Lake** ◎ Manitoba, C Canada
113 L24 **Kistelek** Csongrád, SE Hungary 46.27N 19.58E
Kistna *see* Krishna
113 M23 **Kisújszállás** Jász-Nagykun-Szolnok, E Hungary 47.13N 20.43E
170 F12 **Kisuki** Shimane, Honshū, SW Japan 35.25N 133.15E
83 H18 **Kisumu** *prev.* Port Florence. Nyanza, W Kenya 0.02N 34.42E
Kisutzaneustadtl *see* Kysucké Nové Mesto
113 O20 **Kisvárda** *Ger.* Kleinwardein. Szabolcs-Szatmár-Bereg, E Hungary 48.13N 22.03E
83 J24 **Kiswere** Lindi, SE Tanzania 9.24S 39.37E
Kiszucaújhely *see* Kysucké Nové Mesto
78 K12 **Kita** Kayes, W Mali 13.04N 9.29W
207 N14 **Kitaa** ◈ *province* W Greenland
Kitab *see* Kitob
172 N5 **Kitahiyama** Hokkaidō, NE Japan 42.25N 139.55E
171 L15 **Kita-Ibaraki** Ibaraki, Honshū, S Japan 36.48N 140.43E
172 Ss17 **Kita-Iō-jima** *Eng.* San Alessandro. *island* SE Japan
171 Mm11 **Kitakami** Iwate, Honshū, C Japan 39.16N 141.06E
171 M13 **Kitakami-gawa** ≈ Honshū, C Japan
172 N11 **Kitakami-sanchi** ▲▲ Honshū, C Japan
171 L13 **Kitakata** Fukushima, Honshū, C Japan 37.38N 139.51E
170 D12 **Kitakyūshū** *var.* Kitakyûsyû. Fukuoka, Kyūshū, SW Japan 33.51N 130.49E
Kitakyûsyû *see* Kitakyūshū
83 H18 **Kitale** Rift Valley, W Kenya 1.01N 35.01E
172 Q5 **Kitami** Hokkaidō, NE Japan 43.51N 143.50E
172 Pp4 **Kitami-sanchi** ▲▲ Hokkaidō, NE Japan
171 Kk17 **Kita-ura** ◎ Honshū, S Japan
195 O15 **Kitava Island** *island* Kiriwina Islands, SE PNG
39 W5 **Kit Carson** Colorado, C USA 38.45N 102.47W
188 M12 **Kitchener** Western Australia 31.03S 124.00E
12 F16 **Kitchener** Ontario, S Canada 43.28N 80.27W
95 O17 **Kitee** Itä-Suomi, E Finland 62.06N 30.09E
83 G16 **Kitgum** N Uganda 3.16N 32.54E
Kithareng *see* Kanmaw Kyun
Kíthira *see* Kýthira
Kíthnos *see* Kýthnos
8 J13 **Kitimat** British Columbia, SW Canada 54.04N 128.37W
94 L11 **Kitinen** ≈ N Finland
153 N12 **Kitob** *Rus.* Kitab. Qashqadaryo Wiloyati, S Uzbekistan 39.06N 66.46E
118 K7 **Kitsman'** *Ger.* Kotzman, *Rom.* Cozmeni, *Rus.* Kitsman. Chernivets'ka Oblast', W Ukraine 48.27N 25.46E
170 Dd14 **Kitsuki** *var.* Kituki. Ōita, Kyūshū, SW Japan 33.25N 131.37E
20 C14 **Kittanning** Pennsylvania, NE USA 40.48N 79.28W
21 P10 **Kittery** Maine, NE USA 43.05N 70.44W
94 L11 **Kittilä** Lappi, N Finland 67.39N 24.52E
111 Z4 **Kittsee** Burgenland, E Austria 48.05N 17.05E
83 J19 **Kitui** Eastern, S Kenya 1.25S 38.00E
Kituki *see* Kitsuki
83 G22 **Kitunda** Tabora, C Tanzania 6.47S 33.13E
8 K13 **Kitwanga** British Columbia, SW Canada 55.07N 128.03W
84 J13 **Kitwe** *var.* Kitwe-Nkana. Copperbelt, C Zambia 12.48S 28.13E
Kitwe-Nkana *see* Kitwe
111 O7 **Kitzbühel** Tirol, W Austria 47.27N 12.22E
111 O7 **Kitzbüheler Alpen** ▲▲ W Austria
103 J19 **Kitzingen** Bayern, SE Germany 49.43N 10.10E
159 Q14 **Kiul** Bihār, NE India 25.10N 86.06E
194 E12 **Kiunga** Western, SW PNG 6.06S 141.12E
95 M16 **Kiuruvesi** Itä-Suomi, C Finland 63.37N 26.40E
40 M7 **Kivalina** Alaska, USA 67.43N 164.31W
94 L13 **Kivalo** *ridge* C Finland
118 J3 **Kivertsi** *Pol.* Kiwerce, *Rus.* Kivertsy. Volyns'ka Oblast', NW Ukraine 50.49N 25.31E
Kivertsy *see* Kivertsi
95 L16 **Kivijärvi** Länsi-Suomi, W Finland 63.09N 25.04E
97 L23 **Kivik** Skåne, S Sweden 55.40N 14.15E
120 J3 **Kiviõli** Ida-Virumaa, NE Estonia 59.20N 27.00E
Kivu, Lac *see* Kivu, Lake
69 U10 **Kivu, Lake** *Fr.* Lac Kivu. ◎ Rwanda/Dem. Rep. Congo (Zaire)
194 G15 **Kiwai Island** *island* SW PNG
41 N8 **Kiwalik** Alaska, USA 66.01N 161.50W
Kiwerce *see* Kivertsi
Kiyev *see* Kyyiv
151 R10 **Kiyevka** Karaganda, C Kazakhstan 50.15N 71.33E
Kiyevskaya Oblast' *see* Kyyivs'ka Oblast'
Kiyevskoye Vodokhranilishche *see* Kyyivs'ke Vodoskhovyshche
142 D10 **Kıyıköy** Kırklareli, NW Turkey 41.37N 28.07E
151 O9 **Kiyma** Akmola, C Kazakhstan 51.37N 67.31E
129 V13 **Kizel** Permskaya Oblast', NW Russian Federation 58.59N 57.37E
129 O12 **Kizema** *var.* Kizëma. Arkhangel'skaya Oblast', NW Russian Federation 61.06N 44.51E
Kizilagach *see* Elkhovo
142 H12 **Kızılcahamam** Ankara, N Turkey 40.28N 32.37E
142 J10 **Kızıl Irmak** ≈ C Turkey
Kızılkoca *see* Şefaatli
Kizil Kum *see* Kyzyl Kum
143 P16 **Kızıltepe** Mardin, SE Turkey 37.12N 40.36E
Ki Zil Uzen *see* Qezel Owzan
131 Q16 **Kizilyurt** Respublika Dagestan, SW Russian Federation 43.13N 46.54E
131 Q15 **Kizlyar** Respublika Dagestan, SW Russian Federation 43.51N 46.39E
131 S3 **Kizner** Udmurtskaya Respublika, NW Russian Federation 56.19N 51.37E
Kizyl-Arvat *see* Gyzylarbat
152 B13 **Kizyl-Atrek** *Turkm.* Gyzyletrek. Balkanskiy Velayat, W Turkmenistan 37.40N 54.44E
152 D10 **Kizyl-Kaya** *Turkm.* Gyzylgaya. Balkanskiy Velayat, NW Turkmenistan 40.37N 55.15E
152 A10 **Kizyl-Su** *Turkm.* Gyzylsu. Balkanskiy Velayat, W Turkmenistan 39.49N 53.00E
97 H16 **Kjerkøy** *island* S Norway
Kjølen *see* Kölen
94 L7 **Kjøllefjord** Finnmark, N Norway 70.55N 27.19E
94 H11 **Kjøpsvik** Nordland, C Norway 68.07N 16.22E
174 Ii9 **Klabat, Teluk** *bay* Pulau Bangka, W Indonesia
114 I12 **Kladanj** Federacija Bosan I Hercegovina, C Bosnia and Herzegovina 44.14N 18.42E
176 Xx16 **Kladar** Irian Jaya, E Indonesia 8.14S 137.46E
113 C16 **Kladno** Středočeský Kraj, NW Czech Republic 50.10N 14.04E
114 P11 **Kladovo** Serbia, E Yugoslavia 44.37N 22.36E
178 Hh12 **Klaeng** Rayong, S Thailand 12.48N 101.41E
111 T9 **Klagenfurt** *Slvn.* Celovec. Kärnten, S Austria 46.37N 14.19E
120 B11 **Klaipėda** *Ger.* Memel. Klaipėda, NW Lithuania 55.42N 21.09E
174 M15 **Klakah** Jawa, C Indonesia 7.55S 113.12E
97 B18 **Klaksvík** *Dan.* Klaksvig Faeroe Islands 62.13N 6.43W
36 L2 **Klamath** California, W USA 41.31N 124.02W
34 H16 **Klamath Falls** Oregon, NW USA 42.13N 121.46W
36 M1 **Klamath Mountains** ▲▲ California/Oregon, W USA
36 L2 **Klamath River** ≈ California/Oregon, W USA
174 Gg5 **Klang** *var.* Kelang; *prev.* Port Swettenham. Selangor, Peninsular Malaysia 3.01N 101.27E
96 J13 **Klarälven** ≈ Norway/Sweden
113 B15 **Klášterec nad Ohří** *Ger.* Klösterle an der Eger. Ústecký Kraj, NW Czech Republic 50.24N 13.10E
174 L15 **Klaten** Jawa, C Indonesia 7.40S 110.31E
113 B18 **Klatovy** *Ger.* Klattau. Plzeňský Kraj, W Czech Republic 49.24N 13.16E
Klattau *see* Klatovy
Klausenburg *see* Cluj-Napoca
41 Y14 **Klawock** Prince of Wales Island, Alaska, USA 55.33N 133.06W
100 P8 **Klazienaveen** Drenthe, NE Netherlands 52.43N 7.00E
Kleck *see* Klyetsk
112 H11 **Kłecko** Wielkolpolskie, C Poland 52.37N 17.27E
112 I11 **Kleczew** Wielkopolskie, C Poland 52.22N 18.12E
8 L15 **Kleena Kleene** British Columbia, SW Canada 51.55N 124.54W
85 D20 **Klein Aub** Hardap, C Namibia 23.48S 16.39E
Kleine Donau *see* Mosoni-Duna
103 O14 **Kleine Elster** ≈ E Germany
Kleine Kokel *see* Târnava Mică
101 I16 **Kleine Nete** ≈ N Belgium
Kleines Ungarisches Tiefland *see* Little Alföld
85 E22 **Klein Karas** Karas, S Namibia 27.37S 18.05E
Kleinkopisch *see* Copşa Mică
Klein-Marien *see* Väike-Maarja
Kleinschlatten *see* Zlatna
85 D23 **Kleinsee** Northern Cape, W South Africa 29.43S 17.03E
Kleinwardein *see* Kisvárda
117 C16 **Kleisoúra** Ípeiros, W Greece 39.21N 20.52E
97 C17 **Klepp** Rogaland, S Norway 58.46N 5.39E
85 I22 **Klerksdorp** North-West, N South Africa 26.52S 26.39E
130 I5 **Kletnya** Bryanskaya Oblast', W Russian Federation 53.25N 32.58E
Kletsk *see* Klyetsk
103 D14 **Kleve** *Eng.* Cleves, *Fr.* Clèves; *prev.* Cleve. Nordrhein-Westfalen, W Germany 51.46N 6.07E
115 J16 **Kličevo** Montenegro, SW Yugoslavia 42.45N 18.58E
121 M16 **Klichaw** *Rus.* Klichev. Mahilyowskaya Voblasts', E Belarus 53.28N 29.21E
Klichev *see* Klichaw
121 Q16 **Klimavichy** *Rus.* Klimovichi. Mahilyowskaya Voblasts', E Belarus 53.37N 31.58E
116 M7 **Kliment** Shumen, NE Bulgaria 43.37N 27.00E
Klimovichi *see* Klimavichy
95 G14 **Klimpfjäll** Västerbotten, N Sweden 65.04N 14.49E
130 K3 **Klin** Moskovskaya Oblast', W Russian Federation 56.19N 36.45E
115 M16 **Klina** Serbia, S Yugoslavia 42.38N 20.35E
113 B15 **Klínovec** *Ger.* Keilberg. ▲ NW Czech Republic 50.23N 12.57E
97 P19 **Klintehamn** Gotland, SE Sweden 57.22N 18.15E
131 R8 **Klintsovka** Saratovskaya Oblast', W Russian Federation 51.42N 49.17E
130 H6 **Klintsy** Bryanskaya Oblast', W Russian Federation 52.46N 32.20E
97 K22 **Klippan** Skåne, S Sweden 56.07N 13.10E
94 G13 **Klippen** Västerbotten, N Sweden 65.50N 15.07E
124 Nn3 **Klírou** W Cyprus 35.01N 33.11E
116 I9 **Klisura** Plovdiv, C Bulgaria 42.42N 24.28E
97 F20 **Klitmøller** Viborg, NW Denmark 57.01N 8.29E
114 F11 **Ključ** Federacija Bosna I Hercegovina, NW Bosnia and Herzegovina 44.32N 16.46E
113 J14 **Kłobuck** Śląskie, S Poland 50.55N 18.54E
112 J11 **Kłodawa** Wielkopolskie, C Poland 52.14N 18.55E
113 G16 **Kłodzko** *Ger.* Glatz. Dolnośląskie, SW Poland 50.27N 16.37E
97 I14 **Kløfta** Akershus, S Norway 60.04N 11.09E
114 P12 **Klokočevac** Serbia, E Yugoslavia 44.19N 22.11E
120 G3 **Klooga** *Ger.* Lodensee. Harjumaa, NW Estonia 59.18N 24.15E
101 F15 **Kloosterzande** Zeeland, SW Netherlands 51.22N 4.01E
115 L19 **Klos** *var.* Klosi. Dibër, C Albania 41.30N 20.07E
Klosi *see* Klos
Klösterle an der Eger *see* Klášterec nad Ohří
111 X3 **Klosterneuburg** Niederösterreich, NE Austria 48.19N 16.19E
110 J9 **Klosters** Graubünden, SE Switzerland 46.54N 9.52E
110 G7 **Kloten** Zürich, N Switzerland 47.27N 8.34E
110 G7 **Kloten** ✈ (Zürich) Zürich, N Switzerland 47.25N 8.36E
102 K12 **Klötze** Sachsen-Anhalt, C Germany 52.37N 11.09E
10 K3 **Klotz, Lac** ◎ Quebec, NE Canada
103 O15 **Klotzsche** ✈ (Dresden) Sachsen, E Germany 51.06N 13.44E
8 H7 **Kluane Lake** ◎ Yukon Territory, W Canada
Kluang *see* Keluang
113 I14 **Kluczbork** *Ger.* Kreuzburg, Kreuzburg in Oberschlesien. Opolskie, S Poland 50.59N 18.13E
41 W12 **Klukwan** Alaska, USA 59.24N 135.49W
Klyastitsy *see* Klyastsitsy
120 L11 **Klyastsitsy** *Rus.* Klyastitsy. Vitsyebskaya Voblasts', N Belarus 55.54N 28.38E
131 T5 **Klyavlino** Samarskaya Oblast', W Russian Federation 54.21N 52.12E
86 K9 **Klyaz'in** ≈ W Russian Federation
131 N3 **Klyaz'ma** ≈ W Russian Federation
121 J17 **Klyetsk** *Pol.* Kleck, *Rus.* Kletsk. Minskaya Voblasts', SW Belarus 53.04N 26.38E
153 S8 **Klyuchevka** Talasskaya Oblast', NW Kyrgyzstan 42.33N 71.45E
127 Pp10 **Klyuchevskaya Sopka, Vulkan** 🌋 E Russian Federation 56.03N 160.37E
127 Pp10 **Klyuchi** Kamchatskaya Oblast', E Russian Federation 56.18N 160.44E
97 D17 **Knaben** Vest-Agder, S Norway 58.46N 7.04E
Knanzi *see* Ghanzi
97 K21 **Knäred** Halland, S Sweden 56.30N 13.21E
99 M16 **Knaresborough** N England, UK 54.01N 1.35W
116 H8 **Knezha** Vratsa , NW Bulgaria 43.29N 24.04E
27 O9 **Knickerbocker** Texas, SW USA 31.18N 100.35W
30 K5 **Knife River** ≈ North Dakota, N USA
8 K16 **Knight Inlet** *inlet* British Columbia, W Canada
41 S12 **Knight Island** *island* Alaska, USA
99 K20 **Knighton** E Wales, UK 52.20N 3.00W
37 O7 **Knights Landing** California, W USA 38.47N 121.43W
114 E13 **Knin** Šibenik-Knin, S Croatia 44.03N 16.12E
27 Q12 **Knippal** Texas, SW USA
111 U7 **Knittelfeld** Steiermark, C Austria 47.13N 14.51E
97 O15 **Knivsta** Uppsala, C Sweden 59.43N 17.49E
115 P14 **Knjaževac** Serbia, E Yugoslavia 43.34N 22.16E
29 S4 **Knob Noster** Missouri, C USA 38.47N 93.33W
101 D15 **Knokke-Heist** West-Vlaanderen, NW Belgium 51.21N 3.19E
97 H20 **Knøsen** *hill* N Denmark 57.09N 10.15E
Knosós *see* Knossos
117 J25 **Knossos** *Gk.* Knosós. *prehistoric site* Kríti, Greece, E Mediterranean Sea 35.17N 25.10E
27 N7 **Knott** Texas, SW USA 32.21N 101.35W
204 K5 **Knowles, Cape** *headland* Antarctica 71.45S 60.19W
33 O11 **Knox** Indiana, N USA 41.16N 86.37W
31 O3 **Knox** North Dakota, N USA 48.19N 99.43W
20 C13 **Knox** Pennsylvania, NE USA 41.13N 79.33W
201 X8 **Knox Atoll** *var.* Nadikdik, Narikrik. *atoll* Ratak Chain, SE Marshall Islands
8 H13 **Knox, Cape** *headland* Graham Island, British Columbia, SW Canada 54.05N 133.02W
27 P5 **Knox City** Texas, SW USA 33.25N 99.49W
205 Y11 **Knox Coast** *physical region* Antarctica
33 T12 **Knox Lake** ⊠ Ohio, N USA
25 T5 **Knoxville** Georgia, SE USA 32.44N 83.58W
32 K12 **Knoxville** Illinois, N USA 40.54N 90.16W
31 W15 **Knoxville** Iowa, C USA 41.19N 93.06W
23 N9 **Knoxville** Tennessee, S USA 35.57N 83.55W
207 P11 **Knud Rasmussen Land** *physical region* N Greenland
Knüll *see* Knüllgebirge
103 I16 **Knüllgebirge** *var.* Knüll. ▲▲ C Germany
Knyazhevo *see* Sredishte
Knyazhitsy *see* Knyazhytsy
121 O15 **Knyazhytsy** *Rus.* Knyazhitsy. Mahilyowskaya Voblasts', E Belarus 54.10N 30.27E
85 G26 **Knysna** Western Cape, SW South Africa 34.01S 23.05E
176 V10 **Koagas** Irian Jaya, E Indonesia 2.40S 132.16E
Koartac *see* Quaqtaq
174 J10 **Koba** Pulau Bangka, W Indonesia 2.29S 106.22E
170 C16 **Kobayashi** *var.* Kobayasi. Miyazaki, Kyūshū, SW Japan 32.01N 130.55E
Kobayasi *see* Kobayashi
171 Gg14 **Kōbe** Hyōgo, Honshū, SW Japan 34.39N 135.10E
Kobelyaki *see* Kobelyaky
119 T6 **Kobelyaky** *Rus.* Kobelyaki. Poltavs'ka Oblast', NE Ukraine 49.10N 34.13E
97 J22 **København** *Eng.* Copenhagen; *anc.* Hafnia. ● (Denmark) Sjælland, København, E Denmark 55.43N 12.34E
97 J23 **København** *off.* Københavns Amt. ◈ *county* E Denmark
78 K10 **Kobenni** Hodh el Gharbi, S Mauritania 15.58N 9.24W
176 U11 **Kobi** Pulau Seram, E Indonesia 2.56S 129.53E
103 F17 **Koblenz** *prev.* Coblenz, *Fr.* Coblence, *anc.* Confluentes. Rheinland-Pfalz, W Germany 50.21N 7.36E
110 F6 **Koblenz** Aargau, N Switzerland 47.34N 8.16E
176 Ww11 **Kobowre, Pegunungan** ▲▲ Irian Jaya, E Indonesia
Kobrin *see* Kobryn
176 W14 **Kobroor, Pulau** *island* Kepulauan Aru, E Indonesia
121 G19 **Kobryn** *Pol.* Kobryn, *Rus.* Kobrin. Brestskaya Voblasts', SW Belarus 52.13N 24.21E
41 O7 **Kobuk** Alaska, USA 66.54N 156.52W
41 O7 **Kobuk River** ≈ Alaska, USA
143 Q10 **K'obulet'i** W Georgia 41.47N 41.46E
126 Ll10 **Kobyay** Respublika Sakha (Yakutiya), NE Russian Federation 63.36N 126.33E
142 E11 **Kocaeli** ◈ *province* NW Turkey
115 P18 **Kočani** NE FYR Macedonia 41.55N 22.25E
114 K12 **Koceljevo** Serbia, W Yugoslavia 44.28N 19.49E
111 U12 **Kočevje** *Ger.* Gottschee. S Slovenia 45.41N 14.47E
159 T12 **Koch Bihār** West Bengal, NE India 26.19N 89.25E
126 J10 **Kochechum** ≈ N Russian Federation
103 I20 **Kocher** ≈ SW Germany
129 T13 **Kochevo** Komi-Permyatskiy Avtonomnyy Okrug, NW Russian Federation 59.37N 54.16E
170 Ee15 **Kōchi** *var.* Kôti. Kōchi, Shikoku, SW Japan 33.31N 133.30E
170 Ee15 **Kōchi** *off.* Kōchi-ken, *var.* Kôti. ◈ *prefecture* Shikoku, SW Japan
Kochi *see* Cochin
Kochiu *see* Gejiu
Kochkor *see* Kochkorka
153 V8 **Kochkorka** *Kir.* Kochkor. Narynskaya Oblast', C Kyrgyzstan 42.09N 75.42E
129 V5 **Kochmes** Respublika Komi, NW Russian Federation 66.10N 60.46E
131 P15 **Kochubey** Respublika Dagestan, SW Russian Federation 44.25N 46.33E
117 I17 **Kochýlas** ▲ Skýros, Vóreioi Sporádes, Greece, Aegean Sea 38.50N 24.35E
112 O13 **Kock** Lubelskie, E Poland 51.39N 22.26E
83 J19 **Kodacho** *spring/well* S Kenya 1.52S 39.22E
161 K24 **Koddiyar Bay** *bay* NE Sri Lanka
41 Q14 **Kodiak** Kodiak Island, Alaska, USA 57.47N 152.24W
41 Q14 **Kodiak Island** *island* Alaska, USA
160 B12 **Kodīnār** Gujarāt, W India 20.43N 70.46E
128 M9 **Kodino** Arkhangel'skaya Oblast', NW Russian Federation 63.36N 39.54E
126 Ii13 **Kodinsk** Krasnoyarskiy Kray, C Russian Federation 58.37N 99.18E
82 F12 **Kodok** Upper Nile, SE Sudan 9.51N 32.07E
119 N8 **Kodyma** Odes'ka Oblast', SW Ukraine 48.05N 29.09E
101 B17 **Koekelare** West-Vlaanderen, W Belgium 51.07N 2.58E
Koeln *see* Köln
Koepang *see* Kupang
Ko-erh-mu *see* Golmud
101 J17 **Koersel** Limburg, NE Belgium 51.04N 5.17E
85 E21 **Koës** Karas, SE Namibia 25.57S 19.04E
Koetai *see* Mahakam, Sungai
Koetaradja *see* Bandaaceh
38 I14 **Kofa Mountains** ▲▲ Arizona, SW USA
176 Z15 **Kofarau** Irian Jaya, E Indonesia 7.29S 140.28E
153 P13 **Kofarnihon** *Rus.* Kofarnikhon; *prev.* Ordzhonikidzeabad, *Taj.* Orjonikidzeobod, Yangi-Bazar. W Tajikistan 38.32N 68.56E
153 P14 **Kofarnihon** *Rus.* Kafirnigan. ≈ SW Tajikistan
Kofarnikhon *see* Kofarnihon
116 M11 **Kofçaz** Kırklareli, NW Turkey 41.57N 27.07E
176 U9 **Kofiau, Pulau** *var.* Kafiau. *island* Kepulauan Raja Ampat, E Indonesia
117 J25 **Kófinas** ▲ Kríti, Greece, E Mediterranean Sea 34.58N 25.03E
124 Nn4 **Kofínou** *var.* Kophinou. S Cyprus 34.49N 33.24E
111 V8 **Köflach** Steiermark, SE Austria 47.04N 15.04E
79 Q17 **Koforidua** SE Ghana 6.04N 0.17W
170 Ff12 **Kōfu** Tottori, Honshū, SW Japan 35.16N 133.31E
171 J15 **Kōfu** *var.* Kôhu. Yamanashi, Honshū, S Japan 35.40N 138.33E
171 K16 **Koga** Ibaraki, Honshū, S Japan 36.12N 139.42E
83 F22 **Koga** Tabora, C Tanzania 6.08S 32.20E
Kogălniceanu *see* Mihail Kogălniceanu
11 P6 **Kogaluk** ≈ Newfoundland, E Canada
10 J4 **Kogaluk** ≈ Quebec, NE Canada
126 Gg10 **Kogalym** Khanty-Mansiyskiy Avtonomnyy Okrug, C Russian Federation 62.13N 74.34E

◆ Country
● Country Capital
◇ Dependent Territory
○ Dependent Territory Capital
◈ Administrative Region
✈ International Airport
▲ Mountain
▲▲ Mountain Range
🌋 Volcano
≈ River
◎ Lake
⊠ Reservoir

KØGE – KOSOVO AND METOHIJA, AUTONOMOUS PROVINCE OF

97 J23 **Køge** Roskilde, E Denmark *55.28N 12.12E*
97 J23 **Køge Bugt** *bay* E Denmark
79 U16 **Kogi** ◈ *state* C Nigeria
152 L11 **Kogon** ***Rus.*** Kagan. Bukhoro Wiloyati, C Uzbekistan *39.46N 64.28E*
169 Y17 **Kögüm-do** *island* S South Korea
Kőhalom *see* Rupea
155 T6 **Kohāt** North-West Frontier Province, NW Pakistan *33.37N 71.30E*
120 G4 **Kohila** ***Ger.*** Koil. Raplamaa, NW Estonia *59.07N 24.46E*
159 X13 **Kohīma** Nāgāland, E India *25.40N 94.07E*
Koh I Noh *see* Büyükağrı Dağı
148 L10 **Kohkīlūyeh va Būyer Aḥmadī** ***off.*** Ostān-e Kohkīlūyeh va Būyer Aḥmadī, ***var.*** Boyer Ahmadī va Kohkīlūyeh. ◈ *province* SW Iran
Kohsān *see* Kūhestān
120 J3 **Kohtla-Järve** Ida-Virumaa, NE Estonia *59.22N 27.21E*
Kôhu *see* Kōfu
119 N10 **Kohyl'nyk** ***Rom.*** Cogîlnic. ≈ Moldova/Ukraine
171 K13 **Koide** Niigata, Honshū, C Japan *37.13N 138.58E*
8 G7 **Koidern** Yukon Territory, W Canada *61.55N 140.22W*
78 J15 **Koidu** E Sierra Leone *8.39N 11.01W*
120 I4 **Koigi** Järvamaa, C Estonia *58.51N 25.45E*
Koil *see* Kohila
180 H13 **Koimbani** Grande Comore, NW Comoros *11.37S 43.22E*
145 T3 **Koi Sanjaq** ***var.*** Koysanjaq, Küysanjaq. N Iraq *36.04N 44.37E*
95 O16 **Koitere** ◎ E Finland
Koivisto *see* Primorsk
169 Z16 **Kōje-do** ***Jap.*** Kyōsai-tō. *island* S South Korea
82 J13 **K'ok'a Hāyk'** ◎ C Ethiopia
Kokand *see* Qŭqon
190 F6 **Kokatha** South Australia *31.17S 135.16E*
Kokcha *see* Kŭkcha
Kokchetav *see* Kokshetau
95 K18 **Kokemäenjoki** ≈ SW Finland
176 X12 **Kokenau** ***var.*** Kokonau. Irian Jaya, E Indonesia *4.38S 136.24E*
85 E22 **Kokerboom** Karas, SE Namibia *28.10S 19.25E*
121 N14 **Kokhanava** ***Rus.*** Kokhanovo. Vitsyebskaya Voblasts', NE Belarus *54.28N 29.58E*
Kokhanovichi *see* Kakhanavichy
Kokhanovo *see* Kokhanava
Kök-Janggak *see* Kok-Yangak
95 K16 **Kokkola** ***Swe.*** Karleby; ***prev. Swe.*** Gamlakarleby. Länsi-Suomi, W Finland *63.49N 23.10E*
164 L3 **Kok Kuduk** *well* N China *46.03N 87.34E*
120 H9 **Koknese** Aizkraukle, C Latvia *56.38N 25.27E*
79 T13 **Koko** Kebbi, W Nigeria *11.25N 4.33E*
194 K15 **Kokoda** Northern, S PNG *8.51S 147.37E*
78 K12 **Kokofata** Kayes, W Mali *12.48N 9.56W*
41 N6 **Kokolik River** ≈ Alaska, USA
33 O13 **Kokomo** Indiana, N USA *40.29N 86.07W*
Kokonau *see* Kokenau
Koko Nor *see* Qinghai Hu, China
Koko Nor *see* Qinghai, China
195 P10 **Kokopo** ***var.*** Kopopo; ***prev.*** Herbertshöhe. New Britain, E PNG *4.19S 152.13E*
151 X10 **Kokpekti** ***Kaz.*** Kökpekti. Vostochnyy Kazakhstan, E Kazakhstan *48.45N 82.24E*
151 X11 **Kokpekti** ≈ E Kazakhstan
41 P9 **Kokrines** Alaska, USA *64.57N 154.42W*
41 P9 **Kokrines Hills** ▲▲ Alaska, USA
151 P17 **Koksaray** Yuzhnyy Kazakhstan, S Kazakhstan *42.40N 68.09E*
153 X9 **Kokshaal-Tau** ***Rus.*** Khrebet Kakshaal-Too. ▲▲ China/Kyrgyzstan
151 P7 **Kokshetau** ***Kaz.*** Kökshetaū; ***prev.*** Kokchetav. Severnyy Kazakhstan, N Kazakhstan *53.18N 69.25E*
101 A17 **Koksijde** West-Vlaanderen, W Belgium *51.07N 2.39E*
10 M5 **Koksoak** ≈ Quebec, E Canada
85 K24 **Kokstad** KwaZulu/Natal, E South Africa *30.23S 29.22E*
151 W15 **Koktal** ***Kaz.*** Köktal. Almaty, SE Kazakhstan *44.04N 79.43E*
151 Q12 **Koktas** ≈ C Kazakhstan
Kök-Tash *see* Këk-Tash
Koktokay *see* Fuyun
170 C16 **Kokubu** Kagoshima, Kyūshū, SW Japan *31.44N 130.44E*
126 L15 **Kokuy** Chitinskaya Oblast', S Russian Federation *52.13N 117.18E*
153 T9 **Kok-Yangak** ***Kir.*** Kök-Janggak. Dzhalal-Abadskaya Oblast', W Kyrgyzstan *41.02N 73.11E*
164 F9 **Kokyar** Xinjiang Uygur Zizhiqu, W China *37.24N 77.15E*
155 O13 **Kolāchi** ***var.*** Kulachi. ≈ SW Pakistan
78 J15 **Kolahun** N Liberia *8.24N 10.01W*
175 Q12 **Kolaka** Sulawesi, C Indonesia *4.04S 121.37E*
Kolam *see* Quilon
K'o-la-ma-i *see* Karamay
Kola Peninsula *see* Kol'skiy Poluostrov
161 H19 **Kolār** Karnātaka, E India *13.10N 78.10E*
161 H19 **Kolār Gold Fields** Karnātaka, E India *12.56N 78.16E*
94 K11 **Kolari** Lappi, NW Finland *67.19N 23.51E*
113 I21 **Kolárovo** ***Ger.*** Gutta; ***prev.*** Guta, ***Hung.*** Gúta. Nitriansky Kraj, SW Slovakia *47.54N 18.00E*
115 K16 **Kolašin** Montenegro, SW Yugoslavia *42.49N 19.32E*
158 F11 **Kolāyat** Rājasthān, NW India *27.55N 73.01E*
97 N15 **Kolbäck** Västmanland, C Sweden *59.33N 16.15E*
Kolbcha *see* Kowbcha
207 Q15 **Kolbeinsey Ridge** *undersea feature* Denmark Strait/Norwegian Sea
Kolberg *see* Kołobrzeg
97 H15 **Kolbotn** Akershus, S Norway *62.15N 10.24E*
113 N16 **Kolbuszowa** Podkarpackie, SE Poland *50.12N 22.07E*
130 L3 **Kol'chugino** Vladimirskaya Oblast', W Russian Federation *56.19N 39.24E*
78 H12 **Kolda** S Senegal *12.58N 14.58W*
97 G23 **Kolding** Vejle, C Denmark *55.28N 9.30E*
81 M17 **Kole** Orientale, N Dem. Rep. Congo (Zaire) *2.09N 25.17E*
81 K20 **Kole** Kasai Oriental, SW Dem. Rep. Congo (Zaire) *3.27S 22.28E*
Kōle *see* Kili Island
86 F6 **Kölen** ***Nor.*** Kjølen. ▲▲ Norway/Sweden
Kolepom, Pulau *see* Yos Sudarso, Pulau
120 H3 **Kolga Laht** ***Ger.*** Kolko-Wiek. *bay* N Estonia
129 Q3 **Kolguyev, Ostrov** *island* NW Russian Federation
161 E16 **Kolhāpur** Mahārāshtra, SW India *16.42N 74.13E*
157 K21 **Kolhumadulu Atoll** ***var.*** Kolumadulu Atoll, Thaa Atoll. *atoll* S Maldives
95 O16 **Koli** ***var.*** Kolinkylä. Itä-Suomi, E Finland *63.06N 29.45E*
41 O13 **Koliganek** Alaska, USA *59.43N 157.16W*
113 E16 **Kolín** ***Ger.*** Kolin. Středočeský Kraj, C Czech Republic *50.01N 15.10E*
Kolinkylä *see* Koli
202 E12 **Koliu** Île Futuna, W Wallis and Futuna
120 E7 **Kolka** Talsi, NW Latvia *57.43N 22.33E*
120 E7 **Kolkasrags** ***prev. Eng.*** Cape Domesnes. *headland* NW Latvia *57.45N 22.35E*
Kolkata *see* Calcutta
Kolkhozabad *see* Kolkhozobod
153 P14 **Kolkhozobod** ***Rus.*** Kolkhozabad; ***prev.*** Kaganovichabad, Tugalan. SW Tajikistan *37.33N 68.34E*
Kolki/Kołki *see* Kolky
Kolko-Wiek *see* Kolga Laht
118 K3 **Kolky** ***Pol.*** Kołki, ***Rus.*** Kolki. Volyns'ka Oblast', NW Ukraine *51.05N 25.40E*
Kollam *see* Quilon
161 G20 **Kollegāl** Karnātaka, W India *12.07N 77.06E*
100 M5 **Kollum** Friesland, N Netherlands *53.16N 6.09E*
Kolmar *see* Colmar
103 E16 **Köln** ***var.*** Koeln, ***Eng./Fr.*** Cologne; ***prev.*** Cöln, ***anc.*** Colonia Agrippina, Oppidum Ubiorum. Nordrhein-Westfalen, W Germany *50.57N 6.57E*
112 N9 **Kolno** Podlaskie, NE Poland *53.24N 21.57E*
112 J12 **Koło** Wielkopolskie, C Poland *52.10N 18.39E*
40 B8 **Koloa** ***Haw.*** Kōloa. Kauai, Hawaii, USA, C Pacific Ocean *21.54N 159.28W*
112 E7 **Kołobrzeg** ***Ger.*** Kolberg. Zachodniopomorskie, NW Poland *54.10N 15.33E*
130 H4 **Kolodnya** Smolenskaya Oblast', W Russian Federation *54.57N 32.22E*
202 E13 **Kolofau, Mont** ⩘ Île Alofi, S Wallis and Futuna *14.21S 178.01W*
129 O14 **Kologriv** Kostromskaya Oblast', NW Russian Federation *58.49N 44.22E*
78 L12 **Kolokani** Koulikoro, W Mali *13.34N 8.01W*
79 N13 **Koloko** W Burkina *11.06N 5.18W*
195 U14 **Kolombangara** ***var.*** Kilimbangara, Nduke. *island* New Georgia Islands, NW Solomon Islands
Kolomea *see* Kolomyya
130 L4 **Kolomna** Moskovskaya Oblast', W Russian Federation *55.02N 38.52E*
118 J7 **Kolomyya** ***Ger.*** Kolomea. Ivano-Frankivs'ka Oblast', W Ukraine *48.31N 25.00E*
78 M13 **Kolondiéba** Sikasso, SW Mali *11.04N 6.55W*
200 R15 **Kolonga** Tongatapu, S Tonga *21.07S 175.04W*
201 U16 **Kolonia** ***var.*** Colonia. Pohnpei, E Micronesia *6.57N 158.12E*
Kolonja *see* Kolonjë
115 K21 **Kolonjë** ***var.*** Kolonja. Fier, C Albania *40.49N 19.37E*
Kolonjë *see* Ersekë
Kolotambu *see* Avuavu
200 Q15 **Kolovai** Tongatapu, S Tonga *21.05S 175.20W*
175 R13 **Kolowanawatobo, Teluk** *bay* Pulau Buton, C Indonesia
Kolozsvár *see* Cluj-Napoca
114 C9 **Kolpa** ***Ger.*** Kulpa, ***SCr.*** Kupa. ≈ Croatia/Slovenia
126 H12 **Kolpashevo** Tomskaya Oblast', C Russian Federation *58.21N 82.44E*
128 H13 **Kolpino** Leningradskaya Oblast', NW Russian Federation *59.43N 30.39E*
102 M10 **Kölpinsee** ◎ NE Germany
128 K5 **Kol'skiy Poluostrov** ***Eng.*** Kola Peninsula. *peninsula* NW Russian Federation
131 T6 **Koltubanovskiy** Orenburgskaya Oblast', W Russian Federation *53.00N 52.00E*
114 L11 **Kolubara** ≈ C Yugoslavia
Kolupchii *see* Gurkovo
112 K13 **Koluszki** Łodzkie, C Poland *51.43N 19.49E*
129 T6 **Kolva** ≈ NW Russian Federation
95 E14 **Kolvereid** Nord-Trøndelag, W Norway *64.47N 11.22E*
154 L15 **Kolwa** Baluchistān, SW Pakistan *26.03N 64.00E*
81 M24 **Kolwezi** Katanga, S Dem. Rep. Congo (Zaire) *10.43S 25.29E*
127 Nn7 **Kolyma** ≈ NE Russian Federation
Kolyma Lowland *see* Kolymskaya Nizmennost'
Kolyma Range/Kolymskiy, Khrebet *see* Kolymskoye Nagor'ye
127 Nn6 **Kolymskaya Nizmennost'** ***Eng.*** Kolyma Lowland. *lowlands* NE Russian Federation
127 Nn6 **Kolymskoye** Respublika Sakha (Yakutiya), NE Russian Federation *68.42N 158.46E*
127 N17 **Kolymskoye Nagor'ye** ***var.*** Khrebet Kolymskiy, ***Eng.*** Kolyma Range. ▲▲ E Russian Federation
127 N17 **Kolyuchinskaya Guba** *bay* NE Russian Federation
151 W15 **Kol'zhat** Almaty, SE Kazakhstan *43.30N 80.37E*
116 G8 **Kom** ▲ NW Bulgaria *43.10N 23.02E*
82 I13 **Koma** Oromo, C Ethiopia *8.19N 36.48E*
79 X12 **Komadugu Gana** ≈ NE Nigeria
171 Ii15 **Komagane** Nagano, Honshū, S Japan *35.46N 137.56E*
81 P17 **Komanda** Orientale, NE Dem. Rep. Congo (Zaire) *1.23N 29.44E*
207 U1 **Komandorskaya Basin** ***var.*** Kamchatka Basin. *undersea feature* SW Bering Sea
129 Pp9 **Komandorskiye Ostrova** ***Eng.*** Commander Islands. *island group* E Russian Federation
Kománfalva *see* Comănești
113 I22 **Komárno** ***Ger.*** Komorn, ***Hung.*** Komárom. Nitriansky Kraj, SW Slovakia *47.46N 18.07E*
113 I22 **Komárom** Komárom-Esztergom, NW Hungary *47.44N 18.06E*
Komárom *see* Komárno
113 I22 **Komárom-Esztergom** ***off.*** Komárom-Esztergom Megye. ◈ *county* N Hungary
171 I13 **Komatsu** ***var.*** Komatu. Ishikawa, Honshū, SW Japan *36.24N 136.27E*
170 Ff15 **Komatsushima** Tokushima, Shikoku, SW Japan *34.00N 134.36E*
Komatu *see* Komatsu
85 D17 **Kombat** Otjozondjupa, N Namibia *19.42S 17.45E*
Kombissiguiri *see* Kombissiri
79 P13 **Kombissiri** ***var.*** Kombissiguiri. C Burkina *12.03N 1.14W*
196 E10 **Komebail Lagoon** *lagoon* N Palau
83 F20 **Kome Island** *island* N Tanzania
Komeyo *see* Wandai
176 W13 **Komfane** Pulau Wokam, E Indonesia *5.36S 134.42E*
119 P10 **Kominternivs'ke** Odes'ka Oblast', SW Ukraine *46.52N 30.56E*
129 R12 **Komi-Permyatskiy Avtonomnyy Okrug** ◈ *autonomous district* W Russian Federation
129 R8 **Komi, Respublika** ◈ *autonomous republic* NW Russian Federation
113 I25 **Komló** Baranya, SW Hungary *46.11N 18.19E*
Kommunarsk *see* Alchevs'k
153 S12 **Kommunizm, Qullai** ▲ E Tajikistan
194 G12 **Komo** Southern Highlands, W PNG *6.06S 142.52E*
175 P16 **Komodo** Pulau Komodo, S Indonesia *8.35S 119.27E*
175 P16 **Komodo, Pulau** *island* Nusa Tenggara, S Indonesia
79 N15 **Komoé** ***var.*** Komoé Fleuve. ≈ E Ivory Coast
Komoé Fleuve *see* Komoé
77 X11 **Kôm Ombo** ***var.*** Kawm Umbū. SE Egypt *24.23N 32.58E*
81 F20 **Komono** La Lékoumou, SW Congo *3.15S 13.13E*
176 Y16 **Komoran** Irian Jaya, E Indonesia *8.14S 138.51E*
176 Y16 **Komoran, Pulau** *island* E Indonesia
Komorn *see* Komárno
Komornok *see* Comorâște
171 J14 **Komoro** Nagano, Honshū, S Japan *36.22N 138.25E*
Komosolabad *see* Komsomolobod
Komotau *see* Chomutov
116 K13 **Komotiní** ***var.*** Gümüljina, ***Turk.*** Gümülcine. Anatolikí Makedonía kai Thráki, NE Greece *41.06N 25.27E*
115 K16 **Komovi** ▲▲ SW Yugoslavia
119 R8 **Kompaniyivka** Kirovohrads'ka Oblast', C Ukraine *48.16N 32.12E*
194 H12 **Kompiam** Enga, W PNG *5.23S 143.54E*
Kompong *see* Kâmpóng Chhnăng
Kompong Cham *see* Kâmpóng Cham
Kompong Kleang *see* Kâmpóng Khleăng
Kompong Som *see* Kâmpóng Saôm
Kompong Speu *see* Kâmpóng Spoe
Komrat *see* Comrat
Komsomol *see* Komsomol'skiy, Atyrau, Kazakhstan
Komsomol *see* Komsomolets, Kostanay, Kazakhstan
150 L7 **Komsomolets** ***Kaz.*** Komsomol. Kostanay, N Kazakhstan *53.48N 61.58E*
126 Ii2 **Komsomolets, Ostrov** *island* Severnaya Zemlya, N Russian Federation
150 F13 **Komsomolets, Zaliv** *lake gulf* SW Kazakhstan
153 Q12 **Komsomolobod** ***Rus.*** Komosolabad. C Tajikistan *38.51N 69.54E*
128 M16 **Komsomol'sk** Ivanovskaya Oblast', W Russian Federation *56.58N 40.15E*
119 S6 **Komsomol's'k** Poltavs'ka Oblast', C Ukraine *49.01N 33.37E*
152 M11 **Komsomol'sk** Nawoiy Wiloyati, N Uzbekistan *40.14N 65.10E*
150 G12 **Komsomol'skiy** ***Kaz.*** Komsomol. Atyrau, W Kazakhstan *47.18N 53.37E*
129 W4 **Komsomol'skiy** Respublika Komi, NW Russian Federation *67.33N 64.00E*
127 Nn15 **Komsomol'sk-na-Amure** Khabarovskiy Kray, SE Russian Federation *50.31N 136.58E*
Komsomol'sk-na-Ustyurte *see* Komsomol'sk-Ustyurt
150 K10 **Komsomol'skoye** Aktyubinsk, NW Kazakhstan
131 Q8 **Komsomol'skoye** Saratovskaya Oblast', W Russian Federation *50.45N 47.00E*
152 G6 **Komsomol'sk-Ustyurt** ***Rus.*** Komsomol'sk-na-Ustyurte. Qoraqalpoghiston Respublikasi, NW Uzbekistan *44.06N 58.14E*
151 P10 **Kon** ≈ C Kazakhstan
Kona *see* Kailua
128 K16 **Konakovo** Tverskaya Oblast', W Russian Federation *56.42N 36.44E*
149 V15 **Konārak** Sīstān va Balūchestān, SE Iran *25.26N 60.22E*
Konarhā *see* Kunar
29 O11 **Konawa** Oklahoma, C USA *34.57N 96.45W*
176 V9 **Konda** Irian Jaya, E Indonesia *1.34S 131.58E*
125 Ff11 **Konda** ≈ C Russian Federation
160 L13 **Kondagaon** Madhya Pradesh, C India *19.38N 81.41E*
12 K10 **Kondiaronk, Lac** ◎ Quebec, SE Canada
188 J13 **Kondinin** Western Australia *32.31S 118.15E*
83 H21 **Kondoa** Dodoma, C Tanzania *4.54S 35.46E*
131 P6 **Kondol'** Penzenskaya Oblast', W Russian Federation *52.49N 45.03E*
116 N10 **Kondolovo** Burgas, E Bulgaria *42.07N 27.43E*
176 Z16 **Kondomirat** Irian Jaya, E Indonesia *8.57S 140.55E*
128 J10 **Kondopoga** Respublika Kareliya, NW Russian Federation *62.12N 34.16E*
Kondoz *see* Kunduz
161 J17 **Kondukūr** ***var.*** Kandukur. Andhra Pradesh, E India *15.17N 79.49E*
Kondūz *see* Kunduz
197 H6 **Koné** Province Nord, W New Caledonia *21.04S 164.51E*
Könekesir *see* Kënekesir
Köneürgench *see* Këneurgench
79 N15 **Kong** N Ivory Coast *9.06N 4.34W*
41 S5 **Kongakut River** ≈ Alaska, USA
207 O14 **Kong Christian IX Land** ***Eng.*** King Christian IX Land. *physical region* SE Greenland
207 P13 **Kong Christian X Land** ***Eng.*** King Christian X Land. *physical region* E Greenland
207 N13 **Kong Frederik IX Land** ***Eng.*** King Frederik IX Land. *physical region* SW Greenland
207 Q12 **Kong Frederik VIII Land** ***Eng.*** King Frederik VIII Land. *physical region* NE Greenland
207 N15 **Kong Frederik VI Kyst** ***Eng.*** King Frederik VI Coast. *physical region* SE Greenland
178 I13 **Kŏng, Kaôh** ***prev.*** Kas Kong. *island* SW Cambodia
94 P2 **Kong Karls Land** ***Eng.*** King Charles Islands. *island group* SE Svalbard
83 G14 **Kong Kong** ≈ SE Sudan
Kongo *see* Congo (river)
85 G16 **Kongola** Caprivi, NE Namibia *17.47S 23.24E*
81 N21 **Kongolo** Katanga, E Dem. Rep. Congo (Zaire) *5.20S 26.57E*
83 F14 **Kongor** Jonglei, SE Sudan *7.09N 31.44E*
207 Q14 **Kong Oscar Fjord** *fjord* E Greenland
79 P12 **Kongoussi** N Burkina *13.19N 1.31W*
97 G15 **Kongsberg** Buskerud, S Norway *59.39N 9.37E*
94 Q2 **Kongsøya** *island* Kong Karls Land, E Svalbard
97 I14 **Kongsvinger** Hedmark, S Norway *60.10N 12.00E*
178 Jj11 **Kông, Tônle** ***Lao.*** Xê Kong. ≈ Cambodia/Laos
164 E8 **Kongur Shan** ▲ NW China *38.39N 75.21E*
83 I22 **Kongwa** Dodoma, C Tanzania *6.13S 36.28E*
Kong, Xê *see* Kông, Tônle
Konia *see* Konya
153 R11 **Konibodom** ***Rus.*** Kanibadam. N Tajikistan *40.16N 70.20E*
113 K15 **Koniecpol** Śląskie, S Poland *50.47N 19.45E*
Konieh *see* Konya
Königgrätz *see* Hradec Králové
Königinhof an der Elbe *see* Dvůr Králové nad Labem
103 K23 **Königsbrunn** Bayern, S Germany *48.16N 10.52E*
Königshütte *see* Chorzów
103 O24 **Königssee** ◎ SE Germany
111 S8 **Königstuhl** ▲ S Austria *46.57N 13.47E*
111 U3 **Konigswiesen** Oberösterreich, N Austria *48.25N 14.48E*
103 E17 **Königswinter** Nordrhein-Westfalen, W Germany *50.40N 7.12E*
152 M11 **Konimekh** ***Rus.*** Kenimekh. Nawoiy Wiloyati, N Uzbekistan *40.14N 65.10E*
112 I12 **Konin** ***Ger.*** Kuhnau. Wielkopolskie, C Poland *52.13N 18.16E*
Koninkrijk der Nederlanden *see* Netherlands
115 L24 **Konispol** ***var.*** Konispoli. Vlorë, S Albania *39.40N 20.10E*
Konispoli *see* Konispol
117 C15 **Kónitsa** Ípeiros, W Greece *40.04N 20.48E*
Konitz *see* Chojnice
110 D8 **Köniz** Bern, W Switzerland *46.55N 7.26E*
115 H14 **Konjic** Federacija Bosna I Hercegovina, C Bosnia and Herzegovina *43.39N 17.55E*
94 J10 **Könkämäälven** ≈ Finland/Sweden
161 D14 **Konkan** W India
85 D22 **Konkiep** ≈ S Namibia
78 I14 **Konkouré** ≈ W Guinea
79 O11 **Konna** Mopti, S Mali *14.58N 3.49W*
195 P10 **Konogaiang, Mount** ▲ New Ireland, NE PNG *4.05S 152.43E*
195 P10 **Konogogo** New Ireland, NE PNG *3.25S 152.09E*
110 E9 **Konolfingen** Bern, W Switzerland *46.53N 7.36E*
79 P16 **Konongo** C Ghana *6.39N 1.06W*
195 O9 **Konos** New Ireland, NE PNG *3.07S 151.43E*
128 M12 **Konosha** Arkhangel'skaya Oblast', NW Russian Federation *60.58N 40.09E*
119 R3 **Konotop** Sums'ka Oblast', NE Ukraine *51.15N 33.13E*
164 L7 **Konqi He** ≈ NW China
113 L14 **Końskie** Świętokrzyskie, C Poland *51.12N 20.26E*
Konstantinovka *see* Kostyantynivka
130 M11 **Konstantinovsk** Rostovskaya Oblast', SW Russian Federation *47.37N 41.07E*
103 H24 **Konstanz** ***var.*** Constanz, ***Eng.*** Constance; ***hist.*** Kostnitz, ***anc.*** Constantia. Baden-Württemberg, S Germany *47.40N 9.10E*
Konstanza *see* Constanța
79 T14 **Kontagora** Niger, W Nigeria *10.25N 5.29E*
80 E13 **Kontcha** Nord, N Cameroon *8.00N 12.13E*
101 G17 **Kontich** Antwerpen, N Belgium *51.07N 4.27E*
95 O16 **Kontiolahti** Itä-Suomi, E Finland *62.46N 29.51E*
95 M15 **Kontiomäki** Oulu, C Finland *64.20N 28.09E*
178 K11 **Kon Tum** ***var.*** Kontum. Kon Tum, C Vietnam *14.23N 108.00E*
Konur *see* Sulakyurt
142 H15 **Konya** ***var.*** Konieh; ***prev.*** Konia, ***anc.*** Iconium. Konya, C Turkey *37.51N 32.30E*
142 H15 **Konya** ***var.*** Konia, Konieh. ◈ *province* C Turkey
151 T13 **Konyrat** ***var.*** Kounradskiy, ***Kaz.*** Qongyrat. Karaganda, C Kazakhstan *46.58N 74.54E*
151 W15 **Konyrolen** Almaty, SE Kazakhstan *44.16N 79.18E*
83 I19 **Konza** Eastern, S Kenya *1.44S 37.07E*
100 I9 **Koog aan den Zaan** Noord-Holland, C Netherlands *52.28N 4.49E*
190 E7 **Koonibba** South Australia *31.55S 133.23E*
33 O11 **Koontz Lake** Indiana, N USA *41.25N 86.24W*
176 V8 **Koor** Irian Jaya, E Indonesia *0.21S 132.28E*
191 R9 **Koorawatha** New South Wales, SE Australia *34.03S 148.33E*
120 J5 **Koosa** Tartumaa, E Estonia *58.31N 27.06E*
35 N7 **Kootenai** ***var.*** Kootenay. ≈ Canada/USA ***see also*** Kootenay
9 P17 **Kootenay** ***var.*** Kootenai. ≈ Canada/USA ***see also*** Kootenai
85 F24 **Kootjieskolk** Northern Cape, W South Africa *31.16S 20.21E*
115 M15 **Kopaonik** ▲▲ S Yugoslavia
Kopar *see* Koper
94 K1 **Kópasker** Nordhurland Eystra, N Iceland *66.15N 16.23W*
94 H4 **Kópavogur** Reykjanes, W Iceland *64.06N 21.47W*
111 S13 **Koper** ***It.*** Capodistria; ***prev.*** Kopar. SW Slovenia *45.32N 13.42E*
97 C16 **Kopervik** Rogaland, S Norway *59.16N 5.18E*
Kopetdag, Khrebet *see* Koppeh Dāgh
125 Ee12 **Kopeysk** Kurganskaya Oblast', C Russian Federation *55.06N 61.31E*
Kophinou *see* Kofínou
190 G8 **Kopi** South Australia *33.24S 135.40E*
Kopiago *see* Lake Copiago
159 W12 **Kopili** ≈ NE India
97 M15 **Köping** Västmanland, C Sweden *59.31N 16.00E*
115 K17 **Koplik** ***var.*** Kopliku. Shkodër, NW Albania *42.12N 19.26E*
Kopliku *see* Koplik
Kopopo *see* Kokopo
96 I11 **Koppang** Hedmark, S Norway *61.34N 11.01E*
Kopparberg *see* Dalarna
149 S3 **Koppeh Dāgh** ***var.*** Khrebet Kopetdag. ▲▲ Iran/Turkmenistan
Koppename *see* Coppename Rivier
97 J15 **Koppom** Värmland, C Sweden *59.42N 12.07E*
Kopreinitz *see* Koprivnica
116 K9 **Koprinka, Yazovir** ***prev.*** Yazovir Georgi Dimitrov. ⊠ C Bulgaria
114 F7 **Koprivnica** ***Ger.*** Kopreinitz, ***Hung.*** Kaproncza. Koprivnica-Križevci, N Croatia *46.10N 16.49E*
114 F8 **Koprivnica-Križevci** ***off.*** Koprivničko-Križevačka Županija. ◈ *province* N Croatia
113 I17 **Kopřivnice** ***Ger.*** Nesselsdorf. Ostravský Kraj, E Czech Republic *49.36N 18.09E*
Köprülü *see* Veles
Koptsevichi *see* Kaptsevichy
Kopyl' *see* Kapyl'
121 O14 **Kopys'** ***Rus.*** Kopys'. Vitsyebskaya Voblasts', NE Belarus *54.21N 30.21E*
115 M18 **Korab** ▲ Albania/FYR Macedonia *41.48N 20.33E*
Korabavur Pastligi *see* Karabaur', Uval
83 M14 **K'orahē** Somali, E Ethiopia *6.36N 44.21E*
117 L16 **Kórakas, Akrotírio** *headland* Lésvos, E Greece *39.20N 26.20E*
114 D9 **Korana** ≈ C Croatia
161 L14 **Korāput** Orissa, E India *18.49N 82.43E*
Korat *see* Nakhon Ratchasima
178 Ii9 **Korat Plateau** *plateau* E Thailand
145 T1 **Kōrāwa, Sar-i** ▲ NE Iraq *37.07N 44.39E*
160 L11 **Korba** Madhya Pradesh, C India *22.25N 82.43E*
103 H15 **Korbach** Hessen, C Germany *51.16N 8.52E*
Korça *see* Korçë
115 M21 **Korçë** ***var.*** Korça, ***Gk.*** Korytsa, ***It.*** Corriza; ***prev.*** Koritsa. Korçë, SE Albania *40.37N 20.46E*
115 M21 **Korçë** ◈ *district* SE Albania
115 G15 **Korčula** ***It.*** Curzola. Dubrovnik-Neretva, S Croatia *42.57N 17.08E*
115 F15 **Korčula** ***It.*** Curzola; ***anc.*** Corcyra Nigra. *island* S Croatia
115 F15 **Korčulanski Kanal** *channel* S Croatia
151 T6 **Korday** ***prev.*** Georgiyevka. Zhambyl, SE Kazakhstan *43.06N 74.42E*
148 J5 **Kordestān** ***off.*** Ostān-e Kordestān, ***var.*** Kurdestan. ◈ *province* W Iran
149 P4 **Kord Kūy** ***var.*** Kurd Kui. Golestān, N Iran *36.49N 54.04E*
169 V13 **Korea Bay** *bay* China/North Korea
Korea, Democratic People's Republic of *see* North Korea
176 Uu15 **Koreare** Pulau Yamdena, E Indonesia *7.33S 131.13E*
Korea, Republic of *see* South Korea
169 Z17 **Korea Strait** ***Jap.*** Chōsen-kaikyō, ***Kor.*** Taehan-haehyŏp. *channel* Japan/South Korea
Korelichi/Korelicze *see* Karelichy
82 J11 **Korem** Tigray, N Ethiopia *12.32N 39.29E*
79 U11 **Korén Adoua** ≈ C Niger
130 I7 **Korenevo** Kurskaya Oblast', W Russian Federation *51.21N 34.53E*
130 L13 **Korenovsk** Krasnodarskiy Kray, SW Russian Federation *45.28N 39.25E*
118 L4 **Korets'** ***Pol.*** Korzec, ***Rus.*** Korets. Rivnens'ka Oblast', NW Ukraine *50.38N 27.12E*
127 Pp8 **Korf** Koryakskiy Avtonomnyy Okrug, E Russian Federation *60.20N 165.37E*
204 L7 **Korff Ice Rise** *ice cap* Antarctica
94 G13 **Korgen** Troms, N Norway *66.04N 13.51E*
153 R9 **Korgon-Dëbë** Dzhalal-Abadskaya Oblast', W Kyrgyzstan *41.51N 70.52E*
78 M14 **Korhogo** N Ivory Coast *9.28N 5.38W*
117 F19 **Korinthiakós Kólpos** ***Eng.*** Gulf of Corinth; ***anc.*** Corinthiacus Sinus. *gulf* C Greece
117 F19 **Kórinthos** ***Eng.*** Corinth; ***anc.*** Corinthus. Pelopónnisos, S Greece *37.55N 22.55E*
115 M18 **Koritnik** ▲ S Yugoslavia *42.06N 20.34E*
Koritsa *see* Korçë
171 L14 **Kōriyama** Fukushima, Honshū, C Japan *37.25N 140.20E*
142 E16 **Korkuteli** Antalya, SW Turkey *37.04N 30.12E*
164 K6 **Korla** ***Chin.*** K'u-erh-lo. Xinjiang Uygur Zizhiqu, NW China *41.48N 86.10E*
126 H11 **Korliki** Khanty-Mansiyskiy Avtonomnyy Okrug, C Russian Federation *61.28N 82.12E*
Körlin an der Persante *see* Karlino
Korma *see* Karma
12 D8 **Kormak** Ontario, S Canada *47.38N 83.00W*
Kormakíti, Akrotíri/Kormakiti, Cape/Kormakítis *see* Koruçam Burnu
113 G23 **Körmend** Vas, W Hungary *47.01N 16.34E*
145 T5 **Kōrmōr** E Iraq *35.06N 44.47E*
114 C13 **Kornat** ***It.*** Incoronata. *island* W Croatia
Korneshty *see* Cornești
111 X3 **Korneuburg** Niederösterreich, NE Austria *48.22N 16.20E*
151 P7 **Korneyevka** Severnyy Kazakhstan, N Kazakhstan *54.01N 68.30E*
97 I17 **Kornsjø** Østfold, S Norway *58.55N 11.40E*
79 O11 **Koro** Mopti, S Mali *14.05N 3.06W*
197 J14 **Koro** *island* C Fiji
194 F12 **Koroba** Southern Highlands, W PNG *5.46S 142.48E*
130 K8 **Korocha** Belgorodskaya Oblast', W Russian Federation *50.49N 37.08E*
142 H12 **Köroğlu Dağları** ▲▲ C Turkey
191 V6 **Korogoro Point** *headland* New South Wales, SE Australia *31.03S 153.04E*
83 J21 **Korogwe** Tanga, E Tanzania *5.12S 38.26E*
190 L13 **Koroit** Victoria, SE Australia *38.17S 142.22E*
197 H15 **Korolevu** Viti Levu, W Fiji *18.12S 177.44E*
202 I17 **Koromiri** *island* S Cook Islands
179 R16 **Koronadal** Mindanao, S Philippines *6.23N 124.54E*
117 E22 **Koróni** Pelopónnisos, S Greece *36.46N 21.57E*
116 G13 **Korónia, Límni** ◎ N Greece
112 I9 **Koronowo** ***Ger.*** Krone an der Brahe. Kujawski-pomorskie, C Poland *53.18N 17.56E*
119 R2 **Korop** Chernihivs'ka Oblast', N Ukraine *51.35N 32.57E*
117 H19 **Koropí** Attikí, C Greece *37.54N 23.52E*
Koror *see* Oreor
Kőrös *see* Križevci
113 L23 **Körös** ≈ E Hungary
Körösbánya *see* Baia de Criș
197 J14 **Koro Sea** *sea* C Fiji
Koroška *see* Kärnten
119 N3 **Korosten'** Zhytomyrs'ka Oblast', NW Ukraine *50.56N 28.39E*
Korostyshev *see* Korostyshiv
119 N4 **Korostyshiv** ***Rus.*** Korostyshev. Zhytomyrs'ka Oblast', N Ukraine *50.18N 29.04E*
129 V3 **Korotaikha** ≈ NW Russian Federation
126 H9 **Korotchayevo** Yamalo-Nenetskiy Avtonomnyy Okrug, N Russian Federation *66.00N 78.11E*
80 I8 **Koro Toro** Borkou-Ennedi-Tibesti, N Chad *16.01N 18.27E*
41 N16 **Korovin Island** *island* Shumagin Islands, Alaska, USA
197 I14 **Korovou** Viti Levu, W Fiji *17.48S 178.32E*
95 M17 **Korpilahti** Länsi-Suomi, W Finland *62.01N 25.34E*
94 K12 **Korpilombolo** Norrbotten, N Sweden *66.51N 23.00E*
127 Oo16 **Korsakov** Ostrov Sakhalin, Sakhalinskaya Oblast', SE Russian Federation *46.41N 142.45E*
95 J16 **Korsholm** ***Fin.*** Mustasaari. Länsi-Suomi, W Finland *63.07N 21.45E*
97 I23 **Korsør** Vestsjælland, E Denmark *55.19N 11.09E*
Korsovka *see* Kārsava
119 P6 **Korsun'-Shevchenkivs'kyy** ***Rus.*** Korsun'-Shevchenkovskiy. Cherkas'ka Oblast', C Ukraine *49.25N 31.15E*
Korsun'-Shevchenkovskiy *see* Korsun'-Shevchenkivs'kyy
101 C17 **Kortemark** West-Vlaanderen, W Belgium *51.03N 3.03E*
101 H18 **Kortenberg** Vlaams Brabant, C Belgium *50.52N 4.33E*
101 K18 **Kortessem** Limburg, NE Belgium *50.52N 5.22E*
101 E14 **Kortgene** Zeeland, SW Netherlands *51.34N 3.48E*
82 F8 **Korti** Northern, N Sudan *18.06N 31.33E*
101 C18 **Kortrijk** ***Fr.*** Courtrai. West-Vlaanderen, W Belgium *50.49N 3.16E*
124 N2 **Koruçam Burnu** ***var.*** Cape Kormakiti, Kormakítis, ***Gk.*** Akrotíri Kormakíti. *headland* N Cyprus *35.24N 32.55E*
191 O13 **Korumburra** Victoria, SE Australia *38.27S 145.48E*
Koryak Range *see* Koryakskoye Nagor'ye
127 P8 **Koryakskiy Avtonomnyy Okrug** ◈ *autonomous district* E Russian Federation
Koryakskiy Khrebet *see* Koryakskoye Nagor'ye
127 Pp7 **Koryakskoye Nagor'ye** ***var.*** Koryakskiy Khrebet, ***Eng.*** Koryak Range. ▲▲ NE Russian Federation
129 P11 **Koryazhma** Arkhangel'skaya Oblast', NW Russian Federation *61.16N 47.06E*
Kōryō *see* Kangnŭng
Korytsa *see* Korçë
119 Q2 **Koryukivka** Chernihivs'ka Oblast', N Ukraine *51.45N 32.16E*
Korzec *see* Korets'
117 N21 **Kos** Kos, Dodekánisos, Greece, Aegean Sea *36.53N 27.18E*
117 M21 **Kos** ***It.*** Coo; ***anc.*** Cos. *island* Dodekánisos, Greece, Aegean Sea
129 T12 **Kosa** Komi-Permyatskiy Avtonomnyy Okrug, NW Russian Federation *59.55N 54.54E*
129 T13 **Kosa** ≈ NW Russian Federation
170 C11 **Kō-saki** *headland* Nagasaki, Tsushima, SW Japan *34.06N 129.13E*
169 X13 **Kosan** SE North Korea *38.50N 127.26E*
121 H18 **Kosava** ***Rus.*** Kosovo. Brestskaya Voblasts', SW Belarus *52.45N 25.16E*
Kosch *see* Kose
150 G12 **Koschagyl** ***Kaz.*** Qosshaghyl. Atyrau, W Kazakhstan *46.52N 53.46E*
112 G12 **Kościan** ***Ger.*** Kosten. Wielkopolskie, C Poland *52.04N 16.37E*
112 I7 **Kościerzyna** Pomorskie, NW Poland *54.06N 17.55E*
24 L4 **Kosciusko** Mississippi, S USA *33.03N 89.35W*
Kosciusko, Mount *see* Kosciuszko, Mount
191 R11 **Kosciuszko, Mount** ***prev.*** Mount Kosciusko ▲ New South Wales, SE Australia *36.28S 148.15E*
120 H4 **Kose** ***Ger.*** Kosch. Harjumaa, NW Estonia *59.10N 25.10E*
116 G6 **Koshava** Vidin, NW Bulgaria *44.03N 23.00E*
153 U9 **Kosh-Dëbë** ***var.*** Koshtebë. Narynskaya Oblast', C Kyrgyzstan *41.03N 74.08E*
171 K16 **Koshigaya** ***var.*** Kosigaya. Saitama, Honshū, S Japan *35.54N 139.46E*
K'o-shih *see* Kashi
170 B15 **Koshikijima-rettō** ***var.*** Kosikizima Rettô. *island group* SW Japan
151 W13 **Koshkarkol', Ozero** ◎ SE Kazakhstan
32 L9 **Koshkonong, Lake** ◎ Wisconsin, N USA
152 B10 **Koshoba** ***Turkm.*** Goshoba. Balkanskiy Velayat, NW Turkmenistan *40.28N 54.11E*
171 J14 **Kōshoku** ***var.*** Kôsyoku. Nagano, Honshū, S Japan *36.31N 138.07E*
Koshtebë *see* Kosh-Dëbë
Kōshū *see* Kwangju
113 N19 **Košice** ***Ger.*** Kaschau, ***Hung.*** Kassa. Košický Kraj, E Slovakia *48.43N 21.15E*
113 M20 **Košický Kraj** ◈ *region* E Slovakia
Kosigaya *see* Koshigaya
Kosikizima Rettô *see* Koshikijima-retto
159 R12 **Kosi Reservoir** ⊠ E Nepal
118 J8 **Kosiv** Ivano-Frankivs'ka Oblast', W Ukraine *48.19N 25.04E*
151 O11 **Koskol'** Zhezkazgan, C Kazakhstan *49.34N 67.03E*
129 Q9 **Koslan** Respublika Komi, NW Russian Federation *63.27N 48.52E*
Köslin *see* Koszalin
152 M12 **Koson** ***Rus.*** Kasan. Qashqadaryo Wiloyati, S Uzbekistan *39.03N 65.34E*
169 Y13 **Kosŏng** SE North Korea *38.40N 128.13E*
153 S9 **Kosonsoy** ***Rus.*** Kasansay. Namangan Wiloyati, E Uzbekistan *41.15N 71.28E*
115 M16 **Kosovo** ***prev.*** Autonomous Province of Kosovo and Metohija. *region* S Yugoslavia
Kosovo *see* Kosava
Kosovo and Metohija, Autonomous Province of *see* Kosovo

◆ Country
● Country Capital
◇ Dependent Territory
○ Dependent Territory Capital
◈ Administrative Region
✕ International Airport
▲ Mountain
▲▲ Mountain Range
⩘ Volcano
≈ River
◎ Lake
⊠ Reservoir

KOSOVO POLJE – KSIĄŻ WIELKOPOLSKI

115 N16 **Kosovo Polje** Serbia, S Yugoslavia *42.40N 21.07E*
115 O16 **Kosovska Kamenica** Serbia, SE Yugoslavia *42.37N 21.33E*
115 M16 **Kosovska Mitrovica** *Alb.* Mitrovicë; *prev.* Mitrovica, Titova Mitrovica. Serbia, S Yugoslavia *42.54N 20.52E*
201 X17 **Kosrae** ◆ *state* E Micronesia
201 Y14 **Kosrae** *prev.* Kusaie. *island* Caroline Islands, E Micronesia
27 U9 **Kosse** Texas, SW USA *31.16N 96.38W*
111 P6 **Kössen** Tirol, W Austria *47.40N 12.24E*
78 M16 **Kossou, Lac de** ◎ C Ivory Coast
Kossukavak *see* Krumovgrad
Kostajnica *see* Hrvatska Kostajnica
150 M7 **Kostanay** *var.* Kustanay, *Kaz.* Qostanay. N Kazakhstan *53.15N 63.34E*
150 L8 **Kostanay** *var.* Kostanayskaya Oblast, *Kaz.* Qostanay Oblysy. ◆ *province* N Kazakhstan
Kostanayskaya Oblast *see* Kostanay
Kostamus *see* Kostomuksha
Kosten *see* Kościan
116 H10 **Kostenets** *prev.* Georgi Dimitrov. Sofiya, W Bulgaria *42.17N 23.52E*
82 F10 **Kosti** White Nile, C Sudan *13.10N 32.37E*
Kostnitz *see* Konstanz
128 H7 **Kostomuksha** *Fin.* Kostamus. Respublika Kareliya, NW Russian Federation *64.33N 30.28E*
118 K3 **Kostopil'** *Rus.* Kostopol'. Rivnens'ka Oblast', NW Ukraine *50.20N 26.28E*
Kostopol' *see* Kostopil'
128 M15 **Kostroma** Kostromskaya Oblast', NW Russian Federation *57.46N 40.59E*
129 N14 **Kostroma** ∽ NW Russian Federation
129 N14 **Kostromskaya Oblast'** ◆ *province* NW Russian Federation
112 D11 **Kostrzyn** *Ger.* Cüstrin, Küstrin. Lubuskie, W Poland *52.35N 14.39E*
112 H11 **Kostrzyn** Wielkolpolskie, C Poland *52.23N 17.13E*
119 X7 **Kostyantynivka** *Rus.* Konstantinovka. Donets'ka Oblast', SE Ukraine *48.30N 37.45E*
Kostyukovichi *see* Kastsyukovichy
Kostyukovka *see* Kastsyukowka
Kôsyoku *see* Kōshoku
129 U6 **Kos'yu** Respublika Komi, NW Russian Federation *65.39N 59.01E*
129 U6 **Kos'yu** ∽ NW Russian Federation
112 F7 **Koszalin** *Ger.* Köslin. Koszalin, NW Poland *54.11N 16.10E*
113 F22 **Kőszeg** *Ger.* Güns. Vas, W Hungary *47.24N 16.33E*
158 H13 **Kota** *prev.* Kotah. Rājasthān, N India *25.13N 75.51E*
174 H9 **Kota Baru** Sumatera, W Indonesia *1.07S 101.43E*
175 Nn11 **Kotabaru** Pulau Laut, C Indonesia *3.15S 116.15E*
Kotabaru *see* Jayapura
174 H2 **Kota Bharu** *var.* Kota Baharu, Kota Bahru. Kelantan, Peninsular Malaysia *6.07N 102.15E*
Kotaboemi *see* Kotabumi
174 Ii12 **Kotabumi** *prev.* Kotaboemi. Sumatera, W Indonesia *4.49S 104.54E*
155 S10 **Kot Addu** Punjab, E Pakistan *30.25N 70.54E*
Kotah *see* Kota
175 Nn2 **Kota Kinabalu** *prev.* Jesselton. Sabah, East Malaysia *5.58N 116.04E*
175 Nn2 **Kota Kinabalu** ✈ Sabah, East Malaysia *5.58N 116.04E*
94 M12 **Kotala** Lappi, N Finland *67.01N 29.00E*
Kotamobagoe *see* Kotamobagu
175 Rr7 **Kotamobagu** *prev.* Kotamobagoe. Sulawesi, C Indonesia *0.46N 124.21E*
161 L14 **Kotapad** *var.* Kotapārh. Orissa, E India *19.10N 82.23E*
Kotapārh *see* Kotapad
178 Gg17 **Ko Ta Ru Tao** *island* SW Thailand
174 L11 **Kotawaringin, Teluk** *bay* Borneo, C Indonesia
155 Q13 **Kot Diji** Sind, SE Pakistan *27.16N 68.43E*
158 K9 **Kotdwāra** Uttar Pradesh, N India *29.43N 78.33E*
129 Q14 **Kotel'nich** Kirovskaya Oblast', NW Russian Federation *58.19N 48.12E*
131 N12 **Kotel'nikovo** Volgogradskaya Oblast', SW Russian Federation *47.37N 43.07E*
126 Ll4 **Kotel'nyy, Ostrov** *island* Novosibirskiye Ostrova, N Russian Federation
119 T5 **Kotel'va** Poltavs'ka Oblast', C Ukraine *50.04N 34.46E*
103 M14 **Köthen** *var.* Cöthen. Sachsen-Anhalt, C Germany *51.46N 11.58E*
Kôti *see* Kōchi
83 G17 **Kotido** NE Uganda *3.03N 34.07E*
95 M19 **Kotka** Etelä-Suomi, S Finland *60.28N 26.54E*
129 P11 **Kotlas** Arkhangel'skaya Oblast', NW Russian Federation *61.13N 46.43E*
40 M10 **Kotlik** Alaska, USA *63.01N 163.33W*
79 Q17 **Kotoka** ✈ (Accra) S Ghana *5.41N 0.10W*
Kotonu *see* Cotonou
115 J17 **Kotor** *It.* Cattaro. Montenegro, SW Yugoslavia *42.25N 18.47E*
Kotor *see* Kotoriba
114 F7 **Kotoriba** *Hung.* Kotor. Medimurje, N Croatia *46.20N 16.47E*
115 I17 **Kotorska, Boka** *It.* Bocche di Cattaro. *bay* Montenegro, SW Yugoslavia
114 H11 **Kotorsko** Republika Srpska, N Bosnia and Herzegovina *44.50N 18.03E*
114 G11 **Kotor Varoš** Republika Srpska, N Bosnia and Herzegovina *44.37N 17.24E*
Koto Sho/Kotosho *see* Lan Yü
130 M7 **Kotovsk** Tambovskaya Oblast', W Russian Federation *52.39N 41.31E*
119 O9 **Kotovs'k** *Rus.* Kotovsk. Odes'ka Oblast', SW Ukraine *47.42N 29.30E*
Kotovsk *see* Hînceşti
121 G16 **Kotra** *Rus.* Kotra. ∽ W Belarus
155 P16 **Kotri** Sind, SE Pakistan *25.22N 68.16E*
111 Q9 **Kötschach** Kärnten, S Austria *46.41N 12.57E*
161 K15 **Kottagūdem** Andhra Pradesh, E India *17.36N 80.40E*
161 F21 **Kottappadi** Kerala, SW India *11.38N 76.03E*
161 G23 **Kottayam** Kerala, SW India *9.37N 76.31E*
Kottbus *see* Cottbus
Kotte *see* Sri Jayawardanapura
81 K15 **Kotto** ∽ Central African Republic/Dem. Rep. Congo (Zaire)
200 S13 **Kotu Group** *island group* W Tonga
152 B11 **Koturdepe** *Turkm.* Goturdepe. Balkanskiy Velayat, W Turkmenistan *39.32N 53.39E*
126 J9 **Kotuy** ∽ N Russian Federation
85 M16 **Kotwa** Mashonaland East, NE Zimbabwe *16.58S 32.46E*
41 N7 **Kotzebue** Alaska, USA *66.54N 162.36W*
40 M7 **Kotzebue Sound** *inlet* Alaska, USA
Kotzenan *see* Chocianów
Kotzman *see* Kitsman'
79 R14 **Kouandé** NW Benin *10.19N 1.42E*
81 J15 **Kouango** Ouaka, S Central African Republic *5.00N 20.01E*
79 O13 **Koudougou** C Burkina *12.15N 2.22W*
100 K7 **Koudum** Friesland, N Netherlands *52.55N 5.26E*
117 L25 **Koufonísi** *island* SE Greece
117 K21 **Koufonísi** *island* Kykládes, Greece, Aegean Sea
40 M8 **Kougarok Mountain** ▲ Alaska, USA *65.41N 165.29W*
81 E20 **Kouilou** ∽ S Congo
16 N3 **Koukdjuak** ∽ Baffin Island, Nunavut, NE Canada
124 N4 **Koúklia** SW Cyprus *34.42N 32.35E*
81 E19 **Koulamoutou** Ogooué-Lolo, C Gabon *1.06S 12.26E*
78 L12 **Koulikoro** Koulikoro, SW Mali *12.55N 7.35W*
78 L11 **Koulikoro** ◆ *region* SW Mali
197 H5 **Koumac** Province Nord, W New Caledonia *20.34S 164.18E*
171 J15 **Koumi** Nagano, Honshū, S Japan *36.06N 138.27E*
80 I13 **Koumra** Moyen-Chari, S Chad *8.55N 17.31E*
Kounadougou *see* Koundougou
78 M15 **Kounahiri** C Ivory Coast *7.47N 5.51W*
78 I12 **Koundâra** Moyenne-Guinée, NW Guinea *12.28N 13.15W*
79 N13 **Koundougou** *var.* Kounadougou. C Burkina *11.43N 4.40W*
78 H11 **Koungheul** C Senegal *14.00N 14.48W*
Kounradskiy *see* Konyrat
27 X10 **Kountze** Texas, SW USA *30.22N 94.18W*
79 Q13 **Koupéla** C Burkina *12.09N 0.23W*
79 N13 **Kouri** Sikasso, SW Mali *12.09N 4.46W*
57 Y9 **Kourou** N French Guiana *5.07N 52.37W*
116 J12 **Kouroú** ∽ NE Greece
78 K14 **Kouroussa** Haute-Guinée, C Guinea *10.40N 9.49W*
Kousseir *see* Al Quşayr
80 G11 **Kousséri** *prev.* Fort-Foureau. Extrême-Nord, NE Cameroon *12.01N 15.03E*
Kouteifé *see* Al Quţayfah
78 M13 **Koutiala** Sikasso, S Mali *12.24N 5.30W*
78 M14 **Kouto** NW Ivory Coast *9.51N 6.25W*
95 M19 **Kouvola** Etelä-Suomi, S Finland *60.50N 26.48E*
81 G18 **Kouyou** ∽ C Congo
114 M10 **Kovačica** *Hung.* Antafalva; *prev.* Kovacsicza. Serbia, N Yugoslavia *45.08N 20.36E*
Kovacsicza *see* Kovačica
Kövárhosszúfalu *see* Satulung
Kovászna *see* Covasna
128 I4 **Kovdor** Murmanskaya Oblast', NW Russian Federation *67.32N 30.27E*
128 I5 **Kovdozero, Ozero** ◎ NW Russian Federation
118 J3 **Kovel'** *Pol.* Kowel. Volyns'ka Oblast', NW Ukraine *51.13N 24.42E*
114 M11 **Kovin** *Hung.* Kevevára; *prev.* Temes-Kubin. Serbia, NE Yugoslavia *44.45N 20.59E*
Kovno *see* Kaunas
131 N3 **Kovrov** Vladimirskaya Oblast', W Russian Federation *56.24N 41.21E*
131 O5 **Kovylkino** Respublika Mordoviya, W Russian Federation *54.03N 43.52E*
112 J11 **Kowal** Kujawsko-pomorskie, C Poland *52.31N 19.08E*
112 J9 **Kowalewo Pomorskie** *Ger.* Schönsee. Kujawsko-pomorskie, C Poland *53.07N 18.48E*
Kowasna *see* Covasna
121 M16 **Kowbcha** *Rus.* Kolbcha. Mahilyowskaya Voblasts', E Belarus *53.40N 29.13E*
Koweit *see* Kuwait
Kowel *see* Kovel'
193 F17 **Kowhitirangi** West Coast, South Island, NZ *42.54S 171.01E*
167 O15 **Kowloon** *Chin.* Jiulong. Hong Kong, S China
Kowno *see* Kaunas
165 N7 **Kox Kuduk** *well* NW China *40.32N 92.30E*
142 D16 **Köyceğiz** Muğla, SW Turkey *36.58N 28.38E*
129 N6 **Koyda** Arkhangel'skaya Oblast', NW Russian Federation *66.22N 42.42E*
152 D10 **Koymat** *Turkm.* Goymat. Balkanskiy Velayat, NW Turkmenistan *40.23N 55.45E*
152 D10 **Koymatdag, Gory** *Turkm.* Goymatdag. *hill range* NW Turkmenistan
Koyna Reservoir *see* Shivāji Sāgar
171 M11 **Koyoshi-gawa** ∽ Honshū, C Japan
Koysanjaq *see* Koi Sanjaq
Koytash *see* Qŭytosh
41 N9 **Koyuk** Alaska, USA *64.55N 161.09W*
41 N9 **Koyuk River** ∽ Alaska, USA
41 O9 **Koyukuk** Alaska, USA *64.52N 157.42W*
41 O9 **Koyukuk River** ∽ Alaska, USA
142 J13 **Kozaklı** Nevşehir, C Turkey *39.13N 34.51E*
170 F13 **Kōzan** Hiroshima, Honshū, SW Japan *34.35N 133.02E*
142 K16 **Kozan** Adana, S Turkey *37.27N 35.46E*
117 E14 **Kozáni** Dytikí Makedonía, N Greece *40.18N 21.48E*
114 F10 **Kozara** ▲▲ NW Bosnia and Herzegovina
Kozarska Dubica *see* Bosanska Dubica
119 P3 **Kozelets'** *Rus.* Kozelets. Chernihivs'ka Oblast', NE Ukraine *50.54N 31.09E*
119 S6 **Kozel'shchyna** Poltavs'ka Oblast', C Ukraine *49.13N 33.49E*
130 J5 **Kozel'sk** Kaluzhskaya Oblast', W Russian Federation *54.04N 35.51E*
Kozhikode *see* Calicut
129 V9 **Kozhimiz, Gora** ▲ NW Russian Federation *63.13N 58.54E*
128 L9 **Kozhozero, Ozero** ◎ NW Russian Federation
129 T7 **Kozhva** *var.* Kozya. Respublika Komi, NW Russian Federation *65.06N 57.00E*
129 T7 **Kozhva** ∽ NW Russian Federation
129 U6 **Kozhym** Respublika Komi, NW Russian Federation *65.43N 59.25E*
112 N13 **Kozienice** Mazowieckie, C Poland *51.37N 21.30E*
111 S13 **Kozina** SW Slovenia *45.36N 13.56E*
116 H7 **Kozloduy** Vratsa, NW Bulgaria *43.47N 23.42E*
131 Q3 **Kozlovka** Chuvashskaya Respublika, W Russian Federation *55.53N 48.07E*
Kozlovshchina/Kozlowszczyzna *see* Kazlowshchyna
131 P3 **Koz'modem'yansk** Respublika Mariy El, W Russian Federation *56.19N 46.33E*
118 J6 **Kozova** Ternopil's'ka Oblast', W Ukraine *49.25N 25.09E*
115 P20 **Kožuf** ▲ S FYR Macedonia *41.10N 22.14E*
172 S13 **Kōzu-shima** *island* E Japan
Kozya *see* Kozhva
Koz'yany *see* Kaz'yany
119 N5 **Kozyatyn** *Rus.* Kazatin. Vinnyts'ka Oblast', C Ukraine *49.40N 28.48E*
79 Q16 **Kpalimé** *var.* Palimé. SW Togo *6.54N 0.37E*
79 Q16 **Kpandu** E Ghana *7.00N 0.18E*
101 F15 **Krabbendijke** Zeeland, SW Netherlands *51.25N 4.07E*
178 Gg16 **Krabi** *var.* Muang Krabi. Krabi, SW Thailand *8.04N 98.52E*
178 Gg14 **Kra Buri** Ranong, SW Thailand *10.25N 98.48E*
178 Jj13 **Krâchéh** *prev.* Kratie. Krâchéh, E Cambodia *12.28N 106.01E*
97 G17 **Kragerø** Telemark, S Norway *58.53N 9.22E*
114 M13 **Kragujevac** Serbia, C Yugoslavia *44.01N 20.54E*
Krainburg *see* Kranj
178 Gg14 **Kra, Isthmus of** *isthmus* Malaysia/Thailand
114 D12 **Krajina** *cultural region* SW Croatia
Krakatau, Pulau *see* Rakata, Pulau
Krakau *see* Małopolskie
113 L16 **Kraków** *Eng.* Cracow, *Ger.* Krakau; *anc.* Cracovia. Małopolskie, S Poland *50.03N 19.58E*
102 L9 **Krakower See** ◎ NE Germany
178 Ii12 **Krâlănh** Siĕmréab, NW Cambodia *13.35N 103.27E*
47 Q16 **Kralendijk** Bonaire, E Netherlands Antilles *12.07N 68.13W*
114 B10 **Kraljevica** *It.* Porto Re. Primorje-Gorski Kotar, NW Croatia *45.15N 14.36E*
114 M13 **Kraljevo** *prev.* Rankovićevo. Serbia, C Yugoslavia *43.44N 20.40E*
Kralup an der Moldau *see* Kralupy nad Vltavou
113 C16 **Kralupy nad Vltavou** *Ger.* Kralup an der Moldau. Středočeský Kraj, NW Czech Republic *50.13N 14.17E*
119 W7 **Kramators'k** *Rus.* Kramatorsk. Donets'ka Oblast', SE Ukraine *48.43N 37.34E*
95 H17 **Kramfors** Västernorrland, C Sweden *62.55N 17.49E*
117 D15 **Kranéa** Dytikí Makedonía, N Greece *39.54N 21.21E*
110 M7 **Kranebitten** ✈ (Innsbruck) Tirol, W Austria *47.18N 11.21E*
117 G20 **Kranídi** Pelopónnisos, S Greece *37.21N 23.09E*
111 T11 **Kranj** *Ger.* Krainburg. NW Slovenia *46.16N 14.16E*
117 F16 **Krannón** *battleground* Thessalía, C Greece *39.32N 22.20E*
Kranz *see* Zelenogradsk
114 D7 **Krapina** Krapina-Zagorje, N Croatia *46.12N 15.52E*
114 E8 **Krapina** ∽ N Croatia
114 D8 **Krapina-Zagorje** *off.* Krapinsko-Zagorska Županija. ◆ *province* N Croatia
116 L7 **Krapinets** ∽ NE Bulgaria
113 I15 **Krapkowice** *Ger.* Krappitz. Opolskie, S Poland *50.28N 17.55E*
Krappitz *see* Krapkowice
129 O12 **Krasavino** Vologodskaya Oblast', NW Russian Federation *60.56N 46.27E*
125 Ff5 **Krasino** Novaya Zemlya, Arkhangel'skaya Oblast', N Russian Federation *70.45N 54.16E*
127 N18 **Kraskino** Primorskiy Kray, SE Russian Federation *42.40N 130.51E*
120 J11 **Krāslava** Krāslava, SE Latvia *55.56N 27.08E*
121 M14 **Krasnaluki** *Rus.* Krasnoluki. Vitsyebskaya Voblasts', N Belarus *54.37N 28.49E*
121 P17 **Krasnapollye** *Rus.* Krasnopol'ye. Mahilyowskaya Voblasts', E Belarus *53.19N 31.24E*
130 L15 **Krasnaya Polyana** Krasnodarskiy Kray, SW Russian Federation *43.40N 40.13E*
121 J18 **Krasnaya Slabada** *var.* Chyrvonaya Slabada, *Rus.* Krasnaya Sloboda. Minskaya Voblasts', S Belarus *52.51N 27.10E*
Krasnaya Sloboda *see* Krasnaya Slabada
121 J15 **Krasnaye** *Rus.* Krasnoye. Minskaya Voblasts', C Belarus *54.13N 27.04E*
113 O14 **Kraśnik** *Ger.* Kratznick. Lubelskie, E Poland *50.55N 22.13E*
113 O14 **Kraśnik Fabryczny** Lubelskie, SE Poland *50.57N 22.07E*
119 O9 **Krasni Okny** Odes'ka Oblast', SW Ukraine *47.33N 29.28E*
151 P7 **Krasnoarmeisk** Severnyy Kazakhstan, N Kazakhstan *53.52N 69.51E*
131 P8 **Krasnoarmeysk** Saratovskaya Oblast', W Russian Federation *51.01N 45.42E*
Krasnoarmeysk *see* Krasnoarmiys'k/Tayynsha
127 Oo4 **Krasnoarmeyskiy** Chukotskiy Avtonomnyy Okrug, NE Russian Federation *69.30N 171.44E*
119 W7 **Krasnoarmiys'k** *Rus.* Krasnoarmeysk. Donets'ka Oblast', SE Ukraine *48.16N 37.13E*
129 P11 **Krasnoborsk** Arkhangel'skaya Oblast', NW Russian Federation *61.31N 45.57E*
130 K14 **Krasnodar** *prev.* Ekaterinodar, Yekaterinodar. Krasnodarskiy Kray, SW Russian Federation *45.02N 39.00E*
130 K13 **Krasnodarskiy Kray** ◆ *territory* SW Russian Federation
119 Z7 **Krasnodon** Luhans'ka Oblast', E Ukraine *48.16N 39.45E*
Krasnogor *see* Kallaste
131 T2 **Krasnogorskoye** *Latv.* Sarkaņi. Udmurtskaya Respublika, NW Russian Federation *57.42N 52.29E*
Krasnograd *see* Krasnohrad
Krasnogvardeyskiy *see* Bulunghur
130 M13 **Krasnogvardeyskoye** Stavropol'skiy Kray, SW Russian Federation *45.49N 41.31E*
Krasnogvardeyskoye *see* Krasnohvardiys'ke
119 U6 **Krasnohrad** *Rus.* Krasnograd. Kharkivs'ka Oblast', E Ukraine *49.22N 35.27E*
119 S12 **Krasnohvardiys'ke** *Rus.* Krasnogvardeyskoye. Respublika Krym, S Ukraine *45.30N 34.19E*
126 L16 **Krasnokamensk** Chitinskaya Oblast', S Russian Federation *50.03N 118.01E*
129 U14 **Krasnokamsk** Permskaya Oblast', W Russian Federation *58.07N 55.48E*
131 U8 **Krasnokholm** Orenburgskaya Oblast', W Russian Federation *51.34N 54.11E*
119 U5 **Krasnokuts'k** *Rus.* Krasnokutsk. Kharkivs'ka Oblast', E Ukraine *50.01N 35.03E*
130 L7 **Krasnolesnyy** Voronezhskaya Oblast', W Russian Federation *51.53N 39.37E*
Krasnoluki *see* Krasnaluki
Krasnoosol'skoye Vodokhranilishche *see* Chervonooskil's'ke Vodoskhovyshche
119 S11 **Krasnoperekops'k** *Rus.* Krasnoperekopsk. Respublika Krym, S Ukraine *45.56N 33.46E*
119 U4 **Krasnopillya** Sums'ka Oblast', NE Ukraine *50.46N 35.17E*
Krasnopol'ye *see* Krasnapollye
126 H9 **Krasnosel'kup** Yamalo-Nenetskiy Avtonomnyy Okrug, N Russian Federation *65.46N 82.11E*
128 L5 **Krasnoshchel'ye** Murmanskaya Oblast', NW Russian Federation *67.22N 37.03E*
131 O5 **Krasnoslobodsk** Respublika Mordoviya, W Russian Federation *54.24N 43.51E*
131 T2 **Krasnoslobodsk** Volgogradskaya Oblast', SW Russian Federation *48.41N 44.34E*
Krasnostav *see* Krasnystaw
125 F10 **Krasnotur'insk** Sverdlovskaya Oblast', C Russian Federation *59.45N 60.19E*
125 E11 **Krasnoufimsk** Sverdlovskaya Oblast', C Russian Federation *56.43N 57.39E*
125 Ee10 **Krasnoural'sk** Sverdlovskaya Oblast', C Russian Federation *58.24N 59.44E*
131 V5 **Krasnousol'skiy** Respublika Bashkortostan, W Russian Federation *53.55N 56.22E*
129 U12 **Krasnovishersk** Permskaya Oblast', NW Russian Federation *60.22N 57.04E*
Krasnovodsk *see* Türkmenbashi
152 A10 **Krasnovodskiy Zaliv** *Turkm.* Krasnowodsk Aylagy. *lake gulf* W Turkmenistan
152 B10 **Krasnovodskoye Plato** *Turkm.* Krasnowodsk Platosy. *plateau* NW Turkmenistan
Krasnowodsk Aylagy *see* Krasnovodskiy Zaliv
Krasnowodsk Platosy *see* Krasnovodskoye Plato
126 Hh14 **Krasnoyarsk** Krasnoyarskiy Kray, S Russian Federation
131 X7 **Krasnoyarskiy** Orenburgskaya Oblast', W Russian Federation *51.56N 59.54E*
126 I12 **Krasnoyarskiy Kray** ◆ *territory* C Russian Federation
126 I14 **Krasnoyarskoye Vodokhranilishche** ☒ S Russian Federation
Krasnoye *see* Krasnaye
152 J15 **Krasnoye Znamya** *Turkm.* Gyzylbaydak. Maryyskiy Velayat, S Turkmenistan *36.51N 62.24E*
129 R11 **Krasnozatonskiy** Respublika Komi, NW Russian Federation *61.39N 51.00E*
120 D13 **Krasnoznamensk** *prev.* Lasdehnen, *Ger.* Haselberg. Kaliningradskaya Oblast', W Russian Federation *54.57N 22.28E*
119 R11 **Krasnoznam"yans'kyy Kanal** *canal* S Ukraine
113 P14 **Krasnystaw** *Rus.* Krasnostav. Lubelskie, SE Poland *51.00N 23.10E*
130 H4 **Krasnyy** Smolenskaya Oblast', W Russian Federation *54.36N 31.27E*
131 P2 **Krasnyye Baki** Nizhegorodskaya Oblast', W Russian Federation *57.07N 45.12E*
131 Q13 **Krasnyye Barrikady** Astrakhanskaya Oblast', SW Russian Federation *46.14N 47.48E*
128 K15 **Krasnyy Kholm** Tverskaya Oblast', W Russian Federation *58.04N 37.05E*
131 Q8 **Krasnyy Kut** Saratovskaya Oblast', W Russian Federation *50.54N 46.58E*
Krasnyy Liman *see* Krasnyy Lyman
119 Y7 **Krasnyy Luch** *prev.* Krindachevka. Luhans'ka Oblast', E Ukraine *48.08N 38.52E*
119 X6 **Krasnyy Lyman** *Rus.* Krasnyy Liman. Donets'ka Oblast', SE Ukraine *49.00N 37.50E*
131 R3 **Krasnyy Steklovar** Respublika Mariy El, W Russian Federation *56.14N 48.49E*
131 P8 **Krasnyy Tekstil'shchik** Saratovskaya Oblast', W Russian Federation *51.35N 45.49E*
131 R13 **Krasnyy Yar** Astrakhanskaya Oblast', SW Russian Federation *46.33N 48.21E*
Krassóvár *see* Caraşova
118 L5 **Krasyliv** Khmel'nyts'ka Oblast', W Ukraine *49.38N 26.59E*
113 O21 **Kraszna** *Rom.* Crasna. ∽ Hungary/Romania
Kratie *see* Krâchéh
194 I13 **Kratke Range** ▲▲ C PNG
115 P17 **Kratovo** NE FYR Macedonia *42.04N 22.08E*
Kratznick *see* Kraśnik
176 Yy11 **Krau** Irian Jaya, E Indonesia *3.15S 140.07E*
178 Ii13 **Krâvanh, Chuŏr Phnum** *Eng.* Cardamom Mountains, *Fr.* Chaîne des Cardamomes. ▲▲ W Cambodia
Kravasta Lagoon *see* Karavastasë, Laguna e
Krawang *see* Karawang
Kraxatau *see* Rakata, Pulau
131 Q15 **Kraynovka** Respublika Dagestan, SW Russian Federation *43.58N 47.24E*
120 D12 **Kražiai** Kelmė, C Lithuania *55.36N 22.41E*
29 P11 **Krebs** Oklahoma, C USA *34.55N 95.43W*
103 D15 **Krefeld** Nordrhein-Westfalen, W Germany *51.19N 6.34E*
Kreisstadt *see* Krosno Odrzańskie
117 D17 **Kremastón, Technití Límni** ☒ C Greece
Kremenchug *see* Kremenchuk
Kremenchugskoye Vodokhranilishche/Kremenchuk Reservoir *see* Kremenchuts'ke Vodoskhovyshche
119 S6 **Kremenchuk** *Rus.* Kremenchug. Poltavs'ka Oblast', NE Ukraine *49.03N 33.27E*
119 R6 **Kremenchuts'ke Vodoskhovyshche** *Eng.* Kremenchuk Reservoir, *Rus.* Kremenchugskoye Vodokhranilishche. ☒ C Ukraine
118 K5 **Kremenets'** *Pol.* Krzemieniec, *Rus.* Kremenets. Ternopil's'ka Oblast', W Ukraine *50.05N 25.43E*
Kremennaya *see* Kreminna
119 X6 **Kreminna** *Rus.* Kremennaya. Luhans'ka Oblast', E Ukraine *49.03N 38.14E*
39 R4 **Kremmling** Colorado, C USA *40.03N 106.23W*
111 V3 **Krems** ∽ NE Austria
Krems *see* Krems an der Donau
111 W3 **Krems an der Donau** *var.* Krems. Niederösterreich, N Austria *48.25N 15.34E*
Kremsier *see* Kroměříž
111 S4 **Kremsmünster** Oberösterreich, N Austria *48.04N 14.08E*
40 M17 **Krenitzin Islands** *island* Aleutian Islands, Alaska, USA
Kresena *see* Kresna
116 G11 **Kresna** *var.* Kresena. Blagoevgrad, SW Bulgaria *41.43N 23.12E*
114 O12 **Krespoljin** Serbia, E Yugoslavia *44.37N 21.36E*
27 N4 **Kress** Texas, SW USA *34.21N 101.43W*
127 Pp4 **Kresta, Zaliv** *bay* E Russian Federation
117 D20 **Kréstena** *prev.* Selinoús. Dytikí Ellás, S Greece *37.36N 21.36E*
128 H14 **Krestsy** Novgorodskaya Oblast', W Russian Federation *58.15N 32.28E*
126 Kk11 **Krestyakh** Respublika Sakha (Yakutiya), NE Russian Federation *62.10N 116.24E*
Kretikon Delagos *see* Kritikó Pélagos
120 C11 **Kretinga** *Ger.* Krottingen. Kretinga, NW Lithuania *55.53N 21.13E*
Kreutz *see* Cristuru Secuiesc
Kreuz *see* Križevci, Croatia
Kreuz *see* Risti, Estonia
Kreuzburg/Kreuzburg in Oberschlesien *see* Kluczbork
Kreuzingen *see* Bol'shakovo
110 H6 **Kreuzlingen** Thurgau, NE Switzerland *47.37N 9.10E*
103 K25 **Kreuzspitze** ▲ S Germany *47.30N 10.55E*
103 F16 **Kreuztal** Nordrhein-Westfalen, W Germany *50.58N 8.00E*
121 I15 **Kreva** *Rus.* Krevo. Hrodzyenskaya Voblasts', W Belarus *54.19N 26.16E*
Krevo *see* Kreva
Kría Vrísi *see* Krýa Vrýsi
81 D16 **Kribi** Sud, SW Cameroon *2.53N 9.57E*
Krichëv *see* Krychaw
Krickerhäu/Kriegerhaj *see* Handlová
111 W6 **Krieglach** Steiermark, E Austria *47.33N 15.37E*
110 F8 **Kriens** Luzern, W Switzerland *47.01N 8.16E*
Krimmitschau *see* Crimmitschau
100 H12 **Krimpen aan den IJssel** Zuid-Holland, SW Netherlands *51.56N 4.39E*
Krindachevka *see* Krasnyy Luch
117 G25 **Kríos, Akrotírio** *headland* Kríti, Greece, E Mediterranean Sea *35.17N 23.31E*
161 J16 **Krishna** *prev.* Kistna. ∽ C India
161 H20 **Krishnagiri** Tamil Nādu, SE India *12.33N 78.10E*
161 K17 **Krishna, Mouths of the** *delta* SE India
159 S15 **Krishnanagar** West Bengal, N India *23.22N 88.31E*
161 G20 **Krishnarājāsāgara Reservoir** ☒ W India
97 N19 **Kristdala** Kalmar, S Sweden *57.24N 16.12E*
Kristiania *see* Oslo
97 E18 **Kristiansand** *var.* Christiansand. Vest-Agder, S Norway *58.07N 7.52E*
97 L22 **Kristianstad** Skåne, S Sweden *56.01N 14.10E*
96 F8 **Kristiansund** *var.* Christiansund. Møre og Romsdal, S Norway *63.07N 7.45E*
Kristiinankaupunki *see* Kristinestad
95 I14 **Kristineberg** Västerbotten, N Sweden *65.07N 18.36E*
97 L16 **Kristinehamn** Värmland, C Sweden *59.16N 14.09E*
95 J17 **Kristinestad** *Fin.* Kristiinankaupunki. Länsi-Suomi, W Finland *62.15N 21.24E*
Kristyor *see* Crişcior
117 J25 **Kríti** *Eng.* Crete. ◆ *region* Greece, Aegean Sea
117 J24 **Kríti** *Eng.* Crete. *island* Greece, Aegean Sea
117 J23 **Kritikó Pélagos** *var.* Kretikon Delagos, *Eng.* Sea of Crete; *anc.* Mare Creticum. *sea* Greece, Aegean Sea
Kriulyany *see* Criuleni
114 I12 **Krivaja** ∽ NE Bosnia and Herzegovina
Krivaja *see* Mali Idoš
115 P17 **Kriva Palanka** *Turk.* Eğri Palanka. NE FYR Macedonia *42.13N 22.19E*
Krivichi *see* Kryvychy
116 H8 **Krivodol** Vratsa, NW Bulgaria *43.23N 23.30E*
130 M10 **Krivorozh'ye** Rostovskaya Oblast', SW Russian Federation *48.51N 40.49E*
Krivoshin *see* Kryvoshyn
Krivoy Rog *see* Kryvyy Rih
114 F7 **Križevci** *Ger.* Kreuz, *Hung.* Körös. Varaždin, NE Croatia *46.02N 16.32E*
114 B10 **Krk** *It.* Veglia. Primorje-Gorski Kotar, NW Croatia *45.01N 14.36E*
114 B10 **Krk** *It.* Veglia; *anc.* Curieta. *island* NW Croatia
111 V12 **Krka** ∽ SE Slovenia
Krka *see* Gurk
111 R11 **Krn** ▲ NW Slovenia *46.15N 13.37E*
113 H16 **Krnov** *Ger.* Jägerndorf. Ostravský Kraj, E Czech Republic *50.05N 17.42E*
Kroatien *see* Croatia
97 G14 **Krøderen** Buskerud, S Norway *60.06N 9.48E*
97 G14 **Krøderen** ◎ S Norway
Kroi *see* Krui
97 N17 **Krokek** Östergötland, S Sweden *58.40N 16.25E*
Krokodil *see* Crocodile
95 G16 **Krokom** Jämtland, C Sweden *63.19N 14.30E*
119 S2 **Krolevets'** *Rus.* Krolevets. Sums'ka Oblast', NE Ukraine *51.34N 33.24E*
Królewska Huta *see* Chorzów
113 H18 **Kroměříž** *Ger.* Kremsier. Zlínský Kraj, E Czech Republic *49.18N 17.24E*
100 I9 **Krommenie** Noord-Holland, C Netherlands *52.30N 4.46E*
130 J6 **Kromy** Orlovskaya Oblast', W Russian Federation *52.41N 35.45E*
103 L18 **Kronach** Bayern, E Germany *50.14N 11.19E*
Krone an der Brahe *see* Koronowo
178 I13 **Krŏng Kaôh Kŏng** Kaôh Kŏng, SW Cambodia *11.37N 102.58E*
97 K21 **Kronoberg** ◆ *county* S Sweden
127 Pp11 **Kronotskiy Zaliv** *bay* E Russian Federation
205 O2 **Kronprinsesse Märtha Kyst** *physical region* Antarctica
205 V3 **Kronprins Olav Kyst** *physical region* Antarctica
128 G12 **Kronshtadt** Leningradskaya Oblast', NW Russian Federation *60.01N 29.42E*
Kronstadt *see* Braşov
85 I22 **Kroonstad** Free State, C South Africa *27.40S 27.15E*
126 Kk13 **Kropotkin** Irkutskaya Oblast', C Russian Federation *58.30N 115.21E*
130 L14 **Kropotkin** Krasnodarskiy Kray, SW Russian Federation *45.28N 40.30E*
112 J11 **Krośniewice** Łódzkie, C Poland *52.14N 19.10E*
113 N17 **Krosno** *Ger.* Krossen. Podkarpackie, SE Poland *49.40N 21.46E*
112 E12 **Krosno Odrzańskie** *Ger.* Crossen, Kreisstadt. Lubuskie, W Poland *52.02N 15.06E*
Krossen *see* Krosno
Krotoschin *see* Krotoszyn
112 H13 **Krotoszyn** *Ger.* Krotoschin. Wielkopolskie, C Poland *51.43N 17.24E*
Krottingen *see* Kretinga
Krousón *see* Krousónas
117 J25 **Krousónas** *prev.* Krousón, Kroussón. Kríti, Greece, E Mediterranean Sea *35.13N 24.58E*
Kroussón *see* Krousónas
Krraba *see* Krrabë
115 L20 **Krrabë** *var.* Krraba. Tiranë, C Albania *41.15N 19.56E*
115 L17 **Krrabit, Mali i** ▲▲ N Albania
111 W12 **Krško** *Ger.* Gurkfeld; *prev.* Videm-Krško. E Slovenia *45.57N 15.31E*
85 K19 **Kruger National Park** *national park* Northern, N South Africa
85 J21 **Krugersdorp** Gauteng, NE South Africa *26.05S 27.46E*
40 D16 **Krugloi Point** *headland* Agattu Island, Alaska, USA *52.30N 173.46E*
Krugloye *see* Kruhlaye
121 N15 **Kruhlaye** *Rus.* Krugloye. Mahilyowskaya Voblasts', E Belarus *54.15N 29.48E*
174 I13 **Krui** *var.* Kroi. Sumatera, SW Indonesia *5.11S 103.55E*
101 G16 **Kruibeke** Oost-Vlaanderen, N Belgium *51.10N 4.18E*
85 G25 **Kruidfontein** Western Cape, SW South Africa *32.50S 21.59E*
101 F15 **Kruiningen** Zeeland, SW Netherlands *51.28N 4.01E*
Kruja *see* Krujë
115 L19 **Krujë** *var.* Kruja, *It.* Croia. Durrës, C Albania *41.30N 19.48E*
Krulevshchina *see* Krulewshchyna
120 K13 **Krulewshchyna** *Rus.* Krulevshchina. Vitsyebskaya Voblasts', N Belarus *55.01N 27.46E*
27 T6 **Krum** Texas, SW USA *33.15N 97.14W*
103 J23 **Krumbach** Bayern, S Germany *48.12N 10.21E*
115 M17 **Krumë** Kukës, NE Albania *42.11N 20.25E*
Krummau *see* Český Krumlov
116 K12 **Krumovgrad** *prev.* Kossukavak. Kŭrdzhali, S Bulgaria *41.27N 25.40E*
116 K12 **Krumovitsa** ∽ S Bulgaria
116 L10 **Krumovo** Yambol, E Bulgaria *42.16N 26.25E*
178 Hh11 **Krung Thep** *var.* Krung Thep Mahanakhon, *Eng.* Bangkok. ● (Thailand) Bangkok, C Thailand *13.43N 100.30E*
178 Hh12 **Krung Thep, Ao** *var.* Bight of Bangkok. *bay* S Thailand
Krung Thep Mahanakhon *see* Krung Thep
Krupa/Krupa na Uni *see* Bosanska Krupa
121 M15 **Krupki** *Rus.* Krupki. Minskaya Voblasts', C Belarus *54.19N 29.07E*
97 G24 **Kruså** *var.* Krusaa. Sønderjylland, SW Denmark *54.49N 9.25E*
Krusaa *see* Kruså
15 I4 **Krusenstern, Cape** *headland* Nunavut, NW Canada *68.17N 114.00W*
115 N14 **Kruševac** Serbia, C Yugoslavia *43.36N 21.19E*
115 N19 **Kruševo** SW FYR Macedonia *41.22N 21.15E*
113 A15 **Krušné Hory** *Eng.* Ore Mountains, *Ger.* Erzgebirge. ▲▲ Czech Republic/Germany *see also* Erzgebirge
41 W13 **Kruzof Island** *island* Alexander Archipelago, Alaska, USA
116 F13 **Krýa Vrýsi** *var.* Kría Vrísi. Kentrikí Makedonía, N Greece *40.40N 22.18E*
121 P16 **Krychaw** *Rus.* Krichëv. Mahilyowskaya Voblasts', E Belarus *53.42N 31.43E*
66 K11 **Krylov Seamount** *undersea feature* E Atlantic Ocean *17.34N 30.07W*
Krym *see* Krym, Respublika
119 S13 **Krym, Respublika** *var.* Krym, *Eng.* Crimea, Crimean Oblast; *prev. Rus.* Krymskaya ASSR, Krymskaya Oblast'. ◆ *province* SE Ukraine
130 K14 **Krymsk** Krasnodarskiy Kray, SW Russian Federation *44.56N 38.02E*
Krymskaya ASSR/Krymskaya Oblast' *see* Krym, Respublika
119 T13 **Kryms'ki Hory** ▲▲ S Ukraine
119 T13 **Kryms'kyy Pivostriv** *peninsula* S Ukraine
113 M18 **Krynica** *Ger.* Tannenhof. Małopolskie, S Poland *49.26N 20.57E*
119 P8 **Kryve Ozero** Odes'ka Oblast', SW Ukraine *47.54N 30.19E*
121 I18 **Kryvoshyn** *Rus.* Krivoshin. Brestskaya Voblasts', SW Belarus *52.52N 26.07E*
121 K14 **Kryvychy** *Rus.* Krivichi. Minskaya Voblasts', C Belarus *54.43N 27.16E*
119 S8 **Kryvyy Rih** *Rus.* Krivoy Rog. Dnipropetrovs'ka Oblast', SE Ukraine *47.53N 33.24E*
119 N8 **Kryzhopil'** Vinnyts'ka Oblast', C Ukraine *48.22N 28.51E*
Krzemieniec *see* Kremenets'
113 J14 **Krzepice** Śląskie, S Poland *50.58N 18.42E*
112 F10 **Krzyż Wielkopolski** Wielkopolskie, C Poland *52.52N 16.03E*
Ksar al Kabir *see* Ksar-el-Kebir
Ksar al Soule *see* Er-Rachidia
76 J5 **Ksar El Boukhari** N Algeria *35.57N 2.49E*
76 G5 **Ksar-el-Kebir** *var.* Ksar al Kabir, Ksar-el-Kébir, *Ar.* Al-Kasr al-Kebir, Al-Qsar al-Kbir, *Sp.* Alcazarquivir. NW Morocco *35.04N 5.55W*
112 H12 **Książ Wielkopolski** *Ger.* Xions. Wielkopolskie, C Poland *52.03N 17.10E*

◆ COUNTRY ● COUNTRY CAPITAL ◇ DEPENDENT TERRITORY ○ DEPENDENT TERRITORY CAPITAL ◆ ADMINISTRATIVE REGION ✈ INTERNATIONAL AIRPORT ▲ MOUNTAIN ▲▲ MOUNTAIN RANGE ⛰ VOLCANO ∽ RIVER ◎ LAKE ☒ RESERVOIR

Kstovo – Ky Anh

131 O3 **Kstovo** Nizhegorodskaya Oblast', W Russian Federation *56.07N 44.12E*
174 Mm4 **Kuala Belait** W Brunei *4.48N 114.12E*
Kuala Dungun *see* Dungun
174 M7 **Kualakerian** Borneo, C Indonesia
174 M10 **Kualakuayan** Borneo, C Indonesia *2.01S 112.34E*
174 H4 **Kuala Lipis** Pahang, Peninsular Malaysia *04.11N 102.00E*
174 H5 **Kuala Lumpur** ● (Malaysia) Kuala Lumpur, Peninsular Malaysia *3.07N 101.42E*
Kuala Pelabohan Kelang *see* Pelabuhan Klang
175 Nn3 **Kuala Penyu** Sabah, East Malaysia *5.37N 115.36E*
40 E9 **Kualapuu** *Haw.* Kualapu'u. Molokai, Hawaii, USA, C Pacific Ocean *21.09N 157.02W*
173 G6 **Kuala, Sungai** ≈ Sumatera, W Indonesia
174 Hh3 **Kuala Terengganu** *var.* Kuala Trengganu. Terengganu, Peninsular Malaysia *5.19N 103.07E*
174 Hh9 **Kualatungkal** Sumatera, W Indonesia *0.49S 103.22E*
175 O3 **Kuamut, Sungai** ≈ East Malaysia
175 Qq7 **Kuandang** Sulawesi, N Indonesia *0.50N 122.55E*
175 Qq7 **Kuandang, Teluk** *bay* Sulawesi, N Indonesia
169 V12 **Kuandian** Liaoning, NE China *40.41N 124.46E*
Kuando-Kubango *see* Cuando Cubango
Kuang-chou *see* Guangzhou
Kuang-hsi *see* Guangxi Zhuangzu Zizhiqu
Kuang-tung *see* Guangdong
Kuang-yuan *see* Guangyuan
174 Hh4 **Kuantan** Pahang, Peninsular Malaysia *3.49N 103.19E*
Kuantan, Batang *see* Indragiri, Sungai
Kuanza Norte *see* Cuanza Norte
Kuanza Sul *see* Cuanza Sul
Kuba *see* Quba
125 Aa12 **Kuban'** *var.* Hypanis. ≈ SW Russian Federation
Kubango *see* Cubango/Okavango
147 X8 **Kubārah** NW Oman *23.03N 56.52E*
95 H16 **Kubbe** Västernorrland, C Sweden *63.31N 18.04E*
82 A11 **Kubbum** Southern Darfur, W Sudan *11.46N 23.46E*
128 L13 **Kubenskoye, Ozero** ◎ NW Russian Federation
170 Ee16 **Kubokawa** Kōchi, Shikoku, SW Japan *33.22N 133.14E*
116 L7 **Kubrat** *prev.* Balbunar. Razgrad, N Bulgaria *43.48N 26.31E*
175 Oo15 **Kubu** Sumbawa, S Indonesia *8.15S 115.30E*
114 O13 **Kučajske Planine** ▲▲ E Yugoslavia
172 Pp2 **Kuccharo-ko** ◎ Hokkaidō, N Japan
114 O11 **Kučevo** Serbia, NE Yugoslavia *44.29N 21.42E*
Kuchan *see* Qūchān
174 L6 **Kuching** *prev.* Sarawak. Sarawak, East Malaysia *1.31N 110.19E*
174 L7 **Kuching** ✕ Sarawak, East Malaysia *1.31N 110.19E*
170 Aa17 **Kuchinoerabu-jima** *island* Nansei-shotō, SW Japan
170 C13 **Kuchinotsu** Nagasaki, Kyūshū, SW Japan *32.36N 130.11E*
111 Q6 **Kuchl** Salzburg, NW Austria *47.37N 13.12E*
154 L9 **Kūchnay Darweyshān** Helmand, S Afghanistan *31.01N 64.09E*
Kuchurgan *see* Kuchurhan
119 O9 **Kuchurhan** *Rus.* Kuchurgan. ≈ NE Ukraine
Kuçova *see* Kuçovë
115 L21 **Kuçovë** *var.* Kuçova; *prev.* Qyteti Stalin. Berat, C Albania *40.48N 19.55E*
142 D11 **Küçük Çekmece** İstanbul, NW Turkey *41.01N 28.46E*
170 Dd13 **Kudamatsu** *var.* Kudamatu. Yamaguchi, Honshū, SW Japan *34.00N 131.53E*
Kudamatu *see* Kudamatsu
Kudara *see* Ghūdara
175 O1 **Kudat** Sabah, East Malaysia *6.54N 116.46E*
Küddow *see* Gwda
161 G17 **Kūdligi** Karnātaka, W India *14.58N 76.24E*
Kudowa *see* Kudowa-Zdrój
113 F16 **Kudowa-Zdrój** *Ger.* Kudowa. Wałbrzych, SW Poland *50.27N 16.13E*
119 P9 **Kudryavtsivka** Mykolayivs'ka Oblast', S Ukraine *47.18N 31.02E*
174 L14 **Kudus** *prev.* Koedoes. Jawa, C Indonesia *6.46S 110.48E*
129 T13 **Kudymkar** Komi-Permyatskiy Avtonomnyy Okrug, NW Russian Federation *59.01N 54.40E*
Kudzsir *see* Cugir
Kuei-chou *see* Guizhou
Kuei-lin *see* Guilin
Kuei-yang *see* Guiyang
K'u-erh-lo *see* Korla
Kueyang *see* Guiyang
Kufa *see* Al Kūfah
142 E14 **Kūfiçayı** ≈ C Turkey
111 O6 **Kufstein** Tirol, W Austria *47.36N 12.10E*
151 V14 **Kugaly** *Kaz.* Qoghaly. Almaty, SE Kazakhstan *44.30N 78.40E*
15 I4 **Kugluktuk** *var.* Qurlurtuuq *prev.* Coppermine. Nunavut, NW Canada *67.49N 115.12W*
149 Y13 **Kūhak** Sīstān va Balūchestān, SE Iran *27.10N 63.15E*
149 R9 **Kūhbonān** Kermān, C Iran *31.22N 56.16E*
154 J5 **Kūhestān** *var.* Kohsān. Herāt, W Afghanistan *34.40N 61.10E*
95 N15 **Kuhmo** Oulu, E Finland *64.04N 29.34E*
95 L18 **Kuhmoinen** Länsi-Suomi, W Finland *61.32N 25.09E*
Kuhnau *see* Konin
Kühnö *see* Kihnu
149 O8 **Kūhpāyeh** Eşfahān, C Iran *32.42N 52.25E*
178 H13 **Kui Buri** *var.* Ban Kui Nua. Prachuap Khiri Khan, SW Thailand *12.10N 99.49E*
Kuibyshev *see* Kuybyshevskoye Vodokhranilishche
84 D13 **Kuito** *Port.* Silva Porto. Bié, C Angola *12.21S 16.54E*
41 X14 **Kuiu Island** *island* Alexander Archipelago, Alaska, USA
94 L13 **Kuivaniemi** Oulu, C Finland *65.34N 25.13E*
79 V14 **Kujama** Kaduna, C Nigeria *10.27N 7.39E*
112 I10 **Kujawsko-pomorskie** ◆ *province*, C Poland
172 N10 **Kuji** *var.* Kuzi. Iwate, Honshū, C Japan *40.12N 141.47E*
Kujto, Ozero *see* Kuyto, Ozero
Kujū-renzan *see* Kujū-san
170 D14 **Kujū-san** *var.* Kujū-renzan. ▲ Kyūshū, SW Japan *33.07N 131.13E*
45 N7 **Kukalaya, Rio** *var.* Rio Cuculaya, Rio Kukulaya. ≈ NE Nicaragua
115 O16 **Kukavica** *var.* Vlajna. ▲ SE Yugoslavia *42.46N 21.58E*
152 M10 **Kŭkcha** *Rus.* Kokcha. Bukhoro Wiloyati, C Uzbekistan *40.30N 64.58E*
115 M18 **Kukës** *var.* Kukësi. Kukës, NE Albania *42.03N 20.25E*
115 L18 **Kukës** ◆ *district* NE Albania
Kukësi *see* Kukës
194 J14 **Kukipi** Gulf, S PNG *8.10S 146.09E*
131 S3 **Kukmor** Respublika Tatarstan, W Russian Federation *56.11N 50.56E*
Kukong *see* Shaoguan
41 N6 **Kukpowruk River** ≈ Alaska, USA
40 M6 **Kukpuk River** ≈ Alaska, USA
Kukukhoto *see* Hohhot
Kukulaya, Rio *see* Kukalaya, Rio
174 Hh7 **Kukup** Johor, Peninsular Malaysia *1.18N 103.27E*
201 W12 **Kuku Point** *headland* NW Wake Island *19.19N 166.36E*
152 G11 **Kukurtli** Akhalskiy Velayat, C Turkmenistan *39.58N 58.47E*
Kül *see* Kül, Rūd-e
116 F7 **Kula** Vidin, NW Bulgaria *43.55N 22.32E*
142 D14 **Kula** Manisa, W Turkey *38.33N 28.36E*
114 K9 **Kula** Serbia, NW Yugoslavia *45.37N 19.31E*
155 S8 **Kulāchi** North-West Frontier Province, NW Pakistan *31.58N 70.30E*
Kulachi *see* Kolāchi
150 F11 **Kulagino** *Kaz.* Külagīno. Atyrau, W Kazakhstan *48.30N 51.33E*
174 Hh6 **Kulai** Johor, Peninsular Malaysia *1.40N 103.33E*
116 M7 **Kulak** ≈ NE Bulgaria
159 T11 **Kula Kangri** *var.* Kulhakangri. ▲ Bhutan/China *28.06N 90.19E*
150 E13 **Kulaly, Ostrov** *island* SW Kazakhstan
153 V9 **Kulanak** Narynskaya Oblast', C Kyrgyzstan *41.18N 75.38E*
152 B8 **Kulandag** ▲▲ W Turkmenistan
151 S16 **Kulan** *Kaz.* Qulan; *prev.* Lugovoy, Lugovoye. Zhambyl, S Kazakhstan *42.55N 72.49E*
159 V14 **Kulaura** Chittagong, NE Bangladesh *24.31N 92.01E*
120 D9 **Kuldīga** *Ger.* Goldingen. Kuldīga, W Latvia *56.57N 21.59E*
Kuldja *see* Yining
Kul'dzhuktau, Gory *see* Quljuqtov-Toghi
131 N4 **Kulebaki** Nizhegorodskaya Oblast', W Russian Federation *55.25N 42.31E*
114 E11 **Kulen Vakuf** *var.* Spasovo. Federacija Bosna I Hercegovina, NW Bosnia and Herzegovina *44.32N 16.05E*
189 Q9 **Kulgera Roadhouse** Northern Territory, N Australia *25.49S 133.30E*
Kulhakangri *see* Kula Kangri
131 T1 **Kuliga** Udmurtskaya Respublika, NW Russian Federation *58.14N 53.49E*
Kulkuduk *see* Kalquduq
120 G4 **Kullamaa** Läänemaa, W Estonia *58.52N 24.05E*
207 O12 **Kullorsuaq** *var.* Kuvdlorssuak. Kitaa, C Greenland *74.57N 57.07W*
31 O6 **Kulm** North Dakota, N USA *46.18N 98.57W*
Kulm *see* Chełmno
152 D12 **Kul'mach** Balkanskiy Velayat, W Turkmenistan *39.04N 55.49E*
103 L18 **Kulmbach** Bayern, SE Germany *50.07N 11.27E*
Kulmsee *see* Chełmża
153 Q14 **Kŭlob** *Rus.* Kulyab. SW Tajikistan *37.55N 68.46E*
94 M13 **Kuloharju** Lappi, N Finland *65.51N 28.10E*
129 N7 **Kuloy** Arkhangel'skaya Oblast', NW Russian Federation *64.55N 43.35E*
129 N7 **Kuloy** ≈ NW Russian Federation
143 Q14 **Kulp** Dıyarbakır, SE Turkey *38.31N 41.01E*
Kulpa *see* Kolpa
79 P14 **Kulpawn** ≈ N Ghana
149 R13 **Kül, Rūd-e** *var.* Kül. ≈ S Iran
150 G12 **Kul'sary** *Kaz.* Qulsary. Atyrau, W Kazakhstan *46.58N 53.58E*
159 R15 **Kulti** West Bengal, NE India *23.45N 86.49E*
95 G14 **Kultsjön** ◎ N Sweden
142 I14 **Kulu** Konya, W Turkey *39.06N 33.01E*
127 Nn10 **Kulu** ≈ E Russian Federation
125 G14 **Kulunda** Altayskiy Kray, S Russian Federation *52.33N 79.04E*
151 T7 **Kulunda Steppe** *Kaz.* Qulyndy Zhazyghy, *Rus.* Kulundinskaya Ravnina. *grassland* Kazakhstan/Russian Federation
Kulundinskaya Ravnina *see* Kulunda Steppe
190 M9 **Kulwin** Victoria, SE Australia *35.04S 142.37E*
Kulyab *see* Kŭlob
119 Q3 **Kulykivka** Chernihivs'ka Oblast', N Ukraine *51.23N 31.39E*
Kum *see* Qom
170 Ee15 **Kuma** Ehime, Shikoku, SW Japan *33.36N 132.53E*
131 P14 **Kuma** ≈ SW Russian Federation
Kumafa *see* Kumawa, Pegunungan
171 K15 **Kumagaya** Saitama, Honshū, S Japan *36.10N 139.22E*
172 N6 **Kumaishi** Hokkaidō, NE Japan *42.08N 139.57E*
174 Ll11 **Kumai, Teluk** *bay* Borneo, C Indonesia
131 Y7 **Kumak** Orenburgskaya Oblast', W Russian Federation *51.16N 60.06E*
176 Y9 **Kumamba, Kepulauan** *island group* E Indonesia
170 Cc14 **Kumamoto** Kumamoto, Kyūshū, SW Japan *32.49N 130.40E*
170 C14 **Kumamoto** *off.* Kumamoto-ken. ◆ *prefecture* Kyūshū, SW Japan
171 Gg17 **Kumano** Mie, Honshū, SW Japan *33.54N 136.03E*
Kumanova *see* Kumanovo
115 O17 **Kumanovo** *Turk.* Kumanova. N FYR Macedonia *42.08N 21.42E*
193 G17 **Kumara** West Coast, South Island, NZ *42.39S 171.12E*
188 J8 **Kumarina Roadhouse** Western Australia *24.46S 119.39E*
159 T15 **Kumarkhali** Khulna, W Bangladesh *23.52N 89.13E*
79 P16 **Kumasi** *prev.* Coomassie. C Ghana *6.40N 1.39W*
176 Vv11 **Kumawa, Pegunungan** *var.* Kumafa. ▲▲ Irian Jaya, E Indonesia
Kumayri *see* Gyumri
81 D15 **Kumba** Sud-Ouest, W Cameroon *4.39N 9.25E*
116 N13 **Kumbağ** Tekirdağ, NW Turkey *40.51N 27.26E*
161 J21 **Kumbakonam** Tamil Nādu, SE India *10.58N 79.24E*
176 Z16 **Kumbe, Sungai** ≈ Irian Jaya, E Indonesia
Kum-Dag *see* Gumdag
172 O14 **Kume-jima** *island* Nansei-shotō, SW Japan
131 V6 **Kumertau** Respublika Bashkortostan, W Russian Federation *52.48N 55.48E*
125 F11 **Kuminskiy** Khanty-Mansiyskiy Avtonomnyy Okrug, C Russian Federation *58.42N 65.56E*
37 R4 **Kumiva Peak** ▲ Nevada, W USA *40.24N 119.16W*
165 N8 **Kum Kuduk** *well* NW China *40.21N 91.43E*
165 N7 **Kumkuduk** Xinjiang Uygur Zizhiqu, W China *40.15N 91.55E*
Kumkurgan *see* Qumqurghon
97 M16 **Kumla** Örebro, C Sweden *59.51N 16.40E*
142 E17 **Kumluca** Antalya, SW Turkey *36.22N 30.16E*
102 N9 **Kummerower See** ◎ NE Germany
79 X14 **Kumo** Gombe, E Nigeria *10.03N 11.13E*
151 O13 **Kumola** ≈ C Kazakhstan
178 H1 **Kumon Range** ▲▲ N Burma
126 K14 **Kumora** Respublika Buryatiya, S Russian Federation *55.43N 110.47E*
85 F22 **Kums** Karas, SE Namibia *28.07S 19.40E*
161 E18 **Kumta** Karnātaka, W India *14.25N 74.24E*
164 L6 **Kümük** Xinjiang Uygur Zizhiqu, W China
40 H12 **Kumukahi, Cape** *headland* Hawaii, USA, C Pacific Ocean *19.31N 154.48W*
131 Q17 **Kumukh** Respublika Dagestan, SW Russian Federation *42.10N 47.07E*
Kumul *see* Hami
131 N9 **Kumylzhenskaya** Volgogradskaya Oblast', SW Russian Federation *49.54N 42.35E*
147 W6 **Kumzār** N Oman *26.19N 56.26E*
155 S4 **Kunar** *Per.* Konarhā. ◆ *province* E Afghanistan
Kunashiri *see* Kunashir, Ostrov
127 P16 **Kunashir, Ostrov** *var.* Kunashiri. *island* Kuril'skiye Ostrova, SE Russian Federation
120 I3 **Kunda** Lääne-Virumaa, NE Estonia *59.31N 26.32E*
158 M13 **Kunda** Uttar Pradesh, N India *25.43N 81.31E*
161 E19 **Kundāpura** *var.* Coondapoor. Karnātaka, W India *13.39N 74.41E*
81 O24 **Kundelungu, Monts** ▲ S Dem. Rep. Congo (Zaire)
Kundert *see* Hernád
194 I12 **Kundiawa** Chimbu, W PNG *06.00S 144.57E*
Kundla *see* Sāvarkundla
174 Hh7 **Kundur, Pulau** *island* W Indonesia
155 Q2 **Kunduz** *var.* Kondoz, Kundūz, Qondūz, *Per.* Kondūz. Kunduz, NE Afghanistan *36.48N 68.50E*
155 Q2 **Kunduz** *Per.* Kondūz. ◆ *province* NE Afghanistan
Kuneitra *see* Al Qunayţirah
85 B18 **Kunene** ◆ *district* NE Namibia
85 A16 **Kunene** *var.* Cunene. ≈ Angola/Namibia ***see also*** Cunene
Künes *see* Xinyuan
164 J5 **Künes He** ≈ NW China
97 I19 **Kungälv** Västra Götaland, S Sweden *57.54N 12.00E*
153 W7 **Kungei Ala-Tau** *Rus.* Khrebet Kyungëy Ala-Too, *Kir.* Küngöy Ala-Too. ▲▲ Kazakhstan/Kyrgyzstan
Küngöy Ala-Too *see* Kungei Ala-Tau
Kungrad *see* Qŭnghirot
97 J19 **Kungsbacka** Halland, S Sweden *57.30N 12.04E*
97 I18 **Kungshamn** Västra Götaland, S Sweden *58.21N 11.15E*
97 M16 **Kungsör** Västmanland, C Sweden *59.25N 16.21E*
81 J16 **Kungu** Equateur, NW Dem. Rep. Congo (Zaire) *2.46N 19.12E*
129 V15 **Kungur** Permskaya Oblast', NW Russian Federation *57.24N 56.56E*
177 G9 **Kungyangon** Yangon, SW Burma *16.27N 96.00E*
113 M22 **Kunhegyes** Jász-Nagykun-Szolnok, E Hungary *47.23N 20.37E*
178 H5 **Kunhing** Shan State, E Burma *21.17N 98.26E*
170 Cc15 **Kunimi-dake** ▲ Kyūshū, SW Japan *32.31N 131.01E*
164 D9 **Kunjirap Daban** *var.* Khūnjerāb Pass. *pass* China/Pakistan ***see also*** Khūnjerāb Pass *36.46N 75.16E*
Kunlun Mountains *see* Kunlun Shan
164 H10 **Kunlun Shan** *Eng.* Kunlun Mountains. ▲▲ NW China
165 P11 **Kunlun Shankou** *pass* C China *35.45N 93.59E*
166 G13 **Kunming** *var.* K'un-ming; *prev.* Yunnan. Yunnan, SW China *25.04N 102.40E*
172 N6 **Kunnui** Hokkaidō, NE Japan *42.26N 140.18E*
97 B18 **Kunoy** *Dan.* Kunø *Island* Faeroe Islands *62.18N 6.40W*
169 X16 **Kunsan** *var.* Gunsan, *Jap.* Gunzan. W South Korea *35.58N 126.42E*
113 L24 **Kunszentmárton** Jász-Nagykun-Szolnok, E Hungary *46.49N 20.15E*
113 J23 **Kunszentmiklós** Bács-Kiskun, C Hungary *47.02N 19.05E*
189 N3 **Kununurra** Western Australia *15.49S 128.43E*
Kunya-Urgench *see* Këneurgench
Kunyé *see* Pins, Île des
174 Mm8 **Kunyi** Borneo, C Indonesia *3.22S 119.19E*
103 I20 **Künzelsau** Baden-Württemberg, S Germany *49.22N 9.43E*
167 S10 **Kuocang Shan** ▲▲ SE China
128 H5 **Kuolayarvi** *var.* Luolajarvi. Murmanskaya Oblast', NW Russian Federation *66.58N 29.13E*
95 N16 **Kuopio** Itä-Suomi, C Finland *62.54N 27.41E*
95 K17 **Kuortane** Länsi-Suomi, W Finland *62.48N 23.30E*
95 M18 **Kuortti** Itä-Suomi, E Finland *61.25N 26.25E*
Kupa *see* Kolpa
175 R17 **Kupang** *prev.* Koepang. Timor, C Indonesia *10.13S 123.37E*
41 Q5 **Kuparuk River** ≈ Alaska, USA
Kupchino *see* Cupcina
194 L16 **Kupiano** Central, S PNG *10.04S 148.16E*
188 M4 **Kupingarri** Western Australia *16.46S 125.57E*
125 G14 **Kupino** Novosibirskaya Oblast', C Russian Federation *54.22N 77.09E*
120 H11 **Kupiškis** Kupiškis, NE Lithuania *55.51N 24.58E*
116 L13 **Küplü** Edirne, NW Turkey *41.06N 26.23E*
41 X13 **Kupreanof Island** *island* Alexander Archipelago, Alaska, USA
41 O16 **Kupreanof Point** *headland* Alaska, USA *55.34N 159.36W*
114 G13 **Kupres** Federacija Bosna I Hercegovina, SW Bosnia and Herzegovina *44.00N 17.15E*
119 W5 **Kup"yans'k** *Rus.* Kupyansk. Kharkivs'ka Oblast', E Ukraine *49.42N 37.36E*
119 W5 **Kup"yans'k-Vuzlovyy** Kharkivs'ka Oblast', E Ukraine *49.40N 37.41E*
164 I6 **Kuqa** Xinjiang Uygur Zizhiqu, NW China *41.43N 82.58E*
Kür *see* Kura
143 W11 **Kura** *Az.* Kür, *Geor.* Mtkvari, *Turk.* Kura Nehri. ≈ SW Asia
57 R8 **Kuracki** NW Guyana *6.52N 60.13W*
170 Ee13 **Kurahashi-jima** *island* SW Japan
Kura Kurk *see* Irbe Strait
153 Q10 **Kurama Range** *Rus.* Kuraminskiy Khrebet. ▲▲ Tajikistan/Uzbekistan
Kuraminskiy Khrebet *see* Kurama Range
Kura Nehri *see* Kura
176 Ww10 **Kuran, Kepulauan** *island group* E Indonesia
121 J14 **Kuranyets** *Rus.* Kurenets. Minskaya Voblasts', C Belarus *54.34N 26.58E*
170 Ff14 **Kurashiki** *var.* Kurasiki. Okayama, Honshū, SW Japan *34.35N 133.44E*
160 L10 **Kurasia** Madhya Pradesh, C India *23.11N 82.16E*
Kurasiki *see* Kurashiki
170 G12 **Kurayoshi** *var.* Kurayosi. Tottori, Honshū, SW Japan *35.25N 133.51E*
Kurayosi *see* Kurayoshi
169 X6 **Kurbin He** ≈ NE China
151 X10 **Kurchum** *Kaz.* Kürshim. Vostochnyy Kazakhstan, E Kazakhstan *48.35N 83.37E*
151 Y10 **Kurchum** ≈ E Kazakhstan
143 X11 **Kürdämir** *Rus.* Kyurdamir. C Azerbaijan *40.21N 48.08E*
Kurdestan *see* Kordestān
145 S1 **Kurdistan** *cultural region* SW Asia
Kurd Kui *see* Kord Küy
161 F15 **Kurduvādi** Mahārāshtra, W India *18.06N 75.31E*
116 J11 **Kŭrdzhali** *var.* Kirdzhali. Kŭrdzhali, S Bulgaria *41.39N 25.23E*
116 K11 **Kŭrdzhali** ◆ *province* S Bulgaria
116 J11 **Kŭrdzhali, Yazovir** ⊠ S Bulgaria
170 Ee13 **Kure** Hiroshima, Honshū, SW Japan *34.15N 132.33E*
199 J5 **Kure Atoll** *var.* Ocean Island. *atoll* Hawaiian Islands, Hawaii, USA, C Pacific Ocean
142 J10 **Küre Dağları** ▲▲ N Turkey
Kurenets *see* Kuranyets
120 E6 **Kuressaare** *Ger.* Arensburg; *prev.* Kingissepp. Saaremaa, W Estonia *58.14N 22.27E*
126 I9 **Kureyka** Krasnoyarskiy Kray, N Russian Federation *66.22N 87.21E*
126 I9 **Kureyka** ≈ N Russian Federation
151 P10 **Kurgal'dzhin, Ozero** ◎ C Kazakhstan
151 Q10 **Kurgal'dzhinskiy** *see* Kurgal'dzhino
151 Q10 **Kurgal'dzhino** *var.* Kurgal'dzhinskiy, *Kaz.* Qorgazhyn. Akmola, C Kazakhstan *50.33N 69.58E*
125 F12 **Kurgan** Kurganskaya Oblast', C Russian Federation *55.30N 65.19E*
130 L14 **Kurganinsk** Krasnodarskiy Kray, SW Russian Federation *44.55N 40.45E*
125 Ee12 **Kurganskaya Oblast'** ◆ *province* C Russian Federation
Kurgan-Tyube *see* Qŭrghonteppa
203 O2 **Kuria** *prev.* Woodle Island. *island* Tungaru, W Kiribati
Kuria Muria Bay *see* Ḩalānīyāt, Khalīj al
Kuria Muria Islands *see* Ḩalānīyāt, Juzur al
159 T13 **Kurigram** Rajshahi, N Bangladesh *25.49N 89.37E*
176 Yy16 **Kurik** Irian Jaya, E Indonesia *8.12S 140.15E*
95 K17 **Kurikka** Länsi-Suomi, W Finland *62.36N 22.25E*
171 M12 **Kurikoma-yama** ▲ Honshū, C Japan *38.57N 140.44E*
199 Hh3 **Kurile Basin** *undersea feature* NW Pacific Ocean
Kurile Islands *see* Kuril'skiye Ostrova
Kurile-Kamchatka Depression *see* Kurile Trench
199 Hh6 **Kurile Trench** *var.* Kurile-Kamchatka Depression. *undersea feature* NW Pacific Ocean
131 Q9 **Kurilovka** Saratovskaya Oblast', W Russian Federation *50.39N 48.02E*
127 P15 **Kuril'sk** Kuril'skiye Ostrova, Sakhalinskaya Oblast', SE Russian Federation *45.10N 147.51E*
127 Pp15 **Kuril'skiye Ostrova** *Eng.* Kurile Islands. *island group* SE Russian Federation
44 M9 **Kurinwas, Río** ≈ E Nicaragua
Kurisches Haff *see* Courland Lagoon
Kurkund *see* Kilingi-Nõmme
130 M4 **Kurlovskiy** Vladimirskaya Oblast', W Russian Federation *55.25N 40.39E*
82 G12 **Kurmuk** Blue Nile, SE Sudan *10.36N 34.16E*
Kurna *see* Al Qurnah
161 H17 **Kurnool** *var.* Karnul. Andhra Pradesh, S India *15.51N 78.01E*
171 J13 **Kurobe** Toyama, Honshū, SW Japan *36.52N 137.26E*
170 Cc13 **Kurogi** Fukuoka, Kyūshū, SW Japan *33.09N 130.45E*
171 Mm9 **Kuroishi** *var.* Kuroisi. Aomori, Honshū, C Japan *40.40N 140.34E*
Kuroisi *see* Kuroishi
171 Kk14 **Kuroiso** Tochigi, Honshū, S Japan *36.58N 140.01E*
172 N5 **Kuromatsunai** Hokkaidō, NE Japan *42.40N 140.18E*
172 Oo17 **Kuro-shima** *island* SW Japan
171 H16 **Kuroso-yama** ▲ Honshū, SW Japan *34.31N 136.10E*
193 F21 **Kurow** Canterbury, South Island, NZ *44.44S 170.29E*
176 Uu13 **Kur, Pulau** *island* E Indonesia
131 N15 **Kursavka** Stavropol'skiy Kray, SW Russian Federation *44.28N 42.31E*
120 E11 **Kuršėnai** Šiauliai, N Lithuania *56.00N 22.56E*
Kürshim *see* Kurchum
Kurshskaya Kosa/Kuršiu Nerija *see* Courland Spit
130 J7 **Kursk** Kurskaya Oblast', W Russian Federation *51.43N 36.46E*
130 I7 **Kurskaya Oblast'** ◆ *province* W Russian Federation
Kurskiy Zaliv *see* Courland Lagoon
115 N15 **Kuršumlija** Serbia, S Yugoslavia *43.09N 21.16E*
143 R15 **Kurtalan** Siirt, SE Turkey *37.56N 41.43E*
125 Ee12 **Kurtamysh** Kurganskaya Oblast', C Russian Federation *54.51N 64.46E*
Kurtbunar *see* Tervel
Kurt-Dere *see* Vŭlchidol
Kurtitsch/Kürtös *see* Curtici
151 U15 **Kurtty** ≈ SE Kazakhstan
95 L18 **Kuru** Länsi-Suomi, W Finland *61.51N 23.46E*
82 C13 **Kuru** ≈ W Sudan
116 M13 **Kuru Dağı** ▲▲ NW Turkey
164 L7 **Kuruktag** ▲▲ NW China
85 G22 **Kuruman** Northern Cape, N South Africa *27.28S 23.27E*
69 T14 **Kuruman** ≈ W South Africa
170 Cc13 **Kurume** Fukuoka, Kyūshū, SW Japan *33.15N 130.27E*
126 K15 **Kurumkan** Respublika Buryatiya, S Russian Federation *54.13N 110.21E*
161 J25 **Kurunegala** North Western Province, C Sri Lanka *7.28N 80.22E*
57 T10 **Kurupukari** C Guyana *4.39N 58.39W*
129 U10 **Kur"ya** Respublika Komi, NW Russian Federation *61.38N 57.12E*
150 E15 **Kuryk** *prev.* Yeraliyev. Mangistau, SW Kazakhstan *43.12N 51.43E*
142 B15 **Kuşadası** Aydın, SW Turkey *37.51N 27.15E*
117 M19 **Kuşadası Körfezi** *gulf* SW Turkey
170 Aa16 **Kusagaki-guntō** *island* SW Japan
Kusaie *see* Kosrae
151 T12 **Kusak** ≈ C Kazakhstan
Kusary *see* Qusar
178 Hh8 **Ku Sathan, Doi** ▲ NW Thailand *18.22N 100.31E*
171 H15 **Kusatsu** *var.* Kusatu. Shiga, Honshū, SW Japan *35.02N 135.58E*
Kusatu *see* Kusatsu
144 F11 **Kuseifa** Southern, C Israel *31.15N 35.01E*
142 C12 **Kuş Gölü** ◎ NW Turkey
130 L12 **Kushchevskaya** Krasnodarskiy Kray, SW Russian Federation *46.35N 39.40E*
171 H16 **Kushida-gawa** ≈ Honshū, SW Japan
170 Bb15 **Kushikino** *var.* Kusikino. Kagoshima, Kyūshū, SW Japan *31.42N 130.13E*
170 C17 **Kushima** *var.* Kusima. Miyazaki, Kyūshū, SW Japan *31.27N 131.11E*
170 G17 **Kushimoto** Wakayama, Honshū, SW Japan *33.28N 135.45E*
172 Q7 **Kushiro** *var.* Kusiro. Hokkaidō, NE Japan *42.58N 144.24E*
154 K4 **Kūshk** Herāt, W Afghanistan *34.54N 62.09E*
152 J17 **Kushka** ≈ S Turkmenistan
Kushka *see* Gushgy
151 N8 **Kushmurun** *Kaz.* Qusmuryn. Kostanay, N Kazakhstan *52.27N 64.31E*
151 N8 **Kushmurun, Ozero** *Kaz.* Qusmuryn. ◎ N Kazakhstan
131 U4 **Kushnarenkovo** Respublika Bashkortostan, W Russian Federation *55.07N 55.24E*
Kushrabat *see* Qŭshrabot
159 T15 **Kushtia** *var.* Kustia. Khulna, W Bangladesh *23.54N 89.07E*
125 Ee10 **Kushva** Sverdlovskaya Oblast', C Russian Federation *58.14N 59.36E*
Kusikino *see* Kushikino
Kusima *see* Kushima
Kusiro *see* Kushiro
40 M13 **Kuskokwim Bay** *bay* Alaska, USA
41 P11 **Kuskokwim Mountains** ▲▲ Alaska, USA
41 N12 **Kuskokwim River** ≈ Alaska, USA
110 G7 **Küsnacht** Zürich, N Switzerland *47.21N 8.32E*
172 Qq6 **Kussharo-ko** *var.* Kussyaro. ◎ Hokkaidō, NE Japan
Küssnacht *see* Küssnacht am Rigi
110 F8 **Küssnacht am Rigi** *var.* Küssnacht. Schwyz, C Switzerland *47.03N 8.25E*
Kussyaro *see* Kussharo-ko
Kustanay *see* Kostanay
Küstence/Küstendje *see* Constanţa
102 F11 **Küstenkanal** *var.* Ems-Hunte Canal. *canal* NW Germany
Küstrin *see* Kostrzyn
Kustia *see* Kushtia
175 T7 **Kusu** Pulau Halmahera, E Indonesia *0.51N 127.41E*
175 Nn16 **Kuta** Pulau Lombok, S Indonesia *8.52S 116.15E*
145 T4 **Kutabān** N Iraq *35.21N 44.45E*
142 E13 **Kütahya** *prev.* Kutaiah. Kütahya, W Turkey *39.25N 29.55E*
142 E13 **Kütahya** *var.* Kutaia. ◆ *province* W Turkey
Kutai *see* Mahakam, Sungai
Kutaia *see* Kütahya
143 R9 **K'ut'aisi** W Georgia *42.15N 42.42E*
Kūt al 'Amārah *see* Al Kūt
Kut al Hai/Kūt al Ḩayy *see* Al Ḩayy
Kut al Imara *see* Al Kūt
126 M12 **Kutana** Respublika Sakha (Yakutiya), NE Russian Federation *59.05N 131.43E*
Kutaradja/Kutaraja *see* Bandaaceh
172 Nn5 **Kutchan** Hokkaidō, NE Japan *42.54N 140.46E*
Kutch, Gulf of *see* Kachchh, Gulf of
Kutch, Rann of *see* Kachchh, Rann of
114 F9 **Kutina** Sisak-Moslavina, NE Croatia *45.29N 16.45E*
114 H9 **Kutjevo** Požega-Slavonija, NE Croatia *45.26N 17.54E*
113 E17 **Kutná Hora** *Ger.* Kuttenberg. Středočeský Kraj, C Czech Republic *49.57N 15.15E*
112 K12 **Kutno** Łódzkie, C Poland *52.13N 19.23E*
Kuttenberg *see* Kutná Hora
81 I20 **Kutu** Bandundu, W Dem. Rep. Congo (Zaire) *2.42S 18.07E*
159 V17 **Kutubdia Island** *island* SE Bangladesh
82 B10 **Kutum** Northern Darfur, W Sudan *14.10N 24.40E*
153 Y7 **Kuturgu** Issyk-Kul'skaya Oblast', E Kyrgyzstan *42.45N 78.04E*
10 M5 **Kuujjuaq** *prev.* Fort-Chimo. Quebec, E Canada *58.10N 68.15W*
10 I7 **Kuujjuarapik** Quebec, C Canada *55.07N 78.09W*
152 A10 **Kuuli-Mayak** *Turkm.* Guwlumayak. Balkanskiy Velayat, NW Turkmenistan *40.14N 52.43E*
120 I6 **Kuulse magi** ▲ S Estonia
94 N13 **Kuusamo** Oulu, E Finland *65.57N 29.15E*
95 M19 **Kuusankoski** Etelä-Suomi, S Finland *60.51N 26.40E*
131 W7 **Kuvandyk** Orenburgskaya Oblast', W Russian Federation *51.27N 57.18E*
Kuvango *see* Cubango
Kuvasay *see* Quwasoy
Kuvdlorssuak *see* Kullorsuaq
128 I16 **Kuvshinovo** Tverskaya Oblast', W Russian Federation *57.03N 34.09E*
147 Q4 **Kuwait** *off.* State of Kuwait, *var.* Dawlat al Kuwait, Koweit, Kuweit. ◆ *monarchy* SW Asia
Kuwait *see* Al Kuwayt
Kuwait Bay *see* Kuwayt, Jūn al
Kuwait City *see* Al Kuwayt
Kuwait, Dawlat al *see* Kuwait
Kuwajleen *see* Kwajalein Atoll
171 H15 **Kuwana** Mie, Honshū, SW Japan *35.03N 136.40E*
176 V9 **Kuwawin** Irian Jaya, E Indonesia *1.10S 132.40E*
145 X9 **Kuwayt** E Iraq *32.26N 47.12E*
148 K11 **Kuwayt, Jūn al** *var.* Kuwait Bay. *bay* E Kuwait
Kuweit *see* Kuwait
119 P10 **Kuyal'nyts'kyy Lyman** ◎ SW Ukraine
125 G13 **Kuybyshev** Novosibirskaya Oblast', C Russian Federation *55.28N 77.55E*
Kuybyshev *see* Bolgar, Respublika Tatarstan, Russian Federation
Kuybyshev *see* Samara
119 W9 **Kuybysheve** *Rus.* Kuybyshevo. Zaporiz'ka Oblast', SE Ukraine *47.20N 36.41E*
Kuybyshevo *see* Kuybysheve
Kuybyshev Reservoir *see* Kuybyshevskoye Vodokhranilishche
Kuybyshevskaya Oblast' *see* Samarskaya Oblast'
151 O7 **Kuybyshevskiy** Severnyy Kazakhstan, N Kazakhstan *53.16N 66.53E*
131 R4 **Kuybyshevskoye Vodokhranilishche** *var.* Kuibyshev, *Eng.* Kuybyshev Reservoir. ⊠ W Russian Federation
127 N9 **Kuydusun** Respublika Sakha (Yakutiya), NE Russian Federation *63.15N 143.10E*
129 U16 **Kuyeda** Permskaya Oblast', NW Russian Federation *56.23N 55.19E*
Küysanjaq *see* Koi Sanjaq
128 I7 **Kuyto, Ozero** *var.* Ozero Kujto. ◎ NW Russian Federation
164 J4 **Kuytun** Xinjiang Uygur Zizhiqu, NW China *44.25N 84.55E*
126 J15 **Kuytun** Irkutskaya Oblast', S Russian Federation *54.18N 101.28E*
126 Ii12 **Kuyumba** Evenkiyskiy Avtonomnyy Okrug, C Russian Federation *61.00N 97.07E*
57 S12 **Kuyuwini Landing** S Guyana *2.06N 59.14W*
Kuzi *see* Kuji
40 M9 **Kuzitrin River** ≈ Alaska, USA
131 P6 **Kuznetsk** Penzenskaya Oblast', W Russian Federation *53.06N 46.27E*
118 K3 **Kuznetsovs'k** Rivnens'ka Oblast', NW Ukraine *51.21N 25.51E*
128 K6 **Kuzomen'** Murmanskaya Oblast', NW Russian Federation *66.16N 36.47E*
172 N10 **Kuzumaki** Iwate, Honshū, C Japan *40.04N 141.26E*
94 H9 **Kvaløya** *island* N Norway
94 K8 **Kvalsund** Finnmark, N Norway *70.30N 23.56E*
96 G11 **Kvam** Oppland, S Norway *61.42N 9.43E*
131 X7 **Kvarkeno** Orenburgskaya Oblast', W Russian Federation *52.09N 59.44E*
95 G15 **Kvarnbergsvattnet** *var.* Frostviken. ◎ N Sweden
114 A11 **Kvarner** *var.* Carnaro, *It.* Quarnero. *gulf* W Croatia
114 B11 **Kvarnerić** *channel* W Croatia
41 O14 **Kvichak Bay** *bay* Alaska, USA
94 H12 **Kvikkjokk** Norrbotten, N Sweden *66.58N 17.45E*
97 D17 **Kvina** ≈ S Norway
94 Q1 **Kvitøya** *island* NE Svalbard
97 F16 **Kvitseid** Telemark, S Norway *59.23N 8.31E*
97 H24 **Kværndrup** Fyn, C Denmark *55.10N 10.31E*
81 H20 **Kwa** ≈ W Dem. Rep. Congo (Zaire)
79 Q15 **Kwadwokurom** C Ghana *7.49N 0.15W*
195 X14 **Kwailibesi** Malaita, N Solomon Islands *8.25S 160.48E*
201 S6 **Kwajalein Atoll** *var.* Kuwajleen. *atoll* Ralik Chain, C Marshall Islands
57 W9 **Kwakoegron** Brokopondo, N Surinam *5.13N 55.19W*
83 J21 **Kwale** Coast, S Kenya *4.11S 39.30E*
79 U17 **Kwale** Delta, S Nigeria *5.51N 6.29E*
81 H20 **Kwamouth** Bandundu, W Dem. Rep. Congo (Zaire) *3.10S 16.16E*
Kwando *see* Cuando
Kwangchow *see* Guangzhou
Kwangchu *see* Kwangju
169 X16 **Kwangju** *off.* Kwangju-gwangyŏksi, *var.* Guangju, Kwangchu, *Jap.* Kōshū. SW South Korea *35.09N 126.52E*
81 H20 **Kwango** *Port.* Cuango. ≈ Angola/Dem. Rep. Congo (Zaire) ***see also*** Cuango
Kwangsi/Kwangsi Chuang Autonomous Region *see* Guangxi Zhuangzu Zizhiqu
Kwangtung *see* Guangdong
Kwangyuan *see* Guangyuan
83 F17 **Kwania, Lake** ◎ C Uganda
Kwanza *see* Cuanza
79 S15 **Kwara** ◆ *state* SW Nigeria
176 Ww11 **Kwatisore** Irian Jaya, E Indonesia *3.14S 134.57E*
85 K22 **KwaZulu/Natal** *off.* KwaZulu/Natal Province; *prev.* Natal. ◆ *province* E South Africa
Kweichow *see* Guizhou
Kweichu *see* Guiyang
Kweilin *see* Guilin
Kweisui *see* Hohhot
Kweiyang *see* Guiyang
85 K17 **Kwekwe** *prev.* Que Que. Midlands, C Zimbabwe *18.55S 29.48E*
85 G20 **Kweneng** ◆ *district* S Botswana
Kwesui *see* Hohhot
41 N12 **Kwethluk** Alaska, USA *60.48N 161.26W*
41 N12 **Kwethluk River** ≈ Alaska, USA
112 J8 **Kwidzyń** *Ger.* Marienwerder. Pomorskie, N Poland *53.44N 18.55E*
40 M13 **Kwigillingok** Alaska, USA *59.51N 163.07W*
194 K16 **Kwikila** Central, S PNG *9.48S 147.37E*
81 I20 **Kwilu** ≈ W Dem. Rep. Congo (Zaire)
Kwito *see* Cuito
176 V8 **Kwoka, Gunung** ▲ Irian Jaya, E Indonesia *0.34S 132.25E*
80 I12 **Kyabé** Moyen-Chari, S Chad *9.28N 18.54E*
191 O11 **Kyabram** Victoria, SE Australia *36.21S 145.04E*
178 Gg9 **Kyaikkami** *prev.* Amherst. Mon State, S Burma *16.02N 97.36E*
177 F9 **Kyaiklat** Irrawaddy, SW Burma *16.25N 95.42E*
177 G8 **Kyaikto** Mon State, S Burma *17.16N 97.01E*
126 Jj16 **Kyakhta** Respublika Buryatiya, S Russian Federation *50.24N 106.12E*
190 G8 **Kyancutta** South Australia *33.10S 135.33E*
177 Ff7 **Kyangin** Irrawaddy, SW Burma *18.19N 95.15E*
178 Jj8 **Ky Anh** Ha Tinh, N Vietnam *18.05N 106.16E*

◆ Country ● Country Capital ◇ Dependent Territory ○ Dependent Territory Capital ◆ Administrative Region ✕ International Airport ▲ Mountain ▲▲ Mountain Range Volcano ≈ River ◎ Lake ⊠ Reservoir

◆ COUNTRY ◇ DEPENDENT TERRITORY ◆ ADMINISTRATIVE REGION ▲ MOUNTAIN ▲ VOLCANO ◎ LAKE
● COUNTRY CAPITAL ◉ DEPENDENT TERRITORY CAPITAL ✈ INTERNATIONAL AIRPORT ▲ MOUNTAIN RANGE ✍ RIVER ◙ RESERVOIR

LAKHVA – LASIHAO

121 K19 Lakhva Rus. Lakhva. Brestskaya Voblasts', SW Belarus 52.13N 27.15E
28 I6 Lakin Kansas, C USA 37.56N 101.18W
155 S7 Lakki Marwat North-West Frontier Province, NW Pakistan 32.36N 70.55E
117 F21 Lakonía historical region S Greece
117 F22 Lakonikós Kólpos gulf S Greece
78 M17 Lakota S Ivory Coast 5.52N 5.42W
31 U11 Lakota Iowa, C USA 43.22N 94.04W
31 P3 Lakota North Dakota, N USA 48.02N 98.20W
Lak Sao see Ban Lakxao
94 L8 Laksefjorden fjord N Norway
94 K8 Lakselv Finnmark, N Norway 70.01N 24.57E
161 B21 Lakshadweep prev. the Laccadive, Minicoy and Amindivi Islands. ◈ union territory India, N Indian Ocean
161 C22 Lakshadweep Eng. Laccadive Islands. island group India, N Indian Ocean
159 S17 Lakshmikāntapur West Bengal, NE India 22.04N 88.19E
114 G11 Laktaši Republika Srpska, N Bosnia and Herzegovina 44.54N 17.16E
155 V7 Lāla Mūsa Punjab, NE Pakistan 32.40N 74.01E
la Laon see Laon
116 M11 Lalapaşa Edirne, NW Turkey 41.52N 26.43E
85 P14 Lalaua Nampula, N Mozambique 14.21S 38.16E
107 S10 L'Alcúdia var. L'Alcudia. País Valenciano, E Spain 39.10N 0.30W
82 J11 Lalibela Amhara, N Ethiopia, 12.01N 39.05E
159 T12 Lalmanirhat Rajshahi, N Bangladesh 25.51N 89.34E
81 F20 La Lékoumou ◈ province SW Congo
44 E8 La Libertad La Libertad, SW El Salvador 13.28N 89.17W
44 E3 La Libertad Petén, N Guatemala 16.46N 90.07W
44 H6 La Libertad Comayagua, SW Honduras 14.44N 87.37W
42 E4 La Libertad var. Puerto Libertad. Sonora, NW Mexico 29.52N 112.39W
44 K10 La Libertad Chontales, S Nicaragua 12.14N 85.15W
44 A9 La Libertad ◈ department SW El Salvador
58 B11 La Libertad off. Departamento de la Libertad. ◈ department W Peru
64 G11 La Ligua Valparaíso, C Chile 32.23S 71.16W
145 U5 La'li Khān E Iraq 34.58N 45.36E
81 H16 La Likouala ◈ province NE Congo
106 H3 Lalín Galicia, NW Spain 42.40N 8.06W
104 L13 Lalinde Dordogne, SW France 44.52N 0.42E
106 K16 La Línea var. La Línea de la Concepción. Andalucía, S Spain 36.10N 5.21W
La Línea de la Concepción see La Línea
158 J14 Lalitpur Uttar Pradesh, N India 24.42N 78.24E
159 P11 Lalitpur Central, C Nepal 27.45N 85.17E
158 K10 Lālkua Uttar Pradesh, N India 29.04N 79.31E
9 R12 La Loche Saskatchewan, C Canada 56.31N 109.27W
104 M6 la Loupe Eure-et-Loir, C France 48.30N 1.04E
101 G20 La Louvière Hainaut, S Belgium 50.28N 4.15E
L'Altissima see Hochwilde
106 L14 La Luisiana Andalucía, S Spain 37.30N 5.14W
39 S14 La Luz New Mexico, SW USA 32.58N 105.56W
109 D16 la Maddalena Sardegna, Italy, C Mediterranean Sea 41.13N 9.25E
64 J7 La Madrid Tucumán, N Argentina 27.37S 65.16W
Lama-Kara see Kara
175 R16 Lamakera, Selat strait Nusa Tenggara, S Indonesia
13 S8 La Malbaie Quebec, SE Canada 47.39N 70.10W
178 Jj10 Lamam Xékong, S Laos 15.22N 106.40E
107 P10 La Mancha physical region C Spain
la Manche see English Channel
197 C13 Lamap Malekula, C Vanuatu 16.26S 167.47E
39 W6 Lamar Colorado, C USA 38.03N 102.36W
29 S7 Lamar Missouri, C USA 37.30N 94.16W
23 S12 Lamar South Carolina, SE USA 34.10N 80.03W
109 C19 La Marmora, Punta ▲ Sardegna, Italy, C Mediterranean Sea 39.58N 9.20E
15 H7 La Martre, Lac ◎ Northwest Territories, NW Canada
58 D10 Lamas San Martín, N Peru 6.27S 76.32W
44 I5 La Masica Atlántida, NW Honduras 15.37N 87.04W
105 R12 Lamastre Ardèche, E France 45.00N 4.32E
La Matepec see Santa Ana, Volcán de
46 I7 La Maya Santiago de Cuba, E Cuba 20.09N 75.40W
111 S5 Lambach Oberösterreich, N Austria 48.06N 13.52E
173 Ff8 Lambak Pulau Pini, W Indonesia 0.08N 98.36E
104 H5 Lamballe Côtes d'Armor, NW France 48.28N 2.31W
81 D18 Lambaréné Moyen-Ogooué, W Gabon 0.40S 10.13E
Lambasa see Labasa
175 Q12 Lambasina Besar, Pulau island C Indonesia
58 B11 Lambayeque Lambayeque, W Peru 6.39S 79.54W
58 A10 Lambayeque off. Departamento de Lambayeque. ◈ department NW Peru
99 G17 Lambay Island Ir. Reachrainn. island E Ireland
195 O10 Lambert, Cape headland New Britain, E PNG 4.15S 151.31E
205 W6 Lambert Glacier glacier Antarctica
31 T10 Lamberton Minnesota, N USA 44.14N 95.15W
29 X4 Lambert-Saint Louis ✕ Missouri, C USA 38.43N 90.19W
33 R11 Lambertville Michigan, N USA 41.46N 83.37W
20 J15 Lambertville New Jersey, NE USA 40.20N 74.55W
175 Pp9 Lambogo Sulawesi, N Indonesia 0.57S 120.23E
108 D8 Lambro ≈ N Italy
15 H2 Lambton, Cape headland Banks Island, Northwest Territories, NW Canada 71.04N 123.07W
35 W11 Lame Deer Montana, NW USA 45.37N 106.37W
106 H6 Lamego Viseu, N Portugal 41.04N 7.49W
197 C13 Lamen Bay Épi, C Vanuatu 16.36S 168.10E
47 X6 Lamentin Basse Terre, N Guadeloupe 16.16N 61.37W
Lamentin see le Lamentin
190 K10 Lameroo South Australia 35.22S 140.30E
56 F10 La Mesa Cundinamarca, C Colombia 4.39N 74.24W
37 U17 La Mesa California, W USA 32.44N 117.00W
39 R16 La Mesa New Mexico, SW USA 32.03N 106.41W
27 N6 Lamesa Texas, SW USA 32.43N 101.57W
197 I15 Lami Viti Levu, C Fiji 18.07S 178.25E
117 F17 Lamía Stereá Ellás, C Greece 38.54N 22.26E
179 Q17 Lamitan Basilan Island, SW Philippines 6.40N 122.07E
197 J14 Lamiti Gau, C Fiji 18.00S 179.20E
176 Uu8 Lamlam Irian Jaya, E Indonesia 0.03S 130.46E
196 B16 Lamlam, Mount ▲ SW Guam 13.19N 144.40E
111 Q6 Lammer ≈ E Austria
193 E23 Lammerlaw Range ▲▲ South Island, NZ
97 L20 Lammhult Kronoberg, S Sweden 57.09N 14.34E
95 L18 Lammi Etelä-Suomi, S Finland 61.06N 25.00E
201 U11 Lamoil island Chuuk, C Micronesia
37 W3 Lamoille Nevada, W USA 40.47N 115.37W
20 M7 Lamoille River ≈ Vermont, NE USA
32 J13 La Moine River ≈ Illinois, N USA
179 Pp10 Lamon Bay bay Luzon, N Philippines
31 V16 Lamoni Iowa, C USA 40.37N 93.56W
37 R13 Lamont California, W USA 35.15N 118.54W
29 N8 Lamont Oklahoma, C USA 36.41N 97.33W
56 E13 La Montañita var. Montañita. Caquetá, S Colombia 1.23N 75.28W
45 N8 La Mosquitia var. Miskito Coast, Eng. Mosquito Coast. coastal region E Nicaragua
104 I9 la Mothe-Achard Vendée, NW France 46.37N 1.37W
196 L15 Lamotrek Atoll atoll Caroline Islands, C Micronesia
31 P6 La Moure North Dakota, N USA 46.21N 98.17W
178 H8 Lampang var. Muang Lampang. Lampang, NW Thailand 18.16N 99.30E
178 Ii9 Lam Pao Reservoir ⊠ E Thailand
27 S9 Lampasas Texas, SW USA 31.03N 98.10W
27 S9 Lampasas River ≈ Texas, SW USA
43 N7 Lampazos var. Lampazos de Naranjo. Nuevo León, NE Mexico 27.00N 100.28W
Lampazos de Naranjo see Lampazos
117 E19 Lámpeia Dytikí Ellás, S Greece 37.51N 21.48E
103 G19 Lampertheim Hessen, W Germany 49.36N 8.28E
99 I20 Lampeter SW Wales, UK 52.07N 4.03W
178 H7 Lamphun var. Lampun, Muang Lamphun. Lamphun, NW Thailand 18.36N 99.01E
9 X10 Lamprey Manitoba, C Canada 58.18N 94.06W
Lampun see Lamphun
174 I13 Lampung off. Propinsi Lampung. ◈ province SW Indonesia
174 Ii13 Lampung, Teluk bay Sumatera, SW Indonesia
130 K6 Lamskoye Lipetskaya Oblast', W Russian Federation 52.57N 38.04E
83 K20 Lamu Coast, SE Kenya 2.17S 40.49E
45 N14 La Muerte, Cerro ▲ C Costa Rica 9.33N 83.47W
105 S13 la Mure Isère, E France 44.54N 5.48E
39 S10 Lamy New Mexico, SW USA 35.27N 105.52W
121 J18 Lan' Rus. Lan'. ≈ C Belarus
40 E10 Lanai Haw. Lāna'i. island Hawaii, USA, C Pacific Ocean
40 E10 Lanai City Lanai, Hawaii, USA, C Pacific Ocean 20.49N 156.55W
101 L18 Lanaken Limburg, NE Belgium 50.52N 5.39E
179 R15 Lanao, Lake var. Lake Sultan Alonto. ◎ Mindanao, S Philippines
98 J12 Lanark S Scotland, UK 55.38N 4.24W
98 I13 Lanark cultural region C Scotland, UK
106 L9 La Nava de Ricomalillo Castilla-La Mancha, C Spain 39.40N 4.58W
178 Gg13 Lanbi Kyun prev. Sullivan Island. island Mergui Archipelago, S Burma
Lancang Jiang see Mekong
99 K17 Lancashire cultural region NW England, UK
13 N13 Lancaster Ontario, SE Canada 45.10N 74.31W
99 K16 Lancaster NW England, UK 54.03N 2.48W
37 T14 Lancaster California, W USA 34.42N 118.08W
22 M6 Lancaster Kentucky, S USA 37.35N 84.34W
29 U1 Lancaster Missouri, C USA 40.30N 92.31W
21 O7 Lancaster New Hampshire, NE USA 44.28N 71.34W
20 D10 Lancaster New York, NE USA 42.54N 78.40W
33 T14 Lancaster Ohio, N USA 39.42N 82.36W
20 H16 Lancaster Pennsylvania, NE USA 40.03N 76.18W
23 R11 Lancaster South Carolina, SE USA 34.43N 80.46W
27 U7 Lancaster Texas, SW USA 32.35N 96.45W
23 X5 Lancaster Virginia, NE USA 37.45N 76.25W
32 J9 Lancaster Wisconsin, N USA 42.52N 90.43W
207 N10 Lancaster Sound sound Nunavut, N Canada
Lan-chou/Lan-chow/Lanchow see Lanzhou
109 K14 Lanciano Abruzzo, C Italy 42.15N 14.22E
113 O16 Łańcut Podkarpackie, SE Poland 50.04N 22.13E
174 Kk8 Landak, Sungai ≈ Borneo, N Indonesia
Landao see Lantau Island
Landau see Landau an der Isar, Bayern, Germany
Landau see Landau in der Pfalz, Rheinland-Pfalz, Germany
103 N22 Landau an der Isar var. Landau. Bayern, SE Germany 48.40N 12.41E
103 F20 Landau in der Pfalz var. Landau. Rheinland-Pfalz, SW Germany 49.12N 8.07E
Land Burgenland see Burgenland
110 K8 Landeck Tirol, W Austria 47.09N 10.34E
101 J19 Landen Vlaams Brabant, C Belgium 50.45N 5.04E
35 U15 Lander Wyoming, C USA 42.49N 108.43W
104 F5 Landerneau Finistère, NW France 48.27N 4.16W
97 K20 Landeryd Halland, S Sweden 57.04N 13.15E
104 J15 Landes ◈ department SW France
Landeshut/Landeshut in Schlesien see Kamienna Góra
107 R9 Landete Castilla-La Mancha, C Spain 39.54N 1.22W
101 M18 Landgraaf Limburg, SE Netherlands 50.55N 6.04E
104 F5 Landivisiau Finistère, NW France 48.31N 4.03W
Land of Enchantment see New Mexico
Land of Opportunity see Arkansas
Land of Steady Habits see Connecticut
Land of the Midnight Sun see Alaska
110 I8 Landquart Graubünden, SE Switzerland 46.58N 9.35E
110 J9 Landquart ≈ Austria/Switzerland
23 P10 Landrum South Carolina, SE USA 35.10N 82.11W
Landsberg see Gorówo Iławeckie, Warmińsko-Mazurskie, NE Poland
Landsberg see Gorzów Wielkopolski, Gorzów, Poland
103 K23 Landsberg am Lech Bayern, S Germany 48.03N 10.52E
Landsberg an der Warthe see Gorzów Wielkopolski
99 G25 Land's End headland SW England, UK 50.02N 5.41W
103 M22 Landshut Bayern, SE Germany 48.31N 12.09E
Landskron see Lanškroun
97 J22 Landskrona Skåne, S Sweden 55.52N 12.52E
100 I10 Landsmeer Noord-Holland, C Netherlands 52.25N 4.55E
97 J19 Landvetter ✕ (Göteborg) Västra Götaland, S Sweden 57.39N 12.22E
Landwarów see Lentvaris
25 R5 Lanett Alabama, S USA 32.52N 85.11W
110 C8 La Neuveville var. Neuveville, Ger. Neuenstadt. Neuchâtel, W Switzerland 47.05N 7.03E
97 G21 Langå var. Langaa. Århus, C Denmark 56.22N 9.55E
Langaa see Langå
164 G14 La'nga Co ◎ W China
Langada see Lagkáda
Langades/Langadhás see Lagkádas
Langádhia/Langadia see Lagkádia
153 T14 Langar Rus. Lyangar. SE Tajikistan 37.04N 72.39E
152 M10 Langar Rus. Lyangar. Nawoiy Wiloyati, C Uzbekistan 40.27N 65.54E
148 M3 Langarūd Gīlān, NW Iran 37.12N 50.10E
9 V16 Langbank Saskatchewan, S Canada 50.01N 102.16W
31 P2 Langdon North Dakota, N USA 48.45N 98.22W
105 P12 Langeac Haute-Loire, C France 45.06N 3.31E
104 L8 Langeais Indre-et-Loire, C France 47.22N 0.27E
82 I8 Langeb, Wadi ≈ NE Sudan
Långed see Dals Långed
97 G25 Langeland island S Denmark
101 B18 Langemark West-Vlaanderen, W Belgium 50.55N 2.55E
103 G18 Langen Hessen, W Germany 49.58N 8.40E
103 J22 Langenau Baden-Württemberg, S Germany 48.30N 10.08E
9 V16 Langenburg Saskatchewan, S Canada 50.49N 101.43W
103 E16 Langenfeld Nordrhein-Westfalen, W Germany 51.06N 6.57E
110 L8 Längenfeld Tirol, W Austria 47.04N 10.59E
102 I12 Langenhagen Niedersachsen, N Germany 52.25N 9.43E
102 I12 Langenhagen ✕ (Hannover) Niedersachsen, NW Germany 52.28N 9.40E
111 W3 Langenlois Niederösterreich, NE Austria 48.28N 15.42E
110 E7 Langenthal Bern, NW Switzerland 47.13N 7.46E
111 W6 Langenwang Steiermark, E Austria 47.34N 15.39E
111 X3 Langenzersdorf Niederösterreich, E Austria 48.19N 16.22E
102 F9 Langeoog island NW Germany
126 Gg11 Langepas Khanty-Mansiyskiy Avtonomnyy Okrug, C Russian Federation 61.12N 75.24E
97 H23 Langeskov Fyn, C Denmark 55.22N 10.36E
97 G16 Langesund Telemark, S Norway 59.00N 9.43E
97 G17 Langesundsfjorden fjord S Norway
96 D10 Langevågen Møre og Romsdal, S Norway 62.25N 6.13E
167 P3 Langfang Hebei, E China 39.30N 116.39E
96 E9 Langfjorden fjord S Norway
31 Q8 Langford South Dakota, N USA 45.36N 97.48W
173 G6 Langgapayung Sumatera, W Indonesia 1.42N 99.57E
108 E9 Langhirano Emilia-Romagna, C Italy 44.37N 10.16E
99 K14 Langholm S Scotland, UK 55.13N 3.11W
94 I3 Langjökull glacier C Iceland
173 Ff2 Langkawi, Pulau island Peninsular Malaysia
175 R13 Langkesi, Kepulauan island group C Indonesia
178 Gg15 Langkha Tuk, Khao ▲ SW Thailand 9.19N 98.39E
12 L8 Langlade Quebec, SE Canada 48.13N 75.58W
8 M17 Langley British Columbia, SW Canada 49.07N 122.39W
178 Jj7 Lang Mô Thanh Hoa, N Vietnam 19.36N 105.30E
Langnau see Langnau im Emmental
110 E8 Langnau im Emmental var. Langnau. Bern, W Switzerland 46.57N 7.46E
105 Q13 Langogne Lozère, S France 44.40N 3.52E
164 K16 Langoi Kangri ▲ W China 28.51N 87.28E
104 K13 Langon Gironde, SW France 47.43N 1.49W
La Ngounié see Ngounié
94 G10 Langøya island C Norway
164 G14 Langqên Zangbo ≈ China/India
106 K2 Langreo var. Sama de Langreo. Asturias, N Spain 43.18N 5.40W
105 S7 Langres Haute-Marne, N France 47.52N 5.19E
105 R8 Langres, Plateau de plateau C France
173 F4 Langsa Sumatera, W Indonesia 4.29N 97.53E
95 H16 Långsele Västernorrland, C Sweden 63.10N 17.04E
168 L12 Lang Shan ▲▲ N China
97 M14 Långshyttan Dalarna, C Sweden 60.25N 16.01E
178 K5 Lang Sơn var. Langson. Lang Sơn, N Vietnam 21.49N 106.45E
178 Gg14 Lang Suan Chumphon, SW Thailand 9.52N 99.03E
95 J14 Långträsk Norrbotten, N Sweden 65.22N 20.19E
27 N11 Langtry Texas, SW USA 29.46N 101.25W
105 P16 Languedoc cultural region S France
105 P15 Languedoc-Roussillon ◈ region S France
29 X10 L'Anguille River ≈ Arkansas, C USA
95 I16 Långviksmon Västernorrland, N Sweden 63.39N 18.45E
103 K22 Langweid Bayern, S Germany 48.29N 10.50E
166 J8 Langzhong Sichuan, C China 31.46N 105.55E
Lan Hsü see Lan Yü
9 U15 Lanigan Saskatchewan, S Canada 51.49N 105.01W
118 K5 Lanivtsi Ternopil's'ka Oblast', W Ukraine 49.52N 26.05E
143 Y13 Länkäran Rus. Lenkoran'. S Azerbaijan 38.46N 48.50E
104 L16 Lannemezan Hautes-Pyrénées, S France 43.07N 0.22E
104 G5 Lannion Côtes d'Armor, NW France 48.43N 3.27W
12 M11 L'Annonciation Quebec, SE Canada 46.22N 74.51W
107 V5 L'Anoia ≈ NE Spain
20 I15 Lansdale Pennsylvania, NE USA 40.14N 75.13W
12 L14 Lansdowne Ontario, SE Canada 44.25N 76.00W
158 K9 Lansdowne Uttar Pradesh, N India 29.49N 78.42E
32 M3 L'Anse Michigan, N USA 46.45N 88.27W
13 S7 L'Anse-St-Jean Quebec, SE Canada 48.14N 70.13W
95 K18 Länsi-Suomi ◈ province W Finland
31 Y11 Lansing Iowa, C USA 43.22N 91.11W
29 R4 Lansing Kansas, C USA 39.15N 94.54W
33 Q9 Lansing state capital Michigan, N USA 42.43N 84.33W
94 J12 Lansjärv Norrbotten, N Sweden 66.39N 22.10E
113 G17 Lanškroun Ger. Landskron. Pardubický Kraj, C Czech Republic 49.53N 16.34E
178 Gg16 Lanta, Ko island S Thailand
167 O15 Lantau Island Cant. Tai Yue Shan, Chin. Landao. island Hong Kong, S China
Lan-ts'ang Chiang see Mekong
175 Q7 Lanu Sulawesi, N Indonesia 1.00N 121.33E
109 D19 Lanusei Sardegna, Italy, C Mediterranean Sea 39.55N 9.31E
104 H7 Lanvaux, Landes de physical region NW France
169 W8 Lanxi Heilongjiang, NE China 46.18N 126.49E
167 R10 Lanxi Zhejiang, SE China 29.13N 119.30E
La Nyanga see Nyanga
167 T15 Lan Yü var. Huoshao Tao, var. Hungt'ou, Lan Hsü, Lanyü, Eng. Orchid Island; prev. Kotosho, Koto Sho. island SE Taiwan
66 P11 Lanzarote island Islas Canarias, Spain, NE Atlantic Ocean
165 V10 Lanzhou var. Lan-chou, Lanchow, Lan-chow; prev. Kaolan. Gansu, C China 36.01N 103.52E
108 B8 Lanzo Torinese Piemonte, NE Italy 45.18N 7.26E
179 P8 Laoag Luzon, N Philippines 18.11N 120.34E
179 R12 Laoang Samar, C Philippines 12.29N 125.01E
178 I5 Lao Cai Lao Cai, N Vietnam 22.29N 104.00E
Laodicea/Laodicea ad Mare see Al Lādhiqīyah
Laoet see Laut, Pulau
169 T11 Laoha He ≈ NE China
166 M8 Laohekou prev. Guanghua. Hubei, C China 32.21N 111.40E
Laoi, An see Lee
99 E19 Laois prev. Leix, Queen's County. cultural region C Ireland
Laojunmiao see Yumen
169 W12 Lao Ling ▲▲ N China
66 Q11 La Oliva var. Oliva. Fuerteventura, Islas Canarias, Spain, NE Atlantic Ocean 28.36N 13.52W
Lao, Loch see Belfast Lough
Lao Mangnai see Mangnai
105 P3 Laon var. la Laon; anc. Laudunum. Aisne, N France 49.34N 3.37E
Lao People's Democratic Republic see Laos
56 M3 La Orchila, Isla island N Venezuela
66 O11 La Orotava Tenerife, Islas Canarias, Spain, NE Atlantic Ocean 28.22N 16.31W
59 E14 La Oroya Junín, C Peru 11.29S 75.57W
178 Ii7 Laos off. Lao People's Democratic Republic. ◆ republic SE Asia
167 S5 Laoshan Wan bay E China
169 Y10 Laoye Ling ▲▲ NE China
62 J12 Lapa Paraná, S Brazil 25.46S 49.43W
105 P10 Lapalisse Allier, C France 46.13N 3.39E
56 F9 La Palma Cundinamarca, C Colombia 5.22N 74.24W
44 F7 La Palma Chalatenango, N El Salvador 14.19N 89.10W
45 W16 La Palma Darién, SE Panama 8.24N 78.09W
66 N11 La Palma island Islas Canarias, Spain, NE Atlantic Ocean
106 J14 La Palma del Condado Andalucía, S Spain 37.22N 6.33W
63 F18 La Paloma Durazno, C Uruguay 34.37S 54.07W
63 G20 La Paloma Rocha, E Uruguay 34.37S 54.07W
63 A21 La Pampa off. Provincia de La Pampa. ◈ province C Argentina
57 P8 La Paragua Bolívar, E Venezuela 6.53N 63.16W
121 O16 Lapatsichy Rus. Lopatichi. Mahilyowskaya Voblasts', E Belarus 53.34N 30.53E
63 C16 La Paz Entre Ríos, E Argentina 30.45S 59.36W
64 I11 La Paz Mendoza, C Argentina 33.27S 67.35W
59 J18 La Paz var. La Paz de Ayacucho. ● (Bolivia-legislative and administrative capital) La Paz, W Bolivia 16.30S 68.12W
44 H6 La Paz La Paz, SW Honduras 14.27N 87.41W
42 F9 La Paz Baja California Sur, NW Mexico 24.06N 110.18W
63 F20 La Paz Canelones, S Uruguay 34.46S 56.13W
59 J16 La Paz ◈ department W Bolivia
44 B9 La Paz ◈ department S El Salvador
44 G7 La Paz ◈ department SW Honduras
La Paz see El Alto, Bolivia
La Paz see Robles, Colombia
La Paz see La Paz Centro, Nicaragua
42 F9 La Paz, Bahía de bay W Mexico
44 I10 La Paz Centro var. La Paz. León, W Nicaragua 12.19N 86.40W
La Paz de Ayacucho see La Paz
56 J15 La Pedrera Amazonas, SE Colombia 1.19S 69.31W
33 S9 Lapeer Michigan, N USA 43.03N 83.19W
42 K6 La Perla Chihuahua, N Mexico 28.11N 104.28W
172 Pp1 La Perouse Strait Jap. Sōya-kaikyō, Rus. Proliv Laperuza. strait Japan/Russian Federation
65 I14 La Perra, Salitral de salt lake C Argentina
Laperuza, Proliv see La Perouse Strait
43 Q10 La Pesca Tamaulipas, C Mexico 23.49N 97.45W
42 M13 La Piedad Cavadas Michoacán de Ocampo, C Mexico 20.19N 102.01W
Lapines see Lafnitz
95 M16 Lapinlahti Itä-Suomi, C Finland 63.21N 27.25E
Lápithos see Lapta
24 K9 Laplace Louisiana, S USA 30.04N 90.28W
47 X12 La Plaine SE Dominica 15.19N 61.15W
181 P16 la Plaine-des-Palmistes C Réunion
94 K11 Lapland Fin. Lappi, Swe. Lappland. cultural region N Europe
30 M8 La Plant South Dakota, N USA 45.06N 100.40W
63 D20 La Plata Buenos Aires, E Argentina 34.56S 57.55W
56 D12 La Plata Huila, SW Colombia 2.25N 75.47W
23 W4 La Plata Maryland, NE USA 38.28N 76.55W
La Plata see Sucre
47 U6 la Plata, Río de ≈ C Puerto Rico
107 W4 La Pobla de Lillet Cataluña, NE Spain 42.15N 1.57E
107 U4 La Pobla de Segur Cataluña, NE Spain 42.15N 0.58E
13 S9 La Pocatière Quebec, SE Canada 47.17N 70.04W
106 L3 La Pola de Gordón Castilla-León, N Spain 42.50N 5.38W
33 O11 La Porte Indiana, N USA 41.36N 86.43W
20 H13 Laporte Pennsylvania, NE USA 41.25N 76.28W
31 X13 La Porte City Iowa, C USA 42.19N 92.11W
64 J8 La Posta Catamarca, C Argentina 27.59S 65.32W
42 E8 La Poza Grande Baja California Sur, W Mexico 25.45N 111.58W
95 K16 Lappajärvi Länsi-Suomi, W Finland 63.11N 23.37E
95 L16 Lappajärvi ◎ W Finland
95 N18 Lappeenranta Swe. Villmanstrand. Etelä-Suomi, S Finland 61.04N 28.15E
95 J17 Lappfjärd Fin. Lapväärtti. Länsi-Suomi, W Finland 62.13N 21.34E
94 L12 Lappi Swe. Lappland. ◈ province N Finland
Lappi see Lapland
Lappland see Lappi
Lappland see Lapland, N Europe
Lappo see Lapua
63 C23 Laprida Buenos Aires, E Argentina 37.33S 60.46W
27 P13 La Pryor Texas, SW USA 28.56N 99.51W
142 B11 Lâpseki Çanakkale, NW Turkey 40.17N 26.36E
124 Nn2 Lapta Gk. Lápithos. NW Cyprus 35.19N 33.11E
Laptev Sea see Laptevykh, More
126 Kk5 Laptevykh, More Eng. Laptev Sea. sea Arctic Ocean
95 K16 Lapua Swe. Lappo. Länsi-Suomi, W Finland 62.57N 23.00E
107 P3 La Puebla de Arganzón País Vasco, N Spain 42.45N 2.49W
106 L14 La Puebla de Cazalla Andalucía, S Spain 37.13N 5.18W
106 M9 La Puebla de Montalbán Castilla-La Mancha, C Spain 39.52N 4.22W
56 I6 La Puerta Trujillo, NW Venezuela 9.09N 70.44W
179 Qq13 Lapu-Lapu C Philippines 10.18N 123.58E
Lapurdum see Bayonne
42 E7 La Purísima Baja California Sur, W Mexico 26.10N 112.04W
Lapväärtti see Lappfjärd
112 O10 Łapy Podlaskie, NE Poland 53.00N 22.50E
82 D6 Laqiya Arba'in Northern, NW Sudan 20.01N 28.01E
64 J4 La Quiaca Jujuy, N Argentina 22.12S 65.36W
109 J14 L'Aquila var. Aquila, Aquila degli Abruzzo. Abruzzo, C Italy 42.21N 13.24E
149 Q13 Lār Fārs, S Iran 27.42N 54.19E
56 J5 Lara off. Estado Lara. ◈ state NW Venezuela
106 G2 Laracha Galicia, NW Spain 43.14N 8.34W
76 G5 Larache var. al Araïch, El Araïch, El Araïche, anc. Lixus. NW Morocco 35.16N 6.07W
105 T14 Laragne-Montéglin Hautes-Alpes, SE France 44.21N 5.46E
106 M13 La Rambla Andalucía, S Spain 37.37N 4.44W
35 Y17 Laramie Wyoming, C USA 41.18N 105.35W
35 X15 Laramie Mountains ▲▲ Wyoming, C USA
35 Y16 Laramie River ≈ Wyoming, C USA
62 H12 Laranjeiras do Sul Paraná, S Brazil 25.23S 52.22W
Larantoeka see Larantuka
175 Qq16 Larantuka prev. Larantoeka. Flores, C Indonesia 8.20S 123.00E
176 V15 Larat Pulau Larat, E Indonesia 7.07S 131.46E
176 V15 Larat, Pulau island Kepulauan Tanimbar, E Indonesia
97 P19 Lärbro Gotland, SE Sweden 57.46N 18.49E
108 A9 Larche, Col de pass France/Italy 44.26N 6.54E
12 H8 Larder Lake Ontario, S Canada 48.06N 79.43W
107 O2 Laredo Cantabria, N Spain 43.22N 3.22W
27 Q15 Laredo Texas, SW USA 27.30N 99.30W
42 H9 La Reforma Sinaloa, W Mexico 25.04N 108.03W
100 N11 Laren Gelderland, E Netherlands 52.12N 6.22E
100 J11 Laren Noord-Holland, C Netherlands 52.15N 5.13E
104 K13 la Réole Gironde, SW France 44.34N 0.00W
La Réunion see Réunion
Largeau see Faya
105 U13 l'Argentière-la-Bessée Hautes-Alpes, SE France 44.49N 6.34E
155 O4 Lar Gerd var. Largird. Balkh, N Afghanistan 35.36N 66.48E
Largird see Lar Gerd
25 V12 Largo Florida, SE USA 27.54N 82.47W
39 Q9 Largo, Canon valley New Mexico, SW USA
46 D6 Largo, Cayo island W Cuba
25 Z17 Largo, Key island Florida Keys, Florida, SE USA
98 H12 Largs W Scotland, UK 55.47N 4.50W
104 I16 la Rhune var. Larrún. ▲ France/Spain see also Larrún 43.19N 1.36W
la Riege see Ariège
31 Q4 Larimore North Dakota, N USA 47.54N 97.37W
109 L15 Larino Molise, C Italy 41.46N 14.50E
Lario see Como, Lago di
64 J9 La Rioja La Rioja, NW Argentina 29.25S 66.49W
64 I9 La Rioja off. Provincia de La Rioja. ◈ province NW Argentina
107 O4 La Rioja ◈ autonomous community N Spain
117 F16 Lárisa var. Larissa. Thessalía, C Greece 39.38N 22.27E
Larissa see Lárisa
155 Q13 Lārkāna var. Larkhana. Sind, SE Pakistan 27.31N 68.18E
Larkhana see Lārkāna
Larnaca see Lárnaka
124 Nn3 Lárnaka var. Larnaca, Larnax. SE Cyprus 34.54N 33.38E
124 Nn3 Lárnaka ✕ SE Cyprus 34.52N 33.38E
Larnax see Lárnaka
99 G14 Larne Ir. Latharna. E Northern Ireland, UK 54.51N 5.49W
28 L5 Larned Kansas, C USA 38.10N 99.06W
106 L3 La Robla Castilla-León, N Spain 42.48N 5.37W
106 J10 La Roca de la Sierra Extremadura, W Spain 39.06N 6.41W
101 K22 La Roche-en-Ardenne Luxembourg, SE Belgium 50.11N 5.35E
104 L11 la Rochefoucauld Charente, W France 45.43N 0.23E
104 J10 la Rochelle anc. Rupella. Charente-Maritime, W France 46.09N 1.07W
104 I9 la Roche-sur-Yon prev. Bourbon Vendée, Napoléon-Vendée. Vendée, NW France 46.40N 1.25W
107 Q10 La Roda Castilla-La Mancha, C Spain 39.13N 2.10W
106 L14 La Roda de Andalucía Andalucía, S Spain 37.12N 4.45W
47 P9 La Romana E Dominican Republic 18.25N 69.00W
9 T13 La Ronge Saskatchewan, C Canada 55.07N 105.18W
9 U13 La Ronge, Lac ◎ Saskatchewan, C Canada
24 K10 Larose Louisiana, S USA 29.34N 90.22W
44 M7 La Rosita Región Autónoma Atlántico Norte, NE Nicaragua 13.55N 84.23W
189 Q3 Larrimah Northern Territory, N Australia 15.30S 133.12E
64 N11 Larroque Entre Ríos, E Argentina 33.05S 59.06W
107 Q2 Larrún Fr. la Rhune. ▲ France/Spain see also la Rhune 43.18N 1.35W
205 X6 Lars Christensen Coast physical region Antarctica
41 Q14 Larsen Bay Kodiak Island, Alaska, USA 57.32N 153.58W
204 I5 Larsen Ice Shelf ice shelf Antarctica
15 K3 Larsen Sound sound Nunavut, N Canada
La Rúa see A Rúa
104 K16 Laruns Pyrénées-Atlantiques, SW France 43.00N 0.25W
97 G16 Larvik Vestfold, S Norway 59.03N 10.01E
126 H11 Lar'yak Khanty-Mansiyskiy Avtonomnyy Okrug, C Russian Federation 61.09N 80.01E
La-sa see Lhasa
175 Tt11 Lasahata Pulau Seram, E Indonesia 2.52S 128.27E
Lasahau see Lasihao
39 O6 La Sal Utah, W USA 38.19N 109.14W
12 C17 La Salle Ontario, S Canada 42.13N 83.05W
32 L11 La Salle Illinois, N USA 41.19N 89.06W
47 O9 Las Americas ✕ (Santo Domingo) S Dominican Republic 18.24N 69.38W
81 G17 La Sangha ◈ province N Congo
39 V6 Las Animas Colorado, C USA 38.04N 103.13W
110 D10 La Sarine var. Sarine. ≈ SW Switzerland
110 B9 La Sarraz Vaud, W Switzerland 46.40N 6.32E
10 H12 La Sarre Quebec, SE Canada 48.49N 79.12W
56 L3 Las Aves, Islas var. Islas de Aves. island group N Venezuela
57 N7 Las Bonitas Bolívar, C Venezuela 7.50N 65.40W
106 K15 Las Cabezas de San Juan Andalucía, S Spain 36.58N 5.55W
63 G19 Lascano Rocha, E Uruguay 33.40S 54.12W
64 I5 Lascar, Volcán ▲ N Chile 23.22S 67.33W
43 T15 Las Choapas var. Choapas. Veracruz-Llave, SE Mexico 17.51N 94.00W
39 R15 Las Cruces New Mexico, SW USA 32.19N 106.49W
Lasdehnen see Krasnoznamensk
107 V4 La See d'Urgel var. La Seu d'Urgell, Seo de Urgel. Cataluña, NE Spain 42.22N 1.27E
La Selle see Selle, Pic de la
64 G9 La Serena Coquimbo, C Chile 29.54S 71.18W
106 K11 La Serena physical region W Spain
La Seu d'Urgell see La See d'Urgel
105 T16 la Seyne-sur-Mer Var, SE France 43.07N 5.52E
63 D21 Las Flores Buenos Aires, E Argentina 36.03S 59.07W
64 H9 Las Flores San Juan, W Argentina 30.14S 69.10W
9 S14 Lashburn Saskatchewan, S Canada 53.09N 109.37W
64 I11 Las Heras Mendoza, W Argentina 32.46S 68.51W
178 Gg4 Lashio Shan State, E Burma 22.58N 97.48E
154 M8 Lashkar Gāh var. Lash-Kar-Gar'. Helmand, S Afghanistan 31.34N 64.21E
Lash-Kar-Gar' see Lashkar Gāh
175 Qq13 Lasihao var. Lasahau. Pulau Muna, C Indonesia 5.01S 122.23E

◆ Country ● Country Capital ◇ Dependent Territory ○ Dependent Territory Capital ◈ Administrative Region ✕ International Airport ▲ Mountain ▲▲ Mountain Range ⅄ Volcano ≈ River ◎ Lake ⊠ Reservoir

La Sila – Lenhovda

109 N21 **La Sila** ▲▲ SW Italy
65 H23 **La Silueta, Cerro** ▲ S Chile *52.22S 72.09W*
44 L9 **La Sirena** Región Autónoma Atlántico Sur, E Nicaragua *12.58N 84.42W*
112 J13 **Łask** Łódzkie, C Poland *51.36N 19.06E*
111 V11 **Laško** *Ger.* Tüffer. C Slovenia *46.08N 15.13E*
65 H14 **Las Lajas** Neuquén, W Argentina *38.31S 70.22W*
65 H15 **Las Lajas, Cerro** ▲ W Argentina *38.49S 70.42W*
64 M6 **Las Lomitas** Formosa, N Argentina *24.44S 60.34W*
43 V16 **Las Margaritas** Chiapas, SE Mexico *16.15N 91.58W*
Las Marismas *see* Guadalquivir, Marismas del
56 M6 **Las Mercedes** Guárico, N Venezuela *9.06N 66.22W*
44 F6 **Las Minas, Cerro** ▲ W Honduras *14.33N 88.41W*
107 O11 **La Solana** Castilla-La Mancha, C Spain *38.55N 3.13W*
47 Q14 **La Soufrière** ⋏ Saint Vincent, Saint Vincent and the Grenadines *13.20N 61.11W*
104 M10 **la Souterraine** Creuse, C France *46.15N 1.28E*
64 N7 **Las Palmas** Chaco, N Argentina *27.07S 58.45W*
45 Q16 **Las Palmas** Veraguas, W Panama *8.09N 81.28W*
66 P12 **Las Palmas** *var.* Las Palmas de Gran Canaria. Gran Canaria, Islas Canarias, Spain, NE Atlantic Ocean *28.07N 15.27W*
66 P12 **Las Palmas** ◐ *province* Islas Canarias, Spain, NE Atlantic Ocean
66 Q12 **Las Palmas** ✕ Gran Canaria, Islas Canarias, Spain, NE Atlantic Ocean
Las Palmas de Gran Canaria *see* Las Palmas
42 D6 **Las Palomas** Baja California Sur, W Mexico *31.43N 107.37W*
107 P10 **Las Pedroñeras** Castilla-La Mancha, C Spain *39.27N 2.40W*
108 E10 **La Spezia** Liguria, NW Italy *44.07N 9.49E*
63 F20 **Las Piedras** Canelones, S Uruguay *34.42S 56.13W*
65 J18 **Las Plumas** Chubut, S Argentina *43.46S 67.15W*
63 B18 **Las Rosas** Santa Fe, C Argentina *32.27S 61.30W*
Lassa *see* Lhasa
37 O4 **Lassen Peak** ▲ California, W USA *40.27N 121.28W*
204 K6 **Lassiter Coast** *physical region* Antarctica
111 V9 **Lassnitz** ≈ SE Austria
13 O12 **L'Assomption** Quebec, SE Canada *45.48N 73.27W*
13 N11 **L'Assomption** ≈ Quebec, SE Canada
45 S17 **Las Tablas** Los Santos, S Panama *7.45N 80.17W*
Lastarria, Volcán *see* Azufre, Volcán
39 V4 **Last Chance** Colorado, C USA *39.41N 103.34W*
Last Frontier, The *see* Alaska
9 U16 **Last Mountain Lake** ◎ Saskatchewan, S Canada
64 H9 **Las Tórtolas, Cerro** ▲ W Argentina *29.57S 69.49W*
63 C14 **Las Toscas** Santa Fe, C Argentina *28.22S 59.19W*
81 F19 **Lastoursville** Ogooué-Lolo, E Gabon *0.49S 12.43E*
115 F16 **Lastovo** *It.* Lagosta. *island* SW Croatia
115 F16 **Lastovski Kanal** *channel* SW Croatia
42 E6 **Las Tres Vírgenes, Volcán** ⋏ W Mexico *27.27N 112.34W*
42 F4 **Las Trincheras** Sonora, NW Mexico *30.21N 111.27W*
57 N8 **Las Trincheras** Bolívar, E Venezuela *6.57N 64.49W*
46 H7 **Las Tunas** *var.* Victoria de las Tunas. Las Tunas, E Cuba *20.58N 76.58W*
La Suisse *see* Switzerland
42 I5 **Las Varas** Chihuahua, N Mexico *29.35N 108.01W*
42 J12 **Las Varas** Nayarit, C Mexico *21.11N 105.09W*
64 L10 **Las Varillas** Córdoba, E Argentina *31.54S 62.45W*
37 X11 **Las Vegas** Nevada, W USA *36.09N 115.10W*
39 T10 **Las Vegas** New Mexico, SW USA *35.35N 105.15W*
195 W8 **Lata** Nendö, Solomon Islands *10.45S 165.43E*
11 R10 **La Tabatière** Quebec, E Canada *50.51N 58.58W*
58 C6 **Latacunga** Cotopaxi, C Ecuador *0.58S 78.36W*
204 I7 **Latady Island** *island* Antarctica
56 E14 **La Tagua** Putumayo, S Colombia *0.04S 74.39W*
Latakia *see* Al Lādhiqīyah
94 J10 **Lätäseno** ≈ NW Finland
12 H9 **Latchford** Ontario, S Canada *47.20N 79.45W*
12 J13 **Latchford Bridge** Ontario, SE Canada *45.16N 77.29W*
200 Ss12 **Late** *island* Vava'u Group, N Tonga
159 P15 **Lātehār** Bihār, N India *23.48N 84.28E*
13 R7 **Laterrière** Quebec, SE Canada *48.17N 71.10W*
104 J13 **la Teste** Gironde, SW France *44.37N 1.04W*
27 V8 **Latexo** Texas, SW USA *31.24N 95.28W*
20 L10 **Latham** New York, NE USA *42.45N 73.45W*
Latharna *see* Larne
110 B9 **La Thielle** *var.* Thièle. ≈ W Switzerland
29 R3 **Lathrop** Missouri, C USA *39.33N 94.19W*
109 I16 **Latina** *prev.* Littoria. Lazio, C Italy *41.28N 12.52E*
43 R14 **La Tinaja** Veracruz-Llave, S Mexico
108 J7 **Latisana** Friuli-Venezia Giulia, NE Italy *45.47N 13.01E*
Latium *see* Lazio
117 K25 **Lató** *site of ancient city* Kríti, Greece, E Mediterranean Sea *35.09N 25.40E*
197 J7 **La Tontouta** ✕ (Noumea) Province Sud, S New Caledonia *22.06S 166.12E*
57 N4 **La Tortuga, Isla** *var.* Isla Tortuga. *island* N Venezuela
110 C10 **La Tour-de-Peilz** *var.* La Tour de Peilz. Vaud, SW Switzerland *46.28N 6.52E*
105 S11 **la Tour-du-Pin** Isère, E France *45.34N 5.25E*
104 J11 **la Tremblade** Charente-Maritime, W France *45.45N 1.07W*
104 L10 **la Trimouille** Vienne, W France *46.27N 1.02E*
44 J9 **La Trinidad** Estelí, NW Nicaragua *12.57N 86.13W*
179 P9 **La Trinidad** Luzon, N Philippines *16.30N 120.39E*
43 V16 **La Trinitaria** Chiapas, SE Mexico *16.02N 92.00W*
47 Q11 **la Trinité** E Martinique *14.43N 60.57W*
13 U7 **La Trinité-des-Monts** Quebec, SE Canada *48.07N 68.31W*
20 C15 **Latrobe** Pennsylvania, NE USA *40.18N 79.19W*
191 P13 **La Trobe River** ≈ Victoria, SE Australia
Lattakia/Lattaquié *see* Al Lādhiqīyah
175 Tt11 **Latu** Pulau Seram, E Indonesia *3.24S 128.37E*
13 P9 **La Tuque** Quebec, SE Canada *47.25N 72.46W*
161 G14 **Lātūr** Mahārāshtra, C India *18.24N 76.34E*
120 G8 **Latvia** *off.* Republic of Latvia, *Ger.* Lettland, *Latv.* Latvija, Latvijas Republika; *prev.* Latvian SSR, *Rus.* Latviyskaya SSR. ◆ *republic* NE Europe
Latvian SSR/Latvija/Latvijas Republika/Latviyskaya SSR *see* Latvia
195 O12 **Lau** New Britain, E PNG *5.46S 151.21E*
183 R9 **Lau Basin** *undersea feature* S Pacific Ocean
103 O15 **Lauchhammer** Brandenburg, E Germany *51.27N 13.32E*
Laudunum *see* Laon
Laudus *see* St-Lô
Lauenburg/Lauenburg in Pommern *see* Lębork
103 L20 **Lauf an der Pegnitz** Bayern, SE Germany *49.31N 11.16E*
110 D7 **Laufen** Basel, NW Switzerland *47.25N 7.31E*
111 P5 **Lauffen** Salzburg, NW Austria *47.54N 12.57E*
94 I2 **Laugarbakki** Nordhurland Vestra, N Iceland *65.18N 20.51W*
94 I4 **Laugarvatn** Sudhurland, SW Iceland *64.09N 20.43W*
33 O3 **Laughing Fish Point** *headland* Michigan, N USA *46.31N 87.01W*
197 L14 **Lau Group** *island group* E Fiji
Lauis *see* Lugano
95 M17 **Laukaa** Länsi-Suomi, W Finland *62.27N 25.58E*
120 D12 **Laukuva** Šilalė, W Lithuania *55.37N 22.12E*
Laun *see* Louny
191 P16 **Launceston** Tasmania, SE Australia *41.25S 147.07E*
99 I24 **Launceston** *anc.* Dunheved. SW England, UK *50.37N 4.21W*
56 C13 **La Unión** Nariño, SW Colombia *1.34N 77.09W*
44 H8 **La Unión** La Unión, SE El Salvador *13.19N 87.52W*
44 I6 **La Unión** Olancho, C Honduras *15.02N 86.40W*
42 M15 **La Unión** Guerrero, S Mexico *17.59N 101.48W*
43 Y14 **La Unión** Quintana Roo, E Mexico *18.00N 101.48W*
107 S13 **La Unión** Murcia, SE Spain *37.37N 0.53W*
56 L7 **La Unión** Barinas, C Venezuela *8.12N 67.46W*
44 B10 **La Unión** ◐ *department* E El Salvador
40 H11 **Laupahoehoe** *Haw.* Laupāhoehoe. Hawaii, USA, C Pacific Ocean *20.00N 155.15W*
103 I23 **Laupheim** Baden-Württemberg, S Germany *48.13N 9.54E*
189 W3 **Laura** Queensland, NE Australia *15.37S 144.34E*
201 X2 **Laura** *atoll* Majuro Atoll, SE Marshall Islands
Laurana *see* Lovran
56 L8 **La Urbana** Bolívar, C Venezuela *7.05N 66.58W*
23 Y4 **Laurel** Delaware, NE USA *38.33N 75.34W*
25 V14 **Laurel** Florida, SE USA *27.07N 82.27W*
23 W3 **Laurel** Maryland, NE USA *39.06N 76.51W*
24 M6 **Laurel** Mississippi, S USA *31.41N 89.10W*
35 U11 **Laurel** Montana, NW USA *45.40N 108.46W*
31 R13 **Laurel** Nebraska, C USA *42.25N 97.04W*
20 H15 **Laureldale** Pennsylvania, NE USA *40.24N 75.52W*
20 C16 **Laurel Hill** *ridge* Pennsylvania, NE USA
31 T12 **Laurens** Iowa, C USA *42.51N 94.51W*
23 P11 **Laurens** South Carolina, SE USA *34.29N 82.01W*
Laurentian Highlands *see* Laurentian Mountains
13 P10 **Laurentian Mountains** *var.* Laurentian Highlands, *Fr.* Les Laurentides. *plateau* Newfoundland/Quebec, Canada
13 O12 **Laurentides** Quebec, SE Canada *45.51N 73.49W*
Laurentides, Les *see* Laurentian Mountains
109 M19 **Lauria** Basilicata, S Italy *40.03N 15.49E*
204 I1 **Laurie Island** *island* Antarctica
23 T11 **Laurinburg** North Carolina, SE USA *34.51N 79.40W*
32 M2 **Laurium** Michigan, N USA *47.14N 88.26W*
Lauru *see* Choiseul
110 B9 **Lausanne** *It.* Losanna. Vaud, SW Switzerland *46.31N 6.39E*
103 Q16 **Lausche** *Cz.* Luže. ▲ Czech Republic/Germany *see also* Luže *50.52N 14.39E*
103 Q16 **Lausitzer Bergland** *var.* Lausitzer Gebirge, *Cz.* Gory Lużyckie, Lužické Hory, *Eng.* Lusatian Mountains. ▲▲ E Germany
Lausitzer Gebirge *see* Lausitzer Bergland
Lausitzer Neisse *see* Neisse
105 T12 **Lautaret, Col du** *pass* SE France *45.03N 6.23E*
65 G15 **Lautaro** Araucanía, C Chile *38.31S 72.27W*
103 F21 **Lauter** ≈ W Germany
110 I7 **Lauterach** Vorarlberg, NW Austria *47.28N 9.43E*
103 I17 **Lauterbach** Hessen, C Germany *50.37N 9.24E*
110 E9 **Lauterbrunnen** Bern, C Switzerland *46.36N 7.52E*
175 Nn12 **Laut Kecil, Kepulauan** *island group* N Indonesia
197 H14 **Lautoka** Viti Levu, W Fiji *17.40S 177.25E*
175 Nn11 **Laut, Pulau** *prev.* Laoet. *island* Borneo, C Indonesia
174 Jj4 **Laut, Pulau** *island* Kepulauan Natuna, W Indonesia
175 Nn11 **Laut, Selat** *strait* Borneo, C Indonesia
173 F4 **Laut Tawar, Danau** ◎ Sumatera, NW Indonesia
201 V14 **Lauvergne Island** *island* Chuuk, C Micronesia
100 M5 **Lauwers Meer** ◎ N Netherlands
100 M4 **Lauwersoog** Groningen, NE Netherlands *53.25N 6.14E*
104 M14 **Lauzerte** Tarn-et-Garonne, S France *44.15N 1.08E*
27 U13 **Lavaca Bay** *bay* Texas, SW USA
27 U12 **Lavaca River** ≈ Texas, SW USA
13 O12 **Laval** Quebec, SE Canada *45.32N 73.44W*
104 J6 **Laval** Mayenne, NW France *48.04N 0.46W*
13 T6 **Laval** ≈ Quebec, SE Canada
63 F19 **Lavalleja** ◐ *department* S Uruguay
13 O12 **Lavaltrie** Quebec, SE Canada *45.56N 73.14W*
195 X17 **Lavanggu** Rennell, S Solomon Islands *11.39S 160.13E*
149 O14 **Lāvān, Jazīreh-ye** *island* S Iran
111 U8 **Lavant** ≈ S Austria
120 G5 **Lavassaare** *Ger.* Lawassaar. Pärnumaa, SW Estonia *58.31N 24.22E*
106 L3 **La Vecilla de Curueño** Castilla-León, N Spain *42.51N 5.24W*
47 N8 **La Vega** *var.* Concepción de la Vega. C Dominican Republic *19.15N 70.32W*
La Vela *see* La Vela de Coro
56 J4 **La Vela de Coro** *var.* La Vela. Falcón, N Venezuela *11.26N 69.35W*
105 N17 **Lavelanet** Ariège, S France *42.55N 1.49E*
109 M17 **Lavello** Basilicata, S Italy *41.03N 15.48E*
38 J8 **La Verkin** Utah, W USA *37.12N 113.16W*
28 J8 **Laverne** Oklahoma, C USA *36.42N 99.53W*
27 S12 **La Vernia** Texas, SW USA *29.19N 98.07W*
95 K18 **Lavia** Länsi-Suomi, W Finland *61.36N 22.34E*
12 I12 **Lavieille, Lake** ◎ Ontario, SE Canada
96 C12 **Lavik** Sogn og Fjordane, S Norway *61.06N 5.25E*
La Vila Jojosa *see* Villajoyosa
35 U10 **Lavina** Montana, NW USA *46.18N 108.55W*
204 H5 **Lavoisier Island** *island* Antarctica
25 U2 **Lavonia** Georgia, SE USA *34.26N 83.06W*
105 R13 **la Voulte-sur-Rhône** Ardèche, E France *44.49N 4.46E*
127 Q3 **Lavrentiya** Chukotskiy Avtonomnyy Okrug, NE Russian Federation *65.33N 171.12W*
117 H20 **Lávrio** *prev.* Lávrion. Attikí, C Greece *37.43N 24.03E*
Lávrion *see* Lávrio
85 L22 **Lavumisa** *prev.* Gollel. SE Swaziland *27.20S 31.51E*
155 T4 **Lawarai Pass** *pass* N Pakistan *35.22N 71.48E*
Lawassaar *see* Lavassaare
147 P16 **Lawdar** SW Yemen *13.49N 45.54E*
27 Q7 **Lawn** Texas, SW USA *32.07N 99.45W*
205 Y4 **Law Promontory** *headland* Antarctica
79 O14 **Lawra** NW Ghana *10.40N 2.55W*
193 E23 **Lawrence** Otago, South Island, NZ *45.53S 169.43E*
33 P14 **Lawrence** Indiana, N USA *39.49N 86.01W*
29 Q4 **Lawrence** Kansas, C USA *38.58N 95.14W*
21 O10 **Lawrence** Massachusetts, NE USA *42.42N 71.09W*
22 L5 **Lawrenceburg** Kentucky, S USA *38.02N 84.54W*
22 I10 **Lawrenceburg** Tennessee, S USA *35.14N 87.19W*
25 T3 **Lawrenceville** Georgia, SE USA *33.57N 83.59W*
33 N15 **Lawrenceville** Illinois, N USA *38.43N 87.40W*
23 V7 **Lawrenceville** Virginia, NE USA *36.45N 77.51W*
29 S3 **Lawson** Missouri, C USA *39.26N 94.12W*
28 L12 **Lawton** Oklahoma, C USA *34.35N 98.19W*
146 I4 **Lawz, Jabal al** ▲ NW Saudi Arabia *28.45N 35.20E*
97 L16 **Laxå** Örebro, C Sweden *59.00N 14.37E*
129 T5 **Laya** ≈ NW Russian Federation
59 I19 **La Yarada** Tacna, SW Peru *18.14S 70.30W*
147 S15 **Layjūn** C Yemen *15.27N 49.16E*
147 Q9 **Laylā** *var.* Laila. Ar Riyāḍ, C Saudi Arabia *22.13N 46.39E*
25 P4 **Lay Lake** ⊠ Alabama, S USA
47 P14 **Layou** Saint Vincent, Saint Vincent and the Grenadines *13.11N 61.16W*
La Youne *see* El Ayoun
199 Jj5 **Laysan Island** *island* Hawaiian Islands, Hawaii, USA, C Pacific Ocean
38 L2 **Layton** Utah, W USA *41.03N 112.00W*
36 L5 **Laytonville** California, N USA *39.39N 123.30W*
180 H17 **Lazare, Pointe** *headland* Mahé, NE Seychelles *4.46S 55.28E*
127 O14 **Lazarev** Khabarovskiy Kray, SE Russian Federation *52.11N 141.18E*
114 L12 **Lazarevac** Serbia, C Yugoslavia *44.25N 20.17E*
67 N22 **Lazarev Sea** *sea* Antarctica
42 M15 **Lázaro Cárdenas** Michoacán de Ocampo, SW Mexico *17.55N 102.12W*
121 F15 **Lazdijai** Lazdijai, S Lithuania *54.13N 23.33E*
109 H15 **Lazio** *anc.* Latium. ◐ *region* C Italy
113 A16 **Lázně Kynžvart** *Ger.* Bad Königswart. Karlovarský Kraj, W Czech Republic *50.00N 12.40E*
Lazovsk *see* Sîngerei
178 Ii13 **Leach** Poŭthĭsăt, W Cambodia *12.19N 103.45E*
29 X9 **Leachville** Arkansas, C USA *35.56N 90.15W*
30 I9 **Lead** South Dakota, N USA *44.21N 103.45W*
9 S16 **Leader** Saskatchewan, S Canada *50.55N 109.31W*
21 S6 **Lead Mountain** ▲ Maine, NE USA *44.53N 68.07W*
39 R5 **Leadville** Colorado, C USA *39.15N 106.17W*
9 V12 **Leaf Rapids** Manitoba, C Canada *56.30N 100.01W*
24 M7 **Leaf River** ≈ Mississippi, S USA
27 W11 **League City** Texas, SW USA *29.30N 95.05W*
25 N7 **Leakesville** Mississippi, S USA *31.09N 88.33W*
27 Q11 **Leakey** Texas, SW USA *29.43N 99.45W*
Leal *see* Lihula
85 G15 **Lealui** Western, W Zambia *15.12S 22.58E*
Leamhcán *see* Lucan
12 C18 **Leamington** Ontario, S Canada *42.03N 82.34W*
Leamington/Leamington Spa *see* Royal Leamington Spa
Leammi *see* Lemmenjoki
27 S10 **Leander** Texas, SW USA *30.34N 97.51W*
62 F13 **Leandro N.Alem** Misiones, NE Argentina *27.34S 55.15W*
99 A20 **Leane, Lough** *Ir.* Loch Léin. ◎ SW Ireland
188 G8 **Learmouth** Western Australia *22.17S 114.03E*
Leau *see* Zoutleeuw
L'Eau d'Heure *see* Plate Taille, Lac de la
202 D12 **Leava** Île Futuna, S Wallis and Futuna
29 R3 **Leavenworth** Kansas, C USA *39.17N 94.55W*
34 I8 **Leavenworth** Washington, NW USA *47.36N 120.39W*
94 L8 **Leavvajohka** *var.* Levajok, Lœvvajok. Finnmark, N Norway *69.57N 26.18E*
29 R4 **Leawood** Kansas, C USA *38.57N 94.37W*
112 H6 **Łeba** *Ger.* Leba. Pomorskie, N Poland *54.45N 17.31E*
112 I6 **Łeba** *Ger.* Leba. ≈ N Poland
103 D20 **Lebach** Saarland, SW Germany *49.25N 6.54E*
Łeba, Jezioro *see* Łebsko, Jezioro
179 R17 **Lebak** Mindanao, S Philippines *6.28N 124.03E*
175 Oo11 **Lebani,Teluk** *bay* Sulawesi, C Indonesia
33 O13 **Lebanon** Indiana, N USA *40.03N 86.28W*
22 L6 **Lebanon** Kentucky, S USA *37.34N 85.15W*
29 U6 **Lebanon** Missouri, C USA *37.40N 92.39W*
21 N9 **Lebanon** New Hampshire, NE USA *43.40N 72.15W*
34 G12 **Lebanon** Oregon, NW USA *44.32N 122.54W*
20 H15 **Lebanon** Pennsylvania, NE USA *40.20N 76.24W*
22 J8 **Lebanon** Tennessee, S USA *36.13N 86.16W*
23 P7 **Lebanon** Virginia, NE USA *36.54N 82.04W*
144 G6 **Lebanon** *off.* Republic of Lebanon, *Ar.* Al Lubnān, *Fr.* Liban. ◆ *republic* SW Asia
22 K6 **Lebanon Junction** Kentucky, S USA *37.49N 85.43W*
Lebanon, Mount *see* Liban, Jebel
152 J10 **Lebap** Lebapskiy Velayat, NE Turkmenistan *41.04N 61.49E*
152 H11 **Lebapskiy Velayat** *Turkm.* Lebap Welaýaty; *prev. Rus.* Chardzhevskaya Oblast', *Turkm.* Chärjew Oblasty. ◐ *province* E Turkmenistan
Lebap Welaýaty *see* Lebapskiy Velayat
Lebasee *see* Łebsko, Jezioro
101 F17 **Lebbeke** Oost-Vlaanderen, NW Belgium *51.00N 4.08E*
37 S14 **Lebec** California, W USA *34.51N 118.52W*
Lebedin *see* Lebedyn
126 Ll12 **Lebedinyy** Respublika Sakha (Yakutiya), NE Russian Federation *58.23N 125.24E*
130 L6 **Lebedyan'** Lipetskaya Oblast', W Russian Federation *53.00N 39.11E*
119 T4 **Lebedyn** *Rus.* Lebedin. Sums'ka Oblast', NE Ukraine *50.36N 34.30E*
10 I12 **Lebel-sur-Quévillon** Quebec, SE Canada *49.01N 76.55W*
94 L8 **Lebesby** Finnmark, N Norway *70.31N 27.00E*
104 M9 **le Blanc** Indre, C France *46.38N 1.04E*
29 P5 **Lebo** Kansas, C USA *38.22N 95.50W*
81 L15 **Lebo** Orientale, N Dem. Rep. Congo (Zaire) *4.30N 23.58E*
112 H6 **Lębork** *var.* Lębórk, *Ger.* Lauenburg, Lauenburg in Pommern. Pomorskie, N Poland *54.31N 17.43E*
105 O17 **le Boulou** Pyrénées-Orientales, S France *42.31N 2.49E*
110 A9 **Le Brassus** Vaud, W Switzerland *46.35N 6.14E*
106 J15 **Lebrija** Andalucía, S Spain *36.55N 6.04W*
112 G6 **Łebsko, Jezioro** *Ger.* Lebasee; *prev.* Jezioro Łeba. ◎ N Poland
65 F14 **Lebu** Bío Bío, C Chile *37.34S 73.37W*
Lebyazh'ye *see* Akku
106 F6 **Leça da Palmeira** Porto, N Portugal *41.12N 8.43W*
105 U15 **le Cannet** Alpes-Maritimes, SE France *43.35N 7.00E*
Le Cap *see* Cap-Haïtien
105 P2 **le Cateau-Cambrésis** Nord, N France *50.05N 3.32E*
109 Q18 **Lecce** Puglia, SE Italy *40.22N 18.10E*
108 D7 **Lecco** Lombardia, N Italy *45.49N 9.27E*
31 V10 **Le Center** Minnesota, N USA *44.23N 93.43W*
110 J7 **Lech** Vorarlberg, W Austria *47.14N 10.10E*
103 K22 **Lech** ≈ Austria/Germany
117 D19 **Lechainá** *var.* Lehena, Lekhainá. Dytikí Ellás, S Greece *37.56N 21.16E*
104 J11 **le Château d'Oléron** Charente-Maritime, W France *45.53N 1.12W*
105 R3 **le Chesne** Ardennes, N France *49.33N 4.42E*
105 R13 **le Cheylard** Ardèche, E France *44.55N 4.27E*
110 K7 **Lechtaler Alpen** ▲▲ W Austria
102 H6 **Leck** Schleswig-Holstein, N Germany *54.45N 9.00E*
12 L9 **Lecointre, Lac** ◎ Quebec, SE Canada
24 H7 **Lecompte** Louisiana, S USA *31.05N 92.24W*
105 Q9 **le Creusot** Saône-et-Loire, C France *46.48N 4.25E*
Lecumberri *see* Lekunberri
112 P13 **Łęczna** Lubelskie, E Poland *51.18N 22.51E*
112 J12 **Łęczyca** *Ger.* Lentschiza, *Rus.* Lenchitsa. Łódzkie, C Poland *52.03N 19.10E*
102 F10 **Leda** ≈ NW Germany
101 F17 **Lede** Oost-Vlaanderen, NW Belgium *50.58N 3.58E*
106 K6 **Ledesma** Castilla-León, N Spain *41.05N 6.00W*
47 Q12 **le Diamant** SW Martinique *14.28N 61.02W*
180 J16 **Le Digue** *island* Inner Islands, NE Seychelles
105 Q10 **le Donjon** Allier, C France *46.19N 3.50E*
104 M10 **le Dorat** Haute-Vienne, C France *46.14N 1.05E*
Ledo Salinarius *see* Lons-le-Saunier
9 Q14 **Leduc** Alberta, SW Canada *53.16N 113.30W*
127 Pp7 **Ledyanaya, Gora** ▲ E Russian Federation *61.51N 171.03E*
99 C21 **Lee** *Ir.* An Laoi. ≈ SW Ireland
31 U5 **Leech Lake** ◎ Minnesota, N USA
28 K10 **Leedey** Oklahoma, C USA *35.54N 99.21W*
99 M17 **Leeds** N England, UK *53.49N 1.34W*
25 P4 **Leeds** Alabama, S USA *33.33N 86.32W*
31 O3 **Leeds** North Dakota, N USA *48.19N 99.43W*
100 N6 **Leek** Groningen, NE Netherlands *53.10N 6.24E*
101 K15 **Leende** Noord-Brabant, SE Netherlands *51.21N 5.34E*
102 F10 **Leer** Niedersachsen, NW Germany *53.14N 7.25E*
100 J13 **Leerdam** Zuid-Holland, C Netherlands *51.54N 5.06E*
100 K12 **Leersum** Utrecht, C Netherlands *52.01N 5.25E*
25 W11 **Leesburg** Florida, SE USA *28.48N 81.52W*
23 V3 **Leesburg** Virginia, NE USA *39.07N 77.33W*
29 R4 **Lees Summit** Missouri, C USA *38.55N 94.21W*
24 G7 **Leesville** Louisiana, S USA *31.08N 93.15W*
27 S12 **Leesville** Texas, SW USA *29.22N 97.45W*
33 U13 **Leesville Lake** ⊠ Ohio, N USA
Leesville Lake *see* Smith Mountain Lake
191 P9 **Leeton** New South Wales, SE Australia *34.33S 146.24E*
100 L6 **Leeuwarden** *Fris.* Ljouwert. Friesland, N Netherlands *53.15N 5.48E*
188 I14 **Leeuwin, Cape** *headland* Western Australia *34.18S 115.03E*
37 R8 **Lee Vining** California, W USA *37.57N 119.07W*
47 V8 **Leeward Islands** *island group* E West Indies
Leeward Islands *see* Vent, Îles Sous le, W French Polynesia
Leeward Islands *see* Sotavento, Ilhas de, Cape Verde
81 G20 **Léfini** ≈ SE Congo
Léfka *see* Lefke
117 C17 **Lefkáda** *prev.* Levkás. Lefkáda, Iónioi Nísoi, Greece, C Mediterranean Sea *38.50N 20.43E*
117 B17 **Lefkáda** *It.* Santa Maura; *prev.* Levkás, *anc.* Leucas. *island* Iónioi Nísoi, Greece, C Mediterranean Sea
117 H25 **Lefká Óri** ▲▲ Kríti, Greece, E Mediterranean Sea
124 N3 **Lefke** *Gk.* Léfka. W Cyprus *35.06N 32.52E*
117 B16 **Lefkímmi** *var.* Levkímmi. Kérkyra, Iónioi Nísoi, Greece, C Mediterranean Sea *39.25N 20.03E*
Lefkonico/Lefkónikon *see* Geçitkale
Lefkoşa/Lefkosía *see* Nicosia
27 O2 **Lefors** Texas, SW USA *35.26N 100.48W*
47 R12 **le François** E Martinique *14.36N 60.54W*
188 L12 **Lefroy, Lake** *salt lake* Western Australia
Legaceaster *see* Chester
107 N8 **Leganés** Madrid, C Spain *40.19N 3.46W*
179 Q11 **Legaspi** *off.* Legaspi City. Luzon, N Philippines *13.06N 123.43E*
Leghorn *see* Livorno
112 M11 **Legionowo** Mazowieckie, C Poland *52.23N 20.55E*
101 K24 **Léglise** Luxembourg, SE Belgium *49.48N 5.31E*
108 G8 **Legnago** Lombardia, NE Italy *45.13N 11.18E*
108 D7 **Legnano** Veneto, NE Italy *45.36N 8.54E*
113 F14 **Legnica** *Ger.* Liegnitz. Dolnośląskie, SW Poland *51.12N 16.11E*
37 Q9 **Le Grand** California, W USA *37.12N 120.15W*
105 Q15 **le Grau-du-Roi** Gard, S France *43.32N 4.10E*
191 U3 **Legume** New South Wales, SE Australia *28.24S 152.20E*
104 L4 **le Havre** *Eng.* Havre; *prev.* le Havre-de-Grâce. Seine-Maritime, N France *49.30N 0.07E*
le Havre-de-Grâce *see* le Havre
Lehena *see* Lechainá
38 L3 **Lehi** Utah, W USA *40.23N 111.51W*
20 I14 **Lehighton** Pennsylvania, NE USA *40.49N 75.42W*
31 O6 **Lehr** North Dakota, N USA *46.15N 99.21W*
40 A8 **Lehua Island** *island* Hawaiian Islands, Hawaii, USA, C Pacific Ocean
155 S9 **Leiāh** Punjab, NE Pakistan *30.58N 70.53E*
111 W9 **Leibnitz** Steiermark, SE Austria *46.48N 15.33E*
99 M19 **Leicester** *Lat.* Batae Coritanorum. C England, UK *52.37N 1.04W*
99 M19 **Leicestershire** *cultural region* C England, UK
100 H11 **Leiden** *prev.* Leyden, *anc.* Lugdunum Batavorum. Zuid-Holland, W Netherlands *52.09N 4.30E*
100 H11 **Leiderdorp** Zuid-Holland, W Netherlands *52.07N 4.31E*
100 G11 **Leidschendam** Zuid-Holland, W Netherlands *52.04N 4.24E*
101 D18 **Leie** *Fr.* Lys. ≈ Belgium/France
Leifear *see* Lifford
192 L4 **Leigh** Auckland, North Island, NZ *36.17S 174.48E*
99 K17 **Leigh** NW England, UK *53.30N 2.33W*
190 I5 **Leigh Creek** South Australia *30.27S 138.23E*
25 O2 **Leighton** Alabama, S USA *34.42N 87.31W*
99 M21 **Leighton Buzzard** E England, UK *51.55N 0.40W*
Léim an Bhradáin *see* Leixlip
Léim an Mhadaidh *see* Limavady
Léime, Ceann *see* Loop Head, Ireland
Léime, Ceann *see* Slyne Head, Ireland
103 G20 **Leimen** Baden-Württemberg, SW Germany *49.21N 8.40E*
102 I13 **Leine** ≈ NW Germany
103 J15 **Leinefelde** Thüringen, C Germany *51.22N 10.19E*
Léin, Loch *see* Leane, Lough
99 D19 **Leinster** *Ir.* Cúige Laighean. *cultural region* E Ireland
99 F19 **Leinster, Mount** *Ir.* Stua Laighean. ▲ SE Ireland *52.36N 6.45W*
121 F15 **Leipalingis** Lazdijai, S Lithuania *54.05N 23.52E*
94 J12 **Leipojärvi** Norrbotten, N Sweden *67.03N 21.15E*
33 R12 **Leipsic** Ohio, N USA *41.06N 83.58W*
Leipsic *see* Leipzig
117 M20 **Leipsoí** *island* Dodekánisos, Greece, Aegean Sea
103 M15 **Leipzig** *Pol.* Lipsk; *hist.* Leipsic, *anc.* Lipsia. Sachsen, E Germany *51.19N 12.24E*
103 M15 **Leipzig Halle** ✕ Sachsen, E Germany *51.26N 12.14E*
106 G9 **Leiria** *anc.* Collipo. Leiria, C Portugal *39.45N 8.49W*
106 F9 **Leiria** ◐ *district* C Portugal
97 C15 **Leirvik** Hordaland, S Norway *59.48N 5.26E*
120 E5 **Leisi** *Ger.* Laisberg. Saaremaa, W Estonia *58.35N 22.42E*
106 J3 **Leitariegos, Puerto de** *pass* NW Spain *43.02N 6.26W*
22 J6 **Leitchfield** Kentucky, S USA *37.28N 86.17W*
111 Y5 **Leitha** *Hung.* Lajta. ≈ Austria/Hungary
Leitir Ceanainn *see* Letterkenny
Leitmeritz *see* Litoměřice
Leitomischl *see* Litomyšl
99 D16 **Leitrim** *Ir.* Liatroim. *cultural region* NW Ireland
117 F18 **Leivádia** *prev.* Levádhia. Stereá Ellás, C Greece *38.24N 22.51E*
Leix *see* Laois
99 F18 **Leixlip** *Eng.* Salmon Leap, *Ir.* Léim an Bhradáin. E Ireland *53.22N 6.31W*
66 N8 **Leixões** Porto, N Portugal *41.10N 8.40W*
167 N12 **Leiyang** Hunan, S China *26.23N 112.49E*
166 L16 **Leizhou** *var.* Haikang. Guangdong, S China *20.54N 110.04E*
166 L16 **Leizhou Bandao** *var.* Luichow Peninsula. *peninsula* S China
100 H13 **Lek** ≈ SW Netherlands
116 I13 **Lekánis** ▲▲ NE Greece
180 H13 **Le Kartala** ▲ Grande Comore, NW Comoros
Le Kef *see* El Kef
81 G20 **Lékéti, Monts de la** ▲▲ S Congo
Lekhainá *see* Lechainá
116 H8 **Lekhchevo** Montana, NW Bulgaria *43.32N 23.31E*
94 G11 **Leknes** Nordland, C Norway *68.07N 13.36E*
81 E21 **Le Kouilou** ◐ *province* SW Congo
96 L13 **Leksand** Dalarna, C Sweden *60.44N 15.00E*
128 H8 **Leksozero, Ozero** ◎ NW Russian Federation
107 Q3 **Lekunberri** *var.* Lecumberri. Navarra, N Spain *43.00N 1.54W*
175 Tt6 **Lelai, Tanjung** *headland* Pulau Halmahera, N Indonesia *1.31N 128.43E*
47 Q12 **le Lamentin** *var.* Lamentin. C Martinique *14.37N 61.01W*
47 Q12 **le Lamentin** ✕ (Fort-de-France) C Martinique *14.34N 61.00W*
33 P6 **Leland** Michigan, N USA *44.59N 85.45W*
24 J4 **Leland** Mississippi, S USA *33.24N 90.54W*
97 J16 **Lelång** *var.* Lelången. ◎ S Sweden
Lelången *see* Lelång
Lel'chitsy *see* Lyel'chytsy
le Léman *see* Geneva, Lake
27 O3 **Lelia Lake** Texas, SW USA *34.52N 100.42W*
115 I14 **Lelija** ▲ SE Bosnia and Herzegovina *43.25N 18.31E*
110 C8 **Le Locle** Neuchâtel, W Switzerland *47.04N 6.45E*
201 Y14 **Lelu** Kosrae, E Micronesia
Lelu *see* Lelu Island
201 Y14 **Lelu Island** *var.* Lelu. *island* Kosrae, E Micronesia
57 W9 **Lelydorp** Wanica, N Surinam *5.36N 55.04W*
100 K9 **Lelystad** Flevoland, C Netherlands *52.30N 5.25E*
65 K25 **Le Maire, Estrecho de** *strait* S Argentina
174 Hh7 **Lemang** Pulau Rangsang, W Indonesia *1.04N 102.44E*
195 R11 **Lemankoa** Buka Island, NE PNG *5.04S 154.37E*
Léman, Lac *see* Geneva, Lake
104 L6 **le Mans** Sarthe, NW France *48.00N 0.12E*
31 S12 **Le Mars** Iowa, C USA *42.47N 96.10W*
174 I11 **Lematan, Air** ≈ Sumatera, W Indonesia
111 S3 **Lembach im Mühlkreis** Oberösterreich, N Austria *48.28N 13.53E*
103 G23 **Lemberg** ▲ SW Germany *48.09N 8.47E*
Lemberg *see* L'viv
Lemdiyya *see* Médéa
124 Qq12 **Lemesós** *var.* Limassol. SW Cyprus *34.40N 33.02E*
102 H13 **Lemgo** Nordrhein-Westfalen, W Germany *52.01N 8.54E*
35 P13 **Lemhi Range** ▲▲ Idaho, NW USA
16 Oo2 **Lemieux Islands** *island group* Nunavut, NE Canada
175 Q7 **Lemito** Sulawesi, N Indonesia *0.34N 121.31E*
94 L10 **Lemmenjoki** *Lapp.* Leammi. ≈ NE Finland
100 L7 **Lemmer** *Fris.* De Lemmer. Friesland, N Netherlands *52.49N 5.43E*
30 L7 **Lemmon** South Dakota, N USA *45.54N 102.08W*
38 M15 **Lemmon, Mount** ▲ Arizona, SW USA *32.26N 110.47W*
Lemnos *see* Límnos
33 O14 **Lemon, Lake** ◎ Indiana, N USA
104 J5 **le Mont St-Michel** *castle* Manche, N France *48.37N 1.31W*
37 Q11 **Lemoore** California, W USA *36.16N 119.48W*
201 T13 **Lemotol Bay** *bay* Chuuk Islands, C Micronesia
47 Y5 **le Moule** *var.* Moule. Grande Terre, NE Guadeloupe *16.20N 61.20W*
Lemovices *see* Limoges
Le Moyen-Ogooué *see* Moyen-Ogooué
10 M6 **le Moyne, Lac** ◎ Quebec, E Canada
95 L18 **Lempäälä** Länsi-Suomi, W Finland *61.13N 23.46E*
44 E7 **Lempa, Río** ≈ Central America
44 F7 **Lempira** *prev.* Gracias. ◐ *department* SW Honduras
Lemsalu *see* Limbaži
109 N17 **Le Murge** ▲▲ SE Italy
129 V6 **Lemva** ≈ NW Russian Federation
97 F21 **Lemvig** Ringkøbing, W Denmark *56.31N 8.19E*
177 Ff8 **Lemyethna** Irrawaddy, SW Burma *17.36N 95.07E*
32 K10 **Lena** Illinois, N USA *42.22N 89.49W*
133 V4 **Lena** ≈ NE Russian Federation
181 N13 **Lena Tablemount** *undersea feature* S Indian Ocean *51.06S 56.54E*
Lenchitsa *see* Łęczyca
61 N17 **Lençóis** Bahia, E Brazil *12.36S 41.24W*
62 K9 **Lençóis Paulista** São Paulo, S Brazil *22.35S 48.51W*
178 Mm15 **Len Dao** *island* S Spratly Islands
111 Y9 **Lendava** *Hung.* Lendva, *Ger.* Unterlimbach; *prev.* Dolnja Lendava. NE Slovenia *46.33N 16.27E*
85 F20 **Lendepas** Hardap, SE Namibia *24.41S 19.58E*
128 H9 **Lendery** Respublika Kareliya, NW Russian Federation *63.20N 31.18E*
Lendum *see* Lens
Lendva *see* Lendava
29 R4 **Lenexa** Kansas, C USA *38.57N 94.43W*
111 Q5 **Lengau** Oberösterreich, N Austria *48.01N 13.17E*
151 Q17 **Lenger** Yuzhnyy Kazakhstan, S Kazakhstan *42.10N 69.54E*
165 O9 **Lenghu** Qinghai, C China *38.50N 93.25E*
165 T9 **Lenglong Ling** ▲ N China *37.40N 102.13E*
110 D7 **Lengnau** Bern, W Switzerland *47.12N 7.22E*
166 M12 **Lengshuitan** Hunan, S China *26.31N 111.38E*
97 M20 **Lenhovda** Kronoberg, S Sweden *57.00N 15.16E*

◆ Country
● Country Capital
◇ Dependent Territory
○ Dependent Territory Capital
◐ Administrative Region
✕ International Airport
▲ Mountain
▲▲ Mountain Range
⋏ Volcano
≈ River
◎ Lake
⊠ Reservoir

LE NIARI – LIMBOURG

81 E20 **Le Niari** ◈ province SW Congo
Lenīn see Leninskoye, Kazakhstan
Lenin see Akdepe, Turkmenistan
Leninabad see Khŭjand
Leninakan see Gyumri
Lenina, Pik see Lenin Peak
119 V12 **Lenine** Rus. Lenino. Respublika Krym, S Ukraine 45.18N 35.47E
Lenīngor see Leninogorsk
153 Q13 **Leningrad** Rus. Leningradskiy; prev. Mŭ'minobod, Rus. Muminabad. SW Tajikistan 38.03N 69.50E
Leningrad see Sankt-Peterburg
130 L13 **Leningradskaya** Krasnodarskiy Kray, SW Russian Federation 46.19N 39.23E
205 S16 **Leningradskaya** Russian research station Antarctica 69.30S 159.51E
128 H12 **Leningradskaya Oblast'** ◈ province NW Russian Federation
Leningradskiy see Leningrad
Lenino see Lenine, Ukraine
Lenino see Lyenina, Belarus
Leninobod see Khŭjand
151 X9 **Leninogorsk** Kaz. Lenīngor. Vostochnyy Kazakhstan, E Kazakhstan 50.20N 83.33E
131 T5 **Leninogorsk** Respublika Tatarstan, W Russian Federation 54.34N 52.27E
153 T12 **Lenin Peak** Rus. Pik Lenina, Taj. Qullai Lenin. ▲ Kyrgyzstan/Tajikistan 39.20N 72.50E
153 S8 **Leninpol'** Talasskaya Oblast', NW Kyrgyzstan 42.29N 71.54E
Lenin, Qullai see Lenin Peak
131 P11 **Leninsk** Volgogradskaya Oblast', SW Russian Federation 48.41N 45.18E
Leninsk see Akdepe, Turkmenistan
Leninsk see Asaka, Uzbekistan
Leninsk see Baykonyr, Kazakhstan
151 T8 **Leninskiy** Pavlodar, E Kazakhstan 52.18N 76.48E
126 H14 **Leninsk-Kuznetskiy** Kemerovskaya Oblast', S Russian Federation 54.42N 86.16E
151 N7 **Leninskoye** Kaz. Lenīn. Kostanay, N Kazakhstan 54.04N 65.22E
129 P15 **Leninskoye** Kirovskaya Oblast', NW Russian Federation 58.19N 47.03E
Leninsk-Turkmenski see Chardzhev
Leninváros see Tiszaújváros
Lenkoran' see Länkäran
103 F15 **Lenne** ∽ W Germany
103 G16 **Lennestadt** Nordrhein-Westfalen, W Germany 51.07N 8.04E
31 R11 **Lennox** South Dakota, N USA 43.21N 96.53W
65 J25 **Lennox, Isla** Eng. Lennox Island. island S Chile
Lennox Island see Lennox, Isla
23 Q9 **Lenoir** North Carolina, SE USA 35.54N 81.32W
22 M9 **Lenoir City** Tennessee, S USA 35.48N 84.15W
110 C7 **Le Noirmont** Jura, NW Switzerland 47.14N 6.57E
12 L9 **Lenôtre, Lac** ◎ Quebec, SE Canada
31 U15 **Lenox** Iowa, C USA 40.52N 94.33W
105 O2 **Lens** anc. Lendum, Lentium. Pas-de-Calais, N France 50.25N 2.49E
126 Kk12 **Lensk** Respublika Sakha (Yakutiya), NE Russian Federation 60.43N 115.16E
113 F24 **Lenti** Zala, SW Hungary 46.38N 16.30E
Lentia see Linz
95 N14 **Lentiira** Oulu, E Finland 64.22N 29.52E
109 L25 **Lentini** anc. Leontini. Sicilia, Italy, C Mediterranean Sea 37.17N 15.00E
Lentium see Lens
Lentschiza see Łęczyca
95 N15 **Lentua** ◎ E Finland
121 H14 **Lentvaris** Pol. Landwarów. Trakai, SE Lithuania 24.39N 24.58E
110 F7 **Lenzburg** Aargau, N Switzerland 47.24N 8.09E
111 R5 **Lenzing** Oberösterreich, N Austria 47.58N 13.34E
79 P13 **Léo** SW Burkina 11.09N 2.04W
111 V7 **Leoben** Steiermark, C Austria 47.22N 15.06E
Leobschütz see Głubczyce
46 L9 **Léogâne** S Haiti 18.28N 72.39W
175 Q7 **Leok** Sulawesi, N Indonesia 1.10N 121.20E
31 O7 **Leola** South Dakota, N USA 45.41N 98.58W
99 K20 **Leominster** W England, UK 52.09N 2.18W
21 N11 **Leominster** Massachusetts, NE USA 42.29N 71.43W
31 V16 **Leon** Iowa, C USA 40.44N 93.45W
42 M12 **León** var. León de los Aldamas. Guanajuato, C Mexico 21.05N 101.43W
44 I10 **León** León, NW Nicaragua 12.24N 86.52W
106 L4 **León** Castilla-León, NW Spain 42.34N 5.33W
44 I9 **León** ◈ department W Nicaragua
106 K4 **León** ◈ province Castilla-León, NW Spain
León see Cotopaxi
104 I15 **Léon** Landes, SW France 43.54N 1.17W
27 V9 **Leona** Texas, SW USA 31.09N 95.58W
188 K11 **Leonara** Western Australia 28.52S 121.16E
27 U5 **Leonard** Texas, SW USA 33.22N 96.15W
Leonard Murray Mountains see Murray Range
109 H15 **Leonardo da Vinci** prev. Fiumicino. ✕ (Roma) Lazio, C Italy 41.48N 12.15E
23 X5 **Leonardtown** Maryland, NE USA 38.17N 76.35W
27 Q13 **Leona River** ∽ Texas, SW USA
43 Z11 **Leona Vicario** Quintana Roo, SE Mexico 20.57N 87.06W
103 H21 **Leonberg** Baden-Württemberg, SW Germany 48.48N 9.01E
64 M3 **León, Cerro** ▲ NW Paraguay 20.21S 60.16W
León de los Aldamas see León
111 T4 **Leonding** Oberösterreich, N Austria 48.17N 14.15E
109 I14 **Leonessa** Lazio, C Italy 42.36N 12.56E
109 K24 **Leonforte** Sicilia, Italy, C Mediterranean Sea 37.37N 14.22E
191 O13 **Leongatha** Victoria, SE Australia 38.30S 145.56E
117 F21 **Leonídi** Pelopónnisos, S Greece 37.10N 22.50E
106 J4 **León, Montes de** ▲ NW Spain
27 S8 **Leon River** ∽ Texas, SW USA
Leontini see Lentini
Léopold II, Lac see Mai-Ndombe, Lac
101 J17 **Leopoldsburg** Limburg, NE Belgium 51.07N 5.16E
Léopoldville see Kinshasa
28 I5 **Leoti** Kansas, C USA 38.28N 101.21W
118 M11 **Leova** Rus. Leovo. SW Moldova 46.31N 28.16E
Leovo see Leova
104 G8 **le Palais** Morbihan, NW France 47.20N 3.08W
29 X10 **Lepanto** Arkansas, C USA 35.34N 90.21W
174 J11 **Lepar, Pulau** island W Indonesia
106 I14 **Lepe** Andalucía, S Spain 37.15N 7.12W
Lepel' see Lyepyel'
85 I19 **Lephepe** Kweneng, SE Botswana 23.17S 25.48E
167 Q10 **Leping** Jiangxi, S China 29.01N 117.07E
Lépontiennes, Alpes/Lepontine, Alpi see Lepontine Alps
110 G10 **Lepontine Alps** Fr. Alpes Lépontiennes, It. Alpi Lepontine. ▲ Italy/Switzerland
81 G20 **Le Pool** ◈ province S Congo
181 O16 **le Port** NW Réunion
105 N1 **le Portel** Pas-de-Calais, N France 50.42N 1.34E
95 N17 **Leppävirta** Itä-Suomi, C Finland 62.30N 27.49E
47 Q11 **le Prêcheur** NW Martinique 14.48N 61.13W
Lepsi see Lepsy
151 V13 **Lepsy** Kaz. Lepsi. Almaty, SE Kazakhstan 46.13N 78.55E
151 V13 **Lepsy** Kaz. Lepsi. ∽ SE Kazakhstan
Le Puglie see Puglia
105 Q12 **le Puy** prev. le Puy-en-Velay, hist. Anicium, Podium Anicensis. Haute-Loire, C France 45.03N 3.52E
le Puy-en-Velay see le Puy
Le Raizet see le Raizet
47 X11 **le Raizet** var. Le Raizet. ✕ (Pointe-à-Pitre) Grande Terre, C Guadeloupe 16.16N 61.31W
109 J24 **Lercara Friddi** Sicilia, Italy, C Mediterranean Sea 37.45N 13.37E
80 G12 **Léré** Mayo-Kébbi, SW Chad 9.40N 14.16E
Leribe see Hlotse
108 E10 **Lerici** Liguria, NW Italy 44.06N 9.53E
56 I14 **Lérida** Vaupés, SE Colombia 0.01S 70.28W
Lérida see Lleida
107 N5 **Lerma** Castilla-León, N Spain 42.01N 3.46W
42 M13 **Lerma, Río** ∽ C Mexico
117 F20 **Lérna** prehistoric site Pelopónnisos, S Greece 37.31N 22.43E
47 R11 **le Robert** E Martinique 14.40N 60.56W
117 M21 **Léros** island Dodekánisos, Greece, Aegean Sea
32 L13 **Le Roy** Illinois, N USA 40.21N 88.45W
29 Q6 **Le Roy** Kansas, C USA 38.04N 95.37W
31 W11 **Le Roy** Minnesota, N USA 43.30N 92.30W
20 E10 **Le Roy** New York, NE USA 42.58N 77.58W
Lerrnayin Gharabakh see Nagornyy Karabakh
97 J19 **Lerum** Västra Götaland, S Sweden 57.46N 12.12E
98 M2 **Lerwick** NE Scotland, UK 60.09N 1.09W
47 Y6 **les Abymes** var. Abymes. Grande Terre, C Guadeloupe 16.16N 61.30W
les Albères see Albères, Chaîne des
104 M4 **les Andelys** Eure, N France 49.15N 1.27E
47 Q12 **les Anses-d'Arlets** SW Martinique 14.29N 61.05W
107 U6 **Les Borges Blanques** var. Borjas Blancas. Cataluña, NE Spain 41.31N 0.52E
Lesbos see Lésvos
Les Cayes see Cayes
33 Q4 **Les Cheneaux Islands** island Michigan, N USA
105 T12 **les Écrins** ▲ E France 44.54N 6.25E
110 C10 **Le Sépey** Vaud, W Switzerland 46.21N 7.04E
13 T7 **Les Escoumins** Quebec, SE Canada 48.21N 69.25W
Les Gonaïves see Gonaïves
Lesh/Leshi see Lezhë
166 H9 **Leshan** Sichuan, C China 29.42N 103.43E
110 D11 **Les Haudères** Valais, SW Switzerland 46.02N 7.27E
104 J9 **les Herbiers** Vendée, NW France 46.52N 1.01W
129 O8 **Leshukonskoye** Arkhangel'skaya Oblast', NW Russian Federation 64.54N 45.48E
Lesina see Hvar
109 M15 **Lesina, Lago di** ◎ SE Italy
116 K13 **Lesítse** ▲ NE Greece
96 G10 **Lesja** Oppland, S Norway 62.07N 8.56E
97 L15 **Lesjöfors** Värmland, C Sweden 59.57N 14.12E
113 O18 **Lesko** Podkarpackie, SE Poland 49.28N 22.19E
115 O15 **Leskovac** Serbia, SE Yugoslavia 43.00N 21.58E
115 M22 **Leskovik** var. Leskoviku. Korçë, S Albania 40.09N 20.39E
Leskoviku see Leskovik
35 P14 **Leslie** Idaho, NW USA 43.51N 113.28W
33 Q10 **Leslie** Michigan, N USA 42.27N 84.25W
Leśna/Lesnaya see Lyasnaya
104 F5 **Lesneven** Finistère, NW France 48.35N 4.19W
114 J11 **Lešnica** Serbia, W Yugoslavia 44.40N 19.18E
129 S13 **Lesnoy** Kirovskaya Oblast', NW Russian Federation 59.49N 52.07E
126 I13 **Lesosibirsk** Krasnoyarskiy Kray, C Russian Federation 58.12N 92.22E
85 J23 **Lesotho** off. Kingdom of Lesotho; prev. Basutoland. ◆ monarchy S Africa
127 Nn17 **Lesozavodsk** Primorskiy Kray, SE Russian Federation 45.23N 133.15E
104 J12 **Lesparre-Médoc** Gironde, SW France 45.18N 0.57W
110 C8 **Les Ponts-de-Martel** Neuchâtel, W Switzerland 47.00N 6.45E
104 I9 **les Sables-d'Olonne** Vendée, NW France 46.30N 1.46W
105 P1 **Lesquin** ✕ Nord, N France 50.34N 3.07E
111 S7 **Lessach** var. Lessachbach. ∽ E Austria
Lessachbach see Lessach
47 W11 **les Saintes** var. Îles des Saintes. island group S Guadeloupe
76 L5 **Les Salines** ✕ (Annaba) NE Algeria 36.45N 7.57E
101 J22 **Lesse** ∽ SE Belgium
97 M21 **Lessebo** Kronoberg, S Sweden 56.45N 15.19E
204 M10 **Lesser Antarctica** var. West Antarctica. physical region Antarctica
47 P15 **Lesser Antilles** island group E West Indies
143 T10 **Lesser Caucasus** Rus. Malyy Kavkaz. ▲ SW Asia
Lesser Khingan Range see Xiao Hinggan Ling
9 P13 **Lesser Slave Lake** ◎ Alberta, W Canada
Lesser Sunda Islands see Nusa Tenggara
101 E19 **Lessines** Hainaut, SW Belgium 50.43N 3.49E
105 R16 **les Stes-Maries-de-la-Mer** Bouches-du-Rhône, SE France 43.27N 4.26E
12 G15 **Lester B.Pearson** var. Toronto. ✕ (Toronto) Ontario, S Canada 43.59N 81.30W
31 U9 **Lester Prairie** Minnesota, N USA 44.52N 94.02W
95 L16 **Lestijärvi** Länsi-Suomi, W Finland 63.29N 24.41E
L'Estuaire see Estuaire
31 U9 **Le Sueur** Minnesota, N USA 44.27N 93.53W
110 B8 **Les Verrières** Neuchâtel, W Switzerland 46.54N 6.29E
117 L17 **Lésvos** anc. Lesbos. island E Greece
112 G12 **Leszno** Ger. Lissa. Wielkopolskie, C Poland 51.51N 16.34E
85 L20 **Letaba** Northern, NE South Africa 23.44S 31.29E
181 P17 **le Tampon** SW Réunion
99 O21 **Letchworth** E England, UK 51.58N 0.13W
113 G25 **Letenye** Zala, SW Hungary 46.25N 16.42E
9 Q17 **Lethbridge** Alberta, SW Canada 49.43N 112.48W
57 S11 **Lethem** S Guyana 3.24N 59.45W
85 H18 **Letiahau** ∽ W Botswana
56 J18 **Leticia** Amazonas, S Colombia 4.09S 69.57W
175 T15 **Leti, Kepulauan** island group E Indonesia
85 I18 **Letlhakane** Central, C Botswana 21.28S 25.39E
85 H20 **Letlhakeng** Kweneng, SE Botswana 24.04S 25.03E
116 J8 **Letnitsa** Lovech, N Bulgaria 43.19N 25.02E
105 N1 **le Touquet-Paris-Plage** Pas-de-Calais, N France 50.31N 1.34E
177 G8 **Letpadan** Pegu, SW Burma 17.22N 94.10E
177 Ff6 **Letpan** Arakan State, W Burma 19.22N 94.11E
104 M2 **le Tréport** Seine-Maritime, N France 50.03N 1.21E
178 Gg13 **Letsôk-aw Kyun** var. Letsutan Island; prev. Domel Island. island Mergui Archipelago, S Burma
Letsutan Island see Letsôk-aw Kyun
99 E14 **Letterkenny** Ir. Leitir Ceanainn. NW Ireland 54.57N 7.43W
Lettland see Latvia
118 M6 **Letychiv** Khmel'nyts'ka Oblast', W Ukraine 49.24N 27.39E
Lëtzebuerg see Luxembourg
118 H14 **Leu** Dolj, SW Romania 44.10N 24.01E
Leucas see Lefkáda
105 P17 **Leucate** Aude, S France 42.55N 3.03E
105 P17 **Leucate, Étang de** ◎ S France
110 E10 **Leuk** Valais, SW Switzerland 46.18N 7.46E
110 E10 **Leukerbad** Valais, SW Switzerland 46.22N 7.47E
Leusden see Leusden-Centrum
100 K11 **Leusden-Centrum** var. Leusden. Utrecht, C Netherlands 52.07N 5.25E
Leutensdorf see Litvínov
Leutschau see Levoča
101 H18 **Leuven** Fr. Louvain, Ger. Löwen. Vlaams Brabant, C Belgium 50.52N 4.42E
101 I20 **Leuze** Namur, C Belgium 50.33N 4.55E
Leuze see Leuze-en-Hainaut
101 E19 **Leuze-en-Hainaut** var. Leuze. Hainaut, SW Belgium 50.36N 3.37E
Léva see Levice
Levádhia see Leivádia
Levajok see Leavvajohka
38 L4 **Levan** Utah, W USA 39.33N 111.51W
95 E16 **Levanger** Nord-Trøndelag, C Norway 63.45N 11.18E
124 P14 **Levantine Basin** undersea feature E Mediterranean Sea
108 D10 **Levanto** Liguria, W Italy 44.12N 9.33E
109 H23 **Levanzo, Isola di** island Isole Egadi, S Italy
131 Q17 **Levashi** Respublika Dagestan, SW Russian Federation 42.27N 47.19E
26 M5 **Levelland** Texas, SW USA 33.35N 102.22W
41 P13 **Levelock** Alaska, USA 59.07N 156.51W
103 E16 **Leverkusen** Nordrhein-Westfalen, W Germany 51.01N 7.00E
113 J21 **Levice** Ger. Lewentz, Lewenz, Hung. Léva. Nitriansky Kraj, SW Slovakia 48.13N 18.37E
108 G6 **Levico Terme** Trentino-Alto Adige, N Italy 46.02N 11.19E
117 E20 **Levídi** Pelopónnisos, S Greece 37.39N 22.13E
105 P14 **le Vigan** Gard, S France 43.00N 3.36E
192 L13 **Levin** Manawatu-Wanganui, North Island, NZ 40.37S 175.17E
13 R10 **Lévis** var. Levis. Quebec, SE Canada 46.46N 71.10W
23 P6 **Levisa Fork** ∽ Kentucky/Virginia, S USA
117 L21 **Levítha** island Kykládes, Greece, Aegean Sea
20 L14 **Levittown** Long Island, New York, NE USA 40.42N 73.29W
20 J15 **Levittown** Pennsylvania, NE USA 40.09N 74.50W
Levkás see Lefkáda
Levkímmi see Lefkímmi
113 L19 **Levoča** Ger. Leutschau, Hung. Locse. Prešovský Kraj, E Slovakia 49.01N 20.34E
Lévrier, Baie du see Nouâdhibou, Dakhlet
105 N9 **Levroux** Indre, C France 47.00N 1.37E
116 J8 **Levski** Pleven, N Bulgaria 43.22N 25.10E
Levskigrad see Karlovo
130 L6 **Lev Tolstoy** Lipetskaya Oblast', W Russian Federation 53.12N 39.28E
197 I14 **Levuka** Ovalau, C Fiji 17.42S 178.49E
177 G6 **Lewe** Mandalay, C Burma 19.40N 96.04E
Lewentz/Lewenz see Levice
99 O23 **Lewes** SE England, UK 50.52N 0.01E
23 Z4 **Lewes** Delaware, NE USA 38.46N 75.08W
31 Q12 **Lewis and Clark Lake** ▣ Nebraska/South Dakota, N USA
20 G14 **Lewisburg** Pennsylvania, NE USA 40.57N 76.52W
22 J10 **Lewisburg** Tennessee, S USA 35.27N 86.47W
23 S6 **Lewisburg** West Virginia, NE USA 37.48N 80.27W
98 F6 **Lewis, Butt of** headland NW Scotland, UK 58.31N 6.18W
98 F7 **Lewis, Isle of** island NW Scotland, UK
37 U4 **Lewis, Mount** ▲ Nevada, W USA 40.22N 116.50W
193 H16 **Lewis Pass** pass South Island, NZ 42.23S 172.21E
35 P7 **Lewis Range** ▲ Montana, NW USA
25 O3 **Lewis Smith Lake** ▣ Alabama, S USA
34 M10 **Lewiston** Idaho, NW USA 46.25N 117.01W
21 P7 **Lewiston** Maine, NE USA 44.07N 70.13W
31 X10 **Lewiston** Minnesota, N USA 43.58N 91.52W
20 D9 **Lewiston** New York, NE USA 43.10N 79.02W
38 L1 **Lewiston** Utah, W USA 41.58N 111.52W
32 K13 **Lewistown** Illinois, N USA 40.23N 90.09W
35 T9 **Lewistown** Montana, NW USA 47.04N 109.25W
29 T14 **Lewisville** Arkansas, C USA 33.21N 93.34W
27 T6 **Lewisville** Texas, SW USA 33.00N 96.57W
27 T6 **Lewisville, Lake** ▣ Texas, SW USA
Le Woleu-Ntem see Woleu-Ntem
25 U3 **Lexington** Georgia, SE USA 33.51N 83.04W
22 M5 **Lexington** Kentucky, S USA 38.03N 84.30W
24 L4 **Lexington** Mississippi, S USA 33.06N 90.03W
29 S4 **Lexington** Missouri, C USA 39.10N 93.52W
31 N16 **Lexington** Nebraska, C USA 40.46N 99.44W
22 S9 **Lexington** North Carolina, SE USA 35.49N 80.15W
29 N11 **Lexington** Oklahoma, C USA 35.00N 97.20W
23 R12 **Lexington** South Carolina, SE USA 33.58N 81.14W
22 G9 **Lexington** Tennessee, S USA 35.39N 88.23W
27 T10 **Lexington** Texas, SW USA 30.25N 97.00W
23 T6 **Lexington** Virginia, NE USA 37.46N 79.26W
23 X5 **Lexington Park** Maryland, NE USA 38.16N 76.27W
Leyden see Leiden
104 J14 **Leyre** ∽ SW France
179 R13 **Leyte** island C Philippines
179 R13 **Leyte Gulf** gulf E Philippines
113 O16 **Leżajsk** Podkarpackie, SE Poland 50.15N 22.24E
Lezha see Lezhë
115 K18 **Lezhë** var. Lezha; prev. Lesh, Leshi. Lezhë, NW Albania 41.46N 19.40E
115 K18 **Lezhë** ◈ district NW Albania
105 O16 **Lézignan-Corbières** Aude, S France 43.12N 2.46E
130 J7 **L'gov** Kurskaya Oblast', W Russian Federation 51.38N 35.17E
165 P15 **Lhari** Xizang Zizhiqu, W China 30.34N 93.40E
165 N16 **Lhasa** var. La-sa, Lassa. Xizang Zizhiqu, W China 29.40N 91.10E
165 O15 **Lhasa He** ∽ W China
164 K16 **Lhazê** Xizang Zizhiqu, W China 29.07N 87.32E
164 K14 **Lhazhong** Xizang Zizhiqu, W China 31.58N 86.43E
173 F3 **Lhoksukon** Sumatera, W Indonesia 5.04N 97.19E
165 Q15 **Lhorong** Xizang Zizhiqu, W China 30.51N 95.41E
107 W6 **L'Hospitalet de Llobregat** var. Hospitalet. Cataluña, NE Spain 41.21N 2.06E
159 R11 **Lhotse** ▲ China/Nepal 28.00N 86.55E
165 N17 **Lhozhag** Xizang Zizhiqu, W China 28.21N 90.47E
165 O16 **Lhünzê** Xizang Zizhiqu, W China 28.25N 92.30E
165 N15 **Lhünzhub** var. Poindo. Xizang Zizhiqu, W China 30.14N 91.20E
178 H8 **Li** Lamphun, NW Thailand 17.46N 98.54E
Liancheng see Qinglong
179 Rr14 **Lianga** Mindanao, S Philippines 8.36N 126.04E
167 P12 **Liangcheng** Fujian, SE China 25.47N 116.42E
166 K9 **Liangping** Chongqing Shi, C China 30.40N 107.46E
Liangzhou see Wuwei
167 O9 **Liangzi Hu** ▣ C China
167 R12 **Lianjiang** Fujian, SE China 26.13N 119.33E
166 L15 **Lianjiang** Guangdong, S China 21.41N 110.12E
167 O13 **Lianping** Guangdong, S China 24.22N 114.23E
169 T13 **Lianshan** prev. Jinxi. Liaoning, NE China 40.42N 120.52E
Lian Xian see Lianzhou
166 M11 **Lianyuan** prev. Lantian. Hunan, S China 27.51N 111.44E
167 Q6 **Lianyungang** var. Xinpu. Jiangsu, E China 34.37N 119.12E
167 N13 **Lianzhou** var. Linxian; prev. Lian Xian. Guangdong, S China 24.48N 112.20E
Liao see Liaoning
167 P5 **Liaocheng** Shandong, E China 36.31N 115.59E
169 U13 **Liaodong Bandao** var. Liaotung Peninsula. peninsula NE China
169 T13 **Liaodong Wan** Eng. Gulf of Lantung, Gulf of Liaotung. gulf NE China
169 U11 **Liao He** ∽ NE China
169 W12 **Liao Ling** ▲ NE China
169 U12 **Liaoning** var. Liao, Liaoning Sheng, Shengking; hist. Fengtien, Shenking. ◈ province NE China
Liaoning Sheng see Liaoning
Liaotung, Gulf of see Liaodong Wan
Liaotung Peninsula see Liaodong Bandao
169 V12 **Liaoyang** var. Liao-yang. Liaoning, NE China 41.16N 123.12E
169 V11 **Liaoyuan** var. Dongliao, Shuang-liao, Jap. Chengchiatun. Jilin, NE China 42.51N 125.09E
169 U12 **Liaozhong** Liaoning, NE China 41.33N 122.54E
Liaqatabad see Piplān
8 M10 **Liard** ∽ W Canada
Liard see Fort Liard
8 L10 **Liard River** British Columbia, W Canada 59.22N 126.04W
155 O15 **Liāri** Baluchistān, SW Pakistan 25.43N 66.28E
Liatroim see Leitrim
201 S6 **Lib** var. Ellep. island Ralik Chain, C Marshall Islands
Liban see Lebanon
144 H6 **Liban, Jebel** Ar. Jabal al Gharbt, Jabal Lubnān, Eng. Mount Lebanon. ▲ C Lebanon
Libau see Liepāja
35 N7 **Libby** Montana, NW USA 48.25N 115.33W
81 I16 **Libenge** Equateur, NW Dem. Rep. Congo (Zaire) 3.39N 18.39E
28 I7 **Liberal** Kansas, C USA 37.01N 100.55W
29 R7 **Liberal** Missouri, C USA 37.33N 94.31W
Liberalitas Julia see Évora
113 D15 **Liberec** Ger. Reichenberg. Liberecký Kraj, N Czech Republic 50.44N 15.04E
113 D15 **Liberecký Kraj** ◈ region N Czech Republic
44 K12 **Liberia** Guanacaste, NW Costa Rica 10.36N 85.26W
78 K17 **Liberia** off. Republic of Liberia. ◆ republic W Africa
63 D16 **Libertad** Corrientes, NE Argentina 30.01S 57.51W
63 E20 **Libertad** San José, S Uruguay 34.37S 56.39W
56 I7 **Libertad** Barinas, NW Venezuela 8.21N 69.39W
56 K6 **Libertad** Cojedes, N Venezuela 9.19N 68.43W
64 G12 **Libertador** off. Región del Libertador General Bernardo O'Higgins. ◈ region C Chile
Libertador General San Martín see Ciudad de Libertador General San Martín
22 L6 **Liberty** Kentucky, S USA 37.19N 84.54W
24 J7 **Liberty** Mississippi, S USA 31.09N 90.49W
29 R4 **Liberty** Missouri, C USA 39.15N 94.22W
20 J12 **Liberty** New York, NE USA 41.48N 74.45W
23 T9 **Liberty** North Carolina, SE USA 35.49N 79.34W
Libian Desert see Libyan Desert
101 J23 **Libin** Luxembourg, SE Belgium 50.01N 5.13E
166 K13 **Libo** Guizhou, S China 25.28N 107.52E
Libohova see Libohovë
115 L23 **Libohovë** var. Libohova. Gjirokastër, S Albania 40.03N 20.13E
83 K18 **Liboi** North Eastern, E Kenya 0.23N 40.55E
104 K13 **Libourne** Gironde, SW France 44.55N 0.13W
101 K23 **Libramont** Luxembourg, SE Belgium 49.55N 5.21E
115 M20 **Librazhd** var. Librazhdi. Elbasan, E Albania 41.10N 20.22E
Librazhdi see Librazhd
81 C18 **Libreville** ● (Gabon) Estuaire, NW Gabon 0.25N 9.29E
179 Rr15 **Libuganon** ∽ Mindanao, S Philippines
77 P10 **Libya** off. Socialist People's Libyan Arab Jamahiriya, Ar. Al Jamāhīrīyah al 'Arabīyah al Lībīyah ash Sha'bīyah al Ishtirākīyah; prev. Libyan Arab Republic. ◆ Islamic state N Africa
77 T11 **Libyan Desert** var. Libian Desert, Ar. Aş Şahrā' al Lībīyah. desert N Africa
77 T8 **Libyan Plateau** var. Aḍ Ḍiffah. plateau Egypt/Libya
Lībīyah, Aş Şahrā' al see Libyan Desert
64 G12 **Licantén** Maule, C Chile 35.00S 72.00W
109 J25 **Licata** anc. Phintias. Sicilia, Italy, C Mediterranean Sea 37.07N 13.56E
143 P14 **Lice** Dıyarbakır, SE Turkey 38.28N 40.39E
99 L19 **Lichfield** C England, UK 52.42N 1.48W
85 N14 **Lichinga** Niassa, N Mozambique 13.17S 35.15E
111 V3 **Lichtenau** Niederösterreich, N Austria 48.29N 15.24E
85 I21 **Lichtenburg** North-West, N South Africa 26.06S 26.08E
103 K18 **Lichtenfels** Bayern, SE Germany 50.09N 11.03E
100 O12 **Lichtenvoorde** Gelderland, E Netherlands 51.58N 6.34E
Lichtenwald see Sevnica
101 C17 **Lichtervelde** West-Vlaanderen, W Belgium 51.01N 3.09E
166 L9 **Lichuan** Hubei, C China 30.19N 108.55E
29 V7 **Licking** Missouri, C USA 37.30N 91.51W
22 M4 **Licking River** ∽ Kentucky, S USA
114 C11 **Lički Osik** Lika-Senj, C Croatia 44.36N 15.24E
Ličko-Senjska Županija see Lika-Senj
109 K19 **Licosa, Punta** headland S Italy 40.15N 14.54E
121 H16 **Lida** Rus. Lida. Hrodzyenskaya Voblasts', W Belarus 53.53N 25.19E
95 H17 **Liden** Västernorrland, C Sweden 62.43N 16.49E
31 R7 **Lidgerwood** North Dakota, N USA 46.04N 97.09W
Lidhorikíon see Lidoríki
97 K21 **Lidhult** Kronoberg, S Sweden 56.49N 13.25E
97 P16 **Lidingö** Stockholm, C Sweden 59.22N 18.10E
97 K17 **Lidköping** Västra Götaland, S Sweden 58.30N 13.10E
Lido di Iesolo see Lido di Jesolo
108 I8 **Lido di Jesolo** var. Lido di Iesolo. Veneto, NE Italy 45.30N 12.37E
109 H15 **Lido di Ostia** Lazio, C Italy 41.42N 12.19E
Lidokhorikion see Lidoríki
117 E18 **Lidoríki** prev. Lidhorikíon, Lidokhorikion. Stereá Ellás, C Greece 38.31N 22.12E
112 K9 **Lidzbark** Warmińsko-Mazurskie, NE Poland 53.15N 19.49E
112 L7 **Lidzbark Warmiński** Ger. Heilsberg. Warmińsko-Mazurskie, NE Poland, 54.07N 20.34E
111 U3 **Liebenau** Oberösterreich, N Austria 48.33N 14.48E
189 P7 **Liebig, Mount** ▲ Northern Territory, C Australia 23.19S 131.30E
111 V8 **Lieboch** Steiermark, SE Austria 47.00N 15.21E
110 I8 **Liechtenstein** off. Principality of Liechtenstein. ◆ principality C Europe
101 F18 **Liedekerke** Vlaams Brabant, C Belgium 50.51N 4.05E
101 K19 **Liège** Dut. Luik, Ger. Lüttich. Liège, E Belgium 50.37N 5.34E
101 K20 **Liège** Dut. Luik. ◈ province E Belgium
Liegnitz see Legnica
95 O16 **Lieksa** Itä-Suomi, E Finland 63.20N 30.00E
120 F10 **Lielupe** ∽ Latvia/Lithuania
120 G9 **Lielvārde** Ogre, C Latvia 56.45N 24.48E
178 Kk14 **Liên Hương** var. Tuy Phong. Binh Thuân, S Vietnam 11.13N 108.40E
Liên Nghia see Đưc Trong
111 P9 **Lienz** Tirol, W Austria 46.49N 12.45E
120 B10 **Liepāja** Ger. Libau. Liepāja, W Latvia 56.31N 21.02E
101 H17 **Lier** Fr. Lierre. Antwerpen, N Belgium 51.07N 4.34E
97 H15 **Lierbyen** Buskerud, S Norway 59.46N 10.13E
101 L21 **Lierneux** Liège, E Belgium 50.12N 5.51E
Lierre see Lier
103 D18 **Lieser** ∽ W Germany
111 U7 **Liesing** ∽ E Austria
110 E6 **Liestal** Basel-Land, N Switzerland 47.28N 7.43E
Lietuva see Lithuania
Lievenhof see Līvāni
105 O2 **Liévin** Pas-de-Calais, N France 50.25N 2.48E
12 M9 **Lièvre, Rivière du** ∽ Quebec, SE Canada
111 T6 **Liezen** Steiermark, C Austria 47.34N 14.12E
99 E14 **Lifford** Ir. Leifear. NW Ireland 54.49N 7.28W
197 K5 **Lifou** island Îles Loyauté, E New Caledonia
200 Ss13 **Lifuka** island Ha'apai Group, C Tonga
179 Q11 **Ligao** Luzon, N Philippines 13.16N 123.30E
Liger see Loire
44 H2 **Lighthouse Reef** reef E Belize
191 Q4 **Lightning Ridge** New South Wales, SE Australia 29.29S 148.00E
105 N9 **Lignières** Cher, C France 46.45N 2.10E
105 S5 **Ligny-en-Barrois** Meuse, NE France 48.42N 5.22E
85 P15 **Ligonha** ∽ NE Mozambique
33 P11 **Ligonier** Indiana, N USA 41.25N 85.33W
83 I25 **Ligunga** Ruvuma, S Tanzania 10.51S 37.10E
108 D9 **Ligure, Appennino** Eng. Ligurian Mountains. ▲ NW Italy
Ligure, Mar see Ligurian Sea
108 C9 **Liguria** ◈ region NW Italy
Ligurian Mountains see Ligure, Appennino
123 K6 **Ligurian Sea** Fr. Mer Ligurienne, It. Mar Ligure. sea N Mediterranean Sea
Ligurienne, Mer see Ligurian Sea
195 P9 **Lihir Group** island group NE PNG
195 P9 **Lihir Island** island Lihir Group, N PNG
40 B8 **Lihue** Haw. Līhu'e. Kauai, Hawaii, USA, C Pacific Ocean 21.58N 159.22W
120 F5 **Lihula** Ger. Leal. Läänemaa, W Estonia 58.43N 23.52E
128 I2 **Liinakhamari** var. Linacmamari. Murmanskaya Oblast', NW Russian Federation 69.40N 31.27E
Liivi Laht see Riga, Gulf of
166 F11 **Lijiang** var. Dayan, Lijiang Naxizu Zizhixian. Yunnan, SW China 26.52N 100.10E
114 C11 **Lika-Senj** off. Ličko-Senjska Županija. ◈ province W Croatia
81 N25 **Likasi** prev. Jadotville. Katanga, SE Dem. Rep. Congo (Zaire) 11.01S 26.51E
81 L16 **Likati** Orientale, N Dem. Rep. Congo (Zaire) 3.28N 23.45E
8 M15 **Likely** British Columbia, SW Canada 52.40N 121.34W
159 Y11 **Likhapāni** Assam, NE India 27.24N 95.51E
128 J16 **Likhoslavl'** Tverskaya Oblast', W Russian Federation 57.08N 35.27E
201 U5 **Likiep Atoll** atoll Ratak Chain, C Marshall Islands
97 D18 **Liknes** Vest-Agder, S Norway 58.19N 6.58E
81 H18 **Likouala** ∽ N Congo
81 H18 **Likouala aux Herbes** ∽ E Congo
202 B16 **Liku** E Niue 19.01S 169.46E
Likupang, Selat see Bangka, Selat
29 Y8 **Lilbourn** Missouri, C USA 36.35N 89.37W
105 X14 **l'Île-Rousse** Corse, France, C Mediterranean Sea 42.39N 8.59E
111 W5 **Lilienfeld** Niederösterreich, NE Austria 48.01N 15.36E
167 N11 **Liling** Hunan, S China 27.42N 113.49E
97 J18 **Lilla Edet** Västra Götaland, S Sweden 58.07N 12.07E
105 P1 **Lille** var. l'Isle, Dut. Rijssel, Flem. Ryssel; prev. Lisle, anc. Insula. Nord, N France 50.37N 3.04E
97 G24 **Lillebælt** var. Lille Bælt, Eng. Little Belt. strait S Denmark
104 L3 **Lillebonne** Seine-Maritime, N France 49.30N 0.34E
96 H12 **Lillehammer** Oppland, S Norway 61.07N 10.28E
105 O1 **Lillers** Pas-de-Calais, N France 50.34N 2.26E
97 F18 **Lillesand** Aust-Agder, S Norway 58.13N 8.22E
97 I15 **Lillestrøm** Akershus, S Norway 59.58N 11.04E
95 F18 **Lillhärdal** Jämtland, C Sweden 61.51N 14.04E
23 U10 **Lillington** North Carolina, SE USA 35.24N 78.49W
107 O9 **Lillo** Castilla-La Mancha, C Spain 39.43N 3.19W
8 M16 **Lillooet** British Columbia, SW Canada 50.40N 121.58W
85 M14 **Lilongwe** ● (Malawi) Central, W Malawi 13.58S 33.48E
85 M14 **Lilongwe** ✕ Central, W Malawi 13.46S 33.44E
85 M14 **Lilongwe** ∽ W Malawi
179 Q15 **Liloy** Mindanao, S Philippines 8.04N 122.42E
Lilybaeum see Marsala
190 J7 **Lilydale** South Australia 32.57S 140.00E
191 P16 **Lilydale** Tasmania, SE Australia 41.17S 147.13E
115 J14 **Lim** ∽ Bosnia and Herzegovina/Yugoslavia
59 D15 **Lima** ● (Peru) Lima, W Peru 12.05S 78.00W
96 K13 **Lima** Dalarna, C Sweden 60.55N 13.19E
33 R12 **Lima** Ohio, NE USA 40.43N 84.06W
59 D14 **Lima** ◈ department W Peru
Lima see Jorge Chávez International
106 G5 **Lima, Rio** Sp. Limia ∽ Portugal / Spain see also Limia
113 L17 **Limanowa** Małopolskie, S Poland 49.43N 20.25E
174 I8 **Limas** Pulau Sebangka, W Indonesia 0.09N 104.31E
Limassol see Lemesós
99 F14 **Limavady** Ir. Léim an Mhadaidh. NW Northern Ireland, UK 55.03N 6.57W
65 J14 **Limay Mahuida** La Pampa, C Argentina 37.09S 66.40W
65 H15 **Limay, Río** ∽ W Argentina
103 N16 **Limbach-Oberfrohna** Sachsen, E Germany 50.52N 12.46E
83 F22 **Limba Limba** ∽ C Tanzania
109 C17 **Limbara, Monte** ▲ Sardegna, Italy, C Mediterranean Sea 40.50N 9.10E
120 G7 **Limbaži** Est. Lemsalu. Limbaži, N Latvia 57.33N 24.46E
46 M8 **Limbé** N Haiti 19.40N 72.25W
175 Qq7 **Limboto, Danau** ◎ Sulawesi, N Indonesia
101 L19 **Limbourg** Liège, E Belgium 50.37N 5.55E

◆ Country ● Country Capital ◇ Dependent Territory ○ Dependent Territory Capital ◈ Administrative Region ✕ International Airport ▲ Mountain ▲ Mountain Range Volcano ∽ River ◎ Lake ▣ Reservoir

LIMBURG – LOGONE-ORIENTAL

101 K17 **Limburg** ◐ *province* NE Belgium
101 L16 **Limburg** ◐ *province* SE Netherlands
103 F17 **Limburg an der Lahn** Hessen, W Germany *50.22N 8.04E*
96 K13 **Limedsforsen** Dalarna, C Sweden *60.52N 13.25E*
62 L9 **Limeira** São Paulo, S Brazil *22.34S 47.25W*
99 C19 **Limerick** *Ir.* Luimneach. SW Ireland *52.40N 8.37W*
99 C20 **Limerick** *Ir.* Luimneach. *cultural region* SW Ireland
21 S2 **Limestone** Maine, NE USA *46.52N 67.49W*
27 U9 **Limestone, Lake** ◎ Texas, SW USA
41 P12 **Lime Village** Alaska, USA *61.21N 155.26W*
97 F20 **Limfjorden** *fjord* N Denmark
97 J23 **Limhamn** Skåne, S Sweden *55.34N 12.57E*
106 H5 **Limia** *Port.* Rio Lima ≈ Portugal/ Spain *see also* Lima, Rio
95 L14 **Liminka** Oulu, C Finland *64.48N 25.19E*
Limín Vathéos *see* Sámos
117 G17 **Límni** Évvoia, C Greece *38.46N 23.20E*
117 J15 **Límnos** *anc.* Lemnos. *island* E Greece
104 M11 **Limoges** *anc.* Augustoritum Lemovicensium, Lemovices. Haute-Vienne, C France *45.50N 1.16E*
39 U5 **Limon** Colorado, C USA *39.15N 103.41W*
45 O13 **Limón** *var.* Puerto Limón. Limón, E Costa Rica *9.59N 83.02W*
44 K4 **Limón** Colón, NE Honduras *15.51N 85.30W*
45 N13 **Limón** *off.* Provincia de Limón. ◐ *province* E Costa Rica
108 A10 **Limone Piemonte** Piemonte, NE Italy *44.12N 7.37E*
Limones *see* Valdéz
Limonum *see* Poitiers
105 N11 **Limousin** ◐ *region* C France
105 N16 **Limoux** Aude, S France *43.03N 2.13E*
85 L19 **Limpopo** *var.* Crocodile. ≈ S Africa
166 K17 **Limu Ling** ▲▲ S China
115 M20 **Lin** *var.* Lini. Elbasan, E Albania *41.03N 20.37E*
Linacmamari *see* Liinakhamari
179 P13 **Linapacan Island** *island* W Philippines
64 G13 **Linares** Maule, C Chile *35.49S 71.37W*
56 C13 **Linares** Nariño, SW Colombia *1.23N 77.33W*
43 O9 **Linares** Nuevo León, NE Mexico *24.50N 99.33W*
107 N12 **Linares** Andalucía, S Spain *38.04N 3.37W*
109 G15 **Linaro, Capo** *headland* C Italy *42.01N 11.49E*
108 D8 **Linate** ✕ (Milano) Lombardia, N Italy *45.27N 9.18E*
166 F13 **Lincang** Yunnan, SW China *23.55N 100.03E*
167 P11 **Linchuan** *var.* Fuzhou. Jiangxi, S China *27.58N 116.19E*
63 B20 **Lincoln** Buenos Aires, E Argentina *34.50S 61.32W*
193 H19 **Lincoln** Canterbury, South Island, NZ *43.37S 172.30E*
99 N18 **Lincoln** *anc.* Lindum, Lindum Colonia. E England, UK *53.13N 0.33W*
37 O6 **Lincoln** California, W USA *38.52N 121.18W*
32 L13 **Lincoln** Illinois, N USA *40.09N 89.21W*
28 M4 **Lincoln** Kansas, C USA *39.03N 98.09W*
21 S5 **Lincoln** Maine, NE USA *45.22N 68.30W*
29 T5 **Lincoln** Missouri, C USA *38.23N 93.19W*
31 R16 **Lincoln** *state capital* Nebraska, C USA *40.46N 96.42W*
34 F11 **Lincoln City** Oregon, NW USA *44.57N 124.01W*
178 M10 **Lincoln Island** *island* E Paracel Islands
207 Q11 **Lincoln Sea** *sea* Arctic Ocean
99 N18 **Lincolnshire** *cultural region* E England, UK
23 R10 **Lincolnton** North Carolina, SE USA *35.28N 81.15W*
27 V7 **Lindale** Texas, SW USA *32.31N 95.24W*
103 I25 **Lindau** *var.* Lindau am Bodensee. Bayern, S Germany *47.33N 9.40E*
Lindau am Bodensee *see* Lindau
126 L9 **Linde** ≈ NE Russian Federation
57 T9 **Linden** E Guyana *5.58N 58.11W*
25 O6 **Linden** Alabama, S USA *32.18N 87.48W*
22 H9 **Linden** Tennessee, S USA *35.37N 87.50W*
27 X6 **Linden** Texas, SW USA *33.01N 94.22W*
20 J16 **Lindenwold** New Jersey, NE USA *39.47N 74.58W*
97 M15 **Lindesberg** Örebro, C Sweden *59.36N 15.15E*
97 D18 **Lindesnes** *headland* S Norway *57.58N 7.03E*
Líndhos *see* Líndos
83 K24 **Lindi** Lindi, SE Tanzania *10.00S 39.41E*
83 J24 **Lindi** ◐ *region* SE Tanzania
81 N17 **Lindi** ≈ NE Dem. Rep. Congo (Zaire)
169 V7 **Lindian** Heilongjiang, NE China *47.10N 124.51E*
193 E21 **Lindis Pass** *pass* South Island, NZ *44.33S 169.40E*
85 J22 **Lindley** Free State, C South Africa *27.48S 27.57E*
97 J19 **Lindome** Västra Götaland, S Sweden *57.34N 12.04E*
Lindong *see* Bairin Zuoqi
117 O23 **Líndos** *var.* Líndhos. Ródos, Dodekánisos, Greece, Aegean Sea *36.04N 28.04E*
12 I14 **Lindsay** Ontario, SE Canada *44.21N 78.43W*
37 R11 **Lindsay** California, W USA *36.11N 119.06W*
35 X8 **Lindsay** Montana, NW USA *47.13N 105.10W*
29 N11 **Lindsay** Oklahoma, C USA *34.50N 97.37W*
29 N5 **Lindsborg** Kansas, C USA *38.34N 97.39W*
97 N21 **Lindsdal** Kalmar, S Sweden *56.43N 16.18E*
175 Pp9 **Lindu, Danau** ◎ Sulawesi, N Indonesia
Lindum/Lindum Colonia *see* Lincoln
203 W3 **Line Islands** *island group* E Kiribati
Linëvo *see* Linova
166 M5 **Linfen** *var.* Lin-fen. Shanxi, C China *36.07N 111.34E*
161 F18 **Linganamakki Reservoir** ⊠ SW India
166 L17 **Lingao** Hainan, S China *19.44N 109.23E*
179 Oo9 **Lingayen** Luzon, N Philippines *16.00N 120.12E*
179 Oo9 **Lingayen Gulf** *gulf* Luzon, N Philippines
166 M6 **Lingbao** *var.* Guolüezhen. Henan, C China *34.34N 110.50E*
96 N12 **Lingbo** Gävleborg, C Sweden *61.04N 16.45E*
Lingeh *see* Bandar-e Langeh
102 E12 **Lingen** *var.* Lingen an der Ems. Niedersachsen, NW Germany *52.31N 7.19E*
Lingen an der Ems *see* Lingen
174 Ii8 **Lingga, Kepulauan** *island group* W Indonesia
174 I8 **Lingga, Pulau** *island* Kepulauan Lingga, W Indonesia
12 J14 **Lingham Lake** ◎ Ontario, SE Canada
96 M13 **Linghed** Dalarna, C Sweden *60.48N 15.55E*
35 Z15 **Lingle** Wyoming, C USA *42.07N 104.21W*
20 G15 **Linglestown** Pennsylvania, NE USA *40.20N 76.46W*
81 K18 **Lingomo II** Equateur, NW Dem. Rep. Congo (Zaire) *0.42N 21.59E*
166 L15 **Lingshan** Guangxi Zhuangzu Zizhiqu, S China *22.28N 109.19E*
166 L17 **Lingshui** Hainan, S China *18.35N 110.03E*
161 G16 **Lingsugūr** Karnātaka, C India *16.13N 76.33E*
109 L23 **Linguaglossa** Sicilia, Italy, C Mediterranean Sea *37.51N 15.06E*
78 H10 **Linguère** N Senegal *15.24N 15.06W*
165 W8 **Lingwu** Ningxia, N China *38.04N 106.21E*
Lingxi *see* Yongshun
167 O12 **Lingxian** *var.* Ling Xian. Hunan, S China *26.32N 113.48E*
169 S12 **Lingyuan** Liaoning, NE China *41.09N 119.24E*
169 U4 **Linhai** Heilongjiang, NE China *51.30N 124.18E*
167 S10 **Linhai** *var.* Taizhou. Zhejiang, SE China *28.53N 121.10E*
61 O20 **Linhares** Espírito Santo, SE Brazil *19.22S 40.04W*
168 M13 **Linhe** Nei Mongol Zizhiqu, N China *40.46N 107.27E*
Lini *see* Lin
145 S1 **Linik, Chiyā-ē** ▲ N Iraq
97 M18 **Linköping** Östergötland, S Sweden *58.25N 15.37E*
169 Y8 **Linkou** Heilongjiang, NE China *45.18N 130.16E*
120 F11 **Linkuva** Pakruojis, N Lithuania *56.06N 23.58E*
29 V5 **Linn** Missouri, C USA *38.29N 91.51W*
27 S16 **Linn** Texas, SW USA *26.32N 98.06W*
29 T2 **Linneus** Missouri, C USA *39.53N 93.10W*
98 H10 **Linnhe, Loch** *inlet* W Scotland, UK
121 G19 **Linova** *Rus.* Linëvo. Brestskaya Voblasts', SW Belarus *52.28N 24.33E*
167 O5 **Linqing** Shandong, E China *36.49N 115.39E*
167 N6 **Linruzhen** Henan, C China *34.10N 112.51E*
62 K8 **Lins** São Paulo, S Brazil *21.40S 49.43W*
95 F17 **Linsell** Jämtland, C Sweden *62.10N 14.00E*
166 J9 **Linshui** Sichuan, C China *30.24N 106.54E*
46 K12 **Linstead** C Jamaica *18.07N 77.01W*
165 U11 **Lintan** Gansu, N China *34.43N 101.27E*
165 V11 **Lintao** Gansu, C China *35.23N 103.54E*
13 S12 **Lintère** ≈ Quebec, SE Canada
110 H8 **Linth** ≈ NW Switzerland
110 H8 **Linthal** Glarus, NE Switzerland *46.59N 8.57E*
33 N15 **Linton** Indiana, N USA *39.01N 87.10W*
31 N6 **Linton** North Dakota, N USA *46.16N 100.13W*
169 R11 **Linxi** Nei Mongol Zizhiqu, N China *43.29N 117.59E*
165 U11 **Linxia** *var.* Linxia Huizu Zizhizhou. Gansu, C China *35.33N 103.08E*
Linxia Huizu Zizhizhou *see* Linxia
Linxian *see* Lianzhou
167 Q6 **Linyi** Shandong, S China *37.12N 116.54E*
167 P4 **Linyi** Shandong, E China *37.13N 116.56E*
166 M6 **Linyi** Shanxi, C China *35.10N 110.45E*
111 T4 **Linz** *anc.* Lentia. Oberösterreich, N Austria *48.19N 14.18E*
165 S8 **Linze** *var.* Shahepu. Gansu, N China *39.06N 100.03E*
46 J13 **Lionel Town** C Jamaica *17.49N 77.13W*
105 Q16 **Lion, Golfe du** *Eng.* Gulf of Lion, Gulf of Lions; *anc.* Sinus Gallicus. *gulf* S France
Lion, Gulf of/Lions, Gulf of *see* Lion, Golfe du
85 K16 **Lions Den** Mashonaland West, N Zimbabwe *17.16S 30.00E*
12 F13 **Lion's Head** Ontario, S Canada *44.59N 81.16W*
Lios Ceannúir, Bá *see* Liscannor Bay
Lios Mór *see* Lismore
Lios na gCearrbhach *see* Lisburn
Lios Tuathail *see* Listowel
81 G17 **Liouesso** La Sangha, N Congo *1.01N 15.43E*
Liozno *see* Lyozna
179 P11 **Lipa** *off.* Lipa City. Luzon, N Philippines *13.57N 121.10E*
27 S7 **Lipan** Texas, SW USA *32.31N 98.03W*
Lipari Islands/Lipari, Isole *see* Eolie, Isole
109 L22 **Lipari, Isola** *island* Isole Eolie, S Italy
118 L8 **Lipcani** *Rus.* Lipkany. N Moldova *48.16N 26.47E*
95 N17 **Liperi** Itä-Suomi, E Finland *62.30N 29.25E*
130 L7 **Lipetsk** Lipetskaya Oblast', W Russian Federation *52.37N 39.37E*
130 K6 **Lipetskaya Oblast'** ◐ *province* W Russian Federation
59 K22 **Lipez, Cordillera de** ▲▲ SW Bolivia
112 E10 **Lipiany** *Ger.* Lippehne. Zachodniopomorskie, W Poland *53.00N 14.58E*
114 G9 **Lipik** Požega-Slavonija, NE Croatia *45.24N 17.08E*
128 L12 **Lipin Bor** Vologodskaya Oblast', NW Russian Federation *60.12N 38.04E*
166 L12 **Liping** Guizhou, S China *26.16N 109.07E*
Lipkany *see* Lipcani
121 H15 **Lipnishki** *Rus.* Lipnishki. Hrodzyenskaya Voblasts', W Belarus *54.01N 25.39E*
112 J10 **Lipno** Kujawsko-pomorskie, C Poland *52.51N 19.11E*
118 F11 **Lipova** *Hung.* Lippa. Arad, W Romania *46.06N 21.40E*
Lipovets *see* Lypovets'
Lippa *see* Lipova
103 E14 **Lippe** ≈ W Germany
Lippehne *see* Lipiany
103 G14 **Lippstadt** Nordrhein-Westfalen, W Germany *51.40N 8.21E*
27 P1 **Lipscomb** Texas, SW USA *36.12N 100.13W*
Lipsia/Lipsk *see* Leipzig
Liptau-Sankt-Nikolaus/Liptószentmiklós *see* Liptovský Mikuláš
113 K19 **Liptovský Mikuláš** *Ger.* Liptau-Sankt-Nikolaus, *Hung.* Liptószentmiklós. Žilinský Kraj, N Slovakia *49.06N 19.36E*
191 O13 **Liptrap, Cape** *headland* Victoria, SE Australia *38.55S 145.58E*
166 L13 **Lipu** Guangxi Zhuangzu Zizhiqu, S China *24.29N 110.24E*
147 X12 **Liqbi** S Oman *18.27N 56.37E*
83 G17 **Lira** N Uganda *2.15N 32.55E*
59 F15 **Lircay** Huancavelica, C Peru *12.58S 74.43W*
109 J15 **Liri** ≈ C Italy
150 M8 **Lisakovsk** Kostanay, NW Kazakhstan *52.37N 62.34E*
81 K17 **Lisala** Equateur, N Dem. Rep. Congo (Zaire) *2.10N 21.28E*
106 F11 **Lisboa** *Eng.* Lisbon; *anc.* Felicitas Julia, Olisipo. ● (Portugal) Lisboa, W Portugal *38.43N 9.07W*
106 F10 **Lisboa** ◐ *Eng.* Lisbon. *district* C Portugal
21 N7 **Lisbon** New Hampshire, NE USA *44.11N 71.52W*
31 Q6 **Lisbon** North Dakota, N USA *46.27N 97.42W*
Lisbon *see* Lisboa
21 Q8 **Lisbon Falls** Maine, NE USA *44.00N 70.03W*
99 G15 **Lisburn** *Ir.* Lios na gCearrbhach. E Northern Ireland, UK *54.31N 6.03W*
40 L6 **Lisburne, Cape** *headland* Alaska, USA *68.52N 166.13W*
99 B19 **Liscannor Bay** *Ir.* Bá Lios Ceannúir. *inlet* W Ireland
115 Q18 **Lisec** ▲ E FYR Macedonia *41.46N 22.30E*
166 F13 **Lishe Jiang** ≈ SW China
166 M4 **Lishi** Shanxi, C China *37.27N 111.05E*
169 V10 **Lishu** Jilin, NE China *43.25N 124.19E*
167 R10 **Lishui** Zhejiang, SE China *28.27N 119.25E*
199 Jj5 **Lisianski Island** *island* Hawaiian Islands, Hawaii, USA, C Pacific Ocean
Lisichansk *see* Lysychans'k
104 L4 **Lisieux** *anc.* Noviomagus. Calvados, N France *49.09N 0.13E*
130 L8 **Liski** *prev.* Georgiu-Dezh. Voronezhskaya Oblast', W Russian Federation *51.00N 39.36E*
Lisle/l'Isle *see* Lille
105 N4 **l'Isle-Adam** Val-d'Oise, N France *49.07N 2.13E*
105 R15 **l'Isle-sur-la-Sorgue** Vaucluse, SE France *43.55N 5.03E*
13 S9 **L'Islet** Quebec, SE Canada *47.07N 70.18W*
190 M12 **Lismore** Victoria, SE Australia *37.59S 143.18E*
99 D20 **Lismore** *Ir.* Lios Mór. S Ireland *52.10N 7.10W*
Lissa *see* Vis, Croatia
Lissa *see* Leszno, Poland
100 H11 **Lisse** Zuid-Holland, W Netherlands *52.15N 4.33E*
97 D18 **Lista** *peninsula* S Norway
97 D18 **Listafjorden** *fjord* S Norway
205 R13 **Lister, Mount** ▲ Antarctica *78.12S 161.46E*
130 M8 **Listopadovka** Voronezhskaya Oblast', W Russian Federation *51.54N 41.08E*
12 F15 **Listowel** Ontario, S Canada *43.44N 80.57W*
99 B20 **Listowel** *Ir.* Lios Tuathail. SW Ireland *52.27N 9.28W*
166 L14 **Litang** Guangxi Zhuangzu Zizhiqu, S China *23.09N 109.07E*
166 F9 **Litang** Sichuan, C China *30.03N 100.12E*
166 F10 **Litang Qu** ≈ C China
57 X12 **Litani** *var.* Itany. ≈ French Guiana/Surinam
144 G8 **Lītani, Nahr el** *var.* Nahr al Litant. ≈ C Lebanon
Litant, Nahr al *see* Lītani, Nahr el
Litauen *see* Lithuania
32 K14 **Litchfield** Illinois, N USA *39.17N 89.52W*
31 U8 **Litchfield** Minnesota, N USA *45.09N 94.31W*
38 K13 **Litchfield Park** Arizona, SW USA *33.29N 112.21W*
191 S8 **Lithgow** New South Wales, SE Australia *33.30S 150.09E*
117 I26 **Líthino, Akrotírio** *headland* Kríti, Greece, E Mediterranean Sea *34.55N 24.43E*
120 D12 **Lithuania** *off.* Republic of Lithuania, *Ger.* Litauen, *Lith.* Lietuva, *Pol.* Litwa, *Rus.* Litva; *prev.* Lithuanian SSR, *Rus.* Litovskaya SSR. ◆ *republic* NE Europe
Lithuanian SSR *see* Lithuania
111 U11 **Litija** *Ger.* Littai. C Slovenia *46.03N 14.50E*
20 H15 **Lititz** Pennsylvania, NE USA *40.09N 76.18W*
117 F15 **Litóchoro** *var.* Litohoro, Litókhoron. Kentrikí Makedonía, N Greece *40.06N 22.30E*
Litohoro/Litókhoron *see* Litóchoro
113 C15 **Litoměřice** *Ger.* Leitmeritz. Ústecký Kraj, NW Czech Republic *50.32N 14.09E*
113 F17 **Litomyšl** *Ger.* Leitomischl. Pardubický Kraj, C Czech Republic *49.52N 16.16E*
113 G17 **Litovel** *Ger.* Littau. Olomoucký Kraj, E Czech Republic *49.42N 17.04E*
127 Nn15 **Litovko** Khabarovskiy Kray, SE Russian Federation *49.22N 135.10E*
Litovskaya SSR *see* Lithuania
Littai *see* Litija
Littau *see* Litovel
46 G1 **Little Abaco** *var.* Abaco Island. *island* N Bahamas
113 I21 **Little Alföld** *Ger.* Kleines Ungarisches Tiefland, *Hung.* Kisalföld, *Slvk.* Podunajská Rovina. *plain* Hungary/Slovakia
157 Q20 **Little Andaman** *island* Andaman Islands, India, NE Indian Ocean
28 M5 **Little Arkansas River** ≈ Kansas, C USA
192 L4 **Little Barrier Island** *island* N NZ
Little Belt *see* Lillebælt
40 M11 **Little Black River** ≈ Alaska, USA
29 O2 **Little Blue River** ≈ Kansas/Nebraska, C USA
46 D8 **Little Cayman** *island* E Cayman Islands
9 X11 **Little Churchill** ≈ Manitoba, C Canada
177 Ee10 **Little Coco Island** *island* SW Burma
38 L10 **Little Colorado River** ≈ Arizona, SW USA
12 E11 **Little Current** Manitoulin Island, Ontario, S Canada *45.57N 81.55W*
10 E11 **Little Current** ≈ Ontario, S Canada
40 L8 **Little Diomede Island** *island* Alaska, USA
46 I4 **Little Exuma** *island* C Bahamas
31 U7 **Little Falls** Minnesota, N USA *45.59N 94.21W*
20 J10 **Little Falls** New York, NE USA *43.02N 74.51W*
26 M5 **Littlefield** Texas, SW USA *33.55N 102.19W*
31 V3 **Littlefork** Minnesota, N USA *48.24N 93.33W*
31 V3 **Little Fork River** ≈ Minnesota, N USA
9 N16 **Little Fort** British Columbia, SW Canada *51.27N 120.15W*
9 Y14 **Little Grand Rapids** Manitoba, C Canada *52.06N 95.29W*
99 N23 **Littlehampton** SE England, UK *50.48N 0.33W*
37 T2 **Little Humboldt River** ≈ Nevada, W USA
46 K6 **Little Inagua** *var.* Inagua Islands. *island* S Bahamas
23 Q4 **Little Kanawha River** ≈ West Virginia, NE USA
85 F25 **Little Karoo** *plateau* S South Africa
41 O16 **Little Koniuji Island** *island* Shumagin Islands, Alaska, USA
46 H12 **Little London** W Jamaica *18.14N 78.13W*
11 R10 **Little Mecatina** *Fr.* Rivière du Petit Mécatina. ≈ Newfoundland/Quebec, E Canada
98 F8 **Little Minch, The** *strait* NW Scotland, UK
29 T13 **Little Missouri River** ≈ Arkansas, USA
30 J7 **Little Missouri River** ≈ NW USA
30 J3 **Little Muddy River** ≈ North Dakota, N USA
157 Q22 **Little Nicobar** *island* Nicobar Islands, India, NE Indian Ocean
29 R6 **Little Osage River** ≈ Missouri, C USA
99 P20 **Little Ouse** ≈ E England, UK
155 V2 **Little Pamir** *Pash.* Pāmīr-e Khord, *Rus.* Malyy Pamir. ▲▲ Afghanistan/Tajikistan
23 U12 **Little Pee Dee River** ≈ North Carolina/South Carolina, SE USA
29 V10 **Little Red River** ≈ Arkansas, C USA
Little Rhody *see* Rhode Island
193 I19 **Little River** Canterbury, South Island, NZ *43.45S 172.49E*
23 U12 **Little River** South Carolina, SE USA *33.52N 78.36W*
29 Y9 **Little River** ≈ Arkansas/Missouri, C USA
29 R13 **Little River** ≈ Arkansas/Oklahoma, USA
25 T7 **Little River** ≈ Georgia, SE USA
24 H6 **Little River** ≈ Louisiana, S USA
27 T10 **Little River** ≈ Texas, SW USA
29 V12 **Little Rock** *state capital* Arkansas, C USA *34.45N 92.17W*
33 N8 **Little Sable Point** *headland* Michigan, N USA *43.38N 86.32W*
105 U11 **Little Saint Bernard Pass** *Fr.* Col du Petit St-Bernard, *It.* Colle di Piccolo San Bernardo. *pass* France/Italy *45.41N 6.54E*
38 K7 **Little Salt Lake** ◎ Utah, W USA
188 K8 **Little Sandy Desert** *desert* Western Australia
31 S13 **Little Sioux River** ≈ Iowa, C USA
40 E17 **Little Sitkin Island** *island* Aleutian Islands, Alaska, USA
9 O13 **Little Smoky** Alberta, W Canada *54.35N 117.06W*
9 O14 **Little Smoky** ≈ Alberta, W Canada
39 P3 **Little Snake River** ≈ Colorado, C USA
66 A12 **Little Sound** *bay* Bermuda, NW Atlantic Ocean
39 T4 **Littleton** Colorado, C USA *39.36N 105.01W*
21 N7 **Littleton** New Hampshire, NE USA *44.18N 71.46W*
20 D11 **Little Valley** New York, NE USA *42.15N 78.46W*
32 M15 **Little Wabash River** ≈ Illinois, N USA
12 D10 **Little White River** ≈ Ontario, S Canada
30 M12 **Little White River** ≈ South Dakota, N USA
27 R5 **Little Wichita River** ≈ Texas, SW USA
148 I4 **Little Zab** *Ar.* Nahraz Zāb aş Şaghīr, *Kurd.* Zē-i Kōya, *Per.* Rūdkhāneh-ye Zāb-e Kūchek. ≈ Iran/Iraq
81 D15 **Littoral** ◐ *province* W Cameroon
Littoria *see* Latina
Litva/Litwa *see* Lithuania
113 B15 **Litvínov** *Ger.* Leutensdorf. Ústecký Kraj, NW Czech Republic *50.37N 13.37E*
118 M6 **Lityn** Vinnyts'ka Oblast', C Ukraine *49.19N 28.06E*
Liu-chou/Liuchow *see* Liuzhou
169 W11 **Liuhe** Jilin, NE China *42.15N 125.49E*
Liukang Tenggaya, Kepulauan *see* Sabalana, Kepulauan
85 Q15 **Liúpo** Nampula, NE Mozambique *15.36S 39.57E*
85 G14 **Liuwa Plain** *plain* W Zambia
166 L13 **Liuzhou** *var.* Liu-chou, Liuchow. Guangxi Zhuangzu Zizhiqu, S China *24.09N 108.54E*
118 H8 **Livada** *Hung.* Sárköz. Satu Mare, NW Romania *47.52N 23.03E*
117 J20 **Liváda, Akrotírio** *headland* Tínos, Kykládes, Greece, Aegean Sea *37.36N 25.15E*
117 L21 **Livádi** *island* Kykládes, Greece, Aegean Sea
Livanátai *see* Livanátes
117 G18 **Livanátes** *prev.* Livanátai. Stereá Ellás, C Greece *38.43N 23.01E*
120 I10 **Līvāni** *Ger.* Lievenhof. Preiļi, SE Latvia *56.22N 26.12E*
67 E25 **Lively Island** *island* SE Falkland Islands
67 D25 **Lively Sound** *sound* SE Falkland Islands
41 R8 **Livengood** Alaska, USA *65.31N 148.32W*
108 I7 **Livenza** ≈ NE Italy
37 O6 **Live Oak** California, W USA *39.17N 121.41W*
25 U9 **Live Oak** Florida, SE USA *30.18N 82.59W*
37 O9 **Livermore** California, W USA *37.40N 121.46W*
22 I6 **Livermore** Kentucky, S USA *37.31N 87.08W*
21 Q7 **Livermore Falls** Maine, NE USA *44.30N 70.09W*
26 J10 **Livermore, Mount** ▲ Texas, SW USA *30.37N 104.10W*
11 P16 **Liverpool** Nova Scotia, SE Canada *44.03N 64.43W*
99 K17 **Liverpool** NW England, UK *53.25N 2.55W*
191 S7 **Liverpool Range** ▲▲ New South Wales, SE Australia
98 J12 **Livingston** C Scotland, UK *55.51N 3.31W*
25 N5 **Livingston** Alabama, S USA *32.34N 88.12W*
37 P9 **Livingston** California, W USA *37.22N 120.45W*
24 J8 **Livingston** Louisiana, S USA *30.30N 90.45W*
35 S11 **Livingston** Montana, NW USA *45.40N 110.33W*
22 L8 **Livingston** Tennessee, S USA *36.22N 85.19W*
27 W9 **Livingston** Texas, SW USA *30.42N 94.55W*
44 F4 **Lívingston** Izabal, E Guatemala *15.49N 88.46W*
85 I16 **Livingstone** *var.* Maramba. Southern, S Zambia *17.51S 25.48E*
193 B22 **Livingstone Mountains** ▲ South Island, NZ
82 K13 **Livingstone Mountains** ▲ S Tanzania
84 N12 **Livingstonia** Northern, N Malawi *10.29S 34.06E*
204 G4 **Livingston Island** *island* Antarctica
27 W9 **Livingston, Lake** ⊠ Texas, SW USA
114 F13 **Livno** Federacija Bosna I Hercegovina, SW Bosnia and Herzegovina *43.49N 17.00E*
130 K7 **Livny** Orlovskaya Oblast', W Russian Federation *52.25N 37.42E*
95 M14 **Livojoki** ≈ C Finland
33 R10 **Livonia** Michigan, N USA *42.22N 83.22W*
108 E11 **Livorno** *Eng.* Leghorn. Toscana, C Italy *43.31N 10.18E*
Livramento *see* Santana do Livramento
147 U8 **Liwā** *var.* Al Liwā'. *oasis region* S UAE
83 I24 **Liwale** Lindi, SE Tanzania *9.46S 37.55E*
165 W9 **Liwangbu** Ningxia, N China *36.42N 106.04E*
85 N15 **Liwonde** Southern, S Malawi *15.04S 35.12E*
165 V11 **Lixian** *var.* Li Xian. Gansu, C China *34.15N 105.07E*
166 H8 **Lixian** *var.* Li Xian; *prev.* Zagunao. Sichuan, C China *31.27N 103.06E*
Lixian Jiang *see* Black River
117 B18 **Lixoúri** *prev.* Lixoúrion. Kefallinía, Iónioi Nísoi, Greece, C Mediterranean Sea *38.12N 20.25E*
Lixoúrion *see* Lixoúri
Lixus *see* Larache
Lizarra *see* Estella-Lizarra
35 U15 **Lizard Head Peak** ▲ Wyoming, C USA *42.47N 109.12W*
99 H25 **Lizard Point** *headland* SW England, UK *49.57N 5.12W*
114 L12 **Ljig** Serbia, C Yugoslavia *44.14N 20.16E*
Ljouwert *see* Leeuwarden
Ljubelj *see* Loibl Pass
111 U11 **Ljubljana** *Ger.* Laibach, *It.* Lubiana; *anc.* Aemona, Emona. ● (Slovenia) C Slovenia *46.03N 14.28E*
111 T11 **Ljubljana** ✕ C Slovenia *46.14N 14.26E*
115 N17 **Ljuboten** ▲ S Yugoslavia *42.12N 21.06E*
97 P19 **Ljugarn** Gotland, SE Sweden *57.23N 18.45E*
86 G7 **Ljungan** ≈ N Sweden
95 F17 **Ljungan** ≈ C Sweden
97 K21 **Ljungby** Kronoberg, S Sweden *56.49N 13.55E*
97 M17 **Ljungsbro** Östergötland, S Sweden *58.31N 15.30E*
97 I18 **Ljungskile** Västra Götaland, S Sweden *58.13N 11.55E*
96 M11 **Ljusdal** Gävleborg, C Sweden *61.49N 16.10E*
96 M11 **Ljusnan** ≈ C Sweden
96 N12 **Ljusne** Gävleborg, C Sweden *61.11N 17.07E*
97 P15 **Ljusterö** Stockholm, C Sweden *59.31N 18.40E*
111 X9 **Ljutomer** *Ger.* Luttenberg. NE Slovenia *46.31N 16.12E*
65 G15 **Llaima, Volcán** ▲ S Chile *39.01S 71.38W*
107 X4 **Llançà** *var.* Llansá. Cataluña, NE Spain *42.23N 3.08E*
99 J21 **Llandovery** C Wales, UK *52.01N 3.47W*
99 J20 **Llandrindod Wells** E Wales, UK *52.15N 3.22W*
99 J18 **Llandudno** N Wales, UK *53.19N 3.49W*
99 I21 **Llanelli** *prev.* Llanelly. SW Wales, UK *51.41N 4.11W*
Llanelly *see* Llanelli
106 M2 **Llanes** Asturias, N Spain *43.24N 4.46W*
99 K19 **Llangollen** NE Wales, UK *52.58N 3.10W*
27 R10 **Llano** Texas, SW USA *30.45N 98.40W*
27 Q10 **Llano River** ≈ Texas, SW USA
56 I9 **Llanos** *physical region* Colombia/Venezuela
65 G16 **Llanquihue, Lago** ◎ S Chile
Llansá *see* Llançà
107 U5 **Lleida** *Cast.* Lérida; *anc.* Ilerda. Cataluña, NE Spain *41.37N 0.36E*
107 U5 **Lleida** *Cast.* Lérida ◐ *province* Cataluña, NE Spain
106 K12 **Llerena** Extremadura, W Spain *38.13N 6.00W*
107 S9 **Llíria** País Valenciano, E Spain *39.37N 0.36W*
107 W4 **Llívia** Cataluña, NE Spain *42.27N 2.00E*
107 O3 **Llodio** País Vasco, N Spain *43.07N 2.58W*
107 X5 **Lloret de Mar** Cataluña, NE Spain *41.42N 2.51E*
Llorri *see* Tossal de l'Orri
8 L11 **Lloyd George, Mount** ▲ British Columbia, W Canada *57.46N 124.57W*
9 R14 **Lloydminster** Alberta/Saskatchewan, SW Canada *53.18N 110.00W*
38 L6 **Loa** Utah, W USA *38.24N 111.38W*
174 Mm4 **Loagan Bunut** ◎ East Malaysia
178 Mm14 **Loaita Island** *island* W Spratly Islands
40 G12 **Loa, Mauna** ▲ Hawaii, USA, C Pacific Ocean *19.28N 155.39W*
Loanda *see* Luanda
81 J22 **Loange** ≈ S Dem. Rep. Congo (Zaire)
81 E21 **Loango** Le Kouilou, S Congo *4.37S 11.49E*
108 B10 **Loano** Liguria, NW Italy *44.07N 8.15E*
64 H5 **Loa, Río** ≈ N Chile
85 I20 **Lobatse** *var.* Lobatsi. Kgatleng, SE Botswana *25.10S 25.40E*
Lobatsi *see* Lobatse
103 Q15 **Löbau** Sachsen, E Germany *51.06N 14.39E*
81 H16 **Lobaye** ◐ *prefecture* SW Central African Republic
81 I16 **Lobaye** ≈ SW Central African Republic
101 G21 **Lobbes** Hainaut, S Belgium *50.21N 4.16E*
63 D23 **Lobería** Buenos Aires, E Argentina *38.07S 58.48W*
112 F8 **Łobez** *Ger.* Labes. Zachodniopomorskie, NW Poland *53.29N 15.39E*
84 A13 **Lobito** Benguela, W Angola *12.19S 13.34E*
Lobkovichi *see* Labkovichy
Lob Nor *see* Lop Nur
176 W11 **Lobo** Irian Jaya, E Indonesia *3.41S 134.06E*
106 J11 **Lobón** Extremadura, W Spain *38.51N 6.37W*
63 D20 **Lobos** Buenos Aires, E Argentina *35.10S 59.07W*
42 E4 **Lobos, Cabo** *headland* NW Mexico *29.53N 112.43W*
42 F6 **Lobos, Isla** *island* NW Mexico
Lobositz *see* Lovosice
Lobsens *see* Łobżenica
Loburi *see* Lop Buri
112 H9 **Łobżenica** *Ger.* Lobsens. Wielkopolskie, C Poland *53.19N 17.11E*
110 G11 **Locarno** *Ger.* Luggarus Ticino, S Switzerland *46.10N 8.47E*
98 E9 **Lochboisdale** NW Scotland, UK *57.08N 7.17W*
100 N11 **Lochem** Gelderland, E Netherlands *52.10N 6.25E*
104 M8 **Loches** Indre-et-Loire, C France *47.08N 1.00E*
Loch Garman *see* Wexford
98 H12 **Lochgilphead** W Scotland, UK *56.02N 5.27W*
98 H7 **Lochinver** N Scotland, UK *58.10N 5.14W*
98 F8 **Lochmaddy** NW Scotland, UK *57.35N 7.10W*
98 J10 **Lochnagar** ▲ C Scotland, UK *56.58N 3.09W*
101 E17 **Lochristi** Oost-Vlaanderen, NW Belgium *51.07N 3.49E*
98 H9 **Lochy, Loch** ◎ N Scotland, UK
190 G8 **Lock** South Australia *33.37S 135.45E*
99 J14 **Lockerbie** S Scotland, UK *55.10N 3.27W*
29 S13 **Lockesburg** Arkansas, C USA *33.58N 94.10W*
191 P10 **Lockhart** New South Wales, SE Australia *35.15S 146.43E*
27 S11 **Lockhart** Texas, SW USA *29.52N 97.40W*
20 F13 **Lock Haven** Pennsylvania, NE USA *41.08N 77.27W*
27 N4 **Lockney** Texas, SW USA *34.06N 101.27W*
102 O12 **Löcknitz** ≈ NE Germany
20 E9 **Lockport** New York, NE USA *43.09N 78.40W*
178 Jj13 **Lôc Ninh** Sông Be, S Vietnam *11.51N 106.34E*
109 N23 **Locri** Calabria, SW Italy *38.16N 16.16E*
Locse *see* Levoča
29 T2 **Locust Creek** ≈ Missouri, C USA
25 P3 **Locust Fork** ≈ Alabama, S USA
29 Q9 **Locust Grove** Oklahoma, C USA *36.12N 95.10W*
96 E11 **Lodalskåpa** ▲ S Norway *61.47N 7.10E*
191 N10 **Loddon River** ≈ Victoria, SE Australia
Lodensee *see* Klooga
105 P15 **Lodève** *anc.* Luteva. Hérault, S France *43.43N 3.19E*
128 I12 **Lodeynoye Pole** Leningradskaya Oblast', NW Russian Federation *60.41N 33.29E*
35 V11 **Lodge Grass** Montana, NW USA *45.19N 107.20W*
30 J15 **Lodgepole Creek** ≈ Nebraska/Wyoming, C USA
155 T11 **Lodhrān** Punjab, E Pakistan *29.36N 71.34E*
108 D8 **Lodi** Lombardia, NW Italy *45.15N 9.36E*
37 O8 **Lodi** California, W USA *38.07N 121.17W*
33 T12 **Lodi** Ohio, N USA *41.00N 82.01W*
94 H10 **Lødingen** Nordland, C Norway *68.24N 15.55E*
81 L20 **Lodja** Kasai Oriental, C Dem. Rep. Congo (Zaire) *3.28S 23.24E*
39 O3 **Lodore, Canyon of** *canyon* Colorado, C USA
107 Q4 **Lodosa** Navarra, N Spain *42.25N 2.04W*
83 H16 **Lodwar** Rift Valley, NW Kenya *3.06N 35.37E*
112 K13 **Łódź** *Rus.* Lodz. Łódź, C Poland *51.51N 19.26E*
112 J13 **Łódzkie** ◐ *province* C Poland *51.51N 19.26E*
178 I8 **Loei** *var.* Loey, Muang Loei. Loei, C Thailand *17.28N 101.42E*
100 I11 **Loenen** Utrecht, C Netherlands *52.13N 5.01E*
178 J9 **Loeng Nok Tha** Yasothon, E Thailand *16.12N 104.31E*
85 F24 **Loeriesfontein** Northern Cape, W South Africa *30.53S 19.28E*
97 H20 **Læsø** *island* N Denmark
Loewoek *see* Luwuk
Loey *see* Loei
78 J16 **Lofa** ≈ N Liberia
111 P6 **Lofer** Salzburg, C Austria *47.37N 12.42E*
94 F11 **Lofoten** *var.* Lofoten Islands. *island group* C Norway
Lofoten Islands *see* Lofoten
97 N18 **Loftahammar** Kalmar, S Sweden *57.55N 16.45E*
131 O10 **Log** Volgogradskaya Oblast', SW Russian Federation *49.32N 43.52E*
79 S12 **Loga** Dosso, SW Niger *13.33N 3.18E*
31 S14 **Logan** Iowa, C USA *41.38N 95.47W*
28 K3 **Logan** Kansas, C USA *39.39N 99.34W*
33 T14 **Logan** Ohio, N USA *39.32N 82.24W*
38 L1 **Logan** Utah, W USA *41.45N 111.50W*
23 P6 **Logan** West Virginia, NE USA *37.51N 81.59W*
37 Y10 **Logandale** Nevada, W USA *36.36N 114.28W*
21 O11 **Logan International** ✕ (Boston) Massachusetts, NE USA *42.22N 71.00W*
9 N16 **Logan Lake** British Columbia, SW Canada *50.28N 120.42W*
25 Q4 **Logan Martin Lake** ⊠ Alabama, S USA
8 G8 **Logan, Mount** ▲ Yukon Territory, W Canada *60.32N 140.34W*
34 I7 **Logan, Mount** ▲ Washington, NW USA *48.32N 120.57W*
35 P7 **Logan Pass** *pass* Montana, NW USA *48.43N 113.44W*
33 O12 **Logansport** Indiana, N USA *40.44N 86.25W*
24 F6 **Logansport** Louisiana, S USA *31.58N 94.00W*
Logar *see* Lowgar
69 R11 **Loge** ≈ NW Angola
Logishin *see* Lahishyn
Log na Coille *see* Lugnaquillia Mountain
80 G11 **Logone** *var.* Logone. ≈ Cameroon/Chad
80 G13 **Logone-Occidental** *off.* Préfecture du Logone-Occidental. ◐ *prefecture* SW Chad
80 H13 **Logone Occidental** ≈ SW Chad
80 G13 **Logone-Oriental** *off.* Préfecture du Logone-Oriental. ◐ *prefecture* SW Chad

◆ Country ● Country Capital ◇ Dependent Territory ○ Dependent Territory Capital ◐ Administrative Region ✕ International Airport ▲ Mountain ▲▲ Mountain Range Volcano ≈ River ◎ Lake ⊠ Reservoir

LOGONE ORIENTAL – LUBUDI

80 H13 **Logone Oriental** ≈ SW Chad
Logone Oriental *see* Pendé
L'Ogooué-Ivindo *see* Ogooué-Ivindo
L'Ogooué-Lolo *see* Ogooué-Lolo
L'Ogooué-Maritime *see* Ogooué-Maritime
Logoysk *see* Lahoysk
107 P4 **Logroño** ***anc.*** Vareia, ***Lat.*** Juliobriga. La Rioja, N Spain *42.28N 2.25W*
106 L10 **Logrosán** Extremadura, W Spain *39.21N 5.28W*
97 G20 **Løgstør** Nordjylland, N Denmark *56.57N 9.19E*
97 H22 **Løgten** Århus, C Denmark *56.16N 10.19E*
97 F24 **Løgumkloster** Sønderjylland, SW Denmark *55.04N 8.58E*
Lögurinn *see* Lagarfljót
197 B10 **Loh** *island* Torres Islands, N Vanuatu
159 P15 **Lohārdaga** Bihār, N India *23.27N 84.42E*
158 H10 **Lohāru** Haryāna, N India *28.27N 75.53E*
103 D15 **Lohausen** ✈ (Düsseldorf) Nordrhein-Westfalen, W Germany *51.18N 6.51E*
201 O14 **Lohd** Pohnpei, E Micronesia
194 I14 **Lohiki** ≈ S PNG
94 L12 **Lohiniva** Lappi, N Finland *67.09N 25.04E*
Lohiszyn *see* Lahishyn
95 L20 **Lohja** ***var.*** Lojo. Etelä-Suomi, S Finland *60.14N 24.07E*
175 O8 **Lohjanan** Borneo, C Indonesia
27 Q9 **Lohn** Texas, SW USA *31.15N 99.22W*
102 G12 **Lohne** Niedersachsen, NW Germany *52.40N 8.13E*
Lohr *see* Lohr am Main
103 I18 **Lohr am Main** ***var.*** Lohr. Bayern, C Germany *50.00N 9.30E*
111 T10 **Loibl Pass** ***Ger.*** Loiblpass, ***Slvn.*** Ljubelj. *pass* Austria/Slovenia *46.25N 14.15E*
178 Gg6 **Loi-Kaw** Kayah State, C Burma *19.40N 97.12E*
95 K19 **Loimaa** Länsi-Suomi, W Finland *60.51N 23.03E*
105 O6 **Loing** ≈ C France
178 Ii6 **Loi, Phou** ▲ N Laos *20.18N 103.14E*
104 L7 **Loir** ≈ C France
105 Q11 **Loire** ◐ *department* E France
104 M7 **Loire** ***var.*** Liger. ≈ C France
104 I7 **Loire-Atlantique** ◐ *department* NW France
105 O7 **Loiret** ◐ *department* C France
104 M8 **Loir-et-Cher** ◐ *department* C France
103 L24 **Loisach** ≈ SE Germany
58 B9 **Loja** Loja, S Ecuador *3.58S 79.16W*
106 M14 **Loja** Andalucía, S Spain *37.10N 4.09W*
58 B9 **Loja** ◐ *province* S Ecuador
Lojo *see* Lohja
118 J4 **Lokachi** Volyns'ka Oblast', NW Ukraine *50.44N 24.39E*
81 M20 **Lokandu** Maniema, C Dem. Rep. Congo (Zaire) *2.34S 25.43E*
94 M11 **Lokan Tekojärvi** ◎ NE Finland
143 Z11 **Lökbatan** ***Rus.*** Lokbatan. E Azerbaijan *40.21N 49.43E*
101 F17 **Lokeren** Oost-Vlaanderen, NW Belgium *51.06N 3.58E*
Lokhvitsa *see* Lokhvytsya
119 S4 **Lokhvytsya** ***Rus.*** Lokhvitsa. Poltavs'ka Oblast', NE Ukraine *50.21N 33.15E*
83 H17 **Lokichar** Rift Valley, NW Kenya *2.22N 35.40E*
83 G16 **Lokichokio** Rift Valley, NW Kenya *4.16N 34.22E*
83 H16 **Lokitaung** Rift Valley, NW Kenya *4.15N 35.45E*
94 M11 **Lokka** Lappi, N Finland *67.47N 27.40E*
96 G8 **Løkken Verk** Sør-Trøndelag, S Norway *63.07N 9.40E*
128 G16 **Loknya** Pskovskaya Oblast', W Russian Federation *56.48N 30.08E*
79 V15 **Loko** Nassarawa, C Nigeria *8.00N 7.48E*
79 U15 **Lokoja** Kogi, C Nigeria *7.47N 6.44E*
83 H17 **Lokori** Rift Valley, W Kenya *1.55N 36.03E*
79 R16 **Lokossa** S Benin *6.37N 1.43E*
120 I3 **Loksa** ***Ger.*** Loxa. Harjumaa, NW Estonia *59.36N 25.43E*
16 P3 **Loks Land** *island* Nunavut, NE Canada
82 C13 **Lol** ≈ S Sudan
78 K15 **Lola** Guinée-Forestière, SE Guinea *7.52N 8.28W*
37 Q5 **Lola, Mount** ▲ California, W USA *39.27N 120.20W*
83 H20 **Loliondo** Arusha, NE Tanzania *2.03S 35.46E*
97 H25 **Lolland** ***prev.*** Laaland. *island* S Denmark
195 O11 **Lolobau Island** *island* E PNG
175 T6 **Loloda Utara, Kepulauan** *island group* E Indonesia
81 E16 **Lolodorf** Sud, SW Cameroon *3.16N 10.49E*
116 G7 **Lom** ***prev.*** Lom-Palanka. Oblast Montana, NW Bulgaria *43.48N 23.16E*
116 G7 **Lom** ≈ Montana, NW Bulgaria
81 M19 **Lomami** ≈ C Dem. Rep. Congo (Zaire)
59 F17 **Lomas** Arequipa, SW Peru *15.29S 74.54W*
65 I23 **Lomas, Bahía** *bay* S Chile
63 D20 **Lomas de Zamora** Buenos Aires, E Argentina *34.52S 58.26W*
63 D20 **Loma Verde** Buenos Aires, E Argentina *35.16S 58.24W*
188 K4 **Lombadina** Western Australia *16.39S 122.54E*
108 E6 **Lombardia** ***Eng.*** Lombardy. ◐ *region* N Italy
Lombardy *see* Lombardia
104 M15 **Lombez** Gers, S France *43.28N 0.54E*
175 R15 **Lomblen, Pulau** *island* Nusa Tenggara, S Indonesia
181 W7 **Lombok Basin** *undersea feature* E Indian Ocean
175 Nn16 **Lombok, Pulau** *island* Nusa Tenggara, C Indonesia
175 Nn16 **Lombok, Selat** *strait* S Indonesia
79 Q16 **Lomé** ● (Togo) S Togo *6.08N 1.13E*
79 Q16 **Lomé** ✈ S Togo *6.08N 1.13E*
81 L19 **Lomela** Kasai Oriental, C Dem. Rep. Congo (Zaire) *2.19S 23.15E*
27 R9 **Lometa** Texas, SW USA *31.13N 98.23W*
81 F16 **Lomié** Est, SE Cameroon *3.09N 13.34E*
32 M8 **Lomira** Wisconsin, N USA *43.36N 88.26W*
97 K23 **Lomma** Skåne, S Sweden *55.40N 13.04E*
101 J16 **Lommel** Limburg, N Belgium *51.13N 5.19E*
98 I11 **Lomond, Loch** ◎ C Scotland, UK
207 R9 **Lomonosov Ridge** ***var.*** Harris Ridge, ***Rus.*** Khrebet Lomonsova. *undersea feature* Arctic Ocean
Lomonsova, Khrebet *see* Lomonosov Ridge
Lom-Palanka *see* Lom
Lomphat *see* Lumphăt
37 P14 **Lompoc** California, W USA *34.39N 120.29W*
178 Hh9 **Lom Sak** ***var.*** Muang Lom Sak. Phetchabun, C Thailand *16.45N 101.12E*
112 N9 **Łomża** ***Rus.*** Lomzha. Podlaskie, NE Poland *53.10N 22.04E*
Lomzha *see* Łomża
161 D14 **Lonāvale** ***prev.*** Lonaula. Mahārāshtra, W India *18.45N 73.27E*
65 G15 **Loncoche** Araucanía, C Chile *39.21S 72.34W*
65 H14 **Loncopue** Neuquén, W Argentina *38.06S 70.36W*
101 G17 **Londerzeel** Vlaams Brabant, C Belgium *51.00N 4.19E*
Londinium *see* London
12 E16 **London** Ontario, S Canada *42.59N 81.12W*
203 Y2 **London** Kiritimati, E Kiribati *02.00N 157.28W*
99 O22 **London** ***anc.*** Augusta, ***Lat.*** Londinium. ● (UK) SE England, UK *51.30N 0.10W*
23 N7 **London** Kentucky, S USA *37.06N 84.03W*
33 S13 **London** Ohio, NE USA *39.52N 83.27W*
27 Q10 **London** Texas, SW USA *30.40N 99.33W*
99 O22 **London City** ✈ SE England, UK *51.31N 0.07E*
99 E14 **Londonderry** ***var.*** Derry, ***Ir.*** Doire. NW Northern Ireland, UK *55.00N 7.19W*
99 F14 **Londonderry** *cultural region* NW Northern Ireland, UK
188 M2 **Londonderry, Cape** *headland* Western Australia *13.46S 126.56E*
65 H25 **Londonderry, Isla** *island* S Chile
45 O7 **Londres, Cayos** *reef* NE Nicaragua
62 I10 **Londrina** Paraná, S Brazil *23.18S 51.13W*
29 N13 **Lone Grove** Oklahoma, C USA *34.11N 97.15W*
12 E12 **Lonely Island** *island* Ontario, S Canada
37 T8 **Lone Mountain** ▲ Nevada, W USA *38.01N 117.28W*
27 V6 **Lone Oak** Texas, SW USA *33.02N 95.58W*
37 T11 **Lone Pine** California, W USA *36.36N 118.04W*
Lone Star State *see* Texas
85 D14 **Longa** Cuando Cubango, C Angola *14.37S 18.27E*
84 B12 **Longa** ≈ W Angola
85 E15 **Longa** ≈ SE Angola
169 W11 **Longang Shan** ▲▲ NE China
207 S4 **Longa, Proliv** ***Eng.*** Long Strait. *strait* NE Russian Federation
46 J13 **Long Bay** *bay* W Jamaica
23 V13 **Long Bay** *bay* North Carolina/South Carolina, E USA
37 T16 **Long Beach** California, W USA *33.46N 118.11W*
24 M9 **Long Beach** Mississippi, S USA *30.21N 89.09W*
20 L14 **Long Beach** Long Island, New York, NE USA *40.34N 73.38W*
34 F9 **Long Beach** Washington, NW USA *46.21N 124.03W*
20 K16 **Long Beach Island** *island* New Jersey, NE USA
67 M25 **Longbluff** *headland* SW Tristan da Cunha
25 U13 **Longboat Key** *island* Florida, SE USA
20 K15 **Long Branch** New Jersey, NE USA *40.18N 73.59W*
46 J5 **Long Cay** *island* SE Bahamas
167 P14 **Longchuan** ***prev.*** Laolong. Guangdong, S China *24.07N 115.10E*
Longchuan Jiang *see* Shweli
34 K12 **Long Creek** Oregon, NW USA *44.40N 119.07W*
165 W10 **Longde** Ningxia, N China *35.37N 106.07E*
191 P16 **Longford** Tasmania, SE Australia *41.41S 147.03E*
99 D17 **Longford** ***Ir.*** An Longfort. C Ireland *53.44N 7.49W*
99 E17 **Longford** ***Ir.*** An Longfort. *cultural region* C Ireland
167 P1 **Longhua** Hebei, E China *41.18N 117.43E*
175 Nn8 **Longiram** Borneo, C Indonesia *0.01S 115.36E*
46 J4 **Long Island** *island* C Bahamas
10 H8 **Long Island** *island* Nunavut, C Canada
194 K11 **Long Island** ***var.*** Arop Island. *island* N PNG
20 L14 **Long Island** *island* New York, NE USA
Long Island *see* Bermuda
20 M14 **Long Island Sound** *sound* NE USA
166 K13 **Long Jiang** ≈ S China
169 U7 **Longjiang** Heilongjiang, NE China *47.20N 123.09E*
169 Y10 **Longjing** ***var.*** Yanji. Jilin, NE China *42.48N 129.26E*
167 R4 **Longkou** Shandong, E China *37.40N 120.21E*
10 E11 **Longlac** Ontario, S Canada *49.46N 86.34W*
21 S1 **Long Lake** ◎ Maine, NE USA
33 O6 **Long Lake** ◎ Michigan, N USA
33 R5 **Long Lake** ◎ Michigan, N USA
31 N6 **Long Lake** ◎ North Dakota, N USA
32 J4 **Long Lake** ▣ Wisconsin, N USA
101 K23 **Longlier** Luxembourg, SE Belgium *49.51N 5.27E*
166 I13 **Longlin** ***var.*** Longlin Gezu Zizhixian. Guangxi Zhuangzu Zizhiqu, S China *24.46N 105.19E*
39 T3 **Longmont** Colorado, C USA *40.09N 105.07W*
31 N13 **Long Pine** Nebraska, C USA *42.32N 99.42W*
Longping *see* Luodian
12 F17 **Long Point** *headland* Ontario, S Canada *42.33N 80.15W*
12 K15 **Long Point** *headland* Ontario, SE Canada *43.56N 76.53W*
192 P10 **Long Point** *headland* North Island, NZ *39.07S 177.41E*
32 L2 **Long Point** *headland* Michigan, N USA *47.50N 89.09W*
12 G17 **Long Point Bay** *lake bay* Ontario, S Canada
31 T7 **Long Prairie** Minnesota, N USA *45.58N 94.52W*
11 S11 **Long Range Mountains** *hill range* Newfoundland, E Canada
67 H25 **Long Range Point** *headland* SE Saint Helena *16.00S 05.41W*
189 V8 **Longreach** Queensland, E Australia *23.31S 144.18E*
166 H7 **Longriba** Sichuan, C China *32.32N 102.20E*
166 L10 **Longshan** Hunan, S China *29.25N 109.28E*
39 S3 **Longs Peak** ▲ Colorado, C USA *40.15N 105.37W*
Long Strait *see* Longa, Proliv
104 K8 **Longué** Maine-et-Loire, NW France *47.23N 0.07W*
11 P11 **Longue-Pointe** Quebec, E Canada *50.20N 64.13W*
105 S4 **Longuyon** Meurthe-et-Moselle, NE France *49.25N 5.37E*
27 W7 **Longview** Texas, SW USA *32.30N 94.44W*
34 G10 **Longview** Washington, NW USA *46.08N 122.56W*
67 H25 **Longwood** C Saint Helena
27 P7 **Longworth** Texas, SW USA *32.37N 100.20W*
105 S3 **Longwy** Meurthe-et-Moselle, NE France *49.31N 5.46E*
165 V11 **Longxi** Gansu, C China *35.00N 104.34E*
178 J14 **Long Xuyên** ***var.*** Longxuyen. An Giang, S Vietnam *10.22N 105.25E*
167 Q13 **Longyan** Fujian, SE China *25.06N 117.01E*
94 O3 **Longyearbyen** ○ (Svalbard) Spitsbergen, W Svalbard *78.12N 15.39E*
166 J15 **Longzhou** Guangxi Zhuangzu Zizhiqu, S China *22.22N 106.46E*
102 F12 **Löningen** Niedersachsen, NW Germany *52.43N 7.42E*
29 V11 **Lonoke** Arkansas, C USA *34.46N 91.54W*
97 L21 **Lönsboda** Skåne, S Sweden *56.24N 14.19E*
105 S9 **Lons-le-Saunier** ***anc.*** Ledo Salinarius. Jura, E France *46.40N 5.31E*
33 O15 **Loogootee** Indiana, N USA *38.40N 86.54W*
33 Q9 **Looking Glass River** ≈ Michigan, N USA
23 X11 **Lookout, Cape** *headland* North Carolina, SE USA *34.36N 76.31W*
41 O6 **Lookout Ridge** *ridge* Alaska, USA
189 N11 **Loongana** Western Australia *30.53S 127.15E*
101 I14 **Loon op Zand** Noord-Brabant, S Netherlands *51.37N 5.04E*
99 A19 **Loop Head** ***Ir.*** Ceann Léime. *headland* W Ireland *52.55N 10.33W*
111 V4 **Loosdorf** Niederösterreich, NE Austria *48.13N 15.25E*
164 G10 **Lop** Xinjiang Uygur Zizhiqu, NW China *37.06N 80.12E*
114 J11 **Lopare** Republika Srpska, NE Bosnia and Herzegovina *44.39N 18.49E*
Lopatichi *see* Lapatsichy
131 Q15 **Lopatin** Respublika Dagestan, SW Russian Federation *43.52N 47.40E*
131 P7 **Lopatino** Penzenskaya Oblast', W Russian Federation *52.38N 45.46E*
178 Hh10 **Lop Buri** ***var.*** Loburi. Lop Buri, C Thailand *14.46N 100.40E*
27 R16 **Lopeno** Texas, SW USA *26.42N 99.06W*
197 D13 **Lopevi** ***var.*** Ulveah. *Island* C Vanuatu
81 C18 **Lopez, Cap** *headland* W Gabon *0.39S 8.44E*
100 I12 **Lopik** Utrecht, C Netherlands *51.58N 4.57E*
Lop Nor *see* Lop Nur
164 M7 **Lop Nur** ***var.*** Lob Nor, Lop Nor, Lo-pu Po. *seasonal lake* NW China
Lopnur *see* Yuli
81 K17 **Lopori** ≈ NW Dem. Rep. Congo (Zaire)
100 O5 **Loppersum** Groningen, NE Netherlands *53.19N 6.45E*
94 I8 **Lopphavet** *sound* N Norway
Lo-pu Po *see* Lop Nur
Lora *see* Lowrah
190 F3 **Lora Creek** *seasonal river* South Australia
106 K13 **Lora del Río** Andalucía, S Spain *37.39N 5.31W*
154 M11 **Lora, Hāmūn-i** *wetland* SW Pakistan
33 T11 **Lorain** Ohio, N USA *41.27N 82.10W*
27 O7 **Loraine** Texas, SW USA *32.24N 100.42W*
33 R13 **Loramie, Lake** ▣ Ohio, N USA
107 Q13 **Lorca** ***Ar.*** Lurka; ***anc.*** Eliocroca, ***Lat.*** Illur co. Murcia, S Spain *37.40N 1.40W*
199 I12 **Lord Howe Island** *island* E Australia
Lord Howe Island *see* Ontong Java Atoll
183 O10 **Lord Howe Rise** *undersea feature* SW Pacific Ocean
199 I12 **Lord Howe Seamounts** *undersea feature* W Pacific Ocean
39 P15 **Lordsburg** New Mexico, SW USA *32.19N 108.42W*
194 K8 **Lorengau** ***var.*** Lorungau. Manus Island, N PNG *2.03S 147.16E*
27 N5 **Lorenzo** Texas, SW USA *33.40N 101.31W*
148 K7 **Lorestān** ***off.*** Ostān-e Lorestān, ***var.*** Luristan. ◐ *province* W Iran
59 M17 **Loreto** Beni, N Bolivia *15.19S 64.40W*
108 J12 **Loreto** Marche, C Italy *43.25N 13.37E*
42 F8 **Loreto** Baja California Sur, W Mexico *25.59N 111.21W*
42 M11 **Loreto** Zacatecas, C Mexico *22.15N 102.00W*
58 E9 **Loreto** ***off.*** Departamento de Loreto. ◐ *department* NE Peru
83 K18 **Lorian Swamp** *swamp* E Kenya
56 E6 **Lorica** Córdoba, NW Colombia *9.13N 75.49W*
104 G7 **Lorient** ***prev.*** l'Orient. Morbihan, NW France *47.45N 3.22W*
113 K22 **Lőrinci** Heves, NE Hungary *47.43N 19.39E*
12 G11 **Loring** Ontario, S Canada *45.55N 79.59W*
35 V6 **Loring** Montana, NW USA *48.49N 107.48W*
105 R13 **Loriol-sur-Drôme** Drôme, E France *44.46N 4.51E*
23 U12 **Loris** South Carolina, SE USA *34.03N 78.53W*
59 I18 **Loriscota, Laguna** ◎ S Peru
191 N13 **Lorne** Victoria, SE Australia *38.33S 143.57E*
98 G11 **Lorn, Firth of** *inlet* W Scotland, UK
Loro Sae *see* East Timor
103 F24 **Lörrach** Baden-Württemberg, S Germany *47.37N 7.40E*
105 T5 **Lorraine** ◐ *region* NE France
Lorungau *see* Lorengau
96 L11 **Los** Gävleborg, C Sweden *61.42N 15.15E*
37 P14 **Los Alamos** California, W USA *34.44N 120.16W*
39 S10 **Los Alamos** New Mexico, SW USA *35.52N 106.17W*
44 F5 **Los Amates** Izabal, E Guatemala *15.16N 89.07W*
37 S15 **Los Angeles** California, W USA *34.03N 118.14W*
37 S15 **Los Angeles** ✈ California, W USA *33.54N 118.24W*
65 G14 **Los Ángeles** Bío Bío, C Chile *37.29S 72.18W*
37 T13 **Los Angeles Aqueduct** *aqueduct* California, W USA
Losanna *see* Lausanne
65 H20 **Los Antiguos** Santa Cruz, SW Argentina *46.36S 71.31W*
201 Q16 **Losap Atoll** *atoll* C Micronesia
37 P10 **Los Banos** California, W USA *37.00N 120.39W*
106 K16 **Los Barrios** Andalucía, S Spain *36.10N 5.30W*
64 L5 **Los Blancos** Salta, N Argentina *23.39S 62.36W*
44 L12 **Los Chiles** Alajuela, NW Costa Rica *11.00N 84.42W*
107 O2 **Los Corrales de Buelna** Cantabria, N Spain *43.15N 4.04W*
27 T17 **Los Fresnos** Texas, SW USA *26.03N 97.28W*
37 N9 **Los Gatos** California, W USA *37.13N 121.58W*
112 O11 **Łosice** Mazowieckie, E Poland *52.13N 22.42E*
114 B11 **Lošinj** ***Ger.*** Lussin, ***It.*** Lussino. *island* W Croatia
Los Jardines *see* Ngetik Atoll
65 G15 **Los Lagos** Los Lagos, C Chile *39.52S 72.52W*
65 F17 **Los Lagos** ***off.*** Región de los Lagos. ◐ *region* C Chile
Loslau *see* Wodzisław Śląski
66 N11 **Los Llanos** ***var.*** Los Llanos de Aridane. La Palma, Islas Canarias, Spain, NE Atlantic Ocean *28.39N 17.54W*
Los Llanos de Aridane *see* Los Llanos
39 R11 **Los Lunas** New Mexico, SW USA *34.48N 106.43W*
65 I16 **Los Menucos** Río Negro, C Argentina *40.52S 68.07W*
42 H8 **Los Mochis** Sinaloa, C Mexico *25.48N 108.57W*
37 N4 **Los Molinos** California, W USA *40.00N 122.05W*
106 M9 **Los Navalmorales** Castilla-La Mancha, C Spain *39.43N 4.37W*
27 S15 **Los Olmos Creek** ≈ Texas, SW USA
Losonc/Losontz *see* Lučenec
178 Jj5 **Lô, Sông** ***Chin.*** Panlong Jiang. ≈ China/Vietnam
46 B5 **Los Palacios** Pinar del Río, W Cuba *22.30N 83.19W*
106 K14 **Los Palacios y Villafranca** Andalucía, S Spain *37.10N 5.55W*
175 Ss16 **Lospalos** E East Timor *8.28S 126.56E*
39 R12 **Los Pinos Mountains** ▲▲ New Mexico, SW USA
39 R11 **Los Ranchos De Albuquerque** New Mexico, SW USA *35.09N 106.37W*
42 M14 **Los Reyes** Michoacán de Ocampo, SW Mexico *19.36N 102.29W*
58 B7 **Los Ríos** ◐ *province* C Ecuador
66 O11 **Los Rodeos** ✈ (Santa Cruz de Ternerife) Tenerife, Islas Canarias, Spain, NE Atlantic Ocean *28.27N 16.19W*
56 L4 **Los Roques, Islas** *island group* N Venezuela
45 S17 **Los Santos** Los Santos, S Panama *7.55N 80.25W*
45 S17 **Los Santos** ***off.*** Provincia de Los Santos. ◐ *province* S Panama
Los Santos *see* Los Santos de Maimona
106 J12 **Los Santos de Maimona** ***var.*** Los Santos. Extremadura, W Spain *38.27N 6.22W*
100 P10 **Losser** Overijssel, E Netherlands *52.16N 7.01E*
98 J8 **Lossiemouth** NE Scotland, UK *57.43N 3.18W*
63 B14 **Los Tábanos** Santa Fe, C Argentina *28.27S 59.57W*
56 J4 **Los Taques** Falcón, N Venezuela *11.49N 70.16W*
12 G11 **Lost Channel** Ontario, S Canada *45.54N 80.20W*
56 L5 **Los Teques** Miranda, N Venezuela *10.23N 67.01W*
37 Q12 **Lost Hills** California, W USA *35.35N 119.40W*
38 I7 **Lost Peak** ▲ Utah, W USA *37.30N 113.57W*
35 P11 **Lost Trail Pass** *pass* Montana, NW USA *45.40N 113.58W*
195 N15 **Losuia** Kiriwina Island, SE PNG *8.30S 151.04E*
64 G10 **Los Vilos** Coquimbo, C Chile *31.52S 71.28W*
107 N10 **Los Yébenes** Castilla-La Mancha, C Spain *39.34N 3.52W*
105 N13 **Lot** ◐ *department* S France
105 N13 **Lot** ≈ S France
65 F14 **Lota** Bío Bío, C Chile *37.08S 73.07W*
83 G15 **Lotagipi Swamp** *wetland* Kenya/Sudan
104 K14 **Lot-et-Garonne** ◐ *department* SW France
85 K21 **Lothair** Mpumalanga, NE South Africa *26.22S 30.25E*
35 R7 **Lothair** Montana, NW USA *48.28N 111.15W*
81 L20 **Loto** Kasai Oriental, C Dem. Rep. Congo (Zaire) *2.48S 22.30E*
198 B8 **Lotofagā** Upolu, SE Samoa *13.57S 171.51W*
110 E10 **Lötschbergtunnel** *tunnel* Valais, SW Switzerland
27 T9 **Lott** Texas, SW USA *31.12N 97.02W*
128 H3 **Lotta** ***var.*** Lutto. ≈ Finland/Russian Federation
192 Q7 **Lottin Point** *headland* North Island, NZ *37.26S 178.07E*
Lötzen *see* Giżycko
Loualaba *see* Lualaba
178 I6 **Louangnamtha** ***var.*** Luong Nam Tha. Louang Namtha, N Laos *20.55N 101.24E*
178 I7 **Louangphabang** ***var.*** Louangphrabang, Luang Prabang. Louangphabang, N Laos *19.51N 102.08E*
Louangphrabang *see* Louangphabang
204 H5 **Loubet Coast** *physical region* Antarctica
Loubomo *see* Dolisie
Louch *see* Loukhi
104 H6 **Loudéac** Côtes d'Armor, NW France *48.10N 2.45W*
166 M11 **Loudi** Hunan, S China *27.51N 111.58E*
81 F21 **Loudima** La Bouenza, S Congo *4.06S 13.04E*
22 M9 **Loudon** Tennessee, S USA *35.43N 84.19W*
33 T12 **Loudonville** Ohio, N USA *40.38N 82.13W*
104 L8 **Loudun** Vienne, W France *47.01N 0.04E*
104 K7 **Loué** Sarthe, NW France *48.00N 0.14W*
78 G10 **Louga** NW Senegal *15.36N 16.14W*
99 M19 **Loughborough** C England, UK *52.46N 1.10W*
99 C18 **Loughrea** ***Ir.*** Baile Locha Riach. W Ireland *53.12N 8.34W*
105 S9 **Louhans** Saône-et-Loire, C France *46.38N 5.12E*
23 P5 **Louisa** Kentucky, S USA *38.06N 82.40W*
23 V5 **Louisa** Virginia, NE USA *38.02N 78.00W*
23 V9 **Louisburg** North Carolina, SE USA *36.05N 78.18W*
27 U12 **Louise** Texas, SW USA *29.07N 96.22W*
13 P11 **Louiseville** Quebec, SE Canada *46.15N 72.54W*
195 Q17 **Louisiade Archipelago** *island group* SE PNG
29 W3 **Louisiana** Missouri, C USA *39.25N 91.03W*
24 G8 **Louisiana** ***off.*** State of Louisiana; also known as Creole State, Pelican State. ◐ *state* S USA
194 K9 **Lou Island** *island* N PNG
85 K19 **Louis Trichardt** Northern, NE South Africa *23.06S 29.55E*
25 V4 **Louisville** Georgia, SE USA *33.00N 82.24W*
32 M15 **Louisville** Illinois, N USA *38.46N 88.32W*
22 K5 **Louisville** Kentucky, S USA *38.15N 85.45W*
24 M4 **Louisville** Mississippi, S USA *33.07N 89.03W*
31 S15 **Louisville** Nebraska, C USA *41.00N 96.09W*
199 Jj12 **Louisville Ridge** *undersea feature* S Pacific Ocean
128 J6 **Loukhi** ***var.*** Louch. Respublika Kareliya, NW Russian Federation *66.05N 33.04E*
81 H19 **Loukoléla** Cuvette, E Congo *1.04S 17.10E*
106 G14 **Loulé** Faro, S Portugal *37.07N 8.01W*
113 C16 **Louny** ***Ger.*** Laun. Ústecký kraj NW Czech Republic *50.22N 13.49E*
31 O15 **Loup City** Nebraska, C USA *41.16N 98.58W*
31 P15 **Loup River** ≈ Nebraska, C USA
13 S9 **Loup, Rivière du** ≈ Quebec, SE Canada
10 K7 **Loups Marins, Lacs des** *lakes* Quebec, NE Canada
104 K16 **Lourdes** Hautes-Pyrénées, S France *43.06N 0.03W*
Lourenço Marques *see* Maputo
106 F11 **Loures** Lisboa, C Portugal *38.49N 9.10W*
106 F10 **Lourinhã** Lisboa, C Portugal *39.13N 9.19W*
117 C16 **Loúros** ≈ W Greece
106 G8 **Lousã** Coimbra, N Portugal *40.07N 8.15W*
166 M10 **Lou Shui** ≈ C China
191 O5 **Louth** New South Wales, SE Australia *30.34S 145.07E*
99 O18 **Louth** E England, UK *53.18N 0.00W*
99 F17 **Louth** ***Ir.*** Lú. *cultural region* NE Ireland
117 H15 **Loutrá** Kentrikí Makedonía, N Greece *39.55N 23.37E*
117 G19 **Loutráki** Pelopónnisos, S Greece *37.55N 22.55E*
Louvain *see* Leuven
101 H19 **Louvain-la Neuve** Wallon Brabant, C Belgium *50.39N 4.36E*
12 J8 **Louvicourt** Quebec, SE Canada *48.04N 77.22W*
104 M4 **Louviers** Eure, N France *49.13N 1.10E*
32 K14 **Lou Yaeger, Lake** ▣ Illinois, N USA
95 J15 **Lövånger** Västerbotten, N Sweden *64.22N 21.19E*
128 J14 **Lovat'** ≈ NW Russian Federation
115 J17 **Lovćen** ▲ S Yugoslavia *42.22N 18.49E*
116 I8 **Lovech** Lovech, N Bulgaria *43.09N 24.42E*
116 I9 **Lovech** ◐ *province* N Bulgaria
27 V9 **Lovelady** Texas, SW USA *31.07N 95.27W*
39 T3 **Loveland** Colorado, C USA *40.24N 105.04W*
35 U12 **Lovell** Wyoming, C USA *44.50N 108.23W*
Lovello, Monte *see* Grosser Löffler
37 S4 **Lovelock** Nevada, W USA *40.11N 118.30W*
108 E7 **Lovere** Lombardia, N Italy *45.51N 10.06E*
32 L10 **Loves Park** Illinois, N USA *42.19N 89.03W*
28 M2 **Lovewell Reservoir** ▣ Kansas, C USA
95 M19 **Loviisa** ***Swe.*** Lovisa. Etelä-Suomi, S Finland *60.27N 26.15E*
39 V15 **Loving** New Mexico, SW USA *32.17N 104.06W*
23 U6 **Lovingston** Virginia, NE USA *37.45N 78.47W*
39 V14 **Lovington** New Mexico, SW USA *32.56N 103.21W*
Lovisa *see* Loviisa
113 C15 **Lovosice** ***Ger.*** Lobositz. Ústecký Kraj, NW Czech Republic *50.29N 14.01E*
128 K4 **Lovozero** Murmanskaya Oblast', NW Russian Federation *68.00N 35.03E*
128 K4 **Lovozero, Ozero** ◎ NW Russian Federation
114 B9 **Lovran** ***It.*** Laurana. Primorje-Gorski Kotar, NW Croatia *45.16N 14.15E*
118 E11 **Lovrin** ***Ger.*** Lowrin. Timiş, W Romania *45.58N 20.48E*
84 E10 **Lóvua** Lunda Norte, NE Angola *7.21S 20.09E*
84 G12 **Lóvua** Moxico, E Angola *11.33S 23.35E*
67 D25 **Low Bay** *bay* East Falkland, Falkland Islands
15 M6 **Low, Cape** *headland* Nunavut, E Canada *63.05N 85.27W*
35 N10 **Lowell** Idaho, NW USA *46.07N 115.36W*
21 O10 **Lowell** Massachusetts, NE USA *42.37N 71.19W*
Löwen *see* Leuven
Löwenberg in Schlesien *see* Lwówek Śląski
Lower Austria *see* Niederösterreich
Lower Bann *see* Bann
Lower California *see* Baja California
Lower Danube *see* Niederösterreich
193 L14 **Lower Hutt** Wellington, North Island, NZ *41.13S 174.51E*
41 N11 **Lower Kalskag** Alaska, USA *61.30N 160.28W*
37 O1 **Lower Klamath Lake** ◎ California, W USA
37 Q2 **Lower Lake** ◎ California/Nevada, W USA
99 E15 **Lower Lough Erne** ◎ SW Northern Ireland, UK
Lower Lusatia *see* Niederlausitz
Lower Normandy *see* Basse-Normandie, France
8 K9 **Lower Post** British Columbia, W Canada *59.53N 128.19W*
31 T4 **Lower Red Lake** ◎ Minnesota, N USA
Lower Rhine *see* Neder Rijn
Lower Saxony *see* Niedersachsen
Lower Tunguska *see* Nizhnyaya Tunguska
99 Q19 **Lowestoft** E England, UK *52.28N 1.45E*
155 Q5 **Lowgar** ***var.*** Logar. ◐ *province* E Afghanistan
190 H7 **Low Hill** South Australia *32.17S 136.46E*
112 K12 **Łowicz** Łódzkie, C Poland *52.06N 19.55E*
35 N13 **Lowman** Idaho, NW USA *44.04N 115.37W*
155 P8 **Lowrah** ***var.*** Lora. ≈ SE Afghanistan
Lowrin *see* Lovrin
191 N17 **Low Rocky Point** *headland* Tasmania, SE Australia *42.59S 145.28E*
20 I8 **Lowville** New York, NE USA *43.47N 75.29W*
Loxa *see* Loksa
190 K9 **Loxton** South Australia *34.30S 140.36E*
83 G21 **Loya** Tabora, C Tanzania *4.57S 33.53E*
32 K6 **Loyal** Wisconsin, N USA *44.45N 90.30W*
20 G13 **Loyalsock Creek** ≈ Pennsylvania, NE USA
37 Q5 **Loyalton** California, W USA *39.39N 120.16W*
Lo-yang *see* Luoyang
197 J6 **Loyauté, Îles** *island group* S New Caledonia
Loyev *see* Loyew
121 O20 **Loyew** ***Rus.*** Loyev. Homyel'skaya Voblasts', SE Belarus *51.55N 30.48E*
129 S13 **Loyno** Kirovskaya Oblast', NW Russian Federation *59.44N 52.42E*
105 P13 **Lozère** ◐ *department* S France
105 Q14 **Lozère, Mont** ▲ S France *44.27N 3.44E*
114 J11 **Loznica** Serbia, W Yugoslavia *44.32N 19.13E*
119 V7 **Lozova** ***Rus.*** Lozovaya. Kharkivs'ka Oblast', E Ukraine *48.54N 36.22E*
Lozovaya *see* Lozova
107 N7 **Lozoyuela** Madrid, C Spain *40.55N 3.36W*
Lœvvajok *see* Leavvajohka
Lu *see* Shandong, China
Lú *see* Louth, Ireland
84 F12 **Luacano** Moxico, E Angola *11.19S 21.30E*
81 N21 **Lualaba** ***Fr.*** Loualaba. ≈ SE Dem. Rep. Congo (Zaire)
85 H14 **Luampa** Western, NW Zambia *15.02S 24.27E*
85 H15 **Luampa Kuta** Western, W Zambia *15.22S 24.40E*
167 P8 **Lu'an** Anhui, E China *31.46N 116.31E*
106 K2 **Luanco** Asturias, N Spain *43.36N 5.48W*
84 A11 **Luanda** ***var.*** Loanda, ***Port.*** São Paulo de Loanda. ● (Angola) Luanda, NW Angola *8.48S 13.17E*
84 A11 **Luanda** ◐ *province* NW Angola
84 A11 **Luanda** ✈ Luanda, NW Angola *8.49S 13.16E*
84 D12 **Luando** ≈ C Angola
Luang *see* Tapi, Mae Nam
85 G14 **Luanginga** ***var.*** Luanguinga. ≈ Angola/Zambia
178 Gg15 **Luang, Khao** ▲ SW Thailand *8.21N 99.46E*
Luang Prabang *see* Louangphabang
178 I8 **Luang Prabang Range** ***Th.*** Thiukhaoluang Phrahang. ▲▲ Laos/Thailand
178 H16 **Luang, Thale** *lagoon* S Thailand
Luangua, Rio *see* Luangwa
84 E11 **Luangue** ≈ NE Angola
Luanguinga *see* Luanginga
85 K15 **Luangwa** ***var.*** Aruângua. Lusaka, C Zambia *15.34S 30.23E*
85 K14 **Luangwa** ***var.*** Aruângua, Rio Luangua. ≈ Mozambique/Zambia
167 Q2 **Luan He** ≈ E China
202 G11 **Luaniva, Île** *island* E Wallis and Futuna
167 P2 **Luanping** ***var.*** Anjiangying. Hebei, E China *40.55N 117.19E*
84 J13 **Luanshya** Copperbelt, C Zambia *13.09S 28.24E*
64 K13 **Luan Toro** La Pampa, C Argentina *36.14S 65.08W*
167 Q2 **Luanxian** ***var.*** Luan Xian. Hebei, E China *39.47N 118.46E*
84 J12 **Luapula** ◐ *province* N Zambia
81 O25 **Luapula** ≈ Dem. Rep. Congo (Zaire)/Zambia
106 J2 **Luarca** Asturias, N Spain *43.33N 6.31W*
174 Ll7 **Luar, Danau** ◎ Borneo, N Indonesia
81 L25 **Luashi** Katanga, S Dem. Rep. Congo (Zaire) *10.54S 23.55E*
84 G12 **Luau** ***Port.*** Vila Teixeira de Sousa. Moxico, NE Angola *10.43S 22.07E*
81 C16 **Luba** ***prev.*** San Carlos. Isla de Bioco, NW Equatorial Guinea *3.26N 8.36E*
44 F4 **Lubaantun** *ruins* Toledo, S Belize *16.18N 88.57W*
113 P16 **Lubaczów** ***var.*** Lúbaczów. Podkarpackie, SE Poland *50.09N 23.08E*
Lubale *see* Lubalo
84 E11 **Lubalo** Lunda Norte, NE Angola *9.02S 19.11E*
84 E11 **Lubalo** ***var.*** Lubale. ≈ Angola/Zaire
120 J9 **Lubāna** Madona, E Latvia *56.55N 29.43E*
Lubānas Ezers *see* Lubāns
179 P11 **Lubang Island** *island* N Philippines
85 B15 **Lubango** ***Port.*** Sá da Bandeira. Huíla, SW Angola *14.54S 13.33E*
120 J9 **Lubāns** ***var.*** Lubānas Ezers. ◎ E Latvia
81 M21 **Lubao** Kasai Oriental, C Dem. Rep. Congo (Zaire) *5.21S 25.42E*
112 O13 **Lubartów** ***Ger.*** Qumälisch. Lubelskie, E Poland *51.26N 22.36E*
102 G13 **Lübbecke** Nordrhein-Westfalen, NW Germany *52.18N 8.37E*
102 O13 **Lübben** Brandenburg, E Germany *51.55N 13.51E*
103 P14 **Lübbenau** Brandenburg, E Germany *51.52N 13.57E*
27 N5 **Lubbock** Texas, SW USA *33.34N 101.51W*
Lubcz *see* Lyubcha
21 U6 **Lubec** Maine, NE USA *44.49N 67.00W*
102 K9 **Lübeck** Schleswig-Holstein, N Germany *53.52N 10.40E*
102 K8 **Lübecker Bucht** *bay* N Germany
81 M21 **Lubefu** Kasai Oriental, C Dem. Rep. Congo (Zaire) *4.43S 24.25E*
113 O14 **Lubelska, Wyżyna** *plateau* SE Poland
113 O14 **Lubelskie** ◐ *province* E Poland
Lubembe *see* Luembe
Lüben *see* Lubin
150 H9 **Lubenka** Zapadnyy Kazakhstan, W Kazakhstan *50.27N 54.07E*
81 P18 **Lubero** Nord Kivu, E Dem. Rep. Congo (Zaire) *0.10S 29.12E*
81 L22 **Lubi** ≈ S Dem. Rep. Congo (Zaire)
Lubiana *see* Ljubljana
112 J11 **Lubień Kujawski** Kujawskio-pomorskie, C Poland *52.25N 19.10E*
69 T11 **Lubilandji** ≈ S Dem. Rep. Congo (Zaire)
112 F13 **Lubin** ***Ger.*** Lüben. Dolnośląskie, SW Poland *51.22N 16.12E*
113 O14 **Lublin** ***Rus.*** Lyublin. Lubelskie, E Poland *51.15N 22.33E*
113 J15 **Lubliniec** Śląskie, S Poland *50.40N 18.40E*
Lubnān, Jabal *see* Liban, Jebel
119 R5 **Lubny** Poltavs'ka Oblast', NE Ukraine *50.00N 33.00E*
Luboml *see* Lyuboml'
112 G11 **Luboń** ***Ger.*** Peterhof. Wielkolpolskie, C Poland *52.22N 16.54E*
112 D12 **Lubsko** ***Ger.*** Sommerfeld. Lubuskie, W Poland *51.46N 14.56E*
81 N24 **Lubudi** Katanga, SE Dem. Rep. Congo (Zaire) *9.57S 25.58E*

◆ Country
● Country Capital
◇ Dependent Territory
○ Dependent Territory Capital
◐ Administrative Region
✈ International Airport
▲ Mountain
▲▲ Mountain Range
Volcano
≈ River
◎ Lake
▣ Reservoir

LUBUKLINGGAU – MACERATA

174 Hh11 **Lubuklinggau** Sumatera, W Indonesia 3.15S 102.51E
81 N25 **Lubumbashi** prev. Élisabethville. Katanga, SE Dem. Rep. Congo (Zaire) 11.39S 27.31E
85 I14 **Lubungu** Central, C Zambia 14.28S 26.30E
112 E12 **Lubuskie** ⬖ province W Poland
81 N18 **Lubutu** Maniema, E Dem. Rep. Congo (Zaire) 0.42S 26.31E
Luca see Lucca
84 C11 **Lucala** ~ W Angola
12 E16 **Lucan** Ontario, S Canada 43.10N 81.22W
99 F18 **Lucan** Ir. Leamhcán. E Ireland 53.22N 6.27W
Lucanian Mountains see Lucano, Appennino
109 M18 **Lucano, Appennino** Eng. Lucanian Mountains. ▲▲ S Italy
84 F11 **Lucapa** var. Lukapa. Lunda Norte, NE Angola 8.23S 20.42E
31 V15 **Lucas** Iowa, C USA 41.01N 93.26W
63 C18 **Lucas González** Entre Ríos, E Argentina 32.25S 59.33W
67 C25 **Lucas Point** headland West Falkland, Falkland Islands 52.10S 60.22W
33 S15 **Lucasville** Ohio, N USA 38.52N 83.00W
108 F11 **Lucca** anc. Luca. Toscana, C Italy 43.49N 10.30E
46 H12 **Lucea** W Jamaica 18.26N 78.10W
99 H15 **Luce Bay** inlet SW Scotland, UK
24 M8 **Lucedale** Mississippi, S USA 30.55N 88.35W
179 Pp11 **Lucena** off. Lucena City. Luzon, N Philippines 13.57N 121.38E
106 M14 **Lucena** Andalucía, S Spain 37.25N 4.28W
107 S8 **Lucena del Cid** País Valenciano, E Spain 40.07N 0.15W
113 D15 **Lučenec** Ger. Losontz, Hung. Losonc. Banskobystrický Kraj, C Slovakia 48.21N 19.36E
Lucentum see Alicante
109 M16 **Lucera** Puglia, SE Italy 41.30N 15.19E
Lucerna/Lucerne see Luzern
Lucerne, Lake of see Vierwaldstätter See
42 J4 **Lucero** Chihuahua, N Mexico 30.51N 106.27W
127 Nn17 **Luchegorsk** Primorskiy Kray, SE Russian Federation 46.26N 134.10E
107 Q13 **Luchena** ~ SE Spain
84 N13 **Lucheringo** var. Luchulingo. ~ N Mozambique
Luchesa see Luchosa
Luchin see Luchyn
120 N13 **Luchosa** Rus. Luchesa. ~ N Belarus
Luchow see Hefei
102 K11 **Lüchow** Mecklenburg-Vorpommern, N Germany 52.57N 11.10E
Luchulingo see Lucheringo
121 N17 **Luchyn** Rus. Luchin. Homyel'skaya Voblasts', SE Belarus 53.01N 30.01E
57 U11 **Lucie Rivier** ~ W Surinam
190 K11 **Lucindale** South Australia 36.57S 140.20E
175 T13 **Lucipara, Kepulauan** island group E Indonesia
85 A14 **Lucira** Namibe, SW Angola 13.51S 12.35E
Łuck see Luts'k
103 O14 **Luckau** Brandenburg, E Germany 51.50N 13.42E
102 N13 **Luckenwalde** Brandenburg, E Germany 52.06N 13.11E
12 E15 **Lucknow** Ontario, S Canada 43.58N 81.30W
158 L12 **Lucknow** var. Lakhnau. Uttar Pradesh, N India 26.49N 80.54E
104 J10 **Luçon** Vendée, NW France 46.27N 1.10W
46 I7 **Lucrecia, Cabo** headland E Cuba 21.00N 75.34W
84 F13 **Lucusse** Moxico, E Angola 12.32S 20.46E
Lüda see Dalian
116 M9 **Luda Kamchiya** ~ E Bulgaria
Ludasch see Luduş
116 I10 **Luda Yana** ~ C Bulgaria
114 F7 **Ludbreg** Varaždin, N Croatia 46.15N 16.36E
31 P7 **Ludden** North Dakota, N USA 45.58N 98.07W
103 F15 **Lüdenscheid** Nordrhein-Westfalen, W Germany 51.13N 7.37E
85 C21 **Lüderitz** prev. Angra Pequena. Karas, SW Namibia 26.37S 15.10E
158 H8 **Ludhiāna** Punjab, N India 30.55N 75.52E
33 O7 **Ludington** Michigan, N USA 43.58N 86.27W
99 K20 **Ludlow** W England, UK 52.19N 2.27W
37 W14 **Ludlow** California, W USA 34.43N 116.07W
30 J7 **Ludlow** South Dakota, N USA 45.48N 103.21W
20 M9 **Ludlow** Vermont, NE USA 43.24N 72.39W
116 L7 **Ludogorie** physical region NE Bulgaria
25 W6 **Ludowici** Georgia, SE USA 31.42N 81.44W
Ludsan see Ludza
118 I10 **Luduş** Ger. Ludasch, Hung. Marosludas. Mureş, C Romania 46.27N 24.04E
97 M14 **Ludvika** Dalarna, C Sweden 60.07N 15.13E
103 H21 **Ludwigsburg** Baden-Württemberg, SW Germany 48.54N 9.12E
102 O13 **Ludwigsfelde** Brandenburg, NE Germany 52.17N 13.15E
103 G20 **Ludwigshafen** var. Ludwigshafen am Rhein. Rheinland-Pfalz, W Germany 49.28N 8.24E
Ludwigshafen am Rhein see Ludwigshafen
103 L20 **Ludwigskanal** canal SE Germany
102 L10 **Ludwigslust** Mecklenburg-Vorpommern, N Germany 53.19N 11.28E
120 K10 **Ludza** Ger. Ludsan. Ludza, E Latvia 56.32N 27.41E
81 K21 **Luebo** Kasai Occidental, SW Dem. Rep. Congo (Zaire) 5.19S 21.21E
27 Q6 **Lueders** Texas, SW USA 32.46N 99.38W
81 N20 **Lueki** Maniema, C Dem. Rep. Congo (Zaire) 3.25S 25.49E
84 F10 **Luembe** var. Lubembe. ~ Angola/Dem. Rep. Congo (Zaire)
84 E13 **Luena** var. Lwena, Port. Luso. Moxico, E Angola 11.46S 19.52E
81 M24 **Luena** Katanga, SE Dem. Rep. Congo (Zaire) 9.28S 25.45E
84 K12 **Luena** Northern, NE Zambia 10.31S 30.12E
84 F13 **Luena** ~ E Angola
85 F16 **Luengue** ~ SE Angola
69 V13 **Luenha** ~ W Mozambique
85 G15 **Lueti** ~ Angola/Zambia
166 J7 **Lüeyang** Shaanxi, C China 33.12N 106.31E
167 P14 **Lufeng** Guangdong, S China 22.58N 115.36E
81 N24 **Lufira** ~ SE Dem. Rep. Congo (Zaire)
81 N25 **Lufira, Lac de Retenue de la** var. Lac Tshangalele. ◎ SE Dem. Rep. Congo (Zaire)
27 W8 **Lufkin** Texas, SW USA 31.20N 94.43W
84 L11 **Lufubu** ~ N Zambia
128 G14 **Luga** Leningradskaya Oblast', NW Russian Federation 58.43N 29.46E
128 G13 **Luga** ~ NW Russian Federation
Luganer See see Lugano, Lago di
110 H11 **Lugano** Ger. Lauis. Ticino, S Switzerland 46.01N 8.57E
110 H12 **Lugano, Lago di** var. Ceresio, Ger. Luganer See. ◎ S Switzerland
Lugansk see Luhans'k
197 B12 **Luganville** Espiritu Santo, C Vanuatu 15.31S 167.12E
Lugdunum see Lyon
Lugdunum Batavorum see Leiden
85 O15 **Lugela** Zambézia, NE Mozambique 16.27S 36.47E
85 O16 **Lugela** ~ C Mozambique
84 P13 **Lugenda, Rio** ~ N Mozambique
Luggarus see Locarno
Lugh Ganana see Luuq
99 G19 **Lugnaquillia Mountain** Ir. Log na Coille. ▲ E Ireland 52.58N 6.27W
108 H10 **Lugo** Emilia-Romagna, N Italy 44.25N 11.52E
106 I3 **Lugo** anc. Lugus Augusti. Galicia, NW Spain 43.00N 7.33W
106 I3 **Lugo** ⬖ province Galicia, NW Spain
23 R12 **Lugoff** South Carolina, SE USA 34.13N 80.41W
118 F12 **Lugoj** Ger. Lugosch, Hung. Lugos. Timiş, W Romania 45.40N 21.56E
Lugos/Lugosch see Lugoj
Lugovoy/Lugovoye see Kulan
164 I13 **Lugu** Xizang Zizhiqu, W China 33.26N 84.10E
Lugus Augusti see Lugo
Luguvallium/Luguvallum see Carlisle
119 Y7 **Luhans'k** Rus. Lugansk; prev. Voroshilovgrad. Luhans'ka Oblast', E Ukraine 48.32N 39.21E
119 Y7 **Luhans'k** ✕ Luhans'ka Oblast', E Ukraine 48.25N 39.24E
119 X6 **Luhans'ka Oblast'** var. Luhans'k; prev. Voroshilovgrad, Rus. Voroshilovgradskaya Oblast'. ⬖ province E Ukraine
167 Q7 **Luhe** Jiangsu, E China 32.22N 118.51E
175 T11 **Luhu** Pulau Seram, E Indonesia 3.20S 127.58E
166 G8 **Luhuo** var. Zhaggo. Sichuan, C China 31.25N 100.39E
118 M3 **Luhyny** Zhytomyrs'ka Oblast', N Ukraine 51.06N 28.24E
85 G15 **Lui** ~ W Zambia
85 G16 **Luiana** ~ SE Angola
85 L15 **Luia, Rio** var. Ruya. ~ Mozambique/Zimbabwe
Luichow Peninsula see Leizhou Bandao
Luik see Liège
84 C13 **Luimbale** Huambo, C Angola 12.15S 15.19E
Luimneach see Limerick
108 D6 **Luino** Lombardia, N Italy 46.00N 8.45E
84 E13 **Luio** ~ E Angola
94 L11 **Luiro** ~ NE Finland
81 N25 **Luishia** Katanga, SE Dem. Rep. Congo (Zaire) 11.18S 27.08E
61 M19 **Luislândia do Oeste** Minas Gerais, SE Brazil 17.59S 45.35W
42 K5 **Luis L.León, Presa** ⊠ N Mexico
Luis Muñoz Marin see San Juan
205 N5 **Luitpold Coast** physical region Antarctica
81 K22 **Luiza** Kasai Occidental, S Dem. Rep. Congo (Zaire) 7.10S 22.27E
63 D20 **Luján** Buenos Aires, E Argentina 34.34S 59.07W
81 N24 **Lukafu** Katanga, SE Dem. Rep. Congo (Zaire) 10.28S 27.31E
Lukapa see Lucapa
114 I11 **Lukavac** Federacija Bosna I Hercegovina, NE Bosnia and Herzegovina 44.33N 18.31E
81 I20 **Lukenie** ~ C Dem. Rep. Congo (Zaire)
81 H19 **Lukolela** Equateur, W Dem. Rep. Congo (Zaire) 1.03S 17.07E
121 M14 **Lukoml'skaye, Vozyera** Rus. Ozero Lukoml'skoye. ◎ N Belarus
Lukoml'skoye, Ozero see Lukoml'skaye, Vozyera
116 I8 **Lukovit** Lovech, N Bulgaria 43.13N 24.10E
112 O12 **Łuków** Ger. Bogendorf. Lubelskie, E Poland 51.57N 22.22E
131 O4 **Lukoyanov** Nizhegorodskaya Oblast', W Russian Federation 55.02N 44.26E
81 N22 **Lukuga** ~ SE Dem. Rep. Congo (Zaire)
81 F21 **Lukula** Bas-Congo, SW Dem. Rep. Congo (Zaire) 5.22S 12.57E
85 G14 **Lukulu** Western, NW Zambia 14.24S 23.12E
201 R17 **Lukunor Atoll** atoll Mortlock Islands, C Micronesia
84 J12 **Lukwesa** Luapula, NE Zambia 10.03S 28.42E
95 K14 **Luleå** Norrbotten, N Sweden 65.34N 22.10E
94 J13 **Luleälven** ~ N Sweden
142 C10 **Lüleburgaz** Kırklareli, NW Turkey 41.25N 27.22E
166 M4 **Lüliang Shan** ▲▲ C China
81 O21 **Lulimba** Maniema, E Dem. Rep. Congo (Zaire) 4.42S 28.37E
24 K9 **Luling** Louisiana, S USA 29.55N 90.22W
27 T11 **Luling** Texas, SW USA 29.40N 97.39W
81 I18 **Lulonga** ~ NW Dem. Rep. Congo (Zaire)
81 K22 **Lulua** ~ S Dem. Rep. Congo (Zaire)
Luluabourg see Kananga
198 Dd8 **Luma** Ta'ū, E American Samoa 14.15S 169.30W
174 M16 **Lumajang** Jawa, C Indonesia 8.06S 113.13E
164 G12 **Lumajangdong Co** ◎ W China
84 G13 **Lumbala Kaquengue** Moxico, E Angola 12.40S 22.34E
85 F14 **Lumbala N'Guimbo** var. Nguimbo, Port. Gago Coutinho, Vila Gago Coutinho. Moxico, E Angola 14.04S 21.25E
23 T11 **Lumber River** ~ North Carolina/South Carolina, SE USA
Lumber State see Maine
24 L8 **Lumberton** Mississippi, S USA 31.00N 89.27W
23 U11 **Lumberton** North Carolina, SE USA 34.37N 79.00W
107 R4 **Lumbier** Navarra, N Spain 42.39N 1.19W
85 Q15 **Lumbo** Nampula, NE Mozambique 15.00S 40.40E
128 M4 **Lumbovka** Murmanskaya Oblast', NW Russian Federation 67.41N 40.31E
106 J7 **Lumbrales** Castilla-León, N Spain 40.57N 6.43W
159 W13 **Lumding** Assam, NE India 25.46N 93.10E
84 F12 **Lumege** var. Lumeje. Moxico, E Angola 11.30S 20.57E
Lumeje see Lumege
194 F10 **Lumi** Sandaun, NW PNG 3.30S 142.04E
101 J17 **Lummen** Limburg, NE Belgium 50.58N 5.12E
95 J20 **Lumparland** Åland, SW Finland 60.06N 20.15E
178 K12 **Lumphăt** prev. Lomphat. Rôtânôkiri, NE Cambodia 13.30N 106.57E
9 U16 **Lumsden** Saskatchewan, S Canada 50.39N 104.52W
193 C23 **Lumsden** Southland, South Island, NZ 45.43S 168.26E
174 J11 **Lumut, Tanjung** headland Sumatera, W Indonesia 3.47S 105.55E
163 P4 **Lün** Töv, C Mongolia 47.51N 105.11E
166 H13 **Lunan** var. Lunan Yizu Zizhixian. Yunnan, SW China 24.46N 103.12E
Lunan Yizu Zizhixian see Lunan
118 I13 **Lunca Corbului** Argeş, S Romania 44.41N 24.46E
97 K23 **Lund** Skåne, S Sweden 55.42N 13.10E
37 X6 **Lund** Nevada, W USA 38.50N 115.00W
84 D11 **Lunda Norte** ⬖ province NE Angola
84 E12 **Lunda Sul** ⬖ province NE Angola
84 M13 **Lundazi** Eastern, NE Zambia 12.19S 33.10E
97 G16 **Lunde** Telemark, S Norway 61.31N 6.37E
Lundenburg see Břeclav
97 C17 **Lundevatnet** ◎ S Norway
Lundi see Runde
99 I23 **Lundy** island SW England, UK
102 J10 **Lüneburg** Niedersachsen, N Germany 53.15N 10.25E
102 J11 **Lüneburger Heide** heathland NW Germany
105 Q15 **Lunel** Hérault, S France 43.40N 4.08E
103 F14 **Lünen** Nordrhein-Westfalen, W Germany 51.37N 7.31E
11 P16 **Lunenburg** Nova Scotia, SE Canada 44.22N 64.21W
23 V7 **Lunenburg** Virginia, NE USA 36.56N 78.15W
105 T5 **Lunéville** Meurthe-et-Moselle, NE France 48.34N 6.30E
85 I14 **Lunga** ~ C Zambia
Lunga, Isola see Dugi Otok
164 H12 **Lungdo** Xizang Zizhiqu, W China 33.45N 82.09E
164 I14 **Lunggar** Xizang Zizhiqu, W China 31.10N 84.01E
78 I15 **Lungi** ✕ (Freetown) W Sierra Leone 8.36N 13.10W
Lungkiang see Qiqihar
Lungleh see Lunglei
159 W15 **Lunglei** prev. Lungleh. Mizoram, NE India 22.55N 92.49E
164 L15 **Lungsang** Xizang Zizhiqu, W China 29.49N 88.27E
84 E13 **Lungué-Bungo** var. Lungwebungu. ~ Angola/Zambia see also Lungwebungu
85 G14 **Lungwebungu** var. Lungué-Bungo. ~ Angola/Zambia see also Lungué-Bungo
158 F12 **Lūni** Rājasthān, N India 26.03N 73.00E
158 F12 **Lūni** ~ N India
Luninets see Luninyets
37 S7 **Luning** Nevada, W USA 38.29N 118.10W
Łuniniec see Luninyets
131 P6 **Lunino** Penzenskaya Oblast', W Russian Federation 53.35N 45.12E
121 J19 **Luninyets** Pol. Łuniniec, Rus. Luninets. Brestskaya Voblasts', SW Belarus 52.15N 26.49E
158 F10 **Lünkaransar** Rājasthān, NW India 28.31N 73.49E
121 G17 **Lunna** Pol. Łunna, Rus. Lunna. Hrodzyenskaya Voblasts', W Belarus 53.27N 24.16E
78 I15 **Lunsar** W Sierra Leone 8.40N 12.31W
85 K14 **Lunsemfwa** ~ C Zambia
164 J6 **Luntai** var. Bügür. Xinjiang Uygur Zizhiqu, NW China 41.48N 84.14E
100 K11 **Lunteren** Gelderland, C Netherlands 52.04N 5.37E
175 O16 **Lunyuk** Sumbawa, S Indonesia 8.56S 117.15E
111 U5 **Lunz am See** Niederösterreich, C Austria 47.54N 15.01E
169 Y7 **Luobei** var. Fengxiang. Heilongjiang, NE China 47.35N 130.51E
166 J13 **Luodian** var. Longping. Guizhou, S China 25.25N 106.49E
166 M15 **Luoding** Guangdong, S China 22.44N 111.28E
166 M6 **Luo He** ~ C China
166 L5 **Luo He** ~ C China
167 N7 **Luohe** Henan, C China 33.37N 114.00E
Luolajarvi see Kuoloyarvi
Luong Nam Tha see Louangnamtha
166 L13 **Luoqing Jiang** ~ S China
167 O8 **Luoshan** Henan, C China 32.12N 114.30E
167 O12 **Luoxiao Shan** ▲▲ S China
167 N6 **Luoyang** var. Honan, Lo-yang. Henan, C China 34.40N 112.25E
167 R12 **Luoyuan** Fujian, SE China 26.29N 119.32E
81 F21 **Luozi** Bas-Congo, W Dem. Rep. Congo (Zaire) 4.57S 14.07E
85 J17 **Lupane** Matabeleland North, W Zimbabwe 18.46S 27.47E
166 I12 **Lupanshui** prev. Shuicheng. Guizhou, S China 26.38N 104.49E
174 Ll7 **Lupar, Batang** ~ East Malaysia
Lupatia see Altamura
118 G12 **Lupeni** Hung. Lupény. Hunedoara, SW Romania 45.20N 23.07E
Lupény see Lupeni
84 N13 **Lupiliche** Niassa, N Mozambique 11.36S 35.15E
85 E14 **Lupire** Cuando Cubango, E Angola 14.39S 19.39E
179 Rr16 **Lupon** Mindanao, S Philippines 6.53N 126.00E
81 L22 **Luputa** Kasai Oriental, S Dem. Rep. Congo (Zaire) 7.07S 23.43E
123 Jj17 **Luqa** ✕ (Valletta) S Malta 35.53N 14.27E
165 U11 **Luqu** Gansu, C China 34.34N 102.27E
47 U5 **Luquillo, Sierra de** ▲▲ E Puerto Rico
28 L4 **Luray** Kansas, C USA 39.06N 98.41W
23 U4 **Luray** Virginia, NE USA 38.40N 78.27W
105 T7 **Lure** Haute-Saône, E France 47.42N 6.30E
84 D11 **Luremo** Lunda Norte, NE Angola 8.32S 17.55E
99 F15 **Lurgan** Ir. An Lorgain. S Northern Ireland, UK 54.28N 6.19W
59 K18 **Luribay** La Paz, W Bolivia 17.05S 67.39W
85 Q14 **Lúrio** Nampula, NE Mozambique 13.32S 40.33E
85 P14 **Lúrio, Rio** ~ NE Mozambique
Luristan see Lorestān
Lurka see Lorca
85 J15 **Lusaka** ● (Zambia) Lusaka, SE Zambia 15.23S 28.16E
85 J15 **Lusaka** ⬖ province C Zambia
85 J15 **Lusaka** ✕ Lusaka, C Zambia 15.10S 28.22E
81 L21 **Lusambo** Kasai Oriental, C Dem. Rep. Congo (Zaire) 4.54S 23.25E
195 N14 **Lusancay Islands and Reefs** island group SE PNG
81 I21 **Lusanga** Bandundu, SW Dem. Rep. Congo (Zaire) 4.55S 18.40E
81 N21 **Lusangi** Maniema, E Dem. Rep. Congo (Zaire) 4.39S 27.10E
Lusatian Mountains see Lausitzer Bergland
Lushnja see Lushnjë
115 K21 **Lushnjë** var. Lushnja. Fier, C Albania 40.54N 19.43E
83 J21 **Lushoto** Tanga, E Tanzania 4.48S 38.19E
104 L10 **Lusignan** Vienne, W France 46.25N 0.06E
35 Z15 **Lusk** Wyoming, C USA 42.45N 104.27W
Luso see Luena
104 L10 **Lussac-les-Châteaux** Vienne, W France 46.23N 0.44E
Lussin/Lussino see Lošinj
Lussinpiccolo see Mali Lošinj
110 I7 **Lustenau** Vorarlberg, W Austria 47.26N 9.39E
167 T14 **Lü Tao** var. Huoshao Dao, Lütao, Eng. Green Island. island SE Taiwan
Lūt, Baḩrat/Lut, Bahret see Dead Sea
24 K9 **Lutcher** Louisiana, S USA 30.02N 90.42W
149 T9 **Lūt, Dasht-e** var. Kavīr-e Lūt. desert E Iran
85 F14 **Lutembo** Moxico, E Angola 13.30S 21.21E
Lutetia/Lutetia Parisiorum see Paris
Luteva see Lodève
12 G15 **Luther Lake** ◎ Ontario, S Canada
195 U13 **Luti** Choiseul Island, NW Solomon Islands 7.13S 157.01E
Lūt, Kavīr-e see Lūt, Dasht-e
99 N21 **Luton** SE England, UK 51.53N 0.25W
99 N21 **Luton** ✕ (London) SE England, UK 51.54N 0.24W
110 B10 **Lutry** Vaud, SW Switzerland 46.31N 6.31E
15 I18 **Łutselk'e** prev. Snowdrift. Northwest Territories, W Canada 62.24N 110.42W
31 Y4 **Lutsen** Minnesota, N USA 47.39N 90.37W
118 J4 **Luts'k** Pol. Łuck, Rus. Lutsk. Volyns'ka Oblast', NW Ukraine 50.45N 25.22E
Luttenberg see Ljutomer
Lüttich see Liège
85 G25 **Luttig** Western Cape, SW South Africa 32.33S 22.13E
Lutto see Lotta
84 E13 **Lutuai** Moxico, E Angola 12.38S 20.06E
119 Y7 **Lutuhyne** Luhans'ka Oblast', E Ukraine 48.24N 39.12E
176 Ww13 **Lutur, Pulau** island Kepulauan Aru, E Indonesia
25 V12 **Lutz** Florida, SE USA 28.09N 82.27W
Lutzow-Holm Bay see Lützow Holmbukta
205 V2 **Lützow Holmbukta** var. Lutzow-Holm Bay. bay Antarctica
83 L16 **Luuq** It. Lugh Ganana. Gedo, SW Somalia 3.42N 42.34E
94 M12 **Luusua** Lappi, NE Finland 66.28N 27.16E
25 Q6 **Luverne** Alabama, S USA 31.43N 86.15W
31 S11 **Luverne** Minnesota, N USA 43.39N 96.12W
81 O22 **Luvua** ~ SE Dem. Rep. Congo (Zaire)
84 F13 **Luvuei** Moxico, E Angola 13.08S 21.09E
83 H24 **Luwego** ~ S Tanzania
84 K12 **Luwingu** Northern, NE Zambia 10.13S 29.55E
175 Qq9 **Luwuk** prev. Loewoek. Sulawesi, C Indonesia 0.55S 122.46E
25 N3 **Luxapallila Creek** ~ Alabama/Mississippi, S USA
101 M25 **Luxembourg** ● (Luxembourg) Luxembourg, S Luxembourg 49.37N 6.07E
101 M25 **Luxembourg** off. Grand Duchy of Luxembourg, var. Lëtzebuerg, Luxemburg. ◆ monarchy NW Europe
101 J23 **Luxembourg** ⬖ province SE Belgium
101 L24 **Luxembourg** ⬖ district S Luxembourg
33 N6 **Luxemburg** Wisconsin, N USA 44.32N 87.42W
Luxemburg see Luxembourg
105 U7 **Luxeuil-les-Bains** Haute-Saône, E France 47.49N 6.22E
166 E13 **Luxi** prev. Mangshi. Yunnan, SW China 24.27N 98.31E
84 E10 **Luxico** ~ Angola/Dem. Rep. Congo (Zaire)
77 X10 **Luxor** Ar. Al Uqşur. E Egypt 25.39N 32.39E
77 X10 **Luxor** ✕ C Egypt 25.39N 32.48E
166 M4 **Luya Shan** ▲▲ C China
104 J15 **Luy de Béarn** ~ SW France
104 J15 **Luy de France** ~ SW France
129 P12 **Luza** Kirovskaya Oblast', NW Russian Federation 60.37N 47.13E
129 Q12 **Luza** ~ NW Russian Federation
106 I16 **Luz, Costa de la** coastal region SW Spain
113 K20 **Luže** var. Lausche. ▲ Czech Republic/Germany see also Lausche 50.51N 14.40E
110 F8 **Luzern** Fr. Lucerne, It. Lucerna. Luzern, C Switzerland 47.03N 8.16E
110 E8 **Luzern** Fr. Lucerne. ⬖ canton C Switzerland
166 L13 **Luzhai** Guangxi Zhuangzu Zizhiqu, S China 24.33N 109.46E
120 K12 **Luzhki** Rus. Luzhki. Vitsyebskaya Voblasts', N Belarus 55.20N 27.54E
166 I10 **Luzhou** Sichuan, C China 28.55N 105.28E
Lužická Nisa see Neisse
Lužické Hory see Lausitzer Bergland
Lužnice see Lainsitz
179 Pp9 **Luzon** island N Philippines
179 Oo6 **Luzon Strait** strait Philippines/Taiwan
118 I5 **L'viv** Ger. Lemberg, Pol. Lwów, Rus. L'vov. L'vivs'ka Oblast', W Ukraine 49.49N 24.04E
L'viv see L'vivs'ka Oblast'
118 I4 **L'vivs'ka Oblast'** var. L'viv, Rus. L'vovskaya Oblast'. ⬖ province NW Ukraine
L'vov see L'viv
L'vovskaya Oblast' see L'vivs'ka Oblast'
Lwena see Luena
Lwów see L'viv
112 F11 **Lwówek** Ger. Neustadt bei Pinne. Wielkolpolskie, C Poland 52.27N 16.10E
113 E14 **Lwówek Śląski** Ger. Löwenberg in Schlesien. Dolnośląskie, SW Poland 51.06N 15.35E
121 I18 **Lyakhavichy** Rus. Lyakhovichi. Brestskaya Voblasts', SW Belarus 53.01N 26.15E
Lyakhovichi see Lyakhavichy
193 B22 **Lyall, Mount** ▲ South Island, NZ 45.14S 167.31E
Lyallpur see Faisalābād
125 G10 **Lyamin** ~ C Russian Federation
Lyangar see Langar
125 G10 **Lyantor** Khanty-Mansiyskiy Avtonomnyy Okrug, C Russian Federation 61.40N 72.21E
128 H11 **Lyaskelya** Respublika Kareliya, NW Russian Federation 61.42N 31.06E
121 I18 **Lyasnaya** Rus. Lesnaya. Brestskaya Voblasts', SW Belarus 52.58N 25.46E
121 F19 **Lyasnaya** Pol. Leśna, Rus. Lesnaya. ~ SW Belarus
128 H15 **Lychkovo** Novgorodskaya Oblast', W Russian Federation 57.55N 32.24E
Lyck see Ełk
95 I15 **Lycksele** Västerbotten, N Sweden 64.34N 18.40E
20 G13 **Lycoming Creek** ~ Pennsylvania, NE USA
Lycopolis see Asyūt
205 N3 **Lyddan Island** island Antarctica
85 K20 **Lydenburg** Mpumalanga, NE South Africa 25.01S 30.27E
121 L20 **Lyel'chytsy** Rus. Lel'chitsy. Homyel'skaya Voblasts', SE Belarus 51.46N 28.19E
121 P14 **Lyenina** Rus. Lenino. Mahilyowskaya Voblasts', E Belarus 54.26N 31.07E
120 L13 **Lyepyel'** Rus. Lepel'. Vitsyebskaya Voblasts', N Belarus 54.54N 28.43E
27 S17 **Lyford** Texas, SW USA 26.24N 97.47W
97 E17 **Lygna** ~ S Norway
20 G14 **Lykens** Pennsylvania, NE USA 40.33N 76.42W
117 E21 **Lykódimo** ▲ S Greece 36.56N 21.49E
99 K24 **Lyme Bay** bay S England, UK
99 K24 **Lyme Regis** S England, UK 50.44N 2.55W
112 L7 **Łyna** Ger. Alle. ~ N Poland
31 P12 **Lynch** Nebraska, C USA 42.49N 98.27W
22 J10 **Lynchburg** Tennessee, S USA 35.15N 86.22W
23 T6 **Lynchburg** Virginia, NE USA 37.24N 79.08W
23 T12 **Lynches River** ~ South Carolina, SE USA
34 H6 **Lynden** Washington, NW USA 48.57N 122.27W
190 I5 **Lyndhurst** South Australia 30.19S 138.20E
29 Q5 **Lyndon** Kansas, C USA 38.37N 95.40W
21 N7 **Lyndonville** Vermont, NE USA 44.31N 71.58W
97 D18 **Lyngdal** Vest-Agder, S Norway 58.07N 7.04E
94 I9 **Lyngen** inlet Arctic Ocean
97 G17 **Lyngør** Aust-Agder, S Norway 58.38N 9.05E
94 I9 **Lyngseidet** Troms, N Norway 69.36N 20.07E
21 P11 **Lynn** Massachusetts, NE USA 42.28N 70.57W
Lynn see King's Lynn
25 R9 **Lynn Haven** Florida, SE USA 30.15N 85.39W
9 V11 **Lynn Lake** Manitoba, C Canada 56.51N 101.01W
Lynn Regis see King's Lynn
120 I13 **Lyntupy** Rus. Lyntupy. Vitsyebskaya Voblasts', NW Belarus 55.03N 26.19E
105 R11 **Lyon** Eng. Lyons; anc. Lugdunum. Rhône, E France 45.46N 4.49E
15 H3 **Lyon, Cape** headland Northwest Territories, NW Canada 69.47N 123.10W
20 K6 **Lyon Mountain** ▲ New York, NE USA 44.42N 73.52W
105 Q11 **Lyonnais, Monts du** ▲▲ C France
67 N25 **Lyon Point** headland SE Tristan da Cunha 37.06S 12.13W
190 E5 **Lyons** South Australia 30.40S 133.50E
39 T3 **Lyons** Colorado, C USA 40.13N 105.16W
25 V6 **Lyons** Georgia, SE USA 32.12N 82.19W
28 M5 **Lyons** Kansas, C USA 38.21N 98.12W
31 R14 **Lyons** Nebraska, C USA 41.56N 96.28W
20 G10 **Lyons** New York, NE USA 43.03N 76.58W
Lyons see Lyon
120 O13 **Lyozna** Rus. Liozno. Vitsyebskaya Voblasts', NE Belarus 55.01N 30.48E
119 S4 **Lypova Dolyna** Sums'ka Oblast', NE Ukraine 50.36N 33.50E
119 N6 **Lypovets'** Rus. Lipovets. Vinnyts'ka Oblast', C Ukraine 49.13N 29.06E
Lys see Leie
113 I18 **Lysá Hora** ▲ E Czech Republic 49.31N 18.27E
97 D16 **Lysefjorden** fjord S Norway
97 I18 **Lysekil** Västra Götaland, S Sweden 58.16N 11.25E
Lýsi see Akdoğan
35 V14 **Lysite** Wyoming, C USA 43.16N 107.42W
131 P3 **Lyskovo** Nizhegorodskaya Oblast', W Russian Federation 56.04N 45.01E
110 D8 **Lyss** Bern, W Switzerland 47.04N 7.19E
97 H22 **Lystrup** Århus, C Denmark 56.13N 10.13E
129 V14 **Lys'va** Permskaya Oblast', NW Russian Federation 58.04N 57.48E
119 P6 **Lysyanka** Cherkas'ka Oblast', C Ukraine 49.15N 30.50E
119 X6 **Lysychans'k** Rus. Lisichansk. Luhans'ka Oblast', E Ukraine 48.52N 38.27E
99 K17 **Lytham St Anne's** NW England, UK 53.45N 3.01W
193 I19 **Lyttelton** Canterbury, South Island, NZ 43.35S 172.44E
8 M17 **Lytton** British Columbia, SW Canada 50.12N 121.34W
121 L18 **Lyuban'** Rus. Lyuban'. Minskaya Voblasts', S Belarus 52.48N 28.00E
121 L18 **Lyubanskaye Vodaskhovishcha** ⊠ C Belarus
118 M5 **Lyubar** Zhytomyrs'ka Oblast', N Ukraine 49.54N 27.48E
Lyubashëvka see Lyubashivka
119 O8 **Lyubashivka** Rus. Lyubashëvka. Odes'ka Oblast', SW Ukraine 47.49N 30.18E
121 I16 **Lyubcha** Pol. Lubcz, Rus. Lyubcha. Hrodzyenskaya Voblasts', W Belarus 53.46N 26.04E
130 L4 **Lyubertsy** Moskovskaya Oblast', W Russian Federation 55.37N 38.02E
118 K2 **Lyubeshiv** Volyns'ka Oblast', NW Ukraine 51.46N 25.33E
128 M14 **Lyubim** Yaroslavskaya Oblast', NW Russian Federation 58.21N 40.46E
116 K11 **Lyubimets** Khaskovo, S Bulgaria 41.51N 26.03E
Lyublin see Lublin
118 I3 **Lyuboml'** Pol. Luboml. Volyns'ka Oblast', NW Ukraine 51.12N 24.01E
Lyubotin see Lyubotyn
119 U5 **Lyubotyn** Rus. Lyubotin. Kharkivs'ka Oblast', E Ukraine 49.57N 35.57E
130 I5 **Lyudinovo** Kaluzhskaya Oblast', W Russian Federation 53.52N 34.28E
131 T2 **Lyuk** Udmurtskaya Respublika, NW Russian Federation 56.55N 52.45E
116 M9 **Lyulyakovo** prev. Keremitlik. Burgas, E Bulgaria 42.53N 27.05E
121 I18 **Lyusina** Rus. Lyusino. Brestskaya Voblasts', SW Belarus 52.37N 26.31E
Lyusino see Lyusina

M

144 G9 **Ma'ād** Irbid, N Jordan 32.37N 35.36E
Maalahti see Malax
Maale see Male'
144 G13 **Ma'ān** Ma'ān, SW Jordan 30.10N 35.45E
144 H13 **Ma'ān** off. Muḩāfaẓat Ma'ān, var. Ma'an, Ma'ān. ⬖ governorate S Jordan
95 M16 **Maaninka** Itä-Suomi, C Finland 63.10N 27.19E
168 K7 **Maanīt** Bulgan, C Mongolia 48.17N 103.29E
168 M8 **Maanīt** Töv, C Mongolia 47.14N 107.34E
95 N15 **Maanselkä** Oulu, C Finland 63.53N 28.27E
167 Q8 **Ma'anshan** Anhui, E China 31.45N 118.31E
196 F16 **Maap** island Caroline Islands, W Micronesia
120 H3 **Maardu** Ger. Maart. Harjumaa, NW Estonia 59.28N 25.01E
Ma'aret-en-Nu'man see Ma'arrat an Nu'mān
101 K16 **Maarheeze** Noord-Brabant, SE Netherlands 51.19N 5.37E
Maarianhamina see Mariehamn
144 I4 **Ma'arrat an Nu'mān** var. Ma'aret-en-Nu'man, Fr. Maarret enn Naamâne. Idlib, NW Syria 35.40N 36.40E
Maarret enn Naamâne see Ma'arrat an Nu'mān
100 I11 **Maarssen** Utrecht, C Netherlands 52.07N 5.03E
Maart see Maardu
101 L17 **Maas** Fr. Meuse. ~ W Europe see also Meuse
101 M15 **Maasbree** Limburg, SE Netherlands 51.22N 6.03E
101 L17 **Maaseik** prev. Maeseyck. Limburg, NE Belgium 51.04N 5.48E
179 R13 **Maasin** Leyte, C Philippines 10.10N 124.55E
101 L17 **Maasmechelen** Limburg, NE Belgium 50.58N 5.42E
100 G12 **Maassluis** Zuid-Holland, SW Netherlands 51.55N 4.15E
101 L18 **Maastricht** var. Maestricht; anc. Traietum ad Mosam, Traiectum Tungorum. Limburg, SE Netherlands 50.51N 5.42E
191 N18 **Maatsuyker Group** island group Tasmania, SE Australia
Maba see Qujiang
85 L20 **Mabalane** Gaza, S Mozambique 23.43S 32.37E
27 V7 **Mabank** Texas, SW USA 32.22N 96.06W
172 N10 **Mabechi-gawa** var. Mabuchi-gawa. ~ Honshū, C Japan
99 O18 **Mablethorpe** E England, UK 53.20N 0.14E
176 W9 **Maboi** Irian Jaya, E Indonesia 1.00S 134.02E
85 M19 **Mabote** Inhambane, S Mozambique 22.03S 34.09E
34 J10 **Mabton** Washington, NW USA 46.13N 120.00W
Mabuchi-gawa see Mabechi-gawa
85 H20 **Mabutsane** Southern, S Botswana 24.22S 23.34E
65 G19 **Macá, Cerro** ▲ S Chile 45.07S 73.11W
62 Q9 **Macaé** Rio de Janeiro, SE Brazil 22.21S 41.48W
84 N13 **Macaloge** Niassa, N Mozambique 12.30S 35.25E
Macan see Bonerate, Kepulauan
167 N15 **Macao** Chin. Aomen, Port. Macau. S China
106 H9 **Mação** Santarém, C Portugal 39.33N 8.00W
60 J11 **Macapá** state capital Amapá, N Brazil 0.04N 51.04W
45 S17 **Macaracas** Los Santos, S Panama 7.43N 80.33W
57 P6 **Macare, Caño** ~ NE Venezuela
57 Q6 **Macareo, Caño** ~ NE Venezuela
Macarsca see Makarska
MacArthur see Ormoc
190 L12 **Macarthur** Victoria, SE Australia 38.04S 142.02E
58 C7 **Macas** Morona Santiago, SE Ecuador 2.22S 78.07W
Macassar see Ujungpandang
61 Q14 **Macau** Rio Grande do Norte, E Brazil 5.04S 36.37W
Macau see Macao
Macáu see Makó, Hungary
67 E24 **Macbride Head** headland East Falkland, Falkland Islands 51.25S 57.55W
25 V9 **Macclenny** Florida, SE USA 30.16N 82.07W
99 L18 **Macclesfield** C England, UK 53.16N 2.07W
198 F6 **Macclesfield Bank** undersea feature N South China Sea
MacCluer Gulf see Berau, Teluk
189 N7 **Macdonald, Lake** salt lake Western Australia
189 Q7 **Macdonnell Ranges** ▲▲ Northern Territory, C Australia
98 K8 **Macduff** NE Scotland, UK 57.39N 2.28W
106 I6 **Macedo de Cavaleiros** Bragança, N Portugal 41.31N 6.57W
Macedonia Central see Kentrikí Makedonía
Macedonia East and Thrace see Anatolikí Makedonía kai Thráki
115 O19 **Macedonia, FYR** off. the Former Yugoslav Republic of Macedonia, var. Macedonia, Mac. Makedonija, abbrev. FYR Macedonia, FYROM. ◆ republic SE Europe
Macedonia West see Dytikí Makedonía
61 Q16 **Maceió** state capital Alagoas, E Brazil 9.40S 35.43W
78 K15 **Macenta** Guinée-Forestière, SE Guinea 8.31N 9.31W
108 J12 **Macerata** Marche, C Italy 43.19N 13.28E

◆ Country ● Country Capital ◇ Dependent Territory ○ Dependent Territory Capital ⬖ Administrative Region ✕ International Airport ▲ Mountain ▲▲ Mountain Range ✱ Volcano ~ River ◎ Lake ⊠ Reservoir

MacFarlane – Makkah

9 S11 **MacFarlane** ≈ Saskatchewan, C Canada
190 H7 **Macfarlane, Lake** *var.* Lake Mcfarlane. ◎ South Australia
Macgillicuddy's Reeks Mountains *see* Macgillycuddy's Reeks
99 B21 **Macgillycuddy's Reeks** *var.* Macgillicuddy's Reeks Mountains, *Ir.* Na Cruacha Dubha. ▲▲ SW Ireland
9 X16 **MacGregor** Manitoba, S Canada *49.58N 98.49W*
155 O10 **Mach** Baluchistān, SW Pakistan *29.52N 67.19E*
58 C6 **Machachi** Pichincha, C Ecuador *0.33S 78.34W*
85 M19 **Machaila** Gaza, S Mozambique *22.15S 32.57E*
Machaire Fíolta *see* Magherafelt
Machaire Rátha *see* Maghera
83 I19 **Machakos** Eastern, S Kenya *1.33S 37.17E*
58 B8 **Machala** El Oro, SW Ecuador *3.19S 79.57W*
85 J19 **Machaneng** Central, SE Botswana *23.12S 27.28E*
85 M18 **Machanga** Sofala, E Mozambique *20.55S 35.03E*
82 G13 **Machar Marshes** *wetland* SE Sudan
104 I8 **Machecoul** Loire-Atlantique, NW France *46.59N 1.51W*
167 O8 **Macheng** Hubei, C China *31.10N 115.00E*
161 J16 **Mācherla** Andhra Pradesh, C India *16.28N 79.25E*
159 O11 **Machhapuchhre** ▲ C Nepal *28.30N 83.57E*
21 T6 **Machias** Maine, NE USA *44.43N 67.28W*
21 R3 **Machias River** ≈ Maine, NE USA
21 T6 **Machias River** ≈ Maine, NE USA
66 P5 **Machico** Madeira, Portugal, NE Atlantic Ocean *32.43N 16.46W*
161 K16 **Machilīpatnam** *var.* Bandar Masulipatnam. Andhra Pradesh, E India *16.12N 81.10E*
56 G5 **Machiques** Zulia, NW Venezuela *10.01N 72.40W*
59 G15 **Machupicchu** Cusco, C Peru *13.07S 72.30W*
85 M20 **Macia** *var.* Vila de Macia. Gaza, S Mozambique *25.01S 33.05E*
Macías Nguema Biyogo *see* Bioco, Isla de
118 M13 **Măcin** Tulcea, SE Romania *45.15N 28.09E*
191 T4 **Macintyre River** ≈ New South Wales/Queensland, SE Australia
189 Y7 **Mackay** Queensland, NE Australia *21.10S 149.10E*
189 O7 **Mackay, Lake** *salt lake* Northern Territory/Western Australia
8 M13 **Mackenzie** British Columbia, W Canada *55.18N 123.09W*
15 Gg6 **Mackenzie** ≈ Northwest Territories, NW Canada
205 Y6 **Mackenzie Bay** *bay* Antarctica
8 J1 **Mackenzie Bay** *bay* NW Canada
2 D9 **Mackenzie Delta** *delta* Northwest Territories, NW Canada
207 P8 **Mackenzie King Island** *island* Queen Elizabeth Islands, Northwest Territories, N Canada
14 G5 **Mackenzie Mountains** ▲▲ Northwest Territories, NW Canada
33 Q5 **Mackinac, Straits of** ◎ Michigan, N USA
204 K5 **Mackintosh, Cape** *headland* Antarctica *72.52S 60.00W*
9 R15 **Macklin** Saskatchewan, S Canada *52.19N 109.51W*
191 V6 **Macksville** New South Wales, SE Australia *30.39S 152.54E*
191 V5 **Maclean** New South Wales, SE Australia *29.30S 153.15E*
85 J24 **Maclear** Eastern Cape, SE South Africa *31.04S 28.22E*
191 U6 **Macleay River** ≈ New South Wales, SE Australia
MacLeod *see* Fort Macleod
188 G9 **Macleod, Lake** ◎ Western Australia
8 I6 **Macmillan** ≈ Yukon Territory, NW Canada
32 J12 **Macomb** Illinois, N USA *40.27N 90.40W*
109 B18 **Macomer** Sardegna, Italy, C Mediterranean Sea *40.14N 8.46E*
84 Q13 **Macomia** Cabo Delgado, NE Mozambique *12.15S 40.06E*
25 T5 **Macon** Georgia, SE USA *32.48N 83.41W*
25 N4 **Macon** Mississippi, S USA *33.06N 88.33W*
29 U3 **Macon** Missouri, C USA *39.44N 92.28W*
105 R10 **Mâcon** *anc.* Matisco, Matisco Ædourum. Saône-et-Loire, C France *46.19N 4.48E*
24 J6 **Macon, Bayou** ≈ Arkansas/Louisiana, S USA
84 G13 **Macondo** Moxico, E Angola *12.31S 23.45E*
85 M16 **Macossa** Manica, C Mozambique *17.51S 33.54E*
9 T12 **Macoun Lake** ◎ Saskatchewan, C Canada
32 K14 **Macoupin Creek** ≈ Illinois, N USA
Macouria *see* Tonate
85 N18 **Macovane** Inhambane, SE Mozambique *21.30S 35.07E*
191 N17 **Macquarie Harbour** *inlet* Tasmania, SE Australia
199 Ii15 **Macquarie Island** *island* NZ, SW Pacific Ocean
191 T8 **Macquarie, Lake** *lagoon* New South Wales, SE Australia
191 Q6 **Macquarie Marshes** *wetland* New South Wales, SE Australia
183 O13 **Macquarie Ridge** *undersea feature* SW Pacific Ocean
191 Q6 **Macquarie River** ≈ New South Wales, SE Australia
191 P17 **Macquarie River** ≈ Tasmania, SE Australia
205 V5 **Mac. Robertson Land** *physical region* Antarctica
99 C21 **Macroom** *Ir.* Maigh Chromtha. SW Ireland *51.54N 8.57W*
44 G5 **Macuelizo** Santa Bárbara, NW Honduras *15.21N 88.31W*
190 G2 **Macumba River** ≈ South Australia
59 I16 **Macusani** Puno, S Peru *14.07S 70.27W*
58 E8 **Macusari, Río** ≈ N Peru
43 U15 **Macuspana** Tabasco, SE Mexico *17.43N 92.36W*
144 G10 **Ma'dabā** *var.* Mādabā, Madeba; *anc.* Medeba. 'Ammān, NW Jordan *31.43N 35.48E*
180 G2 **Madagascar** *off.* Democratic Republic of Madagascar, *Malg.* Madagasikara; *prev.* Malagasy Republic. ◆ *republic* W Indian Ocean
180 I5 **Madagascar** *island* W Indian Ocean
132 L17 **Madagascar Basin** *undersea feature* W Indian Ocean
132 L16 **Madagascar Plain** *undersea feature* W Indian Ocean
69 Y14 **Madagascar Plateau** *var.* Madagascar Ridge, Madagascar Rise, *Rus.* Madagaskarskiy Khrebet. *undersea feature* W Indian Ocean
Madagascar Ridge/Madagascar Rise *see* Madagascar Plateau
Madagasikara *see* Madagascar
Madagaskarskiy Khrebet *see* Madagascar Plateau
66 N2 **Madalena** Pico, Azores, Portugal, NE Atlantic Ocean *38.31N 28.15W*
79 Y6 **Madama** Agadez, NE Niger *21.54N 13.43E*
116 J12 **Madan** Smolyan, S Bulgaria *41.30N 24.58E*
161 I19 **Madanapalle** Andhra Pradesh, E India *13.33N 78.31E*
194 I11 **Madang** Madang, N PNG *5.09S 145.48E*
194 I11 **Madang** ◈ *province* N PNG
152 G7 **Madaniyat** *Rus.* Madeniyet. Qoraqalpoghiston Respublikasi, W Uzbekistan *42.48N 59.00E*
Madanīyīn *see* Médenine
79 U11 **Madaoua** Tahoua, SW Niger *14.06N 6.01E*
Madaras *see* Vtáčnik
159 U15 **Madaripur** Dhaka, C Bangladesh *23.09N 90.10E*
79 U12 **Madarounfa** Maradi, S Niger *13.16N 7.07E*
Mađarska *see* Hungary
152 B13 **Madau** *Turkm.* Madaw. Balkanskiy Velayat, W Turkmenistan *38.11N 54.46E*
195 P15 **Madau Island** *island* SE PNG
Madaw *see* Madau
21 S1 **Madawaska** Maine, NE USA *47.19N 68.19W*
12 J13 **Madawaska** ≈ Ontario, SE Canada
Madawaska Highlands *see* Haliburton Highlands
177 G4 **Madaya** Mandalay, C Burma *22.12N 96.04E*
109 K17 **Maddaloni** Campania, S Italy *41.03N 14.22E*
31 O3 **Maddock** North Dakota, N USA *47.57N 99.31W*
101 I14 **Made** Noord-Brabant, S Netherlands *51.40N 4.48E*
Madeba *see* Ma'dabā
66 L9 **Madeira** *var.* Ilha de Madeira. *island* Madeira, Portugal, NE Atlantic Ocean
Madeira, Ilha de *see* Madeira
66 O5 **Madeira Islands** *Port.* Região Autoónoma da Madeira. ◈ *autonomous region* Madeira, Portugal, NE Atlantic Ocean
66 L9 **Madeira Plain** *undersea feature* E Atlantic Ocean
66 L9 **Madeira Ridge** *undersea feature* E Atlantic Ocean
61 F14 **Madeira, Rio** *Sp.* Río Madera. ≈ Bolivia/Brazil ***see also*** Madera, Río
103 J25 **Mädelegabel** ▲ Austria/Germany *47.18N 10.19E*
13 X6 **Madeleine** ≈ Quebec, SE Canada
13 X5 **Madeleine, Cap de la** *headland* Quebec, SE Canada *49.13N 65.20W*
11 Q13 **Madeleine, Îles de la** *Eng.* Magdalen Islands. *island group* Quebec, E Canada
31 U10 **Madelia** Minnesota, N USA *44.03N 94.26W*
37 P3 **Madeline** California, W USA *41.02N 120.28W*
32 K3 **Madeline Island** *island* Apostle Islands, Wisconsin, N USA
143 O15 **Maden** Elâzığ, SE Turkey *38.24N 39.42E*
151 V12 **Madeniyet** Vostochnyy Kazakhstan, E Kazakhstan *47.51N 78.37E*
Madeniyet *see* Madaniyat
42 H5 **Madera** Chihuahua, N Mexico *29.10N 108.10W*
37 Q10 **Madera** California, W USA *36.57N 120.02W*
58 L13 **Madera, Río** *Port.* Rio Madeira. ≈ Bolivia/Brazil ***see also*** Madeira, Rio
108 D6 **Madesimo** Lombardia, N Italy *46.20N 9.26E*
147 O14 **Madhāb, Wādī** *dry watercourse* NW Yemen
159 R13 **Madhepura** *prev.* Madhipure. Bihār, NE India *25.55N 86.48E*
Madhipure *see* Madhepura
159 Q13 **Madhubani** Bihār, N India *26.21N 86.04E*
159 Q15 **Madhupur** Bihār, NE India *24.16N 86.37E*
158 K15 **Madhya Pradesh** *prev.* Central Provinces and Berar. ◈ *state* C India
59 K15 **Madidi, Río** ≈ W Bolivia
161 F20 **Madikeri** *prev.* Mercara. Karnātaka, W India *12.28N 75.40E*
29 O13 **Madill** Oklahoma, C USA *34.05N 96.46W*
81 G21 **Madimba** Bas-Congo, SW Dem. Rep. Congo (Zaire) *4.58S 15.07E*
144 M4 **Ma'dīn** Ar Raqqah, C Syria *35.45N 39.36E*
Madīnah, Minṭaqat al *see* Al Madīnah
78 M14 **Madinani** NW Ivory Coast *9.37N 6.57W*
147 O17 **Madīnat ash Sha'b** *prev.* Al Ittiḥād. SW Yemen *12.52N 44.55E*
144 K3 **Madīnat ath Thawrah** *var.* Ath Thawrah. Ar Raqqah, N Syria Asia *35.36N 39.00E*
181 C6 **Madingley Rise** *undersea feature* W Indian Ocean
81 E21 **Madingo-Kayes** Le Kouilou, S Congo *4.22S 11.40E*
81 F21 **Madingou** La Bouenza, S Congo *4.10S 13.33E*
Madioen *see* Madiun
25 U8 **Madison** Florida, SE USA *30.27N 83.24W*
25 T3 **Madison** Georgia, SE USA *33.37N 83.28W*
33 P15 **Madison** Indiana, N USA *38.44N 85.22W*
29 F6 **Madison** Kansas, C USA *38.08N 96.08W*
21 Q6 **Madison** Maine, NE USA *44.48N 69.52W*
31 S9 **Madison** Minnesota, N USA *45.00N 96.12W*
24 K5 **Madison** Mississippi, S USA *32.27N 90.07W*
31 Q14 **Madison** Nebraska, C USA *41.49N 97.27W*
31 R10 **Madison** South Dakota, N USA *44.00N 97.06W*
23 V5 **Madison** Virginia, NE USA *38.24N 78.12W*
23 Q5 **Madison** West Virginia, NE USA *38.04N 81.49W*
32 L9 **Madison** *state capital* Wisconsin, N USA *43.04N 89.22W*
23 T6 **Madison Heights** Virginia, NE USA *37.25N 79.07W*
22 I6 **Madisonville** Kentucky, S USA *37.19N 87.30W*
22 M10 **Madisonville** Tennessee, S USA *35.31N 84.21W*
27 V9 **Madisonville** Texas, SW USA *30.57N 95.54W*
174 Ll15 **Madiun** *prev.* Madioen. Jawa, C Indonesia *7.37S 111.33E*
Madjene *see* Majene
12 J14 **Madoc** Ontario, SE Canada *44.31N 77.27W*
Madoera *see* Madura, Pulau
83 J18 **Mado Gashi** North Eastern, E Kenya *0.40N 39.09E*
165 R11 **Madoi** Qinghai, C China *34.53N 98.07E*
201 O13 **Madolenihmw** Pohnpei, E Micronesia
120 I9 **Madona** *Ger.* Modohn. Madona, E Latvia *56.51N 26.10E*
109 J23 **Madonie** ▲▲ Sicilia, Italy, C Mediterranean Sea
147 Y11 **Madrakah, Ra's** *headland* E Oman *18.56N 57.54E*
34 I12 **Madras** Oregon, NW USA *44.37N 121.07W*
Madras *see* Chennai
59 H14 **Madre de Dios** *off.* Departamento de Madre de Dios. ◈ *department* E Peru
65 F22 **Madre de Dios, Isla** *island* S Chile
59 J14 **Madre de Dios, Río** ≈ Bolivia/Peru
27 T16 **Madre, Laguna** ◎ Texas, SW USA
43 Q9 **Madre, Laguna** *lagoon* NE Mexico
39 Q12 **Madre Mount** ▲ New Mexico, SW USA *34.18N 107.54W*
107 N8 **Madrid** ● (Spain) Madrid, C Spain *40.25N 3.43W*
31 V14 **Madrid** Iowa, C USA *41.52N 93.49W*
107 N7 **Madrid** ◈ *autonomous community* C Spain
107 N10 **Madridejos** Castilla-La Mancha, C Spain *39.28N 3.31W*
106 L7 **Madrigal de las Altas Torres** Castilla-León, N Spain *41.05N 5.00W*
106 K10 **Madrigalejo** Extremadura, W Spain *39.08N 5.36W*
36 L3 **Mad River** ≈ California, W USA
44 J8 **Madriz** ◈ *department* NW Nicaragua
106 K10 **Madroñera** Extremadura, W Spain *39.25N 5.46W*
189 N12 **Madura** Western Australia *31.52S 127.01E*
Madura *see* Madurai
161 H22 **Madurai** *prev.* Madura, Mathurai. Tamil Nādu, S India *9.55N 78.07E*
174 M15 **Madura, Pulau** *prev.* Madoera. *island* C Indonesia
174 Mm15 **Madura, Selat** *strait* C Indonesia
131 Q17 **Madzhalis** Respublika Dagestan, SW Russian Federation *42.12N 47.46E*
116 K12 **Madzharovo** Khaskovo, S Bulgaria *41.36N 25.52E*
85 M14 **Madzimoyo** Eastern, E Zambia *13.39S 32.31E*
171 K15 **Maebashi** *var.* Maebasi, Mayebashi. Gunma, Honshū, S Japan *36.24N 139.01E*
Maebasi *see* Maebashi
178 Hh6 **Mae Chan** Chiang Rai, NW Thailand *20.13N 99.52E*
178 Gg7 **Mae Hong Son** *var.* Maehongson, Muai To. Mae Hong Son, NW Thailand *19.16N 97.55E*
Mae Nam Khong *see* Mekong
178 Hh7 **Mae Nam Nan** ≈ NW Thailand
178 H10 **Mae Nam Tha Chin** ≈ W Thailand
178 Hh7 **Mae Nam Yom** ≈ W Thailand
178 H7 **Mae Sariang** Mae Hong Son, NW Thailand *18.07N 97.57E*
39 O3 **Maeser** Utah, W USA *40.28N 109.35W*
Maeseyck *see* Maaseik
178 Gg9 **Mae Sot** *var.* Ban Mae Sot. Tak, W Thailand *16.43N 98.31E*
Maestricht *see* Maastricht
178 H7 **Mae Suai** *var.* Ban Mae Suai. Chiang Rai, NW Thailand *19.36N 99.32E*
178 H7 **Mae Tho, Doi** ▲ NW Thailand *18.56N 99.20E*
180 I4 **Maevatanana** Mahajanga, C Madagascar *16.57S 46.49E*
197 C12 **Maéwo** *prev.* Aurora. *island* C Vanuatu
175 T8 **Mafa** Pulau Halmahera, E Indonesia *0.01N 127.49E*
85 I23 **Mafeteng** W Lesotho *29.48S 27.15E*
101 J21 **Maffe** Namur, SE Belgium *50.21N 5.19E*
176 Y10 **Maffin** Irian Jaya, E Indonesia *1.57S 138.48E*
191 P12 **Maffra** Victoria, SE Australia *37.59S 147.03E*
83 K23 **Mafia** *island* E Tanzania
83 J23 **Mafia Channel** *sea waterway* E Tanzania
85 I21 **Mafikeng** North-West, N South Africa *25.52S 25.39E*
62 J12 **Mafra** Santa Catarina, S Brazil *26.07S 49.46W*
106 F10 **Mafra** Lisboa, C Portugal *38.57N 9.19W*
149 Q17 **Mafraq** Abū Ẓaby, C UAE *24.21N 54.33E*
Mafraq/Mafraq, Muḥāfaẓat al *see* Al Mafraq
127 O10 **Magadan** Magadanskaya Oblast', E Russian Federation *59.37N 150.49E*
127 Nn8 **Magadanskaya Oblast'** ◈ *province* E Russian Federation
110 G11 **Magadino** Ticino, S Switzerland *46.09N 8.50E*
65 G23 **Magallanes** *off.* Región de Magallanes y de la Antártica Chilena. ◈ *region* S Chile
Magallanes *see* Punta Arenas
Magallanes, Estrecho de *see* Magellan, Strait of
12 I10 **Maganasipi, Lac** ◎ Quebec, SE Canada
56 F6 **Magangué** Bolívar, N Colombia *9.13N 74.46W*
Magareva *see* Mangareva
79 V12 **Magaria** Zinder, S Niger *13.00N 8.55E*
194 M16 **Magarida** Central, SW PNG *10.13S 149.17E*
179 Pp9 **Magat** ≈ Luzon, N Philippines
29 T11 **Magazine Mountain** ▲ Arkansas, C USA *35.10N 93.38W*
78 I15 **Magburaka** C Sierra Leone *8.43N 11.57W*
126 M14 **Magdagachi** Amurskaya Oblast', SE Russian Federation *53.25N 125.41E*
64 O12 **Magdalena** Buenos Aires, E Argentina *35.04S 57.30W*
59 M15 **Magdalena** Beni, N Bolivia *13.22S 64.07W*
42 F4 **Magdalena** Sonora, NW Mexico *30.37N 110.58W*
39 Q13 **Magdalena** New Mexico, SW USA *34.07N 107.14W*
56 F5 **Magdalena** *off.* Departamento del Magdalena. ◈ *province* N Colombia
42 E9 **Magdalena, Bahía** *bay* W Mexico
65 G19 **Magdalena, Isla** *island* Archipiélago de los Chonos, S Chile
42 D8 **Magdalena, Isla** *island* W Mexico
49 P6 **Magdalena, Río** ≈ C Colombia
42 F4 **Magdalena, Río** ≈ NW Mexico
Magdalen Islands *see* Madeleine, Îles de la
102 L13 **Magdeburg** Sachsen-Anhalt, C Germany *52.07N 11.39E*
24 L6 **Magee** Mississippi, S USA *31.52N 89.43W*
174 Kk15 **Magelang** Jawa, C Indonesia *7.28S 110.10E*
199 J7 **Magellan Rise** *undersea feature* C Pacific Ocean
65 H24 **Magellan, Strait of** *Sp.* Estrecho de Magallanes. *strait* Argentina/Chile
108 D7 **Magenta** Lombardia, NW Italy *45.28N 8.52E*
Magerøy *see* Magerøya
94 K7 **Magerøya** *var.* Magerøy. *island* N Norway
170 B17 **Mage-shima** *island* Nansei-shotō, SW Japan
110 G11 **Maggia** Ticino, S Switzerland *46.15N 8.42E*
110 G10 **Maggia** ≈ SW Switzerland
Maggiore, Lago *see* Maggiore, Lake
108 C6 **Maggiore, Lake** *It.* Lago Maggiore. ◎ Italy/Switzerland
46 I12 **Maggotty** W Jamaica *18.09N 77.46W*
78 I10 **Maghama** Gorgol, S Mauritania *15.31N 12.49W*
99 F14 **Maghera** *Ir.* Machaire Rátha. C Northern Ireland, UK *54.51N 6.40W*
99 F15 **Magherafelt** *Ir.* Machaire Fíolta. C Northern Ireland, UK *54.45N 6.36W*
196 H6 **Magicienne Bay** *bay* Saipan, S Northern Mariana Islands
107 O13 **Magina** ▲ S Spain *37.43N 3.24W*
83 H24 **Magingo** Ruvuma, S Tanzania *9.57S 35.23E*
126 Jj14 **Magistral'nyy** Irkutskaya Oblast', S Russian Federation *56.18N 107.27E*
114 H11 **Maglaj** Federacija Bosna I Hercegovina, N Bosnia and Herzegovina *44.32N 18.03E*
109 Q19 **Maglie** Puglia, SE Italy *40.07N 18.18E*
38 L2 **Magna** Utah, W USA *40.42N 112.06W*
Magnesia *see* Manisa
12 G12 **Magnetawan** ≈ Ontario, S Canada
125 Dd12 **Magnitogorsk** Chelyabinskaya Oblast', C Russian Federation *53.28N 59.06E*
29 T14 **Magnolia** Arkansas, C USA *33.16N 93.14W*
24 K7 **Magnolia** Mississippi, S USA *31.08N 90.27W*
27 V10 **Magnolia** Texas, SW USA *30.12N 95.46W*
Magnolia State *see* Mississippi
97 J15 **Magnor** Hedmark, S Norway *59.57N 12.14E*
197 K14 **Mago** *prev.* Mango. *island* Lau Group, E Fiji
85 L15 **Màgoé** Tete, NW Mozambique *15.51S 31.49E*
13 Q13 **Magog** Quebec, SE Canada *45.16N 72.09W*
85 J15 **Magoye** Southern, S Zambia *16.01S 27.37E*
43 Q12 **Magozal** Veracruz-Llave, C Mexico *21.33N 97.57W*
12 B7 **Magpie** ≈ Ontario, S Canada
9 Q17 **Magrath** Alberta, SW Canada *49.27N 112.52W*
107 R10 **Magro** ≈ E Spain
78 I9 **Magṭa' Laḥjar** *var.* Magta Lahjar, Magta' Lahjar, Magtá Lahjar. Brakna, SW Mauritania *17.27N 13.07W*
85 L20 **Magude** Maputo, S Mozambique *25.01S 32.40E*
79 Y12 **Magumeri** Borno, NE Nigeria *12.07N 12.48E*
201 O14 **Magur Islands** *island group* Caroline Islands, C Micronesia
Magway *see* Magwe
177 Ff6 **Magwe** *var.* Magway. Magwe, W Burma *20.07N 94.59E*
177 Ff6 **Magwe** *var.* Magway. ◈ *division* C Burma
Magyar-Becse *see* Bečej
Magyarkanizsa *see* Kanjiža
Magyarország *see* Hungary
Magyarzsombor *see* Zimbor
148 J4 **Mahābād** *var.* Mehabad; *prev.* Sāūjbulāgh. Āžarbāyjān-e Bākhtarī, NW Iran *36.43N 45.43E*
180 H5 **Mahabo** Toliara, W Madagascar *20.22S 44.39E*
Maha Chai *see* Samut Sakhon
161 D14 **Mahād** Mahārāshtra, W India *18.04N 73.21E*
83 N17 **Mahadday Weyne** Shabeellaha Dhexe, C Somalia *2.55N 45.30E*
81 Q17 **Mahagi** Orientale, NE Dem. Rep. Congo (Zaire) *2.16N 30.58E*
Mahāil *see* Muhāyil
180 I4 **Mahajamba** *seasonal river* NW Madagascar
158 G10 **Mahājan** Rājasthān, NW India *28.46N 73.49E*
180 I3 **Mahajanga** *var.* Majunga. Mahajanga, NW Madagascar *15.40S 46.19E*
180 I3 **Mahajanga** ◈ *province* W Madagascar
180 I3 **Mahajanga** ✕ Mahajanga, NW Madagascar *15.40S 46.19E*
175 N7 **Mahakam, Sungai** *var.* Koetai, Kutai. ≈ Borneo, C Indonesia
85 I19 **Mahalapye** *var.* Mahalatswe. Central, SE Botswana *23.01S 26.52E*
Mahalatswe *see* Mahalapye
Mahalla el Kubra *see* El Maḥalla el Kubra
175 Q10 **Mahalona** Sulawesi, C Indonesia *2.37S 121.26E*
Mahameru *see* Semeru, Gunung
149 S11 **Mahān** Kermān, E Iran *30.07N 57.15E*
160 N12 **Mahānadi** ≈ E India
180 J5 **Mahanoro** Toamasina, E Madagascar *19.52S 48.48E*
159 P13 **Mahārājganj** Bihār, N India *26.07N 84.31E*
160 G13 **Mahārāshtra** ◈ *state* W India
180 I4 **Mahavavy** *seasonal river* N Madagascar
161 K24 **Mahaweli Ganga** ≈ C Sri Lanka
Mahbés *see* El Mahbas
161 J15 **Mahbūbābād** Andhra Pradesh, E India *17.35N 80.00E*
161 H16 **Mahbūbnagar** Andhra Pradesh, C India *16.45N 78.01E*
146 M8 **Mahd adh Dhahab** Al Madīnah, W Saudi Arabia *23.33N 40.56E*
57 S9 **Mahdia** C Guyana *5.16N 59.08W*
77 N6 **Mahdia** *var.* Al Mahdīyah, Mehdia. NE Tunisia *35.14N 11.06E*
161 F20 **Mahe** *Fr.* Mahé; *prev.* Mayyali. Pondicherry, SW India *11.44N 75.33E*
180 I16 **Mahé** ✕ Mahé, NE Seychelles *4.37S 55.27E*
180 H16 **Mahé** *island* Inner Islands, NE Seychelles
181 Y17 **Mahebourg** SE Mauritius *20.24S 57.42E*
158 L10 **Mahendranagar** Far Western, W Nepal *28.58N 80.13E*
83 I23 **Mahenge** Morogoro, SE Tanzania *8.40S 36.40E*
193 F22 **Maheno** Otago, South Island, NZ *45.10S 170.51E*
160 D9 **Mahesāna** Gujarāt, W India *23.37N 72.28E*
160 F11 **Maheshwar** Madhya Pradesh, C India *22.12N 75.40E*
157 F14 **Mahi** ≈ N India
192 Q10 **Mahia Peninsula** *peninsula* North Island, NZ
121 O16 **Mahilyow** *Rus.* Mogilëv. Mahilyowskaya Voblasts', E Belarus *53.54N 30.23E*
121 M16 **Mahilyowskaya Voblasts'** *prev. Rus.* Mogilëvskaya Oblast'. ◈ *province* E Belarus
203 P7 **Mahina** Tahiti, W French Polynesia *17.28S 149.27W*
193 E23 **Mahinerangi, Lake** ◎ South Island, NZ
85 L22 **Mahlabatini** KwaZulu/Natal, E South Africa *28.10S 31.27E*
177 G5 **Mahlaing** Mandalay, C Burma *21.03N 95.43E*
111 X8 **Mahldorf** Steiermark, SE Austria *46.54N 15.55E*
Mahmūd-e 'Erāqī *see* Maḥmūd-e Rāqī
155 R4 **Maḥmūd-e Rāqī** *var.* Mahmūd-e 'Erāqī. Kāpīsā, NE Afghanistan *35.01N 69.19E*
Mahmudiya *see* Al Maḥmūdīyah
31 S5 **Mahnomen** Minnesota, N USA *47.19N 95.58W*
158 K14 **Mahoba** Uttar Pradesh, N India *25.18N 79.52E*
107 Z9 **Mahón** *Cat.* Maó, *Eng.* Port Mahon; *anc.* Portus Magonis. Menorca, Spain, W Mediterranean Sea *39.54N 4.15E*
20 D14 **Mahoning Creek Lake** ▣ Pennsylvania, NE USA
107 Q10 **Mahora** Castilla-La Mancha, C Spain *39.13N 1.43W*
Mähren *see* Moravia
Mährisch-Budwitz *see* Moravské Budějovice
Mährisch-Kromau *see* Moravský Krumlov
Mährisch-Neustadt *see* Uničov
Mährisch-Schönberg *see* Šumperk
Mährisch-Trübau *see* Moravská Třebová
Mährisch-Weisskirchen *see* Hranice
Māh-Shahr *see* Bandar-e Māhshahr
81 N19 **Mahulu** Maniema, E Dem. Rep. Congo (Zaire) *1.04S 27.10E*
160 C12 **Mahuva** Gujarāt, W India *21.06N 71.46E*
116 N11 **Mahya Dağı** ▲ NW Turkey *41.47N 27.34E*
107 T6 **Maials** *var.* Mayals. Cataluña, NE Spain *41.22N 0.30E*
203 O2 **Maiana** *prev.* Hall Island. *atoll* Tungaru, W Kiribati
203 S11 **Maiao** *var.* Tapuaemanu, Tubuai-Manu. *island* Îles du Vent, W French Polynesia
56 H4 **Maicao** La Guajira, N Colombia *11.25N 72.15W*
Mai Ceu/Mai Chio *see* Maych'ew
105 U8 **Maîche** Doubs, E France *47.15N 6.43E*
99 N22 **Maidenhead** S England, UK *51.31N 0.43W*
9 S15 **Maidstone** Saskatchewan, S Canada *53.06N 109.21W*
99 P22 **Maidstone** SE England, UK *51.16N 0.31E*
79 Y13 **Maiduguri** Borno, NE Nigeria *11.51N 13.09E*
110 I8 **Maienfeld** Sankt Gallen, NE Switzerland *47.01N 9.30E*
118 J12 **Măieruș** *Hung.* Szászmagyarós. Brașov, C Romania *45.55N 25.30E*
Maigh Chromtha *see* Macroom
Maigh Eo *see* Mayo
57 N9 **Maigualida, Sierra** ▲▲ S Venezuela
160 K9 **Maihar** Madhya Pradesh, C India *24.18N 80.46E*
160 K11 **Maikala Range** ▲▲ C India
69 T10 **Maiko** ≈ W Dem. Rep. Congo (Zaire)
Mailand *see* Milano
158 L11 **Mailāni** Uttar Pradesh, N India *28.16N 80.19E*
155 U10 **Māilsi** Punjab, E Pakistan *29.46N 72.15E*
153 R8 **Maimak** Talasskaya Oblast', NW Kyrgyzstan *42.40N 71.12E*
Maimāna *see* Meymaneh
Maimansingh *see* Mymensingh
176 Vv11 **Maimawa** Irian Jaya, E Indonesia *3.21S 133.36E*
Maimuna *see* Al Maymūnah
103 G18 **Main** ≈ C Germany
117 F22 **Maïna** *ancient monument* Pelopónnisos, S Greece *36.24N 22.28E*
117 E20 **Maínalo** ▲▲ S Greece
103 L22 **Mainburg** Bayern, SE Germany *48.40N 11.48E*
Main Camp *see* Banana
12 E12 **Main Channel** *lake channel* Ontario, S Canada
81 I20 **Mai-Ndombe, Lac** *prev.* Lac Léopold II. ◎ W Dem. Rep. Congo (Zaire)
103 K20 **Main-Donau-Kanal** *canal* SE Germany
21 R6 **Maine** *off.* State of Maine; also known as Lumber State, Pine Tree State. ◈ *state* NE USA
104 K6 **Maine** *cultural region* NW France
104 J7 **Maine-et-Loire** ◈ *department* NW France
21 Q9 **Maine, Gulf of** *gulf* NE USA
79 X12 **Maïné-Soroa** Diffa, SE Niger *13.13N 12.05E*
178 Gg1 **Maingkwan** *var.* Mungkawn. Kachin State, N Burma *26.19N 96.37E*
Main Island *see* Bermuda
Mainistir Fhear Maí *see* Fermoy
Mainistirna Búille *see* Boyle
Mainistir na Corann *see* Midleton
Mainistir na Féile *see* Abbeyfeale
98 J5 **Mainland** *island* Orkney, N Scotland, UK
98 L2 **Mainland** *island* Shetland, NE Scotland, UK
165 P16 **Mainling** Xizang Zizhiqu, W China *29.12N 94.06E*
158 K12 **Mainpuri** Uttar Pradesh, N India *27.13N 79.01E*
105 N5 **Maintenon** Eure-et-Loir, C France *48.35N 1.34E*
180 H4 **Maintirano** Mahajanga, W Madagascar *18.01S 44.03E*
95 M15 **Mainua** Oulu, C Finland *64.05N 27.28E*
103 G18 **Mainz** *Fr.* Mayence. Rheinland-Pfalz, SW Germany *50.00N 8.16E*
78 I9 **Maio** *var.* Vila do Maio. Maio, S Cape Verde *15.07N 23.12W*
78 E10 **Maio** *var.* Mayo. *island* Ilhas de Sotavento, SE Cape Verde
64 G12 **Maipo, Río** ≈ C Chile
64 H12 **Maipo, Volcán** ▲ W Argentina *34.09S 69.51W*
63 E22 **Maipú** Buenos Aires, E Argentina *36.52S 57.52W*
64 I11 **Maipú** Mendoza, E Argentina *33.00S 68.46W*
64 H11 **Maipú** Santiago, C Chile *33.30S 70.52W*
56 L5 **Maiquetía** Distrito Federal, N Venezuela *10.36N 66.57W*
110 I10 **Maira** *It.* Mera. ≈ Italy/Switzerland
108 A9 **Maira** ≈ NW Italy
159 V12 **Mairābari** Assam, NE India *26.28N 92.22E*
46 K7 **Maisí** Guantánamo, E Cuba *20.13N 74.08W*
120 H13 **Maišiagala** Vilnius, SE Lithuania *54.52N 25.03E*
159 V17 **Maiskhal Island** *island* SE Bangladesh
178 Gg13 **Mai Sombun** Chumphon, SW Thailand *10.49N 99.13E*
Maisur *see* Karnātaka, India
Maisur *see* Mysore, India
191 T8 **Maitland** New South Wales, SE Australia *32.47S 151.31E*
190 I9 **Maitland** South Australia *34.21S 137.42E*
12 F15 **Maitland** ≈ Ontario, S Canada
205 R1 **Maitri** *Indian research station* Antarctica *70.03S 8.59E*
165 N15 **Maizhokunggar** Xizang Zizhiqu, W China *29.49N 91.40E*
45 O10 **Maíz, Islas del** *var.* Corn Islands. *island group* SE Nicaragua
171 H14 **Maizuru** Kyōto, Honshū, SW Japan *35.28N 135.21E*
56 F6 **Majagual** Sucre, N Colombia *8.36N 74.30W*
43 Z13 **Majahual** Quintana Roo, E Mexico *18.43N 87.43W*
Majardah, Wādī *see* Medjerda, Oued/Mejerda
Mājeej *see* Mejit Island
175 P11 **Majene** *prev.* Madjene. Sulawesi, C Indonesia *3.33S 118.58E*
45 V15 **Majé, Serranía de** ▲▲ E Panama
114 I11 **Majevica** ▲▲ NE Bosnia and Herzegovina
83 H15 **Majī** Southern, S Ethiopia *6.11N 35.32E*
147 X7 **Majīs** NW Oman *24.25N 56.34E*
Majorca *see* Mallorca
Mājro *see* Majuro Atoll
Majunga *see* Mahajanga
201 Y3 **Majuro** ✕ Majuro Atoll, SE Marshall Islands *7.04N 171.07E*
201 Y2 **Majuro Atoll** *var.* Mājro. *atoll* Ratak Chain, SE Marshall Islands
201 X2 **Majuro Lagoon** *lagoon* Majuro Atoll, SE Marshall Islands
78 H11 **Maka** C Senegal *13.39N 14.25W*
81 F20 **Makabana** Le Niari, SW Congo *3.28S 12.36E*
40 D9 **Makaha** *Haw.* Mākaha. Oahu, Hawaii, USA, C Pacific Ocean *21.28N 158.13W*
40 B8 **Makahuena Point** *headland* Kauai, Hawaii, USA, C Pacific Ocean *21.52N 159.28W*
40 D9 **Makakilo City** Oahu, Hawaii, USA, C Pacific Ocean *21.21N 158.05W*
85 H18 **Makalamabedi** Central, C Botswana *20.18S 23.52E*
Makale *see* Mek'elē
164 K17 **Makalu** *Chin.* Makaru Shan. ▲ China/Nepal *27.53N 87.09E*
83 G23 **Makampi** Mbeya, S Tanzania *8.00S 33.17E*
151 X12 **Makanchi** *Kaz.* Maqanshy. Vostochnyy Kazakhstan, E Kazakhstan *46.47N 82.00E*
44 M8 **Makantaka** Región Autónoma Atlántico Norte, NE Nicaragua *13.13N 84.04W*
202 B16 **Makapu Point** *headland* W Niue *18.58S 169.55E*
193 C24 **Makarewa** Southland, South Island, NZ *46.17S 168.16E*
119 O4 **Makariv** Kyyivs'ka Oblast', N Ukraine *50.28N 29.49E*
193 D20 **Makarora** ≈ South Island, NZ
127 Oo15 **Makarov** Ostrov Sakhalin, Sakhalinskaya Oblast', SE Russian Federation *48.24N 142.37E*
207 R9 **Makarov Basin** *undersea feature* Arctic Ocean
199 Hh4 **Makarov Seamount** *undersea feature* W Pacific Ocean *29.30N 153.30E*
115 F15 **Makarska** *It.* Macarsca. Split-Dalmacija, SE Croatia *43.18N 17.00E*
Makaru Shan *see* Makalu
129 O15 **Makar'yev** Kostromskaya Oblast', NW Russian Federation *57.52N 43.46E*
84 L11 **Makasa** Northern, NE Zambia *9.42S 31.54E*
Makasar *see* Ujungpandang
Makasar, Selat *see* Makassar Straits
Makassar *see* Ujungpandang
198 Ff8 **Makassar Straits** *Ind.* Selat Makasar. *strait* C Indonesia
150 G12 **Makat** *Kaz.* Maqat. Atyrau, SW Kazakhstan *47.41N 53.24E*
203 T10 **Makatea** *island* Îles Tuamotu, C French Polynesia
145 U7 **Makātū** E Iraq *33.55N 45.25E*
180 H6 **Makay** *var.* Massif du Makay. ▲▲ SW Madagascar
116 J12 **Makaza** *pass* Bulgaria/Greece *41.16N 25.26E*
176 Uu9 **Makbon** Irian Jaya, E Indonesia *0.43S 131.30E*
Makedonija *see* Macedonia, FYR
202 B16 **Makefu** W Niue *18.58S 169.55W*
203 V10 **Makemo** *atoll* Îles Tuamotu, C French Polynesia
78 I15 **Makeni** C Sierra Leone *8.57N 12.01W*
Makenzen *see* Orlyak
Makeyevka *see* Makiyivka
131 Q16 **Makhachkala** *prev.* Petrovsk-Port. Respublika Dagestan, SW Russian Federation *42.58N 47.30E*
150 F11 **Makhambet** Atyrau, W Kazakhstan *47.35N 51.35E*
Makharadze *see* Ozurget'i
145 W13 **Makhfar Al Buṣayyah** S Iraq *30.09N 46.09E*
145 R4 **Makhmūr** N Iraq *35.46N 43.31E*
144 I11 **Makhrūq, Wadi al** *dry watercourse* E Jordan
145 R4 **Makḥūl, Jabal** ▲▲ C Iraq
147 R13 **Makhyah, Wādī** *dry watercourse* N Yemen
176 W11 **Maki** Irian Jaya, E Indonesia *3.00S 134.10E*
175 Ss8 **Makian, Pulau** *island* Maluku, E Indonesia
193 G21 **Makikihi** Canterbury, South Island, NZ *44.36S 171.09E*
203 O2 **Makin** *prev.* Pitt Island. *atoll* Tungaru, W Kiribati
83 I20 **Makindu** Eastern, S Kenya *2.15S 37.49E*
151 Q8 **Makinsk** Akmola, N Kazakhstan *52.37N 70.26E*
195 Y17 **Makira** *off.* Makira Province. ◈ *province* SE Solomon Islands
Makira *see* San Cristobal
119 X8 **Makiyivka** *Rus.* Makeyevka; *prev.* Dmitriyevsk. Donets'ka Oblast', E Ukraine *47.57N 37.47E*
146 L10 **Makkah** *Eng.* Mecca. Makkah, W Saudi Arabia *21.27N 39.50E*

◆ Country ● Country Capital ◇ Dependent Territory ○ Dependent Territory Capital ◈ Administrative Region ✕ International Airport ▲ Mountain ▲▲ Mountain Range Volcano ≈ River ◎ Lake ▣ Reservoir

MAKKAH – MANKATO

146 M10 **Makkah** var. Minţaqat Makkah. ◐ province W Saudi Arabia
11 R7 **Makkovik** Newfoundland, NE Canada 55.06N 59.06W
100 K6 **Makkum** Friesland, N Netherlands 53.03N 5.25E
Mako see Makung
113 M25 **Makó** Rom. Macău. Csongrád, SE Hungary 46.14N 20.28E
12 G9 **Makobe Lake** ◎ Ontario, S Canada
197 I14 **Makogai** island C Fiji
81 F18 **Makokou** Ogooué-Ivindo, NE Gabon 0.37N 12.46E
83 G23 **Makongolosi** Mbeya, S Tanzania 8.24S 33.09E
83 E19 **Makota** SW Uganda 0.37S 30.12E
81 G18 **Makoua** Cuvette, C Congo 0.01S 15.40E
112 M10 **Maków Mazowiecki** Mazowieckie, C Poland 52.51N 21.06E
113 K17 **Maków Podhalański** Małopolskie, S Poland 49.43N 19.40E
149 V14 **Makran** cultural region Iran/Pakistan
158 G12 **Makrāna** Rājasthān, N India 27.01N 74.43E
149 U15 **Makran Coast** coastal region SE Iran
121 F20 **Makrany** Rus. Mokrany. Brestskaya Voblasts', SW Belarus 51.49N 24.15E
Makrinoros see Makrynóros
117 H20 **Makrónisosi** island Kykládes, Greece, Aegean Sea
117 D17 **Makrynóros** var. Makrinoros. ▲▲ C Greece
117 G19 **Makryplági** ▲ C Greece 38.00N 23.06E
Maksamaa see Maxmo
128 J15 **Maksatikha** var. Maksatha, Maksaticha. Tverskaya Oblast', W Russian Federation 57.49N 35.46E
160 G10 **Maksi** Madhya Pradesh, C India 23.18N 76.09E
148 I1 **Mākū** Āžarbāyjān-e Bākhtarī, NW Iran 39.16N 44.33E
159 Y11 **Mākum** Assam, NE India 27.28N 95.28E
Makun see Makung
167 R14 **Makung** prev. Mako, Makun. W Taiwan 23.34N 119.34E
170 Bb16 **Makurazaki** Kagoshima, Kyūshū, SW Japan 31.15N 130.15E
79 V15 **Makurdi** Benue, C Nigeria 7.41N 8.35E
125 F12 **Makushino** Kurganskaya Oblast', C Russian Federation 55.11N 67.16E
40 L17 **Makushin Volcano** ▲ Unalaska Island, Alaska, USA 53.53N 166.55W
85 K16 **Makwiro** Mashonaland West, N Zimbabwe 17.52S 30.24E
59 D15 **Mala** Lima, W Peru 12.45S 76.38W
Mala see Mallow, Ireland
Mala see Malaita, Solomon Islands
95 I14 **Malå** Västerbotten, N Sweden 65.12N 18.45E
202 G12 **Mala'atoli** Île Uvea, E Wallis and Futuna
179 Qq15 **Malabang** E Mindanao, S Philippines 7.37N 124.04E
161 E21 **Malabār Coast** coast SW India
81 C16 **Malabo** prev. Santa Isabel. ● (Equatorial Guinea) Isla de Bioco, NW Equatorial Guinea 3.43N 8.51E
81 C16 **Malabo** ✕ Isla de Bioco, N Equatorial Guinea 3.44N 8.51E
Malaca see Málaga
Malacca see Melaka
173 G4 **Malacca, Strait of** Ind. Selat Malaka. strait Indonesia/Malaysia
Malacka see Malacky
113 G20 **Malacky** Hung. Malacka. Bratislavský Kraj, W Slovakia 48.25N 17.01E
35 R16 **Malad City** Idaho, NW USA 42.10N 112.16W
119 Q4 **Mala Divytsya** Chernihivs'ka Oblast', N Ukraine 50.40N 32.13E
121 J15 **Maladzyechna** Pol. Molodeczno, Rus. Molodechno. Minskaya Voblasts', C Belarus 54.19N 26.51E
202 D12 **Malaee** Île Futuna, N Wallis and Futuna
39 V15 **Malaga** New Mexico, SW USA 32.10N 104.04W
56 G8 **Málaga** Santander, C Colombia 6.42N 72.43W
106 M15 **Málaga** anc. Malaca. Andalucía, S Spain 36.43N 4.25W
106 L15 **Málaga** ◐ province Andalucía, S Spain
106 M15 **Málaga** ✕ Andalucía, S Spain 36.38N 4.36W
Malagasy Republic see Madagascar
107 N10 **Malagón** Castilla-La Mancha, C Spain 39.10N 3.51W
99 G18 **Malahide** Ir. Mullach Íde. E Ireland 53.27N 6.09W
195 Y14 **Malaita** off. Malaita Province. ◐ province N Solomon Islands
195 Y15 **Malaita** var. Mala. island N Solomon Islands
82 F13 **Malakal** Upper Nile, S Sudan 9.31N 31.40E
114 C10 **Mala Kapela** ▲▲ NW Croatia
27 V7 **Malakoff** Texas, SW USA 32.10N 96.00W
Malakula see Malekula
155 V7 **Malakwāl** var. Mālikwāla. Punjab, E Pakistan 32.31N 73.18E
194 J12 **Malalamai** Madang, W PNG 5.47S 146.40E
194 J14 **Malalaua** Gulf, S PNG 8.04S 146.09E
175 Q11 **Malamala** Sulawesi, C Indonesia 3.21S 120.58E
174 M15 **Malang** Jawa, C Indonesia 7.58S 112.45E
85 O14 **Malanga** Niassa, N Mozambique 13.27S 36.05E
Malange see Malanje
94 I9 **Malangen** sound N Norway
84 C11 **Malanje** var. Malange. Malanje, NW Angola 9.33S 16.25E
84 C11 **Malanje** var. Malange. ◐ province N Angola
154 M16 **Malān, Rās** headland SW Pakistan 25.13N 63.31E
79 S13 **Malanville** NE Benin 11.49N 3.22E
Malapane see Ozimek
161 F21 **Malappuram** Kerala, SW India 11.00N 76.02E
45 T17 **Mala, Punta** headland S Panama 7.28N 79.58W
97 N16 **Mälaren** ◎ C Sweden
64 H13 **Malargüe** Mendoza, W Argentina 35.31S 69.34W
12 J8 **Malartic** Quebec, SE Canada 48.09N 78.09W
121 F20 **Malaryta** Pol. Maloryta, Rus. Malorita. Brestskaya Voblasts', SW Belarus 51.46N 24.04E
65 J19 **Malaspina** Chubut, SE Argentina 44.56S 66.52W
41 U12 **Malaspina Glacier** glacier Alaska, USA
143 N15 **Malatya** anc. Melitene. Malatya, SE Turkey 38.22N 38.18E
142 M14 **Malatya** ◐ province C Turkey
119 Q7 **Mala Vyska** Rus. Malaya Viska. Kirovohrads'ka Oblast', S Ukraine 48.37N 31.36E
85 M14 **Malawi** off. Republic of Malaŵi; prev. Nyasaland, Nyasaland Protectorate. ◆ republic S Africa
Malawi, Lake see Nyasa, Lake
95 J17 **Malax** Fin. Maalahti. Länsi-Suomi, W Finland 62.55N 21.30E
128 H14 **Malaya Vishera** Novgorodskaya Oblast', W Russian Federation 58.52N 32.12E
Malaya Viska see Mala Vyska
179 R15 **Malaybalay** Mindanao, S Philippines 8.10N 125.08E
148 L6 **Malāyer** prev. Daulatabad. Hamadān, W Iran 34.19N 48.46E
174 Gg3 **Malay Peninsula** peninsula Malaysia/Thailand
174 I3 **Malaysia** var. Federation of Malaysia; prev. the separate territories of Federation of Malaya, Sarawak and Sabah (North Borneo) and Singapore. ◆ monarchy SE Asia
143 R14 **Malazgirt** Muş, E Turkey 39.09N 42.30E
13 R8 **Malbaie** ≈ Quebec, SE Canada
79 T12 **Malbaza** Tahoua, S Niger 13.57N 5.32E
112 J7 **Malbork** Ger. Marienburg, Marienburg in Westpreussen. Pomorskie, N Poland 54.01N 19.02E
102 N9 **Malchin** Mecklenburg-Vorpommern, N Germany 53.43N 12.46E
102 M9 **Malchiner See** ◎ NE Germany
101 D16 **Maldegem** Oost-Vlaanderen, NW Belgium 51.12N 3.27E
100 L13 **Malden** Gelderland, SE Netherlands 51.46N 5.51E
21 O11 **Malden** Massachusetts, NE USA 42.25N 71.04W
29 Y8 **Malden** Missouri, C USA 36.33N 89.58W
203 X4 **Malden Island** prev. Independence Island. atoll E Kiribati
181 Q6 **Maldives** off. Maldivian Divehi, Republic of Maldives. ◆ republic N Indian Ocean
Maldivian Divehi see Maldives
99 P21 **Maldon** E England, UK 51.43N 0.40E
63 G20 **Maldonado** Maldonado, S Uruguay 34.57S 54.58W
63 G20 **Maldonado** ◐ department S Uruguay
43 P17 **Maldonado, Punta** headland S Mexico 16.18N 98.31W
157 K19 **Male'** Div. Maale ● (Maldives) Male' Atoll, C Maldives 4.10N 73.29E
108 G6 **Malè** Trentino-Alto Adige, N Italy 46.21N 10.51E
78 K13 **Maléa** var. Maléya. Haute-Guinée, NE Guinea 11.46N 9.43W
117 G22 **Maléas, Akrotírio** headland S Greece 36.25N 23.11E
117 L17 **Maléas, Akrotírio** headland Lésvos, E Greece 39.01N 26.36E
157 K19 **Male' Atoll** var. Kaafu Atoll. atoll C Maldives
Malebo, Pool see Stanley Pool
160 E12 **Mālegaon** Mahārāshtra, W India 20.33N 74.31E
83 F15 **Malek** Jonglei, S Sudan 6.04N 31.36E
197 B13 **Malekula** var. Malakula; prev. Mallicolo. island W Vanuatu
201 Y15 **Malem** Kosrae, E Micronesia 5.16N 163.01E
85 O15 **Malema** Nampula, N Mozambique 14.57S 37.28E
81 N23 **Malemba-Nkulu** Katanga, SE Dem. Rep. Congo (Zaire) 8.01S 26.48E
195 Q10 **Malendok Island** island Tanga Islands, NE PNG
128 K9 **Malen'ga** Respublika Kareliya, NW Russian Federation 63.50N 36.21E
97 M20 **Målerås** Kalmar, S Sweden 56.55N 15.34E
105 O6 **Malesherbes** Loiret, C France 48.18N 2.25E
117 G18 **Malesína** Stereá Ellás, E Greece 38.37N 23.15E
Maléya see Maléa
131 O15 **Malgobek** Chechenskaya Respublika, SW Russian Federation 43.34N 44.34E
107 X5 **Malgrat de Mar** Cataluña, NE Spain 41.39N 2.45E
82 C9 **Malha** Northern Darfur, W Sudan 15.07N 26.00E
145 Q5 **Malḥāt** C Iraq 34.44N 42.41E
34 K14 **Malheur Lake** ◎ Oregon, NW USA
34 L14 **Malheur River** ≈ Oregon, NW USA
78 I13 **Mali** Moyenne-Guinée, NW Guinea 12.07N 12.28W
79 O9 **Mali** off. Republic of Mali, Fr. République du Mali; prev. French Sudan, Sudanese Republic. ◆ republic W Africa
175 S16 **Maliana** W East Timor 8.57S 125.25E
178 H1 **Mali Hka** ≈ N Burma
Mali Idjoš see Mali Iđoš
114 K8 **Mali Iđoš** var. Mali Idjoš, Hung. Kishegyes; prev. Krivaja. Serbia, N Yugoslavia 45.43N 19.40E
114 K9 **Mali Kanal** canal N Yugoslavia
175 R8 **Maliku** Sulawesi, N Indonesia 0.36S 123.13E
Malik, Wadi al see Milk, Wadi el
Mālikwāla see Malakwāl
178 Gg12 **Mali Kyun** var. Tavoy Island. island Mergui Archipelago, S Burma
97 M19 **Målilla** Kalmar, S Sweden 57.24N 15.49E
114 B11 **Mali Lošinj** It. Lussinpiccolo. Primorje-Gorski Kotar, W Croatia 44.31N 14.28E
Malin see Malyn
179 Q15 **Malindang, Mount** ▲ Mindanao, S Philippines 8.12N 123.37E
83 K20 **Malindi** Coast, SE Kenya 3.13S 40.04E
Malines see Mechelen
98 E13 **Malin Head** Ir. Cionn Mhálanna. headland NW Ireland 55.37N 7.37W
175 Pp7 **Malino, Gunung** ▲ Sulawesi, N Indonesia 0.44N 120.45E
115 M21 **Maliq** var. Maliqi. Korçë, SE Albania 40.45N 20.45E
Maliqi see Maliq
179 Rr16 **Malita** Mindanao, S Philippines 6.13N 125.39E
160 G12 **Malkāpur** Mahārāshtra, C India 20.52N 76.18E
142 B10 **Malkara** Tekirdağ, NW Turkey 40.55N 26.56E
121 J19 **Mal'kavichy** Rus. Mal'kovichi. Brestskaya Voblasts', SW Belarus 52.28N 26.39E
Malkiye see Al Mālikīyah
116 L11 **Malko Sharkovo, Yazovir** ⊠ SE Bulgaria
116 N11 **Malko Tŭrnovo** Burgas, E Bulgaria 42.00N 27.33E
Mal'kovichi see Mal'kavichy
191 R12 **Mallacoota** Victoria, SE Australia 37.34S 149.45E
98 G10 **Mallaig** N Scotland, UK 57.03N 5.48W
190 I9 **Mallala** South Australia 34.29S 138.30E
77 W9 **Mallawi** C Egypt 27.49N 30.43E
107 R5 **Mallén** Aragón, NE Spain 41.52N 1.25W
108 F5 **Malles Venosta** Trentino-Alto Adige, N Italy 46.40N 10.37E
Mallicolo see Malekula
111 Q8 **Mallnitz** Salzburg, S Austria 46.58N 13.09E
107 W9 **Mallorca** Eng. Majorca; anc. Baleares Major. island Islas Baleares, Spain, W Mediterranean Sea
99 C20 **Mallow** Ir. Mala. SW Ireland 52.07N 8.39W
95 E15 **Malm** Nord-Trøndelag, C Norway 64.04N 11.12E
97 L19 **Malmbäck** Jönköping, S Sweden 57.34N 14.30E
94 J12 **Malmberget** Norrbotten, N Sweden 67.09N 20.39E
101 M20 **Malmédy** Liège, E Belgium 50.25N 6.01E
85 E25 **Malmesbury** Western Cape, SW South Africa 33.28S 18.43E
97 N16 **Malmköping** Södermanland, C Sweden 59.07N 16.49E
97 K23 **Malmö** Skåne, S Sweden 55.35N 13.00E
97 K23 **Malmo** ✕ Skåne, S Sweden 55.33N 13.23E
47 Q16 **Malmok** headland Bonaire, S Netherlands Antilles 12.16N 68.21W
97 M18 **Malmslätt** Östergötland, S Sweden 58.25N 15.30E
129 R16 **Malmyzh** Kirovskaya Oblast', NW Russian Federation 56.30N 50.37E
197 B12 **Malo** island W Vanuatu
130 J7 **Maloarkhangel'sk** Orlovskaya Oblast', W Russian Federation 52.25N 36.37E
Maloelap see Maloelap Atoll
201 V6 **Maloelap Atoll** var. Maļoeļap. atoll E Marshall Islands
Maloenda see Malunda
110 I10 **Maloja** Graubünden, S Switzerland 46.25N 9.42E
84 L12 **Malole** Northern, NE Zambia 10.05S 31.37E
197 H13 **Malolo** island Mamanuca Group, W Fiji
197 H13 **Malolo Barrier Reef** var. Ro Ro Reef. reef W Fiji
179 P10 **Malolos** Luzon, N Philippines 14.51N 120.49E
20 K6 **Malone** New York, NE USA 44.51N 74.18W
81 K25 **Malonga** Katanga, S Dem. Rep. Congo (Zaire) 10.30S 23.06E
113 L15 **Małopolska** plateau S Poland
113 K17 **Małopolskie** ◐ province S Poland
Malorita/Maloryta see Malaryta
128 K9 **Maloshuyka** Arkhangel'skaya Oblast', NW Russian Federation 63.43N 37.20E
116 G10 **Mal'ovitsa** ▲ W Bulgaria 42.12N 23.19E
151 V15 **Malovodnoye** Almaty, SE Kazakhstan 43.31N 77.42E
96 C10 **Måløy** Sogn og Fjordane, S Norway 61.55N 5.06E
130 K4 **Maloyaroslavets** Kaluzhskaya Oblast', W Russian Federation 55.03N 36.31E
125 F6 **Malozemel'skaya Tundra** physical region NW Russian Federation
106 J10 **Malpartida de Cáceres** Extremadura, W Spain 39.25N 6.30W
106 K9 **Malpartida de Plasencia** Extremadura, W Spain 39.58N 6.03W
108 C7 **Malpensa** ✕ (Milano) Lombardia, N Italy 45.41N 8.40E
78 J6 **Malqteïr** desert N Mauritania
120 J10 **Malta** Rēzekne, SE Latvia 56.19N 27.11E
35 V7 **Malta** Montana, NW USA 48.21N 107.52W
123 Jj14 **Malta** off. Republic of Malta. ◆ republic C Mediterranean Sea
111 R8 **Malta** var. Maltabach. ≈ S Austria
123 L11 **Malta** island Malta, C Mediterranean Sea
Maltabach see Malta
Malta, Canale di see Malta Channel
123 L12 **Malta Channel** It. Canale di Malta. strait Italy/Malta
85 D20 **Maltahöhe** Hardap, SW Namibia 24.49S 16.58E
99 N16 **Malton** N England, UK 54.07N 0.49W
175 T11 **Maluku** off. Propinsi Maluku, Dut. Molukken, Eng. Moluccas. ◐ province E Indonesia
175 Ss9 **Maluku** Dut. Molukken, Eng. Moluccas; prev. Spice Islands. island group E Indonesia
Maluku, Laut see Molucca Sea
79 V13 **Malumfashi** Katsina, N Nigeria 11.51N 7.39E
175 P11 **Malunda** prev. Maloenda. Sulawesi, C Indonesia 2.58S 118.52E
96 K13 **Malung** Dalarna, C Sweden 60.40N 13.45E
96 K13 **Malungsfors** Dalarna, C Sweden 60.43N 13.34E
195 X14 **Maluu** var. Malu'u. Malaita, N Solomon Islands 8.22S 160.39E
161 D16 **Mālvan** Mahārāshtra, W India 16.05N 73.28E
Malventum see Benevento
29 U12 **Malvern** Arkansas, C USA 34.21N 92.48W
31 S15 **Malvern** Iowa, C USA 40.59N 95.36W
46 I13 **Malvern** ▲ W Jamaica 17.59N 77.42W
Malvinas, Islas see Falkland Islands
119 N4 **Malyn** Rus. Malin. Zhytomyrs'ka Oblast', N Ukraine 50.46N 29.14E
127 O5 **Malyy Anyuy** ≈ NE Russian Federation
131 O11 **Malyye Derbety** Respublika Kalmykiya, SW Russian Federation 47.57N 44.39E
Malyy Kavkaz see Lesser Caucasus
126 M5 **Malyy Lyakhovskiy, Ostrov** island NE Russian Federation
Malyy Pamir see Little Pamir
126 Jj4 **Malyy Taymyr, Ostrov** island Severnaya Zemlya, N Russian Federation
150 E10 **Malyy Uzen'** Kaz. Kishiözen. ≈ Kazakhstan/Russian Federation
126 I16 **Malyy Yenisey** var. Ka-Krem. ≈ S Russian Federation
126 K13 **Mama** Irkutskaya Oblast', C Russian Federation 58.13N 112.45E
131 S3 **Mamadysh** Respublika Tatarstan, W Russian Federation 55.46N 51.22E
119 N14 **Mamaia** Constanța, E Romania 44.13N 28.37E
197 G14 **Mamanuca Group** island group Yasawa Group, W Fiji
152 L13 **Mamash** Lebapskiy Velayat, E Turkmenistan 38.24N 64.12E
176 W11 **Mamasiware** Irian Jaya, E Indonesia 2.46S 134.26E
194 L14 **Mambare** ≈ S PNG
81 O17 **Mambasa** Orientale, NE Dem. Rep. Congo (Zaire) 1.22N 29.02E
176 Xx10 **Mamberamo, Sungai** ≈ Irian Jaya, E Indonesia
81 G15 **Mambéré** ≈ SW Central African Republic
81 G15 **Mambéré-Kadéï** ◐ prefecture SW Central African Republic
176 X9 **Mambetaloi** Irian Jaya, E Indonesia 1.38S 136.12E
Mambij see Manbij
81 H18 **Mambili** ≈ W Congo
85 N18 **Mambone** var. Nova Mambone. Inhambane, E Mozambique 20.59S 35.04E
179 P11 **Mamburao** Mindoro, N Philippines 13.16N 120.36E
180 I16 **Mamelles** island Inner Islands, NE Seychelles
101 M25 **Mamer** Luxembourg, SW Luxembourg 49.37N 6.01E
104 L6 **Mamers** Sarthe, NW France 48.21N 0.22E
81 D15 **Mamfe** Sud-Ouest, W Cameroon 5.46N 9.18E
151 P6 **Mamlyutka** Severnyy Kazakhstan, N Kazakhstan 54.55N 68.31E
38 M15 **Mammoth** Arizona, SW USA 32.43N 110.38W
35 S12 **Mammoth Hot Springs** Wyoming, C USA 44.57N 110.40W
Mamoedjoe see Mamuju
121 A14 **Mamonovo** Ger. Heiligenbeil. Kaliningradskaya Oblast', W Russian Federation 54.28N 19.57E
59 L14 **Mamoré, Rio** ≈ Bolivia/Brazil
78 I14 **Mamou** Moyenne-Guinée, W Guinea 10.34N 12.45W
24 H8 **Mamou** Louisiana, S USA 30.37N 92.25W
180 I14 **Mamoudzou** ○ (Mayotte) C Mayotte 12.48S 45.00E
180 I3 **Mampikony** Mahajanga, N Madagascar 16.03S 47.39E
79 P16 **Mampong** C Ghana 7.01N 1.36W
112 M7 **Mamry, Jezioro** Ger. Mauersee. ◎ NE Poland
175 P10 **Mamuju** prev. Mamoedjoe. Sulawesi, S Indonesia 2.40S 118.51E
175 Oo10 **Mamuju, Teluk** bay Sulawesi, C Indonesia
85 F19 **Mamuno** Ghanzi, W Botswana 22.15S 20.01E
115 K19 **Mamuras** var. Mamurasi, Mamurras. Lezhë, C Albania 41.34N 19.42E
Mamurasi/Mamurras see Mamuras
78 L16 **Man** W Ivory Coast 7.24N 7.33W
57 X9 **Mana** NW French Guiana 5.40N 53.49W
58 A6 **Manabí** ◐ province W Ecuador
44 G4 **Manabique, Punta** var. Cabo Tres Puntas. headland E Guatemala 15.57N 88.37W
56 G11 **Manacacías, Río** ≈ C Colombia
60 F13 **Manacapuru** Amazonas, N Brazil 3.16S 60.37W
175 Rr6 **Manado** prev. Menado. Sulawesi, C Indonesia 1.31N 124.55E
196 H5 **Managaha** island S Northern Mariana Islands
101 G20 **Manage** Hainaut, S Belgium 50.30N 4.13E
44 J10 **Managua** ● (Nicaragua) Managua, W Nicaragua 12.07N 86.15W
44 J10 **Managua** ◐ department W Nicaragua
44 J10 **Managua** ✕ Managua, W Nicaragua 12.07N 86.11W
44 J10 **Managua, Lago de** var. Xolotlán. ◎ W Nicaragua
Manah see Bilād Manaḥ
20 K16 **Manahawkin** New Jersey, NE USA 39.39N 74.12W
192 K11 **Manaia** Taranaki, North Island, NZ 39.32S 174.04E
180 J6 **Manakara** Fianarantsoa, SE Madagascar 22.09S 48.00E
158 J7 **Manāli** Himāchal Pradesh, NW India 32.18N 77.12E
133 U12 **Ma, Nam** Vtn. Sông Mã. ≈ Laos/Vietnam
Manama see Al Manāmah
194 I10 **Manam Island** island N PNG
69 Y13 **Mananara** ≈ SE Madagascar
190 M9 **Manangatang** Victoria, SE Australia 35.04S 142.53E
180 J6 **Mananjary** Fianarantsoa, SE Madagascar 21.13S 48.19E
78 L14 **Manankoro** Sikasso, SW Mali 10.33N 7.25W
78 J12 **Manantali, Lac de** ⊠ W Mali
Manáos see Manaus
193 B23 **Manapouri** Southland, South Island, NZ 45.33S 167.38E
193 B23 **Manapouri, Lake** ◎ South Island, NZ
60 F13 **Manaquiri** Amazonas, NW Brazil 3.27S 60.37W
Manar see Mannar
164 K5 **Manas** Xinjiang Uygur Zizhiqu, NW China 44.16N 86.12E
159 U12 **Manās** var. Dangme Chu. ≈ Bhutan/India
153 R8 **Manas, Gora** ▲ Kyrgyzstan/Uzbekistan 42.17N 71.04E
164 K3 **Manas Hu** ◎ NW China
159 P10 **Manaslu** ▲ C Nepal 28.33N 84.33E
39 S8 **Manassa** Colorado, C USA 37.10N 105.56W
23 W4 **Manassas** Virginia, NE USA 38.45N 77.28W
47 T5 **Manatí** C Puerto Rico 18.26N 66.29W
175 S16 **Manatuto** N East Timor 8.31S 126.00E
194 L14 **Manau** Northern, S PNG 8.05S 147.57E
56 H4 **Manaure** La Guajira, N Colombia 11.46N 72.28W
60 F12 **Manaus** prev. Manáos. state capital Amazonas, NW Brazil 03.06S 60.00W
142 G17 **Manavgat** Antalya, SW Turkey 36.46N 31.28E
192 M13 **Manawatu** ≈ North Island, NZ
192 L11 **Manawatu-Wanganui** off. Manawatu-Wanganui Region. ◐ region North Island, NZ
176 Uu12 **Manawoka, Pulau** island Kepulauan Gorong, E Indonesia
179 Rr16 **Manay** Mindanao, S Philippines 7.12N 126.29E
144 K2 **Manbij** var. Mambij, Fr. Membidj. Ḥalab, N Syria 36.31N 37.55E
107 N13 **Mancha Real** Andalucía, S Spain 37.46N 3.37W
104 I4 **Manche** ◐ department N France
99 L17 **Manchester** Lat. Mancunium. NW England, UK 53.30N 2.15W
25 S5 **Manchester** Georgia, SE USA 32.51N 84.37W
31 Y13 **Manchester** Iowa, C USA 42.28N 91.27W
23 N7 **Manchester** Kentucky, S USA 37.10N 83.40W
21 O10 **Manchester** New Hampshire, NE USA 42.58N 71.25W
22 K10 **Manchester** Tennessee, S USA 35.28N 86.05W
20 M9 **Manchester** Vermont, NE USA 43.09N 73.03W
99 L18 **Manchester** ✕ NW England, UK 53.21N 2.16W
155 P15 **Manchhar Lake** ◎ SE Pakistan
Man-chou-li see Manzhouli
133 X7 **Manchurian Plain** plain NE China
Máncio Lima see Japiim
Mancunium see Manchester
154 J15 **Mand** Baluchistān, SW Pakistan 26.06N 61.58E
Mand see Mand, Rūd-e
83 H25 **Manda** Iringa, SW Tanzania 10.25S 34.38E
180 H6 **Mandabe** Toliara, W Madagascar 21.01S 44.55E
168 I5 **Mandal** Hövsgöl, N Mongolia 49.55N 99.21E
168 L7 **Mandal** Töv, C Mongolia 48.24N 106.47E
97 E18 **Mandal** Vest-Agder, S Norway 58.01N 7.27E
177 G5 **Mandalay** Mandalay, C Burma 21.57N 96.04E
177 G6 **Mandalay** ◐ division C Burma
168 L9 **Mandalgovĭ** Dundgovĭ, C Mongolia 45.47N 106.18E
145 V7 **Mandalī** E Iraq 33.43N 45.33E
97 E18 **Mandalselva** ≈ S Norway
30 M5 **Mandan** North Dakota, N USA 46.49N 100.53W
Mandargiri Hill see Mandār Hill
159 R14 **Mandār Hill** prev. Mandargiri Hill. Bihār, NE India 24.51N 87.03E
175 P11 **Mandar, Teluk** bay Sulawesi, C Indonesia
109 C19 **Mandas** Sardegna, Italy, C Mediterranean Sea 39.40N 9.07E
Mandasor see Mandsaur
83 L16 **Mandera** North Eastern, NE Kenya 3.55N 41.52E
35 V13 **Manderson** Wyoming, C USA 44.13N 107.55W
46 J12 **Mandeville** C Jamaica 18.01N 77.31W
24 K9 **Mandeville** Louisiana, S USA 30.21N 90.04W
158 I7 **Mandi** Himāchal Pradesh, NW India 31.40N 76.58E
78 K14 **Mandiana** Haute-Guinée, E Guinea 10.37N 8.39W
155 U10 **Mandi Būrewāla** var. Būrewāla. Punjab, E Pakistan 30.04N 72.46E
158 G9 **Mandi Dabwāli** Haryāna, NW India 29.55N 74.40E
Mandidzudzure see Chimanimani
85 M15 **Mandié** Manica, NW Mozambique 16.27S 33.28E
85 N14 **Mandimba** Niassa, N Mozambique 14.21S 35.40E
175 Ss9 **Mandioli, Pulau** island Kepulauan Bacan, E Indonesia
59 Q19 **Mandioré, Laguna** ◎ E Bolivia
160 J10 **Mandla** Madhya Pradesh, C India 22.39N 80.21E
85 M20 **Mandlakazi** var. Manjacaze. Gaza, S Mozambique 24.43S 33.57E
97 E24 **Mandø** var. Manø. island W Denmark
176 Ww9 **Mandori** Irian Jaya, E Indonesia 1.01S 134.58E
Mandoúdhion/Mandoudi see Mantoúdi
117 G19 **Mándra** Attikí, C Greece 38.04N 23.31E
180 I7 **Mandrare** ≈ S Madagascar
116 M10 **Mandra, Yazovir** salt lake SE Bulgaria
109 L23 **Mandrazzi, Portella** pass Sicilia, Italy, C Mediterranean Sea 37.57N 15.02E
180 J3 **Mandritsara** Mahajanga, N Madagascar 15.49S 48.49E
149 O13 **Mand, Rūd-e** var. Mand. ≈ S Iran
160 F9 **Mandsaur** prev. Mandasor. Madhya Pradesh, C India 24.05N 75.04E
160 F11 **Māndu** Madhya Pradesh, C India 22.22N 75.24E
175 Oo5 **Mandul, Pulau** island N Indonesia
85 G15 **Mandundu** Western, W Zambia 16.34S 22.18E
188 I13 **Mandurah** Western Australia 32.31S 115.40E
109 P18 **Manduria** Puglia, SE Italy 40.24N 17.37E
161 G20 **Mandya** Karnātaka, C India 12.34N 76.55E
79 P12 **Mané** C Burkina 12.59N 1.21W
108 E8 **Manerbio** Lombardia, NW Italy 45.22N 10.09E
Manevichi see Manevychi
118 K3 **Manevychi** Pol. Maniewicze, Rus. Manevichi. Volyns'ka Oblast', NW Ukraine 51.18N 25.29E
109 N16 **Manfredonia** Puglia, SE Italy 41.38N 15.54E
109 N16 **Manfredonia, Golfo di** gulf Adriatic Sea, N Mediterranean Sea
79 P13 **Manga** C Burkina 11.40N 1.04W
61 L16 **Mangabeiras, Chapada das** ▲▲ E Brazil
81 J20 **Mangai** Bandundu, W Dem. Rep. Congo (Zaire) 3.57S 19.32E
202 L17 **Mangaia** island group S Cook Islands
192 M9 **Mangakino** Waikato, North Island, NZ 38.22S 175.45E
118 M15 **Mangalia** anc. Callatis. Constanța, SE Romania 43.46N 28.34E
80 J11 **Mangalmé** Guéra, SE Chad 12.25N 19.37E
161 E19 **Mangalore** Karnātaka, W India 12.54N 74.51E
203 Y13 **Mangareva** var. Magareva. island Îles Tuamotu, SE French Polynesia
85 I23 **Mangaung** Free State, C South Africa 29.10S 26.19E
Mangaung see Bloemfontein
160 K9 **Mangawān** Madhya Pradesh, C India 24.39N 81.33E
192 M11 **Mangaweka** Manawatu-Wanganui, North Island, NZ 39.49S 175.47E
192 N11 **Mangaweka** ▲ North Island, NZ 39.51S 176.06E
81 P17 **Mangbwalu** Orientale, NE Dem. Rep. Congo (Zaire) 2.06N 30.04E
102 L24 **Mangfall** ≈ SE Germany
174 K11 **Manggar** Pulau Belitung, W Indonesia 2.51S 108.14E
176 Vv12 **Manggawitu** Irian Jaya, E Indonesia 4.11S 133.28E
152 H8 **Manghit** Rus. Mangit. Qoraqalpoghiston Respublikasi, W Uzbekistan 42.06N 60.02E
177 G2 **Mangin Range** ▲▲ N Burma
145 R1 **Mangish** N Iraq 37.03N 43.04E
150 F15 **Mangistau** Kaz. Mangqystaū Oblysy; prev. Mangyshlaskaya. ◐ province SW Kazakhstan
Mangit see Manghit
56 A13 **Manglares, Cabo** headland SW Colombia 1.36N 79.01W
155 V6 **Mangla Reservoir** ⊠ NE Pakistan
165 N9 **Mangnai** var. Lao Mangnai. Qinghai, C China 37.52N 91.39E
Mango see Mago, Fiji
Mango see Sansanné-Mango, Togo
Mangoche see Mangochi
85 N14 **Mangochi** var. Mangoche; prev. Fort Johnston. Southern, SE Malawi 14.27S 35.15E
79 N14 **Mangodara** SW Burkina 9.49N 4.22W
180 H6 **Mangoky** ≈ W Madagascar
175 S10 **Mangole, Pulau** island Kepulauan Sula, E Indonesia
192 J2 **Mangonui** Northland, North Island, NZ 35.00S 173.30E
Mangqystaū Oblysy see Mangistau
Mangqystaū Shyghanaghy see Mangyshlakskiy Zaliv
106 H7 **Mangualde** Viseu, N Portugal 40.36N 7.46W
63 H18 **Mangueira, Lagoa** ◎ S Brazil
79 X6 **Manguéni, Plateau du** ▲ NE Niger
28 K11 **Mangum** Oklahoma, C USA 34.52N 99.30W
81 O18 **Mangurdjipa** Nord Kivu, E Dem. Rep. Congo (Zaire) 0.28N 28.33E
85 L16 **Mangwendi** Mashonaland East, E Zimbabwe 18.22S 31.24E
150 F15 **Mangyshlak, Plato** plateau SW Kazakhstan
150 E14 **Mangyshlakskiy Zaliv** Kaz. Mangqystaū Shyghanaghy. gulf SW Kazakhstan
Mangyshlaskaya see Mangistau
168 I5 **Manhan** Hövsgöl, N Mongolia 50.05N 100.01E
29 O4 **Manhattan** Kansas, C USA 39.11N 96.33W
101 L21 **Manhay** Luxembourg, SE Belgium 50.13N 5.43E
85 L21 **Manhiça** prev. Vila de Manhiça. Maputo, S Mozambique 25.20S 32.49E
85 L21 **Manhoca** Maputo, S Mozambique 26.47S 32.37E
61 N20 **Manhuaçu** Minas Gerais, SE Brazil 20.16S 42.01W
149 R11 **Mānī** Kermān, C Iran
56 H10 **Maní** Casanare, C Colombia 4.49N 72.15W
58 A6 **Manía, Bahía de** bay W Ecuador
85 M17 **Manica** var. Vila de Manica. Manica, W Mozambique 18.51S 32.50E
85 M17 **Manica** off. Província de Manica. ◐ province W Mozambique
85 L17 **Manicaland** ◐ province E Zimbabwe
13 U5 **Manic Deux, Réservoir** ⊠ Quebec, SE Canada
Manich see Manych
61 F14 **Manicoré** Amazonas, N Brazil 5.48S 61.16W
11 N11 **Manicouagan** Quebec, SE Canada 50.40N 68.46W
11 N11 **Manicouagan** ≈ Quebec, SE Canada
13 U6 **Manicouagan, Péninsule de** peninsula Quebec, SE Canada
11 N11 **Manicouagan, Réservoir** ◎ Quebec, E Canada
13 T4 **Manic Trois, Réservoir** ⊠ Quebec, SE Canada
81 M20 **Maniema** off. Région du Maniema. ◐ region E Dem. Rep. Congo (Zaire)
Maniewicze see Manevychi
166 F8 **Maniganggo** Sichuan, C China 32.01N 99.04E
9 Y15 **Manigotagan** Manitoba, S Canada 51.06N 96.18W
159 R13 **Manihāri** Bihār, N India 25.21N 87.37E
203 U9 **Manihi** island Îles Tuamotu, C French Polynesia
202 L13 **Manihiki** atoll N Cook Islands
183 U8 **Manihiki Plateau** undersea feature C Pacific Ocean
206 M14 **Maniitsoq** var. Manîtsoq, Dan. Sukkertoppen. Kita, S Greenland 65.12N 52.05W
159 T15 **Manikganj** Dhaka, C Bangladesh 23.52N 90.00E
158 M14 **Mānikpur** Uttar Pradesh, N India 25.04N 81.06E
179 P11 **Manila** off. City of Manila. ● (Philippines) Luzon, N Philippines 14.34N 120.58E
29 Y9 **Manila** Arkansas, C USA 35.52N 90.10W
201 N16 **Manila Reef** reef W Micronesia
191 T6 **Manilla** New South Wales, SE Australia 30.44S 150.43E
200 Qq14 **Maniloa** island Tongatapu Group, S Tonga
127 P7 **Manily** Koryakskiy Avtonomnyy Okrug, E Russian Federation 62.33N 165.03E
176 Ww9 **Manim, Pulau** island E Indonesia
173 Ff8 **Maninjau, Danau** ◎ Sumatera, W Indonesia
159 W13 **Manipur** ◐ state NE India
159 X14 **Manipur Hills** hill range E India
142 C14 **Manisa** var. Manissa; prev. Saruhan, anc. Magnesia. Manisa, W Turkey 38.36N 27.28E
142 C13 **Manisa** var. Manissa. ◐ province W Turkey
Manissa see Manisa
33 O7 **Manistee** Michigan, N USA 44.14N 86.19W
33 P7 **Manistee River** ≈ Michigan, N USA
33 O4 **Manistique** Michigan, N USA 45.57N 86.15W
33 P4 **Manistique Lake** ◎ Michigan, N USA
9 W13 **Manitoba** ◐ province S Canada
9 X16 **Manitoba, Lake** ◎ Manitoba, S Canada
9 X17 **Manitou** Manitoba, S Canada 49.12N 98.28W
33 N2 **Manitou Island** island Michigan, N USA
12 H11 **Manitou Lake** ◎ Ontario, SE Canada
10 G15 **Manitoulin Island** island Ontario, S Canada
39 T5 **Manitou Springs** Colorado, C USA 38.51N 104.56W
12 G12 **Manitouwabing Lake** ◎ Ontario, S Canada
10 E12 **Manitouwadge** Ontario, S Canada 49.13N 85.51W
10 G15 **Manitowaning** Manitoulin Island, Ontario, S Canada 45.43N 81.49W
12 B7 **Manitowik Lake** ◎ Ontario, S Canada
33 N7 **Manitowoc** Wisconsin, N USA 44.04N 87.40W
Manîtsoq see Maniitsoq
145 O7 **Mānī', Wādī al** dry watercourse W Iraq
10 J14 **Maniwaki** Quebec, SE Canada 46.24N 75.58W
176 X11 **Maniwori** Irian Jaya, E Indonesia 2.49S 136.00E
56 E10 **Manizales** Caldas, W Colombia 5.03N 75.32W
114 F11 **Manjača** ▲▲ NW Bosnia and Herzegovina
Manjacaze see Mandlakazi
188 J14 **Manjimup** Western Australia 34.18S 116.14E
111 V4 **Mank** Niederösterreich, C Austria 48.06N 15.13E
81 I17 **Mankanza** Equateur, NW Dem. Rep. Congo (Zaire) 1.40N 19.08E
159 N12 **Mankāpur** Uttar Pradesh, N India 27.03N 82.12E
28 M3 **Mankato** Kansas, C USA 39.45N 98.10W
31 U10 **Mankato** Minnesota, N USA 44.10N 94.00W

◆ Country ● Country Capital ◇ Dependent Territory ○ Dependent Territory Capital ◐ Administrative Region ✕ International Airport ▲ Mountain ▲▲ Mountain Range ▲ Volcano ≈ River ◎ Lake ⊠ Reservoir

MAN'KIVKA – MARQUETTE

119 O7 **Man'kivka** Cherkas'ka Oblast', C Ukraine 48.58N 30.10E
78 M15 **Mankono** C Ivory Coast 8.06N 6.07W
9 T17 **Mankota** Saskatchewan, S Canada 49.25N 107.04W
161 K23 **Mankulam** Northern Province, N Sri Lanka 9.09N 80.27E
41 Q9 **Manley Hot Springs** Alaska, USA 65.00N 150.37W
20 H10 **Manlius** New York, NE USA 43.00N 75.58W
107 W5 **Manlleu** Cataluña, NE Spain 41.58N 2.16E
31 V11 **Manly** Iowa, C USA 43.17N 93.12W
160 E13 **Manmād** Mahārāshtra, W India 20.15N 74.28E
190 J7 **Mannahill** South Australia 32.29S 139.58E
161 J23 **Mannar** *var.* Manar. Northern Province, NW Sri Lanka 9.01N 79.53E
161 I24 **Mannar, Gulf of** *gulf* India/Sri Lanka
161 J23 **Mannar Island** *island* N Sri Lanka
Mannersdorf *see* Mannersdorf am Leithagebirge
111 Y5 **Mannersdorf am Leithagebirge** *var.* Mannersdorf. Niederösterreich, E Austria 47.58N 16.36E
111 Y6 **Mannersdorf an der Rabnitz** Burgenland, E Austria 47.25N 16.32E
103 G20 **Mannheim** Baden-Württemberg, SW Germany 49.28N 8.29E
9 O12 **Manning** Alberta, W Canada 56.52N 117.39W
31 T14 **Manning** Iowa, C USA 41.54N 95.03W
30 K5 **Manning** North Dakota, N USA 47.13N 102.46W
23 S13 **Manning** South Carolina, SE USA 33.42N 80.12W
203 Y2 **Manning, Cape** *headland* Kiritimati, NE Kiribati 2.01N 157.25W
195 V13 **Manning Strait** *strait* NW Solomon Islands
23 S3 **Mannington** West Virginia, NE USA 39.31N 80.20W
190 A1 **Mann Ranges** ▲▲ South Australia
109 C19 **Mannu** ≈ Sardegna, Italy, C Mediterranean Sea
9 R14 **Mannville** Alberta, SW Canada 53.19N 111.08W
78 J15 **Mano** ≈ Liberia/Sierra Leone
Manø *see* Mandø
41 O13 **Manokotak** Alaska, USA 59.00N 158.58W
176 W9 **Manokwari** Irian Jaya, E Indonesia 0.49S 134.04E
81 N22 **Manono** Shabo, SE Dem. Rep. Congo (Zaire) 7.18S 27.25E
27 T10 **Manor** Texas, SW USA 30.20N 97.33W
99 D16 **Manorhamilton** *Ir.* Cluainín. NW Ireland 54.18N 8.10W
105 S15 **Manosque** Alpes-de-Haute-Provence, SE France 43.49N 5.46E
10 L11 **Manouane, Lac** ◎ Quebec, SE Canada
169 W12 **Manp'o** *var.* Manp'ojin. NW North Korea 41.10N 126.24E
Manp'ojin *see* Manp'o
203 T4 **Manra** *prev.* Sydney Island. *atoll* Phoenix Islands, C Kiribati
107 V5 **Manresa** Cataluña, NE Spain 41.44N 1.52E
158 H9 **Mānsa** Punjab, NW India 30.00N 75.25E
84 J12 **Mansa** *prev.* Fort Rosebery. Luapula, N Zambia 11.13S 28.55E
78 G12 **Mansa Konko** C Gambia 13.26N 15.29W
13 Q11 **Manseau** Quebec, SE Canada 46.23N 71.59W
155 U5 **Mānsehra** North-West Frontier Province, NW Pakistan 34.22N 73.18E
15 Mm6 **Mansel Island** *island* Nunavut, NE Canada
191 O12 **Mansfield** Victoria, SE Australia 37.04S 146.06E
99 M18 **Mansfield** C England, UK 53.09N 1.10W
29 S11 **Mansfield** Arkansas, C USA 35.03N 94.15W
24 G6 **Mansfield** Louisiana, S USA 32.02N 93.42W
21 O12 **Mansfield** Massachusetts, NE USA 42.00N 71.11W
33 T12 **Mansfield** Ohio, N USA 40.45N 82.31W
20 G12 **Mansfield** Pennsylvania, NE USA 41.46N 77.02W
20 M7 **Mansfield, Mount** ▲ Vermont, NE USA 44.31N 72.49W
61 M16 **Mansidão** Bahia, E Brazil 10.46S 44.03W
104 L11 **Mansle** Charente, W France 45.52N 0.11E
78 G12 **Mansôa** C Guinea-Bissau 12.07N 15.18W
49 V8 **Manso, Rio** ≈ C Brazil
Manşûra *see* El Manşûra
Mansurabad *see* Mehrān, Rūd-e
58 A6 **Manta** Manabí, W Ecuador 0.57S 80.39W
59 F14 **Mantaro, Río** ≈ C Peru
37 O8 **Manteca** California, W USA 37.48N 121.13W
56 J7 **Mantecal** Apure, C Venezuela 7.34N 69.07W
33 N11 **Manteno** Illinois, N USA 41.15N 87.49W
23 Y9 **Manteo** Roanoke Island, North Carolina, SE USA 35.53N 75.39W
Mantes-Gassicourt *see* Mantes-la-Jolie
105 N5 **Mantes-la-Jolie** *prev.* Mantes-Gassicourt, Mantes-sur-Seine, *anc.* Medunta. Yvelines, N France 48.58N 1.42E
Mantes-sur-Seine *see* Mantes-la-Jolie
38 L5 **Manti** Utah, W USA 39.16N 111.38W
Mantinea *see* Mantíneia
117 F20 **Mantíneia** *anc.* Mantinea. *site of ancient city* Pelopónnisos, S Greece 37.36N 22.22E
61 M21 **Mantiqueira, Serra da** ▲▲ S Brazil
31 W10 **Mantorville** Minnesota, N USA 44.04N 92.45W
117 G17 **Mantoúdi** *var.* Mandoudi; *prev.* Mandoúdhion. Évvoia, C Greece 38.46N 23.28E
Mantoue *see* Mantova
108 F8 **Mantova** *Eng.* Mantua, *Fr.* Mantoue. Lombardia, NW Italy 45.10N 10.46E
95 M19 **Mäntsälä** Etelä-Suomi, S Finland 60.38N 25.21E
95 L17 **Mänttä** Länsi-Suomi, W Finland 62.00N 24.36E
Mantua *see* Mantova
129 O14 **Manturovo** Kostromskaya Oblast', NW Russian Federation 58.19N 44.42E
95 M18 **Mäntyharju** Ita-Suomi, SE Finland 61.25N 26.52E
94 M13 **Mäntyjärvi** Lappi, N Finland 66.00N 27.35E
202 L16 **Manuae** *island* S Cook Islands
203 Q10 **Manuae** *atoll* Îles Sous le Vent, W French Polynesia
198 Dd8 **Manua Islands** *island group* E American Samoa
42 L5 **Manuel Benavides** Chihuahua, N Mexico 29.07N 103.52W
63 D21 **Manuel J.Cobo** Buenos Aires, E Argentina 35.49S 57.54W
60 M12 **Manuel Luís, Recife** *reef* E Brazil
63 F15 **Manuel Viana** Rio Grande do Sul, S Brazil 29.33S 55.28W
61 I14 **Manuel Zinho** Pará, N Brazil 7.21S 54.47W
203 V11 **Manuhangi** *atoll* Îles Tuamotu, C French Polynesia
193 E22 **Manuherikia** ≈ South Island, NZ
175 R11 **Manui, Pulau** *island* N Indonesia
Manukau *see* Manurewa
192 L6 **Manukau Harbour** *harbor* North Island, NZ
174 K14 **Manuk, Ci** ≈ Jawa, S Indonesia
176 U12 **Manuk, Pulau** *island* Maluku, E Indonesia
203 Z2 **Manulu Lagoon** ◎ Kiritimati, E Kiribati
190 J7 **Manunda Creek** *seasonal river* South Australia
59 K15 **Manupari, Río** ≈ N Bolivia
192 L6 **Manurewa** *var.* Manukau. Auckland, North Island, NZ 37.03S 174.55E
59 K15 **Manurimi, Río** ≈ NW Bolivia
194 I8 **Manus** ◐ *province* N PNG
194 J8 **Manus Island** *var.* Great Admiralty Island. *island* N PNG
176 U15 **Manuwui** Pulau Babar, E Indonesia 7.47S 129.39E
31 Q3 **Manvel** North Dakota, N USA 48.07N 97.15W
35 Z14 **Manville** Wyoming, C USA 42.45N 104.38W
24 G6 **Many** Louisiana, S USA 31.34N 93.28W
83 H21 **Manyara, Lake** ◎ NE Tanzania
130 L12 **Manych** *var.* Manich. ≈ SW Russian Federation
131 N13 **Manych-Gudilo, Ozero** *salt lake* SW Russian Federation
85 H14 **Manyinga** North Western, NW Zambia 13.28S 24.18E
107 O11 **Manzanares** Castilla-La Mancha, C Spain 39.00N 3.23W
46 H7 **Manzanillo** Granma, E Cuba 20.21N 77.07W
42 K14 **Manzanillo** Colima, SW Mexico 19.00N 104.18W
42 K14 **Manzanillo, Bahía** *bay* SW Mexico
39 S11 **Manzano Mountains** ▲▲ New Mexico, SW USA
39 R12 **Manzano Peak** ▲ New Mexico, SW USA 34.35N 106.27W
169 R6 **Manzhouli** *var.* Man-chou-li. Nei Mongol Zizhiqu, N China 49.36N 117.28E
Manzil Bū Ruqaybah *see* Menzel Bourguiba
145 X9 **Manzilīyah** E Iraq 32.26N 47.01E
85 L21 **Manzini** *prev.* Bremersdorp. C Swaziland 26.30S 31.33E
85 L21 **Manzini** ✈ (Mbabane) C Swaziland 26.36S 31.25E
80 G10 **Mao** Kanem, W Chad 14.06N 15.16E
47 N8 **Mao** NW Dominican Republic 19.33N 71.09W
Maó *see* Mahón
Maoemere *see* Maumere
165 W9 **Maojing** Gansu, N China 36.25N 106.36E
176 Xx12 **Maoke, Pegunungan** *Dut.* Sneeuw-gebergte, *Eng.* Snow Mountains. ▲▲ Irian Jaya, E Indonesia
Maol Réidh, Caoc *see* Mweelrea
166 M15 **Maoming** Guangdong, S China 21.45N 110.50E
166 H8 **Maoxian** *var.* Mao Xian; *prev.* Fengyizhen. Sichuan, C China 31.42N 103.48E
85 L19 **Mapai** Gaza, SW Mozambique 22.52S 32.00E
164 H15 **Mapam Yumco** ◎ W China
85 I15 **Mapanza** Southern, S Zambia 16.16S 26.54E
56 J4 **Mapararí** Falcón, N Venezuela 10.47N 69.26W
43 U17 **Mapastepec** Chiapas, SE Mexico 15.24N 92.55W
175 O5 **Mapat, Pulau** *island* N Indonesia
176 Yy14 **Mapi** Irian Jaya, E Indonesia 7.02S 139.24E
176 Vv7 **Mapia, Kepulauan** *island group* E Indonesia
42 L8 **Mapimí** Durango, C Mexico 25.50N 103.50W
85 N19 **Mapinhane** Inhambane, SE Mozambique 22.14S 35.07E
57 N7 **Mapire** Monagas, NE Venezuela 7.48N 64.40W
9 S17 **Maple Creek** Saskatchewan, S Canada 49.55N 109.28W
33 Q9 **Maple River** ≈ Michigan, N USA
31 P7 **Maple River** ≈ North Dakota/South Dakota, N USA
31 S13 **Mapleton** Iowa, C USA 42.10N 95.47W
31 U10 **Mapleton** Minnesota, N USA 43.55N 93.57W
31 R5 **Mapleton** North Dakota, N USA 46.51N 97.04W
34 F13 **Mapleton** Oregon, NW USA 44.01N 123.56W
38 L3 **Mapleton** Utah, W USA 40.07N 111.37W
199 Ii5 **Mapmaker Seamounts** *undersea feature* N Pacific Ocean
194 G10 **Maprik** East Sepik, NW PNG 3.35S 143.03E
85 L21 **Maputo** *prev.* Lourenço Marques. ● (Mozambique) Maputo, S Mozambique 25.58S 32.34E
85 L21 **Maputo** ◐ *province* S Mozambique
85 L21 **Maputo** ✈ Maputo, S Mozambique 25.47S 32.36E
69 V14 **Maputo** ≈ S Mozambique
Maqanshy *see* Makanchi
Maqat *see* Makat
115 K19 **Maqë** ≈ NW Albania
115 M19 **Maqellarë** Dibër, C Albania 41.36N 20.29E
165 S12 **Maqên** *var.* Dawu. Qinghai, C China 34.32N 100.17E
165 S11 **Maqên Gangri** ▲ C China 34.44N 99.25E
165 U12 **Maqu** Gansu, C China 34.02N 102.00E
106 M9 **Maqueda** Castilla-La Mancha, C Spain 40.04N 4.22W
84 B9 **Maquela do Zombo** Uíge, NW Angola 6.03S 15.05E
65 I16 **Maquinchao** Río Negro, C Argentina 41.19S 68.46W
31 Z13 **Maquoketa** Iowa, C USA 42.03N 90.42W
31 Y13 **Maquoketa River** ≈ Iowa, C USA
12 F13 **Mar** Ontario, S Canada 44.48N 81.12W
97 F14 **Mår** ◎ S Norway
83 G19 **Mara** ◐ *region* N Tanzania
203 P8 **Maraa** Tahiti, W French Polynesia 17.43S 149.34W
60 D12 **Maraã** Amazonas, NW Brazil 1.48S 65.21W
203 O8 **Maraa, Pointe** *headland* Tahiti, W French Polynesia 17.43S 149.34W
61 K14 **Marabá** Pará, NE Brazil 5.22S 49.10W
56 H5 **Maracaibo** Zulia, NW Venezuela 10.39N 71.39W
Maracaibo, Gulf of *see* Venezuela, Golfo de
56 H5 **Maracaibo, Lago de** *var.* Lake Maracaibo. *inlet* NW Venezuela
Maracaibo, Lake *see* Maracaibo, Lago de
60 K10 **Maracá, Ilha de** *island* NE Brazil
61 H20 **Maracaju, Serra de** ▲▲ S Brazil
60 I11 **Maracanaquará, Planalto** ▲▲ NE Brazil
56 L5 **Maracay** Aragua, N Venezuela 10.15N 67.36W
Marada *see* Marādah
77 R9 **Marādah** *var.* Marada. N Libya 29.15N 19.28E
79 U12 **Maradi** Maradi, S Niger 13.30N 7.05E
79 U11 **Maradi** ◐ *department* S Niger
83 E21 **Maragarazi** *var.* Muragarazi. ≈ Burundi/Tanzania
Maragha *see* Marāgheh
148 J3 **Marāgheh** *var.* Maragha. Āžarbāyjān-e Khāvarī, NW Iran 37.21N 46.13E
147 P7 **Marāh** *var.* Marrāt. Ar Riyāḑ, C Saudi Arabia 25.04N 45.30E
57 N11 **Marahuaca, Cerro** ▲ S Venezuela 3.37N 65.25W
29 R5 **Marais des Cygnes River** ≈ Kansas/Missouri, C USA
60 L11 **Marajó, Baía de** *bay* N Brazil
61 K12 **Marajó, Ilha de** *island* N Brazil
203 O2 **Marakei** *atoll* Tungaru, W Kiribati
Marakesh *see* Marrakech
83 I18 **Maralal** Rift Valley, C Kenya 1.04N 36.42E
85 G21 **Maralaleng** Kgalagadi, S Botswana 25.42S 22.39E
151 U8 **Maraldy, Ozero** ◎ NE Kazakhstan
190 C5 **Maralinga** South Australia 30.16S 131.35E
179 R15 **Maramag** Mindanao, S Philippines 7.45N 124.58E
Máramarossziget *see* Sighetu Marmației
195 Y16 **Maramasike** *var.* Small Malaita. *island* N Solomon Islands
Maramba *see* Livingstone
204 H3 **Marambio** *Argentinian research station* Antarctica 64.22S 57.18W
118 H9 **Maramureș** ◐ *county* NW Romania
38 L15 **Marana** Arizona, SW USA 32.24N 111.12W
107 P7 **Maranchón** Castilla-La Mancha, C Spain 41.01N 2.10W
148 J2 **Marand** *var.* Merend. Āžarbāyjān-e Khāvarī, NW Iran 38.23N 45.48E
Marandellas *see* Marondera
60 L13 **Maranhão** *off.* Estado do Maranhão. ◐ *state* E Brazil
106 H10 **Maranhão, Barragem do** ⊠ C Portugal
155 O11 **Mārān, Koh-i** ▲ SW Pakistan 29.24N 66.50E
108 J7 **Marano, Laguna di** *lagoon* NE Italy
58 E9 **Marañón, Río** ≈ N Peru
104 J10 **Marans** Charente-Maritime, W France 46.19N 0.58W
85 M20 **Marão** Inhambane, S Mozambique 24.15S 34.09E
193 B23 **Mararoa** ≈ South Island, NZ
Maraş/Marash *see* Kahramanmaraş
109 M19 **Maratea** Basilicata, S Italy 39.57N 15.44E
106 G11 **Marateca** Setúbal, S Portugal 38.34N 8.40W
117 B20 **Marathiá, Akrotírio** *headland* Zákynthos, Iónioi Nísoi, Greece, C Mediterranean Sea 37.39N 20.49E
10 E12 **Marathon** Ontario, S Canada 48.43N 86.22W
25 Y17 **Marathon** Florida Keys, Florida, SE USA 24.42N 81.05W
26 L10 **Marathon** Texas, SW USA 30.10N 103.14W
Marathón *see* Marathónas
117 H19 **Marathónas** *prev.* Marathón. Attikí, C Greece 38.09N 23.58E
175 Oo6 **Maratua, Pulau** *island* N Indonesia
61 O18 **Maraú** Bahia, SE Brazil 14.07S 39.02W
149 R3 **Marāveh Tappeh** Golestān, N Iran 37.52N 55.57E
26 L11 **Maravillas Creek** ≈ Texas, SW USA
194 J13 **Marawaka** Eastern Highlands, C PNG 6.56S 145.54E
179 R15 **Marawi** Mindanao, S Philippines 7.58N 124.16E
Marbat *see* Mirbāţ
106 L16 **Marbella** Andalucía, S Spain 36.31N 4.49W
188 J7 **Marble Bar** Western Australia 21.13S 119.48E
38 L9 **Marble Canyon** *canyon* Arizona, SW USA
27 S10 **Marble Falls** Texas, SW USA 30.34N 98.16W
29 Y7 **Marble Hill** Missouri, C USA 37.18N 89.58W
35 T15 **Marbleton** Wyoming, C USA 45.31N 110.06W
Marburg *see* Maribor
Marburg *see* Marburg an der Lahn, Germany
103 H16 **Marburg an der Lahn** *hist.* Marburg. Hessen, W Germany 50.49N 8.46E
113 H23 **Marcal** ≈ W Hungary
44 G7 **Marcala** La Paz, SW Honduras 14.13N 88.02W
113 H24 **Marcali** Somogy, SW Hungary 46.33N 17.24E
85 A16 **Marca, Ponta da** *headland* SW Angola 16.31S 11.42E
61 I16 **Marcelândia** Mato Grosso, W Brazil 11.18S 54.49W
29 T3 **Marceline** Missouri, C USA 39.42N 92.57W
62 I13 **Marcelino Ramos** Rio Grande do Sul, S Brazil 27.31S 51.57W
57 Y12 **Marcel, Mont** ▲ S French Guiana 2.32N 53.00W
99 O19 **March** E England, UK 52.37N 0.13E
111 Z3 **March** *var.* Morava. ≈ C Europe *see also* Morava
108 I12 **Marche** *Eng.* Marches. ◐ *region* C Italy
105 N11 **Marche** *cultural region* C France
101 J21 **Marche-en-Famenne** Luxembourg, SE Belgium 50.13N 5.21E
106 K14 **Marchena** Andalucía, S Spain 37.19N 5.24W
59 B17 **Marchena, Isla** *var.* Bindloe Island. *island* Galapagos Islands, Ecuador, E Pacific Ocean
Marches *see* Marche
101 J20 **Marchin** Liège, E Belgium 50.30N 5.17E
189 S1 **Marchinbar Island** *island* Wessel Islands, Northern Territory, N Australia
64 L9 **Mar Chiquita, Laguna** ◎ C Argentina
105 Q10 **Marcigny** Saône-et-Loire, C France 46.16N 4.04E
25 W16 **Marco** Florida, SE USA 25.56N 81.43W
Marcodurum *see* Düren
61 O15 **Marcolândia** Pernambuco, E Brazil 7.21S 40.40W
108 I8 **Marco Polo** ✈ (Venezia) Veneto, NE Italy 45.30N 12.21E
Marcq *see* Mark
118 M8 **Mărculești** *Rus.* Markuleshty. N Moldova 47.54N 28.14E
31 S12 **Marcus** Iowa, C USA 42.49N 95.48W
41 S11 **Marcus Baker, Mount** ▲ Alaska, USA 61.26N 147.45W
199 Hh5 **Marcus Island** *var.* Minami Tori Shima. *island* E Japan
20 K8 **Marcy, Mount** ▲ New York, NE USA 44.06N 73.55W
155 T5 **Mardān** North-West Frontier Province, N Pakistan 34.13N 71.59E
65 N14 **Mar del Plata** Buenos Aires, E Argentina 37.59S 57.31W
143 Q16 **Mardin** Mardin, SE Turkey 37.19N 40.43E
143 Q16 **Mardin** ◐ *province* SE Turkey
143 Q16 **Mardin Dağları** ▲▲ SE Turkey
168 J9 **Mardzad** Övörhangay, C Mongolia 45.58N 102.06E
197 L6 **Maré** *island* Îles Loyauté, E New Caledonia
Marea Neagră *see* Black Sea
107 Z8 **Mare de Déu del Toro** ▲ Menorca, Spain, W Mediterranean Sea 39.59N 4.06E
189 W4 **Mareeba** Queensland, NE Australia 17.03S 145.30E
98 G8 **Maree, Loch** ◎ N Scotland, UK
Mareeq *see* Mereeg
Marek *see* Dupnitsa
78 J11 **Maréna** Kayes, W Mali 14.36N 10.57W
202 I2 **Marenanuka** *atoll* Tungaru, W Kiribati
31 X14 **Marengo** Iowa, C USA 41.48N 92.04W
104 J11 **Marennes** Charente-Maritime, W France 45.47N 1.04W
109 G23 **Marettimo, Isola** *island* Isole Egadi, S Italy
26 K10 **Marfa** Texas, SW USA 30.18N 104.01W
59 P17 **Marfil, Laguna** ◎ E Bolivia
Marganets *see* Marhanets'
27 Q4 **Margaret** Texas, SW USA 34.00N 99.38W
188 I14 **Margaret River** Western Australia 33.58S 115.10E
194 G12 **Margarima** Southern Highlands, W PNG 5.57S 143.22E
57 N4 **Margarita, Isla de** *island* N Venezuela
117 I25 **Margarítes** Kríti, Greece, E Mediterranean Sea 35.19N 24.40E
99 Q22 **Margate** *prev.* Mergate. SE England, UK 51.24N 1.24E
25 Z15 **Margate** Florida, SE USA 26.14N 80.12W
Margelan *see* Marghilon
105 P13 **Margeride, Montagnes de la** ▲▲ C France
Margherita *see* Jamaame
109 N16 **Margherita di Savoia** Puglia, SE Italy 41.22N 16.09E
Margherita, Lake *see* Ābaya Hāyk'
83 E18 **Margherita Peak** *Fr.* Pic Marguerite. ▲ Uganda/Dem. Rep. Congo (Zaire) 0.28N 29.58E
155 O4 **Marghī** Bāmīān, N Afghanistan 35.10N 66.26E
153 S10 **Marghilon** *var.* Margelan, *Rus.* Margilan. Farghona Wiloyati, E Uzbekistan 40.29N 71.43E
118 G9 **Marghita** *Hung.* Margitta. Bihor, NW Romania 47.20N 22.19E
Margilan *see* Marghilon
118 K8 **Marginea** Suceava, NE Romania 47.49N 25.47E
Margitta *see* Marghita
154 K9 **Māragow, Dasht-e** *desert* SW Afghanistan
101 L18 **Margraten** Limburg, SE Netherlands 50.49N 5.49E
8 M15 **Marguerite** British Columbia, SW Canada 52.17N 122.10W
204 I6 **Marguerite Bay** *bay* Antarctica
Marguerite, Pic *see* Margherita Peak
119 T9 **Marhanets'** *Rus.* Marganets. Dnipropetrovs'ka Oblast', E Ukraine 47.34N 34.37E
194 E15 **Mari** Western, SW PNG 9.10S 141.39E
203 R12 **Maria** *island* Îles Australes, SW French Polynesia
203 Y12 **Maria** *atoll* Groupe Actéon, SE French Polynesia
42 I12 **María Cleofas, Isla** *island* C Mexico
64 H4 **María Elena** *var.* Oficina María Elena. Antofagasta, N Chile 22.18S 69.40W
97 G21 **Mariager** Århus, C Denmark 56.39N 9.58E
63 C22 **María Ignacia** Buenos Aires, E Argentina 37.24S 59.30W
191 P17 **Maria Island** *island* Tasmania, SE Australia
42 H12 **María Madre, Isla** *island* C Mexico
42 I12 **María Magdalena, Isla** *island* C Mexico
199 H6 **Mariana Islands** *island group* Guam/Northern Mariana Islands
183 N3 **Mariana Trench** *var.* Challenger Deep. *undersea feature* W Pacific Ocean
159 X12 **Mariāni** Assam, NE India 26.39N 94.18E
29 X11 **Marianna** Arkansas, C USA 34.46N 90.45W
25 R8 **Marianna** Florida, SE USA 30.46N 85.13W
180 J16 **Marianne** *island* Inner Islands, NE Seychelles
97 M19 **Mariannelund** Jönköping, S Sweden 57.37N 15.33E
63 D15 **Mariano I.Loza** Corrientes, NE Argentina 29.22S 58.12W
Mariano Machado *see* Ganda
113 A16 **Mariánské Lázně** *Ger.* Marienbad. Karlovarský Kraj, W Czech Republic 49.57N 12.42E
Máriaradna *see* Radna
35 S7 **Marias River** ≈ Montana, NW USA
Maria-Theresiopel *see* Subotica
Máriatölgyes *see* Dubnica nad Váhom
192 H1 **Maria van Diemen, Cape** *headland* North Island, NZ 34.27S 172.38E
111 V5 **Mariazell** Steiermark, E Austria 47.45N 15.17E
147 P15 **Mar'ib** W Yemen 15.28N 45.25E
97 I25 **Maribo** Storstrøm, S Denmark 54.46N 11.30E
111 W9 **Maribor** *Ger.* Marburg. NE Slovenia 46.33N 15.40E
Marica *see* Maritsa
37 R13 **Maricopa** California, W USA 35.03N 119.24W
Maricourt *see* Kangiqsujuaq
83 D15 **Maridi** Western Equatoria, SW Sudan 4.55N 29.30E
204 M11 **Marie Byrd Land** *physical region* Antarctica
199 Ll16 **Marie Byrd Seamount** *undersea feature* N Amundsen Sea 70.00S 118.00W
47 X11 **Marie-Galante** *var.* Ceyre to the Caribs. *island* SE Guadeloupe
47 Y6 **Marie-Galante, Canal de** *channel* S Guadeloupe
95 J20 **Mariehamn** *Fin.* Maarianhamina. Åland, SW Finland 60.04N 19.55E
46 C4 **Mariel** La Habana, W Cuba 22.58N 82.49W
101 H22 **Mariembourg** Namur, S Belgium 50.07N 4.30E
Marienbad *see* Mariánské Lázně
Marienburg *see* Alūksne, Latvia
Marienburg *see* Malbork, Poland
Marienburg *see* Feldioara, Romania
Marienburg in Westpreussen *see* Malbork
Marienhausen *see* Viļaka
85 D20 **Mariental** Hardap, SW Namibia 24.35S 17.55E
20 D13 **Marienville** Pennsylvania, NE USA 41.27N 79.07W
Marienwerder *see* Kwidzyń
60 C12 **Marié, Rio** ≈ NW Brazil
97 K17 **Mariestad** Västra Götaland, S Sweden 58.42N 13.49E
25 S3 **Marietta** Georgia, SE USA 33.57N 84.34W
33 U14 **Marietta** Ohio, N USA 39.25N 81.27W
29 N13 **Marietta** Oklahoma, C USA 33.56N 97.07W
83 H18 **Marigat** Rift Valley, W Kenya 0.28S 35.58E
105 S16 **Marignane** Bouches-du-Rhône, SE France 43.25N 5.12E
Marignano *see* Melegnano
47 O11 **Marigot** NE Dominica 15.31N 61.17W
126 Hh14 **Mariinsk** Kemerovskaya Oblast', S Russian Federation 56.13N 87.27E
131 Q3 **Mariinskiy Posad** Respublika Mariy El, W Russian Federation 56.07N 47.44E
121 E14 **Marijampolė** *prev.* Kapsukas. Marijampolė, S Lithuania 54.33N 23.21E
116 G12 **Marikostenovo** Blagoevgrad, SW Bulgaria 41.25N 23.21E
62 J9 **Marília** São Paulo, S Brazil 22.13S 49.58W
84 D11 **Marimba** Malanje, NW Angola 8.18S 16.58E
145 T1 **Marī Mīlā** E Iraq 36.58N 44.42E
106 G4 **Marín** Galicia, NW Spain 42.22N 8.42W
37 N10 **Marina** California, W USA 36.40N 121.48W
Marina di Catanzaro *see* Catanzaro Marina
Mar'ina Gorka *see* Mar"ina Horka
121 L17 **Mar"ina Horka** *Rus.* Mar'ina Gorka. Minskaya Voblasts', C Belarus 53.30N 28.09E
179 Pp11 **Marinduque** *island* C Philippines
33 S9 **Marine City** Michigan, N USA 42.43N 82.29W
33 N6 **Marinette** Wisconsin, N USA 45.06N 87.37W
62 I10 **Maringá** Paraná, S Brazil 23.25S 51.55W
85 N16 **Maringuè** Sofala, C Mozambique 17.57S 34.23E
106 F9 **Marinha Grande** Leiria, C Portugal 39.45N 8.55W
109 I15 **Marino** Lazio, C Italy 41.46N 12.40E
61 A15 **Mário Lobão** Acre, W Brazil 8.21S 72.58W
25 O5 **Marion** Alabama, S USA 32.37N 87.19W
29 Y11 **Marion** Arkansas, C USA 35.12N 90.12W
32 L17 **Marion** Illinois, N USA 37.43N 88.55W
33 P13 **Marion** Indiana, N USA 40.31N 85.40W
31 X13 **Marion** Iowa, C USA 42.01N 91.36W
29 O5 **Marion** Kansas, C USA 38.21N 97.01W
22 H6 **Marion** Kentucky, S USA 37.19N 88.04W
23 P9 **Marion** North Carolina, SE USA 35.43N 82.00W
33 S12 **Marion** Ohio, N USA 40.34N 83.07W
23 T12 **Marion** South Carolina, SE USA 34.10N 79.24W
23 Q7 **Marion** Virginia, NE USA 36.49N 81.31W
29 O5 **Marion Lake** ⊠ Kansas, C USA
23 S13 **Marion, Lake** ⊠ South Carolina, SE USA
29 S8 **Marionville** Missouri, C USA 37.00N 93.38W
57 N7 **Maripa** Bolívar, E Venezuela 7.27N 65.10W
57 X11 **Maripasoula** W French Guiana 3.43N 54.04W
37 Q9 **Mariposa** California, W USA 37.28N 119.59W
63 G19 **Mariscala** Lavalleja, S Uruguay 34.03S 54.46W
64 M4 **Mariscal Estigarribia** Boquerón, NW Paraguay 22.02S 60.39W
58 C6 **Mariscal Sucre** *var.* Quito. ✈ (Quito) Pichincha, C Ecuador 0.21S 78.37W
32 K16 **Marissa** Illinois, N USA 38.15N 89.45W
105 U14 **Maritime Alps** *Fr.* Alpes Maritimes, *It.* Alpi Marittime. ▲▲ France/Italy
Maritimes, Alpes *see* Maritime Alps
Maritime Territory *see* Primorskiy Kray
116 K11 **Maritsa** *var.* Marica, *Gk.* Évros, *Turk.* Meriç; *anc.* Hebrus. ≈ SW Europe *see also* Évros/Meriç
Maritsa *see* Simeonovgrad
Marittime, Alpi *see* Maritime Alps
Maritzburg *see* Pietermaritzburg
119 X9 **Mariupol'** *prev.* Zhdanov. Donets'ka Oblast', SE Ukraine 47.06N 37.33E
57 Q6 **Mariusa, Caño** ≈ NE Venezuela
148 J5 **Marīvān** *prev.* Dezh Shāhpūr. Kordestān, W Iran 35.30N 46.09E
125 A16 **Mariy El, Respublika** *prev.* Mariyskaya ASSR. ◐ *autonomous republic* W Russian Federation
131 R3 **Mariyets** Respublika Mariy El, W Russian Federation 56.31N 49.48E
Mariyskaya ASSR *see* Mariy El, Respublika
120 G4 **Märjamaa** *Ger.* Merjama. Raplamaa, NW Estonia 58.53N 24.24E
101 I15 **Mark** *Fr.* Marcq. ≈ Belgium/Netherlands
83 N17 **Marka** *var.* Merca. Shabeellaha Hoose, S Somalia 1.43N 44.45E
151 Z10 **Markakol', Ozero** *Kaz.* Marqaköl. ◎ E Kazakhstan
78 M12 **Markala** Ségou, W Mali 13.38N 6.07W
165 S15 **Markam** *var.* Gartog. Xizang Zizhiqu, W China 29.40N 98.33E
97 K21 **Markaryd** Kronoberg, S Sweden 56.25N 13.34E
148 L7 **Markazī** *off.* Ostān-e Markazī. ◐ *province* W Iran
12 F14 **Markdale** Ontario, S Canada 44.19N 80.37W
29 X10 **Marked Tree** Arkansas, C USA 35.31N 90.25W
100 N11 **Markelo** Overijssel, E Netherlands 52.15N 6.30E
100 J9 **Markermeer** ◎ C Netherlands
99 N20 **Market Harborough** C England, UK 52.30N 0.57W
99 N18 **Market Rasen** E England, UK 53.23N 0.21W
126 Kk10 **Markha** ≈ NE Russian Federation
10 H16 **Markham** Ontario, S Canada 43.53N 79.13W
27 V12 **Markham** Texas, SW USA 28.57N 96.04W
194 J13 **Markham** ≈ C PNG
205 Q11 **Markham, Mount** ▲ Antarctica 82.58S 163.30E
112 M11 **Marki** Mazowieckie, C Poland 52.19N 21.07E
164 F8 **Markit** Xinjiang Uygur Zizhiqu, NW China 38.55N 77.40E
119 Y5 **Markivka** *Rus.* Markovka. Luhans'ka Oblast', E Ukraine 49.34N 39.35E
37 Q7 **Markleeville** California, W USA 38.41N 119.47W
100 L8 **Marknesse** Flevoland, N Netherlands 52.44N 5.54E
81 H14 **Markounda** *var.* Marcounda. Ouham, NW Central African Republic 7.37N 17.00E
Markovka *see* Markivka
127 P6 **Markovo** Chukotskiy Avtonomnyy Okrug, NE Russian Federation 64.43N 170.13E
131 P8 **Marks** Saratovskaya Oblast', W Russian Federation 51.40N 46.44E
24 K2 **Marks** Mississippi, S USA 34.15N 90.16W
24 I7 **Marksville** Louisiana, S USA 31.07N 92.04W
103 I19 **Marktheidenfeld** Bayern, C Germany 49.50N 9.36E
103 J24 **Marktoberdorf** Bayern, S Germany 47.45N 10.36E
103 M18 **Marktredwitz** Bayern, E Germany 50.00N 12.04E
Markt-Übelbach *see* Ubelbach
29 V3 **Mark Twain Lake** ⊠ Missouri, C USA
Markuleshty *see* Mărculești
103 E14 **Marl** Nordrhein-Westfalen, W Germany 51.40N 7.06E
190 E2 **Marla** South Australia 27.19S 133.35E
189 Y8 **Marlborough** Queensland, E Australia 22.55S 150.07E
99 M22 **Marlborough** S England, UK 51.25N 1.44W
193 I15 **Marlborough** *off.* Marlborough District. ◐ *unitary authority* South Island, NZ
105 P3 **Marle** Aisne, N France 49.54N 3.48E
33 S8 **Marlette** Michigan, N USA 43.20N 83.05W
27 T9 **Marlin** Texas, SW USA 31.18N 96.54W
23 S5 **Marlinton** West Virginia, NE USA 38.13N 80.05W
28 M12 **Marlow** Oklahoma, C USA 34.39N 97.57W
161 E17 **Marmagao** Goa, W India 15.22N 73.53E
Marmanda *see* Marmande
104 L13 **Marmande** *anc.* Marmanda. Lot-et-Garonne, SW France 44.30N 0.10E
142 C11 **Marmara** Balıkesir, NW Turkey 40.36N 27.34E
142 D11 **Marmara Denizi** *Eng.* Sea of Marmara. *sea* NW Turkey
116 N13 **Marmaraereğlisi** Tekirdağ, NW Turkey 40.58N 27.57E
Marmara, Sea of *see* Marmara Denizi
142 C16 **Marmaris** Muğla, SW Turkey 36.52N 28.16E
30 J6 **Marmarth** North Dakota, N USA 46.17N 103.55W
23 Q5 **Marmet** West Virginia, NE USA 38.12N 81.31W
108 H5 **Marmolada, Monte** ▲ N Italy 46.36N 11.58E
106 M13 **Marmolejo** Andalucía, S Spain 38.03N 4.10W
12 J14 **Marmora** Ontario, SE Canada 44.28N 77.40W
41 Q14 **Marmot Bay** *bay* Alaska, USA
105 Q4 **Marne** ◐ *department* N France
105 Q4 **Marne** ≈ N France
143 U10 **Marneuli** *prev.* Borchalo, Sarvani. S Georgia 41.28N 44.45E
80 I13 **Maro** Moyen-Chari, S Chad 8.25N 18.46E
56 L12 **Maroa** Amazonas, S Venezuela 2.40N 67.33W
180 J3 **Maroantsetra** Toamasina, NE Madagascar 15.22S 49.43E
203 W11 **Marokau** *atoll* Îles Tuamotu, C French Polynesia
180 J5 **Marolambo** Toamasina, E Madagascar 20.03S 48.07E
180 J2 **Maromokotro** ▲ N Madagascar
85 L16 **Marondera** *prev.* Marandellas. Mashonaland East, NE Zimbabwe 18.10S 31.33E
57 X9 **Maroni** *Dut.* Marowijne. ≈ French Guiana/Surinam
191 V2 **Maroochydore-Mooloolaba** Queensland, E Australia 26.36S 153.04E
175 P13 **Maros** Sulawesi, C Indonesia 4.58S 119.34E
118 H11 **Maros** *var.* Mureș, Mureșul, *Ger.* Marosch, Mieresch. ≈ Hungary/Romania *see also* Mureș
Marosch *see* Maros/Mureș
Maroshévíz *see* Toplița
Marosillye *see* Ilia
Marosludas *see* Luduș
Marosújvár/Marosújvárakna *see* Ocna Mureș
Marosvásárhely *see* Târgu Mureș
203 V14 **Marotiri** *var.* Îlots de Bass, Morotiri. *island group* Îles Australes, SW French Polynesia
80 G12 **Maroua** Extrême-Nord, N Cameroon 10.34N 14.19E
57 X12 **Marouini Rivier** ≈ SE Surinam
180 I3 **Marovoay** Mahajanga, NW Madagascar 16.04S 46.40E
57 W9 **Marowijne** ◐ *district* NE Surinam
Marowijne *see* Maroni
Marqaköl *see* Markakol', Ozero
199 M9 **Marquesas Fracture Zone** *tectonic feature* E Pacific Ocean
Marquesas Islands *see* Marquises, Îles
25 W17 **Marquesas Keys** *island group* Florida, SE USA
31 Y12 **Marquette** Iowa, C USA 43.02N 91.10W
33 N3 **Marquette** Michigan, N USA 46.32N 87.24W

◆ Country ● Country Capital ◇ Dependent Territory ○ Dependent Territory Capital ◐ Administrative Region ✈ International Airport ▲ Mountain ▲▲ Mountain Range ⩚ Volcano ≈ River ◎ Lake ⊠ Reservoir

MARQUISE – MAYENNE

105 N1 **Marquise** Pas-de-Calais, N France 50.49N 1.42E
203 X7 **Marquises, Îles** *Eng.* Marquesas Islands. *island group* N French Polynesia
191 Q6 **Marra Creek** ≈ New South Wales, SE Australia
82 B10 **Marra Hills** *plateau* W Sudan
82 B11 **Marra, Jebel** ▲ W Sudan 12.59N 24.16E
76 E7 **Marrakech** *var.* Marakesh, *Eng.* Marrakesh; *prev.* Morocco. W Morocco 31.39N 7.57W
Marrakesh *see* Marrakech
Marrāt *see* Marāh
191 N15 **Marrawah** Tasmania, SE Australia 40.55S 144.41E
190 I4 **Marree** South Australia 29.39S 138.06E
83 L17 **Marrehan** ⛰ SW Somalia
85 N17 **Marromeu** Sofala, C Mozambique 18.18S 35.58E
106 J17 **Marroquí, Punta** *headland* SW Spain 36.01N 5.39W
191 N8 **Marrowie Creek** *seasonal river* New South Wales, SE Australia
85 O14 **Marrupa** Niassa, N Mozambique 13.13S 37.30E
190 D1 **Marryat** South Australia 26.22S 133.22E
77 Y10 **Marsa ʿAlam** SE Egypt 25.01N 34.52E
77 R8 **Marsá al Burayqah** *var.* Al Burayqah. N Libya 30.21N 19.37E
83 J17 **Marsabit** Eastern, N Kenya 2.19N 37.58E
109 H23 **Marsala** *anc.* Lilybaeum. Sicilia, Italy, C Mediterranean Sea 37.48N 12.26E
123 Jj17 **Marsaxlokk Bay** *bay* SE Malta
67 G15 **Mars Bay** *bay* Ascension Island, C Atlantic Ocean
103 H15 **Marsberg** Nordrhein-Westfalen, W Germany 51.28N 8.51E
9 R15 **Marsden** Saskatchewan, S Canada 52.50N 109.45W
100 H7 **Marsdiep** *strait* NW Netherlands
105 R16 **Marseille** *Eng.* Marseilles; *anc.* Massilia. Bouches-du-Rhône, SE France 43.19N 5.21E
Marseille-Marignane *see* Provence
32 M11 **Marseilles** Illinois, N USA 41.19N 88.42W
Marseilles *see* Marseille
78 J16 **Marshall** W Liberia 6.10N 10.22W
41 N11 **Marshall** Alaska, USA 61.52N 162.04W
29 U9 **Marshall** Arkansas, C USA 35.54N 92.37W
33 N14 **Marshall** Illinois, N USA 39.23N 87.41W
33 Q10 **Marshall** Michigan, N USA 42.16N 84.57W
31 S9 **Marshall** Minnesota, N USA 44.26N 95.48W
29 T4 **Marshall** Missouri, C USA 39.07N 93.12W
23 O9 **Marshall** North Carolina, SE USA 35.49N 82.41W
27 X6 **Marshall** Texas, SW USA 32.32N 94.22W
201 S4 **Marshall Islands** *off.* Republic of the Marshall Islands. ◆ *republic* W Pacific Ocean
183 Q3 **Marshall Islands** *island group* W Pacific Ocean
199 Ii7 **Marshall Seamounts** *undersea feature* SW Pacific Ocean
31 W13 **Marshalltown** Iowa, C USA 42.01N 92.54W
21 P12 **Marshfield** Massachusetts, NE USA 42.04N 70.40W
29 T7 **Marshfield** Missouri, C USA 37.20N 92.54W
32 K6 **Marshfield** Wisconsin, N USA 44.41N 90.12W
46 H1 **Marsh Harbour** Great Abaco, W Bahamas 26.31N 77.03W
21 S3 **Mars Hill** Maine, NE USA 46.31N 67.51W
23 P9 **Mars Hill** North Carolina, SE USA 35.49N 82.33W
24 H10 **Marsh Island** *island* Louisiana, S USA
23 S11 **Marshville** North Carolina, SE USA 34.59N 80.22W
13 W5 **Marsoui** Quebec, SE Canada 49.12N 65.58W
13 R8 **Mars, Rivière à** ≈ Quebec, SE Canada
97 O15 **Märsta** Stockholm, C Sweden 59.37N 17.52E
97 H24 **Marstal** Fyn, C Denmark 54.52N 10.31E
97 I19 **Marstrand** Västra Götaland, S Sweden 57.54N 11.31E
27 U8 **Mart** Texas, SW USA 31.32N 96.49W
178 Gg9 **Martaban** *var.* Moktama. Mon State, S Burma 16.31N 97.34E
177 G9 **Martaban, Gulf of** *gulf* S Burma
109 Q19 **Martano** Puglia, SE Italy 40.12N 18.19E
Martapoera *see* Martapura
175 N11 **Martapura** *prev.* Martapoera. Borneo, C Indonesia 3.25S 114.51E
101 L23 **Martelange** Luxembourg, SE Belgium 49.50N 5.43E
116 L7 **Marten** Ruse, N Bulgaria 43.57N 26.08E
12 H10 **Marten River** Ontario, S Canada 46.43N 79.45W
9 T15 **Martensville** Saskatchewan, S Canada 52.15N 106.42W
Marteskirch *see* Târnăveni
Martes Tolosane *see* Martres-Tolosane
117 K25 **Mártha** Kríti, Greece, E Mediterranean Sea 35.03N 25.22E
191 Q6 **Marthaguy Creek** ≈ New South Wales, SE Australia
21 P13 **Martha's Vineyard** *island* Massachusetts, NE USA
110 C11 **Martigny** Valais, SW Switzerland 46.06N 7.03E
105 R16 **Martigues** Bouches-du-Rhône, SE France 43.24N 5.03E
113 J19 **Martin** *Ger.* Sankt Martin, *Hung.* Turócszentmárton; *prev.* Turčiansky Svätý Martin. Žilinský Kraj, N Slovakia 49.03N 18.54E
30 L11 **Martin** South Dakota, N USA 43.10N 101.43W
22 G8 **Martin** Tennessee, S USA 36.20N 88.51W
107 S7 **Martín** ≈ E Spain
109 P18 **Martina Franca** Puglia, SE Italy 40.42N 17.19E
193 M14 **Martinborough** Wellington, North Island, NZ 41.15S 175.28E
27 S11 **Martindale** Texas, SW USA 29.49N 97.49W
37 N8 **Martinez** California, W USA 38.00N 122.12W
25 V3 **Martinez** Georgia, SE USA 33.31N 82.04W
43 Q13 **Martínez de La Torre** Veracruz-Llave, E Mexico 20.06N 97.03W
47 Y12 **Martinique** ◇ *French overseas department* E West Indies
1 O15 **Martinique** *island* E West Indies
Martinique Channel *see* Martinique Passage
47 X12 **Martinique Passage** *var.* Dominica Channel, Martinique Channel. *channel* Dominica/Martinique
25 Q5 **Martin Lake** ⊡ Alabama, S USA
117 G18 **Martíno** *prev.* Martínon. Stereá Ellás, C Greece 38.34N 23.13E
Martínon *see* Martíno
204 J11 **Martin Peninsula** *peninsula* Antarctica
41 S5 **Martin Point** *headland* Alaska, USA 70.06N 143.04W
111 V3 **Martinsberg** Niederösterreich, NE Austria 48.23N 15.09E
23 V3 **Martinsburg** West Virginia, NE USA 39.25N 77.55W
33 V13 **Martins Ferry** Ohio, N USA 40.06N 80.43W
Martinskirch *see* Târnăveni
33 O14 **Martinsville** Indiana, N USA 39.25N 86.25W
23 S8 **Martinsville** Virginia, NE USA 36.41N 79.52W
67 K16 **Martin Vaz, Ilhas** *island group* E Brazil
Martök *see* Martuk
192 M12 **Marton** Manawatu-Wanganui, North Island, NZ 40.05S 175.22E
107 N13 **Martos** Andalucía, S Spain 37.43N 3.58W
104 M16 **Martres-Tolosane** *var.* Martes Tolosane. Haute-Garonne, S France 43.13N 1.00E
94 M11 **Martti** Lappi, NE Finland 67.28N 28.19E
150 I9 **Martuk** *Kaz.* Martök. Aktyubinsk, NW Kazakhstan 50.45N 56.30E
143 U12 **Martuni** E Armenia 40.07N 45.20E
60 L11 **Marudá** Pará, E Brazil 5.25S 49.04W
175 O2 **Marudu, Teluk** *bay* East Malaysia
155 O8 **Maʿrūf** Kandahār, SE Afghanistan 31.37N 67.08E
170 F14 **Marugame** Kagawa, Shikoku, SW Japan 34.16N 133.46E
193 H16 **Maruia** ≈ South Island, NZ
100 M6 **Marum** Groningen, NE Netherlands 53.07N 6.16E
197 C13 **Marum, Mount** ▲ Ambrym, C Vanuatu 16.15S 168.07E
81 P23 **Marungu** ⛰ SE Dem. Rep. Congo (Zaire)
203 Y12 **Marutea** *atoll* Groupe Actéon, C French Polynesia
149 O11 **Marv Dasht** *var.* Mervdasht. Fārs, S Iran 29.51N 52.44E
105 P13 **Marvejols** Lozère, S France 44.35N 3.16E
29 X12 **Marvell** Arkansas, C USA 34.33N 90.52W
38 L6 **Marvine, Mount** ▲ Utah, W USA 38.40N 111.38W
145 Q7 **Marwānīyah** C Iraq 33.58N 42.31E
158 F13 **Mārwār** *var.* Marwar Junction. Rājasthān, N India 25.43N 73.39E
Marwar Junction *see* Mārwār
9 R14 **Marwayne** Alberta, SW Canada 53.30N 110.25W
152 I14 **Mary** *prev.* Merv. Maryyskiy Velayat, S Turkmenistan 37.24N 61.48E
Mary *see* Maryyskiy Velayat
189 Z9 **Maryborough** Queensland, E Australia 25.31S 152.36E
190 M11 **Maryborough** Victoria, SE Australia 37.04S 143.43E
Maryborough *see* Port Laoise
85 G23 **Marydale** Northern Cape, W South Africa 29.25S 22.06E
119 W8 **Marʺyinka** Donetsʹka Oblastʹ, E Ukraine 47.57N 37.27E
Mary Island *see* Kanton
23 W4 **Maryland** *off.* State of Maryland; *also known as* America in Miniature, Cockade State, Free State, Old Line State. ◐ *state* NE USA
27 P7 **Maryneal** Texas, SW USA 32.12N 100.25W
99 J15 **Maryport** NW England, UK 54.44N 3.28W
11 U13 **Marystown** Newfoundland, SE Canada 47.10N 55.10W
38 K6 **Marysvale** Utah, W USA 38.26N 112.14W
37 O6 **Marysville** California, W USA 39.07N 121.35W
29 O3 **Marysville** Kansas, C USA 39.48N 96.37W
33 S13 **Marysville** Michigan, N USA 42.54N 82.29W
33 S9 **Marysville** Ohio, NE USA 40.13N 83.22W
34 H7 **Marysville** Washington, NW USA 48.03N 122.10W
29 R2 **Maryville** Missouri, C USA 40.20N 94.52W
23 N9 **Maryville** Tennessee, S USA 35.45N 83.58W
Mary Welayaty *see* Maryyskiy Velayat
152 I15 **Maryyskiy Velayat** *var.* Mary, *Turkm.* Mary Welayaty. ◐ *province* S Turkmenistan
Marzūq *see* Murzuq
176 V11 **Mas** Irian Jaya, E Indonesia 3.28S 132.40E
44 J11 **Masachapa** *var.* Puerto Masachapa. Managua, W Nicaragua 11.47N 86.31W
83 G19 **Masai Mara National Reserve** *reserve* C Kenya
83 I21 **Masai Steppe** *grassland* NW Tanzania
83 F19 **Masaka** SW Uganda 0.19S 31.46E
175 N13 **Masalembo Besar, Pulau** *island* S Indonesia
143 Y13 **Masallı** *Rus.* Masally. S Azerbaijan 39.03N 48.39E
Masally *see* Masallı
175 Pp10 **Masamba** Sulawesi, C Indonesia 2.33S 120.19E
Masampo *see* Masan
169 Y16 **Masan** *prev.* Masampo. S South Korea 35.10N 128.36E
Masandam Peninsula *see* Musandam Peninsula
83 J25 **Masasi** Mtwara, SE Tanzania 10.43S 38.48E
Masawa *see* Massawa
44 J10 **Masaya** Masaya, W Nicaragua 11.58N 86.06W
44 J10 **Masaya** ◐ *department* W Nicaragua
179 Q12 **Masbate** Masbate, N Philippines 12.21N 123.34E
179 Qq12 **Masbate** *island* C Philippines
76 I6 **Mascara** *var.* Mouaskar. NW Algeria 35.25N 0.10E
181 O7 **Mascarene Basin** *undersea feature* W Indian Ocean
181 O9 **Mascarene Islands** *island group* W Indian Ocean
181 N9 **Mascarene Plain** *undersea feature* W Indian Ocean
181 O7 **Mascarene Plateau** *undersea feature* W Indian Ocean
204 H5 **Mascart, Cape** *headland* Adelaide Island, Antarctica
64 J10 **Mascasín, Salinas de** *salt lake* C Argentina
42 K13 **Mascota** Jalisco, C Mexico 20.31N 104.46W
13 O12 **Mascouche** Quebec, SE Canada 45.46N 73.37W
128 J9 **Maselʹgskaya** Respublika Kareliya, NW Russian Federation 63.09N 34.22E
85 J23 **Maseru** ● (Lesotho) W Lesotho 29.21S 27.34E
85 J23 **Maseru** ✕ W Lesotho 29.27S 27.37E
Mashaba *see* Mashava
166 K14 **Mashan** Guangxi Zhuangzu Zizhiqu, S China 23.40N 108.10E
85 K17 **Mashava** *prev.* Mashaba. Masvingo, SE Zimbabwe 20.03S 30.28E
149 U4 **Mashhad** *var.* Meshed. Khorāsān, NE Iran 36.16N 59.34E
172 Oo4 **Mashike** Hokkaidō, NE Japan 43.51N 141.30E
Mashīz *see* Bardsīr
155 N14 **Mashkai** ≈ SW Pakistan
149 X13 **Māshkel** *var.* Rūd-i Māshkel, Rūd-e Māshkīd. ≈ Iran/Pakistan
154 K12 **Māshkel, Hāmūn-i** *salt marsh* SW Pakistan
Māshkel, Rūd-i/Māshkīd, Rūd-e *see* Māshkel
85 K15 **Mashonaland Central** ◐ *province* N Zimbabwe
85 K16 **Mashonaland East** ◐ *province* NE Zimbabwe
85 J16 **Mashonaland West** ◐ *province* NW Zimbabwe
Mashtagi *see* Maştağa
172 Qq6 **Mashū-ko** *var.* Masyû Ko. ◎ Hokkaidō, NE Japan
147 S14 **Masīlah, Wādī al** *dry watercourse* SE Yemen
81 I21 **Masi-Manimba** Bandundu, SW Dem. Rep. Congo (Zaire) 4.44S 17.56E
83 F17 **Masindi** W Uganda 1.40N 31.45E
83 I19 **Masinga Reservoir** ⊡ S Kenya
179 Oo10 **Masinloc** Luzon, N Philippines 15.35N 119.57E
Masīra *see* Maşīrah, Jazīrat
Masira, Gulf of *see* Maşīrah, Khalīj
147 Y10 **Maşīrah, Jazīrat** *var.* Masīra. *island* E Oman
147 Y10 **Maşīrah, Khalīj** *var.* Gulf of Masira. *bay* E Oman
Masis *see* Büyükağrı Dağı
81 O19 **Masisi** Nord Kivu, E Dem. Rep. Congo (Zaire) 1.25S 28.49E
176 U11 **Masiwang** ≈ Pulau Seram, E Indonesia
Masjed-e Soleymān *see* Masjed Soleymān
148 L9 **Masjed Soleymān** *var.* Masjed-e Soleymān, Masjid-i Sulaiman. Khūzestān, SW Iran 31.58N 49.17E
Masjid-i Sulaiman *see* Masjed Soleymān
Maskat *see* Masqaţ
145 Q7 **Maskhān** C Iraq 33.41N 42.46E
147 X8 **Maskin** *var.* Miskin. NW Oman 23.28N 56.46E
99 B17 **Mask, Lough** *Ir.* Loch Measca. ◎ W Ireland
116 N10 **Maslen Nos** *headland* E Bulgaria 42.19N 27.47E
180 K3 **Masoala, Tanjona** *headland* NE Madagascar 15.58N 50.13E
Masohi *see* Amahai
33 Q9 **Mason** Michigan, N USA 42.33N 84.25W
33 R14 **Mason** Ohio, N USA 39.21N 84.18W
27 Q10 **Mason** Texas, SW USA 30.44N 99.15W
23 P4 **Mason** West Virginia, NE USA 39.01N 82.01W
193 B25 **Mason Bay** *bay* Stewart Island, NZ
32 K13 **Mason City** Illinois, N USA 40.12N 89.42W
31 V12 **Mason City** Iowa, C USA 43.09N 93.12W
Mă, Sông *see* Ma, Nam
20 B16 **Masontown** Pennsylvania, NE USA 39.49N 79.53W
147 Y8 **Masqaţ** *var.* Maskat, *Eng.* Muscat. ● (Oman) NE Oman 23.34N 58.36E
108 E10 **Massa** Toscana, C Italy 44.01N 10.07E
20 M11 **Massachusetts** *off.* Commonwealth of Massachusetts; *also known as* Bay State, Old Bay State, Old Colony State. ◐ *state* NE USA
21 P11 **Massachusetts Bay** *bay* Massachusetts, NE USA
37 R2 **Massacre Lake** ◎ Nevada, W USA
109 O18 **Massafra** Puglia, SE Italy 40.35N 17.05E
110 G11 **Massagno** Ticino, S Switzerland 46.01N 8.55E
80 G11 **Massaguet** Chari-Baguirmi, W Chad 12.28N 15.25E
Massakori *see* Massakory
80 G10 **Massakory** *var.* Massakori; *prev.* Dagana. Chari-Baguirmi, W Chad 13.01N 15.43E
80 H11 **Massalassef** Chari-Baguirmi, SW Chad 11.37N 17.09E
108 F13 **Massa Marittima** Toscana, C Italy 43.03N 10.55E
84 B11 **Massangano** Cuanza Norte, NW Angola 9.36S 14.19E
85 M18 **Massangena** Gaza, S Mozambique 21.34S 32.57E
82 J9 **Massawa** *var.* Masawa, *Amh.* Mitsʼiwa. E Eritrea 15.37N 39.27E
82 K9 **Massawa Channel** *channel* E Eritrea
20 J6 **Massena** New York, NE USA 44.55N 74.53W
80 H11 **Massenya** Chari-Baguirmi, SW Chad 11.21N 16.09E
8 I13 **Masset** Graham Island, British Columbia, SW Canada 54.00N 132.09W
104 L16 **Masseube** Gers, S France 43.26N 0.33E
12 E11 **Massey** Ontario, S Canada 46.13N 82.06W
105 P12 **Massiac** Cantal, C France 45.16N 3.13E
105 P12 **Massif Central** *plateau* C France
Massilia *see* Marseille
33 U12 **Massillon** Ohio, N USA 40.48N 81.31W
79 N12 **Massina** Ségou, W Mali 13.58N 5.24W
85 N19 **Massinga** Inhambane, SE Mozambique 23.16S 35.23E
85 L20 **Massingir** Gaza, SW Mozambique 23.57S 32.12E
205 Z10 **Masson Island** *island* Antarctica
Massoukou *see* Franceville
143 Z11 **Maştağa** *Rus.* Mashtagi, Mastaga. E Azerbaijan 40.31N 50.01E
Mastanli *see* Momchilgrad
192 M13 **Masterton** Wellington, North Island, NZ 40.56S 175.39E
20 M14 **Mastic** Long Island, New York, NE USA 40.48N 72.50W
155 O10 **Mastung** Baluchistān, SW Pakistan 29.46N 66.48E
121 J20 **Mastva** *Rus.* Mostva. ≈ SW Belarus
121 G17 **Masty** *Rus.* Mosty. Hrodzyenskaya Voblastsʹ, W Belarus 53.25N 24.30E
170 E12 **Masuda** Shimane, Honshū, SW Japan 34.40N 131.50E
94 J11 **Masugnsbyn** Norrbotten, N Sweden 67.28N 22.01E
Masuku *see* Franceville
85 K17 **Masvingo** *prev.* Fort Victoria, Nyanda, Victoria. Masvingo, SE Zimbabwe 20.04S 30.49E
85 K18 **Masvingo** *prev.* Victoria. ◐ *province* SE Zimbabwe
176 W10 **Maswaar, Pulau** *island* East Indies
144 H5 **Maşyāf** *Fr.* Misiaf. Ḩamāh, C Syria 35.04N 36.21E
Masyû Ko *see* Mashū-ko
112 E9 **Maszewo** Zachodniopomorskie, NW Poland 53.29N 15.01E
85 I17 **Matabeleland North** ◐ *province* W Zimbabwe
85 J18 **Matabeleland South** ◐ *province* S Zimbabwe
84 O13 **Mataca** Niassa, N Mozambique 12.27S 36.13E
197 G13 **Matacawa Levu** *island* Yasawa Group, NW Fiji
12 G8 **Matachewan** Ontario, S Canada 47.57N 80.39W
81 F22 **Matadi** Bas-Congo, W Dem. Rep. Congo (Zaire) 5.49S 13.31E
27 O4 **Matador** Texas, SW USA 34.01N 100.50W
44 J9 **Matagalpa** Matagalpa, C Nicaragua 12.53N 85.55W
44 K9 **Matagalpa** ◐ *department* W Nicaragua
10 I12 **Matagami** Quebec, S Canada 49.46N 77.37W
27 U13 **Matagorda** Texas, SW USA 28.40N 96.57W
27 U13 **Matagorda Bay** *inlet* Texas, SW USA
27 U14 **Matagorda Island** *island* Texas, SW USA
27 V13 **Matagorda Peninsula** *headland* Texas, SW USA 28.34N 96.01W
203 Q8 **Mataiea** Tahiti, W French Polynesia 17.46S 149.25W
203 T9 **Mataiva** *atoll* Îles Tuamotu, C French Polynesia
191 O7 **Matakana** New South Wales, SE Australia 32.59S 145.53E
192 N7 **Matakana Island** *island* NE NZ
85 C15 **Matala** Huíla, SW Angola 14.45S 15.01E
202 G12 **Matalaʿa Pointe** *headland* Île Uvea, N Wallis and Futuna 13.19S 176.07W
161 K25 **Matale** Central Province, C Sri Lanka 7.28N 80.37E
202 E12 **Matalesina, Pointe** *headland* Île Alofi, W Wallis and Futuna
78 I10 **Matam** NE Senegal 15.40N 13.18W
192 M8 **Matamata** Waikato, North Island, NZ 37.49S 175.45E
79 V12 **Matameye** Zinder, S Niger 13.27N 8.27E
42 L8 **Matamoros** Coahuila de Zaragoza, NE Mexico 25.34N 103.12W
43 P15 **Matamoros** *var.* Izúcar de Matamoros. Puebla, S Mexico 18.36N 98.30W
43 Q8 **Matamoros** Tamaulipas, C Mexico 25.49N 97.31W
175 Q10 **Matana, Danau** ◎ Sulawesi, C Indonesia
77 S13 **Maʿţan as Sārah** SE Libya 21.45N 21.55E
84 J12 **Matanda** Luapula, N Zambia 11.24S 28.25E
83 J24 **Matandu** ≈ S Tanzania
13 V6 **Matane** Quebec, SE Canada 48.48N 67.31W
13 V6 **Matane** ≈ Quebec, SE Canada
79 S12 **Matankari** Dosso, SW Niger 13.39N 4.03E
41 R11 **Matanuska River** ≈ Alaska, USA
56 G7 **Matanza** Santander, N Colombia 7.22N 73.01W
46 D4 **Matanzas** Matanzas, NW Cuba 23.00N 81.32W
13 V7 **Matapédia** ≈ Quebec, SE Canada
13 V6 **Matapédia, Lac** ◎ Quebec, SE Canada
202 B17 **Mata Point** *headland* SE Niue 19.07S 169.51E
202 D12 **Matapu, Pointe** *headland* Île Futuna, W Wallis and Futuna
64 G12 **Mataquito, Río** ≈ C Chile
161 K26 **Matara** Southern Province, S Sri Lanka 5.57N 80.33E
117 D18 **Matarágka** *var.* Mataránga. Dytikí Ellás, C Greece 38.31N 21.32E
175 Nn16 **Mataram** Pulau Lombok, C Indonesia 8.36S 116.07E
Mataránga *see* Matarágka
189 Q3 **Mataranka** Northern Territory, N Australia 14.55S 133.03E
107 W6 **Mataró** *anc.* Illuro. Cataluña, E Spain 41.31N 2.27E
192 O8 **Matata** Bay of Plenty, North Island, NZ 37.54S 176.45E
198 Cc8 **Matātula, Cape** *headland* Tutuila, W American Samoa 14.15S 170.34W
193 D24 **Mataura** Southland, South Island, NZ 46.11S 168.53E
193 D24 **Mataura** ≈ South Island, NZ
Mata Uta *see* Matāʿutu
202 G11 **Matāʿutu** *var.* Mata Uta. ○ (Wallis and Futuna) Île Uvea, Wallis and Futuna 13.22S 176.12W
198 B8 **Matāutu** Upolu, C Samoa 13.57S 171.55W
202 G12 **Matāʿutu, Baie de** *bay* Île Uvea, Wallis and Futuna
203 P7 **Matavai, Baie de** *bay* Tahiti, W French Polynesia
202 I16 **Matavera** Rarotonga, S Cook Islands 21.13S 159.43W
203 V16 **Mataveri** Easter Island, Chile, E Pacific Ocean 27.10S 109.27W
203 V17 **Mataveri** ✕ (Easter Island) Easter Island, Chile, E Pacific Ocean 27.10S 109.27W
192 P9 **Matawai** Gisborne, North Island, NZ 38.23S 177.31E
13 O10 **Matawin** ≈ Quebec, SE Canada
151 V13 **Matay** Almaty, SE Kazakhstan 45.52N 78.45E
12 K8 **Matchi-Manitou, Lac** ◎ Quebec, SE Canada
43 O10 **Matehuala** San Luis Potosí, C Mexico 23.40N 100.37W
47 V13 **Matelot** Trinidad, Trinidad and Tobago 10.48N 61.06W
85 M15 **Matenge** Tete, NW Mozambique 15.22S 33.47E
109 O18 **Matera** Basilicata, S Italy 40.39N 16.34E
113 O21 **Mátészalka** Szabolcs-Szatmár-Bereg, E Hungary 47.57N 22.16E
176 Y10 **Matewar** Irian Jaya, E Indonesia 1.44S 138.26E
95 H17 **Matfors** Västernorrland, C Sweden 62.22N 16.59E
104 K11 **Matha** Charente-Maritime, W France 45.50N 0.13W
(0) F15 **Mathematicians Seamounts** *undersea feature* E Pacific Ocean
23 X6 **Mathews** Virginia, NE USA 37.24N 76.17W
27 S14 **Mathis** Texas, SW USA 28.05N 97.49W
158 J11 **Mathura** *prev.* Muttra. Uttar Pradesh, N India 27.30N 77.42E
Mathurai *see* Madurai
179 Rr16 **Mati** Mindanao, S Philippines 6.58N 126.11E
Matianus *see* Orūmīyeh, Daryācheh-ye
Matiara *see* Matiāri
155 Q15 **Matiāri** *var.* Matiara. Sind, SE Pakistan 25.37N 68.28E
43 S16 **Matías Romero** Oaxaca, SE Mexico 16.52N 94.57W
45 O13 **Matina** Limón, E Costa Rica 10.02N 83.15W
12 D10 **Matinenda Lake** ◎ Ontario, S Canada
21 R8 **Matinicus Island** *island* Maine, NE USA
Matisco/Matisco Ædourum *see* Mâcon
155 Q16 **Mātli** Sind, SE Pakistan 25.06N 68.37E
99 M18 **Matlock** C England, UK 53.07N 1.31W
61 F18 **Mato Grosso** *prev.* Vila Bela da Santissima Trindade. Mato Grosso, W Brazil 14.52S 59.58W
61 G17 **Mato Grosso** *off.* Estado de Mato Grosso; *prev.* Matto Grosso. ◐ *state* W Brazil
62 H8 **Mato Grosso do Sul** *off.* Estado de Mato Grosso do Sul. ◐ *state* S Brazil
61 I18 **Mato Grosso, Planalto de** *plateau* C Brazil
106 G6 **Matosinhos** *prev.* Matozinhos. Porto, NW Portugal 41.10N 8.42W
57 Z10 **Matoury** NE French Guiana 4.49N 52.17W
Matozinhos *see* Matosinhos
113 L21 **Mátra** ⛰ N Hungary
147 Y8 **Maţraḩ** *var.* Mutrah. NE Oman 23.35N 58.30E
118 L12 **Mărășeşti** Vrancea, E Romania 45.52N 27.13E
110 M8 **Matrei Am Brenner** Tirol, W Austria 47.09N 11.28E
111 P8 **Matrei in Osttirol** Tirol, W Austria 47.04N 12.31E
78 I15 **Matru** SW Sierra Leone 7.37N 12.07W
77 U7 **Maţrūḩ** *var.* Mersa Matrûh; *anc.* Paraetonium. NW Egypt 31.20N 27.15E
172 Q13 **Matsubara** *var.* Matubara. Kagoshima, Tokuno-shima, SW Japan 32.58N 129.55E
171 K16 **Matsudo** *var.* Matudo. Chiba, Honshū, S Japan 35.45N 139.49E
170 F11 **Matsue** *var.* Matsuye, Matue. Shimane, Honshū, SW Japan 35.27N 133.03E
171 Mm7 **Matsumae** Hokkaidō, NE Japan 41.27N 140.04E
171 J14 **Matsumoto** *var.* Matumoto. Nagano, Honshū, S Japan 36.18N 137.58E
171 H16 **Matsusaka** *var.* Matsuzaka, Matusaka. Mie, Honshū, SW Japan 34.34N 136.30E
167 S12 **Matsu Tao** *Chin.* Mazu Dao. *island* NW Taiwan
Matsutō *see* Mattō
170 C12 **Matsuura** *var.* Matuura. Nagasaki, Kyūshū, SW Japan 33.21N 129.40E
170 Ee14 **Matsuyama** *var.* Matuyama. Ehime, Shikoku, SW Japan 33.49N 132.46E
Matsuye *see* Matsue
Matsuzaka *see* Matsusaka
171 J17 **Matsuzaki** Shizuoka, Honshū, S Japan 34.43N 138.45E
12 F8 **Mattagami** ≈ Ontario, S Canada
12 F8 **Mattagami Lake** ◎ Ontario, S Canada
64 K12 **Mattaldi** Córdoba, C Argentina 34.32S 64.18W
23 Y9 **Mattamuskeet, Lake** ◎ North Carolina, SE USA
23 W6 **Mattaponi River** ≈ Virginia, NE USA
12 I11 **Mattawa** Ontario, SE Canada 46.19N 78.42W
12 I11 **Mattawa** ≈ Ontario, SE Canada
21 S5 **Mattawamkeag** Maine, NE USA 45.30N 68.20W
21 S4 **Mattawamkeag Lake** ◎ Maine, NE USA
110 D11 **Matterhorn** *It.* Monte Cervino. ▲ Italy/Switzerland *see also* Cervino, Monte 45.58N 7.36E
37 W1 **Matterhorn** ▲ Nevada, W USA 41.48N 115.22W
34 L12 **Matterhorn** *var.* Sacajawea Peak. ▲ Oregon, NW USA 45.12N 117.18W
37 R8 **Matterhorn Peak** ▲ California, W USA 38.06N 119.19W
111 Y5 **Mattersburg** Burgenland, E Austria 47.44N 16.23E
110 E11 **Matter Vispa** ≈ S Switzerland
57 R7 **Matthews Ridge** N Guyana 7.30N 60.07W
46 K7 **Matthew Town** Great Inagua, S Bahamas 20.56N 73.40W
111 Q4 **Mattighofen** Oberösterreich, NW Austria 48.07N 13.09E
109 N16 **Mattinata** Puglia, SE Italy 41.41N 16.01E
147 T9 **Maţţī, Sabkhat** *salt flat* Saudi Arabia/UAE
20 M14 **Mattituck** Long Island, New York, NE USA 40.59N 72.31W
171 I13 **Mattō** *var.* Matsutō. Ishikawa, Honshū, SW Japan 36.31N 136.34E
Matto Grosso *see* Mato Grosso
32 M14 **Mattoon** Illinois, N USA 39.28N 88.22W
59 L16 **Mattos, Río** ≈ C Bolivia
Matu *see* Metu
174 L15 **Matu** Sarawak, East Malaysia 2.39N 111.31E
59 E14 **Matucana** Lima, W Peru 11.53S 76.23W
Matudo *see* Matsudo
Matue *see* Matsue
197 J16 **Matuku** *island* S Fiji
114 B9 **Matulji** Primorje-Gorski Kotar, NW Croatia 45.21N 14.18E
Matumoto *see* Matsumoto
57 P5 **Maturín** Monagas, NE Venezuela 9.45N 63.10W
Matusaka *see* Matsusaka
Matuura *see* Matsuura
Matuyama *see* Matsuyama
130 K11 **Matveyev Kurgan** Rostovskaya Oblastʹ, SW Russian Federation 47.31N 38.55E
131 O8 **Matyshevo** Volgogradskaya Oblastʹ, SW Russian Federation 50.53N 44.09E
159 O13 **Mau** *var.* Maunāth Bhanjan. Uttar Pradesh, N India 25.57N 83.33E
85 O14 **Maúa** Niassa, N Mozambique 13.54S 37.13E
104 M17 **Maubermé, Pic de** *var.* Tuc de Moubermé, *Sp.* Pico Mauberme; *prev.* Tuc de Maubermé. ▲ France/Spain *see also* Moubermé, Tuc de 42.48N 0.54E
Mauberme, Pico *see* Maubermé, Pic de/Moubermé, Tuc de
Maubermé, Tuc de *see* Maubermé, Pic de/Moubermé, Tuc de
105 Q2 **Maubeuge** Nord, N France 50.16N 4.00E
177 Ff8 **Maubin** Irrawaddy, SW Burma 16.43N 95.37E
158 L13 **Maudaha** Uttar Pradesh, N India 25.40N 80.07E
191 N9 **Maude** New South Wales, SE Australia 34.30S 144.20E
205 P3 **Maudheimvidda** *physical region* Antarctica
67 N22 **Maud Rise** *undersea feature* S Atlantic Ocean
111 Q4 **Mauerkirchen** Oberösterreich, NW Austria 48.10N 13.07E
Mauersee *see* Mamry, Jezioro
196 K2 **Maug Islands** *island group* N Northern Mariana Islands
105 Q15 **Mauguio** Hérault, S France 43.37N 4.01E
199 Kk6 **Maui** *island* Hawaii, USA, C Pacific Ocean
202 M16 **Mauke** *atoll* S Cook Islands
64 G13 **Maule** *off.* Región del Maule. ◐ *region* C Chile
104 J9 **Mauléon** Deux-Sèvres, W France 46.55N 0.45W
104 J16 **Mauléon-Licharre** Pyrénées-Atlantiques, SW France 43.14N 0.51W
64 G13 **Maule, Río** ≈ C Chile
65 G17 **Maullín** Los Lagos, S Chile 41.37S 73.34W
Maulmain *see* Moulmein
33 R11 **Maumee** Ohio, N USA 41.34N 83.40W
33 Q12 **Maumee River** ≈ Indiana/Ohio, N USA
29 U11 **Maumelle** Arkansas, C USA 34.51N 92.24W
29 T11 **Maumelle, Lake** ⊡ Arkansas, C USA
175 Qq16 **Maumere** *prev.* Maoemere. Flores, S Indonesia 8.34S 122.13E
85 G17 **Maun** Ngamiland, C Botswana 20.00S 23.25E
Maunāth Bhanjan *see* Mau
Maunawai *see* Waimea
202 H16 **Maungaroa** ▲ Rarotonga, S Cook Islands 21.13S 159.48W
192 K3 **Maungatapere** Northland, North Island, NZ 35.46S 174.10E
192 K4 **Maungaturoto** Northland, North Island, NZ 36.06S 174.21E
203 R10 **Maupiti** *var.* Maurua. *island* Îles Sous le Vent, W French Polynesia
158 K14 **Mau Rānīpur** Uttar Pradesh, N India 25.13N 79.07E
24 K9 **Maurepas, Lake** ◎ Louisiana, S USA
105 T16 **Maures** ⛰ SE France
105 O12 **Mauriac** Cantal, C France 45.13N 2.21E
Maurice *see* Mauritius
67 J20 **Maurice Ewing Bank** *undersea feature* SW Atlantic Ocean
190 C4 **Maurice, Lake** *salt lake* South Australia
20 I17 **Maurice River** ≈ New Jersey, NE USA
27 Y10 **Mauriceville** Texas, SW USA 30.13N 93.52W
100 K12 **Maurik** Gelderland, C Netherlands 51.57N 5.25E
78 H8 **Mauritania** *off.* Islamic Republic of Mauritania, *Ar.* Mūrītānīyah. ◆ *republic* W Africa
181 W15 **Mauritius** *off.* Republic of Mauritius, *Fr.* Maurice. ◆ *republic* W Indian Ocean
132 M17 **Mauritius** *island* W Indian Ocean
181 N9 **Mauritius Trench** *undersea feature* W Indian Ocean
104 H6 **Mauron** Morbihan, NW France 48.06N 2.16W
105 N13 **Maurs** Cantal, C France 44.45N 2.12E
Maurua *see* Maupiti
Maury Mid-Ocean Channel *see* Maury Seachannel
66 L6 **Maury Seachannel** *var.* Maury Mid-Ocean Channel. *undersea feature* N Atlantic Ocean
32 K8 **Mauston** Wisconsin, N USA 43.45N 90.01W
111 R8 **Mauterndorf** Salzburg, NW Austria 47.09N 13.39E
111 T4 **Mauthausen** Oberösterreich, N Austria 48.13N 14.30E
111 Q9 **Mauthen** Kärnten, S Austria 46.39N 12.58E
85 F15 **Mavinga** Cuando Cubango, SE Angola 15.49S 20.23E
85 M17 **Mavita** Manica, W Mozambique 19.31S 33.09E
117 K22 **Mavrópetra, Akrotírio** *headland* Thíra, Kykládes, Greece, Aegean Sea 36.28N 25.22E
117 F16 **Mavrovoúni** ▲ C Greece 39.37N 22.45E
192 Q8 **Mawhai Point** *headland* North Island, NZ 38.08S 178.24E
177 Ff3 **Mawlaik** Sagaing, C Burma 23.40N 94.25E
Mawlamyine *see* Moulmein
147 N14 **Mawr, Wādī** *dry watercourse* NW Yemen
205 X5 **Mawson** *Australian research station* Antarctica 67.24S 63.16E
205 X5 **Mawson Coast** *physical region* Antarctica
30 M4 **Max** North Dakota, N USA 47.48N 101.18W
43 W12 **Maxcanú** Yucatán, SE Mexico 20.35N 90.00W
Maxesibebi *see* Mount Ayliff
111 Q5 **Maxglan** ✕ (Salzburg) Salzburg, W Austria 47.46N 13.00E
95 K16 **Maxmo** *Fin.* Maksamaa. Länsi-Suomi, W Finland 63.13N 22.04E
23 T11 **Maxton** North Carolina, SE USA 34.47N 79.34W
27 R8 **May** Texas, SW USA 31.58N 98.54W
194 E10 **May** ≈ NW PNG
127 N17 **Maya** ≈ E Russian Federation
157 Q19 **Māyābandar** Andaman and Nicobar Islands, India, E Indian Ocean 12.43N 92.52E
Mayadin *see* Al Mayādīn
46 L5 **Mayaguana** *island* SE Bahamas
46 L5 **Mayaguana Passage** *passage* SE Bahamas
47 S6 **Mayagüez** W Puerto Rico 18.12N 67.08W
47 R6 **Mayagüez, Bahía de** *bay* W Puerto Rico
Mayals *see* Maials
81 G20 **Mayama** Le Pool, SE Congo 3.49S 14.52E
39 V8 **Maya, Mesa De** ▲ Colorado, C USA 37.06N 103.30W
149 R4 **Mayamey** Semnān, N Iran 36.26N 55.49E
44 F3 **Maya Mountains** *Sp.* Montañas Mayas. ⛰ Belize/Guatemala
46 I7 **Mayarí** Holguín, E Cuba 20.40N 75.42W
Mayas, Montañas *see* Maya Mountains
20 I17 **May, Cape** *headland* New Jersey, NE USA 38.55N 74.57W
82 J11 **Maychʼew** *var.* Mai Chio, *It.* Mai Ceu. Tigray, N Ethiopia 12.55N 39.30E
144 I2 **Maydān Ikbiz** Ḩalab, N Syria 36.51N 36.40E
155 Q5 **Maydān Shahr** Wardag, E Afghanistan 34.27N 68.48E
82 O12 **Maydh** Sanaag, N Somalia 10.57N 47.07E
Maydi *see* Midī
Mayebashi *see* Maebashi
Mayence *see* Mainz
104 K6 **Mayenne** Mayenne, NW France 48.18N 0.37W
104 J6 **Mayenne** ◐ *department* NW France
104 J7 **Mayenne** ≈ N France

◆ Country ● Country Capital ◇ Dependent Territory ○ Dependent Territory Capital ◐ Administrative Region ✕ International Airport ▲ Mountain ⛰ Mountain Range Volcano ≈ River ◎ Lake ⊡ Reservoir

MAYER – MELVIN

38 K12 Mayer Arizona, SW USA 34.25N 112.15W
24 J4 Mayersville Mississippi, S USA 32.54N 91.04W
9 P14 Mayerthorpe Alberta, SW Canada 53.58N 115.06W
23 S12 Mayesville South Carolina, SE USA 34.00N 80.10W
193 G19 Mayfield Canterbury, South Island, NZ 43.50S 171.24E
35 N14 Mayfield Idaho, NW USA 43.24N 115.56W
22 G7 Mayfield Kentucky, S USA 36.44N 88.38W
38 L5 Mayfield Utah, W USA 39.06N 111.42W
168 K9 Mayhan Övörhangay, C Mongolia 46.02N 104.00E
39 T14 Mayhill New Mexico, SW USA 32.52N 105.28W
151 T9 Maykain Kaz. Mayqayyng. Pavlodar, NE Kazakhstan 51.24N 75.46E
130 L14 Maykop Respublika Adygeya, SW Russian Federation 44.36N 40.06E
Maylibash see Maylybas
Mayli-Say see Mayluu-Suu
153 T9 Mayluu-Suu prev. Mayli-Say, Kir. Mayly-Say. Dzhalal-Abadskaya Oblast', W Kyrgyzstan 41.16N 72.27E
150 L14 Maylybas prev. Maylibash. Kzyzlorda, S Kazakhstan 45.51N 62.37E
Mayly-Say see Mayluu-Suu
Maymana see Meymaneh
178 Gg5 Maymyo Mandalay, C Burma 22.03N 96.30E
127 P6 Mayn ≈ NE Russian Federation
131 Q5 Mayna Ul'yanovskaya Oblast', W Russian Federation 54.04N 47.20E
23 N8 Maynardville Tennessee, S USA 36.15N 83.48W
12 J13 Maynooth Ontario, SE Canada 45.14N 77.54W
8 I6 Mayo Yukon Territory, NW Canada 63.37N 135.48W
25 U9 Mayo Florida, SE USA 30.03N 83.10W
99 B16 Mayo Ir. Maigh Eo. cultural region W Ireland
Mayo see Maio
80 G12 Mayo-Kébbi off. Préfecture du Mayo-Kébbu, var. Mayo-Kébi. ◈ prefecture SW Chad
Mayo-Kébi see Mayo-Kébbi
81 F19 Mayoko Le Niari, SW Congo 2.18S 12.45E
179 Q11 Mayon Volcano ▲ Luzon, N Philippines 13.15N 123.40E
63 A24 Mayor Buratovich Buenos Aires, E Argentina 39.12S 62.41W
106 L4 Mayorga Castilla-León, N Spain 42.10N 5.16W
192 N6 Mayor Island island NE NZ
Mayor Pablo Lagerenza see Capitán Pablo Lagerenza
181 I14 Mayotte ◇ French territorial collectivity E Africa
Mayoumba see Mayumba
46 J13 May Pen C Jamaica 17.58N 77.15W
Mayqayyng see Maykain
179 P7 Mayraira Point headland Luzon, N Philippines 18.36N 120.47E
111 N8 Mayrhofen Tirol, W Austria 47.09N 11.52E
194 F10 May River East Sepik, NW PNG 4.10S 141.51E
126 Mm15 Mayskiy Amurskaya Oblast', SE Russian Federation 52.13N 129.30E
131 O15 Mayskiy Kabardino-Balkarskaya Respublika, SW Russian Federation 43.37N 44.04E
151 U9 Mayskoye Pavlodar, NE Kazakhstan 50.55N 78.11E
20 J17 Mays Landing New Jersey, NE USA 39.27N 74.43W
23 N4 Maysville Kentucky, S USA 38.39N 83.44W
29 R2 Maysville Missouri, C USA 39.53N 94.21W
176 Y14 Mayu channel Irian Jaya, E Indonesia
81 D20 Mayumba var. Mayoumba. Nyanga, S Gabon 3.22S 10.37E
175 Ss7 Mayu, Pulau island Maluku, E Indonesia
33 S8 Mayville Michigan, N USA 43.18N 83.16W
20 C11 Mayville New York, NE USA 42.15N 79.31W
31 Q4 Mayville North Dakota, N USA 47.27N 97.17W
126 M11 Mayya Respublika Sakha (Yakutiya), NE Russian Federation 61.45N 130.16E
Mayyali see Mahe
Mayyit, Al Baḩr al see Dead Sea
85 J15 Mazabuka Southern, S Zambia 15.52S 27.46E
Mazaca see Kayseri
Mazagan see El-Jadida
34 J7 Mazama Washington, NW USA 48.34N 120.26W
105 O15 Mazamet Tarn, S France 43.30N 2.21E
149 O4 Māzandarān off. Ostān-e Māzandarān. ◈ province N Iran
162 F7 Mazar Xinjiang Uygur Zizhiqu, NW China 36.31N 76.59E
109 H24 Mazara del Vallo Sicilia, Italy, C Mediterranean Sea 37.39N 12.36E
155 O2 Mazār-e Sharif var. Mazār-i Sharif. Balkh, N Afghanistan 36.44N 67.06E
Mazār-i Sharif see Mazār-e Sharif
107 R13 Mazarrón Murcia, SE Spain 37.36N 1.19W
107 R14 Mazarrón, Golfo de gulf SE Spain
57 S9 Mazaruni River ≈ N Guyana
44 B6 Mazatenango Suchitepéquez, SW Guatemala 14.31N 91.28W
42 I10 Mazatlán Sinaloa, C Mexico 23.15N 106.24W
38 L12 Mazatzal Mountains ▲ Arizona, SW USA
120 D10 Mažeikiai Mažeikiai, NW Lithuania 56.19N 22.21E
120 D7 Mazirbe Talsi, NW Latvia 57.39N 22.16E
42 G5 Mazocahui Sonora, NW Mexico 29.34N 110.07W
59 I18 Mazocruz Puno, S Peru 16.41S 69.42W
Mazoe, Rio see Mazowe
81 N21 Mazomeno Maniema, E Dem. Rep. Congo (Zaire) 4.54S 27.13E
165 Q6 Mazong Shan ▲ N China 41.40N 97.10E
85 L16 Mazowe var. Rio Mazoe. ≈ Mozambique/Zimbabwe
112 L11 Mazowieckie ◈ province C Poland
Mazra'a see Al Mazra'ah
144 G6 Mazraat Kfar Debiâne C Lebanon 34.00N 35.51E
120 H7 Mazsalaca Est. Väike-Salatsi, Ger. Salisburg. Valmiera, N Latvia 57.52N 25.03E
112 L9 Mazury physical region NE Poland
121 M20 Mazyr Rus. Mozyr'. Homyel'skaya Voblasts', SE Belarus 52.03N 29.14E
109 K25 Mazzarino Sicilia, Italy, C Mediterranean Sea 37.18N 14.13E
Mba see Ba
85 L21 Mbabane ● (Swaziland) NW Swaziland 26.24S 31.13E
Mbacké see Mbaké
79 N16 Mbahiakro E Ivory Coast 7.25N 4.18W
81 I16 Mbaïki var. M'Baiki. Lobaye, SW Central African Republic 3.52N 17.58E
81 F14 Mbakaou, Lac de ◎ C Cameroon
78 G11 Mbaké var. Mbacké. W Senegal 14.50N 15.52W
84 L11 Mbala prev. Abercorn. Northern, NE Zambia 8.49S 31.22E
85 J18 Mbalabala prev. Balla Balla. Matabeleland South, SW Zimbabwe 20.27S 29.03E
83 G18 Mbale E Uganda 1.04N 34.12E
81 E16 Mbalmayo var. M'Balmayo. Centre, S Cameroon 3.30N 11.31E
83 H25 Mbamba Bay Ruvuma, S Tanzania 11.15S 34.44E
81 I18 Mbandaka prev. Coquilhatville. Equateur, NW Dem. Rep. Congo (Zaire) 0.07N 18.11E
84 B9 M'Banza Congo var. Mbanza Congo; prev. São Salvador, São Salvador do Congo. Zaire, NW Angola 6.10S 14.16E
81 G21 Mbanza-Ngungu Bas-Congo, W Dem. Rep. Congo (Zaire) 5.19S 14.45E
69 V11 Mbarangandu ≈ E Tanzania
83 E19 Mbarara SW Uganda 0.36S 30.40E
81 L15 Mbari ≈ SE Central African Republic
83 J24 Mbarika Mountains ▲ S Tanzania
85 J24 Mbashe ≈ S South Africa
Mbatiki see Batiki
80 F13 Mbé Nord, N Cameroon 7.51N 13.36E
83 J24 Mbemkuru var. Mbwemkuru. ≈ S Tanzania
Mbengga see Beqa
180 H13 Mbéni Grande Comore, NW Comoros
85 K18 Mberengwa Midlands, S Zimbabwe 20.25S 29.57E
83 G24 Mbeya Mbeya, SW Tanzania 8.54S 33.28E
83 G23 Mbeya ◈ region S Tanzania
81 E19 Mbigou Ngounié, C Gabon 01.54S 12.00E
Mbilua see Vella Lavella
81 F19 Mbinda Le Niari, SW Congo 2.07S 12.52E
81 D17 Mbini W Equatorial Guinea 1.34N 9.39E
Mbini see Uolo, Rio
85 L18 Mbizi Masvingo, SE Zimbabwe 21.23S 30.54E
83 G23 Mbogo Mbeya, W Tanzania 7.24S 33.26E
81 N15 Mboki Haut-Mbomou, SE Central African Republic 5.18N 25.52E
81 G18 Mbomo Cuvette, NW Congo 0.25N 14.42E
81 L15 Mbomou ◈ prefecture SE Central African Republic
Mbomou/M'Bomu/Mbomu see Bomu
78 F11 Mbour W Senegal 14.24N 16.58W
78 I10 Mbout Gorgol, S Mauritania 16.01N 12.37W
81 J14 Mbrès var. Mbrés. Nana-Grébizi, C Central African Republic 6.40N 19.46E
81 L22 Mbuji-Mayi prev. Bakwanga. Kasai Oriental, S Dem. Rep. Congo (Zaire) 6.04S 23.30E
194 J9 M'buke Islands island group N PNG
83 H21 Mbulu Arusha, N Tanzania 3.45S 35.33E
194 K8 M'bunai var. Bunai. Manus Island, N PNG 2.09S 147.11E
64 N8 Mburucuyá Corrientes, NE Argentina 28.03S 58.15W
Mbutha see Buca
Mbwemkuru see Mbemkuru
83 G21 Mbwikwe Singida, C Tanzania 5.19S 34.09E
11 O15 McAdam New Brunswick, SE Canada 45.34N 67.19W
27 O5 McAdoo Texas, SW USA 33.41N 100.58W
37 V2 McAfee Peak ▲ Nevada, W USA 41.31N 115.57W
29 P11 McAlester Oklahoma, C USA 34.55N 95.46W
27 S17 McAllen Texas, SW USA 26.12N 98.13W
23 S11 McBee South Carolina, SE USA 34.30N 80.12W
9 N14 McBride British Columbia, SW Canada 53.21N 120.19W
26 M9 McCamey Texas, SW USA 31.08N 102.13W
35 R15 McCammon Idaho, NW USA 42.38N 112.10W
37 X11 McCarran ✕ (Las Vegas) Nevada, W USA 36.04N 115.07W
41 T11 McCarthy Alaska, USA 61.25N 142.55W
32 M5 McCaslin Mountain hill Wisconsin, N USA 45.24N 88.24W
27 O2 McClellan Creek ≈ Texas, SW USA
23 T14 McClellanville South Carolina, SE USA 33.07N 79.27W
15 Jj2 McClintock Channel channel Nunavut, N Canada
205 R12 McClintock, Mount ▲ Antarctica 80.09S 156.42E
37 N2 McCloud California, W USA 41.15N 122.09W
37 N3 McCloud River ≈ California, W USA
37 Q9 McClure, Lake ▣ California, W USA
207 G8 McClure Strait strait Northwest Territories, N Canada
31 N4 McClusky North Dakota, N USA 47.27N 100.25W
23 T11 McColl South Carolina, SE USA 34.40N 79.33W
24 K7 McComb Mississippi, S USA 31.14N 90.27W
20 E16 McConnellsburg Pennsylvania, NE USA 39.56N 78.00W
33 T14 McConnelsville Ohio, N USA 39.39N 81.51W
30 M17 McCook Nebraska, C USA 40.12N 100.37W
23 F13 McCormick South Carolina, SE USA 33.54N 82.17W
9 W16 McCreary Manitoba, S Canada 50.48N 99.34W
29 W11 McCrory Arkansas, C USA 35.15N 91.12W
27 T10 McDade Texas, SW USA 30.15N 97.15W
25 O8 McDavid Florida, SE USA 30.51N 87.18W
37 T1 McDermitt Nevada, W USA 41.57N 117.43W
25 S4 McDonough Georgia, SE USA 33.27N 84.09W
38 L12 McDowell Mountains ▲ Arizona, SW USA
22 H8 McEwen Tennessee, S USA 36.06N 87.37W
37 R12 McFarland California, W USA 35.41N 119.14W
Mcfarlane, Lake see Macfarlane, Lake
29 P12 McGee Creek Lake ▣ Oklahoma, C USA
29 W13 McGehee Arkansas, C USA 33.37N 91.24W
37 X5 Mcgill Nevada, W USA 39.24N 114.46W
12 K11 McGillivray, Lac ◎ Quebec, SE Canada
41 P10 Mcgrath Alaska, USA 62.57N 155.36W
27 T8 McGregor Texas, SW USA 31.26N 97.24W
35 O12 McGuire, Mount ▲ Idaho, NW USA 45.10N 114.36W
85 M14 Mchinji prev. Fort Manning. Central, W Malawi 13.47S 32.51E
30 M7 McIntosh South Dakota, N USA 45.52N 101.19W
16 O3 McKeand ≈ Baffin Island, Nunavut, NE Canada
203 R4 McKean Island island Phoenix Islands, C Kiribati
31 J13 McKee Creek ≈ Illinois, N USA
20 C15 Mckeesport Pennsylvania, NE USA 40.18N 79.48W
23 V7 McKenney Virginia, NE USA 36.57N 77.42W
22 G8 McKenzie Tennessee, S USA 36.07N 88.31W
193 B20 McKerrow, Lake ◎ South Island, NZ
41 Q10 McKinley, Mount var. Denali. ▲ Alaska, USA 63.04N 151.00W
41 R10 McKinley Park Alaska, USA 63.42N 149.01W
36 K3 McKinleyville California, W USA 40.56N 124.06W
27 U6 McKinney Texas, SW USA 33.12N 96.37W
28 I5 McKinney, Lake ◎ Kansas, C USA
30 M7 McLaughlin South Dakota, N USA 45.48N 100.48W
27 O2 McLean Texas, SW USA 35.13N 100.36W
32 M16 Mcleansboro Illinois, N USA 38.05N 88.32W
9 O13 McLennan Alberta, W Canada 55.42N 116.49W
12 L9 McLennan, Lac ◎ Quebec, SE Canada
8 M13 McLeod Lake British Columbia, W Canada 55.03N 123.02W
29 N10 McLoud Oklahoma, C USA 35.26N 97.05W
34 G15 McLoughlin, Mount ▲ Oregon, NW USA 42.27N 122.18W
39 U15 McMillan, Lake ▣ New Mexico, SW USA
34 G11 McMinnville Oregon, NW USA 45.13N 123.12W
22 K9 McMinnville Tennessee, S USA 35.42N 85.46W
205 R13 McMurdo US research station Antarctica 77.40S 167.16E
26 H9 McNary Texas, SW USA 31.15N 105.46W
39 N13 Mcnary Arizona, SW USA 34.04N 109.51W
29 N5 McPherson Kansas, C USA 38.22N 97.39W
McPherson see Fort McPherson
25 U6 McRae Georgia, SE USA 32.04N 82.54W
31 P4 McVille North Dakota, N USA 47.45N 98.10W
85 J25 Mdantsane Eastern Cape, SE South Africa 32.54S 27.39E
178 Jj6 Me Ninh Binh, N Vietnam 20.21N 105.49E
29 J7 Meade Kansas, C USA 37.17N 100.20W
41 O5 Meade River ≈ Alaska, USA
37 Y11 Mead, Lake ▣ Arizona/Nevada, W USA
26 M5 Meadow Texas, SW USA 33.20N 102.12W
9 S14 Meadow Lake Saskatchewan, C Canada 55.08N 108.25W
37 Y10 Meadow Valley Wash ≈ Nevada, W USA
24 J7 Meadville Mississippi, S USA 31.28N 90.51W
20 B12 Meadville Pennsylvania, NE USA 41.38N 80.09W
12 F14 Meaford Ontario, S Canada 44.35N 80.35W
Meáin, Inis see Inishmaan
106 G8 Mealhada Aveiro, N Portugal 40.22N 8.27W
11 R8 Mealy Mountains ▲ Newfoundland, E Canada
9 O10 Meander River Alberta, W Canada 59.01N 117.42W
34 E11 Meares, Cape headland Oregon, NW USA 45.29N 123.59W
49 V6 Mearim, Rio ≈ NE Brazil
Measca, Loch see Mask, Lough
99 F17 Meath Ir. An Mhí. cultural region E Ireland
9 T14 Meath Park Saskatchewan, S Canada 53.25N 105.18W
105 O5 Meaux Seine-et-Marne, N France 48.58N 2.54E
23 T9 Mebane North Carolina, SE USA 36.06N 79.16W
176 W9 Mebo, Gunung ▲ Irian Jaya, E Indonesia 1.10S 133.53E
96 I8 Mebonden Sør-Trøndelag, S Norway 63.13N 11.00E
84 A10 Mebridege ≈ NW Angola
37 W16 Mecca California, W USA 33.34N 116.04W
Mecca see Makkah
31 Y14 Mechanicsville Iowa, C USA 41.54N 91.15W
20 L10 Mechanicville New York, NE USA 42.54N 73.41W
101 H17 Mechelen Eng. Mechlin, Fr. Malines. Antwerpen, C Belgium 51.01N 4.28E
196 C8 Mecherchar var. Eil Malk. island Palau Islands, Palau
103 D17 Mechernich Nordrhein-Westfalen, W Germany 50.36N 6.39E
130 L12 Mechetinskaya Rostovskaya Oblast', SW Russian Federation 46.46N 40.30E
116 J11 Mechka ≈ S Bulgaria
Mechlin see Mechelen
63 D23 Mechongué Buenos Aires, E Argentina 38.09S 58.13W
117 L14 Mecidiye Edirne, NW Turkey 40.39N 26.33E
103 I24 Meckenbeuren Baden-Württemberg, S Germany 47.42N 9.34E
102 L8 Mecklenburger Bucht bay N Germany
102 M10 Mecklenburgische Seenplatte wetland NE Germany
102 L9 Mecklenburg-Vorpommern ◈ state NE Germany
85 Q15 Meconta Nampula, NE Mozambique 15.01S 39.52E
113 I25 Mecsek ▲ SW Hungary
85 P14 Mecubúri ≈ N Mozambique
85 Q14 Mecúfi Cabo Delgado, NE Mozambique 13.18S 40.33E
84 O13 Mecula Niassa, N Mozambique 12.03S 37.37E
173 Ff5 Medan Sumatera, E Indonesia 3.34N 98.39E
63 A24 Médanos var. Medanos. Buenos Aires, E Argentina 38.51S 62.44W
63 C19 Médanos Entre Ríos, E Argentina 33.25S 59.03W
161 K24 Medawachchiya North Central Province, N Sri Lanka 8.32N 80.30E
108 C8 Mede Lombardia, N Italy 45.06N 8.43E
76 J5 Médéa var. El Mediyya, Lemdiyya. N Algeria 36.24N 2.42E
Mededa see Ma'dabā
56 E8 Medellín Antioquia, NW Colombia 6.15N 75.36W
102 H9 Medem ≈ NW Germany
100 J8 Medemblik Noord-Holland, NW Netherlands 52.46N 5.06E
77 N7 Médenine var. Madanīyīn. SE Tunisia 33.23N 10.30E
78 G9 Mederdra Trarza, SW Mauritania 16.55N 15.40W
Medeshamstede see Peterborough
44 F4 Medesto Mendez Izabal, NE Guatemala 15.54N 89.13W
21 O11 Medford Massachusetts, NE USA 42.25N 71.08W
29 N8 Medford Oklahoma, C USA 36.49N 97.45W
34 G15 Medford Oregon, NW USA 42.19N 122.52W
32 K6 Medford Wisconsin, N USA 45.07N 90.22W
41 P10 Medfra Alaska, USA 63.06N 154.42W
118 M14 Medgidia Constanţa, SE Romania 44.16N 28.13E
Medgyes see Mediaş
45 O5 Media Luna, Arrecifes de la reef E Honduras
62 G11 Medianeira Paraná, S Brazil 25.15S 54.07W
31 Y15 Mediapolis Iowa, C USA 41.00N 91.09W
118 I11 Mediaş Ger. Mediasch, Hung. Medgyes. Sibiu, C Romania 46.09N 24.20E
43 S15 Medias Aguas Veracruz-Llave, SE Mexico 17.40N 95.01W
Mediasch see Mediaş
108 G10 Medicina Emilia-Romagna, C Italy 44.29N 11.41E
35 X16 Medicine Bow Wyoming, C USA 41.52N 106.11W
39 S2 Medicine Bow Mountains ▲ Colorado/Wyoming, C USA
35 X16 Medicine Bow River ≈ Wyoming, C USA
9 R17 Medicine Hat Alberta, SW Canada 50.03N 110.40W
28 L7 Medicine Lodge Kansas, C USA 37.14N 98.33W
28 L7 Medicine Lodge River ≈ Kansas/Oklahoma, C USA
114 E7 Međimurje off. Međimurska Županija. ◈ province N Croatia
Međimurska Županija see Međimurje
56 G10 Medina Cundinamarca, C Colombia 4.31N 73.21W
20 E9 Medina New York, NE USA 43.13N 78.23W
31 O5 Medina North Dakota, N USA 46.53N 99.18W
33 T11 Medina Ohio, N USA 41.08N 81.51W
27 Q11 Medina Texas, SW USA 29.46N 99.14W
Medina see Al Madīnah
123 Ll12 Medina Bank undersea feature C Mediterranean Sea
107 P6 Medinaceli Castilla-León, N Spain 41.10N 2.25W
106 L6 Medina del Campo Castilla-León, N Spain 41.18N 4.55W
106 L5 Medina de Ríoseco Castilla-León, N Spain 41.52N 5.03W
Médina Gonassé see Médina Gounas
78 H12 Médina Gounas var. Médina Gonassé. S Senegal 13.06N 13.49W
27 S12 Medina River ≈ Texas, SW USA
106 K16 Medina Sidonia Andalucía, S Spain 36.28N 5.55W
Medinat Israel see Israel
121 H14 Medininkai Vilnius, SE Lithuania 54.31N 25.39E
159 R16 Medinīpur West Bengal, NE India 22.27N 87.19E
Mediolanum see Saintes, France
Mediolanum see Milano, Italy
Mediomatrica see Metz
124 O13 Mediterranean Ridge undersea feature C Mediterranean Sea
123 L11 Mediterranean Sea Fr. Mer Méditerranée. sea Africa/Asia/Europe
Méditerranée, Mer see Mediterranean Sea
81 N17 Medje Orientale, NE Dem. Rep. Congo (Zaire) 2.27N 27.14E
123 K11 Medjerda, Oued var. Mejerda, Wādī Majardah. ≈ Algeria/Tunisia see also Mejerda
116 G7 Medkovets Montana, NW Bulgaria 43.39N 23.22E
95 J15 Medle Västerbotten, N Sweden 64.45N 20.45E
131 W7 Mednogorsk Orenburgskaya Oblast', W Russian Federation 51.24N 57.37E
127 Qq9 Mednyy, Ostrov island E Russian Federation
104 J12 Médoc cultural region SW France
165 Q16 Mêdog Xizang Zizhiqu, W China 29.25N 95.25E
30 J5 Medora North Dakota, N USA 46.52N 103.32W
81 E17 Médouneu Woleu-Ntem, N Gabon 0.58N 10.49E
108 I7 Meduna ≈ NE Italy
Medunta see Mantes-la-Jolie
Medvedica see Medveditsa
128 J16 Medveditsa var. Medvedica. ≈ W Russian Federation
131 O9 Medveditsa ≈ SW Russian Federation
114 E8 Medvednica ▲ NE Croatia
129 R15 Medvedok Kirovskaya Oblast', NW Russian Federation 57.23N 50.01E
127 Nn5 Medvezh'i, Ostrova island group NE Russian Federation
128 J9 Medvezh'yegorsk Respublika Kareliya, NW Russian Federation 62.56N 34.26E
111 T11 Medvode Ger. Zwischenwässern. NW Slovenia 46.09N 14.21E
130 J4 Medyn' Kaluzhskaya Oblast', W Russian Federation 54.59N 35.52E
188 J10 Meekatharra Western Australia 26.36S 118.34E
39 Q4 Meeker Colorado, C USA 40.02N 107.54W
11 T12 Meelpaeg Lake ◎ Newfoundland, E Canada
Meenen see Menen
103 M16 Meerane Sachsen, E Germany 50.49N 12.28E
103 D15 Meerbusch Nordrhein-Westfalen, W Germany 51.19N 6.43E
100 I12 Meerkerk Zuid-Holland, C Netherlands 51.55N 5.00E
101 L18 Meerssen var. Mersen. Limburg, SE Netherlands 50.52N 5.45E
158 J10 Meerut Uttar Pradesh, N India 29.01N 77.40E
35 U13 Meeteetse Wyoming, C USA 44.10N 108.53W
101 K17 Meeuwen Limburg, NE Belgium 51.04N 5.36E
83 J16 Mēga Oromo, C Ethiopia 4.03N 38.15E
83 J16 Mēga Escarpment escarpment S Ethiopia
Megála Kalívia see Megála Kalývia
117 E16 Megála Kalývia var. Megála Kalívia. Thessalía, C Greece 39.30N 21.48E
117 H14 Megáli Panagiá var. Megáli Panayía. Kentrikí Makedonía, N Greece 40.24N 23.42E
Megáli Panayía see Megáli Panagiá
Megáli Préspa, Límni see Prespa, Lake
116 K12 Megálo Livádi ▲ Bulgaria/Greece 41.18N 25.51E
117 E20 Megalópoli prev. Megalópolis. Pelopónnisos, S Greece 37.23N 22.08E
Megalópolis see Megalópoli
176 V9 Megamo Irian Jaya, E Indonesia 0.55S 131.46E
117 C18 Meganísi island Iónioi Nísoi, Greece, C Mediterranean Sea
Meganom, Mys see Mehanom, Mys
Mégantic see Lac-Mégantic
13 R12 Mégantic, Mont ▲ Quebec, SE Canada 45.27N 71.09W
117 G19 Mégara Attikí, C Greece 38.00N 23.20E
27 R5 Megargel Texas, SW USA 33.27N 98.55W
100 K13 Megen Noord-Brabant, S Netherlands 51.49N 5.34E
159 U13 Meghālaya ◈ state NE India
159 U16 Meghna ≈ S Bangladesh
143 V14 Meghri Rus. Megri. SE Armenia 38.57N 46.15E
126 Gg11 Megion Khanty-Mansiyskiy Avtonomnyy Okrug, C Russian Federation 61.01N 76.15E
117 Q23 Megísti var. Kastellórizon. island SE Greece
Megri see Meghri
Mehabad see Mahābād
118 F13 Mehadia Hung. Mehádia. Caraş-Severin, SW Romania 44.53N 22.20E
94 L7 Mehamn Finnmark, N Norway 71.01N 27.46E
119 U13 Mehanom, Mys Rus. Mys Meganom. headland S Ukraine 44.48N 35.04E
155 P14 Mehar Sind, SE Pakistan 27.10N 67.56E
188 J8 Meharry, Mount ▲ Western Australia 23.17S 118.48E
Mehdia see Mahdia
118 G14 Mehedinţi ◈ county SW Romania
159 S15 Meherpur Khulna, W Bangladesh 23.46N 88.40E
23 W8 Meherrin River ≈ North Carolina/Virginia, SE USA
Meheso see Mī'ēso
203 T11 Mehetia island Îles du Vent, W French Polynesia
120 K6 Mehikoorma Tartumaa, E Estonia 58.14N 27.29E
Me Hka see Nmai Hka
149 N5 Mehrabad ✕ (Tehrān) Tehrān, N Iran 35.46N 51.07E
148 J7 Mehrān Īlām, W Iran 33.07N 46.10E
149 Q14 Mehrān, Rūd-e prev. Mansurabad. ≈ W Iran
149 Q9 Mehrīz Yazd, C Iran 31.31N 54.28E
155 R5 Mehtarlām var. Mehtar Lām, Meterlam, Methariam, Metharlam. Laghmān, E Afghanistan 34.39N 70.10E
105 N8 Mehun-sur-Yèvre Cher, C France 47.09N 2.15E
81 G14 Meiganga Adamaoua, NE Cameroon 6.31N 14.07E
166 H10 Meigu Sichuan, C China 28.22N 103.07E
169 W11 Meihekou var. Hailong. Jilin, NE China 42.31N 125.40E
101 L15 Meijel Limburg, SE Netherlands 51.22N 5.52E
177 G5 Meiktila Mandalay, C Burma 20.52N 95.54E
Meilbhe, Loch see Melvin, Lough
110 G7 Meilen Zürich, N Switzerland 47.16N 8.39E
Meilu see Wuchuan
167 T12 Meinhua Yu island N Taiwan
103 J17 Meiningen Thüringen, C Germany 50.34N 10.25E
110 F9 Meiringen Bern, S Switzerland 46.42N 8.13E
103 O15 Meissen var. Meißen. Sachsen, E Germany 51.10N 13.28E
Meißen see Meissen
103 I15 Meissner ▲ C Germany 51.13N 9.52E
101 K25 Meix-devant-Virton Luxembourg, SE Belgium 49.36N 5.27E
Mei Xian see Meizhou
167 P13 Meizhou var. Meixian, Mei Xian. Guangdong, S China 24.21N 116.05E
69 P2 Mejerda var. Oued Medjerda, Wādī Majardah. ≈ Algeria/Tunisia see also Medjerda, Oued
44 F7 Mejicanos San Salvador, C El Salvador 13.50N 89.13W
Méjico see Mexico
64 G5 Mejillones Antofagasta, N Chile 23.03S 70.25W
201 V5 Mejit Island var. Mājeej. island Ratak Chain, NE Marshall Islands
81 F17 Mékambo Ogooué-Ivindo, NE Gabon 1.03N 13.49E
82 J10 Mek'elē var. Makale. Tigray, N Ethiopia 13.36N 39.28E
76 I10 Mekerrhane, Sebkha var. Sebkha Meqerghane, Sebkra Mekerrhane. salt flat C Algeria
Mekerrhane, Sebkra see Mekerrhane, Sebkha
78 G10 Mékhé NW Senegal 15.08N 16.42W
152 G14 Mekhinli Akhalskiy Velayat, C Turkmenistan 37.28N 59.20E
13 P9 Mékinac, Lac ◎ Quebec, SE Canada
Meklong see Samut Songhram
76 G6 Meknès N Morocco 33.54N 5.27W
133 U12 Mekong var. Lan-ts'ang Chiang, Cam. Mékôngk, Chin. Lancang Jiang, Lao. Mènam Khong, Th. Mae Nam Khong, Tib. Dza Chu, Vtn. Sông Tiên Giang. ≈ SE Asia
Mekongga, Pegunungan see Mengkoka, Pegunungan
Mékôngk see Mekong
178 K15 Mekong, Mouths of the delta S Vietnam
40 L12 Mekoryuk Nunivak Island, Alaska, USA 60.23N 166.11W
79 R14 Mékrou ≈ N Benin
174 H6 Melaka var. Malacca. Melaka, Peninsular Malaysia 2.13N 102.13E
174 H6 Melaka var. Malacca. ◈ state Peninsular Malaysia
Melaka, Selat see Malacca, Strait of
183 O6 Melanesia island group W Pacific Ocean
183 P5 Melanesian Basin undersea feature W Pacific Ocean
175 Ss4 Melanguane Pulau Karakelang, N Indonesia 4.02N 126.43E
174 Ll8 Melawi, Sungai ≈ Borneo, N Indonesia
191 N12 Melbourne state capital Victoria, SE Australia 37.51S 144.56E
29 V9 Melbourne Arkansas, C USA 36.03N 91.54W
25 Y12 Melbourne Florida, SE USA 28.04N 80.36W
31 W14 Melbourne Iowa, C USA 41.57N 93.07W
94 G10 Melbu Nordland, C Norway 68.30N 14.46E
Melchor de Mencos see Ciudad Melchor de Mencos
65 F19 Melchor, Isla island Archipiélago de los Chonos, S Chile
42 M9 Melchor Ocampo Zacatecas, C Mexico 24.45N 101.38W
12 C11 Meldrum Bay Manitoulin Island, Ontario, S Canada 45.55N 83.06W
Meleda see Mljet
108 D8 Melegnano prev. Marignano. Lombardia, N Italy 45.22N 9.19E
196 F9 Melekeok var. Melekeiok. Babeldaob, N Palau 7.30N 134.39E
114 L9 Melenci Hung. Melencze. Serbia, N Yugoslavia 45.32N 20.18E
Melencze see Melenci
131 N4 Melenki Vladimirskaya Oblast', W Russian Federation 55.21N 41.37E
131 V6 Meleuz Respublika Bashkortostan, W Russian Federation 52.55N 55.54E
10 L6 Mélèzes, Rivière aux ≈ Quebec, C Canada
80 I11 Melfi Guéra, S Chad 11.04N 17.57E
109 M17 Melfi Basilicata, S Italy 41.00N 15.33E
9 U14 Melfort Saskatchewan, S Canada 52.52N 104.37W
106 H4 Melgaço Viana do Castelo, N Portugal 42.07N 8.15W
107 N4 Melgar de Fernamental Castilla-León, N Spain 42.24N 4.15W
76 L6 Melghir, Chott var. Chott Melrhir. salt lake E Algeria
96 H8 Melhus Sør-Trøndelag, S Norway 63.16N 10.16E
106 H3 Melide Galicia, NW Spain 42.54N 8.01W
Meligalá see Meligalás
117 E21 Meligalás prev. Meligalá. Pelopónnisos, S Greece 37.13N 21.58E
62 L12 Mel, Ilha do island S Brazil
122 G11 Melilla anc. Rusaddir, Russadir. Melilla, Spain, N Africa 35.18N 2.55W
73 N1 Melilla enclave Spain, N Africa
65 G18 Melimoyu, Monte ▲ S Chile 44.06S 72.49W
175 N8 Melintang, Danau ◎ Borneo, N Indonesia
119 U7 Melioratyvne Dnipropetrovs'ka Oblast', E Ukraine 48.35N 35.18E
64 G11 Melipilla Santiago, C Chile 33.33S 71.34W
117 I25 Mélissa, Akrotírio headland Kríti, Greece, E Mediterranean Sea 35.06N 24.33E
15 Kk16 Melita Manitoba, S Canada 49.16N 100.58W
Melita see Mljet
Melitene see Malatya
109 M23 Melito di Porto Salvo Calabria, SW Italy 37.55N 15.48E
119 U10 Melitopol' Zaporiz'ka Oblast', SE Ukraine 46.49N 35.22E
111 V4 Melk Niederösterreich, NE Austria 48.12N 15.20E
97 K15 Mellan-Fryken ◎ C Sweden
101 E17 Melle Oost-Vlaanderen, NW Belgium 51.00N 3.48E
102 G13 Melle Niedersachsen, NW Germany 52.12N 8.19E
97 J17 Mellerud Västra Götaland, S Sweden 58.42N 12.27E
104 K10 Melle-sur-Bretonne Deux-Sèvres, W France 46.13N 0.07W
31 P8 Mellette South Dakota, N USA 45.07N 98.29W
123 J16 Mellieha E Malta 35.58N 14.21E
82 B10 Mellit Northern Darfur, W Sudan 14.07N 25.34E
77 N7 Mellita ✕ SE Tunisia 33.47N 10.51E
65 G21 Mellizo Sur, Cerro ▲ S Chile 48.27S 73.10W
102 G9 Mellum island NW Germany
85 L22 Melmoth KwaZulu/Natal, E South Africa 28.30S 31.23E
113 D16 Mělník Ger. Melnik. Středočeský Kraj, NW Czech Republic 50.21N 14.30E
126 H13 Mel'nikovo Tomskaya Oblast', C Russian Federation 56.35N 84.11E
63 G18 Melo Cerro Largo, NE Uruguay 32.22S 54.10W
Melodunum see Melun
Melrhir, Chott see Melghir, Chott
191 P7 Melrose New South Wales, SE Australia 32.41S 146.58E
190 I7 Melrose South Australia 32.52S 138.16E
31 T7 Melrose Minnesota, N USA 45.40N 94.46W
35 Q11 Melrose Montana, NW USA 45.33N 112.41W
39 V12 Melrose New Mexico, SW USA 34.25N 103.37W
110 I8 Mels Sankt Gallen, NE Switzerland 47.03N 9.25E
Melsetter see Chimanimani
35 V9 Melstone Montana, NW USA 46.37N 107.49W
103 I16 Melsungen Hessen, C Germany 51.07N 9.33E
94 L12 Meltaus Lappi, NW Finland 66.54N 25.18E
99 N19 Melton Mowbray C England, UK 52.46N 1.03W
84 Q13 Meluco Cabo Delgado, NE Mozambique 12.39S 39.35E
105 O5 Melun anc. Melodunum. Seine-et-Marne, N France 48.31N 2.40E
82 F12 Melut Upper Nile, SE Sudan 10.27N 32.13E
29 P5 Melvern Lake ▣ Kansas, C USA
9 V16 Melville Saskatchewan, S Canada 50.57N 102.49W
Melville Bay/Melville Bugt see Qimusseriarsuaq
47 O11 Melville Hall ✕ (Dominica) NE Dominica 15.33N 61.19W
189 O1 Melville Island island Northern Territory, N Australia
207 O8 Melville Island island Parry Islands, Northwest Territories, NW Canada
16 R7 Melville, Lake ◎ Newfoundland, E Canada
15 Ll2 Melville Peninsula peninsula Nunavut, NE Canada
Melville Sound see Viscount Melville Sound
27 Q9 Melvin Texas, SW USA 31.12N 99.34W

◆ Country ● Country Capital ◇ Dependent Territory ○ Dependent Territory Capital ◈ Administrative Region ✕ International Airport ▲ Mountain ▲ Mountain Range Volcano ≈ River ◎ Lake ▣ Reservoir

◆ COUNTRY ◇ DEPENDENT TERRITORY ◇ ADMINISTRATIVE REGION ▲ MOUNTAIN ⊠ VOLCANO ⊚ LAKE
● COUNTRY CAPITAL ○ DEPENDENT TERRITORY CAPITAL × INTERNATIONAL AIRPORT ▲ MOUNTAIN RANGE ⚡ RIVER ⊞ RESERVOIR

293

294

◆ COUNTRY ◇ DEPENDENT TERRITORY ◆ ADMINISTRATIVE REGION ▲ MOUNTAIN ▼ VOLCANO ◎ LAKE
● COUNTRY CAPITAL ○ DEPENDENT TERRITORY CAPITAL × INTERNATIONAL AIRPORT ▲ MOUNTAIN RANGE ✎ RIVER ▢ RESERVOIR

MIZHI – MONTENEGRO

166 L4 **Mizhi** Shaanxi, C China 37.43N 110.13E
118 K13 **Mizil** Prahova, SE Romania 45.00N 26.29E
116 H7 **Miziya** Vratsa, NW Bulgaria 43.42N 23.52E
159 W15 **Mizo Hills** hill range E India
159 W15 **Mizoram** ◈ state NE India
144 F12 **Mizpé Ramon** var. Mitspe Ramon. Southern, S Israel 30.37N 34.46E
59 L19 **Mizque** Cochabamba, C Bolivia 17.58S 65.18W
59 M19 **Mizque, Río** ≈ C Bolivia
171 I15 **Mizunami** Gifu, Honshū, SW Japan 35.19N 137.12E
171 Mm12 **Mizusawa** Iwate, Honshū, C Japan 39.09N 141.07E
97 M18 **Mjölby** Östergötland, S Sweden 58.19N 15.10E
97 G15 **Mjøndalen** Buskerud, S Norway 59.45N 9.58E
97 J19 **Mjörn** ◎ S Sweden
96 I13 **Mjøsa** var. Mjøsen. ◎ S Norway
Mjøsen see Mjøsa
83 G21 **Mkalama** Singida, C Tanzania 4.09S 34.34E
82 K13 **Mkata** ≈ C Tanzania
85 K14 **Mkushi** Central, C Zambia 13.37S 29.27E
85 L22 **Mkuze** KwaZulu/Natal, E South Africa 27.40S 32.05E
83 J22 **Mkwaja** Tanga, E Tanzania 5.42S 38.48E
113 D16 **Mladá Boleslav** Ger. Jungbunzlau. Středočeský Kraj, N Czech Republic 50.24N 14.55E
114 M12 **Mladenovac** Serbia, C Yugoslavia 44.27N 20.42E
116 L11 **Mladinovo** Khaskovo, S Bulgaria 41.57N 26.13E
115 O17 **Mlado Nagoričane** N FYR Macedonia 42.11N 21.49E
Mlanje see Mulanje
114 N12 **Mlava** ≈ E Yugoslavia
112 L9 **Mława** Mazowieckie, C Poland 53.07N 20.23E
115 G16 **Mljet** It. Meleda; anc. Melita. island S Croatia
118 K4 **Mlyniv** Rivnens'ka Oblast', NW Ukraine 50.31N 25.36E
85 I21 **Mmabatho** North-West, N South Africa 25.51S 25.37E
85 I19 **Mmashoro** Central, E Botswana 21.56S 26.39E
46 J7 **Moa** Holguín, E Cuba 20.38N 74.36W
78 J15 **Moa** ≈ Guinea/Sierra Leone
39 O6 **Moab** Utah, W USA 38.34N 109.34W
189 V1 **Moa Island** island Queensland, NE Australia
197 J15 **Moala** island S Fiji
85 L21 **Moamba** Maputo, SW Mozambique 25.33S 32.15E
81 F19 **Moanda** var. Mouanda. Haut-Ogooué, SE Gabon 1.31S 13.07E
175 T16 **Moa, Pulau** island Kepulauan Leti, E Indonesia
85 M15 **Moatize** Tete, NW Mozambique 16.03S 33.49E
81 P22 **Moba** Katanga, E Dem. Rep. Congo (Zaire) 7.03S 29.51E
171 K17 **Mobara** Chiba, Honshū, S Japan 35.25N 140.19E
Mobay see Montego Bay
81 K15 **Mobaye** Basse-Kotto, S Central African Republic 4.19N 21.17E
81 K15 **Mobayi-Mbongo** Equateur, NW Dem. Rep. Congo (Zaire) 4.19N 21.18E
27 P2 **Mobeetie** Texas, SW USA 35.33N 100.25W
29 U3 **Moberly** Missouri, C USA 39.25N 92.26W
25 N8 **Mobile** Alabama, S USA 30.41N 88.02W
25 N9 **Mobile Bay** bay Alabama, S USA
25 N8 **Mobile River** ≈ Alabama, S USA
31 N8 **Mobridge** South Dakota, N USA 45.32N 100.25W
Mobutu Sese Seko, Lac see Albert, Lake
47 N8 **Moca** N Dominican Republic 19.23N 70.31W
Moçâmedes see Namibe
178 J6 **Môc Châu** Sơn La, N Vietnam 20.52N 104.38E
197 L15 **Moce** island Lau Group, E Fij
85 Q15 **Moçambique** Nampula, NE Mozambique 15.00S 40.44E
Mocha see Al Mukhā
200 Oo13 **Mocha Fracture Zone** tectonic feature SE Pacific Ocean
65 F14 **Mocha, Isla** island C Chile
58 C12 **Moche, Río** ≈ W Peru
178 J14 **Môc Hoa** Long An, S Vietnam 10.46N 105.55E
85 I20 **Mochudi** Kgatleng, SE Botswana 24.25S 26.07E
84 Q13 **Mocímboa da Praia** var. Vila de Mocímboa da Praia. Cabo Delgado, N Mozambique 11.16S 40.21E
96 L13 **Mockfjärd** Dalarna, C Sweden 60.30N 14.57E
23 R9 **Mocksville** North Carolina, SE USA 35.53N 80.33W
34 F8 **Moclips** Washington, NW USA 47.11N 124.13W
84 C13 **Môco** var. Morro de Môco. ▲ W Angola 12.36S 15.09E
56 D13 **Mocoa** Putumayo, SW Colombia 1.07N 76.37W
62 M8 **Mococa** São Paulo, S Brazil 21.30S 47.00W
Môco, Morro de see Môco
42 H8 **Mocorito** Sinaloa, C Mexico 25.24N 107.55W
42 J4 **Moctezuma** Chihuahua, N Mexico 30.10N 106.24W
43 N11 **Moctezuma** San Luis Potosí, C Mexico 22.44N 101.04W
42 G4 **Moctezuma** Sonora, NW Mexico 29.49N 109.40W
43 P12 **Moctezuma, Río** ≈ C Mexico
Mó, Cuan see Clew Bay
85 O16 **Mocuba** Zambézia, NE Mozambique 16.49S 37.01E
105 U12 **Modane** Savoie, E France 45.14N 6.41E
108 F9 **Modena** anc. Mutina. Emilia-Romagna, N Italy 44.39N 10.55E
38 I7 **Modena** Utah, W USA 37.46N 113.54W
37 O9 **Modesto** California, W USA 37.38N 121.01W
109 L25 **Modica** anc. Motyca. Sicilia, Italy, C Mediterranean Sea 36.52N 14.45E
81 K17 **Modjamboli** Equateur, N Dem. Rep. Congo (Zaire) 2.27N 22.03E
111 X4 **Mödling** Niederösterreich, NE Austria 48.07N 16.15E
Modohn see Madona
169 N8 **Modot** Hentiy, C Mongolia 47.45N 109.03E
176 W12 **Modowi** Irian Jaya, E Indonesia 4.05S 134.39E
114 I12 **Modračko Jezero** ▣ NE Bosnia and Herzegovina
114 I10 **Modriča** Republika Srpska, N Bosnia and Herzegovina 44.57N 18.17E
191 O13 **Moe** Victoria, SE Australia 38.10S 146.18E
Moearatewe see Muaratewe
Moei, Mae Nam see Thaungyin
96 H13 **Moelv** Hedmark, S Norway 60.55N 10.47E
94 I10 **Moen** Troms, N Norway 69.08N 18.35E
Moen see Weno, Micronesia
Möen see Møn, Denmark
Moena see Muna, Pulau
38 M10 **Moenkopi Wash** ≈ Arizona, SW USA
193 F22 **Moeraki Point** headland South Island, NZ 45.23S 170.52E
101 F16 **Moerbeke** Oost-Vlaanderen, NW Belgium 51.11N 3.57E
101 H14 **Moerdijk** Noord-Brabant, S Netherlands 51.42N 4.37E
Moero, Lac see Mweru, Lake
103 D15 **Moers** var. Mörs. Nordrhein-Westfalen, W Germany 51.27N 6.37E
Moesi see Musi, Air
Moeskroen see Mouscron
98 J13 **Moffat** S Scotland, UK 55.28N 3.36W
193 C22 **Moffat Peak** ▲ South Island, NZ 44.57S 168.10E
158 H8 **Moga** Punjab, N India 30.49N 75.13E
81 N19 **Moga** Sud Kivu, E Dem. Rep. Congo (Zaire) 2.16S 26.54E
Mogadiscio/Mogadishu see Muqdisho
Mogador see Essaouira
106 J6 **Mogadouro** Bragança, N Portugal 41.19N 6.43W
171 Ll12 **Mogami-gawa** ≈ Honshū, C Japan
178 Gg2 **Mogaung** Kachin State, N Burma 25.19N 96.54E
112 L13 **Mogielnica** Mazowieckie, C Poland 51.40N 20.42E
Mogilëv see Mahilyow
Mogilev-Podol'skiy see Mohyliv-Podil's'kyy
Mogilëvskaya Oblast' see Mahilyowskaya Voblasts'
112 I11 **Mogilno** Kujawsko-pomorskie, C Poland 52.39N 17.58E
62 L9 **Mogi-Mirim** var. Moji-Mirim. São Paulo, S Brazil 22.26S 46.55W
85 Q15 **Mogincual** Nampula, NE Mozambique 15.33S 40.28E
116 E13 **Moglenítsas** ≈ N Greece
108 H8 **Mogliano Veneto** Veneto, NE Italy 45.34N 12.13E
115 M21 **Moglicë** Korçë, SE Albania 40.43N 20.22E
126 L15 **Mogocha** Chitinskaya Oblast', S Russian Federation 53.39N 119.47E
126 H13 **Mogochin** Tomskaya Oblast', C Russian Federation 57.42N 83.24E
82 F13 **Mogogh** Jonglei, SE Sudan 8.25N 31.19E
176 Vv10 **Mogoi** Irian Jaya, E Indonesia 1.44S 133.13E
178 Gg4 **Mogok** Mandalay, C Burma 22.55N 96.28E
39 P14 **Mogollon Mountains** ▲▲ New Mexico, SW USA
38 M12 **Mogollon Rim** cliff Arizona, SW USA
63 E23 **Mogotes, Punta** headland E Argentina 38.03S 57.31W
44 J8 **Mogotón** ▲ NW Nicaragua 13.45N 86.22W
106 I14 **Moguer** Andalucía, S Spain 37.15N 6.52W
113 J26 **Mohács** Baranya, SW Hungary 46.00N 18.40E
193 C20 **Mohaka** ≈ North Island, NZ
30 M2 **Mohall** North Dakota, N USA 48.45N 101.30W
Moḥammadābād see Dargaz
76 F6 **Mohammedia** prev. Fédala. NW Morocco 33.46N 7.16W
76 F6 **Mohammed V** ✈ (Casablanca) W Morocco 33.07N 8.28W
Mohammerah see Khorramshahr
38 H10 **Mohave, Lake** ▣ Arizona/Nevada, W USA
38 I12 **Mohave Mountains** ▲▲ Arizona, SW USA
38 I15 **Mohawk Mountains** ▲▲ Arizona, SW USA
20 J10 **Mohawk River** ≈ New York, NE USA
169 T3 **Mohe** Heilongjiang, NE China 53.00N 122.33E
97 L20 **Moheda** Kronoberg, S Sweden 57.00N 14.34E
180 H13 **Mohéli** var. Mwali, Mohilla, Mohila, Fr. Moili. island S Comoros
158 I11 **Mohendergarh** Haryāna, N India 28.16N 76.13E
40 K12 **Mohican, Cape** headland Nunivak Island, Alaska, USA 60.12N 167.25W
Mohn see Muhu
103 G15 **Möhne** ≈ W Germany
103 G15 **Möhne-Stausee** ▣ W Germany
94 P2 **Mohn, Kapp** headland NW Svalbard 79.26N 25.44E
207 S14 **Mohns Ridge** undersea feature Greenland Sea/Norwegian Sea
59 I17 **Moho** Puno, SW Peru 15.21S 69.32W
Mohokare see Caledon
97 L17 **Moholm** Västra Götaland, S Sweden 58.37N 14.04E
38 J11 **Mohon Peak** ▲ Arizona, SW USA 34.55N 113.07W
83 J23 **Mohoro** Pwani, E Tanzania 8.09S 39.10E
Mohra see Moravice
Mohrungen see Morąg
118 M7 **Mohyliv-Podil's'kyy** Rus. Mogilev-Podol'skiy. Vinnyts'ka Oblast', C Ukraine 48.28N 27.49E
97 D17 **Moi** Rogaland, S Norway 58.27N 6.31E
197 I6 **Moindou** Province Sud, C New Caledonia 21.42S 165.40E
118 K11 **Moinești** Hung. Mojnest. Bacău, E Romania 46.27N 26.31E
Móinteach Mílic see Mountmellick
12 J14 **Moira** ≈ Ontario, SE Canada
94 G13 **Mo i Rana** Nordland, C Norway 66.19N 14.10E
159 X14 **Moirāng** Manipur, NE India 24.28N 93.45E
117 J25 **Moíres** Kríti, Greece, E Mediterranean Sea 35.03N 24.51E
120 H6 **Mõisaküla** Ger. Moiseküll. Viljandimaa, S Estonia 58.05N 25.11E
Moiseküll see Mõisaküla
13 W4 **Moisie** Quebec, E Canada 50.12N 66.06W
13 W3 **Moisie** ≈ Quebec, SE Canada
104 M14 **Moissac** Tarn-et-Garonne, S France 44.07N 1.04E
80 I13 **Moïssala** Moyen-Chari, S Chad 8.21N 17.46E
57 O7 **Moitaco** Bolívar, E Venezuela 8.00N 64.22W
97 P15 **Möja** Stockholm, C Sweden 59.25N 18.55E
107 Q14 **Mojácar** Andalucía, S Spain 37.09N 1.49W
37 T13 **Mojave** California, W USA 35.03N 118.10W
37 V13 **Mojave Desert** plain California, W USA
37 V13 **Mojave River** ≈ California, W USA
Moji-Mirim see Mogi-Mirim
115 K15 **Mojkovac** Montenegro, SW Yugoslavia 42.57N 19.34E
Mojnest see Moinești
174 Ll15 **Mojokerto** prev. Modjokerto. Jawa, C Indonesia 7.25S 112.31E
Mōka see Mooka
159 Q13 **Mokāma** prev. Mokameh, Mukama. Bihār, N India 25.24N 85.55E
81 O25 **Mokambo** Katanga, SE Dem. Rep. Congo (Zaire) 12.23S 28.21E
Mokameh see Mokāma
40 D9 **Mokapu Point** headland Oahu, Hawaii, USA, C Pacific Ocean 21.27N 157.43W
192 L9 **Mokau** Waikato, North Island, NZ 38.42S 174.37E
192 L9 **Mokau** ≈ North Island, NZ
37 P7 **Mokelumne River** ≈ California, W USA
85 J23 **Mokhotlong** NE Lesotho 29.19S 29.06E
Mokil Atoll see Mwokil Atoll
97 N14 **Möklinta** Västmanland, C Sweden 60.04N 16.34E
192 L4 **Mokohinau Islands** island group N NZ
159 X12 **Mokokchūng** Nāgāland, NE India 26.19N 94.30E
80 F12 **Mokolo** Extrême-Nord, N Cameroon 10.49N 13.54E
193 D24 **Mokoreta** ≈ South Island, NZ
169 X17 **Mokp'o** Jap. Moppo. SW South Korea 34.49N 126.26E
115 L16 **Mokra Gora** ▲▲ S Yugoslavia
Mokrany see Makrany
131 O5 **Moksha** ≈ W Russian Federation
Moktama see Martaban
79 T14 **Mokwa** Niger, W Nigeria 9.19N 5.01E
101 J16 **Mol** prev. Moll. Antwerpen, N Belgium 51.10N 5.07E
109 O17 **Mola di Bari** Puglia, SE Italy 41.03N 17.04E
Molai see Moláoi
43 P13 **Molango** Hidalgo, C Mexico 20.48N 98.43W
117 F22 **Moláoi** var. Molai. Pelopónnisos, S Greece 36.47N 22.50E
43 Z12 **Molas del Norte, Punta** var. Punta Molas. headland SE Mexico 20.34N 86.43W
Molas, Punta see Molas del Norte, Punta
107 R11 **Molatón** ▲ C Spain 38.58N 1.19W
99 K18 **Mold** NE Wales, UK 53.10N 3.07W
Moldau see Moldova
Moldau see Vltava, Czech Republic
Moldavia see Moldova
Moldavian SSR/Moldavskaya SSR see Moldova
96 E9 **Molde** Møre og Romsdal, S Norway 62.43N 7.07E
Moldotau, Khrebet see Moldo-Too, Khrebet
153 V9 **Moldo-Too, Khrebet** prev. Khrebet Moldotau. ▲▲ C Kyrgyzstan
118 K9 **Moldova** ≈ N Romania
118 K9 **Moldova** Eng. Moldavia, Ger. Moldau. former province NE Romania
118 L9 **Moldova** off. Republic of Moldova, var. Moldavia; prev. Moldavian SSR, Rus. Moldavskaya SSR. ◆ republic SE Europe
118 F13 **Moldova Nouă** Ger. Neumoldowa, Hung. Újmoldova. Caraș-Severin, SW Romania 44.45N 21.39E
118 F13 **Moldova Veche** Ger. Altmoldowa, Hung. Ómoldova. Caraș-Severin, SW Romania 44.45N 21.13E
Moldoveanul see Vârful Moldoveanu
85 I20 **Molepolole** Kweneng, SE Botswana 24.25S 25.30E
46 L8 **Môle-St-Nicolas** NW Haiti 19.46N 73.19W
120 H13 **Molėtai** Molėtai, E Lithuania 55.14N 25.25E
109 O17 **Molfetta** Puglia, SE Italy 41.12N 16.34E
175 R8 **Molibagu** Sulawesi, N Indonesia 0.25N 123.57E
64 G12 **Molina** Maule, C Chile 35.06S 71.18W
107 Q7 **Molina de Aragón** Castilla-La Mancha, C Spain 40.49N 1.54W
107 R13 **Molina de Segura** Murcia, SE Spain 38.03N 1.10W
32 J11 **Moline** Illinois, N USA 41.30N 90.31W
29 P7 **Moline** Kansas, C USA 37.21N 96.18W
81 P23 **Moliro** Katanga, SE Dem. Rep. Congo (Zaire) 8.10S 30.31E
109 K16 **Molise** ◈ region S Italy
97 K15 **Molkom** Värmland, C Sweden 59.36N 13.43E
Moll see Mol
111 Q9 **Möll** ≈ S Austria
97 J22 **Mölle** Skåne, S Sweden 56.15N 12.19E
59 H18 **Mollendo** Arequipa, SW Peru 17.01S 72.01W
107 U5 **Mollerussa** Cataluña, NE Spain 41.37N 0.52E
110 H8 **Mollis** Glarus, NE Switzerland 47.05N 9.03E
97 J19 **Mölndal** Västra Götaland, S Sweden 57.39N 12.05E
97 J19 **Mölnlycke** Västra Götaland, S Sweden 57.42N 12.19E
119 U9 **Molochans'k** Rus. Molochansk. Zaporiz'ka Oblast', SE Ukraine 47.10N 35.38E
119 U10 **Molochna** Rus. Molochnaya. ≈ S Ukraine
Molochnaya see Molochna
119 U10 **Molochnyy Lyman** bay N Black Sea
Molodechno/Molodeczno see Maladzyechna
205 V3 **Molodezhnaya** Russian research station Antarctica 67.33S 46.12E
128 J14 **Mologa** ≈ NW Russian Federation
40 E9 **Molokai** Haw. Moloka'i. island Hawaii, USA, C Pacific Ocean
183 X3 **Molokai Fracture Zone** tectonic feature NE Pacific Ocean
128 K15 **Molokovo** Tverskaya Oblast', W Russian Federation 58.10N 36.43E
129 Q14 **Moloma** ≈ NW Russian Federation
191 R8 **Molong** New South Wales, SE Australia 33.07S 148.52E
85 H21 **Molopo** seasonal river Botswana/South Africa
117 F17 **Mólos** Stereá Ellás, C Greece 38.48N 22.40E
175 Q7 **Molosipat** Sulawesi, N Indonesia 0.28N 121.08E
Molotov see Severodvinsk, Arkhangel'skaya Oblast', Russian Federation
Molotov see Perm', Permskaya Oblast', Russian Federation
81 G17 **Moloundou** Est, SE Cameroon 2.03N 15.13E
105 U5 **Molsheim** Bas-Rhin, NE France 48.33N 7.30E
15 L12 **Molson Lake** ◎ Manitoba, C Canada
Moluccas see Maluku
175 Rr8 **Molucca Sea** Ind. Laut Maluku. sea E Indonesia
Molukken see Maluku
85 O15 **Molumbo** Zambézia, N Mozambique 15.33S 36.19E
176 Uu14 **Molu, Pulau** island Maluku, E Indonesia
85 P16 **Moma** Nampula, NE Mozambique 16.42S 39.12E
176 Xx13 **Momats** ≈ Irian Jaya, E Indonesia
44 J11 **Mombacho, Volcán** ⛰ SW Nicaragua 11.49N 85.58W
83 K21 **Mombasa** Coast, SE Kenya 4.04N 39.40E
83 J21 **Mombasa** ✈ Coast, SE Kenya 4.01S 39.31E
Mombetsu see Monbetsu
176 Y16 **Mombum** Irian Jaya, E Indonesia 8.16S 138.51E
116 J12 **Momchilgrad** prev. Mastanli. Kŭrdzhali, S Bulgaria 41.33N 25.25E
101 F23 **Momignies** Hainaut, S Belgium 50.02N 4.10E
56 E6 **Momil** Córdoba, NW Colombia 9.15N 75.40W
44 I10 **Momotombo, Volcán** ⛰ W Nicaragua 12.25N 86.33W
58 B5 **Mompiche, Ensenada de** bay NW Ecuador
81 K18 **Mompono** Equateur, NW Dem. Rep. Congo (Zaire) 0.11N 21.31E
56 F6 **Mompós** Bolívar, NW Colombia 9.10N 74.21W
97 J24 **Møn** prev. Möen. island SE Denmark
38 L4 **Mona** Utah, W USA 39.49N 111.52W
Mona, Canal de la see Mona Passage
98 E8 **Monach Islands** island group NW Scotland, UK
105 V14 **Monaco** var. Monaco-Ville; anc. Monoecus. ● (Monaco) S Monaco 43.46N 7.22E
105 V14 **Monaco** off. Principality of Monaco. ◆ monarchy W Europe
Monaco see München
Monaco Basin see Canary Basin
Monaco-Ville see Monaco
98 I9 **Monadhliath Mountains** ▲▲ N Scotland, UK
57 O6 **Monagas** off. Estado Monagas. ◈ state NE Venezuela
99 F16 **Monaghan** Ir. Muineachán. N Ireland 54.15N 6.58W
99 E16 **Monaghan** Ir. Muineachán. cultural region N Ireland
45 S16 **Monagrillo** Herrera, S Panama 7.58N 80.23W
26 L8 **Monahans** Texas, SW USA 31.33N 102.52W
47 Q9 **Mona, Isla** island W Puerto Rico
47 Q9 **Mona Passage** Sp. Canal de la Mona. channel Dominican Republic/Puerto Rico
45 O14 **Mona, Punta** headland E Costa Rica 9.44N 82.48W
161 K25 **Monaragala** Uva Province, SE Sri Lanka 6.52N 81.22E
35 S9 **Monarch** Montana, NW USA 47.04N 110.51W
14 Ff14 **Monarch Mountain** ▲ British Columbia, SW Canada 51.59N 125.56W
Monasterio see Monesterio
Monasterzyska see Monastyrys'ka
Monastir see Bitola
Monastyriska see Monastyrys'ka
119 O7 **Monastyryshche** Cherkas'ka Oblast', C Ukraine 48.59N 29.47E
118 J6 **Monastyrys'ka** Pol. Monasterzyska, Rus. Monastyriska. Ternopil's'ka Oblast', W Ukraine 49.04N 25.10E
81 E15 **Monatélé** Centre, SW Cameroon 4.16N 11.12E
172 Q4 **Monbetsu** var. Mombetsu, Monbetu. Hokkaidō, NE Japan 44.22N 143.22E
Monbetu see Monbetsu
108 B8 **Moncalieri** Piemonte, NW Italy 45.00N 7.41E
106 G4 **Monção** Viana do Castelo, N Portugal 42.03N 8.29W
107 Q5 **Moncayo** ▲ N Spain 41.43N 1.51W
107 Q5 **Moncayo, Sierra del** ▲▲ N Spain
128 J4 **Monchegorsk** Murmanskaya Oblast', NW Russian Federation 67.55N 32.46E
103 D15 **Mönchengladbach** prev. München-Gladbach. Nordrhein-Westfalen, W Germany 51.12N 6.25E
106 F14 **Monchique** Faro, S Portugal 37.19N 8.33W
106 G14 **Monchique, Serra de** ▲▲ S Portugal
23 S14 **Moncks Corner** South Carolina, SE USA 33.12N 80.00W
43 N7 **Monclova** Coahuila de Zaragoza, NE Mexico 26.55N 101.25W
Moncorvo see Torre de Moncorvo
11 P14 **Moncton** New Brunswick, SE Canada 46.04N 64.49W
106 F8 **Mondego, Cabo** headland N Portugal 40.10N 8.58W
106 G8 **Mondego, Rio** ≈ N Portugal
106 I2 **Mondoñedo** Galicia, NW Spain 43.25N 7.22W
101 N25 **Mondorf-les-Bains** Grevenmacher, SE Luxembourg 49.30N 6.16E
104 M7 **Mondoubleau** Loir-et-Cher, C France 48.00N 0.49E
32 J6 **Mondovi** Wisconsin, N USA 44.34N 91.40W
108 B9 **Mondovì** Piemonte, NW Italy 44.22N 7.55E
107 P3 **Mondragón** var. Arrasate. País Vasco, N Spain 43.04N 2.30W
109 J17 **Mondragone** Campania, S Italy 41.07N 13.52E
111 R5 **Mondsee** ◎ N Austria
126 J16 **Mondy** Respublika Buryatiya, S Russian Federation 51.41N 101.03E
117 G22 **Monemvasía** Pelopónnisos, S Greece 36.22N 23.03E
20 B15 **Monessen** Pennsylvania, NE USA 40.07N 79.51W
106 J12 **Monesterio** var. Monasterio. Extremadura, W Spain 38.04N 6.16W
12 L8 **Monet** Quebec, SE Canada 48.09N 75.37W
29 S8 **Monett** Missouri, C USA 36.55N 93.55W
29 X9 **Monette** Arkansas, C USA 35.53N 90.20W
12 G11 **Monetville** Ontario, S Canada 46.08N 80.24W
108 J7 **Monfalcone** Friuli-Venezia Giulia, NE Italy 45.49N 13.31E
106 H10 **Monforte** Portalegre, C Portugal 39.03N 7.25W
106 I4 **Monforte** Galicia, NW Spain 42.31N 7.30W
83 I24 **Monga** Lindi, SE Tanzania 9.05S 37.51E
81 L16 **Monga** Orientale, N Dem. Rep. Congo (Zaire) 4.12N 22.49E
83 F15 **Mongalla** Bahr el Gabel, S Sudan 5.12N 31.42E
159 U11 **Mongar** E Bhutan 27.16N 91.07E
178 K6 **Mong Cai** Quang Ninh, N Vietnam 21.33N 107.56E
188 I11 **Mongers Lake** salt lake Western Australia
195 U14 **Mongga** Kolombangara, NW Solomon Islands 7.51S 157.00E
178 Hh6 **Möng Hpayak** Shan State, E Burma 20.56N 100.00E
Monghyr see Munger
108 B10 **Mongioie** ▲ NW Italy 44.13N 7.46E
178 Gg5 **Möng Küng** Shan State, E Burma 21.39N 97.31E
Mongla see Mungla
196 C15 **Mongmong** C Guam
178 Gg6 **Möng Nai** Shan State, E Burma 20.28N 97.51E
80 I11 **Mongo** Guéra, C Chad 12.11N 18.39E
78 I14 **Mongo** ≈ N Sierra Leone
169 I8 **Mongolia** Mong. Mongol Uls. ◆ republic E Asia
133 V8 **Mongolia, Plateau of** plateau E Mongolia
Mongolküre see Zhaosu
Mongol Uls see Mongolia
81 E17 **Mongomo** E Equatorial Guinea 1.39N 11.18E
79 Y12 **Mongonu** var. Monguno. Borno, NE Nigeria 12.42N 13.37E
Mongora see Mingāora
80 K11 **Mongororo** Ouaddaï, SE Chad 12.03N 22.26E
Mongos, Chaîne des see Bongo, Massif des
81 I16 **Mongoumba** Lobaye, SW Central African Republic 3.39N 18.30E
Mongrove, Punta see Cayacal, Punta
85 G15 **Mongu** Western, W Zambia 15.13S 23.09E
78 I10 **Mônguel** Gorgol, SW Mauritania 16.25N 13.07W
Monguno see Mongonu
178 H4 **Möng Yai** Shan State, E Burma 22.25N 98.02E
178 Hh5 **Möng Yang** Shan State, E Burma 21.52N 99.31E
178 H3 **Möng Yu** Shan State, E Burma 24.00N 97.57E
168 K8 **Mönhbulag** Övörhangay, C Mongolia 46.48N 103.25E
Mönh Sarĭdag see Munku-Sardyk, Gora
194 L15 **Moni** ≈ S Papau New Guinea
117 I15 **Moní Megístis Lávras** monastery Kentrikí Makedonía, N Greece 40.10N 24.22E
117 F18 **Moní Osíou Loúkas** monastery Stereá Ellás, C Greece 38.22N 22.42E
56 F9 **Moniquirá** Boyacá, C Colombia 5.57N 73.35W
105 Q12 **Monistrol-sur-Loire** Haute-Loire, C France 45.19N 4.12E
37 V7 **Monitor Range** ▲▲ Nevada, W USA
117 I14 **Moní Vatopedíou** monastery Kentrikí Makedonía, N Greece 40.19N 24.13E
179 Rr15 **Monkayo** Mindanao, S Philippines 7.45N 125.58E
Monkchester see Newcastle upon Tyne
85 N14 **Monkey Bay** Southern, SE Malawi 14.09S 34.53E
45 N11 **Monkey Point** var. Punta Mico, Punte Mono, Punto Mico. headland SE Nicaragua 11.37N 83.39W
Monkey River see Monkey River Town
44 G3 **Monkey River Town** var. Monkey River. Toledo, SE Belize 16.22N 88.28W
12 M13 **Monkland** Ontario, SE Canada 45.11N 74.51W
81 J19 **Monkoto** Equateur, NW Dem. Rep. Congo (Zaire) 1.35S 20.43E
99 K21 **Monmouth** Wel. Trefynwy. SE Wales, UK 51.49N 2.43W
32 J12 **Monmouth** Illinois, N USA 40.54N 90.39W
34 F12 **Monmouth** Oregon, NW USA 44.51N 123.13W
99 K21 **Monmouth** cultural region SE Wales, UK
100 I10 **Monnickendam** Noord-Holland, C Netherlands 52.28N 5.01E
79 R15 **Mono** ≈ C Togo
Monoecus see Monaco
37 R8 **Mono Lake** ◎ California, W USA
117 O23 **Monólithos** Ródos, Dodekánisos, Greece, Aegean Sea 36.08N 27.45E
21 Q12 **Monomoy Island** island Massachusetts, NE USA
33 O12 **Monon** Indiana, N USA 40.52N 86.54W
31 Y12 **Monona** Iowa, C USA 43.03N 91.23W
32 L9 **Monona** Wisconsin, N USA 43.03N 89.18W
20 B15 **Monongahela** Pennsylvania, NE USA 40.10N 79.54W
20 B16 **Monongahela River** ≈ NE USA
109 P17 **Monopoli** Puglia, SE Italy 40.57N 17.18E
Mono, Punte see Monkey Point
113 K23 **Monor** Pest, C Hungary 47.19N 19.28E
Monostor see Beli Manastir
80 K8 **Monou** Borkou-Ennedi-Tibesti, NE Chad 16.22N 22.15E
107 S12 **Monóvar** País Valenciano, E Spain 38.25N 0.49W
107 R7 **Monreal del Campo** Aragón, NE Spain 40.46N 1.19W
109 I23 **Monreale** Sicilia, Italy, C Mediterranean Sea 38.04N 13.16E
25 T3 **Monroe** Georgia, SE USA 33.47N 83.42W
31 W14 **Monroe** Iowa, C USA 41.31N 93.06W
24 I5 **Monroe** Louisiana, S USA 32.31N 92.06W
33 S10 **Monroe** Michigan, N USA 41.55N 83.24W
20 K13 **Monroe** New York, NE USA 41.18N 74.09W
23 S11 **Monroe** North Carolina, SE USA 34.59N 80.33W
38 L6 **Monroe** Utah, W USA 38.37N 112.07W
34 H7 **Monroe** Washington, NW USA 47.51N 121.58W
32 L9 **Monroe** Wisconsin, N USA 42.34N 89.39W
29 V3 **Monroe City** Missouri, C USA 39.39N 91.43W
33 O15 **Monroe Lake** ▣ Indiana, N USA
25 O7 **Monroeville** Alabama, S USA 31.31N 87.19W
20 C15 **Monroeville** Pennsylvania, NE USA 40.24N 79.44W
78 J16 **Monrovia** ● (Liberia) W Liberia 6.18N 10.48W
78 J16 **Monrovia** ✈ W Liberia 6.22N 10.50W
107 T7 **Monroyo** Aragón, NE Spain 40.46N 0.03W
101 F20 **Mons** Dut. Bergen. Hainaut, S Belgium 50.28N 3.58E
106 I8 **Monsanto** Castelo Branco, C Portugal 40.01N 7.07W
108 H8 **Monselice** Veneto, NE Italy 45.15N 11.47E
178 Gg9 **Mon State** ◈ state S Burma
100 G12 **Monster** Zuid-Holland, W Netherlands 52.01N 4.10E
97 N20 **Mönsterås** Kalmar, S Sweden 57.03N 16.27E
103 F17 **Montabaur** Rheinland-Pfalz, W Germany 50.25N 7.48E
108 G8 **Montagnana** Veneto, NE Italy 45.14N 11.31E
37 N1 **Montague** California, W USA 41.43N 122.31W
27 S5 **Montague** Texas, SW USA 33.39N 97.41W
191 S11 **Montague Island** island New South Wales, SE Australia
41 S12 **Montague Island** island Alaska, USA
41 S13 **Montague Strait** strait N Gulf of Alaska
104 J8 **Montaigu** Vendée, NW France 46.58N 1.18W
Montaigu see Scherpenheuvel
107 S7 **Montalbán** Aragón, NE Spain 40.49N 0.48W
108 G13 **Montalcino** Toscana, C Italy 43.01N 11.34E
106 H5 **Montalegre** Vila Real, N Portugal 41.49N 7.48W
116 G8 **Montana** prev. Ferdinand, Mikhaylovgrad. Montana, NW Bulgaria 43.25N 23.14E
110 D10 **Montana** Valais, SW Switzerland 46.23N 7.29E
41 R11 **Montana** Alaska, USA 62.06N 150.03W
116 G8 **Montana** ◈ province NW Bulgaria
35 T9 **Montana** off. State of Montana; also known as Mountain State, Treasure State. ◈ state NW USA
106 J10 **Montánchez** Extremadura, W Spain 39.15N 6.07W
Montañita see La Montañita
13 Q8 **Mont-Apica** Quebec, SE Canada 47.57N 71.24W
106 G10 **Montargil** Portalegre, C Portugal 39.04N 8.10W
106 G10 **Montargil, Barragem de** ▣ C Portugal
105 O7 **Montargis** Loiret, C France 48.00N 2.43E
105 O4 **Montataire** Oise, N France 49.16N 2.24E
104 M14 **Montauban** Tarn-et-Garonne, S France 44.01N 1.19E
21 N14 **Montauk** Long Island, New York, NE USA 41.01N 71.58W
21 N14 **Montauk Point** headland Long Island, New York, NE USA 41.04N 71.51W
105 Q7 **Montbard** Côte d'Or, C France 47.35N 4.25E
105 U7 **Montbéliard** Doubs, E France 47.31N 6.49E
27 W11 **Mont Belvieu** Texas, SW USA 29.51N 94.53W
107 U6 **Montblanc** var. Montblanch. Cataluña, NE Spain 41.22N 1.10E
Montblanch see Montblanc
105 Q11 **Montbrison** Loire, E France 45.37N 4.04E
Montcalm, Lake see Dogai Coring
105 Q9 **Montceau-les-Mines** Saône-et-Loire, C France 46.40N 4.19E
105 U12 **Mont Cenis, Col du** pass E France 45.16N 6.54E
104 K15 **Mont-de-Marsan** Landes, SW France 43.54N 0.30W
105 O3 **Montdidier** Somme, N France 49.39N 2.34E
197 J7 **Mont-Dore** Province Sud, S New Caledonia 22.18S 166.34E
22 K10 **Monteagle** Tennessee, S USA 35.15N 85.47W
59 M20 **Monteagudo** Chuquisaca, S Bolivia 19.48S 63.57W
43 R16 **Monte Albán** ruins Oaxaca, S Mexico 17.01N 96.46W
107 R11 **Montealegre del Castillo** Castilla-La Mancha, C Spain 38.48N 1.18W
61 N18 **Monte Azul** Minas Gerais, SE Brazil 15.13S 42.52W
12 M12 **Montebello** Quebec, SE Canada 45.40N 74.55W
108 H7 **Montebelluna** Veneto, NE Italy 45.46N 12.03E
62 G13 **Montecarlo** Misiones, NE Argentina 26.37S 54.45W
63 D16 **Monte Caseros** Corrientes, NE Argentina 30.15S 57.39W
62 J13 **Monte Castelo** Santa Catarina, S Brazil 26.34S 50.12W
108 F11 **Montecatini Terme** Toscana, C Italy 43.52N 10.46E
44 H7 **Montecillos, Cordillera de** ▲▲ W Honduras
64 I12 **Monte Comén** Mendoza, W Argentina 34.34S 67.52W
46 M8 **Monte Cristi** var. San Fernando de Monte Cristi. NW Dominican Republic 19.52N 71.39W
60 C13 **Monte Cristo** Amazonas, W Brazil 3.13S 68.00W
109 E14 **Montecristo, Isola di** island Archipelago Toscano, C Italy
Monte Croce Carnico, Passo di see Plöcken Pass
60 J12 **Monte Dourado** Pará, NE Brazil 0.48S 52.32W
42 L11 **Monte Escobedo** Zacatecas, C Mexico 22.19N 103.30W
108 I13 **Montefalco** Umbria, C Italy 42.54N 12.40E
109 H14 **Montefiascone** Lazio, C Italy 42.33N 12.01E
107 N14 **Montefrío** Andalucía, S Spain 37.19N 4.00W
46 I11 **Montego Bay** var. Mobay. W Jamaica 18.28N 77.55W
Montego Bay see Sangster
106 J8 **Montehermoso** Extremadura, W Spain 40.04N 6.19W
106 F10 **Montejunto, Serra de** ▲ C Portugal 39.10N 9.01W
Monteleone di Calabria see Vibo Valentia
56 E7 **Montelíbano** Córdoba, NW Colombia 7.58N 75.24W
105 R13 **Montélimar** anc. Acunum Acusio, Montilium Adhemari. Drôme, E France 44.33N 4.45E
106 K15 **Montellano** Andalucía, S Spain 37.00N 5.34W
37 Y2 **Montello** Nevada, W USA 41.18N 114.10W
32 L8 **Montello** Wisconsin, N USA 43.46N 89.19W
65 J18 **Montemayor, Meseta de** plain SE Argentina
43 O9 **Montemorelos** Nuevo León, NE Mexico 25.10N 99.51W
106 G11 **Montemor-o-Novo** Évora, S Portugal 38.37N 8.13W
106 G8 **Montemor-o-Velho** var. Montemor-o-Vélho. Coimbra, N Portugal 40.10N 8.40W
106 H7 **Montemuro, Serra de** ▲ N Portugal 40.59N 7.59W
104 K12 **Montendre** Charente-Maritime, W France 45.17N 0.24W
63 I15 **Montenegro** Rio Grande do Sul, S Brazil 29.40S 51.32W
115 J16 **Montenegro** Serb. Crna Gora. ◈ republic SW Yugoslavia

◆ Country
● Country Capital
◇ Dependent Territory
○ Dependent Territory Capital
◈ Administrative Region
✈ International Airport
▲ Mountain
▲▲ Mountain Range
⛰ Volcano
≈ River
◎ Lake
▣ Reservoir

MONTE PATRIA – MOUNTAIN PARK

64 G10 **Monte Patria** Coquimbo, N Chile 30.40S 71.00W
47 O9 **Monte Plata** E Dominican Republic 18.46N 69.43W
85 P14 **Montepuez** Cabo Delgado, N Mozambique 13.11S 38.59E
85 P14 **Montepuez** N Mozambique
108 G13 **Montepulciano** Toscana, C Italy 43.02N 11.51E
64 L6 **Monte Quemado** Santiago del Estero, N Argentina 25.46S 62.51W
105 O6 **Montereau-Faut-Yonne** *anc.* Condate. Seine-St-Denis, N France 48.22N 2.57E
37 N11 **Monterey** California, W USA 36.36N 121.53W
22 L9 **Monterey** Tennessee, S USA 36.09N 85.16W
23 T5 **Monterey** Virginia, NE USA 38.24N 79.33W
Monterey *see* Monterrey
37 N10 **Monterey Bay** *bay* California, W USA
56 D6 **Montería** Córdoba, NW Colombia 8.45N 75.54W
59 N18 **Montero** Santa Cruz, C Bolivia 17.19S 63.15W
64 J7 **Monteros** Tucumán, C Argentina 27.12S 65.30W
106 I5 **Monterrei** Galicia, NW Spain 41.55N 7.27W
43 O8 **Monterrey** *var.* Monterey. Nuevo León, NE Mexico 25.40N 100.16W
34 F9 **Montesano** Washington, NW USA 46.58N 123.37W
109 M19 **Montesano sulla Marcellana** Campania, S Italy 40.15N 15.41E
109 N16 **Monte Sant' Angelo** Puglia, SE Italy 41.43N 15.58E
61 O16 **Monte Santo** Bahia, E Brazil 10.25S 39.18W
109 D18 **Monte Santu, Capo di** *headland* Sardegna, Italy, C Mediterranean Sea 40.05N 9.43E
61 M19 **Montes Claros** Minas Gerais, SE Brazil 16.45S 43.52W
109 K14 **Montesilvano Marina** Abruzzo, C Italy 42.28N 14.07E
25 P4 **Montevallo** Alabama, S USA 33.06N 86.51W
108 G12 **Montevarchi** Toscana, C Italy 43.31N 11.34E
31 S9 **Montevideo** Minnesota, N USA 44.56N 95.43W
63 F20 **Montevideo** ● (Uruguay) Montevideo, S Uruguay 34.55S 56.10W
39 S7 **Monte Vista** Colorado, C USA 37.33N 106.08W
25 T5 **Montezuma** Georgia, SE USA 32.18N 84.01W
31 W14 **Montezuma** Iowa, C USA 41.35N 92.31W
28 J6 **Montezuma** Kansas, C USA 37.33N 100.25W
105 U12 **Montgenèvre, Col de** *pass* France/Italy 44.56N 6.45E
99 K20 **Montgomery** E Wales, UK 52.37N 3.05W
25 Q5 **Montgomery** *state capital* Alabama, S USA 32.22N 86.18W
31 V9 **Montgomery** Minnesota, N USA 44.26N 93.34W
20 G13 **Montgomery** Pennsylvania, NE USA 41.08N 76.52W
23 Q5 **Montgomery** West Virginia, NE USA 38.07N 81.19W
99 K19 **Montgomery** *cultural region* E Wales, UK
Montgomery *see* Sāhīwāl
29 V4 **Montgomery City** Missouri, C USA 38.58N 91.30W
37 S8 **Montgomery Pass** *pass* Nevada, W USA 37.57N 118.21W
104 K12 **Montguyon** Charente-Maritime, W France 45.12N 0.13W
110 C10 **Monthey** Valais, SW Switzerland 46.15N 6.55E
29 V13 **Monticello** Arkansas, C USA 33.37N 91.44W
25 T4 **Monticello** Florida, SE USA 30.33N 83.52W
25 T8 **Monticello** Georgia, SE USA 33.18N 83.40W
32 M13 **Monticello** Illinois, N USA 40.01N 88.34W
33 O12 **Monticello** Indiana, N USA 40.45N 86.46W
31 Y13 **Monticello** Iowa, C USA 42.14N 91.11W
22 L7 **Monticello** Kentucky, S USA 36.51N 84.51W
31 V8 **Monticello** Minnesota, N USA 45.19N 93.45W
24 K7 **Monticello** Mississippi, S USA 31.33N 90.06W
29 V2 **Monticello** Missouri, C USA 40.07N 91.42W
20 J12 **Monticello** New York, NE USA 41.39N 74.41W
39 O7 **Monticello** Utah, W USA 37.52N 109.20W
108 F8 **Montichiari** Lombardia, N Italy 45.24N 10.27E
104 M12 **Montignac** Dordogne, SW France 45.24N 0.54E
101 G21 **Montignies-le-Tilleul** *var.* Montigny-le-Tilleul. Hainaut, S Belgium 50.22N 4.22E
12 J8 **Montigny, Lac de** ◎ Quebec, SE Canada
105 S6 **Montigny-le-Roi** Haute-Marne, N France 48.02N 5.28E
Montigny-le-Tilleul *see* Montignies-le-Tilleul
45 R16 **Montijo** Veraguas, S Panama 7.58N 81.12W
106 F11 **Montijo** Setúbal, W Portugal 38.42N 8.58W
106 J11 **Montijo** Extremadura, W Spain 38.55N 6.37W
Montilium Adhemari *see* Montélimar
106 M13 **Montilla** Andalucía, S Spain 37.36N 4.39W
104 L3 **Montivilliers** Seine-Maritime, N France 49.31N 0.10E
13 U7 **Mont-Joli** Quebec, SE Canada 48.33N 68.12W
12 M10 **Mont-Laurier** Quebec, SE Canada 46.33N 75.31W
13 X5 **Mont-Louis** Quebec, SE Canada 49.13N 65.44W
105 N17 **Mont-Louis** *var.* Mont Louis. Pyrénées-Orientales, S France 42.30N 2.07E
105 O10 **Montluçon** Allier, C France 46.21N 2.37E
13 R10 **Montmagny** Quebec, SE Canada 47.00N 70.31W
105 S3 **Montmédy** Meuse, NE France 49.31N 5.21E
105 P5 **Montmirail** Marne, N France 48.53N 3.31E
13 R9 **Montmorency** Quebec, SE Canada
104 M10 **Montmorillon** Vienne, W France 46.25N 0.52E
109 J14 **Montorio al Vomano** Abruzzo, C Italy 42.31N 13.39E
106 M13 **Montoro** Andalucía, S Spain 38.00N 4.21W
35 S16 **Montpelier** Idaho, NW USA 42.19N 111.18W
31 P6 **Montpelier** North Dakota, N USA 46.40N 98.34W
20 M7 **Montpelier** *state capital* Vermont, NE USA 44.15N 72.32W
105 Q15 **Montpellier** Hérault, S France 43.37N 3.52E
104 L12 **Montpon-Ménestérol** Dordogne, SW France 45.01N 0.10E
12 G8 **Montreal** Ontario, S Canada
12 C8 **Montreal** Ontario, S Canada
Montreal *see* Mirabel
10 K15 **Montréal** *Eng.* Montreal. Quebec, SE Canada 45.30N 73.36W
9 T14 **Montreal Lake** ◎ Saskatchewan, C Canada
12 B9 **Montreal River** Ontario, S Canada 47.13N 84.36W
105 N2 **Montreuil** Pas-de-Calais, N France 50.28N 1.46E
104 K8 **Montreuil-Bellay** Maine-et-Loire, NW France 47.07N 0.10W
110 C10 **Montreux** Vaud, SW Switzerland 46.27N 6.55E
110 B9 **Montricher** Vaud, SW Switzerland 46.37N 6.24E
98 K10 **Montrose** E Scotland, UK 56.43N 2.28W
29 W14 **Montrose** Arkansas, C USA 33.18N 91.29W
39 Q6 **Montrose** Colorado, C USA 38.28N 107.52W
31 Y16 **Montrose** Iowa, C USA 40.31N 91.24W
20 H12 **Montrose** Pennsylvania, NE USA 41.49N 75.52W
23 X5 **Montross** Virginia, NE USA 38.04N 76.50W
13 O12 **Mont-St-Hilaire** Quebec, SE Canada 45.34N 73.10W
105 S3 **Mont-St-Martin** Meurthe-et-Moselle, NE France 49.31N 5.51E
47 V10 **Montserrat** *var.* Emerald Isle. ◇ *UK dependent territory* E West Indies
107 V5 **Montserrat** ▲ NE Spain 41.39N 1.44E
106 M7 **Montuenga** Castilla-León, N Spain 41.04N 4.37W
101 M19 **Montzen** Liège, E Belgium 50.42N 5.59E
39 N8 **Monument Valley** *valley* Arizona/Utah, SW USA
177 G4 **Monywa** Sagaing, C Burma 22.04N 95.12E
108 D7 **Monza** Lombardia, N Italy 45.34N 9.16E
85 J15 **Monze** Southern, S Zambia 16.19S 27.29E
107 T5 **Monzón** Aragón, NE Spain 41.54N 0.12E
27 T9 **Moody** Texas, SW USA 31.18N 97.21W
100 L13 **Mook** Limburg, SE Netherlands 51.45N 5.52E
171 Kk15 **Mooka** *var.* Mōka. Tochigi, Honshū, S Japan 36.28N 140.01E
190 K3 **Moomba** South Australia 28.07S 140.12E
12 G13 **Moon** Ontario, S Canada
Moon *see* Muhu
189 Y10 **Moonie** Queensland, E Australia 27.45S 150.22E
198 B10 **Moonless Mountains** *undersea feature* E Pacific Ocean
190 L13 **Moonlight Head** *headland* Victoria, SE Australia 38.47S 143.12E
Moon-Sund *see* Väinameri
190 H8 **Moonta** South Australia 34.03S 137.36E
Moor *see* Mór
188 I12 **Moora** Western Australia 30.22S 116.04E
100 H12 **Moordrecht** Zuid-Holland, C Netherlands 51.58N 4.40E
35 T9 **Moore** Montana, NW USA 47.00N 109.40W
29 N11 **Moore** Oklahoma, C USA 35.20N 97.29W
27 R12 **Moore** Texas, SW USA 29.03N 99.01W
203 S10 **Moorea** *island* Îles du Vent, W French Polynesia
23 U3 **Moorefield** West Virginia, NE USA 39.03N 78.58W
25 X14 **Moore Haven** Florida, SE USA 26.49N 81.05W
188 J11 **Moore, Lake** ◎ Western Australia
21 N7 **Moore Reservoir** ⊡ New Hampshire/Vermont, NE USA
46 G1 **Moores Island** *island* N Bahamas
23 R10 **Mooresville** North Carolina, SE USA 35.34N 80.48W
31 R5 **Moorhead** Minnesota, N USA 46.51N 96.43W
24 K4 **Moorhead** Mississippi, S USA 33.27N 90.30W
176 Ww10 **Moor, Kepulauan** *island group* E Indonesia
101 F18 **Moorsel** Oost-Vlaanderen, C Belgium 50.58N 4.06E
101 C18 **Moorslede** West-Vlaanderen, W Belgium 50.53N 3.03E
20 L8 **Moosalamoo, Mount** ▲ Vermont, NE USA 43.55N 73.03W
103 M22 **Moosburg** Bayern, SE Germany 48.28N 11.55E
35 S14 **Moose** Wyoming, C USA 43.38N 110.42W
10 H11 **Moose** Ontario, SE Canada
10 H10 **Moose Factory** Ontario, S Canada 51.16N 80.31W
21 Q4 **Moosehead Lake** ◎ Maine, NE USA
9 U16 **Moose Jaw** Saskatchewan, S Canada 50.25N 105.29W
9 V14 **Moose Lake** Manitoba, C Canada 53.42N 100.22W
31 W6 **Moose Lake** Minnesota, N USA 46.28N 92.46W
21 P6 **Mooselookmeguntic Lake** ◎ Maine, NE USA
41 R12 **Moose Pass** Alaska, USA 60.28N 149.21W
21 P5 **Moose River** Maine, NE USA
20 J9 **Moose River** New York, NE USA
9 V16 **Moosomin** Saskatchewan, S Canada 50.09N 101.40W
10 H10 **Moosonee** Ontario, SE Canada 51.18N 80.40W
21 N12 **Moosup** Connecticut, NE USA 41.42N 71.51W
85 N16 **Mopeia** Zambézia, NE Mozambique 17.58S 35.43E
85 H18 **Mopipi** Central, C Botswana 21.10S 24.54E
Moppo *see* Mokp'o
79 N11 **Mopti** Mopti, C Mali 14.30N 4.15W
79 O11 **Mopti** ◐ *region* S Mali
59 H18 **Moquegua** Moquegua, SE Peru 17.12S 70.55W
59 H18 **Moquegua** *off.* Departamento de Moquegua. ◐ *department* S Peru
113 I23 **Mór** *Ger.* Moor. Fejér, C Hungary 47.21N 18.13E
80 G11 **Mora** Extrême-Nord, N Cameroon 11.01N 14.07E
106 G11 **Mora** Évora, S Portugal 38.55N 8.10W
107 N9 **Mora** Castilla-La Mancha, C Spain 39.40N 3.46W
96 L12 **Mora** Dalarna, C Sweden 61.00N 14.30E
31 V7 **Mora** Minnesota, N USA 45.52N 93.18W
39 T10 **Mora** New Mexico, SW USA 35.56N 105.16W
115 J17 **Morača** SW Yugoslavia
158 K10 **Morādābād** Uttar Pradesh, N India 28.49N 78.45E
107 U6 **Móra d'Ebre** *var.* Mora de Ebro. Cataluña, NE Spain 41.04N 0.37E
Mora de Ebro *see* Móra d'Ebre
107 S8 **Mora de Rubielos** Aragón, NE Spain 40.15N 0.45W
180 H4 **Morafenobe** Mahajanga, W Madagascar 17.49S 44.54E
112 K8 **Morąg** *Ger.* Mohrungen. Warmińsko-Mazurskie, NE Poland, 53.55N 19.55E
113 L25 **Mórahalom** Csongrád, S Hungary 46.13N 19.51E
107 N11 **Moral de Calatrava** Castilla-La Mancha, C Spain 38.49N 3.34W
65 G19 **Moraleda, Canal** *strait* SE Pacific Ocean
56 J3 **Morales** Bolívar, N Colombia 8.16N 73.52W
56 D12 **Morales** Cauca, SW Colombia 2.43N 76.36W
44 F5 **Morales** Izabal, E Guatemala 15.29N 88.46W
180 J5 **Moramanga** Toamasina, E Madagascar 18.57S 48.13E
29 Q6 **Moran** Kansas, C USA 37.55N 95.10W
27 Q7 **Moran** Texas, SW USA 32.33N 99.10W
189 X7 **Moranbah** Queensland, NE Australia 22.01S 148.07E
46 L13 **Morant Bay** E Jamaica 17.52N 76.24W
98 G10 **Morar, Loch** ◎ N Scotland, UK
Morata *see* Goodenough Island
107 Q12 **Moratalla** Murcia, SE Spain 38.10N 1.52W
110 C8 **Morat, Lac de** *Ger.* Murtensee. ◎ W Switzerland
86 I11 **Morava** *var.* March. C Europe
see also March
Morava *see* Moravia, Czech Republic
Morava *see* Velika Morava, Yugoslavia
31 W15 **Moravia** Iowa, C USA 40.53N 92.49W
113 F18 **Moravia** *Cz.* Morava, *Ger.* Mähren. *cultural region* E Czech Republic
113 H17 **Moravice** *Ger.* Mohra. NE Czech Republic
118 E12 **Moravița** Timiș, SW Romania 45.15N 21.17E
113 G17 **Moravská Třebová** *Ger.* Mährisch-Trübau. Pardubický Kraj, C Czech Republic 49.45N 16.40E
113 E19 **Moravské Budějovice** *Ger.* Mährisch-Budwitz. Jihlavský Kraj, C Czech Republic 49.03N 15.48E
113 F19 **Moravský Krumlov** *Ger.* Mährisch-Kromau. Brněnský Kraj, SE Czech Republic 48.58N 16.30E
98 J8 **Moray** *cultural region* N Scotland, UK
98 J8 **Moray Firth** *inlet* N Scotland, UK
44 B10 **Morazán** ◐ *department* NE El Salvador
160 C10 **Morbi** Gujarāt, W India 22.51N 70.49E
104 G7 **Morbihan** ◐ *department* NW France
Mörbisch *see* Mörbisch am See
111 Y5 **Mörbisch am See** *var.* Mörbisch. Burgenland, E Austria 47.43N 16.40E
97 N21 **Mörbylånga** Kalmar, S Sweden 56.31N 16.25E
104 J14 **Morcenx** Landes, SW France 44.04N 0.55W
Morcheh Khort *see* Mūrcheh Khvort
15 L16 **Morden** Manitoba, S Canada 49.12N 98.04W
Mordovskaya ASSR/Mordvinia *see* Mordoviya, Respublika
131 N5 **Mordoviya, Respublika** *prev.* Mordovskaya ASSR, *Eng.* Mordovia, Mordvinia. ◐ *autonomous republic* W Russian Federation
130 M7 **Mordovo** Tambovskaya Oblast', W Russian Federation 52.05N 40.49E
Morea *see* Pelopónnisos
30 K8 **Moreau River** South Dakota, N USA
99 K16 **Morecambe** NW England, UK 54.04N 2.52W
99 K16 **Morecambe Bay** *inlet* NW England, UK
191 S4 **Moree** New South Wales, SE Australia 29.28S 149.52E
194 E15 **Morehead** Western, SW PNG 8.42S 141.37E
23 N5 **Morehead** Kentucky, S USA 38.11N 83.27W
194 E15 **Morehead** SW PNG
23 X11 **Morehead City** North Carolina, SE USA 34.43N 76.43W
29 Y8 **Morehouse** Missouri, C USA 36.51N 89.41W
110 E10 **Mörel** Valais, SW Switzerland 46.22N 8.03E
56 D13 **Morelia** Caquetá, S Colombia 1.27N 75.46W
43 N14 **Morelia** Michoacán de Ocampo, S Mexico 19.40N 101.10W
107 T7 **Morella** País Valenciano, E Spain 40.37N 0.06W
42 I7 **Morelos** Chihuahua, N Mexico 26.37N 107.37W
43 O15 **Morelos** ◐ *state* S Mexico
160 H7 **Morena** Madhya Pradesh, C India 26.35N 77.59E
106 L12 **Morena, Sierra** ▲ S Spain
38 L14 **Morenci** Arizona, SW USA 33.05N 109.21W
33 R11 **Morenci** Michigan, N USA 41.43N 84.13W
118 J13 **Moreni** Dâmbovița, S Romania 44.58N 25.39E
96 D9 **Møre og Romsdal** ◐ *county* S Norway
14 Ee12 **Moresby Island** *island* Queen Charlotte Islands, British Columbia, SW Canada
191 W2 **Moreton Island** *island* Queensland, E Australia
105 O3 **Moreuil** Somme, N France 49.47N 2.28E
37 V7 **Morey Peak** ▲ Nevada, W USA 38.40N 116.16W
129 U4 **More-Yu** NW Russian Federation
105 T9 **Morez** Jura, E France 46.33N 6.01E
Mórfou *see* Güzelyurt
Morfou Bay/Mórfou, Kólpos *see* Güzelyurt Körfezi
190 J8 **Morgan** South Australia 34.02S 139.39E
25 S7 **Morgan** Georgia, SE USA 31.31N 84.34W
27 S8 **Morgan** Texas, SW USA 32.01N 97.36W
24 J10 **Morgan City** Louisiana, S USA 29.42N 91.12W
22 H6 **Morganfield** Kentucky, S USA 37.40N 87.55W
37 O10 **Morgan Hill** California, W USA 37.05N 121.38W
23 Q9 **Morganton** North Carolina, SE USA 35.45N 81.41W
22 J7 **Morgantown** Kentucky, S USA 37.13N 86.40W
23 S2 **Morgantown** West Virginia, NE USA 39.37N 79.57W
110 B10 **Morges** Vaud, SW Switzerland 46.30N 6.24E
154 M4 **Morghāb, Daryā-ye** *var.* Murgab, Murghab, *Turkm.* Murgap Deryasy. Afghanistan/Turkmenistan *see also* Murgab
Morghāb, Daryā-ye *see* Murgab
98 I9 **Mor, Glen** *var.* Glen Albyn, Great Glen. *valley* N Scotland, UK
105 T5 **Morhange** Moselle, NE France 48.56N 6.37E
164 M5 **Mori** *var.* Mori Kazak Zizhixian. Xinjiang Uygur Zizhiqu, NW China 43.48N 90.21E
172 Nn6 **Mori** Hokkaidō, NE Japan 42.04N 140.35E
37 Y6 **Moriah, Mount** ▲ Nevada, W USA 39.16N 114.10W
39 S11 **Moriarty** New Mexico, SW USA 34.59N 106.03W
56 J12 **Morichal** Guainía, E Colombia 2.18N 69.54W
194 H14 **Morigio Island** *island* S PNG
Mori Kazak Zizhixian *see* Mori
169 U7 **Morin Dawa** *var.* Morin Dawa Daurzu Zizhiqi. Nei Mongol Zizhiqu, N China 48.21N 124.32E
Morin Dawa Daurzu Zizhiqi *see* Morin Dawa
15 I13 **Morinville** Alberta, SW Canada 53.48N 113.37W
171 Mm11 **Morioka** Iwate, Honshū, C Japan 39.42N 141.08E
191 T8 **Morisset** New South Wales, SE Australia 33.07S 151.32E
171 Mm10 **Moriyoshi-yama** ▲ Honshū, C Japan 39.58N 140.32E
94 K13 **Morjärv** Norrbotten, N Sweden 66.03N 22.45E
131 R3 **Morki** Respublika Mariy El, W Russian Federation 56.27N 49.01E
126 K10 **Morkoka** NE Russian Federation
104 F5 **Morlaix** Finistère, NW France 48.34N 3.49W
97 M20 **Mörlunda** Kalmar, S Sweden 57.19N 15.52E
109 N19 **Mormanno** Calabria, SW Italy 39.54N 15.58E
38 L11 **Mormon Lake** ◎ Arizona, SW USA
37 Y10 **Mormon Peak** ▲ Nevada, W USA 36.59N 114.25W
Mormon State *see* Utah
47 Y5 **Morne-à-l'Eau** Grande Terre, N Guadeloupe 16.20N 61.28W
31 Y15 **Morning Sun** Iowa, C USA 41.06N 91.15W
200 O14 **Mornington Abyssal Plain** *undersea feature* SE Pacific Ocean
65 F22 **Mornington, Isla** *island* S Chile
189 T4 **Mornington Island** *island* Wellesley Islands, Queensland, N Australia
117 E18 **Mórnos** C Greece
155 P14 **Moro** Sind, SE Pakistan 26.36N 67.58E
34 I11 **Moro** Oregon, NW USA 45.28N 120.44W
194 K14 **Morobe** Morobe, C PNG 7.46S 147.35E
194 J14 **Morobe** ◐ *province* C PNG
33 N12 **Morocco** Indiana, N USA 40.57N 87.27W
76 E8 **Morocco** *off.* Kingdom of Morocco, *Ar.* Al Mamlakah. ◆ *monarchy* N Africa
Morocco *see* Marrakech
83 I22 **Morogoro** Morogoro, E Tanzania 6.49S 37.40E
83 H24 **Morogoro** ◐ *region* SE Tanzania
179 Qq16 **Moro Gulf** *gulf* S Philippines
43 N13 **Moroleón** Guanajuato, C Mexico 20.00N 101.13W
180 H6 **Morombe** Toliara, W Madagascar 21.46S 43.21E
46 G5 **Morón** Ciego de Ávila, C Cuba 22.04N 78.39W
56 K5 **Morón** Carabobo, N Venezuela 10.28N 68.10W
Morón *see* Morón de la Frontera
169 N8 **Mörön** Hentiy, C Mongolia 47.21N 110.21E
168 I6 **Mörön** Hövsgöl, N Mongolia 49.38N 100.07E
58 D8 **Morona, Río** N Peru
58 C8 **Morona Santiago** ◐ *province* E Ecuador
180 H5 **Morondava** Toliara, W Madagascar 20.19S 44.16E
106 K14 **Morón de la Frontera** *var.* Morón. Andalucía, S Spain 37.07N 5.27W
180 G13 **Moroni** ● (Comoros) Grande Comore, NW Comoros 11.40S 43.16E
175 Tt6 **Morotai, Pulau** *island* Maluku, E Indonesia
175 T6 **Morotai, Selat** *strait* Maluku, E Indonesia
Morotiri *see* Marotiri
83 H17 **Moroto** NE Uganda 2.31N 34.40E
Morozov *see* Bratan
130 M11 **Morozovsk** Rostovskaya Oblast', SW Russian Federation 48.21N 41.54E
99 L14 **Morpeth** N England, UK 55.10N 1.40W
Morphou *see* Güzelyurt
Morphou Bay *see* Güzelyurt Körfezi
30 I13 **Morrill** Nebraska, C USA 41.57N 103.55W
29 U11 **Morrilton** Arkansas, C USA 35.09N 92.44W
9 Q16 **Morrin** Alberta, SW Canada 51.40N 112.45W
192 M7 **Morrinsville** Waikato, North Island, NZ 37.40S 175.32E
9 X16 **Morris** Manitoba, S Canada 49.21N 97.21W
32 M11 **Morris** Illinois, N USA 41.21N 88.25W
31 S8 **Morris** Minnesota, N USA 45.31N 95.52W
12 M13 **Morrisburg** Ontario, SE Canada 44.55N 75.07W
207 R11 **Morris Jesup, Kap** *headland* N Greenland 83.33N 32.40W
190 B1 **Morris, Mount** ▲ South Australia 26.04S 131.03E
32 K10 **Morrison** Illinois, N USA 41.48N 89.58W
38 K13 **Morristown** Arizona, SW USA 33.48N 112.34W
20 J14 **Morristown** New Jersey, NE USA 40.48N 74.28W
23 O8 **Morristown** Tennessee, S USA 36.12N 83.18W
44 L11 **Morrito** Río San Juan, SW Nicaragua 11.37N 85.03W
37 P13 **Morro Bay** California, W USA 35.21N 120.51W
97 L22 **Mörrum** Blekinge, S Sweden 56.10N 14.45E
85 N16 **Morrumbala** Zambézia, NE Mozambique 17.16S 35.34E
85 N20 **Morrumbene** Inhambane, SE Mozambique 23.38S 35.22E
97 F21 **Mors** *island* NW Denmark
Mörs *see* Moers
27 N1 **Morse** Texas, SW USA 36.03N 101.28W
131 N6 **Morshansk** Tambovskaya Oblast', W Russian Federation 53.27N 41.46E
104 L5 **Mortagne-au-Perche** Orne, N France 48.32N 0.31E
104 J8 **Mortagne-sur-Sèvre** Vendée, NW France 47.00N 0.57W
106 G8 **Mortágua** Viseu, N Portugal 40.24N 8.13W
104 J5 **Mortain** Manche, N France 48.39N 0.51W
108 C8 **Mortara** Lombardia, N Italy 45.15N 8.43E
61 J17 **Mortes, Rio das** C Brazil
190 M12 **Mortlake** Victoria, SE Australia 38.06S 142.48E
Mortlock Group *see* Takuu Islands
201 Q17 **Mortlock Islands** *prev.* Nomoi Islands. *island group* C Micronesia
31 T9 **Morton** Minnesota, N USA 44.33N 94.58W
24 L5 **Morton** Mississippi, S USA 32.21N 89.39W
26 M5 **Morton** Texas, SW USA 33.40N 102.45W
34 H9 **Morton** Washington, NW USA 46.33N 122.16W
(0) D7 **Morton Seamount** *undersea feature* NE Pacific Ocean 50.15N 142.45W
47 U15 **Moruga** Trinidad, Trinidad and Tobago 10.04N 61.16W
191 P9 **Morundah** New South Wales, SE Australia 34.57S 146.18E
Moruroa *see* Mururoa
191 S11 **Moruya** New South Wales, SE Australia 35.55S 150.04E
105 Q8 **Morvan** *physical region* C France
193 G21 **Morven** Canterbury, South Island, NZ 44.51S 171.07E
191 O13 **Morwell** Victoria, SE Australia 38.13S 146.25E
129 N6 **Morzhovets, Ostrov** *island* NW Russian Federation
106 G4 **Mos** Galicia, NW Spain 42.10N 8.37W
130 J4 **Mosal'sk** Kaluzhskaya Oblast', W Russian Federation 54.30N 34.55E
103 H20 **Mosbach** Baden-Württemberg, SW Germany 49.21N 9.06E
97 E18 **Mosby** Vest-Agder, S Norway 58.12N 7.55E
35 V9 **Mosby** Montana, NW USA 46.58N 107.53W
34 M9 **Moscow** Idaho, NW USA 46.43N 117.00W
22 F10 **Moscow** Tennessee, S USA 35.04N 89.27W
Moscow *see* Moskva
103 D19 **Mosel** *Fr.* Moselle. W Europe
see also Moselle
105 T4 **Moselle** ◐ *department* NE France
105 T5 **Moselle** *Ger.* Mosel. W Europe
see also Mosel
34 K9 **Moses Lake** ◎ Washington, NW USA
85 I18 **Mosetse** Central, E Botswana 20.40S 26.37E
94 H4 **Mosfellsbær** Sudhurland, SW Iceland 65.09N 21.43W
193 F23 **Mosgiel** Otago, South Island, NZ 45.51S 170.21E
128 M11 **Mosha** NW Russian Federation
83 I20 **Moshi** Kilimanjaro, NE Tanzania 3.21S 37.19E
112 G12 **Mosina** Wielkolpolskie, C Poland 52.13N 16.48E
32 L6 **Mosinee** Wisconsin, N USA 44.45N 89.39W
94 F13 **Mosjøen** Nordland, C Norway 65.49N 13.12E
127 Nn13 **Moskal'vo** Ostrov Sakhalin, Sakhalinskaya Oblast', SE Russian Federation 53.36N 142.31E
94 I13 **Moskosel** Norrbotten, N Sweden 65.52N 19.30E
130 K4 **Moskovskaya Oblast'** ◐ *province* W Russian Federation
Moskovskiy *see* Moskva
130 J3 **Moskva** *Eng.* Moscow. ● (Russian Federation) Gorod Moskva, W Russian Federation 55.45N 37.42E
153 Q14 **Moskva** *Rus.* Moskovskiy; *prev.* Chubek. SW Tajikistan 37.41N 69.33E
130 L4 **Moskva** W Russian Federation
85 I20 **Mosomane** Kgatleng, SE Botswana 24.03S 26.16E
Moson and Magyaróvár *see* Mosonmagyaróvár
113 H21 **Mosoni-Duna** *Ger.* Kleine Donau. NW Hungary
113 H21 **Mosonmagyaróvár** *Ger.* Wieselburg-Ungarisch-Altenburg; *prev.* Moson and Magyaróvár, *Ger.* Wieselburg and Ungarisch-Altenburg. Győr-Moson-Sopron, NW Hungary 47.51N 17.15E
Mospino *see* Mospyne
119 X8 **Mospyne** *Rus.* Mospino. Donets'ka Oblast', E Ukraine 47.53N 38.03E
56 B12 **Mosquera** Nariño, SW Colombia 2.31N 78.24W
39 U10 **Mosquero** New Mexico, SW USA 35.46N 103.57W
Mosquito Coast *see* La Mosquitia
33 U11 **Mosquito Creek Lake** ⊡ Ohio, N USA
Mosquito Gulf *see* Mosquitos, Golfo de los
25 X11 **Mosquito Lagoon** *wetland* Florida, SE USA
45 N10 **Mosquito, Punta** *headland* E Nicaragua 12.18N 83.38W
45 W14 **Mosquito, Punta** *headland* NE Panama 9.06N 77.52W
45 Q15 **Mosquitos, Golfo de los** *Eng.* Mosquito Gulf. *gulf* N Panama
97 H16 **Moss** Østfold, S Norway 59.25N 10.40E
Mossâmedes *see* Namibe
24 G8 **Moss Bluff** Louisiana, S USA 30.18N 93.11W
193 C23 **Mossburn** Southland, South Island, NZ 45.40S 168.15E
85 G26 **Mosselbaai** *var.* Mosselbai, *Eng.* Mossel Bay. Western Cape, SW South Africa 34.10S 22.07E
Mosselbai/Mossel Bay *see* Mosselbaai
81 F20 **Mossendjo** Le Niari, SW Congo 2.57S 12.39E
191 N8 **Mossgiel** New South Wales, SE Australia 33.16S 144.34E
103 H22 **Mössingen** Baden-Württemberg, S Germany 48.22N 9.01E
189 W4 **Mossman** Queensland, NE Australia 16.34S 145.27E
61 P14 **Mossoró** Rio Grande do Norte, NE Brazil 5.10S 37.19W
25 N9 **Moss Point** Mississippi, S USA 30.24N 88.31W
191 S9 **Moss Vale** New South Wales, SE Australia 34.33S 150.22E
34 G9 **Mossyrock** Washington, NW USA 46.32N 122.30W
113 B15 **Most** *Ger.* Brüx. Ústecký Kraj, NW Czech Republic 50.30N 13.37E
123 Jj16 **Mosta** *var.* Musta. C Malta 35.54N 14.25E
76 I5 **Mostaganem** *var.* Mestghanem. NW Algeria 35.55N 0.08E
115 H14 **Mostar** Federacija Bosna I Hercegovina, S Bosnia and Herzegovina 43.20N 17.47E
63 J17 **Mostardas** Rio Grande do Sul, S Brazil 31.06S 50.52W
118 K14 **Mostiștea** S Romania
Mostva *see* Mastva
Mosty *see* Masty
118 H5 **Mostys'ka** L'vivs'ka Oblast', W Ukraine 49.47N 23.09E
Mosul *see* Al Mawșil
97 F15 **Møsvatnet** ◎ S Norway
82 J12 **Mot'a** Amhara, N Ethiopia 11.03N 38.03E
197 C10 **Mota** *island* Banks Islands, N Vanuatu
81 H16 **Motaba** N Congo
107 O10 **Mota del Cuervo** Castilla-La Mancha, C Spain 39.30N 2.52W
106 L5 **Mota del Marqués** Castilla-León, N Spain 41.37N 5.10W
44 F5 **Motagua, Río** Guatemala/Honduras
121 H19 **Motal'** Brestskaya Voblasts', SW Belarus 52.13N 25.34E
97 L17 **Motala** Östergötland, S Sweden 58.33N 15.05E
197 C10 **Mota Lava** *island* Banks Islands, N Vanuatu
203 X7 **Motane** *var.* Mohotani. *island* Îles Marquises, NE French Polynesia
158 K13 **Moth** Uttar Pradesh, N India 25.43N 78.55E
Mother of Presidents/Mother of States *see* Virginia
98 I12 **Motherwell** C Scotland, UK 55.48N 4.00W
159 P12 **Motīhāri** Bihār, N India 26.40N 84.55E
107 Q10 **Motilla del Palancar** Castilla-La Mancha, C Spain 39.34N 1.55W
192 N7 **Motiti Island** *island* NE NZ
67 E25 **Motley Island** *island* SE Falkland Islands
85 J19 **Motloutse** E Botswana
43 V17 **Motozintla de Mendoza** Chiapas, SE Mexico 15.22N 92.11W
107 N15 **Motril** Andalucía, S Spain 36.45N 3.29W
118 G13 **Motru** Gorj, SW Romania 44.49N 22.55E
171 Mm5 **Motsuta-misaki** *headland* Hokkaidō, NE Japan 42.36N 139.48E
30 L6 **Mott** North Dakota, N USA 46.21N 102.17W
Möttling *see* Metlika
109 O18 **Mottola** Puglia, SE Italy 40.37N 17.01E
192 P8 **Motu** North Island, NZ
193 I14 **Motueka** Tasman, South Island, NZ 41.08S 173.01E
193 I14 **Motueka** South Island, NZ
Motu Iti *see* Tupai
43 X12 **Motul** *var.* Motul de Felipe Carrillo Puerto. Yucatán, SE Mexico 21.06N 89.16W
Motul de Felipe Carrillo Puerto *see* Motul
203 U17 **Motu Nui** *island* Easter Island, Chile, E Pacific Ocean
203 Q10 **Motu One** *var.* Bellingshausen. *atoll* Îles Sous le Vent, W French Polynesia
202 I16 **Motutapu** *island* E Cook Islands
200 R15 **Motu Tapu** *island* Tongatapu Group, S Tonga
192 L5 **Motutapu Island** *island* N NZ
Motyca *see* Modica
126 I13 **Motygino** Krasnoyarskiy Kray, C Russian Federation 58.09N 94.35E
Mouanda *see* Moanda
Mouaskar *see* Mascara
107 U3 **Moubermé, Tuc de** *Fr.* Pic de Maubermé, *Sp.* Pico Mauberme; *prev.* Tuc de Maubermé. ▲ France/Spain *see also* Maubermé, Pic de 42.48N 0.57E
47 N7 **Mouchoir Passage** *passage* SE Turks and Caicos Islands
78 I9 **Moudjéria** Tagant, SW Mauritania 17.52N 12.19W
110 C9 **Moudon** Vaud, W Switzerland 46.41N 6.49E
Mouhoun *see* Black Volta
81 E19 **Mouila** Ngounié, C Gabon 1.49S 11.01E
81 K14 **Mouka** Haute-Kotto, C Central African Republic 7.12N 21.52E
Moukden *see* Shenyang
191 N10 **Moulamein** New South Wales, SE Australia 35.06S 144.03E
Moulamein Creek *see* Billabong Creek
76 F6 **Moulay-Bousselham** NW Morocco 34.54N 6.15W
Moule *see* le Moule
82 M11 **Moulhoulé** N Djibouti 12.34N 43.06E
105 P9 **Moulins** Allier, C France 46.34N 3.19E
178 Gg9 **Moulmein** *var.* Maulmain, Mawlamyine. Mon State, S Burma 16.30N 97.39E
177 F9 **Moulmeingyun** Irrawaddy, SW Burma 16.24N 95.15E
76 G6 **Moulouya** *var.* Mulucha, Muluya, Mulwiya. *seasonal river* NE Morocco
25 O2 **Moulton** Alabama, S USA 34.28N 87.16W
31 W16 **Moulton** Iowa, C USA 40.41N 92.40W
27 T11 **Moulton** Texas, SW USA 29.34N 97.08W
25 T7 **Moultrie** Georgia, SE USA 31.10N 83.47W
23 S14 **Moultrie, Lake** ◎ South Carolina, SE USA
24 K3 **Mound Bayou** Mississippi, S USA 33.52N 90.43W
32 L17 **Mound City** Illinois, N USA 37.06N 89.09W
29 R6 **Mound City** Kansas, C USA 38.08N 94.48W
29 Q2 **Mound City** Missouri, C USA 40.07N 95.13W
31 N7 **Mound City** South Dakota, N USA 45.42N 100.04W
80 H13 **Moundou** Logone-Occidental, SW Chad 8.34N 16.01E
29 P10 **Mounds** Oklahoma, C USA 35.52N 96.03W
23 R2 **Moundsville** West Virginia, NE USA 39.55N 80.44W
178 Ii12 **Moŭng Roessei** Bătdâmbâng, W Cambodia 12.46N 103.28E
Moun Hou *see* Black Volta
14 G5 **Mountain** Northwest Territories, NW Canada
39 S12 **Mountainair** New Mexico, SW USA 34.31N 106.14W
37 V1 **Mountain City** Nevada, W USA 41.48N 115.58W
23 Q8 **Mountain City** Tennessee, S USA 36.28N 81.48W
29 U7 **Mountain Grove** Missouri, C USA 37.07N 92.15W
29 U9 **Mountain Home** Arkansas, C USA 36.19N 92.24W
35 N15 **Mountain Home** Idaho, NW USA 43.07N 115.42W
27 Q11 **Mountain Home** Texas, SW USA 30.11N 99.19W
31 W4 **Mountain Iron** Minnesota, N USA 47.31N 92.37W
31 T10 **Mountain Lake** Minnesota, N USA 43.57N 94.54W
25 S3 **Mountain Park** Georgia, SE USA 34.04N 84.24W

◆ Country ● Country Capital ◇ Dependent Territory ○ Dependent Territory Capital ◐ Administrative Region ✈ International Airport ▲ Mountain ▲ Mountain Range Volcano River ◎ Lake ⊡ Reservoir

MOUNTAIN PASS – MURGASH

37 W12 **Mountain Pass** pass California, W USA 35.28N 115.31W
29 T12 **Mountain Pine** Arkansas, C USA 34.34N 93.10W
41 Y14 **Mountain Point** Annette Island, Alaska, USA 55.17N 131.31W
Mountain State see Montana, USA
Mountain State see West Virginia, USA
29 V7 **Mountain View** Arkansas, C USA 35.52N 92.07W
40 H12 **Mountain View** Hawaii, USA, C Pacific Ocean 19.31N 155.03W
29 V10 **Mountain View** Missouri, C USA 37.00N 91.42W
40 M11 **Mountain Village** Alaska, USA 62.06N 163.42W
23 R8 **Mount Airy** North Carolina, SE USA 36.30N 80.36W
85 K24 **Mount Ayliff** ***Xh.*** Maxesibebi. Eastern Cape, SE South Africa 30.48S 29.22E
31 U16 **Mount Ayr** Iowa, C USA 40.42N 94.14W
190 J9 **Mount Barker** South Australia 35.06S 138.52E
188 J14 **Mount Barker** Western Australia 34.42S 117.40E
191 P11 **Mount Beauty** Victoria, SE Australia 36.47S 147.12E
12 E16 **Mount Brydges** Ontario, S Canada 42.54N 81.29W
33 N16 **Mount Carmel** Illinois, N USA 38.23N 87.46W
32 K10 **Mount Carroll** Illinois, N USA 42.04N 89.58W
33 S9 **Mount Clemens** Michigan, N USA 42.36N 82.52W
193 E19 **Mount Cook** Canterbury, South Island, NZ 43.46S 170.06E
85 L16 **Mount Darwin** Mashonaland Central, NE Zimbabwe 16.45S 31.32E
21 S7 **Mount Desert Island** island Maine, NE USA
25 W11 **Mount Dora** Florida, SE USA 28.48N 81.38W
190 G5 **Mount Eba** South Australia 30.11S 135.40E
27 W8 **Mount Enterprise** Texas, SW USA 31.53N 94.40W
190 J4 **Mount Fitton** South Australia 29.55S 139.26E
85 J24 **Mount Fletcher** Eastern Cape, SE South Africa 30.40S 28.30E
12 F15 **Mount Forest** Ontario, S Canada 43.58N 80.43W
190 K12 **Mount Gambier** South Australia 37.47S 140.48E
189 W5 **Mount Garnet** Queensland, NE Australia 17.41S 145.07E
23 P6 **Mount Gay** West Virginia, NE USA 37.49N 82.00W
33 S12 **Mount Gilead** Ohio, N USA 40.33N 82.49W
194 H12 **Mount Hagen** Western Highlands, C PNG 5.53S 144.12E
20 J16 **Mount Holly** New Jersey, NE USA 39.59N 74.46W
23 R10 **Mount Holly** North Carolina, SE USA 35.18N 81.01W
29 T12 **Mount Ida** Arkansas, C USA 34.33N 93.37W
189 T6 **Mount Isa** Queensland, C Australia 20.48S 139.32E
23 U4 **Mount Jackson** Virginia, NE USA 38.45N 78.38W
20 D12 **Mount Jewett** Pennsylvania, NE USA 41.43N 78.37W
20 L13 **Mount Kisco** New York, NE USA 41.12N 73.42W
20 B15 **Mount Lebanon** Pennsylvania, NE USA 40.21N 80.03W
190 J8 **Mount Lofty Ranges** ▲▲ South Australia
188 J10 **Mount Magnet** Western Australia 28.09S 117.52E
192 N7 **Mount Maunganui** Bay of Plenty, North Island, NZ 37.39S 176.11E
99 E18 **Mountmellick** ***Ir.*** Móinteach Mílic. C Ireland 53.07N 7.19W
32 L10 **Mount Morris** Illinois, N USA 42.03N 89.25W
33 R9 **Mount Morris** Michigan, N USA 43.07N 83.42W
20 F10 **Mount Morris** New York, NE USA 42.43N 77.51W
20 B16 **Mount Morris** Pennsylvania, NE USA 39.43N 80.06W
32 K15 **Mount Olive** Illinois, N USA 39.04N 89.43W
23 V10 **Mount Olive** North Carolina, SE USA 35.12N 78.03W
23 N4 **Mount Olivet** Kentucky, S USA 38.32N 84.01W
31 Y15 **Mount Pleasant** Iowa, C USA 40.57N 91.33W
33 Q8 **Mount Pleasant** Michigan, N USA 43.36N 84.46W
20 C15 **Mount Pleasant** Pennsylvania, NE USA 40.07N 79.33W
23 T14 **Mount Pleasant** South Carolina, SE USA 32.47N 79.51W
22 I9 **Mount Pleasant** Tennessee, S USA 35.32N 87.11W
27 W6 **Mount Pleasant** Texas, SW USA 33.10N 94.49W
38 L4 **Mount Pleasant** Utah, W USA 39.33N 111.27W
65 N23 **Mount Pleasant** ✈ (Stanley) East Falkland, Falkland Islands
99 G25 **Mount's Bay** inlet SW England, UK
37 N2 **Mount Shasta** California, W USA 41.18N 122.19W
32 J13 **Mount Sterling** Illinois, N USA 39.59N 90.44W
23 N5 **Mount Sterling** Kentucky, S USA 38.03N 83.56W
20 E15 **Mount Union** Pennsylvania, NE USA 40.21N 77.51W
25 V6 **Mount Vernon** Georgia, SE USA 32.10N 82.35W
32 L16 **Mount Vernon** Illinois, N USA 38.19N 88.54W
22 M6 **Mount Vernon** Kentucky, S USA 37.22N 84.22W
29 S7 **Mount Vernon** Missouri, C USA 37.06N 93.49W
33 T13 **Mount Vernon** Ohio, N USA 40.23N 82.29W
34 K13 **Mount Vernon** Oregon, NW USA 44.22N 119.07W
27 W6 **Mount Vernon** Texas, SW USA 33.11N 95.13W
34 H7 **Mount Vernon** Washington, NW USA 48.25N 122.19W
22 L5 **Mount Washington** Kentucky, S USA 38.03N 85.33W
190 F8 **Mount Wedge** South Australia 33.29S 135.08E
32 L14 **Mount Zion** Illinois, N USA 39.46N 88.52W
189 Y9 **Moura** Queensland, NE Australia 24.34S 149.57E
60 F12 **Moura** Amazonas, NW Brazil 1.32S 61.43W
106 H12 **Moura** Beja, S Portugal 38.07N 7.27W
106 I12 **Mourão** Évora, S Portugal 38.22N 7.19W
78 L11 **Mourdiah** Koulikoro, W Mali 14.28N 7.31W
80 K7 **Mourdi, Dépression du** desert lowland Chad/Sudan
104 J16 **Mourenx** Pyrénées-Atlantiques, SW France 43.24N 0.37W
Mourgana see Mourgkána
117 C15 **Mourgkána** ***var.*** Mourgana. ▲ Albania/Greece 39.48N 20.24E
99 G16 **Mourne Mountains** ***Ir.*** Beanna Boirche. ▲▲ SE Northern Ireland, UK
117 I15 **Moúrtzeflos, Akrotírio** headland Límnos, E Greece 40.00N 25.02E
101 C19 **Mouscron** ***Dut.*** Moeskroen. Hainaut, W Belgium 50.43N 3.13E
Mouse River see Souris River
80 H10 **Moussoro** Kanem, W Chad 13.40N 16.31E
105 T11 **Moûtiers** Savoie, E France 45.28N 6.31E
180 J14 **Moutsamoudou** ***var.*** Mutsamudu. Anjouan, SE Comoros 12.10S 44.25E
76 K11 **Mouydir, Monts de** ▲▲ S Algeria
81 F20 **Mouyondzi** La Bouenza, S Congo 3.58S 13.57E
117 E16 **Mouzáki** ***prev.*** Mouzákion. Thessalía, C Greece 39.25N 21.40E
Mouzákion see Mouzáki
31 S13 **Moville** Iowa, C USA 42.30N 96.04W
84 E13 **Moxico** ◐ province E Angola
180 I14 **Moya** Anjouan, SE Comoros 12.18S 44.27E
42 L12 **Moyahua** Zacatecas, C Mexico 21.19N 103.10W
83 J16 **Moyalē** Oromo, C Ethiopia 3.34N 38.58E
78 I15 **Moyamba** W Sierra Leone 8.04N 12.30W
76 G7 **Moyen Atlas** ***Eng.*** Middle Atlas. ▲▲ N Morocco
80 H13 **Moyen-Chari** ***off.*** Préfecture du Moyen-Chari. ◐ prefecture S Chad
Moyen-Congo see Congo (Republic of)
85 J24 **Moyeni** ***var.*** Quthing. SW Lesotho 30.25S 27.43E
78 H13 **Moyenne-Guinée** ◐ state NW Guinea
81 D18 **Moyen-Ogooué** ***off.*** Province du Moyen-Ogooué, ***var.*** Le Moyen-Ogooué. ◐ province C Gabon
105 S4 **Moyeuvre-Grande** Moselle, NE France 49.15N 6.03E
35 N7 **Moyie Springs** Idaho, NW USA 48.43N 116.15W
151 S15 **Moynnkum** ***prev.*** Fumanovka, ***Kaz.*** Fūrmanov. Zhambyl, S Kazakhstan 44.15N 72.55E
83 F16 **Moyo** NW Uganda 3.37N 31.43E
58 D10 **Moyobamba** San Martín, NW Peru 6.04S 76.55W
175 O16 **Moyo, Pulau** island S Indonesia
80 H10 **Moyto** Chari-Baguirmi, W Chad 12.34N 16.33E
164 G9 **Moyu** ***var.*** Karakax. Xinjiang Uygur Zizhiqu, NW China 37.16N 79.39E
126 Jj9 **Moyyero** ≈ N Russian Federation
151 Q15 **Moyynkum, Peski** ***Kaz.*** Moyynqum. desert S Kazakhstan
Moyynqum see Moyynkum, Peski
151 S12 **Moyynty** Zhezkazgan, C Kazakhstan 47.10N 73.24E
151 S12 **Moyynty** ≈ C Kazakhstan
Mozambika, Lakandranon' i see Mozambique Channel
85 M18 **Mozambique** ***off.*** Republic of Mozambique; ***prev.*** People's Republic of Mozambique, Portuguese East Africa. ◆ republic S Africa
Mozambique Basin see Natal Basin
Mozambique, Canal de see Mozambique Channel
85 P17 **Mozambique Channel** ***Fr.*** Canal de Mozambique, ***Mal.*** Lakandranon' i Mozambika. strait W Indian Ocean
180 L11 **Mozambique Escarpment** ***var.*** Mozambique Scarp. undersea feature SW Indian Ocean
180 L10 **Mozambique Plateau** ***var.*** Mozambique Rise. undersea feature SW Indian Ocean
Mozambique Rise see Mozambique Plateau
Mozambique Scarp see Mozambique Escarpment
131 O15 **Mozdok** Respublika Severnaya Osetiya, SW Russian Federation 43.48N 44.42E
59 K17 **Mozetenes, Serranías de** ▲▲ C Bolivia
130 J4 **Mozhaysk** Moskovskaya Oblast', W Russian Federation 55.31N 36.01E
131 T3 **Mozhga** Udmurtskaya Respublika, NW Russian Federation 56.24N 52.13E
Mozyr' see Mazyr
81 P22 **Mpala** Katanga, E Dem. Rep. Congo (Zaire) 6.43S 29.28E
81 G19 **Mpama** ≈ C Congo
83 E22 **Mpanda** Rukwa, W Tanzania 6.21S 31.01E
84 L11 **Mpande** Northern, NE Zambia 9.13S 31.42E
85 J18 **Mphoengs** Matabeleland South, SW Zimbabwe 21.04S 27.56E
83 F18 **Mpigi** S Uganda 0.13N 32.19E
84 L13 **Mpika** Northern, NE Zambia 11.49S 31.27E
85 J14 **Mpima** Central, C Zambia 14.25S 28.34E
84 J13 **Mpongwe** Copperbelt, C Zambia 13.25S 28.13E
84 K11 **Mporokoso** Northern, N Zambia 9.22S 30.06E
81 H20 **Mpouya** Plateaux, SE Congo 2.39S 16.12E
79 P16 **Mpraeso** C Ghana 6.46N 0.41W
84 L11 **Mpulungu** Northern, N Zambia 8.47S 31.09E
85 K21 **Mpumalanga** ***prev.*** Eastern Transvaal, ***Afr.*** Oos-Transvaal. ◐ province NE South Africa
85 D16 **Mpungu** Okavango, N Namibia 17.36S 18.16E
83 I22 **Mpwapwa** Dodoma, C Tanzania 6.21S 36.28E
Mqinvartsveri see Kazbek
112 M8 **Mrągowo** ***Ger.*** Sensburg. Warmińsko-Mazurskie, NE Poland, 53.52N 21.19E
131 V6 **Mrakovo** Respublika Bashkortostan, W Russian Federation 52.43N 56.36E
180 I13 **Mramani** Anjouan, E Comoros 12.18S 44.39E
114 F12 **Mrkonjić Grad** Republika Srpska, W Bosnia and Herzegovina 44.25N 17.04E
112 H9 **Mrocza** Kujawsko-pomorskie, NW Poland 53.15N 17.38E
128 I14 **Msta** ≈ NW Russian Federation
Mtkvari see Kura
Mtoko see Mutoko
130 K6 **Mtsensk** Orlovskaya Oblast', W Russian Federation 53.17N 36.34E
83 K24 **Mtwara** Mtwara, SE Tanzania 10.16S 40.10E
83 J25 **Mtwara** ◐ region SE Tanzania
106 G14 **Mu** ▲ S Portugal 37.24N 8.04W
200 Qq15 **Mu'a** Tongatapu, S Tonga 21.11S 175.07W
Muai To see Mae Hong Son
85 P16 **Mualama** Zambézia, NE Mozambique 16.51S 38.21E
Mualo see Messalo, Rio
81 E22 **Muanda** Bas-Congo, SW Dem. Rep. Congo (Zaire) 5.53S 12.17E
Muang Chiang Rai see Chiang Rai
178 J6 **Muang Ham** Houaphan, N Laos 20.19N 104.00E
178 J9 **Muang Hinboun** Khammouan, C Laos 17.37N 104.37E
Muang Kalasin see Kalasin
Muang Khammouan see Thakhèk
178 Jj11 **Muang Không** Champasak, S Laos 14.08N 105.48E
178 Jj10 **Muang Khôngxédôn** ***var.*** Khong Sedone. Salavan, S Laos 15.34N 105.46E
Muang Khon Kaen see Khon Kaen
178 Ii6 **Muang Khoua** Phôngsali, N Laos 21.07N 102.31E
Muang Krabi see Krabi
Muang Lampang see Lampang
Muang Lamphun see Lamphun
Muang Loei see Loei
Muang Lom Sak see Lom Sak
Muang Nakhon Sawan see Nakhon Sawan
178 I6 **Muang Namo** Oudômxai, N Laos 20.58N 101.46E
Muang Nan see Nan
178 Ii6 **Muang Ngoy** Louangphabang, N Laos 20.43N 102.42E
178 I5 **Muang Ou Tai** Phôngsali, N Laos 22.06N 101.59E
Muang Pak Lay see Pak Lay
Muang Pakxan see Pakxan
178 Jj10 **Muang Pakxong** Champasak, S Laos 15.10N 106.17E
178 Jj9 **Muang Phalan** ***var.*** Muang Phalane. Savannakhét, S Laos 16.40N 105.33E
Muang Phalane see Muang Phalan
Muang Phan see Phan
Muang Phayao see Phayao
Muang Phichit see Phichit
178 Jj9 **Muang Phin** Savannakhét, S Laos 16.31N 106.01E
Muang Phitsanulok see Phitsanulok
Muang Phrae see Phrae
Muang Roi Et see Roi Et
Muang Sakon Nakhon see Sakon Nakhon
Muang Samut Prakan see Samut Prakan
178 I6 **Muang Sing** Louang Namtha, N Laos 21.12N 101.09E
Muang Ubon see Ubon Ratchathani
Muang Uthai Thani see Uthai Thani
178 I7 **Muang Vangviang** Viangchan, C Laos 18.53N 102.27E
Muang Xaignabouri see Xaignabouli
Muang Xay see Xai
178 Jj9 **Muang Xépôn** ***var.*** Sepone. Savannakhét, S Laos 16.40N 106.15E
174 H6 **Muar** ***var.*** Bandar Maharani. Johor, Peninsular Malaysia 2.01N 102.34E
173 Ff6 **Muara** Sumatera, W Indonesia 2.18N 98.54E
174 Hh11 **Muarabeliti** Sumatera, W Indonesia 3.13S 103.00E
174 H9 **Muarabungo** Sumatera, W Indonesia 1.36S 103.37E
174 I11 **Muaraenim** Sumatera, W Indonesia 3.36S 103.43E
174 Mm8 **Muarajuloi** Borneo, C Indonesia 0.12S 114.03E
175 Nn9 **Muarakaman** Borneo, C Indonesia 0.09S 116.43E
173 Ff9 **Muarasigep** Pulau Siberut, W Indonesia 1.01S 98.48E
174 Hh9 **Muaratembesi** Sumatera, W Indonesia 1.42S 103.07E
175 N9 **Muaratewe** ***var.*** Muarateweh; ***prev.*** Moearatewe. Borneo, C Indonesia 0.58S 114.52E
Muarateweh see Muaratewe
175 O7 **Muarawahau** Borneo, N Indonesia 1.03N 116.48E
144 G13 **Mubārak, Jabal** ▲ S Jordan 29.19N 35.13E
159 N13 **Mubārakpur** Uttar Pradesh, N India 26.05N 83.19E
Mubarek see Muborak
83 F18 **Mubende** SW Uganda 0.34N 31.24E
79 Y14 **Mubi** Adamawa, NE Nigeria 10.15N 13.18E
152 M12 **Muborak** ***Rus.*** Mubarek. Qashqadaryo Wiloyati, S Uzbekistan 39.17N 65.10E
176 Vv9 **Mubrani** Irian Jaya, E Indonesia 0.42S 133.25E
69 U12 **Muchinga Escarpment** escarpment NE Zambia
131 N7 **Muchkapskiy** Tambovskaya Oblast', W Russian Federation 51.51N 42.25E
98 G10 **Muck** island W Scotland, UK
84 Q13 **Mucojo** Cabo Delgado, N Mozambique 12.04S 40.30E
84 F12 **Muconda** Lunda Sul, NE Angola 10.37S 21.19E
56 I10 **Muco, Río** ≈ E Colombia
85 O16 **Mucubela** Zambézia, NE Mozambique 16.51S 37.48E
44 J5 **Mucupina, Monte** ▲ N Honduras 15.07N 86.36W
142 J14 **Mucur** Kirşehir, C Turkey 39.04N 34.25E
149 U8 **Mūd** Khorāsān, E Iran 32.40N 59.30E
169 Y9 **Mudanjiang** ***var.*** Mu-tan-chiang. Heilongjiang, NE China 44.33N 129.40E
169 Y9 **Mudan Jiang** ≈ NE China
142 D11 **Mudanya** Bursa, NW Turkey 40.22N 28.52E
30 K8 **Mud Butte** South Dakota, N USA 45.00N 102.51W
161 G16 **Muddebihāl** Karnātaka, C India 16.26N 76.07E
29 P12 **Muddy Boggy Creek** ≈ Oklahoma, C USA
38 M6 **Muddy Creek** ≈ Utah, W USA
39 V7 **Muddy Creek Reservoir** ⊠ Colorado, C USA
35 W15 **Muddy Gap** Wyoming, C USA 42.21N 107.27W
37 Y11 **Muddy Peak** ▲ Nevada, W USA 36.17N 114.40W
191 R7 **Mudgee** New South Wales, SE Australia 32.37S 149.34E
31 S3 **Mud Lake** ◎ Minnesota, N USA
31 P7 **Mud Lake Reservoir** ⊠ South Dakota, N USA
178 Gg9 **Mudon** Mon State, S Burma 16.14N 97.46E
83 O14 **Mudug** ***off.*** Gobolka Mudug. ◐ region NE Somalia
83 O14 **Mudug** ***var.*** Mudugh. plain N Somalia
Mudugh see Mudug
85 Q15 **Muecate** Nampula, NE Mozambique 14.56S 39.38E
84 Q13 **Mueda** Cabo Delgado, NE Mozambique 11.40S 39.36E
44 L10 **Muelle de los Bueyes** Región Autónoma Atlántico Sur, SE Nicaragua 12.03N 84.34W
Muenchen see München
85 M14 **Muende** Tete, NW Mozambique 14.22S 33.00E
27 T5 **Muenster** Texas, SW USA 33.39N 97.22W
Muenster see Münster
45 O6 **Muerto, Cayo** reef NE Nicaragua
43 T17 **Muerto, Mar** lagoon SE Mexico
66 F11 **Muertos Trough** undersea feature N Caribbean Sea
85 H14 **Mufaya Kuta** Western, NW Zambia 14.30S 24.18E
84 J13 **Mufulira** Copperbelt, C Zambia 12.33S 28.15E
167 O10 **Mufu Shan** ▲▲ C China
Mugalzhar Taūlary see Mugodzhary, Gory
143 Y12 **Muğan Düzü** ***Rus.*** Muganskaya Ravnina, Muganskaya Step'. physical region S Azerbaijan
Muganskaya Ravnina/Muganskaya Step' see Muğan Düzü
108 K8 **Múggia** Friuli-Venezia Giulia, NE Italy 45.36N 13.48E
159 N14 **Mughal Sarāi** Uttar Pradesh, N India 25.18N 83.07E
Mughla see Muğla
147 W11 **Mughshin** ***var.*** Muqshin. S Oman 19.25N 54.38E
153 S12 **Mughsu** ***Rus.*** Muksu. ≈ C Tajikistan
170 Ff16 **Mugi** Tokushima, Shikoku, SW Japan 33.39N 134.24E
142 C16 **Muğla** ***var.*** Mughla. Muğla, SW Turkey 37.13N 28.22E
142 C16 **Muğla** ***var.*** Mughla. ◐ province SW Turkey
150 J11 **Mugodzhary, Gory** ***Kaz.*** Mugalzhar Taūlary. ▲▲ W Kazakhstan
85 O15 **Mugulama** Zambézia, NE Mozambique 16.01S 37.33E
145 U9 **Muḩammad** E Iraq 32.46N 45.14E
145 R8 **Muḩammadīyah** C Iraq 33.22N 42.48E
82 I6 **Muhammad Qol** Red Sea, NE Sudan 20.52N 37.09E
77 Y9 **Muhammad, Râs** headland E Egypt 27.45N 34.18E
Muhammerah see Khorramshahr
146 M12 **Muhāyil** ***var.*** Mahāil. 'Asīr, SW Saudi Arabia 18.34N 42.01E
145 O7 **Muḩaywīr** W Iraq 33.34N 41.06E
103 H21 **Mühlacker** Baden-Württemberg, SW Germany 48.57N 8.51E
Mühlbach see Sebeş
Mühldorf see Mühldorf am Inn
103 N23 **Mühldorf am Inn** ***var.*** Mühldorf. Bayern, SE Germany 48.14N 12.32E
103 J15 **Mühlhausen** ***var.*** Mühlhausen in Thüringen. Thüringen, C Germany 51.13N 10.28E
Mühlhausen in Thüringen see Mühlhausen
205 Q2 **Mühlig-Hofmann Mountains** ▲▲ Antarctica
95 L14 **Muhos** Oulu, C Finland 64.48N 26.00E
144 K6 **Mūḩ, Sabkhat al** ◎ C Syria
120 E5 **Muhu** ***Ger.*** Mohn, Moon. island W Estonia
83 F19 **Muhutwe** Kagera, NW Tanzania 1.31S 31.40E
Muhu Väin see Väinameri
100 J10 **Muiden** Noord-Holland, C Netherlands 52.19N 5.04E
200 R15 **Mui Hopohoponga** headland Tongatapu, S Tonga 21.09S 175.01W
171 K14 **Muika** ***var.*** Muikamachi. Niigata, Honshū, C Japan 37.04N 138.53E
Muikamachi see Muika
Muinchille see Cootehill
Muineachán see Monaghan
99 F19 **Muine Bheag** ***Eng.*** Bagenalstown. SE Ireland 52.42N 6.57W
58 B5 **Muisne** Esmeraldas, NW Ecuador 0.34N 79.58W
85 P14 **Muite** Nampula, NE Mozambique 14.02S 39.06E
43 Z11 **Mujeres, Isla** island E Mexico
118 G7 **Mukacheve** ***Hung.*** Munkács, ***Rus.*** Mukachevo. Zakarpats'ka Oblast', W Ukraine 48.26N 22.44E
Mukachevo see Mukacheve
174 Ll5 **Mukah** Sarawak, East Malaysia 2.55N 112.01E
Mukalla see Al Mukallā
Mukama see Mokāma
Mukāshafa/Mukashshafah see Mukayshīfah
172 Oo6 **Mu-kawa** ≈ Hokkaidō, NE Japan
145 S6 **Mukayshīfah** ***var.*** Mukāshafa, Mukashshafah. N Iraq 34.24N 43.44E
178 J9 **Mukdahan** Mukdahan, E Thailand 16.31N 104.43E
Mukden see Shenyang
172 Ss16 **Mukojima-rettō** ***Eng.*** Parry group. island group SE Japan
152 M14 **Mukry** Lebapskiy Velayat, E Turkmenistan 37.39N 65.37E
Muksu see Mughsu
159 U14 **Muktagacha** ***var.*** Muktagachha Dhaka, N Bangladesh 24.46N 90.16E
Muktagachha see Muktagacha
84 K13 **Mukuku** Central, C Zambia 12.10S 29.50E
84 K11 **Mukupa Kaoma** Northern, NE Zambia 9.55S 30.19E
83 I18 **Mukutan** Rift Valley, W Kenya 1.06N 36.16E
85 F16 **Mukwe** Caprivi, NE Namibia 18.01S 21.24E
107 R13 **Mula** Murcia, SE Spain 38.01N 1.28W
157 K20 **Mulaku Atoll** ***var.*** Meemu Atoll. atoll C Maldives
85 J15 **Mulalika** Lusaka, C Zambia 15.37S 28.48E
169 X8 **Mulan** Heilongjiang, NE China 45.57N 128.00E
85 N15 **Mulanje** ***var.*** Mlanje. Southern, S Malawi 16.04S 35.35E
42 H5 **Mulatos** Sonora, NW Mexico 28.42N 108.44W
25 P3 **Mulberry Fork** ≈ Alabama, S USA
41 P12 **Mulchatna River** ≈ Alaska, USA
129 W4 **Mul'da** Respublika Komi, NW Russian Federation 67.29N 63.55E
103 M14 **Mulde** ≈ E Germany
29 R10 **Muldrow** Oklahoma, C USA 35.25N 94.34W
42 E7 **Mulegé** Baja California Sur, W Mexico 26.54N 112.00W
110 I10 **Mulegns** Graubünden, S Switzerland 46.30N 9.36E
81 M21 **Mulenda** Kasai Oriental, C Dem. Rep. Congo (Zaire) 4.19S 24.55E
26 M4 **Muleshoe** Texas, SW USA 34.13N 102.43W
85 O15 **Mulevala** Zambézia, NE Mozambique 16.18S 37.40E
191 P5 **Mulgoa Creek** seasonal river New South Wales, SE Australia
107 O15 **Mulhacén** ***var.*** Cerro de Mulhacén. ▲ S Spain 37.07N 3.11W
Mulhacén, Cerro de see Mulhacén
Mülhausen see Mulhouse
103 E24 **Mülheim** Baden-Württemberg, SW Germany 47.49N 7.36E
103 E15 **Mülheim** ***var.*** Mulheim an der Ruhr. Nordrhein-Westfalen, W Germany 51.25N 6.52E
Mulheim an der Ruhr see Mülheim
105 U7 **Mulhouse** ***Ger.*** Mülhausen. Haut-Rhin, NE France 47.45N 7.19E
166 G11 **Muli** ***var.*** Bowa, Muli Zangzu Zizhixian. Sichuan, C China 27.49N 101.10E
176 Y15 **Muli** channel Irian Jaya, E Indonesia
169 Y9 **Muling** Heilongjiang, NE China 44.54N 130.35E
Mullach Íde see Malahide
Mullaitivu see Mullaittivu
161 K23 **Mullaittivu** ***var.*** Mullaitivu. Northern Province, N Sri Lanka 9.15N 80.48E
35 N8 **Mullan** Idaho, NW USA 47.28N 115.48W
30 M13 **Mullen** Nebraska, C USA 42.02N 101.01W
191 Q6 **Mullengudgery** New South Wales, SE Australia 31.42S 147.24E
23 Q6 **Mullens** West Virginia, NE USA 37.34N 81.22W
Müller-gerbergte see Muller, Pegunungan
174 Mm7 **Muller, Pegunungan** ***Dut.*** Müller-gerbergte. ▲▲ Borneo, C Indonesia
194 F12 **Muller Range** ▲▲ W PNG
33 Q5 **Mullett Lake** ◎ Michigan, N USA
20 J16 **Mullica River** ≈ New Jersey, NE USA
27 R8 **Mullin** Texas, SW USA 31.33N 98.40W
99 E17 **Mullingar** ***Ir.*** An Muileann gCearr. C Ireland 53.31N 7.19W
23 T12 **Mullins** South Carolina, SE USA 34.12N 79.15W
98 G11 **Mull, Isle of** island W Scotland, UK
131 R5 **Mullovka** Ul'yanovskaya Oblast', W Russian Federation 54.13N 49.19E
97 K19 **Mullsjö** Västra Götaland, S Sweden 57.55N 13.55E
191 V4 **Mullumbimby** New South Wales, SE Australia 28.34S 153.28E
85 H15 **Mulobezi** Western, SW Zambia 16.48S 25.10E
85 C15 **Mulondo** Huíla, SW Angola 15.41S 15.09E
85 G15 **Mulonga Plain** plain W Zambia
81 N23 **Mulongo** Katanga, SE Dem. Rep. Congo (Zaire) 7.44S 26.57E
155 T10 **Multān** Punjab, E Pakistan 30.12N 71.29E
95 L17 **Multia** Länsi-Suomi, W Finland 62.27N 24.49E
Mulucha see Moulouya
85 J14 **Mulungushi** Central, C Zambia 14.15S 28.27E
85 K14 **Mulungwe** Central, C Zambia 13.57S 29.51E
Muluya see Moulouya
29 N7 **Mulvane** Kansas, C USA 37.28N 97.14W
191 O10 **Mulwala** New South Wales, SE Australia 35.59S 146.00E
Mulwiya see Moulouya
190 K6 **Mulyungarie** South Australia 31.29S 140.45E
160 D13 **Mumbai** ***prev.*** Bombay. Mahārāshtra, W India 18.55N 72.51E
160 D13 **Mumbai** ✈ Mahārāshtra, W India 19.10N 72.51E
85 D14 **Mumbué** Bié, C Angola 13.52S 17.15E
194 J13 **Mumeng** Morobe, C PNG 6.57S 146.37E
176 W9 **Mumi** Irian Jaya, E Indonesia 1.33S 134.09E
Muminabad/Mŭ'minobod see Leningrad
131 Q13 **Mumra** Astrakhanskaya Oblast', SW Russian Federation 45.46N 47.46E
43 X12 **Muna** Yucatán, SE Mexico 20.28N 89.45W
126 Kk9 **Muna** ≈ NE Russian Federation
158 C12 **Munābāo** Rājasthān, NW India 25.46N 70.19E
Munamägi see Suur Munamägi
175 Qq13 **Muna, Pulau** ***prev.*** Moena. island C Indonesia
175 Qq13 **Muna, Selat** strait Sulawesi, C Indonesia
103 L18 **Münchberg** Bayern, E Germany 50.10N 11.49E
103 L23 **München** ***var.*** Muenchen, ***Eng.*** Munich, ***It.*** Monaco. Bayern, SE Germany 48.08N 11.34E
München-Gladbach see Mönchengladbach
110 E6 **Münchenstein** Basel-Land, NW Switzerland 47.31N 7.37E
8 L10 **Muncho Lake** British Columbia, W Canada 58.52N 125.40W
33 P13 **Muncie** Indiana, N USA 40.10N 85.22W
20 G13 **Muncy** Pennsylvania, NE USA 41.10N 76.46W
195 U14 **Munda** New Georgia, NW Solomon Islands 8.15S 157.15E
9 Q14 **Mundare** Alberta, SW Canada 53.34N 112.20W
27 Q5 **Munday** Texas, SW USA 33.27N 99.37W
33 N10 **Mundelein** Illinois, N USA 42.15N 88.00W
103 I15 **Münden** Niedersachsen, C Germany 52.16N 8.54E
107 Q12 **Mundo** ≈ S Spain
194 L11 **Mundua Island** island Witu Islands, C PNG
84 B12 **Munenga** Cuanza Sul, NW Angola 10.05S 14.35E
107 P11 **Munera** Castilla-La Mancha, C Spain 39.03N 2.28W
22 E9 **Munford** Tennessee, S USA 35.27N 89.49W
22 K7 **Munfordville** Kentucky, S USA 37.15N 85.53W
190 D5 **Mungala** South Australia 30.36S 132.57E
85 M16 **Mungári** Manica, C Mozambique 17.09S 33.33E
81 O16 **Mungbere** Orientale, NE Dem. Rep. Congo (Zaire) 2.37N 28.30E
159 Q13 **Munger** ***prev.*** Monghyr. Bihār, NE India 25.22N 86.28E
190 I2 **Mungeranie** South Australia 28.02S 138.42E
Mu Nggava see Rennell
174 K6 **Mungguresak, Tanjung** headland Borneo, N Indonesia 1.57N 109.19E
Mungiki see Bellona
191 R4 **Mungindi** New South Wales, SE Australia 28.59S 149 00E
Mungkawn see Maingkwan
159 T16 **Mungla** ***var.*** Mongla. Khulna, S Bangladesh 22.18N 89.34E
84 C13 **Mungo** Huambo, W Angola 11.46S 16.13E
196 F16 **Munguuy Bay** bay Yap, W Micronesia
84 E13 **Munhango** Bié, C Angola 12.12S 18.34E
197 L14 **Munia** island Lau Group, E Fiji
Munich see München
107 S7 **Muniesa** Aragón, NE Spain 41.01N 0.49W
33 O4 **Munising** Michigan, N USA 46.24N 86.39W
Munkács see Mukacheve
97 I17 **Munkedal** Västra Götaland, S Sweden 58.28N 11.37E
97 K15 **Munkfors** Värmland, C Sweden 59.49N 13.34E
126 J16 **Munku-Sardyk, Gora** ***var.*** Mönh Sarïdag. ▲ Mongolia/Russian Federation 51.45N 100.22E
101 E18 **Munkzwalm** Oost-Vlaanderen, NW Belgium 50.53N 3.44E
178 J10 **Mun, Mae Nam** ≈ E Thailand
159 U15 **Munshiganj** Dhaka, C Bangladesh 23.31N 90.31E
110 D8 **Münsingen** Bern, W Switzerland 46.52N 7.36E
105 U6 **Munster** Haut-Rhin, NE France 48.03N 7.09E
102 J11 **Munster** Niedersachsen, NW Germany 52.58N 10.06E
99 B20 **Munster** ***Ir.*** Cúige Mumhan. cultural region S Ireland
102 F13 **Münster** ***var.*** Muenster, Münster in Westfalen. Nordrhein-Westfalen, W Germany 51.58N 7.37E
110 F10 **Münster** Valais, S Switzerland 46.31N 8.18E
Münsterberg in Schlesien see Ziębice
Münster in Westfalen see Münster
102 E13 **Münsterland** cultural region NW Germany
102 F13 **Münster-Osnabruck** ✈ Nordrhein-Westfalen, NW Germany 52.08N 7.41E
33 R4 **Munuscong Lake** ◎ Michigan, N USA
85 K17 **Munyati** ≈ C Zimbabwe
111 R3 **Münzkirchen** Oberösterreich, N Austria 48.29N 13.37E
94 K11 **Muodoslompolo** Norrbotten, N Sweden 67.57N 23.31E
94 M13 **Muojärvi** ◎ NE Finland
178 J6 **Mương Khên** Hoa Binh, N Vietnam 20.34N 105.18E
Muong Sai see Xai
178 I7 **Muong Xiang Ngeun** ***var.*** Xieng Ngeun. Louangphabang, N Laos 19.43N 102.09E
94 K11 **Muonio** Lappi, N Finland 67.58N 23.40E
Muonioälv/Muoniojoki see Muonionjoki
94 K11 **Muonionjoki** ***var.*** Muoniojoki, ***Swe.*** Muonioälv. ≈ Finland/Sweden
85 N17 **Mupa** ≈ C Mozambique
85 E16 **Mupini** Okavango, NE Namibia 17.55S 19.34E
82 F8 **Muqaddam, Wadi** ≈ N Sudan
144 K9 **Muqāţ** Al Mafraq, E Jordan 32.28N 38.04E
147 X7 **Muqaz** N Oman 24.13N 56.48E
83 N17 **Muqdisho** ***Eng.*** Mogadishu, ***It.*** Mogadiscio. ● (Somalia) Banaadir, S Somalia 2.06N 45.27E
83 N17 **Muqdisho** ✈ Banaadir, E Somalia 1.58N 45.18E
Muqshin see Mughshin
111 T8 **Mur** ***SCr.*** Mura. ≈ C Europe
Mura see Mur
143 T14 **Muradiye** Van, E Turkey 39.00N 43.44E
Muragarazi see Maragarazi
171 L12 **Murakami** Niigata, Honshū, C Japan 38.13N 139.28E
65 G22 **Murallón, Cerro** ▲ S Argentina 49.49S 73.25W
83 E20 **Muramvya** C Burundi 3.18S 29.41E
83 I19 **Murang'a** ***prev.*** Fort Hall. Central, SW Kenya 0.43S 37.10E
83 H16 **Murangering** Rift Valley, NW Kenya 3.48N 35.29E
Murapara see Murupara
146 M5 **Murār, Bi'r al** well NW Saudi Arabia 27.20N 40.21E
129 Q13 **Murashi** Kirovskaya Oblast', NW Russian Federation 59.27N 48.02E
105 O12 **Murat** Cantal, C France 45.07N 2.52E
116 N12 **Muratlı** Tekirdağ, NW Turkey 41.12N 27.30E
143 R14 **Murat Nehri** ***var.*** Eastern Euphrates; ***anc.*** Arsanias. ≈ NE Turkey
109 D20 **Muravera** Sardegna, Italy, C Mediterranean Sea 39.24N 9.34E
171 Ll12 **Murayama** Yamagata, Honshū, C Japan 38.29N 140.21E
124 Oo15 **Muraysah, Ra's al** headland N Libya 31.58N 25.00E
106 I6 **Murça** Vila Real, N Portugal 41.24N 7.28W
82 Q11 **Murcanyo** Bari, NE Somalia 11.39N 50.27E
149 N8 **Mūrcheh Khvort** ***var.*** Morcheh Khort. Eşfahān, C Iran 33.07N 51.26E
193 H15 **Murchison** Tasman, South Island, NZ 41.48S 172.19E
193 B22 **Murchison Mountains** ▲▲ South Island, NZ
188 I10 **Murchison River** ≈ Western Australia
107 R13 **Murcia** Murcia, SE Spain 37.58N 1.07W
107 Q13 **Murcia** ◐ autonomous community SE Spain
105 O13 **Mur-de-Barrez** Aveyron, S France 44.48N 2.39E
190 G8 **Murdinga** South Australia 33.46S 135.46E
30 M10 **Murdo** South Dakota, N USA 43.53N 100.42W
13 X6 **Murdochville** Quebec, SE Canada 48.57N 65.30W
111 W9 **Mureck** Steiermark, SE Austria 46.42N 15.46E
116 M13 **Mürefte** Tekirdağ, NW Turkey 40.40N 27.15E
118 I10 **Mureş** ◐ county N Romania
86 J11 **Mureş** ***var.*** Maros, Mureşul, ***Ger.*** Marosch, Mieresch. ≈ Hungary/Romania **see also** Maros
Mureşul see Maros/Mureş
104 M16 **Muret** Haute-Garonne, S France 43.28N 1.19E
29 T13 **Murfreesboro** Arkansas, C USA 34.03N 93.41W
23 W8 **Murfreesboro** North Carolina, SE USA 36.26N 77.06W
22 J9 **Murfreesboro** Tennessee, S USA 35.51N 86.23W
152 I14 **Murgab** ***prev.*** Murgap see also Morghāb, Daryā-ye. Maryyskiy Velayat, S Turkmenistan 37.19N 61.48E
152 J16 **Murgab** ***var.*** Murghab, ***Pash.*** Daryā-ye Morghāb, ***Turkm.*** Murgap Deryasy. ≈ Afghanistan/Turkmenistan see also Morghāb, Daryā-ye
Murgab see Murghob
Murgap see Murgab
Murgap Deryasy see Morghāb, Daryā-ye/Murgab
116 H9 **Murgash** ▲ W Bulgaria 42.51N 23.58E

◆ Country
● Country Capital
◇ Dependent Territory
○ Dependent Territory Capital
◐ Administrative Region
✈ International Airport
▲ Mountain
▲▲ Mountain Range
Volcano
≈ River
◎ Lake
⊠ Reservoir

MURGHAB – NAKSKOV

Murghab *see* Morghāb, Daryā-ye /Murgab
153 *U13* **Murghob** ***Rus.*** Murgab. SE Tajikistan *38.11N 73.59E*
153 *U13* **Murghob** ***Rus.*** Murgab. ≈ SE Tajikistan
189 *Z10* **Murgon** Queensland, E Australia *26.07S 152.03E*
202 *I16* **Muri** Rarotonga, S Cook Islands *21.15S 159.43W*
110 *F7* **Muri** Aargau, W Switzerland *47.16N 8.21E*
110 *D8* **Muri** ***var.*** Muri bei Bern. Bern, W Switzerland *46.55N 7.30E*
106 *K3* **Murias de Paredes** Castilla-León, N Spain *42.51N 6.11W*
Muri bei Bern *see* Muri
84 *F11* **Muriege** Lunda Sul, NE Angola *9.55S 21.12E*
201 *P14* **Murilo Atoll** *atoll* Hall Islands, C Micronesia
Mūrītānīyah *see* Mauritania
102 *N10* **Müritz** ***var.*** Müritzee. ◎ NE Germany
Müritzee *see* Müritz
102 *L10* **Müritz-Elde-Kanal** *canal* N Germany
192 *K6* **Muriwai Beach** Auckland, North Island, NZ *36.56S 174.28E*
94 *J13* **Murjek** Norrbotten, N Sweden *66.27N 20.54E*
128 *J3* **Murmansk** Murmanskaya Oblast', NW Russian Federation *68.58N 33.07E*
128 *I4* **Murmanskaya Oblast'** ◐ *province* NW Russian Federation
207 *V14* **Murmansk Rise** *undersea feature* SW Barents Sea
128 *J3* **Murmashi** Murmanskaya Oblast', NW Russian Federation *68.49N 32.42E*
130 *M5* **Murmino** Ryazanskaya Oblast', W Russian Federation *54.31N 40.01E*
103 *K24* **Murnau** Bayern, SE Germany *47.41N 11.12E*
105 *X16* **Muro, Capo di** *headland* Corse, France, C Mediterranean Sea *41.45N 8.40E*
109 *M18* **Muro Lucano** Basilicata, S Italy *40.48N 15.33E*
131 *N4* **Murom** Vladimirskaya Oblast', W Russian Federation *55.33N 42.03E*
125 *G13* **Muromtsevo** Omskaya Oblast', C Russian Federation *56.18N 75.15E*
172 *Nn6* **Muroran** Hokkaidō, NE Japan *42.19N 140.58E*
106 *G3* **Muros** Galicia, NW Spain *42.46N 9.03W*
106 *F3* **Muros e Noia, Ría de** *estuary* NW Spain
170 *F16* **Muroto** Kōchi, Shikoku, SW Japan *33.18N 134.07E*
170 *F16* **Muroto-zaki** *headland* Shikoku, SW Japan *33.15N 134.09E*
118 *L7* **Murovani Kurylivtsi** Vinnyts'ka Oblast', C Ukraine *48.43N 27.31E*
112 *G11* **Murowana Goślina** Wielkolpolskie, C Poland *52.33N 16.59E*
34 *M14* **Murphy** Idaho, NW USA *43.14N 116.36W*
23 *N10* **Murphy** North Carolina, SE USA *35.05N 84.01W*
37 *P8* **Murphys** California, W USA *38.07N 120.27W*
32 *L17* **Murphysboro** Illinois, N USA *37.45N 89.20W*
31 *V15* **Murray** Iowa, C USA *41.03N 93.56W*
22 *H8* **Murray** Kentucky, S USA *36.36N 88.18W*
190 *J10* **Murray Bridge** South Australia *35.06S 139.15E*
183 *X2* **Murray Fracture Zone** *tectonic feature* NE Pacific Ocean
194 *E13* **Murray, Lake** ◎ SW PNG
23 *P12* **Murray, Lake** ▣ South Carolina, SE USA
8 *K8* **Murray, Mount** ▲ Yukon Territory, NW Canada *60.49N 128.57W*
194 *H13* **Murray Range** ***var.*** Leonard Murray Mountains. ▲▲ W PNG
Murray Range *see* Murray Ridge
181 *O3* **Murray Ridge** ***var.*** Murray Range. *undersea feature* N Arabian Sea
191 *N10* **Murray River** ≈ SE Australia
190 *K10* **Murrayville** Victoria, SE Australia *35.17S 141.12E*
155 *U5* **Murree** Punjab, E Pakistan *33.55N 73.25E*
103 *I21* **Murrhardt** Baden-Württemberg, S Germany *49.00N 9.34E*
191 *O9* **Murrumbidgee River** ≈ New South Wales, SE Australia
85 *P15* **Murrupula** Nampula, NE Mozambique *15.26S 38.46E*
191 *T7* **Murrurundi** New South Wales, SE Australia *31.47S 150.51E*
111 *X9* **Murska Sobota** ***Ger.*** Olsnitz. NE Slovenia *46.40N 16.09E*
160 *G12* **Murtajāpur** ***prev.*** Murtazapur. Mahārāshtra, C India *20.43N 77.28E*
79 *S16* **Murtala Muhammed** ✈ (Lagos) Ogun, SW Nigeria *6.31N 3.12E*
Murtazapur *see* Murtajāpur
110 *C8* **Murten** Neuchâtel, W Switzerland *46.55N 7.06E*
Murtensee *see* Morat, Lac de
190 *L11* **Murtoa** Victoria, SE Australia *36.39S 142.27E*
94 *N13* **Murtovaara** Oulu, E Finland *65.40N 29.25E*
Murua Island *see* Woodlark Island
161 *D14* **Murud** Mahārāshtra, W India *18.27N 72.56E*
192 *O9* **Murupara** ***var.*** Murapara. Bay of Plenty, North Island, NZ *38.27S 176.40E*
203 *X12* **Mururoa** ***var.*** Moruroa. *atoll* Îles Tuamotu, SE French Polynesia
Murviedro *see* Sagunto
160 *J9* **Murwāra** Madhya Pradesh, N India *23.50N 80.23E*
191 *V4* **Murwillumbah** New South Wales, SE Australia *28.19S 153.24E*
152 *H11* **Murzechirla** ***prev.*** Mirzachirla. Akhalskiy Velayat, C Turkmenistan *39.33N 60.02E*
Murzuk *see* Murzuq
77 *O11* **Murzuq** ***var.*** Marzūq, Murzuk. SW Libya *25.55N 13.55E*
Murzuq, Edeyin *see* Murzuq, Idhān
77 *N11* **Murzuq, Ḩamādat** *plateau* W Libya
77 *O11* **Murzuq, Idhān** ***var.*** Edeyin Murzuq. *desert* SW Libya
111 *W6* **Mürzzuschlag** Steiermark, E Austria *47.34N 15.40E*
143 *Q14* **Muş** ***var.*** Mush. Muş, E Turkey *38.45N 41.30E*
143 *Q14* **Muş** ***var.*** Mush. ◐ *province* E Turkey
194 *L16* **Musa** ≈ S PNG
120 *G11* **Mūša** ≈ Latvia/Lithuania
77 *X8* **Mûsa, Gebel** ▲ NE Egypt *28.33N 33.51E*
Musaiyib *see* Al Musayyib
Musa Khel *see* Mūsā Khel Bazār
155 *R9* **Musā Khel Bazār** ***var.*** Musa Khel. Baluchistān, SW Pakistan *30.52N 69.46E*
116 *H10* **Musala** ▲ W Bulgaria *42.12N 23.36E*
173 *F6* **Musala, Pulau** *island* W Indonesia
85 *I15* **Musale** Southern, S Zambia *15.27S 26.50E*
147 *Y9* **Muşalla** NE Oman *22.19N 58.03E*
147 *W6* **Musandam Peninsula** ***Ar.*** Masandam Peninsula. *peninsula* N Oman
Musay'id *see* Umm Sa'īd
Muscat *see* Masqaţ
Muscat and Oman *see* Oman
31 *Y14* **Muscatine** Iowa, C USA *41.25N 91.03W*
Muscat Sīb Airport *see* Seeb
33 *O15* **Muscatuck River** ≈ Indiana, N USA
194 *G10* **Muschu Island** *island* NW PNG
32 *K8* **Muscoda** Wisconsin, N USA *43.11N 90.27W*
193 *F19* **Musgrave, Mount** ▲ South Island, NZ *43.48S 170.43E*
189 *P9* **Musgrave Ranges** ▲▲ South Australia
Mush *see* Muş
144 *H12* **Mushayyish, Qaşr al** *castle* Ma'ān, C Jordan *30.58N 36.41E*
81 *H20* **Mushie** Bandundu, W Dem. Rep. Congo (Zaire) *3.00S 16.55E*
174 *I11* **Musi, Air** ***prev.*** Moesi. ≈ Sumatera, W Indonesia
199 *K5* **Musicians Seamounts** *undersea feature* N Pacific Ocean
56 *D8* **Musinga, Alto** ▲ NW Colombia *6.49N 76.24W*
31 *T2* **Muskeg Bay** *lake bay* Minnesota, N USA
33 *O8* **Muskegon** Michigan, N USA *43.13N 86.15W*
33 *O8* **Muskegon Heights** Michigan, N USA *43.12N 86.14W*
33 *P8* **Muskegon River** ≈ Michigan, N USA
33 *T14* **Muskingum River** ≈ Ohio, N USA
97 *P16* **Muskö** Stockholm, C Sweden *58.58N 18.10E*
Muskogean *see* Tallahassee
29 *Q10* **Muskogee** Oklahoma, C USA *35.45N 95.22W*
12 *H13* **Muskoka, Lake** ◎ Ontario, S Canada
82 *H8* **Musmar** Red Sea, NE Sudan *18.13N 35.40E*
85 *K14* **Musofu** Central, C Zambia *13.31S 29.03E*
83 *G19* **Musoma** Mara, N Tanzania *1.31S 33.49E*
84 *L13* **Musoro** Central, C Zambia *13.21S 31.04E*
194 *M8* **Mussau Island** *island* NE PNG
100 *P7* **Musselkanaal** Groningen, NE Netherlands *52.55N 7.01E*
35 *V9* **Musselshell River** ≈ Montana, NW USA
84 *C12* **Mussende** Cuanza Sul, NW Angola *10.33S 16.01E*
104 *L12* **Mussidan** Dordogne, SW France *45.03N 0.22E*
101 *L25* **Musson** Luxembourg, SE Belgium *49.33N 5.42E*
158 *J9* **Mussoorie** Uttar Pradesh, N India *30.25N 78.04E*
Musta *see* Mosta
158 *M13* **Mustafābād** Uttar Pradesh, N India *25.54N 81.16E*
142 *D12* **Mustafakemalpaşa** Bursa, NW Turkey *40.03N 28.25E*
Mustafa-Pasha *see* Svilengrad
83 *M15* **Mustahīl** Somali, E Ethiopia *5.18N 44.34E*
26 *M7* **Mustang Draw** *valley* Texas, SW USA
27 *T14* **Mustang Island** *island* Texas, SW USA
Mustasaari *see* Korsholm
Mustér *see* Disentis
65 *I19* **Musters, Lago** ◎ S Argentina
47 *Y14* **Mustique** *island* C Saint Vincent and the Grenadines
120 *I6* **Mustla** Viljandimaa, S Estonia *58.12N 25.51E*
120 *J4* **Mustvee** ***Ger.*** Tschorna. Jõgevamaa, E Estonia *58.51N 26.57E*
44 *L9* **Musún, Cerro** ▲ NE Nicaragua *13.01N 85.02W*
191 *T7* **Muswellbrook** New South Wales, SE Australia *32.16S 150.55E*
113 *M18* **Muszyna** Małopolskie, SE Poland *49.21N 20.54E*
142 *I17* **Mut** İçel, S Turkey *36.37N 33.27E*
77 *V10* **Mût** ***var.*** Mut. C Egypt *25.34N 28.58E*
111 *V9* **Muta** N Slovenia *46.37N 15.09E*
202 *B15* **Mutalau** N Niue *18.55S 169.49E*
Mu-tan-chiang *see* Mudanjiang
84 *I13* **Mutanda** North Western, NW Zambia *12.22S 26.15E*
61 *O17* **Mutá, Ponta do** *headland* E Brazil *13.54S 38.54W*
85 *L17* **Mutare** ***var.*** Mutari; ***prev.*** Umtali. Manicaland, E Zimbabwe *18.54S 32.36E*
Mutari *see* Mutare
56 *D8* **Mutatá** Antioquia, NW Colombia *7.16N 76.31W*
Mutina *see* Modena
176 *Z15* **Muting** Irian Jaya, E Indonesia *7.10S 140.41E*
85 *L16* **Mutoko** ***prev.*** Mtoko. Mashonaland East, NE Zimbabwe *17.24S 32.13E*
83 *J20* **Mutomo** Eastern, S Kenya *1.49S 38.13E*
126 *J12* **Mutoray** Evenkiyskiy Avtonomnyy Okrug, C Russian Federation *61.30N 101.00E*
Mutrah *see* Maţraḩ
81 *M24* **Mutshatsha** Katanga, S Dem. Rep. Congo (Zaire) *10.40S 24.25E*
172 *Nn8* **Mutsu** ***var.*** Mutu. Aomori, Honshū, N Japan *41.18N 141.11E*
172 *N8* **Mutsu-wan** *bay* N Japan
110 *E6* **Muttenz** Basel-Land, NW Switzerland *47.31N 7.39E*
193 *A26* **Muttonbird Islands** *island group* SW NZ
Mutu *see* Mutsu
85 *O15* **Mutuáli** Nampula, N Mozambique *14.51S 37.01E*
84 *D13* **Mutumbo** Bié, C Angola *13.10S 17.22E*
201 *Y14* **Mutunte, Mount** ***var.*** Mount Buache. ▲ Kosrae, E Micronesia *5.21N 163.00E*
161 *K24* **Mutur** Eastern Province, E Sri Lanka *8.27N 81.15E*
94 *L13* **Muurola** Lappi, NW Finland *66.21N 25.19E*
168 *M14* **Mu Us Shamo** ***var.*** Ordos Desert. *desert* N China
84 *B11* **Muxima** Bengo, NW Angola *9.27S 13.58E*
128 *I8* **Muyezerskiy** Respublika Kareliya, NW Russian Federation *63.54N 32.00E*
83 *E20* **Muyinga** NE Burundi *2.54S 30.19E*
44 *K9* **Muy Muy** Matagalpa, C Nicaragua *12.43N 85.37W*
Muynak *see* Mŭynoq
152 *G6* **Mŭynoq** ***Rus.*** Muynak. Qoraqalpoghiston Respublikasi, NW Uzbekistan *43.45N 59.03E*
81 *N22* **Muyumba** Katanga, SE Dem. Rep. Congo (Zaire) *7.13S 27.02E*
155 *V5* **Muzaffarābād** Jammu and Kashmir, NE Pakistan *34.24N 73.30E*
155 *S10* **Muzaffargarh** Punjab, E Pakistan *30.04N 71.10E*
158 *J9* **Muzaffarnagar** Uttar Pradesh, N India *29.28N 77.42E*
159 *P13* **Muzaffarpur** Bihār, N India *26.07N 85.22E*
164 *H6* **Muzat He** ≈ W China
85 *L15* **Muze** Tete, NW Mozambique *15.05S 31.16E*
125 *Ff8* **Muzhi** Yamalo-Nenetskiy Avtonomnyy Okrug, N Russian Federation *65.25N 64.28E*
104 *H7* **Muzillac** Morbihan, NW France *47.34N 2.30W*
Muzkol, Khrebet *see* Muzqŭl, Qatorkŭhi
114 *L9* **Mužlja** ***Hung.*** Felsőmuzslya; ***prev.*** Gornja Mužlja. Serbia, N Yugoslavia *45.21N 20.25E*
56 *F9* **Muzo** Boyacá, C Colombia *5.34N 74.07W*
85 *J15* **Muzoka** Southern, S Zambia *16.39S 27.21E*
41 *Y15* **Muzon, Cape** *headland* Dall Island, Alaska, USA *54.39N 132.41W*
42 *M6* **Múzquiz** Coahuila de Zaragoza, NE Mexico *27.52N 101.31W*
153 *U13* **Muzqŭl, Qatorkŭhi** ***Rus.*** Khrebet Muzkol. ▲▲ SE Tajikistan
164 *G10* **Muztag** ▲ NW China *36.02N 80.13E*
164 *D8* **Muztagata** ▲ NW China *38.16N 75.03E*
164 *K10* **Muztag Feng** ***var.*** Ulugh Muztag. ▲ W China *36.26N 87.15E*
85 *K17* **Mvuma** ***prev.*** Umvuma. Midlands, C Zimbabwe *19.16S 30.31E*
84 *L13* **Mwanya** Eastern, E Zambia *12.40S 32.15E*
83 *G20* **Mwanza** Mwanza, NW Tanzania *2.31S 32.55E*
81 *N23* **Mwanza** Katanga, SE Dem. Rep. Congo (Zaire) *7.49S 26.49E*
83 *F20* **Mwanza** ◐ *region* N Tanzania
84 *M13* **Mwase Lundazi** Eastern, E Zambia *12.26S 33.20E*
99 *B17* **Mweelrea** ***Ir.*** Caoc Maol Réidh. ▲ W Ireland *53.37N 9.47W*
81 *K21* **Mweka** Kasai Occidental, C Dem. Rep. Congo (Zaire) *4.51S 21.37E*
84 *K12* **Mwenda** Luapula, N Zambia *10.25S 29.10E*
81 *L22* **Mwene-Ditu** Kasai Oriental, S Dem. Rep. Congo (Zaire) *7.05S 23.33E*
85 *L18* **Mwenezi** ≈ S Zimbabwe
81 *O20* **Mwenga** Sud Kivu, E Dem. Rep. Congo (Zaire) *3.00S 28.28E*
84 *K11* **Mweru, Lake** ***var.*** Lac Moero. ◎ Dem. Rep. Congo (Zaire)/Zambia
84 *H13* **Mwinilunga** North Western, NW Zambia *11.43S 24.24E*
201 *V16* **Mwokil Atoll** ***var.*** Mokil Atoll. *atoll* Caroline Islands, E Micronesia
Myadel' *see* Myadzyel
120 *J13* **Myadzyel** ***Pol.*** Miadzioł Nowy, ***Rus.*** Myadel'. Minskaya Voblasts', N Belarus *54.51N 26.51E*
158 *C12* **Myājlār** ***var.*** Miajlar. Rājasthān, NW India *26.16N 70.21E*
127 *O9* **Myakit** Magadanskaya Oblast', E Russian Federation *61.23N 151.58E*
25 *W13* **Myakka River** ≈ Florida, SE USA
128 *L14* **Myaksa** Vologodskaya Oblast', NW Russian Federation *58.54N 38.15E*
191 *U8* **Myall Lake** ◎ New South Wales, SE Australia
177 *Ff7* **Myanaung** Irrawaddy, SW Burma *18.16N 95.19E*
178 *Gg4* **Myanmar** *see* Burma
177 *F9* **Myaungmya** Irrawaddy, SW Burma *16.33N 94.55E*
120 *N11* **Myazha** ***Rus.*** Mezha. Vitsyebskaya Voblasts', NE Belarus *55.40N 30.25E*
121 *O18* **Myerkulavichy** ***Rus.*** Merkulovichi. Homyel'skaya Voblasts', SE Belarus *52.57N 30.33E*
121 *N14* **Myezhava** ***Rus.*** Mezhëvo. Vitsyebskaya Voblasts', NE Belarus *54.39N 30.18E*
177 *Ff5* **Myingyan** Mandalay, C Burma *21.25N 95.19E*
177 *G5* **Myinmu** Sagaing, C Burma *21.58N 95.34E*
178 *Gg2* **Myitkyina** Kachin State, N Burma *25.24N 97.25E*
177 *G5* **Myittha** Mandalay, C Burma *21.21N 96.06E*
113 *H19* **Myjava** ***Hung.*** Miava. Trenčiansky Kraj, W Slovakia *48.48N 17.31E*
Myjeldino *see* Myyëldino
119 *U9* **Mykhaylivka** ***Rus.*** Mikhaylovka. Zaporiz'ka Oblast', SE Ukraine *47.16N 35.14E*
97 *A18* **Mykines** ***Dan.*** Myggenaes *Island* Faeroe Islands *62.07N 7.38W*
118 *I5* **Mykolayiv** L'vivs'ka Oblast', W Ukraine *49.34N 23.58E*
119 *Q10* **Mykolayiv** ***Rus.*** Nikolayev. Mykolayivs'ka Oblast', S Ukraine *46.57N 31.58E*
119 *Q10* **Mykolayiv** ✈ Mykolayivs'ka Oblast', S Ukraine *47.02N 31.54E*
Mykolayiv *see* Mykolayivs'ka Oblast'
119 *P9* **Mykolayivka** Odes'ka Oblast', SW Ukraine *47.34N 30.48E*
119 *S13* **Mykolayivka** Respublika Krym, S Ukraine *44.58N 33.37E*
119 *P9* **Mykolayivs'ka Oblast'** ***var.*** Mykolayiv, ***Rus.*** Nikolayevskaya Oblast'. ◐ *province* S Ukraine
117 *J20* **Mýkonos** Mýkonos, Kykládes, Greece, Aegean Sea *37.27N 25.20E*
117 *K20* **Mýkonos** ***var.*** Míkonos. *island* Kykládes, Greece, Aegean Sea
129 *R7* **Myla** Respublika Komi, NW Russian Federation *65.24N 50.51E*
Mylae *see* Milazzo
95 *M19* **Myllykoski** Etelä-Suomi, S Finland *60.45N 26.52E*
Mymensing *see* Mymensingh
159 *U14* **Mymensingh** ***var.*** Maimansingh, Mymensing; ***prev.*** Nasirābād. Dhaka, N Bangladesh *24.45N 90.22E*
95 *K19* **Mynämäki** Länsi-Suomi, W Finland *60.41N 22.00E*
151 *S14* **Mynaral** ***Kaz.*** Myngaral. Zhambyl, S Kazakhstan *45.25N 73.37E*
Mynbulak *see* Mingbuloq
Mynbulak, Vpadina *see* Mingbuloq Botighi
Myngaral *see* Mynaral
177 *F5* **Myohaung** Arakan State, W Burma *20.34N 93.12E*
169 *W13* **Myohyang-sanmaek** ▲▲ C North Korea
171 *Jj13* **Myōkō-san** ▲ Honshū, S Japan *36.54N 138.05E*
85 *J15* **Myooye** Central, C Zambia *15.10S 27.24E*
120 *K12* **Myory** ***prev.*** Miyory. Vitsyebskaya Voblasts', N Belarus *55.39N 27.39E*
94 *J4* **Mýrdalsjökull** *glacier* S Iceland
94 *G10* **Myre** Nordland, C Norway *68.54N 15.04E*
119 *S5* **Myrhorod** ***Rus.*** Mirgorod. Poltavs'ka Oblast', NE Ukraine *49.57N 33.36E*
117 *J15* **Mýrina** ***var.*** Mírina. Límnos, SE Greece *39.52N 25.04E*
119 *P5* **Myronivka** ***Rus.*** Mironovka. Kyyivs'ka Oblast', N Ukraine *49.40N 30.58E*
23 *U13* **Myrtle Beach** South Carolina, SE USA *33.41N 78.53W*
34 *F14* **Myrtle Creek** Oregon, NW USA *43.01N 123.19W*
191 *P11* **Myrtleford** Victoria, SE Australia *36.34S 146.45E*
34 *E14* **Myrtle Point** Oregon, NW USA *43.04N 124.08W*
117 *K25* **Mýrtos** Kríti, Greece, E Mediterranean Sea *35.00N 25.34E*
Myrtoum Mare *see* Mirtóo Pélagos
95 *G17* **Myrviken** Jämtland, C Sweden *62.59N 14.19E*
97 *I15* **Mysen** Østfold, S Norway *59.33N 11.19E*
128 *L15* **Myshkin** Yaroslavskaya Oblast', NW Russian Federation *57.47N 38.28E*
113 *K17* **Myślenice** Małopolskie, S Poland *49.49N 19.55E*
112 *D10* **Myślibórz** Zachodniopomorskie, NW Poland *52.55N 14.51E*
161 *G20* **Mysore** ***var.*** Maisur. Karnātaka, W India *12.18N 76.37E*
Mysore *see* Karnātaka
117 *F21* **Mystrás** ***var.*** Mistras. Pelopónnisos, S Greece *37.03N 22.22E*
129 *T12* **Mysy** Komi-Permyatskiy Avtonomnyy Okrug, NW Russian Federation *60.40N 53.59E*
113 *K15* **Myszków** Śląskie, S Poland *50.35N 19.16E*
178 *Jj14* **My Tho** ***var.*** Mi Tho. Tiên Giang, S Vietnam *10.21N 106.21E*
Mytilene *see* Mytilíni
117 *L17* **Mytilíni** ***var.*** Mitilíni; ***anc.*** Mytilene. Lésvos, E Greece *39.05N 26.33E*
130 *K3* **Mytishchi** Moskovskaya Oblast', W Russian Federation *56.00N 37.51E*
39 *N3* **Myton** Utah, W USA *40.11N 110.03W*
94 *K2* **Mývatn** ◎ C Iceland
129 *T11* **Myyëldino** ***var.*** Myjeldino. Respublika Komi, NW Russian Federation *61.46N 54.48E*
84 *M13* **Mzimba** Northern, NW Malawi *11.56S 33.36E*
84 *M12* **Mzuzu** Northern, N Malawi *11.23S 34.03E*
178 *Jj6* **Mương Khên** Hoa Binh, N Vietnam *20.34N 105.18E*

N

103 *M19* **Naab** ≈ SE Germany
100 *G12* **Naaldwijk** Zuid-Holland, W Netherlands *52.00N 4.13E*
40 *G12* **Naalehu** ***var.*** Nā'ālehu. Hawaii, USA, C Pacific Ocean *19.04N 155.36W*
95 *K19* **Naantali** ***Swe.*** Nådendal. Länsi-Suomi, W Finland *60.25N 22.10E*
100 *J10* **Naarden** Noord-Holland, C Netherlands *52.18N 5.10E*
111 *U4* **Naarn** ≈ N Austria
99 *F18* **Naas** ***Ir.*** An Nás, Nás na Ríogh. C Ireland *53.13N 6.39W*
94 *M9* **Näätämöjoki** ***Lapp.*** Njávdám. ≈ NE Finland
85 *E23* **Nababeep** ***var.*** Nababiep. Northern Cape, W South Africa *29.36S 17.46E*
Nababiep *see* Nababeep
Nabadwip *see* Navadwīp
171 *H16* **Nabari** Mie, Honshū, SW Japan *34.37N 136.06E*
Nabatié *see* Nabatîyé
144 *G8* **Nabatîyé** ***var.*** An Nabatīyah at Taḩtā, Nabatié, Nabatiyet et Tahta. SW Lebanon *33.18N 35.36E*
Nabatiyet et Tahta *see* Nabatîyé
197 *I13* **Nabavatu** Vanua Levu, N Fiji *16.35S 178.55E*
202 *I2* **Nabeina** *island* Tungaru, W Kiribati
131 *T4* **Naberezhnyye Chelny** ***prev.*** Brezhnev. Respublika Tatarstan, W Russian Federation *55.43N 52.21E*
41 *T10* **Nabesna** Alaska, USA *62.22N 143.00W*
41 *T10* **Nabesna River** ≈ Alaska, USA
77 *N5* **Nabeul** ***var.*** Nābul. NE Tunisia *36.32N 10.45E*
158 *I9* **Nābha** Punjab, NW India *30.22N 76.12E*
176 *Ww11* **Nabire** Irian Jaya, E Indonesia *3.22S 135.31E*
147 *O15* **Nabī Shu'ayb, Jabal an** ▲ W Yemen *15.24N 44.04E*
197 *I13* **Nabiti** Vanua Levu, N Fiji *16.37S 178.54E*
144 *F10* **Nablus** ***var.*** Nābulus, ***Heb.*** Shekhem; ***anc.*** Neapolis, ***Bibl.*** Shechem. N West Bank *32.14N 35.16E*
197 *I13* **Nabouwalu** Vanua Levu, N Fiji *17.00S 178.43E*
Nābul *see* Nabeul
Nābulus *see* Nablus
197 *J13* **Nabuna** Vanua Levu, N Fiji *16.13S 179.46E*
179 *Rr15* **Nabunturan** Mindanao, S Philippines *7.34N 125.54E*
85 *Q14* **Nacala** Nampula, NE Mozambique *14.30S 40.37E*
44 *H8* **Nacaome** Valle, S Honduras *13.30N 87.31W*
Na Cealla Beaga *see* Killybegs
Na-ch'ii *see* Nagqu
171 *Gg17* **Nachikatsuura** ***var.*** Nachi-Katsuura. Wakayama, Honshū, SE Japan *33.37N 135.54E*
83 *J24* **Nachingwea** Lindi, SE Tanzania *10.21S 38.46E*
113 *F16* **Náchod** Hradecký Kraj, N Czech Republic *50.25N 16.09E*
Na Clocha Liatha *see* Greystones
42 *G3* **Naco** Sonora, NW Mexico *31.16N 109.56W*
27 *X8* **Nacogdoches** Texas, SW USA *31.36N 94.40W*
42 *G4* **Nacozari de García** Sonora, NW Mexico *30.27N 109.43W*
197 *H13* **Nacula** ***prev.*** Nathula. *island* Yasawa Group, NW Fiji
Nada *see* Danzhou
79 *O14* **Nadawli** NW Ghana *10.30N 2.40W*
106 *I3* **Nadela** Galicia, NW Spain *42.58N 7.33W*
Nådendal *see* Naantali
150 *M7* **Nadezhdinka** ***prev.*** Nadezhdinskiy. Kostanay, N Kazakhstan *53.46N 63.43E*
Nadezhdinskiy *see* Nadezhdinka
Nadgan *see* Nadqān, Qalamat
197 *H14* **Nadi** ***prev.*** Nandi. Viti Levu, W Fiji *17.48S 177.25E*
197 *H14* **Nadi** ***prev.*** Nandi. ✈ Viti Levu, W Fiji *17.46S 177.28E*
160 *D10* **Nadiād** Gujarāt, W India *22.42N 72.54E*
Ņadikdik *see* Knox Atoll
118 *E11* **Nădlac** ***Ger.*** Nadlak, ***Hung.*** Nagylak. Arad, W Romania *46.10N 20.47E*
Nadlak *see* Nădlac
76 *H6* **Nador** ***prev.*** Villa Nador. NE Morocco *35.15N 2.56W*
147 *S9* **Nadqān, Qalamat** ***var.*** Nadgan. *well* E Saudi Arabia *23.10N 50.08E*
113 *N22* **Nádudvar** Hajdú-Bihar, E Hungary *47.26N 21.09E*
123 *J16* **Nadur** Gozo, N Malta *36.03N 14.18E*
197 *J13* **Naduri** ***prev.*** Nanduri. Vanua Levu, N Fiji *16.27S 179.10E*
118 *I7* **Nadvirna** ***Pol.*** Nadwórna, ***Rus.*** Nadvornaya. Ivano-Frankivs'ka Oblast', W Ukraine *48.27N 24.30E*
128 *J8* **Nadvoitsy** Respublika Kareliya, NW Russian Federation *63.52N 34.17E*
Nadvornaya/Nadwórna *see* Nadvirna
126 *Gg9* **Nadym** Yamalo-Nenetskiy Avtonomnyy Okrug, N Russian Federation *65.25N 72.40E*
126 *Gg9* **Nadym** ≈ C Russian Federation
194 *J13* **Nadzab** Morobe, C PNG *6.36S 146.45E*
79 *X13* **Nafada** Gombe, E Nigeria *11.02N 11.18E*
110 *H8* **Näfels** Glarus, NE Switzerland *47.06N 9.04E*
117 *E18* **Náfpaktos** ***var.*** Návpaktos. Dytikí Ellás, C Greece *38.22N 21.49E*
117 *F20* **Náfplio** ***prev.*** Návplion. Pelopónnisos, S Greece *37.33N 22.50E*
145 *U6* **Naft Khāneh** E Iraq *34.01N 45.26E*
155 *N13* **Nāg** Baluchistān, SW Pakistan *27.43N 65.31E*
179 *Q11* **Naga** ***off.*** Naga City; ***prev.*** Nueva Caceres. Luzon, N Philippines *13.36N 123.10E*
Nagaarzê *see* Nagarzê
10 *F11* **Nagagami** ≈ Ontario, S Canada
170 *E14* **Nagahama** Ehime, Shikoku, SW Japan *33.36N 132.29E*
171 *Hh14* **Nagahama** Shiga, Honshū, SW Japan *35.22N 136.16E*
159 *X12* **Nāga Hills** ▲▲ NE India
171 *Ll13* **Nagai** Yamagata, Honshū, C Japan *38.07N 140.02E*
Na Gaibhlte *see* Galty Mountains
41 *N16* **Nagai Island** *island* Shumagin Islands, Alaska, USA
159 *X12* **Nāgāland** ◐ *state* NE India
171 *Jj13* **Nagano** Nagano, Honshū, S Japan *36.39N 138.10E*
171 *J14* **Nagano** ***off.*** Nagano-ken. ◐ *prefecture* Honshū, S Japan
171 *K13* **Nagaoka** Niigata, Honshū, C Japan *37.26N 138.48E*
159 *W12* **Nagaon** ***prev.*** Nowgong. Assam, NE India *26.21N 92.41E*
161 *J21* **Nāgappattinam** ***var.*** Negapatam, Negapattinam. Tamil Nādu, SE India *10.45N 79.49E*
Nagara Nayok *see* Nakhon Nayok
Nagara Panom *see* Nakhon Phanom
Nagara Pathom *see* Nakhon Pathom
Nagara Sridharmaraj *see* Nakhon Si Thammarat
Nagara Svarga *see* Nakhon Sawan
161 *H16* **Nāgārjuna Sāgar** ▣ E India
44 *I10* **Nagarote** León, SW Nicaragua *12.16N 86.33W*
164 *M16* **Nagarzê** ***var.*** Nagaarzê. Xizang Zizhiqu, W China *28.57N 90.25E*
170 *Bb13* **Nagasaki** Nagasaki, Kyūshū, SW Japan *32.45N 129.52E*
170 *Bb12* **Nagasaki** ***off.*** Nagasaki-ken. ◐ *prefecture* Kyūshū, SW Japan
170 *Bb14* **Naga-shima** *island* SW Japan
170 *Dd13* **Naga-shima** *island* SW Japan
Nagashima *see* Kii-Nagashima
170 *Dd12* **Nagato** Yamaguchi, Honshū, SW Japan *34.22N 131.10E*
158 *F11* **Nāgaur** Rājasthān, NW India *27.12N 73.43E*
160 *F10* **Nāgda** Madhya Pradesh, C India *23.28N 75.27E*
100 *L8* **Nagele** Flevoland, N Netherlands *52.39N 5.43E*
161 *H24* **Nāgercoil** Tamil Nādu, SE India *8.10N 77.30E*
159 *X12* **Nāginimāra** Nāgāland, NE India *26.43N 94.51E*
Na Gleannta *see* Glenties
172 *P14* **Nago** Okinawa, Okinawa, SW Japan *26.36N 127.58E*
160 *K9* **Nāgod** Madhya Pradesh, C India *24.36N 80.35E*
161 *J26* **Nagoda** Southern Province, S Sri Lanka *6.13N 80.13E*
103 *G22* **Nagold** Baden-Württemberg, SW Germany *48.33N 8.43E*
Nagorno-Karabakhskaya Avtonomnaya Oblast *see* Nagornyy Karabakh
126 *Ll13* **Nagornyy** Respublika Sakha (Yakutiya), NE Russian Federation *55.53N 124.58E*
143 *V12* **Nagornyy Karabakh** ***var.*** Nagorno-Karabakhskaya Avtonomnaya Oblast , ***Arm.*** Lerrnayin Gharabakh, ***Az.*** Dağliq Qarabağ. *former autonomous region* SW Azerbaijan
129 *R13* **Nagorsk** Kirovskaya Oblast', NW Russian Federation *59.18N 50.49E*
171 *Hh15* **Nagoya** Aichi, Honshū, SW Japan *35.10N 136.52E*
160 *I12* **Nāgpur** Mahārāshtra, C India *21.09N 79.06E*
162 *K10* **Nagqu** ***Chin.*** Na-ch'ii; ***prev.*** Hei-ho. Xizang Zizhiqu, W China *31.30N 91.57E*
158 *J8* **Nāg Tibba Range** ▲▲ N India
47 *O8* **Nagua** NE Dominican Republic *19.18N 69.48W*
113 *H25* **Nagyatád** Somogy, SW Hungary *46.14N 17.19E*
Nagybánya *see* Baia Mare
Nagybecskerek *see* Zrenjanin
Nagydisznód *see* Cisnădie
Nagyenyed *see* Aiud
113 *N21* **Nagykálló** Szabolcs-Szatmár-Bereg, E Hungary *47.49N 21.47E*
113 *G25* **Nagykanizsa** ***Ger.*** Grosskanizsa. Zala, SW Hungary *46.27N 17.00E*
Nagykároly *see* Carei
113 *K22* **Nagykáta** Pest, C Hungary *47.24N 19.43E*
Nagykikinda *see* Kikinda
113 *K23* **Nagykőrös** Pest, C Hungary *47.04N 19.45E*
Nagy-Küküllő *see* Târnava Mare
Nagylak *see* Nădlac
Nagymihály *see* Michalovce
Nagyrőce *see* Revúca
Nagysomkút *see* Şomcuta Mare
Nagysurány *see* Šurany
Nagyszalonta *see* Salonta
Nagyszeben *see* Sibiu
Nagyszentmiklós *see* Sânnicolau Mare
Nagyszöllös *see* Vynohradiv
Nagyszombat *see* Trnava
Nagytapolcsány *see* Topoľčany
Nagyvárad *see* Oradea
172 *Oo15* **Naha** Okinawa, Okinawa, SW Japan *26.10N 127.40E*
158 *J8* **Nāhan** Himāchal Pradesh, NW India *30.33N 77.18E*
Nahang, Rūd-e *see* Nihing
Nahariya *see* Nahariyya
144 *F8* **Nahariyya** ***var.*** Nahariya. Northern, N Israel *33.01N 35.04E*
148 *L6* **Nahāvand** ***var.*** Nehavend. Hamadān, W Iran *34.13N 48.21E*
103 *F19* **Nahe** ≈ SW Germany
Na h-Iarmhidhe *see* Westmeath
201 *O13* **Nahnalaud** ▲ Pohnpei, E Micronesia
Nahoi, Cape *see* Cumberland, Cape
65 *H16* **Nahuel Huapi, Lago** ◎ W Argentina
25 *W7* **Nahunta** Georgia, SE USA *31.11N 81.58W*
42 *J6* **Naica** Chihuahua, N Mexico *27.53N 105.30W*
9 *U15* **Naicam** Saskatchewan, S Canada *52.26N 104.30W*
169 *T11* **Naiman Qi** Nei Mongol Zizhiqu, N China *42.51N 120.41E*
164 *M4* **Naimin Bulak** *spring* NW China *44.57N 90.29E*
11 *P6* **Nain** Newfoundland, NE Canada *56.33N 61.45W*
149 *P8* **Nā'īn** Eşfahān, C Iran *32.52N 53.04E*
158 *K10* **Naini Tāl** Uttar Pradesh, N India *29.22N 79.25E*
160 *J11* **Nainpur** Madhya Pradesh, C India *22.25N 80.10E*
197 *J14* **Nairai** *island* C Fiji
98 *J8* **Nairn** N Scotland, UK *57.36N 3.51W*
98 *I8* **Nairn** *cultural region* NE Scotland, UK
83 *I19* **Nairobi** ● (Kenya) Nairobi Area, S Kenya *1.16S 36.49E*
83 *I19* **Nairobi** ✈ Nairobi Area, S Kenya *1.21S 37.01E*
84 *P13* **Nairoto** Cabo Delgado, NE Mozambique *12.22S 39.05E*
120 *G3* **Naissaar** *island* N Estonia
Naissus *see* Niš
197 *K13* **Naitaba** ***var.*** Naitauba; ***prev.*** Naitamba. *island* Lau Group, E Fiji
Naitamba/Naitauba *see* Naitaba
83 *I19* **Naivasha** Rift Valley, SW Kenya *0.43S 36.25E*
83 *H19* **Naivasha, Lake** ◎ SW Kenya
Najaf *see* An Najaf
149 *N8* **Najafābād** ***var.*** Nejafabad. Eşfahān, C Iran *32.37N 51.22E*
147 *N7* **Najd** ***var.*** Nejd. *cultural region* C Saudi Arabia
107 *O4* **Nájera** La Rioja, N Spain *42.25N 2.45W*
107 *P4* **Najerilla** ≈ N Spain
158 *J9* **Najībābād** Uttar Pradesh, N India *29.37N 78.19E*
Najima *see* Fukuoka
169 *Y11* **Najin** NE North Korea *42.13N 130.15E*
145 *T9* **Najm al Ḩassūn** C Iraq *32.24N 44.13E*
147 *O13* **Najrān** ***var.*** Abā as Su'ūd. Najrān, S Saudi Arabia *17.31N 44.08E*
147 *P12* **Najrān** ***off.*** Minţaqat al Najrān. ◐ *province* S Saudi Arabia
170 *Bb12* **Nakadōri-jima** *island* Gotō-rettō, SW Japan
172 *Pp3* **Nakagawa** Hokkaidō, NE Japan *44.49N 142.04E*
171 *Kk15* **Naka-gawa** ≈ Honshū, S Japan
40 *F9* **Nakalele Pont** *headland* Maui, Hawaii, USA, C Pacific Ocean *21.01N 156.35W*
170 *D12* **Nakama** Fukuoka, Kyūshū, SW Japan *33.49N 130.42E*
Nakambé *see* White Volta
Nakamti *see* Nek'emtē
170 *E15* **Nakamura** Kōchi, Shikoku, SW Japan *33.00N 132.54E*
195 *O12* **Nakanai Mountains** ▲▲ New Britain, E PNG
171 *Jj14* **Nakano** Nagano, Honshū, S Japan *36.43N 138.22E*
170 *Ff11* **Nakano-shima** *island* Oki-shotō, SW Japan
170 *Ff12* **Nakano-umi** ***var.*** Naka-umi. ◎ Honshū, SW Japan
171 *Mm8* **Nakasato** Aomori, Honshū, C Japan *40.58N 140.26E*
172 *P7* **Nakasatsunai** Hokkaidō, NE Japan *42.42N 143.09E*
172 *Qq7* **Nakashibetsu** Hokkaidō, NE Japan *43.31N 144.58E*
83 *F18* **Nakasongola** C Uganda *1.19N 32.28E*
172 *Pp3* **Nakatonbetsu** Hokkaidō, NE Japan *44.58N 142.18E*
170 *D13* **Nakatsu** ***var.*** Nakatu. Ōita, Kyūshū, SW Japan *33.34N 131.12E*
171 *I15* **Nakatsugawa** ***var.*** Nakatugawa. Gifu, Honshū, SW Japan *35.30N 137.29E*
Nakatu *see* Nakatsu
Nakatugawa *see* Nakatsugawa
Naka-umi *see* Nakano-umi
172 *O5* **Nakayama-tōge** *pass* Hokkaidō, NE Japan *42.51N 141.05E*
Nakdong *see* Naktong-gang
Nakel *see* Nakło nad Notecią
82 *J8* **Nakfa** N Eritrea *16.38N 38.26E*
Nakhichevan' *see* Naxçıvan
127 *Nn18* **Nakhodka** Primorskiy Kray, SE Russian Federation *42.46N 132.47E*
126 *H8* **Nakhodka** Yamalo-Nenetskiy Avtonomnyy Okrug, N Russian Federation *67.48N 77.48E*
Nakhon Navok *see* Nakhon Nayok
178 *Hh11* **Nakhon Nayok** ***var.*** Nagara Nayok, Nakhon Navok. Nakhon Nayok, C Thailand *14.12N 101.08E*
178 *H11* **Nakhon Pathom** ***var.*** Nagara Pathom, Nakorn Pathom. Nakhon Pathom, W Thailand *13.49N 100.06E*
178 *J9* **Nakhon Phanom** ***var.*** Nagara Panom. Nakhon Phanom, E Thailand *17.22N 104.46E*
178 *Hh10* **Nakhon Ratchasima** ***var.*** Khorat, Korat. Nakhon Ratchasima, E Thailand *15.00N 102.06E*
178 *H10* **Nakhon Sawan** ***var.*** Muang Nakhon Sawan, Nagara Svarga. Nakhon Sawan, W Thailand *15.42N 100.06E*
178 *H15* **Nakhon Si Thammarat** ***var.*** Nagara Sridharmaraj, Nakhon Sithamnaraj. Nakhon Si Thammarat, SW Thailand *8.24N 99.58E*
Nakhon Sithamnaraj *see* Nakhon Si Thammarat
145 *Y11* **Nakhrash** SE Iraq *31.13N 47.24E*
8 *I9* **Nakina** British Columbia, W Canada *59.12N 132.48W*
112 *H9* **Nakło nad Notecią** ***Ger.*** Nakel. Kujawsko-pomorskie, C Poland *53.07N 17.34E*
41 *P13* **Naknek** Alaska, USA *58.45N 157.01W*
158 *H8* **Nakodar** Punjab, NW India *31.06N 75.31E*
84 *M11* **Nakonde** Northern, NE Zambia *9.22S 32.45E*
Nakorn Pathom *see* Nakhon Pathom
97 *H24* **Nakskov** Storstrøm, SE Denmark *54.50N 11.05E*

◆ Country ● Country Capital ◇ Dependent Territory ○ Dependent Territory Capital ◐ Administrative Region ✈ International Airport ▲ Mountain ▲▲ Mountain Range ⛰ Volcano ≈ River ◎ Lake ▣ Reservoir

◆ COUNTRY   ◇ DEPENDENT TERRITORY   ◉ ADMINISTRATIVE REGION   ▲ MOUNTAIN   ✕ VOLCANO   ⊕ LAKE
◆ COUNTRY CAPITAL   ◇ DEPENDENT TERRITORY CAPITAL   ✕ INTERNATIONAL AIRPORT   ▲ MOUNTAIN RANGE   ≈ RIVER   ⊞ RESERVOIR

299

NDEKE – NEWPORT

83 E18 **Ndeke** SW Uganda 0.11S 30.04E
80 J13 **Ndélé** Bamingui-Bangoran, N Central African Republic 8.24N 20.40E
81 E19 **Ndendé** Ngounié, S Gabon 2.21S 11.19E
81 E20 **Ndindi** Nyanga, S Gabon 3.46S 11.06E
80 G11 **Ndjamena** var. N'Djamena; prev. Fort-Lamy. ● (Chad) Chari-Baguirmi, W Chad 12.08N 15.01E
80 G11 **Ndjamena** ✕ Chari-Baguirmi, W Chad 12.09N 15.00E
81 D18 **Ndjolé** Moyen-Ogooué, W Gabon 0.07S 10.45E
84 J13 **Ndola** Copperbelt, C Zambia 12.58S 28.35E
Ndrhamcha, Sebkha de see Te-n-Dghâmcha, Sebkhet
81 L15 **Ndu** Orientale, N Dem. Rep. Congo (Zaire) 4.46N 22.54E
83 H21 **Nduguti** Singida, C Tanzania 4.19S 34.40E
195 X16 **Nduindui** Guadalcanal, C Solomon Islands 9.46S 159.54E
Nduke see Kolombangara
117 F16 **Néa Anchiálos** var. Nea Anhialos, Néa Ankhíalos. Thessalía, C Greece 39.18N 22.49E
Nea Anhialos/Néa Ankhíalos see Néa Anchiálos
117 H18 **Néa Artáki** Évvoia, C Greece 38.31N 23.39E
99 F15 **Neagh, Lough** ◎ E Northern Ireland, UK
34 F7 **Neah Bay** Washington, NW USA 48.21N 124.39W
117 J22 **Nea Kaméni** island Kykládes, Greece, Aegean Sea
189 O8 **Neale, Lake** ◎ Northern Territory, C Australia
190 G2 **Neales River** seasonal river South Australia
117 G14 **Néa Moudanía** var. Néa Moudhaniá. Kentrikí Makedonía, N Greece 40.15N 23.19E
Néa Moudhaniá see Néa Moudanía
118 K10 **Neamţ** ◈ county NE Romania
Neapel see Napoli
117 D14 **Neápoli** prev. Neápolis. Dytikí Makedonía, N Greece 40.18N 21.23E
117 K25 **Neápoli** Kríti, Greece, E Mediterranean Sea 35.15N 25.37E
117 G22 **Neápoli** Pelopónnisos, S Greece 36.29N 23.05E
Neapolis see Napoli, Italy
Neapolis see Nablus, West Bank
Neápolis see Neápoli, Greece
40 D16 **Near Islands** island group Aleutian Islands, Alaska, USA
99 J21 **Neath** S Wales, UK 51.39N 3.48W
116 H13 **Néa Zíchni** var. Néa Zíkhni; prev. Néa Zíkhna. Kentrikí Makedonía, NE Greece 41.02N 23.51E
Néa Zíkhna/Néa Zíkhni see Néa Zíchni
44 C5 **Nebaj** Quiché, W Guatemala 15.25N 91.05W
79 P13 **Nebbou** S Burkina 11.22N 1.49W
152 B11 **Nebitdag** Balkanskiy Velayat, W Turkmenistan 39.33N 54.19E
56 M13 **Neblina, Pico da** ▲ NW Brazil 0.49N 66.31W
128 I13 **Nebolchi** Novgorodskaya Oblast', W Russian Federation 59.08N 33.19E
38 L4 **Nebo, Mount** ▲ Utah, W USA 39.47N 111.46W
30 L14 **Nebraska** off. State of Nebraska; also known as Blackwater State, Cornhusker State, Tree Planters State. ◈ state C USA
31 S16 **Nebraska City** Nebraska, C USA 40.38N 95.52W
109 K23 **Nebrodi, Monti** var. Monti Caronie. ▲▲ Sicilia, Italy, C Mediterranean Sea
8 L14 **Nechako** ≈ British Columbia, SW Canada
31 Q2 **Neche** North Dakota, N USA 48.57N 97.33W
27 V8 **Neches** Texas, SW USA 31.51N 95.28W
27 W8 **Neches River** ≈ Texas, SW USA
103 H20 **Neckar** ≈ SW Germany
103 H20 **Neckarsulm** Baden-Württemberg, SW Germany 49.12N 9.13E
199 K5 **Necker Island** island C British Virgin Islands
183 U3 **Necker Ridge** undersea feature N Pacific Ocean
63 D23 **Necochea** Buenos Aires, E Argentina 38.33S 58.42W
106 H2 **Neda** Galicia, NW Spain 43.28N 8.09W
117 E20 **Nédas** ≈ S Greece
27 Y11 **Nederland** Texas, SW USA 29.58N 93.59W
Nederland see Netherlands
100 K12 **Neder Rijn** Eng. Lower Rhine. ≈ C Netherlands
101 L16 **Nederweert** Limburg, SE Netherlands 51.16N 5.45E
97 G16 **Nedre Tokke** ◎ S Norway
Nedrigaylov see Nedryhayliv
119 S3 **Nedryhayliv** Rus. Nedrigaylov. Sums'ka Oblast', NE Ukraine 50.51N 33.52E
100 O11 **Neede** Gelderland, E Netherlands 52.07N 6.36E
35 T13 **Needle Mountain** ▲ Wyoming, C USA 44.03N 109.33W
37 Y14 **Needles** California, W USA 34.50N 114.37W
99 M24 **Needles, The** rocks Isle of Wight, S England, UK
64 O7 **Ñeembucú** off. Departamento de Ñeembucú. ◈ department SW Paraguay
32 M7 **Neenah** Wisconsin, N USA 44.09N 88.26W
9 W16 **Neepawa** Manitoba, S Canada 50.13N 99.28W
101 K16 **Neerpelt** Limburg, NE Belgium 51.13N 5.25E
76 M6 **Nefta** ✕ W Tunisia 34.03N 8.05E
130 L15 **Neftegorsk** Krasnodarskiy Kray, SW Russian Federation 44.21N 39.40E
131 U3 **Neftekamsk** Respublika Bashkortostan, W Russian Federation 56.06N 54.12E
131 O14 **Neftekumsk** Stavropol'skiy Kray, SW Russian Federation 44.45N 45.00E
125 G11 **Nefteyugansk** Khanty-Mansiyskiy Avtonomnyy Okrug, C Russian Federation 61.07N 72.18E
Neftezavodsk see Seydi
84 C10 **Negage** var. N'Gage. Uíge, NW Angola 7.46S 15.27E
Negapatam/Negapattinam see Nāgappattinam
175 N16 **Negara** Bali, Indonesia 8.21S 114.34E
175 N10 **Negara** Borneo, C Indonesia 2.40S 115.04E
Negara Brunei Darussalam see Brunei
33 N4 **Negaunee** Michigan, N USA 46.30N 87.36W
83 J15 **Negēlē** var. Negelli, It. Neghelli. Oromo, C Ethiopia 5.13N 39.43E
Negelli see Negēlē
Negeri Pahang Darul Makmur see Pahang
Negeri Selangor Darul Ehsan see Selangor
174 H5 **Negeri Sembilan** var. Negri Sembilan. ◈ state Peninsular Malaysia
94 P3 **Negerpynten** headland S Svalbard 77.15N 22.40E
Negev see HaNegev
Neghelli see Negēlē
118 I12 **Negoiu** var. Negoiul. ▲ S Romania 45.34N 24.34E
Negoiul see Negoiu
84 P13 **Negomane** var. Negomano. Cabo Delgado, N Mozambique 11.22S 38.32E
Negomano see Negomane
161 J25 **Negombo** Western Province, SW Sri Lanka 7.13N 79.51E
Negoreloye see Nyeharelaye
114 P12 **Negotin** Serbia, E Yugoslavia 44.13N 22.31E
115 P19 **Negotino** C FYR Macedonia 41.29N 22.04E
58 A10 **Negra, Punta** headland NW Peru 6.03S 81.08W
106 G3 **Negreira** Galicia, NW Spain 42.54N 8.46W
118 L10 **Negreşti** Vaslui, E Romania 46.49N 27.28E
Negreşti see Negreşti-Oaş
118 H8 **Negreşti-Oaş** Hung. Avasfelsőfalu; prev. Negreşti. Satu Mare, NE Romania 47.56N 23.21E
46 H12 **Negril** W Jamaica 18.16N 78.21W
Negri Sembilan see Negeri Sembilan
65 K15 **Negro, Río** ≈ E Argentina
64 N7 **Negro, Río** ≈ NE Argentina
59 N17 **Negro, Río** ≈ E Bolivia
64 O5 **Negro, Río** ≈ C Paraguay
50 F6 **Negro, Río** ≈ N South America
63 E18 **Negro, Río** ≈ Brazil/Uruguay
Negro, Río see Sico Tinto, Río, Honduras
Negro, Río see Chixoy, Río, Guatemala/Mexico
179 Q14 **Negros** island C Philippines
118 M15 **Negru Vodă** Constanţa, SE Romania 43.47N 28.10E
11 P13 **Neguac** New Brunswick, SE Canada 47.16N 65.04W
12 B7 **Negwazu, Lake** ◎ Ontario, S Canada
Négyfalu see Săcele
34 F10 **Nehalem** Oregon, NW USA 45.42N 123.55W
34 F10 **Nehalem River** ≈ Oregon, NW USA
Nehavend see Nahāvand
149 V9 **Nehbandān** Khorāsān, E Iran 31.33N 60.01E
169 V6 **Nehe** Heilongjiang, NE China 48.28N 124.52E
200 Ss12 **Neiafu** 'Uta Vava'u, N Tonga 18.36S 173.58W
47 N9 **Neiba** var. Neyba. SW Dominican Republic 18.27N 71.28W
Néid, Carn Uí see Mizen Head
94 M9 **Neiden** Finnmark, N Norway 69.40N 29.22E
Neidín see Kenmare
Néifinn see Nephin
105 S10 **Neige, Crêt de la** ▲ E France 46.18N 5.58E
181 O16 **Neiges, Piton des** ▲ C Réunion 21.04S 55.28E
13 R9 **Neiges, Rivière des** ≈ Quebec, SE Canada
166 I10 **Neijiang** Sichuan, C China 29.31N 105.03E
32 K6 **Neillsville** Wisconsin, N USA 44.34N 90.36W
Nei Monggol Zizhiqu/Nei Mongol see Nei Mongol Zizhiqu
169 Q10 **Nei Mongol Gaoyuan** plateau NE China
169 O12 **Nei Mongol Zizhiqu** var. Nei Mongol, Eng. Inner Mongolia, Inner Mongolian Autonomous Region; prev. Nei Monggol Zizhiqu. ◈ autonomous region N China
167 O4 **Neiqiu** Hebei, E China 37.22N 114.34E
Neiriz see Neyrīz
103 Q16 **Neisse** Cz. Lužická Nisa, Ger. Lausitzer Neisse, Pol. Nisa, Nysa Łużycka. ≈ C Europe
Neisse see Nysa
56 E11 **Neiva** Huila, S Colombia 2.58N 75.15W
166 M7 **Neixiang** Henan, C China 33.07N 111.49E
Nejafabad see Najafābād
9 V9 **Nejanilini Lake** ◎ Manitoba, C Canada
Nejd see Najd
82 I13 **Nek'emtē** var. Lakemti, Nakamti. Oromo, C Ethiopia 9.06N 36.31E
130 M9 **Nekhayevskiy** Volgogradskaya Oblast', SW Russian Federation 50.25N 41.44E
32 K7 **Nekoosa** Wisconsin, N USA 44.19N 89.54W
97 M24 **Nekso** Bornholm, E Denmark 55.04N 15.05E
117 C16 **Nekyomanteío** ancient monument Épeiros, W Greece 39.13N 20.31E
106 H7 **Nelas** Viseu, N Portugal 40.31N 7.52W
128 H16 **Nelidovo** Tverskaya Oblast', W Russian Federation 56.13N 32.45E
31 P13 **Neligh** Nebraska, C USA 42.07N 98.01W
127 N12 **Nel'kan** Khabarovskiy Kray, E Russian Federation 57.44N 136.09E
94 M10 **Nellim** var. Nellimö, Lapp. Njellim. Lappi, N Finland 68.49N 28.18E
Nellimö see Nellim
161 J18 **Nellore** Andhra Pradesh, E India 14.29N 80.00E
127 O16 **Nel'ma** Khabarovskiy Kray, SE Russian Federation 47.43N 139.08E
63 B17 **Nelson** Santa Fe, C Argentina 31.16S 60.45W
9 O17 **Nelson** British Columbia, SW Canada 49.29N 117.13W
193 I14 **Nelson** Nelson, South Island, NZ 41.16S 173.16E
99 L17 **Nelson** NW England, UK 53.51N 2.13W
31 P17 **Nelson** Nebraska, C USA 40.12N 98.04W
193 J14 **Nelson** ◈ unitary authority South Island, NZ
9 X12 **Nelson** ≈ Manitoba, C Canada
191 U8 **Nelson Bay** New South Wales, SE Australia 32.45S 152.09E
190 K13 **Nelson, Cape** headland Victoria, SE Australia 38.25S 141.33E
194 M15 **Nelson, Cape** headland S PNG 8.57S 149.19E
65 G23 **Nelson, Estrecho** strait SE Pacific Ocean
9 W12 **Nelson House** Manitoba, C Canada 55.49N 98.51W
32 J4 **Nelson Lake** ◎ Wisconsin, N USA
33 T14 **Nelsonville** Ohio, N USA 39.27N 82.13W
29 S2 **Nelsoon River** ≈ Iowa/Missouri, C USA
85 K21 **Nelspruit** Mpumalanga, NE South Africa 25.28S 30.58E
78 L10 **Néma** Hodh ech Chargui, SE Mauritania 16.31N 7.12W
120 D13 **Neman** Ger. Ragnit. Kaliningradskaya Oblast', W Russian Federation 55.01N 22.00E
86 I9 **Neman** Bel. Nyoman, Ger. Memel, Lith. Nemunas, Pol. Niemen, Rus. Neman. ≈ NE Europe
Nemausus see Nîmes
117 F19 **Neméa** Pelopónnisos, S Greece 37.49N 22.40E
Německý Brod see Havlíčkův Brod
12 D7 **Nemegosenda** ≈ Ontario, S Canada
12 D8 **Nemegosenda Lake** ◎ Ontario, S Canada
121 H14 **Nemenčinė** Vilnius, SE Lithuania 54.50N 25.29E
Nemetocenna see Arras
Nemirov see Nemyriv
105 O6 **Nemours** Seine-et-Marne, N France 48.16N 2.40E
Nemunas see Neman
172 R7 **Nemuro** Hokkaidō, NE Japan 43.19N 145.34E
172 R7 **Nemuro-hantō** peninsula Hokkaidō, NE Japan
172 R6 **Nemuro-kaikyō** strait Japan/Russian Federation
172 R7 **Nemuro-wan** bay N Japan
118 H5 **Nemyriv** Rus. Nemirov. L'vivs'ka Oblast', NW Ukraine 50.07N 23.27E
119 N7 **Nemyriv** Rus. Nemirov. Vinnyts'ka Oblast', C Ukraine 48.57N 28.51E
99 D19 **Nenagh** Ir. An tAonach. C Ireland 52.52N 8.12W
41 R9 **Nenana** Alaska, USA 64.33N 149.05W
41 R9 **Nenana River** ≈ Alaska, USA
195 W8 **Nendö** var. Swallow Island. island Santa Cruz Islands, E Solomon Islands
99 O19 **Nene** ≈ E England, UK
129 R4 **Nenetskiy Avtonomnyy Okrug** ◈ autonomous district NW Russian Federation
203 W11 **Nengonengo** atoll Îles Tuamotu, C French Polynesia
169 U6 **Nen Jiang** var. Nonni. ≈ NE China
169 V6 **Nenjiang** Heilongjiang, NE China 49.10N 125.18E
201 P16 **Neoch** atoll Caroline Islands, C Micronesia
117 D18 **Neochóri** Dytikí Ellás, C Greece 38.23N 21.14E
29 Q7 **Neodesha** Kansas, C USA 37.25N 95.40W
31 S14 **Neola** Iowa, C USA 41.27N 95.40W
117 M19 **Néon Karlovási** var. Néon Karlovásion. Sámos, Dodekánisos, Greece, Aegean Sea 37.48N 26.42E
Néon Karlovásion see Néon Karlovási
117 E16 **Néon Monastíri** Thessalía, C Greece 39.22N 21.55E
29 R8 **Neosho** Missouri, C USA 36.52N 94.22W
29 Q7 **Neosho River** ≈ Kansas/Oklahoma, C USA
127 N17 **Nepa** ≈ C Russian Federation
159 N10 **Nepal** off. Kingdom of Nepal. ◆ monarchy S Asia
158 M11 **Nepalganj** Mid Western, SW Nepal 28.04N 81.37E
12 L13 **Nepean** Ontario, SE Canada 45.19N 75.53W
38 L4 **Nephi** Utah, W USA 39.43N 111.49W
99 B16 **Nephin** Ir. Néifinn. ▲ W Ireland 54.00N 9.21W
69 T9 **Nepoko** ≈ NE Dem. Rep. Congo (Zaire)
20 K15 **Neptune** New Jersey, NE USA 40.10N 74.03W
190 G10 **Neptune Islands** island group South Australia
109 I14 **Nera** anc. Nar. ≈ C Italy
104 L14 **Nérac** Lot-et-Garonne, SW France 44.08N 0.21E
113 D16 **Neratovice** Ger. Neratowitz. Středočeský Kraj, C Czech Republic 50.16N 14.31E
Neratowitz see Neratovice
126 L15 **Nercha** ≈ S Russian Federation
126 L15 **Nerchinsk** Chitinskaya Oblast', S Russian Federation 52.01N 116.25E
126 L16 **Nerchinskiy Zavod** Chitinskaya Oblast', S Russian Federation 51.13N 119.25E
128 M15 **Nerekhta** Kostromskaya Oblast', NW Russian Federation 57.27N 40.33E
120 H10 **Nereta** Aizkraukle, S Latvia 56.12N 25.18E
108 K13 **Nereto** Abruzzo, C Italy 42.49N 13.50E
115 H15 **Neretva** ≈ Bosnia and Herzegovina/Croatia
117 C17 **Nerikós** ruins Lefkáda, Iónioi Nísoi, Greece, C Mediterranean Sea 38.48N 20.43E
120 B12 **Neringa** Ger. Nidden; prev. Nida. Neringa, SW Lithuania 55.19N 21.00E
85 F15 **Neriquinha** Cuando Cubango, SE Angola 15.44S 21.34E
120 I13 **Neris** Bel. Viliya, Pol. Wilia; prev. Pol. Wilja. ≈ Belarus/Lithuania
Neris see Viliya
107 N15 **Nerja** Andalucía, S Spain 36.45N 3.34W
128 L16 **Nerl'** ≈ W Russian Federation
176 Vv13 **Nerong, Selat** strait Kepulauan Kai, E Indonesia
107 P12 **Nerpio** Castilla-La Mancha, C Spain 38.08N 2.18W
106 J13 **Nerva** Andalucía, S Spain 37.39N 6.31W
126 Ll13 **Neryungri** Respublika Sakha (Yakutiya), NE Russian Federation 56.37N 124.19E
100 L4 **Nes** Friesland, N Netherlands 53.28N 5.46E
96 G13 **Nesbyen** Buskerud, S Norway 60.34N 9.39E
94 L2 **Neskaupstadhur** Austurland, E Iceland 65.08N 13.45W
94 F13 **Nesna** Nordland, C Norway 66.11N 12.54E
28 K5 **Ness City** Kansas, C USA 38.27N 99.54W
Nesselsdorf see Kopřivnice
110 H7 **Nesslau** Sankt Gallen, NE Switzerland 47.13N 9.12E
98 I9 **Ness, Loch** ◎ N Scotland, UK
Nesterov see Zhovkva
116 I12 **Néstos** Bul. Mesta, Turk. Kara Su. ≈ Bulgaria/Greece see also Mesta
97 C14 **Nesttun** Hordaland, S Norway 60.19N 5.16E
Nesvizh see Nyasvizh
144 F9 **Netanya** var. Natanya, Nathanya. Central, C Israel 32.19N 34.51E
100 I9 **Netherlands** off. Kingdom of the Netherlands, var. Holland, Dut. Koninkrijk der Nederlanden, Nederland. ◆ monarchy NW Europe
47 S9 **Netherlands Antilles** prev. Dutch West Indies. ◇ Dutch autonomous region S Caribbean Sea
Netherlands East Indies see Indonesia
Netherlands Guiana see Surinam
Netherlands New Guinea see Irian Jaya
118 L4 **Netishyn** Khmel'nyts'ka Oblast', W Ukraine 50.20N 26.38E
144 E11 **Netivot** Southern, S Israel 31.25N 34.36E
109 O21 **Neto** ≈ S Italy
16 N2 **Nettilling Lake** ◎ Baffin Island, Nunavut, N Canada
31 V3 **Nett Lake** ◎ Minnesota, N USA
109 I16 **Nettuno** Lazio, C Italy 41.26N 12.40E
Netum see Noto
43 U16 **Netzahualcóyotl, Presa** ⊡ SE Mexico
Netze see Noteć
Neu Amerika see Puławy
Neubetsche see Novi Bečej
Neubidschow see Nový Bydžov
Neubistritz see Nová Bystřice
102 N9 **Neubrandenburg** Mecklenburg-Vorpommern, NE Germany 53.33N 13.16E
103 K22 **Neuburg an der Donau** Bayern, S Germany 48.43N 11.10E
110 C8 **Neuchâtel** Ger. Neuenburg. Neuchâtel, W Switzerland 46.58N 6.55E
110 C8 **Neuchâtel** Ger. Neuenburg. ◈ canton W Switzerland
110 C8 **Neuchâtel, Lac de** Ger. Neuenburger See. ◎ W Switzerland
Neudorf see Spišská Nová Ves
102 L10 **Neue Elde** canal N Germany
Neuenburg see Neuchâtel
Neuenburg an der Elbe see Nymburk
Neuenburger See see Neuchâtel, Lac de
110 F7 **Neuenhof** Aargau, N Switzerland 47.27N 8.17E
102 H11 **Neuenland** ✕ (Bremen) Bremen, NW Germany 53.03N 8.46E
Neuenstadt see La Neuveville
103 C18 **Neuerburg** Rheinland-Pfalz, W Germany 50.01N 6.13E
101 K24 **Neufchâteau** Luxembourg, SE Belgium 49.49N 5.25E
105 S6 **Neufchâteau** Vosges, NE France 48.21N 5.42E
104 M3 **Neufchâtel-en-Bray** Seine-Maritime, N France 49.44N 1.26E
111 S3 **Neufelden** Oberösterreich, N Austria 48.27N 14.01E
Neugradisk see Nova Gradiška
Neuhaus see Jindřichův Hradec
Neuhäusel see Nové Zámky
110 G6 **Neuhausen** var. Neuhausen am Rheinfall. Schaffhausen, N Switzerland 47.24N 8.37E
Neuhausen am Rheinfall see Neuhausen
103 I17 **Neuhof** Hessen, C Germany 50.26N 9.34E
Neuhof see Zgierz
Neukuhren see Pionerskiy
Neu-Langenburg see Tukuyu
111 W4 **Neulengbach** Niederösterreich, NE Austria 48.10N 15.53E
115 G15 **Neum** Federacija Bosna I Hercegovina, S Bosnia and Herzegovina 42.57N 17.33E
Neumark see Nowy Targ, Nowy Sącz, Poland
Neumark see Nowe Miasto Lubawskie, Toruń, Poland
Neumarkt see Neumarkt im Hausruckkreis, Oberösterreich, Austria
Neumarkt see Neumarkt Am Wallersee, Salzburg, Austria
Neumarkt see Środa Śląska, Wrocław, Poland
Neumarkt see Târgu Secuiesc, Covasna, Romania
Neumarkt see Târgu Mureş, Mureş, Romania
111 Q5 **Neumarkt am Wallersee** var. Neumarkt. Salzburg, NW Austria 47.55N 13.16E
111 R4 **Neumarkt im Hausruckkreis** var. Neumarkt. Oberösterreich, N Austria 48.16N 13.40E
103 L20 **Neumarkt in der Oberpfalz** Bayern, SE Germany 49.16N 11.28E
Neumarktl see Tržič
Neumoldowa see Moldova Nouă
102 J8 **Neumünster** Schleswig-Holstein, N Germany 54.04N 9.58E
111 X5 **Neunkirchen** var. Neunkirchen am Steinfeld. Niederösterreich, E Austria 47.43N 16.04E
103 E20 **Neunkirchen** Saarland, SW Germany 49.21N 7.10E
Neunkirchen am Steinfeld see Neunkirchen
Neuoderberg see Bohumín
65 I15 **Neuquén** Neuquén, SE Argentina 39.03S 68.36W
65 H14 **Neuquén** off. Provincia de Neuquén. ◈ province W Argentina
65 H14 **Neuquén, Río** ≈ W Argentina
Neurode see Nowa Ruda
102 N11 **Neuruppin** Brandenburg, NE Germany 52.55N 12.49E
Neusalz an der Oder see Nowa Sól
Neu Sandec/Neusandez see Małopolskie
103 K22 **Neusäss** Bayern, S Germany 48.24N 10.49E
Neusatz see Novi Sad
Neuschliss see Gherla
23 N8 **Neuse River** ≈ North Carolina, SE USA
111 Z5 **Neusiedl am See** Burgenland, E Austria 47.56N 16.51E
113 G22 **Neusiedler See** Hung. Fertő. ◎ Austria/Hungary
Neusohl see Banská Bystrica
103 D15 **Neuss** anc. Novaesium, Novesium. Nordrhein-Westfalen, W Germany 51.12N 6.40E
Neuss see Nyon
Neustadt see Neustadt an der Aisch, Bayern, Germany
Neustadt see Neustadt bei Coburg, Bayern, Germany
Neustadt see Prudnik, Opole, Poland
Neustadt see Baia Mare, Maramureş, Romania
102 I12 **Neustadt am Rübenberge** Niedersachsen, N Germany 52.30N 9.28E
103 J19 **Neustadt an der Aisch** var. Neustadt. Bayern, C Germany 49.34N 10.36E
Neustadt an der Haardt see Neustadt an der Weinstrasse
103 F20 **Neustadt an der Weinstrasse** prev. Neustadt an der Haardt, hist. Niewenstat, anc. Nova Civitas. Rheinland-Pfalz, SW Germany 49.21N 8.09E
103 K18 **Neustadt bei Coburg** var. Neustadt. Bayern, C Germany 50.19N 11.06E
Neustadt bei Pinne see Lwówek
Neustadt in Oberschlesien see Prudnik
Neustadtl see Novo mesto
Neustadtl in Mähren see Nové Město na Moravě
Neustettin see Szczecinek
110 M8 **Neustift im Stubaital** var. Stubaital. Tirol, W Austria 47.07N 11.26E
102 N10 **Neustrelitz** Mecklenburg-Vorpommern, NE Germany 53.22N 13.04E
Neutitschein see Nový Jičín
Neutra see Nitra
103 J22 **Neu-Ulm** Bayern, S Germany 48.23N 10.01E
Neuveville see La Neuveville
105 N12 **Neuvic** Corrèze, C France 45.23N 2.16E
Neuwarp see Nowe Warpno
102 G5 **Neuwerk** island NW Germany
103 E17 **Neuwied** Rheinland-Pfalz, W Germany 50.25N 7.28E
Neuzen see Terneuzen
128 H12 **Neva** ≈ NW Russian Federation
31 V14 **Nevada** Iowa, C USA 42.01N 93.27W
29 R6 **Nevada** Missouri, C USA 37.50N 94.21W
37 R5 **Nevada** off. State of Nevada; also known as Battle Born State, Sagebrush State, Silver State. ◈ state W USA
37 P6 **Nevada City** California, W USA 39.15N 121.02W
128 G16 **Nevel'** Pskovskaya Oblast', W Russian Federation 56.01N 29.54E
127 Oo16 **Nevel'sk** Ostrov Sakhalin, Sakhalinskaya Oblast', SE Russian Federation 46.41N 141.54E
126 Ll14 **Never** Amurskaya Oblast', SE Russian Federation 53.58N 124.04E
131 Q6 **Neverkino** Penzenskaya Oblast', W Russian Federation 52.53N 46.46E
105 P8 **Nevers** anc. Noviodunum. Nièvre, C France 47.00N 3.09E
20 J12 **Neversink River** ≈ New York, NE USA
191 Q6 **Nevertire** New South Wales, SE Australia 31.52S 147.42E
115 H15 **Nevesinje** Republika Srpska, S Bosnia and Herzegovina 43.15N 18.09E
120 G12 **Nevežis** ≈ C Lithuania
130 M14 **Nevinnomyssk** Stavropol'skiy Kray, SW Russian Federation 44.39N 41.57E
47 W10 **Nevis** island Saint Kitts and Nevis
Nevoso, Monte see Veliki Snežnik
Nevrokop see Gotse Delchev
142 J14 **Nevşehir** var. Nevshehr. Nevşehir, C Turkey 38.37N 34.43E
142 J14 **Nevşehir** var. Nevshehr. ◈ province C Turkey
Nevshehr see Nevşehir
125 Ee11 **Nev'yansk** Sverdlovskaya Oblast', C Russian Federation 57.26N 60.15E
83 J25 **Newala** Mtwara, SE Tanzania 10.58S 39.18E
33 P16 **New Albany** Indiana, N USA 38.16N 85.49W
24 M2 **New Albany** Mississippi, S USA 34.29N 89.00W
31 Y11 **New Albin** Iowa, C USA 43.30N 91.17W
57 U8 **New Amsterdam** E Guyana 6.17N 57.30W
191 Q4 **New Angledool** New South Wales, SE Australia 29.06S 147.54E
23 Y2 **Newark** Delaware, NE USA 39.40N 75.45W
20 K14 **Newark** New Jersey, NE USA 40.42N 74.12W
20 G10 **Newark** New York, NE USA 43.01N 77.04W
33 T13 **Newark** Ohio, N USA 40.03N 82.24W
Newark see Newark-on-Trent
37 W5 **Newark Lake** ◎ Nevada, W USA
99 N18 **Newark-on-Trent** var. Newark. C England, UK 53.04N 0.49W
24 M7 **New Augusta** Mississippi, S USA 31.12N 89.03W
21 P12 **New Bedford** Massachusetts, NE USA 41.37N 70.55W
34 G11 **Newberg** Oregon, NW USA 45.18N 122.58W
23 X10 **New Bern** North Carolina, SE USA 35.07N 77.03W
22 F8 **Newbern** Tennessee, S USA 36.06N 89.15W
33 P4 **Newberry** Michigan, N USA 46.21N 85.30W
23 Q12 **Newberry** South Carolina, SE USA 34.16N 81.37W
20 F15 **New Bloomfield** Pennsylvania, NE USA 40.24N 77.08W
27 X5 **New Boston** Texas, SW USA 33.27N 94.25W
27 S11 **New Braunfels** Texas, SW USA 29.43N 98.09W
33 Q13 **New Bremen** Ohio, N USA 40.26N 84.22W
99 F18 **Newbridge** Ir. An Droichead Nua. C Ireland 53.10N 6.48W
20 B14 **New Brighton** Pennsylvania, NE USA 40.44N 80.18W
20 M12 **New Britain** Connecticut, NE USA 41.37N 72.45W
195 N13 **New Britain** island E PNG
199 Hh9 **New Britain Trench** undersea feature W Pacific Ocean
20 J15 **New Brunswick** New Jersey, NE USA 40.29N 74.27W
13 V8 **New Brunswick** Fr. Nouveau-Brunswick. ◈ province SE Canada
20 K13 **Newburgh** New York, NE USA 41.30N 74.00W
99 M22 **Newbury** S England, UK 51.25N 1.19W
21 P10 **Newburyport** Massachusetts, NE USA 42.49N 70.53W
79 T14 **New Bussa** Niger, W Nigeria 9.50N 4.32E
197 J4 **New Caledonia** var. Kanaky, Fr. Nouvelle-Calédonie. ◇ French overseas territory SW Pacific Ocean
197 H5 **New Caledonia** island SW Pacific Ocean
183 O10 **New Caledonia Basin** undersea feature W Pacific Ocean
191 T8 **Newcastle** New South Wales, SE Australia 32.55S 151.46E
11 O14 **Newcastle** New Brunswick, SE Canada 47.01N 65.36W
12 I15 **Newcastle** Ontario, SE Canada 43.55N 78.35W
99 C20 **Newcastle** Ir. An Caisleán Nua. SW Ireland 52.25N 9.04W
85 K22 **Newcastle** KwaZulu/Natal, E South Africa 27.45S 29.59E
99 G16 **Newcastle** Ir. An Caisleán Nua. SE Northern Ireland, UK 54.12N 5.54W
33 P13 **New Castle** Indiana, N USA 39.55N 85.21W
22 L5 **New Castle** Kentucky, S USA 38.22N 85.09W
29 N11 **Newcastle** Oklahoma, C USA 35.15N 97.36W
20 B13 **New Castle** Pennsylvania, NE USA 40.59N 80.19W
27 R6 **Newcastle** Texas, SW USA 33.11N 98.44W
38 J7 **Newcastle** Utah, W USA 37.40N 113.31W
23 S6 **New Castle** Virginia, NE USA 37.29N 80.06W
35 Z13 **Newcastle** Wyoming, C USA 43.52N 104.13W
47 W10 **Newcastle** ✕ Nevis, Saint Kitts and Nevis 17.08N 62.36W
99 L14 **Newcastle** ✕ NE England, UK 55.03N 1.42W
Newcastle see Newcastle upon Tyne
99 L18 **Newcastle-under-Lyme** C England, UK 53.00N 2.14W
99 M14 **Newcastle upon Tyne** var. Newcastle; hist. Monkchester, Lat. Pons Aelii. NE England, UK 54.58N 1.34W
189 Q4 **Newcastle Waters** Northern Territory, N Australia 17.20S 133.26E
Newchwang see Yingkou
20 K13 **New City** New York, NE USA 41.08N 73.57W
33 U13 **Newcomerstown** Ohio, N USA 40.16N 81.36W
20 G15 **New Cumberland** Pennsylvania, NE USA 40.13N 76.52W
23 R1 **New Cumberland** West Virginia, NE USA 40.30N 80.35W
158 I10 **New Delhi** ● (India) Delhi, N India 28.34N 77.14E
9 O17 **New Denver** British Columbia, SW Canada 49.58N 117.21W
30 J9 **Newell** South Dakota, N USA 44.42N 103.25W
23 Q13 **New Ellenton** South Carolina, SE USA 33.25N 81.41W
24 J6 **Newellton** Louisiana, S USA 32.04N 91.14W
30 K6 **New England** North Dakota, N USA 46.32N 102.52W
21 P8 **New England** cultural region NE USA
New England of the West see Minnesota
191 U5 **New England Range** ▲▲ New South Wales, SE Australia
66 G9 **New England Seamounts** var. Bermuda-New England Seamount Arc. undersea feature W Atlantic Ocean
40 M14 **Newenham, Cape** headland Alaska, USA 58.39N 162.10W
144 F11 **Newè Zohar** Southern, E Israel 31.07N 35.23E
20 D9 **Newfane** New York, NE USA 43.16N 78.40W
99 M23 **New Forest** physical region S England, UK
16 S8 **Newfoundland** Fr. Terre-Neuve. island Newfoundland, SE Canada
11 R9 **Newfoundland** Fr. Terre Neuve. ◈ province E Canada
67 J8 **Newfoundland Basin** undersea feature NW Atlantic Ocean
66 I8 **Newfoundland Ridge** undersea feature NW Atlantic Ocean
66 J8 **Newfoundland Seamounts** undersea feature N Sargasso Sea
20 G16 **New Freedom** Pennsylvania, NE USA 39.43N 76.41W
195 U14 **New Georgia** island New Georgia Islands, NW Solomon Islands
195 T15 **New Georgia Islands** island group NW Solomon Islands
195 U14 **New Georgia Sound** var. The Slot. sound E Solomon Sea
32 L9 **New Glarus** Wisconsin, N USA 42.50N 89.38W
11 Q15 **New Glasgow** Nova Scotia, SE Canada 45.36N 62.37W
New Goa see Panaji
194 D11 **New Guinea** Dut. Nieuw Guinea, Ind. Irian. island Indonesia/PNG
199 H9 **New Guinea Trench** undersea feature SW Pacific Ocean
34 I6 **Newhalem** Washington, NW USA 48.40N 121.18W
41 P13 **Newhalen** Alaska, USA 59.43N 154.54W
31 X13 **Newhall** Iowa, C USA 42.00N 91.58W
12 F16 **New Hamburg** Ontario, S Canada 43.24N 80.37W
21 N9 **New Hampshire** off. State of New Hampshire; also known as The Granite State. ◈ state NE USA
31 W12 **New Hampton** Iowa, C USA 43.03N 92.19W
195 N9 **New Hanover** island NE PNG
20 M13 **New Haven** Connecticut, NE USA 41.18N 72.55W
33 Q12 **New Haven** Indiana, N USA 41.02N 84.59W
29 W5 **New Haven** Missouri, C USA 38.34N 91.15W
99 P23 **Newhaven** SE England, UK 50.48N 0.00W
8 K13 **New Hazelton** British Columbia, SW Canada 55.15N 127.30W
New Hebrides see Vanuatu
183 P9 **New Hebrides Trench** undersea feature N Coral Sea
20 H15 **New Holland** Pennsylvania, NE USA 40.06N 76.05W
24 I9 **New Iberia** Louisiana, S USA 30.00N 91.51W
195 N10 **New Ireland** ◈ province NE PNG
195 P10 **New Ireland** island NE PNG
67 A24 **New Island** island W Falkland Islands
20 J15 **New Jersey** off. State of New Jersey; also known as The Garden State. ◈ state NE USA
20 C14 **New Kensington** Pennsylvania, NE USA 40.33N 79.45W
23 W6 **New Kent** Virginia, NE USA 37.31N 76.58W
29 O8 **Newkirk** Oklahoma, C USA 36.52N 97.03W
23 Q9 **Newland** North Carolina, SE USA 36.04N 81.50W
30 L6 **New Leipzig** North Dakota, N USA 46.21N 101.54W
12 H9 **New Liskeard** Ontario, S Canada 47.31N 79.40W
24 G7 **Newllano** Louisiana, S USA 31.06N 93.16W
21 N13 **New London** Connecticut, NE USA 41.21N 72.04W
31 Y15 **New London** Iowa, C USA 40.55N 91.24W
31 T8 **New London** Minnesota, N USA 45.18N 94.56W
29 V3 **New London** Missouri, C USA 39.35N 91.24W
32 M7 **New London** Wisconsin, N USA 44.25N 88.44W
29 Y8 **New Madrid** Missouri, C USA 36.35N 89.31W
188 J8 **Newman** Western Australia 23.18S 119.45E
204 M13 **Newman Island** island Antarctica
12 H15 **Newmarket** Ontario, S Canada 44.03N 79.26W
99 P20 **Newmarket** E England, UK 52.17N 0.28E
21 P10 **Newmarket** New Hampshire, NE USA 43.04N 70.53W
23 U4 **New Market** Virginia, NE USA 38.39N 78.40W
23 R2 **New Martinsville** West Virginia, NE USA 39.37N 80.48W
33 U14 **New Matamoras** Ohio, N USA 39.32N 81.04W
34 M12 **New Meadows** Idaho, NW USA 44.57N 116.16W
28 R12 **New Mexico** off. State of New Mexico; also known as Land of Enchantment, Sunshine State. ◈ state SW USA
155 V6 **New Mirpur** var. Mīrpur. Sind, SE Pakistan 33.09N 73.42E
157 T17 **New Moore Island** island E India
25 S4 **Newnan** Georgia, SE USA 33.22N 84.48W
191 P17 **New Norfolk** Tasmania, SE Australia 42.46S 147.01E
24 K9 **New Orleans** Louisiana, S USA 30.00N 90.01W
24 K9 **New Orleans** ✕ Louisiana, S USA 29.59N 90.17W
20 K12 **New Paltz** New York, NE USA 41.44N 74.04W
33 U12 **New Philadelphia** Ohio, N USA 40.29N 81.27W
192 K10 **New Plymouth** Taranaki, North Island, NZ 39.04S 174.06E
99 M24 **Newport** S England, UK 50.42N 1.18W
99 K22 **Newport** SE Wales, UK 51.35N 3.00W
29 W10 **Newport** Arkansas, C USA 35.36N 91.16W

◆ Country ● Country Capital ◇ Dependent Territory ○ Dependent Territory Capital ◈ Administrative Region ✕ International Airport ▲ Mountain ▲▲ Mountain Range ✲ Volcano ≈ River ◎ Lake ⊡ Reservoir

NEWPORT – NŌGATA

33 N13 Newport Indiana, N USA 39.52N 87.24W
22 M3 Newport Kentucky, S USA 39.05N 84.30W
31 W9 Newport Minnesota, N USA 44.52N 93.00W
34 F12 Newport Oregon, NW USA 44.38N 124.03W
21 O13 Newport Rhode Island, NE USA 41.29N 71.17W
23 O9 Newport Tennessee, S USA 35.58N 83.11W
21 N6 Newport Vermont, NE USA 44.55N 72.13W
34 M7 Newport Washington, NW USA 48.08N 117.05W
23 X7 Newport News Virginia, NE USA 36.58N 76.25W
99 N20 Newport Pagnell SE England, UK 52.04N 0.43W
25 U12 New Port Richey Florida, SE USA 28.14N 82.42W
31 V9 New Prague Minnesota, N USA 44.32N 93.34W
46 H3 New Providence island N Bahamas
99 H24 Newquay SW England, UK 50.27N 5.03W
99 I20 New Quay SW Wales, UK 52.13N 4.22W
31 V10 New Richland Minnesota, N USA 43.53N 93.29W
13 X7 New-Richmond Quebec, SE Canada 48.10N 65.54W
33 R15 New Richmond Ohio, N USA 38.57N 84.16W
32 I5 New Richmond Wisconsin, N USA 45.09N 92.31W
44 G1 New River ≈ N Belize
57 T12 New River ≈ SE Guyana
23 R6 New River ≈ West Virginia, NE USA
44 G1 New River Lagoon ◎ N Belize
24 J8 New Roads Louisiana, S USA 30.42N 91.26W
20 L14 New Rochelle New York, NE USA 40.55N 73.44W
31 O4 New Rockford North Dakota, N USA 47.40N 99.08W
99 P23 New Romney SE England, UK 50.58N 0.57E
99 F20 New Ross Ir. Ros Mhic Thriúin. SE Ireland 52.24N 6.55W
99 F16 Newry Ir. An tIúr. SE Northern Ireland, UK 54.10N 6.19W
30 M5 New Salem North Dakota, N USA 46.51N 101.24W
New Sarum see Salisbury
31 W14 New Sharon Iowa, C USA 41.28N 92.39W
New Siberian Islands see Novosibirskiye Ostrova
25 X11 New Smyrna Beach Florida, SE USA 29.01N 80.55W
191 O7 New South Wales ◐ state SE Australia
41 O13 New Stuyahok Alaska, USA 59.27N 95.18W
23 N8 New Tazewell Tennessee, S USA 36.26N 83.36W
40 M12 Newtok Alaska, USA 60.56N 164.37W
25 S7 Newton Georgia, SE USA 31.18N 84.20W
31 W14 Newton Iowa, C USA 41.42N 93.03W
29 N6 Newton Kansas, C USA 38.03N 97.20W
21 O11 Newton Massachusetts, NE USA 42.19N 71.10W
24 M5 Newton Mississippi, S USA 32.19N 89.09W
20 J14 Newton New Jersey, NE USA 41.03N 74.45W
23 R9 Newton North Carolina, SE USA 35.40N 81.13W
27 Y9 Newton Texas, SW USA 30.51N 93.45W
99 J24 Newton Abbot SW England, UK 50.33N 3.34W
98 K13 Newton St Boswells SE Scotland, UK 55.34N 2.40W
99 I14 Newton Stewart S Scotland, UK 54.58N 4.30W
94 O2 Newtontoppen ▲ C Svalbard 78.57N 17.34E
30 K3 New Town North Dakota, N USA 47.58N 102.30W
99 J20 Newtown E Wales, UK 52.31N 3.19W
99 G15 Newtownabbey Ir. Baile na Mainistreach. E Northern Ireland, UK 54.40N 5.57W
99 G15 Newtownards Ir. Baile Nua na hArda. SE Northern Ireland, UK 54.36N 5.40W
31 U10 New Ulm Minnesota, N USA 44.20N 94.28W
30 K10 New Underwood South Dakota, N USA 44.05N 102.46W
27 V10 New Waverly Texas, SW USA 30.32N 95.28W
20 K14 New York New York, NE USA 40.44N 73.57W
20 G10 New York ◐ state NE USA
37 X13 New York Mountains ▲ California, W USA
192 K12 New Zealand abbrev. NZ. ◆ commonwealth republic SW Pacific Ocean
129 O15 Neya Kostromskaya Oblast', NW Russian Federation 58.19N 43.51E
Neyba see Neiba
149 Q12 Neyrīz var. Neiriz, Niriz. Fārs, S Iran 29.13N 54.18E
149 T4 Neyshābūr var. Nishapur. Khorāsān, NE Iran 36.14N 58.46E
161 J21 Neyveli Tamil Nādu, SE India 11.36N 79.25E
Nezhin see Nizhyn
35 N10 Nezperce Idaho, NW USA 46.14N 116.15W
24 H8 Nezpique, Bayou ≈ Louisiana, S USA
176 W14 Ngabordamlu, Tanjung headland Pulau Trangan, SE Indonesia 6.58S 134.13E
79 Y13 Ngadda ≈ NE Nigeria
N'Gage see Negage
193 G16 Ngahere West Coast, South Island, NZ 42.22S 171.29E
79 Z12 Ngala Borno, NE Nigeria 12.19N 14.11E
85 G17 Ngamiland ◐ district N Botswana
164 K16 Ngamring Xizang Zizhiqu, W China 29.16N 87.10E
83 K19 Ngangerabeli Plain plain SE Kenya
164 I14 Ngangla Ringco ◎ W China
164 G13 Nganglong Kangri ▲ W China 32.55N 81.00E
164 K15 Ngangzê Co ◎ W China
81 F14 Ngaoundéré var. N'Gaoundéré. Adamaoua, N Cameroon 7.19N 13.34E
83 E20 Ngara Kagera, NW Tanzania 2.30S 30.40E
196 F8 Ngardmau Bay bay Babeldaob, N Palau
196 F7 Ngaregur island Palau Islands, N Palau
192 L7 Ngaruawahia Waikato, North Island, NZ 37.41S 175.09E
192 N11 Ngaruroro ≈ North Island, NZ
202 I16 Ngatangiia Rarotonga, S Cook Islands 21.13S 159.43W
192 M6 Ngatea Waikato, North Island, NZ 37.16S 175.29E
177 F8 Ngathainggyaung Irrawaddy, SW Burma 17.22N 95.04E
Ngatik see Ngetik Atoll
Ngau see Gau
174 Ll15 Ngawi Jawa, S Indonesia 7.22S 111.22E
196 C7 Ngcheangel var. Kayangel Islands. island Palau Islands, N Palau
196 E10 Ngchemiangel Babeldaob, N Palau
196 C8 Ngeaur var. Angaur. island Palau Islands, S Palau
196 E10 Ngerkeai Babeldaob, N Palau
196 F9 Ngermechau Babeldaob, N Palau 7.34N 134.39E
196 C8 Ngeruktabel prev. Urukthapel. island Palau Islands, S Palau
196 F8 Ngetbong Babeldaob, N Palau 7.37N 134.34E
201 T17 Ngetik Atoll var. Ngatik; prev. Los Jardines. atoll Caroline Islands, E Micronesia
196 E10 Ngetkip Babeldaob, N Palau
Nggamea see Qamea
195 V15 Nggatokae island New Georgia Islands, NW Solomon Islands
85 C16 N'Giva var. Ondjiva, Port. Vila Pereira de Eça. Cunene, S Angola 17.01S 15.41E
81 G20 Ngo Plateaux, SE Congo 2.28S 15.43E
178 Jj7 Ngoc Lac Thanh Hoa, N Vietnam 20.06N 105.21E
81 G17 Ngoko ≈ Cameroon/Congo
176 W14 Ngonì, Tanjung headland Maluku, Kepulauan Aru, SE Indonesia 6.10S 134.04E
83 H19 Ngorengore Rift Valley, SW Kenya 1.01S 35.26E
165 Q11 Ngoring Hu ◎ C China
Ngorolaka see Banifing
83 H20 Ngorongoro Crater crater N Tanzania 3.10S 35.34E
81 D19 Ngounié off. Province de la Ngounié, var. La Ngounié. ◐ province S Gabon
81 D19 Ngounié ≈ Congo/Gabon
80 H10 Ngoura var. NGoura. Chari-Baguirmi, W Chad 12.52N 16.27E
80 G10 Ngouri var. NGouri; prev. Fort-Millot. Lac, W Chad 13.40N 15.24E
79 Y10 Ngourti Diffa, E Niger 15.22N 13.13E
79 Y11 Nguigmi var. N'Guigmi. Diffa, SE Niger 14.16N 13.07E
Nguimbo see Lumbala N'Guimbo
196 F15 Ngulu Atoll atoll Caroline Islands, W Micronesia
197 C14 Nguna island C Vanuatu
N'Gunza see Sumbe
175 N16 Ngurah Rai ✕ (Bali) Bali, S Indonesia
79 W12 Nguru Yobe, NE Nigeria 12.55N 10.30E
Ngwaketze see Southern
85 I16 Ngweze ≈ S Zambia
85 M17 Nhamatanda Sofala, C Mozambique 19.16S 34.10E
60 G12 Nhamundá, Rio var. Jamundá, Yamundá. ≈ N Brazil
62 J7 Nhandeara São Paulo, S Brazil 20.40S 50.03W
N'Harea see Nharêa
84 D12 Nharêa var. N'Harea, Nhareia. Bié, W Angola 11.28S 16.57E
Nhareia see Nharêa
178 Kk13 Nha Trang Khanh Hoa, S Vietnam 12.15N 109.10E
190 L11 Nhill Victoria, SE Australia 36.21S 141.38E
85 L22 Nhlangano prev. Goedgegun. SW Swaziland 27.01S 31.11E
189 S1 Nhulunbuy Northern Territory, N Australia 12.15S 136.46E
79 N10 Niafounké Tombouctou, W Mali 15.54N 3.58W
33 N5 Niagara Wisconsin, N USA 45.45N 87.57W
12 H16 Niagara ≈ Ontario, S Canada
12 G15 Niagara Escarpment hill range Ontario, S Canada
12 H16 Niagara Falls Ontario, S Canada 43.04N 79.06W
20 D9 Niagara Falls New York, NE USA 43.06N 79.04W
16 Pp17 Niagara Falls waterfall Canada/USA 43.04N 79.04W
78 K12 Niagassola var. Nyagassola. Haute-Guinée, NE Guinea 12.22N 9.07W
79 R12 Niamey ● (Niger) Niamey, SW Niger 13.28N 2.03E
79 R12 Niamey ✕ Niamey, SW Niger 13.28N 2.14E
79 R14 Niamtougou N Togo 9.49N 1.07E
81 O16 Niangara Orientale, NE Dem. Rep. Congo (Zaire) 3.45N 27.54E
79 O10 Niangay, Lac ◎ E Mali
79 N14 Niangoloko SW Burkina 10.15N 4.53W
29 U6 Niangua River ≈ Missouri, C USA
81 O17 Nia-Nia Orientale, NE Dem. Rep. Congo (Zaire) 1.26N 27.38E
21 N13 Niantic Connecticut, NE USA 41.19N 72.11W
169 U7 Nianzishan Heilongjiang, NE China 47.31N 122.52E
173 F7 Nias, Pulau island W Indonesia
84 O13 Niassa off. Província do Niassa. ◐ province N Mozambique
203 U10 Niau island Îles Tuamotu, C French Polynesia
97 G20 Nibe Nordjylland, N Denmark 56.58N 9.39E
201 Q8 Nibok N Nauru 0.31S 166.55E
120 C10 Nīca Liepāja, W Latvia 56.21N 21.03E
Nicaea see Nice
44 J9 Nicaragua off. Republic of Nicaragua. ◆ republic Central America
44 K11 Nicaragua, Lago de var. Cocibolca, Gran Lago, Eng. Lake Nicaragua. ◎ S Nicaragua
Nicaragua, Lake see Nicaragua, Lago de
66 D11 Nicaraguan Rise undersea feature NW Caribbean Sea
Nicaria see Ikaría
109 N21 Nicastro Calabria, SW Italy 38.58N 16.19E
105 V15 Nice It. Nizza; anc. Nicaea. Alpes-Maritimes, SE France 43.43N 7.13E
Nice see Côte d'Azur
Nicephorium see Ar Raqqah
10 M9 Nichicun, Lac ◎ Quebec, E Canada
170 C17 Nichinan var. Nitinan. Miyazaki, Kyūshū, SW Japan 31.36N 131.22E
46 E4 Nicholas Channel channel N Cuba
Nicholas II Land see Severnaya Zemlya
155 U2 Nicholas Range Pash. Selseleh-ye Kūh-e Vākhān, Taj. Qatorkŭhi Vakhon. ▲▲ Afghanistan/Tajikistan
22 M6 Nicholasville Kentucky, S USA 37.52N 84.34W
46 G2 Nicholls Town Andros Island, NW Bahamas 25.07N 78.01W
23 U12 Nichols South Carolina, SE USA 34.13N 79.09W
57 U9 Nickerie ◐ district NW Surinam
57 V9 Nickerie Rivier ≈ NW Surinam
157 P22 Nicobar Islands island group India, E Indian Ocean
118 L9 Nicolae Bălcescu Botoşani, NE Romania 47.33N 26.52E
13 P11 Nicolet Quebec, SE Canada 46.13N 72.37W
13 Q12 Nicolet ≈ Quebec, SE Canada
33 Q4 Nicolet, Lake ◎ Michigan, N USA
31 U10 Nicollet Minnesota, N USA 44.16N 94.11W
63 F19 Nico Pérez Florida, S Uruguay 33.30S 55.10W
Nicopolis see Nikopol, Bulgaria
Nicopolis see Nikópoli, Greece
124 R12 Nicosia Gk. Lefkosía, Turk. Lefkoşa. ● (Cyprus) C Cyprus 35.10N 33.22E
109 K24 Nicosia Sicilia, Italy, C Mediterranean Sea 37.45N 14.24E
109 N22 Nicotera Calabria, SW Italy 38.33N 15.55E
44 K13 Nicoya Guanacaste, W Costa Rica 10.06N 85.26W
44 L14 Nicoya, Golfo de gulf W Costa Rica
44 L14 Nicoya, Península de peninsula NW Costa Rica
Nictheroy see Niterói
113 L15 Nida ≈ S Poland
Nida see Neringa
Nidaros see Trondheim
110 D8 Nidau Bern, W Switzerland 47.07N 7.15E
103 H17 Nidda ≈ W Germany
Nidden see Neringa
97 F17 Nidelva ≈ S Norway
126 J10 Nidym Evenkiyskiy Avtonomnyy Okrug, N Russian Federation 64.08N 99.52E
112 L9 Nidzica Ger. Niedenburg. Warmińsko-Mazurskie, NE Poland, 53.22N 20.27E
102 H6 Niebüll Schleswig-Holstein, N Germany 54.47N 8.51E
Niedenburg see Nidzica
101 N25 Niederanven Luxembourg, C Luxembourg 49.39N 6.15E
105 V4 Niederbronn-les-Bains Bas-Rhin, NE France 48.57N 7.37E
Niederdonau see Niederösterreich
111 S7 Niedere Tauern ▲ C Austria
103 P14 Niederlausitz Eng. Lower Lusatia. physical region E Germany
111 U5 Niederösterreich off. Land Niederösterreich, Eng. Lower Austria, Ger. Niederdonau; prev. Lower Danube. ◐ state NE Austria
102 G12 Niedersachsen Eng. Lower Saxony, Fr. Basse-Saxe. ◐ state NW Germany
81 D17 Niefang var. Sevilla de Niefang. NW Equatorial Guinea 1.52N 10.12E
85 G23 Niekerkshoop Northern Cape, W South Africa 29.21S 22.49E
101 G17 Niel Antwerpen, N Belgium 51.07N 4.19E
Niéllé see Niellé
78 M14 Niellé var. Niéllé. N Ivory Coast 10.12N 5.37W
81 O22 Niemba Katanga, E Dem. Rep. Congo (Zaire) 5.58S 28.24E
113 G15 Niemcza Ger. Nimptsch. Dolnośląskie, SW Poland 50.45N 16.52E
Niemen see Neman
94 J13 Niemisel Norrbotten, N Sweden 66.00N 22.00E
113 H15 Niemodlin Ger. Falkenberg. Opolskie, S Poland 50.37N 17.45E
78 M13 Niéna Sikasso, SW Mali 11.24N 6.20W
102 H12 Nienburg Niedersachsen, N Germany 52.37N 9.12E
102 N13 Nieplitz ≈ NE Germany
113 L16 Niepołomice Małopolskie, S Poland 50.02N 20.12E
103 D14 Niers ≈ Germany/Netherlands
103 Q15 Niesky Lus. Niska. Sachsen, E Germany 51.16N 14.49E
Nieśwież see Nyasvizh
Nieuport see Nieuwpoort
100 O8 Nieuw-Amsterdam Drenthe, NE Netherlands 52.43N 6.52E
57 W9 Nieuw Amsterdam Commewijne, NE Surinam 5.52N 55.04W
101 M14 Nieuw-Bergen Limburg, SE Netherlands 51.36N 6.04E
100 O7 Nieuw-Buinen Drenthe, NE Netherlands 52.57N 6.55E
100 J12 Nieuwegein Utrecht, C Netherlands 52.03N 5.06E
100 P6 Nieuwe Pekela Groningen, NE Netherlands 53.04N 6.58E
100 P5 Nieuweschans Groningen, NE Netherlands 53.10N 7.10E
Nieuw Guinea see New Guinea
100 I11 Nieuwkoop Zuid-Holland, C Netherlands 52.09N 4.46E
100 M9 Nieuwleusen Overijssel, S Netherlands 52.34N 6.16E
100 J11 Nieuw-Loosdrecht Utrecht, C Netherlands 52.12N 5.07E
57 U9 Nieuw Nickerie Nickerie, NW Surinam 05.52N 57.00W
100 P5 Nieuwolda Groningen, NE Netherlands 53.15N 6.58E
101 B17 Nieuwpoort var. Nieuport. West-Vlaanderen, W Belgium 51.07N 2.45E
101 G14 Nieuw-Vossemeer Noord-Brabant, S Netherlands 51.34N 4.13E
100 P7 Nieuw-Weerdinge Drenthe, NE Netherlands 52.51N 7.00E
42 L10 Nieves Zacatecas, C Mexico 24.00N 102.57W
66 O11 Nieves, Pico de las ▲ Gran Canaria, Islas Canarias, Spain, NE Atlantic Ocean 27.58N 15.34W
105 P8 Nièvre ◐ department C France
Niewenstat see Neustadt an der Weinstrasse
142 J15 Niğde Niğde, C Turkey 37.58N 34.42E
142 J15 Niğde ◐ province C Turkey
85 J21 Nigel Gauteng, NE South Africa 26.25S 28.28E
79 V10 Niger off. Republic of Niger. ◆ republic W Africa
79 T14 Niger ◐ state C Nigeria
69 P8 Niger ≈ W Africa
Niger Cone see Niger Fan
69 P9 Niger Delta delta S Nigeria
69 P9 Niger Fan var. Niger Cone. undersea feature E Atlantic Ocean
79 T13 Nigeria off. Federal Republic of Nigeria. ◆ federal republic W Africa
79 T17 Niger, Mouths of the delta S Nigeria
193 C24 Nightcaps Southland, South Island, NZ 45.58S 168.03E
12 F7 Night Hawk Lake ◎ Ontario, S Canada
67 M19 Nightingale Island island S Tristan da Cunha, S Atlantic Ocean
40 M12 Nightmute Alaska, USA 60.28N 164.43W
116 G13 Nigríta Kentrikí Makedonía, NE Greece 40.54N 23.28E
154 J15 Nihing Per. Rūd-e Nahang. ≈ Iran/Pakistan
203 V10 Nihiru atoll Îles Tuamotu, C French Polynesia
Nihommatsu see Nihonmatsu
Nihon see Japan
171 L13 Nihonmatsu var. Nihommatsu, Nihonmatu. Fukushima, Honshū, C Japan 37.35N 140.22E
Nihonmatu see Nihonmatsu
64 I12 Nihuil, Embalse del ⊠ W Argentina
171 K12 Niigata Niigata, Honshū, C Japan 37.55N 139.01E
171 K13 Niigata off. Niigata-ken. ◐ prefecture Honshū, C Japan
170 F15 Niihama Ehime, Shikoku, SW Japan 33.57N 133.15E
40 A8 Niihau island Hawaii, USA, C Pacific Ocean
172 Ss13 Nii-jima island E Japan
170 Ff13 Niimi Okayama, Honshū, SW Japan 35.00N 133.27E
171 Kk13 Niitsu var. Niitu. Niigata, Honshū, C Japan 37.48N 139.06E
Niitu see Niitsu
107 P15 Níjar Andalucía, S Spain 36.57N 2.13W
100 K11 Nijkerk Gelderland, C Netherlands 52.13N 5.30E
101 H16 Nijlen Antwerpen, N Belgium 51.10N 4.40E
100 L13 Nijmegen Ger. Nimwegen; anc. Noviomagus. Gelderland, SE Netherlands 51.49N 5.52E
100 N10 Nijverdal Overijssel, E Netherlands 52.22N 6.28E
202 G16 Nikao Rarotonga, S Cook Islands
Nikaria see Ikaría
128 I2 Nikel' Murmanskaya Oblast', NW Russian Federation 69.24N 30.12E
175 Rr17 Nikiniki Timor, S Indonesia 10.00S 124.30E
133 Q15 Nikitin Seamount undersea feature E Indian Ocean 5.48S 84.48E
79 S14 Nikki E Benin 9.55N 3.12E
171 Kk15 Nikkō var. Nikko. Tochigi, Honshū, S Japan 36.45N 139.37E
Niklasmarkt see Gheorgheni
41 P10 Nikolai Alaska, USA 63.00N 154.22W
Nikolaiken see Mikołajki
Nikolainkaupunki see Länsi-Suomi
Nikolayev see Mykolayiv
151 U15 Nikolayevka Almaty, SE Kazakhstan 43.39N 77.10E
151 O6 Nikolayevka Severnyy Kazakhstan, N Kazakhstan
131 P9 Nikolayevsk Volgogradskaya Oblast', SW Russian Federation 50.03N 45.30E
Nikolayevskaya Oblast' see Mykolayivs'ka Oblast'
127 Nn14 Nikolayevsk-na-Amure Khabarovskiy Kray, SE Russian Federation 53.04N 140.39E
131 P6 Nikol'sk Penzenskaya Oblast', W Russian Federation 53.46N 46.03E
129 O13 Nikol'sk Vologodskaya Oblast', NW Russian Federation 59.35N 45.31E
Nikol'sk see Ussuriysk
40 K17 Nikolski Umnak Island, Alaska, USA 52.56N 168.52W
Nikol'skiy see Satpayev
131 V7 Nikol'skoye Orenburgskaya Oblast', W Russian Federation 52.01N 55.48E
Nikol'sk-Ussuriyskiy see Ussuriysk
116 J7 Nikopol anc. Nicopolis. Pleven, N Bulgaria 43.43N 24.55E
119 S9 Nikopol' Dnipropetrovs'ka Oblast', SE Ukraine 47.34N 34.23E
117 C17 Nikópoli anc. Nicopolis. site of ancient city Ípeiros, W Greece 39.01N 20.43E
142 M12 Niksar Tokat, N Turkey 40.36N 36.54E
149 V14 Nīkshahr Sīstān va Balūchestān, SE Iran 26.15N 60.10E
115 J16 Nikšić Montenegro, SW Yugoslavia 42.46N 18.56E
203 R4 Nikumaroro prev. Gardner Island, Kemins Island. atoll Phoenix Islands, C Kiribati
203 P3 Nikunau var. Nukunau; prev. Byron Island. atoll Tungaru, W Kiribati
161 G21 Nilambūr Kerala, SW India 11.16N 76.15E
37 X16 Niland California, W USA 33.14N 115.31W
69 T3 Nile Ar. Nahr an Nīl. ≈ N Africa
82 G8 Nile former province NW Uganda
77 W7 Nile Delta delta N Egypt
69 T3 Nile Fan undersea feature E Mediterranean Sea
33 O11 Niles Michigan, N USA 41.49N 86.15W
33 V11 Niles Ohio, N USA 41.10N 80.46W
161 F20 Nileswaram Kerala, SW India 12.18N 75.07E
12 K10 Nilgaut, Lac ◎ Quebec, SE Canada
164 I5 Nilka Xinjiang Uygur Zizhiqu, NW China 43.46N 82.33E
Nīl, Nahr an see Nile
95 N16 Nilsiä Itä-Suomi, C Finland 63.13N 28.00E
160 F9 Nīmach Madhya Pradesh, C India 24.30N 74.51E
158 G14 Nimbāhera Rājasthān, N India 24.37N 74.45E
78 L15 Nimba, Monts var. Nimba Mountains. ▲ W Africa
Nimba Mountains see Nimba, Monts
Nimburg see Nymburk
105 Q15 Nîmes anc. Nemausus, Nismes. Gard, S France 43.49N 4.19E
158 H11 Nīm ka Thāna Rājasthān, N India 27.44N 75.44E
191 R11 Nimmitabel New South Wales, SE Australia 36.34S 149.18E
Nimptsch see Niemcza
205 R11 Nimrod Glacier glacier Antarctica
Nimroze see Nīmrūz
154 K8 Nīmrūz var. Nimroze; prev. Chakhānsūr. ◐ province SW Afghanistan
83 F16 Nimule Eastern Equatoria, S Sudan 3.33N 32.06E
Nimwegen see Nijmegen
161 C23 Nine Degree Channel channel India/Maldives
20 G9 Ninemile Point headland New York, NE USA 43.31N 76.22W
181 S8 Ninetyeast Ridge undersea feature E Indian Ocean
191 P13 Ninety Mile Beach beach Victoria, SE Australia
192 I2 Ninety Mile Beach beach North Island, NZ
23 P12 Ninety Six South Carolina, SE USA 34.10N 82.01W
169 Y9 Ning'an Heilongjiang, NE China 44.20N 129.28E
167 S9 Ningbo var. Ning-po, Yin-hsien; prev. Ninghsien. Zhejiang, SE China 29.54N 121.33E
167 U12 Ningde Fujian, SE China 26.48N 119.33E
167 P12 Ningdu Jiangxi, S China 26.28N 115.58E
194 E12 Ningerum Western, SW PNG 5.43S 141.09E
167 R9 Ningguo Anhui, E China 30.33N 118.58E
167 S9 Ninghai Zhejiang, SE China 29.19N 121.22E
Ning-hsia see Ningxia
Ninghsien see Ningbo
166 J15 Ningming Guangxi Zhuangzu Zizhiqu, S China 22.07N 106.43E
166 H11 Ningnan Sichuan, C China 26.59N 102.49E
Ning-po see Ningbo
Ningsia/Ningsia Hui/Ningsia Hui Autonomous Region see Ningxia
166 J5 Ningxia off. Ningxia Huizu Zizhiqu, var. Ning-hsia, Ningsia, Eng. Ningsia Hui, Ningsia Hui Autonomous Region. ◐ autonomous region N China
165 X10 Ningxian Gansu, N China 35.30N 108.04E
178 Jj7 Ninh Binh Ninh Binh, N Vietnam 20.12N 105.58E
178 Kk13 Ninh Hoa Khanh Hoa, S Vietnam 12.28N 109.07E
194 H7 Ninigo Group island group N PNG
41 Q12 Ninilchik Alaska, USA 60.03N 151.40W
29 N7 Ninnescah River ≈ Kansas, C USA
205 U16 Ninnis Glacier glacier Antarctica
172 N10 Ninohe Iwate, Honshū, C Japan 40.17N 141.18E
101 F18 Ninove Oost-Vlaanderen, C Belgium 50.49N 4.01E
179 P11 Ninoy Aquino ✕ (Manila) Luzon, N Philippines 14.26N 121.00E
Nio see Íos
31 P12 Niobrara Nebraska, C USA 42.43N 97.59W
30 M12 Niobrara River ≈ Nebraska/Wyoming, C USA
81 I20 Nioki Bandundu, W Dem. Rep. Congo (Zaire) 2.44S 17.42E
78 M11 Niono Ségou, C Mali 14.15N 5.57W
78 K11 Nioro var. Nioro du Sahel. Kayes, W Mali 15.13N 9.38W
78 G11 Nioro du Rip SW Senegal 13.44N 15.48W
Nioro du Sahel see Nioro
104 K10 Niort Deux-Sèvres, W France 46.21N 0.24W
180 H14 Nioumachoua Mohéli, S Comoros 12.21S 43.43E
194 G12 Nipa Southern Highlands, W PNG 6.12S 143.29E
9 U14 Nipawin Saskatchewan, S Canada 53.21N 103.55W
10 D12 Nipigon Ontario, S Canada 49.01N 88.15W
10 D11 Nipigon, Lake ◎ Ontario, S Canada
9 S13 Nipin ≈ Saskatchewan, C Canada
12 G11 Nipissing, Lake ◎ Ontario, S Canada
37 P13 Nipomo California, W USA 35.02N 120.28W
Nippon see Japan
144 K6 Niqniqīyah, Jabal an ▲ C Syria
64 I9 Niquivil San Juan, W Argentina 30.25S 68.42W
176 Yy10 Nirabotong Irian Jaya, E Indonesia 2.35S 140.08E
171 J16 Nirasaki Yamanashi, Honshū, S Japan 35.43N 138.24E
Niriz see Neyrīz
161 I14 Nirmal Andhra Pradesh, C India 19.04N 78.21E
159 Q13 Nirmāli Bihār, N India 26.18N 86.34E
115 O14 Niš Eng. Nish, Ger. Nisch; anc. Naissus. Serbia, SE Yugoslavia 43.20N 21.52E
106 H9 Nisa Portalegre, C Portugal 39.31N 7.39W
Nisa see Neisse
147 P4 Niṣab Al Ḥudūd ash Shamālīyah, N Saudi Arabia 29.10N 44.43E
147 Q15 Niṣāb var. Anṣāb. SW Yemen 14.24N 46.47E
115 P14 Nišava Bul. Nishava. ≈ Bulgaria/Yugoslavia see also Nishava
109 K25 Niscemi Sicilia, Italy, C Mediterranean Sea 37.09N 14.22E
Nisch/Nish see Niš
172 Nn5 Niseko Hokkaidō, NE Japan 42.50N 140.43E
Nishapur see Neyshābūr
116 G9 Nishava var. Nišava. ≈ Bulgaria/Yugoslavia see also Nišava
120 L11 Nishcha Rus. Nishcha. ≈ N Belarus
172 Qq7 Nishibetsu-gawa ≈ Hokkaidō, NE Japan
170 E13 Nishi-gawa ≈ Honshū, SW Japan
170 Ee13 Nishi-Nōmi-jima var. Nōmi-jima. island SW Japan
170 Bb17 Nishinoomote Kagoshima, Tanega-shima, SW Japan 30.42N 130.59E
172 Ss16 Nishino-shima Eng. Rosario. island Ogasawara-shotō, SE Japan
171 Hh16 Nishio var. Nisio. Aichi, Honshū, SW Japan 34.52N 137.01E
170 C13 Nishi-Sonogi-hantō peninsula Kyūshū, SW Japan
171 Gg14 Nishiwaki var. Nisiwaki. Hyōgo, Honshū, SW Japan 35.02N 134.57E
147 U14 Nishtūn SE Yemen 15.47N 52.08E
Nisiros see Nísyros
Nisiwaki see Nishiwaki
Niska see Niesky
115 O14 Niška Banja Serbia, SE Yugoslavia 43.18N 22.01E
10 D6 Niskibi ≈ Ontario, C Canada
113 O15 Nisko Podkarpackie, SE Poland 50.31N 22.09E
8 H7 Nisling ≈ Yukon Territory, W Canada
101 H22 Nismes Namur, S Belgium 50.04N 4.31E
Nismes see Nîmes
118 M10 Nisporeni Rus. Nisporeny. W Moldova 47.04N 28.10E
Nisporeny see Nisporeni
97 K20 Nissan ≈ S Sweden
195 R11 Nissan Island island Green Islands, NE PNG
Nissan Islands see Green Islands
97 F16 Nisser ◎ S Norway
97 E21 Nissum Bredning inlet NW Denmark
31 U6 Nisswa Minnesota, N USA 46.31N 94.17W
Nistru see Dniester
117 M22 Nísyros var. Nisiros. island Dodekánisos, Greece, Aegean Sea
120 H8 Nītaure Cēsis, C Latvia 57.05N 25.12E
62 P10 Niterói prev. Nictheroy. Rio de Janeiro, SE Brazil 22.54S 43.06W
12 F16 Nith ≈ Ontario, S Canada
98 J13 Nith ≈ S Scotland, UK
Nitinan see Nichinan
113 I21 Nitra Ger. Neutra, Hung. Nyitra. Nitriansky Kraj, SW Slovakia 48.19N 18.04E
113 I20 Nitra Ger. Neutra, Hung. Nyitra. ≈ W Slovakia
113 I21 Nitriansky Kraj ◐ region SW Slovakia
23 Q5 Nitro West Virginia, NE USA 38.24N 81.50W
125 F11 Nitsa ≈ C Russian Federation
97 H14 Nittedal Akershus, S Norway 60.08N 10.45E
Niuatobutabu see Niuatoputapu
200 S11 Niuatoputapu var. Niuatobutabu; prev. Keppel Island. island N Tonga
200 Q15 Niu'Aunofa headland Tongatapu, S Tonga 21.03S 175.19W
Niuchwang see Yingkou
202 B16 Niue ◇ self-governing territory in free association with NZ S Pacific Ocean
202 F10 Niulakita var. Nurakita. atoll S Tuvalu
202 E6 Niutao atoll NW Tuvalu
95 L15 Nivala Oulu, C Finland 63.56N 25.00E
104 I15 Nive ≈ SW France
101 G19 Nivelles Wallon Brabant, C Belgium 50.36N 4.04E
105 P8 Nivernais cultural region C France
13 N8 Niverville, Lac ◎ Quebec, SE Canada
29 T7 Nixa Missouri, C USA 37.02N 93.17W
37 R5 Nixon Nevada, W USA 39.48N 119.24W
27 S12 Nixon Texas, SW USA 29.16N 97.45W
Niya see Minfeng
152 K12 Niyazov Lebapskiy Velayat, NE Turkmenistan 39.13N 63.16E
161 H14 Nizāmābād Andhra Pradesh, C India 18.40N 78.04E
161 H15 Nizām Sāgar ◎ C India
129 N16 Nizhegorodskaya Oblast' ◐ province W Russian Federation
126 K14 Nizhneangarsk Respublika Buryatiya, S Russian Federation 55.47N 109.39E
Nizhnegorskiy see Nyzhn'ohirs'kyy
131 S4 Nizhnekamsk Respublika Tatarstan, W Russian Federation 55.36N 51.45E
131 U3 Nizhnekamskoye Vodokhranilishche ⊠ W Russian Federation
127 O5 Nizhnekolymsk Respublika Sakha (Yakutiya), NE Russian Federation 68.32N 161.00E
127 N16 Nizhne Leninskoye Yevreyskaya Avtonomnaya Oblast', SE Russian Federation 47.50N 132.30E
126 Ii14 Nizhneudinsk Irkutskaya Oblast', S Russian Federation 54.48N 98.51E
126 Gg11 Nizhnevartovsk Khanty-Mansiyskiy Avtonomnyy Okrug, C Russian Federation 60.57N 76.40E
126 Ll6 Nizhneyansk Respublika Sakha (Yakutiya), NE Russian Federation 71.25N 135.59E
131 Q11 Nizhniy Baskunchak Astrakhanskaya Oblast', SW Russian Federation 48.15N 46.49E
126 M11 Nizhniy Bestyakh Respublika Sakha (Yakutiya), NE Russian Federation 61.55N 130.07E
131 O6 Nizhniy Lomov Penzenskaya Oblast', W Russian Federation 53.32N 43.39E
131 P3 Nizhniy Novgorod prev. Gor'kiy. Nizhegorodskaya Oblast', W Russian Federation 56.17N 43.59E
129 T8 Nizhniy Odes Respublika Komi, NW Russian Federation 63.42N 54.58E
Nizhniy Pyandzh see Panji Poyon
125 Ee11 Nizhniy Tagil Sverdlovskaya Oblast', C Russian Federation 57.57N 59.51E
129 T9 Nizhnyaya-Omra Respublika Komi, NW Russian Federation 62.46N 55.54E
129 P5 Nizhnyaya Pesha Nenetskiy Avtonomnyy Okrug, NW Russian Federation 66.54N 47.37E
125 F11 Nizhnyaya Tavda Tyumenskaya Oblast', C Russian Federation 57.41N 65.54E
126 Jj12 Nizhnyaya Tunguska Eng. Lower Tunguska. ≈ N Russian Federation
119 Q3 Nizhyn Rus. Nezhin. Chernihivs'ka Oblast', NE Ukraine 51.03N 31.54E
142 M17 Nizip Gaziantep, S Turkey 37.01N 37.46E
147 X8 Nizwá var. Nazwāh. NE Oman 22.50N 57.27E
Nizza see Nice
108 C9 Nizza Monferrato Piemonte, NE Italy 44.47N 8.22E
Njávdám see Näätämöjoki
Njellim see Nellim
83 H24 Njombe Iringa, S Tanzania 9.19S 34.46E
83 G23 Njombe ≈ C Tanzania
94 I10 Njunis ▲ N Norway 68.47N 19.24E
95 H17 Njurunda Västernorrland, C Sweden 62.15N 17.24E
96 N11 Njutånger Gävleborg, C Sweden 61.37N 17.04E
81 D14 Nkambe Nord-Ouest, NW Cameroon 6.34N 10.43E
Nkata Bay see Nkhata Bay
81 F21 Nkayi prev. Jacob. La Bouenza, S Congo 4.10S 13.17E
85 J17 Nkayi Matabeleland North, W Zimbabwe 19.02S 28.55E
84 N13 Nkhata Bay var. Nkata Bay. Northern, N Malawi 11.36S 34.16E
83 E22 Nkonde Kigoma, N Tanzania 6.16S 30.17E
81 D15 Nkongsamba var. N'Kongsamba. Littoral, W Cameroon 4.58N 9.52E
85 E16 Nkurenkuru Okavango, N Namibia 17.39S 18.37E
79 Q15 Nkwanta E Ghana 8.18N 0.27E
178 H1 Nmai Hka var. Me Hka. ≈ N Burma
Noardwâlde see Noordwolde
41 N7 Noatak Alaska, USA 67.34N 162.58W
41 N7 Noatak River ≈ Alaska, USA
Nobeji see Noheji
170 D15 Nobeoka Miyazaki, Kyūshū, SW Japan 32.34N 131.37E
29 N11 Noble Oklahoma, C USA 35.08N 97.23W
33 P13 Noblesville Indiana, N USA 40.03N 86.00W
172 O6 Noboribetsu var. Noboribetu. Hokkaidō, NE Japan 42.27N 141.08E
Noboribetu see Noboribetsu
61 H18 Nobres Mato Grosso, W Brazil 14.43S 56.15W
109 N21 Nocera Terinese Calabria, S Italy 39.03N 16.10E
43 Q16 Nochixtlán var. Asunción Nochixtlán. Oaxaca, SE Mexico 17.28N 97.18W
27 S5 Nocona Texas, SW USA 33.47N 97.43W
65 K21 Nodales, Bahía de los bay S Argentina
29 Q2 Nodaway River ≈ Iowa/Missouri, C USA
29 R8 Noel Missouri, C USA 36.33N 94.29W
97 C17 Nærbø Rogaland, S Norway 58.40N 5.39E
97 I24 Næstved Storstrøm, SE Denmark 55.12N 11.47E
42 H3 Nogales Chihuahua, NW Mexico 18.49N 97.12W
42 F3 Nogales Sonora, NW Mexico 31.16N 110.52W
38 M17 Nogales Arizona, SW USA 31.20N 110.55W
Nogal Valley see Dooxo Nugaaleed
104 K15 Nogaro Gers, S France 43.46N 0.01W
112 J7 Nogat ≈ N Poland
170 D12 Nōgata Fukuoka, Kyūshū, SW Japan 33.42N 130.43E

◆ Country ● Country Capital ◇ Dependent Territory ○ Dependent Territory Capital ◐ Administrative Region ✕ International Airport ▲ Mountain ▲▲ Mountain Range Volcano ≈ River ◎ Lake ⊠ Reservoir

NOGAYSKAYA STEP' – NOUÂDHIBOU, RÂS

131 P15 **Nogayskaya Step'** *steppe* SW Russian Federation
104 M6 **Nogent-le-Rotrou** Eure-et-Loir, C France *48.19N 0.49E*
105 O4 **Nogent-sur-Oise** Oise, N France *49.16N 2.28E*
105 P6 **Nogent-sur-Seine** Aube, N France *48.30N 3.31E*
126 I10 **Noginsk** Evenkiyskiy Avtonomnyy Okrug, N Russian Federation *64.28N 91.09E*
130 L3 **Noginsk** Moskovskaya Oblast', W Russian Federation *55.51N 38.23E*
127 O14 **Nogliki** Ostrov Sakhalin, Sakhalinskaya Oblast', SE Russian Federation *51.44N 143.14E*
171 I14 **Nōgōhaku-san** ▲ Honshū, SW Japan *35.46N 136.30E*
168 D5 **Nogoonnuur** Bayan-Ölgiy, NW Mongolia *49.31N 89.48E*
63 C18 **Nogoyá** Entre Ríos, E Argentina *32.25S 59.49W*
113 K21 **Nógrád** *off.* Nógrád Megye. ◆ *county* N Hungary
107 U5 **Noguera Pallaresa** ≈ NE Spain
107 U4 **Noguera Ribagorçana** ≈ NE Spain
172 N9 **Noheji** *var.* Nobeji. Aomori, Honshū, C Japan *40.51N 141.07E*
103 E19 **Nohfelden** Saarland, SW Germany *49.35N 7.08E*
40 A8 **Nohili Point** *headland* Kauai, Hawaii, USA, C Pacific Ocean *22.03N 159.48W*
106 G3 **Noia** Galicia, NW Spain *42.48N 8.52W*
105 N16 **Noire, Montagne** ▲ S France
13 P12 **Noire, Rivière** ≈ Quebec, SE Canada
12 J10 **Noire, Rivière** ≈ Quebec, SE Canada
Noire, Rivière *see* Black River
104 G6 **Noires, Montagnes** ▲ NW France
104 H8 **Noirmoutier-en-l'Île** Vendée, NW France *47.00N 2.15W*
104 H8 **Noirmoutier, Île de** *island* NW France
171 Jj17 **Nojima-zaki** *headland* Honshū, S Japan *34.54N 139.54E*
195 W8 **Noka** Nendö, E Solomon Islands *10.42S 165.57E*
85 G17 **Nokaneng** Ngamiland, NW Botswana *19.40S 22.12E*
95 L18 **Nokia** Länsi-Suomi, W Finland *61.28N 23.30E*
154 K11 **Nok Kundi** Baluchistān, SW Pakistan *28.49N 62.39E*
32 L14 **Nokomis** Illinois, N USA *39.18N 89.17W*
32 K5 **Nokomis, Lake** ⊞ Wisconsin, N USA
80 G9 **Nokou** Kanem, W Chad *14.36N 14.45E*
197 B12 **Nokuku** Espiritu Santo, W Vanuatu *14.56S 166.34E*
97 J18 **Nol** Västra Götaland, S Sweden *57.55N 12.03E*
81 H16 **Nola** Sangha-Mbaéré, SW Central African Republic *3.28N 16.05E*
27 P7 **Nolan** Texas, SW USA *32.15N 100.15W*
129 R15 **Nolinsk** Kirovskaya Oblast', NW Russian Federation *57.34N 49.54E*
97 B19 **Nólsoy** *Dan.* Nolsø *Island* Faeroe Islands *61.59N 6.39W*
194 F12 **Nomad** Western, SW Papau New Guinea *6.11S 142.13E*
170 B15 **Noma-zaki** *headland* Kyūshū, SW Japan *31.24N 130.07E*
42 K10 **Nombre de Dios** Durango, C Mexico *23.51N 104.13W*
44 I5 **Nombre de Dios, Cordillera** ▲ N Honduras
40 M9 **Nome** Alaska, USA *64.30N 165.24W*
31 Q6 **Nome** North Dakota, N USA *46.39N 97.49W*
40 M9 **Nome, Cape** *headland* Alaska, USA *64.25N 165.00W*
Nōmi-jima *see* Nishi-Nōmi-jima
12 M11 **Nominingue, Lac** ◎ Quebec, SE Canada
Nomoi Islands *see* Mortlock Islands
170 Bb13 **Nomo-zaki** *headland* Kyūshū, SW Japan *32.34N 129.45E*
200 S13 **Nomuka** *island* Nomuka Group, C Tonga
200 S14 **Nomuka Group** *island group* W Tonga
201 Q15 **Nomwin Atoll** *atoll* Hall Islands, C Micronesia
15 I8 **Nonacho Lake** ◎ Northwest Territories, NW Canada
Nondaburi *see* Nonthaburi
41 P12 **Nondalton** Alaska, USA *59.58N 154.51W*
169 V10 **Nong'an** Jilin, NE China *44.23N 125.04E*
178 I10 **Nong Bua Khok** Nakhon Ratchasima, C Thailand *15.23N 101.51E*
178 I9 **Nong Bua Lamphu** Udon Thani, E Thailand *17.11N 102.27E*
178 J7 **Nông Hèt** Xiangkhoang, N Laos *19.27N 104.02E*
Nongkaya *see* Nong Khai
178 I8 **Nong Khai** *var.* Mi Chai, Nongkaya. Nong Khai, E Thailand *17.52N 102.43E*
178 Gg15 **Nong Met** Surat Thani, SW Thailand *9.27N 99.09E*
85 L22 **Nongoma** KwaZulu/Natal, E South Africa *27.54S 31.40E*
178 Hh10 **Nong Phai** Phetchabun, C Thailand *15.58N 101.02E*
159 U13 **Nongstoin** Meghālaya, NE India *25.24N 91.19E*
85 C19 **Nonidas** Erongo, N Namibia *22.36S 14.40E*
Nonni *see* Nen Jiang
42 I7 **Nonoava** Chihuahua, N Mexico *27.24N 106.18W*
203 O3 **Nonouti** *prev.* Sydenham Island. *atoll* Tungaru, W Kiribati
178 Hh11 **Nonthaburi** *var.* Nondaburi, Nontha Buri. Nonthaburi, C Thailand *13.55N 100.33E*
104 L11 **Nontron** Dordogne, SW France *45.34N 0.41E*
189 P1 **Noonamah** Northern Territory, N Australia *12.46S 131.08E*
30 K2 **Noonan** North Dakota, N USA *48.51N 102.57W*
101 E14 **Noord-Beveland** *var.* North Beveland. *island* SW Netherlands
101 J14 **Noord-Brabant** *Eng.* North Brabant. ◆ *province* S Netherlands
100 H7 **Noorder Haaks** *spit* NW Netherlands
100 H9 **Noord-Holland** *Eng.* North Holland. ◆ *province* NW Netherlands
Noordhollandsch Kanaal *see* Noordhollands Kanaal
100 H8 **Noordhollands Kanaal** *var.* Noordhollandsch Kanaal. *canal* NW Netherlands
Noord-Kaap *see* Northern Cape
100 L8 **Noordoostpolder** *island* N Netherlands
47 P16 **Noordpunt** *headland* Curaçao, C Netherlands Antilles *12.21N 69.08W*
100 I8 **Noord-Scharwoude** Noord-Holland, NW Netherlands *52.42N 4.48E*
Noordwes *see* North-West
100 G11 **Noordwijk aan Zee** Zuid-Holland, W Netherlands *52.15N 4.25E*
100 H11 **Noordwijkerhout** Zuid-Holland, W Netherlands *52.16N 4.30E*
100 M7 **Noordwolde** *Fris.* Noardwâlde. Friesland, N Netherlands *52.54N 6.10E*
Noordzee *see* North Sea
100 H10 **Noordzee-Kanaal** *canal* NW Netherlands
95 K18 **Noormarkku** *Swe.* Norrmark. Länsi-Suomi, W Finland *61.34N 21.54E*
41 N8 **Noorvik** Alaska, USA *66.50N 161.01W*
8 J17 **Nootka Sound** *inlet* British Columbia, W Canada
84 A9 **Nóqui** Zaire, NW Angola *5.55S 13.26E*
97 L15 **Nora** Örebro, C Sweden *59.31N 15.01E*
153 Q13 **Norak** *Rus.* Nurek. W Tajikistan *38.23N 69.13E*
16 P14 **Noranda** Quebec, SE Canada *48.16N 79.03W*
31 W12 **Nora Springs** Iowa, C USA *43.08N 93.00W*
97 M14 **Norberg** Västmanland, C Sweden *60.04N 15.34E*
12 K13 **Norcan Lake** ◎ Ontario, SE Canada
207 R12 **Nord** Avannaarsua, N Greenland *81.38N 12.51W*
80 F13 **Nord** *Eng.* North. ◆ *province* N Cameroon
105 P2 **Nord** ◆ *department* N France
94 P1 **Nordaustlandet** *island* NE Svalbard
97 G24 **Nordborg** *Ger.* Nordburg. Sønderjylland, SW Denmark *55.04N 9.40E*
Nordburg *see* Nordborg
97 F23 **Nordby** Ribe, W Denmark *55.27N 8.25E*
9 P15 **Nordegg** Alberta, SW Canada *52.27N 116.06W*
102 E9 **Norden** Niedersachsen, NW Germany *53.36N 7.12E*
102 G10 **Nordenham** Niedersachsen, NW Germany *53.28N 8.27E*
126 Ii4 **Nordenshel'da, Arkhipelag** *island group* N Russian Federation
94 O3 **Nordenskiold Land** *physical region* W Svalbard
102 E9 **Norderney** *island* NW Germany
102 J9 **Norderstedt** Schleswig-Holstein, N Germany *53.42N 9.58E*
96 C11 **Nordfjord** *physical region* S Norway
96 D11 **Nordfjord** *fjord* S Norway
96 D11 **Nordfjordeid** Sogn og Fjordane, S Norway *61.54N 6.01E*
94 G11 **Nordfold** Nordland, C Norway *67.48N 15.16E*
Nordfriesische Inseln *see* North Frisian Islands
102 H7 **Nordfriesland** *cultural region* N Germany
103 K15 **Nordhausen** Thüringen, C Germany *51.31N 10.48E*
27 T13 **Nordheim** Texas, SW USA *28.55N 97.36W*
96 C13 **Nordhordland** *physical region* S Norway
102 E12 **Nordhorn** Niedersachsen, NW Germany *52.25N 7.04E*
94 I1 **Nordhurfjördhur** Vestfirdhir, NW Iceland *66.01N 21.33W*
94 J1 **Nordhurland Eystra** ◆ *region* N Iceland
94 I2 **Nordhurland Vestra** ◆ *region* N Iceland
180 H16 **Nord, Île du** *island* Inner Islands, NE Seychelles
97 F20 **Nordjylland** *off.* Nordjyllands Amt. ◆ *county* N Denmark
94 K7 **Nordkapp** *Eng.* North Cape. *headland* N Norway *71.10N 25.42E*
94 O1 **Nordkapp** *headland* N Svalbard *80.31N 19.58E*
94 L7 **Nordkinn** *headland* N Norway *71.07N 27.40E*
81 N19 **Nord Kivu** *off.* Région du Nord Kivu. ◆ *region* E Dem. Rep. Congo (Zaire)
94 G12 **Nordland** ◆ *county* C Norway
103 J21 **Nördlingen** Bayern, S Germany *48.49N 10.28E*
95 I16 **Nordmaling** Västerbotten, N Sweden *63.34N 19.30E*
97 K15 **Nordmark** Värmland, C Sweden *59.52N 14.04E*
Nord, Mer du *see* North Sea
96 F8 **Nordmøre** *physical region* S Norway
102 I8 **Nord-Ostsee-Kanal** *canal* N Germany
(0) J3 **Nordostrundingen** *headland* NE Greenland *83.00N 10.00W*
81 D14 **Nord-Ouest** *Eng.* North-West. ◆ *province* NW Cameroon
Nord-Ouest, Territoires du *see* Northwest Territories
105 N2 **Nord-Pas-de-Calais** ◆ *region* N France
103 F19 **Nordpfälzer Bergland** ▲ W Germany
Nord, Pointe *see* Fatua, Pointe
197 H5 **Nord, Province** ◆ *province* C New Caledonia
103 D14 **Nordrhein-Westfalen** *Eng.* North Rhine-Westphalia, *Fr.* Rhénanie du Nord-Westphalie. ◆ *state* W Germany
Nordsee/Nordsjøen/Nordsøen *see* North Sea
102 H7 **Nordstrand** *island* N Germany
95 E15 **Nord-Trøndelag** ◆ *county* C Norway
99 E19 **Nore** *Ir.* An Fheoir. ≈ S Ireland
31 Q14 **Norfolk** Nebraska, C USA *42.01N 97.25W*
23 X7 **Norfolk** Virginia, NE USA *36.51N 76.17W*
99 P19 **Norfolk** *cultural region* E England, UK
199 Ii1 **Norfolk Island** ◇ *Australian external territory* SW Pacific Ocean
183 P9 **Norfolk Ridge** *undersea feature* W Pacific Ocean
29 U8 **Norfork Lake** ⊞ Arkansas/Missouri, C USA
100 N6 **Norg** Drenthe, NE Netherlands *53.04N 6.28E*
Norge *see* Norway
97 D14 **Norheimsund** Hordaland, S Norway *60.22N 6.09E*
27 S16 **Norias** Texas, SW USA *26.47N 97.45W*
171 J14 **Norikura-dake** ▲ Honshū, S Japan *36.06N 137.33E*
126 I8 **Noril'sk** Taymyrskiy (Dolgano-Nenetskiy) Avtonomnyy Okrug, N Russian Federation *69.21N 88.01E*
12 I13 **Norland** Ontario, SE Canada *44.46N 78.48W*
23 V8 **Norlina** North Carolina, SE USA *36.26N 78.11W*
32 L13 **Normal** Illinois, N USA *40.30N 88.59W*
29 N11 **Norman** Oklahoma, C USA *35.13N 97.27W*
Norman *see* Tulita
195 O16 **Normanby Island** *island* SE PNG
Normandes, Îles *see* Channel Islands
60 G9 **Normandia** Roraima, N Brazil *3.57N 59.39W*
104 L5 **Normandie** *Eng.* Normandy. *cultural region* N France
104 J5 **Normandie, Collines de** *hill range* NW France
Normandy *see* Normandie
27 V9 **Normangee** Texas, SW USA *31.01N 96.06W*
23 Q10 **Norman, Lake** ⊞ North Carolina, SE USA
46 K13 **Norman Manley** ✈ (Kingston) E Jamaica *17.55N 76.46W*
189 U5 **Norman River** ≈ Queensland, NE Australia
189 U4 **Normanton** Queensland, NE Australia *17.48S 141.07E*
15 Gg5 **Norman Wells** Northwest Territories, NW Canada *65.18N 126.42W*
10 H12 **Normétal** Quebec, S Canada *48.58N 79.22W*
9 V15 **Norquay** Saskatchewan, S Canada *51.51N 102.04W*
96 N11 **Norra Dellen** ◎ C Sweden
95 G15 **Norråker** Jämtland, C Sweden *64.25N 15.40E*
96 N12 **Norrala** Gävleborg, C Sweden *61.22N 17.04E*
Norra Ny *see* Stöllet
94 G13 **Norra Storjfjället** ▲ N Sweden *65.57N 15.15E*
94 I13 **Norrbotten** ◆ *county* N Sweden
Nørre Aaby *see* Nørre Åby
97 G23 **Nørre Åby** *var.* Nørre Aaby. Fyn, C Denmark *55.28N 9.52E*
97 I24 **Nørre Alslev** Storstrøm, SE Denmark *54.54N 11.52E*
97 E23 **Nørre Nebel** Ribe, W Denmark *55.45N 8.16E*
97 G20 **Nørresundby** Nordjylland, N Denmark *57.05N 9.55E*
23 N8 **Norris Lake** ⊞ Tennessee, S USA
20 I15 **Norristown** Pennsylvania, NE USA *40.07N 75.20W*
97 N17 **Norrköping** Östergötland, S Sweden *58.34N 16.10E*
Norrmark *see* Noormarkku
96 N13 **Norrsundet** Gävleborg, C Sweden *60.55N 17.09E*
97 P15 **Norrtälje** Stockholm, C Sweden *59.45N 18.42E*
188 L12 **Norseman** Western Australia *32.16S 121.45E*
95 I14 **Norsjö** Västerbotten, N Sweden *64.55N 19.30E*
97 G16 **Norsjø** ◎ S Norway
126 Mm15 **Norsk** Amurskaya Oblast', SE Russian Federation *52.20N 129.57E*
Norske Havet *see* Norwegian Sea
197 C13 **Norsup** Malekula, C Vanuatu *16.05S 167.24E*
203 V15 **Norte, Cabo** *headland* Easter Island, Chile, E Pacific Ocean *27.03S 109.24W*
56 F7 **Norte de Santander** *off.* Departamento de Norte de Santander. ◆ *province* N Colombia
63 E21 **Norte, Punta** *headland* E Argentina *36.17S 56.46W*
23 R13 **North** South Carolina, SE USA *33.37N 81.06W*
North *see* Nord
20 L10 **North Adams** Massachusetts, NE USA *42.40N 73.06W*
115 L17 **North Albanian Alps** *Alb.* Bjeshkët e Namuna, *SCr.* Prokletije. ▲ Albania/Yugoslavia
99 M15 **Northallerton** N England, UK *54.19N 1.25W*
188 J12 **Northam** Western Australia *31.40S 116.40E*
85 J20 **Northam** Northern, N South Africa *24.56S 27.18E*
1 **North America** *continent*
1 N12 **North American Basin** *undersea feature* W Sargasso Sea
(0) C5 **North American Plate** *tectonic feature*
20 M11 **North Amherst** Massachusetts, NE USA *42.24N 72.31W*
99 N20 **Northampton** C England, UK *52.13N 0.54W*
99 M20 **Northamptonshire** *cultural region* C England, UK
157 P18 **North Andaman** *island* Andaman Islands, India, NE Indian Ocean
67 D25 **North Arm** East Falkland, Falkland Islands *52.06S 59.21W*
23 Q13 **North Augusta** South Carolina, SE USA *33.30N 81.58W*
181 W8 **North Australian Basin** *Fr.* Bassin Nord de l' Australie. *undersea feature* E Indian Ocean
33 R11 **North Baltimore** Ohio, N USA *41.10N 83.40W*
9 T15 **North Battleford** Saskatchewan, S Canada *52.46N 108.19W*
12 H11 **North Bay** Ontario, S Canada *46.19N 79.28W*
10 H6 **North Belcher Islands** *island group* Belcher Islands, Nunavut, C Canada
31 R15 **North Bend** Nebraska, C USA *41.27N 96.46W*
34 E14 **North Bend** Oregon, NW USA *43.24N 124.13W*
98 K12 **North Berwick** SE Scotland, UK *56.03N 2.44W*
North Beveland *see* Noord-Beveland
North Borneo *see* Sabah
191 P5 **North Bourke** New South Wales, SE Australia *30.03S 145.56E*
North Brabant *see* Noord-Brabant
190 F2 **North Branch Neales** *seasonal river* South Australia
46 M6 **North Caicos** *island* NW Turks and Caicos Islands
28 L10 **North Canadian River** ≈ Oklahoma, C USA
33 U12 **North Canton** Ohio, N USA *40.52N 81.24W*
11 R13 **North, Cape** *headland* Cape Breton Island, Nova Scotia, SE Canada *47.06N 60.24W*
192 I1 **North Cape** *headland* North Island, NZ *34.23S 173.02E*
195 N9 **North Cape** *headland* New Ireland, NE PNG *2.33S 150.48E*
North Cape *see* Nordkapp
20 J17 **North Cape May** New Jersey, NE USA *38.59N 74.55W*
10 C9 **North Caribou Lake** ◎ Ontario, C Canada
23 U10 **North Carolina** *off.* State of North Carolina; *also known as* Old North State, Tar Heel State, Turpentine State. ◆ *state* SE USA
North Celebes *see* Sulawesi Utara
161 J24 **North Central Province** ◆ *province* N Sri Lanka
33 S4 **North Channel** *lake channel* Canada/USA
99 G14 **North Channel** *strait* Northern Ireland/Scotland, UK
23 S14 **North Charleston** South Carolina, SE USA *32.51N 79.58W*
33 N10 **North Chicago** Illinois, N USA *42.19N 87.50W*
205 Y10 **Northcliffe Glacier** *glacier* Antarctica
33 Q14 **North College Hill** Ohio, N USA *39.13N 84.33W*
27 O8 **North Concho River** ≈ Texas, SW USA
21 O8 **North Conway** New Hampshire, NE USA *44.03N 71.06W*
29 V14 **North Crossett** Arkansas, C USA *33.10N 91.56W*
30 L4 **North Dakota** *off.* State of North Dakota; *also known as* Flickertail State, Peace Garden State, Sioux State. ◆ *state* N USA
North Devon Island *see* Devon Island
99 O22 **North Downs** *hill range* SE England, UK
20 C11 **North East** Pennsylvania, NE USA *42.13N 79.49W*
85 I18 **North East** ◆ *district* NE Botswana
67 G15 **North East Bay** *bay* Ascension Island, C Atlantic Ocean
40 L10 **Northeast Cape** *headland* Saint Lawrence Island, Alaska, USA *63.16N 168.50W*
178 Mm13 **Northeast Cay** *island* NW Spratly Islands
83 J17 **North Eastern** ◆ *province* Kenya
North East Frontier Agency/North East Frontier Agency of Assam *see* Arunāchal Pradesh
67 E25 **North East Island** *island* E Falkland Islands
201 V11 **Northeast Island** *island* Chuuk, C Micronesia
46 L12 **North East Point** *headland* E Jamaica *18.09N 76.19W*
46 L6 **Northeast Point** *headland* Great Inagua, S Bahamas *21.18N 73.01W*
46 K5 **Northeast Point** *headland* Acklins Island, SE Bahamas *22.43N 73.50W*
203 Z2 **Northeast Point** *headland* Kiritimati, E Kiribati *10.22S 105.45E*
46 H2 **Northeast Providence Channel** *channel* N Bahamas
103 J14 **Northeim** Niedersachsen, C Germany *51.42N 10.00E*
31 X14 **North English** Iowa, C USA *41.30N 92.04W*
144 G8 **Northern** ◆ *district* N Israel
84 M12 **Northern** ◆ *region* N Malawi
194 L15 **Northern** ◆ *province* S PNG
85 J20 **Northern** *off.* Northern Province; *prev.* Northern Transvaal. ◆ *province* NE South Africa
82 D7 **Northern** ◆ *state* N Sudan
84 K12 **Northern** ◆ *province* NE Zambia
82 B13 **Northern Bahr el Ghazal** ◆ *state* SW Sudan
Northern Border Region *see* Al Ḩudūd ash Shamālīyah
85 F24 **Northern Cape** *off.* Northern Cape Province, *Afr.* Noord-Kaap. ◆ *province* W South Africa
202 K14 **Northern Cook Islands** *island group* N Cook Islands
82 B8 **Northern Darfur** ◆ *state* NW Sudan
Northern Dvina *see* Severnaya Dvina
99 F14 **Northern Ireland** *var.* The Six Counties. *political division* UK
82 D9 **Northern Kordofan** ◆ *state* C Sudan
197 K14 **Northern Lau Group** *island group* Lau Group, NE Fiji
196 K3 **Northern Mariana Islands** ◇ *US commonwealth territory* W Pacific Ocean
161 J23 **Northern Province** ◆ *province* N Sri Lanka
Northern Rhodesia *see* Zambia
Northern Sporades *see* Vóreioi Sporádes
190 D1 **Northern Territory** ◆ *territory* N Australia
Northern Transvaal *see* Northern
Northern Ural Hills *see* Severnyye Uvaly
86 I9 **North European Plain** *plain* N Europe
29 V2 **North Fabius River** ≈ Missouri, C USA
67 D24 **North Falkland Sound** *sound* N Falkland Islands
31 V9 **Northfield** Minnesota, N USA *44.27N 93.10W*
21 O9 **Northfield** New Hampshire, NE USA *43.26N 71.34W*
183 Q8 **North Fiji Basin** *undersea feature* N Coral Sea
99 Q22 **North Foreland** *headland* SE England, UK *51.22N 1.26E*
37 P6 **North Fork American River** ≈ California, W USA
41 R7 **North Fork Chandalar River** ≈ Alaska, USA
30 K7 **North Fork Grand River** ≈ North Dakota/South Dakota, N USA
23 O6 **North Fork Kentucky River** ≈ Kentucky, S USA
41 Q7 **North Fork Koyukuk River** ≈ Alaska, USA
41 Q10 **North Fork Kuskokwim River** ≈ Alaska, USA
28 K11 **North Fork Red River** ≈ Oklahoma/Texas, SW USA
28 K3 **North Fork Solomon River** ≈ Kansas, C USA
25 W14 **North Fort Myers** Florida, SE USA *26.40N 81.52W*
33 P5 **North Fox Island** *island* Michigan, N USA
102 G6 **North Frisian Islands** *var.* Nordfriesische Inseln. *island group* N Germany
207 N9 **North Geomagnetic Pole** *pole* Arctic Ocean *78.30N 69.00W*
20 M13 **North Haven** Connecticut, NE USA *41.25N 72.51W*
192 J5 **North Head** *headland* North Island, NZ *36.23S 174.01E*
20 L6 **North Hero** Vermont, NE USA *44.49N 73.14W*
37 O7 **North Highlands** California, W USA *38.40N 121.25W*
North Holland *see* Noord-Holland
83 I16 **North Horr** Eastern, N Kenya *3.17N 37.08E*
157 K21 **North Huvadhu Atoll** *var.* Gaafu Alifu Atoll. *atoll* S Maldives
67 A24 **North Island** *island* W Falkland Islands
192 N9 **North Island** *island* N NZ
23 U14 **North Island** *island* South Carolina, SE USA
33 O11 **North Judson** Indiana, N USA *41.12N 86.44W*
North Kazakhstan *see* Severnyy Kazakhstan
33 V10 **North Kingsville** Ohio, N USA *41.54N 80.41W*
169 Y13 **North Korea** *off.* Democratic People's Republic of Korea, *Kor.* Chosŏn-minjujuŭi-inmin-kanghwaguk. ◆ *republic* E Asia
159 X11 **North Lakhimpur** Assam, NE India *27.10N 94.00E*
192 J3 **Northland** *off.* Northland Region. ◆ *region* North Island, NZ
199 J12 **Northland Plateau** *undersea feature* S Pacific Ocean
37 X11 **North Las Vegas** Nevada, W USA *36.12N 115.07W*
33 O11 **North Liberty** Indiana, N USA *41.36N 86.22W*
31 X14 **North Liberty** Iowa, C USA *41.45N 91.36W*
29 V12 **North Little Rock** Arkansas, C USA *34.46N 92.15W*
30 M13 **North Loup River** ≈ Nebraska, C USA
157 K18 **North Maalhosmadulu Atoll** *var.* North Malosmadulu Atoll, Raa Atoll. *atoll* N Maldives
33 U10 **North Madison** Ohio, N USA *41.48N 81.03W*
33 P12 **North Manchester** Indiana, N USA *41.00N 85.45W*
33 P6 **North Manitou Island** *island* Michigan, N USA
31 U10 **North Mankato** Minnesota, N USA *44.11N 94.03W*
25 Z15 **North Miami** Florida, SE USA *25.54N 80.11W*
157 K18 **North Miladummadulu Atoll** *atoll* N Maldives
North Minch *see* Minch, The
25 W15 **North Naples** Florida, SE USA *26.13N 81.47W*
183 P8 **North New Hebrides Trench** *undersea feature* N Coral Sea
25 Y15 **North New River Canal** ≈ Florida, SE USA
157 K20 **North Nilandhe Atoll** *var.* Faafu Atoll. *atoll* C Maldives
38 L2 **North Ogden** Utah, W USA *41.18N 111.57W*
North Ossetia *see* Severnaya Osetiya-Alaniya, Respublika
37 S10 **North Palisade** ▲ California, W USA *37.06N 118.31W*
201 U11 **North Pass** *passage* Chuuk Islands, C Micronesia
30 M15 **North Platte** Nebraska, C USA *41.07N 100.46W*
35 X17 **North Platte River** ≈ C USA
67 G14 **North Point** *headland* Ascension Island, C Atlantic Ocean
180 I16 **North Point** *headland* Mahé, NE Seychelles *4.22S 55.28E*
33 S6 **North Point** *headland* Michigan, N USA *45.01N 83.16W*
33 R5 **North Point** *headland* Michigan, N USA *45.21N 83.30W*
41 S9 **North Pole** Alaska, USA *64.42N 147.09W*
207 R9 **North Pole** *pole* Arctic Ocean *90.00N 0.00W*
25 O4 **Northport** Alabama, S USA *33.13N 87.34W*
25 W14 **North Port** Florida, SE USA *27.03N 82.15W*
34 L6 **Northport** Washington, NW USA *48.54N 117.48W*
34 L12 **North Powder** Oregon, NW USA *45.00N 117.56W*
31 U13 **North Raccoon River** ≈ Iowa, C USA
North Rhine-Westphalia *see* Nordrhein-Westfalen
99 M16 **North Riding** *cultural region* N England, UK
98 G5 **North Rona** *island* NW Scotland, UK
98 K4 **North Ronaldsay** *island* NE Scotland, UK
38 L2 **North Salt Lake** Utah, W USA *40.51N 111.54W*
9 P15 **North Saskatchewan** ≈ Alberta/Saskatchewan, S Canada
37 X5 **North Schell Peak** ▲ Nevada, W USA *39.25N 114.34W*
North Scotia Ridge *see* South Georgia Ridge
88 D10 **North Sea** *Dan.* Nordsøen, *Dut.* Noordzee, *Fr.* Mer du Nord, *Ger.* Nordsee, *Nor.* Nordsjøen; *prev.* German Ocean, *Lat.* Mare Germanicum. *sea* NW Europe
37 T6 **North Shoshone Peak** ▲ Nevada, W USA *39.08N 117.28W*
North Siberian Lowland/North Siberian Plain *see* Severo-Sibirskaya Nizmennost'
31 R13 **North Sioux City** South Dakota, N USA *42.31N 96.28W*
98 K4 **North Sound, The** *sound* N Scotland, UK
191 T4 **North Star** New South Wales, SE Australia *28.55S 150.25E*
North Star State *see* Minnesota
191 V3 **North Stradbroke Island** *island* Queensland, E Australia
North Sulawesi *see* Sulawesi Utara
North Sumatra *see* Sumatera Utara
12 D17 **North Sydenham** ≈ Ontario, S Canada
20 H9 **North Syracuse** New York, NE USA *43.07N 76.07W*
192 K9 **North Taranaki Bight** *gulf* North Island, NZ
10 H9 **North Twin Island** *island* Nunavut, C Canada
98 E8 **North Uist** *island* NW Scotland, UK
99 L14 **Northumberland** *cultural region* N England, UK
189 Y7 **Northumberland Isles** *island group* Queensland, NE Australia
11 Q14 **Northumberland Strait** *strait* SE Canada
34 G14 **North Umpqua River** ≈ Oregon, NW USA
47 Q13 **North Union** Saint Vincent, Saint Vincent and the Grenadines *13.15N 61.07W*
8 L17 **North Vancouver** British Columbia, SW Canada *49.21N 123.04W*
20 K9 **Northville** New York, NE USA *43.13N 74.08W*
99 Q19 **North Walsham** E England, UK *52.49N 1.22E*
41 T10 **Northway** Alaska, USA *62.57N 141.56W*
85 G21 **North-West** *off.* North-West Province, *Afr.* Noordwes. ◆ *province* N South Africa
North-West *see* Nord-Ouest
66 I6 **Northwest Atlantic Mid-Ocean Canyon** *undersea feature* N Atlantic Ocean
188 G8 **North West Cape** *headland* Western Australia *21.48S 114.10E*
40 J9 **Northwest Cape** *headland* Saint Lawrence Island, Alaska, USA *63.46N 171.45W*
84 H13 **North Western** ◆ *province* W Zambia
161 J24 **North Western Province** ◆ *province* W Sri Lanka
155 U4 **North-West Frontier Province** ◆ *province* NW Pakistan
98 H8 **North West Highlands** ▲ N Scotland, UK
199 Hh4 **Northwest Pacific Basin** *undersea feature* NW Pacific Ocean
203 Y2 **Northwest Point** *headland* Kiritimati, E Kiribati *10.25S 105.34E*
46 G1 **Northwest Providence Channel** *channel* N Bahamas
11 Q8 **North West River** Newfoundland, E Canada *53.30N 60.10W*
15 Ii5 **Northwest Territories** *Fr.* Territoires du Nord-Ouest. ◆ *territory* NW Canada
99 K18 **Northwich** C England, UK *53.16N 2.31W*
27 Q5 **North Wichita River** ≈ Texas, SW USA
20 J17 **North Wildwood** New Jersey, NE USA *39.00N 74.45W*
23 R9 **North Wilkesboro** North Carolina, SE USA *36.09N 81.09W*
21 P8 **North Windham** Maine, NE USA *43.51N 70.25W*
207 Q6 **Northwind Plain** *undersea feature* Arctic Ocean
31 V11 **Northwood** Iowa, C USA *43.26N 93.13W*
31 Q4 **Northwood** North Dakota, N USA *47.43N 97.34W*
99 M15 **North York Moors** *moorland* N England, UK
27 V9 **North Zulch** Texas, SW USA *30.54N 96.06W*
28 K2 **Norton** Kansas, C USA *39.49N 99.53W*
33 S13 **Norton** Ohio, N USA *40.25N 83.04W*
23 P7 **Norton** Virginia, NE USA *36.55N 82.37W*
41 N9 **Norton Bay** *bay* Alaska, USA
Norton de Matos *see* Balombo
33 O9 **Norton Shores** Michigan, N USA *43.10N 86.15W*
40 M10 **Norton Sound** *inlet* Alaska, USA
29 Q3 **Nortonville** Kansas, C USA *39.25N 95.19W*
104 I8 **Nort-sur-Erdre** Loire-Atlantique, NW France *47.27N 1.30W*
205 N2 **Norvegia, Cape** *headland* Antarctica *71.16S 12.25W*
20 L13 **Norwalk** Connecticut, NE USA *41.08N 73.28W*
31 V14 **Norwalk** Iowa, C USA *41.28N 93.40W*
33 S11 **Norwalk** Ohio, N USA *41.14N 82.37W*
21 P7 **Norway** Maine, NE USA *44.13N 70.30W*
33 N5 **Norway** Michigan, N USA *45.47N 87.54W*
95 E17 **Norway** *off.* Kingdom of Norway, *Nor.* Norge. ◆ *monarchy* N Europe
9 X13 **Norway House** Manitoba, C Canada *53.58N 97.49W*
207 R16 **Norwegian Basin** *undersea feature* NW Norwegian Sea
86 D6 **Norwegian Sea** *Nor.* Norske Havet. *sea* NE Atlantic Ocean
207 S17 **Norwegian Trench** *undersea feature* NE North Sea
12 F16 **Norwich** Ontario, S Canada *42.57N 80.37W*
99 Q19 **Norwich** E England, UK *52.37N 1.18E*
21 N13 **Norwich** Connecticut, NE USA *41.30N 72.02W*
20 I11 **Norwich** New York, NE USA *42.31N 75.31W*
31 U9 **Norwood** Minnesota, N USA *44.46N 93.55W*
33 Q15 **Norwood** Ohio, N USA *39.07N 84.27W*
12 H11 **Nosbonsing, Lake** ◎ Ontario, S Canada
Nösen *see* Bistriţa
172 P1 **Noshappu-misaki** *headland* Hokkaidō, NE Japan *45.26N 141.38E*
171 M9 **Noshiro** *var.* Nosiro; *prev.* Noshirominato. Akita, Honshū, C Japan *40.10N 140.01E*
Noshirominato/Nosiro *see* Noshiro
119 Q3 **Nosivka** *Rus.* Nosovka. Chernihivs'ka Oblast', NE Ukraine *50.55N 31.37E*
69 T14 **Nosop** *var.* Nossob, Nossop. ≈ Botswana/Namibia
129 S4 **Nosovaya** Nenetskiy Avtonomnyy Okrug, NW Russian Federation *68.12N 54.33E*
Nosovka *see* Nosivka
149 V11 **Noṣratābād** Sīstān va Balūchestān, E Iran *29.53N 59.57E*
97 J18 **Nossebro** Västra Götaland, S Sweden *58.12N 12.42E*
98 K6 **Noss Head** *headland* N Scotland, UK *58.29N 3.03W*
Nossi-Bé *see* Be, Nosy
85 E20 **Nossob** ≈ E Namibia
Nossob/Nossop *see* Nosop
180 J2 **Nosy Be** ✈ Antsiraňana, N Madagascar *23.36S 47.36E*
180 J6 **Nosy Varika** Fianarantsoa, SE Madagascar *20.36S 48.31E*
12 L10 **Notawassi** ≈ Quebec, SE Canada
12 M9 **Notawassi, Lac** ◎ Quebec, SE Canada
38 J5 **Notch Peak** ▲ Utah, W USA *39.08N 113.24W*
112 G10 **Noteć** *Ger.* Netze. ≈ NW Poland
Nóties Sporádes *see* Dodekánisos
117 J22 **Nótion Aigaíon** *Eng.* Aegean South. ◆ *region* E Greece
117 H18 **Nótios Evvoïkós Kólpos** *gulf* E Greece
117 B16 **Nótio Stenó Kérkyras** *strait* W Greece
109 L25 **Noto** *anc.* Netum. Sicilia, Italy, C Mediterranean Sea *36.52N 15.04E*
171 J12 **Noto** Ishikawa, Honshū, SW Japan *37.18N 137.11E*
97 G15 **Notodden** Telemark, S Norway *59.33N 9.15E*
109 L25 **Noto, Golfo di** *gulf* Sicilia, Italy, C Mediterranean Sea
171 J12 **Noto-hantō** *peninsula* Honshū, SW Japan
171 J12 **Noto-jima** *island* SW Japan
172 Qq5 **Notoro-ko** ◎ Hokkaidō, NE Japan
11 T11 **Notre Dame Bay** *bay* Newfoundland, E Canada
13 P6 **Notre-Dame-de-Lorette** Quebec, SE Canada *49.05N 72.24W*
12 L11 **Notre-Dame-de-Pontmain** Quebec, SE Canada *46.18N 75.37W*
13 T8 **Notre-Dame-du-Lac** Quebec, SE Canada *47.36N 68.48W*
13 Q6 **Notre-Dame-du-Rosaire** Quebec, SE Canada *48.48N 71.27W*
13 U8 **Notre-Dame, Monts** ▲ Quebec, S Canada
79 R16 **Notsé** S Togo *6.53N 1.09E*
172 R7 **Notsuke-suidō** *strait* Japan/Russian Federation
172 R7 **Notsuke-zaki** *headland* Hokkaidō, NE Japan *43.33N 145.18E*
12 G14 **Nottawasaga** ≈ Ontario, S Canada
12 G14 **Nottawasaga Bay** *lake bay* Ontario, S Canada
10 I11 **Nottaway** ≈ Quebec, SE Canada
25 S1 **Nottely Lake** ⊞ Georgia, SE USA
97 H16 **Nøtterøy** *island* S Norway
99 M19 **Nottingham** C England, UK *52.58N 1.10W*
16 N5 **Nottingham Island** *island* Nunavut, NE Canada
99 N18 **Nottinghamshire** *cultural region* C England, UK
23 V7 **Nottoway** Virginia, NE USA *37.07N 78.03W*
23 V7 **Nottoway River** ≈ Virginia, NE USA
78 G7 **Nouâdhibou** *prev.* Port-Étienne. Dakhlet Nouâdhibou, W Mauritania *20.54N 17.01W*
78 G7 **Nouâdhibou** ✈ Dakhlet Nouâdhibou, W Mauritania *20.59N 17.02W*
78 F7 **Nouâdhibou, Dakhlet** *prev.* Baie du Lévrier. *bay* W Mauritania
78 F7 **Nouâdhibou, Râs** *prev.* Cap Blanc. *headland* NW Mauritania *20.48N 17.03W*

◆ Country ● Country Capital ◇ Dependent Territory ○ Dependent Territory Capital ◆ Administrative Region ✈ International Airport ▲ Mountain ▲ Mountain Range Volcano ≈ River ◎ Lake ⊞ Reservoir

Nouakchott – Oahu

78 G9 **Nouakchott** ● (Mauritania) Nouakchott District, SW Mauritania *18.09N 15.58W*
78 G9 **Nouakchott** ✕ Trarza, SW Mauritania *18.18N 15.54W*
123 K13 **Noual, Sebkhet en** *var.* Sabkhat an Nawāl. *salt flat* C Tunisia
78 G8 **Nouâmghâr** *var.* Nouamrhar. Dakhlet Nouâdhibou, W Mauritania *19.22N 16.31W*
Nouamrhar *see* Nouâmghâr
Nouă Sulița *see* Novoselytsya
197 I7 **Nouméa** ○ (New Caledonia) Province Sud, S New Caledonia *22.13S 166.29E*
81 E15 **Noun** ≈ C Cameroon
79 N12 **Nouna** W Burkina *12.43N 3.54W*
85 H24 **Noupoort** Northern Cape, C South Africa *31.10S 24.57E*
Nouveau-Brunswick *see* New Brunswick
Nouveau-Comptoir *see* Wemindji
13 T4 **Nouvel, Lacs** ◎ Quebec, SE Canada
13 W7 **Nouvelle** Quebec, SE Canada *48.07N 66.16W*
13 W7 **Nouvelle** ≈ Quebec, SE Canada
Nouvelle-Calédonie *see* New Caledonia
Nouvelle Écosse *see* Nova Scotia
105 R3 **Nouzonville** Ardennes, N France *49.49N 4.45E*
153 Q11 **Nov** *Rus.* Nau. NW Tajikistan *40.10N 69.16E*
61 I21 **Nova Alvorada** Mato Grosso do Sul, SW Brazil *21.25S 54.19W*
Novabad *see* Navobod
113 D19 **Nová Bystřice** *Ger.* Neubistritz. Budějovický Kraj, S Czech Republic *48.59N 15.05E*
118 H13 **Novaci** Gorj, SW Romania *45.08N 23.39E*
Nova Civitas *see* Neustadt an der Weinstrasse
Novaesium *see* Neuss
62 H10 **Nova Esperança** Paraná, S Brazil *23.09S 52.13W*
108 H11 **Novafeltria** Marche, C Italy *43.54N 12.18E*
62 Q9 **Nova Friburgo** Rio de Janeiro, SE Brazil *22.16S 42.34W*
84 D12 **Nova Gaia** *var.* Cambundi-Catembo. Malanje, NE Angola *10.03S 17.31E*
111 S12 **Nova Gorica** W Slovenia *45.57N 13.40E*
114 G10 **Nova Gradiška** *Ger.* Neugradisk, *Hung.* Újgradiska. Brod-Posavina, NE Croatia *45.15N 17.23E*
62 K7 **Nova Granada** São Paulo, S Brazil *20.33S 49.19W*
62 O10 **Nova Iguaçu** Rio de Janeiro, SE Brazil *22.31S 44.04W*
119 S10 **Nova Kakhovka** *Rus.* Novaya Kakhovka. Khersons'ka Oblast', SE Ukraine *46.45N 33.19E*
Nová Karvinná *see* Karviná
Nova Lamego *see* Gabú
Nova Lisboa *see* Huambo
114 C11 **Novalja** Lika-Senj, W Croatia *44.33N 14.53E*
121 M14 **Novalukoml'** *Rus.* Novolukoml'. Vitsyebskaya Voblasts', N Belarus *54.40N 29.09E*
Nova Mambone *see* Mambone
85 P16 **Nova Nabúri** Zambézia, NE Mozambique *16.47S 38.55E*
119 Q9 **Nova Odesa** *var.* Novaya Odessa. Mykolayivs'ka Oblast', S Ukraine *47.18N 31.45E*
62 H10 **Nova Olímpia** Paraná, S Brazil *23.28S 53.12W*
63 I15 **Nova Prata** Rio Grande do Sul, S Brazil *28.45S 51.37W*
12 H12 **Novar** Ontario, S Canada *45.26N 79.14W*
108 C7 **Novara** *anc.* Novaria. Piemonte, NW Italy *45.27N 8.36E*
Novaria *see* Novara
119 P7 **Novarkanels'k** Kirovohrads'ka Oblast', C Ukraine *48.39N 30.48E*
11 P15 **Nova Scotia** *Fr.* Nouvelle Écosse. ◐ *province* SE Canada
(0) M9 **Nova Scotia** *physical region* SE Canada
36 M8 **Novato** California, W USA *38.06N 122.35W*
199 Jj8 **Nova Trough** *undersea feature* W Pacific Ocean
118 L7 **Nova Ushtsya** Khmel'nyts'ka Oblast', W Ukraine *48.50N 27.16E*
85 M17 **Nova Vanduzi** Manica, C Mozambique *18.54S 33.18E*
119 U5 **Nova Vodolaha** *Rus.* Novaya Vodolaga. Kharkivs'ka Oblast', E Ukraine *49.42N 35.48E*
126 L13 **Novaya Chara** Chitinskaya Oblast', S Russian Federation *56.45N 117.58E*
126 J14 **Novaya Igirma** Irkutskaya Oblast', C Russian Federation *57.08N 103.52E*
Novaya Kakhovka *see* Nova Kakhovka
150 E10 **Novaya Kazanka** Zapadnyy Kazakhstan, W Kazakhstan *48.57N 49.34E*
128 I12 **Novaya Ladoga** Leningradskaya Oblast', NW Russian Federation *60.03N 32.15E*
125 Ee10 **Novaya Lyalya** Sverdlovskaya Oblast, C Russian Federation *59.01N 60.37E*
131 R5 **Novaya Malykla** Ul'yanovskaya Oblast', W Russian Federation *54.13N 49.55E*
Novaya Odessa *see* Nova Odesa
126 M4 **Novaya Sibir', Ostrov** *island* Novosibirskiye Ostrova, NE Russian Federation
Novaya Vodolaga *see* Nova Vodolaha
121 P17 **Novaya Yel'nya** *Rus.* Novaya Yel'nya. Mahilyowskaya Voblasts', E Belarus *53.16N 31.13E*
125 G4 **Novaya Zemlya** *island group* N Russian Federation
Novaya Zemlya Trough *see* East Novaya Zemlya Trough
116 K10 **Nova Zagora** Sliven, C Bulgaria *42.29N 26.00E*
107 S12 **Novelda** País Valenciano, E Spain *38.24N 0.45W*
113 H19 **Nové Mesto nad Váhom** *Ger.* Waagneustadtl, *Hung.* Vágújhely. Trenčiansky Kraj, W Slovakia *48.48N 17.50E*
113 F17 **Nové Město na Moravě** *Ger.* Neustadtl in Mähren. Jihlavský Kraj, C Czech Republic *49.34N 16.04E*
Novesium *see* Neuss
113 I21 **Nové Zámky** *Ger.* Neuhäusel, *Hung.* Érsekújvár. Nitriansky Kraj, SW Slovakia *49.00N 18.10E*
125 C6 **Novgorod** Novgorodskaya Oblast', W Russian Federation *58.31N 31.15E*
Novgorod-Severskiy *see* Novhorod-Sivers'kyy
125 C6 **Novgorodskaya Oblast'** ◐ *province* W Russian Federation
119 R8 **Novhorodka** Kirovohrads'ka Oblast', C Ukraine *48.21N 32.38E*
119 R2 **Novhorod-Sivers'kyy** *Rus.* Novgorod-Severskiy. Chernihivs'ka Oblast', NE Ukraine *52.00N 33.15E*
33 R10 **Novi** Michigan, N USA *42.28N 83.28W*
Novi *see* Novi Vinodolski
114 L9 **Novi Bečej** *prev.* Új-Becse, Vološinovo, *Ger.* Neubetsche, *Hung.* Törökbecse. Serbia, N Yugoslavia *45.36N 20.09E*
27 Q8 **Novice** Texas, SW USA *32.00N 99.38W*
114 A9 **Novigrad** Istra, NW Croatia *45.19N 13.33E*
Novi Grad *see* Bosanski Novi
116 G9 **Novi Iskŭr** Sofiya-Grad, W Bulgaria *42.46N 23.19E*
108 C9 **Novi Ligure** Piemonte, NW Italy *44.46N 8.46E*
101 L22 **Noville** Luxembourg, SE Belgium *50.04N 5.46E*
204 I10 **Noville Peninsula** *peninsula* Thurston Island, Antarctica
Noviodunum *see* Soissons, Aisne, France
Noviodunum *see* Nevers, Nièvre, France
Noviodunum *see* Nyon, Vaud, Switzerland
Noviomagus *see* Lisieux, France
Noviomagus *see* Nijmegen, Netherlands
116 M8 **Novi Pazar** Shumen, NE Bulgaria *43.21N 27.13E*
115 M15 **Novi Pazar** *Turk.* Yenipazar. Serbia, S Yugoslavia *43.09N 20.31E*
114 K10 **Novi Sad** *Ger.* Neusatz, *Hung.* Újvidék. Serbia, N Yugoslavia *45.16N 19.49E*
119 T6 **Novi Sanzhary** Poltavs'ka Oblast', C Ukraine *49.21N 34.18E*
114 H12 **Novi Travnik** *prev.* Pučarevo. Federacija Bosna I Hercegovina, C Bosnia and Herzegovina *44.12N 17.39E*
114 B10 **Novi Vinodolski** *var.* Novi. Primorje-Gorski Kotar, NW Croatia *45.08N 14.46E*
60 F12 **Novo Airão** Amazonas, N Brazil *2.06S 61.19W*
131 N14 **Novoaleksandrovsk** Stavropol'skiy Kray, SW Russian Federation *44.41N 43.01E*
Novoalekseyevka *see* Zhobda
126 H14 **Novoaltaysk** Altayskiy Kray, S Russian Federation *53.22N 83.58E*
131 N9 **Novoanninskiy** Volgogradskaya Oblast', SW Russian Federation *50.31N 42.43E*
60 F13 **Novo Aripuanã** Amazonas, N Brazil *5.04S 60.19W*
119 Y6 **Novoaydar** Luhans'ka Oblast', E Ukraine *49.00N 39.00E*
119 X9 **Novoazovs'k** *Rus.* Novoazovsk. Donets'ka Oblast', E Ukraine *47.07N 38.06E*
126 Mm16 **Novobureyskiy** Amurskaya Oblast', SE Russian Federation *49.42N 129.46E*
131 Q3 **Novocheboksarsk** Chuvashskaya Respublika, W Russian Federation *56.07N 47.32E*
131 R5 **Novocheremshansk** Ul'yanovskaya Oblast', W Russian Federation *54.23N 50.08E*
130 L12 **Novocherkassk** Rostovskaya Oblast', SW Russian Federation *47.23N 40.00E*
131 R6 **Novodevich'ye** Samarskaya Oblast', W Russian Federation *53.33N 48.51E*
128 M8 **Novodvinsk** Arkhangel'skaya Oblast', NW Russian Federation *64.22N 40.48E*
Novograd-Volynskiy *see* Novohrad-Volyns'kyy
Novogrudok *see* Navahrudak
63 I15 **Novo Hamburgo** Rio Grande do Sul, S Brazil *29.42S 51.07W*
61 H16 **Novo Horizonte** Mato Grosso, W Brazil *11.19S 57.11W*
62 K8 **Novo Horizonte** São Paulo, S Brazil *21.27S 49.14W*
118 M4 **Novohrad-Volyns'kyy** *Rus.* Novograd-Volynskiy. Zhytomyrs'ka Oblast', N Ukraine *50.33N 27.31E*
150 L14 **Novokazalinsk** *see* Ayteke Bi
130 M8 **Novokhopersk** Voronezhskaya Oblast', W Russian Federation *51.09N 41.34E*
131 R6 **Novokuybyshevsk** Samarskaya Oblast', W Russian Federation *53.06N 49.56E*
126 H14 **Novokuznetsk** *prev.* Stalinsk. Kemerovskaya Oblast', S Russian Federation *53.45N 87.12E*
205 R1 **Novolazarevskaya** *Russian research station* Antarctica *70.42S 11.31E*
Novolukoml' *see* Novalukoml'
111 V12 **Novo mesto** *Ger.* Rudolfswert; *prev. Ger.* Neustadtl. SE Slovenia *45.48N 15.09E*
130 K15 **Novomikhaylovskiy** Krasnodarskiy Kray, SW Russian Federation *44.18N 38.49E*
114 L8 **Novo Miloševo** Serbia, N Yugoslavia *45.43N 20.20E*
Novomirgorod *see* Novomyrhorod
130 L5 **Novomoskovsk** Tul'skaya Oblast', W Russian Federation *54.04N 38.22E*
119 U7 **Novomoskovs'k** *Rus.* Novomoskovsk. Dnipropetrovs'ka Oblast', E Ukraine *48.37N 35.13E*
119 V8 **Novomykolayivka** Zaporiz'ka Oblast', SE Ukraine *47.58N 35.54E*
119 Q7 **Novomyrhorod** *Rus.* Novomirgorod. Kirovohrads'ka Oblast', S Ukraine *48.46N 31.39E*
126 I12 **Novonazimovo** Krasnoyarskiy Kray, C Russian Federation *59.30N 90.45E*
131 N8 **Novonikolayevskiy** Volgogradskaya Oblast', SW Russian Federation *50.55N 42.24E*
131 P10 **Novonikol'skoye** Volgogradskaya Oblast', SW Russian Federation *49.23N 45.06E*
131 X7 **Novoorsk** Orenburgskaya Oblast', W Russian Federation *51.21N 59.03E*
130 M13 **Novopokrovskaya** Krasnodarskiy Kray, SW Russian Federation *45.58N 40.43E*
Novopolotsk *see* Navapolatsk
119 Y5 **Novopskov** Luhans'ka Oblast', E Ukraine *49.33N 39.07E*
Novoradomsk *see* Radomsko
Novo Redondo *see* Sumbe
131 R8 **Novorepnoye** Saratovskaya Oblast', W Russian Federation *51.04N 48.34E*
130 K14 **Novorossiysk** Krasnodarskiy Kray, SW Russian Federation *44.49N 37.37E*
Novorossiyskiy *see* Novorossiyskoye
150 J10 **Novorossiyskoye** *prev.* Novorossiyskiy. Aktyubinsk, NW Kazakhstan *50.13N 57.57E*
126 Jj6 **Novorybnaya** Taymyrskiy (Dolgano-Nenetskiy) Avtonomnyy Okrug, N Russian Federation *72.48N 105.49E*
128 F15 **Novorzhev** Pskovskaya Oblast', W Russian Federation *57.01N 29.19E*
Novoselitsa *see* Novoselytsya
119 S12 **Novoselivs'ke** Respublika Krym, S Ukraine *45.26N 33.37E*
Novosëlki *see* Navasyolki
116 G6 **Novo Selo** Vidin, NW Bulgaria *44.08N 22.48E*
115 M14 **Novo Selo** Serbia, C Yugoslavia *43.39N 20.54E*
118 K8 **Novoselytsya** *Rom.* Nouă Sulița, *Rus.* Novoselitsa. Chernivets'ka Oblast', W Ukraine *48.13N 26.18E*
131 U7 **Novosergiyevka** Orenburgskaya Oblast', W Russian Federation *52.04N 53.40E*
130 L11 **Novoshakhtinsk** Rostovskaya Oblast', SW Russian Federation *47.48N 39.51E*
126 Gg14 **Novosibirsk** Novosibirskaya Oblast', C Russian Federation *55.04N 83.04E*
125 G13 **Novosibirskaya Oblast'** ◐ *province* C Russian Federation
126 M4 **Novosibirskiye Ostrova** *Eng.* New Siberian Islands. *island group* N Russian Federation
130 K6 **Novosil'** Orlovskaya Oblast', W Russian Federation *53.00N 37.59E*
128 G16 **Novosokol'niki** Pskovskaya Oblast', W Russian Federation *56.21N 30.07E*
131 Q6 **Novospasskoye** Ul'yanovskaya Oblast', W Russian Federation *53.08N 47.48E*
131 X8 **Novotroitsk** Orenburgskaya Oblast', W Russian Federation *51.09N 58.18E*
Novotroitskoye *see* Brlik, Kazakhstan
Novotroitskoye *see* Novotroyits'ke, Ukraine
119 T11 **Novotroyits'ke** *Rus.* Novotroitskoye. Khersons'ka Oblast', S Ukraine *46.21N 34.21E*
Novoukrainka *see* Novoukrayinka
119 Q8 **Novoukrayinka** *Rus.* Novoukrainka. Kirovohrads'ka Oblast', C Ukraine *48.19N 31.33E*
131 Q5 **Novoul'yanovsk** Ul'yanovskaya Oblast', W Russian Federation *54.10N 48.19E*
131 W8 **Novouralets** Orenburgskaya Oblast', W Russian Federation *51.19N 56.57E*
Novo-Urgench *see* Urganch
118 I4 **Novovolyns'k** *Rus.* Novovolynsk. Volyns'ka Oblast', NW Ukraine *50.46N 24.09E*
119 S9 **Novovorontsovka** Khersons'ka Oblast', S Ukraine *47.28N 33.55E*
153 Y7 **Novovoznesenovka** Issyk-Kul'skaya Oblast', E Kyrgyzstan *42.36N 78.44E*
129 R14 **Novovyatsk** Kirovskaya Oblast', NW Russian Federation *58.30N 49.42E*
Novoyel'nya *see* Navayel'nya
119 O6 **Novozhyvotiv** Vinnyts'ka Oblast', C Ukraine *49.16N 29.31E*
130 H6 **Novozybkov** Bryanskaya Oblast', W Russian Federation *52.36N 31.58E*
114 F9 **Novska** Sisak-Moslavina, NE Croatia *45.20N 16.58E*
Nový Bohumín *see* Bohumín
113 D15 **Nový Bor** *Ger.* Haida; *prev.* Bor u České Lípy, Hajda. Liberecký Kraj, N Czech Republic *50.46N 14.32E*
113 E16 **Nový Bydžov** *Ger.* Neubidschow. Hradecký Kraj, N Czech Republic *50.15N 15.27E*
121 G18 **Novy Dvor** *Rus.* Novyy Dvor. Hrodzyenskaya Voblasts', W Belarus *53.49N 24.22E*
113 I17 **Nový Jičín** *Ger.* Neutitschein. Ostravský Kraj, E Czech Republic *49.36N 18.00E*
120 K12 **Novy Pahost** *Rus.* Novyy Pogost. Vitsyebskaya Voblasts', NW Belarus *55.30N 27.28E*
Novyy Bug *see* Novyy Buh
119 R9 **Novyy Buh** *Rus.* Novyy Bug. Mykolayivs'ka Oblast', S Ukraine *47.39N 32.31E*
119 Q4 **Novyy Bykiv** Chernihivs'ka Oblast', N Ukraine *50.36N 31.39E*
Novyy Dvor *see* Novy Dvor
Novyye Aneny *see* Anenii Noi
131 P7 **Novyye Burasy** Saratovskaya Oblast', W Russian Federation *52.10N 46.00E*
Novyy Margilan *see* Farghona
130 K8 **Novyy Oskol** Belgorodskaya Oblast', W Russian Federation *50.43N 37.55E*
Novyy Pogost *see* Novy Pahost
131 R2 **Novyy Tor"yal** Respublika Mariy El, W Russian Federation *56.59N 48.53E*
126 K14 **Novyy Uoyan** Respublika Buryatiya, S Russian Federation *56.06N 111.27E*
126 Gg9 **Novyy Urengoy** Yamalo-Nenetskiy Avtonomnyy Okrug, N Russian Federation *66.06N 76.25E*
127 N15 **Novyy Urgal** Khabarovskiy Kray, E Russian Federation *51.02N 132.45E*
Novyy Uzen' *see* Zhanaozen
125 G12 **Novyy Vasyugan** Tomskaya Oblast', C Russian Federation *58.28N 76.19E*
113 N16 **Nowa Dęba** Podkarpackie, SE Poland *50.31N 21.53E*
113 G15 **Nowa Ruda** *Ger.* Neurode. Dolnośląskie, SW Poland *50.34N 16.30E*
112 F12 **Nowa Sól** *var.* Nowasól, *Ger.* Neusalz an der Oder. Lubuskie, W Poland *51.47N 15.42E*
29 Q8 **Nowata** Oklahoma, C USA *36.42N 95.38W*
148 M6 **Nowbarān** Markazī, W Iran *35.07N 49.51E*
112 J8 **Nowe** Kujawski-pomorskie, C Poland *53.39N 18.44E*
112 K9 **Nowe Miasto Lubawskie** *Ger.* Neumark. Warmińsko-Mazurskie, NE Poland *53.24N 19.36E*
112 L13 **Nowe Miasto nad Pilicą** Mazowieckie, C Poland *51.37N 20.34E*
112 D8 **Nowe Warpno** *Ger.* Neuwarp. Zachodniopomorskie, NW Poland *53.52N 14.12E*
Nowgong *see* Nagaon
112 E8 **Nowogard** *var.* Nowógard, *Ger.* Naugard. Zachodniopomorskie, NW Poland *53.41N 15.09E*
112 N9 **Nowogród** Podlaskie, NE Poland *53.14N 21.52E*
Nowogródek *see* Navahrudak
113 E14 **Nowogrodziec** *Ger.* Naumburg am Queis. Dolnośląskie, SW Poland *51.12N 15.24E*
Nowojelnia *see* Navayel'nya
Nowo-Minsk *see* Mińsk Mazowiecki
35 V13 **Nowood River** ≈ Wyoming, C USA
Nowo-Święciany *see* Švenčionėliai
191 S10 **Nowra-Bomaderry** New South Wales, SE Australia *34.51S 150.41E*
155 T5 **Nowshera** *var.* Naushahra, Naushara. North-West Frontier Province, NE Pakistan *34.00N 72.00E*
112 J7 **Nowy Dwór Gdański** *Ger.* Tiegenhof. Pomorskie, N Poland *54.12N 19.03E*
112 L11 **Nowy Dwór Mazowiecki** Mazowieckie, C Poland *52.25N 20.43E*
113 M17 **Nowy Sącz** *Ger.* Neu Sandec. Małopolskie, S Poland *49.36N 20.41E*
113 L18 **Nowy Targ** *Ger.* Neumark. Małopolskie, S Poland *49.28N 20.00E*
112 F11 **Nowy Tomyśl** *var.* Nowy Tomysl. Wielkopolskie, C Poland *52.18N 16.07E*
154 M7 **Now Zād** *var.* Nauzad. Helmand, S Afghanistan *32.22N 64.31E*
25 N4 **Noxubee River** ≈ Alabama/Mississippi, S USA
126 Gg10 **Noyabr'sk** Yamalo-Nenetskiy Avtonomnyy Okrug, N Russian Federation *63.08N 75.19E*
104 L8 **Noyant** Maine-et-Loire, NW France *47.28N 0.08W*
41 X14 **Noyes Island** *island* Alexander Archipelago, Alaska, USA
105 O3 **Noyon** Oise, N France *49.35N 3.00E*
104 I7 **Nozay** Loire-Atlantique, NW France *47.34N 1.36W*
84 L12 **Nsando** Northern, NE Zambia *10.22S 31.14E*
85 N16 **Nsanje** Southern, S Malawi *16.57S 35.10E*
79 Q17 **Nsawam** SE Ghana *5.46N 0.19W*
81 E16 **Nsimalen** ✕ Centre, C Cameroon *19.15N 81.22W*
84 K12 **Nsombo** Northern, NE Zambia *10.35S 29.58E*
84 H13 **Ntambu** North Western, NW Zambia *12.22S 24.57E*
85 N14 **Ntcheu** *var.* Ncheu. Central, S Malawi *14.49S 34.37E*
81 D17 **Ntem** *prev.* Campo, Kampo. ≈ Cameroon/Equatorial Guinea
85 I14 **Ntemwa** North Western, NW Zambia *14.03S 26.13E*
Ntlenyana, Mount *see* Thabana Ntlenyana
81 I19 **Ntomba, Lac** *var.* Lac Tumba. ◎ NW Dem. Rep. Congo (Zaire)
83 E19 **Ntungamo** SW Uganda *0.54S 30.16E*
83 E18 **Ntusi** SW Uganda *0.03N 31.11E*
85 H18 **Ntwetwe Pan** *salt lake* NE Botswana
95 M15 **Nuasjärvi** ◎ C Finland
82 F11 **Nuba Mountains** ▲▲ C Sudan
70 J9 **Nubian Desert** *desert* NE Sudan
118 G10 **Nucet** *Hung.* Diófás. Bihor, W Romania *46.28N 22.34E*
Nu Chiang *see* Salween
151 U9 **Nuclear Testing Ground** *nuclear site* Pavlodar, E Kazakhstan
58 E9 **Nucuray, Río** ≈ N Peru
27 R14 **Nueces River** ≈ Texas, SW USA
9 V9 **Nueltin Lake** ◎ Manitoba/Nunavut, C Canada
101 K15 **Nuenen** Noord-Brabant, S Netherlands *51.29N 5.36E*
64 G6 **Nuestra Señora, Bahía** *bay* N Chile
63 D14 **Nuestra Señora Rosario de Caa Catí** Corrientes, NE Argentina *27.48S 57.42W*
56 J9 **Nueva Antioquia** Vichada, E Colombia *6.04N 69.30W*
Nueva Caceres *see* Naga
43 O7 **Nueva Ciudad Guerrera** Tamaulipas, C Mexico *26.32N 99.13W*
57 N4 **Nueva Esparta** *off.* Estado Nueva Esparta. ◐ *state* NE Venezuela
46 C5 **Nueva Gerona** Isla de la Juventud, S Cuba *21.49N 82.49W*
44 H8 **Nueva Guadalupe** San Miguel, E El Salvador *13.30N 88.21W*
44 M11 **Nueva Guinea** Región Autónoma Atlántico Sur, SE Nicaragua *11.40N 84.22W*
63 D19 **Nueva Helvecia** Colonia, SW Uruguay *34.16S 57.52W*
65 J25 **Nueva, Isla** *island* S Chile
42 M14 **Nueva Italia** Michoacán de Ocampo, SW Mexico *19.01N 102.06W*
58 D6 **Nueva Loja** *var.* Lago Agrio. Sucumbíos, NE Ecuador
44 F6 **Nueva Ocotepeque** *prev.* Ocotepeque. Ocotepeque, W Honduras *14.25N 89.11W*
63 D19 **Nueva Palmira** Colonia, SW Uruguay *33.52S 58.25W*
43 N6 **Nueva Rosita** Coahuila de Zaragoza, NE Mexico *27.58N 101.10W*
44 E7 **Nueva San Salvador** *prev.* Santa Tecla. La Libertad, SW El Salvador *13.42N 89.18W*
44 J8 **Nueva Segovia** ◐ *department* NW Nicaragua
Nueva Tabarca *see* Plana, Isla
Nueva Villa de Padilla *see* Nuevo Padilla
63 B21 **Nueve de Julio** Buenos Aires, E Argentina *35.29S 60.52W*
46 H6 **Nuevitas** Camagüey, E Cuba *21.34N 77.18W*
63 D18 **Nuevo Berlín** Río Negro, W Uruguay *32.58S 58.03W*
42 I4 **Nuevo Casas Grandes** Chihuahua, N Mexico *30.23N 107.53W*
45 T14 **Nuevo Chagres** Colón, C Panama *9.13N 80.03W*
43 W15 **Nuevo Coahuila** Campeche, E Mexico *17.52N 90.46W*
65 K17 **Nuevo, Golfo** *gulf* S Argentina
43 O7 **Nuevo Laredo** Tamaulipas, NE Mexico *27.27N 99.31W*
43 N8 **Nuevo León** ◐ *state* NE Mexico
43 P10 **Nuevo Padilla** *var.* Nueva Villa de Padilla. Tamaulipas, C Mexico *24.01N 98.48W*
58 E6 **Nuevo Rocafuerte** Napo, E Ecuador *0.55S 75.25W*
168 G6 **Nuga** Dzavhan, W Mongolia *48.17N 95.07E*
82 O13 **Nugaal** *off.* Gobolka Nugaal. ◐ *region* N Somalia
193 E24 **Nugget Point** *headland* South Island, NZ *46.26S 169.49E*
195 R9 **Nuguria Islands** *island group* E PNG
192 P10 **Nuhaka** Hawke's Bay, North Island, NZ *39.03S 177.43E*
144 M10 **Nuhaydayn, Wādī an** *dry watercourse* W Iraq
202 E7 **Nui Atoll** *atoll* W Tuvalu
Nu Jiang *see* Salween
Nûk *see* Nuuk
190 G7 **Nukey Bluff** *hill* South Australia *32.34S 135.36E*
Nukha *see* Şäki
127 O9 **Nukh Yablonevyy, Gora** ▲ E Russian Federation *60.26N 151.45E*
195 T13 **Nukiki** Choiseul Island, NW Solomon Islands *6.45S 94.30E*
194 F10 **Nuku** Sandaun, NW PNG *3.40S 142.29E*
200 R15 **Nuku** *island* Tongatapu Group, NE Tonga
200 Qq15 **Nuku'alofa** Tongatapu, S Tonga *21.09S 175.13W*
200 Qq15 **Nuku'alofa** ● (Tonga) Tongatapu, S Tonga *21.07S 175.13W*
202 G12 **Nukuatea** *island* N Wallis and Futuna
202 F7 **Nukufetau Atoll** *atoll* C Tuvalu
202 G12 **Nukuhifala** *island* E Wallis and Futuna
203 W7 **Nuku Hiva** *island* Îles Marquises, NE French Polynesia
199 Ll9 **Nuku Hiva Island** *island* Îles Marquises, N French Polynesia
202 F9 **Nukulaelae Atoll** *var.* Nukulailai. *atoll* E Tuvalu
Nukulailai *see* Nukulaelae Atoll
202 G11 **Nukuloa** *island* N Wallis and Futuna
195 W10 **Nukumanu Islands** *prev.* Tasman Group. *island group* NE PNG
Nukunau *see* Nikunau
202 J9 **Nukunonu Atoll** *island* C Tokelau
202 J9 **Nukunonu Village** Nukunonu Atoll, C Tokelau
201 S18 **Nukuoro Atoll** *atoll* Caroline Islands, S Micronesia
152 H8 **Nukus** Qoraqalpoghiston Respublikasi, W Uzbekistan *42.28N 59.32E*
202 G11 **Nukutapu** *island* N Wallis and Futuna
41 O9 **Nulato** Alaska, USA *64.43N 158.06W*
41 O10 **Nulato Hills** ▲▲ Alaska, USA
107 T9 **Nules** País Valenciano, E Spain *39.52N 0.10W*
Nuling *see* Sultan Kudarat
190 C6 **Nullarbor** South Australia *31.28S 130.57E*
188 M11 **Nullarbor Plain** *plateau* South Australia/Western Australia
169 S12 **Nulu'erhu Shan** ▲▲ N China
79 X14 **Numan** Adamawa, E Nigeria *9.26N 11.58E*
171 K14 **Numata** Gunma, Honshū, S Japan *36.39N 139.00E*
172 Oo4 **Numata** Hokkaidō, NE Japan *43.48N 141.55E*
83 C15 **Numatinna** ≈ W Sudan
171 J17 **Numazu** Shizuoka, Honshū, S Japan *35.05N 138.52E*
97 F14 **Numedalen** *valley* S Norway
97 G14 **Numedalslågen** *var.* Laagen. ≈ S Norway
95 L19 **Nummela** Etelä-Suomi, S Finland *60.21N 24.19E*
125 G9 **Numto** Khanty-Mansiyskiy Avtonomnyy Okrug, N Russian Federation *63.33N 70.53E*
191 O11 **Numurkah** Victoria, SE Australia *36.04S 145.28E*
206 L16 **Nunap Isua** *var.* Uummannarsuaq, *Dan.* Kap Farvel, *Eng.* Cape Farewell. *headland* S Greenland *59.57N 44.27W*
15 K5 **Nunavut** ◐ *Territory* N Canada
56 H9 **Nunchia** Casanare, C Colombia *5.37N 72.13W*
99 M20 **Nuneaton** C England, UK *52.31N 1.28W*
159 W14 **Nungba** Manipur, NE India *24.46N 93.25E*
40 L12 **Nunivak Island** *island* Alaska, USA
158 I5 **Nun Kun** ▲ NW India *34.01N 76.04E*
100 L10 **Nunspeet** Gelderland, E Netherlands *52.21N 5.45E*
109 C18 **Nuoro** Sardegna, Italy, C Mediterranean Sea *40.19N 9.19E*
77 R12 **Nuqayy, Jabal** *hill range* S Libya
56 C9 **Nuquí** Chocó, W Colombia *5.43N 77.16W*
149 O4 **Nūr** Māzandarān, N Iran *36.34N 52.01E*
151 Q9 **Nura** ≈ N Kazakhstan
149 N11 **Nūrābād** Fārs, C Iran *30.07N 51.30E*
Nurakita *see* Niulakita
Nurata *see* Nurota
Nuratau, Khrebet *see* Nurota Tizmasi
142 L17 **Nur Dağları** ▲▲ S Turkey
Nurek *see* Norak
Nuremberg *see* Nürnberg
142 M15 **Nurhak** Kahramanmaraş, S Turkey *37.57N 37.21E*
190 J9 **Nuriootpa** South Australia *34.28S 139.00E*
131 S5 **Nurlat** Respublika Tatarstan, W Russian Federation *54.26N 50.48E*
95 N15 **Nurmes** Itä-Suomi, E Finland *63.31N 29.10E*
103 K20 **Nürnberg** *Eng.* Nuremberg. Bayern, S Germany *49.27N 11.04E*
103 K20 **Nürnberg** ✕ Bayern, SE Germany *49.29N 11.04E*
152 M10 **Nurota** *Rus.* Nurata. Navoiy Wiloyati, C Uzbekistan *40.40N 65.43E*
153 N10 **Nurota Tizmasi** *Rus.* Khrebet Nuratau. ▲▲ C Uzbekistan
155 T8 **Nūrpur** Punjab, E Pakistan *31.54N 71.55E*
191 P6 **Nurri, Mount** *hill* New South Wales, SE Australia *31.42S 146.03E*
27 T13 **Nursery** Texas, SW USA *28.55N 97.04W*
175 P16 **Nusa Tenggara** *Eng.* Lesser Sunda Islands. *island group* East Timor/ Indonesia
175 O15 **Nusa Tenggara Barat** *off.* Propinsi Nusa Tenggara Barat, *Eng.* West Nusa Tenggara. ◐ *province* S Indonesia
175 Q17 **Nusa Tenggara Timur** *off.* Propinsi Nusa Tenggara Timur, *Eng.* East Nusa Tenggara. ◐ *province* S Indonesia
176 Vv12 **Nusawulan** Irian Jaya, E Indonesia *4.03S 132.56E*
143 Q16 **Nusaybin** *var.* Nisibin. Manisa, SE Turkey *37.07N 41.10E*
41 O14 **Nushagak Bay** *bay* Alaska, USA
41 O13 **Nushagak Peninsula** *headland* Alaska, USA *58.39N 159.03W*
41 O13 **Nushagak River** ≈ Alaska, USA
166 E11 **Nu Shan** ▲▲ SW China
155 N11 **Nushki** Baluchistān, SW Pakistan *29.33N 66.01E*
Nussdorf *see* Năsăud
114 J9 **Nuštar** Vukovar-Srijem, E Croatia *45.20N 18.48E*
101 L18 **Nuth** Limburg, SE Netherlands *50.55N 5.52E*
102 N13 **Nuthe** ≈ NE Germany
Nutmeg State *see* Connecticut
41 T10 **Nutzotin Mountains** ▲▲ Alaska, USA
66 I5 **Nuuk** *var.* Nûk, *Dan.* Godthaab, Godthåb. ○ (Greenland). Kitaa, SW Greenland *64.15N 51.34W*
94 L13 **Nuupas** Lappi, NW Finland *66.01N 26.19E*
203 O7 **Nuupere, Pointe** *headland* Moorea, W French Polynesia *17.34S 149.46W*
203 O7 **Nuuroa, Pointe** *headland* Tahiti, W French Polynesia
168 M8 **Nüürst** Töv, C Mongolia *47.44N 108.22E*
Nuwara *see* Nuwara Eliya
161 K25 **Nuwara Eliya** *var.* Nuwara. Central Province, S Sri Lanka *6.58N 80.46E*
190 E7 **Nuyts Archipelago** *island group* South Australia
85 F17 **Nxaunxau** Ngamiland, NW Botswana *18.57S 21.18E*
41 N12 **Nyac** Alaska, USA *61.00N 159.56W*
125 Ff10 **Nyagan'** Khanty-Mansiyskiy Avtonomnyy Okrug, N Russian Federation *62.10N 65.32E*
Nyagassola *see* Niagassola
83 I18 **Nyahururu** Central, W Kenya *0.04N 36.22E*
190 M10 **Nyah West** Victoria, SE Australia *35.14S 143.18E*
164 M15 **Nyainqêntanglha Feng** ▲ W China *30.20N 90.28E*
165 N15 **Nyainqêntanglha Shan** ▲▲ W China
82 B11 **Nyala** Southern Darfur, W Sudan *12.01N 24.49E*
85 M16 **Nyamapanda** Mashonaland East, NE Zimbabwe *16.57S 32.51E*
83 H25 **Nyamtumbo** Ruvuma, S Tanzania *10.33S 36.07E*
Nyanda *see* Masvingo
128 M11 **Nyandoma** Arkhangel'skaya Oblast', NW Russian Federation *61.39N 40.09E*
85 M16 **Nyanga** *prev.* Inyanga. Manicaland, E Zimbabwe *18.14S 32.42E*
81 D20 **Nyanga** *off.* Province de la Nyanga, *var.* La Nyanga. ◐ *province* SW Gabon
81 E20 **Nyanga** ≈ Congo/Gabon
83 F20 **Nyantakara** Kagera, NW Tanzania *3.04S 31.22E*
83 G19 **Nyanza** ◐ *province* W Kenya
83 E21 **Nyanza-Lac** S Burundi *4.16S 29.38E*
70 J14 **Nyasa, Lake** *var.* Lake Malawi; *prev.* Lago Nyassa. ◎ E Africa
Nyasaland/Nyasaland Protectorate *see* Malawi
Nyassa, Lago *see* Nyasa, Lake
121 J17 **Nyasvizh** *Pol.* Nieśwież, *Rus.* Nesvizh. Minskaya Voblasts', C Belarus *53.13N 26.40E*
177 G8 **Nyaunglebin** Pegu, SW Burma *17.58N 96.43E*
177 G5 **Nyaung-u** Magwe, C Burma *21.03N 95.43E*
97 H24 **Nyborg** Fyn, C Denmark *55.19N 10.48E*
97 N21 **Nybro** Kalmar, S Sweden *56.45N 15.54E*
121 J16 **Nyeharelaye** *Rus.* Negoreloye. Minskaya Voblasts', C Belarus *53.36N 27.05E*
205 W3 **Nye Mountains** ▲▲ Antarctica
83 I19 **Nyeri** Central, C Kenya *0.25S 36.55E*
120 M11 **Nyeshcharda, Vozyera** ◎ N Belarus
94 O2 **Ny-Friesland** *physical region* N Svalbard
97 L14 **Nyhammar** Dalarna, C Sweden *60.19N 14.55E*
166 F7 **Nyikog Qu** ≈ C China
164 L14 **Nyima** Xizang Zizhiqu, W China *31.53N 87.50E*
85 L14 **Nyimba** Eastern, E Zambia *14.33S 30.49E*
165 P16 **Nyingchi** Xizang Zizhiqu, W China *29.34N 94.22E*
113 O21 **Nyírbátor** Szabolcs-Szatmár-Bereg, E Hungary *47.49N 22.06E*
113 N21 **Nyíregyháza** Szabolcs-Szatmár-Bereg, NE Hungary *47.57N 21.43E*
Nyiro *see* Ewaso Ng'iro
Nyitra *see* Nitra
Nyitrabánya *see* Handlová
95 K16 **Nykarleby** *Fin.* Uusikaarlepyy. Länsi-Suomi, W Finland *63.22N 22.30E*
97 I25 **Nykøbing** Storstrøm, SE Denmark *54.46N 11.52E*
97 I22 **Nykøbing** Vestsjælland, C Denmark *55.55N 11.40E*
97 F21 **Nykøbing** Viborg, NW Denmark *56.48N 8.52E*
97 N17 **Nyköping** Södermanland, S Sweden *58.45N 17.03E*
97 L15 **Nykroppa** Värmland, C Sweden *59.37N 14.18E*
85 J20 **Nylstroom** Northern, NE South Africa *24.39S 28.23E*
191 P7 **Nymagee** New South Wales, SE Australia *32.06S 146.19E*
191 V5 **Nymboida** New South Wales, SE Australia *29.57S 152.45E*
191 U5 **Nymboida River** ≈ New South Wales, SE Australia
113 D16 **Nymburk** *var.* Neuenburg an der Elbe, *Ger.* Nimburg. Středočeský Kraj, C Czech Republic *50.12N 15.00E*
97 O16 **Nynäshamn** Stockholm, C Sweden *58.54N 17.55E*
191 Q6 **Nyngan** New South Wales, SE Australia *31.36S 147.07E*
Nyoman *see* Neman
110 A10 **Nyon** *Ger.* Neuss; *anc.* Noviodunum. Vaud, SW Switzerland *46.22N 6.15E*
81 D16 **Nyong** ≈ SW Cameroon
105 S14 **Nyons** Drôme, E France *44.22N 5.06E*
81 D14 **Nyos, Lac** *Eng.* Lake Nyos. ◎ NW Cameroon
Nyos, Lake *see* Nyos, Lac
129 U11 **Nyrob** *var.* Nyrov. Permskaya Oblast', NW Russian Federation *60.41N 56.42E*
Nyrov *see* Nyrob
113 H15 **Nysa** *Ger.* Neisse. Opolskie, S Poland *50.28N 17.20E*
Nysa Łużycka *see* Neisse
Nyslott *see* Savonlinna
34 M13 **Nyssa** Oregon, NW USA *43.52N 116.59W*
Nystad *see* Uusikaupunki
97 I25 **Nysted** Storstrøm, SE Denmark *54.40N 11.41E*
129 U14 **Nytva** Permskaya Oblast', NW Russian Federation *57.56N 55.22E*
171 Ll9 **Nyūdō-zaki** *headland* Honshū, C Japan *39.59N 139.40E*
129 P9 **Nyukhcha** Arkhangel'skaya Oblast', NW Russian Federation *63.24N 46.34E*
128 H8 **Nyuk, Ozero** *var.* Ozero Njuk. ◎ NW Russian Federation
129 O12 **Nyuksenitsa** *var.* Njuksenica. Vologodskaya Oblast', NW Russian Federation *60.25N 44.12E*
81 O22 **Nyunzu** Katanga, SE Dem. Rep. Congo (Zaire) *5.55S 28.00E*
126 Kk11 **Nyurba** Respublika Sakha (Yakutiya), NE Russian Federation *63.17N 118.14E*
126 Kk12 **Nyuya** Respublika Sakha (Yakutiya), NE Russian Federation *60.33N 116.10E*
126 K12 **Nyuya** ≈ NE Russian Federation
119 T10 **Nyzhni Sirohozy** Khersons'ka Oblast', S Ukraine *46.49N 34.21E*
119 U12 **Nyzhn'ohirs'kyy** *Rus.* Nizhnegorskiy. Respublika Krym, S Ukraine *45.26N 34.42E*
83 G21 **Nzega** Tabora, C Tanzania *4.13S 33.10E*
78 K15 **Nzérékoré** Guinée-Forestière, SE Guinea *7.45N 8.49W*
84 A10 **N'Zeto** *prev.* Ambrizete. Zaire, NW Angola *7.13S 12.52E*
81 M24 **Nzilo, Lac** *prev.* Lac Delcommune. ◎ SE Dem. Rep. Congo (Zaire)

O

31 O11 **Oacoma** South Dakota, N USA *43.49N 99.25W*
31 N9 **Oahe Dam** *dam* South Dakota, N USA *44.27N 100.24W*
30 M9 **Oahe, Lake** ⊡ North Dakota/South Dakota, N USA
40 C9 **Oahu** *Haw.* O'ahu. *island* Hawaii, USA, C Pacific Ocean

◆ Country
● Country Capital
◇ Dependent Territory
○ Dependent Territory Capital
◐ Administrative Region
✕ International Airport
▲ Mountain
▲▲ Mountain Range
Volcano
≈ River
◎ Lake
⊡ Reservoir

O-AKAN-DAKE – OLËKMA

172 Qq6 **O-Akan-dake** ▲ Hokkaidō, NE Japan 43.26N 144.09E
190 K8 **Oakbank** South Australia 33.07S 140.36E
21 P13 **Oak Bluffs** Martha's Vineyard, New York, NE USA 41.25N 70.32W
38 K4 **Oak City** Utah, W USA 39.22N 112.19W
39 R3 **Oak Creek** Colorado, C USA 40.16N 106.57W
37 P8 **Oakdale** California, W USA 37.46N 120.51W
24 H8 **Oakdale** Louisiana, S USA 30.49N 92.39W
31 P7 **Oakes** North Dakota, N USA 46.08N 98.05W
24 J4 **Oak Grove** Louisiana, S USA 32.51N 91.25W
99 N19 **Oakham** C England, UK 52.40N 0.45W
34 H7 **Oak Harbor** Washington, NW USA 48.17N 122.38W
23 R5 **Oak Hill** West Virginia, NE USA 37.59N 81.09W
37 N8 **Oakland** California, W USA 37.48N 122.16W
31 T15 **Oakland** Iowa, C USA 41.18N 95.22W
21 Q7 **Oakland** Maine, NE USA 44.32N 69.43W
23 T3 **Oakland** Maryland, NE USA 39.24N 79.24W
31 R14 **Oakland** Nebraska, C USA 41.50N 96.28W
33 N11 **Oak Lawn** Illinois, N USA 41.43N 87.45W
35 P16 **Oakley** Idaho, NW USA 42.13N 113.54W
28 I4 **Oakley** Kansas, C USA 39.06N 100.51W
33 N10 **Oak Park** Illinois, N USA 41.53N 87.46W
9 X16 **Oak Point** Manitoba, S Canada 50.23N 97.00W
34 G13 **Oakridge** Oregon, NW USA 43.45N 122.27W
22 M9 **Oak Ridge** Tennessee, S USA 36.01N 84.12W
192 K10 **Oakura** Taranaki, North Island, NZ 39.07S 173.58E
24 L7 **Oak Vale** Mississippi, S USA 31.26N 89.57W
12 G16 **Oakville** Ontario, S Canada 43.27N 79.40W
27 V8 **Oakwood** Texas, SW USA 31.34N 95.51W
193 F22 **Oamaru** Otago, South Island, NZ 45.10S 170.51E
98 F13 **Oa, Mull of** *headland* W Scotland, UK 55.35N 6.20W
175 Q7 **Oan** Sulawesi, N Indonesia 1.16N 121.25E
193 J17 **Oaro** Canterbury, South Island, NZ 42.29S 173.30E
37 X2 **Oasis** Nevada, W USA 41.01N 114.29W
205 S15 **Oates Land** *physical region* Antarctica
191 P17 **Oatlands** Tasmania, SE Australia 42.21S 147.23E
38 I11 **Oatman** Arizona, SW USA 35.03N 114.19W
43 R16 **Oaxaca** *var.* Oaxaca de Juárez; *prev.* Antequera. Oaxaca, SE Mexico 17.04N 96.40W
43 Q16 **Oaxaca** ◈ *state* SE Mexico
Oaxaca de Juárez *see* Oaxaca
125 G8 **Ob'** ~ C Russian Federation
12 G9 **Obabika Lake** ◎ Ontario, S Canada
Obagan *see* Ubagan
120 M12 **Obal'** *Rus.* Obol'. Vitsyebskaya Voblasts', N Belarus 55.22N 29.16E
81 E16 **Obala** Centre, SW Cameroon 4.09N 11.31E
12 C6 **Oba Lake** ◎ Ontario, S Canada
171 H14 **Obama** Fukui, Honshū, SW Japan 35.29N 135.42E
98 H11 **Oban** W Scotland, UK 56.25N 5.28W
Oban *see* Halfmoon Bay
171 Ll12 **Obanazawa** Yamagata, Honshū, C Japan 38.40N 140.21E
Obando *see* Puerto Inírida
106 I4 **O Barco** *var.* El Barco, El Barco de Valdeorras, O Barco de Valdeorras. Galicia, NW Spain 42.24N 7.00W
O Barco de Valdeorras *see* O Barco
Obbia *see* Hobyo
95 J16 **Obbola** Västerbotten, N Sweden 63.42N 20.18E
Obbrovazzo *see* Obrovac
Obchuga *see* Abchuha
Obdorsk *see* Salekhard
Óbecse *see* Bečej
120 I11 **Obeliai** Rokiškis, NE Lithuania 55.57N 25.47E
62 F13 **Oberá** Misiones, NE Argentina 27.28S 55.07W
110 E8 **Oberburg** Bern, W Switzerland 47.00N 7.37E
111 Q9 **Oberdrauburg** Salzburg, S Austria 46.45N 12.59E
Oberglogau *see* Głogówek
111 W4 **Ober Grafendorf** Niederösterreich, NE Austria 48.09N 15.33E
103 E15 **Oberhausen** Nordrhein-Westfalen, W Germany 51.28N 6.52E
Oberhollabrunn *see* Tulln
Oberlaibach *see* Vrhnika
103 Q15 **Oberlausitz** *physical region* E Germany
28 J2 **Oberlin** Kansas, C USA 39.48N 100.31W
24 H8 **Oberlin** Louisiana, S USA 30.37N 92.45W
33 T11 **Oberlin** Ohio, N USA 41.17N 82.13W
105 U5 **Obernai** Bas-Rhin, NE France 48.28N 7.30E
111 R4 **Obernberg-am-Inn** Oberösterreich, N Austria 48.19N 13.20E
Oberndorf *see* Oberndorf am Neckar
103 G23 **Oberndorf am Neckar** *var.* Oberndorf. Baden-Württemberg, SW Germany 48.18N 8.32E
111 Q5 **Oberndorf bei Salzburg** Salzburg, W Austria 47.57N 12.57E
Oberneustadtl *see* Kysucké Nové Mesto
191 S8 **Oberon** New South Wales, SE Australia 33.42S 149.50E
111 Q4 **Oberösterreich** *off.* Land Oberösterreich, *Eng.* Upper Austria. ◈ *state* NW Austria
Oberpahlen *see* Põltsamaa
103 M19 **Oberpfälzer Wald** ▲▲ SE Germany
111 Y6 **Oberpullendorf** Burgenland, E Austria 47.32N 16.30E
Oberradkersburg *see* Gornja Radgona
103 G18 **Oberursel** Hessen, W Germany 50.12N 8.34E
111 Q8 **Obervellach** Salzburg, S Austria 46.56N 13.10E
111 X7 **Oberwart** Burgenland, SE Austria 47.18N 16.12E
Oberwischau *see* Vişeu de Sus
111 T7 **Oberwölz** *var.* Oberwölz-Stadt. Steiermark, SE Austria 47.12N 14.20E
Oberwölz-Stadt *see* Oberwölz
33 S13 **Obetz** Ohio, N USA 39.52N 82.57W
Ob', Gulf of *see* Obskaya Guba
56 G8 **Obia** Santander, C Colombia 6.16N 73.18W
60 H12 **Óbidos** Pará, NE Brazil 1.52S 55.30W
106 F10 **Óbidos** Leiria, C Portugal 39.21N 9.09W
Obidovichi *see* Abidavichy
153 Q13 **Obigarm** W Tajikistan 38.42N 69.34E
172 P7 **Obihiro** Hokkaidō, NE Japan 42.55N 143.09E
Obi-Khingou *see* Khingov
153 P13 **Obikiik** SW Tajikistan 38.07N 68.36E
115 N16 **Obilić** Serbia, S Yugoslavia 42.50N 20.57E
131 O12 **Obil'noye** Respublika Kalmykiya, SW Russian Federation 47.31N 44.24E
22 F8 **Obion** Tennessee, S USA 36.15N 89.11W
22 F8 **Obion River** ~ Tennessee, S USA
175 T9 **Obi, Pulau** *island* Maluku, E Indonesia
172 Oo4 **Obira** Hokkaidō, NE Japan 44.01N 141.39E
175 T9 **Obi, Selat** *strait* Maluku, E Indonesia
131 N11 **Oblivskaya** Rostovskaya Oblast', SW Russian Federation 48.34N 42.31E
127 N16 **Obluch'ye** Yevreyskaya Avtonomnaya Oblast', SE Russian Federation 48.59N 131.18E
130 K4 **Obninsk** Kaluzhskaya Oblast', W Russian Federation 55.06N 36.40E
116 J8 **Obnova** Pleven, N Bulgaria 43.26N 25.04E
81 N15 **Obo** Haut-Mbomou, E Central African Republic 5.20N 26.28E
82 M11 **Obock** E Djibouti 11.57N 43.09E
Obol' *see* Obal'
Obolyanka *see* Abalyanka
176 Vv11 **Obome** Irian Jaya, E Indonesia 3.42S 133.21E
112 G11 **Oborniki** Wielkolpolskie, C Poland 52.38N 16.48E
81 G19 **Obouya** Cuvette, C Congo 0.55S 15.40E
130 J8 **Oboyan'** Kurskaya Oblast', W Russian Federation 51.12N 36.15E
128 M9 **Obozerskiy** Arkhangel'skaya Oblast', NW Russian Federation 63.26N 40.20E
114 L11 **Obrenovac** Serbia, N Yugoslavia 44.39N 20.12E
114 D12 **Obrovac** *It.* Obbrovazzo. Zadar, SW Croatia 44.12N 15.40E
Obrovo *see* Abrova
37 Q3 **Observation Peak** ▲ California, W USA 40.48N 120.07W
126 H7 **Obskaya Guba** *Eng.* Gulf of Ob'. *gulf* N Russian Federation
181 N13 **Ob' Tablemount** *undersea feature* S Indian Ocean 50.16S 51.59E
181 T10 **Ob' Trench** *undersea feature* E Indian Ocean
79 P16 **Obuasi** S Ghana 6.15N 1.36W
119 P5 **Obukhiv** *Rus.* Obukhov. Kyyivs'ka Oblast', N Ukraine 50.05N 30.37E
Obukhov *see* Obukhiv
129 U14 **Obva** ~ NW Russian Federation
119 V10 **Obytichna Kosa** *spit* SE Ukraine
119 V10 **Obytichna Zatoka** *gulf* SE Ukraine
107 O3 **Oca** ~ N Spain
25 W10 **Ocala** Florida, SE USA 29.11N 82.08W
42 M7 **Ocampo** Coahuila de Zaragoza, NE Mexico 27.18N 102.24W
56 G7 **Ocaña** Norte de Santander, N Colombia 8.16N 73.21W
107 N9 **Ocaña** Castilla-La Mancha, C Spain 39.57N 3.30W
106 H4 **O Carballiño** *Cast.* Carballiño Galicia, NW Spain 42.25N 8.04W
39 T9 **Ocate** New Mexico, SW USA 36.09N 105.03W
Ocavango *see* Okavango
56 D14 **Occidental, Cordillera** ▲▲ W Colombia
59 D14 **Occidental, Cordillera** ▲▲ W S America
23 Q6 **Oceana** West Virginia, NE USA 37.41N 81.37W
23 Z4 **Ocean City** Maryland, NE USA 38.20N 75.05W
20 J17 **Ocean City** New Jersey, NE USA 39.15N 74.33W
8 K15 **Ocean Falls** British Columbia, SW Canada 52.24N 127.42W
Ocean Island *see* Kure Atoll
Ocean Island *see* Banaba
66 J9 **Oceanographer Fracture Zone** *tectonic feature* NW Atlantic Ocean
37 U17 **Oceanside** California, W USA 33.12N 117.22W
24 M9 **Ocean Springs** Mississippi, S USA 30.24N 88.49W
Ocean State *see* Rhode Island
27 O9 **O C Fisher Lake** ▣ Texas, SW USA
119 Q10 **Ochakiv** *Rus.* Ochakov. Mykolayivs'ka Oblast', S Ukraine 46.36N 31.33E
Ochakov *see* Ochakiv
Ochamchira *see* Och'amch'ire
143 Q9 **Och'amch'ire** *Rus.* Ochamchira. W Georgia 42.45N 41.30E
Ochansk *see* Okhansk
129 T15 **Ocher** Permskaya Oblast', NW Russian Federation 57.54N 54.40E
117 I19 **Óchi** ▲ Évvoia, C Greece 38.03N 24.27E
172 R8 **Ochiishi-misaki** *headland* Hokkaidō, NE Japan 43.10N 145.29E
25 S9 **Ochlockonee River** ~ Florida/Georgia, SE USA
46 K12 **Ocho Rios** C Jamaica 18.24N 77.06W
Ochrida *see* Ohrid
Ochrida, Lake *see* Ohrid, Lake
103 J19 **Ochsenfurt** Bayern, C Germany 49.39N 10.03E
25 U7 **Ocilla** Georgia, SE USA 31.35N 83.15W
96 N13 **Ockelbo** Gävleborg, C Sweden 60.51N 16.46E
Ocker *see* Oker
97 I19 **Öckerö** Västra Götaland, S Sweden 57.43N 11.39E
25 U6 **Ocmulgee River** ~ Georgia, SE USA
118 H11 **Ocna Mureş** *Hung.* Marosújvár; *prev.* Ocna Mureşului; *prev. Hung.* Marosújvárakna. Alba, C Romania 46.25N 23.52E
Ocna Mureşului *see* Ocna Mureş
118 H11 **Ocna Sibiului** *Ger.* Salzburg, *Hung.* Vizakna. Sibiu, C Romania 45.52N 23.59E
118 H13 **Ocnele Mari** *prev.* Vioara. Vâlcea, S Romania 45.03N 24.18E
118 L7 **Ocniţa** *Rus.* Oknitsa. N Moldova 48.25N 27.30E
25 U4 **Oconee, Lake** ▣ Georgia, SE USA
25 U5 **Oconee River** ~ Georgia, SE USA
32 M9 **Oconomowoc** Wisconsin, N USA 43.06N 88.29W
32 M6 **Oconto** Wisconsin, N USA 44.55N 87.52W
32 M6 **Oconto Falls** Wisconsin, N USA 44.52N 88.06W
32 M6 **Oconto River** ~ Wisconsin, N USA
106 I3 **O Corgo** Galicia, NW Spain 42.55N 7.25W
43 V16 **Ocosingo** Chiapas, SE Mexico 16.51N 92.06W
44 J8 **Ocotal** Nueva Segovia, NW Nicaragua 13.38N 86.27W
44 F6 **Ocotepeque** ◈ *department* W Honduras
Ocotepeque *see* Nueva Ocotepeque
42 L13 **Ocotlán** Jalisco, SW Mexico 20.18N 102.45W
43 R16 **Ocotlán** *var.* Ocotlán de Morelos. Oaxaca, SE Mexico 16.49N 96.49W
Ocotlán de Morelos *see* Ocotlán
43 U16 **Ocozocuautla** Chiapas, SE Mexico 16.43N 93.19W
23 Y10 **Ocracoke Island** *island* North Carolina, SE USA
104 I3 **Octeville** Manche, N France 49.37N 1.39W
October Revolution Island *see* Oktyabr'skoy Revolyutsii, Ostrov
45 R17 **Ocú** Herrera, S Panama 7.55N 80.47W
85 Q14 **Ocua** Cabo Delgado, NE Mozambique 13.37S 39.44E
Ocumare *see* Ocumare del Tuy
56 M5 **Ocumare del Tuy** *var.* Ocumare. Miranda, N Venezuela 10.07N 66.46W
79 P17 **Oda** SE Ghana 5.54N 1.01W
170 F12 **Ōda** *var.* Oda. Shimane, Honshū, SW Japan 35.09N 132.31E
94 K3 **Ódádhahraun** *lava flow* C Iceland
176 Y14 **Odammun** ~ Irian Jaya, E Indonesia
171 Mm9 **Ōdate** Akita, Honshū, C Japan 40.18N 140.34E
171 J16 **Odawara** Kanagawa, Honshū, S Japan 35.13N 139.07E
97 D14 **Odda** Hordaland, S Norway 60.03N 6.34E
97 G22 **Odder** Århus, C Denmark 55.58N 10.10E
Oddur *see* Xuddur
31 T13 **Odebolt** Iowa, C USA 42.18N 95.15W
106 H14 **Odeleite** Faro, S Portugal 37.01N 7.28W
27 Q4 **Odell** Texas, SW USA 34.19N 99.24W
27 T14 **Odem** Texas, SW USA 27.57N 97.34W
106 F13 **Odemira** Beja, S Portugal 37.34N 8.37W
142 C14 **Ödemiş** İzmir, SW Turkey 38.10N 27.58E
Ödenburg *see* Sopron
85 I22 **Odendaalsrus** Free State, C South Africa 27.52S 26.42E
Odenpäh *see* Otepää
97 H23 **Odense** Fyn, C Denmark 55.24N 10.22E
103 H19 **Odenwald** ▲▲ W Germany
86 H10 **Oder** *Cz./Pol.* Odra. ~ C Europe
Oderberg *see* Bohumín
102 P11 **Oderbruch** *wetland* Germany/Poland
Oderhaff *see* Szczeciński, Zalew
102 O11 **Oder-Havel-Kanal** *canal* NE Germany
Oderhellen *see* Odorheiu Secuiesc
102 P13 **Oder-Spree-Kanal** *canal* NE Germany
Odertal *see* Zdzieszowice
108 I7 **Oderzo** Veneto, NE Italy 45.48N 12.33E
124 Pp4 **Odesa** *Rus.* Odessa. Odes'ka Oblast', SW Ukraine 46.28N 30.43E
Odesa *see* Odes'ka Oblast'
97 L18 **Ödeshög** Östergötland, S Sweden 58.13N 14.40E
119 O9 **Odes'ka Oblast'** *var.* Odesa, *Rus.* Odesskaya Oblast'. ◈ *province* SW Ukraine
26 M8 **Odessa** Texas, SW USA 31.51N 102.22W
34 K8 **Odessa** Washington, NW USA 47.19N 118.41W
Odessa *see* Odesa
Odesskaya Oblast' *see* Odes'ka Oblast'
125 Ff13 **Odesskoye** Omskaya Oblast', C Russian Federation 54.15N 72.45E
Odessus *see* Varna
104 F6 **Odet** ~ NW France
106 I14 **Odiel** ~ SW Spain
78 L14 **Odienné** NW Ivory Coast 9.32N 7.34W
179 Pp12 **Odiongan** Tablas Island, C Philippines 12.23N 122.01E
118 L12 **Odobeşti** Vrancea, E Romania 45.46N 27.06E
112 H13 **Odolanów** *Ger.* Adelnau. Wielkopolskie, C Poland 51.35N 17.42E
178 J13 **Ôdôngk** Kâmpóng Spoe, S Cambodia 11.48N 104.45E
27 N6 **O'donnell** Texas, SW USA 32.57N 101.49W
100 O7 **Odoorn** Drenthe, NE Netherlands 52.52N 6.49E
Odorhei *see* Odorheiu Secuiesc
118 J11 **Odorheiu Secuiesc** *Ger.* Oderhellen, *Hung.* Vámosudvarhely; *prev.* Odorhei; *Ger.* Hofmarkt. Harghita, C Romania 46.18N 25.17E
Odra *see* Oder
114 J9 **Odžaci** *Ger.* Hodschag, *Hung.* Hodság. Serbia, NW Yugoslavia 45.31N 19.15E
61 N14 **Oeiras** Piauí, E Brazil 07.00S 42.07W
106 F11 **Oeiras** Lisboa, C Portugal 38.40N 9.18W
103 G14 **Oelde** Nordrhein-Westfalen, W Germany 51.49N 8.09E
30 J11 **Oelrichs** South Dakota, N USA 43.08N 103.13W
Oels/Oels in Schlesien *see* Oleśnica
103 M17 **Oelsnitz** Sachsen, E Germany 50.22N 12.12E
31 X12 **Oelwein** Iowa, C USA 42.40N 91.54W
Oeniadae *see* Oiniádes
203 N17 **Oeno Island** *atoll* Pitcairn Islands, C Pacific Ocean
Oesel *see* Saaremaa
110 L7 **Oetz** *var.* Ötz. Tirol, W Austria 47.15N 10.56E
143 P11 **Of** Trabzon, NE Turkey 40.57N 40.16E
32 K15 **O'Fallon** Illinois, N USA 38.35N 89.54W
29 W4 **O'Fallon** Missouri, C USA 38.54N 90.31W
109 N16 **Ofanto** ~ S Italy
99 D18 **Offaly** *Ir.* Ua Uíbh Fhailí; *prev.* King's County. *cultural region* C Ireland
103 H18 **Offenbach** *var.* Offenbach am Main. Hessen, W Germany 50.06N 8.46E
Offenbach am Main *see* Offenbach
103 F22 **Offenburg** Baden-Württemberg, SW Germany 48.28N 7.57E
190 C2 **Officer Creek** *seasonal river* South Australia
Oficina María Elena *see* María Elena
Oficina Pedro de Valdivia *see* Pedro de Valdivia
117 K22 **Ofidoússa** *island* Kykládes, Greece, Aegean Sea
Ofiral *see* Sharm el Sheikh
94 H10 **Ofotfjorden** *fjord* N Norway
198 D8 **Ofu** *island* Manua Islands, E American Samoa
171 Mm12 **Ōfunato** Iwate, Honshū, C Japan 39.04N 141.41E
171 M10 **Oga** Akita, Honshū, C Japan 39.54N 139.48E
Ogaadeen *see* Ogadēn
171 M11 **Ogachi** Akita, Honshū, C Japan 39.03N 140.26E
171 M11 **Ogachi-tōge** *pass* Honshū, C Japan 39.00N 140.20E
83 N14 **Ogadēn** *Som.* Ogaadeen. *plateau* Ethiopia/Somalia
171 M10 **Oga-hantō** *peninsula* Honshū, C Japan
171 Hh14 **Ōgaki** Gifu, Honshū, SW Japan 35.21N 136.35E
30 L15 **Ogallala** Nebraska, C USA 41.09N 101.43W
174 I12 **Ogan, Air** ~ Sumatera, W Indonesia
172 T16 **Ogasawara-shotō** *Eng.* Bonin Islands. *island group* SE Japan
12 I9 **Ogascanane, Lac** ◎ Quebec, SE Canada
172 N9 **Ogawara-ko** ◎ Honshū, C Japan
79 T15 **Ogbomosho** Oyo, W Nigeria 8.10N 4.16E
31 U13 **Ogden** Iowa, C USA 42.03N 94.01W
38 L2 **Ogden** Utah, W USA 41.09N 111.58W
20 I6 **Ogdensburg** New York, NE USA 44.42N 75.25W
197 L16 **Ogea Driki** *island* Lau Group, E Fiji
197 L16 **Ogea Levu** *island* Lau Group, E Fiji
25 W5 **Ogeechee River** ~ Georgia, SE USA
Oger *see* Ogre
152 F6 **Oghiyon Shŭrkhogi** *wetland* NW Uzbekistan
171 K12 **Ogi** Niigata, Sado, C Japan 37.49N 138.16E
8 H5 **Ogilvie** Yukon Territory, NW Canada 63.34N 139.43W
8 H4 **Ogilvie** ~ Yukon Territory, NW Canada
8 H5 **Ogilvie Mountains** ▲▲ Yukon Territory, NW Canada
Oginskiy Kanal *see* Ahinski Kanal
152 B10 **Oglanly** Balkanskiy Velayat, W Turkmenistan 39.56N 54.25E
25 T5 **Oglethorpe** Georgia, SE USA 32.17N 84.03W
25 T2 **Oglethorpe, Mount** ▲ Georgia, SE USA 34.29N 84.19W
108 F7 **Oglio** *anc.* Ollius. ~ N Italy
105 T8 **Ognon** ~ E France
175 Pp7 **Ogoamas, Pegunungan** ▲▲ Sulawesi, N Indonesia
127 N14 **Ogodzha** Amurskaya Oblast', S Russian Federation 52.51N 132.49E
79 W16 **Ogoja** Cross River, S Nigeria 6.37N 8.48E
10 C10 **Ogoki** ~ Ontario, S Canada
10 D11 **Ogoki Lake** ◎ Ontario, C Canada
168 K10 **Ögöömör** Ömnögovĭ, S Mongolia 43.47N 104.31E
81 F19 **Ogooué** ~ Congo/Gabon
81 E18 **Ogooué-Ivindo** *off.* Province de l'Ogooué-Ivindo, *var.* L'Ogooué-Ivindo. ◈ *province* N Gabon
81 E19 **Ogooué-Lolo** *off.* Province de l'Ogooué-Lolo, *var.* L'Ogooué-Lolo. ◈ *province* C Gabon
81 C19 **Ogooué-Maritime** *off.* Province de l'Ogooué-Maritime, *var.* L'Ogooué-Maritime. ◈ *province* W Gabon
170 Cc13 **Ogōri** Fukuoka, Kyūshū, SW Japan 33.25N 130.30E
170 Dd13 **Ogōri** Yamaguchi, Honshū, SW Japan 34.05N 131.20E
116 H7 **Ogosta** ~ NW Bulgaria
114 Q9 **Ogražden** *Bul.* Ograzhden. ▲▲ Bulgaria/FYR Macedonia *see also* Ograzhden
116 G12 **Ograzhden** | Mac. Orgražden. ▲▲ Bulgaria/FYR Macedonia *see also* Ogražden
120 G9 **Ogre** *Ger.* Oger. Ogre, C Latvia 56.49N 24.36E
120 H9 **Ogre** ~ C Latvia
114 C10 **Ogulin** Karlovac, NW Croatia 45.15N 15.13E
79 S16 **Ogun** ◈ *state* SW Nigeria
152 A12 **Ogurdzhaly, Ostrov** *Turkm.* Ogurjaly Adasy. *island* W Turkmenistan
Ogurjaly Adasy *see* Ogurdzhaly, Ostrov
79 U16 **Ogwashi-Uku** Delta, S Nigeria 6.08N 6.38E
193 B23 **Ohai** Southland, South Island, NZ 45.56S 167.59E
153 Q10 **Ohangaron** *Rus.* Akhangaran. Toshkent Wiloyati, E Uzbekistan 40.56N 69.37E
153 Q10 **Ohangaron** *Rus.* Akhangaran. ~ E Uzbekistan
85 C16 **Ohangwena** ◈ *district* N Namibia
171 K17 **Ōhara** Chiba, Honshū, S Japan 35.14N 140.19E
32 M10 **O'Hare** ✈ (Chicago) Illinois, N USA 41.59N 87.56W
172 Nn8 **Ōhata** Aomori, Honshū, C Japan 41.23N 141.09E
192 L13 **Ohau** Manawatu-Wanganui, North Island, NZ 40.40S 175.15E
193 E20 **Ohau, Lake** ◎ South Island, NZ
Ohcejohka *see* Utsjoki
101 J20 **Ohey** Namur, SE Belgium 50.26N 5.07E
203 X15 **O'Higgins, Cabo** *headland* Easter Island, Chile, E Pacific Ocean 27.04S 109.15W
O'Higgins, Lago *see* San Martín, Lago
33 S12 **Ohio** *off.* State of Ohio; also known as The Buckeye State. ◈ *state* N USA
(0) L10 **Ohio River** ~ N USA
Ohlau *see* Oława
103 H16 **Ohm** ~ C Germany
200 R16 **Ohonua** 'Eua, E Tonga 21.20S 174.57W
25 V5 **Ohoopee River** ~ Georgia, SE USA
102 L12 **Ohre** *Ger.* Eger. ~ Czech Republic/Germany
Ohri *see* Ohrid
115 M20 **Ohrid** *Turk.* Ochrida, Ohri. SW FYR Macedonia 41.07N 20.48E
115 M20 **Ohrid, Lake** *var.* Lake Ochrida, *Alb.* Liqeni i Ohrit, *Mac.* Ohridsko Ezero. ◎ Albania/FYR Macedonia
Ohridsko Ezero/Ohrit, Liqeni i *see* Ohrid, Lake
192 L9 **Ohura** Manawatu-Wanganui, North Island, NZ 38.51S 174.58E
60 J9 **Oiapoque** Amapá, E Brazil 3.54N 51.46W
60 J10 **Oiapoque, Rio** *var.* Fleuve l'Oyapok, Oyapock. ~ Brazil/French Guiana *see also* Oyapok, Fleuve l'
13 O9 **Oies, Île aux** *island* Quebec, SE Canada
94 L13 **Oijärvi** Oulu, C Finland 65.37N 26.04E
94 L12 **Oikarainen** Lappi, N Finland 66.30N 25.46E
196 F10 **Oikuul** Babeldaob, N Palau
20 C13 **Oil City** Pennsylvania, NE USA 41.25N 79.42W
20 C12 **Oil Creek** ~ Pennsylvania, NE USA
37 R13 **Oildale** California, W USA 35.25N 119.01W
Oileán Ciarral *see* Castleisland
Oil Islands *see* Chagos Archipelago
117 D18 **Oiniádes** *anc.* Oeniadae. *site of ancient city* Dytikí Ellás, W Greece 38.23N 21.13E
117 L18 **Oinoússes** *island* E Greece
Oírr, Inis *see* Inisheer
101 J15 **Oirschot** Noord-Brabant, S Netherlands 51.30N 5.18E
105 N4 **Oise** ◈ *department* N France
105 P3 **Oise** ~ N France
101 J14 **Oisterwijk** Noord-Brabant, S Netherlands 51.34N 5.12E
47 O14 **Oistins** S Barbados 13.04N 59.33W
170 D14 **Ōita** Ōita, Kyūshū, SW Japan 33.15N 131.34E
170 D14 **Ōita** *off.* Ōita-ken. ◈ *prefecture* Kyūshū, SW Japan
117 E17 **Oíti** ▲ C Greece 38.48N 22.12E
172 Oo6 **Oiwake** Hokkaidō, NE Japan 42.54N 141.49E
37 R14 **Ojai** California, W USA 34.25N 119.15W
96 K13 **Öje** Dalarna, C Sweden 60.49N 13.54E
95 J14 **Öjebyn** Norrbotten, N Sweden 65.20N 21.26E
170 Bb12 **Ojika-jima** *island* SW Japan
42 K5 **Ojinaga** Chihuahua, N Mexico 29.30N 104.25W
171 K13 **Ojiya** *var.* Oziya. Niigata, Honshū, C Japan 37.18N 138.47E
42 M11 **Ojo Caliente** *var.* Ojocaliente. Zacatecas, C Mexico 22.39N 102.17W
42 D6 **Ojo de Liebre, Laguna** *var.* Laguna Scammon, Scammon Lagoon. *lagoon* W Mexico
64 I7 **Ojos del Salado, Cerro** ▲ W Argentina 27.04S 68.34W
107 R7 **Ojos Negros** Aragón, NE Spain 40.43N 1.30W
42 M12 **Ojuelos de Jalisco** Aguascalientes, C Mexico 21.52N 101.40W
131 N4 **Oka** ~ W Russian Federation
85 D19 **Okahandja** Otjozondjupa, C Namibia 21.58S 16.55E
192 L9 **Okahukura** Manawatu-Wanganui, North Island, NZ 38.48S 175.13E
192 J3 **Okaihau** Northland, North Island, NZ 35.18S 173.44E
85 D18 **Okakarara** Otjozondjupa, N Namibia 20.34S 17.24E
11 P5 **Okak Islands** *island group* Newfoundland, E Canada
8 M17 **Okanagan** ~ British Columbia, SW Canada
9 N17 **Okanagan Lake** ◎ British Columbia, SW Canada
Ókanizsa *see* Kanjiža
85 C16 **Okankolo** Otjikoto, N Namibia 17.57S 16.28E
34 K6 **Okanogan River** ~ Washington, NW USA
194 I13 **Okapa** Eastern Highlands, C PNG 6.22S 145.29E
85 D18 **Okaputa** Otjozondjupa, N Namibia 20.09S 16.55E
155 V9 **Okāra** Punjab, E Pakistan 30.49N 73.31E
28 M10 **Okarche** Oklahoma, C USA 35.43N 97.58W
152 B13 **Okarem** *Turkm.* Ekerem. Balkanskiy Velayat, W Turkmenistan 38.06N 53.52E
201 X14 **Okat Harbor** *harbor* Kosrae, E Micronesia
24 M5 **Okatibbee Creek** ~ Mississippi, S USA
85 C17 **Okaukuejo** Kunene, N Namibia 19.09S 15.57E
Okavanggo *see* Cubango/Okavango
85 E17 **Okavango** ◈ *district* NW Namibia
85 G17 **Okavango** *var.* Cubango, Kavango, Kavengo, Kubango, Okavanggo, *Port.* Ocavango. ~ S Africa *see also* Cubango
85 G17 **Okavango Delta** *wetland* N Botswana
171 J15 **Okaya** Nagano, Honshū, S Japan 36.04N 138.02E
170 Ff14 **Okayama** Okayama, Honshū, SW Japan 34.40N 133.54E
170 F13 **Okayama** *off.* Okayama-ken. ◈ *prefecture* Honshū, SW Japan
171 I16 **Okazaki** Aichi, Honshū, C Japan 34.58N 137.10E
112 M12 **Okęcie** ✈ (Warszawa) Mazowieckie, C Poland 52.08N 20.57E
25 Y13 **Okeechobee** Florida, SE USA 27.14N 80.49W
25 Y14 **Okeechobee, Lake** ◎ Florida, SE USA
28 M9 **Okeene** Oklahoma, C USA 36.07N 98.19W
25 V8 **Okefenokee Swamp** *wetland* Georgia, SE USA
99 J24 **Okehampton** SW England, UK 50.44N 4.00W
29 P10 **Okemah** Oklahoma, C USA 35.25N 96.18W
79 U16 **Okene** Kogi, S Nigeria 7.31N 6.15E
102 K13 **Oker** *var.* Ocker. ~ NW Germany
103 J14 **Oker-Stausee** ◎ C Germany
127 O13 **Okha** Ostrov Sakhalin, Sakhalinskaya Oblast', SE Russian Federation 53.33N 142.55E
129 U15 **Okhansk** *var.* Ochansk. Permskaya Oblast', NW Russian Federation 57.44N 55.20E
127 N10 **Okhota** ~ E Russian Federation
127 Nn11 **Okhotsk** Khabarovskiy Kray, E Russian Federation 59.21N 143.14E
199 I2 **Okhotsk, Sea of** *sea* NW Pacific Ocean
119 T4 **Okhtyrka** *Rus.* Akhtyrka. Sums'ka Oblast', NE Ukraine 50.19N 34.54E
199 Gg6 **Oki-Daitō Ridge** *undersea feature* W Pacific Ocean
85 E23 **Okiep** Northern Cape, W South Africa 29.39S 17.53E
Oki-guntō *see* Oki-shotō
170 Ff11 **Oki-kaikyō** *strait* SW Japan
172 P15 **Okinawa** Okinawa, SW Japan 26.19N 127.46E
172 Oo14 **Okinawa** *off.* Okinawa-ken. ◈ *prefecture* Okinawa, SW Japan
172 Oo14 **Okinawa** *island* SW Japan
172 Q14 **Okinoerabu-jima** *island* Nansei-shotō, SW Japan
170 Dd15 **Okino-shima** *island* SW Japan
170 Ff11 **Oki-shotō** *var.* Oki-guntō. *island group* SW Japan
79 T16 **Okitipupa** Ondo, SW Nigeria 6.33N 4.43E
177 G8 **Okkan** Pegu, SW Burma 17.31N 95.51E
29 N10 **Oklahoma** *off.* State of Oklahoma; also known as The Sooner State. ◈ *state* C USA
29 N11 **Oklahoma City** *state capital* Oklahoma, C USA 35.28N 97.31W
27 Q4 **Oklaunion** Texas, SW USA 34.07N 99.07W
25 W10 **Oklawaha River** ~ Florida, SE USA
29 P10 **Okmulgee** Oklahoma, C USA 35.37N 95.57W
Oknitsa *see* Ocniţa
24 M3 **Okolona** Mississippi, S USA 34.00N 88.45W
172 Q4 **Okoppe** Hokkaidō, NE Japan 44.27N 143.06E
9 Q16 **Okotoks** Alberta, SW Canada 50.46N 113.57W
82 H6 **Oko, Wadi** ~ NE Sudan
81 G19 **Okoyo** Cuvette, W Congo 1.28S 15.04E
79 S15 **Okpara** ~ Benin/Nigeria
94 J8 **Øksfjord** Finnmark, N Norway 70.13N 22.22E
176 Z12 **Oksibil** Irian Jaya, E Indonesia 4.52S 140.32E
129 R4 **Oksino** Nenetskiy Avtonomnyy Okrug, NW Russian Federation 67.33N 52.15E
94 G13 **Oksskolten** ▲ C Norway 66.00N 14.18E
Oksu *see* Oqsu
150 M8 **Oktaybr'skiy** Kostanay, N Kazakhstan
194 E11 **Ok Tedi** Western, W PNG
Oktemberyan *see* Hoktemberyan
177 G7 **Oktwin** Pegu, C Burma 18.46N 96.21E
131 R6 **Oktyabr'sk** Samarskaya Oblast', W Russian Federation 53.13N 48.36E
Oktyabr'sk *see* Kandyagash
129 N12 **Oktyabr'skiy** Arkhangel'skaya Oblast', NW Russian Federation 61.03N 43.16E
127 Pp12 **Oktyabr'skiy** Kamchatskaya Oblast', E Russian Federation 52.35N 94.18E
131 T5 **Oktyabr'skiy** Respublika Bashkortostan, W Russian Federation 54.28N 53.29E
131 O11 **Oktyabr'skiy** Volgogradskaya Oblast', SW Russian Federation 48.00N 43.35E
Oktyabr'skiy *see* Aktsyabrski
131 V7 **Oktyabr'skoye** Orenburgskaya Oblast', W Russian Federation 52.22N 55.39E
126 J3 **Oktyabr'skoy Revolyutsii, Ostrov** *Eng.* October Revolution Island. *island* Severnaya Zemlya, N Russian Federation
170 C15 **Ōkuchi** *var.* Ôkuti. Kagoshima, Kyūshū, SW Japan 32.03N 130.36E
Okulovka *see* Uglovka
171 Mm5 **Okushiri-tō** *var.* Okusiri Tô. *island* NE Japan
Okusiri Tô *see* Okushiri-tō
79 S15 **Okuta** Kwara, W Nigeria 9.18N 3.09E
Ôkuti *see* Ōkuchi
85 F19 **Okwa** *var.* Chapman's. ~ Botswana/Namibia
127 O10 **Ola** Magadanskaya Oblast', E Russian Federation 59.36N 151.18E
29 T11 **Ola** Arkansas, C USA 35.01N 93.13W
Ola *see* Ala
37 T11 **Olacha Peak** ▲ California, W USA 36.15N 118.07W
94 J1 **Ólafsfjördhur** Nordhurland Eystra, N Iceland 66.04N 18.36W
94 H3 **Ólafsvík** Vesturland, W Iceland 64.52N 23.45W
Oláhbrettye *see* Bretea-Română
Oláhszentgyőrgy *see* Sângeorz-Băi
Oláh-Toplicza *see* Toplița
37 T11 **Olancha** California, W USA 36.16N 118.00W
44 J5 **Olanchito** Yoro, C Honduras 15.27N 86.37W
44 J6 **Olancho** ◈ *department* E Honduras
97 O20 **Öland** *island* S Sweden
97 O19 **Ölands norra udde** *headland* S Sweden 57.21N 17.06E
97 N22 **Ölands södra udde** *headland* S Sweden 56.12N 16.26E
190 K7 **Olary** South Australia 32.18S 140.16E
29 R4 **Olathe** Kansas, C USA 38.52N 94.49W
63 C22 **Olavarría** Buenos Aires, E Argentina 36.57S 60.19W
94 O2 **Olav V Land** *physical region* C Svalbard
113 H14 **Oława** *Ger.* Ohlau. Dolnośląskie, SW Poland 50.57N 17.18E
109 D17 **Olbia** *prev.* Terranova Pausania. Sardegna, Italy, C Mediterranean Sea 40.55N 9.30E
46 G5 **Old Bahama Channel** *channel* Bahamas/Cuba
Old Bay State/Old Colony State *see* Massachusetts
8 H2 **Old Crow** Yukon Territory, NW Canada 67.34N 139.55W
Old Dominion *see* Virginia
Oldeberkeap *see* Oldeberkoop
100 M7 **Oldeberkoop** *Fris.* Oldeberkeap. Friesland, N Netherlands 52.55N 6.07E
100 L10 **Oldebroek** Gelderland, E Netherlands 52.27N 5.54E
100 L8 **Oldemarkt** Overijssel, N Netherlands 52.49N 5.58E
96 E11 **Olden** Sogn og Fjordane, C Norway 61.52N 6.44E
102 G10 **Oldenburg** Niedersachsen, NW Germany 53.09N 8.13E
102 K8 **Oldenburg** Schleswig-Holstein, N Germany 54.17N 10.55E
100 P10 **Oldenzaal** Overijssel, E Netherlands 52.19N 6.52E
20 J8 **Old Forge** New York, NE USA 43.42N 74.59W
Old Goa *see* Goa
99 L17 **Oldham** NW England, UK 53.36N 2.00W
41 Q14 **Old Harbor** Kodiak Island, Alaska, USA 57.12N 153.18W
46 J13 **Old Harbour** C Jamaica 17.55N 77.06W
99 C22 **Old Head of Kinsale** *Ir.* An Seancheann. *headland* SW Ireland 51.37N 8.33W
22 J8 **Old Hickory Lake** ▣ Tennessee, S USA
Old Line State *see* Maryland
Old North State *see* North Carolina
83 I17 **Ol Doinyo Lengeyo** ▲▲ C Kenya
9 Q16 **Olds** Alberta, SW Canada 51.49N 114.06W
21 O7 **Old Speck Mountain** ▲ Maine, NE USA 44.34N 70.55W
21 S6 **Old Town** Maine, NE USA 44.55N 68.39W
9 T17 **Old Wives Lake** ◎ Saskatchewan, S Canada
168 J7 **Öldziyt** Arhangay, C Mongolia 48.30N 101.25E
169 N10 **Öldziyt** Dornogovĭ, SE Mongolia 44.42N 109.10E
196 H6 **Oleai** *var.* San Jose. Saipan, S Northern Mariana Islands
20 E11 **Olean** New York, NE USA 42.04N 78.24W
112 O7 **Olecko** *Ger.* Treuburg. Warmińsko-Mazurskie, NE Poland 54.01N 22.28E
108 C7 **Oleggio** Piemonte, NE Italy 45.36N 8.37E
126 L13 **Olëkma** Amurskaya Oblast', SE Russian Federation 57.00N 120.27E

◆ COUNTRY ● COUNTRY CAPITAL ◇ DEPENDENT TERRITORY ○ DEPENDENT TERRITORY CAPITAL ◈ ADMINISTRATIVE REGION ✈ INTERNATIONAL AIRPORT ▲ MOUNTAIN ▲▲ MOUNTAIN RANGE VOLCANO ~ RIVER ◎ LAKE ▣ RESERVOIR

OLËKMA – ORLANDO

126 L13 **Olëkma** ≈ C Russian Federation
126 L12 **Olëkminsk** Respublika Sakha (Yakutiya), NE Russian Federation 60.25N 120.25E
119 W7 **Oleksandrivka** Donets'ka Oblast', E Ukraine 48.42N 36.56E
119 R7 **Oleksandrivka** *Rus.* Aleksandrovka. Kirovohrads'ka Oblast', C Ukraine 48.58N 32.13E
119 Q9 **Oleksandrivka** Mykolayivs'ka Oblast', S Ukraine 47.42N 31.17E
119 S7 **Oleksandriya** *Rus.* Aleksandriya. Kirovohrads'ka Oblast', C Ukraine 48.42N 33.07E
95 B20 **Ølen** Hordaland, S Norway 59.36N 5.48E
128 J4 **Olenegorsk** Murmanskaya Oblast', NW Russian Federation 68.06N 33.15E
126 K8 **Olenëk** Respublika Sakha (Yakutiya), NE Russian Federation 68.28N 112.18E
126 Jj9 **Olenëk** ≈ NE Russian Federation
126 Kk6 **Olenëkskiy Zaliv** *bay* N Russian Federation
128 K6 **Olenitsa** Murmanskaya Oblast', NW Russian Federation 66.27N 35.21E
104 I11 **Oléron, Île d'** *island* W France
113 H14 **Oleśnica** *Ger.* Oels, Oels in Schlesien. Dolnośląskie, SW Poland 51.13N 17.19E
113 I15 **Olesno** *Ger.* Rosenberg. Opolskie, S Poland 50.53N 18.23E
118 M3 **Olevs'k** *Rus.* Olevsk. Zhytomyrs'ka Oblast', N Ukraine 51.12N 27.38E
127 Nn18 **Ol'ga** Primorskiy Kray, SE Russian Federation 43.41N 135.06E
Olga, Mount *see* Kata Tjuta
94 P2 **Olgastretet** *strait* E Svalbard
168 D5 **Ölgiy** Bayan-Ölgiy, W Mongolia 48.57N 89.59E
97 F23 **Ølgod** Ribe, W Denmark 55.43N 8.37E
106 H14 **Olhão** Faro, S Portugal 37.01N 7.49W
95 L14 **Olhava** Oulu, C Finland 65.28N 25.25E
114 B12 **Olib** *It.* Ulbo. *island* W Croatia
85 B16 **Olifa** Kunene, NW Namibia 17.25S 14.27E
85 E20 **Olifants** *var.* Elephant River. ≈ E Namibia
85 E25 **Olifants** *var.* Elefantes. ≈ SW South Africa
85 G22 **Olifantshoek** Northern Cape, N South Africa 27.52S 22.46E
196 L15 **Olimarao Atoll** *atoll* Caroline Islands, C Micronesia
Ólimbos *see* Ólympos
Olimpo *see* Fuerte Olimpo
61 Q15 **Olinda** Pernambuco, E Brazil 08.00S 34.51W
Olinthos *see* Ólynthos
85 I20 **Oliphants Drift** Kgatleng, SE Botswana 24.13S 26.52E
Olisipo *see* Lisboa
Olita *see* Alytus
107 Q4 **Olite** Navarra, N Spain 42.28N 1.40W
64 K10 **Oliva** Córdoba, C Argentina 32.03S 63.34W
107 T11 **Oliva** País Valenciano, E Spain 38.55N 0.09W
106 I12 **Oliva de la Frontera** Extremadura, W Spain 38.16N 6.54W
Olivares *see* Olivares de Júcar
64 H9 **Olivares, Cerro de** ▲ N Chile 30.25S 69.52W
107 P9 **Olivares de Júcar** *var.* Olivares. Castilla-La Mancha, C Spain 39.45N 2.21W
24 L1 **Olive Branch** Mississippi, S USA 34.58N 89.49W
23 O5 **Olive Hill** Kentucky, S USA 38.18N 83.10W
37 O6 **Olivehurst** California, W USA 39.05N 121.33W
106 G7 **Oliveira de Azeméis** Aveiro, N Portugal 40.49N 8.28W
106 I11 **Olivenza** Extremadura, W Spain 38.40N 7.06W
9 N17 **Oliver** British Columbia, SW Canada 49.10N 119.37W
105 N7 **Olivet** Loiret, C France 47.52N 1.53E
31 Q12 **Olivet** South Dakota, N USA 43.13N 97.40W
31 T9 **Olivia** Minnesota, N USA 44.46N 94.59W
193 C20 **Olivine Range** ▲ South Island, NZ
110 H10 **Olivone** Ticino, S Switzerland 46.32N 8.55E
Ölkeyek *see* Ul'kayak
131 O9 **Ol'khovka** Volgogradskaya Oblast', SW Russian Federation 49.54N 44.36E
113 K16 **Olkusz** Małopolskie, S Poland 50.16N 19.31E
24 I6 **Olla** Louisiana, S USA 31.54N 92.14W
64 I4 **Ollagüe, Volcán** *var.* Oyahue, Volcán Oyahue. ▲ N Chile 21.25S 68.10W
201 U13 **Ollan** *island* Chuuk, C Micronesia
196 F7 **Ollei** Babeldaob, N Palau 7.43N 134.37E
Ollius *see* Oglio
110 C10 **Ollon** Vaud, W Switzerland 46.19N 7.00E
153 Q10 **Olmaliq** *Rus.* Almalyk. Toshkent Wiloyati, E Uzbekistan 40.51N 69.39E
106 M6 **Olmedo** Castilla-León, N Spain 41.16N 4.40W
58 B10 **Olmos** Lambayeque, W Peru 6.00S 79.43W
Olmütz *see* Olomouc
32 M15 **Olney** Illinois, N USA 38.43N 88.05W
27 R5 **Olney** Texas, SW USA 33.22N 98.45W
97 L22 **Olofström** Blekinge, S Sweden 56.16N 14.33E
195 Y15 **Olomburi** Malaita, N Solomon Islands 9.00S 161.09E
113 H17 **Olomouc** *Ger.* Olmütz, *Pol.* Ołomuniec. Olomoucký Kraj, E Czech Republic 49.36N 17.13E
113 H18 **Olomoucký Kraj** ◐ region E Czech Republic
Ołomuniec *see* Olomouc
125 Cc6 **Olonets** Respublika Kareliya, NW Russian Federation 60.58N 33.01E
179 P10 **Olongapo** *off.* Olongapo City. Luzon, N Philippines 14.52N 120.16E
104 J16 **Oloron-Ste-Marie** Pyrénées-Atlantiques, SW France 43.12N 0.34W
198 Dd8 **Olosega** *island* Manua Islands, E American Samoa
107 W4 **Olot** Cataluña, NE Spain 42.10N 2.30E
152 K12 **Olot** *Rus.* Alat. Bukhoro Wiloyati, C Uzbekistan 39.22N 63.42E
114 I12 **Olovo** Federacija Bosna I Hercegovina, E Bosnia and Herzegovina 44.08N 18.35E
126 Kk16 **Olovyannaya** Chitinskaya Oblast', S Russian Federation 50.58N 115.24E
127 Oo6 **Oloy** ≈ NE Russian Federation
103 F16 **Olpe** Nordrhein-Westfalen, W Germany 51.01N 7.51E
111 N8 **Olperer** ▲ SW Austria 47.03N 11.36E
Olshanka *see* Vil'shanka
Ol'shany *see* Al'shany
Olsnitz *see* Murska Sobota
100 M10 **Olst** Overijssel, E Netherlands 52.19N 6.06E
112 L8 **Olsztyn** *Ger.* Allenstein. Warmińsko-Mazurskie, NE Poland, 53.46N 20.28E
112 L8 **Olsztynek** *Ger.* Hohenstein in Ostpreussen. Warmińsko-Mazurskie, NE Poland, 53.34N 20.16E
118 I14 **Olt** ◐ *county* SW Romania
118 I14 **Olt** *var.* Oltul, *Ger.* Alt. ≈ S Romania
110 E7 **Olten** Solothurn, NW Switzerland 47.20N 7.51E
118 K14 **Oltenița** *prev. Eng.* Oltenitsa, *anc.* Constantiola. Călărași, SE Romania 44.04N 26.40E
Oltenitsa *see* Oltenița
118 H14 **Olteț** ≈ S Romania
26 M4 **Olton** Texas, SW USA 34.10N 102.07W
143 R12 **Oltu** Erzurum, NE Turkey 40.34N 41.58E
Oltul *see* Olt
152 G7 **Oltynkŭl** Qoraqalpoghiston Respublikasi, NW Uzbekistan 43.04N 58.51E
167 S15 **Oluan Pi** *Eng.* Cape Olwanpi. *headland* S Taiwan 21.57N 120.48E
Ólubló *see* Stará L'ubovňa
143 R11 **Olur** Erzurum, NE Turkey 40.49N 42.07E
106 L15 **Olvera** Andalucía, S Spain 36.55N 5.15W
Ol'viopol' *see* Pervomays'k
Olwanpi, Cape *see* Oluan Pi
17 G2 **Olympia** *state capital* Washington, NW USA 47.02N 122.54W
117 D20 **Olympía** Dytikí Ellás, S Greece 37.39N 21.36E
190 H5 **Olympic Dam** South Australia 30.25S 136.56E
34 F7 **Olympic Mountains** ▲ Washington, NW USA
124 R12 **Ólympos** *var.* Troodos, *Eng.* Mount Olympus. ▲ C Cyprus 34.55N 32.49E
117 F15 **Ólympos** *var.* Ólimbos, *Eng.* Mount Olympus. ▲ N Greece 40.04N 22.24E
117 L17 **Ólympos** ▲ Lésvos, E Greece 39.03N 26.20E
17 G1 **Olympus, Mount** ▲ Washington, NW USA 47.48N 123.42W
Olympus, Mount *see* Ólympos
117 G14 **Ólynthos** *var.* Olinthos; *anc.* Olynthus. *site of ancient city* Kentrikí Makedonía, N Greece 40.16N 23.21E
Olynthus *see* Ólynthos
119 Q3 **Olyshivka** Chernihivs'ka Oblast', N Ukraine 51.13N 31.19E
127 Q7 **Olyutorskiy, Mys** *headland* E Russian Federation 59.56N 170.22E
127 Pp8 **Olyutorskiy Zaliv** *bay* E Russian Federation
194 F11 **Om** ≈ W PNG
133 S6 **Om'** ≈ N Russian Federation
164 I13 **Oma** Xizang Zizhiqu, W China 32.30N 83.13E
172 N8 **Ōma** Aomori, Honshū, C Japan 41.31N 140.54E
129 P6 **Oma** ≈ NW Russian Federation
171 Jj14 **Ōmachi** *var.* Ōmati. Nagano, Honshū, S Japan 36.33N 137.49E
171 Ii17 **Omae-zaki** *headland* Honshū, S Japan 34.36N 138.12E
171 M11 **Ōmagari** Akita, Honshū, C Japan 39.27N 140.28E
99 E15 **Omagh** *Ir.* An Ómaigh. W Northern Ireland, UK 54.36N 7.18W
31 S15 **Omaha** Nebraska, C USA 41.14N 95.57W
85 E19 **Omaheke** ◐ *district* W Namibia
147 W10 **Oman** *off.* Sultanate of Oman, *Ar.* Salṭanat 'Umān; *prev.* Muscat and Oman. ◆ *monarchy* SW Asia
133 O10 **Oman Basin** *var.* Bassin d'Oman. *undersea feature* N Indian Ocean
Oman, Bassin d' *see* Oman Basin
133 N10 **Oman, Gulf of** *Ar.* Khalīj 'Umān. *gulf* N Arabian Sea
192 J3 **Omapere** Northland, North Island, NZ 35.32S 173.24E
193 E20 **Omarama** Canterbury, South Island, NZ 44.29S 169.57E
114 F11 **Omarska** Republika Srpska, NW Bosnia and Herzegovina 44.53N 16.52E
85 C18 **Omaruru** Erongo, NW Namibia 21.25S 15.57E
85 C19 **Omaruru** ≈ W Namibia
85 E17 **Omatako** ≈ NE Namibia
Ōmati *see* Ōmachi
85 E18 **Omawewozonyanda** Omaheke, E Namibia 21.30S 19.34E
172 N7 **Ōma-zaki** *headland* Honshū, C Japan 41.32N 140.53E
Omba *see* Ambae
Ombai *see* Alor, Pulau
175 Rr16 **Ombai, Selat** *strait* Nusa Tenggara, S Indonesia
85 C16 **Ombalantu** Omusati, N Namibia 17.33S 14.58E
81 H15 **Ombella-Mpoko** ◐ *prefecture* S Central African Republic
Ombetsu *see* Onbetsu
85 B17 **Ombombo** Kunene, NW Namibia 18.43S 13.55E
81 D19 **Omboué** Ogooué-Maritime, W Gabon 1.37S 9.19E
108 G13 **Ombrone** ≈ C Italy
82 F9 **Omdurman** *var.* Umm Durmān. Khartoum, C Sudan 15.37N 32.28E
171 Jj16 **Ōme** Tōkyō, Honshū, S Japan 35.48N 139.10E
108 C6 **Omegna** Piemonte, NE Italy 45.54N 8.25E
191 P12 **Omeo** Victoria, SE Australia 37.09S 147.36E
144 F11 **'Omer** Southern, C Israel 31.16N 34.51E
43 P16 **Ometepec** Guerrero, S Mexico 16.39N 98.22W
44 K11 **Ometepe, Isla de** *island* S Nicaragua
Om Hager *see* Om Hajer
82 I10 **Om Hajer** *var.* Om Hager. SW Eritrea 14.19N 36.46E
171 H14 **Ōmi-Hachiman** *var.* Ōmihachiman. Shiga, Honshū, SW Japan 35.09N 136.04E
8 L12 **Omineca Mountains** ▲ British Columbia, W Canada
115 F14 **Omiš** *It.* Almissa. Split-Dalmacija, S Croatia 43.27N 16.41E
114 B10 **Omišalj** Primorje-Gorski Kotar, NW Croatia 45.10N 14.33E
170 Dd12 **Ōmi-shima** *island* SW Japan
85 D19 **Omitara** Khomas, C Namibia 22.18S 18.01E
43 O16 **Omitlán, Río** ≈ S Mexico
41 X14 **Ommaney, Cape** *headland* Baranof Island, Alaska, USA 56.10N 134.40W
100 N9 **Ommen** Overijssel, E Netherlands 52.31N 6.25E
168 K11 **Ömnögovĭ** ◐ *province* S Mongolia
203 X7 **Omoa** Fatu Hira, NE French Polynesia 10.30S 138.40E
Omo Botego *see* Omo Wenz
Ómoldova *see* Moldova Veche
127 O6 **Omolon** Chukotskiy Avtonomnyy Okrug, NE Russian Federation 65.11N 96.33E
127 O7 **Omolon** ≈ NE Russian Federation
126 Ll8 **Omoloy** ≈ NE Russian Federation
171 M10 **Omono-gawa** ≈ Honshū, C Japan
83 I14 **Omo Wenz** *var.* Omo Botego. ≈ Ethiopia/Kenya
125 Ff13 **Omsk** Omskaya Oblast', C Russian Federation 55.00N 73.22E
125 Ff12 **Omskaya Oblast'** ◐ *province* C Russian Federation
127 O8 **Omsukchan** Magadanskaya Oblast', E Russian Federation 62.25N 155.22E
172 Q4 **Ōmu** Hokkaidō, NE Japan 44.36N 142.55E
112 M9 **Omulew** ≈ NE Poland
118 J12 **Omul, Vârful** *prev.* Vîrful Omu. ▲ C Romania 45.24N 25.26E
85 D16 **Omundaungilo** Ohangwena, N Namibia 17.28S 16.39E
170 C13 **Ōmura** Nagasaki, Kyūshū, SW Japan 32.55N 129.54E
85 B17 **Omusati** ◐ *district* N Namibia
170 Cc13 **Ōmuta** Fukuoka, Kyūshū, SW Japan 33.02N 130.26E
129 S14 **Omutninsk** Kirovskaya Oblast', NW Russian Federation 58.37N 52.08E
Omu, Vîrful *see* Omul, Vârful
31 V7 **Onamia** Minnesota, N USA 46.04N 93.40W
23 Y5 **Onancock** Virginia, NE USA 37.42N 75.45W
12 E10 **Onaping Lake** ◎ Ontario, S Canada
32 M12 **Onarga** Illinois, N USA 40.39N 88.00W
13 R6 **Onatchiway, Lac** ◎ Quebec, SE Canada
31 S14 **Onawa** Iowa, C USA 42.01N 96.06W
172 Pp7 **Onbetsu** *var.* Ombetsu. Hokkaidō, NE Japan 42.52N 143.54E
85 B16 **Oncócua** Cunene, SW Angola 16.37S 13.23E
107 S9 **Onda** País Valenciano, E Spain 39.58N 0.17W
113 N18 **Ondava** ≈ NE Slovakia
Ondjiva *see* N'Giva
79 T16 **Ondo** Ondo, SW Nigeria 7.07N 4.50E
79 T16 **Ondo** ◐ *state* SW Nigeria
169 N8 **Öndörhaan** Hentiy, E Mongolia 47.20N 110.42E
85 D18 **Ondundazongonda** Otjozondjupa, N Namibia 20.28S 18.00E
157 K21 **One and Half Degree Channel** *channel* S Maldives
197 L15 **Oneata** *island* Lau Group, E Fiji
128 L9 **Onega** Arkhangel'skaya Oblast', NW Russian Federation 63.54N 37.58E
125 Dd6 **Onega** ≈ NW Russian Federation
Onega Bay *see* Onezhskaya Guba
Onega, Lake *see* Onezhskoye Ozero
20 I10 **Oneida** New York, NE USA 43.05N 75.39W
22 M8 **Oneida** Tennessee, S USA 36.30N 84.30W
20 H9 **Oneida Lake** ◎ New York, NE USA
31 P13 **O'Neill** Nebraska, C USA 42.28N 98.37W
127 Pp13 **Onekotan, Ostrov** *island* Kuril'skiye Ostrova, SE Russian Federation
25 P3 **Oneonta** Alabama, S USA 33.57N 86.28W
20 J11 **Oneonta** New York, NE USA 42.27N 75.03W
202 I16 **Oneroa** *island* S Cook Islands
118 K11 **Onești** *Hung.* Onyest; *prev.* Gheorghe Gheorghiu-Dej. Bacău, E Romania 46.13N 26.46E
200 Qq15 **Onevai** *island* Tongatapu Group, S Tonga
110 A11 **Onex** Genève, SW Switzerland 46.11N 6.04E
128 K8 **Onezhskaya Guba** *Eng.* Onega Bay. *bay* NW Russian Federation
125 D6 **Onezhskoye Ozero** *Eng.* Lake Onega. ◎ NW Russian Federation
85 C16 **Ongandjera** Omusati, N Namibia 17.49S 15.06E
192 N12 **Ongaonga** Hawke's Bay, North Island, NZ 39.57S 176.21E
168 K9 **Ongi** Dundgovĭ, C Mongolia 45.27N 103.58E
168 J8 **Ongi** Övörhangay, C Mongolia 46.30N 102.18E
169 W14 **Ongjin** SW North Korea 37.55N 125.21E
161 J17 **Ongole** Andhra Pradesh, E India 15.33N 80.03E
168 K8 **Ongon** Övörhangay, C Mongolia 46.58N 103.45E
Ongtüstik Qazaqstan Oblysy *see* Yuzhnyy Kazakhstan
101 I21 **Onhaye** Namur, S Belgium 50.15N 4.51E
177 G8 **Onhne** Pegu, SW Burma 17.02N 96.28E
143 S9 **Oni** N Georgia 42.36N 43.13E
31 N9 **Onida** South Dakota, N USA 44.42N 100.03W
170 E15 **Onigajō-yama** ▲ Shikoku, SW Japan 33.10N 132.37E
180 H7 **Onilahy** ≈ S Madagascar
79 U16 **Onitsha** Anambra, S Nigeria 6.09N 6.48E
171 Gg14 **Ono** Hyōgo, Honshū, SW Japan 34.51N 134.56E
197 I15 **Ono** *island* SW Fiji
171 I14 **Ōno** Fukui, Honshū, SW Japan 35.59N 136.29E
170 D12 **Onoda** Yamaguchi, Honshū, SW Japan 33.59N 131.10E
197 L17 **Ono-i-lau** *island* SE Fiji
170 Cc13 **Ōnojō** *var.* Ōnozyô. Fukuoka, Kyūshū, SW Japan 33.30N 130.30E
126 K16 **Onokhoy** Respublika Buryatiya, S Russian Federation 51.51N 108.17E
170 F14 **Onomichi** *var.* Onomiti. Hiroshima, Honshū, SW Japan 34.25N 133.13E
Onomiti *see* Onomichi
169 O7 **Onon Gol** ≈ N Mongolia
Ononte *see* Orontes
57 N6 **Onoto** Anzoátegui, NE Venezuela 9.36N 65.10W
203 O3 **Onotoa** *prev.* Clerk Island. *atoll* Tungaru, W Kiribati
Ônozyô *see* Ōnojō
97 I19 **Onsala** Halland, S Sweden 57.25N 12.00E
85 E23 **Onseepkans** Northern Cape, W South Africa 28.44S 19.18E
106 F4 **Ons, Illa de** *island* NW Spain
188 H7 **Onslow** Western Australia 21.42S 115.07E
23 W11 **Onslow Bay** *bay* North Carolina, E USA
100 P6 **Onstwedde** Groningen, NE Netherlands 53.01N 7.04E
170 Bb16 **On-take** ▲ Kyūshū, SW Japan 31.35N 130.39E
171 Ii15 **Ontake-san** ▲ Honshū, S Japan 35.54N 137.28E
37 T15 **Ontario** California, W USA 34.03N 117.39W
34 M13 **Ontario** Oregon, NW USA 44.01N 116.57W
10 D10 **Ontario** ◐ *province* S Canada
15 Gg2 **Ontario, Lake** ◎ Canada/USA
(0) L9 **Ontario Peninsula** *peninsula* Canada/USA
Onteniente *see* Ontinyent
107 S11 **Ontinyent** *var.* Onteniente. País Valenciano, E Spain 38.49N 0.37W
95 N15 **Ontojärvi** ◎ E Finland
32 L3 **Ontonagon** Michigan, N USA 46.52N 89.18W
32 L3 **Ontonagon River** ≈ Michigan, N USA
195 W11 **Ontong Java Atoll** *prev.* Lord Howe Island. *atoll* N Solomon Islands
183 N5 **Ontong Java Rise** *undersea feature* W Pacific Ocean
Onuba *see* Huelva
57 W9 **Onverwacht** Para, N Surinam 5.36N 55.12W
Onyest *see* Onești
190 J7 **Oodla Wirra** South Australia 32.52S 139.05E
190 F2 **Oodnadatta** South Australia 27.34S 135.27E
190 C5 **Ooldea** South Australia 30.29S 131.50E
29 Q8 **Oologah Lake** ⊠ Oklahoma, C USA
Oos-Kaap *see* Eastern Cape
Oos-Londen *see* East London
101 E17 **Oostakker** Oost-Vlaanderen, NW Belgium 51.06N 3.46E
101 D15 **Oostburg** Zeeland, SW Netherlands 51.19N 3.30E
100 K9 **Oostelijk-Flevoland** *polder* C Netherlands
101 B16 **Oostende** *Eng.* Ostend, *Fr.* Ostende. West-Vlaanderen, NW Belgium 51.13N 2.55E
101 B16 **Oostende** ✕ West-Vlaanderen, NW Belgium 51.12N 2.55E
100 L12 **Oosterbeek** Gelderland, SE Netherlands 51.58N 5.51E
101 I14 **Oosterhout** Noord-Brabant, S Netherlands 51.37N 4.51E
100 O6 **Oostermoers Vaart** *var.* Hunze. ≈ NE Netherlands
101 F14 **Oosterschelde** *Eng.* Eastern Scheldt. *inlet* SW Netherlands
101 E14 **Oosterscheldedam** *dam* SW Netherlands 51.38N 3.45E
100 M7 **Oosterwolde** *Fris.* Easterwâlde. Friesland, N Netherlands 53.00N 6.15E
100 I9 **Oosthuizen** Noord-Holland, NW Netherlands 52.34N 5.00E
101 H16 **Oostmalle** Antwerpen, N Belgium 51.18N 4.44E
Oos-Transvaal *see* Mpumalanga
101 E15 **Oost-Souburg** Zeeland, SW Netherlands 51.28N 3.36E
101 E17 **Oost-Vlaanderen** *Eng.* East Flanders. ◐ *province* NW Belgium
100 J5 **Oost-Vlieland** Friesland, N Netherlands 53.19N 5.02E
100 F12 **Oostvoorne** Zuid-Holland, SW Netherlands 51.55N 4.06E
Ootacamund *see* Udagamandalam
100 O10 **Ootmarsum** Overijssel, E Netherlands 52.25N 6.55E
8 K14 **Ootsa Lake** ⊠ British Columbia, SW Canada
116 L8 **Opaka** Türgovishte, N Bulgaria 43.26N 26.12E
81 M18 **Opala** Orientale, C Dem. Rep. Congo (Zaire) 0.40S 24.19E
129 Q13 **Oparino** Kirovskaya Oblast', NW Russian Federation 59.52N 48.14E
12 H8 **Opasatica, Lac** ◎ Quebec, SE Canada
114 B9 **Opatija** *It.* Abbazia. Primorje-Gorski Kotar, NW Croatia 45.18N 14.15E
113 N15 **Opatów** Świętokrzyskie, C Poland 50.45N 21.27E
113 I17 **Opava** *Ger.* Troppau. Ostravský Kraj, E Czech Republic 49.55N 17.53E
113 H16 **Opava** *Ger.* Oppa. ≈ NE Czech Republic
Ópazova *see* Stara Pazova
194 L14 **Ope** ≈ S PNG
Ópécska *see* Pecica
12 E8 **Opeepeesway Lake** ◎ Ontario, S Canada
25 R5 **Opelika** Alabama, S USA 32.39N 85.22W
24 I8 **Opelousas** Louisiana, S USA 30.31N 92.04W
195 O11 **Open Bay** *bay* New Britain, E PNG
12 I12 **Opeongo Lake** ◎ Ontario, SE Canada
101 K17 **Opglabbeek** Limburg, NE Belgium 51.04N 5.39E
35 W6 **Opheim** Montana, NW USA 48.50N 106.24W
41 P10 **Ophir** Alaska, USA 63.08N 94.31W
Ophiusa *see* Formentera
81 N18 **Opienge** Orientale, E Dem. Rep. Congo (Zaire) 0.15N 27.25E
193 G20 **Opihi** ≈ South Island, NZ
10 J9 **Opinaca** ≈ Quebec, C Canada
10 J10 **Opinaca, Réservoir** ⊠ Quebec, E Canada
119 T5 **Opishnya** *Rus.* Oposhnya. Poltavs'ka Oblast', NE Ukraine 49.56N 34.36E
100 I8 **Opmeer** Noord-Holland, NW Netherlands 52.43N 4.55E
79 V17 **Opobo** Akwa Ibom, S Nigeria 4.36N 7.37E
128 F16 **Opochka** Pskovskaya Oblast', W Russian Federation 56.42N 28.39E
112 L13 **Opoczno** Łodzkie, C Poland 51.24N 20.18E
113 I15 **Opole** *Ger.* Oppeln. Opolskie, S Poland 50.40N 17.55E
113 H15 **Opolskie** ◐ *province* S Poland
150 G13 **Opornyy** Mangistau, SW Kazakhstan 46.09N 54.32E
Oporto *see* Porto
Oposhnya *see* Opishnya
192 P8 **Opotiki** Bay of Plenty, North Island, NZ 38.02S 177.18E
25 Q7 **Opp** Alabama, S USA 31.16N 86.14W
Oppa *see* Opava
96 G9 **Oppdal** Sør-Trøndelag, S Norway 62.36N 9.41E
Oppeln *see* Opole
109 N23 **Oppido Mamertina** Calabria, SW Italy 38.17N 15.58E
Oppidum Ubiorum *see* Köln
96 F12 **Oppland** ◐ *county* S Norway
120 J12 **Opsa** *Rus.* Opsa. Vitsyebskaya Voblasts', NW Belarus 55.31N 26.49E
28 I8 **Optima Lake** ⊠ Oklahoma, C USA
192 J11 **Opunake** Taranaki, North Island, NZ 39.27S 173.51E
203 N6 **Opunohu, Baie d'** *bay* Moorea, W French Polynesia
85 B17 **Opuwo** Kunene, NW Namibia 18.06S 13.52E
152 H6 **Oqqal'a** *var.* Akkala, *Rus.* Karakala. Qoraqalpoghiston Respublikasi, NW Uzbekistan 43.43N 59.25E
153 V13 **Oqsu** *Rus.* Oksu. ≈ SE Tajikistan
153 P14 **Oqtogh, Qatorkŭhi** *Rus.* Khrebet Aktau. ▲ SW Tajikistan
152 M11 **Oqtosh** *Rus.* Aktash. Samarqand Wiloyati, C Uzbekistan 39.23N 65.45E
153 N11 **Oqtow Tizmasi** *Rus.* Khrebet Aktau. ▲ C Uzbekistan
32 J12 **Oquawka** Illinois, N USA 40.55N 90.55W
150 J10 **Or'** *Kaz.* Or. ≈ Kazakhstan/Russian Federation
38 M15 **Oracle** Arizona, SW USA 32.36N 110.46W
118 F9 **Oradea** *prev.* Oradea Mare, *Ger.* Grosswardein, *Hung.* Nagyvárad. Bihor, NW Romania 47.02N 21.55E
Oradea Mare *see* Oradea
115 M17 **Orahovac** *Alb.* Rahovec. Serbia, S Yugoslavia 42.24N 20.40E
114 H9 **Orahovica** Virovitica-Podravina, NE Croatia 45.33N 17.54E
158 K13 **Orai** Uttar Pradesh, N India 26.00N 79.26E
94 K12 **Orajärvi** Lappi, NW Finland 66.54N 24.04E
Or Akiva *see* Or 'Aqiva
Oral *see* Ural'sk
76 I5 **Oran** *var.* Ouahran, Wahran. NW Algeria 35.42N 0.37W
191 R8 **Orange** New South Wales, SE Australia 33.16S 149.06E
105 R14 **Orange** *anc.* Arausio. Vaucluse, SE France 44.06N 4.52E
27 Y10 **Orange** Texas, SW USA 30.05N 93.44W
23 V5 **Orange** Virginia, NE USA 38.15N 78.06W
23 R13 **Orangeburg** South Carolina, SE USA 33.29N 80.51W
60 J9 **Orange, Cabo** *headland* NE Brazil 4.24N 51.33W
31 S12 **Orange City** Iowa, C USA 43.00N 96.03W
Orange Cone *see* Orange Fan
180 J10 **Orange Fan** *var.* Orange Cone. *undersea feature* SW Indian Ocean
Orange Free State *see* Free State
27 S14 **Orange Grove** Texas, SW USA 27.57N 97.56W
20 K13 **Orange Lake** New York, NE USA 41.32N 74.06W
25 V10 **Orange Lake** ◎ Florida, SE USA
Orange Mouth/Orangemund *see* Oranjemund
25 W9 **Orange Park** Florida, SE USA 30.10N 81.42W
194 M17 **Orangerie Bay** *bay* SE PNG
85 E23 **Orange River** *Afr.* Oranjerivier. ≈ S Africa
12 G15 **Orangeville** Ontario, S Canada 43.55N 80.06W
38 M5 **Orangeville** Utah, W USA 39.14N 111.03W
44 G1 **Orange Walk** Orange Walk, N Belize 18.06N 88.30W
44 F1 **Orange Walk** ◐ *district* NW Belize
102 N11 **Oranienburg** Brandenburg, NE Germany 52.46N 13.15E
100 O7 **Oranjekanaal** *canal* NE Netherlands
85 D23 **Oranjemund** *var.* Orangemund; *prev.* Orange Mouth. Karas, SW Namibia 28.33S 16.27E
Oranjerivier *see* Orange River
47 N16 **Oranjestad** ○ (Aruba) W Aruba 12.31N 70.00W
Oranje Vrystaat *see* Free State
176 W9 **Oransbari** Irian Jaya, E Indonesia 1.18S 134.16E
Orany *see* Varėna
85 H18 **Orapa** Central, C Botswana 21.18S 25.22E
144 F9 **Or 'Aqiva** *var.* Or Akiva. Haifa, W Israel 32.40N 34.58E
114 I10 **Orašje** Federacija Bosna I Hercegovina, N Bosnia and Herzegovina 45.01N 18.42E
118 G11 **Orăștie** *Ger.* Broos, *Hung.* Szászváros. Hunedoara, W Romania 45.49N 23.10E
Orașul Stalin *see* Brașov
113 K18 **Orava** *Hung.* Árva, *Pol.* Orawa. ≈ N Slovakia
Oravainen *see* Oravais
95 K16 **Oravais** *Fin.* Oravainen. Länsi-Suomi, W Finland 63.18N 22.25E
Oravicabánya *see* Oravița
118 F13 **Oravița** *Ger.* Orawitza, *Hung.* Oravicabánya. Caraș-Severin, SW Romania 45.01N 21.43E
Orawa *see* Orava
193 B24 **Orawia** Southland, South Island, NZ 46.03S 167.49E
Orawitza *see* Oravița
105 P16 **Orb** ≈ S France
108 C9 **Orba** ≈ NW Italy
164 H12 **Orba Co** ◎ W China
110 B9 **Orbe** Vaud, W Switzerland 46.42N 6.28E
109 G14 **Orbetello** Toscana, C Italy 42.27N 11.14E
106 K3 **Orbigo** ≈ NW Spain
191 Q12 **Orbost** Victoria, SE Australia 37.44S 148.28E
97 O14 **Örbyhus** Uppsala, C Sweden 60.15N 17.43E
204 I1 **Orcadas** *Argentinian research station* South Orkney Islands, Antarctica 60.37S 44.48W
107 P12 **Orcera** Andalucía, S Spain 38.20N 2.36W
35 P9 **Orchard Homes** Montana, NW USA 46.52N 114.01W
39 P5 **Orchard Mesa** Colorado, C USA 39.02N 108.33W
20 D10 **Orchard Park** New York, NE USA 42.46N 78.44W
Orchid Island *see* Lan Yü
117 G18 **Orchómenos** *var.* Orhomenos, Orkhómenos; *prev.* Skripón, *anc.* Orchomenus. Stereá Ellás, C Greece 38.29N 22.58E
Orchomenus *see* Orchómenos
108 B7 **Orco** ≈ NW Italy
105 R8 **Or, Côte d'** *physical region* C France
31 O14 **Ord** Nebraska, C USA 41.36N 98.55W
Ordat' *see* Ordats'
121 O15 **Ordats'** *Rus.* Ordat'. Mahilyowskaya Voblasts', E Belarus 54.09N 30.42E
38 K8 **Orderville** Utah, W USA 37.16N 112.38W
106 H2 **Ordes** Galicia, NW Spain 43.04N 8.25W
37 V14 **Ord Mountain** ▲ California, W USA 34.41N 116.46W
Ordos Desert *see* Mu Us Shamo
196 B16 **Ordot** C Guam
143 N11 **Ordu** *anc.* Cotyora. Ordu, N Turkey 41.00N 37.52E
142 M11 **Ordu** ◐ *province* N Turkey
143 V14 **Ordubad** SW Azerbaijan 38.55N 46.00E
107 O3 **Orduña** País Vasco, N Spain 43.00N 3.00W
39 U6 **Ordway** Colorado, C USA 38.13N 103.45W
150 L8 **Ordzhonikidze** Kostanay, N Kazakhstan 52.24N 61.40E
119 T9 **Ordzhonikidze** Dnipropetrovs'ka Oblast', E Ukraine 47.39N 34.09E
Ordzhonikidze *see* Vladikavkaz, Russian Federation
Ordzhonikidze *see* Yenakiyeve, Ukraine
Ordzhonikidzeabad *see* Kofarnihon
57 U9 **Orealla** E Guyana 5.13N 57.17W
115 G15 **Orebić** *It.* Sabbioncello. Dubrovnik-Neretva, S Croatia 42.58N 17.12E
97 M16 **Örebro** Örebro, C Sweden 59.18N 15.12E
97 L16 **Örebro** ◐ *county* C Sweden
27 W6 **Ore City** Texas, SW USA 32.48N 94.43W
32 L10 **Oregon** Illinois, N USA 42.00N 89.19W
29 Q2 **Oregon** Missouri, C USA 39.59N 95.08W
33 R11 **Oregon** Ohio, N USA 41.38N 83.29W
34 H13 **Oregon** *off.* State of Oregon; also known as Beaver State, Sunset State, Valentine State, Webfoot State. ◐ *state* NW USA
34 G11 **Oregon City** Oregon, NW USA 45.21N 122.36W
97 P14 **Öregrund** Uppsala, C Sweden 60.19N 18.30E
Orekhov *see* Orikhiv
130 L3 **Orekhovo-Zuyevo** Moskovskaya Oblast', W Russian Federation 55.46N 39.01E
Orekhovsk *see* Arekhawsk
Orel *see* Oril'
130 J6 **Orël** Orlovskaya Oblast', W Russian Federation 52.57N 36.06E
58 E11 **Orellana** Loreto, N Peru 6.55S 75.10W
106 L11 **Orellana, Embalse de** ⊠ W Spain
38 L3 **Orem** Utah, W USA 40.18N 111.41W
Ore Mountains *see* Erzgebirge/Krušné Hory
131 V7 **Orenburg** *prev.* Chkalov. Orenburgskaya Oblast', W Russian Federation 51.45N 55.11E
131 V7 **Orenburg** ✕ Orenburgskaya Oblast', W Russian Federation 51.54N 55.15E
131 T7 **Orenburgskaya Oblast'** ◐ *province* W Russian Federation
Orense *see* Ourense
196 C8 **Oreor** *var.* Koror. ● (Palau) Oreor, N Palau 7.21N 134.28E
196 C8 **Oreor** *var.* Koror. *island* N Palau
193 B24 **Orepuki** Southland, South Island, NZ 46.17S 167.45E
116 L12 **Orestiáda** *prev.* Orestiás. Anatolikí Makedonía kai Thráki, NE Greece 41.30N 26.31E
Orestiás *see* Orestiáda
Öresund/Øresund *see* Sound, The
193 C23 **Oreti** ≈ South Island, NZ
192 L5 **Orewa** Auckland, North Island, NZ 36.36S 174.42E
176 Y14 **Oreyabo** Irian Jaya, E Indonesia 6.57S 139.05E
67 A25 **Orford, Cape** *headland* West Falkland, Falkland Islands 52.00S 61.04W
46 B5 **Órganos, Sierra de los** ▲ W Cuba
39 R15 **Organ Peak** ▲ New Mexico, SW USA 32.17N 106.35W
107 N9 **Orgaz** Castilla-La Mancha, C Spain 39.39N 3.52W
Orgeyev *see* Orhei
168 I6 **Orgil** Hövsgöl, C Mongolia 48.31N 99.19E
107 O15 **Órgiva** *var.* Orjiva. Andalucía, S Spain 36.54N 3.25W
168 I9 **Örgön** Bayanhongor, C Mongolia 44.43N 100.23E
119 N9 **Orhei** *var.* Orheiu, *Rus.* Orgeyev. N Moldova 47.25N 28.48E
Orheiu *see* Orhei
107 R3 **Orhi** *var.* Orhy, Pic d'Orhy, Pic d'Orhy. ▲ France/Spain *see also* Orhy 42.55N 1.01W
Orhomenos *see* Orchómenos
168 L6 **Orhon Gol** ≈ N Mongolia
104 J16 **Orhy** *var.* Orhi, Pic de Orhy, Pic d'Orhy. ▲ France/Spain *see also* Orhi 43.00N 1.00W
Orhy, Pic d'/Orhy, Pico de *see* Orhi/Orhy
36 L2 **Orick** California, W USA 41.16N 124.03W
34 L6 **Orient** Washington, NW USA 48.51N 118.14W
50 D6 **Oriental, Cordillera** ▲ Bolivia/Peru
50 D6 **Oriental, Cordillera** ▲ C Colombia
59 H16 **Oriental, Cordillera** ▲ C Peru
65 M15 **Oriente** Buenos Aires, E Argentina 38.45S 60.37W
107 R12 **Orihuela** País Valenciano, E Spain 38.04N 0.55W
119 V9 **Orikhiv** *Rus.* Orekhov. Zaporiz'ka Oblast', SE Ukraine 47.32N 35.48E
115 K22 **Orikum** *var.* Orikumi. Vlorë, SW Albania 40.20N 19.28E
Orikumi *see* Orikum
119 V6 **Oril'** *Rus.* Orel. ≈ E Ukraine
12 H14 **Orillia** Ontario, S Canada 44.36N 79.25W
95 M19 **Orimattila** Etelä-Suomi, S Finland 60.51N 25.46E
35 Y15 **Orin** Wyoming, C USA 42.39N 105.10W
49 R4 **Orinoco, Río** ≈ Colombia/Venezuela
194 G15 **Oriomo** Western, SW PNG 8.53S 143.13E
32 K11 **Orion** Illinois, N USA 41.21N 90.22W
31 Q5 **Oriska** North Dakota, N USA 46.54N 97.46W
159 P17 **Orissa** ◐ *state* NE India
Orissaar *see* Orissaare
120 E5 **Orissaare** *Ger.* Orissaar. Saaremaa, W Estonia 58.33N 23.05E
109 B19 **Oristano** Sardegna, Italy, C Mediterranean Sea 39.54N 8.34E
109 A19 **Oristano, Golfo di** *gulf* Sardegna, Italy, C Mediterranean Sea
56 D13 **Orito** Putumayo, SW Colombia 0.41N 76.48W
95 L18 **Orivesi** Häme, SW Finland 61.39N 24.21E
95 N17 **Orivesi** ◎ Länsi-Suomi, SE Finland
60 H12 **Oriximiná** Pará, NE Brazil 1.45S 55.49W
43 Q14 **Orizaba** Veracruz-Llave, E Mexico 18.55N 97.57W
43 Q14 **Orizaba, Volcán Pico de** *var.* Citlaltépetl. ▲ S Mexico 19.00N 97.15W
97 I16 **Ørje** Østfold, S Norway 59.28N 11.39E
115 I16 **Orjen** ▲ Bosnia and Herzegovina/Yugoslavia
Orjiva *see* Orgiva
96 G8 **Orkanger** Sør-Trøndelag, S Norway 63.18N 9.51E
96 G8 **Orkdalen** *valley* S Norway
97 K22 **Örkelljunga** Skåne, S Sweden 56.16N 13.19E
Orkhaniye *see* Botevgrad
Orkhómenos *see* Orchómenos
96 H9 **Orkla** ≈ S Norway
Orkney *see* Orkney Islands
67 J22 **Orkney Deep** *undersea feature* Scotia Sea/Weddell Sea
98 J4 **Orkney Islands** *var.* Orkney, Orkneys. *island group* N Scotland, UK
Orkneys *see* Orkney Islands
26 K8 **Orla** Texas, SW USA 31.48N 103.55W
37 N5 **Orland** California, W USA 39.43N 122.12W
25 X11 **Orlando** Florida, SE USA 28.32N 81.22W

◆ Country ● Country Capital ◇ Dependent Territory ○ Dependent Territory Capital ◐ Administrative Region ✕ International Airport ▲ Mountain ▲ Mountain Range ⛰ Volcano ≈ River ◎ Lake ⊠ Reservoir

305

ORLANDO – ÖVT

25 X12 Orlando ✈ Florida, SE USA 28.24N 81.16W
109 K23 Orlando, Capo d' headland Sicilia, Italy, C Mediterranean Sea 38.10N 14.44E
Orlau see Orlová
105 N6 Orléanais cultural region C France
36 L2 Orleans California, W USA 41.16N 123.36W
21 Q12 Orleans Massachusetts, NE USA 41.48N 69.57W
105 N7 Orléans anc. Aurelianum. Loiret, C France 47.54N 1.52E
13 R10 Orléans, Île d' island Quebec, SE Canada
Orléansville see Chlef
113 F16 Orlice Ger. Adler. ≈ NE Czech Republic
126 Ii15 Orlik Respublika Buryatiya, S Russian Federation 52.32N 99.36E
129 Q14 Orlov prev. Khalturin. Kirovskaya Oblast', NW Russian Federation 58.34N 48.57E
113 I17 Orlová Ger. Orlau, Pol. Orłowa. Ostravský Kraj, E Czech Republic 49.52N 18.25E
Orlov, Mys see Orlovskiy, Mys
130 I6 Orlovskaya Oblast' ◐ province W Russian Federation
128 M5 Orlovskiy, Mys var. Mys Orlov. headland NW Russian Federation 67.14N 41.17E
Orłowa see Orlová
105 O5 Orly ✈ (Paris) Essonne, N France 48.43N 2.24E
121 G16 Orlya Rus. Orlya. Hrodzyenskaya Voblasts', W Belarus 53.30N 24.58E
116 M7 Orlyak prev. Makenzen, Trubchular, Rom. Trupcilar. Dobrich, NE Bulgaria 43.39N 27.21E
154 L16 Ormāra Baluchistān, SW Pakistan 25.14N 64.36E
179 Qq13 Ormoc off. Ormoc City, var. MacArthur. Leyte, C Philippines 11.02N 124.35E
25 X10 Ormond Beach Florida, SE USA 29.16N 81.04W
111 X10 Ormož Ger. Friedau. NE Slovenia 46.24N 16.09E
12 J13 Ormsby Ontario, SE Canada 44.52N 77.45W
99 K17 Ormskirk NW England, UK 53.34N 2.54W
Ormsö see Vormsi
13 N13 Ormstown Quebec, SE Canada 45.08N 73.57W
Ormuz, Strait of see Hormuz, Strait of
105 T8 Ornans Doubs, E France 47.06N 6.06E
104 K5 Orne ◐ department N France
104 K5 Orne ≈ N France
97 G12 Ørnes Nordland, C Norway 66.51N 13.43E
112 L7 Orneta Warmińsko-Mazurskie, NE Poland 54.07N 20.10E
97 P16 Ornö Stockholm, C Sweden 59.03N 18.28E
39 Q3 Orno Peak ▲ Colorado, C USA 40.06N 107.06W
95 I16 Örnsköldsvik Västernorrland, C Sweden 63.16N 18.45E
169 X13 Oro E North Korea 39.59N 127.27E
47 T6 Orocovis C Puerto Rico 18.13N 66.22W
56 H10 Orocué Casanare, E Colombia 4.46N 71.22W
79 N13 Orodara SW Burkina 11.00N 4.54W
107 S4 Oroel, Peña de ▲ N Spain 42.30N 0.31W
35 N10 Orofino Idaho, NW USA 46.28N 116.15W
168 I9 Orog Nuur ◎ S Mongolia
37 U14 Oro Grande California, W USA 34.36N 117.19W
39 S15 Orogrande New Mexico, SW USA 32.24N 106.04W
203 Q7 Orohena, Mont ▲ Tahiti, W French Polynesia 17.37S 149.27W
Orolaunum see Arlon
Orol Dengizi see Aral Sea
201 S15 Oroluk Atoll atoll Caroline Islands, C Micronesia
82 J13 Oromo ◐ region C Ethiopia
11 O15 Oromocto New Brunswick, SE Canada 45.49N 66.28W
203 S4 Orona prev. Hull Island. atoll Phoenix Islands, C Kiribati
203 V17 Orongo ancient monument Easter Island, Chile, E Pacific Ocean 27.10S 109.27W
144 I3 Orontes var. Ononte, Ar. Nahr el Aassi, Nahr al 'Aṣī. ≈ SW Asia
106 L9 Oropesa Castilla-La Mancha, C Spain 39.55N 5.10W
107 T8 Oropesa País Valenciano, E Spain 40.06N 0.07E
Oropeza see Cochabamba
169 U5 Oroqen Zizhiqi Nei Mongol Zizhiqu, N China 50.34N 123.40E
179 Qq15 Oroquieta var. Oroquieta City. Mindanao, S Philippines 8.27N 123.46E
42 J8 Oro, Río del ≈ C Mexico
61 O14 Orós, Açude ▣ E Brazil
109 D18 Orosei, Golfo di gulf Tyrrhenian Sea, C Mediterranean Sea
113 M24 Orosháza Békés, SE Hungary 46.33N 20.40E
Orosirá Rodhópis see Rhodope Mountains
113 I22 Oroszlány Komárom-Esztergom, W Hungary 47.31N 18.19E
196 B16 Orote Peninsula peninsula W Guam
127 O9 Orotukan Magadanskaya Oblast', E Russian Federation 62.18N 150.46E
37 O5 Oroville California, W USA 39.29N 121.35W
34 K6 Oroville Washington, NW USA 48.56N 119.25W
37 O5 Oroville, Lake ▣ California, W USA
(0) G15 Orozco Fracture Zone tectonic feature E Pacific Ocean
66 I7 Orphan Knoll undersea feature NW Atlantic Ocean 51.00N 47.00W
31 V3 Orr Minnesota, N USA 48.03N 92.48W
97 M21 Orrefors Kalmar, S Sweden 56.48N 15.45E
190 I7 Orroroo South Australia 32.46S 138.38E
33 T12 Orrville Ohio, N USA 40.50N 81.45W
96 L12 Orsa Dalarna, C Sweden 61.07N 14.40E
Orschowa see Orşova
Orschütz see Orzyc
121 O14 Orsha Rus. Orsha. Vitsyebskaya Voblasts', NE Belarus 54.30N 30.25E
131 Q2 Orshanka Respublika Mariy El, W Russian Federation 56.54N 47.54E
110 C11 Orsières Valais, SW Switzerland 46.00N 7.09E
125 Dd13 Orsk Orenburgskaya Oblast', W Russian Federation 51.13N 58.34E
118 F13 Orşova Ger. Orschowa, Hung. Orsova. Mehedinţi, SW Romania 44.42N 22.22E
96 D10 Ørsta Møre og Romsdal, S Norway 62.12N 6.07E
97 O15 Örsundsbro Uppsala, C Sweden 59.45N 17.19E
142 D16 Ortaca Muğla, SW Turkey 36.49N 28.43E
109 M16 Orta Nova Puglia, SE Italy 41.19N 15.43E
142 I17 Orta Toroslar ▲ S Turkey
56 E11 Ortega Tolima, W Colombia 3.57N 75.10W
106 H1 Ortegal, Cabo headland NW Spain 43.46N 7.54W
Ortelsburg see Szczytno
104 J15 Orthez Pyrénées-Atlantiques, SW France 43.28N 0.46W
59 K14 Orthon, Río ≈ N Bolivia
62 J10 Ortigueira Paraná, S Brazil 24.10S 50.55W
106 H1 Ortigueira Galicia, NW Spain 43.40N 7.50W
108 H5 Ortisei Ger. Sankt-Ulrich. Trentino-Alto Adige, N Italy 46.35N 11.42E
42 F6 Ortiz Sonora, NW Mexico 28.18N 110.40W
56 L5 Ortiz Guárico, N Venezuela 9.37N 67.17W
Ortler see Ortles
108 F5 Ortles Ger. Ortler. ▲ N Italy 46.29N 10.33E
109 K14 Ortona Abruzzo, C Italy 42.21N 14.24E
31 R8 Ortonville Minnesota, N USA 45.18N 96.26W
153 W8 Orto-Tokoy Issyk-Kul'skaya Oblast', NE Kyrgyzstan 42.20N 76.03E
95 I15 Örträsk Västerbotten, N Sweden 64.10N 19.00E
102 J12 Örtze ≈ NW Germany
Oruba see Aruba
148 I3 Orūmīyeh var. Rizaiyeh, Urmia, Urmiyeh; prev. Reẓā'īyeh. Āẕarbāyjān-e Bākhtarī, NW Iran 37.33N 45.06E
148 J3 Orūmīyeh, Daryācheh-ye var. Matianus, Sha Hi, Urumi Yeh, Eng. Lake Urmia; prev. Daryācheh-ye Reẓā'īyeh. ◎ NW Iran
59 K19 Oruro Oruro, W Bolivia 17.57S 67.05W
59 J19 Oruro ◐ department W Bolivia
97 I18 Orust island S Sweden
Orūzgān/Orūzgān see Orūzgān
108 H13 Orvieto anc. Velsuna. Umbria, C Italy 42.43N 12.07E
204 K7 Orville Coast physical region Antarctica
116 H7 Oryakhovo Vratsa, NW Bulgaria 43.43N 23.58E
Oryokko see Yalu
119 R5 Orzhytsya Poltavs'ka Oblast', C Ukraine 49.48N 32.40E
112 M9 Orzyc Ger. Orschütz. ≈ NE Poland
112 N8 Orzysz Ger. Arys. Warmińsko-Mazurskie, NE Poland 53.49N 21.54E
96 I10 Os Hedmark, S Norway 62.29N 11.14E
97 C14 Os Hordaland, S Norway 60.10N 5.30E
129 U15 Osa Permskaya Oblast', NW Russian Federation 57.16N 55.22E
31 W11 Osage Iowa, C USA 43.16N 92.48W
29 U5 Osage Beach Missouri, C USA 38.09N 92.37W
29 P5 Osage City Kansas, C USA 38.37N 95.49W
29 U7 Osage Fork River ≈ Missouri, C USA
29 U5 Osage River ≈ Missouri, C USA
171 Gg15 Ōsaka hist. Naniwa. Ōsaka, Honshū, SW Japan 34.38N 135.27E
171 Gg15 Ōsaka off. Ōsaka-fu, var. Ōsaka Hu. ◐ urban prefecture Honshū, SW Japan
Ōsaka-fu/Ōsaka Hu see Ōsaka
151 R10 Osakarovka Karaganda, C Kazakhstan 50.27N 72.43E
170 G15 Ōsaka-wan bay SW Japan
31 T7 Osakis Minnesota, N USA 45.51N 95.08W
45 N16 Osa, Península de peninsula S Costa Rica
62 M10 Osasco São Paulo, S Brazil 23.31S 46.46W
29 R5 Osawatomie Kansas, C USA 38.30N 94.57W
28 L3 Osborne Kansas, C USA 39.26N 98.41W
181 S8 Osborn Plateau undersea feature E Indian Ocean
97 L21 Osby Skåne, S Sweden 56.24N 14.00E
Osca see Huesca
94 N2 Oscar II Land physical region W Svalbard
29 Y10 Osceola Arkansas, C USA 35.40N 89.58W
31 V15 Osceola Iowa, C USA 41.01N 93.45W
29 S6 Osceola Missouri, C USA 38.03N 93.42W
31 Q15 Osceola Nebraska, C USA 41.09N 97.28W
103 N15 Oschatz Sachsen, E Germany 51.17N 13.10E
102 K13 Oschersleben Sachsen-Anhalt, C Germany 52.02N 11.14E
33 R7 Oscoda Michigan, N USA 44.25N 83.19W
Ösel see Saaremaa
96 H6 Osen Sør-Trøndelag, S Norway 64.17N 10.29E
170 Ac12 Ōse-zaki headland Fukue-jima, SW Japan 32.36N 128.37E
153 T10 Osh Oshskaya Oblast', SW Kyrgyzstan 40.34N 72.46E
85 C16 Oshakati Oshana, N Namibia 17.45S 15.42E
172 Nn6 Oshamambe Hokkaidō, NE Japan 42.31N 140.22E
85 C16 Oshana ◐ district N Namibia
126 Ii12 Osharovo Evenkiyskiy Avtonomnyy Okrug, N Russian Federation 60.16N 98.20E
12 H15 Oshawa Ontario, SE Canada 43.54N 78.50W
171 Mm13 Oshika-hantō peninsula Honshū, C Japan
85 C16 Oshikango Ohangwena, N Namibia 17.28S 15.54E
Oshikoto see Otjikoto
170 Cc12 O-shima island SW Japan
171 M7 Ō-shima island NE Japan
171 Jj7 Ō-shima island S Japan
170 G17 Ō-shima island SW Japan
172 N5 Oshima-hantō ▲ Hokkaidō, NE Japan
85 D17 Oshivelo Otjikoto, N Namibia 18.37S 17.10E
30 K14 Oshkosh Nebraska, C USA 41.25N 102.21W
32 M7 Oshkosh Wisconsin, N USA 44.01N 88.31W
Oshmyany see Ashmyany
Osh Oblasty see Oshskaya Oblast'
79 T16 Oshogbo Osun, W Nigeria 7.42N 4.31E
153 S11 Oshskaya Oblast' Kir. Osh Oblasty. ◐ province SW Kyrgyzstan
81 J20 Oshwe Bandundu, C Dem. Rep. Congo (Zaire) 3.24S 19.31E
Osiek see Osijek
114 I5 Osijek prev. Osiek, Osjek, Ger. Esseg, Hung. Eszék. Osijek-Baranja, E Croatia 45.33N 18.40E
114 I5 Osijek-Baranja off. Osječko-Baranjska Županija. ◐ province E Croatia
108 J12 Osimo Marche, C Italy 43.28N 13.28E
126 H15 Osinniki Kemerovskaya Oblast', S Russian Federation 53.30N 87.25E
126 J14 Osinovka Irkutskaya Oblast', C Russian Federation 56.19N 101.55E
Osintorf see Asintorf
114 N11 Osipaonica Serbia, NE Yugoslavia 44.34N 21.00E
Osipenko see Berdyans'k
Osipovichi see Asipovichy
Osječko-Baranjska Županija see Osijek-Baranja
Osjek see Osijek
31 W15 Oskaloosa Iowa, C USA 41.17N 92.38W
29 Q4 Oskaloosa Kansas, C USA 39.13N 95.18W
97 N20 Oskarshamn Kalmar, S Sweden 57.16N 16.25E
97 J21 Oskarström Halland, S Sweden 56.48N 13.00E
12 M8 Oskélanéo Quebec, SE Canada 48.06N 75.12W
Öskemen see Ust'-Kamenogorsk
Oskil see Oskol
119 W5 Oskol Ukr. Oskil. ≈ Russian Federation/Ukraine
95 E20 Oslo prev. Christiania, Kristiania. ● (Norway) Oslo, S Norway 59.54N 10.43E
95 E20 Oslo ◐ county S Norway
95 E21 Oslofjorden fjord S Norway
161 G15 Osmānābād Mahārāshtra, C India 18.09N 76.06E
142 J11 Osmancık Çorum, N Turkey 40.58N 34.49E
142 L16 Osmaniye Osmaniye, S Turkey 37.04N 36.15E
142 L16 Osmaniye ◐ province S Turkey
97 C16 Ösmo Stockholm, C Sweden 58.58N 17.55E
120 E3 Osmussaar island W Estonia
102 G13 Osnabrück Niedersachsen, NW Germany 52.08N 7.42E
112 D11 Ośno Lubuskie Ger. Drossen. Lubuskie, W Poland 52.28N 14.51E
115 P19 Osogov Mountains var. Osogovske Planine, Osogovski Planina, Mac. Osogovski Planini. ▲ Bulgaria/FYR Macedonia
Osogovske Planine/Osogovski Planina/Osogovski Planini see Osogov Mountains
172 N8 Osore-yama ▲ Honshū, C Japan 41.18N 141.06E
Oşorhei see Târgu Mureş
63 J16 Osório Rio Grande do Sul, S Brazil 29.52S 50.16W
65 G16 Osorno Los Lagos, C Chile 40.38S 73.04W
106 M4 Osorno Castilla-León, N Spain 42.24N 4.22W
9 N17 Osoyoos British Columbia, SW Canada 49.01N 119.31W
56 J6 Ospino Portuguesa, N Venezuela 9.16N 69.25W
100 K13 Oss Noord-Brabant, S Netherlands 51.46N 5.31E
106 H11 Ossa ▲ S Portugal 38.43N 7.33W
117 F15 Óssa ▲ C Greece
25 X6 Ossabaw Island island Georgia, SE USA
25 X6 Ossabaw Sound sound Georgia, SE USA
191 O16 Ossa, Mount ▲ Tasmania, SE Australia 41.55S 146.03E
106 H11 Ossa, Serra d' ▲ SE Portugal
79 U16 Osse ≈ S Nigeria
32 J6 Osseo Wisconsin, N USA 44.33N 91.13W
111 S9 Ossiacher See ◎ S Austria
20 K13 Ossining New York, NE USA 41.10N 73.50W
96 K12 Ossjøen ◎ S Norway
127 P9 Ossora Koryakskiy Avtonomnyy Okrug, E Russian Federation 59.16N 163.01E
128 I15 Ostashkov Tverskaya Oblast', W Russian Federation 57.08N 33.10E
102 H9 Oste ≈ NW Germany
Ostee see Baltic Sea
Ostend/Ostende see Oostende
119 P3 Oster Chernihivs'ka Oblast', N Ukraine 50.57N 30.55E
97 O14 Österbybruk Uppsala, C Sweden 60.13N 17.55E
97 M19 Österbymo Östergotland, S Sweden 57.49N 15.15E
96 K12 Österdalälven ≈ C Sweden
96 I12 Østerdalen valley S Norway
97 L18 Östergötland ◐ county S Sweden
102 H10 Osterholz-Scharmbeck Niedersachsen, NW Germany 53.13N 8.46E
Östermark see Teuva
Östermyra see Seinäjoki
Osterode/Osterode in Ostpreussen see Ostróda
103 J14 Osterode am Harz Niedersachsen, C Germany 51.43N 10.15E
96 C13 Osterøy island S Norway
Österreich see Austria
95 G16 Östersund Jämtland, C Sweden 63.10N 14.43E
97 N14 Östervåla Västmanland, C Sweden 60.10N 17.13E
103 H22 Ostfildern Baden-Württemberg, SW Germany 48.43N 9.16E
97 H16 Østfold ◐ county S Norway
102 E9 Ostfriesische Inseln Eng. East Frisian Islands. island group NW Germany
102 F10 Ostfriesland historical region NW Germany
97 P14 Östhammar Uppsala, C Sweden 60.16N 18.25E
Ostia Aterni see Pescara
108 G8 Ostiglia Lombardia, N Italy 45.03N 11.09E
97 J14 Östmark Värmland, C Sweden 60.15N 12.45E
97 K22 Östra Ringsjön ◎ S Sweden
113 I17 Ostrava Ostravský Kraj, E Czech Republic 49.49N 18.15E
113 H17 Ostravský Kraj ◐ region E Czech Republic
112 K8 Ostróda Ger. Osterode, Osterode in Ostpreussen. Warmińsko-Mazurskie, NE Poland 53.42N 19.58E
Ostrog/Ostróg see Ostroh
130 L8 Ostrogozhsk Voronezhskaya Oblast', W Russian Federation 50.52N 39.00E
118 L4 Ostroh Pol. Ostróg, Rus. Ostrog. Rivnens'ka Oblast', NW Ukraine 50.19N 26.30E
112 N9 Ostrołęka Ger. Wiesenhof, Rus. Ostrolenka. Mazowieckie, C Poland 53.06N 21.33E
113 A16 Ostrov Ger. Schlackenwerth. Karlovarský Kraj, W Czech Republic 50.18N 12.53E
128 F15 Ostrov Latv. Austrava. Pskovskaya Oblast', W Russian Federation 57.21N 28.18E
Ostrovets see Ostrowiec Świętokrzyski
115 M21 Ostrovicës, Mali i ▲ SE Albania 40.36N 20.25E
172 T6 Ostrov Iturup island NE Russian Federation
116 L7 Ostrovo prev. Golema Ada. Razgrad, N Bulgaria 43.40N 26.37E
129 N15 Ostrovskoye Kostromskaya Oblast', NW Russian Federation 57.46N 42.18E
Ostrów see Ostrów Wielkopolski
Ostrowiec see Ostrowiec Świętokrzyski
113 M14 Ostrowiec Świętokrzyski var. Ostrowiec, Rus. Ostrovets. Świętokrzyskie, C Poland 50.54N 21.22E
112 P13 Ostrów Lubelski Lubelskie, E Poland 51.29N 22.57E
112 N10 Ostrów Mazowiecka var. Ostrów Mazowiecki. Mazowieckie, C Poland 52.48N 21.53E
Ostrów Mazowiecki see Ostrów Mazowiecka
Ostrowo see Ostrów Wielkopolski
112 H13 Ostrów Wielkopolski var. Ostrów, Ger. Ostrowo. Wielkopolskie, C Poland 51.40N 17.47E
Ostryna see Astryna
112 I13 Ostrzeszów Wielkopolskie, C Poland 51.25N 17.54E
109 P18 Ostuni Puglia, SE Italy 40.43N 17.34E
Ostyako-Voguls'k see Khanty-Mansiysk
Osum see Osumit, Lumi i
116 I9 Osum ≈ N Bulgaria
170 Bb17 Ōsumi-hantō ▲ Kyūshū, SW Japan
170 Bb17 Ōsumi-kaikyō strait SW Japan
115 L22 Osumit, Lumi i var. Osum. ≈ SE Albania
79 T16 Osun ◐ state SW Nigeria
106 L14 Osuna Andalucía, S Spain 37.13N 5.06W
62 J8 Osvaldo Cruz São Paulo, S Brazil 21.49S 50.52W
Osveya see Asvyeya
20 J7 Oswegatchie River ≈ New York, NE USA
29 Q7 Oswego Kansas, C USA 37.08N 95.07W
20 H9 Oswego New York, NE USA 43.27N 76.13W
99 K19 Oswestry W England, UK 52.50N 3.06W
113 J16 Oświęcim Ger. Auschwitz. Małopolskie, S Poland 50.02N 19.11E
171 K15 Ōta Gunma, Honshū, S Japan 36.17N 139.20E
193 E22 Otago off. Otago Region. ◐ region South Island, NZ
193 F23 Otago Peninsula peninsula South Island, NZ
170 E13 Ōtake Hiroshima, Honshū, SW Japan 34.13N 132.13E
192 L13 Otaki Wellington, North Island, NZ 40.46S 175.08E
171 L14 Ōtakine-yama ▲ Honshū, C Japan 37.23N 140.42E
95 M15 Otanmäki Oulu, C Finland 64.07N 27.04E
151 T15 Otar Zhambyl, SE Kazakhstan 43.34N 75.13E
172 O5 Otaru Hokkaidō, NE Japan 43.13N 140.58E
193 C24 Otatara Southland, South Island, NZ 46.26S 168.18E
193 C24 Otautau Southland, South Island, NZ 46.10S 168.01E
95 M18 Otava Isä-Suomi, E Finland 61.37N 27.07E
113 B18 Otava Ger. Wottawa. ≈ SW Czech Republic
58 C6 Otavalo Imbabura, N Ecuador 0.13N 78.15W
85 D17 Otavi Otjozondjupa, N Namibia 19.34S 17.25E
171 Kk15 Ōtawara Tochigi, Honshū, S Japan 36.52N 140.01E
85 B16 Otchinjau Cunene, SW Angola 16.31S 13.54E
118 F12 Oţelu Roşu Ger. Ferdinandsberg, Hung. Nándorhgy. Caras-Severin, SW Romania 45.30N 22.22E
193 E21 Otematata Canterbury, South Island, NZ 44.37S 170.12E
120 I6 Otepää Ger. Odenpäh. Valgamaa, SE Estonia 58.04N 26.31E
34 K9 Othello Washington, NW USA 46.49N 119.10W
117 A15 Othonoí island Iónioi Nísoi, Greece, C Mediterranean Sea
Othris see Óthrys
117 F17 Óthrys var. Othris. ▲ C Greece
79 Q14 Oti ≈ N Togo
42 K10 Otinapa Durango, C Mexico 24.01N 104.58W
193 G17 Otira West Coast, South Island, NZ 42.51S 171.32E
39 V3 Otis Colorado, C USA 40.09N 102.57W
10 L10 Otish, Monts ▲ Quebec, E Canada
85 C17 Otjikondo Kunene, N Namibia 19.48S 15.28E
85 C17 Otjikoto var. Oshikoto. ◐ district N Namibia
85 E18 Otjinene Omaheke, NE Namibia 21.10S 18.43E
85 D18 Otjiwarongo Otjozondjupa, N Namibia 20.28S 16.36E
85 D18 Otjosondu var. Otjosundu. Otjozondjupa, C Namibia 21.19S 17.51E
Otjosundu see Otjosondu
85 D18 Otjozondjupa ◐ district C Namibia
114 C11 Otočac Lika-Senj, W Croatia 44.52N 15.13E
172 Pp6 Otofuke-gawa ≈ Hokkaidō, NE Japan
168 M14 Otog Qi Nei Mongol Zizhiqu, N China 39.05N 107.58E
172 Pp3 Otoineppu Hokkaidō, NE Japan 44.43N 142.13E
114 J10 Otok Vukovar-Srijem, E Croatia 45.10N 18.52E
118 K14 Otopeni ✈ (Bucureşti) Bucureşti, S Romania 44.34N 26.09E
192 L8 Otorohanga Waikato, North Island, NZ 38.10S 175.13E
10 D9 Otoskwin ≈ Ontario, C Canada
170 F15 Ōtoyo Kōchi, Shikoku, SW Japan 33.45N 133.42E
97 E16 Otra ≈ S Norway
109 R19 Otranto Puglia, SE Italy 40.08N 18.28E
Otranto, Canale d' see Otranto, Strait of
109 Q18 Otranto, Strait of It. Canale d'Otranto. strait Albania/Italy
113 H18 Otrokovice Ger. Otrokowitz. Zlínský Kraj, E Czech Republic 49.13N 17.32E
Otrokowitz see Otrokovice
33 P10 Otsego Michigan, N USA 42.27N 85.42W
33 Q6 Otsego Lake ◎ Michigan, N USA
20 I11 Otselic River ≈ New York, NE USA
171 H15 Ōtsu var. Ōtu. Shiga, Honshū, SW Japan 35.03N 135.49E
171 Jj16 Ōtsuki var. Otuki. Yamanashi, Honshū, S Japan 35.35N 138.53E
96 G11 Otta Oppland, S Norway 61.46N 9.31E
201 U13 Otta island Chuuk, C Micronesia
96 F11 Otta ≈ S Norway
201 U13 Otta Pass passage Chuuk Islands, C Micronesia
97 J22 Ottarp Skåne, S Sweden 55.55N 12.55E
12 L12 Ottawa ● (Canada) Ontario, SE Canada 45.24N 75.40W
32 L11 Ottawa Illinois, N USA 41.21N 88.50W
29 Q5 Ottawa Kansas, C USA 38.37N 95.16W
33 R12 Ottawa Ohio, N USA 41.01N 84.03W
12 L12 Ottawa var. Uplands. ✈ Ontario, SE Canada 45.19N 75.39W
12 M12 Ottawa Fr. Outaouais. ≈ Ontario/Quebec, SE Canada
10 I4 Ottawa Islands island group Nunavut, C Canada
20 L8 Otter Creek ≈ Vermont, NE USA
38 L6 Otter Creek Reservoir ▣ Utah, W USA
100 L11 Otterlo Gelderland, E Netherlands 52.06N 5.46E
96 D9 Otterøya island S Norway
31 S6 Otter Tail Lake ◎ Minnesota, N USA
31 R7 Otter Tail River ≈ Minnesota, C USA
97 H23 Otterup Fyn, C Denmark 55.31N 10.25E
101 H19 Ottignies Wallon Brabant, C Belgium 50.40N 4.34E
103 L23 Ottobrunn Bayern, SE Germany 48.02N 11.40E
194 I12 Otto, Mount ▲ C PNG 5.54S 145.24E
31 X15 Ottumwa Iowa, C USA 41.00N 92.24W
Ōtu see Ōtsu
85 B16 Otuazuma Kunene, NW Namibia 17.52S 13.16E
Otuki see Ōtsuki
79 V16 Oturkpo Benue, S Nigeria 7.12N 8.06E
200 Ss14 Otu Tolu Group island group SE Tonga
190 M13 Otway, Cape headland Victoria, SE Australia 38.52S 143.31E
65 H24 Otway, Seno inlet S Chile
Ötz see Oetz
110 L8 Ötztaler Ache ≈ W Austria
110 L9 Ötztaler Alpen It. Alpi Venoste. ▲ SW Austria
29 T12 Ouachita, Lake ▣ Arkansas, C USA
29 R11 Ouachita Mountains ▲ Arkansas/Oklahoma, C USA
29 U13 Ouachita River ≈ Arkansas/Louisiana, C USA
Ouadaï see Ouaddaï
78 J7 Ouadâne var. Ouadane. Adrar, C Mauritania 20.57N 11.34W
80 K13 Ouadda Haute-Kotto, N Central African Republic 8.02N 22.22E
80 J10 Ouaddaï off. Préfecture du Ouaddaï, var. Ouadaï, Wadai. ◐ prefecture SE Chad
79 P13 Ouagadougou var. Wagadugu. ● (Burkina) C Burkina 12.20N 1.31W
79 P13 Ouagadougou ✈ C Burkina 12.21N 1.27W
79 O12 Ouahigouya NW Burkina 13.31N 2.19W
Ouahran see Oran
81 J14 Ouaka ◐ prefecture C Central African Republic
81 J15 Ouaka ≈ S Central African Republic
Oualam see Ouallam
78 M9 Oualâta var. Oualata. Hodh ech Chargui, SE Mauritania 17.18N 7.00W
79 R11 Ouallam var. Oualam. Tillabéri, W Niger 14.13N 2.07E
180 H14 Ouanani Mohéli, S Comoros 12.19S 94.37E
57 Z10 Ouanary E French Guiana 4.10N 51.40W
80 L13 Ouanda Djallé Vakaga, NE Central African Republic 8.53N 22.47E
81 N14 Ouando Haut-Mbomou, SE Central African Republic 5.57N 25.57E
81 L15 Ouango Mbomou, S Central African Republic 4.19N 22.30E
79 N14 Ouangolodougou var. Wangolodougou. N Ivory Coast 9.58N 5.09W
180 I13 Ouani Anjouan, SE Comoros
81 M15 Ouara ≈ E Central African Republic
78 K7 Ouarâne desert C Mauritania
13 O11 Ouareau ≈ Quebec, SE Canada
76 K7 Ouargla var. Wargla. NE Algeria 32.00N 5.16E
76 F8 Ouarzazate S Morocco 30.54N 6.55W
79 Q11 Ouatagouna Gao, E Mali 15.06N 0.41E
76 G6 Ouazzane var. Ouezzane, Ar. Wazan, Wazzan. N Morocco 34.52N 5.34W
Oubangui see Ubangi
Oubangui-Chari see Central African Republic
Oubari, Edeyen d' see Awbāri, Idhān
100 G13 Oud-Beijerland Zuid-Holland, SW Netherlands 51.49N 4.25E
100 F13 Ouddorp Zuid-Holland, SW Netherlands 51.49N 3.55E
79 P9 Oudeïka oasis C Mali 17.16N 1.42W
100 G13 Oude Maas ≈ SW Netherlands
101 E18 Oudenaarde Fr. Audenarde. Oost-Vlaanderen, SW Belgium 50.49N 3.37E
101 H14 Oudenbosch Noord-Brabant, S Netherlands 51.34N 4.31E
100 P6 Oude Pekela Groningen, NE Netherlands 53.06N 7.00E
Ouderkerk see Ouderkerk aan den Amstel
100 I10 Ouderkerk aan den Amstel var. Ouderkerk. Noord-Holland, C Netherlands 52.18N 4.54E
100 I6 Oudeschild Noord-Holland, NW Netherlands 53.01N 4.51E
101 G14 Oude-Tonge Zuid-Holland, SW Netherlands 51.40N 4.13E
100 I12 Oudewater Utrecht, C Netherlands 52.01N 4.54E
Oudjda see Oujda
100 L5 Oudkerk Friesland, N Netherlands 53.16N 5.52E
104 J7 Oudon ≈ NW France
100 I9 Oudorp Noord-Holland, NW Netherlands 52.39N 4.46E
85 G25 Oudtshoorn Western Cape, SW South Africa 33.32S 22.12E
101 I16 Oud-Turnhout Antwerpen, N Belgium 51.19N 5.01E
76 F7 Oued-Zem C Morocco 32.53N 6.30W
197 H5 Ouégoa Province Nord, C New Caledonia 20.22S 164.25E
78 L13 Ouéléssébougou var. Ouolossébougou. Koulikoro, SW Mali 11.58N 7.51W
79 N16 Ouellé E Ivory Coast 7.18N 4.01W
79 R16 Ouémé ≈ C Benin
197 J7 Ouen, Île island S New Caledonia
79 O13 Ouessa S Burkina 11.02N 2.44W
104 D5 Ouessant, Île d' Eng. Ushant. island NW France
81 H17 Ouésso La Sangha, NW Congo 1.37N 16.03E
81 D15 Ouest Eng. West. ◐ province W Cameroon
202 G11 Ouest, Baie de l' bay Îles Wallis, Wallis and Futuna
13 Y7 Ouest, Pointe de l' headland Quebec, SE Canada 48.08N 64.57W
Ouezzane see Ouazzane
101 K20 Ouffet Liège, E Belgium 50.30N 5.31E
81 H14 Ouham ◐ prefecture NW Central African Republic
80 I13 Ouham ≈ Central African Republic/Chad
81 G14 Ouham-Pendé ◐ prefecture W Central African Republic
79 R16 Ouidah Eng. Whydah, Wida. S Benin 6.22N 2.07E
76 H6 Oujda Ar. Oudjda, Ujda. NE Morocco 34.45N 1.53W
78 I7 Oujeft Adrar, C Mauritania 20.05N 13.00W
95 L15 Oulainen Oulu, C Finland 64.14N 24.50E
Ould Yanja see Ould Yenjé
78 J10 Ould Yenjé var. Ould Yanja. Guidimaka, S Mauritania 15.33N 11.43W
95 L14 Oulu Swe. Uleåborg. Oulu, C Finland 65.01N 25.28E
95 M14 Oulu Swe. Uleåborg. ◐ province N Finland
95 L15 Oulujärvi Swe. Uleträsk. ◎ C Finland
95 M14 Oulujoki Swe. Uleälv. ≈ C Finland
95 L14 Oulunsalo Oulu, C Finland 64.55N 25.19E
108 A8 Oulx Piemonte, NE Italy 45.05N 6.41E
80 J9 Oum-Chalouba Borkou-Ennedi-Tibesti, NE Chad 15.48N 20.46E
78 M16 Oumé C Ivory Coast 6.23N 5.25W
76 F7 Oum er Rbia ≈ C Morocco
80 J10 Oum-Hadjer Batha, E Chad 13.18N 19.40E
94 K10 Ounasjoki ≈ N Finland
80 J7 Ounianga Kébir Borkou-Ennedi-Tibesti, N Chad 19.06N 20.28E
Ouolossébougou see Ouéléssébougou
Oup see Auob
101 K19 Oupeye Liège, E Belgium 50.42N 5.37E
101 N21 Our ≈ NW Europe
39 Q7 Ouray Colorado, C USA 38.01N 107.40W
105 R7 Ource ≈ C France
106 G9 Ourém Santarém, C Portugal 39.40N 8.32W
106 H4 Ourense Cast. Orense; Lat. Aurium. Galicia, NW Spain 42.19N 7.52W
106 I4 Ourense Cast. Orense ◐ province Galicia, NW Spain
61 O15 Ouricuri Pernambuco, E Brazil 7.51S 40.04W
62 J9 Ourinhos São Paulo, S Brazil 22.58S 49.52W
106 G13 Ourique Beja, S Portugal 37.37N 8.13W
61 M20 Ouro Preto Minas Gerais, NE Brazil 20.25S 43.30W
Ours, Grand Lac de l' see Great Bear Lake
101 K20 Ourthe ≈ E Belgium
171 Mm11 Ōu-sanmyaku ▲ Honshū, C Japan
99 M17 Ouse ≈ N England, UK
Ouse see Great Ouse
104 H7 Oust ≈ NW France
Outaouais see Ottawa
13 T4 Outardes Quatre, Réservoir ▣ Quebec, SE Canada
13 T5 Outardes, Rivière aux ≈ Quebec, SE Canada
98 E8 Outer Hebrides var. Western Isles. island group NW Scotland, UK
32 K3 Outer Island island Apostle Islands, Wisconsin, N USA
37 S16 Outer Santa Barbara Passage passage California, SW USA
106 G3 Outes Galicia, NW Spain 42.50N 8.54W
85 C18 Outjo Kunene, N Namibia 20.06S 16.06E
9 T16 Outlook Saskatchewan, S Canada 51.30N 107.03W
95 N16 Outokumpu Itä-Suomi, E Finland 62.43N 29.04E
98 M2 Out Skerries island group NE Scotland, UK
197 J5 Ouvéa island Îles Loyauté, NE New Caledonia
105 S14 Ouvèze ≈ SE France
190 L9 Ouyen Victoria, SE Australia 35.06S 142.18E
41 Q14 Ouzinkie Kodiak Island, Alaska, USA 57.54N 152.27W
143 O13 Ovacık Tunceli, E Turkey 39.22N 39.13E
108 C9 Ovada Piemonte, NE Italy 44.41N 8.39E
197 I14 Ovalau island C Fiji
64 G9 Ovalle Coquimbo, N Chile 30.33S 71.16W
85 C17 Ovamboland physical region N Namibia
56 L10 Ovana, Cerro ▲ S Venezuela 4.41N 66.54W
106 G7 Ovar Aveiro, N Portugal 40.52N 8.37W
116 L10 Ovcharitsa, Yazovir ▣ SE Bulgaria
56 E6 Ovejas Sucre, NW Colombia 9.30N 75.15W
103 E16 Overath Nordrhein-Westfalen, W Germany 50.55N 7.16E
100 F13 Overflakkee island SW Netherlands
101 H19 Overijse Vlaams Brabant, C Belgium 50.46N 4.31E
100 N10 Overijssel ◐ province E Netherlands
100 M9 Overijssels Kanaal canal E Netherlands
94 K13 Överkalix Norrbotten, N Sweden 66.19N 22.49E
29 R4 Overland Park Kansas, C USA 38.57N 94.40W
101 L14 Overloon Noord-Brabant, SE Netherlands 51.35N 5.54E
101 K16 Overpelt Limburg, NE Belgium 51.13N 5.24E
37 Y10 Overton Nevada, W USA 36.32N 114.25W
27 W7 Overton Texas, SW USA 32.16N 94.58W
94 K13 Övertorneå Norrbotten, N Sweden 66.22N 23.38E
97 N18 Överum Kalmar, S Sweden 57.58N 16.19E
94 G13 Överuman ◎ N Sweden
168 H6 Övgödiy Dzavhan, C Mongolia 48.38N 97.39E
119 P11 Ovidiopol' Odes'ka Oblast', SW Ukraine 46.15N 30.27E
118 M14 Ovidiu Constanţa, SE Romania 44.16N 28.34E
47 N10 Oviedo SW Dominican Republic 17.46N 71.22W
106 K2 Oviedo anc. Asturias. Asturias, NW Spain 43.21N 5.49W
106 K2 Oviedo ✈ Asturias, N Spain 43.21N 5.49W
Ovilava see Wels
120 D7 Oviši Ventspils, W Latvia 57.34N 21.43E
169 P10 Ovoot Sühbaatar, SE Mongolia 45.08N 113.51E
163 O4 Övörhangay ◐ province C Mongolia
96 E12 Øvre Årdal Sogn og Fjordane, S Norway 61.17N 7.44E
97 J14 Øvre Fryken ◎ C Sweden
94 J11 Övre Soppero Norrbotten, N Sweden 68.07N 21.40E
119 N3 Ovruch Zhytomyrs'ka Oblast', N Ukraine 51.19N 28.50E
168 J8 Övt Övörhangay, C Mongolia 46.50N 102.15E

◆ Country ● Country Capital ◇ Dependent Territory ○ Dependent Territory Capital ◐ Administrative Region ✈ International Airport ▲ Mountain ▲ Mountain Range ▲ Volcano ≈ River ◎ Lake ▣ Reservoir

OWAKA – PANGI

193 E24 **Owaka** Otago, South Island, NZ 46.27S 169.42E
81 H18 **Owando** *prev.* Fort-Rousset. Cuvette, C Congo 0.28S 15.55E
171 Gg17 **Owase** Mie, Honshū, SW Japan 34.04N 136.10E
29 P9 **Owasso** Oklahoma, C USA 36.16N 95.51W
31 V10 **Owatonna** Minnesota, N USA 44.04N 93.13W
181 O4 **Owen Fracture Zone** *tectonic feature* W Arabian Sea
193 H15 **Owen, Mount** ▲ South Island, NZ 41.32S 172.33E
193 H15 **Owen River** Tasman, South Island, NZ 41.40S 172.28E
46 D8 **Owen Roberts** ✕ Grand Cayman, Cayman Islands 19.15N 81.22W
22 I6 **Owensboro** Kentucky, S USA 37.46N 87.06W
37 T11 **Owens Lake** *salt flat* California, W USA
12 F14 **Owen Sound** Ontario, S Canada 44.34N 80.55W
12 F13 **Owen Sound** ◎ Ontario, S Canada
37 T10 **Owens River** ≈ California, W USA
194 K15 **Owen Stanley Range** ▲▲ S PNG
29 V5 **Owensville** Missouri, C USA 38.21N 91.30W
22 M4 **Owenton** Kentucky, S USA 38.33N 84.51W
79 U17 **Owerri** Imo, S Nigeria 5.19N 7.07E
192 M10 **Owhango** Manawatu-Wanganui, North Island, NZ 39.01S 175.22E
23 N5 **Owingsville** Kentucky, S USA 38.10N 83.42W
152 K10 **Owminzatovo-Toshi** *Rus.* Gory Auminzatau. ▲▲ N Uzbekistan
79 T16 **Owo** Ondo, SW Nigeria 7.10N 5.31E
33 R9 **Owosso** Michigan, N USA 43.00N 84.10W
37 V1 **Owyhee** Nevada, W USA 41.57N 116.07W
34 L14 **Owyhee, Lake** ◎ Oregon, NW USA
34 L15 **Owyhee River** ≈ Idaho/Oregon, NW USA
94 K1 **Öxarfjördhur** *var.* Axarfjördhur. *fjord* N Iceland
96 K12 **Oxberg** Dalarna, C Sweden 61.07N 14.10E
9 V17 **Oxbow** Saskatchewan, S Canada 49.16N 102.12W
97 O17 **Oxelösund** Södermanland, S Sweden 58.40N 17.10E
193 H18 **Oxford** Canterbury, South Island, NZ 43.18S 172.10E
99 M21 **Oxford** *Lat.* Oxonia. S England, UK 51.46N 1.15W
25 Q3 **Oxford** Alabama, S USA 33.36N 85.50W
24 L2 **Oxford** Mississippi, S USA 34.23N 89.30W
31 N16 **Oxford** Nebraska, C USA 40.15N 99.37W
20 I11 **Oxford** New York, NE USA 42.21N 75.39W
23 U8 **Oxford** North Carolina, SE USA 36.18N 78.35W
33 Q14 **Oxford** Ohio, N USA 39.30N 84.45W
20 H16 **Oxford** Pennsylvania, NE USA 39.46N 75.57W
9 X12 **Oxford House** Manitoba, C Canada 54.55N 95.13W
31 Y13 **Oxford Junction** Iowa, C USA 41.58N 90.57W
9 X12 **Oxford Lake** ◎ Manitoba, C Canada
99 M21 **Oxfordshire** *cultural region* S England, UK
Oxia *see* Oxyá
43 X12 **Oxkutzcab** Yucatán, SE Mexico 20.14N 89.20W
37 R15 **Oxnard** California, W USA 34.12N 119.10W
Oxonia *see* Oxford
12 I12 **Oxtongue** ≈ Ontario, SE Canada
Oxus *see* Amu Darya
117 E15 **Oxyá** *var.* Oxia. ▲ C Greece 39.46N 21.56E
171 Ii13 **Oyabe** Toyama, Honshū, SW Japan 36.41N 136.53E
Oyahue/Oyahue, Volcán *see* Ollagüe, Volcán
171 K16 **Oyama** Tochigi, Honshū, S Japan 36.19N 139.46E
49 U5 **Oyapock** ≈ E French Guiana
Oyapock *see* Oiapoque, Rio
57 Z10 **Oyapok, Baie de L'** *bay* Brazil/French Guiana
57 Z11 **Oyapok, Fleuve l'** *var.* Oyapock, Rio Oiapoque. ≈ Brazil/French Guiana *see also* Oiapoque, Rio
81 E17 **Oyem** Woleu-Ntem, N Gabon 1.34N 11.31E
9 R16 **Oyen** Alberta, SW Canada 51.19N 110.28W
97 I15 **Øyeren** ◎ S Norway
168 G6 **Oygon** Dzavhan, N Mongolia 48.57N 96.33E
98 I7 **Oykel** ≈ N Scotland, UK
127 N9 **Oymyakon** Respublika Sakha (Yakutiya), NE Russian Federation 63.28N 142.22E
81 H19 **Oyo** Cuvette, C Congo 1.05S 15.55E
79 S15 **Oyo** Oyo, W Nigeria 7.51N 3.57E
79 S15 **Oyo** ⬖ *state* SW Nigeria
58 D13 **Oyón** Lima, C Peru 10.39S 76.46W
105 S10 **Oyonnax** Ain, E France 46.16N 5.39E
152 L10 **Oyoqighitma** *Rus.* Ayakagytma. Bukhoro Wiloyati, C Uzbekistan 40.37N 64.26E
152 M9 **Oyoqquduq** *Rus.* Ayakkuduk. Nawoiy Wiloyati, N Uzbekistan 41.16N 65.12E
34 F9 **Oysterville** Washington, NW USA 46.33N 124.03W
97 D14 **Øystese** Hordaland, S Norway 60.22N 6.13E
153 U10 **Oy-Tal** Oshskaya Oblast', SW Kyrgyzstan 40.23N 74.04E
153 T10 **Oy-Tal** ≈ SW Kyrgyzstan
151 S16 **Oytal** Zhambyl, S Kazakhstan 42.50N 73.21E
Oyyl *see* Uil
179 Qq15 **Ozamiz** Mindanao, S Philippines 8.09N 123.51E
Ozarichi *see* Azarychy
25 R7 **Ozark** Alabama, S USA 31.27N 85.38W
29 S10 **Ozark** Arkansas, C USA 35.29N 93.49W
29 T8 **Ozark** Missouri, C USA 37.01N 93.12W
29 T8 **Ozark Plateau** *plain* Arkansas/Missouri, C USA
29 T6 **Ozarks, Lake of the** ⊡ Missouri, C USA
199 Jj11 **Ozbourn Seamount** *undersea feature* W Pacific Ocean 26.00S 174.49W
113 L20 **Ózd** Borsod-Abaúj-Zemplén, NE Hungary 48.14N 20.18E
114 D11 **Ozeblin** ▲ C Croatia 44.37N 15.52E
127 Pp12 **Ozernovskiy** Kamchatskaya Oblast', E Russian Federation 51.28N 94.32E
150 M7 **Ozërnoye** *var.* Ozërnyy. Kostanay, N Kazakhstan 53.27N 63.10E
Ozërnyy *see* Ozërnoye
117 D18 **Ozerós, Límni** ◎ W Greece
121 D14 **Ozersk** *prev.* Darkehnen, *Ger.* Angerapp. Kaliningradskaya Oblast', W Russian Federation 54.23N 21.59E
130 L4 **Ozery** Moskovskaya Oblast', W Russian Federation 54.51N 38.37E
Özgön *see* Uzgen
109 C17 **Ozieri** Sardegna, Italy, C Mediterranean Sea 40.34N 9.01E
113 I15 **Ozimek** *Ger.* Malapane. Opolskie, S Poland 50.41N 18.16E
131 R8 **Ozinki** Saratovskaya Oblast', W Russian Federation 51.16N 49.45E
Oziya *see* Ojiya
27 O10 **Ozona** Texas, SW USA 30.42N 101.12W
Ozorkov *see* Ozorków
112 J12 **Ozorków** *Rus.* Ozorkov. Łódź, C Poland 51.58N 19.16E
170 E14 **Ōzu** Ehime, Shikoku, SW Japan 33.31N 132.31E
143 R10 **Ozurget'i** *prev.* Makharadze. W Georgia 41.57N 42.01E

P

101 J17 **Paal** Limburg, NE Belgium 51.03N 5.08E
197 C13 **Paama** *island* C Vanuatu
206 M14 **Paamiut** *var.* Pâmiut, *Dan.* Frederikshåb. Kitaa, S Greenland 62.22N 49.52W
178 Gg9 **Pa-an** Karen State, S Burma 16.51N 97.37E
103 L22 **Paar** ≈ SE Germany
85 E26 **Paarl** Western Cape, SW South Africa 33.45S 18.58E
95 L15 **Paavola** Oulu, C Finland 64.34N 25.15E
98 E8 **Pabbay** *island* NW Scotland, UK
175 P12 **Pabbiring, Kepulauan** *island group* C Indonesia
159 T15 **Pabna** Rajshahi, W Bangladesh 24.02N 89.15E
111 U4 **Pabneukirchen** Oberösterreich, N Austria 48.19N 14.49E
120 H13 **Pabradė** *Pol.* Podbrodzie. Švenčionys, SE Lithuania 54.58N 25.43E
58 L13 **Pacahuaras, Río** ≈ N Bolivia
Pacaraima, Sierra/Pacaraim, Serra *see* Pakaraima Mountains
58 B11 **Pacasmayo** La Libertad, W Peru 7.27S 79.34W
44 D6 **Pacaya, Volcán de** ⛰ S Guatemala 14.19N 90.36W
117 K23 **Pachía** *island* Kykládes, Greece, Aegean Sea
109 L26 **Pachino** Sicilia, Italy, C Mediterranean Sea 36.43N 15.06E
58 F12 **Pachitea, Río** ≈ C Peru
160 I11 **Pachmarhi** Madhya Pradesh, C India 22.36N 78.18E
124 N4 **Páchna** *var.* Pakhna. SW Cyprus 34.47N 32.48E
117 H25 **Páchnes** ▲ Kríti, Greece, E Mediterranean Sea 35.19N 24.00E
56 F9 **Pacho** Cundinamarca, C Colombia 5.07N 74.11W
160 F12 **Pāchora** Mahārāshtra, C India 20.52N 75.28E
43 P13 **Pachuca** *var.* Pachuca de Soto. Hidalgo, C Mexico 20.05N 98.46W
Pachuca de Soto *see* Pachuca
29 W5 **Pacific** Missouri, C USA 38.28N 90.44W
199 Jj15 **Pacific-Antarctic Ridge** *undersea feature* S Pacific Ocean
34 F8 **Pacific Beach** Washington, NW USA 47.09N 124.12W
37 N10 **Pacific Grove** California, W USA 36.35N 121.54W
31 S15 **Pacific Junction** Iowa, C USA 41.01N 95.48W
198-199 **Pacific Ocean** *ocean*
133 Z10 **Pacific Plate** *tectonic feature*
115 J15 **Pačir** ▲ SW Yugoslavia 43.19N 19.07E
190 L5 **Packsaddle** New South Wales, SE Australia 30.42S 141.55E
34 H9 **Packwood** Washington, NW USA 46.37N 121.38W
Padalung *see* Phatthalung
175 Q12 **Padamarang, Pulau** *island* C Indonesia
173 G9 **Padang** Sumatera, W Indonesia 01.00S 100.21E
174 Hh5 **Padang Endau** Pahang, Peninsular Malaysia 2.38N 103.37E
Padangpandjang *see* Padangpanjang
173 G8 **Padangpanjang** *prev.* Padangpandjang. Sumatera, W Indonesia 0.30S 100.25E
173 Ff7 **Padangsidempuan** *prev.* Padangsidimpoean. Sumatera, W Indonesia 1.22N 99.14E
Padangsidimpoean *see* Padangsidempuan
128 I9 **Padany** Respublika Kareliya, NW Russian Federation 63.18N 33.20E
95 M18 **Padasjoki** Etelä-Suomi, S Finland 61.20N 25.20E
59 M22 **Padcaya** Tarija, S Bolivia 21.52S 64.46W
103 H14 **Paderborn** Nordrhein-Westfalen, NW Germany 51.43N 8.45E
Padeşul/Padeş, Vîrful *see* Padeş, Vârful
118 F12 **Padeş, Vârful** *var.* Padeşul; *prev.* Vîrful Padeş. ▲ W Romania 45.39N 22.19E
114 L10 **Padinska Skela** Serbia, N Yugoslavia 44.58N 20.25E
Padma *see* Brahmaputra
159 S14 **Padma** *var.* Ganges. ≈ Bangladesh/India *see also* Ganges
108 H8 **Padova** *Eng.* Padua; *anc.* Patavium. Veneto, NE Italy 45.24N 11.52E
84 A10 **Padrão, Ponta do** *headland* NW Angola 6.06S 12.18E
27 T16 **Padre Island** *island* Texas, SW USA
106 G3 **Padrón** Galicia, NW Spain 42.43N 8.40W
120 K13 **Padsvillye** *Rus.* Podsvil'ye. Vitsyebskaya Voblasts', N Belarus 55.10N 27.58E
190 K11 **Padthaway** South Australia 36.39S 140.30E
Padua *see* Padova
22 G7 **Paducah** Kentucky, S USA 37.09N 88.52W
27 P4 **Paducah** Texas, SW USA 33.59N 100.19W
107 N15 **Padul** Andalucía, S Spain 37.01N 3.37W
203 P8 **Paea** Tahiti, W French Polynesia 17.40S 149.34W
193 L14 **Paekakariki** Wellington, North Island, NZ 41.00S 174.58E
169 X11 **Paektu-san** *var.* Baitou Shan. ▲ China/North Korea 42.00N 128.03W
169 V15 **Paengnyŏng-do** *island* NW South Korea
192 M7 **Paeroa** Waikato, North Island, NZ 37.22S 175.39E
56 D12 **Páez** Cauca, SW Colombia 2.37N 76.00W
123 Mm4 **Páfos** *var.* Paphos. W Cyprus 34.46N 32.25E
123 Mm4 **Páfos** ✕ SW Cyprus 34.46N 32.25E
85 L19 **Pafúri** Gaza, SW Mozambique 22.24S 31.27E
114 C12 **Pag** *It.* Pago. Lika-Senj, W Croatia 44.26N 15.01E
114 B11 **Pag** *It.* Pago. *island* Zadar, SW Croatia
179 Qq16 **Pagadian** Mindanao, S Philippines 7.47N 123.22E
173 G11 **Pagai Selatan, Pulau** *island* Kepulauan Mentawai, W Indonesia
173 Ff10 **Pagai Utara, Pulau** *island* Kepulauan Mentawai, W Indonesia
196 K4 **Pagan** *island* C Northern Mariana Islands
117 G16 **Pagasitikós Kólpos** *gulf* E Greece
38 L8 **Page** Arizona, SW USA 36.54N 111.28W
31 Q5 **Page** North Dakota, N USA 47.09N 97.33W
120 D13 **Pagėgiai** *Ger.* Pogegen. Šilutė, SW Lithuania 55.08N 21.54E
23 S11 **Pageland** South Carolina, SE USA 34.46N 80.23W
83 G16 **Pager** ≈ NE Uganda
155 Q5 **Paghmān** Kābul, E Afghanistan 34.33N 68.55E
Pago *see* Pag
196 C16 **Pago Bay** *bay* E Guam, W Pacific Ocean
117 M20 **Pagóndas** *var.* Pagóndhas. Sámos, Dodekánisos, Greece, Aegean Sea 37.40N 26.49E
Pagóndhas *see* Pagóndas
198 C8 **Pago Pago** ○ (American Samoa) Tutuila, W American Samoa 14.16S 170.43W
39 R8 **Pagosa Springs** Colorado, C USA 37.13N 107.01W
40 H12 **Pahala** *var.* Pāhala. Hawaii, USA, C Pacific Ocean 19.12N 155.28W
174 H4 **Pahang** *off.* Negeri Pahang Darul Makmur. ⬖ *state* Peninsular Malaysia
Pahang *see* Pahang, Sungai
174 Hh5 **Pahang, Sungai** *var.* Pahang, Sungei Pahang. ≈ Peninsular Malaysia
155 S8 **Pahārpur** North-West Frontier Province, NW Pakistan 32.06N 71.00E
193 B24 **Pahia Point** *headland* South Island, NZ 46.19S 167.42E
192 M13 **Pahiatua** Manawatu-Wanganui, North Island, NZ 40.30S 175.48E
40 H12 **Pahoa** *Haw.* Pāhoa. Hawaii, USA, C Pacific Ocean 19.28N 154.55W
25 Y14 **Pahokee** Florida, SE USA 26.49N 80.40W
37 X9 **Pahranagat Range** ▲▲ Nevada, W USA
37 W11 **Pahrump** Nevada, W USA 36.11N 115.58W
Pahsien *see* Chongqing
37 V9 **Pahute Mesa** ▲▲ Nevada, W USA
178 H7 **Pai** Mae Hong Son, NW Thailand 19.24N 98.25E
40 F10 **Paia** *Haw.* Pā'ia. Maui, Hawaii, USA, C Pacific Ocean 20.54N 94.22W
Pai-ch'eng *see* Baicheng
120 H4 **Paide** *Ger.* Weissenstein. Järvamaa, N Estonia 58.54N 25.36E
99 J24 **Paignton** SW England, UK 50.25N 3.34W
192 K3 **Paihia** Northland, North Island, NZ 35.18S 174.06E
95 M18 **Päijänne** ◎ S Finland
116 F13 **Páïko** ▲▲ N Greece
59 M17 **Paila, Río** ≈ C Bolivia
178 I12 **Pailĭn** Bătdâmbâng, W Cambodia 12.51N 102.34E
56 F6 **Pailitas** Cesar, N Colombia 8.58N 73.37W
40 F9 **Pailolo Channel** *channel* Hawaii, USA, C Pacific Ocean
95 K19 **Paimio** *Swe.* Pemar. Länsi-Suomi, W Finland 60.27N 22.42E
172 O17 **Paimi-saki** *var.* Yaeme-saki. *headland* Iriomote-jima, SW Japan 24.18N 123.40E
104 G5 **Paimpol** Côtes d'Armor, NW France 48.46N 3.03W
174 Gg9 **Painan** Sumatera, W Indonesia 1.22S 100.33E
65 G23 **Paine, Cerro** ▲ S Chile 51.01S 72.57W
33 U11 **Painesville** Ohio, N USA 41.43N 81.15W
33 S14 **Paint Creek** ≈ Ohio, N USA
38 L10 **Painted Desert** *desert* Arizona, SW USA
Paint Hills *see* Wemindji
32 M4 **Paint River** ≈ Michigan, N USA
27 P8 **Paint Rock** Texas, SW USA 31.30N 99.55W
23 O6 **Paintsville** Kentucky, S USA 37.48N 82.48W
Paisance *see* Piacenza
98 I12 **Paisley** W Scotland, UK 55.49N 4.25W
34 I15 **Paisley** Oregon, NW USA 42.40N 120.31W
107 R10 **País Valenciano** *var.* Valencia, *Cat.* València; *anc.* Valentia. ⬖ *autonomous community* NE Spain
107 O3 **País Vasco** *Basq.* Euskadi, *Eng.* The Basque Country, *Sp.* Provincias Vascongadas. ⬖ *autonomous community* N Spain
58 A9 **Paita** Piura, NW Peru 5.07S 81.07W
197 J7 **Païta** Province Sud, S New Caledonia 22.06S 166.18E
175 O1 **Paitan, Teluk** *bay* Sabah, East Malaysia
106 H7 **Paiva, Rio** ≈ N Portugal
94 K12 **Pajala** Norrbotten, N Sweden 67.12N 23.19E
106 K3 **Pajares, Puerto de** *pass* NW Spain 43.00N 5.53W
56 G9 **Pajárito** Boyacá, C Colombia 5.18N 72.43W
56 G4 **Pajaro** La Guajira, S Colombia 11.41N 72.37W
Pakanbaru *see* Pekanbaru
57 Q10 **Pakaraima Mountains** *var.* Serra Pacaraim, Sierra Pacaraima. ▲▲ N South America
178 Hh11 **Pak Chong** Nakhon Ratchasima, C Thailand 14.38N 101.22E
127 Pp7 **Pakhachi** Koryakskiy Avtonomnyy Okrug, E Russian Federation 60.36N 168.59E
Pakhna *see* Páchna
153 O11 **Pakhtakor** Jizzakh Wiloyati, C Uzbekistan 40.21N 67.54E
201 U16 **Pakin Atoll** *atoll* Caroline Islands, E Micronesia
155 Q12 **Pakistan** *off.* Islamic Republic of Pakistan, *var.* Islami Jamhuriya e Pakistan. ◆ *republic* S Asia
Pakistan, Islami Jamhuriya e *see* Pakistan
178 I8 **Pak Lay** *var.* Muang Pak Lay. Xaignabouli, C Laos 18.06N 101.21E
Paknam *see* Samut Prakan
177 Ff5 **Pakokku** Magwe, C Burma 21.19N 95.04E
112 I10 **Pakość** *Ger.* Pakosch. Kujawski-pomorskie, C Poland 52.47N 18.03E
Pakosch *see* Pakość
155 V10 **Pākpattan** Punjab, E Pakistan 30.19N 73.27E
178 H16 **Pak Phanang** *var.* Ban Pak Phanang. Nakhon Si Thammarat, SW Thailand 8.19N 100.10E
114 G9 **Pakrac** *Hung.* Pakrácz. Požega-Slavonija, NE Croatia 45.26N 17.09E
Pakrácz *see* Pakrac
120 F11 **Pakruojis** Pakruojis, N Lithuania 55.59N 23.50E
113 J24 **Paks** Tolna, S Hungary 46.37N 18.51E
Pak Sane *see* Pakxan
Paksé *see* Pakxé
178 I11 **Pak Thong Chai** Nakhon Ratchasima, C Thailand 14.43N 102.01E
155 R6 **Paktīā** ⬖ *province* SE Afghanistan
155 Q7 **Paktīkā** ⬖ *province* SE Afghanistan
175 Pp9 **Pakuli** Sulawesi, C Indonesia 1.14S 119.55E
83 F17 **Pakwach** NW Uganda 2.28N 31.28E
178 Ii8 **Pakxan** *var.* Muang Pakxan, Pak Sane. Bolikhamxai, C Laos 18.27N 103.38E
178 Jj10 **Pakxé** *var.* Paksé. Champasak, S Laos 15.09N 105.49E
80 G12 **Pala** Mayo-Kébbi, SW Chad 9.22N 14.54E
63 A17 **Palacios** Santa Fe, C Argentina 30.43S 61.37W
27 V13 **Palacios** Texas, SW USA 28.42N 96.13W
107 X5 **Palafrugell** Cataluña, NE Spain 41.55N 3.10E
109 L24 **Palagonia** Sicilia, Italy, C Mediterranean Sea 37.19N 14.45E
115 E17 **Palagruža** *It.* Pelagosa. *island* SW Croatia
117 G20 **Palaiá Epídavros** Pelopónnisos, S Greece 37.38N 23.09E
124 Nn3 **Palaichóri** *var.* Palekhori. C Cyprus 34.55N 33.06E
117 H25 **Palaiochóra** Kríti, Greece, E Mediterranean Sea 35.14N 23.37E
117 A15 **Palaiolastrítsa** *religious building* Kérkyra, Iónioi Nísoi, Greece, C Mediterranean Sea 39.41N 19.42E
117 J19 **Palaiópoli** Ándros, Kykládes, Greece, Aegean Sea 37.49N 24.49E
105 N5 **Palaiseau** Essonne, N France 48.40N 2.13E
Palakkad *see* Pālghāt
160 N11 **Pāla Laharha** Orissa, E India 21.27N 85.14E
85 G19 **Palamakoloi** Ghanzi, C Botswana 23.10S 22.22E
117 E16 **Palamás** Thessalía, C Greece 39.28N 22.04E
107 X5 **Palamós** Cataluña, NE Spain 41.51N 3.06E
120 J5 **Palamuse** *Ger.* Sankt-Bartholomäi. Jõgevamaa, E Estonia 58.40N 26.34E
191 Q14 **Palana** Tasmania, SE Australia 39.48S 147.54E
127 P9 **Palana** Koryakskiy Avtonomnyy Okrug, E Russian Federation 59.04N 159.58E
120 C11 **Palanga** *Ger.* Polangen. Palanga, NW Lithuania 5.54N 21.05E
149 V10 **Palangān, Kūh-e** ▲▲ E Iran
Palangkaraja *see* Palangkaraya
174 Mm10 **Palangkaraya** *prev.* Palangkaraja. Borneo, C Indonesia 2.16S 113.55E
161 H22 **Palani** Tamil Nādu, SE India 10.30N 77.24E
Palanka *see* Bačka Palanka
160 D9 **Pālanpur** Gujarāt, W India 24.12N 72.28E
Palantia *see* Palencia
85 I19 **Palapye** Central, SE Botswana 22.37S 27.06E
161 J19 **Pālār** ≈ SE India
106 H3 **Palas de Rei** Galicia, NW Spain 42.52N 7.51W
127 O10 **Palatka** Magadanskaya Oblast', E Russian Federation 60.09N 150.33E
25 W10 **Palatka** Florida, SE USA 29.39N 81.38W
196 B9 **Palau** *var.* Belau. ◆ *republic* W Pacific Ocean
133 Y14 **Palau Islands** *var.* Palau. *island group* N Palau
198 Aa8 **Palauli Bay** *bay* Savai'i, Samoa, C Pacific Ocean
178 Gg12 **Palaw** Tenasserim, S Burma 12.57N 98.39E
179 Oo15 **Palawan** *island* W Philippines
179 Oo15 **Palawan Passage** *passage* W Philippines
198 F7 **Palawan Trough** *undersea feature* S South China Sea
179 P10 **Palayan City** Luzon, N Philippines 15.34N 121.34E
161 H23 **Pālayankottai** Tamil Nādu, SE India 8.44N 77.45E
109 L25 **Palazzola Acreide** *anc.* Acrae. Sicilia, Italy, C Mediterranean Sea 37.04N 14.54E
120 G3 **Paldiski** *prev.* Baltiski, *Eng.* Baltic Port, *Ger.* Baltischport. Harjumaa, NW Estonia 59.20N 24.04E
114 I13 **Pale** Republika Srpska, E Bosnia and Herzegovina 43.49N 18.35E
Palekhori *see* Palaichóri
175 Q7 **Paleleh, Pegunungan** ▲▲ Sulawesi, N Indonesia
175 Qq7 **Paleleh, Teluk** *bay* Sulawesi, N Indonesia
174 I11 **Palembang** Sumatera, W Indonesia 2.58S 104.45E
65 G18 **Palena** Los Lagos, S Chile 43.40S 71.49W
65 G18 **Palena, Río** ≈ S Chile
106 M5 **Palencia** *anc.* Palantia, Pallantia. Castilla-León, NW Spain 41.01N 4.31W
106 M3 **Palencia** ⬖ *province* Castilla-León, N Spain
37 X15 **Palen Dry Lake** ◎ California, W USA
43 V15 **Palenque** Chiapas, SE Mexico 17.37N 92.03W
43 V15 **Palenque** *var.* Ruinas de Palenque. *ruins* Chiapas, SE Mexico 17.31N 91.58W
47 O9 **Palenque, Punta** *headland* S Dominican Republic 18.13N 70.08W
Palenque, Ruinas de *see* Palenque
Palerme *see* Palermo
109 I23 **Palermo** *Fr.* Palerme; *anc.* Panhormus, Panormus. Sicilia, Italy, C Mediterranean Sea 38.07N 13.22E
27 V8 **Palestine** Texas, SW USA 31.44N 95.38W
27 V7 **Palestine, Lake** ⊡ Texas, SW USA
109 I15 **Palestrina** Lazio, C Italy 41.49N 12.53E
177 F5 **Paletwa** Chin State, W Burma 21.21N 92.51E
161 G21 **Pālghāt** *var.* Palakkad; *prev.* Pulicat. Kerala, SW India 10.46N 76.42E
158 F13 **Pāli** Rājasthān, N India 25.48N 73.21E
178 Gg16 **Palian** Trang, SW Thailand
201 O12 **Palikir** ● (Micronesia) Pohnpei, E Micronesia 6.58N 158.13E
179 R17 **Palimbang** Mindanao, S Philippines 6.16N 124.10E
Palimé *see* Kpalimé
109 L19 **Palinuro, Capo** *headland* S Italy 40.02N 15.16E
117 H15 **Palioúri, Akrotírio** *var.* Akra Kanestron. *headland* N Greece 39.55N 23.45E
35 R14 **Palisades Reservoir** ⊡ Idaho, NW USA
101 J23 **Paliseul** Luxembourg, SE Belgium 49.55N 5.09E
160 C11 **Pālitāna** Gujarāt, W India 21.30N 71.49E
120 F4 **Palivere** Läänemaa, W Estonia 58.59N 23.58E
43 V14 **Palizada** Campeche, SE Mexico 18.15N 92.03W
95 L18 **Pälkäne** Länsi-Suomi, W Finland 61.21N 24.15E
161 J22 **Palk Strait** *strait* India/Sri Lanka
161 J23 **Pallai** Northern Province, NW Sri Lanka 9.34N 80.19E
Pallantia *see* Palencia
108 C6 **Pallanza** Piemonte, NE Italy 45.57N 8.32E
131 Q9 **Pallasovka** Volgogradskaya Oblast', SW Russian Federation 50.06N 46.52E
Pallene/Pallíni *see* Kassándra
193 L15 **Palliser Bay** *bay* North Island, NZ
193 L15 **Palliser, Cape** *headland* North Island, NZ 41.37S 175.16E
203 U9 **Palliser, Îles** *island group* Îles Tuamotu, C French Polynesia
107 X9 **Palma** *var.* Palma de Mallorca. Mallorca, Spain, W Mediterranean Sea 39.34N 2.39E
107 X9 **Palma** ✕ Mallorca, Spain, W Mediterranean Sea
84 Q12 **Palma** Cabo Delgado, N Mozambique 10.46S 40.30E
107 X10 **Palma, Badia de** *bay* Mallorca, Spain, W Mediterranean Sea
106 L13 **Palma del Río** Andalucía, S Spain 37.42N 5.16W
Palma de Mallorca *see* Palma
109 J25 **Palma di Montechiaro** Sicilia, Italy, C Mediterranean Sea 37.12N 13.46E
108 J7 **Palmanova** Friuli-Venezia Giulia, NE Italy 45.54N 13.20E
56 J7 **Palmarito** Apure, C Venezuela 7.36N 70.11W
45 N15 **Palmar Sur** Puntarenas, SE Costa Rica 8.54N 83.27W
62 I12 **Palmas** Paraná, S Brazil 26.29S 52.00W
61 K16 **Palmas** *var.* Palmas do Tocantins, C Brazil 10.24S 48.19W
Palmas do Tocantins *see* Palmas
56 D11 **Palmaseca** ✕ (Cali) Valle del Cauca, SW Colombia 3.31N 76.27W
109 B21 **Palmas, Golfo di** *gulf* Sardegna, Italy, C Mediterranean Sea
46 I7 **Palma Soriano** Santiago de Cuba, E Cuba 20.10N 76.00W
25 Y12 **Palm Bay** Florida, SE USA 28.01N 80.35W
37 T14 **Palmdale** California, W USA 34.34N 118.07W
63 H14 **Palmeira das Missões** Rio Grande do Sul, S Brazil 27.54S 53.19W
84 A11 **Palmeirinhas, Ponta das** *headland* NW Angola 9.04S 13.02E
41 R11 **Palmer** Alaska, USA 61.36N 149.06W
21 N11 **Palmer** Massachusetts, NE USA 42.09N 72.19W
27 U7 **Palmer** Texas, SW USA 32.25N 96.40W
204 H4 **Palmer** *US research station* Antarctica 64.37S 64.01W
13 R11 **Palmer** ≈ Quebec, SE Canada
39 T5 **Palmer Lake** Colorado, C USA 39.07N 104.55W
204 J6 **Palmer Land** *physical region* Antarctica
12 F15 **Palmerston** Ontario, SE Canada 43.51N 80.49W
193 F22 **Palmerston** Otago, South Island, NZ 45.27S 170.42E
202 K15 **Palmerston** *island* S Cook Islands
Palmerston *see* Darwin
192 M12 **Palmerston North** Manawatu-Wanganui, North Island, NZ 40.19S 175.52E
78 L18 **Palmés, Cap des** *headland* SW Ivory Coast 4.18N 7.31W
25 V13 **Palmetto** Florida, SE USA 27.31N 82.34W
Palmetto State *see* South Carolina
109 M22 **Palmi** Calabria, SW Italy 38.21N 15.51E
56 D11 **Palmira** Valle del Cauca, W Colombia 3.33N 76.15W
58 F8 **Palmira, Río** ≈ N Peru
63 D19 **Palmitas** Soriano, SW Uruguay 33.27S 57.48W
Palmnicken *see* Yantarnyy
37 V15 **Palm Springs** California, W USA 33.48N 116.33W
29 V2 **Palmyra** Missouri, C USA 39.47N 91.31W
20 G10 **Palmyra** New York, NE USA 43.02N 77.13W
20 G15 **Palmyra** Pennsylvania, NE USA 40.18N 76.35W
23 V5 **Palmyra** Virginia, NE USA 37.53N 78.15W
Palmyra *see* Tudmur
199 K7 **Palmyra Atoll** ◇ *US privately owned unincorporated territory* C Pacific Ocean
160 P12 **Palmyras Point** *headland* E India 20.46N 87.00E
37 N9 **Palo Alto** California, W USA 37.26N 122.08W
27 O1 **Palo Duro Creek** ≈ Texas, SW USA
Paloe *see* Palu
Paloe *see* Denpasar, Bali, C Indonesia
174 Hh6 **Paloh** Johor, Peninsular Malaysia 2.10N 103.10E
82 F12 **Paloich** Upper Nile, SE Sudan 10.28N 32.31E
42 I3 **Palomas** Chihuahua, N Mexico 31.45N 107.38W
109 I15 **Palombara Sabina** Lazio, C Italy 42.04N 12.45E
107 S13 **Palos, Cabo de** *headland* SE Spain 37.38N 0.42W
106 I14 **Palos de la Frontera** Andalucía, S Spain 37.13N 6.52W
62 G11 **Palotina** Paraná, S Brazil 24.16S 53.49W
34 M9 **Palouse** Washington, NW USA 46.54N 117.04W
34 L9 **Palouse River** ≈ Washington, NW USA
37 Y16 **Palo Verde** California, W USA 33.25N 114.43W
59 E16 **Palpa** Ica, W Peru 14.33S 75.09W
97 M16 **Pålsboda** Örebro, C Sweden 59.04N 15.21E
95 M15 **Paltamo** Oulu, C Finland 64.25N 27.49E
175 Pp9 **Palu** *prev.* Paloe. Sulawesi, C Indonesia 0.54S 119.52E
143 P14 **Palu** Elâzığ, E Turkey 38.43N 39.55E
175 Q16 **Palu, Pulau** *island* S Indonesia
175 P8 **Palu, Teluk** *bay* Sulawesi, C Indonesia
158 I11 **Palwal** Haryāna, N India 28.15N 77.18E
127 Oo4 **Palyavaam** ≈ NE Russian Federation
79 Q13 **Pama** SE Burkina 11.13N 0.46E
180 J14 **Pamandzi** ✕ (Mamoudzou) Petite-Terre, E Mayotte
Pamangkat *see* Pemangkat
149 R11 **Pā Mazār** Kermān, C Iran
85 N19 **Pambarra** Inhambane, SE Mozambique 21.57S 35.06E
176 Xx10 **Pamdai** Irian Jaya, E Indonesia 1.58S 137.19E
176 X10 **Pami** Irian Jaya, E Indonesia 2.45S 136.02E
105 N16 **Pamiers** Ariège, S France 43.07N 1.36E
153 T14 **Pamir** *var.* Daryā-ye Pāmīr, *Taj.* Dar"yoi Pomir. ≈ Afghanistan/Tajikistan *see also* Pāmīr, Daryā-ye
Pamir/Pāmīr, Daryā-ye *see* Pamirs
155 U1 **Pāmīr, Daryā-ye** *var.* Pamir, *Taj.* Dar"yoi Pomir. ≈ Afghanistan/Tajikistan *see also* Pamir
Pāmīr-e Khord *see* Little Pamir
133 Q8 **Pamirs** *Pash.* Daryā-ye Pāmīr, *Rus.* Pamir. ▲▲ C Asia
Pâmiut *see* Paamiut
23 X10 **Pamlico River** ≈ North Carolina, SE USA
23 Y10 **Pamlico Sound** *sound* North Carolina, SE USA
27 O2 **Pampa** Texas, SW USA 35.31N 100.58W
Pampa Aullagas, Lago *see* Poopó, Lago
63 B21 **Pampa Húmeda** *grassland* E Argentina
58 A10 **Pampa las Salinas** *salt lake* NW Peru
59 F15 **Pampas** Huancavelica, C Peru 12.22S 74.52W
64 K13 **Pampas** *plain* C Argentina
57 O4 **Pampatar** Nueva Esparta, NE Venezuela 10.58N 63.49W
Pampeluna *see* Pamplona
106 H8 **Pampilhosa da Serra** *var.* Pampilhosa de Serra. Coimbra, N Portugal 40.03N 7.58W
181 Y15 **Pamplemousses** N Mauritius 20.06S 57.34E
56 G7 **Pamplona** Norte de Santander, N Colombia 7.24N 72.37W
107 Q3 **Pamplona** *Basq.* Iruña; *prev.* Pampeluna, *anc.* Pompaelo. Navarra, N Spain 42.49N 1.39W
116 I11 **Pamporovo** *prev.* Vasil Kolarov. Smolyan, S Bulgaria 41.39N 24.45E
142 D15 **Pamukkale** Denizli, W Turkey 37.51N 29.13E
23 W5 **Pamunkey River** ≈ Virginia, NE USA
158 K5 **Pamzal** Jammu and Kashmir, NW India 34.16N 78.49E
32 L14 **Pana** Illinois, N USA 39.23N 89.04W
43 Y11 **Panabá** Yucatán, SE Mexico 21.18N 88.15W
37 Y8 **Panaca** Nevada, W USA 37.47N 114.24W
117 E19 **Panachaikó** ▲▲ S Greece
12 F11 **Panache Lake** ◎ Ontario, S Canada
116 I10 **Panagyurishte** Pazardzhik, C Bulgaria 42.30N 24.10E
174 I14 **Panaitan, Pulau** *island* S Indonesia
174 Ii14 **Panaitan, Selat** *strait* Jawa, SW Indonesia
117 D18 **Panaitolikó** ▲▲ C Greece
161 E17 **Panaji** *var.* Pangim, Panjim, New Goa. Goa, W India 15.31N 73.52E
45 T14 **Panama** *off.* Republic of Panama. ◆ *republic* Central America
45 T15 **Panamá** *var.* Ciudad de Panamá, *Eng.* Panama City. ● (Panama) Panamá, C Panama 8.57N 79.33W
45 U14 **Panamá** *off.* Provincia de Panamá. ⬖ *province* E Panama
45 U15 **Panamá, Bahía de** *bay* N Gulf of Panama
200 Oo8 **Panama Basin** *undersea feature* E Pacific Ocean
45 T15 **Panama Canal** *canal* E Panama
25 R9 **Panama City** Florida, SE USA 30.09N 85.39W
45 T14 **Panama City** ✕ Panamá, C Panama 9.02N 79.24W
Panama City *see* Panamá
25 Q9 **Panama City Beach** Florida, SE USA 30.10N 85.48W
45 T17 **Panamá, Golfo de** *var.* Gulf of Panama. *gulf* S Panama
Panama, Gulf of *see* Panamá, Golfo de
Panama, Isthmus of *see* Panamá, Istmo de
45 T15 **Panamá, Istmo de** *Eng.* Isthmus of Panama; *prev.* Isthmus of Darien. *isthmus* E Panama
37 U11 **Panamint Range** ▲▲ California, W USA
109 L22 **Panarea, Isola** *island* Isole Eolie, S Italy
108 G9 **Panaro** ≈ N Italy
179 Q14 **Panay Gulf** *gulf* C Philippines
179 Pp13 **Panay Island** *island* C Philippines
37 W7 **Pancake Range** ▲▲ Nevada, W USA
114 M11 **Pančevo** *Ger.* Pantschowa, *Hung.* Pancsova. Serbia, N Yugoslavia 44.52N 20.39E
115 M15 **Pančićev Vrh** ▲ SW Yugoslavia 43.16N 20.49E
118 L12 **Panciu** Vrancea, E Romania 45.54N 27.07E
118 F10 **Pâncota** *Hung.* Pankota; *prev.* Pîncota. Arad, W Romania 46.19N 21.45E
Pancsova *see* Pančevo
85 N20 **Panda** Inhambane, SE Mozambique 24.04S 34.44E
176 X9 **Pandaidori, Kepulauan** *island group* E Indonesia
27 N11 **Pandale** Texas, SW USA 30.09N 101.34W
174 H7 **Pandang, Pulau** *island* W Indonesia
174 Kk9 **Pandang Tikar, Pulau** *island* N Indonesia
63 F20 **Pan de Azúcar** Maldonado, S Uruguay 34.45S 55.13W
120 H11 **Pandėlys** Rokiškis, NE Lithuania 56.04N 25.18E
161 F15 **Pandharpur** Mahārāshtra, W India 17.42N 75.24E
190 J1 **Pandie Pandie** South Australia 26.06S 139.26E
175 Pp9 **Pandiri** Sulawesi, C Indonesia 1.32S 120.47E
63 F20 **Pando** Canelones, S Uruguay 34.43S 55.58W
59 J14 **Pando** ⬖ *department* N Bolivia
199 Ii10 **Pandora Bank** *undersea feature* W Pacific Ocean
97 G20 **Pandrup** Nordjylland, N Denmark 57.13N 9.42E
159 V12 **Pandu** Assam, NE India 26.08N 91.37E
81 J15 **Pandu** Equateur, NW Dem. Rep. Congo (Zaire) 5.03N 19.14E
Paneas *see* Bāniyās
61 F15 **Panelas** Mato Grosso, W Brazil 9.06S 60.41W
120 G12 **Panevėžys** Panevėžys, C Lithuania 55.44N 24.21E
Panfilov *see* Zharkent
131 N9 **Panfilovo** Volgogradskaya Oblast', SW Russian Federation 50.25N 42.55E
81 N17 **Panga** Orientale, N Dem. Rep. Congo (Zaire) 1.52N 26.18E
200 Ss13 **Pangai** Lifuka, C Tonga 19.49S 174.22W
116 H13 **Pangaío** ▲▲ N Greece
81 G20 **Pangala** Le Pool, S Congo 3.26S 14.38E
83 J22 **Pangani** Tanga, E Tanzania 5.27S 39.00E
83 I21 **Pangani** ≈ NE Tanzania
195 U13 **Panggoe** Choiseul Island, NW Solomon Islands 7.00S 95.05E
81 N20 **Pangi** Maniema, E Dem. Rep. Congo (Zaire) 3.12S 26.39E

◆ Country
● Country Capital
◇ Dependent Territory
○ Dependent Territory Capital
⬖ Administrative Region
✕ International Airport
▲ Mountain
▲▲ Mountain Range
⛰ Volcano
≈ River
◎ Lake
⊡ Reservoir

PANGIA – PAY

194 H12 **Pangia** Southern Highlands, W PNG 6.18S 144.12E
Pangim see Panaji
173 F4 **Pangkalanbrandan** Sumatera, W Indonesia 4.00N 98.15E
Pangkalanbun see Pangkalanbuun
174 I/J10 **Pangkalanbuun** var. Pangkalanbun. Borneo, C Indonesia 2.43S 111.37E
174 J10 **Pangkalpinang** Pulau Bangka, W Indonesia 2.04S 106.09E
9 U17 **Pangman** Saskatchewan, S Canada 49.37N 104.33W
Pang-Nga see Phang-Nga
16 Nn2 **Pangnirtung** Baffin Island, Nunavut, NE Canada 66.04N 65.45W
158 K6 **Pangong Tso** var. Bangong Co. ◎ China/India see also Bangong Co
38 K7 **Panguitch** Utah, W USA 37.49N 112.26W
195 S12 **Panguna** Bougainville Island, NE PNG 6.22S 155.19E
179 Pp17 **Pangutaran Group** island group Sulu Archipelago, SW Philippines
27 N2 **Panhandle** Texas, SW USA 35.18N 101.23W
Panhormus see Palermo
176 X12 **Paniai, Danau** ◎ Irian Jaya, E Indonesia
81 L21 **Pania-Mutombo** Kasai Oriental, C Dem. Rep. Congo (Zaire) 5.09S 23.49E
Panicherevo see Dolno Panicherevo
197 H5 **Panié, Mont** ▲ C New Caledonia 20.33S 164.41E
158 I10 **Pānīpat** Haryāna, N India 29.18N 77.00E
153 Q14 **Panj** Rus. Pyandzh; prev. Kirovabad. SW Tajikistan 37.39N 69.55E
153 P15 **Panj** Rus. Pyandzh. ⤳ Afghanistan/Tajikistan
155 O5 **Panjāb** Bāmīān, C Afghanistan 34.21N 67.00E
153 O12 **Panjakent** Rus. Pendzhikent. W Tajikistan 39.28N 67.33E
154 L14 **Panjgūr** Baluchistān, SW Pakistan 26.58N 64.05E
Panjim see Panaji
169 U12 **Panjin** Liaoning, NE China 41.11N 122.05E
153 P14 **Panji Poyon** Rus. Nizhniy Pyandzh. SW Tajikistan 37.14N 68.32E
155 Q4 **Panjshir** ⤳ E Afghanistan
Pankota see Pâncota
79 W14 **Pankshin** Plateau, C Nigeria 9.21N 9.27E
169 Y10 **Pan Ling** ▲▲ N China
Panlong Jiang see Lô, Sông
160 J9 **Panna** Madhya Pradesh, C India 24.43N 80.10E
101 M16 **Panningen** Limburg, SE Netherlands 51.19N 5.58E
155 R13 **Pāno Āqil** Sind, SE Pakistan 27.56N 69.16E
124 Nn3 **Páno Léfkara** S Cyprus 34.52N 33.18E
124 N3 **Páno Panagiá** var. Pano Panayia. W Cyprus 34.55N 32.38E
Pano Panayia see Páno Panagiá
Panopolis see Akhmîm
31 U14 **Panora** Iowa, C USA 41.41N 94.21W
62 I8 **Panorama** São Paulo, S Brazil 21.22S 51.51W
117 I24 **Pánormos** Kríti, Greece, E Mediterranean Sea 35.24N 24.42E
Panormus see Palermo
169 W11 **Panshi** Jilin, NE China 42.50N 126.06E
61 H19 **Pantanal** var. Pantanalmato-Grossense. swamp SW Brazil
Pantanalmato-Grossense see Pantanal
63 H16 **Pântano Grande** Rio Grande do Sul, S Brazil 30.12S 52.24W
175 R16 **Pantar, Pulau** island Kepulauan Alor, S Indonesia
23 X9 **Pantego** North Carolina, SE USA 35.34N 76.39W
109 G25 **Pantelleria** anc. Cossyra, Cosyra. Sicilia, Italy, C Mediterranean Sea 36.47N 12.00E
109 G25 **Pantelleria, Isola di** island SW Italy
Pante Macassar/Pante Makassar see Pante Makasar
175 Rr17 **Pante Makasar** var. Pante Macassar, Pante Makassar. W East Timor 9.10S 124.27E
158 K10 **Pantnagar** Uttar Pradesh, N India 29.00N 79.28E
117 A15 **Pantokrátoras** ▲ Kérkyra, Iónioi Nísoi, Greece, C Mediterranean Sea 39.45N 19.51E
Pantschowa see Pančevo
179 Rr16 **Pantukan** Mindanao, S Philippines 7.10N 125.55E
43 P11 **Pánuco** Veracruz-Llave, E Mexico 22.01N 98.10W
43 P11 **Pánuco, Río** ⤳ C Mexico
166 I12 **Panxian** Guizhou, S China 25.45N 104.28E
173 G7 **Panyabungan** Sumatera, N Indonesia 0.55N 99.30E
79 W14 **Panyam** Plateau, C Nigeria 9.28N 9.13E
163 N13 **Panzhihua** prev. Dukou, Tu-k'ou. Sichuan, C China 26.35N 101.41E
81 I22 **Panzi** Bandundu, SW Dem. Rep. Congo (Zaire) 7.10S 17.55E
44 E5 **Panzós** Alta Verapaz, E Guatemala 15.21N 89.40W
Pao-chi/Paoki see Baoji
Pao-king see Shaoyang
109 N20 **Paola** Calabria, SW Italy 39.21N 16.03E
123 Jj17 **Paola** E Malta 35.52N 14.30E
29 R5 **Paola** Kansas, C USA 38.34N 94.52W
33 O15 **Paoli** Indiana, N USA 38.31N 86.26W
197 D14 **Paonangisu** Éfaté, C Vanuatu 17.33S 168.23E
175 Tt11 **Paoni** var. Pauni. Pulau Seram, E Indonesia 2.48S 129.03E
39 Q5 **Paonia** Colorado, C USA 38.52N 107.35W
203 O7 **Paopao** Moorea, W French Polynesia 17.28S 149.48W
Pao-shan see Baoshan
Pao-ting see Baoding
Pao-t'ou/Paotow see Baotou
81 H14 **Paoua** Ouham-Pendé, W Central African Republic 7.22N 16.25E
Pap see Pop
113 H23 **Pápa** Veszprém, W Hungary 47.19N 17.27E
44 J12 **Papagayo, Golfo de** gulf NW Costa Rica
40 H11 **Papaikou** var. Pāpa'ikou. Hawaii, USA, C Pacific Ocean 19.45N 155.06W
Papajd see Praid
43 R15 **Papaloapan, Río** ⤳ S Mexico
192 L6 **Papakura** Auckland, North Island, NZ 37.03S 174.57E
43 Q13 **Papantla** var. Papantla de Olarte. Veracruz-Llave, E Mexico 20.27N 97.21W
Papantla de Olarte see Papantla
203 P8 **Papara** Tahiti, W French Polynesia 17.45S 149.33W
192 K4 **Paparoa** Northland, North Island, NZ 36.06S 174.12E
193 G16 **Paparoa Range** ▲▲ South Island, NZ
117 K20 **Pápas, Akrotírio** headland Ikaría, Dodekánisos, Greece, Aegean Sea 37.31N 25.58E
98 L2 **Papa Stour** island NE Scotland, UK
192 L6 **Papatoetoe** Auckland, North Island, NZ 36.58S 174.52E
193 E25 **Papatowai** Otago, South Island, NZ 46.33S 169.33E
98 K4 **Papa Westray** island NE Scotland, UK
203 T10 **Papeete** ○ (French Polynesia) Tahiti, W French Polynesia 17.31S 149.34W
102 F11 **Papenburg** Niedersachsen, NW Germany 53.04N 7.24E
100 H13 **Papendrecht** Zuid-Holland, SW Netherlands 51.49N 4.42E
203 Q7 **Papenoo** Tahiti, W French Polynesia 17.28S 149.25W
203 Q7 **Papenoo Rivière** ⤳ Tahiti, W French Polynesia
203 N7 **Papetoai** Moorea, W French Polynesia 17.28S 149.52W
94 L3 **Papey** island E Iceland
Paphos see Páfos
42 H5 **Papigochic, Río** ⤳ NW Mexico
120 E10 **Papilė** Akmenė, NW Lithuania 56.08N 22.51E
31 S15 **Papillion** Nebraska, C USA 41.09N 96.02W
13 T5 **Papinachois** ⤳ Quebec, SE Canada
194 I15 **Papua, Gulf of** gulf S PNG
194 I15 **Papua New Guinea** off. Independent State of Papua New Guinea; prev. Territory of Papua and New Guinea, abbrev. PNG. ◆ commonwealth republic NW Melanesia
199 H10 **Papua Plateau** undersea feature N Coral Sea
114 G9 **Papuk** ▲▲ NE Croatia
177 G8 **Papun** Karen State, S Burma 18.04N 97.25E
44 L14 **Paquera** Puntarenas, W Costa Rica 9.52N 84.55W
57 V9 **Para** ◆ district N Surinam
60 I13 **Pará** off. Estado do Pará. ◆ state NE Brazil
Pará see Belém
126 H12 **Parabel'** Tomskaya Oblast', C Russian Federation 58.54N 80.45E
188 I8 **Paraburdoo** Western Australia 23.07S 117.40E
59 E16 **Paracas, Península de** peninsula W Peru
61 L19 **Paracatu** Minas Gerais, NE Brazil 17.13S 46.52W
198 F7 **Paracel Islands** ◇ disputed territory SE Asia
190 I6 **Parachilna** South Australia 31.09S 138.23E
155 R6 **Pārachinār** North-West Frontier Province, NW Pakistan 33.55N 70.04E
114 N13 **Paraćin** Serbia, C Yugoslavia 43.51N 21.25E
12 K8 **Paradis** Quebec, SE Canada 48.13N 76.36W
41 N11 **Paradise** var. Paradise Hill. Alaska, USA 62.28N 96.09W
37 O5 **Paradise** California, W USA 39.42N 121.39W
37 X11 **Paradise** Nevada, W USA 36.05N 115.10W
Paradise Hill see Paradise
39 R11 **Paradise Hills** New Mexico, SW USA 35.12N 106.42W
Paradise of the Pacific see Hawaii
38 L13 **Paradise Valley** Arizona, SW USA 33.31N 111.56W
37 T2 **Paradise Valley** Nevada, W USA 41.30N 117.30W
117 O22 **Paradisi** ✕ (Ródos) Ródos, Dodekánisos, Greece, Aegean Sea 36.24N 28.08E
176 X10 **Paradoi** Irian Jaya, E Indonesia 2.10S 136.25E
160 P12 **Pārādwīp** Orissa, E India 20.18N 86.39E
Paraetonium see Maṭrūḥ
119 R4 **Parafiyivka** Chernihivs'ka Oblast', N Ukraine 50.53N 32.40E
38 K7 **Paragonah** Utah, W USA 37.53N 112.46W
29 X9 **Paragould** Arkansas, C USA 36.03N 90.30W
49 X8 **Paraguaçu** var. Paraguassú. ⤳ E Brazil
62 J9 **Paraguaçu Paulista** São Paulo, S Brazil 22.22S 50.35W
56 H4 **Paraguaipoa** Zulia, NW Venezuela 11.21N 71.58W
64 O6 **Paraguarí** Paraguarí, S Paraguay 25.38S 57.09W
64 O7 **Paraguarí** off. Departamento de Paraguarí. ◆ department S Paraguay
57 O8 **Paragua, Río** ⤳ SE Venezuela
59 O16 **Paraguá, Río** ⤳ NE Bolivia
Paraguassú see Paraguaçu
64 N5 **Paraguay** ◆ republic C South America
49 U10 **Paraguay** var. Río Paraguay. ⤳ C South America
Parahiba/Parahyba see Paraíba
61 P15 **Paraíba** off. Estado da Paraíba; prev. Parahiba, Parahyba. ◆ state E Brazil
Paraíba see João Pessoa
62 P9 **Paraíba do Sul, Rio** ⤳ SE Brazil
Parainen see Pargas
45 N14 **Paraíso** Cartago, C Costa Rica 9.50N 83.51W
43 U14 **Paraíso** Tabasco, SE Mexico 18.23N 93.03W
59 O17 **Paraíso, Río** ⤳ E Bolivia
Parajd see Praid
79 S14 **Parakou** C Benin 9.22N 2.40E
124 O3 **Paralimni** E Cyprus 35.01N 34.01E
117 G18 **Paralímni, Límni** ◎ C Greece
194 G15 **Parama Island** island SW PNG
57 W8 **Paramaribo** ● (Surinam) Paramaribo, N Surinam 5.52N 55.13W
57 W9 **Paramaribo** ◆ district N Surinam
57 W9 **Paramaribo** ✕ Paramaribo, N Surinam 5.52N 55.13W
Paramithiá see Paramythiá
58 C13 **Paramonga** Lima, W Peru 10.40S 77.51W
127 Pp13 **Paramushir, Ostrov** island SE Russian Federation
117 C16 **Paramythiá** var. Paramithiá. Ípeiros, W Greece 39.28N 20.31E
64 M10 **Paraná** Entre Ríos, E Argentina 31.48S 60.29W
62 H11 **Paraná** off. Estado do Paraná. ◆ state S Brazil
49 U11 **Paraná** var. Alto Paraná. ⤳ C South America
62 K12 **Paranaguá** Paraná, S Brazil 25.31S 48.36W
61 J20 **Paranaíba, Rio** ⤳ E Brazil
63 C19 **Paraná Ibicuy, Río** ⤳ E Argentina
61 H15 **Paranaíta** Mato Grosso, W Brazil 9.35S 57.01W
62 H9 **Paranapanema, Rio** ⤳ S Brazil
62 K11 **Paranapiacaba, Serra do** ▲▲ S Brazil
62 H9 **Paranavaí** Paraná, S Brazil 23.03S 52.25W
149 N5 **Parandak** Markazī, W Iran 35.19N 50.40E
116 I12 **Paranéstio** Anatolikí Makedonía kai Thráki, NE Greece 41.16N 24.31E
203 W11 **Paraoa** atoll Îles Tuamotu, C French Polynesia
192 L13 **Paraparaumu** Wellington, North Island, NZ 40.55S 175.01E
59 N20 **Parapetí, Río** ⤳ SE Bolivia
56 L10 **Paraque, Cerro** ▲ W Venezuela 6.00S 67.00W
160 I11 **Parasiya** Madhya Pradesh, C India 22.11N 78.47E
117 M23 **Paraspóri, Akrotírio** headland Kárpathos, SE Greece 35.54N 27.15E
62 O10 **Parati** Rio de Janeiro, SE Brazil 23.15S 44.42W
61 K14 **Parauapebas** Pará, N Brazil 6.03S 49.48W
105 Q10 **Paray-le-Monial** Saône-et-Loire, C France 46.27N 4.07E
Parbatsar see Parvatsar
160 G13 **Parbhani** Mahārāshtra, C India 19.16N 76.51E
102 L10 **Parchim** Mecklenburg-Vorpommern, N Germany 53.25N 11.51E
Parchwitz see Prochowice
112 P13 **Parczew** Lubelskie, E Poland 51.39N 22.59E
62 L8 **Pardo, Rio** ⤳ S Brazil
113 E16 **Pardubice** Ger. Pardubitz. Pardubický Kraj, C Czech Republic 50.01N 15.46E
113 E17 **Pardubický Kraj** ◆ region C Czech Republic
Pardubitz see Pardubice
121 F16 **Parechcha** Pol. Porzecze, Rus. Porech'ye. Hrodzyenskaya Voblasts', W Belarus 53.51N 24.07E
61 F17 **Parecis, Chapada dos** var. Serra dos Parecis. ▲▲ W Brazil
Parecis, Serra dos see Parecis, Chapada dos
106 M4 **Paredes de Nava** Castilla-León, N Spain 42.09N 4.42W
201 U12 **Parem** island Chuuk, C Micronesia
201 O12 **Parem Island** island E Micronesia
192 I1 **Parengarenga Harbour** inlet North Island, NZ
13 N8 **Parent** Quebec, SE Canada 47.55N 74.36W
104 J14 **Parentis-en-Born** Landes, SW France 44.22N 1.04W
Parenzo see Poreč
193 G20 **Pareora** Canterbury, South Island, NZ 44.28S 171.12E
175 P12 **Parepare** Sulawesi, C Indonesia 4.00S 119.40E
117 B16 **Párga** Ípeiros, W Greece 39.18N 20.19E
95 K20 **Pargas** Swe. Parainen. Länsi-Suomi, W Finland 60.18N 22.19E
66 O5 **Pargo, Ponta do** headland Madeira, Portugal, NE Atlantic Ocean 32.48N 17.16W
Paria, Golfo de see Paria, Gulf of
57 N6 **Pariaguán** Anzoátegui, NE Venezuela 8.51N 64.43W
47 X17 **Paria, Gulf of** var. Golfo de Paria. gulf Trinidad and Tobago/Venezuela
59 I15 **Pariamanu, Río** ⤳ E Peru
38 L8 **Paria River** ⤳ Utah, W USA
Parichi see Parychy
42 M14 **Paricutín, Volcán** ⛰ C Mexico 19.25N 102.20W
45 P16 **Parida, Isla** island SW Panama
57 T8 **Parika** NE Guyana 6.51N 58.25W
95 O18 **Parikkala** Etelä-Suomi, S Finland 61.33N 29.33E
60 E10 **Parima, Serra** var. Sierra Parima. ▲▲ Brazil/Venezuela see also Parima, Sierra
57 N11 **Parima, Sierra** var. Serra Parima. ▲▲ Brazil/Venezuela see also Parima, Serra
59 F17 **Parinacochas, Laguna** ◎ SW Peru
58 A9 **Pariñas, Punta** headland NW Peru 4.45S 81.22W
60 H12 **Parintins** Amazonas, N Brazil 2.37S 56.45W
105 O5 **Paris** anc. Lutetia, Lutetia Parisiorum, Parisii. ● (France) Paris, N France 48.52N 2.19E
203 Y2 **Paris** Kiritimati, E Kiribati 1.55N 95.30W
29 S11 **Paris** Arkansas, C USA 35.17N 93.43W
35 S16 **Paris** Idaho, NW USA 42.14N 111.24W
33 N14 **Paris** Illinois, N USA 39.36N 87.42W
22 M5 **Paris** Kentucky, S USA 38.12N 84.15W
29 V3 **Paris** Missouri, C USA 39.28N 92.00W
22 H8 **Paris** Tennessee, S USA 36.18N 88.19W
27 V5 **Paris** Texas, SW USA 33.40N 95.33W
Parisii see Paris
45 S16 **Parita** Herrera, S Panama 7.59N 80.31W
45 S16 **Parita, Bahía de** bay S Panama
Parkan/Párkány see Štúrovo
95 K18 **Parkano** Länsi-Suomi, W Finland 62.03N 23.00E
29 N6 **Park City** Kansas, C USA 37.48N 97.19W
38 L3 **Park City** Utah, W USA 40.39N 111.30W
38 I12 **Parker** Arizona, SW USA 34.07N 114.16W
25 R9 **Parker** Florida, SE USA 30.07N 85.36W
31 R11 **Parker** South Dakota, N USA 43.24N 97.08W
37 Z14 **Parker Dam** California, W USA 34.17N 114.08W
31 W13 **Parkersburg** Iowa, C USA 42.34N 92.47W
23 Q3 **Parkersburg** West Virginia, NE USA 39.15N 81.33W
31 T7 **Parkers Prairie** Minnesota, N USA 46.09N 95.19W
179 R17 **Parker Volcano** ⛰ Mindanao, S Philippines 6.09N 124.52E
189 W13 **Parkes** New South Wales, SE Australia 33.09S 148.10E
32 K4 **Park Falls** Wisconsin, N USA 45.57N 90.25W
Parkhar see Farkhor
12 E16 **Parkhill** Ontario, S Canada 43.11N 81.39W
31 T5 **Park Rapids** Minnesota, N USA 46.55N 95.03W
31 Q3 **Park River** North Dakota, N USA 48.24N 97.44W
31 Q11 **Parkston** South Dakota, N USA 43.24N 97.58W
8 L17 **Parksville** Vancouver Island, British Columbia, SW Canada 49.13N 124.13W
39 S3 **Parkview Mountain** ▲ Colorado, C USA 40.19N 106.08W
107 N8 **Parla** Madrid, C Spain 40.13N 3.48W
31 S8 **Parle, Lac qui** ⊟ Minnesota, N USA
117 F20 **Parlía Tyroú** Pelopónnisos, S Greece 37.17N 22.50E
161 G14 **Parli Vaijnāth** Mahārāshtra, C India 18.52N 76.36E
108 F9 **Parma** Emilia-Romagna, N Italy 44.49N 10.19E
33 T11 **Parma** Ohio, N USA 41.24N 81.43W
Parnahyba see Parnaíba
60 N13 **Parnaíba** var. Parnahyba. Piauí, E Brazil 2.58S 41.46W
67 J14 **Parnaíba Ridge** undersea feature C Atlantic Ocean
60 N13 **Parnaíba, Rio** ⤳ NE Brazil
117 F18 **Parnassós** ▲ C Greece
193 J17 **Parnassus** Canterbury, South Island, NZ 42.41S 173.18E
190 H10 **Parndana** South Australia 35.48S 137.13E
117 H19 **Párnitha** ▲▲ C Greece
117 F21 **Párnon** ▲▲ S Greece
120 G5 **Pärnu** Ger. Pernau, Latv. Pērnava; prev. Rus. Pernov. Pärnumaa, SW Estonia 58.23N 24.31E
120 G6 **Pärnu** var. Parnu Jõgi, Ger. Pernau. ⤳ SW Estonia
120 G5 **Pärnu-Jaagupi** Ger. Sankt-Jakobi. Pärnumaa, SW Estonia 58.36N 24.30E
Parnu Jõgi see Pärnu
120 G5 **Pärnu Laht** Ger. Pernauer Bucht. bay SW Estonia
120 F5 **Pärnumaa** off. Pärnu Maakond. ◆ province SW Estonia
159 T11 **Paro** W Bhutan 27.22N 89.31E
159 T11 **Paro** ✕ (Thimphu) W Bhutan 27.22N 89.31E
193 G17 **Paroa** West Coast, South Island, NZ 42.31S 171.10E
169 X14 **P'aro-ho** var. Hwach'ŏn-chŏsuji. ⊟ N South Korea
191 N6 **Paroo River** seasonal river New South Wales/Queensland, SE Australia
Paropamisus Range see Sefīdkūh, Selseleh-ye
117 J21 **Páros** Páros, Kykládes, Greece, Aegean Sea 37.04N 25.09E
117 J21 **Páros** island Kykládes, Greece, Aegean Sea
38 K7 **Parowan** Utah, W USA 37.50N 112.49W
105 U13 **Parpaillon** ▲▲ SE France
110 I9 **Parpan** Graubünden, S Switzerland 46.46N 9.32E
64 G13 **Parral** Maule, C Chile 36.07S 71.47W
Parral see Hidalgo del Parral
191 T9 **Parramatta** New South Wales, SE Australia 33.49S 150.58E
23 Y6 **Parramore Island** island Virginia, NE USA
42 M8 **Parras** var. Parras de la Fuente. Coahuila de Zaragoza, NE Mexico 25.26N 102.07W
Parras de la Fuente see Parras
44 M14 **Parrita** Puntarenas, S Costa Rica 9.33N 84.20W
12 G13 **Parry Island** island Ontario, S Canada
207 O9 **Parry Islands** island group Nunavut, NW Canada
12 G12 **Parry Sound** Ontario, S Canada 45.21N 80.03W
112 F7 **Parsęta** Ger. Persante. ⤳ NW Poland
30 L3 **Parshall** North Dakota, N USA 47.57N 102.07W
29 Q7 **Parsons** Kansas, C USA 37.20N 95.15W
22 H9 **Parsons** Tennessee, S USA 35.39N 88.07W
23 T3 **Parsons** West Virginia, NE USA 39.06N 79.40W
Parsonstown see Birr
102 P11 **Parsteiner See** ◎ NE Germany
109 I24 **Partanna** Sicilia, Italy, C Mediterranean Sea 37.43N 12.54E
110 J8 **Partenen** Graubünden, E Switzerland 46.58N 10.01E
104 K9 **Parthenay** Deux-Sèvres, W France 46.39N 0.13W
97 J19 **Partille** Västra Götaland, S Sweden 57.43N 12.12E
109 I23 **Partinico** Sicilia, Italy, C Mediterranean Sea 38.03N 13.07E
113 I20 **Partizánske** prev. Šimonovany; Hung. Simony. Trenčiansky Kraj, W Slovakia 48.39N 18.22E
60 H11 **Paru de Oeste, Rio** ⤳ N Brazil
190 K9 **Paruna** South Australia 34.45S 140.43E
60 I11 **Paru, Rio** ⤳ N Brazil
Parvān see Parwān
161 M14 **Pārvatīpuram** Andhra Pradesh, E India 17.01N 81.47E
158 G12 **Parvatsar** prev. Parbatsar. Rājasthān, N India 26.52N 74.49E
155 Q5 **Parwān** Per. Parvān. ◆ province E Afghanistan
164 I15 **Paryang** Xizang Zizhiqu, W China 30.04N 83.28E
121 M18 **Parychy** Rus. Parichi. Homyel'skaya Voblasts', SE Belarus 52.48N 29.25E
85 J21 **Parys** Free State, C South Africa 26.51S 27.28E
37 T15 **Pasadena** California, W USA 34.09N 118.08W
27 W11 **Pasadena** Texas, SW USA 29.41N 95.12W
58 B8 **Pasaje** El Oro, SW Ecuador 3.17S 79.45W
143 T9 **P'asanauri** N Georgia 42.21N 44.40E
173 G10 **Pasapuat** Pulau Pagai Utara, W Indonesia 2.36S 99.58E
178 Gg7 **Pasawng** Kayah State, C Burma 18.50N 97.16E
116 L13 **Paşayiğit** Edirne, NW Turkey 40.58N 26.38E
25 N9 **Pascagoula** Mississippi, S USA 30.21N 88.31W
24 M8 **Pascagoula River** ⤳ Mississippi, S USA
118 F12 **Paşcani** Hung. Páskán. Iaşi, NE Romania 47.13N 26.46E
111 T4 **Pasching** Oberösterreich, N Austria 48.16N 14.10E
34 K10 **Pasco** Washington, NW USA 46.13N 119.06W
58 E13 **Pasco** off. Departamento de Pasco. ◆ department C Peru
203 N11 **Pascua, Isla de** var. Rapa Nui, Eng. Easter Island. island E Pacific Ocean
65 G21 **Pascua, Río** ⤳ S Chile
105 N1 **Pas-de-Calais** ◆ department N France
102 P10 **Pasewalk** Mecklenburg-Vorpommern, NE Germany 53.30N 13.58E
9 T10 **Pasfield Lake** ◎ Saskatchewan, C Canada
Pa-shih Hai-hsia see Bashi Channel
Pashkeni see Bolyarovo
Pashmakli see Smolyan
179 P10 **Pasig** Luzon, N Philippines 14.34N 121.04E
159 X10 **Pāsighāt** Arunāchel Pradesh, NE India 28.08N 95.13E
143 Q12 **Pasinler** Erzurum, NE Turkey 39.58N 41.40E
Pasi Oloy, Qatorkŭhi see Zaalayskiy Khrebet
44 E3 **Pasión, Río de la** ⤳ N Guatemala
174 Gg10 **Pasirganting** Sumatera, W Indonesia 2.04S 100.51E
Pasirpangarayan see Bagansiapiapi
174 H2 **Pasir Puteh** var. Pasir Putih. Kelantan, Peninsular Malaysia 5.49N 102.24E
174 L6 **Pasir, Tanjung** headland East Malaysia 2.24N 111.12E
97 N20 **Påskallavik** Kalmar, S Sweden 57.10N 16.25E
Páskán see Paşcani
112 K7 **Pasłęk** Ger. Preußisch Holland. Warmińsko-Mazurskie, NE Poland 54.03N 19.39E
112 K7 **Pasłęka** Ger. Passarge. ⤳ N Poland
154 K16 **Pasni** Baluchistān, SW Pakistan 25.13N 63.30E
65 I18 **Paso de Indios** Chubut, S Argentina 43.52S 69.06W
56 L7 **Paso del Caballo** Guárico, N Venezuela 8.19N 67.07W
63 E15 **Paso de los Libres** Corrientes, NE Argentina 29.39S 57.04W
63 E18 **Paso de los Toros** Tacuarembó, C Uruguay 32.45S 56.30W
37 P12 **Paso Robles** California, W USA 35.37N 120.42W
13 Y7 **Paspébiac** Quebec, SE Canada 48.03N 65.10W
9 U14 **Pasquia Hills** ▲▲ Saskatchewan, S Canada
155 W7 **Pasrūr** Punjab, E Pakistan 32.12N 74.42E
32 M1 **Passage Island** island Michigan, N USA
67 B24 **Passage Islands** island group W Falkland Islands
15 I1 **Passage Point** headland Banks Island, Northwest Territories, NW Canada 73.31N 115.12W
Passarge see Pasłęka
117 C15 **Passarón** ancient monument Ípeiros, W Greece 39.41N 20.43E
Passarowitz see Požarevac
103 O22 **Passau** Bayern, SE Germany 48.34N 13.28E
24 M9 **Pass Christian** Mississippi, S USA 30.19N 89.15W
109 L26 **Passero, Capo** headland Sicilia, Italy, C Mediterranean Sea 36.40N 15.09E
179 Q13 **Passi** Panay Island, C Philippines 11.05N 122.37E
63 H14 **Passo Fundo** Rio Grande do Sul, S Brazil 28.16S 52.19W
62 H13 **Passo Fundo, Barragem de** ⊟ S Brazil
63 H15 **Passo Real, Barragem de** ⊟ S Brazil
61 L20 **Passos** Minas Gerais, NE Brazil 20.45S 46.37W
178 M11 **Passu Keah** island S Paracel Islands
120 J13 **Pastavy** Pol. Postawy, Rus. Postavy. Vitsyebskaya Voblasts', NW Belarus 55.07N 26.50E
58 D7 **Pastaza** ◆ province E Ecuador
58 D9 **Pastaza, Río** ⤳ Ecuador/Peru
63 A21 **Pasteur** Buenos Aires, E Argentina 35.10S 62.13W
13 V3 **Pasteur** ⤳ Quebec, SE Canada
153 Q12 **Pastigav** Rus. Pastigov. W Tajikistan 39.27N 69.16E
Pastigov see Pastigav
56 C13 **Pasto** Nariño, SW Colombia 1.12N 77.16W
40 M10 **Pastol Bay** bay Alaska, USA
39 O8 **Pastora Peak** ▲ Arizona, SW USA 36.48N 109.10W
107 O8 **Pastrana** Castilla-La Mancha, C Spain 40.24N 2.55W
174 M15 **Pasuruan** prev. Pasoeroean. Jawa, C Indonesia 7.37S 112.43E
120 F11 **Pasvalys** Pasvalys, N Lithuania 56.03N 24.24E
113 K21 **Pásztó** Nógrád, N Hungary 47.57N 19.41E
201 U12 **Pata** var. Patta. atoll Chuuk Islands, C Micronesia
38 M16 **Patagonia** Arizona, SW USA 31.32N 110.45W
65 H20 **Patagonia** physical region Argentina/Chile
Patalung see Phatthalung
160 D9 **Pātan** Gujarāt, W India 23.51N 72.10E
160 J10 **Pātan** Madhya Pradesh, C India 23.19N 79.41E
175 T8 **Patani** Pulau Halmahera, E Indonesia 0.19N 128.46E
Patani see Pattani
13 V7 **Patapédia Est** ⤳ Quebec, SE Canada
118 K13 **Pătâriagele** prev. Pătîriagele. Buzău, SE Romania 45.19N 26.21E
Patavium see Padova
190 I5 **Patawarta Hill** ▲ South Australia 30.57S 138.42E
190 L10 **Patchewollock** Victoria, SE Australia 35.24S 142.11E
192 K11 **Patea** Taranaki, North Island, NZ 39.48S 174.35E
192 K11 **Patea** ⤳ North Island, NZ
79 U15 **Pategi** Kwara, C Nigeria 8.39N 5.46E
83 K20 **Pate Island** var. Patta Island. island SE Kenya
107 S10 **Paterna** País Valenciano, E Spain 39.30N 0.24W
111 R9 **Paternion** Slvn. Špatrjan. Kärnten, S Austria 46.40N 13.43E
109 L24 **Paternò** anc. Hybla, Hybla Major. Sicilia, Italy, C Mediterranean Sea 37.34N 14.55E
34 J7 **Pateros** Washington, NW USA 48.01N 119.55W
20 J14 **Paterson** New Jersey, NE USA 40.54N 74.11W
34 J10 **Paterson** Washington, NW USA 45.56N 119.37W
193 C25 **Paterson Inlet** inlet Stewart Island, NZ
100 N6 **Paterswolde** Drenthe, NE Netherlands 53.07N 6.32E
158 H7 **Pathānkot** Himāchal Pradesh, N India 32.16N 75.43E
Pathein see Bassein
35 W15 **Pathfinder Reservoir** ⊟ Wyoming, C USA
178 Hh11 **Pathum Thani** var. Patumdhani, Prathum Thani. Pathum Thani, C Thailand 14.03N 100.28E
174 L14 **Pati** Jawa, C Indonesia 6.45S 111.00E
56 C12 **Patía** var. El Bordo. Cauca, SW Colombia 2.06N 77.02W
158 I9 **Patiāla** var. Puttiala. Punjab, NW India 30.21N 76.27E
56 B12 **Patía, Río** ⤳ SW Colombia
175 T8 **Patinti, Selat** strait Maluku, E Indonesia
196 D15 **Pati Point** headland NE Guam 13.36N 144.39E
Pătîriagele see Pătâriagele
58 C13 **Pativilca** Lima, W Peru 10.40S 77.52W
178 Gg1 **Pātkai Bum** var. Patkai Range. ▲▲ Burma/India
Patkai Range see Pātkai Bum
117 L20 **Pátmos** Pátmos, Dodekánisos, Greece, Aegean Sea 37.18N 26.32E
117 L20 **Pátmos** island Dodekánisos, Greece, Aegean Sea
159 P13 **Patna** var. Azimabad. Bihār, N India 25.36N 85.11E
160 M12 **Patnāgarh** Orissa, E India 20.42N 83.12E
179 Pp13 **Patnongon** Panay Island, C Philippines 10.56N 122.03E
143 S13 **Patnos** Ağrı, E Turkey 39.13N 42.52E
62 H12 **Pato Branco** Paraná, S Brazil 26.15S 52.40W
33 O16 **Patoka Lake** ◎ Indiana, N USA
94 L9 **Patoniva** Lapp. Buoddobohki. Lappi, N Finland 69.44N 27.01E
115 K21 **Patos** var. Patosi. Fier, SW Albania 40.40N 19.37E
Patos see Patos de Minas
61 K19 **Patos de Minas** var. Patos. Minas Gerais, NE Brazil 18.34S 46.31W
Patosi see Patos
63 I17 **Patos, Lagoa dos** lagoon S Brazil
64 J9 **Patquía** La Rioja, C Argentina 30.01S 66.54W
117 E19 **Pátra** Eng. Patras; prev. Pátrai. Dytikí Ellás, S Greece 38.13N 21.45E
Pátrai/Patras see Pátra
117 D18 **Patraïkós Kólpos** gulf S Greece
94 G2 **Patreksfjördhur** Vestfirdhir, W Iceland 65.33N 23.54W
26 M7 **Patricia** Texas, SW USA 32.34N 102.00W
65 F21 **Patricio Lynch, Isla** island S Chile
Patta see Pata
Patta Island see Pate Island
178 Hh17 **Pattani** var. Patani. Pattani, SW Thailand 6.50N 101.18E
178 Hh12 **Pattaya** Chon Buri, S Thailand 12.55N 100.55E
21 S4 **Patten** Maine, NE USA 45.58N 68.27W
37 O9 **Patterson** California, W USA 37.27N 121.07W
24 J10 **Patterson** Louisiana, S USA 29.41N 91.18W
37 R7 **Patterson, Mount** ▲ California, W USA 38.27N 119.16W
33 P4 **Patterson, Point** headland Michigan, N USA 45.58N 85.39W
109 L23 **Patti** Sicilia, Italy, C Mediterranean Sea 38.07N 14.59E
109 L23 **Patti, Golfo di** gulf Sicilia, Italy, C Mediterranean Sea
95 L14 **Pattijoki** Oulu, W Finland 64.41N 24.40E
199 Mm5 **Patton Escarpment** undersea feature E Pacific Ocean
29 S2 **Pattonsburg** Missouri, C USA 40.03N 94.08W
(0) D6 **Patton Seamount** undersea feature NE Pacific Ocean 54.40N 150.30W
8 J12 **Pattullo, Mount** ▲ British Columbia, W Canada 56.18N 129.43W
Patuakhali see Patukhali
44 M5 **Patuca, Río** ⤳ E Honduras
159 U16 **Patukhali** var. Patuakhali. Khulna, S Bangladesh 22.19N 90.19E
Patumdhani see Pathum Thani
42 M14 **Pátzcuaro** Michoacán de Ocampo, SW Mexico 19.30N 101.36W
44 C6 **Patzicía** Chimaltenango, S Guatemala 14.37N 90.54W
104 K16 **Pau** Pyrénées-Atlantiques, SW France 43.18N 0.22W
104 J12 **Pauillac** Gironde, SW France 45.12N 0.44W
177 Ff5 **Pauk** Magwe, W Burma 21.25N 94.30E
15 H3 **Paulatuk** Northwest Territories, NW Canada 69.23N 124.00W
44 K5 **Paulayá, Río** ⤳ NE Honduras
24 M6 **Paulding** Mississippi, S USA 32.01N 89.01W
33 Q12 **Paulding** Ohio, N USA 41.08N 84.34W
31 S12 **Paullina** Iowa, C USA 42.58N 95.41W
61 P15 **Paulo Afonso** Bahia, E Brazil 9.21S 38.13W
40 M16 **Pauloff Harbor** var. Pavlor Harbour. Sanak Island, Alaska, USA 54.26N 162.43W
29 N12 **Pauls Valley** Oklahoma, C USA 34.44N 97.13W
177 Ff7 **Paungde** Pegu, C Burma 18.30N 95.30E
Pauni see Paoni
158 K9 **Pauri** Uttar Pradesh, N India 30.07N 78.48E
Pautalia see Kyustendil
176 Z11 **Pauwasi** ⤳ Irian Jaya, E Indonesia
148 J5 **Pāveh** Kermānshāh, NW Iran 35.01N 46.15E
130 L5 **Pavelets** Ryazanskaya Oblast', W Russian Federation 53.47N 39.22E
108 D8 **Pavia** anc. Ticinum. Lombardia, N Italy 45.10N 9.10E
120 C9 **Pāvilosta** Liepāja, W Latvia 56.52N 21.12E
129 P14 **Pavino** Kostromskaya Oblast', NW Russian Federation 59.10N 46.09E
116 J8 **Pavlikeni** Veliko Tŭrnovo, N Bulgaria 43.15N 25.20E
151 T8 **Pavlodar** Pavlodar, NE Kazakhstan 52.21N 76.58E
151 S9 **Pavlodar** off. Pavlodarskaya Oblast', Kaz. Pavlodar Oblysy. ◆ province NE Kazakhstan
Pavlodar Oblysy/Pavlodarskaya Oblast' see Pavlodar
Pavlograd see Pavlohrad
119 U7 **Pavlohrad** Rus. Pavlograd. Dnipropetrovs'ka Oblast', E Ukraine 48.32N 35.50E
Pavlor Harbour see Pauloff Harbor
151 R9 **Pavlovka** Akmola, C Kazakhstan 51.22N 72.35E
131 V4 **Pavlovka** Respublika Bashkortostan, W Russian Federation 55.28N 56.36E
131 Q7 **Pavlovka** Ul'yanovskaya Oblast', W Russian Federation 52.40N 47.08E
131 N3 **Pavlovo** Nizhegorodskaya Oblast', W Russian Federation 55.59N 43.03E
130 L9 **Pavlovsk** Voronezhskaya Oblast', W Russian Federation 50.26N 40.08E
130 L13 **Pavlovskaya** Krasnodarskiy Kray, SW Russian Federation 46.06N 39.52E
119 S7 **Pavlysh** Kirovohrads'ka Oblast', C Ukraine 48.54N 33.20E
108 F10 **Pavullo nel Frignano** Emilia-Romagna, C Italy 44.19N 10.52E
29 P8 **Pawhuska** Oklahoma, C USA 36.40N 96.20W
23 U13 **Pawleys Island** South Carolina, SE USA 33.27N 79.07W
178 Gg6 **Pawn** ⤳ C Burma
32 K14 **Pawnee** Illinois, N USA 39.35N 89.34W
29 O9 **Pawnee** Oklahoma, C USA 36.18N 96.47W
39 U2 **Pawnee Buttes** ▲ Colorado, C USA 40.49N 103.58W
31 S17 **Pawnee City** Nebraska, C USA 40.06N 96.09W
28 K5 **Pawnee River** ⤳ Kansas, C USA
33 O10 **Paw Paw** Michigan, N USA 42.12N 86.09W
33 O10 **Paw Paw Lake** Michigan, N USA 42.12N 86.16W
21 O12 **Pawtucket** Rhode Island, NE USA 41.52N 71.22W
Pax Augusta see Badajoz
117 I25 **Paximádia** island SE Greece
Pax Julia see Beja
117 B16 **Paxoí** island Iónioi Nísoi, Greece, C Mediterranean Sea
41 S10 **Paxson** Alaska, USA 62.58N 145.27W
32 M13 **Paxton** Illinois, N USA 40.27N 88.06W
128 J11 **Pay** Respublika Kareliya, NW Russian Federation 61.10N 34.24E

◆ Country ● Country Capital ◇ Dependent Territory ○ Dependent Territory Capital ◆ Administrative Region ✕ International Airport ▲ Mountain ▲▲ Mountain Range ⛰ Volcano ⤳ River ◎ Lake ⊟ Reservoir

PAYAGYI – PETAUKE

177 G8 Payagyi Pegu, SW Burma 17.28N 96.31E
110 C9 Payerne Ger. Peterlingen. Vaud, W Switzerland 46.49N 6.57E
34 M13 Payette Idaho, NW USA 44.04N 116.55W
34 M13 Payette River ≈ Idaho, NW USA
129 V2 Pay-Khoy, Khrebet ▲▲ NW Russian Federation
Payne see Kangirsuk
10 K4 Payne, Lac ◎ Quebec, NE Canada
31 T8 Paynesville Minnesota, N USA 45.22N 94.42W
174 M4 Payong, Tanjung headland East Malaysia 3.46N 113.27E
Payo Obispo see Chetumal
63 D18 Paysandú Paysandú, W Uruguay 32.21S 58.04W
63 D17 Paysandú ◈ department W Uruguay
104 I7 Pays de la Loire ◈ region NW France
38 L12 Payson Arizona, SW USA 34.13N 111.19W
38 L4 Payson Utah, W USA 40.02N 111.43W
129 W4 Payyer, Gora ▲ NW Russian Federation 66.49N 64.33E
Payzawat see Jiashi
143 Q11 Pazar Rize, NE Turkey 41.10N 40.52E
142 F10 Pazarbaşı Burnu headland NW Turkey 41.12N 30.18E
142 M16 Pazarcık Kahramanmaraş, S Turkey 37.31N 37.19E
116 I10 Pazardzhik prev. Tatar Pazardzhik.Pazardzhik, C Bulgaria 42.11N 24.21E
66 H11 Pazardzhik ◈ province C Bulgaria 42.11N 24.21E
56 H9 Paz de Ariporo Casanare, E Colombia 5.51N 71.52W
114 A10 Pazin Ger. Mitterburg, It. Pisino. Istra, NW Croatia 45.14N 13.56E
44 D7 Paz, Río ≈ El Salvador/Guatemala
115 O18 Pčinja ≈ N FYR Macedonia
200 Qq15 Pea Tongatapu, S Tonga 21.10S 175.14W
29 O6 Peabody Kansas, C USA 38.10N 97.06W
9 O12 Peace ≈ Alberta/British Columbia, W Canada
Peace Garden State see North Dakota
9 Q10 Peace Point Alberta, C Canada 59.11N 112.12W
9 O12 Peace River Alberta, W Canada 56.15N 117.18W
25 W13 Peace River ≈ Florida, SE USA
9 N17 Peachland British Columbia, SW Canada 49.49N 119.48W
38 J10 Peach Springs Arizona, SW USA 35.33N 113.27W
Peach State see Georgia
25 S4 Peachtree City Georgia, SE USA 33.24N 84.36W
201 Y13 Peacock Point point SE Wake Island 19.16N 166.39E
99 M18 Peak District physical region C England, UK
191 Q7 Peak Hill New South Wales, SE Australia 32.39S 148.12E
67 G15 Peak, The ▲ C Ascension Island
107 O13 Peal de Becerro Andalucía, S Spain 37.55N 3.07W
201 X12 Peale Island island N Wake Island
39 O6 Peale, Mount ▲ Utah, W USA 38.26N 109.13W
41 O4 Peard Bay bay Alaska, USA
25 Q7 Pea River ≈ Alabama/Florida, S USA
27 W11 Pearland Texas, SW USA 29.33N 95.17W
40 D9 Pearl City Oahu, Hawaii, USA, C Pacific Ocean 21.24N 95.58W
40 D9 Pearl Harbor inlet Oahu, Hawaii, USA, C Pacific Ocean
Pearl Islands see Perlas, Archipiélago de las
Pearl Lagoon see Perlas, Laguna de
24 M5 Pearl River ≈ Louisiana/Mississippi, S USA
27 Q13 Pearsall Texas, SW USA 28.53N 99.05W
25 U7 Pearson Georgia, SE USA 31.18N 82.51W
27 P4 Pease River ≈ Texas, SW USA
10 F7 Peawanuk Ontario, C Canada 54.55N 85.31W
85 P16 Pebane Zambézia, NE Mozambique 17.13S 38.10E
67 C23 Pebble Island island N Falkland Islands
67 C23 Pebble Island Settlement Pebble Island, N Falkland Islands 51.19S 59.40W
115 L16 Peć Alb. Pejë, Turk. Ipek. Serbia, S Yugoslavia 42.40N 20.19E
27 R8 Pecan Bayou ≈ Texas, SW USA
24 H10 Pecan Island Louisiana, S USA 29.39N 92.26W
62 L12 Peças, Ilha das island S Brazil
32 L11 Pecatonica River ≈ Illinois/Wisconsin, N USA
110 G10 Peccia Ticino, S Switzerland 46.24N 8.39E
Pechenegi see Pechenihy
Pechenezhskoye Vodokhranilishche see Pechenız'ke Vodoskhovyshche
128 I2 Pechenga Fin. Petsamo. Murmanskaya Oblast', NW Russian Federation 69.34N 31.14E
119 V5 Pechenihy Rus. Pechenegi. Kharkivs'ka Oblast', E Ukraine 49.49N 36.57E
119 V5 Pechenız'ke Vodoskhovyshche Rus. Pechenezhskoye Vodokhranilishche. ⊡ E Ukraine
129 U7 Pechora Respublika Komi, NW Russian Federation 65.08N 57.09E
129 R6 Pechora ≈ NW Russian Federation
Pechora Bay see Pechorskaya Guba
Pechora Sea see Pechorskoye More
129 S3 Pechorskaya Guba Eng. Pechora Bay. bay NW Russian Federation
125 Ff6 Pechorskoye More Eng. Pechora Sea. sea NW Russian Federation
118 E11 Pecica Ger. Petschka, Hung. Ópécska. Arad, W Romania 46.09N 21.06E
26 K8 Pecos Texas, SW USA 31.25N 103.30W
27 N11 Pecos River ≈ New Mexico/Texas, SW USA
113 I25 Pécs Ger. Fünfkirchen; Lat. Sopianae. Baranya, SW Hungary 46.04N 18.11E
45 T17 Pedasí Los Santos, S Panama 7.30N 80.02W
Pedde see Pedja
191 O17 Pedder, Lake ◎ Tasmania, SE Australia
46 M10 Pedernales SW Dominican Republic 17.59N 71.42W
57 Q5 Pedernales Delta Amacuro, NE Venezuela 9.58N 62.15W
27 R10 Pedernales River ≈ Texas, SW USA
64 H6 Pedernales, Salar de salt lake N Chile
Pedhoulas see Pedoulás
57 X11 Pédima var. Malavate. SW French Guiana 3.15N 54.07W
190 F1 Pedirka South Australia 26.41S 135.11E
175 T7 Pediwang Pulau Halmahera, E Indonesia 1.29N 127.57E
120 I5 Pedja var. Pedja Jõgi, Ger. Pedde. ≈ E Estonia
Pedja Jõgi see Pedja
124 N3 Pedoulás var. Pedhoulas. W Cyprus 34.58N 32.51E
61 N18 Pedra Azul Minas Gerais, NE Brazil 16.01S 41.16W
106 I3 Pedrafita, Porto de var. Puerto de Piedrafita. pass NW Spain 42.43N 7.01W
78 E9 Pedra Lume Sal, NE Cape Verde 16.46N 22.54W
45 P16 Pedregal Chiriquí, W Panama 8.21N 82.26W
56 J4 Pedregal Falcón, N Venezuela 11.01N 70.06W
42 L9 Pedriceña Durango, C Mexico 25.08N 103.46W
62 L11 Pedro Barros São Paulo, S Brazil 24.12S 47.22W
41 Q13 Pedro Bay Alaska, USA 59.47N 154.06W
64 H4 Pedro de Valdivia var. Oficina Pedro de Valdivia. Antofagasta, N Chile 22.33S 69.37W
64 P4 Pedro Juan Caballero Amambay, E Paraguay 22.33S 55.40W
65 L15 Pedro Luro Buenos Aires, E Argentina 39.26S 62.40W
107 O10 Pedro Muñoz Castilla-La Mancha, C Spain 39.25N 2.55W
161 J22 Pedro, Point headland NW Sri Lanka 9.54N 80.08E
190 K9 Peebinga South Australia 34.56S 140.56E
98 J13 Peebles SE Scotland, UK 55.39N 3.14W
33 S15 Peebles Ohio, N USA 38.57N 83.23W
98 J12 Peebles cultural region SE Scotland, UK
20 K13 Peekskill New York, NE USA 41.17N 73.54W
99 I16 Peel W Isle of Man 54.13N 4.04W
14 Ff4 Peel ≈ Northwest Territories/Yukon Territory, NW Canada
15 I1 Peel Point headland Victoria Island, Northwest Territories, NW Canada 73.22N 114.33W
15 K1 Peel Sound passage Nunavut, N Canada
102 N9 Peene ≈ NE Germany
101 K17 Peer Limburg, NE Belgium 51.08N 5.28E
12 H14 Pefferlaw Ontario, S Canada 44.18N 79.11W
193 I18 Pegasus Bay bay South Island, NZ
123 Mm3 Pégeia var. Peyia. SW Cyprus 34.52N 32.24E
111 V7 Peggau Steiermark, SE Austria 47.10N 15.20E
103 L19 Pegnitz Bayern, SE Germany 49.45N 11.33E
103 L19 Pegnitz ≈ SE Germany
107 T11 Pego País Valenciano, E Spain 38.51N 0.07W
177 G8 Pegu var. Bago. Pegu, SW Burma 17.18N 96.31E
177 G7 Pegu ◈ division S Burma
176 W7 Pegun, Pulau island Kepulauan Mapia, E Indonesia
201 N13 Pehleng Pohnpei, E Micronesia
116 M12 Pehlivanköy Kırklareli, NW Turkey 41.21N 26.56E
79 R14 Péhonko C Benin 10.14N 1.57E
63 B21 Pehuajó Buenos Aires, E Argentina 35.48S 61.52W
Pei-ching see Beijing/Beijing Shi
102 J13 Peine Niedersachsen, C Germany 52.19N 10.13E
Pei-p'ing see Beijing/Beijing Shi
Peipsi Järv/Peipus-See see Peipus, Lake
120 J5 Peipus, Lake Est. Peipsi Järv, Ger. Peipus-See, Rus. Chudskoye Ozero. ◎ Estonia/Russian Federation
117 H19 Peiraías prev. Piraiévs, Eng. Piraeus. Attikí, C Greece 37.56N 23.39E
Peisern see Pyzdry
62 I8 Peixe, Rio do ≈ S Brazil
61 I16 Peixoto de Azevedo Mato Grosso, W Brazil 10.18S 55.03W
174 J8 Pejantan, Pulau island W Indonesia
Pejë see Peć
114 N11 Pek ≈ E Yugoslavia
178 Ii7 Pèk var. Xieng Khouang; prev. Xiangkhoang. Xiangkhoang, N Laos 19.19N 103.23E
174 Kk14 Pekalongan Jawa, C Indonesia 6.54S 109.37E
174 Gg7 Pekanbaru var. Pakanbaru. Sumatera, W Indonesia 0.31N 101.27E
32 L12 Pekin Illinois, N USA 40.34N 89.38W
Peking see Beijing/Beijing Shi
Pelabohan Kelang/Pelabuhan Kelang see Pelabuhan Klang
173 G5 Pelabuhan Klang var. Kuala Pelabohan Kelang, Pelabohan Kelang, Pelabuhan Kelang, Port Klang, Port Swettenham. Selangor, Peninsular Malaysia 2.57N 101.24E
174 J15 Pelabuhan Ratu, Teluk bay Jawa, SW Indonesia
123 L12 Pelagie, Isole island group SW Italy
Pelagosa see Palagruža
24 L5 Pelahatchie Mississippi, S USA 32.19N 89.48W
175 N11 Pelaihari var. Pleihari. Borneo, C Indonesia 3.48S 114.45E
105 U14 Pelat, Mont ▲ SE France 44.16N 6.46E
118 F12 Peleaga, Vârful prev. Vîrful Peleaga. ▲ W Romania 45.23N 22.52E
Peleaga, Vîrful see Peleaga, Vârful
126 K12 Peleduy Respublika Sakha (Yakutiya), NE Russian Federation 59.39N 112.36E
12 C18 Pelee Island island Ontario, S Canada
47 Q11 Pelée, Montagne ✶ N Martinique 14.47N 61.10W
12 D18 Pelee, Point headland Ontario, S Canada 41.56N 82.30W
175 R9 Pelei Pulau Peleng, N Indonesia 1.26S 123.27E
Peleliu see Beliliou
175 R9 Peleng, Pulau island Kepulauan Banggai, N Indonesia
175 Qq9 Peleng, Selat strait Sulawesi, C Indonesia
25 T7 Pelham Georgia, SE USA 31.07N 84.09W
113 E18 Pelhřimov Ger. Pilgram. Jihlavský Kraj, C Czech Republic 49.25N 15.13E
41 W13 Pelican Chichagof Island, Alaska, USA 57.52N 136.05W
203 Z3 Pelican Lagoon ◎ Kiritimati, E Kiribati
31 U6 Pelican Lake ◎ Minnesota, N USA
31 V3 Pelican Lake ◎ Minnesota, N USA
32 L5 Pelican Lake ◎ Wisconsin, N USA
46 G1 Pelican Point Grand Bahama Island, N Bahamas 26.39N 78.09W
85 B19 Pelican Point headland W Namibia 22.55S 14.25E
31 S6 Pelican Rapids Minnesota, N USA 46.34N 96.04W
Pelican State see Louisiana
9 U13 Pelikan Narrows Saskatchewan, C Canada 55.11N 102.51W
117 L18 Pelinaío ▲ Chíos, E Greece 38.31N 26.01E
Pelinnaeum see Pelinnaío
117 E16 Pelinnaío anc. Pelinnaeum. ruins Thessalía, C Greece 39.33N 21.45E
115 N20 Pelister ▲ SW FYR Macedonia 41.00N 21.12E
115 G15 Pelješac peninsula S Croatia
94 M12 Pelkosenniemi Lappi, NE Finland 67.06N 27.30E
31 W15 Pella Iowa, C USA 41.24N 92.55W
116 F13 Pélla site of ancient city Kentrikí Makedonía, N Greece 40.46N 22.35E
25 Q3 Pell City Alabama, S USA 33.35N 86.17W
63 A22 Pellegrini Buenos Aires, E Argentina 36.16S 63.07W
94 K12 Pello Lappi, NW Finland 66.47N 24.00E
102 G7 Pellworm island N Germany
8 H6 Pelly ≈ Yukon Territory, NW Canada
15 L3 Pelly Bay Nunavut, N Canada 68.37N 89.45W
8 I8 Pelly Mountains ▲▲ Yukon Territory, W Canada
Pélmonostor see Beli Manastir
39 P13 Pelona Mountain ▲ New Mexico, SW USA 33.40N 108.06W
Peloponnese/Peloponnesus see Pelopónnisos
117 E20 Pelopónnisos Eng. Peloponnese. ◈ region S Greece
117 E20 Pelopónnisos var. Morea, Eng. Peloponnese; anc. Peloponnesus. peninsula S Greece
109 L23 Peloritani, Monti anc. Pelorus and Neptunius. ▲▲ Sicilia, Italy, C Mediterranean Sea
109 M22 Peloro, Capo var. Punta del Faro. headland S Italy 38.15N 15.39E
Pelorus and Neptunius see Peloritani, Monti
63 H17 Pelotas Rio Grande do Sul, S Brazil 31.45S 52.19W
63 I14 Pelotas, Rio ≈ S Brazil
94 K10 Peltovuoma Lapp. Bealdovuopmi. Lappi, N Finland 68.23N 24.11E
125 F10 Pelym ≈ C Russian Federation
21 R4 Pemadumcook Lake ◎ Maine, NE USA
174 Kk14 Pemalang Jawa, C Indonesia 6.52S 109.07E
174 K7 Pemangkat var. Pamangkat. Borneo, C Indonesia 1.11N 109.00E
Pemar see Paimio
173 Ff5 Pematangsiantar Sumatera, W Indonesia 2.58N 99.01E
85 Q14 Pemba prev. Port Amelia, Porto Amélia. Cabo Delgado, NE Mozambique 13.00S 40.30E
83 J22 Pemba ◈ region E Tanzania
83 K21 Pemba island E Tanzania
85 Q14 Pemba, Baia de inlet NE Mozambique
83 J21 Pemba Channel channel E Tanzania
188 J14 Pemberton Western Australia 34.27S 116.09E
8 M16 Pemberton British Columbia, SW Canada 50.19N 122.49W
31 Q2 Pembina North Dakota, N USA 48.58N 97.14W
31 Q2 Pembina ≈ Canada/USA
9 P15 Pembina ≈ Alberta, SW Canada
176 Xx15 Pembre Irian Jaya, E Indonesia 7.49S 138.01E
12 K12 Pembroke Ontario, SE Canada 45.49N 77.07W
99 H21 Pembroke SW Wales, UK 51.40N 4.55W
25 W6 Pembroke Georgia, SE USA 32.09N 81.35W
23 U11 Pembroke North Carolina, SE USA 34.40N 79.12W
23 R7 Pembroke Virginia, NE USA 37.19N 80.38W
99 H21 Pembroke cultural region SW Wales, UK
Pembuang, Sungai see Seruyan, Sungai
45 S15 Peña Blanca, Cerro ▲ C Panama 8.39N 80.39W
106 K8 Peña de Francia, Sierra de la ▲▲ W Spain
106 G6 Penafiel var. Peñafiel. Porto, N Portugal 41.12N 8.16W
107 N6 Peñafiel Castilla-León, N Spain 41.36N 4.07W
107 S8 Peñagolosa ▲ E Spain 40.10N 0.15W
107 N7 Peñalara, Pico de ▲ C Spain 40.52N 3.55W
175 Nn5 Penambo, Banjaran var. Banjaran Tama Abu, Penambo Range. ▲▲ Indonesia/Malaysia
Penambo Range see Penambo, Banjaran
43 O10 Peña Nevada, Cerro ▲ C Mexico 23.46N 99.52W
Penang see Pinang, Pulau, Peninsular Malaysia
Penang see Pinang
Penang see George Town
62 J8 Penápolis São Paulo, S Brazil 21.23S 50.02W
106 L7 Peñaranda de Bracamonte Castilla-León, N Spain 40.54N 5.13W
107 S8 Peñarroya ▲ E Spain 40.24N 0.42W
106 L12 Peñarroya-Pueblonuevo Andalucía, S Spain 38.21N 5.18W
99 K22 Penarth S Wales, UK 51.27N 3.10W
106 K1 Peñas, Cabo de headland N Spain 43.39N 5.52W
65 F20 Penas, Golfo de gulf S Chile
Pen-ch'i see Benxi
81 H14 Pendé var. Logone Oriental. ≈ Central African Republic/Chad
78 I14 Pendembu E Sierra Leone 9.06N 12.12W
31 R13 Pender Nebraska, C USA 42.06N 96.42W
Penderma see Bandırma
34 K11 Pendleton Oregon, NW USA 45.40N 118.47W
34 M7 Pend Oreille, Lake ◎ Idaho, NW USA
34 M7 Pend Oreille River ≈ Idaho/Washington, NW USA
Pendzhikent see Panjakent
Peneius see Pineiós
106 G8 Penela Coimbra, N Portugal 40.01N 8.22W
12 G13 Penetanguishene Ontario, S Canada 44.45N 79.55W
157 H15 Penganga ≈ C India
167 T12 P'engchia Yu island N Taiwan
81 M21 Penge Kasai Oriental, C Dem. Rep. Congo (Zaire) 5.29S 24.38E
Penghu Archipelago/P'enghu Ch'üntao/Penghu Islands see P'enghu Liehtao
167 R14 P'enghu Liehtao var. P'enghu Ch'üntao, Penghu Islands, Eng. Penghu Archipelago, Pescadores, Jap. Hoko-guntō, Hoko-shotō. island group W Taiwan
Penghu Shuidao/P'enghu Shuitao see Pescadores Channel
167 R4 Penglai var. Dengzhou. Shandong, E China 37.48N 120.43E
Peng-pu see Bengbu
Penhsihu see Benxi
Penibético, Sistema see Béticos, Sistemas
106 F10 Peniche Leiria, W Portugal 39.21N 9.22W
175 Nn16 Penida, Nusa island S Indonesia
Peninsular State see Florida
107 T8 Peñíscola País Valenciano, E Spain 40.22N 0.24E
42 M13 Pénjamo Guanajuato, C Mexico 20.20N 101.35W
Penki see Benxi
104 F7 Penmarch, Pointe de headland NW France 47.46N 4.34W
109 L15 Penna, Punta della headland C Italy 42.10N 14.43E
109 K14 Penne Abruzzo, C Italy 42.28N 13.57E
Penner see Penneru
161 J18 Penneru var. Penner. ≈ C India
190 I10 Penneshaw South Australia 35.45S 137.57E
20 C14 Penn Hills Pennsylvania, NE USA 40.28N 79.52W
Penninae, Alpes/Pennine, Alpi see Pennine Alps
110 D11 Pennine Alps Fr. Alpes Pennines, It. Alpi Pennine; Lat. Alpes Penninae. ▲▲ Italy/Switzerland
Pennine Chain see Pennines
99 L15 Pennines var. Pennine Chain. ▲▲ N England, UK
Pennines, Alpes see Pennine Alps
23 O8 Pennington Gap Virginia, NE USA 36.45N 83.01W
20 I16 Penns Grove New Jersey, NE USA 39.42N 75.27W
20 I16 Pennsville New Jersey, NE USA 39.37N 75.29W
20 E14 Pennsylvania off. Commonwealth of Pennsylvania; also known as The Keystone State. ◈ state NE USA
20 G10 Penn Yan New York, NE USA 42.39N 77.02W
128 H16 Peno Tverskaya Oblast', W Russian Federation 56.55N 32.44E
21 R7 Penobscot Bay bay Maine, NE USA
21 S5 Penobscot River ≈ Maine, NE USA
190 K12 Penola South Australia 37.24S 140.50E
42 K9 Peñón Blanco Durango, C Mexico 25.12N 100.50W
190 E7 Penong South Australia 31.57S 133.01E
45 S16 Penonomé Coclé, C Panama 8.29N 80.21W
202 L13 Penrhyn atoll N Cook Islands
199 Kk10 Penrhyn Basin undersea feature C Pacific Ocean
191 S9 Penrith New South Wales, SE Australia 33.45S 150.48E
99 K15 Penrith NW England, UK 54.40N 2.43W
25 O9 Pensacola Florida, SE USA 30.25N 87.13W
25 O9 Pensacola Bay bay Florida, SE USA
205 N7 Pensacola Mountains ▲▲ Antarctica
190 L12 Penshurst Victoria, SE Australia 37.54S 142.19E
197 C12 Pentecost Fr. Pentecôte. island C Vanuatu
13 V4 Pentecôte ≈ Quebec, SE Canada
Pentecôte see Pentecost
13 V4 Pentecôte, Lac ◎ Quebec, SE Canada
15 Gg16 Penticton British Columbia, SW Canada 49.28N 119.37W
98 J6 Pentland Firth strait N Scotland, UK
98 J12 Pentland Hills hill range S Scotland, UK
175 Rr10 Penu Pulau Taliabu, E Indonesia 1.43S 125.09E
161 H18 Penukonda Andhra Pradesh, E India 14.04N 77.38E
177 G7 Penwegon Pegu, C Burma 18.13N 96.34E
26 M8 Penwell Texas, SW USA 31.45N 102.32W
99 J21 Pen y Fan ▲ SE Wales, UK 51.52N 3.25W
99 L16 Pen-y-ghent ▲ N England, UK 54.11N 2.15W
175 T12 Penyu, Kepulauan island group E Indonesia
131 O6 Penza Penzenskaya Oblast', W Russian Federation 53.11N 45.00E
99 G25 Penzance SW England, UK 50.07N 5.33W
131 N6 Penzenskaya Oblast' ◈ province W Russian Federation
127 P7 Penzhina ≈ E Russian Federation
127 N17 Penzhinskaya Guba bay E Russian Federation
Penzig see Pieńsk
38 K13 Peoria Arizona, SW USA 33.34N 112.14W
32 L12 Peoria Illinois, N USA 40.41N 89.35W
32 L12 Peoria Heights Illinois, N USA 40.45N 89.34W
33 N11 Peotone Illinois, N USA 41.19N 87.47W
20 J11 Pepacton Reservoir ⊡ New York, NE USA
78 I15 Pepel W Sierra Leone 8.39N 13.04W
32 I6 Pepin, Lake ⊡ Minnesota/Wisconsin, N USA
101 L20 Pepinster Liège, E Belgium 50.34N 5.49E
115 L20 Peqin var. Peqini. Elbasan, C Albania 41.03N 19.46E
Peqini see Peqin
42 D7 Pequeña, Punta headland W Mexico 26.13N 112.34W
174 I11 Perabumulih var. Prabumulih. Sumatera, W Indonesia 3.27S 104.15E
174 Gg4 Perak ◈ state Peninsular Malaysia
174 Gg4 Perak, Sungai ≈ Peninsular Malaysia
107 R7 Perales del Alfambra Aragón, NE Spain 40.38N 1.00W
117 C15 Pérama var. Perama. Ípeiros, W Greece 39.42N 20.51E
94 M13 Perä-Posio Lappi, NE Finland 66.10N 27.56E
13 Z6 Percé Quebec, SE Canada 48.31N 64.15W
13 Z6 Percé, Rocher island Quebec, S Canada
104 L5 Perche, Collines de ▲ N France
111 X4 Perchtoldsdorf Niederösterreich, NE Austria 48.06N 16.16E
188 L6 Percival Lakes lakes Western Australia
107 T3 Perdido, Monte ▲ NE Spain 42.41N 0.01E
25 O8 Perdido River ≈ Alabama/Florida, S USA
Perece Vela Basin see West Mariana Basin
118 G7 Perechyn Zakarpats'ka Oblast', W Ukraine 48.45N 22.28E
56 E10 Pereira Risaralda, W Colombia 4.52N 75.48W
62 I7 Pereira Barreto São Paulo, S Brazil 20.37S 51.07W
61 G15 Pereirinha Pará, N Brazil 8.18S 57.30W
131 N10 Perelazovskiy Volgogradskaya Oblast', SW Russian Federation 49.10N 42.30E
131 S7 Perelyub Saratovskaya Oblast', W Russian Federation 51.52N 50.19E
33 P7 Pere Marquette River ≈ Michigan, N USA
Peremyshl see Przemyśl
118 I5 Peremyshlyany L'vivs'ka Oblast', W Ukraine 49.42N 24.33E
Pereshchepino see Pereshchepyne
118 L9 Pereshchepyne Rus. Pereshchepino. Dnipropetrovs'ka Oblast', E Ukraine 48.59N 35.21E
128 L16 Pereslavl'-Zalesskiy Yaroslavskaya Oblast', W Russian Federation 56.42N 38.45E
119 Y7 Pereval's'k Luhans'ka Oblast', E Ukraine 48.28N 38.54E
131 U7 Perevolotskiy Orenburgskaya Oblast', W Russian Federation 51.54N 54.05E
127 Nn16 Pereyaslavka Khabarovskiy Kray, SE Russian Federation 47.49N 134.56E
Pereyaslav-Khmel'nitskiy see Pereyaslav-Khmel'nyts'kyy
119 Q5 Pereyaslav-Khmel'nyts'kyy Rus. Pereyaslav-Khmel'nitskiy. Kyyivs'ka Oblast', N Ukraine 50.04N 31.28E
111 U4 Perg Oberösterreich, N Austria 48.15N 14.39E
63 B19 Pergamino Buenos Aires, E Argentina 33.55S 60.37W
108 G6 Pergine Valsugana Ger. Persen. Trentino-Alto Adige, N Italy 46.04N 11.13E
31 S6 Perham Minnesota, N USA 46.35N 95.34W
95 L16 Perho Länsi-Suomi, W Finland 63.15N 24.25E
118 E11 Periam Ger. Perjamosch, Hung. Perjámos. Timiş, W Romania 46.01N 20.54E
13 Q6 Péribonca ≈ Quebec, SE Canada
10 L11 Péribonca, Lac ◎ Quebec, SE Canada
13 Q6 Péribonca, Petite Rivière ≈ Quebec, SE Canada
13 Q7 Péribonka Quebec, SE Canada 48.45N 72.01W
42 I9 Pericos Sinaloa, C Mexico 25.04N 107.40W
174 Kk7 Perigi Borneo, C Indonesia
104 L12 Périgueux anc. Vesuna. Dordogne, SW France 45.12N 0.41E
56 G5 Perijá, Serranía de ▲▲ Columbia/Venezuela
117 H17 Peristéra island Vóreioi Sporádes, Greece, Aegean Sea
65 H20 Perito Moreno Santa Cruz, S Argentina 46.35S 71.00W
161 G22 Periyāl var. Periyar. ≈ SW India
Periyar see Periyāl
161 G23 Periyār Lake ◎ S India
Perjámos/Perjamosch see Periam
29 O9 Perkins Oklahoma, C USA 35.58N 97.01W
118 L7 Perkivtsi Chernivets'ka Oblast', W Ukraine 48.28N 26.48E
45 U15 Perlas, Archipiélago de las Eng. Pearl Islands. island group SE Panama
45 O10 Perlas, Cayos de reef SE Nicaragua
45 N9 Perlas, Laguna de Eng. Pearl Lagoon. lagoon E Nicaragua
45 N10 Perlas, Punta de headland E Nicaragua 12.22N 83.30W
102 L11 Perleberg Brandenburg, N Germany 53.04N 11.51E
Perlepe see Prilep
173 G2 Perlis ◈ state Peninsular Malaysia
129 U14 Perm' prev. Molotov. Permskaya Oblast', NW Russian Federation 58.01N 56.10E
115 M22 Përmet var. Përmeti, Prëmet. Gjirokastër, S Albania 40.12N 20.24E
Përmeti see Përmet
129 U15 Permskaya Oblast' ◈ province NW Russian Federation
61 P15 Pernambuco off. Estado de Pernambuco. ◈ state E Brazil
Pernambuco see Recife
Pernambuco Abyssal Plain see Pernambuco Plain
49 Y6 Pernambuco Plain var. Pernambuco Abyssal Plain. undersea feature E Atlantic Ocean
67 K15 Pernambuco Seamounts undersea feature C Atlantic Ocean
190 H6 Pernatty Lagoon salt lake South Australia
Pernau see Pärnu
Pernauer Bucht see Pärnu Laht
Pērnava see Pärnu
116 G9 Pernik prev. Dimitrovo. Pernik, W Bulgaria 42.36N 23.01E
116 G10 Pernik ◈ province W Bulgaria
95 K20 Perniö Swe. Bjärnå. Länsi-Suomi, W Finland 60.13N 23.10E
111 X5 Pernitz Niederösterreich, E Austria 47.54N 15.58E
Pernov see Pärnu
105 O3 Péronne Somme, N France 49.55N 2.57E
12 L8 Péronne, Lac ◎ Quebec, SE Canada
108 A8 Perosa Argentina Piemonte, NE Italy 45.02N 7.10E
43 Q14 Perote Veracruz-Llave, E Mexico 19.31N 97.16W
Pérouse see Perugia
203 W15 Pérouse, Bahía de la bay Easter Island, Chile, E Pacific Ocean
Perovsk see Kyzylorda
105 O17 Perpignan Pyrénées-Orientales, S France 42.40N 2.52E
115 M20 Përrenjas var. Përrenjasi, Prenjas, Prenjasi. Elbasan, E Albania 41.04N 20.34E
Përrenjasi see Përrenjas
94 O2 Perriertoppen ▲ C Svalbard 79.10N 17.01E
27 S6 Perrin Texas, SW USA 32.59N 98.03W
25 Y16 Perrine Florida, SE USA 25.36N 80.21W
39 S12 Perro, Laguna del ◎ New Mexico, SW USA
104 G5 Perros-Guirec Côtes d'Armor, NW France 48.49N 3.28W
25 T9 Perry Florida, SE USA 30.07N 83.34W
25 T5 Perry Georgia, SE USA 32.27N 83.43W
31 U14 Perry Iowa, C USA 41.50N 94.06W
20 E10 Perry New York, NE USA 42.43N 78.00W
29 N9 Perry Oklahoma, C USA 36.17N 97.17W
29 Q3 Perry Lake ⊡ Kansas, C USA
33 R11 Perrysburg Ohio, N USA 41.33N 83.37W
27 O1 Perryton Texas, SW USA 36.24N 100.48W
41 O15 Perryville Alaska, USA 55.55N 159.08W
29 U11 Perryville Arkansas, C USA 35.00N 92.48W
29 Y6 Perryville Missouri, C USA 37.43N 89.51W
Persante see Parsęta
Persen see Pergine Valsugana
Pershay see Pyarshai
119 V7 Pershotravens'k Dnipropetrovs'ka Oblast', E Ukraine 48.19N 36.22E
119 W9 Pershotravneve Donets'ka Oblast', E Ukraine 47.03N 37.20E
Persia see Iran
147 T5 Persian Gulf see Gulf, The
Persis see Fārs
97 K22 Perstorp Skåne, S Sweden 56.07N 13.22E
143 O14 Pertek Tunceli, C Turkey 38.52N 39.19E
191 P16 Perth Tasmania, SE Australia 41.39S 147.11E
188 I13 Perth state capital Western Australia 31.58S 115.49E
12 L13 Perth Ontario, SE Canada 44.54N 76.15W
98 J11 Perth C Scotland, UK 56.24N 3.28W
188 I12 Perth ✕ Western Australia 31.51S 116.06E
98 J10 Perth cultural region C Scotland, UK
181 V10 Perth Basin undersea feature SE Indian Ocean
105 S15 Pertuis Vaucluse, SE France 43.42N 5.30E
105 Y16 Pertusato, Capo headland Corse, France, C Mediterranean Sea 41.22N 9.10E
32 L11 Peru Illinois, N USA 41.18N 89.09W
33 P12 Peru Indiana, N USA 40.45N 86.04W
59 E13 Peru off. Republic of Peru. ◆ republic W South America
Peru see Beru
200 Oo10 Peru Basin undersea feature E Pacific Ocean
200 Oo9 Peru-Chile Trench undersea feature E Pacific Ocean
114 F13 Perućko Jezero ◎ S Croatia
108 H13 Perugia Fr. Pérouse; anc. Perusia. Umbria, C Italy 43.06N 12.24E
Perugia, Lake of see Trasimeno, Lago
63 D15 Perugorría Corrientes, NE Argentina 29.21S 58.34W
62 M11 Peruíbe São Paulo, S Brazil 24.18S 47.01W
161 B21 Perumalpār reef India, N Indian Ocean
Perusia see Perugia
101 D20 Péruwelz Hainaut, SW Belgium 50.30N 3.34E
143 R15 Pervari Siirt, SE Turkey 37.58N 42.30E
131 O4 Pervomaysk Nizhegorodskaya Oblast', W Russian Federation 54.52N 43.49E
119 X7 Pervomays'k Luhans'ka Oblast', E Ukraine 48.37N 38.36E
119 P8 Pervomays'k prev. Ol'viopol'. Mykolayivs'ka Oblast', S Ukraine 48.01N 30.51E
119 S12 Pervomays'ke Respublika Krym, S Ukraine 45.43N 33.49E
131 V7 Pervomayskiy Orenburgskaya Oblast', W Russian Federation 51.32N 54.58E
130 M6 Pervomayskiy Tambovskaya Oblast', W Russian Federation 53.15N 40.20E
119 V6 Pervomays'kyy Kharkivs'ka Oblast', E Ukraine 49.24N 36.12E
125 E10 Pervoural'sk Sverdlovskaya Oblast', C Russian Federation 56.58N 59.50E
127 Pp12 Pervyy Kuril'skiy Proliv strait E Russian Federation
101 I19 Perwez Wallon Brabant, C Belgium 50.39N 4.49E
108 I11 Pesaro anc. Pisaurum. Marche, C Italy 43.55N 12.52E
37 N9 Pescadero California, W USA 37.15N 122.23W
Pescadores see P'enghu Liehtao
167 S14 Pescadores Channel var. Penghu Shuidao, P'enghu Shuitao. channel W Taiwan
109 K14 Pescara anc. Aternum, Ostia Aterni. Abruzzo, C Italy 42.28N 14.13E
109 K15 Pescara ≈ C Italy
108 F11 Pescia Toscana, C Italy 43.54N 10.40E
110 C8 Peseux Neuchâtel, W Switzerland 46.58N 6.52E
129 P6 Pesha ≈ NW Russian Federation
155 T5 Peshāwar North-West Frontier Province, N Pakistan 34.00N 71.33E
155 T6 Peshāwar ✕ North-West Frontier Province, N Pakistan 34.01N 71.40E
115 M19 Peshkopi var. Peshkopia, Peshkopija. Dibër, NE Albania 41.40N 20.25E
Peshkopia/Peshkopija see Peshkopi
116 I11 Peshtera Pazardzhik, C Bulgaria 42.01N 24.18E
33 N6 Peshtigo Wisconsin, N USA 45.04N 87.43W
33 N6 Peshtigo River ≈ Wisconsin, N USA
Peski see Pyeski
129 S13 Peskova Kirovskaya Oblast', NW Russian Federation 59.04N 52.17E
105 S8 Pesmes Haute-Saône, E France 47.17N 5.33E
106 H6 Peso da Régua var. Pêso da Regua. Vila Real, N Portugal 41.10N 7.46W
42 F5 Pesqueira Sonora, NW Mexico 29.22N 110.52W
104 J13 Pessac Gironde, SW France 44.46N 0.42W
113 J23 Pest off. Pest Megye. ◈ county C Hungary
128 J14 Pestovo Novgorodskaya Oblast', W Russian Federation 58.37N 35.48E
42 M15 Petacalco, Bahía bay W Mexico
Petach-Tikva/Petah Tiqva see Petaḥ Tiqwa
144 F10 Petaḥ Tiqwa var. Petach-Tikva, Petah Tiqva, Petakh Tikva. Tel Aviv, C Israel 32.04N 34.52E
Petakh Tikva see Petaḥ Tiqwa
95 L17 Petäjävesi Länsi-Suomi, W Finland 62.16N 25.10E
24 M7 Petal Mississippi, S USA 31.21N 89.15W
117 I19 Petalioí island C Greece
117 H19 Petalión, Kólpos gulf E Greece
117 J19 Pétalo ▲ Ándros, Kykládes, Greece, Aegean Sea 37.51N 24.50E
36 M8 Petaluma California, W USA 38.15N 122.37W
101 L25 Pétange Luxembourg, SW Luxembourg 49.33N 5.52E
56 M5 Petare Miranda, N Venezuela 10.29N 66.47W
43 N16 Petatlán Guerrero, S Mexico 17.31N 101.16W
85 L14 Petauke Eastern, E Zambia 14.12S 31.16E

◆ Country
◈ Country Capital
◇ Dependent Territory
○ Dependent Territory Capital
◈ Administrative Region
✕ International Airport
▲ Mountain
▲▲ Mountain Range
✶ Volcano
≈ River
◎ Lake
⊡ Reservoir

PETAWAWA – PIRAJUÍ

12 J12 **Petawawa** Ontario, SE Canada 45.53N 77.16W
12 J11 **Petawawa** ≈ Ontario, SE Canada
Petchaburi see Phetchaburi
44 D2 **Petén** off. Departamento del Petén. ◈ department N Guatemala
44 D2 **Petén Itzá, Lago** var. Lago de Flores. ◎ N Guatemala
32 K7 **Petenwell Lake** ⊡ Wisconsin, N USA
12 D6 **Peterbell** Ontario, S Canada 48.34N 83.19W
190 I7 **Peterborough** South Australia 32.59S 138.50E
12 I14 **Peterborough** Ontario, SE Canada 44.19N 78.19W
99 N20 **Peterborough** prev. Medeshamstede. E England, UK 52.34N 0.15W
21 N10 **Peterborough** New Hampshire, NE USA 42.51N 71.54W
98 L8 **Peterhead** NE Scotland, UK 57.30N 1.46W
Peterhof see Luboń
199 Mm16 **Peter I Island** ◇ Norwegian dependency Antarctica
204 H9 **Peter I Island** var. Peter I øy. island Antarctica
Peter I øy see Peter I Island
99 M14 **Peterlee** N England, UK 54.45N 1.18W
Peterlingen see Payerne
207 P14 **Petermann Bjerg** ▲ C Greenland 73.16N 27.59W
9 S12 **Peter Pond Lake** ◎ Saskatchewan, C Canada
41 X13 **Petersburg** Mytkof Island, Alaska, USA 56.43N 132.51W
32 K13 **Petersburg** Illinois, N USA 40.01N 89.52W
33 N16 **Petersburg** Indiana, N USA 38.30N 87.16W
31 Q3 **Petersburg** North Dakota, N USA 47.59N 97.59W
27 N5 **Petersburg** Texas, SW USA 33.52N 101.36W
23 V7 **Petersburg** Virginia, NE USA 37.13N 77.24W
23 T4 **Petersburg** West Virginia, NE USA 38.59N 79.07W
102 H12 **Petershagen** Nordrhein-Westfalen, NW Germany 52.22N 8.58E
57 S9 **Peters Mine** var. Peter's Mine. N Guyana 6.13N 59.18W
109 O21 **Petilia Policastro** Calabria, SW Italy 39.07N 16.48E
46 M9 **Pétionville** S Haiti 18.29N 72.16W
47 X6 **Petit-Bourg** Basse Terre, C Guadeloupe 16.11N 61.34W
13 Y5 **Petit-Cap** Quebec, SE Canada 49.00N 64.26W
47 Y6 **Petit Cul-de-Sac Marin** bay C Guadeloupe
10 K7 **Petite Rivière de la Baleine** ≈ Quebec, NE Canada
46 M9 **Petite-Rivière-de-l'Artibonite** C Haiti 19.06N 72.28W
181 X16 **Petite Rivière Noire, Piton de la** ▲ C Mauritius
13 R9 **Petite-Rivière-St-François** Quebec, SE Canada 47.18N 70.34W
46 L9 **Petit-Goâve** S Haiti 18.23N 72.51W
Petitjean see Sidi-Kacem
11 N10 **Petit Lac Manicouagan** ◎ Quebec, E Canada
21 T7 **Petit Manan Point** headland Maine, NE USA 44.23N 67.54W
Petit Mécatina, Rivière du see Little Mecatina
9 N10 **Petitot** ≈ Alberta/British Columbia, W Canada
47 S12 **Petit Piton** ▲ SW Saint Lucia 13.49N 61.03W
Petit-Popo see Aného
Petit St-Bernard, Col du see Little Saint Bernard Pass
11 O8 **Petitsikapau Lake** ◎ Newfoundland, E Canada
94 L11 **Petkula** Lappi, N Finland 67.40N 26.43E
43 X12 **Peto** Yucatán, SE Mexico 20.09N 88.55W
64 G10 **Petorca** Valparaíso, C Chile 32.13S 70.49W
33 Q5 **Petoskey** Michigan, N USA 45.51N 88.03W
144 G14 **Petra** archaeological site Ma'ān, W Jordan 30.19N 35.25E
Petra see Wādī Mūsā
117 F14 **Pétras, Sténa** pass N Greece 40.12N 22.15E
127 Nn18 **Petra Velikogo, Zaliv** bay SE Russian Federation
Petrel see Petrer
12 K15 **Petre, Point** headland Ontario, SE Canada 43.49N 77.07W
107 S12 **Petrer** var. Petrel. País Valenciano, E Spain 38.28N 0.46W
129 U11 **Petretsovo** Permskaya Oblast', NW Russian Federation 61.22N 57.21E
116 G12 **Petrich** Blagoevgrad, SW Bulgaria 41.24N 23.12E
197 H3 **Petrie, Récif** reef N New Caledonia
39 N11 **Petrified Forest** prehistoric site Arizona, SW USA 35.10N 109.49W
Petrikau see Piotrków Trybunalski
Petrikov see Pyetrykaw
118 H12 **Petrila** Hung. Petrilla. Hunedoara, W Romania 45.27N 23.25E
Petrilla see Petrila
114 E9 **Petrinja** Sisak-Moslavina, C Croatia 45.27N 16.14E
Petroaleksandrovsk see Türtkül
Petrőcz see Bački Petrovac
128 G12 **Petrodvorets** Fin. Pietarhovi. Leningradskaya Oblast', NW Russian Federation 59.52N 29.52E
Petrograd see Sankt-Peterburg
Petrokov see Piotrków Trybunalski
56 G6 **Petrólea** Norte de Santander, NE Colombia 8.30N 72.34W
12 D16 **Petrolia** Ontario, S Canada 42.54N 82.07W
27 S4 **Petrolia** Texas, SW USA 34.00N 98.13W
61 O15 **Petrolina** Pernambuco, E Brazil 9.22S 40.30W
47 T6 **Petrona, Punta** headland C Puerto Rico 17.57N 66.23W
Petropavl see Petropavlovsk
119 V7 **Petropavlivka** Dnipropetrovs'ka Oblast', E Ukraine 48.28N 36.28E
151 P6 **Petropavlovsk** Kaz. Petropavl. Severnyy Kazakhstan, N Kazakhstan 54.46N 69.06E
127 Pp11 **Petropavlovsk-Kamchatskiy** Kamchatskaya Oblast', E Russian Federation 53.03N 158.43E
62 P9 **Petrópolis** Rio de Janeiro, SE Brazil 22.30S 43.28W
118 H12 **Petroşani** var. Petroşeni, Ger. Petroschen, Hung. Petrozsény. Hunedoara, W Romania 45.25N 23.22E
Petroschen/Petroşeni see Petroşani
Petroskoi see Petrozavodsk
Petrovac/Petrovácz see Bački Petrovac
115 J17 **Petrovac na Moru** Montenegro, SW Yugoslavia 42.11N 19.00E
119 S8 **Petrove** Kirovohrads'ka Oblast', C Ukraine 48.22N 33.12E
115 O18 **Petrovec** C FYR Macedonia 41.57N 21.37E
Petrovgrad see Zrenjanin
131 P7 **Petrovsk** Saratovskaya Oblast', W Russian Federation 52.20N 45.23E
128 J9 **Petrovskiy Yam** Respublika Kareliya, NW Russian Federation 63.19N 35.14E
Petrovsk-Port see Makhachkala
126 K16 **Petrovsk-Zabaykal'skiy** Chitinskaya Oblast', S Russian Federation 51.15N 108.36E
131 P9 **Petrov Val** Volgogradskaya Oblast', SW Russian Federation 50.10N 45.16E
128 J11 **Petrozavodsk** Fin. Petroskoi. Respublika Kareliya, NW Russian Federation 61.46N 34.19E
Petrozsény see Petroşani
85 D20 **Petrusdal** Hardap, C Namibia 23.42S 17.23E
119 T7 **Petrykivka** Dnipropetrovs'ka Oblast', E Ukraine 48.44N 34.42E
Petsamo see Pechenga
Petschka see Pecica
Pettau see Ptuj
111 S5 **Pettenbach** Oberösterreich, C Austria 47.58N 14.03E
27 S13 **Pettus** Texas, SW USA 28.34N 97.49W
125 F13 **Petukhovo** Kurganskaya Oblast', C Russian Federation 55.04N 67.49E
Petuna see Songyuan
111 R4 **Peuerbach** Oberösterreich, N Austria 48.19N 13.45E
64 G12 **Peumo** Libertador, C Chile 34.22S 71.58W
173 Ee3 **Peusangan, Krueng** ≈ Sumatera, NW Indonesia
127 O4 **Pevek** Chukotskiy Avtonomnyy Okrug, NE Russian Federation 69.40N 170.19E
29 X5 **Pevely** Missouri, C USA 38.16N 90.24W
Peyia see Pégeia
104 J15 **Peyrehorade** Landes, SW France 43.33N 1.04W
128 J14 **Peza** ≈ NW Russian Federation
105 P16 **Pézenas** Hérault, S France 43.28N 3.25E
113 H20 **Pezinok** Ger. Bösing, Hung. Bazin. Bratislavský Kraj, W Slovakia 48.16N 17.15E
103 L22 **Pfaffenhofen an der Ilm** Bayern, SE Germany 48.31N 11.30E
110 G7 **Pfäffikon** Schwyz, C Switzerland 47.11N 8.46E
103 F20 **Pfälzer Wald** hill range W Germany
103 N22 **Pfarrkirchen** Bayern, SE Germany 48.25N 12.56E
103 G21 **Pforzheim** Baden-Württemberg, SW Germany 48.52N 8.42E
103 H24 **Pfullendorf** Baden-Württemberg, S Germany 47.55N 9.16E
110 K8 **Pfunds** Tirol, W Austria 46.56N 10.30E
103 G19 **Pfungstadt** Hessen, W Germany 49.48N 8.36E
85 L20 **Phalaborwa** Northern, NE South Africa 23.50S 31.08E
158 E11 **Phalodi** Rājasthān, NW India 27.06N 72.22E
158 E12 **Phalsund** Rājasthān, NW India 26.22N 71.55E
161 E15 **Phaltan** Mahārāshtra, W India 18.01N 74.31E
178 Hh7 **Phan** var. Muang Phan. Chiang Rai, NW Thailand 19.34N 99.43E
178 H14 **Phangan, Ko** island SW Thailand
178 Gg15 **Phang-Nga** var. Pang-Nga, Phangnga. Phangnga, SW Thailand 8.28N 98.31E
Phan Rang/Phanrang see Phan Rang-Thap Cham
178 Kk13 **Phan Rang-Thap Cham** var. Phanrang, Phan Rang, Phan Rang Thap Cham. Ninh Thuân, S Vietnam 11.34N 109.00E
178 Kk14 **Phan Ri** Binh Thuân, S Vietnam 11.11N 108.31E
178 K14 **Phan Thiêt** Binh Thuân, S Vietnam 10.55N 108.06E
Pharnacia see Giresun
27 S17 **Pharr** Texas, SW USA 26.11N 98.10W
Pharus see Hvar
178 H16 **Phatthalung** var. Padalung, Patalung. Phatthalung, SW Thailand 7.37N 100.04E
178 Hh7 **Phayao** var. Muang Phayao. Phayao, NW Thailand 19.10N 99.55E
9 U10 **Phelps Lake** ◎ Saskatchewan, C Canada
23 X9 **Phelps Lake** ◎ North Carolina, SE USA
25 R5 **Phenix City** Alabama, S USA 32.28N 85.00W
178 Jj8 **Pheo** Quang Binh, C Vietnam 17.42N 105.58E
Phet Buri see Phetchaburi
178 H12 **Phetchaburi** var. Bejraburi, Petchaburi, Phet Buri. Phetchaburi, SW Thailand 13.04N 99.58E
178 Hh9 **Phichit** var. Bichitra, Muang Phichit, Pichit. Phichit, C Thailand 16.28N 100.21E
24 M5 **Philadelphia** Mississippi, S USA 32.45N 89.06W
20 I7 **Philadelphia** New York, NE USA 44.10N 75.40W
20 I15 **Philadelphia** Pennsylvania, NE USA 40.00N 75.10W
20 I15 **Philadelphia** ✕ Pennsylvania, NE USA 39.51N 75.13W
Philadelphia see 'Ammān
30 L10 **Philip** South Dakota, N USA 44.02N 101.39W
101 H22 **Philippeville** Namur, S Belgium 50.12N 4.33E
Philippeville see Skikda
23 S3 **Philippi** West Virginia, NE USA 39.09N 80.02W
Philippi see Fílippoi
205 Y9 **Philippi Glacier** glacier Antarctica
198 G7 **Philippine Basin** undersea feature W Pacific Ocean
133 X12 **Philippine Plate** tectonic feature
179 Q13 **Philippines** off. Republic of the Philippines. ◆ republic SE Asia
133 X13 **Philippines** island group W Pacific Ocean
179 S12 **Philippine Sea** sea W Pacific Ocean
198 G7 **Philippine Trench** undersea feature W Philippine Sea
85 H23 **Philippolis** Free State, C South Africa 30.16S 25.16E
Philippopolis see Plovdiv, Bulgaria
Philippopolis see Shahbā', Syria
47 V9 **Philipsburg** Sint Maarten, N Netherlands Antilles 17.58N 63.02W
35 P19 **Philipsburg** Montana, NW USA 46.19N 113.17W
41 R6 **Philip Smith Mountains** ▲ Alaska, USA
158 H8 **Phillaur** Punjab, N India 31.01N 75.49E
191 N13 **Phillip Island** island Victoria, SE Australia
27 N2 **Phillips** Texas, SW USA 35.39N 101.21W
32 K5 **Phillips** Wisconsin, N USA 45.42N 90.22W
28 K3 **Phillipsburg** Kansas, C USA 39.45N 99.19W
20 I14 **Phillipsburg** New Jersey, NE USA 40.39N 75.09W
23 S7 **Philpott Lake** ⊡ Virginia, NE USA
Phintias see Licata
178 Hh9 **Phitsanulok** var. Bisnulok, Muang Phitsanulok, Pitsanulok. Phitsanulok, C Thailand 16.49N 100.15E
Phlórina see Flórina
Phnom Penh see Phnum Penh
178 J13 **Phnum Penh** var. Phnom Penh. ● (Cambodia) Phnum Penh, S Cambodia 11.34N 104.55E
178 J12 **Phnum Tbêng Meanchey** Preăh Vihéar, N Cambodia 13.45N 104.58E
38 K13 **Phoenix** state capital Arizona, SW USA 33.27N 112.04W
Phoenix Island see Rawaki
203 R3 **Phoenix Islands** island group C Kiribati
20 I15 **Phoenixville** Pennsylvania, NE USA 40.07N 75.31W
85 K22 **Phofung** var. Mont-aux-Sources. ▲ N Lesotho 28.47S 28.52E
178 I10 **Phon** Khon Kaen, E Thailand 15.47N 102.35E
178 I5 **Phôngsali** var. Phong Saly. Phôngsali, N Laos 21.40N 102.04E
Phong Saly see Phôngsali
178 I8 **Phônhông** C Laos 18.29N 102.26E
178 J5 **Phô Rang** Lao Cai, N Vietnam 22.12N 104.27E
Phort Láirge, Cuan see Waterford Harbour
178 Gg10 **Phra Chedi Sam Ong** Kanchanaburi, W Thailand 15.18N 98.26E
178 Hh8 **Phrae** var. Muang Phrae, Prae. Phrae, NW Thailand 18.07N 100.09E
Phra Nakhon Si Ayutthaya see Ayutthaya
177 G15 **Phra Thong, Ko** island SW Thailand
Phu Cuong see Thu Dâu Môt
177 G16 **Phuket** var. Bhuket, Puket, Mal. Ujung Salang; prev. Junkseylon, Salang. Phuket, SW Thailand 7.52N 98.22E
177 G16 **Phuket** ✕ Phuket, SW Thailand 8.03N 98.16E
177 G16 **Phuket, Ko** island SW Thailand
160 N12 **Phulabāni** prev. Phulbani. Orissa, E India 20.30N 84.18E
Phulbani see Phulabāni
178 K10 **Phu Lôc** Th,a Thiên-Huê, C Vietnam 16.13N 107.53E
178 J14 **Phumĭ Banam** Prey Vêng, S Cambodia 11.14N 105.18E
178 Ii13 **Phumĭ Chŏâm** Kâmpóng Spœ, SW Cambodia 11.42N 103.58E
178 Jj11 **Phumĭ Kalêng** Stœng Trêng, NE Cambodia 13.57N 106.17E
178 J12 **Phumĭ Kâmpóng Trâbêk** prev. Phum Kompong Trabek. Kâmpóng Thum, C Cambodia 13.06N 105.16E
178 Ii12 **Phumĭ Koŭk Kduŏch** Bătdâmbâng, NW Cambodia 13.16N 103.08E
178 K12 **Phumĭ Labăng** Rôtânôkiri, NE Cambodia 13.51N 107.01E
178 J11 **Phumĭ Mlu Prey** Preăh Vihéar, N Cambodia 13.48N 105.16E
178 Ii11 **Phumĭ Moŭng** Siĕmréab, NW Cambodia 14.15N 103.35E
178 Ii13 **Phumĭ Prâmaôy** Poŭthĭsăt, W Cambodia 12.13N 103.05E
178 I14 **Phumĭ Samĭt** Kaôh Kŏng, SW Cambodia 10.54N 103.09E
178 Ii11 **Phumĭ Sâmraông** prev. Phum Samrong. Siĕmréab, NW Cambodia 14.09N 103.30E
178 Jj12 **Phumĭ Siĕmbok** Stœng Trêng, N Cambodia 13.28N 105.59E
178 Jj12 **Phumĭ Thalabârivăt** Stœng Trêng, N Cambodia 13.34N 105.57E
178 Ii14 **Phumĭ Veal Renh** Kâmpôt, SW Cambodia 10.43N 103.49E
178 I13 **Phumĭ Yeay Sên** Kaôh Kŏng, SW Cambodia 11.09N 103.09E
Phum Kompong Trabek see Phumĭ Kâmpóng Trâbêk
Phum Samrong see Phumĭ Sâmraông
178 Kk11 **Phu My** Binh Đinh, C Vietnam 14.07N 109.05E
178 J15 **Phung Hiêp** Cân Thơ, S Vietnam 9.49N 105.48E
159 T12 **Phuntsholing** SW Bhutan 26.52N 89.25E
178 J15 **Phươc Long** Minh Hai, S Vietnam 9.27N 105.25E
178 Ii14 **Phu Quôc, Đao** var. Phu Quoc Island. island S Vietnam
Phu Quoc Island see Phu Quôc, Đao
178 J6 **Phu Tho** Vinh Phu, N Vietnam 21.22N 105.13E
Phu Vinh see Tra Vinh
201 T13 **Piaanu Pass** passage Chuuk Islands, C Micronesia
108 E8 **Piacenza** Fr. Paisance; anc. Placentia. Emilia-Romagna, N Italy 45.01N 9.42E
109 K14 **Pianella** Abruzzo, C Italy 42.23N 14.04E
109 M15 **Pianosa, Isola** island Archipelago Toscano, C Italy
176 Vv11 **Piar** Irian Jaya, E Indonesia 2.49S 132.46E
47 U14 **Piarco** var. Port of Spain. ✕ (Port-of-Spain) Trinidad, Trinidad and Tobago 10.36N 61.21W
112 M12 **Piaseczno** Mazowieckie, C Poland 52.04N 21.05E
118 I15 **Piatra** Teleorman, S Romania 43.49N 25.10E
118 L10 **Piatra-Neamţ** Hung. Karácsonkő. Neamţ, NE Romania 46.54N 26.23E
Piauhy see Piauí
61 N15 **Piauí** off. Estado do Piauí; prev. Piauhy. ◈ state E Brazil
108 I7 **Piave** ≈ NE Italy
109 K24 **Piazza Armerina** var. Chiazza. Sicilia, Italy, C Mediterranean Sea 37.22N 14.22E
83 G14 **Pibor** Amh. Pibor Wenz. ≈ Ethiopia/Sudan
83 G14 **Pibor Post** Jonglei, SE Sudan 6.49N 33.06E
Pibor Wenz see Pibor
Pibrans see Příbram
38 K11 **Picacho Butte** ▲ Arizona, SW USA 35.12N 112.44W
42 D4 **Picachos, Cerro** ▲ NW Mexico 29.15N 114.04W
105 O4 **Picardie** Eng. Picardy. ◈ region N France
Picardy see Picardie
24 L8 **Picayune** Mississippi, S USA 30.31N 89.40W
Piccolo San Bernardo, Colle di see Little Saint Bernard Pass
64 K5 **Pichanal** Salta, N Argentina 23.22S 64.11W
153 P12 **Pichandar** W Tajikistan 38.44N 68.51E
29 R8 **Picher** Oklahoma, C USA 36.59N 94.49W
64 G12 **Pichilemu** Libertador, C Chile 34.25S 72.00W
42 F9 **Pichilingue** Baja California Sur, W Mexico 24.19N 110.16W
58 B6 **Pichincha** ◈ province N Ecuador
58 C6 **Pichincha** ▲ N Ecuador 0.12S 78.39W
Pichit see Phichit
43 U15 **Pichucalco** Chiapas, SE Mexico 17.32N 93.07W
24 L5 **Pickens** Mississippi, S USA 32.52N 89.58W
23 O11 **Pickens** South Carolina, SE USA 34.52N 82.42W
12 G11 **Pickerel** ≈ Ontario, S Canada
12 H15 **Pickering** Ontario, S Canada 43.50N 79.03W
99 N16 **Pickering** N England, UK 54.14N 0.46W
33 S13 **Pickerington** Ohio, N USA 39.52N 82.45W
10 C10 **Pickle Lake** Ontario, C Canada 51.30N 90.10W
31 P12 **Pickstown** South Dakota, N USA 43.02N 98.31W
27 V6 **Pickton** Texas, SW USA 33.01N 95.19W
25 N1 **Pickwick Lake** ⊡ S USA
66 N2 **Pico** var. Ilha do Pico. island Azores, Portugal, NE Atlantic Ocean
65 J19 **Pico de Salamanca** Chubut, SE Argentina 45.26S 67.26W
1 P9 **Pico Fracture Zone** tectonic feature NW Atlantic Ocean
Pico, Ilha do see Pico
61 O14 **Picos** Piauí, E Brazil 7.04S 41.24W
65 I20 **Pico Truncado** Santa Cruz, SE Argentina 46.49S 68.01W
191 S9 **Picton** New South Wales, SE Australia 34.12S 150.36E
12 K15 **Picton** Ontario, SE Canada 43.59N 77.09W
193 K14 **Picton** Marlborough, South Island, NZ 41.18S 174.00E
65 H15 **Picún Leufú, Arroyo** ≈ SW Argentina
Pidálion see Gkréko, Akrotíri
161 K25 **Pidurutalagala** ▲ S Sri Lanka 7.03N 80.47E
118 K6 **Pidvolochys'k** Ternopil's'ka Oblast', W Ukraine 49.31N 26.09E
109 K16 **Piedimonte Matese** Campania, S Italy 41.20N 14.30E
29 X7 **Piedmont** Missouri, C USA 37.09N 90.42W
23 P11 **Piedmont** South Carolina, SE USA 34.42N 82.27W
19 Q12 **Piedmont** escarpment E USA
Piedmont see Piemonte
33 U13 **Piedmont Lake** ⊡ Ohio, N USA
106 M11 **Piedrabuena** Castilla-La Mancha, C Spain 39.01N 4.10W
Piedrafita, Puerto de see Pedrafita, Porto de
106 L8 **Piedrahita** Castilla-León, N Spain 40.27N 5.19W
43 N6 **Piedras Negras** var. Ciudad Porfirio Díaz. Coahuila de Zaragoza, NE Mexico 28.40N 100.31W
63 E21 **Piedras, Punta** headland E Argentina 35.27S 57.04W
59 I14 **Piedras, Río de las** ≈ E Peru
113 J16 **Piekary Śląskie** Śląskie, S Poland 50.23N 19.01E
95 M17 **Pieksämäki** Isä-Suomi, E Finland 62.18N 27.10E
111 V5 **Pielach** ≈ NE Austria
95 M16 **Pielavesi** Itä-Suomi, C Finland 63.13N 26.45E
95 N16 **Pielinen** var. Pielisjärvi. ◎ E Finland
Pielisjärvi see Pielinen
108 A8 **Piemonte** Eng. Piedmont. ◈ region NW Italy
113 L18 **Pieniny** ▲ Poland/Slovakia
113 E14 **Pieńsk** Ger. Penzig. Dolnośląskie, SW Poland 51.14N 15.03E
31 Q13 **Pierce** Nebraska, C USA 42.12N 97.31W
9 R14 **Pierceland** Saskatchewan, C Canada
117 E14 **Piéria** ▲ N Greece
31 N10 **Pierre** state capital South Dakota, N USA 44.22N 100.21W
104 K16 **Pierrefitte-Nestalas** Hautes-Pyrénées, S France 42.58N 0.04W
105 R14 **Pierrelatte** Drôme, E France 44.22N 4.40E
13 P11 **Pierreville** Quebec, SE Canada 46.05N 72.48W
13 O7 **Pierriche** ≈ Quebec, SE Canada
113 H20 **Piešt'any** Ger. Pistyan, Hung. Pöstyén. Trnavský, W Slovakia 48.36N 17.48E
111 X5 **Piesting** ≈ E Austria
Pietarhovi see Petrodvorets
Pietari see Sankt-Peterburg
Pietarsaari see Jakobstad
85 K23 **Pietermaritzburg** var. Maritzburg. KwaZulu/Natal, E South Africa 29.34S 30.23E
85 K20 **Pietersburg** Northern. NE South Africa 23.54S 29.22E
109 K24 **Pietraperzia** Sicilia, Italy, C Mediterranean Sea 37.25N 14.07E
109 N22 **Pietra Spada, Passo della** pass SW Italy 38.30N 16.20E
85 K22 **Piet Retief** Mpumalanga, E South Africa 27.00S 30.49E
118 I9 **Pietrosul, Vârful** prev. Vîrful Pietrosu. ▲ N Romania 47.36N 24.39E
118 J10 **Pietrosul, Vârful** prev. Vîrful Pietrosu. ▲ N Romania 47.06N 25.09E
Pietrosu, Vîrful see Pietrosul, Vârful
108 I6 **Pieve di Cadore** Veneto, NE Italy 46.27N 12.22E
12 C18 **Pigeon Bay** lake bay Ontario, S Canada
29 X8 **Piggott** Arkansas, C USA 36.22N 90.11W
85 L21 **Piggs Peak** NW Swaziland 25.58S 31.16E
Pigs, Bay of see Cochinos, Bahía de
63 A23 **Pigüé** Buenos Aires, E Argentina 37.37S 62.24W
43 O12 **Piguícas** ▲ C Mexico 21.08N 99.37W
200 Qq15 **Piha Passage** passage S Tonga
Pihkva Järv see Pskov, Lake
95 N18 **Pihlajavesi** ◎ SE Finland
95 J18 **Pihlava** Länsi-Suomi, W Finland 61.33N 21.36E
95 L16 **Pihtipudas** Länsi-Suomi, W Finland 63.20N 25.37E
42 L14 **Pihuamo** Jalisco, SW Mexico 19.14N 103.21W
201 U11 **Piis Moen** var. Pis. atoll Chuuk Islands, C Micronesia
43 U17 **Pijijiapán** Chiapas, SE Mexico 15.39N 93.13W
100 G12 **Pijnacker** Zuid-Holland, W Netherlands 52.01N 4.25E
44 H5 **Pijol, Pico** ▲ NW Honduras 15.07N 87.39W
Pikaar see Bikar Atoll
128 I13 **Pikalevo** Leningradskaya Oblast', NW Russian Federation 59.33N 34.04E
196 M15 **Pikelot** island Caroline Islands, C Micronesia
32 M5 **Pike River** ≈ Wisconsin, N USA
39 T5 **Pikes Peak** ▲ Colorado, C USA 38.51N 105.06W
23 P6 **Pikeville** Kentucky, S USA 37.28N 82.31W
22 L9 **Pikeville** Tennessee, S USA 35.36N 85.11W
Pikinni see Bikini Atoll
81 H18 **Pikounda** La Sangha, C Congo 0.30N 16.43E
112 G9 **Piła** Ger. Schneidemühl. Wielkopolskie, C Poland 53.09N 16.43E
64 N6 **Pilagá, Riacho** ≈ NE Argentina
63 D20 **Pilar** Buenos Aires, E Argentina 34.28S 58.55W
64 N7 **Pilar** var. Villa del Pilar. Neembucú, S Paraguay 26.55S 58.19W
64 N6 **Pilcomayo, Río** ≈ C South America
153 R12 **Pildon** Rus. Pil'don. C Tajikistan 39.10N 71.00E
Piles see Pylés
Pilgram see Pelhřimov
179 Q11 **Pili** Luzon, N Philippines 13.31N 123.15E
158 L10 **Pilibhit** Uttar Pradesh, N India 28.37N 79.48E
112 M13 **Pilica** ≈ C Poland
117 G16 **Pílio** ▲ C Greece
113 J22 **Pilisvörösvár** Pest, N Hungary 47.37N 18.55E
67 G15 **Pillar Bay** bay Ascension Island, C Atlantic Ocean
191 P17 **Pillar, Cape** headland Tasmania, SE Australia 43.13S 147.58E
Pillau see Baltiysk
191 R5 **Pilliga** New South Wales, SE Australia 30.22S 148.53E
46 H8 **Pilón** Granma, E Cuba 19.54N 77.20W
Pilos see Pýlos
9 W17 **Pilot Mound** Manitoba, S Canada 49.12N 98.49W
23 S8 **Pilot Mountain** North Carolina, SE USA 36.23N 80.28W
41 O14 **Pilot Point** Alaska, USA 57.33N 95.34W
27 T5 **Pilot Point** Texas, SW USA 33.24N 96.57W
34 K11 **Pilot Rock** Oregon, NW USA 45.28N 118.49W
40 M11 **Pilot Station** Alaska, USA 61.56N 162.52W
Pilsen see Plzeň
113 K18 **Pilsko** ▲ N Slovakia 49.31N 19.21E
Pilten see Piltene
120 D8 **Piltene** Ger. Pilten. Ventspils, W Latvia 57.14N 21.41E
113 M16 **Pilzno** Podkarpackie, SE Poland 49.58N 21.18E
Pilzno see Plzeň
39 N14 **Pima** Arizona, SW USA 32.49N 109.50W
60 H13 **Pimenta** Pará, N Brazil 4.32S 56.17W
61 F16 **Pimenta Bueno** Rondônia, W Brazil 11.40S 61.13W
58 B11 **Pimentel** Lambayeque, W Peru 6.51S 79.52W
107 S6 **Pina** Aragón, NE Spain 41.28N 0.31W
121 I20 **Pina** Rus. Pina. ≈ SW Belarus
42 E2 **Pinacate, Sierra del** ▲ NW Mexico 31.49N 113.30W
65 H22 **Pináculo, Cerro** ▲ S Argentina 50.46S 72.07W
203 X11 **Pinaki** atoll Îles Tuamotu, E French Polynesia
39 N15 **Pinaleno Mountains** ▲ Arizona, SW USA
179 Pp12 **Pinamalayan** Mindoro, N Philippines 13.00N 121.30E
174 Kk8 **Pinang** Borneo, C Indonesia 0.36N 109.10W
173 G3 **Pinang** var. Penang. ◈ state Peninsular Malaysia
Pinang see Pinang, Pulau, Peninsular Malaysia
Pinang see George Town
173 G3 **Pinang, Pulau** var. Penang, Pinang; prev. Prince of Wales Island. island Peninsular Malaysia
46 B5 **Pinar del Río** Pinar del Río, W Cuba 22.23N 83.42W
116 N11 **Pınarhisar** Kırklareli, NW Turkey 41.37N 27.30E
179 P10 **Pinatubo, Mount** Ѫ Luzon, N Philippines 15.07N 120.21E
9 Y16 **Pinawa** Manitoba, S Canada 50.09N 95.52W
9 Q17 **Pincher Creek** Alberta, SW Canada 49.31N 113.52W
32 L16 **Pinckneyville** Illinois, N USA 38.04N 89.22W
Pîncota see Pâncota
113 L15 **Pińczów** Świętokrzyskie, C Poland 50.30N 20.31E
155 U7 **Pind Dādan Khān** Punjab, E Pakistan 32.36N 73.07E
Píndhos/Píndhos Óros see Píndos
155 V8 **Pindi Bhattiān** Punjab, E Pakistan 31.54N 73.19E
155 U6 **Pindi Gheb** Punjab, E Pakistan 33.15N 72.16E
117 D15 **Píndos** var. Píndhos Óros, Eng. Pindus Mountains; prev. Píndhos. ▲ C Greece
Pindus Mountains see Píndos
20 J16 **Pine Barrens** physical region New Jersey, NE USA
29 V12 **Pine Bluff** Arkansas, C USA 34.13N 92.01W
25 X11 **Pine Castle** Florida, SE USA 28.28N 81.22W
31 V7 **Pine City** Minnesota, N USA 45.49N 92.55W
189 P2 **Pine Creek** Northern Territory, N Australia 13.51S 131.51E
37 V4 **Pine Creek** ≈ Nevada, W USA
20 F13 **Pine Creek** ≈ Pennsylvania, NE USA
29 Q13 **Pine Creek Lake** ⊡ Oklahoma, C USA
35 T15 **Pinedale** Wyoming, C USA 42.52N 109.51W
9 X15 **Pine Dock** Manitoba, S Canada 51.34N 96.47W
9 Y16 **Pine Falls** Manitoba, S Canada 50.29N 96.12W
37 R10 **Pine Flat Lake** ⊡ California, W USA
129 N8 **Pinega** Arkhangel'skaya Oblast', NW Russian Federation 64.40N 43.24E
129 N8 **Pinega** ≈ NW Russian Federation
13 N12 **Pine Hill** Quebec, SE Canada 45.44N 74.30W
9 T12 **Pinehouse Lake** ◎ Saskatchewan, C Canada
23 T10 **Pinehurst** North Carolina, SE USA 35.12N 79.28W
117 D19 **Pineiós** ≈ S Greece
117 E16 **Pineiós** var. Piniós; anc. Peneius. ≈ C Greece
31 W10 **Pine Island** Minnesota, N USA 44.12N 92.39W
25 V15 **Pine Island** island Florida, SE USA
204 K10 **Pine Island Glacier** glacier Antarctica
27 X9 **Pineland** Texas, SW USA 31.15N 93.58W
25 V13 **Pinellas Park** Florida, SE USA 27.50N 82.42W
8 M13 **Pine Pass** pass British Columbia, W Canada 55.21N 122.43W
15 I9 **Pine Point** Northwest Territories, W Canada 60.52N 114.30W
30 K12 **Pine Ridge** South Dakota, N USA 43.01N 102.33W
31 U6 **Pine River** Minnesota, N USA 46.43N 94.24W
33 Q8 **Pine River** ≈ Michigan, N USA
32 M4 **Pine River** ≈ Wisconsin, N USA
108 A8 **Pinerolo** Piemonte, NE Italy 44.56N 7.21E
27 W6 **Pines, Lake O' the** ⊡ Texas, SW USA
Pines, The Isle of the see Juventud, Isla de la
Pine Tree State see Maine
23 N7 **Pineville** Kentucky, S USA 36.45N 83.42W
24 H7 **Pineville** Louisiana, S USA 31.19N 92.25W
29 R8 **Pineville** Missouri, C USA 36.35N 94.22W
23 R10 **Pineville** North Carolina, SE USA 35.04N 80.53W
23 Q6 **Pineville** West Virginia, NE USA 37.34N 81.32W
35 V8 **Piney Buttes** physical region Montana, NW USA
169 W9 **Ping'an** Jilin, NE China 44.36N 127.13E
166 H14 **Pingbian** var. Pingbian Miaozu Zizhixian. Yunnan, SW China 22.51N 103.28E
163 S9 **Pingdingshan** Henan, C China 33.52N 113.19E
167 R4 **Pingdu** Shandong, E China 36.48N 119.56E
201 W16 **Pingelap Atoll** atoll Caroline Islands, E Micronesia
166 K14 **Pingguo** Guangxi Zhuangzu Zizhiqu, S China 23.22N 107.34E
167 Q13 **Pinghe** Fujian, SE China 24.30N 117.19E
P'ing-hsiang see Pingxiang
167 N10 **Pingjiang** Hunan, S China 28.44N 113.33E
Pingkiang see Harbin
166 L8 **Pingli** Shaanxi, C China 32.24N 109.17E
165 W10 **Pingliang** var. P'ing-liang. Gansu, C China 35.31N 106.46E
165 W8 **Pingluo** Ningxia, N China 38.55N 106.31E
Pingma see Tiandong
178 H9 **Ping, Mae Nam** ≈ W Thailand
167 Q1 **Pingquan** Hebei, E China 41.01N 118.34E
31 P5 **Pingree** North Dakota, N USA 47.07N 98.54W
Pingsiang see Pingxiang
167 S14 **P'ingtung** Jap. Heitō. S Taiwan 22.43N 120.26E
166 I8 **Pingwu** Sichuan, C China 32.33N 104.32E
166 J15 **Pingxiang** Guangxi Zhuangzu Zizhiqu, S China 22.03N 106.43E
167 O11 **Pingxiang** var. P'ing-hsiang; prev. Pingsiang. Jiangxi, S China 27.42N 113.49E
167 S11 **Pingyang** Zhejiang, SE China 27.46N 120.37E
167 P5 **Pingyi** Shandong, E China 35.30N 117.37E
167 P5 **Pingyin** Shandong, E China 36.18N 116.24E
62 H13 **Pinhalzinho** Santa Catarina, S Brazil 26.53S 52.57W
62 I12 **Pinhão** Paraná, S Brazil 25.46S 51.32W
63 H17 **Pinheiro Machado** Rio Grande do Sul, S Brazil 31.34S 53.22W
106 I7 **Pinhel** Guarda, N Portugal 40.46N 7.03W
Piniós see Pineiós
195 R10 **Pinipel Island** island Green Islands, NE PNG
173 Ff8 **Pini, Pulau** island Kepulauan Batu, W Indonesia
111 Y7 **Pinka** ≈ SE Austria
111 X7 **Pinkafeld** Burgenland, SE Austria 47.18N 16.09E
Pinkiang see Harbin
8 M12 **Pink Mountain** British Columbia, W Canada 57.01N 122.36W
177 G3 **Pinlebu** Sagaing, N Burma 24.02N 95.21E
40 J12 **Pinnacle Island** island Alaska, USA
188 I12 **Pinnacles, The** tourist site Western Australia
190 K10 **Pinnaroo** South Australia 35.17S 140.54E
Pinne see Pniewy
102 I9 **Pinneberg** Schleswig-Holstein, N Germany 53.40N 9.48E
117 I15 **Pínnes, Akrotírio** headland N Greece 40.06N 24.19E
Pinos, Isla de see Juventud, Isla de la
37 R14 **Pinos, Mount** ▲ California, W USA 34.48N 119.09W
107 R12 **Pinoso** País Valenciano, E Spain 38.25N 1.01W
107 N14 **Pinos-Puente** Andalucía, S Spain 37.16N 3.46W
43 Q17 **Pinotepa Nacional** var. Santiago Pinotepa Nacional. Oaxaca, SE Mexico 16.19N 98.02W
116 F13 **Pínovo** ▲ N Greece 41.06N 22.19E
197 K7 **Pins, Île des** var. Kunyé. island E New Caledonia
121 I20 **Pinsk** Pol. Pińsk. Brestskaya Voblasts', SW Belarus 52.07N 26.07E
12 D18 **Pins, Pointe aux** headland Ontario, S Canada 42.14N 81.53W
59 B16 **Pinta, Isla** var. Abingdon. island Galapagos Islands, Ecuador, E Pacific Ocean
129 Q12 **Pinyug** Kirovskaya Oblast', NW Russian Federation 60.12N 47.45E
59 B17 **Pinzón, Isla** var. Duncan Island. island Galapagos Islands, Ecuador, E Pacific Ocean
37 Y8 **Pioche** Nevada, W USA 37.54N 114.27W
108 F13 **Piombino** Toscana, C Italy 42.54N 10.30E
(0) C9 **Pioneer Fracture Zone** tectonic feature NE Pacific Ocean
126 I2 **Pioner, Ostrov** island Severnaya Zemlya, N Russian Federation
120 A13 **Pionerskiy** Ger. Neukuhren. Kaliningradskaya Oblast', W Russian Federation 54.57N 20.16E
112 N13 **Pionki** Mazowieckie, C Poland 51.28N 21.27E
192 L9 **Piopio** Waikato, North Island, NZ 38.27S 175.00E
112 K13 **Piotrków Trybunalski** Ger. Petrikau, Rus. Petrokov. Łodzkie, C Poland 51.25N 19.42E
158 F12 **Pīpār Road** Rājasthān, N India 26.25N 73.28E
117 I16 **Pipéri** island Vóreioi Sporádes, Greece, Aegean Sea
31 S10 **Pipestone** Minnesota, N USA 44.00N 96.19W
10 C9 **Pipestone** ≈ Ontario, C Canada
63 E21 **Pipinas** Buenos Aires, E Argentina 35.31S 57.19W
155 T7 **Piplān** prev. Liaqatabad. Punjab, E Pakistan 32.19N 71.21E
13 R5 **Pipmuacan, Réservoir** ⊡ Quebec, SE Canada
Piqan see Shanshan
33 R13 **Piqua** Ohio, N USA 40.08N 84.14W
107 P5 **Piqueras, Puerto de** pass N Spain 42.04N 2.35W
62 H11 **Piquiri, Rio** ≈ S Brazil
62 L9 **Piracicaba** São Paulo, S Brazil 22.44S 47.33W
Piraeus/Piraiévs see Peiraías
62 K10 **Piraju** São Paulo, S Brazil 23.12S 49.24W
62 K9 **Pirajuí** São Paulo, S Brazil 21.58S 49.27W

◆ Country
● Country Capital
◇ Dependent Territory
○ Dependent Territory Capital
◈ Administrative Region
✕ International Airport
▲ Mountain
▲ Mountain Range
Ѫ Volcano
≈ River
◎ Lake
⊡ Reservoir

PIRÁMIDE, CERRO – POMMERSCHE BUCHT

65 G21 **Pirámide, Cerro** ▲ S Chile 49.06S 73.32W
Piramiva *see* Pyramíva
111 R13 **Piran** *It.* Pirano. SW Slovenia 45.31N 13.36E
64 N6 **Pirané** Formosa, N Argentina 25.42S 59.06W
61 J18 **Piranhas** Goiás, S Brazil 16.24S 51.51W
Pirano *see* Piran
148 I4 **Pīrānshahr** Āzarbāyjān-e Bākhtarī, NW Iran 36.46N 45.10E
61 M19 **Pirapora** Minas Gerais, NE Brazil 17.19S 44.54W
62 I9 **Pirapòzinho** São Paulo, S Brazil 22.17S 51.31W
63 G19 **Piraraja** Lavalleja, S Uruguay 33.43S 54.45W
62 L9 **Pirassununga** São Paulo, S Brazil 21.58S 47.23W
47 V6 **Pirata, Monte** ▲ E Puerto Rico 18.06N 65.33W
62 I13 **Piratuba** Santa Catarina, S Brazil 27.26S 51.47W
116 I9 **Pirdop** *prev.* Srednogorie. Sofiya, W Bulgaria 42.44N 24.09E
203 P7 **Pirea** Tahiti, W French Polynesia
61 K18 **Pirenópolis** Goiás, S Brazil 15.48S 49.00W
159 S13 **Pirganj** Rajshahi, NW Bangladesh 25.51N 88.25E
Pirgi *see* Pyrgí
Pírgos *see* Pýrgos
63 F20 **Piriápolis** Maldonado, S Uruguay 34.51S 55.15W
116 G11 **Pirin** ▲▲ SW Bulgaria
Pirineos *see* Pyrenees
60 N13 **Piripiri** Piauí, E Brazil 4.15S 41.46W
120 H4 **Pirita** *var.* Pirita Jõgi. ≈ NW Estonia
Pirita Jõgi *see* Pirita
56 J6 **Píritu** Portuguesa, N Venezuela 9.21N 69.16W
95 L18 **Pirkkala** Länsi-Suomi, W Finland 61.27N 23.47E
103 F20 **Pirmasens** Rheinland-Pfalz, SW Germany 49.12N 7.36E
103 P16 **Pirna** Sachsen, E Germany 50.57N 13.56E
Piroe *see* Piru
115 Q15 **Pirot** Serbia, SE Yugoslavia 43.12N 22.34E
158 H6 **Pīr Panjāl Range** ▲▲ NE India
45 W16 **Pirre, Cerro** ▲ SE Panama 7.54N 77.42W
143 Y11 **Pirsaat** *Rus.* Pirsagat. ≈ E Azerbaijan
Pirsagat *see* Pirsaat
149 V11 **Pīr Shūrān, Selseleh-ye** ▲▲ SE Iran
94 M12 **Pirttikoski** Lappi, N Finland 66.20N 27.08E
Pirttikylä *see* Pörtom
175 T11 **Piru** *prev.* Piroe. Pulau Seram, E Indonesia 3.01S 128.10E
Piryatin *see* Pyryatyn
Pis *see* Piis Moen
108 F11 **Pisa** *var.* Pisae. Toscana, C Italy 43.43N 10.22E
Pisae *see* Pisa
176 Uu10 **Pisang, Kepulauan** *island group* E Indonesia
176 Xx11 **Pisapa** Irian Jaya, E Indonesia 3.25S 137.04E
201 V12 **Pisar** *atoll* Chuuk Islands, C Micronesia
Pisaurum *see* Pesaro
12 M10 **Piscatosine, Lac** ◎ Quebec, SE Canada
111 W7 **Pischeldorf** Steiermark, SE Austria 47.11N 15.48E
Pischk *see* Simeria
109 L19 **Pisciotta** Campania, S Italy 40.07N 15.13E
59 E16 **Pisco** Ica, SW Peru 13.46S 76.12W
118 G9 **Pişcolt** *Hung.* Piskolt. Satu Mare, NW Romania 47.34N 22.18E
59 E16 **Pisco, Río** ≈ E Peru
113 C18 **Písek** Budějovický Kraj, S Czech Republic 49.18N 14.07E
33 R14 **Pisgah** Ohio, N USA 39.19N 84.22W
164 F9 **Pishan** *var.* Guma. Xinjiang Uygur Zizhiqu, NW China 37.36N 78.45E
119 N8 **Pishchanka** Vinnyts'ka Oblast', C Ukraine 48.12N 28.52E
115 K21 **Pishë** Fier, SW Albania 40.40N 19.22E
149 X14 **Pīshīn** Sīstān va Balūchestān, SE Iran 26.05N 61.46E
155 O9 **Pishīn** North-West Frontier Province, NW Pakistan 30.39N 66.52E
155 N11 **Pishin Lora** *var.* Psein Lora, *Pash.* Pseyn Bowr. ≈ SW Pakistan
Pishma *see* Pizhma
Pishpek *see* Bishkek
175 Q13 **Pising** Pulau Kabaena, C Indonesia 5.07S 121.50E
Pisino *see* Pazin
Piski *see* Simeria
Piskolt *see* Pişcolt
153 Q9 **Piskom** *Rus.* Pskem. ≈ E Uzbekistan
Piskom Tizmasi *see* Pskemskiy Khrebet
37 P13 **Pismo Beach** California, W USA 35.08N 120.38W
79 P12 **Pissila** C Burkina 13.07N 0.51W
64 H8 **Pissis, Monte** ▲ N Argentina 27.45S 68.43W
43 X12 **Piste** Yucatán, E Mexico 20.40N 88.34W
109 O18 **Pisticci** Basilicata, S Italy 40.22N 16.33E
108 F11 **Pistoia** *anc.* Pistoria, Pistoriæ. Toscana, C Italy 43.57N 10.52E
34 E15 **Pistol River** Oregon, NW USA 42.13N 124.23W
Pistoria/Pistoriæ *see* Pistoia
13 U5 **Pistuacanis** ≈ Quebec, SE Canada
Pistyan *see* Piešťany
106 M5 **Pisuerga** ≈ N Spain
112 N8 **Pisz** *Ger.* Johannisburg. Warmińsko-Mazurskie, NE Poland 53.37N 21.49E
78 I13 **Pita** Moyenne-Guinée, NW Guinea 11.04N 12.15W
56 D12 **Pitalito** Huila, S Colombia 1.51N 76.01W
62 I11 **Pitanga** Paraná, S Brazil 24.45S 51.43W
190 M9 **Pitarpunga Lake** *salt lake* New South Wales, SE Australia
199 M11 **Pitcairn Island** *island* S Pitcairn Islands
199 M11 **Pitcairn Islands** ◇ *UK dependent territory* C Pacific Ocean
95 J14 **Piteå** Norrbotten, N Sweden 65.19N 21.30E
94 I13 **Piteälven** ≈ N Sweden
118 I13 **Pitești** Argeș, S Romania 44.53N 24.49E
Pithagorio *see* Pythagóreio
188 I12 **Pithara** Western Australia 30.31S 116.38E
105 N6 **Pithiviers** Loiret, C France 48.10N 2.15E
158 L9 **Pithorāgarh** Uttar Pradesh, N India 29.34N 80.12E
196 B16 **Piti** W Guam 13.28N 144.42E
108 G13 **Pitigliano** Toscana, C Italy 42.38N 11.40E
42 F3 **Pitiquito** Sonora, NW Mexico 30.39N 112.00W
Pitkäranta *see* Pitkyaranta
40 M11 **Pitkas Point** Alaska, USA 62.01N 163.17W
128 H11 **Pitkyaranta** *Fin.* Pitkäranta. Respublika Kareliya, NW Russian Federation 61.34N 31.27E
98 J10 **Pitlochry** C Scotland, UK 56.46N 3.48W
20 I16 **Pitman** New Jersey, NE USA 39.43N 75.06W
114 G8 **Pitomača** Virovitica-Podravina, NE Croatia 45.57N 17.14E
37 O2 **Pit River** ≈ California, W USA
65 G15 **Pitrufquén** Araucanía, S Chile 38.58S 72.40W
Pitsanulok *see* Phitsanulok
Pitschen *see* Byczyna
Pitsunda *see* Bichvint'a
111 X6 **Pitten** ≈ E Austria
8 J14 **Pitt Island** *island* British Columbia, W Canada
Pitt Island *see* Makin
24 M3 **Pittsboro** Mississippi, S USA 33.55N 89.20W
23 T9 **Pittsboro** North Carolina, SE USA 35.46N 79.21W
29 R7 **Pittsburg** Kansas, C USA 37.24N 94.42W
27 W6 **Pittsburg** Texas, SW USA 33.00N 94.58W
20 B14 **Pittsburgh** Pennsylvania, NE USA 40.26N 80.00W
32 J14 **Pittsfield** Illinois, N USA 39.36N 90.48W
21 R6 **Pittsfield** Maine, NE USA 44.46N 69.22W
20 L11 **Pittsfield** Massachusetts, NE USA 42.27N 73.15W
191 U3 **Pittsworth** Queensland, E Australia 27.43S 151.36E
64 I8 **Pituil** La Rioja, NW Argentina 28.33S 67.24W
58 A10 **Piura** Piura, NW Peru 5.11S 80.41W
58 A9 **Piura** *off.* Departamento de Piura. ◈ *department* NW Peru
37 S13 **Piute Peak** ▲ California, W USA 35.27N 118.24W
115 J15 **Piva** ≈ SW Yugoslavia
119 V5 **Pivdenne** Kharkivs'ka Oblast', E Ukraine 49.52N 36.04E
119 P8 **Pivdennyy Buh** *Rus.* Yuzhnyy Bug. ≈ S Ukraine
56 F5 **Pivijay** Magdalena, N Colombia 10.28N 74.37W
111 T13 **Pivka** *prev.* Šent Peter, *Ger.* Sankt Peter, *It.* San Pietro del Carso. SW Slovenia 45.41N 14.12E
119 U13 **Pivnichno-Kryms'kyy Kanal** *canal* S Ukraine
115 J15 **Pivsko Jezero** ◎ SW Yugoslavia
113 M18 **Piwniczna** Małopolskie, S Poland 49.26N 20.43E
37 R12 **Pixley** California, W USA 35.58N 119.18W
129 Q15 **Pizhma** *var.* Pishma. ≈ NW Russian Federation
11 U13 **Placentia** Newfoundland, SE Canada 47.12N 53.58W
Placentia *see* Piacenza
11 U13 **Placentia Bay** *inlet* Newfoundland, SE Canada
179 Qq12 **Placer** Masbate, N Philippines 11.54N 123.54E
37 P7 **Placerville** California, W USA 38.42N 120.48W
46 F5 **Placetas** Villa Clara, C Cuba 22.18N 79.40W
115 Q18 **Plačkovica** ▲▲ E FYR Macedonia
38 L2 **Plain City** Utah, W USA 41.18N 112.05W
24 G4 **Plain Dealing** Louisiana, S USA 32.54N 93.42W
33 O14 **Plainfield** Indiana, N USA 39.42N 86.18W
20 K14 **Plainfield** New Jersey, NE USA 40.37N 74.25W
35 O8 **Plains** Montana, NW USA 47.27N 114.52W
26 L6 **Plains** Texas, SW USA 33.11N 102.49W
31 X10 **Plainview** Minnesota, N USA 44.10N 92.10W
31 Q13 **Plainview** Nebraska, C USA 42.21N 97.47W
27 N4 **Plainview** Texas, SW USA 34.12N 101.43W
28 K4 **Plainville** Kansas, C USA 39.13N 99.18W
117 L25 **Pláka, Akrotírio** *headland* Kríti, Greece, E Mediterranean Sea 35.10N 26.19E
117 J15 **Pláka, Akrotírio** *headland* Límnos, E Greece 40.02N 25.25E
115 N19 **Plakenska Planina** ▲▲ SW FYR Macedonia
46 K5 **Plana Cays** *islets* SE Bahamas
107 S12 **Plana, Isla** *var.* Nueva Tabarca. *island* E Spain
61 L18 **Planaltina** Goiás, S Brazil 15.34S 47.27W
85 O14 **Planalto Moçambicano** *plateau* N Mozambique
114 N10 **Plandište** Serbia, NE Yugoslavia 45.13N 21.07E
102 N13 **Plane** ≈ NE Germany
56 E6 **Planeta Rica** Córdoba, NW Colombia 8.24N 75.39W
31 P11 **Plankinton** South Dakota, N USA 43.43N 98.28W
32 M11 **Plano** Illinois, N USA 41.39N 88.32W
27 U6 **Plano** Texas, SW USA 33.01N 96.42W
25 W12 **Plant City** Florida, SE USA 28.01N 82.06W
24 J9 **Plaquemine** Louisiana, S USA 30.17N 91.13W
106 K9 **Plasencia** Extremadura, W Spain 40.01N 6.04W
112 P7 **Płaska** Podlaskie, NE Poland 53.55N 23.18E
114 C10 **Plaški** Karlovac, C Croatia 45.04N 15.21E
115 N19 **Plasnica** SW FYR Macedonia 41.28N 21.07E
125 E12 **Plast** Chelyabinskaya Oblast', C Russian Federation 54.24N 60.51E
11 N14 **Plaster Rock** New Brunswick, SE Canada 46.55N 67.24W
109 J24 **Platani** *anc.* Halycus. ≈ Sicilia, Italy, C Mediterranean Sea
117 G17 **Plataniá** Thessalía, C Greece 39.09N 23.15E
117 G24 **Plátanos** Kríti, Greece, E Mediterranean Sea 35.27N 23.34E
67 H18 **Plata, Río de la** *var.* River Plate. *estuary* Argentina/Uruguay
79 V15 **Plateau** ◈ *state* C Nigeria
81 G19 **Plateaux** *var.* Région des Plateaux. ◈ *province* C Congo
94 P1 **Platen, Kapp** *headland* NE Svalbard 80.30N 22.46E
Plate, River *see* Plata, Río de la
101 G22 **Plate Taille, Lac de la** *var.* L'Eau d'Heure. ◎ SE Belgium
Plathe *see* Płoty
41 N13 **Platinum** Alaska, USA 59.00N 161.49W
56 F5 **Plato** Magdalena, N Colombia 9.47N 74.46W
31 O11 **Platte** South Dakota, N USA 43.20N 98.51W
29 R3 **Platte City** Missouri, C USA 39.22N 94.46W
Plattensee *see* Balaton
29 R3 **Platte River** ≈ Iowa/Missouri, USA
31 Q15 **Platte River** ≈ Nebraska, C USA
39 T3 **Platteville** Colorado, C USA 40.13N 104.49W
32 K9 **Platteville** Wisconsin, N USA 42.44N 90.27W
103 N21 **Plattling** Bayern, SE Germany 48.45N 12.52E
29 R3 **Plattsburg** Missouri, C USA 39.34N 94.27W
20 L6 **Plattsburgh** New York, NE USA 44.42N 73.28W
31 S15 **Plattsmouth** Nebraska, C USA 41.00N 95.52W
103 M17 **Plauen** *var.* Plauen im Vogtland. Sachsen, E Germany 50.30N 12.08E
Plauen im Vogtland *see* Plauen
102 M10 **Plauer See** ◎ NE Germany
115 L16 **Plav** Montenegro, SW Yugoslavia 42.36N 19.57E
120 I10 **Pļaviņas** *Ger.* Stockmannshof. Aizkraukle, S Latvia 56.37N 25.40E
130 K5 **Plavsk** Tul'skaya Oblast', W Russian Federation 53.42N 37.21E
43 Z12 **Playa del Carmen** Quintana Roo, E Mexico 20.37N 87.04W
42 J12 **Playa Los Corchos** Nayarit, SW Mexico 22.31N 105.28W
39 P16 **Playas Lake** ◎ New Mexico, SW USA
43 S15 **Playa Vicenté** Veracruz-Llave, SE Mexico 17.42N 95.01W
178 K11 **Plây Cu** *var.* Pleiku. Gia Lai, C Vietnam 13.57N 108.01E
30 L3 **Plaza** North Dakota, N USA 48.00N 102.00W
65 I15 **Plaza Huincul** Neuquén, C Argentina 38.54S 69.10W
38 L3 **Pleasant Grove** Utah, W USA 40.21N 111.44W
31 V14 **Pleasant Hill** Iowa, C USA 41.34N 93.31W
29 R4 **Pleasant Hill** Missouri, C USA 38.47N 94.16W
Pleasant Island *see* Nauru
38 K13 **Pleasant, Lake** ⊠ Arizona, SW USA
21 P8 **Pleasant Mountain** ▲ Maine, NE USA 44.01N 70.47W
29 R5 **Pleasanton** Kansas, C USA 38.09N 94.43W
27 R12 **Pleasanton** Texas, SW USA 28.58N 98.28W
193 G20 **Pleasant Point** Canterbury, South Island, NZ 44.16S 171.09E
21 R5 **Pleasant River** ≈ Maine, NE USA
20 J17 **Pleasantville** New Jersey, NE USA 39.22N 74.31W
105 N12 **Pléaux** Cantal, C France 45.08N 2.10E
113 B19 **Plechý** *Ger.* Plöckenstein. ▲ Austria/Czech Republic 48.45N 13.50E
Pleebo *see* Plibo
Pleihari *see* Pelaihari
Pleiku *see* Plây Cu
103 M16 **Pleisse** ≈ E Germany
Plencia *see* Plentzia
192 O7 **Plenty, Bay of** *bay* North Island, NZ
35 Y6 **Plentywood** Montana, NW USA 48.46N 104.33W
107 O2 **Plentzia** *var.* Plencia. País Vasco, N Spain 43.25N 2.56W
104 H5 **Plérin** Côtes d'Armor, NW France 48.33N 2.46W
128 M10 **Plesetsk** Arkhangel'skaya Oblast', NW Russian Federation 62.40N 40.14E
Pleshchenitsy *see* Plyeshchanitsy
Pleskau *see* Pskov
Pleskauer See *see* Pskov, Lake
Pleskava *see* Pskov
114 E8 **Pleso International** ✕ (Zagreb) Zagreb, NW Croatia 45.45N 16.00E
Pless *see* Pszczyna
13 Q11 **Plessisville** Quebec, SE Canada 46.14N 71.45W
112 H12 **Pleszew** Wielkopolskie, C Poland 51.54N 17.46E
10 L10 **Plétipi, Lac** ◎ Quebec, SE Canada
103 F15 **Plettenberg** Nordrhein-Westfalen, W Germany 51.13N 7.52E
116 I8 **Pleven** *prev.* Plevna. Pleven, N Bulgaria 43.25N 24.36E
116 I8 **Pleven** ◈ *province* N Bulgaria
Plevlja/Plevlje *see* Pljevlja
Plevna *see* Pleven
Plezzo *see* Bovec
Pliberk *see* Bleiburg
78 L17 **Plibo** *var.* Pleebo. SE Liberia 4.37N 7.40W
124 Oo13 **Pliny Trench** *undersea feature* C Mediterranean Sea
120 K13 **Plisa** *Rus.* Plissa. Vitsyebskaya Voblasts', N Belarus 55.12N 27.58E
Plissa *see* Plisa
114 D11 **Plitvica Selo** Lika-Senj, W Croatia 44.53N 15.36E
114 D11 **Plješevica** ▲▲ C Croatia
115 K14 **Pljevlja** *prev.* Plevlja, Plevlje. Montenegro, N Yugoslavia 43.21N 19.21E
Ploça *see* Ploçë
Plocce *see* Ploče
115 G15 **Ploče** *It.* Plocce; *prev.* Kardeljevo. Dubrovnik-Neretva, SE Croatia 43.02N 17.25E
115 K22 **Ploçë** *var.* Ploça. Vlorë, SW Albania 40.24N 19.41E
112 K11 **Płock** *Ger.* Plozk. Mazowieckie, C Poland 52.31N 19.40E
111 Q10 **Plöcken Pass** *Ger.* Plöckenpass, *It.* Passo di Monte Croce Carnico. *pass* SW Austria 46.36N 12.55E
Plöckenstein *see* Plechý
101 B19 **Ploegsteert** Hainaut, W Belgium 50.45N 2.52E
104 H6 **Ploërmel** Morbihan, NW France 47.57N 2.24W
Ploești *see* Ploiești
118 K13 **Ploiești** *prev.* Ploești. Prahova, SE Romania 44.56N 26.03E
117 L17 **Plomári** *prev.* Plomárion. Lésvos, E Greece 38.58N 26.24E
Plomárion *see* Plomári
105 O12 **Plomb du Cantal** ▲ C France 45.03N 2.48E
191 V6 **Plomer, Point** *headland* New South Wales, SE Australia 31.19S 153.00E
102 J8 **Plön** Schleswig-Holstein, N Germany 54.10N 10.25E
112 L11 **Płońsk** Mazowieckie, C Poland 52.37N 20.22E
121 J20 **Plotnitsa** *Rus.* Plotnitsa. Brestskaya Voblasts', SW Belarus 52.03N 26.39E
112 E8 **Płoty** *Ger.* Plathe. Zachodniopomorskie, NW Poland 53.48N 15.16E
104 G7 **Plouay** Morbihan, NW France 47.54N 3.14W
113 D15 **Ploučnice** *Ger.* Polzen. ≈ NE Czech Republic
116 I10 **Plovdiv** *prev.* Eumolpias, *anc.* Evmolpia, Philippopolis, *Lat.* Trimontium. Plovdiv, C Bulgaria 42.08N 24.47
116 J11 **Plovdiv** ◈ *province* C Bulgaria
32 L6 **Plover** Wisconsin, N USA 44.30N 89.33W
Plozk *see* Płock
29 U11 **Plumerville** Arkansas, C USA 35.09N 92.38W
21 P10 **Plum Island** *island* Massachusetts, NE USA
34 M9 **Plummer** Idaho, NW USA 47.19N 116.54W
85 J18 **Plumtree** Matabeleland South, SW Zimbabwe 20.27S 27.49E
120 D11 **Plungė** Plungė, W Lithuania 55.55N 21.53E
115 J15 **Plužine** Montenegro, SW Yugoslavia 43.08N 18.49E
121 K14 **Plyeshchanitsy** *Rus.* Pleshchenitsy. Minskaya Voblasts', N Belarus 54.25N 27.49E
47 V10 **Plymouth** ○ (Montserrat) SW Montserrat 16.39N 62.11W
99 I24 **Plymouth** SW England, UK 50.22N 4.10W
33 O11 **Plymouth** Indiana, N USA 41.19N 86.19W
21 P12 **Plymouth** Massachusetts, NE USA 41.57N 70.40W
21 N8 **Plymouth** New Hampshire, NE USA 43.43N 71.39W
23 X9 **Plymouth** North Carolina, SE USA 35.52N 76.45W
32 M8 **Plymouth** Wisconsin, N USA 43.48N 87.58W
99 J20 **Plynlimon** ▲ C Wales, UK 52.27N 3.48W
128 G14 **Plyussa** Pskovskaya Oblast', W Russian Federation 58.27N 29.21E
113 B17 **Plzeň** *Ger.* Pilsen, *Pol.* Pilzno. Plzeňský Kraj, W Czech Republic 49.44N 13.22E
113 B17 **Plzeňský Kraj** ◈ *region* W Czech Republic
112 F11 **Pniewy** *Ger.* Pinne. Wielkolpolskie, C Poland 52.31N 16.14E
108 D8 **Po** ≈ N Italy
79 P13 **Pô** S Burkina 11.10N 1.10W
44 M13 **Poás, Volcán** ⊼ NW Costa Rica 10.12N 84.12W
79 S16 **Pobè** S Benin 7.00N 2.41E
127 N8 **Pobeda, Gora** ▲ NE Russian Federation 65.28N 145.44E
Pobeda Peak *see* Pobedy, Pik/Tomur Feng
153 Z7 **Pobedy, Pik** *var.* Pobeda Peak, *Chin.* Tomur Feng. ▲ China/Kyrgyzstan *see also* Tomur Feng 42.02N 80.02E
112 H11 **Pobiedziska** *Ger.* Pudewitz. Wielkolpolskie, C Poland 52.30N 17.19E
Po, Bocche del *see* Po, Foci del
29 W9 **Pocahontas** Arkansas, C USA 36.15N 90.58W
31 U12 **Pocahontas** Iowa, C USA 42.44N 94.40W
35 Q15 **Pocatello** Idaho, NW USA 42.52N 112.27W
178 J13 **Pochentong** ✕ (Phnum Penh) Phnum Penh, S Cambodia 11.24N 104.52E
130 I6 **Pochep** Bryanskaya Oblast', W Russian Federation 52.56N 33.20E
130 H4 **Pochinok** Smolenskaya Oblast', W Russian Federation 54.20N 32.29E
43 R17 **Pochutla** *var.* San Pedro Pochutla. Oaxaca, SE Mexico 15.44N 96.27W
64 I6 **Pocitos, Salar** *var.* Salar Quiróm. *salt lake* NW Argentina
103 O22 **Pocking** Bayern, SE Germany 48.22N 13.17E
195 R17 **Pocklington Reef** *reef* SE PNG
199 Hh9 **Pocklington Trough** *undersea feature* W Pacific Ocean
29 R11 **Pocola** Oklahoma, C USA 35.13N 94.28W
23 Y5 **Pocomoke City** Maryland, NE USA 38.04N 75.34W
61 L21 **Poços de Caldas** Minas Gerais, NE Brazil 21.48S 46.33W
128 H14 **Podberez'ye** Novgorodskaya Oblast', NW Russian Federation 58.42N 31.22E
Podbrodzie *see* Pabradė
129 U8 **Podcher'ye** Respublika Komi, NW Russian Federation 63.55N 57.34E
113 E16 **Poděbrady** *Ger.* Podiebrad. Středočeský Kraj, C Czech Republic 50.09N 15.06E
176 Yy10 **Podena, Kepulauan** *island group* E Indonesia
130 L9 **Podgorenskiy** Voronezhskaya Oblast', W Russian Federation 50.22N 39.43E
115 J17 **Podgorica** *prev.* Titograd. Montenegro, SW Yugoslavia 42.25N 19.16E
115 K17 **Podgorica** ✕ Montenegro, SW Yugoslavia 42.22N 19.16E
111 T13 **Podgrad** SW Slovenia 45.31N 14.09E
Podiebrad *see* Poděbrady
118 M5 **Podil's'ka Vysochina** *plateau* W Ukraine
Podium Anicensis *see* le Puy
126 Ii11 **Podkamennaya Tunguska** *Eng.* Stony Tunguska. ≈ C Russian Federation
113 N17 **Podkarpackie** ◈ *province* SE Poland
Pod Klošter *see* Arnoldstein
112 O9 **Podlaskie** ◈ *province* NE Poland
131 Q8 **Podlesnoye** Saratovskaya Oblast', W Russian Federation 51.51N 47.03E
130 K4 **Podol'sk** Moskovskaya Oblast', W Russian Federation 55.24N 37.30E
78 H10 **Podor** N Senegal 16.40N 14.57W
129 P12 **Podosinovets** Kirovskaya Oblast', NW Russian Federation 60.15N 47.06E
128 I12 **Podporozh'ye** Leningradskaya Oblast', NW Russian Federation 60.52N 34.00E
Podravska Slatina *see* Slatina, Croatia
114 J13 **Podromanlja** Republika Srpska, SE Bosnia & Herzegovina 43.55N 18.46E
Podsvil'ye *see* Padsvillye
118 L9 **Podu Iloaiei** *prev.* Podul Iloaiei. Iași, NE Romania 47.13N 27.16E
115 N15 **Podujevo** Serbia, S Yugoslavia 42.56N 21.13E
Podul Iloaiei *see* Podu Iloaiei
Podunajská Rovina *see* Little Alföld
128 M12 **Podyuga** Arkhangel'skaya Oblast', NW Russian Federation 61.04N 40.46E
58 A9 **Poechos, Embalse** ◎ NW Peru
57 W10 **Poeketi** Sipaliwini, E Surinam
102 L8 **Poel** *island* N Germany
85 M20 **Poelela, Lagoa** ◎ S Mozambique
Poerwodadi *see* Purwodadi
Poetovio *see* Ptuj
85 E23 **Pofadder** Northern Cape, W South Africa 29.03S 19.25E
108 I9 **Po, Foci del** *var.* Bocche del Po. ≈ NE Italy
118 E12 **Pogăniș** ≈ W Romania
Pogegen *see* Pagėgiai
108 G12 **Poggibonsi** Toscana, C Italy 43.28N 11.09E
109 I14 **Poggio Mirteto** Lazio, C Italy 42.17N 12.42E
111 V4 **Pöggstall** Niederösterreich, N Austria 48.19N 15.10E
118 L13 **Pogoanele** Buzău, SE Romania 44.55N 27.00E
Pogónion *see* Delvináki
115 M21 **Pogradec** *var.* Pogradeci. Korçë, SE Albania 40.54N 20.40E
Pogradeci *see* Pogradec
127 N18 **Pogranichnyy** Primorskiy Kray, SE Russian Federation 44.18N 131.33E
40 M16 **Pogromni Volcano** ▲ Unimak Island, Alaska, USA 54.34N 164.41W
169 Z15 **P'ohang** *Jap.* Hokō. E South Korea 36.01N 129.20E
13 T9 **Pohénégamook, Lac** ◎ Quebec, SE Canada
95 L20 **Pohja** *Swe.* Pojo. Etelä-Suomi, SW Finland 60.07N 23.30E
Pohjanlahti *see* Bothnia, Gulf of
201 U16 **Pohnpei** ◈ *state* E Micronesia
201 O12 **Pohnpei** ✕ Pohnpei, E Micronesia
201 O12 **Pohnpei** *prev.* Ponape Ascension Island. *island* E Micronesia
113 F19 **Pohořelice** *Ger.* Pohrlitz. Brněnský Kraj, SE Czech Republic 48.58N 16.30E
111 V10 **Pohorje** *Ger.* Bacher. ▲▲ N Slovenia
119 N6 **Pohrebyshche** Vinnyts'ka Oblast', C Ukraine 49.31N 29.16E
Pohrlitz *see* Pohořelice
175 Qq9 **Poh, Teluk** *bay* Sulawesi, C Indonesia
167 P9 **Po Hu** ⊠ E China
118 G15 **Poiana Mare** Dolj, S Romania 43.55N 23.01E
Poictiers *see* Poitiers
131 N6 **Poim** Penzenskaya Oblast', W Russian Federation 53.03N 43.11E
197 I6 **Poindimié** Province Nord, C New Caledonia 20.55S 165.18E
Poindo *see* Lhünzhub
205 Y13 **Poinsett, Cape** *headland* Antarctica 65.35S 113.00E
31 R9 **Poinsett, Lake** ◎ South Dakota, N USA
24 I10 **Point Au Fer Island** *island* Louisiana, S USA
41 X14 **Point Baker** Prince of Wales Island, Alaska, USA 56.19N 133.31W
27 U13 **Point Comfort** Texas, SW USA 28.40N 96.33W
Point de Galle *see* Galle
46 K10 **Pointe à Gravois** *headland* SW Haiti 18.00N 73.53W
24 L10 **Pointe a la Hache** Louisiana, S USA 29.34N 89.48W
47 Y6 **Pointe-à-Pitre** Grande Terre, C Guadeloupe 16.15N 61.31W
13 U7 **Pointe-au-Père** Quebec, SE Canada 48.31N 68.27W
13 V5 **Pointe-aux-Anglais** Quebec, SE Canada 49.40N 67.09W
47 T10 **Pointe du Cap** *headland* N Saint Lucia 14.06N 60.56W
81 E21 **Pointe-Noire** Le Kouilou, S Congo 4.46S 11.52E
47 X6 **Pointe Noire** Basse Terre, W Guadeloupe 16.13N 61.47W
81 E21 **Pointe-Noire** ✕ Le Kouilou, S Congo 4.45S 11.55E
47 U15 **Point Fortin** Trinidad, Trinidad and Tobago 10.09N 61.41W
40 M6 **Point Hope** Alaska, USA 68.21N 166.48W
41 N5 **Point Lay** Alaska, USA 69.42N 162.57W
20 B16 **Point Marion** Pennsylvania, NE USA 39.44N 79.53W
20 K16 **Point Pleasant** New Jersey, NE USA 40.04N 74.00W
23 P4 **Point Pleasant** West Virginia, NE USA 38.50N 82.08W
47 R14 **Point Salines** ✕ (St.George's) SW Grenada 12.00N 61.47W
104 L9 **Poitiers** *prev.* Poictiers, *anc.* Limonum. Vienne, W France 46.34N 0.19E
104 K9 **Poitou** *cultural region* W France
104 K10 **Poitou-Charentes** ◈ *region* W France
105 N3 **Poix-de-Picardie** Somme, N France 49.47N 1.58E
Pojo *see* Pohja
39 S10 **Pojoaque** New Mexico, SW USA 35.52N 106.01W
158 E11 **Pokaran** Rājasthān, NW India 26.55N 71.55E
191 R4 **Pokataroo** New South Wales, SE Australia 29.37S 148.43E
121 P18 **Pokats'** *Rus.* Pokot'. ≈ SE Belarus
31 V5 **Pokegama Lake** ◎ Minnesota, N USA
192 L6 **Pokeno** Waikato, North Island, NZ 37.15S 175.01E
159 O11 **Pokhara** Western, C Nepal 28.13N 84.00E
131 T6 **Pokhvistnevo** Samarskaya Oblast', W Russian Federation 53.38N 52.07E
57 W10 **Pokigron** Sipaliwini, C Surinam 4.25N 55.24W
94 L10 **Pokka** *Lapp.* Bohkká. Lappi, N Finland 68.10N 25.45E
81 N16 **Poko** Orientale, NE Dem. Rep. Congo (Zaire) 3.07N 26.51E
Pokot' *see* Pokats'
Po-ko-to Shan *see* Bogda Shan
153 S7 **Pokrovka** Talasskaya Oblast', NW Kyrgyzstan 42.45N 71.33E
Pokrovka *see* Kyzyl-Suu
126 M11 **Pokrovsk** Respublika Sakha (Yakutiya), NE Russian Federation 61.40N 129.25E
119 V8 **Pokrovs'ke** *Rus.* Pokrovskoye. Dnipropetrovs'ka Oblast', E Ukraine 47.58N 36.15E
Pokrovskoye *see* Pokrovs'ke
Pola *see* Pula
39 N10 **Polacca** Arizona, SW USA 35.49N 110.21W
106 L2 **Pola de Laviana** Asturias, N Spain 43.15N 5.33W
106 K2 **Pola de Lena** Asturias, N Spain 43.10N 5.49W
106 L2 **Pola de Siero** Asturias, N Spain 43.24N 5.39W
203 Y3 **Poland** Kiritimati, E Kiribati 1.52N 95.33W
112 H12 **Poland** *off.* Republic of Poland, *var.* Polish Republic, *Pol.* Polska, Rzeczpospolita Polska; *prev. Pol.* Polska Rzeczpospolita Ludowa, Polish People's Republic. ◆ *republic* C Europe
Polangen *see* Palanga
112 G7 **Polanów** *Ger.* Pollnow. Zachodniopomorskie, NW Poland 54.07N 16.38E
142 H13 **Polatlı** Ankara, C Turkey 39.34N 32.07E
120 L12 **Polatsk** *Rus.* Polotsk. Vitsyebskaya Voblasts', N Belarus 55.28N 28.46E
112 F8 **Połczyn-Zdrój** *Ger.* Bad Polzin. Zachodniopomorskie, NW Poland 53.43N 16.02E
152 I16 **Polekhatum** *prev.* Pul'-I-Khatum. Akhalskiy Velayat, S Turkmenistan 36.01N 61.08E
155 Q3 **Pol-e Khomrī** *var.* Pul-i-Khumri. Baghlān, NE Afghanistan 35.55N 68.45E
207 S10 **Pole Plain** *undersea feature* Arctic Ocean
149 P5 **Pol-e Safīd** *var.* Pol-e-Sefid, Pul-i-Sefid. Māzandarān, N Iran 36.10N 53.03E
Pol-e-Sefid *see* Pol-e Safīd
120 B13 **Polessk** *Ger.* Labiau. Kaliningradskaya Oblast', W Russian Federation 54.52N 21.06E
Polesskoye *see* Polis'ke
175 P11 **Polewali** Sulawesi, C Indonesia 3.25S 119.22E
116 G11 **Polezhan** ▲ SW Bulgaria 41.42N 23.28E
80 F13 **Poli** Nord, N Cameroon 8.42N 13.09E
Poli *see* Pólis
109 M19 **Policastro, Golfo di** *gulf* S Italy
112 D8 **Police** *Ger.* Politz. Zachodniopomorskie, NW Poland 53.34N 14.34E
180 I17 **Police, Pointe** *headland* Mahé, NE Seychelles 4.48S 55.31E
117 L17 **Polichnítos** *var.* Polihnitos, Políkhnitos. Lésvos, E Greece 39.04N 26.10E
Poligiros *see* Polýgyros
109 P17 **Polignano a Mare** Puglia, SE Italy 40.58N 17.13E
105 S9 **Poligny** Jura, E France 46.51N 5.42E
Polihnitos *see* Polichnítos
Polikastro/Políkastron *see* Polýkastro
Políkhnitos *see* Polichnítos
116 K8 **Polikrayshte** Veliko Tŭrnovo, N Bulgaria 43.12N 25.38E
179 Pp10 **Polillo Islands** *island group* N Philippines
111 Q9 **Polinik** ▲ SW Austria 46.54N 13.10E
123 Mm3 **Pólis** *var.* Poli. W Cyprus 35.02N 32.27E
Polish People's Republic *see* Poland
Polish Republic *see* Poland
119 O3 **Polis'ke** *Rus.* Polesskoye. Kyyivs'ka Oblast', N Ukraine 51.15N 29.27E
109 N22 **Polistena** Calabria, SW Italy 38.25N 16.04E
Politz *see* Police
Políyiros *see* Polýgyros
31 V14 **Polk City** Iowa, C USA 41.46N 93.42W
112 F13 **Polkowice** *Ger.* Heerwegen. Dolnośląskie, SW Poland 51.31N 16.04E
161 G22 **Pollāchi** Tamil Nādu, SE India 10.38N 77.00E
111 W7 **Pöllau** Steiermark, SE Austria 47.18N 15.46E
201 T13 **Polle** *atoll* Chuuk Islands, C Micronesia
Pollnow *see* Polanów
31 N7 **Pollock** South Dakota, N USA 45.53N 100.15W
94 L8 **Polmak** Finnmark, N Norway 70.01N 28.04E
32 L10 **Polo** Illinois, N USA 41.59N 89.34W
200 Qq15 **Poloa** *island* Tongatapu Group, N Tonga
44 E5 **Polochic, Río** ≈ C Guatemala
Pologi *see* Polohy
119 V9 **Polohy** *Rus.* Pologi. Zaporiz'ka Oblast', SE Ukraine 47.29N 36.18E
12 M10 **Polonais, Lac des** ◎ Quebec, SE Canada
63 G20 **Polonio, Cabo** *headland* E Uruguay 34.22S 53.46W
161 K24 **Polonnaruwa** North Central Province, C Sri Lanka 7.55N 81.01E
118 L5 **Polonne** *Rus.* Polonnoye. Khmel'nyts'ka Oblast', NW Ukraine 50.10N 27.30E
Polonnoye *see* Polonne
Polotsk *see* Polatsk
111 T7 **Pöls** *var.* Pölsbach. ≈ E Austria
Pölsbach *see* Pöls
Polska/Polska, Rzeczpospolita/Polska Rzeczpospolita Ludowa *see* Poland
116 L10 **Polski Gradets** Stara Zagora, C Bulgaria 42.12N 26.06E
116 K8 **Polsko Kosovo** Ruse, N Bulgaria 43.26N 25.40E
35 P8 **Polson** Montana, NW USA 47.41N 114.09W
119 T6 **Poltava** Poltavs'ka Oblast', NE Ukraine 49.33N 34.32E
Poltava *see* Poltavs'ka Oblast'
119 R5 **Poltavs'ka Oblast'** *var.* Poltava, *Rus.* Poltavskaya Oblast'. ◈ *province* NE Ukraine
Poltavskaya Oblast' *see* Poltavs'ka Oblast'
Poltoratsk *see* Ashgabat
120 I5 **Põltsamaa** *Ger.* Oberpahlen. Jõgevamaa, E Estonia 58.40N 25.58E
120 I4 **Põltsamaa** *var.* Põltsamaa Jõgi. ≈ C Estonia
Põltsamaa Jõgi *see* Põltsamaa
125 F10 **Polunochnoye** Sverdlovskaya Oblast', C Russian Federation 60.56N 60.15E
125 G8 **Poluy** ≈ N Russian Federation
120 J6 **Põlva** *Ger.* Pölwe. Põlvamaa, SE Estonia 58.03N 27.05E
95 N16 **Polvijärvi** Itä-Suomi, E Finland 62.52N 29.19E
Pölwe *see* Põlva
117 I22 **Polýaigos** *island* Kykládes, Greece, Aegean Sea
117 I22 **Polyaígou Folégandrou, Stenó** *strait* Kykládes, Greece, Aegean Sea
128 J3 **Polyarnyy** Murmanskaya Oblast', NW Russian Federation 69.10N 33.21E
129 W5 **Polyarnyy Ural** ▲▲ NW Russian Federation
117 G14 **Polýgyros** *var.* Poligiros, Políyiros. Kentrikí Makedonía, N Greece 40.21N 23.27E
116 F13 **Polýkastro** *var.* Polikastro; *prev.* Políkastron. Kentrikí Makedonía, N Greece 41.01N 22.33E
199 Kk9 **Polynesia** *island group* C Pacific Ocean
117 J15 **Polýochni** *site of ancient city* Límnos, E Greece 39.51N 25.21E
43 Y13 **Polyuc** Quintana Roo, E Mexico
111 V10 **Polzela** C Slovenia 46.18N 15.04E
Polzen *see* Ploučnice
176 Ww9 **Pom** Irian Jaya, E Indonesia 1.34S 135.39E
58 D12 **Pomabamba** Ancash, C Peru 8.51S 77.13W
193 D23 **Pomahaka** ≈ South Island, NZ
108 F12 **Pomarance** Toscana, C Italy 43.19N 10.53E
106 G9 **Pombal** Leiria, C Portugal 39.55N 8.37W
78 D9 **Pombas** Santo Antão, NW Cape Verde 17.09N 25.02W
85 N19 **Pomene** Inhambane, SE Mozambique 22.57S 35.34E
112 G8 **Pomerania** *cultural region* Germany/Poland
112 D7 **Pomeranian Bay** *Ger.* Pommersche Bucht, *Pol.* Zatoka Pomorska. *bay* Germany/Poland
33 T15 **Pomeroy** Ohio, N USA 39.01N 82.01W
34 L10 **Pomeroy** Washington, NW USA 46.28N 117.36W
119 Q8 **Pomichna** Kirovohrads'ka Oblast', C Ukraine 48.07N 31.25E
195 O12 **Pomio** New Britain, E PNG 5.28S 151.29E
Pomir, Dar"yoi *see* Pamir/Pāmīr, Daryā-ye
29 T6 **Pomme de Terre Lake** ⊠ Missouri, C USA
31 S8 **Pomme de Terre River** ≈ Minnesota, N USA
Pommersche Bucht *see* Pomeranian Bay

◆ Country
● Country Capital
◇ Dependent Territory
○ Dependent Territory Capital
◈ Administrative Region
✕ International Airport
▲ Mountain
▲▲ Mountain Range
⊼ Volcano
≈ River
◎ Lake
⊠ Reservoir

Povorino – Puerto México

131 N8 **Povorino** Voronezhskaya Oblast', W Russian Federation *51.10N 42.16E*
Povungnituk *see* Puvirnituq
10 J3 **Povungnituk, Rivière de** Québec, NE Canada
12 H11 **Powassan** Ontario, S Canada *46.04N 79.21W*
37 U17 **Poway** California, W USA *32.57N 117.02W*
35 W14 **Powder River** Wyoming, C USA *43.01N 106.57W*
35 Y10 **Powder River** Montana/Wyoming, NW USA
34 L12 **Powder River** Oregon, NW USA
35 W13 **Powder River Pass** *pass* Wyoming, C USA *44.08N 107.03W*
35 U12 **Powell** Wyoming, C USA *44.45N 108.45W*
67 I22 **Powell Basin** *undersea feature* NW Weddell Sea
38 M8 **Powell, Lake** ◎ Utah, W USA
39 R4 **Powell, Mount** ▲ Colorado, C USA *39.25N 106.20W*
8 L17 **Powell River** British Columbia, SW Canada *49.54N 124.34W*
33 N5 **Powers** Michigan, N USA *45.40N 87.29W*
30 K2 **Powers Lake** North Dakota, N USA *48.33N 102.37W*
23 V6 **Powhatan** Virginia, NE USA *37.32N 77.55W*
33 V13 **Powhatan Point** Ohio, N USA *39.49N 80.49W*
99 J20 **Powys** *cultural region* E Wales, UK
197 I6 **Poya** Province Nord, C New Caledonia *21.19S 165.07E*
167 P10 **Poyang Hu** ◎ S China
126 Mm16 **Poyarkovo** Amurskaya Oblast', SE Russian Federation *49.37N 128.40E*
32 L7 **Poygan, Lake** ◎ Wisconsin, N USA
111 Y2 **Poysdorf** Niederösterreich, NE Austria *48.40N 16.37E*
114 N11 **Požarevac** *Ger.* Passarowitz. Serbia, NE Yugoslavia *44.37N 21.11E*
43 Q13 **Poza Rica** *var.* Poza Rica de Hidalgo. Veracruz-Llave, E Mexico *20.33N 97.27W*
Poza Rica de Hidalgo *see* Poza Rica
114 L13 **Požega** *Prev.* Slavonska Požega; *Ger.* Poschega, *Hung.* Pozsega. Požega-Slavonija, NE Croatia *43.19N 17.42E*
114 H9 **Požega-Slavonija** *off.* Požeško-Slavonska Županija. ◐ *province* NE Croatia
129 U13 **Pozhva** Komi-Permyatskiy Avtonomnyy Okrug, NW Russian Federation *59.07N 56.04E*
112 G11 **Poznań** *Ger.* Posen, Posnania. Wielkolpolskie, C Poland *52.24N 16.56E*
107 O13 **Pozo Alcón** Andalucía, S Spain *37.43N 2.55W*
64 H3 **Pozo Almonte** Tarapacá, N Chile *20.13S 69.48W*
106 L12 **Pozoblanco** Andalucía, S Spain *38.22N 4.47W*
107 Q11 **Pozo Cañada** Castilla-La Mancha, C Spain *38.49N 1.45W*
64 N5 **Pozo Colorado** Presidente Hayes, C Paraguay *23.25S 58.51W*
65 J20 **Pozos, Punta** *headland* S Argentina *47.55S 65.46W*
Pozsega *see* Požega
Pozsony *see* Bratislava
57 N5 **Pozuelos** Anzoátegui, NE Venezuela *10.10N 64.39W*
109 L26 **Pozzallo** Sicilia, Italy, C Mediterranean Sea *36.43N 14.51E*
109 K17 **Pozzuoli** *anc.* Puteoli. Campania, S Italy *40.49N 14.07E*
79 P17 **Pra** S Ghana
Prabumulih *see* Perabumulih
113 C19 **Prachatice** *Ger.* Prachatitz. Budějovický Kraj, S Czech Republic *49.01N 14.00E*
Prachatitz *see* Prachatice
178 Hh11 **Prachin Buri** *var.* Prachinburi. Prachin Buri, C Thailand *14.05N 101.19E*
Prachuab Girikhand *see* Prachuap Khiri Khan
178 H13 **Prachuap Khiri Khan** *var.* Prachuab Girikhand. Prachuap Khiri Khan, SW Thailand *11.50N 99.45E*
113 H16 **Praděd** *Ger.* Altvater. ▲ NE Czech Republic *50.06N 17.14E*
56 D11 **Pradera** Valle del Cauca, SW Colombia *3.24N 76.19W*
105 O17 **Prades** Pyrénées-Orientales, S France *42.36N 2.22E*
61 O19 **Prado** Bahia, SE Brazil *17.13S 39.15W*
56 E11 **Prado** Tolima, C Colombia *3.38N 74.57W*
Prado del Ganso *see* Goose Green
Prae *see* Phrae
Prag/Praga/Prague *see* Praha
29 O10 **Prague** Oklahoma, C USA *35.29N 96.40W*
113 D16 **Praha** *Eng.* Prague, *Ger.* Prag, *Pol.* Praga. ● (Czech Republic) Středočeský Kraj, NW Czech Republic *50.06N 14.25E*
118 J13 **Prahova** ◐ *county* SE Romania
118 J13 **Prahova** S Romania
78 E10 **Praia** ● (Cape Verde) Santiago, S Cape Verde *14.55N 23.31W*
85 M21 **Praia do Bilene** Gaza, S Mozambique *25.18S 33.10E*
85 M20 **Praia do Xai-Xai** Gaza, S Mozambique *25.04S 33.43E*
118 J10 **Praid** *Hung.* Parajd. Harghita, C Romania *46.33N 25.06E*
28 J3 **Prairie Dog Creek** Kansas/Nebraska, C USA
32 J9 **Prairie du Chien** Wisconsin, N USA *43.01N 91.07W*
29 S9 **Prairie Grove** Arkansas, C USA *35.58N 94.19W*
33 P10 **Prairie River** Michigan, N USA
Prairie State *see* Illinois
27 V11 **Prairie View** Texas, SW USA *30.05N 95.59W*
178 Ii11 **Prakhon Chai** Buri Ram, E Thailand *14.36N 103.04E*
111 R4 **Pram** N Austria
111 S4 **Prambachkirchen** Oberösterreich, N Austria *48.18N 13.50E*
120 H2 **Prangli** *island* N Estonia
160 J13 **Prānhita** C India
180 I15 **Praslin** *island* Inner Islands, NE Seychelles
117 O23 **Prasonísi, Akrotírio** *headland* Ródos, Dodekánisos, Greece, Aegean Sea *35.53N 27.46E*
113 I14 **Praszka** Opolskie, S Poland *51.05N 18.29E*
121 M18 **Pratasy** *Rus.* Protasy. Homyel'skaya Voblasts', SE Belarus *52.48N 29.04E*
178 I10 **Prathai** Nakhon Ratchasima, E Thailand *15.31N 102.42E*
Prathet Thai *see* Thailand
Prathum Thani *see* Pathum Thani
65 F21 **Prat, Isla** *island* S Chile
108 G11 **Prato** Toscana, C Italy *43.52N 11.04E*
105 O17 **Prats-de-Mollo-la-Preste** Pyrénées-Orientales, S France *42.25N 2.28E*
28 L6 **Pratt** Kansas, C USA *37.38N 98.44W*
110 E6 **Pratteln** Basel-Land, NW Switzerland *47.31N 7.42E*
199 L2 **Pratt Seamount** *undersea feature* N Pacific Ocean *56.09N 142.30W*
25 P5 **Prattville** Alabama, S USA *32.27N 86.27W*
Praust *see* Pruszcz Gdański
116 M7 **Pravda** *prev.* Dogrular. Silistra, NE Bulgaria *43.53N 26.58E*
121 B14 **Pravdinsk** *Ger.* Friedland. Kaliningradskaya Oblast', W Russian Federation *54.26N 21.01E*
106 K2 **Pravia** Asturias, N Spain *43.29N 6.06W*
120 L12 **Prazaroki** *Rus.* Prozoroki. Vitsyebskaya Voblasts', N Belarus *55.16N 28.11E*
Prázsmár *see* Prejmer
178 J11 **Preăh Vihéar** Preăh Vihéar, N Cambodia *13.57N 104.48E*
118 J12 **Predeal** *Hung.* Predeál. Braşov, C Romania *45.30N 25.31E*
111 S8 **Predlitz** Steiermark, SE Austria *47.04N 13.54E*
9 V15 **Preeceville** Saskatchewan, S Canada *51.58N 102.40W*
Preenkuln *see* Priekule
104 K6 **Pré-en-Pail** Mayenne, NW France *48.27N 0.15W*
111 T4 **Pregarten** Oberösterreich, N Austria *48.21N 14.31E*
56 H7 **Pregonero** Táchira, NW Venezuela *8.01N 71.45W*
120 J10 **Preiļi** *Ger.* Preli. Preiļi, SE Latvia *56.17N 26.52E*
118 J12 **Prejmer** *Ger.* Tartlau, *Hung.* Prázsmár. Braşov, S Romania *45.42N 25.49E*
115 J16 **Prekornica** ▲ SW Yugoslavia
Preli *see* Preiļi
Prëmet *see* Përmet
102 M12 **Premnitz** Brandenburg, NE Germany *52.33N 12.22E*
27 S15 **Premont** Texas, SW USA *27.21N 98.07W*
115 H14 **Prenj** ▲ S Bosnia and Herzegovina
Prenjas/Prenjasi *see* Përrenjas
24 L7 **Prentiss** Mississippi, S USA *31.36N 89.52W*
Preny *see* Prienai
102 O10 **Prenzlau** Brandenburg, NE Germany *53.19N 13.52E*
126 Jj12 **Preobrazhenka** Irkutskaya Oblast', C Russian Federation *60.01N 108.00E*
177 Ee9 **Preparis Island** *island* SW Burma
Prerau *see* Přerov
113 H18 **Přerov** *Ger.* Prerau. Olomoucký Kraj, E Czech Republic *49.27N 17.27E*
Preschau *see* Prešov
12 M14 **Prescott** Ontario, SE Canada *44.43N 75.33W*
38 K12 **Prescott** Arizona, SW USA *34.33N 112.26W*
29 T13 **Prescott** Arkansas, C USA *33.48N 93.22W*
34 L10 **Prescott** Washington, NW USA *46.17N 118.21W*
32 H6 **Prescott** Wisconsin, N USA *44.46N 92.45W*
193 A24 **Preservation Inlet** *inlet* South Island, NZ
114 O7 **Preševo** Serbia, SE Yugoslavia *42.20N 21.38E*
31 N10 **Presho** South Dakota, N USA *43.54N 100.03W*
60 M13 **Presidente Dutra** Maranhão, E Brazil *5.16S 44.30W*
62 I8 **Presidente Epitácio** São Paulo, S Brazil *21.45S 52.07W*
64 N5 **Presidente Hayes** *off.* Departamento de Presidente Hayes. ◐ *department* C Paraguay
62 I9 **Presidente Prudente** São Paulo, S Brazil *22.09S 51.24W*
Presidente Stroessner *see* Ciudad del Este
Presidente Vargas *see* Itabira
62 I8 **Presidente Venceslau** São Paulo, S Brazil *21.52S 51.51W*
199 L11 **President Thiers Seamount** *undersea feature* C Pacific Ocean *24.39S 145.50W*
26 J11 **Presidio** Texas, SW USA *29.33N 104.22W*
Preslav *see* Veliki Preslav
113 M19 **Prešov** *var.* Preschau, *Ger.* Eperies, *Hung.* Eperjes. Prešovský Kraj, E Slovakia *49.00N 21.13E*
113 M19 **Prešovský Kraj** ◐ *region* E Slovakia
115 N20 **Prespa, Lake** *Alb.* Liqen i Prespës, *Gk.* Límni Megáli Préspa, Limni Prespa, *Mac.* Prespansko Ezero, *Serb.* Prespansko Jezero. ◎ SE Europe
Prespa, Limni/Prespansko Ezero/Prespansko Jezero/Prespës, Liqen i *see* Prespa, Lake
21 S2 **Presque Isle** Maine, NE USA *46.40N 68.01W*
20 B11 **Presque Isle** *headland* Pennsylvania, NE USA *42.09N 80.06W*
Pressburg *see* Bratislava
79 P17 **Prestea** SW Ghana *5.22N 2.07W*
113 B17 **Přeštice** *Ger.* Pschestitz. Plzeňský Kraj, W Czech Republic *49.36N 13.19E*
99 K17 **Preston** NW England, UK *53.46N 2.42W*
25 S6 **Preston** Georgia, SE USA *32.08N 84.35W*
35 R16 **Preston** Idaho, NW USA *42.06N 111.52W*
31 Z13 **Preston** Iowa, C USA *42.03N 90.24W*
31 X11 **Preston** Minnesota, N USA *43.41N 92.06W*
23 O6 **Prestonsburg** Kentucky, S USA *37.40N 82.46W*
98 I13 **Prestwick** W Scotland, UK *55.30N 4.39W*
85 J21 **Pretoria** *var.* Epitoli, Tshwane. ● (South Africa-administrative capital) Gauteng, NE South Africa *25.40S 28.11E*
Pretoria-Witwatersrand-Vereeniging *see* Gauteng
Pretusha *see* Pretushë
115 M21 **Pretushë** *var.* Pretusha. Korçë, SE Albania *40.50N 20.45E*
Preussisch Eylau *see* Bagrationovsk
Preussisch-Stargard *see* Starogard Gdański
Preußisch Holland *see* Pasłęk
117 C17 **Préveza** Ípeiros, W Greece *38.58N 20.43E*
39 V3 **Prewitt Reservoir** ⊡ Colorado, C USA
178 J13 **Prey Vêng** Prey Vêng, S Cambodia *11.30N 105.19E*
150 M12 **Priaral'skiye Karakumy, Peski** *desert* SW Kazakhstan
126 L16 **Priargunsk** Chitinskaya Oblast', S Russian Federation *50.25N 119.12E*
40 K14 **Pribilof Islands** *island group* Alaska, USA
115 K14 **Priboj** Serbia, W Yugoslavia *43.34N 19.33E*
113 C17 **Příbram** *Ger.* Pibrans. Středočeský Kraj, W Czech Republic *49.40N 14.01E*
38 M4 **Price** Utah, W USA *39.34N 110.48W*
39 N5 **Price River** Utah, W USA
25 N8 **Prichard** Alabama, S USA *30.44N 88.04W*
27 R8 **Priddy** Texas, SW USA *31.39N 98.30W*
107 P8 **Priego** Castilla-La Mancha, C Spain *40.25N 2.19W*
106 M14 **Priego de Córdoba** Andalucía, S Spain *37.27N 4.12W*
120 C10 **Priekule** *Ger.* Preenkuln. Liepāja, SW Latvia *56.26N 21.36E*
120 C12 **Priekulė** *Ger.* Prökuls. Gargždai, W Lithuania *55.36N 21.16E*
121 F14 **Prienai** *Pol.* Preny. Prienai, S Lithuania *54.37N 23.56E*
85 G23 **Prieska** Northern Cape, C South Africa *29.40S 22.45E*
34 M7 **Priest Lake** ◎ Idaho, NW USA
34 M7 **Priest River** Idaho, NW USA *48.10N 117.02W*
106 M3 **Prieta, Peña** ▲ N Spain *43.01N 4.42W*
42 J10 **Prieto, Cerro** ▲ C Mexico *24.10N 105.21W*
113 J19 **Prievidza** *var.* Priewitz, *Ger.* Priwitz, *Hung.* Privigye. Trenčiansky Kraj, C Slovakia *48.48N 18.37E*
Priewitz *see* Prievidza
114 F10 **Prijedor** Republika Srpska, NW Bosnia & Herzegovina *45.00N 16.43E*
115 K14 **Prijepolje** Serbia, W Yugoslavia *43.24N 19.39E*
Prikaspiyskaya Nizmennost' *see* Caspian Depression
115 O19 **Prilep** *Turk.* Perlepe. S FYR Macedonia *41.21N 21.33E*
110 B9 **Prilly** Vaud, SW Switzerland *46.32N 6.36E*
Priluki *see* Pryluky
64 L10 **Primero, Río** C Argentina
31 S12 **Primghar** Iowa, C USA *43.05N 95.37W*
114 B9 **Primorje-Gorski Kotar** *off.* Primorsko-Goranska Županija. ◐ *province* NW Croatia
120 A13 **Primorsk** *Ger.* Fischhausen. Kaliningradskaya Oblast', W Russian Federation *54.45N 20.00E*
128 G12 **Primorsk** *Fin.* Koivisto. Leningradskaya Oblast', NW Russian Federation *60.20N 28.39E*
Primorsk/Primorskoye *see* Prymors'k
127 Nn17 **Primorskiy Kray** *prev. Eng.* Maritime Territory. ◐ *territory* SE Russian Federation
116 N10 **Primorsko** *prev.* Keupriya. Burgas, E Bulgaria *42.15N 27.45E*
130 K13 **Primorsko-Akhtarsk** Krasnodarskiy Kray, SW Russian Federation *46.03N 38.44E*
119 U13 **Primors'kyy** Respublika Krym, S Ukraine *45.09N 35.33E*
115 D14 **Primošten** Šibenik-Knin, S Croatia *43.34N 15.57E*
9 R13 **Primrose Lake** ◎ Saskatchewan, C Canada
9 T14 **Prince Albert** Saskatchewan, S Canada *53.08N 105.43W*
85 G25 **Prince Albert** Western Cape, SW South Africa *33.13S 22.03E*
15 I1 **Prince Albert Peninsula** *peninsula* Victoria Island, Northwest Territories, NW Canada
15 J3 **Prince Albert Sound** *inlet* Northwest Territories, N Canada
15 Mm2 **Prince Charles Island** *island* Nunavut, NE Canada
205 W6 **Prince Charles Mountains** ▲ Antarctica
Prince-Édouard, Île-du *see* Prince Edward Island
180 M13 **Prince Edward Fracture Zone** *tectonic feature* SW Indian Ocean
11 P14 **Prince Edward Island** *Fr.* Île-du Prince-Édouard. ◐ *province* SE Canada
11 Q14 **Prince Edward Island** *Fr.* Île-du Prince-Édouard. *island* SE Canada
181 M12 **Prince Edward Islands** *island group* S South Africa
23 X4 **Prince Frederick** Maryland, NE USA *38.32N 76.33W*
8 M14 **Prince George** British Columbia, SW Canada *53.55N 122.49W*
23 W6 **Prince George** Virginia, NE USA *37.13N 77.13W*
207 O8 **Prince Gustaf Adolf Sea** *sea* Nunavut, N Canada
207 Q3 **Prince of Wales, Cape** *headland* Alaska, USA *65.39N 168.12W*
189 V1 **Prince of Wales Island** *island* Queensland, E Australia
15 Jj1 **Prince of Wales Island** *island* Queen Elizabeth Islands, Nunavut, NW Canada
41 Y14 **Prince of Wales Island** *island* Alexander Archipelago, Alaska, USA
Prince of Wales Island *see* Pinang, Pulau
15 I1 **Prince of Wales Strait** *strait* Northwest Territories, N Canada
207 O8 **Prince Patrick Island** *island* Parry Islands, Northwest Territories, NW Canada
15 Kk1 **Prince Regent Inlet** *channel* Nunavut, N Canada
8 J13 **Prince Rupert** British Columbia, SW Canada *54.18N 130.16W*
Prince's Island *see* Príncipe
23 Y5 **Princess Anne** Maryland, NE USA *38.12N 75.48W*
205 R1 **Princess Astrid Kyst** *physical region* Antarctica
189 W2 **Princess Charlotte Bay** *bay* Queensland, NE Australia
205 W7 **Princess Elizabeth Land** *physical region* Antarctica
8 J14 **Princess Royal Island** *island* British Columbia, SW Canada
47 U15 **Princes Town** Trinidad, Trinidad and Tobago *10.16N 61.22W*
9 N17 **Princeton** British Columbia, SW Canada *49.25N 120.34W*
32 L11 **Princeton** Illinois, N USA *41.22N 89.27W*
33 N16 **Princeton** Indiana, N USA *38.21N 87.33W*
31 Z14 **Princeton** Iowa, C USA *41.40N 90.21W*
22 H7 **Princeton** Kentucky, S USA *37.06N 87.52W*
31 V8 **Princeton** Minnesota, N USA *45.34N 93.34W*
29 S1 **Princeton** Missouri, C USA *40.24N 93.34W*
20 J15 **Princeton** New Jersey, NE USA *40.21N 74.39W*
23 R6 **Princeton** West Virginia, NE USA *37.22N 81.06W*
41 S12 **Prince William Sound** *inlet* Alaska, USA
69 P9 **Príncipe** *var.* Príncipe Island, *Eng.* Prince's Island. *island* N Sao Tome and Principe
Príncipe Island *see* Príncipe
34 I13 **Prineville** Oregon, NW USA *44.18N 120.50W*
30 J11 **Pringle** South Dakota, N USA *43.34N 103.34W*
27 N1 **Pringle** Texas, SW USA *35.55N 101.28W*
101 H14 **Prinsenbeek** Noord-Brabant, S Netherlands *51.36N 4.42E*
100 L6 **Prinses Margriet Kanaal** *canal* N Netherlands
205 T2 **Prinsesse Ragnhild Kyst** *physical region* Antarctica
205 U2 **Prins Harald Kyst** *physical region* Antarctica
94 N2 **Prins Karls Forland** *island* W Svalbard
45 N8 **Prinzapolka** Región Autónoma Atlántico Norte, NE Nicaragua *13.19N 83.34W*
44 L8 **Prinzapolka, Río** NE Nicaragua
125 Ff9 **Priob'ye** Khanty-Mansiyskiy Avtonomnyy Okrug, N Russian Federation *62.25N 65.36E*
106 H1 **Prior, Cabo** *headland* NW Spain *43.33N 8.21W*
31 V9 **Prior Lake** Minnesota, N USA *44.42N 93.25W*
128 H11 **Priozersk** *Fin.* Käkisalmi. Leningradskaya Oblast', NW Russian Federation *61.02N 30.07E*
121 J20 **Pripet** *Bel.* Prypyats', *Ukr.* Pryp"yat'. Belarus/Ukraine
121 J20 **Pripet Marshes** *wetland* Belarus/Ukraine
Prishtinë *see* Priština
130 J8 **Pristen'** Kurskaya Oblast', W Russian Federation *51.15N 36.47E*
115 N16 **Priština** *Alb.* Prishtinë. Serbia, S Yugoslavia *42.39N 21.09E*
102 M10 **Pritzwalk** Brandenburg, NE Germany *53.10N 12.11E*
105 R13 **Privas** Ardèche, E France *44.45N 4.34E*
109 I16 **Priverno** Lazio, C Italy *41.28N 13.10E*
Privigye *see* Prievidza
114 C12 **Privlaka** Zadar, SW Croatia *44.15N 15.07E*
128 M15 **Privolzhsk** Ivanovskaya Oblast', NW Russian Federation *57.24N 41.16E*
131 P7 **Privolzhskaya Vozvyshennost'** *var.* Volga Uplands. ▲ W Russian Federation
131 P8 **Privolzhskoye** Saratovskaya Oblast', W Russian Federation *51.08N 45.57E*
Priwitz *see* Prievidza
131 N13 **Priyutnoye** Respublika Kalmykiya, SW Russian Federation *46.08N 43.33E*
115 M17 **Prizren** *Alb.* Prizreni. Serbia, S Yugoslavia *42.13N 20.46E*
Prizreni *see* Prizren
109 I24 **Prizzi** Sicilia, Italy, C Mediterranean Sea *37.43N 13.25E*
115 P18 **Probištip** NE FYR Macedonia *42.00N 22.06E*
174 M15 **Probolinggo** Jawa, C Indonesia *7.45S 113.12E*
Probstberg *see* Wyszków
113 F14 **Prochowice** *Ger.* Parchwitz. Dolnośląskie, SW Poland *51.15N 16.22E*
31 W5 **Proctor** Minnesota, N USA *46.46N 92.13W*
27 R8 **Proctor** Texas, SW USA *31.57N 98.25W*
27 R8 **Proctor Lake** ⊡ Texas, SW USA
161 I18 **Proddatūr** Andhra Pradesh, E India *14.46N 78.39E*
106 H9 **Proença-a-Nova** Castelo Branco, C Portugal *39.45N 7.55W*
97 I24 **Præstø** Storstrøm, SE Denmark *55.07N 12.03E*
101 I21 **Profondeville** Namur, SE Belgium *50.22N 4.52E*
43 W11 **Progreso** Yucatán, SE Mexico *21.14N 89.40W*
126 Mm16 **Progress** Amurskaya Oblast', SE Russian Federation *49.40N 129.30E*
131 O15 **Prokhladnyy** Kabardino-Balkarskaya Respublika, SW Russian Federation *43.48N 44.02E*
Prokletije *see* North Albanian Alps
126 H14 **Prokop'yevsk** Kemerovskaya Oblast', S Russian Federation *53.56N 86.48E*
Prökuls *see* Priekule
115 O15 **Prokuplje** Serbia, SE Yugoslavia *43.15N 21.35E*
128 H14 **Proletariy** Novgorodskaya Oblast', W Russian Federation *58.24N 31.40E*
130 M12 **Proletarsk** Rostovskaya Oblast', SW Russian Federation *46.42N 41.48E*
130 J8 **Proletarskiy** Belgorodskaya Oblast', W Russian Federation *50.48N 35.46E*
177 Ff7 **Prome** *var.* Pyè. Pegu, C Burma *18.49N 95.13E*
62 J8 **Promissão** São Paulo, S Brazil *21.33S 49.51W*
62 J8 **Promissão, Represa de** ⊡ S Brazil
129 V4 **Promyshlennyy** Respublika Komi, NW Russian Federation *67.36N 63.59E*
121 O16 **Pronya** *Rus.* Pronya. E Belarus
8 M11 **Prophet River** British Columbia, W Canada *58.07N 122.39W*
32 K11 **Prophetstown** Illinois, N USA *41.40N 89.56W*
61 P16 **Propriá** Sergipe, E Brazil *10.15S 36.51W*
105 X16 **Propriano** Corse, France, C Mediterranean Sea *41.41N 8.54E*
Prościejów *see* Prostějov
Proskurov *see* Khmel 'nyts'kyy
116 H12 **Prosotsáni** Anatolikí Makedonía kai Thráki, NE Greece *41.10N 23.58E*
179 Rr15 **Prosperidad** Mindanao, S Philippines *8.36N 125.54E*
34 J10 **Prosser** Washington, NW USA *46.12N 119.46W*
Prossnitz *see* Prostějov
113 G18 **Prostějov** *Ger.* Prossnitz, *Pol.* Prościejów. Olomoucký Kraj, E Czech Republic *49.28N 17.07E*
119 V8 **Prosyana** Dnipropetrovs'ka Oblast', E Ukraine *48.07N 36.22E*
113 L16 **Proszowice** Małopolskie, S Poland *50.12N 20.15E*
Protasy *see* Pratasy
180 J11 **Protea Seamount** *undersea feature* SW Indian Ocean *36.49S 18.04E*
117 D21 **Próti** *island* S Greece
116 N8 **Provadiya** Varna, E Bulgaria *43.10N 27.28E*
105 S15 **Provence** *prev.* Marseille-Marignane. ✈ (Marseille) Bouches-du-Rhône, SE France *43.25N 5.15E*
105 T14 **Provence** *cultural region* SE France
105 T14 **Provence-Alpes-Côte d'Azur** ◐ *region* SE France
22 H6 **Providence** Kentucky, S USA *37.23N 87.47W*
21 N12 **Providence** *state capital* Rhode Island, NE USA *41.50N 71.26W*
38 L1 **Providence** Utah, W USA *41.42N 111.49W*
Providence *see* Fort Providence
69 X10 **Providence Atoll** *var.* Providence. *atoll* S Seychelles
12 D12 **Providence Bay** Manitoulin Island, Ontario, S Canada *45.39N 82.16W*
25 R6 **Providence Canyon** *valley* Alabama/Georgia, S USA
24 I5 **Providence, Lake** ◎ Louisiana, S USA
37 X13 **Providence Mountains** ▲ California, W USA
46 L6 **Providenciales** *island* W Turks and Caicos Islands
127 Q4 **Provideniya** Chukotskiy Avtonomnyy Okrug, NE Russian Federation *64.22N 173.14W*
21 Q12 **Provincetown** Massachusetts, NE USA *42.01N 70.10W*
105 P5 **Provins** Seine-et-Marne, N France *48.34N 3.18E*
38 L3 **Provo** Utah, W USA *40.13N 111.39W*
9 R15 **Provost** Alberta, SW Canada *52.24N 110.16W*
114 G13 **Prozor** Federacija Bosna I Hercegovina, SW Bosnia & Herzegovina *43.46N 17.38E*
Prozoroki *see* Prazaroki
62 I11 **Prudentópolis** Paraná, S Brazil *25.12S 50.58W*
41 R5 **Prudhoe Bay** Alaska, USA *70.16N 148.18W*
41 R4 **Prudhoe Bay** *bay* Alaska, USA
113 H16 **Prudnik** *Ger.* Neustadt, Neustadt in Oberschlesien. Opolskie, S Poland *50.19N 17.34E*
121 J16 **Prudy** *Rus.* Prudy. Minskaya Voblasts', C Belarus *53.48N 26.32E*
103 D18 **Prüm** Rheinland-Pfalz, W Germany *50.15N 6.27E*
103 D18 **Prüm** W Germany
Prusa *see* Bursa
112 J7 **Pruszcz Gdański** *Ger.* Praust. Pomorskie, N Poland *54.16N 18.36E*
112 M12 **Pruszków** *Ger.* Kaltdorf. Mazowieckie, C Poland *52.09N 20.49E*
118 K8 **Prut** *Ger.* Pruth. E Europe
Pruth *see* Prut
110 L8 **Prutz** Tirol, W Austria *47.07N 10.42E*
Pružana *see* Pruzhany
121 G19 **Pruzhany** *Pol.* Prużana. Brestskaya Voblasts', SW Belarus *52.33N 24.28E*
128 I11 **Pryazha** Respublika Kareliya, NW Russian Federation *61.42N 33.39E*
119 U10 **Pryazovs'ke** Zaporiz'ka Oblast', SE Ukraine *46.43N 35.39E*
Prychornomors'ka Nyzovyna *see* Black Sea Lowland
Prydniprovs'ka Nyzovyna/Prydnyaprowskaya Nizina *see* Dnieper Lowland
205 Y7 **Prydz Bay** *bay* Antarctica
119 R4 **Pryluky** *Rus.* Priluki. Chernihivs'ka Oblast', NE Ukraine *50.34N 32.23E*
119 V10 **Prymors'k** *Rus.* Primorsk; *prev.* Primorskoye. Zaporiz'ka Oblast', SE Ukraine *46.43N 36.19E*
29 Q9 **Pryor** Oklahoma, C USA *36.18N 95.18W*
35 U11 **Pryor Creek** Montana, NW USA
Pryp"yat'/Prypyats' *see* Pripet
112 M10 **Przasnysz** Mazowieckie, C Poland *53.01N 20.53E*
113 K14 **Przedbórz** Łodzkie, S Poland *51.04N 19.51E*
113 P17 **Przemyśl** *Rus.* Peremyshl. Podkarpackie, SE Poland *49.46N 22.46E*
113 O16 **Przeworsk** Podkarpackie, SE Poland *50.04N 22.30E*
Przheval'sk *see* Karakol
112 L13 **Przysucha** Mazowieckie, SE Poland *51.22N 20.36E*
117 H18 **Psachná** *var.* Psahna, Psakhná. Évvoia, C Greece *38.34N 23.40E*
Psahna/Psakhná *see* Psachná
117 K18 **Psará** *island* E Greece
117 I16 **Psathoúra** *island* Vóreioi Sporádes, Greece, Aegean Sea
Pschestitz *see* Přeštice
Psein Lora *see* Pishin Lora
119 S5 **Psël** Russian Federation/Ukraine
117 M21 **Psérimos** *island* Dodekánisos, Greece, Aegean Sea
Pseyn Bowr *see* Pishin Lora
Pskem *see* Piskom
153 R8 **Pskemskiy Khrebet** *Uzb.* Piskom Tizmasi. ▲ Kyrgyzstan/Uzbekistan
128 F14 **Pskov** *Ger.* Pleskau, *Latv.* Pleskava. Pskovskaya Oblast', W Russian Federation *58.31N 31.15E*
120 K6 **Pskov, Lake** *Est.* Pihkva Järv, *Ger.* Pleskauer See, *Rus.* Pskovskoye Ozero. ◎ Estonia/Russian Federation
128 F15 **Pskovskaya Oblast'** ◐ *province* W Russian Federation
Pskovskoye Ozero *see* Pskov, Lake
114 G9 **Psunj** ▲ NE Croatia
113 J17 **Pszczyna** *Ger.* Pless. Śląskie, S Poland *49.58N 18.56E*
Ptačnik/Ptacsnik *see* Vtáčnik
117 D17 **Ptéri** ▲ C Greece *39.08N 21.32E*
Ptich' *see* Ptsich
117 E14 **Ptolemaïda** *prev.* Ptolemaïs. Dytikí Makedonía, N Greece *40.31N 21.40E*
Ptolemaïs *see* Ptolemaïda, Greece
Ptolemaïs *see* 'Akko, Israel
123 Gg10 **Ptolemy Seamounts** *undersea feature* C Mediterranean Sea
121 M19 **Ptsich** *Rus.* Ptich'. Homyel'skaya Voblasts', SE Belarus *52.10N 28.49E*
121 M18 **Ptsich** *Rus.* Ptich'. SE Belarus
111 X10 **Ptuj** *Ger.* Pettau; *anc.* Poetovio. NE Slovenia *46.26N 15.53E*
194 E9 **Pua** NW PNG
63 A23 **Puán** Buenos Aires, E Argentina *37.34S 62.45W*
198 B7 **Pu'apu'a** Savai'i, C Samoa *13.31S 172.09W*
198 A7 **Puava, Cape** *headland* Savai'i, NW Samoa
58 F12 **Pucallpa** Ucayali, C Peru *8.21S 74.33W*
59 J17 **Pucarani** La Paz, NW Bolivia *16.18S 68.28W*
Pučarevo *see* Novi Travnik
163 U12 **Pucheng** Fujian, SE China *27.54N 118.34E*
166 L6 **Pucheng** Shaanxi, C China *34.55N 109.28E*
129 N16 **Puchezh** Ivanovskaya Oblast', W Russian Federation *56.58N 41.08E*
113 I19 **Púchov** *Hung.* Puhó. Trenčiansky Kraj, W Slovakia *49.06N 18.19E*
118 J13 **Pucioasa** Dâmbovița, S Romania *45.04N 25.22E*
112 I6 **Puck** Pomorskie, N Poland *54.43N 18.24E*
32 L8 **Puckaway Lake** ◎ Wisconsin, N USA
65 G15 **Pucón** Araucanía, S Chile *39.18S 71.52W*
95 M14 **Pudasjärvi** Oulu, C Finland *65.19N 27.01E*
154 L8 **Pūdeh Tal, Shelleh-ye** SW Afghanistan
131 S1 **Pudem** Udmurtskaya Respublika, NW Russian Federation *58.18N 52.08E*
Pudewitz *see* Pobiedziska
128 K11 **Pudozh** Respublika Kareliya, NW Russian Federation *61.48N 36.30E*
99 M17 **Pudsey** N England, UK *53.48N 1.40W*
Puduchcheri *see* Pondicherry
157 H21 **Pudukkottai** Tamil Nādu, SE India *10.22N 78.46E*
176 Z10 **Pue** Irian Jaya, E Indonesia *2.42S 140.36E*
43 P14 **Puebla** *var.* Puebla de Zaragoza. Puebla, S Mexico *19.02N 98.12W*
43 P15 **Puebla** ◐ *state* S Mexico
106 L11 **Puebla de Alcocer** Extremadura, W Spain *38.58N 5.13W*
Puebla de Don Fabrique *see* Puebla de Don Fadrique
107 P13 **Puebla de Don Fadrique** *var.* Puebla de Don Fabrique. Andalucía, S Spain *37.58N 2.25W*
106 J11 **Puebla de la Calzada** Extremadura, W Spain *38.54N 6.37W*
106 J5 **Puebla de Sanabria** Castilla-León, N Spain *42.04N 6.37W*
106 I4 **Puebla de Trives** *see* A Pobla de Trives
Puebla de Zaragoza *see* Puebla
39 T6 **Pueblo** Colorado, C USA *38.15N 104.36W*
39 N10 **Pueblo Colorado Wash** *valley* Arizona, SW USA
63 C16 **Pueblo Libertador** Corrientes, NE Argentina *30.13S 59.22W*
42 J10 **Pueblo Nuevo** Durango, C Mexico *23.24N 105.21W*
44 J8 **Pueblo Nuevo** Estelí, NW Nicaragua *13.24N 86.26W*
56 J3 **Pueblo Nuevo** Falcón, N Venezuela *11.58N 69.57W*
44 B6 **Pueblo Nuevo Tiquisate** *var.* Tiquisate. Escuintla, SW Guatemala *14.16N 91.21W*
43 Q11 **Pueblo Viejo, Laguna de** *lagoon* E Mexico
65 J14 **Puelches** La Pampa, C Argentina *38.08S 65.56W*
106 L14 **Puente-Genil** Andalucía, S Spain *37.23N 4.45W*
107 Q3 **Puente la Reina** Navarra, N Spain *42.40N 1.49W*
106 L12 **Puente Nuevo, Embalse de** ⊡ S Spain
59 D14 **Puente Piedra** Lima, W Peru *11.49S 77.01W*
166 F14 **Pu'er** Yunnan, SW China *23.09N 100.57E*
47 V6 **Puerca, Punta** *headland* E Puerto Rico *18.13N 65.36W*
39 R12 **Puerco, Rio** New Mexico, SW USA
59 J17 **Puerto Acosta** La Paz, W Bolivia *15.33S 69.15W*
65 G19 **Puerto Aisén** Aisén, S Chile *45.24S 72.42W*
43 R17 **Puerto Ángel** Oaxaca, SE Mexico *15.39N 96.29W*
Puerto Argentino *see* Stanley
43 T17 **Puerto Arista** Chiapas, SE Mexico *15.55N 93.47W*
45 O16 **Puerto Armuelles** Chiriquí, SW Panama *8.16N 82.51W*
Puerto Arrecife *see* Arrecife
56 D14 **Puerto Asís** Putumayo, SW Colombia *0.27N 76.27W*
56 L9 **Puerto Ayacucho** Amazonas, SW Venezuela *5.44N 67.36W*
59 C18 **Puerto Ayora** Galapagos Islands, Ecuador, E Pacific Ocean *0.45S 90.19W*
59 C18 **Puerto Baquerizo Moreno** *var.* Baquerizo Moreno. Galapagos Islands, Ecuador, E Pacific Ocean *0.54S 89.37W*
44 G4 **Puerto Barrios** Izabal, E Guatemala *15.42N 88.34W*
Puerto Bello *see* Portobelo
56 F8 **Puerto Berrío** Antioquia, C Colombia *6.25N 74.27W*
56 F9 **Puerto Boyacá** Boyacá, C Colombia *5.58N 74.36W*
56 K4 **Puerto Cabello** Carabobo, N Venezuela *10.27N 68.02W*
45 N7 **Puerto Cabezas** *var.* Bilwi. Región Autónoma Atlántico Norte, NE Nicaragua *14.04N 83.22W*
56 L9 **Puerto Carreño** Vichada, E Colombia *6.08N 67.30W*
56 E4 **Puerto Colombia** Atlántico, N Colombia *10.58N 74.57W*
44 H4 **Puerto Cortés** Cortés, NW Honduras *15.49N 87.55W*
56 J4 **Puerto Cumarebo** Falcón, N Venezuela *11.28N 69.21W*
Puerto de Cabras *see* Puerto del Rosario
57 Q5 **Puerto de Hierro** Sucre, NE Venezuela *10.40N 62.03W*
66 O11 **Puerto de la Cruz** Tenerife, Islas Canarias, Spain, NE Atlantic Ocean *28.24N 16.33W*
66 Q11 **Puerto del Rosario** *var.* Puerto de Cabras. Fuerteventura, Islas Canarias, Spain, NE Atlantic Ocean *28.28N 13.52W*
65 J20 **Puerto Deseado** Santa Cruz, SE Argentina *47.46S 65.52W*
42 F8 **Puerto Escondido** Baja California Sur, W Mexico *25.49N 111.20W*
43 R17 **Puerto Escondido** Oaxaca, SE Mexico *15.48N 96.57W*
62 G12 **Puerto Esperanza** Misiones, NE Argentina *26.01S 54.39W*
58 D6 **Puerto Francisco de Orellana** *var.* Coca. Napo, N Ecuador *0.27S 76.57W*
56 H10 **Puerto Gaitán** Meta, C Colombia *4.19N 72.07W*
Puerto Gallegos *see* Río Gallegos
62 G12 **Puerto Iguazú** Misiones, NE Argentina *25.39S 54.34W*
58 F12 **Puerto Inca** Huánuco, N Peru *9.21S 74.55W*
56 L11 **Puerto Inírida** *var.* Obando. Guainía, E Colombia *3.48N 67.54W*
44 K13 **Puerto Jesús** Guanacaste, NW Costa Rica *10.08N 85.26W*
43 Z11 **Puerto Juárez** Quintana Roo, SE Mexico *21.06N 86.46W*
57 N5 **Puerto La Cruz** Anzoátegui, NE Venezuela *10.13N 64.40W*
56 E14 **Puerto Leguízamo** Putumayo, S Colombia *0.07S 74.51W*
45 N5 **Puerto Lempira** Gracias a Dios, E Honduras *15.13N 83.48W*
Puerto Libertad *see* La Libertad
56 I11 **Puerto Limón** Meta, E Colombia *4.00N 71.09W*
56 D13 **Puerto Limón** Putumayo, SW Colombia *1.01N 76.30W*
Puerto Limón *see* Limón
107 N11 **Puertollano** Castilla-La Mancha, C Spain *38.40N 4.07W*
65 K17 **Puerto Lobos** Chubut, SE Argentina *42.00S 64.58W*
56 I3 **Puerto López** La Guajira, N Colombia *11.54N 71.21W*
107 Q14 **Puerto Lumbreras** Murcia, SE Spain *37.34N 1.49W*
43 V17 **Puerto Madero** Chiapas, SE Mexico *14.43N 92.25W*
65 K17 **Puerto Madryn** Chubut, S Argentina *42.45S 65.01W*
Puerto Magdalena *see* Bahía Magdalena
59 J15 **Puerto Maldonado** Madre de Dios, E Peru *12.37S 69.10W*
Puerto Masachapa *see* Masachapa
Puerto México *see* Coatzacoalcos

◆ Country ● Country Capital ◇ Dependent Territory ○ Dependent Territory Capital ◐ Administrative Region ✈ International Airport ▲ Mountain ▲ Mountain Range Volcano River ◎ Lake ⊡ Reservoir

Puerto Montt – Quakenbrück

65 G17 **Puerto Montt** Los Lagos, C Chile *41.28S 72.57W*
43 Z12 **Puerto Morelos** Quintana Roo, SE Mexico *20.47N 86.54W*
56 L10 **Puerto Nariño** Vichada, E Colombia *4.57N 67.51W*
65 H23 **Puerto Natales** Magallanes, S Chile *51.42S 72.28W*
45 X15 **Puerto Obaldía** San Blas, NE Panama *8.37N 77.25W*
46 H6 **Puerto Padre** Las Tunas, E Cuba *21.13N 76.34W*
56 L9 **Puerto Páez** Apure, C Venezuela *6.10N 67.30W*
42 E3 **Puerto Peñasco** Sonora, NW Mexico *31.21N 113.32W*
57 N5 **Puerto Píritu** Anzoátegui, NE Venezuela *10.02N 65.02W*
47 N8 **Puerto Plata** ***var.*** San Felipe de Puerto Plata. N Dominican Republic *19.46N 70.42W*
47 N8 **Puerto Plata** ✈ N Dominican Republic *19.43N 70.43W*
Puerto Presidente Stroessner *see* Ciudad del Este
179 Oo14 **Puerto Princesa** ***off.*** Puerto Princesa City. Palawan, W Philippines *9.48N 118.43E*
Puerto Princesa City *see* Puerto Princesa
Puerto Príncipe *see* Camagüey
Puerto Quellón *see* Quellón
62 F13 **Puerto Rico** Misiones, NE Argentina *26.48S 54.58W*
59 K14 **Puerto Rico** Pando, N Bolivia *11.09S 67.28W*
56 E12 **Puerto Rico** Caquetá, S Colombia *1.53N 75.08W*
47 U5 **Puerto Rico** ***off.*** Commonwealth of Puerto Rico; ***prev.*** Porto Rico. ◇ *US commonwealth territory* C West Indies
66 F11 **Puerto Rico** *island* C West Indies
66 G11 **Puerto Rico Trench** *undersea feature* NE Caribbean Sea
56 I8 **Puerto Rondón** Arauca, E Colombia *6.16N 71.05W*
Puerto San José *see* San José
65 J21 **Puerto San Julián** ***var.*** San Julián. Santa Cruz, SE Argentina *49.14S 67.40W*
65 I22 **Puerto Santa Cruz** ***var.*** Santa Cruz. Santa Cruz, SE Argentina *50.05S 68.31W*
Puerto Sauce *see* Juan L.Lacaze
59 Q20 **Puerto Suárez** Santa Cruz, E Bolivia *18.58S 57.47W*
56 D13 **Puerto Umbría** Putumayo, SW Colombia *0.52N 76.31W*
42 J13 **Puerto Vallarta** Jalisco, SW Mexico *20.36N 105.15W*
65 G16 **Puerto Varas** Los Lagos, C Chile *41.24S 72.55W*
44 M13 **Puerto Viejo** Heredia, NE Costa Rica *10.27N 84.00W*
Puertoviejo *see* Portoviejo
59 B18 **Puerto Villamil** ***var.*** Villamil. Galapagos Islands, Ecuador, E Pacific Ocean *0.57S 91.00W*
56 F8 **Puerto Wilches** Santander, N Colombia *7.19N 73.55W*
65 H20 **Pueyrredón, Lago** ***var.*** Lago Cochrane. ◎ S Argentina
131 R7 **Pugachëv** Saratovskaya Oblast', W Russian Federation *52.06N 48.50E*
131 T3 **Pugachëvo** Udmurtskaya Respublika, NW Russian Federation *56.38N 53.03E*
34 H8 **Puget Sound** *sound* Washington, NW USA
109 O17 **Puglia** ***var.*** Le Puglie, ***Eng.*** Apulia. ◐ *region* SE Italy
109 N17 **Puglia, Canosa di** ***anc.*** Canusium. Puglia, SE Italy *41.13N 16.04E*
120 I6 **Puhja** ***Ger.*** Kawelecht. Tartumaa, SE Estonia *58.19N 26.19E*
Puhó *see* Púchov
107 V4 **Puigcerdà** Cataluña, NE Spain *42.25N 1.53E*
Puigmal *see* Puigmal d'Err
105 N17 **Puigmal d'Err** ***var.*** Puigmal. ▲ S France *42.24N 2.07E*
78 I16 **Pujehun** S Sierra Leone *7.22N 11.43W*
Puka *see* Pukë
193 E20 **Pukaki, Lake** ◎ South Island, NZ
40 F10 **Pukalani** Maui, Hawaii, USA, C Pacific Ocean *20.50N 94.20W*
202 J13 **Pukapuka** *atoll* N Cook Islands
203 X9 **Pukapuka** *atoll* Îles Tuamotu, E French Polynesia
Pukari Neem *see* Purekkari Neem
203 X11 **Pukarua** ***var.*** Pukaruha. *atoll* Îles Tuamotu, E French Polynesia
Pukaruha *see* Pukarua
12 A7 **Pukaskwa** ≈ Ontario, S Canada
9 V12 **Pukatawagan** Manitoba, C Canada *55.46N 101.13W*
203 X16 **Pukatikei, Maunga** ⛰ Easter Island, Chile, E Pacific Ocean
190 C1 **Pukatja** ***var.*** Ernabella. South Australia *26.18S 132.13E*
169 Y12 **Pukch'ŏng** E North Korea *40.13N 128.19E*
115 L18 **Pukë** ***var.*** Puka. Shkodër, N Albania *42.03N 19.53E*
192 L6 **Pukekohe** Auckland, North Island, NZ *37.12S 174.54E*
192 L7 **Pukemiro** Waikato, North Island, NZ *37.37S 175.02E*
202 D12 **Puke, Mont** ▲ Île Futuna, W Wallis and Futuna
Puket *see* Phuket
193 C20 **Puketeraki Range** ▲▲ South Island, NZ
192 N13 **Puketoi Range** ▲▲ North Island, NZ
193 F21 **Pukeuri Junction** Otago, South Island, NZ *45.01S 171.01E*
121 L16 **Pukhavichy** ***Rus.*** Pukhovichi. Minskaya Voblasts', C Belarus *53.30N 28.15E*
Pukhovichi *see* Pukhavichy
128 M10 **Puksoozero** Arkhangel'skaya Oblast', NW Russian Federation *62.37N 40.29E*
114 A10 **Pula** ***It.*** Pola; ***prev.*** Pulj. Istra, NW Croatia *44.53N 13.51E*
169 U14 **Pulandian** ***var.*** Xinjin. Liaoning, NE China *39.25N 121.58E*
169 T14 **Pulandian Wan** *bay* NE China
179 Rr15 **Pulangi** ≈ Mindanao, S Philippines
201 O15 **Pulap Atoll** *atoll* Caroline Islands, C Micronesia
20 H9 **Pulaski** New York, NE USA *43.34N 76.06W*
22 I10 **Pulaski** Tennessee, S USA *35.11N 87.00W*
23 R7 **Pulaski** Virginia, NE USA *37.03N 80.46W*
176 Yy13 **Pulau, Sungai** ≈ Irian Jaya, E Indonesia
112 N13 **Puławy** ***Ger.*** Neu Amerika. Lubelskie, E Poland *51.25N 21.56E*
103 E16 **Pulheim** Nordrhein-Westfalen, W Germany *51.00N 6.48E*
Pulicat *see* Pālghāt
161 J19 **Pulicat Lake** *lagoon* SE India
194 M12 **Pulie** ≈ New Britain, C PNG
Pul'-I-Khatum *see* Polekhatum
Pul-i-Khumri *see* Pol-e Khomrī
Pul-i-Sefid *see* Pol-e Safīd
Pulj *see* Pula
111 W2 **Pulkau** ≈ NE Austria
95 L15 **Pulkkila** Oulu, C Finland *64.14N 25.52E*
125 Cc6 **Pul'kovo** ✈ (Sankt-Peterburg) Leningradskaya Oblast', NW Russian Federation *60.06N 30.23E*
34 M9 **Pullman** Washington, NW USA *46.43N 117.10W*
110 B10 **Pully** Vaud, SW Switzerland *46.31N 6.40E*
42 F7 **Púlpita, Punta** *headland* W Mexico *26.30N 111.28W*
112 M10 **Pułtusk** Mazowieckie, C Poland *52.41N 21.04E*
164 H10 **Pulu** Xinjiang Uygur Zizhiqu, W China *36.10N 81.28E*
143 P13 **Pülümür** Tunceli, E Turkey *39.30N 39.54E*
201 N16 **Pulusuk** *island* Caroline Islands, C Micronesia
201 N16 **Puluwat Atoll** *atoll* Caroline Islands, C Micronesia
27 N11 **Pumpville** Texas, SW USA *39.55N 101.43W*
203 P7 **Punaauia** ***var.*** Hakapehi. Tahiti, W French Polynesia *17.37S 149.37W*
58 B8 **Puná, Isla** *island* SW Ecuador
193 G16 **Punakaiki** West Coast, South Island, NZ *42.07S 171.21E*
159 T11 **Punakha** C Bhutan *27.37N 89.49E*
59 L18 **Punata** Cochabamba, C Bolivia *17.33S 65.52W*
161 E14 **Pune** ***prev.*** Poona. Mahārāshtra, W India *18.31N 73.52E*
85 M17 **Pungoè, Rio** ***var.*** Púnguè, Pungwe. ≈ C Mozambique
23 X10 **Pungo River** ≈ North Carolina, SE USA
Púnguè/Pungwe *see* Pungoè, Rio
81 N19 **Punia** Maniema, E Dem. Rep. Congo (Zaire) *1.28S 26.25E*
64 H8 **Punilla, Sierra de la** ▲▲ W Argentina
167 P14 **Puning** Guangdong, S China *23.18N 116.12E*
64 G10 **Punitaqui** Coquimbo, C Chile *30.49S 71.13W*
158 H8 **Punjab** ◐ *state* NW India
155 T9 **Punjab** ***prev.*** West Punjab, Western Punjab. ◐ *province* E Pakistan
133 Q9 **Punjab Plains** *plain* N India
95 O17 **Punkaharju** ***var.*** Punkasalmi. Isä-Suomi, E Finland *61.45N 29.21E*
Punkasalmi *see* Punkaharju
59 I17 **Puno** Puno, SE Peru *15.52S 70.03W*
59 H17 **Puno** ***off.*** Departamento de Puno. ◐ *department* S Peru
63 B24 **Punta Alta** Buenos Aires, E Argentina *38.53S 62.00W*
65 H24 **Punta Arenas** ***prev.*** Magallanes. Magallanes, S Chile *53.10S 70.55W*
47 T6 **Punta, Cerro de** ▲ C Puerto Rico *18.10N 66.36W*
45 T15 **Punta Chame** Panamá, C Panama *8.39N 79.42W*
59 G17 **Punta Colorada** Arequipa, SW Peru *16.17S 72.31W*
42 F9 **Punta Coyote** Baja California Sur, W Mexico
64 G8 **Punta de Díaz** Atacama, N Chile *28.03S 70.36W*
63 G20 **Punta del Este** Maldonado, S Uruguay *34.58S 54.58W*
65 K17 **Punta Delgada** Chubut, SE Argentina *42.46S 63.40W*
57 O5 **Punta de Mata** Monagas, NE Venezuela *9.43N 63.39W*
57 O4 **Punta de Piedras** Nueva Esparta, NE Venezuela *10.54N 64.06W*
44 F4 **Punta Gorda** Toledo, SE Belize *16.07N 88.47W*
45 N11 **Punta Gorda** Región Autónoma Atlántico Sur, SE Nicaragua *11.31N 83.46W*
25 W14 **Punta Gorda** Florida, SE USA *26.55N 82.03W*
44 M11 **Punta Gorda, Río** ≈ SE Nicaragua
64 H6 **Punta Negra, Salar de** *salt lake* N Chile
42 D5 **Punta Prieta** Baja California, NW Mexico *28.55N 114.10W*
44 L13 **Puntarenas** Puntarenas, W Costa Rica *9.57N 84.49W*
44 L13 **Puntarenas** ***off.*** Provincia de Puntarenas. ◐ *province* W Costa Rica
56 J4 **Punto Fijo** Falcón, N Venezuela *11.42N 70.13W*
107 S4 **Puntón de Guara** ▲ N Spain *42.18N 0.13W*
20 D14 **Punxsutawney** Pennsylvania, NE USA *40.55N 78.57W*
95 M14 **Puolanka** Oulu, C Finland *64.51N 27.42E*
59 J17 **Pupuya, Nevado** ▲ W Bolivia *15.04S 69.01W*
167 O10 **Puqi** Hubei, C China *29.45N 113.51E*
59 F16 **Puquio** Ayacucho, S Peru *14.43S 74.06W*
126 H9 **Pur** ≈ N Russian Federation
194 I13 **Purari** ≈ S PNG
29 N11 **Purcell** Oklahoma, C USA *35.00N 97.21W*
9 O16 **Purcell Mountains** ▲▲ British Columbia, SW Canada
107 P14 **Purchena** Andalucía, S Spain *37.21N 2.21W*
29 S8 **Purdy** Missouri, C USA *36.49N 93.55W*
120 I2 **Purekkari Neem** ***prev.*** Pukari Neem. *headland* N Estonia *59.33N 24.49E*
39 U7 **Purgatoire River** ≈ Colorado, C USA
Purgstall *see* Purgstall an der Erlauf
111 V5 **Purgstall an der Erlauf** ***var.*** Purgstall. Niederösterreich, NE Austria *48.01N 15.08E*
160 O13 **Puri** ***var.*** Jagannath. Orissa, E India *19.52N 85.49E*
Puriramya *see* Buriram
111 X4 **Purkersdorf** Niederösterreich, NE Austria *48.13N 16.12E*
100 I9 **Purmerend** Noord-Holland, C Netherlands *52.30N 4.55E*
157 G16 **Pūrna** ≈ C India
Purnea *see* Pūrnia
159 R13 **Pūrnia** ***prev.*** Purnea. Bihār, NE India *25.46N 87.28E*
Pursat *see* Poŭthĭsăt, Poŭthĭsăt, W Cambodia
Pursat *see* Poŭthĭsăt, Stœng, W Cambodia
Purulia *see* Puruliya
156 L13 **Puruliya** ***prev.*** Purulia. West Bengal, NE India *23.19N 86.24E*
49 G7 **Purus, Rio** ***Sp.*** Río Purús. ≈ Brazil/Peru
194 G15 **Purutu Island** *island* SW PNG
95 N17 **Puruvesi** ◎ SE Finland
24 L7 **Purvis** Mississippi, S USA *31.08N 89.24W*
116 J11 **Pŭrvomay** ***prev.*** Borisovgrad. Plovdiv, C Bulgaria *42.06N 25.14E*
174 J14 **Purwakarta** ***prev.*** Poerwakarta. Jawa, C Indonesia *6.30S 107.25E*
174 L15 **Purwodadi** ***prev.*** Poerwodadi. Jawa, C Indonesia *7.04S 110.52E*
174 K15 **Purwokerto** ***prev.*** Poerwokerto. Jawa, C Indonesia *7.25S 109.13E*
174 Kk15 **Purworejo** ***prev.*** Poerworedjo. Jawa, C Indonesia *7.45S 110.04E*
22 H8 **Puryear** Tennessee, S USA *36.25N 88.21W*
160 H13 **Pusad** Mahārāshtra, C India *19.56N 77.40E*
169 Z16 **Pusan** ***off.*** Pusan-gwangyŏksi, ***var.*** Busan, ***Jap.*** Fusan. SE South Korea *35.11N 129.04E*
173 Ee4 **Pusatgajo, Pegunungan** ▲▲ Sumatera, NW Indonesia
Puschlav *see* Poschiavo
Pushkin *see* Tsarskoye Selo
131 Q8 **Pushkino** Saratovskaya Oblast', W Russian Federation *51.09N 47.00E*
Pushkino *see* Biläsuvar
113 M22 **Püspökladány** Hajdú-Bihar, E Hungary *47.19N 21.04E*
120 J3 **Püssi** ***Ger.*** Isenhof. Ida-Virumaa, NE Estonia *59.21N 27.05E*
118 I5 **Pustomyty** L'vivs'ka Oblast', W Ukraine *49.43N 23.55E*
128 F16 **Pustoshka** Pskovskaya Oblast', W Russian Federation *56.21N 29.16E*
Pusztakalán *see* Călan
178 H1 **Putao** ***prev.*** Fort Hertz. Kachin State, N Burma *27.22N 97.24E*
192 M8 **Putaruru** Waikato, North Island, NZ *38.02S 175.46E*
Puteoli *see* Pozzuoli
167 R12 **Putian** Fujian, SE China *25.28N 119.01E*
109 O17 **Putignano** Puglia, SE Italy *40.51N 17.07E*
Putivl' *see* Putyvl'
43 Q16 **Putla** ***var.*** Putla de Guerrero. Oaxaca, SE Mexico *16.54N 97.55W*
Putla de Guerrero *see* Putla
21 N12 **Putnam** Connecticut, NE USA *41.56N 71.52W*
27 Q7 **Putnam** Texas, SW USA *32.22N 99.11W*
20 M10 **Putney** Vermont, NE USA *42.59N 72.30W*
113 L20 **Putnok** Borsod-Abaúj-Zemplén, NE Hungary *48.18N 20.25E*
Putorana, Gory/Putorana Mountains *see* Putorana, Plato
126 Ii8 **Putorana, Plato** ***var.*** Gory Putorana, ***Eng.*** Putorana Mountains. ▲▲ N Russian Federation
64 H2 **Putre** Tarapacá, N Chile *18.11S 69.30W*
161 J24 **Puttalam** North Western Province, W Sri Lanka *8.01N 79.54E*
161 J24 **Puttalam Lagoon** *lagoon* W Sri Lanka
101 H17 **Putte** Antwerpen, C Belgium *51.04N 4.39E*
100 K11 **Putten** Gelderland, C Netherlands *52.15N 5.36E*
102 K7 **Puttgarden** Schleswig-Holstein, N Germany *54.30N 11.12E*
Puttiala *see* Patiāla
103 D20 **Püttlingen** Saarland, SW Germany *49.16N 6.52E*
56 D14 **Putumayo** ***off.*** Intendencia del Putumayo. ◐ *province* S Colombia
50 E7 **Putumayo, Río** ***var.*** Rio Içá. ≈ NW South America ***see also*** Içá, Rio
174 K8 **Putus, Tanjung** *headland* Borneo, N Indonesia *0.27S 109.04E*
118 J8 **Putyla** Chernivets'ka Oblast', W Ukraine *47.59N 25.04E*
119 S3 **Putyvl'** ***Rus.*** Putivl'. Sums'ka Oblast', NE Ukraine *51.21N 33.52E*
95 M18 **Puula** ◎ SE Finland
95 N18 **Puumala** Isä-Suomi, E Finland *61.31N 28.12E*
120 I5 **Puurmani** ***Ger.*** Talkhof. Jõgevamaa, E Estonia *58.36N 26.17E*
101 G17 **Puurs** Antwerpen, N Belgium *51.04N 4.16E*
Pu'uUla'ula *see* Red Hill
40 A8 **Puuwai** Niihau, Hawaii, USA, C Pacific Ocean *21.54N 96.11W*
10 J4 **Puvirnituq** ***prev.*** Povungnituk. Quebec, NE Canada *60.10N 77.19W*
34 H8 **Puyallup** Washington, NW USA *47.11N 122.17W*
167 O5 **Puyang** Henan, C China *35.42N 115.03E*
167 R9 **Puyang Jiang** ***var.*** Tsien Tang. ≈ SE China
105 O11 **Puy-de-Dôme** ◐ *department* C France
105 N15 **Puylaurens** Tarn, S France *43.33N 2.01E*
104 M13 **Puy-l'Evêque** Lot, S France *44.31N 1.10E*
105 N17 **Puymorens, Col de** *pass* S France *42.33N 1.50E*
58 C7 **Puyo** Pastaza, C Ecuador *1.30S 77.58W*
193 A24 **Puysegur Point** *headland* South Island, NZ *46.09S 166.38E*
154 J8 **Pūzak, Hāmūn-e** ***Pash.*** Hāmūn-i-Puzak. ◎ SW Afghanistan
Puzak, Hāmūn-i- *see* Pūzak, Hāmūn-e
83 J23 **Pwani** ***Eng.*** Coast. ◐ *region* E Tanzania
81 O23 **Pweto** Katanga, SE Dem. Rep. Congo (Zaire) *8.29S 28.57E*
99 I19 **Pwllheli** NW Wales, UK *52.53N 4.22W*
201 O14 **Pwok** Pohnpei, E Micronesia
126 Gg10 **Pyakupur** ≈ N Russian Federation
128 M6 **Pyalitsa** Murmanskaya Oblast', NW Russian Federation *66.16N 39.55E*
128 K10 **Pyal'ma** Respublika Kareliya, NW Russian Federation *62.24N 35.56E*
Pyandzh *see* Panj
128 I6 **Pyaozero, Ozero** ◎ NW Russian Federation
177 Ff9 **Pyapon** Irrawaddy, SW Burma *16.15N 95.40E*
121 J15 **Pyarshai** ***Rus.*** Pershay. Minskaya Voblasts', C Belarus *54.02N 26.44E*
126 I6 **Pyasina** ≈ N Russian Federation
116 I10 **Pyasŭchnik, Yazovir** ▣ C Bulgaria
125 B13 **Pyatigorsk** Stavropol'skiy Kray, SW Russian Federation *44.01N 43.06E*
Pyatikhatki *see* P"yatykhatky
119 S7 **P"yatykhatky** ***Rus.*** Pyatikhatki. Dnipropetrovs'ka Oblast', E Ukraine *48.22N 33.43E*
177 G6 **Pyawbwe** Mandalay, C Burma *20.39N 96.04E*
131 T3 **Pychas** Udmurtskaya Respublika, NW Russian Federation *56.30N 52.33E*
Pyè *see* Prome
177 F6 **Pyechin** Chin State, W Burma *20.01N 93.36E*
121 G17 **Pyeski** ***Rus.*** Peski. Hrodzyenskaya Voblasts', W Belarus *53.22N 24.37E*
121 L19 **Pyetrykaw** ***Rus.*** Petrikov. Homyel'skaya Voblasts', SE Belarus *52.07N 28.30E*
95 M16 **Pyhajärvi** ◎ C Finland
95 O17 **Pyhäjärvi** ◎ SE Finland
95 L15 **Pyhäjoki** Oulu, W Finland *64.28N 24.15E*
95 L15 **Pyhäjoki** ≈ W Finland
95 M15 **Pyhäntä** Oulu, C Finland *64.07N 26.19E*
95 M16 **Pyhäsalmi** Oulu, C Finland *63.38N 26.00E*
95 O17 **Pyhäselkä** ◎ SE Finland
95 M19 **Pyhtää** ***Swe.*** Pyttis. Etelä-Suomi, S Finland *60.29N 26.40E*
177 G6 **Pyinmana** Mandalay, C Burma *19.45N 96.12E*
117 N24 **Pylés** ***var.*** Piles. Kárpathos, SE Greece *35.31N 27.08E*
117 D21 **Pýlos** ***var.*** Pilos. Pelopónnisos, S Greece *36.55N 21.42E*
20 B12 **Pymatuning Reservoir** ▣ Ohio/Pennsylvania, NE USA
169 X15 **P'yŏngt'aek** NW South Korea *37.00N 127.04E*
169 V14 **P'yŏngyang** ***var.*** P'yŏngyang-si, ***Eng.*** Pyongyang. ● (North Korea) SW North Korea *39.04N 125.46E*
P'yŏngyang-si *see* P'yŏngyang
37 Q4 **Pyramid Lake** ◎ Nevada, W USA
39 P15 **Pyramid Mountains** ▲▲ New Mexico, SW USA
39 R5 **Pyramid Peak** ▲ Colorado, C USA *39.04N 106.57W*
117 D17 **Pyramíva** ***var.*** Piramiva. ▲ C Greece *39.08N 21.18E*
Pyrenaei Montes *see* Pyrenees
88 B12 **Pyrenees** ***Fr.*** Pyrénées, ***Sp.*** Pirineos; ***anc.*** Pyrenaei Montes. ▲▲ SW Europe
104 J16 **Pyrénées-Atlantiques** ◐ *department* SW France
105 N17 **Pyrénées-Orientales** ◐ *department* S France
117 L19 **Pyrgí** ***var.*** Pirgi. Chíos, E Greece *38.13N 26.01E*
117 D20 **Pýrgos** ***var.*** Pírgos. Dytikí Ellás, S Greece *37.40N 21.27E*
Pyritz *see* Pyrzyce
117 E19 **Pýrros** ≈ S Greece
119 R4 **Pyryatyn** ***Rus.*** Piryatin. Poltavs'ka Oblast', NE Ukraine *50.13N 32.31E*
112 D9 **Pyrzyce** ***Ger.*** Pyritz. Zachodniopomorskie, NW Poland *53.09N 14.52E*
128 F15 **Pytalovo** ***Latv.*** Abrene; ***prev.*** Jaunlatgale. Pskovskaya Oblast', W Russian Federation *57.06N 27.55E*
117 M20 **Pythagóreio** ***var.*** Pithagorio. Sámos, Dodekánisos, Greece, Aegean Sea *37.42N 26.57E*
12 L11 **Pythonga, Lac** ◎ Quebec, SE Canada
96 E10 **Pyttegga** ▲ S Norway *62.13N 7.40E*
Pyttis *see* Pyhtää
177 G7 **Pyu** Pegu, C Burma *18.28N 96.25E*
177 G8 **Pyuntaza** Pegu, SW Burma *17.51N 96.43E*
159 N11 **Pyuthan** Mid Western, W Nepal *28.09N 82.50E*
112 H12 **Pyzdry** ***Ger.*** Peisern. Wielkopolskie, C Poland *52.10N 17.42E*

Q

144 H13 **Qā' al Jafr** ◎ S Jordan
207 O11 **Qaanaaq** ***var.*** Qânâq, ***Dan.*** Thule. Avannaarsua, N Greenland *77.34N 69.44W*
144 G7 **Qabb Eliâs** E Lebanon *33.46N 35.49E*
Qabil *see* Al Qābil
Qabırrı *see* Iori
Qābis *see* Gabès
Qābis, Khalīj *see* Gabès, Golfe de
147 S14 **Qabr Hūd** C Yemen *16.02N 49.36E*
Qacentina *see* Constantine
154 L4 **Qādes** Bādghīs, NW Afghanistan *34.52N 63.25E*
145 T11 **Qādisīyah** S Iraq *31.43N 44.28E*
149 O4 **Qā'emshahr** ***prev.*** 'Alīābad, Shāhī. Māzandarān, N Iran *36.31N 52.49E*
149 U7 **Qā'en** ***var.*** Qain, Qāyen. Khorāsān, E Iran *33.43N 59.07E*
147 U13 **Qafa** *spring/well* SW Oman *17.46N 52.55E*
Qafṣah *see* Gafsa
169 V9 **Qagan Nur** ◎ NE China
169 Q11 **Qagan Nur** ◎ N China
Qagan Us *see* Dulan
164 H13 **Qagcaka** Xizang Zizhiqu, W China *32.31N 81.52E*
Qahremānshahr *see* Bākhtarān
165 Q10 **Qaidam He** ≈ C China
162 L8 **Qaidam Pendi** *basin* C China
Qain *see* Qā'en
Qala Āhangarān *see* Chaghcharān
145 U3 **Qal̦ā Diza** ***var.*** Qal 'at Dīzah. NE Iraq *36.10N 45.07E*
Qal'ah Sālih *see* Qal'at Şāliḩ
153 R13 **Qal'aikhum** ***Rus.*** Kalaikhum. S Tajikistan *38.28N 70.49E*
Qala Nau *see* Qal'eh-ye Now
147 V17 **Qalansīyah** Suquṭrā, W Yemen *12.40N 53.30E*
Qala Panja *see* Qal'eh-ye Panjeh
Qala Shāhar *see* Qal'eh Shahr
Qalāt *see* Kalāt
145 W9 **Qal'at Aḩmad** E Iraq *32.24N 46.46E*
147 N11 **Qal'at Bīshah** 'Asīr, SW Saudi Arabia *19.59N 42.38E*
144 H4 **Qal'at Burzay** Ḩamāh, W Syria *35.37N 36.16E*
Qal 'at Dīzah *see* Qal̦ā Diza
145 W9 **Qal'at Ḩusayh** E Iraq *32.19N 46.46E*
145 V10 **Qal'at Majnūnah** S Iraq *31.39N 45.44E*
145 X11 **Qal'at Şāliḩ** ***var.*** Qal'ah Sālih. E Iraq *31.30N 47.24E*
145 V10 **Qal'at Sukkar** SE Iraq *31.52N 46.04E*
Qalba Zhotasy *see* Kalbinskiy Khrebet
149 Q12 **Qal'eh Biābān** Fārs, S Iran
155 N4 **Qal'eh Shahr** ***Pash.*** Qala Shāhar. Sar-e Pol, N Afghanistan *35.34N 65.38E*
154 L4 **Qal'eh-ye Now** ***var.*** Qala Nau. Bādghīs, NW Afghanistan *34.59N 63.07E*
155 T2 **Qal'eh-ye Panjeh** ***var.*** Qala Panja. Badakhshān, NE Afghanistan *36.56N 72.15E*
Qamar Bay *see* Qamar, Ghubbat al
147 U14 **Qamar, Ghubbat al** ***Eng.*** Qamar Bay. *bay* Oman/Yemen
147 V13 **Qamar, Jabal al** ▲▲ SW Oman
Qambar *see* Kambar
165 R14 **Qamdo** Xizang Zizhiqu, W China *31.09N 97.09E*
197 K13 **Qamea** ***prev.*** Nggamea. *island* N Fiji
77 R7 **Qamīnis** NE Libya *31.48N 20.04E*
Qamishly *see* Al Qāmishlī
Qânâq *see* Qaanaaq
Qandahār *see* Kandahār
82 Q11 **Qandala** Bari, NE Somalia *11.30N 50.00E*
Qandyaghash *see* Kandyagash
144 L2 **Qanṭārī** Ar Raqqah, N Syria *36.24N 39.16E*
143 V13 **Qapiciğ Dağı** ***Rus.*** Gora Kapydzhik. ▲ SW Azerbaijan *39.18N 46.00E*
164 H5 **Qapqal** ***var.*** Qapqal Xibe Zizhixian. Xinjiang Uygur Zizhiqu, NW China *43.46N 81.09E*
Qapqal Xibe Zizhixian *see* Qapqal
Qapshagay Böyeni *see* Kapchagayskoye Vodokhranilishche
206 M15 **Qaqortoq** ***Dan.*** Julianehåb. Kitaa, S Greenland *60.51N 46.01W*
77 U8 **Qâra** ***var.*** Qārah. NW Egypt *29.34N 26.28E*
145 T4 **Qara Anjīr** N Iraq *35.30N 44.37E*
Qarabāgh *see* Qarah Bāgh
Qaraböget *see* Karaboget
Qarabulaq *see* Karabulak
Qarabutaq *see* Karabutak
Qaraghandy/Qaraghandy Oblysy *see* Karaganda
Qaraghayly *see* Karagayly
145 U4 **Qara Gol** NE Iraq *35.21N 45.38E*
Qārah *see* Qâra
154 J4 **Qarah Bāgh** ***var.*** Qarabāgh. Herāt, NW Afghanistan *35.06N 61.33E*
144 G7 **Qaraoun, Lac de** ***var.*** Buḩayrat al Qir'awn. ◎ S Lebanon
Qaraoy *see* Karaoy
Qaraqoyyn *see* Karakoyyn, Ozero
Qara Qum *see* Garagumy
Qarasū *see* Karasu
Qaratal *see* Karatal
Qarataū *see* Karatau, Khrebet, Kazakhstan
Qarataū *see* Karatau, Zhambyl, Kazakhstan
Qaraton *see* Karaton
82 P13 **Qardho** ***var.*** Kardh, ***It.*** Gardo. Bari, N Somalia *9.34N 49.30E*
148 M6 **Qareh Chāy** ≈ N Iran
148 K2 **Qareh Sū** ≈ NW Iran
Qariateïne *see* Al Qaryatayn
Qarkilik *see* Ruoqiang
153 O13 **Qarluq** ***Rus.*** Karluk. Surkhondaryo Wiloyati, S Uzbekistan *38.17N 67.39E*
153 U12 **Qarokŭl** ***Rus.*** Karakul'. E Tajikistan *39.07N 73.33E*
153 T12 **Qarokŭl** ***Rus.*** Ozero Karakul'. ◎ E Tajikistan
Qarqan *see* Qiemo
164 K9 **Qarqan He** ≈ NW China
Qarqannah, Juzur *see* Kerkenah, Îles de
Qarqaraly *see* Karkaralinsk
155 O1 **Qarqīn** Jowzjān, N Afghanistan *37.25N 66.03E*
Qars *see* Kars
Qarsaqbay *see* Karsakpay
152 M12 **Qarshi** ***Rus.*** Karshi; ***prev.*** Bek-Budi. Qashqadaryo Wiloyati, S Uzbekistan *38.54N 65.48E*
152 L12 **Qarshi Chŭli** ***Rus.*** Karshinskaya Step. *grassland* S Uzbekistan
152 M13 **Qarshi Kanali** ***Rus.*** Karshinskiy Kanal. *canal* Turkmenistan/Uzbekistan
Qaryatayn *see* Al Qaryatayn
152 M12 **Qashqadaryo Wiloyati** ***Rus.*** Kashkadar'inskaya Oblast'. ◐ *province* S Uzbekistan
Qasigianguit *see* Qasigiannguit
207 N13 **Qasigiannguit** ***var.*** Qasigianguit, ***Dan.*** Christianshåb. Kitaa, C Greenland *68.42N 50.49W*
Qaşīm, Minṭaqat *see* Al Qaşīm
145 P8 **Qaşr 'Amīj** C Iraq *33.30N 41.52E*
145 R9 **Qaşr Darwīshāh** C Iraq *32.36N 43.27E*
148 J6 **Qaşr-e Shīrīn** Kermānshāh, W Iran *34.33N 45.37E*
77 V10 **Qasr Farâfra** W Egypt *27.00N 27.58E*
Qassim *see* Al Qaşīm
147 O16 **Qa'ṭabah** SW Yemen *13.51N 44.42E*
144 H7 **Qaṭanā** ***var.*** Katana. Dimashq, S Syria *33.27N 36.04E*
149 N15 **Qatar** ***off.*** State of Qatar, ***Ar.*** Dawlat Qaṭar. ◆ *monarchy* SW Asia
Qatrana *see* Al Qaṭrānah
149 Q12 **Qaṭrūyeh** Fārs, S Iran
Qattara Depression/Qaṭṭārah, Munkhafaḍ al *see* Qaṭṭâra, Monkhafad el
77 U8 **Qaṭṭâra, Monkhafad el** ***var.*** Munkhafaḍ al Qaṭṭārah, ***Eng.*** Qattara Depression. *desert* NW Egypt
Qaṭṭīnah, Buḩayrat *see* Ḩimş, Buḩayrat
Qaydār *see* Qeydār
Qāyen *see* Qā'en
153 Q11 **Qayroqqum** ***Rus.*** Kayrakkum. NW Tajikistan *40.16N 69.46E*
153 Q10 **Qayroqqum, Obanbori** ***Rus.*** Kayrakkumskoye Vodokhranilishche. ▣ NW Tajikistan
145 U7 **Qazānīyah** ***var.*** Dhū Shaykh. E Iraq *33.39N 45.33E*
Qazaqstan/Qazaqstan Respublikasy *see* Kazakhstan
143 T9 **Qazbegi** ***Rus.*** Kazbegi. NE Georgia *42.39N 44.36E*
155 P15 **Qāzi Ahmad** ***var.*** Kazi Ahmad. Sind, SE Pakistan *26.19N 68.06E*
143 Y12 **Qazimämmäd** ***Rus.*** Kazi Magomed. SE Azerbaijan *40.03N 48.56E*
Qazris *see* Cáceres
148 M4 **Qazvīn** ***var.*** Kazvin. Qazvīn, N Iran *36.16N 50.00E*
148 M5 **Qazvīn** ◐ *province* N Iran
197 K12 **Qelelevu Lagoon** *lagoon* NE Fiji
77 X10 **Qena** ***var.*** Qinā; ***anc.*** Caene, Caenepolis. E Egypt *26.12N 32.49E*
115 L23 **Qeparo** Vlorë, S Albania *40.04N 19.49E*
Qeqertarssuaq *see* Qeqertarsuaq
207 N13 **Qeqertarsuaq** ***var.*** Qeqertarssuaq, ***Dan.*** Godhavn. Kitaa, Greenland *69.27N 52.54W*
206 M13 **Qeqertarsuaq** *island* W Greenland
207 N13 **Qeqertarsuup Tunua** ***Dan.*** Disko Bugt. *inlet* W Greenland
Qerveh *see* Qorveh
149 S14 **Qeshm** Hormozgān, S Iran *26.58N 56.16E*
149 R14 **Qeshm** ***var.*** Jazīreh-ye Qeshm, Qeshm Island. *island* S Iran
Qeshm Island/Qeshm, Jazīreh-ye *see* Qeshm
148 L4 **Qeydār** ***var.*** Qaydār. Zanjān, NW Iran *36.50N 47.40E*
148 K5 **Qezel Owzan** ***var.*** Ki Zil Uzen, Qi Zil Uzun. ≈ NW Iran
148 L5 **Qezel Owzan, Rūd-e** ≈ NW Iran
Qian *see* Guizhou
Qian Gorlo *see* Qian Gorlos
169 V9 **Qian Gorlos** ***var.*** Qian Gorlo, Qian Gorlos Mongolzu Zizhixian, Qianguozhen. Jilin, NE China *45.06N 124.48E*
Qian Gorlos Mongolzu Zizhixian/Qianguozhen *see* Qian Gorlos
167 N9 **Qianjiang** Hubei, C China *30.26N 112.55E*
166 K10 **Qianjiang** Sichuan, C China *29.30N 108.45E*
166 L14 **Qian Jiang** ≈ S China
166 G9 **Qianning** ***var.*** Gartar. Sichuan, C China *30.33N 101.22E*
169 U13 **Qian Shan** ▲▲ NE China
166 H10 **Qianwei** Sichuan, C China *29.15N 103.52E*
166 J11 **Qianxi** Guizhou, S China *27.00N 106.01E*
165 Q7 **Qiaowan** Gansu, N China *40.37N 96.43E*
Qibilī *see* Kebili
164 K9 **Qiemo** ***var.*** Qarqan. Xinjiang Uygur Zizhiqu, NW China *38.09N 85.30E*
166 J10 **Qijiang** Chongqing Shi, C China *29.06N 106.35E*
165 N5 **Qijiaojing** Xinjiang Uygur Zizhiqu, NW China *43.28N 91.34E*
155 P9 **Qila Saifullāh** Baluchistān, SW Pakistan *30.45N 68.08E*
165 S9 **Qilian** Qinghai, C China *38.09N 100.08E*
139 Nn10 **Qilian Shan** ***var.*** Kilien Mountains. ▲▲ N China
207 O11 **Qimusseriarsuaq** ***Dan.*** Melville Bugt, ***Eng.*** Melville Bay. *bay* NW Greenland
Qinā *see* Qena
165 W11 **Qin'an** Gansu, C China *34.49N 105.50E*
Qing *see* Qinghai
169 W7 **Qing'an** Heilongjiang, NE China *46.53N 127.29E*
167 R5 **Qingdao** ***var.*** Ching-Tao, Ch'ing-tao, Tsingtao, Tsintao, ***Ger.*** Tsingtau. Shandong, E China *36.30N 120.55E*
169 V8 **Qinggang** Heilongjiang, NE China *46.40N 126.04E*
Qinggil *see* Qinghe
165 P11 **Qinghai** ***var.*** Chinghai, Koko Nor, Qing, Qinghai Sheng, Tsinghai. ◐ *province* C China
165 S10 **Qinghai Hu** ***var.*** Ch'ing Hai, Tsing Hai, ***Mong.*** Koko **Nor.** ◎ C China
Qinghai Sheng *see* Qinghai
164 M3 **Qinghe** ***var.*** Qinggil. Xinjiang Uygur Zizhiqu, NW China *46.42N 90.19E*
166 L4 **Qingjian** Shaanxi, C China *37.10N 110.09E*
166 L9 **Qing Jiang** ≈ C China
Qingjiang *see* Huaiyin
Qingkou *see* Ganyu
166 I12 **Qinglong** ***var.*** Liancheng. Guizhou, S China *25.49N 105.10E*
167 Q2 **Qinglong** Hebei, E China *40.24N 118.57E*
Qingshan *see* Dedu
165 R12 **Qingshuihe** Qinghai, C China *33.08N 97.19E*
Qingyang *see* Jinjiang
169 V11 **Qingyuan** Liaoning, NE China *42.08N 124.55E*
164 L13 **Qingzang Gaoyuan** ***var.*** Xizang Gaoyuan, ***Eng.*** Plateau of Tibet. *plateau* W China
167 Q4 **Qingzhou** ***prev.*** Yidu. Shandong, E China *36.46N 118.23E*
163 R9 **Qin He** ≈ C China
167 Q2 **Qinhuangdao** Hebei, E China *39.57N 119.31E*
166 K7 **Qin Ling** ▲▲ C China
Qin Xian *see* Qinxian
167 N5 **Qinxian** ***var.*** Qin Xian. Shanxi, C China *36.46N 112.42E*
167 N6 **Qinyang** Henan, C China *35.04N 112.55E*
166 K15 **Qinzhou** Guangxi Zhuangzu Zizhiqu, S China *22.09N 108.36E*
Qiong *see* Hainan
166 L17 **Qionghai** ***prev.*** Jiaji. Hainan, S China *19.12N 110.26E*
166 H9 **Qionglai** Sichuan, C China *30.24N 103.28E*
166 H8 **Qionglai Shan** ▲▲ C China
166 L17 **Qiongzhou Haixia** ***var.*** Hainan Strait. *strait* S China
169 U7 **Qiqihar** ***var.*** Ch'i-ch'i-ha-erh, Tsitsihar; ***prev.*** Lungkiang. Heilongjiang, NE China *47.23N 124.00E*
149 P12 **Qīr** Fārs, S Iran *28.27N 53.04E*
164 H10 **Qira** Xinjiang Uygur Zizhiqu, NW China *37.04N 80.45E*
Qir'awn, Buḩayrat al *see* Qaraoun, Lac de
144 F11 **Qiryat Gat** ***var.*** Kiryat Gat. Southern, C Israel *31.37N 34.46E*
144 G8 **Qiryat Shemona** Northern, N Israel *33.13N 35.34E*
Qishlaq *see* Garmsār
147 U14 **Qishn** SE Yemen *15.28N 51.43E*
144 G9 **Qishon, Naḩal** ≈ N Israel
Qita Ghazzah *see* Gaza Strip
162 K5 **Qitai** Xinjiang Uygur Zizhiqu, NW China *44.00N 89.33E*
169 Y8 **Qitaihe** Heilongjiang, NE China *45.45N 130.53E*
147 W12 **Qitbīt, Wādī** *dry watercourse* S Oman
167 O5 **Qixian** ***var.*** Qi Xian, Zhaoge. Henan, C China *35.34N 114.10E*
Qīzān *see* Jīzān
Qizil Orda *see* Kyzylorda
Qizil Qum/Qizilqum *see* Kyzyl Kum
153 V14 **Qizilrabot** ***Rus.*** Kyzylrabot. SE Tajikistan *37.28N 74.43E*
152 J10 **Qizilrawbe** ***Rus.*** Kyzylrabat. Bukhoro Wiloyati, C Uzbekistan *40.35N 62.09E*
Qi Zil Uzun *see* Qezel Owzan
145 S4 **Qizil Yār** N Iraq *35.26N 44.12E*
152 G7 **Qizqetkan** ***Rus.*** Kazanketken. Qoraqalpoghiston Respublikasi, W Uzbekistan *42.59N 59.21E*
Qoghaly *see* Kugaly
Qogir Feng *see* K2
149 N6 **Qom** ***var.*** Kum, Qum. Qom, N Iran *34.43N 50.53E*
149 N6 **Qom** ◐ *province* N Iran
Qomisheh *see* Shahreẕā
Qomolangma Feng *see* Everest, Mount
148 M7 **Qom, Rūd-e** ≈ C Iran
Qomsheh *see* Shahreẕā
Qomul *see* Hami
Qondūz *see* Kunduz
Qongyrat *see* Konyrat
Qoqek *see* Tacheng
Qorabowur Kirlari *see* Karabaur', Uval
Qoradaryo *see* Karadar'ya
152 G6 **Qorajar** ***Rus.*** Karadzhar. Qoraqalpoghiston Respublikasi, NW Uzbekistan *43.34N 58.35E*
152 K12 **Qorakŭl** ***Rus.*** Karakul'. Bukhoro Wiloyati, C Uzbekistan *39.27N 63.45E*
152 E5 **Qoraqalpoghiston** ***Rus.*** Karakalpakya. Qoraqalpoghiston Respublikasi, NW Uzbekistan *44.45N 56.06E*
152 G7 **Qoraqalpoghiston Respublikasi** ***Rus.*** Respublika Karakalpakstan. ◐ *autonomous republic* NW Uzbekistan
152 H7 **Qoraŭzak** ***Rus.*** Karauzyak. Qoraqalpoghiston Respublikasi, NW Uzbekistan *43.07N 60.03E*
Qorghazhyn *see* Kurgal'dzhino
144 H6 **Qornet es Saouda** ▲ NE Lebanon *36.06N 34.06E*
152 L12 **Qorowulbozor** ***Rus.*** Karaulbazar. Bukhoro Wiloyati, C Uzbekistan *39.28N 64.49E*
148 K5 **Qorveh** ***var.*** Qerveh, Qurveh. Kordestān, W Iran *35.13N 47.46E*
Qosshaghyl *see* Koschagyl
Qostanay/Qostanay Oblysy *see* Kostanay
149 P12 **Qoṭbābād** Fārs, S Iran *28.52N 53.40E*
149 R13 **Qoṭbābād** Hormozgān, S Iran *27.49N 56.00E*
144 H6 **Qoubaïyât** ***var.*** Al Qubayyāt. N Lebanon *37.00N 34.30E*
Qoussantîna *see* Constantine
164 K16 **Qowowuyag** *see* Cho Oyu
152 H6 **Qozoqdaryo** ***Rus.*** Kazakdar'ya. Qoraqalpoghiston Respublikasi, NW Uzbekistan *43.26N 59.47E*
21 N11 **Quabbin Reservoir** ▣ Massachusetts, NE USA
102 F12 **Quakenbrück** Niedersachsen, NW Germany *52.41N 7.57E*

◆ Country
● Country Capital
◇ Dependent Territory
○ Dependent Territory Capital
◐ Administrative Region
✈ International Airport
▲ Mountain
▲▲ Mountain Range
⛰ Volcano
≈ River
◎ Lake
▣ Reservoir

QUAKERTOWN – RANNEYE

20 I15 **Quakertown** Pennsylvania, NE USA 40.26N 75.17W
190 M10 **Quambatook** Victoria, SE Australia 35.52S 143.28E
27 Q4 **Quanah** Texas, SW USA 34.19N 99.45W
178 Kk11 **Quang Ngai** *var.* Quangngai, Quang Nghia. Quang Ngai, C Vietnam 15.09N 108.49E
Quang Nghia *see* Quang Ngai
178 K9 **Quang Tri** Quang Tri, C Vietnam 16.42N 107.15E
Quan Long *see* Ca Mau
158 L4 **Quanshuigou** China/India 35.40N 79.28E
167 R13 **Quanzhou** *var.* Ch'uan-chou, Tsinkiang; *prev.* Chin-chiang. Fujian, SE China 24.56N 118.31E
166 M12 **Quanzhou** Guangxi Zhuangzu Zizhiqu, S China 25.59N 111.01E
9 V16 **Qu'Appelle** ≈ Saskatchewan, S Canada
10 M3 **Quaqtaq** *prev.* Koartac. Quebec, NE Canada 60.49N 69.30W
63 E16 **Quaraí** Rio Grande do Sul, S Brazil 30.24S 56.24W
61 H24 **Quaraí, Rio** *Sp.* Río Cuareim. ≈ Brazil/Uruguay *see also* Cuareim, Río
175 P10 **Quarles, Pegunungan** ▲ Sulawesi, C Indonesia
Quarnero *see* Kvarner
109 C20 **Quartu Sant' Elena** Sardegna, Italy, C Mediterranean Sea 39.15N 9.12E
31 X13 **Quasqueton** Iowa, C USA 42.23N 91.45W
181 X16 **Quatre Bornes** W Mauritius 20.15S 57.28E
180 I17 **Quatre Bornes** Mahé, NE Seychelles
143 X10 **Quba** *Rus.* Kuba. N Azerbaijan 41.22N 48.30E
Qubba *see* Ba'qūbah
149 T3 **Qūchān** *var.* Kuchan. Khorāsān, NE Iran 37.12N 58.28E
191 R10 **Queanbeyan** New South Wales, SE Australia 35.24S 149.16E
13 Q10 **Québec** *var.* Quebec. Quebec, SE Canada 46.49N 71.15W
12 K10 **Quebec** *var.* Quebec. ◐ *province* SE Canada
63 D17 **Quebracho** Paysandú, W Uruguay 31.58S 57.52W
103 K14 **Quedlinburg** Sachsen-Anhalt, C Germany 51.48N 11.09E
144 H10 **Queen Alia** ✕ ('Ammān) 'Ammān, C Jordan
8 L16 **Queen Bess, Mount** ▲ British Columbia, SW Canada 51.15N 124.29W
8 I14 **Queen Charlotte** British Columbia, SW Canada 53.18N 132.04W
67 B24 **Queen Charlotte Bay** *bay* West Falkland, Falkland Islands
8 H14 **Queen Charlotte Islands** *Fr.* Îles de la Reine-Charlotte. *island group* British Columbia, SW Canada
8 I15 **Queen Charlotte Sound** *sea area* British Columbia, W Canada
8 J16 **Queen Charlotte Strait** *strait* British Columbia, W Canada
29 U1 **Queen City** Missouri, C USA 40.24N 92.34W
27 X5 **Queen City** Texas, SW USA 33.09N 94.09W
207 O9 **Queen Elizabeth Islands** *Fr.* Îles de la Reine-Élisabeth. *island group* Nunavut, N Canada
205 Y10 **Queen Mary Coast** *physical region* Antarctica
67 N24 **Queen Mary's Peak** ▲ C Tristan da Cunha
206 M8 **Queen Maud Gulf** *gulf* Arctic Ocean
205 P11 **Queen Maud Mountains** ▲ Antarctica
Queen's County *see* Laois
189 U7 **Queensland** ◐ *state* N Australia
199 Hh10 **Queensland Plateau** *undersea feature* N Coral Sea
191 O16 **Queenstown** Tasmania, SE Australia 42.06S 145.33E
193 C22 **Queenstown** Otago, South Island, NZ 45.03S 168.41E
85 I24 **Queenstown** Eastern Cape, S South Africa 31.52S 26.50E
Queenstown *see* Cobh
34 F8 **Queets** Washington, NW USA 47.31N 124.19W
63 D18 **Queguay Grande, Río** ≈ W Uruguay
61 O16 **Queimadas** Bahia, E Brazil 10.58S 39.37W
84 D11 **Quela** Malanje, NW Angola 9.18S 17.07E
85 O16 **Quelimane** *var.* Kilimane, Kilmain, Quilimane. Zambézia, NE Mozambique 17.52S 36.51E
65 G18 **Quellón** *var.* Puerto Quellón. Los Lagos, S Chile 43.05S 73.38W
Quelpart *see* Cheju-do
39 P12 **Quemado** New Mexico, SW USA 34.18N 108.29W
27 O12 **Quemado** Texas, SW USA 28.58N 100.36W
46 K7 **Quemado, Punta de** *headland* E Cuba 20.13N 74.07W
Quemoy *see* Chinmen Tao
64 K13 **Quemú Quemú** La Pampa, E Argentina 36.03S 63.30W
161 E17 **Quepem** Goa, W India 15.13N 74.03E
44 M14 **Quepos** Puntarenas, S Costa Rica 9.28N 84.10W
Que Que *see* Kwekwe
63 D23 **Quequén** Buenos Aires, E Argentina 38.30S 58.43W
63 D23 **Quequén Grande, Río** ≈ E Argentina
63 C23 **Quequén Salado, Río** ≈ E Argentina
Quera *see* Chur
43 N13 **Querétaro** Querétaro de Arteaga, C Mexico 20.36N 100.24W
42 F4 **Querobabi** Sonora, NW Mexico 30.03N 111.02W
44 M13 **Quesada** *var.* Ciudad Quesada, San Carlos. Alajuela, N Costa Rica 10.17N 84.24W
107 O13 **Quesada** Andalucía, S Spain 37.52N 3.05W
167 O7 **Queshan** Henan, C China 32.48N 114.03E
8 M15 **Quesnel** British Columbia, SW Canada 52.58N 122.30W
39 S9 **Questa** New Mexico, SW USA 36.41N 105.37W
104 H7 **Questembert** Morbihan, NW France 47.39N 2.24W
59 K22 **Quetena, Río** ≈ SW Bolivia
155 O10 **Quetta** Baluchistān, SW Pakistan 30.15N 67.00E
Quetzalcoalco *see* Coatzacoalcos
Quetzaltenango *see* Quezaltenango
58 B6 **Quevedo** Los Ríos, C Ecuador 1.01S 79.27W
44 B6 **Quezaltenango** *var.* Quetzaltenango. Quezaltenango, W Guatemala 14.48N 91.27W
44 A2 **Quezaltenango** *off.* Departamento de Quezaltenango, *var.* Quetzaltenango. ◐ *department* SW Guatemala
44 E6 **Quezaltepeque** Chiquimula, SE Guatemala 14.38N 89.25W
179 O15 **Quezon** Palawan, W Philippines 9.13N 118.01E
179 P10 **Quezon City** Luzon, N Philippines 14.39N 121.01E
167 P5 **Qufu** Shandong, E China 35.37N 117.05E
84 B12 **Quibala** Cuanza Sul, NW Angola 10.44S 14.58E
84 B11 **Quibaxe** *var.* Quibaxi. Cuanza Norte, NW Angola 8.30S 14.36E
Quibaxi *see* Quibaxe
56 D9 **Quibdó** Chocó, W Colombia 5.40N 76.37W
104 G7 **Quiberon** Morbihan, NW France 47.30N 3.07W
104 G7 **Quiberon, Baie de** *bay* NW France
56 J5 **Quíbor** Lara, N Venezuela 9.55N 69.34W
44 C4 **Quiché** *off.* Departamento del Quiché. ◐ *department* W Guatemala
101 E21 **Quiévrain** Hainaut, S Belgium 50.25N 3.40E
42 I9 **Quila** Sinaloa, C Mexico 24.24N 107.11W
85 B14 **Quilengues** Huíla, SW Angola 14.03S 14.03E
Quilimane *see* Quelimane
59 G15 **Quillabamba** Cusco, C Peru 12.48S 72.42W
59 L18 **Quillacollo** Cochabamba, C Bolivia 17.23S 66.15W
64 H4 **Quillagua** Antofagasta, N Chile 21.33S 69.32W
105 N17 **Quillan** Aude, S France 42.52N 2.10E
9 U15 **Quill Lakes** ◎ Saskatchewan, S Canada
64 G11 **Quillota** Valparaíso, C Chile 32.54S 71.16W
161 G23 **Quilon** *var.* Kolam, Kollam. Kerala, SW India 8.57N 76.36E
189 V9 **Quilpie** Queensland, C Australia 26.39S 144.15E
155 O4 **Quil-Qala** Bāmīān, N Afghanistan 35.13N 67.02E
64 L7 **Quimili** Santiago del Estero, C Argentina 27.38S 62.25W
59 O19 **Quimome** Santa Cruz, E Bolivia 17.45S 61.15W
104 F6 **Quimper** *anc.* Quimper Corentin. Finistère, NW France 48.00N 4.05W
Quimper Corentin *see* Quimper
104 G7 **Quimperlé** Finistère, NW France 47.52N 3.33W
34 F8 **Quinault** Washington, NW USA 47.27N 123.53W
34 F8 **Quinault River** ≈ Washington, NW USA
37 P5 **Quincy** California, W USA 39.55N 120.57W
25 S8 **Quincy** Florida, SE USA 30.35N 84.34W
32 I13 **Quincy** Illinois, N USA 39.56N 91.24W
21 O11 **Quincy** Massachusetts, NE USA 42.15N 71.00W
34 J9 **Quincy** Washington, NW USA 47.13N 119.51W
56 E10 **Quindío** *off.* Departamento del Quindío. ◐ *province* C Colombia
56 E10 **Quindío, Nevado del** ▲ C Colombia 4.42N 75.25W
64 J10 **Quines** San Luis, C Argentina 32.15S 65.46W
41 N13 **Quinhagak** Alaska, USA 59.45N 161.55W
78 G13 **Quinhámel** W Guinea-Bissau 11.52N 15.52W
Qui Nhon/Quinhon *see* Quy Nhon
Quinindé *see* Rosa Zárate
27 U6 **Quinlan** Texas, SW USA 32.54N 96.08W
63 H17 **Quinta** Rio Grande do Sul, S Brazil 32.05S 52.18W
107 O10 **Quintanar de la Orden** Castilla-La Mancha, C Spain 39.36N 3.03W
43 X13 **Quintana Roo** ◐ *state* SE Mexico
107 S6 **Quinto** Aragón, NE Spain 41.25N 0.31W
110 G10 **Quinto** Ticino, S Switzerland 46.32N 8.44E
29 Q11 **Quinton** Oklahoma, C USA 35.07N 95.22W
64 K12 **Quinto, Río** ≈ C Argentina
84 A10 **Quinzau** Zaire, NW Angola 6.50S 12.48E
12 H8 **Quinze, Lac des** ◎ Quebec, SE Canada
85 B15 **Quipungo** Huíla, C Angola 14.49S 14.29E
64 G13 **Quirihue** Bío Bío, C Chile 36.15S 72.34W
84 D12 **Quirima** Malanje, NW Angola 10.51S 18.06E
191 T6 **Quirindi** New South Wales, SE Australia 31.29S 150.40E
57 P5 **Quiriquire** Monagas, NE Venezuela 9.58N 63.13W
12 D10 **Quirke Lake** ◎ Ontario, S Canada
63 B21 **Quiroga** Buenos Aires, E Argentina 35.18S 61.22W
106 I4 **Quiroga** Galicia, NW Spain 42.28N 7.15W
Quirom, Salar *see* Pocitos, Salar
58 B9 **Quiroz, Río** ≈ NW Peru
84 Q13 **Quissanga** Cabo Delgado, NE Mozambique 12.21S 40.31E
85 M20 **Quissico** Inhambane, S Mozambique 24.42S 34.43E
27 O4 **Quitaque** Texas, SW USA 34.22N 101.03W
84 Q13 **Quiterajo** Cabo Delgado, NE Mozambique 11.37S 40.22E
25 T6 **Quitman** Georgia, SE USA 30.46N 83.33W
24 M6 **Quitman** Mississippi, S USA 32.02N 88.43W
27 V6 **Quitman** Texas, SW USA 32.48N 95.27W
58 C6 **Quito** ● (Ecuador) Pichincha, N Ecuador 0.13S 78.30W
60 P13 **Quixadá** Ceará, E Brazil 4.57S 39.04W
85 Q15 **Quixaxe** Nampula, NE Mozambique 15.15S 40.07E
166 J9 **Qu Jiang** ≈ C China
167 R10 **Qu Jiang** ≈ SE China
167 N13 **Qujiang** *prev.* Maba. Guangdong, S China 24.47N 113.34E
166 H12 **Qujing** Yunnan, SW China 25.39N 103.52E
Qulan *see* Kulan
152 L10 **Quljuqtov-Toghi** *Rus.* Gory Kul'dzhuktau. ▲ C Uzbekistan
Qulsary *see* Kul'sary
Qulyndy Zhazyghy *see* Kulunda Steppe
Qum *see* Qom
Qumälisch *see* Lubartów
165 P11 **Qumar He** ≈ C China
165 Q12 **Qumarlêb** Qinghai, C China 34.06N 95.54E
Qumisheh *see* Shahreẓā
153 O14 **Qumqurghon** *Rus.* Kumkurgan. Surkhondaryo Wiloyati, S Uzbekistan 37.54N 67.31E
Qunaytirah/Qunayṭirah, Muḥāfaẓat al/Qunaytra *see* Al Qunayṭirah
152 G7 **Qŭnghirot** *Rus.* Kungrad. Qoraqalpoghiston Respublikasi, NW Uzbekistan 43.01N 58.49E
201 V12 **Quoi** *island* Chuuk, C Micronesia
15 Kk6 **Quoich** ≈ Nunavut, NE Canada
85 E26 **Quoin Point** *headland* SW South Africa 34.48S 19.39E
190 I7 **Quorn** South Australia 32.22S 138.03E
153 R10 **Qŭqon** *var.* Khokand, *Rus.* Kokand. Farghona Wiloyati, E Uzbekistan 40.34N 70.55E
Qurein *see* Al Kuwayt
153 P14 **Qŭrghonteppa** *Rus.* Kurgan-Tyube. SW Tajikistan 37.51N 68.42E
Qurlurtuuq *see* Kugluktuk
Qurveh *see* Qorveh
Qusair *see* Quseir
143 X10 **Qusar** *Rus.* Kusary. NE Azerbaijan 41.26N 48.27E
Quṣayr *see* Al Quṣayr
77 Y10 **Quseir** *var.* Al Quṣayr, Qusair. E Egypt 26.05N 34.16E
148 I2 **Qūshchī** Āzarbāyjān-e Bākhtarī, N Iran 37.58N 45.04E
153 N11 **Qŭshrabot** *Rus.* Kushrabat. Samarqand Wiloyati, C Uzbekistan 40.15N 66.40E
Qusmuryn *see* Kushmurun, Kostanay, Kazakhstan
Qusmuryn *see* Kushmurun, Ozero, Kazakhstan
Quṭayfah/Qutayfe/Quteife *see* Al Quṭayfah
Quthing *see* Moyeni
Quwair *see* Guwēr
153 S10 **Quwasoy** *Rus.* Kuvasay. Farghona Wiloyati, E Uzbekistan 40.17N 71.53E
Qu Xian *see* Quzhou
165 N16 **Qüxü** Xizang Zizhiqu, W China 29.25N 90.48E
178 Kk13 **Quy Chanh** Ninh Thuận, S Vietnam 11.28N 108.53E
178 Kk12 **Quy Nhơn** *var.* Quinhon, Qui Nhon. Binh Định, C Vietnam 13.46N 109.10E
153 O11 **Qŭytosh** *Rus.* Koytash. Jizzakh Wiloyati, C Uzbekistan 40.13N 67.19E
167 R10 **Quzhou** *var.* Qu Xian. Zhejiang, SE China 28.55N 118.54E
Qyteti Stalin *see* Kuçovë
Qyzylorda/Qyzylorda Oblysy *see* Kzylorda
Qyzyltū *see* Kishkenekol'
Qyzylzhar *see* Kyzylzhar

R

111 R4 **Raab** Oberösterreich, N Austria 48.19N 13.40E
111 X8 **Raab** *Hung.* Rába. ≈ Austria/Hungary *see also* Rába
Raab *see* Győr
111 V2 **Raabs an der Thaya** Niederösterreich, E Austria 48.51N 15.28E
95 L14 **Raahe** *Swe.* Brahestad. Oulu, W Finland 64.42N 24.30E
100 M10 **Raalte** Overijssel, E Netherlands 52.22N 6.16E
101 I14 **Raamsdonksveer** Noord-Brabant, S Netherlands 51.42N 4.54E
94 L12 **Raanujärvi** Lappi, NW Finland 66.39N 24.40E
98 G9 **Raasay** *island* NW Scotland, UK
120 H3 **Raasiku** *Ger.* Rasik. Harjumaa, NW Estonia 59.22N 25.12E
114 B11 **Rab** *It.* Arbe. Primorje-Gorski Kotar, NW Croatia 44.46N 14.46E
114 B11 **Rab** *It.* Arbe. *island* NW Croatia
175 P16 **Raba** Sumbawa, S Indonesia 8.30S 118.46E
113 G22 **Rába** *Ger.* Raab. ≈ Austria/Hungary *see also* Raab
114 A10 **Rabac** Istra, NW Croatia 45.03N 14.09E
106 I2 **Rábade** Galicia, NW Spain 43.07N 7.37W
82 F10 **Rabak** White Nile, C Sudan 13.12N 32.43E
194 M16 **Rabaraba** Milne Bay, SE PNG 10.02S 149.53E
104 K16 **Rabastens-de-Bigorre** Hautes-Pyrénées, S France 43.22N 0.10E
123 Jj17 **Rabat** W Malta 35.51N 14.25E
76 F6 **Rabat** *var.* al Dar al Baida. ● (Morocco) NW Morocco 34.01N 6.51W
Rabat *see* Victoria
195 P10 **Rabaul** New Britain, E PNG 4.13S 152.10E
Rabbah Ammon/Rabbath Ammon *see* 'Ammān
30 K8 **Rabbit Creek** ≈ South Dakota, N USA
12 H10 **Rabbit Lake** ◎ Ontario, S Canada
197 K13 **Rabi** *prev.* Rambi. *island* N Fiji
146 K9 **Rābigh** Makkah, W Saudi Arabia 22.51N 39.00E
44 D5 **Rabinal** Baja Verapaz, C Guatemala 15.05N 90.23W
173 Ee6 **Rabi, Pulau** *island* NW Indonesia, East Indies
113 L17 **Rabka** Małopolskie, S Poland 49.37N 20.00E
161 F16 **Rabkavi** Karnātaka, W India 16.40N 75.03E
Râbnița *see* Rîbnița
111 Y6 **Rabnitz** ≈ E Austria
128 J7 **Rabocheostrovsk** Respublika Kareliya, NW Russian Federation 64.58N 34.46E
25 U1 **Rabun Bald** ▲ Georgia, SE USA 34.58N 83.18W
77 S11 **Rabyānah** SE Libya 24.07N 21.58E
77 S11 **Rabyānah, Ramlat** *var.* Rebiana Sand Sea, Ṣaḥrā' Rabyānah. *desert* SE Libya
Rabyānah, Ṣaḥrā' *see* Rabyānah, Ramlat
118 L11 **Răcăciuni** Bacău, E Romania 46.20N 27.00E
109 J24 **Racalmuto** Sicilia, Italy, C Mediterranean Sea 37.25N 13.43E
118 J14 **Răcari** Dâmbovița, SE Romania 44.37N 25.43E
Răcari *see* Durankulak
118 F13 **Răcășdia** *Hung.* Rakasd. Caraș-Severin, SW Romania 44.58N 21.36E
108 B9 **Racconigi** Piemonte, NE Italy 44.45N 7.41E
33 T15 **Raccoon Creek** ≈ Ohio, N USA
11 V13 **Race, Cape** *headland* Newfoundland, E Canada 46.40N 53.05W
24 K10 **Raceland** Louisiana, S USA 29.43N 90.36W
21 Q12 **Race Point** *headland* Massachusetts, NE USA 42.03N 70.14W
178 J15 **Rach Gia** Kiên Giang, S Vietnam 10.01N 105.04E
178 J14 **Rach Gia, Vinh** *bay* S Vietnam
78 J8 **Rachid** Tagant, C Mauritania 18.48N 11.40W
112 L10 **Raciąż** Mazowieckie, C Poland 52.46N 20.04E
113 I16 **Racibórz** *Ger.* Ratibor. Śląskie, S Poland 50.06N 18.13E
33 N9 **Racine** Wisconsin, N USA 42.42N 87.49W
12 D7 **Racine Lake** ◎ Ontario, S Canada
113 J23 **Ráckeve** Pest, C Hungary 47.07N 18.57E
Rácz-Becse *see* Bečej
147 O15 **Radā'** *var.* Ridā'. W Yemen 14.24N 44.49E
115 O15 **Radan** ▲ SE Yugoslavia 42.59N 21.31E
65 J19 **Rada Tilly** Chubut, SE Argentina 45.54S 67.33W
118 K8 **Rădăuți** *Ger.* Radautz, *Hung.* Rádóc. Suceava, N Romania 47.49N 25.58E
118 L8 **Rădăuți-Prut** Botoșani, NE Romania 48.14N 26.47E
Radautz *see* Rădăuți
Radbusa *see* Radbuza
113 A17 **Radbuza** *Ger.* Radbusa. ≈ SE Czech Republic
22 K6 **Radcliff** Kentucky, S USA 37.50N 85.57W
145 O2 **Radd, Wādī ar** *dry watercourse* N Syria
97 H16 **Råde** Østfold, S Norway 59.21N 10.52E
111 V11 **Radeče** *Ger.* Ratschach. C Slovenia 46.01N 15.10E
Radein *see* Radenci
118 J4 **Radekhiv** *Pol.* Radziechów, *Rus.* Radekhov. L'vivs'ka Oblast', W Ukraine 50.17N 24.39E
Radekhov *see* Radekhiv
111 X9 **Radenci** *Ger.* Radein; *prev.* Radinci. NE Slovenia 46.36N 16.02E
111 S9 **Radenthein** Kärnten, S Austria 46.48N 13.42E
23 R7 **Radford** Virginia, NE USA 37.07N 80.34W
160 C9 **Rādhanpur** Gujarāt, W India 23.52N 71.49E
Radinci *see* Radenci
131 Q6 **Radishchevo** Ul'yanovskaya Oblast', W Russian Federation 52.49N 47.54E
10 I9 **Radisson** Quebec, E Canada 53.47N 77.35W
9 P16 **Radium Hot Springs** British Columbia, SW Canada 50.39N 116.09W
118 F11 **Radna** *Hung.* Máriaradna. Arad, W Romania 46.04N 21.40E
116 K10 **Radnevo** Stara Zagora, C Bulgaria 42.18N 25.57E
99 J20 **Radnor** *cultural region* E Wales, UK
Radnót *see* Iernut
Radóc *see* Rădăuți
103 H24 **Radolfzell am Bodensee** Baden-Württemberg, S Germany 47.43N 8.58E
112 M13 **Radom** Mazowieckie, C Poland 51.23N 21.07E
118 I14 **Radomirești** Olt, S Romania 44.06N 25.00E
113 K14 **Radomsko** *Rus.* Novoradomsk. Łodzkie, C Poland 51.04N 19.25E
119 N4 **Radomyshl'** Zhytomyrs'ka Oblast', N Ukraine 50.30N 29.16E
115 P19 **Radoviš** *prev.* Radovište. E FYR Macedonia 41.39N 22.26E
Radovište *see* Radoviš
96 B13 **Radøy** *island* S Norway
111 R7 **Radstadt** Salzburg, NW Austria 47.24N 13.31E
190 E8 **Radstock, Cape** *headland* South Australia 33.11S 134.18E
121 G15 **Radun'** *Rus.* Radun'. Hrodzyenskaya Voblasts', W Belarus 54.03N 25.00E
126 Gg11 **Raduzhnyy** Khanty-Mansiyskiy Avtonomnyy Okrug, C Russian Federation 62.03N 77.28E
120 F11 **Radviliškis** Radviliškis, N Lithuania 55.48N 23.32E
9 U17 **Radville** Saskatchewan, S Canada 49.28N 104.19W
146 K7 **Raḍwá, Jabal** ▲ W Saudi Arabia 24.31N 38.21E
113 P16 **Radymno** Podkarpackie, SE Poland 49.57N 22.49E
118 J5 **Radyvyliv** Rivnens'ka Oblast', NW Ukraine 50.07N 25.12E
Radziechów *see* Radekhiv
112 I11 **Radziejów** Kujawsko-pomorskie, C Poland 52.36N 18.33E
112 O12 **Radzyń Podlaski** Lubelskie, E Poland 51.48N 22.36E
15 Hh4 **Rae** ≈ Nunavut, NW Canada
158 M13 **Rāe Bareli** Uttar Pradesh, N India 26.13N 81.13E
Rae-Edzo *see* Edzo
23 T11 **Raeford** North Carolina, SE USA 34.58N 79.13W
101 M19 **Raeren** Liège, E Belgium 50.42N 6.06E
15 Kk3 **Rae Strait** *strait* Nunavut, N Canada
192 L11 **Raetihi** Manawatu-Wanganui, North Island, NZ 39.28S 175.16E
203 U13 **Raevavae** *var.* Raivavae. *island* Îles Australes, SW French Polynesia
Rafa *see* Rafah
64 M10 **Rafaela** Santa Fe, E Argentina 31.16S 61.25W
144 E11 **Rafah** *var.* Rafa, Rafaḥ, *Heb.* Rafiaḥ, Raphiah. SW Gaza Strip 31.17N 34.18E
81 L15 **Rafaï** Mbomou, SE Central African Republic 5.01N 23.51E
147 O4 **Rafḥah** Al Ḥudūd ash Shamālīyah, N Saudi Arabia 29.40N 43.28E
Rafiaḥ *see* Rafah
149 R10 **Rafsanjān** Kermān, C Iran 30.25N 56.00E
82 B13 **Raga** Western Bahr el Ghazal, SW Sudan 8.28N 25.40E
21 S8 **Ragged Island** *island* Maine, NE USA
46 I5 **Ragged Island Range** *island group* S Bahamas
192 L7 **Raglan** Waikato, North Island, NZ 37.48S 174.52E
24 G8 **Ragley** Louisiana, S USA 30.31N 93.13W
Ragnit *see* Neman
109 K25 **Ragusa** Sicilia, Italy, C Mediterranean Sea 36.55N 14.42E
Ragusa *see* Dubrovnik
Ragusavecchia *see* Cavtat
175 Qq12 **Raha** Pulau Muna, C Indonesia 4.49S 122.43E
121 N17 **Rahachow** *Rus.* Rogachëv. Homyel'skaya Voblasts', SE Belarus 53.03N 30.04E
69 U6 **Rahad** *var.* Nahr ar Rahad. ≈ W Sudan
Rahad, Nahr ar *see* Rahad
Rahaeng *see* Tak
144 F11 **Rahat** Southern, C Israel 31.20N 34.43E
146 L8 **Rahaṭ, Ḥarrat** *lavaflow* W Saudi Arabia
155 S12 **Rahimyār Khān** Punjab, SE Pakistan 28.27N 70.21E
97 I14 **Råholt** Akershus, S Norway 60.16N 11.10E
Rahovec *see* Orahovac
203 S10 **Raiatea** *island* Îles Sous le Vent, W French Polynesia
161 H16 **Rāichūr** Karnātaka, C India 16.15N 77.19E
Raidestos *see* Tekirdağ
159 S13 **Rāiganj** West Bengal, NE India 25.37N 88.10E
160 M11 **Raigarh** Madhya Pradesh, C India 21.55N 83.24E
175 Q18 **Raijua, Selat** *strait* Nusa Tenggara, S Indonesia
191 O16 **Railton** Tasmania, SE Australia 41.24S 146.28E
38 L8 **Rainbow Bridge** *natural arch* Utah, W USA
25 Q3 **Rainbow City** Alabama, S USA 33.57N 86.02W
9 N11 **Rainbow Lake** Alberta, W Canada 58.30N 119.24W
23 R5 **Rainelle** West Virginia, NE USA 37.57N 80.46W
34 G10 **Rainier** Oregon, NW USA 46.05N 122.55W
34 H9 **Rainier, Mount** Ж Washington, NW USA 46.51N 121.45W
25 Q2 **Rainsville** Alabama, S USA 34.29N 85.51W
10 B11 **Rainy Lake** ◎ Canada/USA
10 A11 **Rainy River** Ontario, C Canada 48.43N 94.33W
Raippaluoto *see* Replot
160 K12 **Raipur** Madhya Pradesh, C India 21.16N 81.42E
160 H10 **Raisen** Madhya Pradesh, C India 23.21N 77.49E
13 N13 **Raisin** ≈ Ontario, SE Canada
33 R11 **Raisin, River** ≈ Michigan, N USA
Raivavae *see* Raevavae
155 W9 **Rāiwind** Punjab, E Pakistan 31.13N 74.10E
176 U9 **Raja Ampat, Kepulauan** *island group* E Indonesia
161 L16 **Rājahmundry** Andhra Pradesh, E India 17.05N 81.42E
161 I18 **Rājampet** Andhra Pradesh, E India 14.09N 79.10E
Rajang *see* Rajang, Batang
174 Mm6 **Rajang, Batang** *var.* Rajang. ≈ East Malaysia
155 S11 **Rājanpur** Punjab, E Pakistan 29.07N 70.19E
161 H23 **Rājapālaiyam** Tamil Nādu, SE India 9.25N 77.36E
158 E12 **Rājasthān** ◐ *state* NW India
159 T15 **Rajbari** Dhaka, C Bangladesh 23.46N 89.39E
159 R12 **Rajbiraj** Eastern, E Nepal 26.34N 86.52E
160 G9 **Rājgarh** Madhya Pradesh, C India 24.01N 76.42E
158 H10 **Rājgarh** Rājasthān, NW India 28.37N 75.25E
159 P14 **Rājgir** Bihār, N India 25.01N 85.25E
112 O8 **Rajgród** Podlaskie, NE Poland 53.43N 22.40E
160 L12 **Rājim** Madhya Pradesh, C India 20.57N 81.58E
114 C11 **Rajinac, Mali** ▲ W Croatia 44.47N 15.04E
160 B10 **Rājkot** Gujarāt, W India 22.18N 70.46E
159 R14 **Rājmahal** Bihār, NE India 25.03N 87.49E
159 Q14 **Rājmahal Hills** *hill range* N India
160 K12 **Rāj Nāndgaon** Madhya Pradesh, C India 21.06N 81.01E
158 I8 **Rājpura** Punjab, NW India 30.30N 76.36E
159 S14 **Rajshahi** *prev.* Rampur Boalia. Rajshahi, W Bangladesh 24.24N 88.40E
159 S13 **Rajshahi** ◐ *division* NW Bangladesh
202 K13 **Rakahanga** *atoll* N Cook Islands
193 H19 **Rakaia** Canterbury, South Island, NZ 43.45S 172.02E
193 G19 **Rakaia** ≈ South Island, NZ
158 H3 **Rakaposhi** ▲ N India 36.06N 74.31E
Rakasd *see* Răcășdia
174 Ii14 **Rakata, Pulau** *var.* Pulau Krakatau. *island* S Indonesia
164 K16 **Raka Zangbo** ≈ W China
147 U10 **Rakbah, Qalamat ar** *well* SE Saudi Arabia 20.37N 52.45E
Rakhine State *see* Arakan State
118 I8 **Rakhiv** Zakarpats'ka Oblast', W Ukraine 48.05N 24.15E
147 V13 **Rakhyūt** SW Oman 16.41N 53.09E
197 I14 **Rakiraki** Viti Levu, W Fiji 17.21S 178.11E
Rakka *see* Ar Raqqah
120 I4 **Rakke** Lääne-Virumaa, NE Estonia 58.58N 26.14E
97 I16 **Rakkestad** Østfold, S Norway 59.25N 11.19E
112 F12 **Rakoniewice** *Ger.* Rakwitz. Wielkolpolskie, C Poland 52.09N 16.10E
Rakonitz *see* Rakovník
85 H18 **Rakops** Central, C Botswana 21.01S 24.23E
113 C16 **Rakovník** *Ger.* Rakonitz. Středočeský Kraj, W Czech Republic 50.07N 13.43E
116 J10 **Rakovski** Plovdiv, C Bulgaria 42.16N 24.58E
Rakutō-kō *see* Naktong-gang
120 I3 **Rakvere** *Ger.* Wesenberg. Lääne-Virumaa, N Estonia 59.21N 26.19E
Rakwitz *see* Rakoniewice
24 L6 **Raleigh** Mississippi, S USA 32.01N 89.30W
23 U9 **Raleigh** *state capital* North Carolina, SE USA 35.46N 78.38W
23 Y11 **Raleigh Bay** *bay* North Carolina, SE USA
23 U9 **Raleigh-Durham** ✕ North Carolina, SE USA 35.54N 78.45W
201 S6 **Ralik Chain** *island group* Ralik Chain, W Marshall Islands
27 N5 **Ralls** Texas, SW USA 33.40N 101.23W
20 G13 **Ralston** Pennsylvania, NE USA 41.29N 76.57W
147 O16 **Ramādah** W Yemen 13.35N 43.50E
Ramadi *see* Ar Ramādī
107 N2 **Ramales de la Victoria** Cantabria, N Spain 43.15N 3.28W
144 F10 **Ramallah** C West Bank 31.53N 34.49E
63 C19 **Ramallo** Buenos Aires, E Argentina 33.30S 60.01W
161 H20 **Rāmanagaram** Karnātaka, E India 12.45N 77.16E
161 I23 **Rāmanāthapuram** Tamil Nādu, SE India 9.22N 78.52E
160 N12 **Rāmapur** Orissa, E India 21.48N 84.00E
161 I14 **Rāmāreddi** *var.* Kāmāreddi, Kamareddy. Andhra Pradesh, C India 18.19N 78.23E
144 F10 **Ramat Gan** Tel Aviv, W Israel 32.04N 34.48E
105 T6 **Rambervillers** Vosges, NE France 48.15N 6.50E
Rambi *see* Rabi
105 N5 **Rambouillet** Yvelines, N France 48.39N 1.49E
194 L8 **Rambutyo Island** *island* N PNG
159 Q12 **Ramechhap** Central, C Nepal 27.19N 86.04E
191 R12 **Rame Head** *headland* Victoria, SE Australia 37.48S 149.30E
130 L4 **Ramenskoye** Moskovskaya Oblast', W Russian Federation 55.31N 38.24E
128 J15 **Rameshki** Tverskaya Oblast', W Russian Federation 57.21N 36.05E
159 P14 **Rāmgarh** Bihār, N India 23.37N 85.31E
158 D11 **Rāmgarh** Rājasthān, NW India 27.26N 70.35E
148 M9 **Rāmhormoz** *var.* Ram Hormuz, Ramuz. Khūzestān, SW Iran 31.17N 49.37E
Ram Hormuz *see* Rāmhormoz
Ram, Jebel *see* Ramm, Jabal
144 F10 **Ramla** *var.* Ramle, Ramleh, *Ar.* Er Ramle. Central, C Israel 31.55N 34.52E
Ramle/Ramleh *see* Ramla
144 F14 **Ramm, Jabal** *var.* Jebel Ram. ▲ SW Jordan 29.34N 35.24E
158 K10 **Rāmnagar** Uttar Pradesh, N India 29.22N 79.07E
97 N15 **Ramnäs** Västmanland, C Sweden 59.46N 16.16E
Râmnicul-Sărat *see* Râmnicu Sărat
118 L12 **Râmnicu Sărat** *prev.* Râmnicul-Sărat, Rîmnicu-Sărat. Buzău, E Romania 45.24N 27.06E
118 I13 **Râmnicu Vâlcea** *prev.* Rîmnicu Vîlcea. Vâlcea, C Romania 45.04N 24.32E
Ramokgwebana *see* Ramokgwebane
85 J18 **Ramokgwebane** *var.* Ramokgwebana. Central, NE Botswana 20.36S 27.39E
130 L7 **Ramon'** Voronezhskaya Oblast', W Russian Federation 51.51N 39.18E
37 V17 **Ramona** California, W USA 33.02N 116.52W
58 A10 **Ramón, Laguna** ◎ NW Peru
12 G7 **Ramore** Ontario, S Canada 48.26N 80.19W
42 M11 **Ramos** San Luis Potosí, C Mexico 22.48N 101.55W
43 N8 **Ramos Arizpe** Coahuila de Zaragoza, NE Mexico 25.34N 100.58W
42 J9 **Ramos, Río de** ≈ C Mexico
41 R8 **Rampart** Alaska, USA 65.30N 150.10W
14 G5 **Ramparts** ≈ Northwest Territories, NW Canada
158 K10 **Rāmpur** Uttar Pradesh, N India 28.48N 79.03E
160 F9 **Rāmpura** Madhya Pradesh, C India 24.30N 75.25E
Rampur Boalia *see* Rajshahi
177 F6 **Ramree Island** *island* W Burma
147 W6 **Rams** *var.* Ar Rams. Ra's al Khaymah, NE UAE 25.52N 56.01E
149 N4 **Rāmsar** *prev.* Sakhtsar. Māzandarān, N Iran 36.55N 50.39E
95 H16 **Ramsele** Västernorrland, N Sweden 63.33N 16.35E
23 T9 **Ramseur** North Carolina, SE USA 35.43N 79.39W
99 I16 **Ramsey** NE Isle of Man 54.19N 4.24W
99 I16 **Ramsey Bay** *bay* NE Isle of Man
12 E9 **Ramsey Lake** ◎ Ontario, S Canada
99 Q22 **Ramsgate** SE England, UK 51.19N 1.25E
96 M10 **Ramsjö** Gävleborg, C Sweden 62.10N 15.40E
160 I12 **Rāmtek** Mahārāshtra, C India 21.28N 79.28E
Ramtha *see* Ar Ramthā
194 H11 **Ramu** ≈ N PNG
Ramuz *see* Rāmhormoz
120 G12 **Ramygala** Panevėžys, C Lithuania 55.30N 24.18E
94 G12 **Rana** ≈ C Norway
158 H14 **Rāna Pratāp Sāgar** ◎ N India
175 O2 **Ranau** Sabah, East Malaysia 5.55N 116.43E
174 I12 **Ranau, Danau** ◎ Sumatera, W Indonesia
64 H12 **Rancagua** Libertador, C Chile 34.10S 70.45W
101 G22 **Rance** Hainaut, S Belgium 50.09N 4.16E
104 H6 **Rance** ≈ NW France
62 J9 **Rancharia** São Paulo, S Brazil 22.13S 50.53W
159 P15 **Rānchi** Bihār, N India 23.22N 85.19E
63 D21 **Ranchos** Buenos Aires, E Argentina 35.31S 58.22W
39 S9 **Ranchos De Taos** New Mexico, SW USA 36.21N 105.36W
65 G16 **Ranco, Lago** ◎ C Chile
97 C16 **Randaberg** Rogaland, S Norway 59.00N 5.38E
31 U7 **Randall** Minnesota, N USA 46.05N 94.30W
109 L23 **Randazzo** Sicilia, Italy, C Mediterranean Sea 37.52N 14.57E
97 G21 **Randers** Århus, C Denmark 56.28N 10.03E
94 I12 **Randijaure** ◎ N Sweden
23 T9 **Randleman** North Carolina, SE USA 35.49N 79.48W
21 O11 **Randolph** Massachusetts, NE USA 42.09N 71.02W
31 Q13 **Randolph** Nebraska, C USA 42.25N 97.05W
38 M1 **Randolph** Utah, W USA 41.40N 111.10W
102 P9 **Randow** ≈ NE Germany
97 H14 **Randsfjorden** ◎ S Norway
95 J14 **Råneå** Norrbotten, N Sweden 65.52N 22.17E
95 F15 **Ranemsletta** Nord-Trøndelag, C Norway 64.36N 11.55E
78 H10 **Ranérou** C Senegal 15.17N 14.00W
193 E22 **Ranfurly** Otago, South Island, NZ 45.07S 170.06E
178 Hh17 **Rangae** Narathiwat, SW Thailand 6.19N 101.45E
159 V16 **Rangamati** Chittagong, SE Bangladesh 22.40N 92.10E
192 I2 **Rangaunu Bay** *bay* North Island, NZ
21 P6 **Rangeley** Maine, NE USA 44.58N 70.37W
39 O4 **Rangely** Colorado, C USA 40.05N 108.48W
27 R7 **Ranger** Texas, SW USA 32.28N 98.40W
12 C9 **Ranger Lake** Ontario, S Canada 46.51N 83.34W
12 C9 **Ranger Lake** ◎ Ontario, S Canada
159 V12 **Rangia** Assam, NE India 26.27N 91.34E
193 I18 **Rangiora** Canterbury, South Island, NZ 43.19S 172.33E
203 T9 **Rangiroa** *atoll* Îles Tuamotu, W French Polynesia
192 N9 **Rangitaiki** ≈ North Island, NZ
193 F19 **Rangitata** ≈ South Island, NZ
192 M12 **Rangitikei** ≈ North Island, NZ
192 L6 **Rangitoto Island** *island* N NZ
Rangkasbitoeng *see* Rangkasbitung
174 Ii14 **Rangkasbitung** *prev.* Rangkasbitoeng. Jawa, SW Indonesia 6.21S 106.12E
178 Hh9 **Rang, Khao** ▲ C Thailand 16.13N 99.03E
153 V13 **Rangkŭl** *Rus.* Rangkul'. SE Tajikistan 38.30N 74.24E
Rangkul' *see* Rangkŭl
Rangoon *see* Yangon
159 T13 **Rangpur** Rajshahi, N Bangladesh 25.46N 89.20E
174 Hh7 **Rangsang, Pulau** *island* W Indonesia
161 F18 **Rānibennur** Karnātaka, W India 14.36N 75.39E
159 R15 **Rāniganj** West Bengal, NE India 23.34N 87.13E
155 Q13 **Rānīpur** Sind, SE Pakistan 27.16N 68.34E
Rāniyah *see* Rānya
27 N9 **Rankin** Texas, SW USA 31.12N 101.56W
15 L7 **Rankin Inlet** Nunavut, C Canada 62.52N 92.13W
191 P8 **Rankins Springs** New South Wales, SE Australia 33.51S 146.16E
Rankovićevo *see* Kraljevo
110 I7 **Rankweil** Vorarlberg, W Austria 47.16N 9.40E
Rann *see* Brežice
131 T8 **Ranneye** Orenburgskaya Oblast', W Russian Federation 51.28N 52.29E

◆ Country ● Country Capital ◇ Dependent Territory ○ Dependent Territory Capital ◐ Administrative Region ✕ International Airport ▲ Mountain ▲ Mountain Range Ж Volcano ≈ River ◎ Lake ⊡ Reservoir

RANNOCH, LOCH – REYKJANES

98 *I10* **Rannoch, Loch** ◎ C Scotland, UK
203 *U17* **Rano Kau** ***var.*** Rano Kao. *crater* Easter Island, Chile, E Pacific Ocean *27.10S 109.25W*
178 *Gg14* **Ranong** Ranong, SW Thailand *9.58N 98.40E*
195 *T14* **Ranongga** ***var.*** Ghanongga. *island* NW Solomon Islands
203 *W16* **Rano Raraku** *ancient monument* Easter Island, Chile, E Pacific Ocean *27.07S 109.18W*
176 *W9* **Ransiki** Irian Jaya, E Indonesia *1.27S 134.12E*
94 *K12* **Rantajärvi** Norrbotten, N Sweden *66.45N 23.39E*
95 *N17* **Rantasalmi** Isä-Suomi, SE Finland *62.02N 28.22E*
175 *N11* **Rantau** Borneo, C Indonesia *2.55S 115.09E*
174 *Hh7* **Rantau, Pulau** ***var.*** Pulau Tebingtinggi. *island* W Indonesia
175 *Pp11* **Rantepao** Sulawesi, C Indonesia *2.58S 119.58E*
32 *M13* **Rantoul** Illinois, N USA *40.19N 88.08W*
95 *L15* **Rantsila** Oulu, C Finland *64.31N 25.40E*
94 *L13* **Ranua** Lappi, NW Finland *65.55N 26.34E*
145 *T3* **Rānya** ***var.*** Rāniyah. NE Iraq *36.15N 44.52E*
163 *X3* **Raohe** Heilongjiang, NE China *46.49N 134.00E*
76 *H9* **Raoui, Erg er** *desert* W Algeria
199 *L11* **Rapa** *island* Îles Australes, S French Polynesia
203 *V14* **Rapa Iti** *island* Îles Australes, SW French Polynesia
108 *D10* **Rapallo** Liguria, NW Italy *44.21N 9.13E*
Rapa Nui *see* Pascua, Isla de
Raphiah *see* Rafah
23 *V5* **Rapidan River** ≈ Virginia, NE USA
30 *J10* **Rapid City** South Dakota, N USA *44.04N 103.13W*
13 *P8* **Rapide-Blanc** Quebec, SE Canada *47.48N 72.57W*
12 *I8* **Rapide-Deux** Quebec, SE Canada *47.56N 78.33W*
120 *K6* **Räpina** ***Ger.*** Rappin. Põlvamaa, SE Estonia *58.06N 27.27E*
120 *G4* **Rapla** ***Ger.*** Rappel. Raplamaa, NW Estonia *59.00N 24.46E*
120 *G4* **Raplamaa** ***off.*** Rapla Maakond. ◈ *province* NW Estonia
23 *X6* **Rappahonnock River** ≈ Virginia, NE USA
Rappel *see* Rapla
110 *G7* **Rapperswil** Sankt Gallen, NE Switzerland *47.13N 8.49E*
Rappin *see* Räpina
159 *N12* **Rāpti** ≈ N India
59 *K16* **Rapulo, Río** ≈ E Bolivia
Raqqah/Raqqah, Muḩāfaẓat al *see* Ar Raqqah
20 *J8* **Raquette Lake** ◎ New York, NE USA
20 *J6* **Raquette River** ≈ New York, NE USA
203 *V10* **Raraka** *atoll* Îles Tuamotu, C French Polynesia
203 *V10* **Raroia** *atoll* Îles Tuamotu, C French Polynesia
202 *H15* **Rarotonga** ✈ Rarotonga, S Cook Islands, C Pacific Ocean *21.15S 159.45W*
202 *H16* **Rarotonga** *island* S Cook Islands, C Pacific Ocean
153 *P12* **Rarz** W Tajikistan *39.23N 68.43E*
Ras al 'Ain *see* Ra's al 'Ayn
145 *N2* **Ra's al 'Ayn** ***var.*** Ras al 'Ain. Al Ḩasakah, N Syria *36.52N 40.04E*
144 *H3* **Ra's al Basīṭ** Al Lādhiqīyah, W Syria *35.57N 35.55E*
Ra's al-Hafgī *see* Ra's al Khafjī
147 *R5* **Ra's al Khafjī** ***var.*** Ra's al-Hafgī. Ash Sharqīyah, NE Saudi Arabia *28.22N 48.29E*
Ras al-Khaimah/Ras al Khaimah *see* Ra's al Khaymah
149 *R15* **Ra's al Khaymah** ***var.*** Ras al Khaimah. Ra's al Khaymah, NE UAE *25.44N 55.54E*
149 *R15* **Ra's al Khaymah** ***var.*** Ras al-Khaimah. ✈ Ra's al Khaymah, NE UAE *25.37N 55.51E*
144 *G13* **Ra's an Naqb** Ma'ān, S Jordan *30.00N 35.29E*
63 *B26* **Rasa, Punta** *headland* E Argentina *40.50S 62.15W*
176 *W10* **Rasawi** Irian Jaya, E Indonesia *2.04S 134.02E*
Râşcani *see* Rîşcani
82 *J10* **Ras Dashen Terara** ▲ N Ethiopia *13.12N 38.09E*
157 *K19* **Rasdu Atoll** *atoll* C Maldives
120 *E12* **Raseiniai** Raseiniai, C Lithuania *55.23N 23.06E*
77 *X8* **Râs Ghârib** E Egypt *28.16N 33.01E*
168 *D6* **Rashaant** Bayan-Ölgiy, W Mongolia *47.48N 90.45E*
168 *L10* **Rashaant** Dundgovĭ, C Mongolia *44.54N 106.32E*
168 *J6* **Rashaant** Hövsgöl, N Mongolia *49.08N 101.27E*
145 *Y11* **Rashīd** E Iraq *31.15N 47.31E*
77 *V7* **Rashîd** ***Eng.*** Rosetta. N Egypt *31.24N 30.25E*
148 *M3* **Rasht** ***var.*** Resht. Gīlān, NW Iran *37.18N 49.37E*
145 *S2* **Rashwān** N Iraq *36.28N 43.54E*
Rasik *see* Raasiku
115 *M15* **Raška** Serbia, C Yugoslavia *43.18N 20.37E*
121 *P15* **Rasna** ***Rus.*** Ryasna. Mahilyowskaya Voblasts', E Belarus *54.01N 31.12E*
118 *J12* **Râşnov** ***prev.*** Rîşno, Rozsnyó, ***Hung.*** Barcarozsnyó. Braşov, C Romania *45.34N 25.27E*
120 *L11* **Rasony** ***Rus.*** Rossony. Vitsyebskaya Voblasts', N Belarus *55.55N 28.51E*
Ra's Shamrah *see* Ugarit
131 *N7* **Rasskazovo** Tambovskaya Oblast', W Russian Federation *52.42N 41.45E*
121 *O16* **Rasta** ≈ E Belarus
Rastadt *see* Rastatt
Rastâne *see* Ar Rastān
147 *S6* **Ra's Tannūrah** ***Eng.*** Ras Tanura. Ash Sharqīyah, NE Saudi Arabia *26.44N 50.04E*
Ras Tanura *see* Ra's Tannūrah
103 *G21* **Rastatt** ***var.*** Rastadt. Baden-Württemberg, SW Germany *48.52N 8.12E*
Rastenburg *see* Kętrzyn
155 *V7* **Rasūlnagar** Punjab, E Pakistan *32.19N 73.51E*
201 *U6* **Ratak Chain** *island group* Ratak Chain, E Marshall Islands
121 *K15* **Ratamka** ***Rus.*** Ratomka. Minskaya Voblasts', C Belarus *53.57N 27.23E*
95 *G17* **Ratan** Jämtland, C Sweden *62.28N 14.34E*
158 *G11* **Ratangarh** Rājasthān, NW India *28.01N 74.39E*
Rat Buri *see* Ratchaburi
178 *H11* **Ratchaburi** ***var.*** Rat Buri. Ratchaburi, W Thailand *13.30N 99.49E*
31 *W15* **Rathbun Lake** ⊠ Iowa, C USA
Ráth Caola *see* Rathkeale
177 *F5* **Rathedaung** Arakan State, W Burma *20.30N 92.48E*
102 *M12* **Rathenow** Brandenburg, NE Germany *52.34N 12.20E*
99 *C19* **Rathkeale** ***Ir.*** Ráth Caola. SW Ireland *52.31N 8.55W*
98 *F13* **Rathlin Island** ***Ir.*** Reachlainn. *island* N Northern Ireland, UK
99 *C20* **Ráthluirc** ***Ir.*** An Ráth. SW Ireland *52.22N 8.44W*
Ratibor *see* Racibórz
Ratisbon/Ratisbona/Ratisbonne *see* Regensburg
Rätische Alpen *see* Rhaetian Alps
40 *E17* **Rat Island** *island* Aleutian Islands, Alaska, USA
40 *E17* **Rat Islands** *island group* Aleutian Islands, Alaska, USA
160 *F10* **Ratlām** ***prev.*** Rutlam. Madhya Pradesh, C India *23.23N 75.03E*
161 *D15* **Ratnāgiri** Mahārāshtra, W India *17.00N 73.20E*
161 *K26* **Ratnapura** Sabaragamuwa Province, S Sri Lanka *6.40N 80.25E*
118 *J2* **Ratne** ***Rus.*** Ratno. Volyns'ka Oblast', NW Ukraine *51.40N 24.33E*
Ratno *see* Ratne
Ratomka *see* Ratamka
39 *U8* **Raton** New Mexico, SW USA *36.54N 104.27W*
145 *O7* **Ratqah, Wādī ar** *dry watercourse* W Iraq
Ratschach *see* Radeče
178 *H17* **Rattaphum** Songkhla, SW Thailand *7.07N 100.16E*
28 *L6* **Rattlesnake Creek** ≈ Kansas, C USA
96 *L13* **Rättvik** Dalarna, C Sweden *60.53N 15.12E*
102 *K9* **Ratzeburg** Mecklenburg-Vorpommern, N Germany *53.41N 10.48E*
102 *K9* **Ratzeburger See** ◎ N Germany
8 *J10* **Ratz, Mount** ▲ British Columbia, SW Canada *57.22N 132.17W*
63 *D22* **Rauch** Buenos Aires, E Argentina *36.47S 59.06W*
43 *U16* **Raudales** Chiapas, SE Mexico
Raudhatain *see* Ar Rawḑatayn
Raudnitz an der Elbe *see* Roudnice nad Labem
94 *K1* **Raufarhöfn** Nordhurland Eystra, NE Iceland *66.26N 15.57W*
96 *H13* **Raufoss** Oppland, S Norway *60.43N 10.36E*
Raukawa *see* Cook Strait
192 *Q8* **Raukumara** ▲ North Island, NZ *37.46S 178.07E*
199 *J12* **Raukumara Plain** *undersea feature* N Coral Sea
192 *P8* **Raukumara Range** ▲▲ North Island, NZ
160 *N11* **Rāulakela** ***var.*** Raurkela; ***prev.*** Rourkela. Orissa, E. India *22.13N 84.52E*
97 *F15* **Rauland** Telemark, S Norway *59.41N 7.57E*
95 *J19* **Rauma** ***Swe.*** Raumo. Länsi-Suomi, W Finland *61.09N 21.30E*
96 *F10* **Rauma** ≈ S Norway
Raumo *see* Rauma
120 *H8* **Rauna** Cēsis, C Latvia *57.19N 25.34E*
174 *Mm16* **Raung, Gunung** ▲ Jawa, S Indonesia *8.00S 114.07E*
Rāurkela *see* Rāulakela
97 *J22* **Raus** Skåne, S Sweden *56.01N 12.48E*
172 *R6* **Rausu** Hokkaidō, NE Japan *44.00N 145.06E*
172 *R6* **Rausu-dake** ▲ Hokkaidō, NE Japan *44.06N 145.04E*
95 *M17* **Rautalampi** Itä-Suomi, C Finland *62.37N 26.48E*
95 *N16* **Rautavaara** Itä-Suomi, C Finland *63.30N 28.19E*
118 *M9* **Raŭtel** ≈ C Moldova
95 *O18* **Rautjärvi** Etelä-Suomi, S Finland *61.21N 29.20E*
Rautu *see* Sosnovo
203 *V11* **Ravahere** *atoll* Îles Tuamotu, C French Polynesia
109 *J25* **Ravanusa** Sicilia, Italy, C Mediterranean Sea *37.16N 13.57E*
149 *S9* **Rāvar** Kermān, C Iran *31.15N 56.51E*
153 *Q11* **Ravat** Oshskaya Oblast', SW Kyrgyzstan *39.54N 70.06E*
20 *K11* **Ravena** New York, NE USA *42.28N 73.49W*
108 *H10* **Ravenna** Emilia-Romagna, N Italy *44.28N 12.15E*
31 *O15* **Ravenna** Nebraska, C USA *41.01N 98.54W*
33 *U11* **Ravenna** Ohio, N USA *41.09N 81.14W*
103 *I24* **Ravensburg** Baden-Württemberg, S Germany *47.46N 9.37E*
189 *W4* **Ravenshoe** Queensland, NE Australia *17.29S 145.28E*
188 *K13* **Ravensthorpe** Western Australia *33.37S 120.03E*
23 *Q4* **Ravenswood** West Virginia, NE USA *38.57N 81.45W*
155 *U9* **Rāvi** ≈ India/Pakistan
114 *C9* **Ravna Gora** Primorje-Gorski Kotar, NW Croatia *45.20N 14.54E*
111 *U10* **Ravne na Koroškem** ***Ger.*** Gutenstein. N Slovenia *46.33N 14.57E*
145 *P6* **Rāwah** W Iraq *34.32N 41.54E*
203 *T4* **Rawaki** ***prev.*** Phoenix Island. *atoll* Phoenix Islands, C Kiribati
155 *U6* **Rāwalpindi** Punjab, NE Pakistan *33.38N 73.06E*
112 *L13* **Rawa Mazowiecka** Łódzkie, C Poland *51.46N 20.15E*
145 *T2* **Ŗawāndiz** ***var.*** Rawandoz, Rawāndūz. N Iraq *36.37N 44.31E*
Rawandoz/Rawāndūz *see* Ŗawāndiz
176 *Vv9* **Rawarra** ≈ Irian Jaya, E Indonesia
176 *V9* **Rawas** Irian Jaya, E Indonesia *1.07S 132.12E*
145 *O4* **Rawḑah** ◎ E Syria
112 *G13* **Rawicz** ***Ger.*** Rawitsch. Wielkopolskie, C Poland *51.37N 16.51E*
Rawitsch *see* Rawicz
188 *M11* **Rawlinna** Western Australia *31.00S 125.35E*
35 *W16* **Rawlins** Wyoming, C USA *41.47N 107.14W*
65 *K17* **Rawson** Chubut, SE Argentina *43.22S 65.01W*
165 *R16* **Rawu** Xizang Zizhiqu, W China *29.30N 96.42E*
159 *P12* **Raxaul** Bihār, N India *26.58N 84.51E*
30 *K3* **Ray** North Dakota, N USA *48.19N 103.11W*
174 *M9* **Raya, Bukit** ▲ Borneo, C Indonesia *0.40S 112.40E*
161 *I18* **Rāyachoti** Andhra Pradesh, E India *14.03N 78.43E*
Rāyadrug *see* Rāyagarha
161 *M14* **Rāyagarha** ***prev.*** Rāyadrug. Orissa, E India *19.11N 83.22E*
144 *H7* **Rayak** ***var.*** Rayaq, Riyāq. E Lebanon *33.51N 36.03E*
Rayaq *see* Rayak
145 *T2* **Ŗāyat** E Iraq *36.39N 44.56E*
174 *J10* **Raya, Tanjung** *headland* Pulau Bangka, W Indonesia *1.49S 106.04E*
11 *R13* **Ray, Cape** *headland* Newfoundland, E Canada *47.38N 59.15W*
126 *Mm16* **Raychikhinsk** Amurskaya Oblast', SE Russian Federation *49.47N 129.19E*
131 *U5* **Rayevskiy** Respublika Bashkortostan, W Russian Federation *54.04N 54.58E*
9 *Q17* **Raymond** Alberta, SW Canada *49.30N 112.40W*
24 *K6* **Raymond** Mississippi, S USA *32.15N 90.25W*
34 *F9* **Raymond** Washington, NW USA *46.41N 123.43W*
191 *T8* **Raymond Terrace** New South Wales, SE Australia *32.46S 151.45E*
27 *T17* **Raymondville** Texas, SW USA *26.27N 97.45W*
9 *U16* **Raymore** Saskatchewan, S Canada *51.24N 104.34W*
41 *Q8* **Ray Mountains** ▲▲ Alaska, USA
24 *H9* **Rayne** Louisiana, S USA *30.13N 92.15W*
43 *O12* **Rayón** San Luis Potosí, C Mexico *21.54N 99.33W*
42 *G4* **Rayón** Sonora, NW Mexico *29.45N 110.33W*
178 *Hh12* **Rayong** Rayong, S Thailand *12.42N 101.16E*
27 *T5* **Ray Roberts, Lake** ◎ Texas, SW USA
20 *E15* **Raystown Lake** ⊠ Pennsylvania, NE USA
147 *V13* **Raysūt** SW Oman *16.58N 54.01E*
29 *R4* **Raytown** Missouri, C USA *39.00N 94.27W*
24 *I5* **Rayville** Louisiana, S USA *32.29N 91.45W*
148 *L5* **Razan** Hamadān, W Iran *35.22N 48.58E*
145 *S9* **Razāzah, Buḩayrat ar** ***var.*** Baḩr al Milḩ. ◎ C Iraq
116 *L9* **Razboyna** ▲ E Bulgaria *42.54N 26.31E*
Razdan *see* Hrazdan
Razdolnoye *see* Rozdol'ne
Razelm, Lacul *see* Razim, Lacul
145 *U2* **Ŗazga** E Iraq *36.25N 45.06E*
116 *L8* **Razgrad** Razgrad, N Bulgaria *43.33N 26.31E*
116 *L8* **Razgrad** ◈ *province* N Bulgaria
119 *N13* **Razim, Lacul** ***prev.*** Lacul Razelm. *lagoon* NW Black Sea
116 *G11* **Razlog** Blagoevgrad, SW Bulgaria *41.52N 23.28E*
120 *K10* **Rāznas Ezers** ◎ SE Latvia
104 *E6* **Raz, Pointe du** *headland* NW France *48.06N 4.52W*
Reachlainn *see* Rathlin Island
Reachrainn *see* Lambay Island
99 *N22* **Reading** S England, UK *51.28N 0.58W*
20 *H15* **Reading** Pennsylvania, NE USA *40.19N 75.55W*
50 *C7* **Real, Cordillera** ▲▲ C Ecuador
64 *K12* **Realicó** La Pampa, C Argentina *35.01S 64.13W*
27 *R15* **Realitos** Texas, SW USA *27.26N 98.31W*
110 *G9* **Realp** Uri, C Switzerland *46.36N 8.32E*
178 *Ii12* **Reăng Kesei** Bătdâmbâng, W Cambodia *12.57N 103.15E*
203 *Y11* **Reao** *atoll* Îles Tuamotu, E French Polynesia
Reate *see* Rieti
188 *L11* **Rebecca, Lake** ◎ Western Australia
Rebiana Sand Sea *see* Rabyānah, Ramlat
128 *H8* **Reboly** Respublika Kareliya, NW Russian Federation *63.51N 30.49E*
172 *P1* **Rebun** Rebun-tō, NE Japan *45.19N 141.02E*
172 *P1* **Rebun-suidō** *strait* E Sea of Japan
172 *P1* **Rebun-tō** *island* NE Japan
108 *J12* **Recanati** Marche, C Italy *43.23N 13.34E*
Rechitsa *see* Rechytsa
111 *Y7* **Rechnitz** Burgenland, SE Austria *47.18N 16.26E*
121 *J20* **Rechytsa** ***Rus.*** Rechitsa. Brestskaya Voblasts', SW Belarus *51.51N 26.49E*
121 *O19* **Rechytsa** ***Rus.*** Rechitsa. Homyel'skaya Voblasts', SE Belarus *52.22N 30.22E*
61 *Q15* **Recife** ***prev.*** Pernambuco. *state capital* Pernambuco, E Brazil *8.06S 34.52W*
85 *I26* **Recife, Cape** ***Afr.*** Kaap Recife. *headland* S South Africa *34.03S 25.37E*
Recife, Kaap *see* Recife, Cape
180 *I16* **Récifs, Îles aux** *island* Inner Islands, NE Seychelles
103 *E14* **Recklinghausen** Nordrhein-Westfalen, W Germany *51.37N 7.12E*
102 *M8* **Recknitz** ≈ NE Germany
101 *K23* **Recogne** Luxembourg, SE Belgium *49.56N 5.20E*
63 *C15* **Reconquista** Santa Fe, C Argentina *29.10S 59.41W*
205 *O6* **Recovery Glacier** *glacier* Antarctica
61 *G15* **Recreio** Mato Grosso, W Brazil *8.13S 58.15W*
29 *X9* **Rector** Arkansas, C USA *36.15N 90.17W*
112 *E9* **Recz** ***Ger.*** Reetz Neumark. Zachodniopomorskie, NW Poland *53.16N 15.32E*
101 *L24* **Redange** ***var.*** Redange-sur-Attert. Diekirch, W Luxembourg *49.46N 5.52E*
Redange-sur-Attert *see* Redange
20 *C13* **Redbank Creek** ≈ Pennsylvania, NE USA
11 *S9* **Red Bay** Quebec, E Canada *51.40N 56.37W*
25 *N2* **Red Bay** Alabama, S USA *34.26N 88.08W*
37 *N4* **Red Bluff** California, W USA *40.09N 122.14W*
26 *J8* **Red Bluff Reservoir** ◎ New Mexico/Texas, SW USA
32 *K16* **Red Bud** Illinois, N USA *38.12N 89.59W*
32 *J5* **Red Cedar River** ≈ Wisconsin, N USA
9 *R17* **Redcliff** Alberta, SW Canada *50.06N 110.48W*
85 *K17* **Redcliff** Midlands, C Zimbabwe *19.01S 29.43E*
190 *L9* **Red Cliffs** Victoria, SE Australia *34.21S 142.12E*
31 *P17* **Red Cloud** Nebraska, C USA *40.05N 98.31W*
24 *L8* **Red Creek** ≈ Mississippi, S USA
9 *P15* **Red Deer** Alberta, SW Canada *52.15N 113.48W*
9 *Q16* **Red Deer** ≈ Alberta, SW Canada
41 *O11* **Red Devil** Alaska, USA *61.45N 95.18W*
37 *N3* **Redding** California, W USA *40.33N 122.26W*
99 *L20* **Redditch** W England, UK *52.19N 1.55W*
31 *P9* **Redfield** South Dakota, N USA *44.51N 98.31W*
26 *J12* **Redford** Texas, SW USA *29.31N 104.19W*
47 *V13* **Redhead** Trinidad, Trinidad and Tobago *10.48N 60.56W*
190 *I8* **Red Hill** South Australia *33.34S 138.13E*
40 *F10* **Red Hill** ***Haw.*** Pu'uUla'ula. ▲ Maui, Hawaii, USA, C Pacific Ocean *20.42N 94.16W*
28 *K7* **Red Hills** *hill range* Kansas, C USA
11 *T12* **Red Indian Lake** ◎ Newfoundland, E Canada
128 *J16* **Redkino** Tverskaya Oblast', W Russian Federation *56.41N 36.07E*
10 *A10* **Red Lake** Ontario, C Canada *51.00N 93.55W*
38 *I10* **Red Lake** *salt flat* Arizona, SW USA
31 *S4* **Red Lake Falls** Minnesota, N USA *47.52N 96.16W*
31 *R4* **Red Lake River** ≈ Minnesota, N USA
37 *U15* **Redlands** California, W USA *34.03N 117.10W*
20 *G16* **Red Lion** Pennsylvania, NE USA *39.53N 76.36W*
35 *U11* **Red Lodge** Montana, NW USA *45.11N 109.15W*
34 *H13* **Redmond** Oregon, NW USA *44.16N 121.10W*
38 *L5* **Redmond** Utah, W USA *39.00N 111.51W*
34 *H8* **Redmond** Washington, NW USA *47.40N 122.07W*
Rednitz *see* Regnitz
31 *T15* **Red Oak** Iowa, C USA *41.00N 95.10W*
20 *K12* **Red Oaks Mill** New York, NE USA *41.39N 73.52W*
104 *I7* **Redon** Ille-et-Vilaine, NW France *47.39N 2.04W*
47 *W10* **Redonda** *island* SW Antigua and Barbuda
106 *G4* **Redondela** Galicia, NW Spain *42.16N 8.36W*
106 *H11* **Redondo** Évora, S Portugal *38.37N 7.31W*
41 *Q12* **Redoubt Volcano** ▲ Alaska, USA *60.29N 152.44W*
9 *Y16* **Red River** ≈ Canada/USA
133 *U12* **Red River** ***var.*** Yuan, ***Chin.*** Yuan Jiang, ***Vtn.*** Sông Hông Hà. ≈ China/Vietnam
27 *W4* **Red River** ≈ S USA
24 *H7* **Red River** ≈ Louisiana, S USA
32 *M6* **Red River** ≈ Wisconsin, N USA
Red Rock, Lake *see* Red Rock Reservoir
31 *W14* **Red Rock Reservoir** ***var.*** Lake Red Rock. ⊠ Iowa, C USA
194 *J15* **Redscar Bay** *bay* S PNG
82 *H7* **Red Sea** ◈ *state* NE Sudan
77 *Y9* **Red Sea** ***anc.*** Sinus Arabicus. *sea* Africa/Asia
23 *T11* **Red Springs** North Carolina, SE USA *34.49N 79.10W*
15 *Gg6* **Redstone** ≈ Northwest Territories, NW Canada
9 *V17* **Redvers** Saskatchewan, S Canada *49.31N 101.33W*
79 *P13* **Red Volta** ***var.*** Nazinon, ***Fr.*** Volta Rouge. ≈ Burkina/Ghana
9 *Q14* **Redwater** Alberta, SW Canada *53.57N 113.06W*
30 *M16* **Red Willow Creek** ≈ Nebraska, C USA
31 *W9* **Red Wing** Minnesota, N USA *44.33N 92.31W*
37 *N9* **Redwood City** California, W USA *37.29N 122.13W*
31 *T9* **Redwood Falls** Minnesota, N USA *44.33N 95.07W*
198 *Ff7* **Reed Bank** *undersea feature* C South China Sea
33 *P7* **Reed City** Michigan, N USA *43.52N 85.30W*
30 *K6* **Reeder** North Dakota, N USA *46.03N 102.55W*
37 *R11* **Reedley** California, W USA *36.35N 119.27W*
35 *T11* **Reedpoint** Montana, NW USA *45.41N 109.33W*
32 *K8* **Reedsburg** Wisconsin, N USA *43.33N 90.03W*
34 *E13* **Reedsport** Oregon, NW USA *43.42N 124.06W*
195 *X8* **Reef Islands** *island group* Santa Cruz Islands, E Solomon Islands
193 *H16* **Reefton** West Coast, South Island, NZ *42.07S 171.52E*
22 *F8* **Reelfoot Lake** ◎ Tennessee, S USA
99 *D17* **Ree, Lough** ***Ir.*** Loch Rí. ◎ C Ireland
Reengus *see* Rīngas
37 *U4* **Reese River** ≈ Nevada, W USA
100 *M8* **Reest** ≈ E Netherlands
Reetz Neumark *see* Recz
143 *N13* **Refahiye** Erzincan, C Turkey *39.54N 38.45E*
25 *N4* **Reform** Alabama, S USA *33.22N 88.01W*
97 *K20* **Reftele** Jönköping, S Sweden *57.10N 13.34E*
27 *T14* **Refugio** Texas, SW USA *28.18N 97.16W*
112 *E8* **Rega** ≈ NW Poland
Regar *see* Tursunzoda
103 *O21* **Regen** Bayern, SE Germany *48.57N 13.10E*
103 *M20* **Regen** ≈ SE Germany
103 *M21* **Regensburg** ***Eng.*** Ratisbon, ***Fr.*** Ratisbonne; ***hist.*** Ratisbona, ***anc.*** Castra Regina, Reginum. Bayern, SE Germany *49.01N 12.06E*
103 *M21* **Regenstauf** Bayern, SE Germany *49.06N 12.07E*
76 *I10* **Reggane** C Algeria *26.45N 0.10E*
100 *N9* **Regge** ≈ E Netherlands
Reggio *see* Reggio nell' Emilia
Reggio Calabria *see* Reggio di Calabria
109 *M23* **Reggio di Calabria** ***var.*** Reggio Calabria, ***Gk.*** Rhegion; ***anc.*** Regium, Rhegium. Calabria, SW Italy *38.06N 15.39E*
Reggio Emilia *see* Reggio nell' Emilia
108 *F9* **Reggio nell' Emilia** ***var.*** Reggio Emilia, ***abbrev.*** Reggio; ***anc.*** Regium Lepidum. Emilia-Romagna, N Italy *44.42N 10.37E*
118 *I10* **Reghin** ***Ger.*** Sächsisch-Reen, ***Hung.*** Szászrégen; ***prev.*** Reghinul Săsesc, ***Ger.*** Sächsisch-Regen. Mureş, C Romania *46.46N 24.40E*
Reghinul Săsesc *see* Reghin
9 *U16* **Regina** Saskatchewan, S Canada *50.25N 104.39W*
9 *U16* **Regina** ✈ Saskatchewan, S Canada *50.21N 104.43W*
57 *Z10* **Régina** E French Guiana *4.19N 52.07W*
9 *U16* **Regina Beach** Saskatchewan, S Canada *50.44N 105.03W*
Reginum *see* Regensburg
Registan *see* Rīgestān
62 *L11* **Registro** São Paulo, S Brazil *24.30S 47.49W*
Regium *see* Reggio di Calabria
Regium Lepidum *see* Reggio nell' Emilia
103 *K19* **Regnitz** ***var.*** Rednitz. ≈ SE Germany
42 *K10* **Regocijo** Durango, W Mexico *23.34N 105.10W*
106 *H12* **Reguengos de Monsaraz** Évora, S Portugal *38.25N 7.31W*
103 *M18* **Rehau** Bayern, E Germany *50.15N 12.03E*
85 *D19* **Rehoboth** Hardap, C Namibia *23.18S 17.03E*
Rehoboth/Rehovoth *see* Reḥovot
23 *Z4* **Rehoboth Beach** Delaware, NE USA *38.42N 75.03W*
144 *F10* **Reḥovot** ***var.*** Rehoboth, Rekhovot, Rehovoth. Central, C Israel *31.54N 34.49E*
83 *J20* **Rei** *spring/well* S Kenya *3.24S 39.18E*
Reichenau *see* Rychnov nad Kněžnou, Czech Republic
Reichenau *see* Bogatynia, Poland
103 *M17* **Reichenbach** ***var.*** Reichenbach im Vogtland. Sachsen, E Germany *50.36N 12.18E*
Reichenbach *see* Dzierżoniów
Reichenbach im Vogtland *see* Reichenbach
Reichenberg *see* Liberec
189 *O11* **Reid** Western Australia *30.48S 128.24E*
25 *V6* **Reidsville** Georgia, SE USA *32.05N 82.07W*
23 *T8* **Reidsville** North Carolina, SE USA *36.21N 79.39W*
Reifnitz *see* Ribnica
99 *O22* **Reigate** SE England, UK *51.13N 0.13W*
Reikjavik *see* Reykjavík
104 *I10* **Ré, Île de** *island* W France
39 *N15* **Reiley Peak** ▲ Arizona, SW USA *32.24N 110.09W*
105 *Q4* **Reims** ***Eng.*** Rheims; ***anc.*** Durocortorum, Remi. Marne, N France *49.16N 4.01E*
65 *G23* **Reina Adelaida, Archipiélago** *island group* S Chile
47 *O16* **Reina Beatrix** ✈ (Oranjestad) C Aruba *12.30N 69.57W*
110 *F7* **Reinach** Aargau, W Switzerland *47.15N 8.12E*
110 *E6* **Reinach** Basel-Land, NW Switzerland *47.30N 7.36E*
66 *O11* **Reina Sofía** ✈ (Tenerife) Tenerife, Islas Canarias, Spain, NE Atlantic Ocean
31 *W13* **Reinbeck** Iowa, C USA *42.19N 92.36W*
102 *J10* **Reinbek** Schleswig-Holstein, N Germany *53.31N 10.15E*
9 *U12* **Reindeer** ≈ Saskatchewan, C Canada
9 *U11* **Reindeer Lake** ◎ Manitoba/Saskatchewan, C Canada
Reine-Charlotte, Îles de la *see* Queen Charlotte Islands
Reine-Élisabeth, Îles de la *see* Queen Elizabeth Islands
96 *F13* **Reineskarvet** ▲ S Norway *60.38N 7.48E*
192 *H1* **Reinga, Cape** *headland* North Island, NZ *34.24S 172.40E*
107 *N3* **Reinosa** Cantabria, N Spain *43.01N 4.09W*
111 *R8* **Reisseck** ▲ S Austria *46.57N 13.21E*
23 *W3* **Reisterstown** Maryland, NE USA *39.27N 76.46W*
Reisui *see* Yŏsu
100 *N5* **Reitdiep** ≈ NE Netherlands
203 *V10* **Reitoru** *atoll* Îles Tuamotu, C French Polynesia
97 *M17* **Rejmyre** Östergötland, S Sweden *58.49N 15.55E*
Reka *see* Rijeka
Reka Ili *see* Ili
97 *N16* **Rekarne** Västmanland, C Sweden *59.25N 16.04*
Rekhovot *see* Reḥovot
15 *Ii7* **Reliance** Northwest Territories, C Canada *62.45N 109.07W*
35 *U16* **Reliance** Wyoming, C USA *41.42N 109.13W*
76 *I5* **Relizane** ***var.*** Ghelîzâne, Ghilizane. NW Algeria *35.45N 0.39E*
190 *I7* **Remarkable, Mount** ▲ South Australia *32.46S 138.08E*
56 *E8* **Remedios** Antioquia, N Colombia *7.01N 74.42W*
45 *Q16* **Remedios** Veraguas, W Panama *8.12N 81.49W*
44 *D8* **Remedios, Punta** *headland* SW El Salvador *13.31N 89.48W*
Remi *see* Reims
101 *N25* **Remich** Grevenmacher, SE Luxembourg *49.33N 6.22E*
101 *J19* **Remicourt** Liège, E Belgium *50.40N 5.19E*
12 *H8* **Rémigny, Lac** ◎ Quebec, SE Canada
57 *Z10* **Rémire** NE French Guiana *4.52N 52.16W*
131 *N13* **Remontnoye** Rostovskaya Oblast', SW Russian Federation *46.35N 43.38E*
176 *V13* **Remoon** Pulau Kur, E Indonesia *5.18S 131.59E*
101 *L20* **Remouchamps** Liège, E Belgium *50.29N 5.43E*
105 *R15* **Remoulins** Gard, S France *43.56N 4.34E*
181 *X16* **Rempart, Mont du** ***var.*** Mount Rempart. *hill* W Mauritius
103 *E15* **Remscheid** Nordrhein-Westfalen, W Germany *51.10N 7.10E*
31 *S12* **Remsen** Iowa, C USA *42.48N 95.58W*
96 *I12* **Rena** Hedmark, S Norway *61.07N 11.21E*
96 *I11* **Rena** ≈ S Norway
Renaix *see* Ronse
120 *H7* **Rencēni** Valmiera, N Latvia *57.43N 25.25E*
120 *D9* **Renda** Kuldīga, W Latvia *57.04N 22.18E*
109 *N20* **Rende** Calabria, SW Italy *39.19N 16.10E*
101 *K21* **Rendeux** Luxembourg, SE Belgium *50.15N 5.28E*
Rendina *see* Rentína
32 *L16* **Rend Lake** ⊠ Illinois, N USA
195 *U15* **Rendova** *island* New Georgia Islands, NW Solomon Islands
102 *I8* **Rendsburg** Schleswig-Holstein, N Germany *54.18N 9.40E*
110 *B9* **Renens** Vaud, SW Switzerland *46.31N 6.36E*
12 *K12* **Renfrew** Ontario, SE Canada *45.28N 76.42W*
98 *I12* **Renfrew** *cultural region* SW Scotland, UK
174 *H8* **Rengat** Sumatera, W Indonesia *0.25S 102.38E*
159 *W12* **Rengma Hills** ▲▲ NE India
64 *H12* **Rengo** Libertador, C Chile *34.26S 70.53W*
118 *M12* **Reni** Odes'ka Oblast', SW Ukraine *45.30N 28.24E*
82 *F11* **Renk** Upper Nile, E Sudan *11.48N 32.49E*
95 *L19* **Renko** Etelä-Suomi, S Finland *60.52N 24.16E*
100 *L12* **Renkum** Gelderland, SE Netherlands *51.58N 5.43E*
190 *K9* **Renmark** South Australia *34.12S 140.43E*
195 *W17* **Rennell** ***var.*** Mu Nggava. *island* S Solomon Islands
189 *Q4* **Renner Springs Roadhouse** Northern Territory, N Australia *18.12S 133.48E*
104 *I6* **Rennes** ***Bret.*** Roazon; ***anc.*** Condate. Ille-et-Vilaine, NW France *48.07N 1.40W*
205 *S16* **Rennick Glacier** *glacier* Antarctica
9 *Y16* **Rennie** Manitoba, S Canada *49.51N 95.28W*
37 *Q5* **Reno** Nevada, W USA *39.31N 119.48W*
108 *H10* **Reno** ≈ N Italy
37 *Q5* **Reno-Cannon** ✈ Nevada, W USA *39.26N 119.42W*
85 *F24* **Renoster** ≈ SW South Africa
13 *T5* **Renouard, Lac** ◎ Quebec, SE Canada
20 *F13* **Renovo** Pennsylvania, NE USA *41.19N 77.42W*
167 *O3* **Renqiu** Hebei, E China *38.49N 116.02E*
166 *I9* **Renshou** Sichuan, C China *29.58N 104.06E*
33 *N12* **Rensselaer** Indiana, N USA *40.55N 87.10W*
20 *L11* **Rensselaer** New York, NE USA *42.38N 73.44W*
107 *Q2* **Rentería** ***Basq.*** Errenteria. País Vasco, N Spain *43.17N 1.54W*
117 *E17* **Rentína** ***var.*** Rendina. Thessalía, C Greece *39.04N 21.58E*
31 *T9* **Renville** Minnesota, N USA *44.48N 95.13W*
79 *O13* **Réo** W Burkina *12.19N 2.28W*
13 *O12* **Repentigny** Quebec, SE Canada *45.42N 73.28W*
152 *K13* **Repetek** Lebapskiy Velayat, E Turkmenistan *38.40N 63.12E*
95 *J16* **Replot** ***Fin.*** Raippaluoto. *island* W Finland
Reppen *see* Rzepin
Reps *see* Rupea
29 *T7* **Republic** Missouri, C USA *37.07N 93.28W*
34 *K7* **Republic** Washington, NW USA *48.39N 118.44W*
29 *N3* **Republican River** ≈ Kansas/Nebraska, C USA
15 *Ll4* **Repulse Bay** Northwest Territories, N Canada *66.34N 86.19W*
58 *F9* **Requena** Loreto, NE Peru *5.02S 73.47W*
107 *R10* **Requena** País Valenciano, E Spain *39.28N 1.07W*
105 *O14* **Réquista** Aveyron, S France *44.00N 2.31E*
142 *M12* **Reşadiye** Tokat, N Turkey *40.24N 37.19E*
Reschenpass *see* Resia, Passo di
Reschitza *see* Reşiţa
115 *N20* **Resen** ***Turk.*** Resne. SW FYR Macedonia *41.07N 21.00E*
62 *J11* **Reserva** Paraná, S Brazil *24.40S 50.52W*
9 *V15* **Reserve** Saskatchewan, S Canada *52.24N 102.37W*
39 *P13* **Reserve** New Mexico, SW USA *33.42N 108.45W*
Reshetilovka *see* Reshetylivka
119 *S6* **Reshetylivka** ***Rus.*** Reshetilovka. Poltavs'ka Oblast', NE Ukraine *49.34N 34.04E*
Resht *see* Rasht
108 *F5* **Resia, Passo di** ***Ger.*** Reschenpass. *pass* Austria/Italy *46.51N 10.32E*
Resicabánya *see* Reşiţa
64 *N7* **Resistencia** Chaco, NE Argentina *27.27S 58.55W*
118 *F12* **Reşiţa** ***Ger.*** Reschitza, ***Hung.*** Resicabánya. Caraş-Severin, W Romania *45.13N 21.58E*
Resne *see* Resen
207 *N9* **Resolute** Cornwallis Island, Nunavut, N Canada *74.40N 94.54W*
Resolution *see* Fort Resolution
16 *P4* **Resolution Island** *island* Nunavut, NE Canada
193 *A23* **Resolution Island** *island* SW NZ
13 *W7* **Restigouche** Quebec, SE Canada *48.01N 66.42W*
9 *W17* **Reston** Manitoba, S Canada *49.33N 101.03W*
12 *H11* **Restoule Lake** ◎ Ontario, S Canada
56 *F10* **Restrepo** Meta, C Colombia *4.20N 73.29W*
44 *B6* **Retalhuleu** Retalhuleu, SW Guatemala *14.30N 91.41W*
44 *A1* **Retalhuleu** ***off.*** Departamento de Retalhuleu. ◈ *department* SW Guatemala
99 *N18* **Retford** C England, UK *53.18N 0.52W*
105 *Q3* **Rethel** Ardennes, N France *49.31N 4.22E*
Rethimno/Réthimnon *see* Réthymno
117 *I25* **Réthymno** ***var.*** Rethimno; ***prev.*** Réthimnon. Kríti, Greece, E Mediterranean Sea *35.21N 24.28E*
Retiche, Alpi *see* Rhaetian Alps
101 *J16* **Retie** Antwerpen, N Belgium *51.18N 5.05E*
113 *J21* **Rétság** Nógrád, N Hungary *47.57N 19.07E*
111 *W2* **Retz** Niederösterreich, NE Austria *48.46N 15.58E*
181 *N15* **Réunion** ***off.*** La Réunion. ◇ *French overseas department* W Indian Ocean
132 *L17* **Réunion** *island* W Indian Ocean
107 *U6* **Reus** Cataluña, E Spain *41.10N 1.06E*
101 *J15* **Reusel** Noord-Brabant, S Netherlands *51.21N 5.10E*
110 *F7* **Reuss** ≈ NW Switzerland
Reuţel *see* Ciuhuru
103 *H22* **Reutlingen** Baden-Württemberg, S Germany *48.30N 9.13E*
110 *L7* **Reutte** Tirol, W Austria *47.30N 10.43E*
101 *M16* **Reuver** Limburg, SE Netherlands *51.16N 6.04E*
30 *K7* **Reva** South Dakota, N USA *45.30N 103.03W*
Reval/Revel' *see* Tallinn
128 *J4* **Revda** Murmanskaya Oblast', NW Russian Federation *67.57N 34.29E*
125 *Ee11* **Revda** Sverdlovskaya Oblast', C Russian Federation *56.48N 59.42E*
105 *N16* **Revel** Haute-Garonne, S France *43.27N 1.58E*
9 *O16* **Revelstoke** British Columbia, SW Canada *51.01N 118.12W*
45 *N13* **Reventazón, Río** ≈ E Costa Rica
108 *G9* **Revere** Lombardia, N Italy *45.03N 11.07E*
41 *Y14* **Revillagigedo Island** *island* Alexander Archipelago, Alaska, USA
199 *Mm7* **Revillagigedo Islands** *island group* NW Mexico
105 *R3* **Revin** Ardennes, N France *49.57N 4.39E*
94 *O3* **Revnosa** *headland* C Svalbard *78.03N 18.52E*
Revolyutsii, Pik *see* Revolyutsiya, Qullai
153 *T13* **Revolyutsiya, Qullai** ***Rus.*** Pik Revolyutsii. ▲ SE Tajikistan *38.40N 72.26E*
113 *L19* **Revúca** ***Ger.*** Grossrauschenbach, ***Hung.*** Nagyrőce. Banskobystrický Kraj, C Slovakia *48.40N 20.10E*
160 *K9* **Rewa** Madhya Pradesh, C India *24.31N 81.18E*
158 *I11* **Rewāri** Haryāna, N India *28.13N 76.37E*
35 *R14* **Rexburg** Idaho, NW USA *43.49N 111.47W*
80 *G13* **Rey Bouba** Nord, NE Cameroon *8.40N 14.10E*
94 *L3* **Reydharfjördhur** Austurland, E Iceland *65.02N 14.12W*
59 *K16* **Reyes** Beni, NW Bolivia *14.17S 67.18W*
36 *L8* **Reyes, Point** *headland* California, W USA *37.58N 123.01W*
56 *B12* **Reyes, Punta** *headland* SW Colombia *2.43N 78.07W*
142 *L17* **Reyhanlı** Hatay, S Turkey *36.16N 36.33E*
45 *U16* **Rey, Isla del** *island* Archipiélago de las Perlas, SE Panama
94 *H2* **Reykhólar** Vestfirdhir, W Iceland *65.28N 22.12W*
94 *K2* **Reykjahlídh** Nordhurland Eystra, NE Iceland *65.37N 16.54W*
94 *I4* **Reykjanes** ◈ *region* SW Iceland

◆ Country ◇ Dependent Territory ◈ Administrative Region ▲ Mountain Volcano ◎ Lake
● Country Capital ○ Dependent Territory Capital ✈ International Airport ▲▲ Mountain Range ≈ River ⊠ Reservoir

Reykjanes Basin – Rockland

207 O16 **Reykjanes Basin** *var.* Irminger Basin. *undersea feature* N Atlantic Ocean
207 N17 **Reykjanes Ridge** *undersea feature* N Atlantic Ocean
94 H4 **Reykjavík** *var.* Reikjavik. ● (Iceland) Höfudhborgarsvaedhi, W Iceland 64.07N 21.54W
20 D13 **Reynoldsville** Pennsylvania, NE USA 41.04N 78.51W
43 P8 **Reynosa** Tamaulipas, C Mexico 26.03N 98.19W
Reẕā'īyeh *see* Orūmīyeh
Reẕā'īyeh, Daryācheh-ye *see* Orūmīyeh, Daryācheh-ye
104 I8 **Rezé** Loire-Atlantique, NW France 47.10N 1.36W
120 K10 **Rēzekne** *Ger.* Rositten; *prev. Rus.* Rezhitsa. Rēzekne, SE Latvia 56.31N 27.22E
Rezhitsa *see* Rēzekne
119 N9 **Rezina** NE Moldova 47.44N 28.58E
116 N11 **Rezovo** *Turk.* Rezve. Burgas, E Bulgaria 42.00N 28.00E
116 N11 **Rezovska Reka** *Turk.* Rezve Deresi. ≈ Bulgaria/Turkey *see also* Rezve Deresi
Rezve *see* Rezovo
116 N11 **Rezve Deresi** *Bul.* Rezovska Reka. ≈ Bulgaria/Turkey *see also* Rezovska Reka
Rhadames *see* Ghadāmis
Rhaedestus *see* Tekirdağ
110 J10 **Rhaetian Alps** *Fr.* Alpes Rhétiques, *Ger.* Rätische Alpen, *It.* Alpi Retiche. ▲ C Europe
110 I8 **Rhätikon** ▲ C Europe
103 G14 **Rheda-Wiedenbrück** Nordrhein-Westfalen, W Germany 51.51N 8.19E
100 M12 **Rheden** Gelderland, E Netherlands 52.01N 6.03E
Rhegion/Rhegium *see* Reggio di Calabria
Rheims *see* Reims
Rhein *see* Rhine
103 E17 **Rheinbach** Nordrhein-Westfalen, W Germany 50.37N 6.57E
102 F13 **Rheine** *var.* Rheine in Westfalen. Nordrhein-Westfalen, NW Germany 52.16N 7.27E
Rheine in Westfalen *see* Rheine
Rheinfeld *see* Rheinfelden
103 F24 **Rheinfelden** Baden-Württemberg, S Germany 47.34N 7.46E
110 E6 **Rheinfelden** *var.* Rheinfeld. Aargau, N Switzerland 47.33N 7.46E
103 E17 **Rheinisches Schiefergebirge** *var.* Rhine State Uplands, *Eng.* Rhenish Slate Mountains. ▲ W Germany
103 D18 **Rheinland-Pfalz** *Eng.* Rhineland-Palatinate, *Fr.* Rhénanie-Palatinat. ◆ *state* W Germany
103 G18 **Rhein/Main** ✈ (Frankfurt am Main) Hessen, W Germany 50.03N 8.33E
Rhénanie du Nord-Westphalie *see* Nordrhein-Westfalen
Rhénanie-Palatinat *see* Rheinland-Pfalz
100 K12 **Rhenen** Utrecht, C Netherlands 51.57N 5.34E
Rhenish Slate Mountains *see* Rheinisches Schiefergebirge
Rhétiques, Alpes *see* Rhaetian Alps
102 N10 **Rhin** ≈ NE Germany
Rhin *see* Rhine
86 F10 **Rhine** *Dut.* Rijn, *Fr.* Rhin, *Ger.* Rhein. ≈ W Europe
32 L5 **Rhinelander** Wisconsin, N USA 45.39N 89.22W
Rhineland-Palatinate *see* Rheinland-Pfalz
Rhine State Uplands *see* Rheinisches Schiefergebirge
102 N11 **Rhinkanal** *canal* NE Germany
83 F17 **Rhino Camp** NW Uganda 2.58N 31.24E
76 D7 **Rhir, Cap** *headland* W Morocco 30.40N 9.54W
108 D7 **Rho** Lombardia, N Italy 45.31N 9.01E
21 N12 **Rhode Island** *off.* State of Rhode Island and Providence Plantations; *also known as* Little Rhody, Ocean State. ◆ *state* NE USA
21 O13 **Rhode Island** *island* Rhode Island, NE USA
21 O13 **Rhode Island Sound** *sound* Maine/Rhode Island, NE USA
Rhodes *see* Ródos
Rhode-Saint-Genèse *see* Sint-Genesius-Rode
86 L14 **Rhodes Basin** *undersea feature* E Mediterranean Sea
Rhodesia *see* Zimbabwe
116 I12 **Rhodope Mountains** *var.* Rodhópi Óri, *Bul.* Rhodope Planina, Rodopi, *Gk.* Orosirá Rodhópis, *Turk.* Dospad Dagh. ▲ Bulgaria/Greece
Rhodope Planina *see* Rhodope Mountains
Rhodos *see* Ródos
103 I18 **Rhön** ▲ C Germany
105 Q10 **Rhône** ◆ *department* E France
88 C12 **Rhône** ≈ France/Switzerland
105 R12 **Rhône-Alpes** ◆ *region* E France
123 J6 **Rhône Fan** *undersea feature* W Mediterranean Sea
100 G13 **Rhoon** Zuid-Holland, SW Netherlands 51.52N 4.25E
98 G9 **Rhum** *var.* Rum. *island* W Scotland, UK
Rhuthun *see* Ruthin
99 J18 **Rhyl** NE Wales, UK 53.19N 3.28W
61 K18 **Rialma** Goiás, S Brazil 15.22S 49.35W
106 L3 **Riaño** Castilla-León, N Spain 42.59N 5.00W
107 O9 **Riansáres** ≈ C Spain
158 H6 **Riāsi** Jammu and Kashmir, NW India 33.03N 74.51E
174 Gg7 **Riau** *off.* Propinsi Riau. ◆ *province* W Indonesia
Riau Archipelago *see* Riau, Kepulauan
174 I8 **Riau, Kepulauan** *var.* Riau Archipelago, *Dut.* Riouw-Archipel. *island group* W Indonesia
107 O6 **Riaza** Castilla-León, N Spain 41.17N 3.29W
107 N6 **Riaza** ≈ N Spain
83 K17 **Riba** *spring/well* NE Kenya 1.56N 40.38E
106 H4 **Ribadavia** Galicia, NW Spain 42.16N 8.07W
106 J2 **Ribadeo** Galicia, NW Spain 43.31N 7.04W
106 L2 **Ribadesella** Asturias, N Spain 43.27N 5.04W
106 G10 **Ribatejo** *former province* C Portugal
149 Q8 **Ribāṭ-e Rīzāb** Yazd, C Iran
85 P15 **Ribáuè** Nampula, N Mozambique 14.56S 38.19E
99 K17 **Ribble** ≈ NW England, UK
97 F23 **Ribe** Ribe, W Denmark 55.19N 8.46E
97 F23 **Ribe** *off.* Ribe Amt, *var.* Ripen. ◆ *county* W Denmark
106 G3 **Ribeira** Galicia, NW Spain 42.33N 9.01W
66 O5 **Ribeira Brava** Madeira, Portugal, NE Atlantic Ocean 32.39N 17.04W
66 P3 **Ribeira Grande** São Miguel, Azores, Portugal, NE Atlantic Ocean 37.34N 25.31W
62 L8 **Ribeirão Preto** São Paulo, S Brazil 21.09S 47.48W
62 L11 **Ribeira, Rio** ≈ S Brazil
109 I24 **Ribera** Sicilia, Italy, C Mediterranean Sea 37.31N 13.16E
59 L14 **Riberalta** Beni, N Bolivia 11.00S 66.04W
107 W4 **Ribes de Freser** Cataluña, NE Spain 42.18N 2.11E
32 L6 **Rib Mountain** ▲ Wisconsin, N USA 44.55N 89.41W
111 U12 **Ribnica** *Ger.* Reifnitz. S Slovenia 45.46N 14.40E
119 N9 **Rîbniţa** *var.* Râbniţa, *Rus.* Rybnitsa. NE Moldova 47.46N 29.01E
102 M8 **Ribnitz-Damgarten** Mecklenburg-Vorpommern, NE Germany 54.14N 12.25E
113 D16 **Říčany** *Ger.* Ritschan. Středočeský Kraj, W Czech Republic 49.58N 14.39E
31 U7 **Rice** Minnesota, N USA 45.42N 94.10W
32 J5 **Rice Lake** Wisconsin, N USA 45.33N 91.43W
12 I15 **Rice Lake** ◎ Ontario, SE Canada
12 E8 **Rice Lake** ◎ Ontario, S Canada
25 V3 **Richard B.Russell Lake** ⊡ Georgia, SE USA
27 U6 **Richardson** Texas, SW USA 32.57N 96.43W
9 R11 **Richardson** ≈ Alberta, C Canada
8 I3 **Richardson Mountains** ▲ Yukon Territory, NW Canada
193 C21 **Richardson Mountains** ▲ South Island, NZ
44 F3 **Richardson Peak** ▲ SE Belize 16.34N 88.46W
78 G10 **Richard Toll** N Senegal 16.27N 15.44W
30 L5 **Richardton** North Dakota, N USA 46.52N 102.19W
12 F13 **Rich, Cape** *headland* Ontario, S Canada 44.42N 80.37W
104 L8 **Richelieu** Indre-et-Loire, C France 47.01N 0.18E
35 P15 **Richfield** Idaho, NW USA 43.03N 114.11W
38 K5 **Richfield** Utah, W USA 38.46N 112.06W
20 J10 **Richfield Springs** New York, NE USA 42.52N 74.57W
20 M6 **Richford** Vermont, NE USA 44.59N 72.37W
29 R6 **Rich Hill** Missouri, C USA 38.06N 94.22W
11 P14 **Richibucto** New Brunswick, SE Canada 46.42N 64.54W
110 G8 **Richisau** Glarus, NE Switzerland 47.00N 8.54E
25 S6 **Richland** Georgia, SE USA 32.05N 84.40W
29 U6 **Richland** Missouri, C USA 37.51N 92.24W
27 U8 **Richland** Texas, SW USA 31.55N 96.25W
34 K10 **Richland** Washington, NW USA 46.17N 119.16W
32 K8 **Richland Center** Wisconsin, N USA 43.22N 90.22W
23 W11 **Richlands** North Carolina, SE USA 34.52N 77.33W
23 Q7 **Richlands** Virginia, NE USA 37.05N 81.47W
27 R9 **Richland Springs** Texas, SW USA 31.16N 98.56W
191 S8 **Richmond** New South Wales, SE Australia 33.36S 150.43E
8 L17 **Richmond** British Columbia, SW Canada 49.07N 123.09W
12 L13 **Richmond** Ontario, SE Canada 45.12N 75.49W
13 Q12 **Richmond** Quebec, SE Canada 45.39N 72.07W
193 I14 **Richmond** Tasman, South Island, NZ 41.24S 173.04E
37 N8 **Richmond** California, W USA 37.57N 122.22W
33 Q14 **Richmond** Indiana, N USA 39.48N 84.52W
22 M6 **Richmond** Kentucky, S USA 37.45N 84.17W
29 S4 **Richmond** Missouri, C USA 39.16N 93.58W
27 V11 **Richmond** Texas, SW USA 29.34N 95.45W
38 L1 **Richmond** Utah, W USA 41.55N 111.51W
23 W6 **Richmond** *state capital* Virginia, NE USA 37.33N 77.27W
12 H15 **Richmond Hill** Ontario, S Canada 43.51N 79.24W
193 J15 **Richmond Range** ▲ South Island, NZ
29 S12 **Rich Mountain** ▲ Arkansas, C USA 34.37N 94.17W
33 S13 **Richwood** Ohio, N USA 40.25N 83.18W
23 R5 **Richwood** West Virginia, NE USA 38.13N 80.31W
106 K5 **Ricobayo, Embalse de** ⊡ NW Spain
Ricomagus *see* Riom
Ridā' *see* Radā'
100 H13 **Ridderkerk** Zuid-Holland, SW Netherlands 51.52N 4.34E
35 N16 **Riddle** Idaho, NW USA 42.07N 116.09W
34 F14 **Riddle** Oregon, NW USA 42.57N 123.21W
12 L13 **Rideau** ≈ Ontario, SE Canada
37 T12 **Ridgecrest** California, W USA 35.37N 117.40W
20 L13 **Ridgefield** Connecticut, NE USA 41.16N 73.30W
24 K5 **Ridgeland** Mississippi, S USA 32.25N 90.07W
23 R15 **Ridgeland** South Carolina, SE USA 32.28N 80.58W
22 F8 **Ridgely** Tennessee, S USA 36.15N 89.29W
12 D17 **Ridgetown** Ontario, S Canada 42.27N 81.52W
Ridgeway *see* Ridgway
23 R12 **Ridgeway** South Carolina, SE USA 34.17N 80.56W
20 D13 **Ridgway** *var.* Ridgeway. Pennsylvania, NE USA 41.24N 78.40W
9 W16 **Riding Mountain** ▲ Manitoba, S Canada
Ried *see* Ried im Innkreis
111 R4 **Ried im Innkreis** *var.* Ried. Oberösterreich, NW Austria 48.13N 13.28E
111 X8 **Riegersburg** Steiermark, SE Austria 47.03N 15.52E
110 E6 **Riehen** Basel-Stadt, NW Switzerland 47.34N 7.39E
94 J9 **Riehppegáisá** *var.* Rieppe. ▲ N Norway 69.38N 21.31E
101 K18 **Riemst** Limburg, NE Belgium 50.49N 5.35E
Rieppe *see* Riehppegáisá
103 O15 **Riesa** Sachsen, E Germany 51.18N 13.18E
65 H24 **Riesco, Isla** *island* S Chile
109 K25 **Riesi** Sicilia, Italy, C Mediterranean Sea 37.16N 14.04E
85 F25 **Riet** ≈ SW South Africa
85 I23 **Riet** ≈ SW South Africa
120 D11 **Rietavas** Plungė, W Lithuania 55.43N 21.56E
85 F19 **Rietfontein** Omaheke, E Namibia 21.54S 20.57E
109 I14 **Rieti** *anc.* Reate. Lazio, C Italy 42.22N 12.49E
86 D14 **Rif** *var.* Er Rif, Er Riff, Riff. ▲ N Morocco
Riff *see* Rif
39 Q4 **Rifle** Colorado, C USA 39.30N 107.46W
33 R7 **Rifle River** ≈ Michigan, N USA
83 H18 **Rift Valley** ◆ *province* Kenya
Rift Valley *see* Great Rift Valley
120 F9 **Rīga** *Eng.* Riga. ● (Latvia) Rīga, C Latvia 56.57N 24.07E
Rigaer Bucht *see* Riga, Gulf of
120 F6 **Riga, Gulf of** *Est.* Liivi Laht, *Ger.* Rigaer Bucht, *Latv.* Rīgas Jūras Līcis, *Rus.* Rizhskiy Zaliv; *prev. Est.* Riia Laht. *gulf* Estonia/Latvia
149 U12 **Rīgān** Kermān, SE Iran 28.39N 59.01E
Rīgas Jūras Līcis *see* Riga, Gulf of
13 N12 **Rigaud** ≈ Ontario/Quebec, SE Canada
35 R14 **Rigby** Idaho, NW USA 43.40N 111.54W
154 M10 **Rīgestān** *var.* Registan. *desert region* S Afghanistan
34 M11 **Riggins** Idaho, NW USA 45.24N 116.18W
11 R8 **Rigolet** Newfoundland, NE Canada 54.10N 58.25W
80 G9 **Rig-Rig** Kanem, W Chad 14.19N 14.19E
120 F4 **Riguldi** Läänemaa, W Estonia 59.07N 23.34E
Riia Laht *see* Riga, Gulf of
95 L19 **Riihimäki** Etelä-Suomi, S Finland 60.45N 24.45E
205 O2 **Riiser-Larsen Ice Shelf** *ice shelf* Antarctica
205 U2 **Riiser-Larsen Peninsula** *peninsula* Antarctica
67 P22 **Riiser-Larsen Sea** *sea* Antarctica
42 D2 **Riíto** Sonora, NW Mexico 32.06N 114.57W
114 B9 **Rijeka** *Ger.* Sankt Veit am Flaum, *It.* Fiume, *Slvn.* Reka; *anc.* Tarsatica. Primorje-Gorski Kotar, NW Croatia 45.20N 14.25E
101 I14 **Rijen** Noord-Brabant, S Netherlands 51.34N 4.55E
101 H15 **Rijkevorsel** Antwerpen, N Belgium 51.23N 4.43E
Rijn *see* Rhine
100 G11 **Rijnsburg** Zuid-Holland, W Netherlands 52.12N 4.27E
Rijssel *see* Lille
100 N10 **Rijssen** Overijssel, E Netherlands 52.19N 6.30E
100 G12 **Rijswijk** *Eng.* Ryswick. Zuid-Holland, W Netherlands 52.04N 4.22E
94 I10 **Riksgränsen** Norrbotten, N Sweden 68.24N 18.15E
172 Q6 **Rikubetsu** Hokkaidō, NE Japan 43.30N 143.43E
171 Mm12 **Rikuzen-Takata** Iwate, Honshū, C Japan 39.01N 141.37E
29 O4 **Riley** Kansas, C USA 39.18N 96.49W
101 I17 **Rillaar** Vlaams Brabant, C Belgium 50.58N 4.58E
Rí, Loch *see* Ree, Lough
116 G11 **Rilska Reka** ≈ W Bulgaria
79 T12 **Rima** ≈ N Nigeria
147 N7 **Rimah, Wādī ar** *var.* Wādī ar Rummah. *dry watercourse* C Saudi Arabia
Rimaszombat *see* Rimavská Sobota
203 R12 **Rimatara** *island* Îles Australes, SW French Polynesia
113 L20 **Rimavská Sobota** *Ger.* Gross-Steffelsdorf, *Hung.* Rimaszombat. Banskobystrický Kraj, C Slovakia 48.24N 20.01E
9 Q15 **Rimbey** Alberta, SW Canada 52.39N 114.10W
97 P15 **Rimbo** Stockholm, C Sweden 59.43N 18.21E
97 M18 **Rimforsa** Östergötland, S Sweden 58.06N 15.40E
108 I11 **Rimini** *anc.* Ariminum. Emilia-Romagna, N Italy 44.03N 12.33E
Rîmnicu-Sărat *see* Râmnicu Sărat
Rîmnicu Vîlcea *see* Râmnicu Vâlcea
155 Y3 **Rimo Muztāgh** ▲ India/Pakistan
13 U7 **Rimouski** Quebec, SE Canada 48.25N 68.31W
164 M16 **Rinbung** Xizang Zizhiqu, W China 29.15N 89.40E
168 I5 **Rinchinlhümbe** Hövsgöl, N Mongolia 51.06N 99.40E
64 I5 **Rincón, Cerro** ▲ N Chile 24.01S 67.19W
106 M15 **Rincón de la Victoria** Andalucía, S Spain 36.43N 4.18W
Rincón del Bonete, Lago Artificial de *see* Río Negro, Embalse del
107 Q4 **Rincón de Soto** La Rioja, N Spain 42.15N 1.49W
96 G8 **Rindal** Møre og Romsdal, S Norway 63.02N 9.09E
117 J20 **Ríneia** *island* Kykládes, Greece, Aegean Sea
158 H11 **Ringas** *prev.* Reengus, Rīngus. Rājasthān, N India 27.18N 75.27E
97 H24 **Ringe** Fyn, C Denmark 55.13N 10.30E
96 H11 **Ringebu** Oppland, S Norway 61.31N 10.09E
Ringen *see* Rõngu
195 U14 **Ringgi** Kolombangara, NW Solomon Islands 8.03S 95.08E
25 R1 **Ringgold** Georgia, SE USA 34.55N 85.06W
24 G5 **Ringgold** Louisiana, S USA 32.19N 93.16W
27 S5 **Ringgold** Texas, SW USA 33.47N 97.56W
97 E22 **Ringkøbing** Ringkøbing, W Denmark 56.04N 8.22E
97 E21 **Ringkøbing** *off.* Ringkøbing Amt. ◆ *county* W Denmark
97 E22 **Ringkøbing Fjord** *fjord* W Denmark
35 S10 **Ringling** Montana, NW USA 46.15N 110.48W
29 N13 **Ringling** Oklahoma, C USA 34.12N 97.35W
96 H13 **Ringsaker** Hedmark, S Norway 60.54N 10.45E
97 I23 **Ringsted** Vestsjælland, E Denmark 55.28N 11.48E
Ringus *see* Ringas
94 I9 **Ringvassøya** *island* N Norway
20 K13 **Ringwood** New Jersey, NE USA 41.06N 74.15W
Rinn Duáin *see* Hook Head
102 H13 **Rinteln** Niedersachsen, NW Germany 52.10N 9.04E
Rio *see* Rio de Janeiro
117 E18 **Río** Dytikí Ellás, S Greece 38.18N 21.48E
58 C7 **Riobamba** Chimborazo, C Ecuador 1.38S 78.40W
62 P9 **Rio Bonito** Rio de Janeiro, SE Brazil 22.42S 42.38W
61 C16 **Rio Branco** *state capital* Acre, W Brazil 9.58S 67.49W
63 H18 **Río Branco** Cerro Largo, NE Uruguay 32.34S 53.21W
Rio Branco, Território de *see* Roraima
43 P8 **Río Bravo** Tamaulipas, C Mexico 25.57N 98.03W
65 G16 **Río Bueno** Los Lagos, C Chile 40.19S 72.55W
57 P5 **Río Caribe** Sucre, NE Venezuela 10.40N 63.07W
56 M5 **Río Chico** Miranda, N Venezuela 10.18N 66.00W
65 H18 **Río Cisnes** Aisén, S Chile 44.29S 71.15W
62 L9 **Rio Claro** São Paulo, S Brazil 22.22S 47.31W
47 V14 **Rio Claro** Trinidad, Trinidad and Tobago 10.18N 61.10W
56 J5 **Río Claro** Lara, N Venezuela 9.54N 69.22W
65 K15 **Río Colorado** Río Negro, E Argentina 39.04S 64.04W
64 K11 **Río Cuarto** Córdoba, C Argentina 33.06S 64.20W
62 P10 **Rio de Janeiro** *var.* Rio. *state capital* Rio de Janeiro, SE Brazil 22.53S 43.16W
62 P9 **Rio de Janeiro** *off.* Estado do Rio de Janeiro. ◆ *state* SE Brazil
45 R17 **Río de Jesús** Veraguas, S Panama 7.57N 81.09W
36 K3 **Rio Dell** California, W USA 40.30N 124.07W
62 K13 **Rio do Sul** Santa Catarina, S Brazil 27.15S 49.37W
65 I23 **Río Gallegos** *var.* Gallegos, Puerto Gallegos. Santa Cruz, S Argentina 51.39S 69.21W
63 I18 **Rio Grande** *var.* São Pedro do Rio Grande do Sul. Rio Grande do Sul, S Brazil 32.03S 52.07W
26 I9 **Rio Grande** ≈ Texas, SW USA
65 J24 **Río Grande** Tierra del Fuego, S Argentina 53.45S 67.46W
42 L10 **Río Grande** Zacatecas, C Mexico 23.48N 103.03W
44 J9 **Río Grande** León, NW Nicaragua 12.57N 86.31W
47 V5 **Río Grande** E Puerto Rico 18.22N 65.49W
27 R17 **Rio Grande City** Texas, SW USA 26.22N 98.49W
61 P14 **Rio Grande do Norte** *off.* Estado do Rio Grande do Norte. ◆ *state* E Brazil
63 G15 **Rio Grande do Sul** *off.* Estado do Rio Grande do Sul. ◆ *state* S Brazil
67 M17 **Rio Grande Fracture Zone** *tectonic feature* C Atlantic Ocean
67 J18 **Rio Grande Gap** *undersea feature* S Atlantic Ocean
Rio Grande Plateau *see* Rio Grande Rise
67 J18 **Rio Grande Rise** *var.* Rio Grande Plateau. *undersea feature* SW Atlantic Ocean
56 G4 **Ríohacha** La Guajira, N Colombia 11.22N 72.46W
45 S16 **Río Hato** Coclé, C Panama 8.22N 80.09W
27 T17 **Rio Hondo** Texas, SW USA 26.14N 97.34W
58 D10 **Rioja** San Martín, N Peru 6.03S 77.05W
43 Y11 **Río Lagartos** Yucatán, SE Mexico 21.34N 88.07W
105 P11 **Riom** *anc.* Ricomagus. Puy-de-Dôme, C France 45.54N 3.06E
106 F10 **Rio Maior** Santarém, C Portugal 39.19N 8.55W
105 O12 **Riom-ès-Montagnes** Cantal, C France 45.15N 2.39E
62 J12 **Rio Negro** Paraná, S Brazil 26.06S 49.46W
65 I15 **Río Negro** *off.* Provincia de Río Negro. ◆ *province* C Argentina
63 D18 **Río Negro** ◆ *department* W Uruguay
49 V12 **Río Negro, Embalse del** *var.* Lago Artificial de Rincón del Bonete. ⊡ C Uruguay
109 M17 **Rionero in Vulture** Basilicata, S Italy 40.55N 15.40E
143 S9 **Rioni** ≈ W Georgia
107 P12 **Riópar** Castilla-La Mancha, C Spain 38.31N 2.27W
63 H16 **Rio Pardo** Rio Grande do Sul, S Brazil 29.41S 52.25W
39 R11 **Rio Rancho Estates** New Mexico, SW USA 35.14N 106.40W
44 L11 **Río San Juan** ◆ *department* S Nicaragua
56 E9 **Riosucio** Caldas, W Colombia 5.25N 75.43W
56 C7 **Riosucio** Chocó, NW Colombia 7.24N 77.09W
64 K10 **Río Tercero** Córdoba, C Argentina 32.12S 64.03W
56 J5 **Río Tocuyo** Lara, N Venezuela 10.12N 69.58W
Riouw-Archipel *see* Riau, Kepulauan
61 J19 **Rio Verde** Goiás, C Brazil 17.49S 50.55W
43 O12 **Río Verde** *var.* Rioverde. San Luis Potosí, C Mexico 21.58N 100.00W
37 O8 **Rio Vista** California, W USA 38.09N 121.42W
114 M11 **Ripanj** Serbia, N Yugoslavia 44.37N 20.30E
108 J13 **Ripatransone** Marche, C Italy 43.00N 13.45E
Ripen *see* Ribe
24 M2 **Ripley** Mississippi, S USA 34.43N 88.57W
33 R15 **Ripley** Ohio, N USA 38.45N 83.51W
22 F9 **Ripley** Tennessee, S USA 35.45N 89.31W
23 Q4 **Ripley** West Virginia, NE USA 38.49N 81.42W
107 W4 **Ripoll** Cataluña, NE Spain 42.12N 2.12E
99 M16 **Ripon** N England, UK 54.07N 1.31W
32 M7 **Ripon** Wisconsin, N USA 43.52N 88.48W
109 L24 **Riposto** Sicilia, Italy, C Mediterranean Sea 37.43N 15.13E
101 L14 **Rips** Noord-Brabant, SE Netherlands 51.31N 5.49E
56 D9 **Risaralda** *off.* Departamento de Risaralda. ◆ *province* C Colombia
118 L8 **Rîşcani** *var.* Râşcani, *Rus.* Ryshkany. NW Moldova 47.55N 27.31E
158 J9 **Rishikesh** Uttar Pradesh, N India 30.06N 78.16E
172 P2 **Rishiri-suidō** *strait* E Sea of Japan
172 Oo2 **Rishiri-tō** *var.* Risiri Tô. *island* NE Japan
172 P2 **Rishiri-yama** ▲ Rishiri-tō, NE Japan 45.11N 141.11E
27 R7 **Rising Star** Texas, SW USA 32.06N 98.57W
33 Q15 **Rising Sun** Indiana, N USA 38.58N 84.52W
Risiri Tô *see* Rishiri-tō
104 L4 **Risle** ≈ N France
Rîşno *see* Râşnov
29 V13 **Rison** Arkansas, C USA 33.57N 92.11W
97 G17 **Risør** Aust-Agder, S Norway 58.43N 9.13E
94 H10 **Risøyhamn** Nordland, C Norway 69.00N 15.37E
103 I23 **Riss** ≈ S Germany
120 G4 **Risti** *Ger.* Kreuz. Läänemaa, W Estonia 59.03N 24.11E
13 V8 **Ristigouche** ≈ Quebec, SE Canada
95 N18 **Ristiina** Isä-Suomi, E Finland 61.31N 27.15E
95 N14 **Ristijärvi** Oulu, C Finland 64.30N 28.15E
196 C14 **Ritidian Point** *headland* N Guam 13.39N 144.51E
Ritschan *see* Říčany
37 R9 **Ritter, Mount** ▲ California, W USA 37.40N 119.10W
33 T12 **Rittman** Ohio, N USA 40.58N 81.46W
34 L9 **Ritzville** Washington, NW USA 47.07N 118.22W
Riva *see* Riva del Garda
63 A21 **Rivadavia** Buenos Aires, E Argentina 35.28S 62.58W
108 F7 **Riva del Garda** *var.* Riva. Trentino-Alto Adige, N Italy 45.54N 10.50E
108 B8 **Rivarolo Canavese** Piemonte, W Italy 45.21N 7.42E
44 K11 **Rivas** Rivas, SW Nicaragua 11.25N 85.49W
44 J11 **Rivas** ◆ *department* SW Nicaragua
105 R11 **Rive-de-Gier** Loire, E France 45.31N 4.36E
63 A22 **Rivera** Buenos Aires, E Argentina 37.13S 63.13W
63 F16 **Rivera** Rivera, NE Uruguay 30.54S 55.31W
63 F17 **Rivera** ◆ *department* NE Uruguay
37 P9 **Riverbank** California, W USA 37.43N 120.59W
78 K17 **River Cess** SW Liberia 5.28N 9.31W
30 M4 **Riverdale** North Dakota, N USA 47.29N 101.22W
32 I6 **River Falls** Wisconsin, N USA 44.52N 92.38W
9 T16 **Riverhurst** Saskatchewan, S Canada 50.52N 106.49W
191 O10 **Riverina** *physical region* New South Wales, SE Australia
82 G8 **River Nile** ◆ *state* NE Sudan
65 F19 **Rivero, Isla** *island* Archipiélago de los Chonos, S Chile
9 W16 **Rivers** Manitoba, S Canada 50.01N 100.13W
79 U17 **Rivers** ◆ *state* S Nigeria
193 D23 **Riversdale** Southland, South Island, NZ 45.54S 168.44E
85 F26 **Riversdale** Western Cape, SW South Africa 34.04S 21.15E
37 U15 **Riverside** California, W USA 33.57N 117.24W
27 W9 **Riverside** Texas, SW USA 30.51N 95.24W
39 U3 **Riverside Reservoir** ⊡ Colorado, C USA
8 K15 **Rivers Inlet** British Columbia, SW Canada 51.43N 127.19W
8 K15 **Rivers Inlet** *inlet* British Columbia, SW Canada
9 X15 **Riverton** Manitoba, S Canada 51.00N 97.00W
193 C24 **Riverton** Southland, South Island, NZ 46.19S 168.02E
32 L13 **Riverton** Illinois, N USA 39.50N 89.31W
38 L3 **Riverton** Utah, W USA 40.32N 111.57W
35 V15 **Riverton** Wyoming, C USA 43.01N 108.22W
12 G10 **River Valley** Ontario, S Canada 46.36N 80.09W
11 P14 **Riverview** New Brunswick, SE Canada 46.03N 64.46W
105 O17 **Rivesaltes** Pyrénées-Orientales, S France 42.46N 2.48E
38 H11 **Riviera** Arizona, SW USA 35.06N 114.36W
27 S15 **Riviera** Texas, SW USA 27.15N 97.48W
25 Z14 **Riviera Beach** Florida, SE USA 26.46N 80.03W
13 Q10 **Rivière-à-Pierre** Quebec, SE Canada 46.59N 72.12W
13 T9 **Rivière-Bleue** Quebec, SE Canada 47.25N 69.01W
13 T8 **Rivière-du-Loup** Quebec, SE Canada 47.49N 69.31W
181 Y15 **Rivière du Rempart** NE Mauritius 20.06S 57.40E
47 R12 **Rivière-Pilote** S Martinique 14.29N 60.54W
181 O17 **Rivière St-Etienne, Point de la** *headland* SW Réunion
11 S10 **Rivière-St-Paul** Quebec, E Canada 51.26N 57.52W
Rivière Sèche *see* Bel Air
118 K4 **Rivne** *Pol.* Równe, *Rus.* Rovno. Rivnens'ka Oblast', NW Ukraine 50.37N 26.15E
Rivne *see* Rivnens'ka Oblast'
118 K3 **Rivnens'ka Oblast'** *var.* Rivne, *Rus.* Rovenskaya Oblast'. ◆ *province* NW Ukraine
108 B8 **Rivoli** Piemonte, NW Italy 45.04N 7.31E
165 Q14 **Riwoqê** Xizang Zizhiqu, W China 31.10N 96.25E
101 H19 **Rixensart** Wallon Brabant, C Belgium 50.43N 4.31E
Riyadh/Riyāḍ, Minṭaqat ar *see* Ar Riyāḍ
Riyāq *see* Rayak
Rizaiyeh *see* Orūmīyeh
143 P11 **Rize** Rize, NE Turkey 41.02N 40.33E
143 P11 **Rize** *prev.* Çoruh. ◆ *province* NE Turkey
167 R5 **Rizhao** Shandong, E China 35.23N 119.31E
Rizhskiy Zaliv *see* Riga, Gulf of
Rizokarpaso/Rizokárpason *see* Dipkarpaz
109 O21 **Rizzuto, Capo** *headland* S Italy 38.54N 17.05E
97 F15 **Rjukan** Telemark, S Norway 59.52N 8.37E
97 D16 **Rjuven** ▲ S Norway
78 H9 **Rkîz** Trarza, W Mauritania 16.49N 15.19W
97 H14 **Roa** Oppland, S Norway 60.16N 10.38E
107 N5 **Roa** Castilla-León, N Spain 41.42N 3.55W
47 T9 **Road Town** ○ (British Virgin Islands) Tortola, C British Virgin Islands 18.28N 64.38W
98 F6 **Roag, Loch** *inlet* NW Scotland, UK
39 O5 **Roan Cliffs** *cliff* Colorado/Utah, W USA
23 P9 **Roan High Knob** *var.* Roan Mountain. ▲ North Carolina/Tennessee, SE USA 36.09N 82.07W
Roan Mountain *see* Roan High Knob
105 Q10 **Roanne** *anc.* Rodunma. Loire, E France 46.03N 4.04E
25 R4 **Roanoke** Alabama, S USA 33.09N 85.22W
23 S7 **Roanoke** Virginia, NE USA 37.16N 79.56W
23 Z9 **Roanoke Island** *island* North Carolina, SE USA
23 W8 **Roanoke Rapids** North Carolina, SE USA 36.27N 77.39W
23 X9 **Roanoke River** ≈ North Carolina/Virginia, SE USA
39 O4 **Roan Plateau** *plain* Utah, W USA
39 R5 **Roaring Fork River** ≈ Colorado, C USA
27 O5 **Roaring Springs** Texas, SW USA 33.54N 100.51W
44 J4 **Roatán** *var.* Coxen Hole, Coxin Hole. Islas de la Bahía, N Honduras 16.18N 86.32W
44 I4 **Roatán, Isla de** *island* Islas de la Bahía, N Honduras
Roat Kampuchea *see* Cambodia
Roazon *see* Rennes
149 T7 **Robāṭ-e Chāh Gonbad** Khorāsān, E Iran
149 R7 **Robāṭ-e Khān** Khorāsān, C Iran 33.24N 56.04E
149 T7 **Robāṭ-e Khvosh Āb** Khorāsān, E Iran
149 R8 **Robāṭ-e Posht-e Bādām** Khorāsān, NE Iran 33.01N 55.34E
183 S8 **Robbie Ridge** *undersea feature* W Pacific Ocean
23 T10 **Robbins** North Carolina, SE USA 35.25N 79.35W
191 N15 **Robbins Island** *island* Tasmania, SE Australia
23 N10 **Robbinsville** North Carolina, SE USA 35.19N 83.48W
190 J12 **Robe** South Australia 37.11S 139.48E
23 W9 **Robersonville** North Carolina, SE USA 35.49N 77.15W
27 P8 **Robert Lee** Texas, SW USA 31.54N 100.26W
37 V5 **Roberts Creek Mountain** ▲ Nevada, W USA 39.52N 116.16W
95 J15 **Robertsfors** Västerbotten, N Sweden 64.12N 20.49E
29 R11 **Robert S.Kerr Reservoir** ⊡ Oklahoma, C USA
40 L12 **Roberts Mountain** ▲ Nunivak Island, Alaska, USA 60.01N 166.15W
85 F26 **Robertson** Western Cape, SW South Africa 33.48S 19.52E
204 H4 **Robertson Island** *island* Antarctica
78 J16 **Robertsport** W Liberia 6.45N 11.15W
190 J8 **Robertstown** South Australia 34.00S 139.04E
Robert Williams *see* Caála
13 P7 **Roberval** Quebec, SE Canada 48.31N 72.16W
33 N15 **Robinson** Illinois, N USA 39.00N 87.44W
200 Oo12 **Róbinson Crusoe, Isla** *island* Islas Juan Fernández, Chile, E Pacific Ocean
188 J9 **Robinson Range** ▲ Western Australia
194 L16 **Robinson River** Central, S PNG 10.06S 148.51E
190 M9 **Robinvale** Victoria, SE Australia 34.37S 142.45E
107 P11 **Robledo** Castilla-La Mancha, C Spain 38.45N 2.27W
56 G5 **Robles** *var.* La Paz, Robles La Paz. Cesar, N Colombia 10.24N 73.10W
Robles La Paz *see* Robles
9 V15 **Roblin** Manitoba, S Canada 51.15N 101.19W
195 U13 **Rob Roy** *island* NW Solomon Islands
9 S17 **Robsart** Saskatchewan, S Canada 49.22N 109.15W
9 N15 **Robson, Mount** ▲ British Columbia, SW Canada 53.09N 119.16W
27 T14 **Robstown** Texas, SW USA 27.47N 97.40W
27 P6 **Roby** Texas, SW USA 32.43N 100.22W
106 E11 **Roca, Cabo da** *headland* C Portugal 38.47N 9.32W
Rocadas *see* Xangongo
43 S14 **Roca Partida, Punta** *headland* C Mexico 18.43N 95.11W
49 X6 **Rocas, Atol das** *island* E Brazil
109 L18 **Roccadaspide** *var.* Rocca d'Aspide. Campania, S Italy 40.25N 15.12E
109 K15 **Roccaraso** Abruzzo, C Italy 41.49N 14.01E
108 H10 **Rocca San Casciano** Emilia-Romagna, C Italy 44.06N 11.51E
108 G13 **Roccastrada** Toscana, C Italy 43.00N 11.09E
63 G20 **Rocha** Rocha, E Uruguay 34.30S 54.22W
63 G19 **Rocha** ◆ *department* E Uruguay
99 L17 **Rochdale** NW England, UK 53.37N 2.09W
104 L11 **Rochechouart** Haute-Vienne, C France 45.49N 0.49E
101 J22 **Rochefort** Namur, SE Belgium 50.10N 5.13E
104 J11 **Rochefort** *var.* Rochefort sur Mer. Charente-Maritime, W France 45.57N 0.58W
Rochefort sur Mer *see* Rochefort
129 N10 **Rochegda** Arkhangel'skaya Oblast', NW Russian Federation 62.37N 43.21E
32 L10 **Rochelle** Illinois, N USA 41.54N 89.03W
27 Q9 **Rochelle** Texas, SW USA 31.13N 99.10W
11 P13 **Rocher Percé** *island* Rocher Percé, Quebec, E Canada
13 V3 **Rochers Ouest, Rivière aux** ≈ Quebec, SE Canada
99 O22 **Rochester** *anc.* Durobrivae. SE England, UK 51.24N 0.30E
33 O12 **Rochester** Indiana, N USA 41.03N 86.13W
31 W10 **Rochester** Minnesota, N USA 44.01N 92.28W
21 O9 **Rochester** New Hampshire, NE USA 43.18N 70.58W
20 F9 **Rochester** New York, NE USA 43.09N 77.37W
27 P5 **Rochester** Texas, SW USA 33.19N 99.51W
33 S9 **Rochester Hills** Michigan, N USA 42.39N 83.04W
Rocheuses, Montagnes/Rockies *see* Rocky Mountains
66 M6 **Rockall** *island* UK, N Atlantic Ocean
66 L6 **Rockall Bank** *undersea feature* N Atlantic Ocean
86 B8 **Rockall Rise** *undersea feature* N Atlantic Ocean
86 C9 **Rockall Trough** *undersea feature* N Atlantic Ocean
37 U2 **Rock Creek** ≈ Nevada, W USA
27 T10 **Rockdale** Texas, SW USA 30.39N 96.58W
205 N12 **Rockefeller Plateau** *plateau* Antarctica
32 K11 **Rock Falls** Illinois, N USA 41.46N 89.41W
25 Q5 **Rockford** Alabama, S USA 32.53N 86.11W
32 L10 **Rockford** Illinois, N USA 42.16N 89.05W
13 Q12 **Rock Forest** Quebec, SE Canada 45.21N 71.58W
9 T17 **Rockglen** Saskatchewan, S Canada 49.10N 105.57W
189 Y8 **Rockhampton** Queensland, E Australia 23.31S 150.31E
23 R11 **Rock Hill** South Carolina, SE USA 34.55N 80.59W
188 I13 **Rockingham** Western Australia 32.16S 115.21E
23 T11 **Rockingham** North Carolina, SE USA 34.56N 79.46W
32 J11 **Rock Island** Illinois, N USA 41.30N 90.34W
27 U12 **Rock Island** Texas, SW USA 29.31N 96.33W
12 C10 **Rock Lake** Ontario, S Canada 46.25N 83.49W
31 O2 **Rock Lake** North Dakota, N USA 48.45N 99.12W
12 I12 **Rock Lake** ◎ Ontario, SE Canada
12 M12 **Rockland** Ontario, SE Canada 45.33N 75.16W

◆ Country ● Country Capital ◇ Dependent Territory ○ Dependent Territory Capital ◆ Administrative Region ✈ International Airport ▲ Mountain ▲ Mountain Range ▲ Volcano ≈ River ◎ Lake ⊡ Reservoir

ROCKLAND – RUBTSOVSK

21 R7 **Rockland** Maine, NE USA 44.08N 69.06W
190 L11 **Rocklands Reservoir** ⊠ Victoria, SE Australia
37 O7 **Rocklin** California, W USA 38.48N 121.13W
25 R3 **Rockmart** Georgia, SE USA 34.00N 85.02W
33 N16 **Rockport** Indiana, N USA 37.52N 87.04W
29 Q1 **Rock Port** Missouri, C USA 40.26N 95.30W
27 T14 **Rockport** Texas, SW USA 28.01N 97.03W
34 I7 **Rockport** Washington, NW USA 48.28N 121.36W
31 S11 **Rock Rapids** Iowa, C USA 43.25N 96.10W
32 K11 **Rock River** ≈ Illinois/Wisconsin, N USA
46 I3 **Rock Sound** Eleuthera Island, C Bahamas 24.51N 76.09W
35 U17 **Rock Springs** Wyoming, C USA 41.35N 109.12W
27 P11 **Rocksprings** Texas, SW USA 30.01N 100.12W
57 T9 **Rockstone** C Guyana 5.58N 58.33W
31 S12 **Rock Valley** Iowa, C USA 43.12N 96.17W
33 N14 **Rockville** Indiana, N USA 39.45N 87.13W
23 W3 **Rockville** Maryland, NE USA 39.04N 77.04W
27 U6 **Rockwall** Texas, SW USA 32.55N 96.27W
31 U13 **Rockwell City** Iowa, C USA 42.24N 94.37W
33 S10 **Rockwood** Michigan, N USA 42.04N 83.15W
22 M9 **Rockwood** Tennessee, S USA 35.52N 84.41W
27 Q8 **Rockwood** Texas, SW USA 31.29N 99.23W
39 U6 **Rocky Ford** Colorado, C USA 38.03N 103.45W
12 D9 **Rocky Island Lake** ◎ Ontario, S Canada
23 V9 **Rocky Mount** North Carolina, SE USA 35.56N 77.47W
23 S7 **Rocky Mount** Virginia, NE USA 37.00N 79.53W
35 Q8 **Rocky Mountain** ▲ Montana, NW USA 47.45N 112.46W
9 P15 **Rocky Mountain House** Alberta, SW Canada 52.24N 114.52W
39 T3 **Rocky Mountain National Park** national park Colorado, C USA
2 E12 **Rocky Mountains** var. Rockies, Fr. Montagnes Rocheuses. ▲▲ Canada/USA
44 H1 **Rocky Point** headland NE Belize 18.21N 88.04W
85 A17 **Rocky Point** headland NW Namibia 19.01S 12.27E
97 F14 **Rødberg** Buskerud, S Norway 60.16N 9.00E
97 I25 **Rødby** Storstrøm, SE Denmark 54.42N 11.24E
97 I25 **Rødbyhavn** Storstrøm, SE Denmark 54.39N 11.24E
11 T10 **Roddickton** Newfoundland, SE Canada 50.51N 56.03W
97 F23 **Rødding** Sønderjylland, SW Denmark 55.22N 9.04E
97 M22 **Rödeby** Blekinge, S Sweden 56.16N 15.34E
100 N6 **Roden** Drenthe, NE Netherlands 53.07N 6.25E
64 H9 **Rodeo** San Juan, W Argentina 30.12S 69.06W
105 O14 **Rodez** anc. Segodunum. Aveyron, S France 44.21N 2.34E
Rodholívos see Rodolívos
Rodhópi Óri see Rhodope Mountains
Ródhos/Rodi see Ródos
109 N15 **Rodi Gargancio** Puglia, SE Italy 41.54N 15.51E
103 N20 **Roding** Bayern, SE Germany 49.12N 12.30E
115 J19 **Rodinit, Kepi i** headland W Albania 41.35N 19.27E
118 I9 **Rodnei, Munții** ▲▲ N Romania
192 L4 **Rodney, Cape** headland North Island, NZ 36.16S 174.48E
40 L9 **Rodney, Cape** headland Alaska, USA 64.39N 166.24W
128 M16 **Rodniki** Ivanovskaya Oblast', W Russian Federation 57.04N 41.45E
121 Q16 **Rodnya** Rus. Rodnya. Mahilyowskaya Voblasts', E Belarus 53.30N 32.12E
Rodó see José Enrique Rodó
116 H13 **Rodolívos** var. Rodholívos. Kentrikí Makedonía, NE Greece 40.55N 23.59E
Rodopi see Rhodope Mountains
117 O22 **Ródos** var. Ródhos, Eng. Rhodes, It. Rodi. Ródos, Dodekánisos, Greece, Aegean Sea 36.25N 28.13E
117 O22 **Ródos** var. Ródhos, Eng. Rhodes, It. Rodi; anc. Rhodos. island Dodekánisos, Greece, Aegean Sea
Rodosto see Tekirdağ
61 A14 **Rodrigues** Amazonas, W Brazil 6.50S 73.45W
181 P8 **Rodrigues** var. Rodriquez. island E Mauritius
Rodriquez see Rodrigues
Rodunma see Roanne
188 I7 **Roebourne** Western Australia 20.49S 117.04E
85 J20 **Roedtan** Northern, NE South Africa 24.37S 29.04E
100 H11 **Roelofarendsveen** Zuid-Holland, W Netherlands 52.12N 4.37E
Roepat see Rupat, Pulau
Roer see Rur
101 M16 **Roermond** Limburg, SE Netherlands 51.12N 6.00E
101 C18 **Roeselare** Fr. Roulers; prev. Rousselaere. West-Vlaanderen, W Belgium 50.57N 3.07E
15 Ll5 **Roes Welcome Sound** strait Nunavut, N Canada
Roeteng see Ruteng
Rofreit see Rovereto
Rogachëv see Rahachow
59 L15 **Rogagua, Laguna** ◎ NW Bolivia
97 C16 **Rogaland** ⬖ county S Norway
27 Y9 **Roganville** Texas, SW USA 30.49N 93.54W
111 W11 **Rogaška Slatina** Ger. Rohitsch-Sauerbrunn; prev. Rogatec-Slatina. E Slovenia 46.13N 15.38E
Rogatec-Slatina see Rogaška Slatina
114 J13 **Rogatica** Republica Srpska, SE Bosnia & Herzegovina 43.50N 18.55E
Rogatin see Rohatyn
95 F17 **Rogen** ◎ C Sweden
29 S9 **Rogers** Arkansas, C USA 36.19N 94.07W
31 P5 **Rogers** North Dakota, N USA 47.03N 98.12W
27 T9 **Rogers** Texas, SW USA 30.53N 97.10W
33 R5 **Rogers City** Michigan, N USA 45.25N 83.49W
Roger Simpson Island see Abemama
37 T14 **Rogers Lake** salt flat California, W USA
23 Q8 **Rogers, Mount** ▲ Virginia, NE USA 36.39N 81.32W
35 O16 **Rogerson** Idaho, NW USA 42.11N 114.36W
9 O16 **Rogers Pass** pass British Columbia, SW Canada 51.18N 117.36W
23 O8 **Rogersville** Tennessee, S USA 36.26N 83.01W
101 L16 **Roggel** Limburg, SE Netherlands 51.16N 5.55E
Roggeveen see Roggewein, Cabo
200 Nn12 **Roggeveen Basin** undersea feature E Pacific Ocean
203 X16 **Roggewein, Cabo** var. Roggeveen. headland Easter Island, Chile, E Pacific Ocean 27.07S 109.15W
105 Y13 **Rogliano** Corse, France, C Mediterranean Sea 42.58N 9.25E
109 N21 **Rogliano** Calabria, SW Italy 39.09N 16.18E
94 G12 **Rognan** Nordland, C Norway 67.04N 15.21E
102 K10 **Rögnitz** ≈ N Germany
Rogozhina/Rogozhinë see Rrogozhinë
112 G10 **Rogoźno** Wielkopolskie, C Poland 52.46N 16.57E
34 E15 **Rogue River** ≈ Oregon, NW USA
118 I6 **Rohatyn** Rus. Rogatin. Ivano-Frankivs'ka Oblast', W Ukraine 49.25N 24.35E
201 O14 **Rohi** Pohnpei, E Micronesia
Rohitsch-Sauerbrunn see Rogaška Slatina
155 Q13 **Rohri** Sind, SE Pakistan 27.40N 68.52E
158 I10 **Rohtak** Haryāna, N India 28.55N 76.32E
Roi Ed see Roi Et
178 Ii10 **Roi Et** var. Muang Roi Et, Roi Ed. Roi Et, E Thailand 16.04N 103.37E
203 U9 **Roi Georges, Îles du** island group Îles Tuamotu, C French Polynesia
159 Y10 **Roing** Arunāchal Pradesh, NE India 28.06N 95.46E
120 E7 **Roja** Talsi, NW Latvia 57.31N 22.44E
63 B20 **Rojas** Buenos Aires, E Argentina 34.13S 60.41W
155 R12 **Rojhān** Punjab, E Pakistan 28.44N 70.01E
43 Q12 **Rojo, Cabo** headland C Mexico 21.33N 97.19W
47 Q10 **Rojo, Cabo** headland W Puerto Rico 17.57N 67.10W
173 G7 **Rokan Kanan, Sungai** ≈ Sumatera, W Indonesia
173 G7 **Rokan Kiri, Sungai** ≈ Sumatera, W Indonesia
Rokha see Rokhah
155 R4 **Rokhah** var. Rokha. Kāpīsā, E Afghanistan 35.16N 69.28E
120 I11 **Rokiškis** Rokiškis, NE Lithuania 55.58N 25.34E
172 Nn9 **Rokkasho** Aomori, Honshū, C Japan 40.59N 141.22E
113 B17 **Rokycany** Ger. Rokytzan. Plzeňský Kraj, NW Czech Republic 49.45N 13.36E
119 P6 **Rokytne** Kyyivs'ka Oblast', N Ukraine 49.40N 30.29E
118 L3 **Rokytne** Rivnens'ka Oblast', NW Ukraine 51.19N 27.09E
Rokytzan see Rokycany
164 L11 **Rola Co** ◎ W China
31 V13 **Roland** Iowa, C USA 42.10N 93.30W
97 D15 **Røldal** Hordaland, S Norway 59.52N 6.49E
100 O7 **Rolde** Drenthe, NE Netherlands 52.58N 6.39E
31 O2 **Rolette** North Dakota, N USA 48.39N 99.50W
29 V6 **Rolla** Missouri, C USA 37.57N 91.46W
31 O2 **Rolla** North Dakota, N USA 48.51N 99.37W
110 A10 **Rolle** Vaud, W Switzerland 46.27N 6.19E
189 X8 **Rolleston** Queensland, E Australia 24.30S 148.36E
193 H19 **Rolleston** Canterbury, South Island, NZ 43.34S 172.24E
193 G18 **Rolleston Range** ▲▲ South Island, NZ
12 H8 **Rollet** Quebec, SE Canada 47.56N 79.14W
24 J4 **Rolling Fork** Mississippi, S USA 32.54N 90.52W
22 L6 **Rolling Fork** ≈ Kentucky, S USA
12 J11 **Rolphton** Ontario, SE Canada 46.09N 77.43W
Röm see Rømø
189 X10 **Roma** Queensland, E Australia 26.36S 148.53E
109 I15 **Roma** Eng. Rome. ● (Italy) Lazio, C Italy 41.52N 12.30E
97 P19 **Roma** Gotland, SE Sweden 57.31N 18.28E
23 T14 **Romain, Cape** headland South Carolina, SE USA 33.00N 79.21W
11 P11 **Romaine** ≈ Newfoundland/Quebec, E Canada
27 R17 **Roma Los Saenz** Texas, SW USA 26.24N 99.01W
116 H8 **Roman** Vratsa, NW Bulgaria 43.09N 23.56E
118 L10 **Roman** Hung. Románvásár. Neamț, NE Romania 46.46N 26.55E
66 M13 **Romanche Fracture Zone** tectonic feature E Atlantic Ocean
63 C15 **Romang** Santa Fe, C Argentina 29.30S 59.46W
175 T15 **Romang, Pulau** var. Pulau Roma. island Kepulauan Damar, E Indonesia
175 Ss15 **Romang, Selat** strait Nusa Tenggara, S Indonesia
118 J11 **Romania** Bul. Rumŭniya, Ger. Rumänien, Hung. Románia, Rom. România, SCr. Rumunjska, Ukr. Rumuniya; prev. Republica Socialistă România, Roumania, Rumania, Socialist Republic of Romania, Rom. Romînia. ◆ republic SE Europe
119 T14 **Roman-Kash** ▲ S Ukraine 44.37N 34.13E
25 W16 **Romano, Cape** headland Florida, SE USA 25.51N 81.40W
46 G5 **Romano, Cayo** island C Cuba
126 Kk15 **Romanovka** Respublika Buryatiya, S Russian Federation 53.10N 112.34E
131 N8 **Romanovka** Saratovskaya Oblast', W Russian Federation 51.45N 42.45E
110 I6 **Romanshorn** Thurgau, NE Switzerland 47.33N 9.21E
105 R12 **Romans-sur-Isère** Drôme, E France 45.03N 5.03E
201 U12 **Romanum** island Chuuk, C Micronesia
Románvásár see Roman
41 S5 **Romanzof Mountains** ▲▲ Alaska, USA
Roma, Pulau see Romang, Pulau
105 S4 **Rombas** Moselle, NE France 49.15N 6.04E
176 Xx10 **Rombebai, Danau** ◎ Irian Jaya, E Indonesia
25 R2 **Rome** Georgia, SE USA 34.01N 85.01W
20 I9 **Rome** New York, NE USA 43.13N 75.28W
Rome see Roma
33 S9 **Romeo** Michigan, N USA 42.48N 83.00W
Römerstadt see Rýmařov
Rometan see Romitan
105 P5 **Romilly-sur-Seine** Aube, N France 48.31N 3.43E
Romînia see Romania
152 L11 **Romitan** Rus. Rometan. Bukhoro Wiloyati, C Uzbekistan 39.56N 64.21E
23 U3 **Romney** West Virginia, NE USA 39.20N 78.45W
119 S4 **Romny** Sums'ka Oblast', NE Ukraine 50.45N 33.30E
97 E24 **Rømø** Ger. Röm. island SW Denmark
119 S5 **Romodan** Poltavs'ka Oblast', NE Ukraine 50.00N 33.20E
131 P5 **Romodanovo** Respublika Mordoviya, W Russian Federation 54.25N 45.24E
Romorantin see Romorantin-Lanthenay
105 N8 **Romorantin-Lanthenay** var. Romorantin. Loir-et-Cher, C France 47.22N 1.43E
174 Hh5 **Rompin, Sungai** ≈ Peninsular Malaysia
96 F9 **Romsdal** physical region S Norway
96 F10 **Romsdalen** valley S Norway
96 E9 **Romsdalsfjorden** fjord S Norway
35 P8 **Ronan** Montana, NW USA 47.31N 114.06W
61 M14 **Roncador** Maranhão, E Brazil 5.48S 45.08W
195 W12 **Roncador Reef** reef N Solomon Islands
61 J17 **Roncador, Serra do** ▲▲ C Brazil
23 S6 **Ronceverte** West Virginia, NE USA 37.45N 80.27W
109 H14 **Ronciglione** Lazio, C Italy 42.16N 12.15E
106 L15 **Ronda** Andalucía, S Spain 36.45N 5.10W
96 G11 **Rondane** ▲▲ S Norway
106 L15 **Ronda, Serranía de** ▲▲ S Spain
97 H22 **Rønde** Århus, C Denmark 56.18N 10.28E
Rōņdik see Rongrik Atoll
61 E16 **Rondônia** off. Estado de Rondônia; prev. Território de Rondônia. ⬖ state W Brazil
61 I18 **Rondonópolis** Mato Grosso, W Brazil 16.28S 54.37W
96 G11 **Rondslottet** ▲ S Norway 61.54N 9.48E
97 P20 **Ronehamn** Gotland, SE Sweden 57.10N 18.30E
166 L13 **Rong'an** var. Chang'an, Rongan. Guangxi Zhuangzu Zizhiqu, S China 25.13N 109.19E
201 R4 **Rongelap Atoll** var. Rōņļap. atoll Ralik Chain, NW Marshall Islands
Rongerik see Rongrik Atoll
166 L13 **Rong Jiang** ≈ S China
166 K12 **Rongjiang** prev. Guzhou. Guizhou, S China 25.59N 108.27E
Rong, Kas see Rŭng, Kaôh
178 Hh8 **Rong Kwang** Phrae, NW Thailand 18.19N 100.18E
201 T4 **Rongrik Atoll** var. Rōņdik, Rongerik. atoll Ralik Chain, N Marshall Islands
201 X2 **Rongrong** island SE Marshall Islands
166 L13 **Rongshui** var. Rongshui Miaozu Zizhixian. Guangxi Zhuangzu Zizhiqu, S China 25.08N 109.15E
Rongshui Miaozu Zizhixian see Rongshui
120 I6 **Rõngu** Ger. Ringen. Tartumaa, SE Estonia 58.10N 26.17E
166 L15 **Rongxian** var. Rong Xian. Guangxi Zhuangzu Zizhiqu, S China 22.52N 110.33E
Roniu see Ronui, Mont
201 N13 **Ronkiti** Pohnpei, E Micronesia 6.48N 158.10E
Rōņļap see Rongelap Atoll
97 L24 **Rønne** Bornholm, E Denmark 55.07N 14.43E
97 M22 **Ronneby** Blekinge, S Sweden 56.12N 15.18E
204 J7 **Ronne Entrance** inlet Antarctica
204 L6 **Ronne Ice Shelf** ice shelf Antarctica
101 E19 **Ronse** Fr. Renaix. Oost-Vlaanderen, SW Belgium 50.45N 3.36E
203 R8 **Ronui, Mont** var. Roniu. ⛰ Tahiti, W French Polynesia 17.49S 149.12W
32 K14 **Roodhouse** Illinois, N USA 39.28N 90.22W
85 C19 **Rooibank** Erongo, W Namibia 23.04S 14.34E
Rooke Island see Umboi Island
67 N24 **Rookery Point** headland NE Tristan da Cunha 37.03S 12.15W
176 W10 **Roon, Pulau** island E Indonesia
181 V7 **Roo Rise** undersea feature E Indian Ocean
158 J9 **Roorkee** Uttar Pradesh, N India 29.51N 77.54E
101 H15 **Roosendaal** Noord-Brabant, S Netherlands 51.31N 4.28E
27 P10 **Roosevelt** Texas, SW USA 30.28N 100.06W
39 N3 **Roosevelt** Utah, W USA 40.18N 109.59W
49 T8 **Roosevelt** ≈ W Brazil
205 O13 **Roosevelt Island** island Antarctica
8 L10 **Roosevelt, Mount** ▲ British Columbia, W Canada 58.28N 125.22W
9 P17 **Roosville** British Columbia, SW Canada 48.59N 115.03W
31 X10 **Root River** ≈ Minnesota, N USA
113 N16 **Ropczyce** Podkarpackie, SE Poland 50.03N 21.36E
189 Q3 **Roper Bar** Northern Territory, N Australia 14.45S 134.30E
26 M5 **Ropesville** Texas, SW USA 33.24N 102.09W
104 K14 **Roquefort** Landes, SW France 44.01N 0.18W
63 C21 **Roque Pérez** Buenos Aires, E Argentina 35.25S 59.24W
60 E10 **Roraima** off. Estado de Roraima; prev. Território de Rio Branco, Território de Roraima. ⬖ state N Brazil
60 F9 **Roraima, Mount** ▲ N South America 5.10N 60.36W
176 X10 **Rori** Irian Jaya, E Indonesia 1.44S 136.49E
Ro Ro Reef see Malolo Barrier Reef
96 I9 **Røros** Sør-Trøndelag, S Norway 62.37N 11.25E
110 I7 **Rorschach** Sankt Gallen, NE Switzerland 47.28N 9.30E
95 E14 **Rørvik** Nord-Trøndelag, C Norway 64.52N 11.13E
121 G17 **Ros'** Rus. Ross'. Hrodzyenskaya Voblasts', W Belarus 53.20N 24.25E
121 G17 **Ros'** Rus. Ross'. ≈ W Belarus
119 O6 **Ros'** ≈ N Ukraine
46 K7 **Rosa, Lake** ◎ Great Inagua, S Bahamas
34 M9 **Rosalia** Washington, NW USA 47.14N 117.22W
203 W15 **Rosalia, Punta** headland Easter Island, Chile, E Pacific Ocean 27.04S 109.19W
47 P12 **Rosalie** E Dominica 15.22N 61.15W
37 T14 **Rosamond** California, W USA 34.51N 118.09W
37 S14 **Rosamond Lake** salt flat California, W USA
63 B18 **Rosario** Santa Fe, C Argentina 32.56S 60.38W
42 J11 **Rosario** Sinaloa, C Mexico 23.00N 105.51W
42 G6 **Rosario** Sonora, NW Mexico 27.53N 109.18W
64 O6 **Rosario** San Pedro, C Paraguay 24.26S 57.06W
63 E20 **Rosario** Colonia, SW Uruguay 34.19S 57.18W
56 H5 **Rosario** Zulia, NW Venezuela 10.18N 72.19W
Rosario see Rosarito
42 B4 **Rosario, Bahía del** bay NW Mexico
64 K6 **Rosario de la Frontera** Salta, N Argentina 25.50S 65.00W
63 C18 **Rosario del Tala** Entre Ríos, E Argentina 32.19S 59.10W
63 F16 **Rosário do Sul** Rio Grande do Sul, S Brazil 30.15S 54.55W
61 H18 **Rosário Oeste** Mato Grosso, W Brazil 14.49S 56.25W
42 E7 **Rosarito** Baja California, NW Mexico 26.27N 111.37W
42 B1 **Rosarito** var. Rosario. Baja California, NW Mexico 32.25N 117.03W
42 E7 **Rosarito** Baja California Sur, W Mexico 26.28N 111.40W
106 L9 **Rosarito, Embalse del** ⊠ W Spain
109 N22 **Rosarno** Calabria, SW Italy 38.28N 15.58E
58 B5 **Rosa Zárate** var. Quinindé. Esmeraldas, SW Ecuador 0.18N 79.28W
Roscianum see Rossano
31 O8 **Roscoe** South Dakota, N USA 45.24N 99.19W
27 P7 **Roscoe** Texas, SW USA 32.27N 100.32W
104 F5 **Roscoff** Finistère, NW France 48.43N 4.00W
Ros Comáin see Roscommon
99 C17 **Roscommon** Ir. Ros Comáin. C Ireland 53.37N 8.10W
33 Q7 **Roscommon** Michigan, N USA 44.30N 84.34W
99 C17 **Roscommon** Ir. Ros Comáin. cultural region C Ireland
Ros. Cré see Roscrea
99 D19 **Roscrea** Ir. Ros. Cré. C Ireland 52.57N 7.46W
47 X12 **Roseau** prev. Charlotte Town. ● (Dominica) SW Dominica 15.16N 61.22W
31 S2 **Roseau** Minnesota, N USA 48.51N 95.45W
181 Y16 **Rose Belle** SE Mauritius 20.24S 57.36E
191 O16 **Rosebery** Tasmania, SE Australia 41.51S 145.33E
23 U11 **Roseboro** North Carolina, SE USA 34.58N 78.31W
27 T9 **Rosebud** Texas, SW USA 31.04N 96.58W
35 W10 **Rosebud Creek** ≈ Montana, NW USA
34 F14 **Roseburg** Oregon, NW USA 43.13N 123.20W
24 J3 **Rosedale** Mississippi, S USA 33.51N 91.01W
101 H21 **Rosée** Namur, S Belgium 50.15N 4.43E
57 U8 **Rose Hall** E Guyana 6.14N 57.30W
181 X16 **Rose Hill** W Mauritius 20.13S 57.28E
82 H12 **Roseires, Reservoir** var. Lake Rusayris. ⊠ E Sudan
Rosenau see Rožnov pod Radhoštěm, Czech Republic
Rosenau see Rožňava, Slovakia
27 V11 **Rosenberg** Texas, SW USA 29.33N 95.48W
Rosenberg see Olesno, Poland
Rosenberg see Ružomberok, Slovakia
102 I10 **Rosengarten** Niedersachsen, N Germany 53.24N 9.53E
103 M24 **Rosenheim** Bayern, S Germany 47.51N 12.07E
Rosenhof see Zilupe
107 X4 **Roses** Cataluña, NE Spain 42.15N 3.10E
107 X4 **Roses, Golf de** gulf NE Spain
109 K14 **Roseto degli Abruzzi** Abruzzo, C Italy 42.39N 14.01E
9 S16 **Rosetown** Saskatchewan, S Canada 51.34N 107.58W
Rosetta see Rashîd
37 O7 **Roseville** California, W USA 38.44N 121.16W
32 J12 **Roseville** Illinois, N USA 40.42N 90.40W
31 V8 **Roseville** Minnesota, N USA 45.00N 93.09W
31 R7 **Rosholt** South Dakota, N USA 45.51N 96.42W
108 F12 **Rosignano Marittimo** Toscana, C Italy 43.24N 10.28E
118 I14 **Roșiori de Vede** Teleorman, S Romania 44.06N 25.00E
116 K8 **Rositsa** ≈ N Bulgaria
Rositten see Rēzekne
97 J23 **Roskilde** Roskilde, E Denmark 55.39N 12.07E
97 I23 **Roskilde** off. Roskilde Amt. ⬖ county E Denmark
Ros Láir see Rosslare
130 H5 **Roslavl'** Smolenskaya Oblast', W Russian Federation 53.59N 32.57E
34 I8 **Roslyn** Washington, NW USA 47.13N 120.52W
101 K14 **Rosmalen** Noord-Brabant, S Netherlands 51.43N 5.21E
Ros Mhic Thriúin see New Ross
115 P19 **Rosoman** C FYR Macedonia 41.31N 21.55E
104 F6 **Rosporden** Finistère, NW France 47.58N 3.54W
193 F17 **Ross** West Coast, South Island, NZ 42.54S 170.51E
8 J7 **Ross** ≈ Yukon Territory, W Canada
Ross' see Ros'
98 H8 **Ross and Cromarty** cultural region N Scotland, UK
109 O20 **Rossano** anc. Roscianum. Calabria, SW Italy 39.34N 16.37E
24 L5 **Ross Barnett Reservoir** ⊠ Mississippi, S USA
9 W16 **Rossburn** Manitoba, S Canada 50.42N 100.49W
12 H13 **Rosseau** Ontario, S Canada 45.15N 79.38W
12 H13 **Rosseau, Lake** ◎ Ontario, S Canada
195 R17 **Rossel Island** prev. Yela Island. island SE PNG
205 P12 **Ross Ice Shelf** ice shelf Antarctica
11 P16 **Rossignol, Lake** ◎ Nova Scotia, SE Canada
85 C19 **Rössing** Erongo, W Namibia 22.27S 14.52E
205 Q14 **Ross Island** island Antarctica
Rossitten see Rybachiy
Rossiyskaya Federatsiya see Russian Federation
9 N17 **Rossland** British Columbia, SW Canada 49.03N 117.49W
99 F20 **Rosslare** Ir. Ros Láir. SE Ireland 52.15N 6.22W
99 F20 **Rosslare Harbour** Wexford, SE Ireland 52.15N 6.19W
103 M14 **Rosslau** Sachsen-Anhalt, E Germany 51.52N 12.15E
78 G10 **Rosso** Trarza, SW Mauritania 16.36N 15.49W
105 X14 **Rosso, Cap** headland Corse, France, C Mediterranean Sea 42.25N 8.22E
95 H16 **Rosson** Jämtland, C Sweden 63.54N 16.21E
99 K21 **Ross-on-Wye** W England, UK 51.55N 2.34W
Rossony see Rasony
130 L9 **Rossosh'** Voronezhskaya Oblast', W Russian Federation 50.09N 39.34E
189 Q7 **Ross River** Northern Territory, N Australia 23.36S 134.30E
8 J7 **Ross River** Yukon Territory, W Canada 61.57N 132.26W
205 O15 **Ross Sea** sea Antarctica
94 G13 **Røssvatnet** ◎ C Norway
25 R1 **Rossville** Georgia, SE USA 34.59N 85.22W
Rostak see Ar Rustāq
149 P14 **Rostāq** Hormozgān, S Iran 26.48N 53.50E
119 N5 **Rostavytsya** ≈ N Ukraine
9 T15 **Rosthern** Saskatchewan, S Canada 52.40N 106.19W
102 M8 **Rostock** Mecklenburg-Vorpommern, NE Germany 54.04N 12.07E
128 L16 **Rostov** Yaroslavskaya Oblast', W Russian Federation 57.11N 39.19E
Rostov see Rostov-na-Donu
130 L12 **Rostov-na-Donu** var. Rostov, Eng. Rostov-on-Don. Rostovskaya Oblast', SW Russian Federation 47.16N 39.45E
Rostov-on-Don see Rostov-na-Donu
130 L10 **Rostovskaya Oblast'** ⬖ province SW Russian Federation
95 J14 **Rosvik** Norrbotten, N Sweden 65.26N 21.48E
25 S3 **Roswell** Georgia, SE USA 34.01N 84.21W
39 U14 **Roswell** New Mexico, SW USA 33.23N 104.31W
96 K12 **Rot** Dalarna, C Sweden 61.16N 14.04E
103 I23 **Rot** ≈ S Germany
106 J15 **Rota** Andalucía, S Spain 36.39N 6.20W
196 K9 **Rota** island S Northern Mariana Islands
27 P6 **Rotan** Texas, SW USA 32.51N 100.28W
Rotcher Island see Tamana
102 I11 **Rotenburg** Niedersachsen, NW Germany 53.06N 9.25E
Rotenburg see Rotenburg an der Fulda
103 I16 **Rotenburg an der Fulda** var. Rotenburg. Thüringen, C Germany 51.00N 9.43E
103 L18 **Roter Main** ≈ E Germany
103 K20 **Roth** Bayern, SE Germany 49.15N 11.06E
103 G16 **Rothaargebirge** ▲▲ W Germany
Rothenburg see Rothenburg ob der Tauber
103 J20 **Rothenburg ob der Tauber** var. Rothenburg. Bayern, S Germany 49.23N 10.10E
204 H6 **Rothera** UK research station Antarctica 67.28S 68.31W
193 I17 **Rotherham** Canterbury, South Island, NZ 42.42S 172.56E
99 M17 **Rotherham** N England, UK 53.25N 1.19W
98 H12 **Rothesay** W Scotland, UK 55.49N 5.03W
110 E7 **Rothrist** Aargau, N Switzerland 47.18N 7.54E
204 H6 **Rothschild Island** island Antarctica
175 Qq18 **Roti, Pulau** island S Indonesia
175 R18 **Roti, Selat** strait Nusa Tenggara, S Indonesia
191 O8 **Roto** New South Wales, SE Australia 33.04S 145.27E
192 N8 **Rotoiti, Lake** ◎ North Island, NZ
Rotomagus see Rouen
109 N19 **Rotondella** Basilicata, S Italy 40.12N 16.30E
105 X15 **Rotondo, Monte** ▲ Corse, France, C Mediterranean Sea 42.15N 9.03E
193 I15 **Rotoroa, Lake** ◎ South Island, NZ
192 N8 **Rotorua** Bay of Plenty, North Island, NZ 38.09S 176.13E
192 N8 **Rotorua, Lake** ◎ North Island, NZ
103 N22 **Rott** ≈ SE Germany
110 F10 **Rotten** ≈ S Switzerland
111 T6 **Rottenmann** Steiermark, E Austria 47.31N 14.18E
100 H12 **Rotterdam** Zuid-Holland, SW Netherlands 51.55N 4.30E
20 K10 **Rotterdam** New York, NE USA 42.46N 73.57W
97 M21 **Rottnen** ◎ S Sweden
100 N4 **Rottumeroog** island Waddeneilanden, NE Netherlands
100 N4 **Rottumerplaat** island Waddeneilanden, NE Netherlands
103 G23 **Rottweil** Baden-Württemberg, S Germany 48.10N 8.37E
203 O7 **Rotui, Mont** ⛰ Moorea, W French Polynesia 17.30S 149.49W
105 P1 **Roubaix** Nord, N France 50.42N 3.10E
113 C15 **Roudnice nad Labem** Ger. Raudnitz an der Elbe. Ústecký Kraj, NW Czech Republic 50.25N 14.13E
104 M4 **Rouen** anc. Rotomagus. Seine-Maritime, N France 49.25N 1.04E
176 Y11 **Rouffaer Reserves** reserve Irian Jaya, E Indonesia
13 N10 **Rouge, Rivière** ≈ Quebec, SE Canada
22 J6 **Rough River** ≈ Kentucky, S USA
22 J6 **Rough River Lake** ⊠ Kentucky, S USA
Rouhaïbé see Ar Ruḩaybah
104 K11 **Rouillac** Charente, W France 45.46N 0.04W
Roulers see Roeselare
Roumania see Romania
181 Y15 **Round Island** var. Île Ronde. island NE Mauritius
12 J12 **Round Lake** ◎ Ontario, SE Canada
37 U7 **Round Mountain** Nevada, W USA 38.42N 117.04W
27 R10 **Round Mountain** Texas, SW USA 30.25N 98.20W
191 U5 **Round Mountain** ▲ New South Wales, SE Australia 30.22S 152.13E
27 S10 **Round Rock** Texas, SW USA 30.30N 97.40W
35 U10 **Roundup** Montana, NW USA 46.27N 108.32W
57 Y10 **Roura** NE French Guiana 4.45N 52.18W
Rourkela see Rāulakela
98 J4 **Rousay** island N Scotland, UK
Rousselaere see Roeselare
105 O17 **Roussillon** cultural region S France
13 V7 **Routhierville** Quebec, SE Canada 48.09N 67.07W
101 K25 **Rouvroy** Luxembourg, SE Belgium 49.33N 5.28E
12 I7 **Rouyn-Noranda** Quebec, SE Canada 48.16N 79.01W
Rouyuanchengzi see Huachi
94 L12 **Rovaniemi** Lappi, N Finland 66.28N 25.40E
108 E7 **Rovato** Lombardia, N Italy 45.34N 10.03E
129 N11 **Rovdino** Arkhangel'skaya Oblast', NW Russian Federation 61.36N 42.28E
Roven'ki see Roven'ky
119 Y8 **Roven'ky** var. Roven'ki. Luhans'ka Oblast', E Ukraine 48.04N 39.19E
Rovenskaya Oblast' see Rivnens'ka Oblast'
Rovenskaya Sloboda see Rovyenskaya Slabada
108 G7 **Rovereto** Ger. Rofreit. Trentino-Alto Adige, N Italy 45.52N 11.03E
178 J12 **Rôviĕng Tbong** Preăh Vihéar, N Cambodia 13.18N 105.06E
Rovigno see Rovinj
108 H8 **Rovigo** Veneto, NE Italy 45.04N 11.48E
114 A10 **Rovinj** It. Rovigno. Istra, NW Croatia 45.06N 13.39E
56 E10 **Rovira** Tolima, C Colombia 4.15N 75.15W
Rovno see Rivne
131 P9 **Rovnoye** Saratovskaya Oblast', W Russian Federation 50.43N 46.03E
84 Q12 **Rovuma, Rio** var. Ruvuma. ≈ Mozambique/Tanzania see also Ruvuma
121 O19 **Rovyenskaya Slabada** Rus. Rovenskaya Sloboda. Homyel'skaya Voblasts', SE Belarus 52.12N 30.19E
191 R5 **Rowena** New South Wales, SE Australia 29.51S 148.55E
23 T11 **Rowland** North Carolina, SE USA 34.32N 79.17W
15 M1 **Rowley** ≈ Baffin Island, Nunavut, NE Canada
15 M2 **Rowley Island** island Nunavut, NE Canada
181 W8 **Rowley Shoals** reef NW Australia
179 Pp12 **Roxas** Mindoro, N Philippines 12.36N 121.29E
179 Q13 **Roxas City** Panay Island, C Philippines 11.33N 122.43E
23 U8 **Roxboro** North Carolina, SE USA 36.23N 78.58W
193 D23 **Roxburgh** Otago, South Island, NZ 45.32S 169.18E
98 K13 **Roxburgh** cultural region SE Scotland, UK
190 H5 **Roxby Downs** South Australia 30.29S 136.56E
97 M17 **Roxen** ◎ S Sweden
27 V5 **Roxton** Texas, SW USA 33.33N 95.43W
13 P12 **Roxton-Sud** Quebec, SE Canada 45.30N 72.35W
35 U8 **Roy** Montana, NW USA 47.19N 108.55W
39 U10 **Roy** New Mexico, SW USA 35.56N 104.12W
99 E17 **Royal Canal** Ir. An Chanáil Ríoga. canal C Ireland
32 L1 **Royale, Isle** island Michigan, N USA
39 S6 **Royal Gorge** valley Colorado, C USA
99 M20 **Royal Leamington Spa** var. Leamington, Leamington Spa. C England, UK 52.18N 1.31W
99 O23 **Royal Tunbridge Wells** var. Tunbridge Wells. SE England, UK 51.07N 0.16E
26 L9 **Royalty** Texas, SW USA 31.21N 102.51W
104 J11 **Royan** Charente-Maritime, W France 45.37N 1.01W
67 B24 **Roy Cove Settlement** West Falkland, Falkland Islands 51.31S 60.22W
105 O3 **Roye** Somme, N France 49.42N 2.46E
97 H15 **Røyken** Buskerud, S Norway 59.47N 10.21E
95 F14 **Røyrvik** Nord-Trøndelag, C Norway 64.53N 13.30E
27 U6 **Royse City** Texas, SW USA 32.58N 96.19W
99 O21 **Royston** E England, UK 52.05N 0.01W
25 U2 **Royston** Georgia, SE USA 34.17N 83.06W
116 L10 **Roza** prev. Gyulovo. Yambol, E Bulgaria 42.29N 26.30E
115 L16 **Rožaje** Montenegro, SW Yugoslavia 42.51N 20.11E
112 M10 **Różan** Mazowieckie, C Poland 52.36N 21.27E
119 O10 **Rozdil'na** Odes'ka Oblast', SW Ukraine 46.51N 30.03E
119 S12 **Rozdol'ne** Rus. Razdolnoye. Respublika Krym, S Ukraine 45.45N 33.27E
151 Q9 **Rozhdestvenka** Akmola, C Kazakhstan 50.51N 71.25E
118 I6 **Rozhnyativ** Ivano-Frankivs'ka Oblast', W Ukraine 48.58N 24.07E
118 J3 **Rozhyshche** Volyns'ka Oblast', NW Ukraine 50.54N 25.16E
Roznau am Radhost see Rožnov pod Radhoštěm
113 L19 **Rožňava** Ger. Rosenau, Hung. Rozsnyó. Košický Kraj, E Slovakia 48.40N 20.31E
118 K10 **Roznov** Neamț, NE Romania 46.46N 26.33E
113 I18 **Rožnov pod Radhoštěm** Ger. Rosenau, Roznau am Radhost. Zlínský Kraj, E Czech Republic 49.28N 18.09E
Rózsahegy see Ružomberok
Rozsnyó see Râșnov, Romania
Rozsnyó see Rožňava, Slovakia
115 K18 **Rranxë** Shkodër, NW Albania 41.58N 19.27E
115 L18 **Rrëshen** var. Rresheni, Rrshen. Lezhë, C Albania 41.46N 19.54E
Rresheni see Rrëshen
Rrogozhina see Rrogozhinë
115 K20 **Rrogozhinë** var. Rogozhina, Rogozhinë, Rrogozhina. Tiranë, W Albania 41.04N 19.40E
Rrshen see Rrëshen
114 O13 **Rtanj** ▲ E Yugoslavia 43.45N 21.54E
131 O7 **Rtishchevo** Saratovskaya Oblast', W Russian Federation 52.16N 43.46E
192 N12 **Ruahine Range** var. Ruarine. ▲▲ North Island, NZ
193 L14 **Ruamahanga** ≈ North Island, NZ
Ruanda see Rwanda
192 M10 **Ruapehu, Mount** ▲ North Island, NZ 39.15S 175.33E
193 C25 **Ruapuke Island** island SW NZ
Ruarine see Ruahine Range
192 O9 **Ruatahuna** Bay of Plenty, North Island, NZ 38.38S 176.56E
192 Q8 **Ruatoria** Gisborne, North Island, NZ 37.54S 178.18E
192 K4 **Ruawai** Northland, North Island, NZ 36.08S 174.03E
13 N8 **Ruban** ≈ Quebec, SE Canada
83 I22 **Rubeho Mountains** ▲▲ C Tanzania
172 Q5 **Rubeshibe** Hokkaidō, NE Japan 43.49N 143.37E
Rubezhnoye see Rubizhne
115 L18 **Rubik** Lezhë, C Albania 41.46N 19.48E
56 H7 **Rubio** Táchira, W Venezuela 7.42N 72.22W
119 X6 **Rubizhne** Rus. Rubezhnoye. Luhans'ka Oblast', E Ukraine 49.01N 38.22E
83 F20 **Rubondo Island** island N Tanzania
126 Gg15 **Rubtsovsk** Altayskiy Kray, S Russian Federation 51.34N 81.10E

◆ Country
● Country Capital
◇ Dependent Territory
○ Dependent Territory Capital
⬖ Administrative Region
✕ International Airport
▲ Mountain
▲▲ Mountain Range
⛰ Volcano
≈ River
◎ Lake
⊠ Reservoir

RUBY – SAIMAAN KANAVA

41 P9 Ruby Alaska, USA 64.44N 155.29W
37 W3 Ruby Dome ▲ Nevada, W USA 40.35N 115.25W
37 W4 Ruby Lake ◎ Nevada, W USA
37 W4 Ruby Mountains ▲▲ Nevada, W USA
35 Q12 Ruby Range ▲▲ Montana, NW USA
120 C10 Rucava Liepāja, SW Latvia 56.09N 21.10E
Rūdān see Dehbārez
Rudelstadt see Ciechanowiec
Rudensk see Rudzyensk
121 G14 Rūdiškės Trakai, S Lithuania 54.31N 24.49E
97 H24 Rudkøbing Fyn, C Denmark 54.57N 10.43E
127 Nn17 Rudnaya Pristan' Primorskiy Kray, SE Russian Federation 44.19N 135.42E
151 V14 Rudnichnyy Kaz. Rūdnīchnyy. Almaty, SE Kazakhstan 44.39N 78.57E
129 S13 Rudnichnyy Kirovskaya Oblast', NW Russian Federation 59.37N 52.28E
116 N9 Rudnik Varna, E Bulgaria 42.57N 27.46E
Rudny see Rudnyy
130 H4 Rudnya Smolenskaya Oblast', W Russian Federation 54.55N 31.10E
131 O8 Rudnya Volgogradskaya Oblast', SW Russian Federation 50.54N 44.27E
150 M7 Rudnyy var. Rudny. Kostanay, N Kazakhstan 53.00N 63.05E
126 Hh1 Rudol'fa, Ostrov island Zemlya Frantsa-Iosifa, NW Russian Federation
83 H16 Rudolf, Lake var. Lake Turkana. ◎ N Kenya
Rudolfswert see Novo mesto
103 L17 Rudolstadt Thüringen, C Germany 50.43N 11.19E
33 Q4 Rudyard Michigan, N USA 46.15N 84.36W
35 S7 Rudyard Montana, NW USA 48.33N 110.37W
121 K16 Rudzyensk Rus. Rudensk. Minskaya Voblasts', C Belarus 53.36N 27.52E
106 L6 Rueda Castilla-León, N Spain 41.24N 4.58W
116 F10 Ruen ▲ Bulgaria/FYR Macedonia 42.10N 22.31E
82 G10 Rufa'a Gezira, C Sudan 14.49N 33.21E
104 L10 Ruffec Charente, W France 46.01N 0.10E
23 R14 Ruffin South Carolina, SE USA 33.00N 80.48W
83 J23 Rufiji ∽ E Tanzania
63 A20 Rufino Santa Fe, C Argentina 34.15S 62.40W
78 F11 Rufisque W Senegal 14.44N 17.18W
85 K14 Rufunsa Lusaka, C Zambia 15.03S 29.36E
120 J9 Rugāji Balvi, E Latvia 57.01N 27.07E
167 R7 Rugao Jiangsu, E China 32.25N 120.39E
99 M20 Rugby C England, UK 52.22N 1.18W
31 N3 Rugby North Dakota, N USA 48.24N 100.00W
102 N7 Rügen headland NE Germany 54.25N 13.21E
Ruhaybeh see Ar Ruḩaybah
167 N7 Ru He ∽ C China
83 E19 Ruhengeri NW Rwanda 1.39S 29.16E
Ruhja see Rūjiena
102 M10 Ruhner Berg hill N Germany 53.17N 12.00E
120 F7 Ruhnu var. Ruhnu Saar, Swe. Runö. island SW Estonia
Ruhnu Saar see Ruhnu
103 G15 Ruhr ∽ W Germany
93 W6 Ruhr Valley industrial region W Germany
167 S11 Rui'an var. Rui an. Zhejiang, SE China 27.48N 120.36E
167 P10 Ruichang Jiangxi, S China 29.46N 115.37E
26 J11 Ruidosa Texas, SW USA 30.00N 104.40W
39 S14 Ruidoso New Mexico, SW USA 33.19N 105.40W
167 P12 Ruijin Jiangxi, S China 25.52N 116.01E
166 D13 Ruili Yunnan, SW China 24.04N 97.49E
100 N8 Ruinen Drenthe, NE Netherlands 52.46N 6.19E
101 D17 Ruiselede West-Vlaanderen, W Belgium 51.03N 3.21E
66 P5 Ruivo de Santana, Pico ▲ Madeira, Portugal, NE Atlantic Ocean 32.46N 16.57W
42 J12 Ruiz Nayarit, SW Mexico 22.00N 105.09W
56 E10 Ruiz, Nevado del ※ W Colombia 4.52N 75.22W
144 J9 Rujaylah, Ḩarrat ar salt lake N Jordan
Rujen see Rūjiena
120 H7 Rūjiena Est. Ruhja, Ger. Rujen. Valmiera, N Latvia 57.54N 25.22E
81 I18 Ruki ∽ W Dem. Rep. Congo (Zaire)
83 E22 Rukwa ◐ region SW Tanzania
83 F23 Rukwa, Lake ◎ SE Tanzania
27 P6 Rule Texas, SW USA 33.10N 99.53W
24 K3 Ruleville Mississippi, S USA 33.43N 90.33W
Rum see Rhum
114 K10 Ruma Serbia, N Yugoslavia 45.02N 19.51E
Rumadiya see Ar Ramādī
147 Q7 Rumāḩ Ar Riyāḑ, C Saudi Arabia 25.35N 47.09E
Rumaitha see Ar Rumaythah
Rumania/Rumänien see Romania
Rumänisch-Sankt-Georgen see Sângeorz-Băi
145 Y13 Rumaylah SE Iraq 30.16N 47.22E
145 P2 Rumaylah, Wādī dry watercourse NE Syria
176 V10 Rumbati Irian Jaya, E Indonesia 2.44S 132.04E
83 E14 Rumbek El Buhayrat, S Sudan 6.49N 29.42E
176 W10 Rumberpon, Pulau island E Indonesia
Rumburg see Rumburk
113 D14 Rumburk Ger. Rumburg. Ústecký Kraj, NW Czech Republic 50.59N 14.31E
46 J4 Rum Cay island C Bahamas
101 M26 Rumelange Luxembourg, S Luxembourg 49.28N 6.01E
101 D20 Rumes Hainaut, SW Belgium 50.33N 3.19E
21 P7 Rumford Maine, NE USA 44.31N 70.31W
112 I6 Rumia Pomorskie, N Poland 54.35N 18.21E
115 J17 Rumija ▲▲ SW Yugoslavia
105 T11 Rumilly Haute-Savoie, E France 45.52N 5.57E
145 O6 Rūmiyah W Iraq 34.28N 41.17E
Rummah, Wādī ar see Rimah, Wādī ar
Rummelsburg in Pommern see Miastko
172 Oo4 Rumoi Hokkaidō, NE Japan 43.55N 141.37E
84 M12 Rumphi var. Rumpi. Northern, N Malawi 11.00S 33.51E
Rumpi see Rumphi
31 V7 Rum River ∽ Minnesota, N USA
196 F16 Rumung island Caroline Islands, W Micronesia
Rumuniya/Rumŭniya/Rumunjska see Romania
193 G16 Runanga West Coast, South Island, NZ 42.24S 171.15E
192 P7 Runaway, Cape headland North Island, NZ 37.33S 177.59E
99 K18 Runcorn C England, UK 53.19N 2.43W
120 K10 Rundāni Ludza, E Latvia 56.19N 27.51E
85 L18 Runde var. Lundi. ∽ SE Zimbabwe
85 E16 Rundu var. Runtu. Okavango, NE Namibia 17.55S 19.45E
95 I16 Rundvik Västerbotten, N Sweden 63.31N 19.22E
83 G20 Runere Mwanza, N Tanzania 3.06S 33.18E
27 S13 Runge Texas, SW USA 28.52N 97.42W
178 I14 Rŭng, Kaôh prev. Kas Rong. island SW Cambodia
81 O16 Rungu Orientale, NE Dem. Rep. Congo (Zaire) 3.09N 27.58E
83 F23 Rungwa Rukwa, W Tanzania 7.18S 31.40E
83 G22 Rungwa Singida, C Tanzania 6.54S 33.33E
96 M13 Runn ◎ C Sweden
26 M4 Running Water Draw valley New Mexico/Texas, SW USA
Runö see Ruhnu
Runtu see Rundu
201 V12 Ruo island Caroline Islands, C Micronesia
164 L9 Ruoqiang var. Jo-ch'iang, Uigh. Charkhlik, Charkhliq, Qarkilik. Xinjiang Uygur Zizhiqu, NW China 38.59N 88.07E
165 S7 Ruo Shui ∽ N China
94 L8 Ruostefjelbma var. Rustefjelbma Finnmark, N Norway 70.25N 28.10E
95 L18 Ruovesi Länsi-Suomi, W Finland 61.58N 24.04E
114 B9 Rupa Primorje-Gorski Kotar, NW Croatia 45.29N 14.15E
190 M11 Rupanyup Victoria, SE Australia 36.38S 142.37E
174 H6 Rupat, Pulau prev. Roepat. island W Indonesia
174 Gg6 Rupat, Selat strait Sumatera, W Indonesia
118 J11 Rupea Ger. Reps, Hung. Kőhalom; prev. Cohalm. Braşov, C Romania 46.01N 25.13E
101 G17 Rupel ∽ N Belgium
Rupella see la Rochelle
35 P15 Rupert Idaho, NW USA 42.37N 113.40W
23 R5 Rupert West Virginia, NE USA 37.57N 80.40W
Rupert House see Fort Rupert
10 J10 Rupert, Rivière de ∽ Quebec, C Canada
204 M13 Ruppert Coast physical region Antarctica
102 N11 Ruppiner Kanal canal NE Germany
57 S11 Rupununi River ∽ S Guyana
103 D16 Rur Dut. Roer. ∽ Germany/Netherlands
60 H13 Rurópolis Presidente Medici Pará, N Brazil 4.05S 55.26W
203 S12 Rurutu island Îles Australes, SW French Polynesia
Rusaddir see Melilla
85 L17 Rusape Manicaland, E Zimbabwe 18.31S 32.07E
Rusayris, Lake see Roseires, Reservoir
Ruschuk/Rusçuk see Ruse
116 K7 Ruse var. Ruschuk, Rustchuk, Turk. Rusçuk. Ruse, N Bulgaria 43.49N 25.58E
116 L7 Ruse ◐ province N Bulgaria
111 W10 Ruše NE Slovenia 46.31N 15.30E
116 K7 Rusenski Lom ∽ N Bulgaria
99 G17 Rush Ir. An Ros. E Ireland 53.31N 6.06W
167 S4 Rushan var. Xiacun. Shandong, E China 36.57N 121.33E
Rushan see Rŭshon
Rushanskiy Khrebet see Rushon, Qatorkŭhi
31 V7 Rush City Minnesota, N USA 45.41N 92.56W
39 V5 Rush Creek ∽ Colorado, C USA
31 X10 Rushford Minnesota, N USA 43.48N 91.45W
160 N13 Rushikulya ∽ E India
12 D8 Rush Lake ◎ Ontario, S Canada
32 M7 Rush Lake ◎ Wisconsin, N USA
30 J10 Rushmore, Mount ▲ South Dakota, N USA 43.52N 103.27W
153 S13 Rŭshon Rus. Rushan. S Tajikistan 37.58N 71.31E
153 S14 Rushon, Qatorkŭhi Rus. Rushanskiy Khrebet. ▲▲ SE Tajikistan
28 M12 Rush Springs Oklahoma, C USA 34.46N 97.57W
47 V15 Rushville Trinidad, Trinidad and Tobago 10.07N 61.03W
32 J13 Rushville Illinois, N USA 40.07N 90.33W
30 K12 Rushville Nebraska, C USA 42.41N 102.28W
191 O11 Rushworth Victoria, SE Australia 36.36S 145.03E
27 W8 Rusk Texas, SW USA 31.48N 95.09W
95 I14 Rusksele Västerbotten, N Sweden 64.49N 18.55E
120 C12 Rusnė Šilutė, W Lithuania 55.18N 21.19E
116 M10 Rusokastrenska Reka ∽ E Bulgaria
Russadir see Melilla
111 X3 Russbach ∽ NE Austria
9 V16 Russell Manitoba, S Canada 50.46N 101.16W
192 K2 Russell Northland, North Island, NZ 35.17S 174.07E
28 L4 Russell Kansas, C USA 38.54N 98.51W
23 O4 Russell Kentucky, S USA 38.30N 82.43W
195 W15 Russell Islands island group C Solomon Islands
22 L7 Russell Springs Kentucky, S USA 37.02N 85.03W
25 O2 Russellville Alabama, S USA 34.30N 87.43W
29 T11 Russellville Arkansas, C USA 35.16N 93.07W
22 J7 Russellville Kentucky, S USA 36.51N 86.53W
103 G18 Rüsselsheim Hessen, W Germany 50.00N 8.25E
94 K8 Russenes Finnmark, N Norway 70.29N 24.58E
Russia see Russian Federation
Russian America see Alaska
127 N17 Russian Federation off. Russian Federation, var. Russia, Latv. Krievija, Rus. Rossiyskaya Federatsiya. ◆ republic Asia/Europe
41 N11 Russian Mission Alaska, USA 61.48N 161.23W
36 M7 Russian River ∽ California, W USA
204 L13 Russkaya Russian research station Antarctica 74.45S 135.24W
126 H3 Russkaya Gavan' Novaya Zemlya, Arkhangel'skaya Oblast', N Russian Federation 76.13N 62.48E
126 J4 Russkiy, Ostrov island N Russian Federation
111 Y5 Rust Burgenland, E Austria 47.48N 16.42E
Rustaq see Ar Rustāq
143 U10 Rust'avi SE Georgia 41.36N 45.00E
23 T7 Rustburg Virginia, NE USA 37.16N 79.04W
Rustchuk see Ruse
Rustefjelbma see Ruostefjelbma
85 I21 Rustenburg North-West, N South Africa 25.40S 27.15E
24 H5 Ruston Louisiana, S USA 32.31N 92.38W
83 E21 Rutana SE Burundi 4.01S 30.01E
64 I4 Rutana, Volcán ▲ N Chile 22.43S 67.52W
Rutanzige, Lake see Edward, Lake
Rutba see Ar Ruṭbah
106 M14 Rute Andalucía, S Spain 37.19N 4.22W
175 Pp16 Ruteng prev. Roeteng. Flores, C Indonesia 8.34S 120.28E
204 L8 Rutford Ice Stream ice feature Antarctica
37 X6 Ruth Nevada, W USA 39.15N 115.00W
103 G15 Rüthen Nordrhein-Westfalen, W Germany 51.30N 8.28E
12 D17 Rutherford Ontario, S Canada 42.39N 82.06W
23 Q10 Rutherfordton North Carolina, SE USA 35.22N 81.57W
99 J18 Ruthin Wel. Rhuthun. NE Wales, UK 53.05N 3.18W
110 G7 Rüti Zürich, N Switzerland 47.16N 8.51E
Rutlam see Ratlām
20 M9 Rutland Vermont, NE USA 43.37N 72.58W
99 N19 Rutland cultural region C England, UK
23 N8 Rutledge Tennessee, S USA 36.16N 83.31W
164 G12 Rutog var. Rutok. Xizang Zizhiqu, W China 33.27N 79.43E
Rutok see Rutog
81 P19 Rutshuru Nord Kivu, E Dem. Rep. Congo (Zaire) 1.13S 29.27E
100 L8 Rutten Flevoland, N Netherlands 52.49N 5.44E
131 Q17 Rutul Respublika Dagestan, SW Russian Federation 41.35N 47.30E
95 L14 Ruukki Oulu, C Finland 64.40N 25.35E
100 N11 Ruurlo Gelderland, E Netherlands 52.04N 6.27E
149 S15 Ru'ūs al Jibāl headland Oman/UAE 26.13N 56.23E
144 I7 Ru'ūs aṭ Ṭiwāl, Jabal ▲ W Syria
83 H23 Ruvuma ◐ region SE Tanzania
83 I25 Ruvuma var. Rio Rovuma. ∽ Mozambique/Tanzania see also Rovuma, Rio
Ruwais see Ar Ruways
144 L9 Ruwayshid, Wadi ar dry watercourse NE Jordan
147 Z10 Ruways, Ra's ar headland E Oman 20.58N 59.00E
81 P18 Ruwenzori ▲▲ Uganda/Dem. Rep. Congo (Zaire)
147 Y8 Ruwi NE Oman 23.33N 58.31E
116 F9 Ruy ▲ Bulgaria/Yugoslavia 42.52N 22.35E
Ruya see Luia, Rio
83 E20 Ruyigi E Burundi 3.28S 30.19E
131 P5 Ruzayevka Respublika Mordoviya, W Russian Federation 54.04N 44.56E
121 G18 Ruzhany Rus. Ruzhany. Brestskaya Voblasts', SW Belarus 52.52N 24.52E
116 I10 Rŭzhevo Konare var. Rŭzhevo Konare. Plovdiv, C Bulgaria 42.16N 24.58E
Ruzhin see Ruzhyn
116 G7 Ruzhintsi Vidin, NW Bulgaria 43.38N 22.50E
119 N5 Ruzhyn Rus. Ruzhin. Zhytomyrs'ka Oblast', N Ukraine 49.42N 29.01E
113 K19 Ružomberok Ger. Rosenberg, Hung. Rózsahegy. Žilinský Kraj, N Slovakia 49.03N 19.18E
113 C16 Ruzyně ✕ (Praha) Praha, C Czech Republic 50.06N 14.16E
83 D19 Rwanda off. Rwandese Republic; prev. Ruanda. ◆ republic C Africa
Rwandese Republic see Rwanda
97 G22 Ry Århus, C Denmark 56.06N 9.46E
Ryasna see Rasna
130 L5 Ryazan' Ryazanskaya Oblast', W Russian Federation 54.37N 39.37E
130 L5 Ryazanskaya Oblast' ◐ province W Russian Federation
130 M6 Ryazhsk Ryazanskaya Oblast', W Russian Federation 53.42N 40.09E
120 B13 Rybachiy Ger. Rossitten. Kaliningradskaya Oblast', W Russian Federation 55.09N 20.49E
128 J2 Rybachiy, Poluostrov peninsula NW Russian Federation
Rybach'ye see Balykchy
128 L15 Rybinsk prev. Andropov. Yaroslavskaya Oblast', W Russian Federation 58.03N 38.52E
128 K14 Rybinskoye Vodokhranilishche Eng. Rybinsk Reservoir, Rybinsk Sea. ⊠ W Russian Federation
Rybinsk Reservoir/Rybinsk Sea see Rybinskoye Vodokhranilishche
113 I16 Rybnik Śląskie, S Poland 50.05N 18.30E
Rybnitsa see Rîbniţa
113 F16 Rychnov nad Kněžnou Ger. Reichenau. Hradecký Kraj, N Czech Republic 50.09N 16.15E
112 I12 Rychwał Wielkolpolskie, C Poland 52.04N 18.09E
9 O13 Rycroft Alberta, W Canada 55.45N 118.42W
97 L21 Ryd Kronoberg, S Sweden 56.27N 14.44E
97 L20 Rydaholm Jönköping, S Sweden 56.57N 14.19E
204 I8 Rydberg Peninsula peninsula Antarctica
99 P23 Rye SE England, UK 50.57N 0.42E
35 T10 Ryegate Montana, NW USA 46.21N 109.12W
37 S3 Rye Patch Reservoir ⊠ Nevada, W USA
97 D15 Ryfylke physical region S Norway
97 H16 Rygge Østfold, S Norway 59.22N 10.45E
112 N13 Ryki Lubelskie, E Poland 51.37N 21.57E
Rykovo see Yenakiyeve
130 I7 Ryl'sk Kurskaya Oblast', W Russian Federation 51.34N 34.41E
191 S8 Rylstone New South Wales, SE Australia 32.48S 149.58E
113 H17 Rýmařov Ger. Römerstadt. Ostravský Kraj, E Czech Republic 49.57N 17.13E
150 E11 Ryn-Peski desert W Kazakhstan
171 K12 Ryōtsu var. Ryôtu. Niigata, Sado, C Japan 38.02N 138.23E
Ryôtu see Ryōtsu
112 K10 Rypin Kujawsko-pomorskie, C Poland 53.03N 19.25E
Ryshkany see Rîşcani
Ryssel see Lille
Ryswick see Rijswijk
97 M24 Rytterknægten hill E Denmark 55.07N 14.53E
171 Kk16 Ryūgasaki Ibaraki, Honshū, S Japan 35.54N 140.11E
198 G5 Ryukyu Trench var. Nansei Syotō Trench. undersea feature S East China Sea
112 D11 Rzepin Ger. Reppen. Lubuskie, W Poland 52.20N 14.48E
113 N16 Rzeszów Podkarpackie, SE Poland 50.04N 22.00E
128 I16 Rzhev Tverskaya Oblast', W Russian Federation 56.16N 34.21E
Rzhishchev see Rzhyshchiv
119 P5 Rzhyshchiv Rus. Rzhishchev. Kyyivs'ka Oblast', N Ukraine 49.58N 31.01E

S

144 E11 Sa'ad Southern, W Israel 31.27N 34.31E
111 P7 Saalach ∽ W Austria
103 L14 Saale ∽ C Germany
103 L17 Saalfeld var. Saalfeld an der Saale. Thüringen, C Germany 50.39N 11.22E
Saalfeld see Zalewo
Saalfeld an der Saale see Saalfeld
110 C8 Saane ∽ W Switzerland
103 D19 Saar Fr. Sarre. ∽ France/Germany
103 E20 Saarbrücken Fr. Sarrebruck. Saarland, SW Germany 49.13N 7.01E
Saarburg see Sarrebourg
Saare see Saaremaa
120 D6 Sääre var. Sjar. Saaremaa, W Estonia 57.55N 22.03E
120 D5 Saaremaa off. Saare Maakond. ◐ province W Estonia
120 E6 Saaremaa Ger. Oesel, Ösel; prev. Saare. island W Estonia
94 L12 Saarenkylä Lappi, N Finland 66.31N 25.51E
Saargemund see Sarreguemines
95 L17 Saarijärvi Länsi-Suomi, W Finland 62.42N 25.16E
Saar in Mähren see Žďár nad Sázavou
94 M10 Saariselkä Lapp. Suoločielgi. Lappi, N Finland 68.26N 27.28E
94 L10 Saariselkä hill range NE Finland
103 D20 Saarland Fr. Sarre. ◐ state SW Germany
Saarlautern see Saarlouis
103 D20 Saarlouis prev. Saarlautern. Saarland, SW Germany 49.18N 6.49E
110 E11 Saaser Vispa ∽ S Switzerland
143 X12 Saatlı Rus. Saatly. C Azerbaijan 39.57N 48.24E
Saatly see Saatlı
Saaz see Žatec
176 X9 Saba Irian Jaya, E Indonesia 1.04S 136.15E
47 V9 Saba island N Netherlands Antilles
144 J7 Sab' Ābār var. Sab'a Biyar, Sa'b Bi'ār. Ḩimş, C Syria 33.46N 37.40E
Sab'a Biyar see Sab' Ābār
114 K11 Šabac Serbia, W Yugoslavia 44.45N 19.42E
107 W5 Sabadell Cataluña, E Spain 41.33N 2.07E
171 Hh13 Sabae Fukui, Honshū, SW Japan 36.00N 136.12E
175 O3 Sabah prev. British North Borneo, North Borneo. ◐ state East Malaysia
174 Gg4 Sabak var. Sabak Bernam. Selangor, Peninsular Malaysia 3.45N 100.58E
Sabak Bernam see Sabak
40 D16 Sabak, Cape headland Agattu Island, Alaska, USA 52.21N 173.43E
83 J20 Sabaki ∽ S Kenya
175 P14 Sabalana, Kepulauan var. Kepulauan Liukang Tenggaya. island group C Indonesia
148 L2 Sabalān, Kuhhā-ye ▲ NW Iran 38.21N 47.47E
160 H7 Sabalgarh Madhya Pradesh, C India 26.18N 77.28E
46 E4 Sabana, Archipiélago de island group C Cuba
44 H7 Sabanagrande var. Sabana Grande. Francisco Morazán, S Honduras 13.48N 87.15W
56 E5 Sabanalarga Atlántico, N Colombia 10.37N 74.55W
43 W14 Sabancuy Campeche, SE Mexico 18.56N 91.08W
47 N8 Sabaneta NW Dominican Republic 19.27N 71.22W
56 J4 Sabaneta Falcón, N Venezuela 11.15N 70.04W
196 H4 Sabaneta, Puntan prev. Ushi Point. headland Saipan, S Northern Mariana Islands 15.17N 145.49E
176 Y12 Sabang Irian Jaya, E Indonesia 4.33S 138.42E
118 L10 Săbăoani Neamţ, NE Romania 47.01N 26.51E
161 J26 Sabaragamuwa Province ◐ province C Sri Lanka
Sabaria see Szombathely
160 D10 Sābarmati ∽ NW India
175 T6 Sabatai Pulau Morotai, E Indonesia 2.04N 128.23E
147 Q15 Sab'atayn, Ramlat as desert C Yemen
109 I16 Sabaudia Lazio, C Italy 41.17N 13.02E
59 J19 Sabaya Oruro, S Bolivia 19.09S 68.20W
Sa'b Bi'ār see Sab' Ābār
Sabbioncello see Orebić
154 I8 Şāberī, Hāmūn-e var. Daryācheh-ye Hāmūn, Daryācheh-ye Sīstān. ◎ Afghanistan/Iran see also Sīstān, Daryācheh-ye
29 P2 Sabetha Kansas, C USA 39.54N 95.48W
77 P10 Sabhā C Libya 27.01N 14.25E
69 V13 Sabi var. Rio Save. ∽ Mozambique/Zimbabwe see also Save, Rio
120 E8 Sabile Ger. Zabeln. Talsi, NW Latvia 57.03N 22.33E
33 R14 Sabina Ohio, N USA 39.29N 83.38W
42 I3 Sabinal Chihuahua, N Mexico 30.59N 107.29W
27 Q12 Sabinal Texas, SW USA 29.19N 99.28W
27 Q11 Sabinal River ∽ Texas, SW USA
107 S4 Sabiñánigo Aragón, NE Spain 42.31N 0.22W
43 N6 Sabinas Coahuila de Zaragoza, NE Mexico 27.52N 101.04W
43 O8 Sabinas Hidalgo Nuevo León, NE Mexico 26.28N 100.08W
43 N6 Sabinas, Río ∽ NE Mexico
24 F9 Sabine Lake ◎ Louisiana/Texas, S USA
94 O3 Sabine Land physical region C Svalbard
27 W7 Sabine River ∽ Louisiana/Texas, SW USA
143 X12 Sabirabad C Azerbaijan 40.00N 48.27E
Sabkha see As Sabkhah
179 P12 Sablayan Mindoro, N Philippines 12.48N 120.48E
11 P16 Sable, Cape headland Newfoundland, SE Canada 43.21N 65.40W
25 X17 Sable, Cape headland Florida, SE USA 25.12N 81.06W
11 R16 Sable Island island Nova Scotia, SE Canada
12 L11 Sables, Lac des ◎ Quebec, SE Canada
12 E10 Sables, Rivière aux ∽ Ontario, S Canada
104 K7 Sable-sur-Sarthe Sarthe, NW France 47.49N 0.19W
129 U7 Sablya, Gora ▲ NW Russian Federation 64.46N 58.52E
79 U14 Sabon Birnin Gwari Kaduna, C Nigeria 10.43N 6.39E
79 V11 Sabon Kafi Zinder, C Niger 14.37N 8.46E
106 I6 Sabor, Rio ∽ N Portugal
12 J8 Sabourin, Lac ◎ Quebec, SE Canada
104 J14 Sabres Landes, SW France 44.07N 0.46W
205 X13 Sabrina Coast physical region Antarctica
146 M11 Sabt al Ulayā 'Asīr, SW Saudi Arabia 19.33N 41.58E
106 I8 Sabugal Guarda, N Portugal 40.19N 7.04W
31 Z13 Sabula Iowa, C USA 42.04N 90.10W
147 N13 Şabyā Jīzān, SW Saudi Arabia 17.49N 42.49E
Sabzawar see Sabzevār
Sabzawaran see Sabzvārān
149 S4 Sabzevār var. Sabzawar. Khorāsān, NE Iran 36.13N 57.37E
149 T12 Sabzvārān var. Sabzawaran; prev. Jiroft. Kermān, SE Iran 28.40N 57.40E
Sacajawea Peak see Matterhorn
84 C9 Sacandica Uíge, NW Angola 6.01S 15.57E
44 A2 Sacatepéquez off. Departamento de Sacatepéquez. ◐ department S Guatemala
106 F11 Sacavém Lisboa, W Portugal 38.46N 9.06W
31 T13 Sac City Iowa, C USA 42.25N 94.59W
107 P8 Sacedón Castilla-La Mancha, C Spain 40.28N 2.43W
118 J12 Săcele Ger. Vierdörfer, Hung. Négyfalu; prev. Ger. Sieben Dörfer, Hung. Hétfalu. Braşov, C Romania 45.36N 25.40E
10 C8 Sachigo Ontario, C Canada 53.52N 92.16W
10 C7 Sachigo ∽ Ontario, C Canada
10 C8 Sachigo Lake ◎ Ontario, C Canada
169 Y16 Sach'ŏn Jap. Sansenhō; prev. Samch'ŏnpŏ. S South Korea 34.55N 128.07E
103 O15 Sachsen Eng. Saxony, Fr. Saxe. ◐ state E Germany
103 K14 Sachsen-Anhalt Eng. Saxony-Anhalt. ◐ state C Germany
111 R9 Sachsenburg Salzburg, S Austria 46.49N 13.23E
Sachsenfeld see Žalec
15 H1 Sachs Harbour Banks Island, Northwest Territories, N Canada 72.00N 125.13W
Sächsisch-Reen/Sächsisch-Regen see Reghin
20 H8 Sackets Harbor New York, NE USA 43.57N 76.06W
11 P14 Sackville New Brunswick, SE Canada 45.54N 64.22W
21 P9 Saco Maine, NE USA 43.32N 70.25W
21 P8 Saco River ∽ Maine/New Hampshire, NE USA
37 O7 Sacramento state capitol California, W USA 38.34N 121.29W
39 T14 Sacramento Mountains ▲▲ New Mexico, SW USA
37 N6 Sacramento River ∽ California, W USA
37 N5 Sacramento Valley valley California, W USA
38 I10 Sacramento Wash valley Arizona, SW USA
107 N15 Sacratif, Cabo headland S Spain 36.41N 3.30W
118 F9 Săcueni prev. Săcuieni, Hung. Székelyhíd. Bihor, W Romania 47.19N 22.04E
Săcuieni see Săcueni
107 R4 Sádaba Aragón, NE Spain 42.15N 1.16W
Sá da Bandeira see Lubango
144 I6 Şadad Ḩimş, W Syria 34.19N 36.52E
147 O13 Şa'dah NW Yemen 16.59N 43.45E
170 Dd14 Sadamisaki-hantō peninsula Shikoku, SW Japan
175 P12 Sadang, Sungai ∽ Sulawesi, C Indonesia
178 H17 Sadao Songkhla, SW Thailand 6.34N 100.22E
148 L8 Sadd-e Dez, Daryācheh-ye ◎ W Iran
21 S3 Saddleback Mountain hill Maine, NE USA 46.25N 68.00W
21 P6 Saddleback Mountain ▲ Maine, NE USA 44.57N 70.27W
178 J114 Sa Dec Đông Thap, S Vietnam 10.19N 105.45E
147 W13 Şadh S Oman 17.10N 55.07E
78 J11 Sadiola Kayes, W Mali 13.48N 11.47W
155 R12 Sādiqābād Punjab, E Pakistan 28.16N 70.10E
159 Y10 Sadiya Assam, NE India 27.49N 95.37E
145 W9 Sa'diyah, Hawr as ◎ E Iraq
171 K12 Sado var. Sadoga-shima. island C Japan
Sadoga-shima see Sado
106 F12 Sado, Rio ∽ S Portugal
116 I8 Sadovets Pleven, N Bulgaria 43.19N 24.21E
131 O11 Sadovoye Respublika Kalmykiya, SW Russian Federation 47.51N 44.34E
107 W9 Sa Dragonera var. Isla Dragonera. island Islas Baleares, Spain, W Mediterranean Sea
97 H20 Sæby Nordjylland, N Denmark 57.19N 10.33E
107 P9 Saelices Castilla-La Mancha, C Spain 39.55N 2.49W
Saena Julia see Siena
Saetabicula see Alzira
116 O12 Safaalan Tekirdağ, NW Turkey 41.26N 28.07E
Safad see Ẕefat
Şafāqis see Sfax
198 B8 Safata Bay bay Upolu, Samoa, C Pacific Ocean
Safed see Ẕefat
Safed, Āb-i- see Sefid, Darya-ye
145 X11 Şaffāf, Ḩawr aş wetland S Iraq
97 J16 Säffle Värmland, C Sweden 59.07N 12.55E
39 N15 Safford Arizona, SW USA 32.46N 109.41W
76 E7 Safi W Morocco 32.19N 9.14W
149 V9 Safīdābeh Khorāsān, E Iran 31.04N 60.30E
148 M4 Safīd, Rūd-e ∽ NW Iran
130 I4 Safonovo Smolenskaya Oblast', W Russian Federation 55.05N 33.12E
142 H11 Safranbolu Karabük, N Turkey 41.16N 32.40E
145 Y13 Safwān SE Iraq 30.06N 47.43E
164 J16 Saga var. Gya'gya. Xizang Zizhiqu, W China 29.22N 85.19E
170 Cc13 Saga Saga, Kyūshū, SW Japan 33.14N 130.16E
170 Cc13 Saga off. Saga-ken. ◐ prefecture Kyūshū, SW Japan
171 Ll12 Sagae Yamagata, Honshū, C Japan 38.22N 140.13E
177 G5 Sagaing Sagaing, C Burma 21.55N 95.55E
177 G3 Sagaing ◐ division N Burma
171 Jj16 Sagamihara Kanagawa, Honshū, S Japan 35.32N 139.23E
171 Jj17 Sagami-nada inlet SW Japan
171 Jj17 Sagami-wan bay SW Japan
Sagan see Żagań
31 Y3 Saganaga Lake ◎ Minnesota, N USA
161 F18 Sāgar Karnātaka, W India 14.09N 75.02E
160 I9 Sāgar prev. Saugor. Madhya Pradesh, C India 23.52N 78.46E
13 S8 Sagard Quebec, SE Canada 48.01N 70.03W
Sagarmatha see Everest, Mount
179 Qq13 Sagay Negros, C Philippines 10.54N 123.26E
Sagebrush State see Nevada
149 V11 Sāghand Yazd, C Iran 32.33N 55.12E
21 N14 Sag Harbor Long Island, New York, NE USA 40.59N 72.15W
Saghez see Saqqez
33 R8 Saginaw Michigan, N USA 43.25N 83.57W
33 R8 Saginaw Bay lake bay Michigan, N USA
150 H11 Sagiz Atyrau, W Kazakhstan 48.12N 54.55E
66 H6 Saglek Bank undersea feature W Labrador Sea
11 P5 Saglek Bay bay SW Labrador Sea
Saglouc/Sagluk see Salluit
105 X15 Sagonne, Golfe de gulf Corse, France, C Mediterranean Sea
107 P13 Sagra ▲ S Spain 37.59N 2.33W
106 F14 Sagres Faro, S Portugal 37.01N 8.55W
39 S7 Saguache Colorado, C USA 38.05N 106.05W
46 J7 Sagua de Tánamo Holguín, E Cuba 20.34N 75.14W
46 E5 Sagua la Grande Villa Clara, C Cuba 22.48N 80.06W
13 R7 Saguenay ∽ Quebec, SE Canada
76 C9 Saguia al Hamra var. As Saqia al Hamra. ∽ N Western Sahara
Sagunt/Saguntum see Sagunto
107 S9 Sagunto var. Sagunt, Ar. Murviedro; anc. Saguntum. País Valenciano, E Spain 39.40N 0.16W
144 H10 Saḩāb 'Ammān, NW Jordan 31.52N 36.00E
56 E6 Sahagún Córdoba, NW Colombia 8.57N 75.26W
106 L4 Sahagún Castilla-León, N Spain 42.22N 5.01W
147 X8 Saḩam N Oman 24.06N 56.52E
70 F9 Sahara desert Libya/Algeria
77 U9 Sahara el Gharbîya var. Aş Şaḩrā' al Gharbīyah, Eng. Western Desert. desert C Egypt
77 X9 Sahara el Sharqîya var. Aş Şaḩrā' ash Sharqīyah, Eng. Arabian Desert, Eastern Desert. desert E Egypt
Saharan Atlas see Atlas Saharien
158 J9 Sahāranpur Uttar Pradesh, N India 29.58N 77.33E
66 L10 Saharan Seamounts var. Saharian Seamounts. undersea feature E Atlantic Ocean 25.00N 20.00W
159 Q13 Saharsa Bihār, NE India 25.54N 86.36E
69 O7 Sahel physical region C Africa
159 R14 Sāhibganj Bihār, NE India 25.15N 87.40E
145 Q7 Sahīliyah C Iraq 33.43N 42.42E
144 H4 Sāḩilīyah, Jibāl as ▲▲ NW Syria
116 M13 Şahin Tekirdağ, NW Turkey 41.01N 26.51E
155 U8 Sāhīwāl Punjab, E Pakistan 31.57N 72.22E
155 U9 Sāhīwāl prev. Montgomery. Punjab, E Pakistan 30.40N 73.04E
147 W11 Saḩmah, Ramlat as desert C Oman
145 T13 Şaḩrā' al Ḩijārah desert S Iraq
42 H5 Sahuaripa Sonora, NW Mexico 29.02N 109.14W
38 M16 Sahuarita Arizona, SW USA 31.24N 110.55W
42 L13 Sahuayo var. Sahuayo de José María Morelos; prev. Sahuayo de Díaz, Sahuayo de Porfirio Díaz. Michoacán de Ocampo, SW Mexico 20.04N 102.44W
Sahuayo de Díaz/Sahuayo de José María Morelos/Sahuayo de Porfirio Díaz see Sahuayo
181 W8 Sahul Shelf undersea feature N Timor Sea
178 Hh17 Sai Buri Pattani, SW Thailand 6.42N 101.37E
76 I6 Saïda NW Algeria 34.49N 0.10E
144 G7 Saïda var. Şaydā, Sayida; anc. Sidon. W Lebanon 33.20N 35.24E
Sa'īdābād see Sīrjān
82 B13 Sa'īd Bundas Western Bahr el Ghazal, SW Sudan 8.24N 24.53E
194 J12 Saidor Madang, N PNG 5.37S 146.28E
159 S13 Saidpur var. Syedpur. Rajshahi, NW Bangladesh 25.48N 89.00E
110 C7 Saignelégier Jura, NW Switzerland 47.18N 7.03E
170 G11 Saigō Shimane, Dōgo, SW Japan 36.12N 133.18E
Saigon see Hô Chi Minh
168 I12 Saihan Toroi Nei Mongol Zizhiqu, N China 41.44N 100.29E
Saihon Tal see Sonid Youqi
Sai Hun see Syr Darya
94 M11 Saija Lappi, NE Finland 67.07N 28.46E
170 Ee14 Saijō Ehime, Shikoku, SW Japan 33.55N 133.10E
170 Dd15 Saiki Ōita, Kyūshū, SW Japan 32.57N 131.52E
176 Uu9 Saileen Irian Jaya, E Indonesia 1.14S 130.56E
95 N18 Saimaa ◎ SE Finland
95 N18 Saimaa Canal Fin. Saimaan Kanava, Rus. Saymenskiy Kanal. canal Finland/Russian Federation
Saimaan Kanava see Saimaa Canal

◆ Country ● Country Capital ◇ Dependent Territory ○ Dependent Territory Capital ◐ Administrative Region ✕ International Airport ▲ Mountain ▲▲ Mountain Range ※ Volcano ∽ River ◎ Lake ⊠ Reservoir

SAÍN ALTO – SALA Y GOMEZ

42 L10 Saín Alto Zacatecas, C Mexico 23.38N 103.13W
98 L12 St Abb's Head headland SE Scotland, UK 55.54N 2.07W
9 Y16 St.Adolphe Manitoba, S Canada 49.39N 96.55W
105 O15 St-Affrique Aveyron, S France 43.57N 2.52E
13 Q10 St-Agapit Quebec, SE Canada 46.33N 71.25W
99 O21 St Albans anc. Verulamium. E England, UK 51.46N 0.21W
20 L6 Saint Albans Vermont, NE USA 44.49N 73.07W
23 Q5 Saint Albans West Virginia, NE USA 38.21N 81.47W
St Alban's Head see St.Aldhelm's Head
9 Q14 St.Albert Alberta, SW Canada 53.37N 113.37W
99 M24 St. Aldhelm's Head var. St.Alban's Head. headland S England, UK 50.34N 2.04W
13 S8 St-Alexandre Quebec, SE Canada 47.39N 69.36W
13 O11 St-Alexis-des-Monts Quebec, SE Canada 46.30N 73.08W
105 P2 St-Amand-les-Eaux Nord, N France 50.27N 3.25E
105 O9 St-Amand-Montrond var. St-Amand-Mont-Rond. Cher, C France 46.43N 2.28E
13 Q7 St-Ambroise Quebec, SE Canada 48.35N 71.19W
181 P16 St-André NE Réunion
12 M12 St-André-Avellin Quebec, SE Canada 45.45N 75.04W
104 K12 St-André-de-Cubzac Gironde, SW France 45.01N 0.26W
98 K11 St Andrews E Scotland, UK 56.20N 2.48W
25 Q9 Saint Andrews Bay bay Florida, SE USA
25 W7 Saint Andrew Sound sound Georgia, SE USA
Saint Anna Trough see Svyataya Anna Trough
46 J11 St.Ann's Bay C Jamaica 18.25N 77.12W
11 T10 St.Anthony Newfoundland, SE Canada 51.21N 55.34W
35 R13 Saint Anthony Idaho, NW USA 43.56N 111.38W
190 M11 Saint Arnaud Victoria, SE Australia 36.39S 143.15E
193 I15 St.Arnaud Range ▲ South Island, NZ
13 T8 St-Arsène Quebec, SE Canada 47.55N 69.21W
11 R10 St-Augustin Quebec, E Canada 51.13N 58.39W
25 X9 Saint Augustine Florida, SE USA 29.54N 81.19W
99 H24 St Austell SW England, UK 50.21N 4.46W
105 T4 St-Avold Moselle, NE France 49.06N 6.43E
105 N17 St-Barthélemy ▲ S France
104 L17 St-Béat Haute-Garonne, S France 42.55N 0.39E
99 I15 St Bees Head headland NW England, UK 54.30N 3.39W
181 P16 St-Benoit E Réunion
105 T13 St-Bonnet Hautes-Alpes, SE France 44.41N 6.04E
St.Botolph's Town see Boston
99 G21 St Brides Bay inlet SW Wales, UK
104 H5 St-Brieuc Côtes d'Armor, NW France 48.31N 2.45W
104 H5 St-Brieuc, Baie de bay NW France
104 L7 St-Calais Sarthe, NW France 47.55N 0.48E
13 Q10 St-Casimir Quebec, SE Canada 46.40N 72.05W
12 H16 St.Catharines Ontario, S Canada 43.10N 79.15W
47 S14 St.Catherine, Mount ▲ N Grenada 12.10N 61.41W
66 C11 St Catherine Point headland E Bermuda
25 X6 Saint Catherines Island island Georgia, SE USA
99 M24 St Catherine's Point headland S England, UK 50.34N 1.17W
105 N13 St-Céré Lot, S France 44.52N 1.53E
110 A10 St.Cergue Vaud, W Switzerland 46.25N 6.10E
105 R11 St-Chamond Loire, E France 45.28N 4.31E
35 S16 Saint Charles Idaho, NW USA 42.05N 111.23W
29 X4 Saint Charles Missouri, C USA 38.48N 90.28W
105 P13 St-Chély-d'Apcher Lozère, S France 44.51N 3.16E
Saint Christopher-Nevis see Saint Kitts and Nevis
33 S9 Saint Clair Michigan, N USA 42.49N 82.29W
12 D17 St.Clair ≈ Canada/USA
191 O17 St.Clair, Lake ◎ Tasmania, SE Australia
12 C17 St.Clair, Lake var. Lac à L'eau Claire. ◎ Canada/USA
33 S10 Saint Clair Shores Michigan, N USA 42.30N 82.53W
105 S10 St-Claude anc. Condate. Jura, E France 46.22N 5.52E
47 X6 St-Claude Basse Terre, SW Guadeloupe 16.01N 61.41W
25 X12 Saint Cloud Florida, SE USA 28.15N 81.15W
31 U8 Saint Cloud Minnesota, N USA 45.33N 94.09W
47 T9 Saint Croix island S Virgin Islands (US)
32 J4 Saint Croix Flowage ⊡ Wisconsin, N USA
21 T5 Saint Croix River ≈ Canada/USA
31 W7 Saint Croix River ≈ Minnesota/Wisconsin, N USA
47 S14 St.David's SE Grenada 12.01N 61.40W
99 H21 St David's SW Wales, UK 51.53N 5.16W
99 G21 St David's Head headland SW Wales, UK 51.54N 5.19W
66 C12 St David's Island island E Bermuda
181 O16 St-Denis ○ (Réunion) NW Réunion 20.55S 14.33E
105 U6 St-Dié Vosges, NE France 48.16N 6.57E
105 R5 St-Dizier anc. Desiderii Fanum. Haute-Marne, N France 48.39N 5.00E
13 N11 St-Donat Quebec, SE Canada 46.16N 74.12W
13 N11 Ste-Adèle Quebec, SE Canada 45.58N 74.10W
13 N11 Ste-Agathe-des-Monts Quebec, SE Canada 46.03N 74.19W
180 I16 Sainte Anne island Inner Islands, NE Seychelles
9 Y16 Ste.Anne Manitoba, S Canada 49.40N 96.40W
47 R12 Ste-Anne Grande Terre, E Guadeloupe 16.13N 61.22W
47 Y6 Ste-Anne SE Martinique 14.25N 60.53W
13 Q10 Ste-Anne ≈ Quebec, SE Canada
13 W6 Ste-Anne-des-Monts Quebec, SE Canada 49.07N 66.28W
12 M10 Ste-Anne-du-Lac Quebec, SE Canada 46.51N 75.20W
13 U4 Ste-Anne, Lac ◎ Quebec, SE Canada
13 S10 Ste-Apolline Quebec, SE Canada 46.47N 70.15W
13 U7 Ste-Blandine Quebec, SE Canada 48.22N 68.27W
13 R10 Ste-Claire Quebec, SE Canada 46.30N 70.40W
13 Q10 Ste-Croix Quebec, SE Canada 46.36N 71.42W
110 B8 Ste.Croix Vaud, SW Switzerland 46.49N 6.31E
105 P14 Ste-Énimie Lozère, S France 44.21N 3.26E
29 Y6 Sainte Genevieve Missouri, C USA 37.57N 90.01W
105 S12 St-Egrève Isère, E France 45.15N 5.40E
41 T12 Saint Elias, Cape headland Kayak Island, Alaska, USA 59.48N 144.36W
41 U11 Saint Elias, Mount ▲ Alaska, USA 60.18N 140.57W
8 G8 Saint Elias Mountains ▲ Canada/USA
57 Y10 St-Élie N French Guiana 4.49N 53.21W
105 O10 St-Eloy-les-Mines Puy-de-Dôme, C France 46.07N 2.50E
13 S7 Ste-Marguerite Nord-Est ≈ Quebec, SE Canada
13 R7 Ste-Marguerite ≈ Quebec, SE Canada
13 V4 Ste-Marguerite, Pointe headland Quebec, SE Canada 50.01N 66.43W
13 V3 Ste-Marguesite ≈ Quebec, SE Canada
13 R10 Ste-Marie Quebec, SE Canada 46.28N 71.00W
47 Q11 Ste-Marie NE Martinique 14.48N 61.01W
181 P16 Ste-Marie NE Réunion
105 U6 Ste-Marie-aux-Mines Haut-Rhin, NE France 48.16N 7.12E
10 J14 Ste-Marie, Lac ⊡ Quebec, S Canada
180 K4 Sainte Marie, Nosy island E Madagascar
104 L8 Ste-Maure-de-Touraine Indre-et-Loire, C France 47.06N 0.38E
105 R4 Ste-Menehould Marne, NE France 49.06N 4.54E
Ste-Perpétue see Ste-Perpétue-de-l'Islet
13 S9 Ste-Perpétue-de-l'Islet var. Ste-Perpétue. Quebec, SE Canada 47.02N 69.54W
47 X11 Ste-Rose Basse Terre, N Guadeloupe 16.20N 61.41W
181 P16 Ste-Rose E Réunion
9 W15 Ste.Rose du Lac Manitoba, S Canada 51.04N 99.31W
104 J11 Saintes anc. Mediolanum. Charente-Maritime, W France 45.45N 0.37W
47 X7 Saintes, Canal des channel SW Guadeloupe
Saintes, Îles des see les Saintes
181 P16 Ste-Suzanne N Réunion
13 P10 Ste-Thècle Quebec, SE Canada 46.48N 72.31W
105 Q12 St-Étienne Loire, E France 45.25N 4.22E
104 M4 St-Étienne-du-Rouvray Seine-Maritime, N France 49.22N 1.07E
Saint Eustatius see Sint Eustatius
12 M11 Ste-Véronique Quebec, SE Canada 46.30N 74.58W
13 T7 St-Fabien Quebec, SE Canada 48.19N 68.51W
13 P7 St-Félicien Quebec, SE Canada 48.39N 72.28W
13 O11 St-Félix-de-Valois Quebec, SE Canada 46.10N 73.25W
105 Y14 St-Florent Corse, France, C Mediterranean Sea 42.41N 9.19E
105 Y14 St-Florent, Golfe de gulf Corse, France, C Mediterranean Sea
105 P6 St-Florentin Yonne, C France 48.00N 3.46E
105 N9 St-Florent-sur-Cher Cher, C France 47.00N 2.13E
105 P12 St-Flour Cantal, C France 45.01N 3.04E
28 H2 Saint Francis Kansas, C USA 39.45N 101.31W
85 H26 St.Francis, Cape headland S South Africa 34.11S 24.45E
29 X10 Saint Francis River ≈ Arkansas/Missouri, C USA
24 J8 Saint Francisville Louisiana, S USA 30.46N 91.22W
13 Q12 St-François ≈ Quebec, SE Canada
47 Y6 St-François Grande Terre, E Guadeloupe 16.15N 61.16W
13 R11 St-François, Lac ◎ Quebec, SE Canada
29 X7 Saint Francois Mountains ▲ Missouri, C USA
St-Gall/Saint Gall/St.Gallen see Sankt Gallen
104 L16 St-Gaudens Haute-Garonne, S France 43.07N 0.43E
13 R12 St-Gédéon Quebec, SE Canada 45.51N 70.36W
189 X10 Saint George Queensland, E Australia 28.04S 148.39E
66 B12 St George N Bermuda 32.24N 64.42W
40 K15 Saint George Saint George Island, Alaska, USA 56.34N 169.30W
23 S14 Saint George South Carolina, SE USA 33.10N 80.34W
38 J8 Saint George Utah, W USA 37.06N 113.35W
11 R12 St.George, Cape headland Newfoundland, E Canada 48.26N 59.17W
195 P11 St.George, Cape headland New Ireland, NE PNG 4.49S 152.52E
40 J15 Saint George Island island Pribilof Islands, Alaska, USA
25 S10 Saint George Island island Florida, SE USA
101 J19 Saint-Georges Liège, E Belgium 50.36N 5.20E
13 R11 St-Georges Quebec, SE Canada 46.07N 70.40W
57 Z11 St-Georges E French Guiana 3.55N 51.49W
47 R14 St.George's ● (Grenada) SW Grenada 12.03N 61.45W
11 R12 St.George's Bay inlet Newfoundland, E Canada
99 G21 Saint George's Channel channel Ireland/Wales, UK
195 P10 St.George's Channel channel NE PNG
66 B11 St George's Island island E Bermuda
101 I21 Saint-Gérard Namur, S Belgium 50.20N 4.47E
St-Germain see St-Germain-en-Laye
13 P12 St-Germain-de-Grantham Quebec, SE Canada 45.49N 72.32W
105 N5 St-Germain-en-Laye var. St-Germain. Yvelines, N France 48.52N 2.04E
104 H8 St-Gildas, Pointe du headland NW France 47.09N 2.25W
105 R15 St-Gilles Gard, S France 43.41N 4.24E
104 I9 St-Gilles-Croix-de-Vie Vendée, NW France 46.41N 1.55W
181 O16 St-Gilles-les-Bains W Réunion 21.01S 55.13E
104 M16 St-Girons Ariège, S France 42.58N 1.07E
Saint Gotthard see Szentgotthárd
110 G9 St.Gotthard Tunnel tunnel Ticino, S Switzerland
99 H22 St Govan's Head headland SW Wales, UK 51.35N 4.55W
36 M7 Saint Helena California, W USA 38.29N 122.30W
67 F24 Saint Helena ◇ UK dependent territory C Atlantic Ocean
69 O12 Saint Helena island C Atlantic Ocean
85 E25 St.Helena Bay bay SW South Africa
67 M15 Saint Helena Fracture Zone tectonic feature C Atlantic Ocean
36 M7 Saint Helena, Mount ▲ California, W USA 38.40N 122.39W
23 S15 Saint Helena Sound inlet South Carolina, SE USA
33 Q7 Saint Helen, Lake ◎ Michigan, N USA
191 Q16 Saint Helens Tasmania, SE Australia 41.21S 148.15E
99 K18 St Helens NW England, UK 53.28N 2.43W
34 G10 Saint Helens Oregon, NW USA 45.55N 122.51W
34 H13 Saint Helens, Mount ⛰ Washington, NW USA 46.24N 121.49W
99 L26 St Helier ○ (Jersey) S Jersey, Channel Islands 49.12N 2.07W
13 S9 St-Hilarion Quebec, SE Canada 47.34N 70.24W
101 K22 Saint-Hubert Luxembourg, SE Belgium 50.02N 5.23E
13 T8 St-Hubert Quebec, SE Canada 47.46N 69.15W
13 P12 St-Hyacinthe Quebec, SE Canada 45.37N 72.57W
St.Iago de la Vega see Spanish Town
33 Q4 Saint Ignace Michigan, N USA 45.52N 84.43W
13 O10 St-Ignace-du-Lac Quebec, SE Canada 46.43N 73.49W
10 D12 St.Ignace Island island Ontario, S Canada
110 C7 St.Imier Bern, W Switzerland 47.09N 6.55E
99 G25 St Ives SW England, UK 50.12N 5.28W
31 U10 Saint James Minnesota, N USA 43.58N 94.40W
8 I15 Saint James, Cape headland Graham Island, British Columbia, SW Canada 51.57N 131.04W
13 O13 St-Jean var. St-Jean-sur-Richelieu. Quebec, SE Canada 45.15N 73.16W
57 X9 St-Jean NW French Guiana 5.21N 54.09W
13 R8 St-Jean ≈ Quebec, SE Canada
St-Jean-d'Acre see 'Akko
104 K11 St-Jean-d'Angély Charente-Maritime, W France 45.57N 0.31W
105 N7 St-Jean-de-Braye Loiret, C France 47.54N 1.58E
104 I16 St-Jean-de-Luz Pyrénées-Atlantiques, SW France 43.24N 1.40W
105 T12 St-Jean-de-Maurienne Savoie, E France 45.16N 6.21E
104 I9 St-Jean-de-Monts Vendée, NW France 46.45N 2.00W
105 Q14 St-Jean-du-Gard Gard, S France 44.06N 3.49E
13 Q7 St-Jean, Lac ◎ Quebec, SE Canada
104 I16 St-Jean-Pied-de-Port Pyrénées-Atlantiques, SW France 43.10N 1.13W
13 S9 St-Jean-Port-Joli Quebec, SE Canada 47.13N 70.16W
St-Jean-sur-Richelieu see St-Jean
13 N12 St-Jérôme Quebec, SE Canada 45.46N 74.01W
27 T5 Saint Jo Texas, SW USA 33.42N 97.33W
11 O15 St.John New Brunswick, SE Canada 45.16N 66.03W
28 L6 Saint John Kansas, C USA 37.59N 98.44W
78 K16 Saint John ≈ C Liberia
47 T9 Saint John island C Virgin Islands (US)
24 I6 Saint John, Lake ◎ Louisiana, S USA
21 Q2 Saint John Fr. Saint-John. ≈ Canada/USA
47 W10 St John's ● (Antigua and Barbuda) Antigua, Antigua and Barbuda 17.06N 61.50W
11 V12 St.John's Newfoundland, E Canada 47.34N 52.40W
39 O12 Saint Johns Arizona, SW USA 34.28N 109.22W
33 Q9 Saint Johns Michigan, N USA 42.58N 84.31W
11 V12 St.John's ✕ Newfoundland, E Canada 47.22N 52.45W
25 X11 Saint Johns River ≈ Florida, SE USA
47 N12 St.Joseph W Dominica 15.24N 61.25W
181 P17 St-Joseph S Réunion
24 J6 Saint Joseph Louisiana, S USA 31.56N 91.14W
33 O10 Saint Joseph Michigan, N USA 42.04N 86.30W
29 R3 Saint Joseph Missouri, C USA 39.45N 94.49W
22 I10 Saint Joseph Tennessee, S USA 35.02N 87.29W
24 R9 Saint Joseph Bay bay Florida, SE USA
13 R11 St-Joseph-de-Beauce Quebec, SE Canada 46.20N 70.52W
10 C10 St.Joseph, Lake ◎ Ontario, C Canada
33 Q11 Saint Joseph River ≈ N USA
12 C11 Saint Joseph's Island island Ontario, S Canada
13 N11 St-Jovite Quebec, SE Canada 46.07N 74.35W
123 Jj16 St Julian's N Malta 35.55N 14.29E
St-Julien see St-Julien-en-Genevois
105 T10 St-Julien-en-Genevois var. St-Julien. Haute-Savoie, E France 46.07N 6.06E
104 M11 St-Junien Haute-Vienne, C France 45.52N 0.54E
105 Q11 St-Just-St-Rambert Loire, E France 45.30N 4.13E
98 D8 St Kilda island NW Scotland, UK
47 V10 Saint Kitts island Saint Kitts and Nevis
47 U10 Saint Kitts and Nevis off. Federation of Saint Christopher and Nevis, var. Saint Christopher-Nevis. ◆ commonwealth republic E West Indies
9 X16 St.Laurent Manitoba, S Canada 50.20N 97.55W
St-Laurent see St-Laurent-du-Maroni
57 X9 St-Laurent-du-Maroni var. St-Laurent. NW French Guiana 5.28N 54.03W
St-Laurent, Fleuve see St.Lawrence
104 J12 St-Laurent-Médoc Gironde, SW France 45.11N 0.50W
11 N12 St.Lawrence Fr. Fleuve St-Laurent. ≈ Canada/USA
11 Q12 St.Lawrence, Gulf of gulf NW Atlantic Ocean
40 K10 Saint Lawrence Island island Alaska, USA
12 M14 Saint Lawrence River ≈ Canada/USA
101 L25 Saint-Léger Luxembourg, SE Belgium 49.36N 5.39E
11 N14 St.Léonard New Brunswick, SE Canada 47.10N 67.55W
13 P11 St-Léonard Quebec, SE Canada 46.06N 72.18W
181 O17 St-Leu W Réunion 21.09S 55.16E
104 J4 St-Lô anc. Briovera, Laudus. Manche, N France 49.07N 1.08W
9 T15 St.Louis Saskatchewan, S Canada 52.50N 105.43W
105 V7 St-Louis Haut-Rhin, NE France 47.34N 7.34E
181 O17 St-Louis S Réunion
78 G10 Saint Louis NW Senegal 15.58N 16.30W
29 X4 Saint Louis Missouri, C USA 38.38N 90.15W
31 W5 Saint Louis River ≈ Minnesota, N USA
105 T7 St-Loup-sur-Semouse Haute-Saône, E France 47.53N 6.15E
13 O12 St-Luc Quebec, SE Canada 45.19N 73.18W
85 L22 St.Lucia KwaZulu/Natal, E South Africa 28.22S 32.25E
47 X13 Saint Lucia ◆ commonwealth republic SE West Indies
49 S3 Saint Lucia island SE West Indies
85 L22 St.Lucia, Cape headland E South Africa 28.29S 32.26E
47 Y13 Saint Lucia Channel channel Martinique/Saint Lucia
25 Y14 Saint Lucie Canal canal Florida, SE USA
25 Z13 Saint Lucie Inlet inlet Florida, SE USA
98 L2 St Magnus Bay bay N Scotland, UK
104 K10 St-Maixent-l'École Deux-Sèvres, W France 46.24N 0.13W
9 Y16 St.Malo Manitoba, S Canada 49.16N 96.58W
104 I5 St-Malo Ille-et-Vilaine, NW France 48.39N 2.00W
104 H4 St-Malo, Golfe de gulf NW France
46 L9 St-Marc C Haiti 19.05N 72.42W
46 L9 St-Marc, Canal de channel W Haiti
57 Y12 Saint-Marcel, Mont ▲ S French Guiana 2.32N 53.00W
105 S12 St-Marcellin-le-Mollard Isère, E France 45.12N 5.18E
98 K5 St Margaret's Hope NE Scotland, UK 58.49N 2.57W
34 M9 Saint Maries Idaho, NW USA 47.19N 116.37W
25 T9 Saint Marks Florida, SE USA 30.09N 84.12W
110 D11 St.Martin Valais, SW Switzerland 46.09N 7.27E
Saint Martin see Sint Maarten
33 O5 Saint Martin Island island Michigan, N USA
24 I9 Saint Martinville Louisiana, S USA 30.09N 91.51W
193 E20 St.Mary, Mount ▲ South Island, NZ 44.16S 169.42E
194 K14 St.Mary, Mount ▲ S PNG 8.06S 147.00E
190 I6 Saint Mary Peak ▲ South Australia 31.25S 138.39E
191 Q16 Saint Marys Tasmania, SE Australia 41.34S 148.13E
12 E16 St.Marys Ontario, S Canada 43.15N 81.08W
40 M11 Saint Marys Alaska, USA 62.03N 163.10W
25 W8 Saint Marys Georgia, SE USA 30.44N 81.30W
29 P4 Saint Marys Kansas, C USA 39.09N 96.00W
33 Q4 Saint Marys Ohio, N USA 40.31N 84.22W
23 R3 Saint Marys West Virginia, NE USA 39.23N 81.11W
25 W8 Saint Marys River ≈ Florida/Georgia, SE USA
33 Q4 Saint Marys River ≈ Michigan, N USA
104 D6 St-Mathieu, Pointe headland NW France 48.17N 4.56W
40 J12 Saint Matthew Island island Alaska, USA
23 R13 Saint Matthews South Carolina, SE USA 33.40N 80.46W
St.Matthew's Island see Zadetkyi Kyun
194 M8 St.Matthias Group island group NE PNG
110 C11 St.Maurice Valais, SW Switzerland 46.09N 7.28E
13 P9 St-Maurice ≈ Quebec, SE Canada
104 J13 St-Médard-en-Jalles Gironde, SW France 44.54N 0.43W
41 N10 Saint Michael Alaska, USA 63.28N 162.02W
St.Michel see Mikkeli
13 N10 St-Michel-des-Saints Quebec, SE Canada 46.39N 73.54W
105 S5 St-Mihiel Meuse, NE France 48.57N 5.33E
110 J10 St.Moritz Ger. Sankt Moritz, Rmsch. San Murezzan. Graubünden, SE Switzerland 46.30N 9.50E
104 H8 St-Nazaire Loire-Atlantique, NW France 47.16N 2.12W
Saint Nicholas see São Nicolau
Saint-Nicolas see Sint-Niklaas
105 N1 St-Omer Pas-de-Calais, N France 50.45N 2.15E
104 J11 Saintonge cultural region W France
13 S9 St-Pacôme Quebec, SE Canada 47.22N 69.56W
13 S10 St-Pamphile Quebec, SE Canada 46.57N 69.46W
13 S9 St-Pascal Quebec, SE Canada 47.25N 69.51W
12 J11 St-Patrice, Lac ◎ Quebec, SE Canada
9 R14 St.Paul Alberta, SW Canada 54.00N 111.18W
181 O16 St-Paul NW Réunion
40 K14 Saint Paul Saint Paul Island, Alaska, USA 57.08N 170.13W
31 V8 Saint Paul state capital Minnesota, N USA 45.00N 93.10W
31 P15 Saint Paul Nebraska, C USA 41.12N 98.26W
23 P7 Saint Paul Virginia, NE USA 36.53N 82.18W
79 Q17 Saint Paul, Cape headland S Ghana 5.44N 0.55E
105 O17 St-Paul-de-Fenouillet Pyrénées-Orientales, S France 42.49N 2.28E
67 K14 Saint Paul Fracture Zone tectonic feature E Atlantic Ocean
40 J14 Saint Paul Island island Pribilof Islands, Alaska, USA
104 J15 St-Paul-les-Dax Landes, SW France 43.45N 1.01W
23 U11 Saint Pauls North Carolina, SE USA 34.45N 78.56W
Saint Paul's Bay see San Pawl il-Bahar
203 R16 St Paul's Point headland Pitcairn Island, Pitcairn Islands
31 U10 Saint Peter Minnesota, N USA 44.18N 93.59W
99 L26 St Peter Port ○ (Guernsey) C Guernsey, Channel Islands 49.28N 2.33W
25 V13 Saint Petersburg Florida, SE USA 27.46N 82.37W
Saint Petersburg see Sankt-Peterburg
25 V13 Saint Petersburg Beach Florida, SE USA 27.43N 82.43W
181 P17 St-Philippe SE Réunion 21.21S 55.46E
47 Q11 St-Pierre NW Martinique 14.44N 61.10W
181 O17 St-Pierre SW Réunion
11 S13 St-Pierre and Miquelon Fr. Îles St-Pierre et Miquelon. ◇ French territorial collectivity NE North America
13 P11 St-Pierre, Lac ◎ Quebec, SE Canada
104 F5 St-Pol-de-Léon Finistère, NW France 48.42N 4.00W
105 O2 St-Pol-sur-Ternoise Pas-de-Calais, N France 50.22N 2.21E
St. Pons see St-Pons-de-Thomières
105 O16 St-Pons-de-Thomières var. St.Pons. Hérault, S France 43.28N 2.48E
105 P10 St-Pourçain-sur-Sioule Allier, C France 46.19N 3.16E
13 S11 St-Prosper Quebec, SE Canada 46.14N 70.28W
105 P3 St-Quentin Aisne, N France 49.51N 3.16E
13 R10 St-Raphaël Quebec, SE Canada 46.47N 70.46W
105 U15 St-Raphaël Var, SE France 43.25N 6.46E
13 Q10 St-Raymond Quebec, SE Canada 46.53N 71.49W
35 O9 Saint Regis Montana, NW USA 47.18N 115.06W
20 J7 Saint Regis River ≈ New York, NE USA
105 R15 St-Rémy-de-Provence Bouches-du-Rhône, SE France 43.48N 4.49E
13 V6 St-René-de-Matane Quebec, SE Canada 48.42N 67.22W
104 M9 St-Savin Vienne, W France 46.34N 0.53E
13 S8 St-Siméon Quebec, SE Canada 47.49N 69.55W
25 X7 Saint Simons Island island Georgia, SE USA
203 Y2 Saint Stanislas Bay bay Kiritimati, E Kiribati
11 O15 St.Stephen New Brunswick, SE Canada 45.12N 67.18W
41 X12 Saint Terese Alaska, USA 58.28N 134.46W
12 E17 St.Thomas Ontario, S Canada 42.46N 81.12W
31 Q2 Saint Thomas North Dakota, N USA 48.37N 97.28W
47 T9 Saint Thomas island W Virgin Islands (US)
Saint Thomas see São Tomé, Sao Tome and Principe
Saint Thomas see Charlotte Amalie, Virgin Islands (US)
13 P10 St-Tite Quebec, SE Canada 46.42N 72.32W
Saint-Trond see Sint-Truiden
105 U16 St-Tropez Var, SE France 43.16N 6.39E
Saint Ubes see Setúbal
104 L3 St-Valéry-en-Caux Seine-Maritime, N France 49.53N 0.42E
105 Q9 St-Vallier Saône-et-Loire, C France 46.39N 4.19E
108 B7 St-Vincent Valle d'Aosta, NW Italy 45.47N 7.42E
47 Q14 Saint Vincent island N Saint Vincent and the Grenadines
Saint Vincent see São Vicente
47 W14 Saint Vincent and the Grenadines ◆ commonwealth republic SE West Indies
Saint Vincent, Cape see São Vicente, Cabo de
104 I15 St-Vincent-de-Tyrosse Landes, SW France 43.39N 1.16W
190 I9 Saint Vincent, Gulf gulf South Australia
25 R10 Saint Vincent Island island Florida, SE USA
47 T12 Saint Vincent Passage passage Saint Lucia/Saint Vincent and the Grenadines
191 N18 Saint Vincent, Point headland Tasmania, SE Australia 43.19S 145.50E
Saint-Vith see Sankt-Vith
9 S14 St.Walburg Saskatchewan, S Canada 53.37N 109.12W
St Wolfgangsee see Wolfgangsee
104 M11 St-Yrieix-la-Perche Haute-Vienne, C France 45.31N 1.12E
Saint Yves see Setúbal
13 Y5 St-Yvon Quebec, SE Canada 49.09N 64.51W
196 H5 Saipan island ● (Northern Mariana Islands) S Northern Mariana Islands
196 H6 Saipan Channel channel S Northern Mariana Islands
196 H6 Saipan International Airport ✕ Saipan, S Northern Mariana Islands
76 G6 Saïs ✕ (Fès) C Morocco 33.58N 4.48W
Saishū see Cheju
Saishū see Cheju-do
104 J16 Saison ≈ SW France
174 L7 Sai, Sungai ≈ Borneo, N Indonesia
171 Jj16 Saitama off. Saitama-ken. ◐ prefecture Honshū, S Japan
170 Cc16 Saito Miyazaki, Kyūshū, SW Japan 32.07N 131.22E
Saiyid Abid see Sayyid 'Abīd
59 J19 Sajama, Nevado ▲ W Bolivia 17.57S 68.51W
147 V13 Sājir, Ras headland S Oman 16.42N 53.40E
113 M20 Sajószentpéter Borsod-Abaúj-Zemplén, NE Hungary 48.13N 20.43E
85 F24 Sak ≈ SW South Africa
83 J18 Saka Coast, E Kenya 0.11S 39.27E
178 I11 Sa Kaeo Prachin Buri, C Thailand 13.47N 102.03E
171 Gg15 Sakai Ōsaka, Honshū, SW Japan 34.34N 135.28E
170 F14 Sakaide Kagawa, Shikoku, SW Japan 34.19N 133.49E
170 Ff12 Sakaiminato Tottori, Honshū, SW Japan 35.34N 133.12E
146 M3 Sakākah Al Jawf, NW Saudi Arabia 29.55N 40.10E
30 L4 Sakakawea, Lake ⊡ North Dakota, N USA
10 J9 Sakami, Lac ◎ Quebec, C Canada
81 O26 Sakania Katanga, SE Dem. Rep. Congo (Zaire) 12.43S 28.34E
152 K12 Sakar Lebapskiy Velayat, E Turkmenistan 38.57N 63.46E
180 H7 Sakaraha Toliara, SW Madagascar 22.54S 44.31E
152 I14 Sakar-Chaga Turkm. Sakarchäge. Maryyskiy Velayat, C Turkmenistan 37.40N 61.33E
Sakarchäge see Sakar-Chaga
Sak'art'velo see Georgia
142 F11 Sakarya ◐ province NW Turkey
142 F12 Sakarya Nehri ≈ NW Turkey
150 K13 Saksaul'skiy var. Saksaul'skoye Kaz. Seksëuil. Kyzylorda, S Kazakhstan 47.07N 61.06E
Saksaul'skoye see Saksaul'skiy
171 Ll11 Sakata Yamagata, Honshū, C Japan 38.54N 139.51E
126 I9 Sakha (Yakutiya), Respublika var. Respublika Yakutiya, Yakutiya, Eng. Yakutia. ◐ autonomous republic NE Russian Federation
Sakhalin see Sakhalin, Ostrov
127 Oo14 Sakhalin, Ostrov var. Sakhalin. island SE Russian Federation
127 P14 Sakhalinskaya Oblast' ◐ province SE Russian Federation
127 Nn13 Sakhalinskiy Zaliv gulf E Russian Federation
Sakhnovshchina see Sakhnovshchyna
119 U6 Sakhnovshchyna Rus. Sakhnovshchina. Kharkivs'ka Oblast', E Ukraine 49.08N 35.51E
Sakhon Nakhon see Sakon Nakhon
Sakhtsar see Rāmsar
Saki see Saky
143 W10 Şäki Rus. Sheki; prev. Nukha. NW Azerbaijan 41.09N 47.10E
120 E13 Šakiai Ger. Schaken. Šakiai, S Lithuania 54.57N 23.04E
176 Z16 Sakiramke Irian Jaya, E Indonesia 8.36S 140.55E
172 Oo16 Sakishima-shotō var. Sakisima Syotô. island group SW Japan
Sakiz see Saqqez
Sakiz-Adasi see Chíos
161 F19 Sakleshpur Karnātaka, E India 12.58N 75.45E
178 J9 Sakon Nakhon var. Muang Sakon Nakhon, Sakhon Nakhon. Sakon Nakhon, E Thailand 17.10N 104.07E
155 P15 Sakrand Sind, SE Pakistan 26.10N 68.13E
85 F24 Sak River Afr. Sakrivier. Northern Cape, W South Africa 30.49S 20.24E
Sakrivier see Sak River
Saksaul'skiy see Saksaul'skoye
150 K13 Saksaul'skoye prev. Saksaul'skiy, Kaz. Seksëuil. Kzylorda, S Kazakhstan 47.07N 61.06E
97 I25 Sakskøbing Storstrøm, SE Denmark 54.48N 11.39E
171 Jj15 Saku Nagano, Honshū, S Japan 36.15N 138.28E
171 K16 Sakura Chiba, Honshū, S Japan 35.42N 140.16E
119 S13 Saky Rus. Saki. Respublika Krym, S Ukraine 45.08N 33.36E
78 E9 Sal island Ilhas de Barlavento, NE Cape Verde
131 N12 Sal ≈ SW Russian Federation
113 I21 Sal'a Hung. Sellye, Vágsellye. Nitriansky Kraj, SW Slovakia 48.08N 17.55E
97 N15 Sala Västmanland, C Sweden 59.55N 16.37E
175 Qq11 Salabangka, Kepulauan island group N Indonesia
13 N13 Salaberry-de-Valleyfield var. Valleyfield. Quebec, SE Canada 45.15N 74.07W
120 G7 Salacgrīva Est. Salatsi. Limbaži, N Latvia 57.45N 24.21E
109 M18 Sala Consilina Campania, S Italy 40.22N 15.34E
42 C2 Salada, Laguna ◎ NW Mexico
63 D14 Saladas Corrientes, NE Argentina 28.15S 58.40W
63 C21 Saladillo Buenos Aires, E Argentina 35.40S 59.49W
63 B16 Saladillo, Río ≈ C Argentina
27 T9 Salado Texas, SW USA 30.57N 97.32W
65 J16 Salado, Arroyo ≈ SE Argentina
39 Q12 Salado, Río ≈ New Mexico, SW USA
63 D21 Salado, Río ≈ E Argentina
64 J12 Salado, Río ≈ C Argentina
43 N7 Salado, Río ≈ NE Mexico
149 N6 Salafchegān var. Sarafjagān. Qom, N Iran 34.28N 50.28E
79 Q15 Salaga C Ghana 8.31N 0.37W
198 Aa7 Sala'ilua Savai'i, W Samoa 13.39S 172.33W
118 G9 Sălaj ◐ county NW Romania
85 H20 Salajwe Kweneng, SE Botswana 23.40S 24.46E
80 H9 Salal Kanem, W Chad 14.48N 17.12E
82 I6 Salala Red Sea, NE Sudan 21.16N 36.16E
147 V13 Şalālah SW Oman 17.01N 54.03E
44 D5 Salamá Baja Verapaz, C Guatemala 15.06N 90.18W
44 J6 Salamá Olancho, C Honduras 14.48N 86.34W
64 G10 Salamanca Coquimbo, C Chile 31.49S 70.58W
43 N13 Salamanca Guanajuato, C Mexico 20.33N 101.06W
106 K7 Salamanca anc. Helmantica, Salmantica. Castilla-León, NW Spain 40.58N 5.40W
20 D11 Salamanca New York, NE USA 42.09N 78.43W
106 J7 Salamanca ◐ province Castilla-León, W Spain
65 J19 Salamanca, Pampa de plain S Argentina
80 J12 Salamat off. Préfecture du Salamat. ◐ prefecture SE Chad
80 I12 Salamat, Bahr ≈ S Chad
56 F5 Salamina Magdalena, N Colombia 10.28N 74.46W
117 G19 Salamína var. Salamís. Salamína, C Greece 37.58N 23.28E
117 G19 Salamína island C Greece
Salamís see Salamína
144 I5 Salamīyah var. As Salamīyah. Ḩamāh, W Syria 35.01N 37.01E
33 P12 Salamonie Lake ⊡ Indiana, N USA
33 P12 Salamonie River ≈ Indiana, N USA
Salang see Phuket
198 Bb8 Salani Upolu, SE Samoa 14.00S 171.35W
120 C11 Salantai Kretinga, NW Lithuania 56.05N 21.36E
106 K2 Salas Asturias, N Spain 43.25N 6.15W
107 O5 Salas de los Infantes Castilla-León, N Spain 42.01N 3.16W
104 M16 Salat ≈ S France
201 V13 Salat island Chuuk, C Micronesia
174 L15 Salatiga Jawa, C Indonesia 7.15S 110.34E
201 V13 Salat Pass passage W Pacific Ocean
Salatsi see Salacgrīva
178 Jj10 Salavan var. Saravan, Saravane. Salavan, S Laos 15.43N 106.26E
131 V6 Salavat Respublika Bashkortostan, W Russian Federation 53.20N 55.54E
58 C12 Salaverry La Libertad, N Peru 8.15S 78.57W
176 Uu9 Salawati, Pulau island E Indonesia
200 Nn11 Sala y Gomez island Chile, E Pacific Ocean

◆ Country ● Country Capital ◇ Dependent Territory ○ Dependent Territory Capital ◐ Administrative Region ✕ International Airport ▲ Mountain ▲ Mountain Range ⛰ Volcano ≈ River ◎ Lake ⊡ Reservoir

Sala y Gomez Fracture Zone – San Esteban de Gormaz

Sala y Gomez Fracture Zone *see* Sala y Gomez Ridge
200 O11 **Sala y Gomez Ridge** *var.* Sala y Gomez Fracture Zone. *tectonic feature* SE Pacific Ocean
63 A22 **Salazar** Buenos Aires, E Argentina 36.19S 62.10W
56 G7 **Salazar** Norte de Santander, N Colombia 7.46N 72.46W
Salazar *see* N'Dalatando
181 P16 **Salazie** C Réunion 21.01S 55.33E
105 N8 **Salbris** Loir-et-Cher, C France 47.25N 2.02E
59 G15 **Salcantay, Nevado** ▲ C Peru 13.21S 72.31W
47 O8 **Salcedo** N Dominican Republic 19.21N 70.23W
41 S9 **Salcha River** ≈ Alaska, USA
121 H15 **Šalčininkai** Šalčininkai, SE Lithuania 54.19N 25.26E
Saldae *see* Béjaïa
56 E11 **Saldaña** Tolima, C Colombia 3.57N 75.01W
106 M4 **Saldaña** Castilla-León, N Spain 42.31N 4.43W
85 E25 **Saldanha** Western Cape, SW South Africa 33.00S 17.56E
Salduba *see* Zaragoza
63 B23 **Saldungaray** Buenos Aires, E Argentina 38.15S 61.45W
120 D9 **Saldus** *Ger.* Frauenburg. Saldus, W Latvia 56.40N 22.29E
191 P13 **Sale** Victoria, SE Australia 38.06S 147.06E
76 F6 **Salé** NW Morocco 34.07N 6.40W
76 F6 **Salé** ✕ (Rabat) W Morocco 34.09N 6.30W
Salehābād *see* Andīmeshk
174 Ii10 **Saleh, Air** ≈ Sumatera, W Indonesia
175 Oo16 **Saleh, Teluk** *bay* Nusa Tenggara, S Indonesia
125 G8 **Salekhard** *prev.* Obdorsk. Yamalo-Nenetskiy Avtonomnyy Okrug, N Russian Federation 66.33N 66.34E
198 B7 **Sālelologa** Savai'i, C Samoa 13.42S 172.10W
161 H21 **Salem** Tamil Nādu, SE India 11.37N 78.07E
29 V9 **Salem** Arkansas, C USA 36.21N 91.49W
32 L15 **Salem** Illinois, N USA 38.37N 88.57W
33 P15 **Salem** Indiana, N USA 38.37N 86.06W
21 P11 **Salem** Massachusetts, NE USA 42.30N 70.51W
29 V6 **Salem** Missouri, C USA 37.39N 91.32W
20 I16 **Salem** New Jersey, NE USA 39.33N 75.26W
33 U12 **Salem** Ohio, N USA 40.52N 80.51W
34 G12 **Salem** *state capital* Oregon, NW USA 44.57N 123.01W
31 Q11 **Salem** South Dakota, N USA 43.43N 97.23W
38 L4 **Salem** Utah, W USA 40.03N 111.40W
23 S7 **Salem** Virginia, NE USA 37.16N 80.00W
23 R3 **Salem** West Virginia, NE USA 39.15N 80.32W
109 H23 **Salemi** Sicilia, Italy, C Mediterranean Sea 37.48N 12.48E
Salemy *see* As Sālimī
96 K12 **Sälen** Dalarna, C Sweden 61.11N 13.14E
109 Q18 **Salentina, Campi** Puglia, SE Italy 40.22N 18.01E
109 Q18 **Salentina, Penisola** *peninsula* SE Italy
109 L18 **Salerno** *anc.* Salernum. Campania, S Italy 40.40N 14.43E
109 L18 **Salerno, Golfo di** *Eng.* Gulf of Salerno. *gulf* S Italy
Salerno, Gulf of *see* Salerno, Golfo di
Salernum *see* Salerno
99 K17 **Salford** NW England, UK 53.30N 2.16W
Salgir *see* Salhyr
113 K21 **Salgótarján** Nógrád, N Hungary 48.06N 19.46E
61 O15 **Salgueiro** Pernambuco, E Brazil 8.04S 39.04W
96 C13 **Salhus** Hordaland, S Norway 60.30N 5.15E
119 T12 **Salhyr** *Rus.* Salgir. ≈ S Ukraine
175 S4 **Salibabu, Pulau** *island* N Indonesia
39 S6 **Salida** Colorado, C USA 38.29N 105.57W
104 J15 **Salies-de-Béarn** Pyrénées-Atlantiques, SW France 43.28N 0.55W
142 C14 **Salihli** Manisa, W Turkey 38.28N 28.07E
121 K18 **Salihorsk** *Rus.* Soligorsk. Minskaya Voblasts', S Belarus 52.48N 27.31E
121 K18 **Salihorskaye Vodaskhovishcha** ⊡ C Belarus
85 N14 **Salima** Central, C Malawi 13.44S 34.21E
177 Ff5 **Salin** Magwe, W Burma 20.30N 94.40E
29 N4 **Salina** Kansas, C USA 38.50N 97.36W
38 L5 **Salina** Utah, W USA 38.57N 111.54W
43 S17 **Salina Cruz** Oaxaca, SE Mexico 16.10N 95.12W
109 L22 **Salina, Isola** *island* Isole Eolie, S Italy
46 J5 **Salina Point** *headland* Acklins Island, SE Bahamas 22.10N 74.16W
58 A7 **Salinas** Guayas, W Ecuador 2.15S 80.54W
42 M11 **Salinas** *var.* Salinas de Hidalgo. San Luis Potosí, C Mexico 22.36N 101.41W
47 T6 **Salinas** C Puerto Rico 17.58N 66.18W
37 O10 **Salinas** California, W USA 36.40N 121.40W
Salinas, Cabo de *see* Salines, Cap de ses
Salinas de Hidalgo *see* Salinas
84 A13 **Salinas, Ponta das** *headland* W Angola 12.50S 12.57E
47 O10 **Salinas, Punta** *headland* S Dominican Republic 18.11N 70.32W
Salinas, Río *see* Chixoy, Río
37 O11 **Salinas River** ≈ California, W USA
24 H6 **Saline Lake** ◎ Louisiana, S USA
27 R17 **Salineno** Texas, SW USA 26.29N 99.06W
29 V14 **Saline River** ≈ Arkansas, C USA
32 M17 **Saline River** ≈ Illinois, N USA
107 X10 **Salines, Cap de ses** *var.* Cabo de Salinas. *headland* Mallorca, Spain, W Mediterranean Sea 39.15N 3.03E
Salisburg *see* Mazsalaca
47 O12 **Salisbury** *var.* Baroui. W Dominica 15.25N 61.27W
99 M23 **Salisbury** *var.* New Sarum. S England, UK 51.04N 1.48W
23 Y4 **Salisbury** Maryland, NE USA 38.21N 75.36W
29 T3 **Salisbury** Missouri, C USA 39.25N 92.48W
23 S9 **Salisbury** North Carolina, SE USA 35.40N 80.28W
Salisbury *see* Harare
16 N5 **Salisbury Island** *island* Nunavut, NE Canada
Salisbury, Lake *see* Bisina, Lake
99 L23 **Salisbury Plain** *plain* S England, UK
23 R14 **Salkehatchie River** ≈ South Carolina, SE USA
144 I9 **Şalkhad** As Suwaydā', SW Syria 32.28N 36.42E
94 M12 **Salla** Lappi, NE Finland 66.49N 28.40E
105 U11 **Sallanches** Haute-Savoie, E France 45.55N 6.37E
107 V5 **Sallent** Cataluña, NE Spain 41.48N 1.52E
63 A22 **Salliqueló** Buenos Aires, E Argentina 36.42S 62.52W
29 R10 **Sallisaw** Oklahoma, C USA 35.29N 94.47W
82 I7 **Sallom** Red Sea, NE Sudan 19.30N 37.11E
10 J2 **Salluit** *prev.* Saglouc, Sagluk. Quebec, NE Canada 62.10N 75.40W
Sallūm, Khalīj as *see* Salûm, Gulf of
11 S11 **Sally's Cove** Newfoundland, E Canada 49.43N 58.00W
145 W9 **Salmān Bin 'Arāzah** E Iraq 32.33N 46.36E
Salmantica *see* Salamanca
148 I2 **Salmās** *prev.* Dilman, Shāpūr. Āžarbāyjān-e Bākhtarī, NW Iran 38.13N 44.49E
128 I11 **Salmi** Respublika Kareliya, NW Russian Federation 61.21N 31.55E
35 P12 **Salmon** Idaho, NW USA 45.10N 113.54W
9 N16 **Salmon Arm** British Columbia, SW Canada 50.40N 119.18W
199 Jj5 **Salmon Bank** *undersea feature* N Pacific Ocean 26.55N 176.28W
Salmon Leap *see* Leixlip
36 L2 **Salmon Mountains** ▲▲ California, W USA
12 J15 **Salmon Point** *headland* Ontario, SE Canada 43.51N 77.15W
35 N11 **Salmon River** ≈ Idaho, NW USA
20 K6 **Salmon River** ≈ New York, NE USA
35 N12 **Salmon River Mountains** ▲▲ Idaho, NW USA
20 I9 **Salmon River Reservoir** ⊡ New York, NE USA
95 K19 **Salo** Länsi-Suomi, W Finland 60.22N 23.10E
108 F7 **Salò** Lombardia, N Italy 45.37N 10.30E
Salona/Salonae *see* Solin
105 S15 **Salon-de-Provence** Bouches-du-Rhône, SE France 43.39N 5.04E
Salonica/Salonika *see* Thessaloníki
117 I14 **Salonikós, Akrotírio** *headland* Thásos, E Greece 40.34N 24.39E
118 F10 **Salonta** *Hung.* Nagyszalonta. Bihor, W Romania 46.47N 21.37E
106 I9 **Salor** ≈ W Spain
107 U6 **Salou** Cataluña, NE Spain 41.04N 1.07E
78 H11 **Saloum** ≈ C Senegal
44 H4 **Sal, Punta** *headland* NW Honduras 15.55N 87.36W
94 N3 **Salpynten** *headland* W Svalbard 78.12N 12.11E
144 I3 **Salqīn** Idlib, W Syria 36.09N 36.27E
95 F14 **Salsbruket** Nord-Trøndelag, C Norway 64.49N 11.48E
130 M13 **Sal'sk** Rostovskaya Oblast', SW Russian Federation 46.30N 41.30E
109 K25 **Salso** ≈ Sicilia, Italy, C Mediterranean Sea
109 J25 **Salso** ≈ Sicilia, Italy, C Mediterranean Sea
108 E9 **Salsomaggiore Terme** Emilia-Romagna, N Italy 44.49N 9.58E
Salt *see* As Salt
64 J6 **Salta** Salta, NW Argentina 24.47S 65.23W
64 K6 **Salta** *off.* Provincia de Salta. ◐ *province* N Argentina
99 I24 **Saltash** SW England, UK 50.26N 4.13W
26 I8 **Salt Basin** *basin* Texas, SW USA
9 V16 **Saltcoats** Saskatchewan, S Canada 51.06N 102.12W
32 L13 **Salt Creek** ≈ Illinois, N USA
26 J9 **Salt Draw** ≈ Texas, SW USA
99 F21 **Saltee Islands** *island group* SE Ireland
94 G12 **Saltfjorden** *inlet* C Norway
26 I8 **Salt Flat** Texas, SW USA 31.43N 105.05W
29 N8 **Salt Fork Arkansas River** ≈ Oklahoma, C USA
33 T13 **Salt Fork Lake** ◎ Ohio, N USA
28 J11 **Salt Fork Red River** ≈ Oklahoma/Texas, C USA
97 J23 **Saltholm** *island* E Denmark
43 N8 **Saltillo** Coahuila de Zaragoza, NE Mexico 25.30N 101.00W
190 L5 **Salt Lake** *salt lake* New South Wales, SE Australia
39 V15 **Salt Lake** ◎ New Mexico, SW USA
38 K2 **Salt Lake City** *state capital* Utah, W USA 40.44N 111.54W
63 C20 **Salto** Buenos Aires, E Argentina 34.18S 60.17W
63 D17 **Salto** Salto, N Uruguay 31.22S 57.58W
63 E17 **Salto** ◐ *department* N Uruguay
109 I14 **Salto** ≈ C Italy
64 Q6 **Salto del Guairá** Canindeyú, E Paraguay 24.06S 54.22W
63 D17 **Salto Grande, Embalse de** *var.* Lago de Salto Grande. ⊡ Argentina/Uruguay
Salto Grande, Lago de *see* Salto Grande, Embalse de
37 W16 **Salton Sea** ◎ California, W USA
62 I12 **Salto Santiago, Represa de** ⊡ S Brazil
155 U7 **Salt Range** ▲▲ E Pakistan
38 M13 **Salt River** ≈ Arizona, SW USA
22 L5 **Salt River** ≈ Kentucky, S USA
29 V3 **Salt River** ≈ Missouri, C USA
97 F17 **Saltrød** Aust-Agder, S Norway 58.28N 8.49E
97 P16 **Saltsjöbaden** Stockholm, C Sweden 59.15N 18.19E
94 G12 **Saltstraumen** Nordland, C Norway 67.16N 14.42E
23 Q7 **Saltville** Virginia, NE USA 36.52N 81.48W
Saluces/Saluciae *see* Saluzzo
23 Q12 **Saluda** South Carolina, SE USA 34.00N 81.47W
23 X6 **Saluda** Virginia, NE USA 37.36N 76.36W
23 Q12 **Saluda River** ≈ South Carolina, SE USA
175 R10 **Salue Timpaus, Selat** *var.* Selat Banggai. *strait* N Banda Sea
77 T7 **Salûm** *var.* As Sallūm. NW Egypt 31.31N 25.09E
158 F14 **Sālūmbar** Rājasthān, N India 24.16N 74.04E
77 T7 **Salûm, Gulf of** *Ar.* Khalīj as Sallūm. *gulf* Egypt/Libya
175 Q7 **Salumpaga** Sulawesi, N Indonesia 1.18N 120.58E
161 M14 **Sālūr** Andhra Pradesh, E India 18.31N 83.16E
57 Y9 **Salut, Îles du** *island group* N French Guiana
108 A9 **Saluzzo** *Fr.* Saluces; *anc.* Saluciae. Piemonte, NW Italy 44.39N 7.28E
65 F23 **Salvación, Bahía** *bay* S Chile
61 P17 **Salvador** *prev.* São Salvador. Bahia, E Brazil 12.58S 38.28W
67 E24 **Salvador** East Falkland, Falkland Islands 51.28S 58.22W
24 K10 **Salvador, Lake** ◎ Louisiana, S USA
Salvaleón de Higüey *see* Higüey
106 F10 **Salvaterra de Magos** Santarém, C Portugal 39.01N 8.46W
43 N13 **Salvatierra** Guanajuato, C Mexico 20.13N 100.52W
107 P3 **Salvatierra** *Basq.* Agurain. País Vasco, N Spain 42.52N 2.22W
Salwa/Salwah *see* As Salwā
178 F5 **Salween** *Bur.* Thanlwin, *Chin.* Nu Chiang, Nu Jiang. ≈ SE Asia
143 Y12 **Salyan** *Rus.* Sal'yany. SE Azerbaijan 39.36N 48.57E
159 N11 **Salyan** *var.* Sallyana. Mid Western, W Nepal 28.22N 82.10E
Sal'yany *see* Salyan
23 O6 **Salyersville** Kentucky, S USA 37.44N 83.01W
111 V6 **Salza** ≈ E Austria
111 Q7 **Salzach** ≈ Austria/Germany
111 Q6 **Salzburg** *anc.* Juvavum. Salzburg, N Austria 47.48N 13.03E
111 O8 **Salzburg** *off.* Land Salzburg. ◐ *state* C Austria
Salzburg *see* Ocna Sibiului
Salzburg Alps *see* Salzburger Kalkalpen
111 Q7 **Salzburger Kalkalpen** *Eng.* Salzburg Alps. ▲ C Austria
102 J13 **Salzgitter** *prev.* Watenstedt-Salzgitter. Niedersachsen, C Germany 52.06N 10.24E
103 G14 **Salzkotten** Nordrhein-Westfalen, W Germany 51.40N 8.36E
102 K11 **Salzwedel** Sachsen-Anhalt, N Germany 52.51N 11.10E
158 D11 **Sām** Rājasthān, NW India 26.49N 70.30E
Šamac *see* Bosanski Šamac
56 G9 **Samacá** Boyacá, C Colombia 5.26N 73.30W
42 I7 **Samachique** Chihuahua, N Mexico 27.16N 107.28W
147 Y8 **Şamad** NE Oman 22.45N 58.07E
Sama de Langreo *see* Sama
Samaden *see* Samedan
59 M19 **Samaipata** Santa Cruz, C Bolivia 18.09S 63.49W
178 J11 **Samakhixai** *var.* Attapu, Attopeu. Attapu, S Laos 14.48N 106.51E
Samakov *see* Samokov
44 B6 **Samalá, Río** ≈ SW Guatemala
42 J3 **Samalayuca** Chihuahua, N Mexico 31.14N 106.28W
179 Q17 **Samales Group** *island group* Sulu Archipelago, SW Philippines
161 L16 **Sāmalkot** Andhra Pradesh, E India 17.03N 82.15E
47 P8 **Samaná** *var.* Santa Bárbara de Samaná. E Dominican Republic 19.11N 69.19W
47 P8 **Samaná, Bahía de** *bay* E Dominican Republic
46 K4 **Samana Cay** *island* SE Bahamas
142 K17 **Samandağı** Hatay, S Turkey 36.06N 35.56E
155 P3 **Samangān** ◐ *province* N Afghanistan
Samangān *see* Āybak
172 P8 **Samani** Hokkaidō, NE Japan 42.07N 142.57E
56 C13 **Samaniego** Nariño, SW Colombia 1.22N 77.34W
179 R12 **Samar** *island* C Philippines
131 S6 **Samara** *prev.* Kuybyshev. Samarskaya Oblast', W Russian Federation 53.15N 50.15E
131 S6 **Samara** ✕ Samarskaya Oblast', W Russian Federation 53.11N 50.27E
131 T7 **Samara** ≈ W Russian Federation
119 V7 **Samara** ≈ E Ukraine
195 N17 **Samarai** Milne Bay, SE PNG 10.37S 150.39E
Samarang *see* Semarang
144 G9 **Samarian Hills** *hill range* N Israel
56 L9 **Samariapo** Amazonas, C Venezuela 5.13N 67.47W
175 O8 **Samarinda** Borneo, C Indonesia 0.30S 117.09E
Samarkand *see* Samarqand
Samarkandskaya Oblast' *see* Samarqand Wiloyati
Samarkandski/Samarkandskoye *see* Temirtau
Samarobriva *see* Amiens
153 N11 **Samarqand** *Rus.* Samarkand. Samarqand Wiloyati, C Uzbekistan 39.39N 66.55E
152 M11 **Samarqand Wiloyati** *Rus.* Samarkandskaya Oblast'. ◐ *province* C Uzbekistan
145 S6 **Sāmarrā'** C Iraq 34.13N 43.52E
131 R7 **Samarskaya Oblast'** *prev.* Kuybyshevskaya Oblast'. ◐ *province* W Russian Federation
159 Q13 **Samastipur** Bihār, N India 25.52N 85.46E
78 L14 **Samatiguila** NW Ivory Coast 9.51N 7.36W
121 Q17 **Samatsevichy** *Rus.* Samotevichi. Mahilyowskaya Voblasts', E Belarus 53.12N 31.49E
Samawa *see* As Samāwah
143 Y11 **Şamaxı** *Rus.* Shemakha. C Azerbaijan 40.31N 48.54E
158 H6 **Samba** Jammu and Kashmir, NW India 32.31N 75.07E
81 K18 **Samba** Equateur, NW Dem. Rep. Congo (Zaire) 0.13N 21.16E
81 N21 **Samba** Maniema, E Dem. Rep. Congo (Zaire) 4.40S 26.22E
175 Oo6 **Sambaliung, Pegunungan** ▲▲ Borneo, N Indonesia
160 M11 **Sambalpur** Orissa, E India 21.28N 83.04E
69 X12 **Sambao** ≈ W Madagascar
174 Kk7 **Sambas, Sungai** ≈ Borneo, N Indonesia
180 K2 **Sambava** Antsiranana, NE Madagascar 14.16S 50.10E
176 Ww9 **Samberi** Irian Jaya, E Indonesia 1.07S 135.54E
158 J10 **Sambhal** Uttar Pradesh, N India 28.34N 78.34E
158 H12 **Sāmbhar Salt Lake** ◎ N India
109 N21 **Sambiase** Calabria, SW Italy 38.58N 16.16E
118 H5 **Sambir** *Rus.* Sambor. L'vivs'ka Oblast', NW Ukraine 49.29N 23.09E
84 C13 **Sambo** Huambo, C Angola 13.07S 16.06E
Sambor *see* Sambir
63 E21 **Samborombón, Bahía** *bay* NE Argentina
101 H20 **Sambre** ≈ Belgium/France
45 V16 **Sambú, Río** ≈ SE Panama
169 Z14 **Samch'ŏk** *Jap.* Sanchoku. NE South Korea 37.21N 129.12E
Samch'ŏnpŏ *see* Sach'ŏn
83 I21 **Same** Kilimanjaro, NE Tanzania 4.02S 37.46E
110 J10 **Samedan** *Ger.* Samaden. Graubünden, S Switzerland 46.31N 9.51E
84 K12 **Samfya** Luapula, N Zambia 11.25S 29.30E
147 W13 **Samhān, Jabal** ▲ SW Oman
117 C18 **Sámi** Kefallinía, Iónioi Nísoi, Greece, C Mediterranean Sea 38.15N 20.39E
58 F10 **Samiria, Río** ≈ N Peru
Samirum *see* Semīrom
143 V11 **Şämkir** *Rus.* Shamkhor. NW Azerbaijan 40.51N 46.03E
178 J7 **Sam, Nam** *Vtn.* Sông Chu. ≈ Laos/Vietnam
Samnān *see* Semnān
Sam Neua *see* Xam Nua
77 P10 **Samnū** C Libya 27.19N 15.01E
198 Bb7 **Samoa** *off.* Independent State of Samoa, *var.* Sāmoa; *prev.* Western Samoa. ◆ *monarchy* W Polynesia
198 C8 **Sāmoa** *island group* American Samoa
Sāmoa *see* Samoa
183 T9 **Samoa Basin** *undersea feature* W Pacific Ocean
Sāmoa-i-Sisifo *see* Samoa
114 D8 **Samobor** Zagreb, N Croatia 45.48N 15.38E
116 H10 **Samokov** *var.* Samakov. Sofiya, W Bulgaria 42.19N 23.34E
113 H21 **Šamorín** *Ger.* Sommerein, *Hung.* Somorja. Trnavský Kraj, W Slovakia 48.01N 17.18E
117 M19 **Sámos** *prev.* Limín Vathéos. Sámos, Dodekánisos, Greece, Aegean Sea 37.46N 26.58E
117 M20 **Sámos** *island* Dodekánisos, Greece, Aegean Sea
Samosch *see* Szamos
173 Ff5 **Samosir, Pulau** *island* W Indonesia
Samotevichi *see* Samatsevichy
Samothrace *see* Samothráki
117 K14 **Samothráki** Samothráki, NE Greece 40.28N 25.31E
117 J14 **Samothráki** *anc.* Samothrace. *island* NE Greece
117 A15 **Samothráki** *island* Iónioi Nísoi, Greece, C Mediterranean Sea
Samotschin *see* Szamocin
174 M10 **Sampit** Borneo, C Indonesia 2.30S 112.30E
174 M10 **Sampit, Sungai** ≈ Borneo, N Indonesia
Sampoku *see* Sanpoku
195 P11 **Sampun** New Britain, E PNG 5.19S 152.06E
81 N24 **Sampwe** Katanga, SE Dem. Rep. Congo (Zaire) 9.17S 27.22E
27 X8 **Sam Rayburn Reservoir** ⊡ Texas, SW USA
178 Ii6 **Sam Sao, Phou** ▲▲ Laos/Thailand
97 H22 **Samsø** *island* E Denmark
97 H23 **Samsø Bælt** *channel* E Denmark
178 Jj7 **Sâm Sơn** Thanh Hoa, N Vietnam 19.43N 105.52E
142 L11 **Samsun** *anc.* Amisus. Samsun, N Turkey 41.16N 36.22E
142 K11 **Samsun** ◐ *province* N Turkey
143 R9 **Samtredia** W Georgia 42.09N 42.20E
61 E15 **Samuel, Represa de** ⊡ W Brazil
178 H15 **Samui, Ko** *island* SW Thailand
Samundari *see* Samundri
155 U9 **Samundri** *var.* Samundari. Punjab, E Pakistan 31.04N 72.58E
143 X10 **Samur** ≈ Azerbaijan/Russian Federation
143 Y11 **Samur-Abşeron Kanalı** *Rus.* Samur-Apsheronskiy Kanal. *canal* E Azerbaijan
Samur-Apsheronskiy Kanal *see* Samur-Abşeron Kanalı
178 Hh11 **Samut Prakan** *var.* Muang Samut Prakan, Paknam. Samut Prakan, C Thailand 13.33N 100.13E
178 H11 **Samut Sakhon** *var.* Maha Chai, Samut Sakorn, *Tha Chin.* Samut Sakhon, C Thailand 13.31N 100.15E
Samut Sakorn *see* Samut Sakhon
178 H11 **Samut Songhram** *prev.* Meklong. Samut Songkhram, SW Thailand 13.25N 100.01E
79 N12 **San** Ségou, C Mali 13.18N 4.51W
113 O15 **San** ≈ SE Poland
147 O15 **Şan'ā'** *Eng.* Sana. ● (Yemen) W Yemen 15.24N 44.13E
114 F11 **Sana** ≈ NW Bosnia and Herzegovina
82 O12 **Sanaag** *off.* Gobolka Sanaag. ◐ *region* N Somalia
116 J8 **Sanadinovo** Pleven, N Bulgaria 43.33N 25.00E
205 P1 **Sanae** *South African research station* Antarctica 70.19S 1.31W
145 Y10 **Sanāf, Hawr as** ◎ S Iraq
81 E15 **Sanaga** ≈ C Cameroon
56 D12 **San Agustín** Huila, SW Colombia 1.52N 76.13W
179 S16 **San Agustin, Cape** *headland* Mindanao, S Philippines 6.17N 126.12E
39 Q13 **San Agustin, Plains of** *plain* New Mexico, SW USA
40 M16 **Sanak Islands** *island group* Aleutian Islands, Alaska, USA
200 P11 **San Ambrosio, Isla** *Eng.* San Ambrosio Island. *island* W Chile
San Ambrosio Island *see* San Ambrosio, Isla
175 S10 **Sanana** Pulau Sanana, E Indonesia 2.04S 125.58E
175 S10 **Sanana, Pulau** *island* Maluku, E Indonesia
148 K5 **Sanandaj** *prev.* Sinneh. Kordestān, W Iran 35.18N 47.01E
37 P8 **San Andreas** California, W USA 38.10N 120.40W
2 C13 **San Andreas Fault** *fault* W USA
56 G8 **San Andrés** Santander, C Colombia 6.52N 72.52W
63 C20 **San Andrés de Giles** Buenos Aires, E Argentina 34.27S 59.27W
39 R14 **San Andres Mountains** ▲▲ New Mexico, SW USA
43 S15 **San Andrés Tuxtla** *var.* Tuxtla. Veracruz-Llave, E Mexico 18.27N 95.18W
27 P8 **San Angelo** Texas, SW USA 31.27N 100.26W
109 A20 **San Antioco, Isola di** *island* W Italy
44 F4 **San Antonio** Toledo, S Belize 16.13N 89.02W
64 G11 **San Antonio** Valparaíso, C Chile 33.35S 71.34W
196 H6 **San Antonio** Saipan, S Northern Mariana Islands
39 R13 **San Antonio** New Mexico, SW USA 33.53N 106.52W
27 R12 **San Antonio** Texas, SW USA 29.25N 98.29W
56 M11 **San Antonio** Amazonas, S Venezuela 3.31N 66.46W
56 I7 **San Antonio** Barinas, C Venezuela 7.24N 71.28W
57 O5 **San Antonio** Monagas, NE Venezuela 10.03N 63.45W
27 S12 **San Antonio** ✕ Texas, SW USA 29.31N 98.11W
San Antonio *see* San Antonio del Táchira
107 V11 **San Antonio Abad** Eivissa, Spain, W Mediterranean Sea 38.58N 1.18E
27 U13 **San Antonio Bay** *inlet* Texas, SW USA
63 E22 **San Antonio, Cabo** *headland* E Argentina 36.45S 56.40W
46 A5 **San Antonio, Cabo de** *headland* W Cuba 21.51N 84.58W
107 T11 **San Antonio, Cabo de** *headland* E Spain 38.50N 0.09E
56 H7 **San Antonio de Caparo** Táchira, W Venezuela 7.34N 71.28W
64 J5 **San Antonio de los Cobres** Salta, NE Argentina 24.14S 66.17W
56 H7 **San Antonio del Táchira** *var.* San Antonio. Táchira, W Venezuela 7.49N 72.27W
37 T15 **San Antonio, Mount** ▲ California, W USA 34.18N 117.37W
65 K16 **San Antonio Oeste** Río Negro, E Argentina 40.45S 64.58W
27 T13 **San Antonio River** ≈ Texas, SW USA
56 J5 **Sanare** Lara, N Venezuela 9.45N 69.39W
105 T16 **Sanary-sur-Mer** Var, SE France 43.07N 5.48E
27 X8 **San Augustine** Texas, SW USA 31.31N 94.06W
147 T13 **Sanāw** *var.* Sanaw. NE Yemen 18.00N 51.00E
43 O11 **San Bartolo** San Luis Potosí, C Mexico 22.19N 100.04W
109 L16 **San Bartolomeo in Galdo** Campania, S Italy 41.24N 15.01E
108 K13 **San Benedetto del Tronto** Marche, C Italy 42.57N 13.52E
44 E3 **San Benito** Petén, N Guatemala 16.55N 89.58W
27 T17 **San Benito** Texas, SW USA 26.07N 97.37W
56 E6 **San Benito Abad** Sucre, N Colombia 8.55N 75.01W
37 P11 **San Benito Mountain** ▲ California, W USA 36.21N 120.37W
37 O10 **San Benito River** ≈ California, W USA
110 H10 **San Bernardino** Graubünden, S Switzerland 46.21N 9.13E
37 U15 **San Bernardino** California, W USA 34.06N 117.15W
64 H11 **San Bernardo** Santiago, C Chile 33.36S 70.40W
42 J8 **San Bernardo** Durango, C Mexico 25.58N 105.27W
170 F12 **Sanbe-san** ▲ Kyūshū, SW Japan 35.09N 132.36E
42 J12 **San Blas** Nayarit, C Mexico 21.33N 105.17W
42 H8 **San Blas** Sinaloa, C Mexico 26.05N 108.44W
45 V14 **San Blas** *off.* Comarca de San Blas. ◐ *special territory* NE Panama
45 U14 **San Blas, Archipiélago de** *island group* NE Panama
25 Q10 **San Blas, Cape** *headland* Florida, SE USA 29.39N 85.21W
45 V14 **San Blas, Cordillera de** ▲▲ NE Panama
64 J8 **San Blas de los Sauces** Catamarca, NW Argentina 28.18S 67.12W
108 G8 **San Bonifacio** Veneto, NE Italy 45.22N 11.14E
31 S12 **Sanborn** Iowa, C USA 43.10N 95.39W
42 M7 **San Buenaventura** Coahuila de Zaragoza, NE Mexico 27.03N 101.33W
107 S5 **San Caprasio** ▲ N Spain 41.45N 0.26W
64 G13 **San Carlos** Bío Bío, C Chile 36.25S 71.58W
42 E9 **San Carlos** Baja California Sur, W Mexico 24.52N 112.15W
43 N5 **San Carlos** Coahuila de Zaragoza, NE Mexico 29.00N 100.51W
San Carlos, Estrecho de *see* Falkland Sound
43 P9 **San Carlos** Tamaulipas, C Mexico 24.36N 98.42W
44 L12 **San Carlos** Río San Juan, S Nicaragua 11.06N 84.46W
45 T16 **San Carlos** Panamá, C Panama 8.28N 79.58W
179 P9 **San Carlos** *off.* San Carlos City. Luzon, N Philippines 15.57N 120.18E
38 M14 **San Carlos** Arizona, SW USA 33.21N 110.27W
63 G20 **San Carlos** Maldonado, S Uruguay 34.46S 54.58W
56 K5 **San Carlos** Cojedes, N Venezuela 9.39N 68.34W
San Carlos *see* Quesada, Costa Rica
San Carlos *see* Luba, Equatorial Guinea
63 B17 **San Carlos Centro** Santa Fe, C Argentina 31.45S 61.04W
179 Q13 **San Carlos City** Negros, C Philippines 10.34N 123.24E
San Carlos de Ancud *see* Ancud
65 H16 **San Carlos de Bariloche** Río Negro, SW Argentina 41.07S 71.15W
63 B21 **San Carlos de Bolívar** Buenos Aires, E Argentina 36.15S 61.06W
56 H6 **San Carlos del Zulia** Zulia, W Venezuela 9.01N 71.58W
56 L12 **San Carlos de Río Negro** Amazonas, S Venezuela 1.54N 67.54W
San Carlos, Estrecho de *see* Falkland Sound
38 M14 **San Carlos Reservoir** ⊡ Arizona, SW USA
44 M12 **San Carlos, Río** ≈ N Costa Rica
67 D24 **San Carlos Settlement** East Falkland, Falkland Islands
63 C23 **San Cayetano** Buenos Aires, E Argentina 38.19S 59.37W
105 O8 **Sancerre** Cher, C France 47.19N 2.53E
164 G7 **Sanchakou** Xinjiang Uygur Zizhiqu, NW China 39.58N 78.26E
Sanchoku *see* Samch'ŏk
43 O12 **San Ciro** San Luis Potosí, C Mexico 21.40N 99.49W
107 P10 **San Clemente** Castilla-La Mancha, C Spain 39.24N 2.25W
37 T16 **San Clemente** California, W USA 33.25N 117.36W
63 E21 **San Clemente del Tuyú** Buenos Aires, E Argentina 36.25S 56.45W
37 S17 **San Clemente Island** *island* Channel Islands, California, W USA
105 O9 **Sancoins** Cher, C France 46.49N 3.00E
195 Z17 **San Cristobal** *var.* Makira. *island* SE Solomon Islands
63 B16 **San Cristóbal** Santa Fe, C Argentina 30.19S 61.13W
46 B4 **San Cristóbal** Pinar del Río, W Cuba 22.43N 83.03W
47 O9 **San Cristóbal** *var.* Benemérita de San Cristóbal. S Dominican Republic 18.26N 70.07W
56 H7 **San Cristóbal** Táchira, W Venezuela 7.46N 72.15W
San Cristóbal *see* San Cristóbal de Las Casas
43 U16 **San Cristóbal de Las Casas** *var.* San Cristóbal. Chiapas, SE Mexico 16.43N 92.40W
200 Oo8 **San Cristóbal, Isla** *var.* Chatham Island. *island* Galapagos Islands, Ecuador, E Pacific Ocean
44 D5 **San Cristóbal Verapaz** Alta Verapaz, C Guatemala 15.22N 90.25W
46 F6 **Sancti Spíritus** Sancti Spíritus, C Cuba 21.54N 79.27W
105 O11 **Sancy, Puy de** ▲ C France 45.33N 2.48E
97 D15 **Sand** Rogaland, S Norway 59.28N 6.16E
175 Oo2 **Sandakan** Sabah, East Malaysia 5.52N 118.04E
190 K9 **Sandalwood** South Australia 34.51S 140.13E
Sandalwood Island *see* Sumba, Pulau
96 D11 **Sandane** Sogn og Fjordane, S Norway 61.46N 6.13E
116 G12 **Sandanski** *prev.* Sveti Vrach. Blagoevgrad, SW Bulgaria 41.36N 23.18E
78 J11 **Sandaré** Kayes, W Mali 14.36N 10.22W
97 J19 **Sandared** Västra Götaland, S Sweden 57.43N 12.46E
96 N12 **Sandarne** Gävleborg, C Sweden 61.15N 17.15E
194 E10 **Sandaun** *prev.* West Sepik. ◐ *province* NW PNG
98 K4 **Sanday** *island* NE Scotland, UK
179 N14 **Sand Cay** *island* W Spratly Islands
33 P15 **Sand Creek** ≈ Indiana, N USA
97 H15 **Sande** Vestfold, S Norway 59.34N 10.13E
97 H16 **Sandefjord** Vestfold, S Norway 59.07N 10.13E
79 O15 **Sandégué** E Ivory Coast 7.58N 3.33W
79 P14 **Sandema** N Ghana 10.42N 1.17W
39 O11 **Sanders** Arizona, SW USA 35.13N 109.21W
26 M11 **Sanderson** Texas, SW USA 30.08N 102.23W
25 U4 **Sandersville** Georgia, SE USA 32.58N 82.48W
94 H4 **Sandgerdhi** Sudhurland, SW Iceland 64.01N 22.42W
30 K14 **Sand Hills** ▲ Nebraska, C USA
27 S14 **Sandia** Texas, SW USA 27.59N 97.52W
37 T17 **San Diego** California, W USA 32.43N 117.09W
27 S14 **San Diego** Texas, SW USA 27.45N 98.14W
142 F14 **Sandıklı** Afyon, W Turkey 38.28N 30.16E
158 L12 **Sandila** Uttar Pradesh, N India 27.05N 80.37E
123 J15 **San Dimitri, Ras** *var.* San Dimitri Point. *headland* Gozo, NW Malta 36.04N 14.12E
174 Gg11 **Sanding, Selat** *strait* W Indonesia
32 J3 **Sand Island** *island* Apostle Islands, Wisconsin, N USA
97 C16 **Sandnes** Rogaland, S Norway 58.51N 5.45E
94 F13 **Sandnessjøen** Nordland, C Norway 66.00N 12.37E
81 L24 **Sandoa** Katanga, S Dem. Rep. Congo (Zaire) 9.39S 22.58E
113 N15 **Sandomierz** *Rus.* Sandomir. Świętokrzyskie, C Poland 50.42N 21.44E
Sandomir *see* Sandomierz
56 C13 **Sandoná** Nariño, SW Colombia 1.13N 77.29W
108 I7 **San Donà di Piave** Veneto, NE Italy 45.37N 12.34E
128 K14 **Sandovo** Tverskaya Oblast', W Russian Federation 58.26N 36.30E
177 Ff7 **Sandoway** Arakan State, W Burma 18.28N 94.19E
99 M24 **Sandown** S England, UK 50.39N 1.11W
97 B19 **Sandoy** *Dan.* Sandø *Island* Faeroe Islands 61.52N 6.51W
41 N16 **Sand Point** Popof Island, Alaska, USA 55.20N 160.30W
67 N24 **Sand Point** *headland* E Tristan da Cunha
33 R7 **Sand Point** *headland* Michigan, N USA 43.54N 83.24W
34 M7 **Sandpoint** Idaho, NW USA 48.16N 116.33W
95 H14 **Sandsele** Västerbotten, N Sweden 65.16N 17.40E
8 I14 **Sandspit** Moresby Island, British Columbia, SW Canada 53.13N 131.49W
29 P9 **Sand Springs** Oklahoma, C USA 36.08N 96.06W
31 W7 **Sandstone** Minnesota, N USA 46.07N 92.51W
38 K15 **Sand Tank Mountains** ▲▲ Arizona, SW USA
33 S8 **Sandusky** Michigan, N USA 43.24N 82.47W
33 S11 **Sandusky** Ohio, N USA 41.27N 82.42W
33 S12 **Sandusky River** ≈ Ohio, N USA
85 D22 **Sandverhaar** Karas, S Namibia 26.49S 17.25E
97 L24 **Sandvig** Bornholm, E Denmark 55.15N 14.45E
97 H15 **Sandvika** Akershus, S Norway 59.54N 10.28E
96 N13 **Sandviken** Gävleborg, C Sweden 60.37N 16.49E
32 M11 **Sandwich** Illinois, N USA 41.39N 88.37W
Sandwich Island *see* Éfaté
Sandwich Islands *see* Hawaiian Islands
159 V16 **Sandwip Island** *island* SE Bangladesh
9 U12 **Sandy Bay** Saskatchewan, C Canada 55.31N 102.14W
191 N16 **Sandy Cape** *headland* Tasmania, SE Australia 41.27S 144.43E
178 Mm14 **Sandy Cay** *island* NW Spratly Islands
38 L3 **Sandy City** Utah, W USA 40.36N 111.53W
33 U12 **Sandy Creek** ≈ Ohio, N USA
23 O5 **Sandy Hook** Kentucky, S USA 38.09N 83.05W
20 K15 **Sandy Hook** *headland* New Jersey, NE USA 40.27N 73.59W
152 J15 **Sandykachi** *Turkm.* Sandykgachy. Maryyskiy Velayat, S Turkmenistan 36.34N 62.28E
Sandykgachy *see* Sandykachi
152 L13 **Sandykly, Peski** *desert* E Turkmenistan
9 Q13 **Sandy Lake** Alberta, W Canada 55.50N 113.30W
10 B8 **Sandy Lake** Ontario, C Canada 53.00N 93.25W
10 B8 **Sandy Lake** ◎ Ontario, C Canada
25 S3 **Sandy Springs** Georgia, SE USA 33.57N 84.23W
26 H8 **San Elizario** Texas, SW USA 31.35N 106.16W
101 L25 **Sanem** Luxembourg, SW Luxembourg 49.33N 5.55E
44 K5 **San Esteban** Olancho, C Honduras 15.18N 85.45W
107 O6 **San Esteban de Gormaz** Castilla-León, N Spain 41.34N 3.13W

◆ Country ● Country Capital ◇ Dependent Territory ○ Dependent Territory Capital ◐ Administrative Region ✕ International Airport ▲ Mountain ▲▲ Mountain Range Volcano ≈ River ◎ Lake ⊡ Reservoir

SAN ESTEBAN, ISLA – SANTA ANA DE CORO

42 E5 **San Esteban, Isla** *island* NW Mexico
San Eugenio/San Eugenio del Cuareim *see* Artigas
64 H11 **San Felipe** *var.* San Felipe de Aconcagua. Valparaíso, C Chile 32.45S 70.42W
42 D3 **San Felipe** Baja California, NW Mexico 31.02N 114.55W
42 N12 **San Felipe** Guanajuato, C Mexico 21.27N 101.12W
56 K5 **San Felipe** Yaracuy, NW Venezuela 10.25N 68.40W
46 B5 **San Felipe, Cayos de** *island group* W Cuba
San Felipe de Aconcagua *see* San Felipe
San Felipe de Puerto Plata *see* Puerto Plata
39 R11 **San Felipe Pueblo** New Mexico, SW USA 35.25N 106.27W
San Feliú de Guixols *see* Sant Feliu de Guíxols
200 Oo11 **San Félix, Isla** *Eng.* San Felix Island. *island* W Chile
San Felix Island *see* San Félix, Isla
56 L11 **San Fernando de Atabapo** Amazonas, S Venezuela 4.00N 67.42W
42 C4 **San Fernando** *var.* Misión San Fernando. Baja California, NW Mexico 29.58N 115.14W
43 P9 **San Fernando** Tamaulipas, C Mexico 24.51N 98.09W
179 P9 **San Fernando** Luzon, N Philippines 16.45N 120.21E
179 P10 **San Fernando** Luzon, N Philippines 15.01N 120.41E
106 J16 **San Fernando** *prev.* Isla de León. Andalucía, S Spain 36.28N 6.12W
47 U14 **San Fernando** Trinidad, Trinidad and Tobago 10.16N 61.27W
37 S15 **San Fernando** California, W USA 34.16N 118.26W
56 L7 **San Fernando** *var.* San Fernando de Apure. Apure, C Venezuela 7.54N 67.28W
San Fernando de Apure *see* San Fernando
64 L8 **San Fernando del Valle de Catamarca** *var.* Catamarca. Catamarca, NW Argentina 28.28S 65.46W
San Fernando de Monte Cristi *see* Monte Cristi
43 P9 **San Fernando, Río** ≈ C Mexico
25 X11 **Sanford** Florida, SE USA 28.48N 81.16W
21 P9 **Sanford** Maine, NE USA 43.26N 70.46W
23 T10 **Sanford** North Carolina, SE USA 35.28N 79.10W
27 N2 **Sanford** Texas, SW USA 35.42N 101.31W
41 T10 **Sanford, Mount** ▲ Alaska, USA 62.21N 144.12W
44 G8 **San Francisco** *var.* Gotera, San Francisco Gotera. Morazán, E El Salvador 13.40N 88.06W
45 R16 **San Francisco** Veraguas, C Panama 8.14N 80.58W
179 Pp11 **San Francisco** *var.* Aurora. Luzon, N Philippines 13.22N 122.31E
37 L8 **San Francisco** California, W USA 37.46N 122.25W
56 H5 **San Francisco** Zulia, NW Venezuela 10.36N 71.39W
36 M8 **San Francisco** ✈ California, W USA 37.37N 122.23W
37 N9 **San Francisco Bay** *bay* California, W USA
63 C24 **San Francisco de Bellocq** Buenos Aires, E Argentina 38.42S 60.01W
42 I6 **San Francisco de Borja** Chihuahua, N Mexico 27.57N 106.42W
44 J6 **San Francisco de la Paz** Olancho, C Honduras 14.55N 86.13W
42 J7 **San Francisco del Oro** Chihuahua, N Mexico 26.52N 105.49W
42 M12 **San Francisco del Rincón** Jalisco, SW Mexico 20.57N 101.54W
47 O8 **San Francisco de Macorís** C Dominican Republic 19.15N 70.15W
San Francisco de Satipo *see* Satipo
San Francisco Gotera *see* San Francisco
San Francisco Telixtlahuaca *see* Telixtlahuaca
109 K23 **San Fratello** Sicilia, Italy, C Mediterranean Sea 38.00N 14.35E
San Fructuoso *see* Tacuarembó
84 C12 **Sanga** Cuanza Sul, NW Angola 11.10S 15.27E
58 C5 **San Gabriel** Carchi, N Ecuador 0.37N 77.49W
165 S15 **Sa'ngain** Xizang Zizhiqu, W China 30.46N 98.45E
160 E13 **Sangamner** Mahārāshtra, W India 19.37N 74.18E
158 H12 **Sāngāner** Rājasthān, N India 26.48N 75.48E
Sangan, Koh-i- *see* Sangān, Kūh-e
155 N6 **Sangān, Kūh-e** *Pash.* Koh-i-Sangan. ▲ C Afghanistan
126 Ll10 **Sangar** Respublika Sakha (Yakutiya), NE Russian Federation 63.48N 127.37E
175 O8 **Sangasanga** Borneo, C Indonesia 0.36S 117.12E
105 N1 **Sangatte** Pas-de-Calais, N France 50.56N 1.41E
109 B19 **San Gavino Monreale** Sardegna, Italy, C Mediterranean Sea 39.33N 8.47E
59 D16 **Sangayan, Isla** *island* W Peru
32 L14 **Sangchris Lake** ⊡ Illinois, N USA
175 P15 **Sangeang, Pulau** *island* S Indonesia
118 I10 **Sângeorgiu de Pădure** *prev.* Erdăt-Sângeorz, Sîngeorgiu de Pădure, *Hung.* Erdőszentgyörgy. Mureș, C Romania 46.27N 24.49E
118 I9 **Sângeorz-Băi** *var.* Singeroz Băi, *Ger.* Rumänisch-Sankt-Georgen, *Hung.* Oláhszentgyörgy; *prev.* Sîngeorz-Băi. Bistrița-Năsăud, N Romania 47.24N 24.40E
37 R10 **Sanger** California, W USA 36.42N 119.33W
27 T5 **Sanger** Texas, SW USA 33.21N 97.10W
Sângerei *see* Sîngerei
103 L15 **Sangerhausen** Sachsen-Anhalt, C Germany 51.28N 11.18E
47 S6 **San Germán** W Puerto Rico 18.05N 67.02W
San Germano *see* Cassino
167 N2 **Sanggan He** ≈ E China
175 Oo16 **Sanggar, Teluk** *bay* Nusa Tenggara, S Indonesia
174 L8 **Sanggau** Borneo, C Indonesia 0.07N 110.34E
81 H16 **Sangha** ≈ Central African Republic/Congo
81 G16 **Sangha-Mbaéré** ◐ *prefecture* SW Central African Republic
155 Q15 **Sānghar** Sind, SE Pakistan 26.10N 68.58E
117 F22 **Sangiás** ▲ S Greece 36.39N 22.24E
Sangihe, Kepulauan *see* Sangir, Kepulauan
175 S4 **Sangihe, Pulau** *var.* Sangir. *island* N Indonesia
56 G8 **San Gil** Santander, C Colombia 6.34N 73.07W
108 F12 **San Gimignano** Toscana, C Italy 43.30N 11.00E
154 M8 **Sangīn** *var.* Sangin. Helmand, S Afghanistan 32.03N 64.49E
109 O21 **San Giovanni in Fiore** Calabria, SW Italy 39.16N 16.42E
109 M16 **San Giovanni Rotondo** Puglia, SE Italy 41.43N 15.43E
108 G12 **San Giovanni Valdarno** Toscana, C Italy 43.34N 11.31E
Sangir *see* Sangihe, Pulau
175 Rr6 **Sangir, Kepulauan** *var.* Kepulauan Sangihe. *island group* N Indonesia
168 K9 **Sangiyn Dalay** Dundgovĭ, C Mongolia 45.59N 104.58E
168 H9 **Sangiyn Dalay** Govĭ-Altay, C Mongolia 45.12N 97.51E
168 K11 **Sangiyn Dalay** Ömnögovĭ, S Mongolia 42.50N 105.04E
168 K8 **Sangiyn Dalay** Övörhangay, C Mongolia 46.35N 103.18E
169 Y15 **Sangju** *Jap.* Shōshū. C South Korea 36.26N 128.09E
178 Ii11 **Sangkha** Surin, E Thailand 14.36N 103.43E
175 Oo7 **Sangkulirang** Borneo, N Indonesia 1.00N 117.56E
175 Oo7 **Sangkulirang, Teluk** *bay* Borneo, N Indonesia
161 E16 **Sāngli** Mahārāshtra, W India 16.55N 74.37E
81 E16 **Sangmélima** Sud, S Cameroon 2.57N 11.55E
37 V15 **San Gorgonio Mountain** ▲ California, W USA 34.06N 116.50W
39 T8 **Sangre de Cristo Mountains** ▲▲ Colorado/New Mexico, C USA
63 A20 **San Gregorio** Santa Fe, C Argentina 34.18S 62.01W
63 F18 **San Gregorio de Polanco** Tacuarembó, C Uruguay 32.37S 55.49W
47 V14 **Sangre Grande** Trinidad, Trinidad and Tobago 10.35N 61.07W
165 N16 **Sangri** Xizang Zizhiqu, W China 29.17N 92.01E
158 H9 **Sangrūr** Punjab, NW India 30.16N 75.52E
46 I11 **Sangster** *off.* Sir Donald Sangster International Airport, *var.* Montego Bay. ✈ (Montego Bay) W Jamaica 18.30N 77.54W
61 G17 **Sangue, Rio do** ≈ W Brazil
107 R4 **Sangüesa** Navarra, N Spain 42.34N 1.16W
63 C16 **San Gustavo** Entre Ríos, E Argentina 30.40S 59.22W
Sangyuan *see* Wuqiao
42 C6 **San Hipólito, Punta** *headland* W Mexico 26.57N 114.00W
25 W15 **Sanibel** Sanibel Island, Florida, SE USA 26.27N 82.01W
25 V15 **Sanibel Island** *island* Florida, SE USA
62 F13 **San Ignacio** Misiones, NE Argentina 27.13S 55.29W
44 F2 **San Ignacio** *prev.* Cayo, El Cayo. Cayo, W Belize 17.09N 89.02W
59 L16 **San Ignacio** Beni, N Bolivia 14.54S 65.34W
59 O18 **San Ignacio** Santa Cruz, E Bolivia 16.27S 60.57W
44 M14 **San Ignacio** *var.* San Ignacio de Acosta. San José, W Costa Rica 9.46N 84.10W
42 E6 **San Ignacio** Baja California Sur, W Mexico 27.18N 112.51W
42 J10 **San Ignacio** Sinaloa, W Mexico 23.55N 106.25W
58 B9 **San Ignacio** Cajamarca, N Peru 5.03S 79.03W
San Ignacio de Acosta *see* San Ignacio
42 D7 **San Ignacio, Laguna** *lagoon* W Mexico
10 I6 **Sanikiluaq** Belcher Islands, Nunavut, C Canada 55.16N 77.44W
179 Pp9 **San Ildefonso Peninsula** *peninsula* Luzon, N Philippines
Saniquillie *see* Sanniquellie
63 D20 **San Isidro** Buenos Aires, E Argentina 34.28S 58.31W
45 N14 **San Isidro** *var.* San Isidro de El General. San José, SE Costa Rica 9.21N 83.42W
San Isidro de El General *see* San Isidro
56 E5 **San Jacinto** Bolívar, N Colombia 9.52N 75.10W
37 U16 **San Jacinto** California, W USA 33.47N 116.58W
37 V15 **San Jacinto Peak** ▲ California, W USA 33.48N 116.40W
63 F14 **San Javier** Misiones, NE Argentina 27.49S 55.06W
63 C16 **San Javier** Santa Fe, C Argentina 30.34S 59.58W
107 S13 **San Javier** Murcia, SE Spain 37.49N 0.49W
63 D18 **San Javier** Río Negro, W Uruguay 32.40S 58.07W
63 C16 **San Javier, Río** ≈ C Argentina
Sanjiang *see* Jinping
166 L12 **Sanjiang** *var.* Guyi, Sanjiang Dongzu Zizhixian. Guangxi Zhuangzu Zizhiqu, S China 25.49N 109.31E
Sanjiang Dongzu Zizhixian *see* Sanjiang
171 Kk13 **Sanjō** *var.* Sanzyô. Niigata, Honshū, C Japan 37.39N 139.00E
59 M15 **San Joaquín** Beni, N Bolivia 13.03S 64.47W
57 O6 **San Joaquín** Anzoátegui, NE Venezuela 9.21N 64.30W
37 O9 **San Joaquin River** ≈ California, W USA
37 P10 **San Joaquin Valley** *valley* California, W USA
63 A18 **San Jorge** Santa Fe, C Argentina 31.49S 61.49W
195 W15 **San Jorge** *island* N Solomon Islands
42 D3 **San Jorge, Bahía de** *bay* NW Mexico
San Jorge, Isla de *see* Weddell Island
65 J19 **San Jorge, Golfo** *var.* Gulf of San Jorge. *gulf* S Argentina
San Jorge, Gulf of *see* San Jorge, Golfo
196 K8 **San Jose** Tinian, S Northern Mariana Islands 15.00S 145.38E
179 Pp12 **San Jose** Mindoro, N Philippines 12.20N 121.07E
37 N9 **San Jose** California, W USA 37.18N 121.53W
63 F14 **San José** Misiones, NE Argentina 27.46S 55.46W
59 P19 **San José** *var.* San José de Chiquitos. Santa Cruz, E Bolivia 14.13S 68.04W
44 M14 **San José** ● (Costa Rica) San José, C Costa Rica 9.55N 84.05W
44 C7 **San José** *var.* Puerto San José. Escuintla, S Guatemala 13.55N 90.48W
42 G6 **San José** Sonora, NW Mexico 27.31N 110.09W
107 U11 **San José** Eivissa, Spain, W Mediterranean Sea 38.55N 1.18E
56 H5 **San José** Zulia, NW Venezuela 9.58N 72.22W
44 M14 **San José** *off.* Provincia de San José. ◐ *province* W Costa Rica
63 E19 **San José** ◐ *department* S Uruguay
44 M13 **San José** ✈ Alajuela, C Costa Rica 10.03N 84.12W
San José *see* San José del Guaviare, Colombia
San José *see* San José de Mayo, S Uruguay
179 P9 **San Jose City** Luzon, N Philippines 15.49N 120.57E
179 Pp13 **San Jose de Buenavista** Panay Island, C Philippines 10.44N 122.00E
San José de Cúcuta *see* Cúcuta
63 D16 **San José de Feliciano** Entre Ríos, E Argentina 30.21S 58.47W
57 O6 **San José de Guanipa** *var.* El Tigrito. Anzoátegui, NE Venezuela 8.54N 64.10W
64 I9 **San José de Jáchal** San Juan, W Argentina 30.15S 68.46W
42 G10 **San José del Cabo** Baja California Sur, W Mexico 23.01N 109.40W
56 G12 **San José del Guaviare** *var.* San José. Guaviare, S Colombia 2.34N 72.37W
63 E20 **San José de Mayo** *var.* San José. San José, S Uruguay 34.19S 56.42W
56 I10 **San José de Ocuné** Vichada, E Colombia 4.10N 70.21W
43 O9 **San José de Raíces** Nuevo León, NE Mexico 24.32N 100.15W
65 K17 **San José, Golfo** *gulf* E Argentina
42 F9 **San José, Isla** *island* W Mexico
45 U16 **San José, Isla** *island* SE Panama
27 U14 **San Jose Island** *island* Texas, SW USA
64 I10 **San Juan** San Juan, W Argentina 31.36S 68.26W
47 N9 **San Juan** *var.* San Juan de la Maguana. C Dominican Republic 18.46N 71.13W
59 E17 **San Juan** Ica, S Peru 15.22S 75.08W
47 U5 **San Juan** ○ (Puerto Rico) NE Puerto Rico 18.28N 66.06W
64 H10 **San Juan** *off.* Provincia de San Juan. ◐ *province* W Argentina
47 U5 **San Juan** *var.* Luis Muñoz Marin. ✈ NE Puerto Rico 18.27N 66.05W
San Juan *see* San Juan de los Morros
64 O7 **San Juan Bautista** Misiones, S Paraguay 26.39S 57.08W
37 O10 **San Juan Bautista** California, W USA 36.50N 121.34W
San Juan Bautista *see* Villahermosa
San Juan Bautista Cuicatlán *see* Cuicatlán
San Juan Bautista Tuxtepec *see* Tuxtepec
81 C17 **San Juan, Cabo** *headland* S Equatorial Guinea 1.09N 9.25E
107 S12 **San Juan de Alicante** País Valenciano, E Spain 38.25N 0.27W
56 H7 **San Juan de Colón** Táchira, NW Venezuela 8.01N 72.16W
42 L9 **San Juan de Guadalupe** Durango, C Mexico 25.12N 100.50W
San Juan de la Maguana *see* San Juan
56 G4 **San Juan del Cesar** La Guajira, N Colombia 10.45N 73.00W
42 L15 **San Juan de Lima, Punta** *headland* SW Mexico 18.34N 103.40W
44 I8 **San Juan de Limay** Estelí, NW Nicaragua 13.10N 86.36W
45 N12 **San Juan del Norte** *var.* Greytown. Río San Juan, SE Nicaragua 10.54N 83.42W
56 K4 **San Juan de los Cayos** Falcón, N Venezuela 11.06N 68.25W
42 M12 **San Juan de los Lagos** Jalisco, C Mexico 21.15N 102.15W
56 L5 **San Juan de los Morros** *var.* San Juan. Guárico, N Venezuela 9.52N 67.22W
42 K9 **San Juan del Río** Durango, C Mexico 25.12N 100.50W
43 O13 **San Juan del Río** Querétaro de Arteaga, C Mexico 20.21N 100.01W
44 J11 **San Juan del Sur** Rivas, SW Nicaragua 11.14N 85.52W
56 M9 **San Juan de Manapiare** Amazonas, S Venezuela 5.15N 66.04W
42 E7 **San Juanico** Baja California Sur, W Mexico
42 D7 **San Juanico, Punta** *headland* W Mexico 26.01N 112.17W
34 G6 **San Juan Islands** *island group* Washington, NW USA
42 I6 **San Juanito** Chihuahua, N Mexico
42 I12 **San Juanito, Isla** *island* C Mexico
39 R8 **San Juan Mountains** ▲▲ Colorado, C USA
56 E5 **San Juan Nepomuceno** Bolívar, NW Colombia 9.57N 75.06W
46 E5 **San Juan, Pico** ▲ C Cuba 21.58N 80.10W
203 W15 **San Juan, Punta** *headland* Easter Island, Chile, E Pacific Ocean 27.03S 109.22W
44 M12 **San Juan, Río** ≈ Costa Rica/Nicaragua
43 S15 **San Juan, Río** ≈ SE Mexico
39 O8 **San Juan River** ≈ Colorado/Utah, W USA
San Julián *see* Puerto San Julián
63 B17 **San Justo** Santa Fe, C Argentina 30.46S 60.31W
111 W5 **Sankt Aegyd-am-Neuwalde** Niederösterreich, E Austria 47.51N 15.34E
111 U9 **Sankt Andrä** *Slvn.* Šent Andraž. Kärnten, S Austria 46.46N 14.49E
Sankt Andrä *see* Szentendre
Sankt Anna *see* Sântana
110 K8 **Sankt Anton-am-Arlberg** Vorarlberg, W Austria 47.08N 10.11E
103 E16 **Sankt Augustin** Nordrhein-Westfalen, W Germany 50.46N 7.10E
Sankt-Bartholomäi *see* Palamuse
103 F23 **Sankt Blasien** Baden-Württemberg, SW Germany 47.43N 8.09E
111 R3 **Sankt Florian am Inn** Oberösterreich, N Austria 48.24N 13.27E
110 I7 **Sankt Gallen** *var.* St.Gallen, *Eng.* Saint Gall, *Fr.* St-Gall. Sankt Gallen, NE Switzerland 47.25N 9.22E
110 H8 **Sankt Gallen** *var.* St.Gallen, *Eng.* Saint Gall, *Fr.* St-Gall. ◐ *canton* NE Switzerland
110 J8 **Sankt Gallenkirch** Vorarlberg, W Austria 47.00N 10.59E
111 Q5 **Sankt Georgen** Salzburg, N Austria 47.59N 12.57E
Sankt Georgen *see* Đurđevac, Croatia
Sankt-Georgen *see* Sfântu Gheorghe, Romania
111 R6 **Sankt Gilgen** Salzburg, NW Austria 47.46N 13.21E
Sankt Gotthard *see* Szentgotthárd
103 E20 **Sankt Ingbert** Saarland, SW Germany 49.16N 7.07E
Sankt-Jakobi *see* Viru-Jaagupi, Lääne-Virumaa, Estonia
Sankt-Jakobi *see* Pärnu-Jaagupi, Pärnumaa, Estonia
Sankt Johann *see* Sankt Johann in Tirol
111 T7 **Sankt Johann am Tauern** Steiermark, E Austria 47.20N 14.27E
111 Q7 **Sankt Johann im Pongau** Salzburg, NW Austria 47.22N 13.13E
111 P6 **Sankt Johann in Tirol** *var.* Sankt Johann. Tirol, W Austria 47.31N 12.25E
Sankt-Johannis *see* Järva-Jaani
110 L8 **Sankt Leonhard** Tirol, W Austria 47.05N 10.53E
Sankt Margarethen *see* Sankt Margarethen im Burgenland
111 Y5 **Sankt Margarethen im Burgenland** *var.* Sankt Margarethen. Burgenland, E Austria 47.49N 16.37E
Sankt Martin *see* Martin
111 X8 **Sankt Martin an der Raab** Burgenland, SE Austria 46.59N 16.12E
111 U7 **Sankt Michael in Obersteiermark** Steiermark, SE Austria 47.21N 14.59E
Sankt Michel *see* Mikkeli
Sankt Moritz *see* St.Moritz
110 E11 **Sankt Niklaus** Valais, S Switzerland 46.09N 7.48E
111 S7 **Sankt Nikolai** *var.* Sankt Nikolai im Sölktal. Steiermark, SE Austria 47.18N 14.04E
Sankt Nikolai im Sölktal *see* Sankt Nikolai
111 U9 **Sankt Paul** *var.* Sankt Paul im Lavanttal. Kärnten, S Austria 46.42N 14.53E
Sankt Paul im Lavanttal *see* Sankt Paul
Sankt Peter *see* Pivka
111 W9 **Sankt Peter am Ottersbach** Steiermark, SE Austria 46.49N 15.48E
128 J13 **Sankt-Peterburg** *prev.* Leningrad, Petrograd, *Eng.* Saint Petersburg, *Fin.* Pietari. Leningradskaya Oblast', NW Russian Federation 59.55N 30.25E
102 H8 **Sankt Peter-Ording** Schleswig-Holstein, N Germany 54.18N 8.37E
111 V4 **Sankt Pölten** Niederösterreich, N Austria 48.14N 15.37E
111 W7 **Sankt Ruprecht** *var.* Sankt Ruprecht an der Raab. Steiermark, SE Austria 47.10N 15.41E
Sankt Ruprecht an der Raab *see* Sankt Ruprecht
Sankt-Ulrich *see* Ortisei
111 T4 **Sankt Valentin** Niederösterreich, C Austria 48.09N 14.30E
Sankt Veit am Flaum *see* Rijeka
111 T9 **Sankt Veit an der Glan** *Slvn.* Šent Vid. Kärnten, S Austria 46.46N 14.22E
101 M21 **Sankt-Vith** *var.* Saint-Vith. Liège, E Belgium 50.16N 6.07E
103 E20 **Sankt Wendel** Saarland, SW Germany 49.28N 7.10E
111 R6 **Sankt Wolfgang** Salzburg, NW Austria 47.43N 13.30E
81 K21 **Sankuru** ≈ C Dem. Rep. Congo (Zaire)
42 D8 **San Lázaro, Cabo** *headland* W Mexico 24.46N 112.15W
143 O16 **Şanlıurfa** *prev.* Sanli Urfa, Urfa, *anc.* Edessa. Şanlıurfa, S Turkey 37.07N 38.45E
143 O16 **Şanlıurfa** *prev.* Urfa. ◐ *province* SE Turkey
143 O16 **Şanlıurfa Yaylası** *plateau* SE Turkey
63 B18 **San Lorenzo** Santa Fe, C Argentina 32.37S 60.48W
59 M21 **San Lorenzo** Tarija, S Bolivia 21.27S 64.47W
58 C5 **San Lorenzo** Esmeraldas, N Ecuador 1.15N 78.51W
44 H8 **San Lorenzo** Valle, S Honduras 13.25N 87.27W
107 N8 **San Lorenzo de El Escorial** *var.* El Escorial. Madrid, C Spain 40.36N 4.07W
42 E5 **San Lorenzo, Isla** *island* NW Mexico
59 C14 **San Lorenzo, Isla** *island* W Peru
65 G20 **San Lorenzo, Monte** ▲ S Argentina 47.40S 72.12W
42 I9 **San Lorenzo, Río** ≈ C Mexico
106 J15 **Sanlúcar de Barrameda** Andalucía, S Spain 36.46N 6.21W
106 J14 **Sanlúcar la Mayor** Andalucía, S Spain 37.24N 6.13W
42 F11 **San Lucas** Baja California Sur, NW Mexico 22.49N 109.52W
42 E6 **San Lucas** *var.* Cabo San Lucas. Baja California Sur, W Mexico 27.13N 112.15W
42 G11 **San Lucas, Cabo** *var.* San Lucas Cape. *headland* W Mexico 22.52N 109.55W
San Lucas Cape *see* San Lucas, Cabo
64 J11 **San Luis** San Luis, C Argentina 33.18S 66.18W
44 E4 **San Luis** Petén, NE Guatemala 16.16N 89.27W
42 D2 **San Luis** *var.* San Luis Río Colorado. Sonora, NW Mexico 32.25N 114.48W
44 M7 **San Luis** Región Autónoma Atlántico Norte, NE Nicaragua 13.58N 84.10W
38 H15 **San Luis** Arizona, SW USA 32.27N 114.45W
39 T8 **San Luis** Colorado, C USA 37.09N 105.24W
56 J4 **San Luis** Falcón, N Venezuela 11.08N 69.36W
64 J11 **San Luis** *off.* Provincia de San Luis. ◐ *province* C Argentina
43 N12 **San Luis de la Paz** Guanajuato, C Mexico 21.15N 100.33W
42 K8 **San Luis del Cordero** Durango, C Mexico 25.25N 104.09W
42 D4 **San Luis, Isla** *island* NW Mexico
44 E6 **San Luis Jilotepeque** Jalapa, SE Guatemala 14.36N 89.40W
59 M16 **San Luis, Laguna de** ◎ NW Bolivia
37 P13 **San Luis Obispo** California, W USA 35.16N 120.39W
39 R7 **San Luis Peak** ▲ Colorado, C USA 37.59N 106.55W
43 N11 **San Luis Potosí** San Luis Potosí, C Mexico 22.09N 100.57W
43 N11 **San Luis Potosí** ◐ *state* C Mexico
37 O10 **San Luis Reservoir** ⊡ California, W USA
San Luis Río Colorado *see* San Luis
39 S8 **San Luis Valley** *basin* Colorado, C USA
109 C19 **Sanluri** Sardegna, Italy, C Mediterranean Sea 39.34N 8.54E
63 D23 **San Manuel** Buenos Aires, E Argentina 37.46S 58.49W
38 M15 **San Manuel** Arizona, SW USA 32.36N 110.37W
108 F11 **San Marcello Pistoiese** Toscana, C Italy 44.03N 10.46E
109 N20 **San Marco Argentano** Calabria, SW Italy 39.31N 16.07E
56 E6 **San Marcos** Sucre, N Colombia 8.37N 75.12W
44 M14 **San Marcos** San José, C Costa Rica 9.39N 84.00W
44 B5 **San Marcos** San Marcos, W Guatemala 14.57N 91.46W
44 F6 **San Marcos** Ocotepeque, SW Honduras 14.23N 88.57W
43 O16 **San Marcos** Guerrero, S Mexico 16.47N 99.29W
27 S11 **San Marcos** Texas, SW USA 29.52N 97.56W
44 A5 **San Marcos** *off.* Departamento de San Marcos. ◐ *department* W Guatemala
San Marcos de Arica *see* Arica
42 E6 **San Marcos, Isla** *island* W Mexico
108 H11 **San Marino** ● (San Marino) C San Marino 43.53N 12.27E
108 I11 **San Marino** *off.* Republic of San Marino. ◆ *republic* S Europe
64 I11 **San Martín** Mendoza, C Argentina 33.04S 68.28W
56 F11 **San Martín** Meta, C Colombia 3.43N 73.42W
58 D11 **San Martín** *off.* Departamento de San Martín. ◐ *department* C Peru
204 I5 **San Martín** *Argentinian research station* Antarctica 68.18S 67.03W
65 H16 **San Martín de los Andes** Neuquén, W Argentina 40.10S 71.22W
106 M8 **San Martín de Valdeiglesias** Madrid, C Spain 40.21N 4.24W
65 G21 **San Martín, Lago** *var.* Lago O'Higgins. ◎ S Argentina
108 H6 **San Martino di Castrozza** Trentino-Alto Adige, N Italy 46.16N 11.50E
59 N16 **San Martín, Río** ≈ N Bolivia
San Martín Texmelucan *see* Texmelucan
37 N9 **San Mateo** California, W USA 37.33N 122.19W
57 O6 **San Mateo** Anzoátegui, NE Venezuela 9.34N 64.30W
44 B4 **San Mateo Ixtatán** Huehuetenango, W Guatemala 15.48N 91.30W
59 Q18 **San Matías** Santa Cruz, E Bolivia 16.19S 58.23W
65 K16 **San Matías, Golfo** *var.* Gulf of San Matías. *gulf* E Argentina
San Matías, Gulf of *see* San Matías, Golfo
13 O8 **Sanmaur** Quebec, SE Canada 47.52N 73.47W
167 T10 **Sanmen Wan** *bay* E China
166 M6 **Sanmenxia** *var.* Shan Xian. Henan, C China 34.46N 111.16E
Sânmiclăuș Mare *see* Sânnicolau Mare
63 D14 **San Miguel** Corrientes, NE Argentina 28.02S 57.38W
59 L16 **San Miguel** Beni, N Bolivia 16.43S 61.06W
44 G8 **San Miguel** San Miguel, SE El Salvador 13.27N 88.10W
42 L6 **San Miguel** Coahuila de Zaragoza, N Mexico 29.10N 101.28W
42 J9 **San Miguel** *var.* San Miguel de Cruces. Durango, C Mexico 24.25N 105.55W
45 U16 **San Miguel** Panamá, SE Panama 8.26N 78.57W
37 P12 **San Miguel** California, W USA 35.45N 120.42W
44 B9 **San Miguel** ◐ *department* E El Salvador
43 N13 **San Miguel de Allende** Guanajuato, C Mexico 20.54N 100.46W
San Miguel de Cruces *see* San Miguel
San Miguel de Ibarra *see* Ibarra
63 D21 **San Miguel del Monte** Buenos Aires, E Argentina 35.25S 58.49W
64 J7 **San Miguel de Tucumán** *var.* Tucumán. Tucumán, N Argentina 26.46S 65.15W
45 V16 **San Miguel, Golfo de** *gulf* S Panama
37 P15 **San Miguel Island** *island* California, W USA
44 L11 **San Miguelito** Río San Juan, S Nicaragua 11.22N 84.52W
45 T15 **San Miguelito** Panamá, C Panama 8.58N 79.31W
59 N18 **San Miguel, Río** ≈ E Bolivia
58 D6 **San Miguel, Río** ≈ Colombia/Ecuador
42 I7 **San Miguel, Río** ≈ N Mexico
44 G8 **San Miguel, Volcán de** ⛰ SE El Salvador 13.27N 88.18W
167 Q12 **Sanming** Fujian, SE China 26.10N 117.37E
108 F11 **San Miniato** Toscana, C Italy 43.40N 10.53E
San Murezzan *see* St.Moritz
Sannār *see* Sennar
109 M15 **Sannicandro Garganico** Puglia, SE Italy 41.49N 15.31E
42 H6 **San Nicolás** Sonora, NW Mexico 28.31N 109.24W
63 C19 **San Nicolás de los Arroyos** Buenos Aires, E Argentina 33.17S 60.12W
37 R16 **San Nicolas Island** *island* Channel Islands, California, W USA
Sânnicolaul-Mare *see* Sânnicolau Mare
118 E11 **Sânnicolau Mare** *var.* Sânnicolaul-Mare, *Hung.* Nagyszentmiklós; *prev.* Sânmiclăuș Mare, Sînnicolau Mare. Timiș, W Romania 46.05N 20.37E
126 Ll5 **Sannikova, Proliv** *strait* NE Russian Federation
78 K16 **Sanniquellie** *var.* Saniquillie. NE Liberia 7.24N 8.45W
172 N9 **Sannohe** Aomori, Honshū, C Japan 40.23N 141.16E
Sanntaler Alpen *see* Kamniško-Savinjske Alpe
171 K15 **Sano** Tochigi, Honshū, S Japan 36.19N 139.26E
113 O17 **Sanok** Podkarpackie, SE Poland 49.31N 22.14E
56 E5 **San Onofre** Sucre, NW Colombia 9.45N 75.33W
59 K21 **San Pablo** Potosí, S Bolivia 21.43S 66.37W
179 P11 **San Pablo** *off.* San Pablo City. Luzon, N Philippines 14.04N 121.16E
San Pablo Balleza *see* Balleza
37 N8 **San Pablo Bay** *bay* California, W USA
42 C6 **San Pablo, Punta** *headland* W Mexico 27.12N 114.30W
45 R16 **San Pablo, Río** ≈ C Panama
179 Q11 **San Pascual** Burias Island, C Philippines 13.06N 122.59E
123 Jj16 **San Pawl il-Bahar** *Eng.* Saint Paul's Bay. E Malta 35.57N 14.24E
63 C19 **San Pedro** Buenos Aires, E Argentina 33.37S 59.42W
64 K5 **San Pedro** Jujuy, N Argentina 24.13S 64.51W
62 G13 **San Pedro** Misiones, NE Argentina 26.37S 54.12W
44 H1 **San Pedro** Corozal, NE Belize 17.58N 87.55W
42 L8 **San Pedro** *var.* San Pedro de las Colonias. Coahuila de Zaragoza, NE Mexico 25.47N 102.57W
64 O5 **San Pedro** San Pedro, SE Paraguay 24.04S 57.03W
64 O6 **San Pedro** *off.* Departamento de San Pedro. ◐ *department* C Paraguay
79 N16 **San Pedro** ✈ (Yamoussoukro) C Ivory Coast 6.49N 5.14W
46 G6 **San Pedro** ≈ C Cuba
San Pedro *see* San Pedro del Pinatar
78 M17 **San-Pédro** S Ivory Coast 4.45N 6.37W
44 D5 **San Pedro Carchá** Alta Verapaz, C Guatemala 15.30N 90.12W
37 S16 **San Pedro Channel** *channel* California, W USA
64 I5 **San Pedro de Atacama** Antofagasta, N Chile 22.52S 68.10W
San Pedro de Durazno *see* Durazno
42 G5 **San Pedro de la Cueva** Sonora, NW Mexico 29.16N 109.46W
San Pedro de las Colonias *see* San Pedro
58 B11 **San Pedro de Lloc** La Libertad, NW Peru 7.27S 79.34W
107 S13 **San Pedro del Pinatar** *var.* San Pedro. Murcia, SE Spain 37.49N 0.46W
47 P9 **San Pedro de Macorís** SE Dominican Republic 18.28N 69.19W
42 C3 **San Pedro Mártir, Sierra** ▲▲ NW Mexico
San Pedro Pochutla *see* Pochutla
44 D2 **San Pedro, Río** ≈ Guatemala/Mexico
42 K10 **San Pedro, Río** ≈ C Mexico
106 J10 **San Pedro, Sierra de** ▲▲ W Spain
44 G5 **San Pedro Sula** Cortés, NW Honduras 15.25N 88.01W
San Pedro Tapanatepec *see* Tapanatepec
64 I4 **San Pedro, Volcán** ▲ N Chile 21.46S 68.13W
108 E7 **San Pellegrino Terme** Lombardia, N Italy 45.53N 9.42E
27 T16 **San Perlita** Texas, SW USA 26.30N 97.38W
San Pietro *see* Supetar
San Pietro del Carso *see* Pivka
109 A20 **San Pietro, Isola di** *island* W Italy
34 K7 **Sanpoil River** ≈ Washington, NW USA
171 L12 **Sanpoku** *var.* Sampoku. Niigata, Honshū, C Japan 38.32N 139.33E
42 C3 **San Quintín** Baja California, NW Mexico 30.21N 115.58W
42 B3 **San Quintín, Bahía de** *bay* NW Mexico
42 B3 **San Quintín, Cabo** *headland* NW Mexico 30.22N 116.01W
64 I12 **San Rafael** Mendoza, W Argentina 34.43S 68.15W
43 N9 **San Rafael** Nuevo León, NE Mexico 25.01N 100.33W
36 M8 **San Rafael** California, W USA 37.58N 122.31W
39 Q11 **San Rafael** New Mexico, SW USA 35.03N 107.52W
56 H4 **San Rafael** *var.* El Moján. Zulia, NW Venezuela 10.58N 71.45W
44 J8 **San Rafael del Norte** Jinotega, NW Nicaragua 13.10N 86.10W
44 J10 **San Rafael del Sur** Managua, SW Nicaragua 11.51N 86.24W
38 M5 **San Rafael Knob** ▲ Utah, W USA 38.46N 110.45W
37 Q14 **San Rafael Mountains** ▲▲ California, W USA
44 M13 **San Ramón** Alajuela, C Costa Rica 10.04N 84.27W
59 E14 **San Ramón** Junín, C Peru 11.08S 75.19W
63 F19 **San Ramón** Canelones, S Uruguay 34.18S 55.55W
64 K5 **San Ramón de la Nueva Orán** Salta, N Argentina 23.07S 64.19W
59 O16 **San Ramón, Río** ≈ E Bolivia
108 B11 **San Remo** Liguria, NW Italy 43.48N 7.46E
56 J3 **San Román, Cabo** *headland* NW Venezuela 12.10N 70.01W
63 C15 **San Roque** Corrientes, NE Argentina 28.34S 58.45W
196 I4 **San Roque** Saipan, S Northern Mariana Islands 15.15S 85.46E
106 K16 **San Roque** Andalucía, S Spain 36.13N 5.22W
27 R9 **San Saba** Texas, SW USA 31.12N 98.43W
27 Q9 **San Saba River** ≈ Texas, SW USA
63 D17 **San Salvador** Entre Ríos, E Argentina 31.37S 58.30W
44 F7 **San Salvador** ● (El Salvador) San Salvador, SW El Salvador 13.42N 89.12W
44 A10 **San Salvador** ◐ *department* C El Salvador
44 F8 **San Salvador** ✈ La Paz, S El Salvador 13.27N 89.04W
46 K4 **San Salvador** *prev.* Watlings Island. *island* E Bahamas
64 J5 **San Salvador de Jujuy** *var.* Jujuy. Jujuy, N Argentina 24.10S 65.19W
44 F7 **San Salvador, Volcán de** ⛰ C El Salvador 13.58N 89.14W
79 Q14 **Sansanné-Mango** *var.* Mango. N Togo 10.21N 0.28E
47 S5 **San Sebastián** W Puerto Rico 18.21N 67.00W
65 J24 **San Sebastián, Bahía** *bay* S Argentina
Sansenhō *see* Sach'ŏn
108 H12 **Sansepolcro** Toscana, C Italy 43.34N 12.12E
109 M16 **San Severo** Puglia, SE Italy 41.40N 15.22E
114 F11 **Sanski Most** Federacija Bosna I Hercegovina, NW Bosnia & Herzegovina 44.43N 16.40E
176 Ww9 **Sansundi** Irian Jaya, E Indonesia 0.42S 135.48E
106 K11 **Santa Amalia** Extremadura, W Spain 39.00N 6.01W
62 F13 **Santa Ana** Misiones, NE Argentina 27.22S 55.34W
59 L16 **Santa Ana** Beni, N Bolivia 13.43S 65.37W
44 E7 **Santa Ana** Santa Ana, NW El Salvador 13.58N 89.34W
42 F4 **Santa Ana** Sonora, NW Mexico 30.33N 111.07W
37 T16 **Santa Ana** California, W USA 33.45N 117.52W
57 N6 **Santa Ana** Nueva Esparta, NE Venezuela 9.15N 64.39W
44 A9 **Santa Ana** ◐ *department* NW El Salvador
Santa Ana de Coro *see* Coro

◆ Country
● Country Capital
◇ Dependent Territory
○ Dependent Territory Capital
◐ Administrative Region
✈ International Airport
▲ Mountain
▲▲ Mountain Range
⛰ Volcano
≈ River
◎ Lake
⊡ Reservoir

SANTA ANA, VOLCÁN DE – SARIOSIYO

44 E7 Santa Ana, Volcán de var. La Matepec. ✻ W El Salvador 13.49N 89.36W
42 J7 Santa Barbara Chihuahua, N Mexico 26.46N 105.46W
37 Q14 Santa Barbara California, W USA 34.24N 119.40W
44 G6 Santa Bárbara Santa Bárbara, W Honduras 14.57N 88.15W
56 L11 Santa Bárbara Amazonas, S Venezuela 3.55N 67.06W
56 I7 Santa Bárbara Barinas, W Venezuela 7.48N 71.10W
44 F5 Santa Bárbara ◐ department NW Honduras
Santa Bárbara see Iscuandé
37 Q15 Santa Barbara Channel channel California, W USA
Santa Bárbara de Samaná see Samaná
37 R16 Santa Barbara Island island Channel Islands, California, W USA
56 E5 Santa Catalina Bolívar, N Colombia 10.34N 75.22W
45 R15 Santa Catalina Bocas del Toro, W Panama 8.46N 81.18W
37 T17 Santa Catalina, Gulf of gulf California, W USA
42 F8 Santa Catalina, Isla island W Mexico
37 S16 Santa Catalina Island island Channel Islands, California, W USA
43 N8 Santa Catarina Nuevo León, NE Mexico 25.39N 100.30W
62 H13 Santa Catarina off. Estado de Santa Catarina. ◐ state S Brazil
Santa Catarina de Tepehuanes see Tepehuanes
62 L13 Santa Catarina, Ilha de island S Brazil
47 Q16 Santa Catherina Curaçao, C Netherlands Antilles 12.07N 68.46W
46 E5 Santa Clara Villa Clara, C Cuba 22.25N 78.00W
37 N9 Santa Clara California, W USA 37.20N 121.57W
38 J8 Santa Clara Utah, W USA 37.07N 113.39W
Santa Clara see Santa Clara de Olimar
63 F18 Santa Clara de Olimar var. Santa Clara. Cerro Largo, NE Uruguay 32.54S 54.55W
63 A17 Santa Clara de Saguier Santa Fe, C Argentina 31.21S 61.49W
Santa Coloma see Santa Coloma de Gramanet
107 X5 Santa Coloma de Farners var. Santa Coloma de Farnés. Cataluña, NE Spain 41.52N 2.39E
Santa Coloma de Farnés see Santa Coloma de Farners
107 W6 Santa Coloma de Gramanet var. Santa Coloma. Cataluña, NE Spain 41.28N 2.13E
106 G2 Santa Comba Galicia, NW Spain 43.01N 8.49W
Santa Comba see Uaco Cungo
106 H8 Santa Comba Dão Viseu, N Portugal 40.22N 8.07W
84 C10 Santa Cruz Uíge, NW Angola 6.56S 16.25E
59 N19 Santa Cruz var. Santa Cruz de la Sierra. Santa Cruz, C Bolivia 17.49S 63.10W
64 G12 Santa Cruz Libertador, C Chile 34.39S 71.16W
44 K13 Santa Cruz Guanacaste, W Costa Rica 10.15N 85.34W
46 I12 Santa Cruz W Jamaica 18.03N 77.41W
66 P6 Santa Cruz Madeira, Portugal, NE Atlantic Ocean 32.43N 16.46W
37 N10 Santa Cruz California, W USA 36.58N 122.01W
65 H20 Santa Cruz off. Provincia de Santa Cruz. ◐ province S Argentina
59 O18 Santa Cruz ◐ department E Bolivia
Santa Cruz see Viru-Viru
Santa Cruz see Puerto Santa Cruz
Santa Cruz Barillas see Barillas
61 O18 Santa Cruz Cabrália Bahia, E Brazil 16.16S 39.03W
Santa Cruz de El Seibo see El Seibo
66 N11 Santa Cruz de la Palma La Palma, Islas Canarias, Spain, NE Atlantic Ocean 28.40N 17.46W
Santa Cruz de la Sierra see Santa Cruz
107 O9 Santa Cruz de la Zarza Castilla-La Mancha, C Spain 39.59N 3.10W
44 C5 Santa Cruz del Quiché Quiché, W Guatemala 15.01N 91.08W
107 N8 Santa Cruz del Retamar Castilla-La Mancha, C Spain 40.07N 4.13W
Santa Cruz del Seibo see El Seibo
46 G7 Santa Cruz del Sur Camagüey, C Cuba 20.44N 78.00W
107 O11 Santa Cruz de Mudela Castilla-La Mancha, C Spain 38.37N 3.27W
66 Q11 Santa Cruz de Tenerife Tenerife, Islas Canarias, Spain, NE Atlantic Ocean 28.28N 16.15W
66 P11 Santa Cruz de Tenerife ◐ province Islas Canarias, Spain, NE Atlantic Ocean
62 K9 Santa Cruz do Rio Pardo São Paulo, S Brazil 22.52S 49.37W
63 H15 Santa Cruz do Sul Rio Grande do Sul, S Brazil 29.42S 52.25W
59 C17 Santa Cruz, Isla var. Indefatigable Island, Isla Chávez. island Galapagos Islands, Ecuador, E Pacific Ocean
42 F8 Santa Cruz, Isla island W Mexico
37 Q15 Santa Cruz Island island California, W USA
195 X8 Santa Cruz Islands island group E Solomon Islands
65 I22 Santa Cruz, Río ≈ S Argentina
38 L15 Santa Cruz River ≈ Arizona, SW USA
63 C17 Santa Elena Entre Ríos, E Argentina 30.58S 59.46W
44 F2 Santa Elena Cayo, W Belize 17.08N 89.04W
27 R16 Santa Elena Texas, SW USA 26.43N 98.30W
58 A7 Santa Elena, Bahía de bay W Ecuador
57 R10 Santa Elena de Uairén Bolívar, E Venezuela 4.40N 61.03W
44 K12 Santa Elena, Península peninsula NW Costa Rica
58 A7 Santa Elena, Punta headland W Ecuador 2.11S 81.00W
106 L11 Santa Eufemia Andalucía, S Spain 38.36N 4.54W
109 N21 Santa Eufemia, Golfo di gulf S Italy
109 N21 Santa Eufemia Lamezia Terme Calabria, SE Italy 38.54N 16.13E
107 S4 Santa Eulalia de Gállego Aragón, NE Spain 42.16N 0.46W
107 V11 Santa Eulalia del Río Eivissa, Spain, W Mediterranean Sea 39.00N 1.33E
63 B17 Santa Fe Santa Fe, C Argentina 31.36S 60.46W
107 N14 Santa Fe Andalucía, S Spain 37.10N 3.43W
39 S10 Santa Fe state capital New Mexico, SW USA 35.41N 105.56W
63 B15 Santa Fe off. Provincia de Santa Fe. ◐ province C Argentina
Santa Fe see Bogotá
46 C6 Santa Fé var. La Fe. Isla de la Juventud, W Cuba 21.39N 82.45W
45 R16 Santa Fé Veraguas, C Panama 8.28N 81.03W
Santa Fe de Bogotá see Bogotá
62 J7 Santa Fé do Sul São Paulo, S Brazil 20.13S 50.55W
59 B18 Santa Fe, Isla var. Barrington Island. island Galapagos Islands, Ecuador, E Pacific Ocean
25 V9 Santa Fe River ≈ Florida, SE USA
61 M15 Santa Filomena Piauí, E Brazil 9.06S 45.52W
42 G10 Santa Genoveva ▲ W Mexico 23.07N 109.56W
159 S14 Santahar Rajshahi, NW Bangladesh 24.45N 89.03E
62 G11 Santa Helena Paraná, S Brazil 24.53S 54.19W
56 J5 Santa Inés Lara, N Venezuela 10.37N 69.18W
65 G24 Santa Inés, Isla island S Chile
64 J13 Santa Isabel La Pampa, C Argentina 36.11S 66.59W
45 U14 Santa Isabel Colón, N Panama 9.31N 79.12W
195 W14 Santa Isabel var. Bughotu. island N Solomon Islands
Santa Isabel see Malabo
60 D11 Santa Isabel do Rio Negro Amazonas, NW Brazil 0.40S 64.55W
63 C15 Santa Lucia Corrientes, NE Argentina 28.58S 59.05W
59 I17 Santa Lucía Puno, S Peru 15.45S 70.34W
63 F20 Santa Lucía var. Santa Lucia. Canelones, S Uruguay 34.25S 56.25W
44 B6 Santa Lucía Cotzumalguapa Escuintla, SW Guatemala 14.20N 91.00W
109 L23 Santa Lucia del Mela Sicilia, Italy, C Mediterranean Sea 38.07N 15.16E
37 O11 Santa Lucia Range ▲▲ California, W USA
42 D9 Santa Margarita, Isla island W Mexico
63 G15 Santa Maria Rio Grande do Sul, S Brazil 29.40S 53.48W
37 P13 Santa Maria California, W USA 34.56N 120.25W
66 Q4 Santa Maria ✕ Santa Maria, Azores, Portugal, NE Atlantic Ocean
66 P3 Santa Maria island Azores, Portugal, NE Atlantic Ocean
Santa Maria see Gaua.
64 J7 Santa María Catamarca, N Argentina 26.38S 66.01W
Santa María Asunción Tlaxiaco see Tlaxiaco
42 G9 Santa María, Bahía bay W Mexico
85 L21 Santa Maria, Cabo de headland S Mozambique 26.05S 32.58E
106 G15 Santa Maria, Cabo de headland S Portugal 36.57N 7.55W
46 J4 Santa Maria, Cape headland Long Island, C Bahamas 23.40N 75.20W
109 J17 Santa Maria Capua Vetere Campania, S Italy 41.04N 14.15E
61 M17 Santa Maria da Vitória Bahia, E Brazil 13.25S 44.09W
57 N9 Santa Maria de Erebato Bolívar, SE Venezuela 5.09N 64.49W
106 G7 Santa Maria da Feira Aveiro, N Portugal 40.55N 8.31W
57 N6 Santa Maria de Ipire Guárico, C Venezuela 8.51N 65.21W
Santa Maria del Buen Aire see Buenos Aires
42 J8 Santa María del Oro Durango, C Mexico 25.57N 105.22W
43 N12 Santa María del Río San Luis Potosí, C Mexico 21.48N 100.42W
Santa Maria di Castellabate see Castellabate
109 Q20 Santa Maria di Leuca, Capo headland SE Italy 39.48N 18.21E
110 K10 Santa Maria-im-Münstertal Graubünden, SE Switzerland 46.36N 10.25E
59 B18 Santa María, Isla var. Isla Floreana, Charles Island. island Galapagos Islands, Ecuador, E Pacific Ocean
42 J3 Santa María, Laguna de ⊙ N Mexico
63 G16 Santa Maria, Rio ≈ S Brazil
45 R16 Santa María, Río ≈ C Panama
38 J12 Santa Maria River ≈ Arizona, SW USA
109 G15 Santa Marinella Lazio, C Italy 42.01N 11.51E
56 F4 Santa Marta Magdalena, N Colombia 11.13N 74.13W
106 J11 Santa Marta Extremadura, W Spain 38.37N 6.39W
Santa Maura see Lefkáda
37 S15 Santa Monica California, W USA 34.01N 118.29W
118 F10 Sântana Ger. Sankt Anna, Hung. Újszentanna; prev. Sîntana. Arad, W Romania 46.19N 21.30E
63 F16 Santana, Coxilha de hill range S Brazil
63 H16 Santana da Boa Vista Rio Grande do Sul, S Brazil 30.52S 53.03W
63 F16 Santana do Livramento prev. Livramento. Rio Grande do Sul, S Brazil 30.52S 55.30W
107 N2 Santander Cantabria, N Spain 43.28N 3.48W
56 F8 Santander off. Departamento de Santander. ◐ province C Colombia
Santander Jiménez see Jiménez
Sant'Andrea see Svetac
109 B20 Sant'Antioco Sardegna, Italy, C Mediterranean Sea 39.03N 8.28E
106 J13 Santa Olalla del Cala Andalucía, S Spain 37.54N 6.13W
37 R15 Santa Paula California, W USA 34.21N 119.03W
38 L4 Santaquin Utah, W USA 39.58N 111.46W
60 I12 Santarém Pará, N Brazil 2.25S 54.40W
106 G10 Santarém anc. Scalabis. Santarém, W Portugal 39.13N 8.40W
106 G10 Santarém ◐ district C Portugal
46 F4 Santaren Channel channel W Bahamas
56 K10 Santa Rita Vichada, E Colombia 4.51N 68.27W
196 B16 Santa Rita SW Guam
44 H5 Santa Rita Cortés, NW Honduras 15.10N 87.54W
42 E9 Santa Rita Baja California Sur, W Mexico 27.28N 100.33W
56 H5 Santa Rita Zulia, NW Venezuela 10.33N 71.31W
61 I19 Santa Rita de Araguaia Goiás, S Brazil 17.17S 53.13W
Santa Rita de Cassia see Cássia
63 D14 Santa Rosa Corrientes, NE Argentina 28.18S 58.04W
64 K13 Santa Rosa La Pampa, C Argentina 36.37S 64.15W
63 G14 Santa Rosa Rio Grande do Sul, S Brazil 27.49S 54.28W
60 E10 Santa Rosa Roraima, N Brazil 3.41N 62.29W
58 B8 Santa Rosa El Oro, SW Ecuador 3.27S 79.57W
59 I16 Santa Rosa Puno, S Peru 14.38S 70.48W
36 M7 Santa Rosa California, W USA 38.26N 122.42W
39 U11 Santa Rosa New Mexico, SW USA 34.54N 104.43W
57 O6 Santa Rosa Anzoátegui, NE Venezuela 9.36N 64.16W
44 A3 Santa Rosa off. Departamento de Santa Rosa. ◐ department SE Guatemala
Santa Rosa see Santa Rosa de Copán
65 J15 Santa Rosa, Bajo de basin E Argentina
44 F6 Santa Rosa de Copán var. Santa Rosa. Copán, W Honduras 14.46N 88.48W
56 E8 Santa Rosa de Osos Antioquia, C Colombia 6.40N 75.27W
37 Q15 Santa Rosa Island island California, W USA
25 O9 Santa Rosa Island island Florida, SE USA
42 E6 Santa Rosalía Baja California Sur, W Mexico 27.19N 112.16W
56 K6 Santa Rosalía Portuguesa, NW Venezuela 9.01N 69.02W
196 C15 Santa Rosa, Mount ▲ NE Guam
37 V16 Santa Rosa Mountains ▲▲ California, W USA
37 T2 Santa Rosa Range ▲▲ Nevada, W USA
64 M8 Santa Sylvina Chaco, N Argentina 27.49S 61.07W
Santa Tecla see Nueva San Salvador
63 B19 Santa Teresa Santa Fe, C Argentina 33.30S 60.45W
61 O20 Santa Teresa Espírito Santo, SE Brazil 19.51S 40.49W
109 M23 Santa Teresa di Riva Sicilia, Italy, C Mediterranean Sea 38.00N 15.25E
63 E21 Santa Teresita Buenos Aires, E Argentina 36.34S 56.43W
63 H19 Santa Vitória do Palmar Rio Grande do Sul, S Brazil 33.31S 53.25W
37 Q14 Santa Ynez River ≈ California, W USA
Sant Carles de la Rápida see Sant Carles de la Ràpita
107 U7 Sant Carles de la Ràpita var. Sant Carles de la Rápida. Cataluña, NE Spain 40.37N 0.36E
107 W5 Sant Celoni Cataluña, NE Spain 41.39N 2.25E
37 U17 Santee California, W USA 32.50N 116.58W
23 T13 Santee River ≈ South Carolina, SE USA
42 K15 San Telmo, Punta headland SW Mexico 18.19N 103.30W
109 O17 Santeramo in Colle Puglia, SE Italy 40.46N 16.45E
107 X5 Sant Feliu de Guíxols var. San Feliú de Guixols. Cataluña, NE Spain 41.46N 3.01E
107 W6 Sant Feliu de Llobregat Cataluña, NE Spain 41.22N 2.00E
108 C7 Santhià Piemonte, NE Italy 45.21N 8.11E
63 F15 Santiago Rio Grande do Sul, S Brazil 29.10S 54.52W
64 H11 Santiago var. Gran Santiago. ● (Chile) Santiago, C Chile 33.30S 70.40W
47 N8 Santiago var. Santiago de los Caballeros. N Dominican Republic 19.27N 70.42W
42 G10 Santiago Baja California Sur, W Mexico 23.32N 109.45W
43 O8 Santiago Nuevo León, NE Mexico 25.22N 100.09W
45 R16 Santiago Veraguas, S Panama 8.06N 80.58W
59 E16 Santiago Ica, SW Peru 14.13S 75.43W
106 G3 Santiago var. Santiago de Compostela, Eng. Compostella; anc. Campus Stellae. Galicia, NW Spain 42.52N 8.33W
64 H11 Santiago off. Región Metropolitana de Santiago, var. Metropolitan. ◐ region C Chile
64 H11 Santiago ✕ Santiago, C Chile 33.27S 70.40W
106 G3 Santiago ✕ Galicia, NW Spain
78 D10 Santiago var. São Tiago. island Ilhas de Sotavento, S Cape Verde
Santiago see Santiago de Cuba, Cuba
Santiago see Grande de Santiago, Río, Mexico
44 B6 Santiago Atitlán Sololá, SW Guatemala 14.36N 91.13W
45 Q16 Santiago, Cerro ▲ W Panama 8.27N 81.42W
Santiago de Compostela see Santiago
46 I8 Santiago de Cuba var. Santiago. Santiago de Cuba, E Cuba 20.01N 75.50W
Santiago de Guayaquil see Guayaquil
64 K8 Santiago del Estero Santiago del Estero, C Argentina 27.51S 64.15W
63 A15 Santiago del Estero off. Provincia de Santiago del Estero. ◐ province N Argentina
42 I8 Santiago de los Caballeros Sinaloa, W Mexico 25.33N 107.22W
Santiago de los Caballeros see Santiago, Dominican Republic
Santiago de los Caballeros see Guatemala, Guatemala
44 F8 Santiago de María Usulután, SE El Salvador 13.28N 88.28W
106 F12 Santiago do Cacém Setúbal, S Portugal 38.01N 8.42W
42 J12 Santiago Ixcuintla Nayarit, C Mexico 21.49N 105.07W
Santiago Jamiltepec see Jamiltepec
26 L11 Santiago Mountains ▲▲ Texas, SW USA
42 J9 Santiago Papasquiaro Durango, C Mexico 25.03N 105.25W
Santiago Pinotepa Nacional see Pinotepa Nacional
58 C8 Santiago, Río ≈ N Peru
42 M10 San Tiburcio Zacatecas, C Mexico 24.07N 101.28W
107 N2 Santillana Cantabria, N Spain 43.24N 4.06W
56 I5 San Timoteo Zulia, NW Venezuela 9.49N 71.04W
Santi Quaranta see Sarandë
Santissima Trinidad see Chilung
107 O12 Santisteban del Puerto Andalucía, S Spain 38.15N 3.10W
107 U7 Sant Jordi, Golf de gulf NE Spain
107 T8 Sant Mateu País Valenciano, E Spain 40.28N 0.10E
27 S7 Santo Texas, SW USA 32.35N 98.06W
Santo see Espiritu Santo
62 M10 Santo Amaro, Ilha de island SE Brazil
63 G14 Santo Ângelo Rio Grande do Sul, S Brazil 28.16S 54.15W
78 C9 Santo Antão island Ilhas de Barlavento, N Cape Verde
62 J10 Santo Antônio da Platina Paraná, S Brazil 23.20S 50.05W
60 C13 Santo Antônio do Içá Amazonas, N Brazil 3.04S 67.55W
59 Q18 Santo Corazón, Río ≈ E Bolivia
46 E5 Santo Domingo Villa Clara, C Cuba 22.34N 80.15W
47 O9 Santo Domingo prev. Ciudad Trujillo. ● (Dominican Republic) SE Dominican Republic 18.30N 69.57W
42 E8 Santo Domingo Baja California Sur, W Mexico 25.31N 111.54W
42 M10 Santo Domingo San Luis Potosí, C Mexico 23.18N 101.42W
44 L10 Santo Domingo Chontales, S Nicaragua 12.15N 85.06W
107 P4 Santo Domingo de la Calzada La Rioja, N Spain 42.25N 2.57W
58 B6 Santo Domingo de los Colorados Pichincha, NW Ecuador 0.16S 79.11W
Santo Domingo Tehuantepec see Tehuantepec
57 O6 San Tomé Anzoátegui, NE Venezuela 8.54N 64.14W
San Tomé de Guayana see Ciudad Guayana
107 R13 Santomera Murcia, SE Spain 38.03N 1.05W
107 O2 Santoña Cantabria, N Spain 43.27N 3.28W
Santorin/Santoríni see Thíra
62 M10 Santos São Paulo, S Brazil 23.55S 46.22W
67 J17 Santos Plateau undersea feature SW Atlantic Ocean
106 G6 Santo Tirso Porto, N Portugal 41.20N 8.25W
42 B2 Santo Tomás Baja California, NW Mexico 31.31N 116.25W
44 L10 Santo Tomás Chontales, S Nicaragua 12.04N 85.01W
44 G5 Santo Tomás de Castilla Izabal, E Guatemala 15.40N 88.36W
42 B2 Santo Tomás, Punta headland NW Mexico 31.30N 116.40W
59 H16 Santo Tomás, Río ≈ C Peru
59 B18 Santo Tomás, Volcán ✻ Galapagos Islands, Ecuador, E Pacific Ocean 0.46S 91.01W
63 F14 Santo Tomé Corrientes, NE Argentina 28.31S 56.03W
Santo Tomé de Guayana see Ciudad Guayana
100 H10 Santpoort Noord-Holland, W Netherlands 52.25N 4.37E
Santurce see Santurtzi
107 O2 Santurtzi var. Santurce, Santurzi. País Vasco, N Spain 43.19N 3.03W
Santurzi see Santurtzi
65 G20 San Valentín, Cerro ▲ S Chile 46.36S 73.17W
44 F8 San Vicente San Vicente, C El Salvador 13.37N 88.44W
42 C2 San Vicente Baja California, NW Mexico 31.18N 116.12W
196 H6 San Vicente Saipan, S Northern Mariana Islands
44 B9 San Vicente ◐ department E El Salvador
106 I10 San Vicente de Alcántara Extremadura, W Spain 39.21N 7.07W
107 N2 San Vicente de Barakaldo var. Baracaldo. País Vasco, N Spain 43.16N 2.58W
59 E15 San Vicente de Cañete var. Cañete. Lima, W Peru 13.04S 76.25W
106 M2 San Vicente de la Barquera Cantabria, N Spain 43.22N 4.24W
56 E12 San Vicente del Caguán Caquetá, S Colombia 2.07N 74.46W
44 F8 San Vicente, Volcán de ✻ C El Salvador 13.34N 88.50W
45 O15 San Vito Puntarenas, SE Costa Rica 8.49N 82.58W
108 I7 San Vito al Tagliamento Friuli-Venezia Giulia, NE Italy 45.54N 12.55E
109 H23 San Vito, Capo headland Sicilia, Italy, C Mediterranean Sea 38.11N 12.41E
109 P18 San Vito dei Normanni Puglia, SE Italy 40.40N 17.42E
166 L17 Sanya var. Ya Xian. Hainan, S China 18.17N 109.32E
85 J16 Sanyati ≈ N Zimbabwe
27 Q16 San Ygnacio Texas, SW USA 27.04N 99.25W
166 L6 Sanyuan Shaanxi, C China 34.40N 108.55E
126 Ll12 Sanyyakhtakh Respublika Sakha (Yakutiya), NE Russian Federation 60.34N 124.09E
84 C10 Sanza Pombo Uíge, NW Angola 7.20S 16.00E
Sanzyô see Sanjō
106 G14 São Bartolomeu de Messines Faro, S Portugal 37.12N 8.16W
62 M10 São Bernardo do Campo São Paulo, S Brazil 23.41S 46.29W
63 F15 São Borja Rio Grande do Sul, S Brazil 28.34S 56.01W
106 H14 São Brás de Alportel Faro, S Portugal 37.09N 7.55W
62 M10 São Caetano do Sul São Paulo, S Brazil 23.37S 46.34W
62 L9 São Carlos São Paulo, S Brazil 22.01S 47.52W
61 P16 São Cristóvão Sergipe, E Brazil 10.58S 37.10W
63 F15 São Francisco de Assis Rio Grande do Sul, S Brazil 29.31S 55.07W
60 K13 São Félix Pará, NE Brazil 6.43S 51.55W
São Félix see São Félix do Araguaia
61 J16 São Félix do Araguaia var. São Félix. Mato Grosso, W Brazil 11.36S 50.40W
61 J14 São Félix do Xingu Pará, NE Brazil 6.37S 51.58W
62 Q9 São Fidélis Rio de Janeiro, SE Brazil 21.37S 41.40W
78 D10 São Filipe Fogo, S Cape Verde 14.52N 24.28W
62 K12 São Francisco do Sul Santa Catarina, S Brazil 26.16S 48.39W
62 K12 São Francisco, Ilha de island S Brazil
61 P16 São Francisco, Rio ≈ E Brazil
63 G16 São Gabriel Rio Grande do Sul, S Brazil 30.17S 54.17W
62 P10 São Gonçalo Rio de Janeiro, SE Brazil 22.48S 43.02W
83 H23 Sao Hill Iringa, S Tanzania 8.19S 35.10E
62 R9 São João da Barra Rio de Janeiro, SE Brazil 21.39S 41.04W
106 G7 São João da Madeira Aveiro, N Portugal 40.52N 8.28W
60 M12 São João de Cortês Maranhão, E Brazil 2.30S 44.27W
61 M21 São João del Rei Minas Gerais, NE Brazil 21.07S 44.15W
61 N15 São João do Piauí Piauí, E Brazil 8.21S 42.13W
61 N14 São João dos Patos Maranhão, E Brazil 6.28S 43.43W
60 C11 São Joaquim Amazonas, NW Brazil 0.08S 67.10W
63 J14 São Joaquim Santa Catarina, S Brazil 28.20S 49.55W
62 L7 São Joaquim da Barra São Paulo, S Brazil 20.36S 47.50W
66 N2 São Jorge island Azores, Portugal, NE Atlantic Ocean
63 K14 São José Santa Catarina, S Brazil 27.34S 48.39W
62 M8 São José do Rio Pardo São Paulo, S Brazil 21.37S 46.52W
62 K8 São José do Rio Preto São Paulo, S Brazil 20.49S 49.19W
62 N10 São Jose dos Campos São Paulo, S Brazil 23.07S 45.52W
63 I17 São Lourenço do Sul Rio Grande do Sul, S Brazil 31.25S 52.00W
60 F11 São Luís Roraima, N Brazil 1.11N 60.15W
60 M12 São Luís state capital Maranhão, NE Brazil 2.34S 44.16W
60 M12 São Luís, Ilha de island NE Brazil
63 F14 São Luiz Gonzaga Rio Grande do Sul, S Brazil 28.24S 54.58W
106 I10 São Mamede ▲ C Portugal 39.18N 7.19W
São Mandol see São Manuel, Rio
49 U8 São Manuel, Rio ≈ C Brazil
61 H15 São Manuel, Rio var. São Mandol, Teles Pirés. ≈ C Brazil
60 C11 São Marcelino Amazonas, NW Brazil 0.53N 67.16W
60 N12 São Marcos, Baía de bay N Brazil
61 O20 São Mateus Espírito Santo, SE Brazil 18.43S 39.52W
62 J12 São Mateus do Sul Paraná, S Brazil 25.51S 50.24W
66 P3 São Miguel island Azores, Portugal, NE Atlantic Ocean
62 G13 São Miguel d'Oeste Santa Catarina, S Brazil 26.45S 53.34W
47 P9 Saona, Isla island SE Dominican Republic
180 H12 Saondzou ▲ Grande Comore, NW Comoros
105 R10 Saône ≈ E France
105 Q9 Saône-et-Loire ◐ department C France
78 D9 São Nicolau Eng. Saint Nicholas. island Ilhas de Barlavento, N Cape Verde
62 M10 São Paulo state capital São Paulo, S Brazil 23.33S 46.39W
62 K9 São Paulo off. Estado de São Paulo. ◐ state S Brazil
São Paulo de Loanda see Luanda
São Pedro do Rio Grande do Sul see Rio Grande
106 H7 São Pedro do Sul Viseu, N Portugal 40.46N 7.58W
66 K13 São Pedro e São Paulo undersea feature C Atlantic Ocean 1.25N 28.54W
61 M14 São Raimundo das Mangabeiras Maranhão, E Brazil 7.00S 45.30W
61 Q14 São Roque, Cabo de headland E Brazil 5.28S 35.16W
São Salvador/São Salvador do Congo see M'Banza Congo, Angola
São Salvador see Salvador, Brazil
62 N10 São Sebastião, Ilha de island S Brazil
85 N19 São Sebastião, Ponta headland C Mozambique 22.09S 35.33E
106 F13 São Teotónio Beja, S Portugal 37.30N 8.41W
São Tiago see Santiago
81 B18 São Tomé ● (Sao Tome and Principe) São Tomé, S Sao Tome and Principe 0.19N 5.18E
81 B18 São Tomé ✕ São Tomé, S Sao Tome and Principe 0.24N 6.39E
81 B18 São Tomé Eng. Saint Thomas. island S Sao Tome and Principe
81 B17 Sao Tome and Principe off. Democratic Republic of Sao Tome and Principe. ◆ republic E Atlantic Ocean
76 H9 Saoura, Oued ≈ NW Algeria
62 M10 São Vicente Eng. Saint Vincent. São Paulo, S Brazil 23.55S 46.25W
66 O5 São Vicente Madeira, Portugal, NE Atlantic Ocean 32.48N 17.03W
78 C9 São Vicente Eng. Saint Vincent. island Ilhas de Barlavento, N Cape Verde
São Vicente, Cabo de see São Vicente, Cabo de
106 F14 São Vicente, Cabo de Eng. Cape Saint Vincent, Port. Cabo de São Vicente. headland S Portugal 37.01N 9.01W
Sápai see Sápes
Sapaleri, Cerro see Zapaleri, Cerro
175 Tt11 Saparau, Pulau island C Indonesia
Saparoea see Saparua
175 Tt11 Saparua prev. Saparoea. Pulau Saparau, C Indonesia 3.34S 128.37E
174 Hh8 Sapat Sumatera, W Indonesia 0.18S 103.18E
79 U17 Sapele Delta, S Nigeria 5.54N 5.43E
25 X7 Sapelo Island island Georgia, SE USA
25 X7 Sapelo Sound sound Georgia, SE USA
116 K13 Sápes var. Sápai. Anatolikí Makedonía kai Thráki, NE Greece 41.01N 25.42E
175 P16 Sape, Selat strait Nusa Tenggara, S Indonesia
117 D22 Sapiéntza island S Greece
Sapir see Sappir
63 I15 Sapiranga Rio Grande do Sul, S Brazil 29.39S 50.58W
116 K13 Sápka ▲▲ NE Greece
58 D11 Saposoa San Martín, N Peru 6.58S 76.40W
121 F16 Sapotskin Pol. Sopockinie, Rus. Sopotskin. Hrodzyenskaya Voblasts', W Belarus 53.50N 23.41E
79 P13 Sapoui var. Sapouy. S Burkina 11.34N 1.43W
Sapouy see Sapoui
144 F12 Sappir var. Sapir. Southern, S Israel 30.43N 35.11E
172 O5 Sapporo Hokkaidō, NE Japan 43.04N 141.21E
109 M19 Sapri Campania, S Italy 40.04N 15.35E
174 Mm15 Sapudi, Pulau island S Indonesia
29 P9 Sapulpa Oklahoma, C USA 36.00N 96.06W
148 J4 Saqqez var. Saghez, Sakiz, Saqqiz. Kordestān, NW Iran 36.30N 46.16E
Saqqiz see Saqqez
145 U8 Sarābādī E Iraq 33.00N 44.52E
178 Hh11 Sara Buri var. Saraburi. Saraburi, C Thailand 14.30N 100.54E
26 K9 Saragosa Texas, SW USA 31.03N 103.39W
Saragossa see Zaragoza
Saragt see Serakhs
58 B8 Saraguro Loja, S Ecuador 3.42S 79.16W
130 M6 Sarai Ryazanskaya Oblast', W Russian Federation 53.43N 39.59E
Sarai see Saray
160 M12 Saraipāli Madhya Pradesh, C India 21.21N 83.01E
155 T9 Sarāi Sidhu Punjab, E Pakistan 30.34N 71.58E
95 M15 Säräisniemi Oulu, C Finland 64.25N 26.50E
115 I14 Sarajevo ● (Bosnia and Herzegovina) Federacija Bosna I Hercegovina, SE Bosnia and Herzegovina 43.52N 18.24E
114 I13 Sarajevo ✕ Federacija Bosna I Hercegovina, C Bosnia and Herzegovina 43.49N 18.21E
149 V4 Sarakhs Khorāsān, NE Iran 36.41N 61.06E
117 H17 Sarakíniko, Akrotírio headland Évvoia, C Greece 38.46N 23.43E
117 I18 Sarakinó island Vóreioi Sporádes, Greece, Aegean Sea
131 V7 Saraktash Orenburgskaya Oblast', W Russian Federation 51.45N 56.23E
32 L15 Sara, Lake ⊡ Illinois, N USA
25 N8 Saraland Alabama, S USA 30.49N 88.04W
57 V9 Saramacca ◐ district N Surinam
57 V10 Saramacca Rivier ≈ C Surinam
177 G2 Saramati ▲ N Burma 25.46N 95.01E
151 R10 Saran' Kaz. Saran. Karaganda, C Kazakhstan 49.46N 73.01E
20 K7 Saranac Lake New York, NE USA 44.18N 74.06W
20 K7 Saranac River ≈ New York, NE USA
Saranda see Sarandë
115 L23 Sarandë var. Saranda, It. Porto Edda; prev. Santi Quaranta. Vlorë, S Albania 39.53N 19.59E
63 H14 Sarandi Rio Grande do Sul, S Brazil 27.57S 52.58W
63 F19 Sarandí del Yí Durazno, C Uruguay 33.18S 55.37W
63 F19 Sarandí Grande Florida, S Uruguay 33.43S 56.19W
179 Rr17 Sarangani Islands island group S Philippines
131 P5 Saransk Respublika Mordoviya, W Russian Federation 54.10N 45.09E
117 C14 Sarantáporos ≈ N Greece
116 H9 Sarantsi Sofiya, W Bulgaria 42.43N 23.46E
131 T3 Sarapul Udmurtskaya Respublika, NW Russian Federation 56.26N 53.52E
Sarâqeb see Sarāqib
144 I3 Sarāqib Fr. Sarâqeb. Idlib, N Syria 35.52N 36.48E
56 J5 Sarare Lara, N Venezuela 9.46N 69.10W
57 O10 Sarariña Amazonas, S Venezuela 4.10N 64.31W
149 S10 Sar Ashk Kermān, C Iran
25 V13 Sarasota Florida, SE USA 27.20N 82.31W
119 O11 Sarata Odes'ka Oblast', SW Ukraine 46.01N 29.40E
118 I10 Sărăţel Hung. Szeretfalva. Bistriţa-Năsăud, N Romania 47.02N 24.24E
27 X10 Saratoga Texas, SW USA 30.15N 94.31W
20 K10 Saratoga Springs New York, NE USA 43.04N 73.47W
131 P8 Saratov Saratovskaya Oblast', W Russian Federation 51.33N 45.57E
131 P8 Saratovskaya Oblast' ◐ province W Russian Federation
131 Q7 Saratovskoye Vodokhranilishche ⊡ W Russian Federation
Saravan/Saravane see Salavan
194 K12 Sarawaget Range var. Saruwaged Range. ▲ C PNG
174 M5 Sarawak ◐ state East Malaysia
Sarawak see Kuching
145 U6 Saray var. Sarāi. E Iraq 34.06N 45.06E
142 D10 Saray Tekirdağ, NW Turkey 41.27N 27.54E
78 J12 Saraya SE Senegal 12.49N 11.45W
149 W14 Sarbāz Sīstān va Balūchestān, SE Iran 26.37N 61.13E
149 U8 Sarbīsheh Khorāsān, E Iran 32.34N 59.49E
113 J24 Sárbogárd Fejér, C Hungary 46.53N 18.36E
Şărcad see Sarkad
29 S7 Sarcoxie Missouri, C USA 37.04N 94.07W
158 L11 Sārda Nep. Kali. ≈ India/Nepal
158 G10 Sardārshahr Rājasthān, NW India 28.24N 74.32E
109 C18 Sardegna Eng. Sardinia. ◐ region Italy, C Mediterranean Sea
109 A18 Sardegna Eng. Sardinia. island Italy, C Mediterranean Sea
44 K13 Sardinal Guanacaste, NW Costa Rica 10.30N 85.38W
56 G7 Sardinata Norte de Santander, N Colombia 8.05N 72.50W
Sardinia see Sardegna
123 K8 Sardinia-Corsica Trough undersea feature Tyrrhenian Sea, C Mediterranean Sea
24 L2 Sardis Mississippi, S USA 34.25N 89.55W
24 L2 Sardis Lake ⊡ Mississippi, S USA
29 P12 Sardis Lake ⊡ Oklahoma, C USA
94 H12 Sarek ▲ N Sweden
155 N3 Sar-e Pol var. Sar-i-Pul. Sar-e Pol, N Afghanistan 36.16N 65.55E
155 O3 Sar-e Pol ◐ province N Afghanistan
Sar-e Pol see Sar-e Pol-e Ẕahāb
148 J6 Sar-e Pol-e Ẕahāb var. Sar-e Pol, Sar-i Pul. Kermānshāh, W Iran 34.28N 45.52E
153 T13 Sarez, Kŭli Rus. Sarezskoye Ozero. ⊙ SE Tajikistan
Sarezskoye Ozero see Sarez, Kŭli
66 G10 Sargasso Sea sea W Atlantic Ocean
155 U8 Sargodha Punjab, NE Pakistan 32.06N 72.47E
80 I13 Sarh prev. Fort-Archambault. Moyen-Chari, S Chad 9.07N 18.22E
149 P4 Sārī var. Sari, Sāri. Māzandarān, N Iran 36.36N 53.04E
117 N23 Saría island SE Greece
Sariasiya see Sariosiyo
42 F3 Saric Sonora, NW Mexico 31.07N 111.22W
196 K6 Sarigan island C Northern Mariana Islands
142 D14 Sarıgöl Manisa, SW Turkey 38.13N 28.40E
145 T6 Sārihah E Iraq 34.34N 44.38E
143 R12 Sarıkamış Kars, NE Turkey 40.18N 42.36E
174 L6 Sarikei Sarawak, East Malaysia 2.07N 111.30E
153 U12 Sarikol Range Rus. Sarykol'skiy Khrebet. ▲ China/Tajikistan
189 Y7 Sarina Queensland, NE Australia 21.34S 149.12E
Sarine see La Sarine
107 S5 Sariñena Aragón, NE Spain 41.46N 0.10W
153 O13 Sariosiyo Rus. Sariasiya. Surkhondaryo Wiloyati, S Uzbekistan 38.25N 67.51E

◆ COUNTRY ● COUNTRY CAPITAL ◇ DEPENDENT TERRITORY ○ DEPENDENT TERRITORY CAPITAL ◐ ADMINISTRATIVE REGION ✕ INTERNATIONAL AIRPORT ▲ MOUNTAIN ▲▲ MOUNTAIN RANGE ✻ VOLCANO ≈ RIVER ⊙ LAKE ⊡ RESERVOIR

SAR-I-PUL – SCOTTSBLUFF

Sar-i-Pul see Sar-e Pol, Afghanistan
Sar-i Pul see Sar-e Pol-e Žahāb, Iran
Sariqamish Kŭli see Sarykamyshkoye Ozero
155 V1 **Sarī Qūl** Rus. Ozero Zurkul', Taj. Zŭrkŭl. ◎ Afghanistan/Tajikistan see also Zŭrkŭl
77 Q12 **Sarīr Tībistī** var. Serir Tibesti. desert S Libya
27 S15 **Sarita** Texas, SW USA 27.12N 97.48W
169 W14 **Sariwŏn** SW North Korea 38.30N 125.52E
116 P12 **Sarıyer** İstanbul, NW Turkey 41.10N 29.03E
99 L26 **Sark** Fr. Sercq. island Channel Islands
113 N24 **Sarkad** Rom. Şărcad. Békés, SE Hungary 46.42N 21.21E
151 W14 **Sarkand** Almaty, SW Kazakhstan 45.25N 79.53E
Sarkaṇi see Krasnogorskoye
158 D11 **Sarkāri Tala** Rājasthān, NW India 27.39N 70.52E
142 G15 **Şarkîkaraağaç** var. Şarki Karaağaç. Isparta, SW Turkey 38.04N 31.22E
142 L13 **Şarkışla** Sivas, C Turkey 39.21N 36.27E
142 C11 **Şarköy** Tekirdağ, NW Turkey 40.37N 27.07E
Sárköz see Livada
Sarlat see Sarlat-la-Canéda
104 M13 **Sarlat-la-Canéda** var. Sarlat. Dordogne, SW France 44.54N 1.12E
111 S3 **Sarleinsbach** Oberösterreich, N Austria 48.33N 13.55E
176 Y10 **Sarmi** Irian Jaya, E Indonesia 1.51S 138.45E
65 I19 **Sarmiento** Chubut, S Argentina 45.37S 69.06W
65 H25 **Sarmiento, Monte** ▲ S Chile 54.28S 70.49W
96 J11 **Särna** Dalarna, C Sweden 61.40N 13.10E
110 F8 **Sarnen** Obwalden, C Switzerland 46.54N 8.15E
110 F9 **Sarner See** ◎ C Switzerland
12 D16 **Sarnia** Ontario, S Canada 42.57N 82.22W
118 L3 **Sarny** Rivnens'ka Oblast', NW Ukraine 51.20N 26.34E
175 Q10 **Saroako** Sulawesi, C Indonesia 2.31S 121.18E
120 L13 **Sarochyna** Rus. Sorochino. Vitsyebskaya Voblasts', N Belarus 55.12N 28.45E
174 Hh10 **Sarolangun** Sumatera, W Indonesia 2.17S 102.39E
172 Q5 **Saroma** Hokkaidō, NE Japan 44.01N 143.43E
172 Q5 **Saroma-ko** ◎ Hokkaidō, NE Japan
Saronic Gulf see Saronikós Kólpos
117 H20 **Saronikós Kólpos** Eng. Saronic Gulf. gulf S Greece
108 D7 **Saronno** Lombardia, N Italy 45.37N 9.01E
142 B11 **Saros Körfezi** gulf NW Turkey
113 N20 **Sárospatak** Borsod-Abaúj-Zemplén, NE Hungary 48.18N 21.30E
131 P12 **Sarpa** Respublika Kalmykiya, SW Russian Federation 47.00N 45.42E
131 P12 **Sarpa, Ozero** ◎ SW Russian Federation
115 M18 **Šar Planina** ▲▲ FYR Macedonia/Yugoslavia
97 I16 **Sarpsborg** Østfold, S Norway 59.16N 11.07E
145 U5 **Sarqaļā** N Iraq
105 U4 **Sarralbe** Moselle, NE France 49.02N 7.01E
Sarre see Saar, France/Germany
Sarre see Saarland, Germany
105 U5 **Sarrebourg** Ger. Saarburg. Moselle, NE France 48.43N 7.03E
Sarrebruck see Saarbrücken
105 U4 **Sarreguemines** prev. Saargemund. Moselle, NE France 49.06N 7.04E
106 I3 **Sarria** Galicia, NW Spain 42.46N 7.25W
107 S8 **Sarrión** Aragón, NE Spain 40.09N 0.49W
44 F4 **Sarstoon** Sp. Río Sarstún. ≈ Belize/Guatemala
Sarstún, Río see Sarstoon
126 M9 **Sartang** ≈ NE Russian Federation
105 X16 **Sartène** Corse, France, C Mediterranean Sea 41.37N 8.58E
104 K7 **Sarthe** ◐ department NW France
104 K7 **Sarthe** ≈ N France
117 H15 **Sárti** Kentrikí Makedonía, N Greece 40.04N 23.59E
172 Pp2 **Sarufutsu** Hokkaidō, NE Japan 45.20N 142.03E
172 Oo7 **Saru-gawa** ≈ Hokkaidō, NE Japan
Saruhan see Manisa
158 G9 **Sarūpsar** Rājasthān, NW India 29.25N 73.49E
143 U13 **Şärur** prev. Il'ichevsk. SW Azerbaijan 39.30N 44.59E
Saruwaged Range see Sarawaget Range
Sarvani see Marneuli
113 G23 **Sárvár** Vas, W Hungary 47.14N 16.57E
149 P11 **Sarvestān** Fārs, S Iran 29.16N 53.13E
176 X9 **Sarwon** Irian Jaya, E Indonesia 0.58S 136.08E
151 P17 **Saryagach** Kaz. Saryaghash. Yuzhnyy Kazakhstan, S Kazakhstan 41.28N 69.10E
Saryaghash see Saryagach
Saryarqa see Kazakhskiy Melkosopochnik
153 W8 **Sary-Bulak** Narynskaya Oblast', C Kyrgyzstan 41.56N 75.44E
153 U10 **Sary-Bulak** Oshskaya Oblast', SW Kyrgyzstan 40.49N 73.44E
119 S14 **Sarych, Mys** headland S Ukraine 44.23N 33.44E
153 Z7 **Sary-Dzhaz** var. Aksu He. ≈ China/Kyrgyzstan see also Aksu He
151 T14 **Saryesik-Atyrau, Peski** desert E Kazakhstan
150 G13 **Sarykamys** Kaz. Saryqamys. Mangistau, SW Kazakhstan 45.58N 53.30E
152 F8 **Sarykamyshkoye Ozero** Uzb. Sariqamish Kŭli. salt lake Kazakhstan/Uzbekistan
Sarykol'skiy Khrebet see Sarikol Range
150 M10 **Sarykopa, Ozero** ◎ C Kazakhstan
151 V15 **Saryozek** Kaz. Saryözek. Almaty, SE Kazakhstan 44.22N 77.57E
Saryqamys see Sarykamys
151 S13 **Saryshagan** Kaz. Saryshahan. Zhezkazgan, SE Kazakhstan 46.03N 73.36E
Saryshahan see Saryshagan
151 O13 **Sarysu** ≈ S Kazakhstan
153 T11 **Sary-Tash** Oshskaya Oblast', SW Kyrgyzstan 39.43N 73.13E
152 J15 **Saryyazynskoye Vodokhranilishche** ⊠ S Turkmenistan
108 E10 **Sarzana** Liguria, NW Italy 44.07N 9.59E
196 B17 **Sasalaguan, Mount** ▲ S Guam
159 O14 **Sasarām** Bihār, N India 24.58N 84.01E
195 W14 **Sasari, Mount** ▲ Santa Isabel, N Solomon Islands 8.09S 159.32E
170 C12 **Sasebo** Nagasaki, Kyūshū, SW Japan 33.10N 129.42E
12 I9 **Saseginaga, Lac** ◎ Quebec, SE Canada
Saseno see Sazan
9 R13 **Saskatchewan** ◐ province SW Canada
9 U14 **Saskatchewan** ≈ Manitoba/Saskatchewan, C Canada
9 T15 **Saskatoon** Saskatchewan, S Canada 52.10N 106.40W
9 T15 **Saskatoon** ✕ Saskatchewan, S Canada 52.15N 107.05W
126 K7 **Saskylakh** Respublika Sakha (Yakutiya), NE Russian Federation 71.56N 114.07E
44 L7 **Saslaya, Cerro** ▲ N Nicaragua 13.52N 85.06W
40 G17 **Sasmik, Cape** headland Tanaga Island, Alaska, USA 51.36N 105.55W
121 N19 **Sasnovy Bor** Rus. Sosnovyy Bor. Homyel'skaya Voblasts', SE Belarus 52.31N 29.37E
131 N5 **Sasovo** Ryazanskaya Oblast', W Russian Federation 54.19N 41.54E
27 S12 **Saspamco** Texas, SW USA 29.13N 98.18W
111 W9 **Sass** var. Sassbach. ≈ SE Austria
78 M17 **Sassandra** S Ivory Coast 4.58N 6.07W
78 M17 **Sassandra** var. Ibo, Sassandra Fleuve. ≈ S Ivory Coast
Sassandra Fleuve see Sassandra
109 B17 **Sassari** Sardegna, Italy, C Mediterranean Sea 40.43N 8.33E
Sassbach see Sass
100 H11 **Sassenheim** Zuid-Holland, W Netherlands 52.13N 4.31E
Sassmacken see Valdemārpils
102 O7 **Sassnitz** Mecklenburg-Vorpommern, NE Germany 54.32N 13.39E
101 E16 **Sas van Gent** Zeeland, SW Netherlands 51.13N 3.48E
151 W12 **Sasykkol', Ozero** ◎ E Kazakhstan
119 O12 **Sasyk Kunduk, Ozero** ◎ SW Ukraine
78 J12 **Satadougou** Kayes, SW Mali 12.40N 11.25W
107 V11 **Sa Talaiassa** ▲ Eivissa, Spain, W Mediterranean Sea 38.55N 1.17E
170 B17 **Sata-misaki** headland Kyūshū, SW Japan 31.00N 130.39E
28 I7 **Satanta** Kansas, C USA 37.23N 102.00W
161 E15 **Sātāra** Mahārāshtra, W India 17.40N 73.58E
198 Aa7 **Sātaua** Savai'i, NW Samoa 13.25S 172.40W
196 M16 **Satawal** island Caroline Islands, C Micronesia
201 R17 **Satawan Atoll** atoll Mortlock Islands, C Micronesia
25 Y12 **Satellite Beach** Florida, SE USA 28.10N 80.35W
97 M14 **Säter** Dalarna, C Sweden 60.21N 15.45E
Sathmar see Satu Mare
25 V7 **Satilla River** ≈ Georgia, SE USA
59 F14 **Satipo** var. San Francisco de Satipo. Junín, C Peru 11.13S 74.40W
125 E11 **Satka** Chelyabinskaya Oblast', C Russian Federation 55.08N 58.54E
159 T16 **Satkhira** Khulna, SW Bangladesh 22.43N 89.06E
160 K9 **Satna** prev. Sutna. Madhya Pradesh, C India 24.33N 80.49E
105 R11 **Satolas** ✕ (Lyon) Rhône, E France 45.44N 5.01E
113 N20 **Sátoraljaújhely** Borsod-Abaúj-Zemplén, NE Hungary 48.24N 21.39E
151 O12 **Satpayev** prev. Nikol'skiy. Zhezkazgan, C Kazakhstan 47.59N 67.27E
160 G11 **Sātpura Range** ▲▲ C India
170 Bb16 **Satsuma-hantō** peninsula Kyūshū, SW Japan
178 Hh12 **Sattahip** var. Ban Sattahip, Ban Sattahipp. Chon Buri, S Thailand 12.41N 100.55E
94 L11 **Sattanen** Lappi, NE Finland 67.31N 26.35E
Satul see Satun
118 H9 **Satulung** Hung. Kővárhosszúfalu. Maramureş, N Romania 47.34N 23.25E
Satul-Vechi see Staro Selo
118 G8 **Satu Mare** Ger. Sathmar, Hung. Szatmárnémeti. Satu Mare, NW Romania 47.46N 22.54E
118 G8 **Satu Mare** ◐ county NW Romania
178 H17 **Satun** var. Satul, Setul. Satun, SW Thailand 6.34N 100.02E
198 Aa8 **Satupaiteau** Savai'i, W Samoa 13.46S 172.26W
Sau see Sava
12 F14 **Sauble** ≈ Ontario, S Canada
12 F13 **Sauble Beach** Ontario, S Canada 44.36N 81.15W
63 C16 **Sauce** Corrientes, NE Argentina 30.07S 58.50W
Sauce see Juan L.Lacaze
38 K15 **Sauceda Mountains** ▲▲ Arizona, SW USA
63 C17 **Sauce de Luna** Entre Ríos, E Argentina 31.15S 59.09W
65 L15 **Sauce Grande, Río** ≈ E Argentina
42 K6 **Saucillo** Chihuahua, N Mexico 28.01N 105.17W
97 D15 **Sauda** Rogaland, S Norway 59.39N 6.21E
151 Q16 **Saudakent** Kaz. Saūdakent; prev. Baykadam Kaz. Bayqadam. Zhambyl, S Kazakhstan 43.45N 69.52E
94 J2 **Saudhárkrókur** Nordhurland Vestra, N Iceland 65.45N 19.39W
147 P9 **Saudi Arabia** off. Kingdom of Saudi Arabia, Ar. Al 'Arabīyah as Su'ūdīyah, Al Mamlakah al 'Arabīyah as Su'ūdīyah. ◆ monarchy SW Asia
103 D19 **Sauer** var. Sûre. ≈ NW Europe see also Sûre
103 F15 **Sauerland** forest W Germany
12 F14 **Saugeen** ≈ Ontario, S Canada
20 K12 **Saugerties** New York, NE USA 42.04N 73.55W
Saugor see Sāgar
8 K15 **Saugstad, Mount** ▲ British Columbia, SW Canada 52.12N 126.35W
Sāūjbulāgh see Mahābād
104 J11 **Saujon** Charente-Maritime, W France 45.40N 0.54W
31 T7 **Sauk Centre** Minnesota, N USA 45.44N 94.57W
32 L8 **Sauk City** Wisconsin, N USA 43.16N 89.43W
176 Vv8 **Sau Korem** Irian Jaya, E Indonesia 0.30S 133.10E
31 U7 **Sauk Rapids** Minnesota, N USA 45.35N 94.09W
57 Y11 **Saül** C French Guiana 3.37N 53.12W
105 O7 **Sauldre** ≈ C France
103 I23 **Saulgau** Baden-Württemberg, SW Germany 48.03N 9.28E
105 Q8 **Saulieu** Côte d'Or, C France 47.15N 4.15E
120 G8 **Saulkrasti** Rīga, C Latvia 57.13N 24.25E
13 S6 **Sault-aux-Cochons, Rivière du** ≈ Quebec, SE Canada
33 Q4 **Sault Sainte Marie** Michigan, N USA 46.28N 84.22W
10 F14 **Sault Ste.Marie** Ontario, S Canada 46.30N 84.16W
151 P7 **Saumalkol'** prev. Volodarskoye. Severnyy Kazakhstan, N Kazakhstan 53.19N 68.04E
202 E13 **Sauma, Pointe** headland Île Alofi, W Wallis and Futuna 14.21S 105.58W
176 Uu15 **Saumlaki** var. Saumlakki. Pulau Yamdena, E Indonesia 7.53S 131.18E
Saumlakki see Saumlaki
13 R12 **Saumon, Rivière au** ≈ Quebec, SE Canada
104 K8 **Saumur** Maine-et-Loire, NW France 47.16N 0.04W
193 F23 **Saunders, Cape** headland South Island, NZ 45.53S 170.40E
205 N13 **Saunders Coast** physical region Antarctica
67 B23 **Saunders Island** island NW Falkland Islands
67 C24 **Saunders Island Settlement** Saunders Island, NW Falkland Islands 51.22S 60.04W
84 F11 **Saurimo** Port. Henrique de Carvalho, Vila Henrique de Carvalho. Lunda Sul, NE Angola 9.39S 20.24E
57 S11 **Sauriwaunawa** S Guyana 3.10N 59.51W
176 V8 **Sausapor** Irian Jaya, E Indonesia 0.28S 132.09E
84 D12 **Sautar** Malanje, NW Angola 11.10S 18.26E
47 S13 **Sauteurs** N Grenada 12.13N 61.38W
104 K13 **Sauveterre-de-Guyenne** Gironde, SW France 44.43N 0.02W
121 O14 **Sava** Rus. Sava. Mahilyowskaya Voblasts', E Belarus 54.22N 30.47E
86 H11 **Sava** Eng. Save, Ger. Sau, Hung. Száva. ≈ SE Europe
44 J5 **Savá** Colón, N Honduras 15.30N 86.12W
35 Y8 **Savage** Montana, NW USA 47.28N 104.17W
191 N16 **Savage River** Tasmania, SE Australia 41.34S 145.15E
198 Aa7 **Savai'i** island NW Samoa
79 R15 **Savalou** S Benin 7.58N 1.58E
32 K10 **Savanna** Illinois, N USA 42.05N 90.09W
25 X6 **Savannah** Georgia, SE USA 32.01N 81.00W
29 R2 **Savannah** Missouri, C USA 39.56N 94.49W
22 H10 **Savannah** Tennessee, S USA 35.13N 88.15W
23 O12 **Savannah River** ≈ Georgia/South Carolina, SE USA
Savannakhét see Khanthabouli
46 H12 **Savanna-La-Mar** W Jamaica 18.13N 78.07W
10 B10 **Savant Lake** ◎ Ontario, S Canada
161 F17 **Savanūr** Karnātaka, W India 14.58N 75.19E
95 J16 **Sävar** Västerbotten, N Sweden 63.52N 20.33E
Savaria see Szombathely
160 C11 **Sāvarkundla** var. Kundla. Gujarāt, W India 21.21N 71.20E
118 F11 **Săvârşin** Hung. Soborsin; prev. Săvîrşin. Arad, W Romania 46.00N 22.15E
142 C13 **Savaştepe** Balıkesir, W Turkey 39.19N 27.37E
Savat see Sawot
85 N18 **Save** Inhambane, E Mozambique 21.07S 34.35E
104 L16 **Save** ≈ S France
85 L17 **Save** var. Sabi. ≈ Mozambique/Zimbabwe see also Sabi
Save see Sava
79 R15 **Savè** SE Benin 8.04N 2.28E
148 M6 **Sāveh** Markazī, W Iran 35.03N 50.21E
118 L8 **Săveni** Botoşani, NE Romania 47.57N 26.49E
105 N16 **Saverdun** Ariège, S France 43.15N 1.34E
105 U5 **Saverne** var. Zabern; anc. Tres Tabernae. Bas-Rhin, NE France 48.45N 7.22E
Savichi see Savichy
121 O21 **Savichy** Rus. Savichi. Homyel'skaya Voblasts', SE Belarus 51.37N 30.19E
108 B9 **Savigliano** Piemonte, NW Italy 44.39N 7.39E
Savigsivik see Savissivik
Savinichi see Savinichy
121 Q16 **Savinichy** Rus. Savinichi. Mahilyowskaya Voblasts', E Belarus 53.28N 31.46E
Savinski see Savinskiy
125 Dd6 **Savinskiy** var. Savinski. Arkhangel'skaya Oblast', NW Russian Federation 62.54N 40.07E
108 H11 **Savio** ≈ C Italy
Săvîrşin see Săvârşin
207 O11 **Savissivik** var. Savigsivik. Avannaarsua, S Greenland 76.09N 65.24W
95 N18 **Savitaipale** Etelä-Suomi, S Finland 61.12N 27.43E
115 J15 **Šavnik** Montenegro, SW Yugoslavia 42.57N 19.04E
195 W15 **Savo** island C Solomon Islands
110 I9 **Savognin** Graubünden, S Switzerland 46.34N 9.35E
105 T12 **Savoie** ◐ department E France
108 C10 **Savona** Liguria, NW Italy 44.18N 8.28E
95 N17 **Savonlinna** Swe. Nyslott. Itä-Suomi, SE Finland 61.51N 28.55E
95 N17 **Savonranta** Itä-Suomi, SE Finland 62.10N 29.10E
40 K10 **Savoonga** Saint Lawrence Island, Alaska, USA 63.40N 170.29W
32 M13 **Savoy** Illinois, N USA 40.03N 88.15W
119 O8 **Savran'** Odes'ka Oblast', SW Ukraine 48.07N 30.00E
143 R11 **Şavşat** Artvin, NE Turkey 41.15N 42.30E
97 L19 **Sävsjö** Jönköping, S Sweden 57.25N 14.40E
Savu, Kepulauan see Sawu, Kepulauan
94 M11 **Savukoski** Lappi, NE Finland 67.17N 28.14E
Savu, Pulau see Sawu, Pulau
197 J13 **Savusavu** Vanua Levu, N Fiji 16.47S 179.21E
175 Q17 **Savu Sea** Ind. Laut Sawu. sea S Indonesia
85 H17 **Savute** Chobe, N Botswana 18.33S 24.06E
145 N7 **Şawāb 'Uqlat** well W Iraq 33.57N 40.04E
144 M7 **Sawāb, Wādī as** dry watercourse W Iraq
158 H13 **Sawāi Mādhopur** Rājasthān, N India 26.00N 76.22E
175 Tt10 **Sawai, Teluk** bay Pulau Seram, E Indonesia
Sawakin see Suakin
178 Ii9 **Sawang Daen Din** Sakon Nakhon, E Thailand 17.28N 103.27E
178 H8 **Sawankhalok** var. Swankalok. Sukhothai, NW Thailand 17.19N 99.49E
171 Kk17 **Sawara** Chiba, Honshū, S Japan 35.52N 140.29E
171 Jj12 **Sawasaki-bana** headland Sado, C Japan 37.48N 138.11E
39 R5 **Sawatch Range** ▲▲ Colorado, C USA
147 N12 **Sawdā', Jabal** ▲ SW Saudi Arabia 18.15N 42.26E
77 P9 **Sawdā', Jabal as** ▲▲ C Libya
Sawdirī see Sodiri
176 W9 **Saweba, Tanjung** headland Irian Jaya, E Indonesia 0.41S 133.59E
99 F14 **Sawel Mountain** ▲ C Northern Ireland, UK 54.49N 7.04W
Sawhāj see Sohâg
79 O15 **Sawla** N Ghana 9.14N 2.26W
153 P11 **Sawot** Rus. Savat. Sirdaryo Wiloyati, E Uzbekistan 40.03N 68.35E
147 X12 **Şawqirah** var. Suqrah. S Oman 18.16N 56.34E
147 X12 **Şawqirah, Dawḩat** var. Ghubbat Sawqirah, Sukra Bay, Suqrah Bay. bay S Oman
Sawqirah, Ghubbat see Şawqirah, Dawḩat
191 V5 **Sawtell** New South Wales, SE Australia 30.22S 153.04E
144 K7 **Şawt, Wādī aş** dry watercourse S Syria
175 Q18 **Sawu, Kepulauan** var. Kepulauan Savu. island group S Indonesia
Sawu, Laut see Savu Sea
175 Qq18 **Sawu, Pulau** var. Pulau Savu. island Kepulauan Sawu, S Indonesia
107 S12 **Sax** País Valenciano, E Spain 38.33N 0.49W
Saxe see Sachsen
110 C11 **Saxon** Valais, SW Switzerland 46.07N 7.09E
Saxony see Sachsen
Saxony-Anhalt see Sachsen-Anhalt
79 R12 **Say** Niamey, SW Niger 13.02N 2.22E
13 V7 **Sayabec** Quebec, SE Canada 48.33N 67.42W
Sayaboury see Xaignabouli
151 U12 **Sayak** Kaz. Sayaq. Zhezkazgan, E Kazakhstan 46.54N 77.17E
59 D14 **Sayán** Lima, W Peru 11.06S 77.09W
126 Hh15 **Sayanogorsk** Respublika Khakasiya, S Russian Federation 53.07N 91.08E
126 J15 **Sayansk** Irkutskaya Oblast', S Russian Federation 54.06N 102.10E
133 T6 **Sayanskiy Khrebet** ▲▲ S Russian Federation
Sayaq see Sayak
152 K13 **Sayat** Lebapskiy Velayat, E Turkmenistan 38.44N 63.51E
44 D3 **Sayaxché** Petén, N Guatemala 16.31N 90.10W
Şaydā/Sayida see Saïda
147 T15 **Sayḩūt** E Yemen 15.18N 51.15E
31 U14 **Saylorville Lake** ⊠ Iowa, C USA
Saymenskiy Kanal see Saimaa Canal
169 N10 **Saynshand** Dornogovĭ, SE Mongolia 44.51N 110.07E
168 J11 **Saynshand** Ömnögovĭ, S Mongolia 43.30N 102.08E
168 F7 **Sayn-Ust** Govĭ-Altay, W Mongolia 47.23N 94.19E
Say-Ötesh see Say-Utës
144 J7 **Şayqal, Baḩr** ◎ S Syria
Sayrab see Sayrob
164 H4 **Sayram Hu** ◎ NW China
28 K11 **Sayre** Oklahoma, C USA 35.17N 99.38W
20 H12 **Sayre** Pennsylvania, NE USA 41.57N 76.30W
20 K15 **Sayreville** New Jersey, NE USA 40.27N 74.19W
153 N13 **Sayrob** Rus. Sayrab. Surkhondaryo Wiloyati, S Uzbekistan 38.03N 66.54E
42 L13 **Sayula** Jalisco, SW Mexico 19.52N 103.36W
147 R14 **Say 'ūn** var. Saywūn. C Yemen 15.52N 48.31E
150 G14 **Say-Utës** Kaz. Say-Ötesh. Mangistau, SW Kazakhstan 44.20N 53.32E
8 K16 **Sayward** Vancouver Island, British Columbia, SW Canada 50.20N 126.01W
Saywūn see Say 'ūn
Sayyāl see As Sayyāl
145 U8 **Sayyid 'Abīd** var. Saiyid Abid. E Iraq 32.51N 45.07E
115 J22 **Sazan** var. Ishulli i Sazanit, It. Saseno. island SW Albania
Sazanit, Ishulli i see Sazan
Sazau/Sazawa see Sázava
113 E17 **Sázava** var. Sazau, Ger. Sazawa. ≈ C Czech Republic
128 J14 **Sazonovo** Vologodskaya Oblast', NW Russian Federation 59.04N 35.10E
104 G6 **Scaër** Finistère, NW France 48.00N 3.40W
99 J15 **Scafell Pike** ▲ NW England, UK 54.26N 3.10W
Scalabis see Santarém
98 M2 **Scalloway** N Scotland, UK 60.10N 1.17W
40 M11 **Scammon Bay** Alaska, USA 61.50N 165.34W
Scammon Lagoon/Scammon, Laguna see Ojo de Liebre, Laguna
86 F7 **Scandinavia** geophysical region NW Europe
Scania see Skåne
98 K5 **Scapa Flow** sea basin N Scotland, UK
109 K26 **Scaramia, Capo** headland Sicilia, Italy, C Mediterranean Sea 36.46N 14.29E
12 H15 **Scarborough** Ontario, SE Canada 43.46N 79.14W
47 Z16 **Scarborough** prev. Port Louis. Tobago, Trinidad and Tobago 11.10N 60.45W
99 N16 **Scarborough** N England, UK 54.16N 0.24W
193 I17 **Scargill** Canterbury, South Island, NZ 42.57S 172.57E
98 E7 **Scarp** island NW Scotland, UK
Scarpanto see Kárpathos
Scarpanto Strait see Karpathou, Stenó
109 G25 **Scauri** Sicilia, Italy, C Mediterranean Sea 36.45N 12.06E
Scealg, Bá na see Ballinskelligs Bay
Scebeli see Shebeli
102 K10 **Schaale** ≈ N Germany
102 K9 **Schaalsee** ◎ N Germany
101 G18 **Schaerbeek** Brussels, C Belgium 50.51N 4.21E
110 G6 **Schaffhausen** Fr. Schaffhouse. Schaffhausen, N Switzerland 47.42N 8.37E
110 G6 **Schaffhausen** Fr. Schaffhouse. ◐ canton N Switzerland
Schaffhouse see Schaffhausen
100 I8 **Schagen** Noord-Holland, NW Netherlands 52.46N 4.46E
Schaken see Šakiai
100 M10 **Schalkhaar** Overijssel, E Netherlands 52.16N 6.10E
111 R3 **Schärding** Oberösterreich, N Austria 48.27N 13.26E
102 G9 **Scharhörn** island NW Germany
Schässburg see Sighişoara
Schaulen see Šiauliai
32 M10 **Schaumburg** Illinois, N USA 42.01N 88.04W
Schebschi Mountains see Shebshi Mountains
100 P6 **Scheemda** Groningen, NE Netherlands 53.10N 6.58E
102 I10 **Scheessel** Niedersachsen, NW Germany 53.11N 9.32E
11 N8 **Schefferville** Quebec, E Canada 54.50N 67.00W
Schelde see Scheldt
101 D18 **Scheldt** Dut. Schelde, Fr. Escaut. ≈ W Europe
37 X5 **Schell Creek Range** ▲▲ Nevada, W USA
20 K10 **Schenectady** New York, NE USA 42.48N 73.57W
101 I17 **Scherpenheuvel** Fr. Montaigu. Vlaams Brabant, C Belgium 51.00N 4.57E
100 K11 **Scherpenzeel** Gelderland, C Netherlands 52.07N 5.30E
27 S12 **Schertz** Texas, SW USA 29.33N 98.16W
100 G11 **Scheveningen** Zuid-Holland, W Netherlands 52.07N 4.18E
100 G12 **Schiedam** Zuid-Holland, SW Netherlands 51.55N 4.25E
101 M24 **Schieren** Diekirch, NE Luxembourg 49.49N 6.06E
100 M4 **Schiermonnikoog** Fris. Skiermûntseach. Friesland, N Netherlands 53.28N 6.09E
100 M4 **Schiermonnikoog** Fris. Skiermûntseach. island Waddeneilanden, N Netherlands
101 K14 **Schijndel** Noord-Brabant, S Netherlands 51.37N 5.27E
Schil see Jiu
101 H16 **Schilde** Antwerpen, N Belgium 51.13N 4.34E
Schillen see Zhilino
105 V5 **Schiltigheim** Bas-Rhin, NE France 48.37N 7.46E
108 G7 **Schio** Veneto, NE Italy 45.42N 11.21E
100 H10 **Schiphol** ✕ (Amsterdam) Noord-Holland, C Netherlands 52.18N 4.48E
Schippenbeil see Sępopol
Schiria see Şiria
Schivelbein see Świdwin
117 D22 **Schíza** island S Greece
183 U3 **Schjetman Reef** reef Antarctica
Schlackenwerth see Ostrov
111 R7 **Schladming** Steiermark, SE Austria 47.23N 13.37E
Schlan see Slaný
Schlanders see Silandro
102 I7 **Schlei** inlet N Germany
103 D17 **Schleiden** Nordrhein-Westfalen, W Germany 50.31N 6.30E
195 P9 **Schleinitz Range** ▲▲ New Ireland, N PNG
Schlelau see Szydłowiec
102 I7 **Schleswig** Schleswig-Holstein, N Germany 54.31N 9.34E
31 T13 **Schleswig** Iowa, C USA 42.10N 95.27W
102 H8 **Schleswig-Holstein** ◐ state N Germany
Schlettstadt see Sélestat
110 F7 **Schlieren** Zürich, N Switzerland 47.22N 8.27E
Schlochau see Człuchów
Schloppe see Człopa
103 I18 **Schlüchtern** Hessen, C Germany 50.19N 9.27E
103 J17 **Schmalkalden** Thüringen, C Germany 50.42N 10.26E
111 W2 **Schmida** ≈ NE Austria
67 P19 **Schmidt-Ott Seamount** var. Schmitt-Ott Seamount, Schmitt-Ott Tablemount. undersea feature SW Indian Ocean 39.37S 13.00E
Schmiegel see Śmigiel
Schmitt-Ott Seamount/Schmitt-Ott Tablemount see Schmidt-Ott Seamount
13 V3 **Schmon** ≈ Quebec, SE Canada
103 M18 **Schneeberg** ▲ W Germany 50.03N 11.51E
Schneeberg see Veliki Snežnik
Schnee-Eifel see Schneifel
Schneekoppe see Sněžka
Schneidemühl see Piła
103 D18 **Schneifel** var. Schnee-Eifel. plateau W Germany
Schnelle Körös/Schnelle Kreisch see Crişul Repede
102 I11 **Schneverdingen** var. Schneverdingen (Wümme). Niedersachsen, NW Germany 53.07N 9.48E
Schneverdingen (Wümme) see Schneverdingen
Schoden see Skuodas
20 K10 **Schoharie** New York, NE USA 42.40N 74.19W
20 K11 **Schoharie Creek** ≈ New York, NE USA
117 J21 **Schoinoússa** island Kykládes, Greece, Aegean Sea
102 L13 **Schönebeck** Sachsen-Anhalt, C Germany 52.01N 11.45E
Schöneck see Skarszewy
102 O12 **Schönefeld** ✕ (Berlin) Berlin, NE Germany 52.23N 13.29E
103 K24 **Schongau** Bayern, S Germany 47.49N 10.54E
102 K13 **Schöningen** Niedersachsen, C Germany 52.07N 10.58E
Schönlanke see Trzcianka
Schönsee see Kowalewo Pomorskie
33 P10 **Schoolcraft** Michigan, N USA 42.05N 85.39W
100 O8 **Schoonebeek** Drenthe, NE Netherlands 52.39N 6.57E
100 I12 **Schoonhoven** Zuid-Holland, C Netherlands 51.57N 4.51E
100 H8 **Schoorl** Noord-Holland, NW Netherlands 52.42N 4.40E
Schooten see Schoten
103 F24 **Schopfheim** Baden-Württemberg, SW Germany 47.39N 7.49E
103 I21 **Schorndorf** Baden-Württemberg, S Germany 48.48N 9.31E
102 F10 **Schortens** Niedersachsen, NW Germany 53.31N 7.57E
101 H16 **Schoten** var. Schooten. Antwerpen, N Belgium 51.15N 4.30E
191 Q17 **Schouten Island** island Tasmania, SE Australia
194 H9 **Schouten Islands** island group NW PNG
100 E13 **Schouwen** island SW Netherlands
47 Q12 **Schœlcher** W Martinique 14.37N 61.06W
Schreiberhau see Szklarska Poręba
111 U2 **Schrems** Niederösterreich, E Austria 48.49N 15.01E
103 L22 **Schrobenhausen** Bayern, SE Germany 48.33N 11.14E
20 L8 **Schroon Lake** ◎ New York, NE USA
110 J8 **Schruns** Vorarlberg, W Austria 47.04N 9.54E
Schubin see Szubin
27 U11 **Schulenburg** Texas, SW USA 29.40N 96.54W
Schuls see Scuol
110 E8 **Schüpfheim** Luzern, C Switzerland 47.02N 7.23E
37 S6 **Schurz** Nevada, W USA 38.55N 118.48W
103 I24 **Schussen** ≈ S Germany
Schüttenhofen see Sušice
31 R15 **Schuyler** Nebraska, C USA 41.25N 97.04W
20 L10 **Schuylerville** New York, NE USA 43.05N 73.34W
103 K20 **Schwabach** Bayern, SE Germany 49.19N 11.01E
Schwabenalb see Schwäbische Alb
103 I23 **Schwäbische Alb** var. Schwabenalb, Eng. Swabian Jura. ▲▲ S Germany
103 I22 **Schwäbisch Gmünd** var. Gmünd. Baden-Württemberg, SW Germany 48.48N 9.48E
103 I21 **Schwäbisch Hall** var. Hall. Baden-Württemberg, SW Germany 49.07N 9.43E
103 H16 **Schwalm** ≈ C Germany
111 V9 **Schwanberg** Steiermark, SE Austria 46.46N 15.12E
110 H8 **Schwanden** Glarus, E Switzerland 47.02N 9.04E
103 M20 **Schwandorf** Bayern, SE Germany 49.19N 12.07E
111 S5 **Schwanenstadt** Oberösterreich, NW Austria 48.03N 13.45E
174 M9 **Schwaner, Pegunungan** ▲▲ Borneo, N Indonesia
111 W5 **Schwarza** ≈ E Austria
111 P9 **Schwarzach** ≈ S Austria
103 M20 **Schwarzach** Cz. Černice. ≈ Czech Republic/Germany
Schwarzach see Schwarzach im Pongau, Austria
Schwarzach see Svratka, Czech Republic
111 Q7 **Schwarzach im Pongau** var. Schwarzach. Salzburg, NW Austria 47.19N 13.09E
Schwarzawa see Svratka
103 N14 **Schwarze Elster** ≈ E Germany
Schwarze Körös see Crişul Negru
110 D9 **Schwarzenburg** Bern, W Switzerland 46.51N 7.28E
85 D21 **Schwarzrand** ▲▲ S Namibia
103 G23 **Schwarzwald** Eng. Black Forest. ▲▲ SW Germany
Schwarzwasser see Wda
41 P7 **Schwatka Mountains** ▲▲ Alaska, USA
111 N7 **Schwaz** Tirol, W Austria 47.21N 11.43E
111 Y4 **Schwechat** Niederösterreich, NE Austria 48.09N 16.28E
111 Y4 **Schwechat** ✕ (Wien) Wien, E Austria 48.04N 16.31E
102 P11 **Schwedt** Brandenburg, NE Germany 53.04N 14.16E
103 D19 **Schweich** Rheinland-Pfalz, SW Germany 49.49N 6.44E
Schweidnitz see Świdnica
103 J18 **Schweinfurt** Bayern, SE Germany 50.03N 10.13E
Schweiz see Switzerland
102 L9 **Schwerin** Mecklenburg-Vorpommern, N Germany 53.37N 11.25E
Schwerin see Skwierzyna
102 L9 **Schweriner See** ◎ N Germany
Schwertberg see Świecie
103 F15 **Schwerte** Nordrhein-Westfalen, W Germany 51.27N 7.34E
Schwiebus see Świebodzin
102 P13 **Schwielochsee** ◎ NE Germany
Schwihau see Švihov
Schwiz see Schwyz
110 G8 **Schwyz** var. Schwiz. Schwyz, C Switzerland 47.01N 8.39E
110 G8 **Schwyz** var. Schwiz. ◐ canton C Switzerland
12 J11 **Schyan** ≈ Quebec, SE Canada
Schyl see Jiu
109 I24 **Sciacca** Sicilia, Italy, C Mediterranean Sea 37.30N 13.05E
Sciasciamana see Shashemenē
109 L26 **Scicli** Sicilia, Italy, C Mediterranean Sea 36.48N 14.43E
99 F25 **Scilly, Isles of** island group SW England, UK
113 H17 **Ścinawa** Ger. Steinau an der Elbe. Dolnośląskie, SW Poland 51.22N 16.27E
Scio see Chíos
33 S14 **Scioto River** ≈ Ohio, N USA
38 L5 **Scipio** Utah, W USA 39.15N 112.06W
35 X6 **Scobey** Montana, NW USA 48.47N 105.25W
191 T7 **Scone** New South Wales, SE Australia 32.02S 150.51E
Scoresby Sound/Scoresbysund see Ittoqqortoormiit
Scoresby Sund see Kangertittivaq
Scorno, Punta dello see Caprara, Punta
36 K3 **Scotia** California, W USA 40.04N 124.07W
49 Y14 **Scotia Plate** tectonic feature
49 V15 **Scotia Ridge** undersea feature S Atlantic Ocean
204 H2 **Scotia Sea** sea SW Atlantic Ocean
31 Q12 **Scotland** South Dakota, N USA 43.09N 97.43W
27 R5 **Scotland** Texas, SW USA 33.37N 98.27W
98 H11 **Scotland** national region UK
23 W8 **Scotland Neck** North Carolina, SE USA 36.07N 77.25W
205 R13 **Scott Base** NZ research station Antarctica 77.52S 167.18E
8 J16 **Scott, Cape** headland Vancouver Island, British Columbia, SW Canada 50.43N 128.24W
28 I5 **Scott City** Kansas, C USA 38.28N 100.54W
29 Y7 **Scott City** Missouri, C USA 37.13N 89.31W
205 R14 **Scott Coast** physical region Antarctica
20 C15 **Scottdale** Pennsylvania, NE USA 40.05N 79.35W
205 Y11 **Scott Glacier** glacier Antarctica
205 Q17 **Scott Island** island Antarctica
28 L11 **Scott, Mount** ▲ Oklahoma, USA 34.52N 98.34W
34 G15 **Scott, Mount** ▲ Oregon, NW USA 42.53N 122.06W
36 M1 **Scott River** ≈ California, W USA
30 I13 **Scottsbluff** Nebraska, C USA 41.52N 103.40W

◆ Country
● Country Capital
◇ Dependent Territory
○ Dependent Territory Capital
◐ Administrative Region
✕ International Airport
▲ Mountain
▲▲ Mountain Range
Volcano
≈ River
◎ Lake
⊠ Reservoir

Scottsboro – Severodvinsk

25 Q2 Scottsboro Alabama, S USA 34.40N 86.01W
33 P15 Scottsburg Indiana, N USA 38.42N 85.46W
191 P16 Scottsdale Tasmania, SE Australia 41.13S 147.30E
38 L13 Scottsdale Arizona, SW USA 33.30N 111.54W
47 O12 Scotts Head Village var. Cachacrou. S Dominica 15.12N 61.22W
199 J17 Scott Shoal undersea feature S Pacific Ocean
22 K7 Scottsville Kentucky, S USA 36.45N 86.11W
31 U14 Scranton Iowa, C USA 42.01N 94.33W
20 I13 Scranton Pennsylvania, NE USA 41.25N 75.40W
194 G10 Screw ≈ NW PNG
31 R14 Scribner Nebraska, C USA 41.40N 96.40W
Scrobesbyrig' see Shrewsbury
12 I14 Scugog ≈ Ontario, SE Canada
12 I14 Scugog, Lake ◎ Ontario, SE Canada
99 N17 Scunthorpe E England, UK 53.34N 0.39W
110 K9 Scuol Ger. Schuls. Graubünden, E Switzerland 46.51N 10.21E
Scupi see Skopje
Scutari see Shkodër
115 K17 Scutari, Lake Alb. Liqeni i Shkodrës, SCr. Skadarsko Jezero. ◎ Albania/Yugoslavia
Scyros see Skýros
Scythopolis see Bet She'an
27 U13 Seadrift Texas, SW USA 28.25N 96.42W
23 Y4 Seaford var. Seaford City. Delaware, NE USA 38.38N 75.36W
Seaford City see Seaford
12 E15 Seaforth Ontario, S Canada 43.33N 81.25W
26 M6 Seagraves Texas, SW USA 32.56N 102.33W
9 X9 Seal ≈ Manitoba, C Canada
190 M10 Sea Lake Victoria, SE Australia 35.34S 142.51E
85 G26 Seal, Cape headland S South Africa 34.06S 23.18E
67 D26 Sea Lion Islands island group SE Falkland Islands
21 S8 Seal Island island Maine, NE USA
27 V11 Sealy Texas, SW USA 29.46N 96.09W
37 X12 Searchlight Nevada, W USA 35.27N 114.54W
29 V11 Searcy Arkansas, C USA 35.15N 91.44W
21 R7 Searsport Maine, NE USA 44.28N 68.54W
37 N10 Seaside California, W USA 36.36N 121.51W
34 F10 Seaside Oregon, NW USA 45.57N 123.55W
20 K16 Seaside Heights New Jersey, NE USA 39.56N 74.03W
34 H8 Seattle Washington, NW USA 47.34N 122.19W
34 H9 Seattle-Tacoma ✕ Washington, NW USA 47.04N 122.27W
193 J16 Seaward Kaikoura Range ▲▲ South Island, NZ
44 J9 Sébaco Matagalpa, W Nicaragua 12.50N 86.04W
21 P8 Sebago Lake ◎ Maine, NE USA
176 V11 Sebakor, Teluk bay Irian Jaya, E Indonesia
Sebangan, Sungai see Sebangau Besar, Sungai
174 M11 Sebangan, Teluk bay Borneo, C Indonesia
174 Mm11 Sebanganu, Teluk bay Borneo, C Indonesia
174 Mm11 Sebangau Besar, Sungai var. Sungai Sebangan. ≈ Borneo, N Indonesia
174 I8 Sebanglea, Pulau island W Indonesia
Sebaste/Sebastia see Sivas
25 Y12 Sebastian Florida, SE USA 27.55N 80.31W
42 C5 Sebastián Vizcaíno, Bahía bay NW Mexico
21 R6 Sebasticook Lake ◎ Maine, NE USA
36 M7 Sebastopol California, W USA 38.22N 122.50W
Sebastopol see Sevastopol'
175 Oo4 Sebatik, Pulau island N Indonesia
21 R5 Sebec Lake ◎ Maine, NE USA
78 K12 Sébékoro Kayes, W Mali 13.00N 9.03W
Sebenico see Šibenik
42 G6 Seberi, Cerro ▲ NW Mexico 27.49N 110.18W
118 H11 Sebeş Ger. Mühlbach, Hung. Szászsebes; prev. Sebeşu Săsesc. Alba, W Romania 45.57N 23.34E
Sebes-Körös see Crişul Repede
Sebeşu Săsesc see Sebeş
33 R8 Sebewaing Michigan, N USA 43.43N 83.27W
128 F16 Sebezh Pskovskaya Oblast', W Russian Federation 56.19N 28.31E
143 N12 Şebinkarahisar Giresun, N Turkey 40.19N 38.25E
118 F11 Sebiş Hung. Borossebes. Arad, W Romania 46.21N 22.09E
Sebkra Azz el Matti see Azzel Matti, Sebkha
21 Q4 Seboomook Lake ◎ Maine, NE USA
76 G6 Sebou var. Sebu. ≈ N Morocco
22 I6 Sebree Kentucky, S USA 37.34N 87.30W
25 X13 Sebring Florida, SE USA 27.30N 81.26W
Sebta see Ceuta
Sebu see Sebou
175 Nn11 Sebuku, Pulau island N Indonesia
175 Oo4 Sebuku, Teluk bay Borneo, N Indonesia
176 Vv10 Sebyar ≈ Irian Jaya, E Indonesia
108 F10 Secchia ≈ N Italy
8 L17 Sechelt British Columbia, SW Canada 49.25N 123.37W
58 C12 Sechín, Río ≈ W Peru
58 A10 Sechura, Bahía de bay NW Peru
193 A22 Secretary Island island SW NZ
161 I15 Secunderābād var. Sikandarabad. Andhra Pradesh, C India 17.30N 78.33E
59 L17 Sécure, Río ≈ C Bolivia
120 D10 Seda Mažeikiai, NW Lithuania 56.10N 22.04E
29 T5 Sedalia Missouri, C USA 38.42N 93.13W
105 R3 Sedan Ardennes, N France 49.42N 4.55E
29 P7 Sedan Kansas, C USA 37.07N 96.11W
107 N3 Sedano Castilla-León, N Spain 42.43N 3.43W
106 H10 Seda, Ribeira de stream C Portugal
193 K15 Seddon Marlborough, South Island, NZ 41.41S 174.04E
193 H15 Seddonville West Coast, South Island, NZ 41.34S 171.59E
149 U7 Sedeh Khorāsān, E Iran 33.18N 59.12E
144 E11 Sederot Southern, S Israel 31.31N 34.34E
67 B23 Sedge Island island NW Falkland Islands
78 G12 Sédhiou SW Senegal 12.39N 15.33W
9 U16 Sedley Saskatchewan, S Canada 50.06N 103.51W
Sedlez see Siedlce
125 G12 Sednel'nikovo Omskaya Oblast', C Russian Federation 56.54N 75.24E
119 Q2 Sedniv Chernihivs'ka Oblast', N Ukraine 51.39N 31.34E
38 L11 Sedona Arizona, SW USA 34.52N 111.45W
Sedunum see Sion
120 F12 Šeduva Radviliškis, N Lithuania 55.45N 23.46E
147 Y8 Seeb var. Muscat Sib Airport. ✕ (Masqaṭ) NE Oman 23.36N 58.27E
Seeb see As Sīb
110 M7 Seefeld-in-Tirol Tirol, W Austria 47.19N 11.16E
85 E22 Seeheim Noord Karas, S Namibia 26.49S 17.50E
Seeland see Sjælland
205 N9 Seelig, Mount ▲ Antarctica 81.45S 102.15W
Seeonee see Seoni
168 E6 Seer Hovd, W Mongolia 48.18N 92.37E
104 L5 Sées Orne, N France 48.36N 0.11E
103 J14 Seesen Niedersachsen, C Germany 51.54N 10.10E
Seesker Höhe see Szeskie Wzgórza
102 J10 Seevetal Niedersachsen, N Germany 53.24N 10.01E
111 V6 Seewiesen Steiermark, E Austria 47.37N 15.16E
142 J13 Şefaatli var. Kızılkoca. Yozgat, C Turkey 39.31N 34.45E
155 N3 Sefid, Darya-ye Pash. Āb-i-Safed. ≈ N Afghanistan
154 K5 Sefid Kūh, Selseleh-ye Eng. Paropamisus Range. ▲▲ W Afghanistan
76 G6 Sefrou N Morocco 33.51N 4.49W
193 E19 Sefton, Mount ▲ South Island, NZ 43.43S 169.58E
176 U10 Segaf, Kepulauan island group E Indonesia
175 Oo3 Segama, Sungai ≈ East Malaysia
174 Hh6 Segamat Johor, Peninsular Malaysia 2.30N 102.48E
79 S13 Ségbana NE Benin 10.55N 3.42E
Segestica see Sisak
Segesvár see Sighişoara
176 Uu9 Seget Irian Jaya, E Indonesia 1.21S 131.04E
Segewold see Sigulda
128 J9 Segezha Respublika Kareliya, NW Russian Federation 63.39N 34.24E
Seghedin see Szeged
Segna see Senj
109 I16 Segni Lazio, C Italy 41.41N 13.02E
Segodunum see Rodez
107 S9 Segorbe País Valenciano, E Spain 39.51N 0.30W
78 M12 Ségou var. Segu. Ségou, C Mali 13.25N 6.12W
78 M12 Ségou ◐ region SW Mali
56 E8 Segovia Antioquia, N Colombia 7.06N 74.42W
107 N7 Segovia Castilla-León, C Spain 40.57N 4.07W
106 M6 Segovia ◐ province Castilla-León, N Spain
Segoviao Wangkí see Coco, Río
128 J9 Segozero, Ozero ◎ NW Russian Federation
107 U5 Segre ≈ NE Spain
104 J7 Segré Maine-et-Loire, NW France 47.40N 0.51W
Segu see Ségou
40 I17 Seguam Island island Aleutian Islands, Alaska, USA
40 I17 Seguam Pass strait Aleutian Islands, Alaska, USA
79 Y7 Séguédine Agadez, NE Niger 20.12N 13.03E
78 M15 Séguéla W Ivory Coast 8.01N 6.38W
27 S11 Seguin Texas, SW USA 29.34N 97.58W
40 E17 Segula Island island Aleutian Islands, Alaska, USA
64 K10 Segundo, Río ≈ C Argentina
107 Q12 Segura ≈ S Spain
107 P13 Segura, Sierra de ▲▲ S Spain
85 G18 Sehithwa Ngamiland, N Botswana 20.28S 22.43E
160 H10 Sehore Madhya Pradesh, C India 23.12N 77.07E
195 O16 Sehulea Normanby Island, S PNG 9.55S 151.10E
155 P15 Sehwān Sind, SE Pakistan 26.27N 67.46E
111 V8 Seiersberg Steiermark, SE Austria 47.01N 15.22E
28 L9 Seiling Oklahoma, C USA 36.09N 98.55W
105 S9 Seille ≈ E France
101 J20 Seilles Namur, SE Belgium 50.31N 5.12E
95 K17 Seinäjoki Swe. Östermyra. Länsi-Suomi, W Finland 62.45N 22.54E
10 B12 Seine ≈ Ontario, S Canada
104 M4 Seine ≈ N France
104 K4 Seine, Baie de la bay N France
Seine, Banc de la see Seine Seamount
105 O5 Seine-et-Marne ◐ department N France
104 L3 Seine-Maritime ◐ department N France
86 B14 Seine Plain undersea feature E Atlantic Ocean
86 B15 Seine Seamount var. Banc de la Seine. undersea feature E Atlantic Ocean 33.45N 14.25W
104 E6 Sein, Île de island NW France
176 Y12 Seinma Irian Jaya, E Indonesia 4.10S 138.54E
Seisbierrum see Sexbierum
111 U5 Seitenstetten Markt Niederösterreich, C Austria 48.03N 14.41E
Seiyu see Chŏnju
97 H22 Sejerø island E Denmark
112 P7 Sejny Podlaskie, NE Poland 54.09N 23.21E
174 Ii13 Sekampung, Way ≈ Sumatera, SW Indonesia
83 G20 Seke Shinyanga, N Tanzania 3.16S 33.31E
171 I15 Seki Gifu, Honshū, SW Japan 35.25N 136.51E
167 U12 Sekibi-sho island China/Japan/Taiwan
172 Pp5 Sekihoku-tōge pass Hokkaidō, NE Japan 43.40N 143.10E
Sekondi see Sekondi-Takoradi
79 P17 Sekondi-Takoradi var. Sekondi. S Ghana 4.55N 1.45W
82 J11 Sek'ot'a Amhara, N Ethiopia 12.41N 39.05E
Sekseŭil see Saksaul'skiy
34 I9 Selah Washington, NW USA 46.39N 120.31W
174 Gg5 Selangor var. Negeri Selangor Darul Ehsan. ◐ state Peninsular Malaysia
Selânik see Thessaloníki
174 Hh7 Selapanjang Pulau Rantau, W Indonesia 1.00N 102.44E
178 Ii10 Selaphum Roi Et, E Thailand 16.00N 103.54E
176 Uu16 Selaru, Pulau island Kepulauan Tanimbar, E Indonesia
176 Vv11 Selassi Irian Jaya, E Indonesia 3.16S 132.50E
173 G3 Selatan, Selat strait Peninsular Malaysia
41 N8 Selawik Alaska, USA 66.36N 160.00W
41 N8 Selawik Lake ◎ Alaska, USA
175 Pp13 Selayar, Selat strait Sulawesi, C Indonesia
97 C14 Selbjørnsfjorden fjord S Norway
96 H8 Selbusjøen ◎ S Norway
99 M17 Selby N England, UK 53.49N 1.06W
31 N8 Selby South Dakota, N USA 45.30N 100.01W
23 Z4 Selbyville Delaware, NE USA 38.28N 75.12W
142 B15 Selçuk var. Akıncılar. İzmir, SW Turkey 37.55N 27.21E
41 Q13 Seldovia Alaska, USA 59.26N 151.42W
109 M18 Sele anc. Silarus. ≈ S Italy
44 B5 Selegua, Río ≈ W Guatemala
133 X7 Selemdzha ≈ SE Russian Federation
133 U7 Selenga Mong. Selenge Mörön. ≈ Mongolia/Russian Federation
168 K6 Selenge Bulgan, N Mongolia 49.34N 104.18E
168 J6 Selenge Hövsgöl, N Mongolia 49.25N 101.30E
81 I19 Selenge Bandundu, W Dem. Rep. Congo (Zaire) 1.58S 18.10E
168 L6 Selenge ◐ province N Mongolia
Selenge Mörön see Selenga
126 Jj16 Selenginsk Respublika Buryatiya, S Russian Federation 52.00N 106.40E
Selenica see Selenicë
115 K22 Selenicë var. Selenica. Vlorë, SW Albania 40.32N 19.38E
126 M7 Selennyakh ≈ NE Russian Federation
102 J8 Selenter See ◎ N Germany
Sele Sound see Soela Väin
105 U6 Sélestat Ger. Schlettstadt. Bas-Rhin, NE France 48.16N 7.28E
Selety see Sileti
Seleucia see Silifke
94 I4 Selfoss Sudhurland, SW Iceland 63.56N 20.59W
30 M7 Selfridge North Dakota, N USA 46.01N 100.52W
78 I15 Seli ≈ N Sierra Leone
78 I11 Sélibabi var. Sélibaby. Guidimaka, S Mauritania 15.13N 12.10W
Sélibaby see Sélibabi
Selidovka/Selidovo see Selydove
128 I15 Seliger, Ozero ◎ W Russian Federation
38 J11 Seligman Arizona, SW USA 35.20N 112.56W
29 S8 Seligman Missouri, C USA 36.31N 93.56W
82 E6 Selima Oasis oasis N Sudan 21.22N 29.19E
78 L13 Sélingué, Lac de ⊡ S Mali
Selinoús see Kréstena
20 G14 Selinsgrove Pennsylvania, NE USA 40.47N 76.51W
Selishche see Syelishcha
128 I16 Selizharovo Tverskaya Oblast', W Russian Federation 56.50N 33.24E
96 C10 Selje Sogn og Fjordane, S Norway 62.02N 5.22E
9 X16 Selkirk Manitoba, S Canada 50.10N 96.52W
98 K13 Selkirk SE Scotland, UK 55.35N 2.48W
98 K13 Selkirk cultural region SE Scotland, UK
9 O16 Selkirk Mountains ▲▲ British Columbia, SW Canada
200 Oo12 Selkirk Rise undersea feature SE Pacific Ocean
117 F21 Sellasía Pelopónnisos, S Greece 37.14N 22.24E
46 M9 Selle, Pic de la var. La Selle. ▲ SE Haiti 18.18N 71.55W
104 M8 Selles-sur-Cher Loir-et-Cher, C France 47.16N 1.31E
38 K16 Sells Arizona, SW USA 31.54N 111.52W
Sellye see Sal'a
25 P5 Selma Alabama, S USA 32.24N 87.01W
37 Q11 Selma California, W USA 36.33N 119.37W
22 G10 Selmer Tennessee, S USA 35.10N 88.35W
181 N17 Sel, Pointe au headland W Réunion
Selseleh-ye Kūh-e Vākhān see Nicholas Range
131 S2 Selty Udmurtskaya Respublika, NW Russian Federation 57.19N 52.09E
Selukwe see Shurugwi
64 L9 Selva Santiago del Estero, N Argentina 29.46S 62.01W
9 T9 Selwyn Lake ◎ Northwest Territories/Saskatchewan, C Canada
8 K6 Selwyn Mountains ▲▲ Yukon Territory, NW Canada
189 T6 Selwyn Range ▲▲ Queensland, C Australia
119 W8 Selydove var. Selidovka, Rus. Selidovo. Donets'ka Oblast', SE Ukraine 48.06N 37.16E
Selzaete see Zelzate
Seman see Semanit, Lumi i
174 Ii13 Semangka, Teluk bay Sumatera, SW Indonesia
174 I13 Semangka, Way ≈ Sumatera, SW Indonesia
115 D22 Semanit, Lumi i var. Seman. ≈ W Albania
174 Kk14 Semarang var. Samarang. Jawa, C Indonesia 6.58S 110.28E
174 Kk6 Sematan Sarawak, East Malaysia 1.49N 109.43E
175 Qq17 Semau, Pulau island S Indonesia
175 Nn8 Semayang, Danau ◎ Borneo, N Indonesia
175 O4 Sembakung, Sungai ≈ Borneo, N Indonesia
81 G17 Sembé La Sangha, NW Congo 1.37N 14.34E
Semberong see Semberong, Sungai
174 Hh6 Semberong, Sungai var. Semberong. ≈ Peninsular Malaysia
174 M10 Sembulu, Danau ◎ Borneo, N Indonesia
Semendria see Smederevo
119 R1 Semenivka Chernihivs'ka Oblast', N Ukraine 52.10N 32.37E
119 S6 Semenivka Rus. Semenovka. Poltavs'ka Oblast', NE Ukraine 49.36N 33.11E
131 O3 Semenov Nizhegorodskaya Oblast', W Russian Federation 56.47N 44.27E
Semenovka see Semenivka
174 M16 Semeru, Gunung var. Mahameru. ▲ Jawa, S Indonesia 8.01S 112.53E
Semey see Semipalatinsk
Semezhevo see Syemyezhava
130 L7 Semiluki Voronezhskaya Oblast', W Russian Federation 51.46N 39.00E
35 W16 Seminoe Reservoir ⊡ Wyoming, C USA
29 O11 Seminole Oklahoma, C USA 35.13N 96.40W
26 M6 Seminole Texas, SW USA 32.43N 102.38W
25 S8 Seminole, Lake ⊡ Florida/Georgia, SE USA
150 M8 Semiozernoye Kostanay, N Kazakhstan 52.22N 64.06E
151 V9 Semipalatinsk Kaz. Semey. Vostochnyy Kazakhstan, E Kazakhstan 50.25N 80.16E
149 O9 Semīrom var. Samirum. Eşfahān, C Iran 31.19N 51.49E
40 F17 Semisopochnoi Island island Aleutian Islands, Alaska, USA
174 Ll7 Semitau Borneo, C Indonesia 0.30N 111.58E
83 E18 Semliki ≈ Uganda/Dem. Rep. Congo (Zaire)
149 P5 Semnān var. Samnān. Semnān, N Iran 35.37N 53.21E
149 Q5 Semnān off. Ostān-e Semnān. ◐ province N Iran
101 K24 Semois ≈ SE Belgium
110 E8 Sempacher See ◎ C Switzerland
Sena see Vila de Sena
32 L12 Senachwine Lake ◎ Illinois, N USA
61 O14 Senador Pompeu Ceará, E Brazil 5.30S 39.25W
Sena Gallica see Senigallia
61 C15 Sena Madureira Acre, W Brazil 9.04S 68.40W
161 L25 Senanayake Samudra ◎ E Sri Lanka
85 G15 Senanga Western, SW Zambia 16.09S 23.16E
29 Y9 Senath Missouri, C USA 36.07N 90.09W
24 L2 Senatobia Mississippi, S USA 34.37N 89.58W
170 C15 Sendai Kagoshima, Kyūshū, SW Japan 31.48N 130.16E
171 M13 Sendai Miyagi, Honshū, C Japan 38.16N 140.52E
170 Bb15 Sendai-gawa ≈ Kyūshū, SW Japan
171 M14 Sendai-wan bay E Japan
103 J23 Senden Bayern, S Germany 48.18N 10.04E
160 F11 Sendhwa Madhya Pradesh, C India 21.38N 75.04E
113 H21 Senec Ger. Wartberg, Hung. Szenc; prev. Szempcz. Bratislavský Kraj, W Slovakia 48.14N 17.24E
29 P3 Seneca Kansas, C USA 39.47N 96.04W
29 R8 Seneca Missouri, C USA 36.50N 94.36W
34 K13 Seneca Oregon, NW USA 44.06N 118.57W
23 O11 Seneca South Carolina, SE USA 34.41N 82.57W
20 G11 Seneca Lake ◎ New York, NE USA
33 U13 Senecaville Lake ⊡ Ohio, N USA
78 G11 Senegal off. Republic of Senegal, Fr. Sénégal. ◆ republic W Africa
78 H9 Senegal Fr. Sénégal. ≈ W Africa
33 O4 Seney Marsh wetland Michigan, N USA
103 P14 Senftenberg Brandenburg, E Germany 51.31N 14.01E
84 L11 Senga Hill Northern, NE Zambia 9.26S 31.12E
164 G13 Sêngge Zangbo ≈ W China
176 Z11 Senggi Irian Jaya, E Indonesia 3.26S 140.46E
131 R5 Sengiley Ul'yanovskaya Oblast', W Russian Federation 53.54N 48.51E
65 I19 Senguerr, Río ≈ S Argentina
85 J16 Sengwa ≈ C Zimbabwe
Senia see Senj
113 H19 Senica Ger. Senitz, Hung. Szenice. Trnavský Kraj, W Slovakia 48.40N 17.22E
Senica see Sjenica
108 J11 Senigallia anc. Sena Gallica. Marche, C Italy 43.43N 13.13E
142 F15 Senirkent Isparta, SW Turkey 38.07N 30.34E
Senitz see Senica
114 C10 Senj Ger. Zengg, It. Segna; anc. Senia. Lika-Senj, NW Croatia 44.58N 14.55E
169 O10 Senj Dornogovĭ, SE Mongolia 44.34N 110.58E
94 H9 Senja prev. Senjen. island N Norway
Senjen see Senja
167 U12 Senkaku-shotō island group SW Japan
143 R12 Şenkaya Erzurum, NE Turkey 40.33N 42.16E
85 I16 Senkobo Southern, S Zambia 17.34S 25.57E
105 O4 Senlis Oise, N France 49.13N 2.33E
178 K13 Senmonorom Môndól Kiri, E Cambodia 12.27N 107.12E
82 G10 Sennar var. Sannār. Sinnar, C Sudan 13.31N 33.37E
Senno see Syanno
Senones see Sens
111 W11 Senovo E Slovenia 46.01N 15.24E
105 P6 Sens anc. Agendicum, Senones. Yonne, C France 48.12N 3.16E
Sensburg see Mrągowo
178 J12 Sên, Stœng ≈ C Cambodia
44 F7 Sensuntepeque Cabañas, NE El Salvador 13.52N 88.37W
114 L8 Senta Hung. Zenta. Serbia, N Yugoslavia 45.57N 20.04E
Sent Andraž see Sankt Andrä
176 Z10 Sentani, Danau ◎ Irian Jaya, E Indonesia
30 J5 Sentinel Butte ▲ North Dakota, N USA 46.52N 103.50W
8 M13 Sentinel Peak ▲ British Columbia, W Canada 54.51N 122.02W
61 N16 Sento Sé Bahia, E Brazil 9.51S 41.56W
Šent Peter see Pivka
Šent Vid see Sankt Veit an der Glan
194 E10 Senu ≈ NW PNG
Seo de Urgel see La Seu d'Urgel
160 I7 Seondha Madhya Pradesh, C India 26.09N 78.46E
160 J11 Seoni prev. Seeonee. Madhya Pradesh, C India 22.07N 79.33E
Seoul see Sŏul
192 I13 Separation Point headland South Island, NZ 40.46S 172.58E
175 O7 Sepasu Borneo, N Indonesia 0.44N 117.38E
194 F10 Sepik ≈ Indonesia/PNG
Sepone see Muang Xépôn
112 M7 Sępopol Ger. Schippenbeil. Warmińsko-Mazurskie, NE Poland, 54.16N 21.09E
118 F10 Şepreuş Hung. Seprős. Arad, W Romania 46.34N 21.44E
Seprős see Şepreuş
Şepşi-Sângeorz/Sepsiszentgyörgy see Sfântu Gheorghe
13 W4 Sept-Îles Quebec, SE Canada 50.11N 66.18W
107 N6 Sepúlveda Castilla-León, N Spain 41.18N 3.45W
174 Ii12 Seputih, Way ≈ Sumatera, SW Indonesia
106 K8 Sequeros Castilla-León, N Spain 40.31N 6.04W
106 L5 Sequillo ≈ NW Spain
34 G7 Sequim Washington, NW USA 48.04N 123.06W
37 S11 Sequoia National Park national park California, W USA
143 Q14 Şerafettin Dağları ▲▲ E Turkey
131 N10 Serafimovich Volgogradskaya Oblast', SW Russian Federation 49.34N 42.43E
175 Rr6 Serai Sulawesi, N Indonesia 1.45N 124.58E
101 K19 Seraing Liège, E Belgium 50.37N 5.31E
Sêraitang see Baima
Serajgonj see Shirajganj Ghat
152 I15 Serakhs var. Saragt. Akhalskiy Velayat, S Turkmenistan 36.33N 61.10E
176 X10 Serami Irian Jaya, E Indonesia 2.11S 136.46E
Seram, Laut see Ceram Sea
Serampore/Serampur see Shrīrāmpur
175 Tt11 Seram, Pulau var. Serang, Eng. Ceram. island Maluku, E Indonesia
174 J14 Serang Jawa, C Indonesia 6.07S 106.09E
Serang see Seram, Pulau
174 Kk6 Serasan, Pulau island Kepulauan Natuna, W Indonesia
174 Kk6 Serasan, Selat strait Indonesia/Malaysia
114 M12 Serbia Ger. Serbien, Serb. Srbija. ◐ republic Yugoslavia
Serbien see Serbia
Sercq see Sark
Serdica see Sofiya
131 O7 Serdobsk Penzenskaya Oblast', W Russian Federation 52.30N 44.16E
151 X9 Serebryansk Vostochnyy Kazakhstan, E Kazakhstan 49.43N 83.16E
126 Ll13 Serebryanyy Bor Respublika Sakha (Yakutiya), NE Russian Federation 56.40N 124.46E
113 H20 Sered' Hung. Szered. Trnavský Kraj, SW Slovakia 48.17N 17.44E
119 S1 Seredyna-Buda Sums'ka Oblast', NE Ukraine 52.09N 34.00E
120 E13 Seredžius Jurbarkas, C Lithuania 55.04N 23.24E
142 I14 Şereflikoçhisar Ankara, C Turkey 38.55N 33.31E
108 D7 Seregno Lombardia, N Italy 45.39N 9.12E
105 P7 Serein ≈ C France
174 H5 Seremban Negeri Sembilan, Peninsular Malaysia 2.42N 101.54E
83 H20 Serengeti Plain plain N Tanzania
84 K13 Serenje Central, E Zambia 13.12S 30.15E
Seres see Sérres
118 J5 Seret ≈ W Ukraine
Seret/Sereth see Siret
117 I21 Serifopoúla island Kykládes, Greece, Aegean Sea
131 P4 Sergach Nizhegorodskaya Oblast', W Russian Federation 55.31N 45.29E
31 S13 Sergeant Bluff Iowa, C USA 42.24N 96.19W
169 P7 Sergelen Dornod, NE Mongolia 48.31N 114.01E
169 O9 Sergelen Sühbaatar, E Mongolia 46.12N 111.48E
173 F4 Sergeulangit, Pegunungan ▲▲ Sumatera, NW Indonesia
126 I4 Sergeya Kirova, Ostrova island N Russian Federation
Sergeyevichi see Syarhyeyevichy
151 O7 Sergeyevka Severnyy Kazakhstan, N Kazakhstan 53.51N 67.17E
Sergiopol see Ayagoz
61 P16 Sergipe off. Estado de Sergipe. ◐ state E Brazil
130 L3 Sergiyev Posad Moskovskaya Oblast', W Russian Federation 56.21N 38.10E
128 K5 Sergozero, Ozero ◎ NW Russian Federation
174 L7 Serian Sarawak, East Malaysia 1.10N 110.34E
174 J13 Seribu, Kepulauan island group S Indonesia
117 I21 Sérifos anc. Seriphos. island Kykládes, Greece, Aegean Sea
117 I21 Sérifou, Stenó strait SE Greece
142 F16 Serik Antalya, SW Turkey 36.55N 31.06E
108 E7 Serio ≈ N Italy
Seriphos see Sérifos
Serir Tibesti see Sarīr Tibistī
131 S5 Sernovodsk Samarskaya Oblast', W Russian Federation 53.56N 51.16E
131 R2 Sernur Respublika Mariy El, W Russian Federation 56.55N 49.09E
112 M11 Serock Mazowieckie, C Poland 52.30N 21.03E
63 B18 Serodino Santa Fe, C Argentina 32.33S 60.52W
Seroei see Serui
107 P14 Serón Andalucía, S Spain 37.20N 2.28W
101 E14 Serooskerke Zeeland, SW Netherlands 51.42N 3.52E
107 T6 Seròs Cataluña, NE Spain 41.27N 0.24E
125 F10 Serov Sverdlovskaya Oblast', C Russian Federation 59.42N 60.31E
85 I19 Serowe Central, SE Botswana 22.25S 26.43E
106 H13 Serpa Beja, S Portugal 37.55N 7.36W
Serpa Pinto see Menongue
190 A4 Serpentine Lakes salt lake South Australia
47 T15 Serpent's Mouth, The Sp. Boca de la Serpiente. strait Trinidad and Tobago/Venezuela
Serpiente, Boca de la see Serpent's Mouth, The
130 K4 Serpukhov Moskovskaya Oblast', W Russian Federation 54.54N 37.25E
62 K13 Serra do Mar ▲▲ S Brazil
Sérrai see Sérres
109 N22 Serra San Bruno Calabria, SW Italy 38.32N 16.18E
105 S14 Serres Hautes-Alpes, SE France 44.26N 5.42E
116 H13 Sérres var. Seres; prev. Sérrai. Kentrikí Makedonía, NE Greece 41.04N 23.34E
64 J9 Serrezuela Córdoba, C Argentina 30.37S 65.25W
61 O16 Serrinha Bahia, E Brazil 11.37S 38.55W
61 M19 Serro var. Sêrro. Minas Gerais, NE Brazil 18.37S 43.22W
Sêrro see Serro
Sert see Siirt
Sertá see Sertã
106 H9 Sertã var. Sertá. Castelo Branco, C Portugal 39.48N 8.04W
62 L8 Sertãozinho São Paulo, S Brazil 21.04S 47.55W
166 F7 Sêrtar Sichuan, C China 32.18N 100.18E
176 X10 Serui prev. Seroei. Irian Jaya, E Indonesia 1.52S 136.15E
85 J19 Serule Central, E Botswana 21.58S 27.18E
174 Ll10 Seruyan, Sungai var. Sungai Pembuang. ≈ Borneo, N Indonesia
117 E14 Sérvia Dytikí Makedonía, N Greece 40.12N 22.01E
166 E7 Sêrxü Sichuan, C China 32.54N 98.06E
126 Mm15 Seryshevo Amurskaya Oblast', SE Russian Federation 51.03N 128.16E
Sesana see Sežana
175 Nn5 Sesayap, Sungai ≈ Borneo, N Indonesia
Sesdlets see Siedlce
81 N17 Sese Orientale, N Dem. Rep. Congo (Zaire) 2.13N 25.52E
83 F18 Sese Islands island group S Uganda
175 T9 Sesepe Pulau Obi, E Indonesia 1.26S 127.55E
85 H16 Sesheke var. Sesheko. Western, SE Zambia 17.27S 24.19E
Sesheko see Sesheke
108 C8 Sesia anc. Sessites. ≈ NW Italy
106 F11 Sesimbra Setúbal, S Portugal 38.25N 9.06W
117 N22 Sesklió island Dodekánisos, Greece, Aegean Sea
32 L16 Sesser Illinois, N USA 38.05N 89.03W
Sessites see Sesia
108 G11 Sesto Fiorentino Toscana, C Italy 43.49N 11.12E
108 E7 Sesto San Giovanni Lombardia, N Italy 45.31N 9.13E
108 A8 Sestriere Piemonte, NE Italy 45.00N 6.54E
108 D10 Sestri Levante Liguria, NW Italy 44.16N 9.22E
109 C20 Sestu Sardegna, Italy, C Mediterranean Sea 39.15N 9.06E
114 E8 Sesvete Zagreb, N Croatia 45.50N 16.03E
120 G12 Šeta Kaišiadorys, C Lithuania 55.17N 24.16E
Setabis see Xátiva
172 N5 Setana Hokkaidō, NE Japan 42.27N 139.52E
105 Q16 Sète prev. Cette. Hérault, S France 43.24N 3.42E
60 J11 Sete Ilhas Amapá, NE Brazil 1.06N 52.06W
61 L20 Sete Lagoas Minas Gerais, NE Brazil 19.28S 44.15W
62 G10 Sete Quedas, Ilha das island S Brazil
94 I10 Setermoen Troms, N Norway 68.51N 18.19E
97 E17 Setesdal valley S Norway
45 W16 Setetule, Cerro ▲ SE Panama 7.51N 77.37W
23 Q5 Seth West Virginia, NE USA 38.06N 81.40W
Setia see Sezze
76 K5 Sétif var. Stif. N Algeria 36.10N 5.24E
171 I15 Seto Aichi, Honshū, SW Japan 35.13N 137.03E
170 F14 Seto-naikai Eng. Inland Sea. sea S Japan
172 Qq13 Setouchi var. Setoushi. Kagoshima, Amami-Ō-shima, SW Japan 44.19N 142.58E
76 F6 Settat W Morocco 33.03N 7.37W
81 D20 Setté Cama Ogooué-Maritime, SW Gabon 2.31S 9.46E
9 W13 Setting Lake ◎ Manitoba, C Canada
99 L16 Settle N England, UK 54.04N 2.17W
201 Y12 Settlement E Wake Island 19.16N 166.37E
106 F11 Setúbal Eng. Saint Ubes, Saint Yves. Setúbal, W Portugal 38.31N 8.54W
106 F11 Setúbal ◐ district S Portugal
106 F12 Setúbal, Baía de bay W Portugal
Setul see Satun
10 B10 Seul, Lac ◎ Ontario, S Canada
105 R8 Seurre Côte d'Or, C France 47.00N 5.09E
143 U11 Sevan C Armenia 40.31N 44.55E
143 V12 Sevana Lich Eng. Lake Sevan, Rus. Ozero Sevan. ◎ E Armenia
Sevan, Lake/Sevan, Ozero see Sevana Lich
79 N11 Sévaré Mopti, C Mali 14.30N 4.08W
119 S14 Sevastopol' Eng. Sebastopol. Respublika Krym, S Ukraine 44.36N 33.33E
27 R14 Seven Sisters Texas, SW USA 27.57N 98.34W
8 K13 Seven Sisters Peaks ▲ British Columbia, SW Canada 54.57N 128.10W
101 M15 Sevenum Limburg, SE Netherlands 51.25N 6.01E
105 P14 Séverac-le-Château Aveyron, S France 44.18N 3.03E
12 H13 Severn ≈ Ontario, S Canada
99 L21 Severn Wel. Hafren. ≈ England/Wales, UK
129 O11 Severnaya Dvina var. Northern Dvina. ≈ NW Russian Federation
131 N16 Severnaya Osetiya-Alaniya, Respublika Eng. North Ossetia; prev. Respublika Severnaya Osetiya, Severo-Osetinskaya SSR. ◐ autonomous republic SW Russian Federation
Severnaya Osetiya, Respublika see Severnaya Osetiya-Alaniya Respublika
125 F9 Severnaya Sos'va ≈ N Russian Federation
126 J2 Severnaya Zemlya var. Nicholas II Land. island group N Russian Federation
131 T5 Severnoye Orenburgskaya Oblast', W Russian Federation 54.03N 52.31E
37 S3 Severn Troughs Range ▲▲ Nevada, W USA
129 W3 Severnyy Respublika Komi, NW Russian Federation 67.37N 64.12E
150 I13 Severnyy Chink Ustyurta ▲▲ W Kazakhstan
129 Q13 Severnyye Uvaly var. Northern Ural Hills. hill range NW Russian Federation
151 O6 Severnyy Kazakhstan off. Severo-Kazakhstanskaya Oblast', var. North Kazakhstan, Kaz. Soltūstik Qazaqstan Oblysy. ◐ province N Kazakhstan
129 V9 Severnyy Ural ▲▲ NW Russian Federation
Severo-Alichurskiy Khrebet see Alichuri Shimolí, Qatorkŭhi
126 K14 Severobaykal'sk Respublika Buryatiya, S Russian Federation 55.39N 109.17E
Severodonetsk see Syeverodonets'k
128 M8 Severodvinsk prev. Molotov, Sudostroy. Arkhangel'skaya Oblast', NW Russian Federation 64.31N 39.50E

◆ Country ● Country Capital ◇ Dependent Territory ○ Dependent Territory Capital ◐ Administrative Region ✕ International Airport ▲ Mountain ▲▲ Mountain Range ※ Volcano ≈ River ◎ Lake ⊡ Reservoir
325

Severo-Kazakhstanskaya Oblast' – Shimabara-wan

Severo-Kazakhstanskaya Oblast' see Severnyy Kazakhstan
127 Pp13 **Severo-Kuril'sk** Sakhalinskaya Oblast', SE Russian Federation 50.38N 155.57E
128 J3 **Severomorsk** Murmanskaya Oblast', NW Russian Federation 69.00N 33.15E
Severo-Osetinskaya SSR see Severnaya Osetiya-Alaniya, Respublika
126 J6 **Severo-Sibirskaya Nizmennost'** var. North Siberian Plain, Eng. North Siberian Lowland. lowlands N Russian Federation
125 Ee10 **Severoural'sk** Sverdlovskaya Oblast', C Russian Federation 60.09N 59.58E
126 I12 **Severo-Yeniseyskiy** Krasnoyarskiy Kray, C Russian Federation 60.29N 93.13E
130 M11 **Severskiy Donets** Ukr. Sivers'kyy Donets'. ≈ Russian Federation/Ukraine see also Sivers'kyy Donets'
94 M9 **Sevettijärvi** Lappi, N Finland 69.31N 28.40E
38 M5 **Sevier Bridge Reservoir** ⊠ Utah, W USA
38 J4 **Sevier Desert** plain Utah, W USA
38 J5 **Sevier Lake** ◎ Utah, W USA
23 N9 **Sevierville** Tennessee, S USA 35.52N 83.33W
106 J14 **Sevilla** Eng. Seville; anc. Hispalis. Andalucía, SW Spain 37.24N 5.58W
106 J13 **Sevilla** ◈ province Andalucía, SW Spain
Sevilla de Niefang see Niefang
45 O16 **Sevilla, Isla** island SW Panama
Seville see Sevilla
116 J9 **Sevlievo** Gabrovo, N Bulgaria 43.01N 25.07E
Sevluš/Sevlyush see Vynohradiv
111 V11 **Sevnica** Ger. Lichtenwald. E Slovenia 46.00N 15.20E
130 I7 **Sevsk** Bryanskaya Oblast', W Russian Federation 52.03N 34.31E
78 J15 **Sewa** ≈ E Sierra Leone
41 R12 **Seward** Alaska, USA 60.06N 149.26W
31 R15 **Seward** Nebraska, C USA 40.52N 97.06W
8 G8 **Seward Glacier** glacier Yukon Territory, W Canada
207 Q3 **Seward Peninsula** peninsula Alaska, USA
Seward's Folly see Alaska
64 H12 **Sewell** Libertador, C Chile 34.03S 70.16W
100 K5 **Sexbierum** Fris. Seisbierrum. Friesland, N Netherlands 53.13N 5.28E
9 O13 **Sexsmith** Alberta, W Canada 55.18N 118.45W
43 W13 **Seybaplaya** Campeche, SE Mexico 19.39N 90.36W
181 N6 **Seychelles** off. Republic of Seychelles. ◆ republic W Indian Ocean
69 Z9 **Seychelles** island group NE Seychelles
181 N6 **Seychelles Bank** var. Le Banc des Seychelles. undersea feature W Indian Ocean
Seychelles, Le Banc des see Seychelles Bank
180 H17 **Seychellois, Morne** ▲ Mahé, NE Seychelles
94 L2 **Seydhisfjördhur** Austurland, E Iceland 65.15N 14.00W
152 J12 **Seydi** prev. Neftezavodsk. Lebapskiy Velayat, E Turkmenistan 39.30N 62.52E
142 G16 **Seydişehir** Konya, SW Turkey 37.25N 31.51E
142 J13 **Seyfe Gölü** ◎ C Turkey
Seyhan see Adana
142 K16 **Seyhan Barajı** ⊠ S Turkey
142 K17 **Seyhan Nehri** ≈ S Turkey
142 F13 **Seyitgazi** Eskişehir, W Turkey 39.27N 30.42E
130 J7 **Seym** ≈ W Russian Federation
119 S3 **Seym** ≈ N Ukraine
127 O9 **Seymchan** Magadanskaya Oblast', E Russian Federation 62.54N 152.27E
116 N12 **Seymen** Tekirdağ, NW Turkey 41.06N 27.56E
191 O11 **Seymour** Victoria, SE Australia 37.01S 145.10E
85 I25 **Seymour** Eastern Cape, S South Africa 32.31S 26.48E
31 W16 **Seymour** Iowa, C USA 40.40N 93.07W
29 6U7 **Seymour** Missouri, C USA 37.09N 92.46W
27 Q5 **Seymour** Texas, SW USA 33.35N 99.15W
116 M12 **Şeytan Deresi** ≈ NW Turkey
111 S12 **Sežana** It. Sesana. SW Slovenia 45.42N 13.52E
105 P5 **Sézanne** Marne, N France 48.43N 3.41E
109 I16 **Sezze** anc. Setia. Lazio, C Italy 41.28N 13.04E
117 H25 **Sfákia** Kríti, Greece, E Mediterranean Sea 35.12N 24.05E
117 D21 **Sfaktiría** island S Greece
118 J11 **Sfântu Gheorghe** Ger. Sankt-Georgen, Hung. Sepsiszentgyörgy; prev. Şepşi-Sângeorz, Sfintu Gheorghe. Covasna, C Romania 45.52N 25.49E
119 N13 **Sfântu Gheorghe, Braţul** var. Gheorghe Braţul. ≈ E Romania
77 N6 **Sfax** Ar. Şafāqis. E Tunisia 34.45N 10.45E
77 N6 **Sfax** ✕ E Tunisia 34.43N 10.37E
Sfîntu Gheorghe see Sfântu Gheorghe
100 H13 **'s-Gravendeel** Zuid-Holland, SW Netherlands 51.48N 4.36E
100 F11 **'s-Gravenhage** var. Den Haag, Eng. The Hague. Fr. La Haye. ● (Netherlands-seat of government) Zuid-Holland, W Netherlands 52.07N 4.16E
100 G12 **'s-Gravenzande** Zuid-Holland, W Netherlands 52.00N 4.10E
Shaan/Shaanxi Sheng see Shaanxi
165 X11 **Shaanxi** var. Shaan, Shaanxi Sheng, Shan-hsi, Shenshi, Shensi. ◈ province C China
Shaartuz see Shahrtuz
Shabani see Zvishavane
83 N17 **Shabeellaha Dhexe** off. Gobolka Shabeellaha Dhexe. ◈ region E Somalia
83 L17 **Shabeellaha Hoose** off. Gobolka Shabeellaha Hoose. ◈ region S Somalia
Shabeelle, Webi see Shebeli
116 O7 **Shabla** Dobrich, NE Bulgaria 43.33N 28.31E
116 O7 **Shabla, Nos** headland NE Bulgaria 43.30N 28.36E
11 N9 **Shabogama Lake** ◎ Newfoundland, E Canada
81 N20 **Shabunda** Sud Kivu, E Dem. Rep. Congo (Zaire) 2.42S 27.19E
147 Q15 **Shabwah** C Yemen 15.09N 46.46E
164 F8 **Shache** var. Yarkant. Xinjiang Uygur Zizhiqu, NW China 38.27N 77.16E
Shacheng see Huailai
205 R12 **Shackleton Coast** physical region Antarctica
205 Z10 **Shackleton Ice Shelf** ice shelf Antarctica
Shaddādī see Ash Shadādah
30 K7 **Shadehill Reservoir** ⊠ South Dakota, N USA
125 Ee12 **Shadrinsk** Kurganskaya Oblast', C Russian Federation 56.08N 63.18E
33 O12 **Shafer, Lake** ⊠ Indiana, N USA
37 R13 **Shafter** California, W USA 35.27N 119.15W
26 J11 **Shafter** Texas, SW USA 29.49N 104.18W
99 L23 **Shaftesbury** S England, UK 51.01N 2.12W
193 F22 **Shag** ≈ South Island, NZ
151 V9 **Shagan** ≈ E Kazakhstan
41 O11 **Shageluk** Alaska, USA 62.40N 159.33W
126 I16 **Shagonar** Respublika Tyva, S Russian Federation 51.31N 93.06E
193 F22 **Shag Point** headland South Island, NZ 45.28S 170.50E
150 J12 **Shagyray, Plato** plain SW Kazakhstan
Shāhābād see Eslāmābād
174 H5 **Shah Alam** Selangor, Peninsular Malaysia 3.01N 101.31E
119 O12 **Shahany, Ozero** ◎ SW Ukraine
144 H9 **Shahbā'** anc. Philippopolis. As Suwaydā', S Syria 32.49N 36.37E
Shahbān see Ad Dayr
155 P17 **Shāhbandar** Sind, SE Pakistan 23.59N 67.54E
155 P13 **Shāhdād Kot** Sind, SW Pakistan 27.49N 67.49E
149 T10 **Shahdād, Namakzār-e** salt pan E Iran
155 Q15 **Shāhdādpur** Sind, SE Pakistan 25.55N 68.40E
160 K10 **Shahdol** Madhya Pradesh, C India 23.19N 81.25E
167 N7 **Sha He** ≈ C China
Shahepu see Linze
159 N13 **Shāhganj** Uttar Pradesh, N India 26.03N 82.40E
158 C11 **Shāhgarh** Rājasthān, NW India 27.07N 69.55E
Sha Hi see Orūmīyeh, Daryācheh-ye, Iran
Shāhī see Qā'emshahr, Māzandarān, Iran
145 Q6 **Shāhimah** var. Shahma. C Iraq 34.21N 42.19E
Shahjahanabad see Delhi
158 L11 **Shāhjahānpur** Uttar Pradesh, N India 27.52N 79.55E
Shahma see Shāhimah
155 U7 **Shāhpur** Punjab, E Pakistan 32.15N 72.31E
Shāhpur see Shāhpur Chākar
158 G13 **Shāhpura** Rājasthān, N India 25.37N 75.01E
155 Q15 **Shāhpur Chākar** var. Shāhpur. Sind, SE Pakistan 26.09N 68.40E
154 M5 **Shahrak** Ghowr, C Afghanistan 34.09N 64.16E
149 Q11 **Shahr-e Bābak** Kermān, C Iran 30.07N 55.04E
149 N8 **Shahr-e Kord** var. Shahr Kord. Chahār Maḩall va Bakhtīārī, C Iran 32.19N 50.52E
149 O9 **Shahreẓā** var. Qomisheh, Qumisheh, Shahriza; prev. Qomsheh. Eşfahān, C Iran 32.01N 51.51E
153 S10 **Shahrikhon** Rus. Shakhrikhan. Andijon Wiloyati, E Uzbekistan 40.42N 72.03E
153 N12 **Shahrisabz** Rus. Shakhrisabz. Qashqadaryo Wiloyati, S Uzbekistan 39.01N 66.45E
153 P11 **Shahriston** Rus. Shakhristan. NW Tajikistan 39.45N 68.47E
Shahriza see Shahreẓā
Shahr Kord see Shahr-e Kord
153 P14 **Shahrtuz** Rus. Shaartuz. SW Tajikistan 37.13N 68.05E
149 Q4 **Shāhrūd** prev. Emāmrūd, Emāmshahr. Semnān, N Iran 36.30N 54.59E
Shahsavār/Shahsawar see Tonekābon
Shaidara see Step' Nardara
Shaikh Ābid see Shaykh 'Ābid
Shaikh Fāris see Shaykh Fāris
Shaikh Najm see Shaykh Najm
144 K5 **Shā'īr, Jabal** ▲ C Syria 34.51N 37.49E
160 G10 **Shājāpur** Madhya Pradesh, C India 23.27N 76.21E
82 J8 **Shakal, Ras** headland NE Sudan 18.04N 38.34E
Shakhdarinskiy Khrebet see Shokhdara, Qatorkŭhi
Shakhrikhan see Shahrikhon
Shakhrisabz see Shahrisabz
Shakhristan see Shahriston
119 X8 **Shakhtars'k** Rus. Shakhtërsk. Donets'ka Oblast', SE Ukraine 48.02N 38.18E
127 O15 **Shakhtersk** Ostrov Sakhalin, Sakhalinskaya Oblast', SE Russian Federation 49.10N 142.09E
Shakhtërsk see Shakhtars'k
151 R10 **Shakhtinsk** Karaganda, C Kazakhstan 49.40N 72.37E
130 L11 **Shakhty** Rostovskaya Oblast', SW Russian Federation 47.45N 40.14E
131 P2 **Shakhun'ya** Nizhegorodskaya Oblast', W Russian Federation 57.42N 46.36E
79 S15 **Shaki** Oyo, W Nigeria 8.37N 3.25E
83 J15 **Shakiso** Oromo, C Ethiopia 5.33N 38.48E
119 X8 **Shakmars'k** Donets'ka Oblast', E Ukraine 48.04N 38.22E
31 V9 **Shakopee** Minnesota, N USA 44.48N 93.31W
172 Nn5 **Shakotan-hantō** peninsula Hokkaidō, NE Japan
172 O4 **Shakotan-misaki** headland Hokkaidō, NE Japan 43.22N 140.28E
41 N9 **Shaktoolik** Alaska, USA 64.19N 161.05W
83 J14 **Shala Hāyk'** ◎ C Ethiopia
128 M10 **Shalakusha** Arkhangel'skaya Oblast', NW Russian Federation 62.16N 40.16E
151 U8 **Shalday** Pavlodar, NE Kazakhstan 51.57N 78.51E
131 P16 **Shali** Chechenskaya Respublika, SW Russian Federation 43.03N 45.55E
147 W12 **Shalim** var. Shelim. S Oman 18.07N 55.39E
Shaliuhe see Gangca
150 F9 **Shalkar, Ozero** prev. Chelkar, Ozero. ◎ W Kazakhstan
23 V12 **Shallotte** North Carolina, SE USA 33.58N 78.21W
27 N5 **Shallowater** Texas, SW USA 33.41N 102.00W
128 K11 **Shal'skiy** Respublika Kareliya, NW Russian Federation 61.45N 36.02E
166 F9 **Shaluli Shan** ▲▲ C China
83 F22 **Shama** ≈ C Tanzania
9 Z11 **Shamattawa** Manitoba, C Canada 55.52N 92.04W
10 F8 **Shamattawa** ≈ Ontario, C Canada
Shām, Bādiyat ash see Syrian Desert
Shamiya see Ash Shāmīyah
147 X8 **Shām, Jabal ash** var. Jebel Sham. ▲ NW Oman 23.21N 57.08E
Sham, Jebel see Shām, Jabal ash
Shamkhor see Şämkir
20 G14 **Shamokin** Pennsylvania, NE USA 40.47N 76.33W
27 P2 **Shamrock** Texas, SW USA 35.12N 100.15W
Sha'nabī, Jabal ash see Chambi, Jebel
145 Y12 **Shanāwah** E Iraq 30.57N 47.25E
165 T8 **Shandan** Gansu, N China 38.43N 101.12E
Shandi see Shendi
167 Q5 **Shandong** var. Lu, Shandong Sheng, Shantung. ◈ province E China
167 R4 **Shandong Bandao** var. Shantung Peninsula. peninsula E China
Shandong Peninsula see Shandong Bandao
Shandong Sheng see Shandong
145 U8 **Shandrūkh** E Iraq 33.20N 45.19E
85 J17 **Shangani** ≈ W Zimbabwe
167 O15 **Shangchuan Dao** island S China
Shangchuankou see Minhe
169 P12 **Shangdu** Nei Mongol Zizhiqu, N China 41.32N 113.33E
167 O11 **Shanggao** Jiangxi, S China 28.16N 114.52E
167 S8 **Shanghai** var. Shang-hai. Shanghai Shi, E China 31.13N 121.28E
Shanghai see Shanghai Shi
167 S8 **Shanghai Shi** var. Hu, Shanghai. ◈ municipality E China
167 P13 **Shanghang** Fujian, SE China 25.02N 116.21E
166 K14 **Shanglin** Guangxi Zhuangzu Zizhiqu, S China 23.25N 108.31E
85 G15 **Shangombo** Western, W Zambia 16.21S 22.12E
167 O6 **Shangqiu** var. Zhuji. Henan, C China 34.29N 115.39E
167 Q10 **Shangrao** Jiangxi, S China 28.27N 117.57E
167 S9 **Shangyu** var. Baiguan. Zhejiang, SE China 30.03N 120.52E
169 X9 **Shangzhi** Heilongjiang, NE China 45.11N 127.58E
166 L7 **Shangzhou** var. Shang Xian. Shaanxi, C China 33.51N 109.55E
169 W5 **Shanhetun** Heilongjiang, NE China 44.42N 127.12E
Shan-hsi see Shaanxi, China
Shan-hsi see Shanxi, China
165 O6 **Shankou** Xinjiang Uygur Zizhiqu, W China 42.01N 94.07E
192 M13 **Shannon** Manawatu-Wanganui, North Island, NZ 40.33S 175.25E
99 B19 **Shannon** ✕ W Ireland 52.42N 8.57W
99 C17 **Shannon** Ir. An tSionainn. ≈ W Ireland
178 H6 **Shan Plateau** plateau E Burma
164 M6 **Shanshan** var. Piqan. Xinjiang Uygur Zizhiqu, NW China 42.53N 90.18E
Shansi see Shanxi
178 Gg5 **Shan State** ◈ state E Burma
Shantar Islands see Shantarskiye Ostrova
127 N13 **Shantarskiye Ostrova** Eng. Shantar Islands. island group E Russian Federation
167 Q14 **Shantou** var. Shan-t'ou, Swatow. Guangdong, S China 23.22N 116.39E
Shantung see Shandong
Shantung Peninsula see Shandong Bandao
169 O14 **Shanxi** var. Jin, Shan-hsi, Shansi, Shanxi Sheng. ◈ province C China
Shan Xian see Sanmenxia
167 P6 **Shanxian** var. Shan Xian. Shandong, E China 34.51N 116.05E
Shanxi Sheng see Shanxi
166 L7 **Shanyang** Shaanxi, C China 33.35N 109.48E
167 O13 **Shaoguan** var. Shao-kuan, Cant. Kukong; prev. Ch'u-chiang. Guangdong, S China 24.56N 113.37E
Shao-kuan see Shaoguan
167 Q11 **Shaowu** Fujian, SE China 27.24N 117.26E
167 S9 **Shaoxing** Zhejiang, SE China 30.01N 120.34E
166 M12 **Shaoyang** prev. Tangdukou. Hunan, S China 26.54N 111.14E
166 M11 **Shaoyang** var. Baoqing, Shao-yang; prev. Pao-king. Hunan, S China 27.18N 111.33E
98 K5 **Shapinsay** island NE Scotland, UK
129 S4 **Shapkina** ≈ NW Russian Federation
Shāpūr see Salmās
164 M4 **Shaqiuhe** Xinjiang Uygur Zizhiqu, W China 45.00N 88.52E
145 T2 **Shaqlāwa** var. Shaqlāwah. E Iraq 36.24N 44.21E
Shaqlāwah see Shaqlāwa
144 I8 **Shaqqā** As Suwaydā', S Syria 32.55N 36.42E
147 P7 **Shaqrā'** Ar Riyāḑ, C Saudi Arabia 25.10N 45.08E
Shaqrā see Shuqrah
151 W10 **Shar** var. Charsk. Vostochnyy Kazakhstan, E Kazakhstan 49.33N 81.03E
155 O6 **Sharan** Urūzgān, SE Afghanistan 33.28N 66.19E
Sharaqpur see Sharqpur
Sharbaqty see Shcherbakty
147 X12 **Sharbatāt** S Oman 17.57N 56.14E
147 X12 **Sharbithāt, Ras** var. Ra's Sharbatāt. headland S Oman 17.55N 56.30E
12 K14 **Sharbot Lake** Ontario, SE Canada 44.45N 76.46W
151 P17 **Shardara** var. Chardara. Yuzhnyy Kazakhstan, S Kazakhstan 41.17N 68.03E
Shardara Dalasy see Step' Nardara
168 F8 **Sharga** Govĭ-Altay, W Mongolia 46.16N 95.32E
168 H6 **Sharga** Hövsgöl, N Mongolia 49.33N 98.36E
118 M7 **Sharhorod** Vinnyts'ka Oblast', C Ukraine 48.46N 28.05E
168 K10 **Sharhulsan** Ömnögovĭ, S Mongolia 44.43N 104.06E
172 Qq6 **Shari** Hokkaidō, NE Japan 43.54N 144.42E
Shari see Chari
145 T6 **Shārī, Buḩayrat** ◎ C Iraq
Sharjah see Ash Shāriqah
120 K12 **Sharkawshchyna** var. Sharkowshchyna, Pol. Szarkowszczyzna, Rus. Sharkovshchina. Vitsyebskaya Voblasts', NW Belarus 55.21N 27.27E
188 G9 **Shark Bay** bay Western Australia
147 Y9 **Sharkh** E Oman 21.19N 59.04E
Sharkovshchina/Sharkowshchyna see Sharkawshchyna
131 U6 **Sharlyk** Orenburgskaya Oblast', W Russian Federation 52.52N 54.45E
Sharm ash Shaykh see Sharm el Sheikh
77 Y9 **Sharm el Sheikh** var. Ofiral, Sharm ash Shaykh. E Egypt 27.51N 34.16E
20 B13 **Sharon** Pennsylvania, NE USA 41.12N 80.28W
28 H4 **Sharon Springs** Kansas, C USA 38.54N 101.45W
33 Q14 **Sharonville** Ohio, N USA 39.16N 84.24W
Sharourah see Sharūrah
31 O10 **Sharpe, Lake** ⊠ South Dakota, N USA
Sharqī, Al Jabal ash/Sharqi, Jebel esh see Anti-Lebanon
Sharqiyah, Al Minţaqah ash see Ash Sharqīyah
144 I6 **Sharqīyat an Nabk, Jabal** ▲ W Syria
155 W8 **Sharqpur** var. Sharaqpur. Punjab, E Pakistan 31.27N 74.10E
147 Q13 **Sharūrah** var. Sharourah. Najrān, S Saudi Arabia 17.29N 47.04E
129 O14 **Shar'ya** Kostromskaya Oblast', NW Russian Federation 58.22N 45.30E
151 V15 **Sharyn** var. Charyn. ≈ SE Kazakhstan
Sharyn see Charyn
85 J18 **Shashe** Central, NE Botswana 21.25S 27.28E
85 J18 **Shashe** var. Shashi. ≈ Botswana/Zimbabwe
83 J14 **Shashemenē** var. Shashemenne, Shashhamana, It. Sciasciamana. Oromo, C Ethiopia 7.16N 38.38E
Shashemenne/Shashhamana see Shashemenē
Shashi see Shashe
Shashi/Sha-shih/Shasi see Jingzhou
37 N3 **Shasta Lake** ⊠ California, W USA
37 N2 **Shasta, Mount** ▲ California, W USA 41.24N 122.11W
131 O4 **Shatki** Nizhegorodskaya Oblast', W Russian Federation 55.09N 44.04E
152 J13 **Shatlyk** Maryyskiy Velayat, C Turkmenistan 37.55N 61.00E
Shatra see Ash Shaţrah
121 K17 **Shatsk** Rus. Shatsk. Minskaya Voblasts', C Belarus 53.25N 27.44E
131 N5 **Shatsk** Ryazanskaya Oblast', W Russian Federation 54.02N 41.38E
28 J9 **Shattuck** Oklahoma, C USA 36.16N 99.52W
151 P16 **Shaul'der** Yuzhnyy Kazakhstan, S Kazakhstan 42.49N 68.22E
9 S17 **Shaunavon** Saskatchewan, S Canada 49.37N 108.22W
Shavat see Showot
164 K4 **Shawan** Xinjiang Uygur Zizhiqu, NW China 44.19N 85.34E
12 G12 **Shawanaga** Ontario, S Canada 45.29N 80.16W
32 M6 **Shawano** Wisconsin, N USA 44.46N 88.36W
32 M6 **Shawano Lake** ◎ Wisconsin, N USA
13 P10 **Shawinigan** prev. Shawinigan Falls. Quebec, SE Canada 46.35N 72.45W
Shawinigan Falls see Shawinigan
13 P10 **Shawinigan-Sud** Quebec, SE Canada 46.30N 72.43W
144 J5 **Shawmarīyah, Jabal ash** ▲▲ C Syria
29 O11 **Shawnee** Oklahoma, C USA 35.19N 96.55W
12 K12 **Shawville** Quebec, SE Canada 45.37N 76.31W
Shaykh see Ash Shakk
145 W9 **Shaykh 'Ābid** var. Shaikh Ābid. E Iraq 32.40N 46.09E
145 Y10 **Shaykh Fāris** var. Shaikh Fāris. E Iraq 32.06N 47.39E
145 T7 **Shaykh Ḩātim** E Iraq 33.28N 44.15E
Shaykh, Jabal ash see Hermon, Mount
145 X10 **Shaykh Najm** var. Shaikh Najm. E Iraq 32.04N 46.54E
145 W9 **Shaykh Sa'd** E Iraq 32.35N 46.16E
153 T14 **Shazud** SE Tajikistan 37.45N 72.22E
121 N18 **Shchadryn** Rus. Shchedrin. Homyel'skaya Voblasts', SE Belarus 52.55N 29.32E
121 H18 **Shchara** ≈ SW Belarus
Shchedrin see Shchadryn
Shcheglovsk see Kemerovo
130 K5 **Shchëkino** Tul'skaya Oblast', W Russian Federation 53.57N 37.33E
129 S7 **Shchel'yayur** Respublika Komi, NW Russian Federation 65.19N 53.27E
151 U8 **Shcherbakty** Kaz. Sharbaqty. Pavlodar, E Kazakhstan 52.28N 78.00E
130 K7 **Shchigry** Kurskaya Oblast', W Russian Federation 51.53N 36.49E
Shchitkovichi see Shchytkavichy
119 Q2 **Shchors** Chernihivs'ka Oblast', N Ukraine 51.49N 31.58E
119 T8 **Shchors'k** Dnipropetrovs'ka Oblast', E Ukraine 48.20N 34.10E
Shchuchin see Shchuchyn
151 Q7 **Shchuchinsk** prev. Shchuchye. Severnyy Kazakhstan, N Kazakhstan 52.56N 70.09E
Shchuchye see Shchuchinsk
121 G16 **Shchuchyn** Pol. Szczuczyn Nowogródzki, Rus. Shchuchin. Hrodzyenskaya Voblasts', W Belarus 53.38N 24.48E
121 K17 **Shchytkavichy** Rus. Shchitkovichi. Minskaya Voblasts', C Belarus 53.13N 27.58E
126 H15 **Shebalino** Respublika Altay, S Russian Federation 51.16N 85.41E
130 J9 **Shebekino** Belgorodskaya Oblast', W Russian Federation 50.25N 36.54E
Shebelē Wenz, Wabē see Shebeli
83 L14 **Shebeli** Amh. Wabē Shebelē Wenz, It. Scebeli, Som. Webi Shabeelle. ≈ Ethiopia/Somalia
115 M20 **Shebenikut, Maja e** ▲ E Albania 41.13N 20.27E
155 N2 **Sheberghān** var. Shibarghān, Shiberghan, Shiberghān. Jowzjān, N Afghanistan 36.40N 65.45E
150 F14 **Shebir** Mangistau, SW Kazakhstan 44.52N 52.01E
33 N8 **Sheboygan** Wisconsin, N USA 43.46N 87.43W
79 X15 **Shebshi Mountains** var. Schebschi Mountains. ▲▲ E Nigeria
Shechem see Nablus
Shedadi see Ash Shadādah
11 P14 **Shediac** New Brunswick, SE Canada 46.13N 64.34W
130 L15 **Shedok** Krasnodarskiy Kray, SW Russian Federation 44.12N 40.49E
82 N12 **Sheekh** Woqooyi Galbeed, N Somalia 10.01N 45.21E
40 M11 **Sheenjek River** ≈ Alaska, USA
98 D13 **Sheep Haven** Ir. Cuan na gCaorach. inlet N Ireland
37 X10 **Sheep Range** ▲▲ Nevada, W USA
100 M13 **'s-Heerenberg** Gelderland, E Netherlands 51.52N 6.15E
99 P22 **Sheerness** SE England, UK 51.27N 0.45E
11 Q15 **Sheet Harbour** Nova Scotia, SE Canada 44.55N 62.31W
193 H18 **Sheffield** Canterbury, South Island, NZ 43.22S 172.01E
99 M18 **Sheffield** N England, UK 53.22N 1.30W
25 O2 **Sheffield** Alabama, S USA 34.46N 87.42W
31 V12 **Sheffield** Iowa, C USA 42.53N 93.13W
27 N10 **Sheffield** Texas, SW USA 30.42N 101.49W
65 H22 **Shehuen, Río** ≈ S Argentina
Shekhem see Nablus
155 V8 **Shekhūpura** Punjab, NE Pakistan 31.43N 73.58E
Sheki see Şäki
128 L14 **Sheksna** Vologodskaya Oblast', NW Russian Federation 59.11N 38.32E
127 O4 **Shelagskiy, Mys** headland NE Russian Federation 70.04N 170.39E
29 V3 **Shelbina** Missouri, C USA 39.41N 92.02W
11 P16 **Shelburne** Nova Scotia, SE Canada 43.46N 65.19W
12 G14 **Shelburne** Ontario, S Canada 44.04N 80.12W
35 R7 **Shelby** Montana, NW USA 48.30N 111.52W
23 Q10 **Shelby** North Carolina, SE USA 35.17N 81.32W
33 S12 **Shelby** Ohio, N USA 40.52N 82.39W
32 L14 **Shelbyville** Illinois, N USA 39.24N 88.47W
33 P14 **Shelbyville** Indiana, N USA 39.31N 85.46W
22 L5 **Shelbyville** Kentucky, S USA 38.12N 85.13W
29 V2 **Shelbyville** Missouri, C USA 39.48N 92.02W
22 J10 **Shelbyville** Tennessee, S USA 35.28N 86.27W
27 X8 **Shelbyville** Texas, SW USA 31.42N 94.03W
32 L14 **Shelbyville, Lake** ⊠ Illinois, N USA
31 S12 **Sheldon** Iowa, C USA 43.10N 95.51W
40 M11 **Sheldons Point** Alaska, USA 62.31N 165.03W
126 J16 **Shelekhov** Irkutskaya Oblast', C Russian Federation 52.04N 104.03E
Shelekhov Gulf see Shelikhova, Zaliv
127 Oo9 **Shelikhova, Zaliv** Eng. Shelekhov Gulf. gulf E Russian Federation
41 P14 **Shelikof Strait** strait Alaska, USA
Shelim see Shalīm
9 T14 **Shellbrook** Saskatchewan, S Canada 53.13N 106.24W
30 L3 **Shell Creek** ≈ North Dakota, N USA
Shellif see Chelif, Oued
24 I10 **Shell Keys** island group Louisiana, S USA
32 I4 **Shell Lake** Wisconsin, N USA 45.43N 91.55W
31 W12 **Shell Rock** Iowa, C USA 42.42N 92.34W
193 C26 **Shelter Point** headland Stewart Island, NZ 47.04S 168.13E
20 L13 **Shelton** Connecticut, NE USA 41.19N 73.06W
34 G8 **Shelton** Washington, NW USA 47.13N 123.06W
Shemakha see Şamaxı
151 W9 **Shemonaikha** Vostochnyy Kazakhstan, E Kazakhstan 50.39N 81.51E
131 Q4 **Shemursha** Chuvashskaya Respublika, W Russian Federation 54.57N 47.27E
40 D16 **Shemya Island** island Aleutian Islands, Alaska, USA
31 T16 **Shenandoah** Iowa, C USA 40.46N 95.23W
23 U4 **Shenandoah** Virginia, NE USA 38.26N 78.34W
23 U4 **Shenandoah Mountains** ridge West Virginia, NE USA
23 V3 **Shenandoah River** ≈ West Virginia, NE USA
79 W15 **Shendam** Plateau, C Nigeria 8.52N 9.30E
82 G8 **Shendi** var. Shandī. River Nile, NE Sudan 16.40N 33.22E
78 I15 **Shenge** SW Sierra Leone 7.54N 12.54W
151 U15 **Shengel'dy** Almaty, SE Kazakhstan 44.04N 77.31E
115 K18 **Shëngjin** var. Shëngjini. Lezhë, NW Albania 41.49N 19.34E
Shëngjini see Shëngjin
Shengking see Liaoning
Sheng Xian/Shengxian see Shengzhou
167 S9 **Shengzhou** var. Shengxian, Sheng Xian. Zhejiang, SE China 29.36N 120.47E
Shenking see Liaoning
129 N11 **Shenkursk** Arkhangel'skaya Oblast', NW Russian Federation 62.10N 42.58E
166 L3 **Shenmu** Shaanxi, C China 38.49N 110.27E
115 L19 **Shën Noj i Madh** ▲ C Albania 41.23N 20.07E
Shenshi/Shensi see Shaanxi
169 V12 **Shenyang** Chin. Shen-yang, Eng. Moukden, Mukden; prev. Fengtien. Liaoning, NE China 41.49N 123.25E
167 O15 **Shenzhen** Guangdong, S China 22.39N 114.02E
160 G8 **Sheopur** Madhya Pradesh, C India 25.40N 76.42E
118 L5 **Shepetivka** Rus. Shepetovka. Khmel'nyts'ka Oblast', NW Ukraine 50.12N 27.01E
Shepetovka see Shepetivka
27 W10 **Shepherd** Texas, SW USA 30.30N 95.00W
197 D14 **Shepherd Islands** island group C Vanuatu
22 K5 **Shepherdsville** Kentucky, S USA 37.59N 85.43W
191 O11 **Shepparton** Victoria, SE Australia 36.25S 145.25E
99 P22 **Sheppey, Isle of** island SE England, UK
Sherabad see Sherobod
99 L23 **Sherborne** S England, UK 50.57N 2.30W
78 H16 **Sherbro Island** island SW Sierra Leone
13 Q12 **Sherbrooke** Quebec, SE Canada 45.23N 71.54W
31 T11 **Sherburn** Minnesota, N USA 43.39N 94.43W
80 H6 **Sherda** Borkou-Ennedi-Tibesti, N Chad 20.04N 16.48E
82 G7 **Shereik** River Nile, N Sudan 18.43N 33.37E
130 K3 **Sheremet'yevo** ✕ (Moskva) Moskovskaya Oblast', W Russian Federation 56.05N 37.10E
159 P14 **Shergāti** Bihār, N India 24.35N 84.51E
29 U12 **Sheridan** Arkansas, C USA 34.18N 92.24W
35 W12 **Sheridan** Wyoming, C USA 44.47N 106.59W
190 G8 **Sheringa** South Australia 33.51S 135.13E
126 L16 **Sherlovaya Gora** Chitinskaya Oblast', S Russian Federation 50.26N 116.09E
27 U5 **Sherman** Texas, SW USA 33.39N 96.34W
204 I10 **Sherman Island** island Antarctica
21 S4 **Sherman Mills** Maine, NE USA 45.51N 68.23W
31 O15 **Sherman Reservoir** ⊠ Nebraska, C USA
153 N14 **Sherobod** Rus. Sherabad. Surkhondaryo Wiloyati, S Uzbekistan 37.43N 66.59E
153 O13 **Sherobod** Rus. Sherabad. ≈ S Uzbekistan
159 T14 **Sherpur** Dhaka, N Bangladesh 25.00N 90.01E
39 T4 **Sherrelwood** Colorado, C USA 39.49N 105.00W
101 J14 **'s-Hertogenbosch** Fr. Bois-le-Duc, Ger. Herzogenbusch. Noord-Brabant, S Netherlands 51.40N 5.19E
30 M2 **Sherwood** North Dakota, N USA 48.55N 101.36W
9 Q14 **Sherwood Park** Alberta, SW Canada 53.34N 113.04W
58 F13 **Sheshea, Río** ≈ E Peru
149 T5 **Sheshtamad** Khorāsān, NE Iran 36.03N 57.45E
31 S10 **Shetek, Lake** ◎ Minnesota, N USA
98 M2 **Shetland Islands** island group NE Scotland, UK
150 F14 **Shetpe** Mangistau, SW Kazakhstan 44.06N 52.03E
160 C11 **Shetrunji** ≈ W India
Shevchenko see Aktau
119 W5 **Shevchenkove** Kharkivs'ka Oblast', E Ukraine 49.40N 37.13E
83 H14 **Shewa Gimira** Southern, S Ethiopia 7.12N 35.49E
167 Q9 **Shexian** var. Huicheng, She Xian. Anhui, E China 29.52N 118.27E
167 R6 **Sheyang** prev. Hede. Jiangsu, E China 33.49N 120.13E
31 O4 **Sheyenne** North Dakota, N USA 47.49N 99.08W
31 P4 **Sheyenne River** ≈ North Dakota, N USA
98 G7 **Shiant Islands** island group NW Scotland, UK
127 Pp14 **Shiashkotan, Ostrov** island Kuril'skiye Ostrova, SE Russian Federation
33 R9 **Shiawassee River** ≈ Michigan, N USA
147 R14 **Shibām** C Yemen 15.49N 48.24E
Shibarghān see Sheberghān
171 Kk12 **Shibata** var. Sibata. Niigata, Honshū, C Japan 37.57N 139.19E
172 Qq7 **Shibecha** Hokkaidō, NE Japan 43.19N 144.34E
Shiberghan/Shiberghān see Sheberghān
172 Qq6 **Shibetsu** Hokkaidō, N Japan 43.40N 145.10E
172 Pp4 **Shibetsu** var. Sibetu. Hokkaidō, NE Japan 44.12N 142.23E
172 P5 **Shibetsu** var. Sibetu. Hokkaidō, NE Japan 43.57N 142.13E
Shibh Jazīrat Sīnā' see Sinai
Shibīn al Kawm see Shibîn el Kôm
77 W8 **Shibîn el Kôm** var. Shibīn al Kawm. N Egypt 30.33N 30.59E
149 O13 **Shīb, Kūh-e** ▲ S Iran
10 D8 **Shibogama Lake** ◎ Ontario, C Canada
Shibotsu-jima see Zelënyy, Ostrov
171 K14 **Shibukawa** var. Sibukawa. Gunma, Honshū, S Japan 36.31N 138.58E
170 Bb16 **Shibushi** Kagoshima, Kyūshū, SW Japan 31.27N 131.05E
170 C17 **Shibushi-wan** bay SW Japan
172 N9 **Shichinohe** Aomori, Honshū, C Japan 40.40N 141.07E
201 U13 **Shichiyo Islands** island group Chuuk, C Micronesia
Shickshock Mountains see Chic-Chocs, Monts
151 S9 **Shiderti** ≈ N Kazakhstan
151 S8 **Shiderty** Pavlodar, NE Kazakhstan 51.43N 74.34E
98 G10 **Shiel, Loch** ◎ N Scotland, UK
171 H15 **Shiga** off. Shiga-ken, var. Siga. ◈ prefecture Honshū, SW Japan
Shigatse see Xigazê
147 U13 **Shiḩan** oasis NE Yemen 17.46N 52.25E
Shih-chia-chuang/Shihmen see Shijiazhuang
164 K4 **Shihezi** Xinjiang Uygur Zizhiqu, NW China 44.20N 85.59E
Shiichi see Shyichy
115 K19 **Shijak** var. Shijaku. Durrës, W Albania 41.21N 19.34E
Shijaku see Shijak
167 O4 **Shijiazhuang** var. Shih-chia-chuang; prev. Shihmen. Hebei, E China 38.04N 114.28E
172 Nn7 **Shikabe** Hokkaidō, NE Japan 42.03N 140.45E
155 Q13 **Shikārpur** Sind, S Pakistan 27.59N 68.39E
201 V12 **Shiki Islands** island group Chuuk, C Micronesia
170 Ee15 **Shikoku** var. Sikoku. island SW Japan
199 Gg6 **Shikoku Basin** var. Sikoku Basin. undersea feature N Philippine Sea
170 Ee15 **Shikoku-sanchi** ▲▲ Shikoku, SW Japan
172 S7 **Shikotan, Ostrov** Jap. Shikotan-tō. island NE Russian Federation
Shikotan-tō see Shikotan, Ostrov
172 O6 **Shikotsu-ko** var. Sikotu Ko. ◎ Hokkaidō, NE Japan
83 N15 **Shilabo** Somali, E Ethiopia 6.05N 44.48E
131 X7 **Shil'da** Orenburgskaya Oblast', W Russian Federation 51.46N 59.48E
145 V3 **Shilēr, Āw-e** ≈ E Iraq
159 S12 **Shiliguri** prev. Siliguri. West Bengal, NE India 26.45N 88.24E
126 Kk16 **Shilka** Chitinskaya Oblast', S Russian Federation 51.52N 115.49E
133 V7 **Shilka** ≈ S Russian Federation
20 H15 **Shillington** Pennsylvania, NE USA 40.18N 75.57W
159 V13 **Shillong** Meghālaya, NE India 25.36N 91.54E
130 M5 **Shilovo** Ryazanskaya Oblast', W Russian Federation 54.18N 40.53E
170 C14 **Shimabara** var. Simabara. Nagasaki, Kyūshū, SW Japan 32.48N 130.19E
170 C14 **Shimabara-wan** bay SW Japan

◆ Country ● Country Capital ◇ Dependent Territory ○ Dependent Territory Capital ◈ Administrative Region ✕ International Airport ▲ Mountain ▲▲ Mountain Range Volcano ≈ River ◎ Lake ⊠ Reservoir

Shimada – Simeonovgrad

171 Ii17 **Shimada** *var.* Simada. Shizuoka, Honshū, S Japan 34.49N 138.10E
170 Ee12 **Shimane** *off.* Shimane-ken, *var.* Simane. ◐ *prefecture* Honshū, SW Japan
170 F11 **Shimane-hantō** *peninsula* Honshū, SW Japan
126 M15 **Shimanovsk** Amurskaya Oblast', SE Russian Federation 52.00N 127.36E
Shimbir Berris *see* Shimbiris
82 O12 **Shimbiris** *var.* Shimbir Berris. ▲ N Somalia 10.43N 47.10E
172 P6 **Shimizu** Hokkaidō, NE Japan 42.58N 142.54E
171 Ii16 **Shimizu** *var.* Simizu. Shizuoka, Honshū, S Japan 35.01N 138.28E
158 I8 **Shimla** *prev.* Simla. Himāchal Pradesh, N India 31.07N 77.09E
Shimminato *see* Shinminato
171 J18 **Shimoda** *var.* Simoda. Shizuoka, Honshū, S Japan 34.49N 138.09E
171 Kk16 **Shimodate** *var.* Simodate. Ibaraki, Honshū, S Japan 36.18N 139.57E
161 F18 **Shimoga** Karnātaka, W India 13.55N 75.31E
170 Bb14 **Shimo-jima** *island* SW Japan
170 B15 **Shimo-Koshiki-jima** *island* SW Japan
83 J21 **Shimoni** Coast, S Kenya 4.40S 39.22E
170 D12 **Shimonoseki** *var.* Simonoseki; *hist.* Akamagaseki, Bakan. Yamaguchi, Honshū, SW Japan 33.57N 130.54E
171 Kk16 **Shimotsuma** *var.* Simotuma. Ibaraki, Honshū, S Japan 36.10N 139.58E
128 G14 **Shimsk** Novgorodskaya Oblast', NW Russian Federation 58.12N 30.43E
171 Jj14 **Shinano-gawa** *var.* Sinano Gawa. ≈ Honshū, C Japan
147 W7 **Shināş** N Oman 24.45N 56.24E
154 J6 **Shīndand** Farāh, W Afghanistan 33.19N 62.09E
Shinei *see* Hsinying
27 T12 **Shiner** Texas, SW USA 29.25N 97.10W
178 Gg1 **Shingbwiyang** Kachin State, N Burma 26.40N 96.14E
151 W11 **Shingozha** Vostochnyy Kazakhstan, E Kazakhstan 47.46N 80.38E
171 Gg17 **Shingū** *var.* Singû. Wakayama, Honshū, SW Japan 33.40N 135.57E
12 F8 **Shining Tree** Ontario, S Canada 47.36N 81.12W
170 F12 **Shinji-ko** *var.* Sinzi-ko. ◎ Honshū, SW Japan
171 Ll12 **Shinjō** *var.* Sinzyô. Yamagata, Honshū, C Japan 38.46N 140.16E
98 I7 **Shin, Loch** ◎ N Scotland, UK
171 Ii13 **Shinminato** *var.* Shimminato, Sinminato. Toyama, Honshū, SW Japan 36.46N 137.04E
170 Dd12 **Shinnanyō** *var.* Shin-Nan'yō, Sinn'anyô. Yamaguchi, Honshū, SW Japan 34.04N 131.43E
23 S3 **Shinnston** West Virginia, NE USA 39.22N 80.19W
144 I6 **Shinshār** *Fr.* Chinnchâr. Ḩimş, W Syria 34.36N 36.45E
171 I16 **Shinshiro** *var.* Sinsiro. Aichi, Honshū, SW Japan 34.52N 137.29E
Shinshū *see* Chinju
172 P6 **Shintoku** Hokkaidō, NE Japan 43.03N 142.50E
83 G20 **Shinyanga** Shinyanga, NW Tanzania 3.40S 33.25E
83 G20 **Shinyanga** ◐ *region* N Tanzania
171 M13 **Shiogama** *var.* Siogama. Miyagi, Honshū, C Japan 38.19N 140.59E
171 J15 **Shiojiri** *var.* Sioziri. Nagano, Honshū, S Japan 36.07N 137.57E
170 G17 **Shiono-misaki** *headland* Honshū, SW Japan 33.25N 135.45E
171 Ll15 **Shioya-zaki** *headland* Honshū, C Japan 37.00N 140.57E
116 J9 **Shipchenski Prokhod** *pass* C Bulgaria 42.46N 25.21E
166 G14 **Shiping** Yunnan, SW China 23.45N 102.23E
11 P13 **Shippagan** *var.* Shippegan. New Brunswick, SE Canada 47.45N 64.43W
Shippegan *see* Shippagan
20 F15 **Shippensburg** Pennsylvania, NE USA 40.03N 77.31W
39 O9 **Ship Rock** ▲ New Mexico, SW USA 36.41N 108.50W
39 P9 **Shiprock** New Mexico, SW USA 36.47N 108.41W
13 R6 **Shipshaw** ≈ Quebec, SE Canada
127 Pp11 **Shipunskiy, Mys** *headland* E Russian Federation 53.04N 159.57E
166 K7 **Shiquan** Shaanxi, C China 33.06N 108.10E
126 Hh14 **Shira** Respublika Khakasiya, S Russian Federation 54.35N 89.58E
170 G16 **Shirahama** Wakayama, Honshū, SW Japan 33.40N 135.21E
159 T14 **Shirajganj Ghat** *var.* Serajgonj, Sirajganj. Rajshahi, C Bangladesh 24.25N 89.40E
171 Mm7 **Shirakami-misaki** *headland* Hokkaidō, NE Japan 41.26N 140.10E
171 L14 **Shirakawa** *var.* Sirakawa. Fukushima, Honshū, C Japan 37.07N 140.11E
171 Ii13 **Shirakawa** Gifu, Honshū, SW Japan 36.17N 136.52E
171 K14 **Shirane-san** ▲ Honshū, S Japan 36.44N 139.21E
171 J16 **Shirane-san** ▲ Honshū, S Japan 35.39N 138.13E
172 Pp7 **Shiranuka** Hokkaidō, NE Japan 42.57N 144.01E
172 O6 **Shiraoi** Hokkaidō, NE Japan 42.34N 141.24E
205 N12 **Shirase Coast** *physical region* Antarctica
172 Pp5 **Shirataki** Hokkaidō, NE Japan 43.55N 143.14E
149 O11 **Shīrāz** *var.* Shīrāz. Fārs, S Iran 29.37N 52.34E
85 N15 **Shire** *var.* Chire. ≈ Malawi/Mozambique
168 G7 **Shiree** Dzavhan, W Mongolia 47.30N 96.48E
169 O9 **Shireet** Sühbaatar, SE Mongolia 45.33N 112.19E
172 R6 **Shiretoko-hantō** *headland* Hokkaidō, NE Japan 44.06N 145.07E
172 R5 **Shiretoko-misaki** *headland* Hokkaidō, NE Japan 44.20N 145.19E
131 N5 **Shiringushi** Respublika Mordoviya, W Russian Federation 53.50N 42.49E
154 M3 **Shīrīn Tagāb** Fāryāb, N Afghanistan 36.49N 65.01E
155 N2 **Shīrīn Tagāb** ≈ N Afghanistan
172 Nn8 **Shiriya-zaki** *headland* Honshū, C Japan 41.24N 141.27E
150 I12 **Shirkala, Gryada** *plain* W Kazakhstan
171 Ll13 **Shiroishi** *var.* Siroisi. Miyagi, Honshū, C Japan 38.01N 140.37E
Shirokoye *see* Shyroke
171 K12 **Shirone** *var.* Sirone. Niigata, Honshū, C Japan 37.46N 139.00E
171 I14 **Shirotori** Gifu, Honshū, SW Japan 35.53N 136.52E
171 J13 **Shirouma-dake** ▲ Honshū, S Japan 36.46N 137.46E
207 T1 **Shirshov Ridge** *undersea feature* W Bering Sea
Shirshütür *see* Shirshyutyur, Peski
152 K12 **Shirshyutyur, Peski** *Turkm.* Shirshütür. *desert* E Turkmenistan
149 T3 **Shīrvān** *var.* Shirwān. Khorāsān, NE Iran 37.25N 57.55E
Shirwa, Lake *see* Chilwa, Lake
Shirwān *see* Shīrvān
165 N5 **Shisanjianfang** Xinjiang Uygur Zizhiqu, W China 43.10N 91.15E
40 M16 **Shishaldin Volcano** ▲ Unimak Island, Alaska, USA 54.45N 163.58W
Shishchitsy *see* Shyshchytsy
40 M8 **Shishmaref** Alaska, USA 66.15N 166.04W
Shisur *see* Ash Shişar
171 I16 **Shitara** Aichi, Honshū, SW Japan 35.06N 137.33E
158 D12 **Shiv** Rājasthān, NW India 26.10N 71.13E
157 E15 **Shivāji Sāgar** *prev.* Konya Reservoir ⊠ W India
160 H8 **Shivpuri** Madhya Pradesh, C India 25.28N 77.41E
38 J9 **Shivwits Plateau** *plain* Arizona, SW USA
Shiwālik Range *see* Siwalik Range
166 M8 **Shiyan** Hubei, C China 32.39N 110.48E
166 H13 **Shizong** Yunnan, SW China 24.49N 103.59E
171 Mm13 **Shizugawa** Miyagi, Honshū, NE Japan 38.40N 141.26E
165 W8 **Shizuishan** *var.* Dawukou. Ningxia, N China 39.04N 106.22E
172 Oo7 **Shizunai** Hokkaidō, NE Japan 42.20N 142.24E
171 Ii16 **Shizuoka** *var.* Sizuoka. Shizuoka, Honshū, S Japan 34.58N 138.20E
171 Ii16 **Shizuoka** *off.* Shizuoka-ken, *var.* Sizuoka. ◐ *prefecture* Honshū, S Japan
Shklov *see* Shklow
121 N15 **Shklow** *Rus.* Shklov. Mahilyowskaya Voblasts', E Belarus 54.13N 30.16E
115 K18 **Shkodër** *var.* Shkodra, *It.* Scutari, *SCr.* Skadar. Shkodër, NW Albania 42.03N 19.31E
115 K17 **Shkodër** ◐ *district* NW Albania
Shkodra *see* Shkodër
Shkodrës, Liqeni i *see* Scutari, Lake
Shkumbî/Shkumbin *see* Shkumbinit, Lumi i
115 L20 **Shkumbinit, Lumi i** *var.* Shkumbî, Shkumbin. ≈ C Albania
Shligigh, Cuan *see* Sligo Bay
126 Ii2 **Shmidta, Ostrov** *island* Severnaya Zemlya, N Russian Federation
191 S10 **Shoalhaven River** ≈ New South Wales, SE Australia
9 W16 **Shoal Lake** Manitoba, S Canada 50.28N 100.36W
33 O15 **Shoals** Indiana, N USA 38.40N 86.46W
170 F13 **Shōbara** *var.* Syôbara. Hiroshima, Honshū, SW Japan 34.50N 132.58E
170 Ff14 **Shōdo-shima** *island* SW Japan
171 Ii13 **Shō-gawa** ≈ Honshū, SW Japan
Shōka *see* Changhua
126 J3 **Shokal'skogo, Proliv** *strait* N Russian Federation
172 Oo4 **Shokanbetsu-dake** ⛰ Hokkaidō, NE Japan 43.43N 141.33E
153 T14 **Shokhdara, Qatorkŭhi** *Rus.* Shakhdarinskiy Khrebet. ▲▲ SE Tajikistan
151 N9 **Sholaksay** Kostanay, N Kazakhstan 51.45N 64.45E
Sholāpur *see* Solāpur
Sholdaneshty *see* Şoldăneşti
151 P17 **Shollakorgan** *var.* Chulakkurgan. Yuznhyy Kazakhstan, S Kazakhstan 43.48N 69.12E
Shoqpar *see* Chokpar
161 G21 **Shoranūr** Kerala, SW India 10.53N 76.06E
161 G16 **Shorāpur** Karnātaka, C India 16.34N 76.48E
32 M11 **Shorewood** Illinois, N USA 41.31N 88.12W
Shorkazakhly, Solonchak *see* Kazakhlyshor, Solonchak
151 Q9 **Shortandy** Akmola, C Kazakhstan 51.47N 70.55E
Shortepa/Shor Tepe *see* Shūr Tappeh
195 S13 **Shortland Island** *var.* Alu. *island* Shortland Islands, NW Solomon Islands
195 T13 **Shortland Islands** *island group* NW Solomon Islands
Shosambetsu *see* Shosanbetsu
172 P3 **Shosanbetsu** *var.* Shosambetsu. Hokkaidō, NE Japan 44.31N 141.47E
35 O15 **Shoshone** Idaho, NW USA 42.56N 114.24W
37 T6 **Shoshone Mountains** ▲▲ Nevada, W USA
35 U12 **Shoshone River** ≈ Wyoming, C USA
85 I19 **Shoshong** Central, SE Botswana 23.03S 26.33E
35 V14 **Shoshoni** Wyoming, C USA 43.13N 108.06W
Shōshū *see* Sangju
119 S2 **Shostka** Sums'ka Oblast', NE Ukraine 51.51N 33.30E
193 C21 **Shotover** ≈ South Island, NZ
39 N12 **Show Low** Arizona, SW USA 34.15N 110.01W
Show Me State *see* Missouri
152 H9 **Showot** *Rus.* Shavat. Khorazm Wiloyati, W Uzbekistan 41.41N 60.13E
129 O4 **Shoyna** Nenetskiy Avtonomnyy Okrug, NW Russian Federation 67.50N 44.09E
128 M11 **Shozhma** Arkhangel'skaya Oblast', NW Russian Federation 61.57N 40.10E
119 Q7 **Shpola** Cherkas'ka Oblast', N Ukraine 49.00N 31.27E
Shqipëria/Shqipërisë, Republika e *see* Albania
24 G5 **Shreveport** Louisiana, S USA 32.31N 93.45W
99 K19 **Shrewsbury** *hist.* Scrobesbyrig'. W England, UK 52.43N 2.45W
158 D11 **Shri Mohangarh** *prev.* Sri Mohangorh. Rājasthān, NW India 27.16N 71.18E
159 S16 **Shrīrāmpur** *prev.* Serampore, Serampur. West Bengal, NE India 22.43N 88.19E
99 K19 **Shropshire** *cultural region* W England, UK
151 S16 **Shu** *Kaz.* Shū. Zhambyl, SE Kazakhstan 43.34N 73.40E
Shū *see* Chu
166 G13 **Shuangbai** Yunnan, SW China 24.45N 101.38E
169 W9 **Shuangcheng** Heilongjiang, NE China 45.20N 126.21E
166 E14 **Shuangjiang** Yunnan, SW China 23.28N 99.43E
169 U10 **Shuangliao** *var.* Zhengjiatun. Jilin, NE China 43.31N 123.32E
Shuang-liao *see* Liaoyuan
169 Y7 **Shuangyashan** *var.* Shuang-ya-shan. Heilongjiang, NE China 46.37N 131.10E
Shu'aymiah *see* Shu'aymīyah
147 W12 **Shu'aymīyah** *var.* Shu'aymiah. S Oman 17.55N 55.39E
150 I10 **Shubarkuduk** *Kaz.* Shubarqudyq. Aktyubinsk, W Kazakhstan 49.10N 56.28E
Shubarqudyq *see* Shubarkuduk
151 N12 **Shubar-Tengiz, Ozero** ◎ C Kazakhstan
41 S5 **Shublik Mountains** ▲▲ Alaska, USA
Shubrā al Khaymah *see* Shubrâ el Kheima
124 Qq16 **Shubrâ el Kheima** *var.* Shubrā al Khaymah. N Egypt 30.06N 31.15E
164 E8 **Shufu** Xinjiang Uygur Zizhiqu, NW China 39.18N 75.43E
153 S14 **Shughnon, Qatorkŭhi** *Rus.* Shugnanskiy Khrebet. ▲▲ SE Tajikistan
Shugnanskiy Khrebet *see* Shughnon, Qatorkŭhi
167 Q6 **Shu He** ≈ E China
Shuiding *see* Huocheng
Shuiji *see* Laixi
Shū-Ile Taūlary *see* Chu-Iliyskiye Gory
155 T10 **Shujāābād** Punjab, E Pakistan 29.52N 71.22E
169 W9 **Shulan** Jilin, NE China 44.28N 126.57E
164 E8 **Shule** Xinjiang Uygur Zizhiqu, NW China 39.19N 76.06E
Shuleh *see* Shule He
165 Q8 **Shule He** *var.* Shuleh, Sulo. ≈ C China
32 K9 **Shullsburg** Wisconsin, N USA 42.37N 90.12W
41 N16 **Shumagin Islands** *island group* Alaska, USA
152 G7 **Shumanay** Qoraqalpoghiston Respublikasi, W Uzbekistan 42.42N 58.56E
116 M8 **Shumen** Shumen, NE Bulgaria 43.17N 26.57E
116 M8 **Shumen** ◐ *province* NE Bulgaria
131 P4 **Shumerlya** Chuvashskaya Respublika, W Russian Federation 55.31N 46.24E
125 Ee12 **Shumikha** Kurganskaya Oblast', C Russian Federation 55.12N 63.09E
120 M12 **Shumilina** *Rus.* Shumilino. Vitsyebskaya Voblasts', NE Belarus 55.19N 29.33E
Shumilino *see* Shumilina
127 Pp12 **Shumshu, Ostrov** *island* SE Russian Federation
118 K5 **Shums'k** Ternopil's'ka Oblast', W Ukraine 50.06N 26.04E
41 O7 **Shungnak** Alaska, USA 66.53N 157.08W
Shunsen *see* Ch'unch'ŏn
166 M3 **Shuo Xian** Shanxi, NE China 39.19N 112.25E
Shuo Xian/Shuoxian *see* Shuozhou
167 N3 **Shuozhou** *var.* Shuoxian; *prev.* Shuo Xian. Shanxi, C China 39.19N 112.25E
147 P16 **Shuqrah** *var.* Shaqrā. SW Yemen 13.25N 45.43E
Shurab *see* Shŭrob
153 O14 **Shŭrchi** *Rus.* Shurchi. Surkhondaryo Wiloyati, S Uzbekistan 37.58N 67.40E
153 R11 **Shŭrob** *Rus.* Shurab. NW Tajikistan 40.02N 70.31E
149 T10 **Shūr, Rūd-e** ≈ E Iran
155 O2 **Shūr Tappeh** *var.* Shortepa, Shor Tepe. Balkh, N Afghanistan 37.22N 66.49E
85 K17 **Shurugwi** *prev.* Selukwe. Midlands, C Zimbabwe 19.40S 30.00E
148 L8 **Shūsh** *anc.* Susa, *Bibl.* Shushan. Khūzestān, SW Iran 32.11N 48.13E
Shushan *see* Shūsh
148 L9 **Shūshtar** *var.* Shustar, Shushter. Khūzestān, SW Iran 32.03N 48.51E
Shushter/Shustar *see* Shūshtar
147 T9 **Shuṭfah, Qalamat** *well* E Saudi Arabia 22.46N 52.50E
145 V9 **Shuwayjah, Hawr ash** *var.* Hawr as Suwayqiyah. ◎ E Iraq
128 M16 **Shuya** Ivanovskaya Oblast', W Russian Federation 56.51N 41.24E
41 Q14 **Shuyak Island** *island* Alaska, USA
177 G4 **Shwebo** Sagaing, C Burma 22.34N 95.42E
177 Ff7 **Shwedaung** Pegu, W Burma 18.43N 95.15E
177 G8 **Shwegyin** Pegu, SW Burma 17.55N 96.58E
178 Gg4 **Shweli** *Chin.* Longchuan Jiang. ≈ Burma/China
177 G6 **Shwemyo** Mandalay, C Burma 20.04N 96.13E
Shyghys Qazagastan Oblysy *see* Vostochnyy Kazakhstan
Shyghys Qongyrat *see* Shygys Konyrat
151 T12 **Shygys Konyrat** *var.* Vostochno-Kounradskiy, *Kaz.* Shyghys Qongyrat. Karaganda, C Kazakhstan 47.01N 75.05E
121 M19 **Shyichy** *Rus.* Shiichi. Homyel'skaya Voblasts', SE Belarus 52.15N 29.13E
151 Q17 **Shymkent** *prev.* Chimkent. Yuzhnyy Kazakhstan, S Kazakhstan 42.19N 69.36E
Shyngghyrlaū *see* Chingirlau
158 J5 **Shyok** Jammu and Kashmir, NW India 34.13N 78.12E
119 S9 **Shyroke** *Rus.* Shirokoye. Dnipropetrovs'ka Oblast', E Ukraine 47.37N 33.15E
119 O9 **Shyryayeve** Odes'ka Oblast', SW Ukraine 47.21N 30.11E
119 S5 **Shyshaky** Poltavs'ka Oblast', C Ukraine 49.54N 34.00E
121 K17 **Shyshchytsy** *Rus.* Shishchitsy. Minskaya Voblasts', C Belarus 53.12N 27.33E
155 Y3 **Siachen Muztāgh** ▲▲ NE Pakistan
Siadehan *see* Tākestān
154 M13 **Siāhān Range** ▲▲ W Pakistan
148 I1 **Sīāh Chashmeh** Āzarbāyjān-e Bākhtarī, N Iran 39.01N 44.22E
155 W7 **Siālkot** Punjab, NE Pakistan 32.31N 74.33E
194 K12 **Sialum** Morobe, C PNG 6.05S 147.33E
Siam *see* Thailand
Siam, Gulf of *see* Thailand, Gulf of
Sian *see* Xi'an
Siang *see* Brahmaputra
Siangtan *see* Xiangtan
174 J5 **Siantan, Pulau** *island* Kepulauan Anambas, W Indonesia
56 H11 **Siare, Río** ≈ C Colombia
179 Rr13 **Siargao Island** *island* S Philippines
194 K12 **Siassi** Umboi Island, C PNG 5.34S 147.50E
117 D14 **Siátista** Dytikí Makedonía, N Greece 40.16N 21.34E
177 Ff4 **Siatlai** Chin State, W Burma 22.05N 93.36E
179 Q15 **Siaton** Negros, C Philippines 9.03N 123.03E
179 Q15 **Siaton Point** *headland* Negros, C Philippines 9.03N 123.00E
120 F11 **Šiauliai** *Ger.* Schaulen. Šiauliai, N Lithuania 55.54N 23.21E
175 S5 **Siau, Pulau** *island* N Indonesia
85 J15 **Siavonga** Southern, SE Zambia 16.28S 28.45E
Siazan' *see* Siyäzän
Sibah *see* As Sībah
109 N20 **Sibari** Calabria, S Italy 39.45N 16.26E
Sibata *see* Shibata
131 X6 **Sibay** Respublika Bashkortostan, W Russian Federation 52.39N 58.39E
95 M19 **Sibbo** *Fin.* Sipoo. Etelä-Suomi, S Finland 60.22N 25.19E
114 D13 **Šibenik** *It.* Sebenico. Šibenik-Knin, S Croatia 43.43N 15.54E
Šibenik *see* Šibenik-Knin
114 E13 **Šibenik-Knin** *off.* Šibenska Županija. *var.* Šibenik ◐ *province* S Croatia
Šibenska Županija *see* Šibenik-Knin
Siberia *see* Sibir'
Siberoet *see* Siberut, Pulau
173 Ff9 **Siberut, Pulau** *prev.* Siberoet. *island* Kepulauan Mentawai, W Indonesia
173 Ff9 **Siberut, Selat** *strait* W Indonesia
Sibetu *see* Shibetsu
155 P11 **Sibi** Baluchistān, SW Pakistan 29.31N 67.54E
194 F15 **Sibidiri** Western, SW PNG 8.58S 142.14E
126 K10 **Sibir'** *var.* Siberia. *physical region* NE Russian Federation
81 F20 **Sibiti** La Lékoumou, S Congo 3.40S 13.19E
83 G21 **Sibiti** ≈ C Tanzania
118 I12 **Sibiu** *Ger.* Hermannstadt, *Hung.* Nagyszeben. Sibiu, C Romania 45.48N 24.08E
118 I11 **Sibiu** ◐ *county* C Romania
31 S11 **Sibley** Iowa, C USA 43.24N 95.45W
173 Ff6 **Sibolga** Sumatera, W Indonesia 1.42N 98.48E
173 Ff6 **Sibolga, Teluk** *var.* Teluk Tapanuli. *bay* Sumatera, W Indonesia
174 Ll6 **Sibu** Sarawak, East Malaysia 2.18N 111.49E
Sibukawa *see* Shibukawa
44 G2 **Sibun** ≈ E Belize
81 I15 **Sibut** *prev.* Fort-Sibut. Kémo, S Central African Republic 5.44N 19.07E
179 P17 **Sibutu** *island* SW Philippines
179 P17 **Sibutu Passage** *passage* SW Philippines
179 Q12 **Sibuyan Island** *island* C Philippines
179 Q12 **Sibuyan Sea** *sea* C Philippines
201 U1 **Sibylla Island** *island* N Marshall Islands
9 N16 **Sicamous** British Columbia, SW Canada 50.49N 118.52W
Sichelburger Gebirge *see* Gorjanci/Žumberačko Gorje
178 H15 **Sichon** *var.* Ban Sichon, Si Chon. Nakhon Si Thammarat, SW Thailand 9.03N 99.51E
166 H9 **Sichuan** *var.* Chuan, Sichuan Sheng, Ssu-ch'uan, Szechuan, Szechwan. ◐ *province* C China
166 I9 **Sichuan Pendi** *basin* C China
Sichuan Sheng *see* Sichuan
105 S16 **Sicie, Cap** *headland* SE France 43.03N 5.50E
109 J24 **Sicilia** *Eng.* Sicily; *anc.* Trinacria. ◐ *region* Italy, C Mediterranean Sea
109 M24 **Sicilia** *Eng.* Sicily; *anc.* Trinacria. *island* Italy, C Mediterranean Sea
Sicilian Channel *see* Sicily, Strait of
Sicily *see* Sicilia
109 H24 **Sicily, Strait of** *var.* Sicilian Channel. *strait* C Mediterranean Sea
44 K5 **Sico Tinto, Río** *var.* Río Negro. ≈ NE Honduras
59 H16 **Sicuani** Cusco, S Peru 14.18S 71.16W
114 J10 **Šid** Serbia, NW Yugoslavia 45.07N 19.13E
117 A15 **Sidári** Kérkyra, Iónioi Nísoi, Greece, C Mediterranean Sea 39.47N 19.43E
174 Kk8 **Sidas** Borneo, C Indonesia 0.24N 109.46E
100 O5 **Siddeburen** Groningen, NE Netherlands 53.15N 6.52E
160 D9 **Siddhapur** *prev.* Siddhpur, Sidhpur. Gujarāt, W India 23.57N 72.28E
Siddhpur *see* Siddhapur
161 I15 **Siddipet** Andhra Pradesh, C India 18.10N 78.54E
195 O17 **Sideia Island** *island* SE PNG
175 Pp12 **Sidenreng, Danau** ◎ Sulawesi, C Indonesia
79 N14 **Sidéradougou** SW Burkina 10.39N 4.16W
109 N23 **Siderno** Calabria, SW Italy 38.17N 16.19E
Siders *see* Sierre
160 L9 **Sidhi** Madhya Pradesh, C India 24.24N 81.54E
Sidhirókastron *see* Sidirókastro
Sidhpur *see* Siddhapur
Sīdī al Hānī', Sabkhat *see* Sidi el Hani, Sebkhet de
77 U7 **Sîdi Barrâni** NW Egypt 31.33N 25.54E
76 I6 **Sidi Bel Abbès** *var.* Sidi bel Abbès, Sidi-Bel-Abbès. NW Algeria 35.12N 0.42W
76 E7 **Sidi-Bennour** W Morocco 32.39N 8.28W
76 M6 **Sidi Bouzid** *var.* Gammouda, Sīdī Bu Zayd. C Tunisia 35.05N 9.20E
123 K12 **Sidi el Hani, Sebkhet de** *var.* Sabkhat Sīdī al Hānī'. *salt flat* NE Tunisia
76 D8 **Sidi-Ifni** SW Morocco 29.33N 10.04W
76 G6 **Sidi-Kacem** *prev.* Petitjean. N Morocco 34.21N 5.46W
116 G12 **Sidirókastro** *prev.* Sidhirókastron. Kentrikí Makedonía, NE Greece 41.13N 23.24E
204 L12 **Sidley, Mount** ▲ Antarctica 76.39S 124.48W
31 S16 **Sidney** Iowa, C USA 40.45N 95.39W
35 Y7 **Sidney** Montana, NW USA 47.42N 104.10W
30 J15 **Sidney** Nebraska, C USA 41.09N 102.57W
20 I11 **Sidney** New York, NE USA 42.18N 75.21W
33 R13 **Sidney** Ohio, N USA 40.16N 84.09W
25 T2 **Sidney Lanier, Lake** ⊠ Georgia, SE USA
Sidon *see* Saïda
126 Hh9 **Sidorovsk** Yamalo-Nenetskiy Avtonomnyy Okrug, N Russian Federation 66.34N 82.12E
Sidra/Sidra, Gulf of *see* Surt, Khalīj, N Libya
Sidra *see* Surt, N Libya
Sīdī Bu Zayd *see* Sidi Bouzid
Siebenbürgen *see* Transylvania
Sieben Dörfer *see* Săcele
112 O12 **Siedlce** *Ger.* Sedlez, *Rus.* Sesdlets. Mazowieckie, C Poland 52.10N 22.18E
103 E16 **Sieg** ≈ W Germany
103 F16 **Siegen** Nordrhein-Westfalen, W Germany 50.52N 8.01E
111 X4 **Sieghartskirchen** Niederösterreich, E Austria 48.13N 16.01E
112 O11 **Siemiatycze** Podlaskie, NE Poland 52.27N 22.51E
178 Jj11 **Siĕmpang** Stœng Trêng, NE Cambodia 14.07N 106.24E
178 Ii12 **Siĕmréab** *prev.* Siemreap. Siĕmréab, NW Cambodia 13.21N 103.49E
Siemreap *see* Siĕmréab
108 G12 **Siena** *Fr.* Sienne; *anc.* Saena Julia. Toscana, C Italy 43.19N 11.19E
Sienne *see* Siena
94 K12 **Sieppijärvi** Lappi, NW Finland 67.09N 23.58E
112 J13 **Sieradz** Sieradz, C Poland 51.36N 18.42E
112 K10 **Sierpc** Mazowieckie, C Poland 52.51N 19.43E
26 I9 **Sierra Blanca** Texas, SW USA 31.10N 105.21W
39 S14 **Sierra Blanca Peak** ▲ New Mexico, SW USA 33.22N 105.48W
37 P5 **Sierra City** California, W USA 39.34N 120.35W
65 I16 **Sierra Colorada** Río Negro, S Argentina 40.37S 67.48W
64 I13 **Sierra del Nevado** ▲▲ W Argentina
65 J16 **Sierra Grande** Río Negro, E Argentina 41.40S 65.22W
78 G15 **Sierra Leone** *off.* Republic of Sierra Leone. ◆ *republic* W Africa
66 M13 **Sierra Leone Basin** *undersea feature* E Atlantic Ocean
68 K8 **Sierra Leone Fracture Zone** *tectonic feature* E Atlantic Ocean
Sierra Leone Ridge *see* Sierra Leone Rise
66 L13 **Sierra Leone Rise** *var.* Sierra Leone Ridge, Sierra Leone Schwelle. *undersea feature* E Atlantic Ocean
Sierra Leone Schwelle *see* Sierra Leone Rise
43 U17 **Sierra Madre** *var.* Sierra de Soconusco. ▲▲ Guatemala/Mexico
179 Pp9 **Sierra Madre** ▲▲ Luzon, N Philippines
39 R2 **Sierra Madre** ▲▲ Colorado/Wyoming, C USA
(0) H15 **Sierra Madre del Sur** ▲▲ S Mexico
(0) G13 **Sierra Madre Occidental** *var.* Western Sierra Madre. ▲▲ C Mexico
(0) H13 **Sierra Madre Oriental** *var.* Eastern Sierra Madre. ▲▲ C Mexico
46 H8 **Sierra Maestra** ▲▲ E Cuba
42 L7 **Sierra Mojada** Coahuila de Zaragoza, NE Mexico 27.13N 103.42W
107 O14 **Sierra Nevada** ▲▲ S Spain
37 P6 **Sierra Nevada** ▲▲ W USA
56 F4 **Sierra Nevada de Santa Marta** ▲▲ NE Colombia
44 K5 **Sierra Río Tinto** ▲▲ NE Honduras
26 J10 **Sierra Vieja** ▲▲ Texas, SW USA
39 N16 **Sierra Vista** Arizona, SW USA 31.33N 110.18W
110 D10 **Sierre** *Ger.* Siders. Valais, SW Switzerland 46.18N 7.33E
38 L16 **Sierrita Mountains** ▲▲ Arizona, SW USA
Siete Moai *see* Ahu Akivi
78 M15 **Sifié** W Ivory Coast 7.58N 6.55W
117 I21 **Sífnos** *anc.* Siphnos. *island* Kykládes, Greece, Aegean Sea
117 I21 **Sífnou, Stenó** *strait* SE Greece
Siga *see* Shiga
197 H15 **Sigatoka** *prev.* Singatoka. Viti Levu, W Fiji 18.10S 105.30E
105 P16 **Sigean** Aude, S France 43.01N 2.58E
Sighet *see* Sighetu Marmaţiei
Sighetul Marmaţiei *see* Sighetu Marmaţiei
118 I8 **Sighetu Marmaţiei** *var.* Sighet, Sighetul Marmaţiei, *Hung.* Máramarossziget. Maramureş, N Romania 47.55N 23.52E
118 I11 **Sighişoara** *Ger.* Schässburg, *Hung.* Segesvár. Mureş, C Romania 46.12N 24.48E
173 E3 **Sigli** Sumatera, W Indonesia 5.21N 95.55E
94 J1 **Siglufjördhur** Nordhurland Vestra, N Iceland 66.09N 18.55W
103 H23 **Sigmaringen** Baden-Württemberg, S Germany 48.04N 9.12E
103 N20 **Signalberg** ▲ SE Germany 49.30N 12.34E
38 I13 **Signal Peak** ▲ Arizona, SW USA 33.20N 114.03W
Signan *see* Xi'an
204 H1 **Signy** *UK research station* South Orkney Islands, Antarctica 60.27S 45.35W
31 X15 **Sigourney** Iowa, C USA 41.19N 92.12W
117 K17 **Sígri, Akrotírio** *headland* Lésvos, E Greece 39.12N 25.49E
Sigsbee Deep *see* Mexico Basin
49 N2 **Sigsbee Escarpment** *undersea feature* N Gulf of Mexico
58 C8 **Sigsig** Azuay, S Ecuador 3.04S 78.49W
97 O15 **Sigtuna** Stockholm, C Sweden 59.36N 17.43E
44 H6 **Siguatepeque** Comayagua, W Honduras 14.38N 87.52W
107 P7 **Sigüenza** Castilla-La Mancha, C Spain 41.04N 2.37W
107 R4 **Sigües** Aragón, NE Spain 42.39N 1.01W
78 K13 **Siguiri** Haute-Guinée, NE Guinea 11.25N 9.07W
120 G8 **Sigulda** *Ger.* Segewold. Rīga, C Latvia 57.08N 24.51E
Sihanoukville *see* Kâmpóng Saôm
110 G8 **Sihlsee** ◎ NW Switzerland
95 K18 **Siikainen** Länsi-Suomi, W Finland 61.52N 21.49E
95 M16 **Siilinjärvi** Itä-Suomi, C Finland 63.04N 27.40E
143 R15 **Siirt** *var.* Sert; *anc.* Tigranocerta. Siirt, SE Turkey 37.55N 41.55E
143 R15 **Siirt** *var.* Sert. ◐ *province* SE Turkey
195 Z15 **Sikaiana** *var.* Stewert Islands. *island group* W Solomon Islands
Sikandarabad *see* Secunderābād
158 J11 **Sikandra Rao** Uttar Pradesh, N India 27.42N 78.22E
8 M11 **Sikanni Chief** British Columbia, W Canada 57.16N 122.44W
8 M11 **Sikanni Chief** ≈ British Columbia, W Canada
158 H11 **Sīkar** Rājasthān, N India 27.39N 75.09E
78 M13 **Sikasso** Sikasso, S Mali 11.21N 5.42W
78 L13 **Sikasso** ◐ *region* SW Mali
178 Gg3 **Sikaw** Kachin State, C Burma 23.50N 97.04E
85 H14 **Sikelenge** Western, W Zambia 14.51S 24.13E
29 Y7 **Sikeston** Missouri, C USA 36.52N 89.35W
95 J14 **Sikfors** Norrbotten, N Sweden 65.29N 21.17E
127 O16 **Sikhote-Alin', Khrebet** ▲▲ SE Russian Federation
Siking *see* Xi'an
117 J22 **Síkinos** *island* Kykládes, Greece, Aegean Sea
159 S11 **Sikkim** *Tib.* Denjong. ◐ *state* N India
113 I26 **Siklós** Baranya, SW Hungary 45.51N 18.18E
Sikoku *see* Shikoku
Sikoku Basin *see* Shikoku Basin
85 G14 **Sikongo** Western, W Zambia 15.03S 22.07E
Sikotu Ko *see* Shikotsu-ko
Sikouri/Sikoúrion *see* Sykoúri
126 L7 **Siktyakh** Respublika Sakha (Yakutiya), NE Russian Federation 69.45N 124.42E
120 D12 **Šilalė** Šilalė, W Lithuania 55.29N 22.10E
108 G5 **Silandro** *Ger.* Schlanders. Trentino-Alto Adige, N Italy 46.39N 10.55E
43 N12 **Silao** Guanajuato, C Mexico 20.55N 101.24W
Silarius *see* Sele
179 Q13 **Silay** *off.* Silay City. Negros, C Philippines 10.49N 122.58E
159 W14 **Silchar** Assam, NE India 24.49N 92.48E
110 G9 **Silenen** Uri, C Switzerland 46.49N 8.39E
23 T9 **Siler City** North Carolina, SE USA 35.43N 79.27W
35 U11 **Silesia** Montana, NW USA 45.32N 108.52W
112 F13 **Silesia** *physical region* SW Poland
76 K12 **Silet** S Algeria 22.45N 4.51E
151 R8 **Sileti** *var.* Selety. ≈ N Kazakhstan
Siletitengiz *see* Siletiteniz, Ozero
151 R7 **Siletiteniz, Ozero** *Kaz.* Siletitengiz. ◎ N Kazakhstan
180 H16 **Silhouette** *island* Inner Islands, SE Seychelles
142 I17 **Silifke** *anc.* Seleucia. İçel, S Turkey 36.22N 33.57E
Siliguri *see* Shiliguri
162 J10 **Siling Co** ◎ W China
Silinhot *see* Xilinhot
198 Aa7 **Silisili** ▲ Savai'i, C Samoa 13.37S 172.26W
116 M6 **Silistra** *var.* Silistria; *anc.* Durostorum. Silistra, NE Bulgaria 44.07N 27.16E
116 M7 **Silistra** ◐ *province* NE Bulgaria
Silistria *see* Silistra
142 D10 **Silivri** İstanbul, NW Turkey 41.04N 28.15E
96 L13 **Siljan** ◎ C Sweden
97 G22 **Silkeborg** Århus, C Denmark 56.10N 9.34E
110 M8 **Sill** ≈ W Austria
107 S10 **Silla** País Valenciano, E Spain 39.22N 0.25W
64 H3 **Sillajguay, Cordillera** ▲ N Chile 19.45S 68.39W
120 K3 **Sillamäe** *Ger.* Sillamäggi. Ida-Virumaa, NE Estonia 59.23N 27.45E
Sillamäggi *see* Sillamäe
Sillein *see* Žilina
111 P9 **Sillian** Tirol, W Austria 46.45N 12.25E
114 B10 **Šilo** Primorje-Gorski Kotar, NW Croatia 45.09N 14.39E
29 R9 **Siloam Springs** Arkansas, C USA 36.11N 94.32W
27 X10 **Silsbee** Texas, SW USA 30.21N 94.10W
149 W15 **Sīlūp, Rūd-e** ≈ SE Iran
120 C12 **Šilutė** *Ger.* Heydekrug. Šilutė, W Lithuania 55.20N 21.29E
143 Q15 **Sılvan** Dıyarbakır, SE Turkey 38.08N 41.00E
110 J10 **Silvaplana** Graubünden, S Switzerland 46.27N 9.45E
Silva Porto *see* Kuito
60 M12 **Silva, Recife do** *reef* E Brazil
160 D12 **Silvassa** Dādra and Nagar Haveli, W India 20.13N 73.03E
31 X4 **Silver Bay** Minnesota, N USA 47.17N 91.15W
39 P15 **Silver City** New Mexico, SW USA 32.46N 108.16W
20 D10 **Silver Creek** New York, NE USA 42.32N 79.10W
39 N12 **Silver Creek** ≈ Arizona, SW USA
29 P4 **Silver Lake** Kansas, C USA 39.06N 95.51W
34 I14 **Silver Lake** Oregon, NW USA 43.07N 121.04W
37 T9 **Silver Peak Range** ▲▲ Nevada, W USA
23 W3 **Silver Spring** Maryland, NE USA 38.59N 77.01W
Silver State *see* Nevada
Silver State *see* Colorado
39 Q7 **Silverton** Colorado, C USA 37.48N 107.39W
20 K16 **Silverton** New Jersey, NE USA 40.00N 74.09W
34 G11 **Silverton** Oregon, NW USA 45.00N 122.46W
27 N4 **Silverton** Texas, SW USA 34.26N 101.19W
106 G14 **Silves** Faro, S Portugal 37.10N 8.25W
56 D12 **Silvia** Cauca, SW Colombia 2.36N 76.20W
110 J9 **Silvrettagruppe** ▲▲ Austria/Switzerland
Sily-Vajdej *see* Vulcan
110 L7 **Silz** Tirol, W Austria 47.17N 11.00E
180 I13 **Sima** Anjouan, SE Comoros 12.10S 44.18E
Simabara *see* Shimabara
Simada *see* Shimada
85 H15 **Simakando** Western, W Zambia 16.43S 24.46E
Simane *see* Shimane
121 L20 **Simanichy** *Rus.* Simonichi. Homyel'skaya Voblasts', SE Belarus 51.53N 28.04E
166 F14 **Simao** Yunnan, SW China 22.30N 101.06E
159 P12 **Simara** Central, C Nepal 27.14N 85.00E
12 I8 **Simard, Lac** ◎ Quebec, SE Canada
142 D13 **Simav** Kütahya, W Turkey 39.04N 28.58E
142 D13 **Simav Çayı** ≈ NW Turkey
81 L18 **Simba** Orientale, N Dem. Rep. Congo (Zaire) 0.46N 22.54E
194 H11 **Simbai** Madang, N PNG 5.12S 144.33E
195 O9 **Simberi Island** *island* Tabar Islands, N PNG
Simbirsk *see* Ul'yanovsk
12 F17 **Simcoe** Ontario, S Canada 42.50N 80.16W
12 H14 **Simcoe, Lake** ◎ Ontario, S Canada
82 J11 **Sīmēn** ▲▲ N Ethiopia
116 K11 **Simeonovgrad** *prev.* Maritsa. Khaskovo, S Bulgaria 42.03N 25.36E

◆ Country
● Country Capital
◇ Dependent Territory
○ Dependent Territory Capital
◐ Administrative Region
✈ International Airport
▲ Mountain
▲▲ Mountain Range
⛰ Volcano
≈ River
◎ Lake
⊠ Reservoir

SIMERIA – SLIDELL

118 G11 **Simeria** *Ger.* Pischk, *Hung.* Piski. Hunedoara, W Romania *45.51N 23.00E*
109 L24 **Simeto** ~ Sicilia, Italy, C Mediterranean Sea
173 E5 **Simeulue, Pulau** *island* NW Indonesia
119 T13 **Simferopol'** Respublika Krym, S Ukraine *44.55N 33.05E*
119 T13 **Simferopol'** ✕ Respublika Krym, S Ukraine *44.55N 34.04E*
Simi *see* Sými
158 M9 **Simikot** Far Western, NW Nepal *30.02N 81.49E*
56 F7 **Simití** Bolívar, N Colombia *7.57N 73.57W*
116 G11 **Simitla** Blagoevgrad, SW Bulgaria *41.57N 23.06E*
37 S15 **Simi Valley** California, W USA *34.17N 118.52W*
Simizu *see* Shimizu
Simla *see* Shimla
Şimlăul Silvaniei/Şimleul Silvaniei *see* Şimleu Silvaniei
118 G9 **Şimleu Silvaniei** *Hung.* Szilágysomlyó; *prev.* Şimlăul Silvaniei, Şimleul Silvaniei. Sălaj, NW Romania *47.12N 22.49E*
Simmer *see* Simmerbach
103 E19 **Simmerbach** *var.* Simmer. ~ W Germany
103 F18 **Simmern** Rheinland-Pfalz, W Germany *50.00N 7.30E*
24 I7 **Simmesport** Louisiana, S USA *30.58N 91.48W*
121 F14 **Simnas** Alytus, S Lithuania *54.23N 23.40E*
94 L13 **Simo** Lappi, NW Finland *65.40N 25.04E*
Simoda *see* Shimoda
Simodate *see* Shimodate
94 M13 **Simojärvi** ◎ N Finland
94 L13 **Simojoki** ~ NW Finland
43 U15 **Simojovel** *var.* Simojovel de Allende. Chiapas, SE Mexico *17.12N 92.42W*
Simojovel de Allende *see* Simojovel
58 B7 **Simon Bolivar** *var.* Guayaquil. ✕ (Guayaquil) Guayas, W Ecuador *2.16S 79.54W*
56 L5 **Simón Bolívar** ✕ (Caracas) Distrito Federal, N Venezuela
Simonichi *see* Simanichy
12 M12 **Simon, Lac** ◎ Quebec, SE Canada
Simonoseki *see* Shimonoseki
Šimonovany *see* Partizánske
Simonstad *see* Simon's Town
85 E26 **Simon's Town** *var.* Simonstad. Western Cape, SW South Africa *34.12S 18.25E*
Simony *see* Partizánske
Simotuma *see* Shimotsuma
173 F6 **Simpangkanan, Sungai** ~ Sumatera, NW Indonesia
173 F5 **Simpangkiri, Sungai** ~ Sumatera, NW Indonesia
Simpeln *see* Simplon
101 M18 **Simpelveld** Limburg, SE Netherlands *50.49N 5.58E*
110 E11 **Simplon** *var.* Simpeln. Valais, SW Switzerland *46.13N 8.01E*
110 E11 **Simplon Pass** *pass* S Switzerland *46.18N 8.01E*
108 C6 **Simplon Tunnel** *tunnel* Italy/Switzerland
Simpson *see* Fort Simpson
190 G1 **Simpson Desert** *desert* Northern Territory/South Australia
8 J9 **Simpson Peak** ▲ British Columbia, W Canada *59.43N 131.29W*
15 L3 **Simpson Peninsula** *peninsula* Nunavut, NE Canada
23 P11 **Simpsonville** South Carolina, SE USA *34.44N 82.15W*
97 L23 **Simrishamn** Skåne, S Sweden *55.34N 14.20E*
127 Pp15 **Simushir, Ostrov** *island* Kuril'skiye Ostrova, SE Russian Federation
Sinā'/Sinai Peninsula *see* Sinai
173 Ee6 **Sinabang** Sumatera, W Indonesia *2.27N 96.24E*
83 N15 **Sina Dhaqa** Galguduud, C Somalia *5.21N 46.21E*
77 X8 **Sinai** *var.* Sinai Peninsula, *Ar.* Shibh Jazīrat Sīnā', Sīnā'. *physical region* NE Egypt
118 J12 **Sinaia** Prahova, SE Romania *45.19N 25.33E*
196 B16 **Sinajana** C Guam *13.28N 144.45E*
42 H8 **Sinaloa** ◆ *state* C Mexico
56 H4 **Sinamaica** Zulia, NW Venezuela *11.06N 71.52W*
169 X14 **Sinan-ni** SE North Korea *38.37N 127.43E*
Sinano Gawa *see* Shinano-gawa
Sināwan *see* Sīnāwin
77 N8 **Sīnāwin** *var.* Sināwan. NW Libya *31.00N 10.37E*
85 J16 **Sinazongwe** Southern, S Zambia *17.11S 27.20E*
177 Ff6 **Sinbaungwe** Magwe, W Burma *19.43N 95.10E*
177 Ff5 **Sinbyugyun** Magwe, W Burma *20.37N 94.40E*
56 E6 **Since** Sucre, NW Colombia *9.15N 75.12W*
56 E6 **Sincelejo** Sucre, NW Colombia *9.16N 75.22W*
177 F5 **Sinchaingbyin** *var.* Zullapara. Arakan State, W Burma *20.51N 92.23E*
25 U4 **Sinclair, Lake** ⊠ Georgia, SE USA
8 M14 **Sinclair Mills** British Columbia, SW Canada *54.03N 121.37W*
178 Mm15 **Sin Cowe East Island** *island* S Spratly Islands
178 Mm15 **Sin Cowe Island** *island* SW Spratly Islands
155 Q14 **Sind** *var.* Sindh. ◆ *province* SE Pakistan
160 I8 **Sind** ~ N India
97 H19 **Sindal** Nordjylland, N Denmark *57.28N 10.13E*
179 Q15 **Sindañgan** Mindanao, S Philippines *8.09N 122.59E*
81 D19 **Sindara** Ngounié, W Gabon *1.07S 10.40E*
158 E13 **Sindari** *prev.* Sindri. Rājasthān, N India *25.34N 71.57E*
175 Q16 **Sindeh, Teluk** *bay* Nusa Tenggara, C Indonesia
116 N8 **Sindel** Varna, E Bulgaria *43.07N 27.35E*
103 H22 **Sindelfingen** Baden-Württemberg, SW Germany *48.43N 9.01E*
161 G16 **Sindgi** Karnātaka, C India *17.01N 76.22E*
Sindh *see* Sind
120 G5 **Sindi** *Ger.* Zintenhof. Pärnumaa, SW Estonia *58.25N 24.40E*
142 C13 **Sındırgı** Balıkesir, W Turkey *39.15N 28.10E*
79 N14 **Sindou** SW Burkina *10.34N 5.04W*
Sindri *see* Sindari
155 T9 **Sind Sāgar Doāb** *desert* E Pakistan
130 M11 **Sinegorskiy** Rostovskaya Oblast', SW Russian Federation *48.01N 40.52E*
127 O9 **Sinegor'ye** Magadanskaya Oblast', E Russian Federation *62.04N 150.33E*
116 O12 **Sinekli** İstanbul, NW Turkey *41.13N 28.13E*
106 F12 **Sines** Setúbal, S Portugal *37.58N 8.52W*
106 F12 **Sines, Cabo de** *headland* S Portugal *37.57N 8.55W*
94 L12 **Sinettä** Lappi, NW Finland *66.39N 25.25E*
195 P11 **Sinewit, Mount** ▲ New Britain, C PNG *4.42S 151.58E*
82 G11 **Singa** *var.* Sinja, Sinjah. Sinnar, E Sudan *13.07N 33.54E*
80 J12 **Singako** Moyen-Chari, S Chad *9.52N 19.31E*
Singan *see* Xi'an
174 I7 **Singapore** ● (Singapore) S Singapore *1.17N 103.48E*
174 I7 **Singapore** *off.* Republic of Singapore. ◆ *republic* SE Asia
174 I7 **Singapore Strait** *var.* Strait of Singapore, *Mal.* Selat Singapura. *strait* Indonesia/Singapore
Singapore, Strait of/Singapura, Selat *see* Singapore Strait
175 N16 **Singaraja** Bali, C Indonesia *8.06S 115.04E*
Singatoka *see* Sigatoka
178 H10 **Sing Buri** *var.* Singhaburi. Sing Buri, C Thailand *14.55N 100.21E*
103 H24 **Singen** Baden-Württemberg, S Germany *47.46N 8.49E*
Sîngeorgiu de Pădure *see* Sângeorgiu de Pădure
Sîngeorz-Băi/Singeroz Băi *see* Sângeorz-Băi
118 M9 **Sîngerei** *var.* Sângerei; *prev.* Lazovsk. N Moldova *47.38N 28.08E*
Singhaburi *see* Sing Buri
83 H21 **Singida** Singida, C Tanzania *4.45S 34.48E*
83 G22 **Singida** ◆ *region* C Tanzania
Singidunum *see* Beograd
177 G2 **Singkaling Hkamti** Sagaing, N Burma *26.00N 95.43E*
175 Pp12 **Singkang** Sulawesi, C Indonesia *4.09S 119.58E*
174 Gg8 **Singkarak, Danau** ◎ Sumatera, W Indonesia
174 K7 **Singkawang** Borneo, C Indonesia *0.57N 108.57E*
174 I8 **Singkep, Pulau** *island* Kepulauan Lingga, W Indonesia
173 F6 **Singkilbaru** Sumatera, W Indonesia *2.18N 97.47E*
191 T7 **Singleton** New South Wales, SE Australia *32.36S 151.10E*
Singora *see* Songkhla
Singū *see* Shingū
Sining *see* Xining
109 D17 **Siniscola** Sardegna, Italy, C Mediterranean Sea *40.34N 9.42E*
115 F14 **Sinj** Split-Dalmacija, SE Croatia *43.41N 16.37E*
Sinja/Sinjah *see* Singa
Sinjajevina *see* Sinjavina
145 P3 **Sinjār** NW Iraq *36.19N 41.51E*
145 P2 **Sinjār, Jabal** ▲ N Iraq
115 K15 **Sinjavina** *var.* Sinjajevina. ▲ SW Yugoslavia
82 I7 **Sinkat** Red Sea, NE Sudan *18.52N 36.51E*
Sinkiang/Sinkiang Uighur Autonomous Region *see* Xinjiang Uygur Zizhiqu
Sînmartin *see* Târnăveni
169 V13 **Sinmi-do** *island* NW North Korea
Sinminato *see* Shinminato
103 I18 **Sinn** ~ C Germany
Sinnamarie *see* Sinnamary
57 Y9 **Sinnamary** *var.* Sinnamarie. N French Guiana *5.23N 52.57W*
82 G11 **Sinnar** ◆ *state* E Sudan
Sinneh *see* Sanandaj
20 E13 **Sinnemahoning Creek** ~ Pennsylvania, NE USA
Sînnicolau Mare *see* Sânnicolau Mare
Sino/Sinoe *see* Greenville
Sinoe, Lacul *see* Sinoie, Lacul
Sinoia *see* Chinhoyi
119 N14 **Sinoie, Lacul** *prev.* Lacul Sinoe. *lagoon* SE Romania
61 H16 **Sinop** Mato Grosso, W Brazil *11.38S 55.27W*
142 K10 **Sinop** *anc.* Sinope. Sinop, N Turkey *42.01N 35.09E*
142 J10 **Sinop** ◆ *province* N Turkey
142 K10 **Sinop Burnu** *headland* N Turkey *42.02N 35.12E*
Sinope *see* Sinop
169 Y12 **Sinp'o** E North Korea *40.01N 128.09E*
103 H20 **Sinsheim** Baden-Württemberg, SW Germany *49.15N 8.52E*
Sinsiro *see* Shinshiro
Sîntana *see* Sântana
174 L8 **Sintang** Borneo, C Indonesia *0.03N 111.31E*
101 F14 **Sint Annaland** Zeeland, SW Netherlands *51.36N 4.07E*
100 L5 **Sint Annaparochie** Friesland, N Netherlands *53.20N 5.46E*
47 V9 **Sint Eustatius** *Eng.* Saint Eustatius. *island* N Netherlands Antilles
101 G19 **Sint-Genesius-Rode** *Fr.* Rhode-Saint-Genèse. Vlaams Brabant, C Belgium *50.45N 4.21E*
101 F16 **Sint-Gillis-Waas** Oost-Vlaanderen, N Belgium *51.14N 4.08E*
101 H17 **Sint-Katelijne-Waver** Antwerpen, C Belgium *51.05N 4.31E*
101 E18 **Sint-Lievens-Houtem** Oost-Vlaanderen, NW Belgium *50.55N 3.52E*
47 V9 **Sint Maarten** *Eng.* Saint Martin. *island* N Netherlands Antilles
101 F14 **Sint Maartensdijk** Zeeland, SW Netherlands *51.33N 4.05E*
101 L19 **Sint-Martens-Voeren** *Fr.* Fouron-Saint-Martin. Limburg, NE Belgium *50.46N 5.49E*
101 J14 **Sint-Michielsgestel** Noord-Brabant, S Netherlands *51.37N 5.21E*
Sînt-Miclăuș *see* Gheorgheni
47 O16 **Sint Nicholaas** S Aruba *12.25N 69.52W*
101 F16 **Sint-Niklaas** *Fr.* Saint-Nicolas. Oost-Vlaanderen, N Belgium *51.10N 4.09E*
101 K14 **Sint-Oedenrode** Noord-Brabant, S Netherlands *51.34N 5.28E*
27 T14 **Sinton** Texas, SW USA *28.02N 97.30W*
101 G14 **Sint Philipsland** Zeeland, SW Netherlands *51.37N 4.11E*
101 G19 **Sint-Pieters-Leeuw** Vlaams Brabant, C Belgium *50.46N 4.16E*
106 E11 **Sintra** *prev.* Cintra. Lisboa, W Portugal *38.48N 9.22W*
101 J18 **Sint-Truiden** *Fr.* Saint-Trond. Limburg, NE Belgium *50.48N 5.13E*
101 H14 **Sint Willebrord** Noord-Brabant, S Netherlands *51.33N 4.34E*
169 V13 **Sinŭiju** W North Korea *40.08N 124.33E*
82 P13 **Sinujiif** Nugaal, NE Somalia *8.33N 49.05E*
Sinus Aelaniticus *see* Aqaba, Gulf of
Sinus Gallicus *see* Lion, Golfe du
Sinyang *see* Xinyang
Sinyavka *see* Sinyawka
121 I18 **Sinyawka** *Rus.* Sinyavka. Minskaya Voblasts', SW Belarus *52.57N 26.29E*
126 Ll11 **Sinyaya** ~ NE Russian Federation
Sinying *see* Hsinying
Sinyukha *see* Synyukha
Sinzi-ko *see* Shinji-ko
Sinzyô *see* Shinjō
113 I24 **Sió** ~ W Hungary
179 Q16 **Siocon** Mindanao, S Philippines *7.37N 122.09E*
113 I24 **Siófok** Somogy, C Hungary *46.54N 18.03E*
Siogama *see* Shiogama
85 G13 **Sioma** Western, SW Zambia *16.41S 23.34E*
110 D11 **Sion** *Ger.* Sitten; *anc.* Sedunum. Valais, SW Switzerland *46.15N 7.23E*
105 O11 **Sioule** ~ C France
31 S12 **Sioux Center** Iowa, C USA *43.04N 96.10W*
31 R13 **Sioux City** Iowa, C USA *42.30N 96.24W*
31 R11 **Sioux Falls** South Dakota, N USA *43.33N 96.45W*
10 B11 **Sioux Lookout** Ontario, S Canada *49.27N 94.06W*
31 T12 **Sioux Rapids** Iowa, C USA *42.53N 95.09W*
Sioux State *see* North Dakota
Siozirė *see* Shiojiri
179 Q14 **Sipalay** Negros, C Philippines *9.46N 122.25E*
57 V11 **Sipaliwini** ◆ *district* S Surinam
47 U15 **Siparia** Trinidad, Trinidad and Tobago *10.07N 61.33W*
Siphnos *see* Sífnos
169 V11 **Siping** *var.* Ssu-p'ing, Szeping; *prev.* Ssu-p'ing-chieh. Jilin, NE China *43.09N 124.22E*
9 X12 **Sipiwesk** Manitoba, C Canada *55.28N 97.16W*
9 W13 **Sipiwesk Lake** ◎ Manitoba, C Canada
205 O11 **Siple Coast** *physical region* Antarctica
204 K12 **Siple Island** *island* Antarctica
204 K13 **Siple, Mount** ▲ Siple Island, Antarctica *73.25S 126.24W*
Sipoo *see* Sibbo
114 G12 **Šipovo** Republika Srpska, W Bosnia and Herzegovina *44.16N 17.05E*
25 O4 **Sipsey River** ~ Alabama, S USA
173 Ff10 **Sipura, Pulau** *island* W Indonesia
(0) G16 **Siqueiros Fracture Zone** *tectonic feature* E Pacific Ocean
44 L10 **Siquia, Río** ~ SE Nicaragua
179 Qq14 **Siquijor Island** *island* C Philippines
45 N13 **Siquirres** Limón, E Costa Rica *10.06N 83.33W*
56 J5 **Siquisique** Lara, N Venezuela *10.36N 69.38W*
161 G19 **Sira** Karnātaka, W India *13.46N 76.54E*
97 D16 **Sira** ~ S Norway
178 Hh12 **Siracha** *var.* Ban Si Racha, Si Racha. Chon Buri, S Thailand *13.10N 100.57E*
109 L25 **Siracusa** *Eng.* Syracuse. Sicilia, Italy, C Mediterranean Sea *37.04N 15.16E*
Sirajganj *see* Shirajganj Ghat
Sirakawa *see* Shirakawa
9 N14 **Sir Alexander, Mount** ▲ British Columbia, W Canada *54.00N 120.33W*
143 O12 **Şiran** Gümüşhane, NE Turkey *40.12N 39.07E*
79 Q12 **Sirba** ~ E Burkina
149 O17 **Şīr Banī Yās** *island* W UAE
97 D17 **Sirdalsvatnet** ◎ S Norway
Sir Darya/Sirdaryo *see* Syr Darya
153 O11 **Sirdaryo Wiloyati** *Rus.* Syrdar'inskaya Oblast'. ◆ *province* E Uzbekistan
Sir Donald Sangster International Airport *see* Sangster
194 H13 **Sirebi** ~ S PNG
189 S3 **Sir Edward Pellew Group** *island group* Northern Territory, NE Australia
118 K8 **Siret** *Ger.* Sereth, *Hung.* Szeret. Suceava, N Romania *47.55N 26.04E*
118 K8 **Siret** *var.* Siretul, *Ger.* Sereth, *Rus.* Seret, *Ukr.* Siret. ~ Romania/Ukraine
Siretul *see* Siret
146 K3 **Sirḥān, Wādī as** *dry watercourse* Jordan/Saudi Arabia
158 I8 **Sirhind** Punjab, N India *30.39N 76.28E*
118 F11 **Şiria** *Ger.* Schiria. Arad, W Romania *46.16N 21.37E*
Siria *see* Syria
149 S14 **Sīrīk** Hormozgān, SE Iran *26.31N 57.06E*
178 Hh8 **Sirikit Reservoir** ◎ N Thailand
60 K12 **Siriituba, Ilha** *island* NE Brazil
176 Ww11 **Siriwo** ~ Irian Jaya, E Indonesia
149 R11 **Sīrjān** *prev.* Sa'īdābād. Kermān, S Iran *29.28N 55.39E*
190 H9 **Sir Joseph Banks Group** *island group* South Australia
94 K11 **Sirkka** Lappi, N Finland *67.49N 24.48E*
Sirna *see* Sýrna
143 R16 **Şırnak** Şırnak, SE Turkey *37.33N 42.27E*
143 S16 **Şırnak** ◆ *province* SE Turkey
Siroisi *see* Shiroishi
161 J14 **Sironcha** Mahārāshtra, C India *18.51N 80.03E*
Sirone *see* Shirone
Síros *see* Sýros
Sirotino *see* Sirotsina
120 M12 **Sirotsina** *Rus.* Sirotino. Vitsyebskaya Voblasts', N Belarus *55.22N 29.34E*
158 H9 **Sirsa** Haryāna, NW India *29.31N 75.04E*
181 Y17 **Sir Seewoosagur Ramgoolam** ✕ (Port Louis) SE Mauritius
161 E18 **Sirsi** Karnātaka, W India *14.46N 74.49E*
Sirte *see* Surt
190 A2 **Sir Thomas, Mount** ▲ South Australia *27.09S 129.49E*
Sirti, Gulf of *see* Surt, Khalīj
148 J5 **Sīrvān, Rūdkhāneh-ye** *var.* Nahr Diyālá, Sirwan. ~ Iran/Iraq *see also* Diyālá, Nahr
120 H13 **Širvintos** Širvintos, SE Lithuania *55.01N 24.58E*
Sirwan *see* Diyālá, Nahr/Sīrvān, Rūdkhāneh-ye
9 N15 **Sir Wilfrid Laurier, Mount** ▲ British Columbia, SW Canada *52.45N 119.51W*
12 M10 **Sir-Wilfrid, Mont** ▲ Quebec, SE Canada *46.57N 75.33W*
Sisačko-Moslavačka Županija *see* Sisak-Moslavina
114 E9 **Sisak** *var.* Siscia, *Ger.* Sissek, *Hung.* Sziszek; *anc.* Segestica. Sisak-Moslavina, C Croatia *45.28N 16.21E*
178 J10 **Si Sa Ket** *var.* Sisaket, Sri Saket. Si Sa Ket, E Thailand *15.07N 104.18E*
114 E9 **Sisak-Moslavina** *off.* Sisačko-Moslavačka Županija. ◆ *province* C Croatia
178 H8 **Si Satchanala** Sukhothai, NW Thailand
Siscia *see* Sisak
176 W10 **Sisember** Irian Jaya, E Indonesia *1.51S 134.09E*
85 G22 **Sishen** Northern Cape, NW South Africa *27.46S 22.58E*
143 V13 **Sisian** SE Armenia *39.31N 46.03E*
207 N13 **Sisimiut** *var.* Holsteinborg, Holsteinsborg, Holstenborg, Holstensborg. Kitaa, S Greenland *67.07N 53.42W*
32 M1 **Siskiwit Bay** *lake bay* Michigan, N USA
36 L1 **Siskiyou Mountains** ▲ California/Oregon, W USA
178 I12 **Sisŏphŏn** Bătdâmbâng, NW Cambodia *13.37N 102.58E*
110 E7 **Sissach** Basel-Land, NW Switzerland *47.27N 7.48E*
194 F9 **Sissano** Sandaun, NW PNG *3.01S 142.01E*
Sissek *see* Sisak
31 R7 **Sisseton** South Dakota, N USA *45.39N 97.03W*
149 W9 **Sīstān, Daryācheh-ye** *var.* Daryācheh-ye Hāmūn, Hāmūn-e Şāberī. ◎ Afghanistan/Iran *see also* Şāberī, Hāmūn-e
149 V12 **Sīstān va Balūchestān** *off.* Ostān-e Sīstān va Balūchestān, *var.* Balūchestān va Sīstān. ◆ *province* SE Iran
105 T14 **Sisteron** Alpes-de-Haute-Provence, SE France *44.12N 5.55E*
34 H13 **Sisters** Oregon, NW USA *44.17N 121.33W*
67 G15 **Sisters Peak** ▲ N Ascension Island *7.55S 14.22W*
23 R3 **Sistersville** West Virginia, NE USA *39.33N 81.00W*
Sistova *see* Svishtov
Sitakund *see* Sitakunda
159 V16 **Sitakunda** *var.* Sitakund. Chittagong, SE Bangladesh *22.35N 91.40E*
159 P12 **Sītāmarhi** Bihār, N India *26.36N 85.30E*
158 L11 **Sītāpur** Uttar Pradesh, N India *27.33N 80.40E*
Sitaș Cristuru *see* Cristuru Secuiesc
117 L25 **Siteía** *var.* Sitía. Kríti, Greece, E Mediterranean Sea *35.13N 26.06E*
107 V6 **Sitges** Cataluña, NE Spain *41.13N 1.49E*
117 H15 **Sithoniá** *peninsula* NE Greece
Sitía *see* Siteía
56 F4 **Sitionuevo** Magdalena, N Colombia *10.41N 74.42W*
41 X13 **Sitka** Baranof Island, Alaska, USA *57.03N 135.19W*
41 Q15 **Sitkinak Island** *island* Trinity Islands, Alaska, USA
177 G7 **Sittang** *var.* Sittoung. ~ S Burma
101 L17 **Sittard** Limburg, SE Netherlands *51.00N 5.52E*
Sitten *see* Sion
110 H7 **Sitter** ~ NW Switzerland
111 U10 **Sittersdorf** Kärnten, S Austria *46.31N 14.34E*
Sittoung *see* Sittang
177 F6 **Sittwe** *var.* Akyab. Arakan State, W Burma *22.09N 92.51E*
174 Mm15 **Situbondo** *prev.* Sitoebondo. Jawa, C Indonesia *7.40S 114.01E*
44 L8 **Siuna** Región Autónoma Atlántico Norte, NE Nicaragua *13.43N 84.46W*
159 R15 **Siuri** West Bengal, NE India *23.54N 87.31E*
Siut *see* Asyût
126 M15 **Sivaki** Amurskaya Oblast', SE Russian Federation *52.39N 126.43E*
142 M13 **Sivas** *anc.* Sebastia, Sebaste. Sivas, C Turkey *39.43N 37.01E*
142 M13 **Sivas** ◆ *province* C Turkey
143 O15 **Siverek** Şanlıurfa, S Turkey *37.46N 39.19E*
119 X6 **Sivers'k** Donets'ka Oblast', E Ukraine *48.52N 38.07E*
128 G13 **Siverskiy** Leningradskaya Oblast', NW Russian Federation *59.21N 30.01E*
119 X6 **Sivers'kyy Donets'** *Rus.* Severskiy Donets. ~ Russian Federation/Ukraine *see also* Severskiy Donets
129 W5 **Sivomaskinskiy** Respublika Komi, NW Russian Federation *66.42N 62.33E*
142 G13 **Sivrihisar** Eskişehir, W Turkey *39.28N 31.29E*
101 F22 **Sivry** Hainaut, S Belgium *50.10N 4.11E*
127 Pp9 **Sivuchiy, Mys** *headland* E Russian Federation *56.45N 163.13E*
77 U9 **Siwa** *var.* Sīwah. NW Egypt *29.11N 25.32E*
Sīwah *see* Siwa
158 J9 **Siwalik Range** *var.* Shiwālik Range. ▲ India/Nepal
159 O13 **Siwān** Bihār, N India *26.13N 84.21E*
45 O14 **Sixaola, Río** ~ Costa Rica/Panama
Six Counties, The *see* Northern Ireland
105 T16 **Six-Fours-les-Plages** Var, SE France *43.04N 5.49E*
167 Q7 **Sixian** *var.* Si Xian. Anhui, E China *33.28N 117.52E*
24 J9 **Six Mile Lake** ◎ Louisiana, S USA
145 V3 **Siyāh Gūz** E Iraq *35.49N 45.45E*
161 L25 **Siyambalanduwa** Uva Province, SE Sri Lanka *6.54N 81.31E*
143 Y10 **Siyäzän** *Rus.* Siazan'. NE Azerbaijan *41.04N 49.04E*
Sizebolu *see* Sozopol
Sizuoka *see* Shizuoka
Sjar *see* Sääre
115 L15 **Sjenica** *Turk.* Seniça. Serbia, SW Yugoslavia *43.16N 20.01E*
96 G11 **Sjoa** ~ S Norway
97 K23 **Sjöbo** Skåne, S Sweden *55.37N 13.45E*
97 I24 **Sjælland** *Eng.* Zealand, *Ger.* Seeland. *island* E Denmark
96 E9 **Sjøholt** Møre og Romsdal, S Norway *62.28N 6.49E*
94 O1 **Sjuøyane** *island group* N Svalbard
Skadar *see* Shkodër
Skadarsko Jezero *see* Scutari, Lake
119 R11 **Skadovs'k** Khersons'ka Oblast', S Ukraine *46.07N 32.53E*
94 I2 **Skagaströnd** *prev.* Höfdhakaupstadhur. Nordhurland Vestra, N Iceland *65.49N 20.18W*
97 H19 **Skagen** Nordjylland, N Denmark *57.43N 11.36E*
Skagerak *see* Skagerrak
97 L16 **Skagern** ◎ C Sweden
207 T17 **Skagerrak** *var.* Skagerak. *channel* N Europe
96 G12 **Skaget** ▲ S Norway *61.19N 9.07E*
34 H7 **Skagit River** ~ Washington, NW USA
41 W12 **Skagway** Alaska, USA *59.27N 135.18W*
94 K8 **Skaidi** Finnmark, N Norway *70.26N 24.31E*
117 F21 **Skála** Pelopónnisos, S Greece *36.51N 22.39E*
118 K6 **Skalat** *Pol.* Skałat. Ternopil's'ka Oblast', W Ukraine *49.27N 25.59E*
97 J22 **Skälderviken** *inlet* Denmark/Sweden
94 I12 **Skalka** ◎ N Sweden
116 I12 **Skalotí** Anatolikí Makedonía kai Thráki, NE Greece *41.24N 24.16E*
97 G22 **Skanderborg** Århus, C Denmark *56.01N 9.57E*
97 K22 **Skåne** *prev. Eng.* Scania. ◆ *county* S Sweden
77 N6 **Skanès** ✕ (Sousse) E Tunisia *35.36N 10.56E*
97 C15 **Skånevik** Hordaland, S Norway *59.43N 6.35E*
97 M18 **Skänninge** Östergötland, S Sweden *58.24N 15.04E*
97 J23 **Skanör** Skåne, S Sweden *55.24N 12.48E*
117 H17 **Skantzoúra** *island* Vóreioi Sporádes, Greece, Aegean Sea
97 K18 **Skara** Västra Götaland, S Sweden *58.22N 13.25E*
97 M17 **Skärblacka** Östergötland, S Sweden *58.34N 15.54E*
97 I18 **Skärhamn** Västra Götaland, S Sweden *57.58N 11.33E*
97 I14 **Skarnes** Hedmark, S Norway *60.13N 11.40E*
121 M21 **Skarodnaye** *Rus.* Skorodnoye. Homyel'skaya Voblasts', SE Belarus *51.38N 28.50E*
112 I8 **Skarszewy** *Ger.* Schöneck. Pomorskie, NW Poland *54.04N 18.25E*
113 M14 **Skarżysko-Kamienna** Świętokrzyskie, C Poland *51.07N 20.52E*
97 K16 **Skattkärr** Värmland, C Sweden *59.25N 13.42E*
120 D12 **Skaudvilė** Tauragė, SW Lithuania *55.25N 22.33E*
94 J12 **Skaulo** Norrbotten, N Sweden *67.21N 21.03E*
113 K17 **Skawina** Małopolskie, S Poland *49.56N 19.49E*
8 K12 **Skeena** ~ British Columbia, SW Canada
8 J11 **Skeena Mountains** ▲ British Columbia, W Canada
99 O18 **Skegness** E England, UK *53.10N 0.21E*
94 J4 **Skeidharársandur** *coast* S Iceland
95 J15 **Skellefteå** Västerbotten, N Sweden *64.45N 20.57E*
95 I14 **Skelleftealven** ~ N Sweden
95 J15 **Skelleftehamn** Västerbotten, N Sweden *64.41N 21.13E*
27 O2 **Skellytown** Texas, SW USA *35.34N 101.10W*
97 J19 **Skene** Västra Götaland, S Sweden *57.30N 12.34E*
99 G17 **Skerries** *Ir.* Na Sceirí. E Ireland *53.34N 6.07W*
97 H15 **Ski** Akershus, S Norway *59.43N 10.49E*
117 G17 **Skíathos** Skíathos, Vóreioi Sporádes, Greece, Aegean Sea *39.10N 23.30E*
117 G17 **Skíathos** *island* Vóreioi Sporádes, Greece, Aegean Sea
29 P9 **Skiatook** Oklahoma, C USA *36.22N 96.00W*
29 P9 **Skiatook Lake** ⊠ Oklahoma, C USA
99 B22 **Skibbereen** *Ir.* An Sciobairín. SW Ireland *51.33N 9.15W*
94 I9 **Skibotn** Troms, N Norway *69.22N 20.18E*
121 F16 **Skidal'** *Rus.* Skidel'. Hrodzyenskaya Voblasts', W Belarus *53.34N 24.12E*
99 K15 **Skiddaw** ▲ NW England, UK *54.37N 3.07W*
Skidel' *see* Skidal'
27 T14 **Skidmore** Texas, SW USA *28.13N 97.40W*
97 G16 **Skien** Telemark, S Norway *59.12N 9.36E*
Skiermûntseach *see* Schiermonnikoog
112 L12 **Skierniewice** Łodzkie, C Poland *51.58N 20.10E*
76 L5 **Skikda** *prev.* Philippeville. NE Algeria *36.51N 7.00E*
32 M16 **Skillet Fork** ~ Illinois, N USA
97 L19 **Skillingaryd** Jönköping, S Sweden *57.27N 14.04E*
117 B19 **Skinári, Akrotírio** *headland* Zákynthos, Iónioi Nísoi, Greece, C Mediterranean Sea *37.55N 20.57E*
97 M15 **Skinnskatteberg** Västmanland, C Sweden *59.49N 15.40E*
190 M12 **Skipton** Victoria, SE Australia *37.44S 143.21E*
99 L16 **Skipton** N England, UK *53.56N 1.59W*
Skiropoula *see* Skyropoúla
Skíros *see* Skýros
97 F21 **Skive** Viborg, NW Denmark *56.34N 9.01E*
96 F11 **Skjåk** Oppland, S Norway *61.52N 8.21E*
94 K2 **Skjálfandafljót** ~ C Iceland
97 F22 **Skjern** Ringkøbing, W Denmark *55.55N 8.30E*
97 F22 **Skjern Å** *var.* Skjern Aa. ~ W Denmark
Skjern Aa *see* Skjern Å
94 G12 **Skjerstad** Nordland, C Norway *67.14N 15.00E*
94 J8 **Skjervøy** Troms, N Norway *70.01N 20.57E*
94 I10 **Skjold** Troms, N Norway *69.03N 19.18E*
113 I17 **Skoczów** Śląskie, S Poland *49.47N 18.46E*
97 I24 **Skælskør** Vestsjælland, E Denmark *55.16N 11.18E*
111 T11 **Škofja Loka** *Ger.* Bischoflack. NW Slovenia *46.12N 14.16E*
96 N12 **Skog** Gävleborg, C Sweden *61.10N 16.49E*
97 K16 **Skoghall** Värmland, C Sweden *59.19N 13.30E*
33 N10 **Skokie** Illinois, N USA *42.01N 87.43W*
118 H6 **Skole** L'vivs'ka Oblast', W Ukraine *49.04N 23.29E*
117 D19 **Skóllis** ▲ S Greece *37.58N 21.33E*
178 J13 **Skon** Kâmpóng Cham, C Cambodia *12.56N 104.36E*
117 H17 **Skópelos** Skópelos, Vóreioi Sporádes, Greece, Aegean Sea *39.07N 23.44E*
117 H17 **Skópelos** *island* Vóreioi Sporádes, Greece, Aegean Sea
130 L5 **Skopin** Ryazanskaya Oblast', W Russian Federation *53.46N 39.37E*
115 N18 **Skopje** *var.* Üsküb, *Turk.* Üsküp; *prev.* Skoplje, *anc.* Scupi. ● (FYR Macedonia) N FYR Macedonia *42.01N 21.27E*
115 O18 **Skopje** ✕ N FYR Macedonia *41.58N 21.35E*
Skoplje *see* Skopje
112 I8 **Skórcz** *Ger.* Skurz. Pomorskie, N Poland *53.46N 18.43E*
Skorodnoye *see* Skarodnaye
95 H16 **Skorped** Västernorrland, C Sweden *63.22N 17.55E*
97 G21 **Skørping** Nordjylland, N Denmark *56.49N 9.55E*
97 K18 **Skövde** Västra Götaland, S Sweden *58.24N 13.52E*
126 Ll14 **Skovorodino** Amurskaya Oblast', SE Russian Federation *54.02N 123.47E*
21 Q6 **Skowhegan** Maine, NE USA *44.46N 69.41W*
9 W15 **Skownan** Manitoba, S Canada *51.55N 99.34W*
96 H13 **Skreia** Oppland, S Norway *60.37N 11.00E*
Skripón *see* Orchómenos
120 H9 **Skriveri** Aizkraukle, S Latvia *56.39N 25.07E*
120 J11 **Skrudaliena** Daugvapils, SE Latvia *55.50N 26.42E*
120 D9 **Skrunda** Kuldīga, W Latvia *56.39N 22.01E*
97 C16 **Skudeneshavn** Rogaland, S Norway *59.09N 5.16E*
85 L20 **Skukuza** Mpumalanga, NE South Africa *24.54S 31.33E*
99 B22 **Skull** *Ir.* An Scoil. SW Ireland *51.32N 9.33W*
24 L3 **Skuna River** ~ Mississippi, S USA
31 X15 **Skunk River** ~ Iowa, C USA
120 C10 **Skuodas** *Ger.* Schoden, *Pol.* Szkudy. Skuodas, NW Lithuania *56.16N 21.30E*
97 K23 **Skurup** Skåne, S Sweden *55.28N 13.30E*
Skurz *see* Skórcz
116 H8 **Skŭt** ~ NW Bulgaria
96 O13 **Skutskär** Uppsala, C Sweden *60.38N 17.29E*
97 B19 **Skúvoy** *Dan.* Skuø *Island* Faeroe Islands *61.46N 6.49W*
Skvira *see* Skvyra
119 O5 **Skvyra** *Rus.* Skvira. Kyyivs'ka Oblast', N Ukraine *49.44N 29.40E*
41 Q11 **Skwentna** Alaska, USA *61.56N 151.03W*
112 E11 **Skwierzyna** *Ger.* Schwerin. Lubuskie, W Poland *52.36N 15.27E*
38 K13 **Sky Harbour** ✕ (Phoenix) Arizona, SW USA *33.26N 112.00W*
98 G9 **Skye, Isle of** *island* NW Scotland, UK
34 I8 **Skykomish** Washington, NW USA *47.40N 121.20W*
Skylge *see* Terschelling
65 F19 **Skyring, Peninsula** *peninsula* S Chile
65 H24 **Skyring, Seno** *inlet* S Chile
117 H17 **Skyropoúla** *var.* Skiropoula. *island* Vóreioi Sporádes, Greece, Aegean Sea
117 I17 **Skýros** *var.* Skíros. Skýros, Vóreioi Sporádes, Greece, Aegean Sea *38.55N 24.34E*
117 I17 **Skýros** *var.* Skíros; *anc.* Scyros. *island* Vóreioi Sporádes, Greece, Aegean Sea
120 J12 **Slabodka** *Rus.* Slobodka. Vitsyebskaya Voblasts', NW Belarus *55.42N 27.10E*
97 I23 **Slagelse** Vestsjælland, E Denmark *55.25N 11.21E*
95 I14 **Slagnäs** Norrbotten, N Sweden *65.36N 18.10E*
174 Kk15 **Slamet, Gunung** ▲ Jawa, S Indonesia *7.12S 109.13E*
41 T10 **Slana** Alaska, USA *62.46N 144.00W*
99 F20 **Slaney** *Ir.* An tSláine. ~ SE Ireland
118 J13 **Slănic** Prahova, SE Romania *45.13N 25.58E*
118 K11 **Slănic Moldova** Bacău, E Romania *46.12N 26.23E*
115 H16 **Slano** Dubrovnik-Neretva, SE Croatia *42.47N 17.54E*
128 F13 **Slantsy** Leningradskaya Oblast', NW Russian Federation *59.06N 28.00E*
113 C16 **Slaný** *Ger.* Schlan. Střední Čechy, NW Czech Republic *50.13N 14.04E*
113 I16 **Śląskie** ◆ *province* S Poland
10 C10 **Slate Falls** Ontario, S Canada *51.11N 91.32W*
29 T4 **Slater** Missouri, C USA *39.13N 93.04W*
114 H9 **Slatina** *Hung.* Szlatina *prev.* Podravska Slatina. Virovitica-Podravina, NE Croatia *45.40N 17.46E*
118 I14 **Slatina** Olt, S Romania *45.27N 24.21E*
27 N5 **Slaton** Texas, SW USA *33.26N 101.38W*
97 H14 **Slattum** Akershus, S Norway *60.00N 10.55E*
9 R10 **Slave** ~ Alberta/Northwest Territories, C Canada
70 E11 **Slave Coast** *coastal region* W Africa
9 P13 **Slave Lake** Alberta, SW Canada *55.16N 114.46W*
125 G14 **Slavgorod** Altayskiy Kray, S Russian Federation *52.55N 78.46E*
Slavgorod *see* Slawharad
Slavonia *see* Slavonija
114 G9 **Slavonija** *Eng.* Slavonia, *Ger.* Slawonien, *Hung.* Szlavonország. *cultural region* NE Croatia
Slavonska Požega *see* Požega
114 H10 **Slavonski Brod** *Ger.* Brod, *Hung.* Bród; *prev.* Brod, Brod na Savi. Brod-Posavina, NE Croatia *45.09N 18.00E*
118 L4 **Slavuta** Khmel'nyts'ka Oblast', NW Ukraine *50.17N 26.52E*
119 P2 **Slavutych** Chernihivs'ka Oblast', N Ukraine *51.31N 30.47E*
127 N18 **Slavyanka** Primorskiy Kray, SE Russian Federation *42.46N 131.19E*
116 J8 **Slavyanovo** Pleven, N Bulgaria *43.28N 24.52E*
Slavyansk *see* Slov"yans'k
130 K14 **Slavyansk-na-Kubani** Krasnodarskiy Kray, SW Russian Federation *45.16N 38.09E*
121 N20 **Slavyechna** *Rus.* Slovechna. ~ Belarus/Ukraine
121 O16 **Slawharad** *Rus.* Slavgorod. Mahilyowskaya Voblasts', E Belarus *53.27N 31.00E*
112 G7 **Sławno** Zachodniopomorskie, NW Poland *54.22N 16.43E*
Slawonien *see* Slavonija
31 S10 **Slayton** Minnesota, N USA *43.59N 95.45W*
99 N18 **Sleaford** E England, UK *52.58N 0.27W*
99 A20 **Slea Head** *Ir.* Ceann Sléibhe. *headland* SW Ireland *52.05N 10.25W*
98 G9 **Sleat, Sound of** *strait* NW Scotland, UK
Sledyuki *see* Slyedzyuki
10 I5 **Sleeper Islands** *island group* Nunavut, C Canada
33 O6 **Sleeping Bear Point** *headland* Michigan, N USA *44.54N 86.02W*
31 T10 **Sleepy Eye** Minnesota, N USA *44.18N 94.43W*
41 O11 **Sleetmute** Alaska, USA *61.42N 157.10W*
Sléibhe, Ceann *see* Slea Head
Slēmānī *see* As Sulaymānīyah
205 O5 **Slessor Glacier** *glacier* Antarctica
24 L9 **Slidell** Louisiana, S USA *30.16N 89.46W*

◆ Country ● Country Capital ◇ Dependent Territory ○ Dependent Territory Capital ◆ Administrative Region ✕ International Airport ▲ Mountain ▲ Mountain Range ⚠ Volcano ~ River ◎ Lake ⊠ Reservoir

Slide Mountain – Sonthofen

20 K12 Slide Mountain ▲ New York, NE USA 42.00N 74.23W
100 I13 Sliedrecht Zuid-Holland, C Netherlands 51.49N 4.45E
123 Jj16 Sliema N Malta 35.54N 14.31E
99 G16 Slieve Donard ▲ SE Northern Ireland, UK 54.10N 5.57W
Sligeach see Sligo
99 D16 Sligo Ir. Sligeach. NW Ireland 54.16N 8.28W
99 C16 Sligo Ir. Sligeach. cultural region NW Ireland
99 C15 Sligo Bay Ir. Cuan Shligigh. inlet NW Ireland
20 B13 Slippery Rock Pennsylvania, NE USA 41.02N 80.02W
97 P19 Slite Gotland, SE Sweden 57.37N 18.46E
116 L9 Sliven var. Slivno. Sliven, C Bulgaria 42.42N 26.20E
116 L10 Sliven ◐ province C Bulgaria
116 G9 Slivnitsa Sofiya, W Bulgaria 42.51N 23.01E
Slivno see Sliven
116 L7 Slivo Pole Ruse, N Bulgaria 43.57N 26.15E
31 S13 Sloan Iowa, C USA 42.13N 96.13W
37 X12 Sloan Nevada, W USA 35.56N 115.13W
Slobodka see Slabodka
129 R14 Slobodskoy Kirovskaya Oblast', NW Russian Federation 58.43N 50.12E
Slobodzeya see Slobozia
119 O10 Slobozia Rus. Slobodzeya. E Moldova 46.45N 29.42E
118 L14 Slobozia Ialomiţa, SE Romania 44.34N 27.22E
100 O5 Slochteren Groningen, NE Netherlands 53.13N 6.48E
121 H17 Slonim Pol. Słonim, Rus. Slonim. Hrodzyenskaya Voblasts', W Belarus 53.04N 25.21E
100 K7 Sloter Meer ◎ N Netherlands
Slot, The see New Georgia Sound
99 N22 Slough S England, UK 51.31N 0.36W
113 J20 Slovakia off. Slovenská Republika, Ger. Slowakei, Hung. Szlovákia, Slvk. Slovensko. ◆ republic C Europe
Slovak Ore Mountains see Slovenské rudohorie
Slovechna see Slavyechna
111 S12 Slovenia off. Republic of Slovenia, Ger. Slowenien, Slvn. Slovenija. ◆ republic SE Europe
Slovenija see Slovenia
111 V10 Slovenj Gradec Ger. Windischgraz. N Slovenia 46.29N 15.05E
111 W10 Slovenska Bistrica Ger. Windischfeistritz. NE Slovenia 46.21N 15.27E
Slovenská Republika see Slovakia
111 W10 Slovenske Konjice E Slovenia 46.21N 15.28E
113 K20 Slovenské rudohorie Eng. Slovak Ore Mountains, Ger. Slowakisches Erzgebirge, Ungarisches Erzgebirge. ▲▲ C Slovakia
Slovensko see Slovakia
119 Y7 Slov"yanoserbs'k Luhans'ka Oblast', E Ukraine 48.41N 39.00E
119 W6 Slov"yans'k Rus. Slavyansk. Donets'ka Oblast', E Ukraine 48.51N 37.38E
Slowakei see Slovakia
Slowakisches Erzgebirge see Slovenské rudohorie
Slowenien see Slovenia
112 D11 Słubice Ger. Frankfurt. Lubuskie, W Poland 52.19N 14.34E
121 K19 Sluch Rus. Sluch'. ≈ C Belarus
118 L4 Sluch ≈ NW Ukraine
101 D16 Sluis Zeeland, SW Netherlands 51.18N 3.22E
114 D10 Slunj Hung. Szluin. Karlovac, C Croatia 45.06N 15.35E
112 I11 Słupca Wielkolpolskie, C Poland 52.16N 17.54E
112 G6 Słupia Ger. Stolpe. ≈ NW Poland
112 G6 Słupsk Ger. Stolp. Pomorskie, N Poland 54.27N 17.01E
121 K18 Slutsk Rus. Slutsk. Minskaya Voblasts', S Belarus 53.01N 27.31E
121 O16 Slyedzyuki Rus. Sledyuki. Mahilyowskaya Voblasts', E Belarus 53.34N 30.19E
99 A17 Slyne Head Ir. Ceann Léime. headland W Ireland 53.25N 10.11W
126 J16 Slyudyanka Irkutskaya Oblast', S Russian Federation 51.36N 103.28E
29 U14 Smackover Arkansas, C USA 33.21N 92.43W
97 L20 Småland cultural region S Sweden
97 K20 Smålandsstenar Jönköping, S Sweden 57.10N 13.24E
Small Malaita see Maramasike
11 O8 Smallwood Reservoir ◎ Newfoundland, S Canada
121 N14 Smalyany Rus. Smolyany. Vitsyebskaya Voblasts', NE Belarus 54.36N 30.04E
121 L15 Smalyavichy Rus. Smolevichi. Minskaya Voblasts', C Belarus 54.01N 28.09E
76 C9 Smara var. Es Semara. N Western Sahara 26.45N 11.43W
121 I14 Smarhon' Pol. Smorgonie, Rus. Smorgon'. Hrodzyenskaya Voblasts', W Belarus 54.28N 26.24E
114 M11 Smederevo Ger. Semendria. Serbia, N Yugoslavia 44.40N 20.55E
114 M12 Smederevska Palanka Serbia, C Yugoslavia 44.23N 20.55E
97 M14 Smedjebacken Dalarna, C Sweden 60.07N 15.25E
118 L13 Smeeni Buzău, SE Romania 45.00N 26.52E
Smela see Smila
109 D16 Smeralda, Costa cultural region Sardegna, Italy, C Mediterranean Sea
113 J22 Smigiel Ger. Schmiegel. Wielkolpolskie, C Poland 52.02N 16.33E
119 Q6 Smila Rus. Smela. Cherkas'ka Oblast', C Ukraine 49.15N 31.54E
100 N7 Smilde Drenthe, NE Netherlands 52.57N 6.28E
9 S16 Smiley Saskatchewan, S Canada 51.40N 109.24W
27 T12 Smiley Texas, SW USA 29.16N 97.38W
Smilten see Smiltene
120 I8 Smiltene Ger. Smilten. Valka, N Latvia 57.25N 25.53E
127 O14 Smirnykh Ostrov Sakhalin, Sakhalinskaya Oblast', SE Russian Federation 49.43N 142.48E
9 Q13 Smith Alberta, W Canada 55.06N 113.57W
41 P4 Smith Bay bay Alaska, USA
10 I3 Smith, Cape headland Quebec, NE Canada 60.50N 78.06W
28 L3 Smith Center Kansas, C USA 39.46N 98.46W
8 K13 Smithers British Columbia, SW Canada 54.45N 127.10W
23 V10 Smithfield North Carolina, SE USA 35.30N 78.20W
38 L1 Smithfield Utah, W USA 41.50N 111.49W
23 X7 Smithfield Virginia, NE USA 36.41N 76.38W
10 I3 Smith Island island Nunavut, C Canada
Smith Island see Sumisu-jima
22 H7 Smithland Kentucky, S USA 37.06N 88.24W
23 T7 Smith Mountain Lake var. Leesville Lake. ⊠ Virginia, NE USA
36 L1 Smith River California, W USA 41.54N 124.09W
35 R9 Smith River ≈ Montana, NW USA
12 L13 Smiths Falls Ontario, SE Canada 44.54N 76.01W
35 N13 Smiths Ferry Idaho, NW USA 44.19N 116.04W
22 K7 Smiths Grove Kentucky, S USA 37.01N 86.14W
191 N15 Smithton Tasmania, SE Australia 40.54S 145.06E
20 L14 Smithtown Long Island, New York, NE USA 40.52N 73.13W
22 K9 Smithville Tennessee, S USA 35.57N 85.48W
27 T11 Smithville Texas, SW USA 30.04N 97.32W
Šmohor see Hermagor
37 Q4 Smoke Creek Desert desert Nevada, W USA
9 O14 Smoky ≈ Alberta, W Canada
190 E7 Smoky Bay South Australia 32.22S 133.57E
191 V6 Smoky Cape headland New South Wales, SE Australia 30.54S 153.06E
28 L4 Smoky Hill River ≈ Kansas, C USA
28 L4 Smoky Hills hill range Kansas, C USA
9 Q14 Smoky Lake Alberta, SW Canada 54.07N 112.25W
96 E8 Smøla island W Norway
130 H4 Smolensk Smolenskaya Oblast', W Russian Federation 54.48N 32.07E
130 H4 Smolenskaya Oblast' ◐ province W Russian Federation
Smolensk-Moscow Upland see Smolensko-Moskovskaya Vozvyshennost'
130 J3 Smolensko-Moskovskaya Vozvyshennost' var. Smolensk-Moscow Upland. ▲▲ W Russian Federation
Smolevichi see Smalyavichy
117 C15 Smolikás ▲ W Greece 40.06N 20.54E
116 I12 Smolyan prev. Pashmakli. Smolyan, S Bulgaria 41.33N 24.46E
116 I12 Smolyan ◐ province S Bulgaria
Smolyany see Smalyany
35 S15 Smoot Wyoming, C USA 42.37N 110.55W
10 G12 Smooth Rock Falls Ontario, S Canada 49.16N 81.37W
Smorgon'/Smorgonie see Smarhon'
97 K23 Smygehamn Skåne, S Sweden 55.19N 13.25E
204 I7 Smyley Island island Antarctica
23 Y3 Smyrna Delaware, NE USA 39.18N 75.36W
25 S3 Smyrna Georgia, SE USA 33.52N 84.30W
22 J9 Smyrna Tennessee, S USA 36.00N 86.30W
Smyrna see İzmir
176 W10 Snabai Irian Jaya, E Indonesia 1.45S 134.14E
99 I16 Snaefell ▲ C Isle of Man 54.15N 4.29W
94 H3 Snaefellsjökull ▲ W Iceland 64.51N 23.51W
8 J4 Snake ≈ Yukon Territory, NW Canada
31 O8 Snake Creek ≈ South Dakota, N USA
191 P13 Snake Island island Victoria, SE Australia
37 Y6 Snake Range ▲▲ Nevada, W USA
34 K10 Snake River ≈ NW USA
31 V6 Snake River ≈ Minnesota, N USA
30 L12 Snake River ≈ Nebraska, C USA
35 Q14 Snake River Plain plain Idaho, NW USA
15 I7 Snare ≈ Northwest Territories, NW Canada
95 F15 Snåsa Nord-Trøndelag, C Norway 64.16N 12.25E
23 O8 Sneedville Tennessee, S USA 36.31N 83.13W
100 K6 Sneek Friesland, N Netherlands 53.01N 5.40E
Sneeuw-gebergte see Maoke, Pegunungan
97 F22 Snejbjerg Ringkøbing, C Denmark 56.07N 8.55E
126 I8 Snezhnogorsk Taymyrskiy (Dolgano-Nenetskiy) Avtonomnyy Okrug, N Russian Federation 68.06N 87.37E
Snezhnoye see Snizhne
113 G15 Sněžka Ger. Schneekoppe. ▲ N Czech Republic 50.42N 15.55E
112 N8 Śniardwy, Jezioro Ger. Spirdingsee. ◎ NE Poland
Sniečkus see Visaginas
119 R10 Snihurivka Mykolayivs'ka Oblast', S Ukraine 47.05N 32.48E
118 I5 Snilov ✕ (L'viv) L'vivs'ka Oblast', W Ukraine 49.45N 23.59E
113 O19 Snina Hung. Szinna. Prešovský Kraj, E Slovakia 49.00N 22.10E
119 Y8 Snizhne Rus. Snezhnoye. Donets'ka Oblast', SE Ukraine 48.01N 38.46E
94 J3 Snækollur ▲ C Iceland 64.38N 19.18W
96 G10 Snøhetta var. Snohetta. ▲ S Norway 62.22N 9.08E
94 G12 Snøtinden ▲ C Norway 66.39N 13.50E
99 I18 Snowdon ▲ NW Wales, UK 53.04N 4.04W
99 I18 Snowdonia ▲▲ NW Wales, UK
15 Ii8 Snowdrift ≈ Northwest Territories, NW Canada
Snowdrift see Lutselk'e
39 N12 Snowflake Arizona, SW USA 34.30N 110.04W
23 Y5 Snow Hill Maryland, NE USA 38.10N 75.23W
23 W10 Snow Hill North Carolina, SE USA 35.25N 77.40W
204 H3 Snowhill Island island Antarctica
9 V13 Snow Lake Manitoba, C Canada 54.55N 100.01W
39 R5 Snowmass Mountain ▲ Colorado, C USA 39.07N 107.04W
20 M10 Snow, Mount ▲ Vermont, NE USA 42.56N 72.52W
36 M5 Snow Mountain ▲ California, W USA 39.44N 123.01W
Snow Mountains see Maoke, Pegunungan
35 N7 Snowshoe Peak ▲ Montana, NW USA 48.15N 115.44W
190 I8 Snowtown South Australia 33.49S 138.13E
38 K1 Snowville Utah, W USA 41.59N 112.42W
37 X3 Snow Water Lake ◎ Nevada, W USA
191 Q11 Snowy Mountains ▲▲ New South Wales/Victoria, SE Australia
191 Q12 Snowy River ≈ New South Wales/Victoria, SE Australia
46 K5 Snug Corner Acklins Island, SE Bahamas 22.31N 73.51W
178 Jj13 Snuŏl Krâchéh, E Cambodia 12.04N 106.25E
118 J7 Snyatyn Rus. Snyatyn. Ivano-Frankivs'ka Oblast', W Ukraine 48.28N 25.33E
28 L12 Snyder Oklahoma, C USA 34.37N 98.56W
27 O6 Snyder Texas, SW USA 32.43N 100.54W
180 H3 Soalala Mahajanga, W Madagascar 16.04S 45.21E
180 J4 Soanierana-Ivongo Toamasina, E Madagascar 16.52S 49.34E
175 Ss7 Soasiu var. Tidore. Pulau Tidore, E Indonesia 0.40N 127.25E
56 G8 Soatá Boyacá, C Colombia 6.14N 72.42W
180 I5 Soavinandriana Antananarivo, C Madagascar 19.09S 46.43E
176 Yy12 Soba Irian Jaya, E Indonesia 4.18S 139.11E
79 V13 Soba Kaduna, C Nigeria 10.58N 8.06E
169 Y16 Sobaek-sanmaek ▲▲ S South Korea
82 F13 Sobat ≈ E Sudan
176 Z12 Sobger, Sungai ≈ Irian Jaya, E Indonesia
176 W10 Sobiei Irian Jaya, E Indonesia 2.31S 134.30E
130 M3 Sobinka Vladimirskaya Oblast', W Russian Federation 56.00N 39.55E
131 S7 Sobolevo Orenburgskaya Oblast', W Russian Federation 51.57N 51.42E
Soborsin see Săvârşin
170 D15 Sobo-san ▲ Kyūshū, SW Japan 32.50N 131.16E
113 G14 Sobótka Dolnośląskie, SW Poland 50.53N 16.48E
61 O15 Sobradinho Bahia, E Brazil 9.33S 40.56W
Sobradinho, Barragem de see Sobradinho, Represa de
61 O16 Sobradinho, Represa de var. Barragem de Sobradinho. ⊠ E Brazil
60 O13 Sobral Ceará, E Brazil 3.45S 40.19W
107 T4 Sobrarbe physical region NE Spain
111 R10 Soča It. Isonzo. ≈ Italy/Slovenia
112 L11 Sochaczew Mazowieckie, C Poland 52.15N 20.15E
130 L15 Sochi Krasnodarskiy Kray, SW Russian Federation 43.34N 39.46E
116 G13 Sochós var. Sohos, Sokhós. Kentrikí Makedonía, N Greece 40.49N 23.22E
203 R11 Société, Archipel de la var. Archipel de Tahiti, Îles de la Société, Eng. Society Islands. island group W French Polynesia
Société, Îles de la/Society Islands see Société, Archipel de la
23 T11 Society Hill South Carolina, SE USA 34.28N 79.54W
183 W9 Society Ridge undersea feature C Pacific Ocean
64 I5 Socompa, Volcán ▲ N Chile 24.18S 68.03W
Soconusco, Sierra de see Sierra Madre
56 G8 Socorro Santander, C Colombia 6.25N 73.13W
39 R13 Socorro New Mexico, SW USA 33.58N 106.55W
Socotra see Suquţrā
178 Jj15 Soc Trăng var. Khanh Hung. Soc Trăng, S Vietnam 9.36N 105.58E
107 P10 Socuéllamos Castilla-La Mancha, C Spain 39.18N 2.48W
37 W13 Soda Lake salt flat California, W USA
94 L11 Sodankylä Lappi, N Finland 67.25N 26.34E
Sodari see Sodiri
35 R15 Soda Springs Idaho, NW USA 42.39N 111.36W
Soddo/Soddu see Sodo
22 L10 Soddy Daisy Tennessee, S USA 35.14N 85.11W
97 N14 Söderfors Uppsala, C Sweden 60.22N 17.19E
96 N12 Söderhamn Gävleborg, C Sweden 61.19N 17.10E
97 N17 Söderköping Östergötland, S Sweden 58.28N 16.19E
97 N17 Södermanland ◐ county C Sweden
97 O16 Södertälje Stockholm, C Sweden 59.10N 17.39E
82 D10 Sodiri var. Sawdirī, Sodari. Northern Kordofan, C Sudan 14.22N 29.06E
83 I14 Sodo var. Soddo, Soddu. Southern, S Ethiopia 6.49N 37.43E
96 N11 Södra Dellen ◎ C Sweden
97 M19 Södra Vi Kalmar, S Sweden 57.45N 15.45E
20 G9 Sodus Point headland New York, NE USA 43.16N 76.59W
175 Rr17 Soe prev. Soë. Timor, C Indonesia 9.51S 124.28E
174 J14 Soekarno-Hatta ✕ (Jakarta) Jawa, S Indonesia
Soëla-Sund see Soela Väin
120 E5 Soela Väin prev. Eng. Sele Sound, Ger. Dagden-Sund, Soëla-Sund. strait W Estonia
Soemba see Sumba, Pulau
Soembawa see Sumbawa
Soemenep see Sumenep
Soengaipenoeh see Sungaipenuh
Soerabaja see Surabaya
103 G14 Soest Nordrhein-Westfalen, W Germany 51.34N 8.07E
100 J11 Soest Utrecht, C Netherlands 52.10N 5.19E
102 F11 Soeste ≈ NW Germany
100 J11 Soesterberg Utrecht, C Netherlands 52.07N 5.16E
117 E16 Sofádes var. Sofádhes. Thessalía, C Greece 39.19N 22.06E
Sofádhes see Sofádes
85 N18 Sofala Sofala, C Mozambique 20.04S 34.43E
85 N17 Sofala ◐ province C Mozambique
85 N18 Sofala, Baia de bay E Mozambique
180 J3 Sofia seasonal river NW Madagascar
Sofia see Sofiya
117 G19 Sofikó Pelopónnisos, S Greece 37.46N 23.04E
Sofi-Kurgan see Sopu-Korgon
116 G10 Sofiya var. Sophia, Eng. Sofia; Lat. Serdica. ● (Bulgaria) Sofiya-Grad, W Bulgaria 42.42N 23.20E
116 G9 Sofiya ✕ Sofiya-Grad, W Bulgaria 42.42N 23.26E
116 H9 Sofiya ◐ province W Bulgaria
116 G9 Sofiya-Grad ◐ municipality W Bulgaria
Sofiyevka see Sofiyivka
119 S8 Sofiyivka Rus. Sofiyevka. Dnipropetrovs'ka Oblast', E Ukraine 48.03N 33.52E
127 Nn14 Sofiysk Khabarovskiy Kray, SE Russian Federation 51.31N 139.46E
127 N14 Sofiysk Khabarovskiy Kray, SE Russian Federation 52.20N 133.37E
128 I6 Sofporog Respublika Kareliya, NW Russian Federation 65.48N 31.30E
172 Ss15 Sōfu-gan island Izu-shotō, SE Japan
Sog see Sog Xian
56 G9 Sogamoso Boyacá, C Colombia 5.43N 72.55W
142 I11 Soğanlı Çayı ≈ N Turkey
96 E12 Sogn physical region S Norway
96 E12 Sogndal var. Sogndalsfjøra. Sogn og Fjordane, S Norway 61.13N 7.06E
Sogndalsfjøra see Sogndal
97 E18 Søgne Vest-Agder, S Norway 58.04N 7.48E
96 D12 Sognefjorden fjord NE North Sea
96 C12 Sogn Og Fjordane ◐ county S Norway
179 R13 Sogod Leyte, C Philippines 10.25N 125.00E
168 I11 Sogo Nur ◎ N China
165 T12 Sogruma Qinghai, W China 32.31N 100.52E
169 X17 Sŏgwip'o S South Korea 33.13N 126.33E
162 K10 Sog Xian var. Sog. Xizang Zizhiqu, W China 31.52N 93.40E
77 X10 Sohâg var. Sawhāj, Suliag. C Egypt 26.27N 31.43E
Sohar see Şuḩār
66 H9 Sohm Plain undersea feature NW Atlantic Ocean
102 H7 Soholmer Au ≈ N Germany
Sohos see Sochós
Sohrau see Żory
101 F20 Soignies Hainaut, SW Belgium 50.34N 4.04E
165 R15 Soila Xizang Zizhiqu, W China 30.40N 97.07E
105 P4 Soissons anc. Augusta Suessionum, Noviodunum. Aisne, N France 49.22N 3.19E
170 Ff14 Sōja Okayama, Honshū, SW Japan 34.41N 133.45E
158 F13 Sojat Rājasthān, N India 25.55N 73.43E
169 W13 Sŏjosŏn-man inlet W North Korea
118 I4 Sokal' Rus. Sokal. L'vivs'ka Oblast', NW Ukraine 50.28N 24.16E
169 Y14 Sokch'o N South Korea 38.07N 128.33E
142 B15 Söke Aydın, SW Turkey 37.45N 27.24E
201 N12 Sokehs Island island E Micronesia
81 M24 Sokele Katanga, SE Dem. Rep. Congo (Zaire) 9.54S 24.38E
153 R11 Sokh Uzb. Sŭkh. ≈ Kyrgyzstan/Uzbekistan
Sokh see Sŭkh
Sokhós see Sochós
143 Q8 Sokhumi Rus. Sukhumi. NW Georgia 43.01N 41.01E
115 O14 Sokobanja Serbia, E Yugoslavia 43.39N 21.51E
79 R15 Sokodé C Togo 8.58N 1.10E
127 O10 Sokol Magadanskaya Oblast', E Russian Federation 59.51N 150.56E
128 M13 Sokol Vologodskaya Oblast', NW Russian Federation 59.26N 40.09E
112 P9 Sokółka Podlaskie, NE Poland 53.24N 23.30E
78 M11 Sokolo Ségou, W Mali 14.43N 6.02W
113 A16 Sokolov Ger. Falkenau an der Eger; prev. Falknov nad Ohří. Karlovarský Kraj, W Czech Republic 50.10N 12.38E
113 O16 Sokołów Małopolski Podkarpackie, SE Poland 50.12N 22.07E
112 O11 Sokołów Podlaski Mazowieckie, E Poland 52.25N 22.14E
78 G11 Sokone W Senegal 13.52N 16.22W
79 T12 Sokoto Sokoto, NW Nigeria 13.05N 5.15E
79 T12 Sokoto ◐ state NW Nigeria
79 S12 Sokoto ≈ NW Nigeria
Sokotra see Suquţrā
153 U7 Sokuluk Chuyskaya Oblast', N Kyrgyzstan 42.53N 74.19E
118 L7 Sokyryany Chernivets'ka Oblast', W Ukraine 48.28N 27.25E
97 C16 Sola Rogaland, S Norway 58.52N 5.37E
197 C10 Sola Vanua Lava, N Vanuatu 13.51S 167.34E
97 C17 Sola ✕ (Stavanger) Rogaland, S Norway 58.54N 5.36E
83 H18 Solai Rift Valley, W Kenya 0.02N 36.03E
176 Y15 Solaka Irian Jaya, E Indonesia 7.52S 138.45E
158 I8 Solan Himāchal Pradesh, N India 30.54N 77.06E
193 A25 Solander Island island SW NZ
Solano see Bahía Solano
161 F15 Solāpur var. Sholāpur. Mahārāshtra, W India 17.42N 75.54E
95 H16 Solberg Västernorrland, C Sweden 63.48N 17.40E
118 K9 Solca Ger. Solka. Suceava, N Romania 47.40N 25.49E
107 O16 Sol, Costa del coastal region S Spain
108 F5 Solda Trentino-Alto Adige, N Italy 46.33N 10.35E
119 N9 Şoldăneşti Rus. Sholdaneshty. N Moldova 47.49N 28.45E
Soldau see Wkra
110 L8 Sölden Tirol, W Austria 46.58N 11.01E
29 P3 Soldier Creek ≈ Kansas, C USA
41 R12 Soldotna Alaska, USA 60.29N 151.03W
112 I10 Solec Kujawski Kujawsko-pomorskie, C Poland 53.04N 18.09E
63 B16 Soledad Santa Fe, C Argentina 30.37S 60.52W
57 E4 Soledad Atlántico, N Colombia 10.54N 74.48W
37 O11 Soledad California, W USA 36.25N 121.19W
57 O7 Soledad Anzoátegui, NE Venezuela 8.10N 63.31W
Soledad see East Falkland
Soledad, Isla see East Falkland
63 H15 Soledade Rio Grande do Sul, S Brazil 28.49S 52.30W
105 Y15 Solenzara Corse, France, C Mediterranean Sea 41.55N 9.24E
Soleure see Solothurn
96 C12 Solheim Hordaland, S Norway 60.54N 5.30E
129 N14 Soligalich Kostromskaya Oblast', NW Russian Federation 59.05N 42.15E
Soligorsk see Salihorsk
99 L20 Solihull C England, UK 52.25N 1.45W
129 U13 Solikamsk Permskaya Oblast', NW Russian Federation 59.37N 56.46E
131 V8 Sol'-Iletsk Orenburgskaya Oblast', W Russian Federation 51.08N 55.05E
59 G17 Solimana, Nevado ▲ S Peru 15.24S 72.49W
60 E13 Solimões, Rio ≈ C Brazil
115 E14 Solin It. Salona; anc. Salonae. Split-Dalmacija, S Croatia 43.33N 16.29E
103 E15 Solingen Nordrhein-Westfalen, W Germany 51.10N 7.04E
Solka see Solca
95 H16 Sollefteå Västernorrland, C Sweden 63.09N 17.15E
97 O15 Sollentuna Stockholm, C Sweden 59.25N 17.55E
96 L13 Sollerön Dalarna, C Sweden 60.55N 14.34E
103 I14 Solling hill range C Germany
97 O16 Solna Stockholm, C Sweden 59.22N 17.58E
130 K3 Solnechnogorsk Moskovskaya Oblast', W Russian Federation 56.07N 37.04E
127 Nn15 Solnechnyy Khabarovskiy Kray, SE Russian Federation 50.41N 136.42E
127 N11 Solnechnyy Respublika Sakha (Yakutiya), NE Russian Federation 60.13N 137.42E
96 H11 Sølnkletten ▲ S Norway 61.52N 11.32E
109 L17 Solofra Campania, S Italy 40.49N 14.48E
174 Gg9 Solok Sumatera, W Indonesia 0.45S 100.42E
44 C6 Sololá Sololá, W Guatemala 14.46N 91.09W
44 A2 Sololá off. Departamento de Sololá. ◐ department SW Guatemala
83 J16 Sololo Eastern, N Kenya 3.31N 38.39E
44 C4 Soloma Huehuetenango, W Guatemala 15.38N 91.25W
40 M9 Solomon Alaska, USA 64.33N 164.26W
29 N4 Solomon Kansas, C USA 38.55N 97.22W
195 U16 Solomon Islands prev. British Solomon Islands Protectorate. ◆ commonwealth republic W Pacific Ocean
195 T12 Solomon Islands island group PNG/Solomon Islands
28 M3 Solomon River ≈ Kansas, C USA
199 Hh9 Solomon Sea sea W Pacific Ocean
33 U11 Solon Ohio, N USA 41.23N 81.26W
119 T8 Solone Dnipropetrovs'ka Oblast', E Ukraine 48.12N 34.49E
175 R16 Solor, Kepulauan island group S Indonesia
130 M4 Solotcha Ryazanskaya Oblast', W Russian Federation 54.43N 39.50E
110 D7 Solothurn Fr. Soleure. Solothurn, NW Switzerland 47.12N 7.28E
110 D7 Solothurn Fr. Soleure. ◐ canton NW Switzerland
128 J7 Solovetskiye Ostrova island group NW Russian Federation
107 V5 Solsona Cataluña, NE Spain 42.00N 1.31E
115 E14 Šolta It. Solta. island S Croatia
Solṭānābād see Kāshmar
148 L4 Solṭānīyeh Zanjān, NW Iran 36.24N 48.49E
102 I11 Soltau Niedersachsen, NW Germany 52.58N 9.49E
128 G14 Sol'tsy Novgorodskaya Oblast', W Russian Federation 58.09N 30.22E
Soltüstik Qazaqstan Oblysy see Severnyy Kazakhstan
Solun see Thessaloníki
115 O19 Solunska Glava ▲ C FYR Macedonia 41.43N 21.24E
97 L22 Sölvesborg Blekinge, S Sweden 56.04N 14.34E
99 J15 Solway Firth inlet England/Scotland, UK
84 I13 Solwezi North Western, NW Zambia 12.10S 26.22E
171 Ll14 Sōma Fukushima, Honshū, C Japan 37.49N 140.52E
142 C13 Soma Manisa, W Turkey 39.11N 27.34E
83 M14 Somali ◐ region E Ethiopia
83 O15 Somalia off. Somali Democratic Republic, Som. Jamuuriyada Demuqraadiga Soomaaliyeed, Soomaaliya; prev. Italian Somaliland, Somaliland Protectorate. ◆ republic E Africa
181 N6 Somali Basin undersea feature W Indian Ocean
69 Y8 Somali Plain undersea feature W Indian Ocean
114 J8 Sombor Hung. Zombor. Serbia, NW Yugoslavia 45.46N 19.07E
101 H20 Sombreffe Namur, S Belgium 50.32N 4.39E
42 L10 Sombrerete Zacatecas, C Mexico 23.36N 103.46W
47 V8 Sombrero island N Anguilla
157 Q21 Sombrero Channel channel Nicobar Islands, India
118 H9 Şomcuta Mare Hung. Nagysomkút; prev. Somcuţa Mare. Maramureş, N Romania 47.28N 23.30E
178 Ii9 Somdet Kalasin, E Thailand 16.41N 103.44E
101 L15 Someren Noord-Brabant, SE Netherlands 51.22N 5.42E
95 L19 Somero Länsi-Suomi, W Finland 60.37N 23.30E
35 P7 Somers Montana, NW USA 48.04N 114.16W
66 A12 Somerset var. Somerset Village. W Bermuda 32.18N 64.52W
39 Q5 Somerset Colorado, C USA 38.55N 107.27W
22 M7 Somerset Kentucky, S USA 37.05N 84.36W
21 O12 Somerset Massachusetts, NE USA 41.46N 71.07W
99 K23 Somerset cultural region SW England, UK
Somerset East see Somerset-Oos
66 A12 Somerset Island island W Bermuda
207 N9 Somerset Island island Queen Elizabeth Islands, Nunavut, NW Canada
Somerset Nile see Victoria Nile
85 I25 Somerset-Oos Eng. Somerset East. Eastern Cape, S South Africa 32.43S 25.34E
85 E26 Somerset-Wes Eng. Somerset West. Western Cape, SW South Africa 34.01S 18.51E
Somerset West see Somerset-Wes
Somers Islands see Bermuda
20 J17 Somers Point New Jersey, NE USA 39.18N 74.34W
21 P9 Somersworth New Hampshire, NE USA 43.15N 70.52W
38 H15 Somerton Arizona, SW USA 32.36N 114.42W
20 J14 Somerville New Jersey, NE USA 40.34N 74.36W
22 F10 Somerville Tennessee, S USA 35.14N 89.21W
27 U10 Somerville Texas, SW USA 30.21N 96.31W
27 T10 Somerville Lake ⊠ Texas, SW USA
Someş/Somesch/Someşul see Szamos
105 N2 Somme ◐ department N France
105 N2 Somme ≈ N France
97 L18 Sommen Jönköping, S Sweden 58.07N 14.58E
97 M18 Sommen ◎ S Sweden
103 K16 Sömmerda Thüringen, C Germany 51.10N 11.07E
Sommerein see Šamorín
Sommerfeld see Lubsko
57 Y11 Sommet Tabulaire var. Mont Itoupé. ▲ S French Guiana
113 H25 Somogy off. Somogy Megye. ◐ county SW Hungary
Somorja see Šamorín
107 N7 Somosierra, Puerto de pass N Spain 41.07N 3.36W
197 J13 Somosomo Taveuni, N Fiji 16.46S 179.57W
44 I9 Somotillo Chinandega, NW Nicaragua 13.01N 86.54W
44 I8 Somoto Madriz, NW Nicaragua 13.28N 86.36W
112 I11 Sompolno Wielkolpolskie, C Poland 52.24N 18.30E
107 S3 Somport var. Puerto de Somport, Fr. Col du Somport; anc. Summus Portus. pass France/Spain see also Somport, Col du 42.48N 0.33W
104 J17 Somport, Col du var. Puerto de Somport, Sp. Somport; anc. Summus Portus. pass France/Spain see also Somport 42.47N 0.33W
Somport, Puerto de see Somport/Somport, Col du
101 K15 Son Noord-Brabant, S Netherlands 51.32N 5.34E
97 H15 Son Akershus, S Norway 59.31N 10.42E
160 L9 Son var. Sone. ≈ C India
45 R16 Soná Veraguas, W Panama 8.00N 81.20W
160 M12 Sonapur prev. Sonepur. Orissa, E India 20.49N 83.58E
176 Vv10 Sonar Irian Jaya, E Indonesia 2.31S 133.01E
97 G24 Sønderborg Ger. Sonderburg. Sønderjylland, SW Denmark 54.55N 9.48E
Sonderburg see Sønderborg
97 F24 Sønderjyllands off. Sønderjyllands Amt. ◐ county SW Denmark
103 K15 Sondershausen Thüringen, C Germany 51.22N 10.52E
Søndre Strømfjord see Kangerlussuaq
108 E6 Sondrio Lombardia, N Italy 46.10N 9.52E
Sone see Son
Sonepur see Sonapur
59 K22 Sonequera ▲ S Bolivia 22.06S 67.10W
178 Kk12 Sông Câu Phu Yên, C Vietnam 13.25N 109.12E
178 J15 Sông Đôc Minh Hai, S Vietnam 9.03N 104.51E
83 H25 Songea Ruvuma, S Tanzania 10.42S 35.39E
176 Z11 Songgato, Sungai ≈ Irian Jaya, E Indonesia
169 X10 Songhua Hu ◎ NE China
169 Y7 Songhua Jiang var. Sungari. ≈ NE China
167 S8 Songjiang Shanghai Shi, E China 31.01N 121.13E
Sŏngjin see Kimch'aek
178 H17 Songkhla var. Songkla, Mal. Singora. Songkhla, SW Thailand 7.12N 100.36E
Songkla see Songkhla
169 T13 Song Ling ▲▲ NE China
169 W14 Songnim SW North Korea 38.43N 125.40E
84 B10 Songo Uíge, NW Angola 7.30S 14.56E
85 M15 Songo Tete, NW Mozambique 15.35S 32.43E
81 F21 Songololo Bas-Congo, SW Dem. Rep. Congo (Zaire) 5.40S 14.04E
166 H7 Songpan prev. Sungpu. Sichuan, C China 32.49N 103.39E
169 Y17 Sŏngsan S South Korea
167 R11 Songxi Fujian, SE China 27.33N 118.46E
166 M6 Songxian var. Song Xian. Henan, C China 34.11N 112.04E
167 R10 Songyin Zhejiang, SE China 28.29N 119.27E
169 V9 Songyuan var. Fu-yü, Petuna; prev. Fuyu. Jilin, NE China 45.10N 124.52E
169 P11 Sonid Youqi var. Saihon Tal. Nei Mongol Zizhiqu, N China 42.45N 112.36E
169 P11 Sonid Zuoqi Nei Mongol Zizhiqu, N China 43.49N 113.36E
158 I10 Sonipat Haryāna, N India 29.00N 77.01E
95 M15 Sonkajärvi Itä-Suomi, C Finland 63.40N 27.30E
178 J6 Sơn La Sơn La, N Vietnam 21.19N 103.55E
155 O16 Sonmiāni Baluchistān, S Pakistan 25.24N 66.37E
155 O16 Sonmiāni Bay bay S Pakistan
103 K18 Sonneberg Thüringen, C Germany 50.22N 11.10E
103 N24 Sonntagshorn ▲ Austria/Germany 47.40N 12.42E
Sonoita see Sonoyta
42 E3 Sonoita, Rio var. Río Sonoyta. ≈ Mexico/USA
37 N7 Sonoma California, W USA 38.16N 122.28W
37 T3 Sonoma Peak ▲ Nevada, W USA 40.50N 117.34W
37 P8 Sonora California, W USA 37.58N 120.22W
27 O10 Sonora Texas, SW USA 30.31N 100.40W
42 F5 Sonora ◐ state NW Mexico
37 X17 Sonoran Desert var. Desierto de Altar. desert Mexico/USA see also Altar, Desierto de
42 G5 Sonora, Río ≈ NW Mexico
42 E2 Sonoyta var. Sonoita. Sonora, NW Mexico 31.49N 112.50W
Sonoyta, Río see Sonoita, Rio
148 K6 Sonqor var. Sunqur. Kermānshāh, W Iran 34.45N 47.39E
107 N9 Sonseca var. Sonseca con Casalgordo. Castilla-La Mancha, C Spain 39.40N 3.58W
Sonseca con Casalgordo see Sonseca
56 E9 Sonsón Antioquia, W Colombia 5.41N 75.15W
44 E7 Sonsonate Sonsonate, W El Salvador 13.43N 89.43W
44 A9 Sonsonate ◐ department SW El Salvador
196 A10 Sonsorol Islands island group S Palau
114 J9 Sonta Hung. Szond; prev. Szonta. Serbia, NW Yugoslavia 45.34N 19.06E
178 Jj6 Sơn Tây var. Sontay. Ha Tây, N Vietnam 21.06N 105.31E
103 J25 Sonthofen Bayern, S Germany 47.31N 10.16E

◆ Country ● Country Capital ◇ Dependent Territory ○ Dependent Territory Capital ◐ Administrative Region ✕ International Airport ▲ Mountain ▲▲ Mountain Range ⚠ Volcano ≈ River ◎ Lake ⊠ Reservoir
329

Soochow – Spruce Pine

Soochow see Suzhou
Soomaaliya/Soomaaliyeed, Jamuuriyada Demuqraadiga see Somalia
Soome Laht see Finland, Gulf of
Sooner State see Oklahoma
25 V5 Soperton Georgia, SE USA 32.22N 82.35W
178 J6 Sop Hao Houaphan, N Laos 20.33N 104.25E
Sophia see Sofiya
175 Tt5 Sopi Pulau Morotai, E Indonesia 2.36N 128.32E
Sopianae see Pécs
176 Vv11 Sopinusa Irian Jaya, E Indonesia 3.31S 132.55E
175 Tt5 Sopi, Tanjung headland Pulau Morotai, N Indonesia 2.39N 128.34E
83 B14 Sopo ~ W Sudan
Sopockinie/Sopotskin see Sapotskino
116 I9 Sopot Plovdiv, C Bulgaria 42.40N 24.45E
112 I7 Sopot Ger. Zoppot. Pomorskie, N Poland 54.25N 18.33E
178 H8 Sop Prap var. Ban Sop Prap. Lampang, NW Thailand 17.55N 99.19E
113 G22 Sopron Ger. Ödenburg. Győr-Moson-Sopron, NW Hungary 47.40N 16.34E
153 U11 Sopu-Korgon var. Sofi-Kurgan. Oshskaya Oblast', SW Kyrgyzstan 40.03N 73.30E
158 H5 Sopur Jammu and Kashmir, NW India 34.19N 74.28E
109 J15 Sora Lazio, C Italy 41.43N 13.37E
160 N13 Sorada Orissa, E India 19.46N 84.28E
95 H17 Söråker Västernorrland, C Sweden 62.31N 17.31E
59 J17 Sorata La Paz, W Bolivia 15.49S 68.39W
Sorau/Sorau in der Niederlausitz see Żary
107 Q14 Sorbas Andalucía, S Spain 37.06N 2.06W
Sord/Sórd Choluim Chille see Swords
13 O11 Sorel Quebec, SE Canada 46.02N 73.06W
191 P17 Sorell Tasmania, SE Australia 42.49S 147.34E
191 O17 Sorell, Lake ◎ Tasmania, SE Australia
108 E8 Soresina Lombardia, N Italy 45.16N 9.51E
97 D14 Sørfjorden fjord S Norway
96 N11 Sörforsa Gävleborg, C Sweden 61.45N 17.00E
105 R14 Sorgues Vaucluse, SE France 44.00N 4.52E
142 K13 Sorgun Yozgat, C Turkey 39.49N 35.10E
107 P5 Soria Castilla-León, N Spain 41.46N 2.26W
107 P6 Soria ◐ province Castilla-León, N Spain
63 D19 Soriano Soriano, SW Uruguay 33.25S 58.21W
63 D19 Soriano ◐ department SW Uruguay
94 O4 Sørkapp headland SW Svalbard 76.34N 16.33E
149 T5 Sorkh, Kūh-e ▲▲ NE Iran
Soro see Ghazal, Bahr el
97 I23 Sorø Vestsjælland, E Denmark 55.25N 11.34E
118 M8 Soroca Rus. Soroki. N Moldova 48.10N 28.18E
62 L10 Sorocaba São Paulo, S Brazil 23.28S 47.27W
Sorochino see Sarochyna
131 T7 Sorochinsk Orenburgskaya Oblast', W Russian Federation 52.26N 53.10E
Soroki see Soroca
196 H15 Sorol atoll Caroline Islands, W Micronesia
176 Uu9 Sorong Irian Jaya, E Indonesia 0.49S 131.16E
83 G17 Soroti C Uganda 1.42N 33.37E
Sørøy see Sørøya
94 J8 Sørøya var. Sørøy. island N Norway
106 G11 Sorraia, Rio ~ C Portugal
94 I10 Sørreisa Troms, N Norway 69.08N 18.09E
109 K18 Sorrento anc. Surrentum. Campania, S Italy 40.37N 14.22E
106 H10 Sor, Ribeira de stream C Portugal
205 T3 Sør Rondane Mountains ▲▲ Antarctica
95 H14 Sorsele Västerbotten, N Sweden 65.31N 17.34E
109 B17 Sorso Sardegna, Italy, C Mediterranean Sea 40.46N 8.33E
179 Qq11 Sorsogon Luzon, N Philippines 12.57N 124.04E
107 U4 Sort Cataluña, NE Spain 42.25N 1.07E
128 H11 Sortavala Respublika Kareliya, NW Russian Federation 61.45N 30.36E
109 L25 Sortino Sicilia, Italy, C Mediterranean Sea 37.10N 15.01E
94 G10 Sortland Nordland, C Norway 68.40N 15.22E
96 G9 Sør-Trøndelag ◐ county S Norway
97 I15 Sørumsand Akershus, S Norway 59.58N 11.13E
120 D6 Sõrve Säär headland SW Estonia 57.54N 22.02E
97 K22 Sösdala Skåne, S Sweden 56.00N 13.36E
107 R4 Sos del Rey Católico Aragón, NE Spain 42.30N 1.13W
95 F15 Sösjöfjällen ▲ C Sweden 63.51N 13.15E
130 K7 Sosna ~ W Russian Federation
64 H12 Sosneado, Cerro ▲ W Argentina 34.44S 69.52W
129 S9 Sosnogorsk Respublika Komi, NW Russian Federation 63.33N 53.55E
128 J8 Sosnovets Respublika Kareliya, NW Russian Federation 64.25N 34.23E
Sosnovets see Sosnowiec
131 Q3 Sosnovka Chuvashskaya Respublika, W Russian Federation 56.18N 47.14E
129 S16 Sosnovka Kirovskaya Oblast', NW Russian Federation 56.15N 51.20E
128 M6 Sosnovka Murmanskaya Oblast', NW Russian Federation 66.28N 40.31E
130 M6 Sosnovka Tambovskaya Oblast', W Russian Federation 53.14N 41.19E
128 H12 Sosnovo Fin. Rautu. Leningradskaya Oblast', NW Russian Federation 60.30N 30.13E
126 K15 Sosnovo-Ozerskoye Respublika Buryatiya, S Russian Federation 52.34N 111.36E
Sosnovyy Bor see Sasnovy Bor
113 J16 Sosnowiec Ger. Sosnowitz, Rus. Sosnovets. Śląskie, S Poland 50.16N 19.07E
Sosnowitz see Sosnowiec
119 R2 Sosnytsya Chernihivs'ka Oblast', N Ukraine 51.31N 32.30E
111 V10 Šoštanj N Slovenia 46.23N 15.03E
125 F10 Sos'va Sverdlovskaya Oblast', C Russian Federation 59.13N 61.58E
56 D12 Sotará, Volcán ‡ S Colombia 2.04N 76.40W
78 D10 Sotavento, Ilhas de var. Leeward Islands. island group S Cape Verde
95 N15 Sotkamo Oulu, C Finland 64.06N 28.30E
43 P10 Soto la Marina Tamaulipas, C Mexico 23.46N 98.12W
43 P10 Soto la Marina, Río ~ C Mexico
43 X12 Sotuta Yucatán, SE Mexico 20.34N 89.00W
81 F17 Souanké La Sangha, NW Congo 2.03N 14.01E
78 M17 Soubré S Ivory Coast 5.49N 6.34W
117 H24 Soúda var. Soúdha, Eng. Suda. Kríti, Greece, E Mediterranean Sea 35.28N 24.04E
Soúdha see Soúda
Soueida see As Suwaydā'
116 L12 Souflí prev. Souflíon. Anatolikí Makedonía kai Thráki, NE Greece 41.12N 26.17E
Souflíon see Souflí
47 S11 Soufrière W Saint Lucia 13.51N 61.03W
47 X6 Soufrière ‡ Basse Terre, S Guadeloupe 16.03N 61.39W
104 M13 Souillac Lot, S France 44.53N 1.29E
181 Y17 Souillac S Mauritius 20.31S 57.31E
76 M5 Souk Ahras NE Algeria 36.14N 8.00E
76 E6 Souk-el-Arba-Rharb var. Souk el Arba du Rharb, Souk-el-Arba-du-Rharb, Souk-el-Arba-el-Rhab. NW Morocco 34.38N 6.00W
Soukhné see As Sukhnah
169 X14 Sŏul off. Sŏul-t'ŭkpyŏlsi, Eng. Seoul, Jap. Keijō; prev. Kyŏngsŏng. ● (South Korea) NW South Korea 37.30N 126.57E
104 J11 Soulac-sur-Mer Gironde, SW France 45.31N 1.06W
101 L19 Soumagne Liège, E Belgium 50.36N 5.48E
20 M14 Sound Beach Long Island, New York, NE USA 40.56N 72.58W
97 J22 Sound, The Dan. Øresund, Swe. Öresund. strait Denmark/Sweden
117 H20 Soúnio, Akrotírio headland C Greece 37.39N 24.01E
144 F8 Soûr var. Şūr; anc. Tyre. SW Lebanon 33.18N 35.30E
Sources, Mont-aux- see Phofung
106 G8 Soure Coimbra, N Portugal 40.04N 8.37W
9 W17 Souris Manitoba, S Canada 49.37N 100.16W
11 Q14 Souris Prince Edward Island, SE Canada 46.22N 62.16W
30 L2 Souris River var. Mouse River. ~ Canada/USA
27 X10 Sour Lake Texas, SW USA 30.08N 94.24W
117 F17 Sourpi Thessalía, C Greece 39.07N 22.54E
106 H11 Sousel Portalegre, C Portugal 38.57N 7.40W
77 N6 Sousse var. Sūsah. NE Tunisia 35.45N 10.37E
12 H11 South ~ Ontario, S Canada
South see Sud
85 G23 South Africa off. Republic of South Africa, Afr. Suid-Afrika. ◆ republic S Africa
48-49 South America continent
2 J17 South American Plate tectonic feature
99 M23 Southampton hist. Hamwih, Lat. Clausentum. S England, UK 50.54N 1.22W
21 N14 Southampton Long Island, New York, NE USA 40.52N 72.22W
15 M5 Southampton Island island Nunavut, NE Canada
157 P20 South Andaman island Andaman Islands, India, NE Indian Ocean
11 Q6 South Aulatsivik Island island Newfoundland, E Canada
190 E4 South Australia ◐ state S Australia
South Australian Abyssal Plain see South Australian Plain
199 Gg13 South Australian Basin undersea feature SW Indian Ocean
181 X12 South Australian Plain var. South Australian Abyssal Plain. undersea feature SE Indian Ocean
39 R13 South Baldy ▲ New Mexico, SW USA 33.59N 107.11W
25 Y14 South Bay Florida, SE USA 26.39N 80.43W
12 E12 South Baymouth Manitoulin Island, Ontario, S Canada 45.33N 82.01W
32 L10 South Beloit Illinois, N USA 42.29N 89.02W
33 O11 South Bend Indiana, N USA 41.40N 86.15W
27 R6 South Bend Texas, SW USA 32.58N 98.39W
34 F9 South Bend Washington, NW USA 46.38N 123.48W
South Beveland see Zuid-Beveland
South Borneo see Kalimantan Selatan
23 U7 South Boston Virginia, NE USA 36.42N 78.54W
190 F2 South Branch Neales seasonal river South Australia
23 U3 South Branch Potomac River ~ West Virginia, NE USA
193 H19 Southbridge Canterbury, South Island, NZ 43.49S 172.17E
21 N12 Southbridge Massachusetts, NE USA 42.03N 72.00W
191 P17 South Bruny Island island Tasmania, SE Australia
20 L7 South Burlington Vermont, NE USA 44.27N 73.08W
46 M6 South Caicos island S Turks and Caicos Islands
South Cape see Ka Lae
25 V3 South Carolina off. State of South Carolina; also known as The Palmetto State. ◐ state SE USA
South Carpathians see Carpaţii Meridionali
South Celebes see Sulawesi Selatan
23 Q5 South Charleston West Virginia, NE USA 38.22N 81.42W
198 F7 South China Basin undersea feature SE South China Sea
198 F7 South China Sea Chin. Nan Hai, Ind. Laut Cina Selatan, Vtn. Biên Đông. sea SE Asia
35 Z10 South Dakota off. State of South Dakota; also known as The Coyote State, Sunshine State. ◐ state N USA
25 X10 South Daytona Florida, SE USA 29.09N 81.01W
39 R10 South Domingo Pueblo New Mexico, SW USA 35.28N 106.24W
99 N23 South Downs hill range SE England, UK
85 I21 South East ◐ district SE Botswana
67 H15 South East Bay bay Ascension Island, C Atlantic Ocean
191 O17 South East Cape headland Tasmania, SE Australia 43.36S 146.52E
40 K10 Southeast Cape headland Saint Lawrence Island, Alaska, USA 62.56N 169.39W
South-East Celebes see Sulawesi Tenggara
198 G14 Southeast Indian Ridge undersea feature Indian Ocean/Pacific Ocean
Southeast Island see Tagula Island
199 Mm16 Southeast Pacific Basin var. Belling Hausen Mulde. undersea feature SE Pacific Ocean
67 H15 South East Point headland SE Ascension Island
191 O14 South East Point headland Victoria, S Australia 39.10S 146.21E
203 Z3 South East Point headland Kiritimati, NE Kiribati 1.42N 157.10W
46 L5 Southeast Point headland Mayaguana, SE Bahamas 22.15N 72.44W
South-East Sulawesi see Sulawesi Tenggara
9 U12 Southend Saskatchewan, C Canada 56.19N 103.13W
99 P22 Southend-on-Sea E England, UK 51.33N 0.43E
85 H20 Southern var. Bangwaketse, Ngwaketze. ◐ district SE Botswana
83 I15 Southern ◐ region S Ethiopia
144 E13 Southern ◐ district S Israel
85 N15 Southern ◐ region S Malawi
85 I15 Southern ◐ province S Zambia
193 E19 Southern Alps ▲▲ South Island, NZ
202 K15 Southern Cook Islands island group S Cook Islands
188 K12 Southern Cross Western Australia 31.17S 119.15E
82 A12 Southern Darfur ◐ state W Sudan
194 F13 Southern Highlands ◐ province W PNG
9 V11 Southern Indian Lake ◎ Manitoba, C Canada
82 E11 Southern Kordofan ◐ state C Sudan
197 L15 Southern Lau Group island group Lau Group, SE Fiji
181 S13 Southern Ocean ocean
23 T10 Southern Pines North Carolina, SE USA 35.10N 79.23W
161 J26 Southern Province ◐ province S Sri Lanka
98 I13 Southern Uplands ▲▲ S Scotland, UK
Southern Urals see Yuzhnyy Ural
191 P16 South Esk River ~ Tasmania, SE Australia
9 U16 Southey Saskatchewan, S Canada 50.53N 104.27W
29 V2 South Fabius River ~ Missouri, C USA
33 S10 Southfield Michigan, N USA 42.28N 83.12W
199 J11 South Fiji Basin undersea feature S Pacific Ocean
99 Q22 South Foreland headland SE England, UK 51.08N 1.22E
37 P7 South Fork American River ~ California, W USA
30 K7 South Fork Grand River ~ South Dakota, N USA
37 T12 South Fork Kern River ~ California, W USA
41 Q7 South Fork Koyukuk River ~ Alaska, USA
41 Q12 South Fork Kuskokwim River ~ Alaska, USA
28 H2 South Fork Republican River ~ C USA
28 L3 South Fork Solomon River ~ Kansas, C USA
33 P5 South Fox Island island Michigan, N USA
22 G8 South Fulton Tennessee, S USA 36.28N 88.53W
205 U10 South Geomagnetic Pole pole Antarctica 78.30S 111.00E
67 J20 South Georgia island South Georgia and the South Sandwich Islands, SW Atlantic Ocean
67 K21 South Georgia and the South Sandwich Islands ◇ UK dependent territory SW Atlantic Ocean
49 Y14 South Georgia Ridge var. North Scotia Ridge. undersea feature SW Atlantic Ocean
189 Q1 South Goulburn Island island Northern Territory, N Australia
159 U16 South Hatia Island island SE Bangladesh
33 O10 South Haven Michigan, N USA 42.24N 86.16W
23 V7 South Hill Virginia, NE USA 36.43N 78.07W
South Holland see Zuid-Holland
23 P8 South Holston Lake ⊡ Tennessee/Virginia, S USA
183 N1 South Honshu Ridge undersea feature W Pacific Ocean
28 M6 South Hutchinson Kansas, C USA 38.01N 97.56W
157 K21 South Huvadhu Atoll var. Gaafu Dhaalu Atoll. atoll S Maldives
181 U14 South Indian Basin undersea feature Indian Ocean/Pacific Ocean
9 W11 South Indian Lake Manitoba, C Canada 56.48N 98.55W
83 I17 South Island island NW Kenya
193 C20 South Island island S NZ
67 B23 South Jason island Jason Islands, NW Falkland Islands
South Kalimantan see Kalimantan Selatan
South Kazakhstan see Yuzhnyy Kazakhstan
169 X15 South Korea off. Republic of Korea, Kor. Taehan Min'guk. ◆ republic E Asia
37 Q6 South Lake Tahoe California, W USA 38.56N 119.57W
27 N6 Southland Texas, SW USA 33.16N 101.31W
193 B23 Southland off. Southland Region. ◐ region South Island, NZ
31 N15 South Loup River ~ Nebraska, C USA
157 K19 South Maalhosmadulu Atoll var. Baa Atoll. atoll N Maldives
12 E15 South Maitland ~ Ontario, S Canada
198 F9 South Makassar Basin undersea feature E Java Sea
33 O6 South Manitou Island island Michigan, N USA
157 K18 South Miladummadulu Atoll atoll N Maldives
23 X8 South Mills North Carolina, SE USA 36.28N 76.18W
14 G7 South Nahanni ~ Northwest Territories, NW Canada
41 P13 South Naknek Alaska, USA 58.39N 157.01W
12 M13 South Nation ~ Ontario, SE Canada
46 F9 South Negril Point headland W Jamaica 18.14N 78.21W
157 K20 South Nilandhe Atoll var. Dhaalu Atoll. atoll C Maldives
38 L2 South Ogden Utah, W USA 41.09N 111.58W
20 M14 Southold Long Island, New York, NE USA 41.03N 72.24W
204 H1 South Orkney Islands island group Antarctica
143 S9 South Ossetia former autonomous region SW Georgia
South Pacific Basin see Southwest Pacific Basin
21 P7 South Paris Maine, NE USA 44.14N 70.29W
35 U15 South Pass pass Wyoming, C USA 42.20N 108.55W
201 U13 South Pass passage Chuuk Islands, C Micronesia
22 K10 South Pittsburg Tennessee, S USA 35.00N 85.42W
30 K15 South Platte River ~ Colorado/Nebraska, C USA
33 T16 South Point Ohio, N USA 38.25N 82.35W
67 G15 South Point headland S Ascension Island
33 R6 South Point headland Michigan, N USA 44.51N 83.17W
South Point see Ka Lae
205 P9 South Pole pole Antarctica 90.00S 0.00E
191 P17 Southport Tasmania, SE Australia 43.26S 146.57E
99 K17 Southport NW England, UK 53.39N 3.01W
23 V12 Southport North Carolina, SE USA 33.55N 78.01W
21 P8 South Portland Maine, NE USA 43.38N 70.14W
12 H12 South River Ontario, S Canada 45.48N 79.21W
23 U11 South River ~ North Carolina, SE USA
98 K5 South Ronaldsay island NE Scotland, UK
38 L2 South Salt Lake Utah, W USA 40.42N 111.52W
67 L21 South Sandwich Islands island group SE South Georgia and South Sandwich Islands
67 K21 South Sandwich Trench undersea feature SW Atlantic Ocean
9 S16 South Saskatchewan ~ Alberta/Saskatchewan, S Canada
67 I21 South Scotia Ridge undersea feature S Scotia Sea
9 V10 South Seal ~ Manitoba, C Canada
204 G4 South Shetland Islands island group Antarctica
67 H22 South Shetland Trough undersea feature Atlantic Ocean/Pacific Ocean
99 M14 South Shields NE England, UK 55.00N 1.25W
31 R13 South Sioux City Nebraska, C USA 42.28N 96.24W
199 I10 South Solomon Trench undersea feature W Pacific Ocean
191 V3 South Stradbroke Island island Queensland, E Australia
South Sulawesi see Sulawesi Selatan
South Sumatra see Sumatera Selatan
192 K11 South Taranaki Bight bight SE Tasman Sea
South Tasmania Plateau see Tasman Plateau
38 M15 South Tucson Arizona, SW USA 32.11N 110.56W
10 H9 South Twin Island island Nunavut, C Canada
98 E9 South Uist island NW Scotland, UK
South-West see Sud-Ouest
South-West Africa/South West Africa see Namibia
67 F15 South West Bay bay Ascension Island, C Atlantic Ocean
191 N18 South West Cape headland Tasmania, SE Australia 43.34S 146.01E
193 B26 South West Cape headland Stewart Island, NZ 47.15S 167.28E
40 J10 Southwest Cape headland Saint Lawrence Island, Alaska, USA 63.19N 171.27W
178 Mm13 Southwest Cay island NW Spratly Islands
Southwest Indian Ocean Ridge see Southwest Indian Ridge
181 N11 Southwest Indian Ridge var. Southwest Indian Ocean Ridge. undersea feature SW Indian Ocean
199 Kk13 Southwest Pacific Basin var. South Pacific Basin. undersea feature SE Pacific Ocean
46 H2 Southwest Point headland Great Abaco, N Bahamas 25.50N 77.12W
203 X3 South West Point headland Kiritimati, NE Kiribati 1.52N 157.34E
67 G25 South West Point headland SW Saint Helena 16.00S 5.48W
27 P5 South Wichita River ~ Texas, SW USA
99 Q20 Southwold E England, UK 52.15N 1.36E
21 Q12 South Yarmouth Massachusetts, NE USA 41.38N 70.09W
118 J10 Sovata Hung. Szováta. Mureş, C Romania 46.36N 25.04E
109 N22 Soverato Calabria, SW Italy 38.40N 16.31E
Sovetabad see Ghafurov
130 C2 Sovetsk Ger. Tilsit. Kaliningradskaya Oblast', W Russian Federation 53.04N 21.52E
129 Q15 Sovetsk Kirovskaya Oblast', NW Russian Federation 57.37N 49.02E
131 N10 Sovetskaya Rostovskaya Oblast', SW Russian Federation 49.00N 42.09E
127 O15 Sovetskaya Gavan' Khabarovskiy Kray, SE Russian Federation 48.54N 140.19E
125 F10 Sovetskiy Khanty-Mansiyskiy Avtonomnyy Okrug, C Russian Federation 61.20N 63.34E
Sovetskoye see Ketchenery
152 I15 Sovet"yab prev. Sovet"yap. Akhalskiy Velayat, S Turkmenistan 36.29N 61.13E
Sovet"yap see Sovet"yab
119 U12 Sovyets'kyy Respublika Krym, S Ukraine 45.20N 34.54E
85 I18 Sowa var. Sua. Central, NE Botswana 20.33S 26.18E
85 I18 Sowa Pan salt lake NE Botswana
176 Ww9 Sowek Irian Jaya, E Indonesia 0.46S 135.31E
85 J21 Soweto Gauteng, NE South Africa 26.08S 27.53E
Sōya-kaikyō see La Perouse Strait
172 Pp1 Sōya-misaki headland Hokkaidō, NE Japan 45.31N 141.55E
129 N7 Soyana ~ NW Russian Federation
152 A8 Soye, Mys var. Mys Suz. headland NW Turkmenistan 41.47N 52.27E
84 A10 Soyo Zaire, NW Angola 6.07S 12.19E
82 J10 Soyra ▲ C Eritrea 14.46N 39.29E
Sozaq see Suzak
121 P16 Sozh Rus. Sozh. ~ NE Europe
116 N10 Sozopol prev. Sizebolu anc. Apollonia. Burgas, E Bulgaria 42.25N 27.42E
180 J15 Sœurs, Les island group Inner Islands, W Seychelles
101 L20 Spa Liège, E Belgium 50.28N 5.52E
204 I7 Spaatz Island island Antarctica
150 M14 Space Launching Centre space station Kzylorda, S Kazakhstan 45.50N 63.20E
107 O7 Spain off. Kingdom of Spain, Sp. España; anc. Hispania, Iberia, Lat. Hispana. ◆ monarchy SW Europe
Spalato see Split
99 O19 Spalding E England, UK 52.48N 0.06W
12 D11 Spanish Ontario, S Canada 46.12N 82.21W
38 L3 Spanish Fork Utah, W USA 40.09N 111.40W
66 B12 Spanish Point headland C Bermuda 32.18N 64.49W
12 E9 Spanish River ~ Ontario, S Canada
46 K13 Spanish Town hist. St.Iago de la Vega. C Jamaica 18.00N 76.57W
117 H24 Spánta, Akrotírio headland Kríti, Greece, E Mediterranean Sea 35.40N 23.44E
37 Q5 Sparks Nevada, W USA 39.32N 119.45W
Sparnacum see Épernay
97 N16 Sparreholm Södermanland, C Sweden 59.04N 16.51E
25 U4 Sparta Georgia, SE USA 33.16N 82.58W
32 K16 Sparta Illinois, N USA 38.07N 89.42W
33 P9 Sparta Michigan, N USA 43.09N 85.42W
23 R8 Sparta North Carolina, SE USA 36.34N 81.21W
22 L9 Sparta Tennessee, S USA 35.55N 85.27W
32 I7 Sparta Wisconsin, N USA 43.57N 90.49W
Sparta see Spárti
23 Q11 Spartanburg South Carolina, SE USA 34.57N 81.55W
122 F10 Spartel, Cap headland N Morocco 35.49N 5.55W
117 F21 Spárti Eng. Sparta. Pelopónnisos, S Greece 37.04N 22.25E
109 B21 Spartivento, Capo headland Sardegna, Italy, C Mediterranean Sea 38.52N 8.50E
9 P17 Sparwood British Columbia, SW Canada 49.45N 114.45W
130 I4 Spas-Demensk Kaluzhskaya Oblast', W Russian Federation 54.22N 34.16E
130 M4 Spas-Klepiki Ryazanskaya Oblast', W Russian Federation 55.08N 40.15E
Spasovo see Kulen Vakuf
127 N17 Spassk-Dal'niy Primorskiy Kray, SE Russian Federation 44.34N 132.52E
130 M5 Spassk-Ryazanskiy Ryazanskaya Oblast', W Russian Federation 54.25N 40.21E
117 H19 Spáta Attikí, C Greece 37.58N 23.55E
124 O12 Spátha, Akrotírio headland Kríti, Greece, E Mediterranean Sea 35.42N 23.43E
Spatrjan see Paternion
30 I9 Spearfish South Dakota, N USA 44.29N 103.51W
27 O1 Spearman Texas, SW USA 36.12N 101.11W
67 C25 Speedwell Island island S Falkland Islands
67 C25 Speedwell Island Settlement S Falkland Islands 52.13S 59.40W
67 G25 Speery Island island S Saint Helena
47 N14 Speightstown NW Barbados 13.13N 59.37W
108 I13 Spello Umbria, C Italy 43.00N 12.41E
41 R12 Spenard Alaska, USA 61.09N 150.03W
Spence Bay see Taloyoak
33 O14 Spencer Indiana, N USA 39.18N 86.46W
31 T12 Spencer Iowa, C USA 43.09N 95.07W
31 P12 Spencer Nebraska, C USA 42.52N 98.42W
23 S9 Spencer North Carolina, SE USA 35.41N 80.26W
22 L9 Spencer Tennessee, S USA 35.46N 85.27W
23 Q4 Spencer West Virginia, NE USA 38.48N 81.21W
32 K6 Spencer Wisconsin, N USA 44.46N 90.17W
190 G10 Spencer, Cape headland South Australia 35.17S 136.52E
41 V13 Spencer, Cape headland Alaska, USA 58.12N 136.39W
190 H9 Spencer Gulf gulf South Australia
20 F9 Spencerport New York, NE USA 43.11N 77.48W
33 Q12 Spencerville Ohio, N USA 40.42N 84.21W
117 E17 Spercheiáda var. Sperhiada, Sperkhiás. Stereá Ellás, C Greece 38.54N 22.07E
117 E17 Spercheiós ~ C Greece
Sperhiada see Spercheiáda
97 G14 Sperillen ◎ S Norway
Sperkhiás see Spercheiáda
103 I18 Spessart hill range C Germany
Spétsai see Spétses
117 G21 Spétses prev. Spétsai. Spétses, S Greece 37.16N 23.09E
117 G21 Spétses island S Greece
98 J8 Spey ~ NE Scotland, UK
103 G20 Speyer Eng. Spires; anc. Civitas Nemetum, Spira. Rheinland-Pfalz, SW Germany 49.19N 8.25E
103 G20 Speyerbach ~ W Germany
109 N20 Spezzano Albanese Calabria, SW Italy 39.40N 16.17E
Spice Islands see Maluku
102 F9 Spiekeroog island NW Germany
111 W9 Spielfeld Steiermark, SE Austria 46.43N 15.36E
67 N21 Spiess Seamount undersea feature S Atlantic Ocean 53.00S 2.00W
110 E9 Spiez Bern, W Switzerland 46.42N 7.40E
100 G13 Spijkenisse Zuid-Holland, SW Netherlands 51.52N 4.19E
41 T6 Spike Mountain ▲ Alaska, USA 67.42N 141.39W
117 I25 Spíli Kríti, Greece, E Mediterranean Sea 35.12N 24.33E
110 D10 Spillgerten ▲ W Switzerland 46.34N 7.25E
120 F9 Spilva ✕ (Rīga) Rīga, C Latvia 56.55N 24.03E
109 N17 Spinazzola Puglia, SE Italy 40.58N 16.06E
155 O9 Spīn Būldak Kandahār, S Afghanistan 31.01N 66.22E
Spira see Speyer
Spirdingsee see Śniardwy, Jezioro
Spires see Speyer
31 T11 Spirit Lake Iowa, C USA 43.25N 95.06W
31 T11 Spirit Lake ◎ Iowa, C USA
9 N13 Spirit River Alberta, W Canada 55.46N 118.51W
9 S14 Spiritwood Saskatchewan, S Canada 53.18N 107.33W
29 R11 Spiro Oklahoma, C USA 35.14N 94.37W
113 L19 Spišská Nová Ves Ger. Neudorf, Zipser Neudorf, Hung. Igló. Košický Kraj, E Slovakia 48.58N 20.34E
143 T11 Spitak NW Armenia 40.51N 44.17E
94 O2 Spitsbergen island NW Svalbard
Spittal see Spittal an der Drau
111 R9 Spittal an der Drau var. Spittal. Kärnten, S Austria 46.48N 13.30E
111 V3 Spitz Niederösterreich, NE Austria 48.24N 15.22E
96 D9 Spjelkavik Møre og Romsdal, S Norway 62.28N 6.22E
27 W10 Splendora Texas, SW USA 30.13N 95.09W
115 E14 Split It. Spalato. Split-Dalmacija, S Croatia 43.31N 16.27E
115 E14 Split ✕ Split-Dalmacija, S Croatia 43.33N 16.19E
115 E14 Split-Dalmacija off. Splitsko-Dalmatinska Županija. ◐ province S Croatia
9 X12 Split Lake ◎ Manitoba, C Canada
Splitsko-Dalmatinska Županija see Split-Dalmacija
110 H10 Splügen Graubünden, S Switzerland 46.33N 9.18E
Spodnji Dravograd see Dravograd
27 P12 Spofford Texas, SW USA 29.10N 100.24W
120 J11 Špoģi Daugvapils, SE Latvia 56.03N 26.47E
34 L8 Spokane Washington, NW USA 47.39N 117.25W
34 L8 Spokane River ~ Washington, NW USA
108 I13 Spoleto Umbria, C Italy 42.43N 12.43E
32 I4 Spooner Wisconsin, N USA 45.51N 91.49W
32 K12 Spoon River ~ Illinois, N USA
23 W5 Spotsylvania Virginia, NE USA 38.13N 77.31W
34 L8 Sprague Washington, NW USA 47.19N 117.55W
178 Ll16 Spratly Island island SW Spratly Islands
198 Ff7 Spratly Islands Chin. Nansha Qundao. ◇ disputed territory SE Asia
34 J12 Spray Oregon, NW USA 44.30N 119.38W
114 I11 Spreča ~ N Bosnia and Herzegovina
102 P13 Spree ~ E Germany
102 P13 Spreewald wetland NE Germany
103 P14 Spremberg Brandenburg, E Germany 51.34N 14.22E
27 W11 Spring Texas, SW USA 30.03N 95.24W
33 Q10 Spring Arbor Michigan, N USA 42.12N 84.33W
85 E23 Springbok Northern Cape, W South Africa 29.38S 17.56E
20 I15 Spring City Pennsylvania, NE USA 40.10N 75.33W
22 L9 Spring City Tennessee, S USA 35.41N 84.51W
38 L4 Spring City Utah, W USA 39.28N 111.30W
37 W3 Spring Creek Nevada, W USA 40.45N 115.40W
29 S9 Springdale Arkansas, C USA 36.11N 94.07W
33 Q14 Springdale Ohio, N USA 39.17N 84.29W
102 I13 Springe Niedersachsen, N Germany 52.13N 9.33E
39 U9 Springer New Mexico, SW USA 36.21N 104.35W
39 W7 Springfield Colorado, C USA 37.24N 102.36W
25 W5 Springfield Georgia, SE USA 32.21N 81.20W
32 K14 Springfield state capital Illinois, N USA 39.48N 89.38W
22 L6 Springfield Kentucky, S USA 37.41N 85.13W
20 M12 Springfield Massachusetts, NE USA 42.06N 72.32W
31 T10 Springfield Minnesota, N USA 44.15N 94.58W
29 T7 Springfield Missouri, C USA 37.13N 93.18W
33 R13 Springfield Ohio, N USA 39.55N 83.48W
34 G13 Springfield Oregon, NW USA 44.03N 123.01W
31 Q12 Springfield South Dakota, N USA 42.51N 97.54W
22 J8 Springfield Tennessee, S USA 36.30N 86.53W
20 M9 Springfield Vermont, NE USA 43.18N 72.27W
32 K14 Springfield, Lake ◎ Illinois, N USA
57 T8 Spring Garden NE Guyana 6.58N 58.34W
32 K8 Spring Green Wisconsin, N USA 43.10N 90.02W
31 X11 Spring Grove Minnesota, N USA 43.33N 91.38W
24 G4 Springhill Louisiana, S USA 33.01N 93.27W
25 V12 Spring Hill Florida, SE USA 28.28N 82.36W
29 R4 Spring Hill Kansas, C USA 38.44N 94.49W
11 P15 Springhill Nova Scotia, SE Canada 45.40N 64.04W
22 I9 Spring Hill Tennessee, S USA 35.46N 86.55W
23 U10 Spring Lake North Carolina, SE USA 35.10N 78.58W
26 M4 Springlake Texas, SW USA 34.13N 102.18W
37 W11 Spring Mountains ▲▲ Nevada, W USA
67 B24 Spring Point West Falkland, Falkland Islands 51.49S 60.27W
29 W9 Spring River ~ Arkansas/Missouri, C USA
29 S7 Spring River ~ Missouri/Oklahoma, C USA
85 J21 Springs Gauteng, NE South Africa 26.13S 28.32E
193 H16 Springs Junction West Coast, South Island, NZ 42.20S 172.10E
189 X8 Springsure Queensland, E Australia 24.09S 148.06E
31 W11 Spring Valley Minnesota, N USA 43.41N 92.23W
20 K13 Spring Valley New York, NE USA 41.10N 73.58W
31 N12 Springview Nebraska, C USA 42.48N 99.45W
20 D11 Springville New York, NE USA 42.27N 78.52W
38 L3 Springville Utah, W USA 40.10N 111.36W
Sprottau see Szprotawa
13 V4 Sproule, Pointe headland Quebec, SE Canada 49.47N 67.02W
9 Q14 Spruce Grove Alberta, SW Canada 53.36N 113.55W
23 T4 Spruce Knob ▲ West Virginia, NE USA 38.40N 79.37W
37 X3 Spruce Mountain ▲ Nevada, W USA 40.33N 114.46W
23 P9 Spruce Pine North Carolina, SE USA 35.55N 82.03W

◆ Country
● Country Capital
◇ Dependent Territory
○ Dependent Territory Capital
◐ Administrative Region
✕ International Airport
▲ Mountain
▲▲ Mountain Range
‡ Volcano
~ River
◎ Lake
⊡ Reservoir

Spui – Stranraer

100 G13 **Spui** ⇝ SW Netherlands
109 O19 **Spulico, Capo** *headland* S Italy *39.57N 16.38E*
27 O5 **Spur** Texas, SW USA *33.28N 100.51W*
99 O17 **Spurn Head** *headland* E England, UK *53.34N 0.06E*
101 H20 **Spy** Namur, S Belgium *50.29N 4.43E*
97 I15 **Spydeberg** Østfold, S Norway *59.36N 11.04E*
193 J17 **Spy Glass Point** *headland* South Island, NZ *42.33S 173.31E*
8 L17 **Squamish** British Columbia, SW Canada *49.40N 123.10W*
21 O8 **Squam Lake** ◎ New Hampshire, NE USA
21 S2 **Squa Pan Mountain** ▲ Maine, NE USA *46.36N 68.09W*
41 N16 **Squaw Harbor** Unga Island, Alaska, USA *55.12N 160.41W*
12 E11 **Squaw Island** *island* Ontario, S Canada
109 O22 **Squillace, Golfo di** *gulf* S Italy
109 Q18 **Squinzano** Puglia, SE Italy *40.25N 18.03E*
174 L15 **Sragen** Jawa, C Indonesia *7.24S 111.00E*
Sráid na Cathrach *see* Milltown Malbay
178 Jj11 **Srâlau** Stœng Trêng, N Cambodia *14.03N 105.46E*
Srath an Urláir *see* Stranorlar
114 G10 **Srbac** Republika Srpska, N Bosnia & Herzegovina *45.06N 17.33E*
Srbinje *see* Foča
Srbija *see* Serbia
Srbobran *see* Donji Vakuf
114 K9 **Srbobran** *var.* Bácsszenttamás, *Hung.* Szenttamás. Serbia, N Yugoslavia *45.33N 19.46E*
178 Ii14 **Srê Âmbêl** Kaôh Kông, SW Cambodia *11.07N 103.46E*
114 K13 **Srebrenica** Republika Srpska, E Bosnia & Herzegovina *44.04N 19.18E*
114 I11 **Srebrenik** Federacija Bosna I Hercegovina, E Bosnia & Herzegovina *44.42N 18.30E*
116 M10 **Sredets** *prev.* Grudovo. Burgas, E Bulgaria *42.21N 27.13E*
116 K10 **Sredets** *prev.* Syulemeshlii. Stara Zagora, C Bulgaria *42.16N 25.40E*
116 M10 **Sredetska Reka** ⇝ SE Bulgaria
127 P9 **Sredinnyy Khrebet** ▲▲ E Russian Federation
116 N7 **Sredishte** *Rom.* Beibunar; *prev.* Knyazhevo. Dobrich, NE Bulgaria *43.51N 27.30E*
116 I10 **Sredna Gora** ▲▲ C Bulgaria
127 N7 **Srednekolymsk** Respublika Sakha (Yakutiya), NE Russian Federation *67.28N 153.52E*
130 K7 **Srednerusskaya Vozvyshennost'** *Eng.* Central Russian Upland. ▲▲ W Russian Federation
126 Ii9 **Srednesibirskoye Ploskogor'ye** *var.* Central Siberian Uplands, *Eng.* Central Siberian Plateau. ▲▲ N Russian Federation
129 V13 **Sredniy Ural** ▲▲ NW Russian Federation
178 Jj13 **Srê Khtûm** Môndól Kiri, E Cambodia *12.10N 106.52E*
112 G12 **Śrem** Wielkolpolskie, C Poland *52.07N 17.00E*
114 K10 **Sremska Mitrovica** *prev.* Mitrovica, *Ger.* Mitrowitz. Serbia, NW Yugoslavia *44.58N 19.37E*
178 Ii11 **Srêng, Stœng** ⇝ NW Cambodia
178 Ii11 **Srê Noy** Siĕmréab, NW Cambodia *13.47N 104.03E*
Srepok, Sông *see* Srêpôk, Tônle
178 K12 **Srêpôk, Tônle** *var.* Sông Srepok. ⇝ Cambodia/Vietnam
126 L15 **Sretensk** Chitinskaya Oblast', S Russian Federation *52.14N 117.33E*
174 Ll7 **Sri Aman** Sarawak, East Malaysia *1.13N 111.25E*
119 R4 **Sribne** Chernihivs'ka Oblast', N Ukraine *50.40N 32.55E*
161 I25 **Sri Jayawardanapura** *var.* Sri Jayawardenepura; *prev.* Kotte. Western Province, W Sri Lanka *6.54N 79.58E*
161 M14 **Srikākulam** Andhra Pradesh, E India *18.18N 83.54E*
161 I25 **Sri Lanka** *off.* Democratic Socialist Republic of Sri Lanka; *prev.* Ceylon. ◆ *republic* S Asia
138 Mm15 **Sri Lanka** *island* S Asia
159 V14 **Srimangal** Chittagong, E Bangladesh *24.19N 91.40E*
Sri Mohangorh *see* Shri Mohangarh
158 H5 **Srinagar** Jammu and Kashmir, N India *34.06N 74.50E*
178 H10 **Srinagarind Reservoir** ◎ W Thailand
161 F19 **Sringeri** Karnātaka, W India *13.25N 75.13E*
161 K25 **Sri Pada** *Eng.* Adam's Peak. ▲ S Sri Lanka *6.49N 80.25E*
Sri Saket *see* Si Sa Ket
113 G14 **Środa Śląska** *Ger.* Neumarkt. Dolnośląskie, SW Poland *51.10N 16.30E*
112 H12 **Środa Wielkopolska** Wielkolpolskie, C Poland *52.13N 17.16E*
Srpska Kostajnica *see* Bosanska Kostajnica
115 G14 **Srpska, Republika** ◐ *republic* Bosnia & Herzegovina
Srpski Brod *see* Bosanski Brod
Ssu-ch'uan *see* Sichuan
Ssu-p'ing/Ssu-p'ing-chieh *see* Siping
Stablo *see* Stavelot
101 G15 **Stabroek** Antwerpen, N Belgium *51.21N 4.22E*
Stackeln *see* Strenči
98 I5 **Stack Skerry** *island* N Scotland, UK
96 C10 **Stad** *peninsula* S Norway
102 I9 **Stade** Niedersachsen, NW Germany *53.36N 9.28E*
111 R5 **Stadl-Paura** Oberösterreich, NW Austria *48.04N 13.52E*
121 L20 **Stadolichy** *Rus.* Stodolichi. Homyel'skaya Voblasts', SE Belarus *51.43N 28.30E*
100 P7 **Stadskanaal** Groningen, NE Netherlands *53.00N 6.55E*
103 H16 **Stadtallendorf** Hessen, C Germany *50.49N 9.01E*
103 K23 **Stadtbergen** Bayern, S Germany *48.21N 10.50E*
110 G7 **Stäfa** Zürich, NE Switzerland *47.14N 8.42E*
97 K23 **Staffanstorp** Skåne, S Sweden *55.37N 13.13E*
103 K18 **Staffelstein** Bayern, C Germany *50.05N 11.00E*
99 L19 **Stafford** C England, UK *52.48N 2.07W*
28 L6 **Stafford** Kansas, C USA *37.57N 98.36W*
23 W4 **Stafford** Virginia, NE USA *38.24N 77.22W*
99 L19 **Staffordshire** *cultural region* C England, UK
21 N12 **Stafford Springs** Connecticut, NE USA *41.57N 72.18W*
117 H14 **Stágira** Kentrikí Makedonía, N Greece *40.31N 23.46E*
120 G7 **Staicele** Limbaži, N Latvia *57.52N 24.48E*
Staierdorf-Anina *see* Anina
111 V8 **Stainz** Steiermark, SE Austria *46.55N 15.18E*
Stájerlakanina *see* Anina
119 Y7 **Stakhanov** Luhans'ka Oblast', E Ukraine *48.30N 38.42E*
110 E11 **Stalden** Valais, SW Switzerland *46.12N 7.55E*
Stalin *see* Varna
Stalinabad *see* Dushanbe
Stalingrad *see* Volgograd
Staliniri *see* Ts'khinvali
Stalino *see* Donets'k
Stalinobod *see* Dushanbe
Stalinov Štít *see* Gerlachovský štít
Stalinsk *see* Novokuznetsk
Stalinskaya Oblast' *see* Donets'ka Oblast'
Stalinski Zaliv *see* Varnenski Zaliv
Stalin, Yazovir *see* Iskŭr, Yazovir
113 N15 **Stalowa Wola** Podkarpackie, SE Poland *50.34N 22.01E*
116 I11 **Stamboliyski** Plovdiv, C Bulgaria *42.08N 24.36E*
116 J8 **Stamboliyski, Yazovir** ◎ N Bulgaria
99 N19 **Stamford** E England, UK *52.39N 0.32W*
20 L14 **Stamford** Connecticut, NE USA *41.03N 73.31W*
27 P6 **Stamford** Texas, SW USA *32.55N 99.49W*
27 Q6 **Stamford, Lake** ◙ Texas, SW USA
110 I10 **Stampa** Graubünden, SE Switzerland *46.21N 9.35E*
Stampalia *see* Astypálaia
29 T14 **Stamps** Arkansas, C USA *33.22N 93.30W*
94 G11 **Stamsund** Nordland, C Norway *68.07N 13.49E*
29 R2 **Stanberry** Missouri, C USA *40.12N 94.33W*
205 O3 **Stancomb-Wills Glacier** *glacier* Antarctica
85 K21 **Standerton** Mpumalanga, E South Africa *26.54S 29.15E*
33 R7 **Standish** Michigan, N USA *43.58N 83.58W*
22 M6 **Stanford** Kentucky, S USA *37.30N 84.39W*
35 S9 **Stanford** Montana, NW USA *47.08N 110.15W*
97 P19 **Stånga** Gotland, SE Sweden *57.16N 18.30E*
96 I13 **Stange** Hedmark, S Norway *60.43N 11.12E*
85 L23 **Stanger** KwaZulu/Natal, E South Africa *29.18S 31.17E*
Stanimaka *see* Asenovgrad
Stanislau *see* Ivano-Frankivs'k
37 P8 **Stanislaus River** ⇝ California, W USA
Stanislav *see* Ivano-Frankivs'k
Stanislavskaya Oblast' *see* Ivano-Frankivs'ka Oblast'
Stanisławów *see* Ivano-Frankivs'k
Stanke Dimitrov *see* Dupnitsa
191 O15 **Stanley** Tasmania, SE Australia *40.48S 145.18E*
67 E24 **Stanley** *var.* Port Stanley, Puerto Argentino ○ (Falkland Islands) East Falkland, Falkland Islands *51.45S 57.55W*
35 O13 **Stanley** Idaho, NW USA *44.12N 114.58W*
30 L3 **Stanley** North Dakota, N USA *48.19N 102.23W*
23 U4 **Stanley** Virginia, NE USA *38.34N 78.30W*
32 J6 **Stanley** Wisconsin, N USA *44.58N 90.54W*
81 G21 **Stanley Pool** *var.* Pool Malebo. ◎ Congo/Dem. Rep. Congo (Zaire)
161 H20 **Stanley Reservoir** ◙ S India
Stanleyville *see* Kisangani
44 G3 **Stann Creek** ◐ *district* SE Belize
Stann Creek *see* Dangriga
127 N17 **Stanovoy Khrebet** ▲▲ SE Russian Federation
110 F8 **Stans** Unterwalden, C Switzerland *46.57N 8.22E*
99 O21 **Stansted** ✕ (London) Essex, E England, UK *51.53N 0.16E*
191 U4 **Stanthorpe** Queensland, E Australia *28.35S 151.52E*
23 N6 **Stanton** Kentucky, S USA *37.51N 83.51W*
33 Q8 **Stanton** Michigan, N USA *43.17N 85.01W*
31 Q14 **Stanton** Nebraska, C USA *41.57N 97.13W*
30 L5 **Stanton** North Dakota, N USA *47.19N 101.22W*
27 N7 **Stanton** Texas, SW USA *32.07N 101.47W*
34 H7 **Stanwood** Washington, NW USA *48.14N 122.22W*
119 Y7 **Stanychno-Luhans'ke** Luhans'ka Oblast', E Ukraine *48.39N 39.30E*
110 K7 **Stanzach** Tirol, W Austria *47.24N 10.36E*
100 M9 **Staphorst** Overijssel, E Netherlands *52.37N 6.12E*
12 D18 **Staples** Ontario, S Canada *42.09N 82.34W*
31 T6 **Staples** Minnesota, N USA *46.21N 94.47W*
30 M14 **Stapleton** Nebraska, C USA *41.28N 100.30W*
27 S8 **Star** Texas, SW USA *31.27N 98.16W*
113 M14 **Starachowice** Świętokrzyskie, C Poland *51.04N 21.02E*
Stara Kanjiža *see* Kanjiža
113 M18 **Stará L'ubovňa** *Ger.* Altlublau, *Hung.* Prešovský Kraj, E Slovakia *49.18N 20.40E*
114 L10 **Stara Pazova** *Ger.* Altpasua, *Hung.* Ópazova. Serbia, N Yugoslavia *44.59N 20.10E*
Stara Planina *see* Balkan Mountains
116 L9 **Stara Reka** ⇝ C Bulgaria
118 M5 **Stara Synyava** Khmel'nyts'ka Oblast', W Ukraine *49.39N 27.39E*
118 I2 **Stara Vyzhivka** Volyns'ka Oblast', NW Ukraine *51.27N 24.25E*
Staraya Belitsa *see* Staraya Byelitsa
121 M14 **Staraya Byelitsa** *Rus.* Staraya Belitsa. Vitsyebskaya Voblasts', NE Belarus *54.42N 29.37E*
131 R5 **Staraya Mayna** Ul'yanovskaya Oblast', W Russian Federation *54.36N 48.57E*
121 O18 **Staraya Rudnya** *Rus.* Staraya Rudnya. Homyel'skaya Voblasts', SE Belarus *52.50N 30.15E*
128 H14 **Staraya Russa** Novgorodskaya Oblast', W Russian Federation *57.59N 31.18E*
116 K10 **Stara Zagora** *Lat.* Augusta Trajana. Stara Zagora, C Bulgaria *42.26N 25.39E*
116 K10 **Stara Zagora** ◐ *province* C Bulgaria
31 S8 **Starbuck** Minnesota, N USA *45.36N 95.31W*
203 W4 **Starbuck Island** *prev.* Volunteer Island. *island* E Kiribati
29 V13 **Star City** Arkansas, C USA *33.56N 91.50W*
114 F13 **Staretina** ▲▲ W Bosnia and Herzegovina
Stargard in Pommern *see* Stargard Szczeciński
112 E9 **Stargard Szczeciński** *Ger.* Stargard in Pommern. Zachodniopomorskie, NW Poland *53.19N 15.01E*
195 Z17 **Star Harbour** *harbor* San Cristobal, SE Solomon Islands
Stari Bečej *see* Bečej
115 F15 **Stari Grad** *It.* Cittavecchia. Split-Dalmacija, S Croatia *43.11N 16.36E*
175 Qq12 **Staring, Teluk** *var.* Teluk Wawosungu. *bay* Sulawesi, C Indonesia
128 J16 **Staritsa** Tverskaya Oblast', W Russian Federation *56.28N 34.51E*
25 V9 **Starke** Florida, SE USA *29.56N 82.07W*
24 M4 **Starkville** Mississippi, S USA *33.27N 88.49W*
194 E11 **Star Mountains** *Ind.* Pegunungan Sterren. ▲▲ Indonesia/PNG
103 L23 **Starnberg** Bayern, SE Germany *48.00N 11.19E*
103 L24 **Starnberger See** ◎ SE Germany
Starobel'sk *see* Starobil's'k
119 X8 **Starobesheve** Donets'ka Oblast', E Ukraine *47.45N 38.01E*
119 Y6 **Starobil's'k** *Rus.* Starobel'sk. Luhans'ka Oblast', E Ukraine *49.16N 38.55E*
Starobin *see* Starobyn
121 K18 **Starobyn** *Rus.* Starobin. Minskaya Voblasts', S Belarus *52.43N 27.28E*
130 H6 **Starodub** Bryanskaya Oblast', W Russian Federation *52.30N 32.56E*
112 I8 **Starogard Gdański** *Ger.* Preussisch-Stargard. Pomorskie, N Poland *53.57N 18.29E*
151 P16 **Staroikan** Yuzhnyy Kazakhstan, S Kazakhstan *43.09N 68.34E*
Starokonstantinov *see* Starokostyantyniv
118 L5 **Starokostyantyniv** *Rus.* Starokonstantinov. Khmel'nyts'ka Oblast', NW Ukraine *49.43N 27.12E*
130 K12 **Starominskaya** Krasnodarskiy Kray, SW Russian Federation *46.31N 39.03E*
116 L7 **Staro Selo** *Rom.* Satul-Vechi; *prev.* Star-Smil. Silistra, NE Bulgaria *43.58N 26.32E*
130 K12 **Staroshcherbinovskaya** Krasnodarskiy Kray, SW Russian Federation *46.36N 38.42E*
131 V6 **Starosubkhangulovo** Respublika Bashkortostan, W Russian Federation *53.05N 57.22E*
37 S4 **Star Peak** ▲ Nevada, W USA *40.31N 118.09W*
Star-Smil *see* Staro Selo
99 J25 **Start Point** *headland* SW England, UK *50.13N 3.38W*
Startsy *see* Kirawsk
Starum *see* Stavoren
121 L18 **Staryya Darohi** *Rus.* Staryye Dorogi. Minskaya Voblasts', S Belarus *53.01N 28.12E*
Staryye Dorogi *see* Staryya Darohi
131 T2 **Staryye Zyatsy** Udmurtskaya Respublika, NW Russian Federation *57.22N 52.42E*
119 U13 **Staryy Krym** Respublika Krym, S Ukraine *45.03N 35.06E*
130 K8 **Staryy Oskol** Belgorodskaya Oblast', W Russian Federation *51.21N 37.52E*
118 H6 **Staryy Sambir** L'vivs'ka Oblast', W Ukraine *49.27N 23.00E*
103 L14 **Stassfurt** *var.* Staßfurt. Sachsen-Anhalt, C Germany *51.51N 11.34E*
113 M15 **Staszów** Świętokrzyskie, C Poland *50.34N 21.08E*
31 W13 **State Center** Iowa, C USA *42.01N 93.09W*
20 E14 **State College** Pennsylvania, NE USA *40.48N 77.52W*
20 K15 **Staten Island** *island* New York, NE USA
Staten Island *see* Estados, Isla de los
25 U8 **Statenville** Georgia, SE USA *30.42N 83.00W*
25 W5 **Statesboro** Georgia, SE USA *32.28N 81.46W*
States, The *see* United States of America
23 R9 **Statesville** North Carolina, SE USA *35.46N 80.53W*
97 G16 **Stathelle** Telemark, S Norway *59.01N 9.40E*
32 K15 **Staunton** Illinois, N USA *39.00N 89.47W*
23 T5 **Staunton** Virginia, NE USA *38.09N 79.04W*
97 C16 **Stavanger** Rogaland, S Norway *58.58N 5.43E*
101 L21 **Stavelot** *Dut.* Stablo. Liège, E Belgium *50.24N 5.55E*
97 G16 **Stavern** Vestfold, S Norway *58.58N 10.01E*
Stavers Island *see* Vostok Island
100 J7 **Stavoren** *Fris.* Starum. Friesland, N Netherlands *52.52N 5.22E*
130 M14 **Stavropol'** *prev.* Voroshilovsk. Stavropol'skiy Kray, SW Russian Federation *45.02N 41.57E*
Stavropol' *see* Tol'yatti
130 M14 **Stavropol'skaya Vozvyshennost'** ▲▲ SW Russian Federation
130 M14 **Stavropol'skiy Kray** ◐ *territory* SW Russian Federation
117 H14 **Stavrós** Kentrikí Makedonía, N Greece *40.39N 23.43E*
117 J24 **Stavrós, Akrotírio** *headland* Kríti, Greece, E Mediterranean Sea *35.25N 24.57E*
117 K21 **Stavrós, Akrotírio** *headland* Náxos, Kykládes, Greece, Aegean Sea *37.12N 25.32E*
116 I12 **Stavroúpoli** *prev.* Stavroúpolis. Anatolikí Makedonía kai Thráki, NE Greece *41.12N 24.42E*
Stavroúpolis *see* Stavroúpoli
119 O6 **Stavyshche** Kyyivs'ka Oblast', N Ukraine *49.23N 30.10E*
190 M11 **Stawell** Victoria, SE Australia *37.03S 142.47E*
112 N9 **Stawiski** Podlaskie, NE Poland *53.22N 22.08E*
12 G14 **Stayner** Ontario, S Canada *44.25N 80.05W*
39 R3 **Steamboat Springs** Colorado, C USA *40.28N 106.51W*
22 M8 **Stearns** Kentucky, S USA *36.39N 84.27W*
41 N10 **Stebbins** Alaska, USA *63.30N 162.15W*
110 K7 **Steeg** Tirol, W Austria *47.15N 10.18E*
29 Y9 **Steele** Missouri, C USA *36.04N 89.49W*
31 N5 **Steele** North Dakota, N USA *46.51N 99.55W*
204 J5 **Steele Island** *island* Antarctica
32 K16 **Steeleville** Illinois, N USA *38.00N 89.39W*
29 W6 **Steelville** Missouri, C USA *37.58N 91.21W*
101 G14 **Steenbergen** Noord-Brabant, S Netherlands *51.34N 4.13E*
Steenkool *see* Bintuni
9 O10 **Steen River** Alberta, W Canada *59.37N 117.16W*
100 M8 **Steenwijk** Overijssel, N Netherlands *52.46N 6.07E*
67 A23 **Steeple Jason** *island* Jason Islands, NW Falkland Islands
182 J8 **Steep Point** *headland* Western Australia *26.09S 113.10E*
118 L9 **Ştefăneşti** Botoşani, NE Romania *47.43N 27.15E*
Stefanie, Lake *see* Ch'ew Bahir
15 J1 **Stefansson Island** *island* Nunavut, N Canada
119 O10 **Ştefan Vodă** *Rus.* Suvorovo. SE Moldova *46.33N 29.39E*
65 H18 **Steffen, Cerro** ▲ S Chile *44.27S 71.42W*
110 D9 **Steffisburg** Bern, C Switzerland *46.46N 7.37E*
97 J24 **Stege** Storstrøm, SE Denmark *54.58N 12.18E*
118 G10 **Ştei** *Hung.* Vaskohsziklás. Bihor, W Romania *46.33N 22.28E*
Steier *see* Steyr
Steierdorf/Steierdorf-Anina *see* Anina
111 T7 **Steiermark** *off.* Land Steiermark, *Eng.* Styria. ◐ *state* C Austria
103 J19 **Steigerwald** *hill range* C Germany
101 L17 **Stein** Limburg, SE Netherlands *50.58N 5.45E*
Stein *see* Stein an der Donau, Austria
Stein *see* Kamnik, Slovenia
110 M8 **Steinach** Tirol, W Austria *47.07N 11.30E*
Steinamanger *see* Szombathely
111 W3 **Stein an der Donau** *var.* Stein. Niederösterreich, NE Austria *48.24N 15.35E*
Steinau an der Elbe *see* Ścinawa
9 Y16 **Steinbach** Manitoba, S Canada *49.31N 96.40W*
Steiner Alpen *see* Kamniško-Savinjske Alpe
101 L24 **Steinfort** Luxembourg, W Luxembourg *49.39N 5.55E*
102 H12 **Steinhuder Meer** ◎ NW Germany
95 E15 **Steinkjer** Nord-Trøndelag, C Norway *64.01N 11.28E*
Stejarul *see* Karapelit
101 F16 **Stekene** Oost-Vlaanderen, NW Belgium *51.13N 4.04E*
85 E26 **Stellenbosch** Western Cape, SW South Africa *33.48S 18.49E*
100 F13 **Stellendam** Zuid-Holland, SW Netherlands *51.48N 4.01E*
41 T12 **Steller, Mount** ▲ Alaska, USA *60.36N 142.49W*
105 Y14 **Stello, Monte** ▲ Corse, France, C Mediterranean Sea *42.49N 9.24E*
108 F5 **Stelvio, Passo dello** *pass* Italy/Switzerland *46.32N 10.27E*
105 R3 **Stenay** Meuse, NE France *49.29N 5.12E*
102 L12 **Stendal** Sachsen-Anhalt, C Germany *52.36N 11.52E*
120 E8 **Stende** Talsi, NW Latvia *57.09N 22.33E*
190 H10 **Stenhouse Bay** South Australia *35.15S 136.58E*
97 J23 **Stenløse** Frederiksborg, E Denmark *55.46N 12.13E*
97 L19 **Stensjön** Jönköping, S Sweden *57.36N 14.42E*
97 K18 **Stenstorp** Västra Götaland, S Sweden *58.15N 13.45E*
97 I18 **Stenungsund** Västra Götaland, S Sweden *58.04N 11.55E*
Stepanakert *see* Xankändi
143 T11 **Step'anavan** N Armenia *41.00N 44.27E*
102 K9 **Stepenitz** ⇝ N Germany
31 O10 **Stephan** South Dakota, N USA *44.12N 99.25W*
31 R3 **Stephen** Minnesota, N USA *48.27N 96.54W*
29 T14 **Stephens** Arkansas, C USA *33.25N 93.04W*
192 J13 **Stephens, Cape** *headland* D'Urville Island, Marlborough, SW NZ *40.42S 173.56E*
23 V3 **Stephens City** Virginia, NE USA *39.03N 78.10W*
190 L6 **Stephens Creek** New South Wales, SE Australia *31.51S 141.30E*
192 K13 **Stephens Island** *island* C NZ
33 N5 **Stephenson** Michigan, N USA *45.27N 87.36W*
11 S12 **Stephenville** Newfoundland, SE Canada *48.33N 58.29W*
27 S7 **Stephenville** Texas, SW USA *32.12N 98.13W*
151 P17 **Step' Nardara** *Kaz.* Shardara Dalasy; *prev.* Shaidara. *grassland* S Kazakhstan
151 R8 **Stepnogorsk** Akmola, C Kazakhstan *52.04N 72.18E*
131 O15 **Stepnoye** Stavropol'skiy Kray, SW Russian Federation *44.18N 44.34E*
151 Q8 **Stepnyak** Severnyy Kazakhstan, N Kazakhstan *52.52N 70.49E*
198 C9 **Steps Point** *headland* Tutuila, W American Samoa *14.22S 170.46W*
117 F17 **Stereá Ellás** *Eng.* Greece Central. ◐ *region* C Greece
85 J24 **Sterkspruit** Eastern Cape, SE South Africa *30.28S 27.24E*
131 U6 **Sterlibashevo** Respublika Bashkortostan, W Russian Federation *53.19N 55.12E*
41 R12 **Sterling** Alaska, USA *60.32N 150.51W*
39 V3 **Sterling** Colorado, C USA *40.37N 103.12W*
32 K11 **Sterling** Illinois, N USA *41.47N 89.42W*
28 M5 **Sterling** Kansas, C USA *38.12N 98.12W*
27 O8 **Sterling City** Texas, SW USA *31.50N 100.58W*
33 S9 **Sterling Heights** Michigan, N USA *42.34N 83.01W*
23 W3 **Sterling Park** Virginia, NE USA *39.00N 77.24W*
39 V2 **Sterling Reservoir** ◙ Colorado, C USA
24 I5 **Sterlington** Louisiana, S USA *32.42N 92.05W*
131 U6 **Sterlitamak** Respublika Bashkortostan, W Russian Federation *53.39N 56.00E*
Sternberg *see* Šternberk
113 H17 **Šternberk** *Ger.* Sternberg. Olomoucký Kraj, E Czech Republic *49.45N 17.19E*
147 V17 **Stěroh** Suquṭrā, S Yemen *12.21N 53.50E*
112 G11 **Stęszew** Wielkolpolskie, C Poland *52.16N 16.41E*
Stettin *see* Szczecin
Stettiner Haff *see* Szczeciński, Zalew
9 Q15 **Stettler** Alberta, SW Canada *52.21N 112.40W*
33 V13 **Steubenville** Ohio, N USA *40.21N 80.37W*
99 O21 **Stevenage** E England, UK *51.55N 0.13W*
25 Q1 **Stevenson** Alabama, S USA *34.52N 85.50W*
34 H11 **Stevenson** Washington, NW USA *45.43N 121.54W*
190 E1 **Stevenson Creek** *seasonal river* South Australia
41 Q13 **Stevenson Entrance** *strait* Alaska, USA
32 L6 **Stevens Point** Wisconsin, N USA *44.31N 89.33W*
41 R8 **Stevens Village** Alaska, USA *66.01N 149.02W*
35 P10 **Stevensville** Montana, NW USA *46.30N 114.05W*
95 E25 **Stevns Klint** *headland* E Denmark *55.15N 12.25E*
8 J12 **Stewart** British Columbia, W Canada *55.58N 129.52W*
8 J6 **Stewart** ⇝ Yukon Territory, NW Canada
8 I6 **Stewart Crossing** Yukon Territory, NW Canada *63.22N 136.37W*
65 H25 **Stewart, Isla** *island* S Chile
193 B25 **Stewart Island** *island* S NZ
189 W6 **Stewart, Mount** ▲ Queensland, E Australia *20.11S 145.29E*
8 H6 **Stewart River** Yukon Territory, NW Canada *63.17N 139.24W*
29 R3 **Stewartsville** Missouri, C USA *39.45N 94.30W*
9 S16 **Stewart Valley** Saskatchewan, S Canada *50.34N 107.47W*
31 W10 **Stewartville** Minnesota, N USA *43.51N 92.29W*
Steyerlak-Anina *see* Anina
111 T5 **Steyr** *var.* Steier. Oberösterreich, N Austria *48.02N 14.26E*
111 T5 **Steyr** ⇝ NW Austria
31 P11 **Stickney** South Dakota, N USA *43.24N 98.23W*
100 L5 **Stiens** Friesland, N Netherlands *53.15N 5.45E*
Stif *see* Sétif
29 Q11 **Stigler** Oklahoma, C USA *35.15N 95.07W*
109 N18 **Stigliano** Basilicata, S Italy *40.24N 16.13E*
97 N17 **Stigtomta** Södermanland, C Sweden *58.48N 16.46E*
8 I11 **Stikine** ⇝ British Columbia, W Canada
Stilida/Stilís *see* Stylida
97 G22 **Stilling** Århus, C Denmark *56.04N 10.00E*
31 W8 **Stillwater** Minnesota, N USA *45.03N 92.48W*
29 O9 **Stillwater** Oklahoma, C USA *36.07N 97.02W*
37 S5 **Stillwater Range** ▲▲ Nevada, W USA
20 I8 **Stillwater Reservoir** ◙ New York, NE USA
109 O22 **Stilo, Punta** *headland* S Italy *38.27N 16.36E*
29 R10 **Stilwell** Oklahoma, C USA *35.48N 94.37W*
115 N17 **Štimlje** Serbia, S Yugoslavia *42.27N 21.03E*
27 N1 **Stinnett** Texas, SW USA *35.49N 101.26W*
115 P18 **Štip** E FYR Macedonia *41.45N 22.10E*
Stira *see* Stýra
98 J12 **Stirling** C Scotland, UK *56.07N 3.57W*
98 I12 **Stirling** *cultural region* C Scotland, UK
188 J14 **Stirling Range** ▲▲ Western Australia
95 E16 **Stjørdal** Nord-Trøndelag, C Norway *63.27N 10.57E*
Stochód *see* Stokhid
103 H24 **Stockach** Baden-Württemberg, S Germany *47.51N 9.01E*
27 S12 **Stockdale** Texas, SW USA *29.14N 97.57W*
111 X3 **Stockerau** Niederösterreich, NE Austria *48.24N 16.13E*
95 H20 **Stockholm** ● (Sweden) Stockholm, C Sweden *59.16N 18.03E*
97 O15 **Stockholm** ◐ *county* C Sweden
Stockmannshof *see* Pļaviņas
99 L18 **Stockport** NW England, UK *53.25N 2.10W*
67 K15 **Stocks Seamount** *undersea feature* C Atlantic Ocean *11.42S 33.48W*
37 O8 **Stockton** California, W USA *37.55N 121.19W*
28 L3 **Stockton** Kansas, C USA *39.25N 99.17W*
29 S6 **Stockton** Missouri, C USA *37.42N 93.48W*
32 K3 **Stockton Island** *island* Apostle Islands, Wisconsin, N USA
29 S7 **Stockton Lake** ◙ Missouri, C USA
99 M15 **Stockton-on-Tees** *var.* Stockton on Tees. N England, UK *54.34N 1.19W*
26 M10 **Stockton Plateau** *plain* Texas, SW USA
30 M16 **Stockville** Nebraska, C USA *40.30N 100.21W*
95 H17 **Stöde** Västernorrland, C Sweden *62.27N 16.34E*
Stodolichi *see* Stadolichy
178 Jj12 **Stœng Trêng** *prev.* Stung Treng. Stœng Trêng, NE Cambodia *13.31N 105.58E*
115 M19 **Stogovo Karaorman** ▲ W FYR Macedonia
Stoke *see* Stoke-on-Trent
99 L19 **Stoke-on-Trent** *var.* Stoke. C England, UK *53.00N 2.10W*
190 M15 **Stokes Point** *headland* Tasmania, SE Australia *40.09S 143.55E*
118 J2 **Stokhid** *Pol.* Stochód, *Rus.* Stokhod. ⇝ NW Ukraine
Stokhod *see* Stokhid
94 I4 **Stokkseyri** Sudhurland, SW Iceland *63.49N 21.00W*
94 G10 **Stokmarknes** Nordland, C Norway *68.33N 14.54E*
Stol *see* Veliki Krš
115 H15 **Stolac** Federacija Bosna I Hercegovina, S Bosnia and Herzegovina *43.04N 17.58E*
Stolbce *see* Stowbtsy
103 D16 **Stolberg** *var.* Stolberg im Rheinland. Nordrhein-Westfalen, W Germany *50.46N 6.13E*
Stolberg im Rheinland *see* Stolberg
126 L5 **Stolbovoy, Ostrov** *island* NE Russian Federation
Stolbtsy *see* Stowbtsy
121 J20 **Stolin** *Rus.* Stolin. Brestskaya Voblasts', SW Belarus *51.52N 26.51E*
97 K14 **Stöllet** *var.* Norra Ny. Värmland, C Sweden *60.24N 13.15E*
Stolp *see* Słupsk
Stolpe *see* Słupia
Stolpmünde *see* Ustka
117 F15 **Stómio** Thessalía, C Greece *39.51N 22.45E*
12 J11 **Stonecliffe** Ontario, SE Canada *46.12N 77.58W*
98 L10 **Stonehaven** NE Scotland, UK *56.58N 2.13W*
99 M23 **Stonehenge** *ancient monument* Wiltshire, S England, UK *51.12N 1.54W*
25 T3 **Stone Mountain** ▲ Georgia, SE USA *33.48N 84.10W*
9 X16 **Stonewall** Manitoba, S Canada *50.07N 97.19W*
23 S3 **Stonewood** West Virginia, NE USA *39.15N 80.18W*
12 D17 **Stoney Point** Ontario, S Canada *42.18N 82.32W*
94 H10 **Stonglandseidet** Troms, N Norway *69.03N 17.06E*
67 N25 **Stonybeach Bay** *bay* Tristan da Cunha, SE Atlantic Ocean
37 N5 **Stony Creek** ⇝ California, W USA
67 N25 **Stonyhill Point** *headland* S Tristan da Cunha
12 I14 **Stony Lake** ◎ Ontario, SE Canada
9 Q14 **Stony Plain** Alberta, SW Canada *53.31N 114.04W*
23 R9 **Stony Point** North Carolina, SE USA *35.51N 81.04W*
20 G8 **Stony Point** *headland* New York, NE USA *43.50N 76.18W*
9 T10 **Stony Rapids** Saskatchewan, C Canada *59.13N 105.48W*
41 P11 **Stony River** Alaska, USA *61.48N 156.37W*
Stony Tunguska *see* Podkamennaya Tunguska
10 G10 **Stooping** ⇝ Ontario, C Canada
102 I9 **Stör** ⇝ N Germany
97 M15 **Storå** Örebro, S Sweden *59.43N 15.10E*
97 J16 **Stora Gla** ◎ C Sweden
97 I16 **Stora Le** *Nor.* Store Le. ◎ Norway/Sweden
94 I12 **Stora Lulevatten** ◎ N Sweden
94 H13 **Storavan** ◎ N Sweden
95 I20 **Storby** Åland, SW Finland *60.12N 19.33E*
96 E10 **Stordalen** Møre og Romsdal, S Norway *62.22N 7.00E*
Storebelt *see* Storebælt
97 H23 **Storebælt** *var.* Store Bælt, *Eng.* Great Belt, Storebelt. *channel* Baltic Sea/Kattegat
97 M19 **Storebro** Kalmar, S Sweden *57.36N 15.30E*
97 J24 **Store Heddinge** Storstrøm, SE Denmark *55.19N 12.24E*
Store Le *see* Stora Le
95 E16 **Støren** Sør-Trøndelag, S Norway *63.01N 10.16E*
97 B14 **Store Sotra** *island* S Norway
94 O4 **Storfjorden** *fjord* S Norway
97 L15 **Storfors** Värmland, C Sweden *59.33N 14.16E*
94 G13 **Storforshei** Nordland, C Norway *66.25N 14.25E*
Storhammer *see* Hamar
102 L10 **Störkanal** *canal* N Germany
95 F16 **Storlien** Jämtland, C Sweden *63.18N 12.10E*
191 P17 **Storm Bay** *inlet* Tasmania, SE Australia
31 T12 **Storm Lake** Iowa, C USA *42.38N 95.12W*
31 S13 **Storm Lake** ◎ Iowa, C USA
98 G7 **Stornoway** NW Scotland, UK *58.13N 6.22W*
Storojineț *see* Storozhynets'
94 P1 **Storøya** *island* NE Svalbard
129 S10 **Storozhevsk** Respublika Komi, NW Russian Federation *61.56N 52.18E*
Storozhinets *see* Storozhynets'
118 K8 **Storozhynets'** *Ger.* Storozynetz, *Rom.* Storojineț, *Rus.* Storozhinets. Chernivets'ka Oblast', W Ukraine *48.09N 25.40E*
Storozynetz *see* Storozhynets'
94 H11 **Storriten** ▲ C Norway *68.09N 17.12E*
21 N12 **Storrs** Connecticut, NE USA *41.48N 72.15W*
96 I11 **Storsjøen** ◎ S Norway
96 N13 **Storsjön** ◎ C Sweden
95 F16 **Storsjön** ◎ C Sweden
94 I9 **Storslett** Troms, N Norway *69.45N 21.03E*
94 I9 **Storsteinnes** Troms, N Norway *69.13N 19.14E*
97 I24 **Storstrøm** *off.* Storstrøms Amt. ◐ *county* SE Denmark
95 J14 **Storsund** Norrbotten, N Sweden *65.36N 20.40E*
95 F16 **Storsylen** ▲ S Norway *63.07N 12.10E*
94 H11 **Stortoppen** ▲ N Sweden *67.28N 17.56E*
95 H14 **Storuman** Västerbotten, N Sweden *65.05N 17.10E*
95 H14 **Storuman** ◎ N Sweden
96 N13 **Storvik** Gävleborg, C Sweden *60.37N 16.30E*
97 O14 **Storvreta** Uppsala, C Sweden *59.58N 17.42E*
31 V13 **Story City** Iowa, C USA *42.10N 93.36W*
9 V17 **Stoughton** Saskatchewan, S Canada *49.40N 103.01W*
21 O11 **Stoughton** Massachusetts, NE USA *42.07N 71.06W*
32 L9 **Stoughton** Wisconsin, N USA *42.56N 89.12W*
99 L23 **Stour** ⇝ E England, UK
99 P21 **Stour** ⇝ S England, UK
29 T5 **Stover** Missouri, C USA *38.26N 92.59W*
97 G21 **Støvring** Nordjylland, N Denmark *56.52N 9.52E*
121 J17 **Stowbtsy** *Pol.* Stołbce, *Rus.* Stolbtsy. Minskaya Voblasts', C Belarus *53.27N 26.44E*
27 X11 **Stowell** Texas, SW USA *29.47N 94.22W*
99 P20 **Stowmarket** E England, UK *52.04N 0.54E*
116 N8 **Stozher** Dobrich, NE Bulgaria *43.27N 27.49E*
99 E14 **Strabane** *Ir.* An Srath Bán. W Northern Ireland, UK *54.49N 7.27W*
123 Gg10 **Strabo Trench** *undersea feature* C Mediterranean Sea
29 T7 **Strafford** Missouri, C USA *37.16N 93.07W*
191 N17 **Strahan** Tasmania, SE Australia *42.10S 145.18E*
113 C18 **Strakonice** *Ger.* Strakonitz. Budějovický Kraj, S Czech Republic *49.13N 13.55E*
Strakonitz *see* Strakonice
102 N8 **Stralsund** Mecklenburg-Vorpommern, NE Germany *54.18N 13.06E*
101 L16 **Stramproy** Limburg, SE Netherlands *51.12N 5.43E*
85 E26 **Strand** Western Cape, SW South Africa *34.06S 18.49E*
96 E10 **Stranda** Møre og Romsdal, S Norway *62.18N 6.55E*
99 G15 **Strangford Lough** *Ir.* Loch Cuan. *inlet* E Northern Ireland, UK
97 N16 **Strängnäs** Södermanland, C Sweden *59.22N 17.01E*
99 E14 **Stranorlar** *Ir.* Srath an Urláir. NW Ireland *54.48N 7.46W*
99 H14 **Stranraer** S Scotland, UK *54.54N 5.01W*

◆ Country
● Country Capital
◇ Dependent Territory
○ Dependent Territory Capital
◐ Administrative Region
✕ International Airport
▲ Mountain
▲▲ Mountain Range
Ж Volcano
⇝ River
◎ Lake
◙ Reservoir

Strasbourg – Support Force Glacier

9 U16 **Strasbourg** Saskatchewan, S Canada 51.04N 104.58W
105 V5 **Strasbourg** *Ger.* Strassburg; *anc.* Argentoratum. Bas-Rhin, NE France 48.34N 7.45E
39 U4 **Strasburg** Colorado, C USA 39.42N 104.13W
31 N7 **Strasburg** North Dakota, N USA 46.07N 100.10W
33 U12 **Strasburg** Ohio, N USA 40.35N 81.31W
23 U3 **Strasburg** Virginia, NE USA 38.59N 78.21W
119 N10 **Străşeni** *var.* Strasheny. C Moldova 47.07N 28.37E
Strasheny *see* Străşeni
111 T8 **Strassburg** Kärnten, S Austria 46.54N 14.21E
Strassburg *see* Strasbourg, France
Strassburg *see* Aiud, Romania
101 M25 **Strassen** Luxembourg, S Luxembourg 49.37N 6.04E
111 R5 **Strasswalchen** Salzburg, C Austria 47.59N 13.19E
12 F16 **Stratford** Ontario, S Canada 43.22N 81.00W
192 K10 **Stratford** Taranaki, North Island, NZ 39.20S 174.15E
37 Q11 **Stratford** California, W USA 36.10N 119.47W
31 V13 **Stratford** Iowa, C USA 42.16N 93.55W
29 O12 **Stratford** Oklahoma, C USA 34.48N 96.57W
27 N1 **Stratford** Texas, SW USA 36.20N 102.04W
32 K6 **Stratford** Wisconsin, N USA 44.53N 90.13W
Stratford *see* Stratford-upon-Avon
99 M20 **Stratford-upon-Avon** *var.* Stratford. C England, UK 52.12N 1.40W
191 O17 **Strathgordon** Tasmania, SE Australia 42.49S 146.04E
9 Q16 **Strathmore** Alberta, SW Canada 51.04N 113.19W
37 R11 **Strathmore** California, W USA 36.07N 119.04W
12 E16 **Strathroy** Ontario, S Canada 42.57N 81.40W
98 I6 **Strathy Point** *headland* N Scotland, UK 58.36N 4.04W
39 W4 **Stratton** Colorado, C USA 39.16N 102.34W
21 P6 **Stratton** Maine, NE USA 45.08N 70.25W
20 M10 **Stratton Mountain** ▲ Vermont, NE USA 43.05N 72.55W
103 N21 **Straubing** Bayern, SE Germany 48.52N 12.34E
102 O12 **Strausberg** Brandenburg, E Germany 52.34N 13.52E
34 K13 **Strawberry Mountain** ▲ Oregon, NW USA 44.18N 118.43W
31 X12 **Strawberry Point** Iowa, C USA 42.40N 91.31W
38 M3 **Strawberry Reservoir** ⊠ Utah, W USA
38 M4 **Strawberry River** Utah, W USA
27 R7 **Strawn** Texas, SW USA 32.33N 98.30W
115 P17 **Straža** ▲ Bulgaria/FYR Macedonia 42.16N 22.13E
113 I19 **Strážov** *Hung.* Sztrazsó. ▲ NW Slovakia 48.59N 18.29E
190 F7 **Streaky Bay** South Australia 32.49S 134.13E
190 E7 **Streaky Bay** *bay* South Australia
32 L12 **Streator** Illinois, N USA 41.07N 88.50W
Streckenbach *see* Świdnik
113 C17 **Středočeský kraj** ◆ *region* C Czech Republic
Strednogorie *see* Pirdop
31 O6 **Streeter** North Dakota, N USA 46.37N 99.23W
27 U8 **Streetman** Texas, SW USA 31.52N 96.19W
118 G13 **Strehaia** Mehedinţi, SW Romania 44.37N 23.10E
Strehlen *see* Strzelin
116 I10 **Strelcha** Pazardzhik, C Bulgaria 42.28N 24.21E
126 I13 **Strelka** Krasnoyarskiy Kray, C Russian Federation 58.04N 92.54E
128 L6 **Strel'na** NW Russian Federation
120 H7 **Strenči** *Ger.* Stackeln. Valka, N Latvia 57.38N 25.42E
110 K8 **Strengen** Tirol, W Austria 47.07N 10.25E
108 C6 **Stresa** Piemonte, NE Italy 45.52N 8.32E
Streshin *see* Streshyn
121 N18 **Streshyn** *Rus.* Streshin. Homyel'skaya Voblasts', SE Belarus 52.42N 30.08E
97 B18 **Streymoy** *Dan.* Strømø *Island* Faeroe Islands 62.10N 7.05W
126 Gg11 **Strezhevoy** Tomskaya Oblast', C Russian Federation 60.39N 77.37E
97 G23 **Strib** Fyn, C Denmark 55.33N 9.46E
113 A17 **Stříbro** *Ger.* Mies. Plzeňský Kraj, W Czech Republic 49.44N 12.55E
194 E13 **Strickland** SW PNG
Striegau *see* Strzegom
Strigonium *see* Esztergom
100 H13 **Strijen** Zuid-Holland, SW Netherlands 51.45N 4.34E
65 H21 **Strobel, Lago** ◎ S Argentina
63 B25 **Stroeder** Buenos Aires, E Argentina 40.10S 62.34W
117 C20 **Strofádes** *island* Iónioi Nísoi, Greece, C Mediterranean Sea
Strofilia *see* Strofyliá
117 G17 **Strofyliá** *var.* Strofilia. Évvoia, C Greece 38.49N 23.25E
102 O10 **Strom** NE Germany
109 L22 **Stromboli** ☒ Isola Stromboli, SW Italy 38.48N 15.13E
109 L22 **Stromboli, Isola** *island* Isole Eolie, S Italy
98 H9 **Stromeferry** N Scotland, UK 57.20N 5.34W
98 J5 **Stromness** N Scotland, UK 58.57N 3.18W
96 N11 **Strömsbruk** Gävleborg, C Sweden 61.52N 17.19E
31 Q15 **Stromsburg** Nebraska, C USA 41.06N 97.36W
97 K21 **Strömsnäsbruk** Kronoberg, S Sweden 56.34N 13.45E
97 I17 **Strömstad** Västra Götaland, S Sweden 58.55N 11.10E
95 G16 **Strömsund** Jämtland, C Sweden 63.51N 15.34E
95 G15 **Ströms Vattudal** *valley* N Sweden
29 V14 **Strong** Arkansas, C USA 33.06N 92.19W
Strongilí *see* Strongylí
109 O21 **Strongoli** Calabria, SW Italy 39.17N 17.03E
33 T11 **Strongsville** Ohio, N USA 41.18N 81.50W
117 Q23 **Strongylí** *var.* Strongilí. *island* SE Greece
98 K5 **Stronsay** *island* NE Scotland, UK
99 L21 **Stroud** C England, UK 51.45N 2.15W
29 O10 **Stroud** Oklahoma, C USA 35.45N 96.39W
20 I14 **Stroudsburg** Pennsylvania, NE USA 40.59N 75.12W
97 F21 **Struer** Ringkøbing, W Denmark 56.28N 8.37E
115 M20 **Struga** SW FYR Macedonia 41.11N 20.40E
Strugi-Kranyse *see* Strugi-Krasnyye
128 G14 **Strugi-Krasnyye** *var.* Strugi-Kranyse. Pskovskaya Oblast', W Russian Federation 58.19N 29.09E
116 G11 **Struma** *Gk.* Strymónas. Bulgaria/Greece *see also* Strymónas
99 G21 **Strumble Head** *headland* SW Wales, UK 52.01N 5.05W
115 Q19 **Strumeshnitsa** | *Mac.* Strumica. Bulgaria/FYR Macedonia
115 Q19 **Strumica** E FYR Macedonia 41.27N 22.39E
Strumica *see* Strumeshnitsa
116 G11 **Strumyani** Blagoevgrad, SW Bulgaria 41.41N 23.13E
33 V12 **Struthers** Ohio, N USA 41.03N 80.36W
116 I10 **Stryama** C Bulgaria
116 G13 **Strymónas** *Bul.* Struma. Bulgaria/Greece *see also* Struma
117 H14 **Strymonikós Kólpos** *gulf* N Greece
118 I6 **Stryy** L'vivs'ka Oblast', NW Ukraine 49.16N 23.51E
118 H6 **Stryy** W Ukraine
113 F14 **Strzegom** *Ger.* Striegau. Wałbrzych, SW Poland 50.58N 16.19E
112 E10 **Strzelce Krajeńskie** *Ger.* Friedeberg Neumark. Lubuskie, W Poland 52.52N 15.30E
113 I15 **Strzelce Opolskie** *Ger.* Gross Strehlitz. Opolskie, S Poland 50.31N 18.19E
190 K3 **Strzelecki Creek** *seasonal river* South Australia
190 J3 **Strzelecki Desert** *desert* South Australia
113 G15 **Strzelin** *Ger.* Strehlen. Dolnośląskie, SW Poland 50.46N 17.03E
112 I11 **Strzelno** Kujawsko-pomorskie, C Poland 52.38N 18.11E
113 N17 **Strzyżów** Podkarpackie, SE Poland 49.52N 21.46E
Stua Laighean *see* Leinster, Mount
25 Y13 **Stuart** Florida, SE USA 27.12N 80.15W
31 U14 **Stuart** Iowa, C USA 41.30N 94.19W
31 O13 **Stuart** Nebraska, C USA 42.36N 99.08W
23 S8 **Stuart** Virginia, NE USA 36.38N 80.16W
8 L13 **Stuart** British Columbia, SW Canada
41 N10 **Stuart Island** *island* Alaska, USA
8 L13 **Stuart Lake** ◎ British Columbia, SW Canada
193 B22 **Stuart Mountains** ▲▲ South Island, NZ
190 F3 **Stuart Range** *hill range* South Australia
Stubaital *see* Neustift im Stubaital
97 I24 **Stubbekøbing** Storstrøm, SE Denmark 54.52N 12.04E
47 P14 **Stubbs** Saint Vincent, Saint Vincent and the Grenadines 13.08N 61.09W
111 V6 **Stübming** E Austria
116 J11 **Studen Kladenets, Yazovir** ⊠ S Bulgaria
193 G21 **Studholme** Canterbury, South Island, NZ 44.44S 171.07E
Stuhlweissenberg *see* Székesfehérvár
Stuhm *see* Sztum
10 C7 **Stull Lake** ◎ Ontario, C Canada
Stung Treng *see* Stœng Trêng
130 L4 **Stupino** Moskovskaya Oblast', W Russian Federation 54.54N 38.06E
29 U4 **Sturgeon** Missouri, C USA 39.13N 92.16W
12 G10 **Sturgeon** Ontario, S Canada
33 N6 **Sturgeon Bay** Wisconsin, N USA 44.51N 87.21W
12 G11 **Sturgeon Falls** Ontario, S Canada 46.22N 79.57W
10 C11 **Sturgeon Lake** ◎ Ontario, S Canada
32 M3 **Sturgeon River** Michigan, N USA
22 H6 **Sturgis** Kentucky, S USA 37.33N 87.58W
33 P11 **Sturgis** Michigan, N USA 41.48N 85.25W
30 J9 **Sturgis** South Dakota, N USA 44.24N 103.30W
114 D10 **Šturlić** Federacija Bosna I Hercegovina, NW Bosnia and Herzegovina 45.03N 15.47E
113 J22 **Štúrovo** *Hung.* Párkány; *prev.* Parkan. Nitriansky Kraj, W Slovakia 47.49N 18.44E
190 L4 **Sturt, Mount** *hill* New South Wales, SE Australia 29.30S 141.41E
189 P4 **Sturt Plain** *plain* Northern Territory, N Australia
189 T9 **Sturt Stony Desert** *desert* South Australia
85 J25 **Stutterheim** Eastern Cape, S South Africa 32.34S 27.25E
103 H21 **Stuttgart** Baden-Württemberg, SW Germany 48.47N 9.12E
29 W12 **Stuttgart** Arkansas, C USA 34.30N 91.33W
94 H2 **Stykkishólmur** Vesturland, W Iceland 65.03N 22.43W
117 F17 **Stylída** *var.* Stilida, Stilís. Stereá Ellás, C Greece 38.55N 22.37E
118 K2 **Styr** *Rus.* Styr'. Belarus/Ukraine
117 I19 **Stýra** *var.* Stira. Évvoia, C Greece 38.10N 24.13E
Styria *see* Steiermark
Su *see* Jiangsu
Sua *see* Sowa
175 S17 **Suai** W East Timor 9.19S 125.16E
56 G9 **Suaita** Santander, C Colombia 6.07N 73.30W
82 I7 **Suakin** *var.* Sawakin. Red Sea, NE Sudan 19.06N 37.17E
167 T13 **Suao** *Jap.* Suō. N Taiwan 24.33N 121.48E
Suao *see* Suau
42 G6 **Suaqui Grande** Sonora, NW Mexico 28.22N 109.52W
63 A16 **Suardi** Santa Fe, C Argentina 30.31S 61.58W
56 D11 **Suárez** Cauca, SW Colombia 2.55N 76.40W
195 N17 **Suau** *var.* Suao. Suaul Island, SE PNG 10.44S 150.18E
120 G12 **Subačius** Kupiškis, NE Lithuania 55.46N 24.45E
174 Jj14 **Subang** *prev.* Soebang. Jawa, C Indonesia 6.31S 107.45E
174 Gg5 **Subang** ✈ (Kuala Lumpur) Pahang, Peninsular Malaysia
133 S10 **Subansiri** NE India
120 I11 **Subate** Daugvapils, SE Latvia 56.00N 25.54E
145 N5 **Subaykhān** Dayr az Zawr, E Syria 34.47N 40.38E
165 P8 **Subei** *var.* Dangchengwan, Subei Mongolzu Zizhixian. Gansu, N China 39.33N 94.50E
Subei Mongolzu Zizhixian *see* Subei
174 K5 **Subi Besar, Pulau** *island* Kepulauan Natuna, W Indonesia
Subiyah *see* Aş Şubayḩīyah
28 I7 **Sublette** Kansas, C USA 37.26N 100.48W
114 K8 **Subotica** *Ger.* Maria-Theresiopel, *Hung.* Szabadka. Serbia, N Yugoslavia 46.06N 19.40E
118 K9 **Suceava** *Ger.* Suczawa, *Hung.* Szucsava. Suceava, NE Romania 47.40N 26.15E
118 J9 **Suceava** ◆ *county* NE Romania
118 K9 **Suceava** *Ger.* Suczawa. N Romania
114 E12 **Sučevići** Zadar, SW Croatia 44.13N 16.04E
113 K17 **Sucha Beskidzka** Małopolskie, S Poland 49.39N 19.11E
113 M14 **Suchedniów** Świętokrzyskie, C Poland 51.01N 20.49E
44 A2 **Suchitepéquez** *off.* Departamento de Suchitepéquez. ◆ *department* SW Guatemala
Su-chou *see* Suzhou
Suchow *see* Suzhou, Jiangsu, China
Suchow *see* Xuzhou, Jiangsu, China
99 D17 **Suck** C Ireland
Sucker State *see* Illinois
194 M16 **Suckling, Mount** ▲ S PNG 9.36S 149.00E
59 L19 **Sucre** *hist.* Chuquisaca, La Plata. ● (Bolivia-legal capital) Chuquisaca, S Bolivia 18.52S 65.24W
56 E6 **Sucre** Santander, N Colombia 8.50N 74.22W
58 A7 **Sucre** Manabí, W Ecuador 1.21S 80.27W
56 E6 **Sucre** *off.* Departamento de Sucre. ◆ *province* N Colombia
57 O5 **Sucre** *off.* Estado Sucre. ◆ *state* NE Venezuela
58 D6 **Sucumbíos** ◆ *province* NE Ecuador
115 G15 **Sućuraj** Split-Dalmacija, S Croatia 43.07N 17.10E
60 K10 **Sucuriju** Amapá, NE Brazil 1.30N 50.00W
Suczawa *see* Suceava
81 E16 **Sud** *Eng.* South. ◆ *province* S Cameroon
128 K13 **Suda** NW Russian Federation
Suda *see* Soúda
119 U13 **Sudak** Respublika Krym, S Ukraine 44.51N 34.55E
26 M4 **Sudan** Texas, SW USA 34.04N 102.31W
82 C10 **Sudan** *off.* Republic of Sudan, *Ar.* Jumhuriyat as-Sudan; *prev.* Anglo-Egyptian *Sudan.* ◆ *republic* N Africa
Sudanese Republic *see* Mali
Sudan, Jumhuriyat as- *see* Sudan
12 F10 **Sudbury** Ontario, S Canada 46.29N 80.59W
99 P20 **Sudbury** E England, UK 52.04N 0.43E
Sud, Canal de *see* Gonâve, Canal de la
82 E13 **Sudd** *swamp region* S Sudan
102 K10 **Sude** N Germany
Sudest Island *see* Tagula Island
113 E15 **Sudeten** *var.* Sudetes, Sudetic Mountains, *Cz./Pol.* Sudety. ▲▲ Czech Republic/Poland
Sudetes/Sudetic Mountains/Sudety *see* Sudeten
94 G1 **Sudhureyri** Vestfirdhir, NW Iceland 66.08N 23.31W
94 J4 **Sudhurland** ◆ *region* S Iceland
97 B19 **Sudhuroy** *Dan.* Suderø *Island* Faeroe Islands 61.60N 6.29W
176 Xx12 **Sudirman, Pegunungan** ▲▲ Irian Jaya, E Indonesia
128 M15 **Sudislavl'** Kostromskaya Oblast', NW Russian Federation 57.55N 41.45E
Südkarpaten *see* Carpaţii Meridionali
81 N20 **Sud Kivu** *off.* Région Sud Kivu. ◆ *region* E Dem. Rep. Congo (Zaire)
Südliche Morava *see* Južna Morava
102 E12 **Süd-Nord-Kanal** *canal* NW Germany
130 M3 **Sudogda** Vladimirskaya Oblast', W Russian Federation 55.58N 40.57E
Sudostroy *see* Severodvinsk
81 C15 **Sud-Ouest** *Eng.* South-West. ◆ *province* W Cameroon
181 X17 **Sud Ouest, Pointe** *headland* SW Mauritius 20.27S 57.18E
197 J7 **Sud, Province** ◆ *province* S New Caledonia
130 J8 **Sudzha** Kurskaya Oblast', W Russian Federation 51.12N 35.19E
83 D15 **Sue** S Sudan
107 S10 **Sueca** País Valenciano, E Spain 39.13N 0.19W
116 I10 **Sŭedinenie** Plovdiv, C Bulgaria 42.14N 24.36E
Suero *see* Alzira
77 X8 **Suez** *Ar.* As Suways, El Suweis. NE Egypt 29.58N 32.33E
77 W7 **Suez Canal** *Ar.* Qanāt as Suways. *canal* NE Egypt
77 X8 **Suez, Gulf of** *Ar.* Khalīj as Suways. *gulf* NE Egypt
9 R17 **Suffield** Alberta, SW Canada 50.15N 111.05W
23 X7 **Suffolk** Virginia, NE USA 36.43N 76.34W
99 P20 **Suffolk** *cultural region* E England, UK
148 J2 **Şūfīān** Āžarbāyjān-e Khāvarī, N Iran 38.15N 45.58E
33 N12 **Sugar Creek** Illinois, N USA
32 L13 **Sugar Creek** Illinois, N USA
33 R3 **Sugar Island** *island* Michigan, N USA
27 V11 **Sugar Land** Texas, SW USA 29.37N 95.37W
21 P6 **Sugarloaf Mountain** ▲ Maine, NE USA 45.01N 70.18W
67 G24 **Sugar Loaf Point** *headland* N Saint Helena 15.54S 5.43W
142 G16 **Suğla Gölü** ◎ SW Turkey
127 O8 **Sugoy** E Russian Federation
164 F7 **Sugun** Xinjiang Uygur Zizhiqu, W China 39.46N 76.45E
153 U11 **Sugut, Gora** ▲ SW Kyrgyzstan 39.52N 73.36E
175 O2 **Sugut, Sungai** East Malaysia
165 O9 **Suhai Hu** ◎ C China
168 K14 **Suhait** Nei Mongol Zizhiqu, N China 39.29N 105.11E
147 X7 **Şuḩār** *var.* Sohar. N Oman 24.20N 56.43E
168 L6 **Sühbaatar** Selenge, N Mongolia 50.11N 106.14E
169 P9 **Sühbaatar** ◆ *province* E Mongolia
103 K17 **Suhl** Thüringen, C Germany 50.37N 10.43E
110 F7 **Suhr** Aargau, N Switzerland 47.22N 8.04E
167 O12 **Suichuan** Jiangxi, S China 26.18N 114.31E
Suid-Afrika *see* South Africa
166 L4 **Suide** Shaanxi, C China 37.30N 110.10E
Suidwes-Afrika *see* Namibia
169 Y9 **Suifenhe** Heilongjiang, NE China 44.22N 131.12E
Suigen *see* Suwŏn
169 W8 **Suihua** Heilongjiang, NE China 46.40N 127.00E
Súilí, Loch *see* Swilly, Lough
167 Q6 **Suining** Jiangsu, E China 33.54N 117.58E
166 I9 **Suining** Sichuan, C China 30.31N 105.33E
105 Q4 **Suippes** Marne, N France 49.08N 4.31E
99 E20 **Suir** *Ir.* An tSiúir. S Ireland
171 Gg15 **Suita** Ōsaka, Honshū, SW Japan 34.39N 135.27E
166 L16 **Suixi** Guangdong, S China 21.22N 110.13E
Sui Xian *see* Suizhou
169 T13 **Suizhong** Liaoning, NE China 40.19N 120.20E
167 N8 **Suizhou** *prev.* Sui Xian. Hubei, C China 31.46N 113.20E
155 P17 **Sujāwal** Sind, SE Pakistan 24.36N 68.06E
174 Jj14 **Sukabumi** *prev.* Soekaboemi. Jawa, C Indonesia 6.55S 106.55E
174 Kk9 **Sukadana, Teluk** *bay* Borneo, W Indonesia
171 Ll14 **Sukagawa** Fukushima, Honshū, C Japan 37.16N 140.19E
Sukarnapura *see* Jayapura
Sukarno, Puntjak *see* Jaya, Puncak
153 R11 **Sŭkh** *Rus.* Sokh. Farghona Wiloyati, E Uzbekistan 39.56N 71.10E
Sŭkh *see* Sokh
116 N8 **Sukha Reka** NE Bulgaria
130 J5 **Sukhinichi** Kaluzhskaya Oblast', W Russian Federation 54.06N 35.22E
Sukhne *see* As Sukhnah
133 Q4 **Sukhona** *var.* Tot'ma. NW Russian Federation
178 H9 **Sukhothai** *var.* Sukotai. Sukhothai, W Thailand 17.00N 99.51E
Sukhumi *see* Sokhumi
Sukkertoppen *see* Maniitsoq
155 Q13 **Sukkur** Sind, SE Pakistan 27.44N 68.46E
Sukotai *see* Sukhothai
Sukra Bay *see* Şawqirah, Dawḩat
129 V15 **Suksun** Permskaya Oblast', NW Russian Federation 57.10N 57.27E
170 E16 **Sukumo** Kōchi, Shikoku, SW Japan 32.55N 132.42E
96 B12 **Sula** *island* S Norway
129 Q5 **Sula** NW Russian Federation
119 R5 **Sula** N Ukraine
44 H6 **Sulaco, Río** NW Honduras
Sulaimaniya *see* As Sulaymānīyah
155 S10 **Sulaimān Range** ▲▲ C Pakistan
131 Q16 **Sulak** Respublika Dagestan, SW Russian Federation 43.19N 47.28E
131 Q16 **Sulak** SW Russian Federation
175 Rr10 **Sula, Kepulauan** *island group* C Indonesia
142 I12 **Sulakyurt** *var.* Konur. Kırıkkale, N Turkey 40.10N 33.42E
175 R17 **Sulamu** Timor, S Indonesia 9.57S 123.33E
98 F5 **Sula Sgeir** *island* NW Scotland, UK
175 Pp10 **Sulawesi** *Eng.* Celebes. *island* C Indonesia
Sulawesi, Laut *see* Celebes Sea
175 P11 **Sulawesi Selatan** *off.* Propinsi Sulawesi Selatan, *Eng.* South Celebes, South Sulawesi. ◆ *province* C Indonesia
175 Q9 **Sulawesi Tengah** *off.* Propinsi Sulawesi Tengah, *Eng.* Central Celebes, Central Sulawesi. ◆ *province* N Indonesia
175 Q11 **Sulawesi Tenggara** *off.* Propinsi Sulawesi Tenggara, *Eng.* South-East Celebes, South-East Sulawesi. ◆ *province* C Indonesia
175 Qq7 **Sulawesi Utara** *off.* Propinsi Sulawesi Utara, *Eng.* North Celebes, North Sulawesi. ◆ *province* N Indonesia
145 T5 **Sulaymān Beg** N Iraq
97 D15 **Suldalsvatnet** ◎ S Norway
112 E12 **Sulechów** *Ger.* Züllichau. Lubuskie, W Poland 52.04N 15.37E
112 E11 **Sulęcin** Lubuskie, W Poland 52.29N 15.06E
79 U14 **Suleja** Niger, C Nigeria 9.15N 7.10E
113 K14 **Sulejów** Łodzkie, S Poland 51.21N 19.57E
98 I5 **Sule Skerry** *island* N Scotland, UK
Suliag *see* Sohâg
78 J16 **Sulima** S Sierra Leone 6.58N 11.34W
119 O13 **Sulina** Tulcea, SE Romania 45.07N 29.40E
119 N13 **Sulina Braţul** SE Romania
102 H12 **Sulingen** Niedersachsen, NW Germany 52.40N 8.48E
94 H12 **Suliskongen** ▲ C Norway 67.10N 16.16E
94 H12 **Sulitjelma** Nordland, C Norway 67.09N 15.59E
58 A9 **Sullana** Piura, NW Peru 4.54S 80.42W
25 N3 **Sulligent** Alabama, S USA 33.54N 88.07W
32 M14 **Sullivan** Illinois, N USA 39.36N 88.36W
33 N15 **Sullivan** Indiana, N USA 39.04N 87.24W
29 W5 **Sullivan** Missouri, C USA 38.12N 91.09W
Sullivan Island *see* Lanbi Kyun
98 M1 **Sullom Voe** NE Scotland, UK 60.24N 1.09W
105 O7 **Sully-sur-Loire** Loiret, C France 47.46N 2.21E
Sulmo *see* Sulmona
109 K15 **Sulmona** *anc.* Sulmo. Abruzzo, C Italy 42.03N 13.55E
Sulo *see* Shule He
116 M11 **Süloğlu** Edirne, NW Turkey 41.46N 26.55E
24 G9 **Sulphur** Louisiana, S USA 30.14N 93.22W
29 O12 **Sulphur** Oklahoma, C USA 34.30N 96.58W
30 K9 **Sulphur Creek** South Dakota, N USA
26 M5 **Sulphur Draw** Texas, SW USA
27 W5 **Sulphur River** Arkansas/Texas, SW USA
27 V6 **Sulphur Springs** Texas, SW USA 33.09N 95.36W
26 M6 **Sulphur Springs Draw** Texas, SW USA
12 D8 **Sultan** Ontario, S Canada 47.34N 82.45W
Sultānābād *see* Arāk
Sultan Alonto, Lake *see* Lanao, Lake
142 G15 **Sultan Dağları** ▲▲ C Turkey
116 N13 **Sultanköy** Tekirdağ, NW Turkey 41.01N 27.58E
179 R16 **Sultan Kudarat** *var.* Nuling. Mindanao, S Philippines 7.20N 124.16E
158 M13 **Sultānpur** Uttar Pradesh, N India 26.15N 82.04E
179 Pp17 **Sulu Archipelago** *island group* SW Philippines
198 Ff7 **Sulu Basin** *undersea feature* SE South China Sea
Sülüktü *see* Sulyukta
Sulu, Laut *see* Sulu Sea
175 Pp1 **Sulu Sea** *Ind.* Laut Sulu. *sea* SW Philippines
151 O15 **Sulutobe** *Kaz.* Sulūtöbe. Kzylorda, S Kazakhstan 44.31N 66.17E
153 Q11 **Sulyukta** *Kir.* Sülüktü. Oshskaya Oblast', SW Kyrgyzstan 39.57N 69.30E
Sulz *see* Sulz am Neckar
103 G22 **Sulz am Neckar** *var.* Sulz. Baden-Württemberg, SW Germany 48.22N 8.37E
103 L20 **Sulzbach-Rosenberg** Bayern, SE Germany 49.30N 11.43E
205 N13 **Sulzberger Bay** *bay* Antarctica
Sumail *see* Summēl
115 F15 **Sumartin** Split-Dalmacija, S Croatia 43.17N 16.52E
34 H6 **Sumas** Washington, NW USA 49.00N 122.15W
174 Gg7 **Sumatera** *Eng.* Sumatra. *island* W Indonesia
173 G9 **Sumatera Barat** *off.* Propinsi Sumatera Barat, *Eng.* West Sumatra. ◆ *province* W Indonesia
174 Hh11 **Sumatera Selatan** *off.* Propinsi Sumatera Selatan, *Eng.* South Sumatra. ◆ *province* W Indonesia
173 Ff6 **Sumatera Utara** *off.* Propinsi Sumatera Utara, *Eng.* North Sumatra. ◆ *province* W Indonesia
Sumatra *see* Sumatera
Šumava *see* Bohemian Forest
Sumayl *see* Summēl
145 U7 **Sumayr al Muḩammad** E Iraq 33.34N 45.06E
175 P17 **Sumba, Pulau** *Eng.* Sandalwood Island; *prev.* Soemba. *island* Nusa Tenggara, C Indonesia
152 D12 **Sumbar** W Turkmenistan
175 P16 **Sumba, Selat** *strait* Nusa Tenggara, S Indonesia
175 Oo16 **Sumbawa** *prev.* Soembawa. *island* Nusa Tenggara, C Indonesia
175 O16 **Sumbawabesar** Sumbawa, S Indonesia 8.30S 117.25E
83 F23 **Sumbawanga** Rukwa, W Tanzania 7.57S 31.36E
84 B12 **Sumbe** *prev.* N'Gunza, *Port.* Novo Redondo. Cuanza Sul, W Angola 11.13S 13.52E
98 M3 **Sumburgh Head** *headland* NE Scotland, UK 59.51N 1.16W
113 H23 **Sümeg** Veszprém, W Hungary 47.00N 17.13E
82 C12 **Sumeih** Southern Darfur, S Sudan 9.49N 27.39E
174 Mm14 **Sumenep** *prev.* Soemenep. Pulau Madura, C Indonesia 7.01S 113.51E
Sumgait *see* Sumqayıt, Azerbaijan
Sumgait *see* Sumqayıtçay, Azerbaijan
172 Ss14 **Sumisu-jima** *Eng.* Smith Island. *island* SE Japan
145 Q2 **Summēl** *var.* Sumail, Sumayl. N Iraq 36.52N 42.51E
33 O5 **Summer Island** *island* Michigan, N USA
34 H15 **Summer Lake** ◎ Oregon, NW USA
9 N17 **Summerland** British Columbia, SW Canada 49.34N 119.45W
11 P14 **Summerside** Prince Edward Island, SE Canada 46.24N 63.46W
23 R5 **Summersville** West Virginia, NE USA 38.16N 80.51W
23 R5 **Summersville Lake** ⊠ West Virginia, NE USA
23 S13 **Summerton** South Carolina, SE USA 33.36N 80.21W
25 R2 **Summerville** Georgia, SE USA 34.28N 85.21W
23 S14 **Summerville** South Carolina, SE USA 33.01N 80.10W
41 R10 **Summit** Alaska, USA 63.21N 148.50W
37 V6 **Summit Mountain** ▲ Nevada, W USA 39.23N 116.25W
39 R8 **Summit Peak** ▲ Colorado, C USA 37.21N 106.42W
Summus Portus *see* Somport, Col du
31 X12 **Sumner** Iowa, C USA 42.51N 92.05W
24 K3 **Sumner** Mississippi, S USA 33.58N 90.22W
193 H17 **Sumner, Lake** ◎ South Island, NZ
39 U12 **Sumner, Lake** ⊠ New Mexico, SW USA
171 Kk13 **Sumon-dake** ▲ Honshū, C Japan 37.24N 139.07E
170 G15 **Sumoto** Hyōgo, Awaji-shima, SW Japan 34.18N 134.52E
113 G17 **Šumperk** *Ger.* Mährisch-Schönberg. Olomoucký Kraj, E Czech Republic 49.59N 16.58E
44 F7 **Sumpul, Río** El Salvador/Honduras
143 Z11 **Sumqayıt** *Rus.* Sumgait. E Azerbaijan 40.33N 49.41E
143 Y11 **Sumqayıtçay** *Rus.* Sumgait. E Azerbaijan
153 R9 **Sumsar** Dzhalal-Abadskaya Oblast', W Kyrgyzstan 41.12N 71.16E
119 S3 **Sums'ka Oblast'** *var.* Sumy, *Rus.* Sumskaya Oblast'. ◆ *province* NE Ukraine
Sumskaya Oblast' *see* Sums'ka Oblast'
128 J8 **Sumskiy Posad** Respublika Kareliya, NW Russian Federation 64.12N 35.22E
23 S12 **Sumter** South Carolina, SE USA 33.55N 80.20W
119 T3 **Sumy** Sums'ka Oblast', NE Ukraine 50.54N 34.48E
Sumy *see* Sums'ka Oblast'
165 Q15 **Sumzom** Xizang Zizhiqu, W China 29.45N 96.13E
129 R15 **Suna** Kirovskaya Oblast', NW Russian Federation 57.53N 50.04E
128 I10 **Suna** NW Russian Federation
172 Oo5 **Sunagawa** Hokkaidō, NE Japan 43.30N 141.55E
159 V13 **Sunamganj** Chittagong, NE Bangladesh 25.04N 91.24E
165 S8 **Sunan** *var.* Hongwan, Sunan Yugurzu Zizhixian. Gansu, N China 38.55N 99.29E
169 W14 **Sunan** ✈ (P'yŏngyang) SW North Korea 39.12N 125.40E
Sunan Yugurzu Zizhixian *see* Sunan
21 N9 **Sunapee Lake** ◎ New Hampshire, NE USA
145 P4 **Sunaysilah** *salt marsh* N Iraq
22 M8 **Sunbright** Tennessee, S USA 36.12N 84.39W
35 R6 **Sunburst** Montana, NW USA 48.51N 111.54W
191 N12 **Sunbury** Victoria, SE Australia 37.36S 144.42E
23 X8 **Sunbury** North Carolina, SE USA 36.27N 76.34W
20 G14 **Sunbury** Pennsylvania, NE USA 40.51N 76.47W
63 A17 **Sunchales** Santa Fe, C Argentina 30.58S 61.34W
169 W13 **Sunch'ŏn** SW North Korea 39.28N 125.58E
169 Y16 **Sunch'ŏn** *Jap.* Junten. S South Korea 34.56N 127.28E
38 K13 **Sun City** Arizona, SW USA 33.36N 112.16W
21 O9 **Suncook** New Hampshire, NE USA 43.07N 71.25W
Sunda Islands *see* Greater Sunda Islands
35 Z12 **Sundance** Wyoming, C USA 44.24N 104.22W
159 T17 **Sundarbans** *wetland* Bangladesh/India
160 M11 **Sundargarh** Orissa, E India 22.07N 84.01E
174 Ii14 **Sunda, Selat** *strait* Jawa/Sumatera, SW Indonesia
133 U15 **Sunda Shelf** *undersea feature* S South China Sea
Sunda Trench *see* Java Trench
133 U17 **Sunda Trough** *undersea feature* E Indian Ocean
97 O16 **Sundbyberg** Stockholm, C Sweden 59.22N 17.58E
99 M14 **Sunderland** *var.* Wearmouth. NE England, UK 54.55N 1.22W
103 F15 **Sundern** Nordrhein-Westfalen, W Germany 51.19N 8.00E
142 F12 **Sündiken Dağları** ▲▲ C Turkey
26 M5 **Sundown** Texas, SW USA 33.27N 102.29W
9 P16 **Sundre** Alberta, SW Canada 51.49N 114.46W
12 H12 **Sundridge** Ontario, S Canada 45.45N 79.25W
95 H17 **Sundsvall** Västernorrland, C Sweden 62.22N 17.19E
28 H4 **Sunflower, Mount** ▲ Kansas, C USA 39.01N 102.02W
Sunflower State *see* Kansas
174 Gg4 **Sungai Bernam** Peninsular Malaysia
174 Ii12 **Sungaibuntu** Sumatera, SW Indonesia 4.04S 105.37E
174 Gg9 **Sungaidareh** Sumatera, W Indonesia 0.58S 101.30E
178 Hh17 **Sungai Kolok** *var.* Sungai Ko-Lok. Narathiwat, SW Thailand 6.01N 101.58E
174 Gg10 **Sungaipenuh** *prev.* Soengaipenoeh. Sumatera, W Indonesia 2.00S 101.28E
174 Kk8 **Sungaipinyuh** Borneo, C Indonesia 0.16N 109.06E
Sungari *see* Songhua Jiang
Sungaria *see* Dzungaria
Sungei Pahang *see* Pahang, Sungai
178 Hh8 **Sung Men** Phrae, NW Thailand 17.59N 100.07E
85 M15 **Sungo** Tete, NW Mozambique 16.31S 33.58E
174 Ii10 **Sungsang** Sumatera, W Indonesia 2.22S 104.50E
116 M9 **Sungurlare** Burgas, E Bulgaria 42.47N 26.46E
142 J12 **Sungurlu** Çorum, N Turkey 40.10N 34.22E
114 F9 **Sunja** Sisak-Moslavina, C Croatia 45.21N 16.33E
159 Q12 **Sun Koshi** E Nepal
96 F9 **Sunndalen** *valley* S Norway
96 F9 **Sunndalsøra** Møre og Romsdal, S Norway 62.40N 8.34E
97 K15 **Sunne** Värmland, C Sweden 59.52N 14.30E
97 O15 **Sunnersta** Uppsala, C Sweden 59.46N 17.40E
96 C11 **Sunnfjord** *physical region* S Norway
97 C15 **Sunnhordland** *physical region* S Norway
96 D10 **Sunnmøre** *physical region* S Norway
39 N4 **Sunnyside** Utah, W USA 39.33N 110.23W
34 J10 **Sunnyside** Washington, NW USA 46.01N 119.58W
37 N9 **Sunnyvale** California, W USA 37.22N 122.02W
32 L8 **Sun Prairie** Wisconsin, N USA 43.12N 89.12W
Sunqur *see* Sonqor
27 N1 **Sunray** Texas, SW USA 36.01N 101.49W
24 I8 **Sunset** Louisiana, S USA 30.24N 92.04W
27 S5 **Sunset** Texas, SW USA 33.24N 97.45W
Sunset State *see* Oregon
189 Z10 **Sunshine Coast** *cultural region* Queensland, E Australia
Sunshine State *see* Florida, USA
Sunshine State *see* New Mexico, USA
Sunshine State *see* South Dakota, USA
126 Kk11 **Suntar** Respublika Sakha (Yakutiya), NE Russian Federation 62.09N 117.34E
41 R10 **Suntrana** Alaska, USA 63.51N 148.51W
154 J15 **Suntsar** Baluchistān, SW Pakistan 25.30N 62.03E
169 W15 **Sunwi-do** *island* SW North Korea
169 W6 **Sunwu** Heilongjiang, NE China 49.23N 127.17E
79 O16 **Sunyani** W Ghana 7.22N 2.18W
Suō *see* Suao
95 M17 **Suolahti** Länsi-Suomi, W Finland 62.32N 25.51E
Suoločielgi *see* Saariselkä
Suomenlahti *see* Finland, Gulf of
Suomen Tasavalta/Suomi *see* Finland
95 N14 **Suomussalmi** Oulu, E Finland 64.54N 29.05E
170 D13 **Suō-nada** *sea* SW Japan
95 M17 **Suonenjoki** Itä-Suomi, C Finland 62.36N 27.06E
178 Jj13 **Suŏng** Kâmpóng Cham, C Cambodia 11.53N 105.41E
128 I10 **Suoyarvi** Respublika Kareliya, NW Russian Federation 62.01N 32.24E
Supanburi *see* Suphan Buri
59 D14 **Supe** Lima, W Peru 10.49S 77.42W
13 V7 **Supérieur, Lac** ◎ Quebec, SE Canada
Supérieur, Lac *see* Superior, Lake
38 M14 **Superior** Arizona, SW USA 33.17N 111.06W
35 O9 **Superior** Montana, NW USA 47.11N 114.53W
31 P17 **Superior** Nebraska, C USA 40.01N 98.04W
32 I3 **Superior** Wisconsin, N USA 46.41N 92.03W
43 S17 **Superior, Laguna** *lagoon* S Mexico
33 N2 **Superior, Lake** *Fr.* Lac Supérieur. ◎ Canada/USA
38 L13 **Superstition Mountains** ▲▲ Arizona, SW USA
115 F14 **Supetar** *It.* San Pietro. Split-Dalmacija, S Croatia 43.22N 16.34E
178 H11 **Suphan Buri** *var.* Supanburi. Suphan Buri, W Thailand 14.28N 100.10E
176 W9 **Supiori, Pulau** *island* E Indonesia
196 K2 **Supply Reef** *reef* N Northern Mariana Islands
205 O7 **Support Force Glacier** *glacier* Antarctica

332

◆ Country ● Country Capital ◇ Dependent Territory ○ Dependent Territory Capital ◆ Administrative Region ✈ International Airport ▲ Mountain ▲▲ Mountain Range ☒ Volcano River ◎ Lake ⊠ Reservoir

Sup'sa – Tacna

143 R10 **Sup'sa** *var.* Supsa. ≈ W Georgia
Sūq 'Abs *see* 'Abs
145 W12 **Sūq ash Shuyūkh** SE Iraq *30.52N 46.28E*
144 H4 **Şuqaylibīyah** Ḩamāh, W Syria *35.21N 36.24E*
167 Q6 **Suqian** Jiangsu, E China *33.57N 118.18E*
Suqrah *see* Şawqirah
Suqrah Bay *see* Şawqirah, Dawḩat
147 V16 **Suquţrā** *var.* Sokotra, *Eng.* Socotra. *island* SE Yemen
147 Z8 **Şūr** NE Oman *22.32N 59.33E*
Şūr *see* Soûr
131 P5 **Sura** Penzenskaya Oblast', W Russian Federation *53.23N 45.03E*
131 P4 **Sura** ≈ W Russian Federation
155 N12 **Sūrāb** Baluchistān, SW Pakistan *28.28N 66.15E*
Surabaja *see* Surabaya
174 M15 **Surabaya** *prev.* Soerabaja, Surabaja. Jawa, C Indonesia *7.13S 112.45E*
97 N15 **Surahammar** Västmanland, C Sweden *59.43N 16.13E*
174 L15 **Surakarta** *Eng.* Solo; *prev.* Soerakarta. Jawa, S Indonesia *7.31S 110.49E*
Surakhany *see* Suraxanı
179 R17 **Surallah** Mindanao, S Philippines *6.16N 124.46E*
143 S10 **Surami** C Georgia *41.59N 43.36E*
149 X13 **Sūrān** Sīstān va Balūchestān, SE Iran *27.18N 61.58E*
113 I21 **Šurany** *Hung.* Nagysurány. Nitriansky Kraj, SW Slovakia *48.05N 18.10E*
160 D12 **Sūrat** Gujarāt, W India *21.10N 72.54E*
Suratdhani *see* Surat Thani
158 G9 **Sūratgarh** Rājasthān, NW India *29.19N 73.58E*
178 Gg15 **Surat Thani** *var.* Suratdhani. Surat Thani, SW Thailand *9.09N 99.19E*
121 Q16 **Suraw** *Rus.* Surov. ≈ E Belarus
143 Z11 **Suraxanı** *Rus.* Surakhany. E Azerbaijan *40.25N 49.59E*
147 Y11 **Şurayr** E Oman *19.55N 57.46E*
144 K2 **Şuraysāt** Ḩalab, N Syria *36.42N 38.01E*
120 O12 **Surazh** *Rus.* Surazh. Vitsyebskaya Voblasts', NE Belarus *55.24N 30.46E*
130 H6 **Surazh** Bryanskaya Oblast', W Russian Federation *53.04N 32.29E*
203 V17 **Sur, Cabo** *headland* Easter Island, Chile, E Pacific Ocean *27.10S 109.25W*
114 L11 **Surčin** Serbia, N Yugoslavia *44.48N 20.19E*
118 H9 **Surduc** *Hung.* Szurduk. Sălaj, NW Romania *47.13N 23.19E*
115 P16 **Surdulica** Serbia, SE Yugoslavia *42.43N 22.10E*
101 L24 **Sûre** *var.* Sauer. ≈ W Europe *see also* Sauer
160 C10 **Surendranagar** Gujarāt, W India *22.43N 71.43E*
20 K16 **Surf City** New Jersey, NE USA *39.21N 74.24W*
191 V3 **Surfers Paradise** Queensland, E Australia *27.54S 153.18E*
23 U13 **Surfside Beach** South Carolina, SE USA *33.36N 78.58W*
104 J10 **Surgères** Charente-Maritime, W France *46.07N 0.44W*
125 G11 **Surgut** Khanty-Mansiyskiy Avtonomnyy Okrug, C Russian Federation *61.13N 73.28E*
126 Hh10 **Surgutikha** Krasnoyarskiy Kray, N Russian Federation *64.44N 87.13E*
100 M6 **Surhuisterveen** Friesland, N Netherlands *53.10N 6.10E*
107 V5 **Súria** Cataluña, NE Spain *41.49N 1.45E*
149 P10 **Sūrīān** Fārs, S Iran
161 J15 **Suriāpet** Andhra Pradesh, C India *17.10N 79.42E*
179 R14 **Surigao** Mindanao, S Philippines *9.43N 125.31E*
178 Ii11 **Surin** Surin, E Thailand *14.52N 103.28E*
Suriname *see* Surinam
57 U11 **Surinam** *off.* Republic of Suriname, *var.* Surinam; *prev.* Dutch Guiana, Netherlands Guiana. ◆ *republic* N South America
Sūrīya/Sūrīyah, Al-Jumhūrīyah al-'Arabīyah as - *see* Syria
Surkhab, Darya-i- *see* Kahmard, Daryā-ye
Surkhandar'inskaya Oblast' *see* Surkhondaryo Wiloyati
Surkhandar'ya *see* Surkhondaryo
Surkhet *see* Birendranagar
153 R12 **Surkhob** ≈ C Tajikistan
153 P13 **Surkhondaryo** *Rus.* Surkhandar'ya. ≈ Tajikistan/Uzbekistan
153 N13 **Surkhondaryo Wiloyati** *Rus.* Surkhandar'inskaya Oblast'. ◐ *province* S Uzbekistan
143 P11 **Sürmene** Trabzon, NE Turkey *40.55N 40.03E*
Surov *see* Suraw
131 N11 **Surovikino** Volgogradskaya Oblast', SW Russian Federation *48.39N 42.46E*
126 Jj14 **Surovo** Irkutskaya Oblast', S Russian Federation *55.45N 105.31E*
37 N11 **Sur, Point** *headland* California, W USA *36.18N 121.54W*
197 F3 **Surprise, Île** *island* N New Caledonia
63 E22 **Sur, Punta** *headland* E Argentina *50.58S 69.10W*
Surrentum *see* Sorrento
30 M3 **Surrey** North Dakota, N USA *48.13N 101.05W*
99 O22 **Surrey** *cultural region* SE England, UK
23 X7 **Surry** Virginia, NE USA *37.08N 76.48W*
110 F8 **Sursee** Luzern, W Switzerland *47.10N 8.07E*
131 P6 **Sursk** Penzenskaya Oblast', W Russian Federation *53.06N 45.46E*
131 P5 **Surskoye** Ul'yanovskaya Oblast', W Russian Federation *54.28N 46.47E*
77 P8 **Surt** *var.* Sidra, Sirte. N Libya *31.13N 16.34E*
97 I19 **Surte** Västra Götaland, S Sweden *57.49N 12.01E*
77 Q8 **Surt, Khalīj** *Eng.* Gulf of Sidra, Gulf of Sirti, Sidra. *gulf* N Libya
94 I5 **Surtsey** *island* S Iceland
143 N17 **Suruç** Şanlıurfa, S Turkey *36.58N 38.24E*
171 Ii17 **Suruga-wan** *bay* SE Japan
174 Hh10 **Surulangun** Sumatera, W Indonesia *2.36S 102.43E*
Süs *see* Susch
108 A8 **Susa** Piemonte, NE Italy *45.09N 7.01E*
170 E12 **Susa** Yamaguchi, Honshū, SW Japan *34.35N 131.34E*
Susa *see* Shūsh
115 E16 **Sušac** *It.* Cazza. *island* SW Croatia
Sūsah *see* Sousse
170 Ee15 **Susaki** Kōchi, Shikoku, SW Japan *33.22N 133.13E*
170 G17 **Susami** Wakayama, Honshū, SW Japan *33.32N 135.32E*
148 K9 **Sūsangerd** *var.* Susangird. Khūzestān, SW Iran *31.40N 48.06E*
Susangird *see* Sūsangerd
37 P4 **Susanville** California, W USA *40.25N 120.39W*
110 J9 **Susch** *var.* Süs. Graubünden, SE Switzerland *46.45N 10.04E*
143 N12 **Suşehri** Sivas, N Turkey *40.10N 38.06E*
Susiana *see* Khūzestān
113 B18 **Sušice** *Ger.* Schüttenhofen. Plzeňský Kraj, W Czech Republic *49.13N 13.31E*
41 R11 **Susitna** Alaska, USA *61.32N 150.30W*
41 R11 **Susitna River** ≈ Alaska, USA
131 Q3 **Suslonger** Respublika Mariy El, W Russian Federation *56.18N 48.16E*
107 N14 **Suspiro del Moro, Puerto del** *pass* S Spain *37.04N 3.39W*
20 H16 **Susquehanna River** ≈ New York/Pennsylvania, NE USA
11 O15 **Sussex** New Brunswick, SE Canada *45.43N 65.31W*
20 J13 **Sussex** New Jersey, NE USA *41.12N 74.34W*
23 W7 **Sussex** Virginia, NE USA *36.54N 77.16W*
99 O23 **Sussex** *cultural region* S England, UK
191 S10 **Sussex Inlet** New South Wales, SE Australia *35.10S 150.35E*
101 L17 **Susteren** Limburg, SE Netherlands *51.04N 5.49E*
8 K12 **Sustut Peak** ▲ British Columbia, W Canada *56.25N 126.34W*
127 Nn9 **Susuman** Magadanskaya Oblast', E Russian Federation *62.46N 148.07E*
196 H6 **Susupe** Saipan, S Northern Mariana Islands
142 D12 **Susurluk** Balıkesir, NW Turkey *39.55N 28.10E*
116 M13 **Susuzmüsellim** Tekirdağ, NW Turkey *41.04N 27.03E*
142 F15 **Sütçüler** Isparta, SW Turkey *37.31N 31.00E*
118 L13 **Şuţeşti** Brăila, SE Romania *45.13N 27.26E*
85 F25 **Sutherland** Western Cape, SW South Africa *32.22S 20.42E*
30 L15 **Sutherland** Nebraska, C USA *41.09N 101.07W*
98 I7 **Sutherland** *cultural region* N Scotland, UK
193 B21 **Sutherland Falls** *waterfall* South Island, NZ *44.49S 167.32E*
34 F14 **Sutherlin** Oregon, NW USA *43.23N 123.18W*
155 V10 **Sutlej** ≈ India/Pakistan
Sutna *see* Satna
37 P7 **Sutter Creek** California, W USA *38.22N 120.49W*
41 R11 **Sutton** Alaska, USA *61.42N 148.53W*
31 Q16 **Sutton** Nebraska, C USA *40.36N 97.52W*
23 R4 **Sutton** West Virginia, NE USA *38.39N 80.42W*
10 F8 **Sutton** ≈ Ontario, C Canada
99 M19 **Sutton Coldfield** C England, UK *52.34N 1.48W*
23 R4 **Sutton Lake** ⊠ West Virginia, NE USA
13 P13 **Sutton, Monts** *hill range* Quebec, SE Canada
10 F8 **Sutton Ridges** ▲▲ Ontario, C Canada
172 Nn5 **Suttsu** Hokkaidō, NE Japan *42.46N 140.12E*
41 P15 **Sutwik Island** *island* Alaska, USA
168 K7 **Süüj** Bulgan, C Mongolia *47.49N 104.06E*
120 H5 **Suure-Jaani** *Ger.* Gross-Sankt-Johannis. Viljandimaa, S Estonia *58.34N 25.26E*
120 J7 **Suur Munamägi** *var.* Munamägi, *Ger.* Eier-Berg. ▲ SE Estonia *57.42N 27.03E*
120 F5 **Suur Väin** *Ger.* Grosser Sund. *strait* W Estonia
153 U8 **Suusamyr** Chuyskaya Oblast', C Kyrgyzstan *42.07N 73.55E*
197 I13 **Suva** ● (Fiji) Viti Levu, W Fiji *18.07S 178.26E*
197 I13 **Suva** ✕ Viti Levu, C Fiji *18.01S 178.30E*
115 N18 **Suva Gora** ▲▲ W FYR Macedonia
120 H11 **Suvainiškis** Rokiškis, NE Lithuania *56.09N 25.15E*
Suvalkai/Suvalki *see* Suwałki
115 P15 **Suva Planina** ▲▲ SE Yugoslavia
115 M17 **Suva Reka** Serbia, S Yugoslavia *42.23N 20.50E*
130 K5 **Suvorov** Tul'skaya Oblast', W Russian Federation *54.08N 36.33E*
119 N12 **Suvorove** Odes'ka Oblast', SW Ukraine *45.35N 28.58E*
Suvorovo *see* Ştefan Vodă
171 J15 **Suwa** Nagano, Honshū, S Japan *36.01N 138.07E*
Suwaik *see* As Suwayq
Suwaira *see* Aş Şuwayrah
112 O7 **Suwałki** *Lith.* Suvalkai, *Rus.* Suvalki. Podlaskie, NE Poland *54.06N 22.55E*
178 Ii10 **Suwannaphum** Roi Et, E Thailand *15.36N 103.46E*
25 V8 **Suwannee River** ≈ Florida/Georgia, SE USA
Şuwār *see* Aş Şuwār
202 K14 **Suwarrow** *atoll* N Cook Islands
Suwaydā/Suwaydā', Muḩāfaẓat as *see* As Suwaydā'
149 R16 **Suwaydān** *var.* Sweiham. Abū Ẓaby, E UAE *24.30N 55.18E*
Suwayqiyah, Hawr as *see* Shuwayjah, Hawr ash
Suways, Khalij as *see* Suez, Gulf of
Suways, Qanāt as *see* Suez Canal
Suweida *see* As Suwaydā'
Suweon *see* Suwŏn
169 X15 **Suwŏn** *var.* Suweon, *Jap.* Suigen. NW South Korea *37.17N 127.03E*
Su Xian *see* Suzhou
149 R14 **Sūzā** Hormozgān, S Iran *26.49N 56.04E*
151 P15 **Suzak** *Kaz.* Sozaq. Yuzhnyy Kazakhstan, S Kazakhstan *44.09N 68.28E*
Suzaka *see* Suzuka
130 M3 **Suzdal'** Vladimirskaya Oblast', W Russian Federation *56.27N 40.29E*
167 P7 **Suzhou** *var.* Su Xian. Anhui, E China *33.39N 116.56E*
167 R8 **Suzhou** *var.* Soochow, Su-chou, Suchow; *prev.* Wuhsien. Jiangsu, E China *31.22N 120.34E*
Suz, Mys *see* Soye, Mys
171 J12 **Suzu** Ishikawa, Honshū, SW Japan *37.24N 137.12E*
171 Hh16 **Suzuka** Mie, Honshū, SW Japan *34.51N 136.31E*
171 Jj14 **Suzuka** *var.* Suzaka. Nagano, Honshū, S Japan *36.39N 138.16E*
171 J12 **Suzu-misaki** *headland* Honshū, SW Japan *37.31N 137.19E*
Svágälv *see* Svågan
96 M10 **Svågan** *var.* Svágälv. ≈ C Sweden
Svalava/Svaljava *see* Svalyava
94 O2 **Svalbard** ◇ *Norwegian dependency* Arctic Ocean
94 J2 **Svalbardhseyri** Nordhurland Eystra, N Iceland *65.43N 18.03W*
97 K22 **Svalöv** Skåne, S Sweden *55.55N 13.06E*
118 H7 **Svalyava** *Cz.* Svalava, Svaljava, *Hung.* Szolyva. Zakarpats'ka Oblast', W Ukraine *48.33N 23.00E*
94 O2 **Svanbergfjellet** ▲ C Svalbard *78.40N 18.10E*
97 M24 **Svaneke** Bornholm, E Denmark *55.07N 15.08E*
97 L22 **Svängsta** Blekinge, S Sweden *56.16N 14.46E*
97 J16 **Svanskog** Värmland, C Sweden *59.10N 12.34E*
97 L16 **Svartå** Örebro, C Sweden *59.13N 14.07E*
97 L15 **Svartälven** ≈ C Sweden
94 G12 **Svartisen** *glacier* C Norway
119 X6 **Svatove** *Rus.* Svatovo. Luhans'ka Oblast', E Ukraine *49.24N 38.10E*
Svatovo *see* Svatove
Sväty Kríž nad Hronom *see* Žiar nad Hronom
178 Ii12 **Svay Chék, Stœng** ≈ Cambodia/Thailand
178 Jj14 **Svay Riĕng** Svay Riĕng, S Cambodia *11.04N 105.48E*
94 O3 **Sveagruva** Spitsbergen, W Svalbard *77.53N 16.42E*
97 K23 **Svedala** Skåne, S Sweden *55.30N 13.15E*
120 H12 **Švėdesai** Anykščiai, NE Lithuania *55.42N 25.22E*
95 G18 **Sveg** Jämtland, C Sweden *62.01N 14.19E*
120 C12 **Švėkšna** Šilutė, W Lithuania *55.31N 21.37E*
96 C11 **Svelgen** Sogn og Fjordane, S Norway *61.46N 5.18E*
97 H15 **Svelvik** Vestfold, S Norway *59.36N 10.22E*
120 I13 **Švenčionėliai** *Pol.* Nowo-Święciany. Švenčionys, SE Lithuania *55.10N 26.00E*
120 I13 **Švenčionys** *Pol.* Święciany. Švenčionys, SE Lithuania *55.08N 26.08E*
97 H24 **Svendborg** Fyn, C Denmark *55.04N 10.37E*
97 K19 **Svenljunga** Västra Götaland, S Sweden *57.30N 13.04E*
94 P2 **Svenskøya** *island* E Svalbard
95 G17 **Svenstavik** Jämtland, C Sweden *62.39N 14.24E*
97 G20 **Svenstrup** Nordjylland, N Denmark *56.58N 9.52E*
120 H12 **Šventoji** ≈ C Lithuania
119 Z8 **Sverdlovs'k** *Rus.* Sverdlovsk; *prev.* Imeni Sverdlova Rudnik. Luhans'ka Oblast', E Ukraine *48.05N 39.37E*
Sverdlovsk *see* Yekaterinburg
131 W2 **Sverdlovskaya Oblast'** ◐ *province* C Russian Federation
126 Hh5 **Sverdrup, Ostrov** *island* N Russian Federation
Sverige *see* Sweden
115 D15 **Svetac** *prev.* Sveti Andrea, *It.* Sant'Andrea. *island* SW Croatia
Sveti Andrea *see* Svetac
Sveti Nikola *see* Sveti Nikole
115 O18 **Sveti Nikole** *prev.* Sveti Nikola. C FYR Macedonia *41.54N 21.55E*
Sveti Vrach *see* Sandanski
127 O16 **Svetlaya** Primorskiy Kray, SE Russian Federation *46.33N 138.20E*
130 B2 **Svetlogorsk** Kaliningradskaya Oblast', W Russian Federation *54.56N 20.09E*
126 I9 **Svetlogorsk** Krasnoyarskiy Kray, N Russian Federation *66.51N 88.29E*
Svetlogorsk *see* Svyetlahorsk
131 N14 **Svetlograd** Stavropol'skiy Kray, SW Russian Federation *45.19N 42.52E*
Svetlovodsk *see* Svitlovods'k
121 A14 **Svetlyy** *Ger.* Zimmerbude. Kaliningradskaya Oblast', W Russian Federation *54.42N 20.07E*
131 Y8 **Svetlyy** Orenburgskaya Oblast', W Russian Federation *50.34N 60.42E*
128 G11 **Svetogorsk** *Fin.* Enso. Leningradskaya Oblast', NW Russian Federation *61.06N 28.52E*
Svetozarevo *see* Jagodina
113 B18 **Švihov** *Ger.* Schwihau. Plzeňský Kraj, W Czech Republic *49.31N 13.18E*
114 E13 **Svilaja** ▲▲ SE Croatia
114 N12 **Svilajnac** Serbia, C Yugoslavia *44.15N 21.12E*
116 L11 **Svilengrad** *prev.* Mustafa-Pasha. Khaskovo, S Bulgaria *41.46N 26.13E*
Svinecea Mare, Munte *see* Svinecea Mare, Vârful
118 F13 **Svinecea Mare, Vârful** *var.* Munte Svinecea Mare. ▲ SW Romania *44.47N 22.10E*
97 B18 **Svínoy** *Dan.* Svinø *Island* Faeroe Islands *62.17N 6.17W*
153 N14 **Svintsovyy Rudnik** *Turkm.* Swintsowyy Rudnik. Lebapskiy Velayat, E Turkmenistan *37.54N 66.25E*
120 I13 **Svir** *Rus.* Svir'. Minskaya Voblasts', NW Belarus *54.51N 26.24E*
128 I12 **Svir'** *canal* NW Russian Federation
Svir', Ozero *see* Svir, Vozyera
121 I14 **Svir, Vozyera** *Rus.* Ozero Svir'. ◎ C Belarus
116 J7 **Svishtov** *prev.* Sistova. Veliko Tŭrnovo, N Bulgaria *43.37N 25.22E*
121 F18 **Svislach** *Pol.* Świsłocz, *Rus.* Svisloch'. Hrodzyenskaya Voblasts', W Belarus *53.01N 24.06E*
121 M17 **Svislach** *Rus.* Svisloch'. Mahilyowskaya Voblasts', E Belarus *53.25N 28.56E*
121 L17 **Svislach** *Rus.* Svisloch'. ≈ E Belarus
Svisloch' *see* Svislach
113 F17 **Svitavy** *Ger.* Zwittau. Pardubický Kraj, C Czech Republic *49.44N 16.27E*
119 S6 **Svitlovods'k** *Rus.* Svetlovodsk. Kirovohrads'ka Oblast', C Ukraine *49.04N 33.15E*
Svizzera *see* Switzerland
126 Mm15 **Svobodnyy** Amurskaya Oblast', SE Russian Federation *51.24N 128.05E*
116 G9 **Svoge** Sofiya, W Bulgaria *42.58N 23.20E*
94 G11 **Svolvær** Nordland, C Norway *68.15N 14.29E*
113 F18 **Svratka** *Ger.* Schwarzach, Schwarzawa. ≈ SE Czech Republic
115 P14 **Svrljig** Serbia, E Yugoslavia *43.26N 22.07E*
207 U10 **Svyataya Anna Trough** *var.* Saint Anna Trough. *undersea feature* N Kara Sea
128 M4 **Svyatoy Nos, Mys** *headland* NW Russian Federation *68.07N 39.49E*
126 M5 **Svyatoy Nos, Mys** *headland* NE Russian Federation *72.49N 140.45E*
121 N18 **Svyetlahorsk** *Rus.* Svetlogorsk. Homyel'skaya Voblasts', SE Belarus *52.39N 29.43E*
Swabian Jura *see* Schwäbische Alb
99 P19 **Swaffham** E England, UK *52.38N 0.40E*
25 V5 **Swainsboro** Georgia, SE USA *32.36N 82.19W*
85 C19 **Swakop** ≈ W Namibia
85 C19 **Swakopmund** Erongo, W Namibia *22.40S 14.34E*
99 M15 **Swale** ≈ N England, UK
Swallow Island *see* Nendö
101 M16 **Swalmen** Limburg, SE Netherlands *51.13N 6.01E*
10 G8 **Swan** ≈ Ontario, C Canada
99 L24 **Swanage** S England, UK *50.37N 1.59W*
190 M10 **Swan Hill** Victoria, SE Australia *35.21S 143.34E*
9 P13 **Swan Hills** Alberta, W Canada *54.40N 116.19W*
67 D24 **Swan Island** *island* C Falkland Islands
Swankalok *see* Sawankhalok
31 U10 **Swan Lake** ◎ Minnesota, N USA
23 Y10 **Swanquarter** North Carolina, SE USA *35.23N 76.17W*
190 J9 **Swan Reach** South Australia *34.39S 139.35E*
9 V15 **Swan River** Manitoba, S Canada *52.06N 101.16W*
191 P17 **Swansea** Tasmania, SE Australia *42.09S 148.03E*
99 J22 **Swansea** *Wel.* Abertawe. S Wales, UK *51.37N 3.57W*
23 R13 **Swansea** South Carolina, SE USA *33.47N 81.06W*
21 S7 **Swans Island** *island* Maine, NE USA
30 L17 **Swanson Lake** ⊠ Nebraska, C USA
33 R11 **Swanton** Ohio, N USA *41.35N 83.53W*
112 G11 **Swarzędz** Poznań, C Poland *52.24N 17.05E*
Swatow *see* Shantou
85 L22 **Swaziland** *off.* Kingdom of Swaziland. ◆ *monarchy* S Africa
95 G18 **Sweden** *off.* Kingdom of Sweden, *Swe.* Sverige. ◆ *monarchy* N Europe
Swedru *see* Agona Swedru
27 V12 **Sweeny** Texas, SW USA *29.02N 95.42W*
35 R6 **Sweetgrass** Montana, NW USA *48.58N 111.58W*
34 G12 **Sweet Home** Oregon, NW USA *44.24N 122.44W*
27 T12 **Sweet Home** Texas, SW USA *29.21N 97.04W*
29 T4 **Sweet Springs** Missouri, C USA *38.57N 93.24W*
22 M10 **Sweetwater** Tennessee, S USA *35.36N 84.27W*
27 P7 **Sweetwater** Texas, SW USA *32.28N 100.24W*
35 V15 **Sweetwater River** ≈ Wyoming, C USA
Sweiham *see* Suwaydān
85 F26 **Swellendam** Western Cape, SW South Africa *34.01S 20.25E*
113 G15 **Świdnica** *Ger.* Schweidnitz. Wałbrzych, SW Poland *50.51N 16.28E*
113 O14 **Świdnik** *Ger.* Streckenbach. Lubelskie, E Poland *51.13N 22.39E*
112 F8 **Świdwin** *Ger.* Schivelbein. Zachodniopomorskie, NW Poland *53.46N 15.43E*
113 F15 **Świebodzice** *Ger.* Freiburg in Schlesien, Swiebodzice. Wałbrzych, SW Poland *50.54N 16.22E*
112 E11 **Świebodzin** *Ger.* Schwiebus. Lubuskie, W Poland *52.15N 15.30E*
Święciany *see* Švenčionys
112 I9 **Świecie** *Ger.* Schwertberg. Kujawsko-pomorskie, N Poland *53.24N 18.24E*
113 L15 **Świętokrzyskie** ◐ *province* C Poland
9 T16 **Swift Current** Saskatchewan, S Canada *50.16N 107.49W*
100 K9 **Swifterbant** Flevoland, C Netherlands *52.36N 5.33E*
191 Q12 **Swifts Creek** Victoria, SE Australia *37.17S 147.41E*
98 E13 **Swilly, Lough** *Ir.* Loch Súilí. *inlet* N Ireland
99 M22 **Swindon** S England, UK *51.34N 1.46W*
Swinemünde *see* Świnoujście
112 D8 **Świnoujście** *Ger.* Swinemünde. Zachodniopomorskie, NW Poland *53.54N 14.12E*
Swintsowyy Rudnik *see* Svintsovyy Rudnik
Świsłocz *see* Svislach
Swiss Confederation *see* Switzerland
110 E9 **Switzerland** *off.* Swiss Confederation, *Fr.* La Suisse, *Ger.* Schweiz, *It.* Svizzera; *anc.* Helvetia. ◆ *federal republic* C Europe
99 F17 **Swords** *Ir.* Sord, Sórd Choluim Chille. E Ireland *53.28N 6.13W*
20 H13 **Swoyersville** Pennsylvania, NE USA *41.18N 75.48W*
128 I10 **Syamozera, Ozero** ◎ NW Russian Federation
128 M13 **Syamzha** Vologodskaya Oblast', NW Russian Federation *60.02N 41.09E*
120 N13 **Syanno** *Rus.* Senno. Vitsyebskaya Voblasts', NE Belarus *54.48N 29.44E*
121 K16 **Syarheyevichy** *Rus.* Sergeyevichi. Minskaya Voblasts', C Belarus *53.30N 27.45E*
128 I12 **Syas'stroy** Leningradskaya Oblast', NW Russian Federation *60.05N 32.37E*
Sycaminum *see* Ḩefa
32 M10 **Sycamore** Illinois, N USA *41.59N 88.41W*
130 J3 **Sychëvka** Smolenskaya Oblast', W Russian Federation *55.52N 34.19E*
113 H14 **Syców** *Ger.* Gross Wartenberg. Dolnośląskie, SW Poland *51.18N 17.42E*
12 E17 **Sydenham** ≈ Ontario, S Canada
Sydenham Island *see* Nonouti
191 T9 **Sydney** *state capital* New South Wales, SE Australia *33.55S 151.10E*
11 R14 **Sydney** Cape Breton Island, Nova Scotia, SE Canada *46.10N 60.10W*
Sydney Island *see* Manra
11 R14 **Sydney Mines** Cape Breton Island, Nova Scotia, SE Canada *46.14N 60.19W*
Syedpur *see* Saidpur
121 K18 **Syelishcha** *Rus.* Selishche. Minskaya Voblasts', C Belarus *53.01N 27.25E*
121 J18 **Syemyezhava** *Rus.* Semezhevo. Minskaya Voblasts', C Belarus *52.57N 27.01E*
Syene *see* Aswān
119 X6 **Syeverodonets'k** *Rus.* Severodonetsk. Luhans'ka Oblast', E Ukraine *48.58N 38.28E*
167 T6 **Syïao Shan** *island* SE China
102 H11 **Syke** Niedersachsen, NW Germany *52.55N 8.49E*
96 D10 **Sykkylven** Møre og Romsdal, S Norway *62.22N 6.34E*
117 F15 **Sykoúri** *var.* Sikouri; *prev.* Sikoúrion. Thessalía, C Greece *39.46N 22.34E*
129 R11 **Syktyvkar** *prev.* Ust'-Sysol'sk. Respublika Komi, NW Russian Federation *61.42N 50.45E*
25 Q4 **Sylacauga** Alabama, S USA *33.10N 86.15W*
Sylarna *see* Sylene
96 J9 **Sylene** *Swe.* Sylarna. ▲ Norway/Sweden *63.00N 12.14E*
159 V14 **Sylhet** Chittagong, NE Bangladesh *24.52N 91.51E*
102 G6 **Sylt** *island* NW Germany
23 O10 **Sylva** North Carolina, SE USA *35.22N 83.13W*
129 V15 **Sylva** ≈ NW Russian Federation
25 W5 **Sylvania** Georgia, SE USA *32.45N 81.38W*
33 R11 **Sylvania** Ohio, N USA *41.43N 83.42W*
9 Q15 **Sylvan Lake** Alberta, SW Canada *52.18N 114.02W*
35 T13 **Sylvan Pass** *pass* Wyoming, C USA *44.29N 110.03W*
25 T7 **Sylvester** Georgia, SE USA *31.31N 83.50W*
27 P6 **Sylvester** Texas, SW USA *32.42N 100.15W*
8 L11 **Sylvia, Mount** ▲ British Columbia, W Canada *58.03N 124.26W*
126 Hh12 **Sym** ≈ C Russian Federation
117 N22 **Sými** *var.* Simi. *island* Dodekánisos, Greece, Aegean Sea
119 U8 **Synel'nykove** Dnipropetrovs'ka Oblast', E Ukraine *48.18N 35.31E*
129 U6 **Synya** Respublika Komi, NW Russian Federation *65.21N 58.01E*
119 P7 **Synyukha** *Rus.* Sinyukha. ≈ S Ukraine
Syôbara *see* Shōbara
205 V2 **Syowa** *Japanese research station* Antarctica *68.58S 40.07E*
28 H6 **Syracuse** Kansas, C USA *38.00N 101.43W*
31 S16 **Syracuse** Nebraska, C USA *40.39N 96.11W*
20 H10 **Syracuse** New York, NE USA *43.03N 76.09W*
Syracuse *see* Siracusa
Syrdar'inskaya Oblast' *see* Sirdaryo Wiloyati
Syrdariya *see* Syr Darya
150 L14 **Syr Darya** *var.* Sai Hun, Sir Darya, Syrdarya, *Kaz.* Syrdariya, *Rus.* Syrdar'ya, *Uzb.* Sirdaryo; *anc.* Jaxartes. ≈ C Asia
153 P10 **Syrdar'ya** Sirdaryo Wiloyati, E Uzbekistan *40.46N 68.34E*
144 J6 **Syria** *off.* Syrian Arab Republic, *var.* Siria, Syrie, *Ar.* Al-Jumhūrīyah al-'Arabīyah as-Sūrīyah, Sūrīya. ◆ *republic* SW Asia
144 L9 **Syrian Desert** *Ar.* Al Hamad, Bādiyat ash Shām. *desert* SW Asia
Syrie *see* Syria
117 L22 **Sýrna** *var.* Sirna. *island* Kykládes, Greece, Aegean Sea
117 I20 **Sýros** *var.* Siros. *island* Kykládes, Greece, Aegean Sea
95 M18 **Sysmä** Etelä-Suomi, S Finland *61.28N 25.37E*
129 R12 **Sysola** ≈ NW Russian Federation
Syulemeshlii *see* Sredets
131 S2 **Syumsi** Udmurtskaya Respublika, NW Russian Federation *57.07N 51.35E*
116 K10 **Syuyutliyka** ≈ C Bulgaria
Syvash, Zaliv *see* Syvash, Zatoka
119 U12 **Syvash, Zatoka** *Rus.* Zaliv Syvash. *inlet* S Ukraine
131 Q6 **Syzran'** Samarskaya Oblast', W Russian Federation *53.10N 48.22E*
Szabadka *see* Subotica
113 N21 **Szabolcs-Szatmár-Bereg** *off.* Szabolcs-Szatmár-Bereg Megye. ◐ *county* E Hungary
112 G10 **Szamocin** *Ger.* Samotschin. Wielkolpolskie, C Poland *53.02N 17.04E*
118 H8 **Szamos** *var.* Someș, Someşul, *Ger.* Samosch, Somesch. ≈ Hungary/Romania
Szamosújvár *see* Gherla
112 G11 **Szamotuły** Poznań, C Poland *52.35N 16.35E*
Szarkowszczyzna *see* Sharkawshchyna
113 M24 **Szarvas** Békés, SE Hungary *46.52N 20.32E*
Szászmagyarós *see* Măieruș
Szászrégen *see* Reghin
Szászsebes *see* Sebeş
Szászváros *see* Orăştie
Szatmárrnémeti *see* Satu Mare
Száva *see* Sava
113 P15 **Szczebrzeszyn** Lubelskie, E Poland *50.43N 23.00E*
112 D9 **Szczecin** *Eng./Ger.* Stettin. Zachodniopomorskie, NW Poland *53.25N 14.31E*
112 G8 **Szczecinek** *Ger.* Neustettin. Zachodniopomorskie, NW Poland *53.42N 16.39E*
112 D8 **Szczeciński, Zalew** *var.* Stettiner Haff, *Ger.* Oderhaff. *bay* Germany/Poland
113 K15 **Szczekociny** Śląskie, S Poland *50.38N 19.46E*
112 N8 **Szczuczyn** Podlaskie, NE Poland *53.34N 22.17E*
Szczuczyn Nowogródzki *see* Shchuchyn
112 M8 **Szczytno** *Ger.* Ortelsburg. Warmińsko-Mazurskie, NE Poland, *53.33N 21.00E*
Szechuan/Szechwan *see* Sichuan
113 K21 **Szécsény** Nógrád, N Hungary *48.04N 19.31E*
113 L25 **Szeged** *Ger.* Szegedin, *Rom.* Seghedin. Csongrád, SE Hungary *46.16N 20.06E*
Szegedin *see* Szeged
113 N23 **Szeghalom** Békés, SE Hungary *47.02N 21.09E*
Székelyhid *see* Săcueni
Székelykeresztúr *see* Cristuru Secuiesc
113 I23 **Székesfehérvár** *Ger.* Stuhlweissenberg; *anc.* Alba Regia. Fejér, W Hungary *47.13N 18.24E*
Szeklerburg *see* Miercurea-Ciuc
Szekler Neumarkt *see* Târgu Secuiesc
113 J25 **Szekszárd** Tolna, S Hungary *46.21N 18.40E*
Szempcz/Szenc *see* Senec
Szenice *see* Senica
Szentágota *see* Agnita
113 J22 **Szentendre** *Ger.* Sankt Andrä. Pest, N Hungary *47.40N 19.04E*
113 L24 **Szentes** Csongrád, SE Hungary *46.40N 20.16E*
113 F23 **Szentgotthárd** *Eng.* Saint Gotthard, *Ger.* Sankt Gotthard. Vas, W Hungary *46.57N 16.18E*
Szentgyörgy *see* Đurđevac
Szenttamás *see* Srbobran
Széphely *see* Jebel
Szeping *see* Siping
Szered *see* Sereď
113 N21 **Szerencs** Borsod-Abaúj-Zemplén, NE Hungary *48.10N 21.10E*
Szeret *see* Siret
Szeretfalva *see* Sărăţel
112 N7 **Szeskie Wzgórza** *Ger.* Seesker Höhe. *hill* NE Poland *54.15N 22.19E*
113 H25 **Szigetvár** Baranya, SW Hungary *46.03N 17.47E*
Szilágysomlyó *see* Şimleu Silvaniei
Szinna *see* Snina
Sziszek *see* Sisak
Szitás-Keresztúr *see* Cristuru Secuiesc
113 E15 **Szklarska Poręba** *Ger.* Schreiberhau. Dolnośląskie, SW Poland *50.50N 15.30E*
Szkudy *see* Skuodas
Szlatina *see* Slatina, Croatia
Szlavonia/Szlavonország *see* Slavonija
Szlovákia *see* Slovakia
Szluin *see* Slunj
113 L23 **Szolnok** Jász-Nagykun-Szolnok, C Hungary *47.10N 20.12E*
Szolyva *see* Svalyava
113 G23 **Szombathely** *Ger.* Steinamanger; *anc.* Sabaria, Savaria. Vas, W Hungary *47.13N 16.37E*
Szond/Szonta *see* Sonta
Szováta *see* Sovata
112 F13 **Szprotawa** *Ger.* Sprottau. Lubuskie, W Poland *51.33N 15.31E*
Sztálinváros *see* Dunaújváros
Sztrazsó *see* Strážov
112 J8 **Sztum** *Ger.* Stuhm. Pomorskie, N Poland *53.54N 19.01E*
112 H10 **Szubin** *Ger.* Schubin. Kujawsko-pomorskie, W Poland *53.04N 17.49E*
Szucsava *see* Suceava
Szurduk *see* Surduc
113 M14 **Szydłowiec** *Ger.* Schlelau. Mazowieckie, C Poland *51.15N 20.51E*

T

Taalintehdas *see* Dalsbruk
179 P11 **Taal, Lake** ◎ Luzon, NW Philippines
Taastrup *see* Tåstrup
113 I24 **Tab** Somogy, W Hungary *46.40N 18.01E*
179 Q11 **Tabaco** Luzon, N Philippines *13.22N 123.42E*
194 M7 **Tabalo** Mussau Island, NE PNG *1.22S 149.37E*
106 K5 **Tábara** Castilla-León, N Spain *41.49N 5.57W*
195 P9 **Tabar Island** *island* Tabar Islands, N PNG
195 P9 **Tabar Islands** *island group* NE PNG
Tabariya, Bahrat *see* Tiberias, Lake
149 S7 **Ţabas** *var.* Golshan. Khorāsān, C Iran *33.37N 56.54E*
45 P15 **Tabasará, Serranía de** ▲▲ W Panama
43 U15 **Tabasco** ◐ *state* SE Mexico
Tabasco *see* Grijalva, Río
131 Q2 **Tabashino** Respublika Mariy El, W Russian Federation *57.00N 47.47E*
60 B13 **Tabatinga** Amazonas, N Brazil *4.13S 69.43W*
76 G9 **Tabelbala** W Algeria *29.22N 3.01W*
9 Q17 **Taber** Alberta, SW Canada *49.48N 112.09W*
176 W14 **Taberfane** Pulau Trangan, E Indonesia *6.14S 134.08E*
97 L19 **Taberg** Jönköping, S Sweden *57.42N 14.04E*
Tabibug *see* Tabibuga
194 H12 **Tabibuga** *var.* Tabibug. Western Highlands, C PNG *5.32S 144.37E*
203 O3 **Tabiteuea** *prev.* Drummond Island. *atoll* Tungaru, W Kiribati
179 Q12 **Tablas Island** *island* C Philippines
179 Pp12 **Tablas Strait** *strait* C Philippines
194 M16 **Table Bay** *bay* SE PNG
192 Q10 **Table Cape** *headland* North Island, NZ *39.07S 178.00E*
11 S13 **Table Mountain** ▲ Newfoundland, E Canada *47.39N 59.15W*
181 P17 **Table, Pointe de la** *headland* SE Réunion *21.19S 55.49E*
29 S8 **Table Rock Lake** ⊠ Arkansas/Missouri, C USA
38 K14 **Table Top** ▲ Arizona, SW USA *32.45N 112.07W*
194 J13 **Tabletop, Mount** ▲ C PNG *6.51S 146.00E*
126 Mm5 **Tabor** Respublika Sakha (Yakutiya), NE Russian Federation *71.14N 150.23E*
31 S15 **Tabor** Iowa, C USA *40.54N 95.40W*
113 D18 **Tábor** Budějovický Kraj, S Czech Republic *49.25N 14.40E*
83 F21 **Tabora** Tabora, W Tanzania *5.04S 32.49E*
83 F21 **Tabora** ◐ *region* C Tanzania
23 U12 **Tabor City** North Carolina, SE USA *34.09N 78.52W*
153 Q10 **Taboshar** NW Tajikistan *40.37N 69.33E*
78 L18 **Tabou** *var.* Tabu. S Ivory Coast *4.28N 7.19W*
148 J2 **Tabrīz** *var.* Tebriz; *anc.* Tauris. Āzarbāyjān-e Khāvarī, NW Iran *38.04N 46.18E*
Tabu *see* Tabou
203 W1 **Tabuaeran** *prev.* Fanning Island. *atoll* Line Islands, E Kiribati
194 E11 **Tabubil** Western, SW PNG *5.13S 141.13E*
179 P8 **Tabuk** Luzon, N Philippines *17.26N 121.25E*
146 J4 **Tabūk** Tabūk, NW Saudi Arabia *28.25N 36.33E*
146 J5 **Tabūk** *off.* Minţaqat Tabūk. ◐ *province* NW Saudi Arabia
197 B12 **Tabwemasana, Mount** ▲ Espiritu Santo, W Vanuatu *15.22S 166.44E*
97 O15 **Täby** Stockholm, C Sweden *59.28N 18.04E*
43 N14 **Tacámbaro** Michoacán de Ocampo, SW Mexico *19.12N 101.27W*
44 A5 **Tacaná, Volcán** ⛰ Guatemala/Mexico *15.07N 92.06W*
45 X16 **Tacarcuna, Cerro** ▲ SE Panama *8.08N 77.15W*
Tachau *see* Tachov
164 J3 **Tacheng** *var.* Qoqek. Xinjiang Uygur Zizhiqu, NW China *46.45N 82.55E*
56 H7 **Táchira** *off.* Estado Táchira. ◐ *state* W Venezuela
167 T13 **Tachoshui** N Taiwan *24.26N 121.43E*
113 A17 **Tachov** *Ger.* Tachau. Plzeňský Kraj, W Czech Republic *49.48N 12.37E*
179 R13 **Tacloban** *off.* Tacloban City. Leyte, C Philippines *11.15N 124.59E*
59 I19 **Tacna** Tacna, SE Peru *18.00S 70.15W*

◆ Country ● Country Capital ◇ Dependent Territory ○ Dependent Territory Capital ◐ Administrative Region ✕ International Airport ▲ Mountain ▲▲ Mountain Range ⛰ Volcano ≈ River ◎ Lake ⊠ Reservoir

TACNA – TANO

59 H18 **Tacna** *off.* Departamento de Tacna. ◆ *department* S Peru
34 H8 **Tacoma** Washington, NW USA *47.15N 122.26W*
20 L11 **Taconic Range** ▲ NE USA
64 L6 **Taco Pozo** Formosa, N Argentina *25.35S 63.15W*
59 M20 **Tacsara, Cordillera de** ▲ S Bolivia
63 F17 **Tacuarembó** *prev.* San Fructuoso. Tacuarembó, C Uruguay *31.42S 56.00W*
63 E18 **Tacuarembó** ◆ *department* C Uruguay
63 F17 **Tacuarembó, Río** ∾ C Uruguay
85 I14 **Tacuali** North Western, NW Zambia *14.17S 26.51E*
179 R16 **Tacurong** Mindanao, S Philippines *6.42N 124.40E*
171 Kk13 **Tadamu-gawa** ∾ Honshū, C Japan
79 V8 **Tadek** ∾ NW Niger
76 J9 **Tademaït, Plateau du** *plateau* C Algeria
197 K6 **Tadine** Province des Îles Loyauté, E New Caledonia *21.33S 167.54E*
82 L11 **Tadjoura** E Djibouti *11.47N 42.51E*
82 M11 **Tadjoura, Golfe de** *Eng.* Gulf of Tajura. *inlet* E Djibouti
Tadmor/Tadmur *see* Tudmur
9 W10 **Tadoule Lake** ◎ Manitoba, C Canada
13 S8 **Tadoussac** Quebec, SE Canada *48.07N 69.55W*
161 H18 **Tādpatri** Andhra Pradesh, E India *14.55N 77.58E*
Tadzhikabad *see* Tojikobod
Tadzhikistan *see* Tajikistan
169 Y14 **T'aebaek-sanmaek** ▲ E South Korea
169 V15 **Taechŏng-do** *island* NW South Korea
169 X13 **Taedong-gang** ∾ C North Korea
169 Y16 **Taegu** *off.* Taegu-gwangyŏksi, *var.* Daegu, *Jap.* Taikyū. SE South Korea *35.55N 128.32E*
Taehan-haehyŏp *see* Korea Strait
Taehan Min'guk *see* South Korea
169 Y15 **Taejŏn** *off.* Taejŏn-gwangyŏksi, *Jap.* Taiden. C South Korea *36.19N 127.28E*
200 T11 **Tafahi** *island* N Tonga
107 Q4 **Tafalla** Navarra, N Spain *42.31N 1.40W*
77 M12 **Tafassâsset, Oued** ∾ SE Algeria
79 W7 **Tafassâsset, Ténéré du** *desert* N Niger
57 U11 **Tafelberg** ▲ S Surinam *3.55N 56.09W*
99 J21 **Taff** ∾ SE Wales, UK
Tafila/Ṭafīlah, Muḥāfaẓat aṭ *see* Aṭ Ṭafīlah
79 N15 **Tafiré** N Ivory Coast *9.04N 5.10W*
148 M6 **Tafresh** Markazī, W Iran *34.40N 50.00E*
149 Q9 **Taft** Yazd, C Iran *31.48N 54.10E*
37 R13 **Taft** California, W USA *35.08N 119.27W*
27 T14 **Taft** Texas, SW USA *27.58N 97.24W*
149 W12 **Taftān, Kūh-e** ▲ SE Iran *28.38N 61.06E*
37 R13 **Taft Heights** California, W USA *35.06N 119.29W*
201 Y14 **Tafunsak** Kosrae, E Micronesia *5.21N 162.58E*
198 Aa8 **Tāga** Savai'i, SW Samoa *13.46S 172.31W*
155 O6 **Tagāb** Kāpīsā, E Afghanistan *33.52N 66.22E*
41 O8 **Tagagawik River** ∾ Alaska, USA
171 M13 **Tagajō** *var.* Tagayō. Miyagi, Honshū, C Japan *38.21N 141.02E*
130 K12 **Taganrog** Rostovskaya Oblast', SW Russian Federation *47.10N 38.54E*
130 K12 **Taganrog, Gulf of** *Rus.* Taganrogskiy Zaliv, *Ukr.* Tahanroz'ka Zatoka. *gulf* Russian Federation/Ukraine
Taganrogskiy Zaliv *see* Taganrog, Gulf of
78 J8 **Tagant** ◆ *region* C Mauritania
154 M14 **Tagas** Baluchistān, SW Pakistan *27.09N 64.36E*
170 D13 **Tagawa** Fukuoka, Kyūshū, SW Japan *33.37N 130.46E*
179 P11 **Tagaytay** Luzon, N Philippines *14.04N 120.55E*
Tagazyô *see* Tagajō
179 Qq14 **Tagbilaran** *var.* Tagbilaran City. Bohol, C Philippines *9.41N 123.54E*
108 B10 **Taggia** Liguria, NW Italy *43.51N 7.48E*
79 V9 **Taghouaji, Massif de** ▲ C Niger *17.13N 8.37E*
109 J15 **Tagliacozzo** Lazio, C Italy *42.03N 13.15E*
108 J7 **Tagliamento** ∾ NE Italy
179 R15 **Tagoloan** Mindanao, S Philippines *8.30N 124.45E*
155 N3 **Tagow Bāy** *var.* Bai. Sar-e Pol, N Afghanistan *35.41N 66.01E*
Tagtabazar *see* Takhtabazar
61 L17 **Taguatinga** Tocantins, C Brazil *12.16S 46.25W*
195 Q17 **Tagula** Tagula Island, SE PNG *11.21S 153.13E*
195 P17 **Tagula Island** *prev.* Southeast Island, Sudest Island. *island* SE PNG
179 Rr15 **Tagum** Mindanao, S Philippines *7.22N 125.51E*
56 C7 **Tagún, Cerro** *elevation* Colombia/Panama *7.57N 77.13W*
107 P7 **Tagus** *Port.* Rio Tejo, *Sp.* Río Tajo. ∾ Portugal/Spain
66 M9 **Tagus Plain** *undersea feature* E Atlantic Ocean
203 S10 **Tahaa** *island* Îles Sous le Vent, W French Polynesia
203 U10 **Tahanea** *atoll* Îles Tuamotu, C French Polynesia
Tahanroz'ka Zatoka *see* Taganrog, Gulf of
171 I16 **Tahara** Aichi, Honshū, SW Japan *34.40N 137.15E*
76 K12 **Tahat** ▲ SE Algeria *23.15N 5.34E*
169 V12 **Ta He** ∾ NE China
169 U4 **Tahe** Heilongjiang, NE China *52.21N 124.42E*
168 G9 **Tahilt** Govĭ-Altay, W Mongolia *45.20N 96.42E*
203 T10 **Tahiti** *island* Îles du Vent, W French Polynesia
Tahiti, Archipel de *see* Société, Archipel de la
120 E4 **Tahkuna nina** *headland* W Estonia *59.06N 22.35E*
154 K12 **Tahlāb** ∾ W Pakistan
154 K12 **Tāhlāb, Dasht-i** *desert* SW Pakistan
29 R10 **Tahlequah** Oklahoma, C USA *35.55N 94.58W*
37 Q6 **Tahoe City** California, W USA *39.09N 120.09W*
37 P6 **Tahoe, Lake** ◎ California/Nevada, W USA
Tahoena *see* Tahuna
27 N6 **Tahoka** Texas, SW USA *33.10N 101.47W*
34 F8 **Taholah** Washington, NW USA *47.19N 124.17W*
79 T11 **Tahoua** Tahoua, W Niger *14.52N 5.18E*
79 T11 **Tahoua** ◆ *department* W Niger
33 P3 **Tahquamenon Falls** *waterfall* Michigan, N USA *46.34N 85.14W*
33 P4 **Tahquamenon River** ∾ Michigan, N USA
145 V10 **Taḥrīr** S Iraq *31.58N 45.34E*
8 K17 **Tahsis** Vancouver Island, British Columbia, SW Canada *49.42N 126.31W*
Tahta *see* Takhta
77 W9 **Ṭahṭa** C Egypt *26.40N 31.27E*
142 L15 **Tahtalı Dağları** ▲ C Turkey
59 I14 **Tahuamanu, Río** ∾ Bolivia/Peru
58 F13 **Tahuanía, Río** ∾ E Peru
203 X7 **Tahuata** *island* Îles Marquises, NE French Polynesia
175 S6 **Tahulandang, Pulau** *island* N Indonesia
175 S5 **Tahuna** *prev.* Tahoena. Pulau Sangihe, N Indonesia *3.33N 125.33E*
176 Yy10 **Tahun, Danau** *see* Tahun, Danau
78 L17 **Taï** SW Ivory Coast *5.52N 7.28W*
167 P5 **Tai'an** Shandong, E China *36.13N 117.12E*
203 R8 **Taiarapu, Presqu'île de** *peninsula* Tahiti, W French Polynesia
Taibad *see* Tāybād
166 K7 **Taibai Shan** ▲ C China *33.57N 107.31E*
107 Q12 **Taibilla, Sierra de** ▲ S Spain
169 Q12 **Taibus Qi** *var.* Baochang. Nei Mongol Zizhiqu, N China *41.55N 115.22E*
Taichū *see* T'aichung
167 S13 **T'aichung** *Jap.* Taichū; *prev.* Taiwan. C Taiwan *24.09N 120.40E*
Taiden *see* Taejŏn
193 E23 **Taieri** ∾ South Island, NZ
117 E21 **Taïgetos** ▲ S Greece
167 N4 **Taihang Shan** ▲ C China
192 M11 **Taihape** Manawatu-Wanganui, North Island, NZ *39.41S 175.46E*
167 O7 **Taihe** Anhui, E China *33.14N 115.35E*
167 O12 **Taihe** Jiangxi, S China *26.50N 114.49E*
Taihoku *see* T'aipei
167 R8 **Tai Hu** ◎ E China
167 P9 **Taihu** Anhui, E China *30.26N 116.13E*
167 O6 **Taikang** Henan, C China *34.06N 114.53E*
172 P7 **Taiki** Hokkaidō, NE Japan *42.29N 143.15E*
177 Ff8 **Taikkyi** Yangon, SW Burma *17.16N 95.55E*
Taikyū *see* Taegu
169 U8 **Tailai** Heilongjiang, NE China *46.25N 123.25E*
173 Ff10 **Taileleo** Pulau Siberut, W Indonesia *1.45S 99.06E*
190 J10 **Tailem Bend** South Australia *35.20S 139.33E*
98 I8 **Tain** N Scotland, UK *57.49N 4.04W*
167 S14 **T'ainan** *Jap.* Tainan; *prev.* Dainan. S Taiwan *23.00N 120.05E*
117 E22 **Taínaro, Akrotírio** *headland* S Greece *36.41N 22.28E*
167 Q11 **Taining** Fujian, SE China *26.55N 117.13E*
203 W7 **Taiohae** *prev.* Madisonville. Nuku Hiva, NE French Polynesia *8.55S 140.04W*
167 T13 **T'aipei** *Jap.* Taihoku; *prev.* Daihoku. ● (Taiwan) N Taiwan *25.01N 121.28E*
174 Gg3 **Taiping** Perak, Peninsular Malaysia *4.54N 100.42E*
169 S8 **Taiping Ling** ▲ NE China *47.27N 120.27E*
172 N6 **Taisei** Hokkaidō, NE Japan *42.13N 139.52E*
170 F12 **Taisha** Shimane, Honshū, SW Japan *35.23N 132.40E*
111 R4 **Taiskirchen** Oberösterreich, NW Austria *48.15N 13.33E*
65 F20 **Taitao, Peninsula de** *peninsula* S Chile
Taitō *see* T'aitung
167 T14 **T'aitung** *Jap.* Taitō. S Taiwan *22.49N 121.04E*
94 M13 **Taivalkoski** Oulu, E Finland *65.34N 28.19E*
95 K19 **Taivassalo** Länsi-Suomi, W Finland *60.35N 21.36E*
167 T14 **Taiwan** *off.* Republic of China, *var.* Formosa, Formo'sa. ◆ *republic* E Asia
139 Q11 **Taiwan** *var.* Formosa. *island* E Asia
Taiwan *see* T'aichung
T'aiwan Haihsia/Taiwan Haixia *see* Taiwan Strait
Taiwan Shan *see* Chungyang Shanmo
167 R13 **Taiwan Strait** *var.* Formosa Strait, *Chin.* T'aiwan Haihsia, Taiwan Haixia. *strait* China/Taiwan
167 N4 **Taiyuan** *prev.* T'ai-yuan, T'ai-yüan, Yangku. Shanxi, C China *37.48N 112.33E*
167 R7 **Taizhou** Jiangsu, E China *32.36N 119.52E*
167 S10 **Taizhou** *prev.* Haimen, Jiaojiang. Zhejiang, SE China *28.36N 121.19E*
Taizhou *see* Linhai
147 O16 **Ta'izz** SW Yemen *13.36N 44.04E*
147 O16 **Ta'izz** ✕ SW Yemen *13.40N 44.10E*
77 P12 **Tajarhī** SW Libya *24.21N 14.28E*
153 P13 **Tajikistan** *off.* Republic of Tajikistan, *Rus.* Tadzhikistan, *Taj.* Jumhurii Tojikiston; *prev.* Tajik S.S.R. ◆ *republic* C Asia
Tajik S.S.R *see* Tajikistan
171 Kk14 **Tajima** Fukushima, Honshū, C Japan *37.10N 139.46E*
Tajoe *see* Tayu
Tajo, Río *see* Tagus
44 B5 **Tajumulco, Volcán** ▲ W Guatemala *15.04N 91.50W*
107 P7 **Tajuña** ∾ C Spain
Tajura, Gulf of *see* Tadjoura, Golfe de
178 H9 **Tak** *var.* Rahaeng. Tak, W Thailand *16.51N 99.07E*
201 U4 **Taka Atoll** *var.* Tōke. *atoll* Ratak Chain, N Marshall Islands
171 L16 **Takahagi** Ibaraki, Honshū, S Japan *36.43N 140.40E*
170 Ff13 **Takahashi** *var.* Takahasi. Okayama, Honshū, SW Japan *34.48N 133.37E*
170 F13 **Takahashi-gawa** ∾ Honshū, SW Japan
Takahasi *see* Takahashi
201 P12 **Takaieu Island** *island* E Micronesia
192 I13 **Takaka** Tasman, South Island, NZ *40.52S 172.49E*
175 P13 **Takalar** Sulawesi, C Indonesia *5.28S 119.24E*
170 Ff14 **Takamatsu** *var.* Takamatu. Kagawa, Shikoku, SW Japan *34.18N 133.58E*
Takamatu *see* Takamatsu
170 Cc14 **Takamori** Kumamoto, Kyūshū, SW Japan *32.50N 131.08E*
170 Cc16 **Takanabe** Miyazaki, Kyūshū, SW Japan *32.13N 131.31E*
175 O16 **Takan, Gunung** ▲ Pulau Sumba, S Indonesia *8.52S 117.32E*
171 M9 **Takanosu** Akita, Honshū, C Japan *40.13N 140.23E*
Takao *see* Kaohsiung
171 Ii13 **Takaoka** Toyama, Honshū, SW Japan *36.43N 137.01E*
192 N12 **Takapau** Hawke's Bay, North Island, NZ *40.01S 176.21E*
203 U9 **Takapoto** *atoll* Îles Tuamotu, C French Polynesia
192 L5 **Takapuna** Auckland, North Island, NZ *36.48S 174.45E*
171 Gg14 **Takarazuka** Hyōgo, Honshū, SW Japan *34.48N 135.18E*
203 U9 **Takaroa** *atoll* Îles Tuamotu, C French Polynesia
171 Jj15 **Takasaki** Gunma, Honshū, S Japan *36.20N 139.00E*
171 Gg15 **Takatsuki** *var.* Takatuki. Ōsaka, Honshū, SW Japan *34.50N 135.36E*
Takatuki *see* Takatsuki
171 Ii14 **Takayama** Gifu, Honshū, SW Japan *36.09N 137.17E*
171 Hh13 **Takefu** *var.* Takehu. Fukui, Honshū, SW Japan *35.55N 136.11E*
170 F14 **Takehara** Hiroshima, Honshū, SW Japan *34.19N 132.52E*
Takehu *see* Takefu
170 C13 **Takeo** Saga, Kyūshū, SW Japan *33.12N 130.01E*
Takeo *see* Takêv
170 B17 **Take-shima** *island* Nansei-shotō, SW Japan
148 M5 **Tākestān** *var.* Takistan; *prev.* Siadehan. Qazvīn, N Iran *36.02N 49.36E*
170 D14 **Taketa** Ōita, Kyūshū, SW Japan *32.56N 131.21E*
178 J14 **Takêv** *prev.* Takeo. Takêv, S Cambodia *10.58N 104.46E*
178 Hh10 **Tak Fah** Nakhon Sawan, C Thailand
145 T13 **Takhādīd** *well* S Iraq *29.56N 44.33E*
155 R3 **Takhār** ◆ *province* NE Afghanistan
Takhiatash *see* Takhiatosh
152 H8 **Takhiatosh** *Rus.* Takhiatash. Qoraqalpoghiston Respublikasi, W Uzbekistan *42.27N 59.26E*
178 J13 **Ta Khmau** Kândal, S Cambodia *11.30N 104.59E*
152 H9 **Takhta** *Turkm.* Tahta. Dashkhovuzskiy Velayat, N Turkmenistan *41.40N 59.51E*
152 J16 **Takhtabazar** *var.* Tagtabazar. Maryyskiy Velayat, S Turkmenistan *35.57N 62.49E*
151 O8 **Takhtabrod** Severnyy Kazakhstan, N Kazakhstan *52.35N 67.37E*
152 H7 **Takhtakŭpir** *Rus.* Takhtakupyr. Qoraqalpoghiston Respublikasi, NW Uzbekistan *43.04N 60.23E*
Takhtakupyr *see* Takhtakŭpir
148 M8 **Takht-e Shāh, Kūh-e** ▲ C Iran
79 V12 **Takiéta** Zinder, S Niger *13.43N 8.33E*
15 I5 **Takijuq Lake** ◎ Nunavut, NW Canada
172 P4 **Takikawa** Hokkaidō, NE Japan *43.34N 141.54E*
172 Pp4 **Takinoue** Hokkaidō, NE Japan *44.10N 143.09E*
Takistan *see* Tākestān
193 B23 **Takitimu Mountains** ▲ South Island, NZ
Takkaze *see* Tekezē
172 N10 **Takko** Aomori, Honshū, C Japan *40.19N 141.11E*
8 L13 **Takla Lake** ◎ British Columbia, SW Canada
Takla Makan Desert *see* Taklimakan Shamo
164 H9 **Taklimakan Shamo** *Eng.* Takla Makan Desert. *desert* NW China
178 Jj12 **Takôk** Môndôl Kiri, E Cambodia *12.37N 106.30E*
175 P9 **Takolekaju, Pegunungan** ▲ Sulawesi, N Indonesia
41 P10 **Takotna** Alaska, USA *62.59N 156.03W*
Takow *see* Kaohsiung
126 Kk14 **Taksimo** Respublika Buryatiya, S Russian Federation *56.18N 114.53E*
170 Cc13 **Taku** Saga, Kyūshū, SW Japan *33.17N 130.07E*
8 I10 **Taku** ∾ British Columbia, W Canada
177 G15 **Takua Pa** *var.* Ban Takua Pa. Phangnga, SW Thailand *8.47N 98.16E*
79 W16 **Takum** Taraba, E Nigeria *7.16N 10.00E*
203 V10 **Takume** *atoll* Îles Tuamotu, C French Polynesia
202 L16 **Takutea** *island* S Cook Islands
195 U11 **Takuu Islands** *prev.* Mortlock Group. *island group* NE PNG
121 L18 **Tal'** *Rus.* Tal'. Minskaya Voblasts', S Belarus *52.52N 27.59E*
42 L13 **Tala** Jalisco, C Mexico *20.39N 103.45W*
63 F19 **Tala** Canelones, S Uruguay *34.24S 55.45W*
Talabriga *see* Aveiro, Portugal
Talabriga *see* Talavera de la Reina, Spain
121 N14 **Talachyn** *Rus.* Tolochin. Vitsyebskaya Voblasts', NE Belarus *54.25N 29.42E*
155 U7 **Talagang** Punjab, E Pakistan *32.55N 72.23E*
161 J23 **Talaimannar** Northern Province, NW Sri Lanka *9.07N 79.45E*
119 R3 **Talalayivka** Chernihivs'ka Oblast', N Ukraine *50.51N 33.09E*
45 O15 **Talamanca, Cordillera de** ▲ S Costa Rica
58 A9 **Talara** Piura, NW Peru *4.31S 81.17W*
106 L11 **Talarrubias** Extremadura, W Spain *39.03N 5.13W*
153 S8 **Talas** Talasskaya Oblast', NW Kyrgyzstan *42.29N 72.21E*
153 S8 **Talas** ∾ NW Kyrgyzstan
195 N11 **Talasea** New Britain, E PNG *5.19S 150.02E*
Talas Oblasty *see* Talasskaya Oblast'
153 S8 **Talasskaya Oblast'** *Kir.* Talas Oblasty. ◆ *province* NW Kyrgyzstan
153 S8 **Talasskiy Alatau, Khrebet** ▲ Kazakhstan/Kyrgyzstan
79 U12 **Talata Mafara** Zamfara, NW Nigeria *12.33N 6.01E*
175 Ss4 **Talaud, Kepulauan** *island group* E Indonesia
106 M9 **Talavera de la Reina** *anc.* Caesarobriga, Talabriga. Castilla-La Mancha, C Spain *39.58N 4.49W*
106 J11 **Talavera la Real** Extremadura, W Spain *38.52N 6.46W*
194 L12 **Talawe, Mount** ▲ New Britain, C PNG *5.30S 148.24E*
25 S5 **Talbotton** Georgia, SE USA *32.40N 84.32W*
191 R7 **Talbragar River** ∾ New South Wales, SE Australia
64 G13 **Talca** Maule, C Chile *35.28S 71.42W*
64 F13 **Talcahuano** Bío Bío, C Chile *36.43S 73.07W*
160 N12 **Tālcher** Orissa, E India *20.57N 85.13E*
27 W5 **Talco** Texas, SW USA *33.21N 95.06W*
151 V14 **Taldykorgan** *Kaz.* Taldyqorghan; *prev.* Taldy-Kurgan. Almaty, SE Kazakhstan *45.00N 78.23E*
Taldy-Kurgan/Taldyqorghan *see* Taldykorgan
153 Y7 **Taldy-Suu** Issyk-Kul'skaya Oblast', E Kyrgyzstan *42.49N 78.33E*
153 U10 **Taldy-Suu** Oshskaya Oblast', SW Kyrgyzstan *40.33N 73.52E*
Tal-e Khosravī *see* Yāsūj
200 Ss14 **Taleki Tonga** *island* Otu Tolu Group, C Tonga
200 Ss13 **Taleki Vavu'u** *island* Otu Tolu Group, C Tonga
104 J13 **Talence** Gironde, SW France *44.49N 0.35W*
151 U16 **Talgar** *Kaz.* Talghar. Almaty, SE Kazakhstan *43.25N 77.07E*
Talghar *see* Talgar
175 Rr10 **Taliabu, Pulau** *island* Kepulauan Sula, C Indonesia
117 L22 **Taliarós, Akrotírio** *headland* Astypálaia, Kykládes, Greece, Aegean Sea *36.31N 26.18E*
Ta-lien *see* Dalian
29 Q12 **Talihina** Oklahoma, C USA *34.45N 95.03W*
Talimardzhan *see* Tollimarjon
Talin *see* T'alin
143 T12 **T'alin** *Rus.* Talin; *prev.* Verin T'alin. W Armenia *40.23N 43.51E*
83 E15 **Tali Post** Bahr el Gabel, S Sudan *5.55N 30.43E*
Taliq-an *see* Tāloqān
Taliş Dağları *see* Talish Mountains
148 L2 **Talish Mountains** *Az.* Taliş Dağları, *Per.* Kūhhā-ye Ṭavālesh, *Rus.* Talyshskiye Gory. ▲ Azerbaijan/Iran
125 F11 **Talitsa** Sverdlovskaya Oblast', C Russian Federation *56.58N 63.34E*
175 O16 **Taliwang** Sumbawa, C Indonesia *8.45S 116.55E*
121 L17 **Tal'ka** *Rus.* Tal'ka. Minskaya Voblasts', C Belarus *53.22N 28.22E*
Talkang *see* Dorbod
41 R11 **Talkeetna** Alaska, USA *62.19N 150.06W*
41 R11 **Talkeetna Mountains** ▲ Alaska, USA
Talkhof *see* Puurmani
94 H2 **Tálknafjörður** Vestfirdhir, W Iceland *65.38N 23.51W*
145 Q3 **Tall 'Abṭah** N Iraq *35.52N 42.40E*
144 M2 **Tall Abyaḍ** *var.* Tell Abiad. Ar Raqqah, N Syria *36.42N 38.56E*
25 Q4 **Talladega** Alabama, S USA *33.26N 86.06W*
145 Q2 **Tall 'Afar** N Iraq *36.22N 42.27E*
25 S8 **Tallahassee** *prev.* Muskogean. *state capital* Florida, SE USA *30.26N 84.16W*
24 L2 **Tallahatchie River** ∾ Mississippi, S USA
Tall al Abyaḍ *see* At Tall al Abyaḍ
145 W12 **Tall al Laḥm** S Iraq *30.46N 46.22E*
191 P11 **Tallangatta** Victoria, SE Australia *36.15S 147.13E*
25 R4 **Tallapoosa River** ∾ Alabama/Georgia, S USA
105 T13 **Tallard** Hautes-Alpes, SE France *44.30N 6.04E*
145 Q3 **Tall ash Sha'īr** N Iraq *36.11N 42.26E*
25 Q5 **Tallassee** Alabama, S USA *32.32N 85.53W*
145 R4 **Tall 'Azbah** NW Iraq *35.47N 43.13E*
144 I5 **Tall Bīsah** Ḥimṣ, W Syria *34.49N 36.43E*
145 R3 **Tall Ḥassūnah** N Iraq *36.05N 43.10E*
145 Q2 **Tall Ḥuqnah** *var.* Tell Huqnah. N Iraq *36.33N 42.34E*
Tallin *see* Tallinn
120 G3 **Tallinn** *Ger.* Reval, *Rus.* Tallin; *prev.* Revel. ● (Estonia) Harjumaa, NW Estonia *59.25N 24.42E*
120 H3 **Tallinn** ✕ Harjumaa, NW Estonia *59.23N 24.52E*
144 H5 **Tall Kalakh** *var.* Tell Kalakh. Ḥimṣ, C Syria *34.40N 36.18E*
145 R2 **Tall Kayf** NW Iraq *36.30N 43.07E*
Tall Kūchak *see* Tall Kūshik
145 P2 **Tall Kūshik** *var.* Tall Kūchak. Al Ḥasakah, E Syria *36.48N 42.01E*
33 U12 **Tallmadge** Ohio, N USA *41.06N 81.26W*
24 J5 **Tallulah** Louisiana, S USA *32.22N 91.12W*
145 Q2 **Tall 'Uwaynāt** NW Iraq *36.43N 42.18E*
145 Q2 **Tall Ẓāhir** N Iraq *36.51N 42.29E*
126 H14 **Tal'menka** Altayskiy Kray, S Russian Federation *53.55N 83.26E*
126 I8 **Talnakh** Taymyrskiy (Dolgano-Nenetskiy) Avtonomnyy Okrug, N Russian Federation *69.26N 88.26E*
119 P7 **Tal'ne** *Rus.* Tal'noye. Cherkas'ka Oblast', C Ukraine *48.54N 30.39E*
Tal'noye *see* Tal'ne
82 E12 **Talodi** Southern Kordofan, C Sudan *10.40N 30.25E*
196 B16 **Talofofo** SE Guam *13.21N 144.45E*
196 B16 **Talofofo Bay** *bay* SE Guam
28 L9 **Taloga** Oklahoma, C USA *36.01N 98.58W*
127 O10 **Talon** Magadanskaya Oblast', E Russian Federation *59.47N 148.46E*
12 H11 **Talon, Lake** ◎ Ontario, S Canada
155 R2 **Tāloqān** *var.* Taliq-an. Takhār, NE Afghanistan *36.43N 69.33E*
130 M8 **Talovaya** Voronezhskaya Oblast', W Russian Federation *51.07N 40.46E*
175 Qq10 **Talowa, Teluk** *bay* Sulawesi, C Indonesia
15 Kk3 **Taloyoak** *prev.* Spence Bay. Nunavut, N Canada *69.30N 93.25W*
27 Q8 **Talpa** Texas, SW USA *31.46N 99.42W*
42 K13 **Talpa de Allende** Jalisco, C Mexico *20.22N 104.51W*
25 S9 **Talquin, Lake** ⊡ Florida, SE USA
Talsen *see* Talsi
168 H9 **Talshand** Govĭ-Altay, C Mongolia *45.21N 98.00E*
120 E8 **Talsi** *Ger.* Talsen. Talsi, NW Latvia *57.14N 22.34E*
149 V11 **Tal Sīāh** Sīstān va Balūchestān, SE Iran *28.19N 57.43E*
64 G6 **Taltal** Antofagasta, N Chile *25.22S 70.27W*
15 I18 **Taltson** ∾ Northwest Territories, NW Canada
174 H8 **Taluk** Sumatera, W Indonesia *0.30S 101.36E*
94 J8 **Talvik** Finnmark, N Norway *70.02N 22.58E*
190 M7 **Talyawalka Creek** ∾ New South Wales, SE Australia
Talyshskiye Gory *see* Talish Mountains
31 W14 **Tama** Iowa, C USA *41.58N 92.34W*
Tama Abu, Banjaran *see* Penambo, Banjaran
175 N5 **Tamabo, Banjaran** ▲ East Malaysia
202 B16 **Tamakautoga** SW Niue *19.04S 169.55W*
131 N7 **Tamala** Penzenskaya Oblast', W Russian Federation *52.32N 43.18E*
79 P15 **Tamale** C Ghana *9.21N 0.54W*
170 Cc13 **Tamana** Kumamoto, Kyūshū, SW Japan *32.54N 130.34E*
203 P3 **Tamana** *prev.* Rotcher Island. *atoll* Tungaru, W Kiribati
170 Ff14 **Tamano** Okayama, Honshū, SW Japan *34.28N 133.53E*
76 K12 **Tamanrasset** *var.* Tamenghest. S Algeria *22.49N 5.31E*
76 J13 **Tamanrasset** *wadi* Algeria/Mali
177 G2 **Tamanthi** Sagaing, N Burma *25.17N 95.18E*
99 I24 **Tamar** ∾ SW England, UK
Tamar *see* Tudmur
56 H9 **Támara** Casanare, C Colombia *5.51N 72.10W*
56 F7 **Tamar, Alto de** ▲ C Colombia *7.25N 74.28W*
181 X16 **Tamarin** E Mauritius *20.19S 57.22E*
107 T5 **Tamarite de Litera** *var.* Tararite de Litera. Aragón, NE Spain *41.52N 0.25E*
113 I24 **Tamási** Tolna, S Hungary *46.39N 18.16E*
Tamatave *see* Toamasina
43 O9 **Tamaulipas** ◆ *state* C Mexico
43 P10 **Tamaulipas, Sierra de** ▲ C Mexico
58 F12 **Tamaya, Río** ∾ E Peru
42 I9 **Tamazula** Durango, C Mexico *24.43N 106.33W*
42 L14 **Tamazula** Jalisco, C Mexico *19.41N 103.18W*
Tamazulápam *see* Tamazulapán
43 Q15 **Tamazulapán** *var.* Tamazulápam. Oaxaca, SE Mexico *17.40N 97.33W*
43 P12 **Tamazunchale** San Luis Potosí, C Mexico *21.17N 98.45W*
78 H11 **Tambacounda** SE Senegal *13.43N 13.43W*
85 M16 **Tambara** Manica, C Mozambique *16.45S 34.14E*
175 Pp9 **Tambarana** Sulawesi, N Indonesia *1.09S 120.30E*
79 T13 **Tambawel** Sokoto, NW Nigeria *12.24N 4.42E*
195 W15 **Tambea** Guadalcanal, C Solomon Islands *9.19S 159.42E*
174 Jj7 **Tambelan, Kepulauan** *island group* W Indonesia
59 E15 **Tambo de Mora** Ica, W Peru *13.43S 76.12W*
175 Oo15 **Tambora, Gunung** ⩕ Sumbawa, S Indonesia *8.16S 117.59E*
63 E17 **Tambores** Paysandú, W Uruguay *31.49S 56.16W*
59 F14 **Tambo, Río** ∾ C Peru
58 F7 **Tamboryacu, Río** ∾ N Peru
130 M7 **Tambov** Tambovskaya Oblast', W Russian Federation *52.43N 41.28E*
130 L6 **Tambovskaya Oblast'** ◆ *province* W Russian Federation
106 H3 **Tambre** ∾ NW Spain
175 Nn3 **Tambunan** Sabah, East Malaysia *5.40N 116.22E*
83 C15 **Tambura** Western Equatoria, SW Sudan *5.37N 27.30E*
175 P8 **Tambu, Teluk** *bay* Sulawesi, C Indonesia
Tamchaket *see* Tâmchekket
78 J9 **Tâmchekket** *var.* Tamchaket. Hodh el Gharbi, S Mauritania *17.12N 10.36W*
178 Jj7 **Tam Điệp** Ninh Binh, N Vietnam *20.09N 105.54E*
Tamdybulak *see* Tomdibuloq
56 H8 **Tame** Arauca, C Colombia *6.27N 71.44W*
106 H6 **Tâmega, Rio** *Sp.* Río Támega. ∾ Portugal/Spain
117 H20 **Tamélos, Akrotírio** *headland* Kéa, Kykládes, Greece, Aegean Sea *37.31N 24.16E*
Tamenghest *see* Tamanrasset
79 V8 **Tamgak, Adrar** ▲ C Niger *19.10N 8.39E*
78 I13 **Tamgue** ▲ NW Guinea *12.14N 12.18W*
43 Q12 **Tamiahua** Veracruz-Llave, E Mexico *21.15N 97.27W*
43 Q12 **Tamiahua, Laguna de** *lagoon* E Mexico
25 Y16 **Tamiami Canal** *canal* Florida, SE USA
196 F17 **Tamil Harbor** *harbor* Yap, W Micronesia
161 H21 **Tamil Nādu** *prev.* Madras. ◆ *state* SE India
101 H20 **Tamines** Namur, S Belgium *50.27N 4.37E*
118 E12 **Tamiš** *Ger.* Temesch, *Hung.* Temes, *SCr.* Tamiš. ∾ Romania/Yugoslavia
178 Kk10 **Tam Kỳ** Quang Nam-Đa Nẵng, C Vietnam *15.31N 108.30E*
Tammerfors *see* Tampere
Tammisaari *see* Ekenäs
97 N14 **Tämnaren** ◎ C Sweden
203 Q7 **Tamotoe, Passe** *passage* Tahiti, W French Polynesia
25 V12 **Tampa** Florida, SE USA *27.57N 82.27W*
25 V12 **Tampa** ✕ Florida, SE USA *27.57N 82.29W*
25 V13 **Tampa Bay** *bay* Florida, SE USA
95 L18 **Tampere** *Swe.* Tammerfors. Länsi-Suomi, W Finland *61.30N 23.45E*
43 Q11 **Tampico** Tamaulipas, C Mexico *22.18N 97.52W*
175 Qq12 **Tampo** Pulau Muna, C Indonesia *4.38S 122.40E*
178 Kk11 **Tam Quan** Bình Định, C Vietnam *14.34N 109.00E*
176 V9 **Tamrau, Pegunungan** ▲ Irian Jaya, E Indonesia
168 J13 **Tamsag Muchang** Nei Mongol Zizhiqu, N China *40.28N 102.34E*
Tamsal *see* Tamsalu
120 I4 **Tamsalu** *Ger.* Tamsal. Lääne-Virumaa, NE Estonia *59.10N 26.07E*
111 S8 **Tamsweg** Salzburg, SW Austria *47.07N 13.49E*
177 Ff3 **Tamu** Sagaing, N Burma *24.11N 94.21E*
43 P12 **Tamuín** San Luis Potosí, C Mexico *21.57N 98.46W*
196 C15 **Tamuning** NW Guam *13.29N 144.47E*
191 T6 **Tamworth** New South Wales, SE Australia *31.07S 150.54E*
99 M19 **Tamworth** C England, UK *52.39N 1.40W*
94 L8 **Tana** Finnmark, N Norway *70.10N 28.06E*
94 M8 **Tana** *var.* Tenojoki, *Fin.* Teno, *Lapp.* Deatnu. ∾ Finland/Norway *see also* Teno
83 K19 **Tana** ∾ SE Kenya
170 G17 **Tanabe** Wakayama, Honshū, SW Japan *33.43N 135.22E*
41 T10 **Tanacross** Alaska, USA *63.30N 143.21W*
94 L7 **Tanafjorden** *fjord* N Norway
40 G17 **Tanaga Island** *island* Aleutian Islands, Alaska, USA
40 G17 **Tanaga Volcano** ▲ Tanaga Island, Alaska, USA *51.53N 178.08W*
109 M18 **Tanagro** ∾ S Italy
82 H11 **T'ana Hāyk'** *Eng.* Lake Tana. ◎ NW Ethiopia
173 F8 **Tanahbela, Pulau** *island* Kepulauan Batu, W Indonesia
175 Pp15 **Tanahjampea, Pulau** *island* W Indonesia
173 Ff8 **Tanahmasa, Pulau** *island* Kepulauan Batu, W Indonesia
Tanais *see* Don
158 L10 **Tanakpur** Uttar Pradesh, N India *29.04N 80.06E*
Tana, Lake *see* T'ana Hāyk'
189 P5 **Tanami Desert** *desert* Northern Territory, N Australia
178 Jj14 **Tân An** Long An, S Vietnam *10.31N 106.24E*
41 Q9 **Tanana** Alaska, USA *65.12N 152.00W*
Tananarive *see* Antananarivo
41 Q9 **Tanana River** ∾ Alaska, USA
97 C16 **Tananger** Rogaland, S Norway *58.55N 5.34E*
196 H5 **Tanapag** Saipan, S Northern Mariana Islands *15.13S 145.45E*
196 H5 **Tanapag, Puetton** *bay* Saipan, S Northern Mariana Islands
108 C9 **Tanaro** ∾ N Italy
169 Y12 **Tanch'ŏn** E North Korea *40.22N 128.49E*
42 M14 **Tancitaro, Cerro** ⩕ C Mexico *19.16N 102.25W*
159 N12 **Tānda** Uttar Pradesh, N India *26.36N 82.39E*
79 O15 **Tanda** E Ivory Coast *7.48N 3.10W*
179 Rr14 **Tandag** Mindanao, S Philippines *9.00N 126.13E*
118 L14 **Ţăndărei** Ialomiţa, SE Romania *44.39N 27.40E*
65 N14 **Tandil** Buenos Aires, E Argentina *37.18S 59.10W*
80 H12 **Tandjilé** *off.* Préfecture du Tandjilé. ◆ *prefecture* SW Chad
Tandjoeng *see* Tanjung
Tandjoengpandan *see* Tanjungpandan
Tandjoengpinang *see* Tanjungpinang
Tandjoengredeb *see* Tanjungredeb
155 Q16 **Tando Allāhyār** Sind, SE Pakistan *25.30N 68.43E*
155 Q17 **Tando Bāgo** Sind, SE Pakistan *24.48N 68.58E*
155 Q16 **Tando Muhammad Khān** Sind, SE Pakistan *25.07N 68.34E*
190 L7 **Tandou Lake** *seasonal lake* New South Wales, SE Australia
96 L11 **Tandsjöborg** Gävleborg, C Sweden *61.40N 14.40E*
161 H15 **Tāndūr** Andhra Pradesh, C India *17.16N 77.37E*
170 Bb17 **Tanega-shima** *island* Nansei-shotō, SW Japan
172 N10 **Taneichi** Iwate, Honshū, C Japan *40.23N 141.42E*
Tanen Taunggyi *see* Tane Range
178 H8 **Tane Range** *Bur.* Tanen Taunggyi. ▲ W Thailand
113 P15 **Tanew** ∾ SE Poland
23 W2 **Taneytown** Maryland, NE USA *39.39N 77.10W*
76 H12 **Tanezrouft** *desert* Algeria/Mali
144 L7 **Ţanf, Jabal aţ** ▲ SE Syria *33.31N 38.43E*
83 J21 **Tanga** Tanga, E Tanzania *5.07S 39.04E*
83 I22 **Tanga** ◆ *region* E Tanzania
159 T14 **Tangail** Dhaka, C Bangladesh *24.15N 89.55E*
195 Q9 **Tanga Islands** *island group* NE PNG
161 K26 **Tangalla** Southern Province, S Sri Lanka *6.01N 80.46E*
Tanganyika and Zanzibar *see* Tanzania
70 I13 **Tanganyika, Lake** ◎ E Africa
58 E7 **Tangarana, Río** ∾ N Peru
195 W16 **Tangarare** Guadalcanal, C Solomon Islands *9.37S 159.40E*
203 V16 **Tangaroa, Maunga** ⩕ Easter Island, Chile, E Pacific Ocean
76 G5 **Tanger** *var.* Tangiers, Tangier, *Fr./Ger.* Tangerk, *Sp.* Tánger; *anc.* Tingis. NW Morocco *35.49N 5.48W*
174 J14 **Tangerang** Jawa, C Indonesia *6.13S 106.36E*
Tangerk *see* Tanger
102 M12 **Tangermünde** Sachsen-Anhalt, C Germany *52.35N 11.57E*
162 K10 **Tanggula Shan** *var.* Dangla, Tangla Range. ▲ W China
165 N13 **Tanggula Shan** ▲ W China *33.18N 91.10E*
Tanggulashan *see* Tuotuoheyan
162 K10 **Tanggula Shankou** *pass* W China *32.52N 91.59E*
167 N7 **Tanghe** Henan, C China *32.40N 112.49E*
155 T5 **Tāngi** North-West Frontier Province, NW Pakistan *34.18N 71.42E*
Tangier *see* Tanger
23 Y5 **Tangier Island** *island* Virginia, NE USA
Tangiers *see* Tanger
24 K8 **Tangipahoa River** ∾ Louisiana, S USA
Tangla Range *see* Tanggula Shan
171 H13 **Tango-hantō** *peninsula* Honshū, SW Japan
162 I10 **Tangra Yumco** *var.* Tangro Tso. ◎ W China
Tangro Tso *see* Tangra Yumco
163 T7 **Tangshan** *var.* T'ang-shan. Hebei, E China *39.38N 118.14E*
179 Qq15 **Tangub** *var.* Tangub City. Mindanao, S Philippines *8.07N 123.42E*
79 R14 **Tanguiéta** NW Benin *10.34N 1.19E*
169 X7 **Tangwang He** ∾ NE China
169 X7 **Tangyuan** Heilongjiang, NE China *46.45N 129.52E*
94 M11 **Tanhua** Lappi, N Finland *67.31N 27.30E*
176 Uu16 **Tanimbar, Kepulauan** *island group* Maluku, E Indonesia
Tanintharyi *see* Tenasserim
145 U4 **Tānjarō** ∾ E Iraq
133 T15 **Tanjong Piai** *headland* Peninsular Malaysia
Tanjore *see* Thanjāvūr
175 N10 **Tanjung** *prev.* Tandjoeng. Borneo, C Indonesia *2.07S 115.22E*
175 Oo6 **Tanjungbatu** Borneo, N Indonesia *2.19N 118.03E*
Tanjungkarang *see* Bandarlampung
174 J11 **Tanjunglabu** Pulau Lepar, W Indonesia *2.57S 106.51E*
174 J10 **Tanjungpandan** *prev.* Tandjoengpandan. Pulau Belitung, W Indonesia *2.43S 107.36E*
174 I7 **Tanjungpinang** *prev.* Tandjoengpinang. Pulau Bintan, W Indonesia *0.55N 104.28E*
175 O6 **Tanjungredeb** *var.* Tanjungredep; *prev.* Tandjoengredeb. Borneo, C Indonesia *2.09N 117.28E*
Tanjungredep *see* Tanjungredeb
155 S8 **Tānk** North-West Frontier Province, NW Pakistan *32.13N 70.28E*
197 D16 **Tanna** *island* S Vanuatu
95 F17 **Tännäs** Jämtland, C Sweden *62.27N 12.40E*
Tannenhof *see* Krynica
110 K7 **Tannheim** Tirol, W Austria *47.30N 10.32E*
Tannu-Tuva *see* Tyva, Respublika
175 Rr10 **Tano** Pulau Taliabu, E Indonesia *1.51S 124.55E*

◆ Country ● Country Capital ◇ Dependent Territory ○ Dependent Territory Capital ◆ Administrative Region ✕ International Airport ▲ Mountain ▲ Mountain Range ⩕ Volcano ∾ River ◎ Lake ⊡ Reservoir

Tano – Tefedest

79 O17 **Tano** ~ S Ghana
158 D10 **Tanot** Rājasthān, NW India *27.49N 70.21E*
79 V11 **Tanout** Zinder, C Niger *14.58N 8.54E*
43 P12 **Tanquián** San Luis Potosí, C Mexico *21.38N 98.39W*
79 R13 **Tansarga** E Burkina *11.51N 1.51E*
178 Jj14 **Tan Son Nhat** ✕ (Hồ Chí Minh) Tây Ninh, S Vietnam *10.52N 106.38E*
77 V8 **Tanta** *var.* Tanṭā, Tantâ. N Egypt *30.42N 31.00E*
76 D8 **Tan-Tan** SW Morocco *28.30N 11.10W*
43 P12 **Tantoyuca** Veracruz-Llave, E Mexico *21.18N 98.12W*
158 J12 **Tāntpur** Uttar Pradesh, N India *26.51N 77.28E*
Tan-tung *see* Dandong
40 M2 **Tanunak** Alaska, USA *60.35N 165.15W*
177 Ff8 **Ta-nyaung** Magwe, W Burma *20.49N 94.40E*
178 J5 **Tân Yên** Tuyên Quang, N Vietnam *22.08N 104.58E*
83 F22 **Tanzania** *off.* United Republic of Tanzania, *Swa.* Jamhuri ya Muungano wa Tanzania; *prev.* German East Africa, Tanganyika and Zanzibar. ◆ *republic* E Africa
Tanzania, Jamhuri ya Muungano wa *see* Tanzania
169 U5 **Tao'an** *var.* Taoan, Taonan. Jilin, NE China *45.19N 122.46E*
169 T8 **Tao'er He** ~ NE China
165 U11 **Tao He** ~ C China
T'aon-an *see* Baicheng
Taongi *see* Bokaak Atoll
109 M23 **Taormina** *anc.* Tauromenium. Sicilia, Italy, C Mediterranean Sea *37.54N 15.18E*
39 S9 **Taos** New Mexico, SW USA *36.24N 105.34W*
Taoudenit *see* Taoudenni
79 O6 **Taoudenni** *var.* Taoudenit. Tombouctou, N Mali *22.46N 3.54W*
76 G6 **Taounate** N Morocco *34.34N 4.35W*
167 S13 **T'aoyüan** *Jap.* Tōen. N Taiwan *25.00N 121.15E*
120 I3 **Tapa** *Ger.* Taps. Lääne-Virumaa, NE Estonia *59.15N 26.00E*
43 V17 **Tapachula** Chiapas, SE Mexico *14.53N 92.18W*
Tapaiu *see* Gvardeysk
61 H14 **Tapajós, Rio** *var.* Tapajóz. ~ NW Brazil
Tapajóz *see* Tapajós, Rio
63 C21 **Tapalqué** *var.* Tapalquén. Buenos Aires, E Argentina *36.21S 60.01W*
Tapalquén *see* Tapalqué
Tapanahoni *see* Tapanahony Rivier
57 W11 **Tapanahony Rivier** *var.* Tapanahoni. ~ E Surinam
43 T15 **Tapanatepec** *var.* San Pedro Tapanatepec. Oaxaca, SE Mexico *16.23N 94.09W*
193 D23 **Tapanui** Otago, South Island, NZ *45.55S 169.16E*
Tapanuli, Teluk *see* Sibolga, Teluk
61 E14 **Tapauá** Amazonas, N Brazil *5.42S 64.15W*
49 R7 **Tapauá, Rio** ~ W Brazil
193 I14 **Tapawera** Tasman, South Island, NZ *41.24S 172.50E*
63 I16 **Tapes** Rio Grande do Sul, S Brazil *30.40S 51.25W*
78 K16 **Tapeta** C Liberia *6.30N 8.53W*
160 H11 **Tāpi** *prev.* Tāpti. ~ W India
106 J2 **Tapia de Casariego** Asturias, N Spain *43.34N 6.55W*
58 F19 **Tapiche, Río** ~ N Peru
178 Gg15 **Tapi, Mae Nam** *var.* Luang. ~ SW Thailand
194 K14 **Tapini** Central, S PNG *8.20S 146.57E*
Tapirapecó, Serra *see* Tapirapecó, Sierra
57 N13 **Tapirapecó, Sierra** *Port.* Serra Tapirapecó. ▲▲ Brazil/Venezuela
79 R13 **Tapoa** ~ Benin/Niger
196 H5 **Tapochau, Mount** ▲ Saipan, S Northern Mariana Islands
113 H24 **Tapolca** Veszprém, W Hungary *46.54N 17.28E*
23 X5 **Tappahannock** Virginia, NE USA *37.55N 76.51W*
33 U13 **Tappan Lake** ⊠ Ohio, N USA
171 Mm17 **Tappi-zaki** *headland* Honshū, C Japan *41.15N 140.19E*
Taps *see* Tapa
Tāpti *see* Tāpi
193 J16 **Tapuaenuku** ▲ South Island, NZ *42.00S 173.39E*
179 Pp17 **Tapul Group** *island group* Sulu Archipelago, SW Philippines
60 F11 **Tapurmcuará** *var.* Tapuruquara. Amazonas, NW Brazil *0.17S 65.00W*
Tapuruquara *see* Tapurmcuará
198 C9 **Taputapu, Cape** *headland* Tutuila, W American Samoa *14.19S 170.51W*
147 W13 **Tāqah** S Oman *17.04N 54.24E*
145 T3 **Taqtaq** N Iraq *35.54N 44.36E*
63 J15 **Taquara** Rio Grande do Sul, S Brazil *29.40S 50.46W*
61 H19 **Taquari, Rio** ~ C Brazil
62 L8 **Taquaritinga** São Paulo, S Brazil *21.22S 48.29W*
125 G12 **Tara** Omskaya Oblast', C Russian Federation *56.54N 74.17E*
85 I15 **Tara** Southern, S Zambia *16.54S 26.47E*
115 J15 **Tara** ~ SW Yugoslavia
114 K13 **Tara** ▲▲ W Yugoslavia
79 W15 **Taraba** ◐ *state* E Nigeria
79 X15 **Taraba** ~ E Nigeria
77 O7 **Țarābulus** *var.* Țarābulus al Gharb, *Eng.* Tripoli. ● (Libya) NW Libya *32.54N 13.10E*
77 O7 **Țarābulus** ✕ NW Libya *32.37N 13.07E*
Țarābulus/Țarābulus ash Shām *see* Tripoli
Țarābulus al Gharb *see* Țarābulus
107 O7 **Taracena** Castilla-La Mancha, C Spain *40.39N 3.07W*
119 N12 **Taraclia** *Rus.* Tarakilya. S Moldova *45.55N 28.40E*
145 V10 **Tarād al Kahf** SE Iraq *31.58N 45.58E*
191 R10 **Tarago** New South Wales, SE Australia *35.04S 149.40E*
174 Jj15 **Taraju** Jawa, S Indonesia *7.27S 107.58E*
176 Vv11 **Tarak** Irian Jaya, E Indonesia *3.21S 132.43E*
175 O5 **Tarakan** Borneo, C Indonesia *3.19N 117.37E*
175 O5 **Tarakan, Pulau** *island* N Indonesia
Tarakilya *see* Taraclia
172 Pp16 **Tarama-jima** *island* Sakishima-shotō, SW Japan
192 K10 **Taranaki** *off.* Taranaki Region. ◐ *region* North Island, NZ
192 K10 **Taranaki, Mount** *var.* Egmont. ▲ North Island, NZ *39.16S 174.04E*
107 O9 **Tarancón** Castilla-La Mancha, C Spain *40.01N 3.01W*
196 M15 **Tarang Reef** *reef* C Micronesia
98 E7 **Taransay** *island* NW Scotland, UK
109 P18 **Taranto** *var.* Tarentum. Puglia, SE Italy *40.30N 17.10E*
109 O19 **Taranto, Golfo di** *Eng.* Gulf of Taranto. *gulf* S Italy
Taranto, Gulf of *see* Taranto, Golfo di
64 G3 **Tarapacá** *off.* Región de Tarapacá. ◐ *region* N Chile
195 Y16 **Tarapaina** Maramasike Island, N Solomon Islands *9.28S 161.24E*
58 D10 **Tarapoto** San Martín, N Peru *6.31S 76.24W*
144 M6 **Taraq an Na'jah** *hill range* E Syria
144 M6 **Taraq Sidāwī** *hill range* E Syria
105 Q11 **Tarare** Rhône, E France *45.54N 4.25E*
Tararite de Llitera *see* Tamarite de Litera
192 M13 **Tararua Range** ▲▲ North Island, NZ
157 Q22 **Tarāsa Dwīp** *island* Nicobar Islands, India, NE Indian Ocean
105 Q15 **Tarascon** Bouches-du-Rhône, SE France *43.48N 4.39E*
104 M17 **Tarascon-sur-Ariège** Ariège, S France *42.51N 1.36E*
119 P6 **Tarashcha** Kyyivs'ka Oblast', N Ukraine *49.34N 30.31E*
59 L18 **Tarata** Cochabamba, C Bolivia *17.34S 66.04W*
59 I18 **Tarata** Tacna, SW Peru *17.30S 70.00W*
202 H2 **Taratai** *atoll* Tungaru, W Kiribati
61 B15 **Tarauacá** Acre, W Brazil *8.06S 70.45W*
61 B15 **Tarauacá, Rio** ~ NW Brazil
203 Q8 **Taravao** Tahiti, W French Polynesia *17.43S 149.19W*
203 R8 **Taravao, Baie de** *bay* Tahiti, W French Polynesia
203 Q8 **Taravao, Isthme de** *isthmus* Tahiti, W French Polynesia
105 X16 **Taravo** ~ Corse, France, C Mediterranean Sea
202 J3 **Tarawa** ✕ Tarawa, W Kiribati *0.52S 169.31E*
202 H2 **Tarawa** *atoll* Tungaru, W Kiribati
192 N10 **Tarawera** Hawke's Bay, North Island, NZ *39.03S 176.34E*
192 N8 **Tarawera, Lake** ◎ North Island, NZ
192 N8 **Tarawera, Mount** ▲ North Island, NZ *38.13S 176.29E*
107 S8 **Tarayuela** ▲ N Spain *40.28N 0.22W*
151 R16 **Taraz** *prev.* Aulie Ata, Auliye-Ata, Dzhambul, Zhambyl. Zhambyl, S Kazakhstan. *42.55N 71.27E*
107 Q5 **Tarazona** Aragón, NE Spain *41.54N 1.43W*
107 Q10 **Tarazona de la Mancha** Castilla-La Mancha, C Spain *39.16N 1.55W*
151 X12 **Tarbagatay, Khrebet** ▲▲ China/Kazakhstan
98 J8 **Tarbat Ness** *headland* N Scotland, UK *57.51N 3.48W*
155 U5 **Tarbela Reservoir** ⊠ N Pakistan
98 H12 **Tarbert** W Scotland, UK *55.52N 5.25W*
98 F7 **Tarbert** Western Isles, NW Scotland, UK *57.53N 6.48W*
104 K16 **Tarbes** *anc.* Bigorra. Hautes-Pyrénées, S France *43.13N 0.04E*
23 W9 **Tarboro** North Carolina, SE USA *35.54N 77.32W*
Tarca *see* Torysa
108 J6 **Tarcento** Friuli-Venezia Giulia, NE Italy *46.13N 13.13E*
190 F5 **Tarcoola** South Australia *30.44S 134.33E*
107 S5 **Tardienta** Aragón, NE Spain *41.58N 0.31W*
104 L11 **Tardoire** ~ W France
191 U7 **Taree** New South Wales, SE Australia *31.55S 152.28E*
94 K12 **Tärendö** Norrbotten, N Sweden *67.10N 22.40E*
Tarentum *see* Taranto
76 C9 **Tarfaya** SW Morocco *27.56N 12.55W*
118 J13 **Târgoviște** *prev.* Tîrgoviște. Dâmbovița, S Romania *44.54N 25.28E*
118 M12 **Târgu Bujor** *prev.* Tîrgu Bujor. Galați, E Romania *45.52N 27.55E*
118 H13 **Târgu Cărbunești** *prev.* Tîrgu. Gorj, SW Romania *44.57N 23.31E*
118 L9 **Târgu Frumos** *prev.* Tîrgu Frumos. Iași, NE Romania *47.12N 27.00E*
118 H13 **Târgu Jiu** *prev.* Tîrgu Jiu. Gorj, W Romania *45.02N 23.19E*
118 H9 **Târgu Lăpuș** *prev.* Tîrgu Lăpuș. Maramureș, N Romania *47.28N 23.54E*
Târgul-Neamț *see* Târgu-Neamț
Târgul-Săcuiesc *see* Târgu Secuiesc
118 I10 **Târgu Mureș** *prev.* Oșorhei, Tîrgu Mures, *Ger.* Neumarkt, *Hung.* Marosvásárhely. Mureș, C Romania *46.33N 24.36E*
118 K9 **Târgu-Neamț** *var.* Târgul-Neamț; *prev.* Tîrgu-Neamț. Neamț, NE Romania *47.12N 26.25E*
118 K11 **Târgu Ocna** *Hung.* Aknavásár; *prev.* Tîrgu Ocna. Bacău, E Romania *46.16N 26.37E*
118 K11 **Târgu Secuiesc** *Ger.* Neumarkt, Szekler Neumarkt, *Hung.* Kezdivásárhely; *prev.* Chezdi-Oșorheiu, Târgul-Săcuiesc, Tîrgu Secuiesc. Covasna, E Romania *46.00N 26.08E*
151 X10 **Targyn** Vostochnyy Kazakhstan, E Kazakhstan *49.31N 82.46E*
Tar Heel State *see* North Carolina
194 G12 **Tari** Southern Highlands, W PNG *5.52S 142.58E*
149 P17 **Țarīf** Abū Ẓaby, C UAE *24.01N 53.46E*
106 K16 **Tarifa** Andalucía, S Spain *36.01N 5.36W*
86 C14 **Tarifa, Punta de** *headland* SW Spain *36.01N 5.39W*
59 M21 **Tarija** Tarija, S Bolivia *21.33S 64.42W*
59 M21 **Tarija** ◐ *department* S Bolivia
147 R14 **Tarim** C Yemen *16.00N 48.50E*
Tarim Basin *see* Tarim Pendi
83 G19 **Tarime** Mara, N Tanzania *1.19S 34.24E*
133 S8 **Tarim He** ~ NW China
165 H8 **Tarim Pendi** *Eng.* Tarim Basin. *basin* NW China
155 N7 **Tarīn Kowt** *var.* Terinkot. Urūzgān, C Afghanistan *32.37N 65.52E*
175 Pp10 **Taripa** Sulawesi, C Indonesia *1.51S 120.46E*
176 Z11 **Taritatu, Sungai** *prev.* Idenburg-rivier. ~ Irian Jaya, E Indonesia
119 Q12 **Tarkhankut, Mys** *headland* S Ukraine *45.20N 32.32E*
29 Q1 **Tarkio** Missouri, C USA *40.25N 95.24W*
126 H9 **Tarko-Sale** Yamalo-Nenetskiy Avtonomnyy Okrug, N Russian Federation *64.55N 77.34E*
79 P17 **Tarkwa** S Ghana *5.16N 1.58W*
179 P10 **Tarlac** Luzon, N Philippines *15.29N 120.34E*
97 F22 **Tarm** Ringkøbing, W Denmark *55.55N 8.31E*
59 E14 **Tarma** Junín, C Peru *11.25S 75.43W*
105 N15 **Tarn** ◐ *department* S France
104 M15 **Tarn** ~ S France
113 L22 **Tarna** ~ C Hungary
94 G13 **Tärnaby** Västerbotten, N Sweden *65.43N 15.19E*
155 P8 **Tarnak Rūd** ~ SE Afghanistan
118 J11 **Târnava Mare** *Ger.* Grosse Kokel, *Hung.* Nagy-Küküllő; *prev.* Tîrnava Mare. ~ S Romania
118 I11 **Târnava Mică** *Ger.* Kleine Kokel, *Hung.* Kis-Küküllo; *prev.* Tîrnava Mică. ~ C Romania
118 I11 **Târnăveni** *Ger.* Marteskirch, Martinskirch, *Hung.* Dicsőszentmárton; *prev.* Sînmartin, Tîrnăveni. Mureș, C Romania *46.19N 24.16E*
104 L14 **Tarn-et-Garonne** ◐ *department* S France
113 P18 **Tarnica** ▲ SE Poland *49.05N 22.43E*
113 N15 **Tarnobrzeg** Podkarpackie, SE Poland *50.34N 21.40E*
129 N12 **Tarnogskiy Gorodok** Vologodskaya Oblast', NW Russian Federation *60.28N 43.45E*
Tarnopol *see* Ternopil'
113 M16 **Tarnów** Małopolskie, SE Poland *50.01N 20.58E*
Tarnowice/Tarnowitz *see* Tarnowskie Góry
113 J16 **Tarnowskie Góry** *var.* Tarnowice, Tarnowskie Gory, *Ger.* Tarnowitz. Śląskie, S Poland *50.27N 18.52E*
97 N14 **Tärnsjö** Västmanland, C Sweden *60.10N 16.57E*
108 E9 **Taro** ~ NW Italy
195 Q10 **Taron** New Ireland, NE PNG *4.22S 153.04E*
76 E8 **Taroudannt** *var.* Taroudant. SW Morocco *30.31N 8.50W*
Taroudant *see* Taroudannt
25 V12 **Tarpon, Lake** ◎ Florida, SE USA
25 V12 **Tarpon Springs** Florida, SE USA *28.09N 82.45W*
109 G14 **Tarquinia** *anc.* Tarquinii; *hist.* Corneto. Lazio, C Italy *42.22N 11.45E*
Tarquinii *see* Tarquinia
Tarraco *see* Tarragona
78 D10 **Tarrafal** Santiago, S Cape Verde *15.16N 23.45W*
107 V6 **Tarragona** *anc.* Tarraco. Cataluña, E Spain *41.07N 1.15E*
107 T7 **Tarragona** ◐ *province* Cataluña, NE Spain
191 O17 **Tarraleah** Tasmania, SE Australia *42.11S 146.29E*
25 P3 **Tarrant City** Alabama, S USA *33.34N 86.45W*
193 D21 **Tarras** Otago, South Island, NZ *44.48S 169.25E*
Tarrasa *see* Terrassa
107 U5 **Tàrrega** *var.* Tarrega. Cataluña, NE Spain *41.39N 1.09E*
23 W9 **Tar River** ~ North Carolina, SE USA
Tarsatica *see* Rijeka
142 J17 **Tarsus** İçel, S Turkey *36.52N 34.52E*
64 K4 **Tartagal** Salta, N Argentina *22.31S 63.49W*
143 V12 **Tärtär** *Rus.* Terter. ~ SW Azerbaijan
104 J15 **Tartas** Landes, SW France *43.52N 0.45W*
145 Q6 **Tartasah** C Iraq *34.18N 42.21E*
Tartlau *see* Prejmer
Tartous/Tartouss *see* Țarțūs
120 J5 **Tartu** *Ger.* Dorpat; *prev. Rus.* Yurev, Yur'yev. Tartumaa, SE Estonia *58.19N 26.43E*
120 I5 **Tartumaa** *off.* Tartu Maakond. ◐ *province* E Estonia
144 H5 **Țarțūs** *Fr.* Tartouss; *anc.* Tortosa. Țarțūs, W Syria *34.55N 35.52E*
144 H5 **Țarțūs** *off.* Muḥāfaẓat Țarțūs, *var.* Tartous, Tartus. ◐ *governorate* W Syria
170 Bb16 **Tarumizu** Kagoshima, Kyūshū, SW Japan *31.30N 130.40E*
130 K4 **Tarusa** Kaluzhskaya Oblast', W Russian Federation *54.45N 37.10E*
173 G9 **Tarusan** Sumatera, W Indonesia *1.13S 100.22E*
119 N11 **Tarutyne** Odes'ka Oblast', SW Ukraine *46.11N 29.09E*
168 I7 **Tarvagatyn Nuruu** ▲▲ N Mongolia
108 J6 **Tarvisio** Friuli-Venezia Giulia, NE Italy *46.31N 13.33E*
Tarvisium *see* Treviso
59 O16 **Tarvo, Río** ~ E Bolivia
12 G8 **Tarzwell** Ontario, S Canada *48.00N 79.58W*
42 K5 **Tasajera, Sierra de la** ▲▲ N Mexico
151 S13 **Tasaral** Zhezkazgan, C Kazakhstan *46.17N 73.54E*
Tasböget *see* Tasbuget
151 N15 **Tasbuget** *Kaz.* Tasböget. Kzylorda, S Kazakhstan *44.49N 65.34E*
110 E11 **Tasch** Valais, SW Switzerland *46.04N 7.43E*
Tasek Kenyir *see* Kenyir, Tasik
126 Hh16 **Tashanta** Respublika Altay, S Russian Federation *49.42N 89.15E*
Tashauz *see* Dashkhovuz
Tashi Chho Dzong *see* Thimphu
159 U11 **Tashigang** E Bhutan *27.19N 91.33E*
143 T11 **Tashir** *prev.* Kalinino. N Armenia *41.07N 44.16E*
149 Q11 **Țashk, Daryācheh-ye** ◎ C Iran
Tashkent *see* Toshkent
Tashkentskaya Oblast' *see* Toshkent Wiloyati
152 J16 **Tashkepri** *Turkm.* Dashköpri. Maryyskiy Velayat, S Turkmenistan *36.15N 62.37E*
Tash-Kömür *see* Tash-Kumyr
153 S9 **Tash-Kumyr** *Kir.* Tash-Kömür. Dzhalal-Abadskaya Oblast', W Kyrgyzstan *41.22N 72.08E*
131 T7 **Tashla** Orenburgskaya Oblast', W Russian Federation *51.42N 52.33E*
Tashqurghan *see* Kholm
126 H15 **Tashtagol** Kemerovskaya Oblast', S Russian Federation *52.49N 88.00E*
174 Jj15 **Tasikmalaya** *prev.* Tasikmalaja. Jawa, C Indonesia *7.19S 108.16E*
97 H24 **Tåsinge** *island* C Denmark
10 M5 **Tasiujaq** Quebec, E Canada *58.43N 69.58W*
127 Nn9 **Taskan** Magadanskaya Oblast', E Russian Federation *63.00N 150.03E*
79 W11 **Tasker** Zinder, C Niger *15.06N 10.42E*
151 W12 **Taskesken** Vostochnyy Kazakhstan, E Kazakhstan *47.15N 80.42E*
142 J10 **Taşköprü** Kastamonu, N Turkey *41.30N 34.12E*
Taskuduk, Peski *see* Goshquduq Qum
195 N9 **Taskul** New Ireland, NE PNG *2.30S 150.22E*
143 S13 **Taşlıçay** Ağrı, E Turkey *39.37N 43.22E*
193 H14 **Tasman** *off.* Tasman District. ◐ *unitary authority* South Island, NZ
199 I14 **Tasman Basin** *var.* East Australian Basin. *undersea feature* S Tasman Sea
193 I14 **Tasman Bay** *inlet* South Island, NZ
199 Hh14 **Tasman Fracture Zone** *tectonic feature* S Indian Ocean
193 E19 **Tasman Glacier** *glacier* South Island, NZ
Tasman Group *see* Nukumanu Islands
191 N15 **Tasmania** *prev.* Van Diemen's Land. ◐ *state* SE Australia
191 Q16 **Tasmania** *island* SE Australia
193 H14 **Tasman Mountains** ▲▲ South Island, NZ
191 P17 **Tasman Peninsula** *peninsula* Tasmania, SE Australia
199 Hh13 **Tasman Plain** *undersea feature* W Tasman Sea
199 Hh14 **Tasman Plateau** *var.* South Tasmania Plateau. *undersea feature* SW Tasman Sea
199 Ii14 **Tasman Sea** *sea* SW Pacific Ocean
118 G9 **Tășnad** *Ger.* Trestenberg, Trestendorf, *Hung.* Tasnád. Satu Mare, NW Romania *47.30N 22.33E*
142 L11 **Taşova** Amasya, N Turkey *40.45N 36.19E*
79 T10 **Tassara** Tahoua, W Niger *16.40N 5.34E*
10 K4 **Tassialouc, Lac** ◎ Quebec, C Canada
Tassili du Hoggar *see* Tassili ta-n-Ahaggar
76 L11 **Tassili-n-Ajjer** *plateau* E Algeria
76 K14 **Tassili ta-n-Ahaggar** *var.* Tassili du Hoggar. *plateau* S Algeria
61 M15 **Tasso Fragoso** Maranhão, E Brazil *8.22S 45.53W*
97 J23 **Tåstrup** *var.* Taastrup. København, E Denmark *55.39N 12.19E*
151 O9 **Tasty-Taldy** Akmola, C Kazakhstan *50.45N 66.35E*
149 W10 **Tāsūkī** Sīstān va Balūchestān, SE Iran
113 I22 **Tata** *Ger.* Totis. Komárom-Esztergom, NW Hungary *47.39N 18.19E*
76 E8 **Tata** SW Morocco *29.38N 8.04W*
Tataaihoa, Pointe *see* Vénus, Pointe
113 I22 **Tatabánya** Komárom-Esztergom, NW Hungary *47.33N 18.22E*
203 X10 **Tatakoto** *atoll* Îles Tuamotu, E French Polynesia
77 N7 **Tataouine** *var.* Taṭāwīn. SE Tunisia *32.48N 10.27E*
57 O5 **Tataracual, Cerro** ▲ NE Venezuela *10.13N 64.20W*
119 O12 **Tatarbunary** Odes'ka Oblast', SW Ukraine *45.50N 29.37E*
121 M17 **Tatarka** *Rus.* Tatarka. Mahilyowskaya Voblasts', E Belarus *53.15N 28.49E*
Tatar Pazardzhik *see* Pazardzhik
125 G13 **Tatarsk** Novosibirskaya Oblast', C Russian Federation *55.08N 75.58E*
Tatarskaya ASSR *see* Tatarstan, Respublika
127 O15 **Tatarskiy Proliv** *Eng.* Tatar Strait. *strait* SE Russian Federation
131 R4 **Tatarstan, Respublika** *prev.* Tatarskaya ASSR. ◐ *autonomous republic* W Russian Federation
Tatar Strait *see* Tatarskiy Proliv
195 O9 **Tatau Island** *island* Tabar Islands, N PNG
Taṭāwīn *see* Tataouine
175 P8 **Tate** Sulawesi, N Indonesia *0.12S 119.44E*
171 Jj17 **Tateyama** Chiba, Honshū, S Japan *35.00N 139.51E*
171 J14 **Tate-yama** ▲ Honshū, S Japan *36.27N 137.32E*
147 N11 **Tathlīth** 'Asīr, S Saudi Arabia *19.37N 43.31E*
147 O11 **Tathlīth, Wādī** *dry watercourse* S Saudi Arabia
191 R11 **Tathra** New South Wales, SE Australia *36.46S 149.58E*
131 P8 **Tatishchevo** Saratovskaya Oblast', W Russian Federation *51.43N 45.35E*
41 S12 **Tatitlek** Alaska, USA *60.49N 146.29W*
8 L15 **Tatla Lake** British Columbia, SW Canada *51.54N 124.39W*
124 O2 **Tatlısu** *Gk.* Akanthoú. N Cyprus *35.21N 33.45E*
9 Z10 **Tatnam, Cape** *headland* Manitoba, C Canada *57.16N 91.03W*
Tatra/Tátra *see* Tatra Mountains
113 K18 **Tatra Mountains** *Ger.* Tatra, *Hung.* Tátra, *Pol./Slvk.* Tatry. ▲▲ Poland/Slovakia
Tatry *see* Tatra Mountains
170 G14 **Tatsuno** *var.* Tatuno. Hyōgo, Honshū, SW Japan *34.51N 134.33E*
151 S16 **Tatti** *var.* Tatty. Zhambyl, S Kazakhstan *43.10N 73.22E*
Tatty *see* Tatti
62 L10 **Tatuí** São Paulo, S Brazil *23.21S 47.49W*
39 V14 **Tatum** New Mexico, SW USA *33.15N 103.19W*
27 X7 **Tatum** Texas, SW USA *32.19N 94.31W*
Ta-t'ung/Tatung *see* Datong
Tatuno *see* Tatsuno
143 R14 **Tatvan** Bitlis, SE Turkey *38.31N 42.15E*
97 C16 **Tau** Rogaland, S Norway *59.04N 5.55E*
198 Dd8 **Ta'ū** *var.* Tau. *island* Manua Islands, E American Samoa
200 R14 **Tau** *island* Tongatapu Group, N Tonga
61 O14 **Tauá** Ceará, E Brazil *6.04S 40.25W*
62 N10 **Taubaté** São Paulo, S Brazil *23.00S 45.36W*
103 I19 **Tauber** ~ SW Germany
103 I19 **Tauberbischofsheim** Baden-Württemberg, C Germany *49.37N 9.39E*
150 E14 **Tauchik** *Kaz.* Taūshyq. Mangistau, SW Kazakhstan *44.17N 51.22E*
203 W10 **Tauere** *atoll* Îles Tuamotu, C French Polynesia
103 H17 **Taufstein** ▲ C Germany *50.31N 9.18E*
202 I17 **Taukoka** *island* SE Cook Islands
151 T15 **Taukum, Peski** *desert* SE Kazakhstan
192 L10 **Taumarunui** Manawatu-Wanganui, North Island, NZ *38.52S 175.14E*
61 A15 **Taumaturgo** Acre, W Brazil *8.54S 72.48W*
29 X6 **Taum Sauk Mountain** ▲ Missouri, C USA *37.34N 90.43W*
85 H22 **Taung** North-West, N South Africa *27.31S 24.47E*
177 G6 **Taungdwingyi** Magwe, C Burma *20.01N 95.34E*
178 Gg6 **Taunggyi** Shan State, C Burma *20.46N 97.06E*
177 G5 **Taungtha** Mandalay, C Burma *21.16N 95.25E*
177 F7 **Taungup** Arakan State, W Burma *18.49N 94.13E*
155 S9 **Taunsa** Punjab, E Pakistan *30.43N 70.40E*
99 K23 **Taunton** SW England, UK *51.01N 3.06W*
21 O12 **Taunton** Massachusetts, NE USA *41.54N 71.03W*
103 F18 **Taunus** ▲▲ W Germany
103 G18 **Taunusstein** Hessen, W Germany *50.09N 8.09E*
192 N9 **Taupo** Waikato, North Island, NZ *38.42S 176.05E*
192 M9 **Taupo, Lake** ◎ North Island, NZ
111 R8 **Taurach** *var.* Taurachbach. ~ E Austria
Taurachbach *see* Taurach
120 D12 **Tauragė** *Ger.* Tauroggen. Tauragė, SW Lithuania *55.15N 22.17E*
56 G10 **Tauramena** Casanare, C Colombia *5.01N 72.48W*
192 N7 **Tauranga** Bay of Plenty, North Island, NZ *37.41S 176.09E*
13 O10 **Taureau, Réservoir** ⊠ Quebec, SE Canada
109 N22 **Taurianova** Calabria, SW Italy *38.22N 16.01E*
Tauris *see* Tabrīz
192 I2 **Tauroa Point** *headland* North Island, NZ *35.09S 173.02E*
Tauroggen *see* Tauragė
Tauromenium *see* Taormina
Taurus Mountains *see* Toros Dağları
Taus *see* Domažlice
Taūshyq *see* Tauchik
107 R5 **Tauste** Aragón, NE Spain *41.55N 1.15W*
203 V16 **Tautara, Motu** *island* Easter Island, Chile, E Pacific Ocean
203 R8 **Tautira** Tahiti, W French Polynesia *17.45S 149.10W*
Tauz *see* Tovuz
Tavālesh, Kūhhā-ye *see* Talish Mountains
142 D15 **Tavas** Denizli, SW Turkey *37.33N 29.04E*
Tavastehus *see* Hämeenlinna
Tavau *see* Davos
125 F11 **Tavda** Sverdlovskaya Oblast', C Russian Federation *58.01N 65.07E*
125 F11 **Tavda** ~ C Russian Federation
107 T11 **Tavernes de la Valldigna** País Valenciano, E Spain *39.03N 0.13W*
83 J20 **Taveta** Coast, S Kenya *3.24S 37.46E*
197 J13 **Taveuni** *island* N Fiji
153 R13 **Tavildara** *Rus.* Tavil'dara, Tovil'-Dora. C Tajikistan *38.42N 70.27E*
168 L8 **Tavin** Dundgovĭ, C Mongolia *46.27N 105.43E*
106 H14 **Tavira** Faro, S Portugal *37.07N 7.39W*
99 I24 **Tavistock** SW England, UK *50.33N 4.07W*
178 Gg11 **Tavoy** *var.* Dawei. Tenasserim, S Burma *14.01N 98.12E*
Tavoy Island *see* Mali Kyun
125 Ff13 **Tavricheskoye** Omskaya Oblast', C Russian Federation *54.34N 73.33E*
117 E16 **Tavropoú, Techníti Límni** ⊠ C Greece
142 E13 **Tavşanlı** Kütahya, NW Turkey *39.34N 29.28E*
197 H14 **Tavua** Viti Levu, W Fiji *17.26S 105.53E*
197 I16 **Tavuki** Kadavu, SW Fiji *19.05S 178.06E*
99 J23 **Taw** ~ SW England, UK
193 L14 **Tawa** Wellington, North Island, NZ *41.11S 174.48E*
27 V6 **Tawakoni, Lake** ⊠ Texas, SW USA
159 V11 **Tawang** Arunāchal Pradesh, NE India *27.34N 91.54E*
174 L16 **Tawang, Teluk** *bay* Jawa, S Indonesia
33 R7 **Tawas Bay** ◎ Michigan, N USA
33 R7 **Tawas City** Michigan, N USA *44.16N 83.33W*
175 Oo4 **Tawau** Sabah, East Malaysia *4.16N 117.54E*
147 U10 **Ṭawīl, Qalamat aṭ** *well* SE Saudi Arabia *21.07N 52.11E*
179 P17 **Tawitawi** *island* Tawitawi Group, SW Philippines
179 Pp17 **Tawitawi Group** *island group* Sulu Archipelago, SW Philippines
Ṭawkar *see* Tokar
Tāwūq *see* Dāqūq
Tawzar *see* Tozeur
43 O15 **Taxco** *var.* Taxco de Alarcón. Guerrero, S Mexico *18.32N 99.37W*
Taxco de Alarcón *see* Taxco
164 D9 **Taxkorgan** *var.* Taxkorgan Tajik Zizhixian. Xinjiang Uygur Zizhiqu, NW China *37.43N 75.13E*
Taxkorgan Tajik Zizhixian *see* Taxkorgan
98 J10 **Tay** ~ C Scotland, UK
176 V13 **Tayandu, Kepulauan** *island group* E Indonesia
149 V6 **Tāybād** *var.* Taibad, Tāyybād, Tayyebāt. Khorāsān, NE Iran *34.48N 60.46E*
Taybert at Turkz *see* Ṭayyibat at Turkī
128 J3 **Taybola** Murmanskaya Oblast', NW Russian Federation *68.30N 33.18E*
83 M16 **Tayeeglow** Bakool, C Somalia *4.01N 44.25E*
98 K11 **Tay, Firth of** *inlet* E Scotland, UK
126 H13 **Tayga** Kemerovskaya Oblast', S Russian Federation *56.02N 85.26E*
168 G8 **Taygan** Govĭ-Altay, C Mongolia *46.20N 97.22E*
127 Oo9 **Taygonos, Mys** *headland* E Russian Federation *60.36N 160.09E*
98 I11 **Tay, Loch** ◎ C Scotland, UK
9 N12 **Taylor** British Columbia, W Canada *56.09N 120.43W*
31 O14 **Taylor** Nebraska, C USA *41.45N 99.22W*
20 I13 **Taylor** Pennsylvania, NE USA *41.22N 75.41W*
27 T10 **Taylor** Texas, SW USA *30.34N 97.24W*
39 Q11 **Taylor, Mount** ▲ New Mexico, SW USA *35.14N 107.36W*
39 R5 **Taylor Park Reservoir** ⊠ Colorado, C USA
39 R6 **Taylor River** ~ Colorado, C USA
23 P11 **Taylors** South Carolina, SE USA *34.55N 82.18W*
22 L5 **Taylorsville** Kentucky, S USA *38.01N 85.21W*
23 R6 **Taylorsville** North Carolina, SE USA *35.55N 81.10W*
32 L14 **Taylorville** Illinois, N USA *39.33N 89.17W*
146 K5 **Taymā'** Tabūk, NW Saudi Arabia *27.39N 38.32E*
126 J11 **Taymura** ~ C Russian Federation
126 Kk6 **Taymylyr** Respublika Sakha (Yakutiya), NE Russian Federation *72.32N 121.54E*
126 J5 **Taymyr, Ozero** ◎ N Russian Federation
126 J5 **Taymyr, Poluostrov** *peninsula* N Russian Federation
126 Ii7 **Taymyrskiy (Dolgano-Nenetskiy) Avtonomnyy Okrug** *var.* Taymyrskiy Avtonomnyy Okrug. ◐ *autonomous district* N Russian Federation
178 Jj13 **Tây Ninh** Tây Ninh, S Vietnam *11.20N 106.03E*
126 Ii14 **Tayshet** Irkutskaya Oblast', S Russian Federation *55.51N 98.04E*
179 Oo13 **Taytay** Palawan, W Philippines *10.49N 119.30E*
174 L14 **Tayu** *prev.* Tajoe. Jawa, C Indonesia *6.31S 111.01E*
Ṭāyybād/Tayyebāt *see* Tāybād
144 L5 **Ṭayyibah** *var.* At Taybé. Ḥimṣ, C Syria *35.13N 38.51E*
144 I4 **Ṭayyibat at Turkī** *var.* Taybert at Turkz. Ḥamāh, W Syria *35.16N 36.55E*
151 P7 **Tayynsha** *prev.* Krasnoarmeysk. Severnyy Kazakhstan, N Kazakhstan *53.52N 69.51E*
126 H9 **Taz** ~ N Russian Federation
76 G6 **Taza** NE Morocco *34.13N 4.06W*
145 T4 **Tāza Khurmātū** E Iraq *35.18N 44.21E*
171 M10 **Tazawa-ko** ◎ Honshū, C Japan
Taz, Bay of *see* Tazovskaya Guba
23 N8 **Tazewell** Tennessee, S USA *36.27N 83.34W*
23 Q7 **Tazewell** Virginia, NE USA *37.06N 81.31W*
77 S11 **Tāzirbū** SE Libya *25.43N 21.16E*
41 S11 **Tazlina Lake** ◎ Alaska, USA
126 H7 **Tazovskaya Guba** *Eng.* Bay of Taz. *bay* N Russian Federation
126 H8 **Tazovskiy** Yamalo-Nenetskiy Avtonomnyy Okrug, N Russian Federation *67.33N 78.21E*
143 U10 **T'bilisi** *Eng.* Tiflis. ● (Georgia) SE Georgia *41.40N 44.54E*
143 T10 **T'bilisi** ✕ S Georgia *41.43N 44.49E*
81 E14 **Tchabal Mbabo** ▲ NW Cameroon *7.12N 12.16E*
Tchad *see* Chad
Tchad, Lac *see* Chad, Lake
79 S15 **Tchaourou** E Benin *8.55N 2.39E*
81 E20 **Tchibanga** Nyanga, S Gabon *2.49S 11.00E*
Tchien *see* Zwedru
79 Z6 **Tchigaï, Plateau du** ▲ NE Niger
79 V9 **Tchighozérine** Agadez, C Niger *17.15N 7.48E*
79 T10 **Tchin-Tabaradene** Tahoua, W Niger *15.57N 5.49E*
80 G13 **Tcholliré** Nord, NE Cameroon *8.48N 14.00E*
Tchongking *see* Chongqing
24 K4 **Tchula** Mississippi, S USA *33.10N 90.13W*
112 I7 **Tczew** *Ger.* Dirschau. Pomorskie, N Poland *54.05N 18.46E*
118 I10 **Teaca** *Ger.* Tekendorf, *Hung.* Teke; *prev. Ger.* Teckendorf. Bistrița-Năsăud, N Romania *46.55N 24.30E*
42 J11 **Teacapán** Sinaloa, C Mexico *22.33N 105.44W*
202 A10 **Teafuafou** *island* Funafuti Atoll, C Tuvalu
27 U8 **Teague** Texas, SW USA *31.37N 96.16W*
203 R9 **Teahupoo** Tahiti, W French Polynesia *17.51S 149.15W*
202 H15 **Te Aiti Point** *headland* Rarotonga, S Cook Islands *21.10S 159.46W*
67 D24 **Teal Inlet** East Falkland, Falkland Islands *51.34S 58.25W*
193 B22 **Te Anau** Southland, South Island, NZ *45.24S 167.44E*
193 B22 **Te Anau, Lake** ◎ South Island, NZ
43 U15 **Teapa** Tabasco, SE Mexico *17.36N 92.57W*
192 Q7 **Te Araroa** Gisborne, North Island, NZ *37.37S 178.21E*
192 M7 **Te Aroha** Waikato, North Island, NZ *37.33S 175.41E*
Teate *see* Chieti
202 A9 **Te Ava Fuagea** *channel* Funafuti Atoll, SE Tuvalu
202 B8 **Te Ava I Te Lape** *channel* Funafuti Atoll, SE Tuvalu
202 B9 **Te Ava Pua Pua** *channel* Funafuti Atoll, SE Tuvalu
192 M8 **Te Awamutu** Waikato, North Island, NZ *37.59S 175.19E*
176 Xx9 **Teba** Irian Jaya, E Indonesia *1.27S 137.54E*
106 L15 **Teba** Andalucía, S Spain *36.59N 4.54W*
130 M15 **Teberda** Karachayevo-Cherkesskaya Respublika, SW Russian Federation *43.28N 41.45E*
76 M6 **Tébessa** NE Algeria *35.21N 8.06E*
64 O7 **Tebicuary, Río** ~ S Paraguay
174 Hh11 **Tebingtinggi** Sumatera, W Indonesia *3.33S 103.00E*
173 Ff5 **Tebingtinggi** Sumatera, N Indonesia *3.19N 99.07E*
Tebingtinggi, Pulau *see* Rantau, Pulau
Tebriz *see* Tabrīz
143 U9 **Tebulos Mt'a** *Rus.* Gora Tebulosmta. ▲ Georgia/Russian Federation *42.33N 45.21E*
Tebulosmta, Gora *see* Tebulos Mt'a
43 Q14 **Tecamachalco** Puebla, S Mexico *18.52N 97.43W*
42 B1 **Tecate** Baja California, NW Mexico *32.33N 116.37W*
142 M13 **Tecer Dağları** ▲▲ C Turkey
105 O17 **Tech** ~ S France
79 P16 **Techiman** W Ghana *7.35N 1.56W*
119 N15 **Techirghiol** Constanța, SE Romania *44.03N 28.37E*
76 A12 **Techla** *var.* Techlé. SW Western Sahara *21.39N 14.57W*
Techlé *see* Techla
65 H18 **Tecka, Sierra de** ▲▲ SW Argentina
Teckendorf *see* Teaca
42 K13 **Tecolotlán** Jalisco, SW Mexico *20.14N 104.01W*
42 K14 **Tecomán** Colima, SW Mexico *18.52N 103.54W*
37 V12 **Tecopa** California, W USA *35.51N 116.14W*
42 G5 **Tecoripa** Sonora, NW Mexico *28.36N 109.57W*
43 N16 **Tecpan** *var.* Tecpan de Galeana. Guerrero, S Mexico *17.11N 100.39W*
Tecpan de Galeana *see* Tecpan
42 J11 **Tecuala** Nayarit, C Mexico *22.24N 105.30W*
118 L12 **Tecuci** Galați, E Romania *45.49N 27.27E*
33 R10 **Tecumseh** Michigan, N USA *42.00N 83.57W*
31 S16 **Tecumseh** Nebraska, C USA *40.22N 96.12W*
29 O11 **Tecumseh** Oklahoma, C USA *35.15N 96.56W*
194 E12 **Tedi** ~ W PNG
152 H14 **Tedzhen** *Turkm.* Tejen. Akhalskiy Velayat, S Turkmenistan *37.23N 60.28E*
152 I15 **Tedzhen** *Per.* Harīrūd, *Turkm.* Tejen. ~ Afghanistan/Iran *see also* Harīrūd
152 H15 **Tedzhenstroy** *Turkm.* Tejenstroy. Akhalskiy Velayat, S Turkmenistan *36.57N 60.49E*
168 I7 **Teel** Arhangay, C Mongolia *48.01N 100.30E*
99 L15 **Tees** ~ N England, UK
12 E15 **Teeswater** Ontario, S Canada *44.00N 81.17W*
202 A10 **Tefala** *island* Funafuti Atoll, C Tuvalu
60 D13 **Tefé** Amazonas, N Brazil *3.24S 64.45W*
76 K11 **Tefedest** ▲▲ S Algeria

◆ Country ● Country Capital ◇ Dependent Territory ○ Dependent Territory Capital ◐ Administrative Region ✕ International Airport ▲ Mountain ▲▲ Mountain Range ⛰ Volcano ~ River ◎ Lake ⊠ Reservoir

Tefenni – Tharthār, Wādī ath

142 E16 Tefenni Burdur, SW Turkey 37.19N 29.45E
60 D13 Tefé, Rio ≈ NW Brazil
174 Kk14 Tegal Jawa, C Indonesia 6.52S 109.07E
102 O12 Tegel ✕ (Berlin) Berlin, NE Germany 52.33N 13.16E
101 M15 Tegelen Limburg, SE Netherlands 51.19N 6.09E
103 L24 Tegernsee ◎ SE Germany
109 M18 Teggiano Campania, S Italy 40.25N 15.28E
79 U14 Tegina Niger, C Nigeria 10.06N 6.10E
197 B10 Tegua island Torres Islands, N Vanuatu
44 I7 Tegucigalpa ● (Honduras) Francisco Morazán, SW Honduras 14.04N 87.10W
44 H7 Tegucigalpa ✕ Central District, C Honduras 14.03N 87.20W
Tegucigalpa see Central District, Honduras
Tegucigalpa see Francisco Morazán, Honduras
79 U9 Teguidda-n-Tessoumt Agadez, C Niger 17.27N 6.40E
66 Q11 Teguise Lanzarote, Islas Canarias, Spain, NE Atlantic Ocean 29.04N 13.37W
126 Hh13 Tegul'det Tomskaya Oblast', C Russian Federation 57.16N 87.58E
37 S13 Tehachapi California, W USA 35.07N 118.27W
37 S13 Tehachapi Mountains ▲ California, W USA
Tehama see Tihāmah
Teheran see Tehrān
79 O14 Téhini NE Ivory Coast 9.36N 3.40W
149 N5 Tehrān var. Teheran. ● (Iran) Tehrān, N Iran 35.43N 51.26E
149 N6 Tehrān off. Ostān-e Tehrān, var. Tehran. ◆ province N Iran
158 K9 Tehri Uttar Pradesh, N India 30.12N 78.28E
Tehri see Tīkamgarh
43 Q15 Tehuacán Puebla, S Mexico 18.28N 97.24W
43 S17 Tehuantepec var. Santo Domingo Tehuantepec. Oaxaca, SE Mexico 16.18N 95.13W
43 S17 Tehuantepec, Golfo de var. Gulf of Tehuantepec. gulf S Mexico
Tehuantepec, Gulf of see Tehuantepec, Golfo de
Tehuantepec, Isthmus of see Tehuantepec, Istmo de
43 T16 Tehuantepec, Istmo de var. Isthmus of Tehuantepec. isthmus SE Mexico
(0) I16 Tehuantepec Ridge undersea feature E Pacific Ocean
43 S16 Tehuantepec, Río ≈ SE Mexico
203 W10 Tehuata atoll Îles Tuamotu, C French Polynesia
66 O11 Teide, Pico de ▲ Gran Canaria, Islas Canarias, Spain, NE Atlantic Ocean 28.16N 16.39W
99 I21 Teifi ≈ SW Wales, UK
82 B9 Teiga Plateau plateau W Sudan
99 J24 Teignmouth SW England, UK 50.34N 3.29W
Teisen see Chech'ŏn
118 H1 Teiuş Ger. Dreikirchen, Hung. Tövis. Alba, C Romania 46.12N 23.40E
175 N16 Tejakula Bali, C Indonesia 8.09S 115.19E
Tejen see Harīrūd/Tedzhen
Tejenstroy see Tedzhenstroy
37 S14 Tejon Pass pass California, W USA 34.46N 118.49W
Tejo, Rio see Tagus
43 O14 Tejupilco var. Tejupilco de Hidalgo. México, S Mexico 18.55N 100.10W
Tejupilco de Hidalgo see Tejupilco
192 P7 Te Kaha Bay of Plenty, North Island, NZ 37.45S 105.42E
31 S14 Tekamah Nebraska, C USA 41.46N 96.13W
192 I1 Te Kao Northland, North Island, NZ 34.39S 172.57E
193 F20 Tekapo ≈ South Island, NZ
193 F19 Tekapo, Lake ◎ South Island, NZ
192 P9 Te Karaka Gisborne, North Island, NZ 38.30S 105.52E
192 L7 Te Kauwhata Waikato, North Island, NZ 37.22S 175.07E
43 X12 Tekax var. Tekax de Álvaro Obregón. Yucatán, SE Mexico 20.07N 89.10W
Tekax de Álvaro Obregón see Tekax
Teke/Tekenderf see Teaca
142 A14 Teke Burnu headland W Turkey 38.06N 26.35E
116 M12 Teke Deresi ≈ NE Turkey
152 D10 Tekedzhik, Gory hill range NW Turkmenistan
151 V14 Tekeli Almaty, SE Kazakhstan 44.49N 78.46E
151 R7 Teke, Ozero ◎ N Kazakhstan
164 I5 Tekes Xinjiang Uygur Zizhiqu, NW China 43.15N 81.43E
151 W16 Tekes Almaty, SE Kazakhstan 42.40N 80.01E
Tekes see Tekes He
164 H5 Tekes He Rus. Tekes. ≈ China/Kazakhstan
82 I10 Tekezē var. Takkaze. ≈ Eritrea/Ethiopia
Tekhtin see Tsyakhtsin
142 C10 Tekirdağ It. Rodosto; anc. Bisanthe, Raidestos, Rhaedestus. Tekirdağ, NW Turkey 40.58N 27.31E
142 C10 Tekirdağ ◆ province NW Turkey
161 N14 Tekkali Andhra Pradesh, E India 18.37N 84.15E
117 K15 Tekke Burnu Turk. İlyasbaba Burnu. headland NW Turkey 40.03N 26.12E
143 Q13 Tekman Erzurum, NE Turkey 39.39N 41.31E
34 M9 Tekoa Washington, NW USA 47.13N 117.05W
202 H16 Te Kou ▲ Rarotonga, S Cook Islands 21.13S 159.46W
Tekrit see Tikrīt
175 R9 Teku Sulawesi, N Indonesia 0.46S 123.25E
192 L9 Te Kuiti Waikato, North Island, NZ 38.21S 175.09E
44 H4 Tela Atlántida, NW Honduras 15.43N 87.27W
144 F12 Telalim Southern, S Israel 30.58N 34.47E
Telanaipura see Jambi
143 U10 T'elavi E Georgia 41.55N 45.29E
144 F10 Tel Aviv ◆ district W Israel
Tel Aviv-Jaffa see Tel Aviv-Yafo
144 F10 Tel Aviv-Yafo var. Tel Aviv-Jaffa. Tel Aviv, C Israel 32.04N 34.46E
144 F10 Tel Aviv-Yafo ✕ Tel Aviv, C Israel 32.04N 34.45E
113 E18 Telč Ger. Teltsch. Jihlavský Kraj, C Czech Republic 49.10N 15.28E
194 E11 Telefomin Sandaun, NW PNG 5.05S 141.40E
8 J10 Telegraph Creek British Columbia, W Canada 57.55N 131.10W
202 B10 Telele island Funafuti Atoll, C Tuvalu
62 J11 Telêmaco Borba Paraná, S Brazil 24.21S 50.39W
97 E15 Telemark ◆ county S Norway
64 J13 Telén La Pampa, C Argentina 36.16S 65.24W
Teleneshty see Teleneşti
118 M9 Teleneşti Rus. Teleneshty. C Moldova 47.35N 28.20E
106 J4 Teleno, El ▲ NW Spain 42.19N 6.21W
175 O8 Telen, Sungai ≈ Borneo, C Indonesia
118 I15 Teleorman ◆ county S Romania
118 I14 Teleorman ≈ S Romania
27 V5 Telephone Texas, SW USA 33.48N 96.00W
37 U11 Telescope Peak ▲ California, W USA 36.09N 117.03W
Teles Pirés see São Manuel, Rio
99 L19 Telford C England, UK 52.42N 2.28W
110 L7 Telfs Tirol, W Austria 47.19N 11.04E
44 I9 Telica León, NW Nicaragua 12.29N 86.51W
44 J6 Telica, Río ≈ C Honduras
78 I13 Télimélé Guinée-Maritime, W Guinea 10.45N 13.01W
45 O14 Telire, Río ≈ Costa Rica/Panama
116 I8 Telish prev. Azizie. Pleven, N Bulgaria 43.20N 24.16E
43 R16 Telixtlahuaca var. San Francisco Telixtlahuaca. Oaxaca, SE Mexico 17.18N 96.54W
8 K13 Telkwa British Columbia, SW Canada 54.39N 126.51W
27 P4 Tell Texas, SW USA 34.18N 100.20W
Tell Abiad see Tall Abyaḍ
Tell Abiad/Tell Abyad see At Tall al Abyaḍ
33 O16 Tell City Indiana, N USA 37.56N 86.47W
40 M9 Teller Alaska, USA 65.15N 166.21W
Tell Huqnah see Tall Ḥuqnah
161 F20 Tellicherry var. Thalassery. Kerala, SW India 11.48N 75.30E
22 M10 Tellico Plains Tennessee, S USA 35.19N 84.18W
Tell Kalakh see Tall Kalakh
Tell Mardikh see Ebla
56 E11 Tello Huila, C Colombia 3.06N 75.07W
Tell Shedadi see Ash Shadādah
39 Q7 Telluride Colorado, C USA 37.56N 107.48W
Tel'man/Tel'mansk see Gubadag
119 X9 Tel'manove Donets'ka Oblast', E Ukraine 47.24N 38.03E
168 H6 Telmen Nuur ◎ NW Mongolia
Teloekbetoeng see Bandarlampung
43 O15 Teloloapán Guerrero, S Mexico 18.21N 99.54W
Telo Martius see Toulon
129 V8 Telposiz, Gora ▲ NW Russian Federation 63.52N 59.15E
Telschen see Telšiai
65 J17 Telsen Chubut, S Argentina 42.27S 66.59W
120 D11 Telšiai Ger. Telschen. Telšiai, NW Lithuania 55.59N 22.21E
Teltsch see Telč
Telukbetung see Bandarlampung
173 F7 Telukdalam Pulau Nias, W Indonesia 0.34N 97.47E
12 H9 Temagami Ontario, S Canada 47.03N 79.47W
12 G9 Temagami, Lake ◎ Ontario, S Canada
202 H16 Te Manga ▲ Rarotonga, S Cook Islands 21.13S 159.45W
Temanggoeng see Temanggung
174 Kk15 Temanggung prev. Temanggoeng. Jawa, S Indonesia 0.22S 110.12E
203 W12 Tematangi atoll Îles Tuamotu, S French Polynesia
43 X11 Temax Yucatán, SE Mexico 21.10N 88.55W
176 X12 Tembagapura Irian Jaya, E Indonesia 4.10S 137.18E
133 U5 Tembenchi ≈ N Russian Federation
174 Hh10 Tembesi, Sungai ≈ Sumatera, W Indonesia
57 P6 Temblador Monagas, NE Venezuela 9.01N 62.38W
107 N9 Tembleque Castilla-La Mancha, C Spain 39.40N 3.30W
Temboni see Mitemele, Río
37 U16 Temecula California, W USA 33.29N 117.09W
174 Gg3 Temengor, Tasik ⊠ Peninsular Malaysia
114 L9 Temerin Serbia, N Yugoslavia 45.25N 19.54E
Temes/Temesch see Tamiš
Temeschburg/Temeschwar see Timişoara
Temes-Kubin see Kovin
Temesvár/Temeswar see Timişoara
Teminaboean see Teminabuan
176 V9 Teminabuan prev. Teminaboean. Irian Jaya, E Indonesia 1.30S 131.58E
151 P17 Temirlanovka Yuzhnyy Kazakhstan, S Kazakhstan 42.36N 69.15E
151 R10 Temirtau prev. Samarkandski, Samarkandskoye. Karaganda, C Kazakhstan 50.04N 72.55E
12 H10 Témiscaming Quebec, SE Canada 46.40N 79.04W
Témiscamingue, Lac see Timiskaming, Lake
13 T8 Témiscouata, Lac ◎ Quebec, SE Canada
131 N5 Temnikov Respublika Mordoviya, W Russian Federation 54.39N 43.09E
203 Y13 Temoe island Îles Gambier, E French Polynesia
191 Q9 Temora New South Wales, SE Australia 34.28S 147.33E
42 H7 Témoris Chihuahua, W Mexico 27.16N 108.15W
42 I5 Temósachic Chihuahua, N Mexico 28.55N 107.42W
195 W8 Temotu off. Temotu Province. ◆ province E Solomon Islands
38 L14 Tempe Arizona, SW USA 33.24N 111.54W
175 P12 Tempe, Danau ◎ Sulawesi, C Indonesia
Tempelburg see Czaplinek
109 C17 Tempio Pausania Sardegna, Italy, C Mediterranean Sea 40.55N 9.07E
44 K12 Tempisque, Río ≈ NW Costa Rica
27 T9 Temple Texas, SW USA 31.06N 97.22W
102 O12 Templehof ✕ (Berlin) Berlin, NE Germany 52.28N 13.24E
99 D19 Templemore Ir. An Teampall Mór. C Ireland 52.48N 7.49W
102 O11 Templin Brandenburg, NE Germany 53.07N 13.31E
43 P12 Tempoal var. Tempoal de Sánchez. Veracruz-Llave, E Mexico 21.27N 98.21W
Tempoal de Sánchez see Tempoal
43 P13 Tempoal, Río ≈ C Mexico
85 E14 Tempué Moxico, C Angola 13.36S 18.56E
130 J14 Temryuk Krasnodarskiy Kray, SW Russian Federation 45.15N 37.26E
101 G17 Temse Oost-Vlaanderen, N Belgium 51.07N 4.13E
65 F15 Temuco Araucanía, C Chile 38.45S 72.37W
193 G20 Temuka Canterbury, South Island, NZ 44.13S 171.16E
201 P13 Temwen Island island E Micronesia
58 C6 Tena Napo, C Ecuador 01.00S 77.48W
43 W13 Tenabo Campeche, E Mexico 20.01N 90.12W
Tenaghau see Aola
27 X7 Tenaha Texas, SW USA 31.56N 94.14W
41 X13 Tenake Chichagof Island, Alaska, USA 57.46N 135.13W
161 K16 Tenāli Andhra Pradesh, E India 16.13N 80.36E
Tenan see Ch'ŏnan
43 O14 Tenancingo var. Tenencingo de Degollado. México, S Mexico 18.57N 99.39W
203 X12 Tenararo island Groupe Actéon, SE French Polynesia
178 Gg12 Tenasserim Tenasserim, S Burma 12.06N 98.55E
178 H11 Tenasserim var. Tanintharyi. ◆ division S Burma
100 O5 Ten Boer Groningen, NE Netherlands 53.16N 6.42E
99 I21 Tenby SW Wales, UK 51.40N 4.43W
82 K11 Tendaho Afar, NE Ethiopia 11.39N 40.59E
105 V14 Tende Alpes Maritimes, SE France 44.04N 7.34E
157 Q20 Ten Degree Channel strait Andaman and Nicobar Islands, India, E Indian Ocean
82 F11 Tendelti White Nile, E Sudan 13.01N 31.55E
78 G8 Te-n-Dghâmcha, Sebkhet var. Sebkha de Ndrhamcha, Sebkra de Ndaghamcha. salt lake W Mauritania
171 Ll12 Tendō Yamagata, Honshū, C Japan 38.22N 140.22E
76 H7 Tendrara NE Morocco 33.06N 1.58W
119 Q11 Tendrivs'ka Kosa spit S Ukraine
119 Q11 Tendrivs'ka Zatoka gulf S Ukraine
Tenencingo de Degollado see Tenancingo
79 N11 Ténenkou Mopti, C Mali 14.28N 4.55W
79 W9 Ténéré physical region C Niger
79 W9 Ténére, Erg du desert C Niger
66 O11 Tenerife island Islas Canarias, Spain, NE Atlantic Ocean
76 J5 Ténès NW Algeria 36.30N 1.18E
175 Oo15 Tengah, Kepulauan island group C Indonesia
175 O8 Tenggarong Borneo, C Indonesia 0.23S 117.00E
168 J15 Tengger Shamo desert N China
174 J4 Tenggul, Pulau island Peninsular Malaysia
Tengiz Köl see Tengiz, Ozero
151 P9 Tengiz, Ozero Kaz. Tengiz Köl. salt lake C Kazakhstan
78 M14 Tengréla var. Tingréla. N Ivory Coast 10.25N 6.25W
166 M14 Tengxian var. Teng Xian. Guangxi Zhuangzu Zizhiqu, S China 23.24N 110.49E
204 H2 Teniente Rodolfo Marsh Chilean research station South Shetland Islands, Antarctica 61.57S 58.23W
34 G9 Tenino Washington, NW USA 46.51N 122.51W
114 I9 Tenja Osijek-Baranja, E Croatia 45.30N 18.45E
196 B16 Tenjo, Mount ▲ W Guam
161 H23 Tenkāsi Tamil Nādu, SE India 8.58N 77.22E
81 N24 Tenke Katanga, SE Dem. Rep. Congo (Zaire) 10.34S 26.12E
Tenke see Tinca
126 M7 Tenkeli Respublika Sakha (Yakutiya), NE Russian Federation 70.09N 140.39E
29 R10 Tenkiller Ferry Lake ⊠ Oklahoma, C USA
79 Q13 Tenkodogo S Burkina 11.43N 0.19W
189 Q5 Tennant Creek Northern Territory, C Australia 19.40S 134.16E
22 G9 Tennessee off. State of Tennessee; also known as The Volunteer State. ◆ state SE USA
39 R5 Tennessee Pass pass Colorado, C USA 39.21N 106.18W
22 H10 Tennessee River ≈ S USA
25 N2 Tennessee Tombigbee Waterway canal Alabama/Mississippi, S USA
101 K22 Tenneville Luxembourg, SE Belgium 50.05N 5.31E
94 M11 Tenniöjoki ≈ NE Finland
94 L9 Teno var. Tenojoki, Lapp. Deatnu, Nor. Tana. ≈ Finland/Norway see also Tana
Tenojoki see Tana/Teno
175 Nn3 Tenom Sabah, East Malaysia 5.07N 115.57E
Tenos see Tínos
43 V15 Tenosique var. Tenosique de Pino Suárez. Tabasco, SE Mexico 17.30N 91.24W
Tenosique de Pino Suárez see Tenosique
171 H15 Tenri Nara, Honshū, SW Japan 34.36N 135.51E
171 I16 Tenryū Shizuoka, Honshū, SW Japan 34.49N 137.48E
172 ii15 Tenryū-gawa ≈ Honshū, C Japan
24 I6 Tensas River ≈ Louisiana, S USA
25 O8 Tensaw River ≈ Alabama, S USA
76 E7 Tensift seasonal river W Morocco
175 Pp10 Tentena var. Tenteno. Sulawesi, C Indonesia 1.46S 120.40E
Tenteno see Tentena
191 U4 Tenterfield New South Wales, SE Australia 29.04S 152.02E
25 X16 Ten Thousand Islands island group Florida, SE USA
62 H9 Teodoro Sampaio São Paulo, S Brazil 22.30S 52.13W
61 N19 Teófilo Otoni var. Theophilo Ottoni. Minas Gerais, NE Brazil 17.52S 41.31W
118 K5 Teofipol' Khmel'nyts'ka Oblast', W Ukraine 50.00N 26.22E
203 Q8 Teohatu Tahiti, W French Polynesia
43 P14 Teotihuacán ruins México, S Mexico 19.49N 98.48W
Teotilán see Teotitlán del Camino
43 Q15 Teotitlán del Camino var. Teotilán. Oaxaca, S Mexico 18.05N 97.04W
202 G12 Tepa Île Uvea, E Wallis and Futuna 13.19S 176.09W
203 P8 Tepaee, Récif reef Tahiti, W French Polynesia
42 L14 Tepalcatepec Michoacán de Ocampo, SW Mexico 19.10N 102.49W
202 A16 Tepa Point headland SW Niue 19.07S 169.55E
42 L13 Tepatitlán var. Tepatitlán de Morelos. Jalisco, SW Mexico 20.54N 102.45W
Tepatitlán de Morelos see Tepatitlán
42 J9 Tepehuanes var. Santa Catarina de Tepehuanes. Durango, C Mexico 25.18N 105.43W
Tepelena see Tepelenë
115 L22 Tepelenë var. Tepelena, It. Tepeleni. Gjirokastër, S Albania 40.18N 20.00E
Tepeleni see Tepelenë
42 K12 Tepic Nayarit, C Mexico 21.29N 104.54W
113 C15 Teplice Ger. Teplitz; prev. Teplice-Šanov, Teplitz-Schönau. Ústecký Kraj, NW Czech Republic 50.37N 13.48E
Teplice-Šanov/Teplitz/Teplitz-Schönau see Teplice
119 O7 Teplyk Vinnyts'ka Oblast', C Ukraine 48.40N 29.46E
126 Mm10 Teplyy Klyuch Respublika Sakha (Yakutiya), NE Russian Federation 62.46N 137.01E
42 E5 Tepoca, Cabo headland NW Mexico 29.19N 112.24W
203 W9 Tepoto island Îles du Désappointement, C French Polynesia
94 L11 Tepsa Lappi, N Finland 67.34N 25.36E
202 B8 Tepuka atoll Funafuti Atoll, C Tuvalu
192 N7 Te Puke Bay of Plenty, North Island, NZ 37.48S 176.19E
42 L13 Tequila Jalisco, SW Mexico 20.52N 103.48W
43 O13 Tequisquiapan Querétaro de Arteaga, C Mexico 20.34N 99.52W
106 J5 Tera ≈ NW Spain
79 Q12 Téra Tillabéri, W Niger 14.01N 0.48E
203 V1 Teraina prev. Washington Island. atoll Line Islands, E Kiribati
83 F15 Terakeka Bahr el Gabel, S Sudan 5.25N 31.45E
109 J14 Teramo anc. Interamna. Abruzzo, C Italy 42.40N 13.43E
100 P7 Ter Apel Groningen, NE Netherlands 52.52N 7.04E
106 H11 Tera, Ribeira de ≈ S Portugal
193 K14 Terawhiti, Cape headland North Island, NZ 41.17S 174.36E
100 N12 Terborg Gelderland, E Netherlands 51.55N 6.22E
143 P13 Tercan Erzincan, NE Turkey 39.46N 40.22E
66 O2 Terceira ✕ Terceira, Azores, Portugal, NE Atlantic Ocean 38.43N 27.13W
66 O2 Terceira var. Ilha Terceira. island Azores, Portugal, NE Atlantic Ocean
Terceira, Ilha see Terceira
118 K6 Terebovlya Ternopil's'ka Oblast', W Ukraine 49.18N 25.43E
131 O15 Terek ≈ SW Russian Federation
Terekhovka see Tsyerakhowka
153 R9 Terek-Say Dzhalal-Abadskaya Oblast', W Kyrgyzstan 41.28N 71.06E
174 Hh3 Terengganu var. Trengganu. ◆ state Peninsular Malaysia
131 X7 Terensay Orenburgskaya Oblast', W Russian Federation 51.35N 59.28E
60 N13 Teresina var. Therezina. state capital Piauí, NE Brazil 5.09S 42.46W
62 P9 Teresópolis Rio de Janeiro, SE Brazil 22.25S 42.59W
112 P12 Terespol Lubelskie, E Poland 52.05N 23.37E
203 V16 Terevaka, Maunga ▲ Easter Island, Chile, E Pacific Ocean 27.04S 109.22W
105 P3 Tergnier Aisne, N France 49.39N 3.18E
45 O14 Teribe, Río ≈ NW Panama
128 K3 Teriberka Murmanskaya Oblast', NW Russian Federation 69.10N 35.18E
Terijoki see Zelenogorsk
Terinkot see Tarīn Kowt
Terisaqqan see Tersakkan
26 K12 Terlingua Texas, SW USA 29.18N 103.36W
26 K11 Terlingua Creek ≈ Texas, SW USA
64 K7 Termas de Río Hondo Santiago del Estero, N Argentina 27.28S 64.52W
142 M11 Terme Samsun, N Turkey 41.11N 36.58E
Termez see Termiz
Termia see Kýthnos
109 J23 Termini Imerese anc. Thermae Himerenses. Sicilia, Italy, C Mediterranean Sea 38.01N 13.55E
43 V14 Términos, Laguna de lagoon SE Mexico
79 X10 Termit-Kaoboul Zinder, C Niger 15.34N 11.31E
153 O14 Termiz Rus. Termez. Surkhondaryo Wiloyati, S Uzbekistan 37.17N 67.12E
109 L15 Termoli Molise, C Italy 42.00N 14.58E
Termonde see Dendermonde
100 P5 Termunten Groningen, NE Netherlands 53.18N 7.02E
175 T7 Ternate Pulau Ternate, E Indonesia 0.50N 127.20E
175 Ss7 Ternate, Pulau island E Indonesia
111 T5 Ternberg Oberösterreich, N Austria 47.57N 14.22E
101 E15 Terneuzen var. Neuzen. Zeeland, SW Netherlands 51.19N 3.49E
127 O17 Terney Primorskiy Kray, SE Russian Federation 45.03N 136.43E
109 I14 Terni anc. Interamna Nahars. Umbria, C Italy 42.34N 12.37E
111 X6 Ternitz Niederösterreich, E Austria 47.43N 16.01E
119 V7 Ternivka Dnipropetrovs'ka Oblast', E Ukraine 48.30N 36.05E
118 K6 Ternopil' Pol. Tarnopol, Rus. Ternopol'. Ternopil's'ka Oblast', W Ukraine 49.32N 25.37E
Ternopil' see Ternopil's'ka Oblast'
118 I6 Ternopil's'ka Oblast' var. Ternopil', Rus. Ternopol'skaya Oblast'. ◆ province NW Ukraine
Ternopol' see Ternopil'
Ternopol'skaya Oblast' see Ternopil's'ka Oblast'
127 Oo15 Terpeniya, Mys headland Ostrov Sakhalin, SE Russian Federation 48.37N 144.40E
127 Oo15 Terpeniya, Zaliv inlet Ostrov Sakhalin, SE Russian Federation
Térraba, Río see Grande de Térraba, Río
8 J13 Terrace British Columbia, W Canada 54.31N 128.31W
10 D12 Terrace Bay Ontario, S Canada 48.46N 87.06W
109 I16 Terracina Lazio, C Italy 41.17N 13.13E
95 F14 Terråk Troms, N Norway 65.03N 12.22E
28 M13 Terral Oklahoma, C USA 33.55N 97.54W
109 B19 Terralba Sardegna, Italy, C Mediterranean Sea 39.47N 8.35E
Terranova di Sicilia see Gela
Terranova Pausania see Olbia
107 W5 Terrassa Cast. Tarrasa. Cataluña, E Spain 41.34N 2.01E
13 O12 Terrebonne Quebec, SE Canada 45.42N 73.37W
24 J11 Terrebonne Bay bay Louisiana, SE USA
33 N14 Terre Haute Indiana, N USA 39.27N 87.24W
27 U6 Terrell Texas, SW USA 32.44N 96.16W
Terre Neuve see Newfoundland
35 Q14 Terreton Idaho, NW USA 43.49N 112.25W
105 T7 Territoire-de-Belfort ◆ department E France
35 X9 Terry Montana, NW USA 46.46N 105.16W
30 I9 Terry Peak ▲ South Dakota, N USA 44.19N 103.49W
142 H14 Tersakan Gölü ◎ C Turkey
151 O10 Tersakkan Kaz. Terisaqqan. ≈ C Kazakhstan
100 J4 Terschelling Fris. Skylge. island Waddeneilanden, N Netherlands
80 H10 Tersef Chari-Baguirmi, C Chad 12.55N 16.49E
153 X8 Terskey Ala-Too, Khrebet ▲ Kazakhstan/Kyrgyzstan
Terter see Tärtär
107 R8 Teruel anc. Turba. Aragón, E Spain 40.21N 1.06W
107 R7 Teruel ◆ province Aragón, E Spain
116 M7 Tervel prev. Kurtbunar, Rom. Curtbunar. Dobrich, NE Bulgaria 43.45N 27.25E
95 M16 Tervo Itä-Suomi, C Finland 62.57N 26.48E
94 L13 Tervola Lappi, NW Finland 66.04N 24.49E
Tervueren see Tervuren
101 H18 Tervuren var. Tervueren. Vlaams Brabant, C Belgium 50.48N 4.28E
114 H11 Tešanj Federacija Bosna I Hercegovina, N Bosnia and Herzegovina 44.37N 18.00E
Teschen see Cieszyn
85 M19 Tesenane Inhambane, S Mozambique 22.48S 34.02E
82 I9 Teseney var. Tessenei. W Eritrea 15.05N 36.42E
41 P5 Teshekpuk Lake ◎ Alaska, USA
168 K6 Teshig Bulgan, N Mongolia 49.51N 102.45E
172 Q6 Teshikaga Hokkaidō, NE Japan 43.29N 144.27E
172 P2 Teshio Hokkaidō, NE Japan 44.49N 141.46E
172 P2 Teshio-gawa var. Tesio Gawa. ≈ Hokkaidō, NE Japan
172 P3 Teshio-sanchi ▲ Hokkaidō, NE Japan
Těšín see Cieszyn
Tesio Gawa see Teshio-gawa
168 F5 Tesiyn Gol var. Tes-Khem. ≈ Mongolia/Russian Federation see also Tes-Khem
133 T7 Tes-Khem var. Tesiyn Gol. ≈ Mongolia/Russian Federation see also Tesiyn Gol
114 H11 Teslić Republika Srpska, N Bosnia and Herzegovina 44.35N 17.50E
8 I9 Teslin Yukon Territory, W Canada 60.12N 132.44W
8 I8 Teslin ≈ British Columbia/Yukon Territory, W Canada
79 Q8 Tessalit Kidal, NE Mali 20.11N 0.58E
79 V12 Tessaoua Maradi, S Niger 13.43N 7.59E
101 J17 Tessenderlo Limburg, NE Belgium 51.04N 5.04E
Tessenei see Teseney
12 L7 Tessier, Lac ◎ Quebec, SE Canada
Tessin see Ticino
99 M23 Test ≈ S England, UK
Testama see Tõstamaa
57 P4 Testigos, Islas los island group N Venezuela
39 S10 Tesuque New Mexico, SW USA 35.45N 105.55W
105 O17 Têt var. Tet. ≈ S France
56 G5 Tetas, Cerro de las ▲ NW Venezuela 9.58N 73.00W
85 M15 Tete Tete, NW Mozambique 16.14S 33.34E
85 M15 Tete off. Província de Tete. ◆ province NW Mozambique
9 N15 Tête Jaune Cache British Columbia, SW Canada 52.52N 119.22W
192 O8 Te Teko Bay of Plenty, North Island, NZ 38.03S 176.48E
195 U15 Tetepare island New Georgia Islands, NW Solomon Islands
Teterev see Teteriv
118 M5 Teteriv Rus. Teterev. ≈ N Ukraine
102 M9 Teterow Mecklenburg-Vorpommern, NE Germany 53.46N 12.34E
116 I9 Teteven Lovech, N Bulgaria 42.54N 24.19E
203 T10 Tetiaroa atoll Îles du Vent, W French Polynesia
107 P14 Tetica de Bacares ▲ S Spain 37.15N 2.31W
Tetiyev see Tetiyiv
119 O6 Tetiyiv Rus. Tetiyev. Kyyivs'ka Oblast', N Ukraine 49.21N 29.40E
41 T10 Tetlin Alaska, USA 63.08N 142.31W
35 R8 Teton River ≈ Montana, NW USA
76 G5 Tétouan var. Tetouan, Tetuán. N Morocco 35.33N 5.22W
Tetova/Tetovë see Tetovo
116 L7 Tetovo Razgrad, N Bulgaria 43.49N 26.21E
115 N18 Tetovo Alb. Tetova, Tetovë, Turk. Kalkandelen. NW FYR Macedonia 42.01N 20.58E
117 E20 Tetrázio ▲ S Greece
Tetschen see Děčín
Tetuán see Tétouan
203 Q8 Tetufera, Mont ▲ Tahiti, W French Polynesia 17.40S 149.25W
131 R4 Tetyushi Respublika Tatarstan, W Russian Federation 54.55N 48.46E
110 I7 Teufen Sankt Gallen, NE Switzerland 47.24N 9.24E
42 L12 Teul var. Teul de Gonzáles Ortega. Zacatecas, C Mexico 21.30N 103.28W
109 B21 Teulada Sardegna, Italy, C Mediterranean Sea 38.58N 8.46E
Teul de Gonzáles Ortega see Teul
9 X16 Teulon Manitoba, S Canada 50.20N 97.14W
44 I7 Teupasenti El Paraíso, S Honduras 14.14N 86.43W
172 Oo3 Teuri-tō island NE Japan
102 G13 Teutoburger Wald Eng. Teutoburg Forest. hill range NW Germany
Teutoburg Forest see Teutoburger Wald
95 K17 Teuva Swe. Östermark. Länsi-Suomi, W Finland 62.28N 21.45E
109 H15 Tevere Eng. Tiber. ≈ C Italy
144 G9 Teverya var. Tiberias, Tverya. Northern, N Israel 32.48N 35.31E
98 K13 Teviot ≈ SE Scotland, UK
Tevli see Tewli
125 Ff12 Tevriz Omskaya Oblast', C Russian Federation 57.30N 72.13E
193 B24 Te Waewae Bay bay South Island, NZ
99 L21 Tewkesbury C England, UK 51.58N 2.09W
121 F19 Tewli Rus. Tevli. Brestskaya Voblasts', SW Belarus 52.20N 24.13E
165 U12 Têwo var. Dêngkagoin. Gansu, C China 34.05N 103.15E
27 U12 Texana, Lake ◎ Texas, SW USA
29 S14 Texarkana Arkansas, C USA 33.26N 94.02W
27 X5 Texarkana Texas, SW USA 33.25N 94.03W
27 N9 Texas off. State of Texas; also known as The Lone Star State. ◆ state S USA
27 W12 Texas City Texas, SW USA 29.22N 94.54W
43 P14 Texcoco México, C Mexico 19.31N 98.52W
100 I6 Texel island Waddeneilanden, NW Netherlands
28 H8 Texhoma Oklahoma, C USA 36.30N 101.46W
27 N1 Texhoma Texas, SW USA 36.30N 101.46W
39 W12 Texico New Mexico, SW USA 34.23N 103.03W
26 L1 Texline Texas, SW USA 36.22N 103.01W
43 P14 Texmelucan var. San Martín Texmelucan. Puebla, S Mexico 19.13N 98.25W
29 O13 Texoma, Lake ⊠ Oklahoma/Texas, C USA
27 N9 Texon Texas, SW USA 31.13N 101.42W
126 I12 Teya Krasnoyarskiy Kray, C Russian Federation 60.27N 92.46E
85 J23 Teyateyaneng NW Lesotho 29.04S 27.51E
128 M16 Teykovo Ivanovskaya Oblast', W Russian Federation 56.49N 40.31E
128 M16 Teza ≈ W Russian Federation
43 Q13 Teziutlán Puebla, S Mexico 19.49N 97.22W
159 W12 Tezpur Assam, NE India 26.39N 92.47E
15 L8 Tha-Anne ≈ Nunavut, NE Canada
85 K23 Thabana Ntlenyana var. Thabantshonyana, Mount Ntlenyana. ▲ E Lesotho 29.26S 29.16E
Thabantshonyana see Thabana Ntlenyana
85 J23 Thaba Putsoa ▲ C Lesotho 29.48S 27.46E
178 I8 Tha Bo Nong Khai, E Thailand 17.52N 102.34E
105 T12 Thabor, Pic du ▲ E France 45.07N 6.34E
Tha Chin see Samut Sakhon
177 G7 Thagaya Pegu, C Burma 19.19N 96.16E
Thai, Ao see Thailand, Gulf of
178 Jj6 Thai Binh Thai Binh, N Vietnam 20.27N 106.19E
178 Jj7 Thai Hoa Nghê An, N Vietnam 19.21N 105.26E
178 Hh10 Thailand off. Kingdom of Thailand, Th. Prathet Thai; prev. Siam. ◆ monarchy SE Asia
178 Hh13 Thailand, Gulf of var. Gulf of Siam, Th. Ao Thai, Vtn. Vinh Thai Lan. gulf SE Asia
Thai Lan, Vinh see Thailand, Gulf of
178 Jj6 Thai Nguyên Băc Thai, N Vietnam 21.36N 105.49E
178 J9 Thakhèk prev. Muang Khammouan. Khammouan, C Laos 17.24N 104.50E
159 S13 Thakurgaon Rajshahi, NW Bangladesh 26.04N 88.34E
155 S6 Thal North-West Frontier Province, NW Pakistan 33.24N 70.31E
177 G16 Thalang Phuket, SW Thailand 08.00N 98.21E
Thalassery see Tellicherry
178 I10 Thalat Khae Nakhon Ratchasima, C Thailand 15.15N 102.24E
111 Q5 Thalgau Salzburg, NW Austria 47.49N 13.19E
110 G7 Thalwil Zürich, NW Switzerland 47.16N 8.34E
85 I20 Thamaga Kweneng, SE Botswana 24.40S 25.31E
Thamarid see Thamarīt
147 V13 Thamarīt var. Thamarīd, Thumrayt. SW Oman 17.39N 54.01E
147 P16 Thamar, Jabal ▲ SW Yemen 13.46N 45.32E
192 M6 Thames Waikato, North Island, NZ 37.10S 175.33E
12 D17 Thames ≈ Ontario, S Canada
99 O22 Thames ≈ S England, UK
192 M6 Thames, Firth of gulf North Island, NZ
12 D17 Thamesville Ontario, S Canada 42.33N 81.58W
147 S13 Thamūd N Yemen 17.17N 49.57E
178 Gg9 Thanbyuzayat Mon State, S Burma 15.58N 97.43E
158 I9 Thānesar Haryāna, NW India 29.58N 76.51E
178 Jj7 Thanh Hoa Thanh Hoa, N Vietnam 19.49N 105.48E
Thanintari Taungdan see Bilauktaung Range
161 I21 Thanjāvūr prev. Tanjore. Tamil Nādu, SE India 10.46N 79.09E
Thanlwin see Salween
105 U7 Thann Haut-Rhin, NE France 47.51N 7.04E
178 H16 Tha Nong Phrom Phatthalung, SW Thailand 7.24N 100.04E
178 H13 Thap Sakae var. Thap Sakau. Prachuap Khiri Khan, SW Thailand 11.30N 99.34E
Thap Sakau see Thap Sakae
100 L10 't Harde Gelderland, E Netherlands 52.25N 5.52E
158 D11 Thar Desert var. Great Indian Desert, Indian Desert. desert India/Pakistan
189 V10 Thargomindah Queensland, C Australia 28.00S 143.47E
156 D11 Thar Pārkar desert SE Pakistan
145 S7 Tharthār al Furāt, Qanāt ath canal C Iraq
145 R7 Tharthār, Buḩayrat ath ◎ C Iraq
145 R5 Tharthār, Wādī ath dry watercourse N Iraq

◆ Country ● Country Capital ◇ Dependent Territory ○ Dependent Territory Capital ◆ Administrative Region ✕ International Airport ▲ Mountain ▲ Mountain Range ▲ Volcano ≈ River ◎ Lake ⊠ Reservoir

THA SAE – TIRUNELVELI

178 Gg14 **Tha Sae** Chumphon, SW Thailand
178 H15 **Tha Sala** Nakhon Si Thammarat, SW Thailand 8.43N 99.54E
116 I13 **Thásos** Thásos, E Greece 40.46N 24.43E
117 I14 **Thásos** *island* E Greece
39 N14 **Thatcher** Arizona, SW USA 32.47N 109.46W
178 J5 **Thât Khê** *var.* Tràng Dinh. Lang Sơn, N Vietnam 22.15N 106.26E
178 Gg9 **Thaton** Mon State, S Burma 16.55N 97.19E
178 J9 **That Phanom** Nakhon Phanom, E Thailand 16.52N 104.41E
178 I10 **Tha Tum** Surin, E Thailand 15.18N 103.39E
105 F16 **Thau, Bassin de** *var.* Étang de Thau. ◎ S France
Thau, Étang de *see* Thau, Bassin de
177 G3 **Thaungdut** Sagaing, N Burma 24.25N 94.45E
178 Gg8 **Thaungyin** *Th.* Mae Nam Moei. ~ Burma/Thailand
178 J9 **Tha Uthen** Nakhon Phanom, E Thailand 17.31N 104.34E
111 W2 **Thaya** *var.* Dyje. ~ Austria/Czech Republic *see also* Dyje
29 V8 **Thayer** Missouri, C USA 36.31N 91.34W
177 Ff7 **Thayetmyo** Magwe, C Burma 19.19N 95.10E
35 S15 **Thayne** Wyoming, C USA 42.54N 111.01W
177 G6 **Thazi** Mandalay, C Burma 20.49N 96.04E
Thebes *see* Thíva
46 L5 **The Carlton** *var.* Abraham Bay. Mayaguana, SE Bahamas 22.21N 72.56W
47 O14 **The Crane** *var.* Crane. S Barbados 13.06N 59.26W
34 I11 **The Dalles** Oregon, NW USA 45.36N 121.10W
30 M14 **Thedford** Nebraska, C USA 41.58N 100.34W
The Hague *see* 's-Gravenhage
Theiss *see* Tisa/Tisza
15 Jj6 **Thelon** ~ Northwest Territories/Nunavut, N Canada
9 V15 **Theodore** Saskatchewan, S Canada 51.25N 103.01W
25 N8 **Theodore** Alabama, S USA 30.33N 88.10W
38 L13 **Theodore Roosevelt Lake** ⊠ Arizona, SW USA
Theodosia *see* Feodosiya
Theophilo Ottoni *see* Teófilo Otoni
15 K13 **The Pas** Manitoba, C Canada 53.49N 101.09W
33 T14 **The Plains** Ohio, N USA 39.22N 82.07W
Thera *see* Thíra
180 H17 **Thérèse, Île** *island* Inner Islands, NE Seychelles
Therezina *see* Teresina
117 L20 **Thérma** Ikaria, Dodekánisos, Greece, Aegean Sea 37.37N 26.18E
Thermae Himerenses *see* Termini Imerese
Thermae Pannonicae *see* Baden
Thermaic Gulf/Thermaicus Sinus *see* Thermaïkós Kólpos
123 Gg10 **Thermaïkós Kólpos** *Eng.* Thermaic Gulf; *anc.* Thermaicus Sinus. *gulf* N Greece
Thermiá *see* Kýthnos
117 L17 **Thermís** Lésvos, E Greece 39.08N 26.32E
117 E18 **Thérmo** Dytikí Ellás, C Greece 38.32N 21.42E
35 V14 **Thermopolis** Wyoming, C USA 43.39N 108.12W
191 F10 **The Rock** New South Wales, SE Australia 35.18S 147.07E
205 O5 **Theron Mountains** ▲ Antarctica
117 G18 **Thespiés** Stereá Ellás, C Greece 38.18N 23.08E
117 E16 **Thessalía** *Eng.* Thessaly. ◆ *region* C Greece
12 C10 **Thessalon** Ontario, S Canada 46.15N 83.32W
117 G14 **Thessaloníki** *Eng.* Salonica, Salonika, *SCr.* Solun, *Turk.* Selânik. Kentrikí Makedonía, N Greece 40.37N 22.58E
117 G14 **Thessaloníki** ✕ Kentrikí Makedonía, N Greece 40.30N 22.58E
Thessaly *see* Thessalía
86 E12 **Theta Gap** *undersea feature* E Atlantic Ocean
99 P20 **Thetford** E England, UK 52.25N 0.45E
13 R11 **Thetford-Mines** Quebec, SE Canada 46.07N 71.16W
115 K17 **Theth** *var.* Thethi. Shkodër, N Albania 42.25N 19.45E
Thethi *see* Theth
101 L20 **Theux** Liège, E Belgium 50.33N 5.48E
47 V9 **The Valley** ○ (Anguilla) E Anguilla 18.12N 63.00W
29 N10 **The Village** Oklahoma, C USA 35.33N 97.33W
27 W10 **The Woodlands** Texas, SW USA 30.09N 95.27E
Thiamis *see* Thýamis
Thian Shan *see* Tien Shan
24 J9 **Thibodaux** Louisiana, S USA 29.48N 90.49W
31 S3 **Thief Lake** ◎ Minnesota, N USA
31 S3 **Thief River** ~ Minnesota, C USA
31 S3 **Thief River Falls** Minnesota, N USA 48.07N 96.10W
Thièle *see* La Thielle
34 G14 **Thielsen, Mount** ▲ Oregon, NW USA 43.09N 122.04W
Thielt *see* Tielt
108 G7 **Thiene** Veneto, NE Italy 45.43N 11.28E
Thienen *see* Tienen
105 P11 **Thiers** Puy-de-Dôme, C France 45.51N 3.33E
78 F11 **Thiès** W Senegal 14.51N 16.51W
83 I19 **Thika** Central, S Kenya 1.03S 37.04E
Thikombia *see* Cikobia
157 K18 **Thiladhunmathi Atoll** *var.* Tiladummati Atoll. *atoll* N Maldives
Thimbu *see* Thimphu
159 T11 **Thimphu** *var.* Thimbu; *prev.* Tashi Chho Dzong. ● (Bhutan) W Bhutan 27.28N 89.37E
94 H2 **Thingeyri** Vestfirdhir, NW Iceland 65.52N 23.28W
94 I3 **Thingvellir** Sudhurland, SW Iceland 64.15N 21.06W
197 J6 **Thio** Province Sud, C New Caledonia 21.37S 166.13E
105 T4 **Thionville** *Ger.* Diedenhofen. Moselle, NE France 49.22N 6.10E
117 K22 **Thíra** Thíra, Kykládes, Greece, Aegean Sea 36.25N 25.26E
117 K22 **Thíra** *prev.* Santorin, Santoríni, *anc.* Thera. *island* Kykládes, Greece, Aegean Sea
117 J22 **Thirasía** *island* Kykládes, Greece, Aegean Sea
99 M16 **Thirsk** N England, UK 54.06N 1.16W
12 F12 **Thirty Thousand Islands** *island group* Ontario, S Canada
Thiruvanathapuram *see* Trivandrum
97 F20 **Thisted** Viborg, NW Denmark 56.58N 8.42E
Thistil Fjord *see* Thistilfjördhur
94 L1 **Thistilfjördhur** *var.* Thistil Fjord. *fjord* NE Iceland
190 G9 **Thistle Island** *island* South Australia
Thithia *see* Cicia
179 N14 **Thitu Island** *island* NW Spratly Islands
Thiukhaoluang Phrahang *see* Luang Prabang Range
117 G18 **Thíva** *Eng.* Thebes; *prev.* Thívai. Stereá Ellás, C Greece 38.19N 23.19E
Thívai *see* Thíva
104 M12 **Thiviers** Dordogne, SW France 45.24N 0.54E
94 J4 **Thjórsá** ~ C Iceland
15 L9 **Thlewiaza** ~ Nunavut, NE Canada
15 J9 **Thoa** ~ Northwest Territories, NW Canada
101 G14 **Tholen** Zeeland, SW Netherlands 51.31N 4.13E
101 F14 **Tholen** *island* SW Netherlands
28 L10 **Thomas** Oklahoma, C USA 35.44N 98.45W
23 T3 **Thomas** West Virginia, NE USA 39.09N 79.28W
29 U3 **Thomas Hill Reservoir** ⊠ Missouri, C USA
25 S5 **Thomaston** Georgia, SE USA 32.53N 84.19W
21 R7 **Thomaston** Maine, NE USA 44.06N 69.10W
27 T12 **Thomaston** Texas, SW USA 28.56N 97.07W
25 O6 **Thomasville** Alabama, S USA 31.54N 87.42W
25 T8 **Thomasville** Georgia, SE USA 30.49N 83.57W
23 S9 **Thomasville** North Carolina, SE USA 35.52N 80.04W
37 N5 **Thomes Creek** ~ California, W USA
9 W12 **Thompson** Manitoba, C Canada 55.45N 97.54W
31 R4 **Thompson** North Dakota, N USA 47.45N 97.07W
(0) F8 **Thompson** ~ Alberta/British Columbia, SW Canada
35 O8 **Thompson Falls** Montana, NW USA 47.36N 115.20W
31 Q10 **Thompson, Lake** ◎ South Dakota, N USA
36 M3 **Thompson Peak** ▲ California, W USA 41.00N 123.01W
29 S2 **Thompson River** ~ Missouri, C USA
193 A22 **Thompson Sound** *sound* South Island, NZ
15 Hh1 **Thomsen** ~ Banks Island, Northwest Territories, NW Canada
25 V4 **Thomson** Georgia, SE USA 33.28N 82.30W
105 T10 **Thonon-les-Bains** Haute-Savoie, E France 46.22N 6.30E
105 O15 **Thoré** *var.* Thore. ~ S France
39 P11 **Thoreau** New Mexico, SW USA 35.24N 108.13W
Thorenburg *see* Turda
94 J3 **Thórisvatn** ◎ C Iceland
94 P4 **Thor, Kapp** *headland* S Svalbard 76.25N 25.01E
94 J4 **Thorlákshöfn** Sudhurland, SW Iceland 63.51N 21.24W
Thorn *see* Toruń
27 T10 **Thorndale** Texas, SW USA 30.36N 97.12W
12 H10 **Thorne** Ontario, S Canada 46.38N 79.04W
99 J14 **Thornhill** S Scotland, UK 55.13N 3.46W
27 U8 **Thornton** Texas, SW USA 31.24N 96.34W
Thornton Island *see* Millennium Island
12 H16 **Thorold** Ontario, S Canada 43.07N 79.15W
34 I9 **Thorp** Washington, NW USA 47.03N 120.40W
205 S3 **Thorshavnheiane** *physical region* Antarctica
94 L1 **Thórshöfn** Nordhurland Eystra, NE Iceland 66.09N 15.18W
Thospitis *see* Van Gölü
178 J14 **Thôt Nôt** Cân Thơ, S Vietnam 10.16N 105.31E
104 K8 **Thouars** Deux-Sèvres, W France 46.58N 0.13W
159 X14 **Thoubal** Manipur, NE India 24.40N 94.00E
104 K9 **Thouet** ~ W France
Thoune *see* Thun
20 H7 **Thousand Islands** *island* Canada/USA
37 S15 **Thousand Oaks** California, W USA 34.10N 118.50W
116 L12 **Thrace** *cultural region* SE Europe
116 J13 **Thracian Sea** *Gk.* Thrakikó Pélagos; *anc.* Thracium Mare. *sea* Greece/Turkey
Thracium Mare/Thrakikó Pélagos *see* Thracian Sea
Thrá Lí, Bá *see* Tralee Bay
35 R11 **Three Forks** Montana, NW USA 45.53N 111.34W
9 Q16 **Three Hills** Alberta, SW Canada 51.43N 113.15W
191 N15 **Three Hummock Island** *island* Tasmania, SE Australia
192 H1 **Three Kings Islands** *island group* N NZ
183 P10 **Three Kings Rise** *undersea feature* W Pacific Ocean
79 O18 **Three Points, Cape** *headland* S Ghana 4.43N 2.03W
33 P10 **Three Rivers** Michigan, N USA 41.56N 85.37W
27 S13 **Three Rivers** Texas, SW USA 28.27N 98.10W
85 G24 **Three Sisters** Northern Cape, SW South Africa 31.51S 23.04E
34 H13 **Three Sisters** ▲ Oregon, NW USA 44.08N 121.46W
195 Z16 **Three Sisters Islands** *island group* SE Solomon Islands
Thrissur *see* Trichūr
27 Q6 **Throckmorton** Texas, SW USA 33.10N 99.10W
188 M10 **Throssell, Lake** *salt lake* Western Australia
117 K25 **Thrýptis** ▲ Kríti, Greece, E Mediterranean Sea 35.06N 25.51E
178 Jj14 **Thu Dâu Môt** *var.* Phu Cương. Sông Be, S Vietnam 10.58N 106.40E
178 Jj6 **Thu Do** ✕ (Ha Nôi) Ha Nôi, N Vietnam 21.13N 105.46E
101 G21 **Thuin** Hainaut, S Belgium 50.21N 4.18E
155 Q12 **Thul** Sind, SE Pakistan 28.13N 68.49E
Thule *see* Qaanaaq
85 J18 **Thuli** *var.* Tuli. ~ S Zimbabwe
Thumrayt *see* Thamarīt
110 D9 **Thun** *Fr.* Thoune. Bern, W Switzerland 46.46N 7.37E
10 C12 **Thunder Bay** Ontario, S Canada 48.27N 89.12W
32 M1 **Thunder Bay** *lake bay* S Canada
33 R6 **Thunder Bay** *lake bay* Michigan, N USA
33 R6 **Thunder Bay River** ~ Michigan, N USA
29 N11 **Thunderbird, Lake** ⊠ Oklahoma, C USA
30 L8 **Thunder Butte Creek** ~ South Dakota, N USA
110 E9 **Thuner See** ◎ C Switzerland
178 H16 **Thung Song** *var.* Cha Mai. Nakhon Si Thammarat, SW Thailand 8.10N 99.40E
110 H7 **Thur** ~ N Switzerland
110 G6 **Thurgau** *Fr.* Thurgovie. ◆ *canton* NE Switzerland
Thurgovie *see* Thurgau
Thuringe *see* Thüringen
110 J7 **Thüringen** Vorarlberg, W Austria 47.12N 9.48E
103 J17 **Thüringen** *Eng.* Thuringia, *Fr.* Thuringe. ◆ *state* C Germany
103 J17 **Thüringer Wald** *Eng.* Thuringian Forest. ▲ C Germany
Thuringia *see* Thüringen
Thuringian Forest *see* Thüringer Wald
99 D19 **Thurles** *Ir.* Durlas. S Ireland 52.40N 7.49W
23 W2 **Thurmont** Maryland, NE USA 39.36N 77.22W
Thurø *see* Thurø By
97 H24 **Thurø By** *var.* Thurø. Fyn, C Denmark 55.03N 10.43E
12 M12 **Thurso** Quebec, SE Canada 45.36N 75.13W
98 J6 **Thurso** N Scotland, UK 58.34N 3.31W
204 I10 **Thurston Island** *island* Antarctica
110 I9 **Thusis** Graubünden, S Switzerland 46.40N 9.27E
117 C15 **Thýamis** *var.* Thiamis. ~ W Greece
97 E21 **Thyborøn** *var.* Tyborøn. Ringkøbing, W Denmark 56.40N 8.12E
205 U3 **Thyer Glacier** *glacier* Antarctica
117 L20 **Thýmaina** *island* Dodekánisos, Greece, Aegean Sea
85 N15 **Thyolo** *var.* Cholo. Southern, S Malawi 16.03S 35.11E
191 U6 **Tia** New South Wales, SE Australia 31.14S 151.51E
56 H5 **Tía Juana** Zulia, NW Venezuela 10.18N 71.22W
166 J14 **Tiandong** *var.* Pingma. Guangxi Zhuangzu Zizhiqu, S China 23.37N 107.06E
167 O3 **Tianjin** *var.* Tientsin. Tianjin Shi, E China 39.13N 117.06E
Tianjin *see* Tianjin Shi
167 P3 **Tianjin Shi** *var.* Jin, Tianjin, T'ien-ching, Tientsin. ◆ *municipality* E China
165 S10 **Tianjun** *var.* Xinyuan. Qinghai, C China 37.16N 99.03E
166 J13 **Tianlin** *prev.* Leli. Guangxi Zhuangzu Zizhiqu, S China 24.27N 106.03E
Tian Shan *see* Tien Shan
165 W11 **Tianshui** Gansu, C China 34.33N 105.51E
156 I7 **Tianshuihai** Xinjiang Uygur Zizhiqu, W China 35.16N 79.30E
167 S10 **Tiantai** Zhejiang, SE China 29.11N 121.01E
166 J14 **Tianyang** Guangxi Zhuangzu Zizhiqu, S China 23.45N 106.54E
165 U9 **Tianzhu** *var.* Tianzhu Zangzu Zizhixian. Gansu, C China 37.01N 103.04E
Tianzhu Zangzu Zizhixian *see* Tianzhu
203 Q7 **Tiarei** Tahiti, W French Polynesia 17.31S 149.19W
76 J6 **Tiaret** *var.* Tihert. NW Algeria 35.23N 1.18E
79 N17 **Tiassalé** S Ivory Coast 5.54N 4.49W
198 Bb8 **Ti'avea** Upolu, SE Samoa 13.58S 171.30W
Tiba *see* Chiba
62 J11 **Tibagi** *var.* Tibají. Paraná, S Brazil 24.28S 50.29W
62 J10 **Tibagi, Rio** *var.* Rio Tibají. ~ S Brazil
Tibají *see* Tibagi
Tibají, Rio *see* Tibagi, Rio
145 Q9 **Tibal, Wādī** *dry watercourse* S Iraq
56 G9 **Tibaná** Boyacá, C Colombia 5.19N 73.25W
81 F14 **Tibati** Adamaoua, N Cameroon 6.28N 12.37E
78 K15 **Tibé, Pic de** ▲ SE Guinea 8.39N 8.58W
Tiber *see* Tivoli, Italy
Tiber *see* Tevere, Italy
Tiberias *see* Teverya
144 G8 **Tiberias, Lake** *var.* Chinnereth, Sea of Bahr Tabariya, Sea of Galilee, *Ar.* Bahrat Tabariya, *Heb.* Yam Kinneret. ◎ N Israel
69 Q5 **Tibesti** *var.* Tibesti Massif, *Ar.* Tibistī. ▲ N Africa
Tibesti Massif *see* Tibesti
Tibetan Autonomous Region *see* Xizang Zizhiqu
Tibet, Plateau of *see* Qingzang Gaoyuan
Tibistī *see* Tibesti
12 K7 **Tiblemont, Lac** ◎ Quebec, SE Canada
145 X9 **Ţīb, Nahr aţ** ~ S Iraq
Tibnī *see* At Tibnī
190 L4 **Tibooburra** New South Wales, SE Australia 29.24S 142.01E
97 L18 **Tibro** Västra Götaland, S Sweden 58.25N 14.10E
42 E5 **Tiburón, Isla** *var.* Isla del Tiburón. *island* NW Mexico
Tiburón, Isla del *see* Tiburón, Isla
25 W14 **Tice** Florida, SE USA 26.40N 81.49W
Tichau *see* Tychy
116 L8 **Ticha, Yazovir** ◎ NE Bulgaria
78 K9 **Tichît** *var.* Tichitt. Tagant, C Mauritania 18.25N 9.31W
Tichitt *see* Tichît
110 G11 **Ticino** *Fr./Ger.* Tessin. ◆ *canton* S Switzerland
108 D8 **Ticino** ~ Italy/Switzerland
110 H11 **Ticino** *Ger.* Tessin. ~ SW Switzerland
Ticinum *see* Pavia
43 X12 **Ticul** Yucatán, SE Mexico 20.21N 89.29W
97 K18 **Tidaholm** Västra Götaland, S Sweden 58.12N 13.55E
Tidjikdja *see* Tidjikja
78 J8 **Tidjikja** *var.* Tidjikdja; *prev.* Fort-Cappolani. Tagant, C Mauritania 18.30N 11.24W
Tidore *see* Soasiu
175 Ss7 **Tidore, Pulau** *island* E Indonesia
Tidra, Ile *see* Et Tidra
79 N16 **Tiébissou** *var.* Tiebissou. C Ivory Coast 7.10N 5.10W
169 V11 **Tiefa** Liaoning, NE China 42.25N 123.29E
110 I9 **Tiefencastel** Graubünden, S Switzerland 46.40N 9.33E
Tiegenhof *see* Nowy Dwór Gdański
T'ieh-ling *see* Tieling
100 K13 **Tiel** Gelderland, C Netherlands 51.54N 5.04E
169 W7 **Tieli** Heilongjiang, NE China 46.57N 128.01E
169 V11 **Tieling** *var.* T'ieh-ling. Liaoning, NE China 42.19N 123.52E
158 L4 **Tielongtan** China/India 35.10N 79.31E
101 D17 **Tielt** *var.* Thielt. West-Vlaanderen, W Belgium 51.00N 3.20E
T'ien-ching *see* Tianjin Shi
101 I18 **Tienen** *var.* Thienen, *Fr.* Tirlemont. Vlaams Brabant, C Belgium 50.48N 4.55E
Tiên Giang, Sông *see* Mekong
153 X9 **Tien Shan** *Chin.* Thian Shan, Tian Shan, T'ien Shan, *Rus.* Tyan'-Shan'. ▲ C Asia
Tientsin *see* Tianjin
Tientsin *see* Tianjin Shi
178 K6 **Tiên Yên** Quang Ninh, N Vietnam 21.19N 107.24E
97 O14 **Tierp** Uppsala, C Sweden 60.19N 17.30E
64 H7 **Tierra Amarilla** Atacama, N Chile 27.28S 70.16W
39 R9 **Tierra Amarilla** New Mexico, SW USA 36.42N 106.31W
43 R15 **Tierra Blanca** Veracruz-Llave, E Mexico 18.28N 96.21W
43 O16 **Tierra Colorada** Guerrero, S Mexico 17.10N 99.36W
65 J17 **Tierra Colorada, Bajo de la** *basin* SE Argentina
65 I25 **Tierra del Fuego** *off.* Provincia de la Tierra del Fuego. ◆ *province* S Argentina
65 J24 **Tierra del Fuego** *island* Argentina/Chile
56 D7 **Tierralta** Córdoba, NW Colombia 8.10N 76.04W
106 K9 **Tiétar** ~ W Spain
62 L10 **Tietê** São Paulo, S Brazil 23.04S 47.40W
62 J8 **Tietê, Rio** ~ S Brazil
34 J9 **Tieton** Washington, NW USA 46.41N 120.43W
34 J6 **Tiffany Mountain** ▲ Washington, NW USA 48.40N 119.55W
33 S12 **Tiffin** Ohio, N USA 41.06N 83.10W
33 Q11 **Tiffin River** ~ Ohio, N USA
Tiflis *see* T'bilisi
25 U7 **Tifton** Georgia, SE USA 31.27N 83.31W
175 Ss11 **Tifu** Pulau Buru, E Indonesia 3.46S 126.36E
197 K6 **Tiga, Île** *island* Îles Loyauté, W New Caledonia
40 L17 **Tigalda Island** *island* Aleutian Islands, Alaska, USA
117 I15 **Tigáni, Akrotírio** *headland* Límnos, E Greece 39.50N 25.03E
175 O1 **Tiga Tarok** Sabah, East Malaysia 6.57N 117.07E
119 O10 **Tighina** *Rus.* Bendery; *prev.* Bender. E Moldova 46.51N 29.27E
127 P10 **Tigil'** Koryakskiy Avtonomnyy Okrug, E Russian Federation 57.43N 158.19E
151 X9 **Tigiretskiy Khrebet** ▲ E Kazakhstan
81 F14 **Tignère** Adamaoua, N Cameroon 7.25N 12.49E
11 P14 **Tignish** Prince Edward Island, SE Canada 46.58N 64.03W
Tigranocerta *see* Siirt
82 I11 **Tigray** ◆ *province* N Ethiopia
43 O11 **Tigre, Cerro del** ▲ C Mexico 23.06N 99.13W
58 F8 **Tigre, Río** ~ N Peru
145 X10 **Tigris** *Ar.* Dijlah, *Turk.* Dicle. ~ Iraq/Turkey
78 G9 **Tiguent** Trarza, SW Mauritania 17.15N 16.00W
76 M10 **Tiguentourine** E Algeria 27.59N 9.16E
79 V10 **Tiguidit, Falaise de** *ridge* C Niger
147 N13 **Tihāmah** *var.* Tehama. *plain* Saudi Arabia/Yemen
Tihert *see* Tiaret
Ti-hua/Tihwa *see* Ürümqi
43 Q13 **Tihuatlán** Veracruz-Llave, E Mexico 20.44N 97.30W
42 B1 **Tijuana** Baja California, NW Mexico 32.31N 117.01W
44 E2 **Tikal** Petén, N Guatemala 17.11N 89.36W
160 I9 **Tīkamgarh** *prev.* Tehri. Madhya Pradesh, C India 24.43N 78.49E
164 L7 **Tikanlik** Xinjiang Uygur Zizhiqu, NW China 40.34N 87.37E
79 P12 **Tikaré** N Burkina 13.16N 1.39W
41 O12 **Tikchik Lakes** *lakes* Alaska, USA
203 T9 **Tikehau** *atoll* Îles Tuamotu, C French Polynesia
203 V9 **Tikei** *island* Îles Tuamotu, C French Polynesia
125 B12 **Tikhoretsk** Krasnodarskiy Kray, SW Russian Federation 45.50N 40.07E
128 I13 **Tikhvin** Leningradskaya Oblast', NW Russian Federation 59.37N 33.29E
199 I10 **Tiki Basin** *undersea feature* S Pacific Ocean
78 K13 **Tikinsso** ~ NE Guinea
192 Q8 **Tikitiki** Gisborne, North Island, NZ 37.49S 178.23E
81 D16 **Tiko** Sud-Ouest, SW Cameroon 4.01N 9.19E
145 S6 **Tikrīt** *var.* Tekrit. N Iraq 34.36N 43.42E
128 I8 **Tiksha** Respublika Kareliya, NW Russian Federation 64.07N 32.31E
128 I6 **Tikshozero, Ozero** ◎ NW Russian Federation
126 L7 **Tiksi** Respublika Sakha (Yakutiya), NE Russian Federation 71.40N 128.46E
173 G8 **Tiku** Sumatera, W Indonesia 0.24S 99.55E
44 A6 **Tilapa** San Marcos, SW Guatemala 14.31N 92.11W
44 L13 **Tilarán** Guanacaste, NW Costa Rica 10.28N 84.57W
101 J14 **Tilburg** Noord-Brabant, S Netherlands 51.34N 5.04E
12 D17 **Tilbury** Ontario, S Canada 42.15N 82.25W
190 K4 **Tilcha** South Australia 29.37S 140.52E
Tilcha Creek *see* Callabonna Creek
31 Q14 **Tilden** Nebraska, C USA 42.03N 97.49W
27 R13 **Tilden** Texas, SW USA 28.28N 98.32W
12 H10 **Tilden Lake** Ontario, S Canada 46.35N 79.36W
118 G9 **Tileagd** *Hung.* Mezötelegd. Bihor, W Romania 47.03N 22.10E
79 Q8 **Tilemsi, Vallée de** ~ C Mali
127 Pp8 **Tilichiki** Koryakskiy Avtonomnyy Okrug, E Russian Federation 60.25N 165.55E
Tiligul *see* Tilihul
Tiligul'skiy Liman *see* Tilihul's'kyy Lyman
119 P9 **Tilihul** *Rus.* Tiligul. ~ SW Ukraine
119 P10 **Tilihul's'kyy Lyman** *Rus.* Tiligul'skiy Liman. ◎ S Ukraine
Tilimsen *see* Tlemcen
Tilio Martius *see* Toulon
79 R11 **Tillabéri** *var.* Tillabéry. Tillabéri. W Niger 14.12N 1.25E
79 R11 **Tillabéri** ◆ *department* SW Niger
Tillabéry *see* Tillabéri
34 F11 **Tillamook** Oregon, NW USA 45.27N 123.50W
34 E11 **Tillamook Bay** *inlet* Oregon, NW USA
157 Q22 **Tillanchang Dwip** *island* Nicobar Islands, India, NE Indian Ocean
97 N15 **Tillberga** Västmanland, C Sweden 59.52N 16.39E
Tillenberg *see* Dyleň
23 S10 **Tillery, Lake** ⊠ North Carolina, SE USA
79 T10 **Tillia** Tahoua, W Niger 16.13N 4.51E
25 N8 **Tillmans Corner** Alabama, S USA 30.35N 88.10W
12 F17 **Tillsonburg** Ontario, S Canada 42.51N 80.41W
117 N22 **Tílos** *island* Dodekánisos, Greece, Aegean Sea
191 N5 **Tilpa** New South Wales, SE Australia 30.56S 144.24E
Tilsit *see* Sovetsk
33 N13 **Tilton** Illinois, N USA 40.06N 87.39W
130 K7 **Tim** Kurskaya Oblast', W Russian Federation 51.39N 37.11E
56 D12 **Timaná** Huila, S Colombia 1.56N 75.57W
Timan Ridge *see* Timanskiy Kryazh
129 Q6 **Timanskiy Kryazh** *Eng.* Timan Ridge. *ridge* NW Russian Federation
193 G20 **Timaru** Canterbury, South Island, NZ 44.22S 171.15E
131 S6 **Timashevo** Samarskaya Oblast', W Russian Federation 53.22N 51.13E
130 K13 **Timashevsk** Krasnodarskiy Kray, SW Russian Federation 45.37N 38.57E
Timbaki/Timbákion *see* Tympáki
24 K10 **Timbalier Bay** *bay* Louisiana, S USA
24 K11 **Timbalier Island** *island* Louisiana, S USA
194 K12 **Timbe** ~ C Papau New Guinea
78 L10 **Timbedgha** *var.* Timbédra. Hodh ech Chargui, SE Mauritania 16.16N 8.13W
Timbédra *see* Timbedgha
34 G10 **Timber** Oregon, NW USA 45.42N 123.19W
189 O3 **Timber Creek** Northern Territory, N Australia 15.35S 130.21E
30 M8 **Timber Lake** South Dakota, N USA 45.25N 101.01W
56 D12 **Timbío** Cauca, SW Colombia 2.22N 76.41W
56 C12 **Timbiquí** Cauca, SW Colombia 2.41N 77.41W
85 O17 **Timbue, Ponta** *headland* C Mozambique 18.49S 36.22E
Timbuktu *see* Tombouctou
176 Vv10 **Timbuni, Sungai** ~ Irian Jaya, E Indonesia
175 Oo4 **Timbun Mata, Pulau** *island* E Malaysia
79 P8 **Timétrine** *var.* Ti-n-Kâr. *oasis* C Mali 19.18N 0.09W
Timfi *see* Týmfi
Timfristos *see* Tymfristós
79 V9 **Timia** Agadez, C Niger 18.07N 8.49E
176 X12 **Timika** Irian Jaya, E Indonesia 4.39S 137.15E
76 I9 **Timimoun** C Algeria 29.18N 0.21E
Timiris, Cap *see* Timirist, Râs
78 F8 **Timirist, Râs** *var.* Cap Timiris. *headland* NW Mauritania 19.18N 16.28W
151 O7 **Timiryazevo** Severnyy Kazakhstan, N Kazakhstan 53.45N 66.33E
118 E11 **Timiş** ◆ *county* SW Romania
12 H9 **Timiskaming, Lake** *Fr.* Lac Témiscamingue. ◎ Ontario/Quebec, SE Canada
118 E11 **Timişoara** *Ger.* Temeschwar, Temeswar, *Hung.* Temesvár; *prev.* Temeschburg. Timiş, W Romania 45.46N 21.16E
118 E11 **Timişoara** ✕ Timiş, W Romania 45.50N 21.21E
Timkovichi *see* Tsimkavichy
79 U8 **Ti-m-Meghsoï** ~ NW Niger
102 K8 **Timmerdorfer Strand** Schleswig-Holstein, N Germany 53.59N 10.50E
12 F7 **Timmins** Ontario, S Canada 48.09N 80.00W
23 S12 **Timmonsville** South Carolina, SE USA 34.07N 79.56W
32 K5 **Timms Hill** ▲ Wisconsin, N USA 45.27N 90.12W
176 Vv9 **Timoforo** ~ Irian Jaya, E Indonesia
114 P12 **Timok** ~ E Yugoslavia
60 N13 **Timon** Maranhão, E Brazil 5.07S 42.52W
175 Rr17 **Timor** *island* East Timor/Indonesia
175 S17 **Timor Sea** *sea* E Indian Ocean
Timor Timur *see* East Timor
Timor Trench *see* Timor Trough
198 G9 **Timor Trough** *var.* Timor Trench. *undersea feature* NE Timor Sea
63 A21 **Timote** Buenos Aires, E Argentina 35.22S 62.13W
56 I6 **Timotes** Mérida, NW Venezuela 8.57N 70.46W
27 X8 **Timpson** Texas, SW USA 31.54N 94.24W
126 Ll13 **Timpton** ~ NE Russian Federation
95 H17 **Timrå** Västernorrland, C Sweden 62.28N 17.19E
22 J10 **Tims Ford Lake** ⊠ Tennessee, S USA
174 Hh7 **Timun** Pulau Kundur, C Indonesia 0.49N 103.23E
174 H3 **Timur, Banjaran** ▲ Peninsular Malaysia
179 R17 **Tinaca Point** *headland* Mindanao, S Philippines 5.35N 125.18E
56 K5 **Tinaco** Cojedes, N Venezuela 9.42N 68.27W
66 Q11 **Tinajo** Lanzarote, Islas Canarias, Spain, NE Atlantic Ocean 29.33N 13.40W
195 W8 **Tinakula** *island* Santa Cruz Islands, E Solomon Islands
56 K5 **Tinaquillo** Cojedes, N Venezuela 9.52N 68.19W
118 F10 **Tinca** *Hung.* Tenke. Bihor, W Romania 46.46N 21.58E
161 J20 **Tindivanam** Tamil Nādu, SE India 12.15N 79.40E
76 E9 **Tindouf** W Algeria 27.43N 8.09W
76 E9 **Tindouf, Sebkha de** *salt lake* W Algeria
106 J2 **Tineo** Asturias, N Spain 43.19N 6.25W
79 R9 **Ti-n-Essako** Kidal, E Mali 18.30N 2.27E
191 T5 **Tingha** New South Wales, SE Australia 29.56S 151.13E
Tingis *see* Tanger
Tinglett *see* Tinglev
97 F24 **Tinglev** *Ger.* Tinglett. Sønderjylland, SW Denmark 54.57N 9.15E
58 E12 **Tingo María** Huánuco, C Peru 9.19S 75.56W
Tingréla *see* Tengréla
164 K16 **Tingri** *var.* Xêgar. Xizang Zizhiqu, W China 28.40N 87.04E
97 M21 **Tingsryd** Kronoberg, S Sweden 56.30N 15.00E
97 P19 **Tingstäde** Gotland, SE Sweden 57.45N 18.36E
64 H12 **Tinguiririca, Volcán** ▲ C Chile 34.52S 70.24W
96 F9 **Tingvoll** Møre og Romsdal, S Norway 62.55N 8.13E
194 M9 **Tingwon Island** *island* N PNG
196 K8 **Tinian** *island* S Northern Mariana Islands
Ti-n-Kâr *see* Timétrine
Tinnevelly *see* Tirunelveli
97 G15 **Tinnoset** Telemark, S Norway 59.43N 9.03E
97 F15 **Tinnsjø** ◎ S Norway
Tino *see* Chino
117 J20 **Tínos** Tínos, Kykládes, Greece, Aegean Sea 37.32N 25.10E
117 J20 **Tínos** *anc.* Tenos. *island* Kykládes, Greece, Aegean Sea
159 R14 **Tinpahar** Bihār, NE India 25.00N 87.43E
124 O14 **Tin, Ra's al** *headland* N Libya 32.36N 23.10E
159 X11 **Tinsukia** Assam, NE India 27.28N 95.19E
78 K10 **Tintâne** Hodh el Gharbi, S Mauritania 16.25N 10.08W
64 L7 **Tintina** Santiago del Estero, N Argentina 27.03S 62.42W
190 K10 **Tintinara** South Australia 35.54S 140.04E
106 I14 **Tinto** ~ SW Spain
79 S8 **Ti-n-Zaouâtene** Kidal, NE Mali 19.56N 2.45E
Tiobraid Árann *see* Tipperary
30 K3 **Tioga** North Dakota, N USA 48.24N 102.56W
20 G12 **Tioga** Pennsylvania, NE USA 41.54N 77.07W
27 T5 **Tioga** Texas, SW USA 33.28N 96.55W
37 Q8 **Tioga Pass** *pass* California, W USA 37.53N 119.15W
20 G12 **Tioga River** ~ New York/Pennsylvania, NE USA
176 Y11 **Tiom** Irian Jaya, E Indonesia 3.49S 138.22E
Tioman Island *see* Tioman, Pulau
174 I5 **Tioman, Pulau** *var.* Tioman Island. *island* Peninsular Malaysia
20 C12 **Tionesta** Pennsylvania, NE USA 41.31N 79.30W
20 D12 **Tionesta Creek** ~ Pennsylvania, NE USA
173 G11 **Tiop** Pulau Pagai Selatan, W Indonesia 3.12S 100.21E
175 Qq12 **Tioro, Selat** *var.* Tiworo. *strait* Sulawesi, C Indonesia
79 O12 **Tiou** NW Burkina 13.42N 2.34W
20 H11 **Tioughnioga River** ~ New York, NE USA
176 U10 **Tip** Irian Jaya, E Indonesia 1.50S 130.04E
76 J5 **Tipasa** *var.* Tipaza. N Algeria 36.34N 2.27E
Tipaza *see* Tipasa
44 J10 **Tipitapa** Managua, W Nicaragua 12.10N 86.04W
33 R13 **Tipp City** Ohio, N USA 39.57N 84.10W
33 O12 **Tippecanoe River** ~ Indiana, N USA
99 D20 **Tipperary** *Ir.* Tiobraid Árann. S Ireland 52.28N 8.10W
99 D19 **Tipperary** *Ir.* Tiobraid Árann. *cultural region* S Ireland
37 R12 **Tipton** California, W USA 36.02N 119.19W
33 P13 **Tipton** Indiana, N USA 40.19N 86.00W
31 Y14 **Tipton** Iowa, C USA 41.46N 91.07W
29 U5 **Tipton** Missouri, C USA 38.39N 92.46W
38 I10 **Tipton, Mount** ▲ Arizona, SW USA 35.32N 114.11W
22 F8 **Tiptonville** Tennessee, S USA 36.22N 89.28W
10 E12 **Tip Top Mountain** ▲ Ontario, S Canada 48.18N 86.06W
161 G19 **Tiptūr** Karnātaka, W India 13.17N 76.31E
Tiquisate *see* Pueblo Nuevo Tiquisate
60 L13 **Tiracambu, Serra do** ▲ E Brazil
Tirana *see* Tiranë
115 K19 **Tirana Rinas** ✕ Durrës, W Albania 41.25N 19.41E
115 L20 **Tiranë** *var.* Tirana. ● (Albania) Tiranë, C Albania 41.19N 19.49E
115 K20 **Tiranë** ◆ *district* W Albania
146 I5 **Tirān, Jazīrat** *island* Egypt/Saudi Arabia
108 F6 **Tirano** Lombardia, N Italy 46.13N 10.10E
190 I2 **Tirari Desert** *desert* South Australia
119 O10 **Tiraspol** *Rus.* Tiraspol'. E Moldova 46.50N 29.34E
192 M8 **Tirau** Waikato, North Island, NZ 37.59S 175.44E
142 C14 **Tire** İzmir, SW Turkey 38.04N 27.45E
143 O11 **Tirebolu** Giresun, N Turkey 41.01N 38.49E
98 F11 **Tiree** *island* W Scotland, UK
Tîrgovişte *see* Târgovişte
Tîrgu *see* Târgu Cărbuneşti
Tîrgu Bujor *see* Târgu Bujor
Tîrgu Frumos *see* Târgu Frumos
Tîrgu Jiu *see* Targu Jui
Tîrgu Lăpuş *see* Târgu Lăpuş
Tîrgu Mures *see* Târgu Mureş
Tîrgu-Neamţ *see* Târgu-Neamţ
Tîrgu Ocna *see* Târgu Ocna
Tîrgu Secuiesc *see* Târgu Secuiesc
155 T3 **Tirich Mir** ▲ NW Pakistan 36.12N 71.51E
78 J5 **Tiris Zemmour** ◆ *region* N Mauritania
Tirlemont *see* Tienen
131 W5 **Tirlyanskiy** Respublika Bashkortostan, W Russian Federation 54.09N 58.32E
Tîrnava Mare *see* Târnava Mare
Tîrnava Mică *see* Târnava Mică
Tîrnăveni *see* Târnăveni
Tírnavos *see* Týrnavos
Tirnovo *see* Veliko Tŭrnovo
160 J11 **Tirodi** Madhya Pradesh, C India 21.40N 79.43E
110 K8 **Tirol** *off.* Land Tirol, *var.* Tyrol, *It.* Tirolo. ◆ *state* W Austria
Tirolo *see* Tirol
Tirreno, Mare *see* Tyrrhenian Sea
109 B19 **Tirso** ~ Sardegna, Italy, C Mediterranean Sea
97 H22 **Tirstrup** ✕ (Århus) Århus, C Denmark 56.17N 10.36E
161 I21 **Tiruchchirāppalli** *prev.* Trichinopoly. Tamil Nādu, SE India 10.49N 78.43E
161 H23 **Tirunelveli** *var.* Tinnevelly. Tamil Nādu, SE India 8.45N 77.43E

◆ Country ● Country Capital ◇ Dependent Territory ○ Dependent Territory Capital ◆ Administrative Region ✕ International Airport ▲ Mountain ▲ Mountain Range ▲ Volcano ~ River ◎ Lake ⊠ Reservoir
337

◆ COUNTRY ◇ DEPENDENT TERRITORY ♦ ADMINISTRATIVE REGION ▲ MOUNTAIN ☒ VOLCANO ☺ LAKE
● COUNTRY CAPITAL ○ DEPENDENT TERRITORY CAPITAL ✕ INTERNATIONAL AIRPORT ▲ MOUNTAIN RANGE ♣ RIVER ☒ RESERVOIR

Torricelli Mountains – Truite, Lac à la

194 F9 **Torricelli Mountains** ▲▲ NW PNG
98 G8 **Torridon, Loch** *inlet* NW Scotland, UK
108 D9 **Torriglia** Liguria, NW Italy *44.31N 9.08E*
106 M9 **Torrijos** Castilla-La Mancha, C Spain *39.58N 4.18W*
20 L12 **Torrington** Connecticut, NE USA *41.48N 73.07W*
35 Z15 **Torrington** Wyoming, C USA *42.04N 104.10W*
95 F16 **Torröjen** *var.* Torrön. ◎ C Sweden
Torrön *see* Torröjen
107 N15 **Torrox** Andalucía, S Spain *36.45N 3.58W*
96 N13 **Torsåker** Gävleborg, C Sweden *60.31N 16.30E*
97 N21 **Torsås** Kalmar, S Sweden *56.24N 16.00E*
97 J14 **Torsby** Värmland, C Sweden *60.07N 13.00E*
97 N16 **Torshälla** Södermanland, C Sweden *59.25N 16.28E*
97 B19 **Tórshavn** ***Dan.*** Thorshavn *Dependent territory capital* Faeroe Islands *62.02N 6.47W*
Torshiz *see* Kāshmar
47 T9 **Tortola** *island* C British Virgin Islands
108 D9 **Tortona** ***anc.*** Dertona. Piemonte, NW Italy *44.54N 8.52E*
109 L23 **Tortorici** Sicilia, Italy, C Mediterranean Sea *38.01N 14.49E*
107 U7 **Tortosa** ***anc.*** Dertosa. Cataluña, E Spain *40.49N 0.31E*
Tortosa *see* Ţarţūs
107 U7 **Tortosa, Cap** *headland* E Spain *40.43N 0.52E*
46 L8 **Tortue, Île de la** ***var.*** Tortuga Island. *island* N Haiti
57 Y10 **Tortue, Montagne** ▲▲ C French Guiana
Tortuga, Isla *see* La Tortuga, Isla
Tortuga Island *see* Tortue, Île de la
56 C11 **Tortugas, Golfo** *gulf* W Colombia
47 T5 **Tortuguero, Laguna** *lagoon* N Puerto Rico
143 Q12 **Tortum** Erzurum, NE Turkey *40.15N 41.30E*
Torugart, Pereval *see* Turugart Shankou
143 O12 **Torul** Gümüşhane, NE Turkey *40.34N 39.18E*
112 J10 **Toruń** ***Ger.*** Thorn. Toruń, Kujawsko-pomorskie, C Poland *53.01N 18.36E*
97 K20 **Torup** Halland, S Sweden *56.57N 13.04E*
120 I6 **Tõrva** ***Ger.*** Törwa. Valgamaa, S Estonia *58.00N 25.54E*
Törwa *see* Tõrva
98 D13 **Tory Island** ***Ir.*** Toraigh. *island* NW Ireland
113 N19 **Torysa** ***Hung.*** Tarca. ∿ NE Slovakia
Törzburg *see* Bran
128 J16 **Torzhok** Tverskaya Oblast', W Russian Federation *57.04N 34.55E*
170 Ee15 **Tosa** Kōchi, Shikoku, SW Japan *33.28N 133.25E*
170 E16 **Tosa-Shimizu** ***var.*** Tosasimizu. Kōchi, Shikoku, SW Japan *32.46N 132.55E*
Tosasimizu *see* Tosa-Shimizu
170 Ee16 **Tosa-wan** *bay* SW Japan
85 H21 **Tosca** North-West, N South Africa *25.51S 23.56E*
108 F12 **Toscana** ***Eng.*** Tuscany. ◐ *region* C Italy
109 E14 **Toscano, Archipelago** ***Eng.*** Tuscan Archipelago. *island group* C Italy
108 G10 **Tosco-Emiliano, Appennino** ***Eng.*** Tuscan-Emilian Mountains. ▲▲ C Italy
Tōsei *see* Tungshih
171 J18 **To-shima** *island* Izu-shotō, SE Japan
153 Q9 **Toshkent** ***Eng./Rus.*** Tashkent. ● (Uzbekistan) Toshkent Wiloyati, E Uzbekistan *41.19N 69.17E*
153 Q9 **Toshkent** ✈ Toshkent Wiloyati, E Uzbekistan *41.13N 69.15E*
153 P9 **Toshkent Wiloyati** ***Rus.*** Tashkentskaya Oblast'. ◐ *province* E Uzbekistan
128 H13 **Tosno** Leningradskaya Oblast', NW Russian Federation *59.34N 30.48E*
165 Q10 **Toson Hu** ◎ C China
168 H6 **Tosontsengel** Dzavhan, NW Mongolia *48.42N 98.14E*
Tosquduq Qumlari *see* Goshquduq Qum
107 U4 **Tossal de l'Orri** ***var.*** Llorri. ▲ NE Spain *42.24N 1.15E*
63 A15 **Tostado** Santa Fe, C Argentina *29.14S 61.43W*
120 F6 **Tõstamaa** ***Ger.*** Testama. Pärnumaa, SW Estonia *58.19N 23.58E*
102 I10 **Tostedt** Niedersachsen, NW Germany *53.16N 9.42E*
142 J11 **Tosya** Kastamonu, N Turkey *41.01N 34.01E*
97 F15 **Totak** ◎ S Norway
107 R13 **Totana** Murcia, SE Spain *37.45N 1.30W*
96 H13 **Toten** *physical region* S Norway
85 G18 **Toteng** Ngamiland, C Botswana *20.19S 22.57E*
104 M3 **Tôtes** Seine-Maritime, N France *49.40N 1.02E*
Totigi *see* Tochigi
Totio *see* Tochio
Totis *see* Tata
201 U13 **Totiw** *island* Chuuk, C Micronesia
129 N13 **Tot'ma** ***var.*** Totma. Vologodskaya Oblast', NW Russian Federation *59.58N 42.42E*
Tot'ma *see* Sukhona
57 V9 **Totness** Coronie, N Surinam *5.51N 56.19W*
44 C5 **Totonicapán** Totonicapán, W Guatemala *14.54N 91.18W*
44 A2 **Totonicapán** ***off.*** Departamento de Totonicapán. ◐ *department* W Guatemala
63 B18 **Totoras** Santa Fe, C Argentina *32.34S 61.10W*
197 K15 **Totoya** *island* S Fiji
191 Q7 **Tottenham** New South Wales, SE Australia *32.16S 147.23E*
171 Gg13 **Tottori** Tottori, Honshū, SW Japan *35.28N 134.14E*
170 Ff13 **Tottori** ***off.*** Tottori-ken. ◐ *prefecture* Honshū, SW Japan
78 I6 **Touâjîl** Tiris Zemmour, N Mauritania *22.03N 12.39W*
78 L15 **Touba** W Ivory Coast *8.16N 7.40W*
78 G11 **Touba** W Senegal *14.55N 15.53W*
76 E7 **Toubkal, Jbel** ▲ W Morocco *31.00N 7.50W*
34 K10 **Touchet** Washington, NW USA *46.03N 118.40W*
105 P7 **Toucy** Yonne, C France *47.45N 3.18E*
79 O12 **Tougan** W Burkina *13.06N 3.03W*
76 L7 **Touggourt** NE Algeria *33.07N 6.04E*
79 Q12 **Tougouri** N Burkina *13.22N 0.25W*
78 J13 **Tougué** Moyenne-Guinée, NW Guinea *11.28N 11.48W*
78 K12 **Toukoto** Kayes, W Mali *13.24N 9.52W*
105 S5 **Toul** Meurthe-et-Moselle, NE France *48.40N 5.54E*
78 L16 **Toulépleu** ***var.*** Toulobli. W Ivory Coast *6.37N 8.27W*
167 S14 **Touliu** C Taiwan *23.44N 120.27E*
13 U3 **Toulnustouc** ∿ Quebec, SE Canada
Toulobli *see* Toulépleu
105 T16 **Toulon** ***anc.*** Telo Martius, Tilio Martius. Var, SE France *43.07N 5.55E*
32 K12 **Toulon** Illinois, N USA *41.04N 89.54W*
104 M15 **Toulouse** ***anc.*** Tolosa. Haute-Garonne, S France *43.36N 1.24E*
104 M15 **Toulouse** ✈ Haute-Garonne, S France *43.38N 1.19E*
79 N16 **Toumodi** C Ivory Coast *6.34N 5.01W*
76 G9 **Tounassine, Hamada** *hill range* W Algeria
177 G7 **Toungoo** Pegu, C Burma *18.57N 96.25E*
104 L8 **Touraine** *cultural region* C France
Tourane *see* Đă Nâng
105 P1 **Tourcoing** Nord, N France *50.43N 3.10E*
106 F2 **Touriñán, Cabo** *headland* NW Spain *43.02N 9.20W*
78 J6 **Tourîne** Tiris Zemmour, N Mauritania *22.22N 11.49W*
104 J3 **Tourlaville** Manche, N France *49.39N 1.34W*
101 D19 **Tournai** ***var.*** Tournay, ***Dut.*** Doornik; ***anc.*** Tornacum. Hainaut, SW Belgium *50.36N 3.24E*
104 L16 **Tournay** Hautes-Pyrénées, S France *43.10N 0.16E*
Tournay *see* Tournai
105 R12 **Tournon** Ardèche, E France *45.04N 4.49E*
105 R9 **Tournus** Saône-et-Loire, C France *46.33N 4.53E*
61 Q14 **Touros** Rio Grande do Norte, E Brazil *5.10S 35.28W*
104 L8 **Tours** ***anc.*** Caesarodunum, Turoni. Indre-et-Loire, C France *47.22N 0.40E*
191 Q17 **Tourville, Cape** *headland* Tasmania, SE Australia *42.09S 148.20E*
168 L8 **Töv** ◐ *province* C Mongolia
56 H7 **Tovar** Mérida, NW Venezuela *8.21N 71.45W*
130 L5 **Tovarkovskiy** Tul'skaya Oblast', W Russian Federation *53.41N 38.18E*
Tovil'-Dora *see* Tavildara
Tövis *see* Teiuş
143 V11 **Tovuz** ***Rus.*** Tauz. W Azerbaijan *40.58N 45.41E*
172 N9 **Towada** Aomori, Honshū, C Japan *40.36N 141.11E*
172 N9 **Towada-ko** ***var.*** Towada Ko. ◎ Honshū, C Japan
192 K3 **Towai** Northland, North Island, NZ *35.29S 174.06E*
20 H12 **Towanda** Pennsylvania, NE USA *41.45N 76.25W*
31 W4 **Tower** Minnesota, N USA *47.48N 92.16W*
175 Pp8 **Towera** Sulawesi, N Indonesia *0.29S 120.01E*
Tower Island *see* Genovesa, Isla
188 M13 **Tower Peak** ▲ Western Australia *33.23S 123.27E*
37 U11 **Towne Pass** *pass* California, W USA
31 N3 **Towner** North Dakota, N USA *48.20N 100.27W*
35 R10 **Townsend** Montana, NW USA *46.19N 111.31W*
189 X6 **Townsville** Queensland, NE Australia *19.24S 146.52E*
Towoeti Meer *see* Towuti, Danau
175 Q10 **Towori, Teluk** *bay* Sulawesi, C Indonesia
154 K4 **Towraghoudī** Herāt, NW Afghanistan *35.12N 62.19E*
23 X3 **Towson** Maryland, NE USA *39.22N 76.33W*
175 Q11 **Towuti, Danau** ***Dut.*** Towoeti Meer. ◎ Sulawesi, C Indonesia
Toxkan He *see* Ak-say
26 K9 **Toyah** Texas, SW USA *31.18N 103.47W*
172 Nn6 **Tōya-ko** ◎ Hokkaidō, NE Japan
171 Ii13 **Toyama** Toyama, Honshū, SW Japan *36.41N 137.12E*
171 Ii13 **Toyama** ***off.*** Toyama-ken. ◐ *prefecture* Honshū, SW Japan
171 J13 **Toyama-wan** *bay* W Japan
170 F16 **Tōyo** Ehime, Shikoku, SW Japan *33.57N 133.02E*
170 Ee14 **Tōyo** Kōchi, Shikoku, SW Japan *33.28N 134.13E*
Toyohara *see* Yuzhno-Sakhalinsk
171 Hh16 **Toyohashi** ***var.*** Toyohasi. Aichi, Honshū, SW Japan *34.45N 137.22E*
Toyohasi *see* Toyohashi
171 I16 **Toyokawa** Aichi, Honshū, SW Japan *34.49N 137.22E*
171 Gg13 **Toyooka** Hyōgo, Honshū, SW Japan *35.33N 134.48E*
171 Kk12 **Toyosaka** Niigata, Honshū, C Japan *37.54N 139.12E*
171 I16 **Toyota** Aichi, Honshū, SW Japan *35.04N 137.09E*
172 Pp2 **Toyotomi** Hokkaidō, NE Japan *45.07N 141.45E*
170 Dd12 **Toyoura** Yamaguchi, Honshū, SW Japan *34.09N 130.55E*
Toytepa *see* Tuytepa
76 M6 **Tozeur** ***var.*** Tawzar. W Tunisia *34.00N 8.09E*
41 Q8 **Tozi, Mount** ▲ Alaska, USA *65.45N 151.01W*
143 Q9 **Tqvarch'eli** ***Rus.*** Tkvarcheli. NW Georgia *42.51N 41.42E*
Trâblous *see* Tripoli
143 O11 **Trabzon** ***Eng.*** Trebizond; ***anc.*** Trapezus. Trabzon, NE Turkey *41.00N 39.43E*
143 O11 **Trabzon** ***Eng.*** Trebizond. ◐ *province* NE Turkey
11 P13 **Tracadie** New Brunswick, SE Canada *47.31N 64.57W*
Trachenberg *see* Żmigród
13 O11 **Tracy** Quebec, SE Canada *45.59N 73.07W*
37 O8 **Tracy** California, W USA *37.43N 121.27W*
31 S10 **Tracy** Minnesota, N USA *44.14N 95.37W*
22 K10 **Tracy City** Tennessee, S USA *35.15N 85.44W*
108 D7 **Tradate** Lombardia, N Italy *45.43N 8.57E*
86 F6 **Traena Bank** *undersea feature* E Norwegian Sea
31 W13 **Traer** Iowa, C USA *42.11N 92.28W*
106 J16 **Trafalgar, Cabo de** *headland* SW Spain *36.10N 6.03W*
Traiectum ad Mosam/Traiectum Tungorum *see* Maastricht
Tráigh Mhór *see* Tramore
9 O17 **Trail** British Columbia, SW Canada *49.04N 117.46W*
60 B11 **Traíra, Serra do** ▲▲ NW Brazil
111 V5 **Traisen** Niederösterreich, NE Austria *48.03N 15.37E*
111 W4 **Traisen** ∿ NE Austria
111 X4 **Traiskirchen** Niederösterreich, NE Austria *48.01N 16.18E*
Trajani Portus *see* Civitavecchia
Trajectum ad Rhenum *see* Utrecht
121 H14 **Trakai** ***Ger.*** Traken, ***Pol.*** Troki. Trakai, SE Lithuania *54.39N 24.58E*
Traken *see* Trakai
99 B20 **Tralee** ***Ir.*** Trá Lí. SW Ireland *52.16N 9.42W*
99 A20 **Tralee Bay** ***Ir.*** Bá Thrá Lí. *bay* SW Ireland
Trá Lí *see* Tralee
Trälleborg *see* Trelleborg
Tralles *see* Aydın
63 J16 **Tramandaí** Rio Grande do Sul, S Brazil *30.01S 50.11W*
110 C7 **Tramelan** Bern, W Switzerland *47.13N 7.07E*
Trá Mhór *see* Tramore
99 E20 **Tramore** ***Ir.*** Tráigh Mhór, Trá Mhór. S Ireland *52.10N 7.10W*
97 L18 **Tranås** Jönköping, S Sweden *58.03N 15.00E*
64 J7 **Trancas** Tucumán, N Argentina *26.10S 65.19W*
106 I7 **Trancoso** Guarda, N Portugal *40.46N 7.21W*
97 H22 **Tranebjerg** Århus, C Denmark *55.51N 10.36E*
97 K19 **Tranemo** Västra Götaland, S Sweden *57.30N 13.19E*
178 Gg16 **Trang** Trang, S Thailand *7.33N 99.36E*
176 W14 **Trangan, Pulau** *island* Kepulauan Aru, E Indonesia
Trâng Dinh *see* Thât Khê
191 Q7 **Trangie** New South Wales, SE Australia *32.01S 147.58E*
96 K12 **Trängslet** Dalarna, C Sweden *61.22N 13.43E*
109 N16 **Trani** Puglia, SE Italy *41.16N 16.24E*
63 F17 **Tranqueras** Rivera, NE Uruguay *31.13S 55.45W*
65 G17 **Tranqui, Isla** *island* S Chile
41 V6 **Trans-Alaska pipeline** *oil pipeline* Alaska, USA
205 Q10 **Transantarctic Mountains** ▲▲ Antarctica
Transcarpathian Oblast *see* Zakarpats'ka Oblast'
Transilvania *see* Transylvania
Transilvaniei, Alpi *see* Carpaţii Meridionali
Transjordan *see* Jordan
180 L11 **Transkei Basin** *undersea feature* SW Indian Ocean
127 N17 **Trans-Siberian Railway** *Railroad* Russian Federation
Transsylvanische Alpen/Transylvanian Alps *see* Carpaţii Meridionali
96 K12 **Transtrand** Dalarna, C Sweden *61.06N 13.19E*
118 G10 **Transylvania** ***Eng.*** Ardeal, Transilvania, ***Ger.*** Siebenbürgen, ***Hung.*** Erdély. *cultural region* NW Romania
178 Jj15 **Tra Ôn** Vinh Long, S Vietnam *9.58N 105.58E*
109 H23 **Trapani** ***anc.*** Drepanum. Sicilia, Italy, C Mediterranean Sea *38.02N 12.31E*
178 J12 **Trâpeăng Vêng** Kâmpóng Thum, C Cambodia *12.37N 104.58E*
Trapezus *see* Trabzon
116 L9 **Trapoklovo** Sliven, C Bulgaria *42.40N 26.36E*
191 P13 **Traralgon** Victoria, SE Australia *38.15S 146.35E*
78 H9 **Trarza** ◐ *region* SW Mauritania
Trasimenischersee *see* Trasimeno, Lago
108 H12 **Trasimeno, Lago** ***Eng.*** Lake of Perugia, ***Ger.*** Trasimenischersee. ◎ C Italy
97 J20 **Träslövsläge** Halland, S Sweden *57.02N 12.18E*
Trás-os-Montes *see* Cucumbi
106 I6 **Trás-os-Montes e Alto Douro** *former province* N Portugal
178 I13 **Trat** ***var.*** Bang Phra. Trat, S Thailand *12.16N 102.30E*
Trá Tholl, Inis *see* Inishtrahull
Traù *see* Trogir
111 T4 **Traun** Oberösterreich, N Austria *48.14N 14.13E*
111 S5 **Traun** ∿ N Austria
Traun, Lake *see* Traunsee
103 N23 **Traunreut** Bayern, SE Germany *47.58N 12.36E*
111 S5 **Traunsee** ***var.*** Gmundner See, ***Eng.*** Lake Traun. ◎ N Austria
Trautenau *see* Trutnov
23 P11 **Travelers Rest** South Carolina, SE USA *34.58N 82.26W*
190 L8 **Travellers Lake** *seasonal lake* New South Wales, SE Australia
33 P6 **Traverse City** Michigan, N USA *44.45N 85.37W*
31 R7 **Traverse, Lake** ◎ Minnesota/South Dakota, N USA
193 I16 **Travers, Mount** ▲ South Island, NZ *42.01S 172.46E*
9 P17 **Travers Reservoir** ⊠ Alberta, SW Canada
178 Jj15 **Tra Vinh** ***var.*** Phu Vinh. Tra Vinh, S Vietnam *9.57N 106.19E*
27 S10 **Travis, Lake** ⊠ Texas, SW USA
114 H12 **Travnik** Federacija Bosna I Hercegovina, C Bosnia and Herzegovina *44.14N 17.40E*
111 V11 **Trbovlje** ***Ger.*** Trifail. C Slovenia *46.09N 15.03E*
25 V13 **Treasure Island** Florida, SE USA *27.46N 82.46W*
Treasure State *see* Montana
195 S14 **Treasury Islands** *island group* NW Solomon Islands
108 D9 **Trebbia** ***anc.*** Trebia. ∿ NW Italy
102 N8 **Trebel** ∿ NE Germany
105 O16 **Trèbes** Aude, S France *43.12N 2.25E*
Trebia *see* Trebbia
113 F18 **Třebíč** ***Ger.*** Trebitsch. Jihlavský Kraj, S Czech Republic *49.13N 15.52E*
115 I16 **Trebinje** Republika Srpska, S Bosnia and Herzegovina *42.42N 18.19E*
Trebišnica *see* Trebišnjica
115 H16 **Trebišnjica** ***var.*** Trebišnica. ∿ S Bosnia and Herzegovina
113 N20 **Trebišov** ***Hung.*** Tőketerebes. Košický Kraj, E Slovakia *48.36N 21.44E*
Trebitsch *see* Třebíč
Trebizond *see* Trabzon
Trebnitz *see* Trzebnica
111 V12 **Trebnje** SE Slovenia *45.54N 15.01E*
113 D19 **Třeboň** ***Ger.*** Wittingau. Budějovický Kraj, S Czech Republic *49.00N 14.46E*
106 J15 **Trebujena** Andalucía, S Spain *36.52N 6.10W*
102 I7 **Treene** ∿ N Germany
Tree Planters State *see* Nebraska
111 S9 **Treffen** Kärnten, S Austria *46.40N 13.51E*
Trefynwy *see* Monmouth
104 G5 **Tréguier** Côtes d'Armor, NW France *48.50N 3.12W*
63 G18 **Treinta y Tres** Treinta y Tres, E Uruguay *33.12S 54.19W*
63 F18 **Treinta y Tres** ◐ *department* E Uruguay
116 F9 **Treklyanska Reka** ∿ W Bulgaria
175 R10 **Treko, Kepulauan** *island group* N Indonesia
104 K8 **Trélazé** Maine-et-Loire, NW France *47.27N 0.28W*
65 K17 **Trelew** Chubut, SE Argentina *43.13S 65.15W*
97 K23 **Trelleborg** ***var.*** Trälleborg. Skåne, S Sweden *55.22N 13.10E*
115 P15 **Trem** ▲ SE Yugoslavia *43.10N 22.12E*
13 N11 **Tremblant, Mont** ▲ Quebec, SE Canada *46.13N 74.34W*
101 H17 **Tremelo** Vlaams Brabant, C Belgium *50.59N 4.34E*
109 M15 **Tremiti, Isole** *island group* SE Italy
32 K12 **Tremont** Illinois, N USA *40.30N 89.31W*
38 L1 **Tremonton** Utah, W USA *41.42N 112.09W*
107 U4 **Tremp** Cataluña, NE Spain *42.09N 0.53E*
32 J7 **Trempealeau** Wisconsin, N USA *44.00N 91.25W*
13 P8 **Trenche** ∿ Quebec, SE Canada
13 O7 **Trenche, Lac** ◎ Quebec, SE Canada
113 I20 **Trenčiansky Kraj** ◐ *region* W Slovakia
113 I19 **Trenčín** ***Ger.*** Trentschin, ***Hung.*** Trencsén. Trenčiansky Kraj, W Slovakia *48.54N 18.03E*
Trencsén *see* Trenčín
Trengganu *see* Terengganu
63 A21 **Trenque Lauquen** Buenos Aires, E Argentina *36.00S 62.46W*
12 J14 **Trent** ∿ Ontario, SE Canada
99 N18 **Trent** ∿ C England, UK
Trent *see* Trento
108 F5 **Trentino-Alto Adige** ***prev.*** Venezia Tridentina. ◐ *region* N Italy
108 G6 **Trento** ***Eng.*** Trent, ***Ger.*** Trient; anc.Tridentum. Trentino-Alto Adige, N Italy *46.04N 11.07E*
12 J15 **Trenton** Ontario, SE Canada *44.06N 77.36W*
25 V10 **Trenton** Florida, SE USA *29.36N 82.49W*
25 R1 **Trenton** Georgia, SE USA *34.52N 85.27W*
33 S10 **Trenton** Michigan, N USA *42.08N 83.10W*
29 S2 **Trenton** Missouri, C USA *40.04N 93.37W*
30 M17 **Trenton** Nebraska, C USA *40.10N 101.00W*
20 J15 **Trenton** *state capital* New Jersey, NE USA *40.13N 74.44W*
23 W10 **Trenton** North Carolina, SE USA *35.03N 77.20W*
22 G9 **Trenton** Tennessee, S USA *35.58N 88.56W*
38 L1 **Trenton** Utah, W USA *41.53N 111.57W*
Trentschin *see* Trenčín
Treptow an der Rega *see* Trzebiatów
63 C23 **Tres Arroyos** Buenos Aires, E Argentina *38.21S 60.16W*
63 J15 **Três Cachoeiras** Rio Grande do Sul, S Brazil *29.21S 49.48W*
108 E7 **Trescore Balneario** Lombardia, N Italy *45.43N 9.52E*
43 V17 **Tres Cruces, Cerro** ▲ SE Mexico *15.28N 92.27W*
59 K18 **Tres Cruces, Cordillera** ▲▲ W Bolivia
115 N18 **Treska** ∿ NW FYR Macedonia
115 I14 **Treskavica** ▲▲ SE Bosnia and Herzegovina
61 J20 **Três Lagoas** Mato Grosso do Sul, SW Brazil *20.46S 51.43W*
42 H12 **Tres Marías, Islas** *island group* C Mexico
61 M19 **Três Marias, Represa** ⊠ SE Brazil
65 F20 **Tres Montes, Península** *headland* S Chile *46.49S 75.29W*
107 O3 **Trespaderne** Castilla-León, N Spain *42.46N 3.24W*
62 G13 **Três Passos** Rio Grande do Sul, S Brazil *27.28S 53.55W*
63 A23 **Tres Picos, Cerro** ▲ E Argentina *38.10S 61.54W*
65 G17 **Tres Picos, Cerro** ▲ SW Argentina *42.22S 71.51W*
62 I12 **Três Pinheiros** Paraná, S Brazil *25.25S 51.57W*
61 M21 **Três Pontas** Minas Gerais, SE Brazil *21.33S 45.18W*
Tres Puntas, Cabo *see* Manabique, Punta
62 P9 **Três Rios** Rio de Janeiro, SE Brazil *22.06S 43.15W*
Tres Tabernae *see* Saverne
Trestenberg/Trestendorf *see* Tăşnad
43 R15 **Tres Valles** Veracruz-Llave, SE Mexico *18.14N 96.03W*
96 H12 **Tretten** Oppland, S Norway *61.19N 10.19E*
Treuburg *see* Olecko
103 K21 **Treuchtlingen** Bayern, S Germany *48.57N 10.55E*
102 N13 **Treuenbrietzen** Brandenburg, E Germany *52.06N 12.52E*
97 F16 **Treungen** Telemark, S Norway *59.00N 8.34E*
65 H17 **Trevelín** Chubut, SW Argentina *43.02S 71.27W*
Treves/Trèves *see* Trier
108 I13 **Trevi** Umbria, C Italy *42.52N 12.46E*
108 E7 **Treviglio** Lombardia, N Italy *45.31N 9.34E*
106 J4 **Trevinca, Peña** ▲ NW Spain *42.10N 6.49W*
107 P3 **Treviño** Castilla-León, N Spain *42.45N 2.41W*
108 I7 **Treviso** ***anc.*** Tarvisium. Veneto, NE Italy *45.40N 12.15E*
99 G24 **Trevose Head** *headland* SW England, UK *50.33N 5.03W*
Trg *see* Feldkirchen in Kärnten
191 P17 **Triabunna** Tasmania, SE Australia *42.33S 147.55E*
23 W4 **Triangle** Virginia, NE USA *38.30N 77.17W*
85 L18 **Triangle** Masvingo, SE Zimbabwe *20.58S 31.28E*
117 L23 **Tría Nisía** *island* Kykládes, Greece, Aegean Sea
Triberg *see* Triberg im Schwarzwald
103 G23 **Triberg im Schwarzwald** ***var.*** Triberg. Baden-Württemberg, SW Germany *48.07N 8.13E*
159 P11 **Tribhuvan** ✈ (Kathmandu) Central, C Nepal
56 C9 **Tribugá, Golfo de** *gulf* W Colombia
189 W4 **Tribulation, Cape** *headland* Queensland, NE Australia *16.14S 145.48E*
110 M8 **Tribulaun** ▲ SW Austria *46.59N 11.18E*
9 U17 **Tribune** Saskatchewan, S Canada *49.16N 103.50W*
28 H5 **Tribune** Kansas, C USA *38.28N 101.45W*
109 N18 **Tricarico** Basilicata, S Italy *40.37N 16.09E*
109 Q19 **Tricase** Puglia, SE Italy *39.56N 18.21E*
Trichinopoly *see* Tiruchchirāppalli
117 D18 **Trichonída, Límni** ◎ C Greece
161 G22 **Trichūr** ***var.*** Thrissur. Kerala, SW India *10.31N 76.13E*
Tricorno *see* Triglav
191 O8 **Trida** New South Wales, SE Australia *33.02S 145.03E*
37 S1 **Trident Peak** ▲ Nevada, W USA *41.52N 118.22W*
Tridentum/Trient *see* Trento
111 T6 **Trieben** Steiermark, SE Austria *47.29N 14.27E*
103 D19 **Trier** ***Eng.*** Treves, ***Fr.*** Trèves; ***anc.*** Augusta Treverorum. Rheinland-Pfalz, SW Germany *49.45N 6.39E*
108 K7 **Trieste** ***Slvn.*** Trst. Friuli-Venezia Giulia, NE Italy *45.39N 13.45E*
Trieste, Golfo di/Triest, Golf von *see* Trieste, Gulf of
108 J8 **Trieste, Gulf of** ***Cro.*** Tršćanski Zaljev, ***Ger.*** Golf von Triest, ***It.*** Golfo di Trieste, ***Slvn.*** Tržaški Zaliv. *gulf* S Europe
111 W4 **Triesting** ∿ W Austria
Trifail *see* Trbovlje
118 L9 **Trifeşti** Iaşi, NE Romania *47.30N 27.31E*
111 S10 **Triglav** ***It.*** Tricorno. ▲ NW Slovenia *46.22N 13.40E*
106 I14 **Trigueros** Andalucía, S Spain *37.24N 6.49W*
117 E16 **Tríkala** ***prev.*** Trikkala. Thessalía, C Greece *39.33N 21.46E*
117 E17 **Trikeriótis** ∿ C Greece
Trikkala *see* Tríkala
Trikomo/Tríkomon *see* İskele
99 F17 **Trim** ***Ir.*** Baile Átha Troim. E Ireland *53.34N 6.46W*
110 E7 **Trimbach** Solothurn, NW Switzerland *47.21N 7.49E*
111 Q5 **Trimmelkam** Oberösterreich, N Austria *48.02N 12.55E*
31 U11 **Trimont** Minnesota, N USA *43.45N 94.42W*
Trimontium *see* Plovdiv
Trinacria *see* Sicilia
161 K24 **Trincomalee** ***var.*** Trinkomali. Eastern Province, NE Sri Lanka *8.34N 81.13E*
67 K16 **Trindade, Ilha da** *island* Brazil, W Atlantic Ocean
49 Y9 **Trindade Spur** *undersea feature* SW Atlantic Ocean
113 J17 **Třinec** ***Ger.*** Trzynietz. Ostravský Kraj, E Czech Republic *49.42N 18.37E*
59 M16 **Trinidad** Beni, N Bolivia *14.52S 64.54W*
56 H9 **Trinidad** Casanare, E Colombia *5.25N 71.39W*
46 E6 **Trinidad** Sancti Spíritus, C Cuba *21.48N 80.00W*
39 U8 **Trinidad** Colorado, C USA *37.10N 104.31W*
63 E19 **Trinidad** Flores, S Uruguay *33.34S 56.54W*
47 Y17 **Trinidad** *island* C Trinidad and Tobago
Trinidad *see* Jose Abad Santos
47 Y16 **Trinidad and Tobago** ***off.*** Republic of Trinidad and Tobago. ◆ *republic* SE West Indies
65 F22 **Trinidad, Golfo** *gulf* S Chile
63 B24 **Trinidad, Isla** *island* E Argentina
109 N16 **Trinitapoli** Puglia, SE Italy *41.22N 16.06E*
57 X10 **Trinité, Montagnes de la** ▲▲ C French Guiana
27 W9 **Trinity** Texas, SW USA *30.57N 95.22W*
11 U12 **Trinity Bay** *inlet* Newfoundland, E Canada
41 P15 **Trinity Islands** *island group* Alaska, USA
37 N2 **Trinity Mountains** ▲▲ California, W USA
37 S4 **Trinity Peak** ▲ Nevada, W USA *40.13N 118.43W*
37 S5 **Trinity Range** ▲▲ Nevada, W USA
37 N2 **Trinity River** ∿ California, W USA
27 V8 **Trinity River** ∿ Texas, SW USA
Trinkomali *see* Trincomalee
181 Y15 **Triolet** NW Mauritius *20.04S 57.31E*
109 O20 **Trionto, Capo** *headland* S Italy *39.37N 16.46E*
173 Ee4 **Tripa, Krueng** ∿ Sumatera, NW Indonesia
117 J16 **Tripití, Akrotírio** *headland* Ágios Efstrátios, E Greece *39.28N 24.58E*
144 G6 **Tripoli** ***var.*** Tarābulus, Ţarābulus ash Shām, Trâblous; ***anc.*** Tripolis. N Lebanon *34.30N 35.42E*
31 X12 **Tripoli** Iowa, C USA *42.48N 92.15W*
Tripoli *see* Ţarābulus
117 F20 **Trípoli** ***prev.*** Trípolis. Pelopónnisos, S Greece *37.31N 22.22E*
Tripolis *see* Tripoli, Lebanon
Trípolis *see* Trípoli, Greece
31 Q12 **Tripp** South Dakota, N USA *43.12N 97.57W*
159 V15 **Tripura** ***var.*** Hill Tippera. ◐ *state* NE India
110 K8 **Trisanna** ∿ W Austria
102 H8 **Trischen** *island* NW Germany
67 M24 **Tristan da Cunha** ◇ *dependency of Saint Helena* SE Atlantic Ocean
69 P15 **Tristan da Cunha** *island* SE Atlantic Ocean
67 L18 **Tristan da Cunha Fracture Zone** *tectonic feature* S Atlantic Ocean
178 J14 **Tri Tôn** An Giang, S Vietnam *10.25N 105.01E*
178 Ll11 **Triton Island** *island* S Paracel Islands
161 G24 **Trivandrum** ***var.*** Thiruvanathapuram. Kerala, SW India *8.30N 76.57E*
113 H20 **Trnava** ***Ger.*** Tyrnau, ***Hung.*** Nagyszombat. Trnavský Kraj, W Slovakia *48.22N 17.36E*
113 H20 **Trnavský Kraj** ◐ *region* W Slovakia
Trnovo *see* Veliko Tŭrnovo
Trobriand Island *see* Kiriwina Island
Trobriand Islands *see* Kiriwina Islands
9 Q16 **Trochu** Alberta, SW Canada *51.48N 113.12W*
111 U7 **Trofaiach** Steiermark, SE Austria *47.24N 14.56E*
95 F14 **Trofors** Troms, N Norway *65.31N 13.19E*
115 E14 **Trogir** ***It.*** Traù. Split-Dalmacija, S Croatia *43.32N 16.13E*
114 F13 **Troglav** ▲ Bosnia and Herzegovina/Croatia *44.00N 16.36E*
109 M16 **Troia** Puglia, SE Italy *41.21N 15.19E*
109 K24 **Troina** Sicilia, Italy, C Mediterranean Sea *37.48N 14.33E*
181 O16 **Trois-Bassins** W Réunion *21.04S 55.18E*
103 E17 **Troisdorf** Nordrhein-Westfalen, W Germany *50.49N 7.09E*
76 H5 **Trois Fourches, Cap des** *headland* NE Morocco *35.27N 2.58W*
13 T8 **Trois-Pistoles** Quebec, SE Canada *48.07N 69.10W*
101 L21 **Trois-Ponts** Liège, E Belgium *50.22N 5.52E*
13 P11 **Trois-Rivières** Quebec, SE Canada *46.21N 72.34W*
57 Y12 **Trois Sauts** S French Guiana *2.15N 52.52W*
101 M22 **Troisvierges** Diekirch, N Luxembourg *50.07N 6.00E*
125 Ee12 **Troitsk** Chelyabinskaya Oblast', S Russian Federation *54.04N 61.31E*
129 T9 **Troitsko-Pechorsk** Respublika Komi, NW Russian Federation *62.39N 56.06E*
131 V7 **Troitskoye** Orenburgskaya Oblast', W Russian Federation *52.23N 56.24E*
Troki *see* Trakai
96 F9 **Trolla** ▲ S Norway *62.41N 9.47E*
97 J18 **Trollhättan** Västra Götaland, S Sweden *58.16N 12.19E*
96 G9 **Trollheimen** ▲▲ S Norway
96 E9 **Trolltindane** ▲ S Norway *62.30N 7.43E*
60 H11 **Trombetas, Rio** ∿ NE Brazil
132 L16 **Tromelin, Île** *island* N Réunion
94 I9 **Troms** ◐ *county* N Norway
94 I9 **Tromsø** ***Fin.*** Tromssa. Troms, N Norway *69.42N 19.00E*
86 F5 **Tromsøflaket** *undersea feature* W Barents Sea
Tromssa *see* Tromsø
96 H10 **Tron** ▲ S Norway *62.12N 10.46E*
37 U12 **Trona** California, W USA *35.46N 117.21W*
65 G16 **Tronador, Cerro** ▲ S Chile *41.12S 71.51W*
96 H8 **Trondheim** ***Ger.*** Drontheim; ***prev.*** Nidaros, Trondhjem. Sør-Trøndelag, S Norway *63.25N 10.24E*
96 H7 **Trondheimsfjorden** *fjord* S Norway
Trondhjem *see* Trondheim
109 J14 **Tronto** ∿ C Italy
Troodos *see* Ólympos
124 N3 **Troódos** ***var.*** Troodos Mountains. ▲▲ C Cyprus
Troodos Mountains *see* Troódos
98 I13 **Troon** W Scotland, UK *55.32N 4.41W*
109 M22 **Tropea** Calabria, SW Italy *38.40N 15.52E*
38 L7 **Tropic** Utah, W USA *37.37N 112.04W*
66 L10 **Tropic Seamount** ***var.*** Banc du Tropique. *undersea feature* E Atlantic Ocean *23.49N 20.40W*
Tropique, Banc du *see* Tropic Seamount
Tropoja *see* Tropojë
115 L17 **Tropojë** ***var.*** Tropoja. Kukës, N Albania *42.25N 20.09E*
Troppau *see* Opava
97 O16 **Trosa** Södermanland, C Sweden *58.54N 17.34E*
120 H12 **Troškūnai** Anykščiai, E Lithuania *55.36N 24.55E*
103 G23 **Trossingen** Baden-Württemberg, SW Germany *48.04N 8.37E*
119 T4 **Trostyanets'** ***Rus.*** Trostyanets. Sums'ka Oblast', NE Ukraine *50.29N 34.58E*
119 N7 **Trostyanets'** ***Rus.*** Trostyanets. Vinnyts'ka Oblast', C Ukraine *48.35N 29.10E*
118 L11 **Trotuş** ∿ E Romania
46 M8 **Trou-du-Nord** N Haiti *19.34N 71.57W*
27 W7 **Troup** Texas, SW USA *32.08N 95.07W*
15 H8 **Trout** ∿ Northwest Territories, NW Canada
35 N8 **Trout Creek** Montana, NW USA *47.51N 115.40W*
34 H10 **Trout Lake** Washington, NW USA *45.59N 121.33W*
10 B9 **Trout Lake** ◎ Ontario, S Canada
35 T12 **Trout Peak** ▲ Wyoming, C USA *44.36N 109.33W*
104 L4 **Trouville** Calvados, N France *49.21N 0.07E*
99 L22 **Trowbridge** S England, UK *51.19N 2.13W*
25 Q6 **Troy** Alabama, S USA *31.48N 85.58W*
29 Q3 **Troy** Kansas, C USA *39.46N 95.05W*
29 W4 **Troy** Missouri, C USA *38.58N 90.58W*
20 L10 **Troy** New York, NE USA *42.43N 73.37W*
23 S10 **Troy** North Carolina, SE USA *35.21N 79.53W*
33 R13 **Troy** Ohio, N USA *40.02N 84.12W*
27 T9 **Troy** Texas, SW USA *31.12N 97.18W*
116 I9 **Troyan** Lovech, N Bulgaria *42.53N 24.43E*
116 I9 **Troyanski Prokhod** *pass* N Bulgaria *42.48N 24.38E*
151 N6 **Troyebratskiy** Severnyy Kazakhstan, N Kazakhstan *54.21N 66.07E*
105 Q6 **Troyes** ***anc.*** Augustobona Tricassium. Aube, N France *48.18N 4.04E*
119 X5 **Troyits'ke** Luhans'ka Oblast', E Ukraine *49.55N 38.18E*
37 W7 **Troy Peak** ▲ Nevada, W USA *38.18N 115.27W*
115 G15 **Trpanj** Dubrovnik-Neretva, S Croatia *43.00N 17.18E*
Tršćanski Zaljev *see* Trieste, Gulf of
Trst *see* Trieste
115 N14 **Trstenik** Serbia, C Yugoslavia *43.38N 21.01E*
130 I6 **Trubchevsk** Bryanskaya Oblast', W Russian Federation *52.33N 33.45E*
Trubchular *see* Orlyak
39 S10 **Truchas Peak** ▲ New Mexico, SW USA *35.57N 105.38W*
149 P16 **Trucial Coast** *physical region* C UAE
Trucial States *see* United Arab Emirates
37 Q6 **Truckee** California, W USA *39.18N 120.10W*
37 R5 **Truckee River** ∿ Nevada, W USA
131 Q13 **Trudfront** Astrakhanskaya Oblast', SW Russian Federation *45.56N 47.42E*
12 I9 **Truite, Lac à la** ◎ Quebec, SE Canada

◆ Country
● Country Capital
◇ Dependent Territory
○ Dependent Territory Capital
◐ Administrative Region
✈ International Airport
▲ Mountain
▲▲ Mountain Range
Volcano
∿ River
◎ Lake
⊠ Reservoir

TRUJILLO – TUSTUMENA LAKE

44 K4 **Trujillo** Colón, NE Honduras 15.59N 85.54W
58 C12 **Trujillo** La Libertad, NW Peru 8.04S 79.02W
106 K10 **Trujillo** Extremadura, W Spain 39.28N 5.52W
56 I6 **Trujillo** Trujillo, NW Venezuela 9.19N 70.37W
56 I6 **Trujillo** *off.* Estado Trujillo. ◈ *state* W Venezuela
Truk *see* Chuuk
Truk Islands *see* Chuuk Islands
31 U10 **Truman** Minnesota, N USA 43.49N 94.26W
29 X10 **Trumann** Arkansas, C USA 35.40N 90.30W
38 J9 **Trumbull, Mount** ▲ Arizona, SW USA 36.22N 113.09W
116 F9 **Trŭn** Pernik, W Bulgaria 42.51N 22.37E
191 Q8 **Trundle** New South Wales, SE Australia 32.55S 147.43E
133 U13 **Trung Phân** *physical region* S Vietnam
Trupcilar *see* Orlyak
11 Q15 **Truro** Nova Scotia, SE Canada 45.20N 63.14W
99 H25 **Truro** SW England, UK 50.16N 5.03W
27 P5 **Truscott** Texas, SW USA 33.43N 99.48W
118 K9 **Truşeşti** Botoşani, NE Romania 47.45N 27.01E
118 H6 **Truskavets'** L'vivs'ka Oblast', W Ukraine 49.15N 23.30E
97 H22 **Trustrup** Århus, C Denmark 56.20N 10.46E
8 M11 **Trutch** British Columbia, W Canada 57.42N 123.00W
39 Q14 **Truth Or Consequences** New Mexico, SW USA 33.07N 107.15W
113 F15 **Trutnov** *Ger.* Trautenau. Hradecký Kraj, NE Czech Republic 50.34N 15.52E
105 P13 **Truyère** ≈ C France
116 K9 **Tryavna** Lovech, N Bulgaria 42.52N 25.30E
30 M14 **Tryon** Nebraska, C USA 41.31N 100.56W
96 I11 **Trysilelva** ≈ S Norway
114 D10 **Tržac** Federacija Bosna I Hercegovina, NW Bosnia and Herzegovina 44.58N 15.48E
Tržaški Zaliv *see* Trieste, Gulf of
112 G10 **Trzcianka** *Ger.* Schönlanke. Piła, Wielkopolskie, C Poland 53.01N 16.24E
112 E7 **Trzebiatów** *Ger.* Treptow an der Rega. Zachodniopomorskie, NW Poland 54.04N 15.14E
113 G14 **Trzebnica** *Ger.* Trebnitz. Dolnośląskie, SW Poland 51.18N 17.03E
111 T10 **Tržič** *Ger.* Neumarktl. NW Slovenia 46.22N 14.17E
Trzynietz *see* Třinec
Tsabong *see* Tshabong
168 G7 **Tsagaanchuluut** Dzavhan, C Mongolia 47.06N 96.40E
169 P7 **Tsagaanders** Dornod, NE Mongolia 48.03N 114.16E
169 S8 **Tsagaannuur** Dornod, E Mongolia 47.30N 118.45E
168 G8 **Tsagaan-Olom** Govĭ-Altay, C Mongolia 46.42N 96.30E
168 J8 **Tsagaan-Ovoo** Övörhangay, C Mongolia 45.57N 101.25E
168 D5 **Tsagaantüngi** Bayan-Ölgiy, NW Mongolia 49.06N 90.26E
131 P12 **Tsagan Aman** Respublika Kalmykiya, SW Russian Federation 47.37N 46.43E
25 V11 **Tsala Apopka Lake** ◎ Florida, SE USA
Tsamkong *see* Zhanjiang
Tsangpo *see* Brahmaputra
168 L9 **Tsant** Dundgovĭ, C Mongolia 46.16N 106.55E
85 G17 **Tsao** Ngamiland, NW Botswana 20.08S 22.29E
180 I4 **Tsaratanana** Mahajanga, C Madagascar 16.46S 47.40E
116 N10 **Tsarevo** *prev.* Michurin. Burgas, E Bulgaria 42.10N 27.51E
Tsarigrad *see* İstanbul
Tsaritsyn *see* Volgograd
128 G13 **Tsarskoye Selo** *prev.* Pushkin. Leningradskaya Oblast', NW Russian Federation 59.42N 30.24E
119 T7 **Tsarychanka** Dnipropetrovs'ka Oblast', E Ukraine 48.56N 34.29E
85 H21 **Tsatsu** Southern, S Botswana 25.21S 24.45E
83 J20 **Tsavo** Coast, S Kenya 2.58S 38.28E
85 E21 **Tsawisis** Karas, S Namibia 26.18S 18.07E
Tschakathurn *see* Čakovec
Tschaslau *see* Čáslav
Tschenstochau *see* Częstochowa
Tschernembl *see* Črnomelj
30 K6 **Tschida, Lake** ⊞ North Dakota, N USA
Tschorna *see* Mustvee
85 I17 **Tsebanana** Central, NE Botswana 19.50S 26.29E
Tsefat *see* Ẕefat
168 G8 **Tseel** Govĭ-Altay, SW Mongolia 45.45N 95.54E
130 M13 **Tselina** Rostovskaya Oblast', SW Russian Federation 46.31N 41.01E
Tselinograd *see* Astana
Tselinogradskaya Oblast' *see* Akmola
168 J6 **Tsengel** Hövsgöl, N Mongolia 49.29N 101.09E
168 E7 **Tsenher** Hovd, W Mongolia 47.07N 92.04E
152 E12 **Tsentral'nyye Nizmennyye Garagumy** *Turkm.* Mencezi Garagum. *desert* C Turkmenistan
85 E21 **Tses** Karas, S Namibia 25.54S 18.09E
Tseshevlya *see* Tsyeshawlya
168 E7 **Tsetsegnuur** Hovd, W Mongolia 46.30N 93.16E
168 J7 **Tsetserleg** Arhangay, C Mongolia 47.28N 101.19E
79 R16 **Tsévié** S Togo 6.25N 1.13E
85 G21 **Tshabong** *var.* Tsabong. Kgalagadi, SW Botswana 26.01S 22.24E
85 G20 **Tshane** Kgalagadi, SW Botswana 24.02S 21.54E
Tshangalele, Lac *see* Lufira, Lac de Retenue de la
85 H17 **Tshauxaba** Central, C Botswana 19.56S 25.09E
81 F21 **Tshela** Bas-Congo, W Dem. Rep. Congo (Zaire) 4.55S 13.01E
81 K22 **Tshibala** Kasai Occidental, S Dem. Rep. Congo (Zaire) 6.53S 22.01E
81 J22 **Tshikapa** Kasai Occidental, SW Dem. Rep. Congo (Zaire) 6.23S 20.47E
81 L22 **Tshilenge** Kasai Oriental, S Dem. Rep. Congo (Zaire) 6.16S 23.48E
81 L24 **Tshimbalanga** Katanga, S Dem. Rep. Congo (Zaire) 9.42S 23.04E
81 L22 **Tshimbulu** Kasai Occidental, S Dem. Rep. Congo (Zaire) 6.27S 22.54E
Tshiumbe *see* Chiumbe
81 M21 **Tshofa** Kasai Oriental, C Dem. Rep. Congo (Zaire) 5.13S 25.13E
81 K18 **Tshuapa** ≈ C Dem. Rep. Congo (Zaire)
Tshwane *see* Pretoria
116 G7 **Tsibritsa** ≈ NW Bulgaria
Tsien Tang *see* Puyang Jiang
116 I12 **Tsigansko Gradishte** ▲ Bulgaria/Greece 41.24N 24.41E
14 G3 **Tsiigehtchic** *prev.* Arctic Red River. Northwest Territories, NW Canada 67.24N 133.40W
129 Q7 **Tsil'ma** ≈ NW Russian Federation
121 J17 **Tsimkavichy** *Rus.* Timkovichi. Minskaya Voblasts', C Belarus 53.04N 26.58E
130 M11 **Tsimlyansk** Rostovskaya Oblast', SW Russian Federation 47.39N 42.05E
131 N11 **Tsimlyanskoye Vodokhranilishche** *var.* Tsimlyansk Vodoskhovshche, *Eng.* Tsimlyansk Reservoir ⊞ SW Russian Federation
Tsimlyansk Reservoir *see* Tsimlyanskoye Vodokhranilishche
Tsimlyansk Vodoskhovshche *see* Tsimlyanskoye Vodokhranilishche
Tsinan *see* Jinan
Tsing Hai *see* Qinghai Hu, China
Tsinghai *see* Qinghai, China
Tsingtao/Tsingtau *see* Qingdao
Tsingyuan *see* Baoding
Tsinkiang *see* Quanzhou
Tsintao *see* Qingdao
85 D17 **Tsintsabis** Otjikoto, N Namibia 18.45S 17.57E
180 H8 **Tsiombe** *var.* Tsihombe. Toliara, S Madagascar
126 Kk14 **Tsipa** ≈ S Russian Federation
180 H5 **Tsiribihina** ≈ W Madagascar
180 I5 **Tsiroanomandidy** Antananarivo, C Madagascar 18.43S 46.01E
201 U13 **Tsis** *island* Chuuk, C Micronesia
Tsitsihar *see* Qiqihar
131 Q3 **Tsivil'sk** Chuvashskaya Respublika, W Russian Federation 55.51N 47.30E
143 T9 **Ts'khinvali** *prev.* Staliniri. C Georgia 42.12N 43.58E
121 J19 **Tsna** ≈ SW Belarus
128 I15 **Tsna** *var.* Zna. ≈ W Russian Federation
168 K11 **Tsoohor** Ömnögovĭ, S Mongolia 43.15N 104.04E
171 H16 **Tsu** *var.* Tu. Mie, Honshū, SW Japan 34.40N 136.30E
171 K13 **Tsubame** *var.* Tubame. Niigata, Honshū, C Japan 37.39N 138.55E
171 Ii13 **Tsubata** Ishikawa, Honshū, SW Japan 36.33N 136.42E
172 Q6 **Tsubetsu** Hokkaidō, NE Japan 43.43N 144.01E
171 Kk16 **Tsuchiura** *var.* Tutiura. Ibaraki, Honshū, S Japan 36.03N 140.09E
172 N7 **Tsugaru-kaikyō** *strait* N Japan
171 Kk13 **Tsugawa** Niigata, Honshū, C Japan 37.40N 139.26E
172 Oo5 **Tsukigata** Hokkaidō, NE Japan 43.18N 141.37E
170 Dd15 **Tsukumi** *var.* Tukumi. Ōita, Kyūshū, SW Japan 33.02N 131.51E
168 E5 **Tsul-Ulaan** Bayan-Ölgiy, W Mongolia 48.51N 91.13E
85 D17 **Tsumeb** Otjikoto, N Namibia 19.13S 17.42E
85 F17 **Tsumkwe** Otjozondjupa, NE Namibia 19.35S 20.26E
170 Cc16 **Tsuno** Miyazaki, Kyūshū, SW Japan 32.43N 131.32E
170 D11 **Tsuno-shima** *island* SW Japan
171 H14 **Tsuruga** *var.* Turuga. Fukui, Honshū, SW Japan 35.38N 136.01E
170 F15 **Tsurugi-san** ▲ Shikoku, SW Japan 33.50N 134.04E
170 Dd15 **Tsurumi-zaki** *headland* Kyūshū, SW Japan 32.55N 132.03E
171 L11 **Tsuruoka** *var.* Turuoka. Yamagata, Honshū, C Japan 38.43N 139.48E
171 Hh15 **Tsushima** *var.* Tusima. Aichi, Honshū, SW Japan 35.10N 136.45E
170 C10 **Tsushima** *var.* Tsushima-tō, Tusima. *island group* SW Japan
Tsushima-tō *see* Tsushima
170 E12 **Tsuwano** Shimane, Honshū, SW Japan 34.28N 131.43E
170 Ff13 **Tsuyama** *var.* Tuyama. Okayama, Honshū, SW Japan 35.03N 133.57E
85 G19 **Tswaane** Ghanzi, W Botswana 22.21S 21.52E
121 N16 **Tsyakhtsin** *Rus.* Tekhtin. Mahilyowskaya Voblasts', E Belarus 53.52N 29.43E
121 P19 **Tsyerakhowka** *Rus.* Terekhovka. Homyel'skaya Voblasts', SE Belarus 52.13N 31.24E
121 I17 **Tsyeshawlya** *Rus.* Cheshevlya, Tseshevlya. Brestskaya Voblasts', SW Belarus 53.13N 25.49E
Tsyurupinsk *see* Tsyurupyns'k
119 R10 **Tsyurupyns'k** *Rus.* Tsyurupinsk. Khersons'ka Oblast', S Ukraine 46.34N 32.42E
Tu *see* Tsu
194 H13 **Tua** ≈ C PNG
Tuaim *see* Tuam
192 L6 **Tuakau** Waikato, North Island, NZ 37.16S 174.56E
99 C17 **Tuam** *Ir.* Tuaim. W Ireland 53.31N 8.49W
193 K14 **Tuamarina** Marlborough, South Island, NZ 41.27S 174.00E
Tuamotu, Archipel des *see* Tuamotu, Îles
199 M10 **Tuamotu Fracture Zone** *tectonic feature* E Pacific Ocean
203 W9 **Tuamotu, Îles** *var.* Archipel des Tuamotu, Dangerous Archipelago, Tuamotu Islands. *island group* N French Polynesia
Tuamotu Islands *see* Tuamotu, Îles
183 X10 **Tuamotu Ridge** *undersea feature* C Pacific Ocean
178 Ii5 **Tuân Giao** Lai Châu, N Vietnam 21.34N 103.24E
179 P8 **Tuao** Luzon, N Philippines 17.42N 121.25E
202 B15 **Tuapa** NW Niue 18.57S 169.58W
45 N7 **Tuapí** Región Autónoma Atlántico Norte, NE Nicaragua 14.10N 83.18W
130 K15 **Tuapse** Krasnodarskiy Kray, SW Russian Federation 44.07N 39.07E
175 Nn2 **Tuaran** Sabah, East Malaysia 6.12N 116.12E
106 I6 **Tua, Rio** ≈ N Portugal
198 B7 **Tuasivi** Savai'i, C Samoa 13.37S 172.07W
193 B24 **Tuatapere** Southland, South Island, NZ 46.09S 167.43E
38 M9 **Tuba City** Arizona, SW USA 36.08N 111.14W
144 H11 **Ṭubah, Qaṣr aṭ** *castle* Ma'ān, C Jordan 31.22N 36.39E
Tubame *see* Tsubame
174 Ll14 **Tuban** *prev.* Toeban. Jawa, C Indonesia 6.55S 112.01E
147 O15 **Tuban, Wādī** *dry watercourse* SW Yemen
63 K14 **Tubarão** Santa Catarina, S Brazil 28.29S 49.00W
100 O19 **Tubbergen** Overijssel, E Netherlands 52.25N 6.46E
Tubeke *see* Tubize
103 H22 **Tübingen** *var.* Tuebingen. Baden-Württemberg, SW Germany 48.31N 9.04E
131 W6 **Tubinskiy** Respublika Bashkortostan, W Russian Federation 52.48N 58.18E
101 G19 **Tubize** *Dut.* Tubeke. Walloon Brabant, C Belgium 50.43N 4.14E
78 J16 **Tubmanburg** NW Liberia 6.50N 10.53W
179 Qq15 **Tubod** Mindanao, S Philippines 7.58N 123.46E
77 T7 **Ṭubruq** *Eng.* Tobruk, *It.* Tobruch. NE Libya 32.04N 23.58E
203 T13 **Tubuai** *island* Îles Australes, SW French Polynesia
Tubuai, Îles/Tubuai Islands *see* Australes, Îles
42 F3 **Tubutama** Sonora, NW Mexico 30.51N 111.31W
56 K4 **Tucacas** Falcón, N Venezuela 10.46N 68.19W
61 P16 **Tucano** Bahia, E Brazil 10.52S 38.48W
59 P19 **Tucavaca, Río** ≈ E Bolivia
112 H8 **Tuchola** Kujawsko-pomorskie, C Poland 53.36N 17.49E
113 M17 **Tuchów** Małopolskie, SE Poland 49.53N 21.04E
25 S3 **Tucker** Georgia, SE USA 33.53N 84.10W
29 W10 **Tuckerman** Arkansas, C USA 35.43N 91.12W
66 B12 **Tucker's Town** E Bermuda 32.19N 64.42W
Tuckum *see* Tukums
38 M15 **Tucson** Arizona, SW USA 32.13N 111.00W
64 J7 **Tucumán** *off.* Provincia de Tucumán. ◈ *province* N Argentina
Tucumán *see* San Miguel de Tucumán
39 V11 **Tucumcari** New Mexico, SW USA 35.10N 103.43W
60 H13 **Tucunaré** Pará, N Brazil 5.15S 55.49W
57 Q6 **Tucupita** Delta Amacuro, NE Venezuela 9.01N 62.04W
60 K13 **Tucuruí, Represa de** ⊞ NE Brazil
112 F9 **Tuczno** Zachodniopomorskie, NW Poland 53.12N 16.08E
Tuddo *see* Tudu
107 Q5 **Tudela** *Basq.* Tutera; *anc.* Tutela. Navarra, N Spain 42.04N 1.37W
106 M6 **Tudela de Duero** Castilla-León, N Spain 41.35N 4.34W
144 K6 **Tudmur** *var.* Tadmur, Tamar, *Gk.* Palmyra; *Bibl.* Tadmor. Ḥimṣ, C Syria 34.36N 38.15E
120 J4 **Tudu** *Ger.* Tuddo. Lääne-Virumaa, NE Estonia 59.12N 26.52E
Tuebingen *see* Tübingen
126 Hh16 **Tuekta** Respublika Altay, S Russian Federation 50.51N 85.52E
106 I5 **Tuela, Rio** ≈ N Portugal
159 X12 **Tuensang** Nāgāland, NE India 26.16N 94.45E
142 L15 **Tufanbeyli** Adana, C Turkey 38.15N 36.13E
Tüffer *see* Laško
194 M15 **Tufi** Northern, S PNG 9.04S 149.15E
199 L3 **Tufts Plain** *undersea feature* N Pacific Ocean
Tugalan *see* Kolkhozobod
69 V14 **Tugela** ≈ SE South Africa
23 P6 **Tug Fork** ≈ S USA
41 P15 **Tugidak Island** *island* Trinity Islands, Alaska, USA
179 P8 **Tuguegarao** Luzon, N Philippines 17.36N 121.47E
127 N13 **Tugur** Khabarovskiy Kray, SE Russian Federation 53.43N 137.00E
167 P4 **Tuhai He** ≈ E China
106 G4 **Tui** Galicia, NW Spain 42.02N 8.37W
79 O13 **Tui** *var.* Grand Balé. ≈ W Burkina
59 J16 **Tuichi, Río** ≈ W Bolivia
66 Q11 **Tuineje** Fuerteventura, Islas Canarias, Spain, NE Atlantic Ocean 28.18N 14.03W
45 X16 **Tuira, Río** ≈ SE Panama
Tuisarkan *see* Tūysarkān
Tujiabu *see* Yongxiu
131 W5 **Tukan** Respublika Bashkortostan, W Russian Federation 53.58N 57.29E
175 R13 **Tukangbesi, Kepulauan** *Dut.* Toekang Besi Eilanden. *island group* C Indonesia
153 V13 **Tŭkhtamish** *Rus.* Toktomush, *prev.* Tokhtamyshbek. SE Tajikistan 37.51N 74.41E
192 O12 **Tukituki** ≈ North Island, NZ
Tu-k'ou *see* Panzhihua
124 N15 **Tūkrah** NE Libya 32.28N 20.36E
14 G2 **Tuktoyaktuk** Northwest Territories, NW Canada 69.27N 133.00W
173 Ff6 **Tuktuk** Pulau Samosir, W Indonesia 2.32N 98.43E
Tukumi *see* Tsukumi
120 E9 **Tukums** *Ger.* Tuckum. Tukums, W Latvia 56.58N 23.12E
83 G24 **Tukuyu** *prev.* Neu-Langenburg. Mbeya, S Tanzania 9.13S 33.39E
Tukzār *see* Tokzār
43 O13 **Tula** *var.* Tula de Allende. Hidalgo, C Mexico 20.01N 99.17W
43 O11 **Tula** Tamaulipas, C Mexico 22.59N 99.43W
130 K5 **Tula** Tul'skaya Oblast', W Russian Federation 54.11N 37.39E
Tulach Mhór *see* Tullamore
Tula de Allende *see* Tula
165 N10 **Tulage Ar Gol** ≈ W China
195 X15 **Tulaghi** *var.* Tulagi. Florida Islands, C Solomon Islands 9.04S 160.09E
Tulagi *see* Tulaghi
43 P13 **Tulancingo** Hidalgo, C Mexico 20.34N 98.24W
37 R11 **Tulare** California, W USA 36.12N 119.21W
31 P9 **Tulare** South Dakota, N USA 44.43N 98.29W
37 Q12 **Tulare Lake Bed** *salt flat* California, W USA
39 S14 **Tularosa** New Mexico, SW USA 33.04N 106.01W
39 P13 **Tularosa Mountains** ▲▲ New Mexico, SW USA
39 S15 **Tularosa Valley** *basin* New Mexico, SW USA
85 E25 **Tulbagh** Western Cape, SW South Africa 33.16S 19.09E
58 C5 **Tulcán** Carchi, N Ecuador 0.44N 77.43W
119 N13 **Tulcea** Tulcea, E Romania 45.11N 28.48E
119 N13 **Tulcea** ◈ *county* SE Romania
Tul'chin *see* Tul'chyn
119 N7 **Tul'chyn** *Rus.* Tul'chin. Vinnyts'ka Oblast', C Ukraine 48.40N 28.48E
Tuléar *see* Toliara
37 O1 **Tulelake** California, W USA 41.57N 121.30W
118 J10 **Tulgheş** *Hung.* Gyergyótölgyes. Harghita, C Romania 46.57N 25.46E
Tul'govichi *see* Tul'havichy
121 N20 **Tul'havichy** *Rus.* Tul'govichi. Homyel'skaya Voblasts', SE Belarus 51.45N 29.41E
Tuli *see* Thuli
27 N4 **Tulia** Texas, SW USA 34.32N 101.45W
15 Gg6 **Tulita** *prev.* Fort Norman, Norman. Northwest Territories, NW Canada 64.55N 125.29W
22 J10 **Tullahoma** Tennessee, S USA 35.21N 86.12W
191 N12 **Tullamarine** ✕ (Melbourne) Victoria, SE Australia 37.40S 144.46E
191 Q7 **Tullamore** New South Wales, SE Australia 32.39S 147.35E
99 E18 **Tullamore** *Ir.* Tulach Mhór. C Ireland 53.16N 7.30W
105 N12 **Tulle** *anc.* Tutela. Corrèze, C France 45.16N 1.46E
111 X3 **Tulln** *var.* Oberhollabrunn. Niederösterreich, NE Austria 48.19N 16.01E
111 W4 **Tulln** ≈ NE Austria
24 H6 **Tullos** Louisiana, S USA 31.48N 92.19W
99 F19 **Tullow** *Ir.* An Tullach. SE Ireland 52.48N 6.43W
189 W5 **Tully** Queensland, NE Australia 18.03S 145.55E
128 J3 **Tuloma** ≈ NW Russian Federation
116 K10 **Tulovo** Stara Zagora, C Bulgaria 42.34N 25.34E
29 P9 **Tulsa** Oklahoma, C USA 36.09N 95.59W
159 N11 **Tulsipur** Mid Western, W Nepal 28.01N 82.22E
130 K6 **Tul'skaya Oblast'** ◈ *province* W Russian Federation
130 L14 **Tul'skiy** Respublika Adygeya, SW Russian Federation 44.26N 40.12E
194 K8 **Tulu** Manus Island, N PNG 1.58S 146.50E
56 D10 **Tuluá** Valle del Cauca, W Colombia 4.01N 76.16W
118 M12 **Tulucești** Galați, E Romania 45.35N 28.01E
41 N12 **Tuluksak** Alaska, USA 61.06N 160.57W
43 Z12 **Tulum, Ruinas de** *ruins* Quintana Roo, SE Mexico 20.13N 87.24W
126 Ii15 **Tulun** Irkutskaya Oblast', S Russian Federation 54.28N 100.18E
174 Ll15 **Tulungagung** *prev.* Toeloengagoeng. Jawa, C Indonesia 8.03S 111.54E
195 S11 **Tulun Islands** *var.* Kilinailau Islands; *prev.* Carteret Islands. *island group* NE PNG
130 M4 **Tuma** Ryazanskaya Oblast', W Russian Federation 55.09N 40.27E
56 B12 **Tumaco** Nariño, SW Colombia 1.51N 78.46W
56 B12 **Tumaco, Bahía de** *bay* SW Colombia
Tuman-gang *see* Tumen
44 L8 **Tuma, Río** ≈ N Nicaragua
97 O16 **Tumba** Stockholm, C Sweden 59.12N 17.49E
Tumba, Lac *see* Ntomba, Lac
174 M9 **Tumbangsenamang** Borneo, C Indonesia 1.16S 112.21E
191 Q10 **Tumbarumba** New South Wales, SE Australia 35.47S 148.03E
58 A8 **Tumbes** Tumbes, NW Peru 3.33S 80.27W
58 A9 **Tumbes** *off.* Departamento de Tumbes. ◈ *department* NW Peru
21 P5 **Tumbledown Mountain** ▲ Maine, NE USA 45.27N 70.28W
9 N13 **Tumbler Ridge** British Columbia, W Canada 55.06N 120.51W
178 I12 **Tumbŏt, Phnum** ▲ W Cambodia 12.23N 102.57E
190 G9 **Tumby Bay** South Australia 34.22S 136.05E
169 Y10 **Tumen** Jilin, NE China 42.58N 129.52E
169 Y11 **Tumen** *Chin.* Tumen Jiang, *Kor.* Tuman-gang, *Rus.* Tumyn'tszyan. ≈ E Asia
Tumen Jiang *see* Tumen
57 Q8 **Tumeremo** Bolívar, E Venezuela 7.19N 61.28W
161 G19 **Tumkūr** Karnātaka, W India 13.19N 77.06E
98 I10 **Tummel** ≈ C Scotland, UK
196 B15 **Tumon Bay** *bay* W Guam
79 P14 **Tumu** NW Ghana 10.51N 1.58W
60 I10 **Tumuc Humac Mountains** *var.* Serra Tumucumaque. ▲▲ N South America
Tumucumaque, Serra *see* Tumuc Humac Mountains
191 Q10 **Tumut** New South Wales, SE Australia 35.19S 148.12E
Tumyn'tszyan *see* Tumen
Tün *see* Ferdows
47 U14 **Tunapuna** Trinidad, Trinidad and Tobago 10.38N 61.23W
62 K11 **Tunas** Paraná, S Brazil 24.57S 49.05W
Tunbridge Wells *see* Royal Tunbridge Wells
116 L11 **Tunca Nehri** *Bul.* Tundzha. ≈ Bulgaria/Turkey *see also* Tundzha
143 O14 **Tunceli** *var.* Kalan. Tunceli, E Turkey 39.07N 39.34E
143 O14 **Tunceli** ◈ *province* C Turkey
158 J12 **Tūndla** Uttar Pradesh, N India 27.13N 78.13E
83 I25 **Tunduru** Ruvuma, S Tanzania 11.07S 37.21E
116 L10 **Tundzha** *Turk.* Tunca Nehri. ≈ Bulgaria/Turkey *see also* Tunca Nehri
161 H17 **Tungabhadra** ≈ S India
161 F17 **Tungabhadra Reservoir** ◎ S India
203 P2 **Tungaru** *prev.* Gilbert Islands. *island group* W Kiribati
179 Q16 **Tungawan** Mindanao, S Philippines 7.33N 122.22E
174 Hh9 **Tungkal** ≈ Sumatera, W Indonesia
T'ung-shan *see* Xuzhou
167 Q16 **Tungsha Tao** *Chin.* Dongsha Qundao, *Eng.* Pratas Island. *island* S Taiwan
167 S13 **Tungshih** *Jap.* Tōsei. N Taiwan 24.13N 120.54E
14 G7 **Tungsten** Northwest Territories, W Canada 62.00N 128.09W
Tung-t'ing Hu *see* Dongting Hu
58 A13 **Tungurahua** ◈ *province* C Ecuador
97 F14 **Tunhovdfjorden** ◎ S Norway
24 K2 **Tunica** Mississippi, S USA 34.40N 90.22W
77 N5 **Tunis** *var.* Tūnis. ● (Tunisia) NE Tunisia 36.52N 10.10E
77 N5 **Tunis, Golfe de** *Ar.* Khalīj Tūnis. *gulf* NE Tunisia
77 N6 **Tunisia** *off.* Republic of Tunisia, *Ar.* Al Jumhūrīyah at Tūnisīyah, *Fr.* République Tunisienne. ◆ *republic* N Africa
Tūnisīyah, Al Jumhūrīyah at *see* Tunisia
Tūnis, Khalīj *see* Tunis, Golfe de
56 G9 **Tunja** Boyacá, C Colombia 5.33N 73.22W
95 F14 **Tunnsjøen** ◎ C Norway
41 N12 **Tuntutuliak** Alaska, USA 60.21N 162.40W
153 U8 **Tunuk** Chuyskaya Oblast', C Kyrgyzstan 42.11N 73.55E
11 Q6 **Tunungayualok Island** *island* Newfoundland, E Canada
64 H11 **Tunuyán** Mendoza, W Argentina 33.28S 69.01W
207 P14 **Tunu** ◈ *province* E Greenland
64 I11 **Tunuyán, Río** ≈ W Argentina
Tunxi *see* Huangshan
37 P9 **Tuolumne River** ≈ California, W USA
Tuong Buong *see* Tương Đương
178 J7 **Tương Đương** *var.* Tuong Buong. Nghê An, N Vietnam 19.14N 104.30E
166 I13 **Tuoniang Jiang** ≈ S China
165 N12 **Tuotuo He** ≈ C China
165 O12 **Tuotuoheyan** *var.* Tanggulashan, Togton-heyan. Qinghai, C China 34.13N 92.25E
Tüp *see* Tyup
62 J9 **Tupã** São Paulo, S Brazil 21.57S 50.28W
203 S10 **Tupai** *var.* Motu Iti. *atoll* Îles Sous le Vent, W French Polynesia
63 G15 **Tupanciretã** Rio Grande do Sul, S Brazil 29.06S 53.48W
24 M2 **Tupelo** Mississippi, S USA 34.15N 88.42W
126 L14 **Tupik** Chitinskaya Oblast', S Russian Federation 54.21N 119.56E
61 K18 **Tupiraçaba** Goiás, S Brazil 14.33S 48.40W
59 L21 **Tupiza** Potosí, S Bolivia 21.27S 65.45W
9 N13 **Tupper** British Columbia, W Canada 55.30N 119.59W
20 J8 **Tupper Lake** ◎ New York, NE USA
64 H11 **Tupungato, Volcán** ▲ W Argentina 33.27S 69.42W
169 T9 **Tuquan** Nei Mongol Zizhiqu, N China 45.21N 121.36E
56 C13 **Túquerres** Nariño, SW Colombia 1.06N 77.37W
159 U13 **Tura** Meghālaya, NE India 25.33N 90.14E
126 J10 **Tura** Evenkiyskiy Avtonomnyy Okrug, N Russian Federation 64.19N 100.16E
125 F11 **Tura** ≈ C Russian Federation
146 M10 **Turabah** Makkah, W Saudi Arabia 21.27N 41.40E
57 O8 **Turagua, Cerro** ▲ C Venezuela 6.59N 64.34W
192 L12 **Turakina** Manawatu-Wanganui, North Island, NZ 40.03S 175.13E
193 K15 **Turakirae Head** *headland* North Island, NZ 41.26S 174.54E
194 G13 **Turama** ≈ S PNG
126 I15 **Turan** Respublika Tyva, S Russian Federation 52.11N 93.40E
192 M10 **Turangi** Waikato, North Island, NZ 39.01S 175.46E
152 F11 **Turan Lowland** *var.* Turan Plain, *Kaz.* Turan Oypaty, *Rus.* Turanskaya Nizmennost', *Turk.* Turan Pesligi, *Uzb.* Turon Pasttekisligi. *plain* C Asia
Turan Oypaty/Turan Pesligi/Turan Plain/Turanskaya Nizmennost' *see* Turan Lowland
144 K7 **Ţurāq al 'Ilab** *hill range* S Syria
121 K20 **Turaw** *Rus.* Turov. Homyel'skaya Voblasts', SE Belarus 52.04N 27.41E
146 L2 **Ţurayf** Al Ḥudūd ash Shamālīyah, NW Saudi Arabia 31.43N 38.39E
Turba *see* Teruel
56 E5 **Turbaco** Bolívar, N Colombia 10.19N 75.25W
154 K15 **Turbat** Baluchistān, SW Pakistan 26.02N 62.56E
Turbat-i-Haidari *see* Torbat-e Ḥeydarīyeh
Turbat-i-Jam *see* Torbat-e Jām
56 D7 **Turbo** Antioquia, NW Colombia 8.06N 76.43W
Turčianský Svätý Martin *see* Martin
118 H10 **Turda** *Ger.* Thorenburg, *Hung.* Torda. Cluj, NW Romania 46.34N 23.49E
148 M7 **Tūreh** Markazī, W Iran 34.02N 49.15E
203 X12 **Tureia** *atoll* Îles Tuamotu, SE French Polynesia
112 I12 **Turek** Wielkopolskie, C Poland 52.01N 18.30E
95 L19 **Turenki** Etelä-Suomi, S Finland 60.55N 24.37E
Turfan *see* Turpan
151 R8 **Turgay** *Kaz.* Torghay. Akmola, W Kazakhstan 51.43N 72.46E
151 N10 **Turgay** *Kaz.* Torgay. ≈ C Kazakhstan
150 M8 **Turgayskaya Stolovaya Strana** *Kaz.* Torgay Ūstirti. *plateau* Kazakhstan/Russian Federation
Turgel *see* Türi
116 L8 **Tŭrgovishte** *prev.* Eski Dzhumaya. Tŭrgovishte, N Bulgaria 43.15N 26.33E
116 L8 **Tŭrgovishte** ◈ *province* N Bulgaria
142 C14 **Turgutlu** Manisa, W Turkey 38.30N 27.43E
142 L12 **Turhal** Tokat, N Turkey 40.22N 36.04E
120 H4 **Türi** *Ger.* Turgel. Järvamaa, N Estonia 58.49N 25.25E
107 S9 **Turia** ≈ E Spain
60 M12 **Turiaçu** Maranhão, E Brazil 1.40S 45.22W
Turin *see* Torino
118 I3 **Turiys'k** Volyns'ka Oblast', NW Ukraine 51.05N 24.31E
Turja *see* Tur"ya
126 K15 **Turka** Respublika Buryatiya, S Russian Federation 53.02N 108.19E
118 H6 **Turka** L'vivs'ka Oblast', W Ukraine 49.07N 23.01E
Turkana, Lake *see* Rudolf, Lake
151 P16 **Turkestan** *Kaz.* Türkistan. Yuzhnyy Kazakhstan, S Kazakhstan 43.18N 68.18E
153 Q12 **Turkestan Range** *Rus.* Turkestanskiy Khrebet. ▲▲ C Asia
Turkestanskiy Khrebet *see* Turkestan Range
113 M23 **Túrkeve** Jász-Nagykun-Szolnok, E Hungary 47.07N 20.48E
27 O4 **Turkey** Texas, SW USA 34.23N 100.54W
142 H14 **Turkey** *off.* Republic of Turkey, *Turk.* Türkiye Cumhuriyeti. ◆ *republic* SW Asia
189 N4 **Turkey Creek** Western Australia 16.54S 128.12E
28 M9 **Turkey Creek** ≈ Oklahoma, C USA
39 T9 **Turkey Mountains** ▲▲ New Mexico, SW USA
31 X11 **Turkey River** ≈ Iowa, C USA
131 N7 **Turki** Saratovskaya Oblast', W Russian Federation 52.00N 43.16E
124 Nn2 **Turkish Republic of Northern Cyprus** ◇ *disputed territory* Cyprus
Türkistan *see* Turkestan
Turkistan, Bandi-i *see* Torkestān, Selseleh-ye Band-e
Türkiye Cumhuriyeti *see* Turkey
Türkmen Aylagy *see* Turkmenskiy Zaliv
152 A10 **Turkmenbashi** *prev.* Krasnovodsk. Balkanskiy Velayat, W Turkmenistan 40.00N 53.04E
Türkmengala *see* Turkmen-kala
152 G13 **Turkmenistan** *off.* Turkmenistan; *prev.* Turkmenskaya Soviet Socialist Republic. ◆ *republic* C Asia
152 J14 **Turkmen-kala** *Turkm.* Türkmengala; *prev.* Turkmen-Kala. Maryyskiy Velayat, S Turkmenistan 37.25N 62.19E
Turkmenskaya Soviet Socialist Republic *see* Turkmenistan
152 A11 **Turkmenskiy Zaliv** *Turkm.* Türkmen Aylagy. *lake gulf* W Turkmenistan
142 L16 **Türkoğlu** Kahramanmaraş, S Turkey 37.24N 36.49E
46 L6 **Turks and Caicos Islands** ◇ *UK dependent territory* N West Indies
66 G10 **Turks and Caicos Islands** *island group* N West Indies
47 N6 **Turks Islands** *island group* SE Turks and Caicos Islands
95 K19 **Turku** *Swe.* Åbo. Länsi-Suomi, W Finland 60.27N 22.16E
83 H17 **Turkwel** *seasonal river* NW Kenya
29 P9 **Turley** Oklahoma, C USA 36.14N 95.58W
37 P9 **Turlock** California, W USA 37.29N 120.52W
120 I12 **Turmantas** Zarasai, NE Lithuania 55.41N 26.27E
56 L5 **Turmero** Aragua, N Venezuela 10.14N 66.40W
Turmberg *see* Wieżyca
192 N13 **Turnagain, Cape** *headland* North Island, NZ 40.30S 176.36E
Turnau *see* Turnov
44 H2 **Turneffe Islands** *island group* E Belize
20 M11 **Turners Falls** Massachusetts, NE USA 42.36N 72.31W
9 P16 **Turner Valley** Alberta, SW Canada 50.43N 114.19W
101 I16 **Turnhout** Antwerpen, N Belgium 51.19N 4.57E
111 V5 **Turnitz** Niederösterreich, E Austria 47.56N 15.26E
9 S12 **Turnor Lake** ◎ Saskatchewan, C Canada
113 E15 **Turnov** *Ger.* Turnau. Liberecký Kraj, N Czech Republic 50.36N 15.10E
Tŭrnovo *see* Veliko Tŭrnovo
118 I15 **Turnu Măgurele** *var.* Turnu-Măgurele. Teleorman, S Romania 43.43N 24.52E
Turnu Severin *see* Drobeta-Turnu Severin
Turócszentmárton *see* Martin
Turoni *see* Tours
Turon Pasttekisligi *see* Turan Lowland
Turov *see* Turaw
Turpakkla *see* Turpoqqal'a
164 M6 **Turpan** *var.* Turfan. Xinjiang Uygur Zizhiqu, NW China 42.54N 89.06E
Turpan Depression *see* Turpan Pendi
164 M6 **Turpan Pendi** *Eng.* Turpan Depression. *depression* NW China
164 M5 **Turpan Zhan** Xinjiang Uygur Zizhiqu, W China 43.10N 89.06E
Turpentine State *see* North Carolina
152 I10 **Turpoqqal'a** *Rus.* Turpakkla. Khorazm Wiloyati, W Uzbekistan 40.52N 62.00E
46 H8 **Turquino, Pico** ▲ E Cuba 19.54N 76.55W
29 Y10 **Turrell** Arkansas, C USA 35.22N 90.13W
45 N14 **Turrialba** Cartago, E Costa Rica 9.52N 83.40W
98 K8 **Turriff** NE Scotland, UK 57.32N 2.28W
145 V7 **Tursāq** E Iraq 33.27N 45.47E
Turshiz *see* Kāshmar
Tursunzade *see* Tursunzoda
153 P13 **Tursunzoda** *Rus.* Tursunzade; *prev.* Regar. W Tajikistan 38.30N 68.10E
168 J4 **Turt** Hövsgöl, N Mongolia 51.30N 100.40E
152 I9 **Türtkŭl** *Rus.* Turtkul'; *prev.* Petroaleksandrovsk. Qoraqalpoghiston Respublikasi, W Uzbekistan 41.34N 61.00E
31 O9 **Turtle Creek** ≈ South Dakota, N USA
32 K4 **Turtle Flambeau Flowage** ⊞ Wisconsin, N USA
9 S14 **Turtleford** Saskatchewan, S Canada 53.21N 108.48W
30 M4 **Turtle Lake** North Dakota, N USA 47.31N 100.53W
94 K12 **Turtola** Lappi, NW Finland 66.39N 23.55E
126 Jj10 **Turu** ≈ N Russian Federation
Turuga *see* Tsuruga
153 V10 **Turugart Pass** *pass* China/Kyrgyzstan 40.33N 74.04E
164 E7 **Turugart Shankou** *var.* Pereval Torugart. *pass* China/Kyrgyzstan 40.33N 75.21E
126 Hh9 **Turukhan** ≈ N Russian Federation
126 I9 **Turukhansk** Krasnoyarskiy Kray, N Russian Federation 65.50N 87.48E
145 N3 **Ţurumbah** *well* NE Syria 36.09N 40.24E
Turuoka *see* Tsuruoka
150 H14 **Turush** Mangistau, SW Kazakhstan 45.24N 56.02E
62 K7 **Turvo, Rio** ≈ S Brazil
118 J2 **Tur"ya** *Pol.* Turja, *Rus.* Tur'ya. ≈ NW Ukraine
25 O4 **Tuscaloosa** Alabama, S USA 33.12N 87.34W
25 O4 **Tuscaloosa, Lake** ◎ Alabama, S USA
Tuscan Archipelago *see* Toscano, Archipelago
Tuscan-Emilian Mountains *see* Tosco-Emiliano, Appennino
Tuscany *see* Toscana
37 V2 **Tuscarora** Nevada, W USA 41.16N 116.13W
20 F15 **Tuscarora Mountain** *ridge* Pennsylvania, NE USA
32 M14 **Tuscola** Illinois, N USA 39.46N 88.19W
27 P7 **Tuscola** Texas, SW USA 32.12N 99.48W
25 O2 **Tuscumbia** Alabama, S USA 34.43N 87.42W
94 O4 **Tusenøyane** *island group* S Svalbard
150 K13 **Tushybas, Zaliv** *prev.* Zaliv Paskevicha. *lake gulf* SW Kazakhstan
Tusima *see* Tsushima
176 Z14 **Tusirah** Irian Jaya, E Indonesia 6.46S 140.19E
25 Q5 **Tuskegee** Alabama, S USA 32.25N 85.41W
96 E8 **Tustna** *island* S Norway
41 R12 **Tustumena Lake** ◎ Alaska, USA

◆ Country ● Country Capital ◇ Dependent Territory ○ Dependent Territory Capital ◈ Administrative Region ✕ International Airport ▲ Mountain ▲▲ Mountain Range ⛰ Volcano ≈ River ◎ Lake ⊞ Reservoir

TUSZYN – UNGARN

112 K13 Tuszyn Łodzkie, C Poland 51.36N 19.31E
143 S13 Tutak Ağrı, E Turkey 39.34N 42.48E
193 C20 Tutamoe Range ▲ North Island, NZ
Tutasev see Tutayev
128 L15 Tutayev var. Tutasev. Yaroslavskaya Oblast', W Russian Federation 57.51N 39.29E
Tutela see Tulle, France
Tutela see Tudela, Spain
Tutera see Tudela
161 H23 Tuticorin Tamil Nādu, SE India 8.48N 78.10E
115 L15 Tutin Serbia, S Yugoslavia 43.00N 20.20E
192 O10 Tutira Hawke's Bay, North Island, NZ 39.14S 176.53E
Tutiura see Tsuchiura
126 Ii10 Tutonchany Evenkiyskiy Avtonomnyy Okrug, N Russian Federation 64.12N 93.52E
116 L6 Tutrakan Silistra, NE Bulgaria 44.03N 26.38E
31 N5 Tuttle North Dakota, N USA 47.07N 99.58W
28 M11 Tuttle Oklahoma, C USA 35.17N 97.48W
29 O3 Tuttle Creek Lake ⊠ Kansas, C USA
103 H23 Tuttlingen Baden-Württemberg, S Germany 47.58N 8.49E
175 Ss16 Tutuala W East Timor 8.23S 127.12E
198 Cc9 Tutuila island W American Samoa
85 I18 Tutume Central, E Botswana 20.27S 26.58E
41 N7 Tututalak Mountain ▲ Alaska, USA 67.51N 161.27W
24 K3 Tutwiler Mississippi, S USA 34.00N 90.25W
168 L8 Tuul Gol ⁓ N Mongolia
95 O16 Tuupovaara Itä-Suomi, E Finland 62.30N 30.40E
Tuva see Tyva, Respublika
202 E7 Tuvalu prev. Ellice Islands. ◆ commonwealth republic SW Pacific Ocean
197 L17 Tuvana-i-Colo prev. Tuvana-i-Tholo. island Lau Group, SE Fiji
197 L18 Tuvana-i-Ra island Lau Group, SE Fiji
Tuvana-i-Tholo see Tuvana-i-Colo
Tuvinskaya ASSR see Tyva, Respublika
197 L14 Tuvuca prev. Tuvutha. island Lau Group, E Fiji
Tuvutha see Tuvuca
147 P9 Ţuwayq, Jabal ▲ C Saudi Arabia
144 H13 Ţuwayyil ash Shihāq desert S Jordan
9 U16 Tuxford Saskatchewan, S Canada 50.33N 105.32W
178 K13 Tu Xoay Đăc Lăc, S Vietnam 12.18N 107.33E
42 L14 Tuxpan Jalisco, C Mexico 19.33N 103.21W
42 J12 Tuxpan Nayarit, C Mexico 21.57N 105.12W
43 Q12 Tuxpán var. Tuxpán de Rodríguez Cano. Veracruz-Llave, E Mexico 20.58N 97.22W
Tuxpán de Rodríguez Cano see Tuxpán
43 R15 Tuxtepec var. San Juan Bautista Tuxtepec. Oaxaca, S Mexico 18.01N 96.05W
43 U16 Tuxtla var. Tuxtla Gutiérrez. Chiapas, SE Mexico 16.43N 93.03W
Tuxtla see San Andrés Tuxtla
Tuxtla Gutiérrez see Tuxtla
Tuyama see Tsuyama
178 Jj5 Tuyên Quang Tuyên Quang, N Vietnam 21.48N 105.10E
178 K14 Tuy Hoa Binh Thuân, S Vietnam 11.03N 108.12E
178 Kk12 Tuy Hoa Phu Yên, S Vietnam 13.01N 109.15E
131 U5 Tuymazy Respublika Bashkortostan, W Russian Federation 54.36N 53.40E
148 L6 Tūysarkān var. Tuisarkan, Tuyserkān. Hamadān, W Iran 34.31N 48.30E
Tuyserkān see Tūysarkān
153 Q10 Tuytepa Rus. Toytepa. Toshkent Wiloyati, E Uzbekistan 41.04N 69.22E
151 W16 Tuyuk Kaz. Tuyyq. Almaty, SE Kazakhstan 43.07N 79.24E
Tuyyq see Tuyuk
142 I14 Tuz Gölü ⊚ C Turkey
129 Q15 Tuzha Kirovskaya Oblast', NW Russian Federation 57.37N 48.02E
115 K17 Tuzi Montenegro, SW Yugoslavia 42.22N 19.21E
145 T5 Ţūz Khurmātū N Iraq 34.55N 44.37E
114 I11 Tuzla Federacija Bosna I Hercegovina, NE Bosnia and Herzegovina 44.33N 18.40E
119 N15 Tuzla Constanţa, SE Romania 43.58N 28.38E
143 T12 Tuzluca Iğdır, NE Turkey 40.01N 43.39E
97 J20 Tvååker Halland, S Sweden 57.04N 12.25E
97 F17 Tvedestrand Aust-Agder, S Norway 58.37N 8.55E
128 J16 Tver' prev. Kalinin. Tverskaya Oblast', W Russian Federation 56.52N 35.52E
Tverya see Teverya
130 I15 Tverskaya Oblast' ◐ province W Russian Federation
128 I15 Tvertsa ⁓ W Russian Federation
112 H13 Twardogóra Ger. Festenberg. Dolnośląskie, SW Poland 51.21N 17.27E
12 J14 Tweed Ontario, SE Canada 44.28N 77.19W
98 K13 Tweed ⁓ England/Scotland, UK
100 O7 Tweede-Exloërmond Drenthe, NE Netherlands 52.55N 6.55E
191 V3 Tweed Heads New South Wales, SE Australia 28.10S 153.32E
100 M11 Twello Gelderland, E Netherlands 52.13N 6.07E
37 W15 Twentynine Palms California, W USA 34.08N 116.03W
27 P9 Twin Buttes Reservoir ⊠ Texas, SW USA
35 O15 Twin Falls Idaho, NW USA 42.33N 114.27W
41 N13 Twin Hills Alaska, USA 59.06N 160.21W
9 O11 Twin Lakes Alberta, W Canada 57.46N 117.30W
35 O12 Twin Peaks ▲ Idaho, NW USA 44.37N 114.24W
193 I14 Twins, The ▲ South Island, NZ 41.14S 172.38E
31 S5 Twin Valley Minnesota, N USA 47.15N 96.15W
102 G11 Twistringen Niedersachsen, NW Germany 52.48N 8.39E
193 E20 Twizel Canterbury, South Island, NZ 44.15S 170.06E
31 X5 Two Harbors Minnesota, N USA 47.01N 91.40W
9 R14 Two Hills Alberta, SW Canada 53.40N 111.43W
33 N7 Two Rivers Wisconsin, N USA 44.10N 87.33W
118 H8 Tyachiv Zakarpats'ka Oblast', W Ukraine 48.02N 23.35E
Tyan'-Shan' see Tien Shan
177 Ff3 Tyao ⁓ Burma/India
119 R6 Tyas'myn ⁓ N Ukraine
25 X6 Tybee Island Georgia, SE USA 32.00N 80.51W
Tyborøn see Thyborøn
113 J16 Tychy Ger. Tichau. Śląskie, S Poland 50.12N 19.01E
113 O16 Tyczyn Podkarpackie, SE Poland 49.58N 22.03E
96 I8 Tydal Sør-Trøndelag, S Norway 63.01N 11.36E
117 H24 Tyflós ⁓ Kríti, Greece, E Mediterranean Sea
23 S3 Tygart Lake ⊠ West Virginia, NE USA
126 M15 Tygda Amurskaya Oblast', SE Russian Federation 53.07N 126.12E
23 Q11 Tyger River ⁓ South Carolina, SE USA
34 I11 Tygh Valley Oregon, NW USA 45.15N 121.12W
96 F12 Tyin ⊚ S Norway
31 S10 Tyler Minnesota, N USA 44.16N 96.07W
27 W7 Tyler Texas, SW USA 32.21N 95.18W
27 W7 Tyler, Lake ⊠ Texas, SW USA
24 K7 Tylertown Mississippi, S USA 31.07N 90.08W
119 P10 Tylihuls'kyy Lyman ⁓ SW Ukraine
Tylos see Bahrain
126 Gg12 Tym ⁓ C Russian Federation
117 C15 Týmfi var. Timfi. ▲ W Greece 39.58N 20.51E
117 E17 Tymfristós var. Timfristos. ▲ C Greece 38.57N 21.49E
127 O14 Tymovskoye Ostrov Sakhalin, Sakhalinskaya Oblast', SE Russian Federation 50.36N 142.45E
117 J25 Tympáki var. Timbaki; prev. Timbákion. Kríti, Greece, E Mediterranean Sea 35.04N 24.46E
126 Ll14 Tynda Amurskaya Oblast', SE Russian Federation 55.09N 124.43E
31 Q12 Tyndall South Dakota, N USA 42.57N 97.52W
99 L14 Tyne ⁓ N England, UK
99 M14 Tynemouth NE England, UK 55.01N 1.24W
99 L14 Tyneside cultural region NE England, UK
96 H10 Tynset Hedmark, S Norway 61.45N 10.48E
41 Q12 Tyonek Alaska, USA 61.04N 151.08W
Tyôsi see Chôshi
Tyras see Dniester, Moldova/Ukraine
Tyras see Bilhorod-Dnistrovs'kyy, Ukraine
Tyre see Soûr
97 G14 Tyrifjorden ⊚ S Norway
97 K22 Tyringe Skåne, S Sweden 56.09N 13.34E
127 N15 Tyrma Khabarovskiy Kray, SE Russian Federation 50.00N 132.04E
Tyrnau see Trnava
117 F15 Týrnavos var. Tírnavos. Thessalía, C Greece 39.45N 22.18E
131 N16 Tyrnyauz Kabardino-Balkarskaya Respublika, SW Russian Federation 43.19N 42.55E
Tyrol see Tirol
20 E14 Tyrone Pennsylvania, NE USA 40.41N 78.12W
99 E15 Tyrone cultural region W Northern Ireland, UK
190 M10 Tyrrell, Lake salt lake Victoria, SE Australia
86 H14 Tyrrhenian Basin undersea feature Tyrrhenian Sea, C Mediterranean Sea
123 L9 Tyrrhenian Sea It. Mare Tirreno. sea N Mediterranean Sea
Tysa see Tisa/Tisza
118 J7 Tysmenytsya Ivano-Frankivs'ka Oblast', W Ukraine 48.54N 24.50E
97 C14 Tysnesøya island S Norway
97 C14 Tysse Hordaland, S Norway 60.23N 5.46E
97 D14 Tyssedal Hordaland, S Norway 60.07N 6.36E
97 O17 Tystberga Södermanland, C Sweden 58.51N 17.15E
120 E12 Tytuvėnai Kelmė, C Lithuania 55.36N 23.14E
150 D14 Tyub-Karagan, Mys headland SW Kazakhstan 44.40N 50.19E
153 V8 Tyugel'-Say Narynskaya Oblast', C Kyrgyzstan 41.57N 74.40E
125 Ff13 Tyukalinsk Omskaya Oblast', C Russian Federation 55.56N 72.02E
131 V7 Tyul'gan Orenburgskaya Oblast', W Russian Federation 52.27N 56.08E
125 F11 Tyumen' Tyumenskaya Oblast', C Russian Federation 57.10N 65.28E
125 Ff10 Tyumenskaya Oblast' ◐ province C Russian Federation
126 Kk10 Tyung ⁓ NE Russian Federation
153 Y7 Tyup Kir. Tüp. Issyk-Kul'skaya Oblast', NE Kyrgyzstan 42.43N 78.18E
126 I16 Tyva, Respublika prev. Tannu-Tuva, Tuva, Tuvinskaya ASSR. ◐ autonomous republic C Russian Federation
119 N7 Tyvriv Vinnyts'ka Oblast', C Ukraine 49.01N 28.28E
99 J21 Tywi ⁓ S Wales, UK
99 I19 Tywyn W Wales, UK 52.34N 4.06W
85 K20 Tzaneen Northern, NE South Africa 23.49S 30.09E
Tzekung see Zigong
43 X12 Tzucacab Yucatán, SE Mexico 20.04N 89.03W

U

84 B12 Uaco Cungo var. Waku Kungo, Port. Santa Comba. Cuanza Sul, C Angola 11.21S 15.04E
UAE see United Arab Emirates
203 X7 Ua Huka island Îles Marquises, NE French Polynesia
60 E10 Uaiacás Roraima, N Brazil 3.28N 63.13W
Uamba see Wamba
Uanle Uen see Wanlaweyn
203 W7 Ua Pu island Îles Marquises, NE French Polynesia
83 L17 Uar Garas spring/well SW Somalia 1.19N 41.22E
60 G12 Uatumã, Rio ⁓ C Brazil
Ua Uíbh Fhailí see Offaly
60 C11 Uaupés, Rio var. Río Vaupés. ⁓ Brazil/Colombia see also Vaupés, Río
151 X9 Uba ⁓ E Kazakhstan
151 N6 Ubagan Kaz. Obagan. ⁓ Kazakhstan/Russian Federation
195 N12 Ubai New Britain, E PNG 5.38S 150.45E
81 J15 Ubangi Fr. Oubangui. ⁓ C Africa
Ubangi-Shari see Central African Republic
118 M3 Ubarts' Ukr. Ubort'. ⁓ Belarus/Ukraine see also Ubort'
56 F9 Ubaté Cundinamarca, C Colombia 5.19N 73.49W
62 N10 Ubatuba São Paulo, S Brazil 23.24S 45.06W
155 R12 Ubauro Sind, SE Pakistan 28.07N 69.43E
179 Qq14 Ubay Bohol, C Philippines 10.02N 124.29E
105 U14 Ubaye ⁓ SE France
Ubayid, Wadi al see Ubayyiḍ, Wādī al
145 N8 Ubaylah W Iraq 33.06N 40.13E
145 O10 Ubayyiḍ, Wādī al var. Wadi al Ubayid. dry watercourse SW Iraq
100 L13 Ubbergen Gelderland, E Netherlands 51.49N 5.54E
170 Dd13 Ube Yamaguchi, Honshū, SW Japan 33.56N 131.14E
107 O13 Ubeda Andalucía, S Spain 38.01N 3.22W
111 V7 Ubelbach var. Markt-Übelbach. Steiermark, SE Austria 47.13N 15.15E
61 L20 Uberaba Minas Gerais, SE Brazil 19.46S 47.57W
59 Q19 Uberaba, Laguna ⊚ E Bolivia
61 K19 Uberlândia Minas Gerais, SE Brazil 18.16S 48.16W
103 H24 Überlingen Baden-Württemberg, S Germany 47.46N 9.10E
79 U16 Ubiaja Edo, S Nigeria 6.39N 6.23E
106 K3 Ubiña, Peña ▲ NW Spain 43.01N 5.58W
59 H17 Ubinas, Volcán ⩕ S Peru 16.16S 70.49W
Ubol Rajadhani/Ubol Ratchathani see Ubon Ratchathani
178 Ii9 Ubolratna Reservoir ⊠ C Thailand
178 J10 Ubon Ratchathani var. Muang Ubon, Ubol Rajadhani, Ubol Ratchathani, Udon Ratchathani. Ubon Ratchathani, E Thailand 15.15N 104.49E
121 L20 Ubort' Bel. Ubarts'. ⁓ Belarus/Ukraine see also Ubarts'
106 K15 Ubrique Andalucía, S Spain 36.42N 5.27W
Ubsu-Nur, Ozero see Uvs Nuur
81 M18 Ubundu Orientale, C Dem. Rep. Congo (Zaire) 0.24S 25.30E
143 X11 Ucar Rus. Udzhary. C Azerbaijan 40.31N 47.40E
58 G13 Ucayali off. Departamento de Ucayali. ◐ department E Peru
58 F10 Ucayali, Río ⁓ C Peru
Uccle see Ukkel
152 J13 Uch-Adzhi Turkm. Üchajy. Maryyskiy Velayat, C Turkmenistan 38.06N 62.44E
Üchajy see Uch-Adzhi
131 X4 Uchaly Respublika Bashkortostan, W Russian Federation 54.19N 59.33E
151 W13 Ucharal Kaz. Üsharal. Almaty, E Kazakhstan 46.07N 80.55E
170 C17 Uchinoura Kagoshima, Kyūshū, SW Japan 31.16N 131.04E
172 Nn6 Uchiura-wan bay NW Pacific Ocean
Uchkuduk see Uchquduq
Uchkurghan see Uchqŭrghon
152 K8 Uchquduq Rus. Uchkuduk. Nawoiy Wiloyati, N Uzbekistan 42.12N 63.27E
153 S9 Uchqŭrghon Rus. Uchkurghan. Namangan Wiloyati, E Uzbekistan 41.06N 72.04E
Uchsay see Uchsoy
152 G6 Uchsoy Rus. Uchsay. Qoraqalpoghiston Respublikasi, NW Uzbekistan 43.51N 58.51E
Uchtagan Gumy see Uchtagan, Peski
152 D10 Uchtagan, Peski Turkm. Uchtagan Gumy. desert NW Turkmenistan
126 Mm12 Uchur ⁓ E Russian Federation
102 O10 Uckermark cultural region E Germany
8 K17 Ucluelet Vancouver Island, British Columbia, SW Canada 48.58N 125.28W
126 Ii14 Uda ⁓ S Russian Federation
126 Mm13 Uda ⁓ E Russian Federation
126 K9 Udachnyy Respublika Sakha (Yakutiya), NE Russian Federation 66.27N 112.18E
161 G21 Udagamandalam var. Udhagamandalam; prev. Ootacamund. Tamil Nādu, SW India 11.28N 76.42E
158 F14 Udaipur prev. Oodeypore. Rājasthān, N India 24.34N 73.40E
Udayadhani see Uthai Thani
149 N16 'Udayd, Khawr al var. Khor al Udeid. inlet Qatar/Saudi Arabia
114 D11 Udbina Lika-Senj, W Croatia 44.33N 15.46E
97 I18 Uddevalla Västra Götaland, S Sweden 58.19N 11.55E
Uddjaur see Uddjaure
94 H13 Uddjaure var. Uddjaur. ⊚ N Sweden
Udeid, Khor al see 'Udayd, Khawr al
101 K14 Uden Noord-Brabant, SE Netherlands 51.40N 5.37E
Uden see Udenhout
101 J14 Udenhout var. Uden. Noord-Brabant, S Netherlands 51.37N 5.09E
161 H14 Udgīr Mahārāshtra, C India 18.23N 77.06E
Udhagamandalam see Udagamandalam
158 H6 Udhampur Jammu and Kashmir, NW India 32.55N 75.07E
145 X14 'Udhaybah, 'Uqlat al well S Iraq 29.46N 46.50E
108 J7 Udine anc. Utina. Friuli-Venezia Giulia, NE Italy 46.04N 13.10E
183 T14 Udintsev Fracture Zone tectonic feature S Pacific Ocean
Udipi see Udupi
Udmurtia see Udmurtskaya Respublika
131 S2 Udmurtskaya Respublika Eng. Udmurtia. ◐ autonomous republic NW Russian Federation
128 J15 Udomlya Tverskaya Oblast', W Russian Federation 57.53N 34.59E
Udon Ratchathani see Ubon Ratchathani
178 Ii9 Udon Thani var. Ban Mak Khaeng, Udorndhani. Udon Thani, N Thailand 17.25N 102.45E
Udorndhani see Udon Thani
201 U12 Udot atoll Chuuk Islands, C Micronesia
127 N13 Udskaya Guba bay E Russian Federation
161 E19 Udupi var. Udipi. Karnātaka, SW India 13.18N 74.46E
Udzhary see Ucar
175 Q9 Uebonti, Teluk bay Sulawesi, C Indonesia
102 O9 Uecker ⁓ NE Germany
102 P9 Ueckermünde Mecklenburg-Vorpommern, NE Germany 53.43N 14.03E
171 J14 Ueda var. Uyeda. Nagano, Honshū, S Japan 36.25N 138.14E
81 L16 Uele var. Welle. ⁓ NE Dem. Rep. Congo (Zaire)
Uele (upper course) see Uolo, Río, Equatorial Guinea/Gabon
Uele (upper course) see Kibali, Dem. Rep. Congo (Zaire)
127 Q3 Uelen Chukotskiy Avtonomnyy Okrug, NE Russian Federation 66.01N 169.52W
102 J11 Uelzen Niedersachsen, N Germany 52.58N 10.34E
171 H15 Ueno Mie, Honshū, SW Japan 34.45N 136.09E
131 V4 Ufa Respublika Bashkortostan, W Russian Federation 54.46N 56.02E
131 V4 Ufa ⁓ W Russian Federation
152 A10 Ufra Balkanskiy Velayat, NW Turkmenistan 40.00N 53.05E
85 C18 Ugab ⁓ C Namibia
120 D8 Ugāle Ventspils, NW Latvia 57.16N 21.58E
83 F17 Uganda off. Republic of Uganda. ◆ republic E Africa
144 G4 Ugarit Ar. Ra's Shamrah. site of ancient city Al Lādhiqīyah, NW Syria 35.34N 35.45E
41 O14 Ugashik Alaska, USA 57.30N 157.24W
109 Q19 Ugento Puglia, SE Italy 39.53N 18.09E
107 O15 Ugíjar Andalucía, S Spain 36.58N 3.03W
105 T11 Ugine Savoie, E France 45.45N 6.25E
127 O15 Uglegorsk Ostrov Sakhalin, Sakhalinskaya Oblast', SE Russian Federation 49.05N 142.06E
129 V13 Ugleural'skiy Permskaya Oblast', NW Russian Federation 58.57N 57.37E
128 L15 Uglich Yaroslavskaya Oblast', W Russian Federation 57.33N 38.23E
128 I14 Uglovka var. Okulovka. Novgorodskaya Oblast', W Russian Federation 58.24N 33.15E
127 Pp5 Ugol'nyye Kopi Chukotskiy Avtonomnyy Okrug, NE Russian Federation 64.43N 105.46E
130 I4 Ugra ⁓ W Russian Federation
153 V9 Ugyut Narynskaya Oblast', C Kyrgyzstan 41.22N 74.49E
113 H19 Uherské Hradiště Ger. Ungarisch-Hradisch. Zilinský kraj, E Czech Republic 49.04N 17.26E
113 H19 Uherský Brod Ger. Ungarisch-Brod. Zilinský kraj, E Czech Republic 49.01N 17.37E
113 B17 Úhlava Ger. Angel. ⁓ W Czech Republic
Uhorshchyna see Hungary
33 T13 Uhrichsville Ohio, N USA 40.23N 81.21W
Uhuru Peak see Kilimanjaro
98 G8 Uig N Scotland, UK 57.35N 6.22W
84 B10 Uíge Port. Carmona, Vila Marechal Carmona. Uíge, NW Angola 7.37S 15.02E
84 B10 Uíge ◐ province N Angola
200 Ss13 Uiha island Ha'apai Group, C Tonga
201 U13 Uijec island Chuuk, C Micronesia
169 X14 Ŭijŏngbu Jap. Giseifu. NW South Korea 37.42N 127.02E
150 H10 Uil Kaz. Oyyl. Aktyubinsk, W Kazakhstan 49.06N 54.41E
150 H10 Uil Kaz. Oyyl. ⁓ W Kazakhstan
38 M3 Uinta Mountains ▲ Utah, W USA
85 C18 Uis Erongo, NW Namibia 21.15S 14.54E
85 I25 Uitenhage Eastern Cape, S South Africa 33.43S 25.27E
100 H9 Uitgeest Noord-Holland, W Netherlands 52.31N 4.43E
100 I11 Uithoorn Noord-Holland, C Netherlands 52.13N 4.49E
100 O4 Uithuizen Groningen, NE Netherlands 53.24N 6.40E
100 O4 Uithuizermeeden Groningen, NE Netherlands 53.25N 6.43E
201 R6 Ujae Atoll var. Wūjae. atoll Ralik Chain, W Marshall Islands
Ujain see Ujjain
113 I16 Ujazd Opolskie, S Poland 50.22N 18.20E
Új-Becse see Novi Bečej
Ujda see Oujda
201 N5 Ujelang Atoll var. Wujlān. atoll Ralik Chain, W Marshall Islands
113 N21 Újfehértó Szabolcs-Szatmár-Bereg, E Hungary 47.48N 21.41E
Újgradiska see Nova Gradiška
171 H15 Uji var. Uzi. Kyōto, Honshū, SW Japan 34.52N 135.47E
170 Aa16 Uji-guntō island Nansei-shotō, SW Japan
83 E21 Ujiji Kigoma, W Tanzania 4.55S 29.39E
160 G10 Ujjain prev. Ujain. Madhya Pradesh, C India 23.10N 75.49E
Újlak see Ilok
'Ujmān see 'Ajmān
Újmoldova see Moldova Nouă
Újszentanna see Sântana
175 P13 Ujungpandang var. Macassar, Makassar; prev. Makasar. Sulawesi, C Indonesia 5.09S 119.28E
Ujung Salang see Phuket
Újvidék see Novi Sad
160 E11 Ukāi Reservoir ⊠ W India
83 G19 Ukara Island island N Tanzania
'Ukash, Wādī see 'Akāsh, Wādī
83 F19 Ukerewe Island island N Tanzania
145 S9 Ukhaydhir C Iraq 32.28N 43.36E
159 X13 Ukhrul Manipur, NE India 25.07N 94.24E
129 S9 Ukhta Respublika Komi, NW Russian Federation 63.30N 53.47E
36 L6 Ukiah California, W USA 39.07N 123.14W
34 K12 Ukiah Oregon, NW USA 45.06N 118.57W
101 G18 Ukkel Fr. Uccle. Brussels, C Belgium 50.47N 4.19E
120 G13 Ukmergė Pol. Wiłkomierz. Ukmergė, C Lithuania 55.16N 24.46E
Ukraina see Ukraine
118 L6 Ukraine off. Ukraine, Rus. Ukraina, Ukr. Ukrayina; prev. Ukrainian Soviet Socialist Republic, Ukrainskaya S.S.R. ◆ republic SE Europe
Ukrainskay S.S.R/Ukrayina see Ukraine
84 B13 Uku Cuanza Sul, NW Angola 11.25S 14.18E
170 Bb12 Uku-jima island Gotō-rettō, SW Japan
85 F20 Ukwi Kgalagadi, SW Botswana 23.41S 20.26E
120 M13 Ula Rus. Ulla. Vitsyebskaya Voblasts', N Belarus 55.13N 29.15E
142 C16 Ula Muğla, SW Turkey 37.07N 28.25E
120 M13 Ula Rus. Ulla. ⁓ N Belarus
168 L7 Ulaanbaatar Eng. Ulan Bator. ● (Mongolia) Töv, C Mongolia 47.54N 106.57E
169 N8 Ulaan-Ereg Hentiy, E Mongolia 46.50N 109.39E
168 E5 Ulaangom Uvs, NW Mongolia 49.56N 92.06E
168 E7 Ulaantolgoy Hovd, W Mongolia 46.39N 92.50E
168 I8 Ulaan-Uul Bayanhongor, C Mongolia 46.03N 100.52E
169 O10 Ulaan-Uul Dornogovi, SE Mongolia 44.21N 111.06E
165 R10 Ulan Qinghai, C China 36.59N 98.21E
Ulan Bator see Ulaanbaatar
168 L13 Ulan Buh Shamo desert N China
Ulanhad see Chifeng
169 T8 Ulanhot Nei Mongol Zizhiqu, N China 46.02N 122.00E
131 Q14 Ulan Khol Respublika Kalmykiya, SW Russian Federation 45.27N 46.48E
168 M13 Ulansuhai Nur ⊚ N China
126 Jj16 Ulan-Ude prev. Verkhneudinsk. Respublika Buryatiya, S Russian Federation 51.55N 107.40E
165 N12 Ulan Ul Hu ⊚ C China
195 Z16 Ulawa Island island SE Solomon Islands
144 J7 'Ulayyānīyah, Bi'r al var. Al Hilbeh. well S Syria 34.01N 38.06E
127 Nn13 Ul'banskiy Zaliv strait E Russian Federation
Ulbo see Olib
115 J18 Ulcinj Montenegro, SW Yugoslavia 41.56N 19.14E
169 O7 Uldz Hentiy, NE Mongolia 48.47N 112.01E
Uleåborg see Oulu
Uleälv see Oulujoki
97 G16 Ulefoss Telemark, S Norway 59.16N 9.16E
Uleträsk see Oulujärvi
115 L19 Ulëz var. Ulëza. Dibër, C Albania 41.42N 19.52E
Ulëza see Ulëz
97 F22 Ulfborg Ringkøbing, W Denmark 56.16N 8.21E
100 N13 Ulft Gelderland, E Netherlands 51.52N 6.22E
168 G7 Uliastay Dzavhan, W Mongolia 47.46N 96.53E
196 F8 Ulimang Babeldaob, N Palau
69 T10 Ulindi ⁓ W Dem. Rep. Congo (Zaire)
196 H14 Ulithi Atoll atoll Caroline Islands, W Micronesia
114 N10 Uljma Serbia, NE Yugoslavia 45.04N 21.08E
150 L11 Ul'kayak Kaz. Ölkeyek. ⁓ C Kazakhstan
151 Q7 Ul'ken-Karoy, Ozero ⊚ N Kazakhstan
Ülkenözen see Bol'shoy Uzen'
Ülkenqobda see Bol'shaya Khobda
106 G3 Ulla ⁓ NW Spain
Ulla see Ula
191 S10 Ulladulla New South Wales, SE Australia 35.22S 150.28E
159 T14 Ullapara Rajshahi, W Bangladesh 24.19N 89.34E
98 H7 Ullapool N Scotland, UK 57.54N 5.10W
97 J20 Ullared Halland, S Sweden 57.07N 12.45E
107 T7 Ulldecona Cataluña, NE Spain 40.36N 0.27E
94 I9 Ullsfjorden fjord N Norway
99 K15 Ullswater ⊚ NW England, UK
103 I22 Ulm Baden-Württemberg, S Germany 48.24N 9.58E
35 R8 Ulm Montana, NW USA 47.27N 111.32W
191 V5 Ulmarra New South Wales, SE Australia 29.37S 153.06E
118 K13 Ulmeni Buzău, C Romania 45.08N 26.43E
118 K14 Ulmeni Călăraşi, S Romania 44.08N 26.43E
44 L7 Ulmukhuás Región Autónoma Atlántico Norte, NE Nicaragua 14.21N 84.34W
196 C8 Ulong var. Aulong. island Palau Islands, N Palau
85 N14 Ulonguè var. Ulongwé. Tete, NW Mozambique 14.42S 34.21E
Ulongwé see Ulonguè
97 K19 Ulricehamn Västra Götaland, S Sweden 57.57N 13.25E
100 N5 Ulrum Groningen, NE Netherlands 53.24N 6.20E
169 Z16 Ulsan Jap. Urusan. SE South Korea 35.33N 129.19E
96 D10 Ulsteinvik Møre og Romsdal, S Norway 62.19N 5.52E
99 D15 Ulster ◐ province Northern Ireland, UK/Ireland
175 S5 Ulu Pulau Siau, N Indonesia 2.46N 125.22E
126 Ll12 Ulu Respublika Sakha (Yakutiya), NE Russian Federation 60.18N 127.27E
44 H5 Ulúa, Río ⁓ NW Honduras
142 D12 Ulubat Gölü ⊚ NW Turkey
142 E12 Uludağ ▲ NW Turkey 40.08N 29.13E
Ulugh Muztag see Muztag Feng
164 D7 Ulugqat Xinjiang Uygur Zizhiqu, W China 39.45N 74.10E
142 J16 Ulukışla Niğde, S Turkey 37.33N 34.28E
201 O15 Ulul island Caroline Islands, C Micronesia
85 L22 Ulundi KwaZulu/Natal, E South Africa 28.18S 31.25E
164 M3 Ulungur He ⁓ NW China
164 K2 Ulungur Hu ⊚ NW China
189 P8 Uluru var. Ayers Rock. rocky outcrop Northern Territory, C Australia 25.20S 130.59E
Ulveah see Lopevi
99 K16 Ulverston NW England, UK 54.12N 3.07W
191 O16 Ulverstone Tasmania, SE Australia 41.13S 146.09E
96 D13 Ulvik Hordaland, S Norway 60.34N 6.53E
95 J18 Ulvila Länsi-Suomi, W Finland 61.25N 21.55E
119 O8 Ulyanivka Rus. Ul'yanovka. Kirovohrads'ka Oblast', C Ukraine 48.18N 30.15E
Ul'yanovka see Ulyanivka
131 Q5 Ul'yanovsk prev. Simbirsk. Ul'yanovskaya Oblast', W Russian Federation 54.17N 48.21E
131 Q5 Ul'yanovskaya Oblast' ◐ province W Russian Federation
151 S10 Ul'yanovskiy Karaganda, C Kazakhstan 50.04N 73.45E
Ul'yanovskiy Kanal see Ul'yanow Kanali
152 M13 Ul'yanow Kanali Rus. Ul'yanovskiy Kanal. canal Turkmenistan/Uzbekistan
Ulyshylanshyq see Uly-Zhylanshyk
28 H6 Ulysses Kansas, C USA 37.34N 101.21W
151 O12 Ulytau, Gory ▲ C Kazakhstan
126 K14 Ulyunkhan Respublika Buryatiya, S Russian Federation 54.48N 111.01E
151 N11 Uly-Zhylanshyk Kaz. Ulyshylanshyq. ⁓ C Kazakhstan
114 A9 Umag It. Umago. Istra, NW Croatia 45.25N 13.32E
Umago see Umag
201 V13 Uman atoll Chuuk Islands, C Micronesia
119 O7 Uman' Rus. Uman. Cherkas'ka Oblast', C Ukraine 48.45N 30.10E
43 W12 Umán Yucatán, SE Mexico 20.51N 89.45W
Umanak/Umanaq see Uummannaq
'Umān, Khalīj see Oman, Gulf of
'Umān, Salţanat see Oman
176 Ww12 Umari Irian Jaya, E Indonesia 4.18S 135.22E
160 K10 Umaria Madhya Pradesh, C India 23.34N 80.49E
155 R16 Umar Kot Sind, SE Pakistan 25.19N 69.46E
196 B17 Umatac SW Guam 13.17N 144.40E
196 A17 Umatac Bay bay SW Guam
145 S6 Umayqah C Iraq 34.32N 43.45E
128 J5 Umba Murmanskaya Oblast', NW Russian Federation 66.39N 34.24E
144 I8 Umbāshī, Khirbat al ruins As Suwaydā', S Syria 33.05N 37.00E
82 A12 Umbelasha ⁓ W Sudan
108 H12 Umbertide Umbria, C Italy 43.16N 12.21E
63 B17 Umberto var. Humberto. Santa Fe, C Argentina 30.52S 61.19W
194 K11 Umboi Island var. Rooke Island. island C PNG
128 J4 Umbozero, Ozero ⊚ NW Russian Federation
108 H13 Umbria ◐ region C Italy
Umbrian-Machigian Mountains see Umbro-Marchigiano, Appennino
108 I12 Umbro-Marchigiano, Appennino Eng. Umbrian-Machigian Mountains. ▲ C Italy
95 J16 Umeå Västerbotten, N Sweden 63.49N 20.15E
95 H14 Umeälven ⁓ N Sweden
41 Q5 Umiat Alaska, USA 69.22N 152.08W
85 K23 Umlazi KwaZulu/Natal, E South Africa 29.58S 30.50E
145 X10 Umm al Baqar, Hawr var. Birkat ad Dawaymah. spring S Iraq 31.43N 46.50E
147 U12 Umm al Ḥayt, Wādī var. Wādī Amilhayt. seasonal river SW Oman
Umm al Qaiwain see Umm al Qaywayn
149 R15 Umm al Qaywayn var. Umm al Qaiwain. Umm al Qaywayn, NE UAE 25.43N 55.54E
145 Q5 Umm al Ţūz C Iraq 34.53N 42.42E
144 J3 Umm 'Āmūd Ḥalab, N Syria 35.57N 37.39E
147 Y10 Umm ar Ruṣāṣ var. Umm Ruṣayṣ. W Oman 20.26N 58.48E
147 X9 Ummas Samīn salt flat C Oman
147 V9 Umm az Zumūl oasis E Saudi Arabia 22.39N 54.45E
82 A9 Umm Buru Western Darfur, W Sudan 15.01N 23.36E
82 A12 Umm Dafag Southern Darfur, W Sudan 10.28N 23.19E
Umm Durmān see Omdurman
144 F9 Umm el Fahm Haifa, N Israel 32.30N 35.06E
82 F9 Umm Inderab Northern Kordofan, C Sudan 15.18N 31.56E
82 C10 Umm Keddada Northern Darfur, W Sudan 13.36N 26.42E
146 J7 Umm Lajj Tabūk, W Saudi Arabia 25.01N 37.19E
144 L10 Umm Maḥfur ⁓ N Jordan
145 Y13 Umm Qaşr SE Iraq 30.01N 47.55E
Umm Ruṣayṣ see Umm ar Ruṣāṣ
82 F11 Umm Ruwaba var. Umm Ruwābah, Um Ruwāba. Northern Kordofan, C Sudan 12.54N 31.13E
Umm Ruwābah see Umm Ruwaba
149 N16 Umm Sa'īd var. Musay'īd. S Qatar 24.57N 51.31E
144 K10 Umm Ţuways, Wādī dry watercourse N Jordan
40 J17 Umnak Island island Aleutian Islands, Alaska, USA
34 F13 Umpqua River ⁓ Oregon, NW USA
84 D13 Umpulo Bié, C Angola 12.43S 17.42E
160 I12 Umred Mahārāshtra, C India 20.54N 79.19E
145 Y10 Umr Sawān, Hawr ⊚ S Iraq
Um Ruwāba see Umm Ruwaba
Umtali see Mutare
85 J24 Umtata Eastern Cape, S South Africa 31.33S 28.47E
79 V17 Umuahia Abia, SW Nigeria 5.30N 7.33E
62 H10 Umuarama Paraná, S Brazil 23.45S 53.19W
Umvuma see Mvuma
85 K18 Umzingwani ⁓ S Zimbabwe
114 D11 Una ⁓ Bosnia and Herzegovina/Croatia
114 E12 Unac ⁓ W Bosnia and Herzegovina
25 T6 Unadilla Georgia, SE USA 32.15N 83.44W
20 I10 Unadilla River ⁓ New York, NE USA
61 L18 Unaí Minas Gerais, SE Brazil 16.24S 46.49W
41 N10 Unalakleet Alaska, USA 63.52N 160.47W
40 K17 Unalaska Island island Aleutian Islands, Alaska, USA
193 I16 Una, Mount ▲ South Island, NZ 42.12S 172.34E
84 N13 Unango Niassa, N Mozambique 12.45S 35.28E
Unao see Unnão
94 L12 Unari Lappi, N Finland 67.07N 25.37E
147 O6 'Unayzah var. Anaiza. Al Qaşim, C Saudi Arabia 26.03N 44.00E
144 L10 'Unayzah, Jabal ▲ Jordan/Saudi Arabia 32.09N 39.10E
Unci see Almería
59 K19 Uncía Potosí, C Bolivia 18.30S 66.29W
39 Q7 Uncompahgre Peak ▲ Colorado, C USA 38.04N 107.27W
39 P6 Uncompahgre Plateau plain Colorado, C USA
97 L17 Unden ⊚ S Sweden
30 M4 Underwood North Dakota, N USA 47.25N 101.09W
176 Uu11 Undur Pulau Seram, E Indonesia 3.41S 130.38E
194 M11 Unea Island island C PNG
130 H6 Unecha Bryanskaya Oblast', W Russian Federation 52.51N 32.38E
41 N16 Unga Unga Island, Alaska, USA 55.14N 160.34W
Ungaria see Hungary
191 P8 Ungarie New South Wales, SE Australia 33.39S 146.54E
Ungarisch-Brod see Uherský Brod
Ungarisches Erzgebirge see Slovenské rudohorie
Ungarisch-Hradisch see Uherské Hradiště
Ungern see Hungary

◆ Country ● Country Capital ◇ Dependent Territory ○ Dependent Territory Capital ◐ Administrative Region ✕ International Airport ▲ Mountain ▲ Mountain Range ⩕ Volcano ⁓ River ⊚ Lake ⊠ Reservoir

UNGAVA BAY – VALDEPEÑAS

10 M4 **Ungava Bay** *bay* Quebec, E Canada
10 J2 **Ungava, Péninsule d'** *peninsula* Quebec, SE Canada
Ungeny *see* Ungheni
118 M9 **Ungheni** ***Rus.*** Ungeny. W Moldova 47.13N 27.48E
Unguja *see* Zanzibar
Üngüz Angyrsyndaky Garagum *see* Zaungukskiye Garagumy
152 H11 **Unguz, Solonchakovyye Vpadiny** *salt marsh* C Turkmenistan
Ungvár *see* Uzhhorod
62 I12 **União da Vitória** Paraná, S Brazil 26.13S 51.04W
113 G17 **Uničov** ***Ger.*** Mährisch-Neustadt. Olomoucký Kraj, E Czech Republic 49.46N 17.05E
112 J12 **Uniejów** Łódzkie, C Poland 51.58N 18.46E
114 A11 **Unije** *island* W Croatia
40 L16 **Unimak Island** *island* Aleutian Islands, Alaska, USA
40 L16 **Unimak Pass** *strait* Aleutian Islands, Alaska, USA
29 W5 **Union** Missouri, C USA 38.27N 91.01W
34 L12 **Union** Oregon, NW USA 45.12N 117.51W
23 Q11 **Union** South Carolina, SE USA 34.40N 81.35W
23 R6 **Union** West Virginia, NE USA 37.33N 80.33W
64 J12 **Unión** San Luis, C Argentina 35.09S 65.55W
63 B25 **Unión, Bahía** *bay* E Argentina
33 Q13 **Union City** Indiana, N USA 40.12N 84.50W
33 Q10 **Union City** Michigan, N USA 42.03N 85.06W
20 C12 **Union City** Pennsylvania, NE USA 41.54N 79.51W
22 G8 **Union City** Tennessee, S USA 36.25N 89.01W
34 G14 **Union Creek** Oregon, NW USA 42.54N 122.26W
85 G25 **Uniondale** Western Cape, SW South Africa 33.40S 23.07E
42 K13 **Unión de Tula** Jalisco, SW Mexico 19.58N 104.20W
32 M9 **Union Grove** Wisconsin, N USA 42.39N 88.03W
47 Y15 **Union Island** *island* S Saint Vincent and the Grenadines
48 K5 **Union Reefs** *reef* SW Mexico
(0) D7 **Union Seamount** *undersea feature* NE Pacific Ocean 49.34N 132.45W
25 Q6 **Union Springs** Alabama, S USA 32.08N 85.43W
22 H6 **Uniontown** Kentucky, S USA 37.46N 87.55W
20 C16 **Uniontown** Pennsylvania, NE USA 39.54N 79.43W
29 T1 **Unionville** Missouri, C USA 40.28N 93.00W
147 V8 **United Arab Emirates** ***Ar.*** Al Imārāt al 'Arabīyah al Muttaḩidah, ***abbrev.*** UAE; ***prev.*** Trucial States. ◆ *federation* SW Asia
United Arab Republic *see* Egypt
99 H14 **United Kingdom** ***off.*** UK of Great Britain and Northern Ireland, ***abbrev.*** UK. ◆ *monarchy* NW Europe
United Mexican States *see* Mexico
United Provinces *see* Uttar Pradesh
18 L9 **United States of America** ***off.*** United States of America, ***var.*** America, The States, ***abbrev.*** U.S., USA. ◆ *federal republic*
128 J10 **Unitsa** Respublika Kareliya, NW Russian Federation 62.31N 34.31E
9 S15 **Unity** Saskatchewan, S Canada 52.27N 109.10W
Unity State *see* Wahda
107 Q8 **Universales, Montes** ▲▲ C Spain
29 X4 **University City** Missouri, C USA 38.40N 90.19W
197 B13 **Unmet** Malekula, C Vanuatu 16.09S 167.16E
103 F15 **Unna** Nordrhein-Westfalen, W Germany 51.31N 7.40E
158 L12 **Unnão** ***prev.*** Unao. Uttar Pradesh, N India 26.31N 80.30E
197 D15 **Unpongkor** Erromango, S Vauautu 18.48S 169.01E
Unruhstadt *see* Kargowa
98 M1 **Unst** *island* NE Scotland, UK
103 K16 **Unstrut** ≈ C Germany
Unterdrauburg *see* Dravograd
Unterlimbach *see* Lendava
103 L23 **Unterschleissheim** Bayern, SE Germany 48.16N 11.34E
103 H24 **Untersee** ◎ Germany/Switzerland
102 O10 **Unterueckersee** ◎ NE Germany
110 F9 **Unterwalden** ⬖ *canton* C Switzerland
57 N12 **Unturán, Sierra de** ▲▲ Brazil/Venezuela
165 N11 **Unuli Horog** Qinghai, W China 35.10N 91.49E
142 M11 **Ünye** Ordu, W Turkey 41.07N 37.14E
Unza *see* Unzha
129 O14 **Unzha** ***var.*** Unza. ≈ NW Russian Federation
81 E17 **Uolo, Río** ***var.*** Eyo (lower course), Mbini, Uele (upper course), Woleu; ***prev.*** Benito. ≈ Equatorial Guinea/Gabon
57 Q10 **Uonán** Bolívar, SE Venezuela 4.33N 62.10W
167 T12 **Uotsuri-shima** *island* China/Japan/Taiwan
171 J13 **Uozu** Toyama, Honshū, SW Japan 36.48N 137.23E
44 L12 **Upala** Alajuela, NW Costa Rica 10.52N 85.00W
57 P7 **Upata** Bolívar, E Venezuela 8.01N 62.25W
81 M23 **Upemba, Lac** ◎ SE Dem. Rep. Congo (Zaire)
207 O12 **Upernavik** ***var.*** Upernivik. Kitaa, C Greenland 73.06N 55.42W
Upernivik *see* Upernavik
85 F22 **Upington** Northern Cape, W South Africa 28.24S 21.13E
Uplands *see* Ottawa
198 Bb8 **Upolu** *island* SE Samoa
40 G11 **Upolu Point** *headland* Hawaii, USA, C Pacific Ocean 20.15N 155.51W
Upper Austria *see* Oberösterreich
Upper Bann *see* Bann
12 M13 **Upper Canada Village** *tourist site* Ontario, SE Canada 44.57N 75.04W
20 I16 **Upper Darby** Pennsylvania, NE USA 39.57N 75.15W
30 L2 **Upper Des Lacs Lake** ⊠ North Dakota, N USA
193 L14 **Upper Hutt** Wellington, North Island, NZ 41.08S 174.58E
31 X11 **Upper Iowa River** ≈ Iowa, C USA
34 H15 **Upper Klamath Lake** ◎ Oregon, NW USA
36 M6 **Upper Lake** California, W USA 39.07N 122.53W
37 Q1 **Upper Lake** ◎ California, W USA
8 K9 **Upper Liard** Yukon Territory, W Canada 60.01N 128.59W
99 E16 **Upper Lough Erne** ◎ SW Northern Ireland, UK
82 F12 **Upper Nile** ⬖ *state* E Sudan
31 T3 **Upper Red Lake** ◎ Minnesota, N USA
33 S12 **Upper Sandusky** Ohio, N USA 40.49N 83.16W
Upper Volta *see* Burkina
97 O15 **Upplandsväsby** ***var.*** Upplands Väsby. Stockholm, C Sweden 59.28N 17.49E
97 O15 **Uppsala** Uppsala, C Sweden 59.52N 17.37E
97 O14 **Uppsala** ⬖ *county* C Sweden
40 J12 **Upright Cape** *headland* Saint Matthew Island, Alaska, USA 60.19N 172.15W
22 K6 **Upton** Kentucky, S USA 37.25N 85.53W
35 Y13 **Upton** Wyoming, C USA 44.06N 104.37W
147 N7 **'Uqlat aş Şuqūr** Al Qaşīm, W Saudi Arabia 25.51N 42.12E
Uqturpan *see* Wushi
56 C7 **Urabá, Golfo de** *gulf* NW Colombia
Uracas *see* Farallon de Pajaros
Uradar'ya *see* Ŭradaryo
153 N13 **Ŭradaryo** ***Rus.*** Uradar'ya. ≈ S Uzbekistan
168 M13 **Urad Qianqi** ***var.*** Xishanzui. Nei Mongol Zizhiqu, N China 40.43N 108.41E
171 Jj17 **Uraga-suidō** *strait* S Japan
172 Pp7 **Urahoro** Hokkaidō, NE Japan 42.47N 143.41E
172 Oo8 **Urakawa** Hokkaidō, NE Japan 42.11N 142.42E
131 X6 **Ural** ***Kaz.*** Zayyq. ≈ Kazakhstan/Russian Federation
191 T6 **Uralla** New South Wales, SE Australia 30.39S 151.30E
Ural Mountains *see* Ural'skiye Gory
150 F8 **Ural'sk** ***Kaz.*** Oral. Zapadnyy Kazakhstan, NW Kazakhstan 51.12N 51.17E
Ural'skaya Oblast' *see* Zapadnyy Kazakhstan
131 W5 **Ural'skiye Gory** ***var.*** Ural'skiy Khrebet, ***Eng.*** Ural Mountains. ▲▲ Kazakhstan/Russian Federation
Ural'skiy Khrebet *see* Ural'skiye Gory
144 I3 **Urām aş Şughrá** Ḩalab, N Syria 36.10N 36.55E
191 P10 **Urana** New South Wales, SE Australia 35.22S 146.16E
9 S10 **Uranium City** Saskatchewan, C Canada 59.30N 108.46W
60 F10 **Uraricoera** Roraima, N Brazil 3.26N 60.54W
49 S5 **Uraricoera, Rio** ≈ N Brazil
Ura-Tyube *see* Ŭroteppa
171 K16 **Urawa** Saitama, Honshū, S Japan 35.51N 139.37E
125 F10 **Uray** Khanty-Mansiyskiy Avtonomnyy Okrug, C Russian Federation 60.07N 64.38E
147 R7 **'Uray'irah** Ash Sharqīyah, E Saudi Arabia 25.59N 48.51E
32 M13 **Urbana** Illinois, N USA 40.06N 88.12W
33 R13 **Urbana** Ohio, N USA 40.04N 83.46W
31 V14 **Urbandale** Iowa, C USA 41.37N 93.42W
108 I11 **Urbania** Marche, C Italy 43.40N 12.33E
176 Uu8 **Urbinasopon** Irian Jaya, E Indonesia 0.19S 131.12E
108 I11 **Urbino** Marche, C Italy 43.45N 12.38E
59 H16 **Urcos** Cusco, S Peru 13.45S 71.37W
150 D10 **Urda** Zapadnyy Kazakhstan, W Kazakhstan 48.52N 47.31E
107 N10 **Urda** Castilla-La Mancha, C Spain 39.25N 3.43W
168 E7 **Urdgol** Hovd, W Mongolia 47.39N 92.46E
Urdunn *see* Jordan
151 X12 **Urdzhar** ***Kaz.*** Ürzhar. Vostochnyy Kazakhstan, E Kazakhstan 47.06N 81.37E
99 L16 **Ure** ≈ N England, UK
121 K18 **Urechcha** ***Rus.*** Urech'ye. Minskaya Voblasts', S Belarus 52.57N 27.54E
Urech'ye *see* Urechcha
131 P2 **Uren'** Nizhegorodskaya Oblast', W Russian Federation 57.29N 45.47E
126 H9 **Urengoy** Yamalo-Nenetskiy Avtonomnyy Okrug, N Russian Federation 65.52N 78.42E
192 K10 **Urenui** Taranaki, North Island, NZ 38.59S 174.25E
197 B10 **Ureparapara** *island* Banks Islands, N Vanuatu
42 G5 **Ures** Sonora, NW Mexico 29.25N 110.24W
Urfa *see* Şanlıurfa
152 H9 **Urganch** ***Rus.*** Urgench; ***prev.*** Novo-Urgench. Khorazm Wiloyati, W Uzbekistan 41.39N 60.32E
Urgench *see* Urganch
142 J14 **Ürgüp** Nevşehir, C Turkey 38.39N 34.55E
153 O12 **Urgut** Samarqand Wiloyati, C Uzbekistan 39.25N 67.15E
164 K3 **Urho** Xinjiang Uygur Zizhiqu, W China 46.04N 84.51E
158 G5 **Uri** Jammu and Kashmir, NW India 34.04N 74.03E
110 G9 **Uri** ⬖ *canton* C Switzerland
56 F11 **Uribe** Meta, C Colombia 3.01N 74.33W
56 H4 **Uribia** La Guajira, N Colombia 11.45N 72.19W
118 G12 **Uricani** ***Hung.*** Hobicaurikány. Hunedoara, SW Romania 45.18N 23.03E
59 M21 **Uriondo** Tarija, S Bolivia 21.40S 64.37W
42 I7 **Urique** Chihuahua, N Mexico 27.16N 107.51W
42 I7 **Urique, Río** ≈ N Mexico
58 E9 **Uritiyacu, Río** ≈ N Peru
151 N7 **Uritskiy** Kostanay, N Kazakhstan 53.21N 65.27E
100 K8 **Urk** Flevoland, N Netherlands 52.40N 5.34E
142 B14 **Urla** İzmir, W Turkey 38.19N 26.46E
118 K13 **Urlaţi** Prahova, SE Romania 44.58N 26.15E
131 V4 **Urman** Respublika Bashkortostan, W Russian Federation 54.53N 56.52E
153 P12 **Urmetan** W Tajikistan 39.27N 68.13E
Urmia *see* Orūmīyeh
Urmia, Lake *see* Orūmīyeh, Daryācheh-ye
Urmiyeh *see* Orūmīyeh
115 N17 **Uroševac** ***Alb.*** Ferizaj. Serbia, S Yugoslavia 42.23N 21.09E
153 P11 **Ŭroteppa** ***Rus.*** Ura-Tyube. NW Tajikistan 39.54N 68.57E
56 D8 **Urrao** Antioquia, W Colombia 6.16N 76.10W
Ursat'yevskaya *see* Khowos
168 I11 **Urt** Ömnögovĭ, S Mongolia 43.16N 101.00E
131 X7 **Urtazym** Orenburgskaya Oblast', W Russian Federation 52.12N 58.48E
61 K18 **Uruaçu** Goiás, C Brazil 14.37S 49.06W
42 M14 **Uruapan** ***var.*** Uruapan del Progreso. Michoacán de Ocampo, SW Mexico 19.25N 102.04W
Uruapan del Progreso *see* Uruapan
59 G15 **Urubamba, Cordillera** ▲▲ C Peru
59 G14 **Urubamba, Río** ≈ C Peru
60 G12 **Urucará** Amazonas, N Brazil 2.30S 57.45W
63 E16 **Uruguaiana** Rio Grande do Sul, S Brazil 29.45S 57.04W
Uruguai, Rio *see* Uruguay
63 E18 **Uruguay** ***off.*** Oriental Republic of Uruguay; ***prev.*** La Banda Oriental. ◆ *republic* E South America
63 E15 **Uruguay** ***var.*** Rio Uruguai, Río Uruguay. ≈ E South America
Uruguay, Río *see* Uruguay
Urumchi *see* Ürümqi
164 L5 **Ürümqi** ***var.*** Tihwa, Urumchi, Urumqi, Urumtsi, Wu-lu-k'o-mu-shi, Wu-lu-mu-ch'i; ***prev.*** Ti-hua. *autonomous region capital* Xinjiang Uygur Zizhiqu, NW China 43.52N 87.31E
Urumtsi *see* Ürümqi
Urundi *see* Burundi
191 V6 **Urunga** New South Wales, SE Australia 30.33S 152.58E
196 C15 **Uruno Point** *headland* NW Guam 13.37N 144.49E
127 P15 **Urup, Ostrov** *island* Kuril'skiye Ostrova, SE Russian Federation
147 P11 **'Uruq al Mawārid** *desert* S Saudi Arabia
Urusan *see* Ulsan
131 T5 **Urussu** Respublika Tatarstan, W Russian Federation 54.34N 53.23E
192 K10 **Uruti** Taranaki, North Island, NZ 38.57S 174.32E
59 K19 **Uru Uru, Lago** ◎ W Bolivia
57 P9 **Uruyén** Bolívar, SE Venezuela 5.40N 62.25W
155 O7 **Ūrūzgān** ***var.*** Oruzgān, Orūzgān. Urūzgān, C Afghanistan 32.58N 66.39E
155 N6 **Urūzgān** ***Per.*** Orūzgān. ⬖ *province* C Afghanistan
172 P6 **Uryū-gawa** ≈ Hokkaidō, NE Japan
172 P4 **Uryū-ko** ◎ Hokkaidō, NE Japan
131 N8 **Uryupinsk** Volgogradskaya Oblast', SW Russian Federation 50.51N 41.59E
Ürzhar *see* Urdzhar
129 R16 **Urzhum** Kirovskaya Oblast', NW Russian Federation 57.09N 49.56E
118 K13 **Urziceni** Ialomiţa, SE Romania 44.43N 26.39E
U.S./USA *see* United States of America
170 D13 **Usa** Ōita, Kyūshū, SW Japan 33.32N 131.20E
121 L16 **Usa** ***Rus.*** Usa. ≈ C Belarus
129 T6 **Usa** ≈ NW Russian Federation
142 E14 **Uşak** ***prev.*** Ushak. Uşak, W Turkey 38.42N 29.25E
142 D14 **Uşak** ***var.*** Ushak. ⬖ *province* W Turkey
85 C19 **Usakos** Erongo, W Namibia 22.01S 15.31E
83 J21 **Usambara Mountains** ▲▲ NE Tanzania
83 G23 **Usangu Flats** *wetland* SW Tanzania
67 D24 **Usborne, Mount** ▲ East Falkland, Falkland Islands 51.34S 58.57W
102 O8 **Usedom** *island* NE Germany
101 M24 **Useldange** Diekirch, C Luxembourg 49.46N 5.58E
120 L12 **Ushacha** ***Rus.*** Ushacha. Vitsyebskaya Voblasts', N Belarus 55.31N 28.30E
Ushachi *see* Ushachy
120 L13 **Ushachy** ***Rus.*** Ushachi. Vitsyebskaya Voblasts', N Belarus 55.09N 28.37E
Ushak *see* Uşak
126 I2 **Ushakova, Ostrov** *island* Severnaya Zemlya, N Russian Federation
Ushant *see* Ouessant, Île d'
Üsharal *see* Ucharal
170 Bb14 **Ushibuka** ***var.*** Usibuka. Kumamoto, Shimo-jima, SW Japan 32.13N 130.01E
Ushi Point *see* Sabaneta, Puntan
151 V14 **Ushtobe** ***Kaz.*** Üshtöbe. Almaty, SE Kazakhstan 45.15N 77.58E
65 I25 **Ushuaia** Tierra del Fuego, S Argentina 54.48S 68.19W
41 R10 **Usibelli** Alaska, USA 63.54N 148.41W
Usibuka *see* Ushibuka
194 I12 **Usino** Madang, N PNG 5.40S 145.31E
129 U6 **Usinsk** Respublika Komi, NW Russian Federation 66.00N 57.37E
99 K22 **Usk** ***Wel.*** Wysg. ≈ SE Wales, UK
Uskočke Planine/Uskokengebirge *see* Gorjanci/Žumberačko Gorje
Uskoplje *see* Gornji Vakuf
Üsküb *see* Skopje
116 M11 **Üsküpdere** Kırklareli, NW Turkey 41.41N 27.21E
130 L7 **Usman'** Lipetskaya Oblast', W Russian Federation 52.04N 39.41E
120 D8 **Usmas Ezers** ◎ NW Latvia
129 U13 **Usol'ye** Permskaya Oblast', NW Russian Federation 59.27N 56.33E
126 J15 **Usol'ye-Sibirskoye** Irkutskaya Oblast', C Russian Federation 52.48N 103.40E
43 T16 **Uspanapa, Río** ≈ SE Mexico
151 R11 **Uspenskiy** Zhezkazgan, C Kazakhstan 48.45N 72.46E
105 O11 **Ussel** Corrèze, C France 45.33N 2.18E
169 Z6 **Ussuri** ***var.*** Usuri, Wusuri, ***Chin.*** Wusuli Jiang. ≈ China/Russian Federation
127 Nn18 **Ussuriysk** ***prev.*** Nikol'sk, Nikol'sk-Ussuriyskiy, Voroshilov. Primorskiy Kray, SE Russian Federation 43.48N 131.58E
142 J10 **Usta Burnu** *headland* N Turkey 41.58N 34.30E
155 P13 **Usta Muhammad** Baluchistān, SW Pakistan 28.07N 68.00E
126 K15 **Ust'-Barguzin** Respublika Buryatiya, S Russian Federation 53.28N 109.00E
127 P12 **Ust'-Bol'sheretsk** Kamchatskaya Oblast', E Russian Federation 52.48N 156.12E
131 N9 **Ust'-Buzulukskaya** Volgogradskaya Oblast', SW Russian Federation 50.12N 42.06E
113 C16 **Ústecký Kraj** ⬖ *region* NW Czech Republic
110 G7 **Uster** Zürich, NE Switzerland 47.20N 8.40E
109 I22 **Ustica, Isola d'** *island* S Italy
126 J13 **Ust'-Ilimsk** Irkutskaya Oblast', C Russian Federation 57.57N 102.30E
113 C15 **Ústí nad Labem** ***Ger.*** Aussig. Ústecký Kraj, NW Czech Republic 50.40N 14.04E
113 F17 **Ústí nad Orlicí** ***Ger.*** Wildenschwert. Pardubický Kraj, E Czech Republic 49.58N 16.24E
Ustinov *see* Izhevsk
115 J14 **Ustiprača** Republika Srpska, SE Bosnia and Herzegovina 43.42N 19.03E
125 Ff12 **Ust'-Ishim** Omskaya Oblast', C Russian Federation 57.42N 70.58E
112 G6 **Ustka** ***Ger.*** Stolpmünde. Pomorskie, N Poland 54.34N 16.50E
127 Pp10 **Ust'-Kamchatsk** Kamchatskaya Oblast', E Russian Federation 56.13N 162.28E
151 X9 **Ust'-Kamenogorsk** ***Kaz.*** Öskemen. Vostochnyy Kazakhstan, E Kazakhstan 49.58N 82.36E
127 Oo10 **Ust'-Khayryuzovo** Koryakskiy Avtonomnyy Okrug, E Russian Federation 57.07N 156.37E
126 H16 **Ust'-Koksa** Respublika Altay, S Russian Federation 50.15N 85.45E
129 S11 **Ust'-Kulom** Respublika Komi, NW Russian Federation 61.42N 53.42E
126 Jj14 **Ust'-Kut** Irkutskaya Oblast', C Russian Federation 56.49N 105.31E
126 M7 **Ust'-Kuyga** Respublika Sakha (Yakutiya), NE Russian Federation 69.59N 135.27E
130 L14 **Ust'-Labinsk** Krasnodarskiy Kray, SW Russian Federation 44.40N 40.46E
126 Mm11 **Ust'-Maya** Respublika Sakha (Yakutiya), NE Russian Federation 60.27N 134.28E
127 N9 **Ust'-Nera** Respublika Sakha (Yakutiya), NE Russian Federation 64.28N 143.01E
126 Ll13 **Ust'-Nyukzha** Amurskaya Oblast', S Russian Federation 56.30N 121.32E
126 Kk6 **Ust'-Olenëk** Respublika Sakha (Yakutiya), NE Russian Federation 73.03N 119.34E
127 O10 **Ust'-Omchug** Magadanskaya Oblast', E Russian Federation 61.07N 149.17E
126 Jj15 **Ust'-Ordynskiy** Ust'-Ordynskiy Buryatskiy Avtonomnyy Okrug, S Russian Federation 52.49N 104.42E
126 J15 **Ust'-Ordynskiy Buryatskiy Avtonomnyy Okrug** ⬖ *autonomous district* S Russian Federation
129 N8 **Ust'-Pinega** Arkhangel'skaya Oblast', NW Russian Federation 64.09N 41.55E
126 Hh8 **Ust'-Port** Taymyrskiy (Dolgano-Nenetskiy) Avtonomnyy Okrug, N Russian Federation 69.42N 84.25E
116 L11 **Ustrem** ***prev.*** Vakav. Yambol, E Bulgaria 42.01N 26.28E
113 O18 **Ustrzyki Dolne** Podkarpackie, SE Poland 49.26N 22.36E
Ust'-Sysol'sk *see* Syktyvkar
129 R7 **Ust'-Tsil'ma** Respublika Komi, NW Russian Federation 65.25N 52.09E
Ust Urt *see* Ustyurt Plateau
129 O11 **Ust'ya** ≈ NW Russian Federation
119 R8 **Ustynivka** Kirovohrads'ka Oblast', C Ukraine 47.58N 32.32E
150 H15 **Ustyurt Plateau** ***var.*** Ust Urt, ***Uzb.*** Ustyurt Platosi. *plateau* Kazakhstan/Uzbekistan
Ustyurt Platosi *see* Ustyurt Plateau
128 K14 **Ustyuzhna** Vologodskaya Oblast', NW Russian Federation 58.50N 36.25E
164 J4 **Usu** Xinjiang Uygur Zizhiqu, NW China 44.27N 84.37E
175 Q10 **Usu** Sulawesi, C Indonesia 2.34S 120.58E
170 Dd14 **Usuki** Ōita, Kyūshū, SW Japan 33.07N 131.46E
44 G8 **Usulután** Usulután, SE El Salvador 13.19N 88.26W
44 B9 **Usulután** ⬖ *department* SE El Salvador
43 W16 **Usumacinta, Río** ≈ Guatemala/Mexico
Usumbura *see* Bujumbura
Usuri *see* Ussuri
176 X12 **Uta** Irian Jaya, E Indonesia 4.28S 136.03E
38 K5 **Utah** ***off.*** State of Utah; also known as Beehive State, Mormon State. ⬖ *state* W USA
38 L3 **Utah Lake** ◎ Utah, W USA
Utaidhani *see* Uthai Thani
95 M14 **Utajärvi** Oulu, C Finland 64.45N 26.25E
Utamboni *see* Mitemele, Río
Utaradit *see* Uttaradit
173 G3 **Utara, Selat** *strait* Peninsular Malaysia
172 P5 **Utashinai** ***var.*** Utasinai. Hokkaidō, NE Japan 43.32N 142.03E
Utasinai *see* Utashinai
176 X12 **Uta, Sungai** ≈ Irian Jaya, E Indonesia
200 Ss12 **'Uta Vava'u** *island* Vava'u Group, N Tonga
39 V9 **Ute Creek** ≈ New Mexico, SW USA
120 H12 **Utena** Utena, E Lithuania 55.30N 25.34E
39 V10 **Ute Reservoir** ⊠ New Mexico, SW USA
178 H10 **Uthai Thani** ***var.*** Muang Uthai Thani, Udayadhani, Utaidhani. Uthai Thani, W Thailand 15.22N 100.03E
155 O15 **Uthal** Baluchistān, SW Pakistan 25.53N 66.37E
20 I10 **Utica** New York, NE USA 43.06N 75.15W
107 R10 **Utiel** País Valenciano, E Spain 39.33N 1.13W
9 O13 **Utikuma Lake** ◎ Alberta, W Canada
44 I4 **Utila, Isla de** *island* Islas de la Bahía, N Honduras
Utina *see* Udine
61 O17 **Utinga** Bahia, E Brazil 12.05S 41.07W
Utirik *see* Utrik Atoll
97 M22 **Utlängan** *island* S Sweden
119 U11 **Utlyuts'kyy Lyman** *bay* S Ukraine
170 Cc14 **Uto** Kumamoto, Kyūshū, SW Japan 32.40N 130.37E
97 P16 **Utö** Stockholm, C Sweden 58.55N 18.19E
27 Q12 **Utopia** Texas, SW USA 29.30N 99.31W
100 J11 **Utrecht** ***Lat.*** Trajectum ad Rhenum. Utrecht, C Netherlands 52.06N 5.07E
85 K22 **Utrecht** KwaZulu/Natal, E South Africa 27.34S 30.19E
100 I11 **Utrecht** ⬖ *province* C Netherlands
106 K14 **Utrera** Andalucía, S Spain 37.10N 5.46W
201 V4 **Utrik Atoll** ***var.*** Utirik, Utrōk, Utrōnk. *atoll* Ratak Chain, N Marshall Islands
Utrōk/Utrōnk *see* Utrik Atoll
97 B16 **Utsira** *island* SW Norway
94 L8 **Utsjoki** ***var.*** Ohcejohka. Lappi, N Finland 69.54N 27.01E
171 Kk15 **Utsunomiya** ***var.*** Utunomiya. Tochigi, Honshū, S Japan 36.36N 139.52E
131 P13 **Utta** Respublika Kalmykiya, SW Russian Federation 46.22N 46.03E
178 Hh8 **Uttaradit** ***var.*** Utaradit. Uttaradit, N Thailand 17.37N 100.04E
158 J8 **Uttarkāshi** Uttar Pradesh, N India 30.45N 78.19E
158 K11 **Uttar Pradesh** ***prev.*** United Provinces, United Provinces of Agra and Oudh. ⬖ *state* N India
47 T5 **Utuado** C Puerto Rico 18.16N 66.43W
164 K3 **Utubulak** Xinjiang Uygur Zizhiqu, W China 46.49N 86.15E
41 N5 **Utukok River** ≈ Alaska, USA
Utunomiya *see* Utsunomiya
195 X9 **Utupua** *island* Santa Cruz Islands, E Soloman Islands
150 G9 **Utva** ≈ NW Kazakhstan
201 Y15 **Utwe** Kosrae, E Micronesia
201 X15 **Utwe Harbor** *harbor* Kosrae, E Micronesia
168 J7 **Uubulan** Arhangay, C Mongolia 48.37N 101.58E
120 G6 **Uulu** Pärnumaa, SW Estonia 58.15N 24.31E
207 N13 **Uummannaq** ***var.*** Umanak, Umanaq. Kitaa, C Greenland 70.37N 52.25W
Uummannarsuaq *see* Nunap Isua
168 E4 **Üüreg Nuur** ◎ NW Mongolia
Uusikaarlepyy *see* Nykarleby
95 J19 **Uusikaupunki** ***Swe.*** Nystad. Länsi-Suomi, W Finland 60.48N 21.25E
131 S2 **Uva** Udmurtskaya Respublika, NW Russian Federation 56.41N 52.15E
115 L14 **Uvac** ≈ W Yugoslavia
27 Q12 **Uvalde** Texas, SW USA 29.13N 99.49W
161 K25 **Uva Province** ⬖ *province* SE Sri Lanka
121 O18 **Uvaravichy** ***Rus.*** Uvarovichi. Homyel'skaya Voblasts', SE Belarus 52.36N 30.43E
56 J11 **Uvá, Río** ≈ E Colombia
Uvarovichi *see* Uvaravichy
131 N7 **Uvarovo** Tambovskaya Oblast', W Russian Federation 51.58N 42.13E
125 Ff11 **Uvat** Tyumenskaya Oblast', C Russian Federation 59.11N 68.37E
202 G12 **Uvea, Île** *island* N Wallis and Futuna
83 E21 **Uvinza** Kigoma, W Tanzania 5.04S 30.24E
81 O20 **Uvira** Sud Kivu, E Dem. Rep. Congo (Zaire) 3.24S 29.04E
168 E5 **Uvs** ⬖ *province* NW Mongolia
168 F5 **Uvs Nuur** ***var.*** Ozero Ubsu-Nur. ◎ Mongolia/Russian Federation
170 E15 **Uwa** Ehime, Shikoku, SW Japan 33.22N 132.29E
170 E15 **Uwajima** ***var.*** Uwazima. Ehime, Shikoku, SW Japan 33.13N 132.32E
82 B5 **'Uwaynāt, Jabal al** ***var.*** Jebel Uweinat. ▲ Libya/Sudan 21.51N 25.01E
Uwazima *see* Uwajima
Uweinat, Jebel *see* 'Uwaynāt, Jabal al
176 Z14 **Uwimmerah, Sungai** ≈ Irian Jaya, E Indonesia
12 H14 **Uxbridge** Ontario, S Canada 44.07N 79.07W
Uxellodunum *see* Issoudun
168 M15 **Uxin Qi** Nei Mongol Zizhiqu, N China 38.29N 108.48E
43 X12 **Uxmal, Ruinas** *ruins* Yucatán, SE Mexico 20.20N 89.46W
133 Q5 **Uy** ≈ Kazakhstan/Russian Federation
150 K15 **Uyaly** Kzylorda, S Kazakhstan 44.22N 61.16E
126 Mm7 **Uyandina** ≈ NE Russian Federation
126 I14 **Uyar** Krasnoyarskiy Kray, S Russian Federation 55.48N 94.12E
168 L10 **Üydzen** Ömnögovĭ, S Mongolia 44.08N 106.48E
Uyeda *see* Ueda
126 Hh3 **Uyedineniya, Ostrov** *island* N Russian Federation
79 V17 **Uyo** Akwa Ibom, S Nigeria 5.00N 7.57E
168 D8 **Üyönch** Hovd, W Mongolia 46.04N 92.05E
151 Q15 **Uyuk** Zhambyl, S Kazakhstan 43.46N 70.55E
147 V13 **'Uyūn** SW Oman 17.12N 53.46E
59 K20 **Uyuni** Potosí, W Bolivia 20.26S 66.48W
59 J20 **Uyuni, Salar de** *wetland* SW Bolivia
152 I9 **Uzbekistan** ***off.*** Republic of Uzbekistan. ◆ *republic* C Asia
164 D8 **Uzbel Shankou** ***Rus.*** Pereval Kyzyl-Dzhiik. *pass* China/Tajikistan 38.33N 73.46E
121 J17 **Uzda** ***Rus.*** Uzda. Minskaya Voblasts', C Belarus 53.29N 27.10E
105 N12 **Uzerche** Corrèze, C France 45.24N 1.35E
105 R14 **Uzès** Gard, S France 44.00N 4.25E
153 T10 **Uzgen** ***Kir.*** Özgön. Oshskaya Oblast', SW Kyrgyzstan 40.42N 73.17E
119 O3 **Uzh** ≈ N Ukraine
Uzhgorod *see* Uzhhorod
118 G7 **Uzhhorod** ***Rus.*** Uzhgorod; ***prev.*** Ungvár. Zakarpats'ka Oblast', W Ukraine 48.36N 22.19E
126 Hh14 **Uzhur** Krasnoyarskiy Kray, S Russian Federation 55.18N 89.36E
Uzi *see* Uji
114 K13 **Užice** ***prev.*** Titovo Užice. Serbia, W Yugoslavia 43.52N 19.51E
Uzin *see* Uzyn
130 L5 **Uzlovaya** Tul'skaya Oblast', W Russian Federation 54.01N 38.15E
110 H7 **Uznach** Sankt Gallen, NE Switzerland 47.12N 9.00E
151 U16 **Uzunagach** Almaty, SE Kazakhstan 43.07N 76.19E
142 B10 **Uzunköprü** Edirne, NW Turkey 41.15N 26.42E
120 D11 **Užventis** Kelmė, C Lithuania 55.49N 22.38E
119 P5 **Uzyn** ***Rus.*** Uzin. Kyyivs'ka Oblast', N Ukraine 49.52N 30.28E

V

Vääksy *see* Asikkala
85 H23 **Vaal** ≈ C South Africa
95 M14 **Vaala** Oulu, C Finland 64.34N 26.49E
95 N19 **Vaalimaa** Etelä-Suomi, SE Finland 60.34N 27.49E
101 M19 **Vaals** Limburg, SE Netherlands 50.46N 6.01E
95 J16 **Vaasa** ***Swe.*** Vasa; ***prev.*** Nikolainkaupunki. Vaasa, W Finland 63.07N 21.39E
100 L10 **Vaassen** Gelderland, E Netherlands 52.18N 5.58E
120 G11 **Vabalninkas** Biržai, NE Lithuania 55.59N 24.45E
Vabkent *see* Wobkent
113 J22 **Vác** ***Ger.*** Waitzen. Pest, N Hungary 47.46N 19.07E
63 I14 **Vacaria** Rio Grande do Sul, S Brazil 28.30S 50.57W
37 N7 **Vacaville** California, W USA 38.21N 121.59W
105 R15 **Vaccarès, Étang de** ◎ SE France
46 L10 **Vache, Île à** *island* SW Haiti
181 Y16 **Vacoas** W Mauritius 20.18S 57.28E
34 G10 **Vader** Washington, NW USA 46.23N 122.58W
96 D12 **Vadheim** Sogn og Fjordane, S Norway 61.12N 5.48E
124 O3 **Vadili** ***Gk.*** Vatilí. C Cyprus 35.09N 33.39E
160 D11 **Vadodara** ***prev.*** Baroda. Gujarāt, W India 22.19N 73.13E
94 M8 **Vadsø** ***Fin.*** Vesisaari. Finnmark, N Norway 70.07N 29.47E
97 L17 **Vadstena** Östergötland, S Sweden 58.25N 14.55E
110 I8 **Vaduz** ● (Liechtenstein) W Liechtenstein 47.07N 9.31E
Vág *see* Váh
129 N12 **Vaga** ≈ NW Russian Federation
96 G11 **Vågåmo** Oppland, S Norway 61.52N 9.06E
114 D12 **Vaganski Vrh** ▲ W Croatia 44.24N 15.32E
97 A19 **Vágar** ***Dan.*** Vågø *Island* Faeroe Islands 62.03N 7.19W
Vágbeszterce *see* Považská Bystrica
97 L19 **Vaggeryd** Jönköping, S Sweden 57.30N 14.10E
195 U14 **Vaghena** ***var.*** Wagina. *island* NW Solomon Islands
97 O16 **Vagnhärad** Södermanland, C Sweden 58.57N 17.31E
106 G7 **Vagos** Aveiro, N Portugal 40.33N 8.42W
Vágsellye *see* Sal'a
94 H10 **Vågsfjorden** *fjord* N Norway
96 C10 **Vågsøy** *island* S Norway
Vágújhely *see* Nové Mesto nad Váhom
113 I21 **Váh** ***Ger.*** Waag, ***Hung.*** Vág. ≈ W Slovakia
95 K16 **Vähäkyrö** Länsi-Suomi, W Finland 63.04N 22.04E
203 X11 **Vahitahi** *atoll* Îles Tuamotu, E French Polynesia
Vaidei *see* Vulcan
24 L4 **Vaiden** Mississippi, S USA 33.19N 89.42W
161 I23 **Vaigai** ≈ SE India
203 V16 **Vaihu** Easter Island, Chile, E Pacific Ocean 27.10S 109.22W
120 I6 **Väike Emajõgi** ≈ S Estonia
120 I4 **Väike-Maarja** ***Ger.*** Klein-Marien. Lääne-Virumaa, NE Estonia 59.07N 26.13E
Väike-Salatsi *see* Mazsalaca
39 R4 **Vail** Colorado, C USA 39.36N 106.20W
200 Qq15 **Vaina** Tongatapu, S Tonga 21.12S 175.10W
120 E5 **Väinameri** ***prev.*** Muhu Väin, ***Ger.*** Moon-Sund. *sea* E Baltic Sea
95 N18 **Vainikkala** Etelä-Suomi, SE Finland 60.54N 28.18E
120 D10 **Vaiņode** Liepāja, SW Latvia 56.25N 21.52E
161 H23 **Vaippār** ≈ SE India
203 W11 **Vairaatea** *atoll* Îles Tuamotu, C French Polynesia
203 R8 **Vairao** Tahiti, W French Polynesia 17.48S 149.16W
105 R14 **Vaison-la-Romaine** Vaucluse, SE France 44.15N 5.04E
202 G11 **Vaitupu** Île Uvea, E Wallis and Futuna 13.13S 176.09W
202 F7 **Vaitupu** *atoll* C Tuvalu
Vajdahunyad *see* Hunedoara
Vajdej *see* Vulcan
80 K12 **Vakaga** ⬖ *prefecture* NE Central African Republic
116 H10 **Vakarel** Sofiya, W Bulgaria 42.34N 23.43E
Vakav *see* Ustrem
143 O11 **Vakfıkebir** Trabzon, NE Turkey 41.03N 39.19E
126 H11 **Vakh** ≈ C Russian Federation
Vakhon, Qatorkŭhi *see* Nicholas Range
153 P14 **Vakhsh** SW Tajikistan 37.46N 68.48E
153 Q12 **Vakhsh** ≈ SW Tajikistan
131 P1 **Vakhtan** Nizhegorodskaya Oblast', W Russian Federation 58.00N 46.43E
96 C13 **Vaksdal** Hordaland, S Norway 60.28N 5.45E
129 O8 **Vashka** ≈ NW Russian Federation
195 O15 **Vakuta Island** *island* Kiriwina Islands, SE PNG
Valachia *see* Wallachia
110 D11 **Valais** ***Ger.*** Wallis. ⬖ *canton* SW Switzerland
115 M21 **Valamarës, Mali i** ▲ SE Albania 40.48N 20.31E
131 S2 **Valamaz** Udmurtskaya Respublika, NW Russian Federation 57.36N 52.07E
115 Q19 **Valandovo** SE FYR Macedonia 41.20N 22.33E
113 I18 **Valašské Meziříčí** ***Ger.*** Wallachisch-Meseritsch, ***Pol.*** Wałeckie Międzyrzecze. Zlínský Kraj, E Czech Republic 49.28N 17.57E
117 I17 **Valáxa** *island* Vóreioi Sporádes, Greece, Aegean Sea
97 K16 **Vålberg** Värmland, C Sweden 59.24N 13.12E
118 H12 **Vâlcea** ***prev.*** Vîlcea. ⬖ *county* SW Romania
65 J16 **Valcheta** Río Negro, E Argentina 40.42S 66.07W
13 P12 **Valcourt** Quebec, SE Canada 45.28N 72.18W
Valdai Hills *see* Valdayskaya Vozvyshennost'
106 M3 **Valdavia** ≈ N Spain
128 I15 **Valday** Novgorodskaya Oblast', W Russian Federation 57.56N 33.19E
128 I15 **Valdayskaya Vozvyshennost'** ***var.*** Valdai Hills. *hill range* W Russian Federation
106 L9 **Valdecañas, Embalse de** ⊠ W Spain
120 E8 **Valdemārpils** ***Ger.*** Sassmacken. Talsi, NW Latvia 57.23N 22.36E
97 N18 **Valdemarsvik** Östergötland, S Sweden 58.13N 16.34E
107 N8 **Valdemoro** Madrid, C Spain 40.12N 3.40W
107 O11 **Valdepeñas** Castilla-La Mancha, C Spain 38.46N 3.24W

◆ Country
● Country Capital
◇ Dependent Territory
○ Dependent Territory Capital
⬖ Administrative Region
✈ International Airport
▲ Mountain
▲▲ Mountain Range
Volcano
≈ River
◎ Lake
⊠ Reservoir

VALDERADUEY – VENEZUELA, GULF OF

106 L5 **Valderaduey** ≈ NE Spain
106 L5 **Valderas** Castilla-León, N Spain 42.04N 5.27W
107 T7 **Valderrobres** *var.* Vall-de-roures. Aragón, NE Spain 40.52N 0.07E
65 K17 **Valdés, Península** *peninsula* SE Argentina
41 S11 **Valdez** Alaska, USA 61.07N 146.21W
58 C5 **Valdéz** *var.* Limones. Esmeraldas, NW Ecuador 1.17N 78.56W
Valdia *see* Weldiya
105 U11 **Val d'Isère** Savoie, E France 45.23N 7.03E
65 G15 **Valdivia** Los Lagos, C Chile 39.49S 73.12W
Valdivia Bank *see* Valdivia Seamount
67 P17 **Valdivia Seamount** *var.* Valdivia Bank. *undersea feature* E Atlantic Ocean 26.15S 6.25E
105 N4 **Val-d'Oise** ◐ *department* N France
12 J8 **Val-d'Or** Quebec, SE Canada 48.05N 77.42W
25 U8 **Valdosta** Georgia, SE USA 30.49N 83.16W
96 G13 **Valdres** *physical region* S Norway
34 L13 **Vale** Oregon, NW USA 43.58N 117.14W
118 F9 **Valea lui Mihai** ***Hung.*** Érmihályfalva. Bihor, NW Romania 47.31N 22.08E
9 N15 **Valemount** British Columbia, SW Canada 52.46N 119.17W
61 O17 **Valença** Bahia, E Brazil 13.22S 39.06W
106 F4 **Valença do Minho** Viana do Castelo, N Portugal 42.01N 8.37W
61 N14 **Valença do Piauí** Piauí, E Brazil 6.25S 41.46W
105 N8 **Valençay** Indre, C France 47.10N 1.31E
105 R13 **Valence** ***anc.*** Valentia, Valentia Julia, Ventia. Drôme, E France 44.55N 4.54E
107 S10 **Valencia** País Valenciano, E Spain 39.28N 0.24W
56 K5 **Valencia** Carabobo, N Venezuela 10.11N 68.02W
107 R10 **Valencia** ***Cat.*** València. ◐ *province* País Valenciano, E Spain
107 S10 **Valencia** ✈ Valencia, E Spain
València/Valencia *see* País Valenciano
106 I10 **Valencia de Alcántara** Extremadura, W Spain 39.25N 7.13W
106 L4 **Valencia de Don Juan** Castilla-León, N Spain 42.16N 5.31W
107 U9 **Valencia, Golfo de** *var.* Gulf of Valencia. *gulf* E Spain
Valencia, Gulf of *see* Valencia, Golfo de
99 A21 **Valencia Island** ***Ir.*** Dairbhre. *island* SW Ireland
105 P2 **Valenciennes** Nord, N France 50.21N 3.31E
118 K13 **Vălenii de Munte** Prahova, SE Romania 45.10N 26.01E
Valentia *see* Valence, France
Valentia *see* País Valenciano
Valentia Julia *see* Valence
105 T8 **Valentigney** Doubs, E France 47.27N 6.49E
30 M12 **Valentine** Nebraska, C USA 42.52N 100.31W
26 J10 **Valentine** Texas, SW USA 30.35N 104.30W
Valentine State *see* Oregon
108 C8 **Valenza** Piemonte, NW Italy 45.01N 8.37E
96 I13 **Våler** Hedmark, S Norway 60.39N 11.52E
56 I6 **Valera** Trujillo, NW Venezuela 9.21N 70.37W
199 K13 **Valerie Guyot** *undersea feature* S Pacific Ocean 33.00S 164.00W
Valetta *see* Valletta
120 I7 **Valga** ***Ger.*** Walk, ***Latv.*** Valka. Valgamaa, S Estonia 57.48N 26.04E
120 I7 **Valgamaa** ***off.*** Valga Maakond. ◐ *province* S Estonia
45 Q15 **Valiente, Península** *peninsula* NW Panama
105 X16 **Valinco, Golfe de** *gulf* Corse, France, C Mediterranean Sea
114 L12 **Valjevo** Serbia, W Yugoslavia 44.16N 19.54E
Valjok *see* Válljohka
120 I7 **Valka** ***Ger.*** Walk. Valka, N Latvia 57.48N 26.01E
Valka *see* Valga
95 L18 **Valkeakoski** Länsi-Suomi, W Finland 61.16N 24.04E
95 M19 **Valkeala** Etelä-Suomi, S Finland 60.55N 26.49E
101 L18 **Valkenburg** Limburg, SE Netherlands 50.52N 5.46E
101 K15 **Valkenswaard** Noord-Brabant, S Netherlands 51.21N 5.28E
121 G15 **Valkininkai** Varėna, S Lithuania 54.22N 24.51E
119 U5 **Valky** Kharkivs'ka Oblast', E Ukraine 49.51N 35.40E
43 Y12 **Valladolid** Yucatán, SE Mexico 20.39N 88.13W
106 M5 **Valladolid** Castilla-León, NW Spain 41.39N 4.45W
106 L5 **Valladolid** ◐ *province* Castilla-León, N Spain
105 U15 **Vallauris** Alpes-Maritimes, SE France 43.34N 7.03E
Vall-de-roures *see* Valderrobres
107 S9 **Vall d'Uxó** País Valenciano, E Spain 39.49N 0.15W
97 E16 **Valle** Aust-Agder, S Norway 59.13N 7.33E
107 N2 **Valle** Cantabria, N Spain 43.14N 4.16W
44 H8 **Valle** ◐ *department* S Honduras
107 N8 **Vallecas** Madrid, C Spain 40.22N 3.37W
39 Q8 **Vallecito Reservoir** ⊠ Colorado, C USA
108 A7 **Valle d'Aosta** ◐ *region* NW Italy
43 O14 **Valle de Bravo** México, S Mexico 19.19N 100.08W
57 N5 **Valle de Guanape** Anzoátegui, N Venezuela 9.49N 65.34W
56 M6 **Valle de La Pascua** Guárico, N Venezuela 09.15N 66.00W
56 B11 **Valle del Cauca** ***off.*** Departamento del Valle del Cauca. ◐ *province* W Colombia
43 N13 **Valle de Santiago** Guanajuato, C Mexico 20.21N 101.13W
42 J7 **Valle de Zaragoza** Chihuahua, N Mexico 27.25N 105.50W
56 G5 **Valledupar** Cesar, N Colombia 10.31N 73.16W
78 G10 **Vallée de Ferlo** ≈ NW Senegal
59 M19 **Vallegrande** Santa Cruz, C Bolivia 18.30S 64.06W
43 P8 **Valle Hermoso** Tamaulipas, C Mexico 25.39N 97.49W
37 N8 **Vallejo** California, W USA 38.07N 122.16W
64 G8 **Vallenar** Atacama, N Chile 28.35S 70.44W
97 O15 **Vallentuna** Stockholm, C Sweden 59.31N 18.04E
123 Ll12 **Valletta** ***prev.*** Valetta. ● (Malta) E Malta 35.54N 14.30E
29 N6 **Valley Center** Kansas, C USA 37.49N 97.22W
31 Q5 **Valley City** North Dakota, N USA 46.57N 97.58W
34 I15 **Valley Falls** Oregon, NW USA 42.28N 120.16W
Valleyfield *see* Salaberry-de-Valleyfield
23 S4 **Valley Head** West Virginia, NE USA 38.33N 80.01W
27 T8 **Valley Mills** Texas, SW USA 31.36N 97.27W
77 W10 **Valley of the Kings** *ancient monument* E Egypt 25.41N 32.30E
31 R11 **Valley Springs** South Dakota, N USA 43.34N 96.28W
22 K5 **Valley Station** Kentucky, S USA 38.06N 85.52W
9 O13 **Valleyview** Alberta, W Canada 55.01N 117.16W
27 T5 **Valley View** Texas, SW USA 33.27N 97.08W
63 C21 **Vallimanca, Arroyo** ≈ E Argentina
94 L9 **Válljohka** ***var.*** Valjok Finnmark, N Norway 69.39N 25.52E
109 M19 **Vallo della Lucania** Campania, S Italy 40.13N 15.15E
110 B9 **Vallorbe** Vaud, W Switzerland 46.43N 6.21E
107 V6 **Valls** Cataluña, NE Spain 41.18N 1.15E
96 N11 **Vallsta** Gävleborg, C Sweden 61.30N 16.25E
96 N12 **Vallvik** Gävleborg, C Sweden 61.10N 17.15E
9 T17 **Val Marie** Saskatchewan, S Canada 49.15N 107.43W
120 H7 **Valmiera** ***Est.*** Volmari, ***Ger.*** Wolmar. Valmiera, N Latvia 57.33N 25.26E
107 N3 **Valnera** ▲ N Spain 43.08N 3.39W
104 J3 **Valognes** Manche, N France 49.31N 1.28W
Valona *see* Vlorë
Valona Bay *see* Vlorës, Gjiri i
106 G6 **Valongo** ***var.*** Valongo de Gaia. Porto, N Portugal 41.10N 8.30W
Valongo de Gaia *see* Valongo
106 M5 **Valoria la Buena** Castilla-León, N Spain 41.48N 4.33W
121 J15 **Valozhyn** ***Pol.*** Wołożyn, ***Rus.*** Volozhin. Minskaya Voblasts', C Belarus 54.07N 26.31E
106 I5 **Valpaços** Vila Real, N Portugal 41.36N 7.16W
25 P8 **Valparaiso** Florida, SE USA 30.30N 86.28W
33 N11 **Valparaiso** Indiana, N USA 41.28N 87.04W
64 G11 **Valparaíso** Valparaíso, C Chile 33.04S 71.18W
42 L11 **Valparaíso** Zacatecas, C Mexico 22.49N 103.28W
64 G11 **Valparaíso** ***off.*** Región de Valparaíso. ◐ *region* C Chile
Valpo *see* Valpovo
114 I9 **Valpovo** ***Hung.*** Valpo. Osijek-Baranja, E Croatia 45.40N 18.25E
105 R14 **Valréas** Vaucluse, SE France 44.22N 5.00E
Vals *see* Vals-Platz
160 D12 **Valsād** ***prev.*** Bulsar. Gujarāt, W India 20.40N 72.55E
Valsbaai *see* False Bay
176 Uu10 **Valse Pisang, Kepulauan** *island group* E Indonesia
110 H9 **Vals-Platz** ***var.*** Vals. Graubünden, S Switzerland 46.39N 9.09E
176 Xx16 **Vals, Tanjung** *headland* Irian Jaya, SE Indonesia 8.25S 137.34E
95 N15 **Valtimo** Itä-Suomi, E Finland 63.39N 28.49E
117 D17 **Váltou** ▲▲ C Greece
131 O12 **Valuyevka** Rostovskaya Oblast', SW Russian Federation 46.48N 43.49E
130 K9 **Valuyki** Belgorodskaya Oblast', W Russian Federation 50.11N 38.07E
38 L2 **Val Verda** Utah, W USA 40.51N 111.53W
66 N12 **Valverde** Hierro, Islas Canarias, Spain, NE Atlantic Ocean 27.48N 17.55W
106 I13 **Valverde del Camino** Andalucía, S Spain 37.34N 6.45W
97 G23 **Vamdrup** Vejle, C Denmark 55.25N 9.18E
96 L12 **Våmhus** Dalarna, C Sweden 61.07N 14.30E
95 K18 **Vammala** Länsi-Suomi, W Finland 61.19N 22.55E
Vámosudvarhely *see* Odorheiu Secuiesc
143 S14 **Van** Van, E Turkey 38.30N 43.22E
27 V7 **Van** Texas, SW USA 32.31N 95.38W
143 T14 **Van** ◐ *province* E Turkey
143 T11 **Vanadzor** ***prev.*** Kirovakan. N Armenia 40.49N 44.28E
27 U5 **Van Alstyne** Texas, SW USA 33.25N 96.34W
35 W10 **Vananda** Montana, NW USA 46.22N 106.58W
118 I11 **Vânători** ***Hung.*** Héjjasfalva; ***prev.*** Vînători. Mureş, C Romania 46.13N 24.56E
203 W12 **Vanavana** *atoll* Îles Tuamotu, SE French Polynesia
Vana-Vändra *see* Vändra
126 J12 **Vanavara** Evenkiyskiy Avtonomnyy Okrug, C Russian Federation 60.19N 102.19E
13 Q8 **Van Bruyssel** Quebec, SE Canada 47.56N 72.08W
29 R10 **Van Buren** Arkansas, C USA 35.26N 94.21W
21 S1 **Van Buren** Maine, NE USA 47.07N 67.57W
29 W7 **Van Buren** Missouri, C USA 37.00N 91.00W
21 T5 **Vanceboro** Maine, NE USA 45.31N 67.25W
23 W10 **Vanceboro** North Carolina, SE USA 35.16N 77.06W
23 O4 **Vanceburg** Kentucky, S USA 38.32N 83.18W
Vanch *see* Vanj
8 L17 **Vancouver** British Columbia, SW Canada 49.13N 123.06W
34 G11 **Vancouver** Washington, NW USA 45.38N 122.39W
8 L17 **Vancouver** ✈ British Columbia, SW Canada 49.03N 123.00W
8 K16 **Vancouver Island** *island* British Columbia, SW Canada
Vanda *see* Vantaa
176 Xx11 **Van Daalen** ≈ Irian Jaya, E Indonesia
32 L15 **Vandalia** Illinois, N USA 38.57N 89.05W
29 V3 **Vandalia** Missouri, C USA 39.18N 91.29W
33 R13 **Vandalia** Ohio, N USA 39.53N 84.12W
27 U13 **Vanderbilt** Texas, SW USA 28.45N 96.37W
33 Q10 **Vandercook Lake** Michigan, N USA 42.11N 84.23W
8 L14 **Vanderhoof** British Columbia, SW Canada 53.54N 124.00W
20 K8 **Vanderwhacker Mountain** ▲ New York, NE USA 43.54N 74.06W
189 P1 **Van Diemen Gulf** *gulf* Northern Territory, N Australia
Van Diemen's Land *see* Tasmania
120 H5 **Vändra** ***Ger.*** Fennern; ***prev.*** Vana-Vändra. Pärnumaa, SW Estonia 58.40N 25.01E
Vandsburg *see* Więcbork
36 L4 **Van Duzen River** ≈ California, W USA
120 F13 **Vandžiogala** Kaunas, C Lithuania 55.07N 23.55E
43 N10 **Vanegas** San Luis Potosí, C Mexico 23.53N 100.55W
Vaner, Lake *see* Vänern
97 K17 **Vänern** ***Eng.*** Lake Vaner; ***prev.*** Lake Vener. ◎ S Sweden
97 J18 **Vänersborg** Västra Götaland, S Sweden 58.16N 12.22E
96 F12 **Vang** Oppland, S Norway 61.07N 8.34E
180 I7 **Vangaindrano** Fianarantsoa, SE Madagascar 23.21S 47.34E
143 S14 **Van Gölü** ***Eng.*** Lake Van; ***anc.*** Thospitis. *salt lake* E Turkey
195 V15 **Vangunu** *island* New Georgia Islands, NW Solomon Islands
26 J9 **Van Horn** Texas, SW USA 31.03N 104.51W
195 X9 **Vanikolo** ***var.*** Vanikoro. *island* Santa Cruz Islands, E Solomon Islands
Vanikoro *see* Vanikolo
194 E9 **Vanimo** Sandaun, NW PNG 2.43S 141.22E
127 O15 **Vanino** Khabarovskiy Kray, SE Russian Federation 49.10N 140.18E
161 G19 **Vānīvilāsa Sāgara** ◎ SW India
153 S13 **Vanj** ***Rus.*** Vanch. S Tajikistan 38.22N 71.27E
118 G14 **Vânju Mare** ***prev.*** Vînju Mare. Mehedinţi, SW Romania 44.25N 22.52E
127 P3 **Vankarem** Chukotskiy Avtonomnyy Okrug, NE Russian Federation 67.48N 176.11W
13 N12 **Vankleek Hill** Ontario, SE Canada 45.32N 74.39W
Van, Lake *see* Van Gölü
95 I16 **Vännäs** Västerbotten, N Sweden 63.54N 19.43E
95 I15 **Vännäsby** Västerbotten, N Sweden 63.55N 19.53E
104 H7 **Vannes** ***anc.*** Dariorigum. Morbihan, NW France 47.40N 2.45W
94 I8 **Vannøya** *island* N Norway
105 T12 **Vanoise, Massif de la** ▲▲ E France
176 Xx10 **Van Rees, Pegunungan** ▲▲ Irian Jaya, E Indonesia
85 E24 **Vanrhynsdorp** Western Cape, SW South Africa 31.33S 18.42E
23 P7 **Vansant** Virginia, NE USA 37.13N 82.03W
96 L13 **Vansbro** Dalarna, C Sweden 60.31N 14.15E
97 D18 **Vanse** Vest-Agder, S Norway 58.04N 6.40E
15 M4 **Vansittart Island** *island* Nunavut, NE Canada
95 M20 **Vantaa** ***Swe.*** Vanda. Etelä-Suomi, S Finland 60.18N 25.01E
95 L19 **Vantaa** ✈ (Helsinki) Etelä-Suomi, S Finland 60.18N 25.01E
34 J9 **Vantage** Washington, NW USA 46.55N 119.55W
197 K14 **Vanua Balavu** ***prev.*** Vanua Mbalavu. *island* Lau Group, E Fiji
197 C10 **Vanua Lava** *island* Banks Islands, N Vanuatu
197 J12 **Vanua Levu** *island* N Fiji
197 I12 **Vanua Levu Barrier Reef** *reef* C Fiji
Vanua Mbalavu *see* Vanua Balavu
197 B10 **Vanuatu** ***off.*** Republic of Vanuatu; ***prev.*** New Hebrides. ◆ *republic* SW Pacific Ocean
183 P8 **Vanuatu** *island group* SW Pacific Ocean
197 K15 **Vanua Vatu** *island* Lau Group, E Fiji
33 Q12 **Van Wert** Ohio, N USA 40.52N 84.34W
197 K7 **Vao** Province Sud, S New Caledonia 22.40S 167.29E
Vapincum *see* Gap
119 N7 **Vapnyarka** Vinnyts'ka Oblast', C Ukraine 48.32N 28.44E
105 T15 **Var** ◐ *department* SE France
105 U14 **Var** ≈ SE France
97 J18 **Vara** Västra Götaland, S Sweden 58.16N 12.57E
Varadinska Županija *see* Varaždin
120 J10 **Varakļani** Madona, C Latvia 56.36N 26.40E
108 C7 **Varallo** Piemonte, NE Italy 45.51N 8.16E
149 O5 **Varāmīn** ***var.*** Veramin. Tehrān, N Iran 35.19N 51.40E
159 N14 **Vārānasi** ***prev.*** Banaras, Benares, ***hist.*** Kasi. Uttar Pradesh, N India 25.20N 83.00E
129 T3 **Varandey** Nenetskiy Avtonomnyy Okrug, NW Russian Federation 68.48N 57.54E
94 M8 **Varangerbotn** Finnmark, N Norway 70.09N 28.28E
94 M8 **Varangerfjorden** *fjord* N Norway
94 M8 **Varangerhalvøya** *peninsula* N Norway
Varannó *see* Vranov nad Topl'ou
109 M15 **Varano, Lago di** ◎ SE Italy
120 J13 **Varapayeva** ***Rus.*** Voropayevo. Vitsyebskaya Voblasts', NW Belarus 55.09N 27.13E
Varasd *see* Varaždin
114 E7 **Varaždin** ***Ger.*** Warasdin, ***Hung.*** Varasd. Varaždin, N Croatia 46.18N 16.20E
114 E7 **Varaždin** ***off.*** Varadinska Županija. ◐ *province* N Croatia
108 C10 **Varazze** Liguria, NW Italy 44.21N 8.35E
97 J20 **Varberg** Halland, S Sweden 57.06N 12.15E
Vardak *see* Wardag
115 Q19 **Vardar** ***Gk.*** Axiós. ≈ FYR Macedonia/Greece ***see also*** Axiós
97 F23 **Varde** Ribe, W Denmark 55.37N 8.31E
143 V12 **Vardenis** E Armenia 40.11N 45.43E
94 N8 **Vardø** ***Fin.*** Vuoreija. Finnmark, N Norway 70.22N 31.04E
117 E18 **Vardoúsia** ▲▲ C Greece
Vareia *see* Logroño
102 G10 **Varel** Niedersachsen, NW Germany 53.24N 8.07E
121 G15 **Varėna** ***Pol.*** Orany. Varėna, S Lithuania 54.13N 24.35E
13 O12 **Varennes** Quebec, SE Canada 45.42N 73.25W
105 P10 **Varennes-sur-Allier** Allier, C France 46.17N 3.24E
114 I12 **Vareš** Federacija Bosna I Hercegovina, E Bosnia and Herzegovina 44.12N 18.19E
108 D7 **Varese** Lombardia, N Italy 45.49N 8.49E
118 J12 **Vârful Moldoveanu** ***var.*** Moldoveanul; ***prev.*** Vîrful Moldoveanu. ▲ C Romania 45.35N 24.48E
Varganzi *see* Warganza
97 J18 **Vårgårda** Västra Götaland, S Sweden 58.00N 12.49E
125 F12 **Vargashi** Kurganskaya Oblast', C Russian Federation 55.22N 65.39E
97 J18 **Vargön** Västra Götaland, S Sweden 58.21N 12.22E
97 C17 **Varhaug** Rogaland, S Norway 58.37N 5.39E
95 N17 **Varkaus** Itä-Suomi, C Finland 62.19N 27.49E
94 J2 **Varmahlidh** Nordhurland Vestra, N Iceland 65.32N 19.33W
97 J15 **Värmland** ◐ *county* C Sweden
97 K16 **Värmlandsnäs** *peninsula* S Sweden
116 N8 **Varna** ***prev.*** Stalin, ***anc.*** Odessus. Varna, E Bulgaria 43.13N 27.55E
116 N8 **Varna** ✈ Varna, E Bulgaria 43.16N 27.52E
116 N8 **Varna** ◐ *province* E Bulgaria
97 L20 **Värnamo** Jönköping, S Sweden 57.10N 14.03E
116 N8 **Varnenski Zaliv** ***prev.*** Stalinski Zaliv. *bay* E Bulgaria
116 N8 **Varnensko Ezero** *estuary* E Bulgaria
120 D11 **Varniai** Telšiai, W Lithuania 55.45N 22.22E
Varnoús *see* Baba
113 D14 **Varnsdorf** ***Ger.*** Warnsdorf. Ústecký Kraj, N Czech Republic 50.55N 14.34E
113 I23 **Várpalota** Veszprém, W Hungary 47.13N 18.07E
Varshava *see* Warszawa
120 K6 **Värska** Põlvamaa, SE Estonia 57.58N 27.37E
100 N12 **Varsseveld** Gelderland, E Netherlands 51.55N 6.28E
117 D19 **Vartholomió** ***prev.*** Vartholomión. Dytikí Ellás, S Greece 37.52N 21.12E
Vartholomión *see* Vartholomió
143 Q14 **Varto** Muş, E Turkey 39.10N 41.28E
97 K18 **Vartofta** Västra Götaland, S Sweden 58.06N 13.40E
95 O17 **Värtsilä** Itä-Suomi, E Finland 62.10N 30.35E
Värtsilä *see* Vyartsilya
119 R4 **Varva** Chernihivs'ka Oblast', NE Ukraine 50.31N 32.43E
61 H18 **Várzea Grande** Mato Grosso, SW Brazil 15.39S 56.07W
108 D9 **Varzi** Lombardia, N Italy 44.51N 9.13E
Varzimanor Ayni *see* Ayní
128 K5 **Varzuga** ≈ NW Russian Federation
105 P8 **Varzy** Nièvre, C France 47.22N 3.22E
113 G23 **Vas** ***off.*** Vas Megye. ◐ *county* W Hungary
Vasa *see* Vaasa
202 A9 **Vasafua** *island* Funafuti Atoll, C Tuvalu
113 O21 **Vásárosnamény** Szabolcs-Szatmár-Bereg, E Hungary 48.07N 22.19E
106 H13 **Vascão, Ribeira de** ≈ S Portugal
118 G10 **Vaşcău** ***Hung.*** Vaskoh. Bihor, NE Romania 46.26N 22.30E
Vascongadas, Provincias *see* País Vasco
Vashess Bay *see* Vaskess Bay
Vāsht *see* Khāsh
Vasilevichi *see* Vasilyevichy
117 G14 **Vasiliká** Kentrikí Makedonía, NE Greece 40.28N 23.07E
117 C18 **Vasilikí** Lefkáda, Iónioi Nísoi, Greece, C Mediterranean Sea 38.36N 20.37E
117 K25 **Vasilikí** Kríti, Greece, E Mediterranean Sea 35.04N 25.49E
121 G16 **Vasilishki** ***Pol.*** Wasiliszki, ***Rus.*** Vasilishki. Hrodzyenskaya Voblasts', W Belarus 53.46N 24.51E
Vasil Kolarov *see* Pamporovo
Vasil'kov *see* Vasyl'kiv
121 N19 **Vasilyevichy** ***Rus.*** Vasilevichi. Homyel'skaya Voblasts', SE Belarus 52.15N 29.49E
203 Y3 **Vaskess Bay** ***var.*** Vashess Bay. *bay* Kiritimati, E Kiribati
Vaskoh *see* Vaşcău
Vaskohsziklás *see* Ştei
118 M10 **Vaslui** Vaslui, C Romania 46.38N 27.44E
118 L11 **Vaslui** ◐ *county* NE Romania
33 R8 **Vassar** Michigan, N USA 43.22N 83.34W
97 E15 **Vassdalseggi** ▲ S Norway 59.47N 7.07E
62 P9 **Vassouras** Rio de Janeiro, SE Brazil 22.24S 43.38W
94 H11 **Vastenjaure** ◎ N Sweden
97 N15 **Västerås** Västmanland, C Sweden 59.37N 16.33E
95 G15 **Västerbotten** ◐ *county* N Sweden
96 K12 **Västerdalälven** ≈ C Sweden
97 O16 **Västerhaninge** Stockholm, C Sweden 59.07N 18.06E
96 M10 **Västernorrland** ◐ *county* C Sweden
97 N19 **Västervik** Kalmar, S Sweden 57.44N 16.40E
97 M15 **Västmanand** ◐ *county* C Sweden
109 L15 **Vasto** ***anc.*** Histonium. Abruzzo, C Italy 42.07N 14.40E
97 J19 **Västra Götaland** ◐ *county* S Sweden
97 J16 **Västra Silen** ◎ S Sweden
113 G23 **Vasvár** ***Ger.*** Eisenburg. Vas, W Hungary 47.04N 16.46E
119 U9 **Vasylivka** Zaporiz'ka Oblast', SE Ukraine 47.26N 35.18E
119 O5 **Vasyl'kiv** ***Rus.*** Vasil'kov. Kyyivs'ka Oblast', N Ukraine 50.10N 30.18E
126 Gg12 **Vasyugan** ≈ C Russian Federation
105 N8 **Vatan** Indre, C France 47.06N 1.49E
Vaté *see* Efate
109 G15 **Vatican City** ***off.*** Vatican City State. ◆ *papal state* S Europe
109 M22 **Vaticano, Capo** *headland* S Italy 38.37N 15.49E
Vatilí *see* Vadili
94 K3 **Vatnajökull** *glacier* SE Iceland
97 P15 **Vätö** Stockholm, C Sweden 59.48N 18.55E
197 L16 **Vatoa** *island* Lau Group, SE Fiji
180 J5 **Vatomandry** Toamasina, E Madagascar 19.19S 48.58E
118 J9 **Vatra Dornei** ***Ger.*** Dorna Watra. Suceava, NE Romania 47.19N 25.21E
118 J9 **Vatra Moldoviţei** Suceava, NE Romania 47.37N 25.36E
Vatter, Lake *see* Vättern
97 L18 **Vättern** ***Eng.*** Lake Vatter; ***prev.*** Lake Vetter. ◎ S Sweden
197 H14 **Vatukoula** Viti Levu, W Fiji 17.33S 105.49E
197 H15 **Vatulele** *island* SW Fiji
119 P7 **Vatutine** Cherkas'ka Oblast', C Ukraine 49.01N 31.04E
197 J14 **Vatu Vara** *island* Lau Group, E Fiji
105 R14 **Vaucluse** ◐ *department* SE France
105 S5 **Vaucouleurs** Meuse, NE France 48.37N 5.38E
110 B9 **Vaud** ***Ger.*** Waadt. ◐ *canton* SW Switzerland
13 N12 **Vaudreuil** Quebec, SE Canada 45.24N 74.01W
39 T12 **Vaughn** New Mexico, SW USA 34.36N 105.12W
56 I14 **Vaupés** ***off.*** Comisaría del Vaupés. ◐ *province* SE Colombia
56 J13 **Vaupés, Río** ***var.*** Rio Uaupés. ≈ Brazil/Colombia ***see also*** Uaupés, Rio
105 Q15 **Vauvert** Gard, S France 43.42N 4.16E
9 R17 **Vauxhall** Alberta, SW Canada 50.04N 112.09W
101 K23 **Vaux-sur-Sûre** Luxembourg, SE Belgium 49.55N 5.34E
180 J4 **Vavatenina** Toamasina, E Madagascar 17.25S 49.10E
200 Ss12 **Vava'u Group** *island group* N Tonga
78 M16 **Vavoua** W Ivory Coast 7.22N 6.28W
131 S2 **Vavozh** Udmurtskaya Respublika, NW Russian Federation 56.48N 51.53E
161 K23 **Vavuniya** Northern Province, N Sri Lanka 8.45N 80.30E
121 G17 **Vawkavysk** ***Pol.*** Wołkowysk, ***Rus.*** Volkovysk. Hrodzyenskaya Voblasts', W Belarus 53.10N 24.28E
121 F17 **Vawkavyskaye Wzvyshsha** ***Rus.*** Volkovyskiye Vysoty. *hill range* W Belarus
97 P15 **Vaxholm** Stockholm, C Sweden 59.43N 18.57E
97 L21 **Växjö** ***var.*** Vexiö. Kronoberg, S Sweden 56.52N 14.49E
129 T1 **Vaygach, Ostrov** *island* NW Russian Federation
143 V13 **Vayk'** ***prev.*** Azizbekov. SE Armenia 39.41N 45.28E
129 P8 **Vazhgort** ***prev.*** Chasovo. Respublika Komi, NW Russian Federation 64.06N 46.44E
47 V10 **V.C.Bird** ✈ (St John's) Antigua, Antigua and Barbuda 17.07N 61.49W
97 C16 **Veavågen** Rogaland, S Norway 59.18N 5.13E
31 Q7 **Veblen** South Dakota, N USA 45.50N 97.17W
100 N9 **Vecht** ***Ger.*** Vechte. ≈ Germany/Netherlands ***see also*** Vechte
102 G12 **Vechta** Niedersachsen, NW Germany 52.44N 8.16E
102 E12 **Vechte** ***Dut.*** Vecht. ≈ Germany/Netherlands ***see also*** Vecht
120 I8 **Vecpiebalga** Cēsis, C Latvia 57.03N 25.47E
120 G9 **Vecumnieki** Bauska, C Latvia 56.36N 24.30E
Vedāvati *see* Hagari
97 J20 **Veddige** Halland, S Sweden 57.16N 12.19E
118 J15 **Vedea** ≈ S Romania
131 P16 **Vedeno** Chechenskaya Respublika, SW Russian Federation 42.57N 46.02E
197 H14 **Ve Drala Reef** *reef* N Fiji
100 O6 **Veendam** Groningen, NE Netherlands 53.04N 6.52E
100 K12 **Veenendaal** Utrecht, C Netherlands 52.03N 5.33E
101 E14 **Veere** Zeeland, SW Netherlands 51.33N 3.40E
26 M2 **Vega** Texas, SW USA 35.14N 102.25W
94 E13 **Vega** *island* C Norway
47 T5 **Vega Baja** C Puerto Rico 18.27N 66.23W
40 D17 **Vega Point** *headland* Kiska Island, Alaska, USA 51.49N 105.19E
97 F17 **Vegår** ◎ S Norway
101 K14 **Veghel** Noord-Brabant, S Netherlands 51.37N 5.33E
Veglia *see* Krk
116 E13 **Vegorítis, Límni** ◎ N Greece
9 Q14 **Vegreville** Alberta, SW Canada 53.30N 112.01W
97 K21 **Veinge** Halland, S Sweden 56.33N 13.04E
63 B21 **Veinticinco de Mayo** ***var.*** 25 de Mayo. Buenos Aires, E Argentina 35.27S 60.11W
65 I14 **Veinticinco de Mayo** La Pampa, C Argentina 37.45S 67.40W
121 F15 **Veisiejai** Lazdijai, S Lithuania 54.06N 23.41E
97 F23 **Vejen** Ribe, W Denmark 55.28N 9.09E
106 K16 **Vejer de la Frontera** Andalucía, S Spain 36.15N 5.58W
97 G23 **Vejle** Vejle, C Denmark 55.43N 9.33E
97 F23 **Vejle** ***off.*** Vejle Amt. ◐ *county* C Denmark
116 M7 **Vekilski** Shumen, NE Bulgaria 43.33N 27.19E
56 G3 **Vela, Cabo de la** *headland* NE Colombia 12.13N 72.13W
Vela Goa *see* Goa
115 F15 **Vela Luka** Dubrovnik-Neretva, S Croatia 42.57N 16.43E
63 G19 **Velázquez** Rocha, E Uruguay 34.04S 54.16W
103 E15 **Velbert** Nordrhein-Westfalen, W Germany 51.19N 7.03E
111 S9 **Velden** Kärnten, S Austria 46.37N 13.59E
Veldes *see* Bled
101 K15 **Veldhoven** Noord-Brabant, S Netherlands 51.24N 5.24E
114 C11 **Velebit** ▲▲ C Croatia
116 N11 **Veleka** ≈ SE Bulgaria
111 V10 **Velenje** ***Ger.*** Wöllan. N Slovenia 46.21N 15.07E
202 E12 **Vele, Pointe** *headland* Île Futuna, S Wallis and Futuna
115 O18 **Veles** ***Turk.*** Köprülü. C FYR Macedonia 41.43N 21.49E
115 M20 **Velešta** SW FYR Macedonia 41.16N 20.37E
117 F16 **Velestíno** ***prev.*** Velestínon. Thessalía, C Greece 39.22N 22.43E
Velestínon *see* Velestíno
Velevshchina *see* Vyelyewshchyna
56 F9 **Vélez** Santander, C Colombia 6.01N 73.37W
107 Q13 **Vélez Blanco** Andalucía, S Spain 37.43N 2.07W
106 M17 **Vélez de la Gomera, Peñon de** *island group* S Spain
107 N15 **Vélez-Málaga** Andalucía, S Spain 36.46N 4.06W
107 Q13 **Vélez Rubio** Andalucía, S Spain 37.39N 2.04W
Velha Goa *see* Goa
Velho *see* Porto Velho
114 E8 **Velika Gorica** Zagreb, N Croatia 45.43N 16.03E
114 C9 **Velika Kapela** ▲▲ NW Croatia
Velika Kikinda *see* Kikinda
114 D10 **Velika Kladuša** Federacija Bosna I Hercegovina, NW Bosnia and Herzegovina 45.10N 15.48E
114 N11 **Velika Morava** ***var.*** Glavn'a Morava, Morava, ***Ger.*** Grosse Morava. ≈ C Yugoslavia
114 N12 **Velika Plana** Serbia, C Yugoslavia 44.20N 21.01E
111 U10 **Velika Raduha** ▲ N Slovenia 46.24N 14.46E
127 Pp5 **Velikaya** ≈ NE Russian Federation
128 F15 **Velikaya** ≈ W Russian Federation
Velikaya Berestovitsa *see* Vyalikaya Byerastavitsa
Velikaya Lepetikha *see* Velyka Lepetykha
Veliki Bečkerek *see* Zrenjanin
114 P12 **Veliki Krš** ***var.*** Stol. ▲ E Yugoslavia 44.10N 22.09E
116 L8 **Veliki Preslav** ***prev.*** Preslav. Shumen, NE Bulgaria 43.09N 26.46E
114 B9 **Veliki Risnjak** ▲ NW Croatia 45.30N 14.31E
111 T13 **Veliki Snežnik** ***Ger.*** Schneeberg, ***It.*** Monte Nevoso. ▲ SW Slovenia 45.36N 14.25E
114 J13 **Veliki Stolac** ▲ E Bosnia and Herzegovina 43.55N 19.15E
Velikiy Bor *see* Vyaliki Bor
128 G16 **Velikiye Luki** Pskovskaya Oblast', W Russian Federation 56.19N 30.27E
129 P12 **Velikiy Ustyug** Vologodskaya Oblast', NW Russian Federation 60.46N 46.18E
114 N11 **Veliko Gradište** Serbia, NE Yugoslavia 44.46N 21.28E
161 I18 **Velikonda Range** ▲▲ SE India
116 K9 **Veliko Tŭrnovo** ***prev.*** Tirnovo, Trnovo, Tŭrnovo. Veliko Tŭrnovo, N Bulgaria 43.04N 25.40E
116 K8 **Veliko Tŭrnovo** ◐ *province* N Bulgaria
Velikovec *see* Völkermarkt
129 R5 **Velikovisochnoye** Nenetskiy Avtonomnyy Okrug, NW Russian Federation 67.13N 52.00E
78 H12 **Vélingara** C Senegal 15.00N 14.39W
78 H11 **Vélingara** S Senegal 13.12N 14.04W
116 H11 **Velingrad** Pazardzhik, C Bulgaria 42.01N 24.00E
130 H3 **Velizh** Smolenskaya Oblast', W Russian Federation 55.30N 31.06E
113 F16 **Velká Deštná** ***var.*** Deštná, Grosskoppe, ***Ger.*** Deschnaer Koppe. ▲ NE Czech Republic 50.18N 16.25E
113 F18 **Velké Meziříčí** ***Ger.*** Grossmeseritsch. Jihlavský Kraj, C Czech Republic 49.22N 16.01E
94 N1 **Velkomstpynten** *headland* NW Svalbard 79.51N 11.37E
113 K21 **Veľký Krtíš** Banskobystrický Kraj, C Slovakia 48.13N 19.21E
195 T14 **Vella Lavella** ***var.*** Mbilua. *island* New Georgia Islands, NW Solomon Islands
109 I15 **Velletri** Lazio, C Italy 41.43N 12.43E
97 K23 **Vellinge** Skåne, S Sweden 55.29N 13.00E
161 I19 **Vellore** Tamil Nādu, SE India 12.55N 79.09E
Velobriga *see* Viana do Castelo
117 G21 **Velopoúla** *island* S Greece
100 M12 **Velp** Gelderland, SE Netherlands 52.00N 5.59E
Velsen *see* Velsen-Noord
100 H9 **Velsen-Noord** ***var.*** Velsen. Noord-Holland, W Netherlands 52.27N 4.40E
129 N12 **Vel'sk** ***var.*** Velsk. Arkhangel'skaya Oblast', NW Russian Federation 61.02N 42.00E
Velsuna *see* Orvieto
100 K10 **Veluwemeer** *lake channel* C Netherlands
30 M3 **Velva** North Dakota, N USA 48.03N 100.55W
117 E14 **Velvendós** ***var.*** Velvendos. Dytikí Makedonía, N Greece 40.15N 22.04E
119 S5 **Velyka Bahachka** Poltavs'ka Oblast', C Ukraine 49.46N 33.44E
119 S9 **Velyka Lepetykha** ***Rus.*** Velikaya Lepetikha. Khersons'ka Oblast', S Ukraine 47.10N 33.55E
119 O10 **Velyka Mykhaylivka** Odes'ka Oblast', SW Ukraine 47.07N 29.49E
119 W8 **Velyka Novosilka** Donets'ka Oblast', E Ukraine 47.49N 36.49E
119 S9 **Velyka Oleksandrivka** Khersons'ka Oblast', S Ukraine 47.17N 33.16E
119 T4 **Velyka Pysanivka** Sums'ka Oblast', NE Ukraine 50.25N 35.28E
118 G6 **Velykyy Bereznyy** Zakarpats'ka Oblast', W Ukraine 48.54N 22.27E
119 W4 **Velykyy Burluk** Kharkivs'ka Oblast', E Ukraine 50.04N 37.25E
Velykyy Tokmak *see* Tokmak
181 P7 **Vema Fracture Zone** *tectonic feature* W Indian Ocean
67 P18 **Vema Seamount** *undersea feature* SW Indian Ocean 31.37S 8.19E
95 F17 **Vemdalen** Jämtland, C Sweden 62.26N 13.50E
97 N19 **Vena** Kalmar, S Sweden 57.31N 16.00E
43 N11 **Venado** San Luis Potosí, C Mexico 22.54N 101.06W
64 L11 **Venado Tuerto** Entre Ríos, E Argentina 33.45S 61.55W
63 A19 **Venado Tuerto** Santa Fe, C Argentina 33.46S 61.57W
109 K16 **Venafro** Molise, C Italy 41.28N 14.03E
57 Q9 **Venamo, Cerro** ▲ E Venezuela 5.56N 61.25W
108 B8 **Venaria** Piemonte, NW Italy 45.09N 7.40E
105 U15 **Vence** Alpes-Maritimes, SE France 43.45N 7.07E
106 H5 **Venda Nova** Vila Real, N Portugal 41.40N 7.58W
106 G11 **Vendas Novas** Évora, S Portugal 38.40N 8.27W
104 J9 **Vendée** ◐ *department* NW France
105 Q6 **Vendeuvre-sur-Barse** Aube, NE France 48.08N 4.17E
104 M7 **Vendôme** Loir-et-Cher, C France 47.48N 1.04E
Venedig *see* Venezia
Vener, Lake *see* Vänern
108 I8 **Veneta, Laguna** *lagoon* NE Italy
Venetia *see* Venezia
41 S7 **Venetie** Alaska, USA 67.00N 146.25W
108 H8 **Veneto** ***var.*** Venezia Euganea. ◐ *region* NE Italy
116 M7 **Venets** Shumen, NE Bulgaria 43.33N 26.56E
130 L5 **Venev** Tul'skaya Oblast', W Russian Federation 54.18N 38.16E
108 I8 **Venezia** ***Eng.*** Venice, ***Fr.*** Venise, ***Ger.*** Venedig; anc. Venetia. Veneto, NE Italy 45.25N 12.19E
Venezia Euganea *see* Veneto
Venezia, Golfo di *see* Venice, Gulf of
Venezia Tridentina *see* Trentino-Alto Adige
56 K8 **Venezuela** ***off.*** Republic of Venezuela; ***prev.*** Estados Unidos de Venezuela, United States of Venezuela. ◆ *republic* N South America
Venezuela, Cordillera de *see* Costa, Cordillera de la
56 I4 **Venezuela, Golfo de** ***Eng.*** Gulf of Maracaibo, Gulf of Venezuela. *gulf* NW Venezuela
Venezuela, Gulf of *see* Venezuela, Golfo de

◆ Country
● Country Capital
◇ Dependent Territory
○ Dependent Territory Capital
◐ Administrative Region
✈ International Airport
▲ Mountain
▲▲ Mountain Range
Volcano
≈ River
◎ Lake
⊠ Reservoir

VENEZUELAN BASIN – VILLALONGA

66 F11 **Venezuelan Basin** *undersea feature* E Caribbean Sea
161 D16 **Vengurla** Mahārāshtra, W India 15.55N 73.39E
41 O15 **Veniaminof, Mount** ▲ Alaska, USA 56.12N 159.24W
25 V14 **Venice** Florida, SE USA 27.06N 82.27W
24 L10 **Venice** Louisiana, S USA 29.15N 89.20W
Venice *see* Venezia
108 J8 **Venice, Gulf of** *It.* Golfo di Venezia, *Slvn.* Beneški Zaliv. *gulf* N Adriatic Sea
Venise *see* Venezia
96 K13 **Venjan** Dalarna, C Sweden 60.58N 13.55E
96 K13 **Venjansjön** ◎ C Sweden
161 J18 **Venkatagiri** Andhra Pradesh, E India 14.00N 79.39E
101 M15 **Venlo** *prev.* Venloo. Limburg, SE Netherlands 51.22N 6.10E
Venloo *see* Venlo
97 E18 **Vennesla** Vest-Agder, S Norway 58.15N 7.58E
109 M17 **Venosa** *anc.* Venusia. Basilicata, S Italy 40.57N 15.49E
Venoste, Alpi *see* Ötztaler Alpen
Venraij *see* Venray
101 M14 **Venray** *var.* Venraij. Limburg, SE Netherlands 51.31N 5.58E
120 C8 **Venta** *Ger.* Windau. ∽ Latvia/Lithuania
Venta Belgarum *see* Winchester
42 G9 **Ventana, Punta Arena de la** *var.* Punta de la Ventana. *headland* W Mexico 24.03N 109.49W
Ventana, Punta de la *see* Ventana, Punta Arena de la
63 B23 **Ventana, Sierra de la** *hill range* E Argentina
Ventia *see* Valence
203 S11 **Vent, Îles du** *var.* Windward Islands. *island group* Archipel de la Société, W French Polynesia
203 R10 **Vent, Îles Sous le** *var.* Leeward Islands. *island group* Archipel de la Société, W French Polynesia
108 B11 **Ventimiglia** Liguria, NW Italy 43.46N 7.37E
99 M24 **Ventnor** S England, UK 50.35N 1.10W
20 J17 **Ventnor City** New Jersey, NE USA 39.19N 74.27W
105 S14 **Ventoux, Mont** ▲ SE France 44.12N 5.21E
120 C8 **Ventspils** *Ger.* Windau. Ventspils, NW Latvia 57.22N 21.34E
56 M10 **Ventuari, Río** ∽ S Venezuela
37 R15 **Ventura** California, W USA 34.15N 119.14W
190 F8 **Venus Bay** South Australia 33.15S 134.42E
Venusia *see* Venosa
203 P7 **Vénus, Pointe** *var.* Pointe Tataaihoa. *headland* Tahiti, W French Polynesia 17.28S 149.28W
43 V16 **Venustiano Carranza** Chiapas, SE Mexico 16.24N 92.04W
43 N7 **Venustiano Carranza, Presa** ⊠ NE Mexico
63 B15 **Vera** Santa Fe, C Argentina 29.28S 60.10W
107 Q14 **Vera** Andalucía, S Spain 37.13N 1.51W
65 K18 **Vera, Bahía** *bay* E Argentina
43 R14 **Veracruz** *var.* Veracruz Llave. Veracruz-Llave, E Mexico 19.09N 96.09W
43 Q13 **Veracruz-Llave** *var.* Veracruz. ◐ *state* E Mexico
45 Q16 **Veraguas** *off.* Provincia de Veraguas. ◐ *province* W Panama
Veramin *see* Varāmīn
160 B12 **Verāval** Gujarāt, W India 20.54N 70.22E
108 C6 **Verbania** Piemonte, NW Italy 45.55N 8.34E
109 N20 **Verbicaro** Calabria, SW Italy 39.44N 15.51E
110 D11 **Verbier** Valais, SW Switzerland 46.06N 7.14E
Vercellae *see* Vercelli
108 C8 **Vercelli** *anc.* Vercellae. Piemonte, NW Italy 45.19N 8.25E
105 S13 **Vercors** *physical region* E France
95 E16 **Verdalsøra** Nord-Trøndelag, C Norway 63.46N 11.27E
Verde, Cabo *see* Cape Verde
46 J5 **Verde, Cape** *headland* Long Island, C Bahamas 22.51N 75.50W
106 M2 **Verde, Costa** *coastal region* N Spain
Verde Grande, Río/Verde Grande y de Belem, Río *see* Verde, Río
102 H11 **Verden** Niedersachsen, NW Germany 52.55N 9.13E
61 J19 **Verde, Río** ∽ SE Brazil
59 P16 **Verde, Río** ∽ Bolivia/Brazil
42 M12 **Verde, Río** *var.* Río Verde Grande, Río Verde Grande y de Belem. ∽ C Mexico
43 Q16 **Verde, Río** ∽ SE Mexico
38 L13 **Verde River** ∽ Arizona, SW USA
Verdhikoúsa/Verdhikoússa *see* Verdikoússa
29 Q8 **Verdigris River** ∽ Kansas/Oklahoma, C USA
117 E15 **Verdikoússa** *var.* Verdhikoúsa, Verdhikoússa. Thessalía, C Greece 39.46N 21.58E
105 S15 **Verdon** ∽ SE France
13 O12 **Verdun** Quebec, SE Canada 45.27N 73.36W
105 S4 **Verdun** *var.* Verdun-sur-Meuse; *anc.* Verodunum. Meuse, NE France 49.09N 5.25E
Verdun-sur-Meuse *see* Verdun
85 J21 **Vereeniging** Gauteng, NE South Africa 26.40S 27.55E
Veremeyki *see* Vyeramyeyki
129 T14 **Vereshchagino** Permskaya Oblast', NW Russian Federation 58.06N 54.38E
78 G14 **Verga, Cap** *headland* W Guinea 10.12N 14.27W
63 G18 **Vergara** Treinta y Tres, E Uruguay 32.58S 53.54W
110 G11 **Vergeletto** Ticino, S Switzerland 46.13N 8.34E
20 L8 **Vergennes** Vermont, NE USA 44.09N 73.13W
Veria *see* Véroia
106 I5 **Verín** Galicia, NW Spain 41.55N 7.25W
Verin T'alin *see* T'alin
120 K6 **Veriora** Põlvamaa, SE Estonia 57.57N 27.23E
119 T7 **Verkhivtseve** Dnipropetrovs'ka Oblast', E Ukraine 48.27N 34.15E
131 W3 **Verkhiye Kigi** Respublika Bashkortostan, W Russian Federation 55.25N 58.40E
Verkhnedvinsk *see* Vyerkhnyadzvinsk
126 Hh11 **Verkhneimbatsk** Krasnoyarskiy Kray, N Russian Federation 63.06N 88.03E
128 I3 **Verkhnetulomskiy** Murmanskaya Oblast', NW Russian Federation 68.37N 31.46E
128 I3 **Verkhnetulomskoye Vodokhranilishche** ⊠ NW Russian Federation
Verkhneudinsk *see* Ulan-Ude
126 L11 **Verkhnevilyuysk** Respublika Sakha (Yakutiya), NE Russian Federation 63.44N 119.59E
131 W5 **Verkhniy Avzyan** Respublika Bashkortostan, W Russian Federation 53.31N 57.26E
131 Q11 **Verkhniy Baskunchak** Astrakhanskaya Oblast', SW Russian Federation 48.14N 46.43E
119 T9 **Verkhniy Rohachyk** Khersons'ka Oblast', S Ukraine 47.16N 34.16E
126 Ll12 **Verkhnyaya Amga** Respublika Sakha (Yakutiya), NE Russian Federation 59.34N 127.07E
129 V6 **Verkhnyaya Inta** Respublika Komi, NW Russian Federation 65.55N 60.07E
126 Ii6 **Verkhnyaya Taymyra** ∽ N Russian Federation
129 O10 **Verkhnyaya Toyma** Arkhangel'skaya Oblast', NW Russian Federation 62.12N 44.57E
130 K6 **Verkhov'ye** Orlovskaya Oblast', W Russian Federation 52.49N 37.20E
118 I8 **Verkhovyna** Ivano-Frankivs'ka Oblast', W Ukraine 48.09N 24.48E
126 M8 **Verkhoyansk** Respublika Sakha (Yakutiya), NE Russian Federation 67.27N 133.27E
126 L8 **Verkhoyanskiy Khrebet** ▲▲ NE Russian Federation
119 T7 **Verkhn'odniprovs'k** Dnipropetrovs'ka Oblast', E Ukraine 48.40N 34.17E
103 G14 **Verl** Nordrhein-Westfalen, NW Germany 51.52N 8.30E
94 N1 **Verlegenhuken** *headland* N Svalbard 80.03N 16.15E
84 A9 **Vermelha, Ponta** *headland* NW Angola 5.40S 12.09E
105 P7 **Vermenton** Yonne, C France 47.40N 3.43E
9 R14 **Vermilion** Alberta, SW Canada 53.21N 110.52W
33 T11 **Vermilion** Ohio, N USA 41.25N 82.21W
24 I10 **Vermilion Bay** *bay* Louisiana, S USA
31 V4 **Vermilion Lake** ◎ Minnesota, N USA
12 F9 **Vermilion River** ∽ Ontario, S Canada
32 L12 **Vermilion River** ∽ Illinois, N USA
31 R12 **Vermillion** South Dakota, N USA 42.46N 96.55W
31 R12 **Vermillion River** ∽ South Dakota, N USA
13 O9 **Vermillon, Rivière** ∽ Quebec, SE Canada
117 E14 **Vérmio** ▲▲ N Greece
20 L8 **Vermont** *off.* State of Vermont; *also known as* The Green Mountain State. ◐ *state* NE USA
115 K16 **Vermosh** *var.* Vermoshi. Shkodër, N Albania 42.37N 19.42E
Vermoshi *see* Vermosh
39 O3 **Vernal** Utah, W USA 40.27N 109.31W
12 G11 **Verner** Ontario, S Canada 46.24N 80.04W
104 M5 **Verneuil-sur-Avre** Eure, N France 48.44N 0.55E
116 D13 **Vérno** ▲▲ N Greece
9 N17 **Vernon** British Columbia, SW Canada 50.16N 119.19W
104 M4 **Vernon** Eure, N France 49.04N 1.28E
25 N3 **Vernon** Alabama, S USA 33.45N 88.06W
33 P15 **Vernon** Indiana, N USA 38.58N 85.39W
27 Q4 **Vernon** Texas, SW USA 34.10N 99.16W
34 G10 **Vernonia** Oregon, NW USA 45.51N 123.11W
12 G12 **Vernon, Lake** ◎ Ontario, S Canada
24 G7 **Vernon Lake** ⊠ Louisiana, S USA
25 Y13 **Vero Beach** Florida, SE USA 27.38N 80.24W
Verőcze *see* Virovitica
Verodunum *see* Verdun
117 E14 **Véroia** *var.* Veria, Vérroia, *Turk.* Karaferiye. Kentrikí Makedonía, N Greece 40.31N 22.14E
108 E8 **Verolanuova** Lombardia, N Italy 45.20N 10.06E
12 K14 **Verona** Ontario, SE Canada 44.30N 76.42W
108 G8 **Verona** Veneto, NE Italy 45.26N 11.00E
31 P6 **Verona** North Dakota, N USA 46.19N 98.03W
32 L9 **Verona** Wisconsin, N USA 42.59N 89.33W
63 E20 **Verónica** Buenos Aires, E Argentina 35.25S 57.16W
24 I9 **Verret, Lake** ◎ Louisiana, S USA
Vérroia *see* Véroia
195 P10 **Verron Range** ▲▲ New Ireland, NE PNG
105 N5 **Versailles** Yvelines, N France 48.48N 2.07E
33 P15 **Versailles** Indiana, N USA 39.04N 85.16W
22 M5 **Versailles** Kentucky, S USA 38.03N 84.43W
29 U5 **Versailles** Missouri, C USA 38.25N 92.50W
33 Q13 **Versailles** Ohio, N USA 40.13N 84.28W
Versecz *see* Vršac
110 A10 **Versoix** Genève, SW Switzerland 46.16N 6.10E
13 Z6 **Verte, Pointe** *headland* Quebec, SE Canada 48.36N 64.10W
113 I22 **Vértes** ▲▲ NW Hungary
46 G6 **Vertientes** Camagüey, C Cuba 21.15N 78.09W
116 G13 **Vertískos** ▲▲ N Greece
104 I8 **Vertou** Loire-Atlantique, NW France 47.10N 1.28W
Verulamium *see* St Albans
101 L19 **Verviers** Liège, E Belgium 50.36N 5.52E
105 Y14 **Vescovato** Corse, France, C Mediterranean Sea 42.30N 9.27E
101 L20 **Vesdre** ∽ E Belgium
119 U10 **Vesele** *Rus.* Veseloye. Zaporiz'ka Oblast', S Ukraine 47.00N 34.52E
113 D18 **Veselí nad Lužnicí** *var.* Weseli an der Lainsitz, *Ger.* Frohenbruck. Budějovický Kraj, S Czech Republic 49.11N 14.40E
116 M9 **Veselinovo** Shumen, E Bulgaria 43.01N 27.02E
130 L12 **Veselovskoye Vodokhranilishche** ⊠ SW Russian Federation
Veseloye *see* Vesele
119 Q9 **Veselynove** Mykolayivs'ka Oblast', S Ukraine 47.21N 31.15E
Veseya *see* Vyasyeya
130 M10 **Veshenskaya** Rostovskaya Oblast', SW Russian Federation 49.37N 41.43E
131 Q5 **Veshkayma** Ul'yanovskaya Oblast', W Russian Federation 54.04N 47.06E
Vesisaari *see* Vadsø
Vesontio *see* Besançon
105 T7 **Vesoul** *anc.* Vesulium, Vesulum. Haute-Saône, E France 47.37N 6.09E
97 J20 **Vessigebro** Halland, S Sweden 56.58N 12.40E
97 D17 **Vest-Agder** ◐ *county* S Norway
25 P4 **Vestavia Hills** Alabama, S USA 33.27N 86.47W
86 F6 **Vesterålen** *island* NW Norway
94 G10 **Vesterålen** *island group* N Norway
89 V3 **Vestervig** Viborg, NW Denmark 56.46N 8.19E
94 H2 **Vestfirdhir** ◐ *region* NW Iceland
94 G11 **Vestfjorden** *fjord* C Norway
97 G16 **Vestfold** ◐ *county* S Norway
97 B19 **Vestmanna** *Dan.* Vestmanhavn Faeroe Islands 62.09N 7.11W
94 I4 **Vestmannaeyjar** Sudhurland, S Iceland 63.26N 20.13W
96 E9 **Vestnes** Møre og Romsdal, S Norway 62.39N 7.00E
97 I23 **Vestsjælland** *off.* Vestsjællands Amt. ◐ *county* E Denmark
94 H3 **Vesturland** ◐ *region* W Iceland
94 G11 **Vestvågøya** *island* C Norway
Vesulium/Vesulum *see* Vesoul
Vesuna *see* Périgueux
109 K17 **Vesuvio** *Eng.* Vesuvius. ⛰ S Italy 40.48N 14.29E
Vesuvius *see* Vesuvio
128 K14 **Ves'yegonsk** Tverskaya Oblast', W Russian Federation 58.40N 37.13E
113 I23 **Veszprém** *Ger.* Veszprim. Veszprém, W Hungary 47.06N 17.54E
113 H23 **Veszprém** *off.* Veszprém Megye. ◐ *county* W Hungary
Veszprim *see* Veszprém
Vetka *see* Vyetka
97 M19 **Vetlanda** Jönköping, S Sweden 57.25N 15.04E
131 P1 **Vetluga** Nizhegorodskaya Oblast', W Russian Federation 57.51N 45.45E
129 P14 **Vetluga** ∽ NW Russian Federation
129 O14 **Vetluzhskiy** Kostromskaya Oblast', NW Russian Federation 58.21N 45.25E
131 P2 **Vetluzhskiy** Nizhegorodskaya Oblast', W Russian Federation 57.10N 45.07E
109 H14 **Vetralla** Lazio, C Italy 42.18N 12.03E
116 M9 **Vetren** *prev.* Zhitarovo. Burgas, E Bulgaria 42.38N 27.22E
116 M8 **Vetrino** Varna, E Bulgaria 43.19N 27.26E
Vetrino *see* Vyetryna
126 Ii6 **Vetrovaya, Gora** ▲ N Russian Federation 73.54N 95.00E
Vetter, Lake *see* Vättern
108 J13 **Vettore, Monte** ▲ C Italy 42.49N 13.15E
101 A17 **Veurne** *var.* Furnes. West-Vlaanderen, W Belgium 51.04N 2.40E
33 Q15 **Vevay** Indiana, N USA 38.45N 85.07W
110 C10 **Vevey** *Ger.* Vivis; *anc.* Vibiscum. Vaud, SW Switzerland 46.28N 6.51E
Vexiö *see* Växjö
105 S13 **Veynes** Hautes-Alpes, SE France 44.33N 5.51E
105 N11 **Vézère** ∽ W France
116 I9 **Vezhen** ▲ C Bulgaria 42.45N 24.22E
142 K11 **Vezirköprü** Samsun, N Turkey 41.09N 35.27E
59 J18 **Viacha** La Paz, W Bolivia 16.40S 68.16W
29 R10 **Vian** Oklahoma, C USA 35.30N 94.56W
Viana de Castelo *see* Viana do Castelo
106 H12 **Viana do Alentejo** Évora, S Portugal 38.20N 8.00W
106 I4 **Viana do Bolo** Galicia, NW Spain 42.10N 7.06W
106 G5 **Viana do Castelo** *var.* Viana de Castelo; *anc.* Velobriga. Viana do Castelo, NW Portugal 41.40N 8.49W
106 G5 **Viana do Castelo** *var.* Viana de Castelo. ◐ *district* N Portugal
100 J12 **Vianen** Zuid-Holland, C Netherlands 52.00N 5.06E
178 Ii8 **Viangchan** *Eng./Fr.* Vientiane. ● (Laos) C Laos 17.57N 102.38E
178 I6 **Viangphoukha** *var.* Vieng Pou Kha. Louang Namtha, N Laos 20.41N 101.03E
106 K13 **Viar** ∽ SW Spain
108 E11 **Viareggio** Toscana, C Italy 43.52N 10.15E
105 O14 **Viaur** ∽ S France
Vibiscum *see* Vevey
97 G21 **Viborg** Viborg, NW Denmark 56.28N 9.25E
31 R12 **Viborg** South Dakota, N USA 43.10N 97.04W
97 F21 **Viborg** *off.* Viborg Amt. ◐ *county* NW Denmark
109 N22 **Vibo Valentia** *prev.* Monteleone di Calabria; *anc.* Hipponium. Calabria, SW Italy 38.40N 16.06E
107 W5 **Vic** *var.* Vich; *anc.* Ausa, Vicus Ausonensis. Cataluña, NE Spain 41.55N 2.16E
104 K16 **Vic-en-Bigorre** Hautes-Pyrénées, S France 43.22N 0.03E
42 K10 **Vicente Guerrero** Durango, C Mexico 23.30N 104.24W
43 P10 **Vicente Guerrero, Presa** *var.* Presa de las Adjuntas. ⊠ NE Mexico
Vicentia *see* Vicenza
108 G8 **Vicenza** *anc.* Vicentia. Veneto, NE Italy 45.31N 11.31E
Vich *see* Vic
56 J10 **Vichada** *off.* Comisaría del Vichada. ◐ *province* E Colombia
56 K10 **Vichada, Río** ∽ E Colombia
63 G17 **Vichadero** Rivera, NE Uruguay 31.45S 54.40W
Vichegda *see* Vychegda
128 M16 **Vichuga** Ivanovskaya Oblast', W Russian Federation 57.13N 41.51E
105 P10 **Vichy** Allier, C France 46.08N 3.26E
28 K9 **Vici** Oklahoma, C USA 36.09N 99.18W
33 P10 **Vicksburg** Michigan, N USA 42.07N 85.31W
24 J5 **Vicksburg** Mississippi, S USA 32.21N 90.52W
105 O12 **Vic-sur-Cère** Cantal, C France 45.00N 2.36E
31 X14 **Victor** Iowa, C USA 41.45N 92.18W
61 I21 **Victor** Mato Grosso do Sul, SW Brazil 21.39S 53.21W
190 I10 **Victor Harbor** South Australia 35.33S 138.37E
63 C18 **Victoria** Entre Ríos, E Argentina 32.36S 60.12W
8 L17 **Victoria** Vancouver Island, British Columbia, SW Canada 48.25N 123.22W
47 R14 **Victoria** NW Grenada 12.11N 61.42W
44 H6 **Victoria** Yoro, NW Honduras 15.01N 87.28W
123 J16 **Victoria** *var.* Rabat. Gozo, NW Malta 36.02N 14.14E
118 I12 **Victoria** *Ger.* Viktoriastadt. Braşov, C Romania 45.43N 24.40E
180 H17 **Victoria** ● (Seychelles) Mahé, SW Seychelles 4.37S 28.28E
27 U13 **Victoria** Texas, SW USA 28.47N 96.58W
191 N12 **Victoria** ◐ *state* SE Australia
182 K7 **Victoria** ∽ Western Australia
Victoria *see* Labuan, East Malaysia
Victoria *see* Masvingo, Zimbabwe
Victoria Bank *see* Vitória Seamount
9 Y15 **Victoria Beach** Manitoba, S Canada 50.40N 96.30W
Victoria de Durango *see* Durango
Victoria de las Tunas *see* Las Tunas
85 I16 **Victoria Falls** Matabeleland North, W Zimbabwe 17.55S 25.48E
85 I16 **Victoria Falls** ✕ Matabeleland North, W Zimbabwe 18.03S 25.48E
85 I16 **Victoria Falls** *waterfall* Zambia/Zimbabwe 18.03S 25.50E
Victoria Falls *see* Iguaçu, Salto do
65 F19 **Victoria, Isla** *island* Archipiélago de los Chonos, S Chile
15 J2 **Victoria Island** *island* Northwest Territories/Nunavut, NW Canada
190 L8 **Victoria, Lake** ◎ New South Wales, SE Australia
70 I12 **Victoria, Lake** *var.* Victoria Nyanza. ◎ E Africa
205 S13 **Victoria Land** *physical region* Antarctica
177 F5 **Victoria, Mount** ▲ W Burma 21.13N 93.53E
197 I14 **Victoria, Mount** ▲ Viti Levu, W Fiji 17.37S 178.00E
194 K15 **Victoria, Mount** ▲ S PNG 8.51S 147.36E
83 F17 **Victoria Nile** *var.* Somerset Nile. ∽ C Uganda
Victoria Nyanza *see* Victoria, Lake
44 G3 **Victoria Peak** ▲ SE Belize 16.50N 88.38W
193 H16 **Victoria Range** ▲▲ South Island, NZ
189 O3 **Victoria River** ∽ Northern Territory, N Australia
189 P3 **Victoria River Roadhouse** Northern Territory, N Australia 15.37S 131.07E
13 Q11 **Victoriaville** Quebec, SE Canada 46.03N 71.55W
Victoria-Wes *see* Victoria West
85 G24 **Victoria West** *Afr.* Victoria-Wes. Northern Cape, W South Africa 31.22S 23.06E
64 J13 **Victorica** La Pampa, C Argentina 36.14S 65.21W
205 T3 **Victor, Mount** ▲ Antarctica 72.49S 33.01E
37 U14 **Victorville** California, W USA 34.32N 117.17W
64 G9 **Vicuña** Coquimbo, N Chile 30.00S 70.44W
64 K11 **Vicuña Mackenna** Córdoba, C Argentina 33.52S 64.25W
Vicus Ausonensis *see* Vic
Vicus Elbii *see* Viterbo
35 X7 **Vida** Montana, NW USA 47.52N 105.30W
25 V6 **Vidalia** Georgia, SE USA 32.13N 82.24W
24 J7 **Vidalia** Louisiana, S USA 31.34N 91.25W
97 F22 **Videbæk** Ringkøbing, C Denmark 56.07N 8.37E
62 I13 **Videira** Santa Catarina, S Brazil 27.00S 51.08W
118 J14 **Videle** Teleorman, S Romania 44.15N 25.27E
Videm-Krško *see* Krško
Vídeň *see* Wien
106 H12 **Vidigueira** Beja, S Portugal 38.12N 7.48W
116 J9 **Vidima** ∽ N Bulgaria
116 G7 **Vidin** *anc.* Bononia. Vidin, NW Bulgaria 44.00N 22.50E
116 F8 **Vidin** ◐ *province* NW Bulgaria
160 H10 **Vidisha** Madhya Pradesh, C India 23.30N 77.49E
27 Y10 **Vidor** Texas, SW USA 30.07N 94.01W
97 L20 **Vidöstern** ◎ S Sweden
94 J13 **Vidsel** Norrbotten, N Sweden 65.49N 20.31E
120 H9 **Vidzemes Augstiene** ▲▲ C Latvia
120 J12 **Vidzy** *Rus.* Vidzy. Vitsyebskaya Voblasts', NW Belarus 55.22N 26.37E
65 L16 **Viedma** Río Negro, E Argentina 40.50S 62.57W
65 H22 **Viedma, Lago** ◎ S Argentina
47 O11 **Vieille Case** *var.* Itassi. N Dominica 15.36N 61.24W
106 M2 **Vieja, Peña** ▲ N Spain 43.09N 4.47W
42 E4 **Viejo, Cerro** ▲ NW Mexico 30.16N 112.18W
58 B9 **Viejo, Cerro** ▲ N Peru 4.54S 79.24W
120 E10 **Viekšniai** Akmenė, NW Lithuania 56.14N 22.33E
107 U3 **Vielha** *var.* Viella. Cataluña, NE Spain 42.40N 0.46E
Viella *see* Vielha
101 L21 **Vielsalm** Luxembourg, E Belgium 50.16N 5.55E
Vieng Pou Kha *see* Viangphoukha
25 T6 **Vienna** Georgia, SE USA 32.05N 83.48W
32 L17 **Vienna** Illinois, N USA 37.22N 88.51W
29 V5 **Vienna** Missouri, C USA 38.11N 91.57W
23 Q3 **Vienna** West Virginia, NE USA 39.19N 81.33W
Vienna *see* Wien, Austria
Vienna *see* Vienne, France
105 R11 **Vienne** *anc.* Vienna. Isère, E France 45.31N 4.52E
104 L10 **Vienne** ◐ *department* W France
104 L9 **Vienne** ∽ W France
Vientiane *see* Viangchan
Vientos, Paso de los *see* Windward Passage
47 V6 **Vieques** *var.* Isabel Segunda. E Puerto Rico 18.08N 65.27W
47 V6 **Vieques, Isla de** *island* E Puerto Rico
47 V6 **Vieques, Pasaje de** *passage* E Puerto Rico
47 V5 **Vieques, Sonda de** *sound* E Puerto Rico
Vierdörfer *see* Săcele
95 M15 **Vieremä** Itä-Suomi, C Finland 63.42N 27.02E
101 M14 **Vierlingsbeek** Noord-Brabant, SE Netherlands 51.36N 6.01E
103 G20 **Viernheim** Hessen, W Germany 49.31N 8.34E
103 D15 **Viersen** Nordrhein-Westfalen, W Germany 51.15N 6.24E
110 G8 **Vierwaldstätter See** *Eng.* Lake of Lucerne. ◎ C Switzerland
105 N8 **Vierzon** Cher, C France 47.13N 2.04E
42 L8 **Viesca** Coahuila de Zaragoza, NE Mexico 25.25N 102.45W
120 H10 **Viesīte** *Ger.* Eckengraf. Jēkabpils, S Latvia 56.21N 25.30E
109 N15 **Vieste** Puglia, SE Italy 41.52N 16.10E
178 Jj9 **Vietnam** *off.* Socialist Republic of Vietnam, *Vtn.* Công Hoa Xa Hôi Chu Nghia Viêt Nam. ◆ *republic* SE Asia
178 J5 **Viêt Quang** Ha Giang, N Vietnam 22.24N 104.48E
Vietri *see* Viêt Tri
178 Jj6 **Viêt Tri** *var.* Vietri. Vinh Phu, N Vietnam 21.19N 105.25E
32 L4 **Vieux Desert, Lac** ◎ Michigan/Wisconsin, N USA
47 Y13 **Vieux Fort** S Saint Lucia 13.43N 60.57W
47 X6 **Vieux-Habitants** Basse Terre, SW Guadeloupe 16.03N 61.45W
121 G14 **Vievis** Kaišiadorys, S Lithuania 54.46N 24.51E
179 P8 **Vigan** Luzon, N Philippines 17.34N 102.21E
108 D8 **Vigevano** Lombardia, N Italy 45.19N 8.51E
109 N18 **Viggiano** Basilicata, S Italy 40.21N 15.54E
60 L12 **Vigia** Pará, NE Brazil 0.49S 48.07W
43 Y12 **Vigía Chico** Quintana Roo, SE Mexico 19.49N 87.31W
47 T11 **Vigie** ✕ (Castries) NE Saint Lucia 14.01N 60.59W
104 K17 **Vignemale** *var.* Pic de Vignemale. ▲ France/Spain 42.48N 0.06W
Vignemale, Pic de *see* Vignemale
108 G10 **Vignola** Emilia-Romagna, C Italy 44.28N 11.00E
106 G4 **Vigo** Galicia, NW Spain 42.15N 8.43W
106 G4 **Vigo, Ría de** *estuary* NW Spain
96 D9 **Vigra** *island* S Norway
97 C17 **Vigrestad** Rogaland, S Norway 58.34N 5.42E
95 L15 **Vihanti** Oulu, C Finland 64.28N 25.00E
155 U10 **Vihāri** Punjab, E Pakistan 30.03N 72.31E
104 K8 **Vihiers** Maine-et-Loire, NW France 47.09N 0.37W
113 O19 **Vihorlat** ▲ E Slovakia 48.54N 22.09E
95 L19 **Vihti** Etelä-Suomi, S Finland 60.25N 24.16E
Viipuri *see* Vyborg
95 M16 **Viitasaari** Länsi-Suomi, W Finland 63.05N 25.52E
120 K3 **Viivikonna** Ida-Virumaa, NE Estonia 59.19N 27.40E
161 K16 **Vijayawāda** *prev.* Bezwada. Andhra Pradesh, SE India 16.34N 80.40E
Vijosa/Vijosë *see* Aóos, Albania/Greece
Vijosa/Vijosë *see* Vjosës, Lumi i, Albania/Greece
Vik *see* Vikøyri
94 J4 **Vík** Sudhurland, S Iceland 63.25N 18.58W
96 L13 **Vika** Dalarna, C Sweden 60.55N 14.30E
94 L12 **Vikajärvi** Lappi, N Finland 66.37N 26.10E
96 L13 **Vikarbyn** Dalarna, C Sweden 60.57N 15.00E
97 J22 **Viken** Skåne, S Sweden 56.09N 12.36E
97 L17 **Viken** ◎ C Sweden
97 G15 **Vikersund** Buskerud, S Norway 59.58N 9.58E
126 J14 **Vikhorevka** Irkutskaya Oblast', S Russian Federation 56.09N 99.09E
116 G11 **Vikhren** ▲ SW Bulgaria 41.45N 23.24E
9 R15 **Viking** Alberta, SW Canada 53.07N 111.49W
86 E7 **Viking Bank** *undersea feature* N North Sea
97 M14 **Vikmanshyttan** Dalarna, C Sweden 60.19N 15.55E
96 D12 **Vikøyri** *var.* Vik. Sogn og Fjordane, S Norway 61.04N 6.34E
95 H17 **Viksjö** Västernorrland, C Sweden 62.45N 17.30E
Viktoriastadt *see* Victoria
Vila *see* Port-Vila
Vila Arriaga *see* Bibala
Vila Artur de Paiva *see* Cubango
Vila Bela da Santissima Trindade *see* Mato Grosso
60 B12 **Vila Bittencourt** Amazonas, NW Brazil 1.25S 69.24W
Vila da Ponte *see* Cubango
66 O2 **Vila da Praia da Vitória** Terceira, Azores, Portugal, NE Atlantic Ocean 38.43N 27.04W
Vila de Aljustrel *see* Cangamba
Vila de Almoster *see* Chiange
Vila de João Belo *see* Xai-Xai
Vila de Macia *see* Macia
Vila de Manhiça *see* Manhiça
Vila de Manica *see* Manica
Vila de Mocímboa da Praia *see* Mocímboa da Praia
85 N16 **Vila de Sena** *var.* Sena. Sofala, C Mozambique 17.25S 34.59E
106 F14 **Vila do Bispo** Faro, S Portugal 37.04N 8.52W
106 G6 **Vila do Conde** Porto, NW Portugal 41.21N 8.45W
Vila do Maio *see* Maio
66 P3 **Vila do Porto** Santa Maria, Azores, Portugal, NE Atlantic Ocean 36.57N 25.10W
85 K15 **Vila do Zumbo** *prev.* Vila do Zumbu, Zumbo. Tete, NW Mozambique 15.36S 30.30E
Vila do Zumbu *see* Vila do Zumbo
106 I6 **Vila Flor** *var.* Vila Flôr. Bragança, N Portugal 41.18N 7.09W
107 V6 **Vilafranca del Penedès** *var.* Villafranca del Panadés. Cataluña, NE Spain 41.21N 1.42E
106 F10 **Vila Franca de Xira** *var.* Vilafranca de Xira. Lisboa, C Portugal 38.57N 8.58W
Vila Gago Coutinho *see* Lumbala N'Guimbo
106 G3 **Vilagarcía de Arousa** *var.* Villagarcía de Arosa. Galicia, NW Spain 42.34N 8.45W
Vila General Machado *see* Camacupa
Vila Henrique de Carvalho *see* Saurimo
104 I7 **Vilaine** ∽ NW France
Vila João de Almeida *see* Chibia
120 K8 **Viļaka** *Ger.* Marienhausen. Balvi, NE Latvia 57.11N 27.42E
106 I2 **Vilalba** Galicia, NW Spain 43.16N 7.40W
Vila Marechal Carmona *see* Uíge
Vila Mariano Machado *see* Ganda
180 G3 **Vilanandro, Tanjona** *headland* W Madagascar 16.10S 44.27E
Vilanculos *see* Vilankulo
120 J10 **Viļāni** Rēzekne, E Latvia 56.33N 26.55E
85 N19 **Vilankulo** *var.* Vilanculos. Inhambane, E Mozambique 22.01S 35.19E
Vila Norton de Matos *see* Balombo
106 G6 **Vila Nova de Famalicão** *var.* Vila Nova de Famalicao. Braga, N Portugal 41.24N 8.31W
106 I6 **Vila Nova de Foz Côa** *var.* Vila Nova de Fozcoa. Guarda, N Portugal 41.04N 7.09W
106 F6 **Vila Nova de Gaia** Porto, NW Portugal 41.07N 8.37W
Vila Nova de Portimão *see* Portimão
107 V6 **Vilanova i La Geltrú** Cataluña, NE Spain 41.15N 1.42E
Vila Pereira de Eça *see* N'Giva
106 H6 **Vila Pouca de Aguiar** Vila Real, N Portugal 41.30N 7.37W
106 H6 **Vila Real** *var.* Vila Real. Vila Real, N Portugal 41.16N 7.45W
106 H6 **Vila Real** ◐ *district* N Portugal
107 T9 **Vila-real de los Infantes** *var.* Villarreal. País Valenciano, E Spain 39.55N 0.07W
106 H14 **Vila Real de Santo António** Faro, S Portugal 37.12N 7.25W
106 J7 **Vilar Formoso** Guarda, N Portugal 40.37N 6.49W
Vila Rial *see* Vila Real
61 J15 **Vila Rica** Mato Grosso, W Brazil 9.52S 50.44W
Vila Robert Williams *see* Caála
Vila Salazar *see* N'Dalatando
Vila Serpa Pinto *see* Menongue
Vila Teixeira da Silva *see* Bailundo
Vila Teixeira de Sousa *see* Luau
106 H9 **Vila Velha de Ródão** Castelo Branco, C Portugal 39.39N 7.40W
106 G5 **Vila Verde** Braga, N Portugal 41.39N 8.27W
106 H11 **Vila Viçosa** Évora, S Portugal 38.46N 7.25W
59 G15 **Vilcabamba, Cordillera de** ▲▲ C Peru
Vîlcea *see* Vâlcea
126 Hh1 **Vil'cheka, Zemlya** *Eng.* Wilczek Land. *island* Zemlya Frantsa-Iosifa, NW Russian Federation
97 F22 **Vildbjerg** Ringkøbing, C Denmark 56.12N 8.46E
Vileyka *see* Vilyeyka
95 H15 **Vilhelmina** Västerbotten, N Sweden 64.37N 16.40E
61 F17 **Vilhena** Rondônia, W Brazil 12.40S 60.07W
117 G19 **Vília** Attikí, C Greece 38.09N 23.21E
Viliya *see* Viliya
121 I14 **Viliya** *Lith.* Neris, *Rus.* Viliya. ∽ W Belarus
Viliya *see* Neris
120 H5 **Viljandi** *Ger.* Fellin. Viljandimaa, S Estonia 58.22N 25.34E
120 H5 **Viljandimaa** *off.* Viljandi Maakond. ◐ *province* SW Estonia
121 E14 **Vilkaviškis** *Pol.* Wyłkowyszki. Vilkaviškis, SW Lithuania 54.39N 23.03E
120 F13 **Vilkija** Kaunas, C Lithuania 55.02N 23.36E
207 V9 **Vil'kitskogo, Proliv** *strait* N Russian Federation
Vilkovo *see* Vylkove
59 L21 **Villa Abecia** Chuquisaca, S Bolivia 21.01S 65.12W
43 N5 **Villa Acuña** *var.* Ciudad Acuña. Coahuila de Zaragoza, NE Mexico 29.17N 100.57W
42 J4 **Villa Ahumada** Chihuahua, N Mexico 30.37N 106.30W
47 O9 **Villa Altagracia** C Dominican Republic 18.37N 70.11W
58 L13 **Villa Bella** Beni, N Bolivia 10.21S 65.25W
106 J3 **Villablino** Castilla-León, N Spain 42.55N 6.21W
56 K6 **Villa Bruzual** Portuguesa, N Venezuela 9.19N 69.06W
107 O9 **Villacañas** Castilla-La Mancha, C Spain 39.37N 3.19W
107 O12 **Villacarrillo** Andalucía, S Spain 38.07N 3.04W
106 M7 **Villacastín** Castilla-León, N Spain 40.46N 4.25W
Villa Cecilia *see* Ciudad Madero
111 S9 **Villach** *Slvn.* Beljak. Kärnten, S Austria 46.36N 13.49E
109 B20 **Villacidro** Sardegna, Italy, C Mediterranean Sea 39.27N 8.43E
Villa Concepción *see* Concepción
106 L4 **Villada** Castilla-León, N Spain 42.15N 4.58W
42 M10 **Villa de Cos** Zacatecas, C Mexico 23.20N 102.20W
56 L5 **Villa de Cura** *var.* Cura. Aragua, N Venezuela 10.00N 67.30W
Villa del Nevoso *see* Ilirska Bistrica
Villa del Pilar *see* Pilar
106 M13 **Villa del Río** Andalucía, S Spain 37.58N 4.16W
Villa de Méndez *see* Méndez
44 H6 **Villa de San Antonio** Comayagua, W Honduras 14.24N 87.37W
107 N4 **Villadiego** Castilla-León, N Spain 42.31N 4.01W
107 T8 **Villafamés** País Valenciano, E Spain 40.07N 0.03W
43 U16 **Villa Flores** Chiapas, SE Mexico 16.12N 93.16W
106 J3 **Villafranca del Bierzo** Castilla-León, N Spain 42.36N 6.49W
107 S8 **Villafranca del Cid** País Valenciano, E Spain 40.25N 0.15W
106 J11 **Villafranca de los Barros** Extremadura, W Spain 38.34N 6.19W
107 N10 **Villafranca de los Caballeros** Castilla-La Mancha, C Spain 39.25N 3.21W
Villafranca del Panadés *see* Vilafranca del Penedès
108 F8 **Villafranca di Verona** Veneto, NE Italy 45.22N 10.51E
109 J23 **Villafrati** Sicilia, Italy, C Mediterranean Sea 37.53N 13.30E
Villagarcía de Arosa *see* Vilagarcía de Arousa
43 O9 **Villagrán** Tamaulipas, C Mexico 24.28N 99.30W
63 C17 **Villaguay** Entre Ríos, E Argentina 31.55S 59.01W
64 O6 **Villa Hayes** Presidente Hayes, S Paraguay 25.04S 57.25W
43 U15 **Villahermosa** *prev.* San Juan Bautista. Tabasco, SE Mexico 17.56N 92.50W
107 O11 **Villahermosa** Castilla-La Mancha, C Spain 38.46N 2.52W
66 O11 **Villahermoso** Gomera, Islas Canarias, Spain, NE Atlantic Ocean 38.46N 2.52W
Villa Hidalgo *see* Hidalgo
107 T12 **Villajoyosa** *var.* La Vila Jojosa. País Valenciano, E Spain 38.31N 0.13W
Villa Juárez *see* Juárez
Villalba *see* Collado Villalba
43 N8 **Villaldama** Nuevo León, NE Mexico 26.29N 100.27W
106 L5 **Villalón de Campos** Castilla-León, N Spain 42.04N 5.03W
63 A25 **Villalonga** Buenos Aires, E Argentina 39.55S 62.34W

◆ Country ● Country Capital ◇ Dependent Territory ○ Dependent Territory Capital ◐ Administrative Region ✕ International Airport ▲ Mountain ▲▲ Mountain Range ⛰ Volcano ∽ River ◎ Lake ⊠ Reservoir

VILLALPANDO – VOYNISHKA REKA

106 L5 **Villalpando** Castilla-León, N Spain 41.51N 5.25W
42 K9 **Villa Madero** *var.* Francisco I.Madero. Durango, C Mexico 24.27N 104.11W
43 O9 **Villa Mainero** Tamaulipas, C Mexico 24.32N 99.39W
Villamaña *see* Villamañán
106 L4 **Villamañán** *var.* Villamaña. Castilla-León, N Spain 42.19N 5.34W
64 L10 **Villa María** Córdoba, C Argentina 32.22S 63.15W
63 C17 **Villa María Grande** Entre Ríos, E Argentina 31.39S 59.54W
59 K21 **Villa Martín** Potosí, SW Bolivia 20.48S 67.36W
106 K15 **Villamartin** Andalucía, S Spain 36.50N 5.39W
64 J8 **Villa Mazán** La Rioja, NW Argentina 28.43S 66.25W
Villa Mercedes *see* Mercedes
Villamil *see* Puerto Villamil
Villa Nador *see* Nador
56 G5 **Villanueva** La Guajira, N Colombia 10.37N 72.58W
44 H5 **Villanueva** Cortés, NW Honduras 15.17N 87.58W
42 L11 **Villanueva** Zacatecas, C Mexico 22.24N 102.52W
44 I9 **Villa Nueva** Chinandega, NW Nicaragua 12.58N 86.46W
39 T11 **Villanueva** New Mexico, SW USA 35.18N 105.20W
106 M12 **Villanueva de Córdoba** Andalucía, S Spain 38.19N 4.37W
107 O12 **Villanueva del Arzobispo** Andalucía, S Spain 38.10N 3.00W
106 K11 **Villanueva de la Serena** Extremadura, W Spain 38.58N 5.48W
106 L5 **Villanueva del Campo** Castilla-León, N Spain 41.58N 5.25W
107 O11 **Villanueva de los Infantes** Castilla-La Mancha, C Spain 38.45N 3.01W
63 C14 **Villa Ocampo** Santa Fe, C Argentina 28.28S 59.22W
42 J8 **Villa Ocampo** Durango, C Mexico 26.26N 105.28W
42 J7 **Villa Orestes Pereyra** Durango, C Mexico 26.30N 105.38W
107 N3 **Villarcayo** Castilla-León, N Spain 42.55N 3.34W
106 L5 **Villardefrades** Castilla-León, N Spain 41.43N 5.15W
107 S9 **Villar del Arzobispo** País Valenciano, E Spain 39.43N 0.49W
107 Q6 **Villaroya de la Sierra** Aragón, NE Spain 41.28N 1.46W
Villarreal *see* Vila-real de los Infantes
64 P6 **Villarrica** Guairá, SE Paraguay 25.45S 56.28W
65 G15 **Villarrica, Volcán** ⛰ S Chile 39.28S 71.57W
107 P10 **Villarrobledo** Castilla-La Mancha, C Spain 39.16N 2.36W
107 N10 **Villarrubia de los Ojos** Castilla-La Mancha, C Spain 39.13N 3.36W
20 J17 **Villas** New Jersey, NE USA 39.01N 74.54W
107 O3 **Villasana de Mena** Castilla-León, N Spain 43.04N 3.16W
109 M23 **Villa San Giovanni** Calabria, S Italy 38.12N 15.39E
63 D18 **Villa San José** Entre Ríos, E Argentina 32.12S 58.15W
Villa Sanjurjo *see* Al-Hoceïma
107 P6 **Villasayas** Castilla-León, N Spain 41.19N 2.36W
109 C20 **Villasimius** Sardegna, Italy, C Mediterranean Sea 39.10N 9.30E
43 N6 **Villa Unión** Coahuila de Zaragoza, NE Mexico 28.18N 100.43W
42 K10 **Villa Unión** Durango, C Mexico 23.58N 104.01W
42 J10 **Villa Unión** Sinaloa, C Mexico 23.13N 106.10W
64 K12 **Villa Valeria** Córdoba, C Argentina 34.21S 64.55W
107 N8 **Villaverde** Madrid, C Spain 40.21N 3.43W
56 F10 **Villavicencio** Meta, C Colombia 4.09N 73.37W
106 L2 **Villaviciosa** Asturias, N Spain 43.28N 5.25W
106 L12 **Villaviciosa de Cordoba** Andalucía, S Spain 38.04N 5.00W
59 L22 **Villazón** Potosí, S Bolivia 22.04S 65.34W
12 J8 **Villebon, Lac** ◎ Quebec, SE Canada
Ville de Kinshasa *see* Kinshasa
104 J5 **Villedieu-les-Poêles** Manche, N France 48.51N 1.12W
Villefranche *see* Villefranche-sur-Saône
105 N16 **Villefranche-de-Lauragais** Haute-Garonne, S France 43.24N 1.42E
105 N14 **Villefranche-de-Rouergue** Aveyron, S France 44.21N 2.01E
105 R10 **Villefranche-sur-Saône** *var.* Villefranche. Rhône, E France 46.00N 4.40E
12 H9 **Ville-Marie** Quebec, SE Canada 47.21N 79.25W
104 M15 **Villemur-sur-Tarn** Haute-Garonne, S France 43.50N 1.32E
107 S11 **Villena** País Valenciano, E Spain 38.39N 0.52W
Villeneuve-d'Agen *see* Villeneuve-sur-Lot
104 L13 **Villeneuve-sur-Lot** *var.* Villeneuve-d'Agen; *hist.* Gajac. Lot-et-Garonne, SW France 44.24N 0.43E
105 P6 **Villeneuve-sur-Yonne** Yonne, C France 48.04N 3.21E
24 H8 **Ville Platte** Louisiana, S USA 30.41N 92.16W
105 R11 **Villeurbanne** Rhône, E France 45.46N 4.54E
103 G23 **Villingen-Schwenningen** Baden-Württemberg, S Germany 48.04N 8.27E
31 T15 **Villisca** Iowa, C USA 40.55N 94.58W
Villmanstrand *see* Lappeenranta
Vilna *see* Vilnius
121 H14 **Vilnius** *Pol.* Wilno, *Ger.* Wilna; *prev. Rus.* Vilna. ● (Lithuania) Vilnius, SE Lithuania 54.41N 25.19E
121 H14 **Vilnius** ✕ Vilnius, SE Lithuania 54.33N 25.17E
119 S7 **Vil'nohirs'k** Dnipropetrovs'ka Oblast', E Ukraine 48.31N 34.01E
119 U8 **Vil'nyans'k** Zaporiz'ka Oblast', SE Ukraine 47.56N 35.22E
95 L17 **Vilppula** Länsi-Suomi, W Finland 62.01N 24.30E
103 M20 **Vils** ∽ SE Germany
120 C5 **Vilsandi Saar** *island* W Estonia
119 P8 **Vil'shanka** *Rus.* Olshanka. Kirovohrads'ka Oblast', C Ukraine 48.12N 30.54E
103 O22 **Vilshofen** Bayern, SE Germany 48.36N 13.10E
161 J20 **Viluppuram** Tamil Nādu, SE India 12.54N 79.40E
115 I16 **Vilusi** Montenegro, SW Yugoslavia 42.44N 18.34E
101 G18 **Vilvoorde** *Fr.* Vilvorde. Vlaams Brabant, C Belgium 50.55N 4.25E
Vilvorde *see* Vilvoorde
121 J14 **Vilyeyka** *Pol.* Wilejka, *Rus.* Vileyka. Minskaya Voblasts', NW Belarus 54.30N 26.54E
126 Kk11 **Vilyuy** ∽ NE Russian Federation
126 L10 **Vilyuysk** Respublika Sakha (Yakutiya), NE Russian Federation 63.42N 121.20E
126 K11 **Vilyuyskoye Vodokhranilishche** ⊠ NE Russian Federation
106 G2 **Vimianzo** Galicia, NW Spain 43.06N 9.03W
97 M19 **Vimmerby** Kalmar, S Sweden 57.40N 15.49E
104 L5 **Vimoutiers** Orne, N France 48.56N 0.10E
95 L16 **Vimpeli** Länsi-Suomi, W Finland 63.10N 23.49E
81 G14 **Vina** ∽ Cameroon/Chad
64 G11 **Viña del Mar** Valparaíso, C Chile 33.01S 71.34W
21 R8 **Vinalhaven Island** *island* Maine, NE USA
107 T8 **Vinaròs** País Valenciano, E Spain 40.28N 0.28E
Vînători *see* Vânători
33 N15 **Vincennes** Indiana, N USA 38.42N 87.30W
205 Y12 **Vincennes Bay** *bay* Antarctica
27 O7 **Vincent** Texas, SW USA 32.30N 101.10W
97 H24 **Vindeby** Fyn, C Denmark 54.55N 11.09E
95 I15 **Vindeln** Västerbotten, N Sweden 64.10N 19.45E
97 F21 **Vinderup** Ringkøbing, C Denmark 56.28N 8.48E
Vindhya Mountains *see* Vindhya Range
159 N14 **Vindhya Range** *var.* Vindhya Mountains. ▲▲ N India
Vindobona *see* Wien
22 K6 **Vine Grove** Kentucky, S USA 37.48N 85.58W
20 J17 **Vineland** New Jersey, NE USA 39.28N 75.01W
118 E11 **Vinga** Arad, W Romania 46.00N 21.14E
97 M16 **Vingåker** Södermanland, C Sweden 59.01N 15.52E
178 Jj8 **Vinh** Nghê An, N Vietnam 18.42N 105.40E
106 I5 **Vinhais** Bragança, N Portugal 41.50N 7.00W
178 K9 **Vinh Linh** Quang Tri, C Vietnam 17.02N 107.03E
Vinh Loi *see* Bac Liêu
178 Jj14 **Vinh Long** *var.* Vinhlong. Vinh Long, S Vietnam 10.15N 105.58E
115 Q18 **Vinica** NE FYR Macedonia 41.53N 22.30E
111 V13 **Vinica** SE Slovenia 45.28N 15.12E
116 G8 **Vinishte** Montana, NW Bulgaria 43.30N 23.04E
29 Q8 **Vinita** Oklahoma, C USA 36.38N 95.09W
Vînju Mare *see* Vânju Mare
100 I11 **Vinkeveen** Utrecht, C Netherlands 52.13N 4.55E
118 L6 **Vin'kivtsi** Khmel'nyts'ka Oblast', W Ukraine 49.02N 27.13E
114 I10 **Vinkovci** *Ger.* Winkowitz, *Hung.* Vinkovcze. Vukovar-Srijem, E Croatia 45.18N 18.45E
Vinkovcze *see* Vinkovci
Vinnitsa *see* Vinnytsya
Vinnitskaya Oblast'/Vinnytsya *see* Vinnyts'ka Oblast'
118 M7 **Vinnyts'ka Oblast'** *var.* Vinnytsya, *Rus.* Vinnitskaya Oblast'. ◆ *province* C Ukraine
119 N6 **Vinnytsya** *Rus.* Vinnitsa. Vinnyts'ka Oblast', C Ukraine 49.14N 28.30E
119 N6 **Vinnytsya** ✕ Vinnyts'ka Oblast', N Ukraine 49.13N 28.40E
Vinogradov *see* Vynohradiv
204 L8 **Vinson Massif** ▲ Antarctica 78.45S 85.19W
96 G11 **Vinstra** Oppland, S Norway 61.36N 9.44E
118 K12 **Vintilă Vodă** Buzău, SE Romania 45.28N 26.44E
31 X13 **Vinton** Iowa, C USA 42.10N 92.01W
24 F9 **Vinton** Louisiana, S USA 30.10N 93.37W
161 J17 **Vinukonda** Andhra Pradesh, E India 16.03N 79.41E
Vioara *see* Ocnele Mari
85 E23 **Vioolsdrif** Northern Cape, SW South Africa 28.50S 17.38E
84 M13 **Viphya Mountains** ▲▲ C Malawi
179 Qq11 **Virac** Catanduanes Island, N Philippines 13.39N 124.17E
128 K8 **Virandozero** Respublika Kareliya, NW Russian Federation 63.59N 36.00E
143 P16 **Viranşehir** Şanlıurfa, SE Turkey 37.13N 39.31E
160 D13 **Virār** Mahārāshtra, W India 19.30N 72.48E
9 W16 **Virden** Manitoba, S Canada 49.49N 100.57W
32 K14 **Virden** Illinois, N USA 39.30N 89.46W
Virdois *see* Virrat
104 J5 **Vire** Calvados, N France 48.49N 0.52W
104 J4 **Vire** ∽ N France
85 A15 **Virei** Namibe, SW Angola 15.43S 12.54E
Vîrful Moldoveanu *see* Vârful Moldoveanu
37 R5 **Virgina Peak** ▲ Nevada, W USA 39.46N 119.26W
47 U9 **Virgin Gorda** *island* C British Virgin Islands
85 I22 **Virginia** Free State, C South Africa 28.04S 26.51E
32 K13 **Virginia** Illinois, N USA 39.57N 90.12W
31 W4 **Virginia** Minnesota, N USA 47.31N 92.32W
23 T6 **Virginia** *off.* Commonwealth of Virginia; also known as Mother of Presidents, Mother of States, Old Dominion. ◆ *state* NE USA
23 Y7 **Virginia Beach** Virginia, NE USA 36.51N 75.58W
35 R11 **Virginia City** Montana, NW USA 45.17N 111.54W
37 Q6 **Virginia City** Nevada, W USA 39.19N 119.39W
12 H8 **Virginiatown** Ontario, S Canada 48.09N 79.35W
Virgin Islands *see* British Virgin Islands
47 T9 **Virgin Islands (US)** *var.* Virgin Islands of the United States; *prev.* Danish West Indies. ◇ *US unincorporated territory* E West Indies
47 T9 **Virgin Passage** *passage* Puerto Rico/Virgin Islands (US)
37 Y10 **Virgin River** ∽ Nevada/Utah, W USA
Virihaur *see* Virihaure
94 H12 **Virihaure** *var.* Virihaur. ◎ N Sweden
178 Jj11 **Virôchey** Rôtânôkiri, NE Cambodia 13.58N 106.49E
95 N19 **Virolahti** Etelä-Suomi, S Finland 60.33N 27.37E
32 J8 **Viroqua** Wisconsin, N USA 43.33N 90.54W
114 G8 **Virovitica** *Ger.* Virovititz, *Hung.* Verőcze; *prev. Ger.* Werowitz. Virovitica-Podravina, NE Croatia 45.49N 17.25E
114 G8 **Virovitica-Podravina** *off.* Virovitičko-Podravska Županija. ◆ *province* NE Croatia
Virovititz *see* Virovitica
115 J17 **Virpazar** Montenegro, SW Yugoslavia 42.15N 19.06E
95 L17 **Virrat** *Swe.* Virdois. Länsi-Suomi, SW Finland 62.13N 23.49E
97 M20 **Virserum** Kalmar, S Sweden 57.17N 15.18E
101 K25 **Virton** Luxembourg, SE Belgium 49.34N 5.31E
120 F5 **Virtsu** *Ger.* Werder. Läänemaa, W Estonia 58.35N 23.32E
58 C12 **Virú** La Libertad, C Peru 8.27S 78.44W
Virudhunagar *see* Virudunagar
161 H23 **Virudunagar** *var.* Virudhunagar. Tamil Nādu, SE India 9.34N 77.57E
120 I3 **Viru-Jaagupi** *Ger.* Sankt-Jakobi. Lääne-Virumaa, NE Estonia 59.13N 26.28E
59 N19 **Viru-Viru** *var.* Santa Cruz. ✕ (Santa Cruz) Santa Cruz, C Bolivia 17.49S 63.12W
115 E15 **Vis** *It.* Lissa; *anc.* Issa. *island* S Croatia
Vis *see* Fish
120 I12 **Visaginas** *prev.* Sniečkus. Ignalina, E Lithuania 55.36N 26.22E
161 M15 **Visākhapatnam** Andhra Pradesh, SE India 17.45N 83.19E
37 R11 **Visalia** California, W USA 36.19N 119.19W
Vişău *see* Vişeu
179 Qq12 **Visayan Sea** *sea* C Philippines
97 P19 **Visby** *Ger.* Wisby. Gotland, SE Sweden 57.37N 18.19E
207 N9 **Viscount Melville Sound** *prev.* Melville Sound. *sound* Northwest Territories/Nunavut, N Canada
101 L19 **Visé** Liège, E Belgium 50.43N 5.42E
114 K13 **Višegrad** Republika Srpska, E Bosnia and Herzegovina 43.46N 19.18E
60 L12 **Viseu** Pará, NE Brazil 1.10S 46.09W
106 H7 **Viseu** *prev.* Vizeu. Viseu, N Portugal 40.40N 7.55W
106 H7 **Viseu** *var.* Vizeu. ◆ *district* N Portugal
118 I8 **Vişeu** *Hung.* Visó; *prev.* Vişău. ∽ NW Romania
118 I8 **Vişeu de Sus** *var.* Vişeul de Sus, *Ger.* Oberwischau, *Hung.* Felsővisó. Maramureş, N Romania 47.43N 23.24E
Vişeul de Sus *see* Vişeu de Sus
129 R10 **Vishera** ∽ NW Russian Federation
97 J19 **Viskafors** Västra Götaland, S Sweden 57.37N 12.49E
97 J20 **Viskan** ∽ S Sweden
97 L21 **Vislanda** Kronoberg, S Sweden 56.46N 14.30E
Vislinskiy Zaliv *see* Vistula Lagoon
Visó *see* Vişeu
114 H13 **Visoko** Federacija Bosna I Hercegovina, C Bosnia and Herzegovina 43.58N 18.12E
108 A9 **Viso, Monte** ▲ NW Italy 44.42N 7.04E
110 E10 **Visp** Valais, SW Switzerland 46.18N 7.52E
110 E10 **Vispa** ∽ S Switzerland
97 M21 **Vissefjärda** Kalmar, S Sweden 56.31N 15.34E
102 I11 **Visselhövede** Niedersachsen, NW Germany 52.58N 9.36E
97 G23 **Vissenbjerg** Fyn, C Denmark 55.22N 10.07E
37 U17 **Vista** California, W USA 33.12N 117.14W
60 C11 **Vista Alegre** Amazonas, NW Brazil 1.23N 68.13W
116 J13 **Vistonída, Límni** ◎ NE Greece
Vistula *see* Wisła
121 A14 **Vistula Lagoon** *Ger.* Frisches Haff, *Pol.* Zalew Wiślany, *Rus.* Vislinskiy Zaliv. *lagoon* Poland/Russian Federation
116 I8 **Vit** ∽ NW Bulgaria
Vitebsk *see* Vitsyebsk
Vitebskaya Oblast' *see* Vitsyebskaya Voblasts'
109 H14 **Viterbo** *anc.* Vicus Elbii. Lazio, C Italy 42.25N 12.07E
114 H12 **Vitez** Federacija Bosna I Hercegovina, C Bosnia and Herzegovina 44.08N 17.47E
178 J15 **Vi Thanh** Cân Thơ, S Vietnam 9.45N 105.28E
Viti *see* Fiji
194 K12 **Vitiaz Strait** *strait* NE PNG
106 J7 **Vitigudino** Castilla-León, N Spain 41.00N 6.26W
197 H15 **Viti Levu** *island* W Fiji
126 Kk14 **Vitim** ∽ C Russian Federation
126 Kk13 **Vitimskiy** Irkutskaya Oblast', C Russian Federation 58.12N 113.10E
111 V2 **Vitis** Niederösterreich, N Austria 48.45N 15.09E
Vitoria *see* Vitoria-Gasteiz
61 O20 **Vitória** Espírito Santo, SE Brazil 20.19S 40.21W
Vitoria Bank *see* Vitória Seamount
61 N18 **Vitória da Conquista** Bahia, E Brazil 14.52S 40.52W
107 P3 **Vitoria-Gasteiz** *var.* Vitoria, *Eng.* Vittoria. País Vasco, N Spain 42.51N 2.40W
67 J16 **Vitória Seamount** *var.* Victoria Bank, Vitoria Bank. *undersea feature* C Atlantic Ocean 18.48S 37.24W
114 F13 **Vitorog** ▲ SW Bosnia and Herzegovina 44.06N 17.03E
104 J6 **Vitré** Ille-et-Vilaine, NW France 48.07N 1.12W
105 R5 **Vitry-le-François** Marne, N France 48.43N 4.36E
116 D13 **Vítsoi** ▲ N Greece 40.39N 21.23E
120 N13 **Vitsyebsk** *Rus.* Vitebsk. Vitsyebskaya Voblasts', NE Belarus 55.11N 30.10E
120 K13 **Vitsyebskaya Voblasts'** *prev. Rus.* Vitebskaya Oblast'. ◆ *province* N Belarus
94 J11 **Vittangi** Norrbotten, N Sweden 67.40N 21.39E
105 R8 **Vitteaux** Côte d'Or, C France 47.24N 4.31E
105 S6 **Vittel** Vosges, NE France 48.13N 5.57E
97 N15 **Vittinge** Västmanland, C Sweden 59.52N 17.04E
109 K25 **Vittoria** Sicilia, Italy, C Mediterranean Sea 36.55N 14.30E
Vittoria *see* Vitoria-Gasteiz
108 I7 **Vittorio Veneto** Veneto, NE Italy 45.58N 12.18E
183 Q9 **Vitu Levu** *island* W Fiji
199 Jj7 **Vityaz Seamount** *undersea feature* C Pacific Ocean 13.30N 173.15W
183 Q7 **Vityaz Trench** *undersea feature* W Pacific Ocean
110 G8 **Vitznau** Luzern, W Switzerland 47.01N 8.28E
106 I1 **Viveiro** Galicia, NW Spain 43.39N 7.34W
107 S9 **Viver** País Valenciano, E Spain 39.55N 0.36W
105 Q13 **Viverais, Monts du** ▲▲ C France
126 Ii10 **Vivi** ∽ N Russian Federation
24 F4 **Vivian** Louisiana, S USA 32.52N 93.59W
31 N10 **Vivian** South Dakota, N USA 43.53N 100.16W
105 R13 **Viviers** Ardèche, E France 44.31N 4.40E
Vivis *see* Vevey
85 K19 **Vivo** Northern, NE South Africa 22.58S 29.13E
104 L10 **Vivonne** Vienne, W France 46.25N 0.15E
197 G14 **Viwa** *island* Yasawa Group, NW Fiji
Vizakna *see* Ocna Sibiului
107 O2 **Vizcaya** *Basq.* Bizkaia. ◆ *province* País Vasco, N Spain
Vizcaya, Golfo de *see* Biscay, Bay of
142 C10 **Vize** Kırklareli, NW Turkey 41.33N 27.49E
126 I2 **Vize, Ostrov** *island* Severnaya Zemlya, N Russian Federation
Vizeu *see* Viseu
161 M15 **Vizianagaram** *var.* Vizianagram. Andhra Pradesh, E India 18.07N 83.25E
Vizianagram *see* Vizianagaram
105 S12 **Vizille** Isère, E France 45.05N 5.46E
129 R11 **Vizinga** Respublika Komi, NW Russian Federation 61.06N 50.09E
118 M13 **Viziru** Brăila, SE Romania 45.00N 27.43E
115 K21 **Vjosës, Lumi i** *var.* Vijosa, Vijosë, *Gk.* Aóos. ∽ Albania/Greece *see also* Aóos
101 H18 **Vlaams Brabant** ◆ *province* C Belgium
Vlaanderen *see* Flanders
100 G12 **Vlaardingen** Zuid-Holland, SW Netherlands 51.55N 4.21E
118 F10 **Vlădeasa, Vârful** *prev.* Vîrful Vlădeasa. ▲ NW Romania 46.45N 22.46E
Vlădeasa, Vîrful *see* Vlădeasa, Vârful
115 P16 **Vladičin Han** Serbia, SE Yugoslavia 42.44N 22.04E
131 O16 **Vladikavkaz** *prev.* Dzaudzhikau, Ordzhonikidze. Respublika Severnaya Osetiya, SW Russian Federation 42.58N 44.41E
130 M3 **Vladimir** Vladimirskaya Oblast', W Russian Federation 56.09N 40.21E
150 M7 **Vladimirovka** Kostanay, N Kazakhstan 53.28N 64.01E
Vladimirovka *see* Yuzhno-Sakhalinsk
130 L3 **Vladimirskaya Oblast'** ◆ *province* W Russian Federation
130 I3 **Vladimirskiy Tupik** Smolenskaya Oblast', W Russian Federation 55.45N 33.25E
Vladimir-Volynskiy *see* Volodymyr-Volyns'kyy
127 Nn18 **Vladivostok** Primorskiy Kray, SE Russian Federation 43.09N 131.52E
119 U13 **Vladyslavivka** Respublika Krym, S Ukraine 45.09N 35.25E
100 P6 **Vlagtwedde** Groningen, NE Netherlands 53.01N 7.07E
Vlajna *see* Kukavica
114 J12 **Vlasenica** Republika Srpska, E Bosnia and Herzegovina 44.10N 18.57E
114 G12 **Vlašić** ▲ C Bosnia and Herzegovina 44.18N 17.40E
113 D17 **Vlašim** *Ger.* Wlaschim. Středočeský Kraj, C Czech Republic 49.42N 14.54E
115 P15 **Vlasotince** Serbia, SE Yugoslavia 42.58N 22.07E
126 Ll7 **Vlasovo** Respublika Sakha (Yakutiya), NE Russian Federation 70.41N 134.49E
100 I11 **Vleuten** Utrecht, C Netherlands 52.07N 5.01E
100 I5 **Vlieland** *Fris.* Flylân. *island* Waddeneilanden, N Netherlands
100 I5 **Vliestroom** *strait* NW Netherlands
101 J14 **Vlijmen** Noord-Brabant, S Netherlands 51.42N 5.13E
101 E15 **Vlissingen** *Eng.* Flushing, *Fr.* Flessingue. Zeeland, SW Netherlands 51.25N 3.34E
Vlodava *see* Włodawa
Vlonë/Vlora *see* Vlorë
115 K22 **Vlorë** *prev.* Vlonë, *It.* Valona, Vlora. Vlorë, SW Albania 40.27N 19.31E
115 K22 **Vlorë** ◆ *district* SW Albania
115 K22 **Vlorës, Gjiri i** *var.* Valona Bay. *bay* SW Albania
Vlotslavsk *see* Włocławek
113 C16 **Vltava** *Ger.* Moldau. ∽ W Czech Republic
130 K3 **Vnukovo** ✕ (Moskva) Gorod Moskva, W Russian Federation 55.30N 36.52E
27 Q9 **Voca** Texas, SW USA 30.58N 99.09W
111 R5 **Vöcklabruck** Oberösterreich, NW Austria 48.01N 13.37E
114 D13 **Vodice** Šibenik-Knin, S Croatia 43.46N 15.46E
128 K10 **Vodlozero, Ozero** ◎ NW Russian Federation
114 A10 **Vodnjan** *It.* Dignano d'Istria. Istra, NW Croatia 44.57N 13.51E
129 S9 **Vodnyy** Respublika Komi, NW Russian Federation 63.31N 53.21E
97 G20 **Vodskov** Nordjylland, N Denmark 57.07N 10.01E
94 H4 **Vogar** Sudhurland, SW Iceland 63.58N 22.20W
195 N16 **Vogel, Cape** *headland* SE PNG 9.42S 150.04E
Vogelkop *see* Doberai, Jazirah
79 X15 **Vogel Peak** *prev.* Dim lang. ▲ E Nigeria 8.16N 11.44E
103 H17 **Vogelsberg** ▲▲ C Germany
108 D8 **Voghera** Lombardia, N Italy 44.58N 9.01E
114 I13 **Vogošća** Federacija Bosna I Hercegovina, SE Bosnia and Herzegovina 43.55N 18.20E
103 M17 **Vogtland** *historical region* E Germany
129 V12 **Vogul'skiy Kamen', Gora** ▲ NW Russian Federation 60.10N 58.41E
197 H6 **Voh** Province Nord, C New Caledonia 20.57S 164.41E
Vohémar *see* Iharaña
180 H8 **Vohimena, Tanjona** *Fr.* Cap Sainte Marie. *headland* S Madagascar 25.20S 45.06E
180 J6 **Vohipeno** Fianarantsoa, SE Madagascar 22.21S 47.51E
120 H5 **Võhma** *Ger.* Wöchma. Viljandimaa, S Estonia 58.37N 25.34E
83 J20 **Voi** Coast, S Kenya 3.22S 38.34E
78 K15 **Voinjama** N Liberia 8.23N 9.48W
105 S12 **Voiron** Isère, E France 45.22N 5.34E
111 V8 **Voitsberg** Steiermark, SE Austria 47.04N 15.09E
97 F24 **Vojens** *Ger.* Woyens. Sønderjylland, SW Denmark 55.15N 9.19E
114 K9 **Vojvodina** *Ger.* Wojwodina. *Region* N Yugoslavia
13 S6 **Volant** ∽ Quebec, SE Canada
Volaterrae *see* Volterra
45 P15 **Volcán** *var.* Hato del Volcán. Chiriquí, W Panama 8.45N 82.38W
Volchansk *see* Vovchans'k
Volchya *see* Vovcha
96 D10 **Volda** Møre og Romsdal, S Norway 62.07N 6.04E
100 J9 **Volendam** Noord-Holland, C Netherlands 52.30N 5.04E
128 L15 **Volga** Yaroslavskaya Oblast', W Russian Federation 57.56N 38.23E
31 R10 **Volga** South Dakota, N USA 44.19N 96.55W
125 Cc11 **Volga** ∽ NW Russian Federation
Volga-Baltic Waterway *see* Volgo-Baltiyskiy Kanal
Volga Hills/Volga Uplands *see* Privolzhskaya Vozvyshennost'
128 L13 **Volgo-Baltiyskiy Kanal** *Eng.* Volga-Baltic Waterway. *canal* NW Russian Federation
130 M12 **Volgodonsk** Rostovskaya Oblast', SW Russian Federation 47.34N 42.03E
131 O10 **Volgograd** *prev.* Stalingrad, Tsaritsyn. Volgogradskaya Oblast', SW Russian Federation 48.42N 44.28E
131 N9 **Volgogradskaya Oblast'** ◆ *province* SW Russian Federation
131 P10 **Volgogradskoye Vodokhranilishche** ⊠ SW Russian Federation
103 J19 **Volkach** Bayern, C Germany 49.51N 10.15E
111 U9 **Völkermarkt** *Slvn.* Velikovec. Kärnten, S Austria 46.39N 14.37E
128 I12 **Volkhov** Leningradskaya Oblast', NW Russian Federation 59.56N 32.19E
103 D20 **Völklingen** Saarland, SW Germany 49.15N 6.51E
Volkovysk *see* Vawkavysk
Volkovyskiye Vysoty *see* Vawkavyskaye Wzvyshsha
85 K22 **Volksrust** Mpumalanga, E South Africa 27.18S 29.53E
100 L8 **Vollenhove** Overijssel, N Netherlands 52.40N 5.58E
121 L16 **Volma** *Rus.* Volma. ∽ C Belarus
Volmari *see* Valmiera
119 W9 **Volnovakha** Donets'ka Oblast', SE Ukraine 47.36N 37.31E
118 K6 **Volochys'k** Khmel'nyts'ka Oblast', W Ukraine 49.32N 26.14E
119 O6 **Volodarka** Kyyivs'ka Oblast', N Ukraine 49.31N 29.55E
119 W9 **Volodars'ke** Donets'ka Oblast', E Ukraine 47.11N 37.19E
131 R13 **Volodarskiy** Astrakhanskaya Oblast', SW Russian Federation 46.23N 48.39E
Volodarskoye *see* Saumalkol'
119 N8 **Volodars'k-Volyns'kyy** Zhytomyrs'ka Oblast', N Ukraine 50.37N 28.28E
118 K3 **Volodymerets'** Rivnens'ka Oblast', NW Ukraine 51.24N 25.52E
118 I3 **Volodymyr-Volyns'kyy** *Pol.* Włodzimierz, *Rus.* Vladimir-Volynskiy. Volyns'ka Oblast', NW Ukraine 50.51N 24.19E
128 L14 **Vologda** Vologodskaya Oblast', W Russian Federation 59.10N 39.55E
128 L12 **Vologodskaya Oblast'** ◆ *province* NW Russian Federation
130 K3 **Volokolamsk** Moskovskaya Oblast', W Russian Federation 56.03N 35.57E
130 K9 **Volokonovka** Belgorodskaya Oblast', W Russian Federation 50.30N 37.54E
117 G16 **Vólos** Thessalía, C Greece 39.21N 22.58E
128 M11 **Voloshka** Arkhangel'skaya Oblast', NW Russian Federation 61.19N 40.06E
Vološinovo *see* Novi Bečej
118 H7 **Volovets'** Zakarpats'ka Oblast', W Ukraine 48.42N 23.12E
116 K7 **Volovo** Ruse, N Bulgaria 43.33N 25.49E
Volozhin *see* Valozhyn
131 Q7 **Vol'sk** Saratovskaya Oblast', W Russian Federation 52.04N 47.19E
79 Q17 **Volta** ∽ SE Ghana
Volta Blanche *see* White Volta
79 P16 **Volta, Lake** ⊠ SE Ghana
Volta Noire *see* Black Volta
62 O9 **Volta Redonda** Rio de Janeiro, SE Brazil 22.31S 44.04W
Volta Rouge *see* Red Volta
108 F12 **Volterra** *anc.* Volaterrae. Toscana, C Italy 43.25N 10.51E
109 K17 **Volturno** ∽ S Italy
115 I15 **Volujak** ▲▲ SW Yugoslavia
Volunteer Island *see* Starbuck Island
67 F24 **Volunteer Point** *headland* East Falkland, Falkland Islands 51.31S 57.43W
Volunteer State *see* Tennessee
116 H13 **Vólvi, Límni** ◎ N Greece
Volyn *see* Volyns'ka Oblast'
118 I3 **Volyns'ka Oblast'** *var.* Volyn, *Rus.* Volynskaya Oblast'. ◆ *province* NW Ukraine
Volynskaya Oblast' *see* Volyns'ka Oblast'
131 Q3 **Volzhsk** Respublika Mariy El, W Russian Federation 55.53N 48.21E
131 O10 **Volzhskiy** Volgogradskaya Oblast', SW Russian Federation 48.48N 44.40E
180 I7 **Vondrozo** Fianarantsoa, SE Madagascar 22.49S 47.19E
116 K9 **Voneshta Voda** Veliko Tŭrnovo, N Bulgaria 42.55N 25.40E
41 P10 **Von Frank Mountain** ▲ Alaska, USA 63.36N 154.29W
117 C17 **Vónitsa** Dytikí Ellás, W Greece 38.55N 20.52E
120 J6 **Võnnu** *Ger.* Wendau. Tartumaa, SE Estonia 58.15N 27.04E
100 G12 **Voorburg** Zuid-Holland, W Netherlands 52.04N 4.22E
100 H11 **Voorschoten** Zuid-Holland, W Netherlands 52.07N 4.25E
100 M11 **Voorst** Gelderland, E Netherlands 52.10N 6.10E
100 K11 **Voorthuizen** Gelderland, C Netherlands 52.12N 5.36E
94 L2 **Vopnafjördhur** Austurland, E Iceland 65.45N 14.51W
94 L2 **Vopnafjördhur** *bay* E Iceland
Vora *see* Vorë
121 H15 **Voranava** *Pol.* Werenów, *Rus.* Voronovo. Hrodzyenskaya Voblasts', W Belarus 54.10N 25.21E
110 I8 **Vorarlberg** *off.* Land Vorarlberg. ◆ *state* W Austria
111 X7 **Vorau** Steiermark, E Austria 47.22N 15.55E
100 N11 **Vorden** Gelderland, E Netherlands 52.07N 6.18E
110 H9 **Vorderrhein** ∽ SE Switzerland
94 J2 **Vordhufell** ▲ N Iceland 65.42N 18.45W
97 I24 **Vordingborg** Storstrøm, SE Denmark 55.01N 11.55E
115 K19 **Vorë** *var.* Vora. Tiranë, W Albania 41.23N 19.37E
117 H17 **Vóreioi Sporádes** *var.* Vórioi Sporádhes, *Eng.* Northern Sporades. *island group* E Greece
117 J17 **Vóreion Aigaíon** *Eng.* Aegean North. ◆ *region* SE Greece
117 G18 **Voreiós Evvoïkós Kólpos** *gulf* E Greece
207 S16 **Voring Plateau** *undersea feature* N Norwegian Sea
Vórioi Sporádhes *see* Vóreioi Sporádes
129 W4 **Vorkuta** Respublika Komi, NW Russian Federation 67.27N 64.00E
97 I14 **Vorma** ∽ S Norway
120 E4 **Vormsi** *var.* Vormsi Saar, *Ger.* Worms, Swed. Ormsö. *island* W Estonia
Vormsi Saar *see* Vormsi
126 Hh12 **Vorogovo** Krasnoyarskiy Kray, C Russian Federation 61.01N 89.25E
131 N7 **Vorona** ∽ W Russian Federation
130 L7 **Voronezh** Voronezhskaya Oblast', W Russian Federation 51.39N 39.13E
130 L7 **Voronezh** ∽ W Russian Federation
130 K8 **Voronezhskaya Oblast'** ◆ *province* W Russian Federation
Voronovitsya *see* Voronovytsya
Voronovo *see* Voranava
119 N6 **Voronovytsya** *Rus.* Voronovitsya. Vinnyts'ka Oblast', C Ukraine 49.06N 28.49E
126 Hh7 **Vorontsovo** Taymyrskiy (Dolgano-Nenetskiy) Avtonomnyy Okrug, N Russian Federation 71.45N 83.31E
128 K3 **Voron'ya** ∽ NW Russian Federation
Voropayevo *see* Varapayeva
Voroshilov *see* Ussuriysk
Voroshilovgrad *see* Luhans'k, Ukraine
Voroshilovgrad *see* Luhans'ka Oblast', Ukraine
Voroshilovgradskaya Oblast' *see* Luhans'ka Oblast'
Voroshilovsk *see* Stavropol', Russian Federation
Voroshilovsk *see* Alchevs'k, Ukraine
143 V13 **Vorotan** *Az.* Bärguşad. ∽ Armenia/Azerbaijan
131 P3 **Vorotynets** Nizhegorodskaya Oblast', W Russian Federation 56.06N 46.06E
119 S3 **Vorozhba** Sums'ka Oblast', NE Ukraine 51.09N 34.16E
119 T5 **Vorskla** ∽ Russian Federation/Ukraine
101 I17 **Vorst** Antwerpen, N Belgium 51.06N 5.01E
85 G21 **Vorstershoop** North-West, N South Africa 25.46S 22.57E
120 H6 **Võrtsjärv** *Ger.* Wirz-See. ◎ SE Estonia
120 J7 **Võru** *Ger.* Werro. Võrumaa, SE Estonia 57.51N 27.00E
153 R11 **Vorukh** N Tajikistan 39.51N 70.34E
120 I7 **Võrumaa** *off.* Võru Maakond. ◆ *province* SE Estonia
85 G24 **Vosburg** Northern Cape, W South Africa 30.33S 22.49E
153 Q14 **Vose'** *Rus.* Vose; *prev.* Aral. SW Tajikistan 37.51N 69.31E
105 S6 **Vosges** ◆ *department* NE France
105 U6 **Vosges** ▲▲ NE France
128 K13 **Voskresenkoye** Vologodskaya Oblast', NW Russian Federation 59.25N 37.56E
130 L4 **Voskresensk** Moskovskaya Oblast', W Russian Federation 55.19N 38.42E
131 P2 **Voskresenskoye** Nizhegorodskaya Oblast', W Russian Federation 57.00N 45.33E
131 V6 **Voskresenskoye** Respublika Bashkortostan, W Russian Federation 53.07N 56.07E
96 D13 **Voss** Hordaland, S Norway 60.37N 6.25E
96 D13 **Voss** *physical region* S Norway
101 I16 **Vosselaar** Antwerpen, N Belgium 51.19N 4.55E
96 D13 **Vosso** ∽ S Norway
Vostochno-Kazakhstanskaya Oblast' *see* Shygys Konyrat
151 T12 **Vostochno-Kounradskiy** *Kaz.* Shyghys Qongyrat. Zhezkazgan, C Kazakhstan 47.01N 75.05E
127 N4 **Vostochno-Sibirskoye More** *Eng.* East Siberian Sea. *sea* Arctic Ocean
151 X10 **Vostochnyy Kazakhstan** *off.* Vostochno-Kazakhstanskaya Oblast', *var.* East Kazakhstan, *Kaz.* Shyghys Qazagastan Oblysy. ◆ *province* E Kazakhstan
Vostochnyy Sayan *see* Eastern Sayans
Vostock Island *see* Vostok Island
205 U10 **Vostok** *Russian research station* Antarctica 77.18S 105.32E
203 X5 **Vostok Island** *var.* Vostock Island; *prev.* Stavers Island. *island* Line Islands, SE Kiribati
131 T2 **Votkinsk** Udmurtskaya Respublika, NW Russian Federation 57.04N 54.00E
129 U15 **Votkinskoye Vodokhranilishche** *var.* Votkinsk Reservoir. ⊠ NW Russian Federation
Votkinsk Reservoir *see* Votkinskoye Vodokhranilishche
62 J7 **Votuporanga** São Paulo, S Brazil 20.25S 49.52W
106 H7 **Vouga, Rio** ∽ N Portugal
117 E14 **Voúrinos** ▲▲ N Greece
117 G24 **Voúxa, Akrotírio** *headland* Kríti, Greece, E Mediterranean Sea 35.37N 23.34E
105 R4 **Vouziers** Ardennes, N France 49.24N 4.42E
119 V7 **Vovcha** *Rus.* Volchya. ∽ E Ukraine
119 V4 **Vovchans'k** *Rus.* Volchansk. Kharkivs'ka Oblast', E Ukraine 50.19N 36.54E
105 N6 **Voves** Eure-et-Loir, C France 48.18N 1.39E
81 M14 **Vovodo** ∽ S Central African Republic
96 M12 **Voxna** Gävleborg, C Sweden 61.20N 15.34E
96 L11 **Voxnan** ∽ C Sweden
116 F7 **Voynishka Reka** ∽ NW Bulgaria

◆ COUNTRY
● COUNTRY CAPITAL
◇ DEPENDENT TERRITORY
○ DEPENDENT TERRITORY CAPITAL
◆ ADMINISTRATIVE REGION
✕ INTERNATIONAL AIRPORT
▲ MOUNTAIN
▲▲ MOUNTAIN RANGE
⛰ VOLCANO
∽ RIVER
◎ LAKE
⊠ RESERVOIR

VOYVOZH – WARBURG

129 T9 **Voyvozh** Respublika Komi, NW Russian Federation 62.54N 54.52E
128 M12 **Vozhega** Vologodskaya Oblast', NW Russian Federation 60.27N 40.11E
128 L12 **Vozhe, Ozero** NW Russian Federation
119 Q9 **Voznesens'k** *Rus.* Voznesensk. Mykolayivs'ka Oblast', S Ukraine 47.33N 31.22E
128 J12 **Voznesen'ye** Leningradskaya Oblast', NW Russian Federation 61.00N 35.24E
150 J14 **Vozrozhdeniya, Ostrov** *Uzb.* Wozrojdeniye Oroli. *island* Kazakhstan/Uzbekistan
97 G20 **Vrå** *var.* Vraa. Nordjylland, N Denmark 57.21N 9.57E
Vraa *see* Vrå
116 H9 **Vrachesh** Sofiya, NW Bulgaria 42.52N 23.45E
117 C19 **Vrachíonas** ▲ Zákynthos, Iónioi Nísoi, Greece, C Mediterranean Sea 37.49N 20.43E
119 P8 **Vradiyivka** Mykolayivs'ka Oblast', S Ukraine 47.51N 30.37E
115 G14 **Vran** ▲ SW Bosnia and Herzegovina 43.35N 17.30E
118 K12 **Vrancea** *county* E Romania
153 T14 **Vrang** SE Tajikistan 37.03N 72.26E
127 Oo2 **Vrangelya, Ostrov** *Eng.* Wrangel Island. *island* NE Russian Federation
114 H13 **Vranica** ▲ C Bosnia and Herzegovina 43.57N 17.43E
115 O16 **Vranje** Serbia, SE Yugoslavia 42.33N 21.55E
Vranov *see* Vranov nad Topl'ou
113 N19 **Vranov nad Topl'ou** *var.* Vranov, *Hung.* Varannó. Prešovský Kraj, E Slovakia 48.54N 21.40E
116 H8 **Vratsa** Vratsa, NW Bulgaria 43.13N 23.33E
116 H8 **Vratsa** *province* NW Bulgaria
116 F10 **Vrattsa** *prev.* Mirovo. Kyustendil, W Bulgaria 42.16N 22.39E
114 G11 **Vrbanja** NW Bosnia and Herzegovina
114 K9 **Vrbas** Serbia, NW Yugoslavia 45.34N 19.39E
114 G13 **Vrbas** N Bosnia and Herzegovina
114 E8 **Vrbovec** Zagreb, N Croatia 45.53N 16.24E
114 C9 **Vrbovsko** Primorje-Gorski Kotar, NW Croatia 45.22N 15.06E
113 E15 **Vrchlabí** *Ger.* Hohenelbe. Hradecký Kraj, NE Czech Republic 50.37N 15.37E
85 J22 **Vrede** Free State, E South Africa 27.25S 29.10E
102 E13 **Vreden** Nordrhein-Westfalen, NW Germany 52.01N 6.50E
85 E25 **Vredenburg** Western Cape, SW South Africa 32.55S 18.00E
101 I23 **Vresse-sur-Semois** Namur, SE Belgium 49.52N 4.56E
97 L16 **Vretstorp** Örebro, C Sweden 59.03N 14.51E
115 G15 **Vrgorac** *prev.* Vrhgorac. Split-Dalmacija, SE Croatia 43.10N 17.24E
Vrhgorac *see* Vrgorac
111 T12 **Vrhnika** *Ger.* Oberlaibach. W Slovenia 45.57N 14.18E
161 I21 **Vriddhāchalam** Tamil Nādu, SE India 11.33N 79.18E
100 N6 **Vries** Drenthe, NE Netherlands 53.04N 6.34E
100 O10 **Vriezenveen** Overijssel, E Netherlands 52.25N 6.39E
97 L20 **Vrigstad** Jönköping, S Sweden 57.19N 14.30E
110 H9 **Vrin** Graubünden, S Switzerland 46.40N 9.06E
114 E13 **Vrlika** Split-Dalmacija, S Croatia 43.54N 16.24E
115 M14 **Vrnjačka Banja** Serbia, C Yugoslavia 43.36N 20.55E
Vrondádhes/Vrondados *see* Vrontádos
117 L18 **Vrontádos** *var.* Vrondados; *prev.* Vrondádhes. Chíos, E Greece 38.25N 26.07E
100 N9 **Vroomshoop** Overijssel, E Netherlands 52.28N 6.34E
114 N10 **Vršac** *Ger.* Werschetz, *Hung.* Versecz. Serbia, NE Yugoslavia 45.08N 21.17E
114 M10 **Vršački Kanal** *canal* N Yugoslavia
85 H21 **Vryburg** North-West, N South Africa 26.57S 24.43E
85 K22 **Vryheid** KwaZulu/Natal, E South Africa 27.45S 30.48E
113 I18 **Vsetín** *Ger.* Wsetin. Zlínský Kraj, E Czech Republic 49.21N 17.57E
113 J20 **Vtáčnik** *Hung.* Madaras, Ptacsnik; *prev.* Ptačnik. ▲ W Slovakia 48.38N 18.38E
Vuadil' *see* Wodil
Vuanggava *see* Vuaqava
197 K15 **Vuaqava** *prev.* Vuanggava. *island* Lau Group, SE Fiji
116 I11 **Vŭcha** SW Bulgaria
115 N16 **Vučitrn** Serbia, S Yugoslavia 42.49N 21.00E
101 J14 **Vught** Noord-Brabant, S Netherlands 51.37N 5.19E
119 W8 **Vuhledar** Donets'ka Oblast', E Ukraine 47.48N 37.11E
114 I9 **Vuka** E Croatia
115 K17 **Vukël** *var.* Vukli. Shkodër, N Albania 42.29N 19.39E
Vukli *see* Vukël
114 J9 **Vukovar** *Hung.* Vukovár. Vukovar-Srijem, E Croatia 45.18N 18.45E
114 I10 **Vukovar-Srijem** *off.* Vukovarsko-Srijemska Županija. *province* E Croatia
129 U8 **Vuktyl** Respublika Komi, NW Russian Federation 63.49N 57.07E
9 Q17 **Vulcan** Alberta, SW Canada 50.27N 113.12W
118 G12 **Vulcan** *Ger.* Wulkan, *Hung.* Zsilyvajdevulkán; *prev.* Crivadia Vulcanului, Vaidei, *Hung.* Sily-Vajdej, Vajdej. Hunedoara, W Romania 45.22N 23.16E
118 M12 **Vulcănești** *Rus.* Vulkaneshty. S Moldova 45.41N 28.25E
109 L22 **Vulcano, Isola** *island* Isole Eolie, S Italy
116 G7 **Vŭlchedrŭm** Montana, NW Bulgaria 43.42N 23.25E
116 N8 **Vŭlchidol** *prev.* Kurt-Dere. Varna, NE Bulgaria 43.25N 27.33E
Vulkaneshty *see* Vulcănești
38 J13 **Vulture Mountains** ▲ Arizona, SW USA
178 K14 **Vung Tau** *prev. Fr.* Cape Saint Jacques, Cap Saint-Jacques. Ba Ria-Vung Tau, S Vietnam 10.21N 107.04E
197 I15 **Vunisea** Kadavu, SE Fiji 19.04S 178.09E
Vuohčču *see* Vuotso
95 N15 **Vuokatti** Oulu, C Finland 64.08N 28.16E
95 M15 **Vuolijoki** Oulu, C Finland 64.09N 27.00E
94 J13 **Vuollerim** Norrbotten, N Sweden 66.24N 20.36E
Vuoreija *see* Vardø
94 L10 **Vuotso** *Lapp.* Vuohčču. Lappi, N Finland 68.04N 27.05E
116 J11 **Vŭrbitsa** *prev.* Filevo. Khaskovo, S Bulgaria 42.02N 25.25E
116 J12 **Vŭrbitsa** S Bulgaria
131 Q4 **Vurnary** Chuvashskaya Respublika, W Russian Federation 55.30N 46.59E
116 G8 **Vŭrshets** Montana, NW Bulgaria 43.14N 23.20E
121 F17 **Vyalikaya Byerastavitsa** *Pol.* Brzostowica Wielka, *Rus.* Bol'shaya Berëstovitsa; *prev.* Velikaya Berestovitsa. Hrodzyenskaya Voblasts', SW Belarus 53.12N 24.03E
121 N20 **Vyaliki Bor** *Rus.* Velikiy Bor. Homyel'skaya Voblasts', SE Belarus 52.01N 29.54E
121 J18 **Vyaliki Rozhan** *Rus.* Bol'shoy Rozhan. Minskaya Voblasts', S Belarus 52.46N 27.07E
128 H10 **Vyartsilya** *Fin.* Värtsilä. Respublika Kareliya, NW Russian Federation 62.07N 30.43E
121 K17 **Vyasyeya** *Rus.* Veseya. Minskaya Voblasts', C Belarus 53.04N 27.40E
129 R15 **Vyatka** NW Russian Federation
Vyatka *see* Kirov
129 S16 **Vyatskiye Polyany** Kirovskaya Oblast', NW Russian Federation 56.15N 51.06E
127 Nn16 **Vyazemskiy** Khabarovskiy Kray, SE Russian Federation 47.28N 134.39E
130 I4 **Vyaz'ma** Smolenskaya Oblast', W Russian Federation 55.09N 34.20E
131 N3 **Vyazniki** Vladimirskaya Oblast', W Russian Federation 56.15N 42.06E
131 O8 **Vyazovka** Volgogradskaya Oblast', SW Russian Federation 50.57N 43.57E
121 J14 **Vyazyn'** *Rus.* Vyazyn'. Minskaya Voblasts', NW Belarus 54.25N 27.10E
128 G11 **Vyborg** *Fin.* Viipuri. Leningradskaya Oblast', NW Russian Federation 60.44N 28.47E
129 P11 **Vychegda** *var.* Vichegda. NW Russian Federation
126 Jj16 **Vydrino** Respublika Buryatiya, S Russian Federation 51.22N 104.34E
121 L14 **Vyelyewshchyna** *Rus.* Velevshchina. Vitsyebskaya Voblasts', N Belarus 54.44N 28.33E
121 P16 **Vyeramyeyki** *Rus.* Veremeyki. Mahilyowskaya Voblasts', E Belarus 53.46N 31.18E
120 K11 **Vyerkhnyadzvinsk** *Rus.* Verkhnedvinsk. Vitsyebskaya Voblasts', N Belarus 55.46N 27.55E
121 P18 **Vyetka** *Rus.* Vetka. Homyel'skaya Voblasts', SE Belarus 52.34N 31.13E
120 L12 **Vyetryna** *Rus.* Vetrino. Vitsyebskaya Voblasts', N Belarus 55.24N 28.28E
Vygonovskoye, Ozero *see* Vyhanawskaye, Vozyera
128 J9 **Vygozero, Ozero** NW Russian Federation
Vyhanashchanskaye Vozyera *see* Vyhanawskaye, Vozyera
121 I18 **Vyhanawskaye, Vozyera** *var.* Vyhanashchanskaye Vozyera, *Rus.* Ozero Vygonovskoye. SW Belarus
131 N4 **Vyksa** Nizhegorodskaya Oblast', W Russian Federation 55.21N 42.10E
119 O12 **Vylkove** *Rus.* Vilkovo. Odes'ka Oblast', SW Ukraine 45.24N 29.37E
129 R9 **Vym'** NW Russian Federation
118 H8 **Vynohradiv** *Cz.* Sevluš, *Hung.* Nagyszöllös, *Rus.* Vinogradov; *prev.* Sevlyush. Zakarpats'ka Oblast', W Ukraine 48.09N 23.01E
128 G13 **Vyritsa** Leningradskaya Oblast', NW Russian Federation 59.25N 30.20E
99 J19 **Vyrnwy** *Wel.* Afon Efyrnwy. E Wales, UK
151 X9 **Vyshe Ivanovskiy Belak, Gora** ▲ E Kazakhstan 50.16N 83.46E
119 P4 **Vyshhorod** Kyyivs'ka Oblast', N Ukraine 50.36N 30.28E
128 I15 **Vyshniy Volochek** Tverskaya Oblast', W Russian Federation 57.37N 34.33E
113 G18 **Vyškov** *Ger.* Wischau. Brněnský Kraz, SE Czech Republic 49.16N 16.58E
113 F17 **Vysoké Mýto** *Ger.* Hohenmauth. Pardubický Kraj, C Czech Republic 49.58N 16.08E
119 S9 **Vysokopillya** Khersons'ka Oblast', S Ukraine 47.28N 33.30E
130 K3 **Vysokovsk** Moskovskaya Oblast', W Russian Federation 56.12N 36.42E
128 K12 **Vytegra** Vologodskaya Oblast', NW Russian Federation 60.59N 36.27E
118 J8 **Vyzhnytsya** Chernivets'ka Oblast', W Ukraine 48.14N 25.10E

W

79 O14 **Wa** NW Ghana 10.07N 2.28W
Waadt *see* Vaud
Waag *see* Váh
Waagbistritz *see* Považská Bystrica
Waagneustadtl *see* Nové Mesto nad Váhom
83 M16 **Waajid** Gedo, SW Somalia 3.37N 43.19E
100 L13 **Waal** S Netherlands
197 G4 **Waala** Province Nord, W New Caledonia 19.46S 163.41E
101 I14 **Waalwijk** Noord-Brabant, S Netherlands 51.42N 5.04E
101 E16 **Waarschoot** Oost-Vlaanderen, NW Belgium 51.09N 3.35E
194 G12 **Wabag** Enga, W PNG 5.28S 143.40E
13 N7 **Wabano** Quebec, SE Canada
9 P11 **Wabasca** Alberta, SW Canada
33 P12 **Wabash** Indiana, N USA 40.46N 85.48W
31 X9 **Wabasha** Minnesota, N USA 44.22N 92.01W
33 N13 **Wabash River** N USA
12 C7 **Wabatongushi Lake** Ontario, S Canada
83 L15 **Wabē Gestro Wenz** SE Ethiopia
12 B9 **Wabos** Ontario, S Canada 46.48N 84.06W
9 W13 **Wabowden** Manitoba, C Canada 54.57N 98.37W
112 J9 **Wąbrzeźno** Kujawsko-pomorskie, N Poland 53.18N 18.55E
194 G14 **Wabuda Island** *island* SW PNG
23 U12 **Waccamaw River** South Carolina, SE USA
25 U11 **Waccasassa Bay** *bay* Florida, SE USA
101 F16 **Wachtebeke** Oost-Vlaanderen, NW Belgium 51.10N 3.52E
27 T8 **Waco** Texas, SW USA 31.33N 97.09W
28 M3 **Waconda Lake** *var.* Great Elder Reservoir. Kansas, C USA
Wadai *see* Ouaddaï
Wad Al-Hajarah *see* Guadalajara
171 Gg13 **Wadayama** Hyōgo, Honshū, SW Japan 35.19N 134.51E
82 D10 **Wad Banda** Western Kordofan, C Sudan 13.07N 27.55E
77 P9 **Waddān** NW Libya 29.10N 16.07E
100 J4 **Waddeneilanden** *Eng.* West Frisian Islands. *island group* N Netherlands
100 J6 **Waddenzee** *var.* Wadden Zee. *sea* SE North Sea
8 L16 **Waddington, Mount** ▲ British Columbia, SW Canada 51.17N 125.16W
100 H12 **Waddinxveen** Zuid-Holland, C Netherlands 52.03N 4.37E
9 U15 **Wadena** Saskatchewan, S Canada 51.57N 103.48W
31 T6 **Wadena** Minnesota, N USA 46.27N 95.07W
110 G7 **Wädenswil** Zürich, N Switzerland 47.13N 8.39E
23 S11 **Wadesboro** North Carolina, SE USA 34.58N 80.04W
161 G16 **Wādi** Karnātaka, C India 17.00N 76.58E
144 G10 **Wādī as Sīr** *var.* Wadi es Sir. 'Ammān, NW Jordan 31.57N 35.49E
Wadi es Sir *see* Wādī as Sīr
82 F5 **Wadi Halfa** *var.* Wādī Ḥalfā'. Northern, N Sudan 21.46N 31.16E
144 G13 **Wādī Mūsā** *var.* Petra. Ma'ān, S Jordan 30.19N 35.28E
25 V4 **Wadley** Georgia, SE USA 32.52N 82.24W
Wad Madanī *see* Wad Medani
82 G10 **Wad Medani** *var.* Wad Madanī. Gezira, C Sudan 14.24N 33.30E
82 F10 **Wad Nimr** White Nile, C Sudan 14.31N 32.10E
172 Q14 **Wadomari** Kagoshima, Okinoerabu-jima, SW Japan 27.25N 128.40E
113 K17 **Wadowice** Małopolskie, S Poland 49.52N 19.30E
37 R5 **Wadsworth** Nevada, W USA 39.39N 119.16W
33 T12 **Wadsworth** Ohio, N USA 41.01N 81.43W
27 T11 **Waelder** Texas, SW USA 29.42N 97.16W
Waereghem *see* Waregem
169 U13 **Wafangdian** *var.* Fuxian, Fu Xian. Liaoning, NE China 39.36N 122.00E
175 S11 **Waflia** Pulau Buru, E Indonesia 3.09S 126.05E
Wagadugu *see* Ouagadougou
100 K12 **Wageningen** Gelderland, SE Netherlands 51.58N 5.40E
57 V9 **Wageningen** Nickerie, NW Surinam 5.43N 56.45W
15 Ll5 **Wager Bay** *inlet* Nunavut, N Canada
176 Y10 **Wageseri** Irian Jaya, E Indonesia 1.48S 138.19E
191 P10 **Wagga Wagga** New South Wales, SE Australia 35.10S 147.22E
188 J13 **Wagin** Western Australia 33.16S 117.25E
Wagina *see* Vaghena
110 H8 **Wägitaler See** SW Switzerland
31 P12 **Wagner** South Dakota, N USA 43.04N 98.17W
29 Q9 **Wagoner** Oklahoma, C USA 35.57N 95.22W
39 U10 **Wagon Mound** New Mexico, SW USA 36.00N 104.42W
34 J14 **Wagontire** Oregon, NW USA 43.15N 119.51W
112 H10 **Wągrowiec** Wielkopolskie, NW Poland 52.49N 17.10E
155 U6 **Wāh** Punjab, NE Pakistan 33.49N 72.43E
176 U10 **Wahai** Pulau Seram, E Indonesia 2.48S 129.28E
175 O7 **Wahau, Sungai** Borneo, C Indonesia
Wahaybah, Ramlat Al *see* Wahībah, Ramlat Āl
82 D13 **Wahda** *var.* Unity State. *state* S Sudan
40 D9 **Wahiawa** *Haw.* Wahiawā. Oahu, Hawaii, USA, C Pacific Ocean 21.30N 158.01W
Wahībah, Ramlat Ahl *see* Wahībah, Ramlat Āl
147 Y9 **Wahībah, Ramlat Āl** *var.* Ramlat Ahl Wahībah, Ramlat Al Wahaybah, *Eng.* Wahibah Sands. *desert* N Oman
Wahibah Sands *see* Wahībah, Ramlat Āl
103 E16 **Wahn** ✕ (Köln) Nordrhein-Westfalen, W Germany 50.51N 7.09E
31 R15 **Wahoo** Nebraska, C USA 41.12N 96.37W
31 R6 **Wahpeton** North Dakota, N USA 46.16N 96.36W
Wahran *see* Oran
38 J6 **Wah Wah Mountains** ▲ Utah, W USA
40 D9 **Waialua** Oahu, Hawaii, USA, C Pacific Ocean 21.34N 158.07W
40 D9 **Waianae** *Haw.* Wai'anae. Oahu, Hawaii, USA, C Pacific Ocean 21.26N 158.11W
192 Q8 **Waiapu** North Island, NZ
193 I17 **Waiau** Canterbury, South Island, NZ 42.39S 173.03E
193 I17 **Waiau** South Island, NZ
193 B23 **Waiau** South Island, NZ
103 H21 **Waiblingen** Baden-Württemberg, S Germany 48.49N 9.19E
Waidhofen *see* Waidhofen an der Ybbs, Niederösterreich, Austria
Waidhofen *see* Waidhofen an der Thaya, Niederösterreich, Austria
111 V2 **Waidhofen an der Thaya** *var.* Waidhofen. Niederösterreich, NE Austria 48.49N 15.16E
111 U5 **Waidhofen an der Ybbs** *var.* Waidhofen. Niederösterreich, E Austria 47.57N 14.47E
176 Uu8 **Waigeo, Pulau** *island* Maluku, E Indonesia
192 L5 **Waiheke Island** *island* N NZ
192 M7 **Waihi** Waikato, North Island, NZ 37.24S 175.49E
193 C20 **Waihou** North Island, NZ
Waikaboebak *see* Waikabubak
175 P17 **Waikabubak** *prev.* Waikaboebak. Pulau Sumba, C Indonesia 9.40S 119.25E
193 D23 **Waikaia** South Island, NZ
193 D23 **Waikaka** Southland, South Island, NZ 45.55S 168.59E
192 L13 **Waikanae** Wellington, North Island, NZ 40.52S 175.04E
192 M7 **Waikare, Lake** North Island, NZ
192 O9 **Waikaremoana, Lake** North Island, NZ
193 I17 **Waikari** Canterbury, South Island, NZ 42.50S 172.41E
192 L8 **Waikato** *off.* Waikato Region. *region* North Island, NZ
192 M8 **Waikato** North Island, NZ
190 J9 **Waikerie** South Australia 34.12S 139.57E
193 F23 **Waikouaiti** Otago, South Island, NZ 45.36S 170.39E
40 H11 **Wailea** Hawaii, USA, C Pacific Ocean 19.53N 155.07W
40 F10 **Wailuku** Maui, Hawaii, USA, C Pacific Ocean 20.53N 156.30W
193 H18 **Waimakariri** South Island, NZ
40 D9 **Waimanalo Beach** Oahu, Hawaii, USA, C Pacific Ocean 21.20N 157.42W
193 G15 **Waimangaroa** West Coast, South Island, NZ 41.41S 171.49E
193 G21 **Waimate** Canterbury, South Island, NZ 44.44S 171.03E
40 G11 **Waimea** *var.* Kamuela. Hawaii, USA, C Pacific Ocean 20.01N 155.39W
40 D9 **Waimea** *var.* Maunawai. Oahu, Hawaii, USA, C Pacific Ocean 21.38N 158.03W
40 B8 **Waimea** Kauai, Hawaii, USA, C Pacific Ocean 21.57N 159.39W
101 M20 **Waimes** Liège, E Belgium 50.25N 6.10E
160 J11 **Wainganga** *var.* Wain River. C India
Waingapoe *see* Waingapu
175 Pp17 **Waingapu** *prev.* Waingapoe. Pulau Sumba, C Indonesia 9.40S 120.16E
57 S7 **Waini** N Guyana
57 S7 **Waini Point** *headland* NW Guyana 8.24N 59.48W
Wain River *see* Wainganga
9 R15 **Wainwright** Alberta, SW Canada 52.49N 110.51W
41 O5 **Wainwright** Alaska, USA 70.38N 160.02W
192 K4 **Waiotira** Northland, North Island, NZ 35.56S 174.11E
192 M11 **Waiouru** Manawatu-Wanganui, North Island, NZ 39.27S 175.40E
176 X11 **Waipa** Irian Jaya, E Indonesia 3.47S 136.16E
192 L8 **Waipa** North Island, NZ
192 P9 **Waipaoa** North Island, NZ
193 D25 **Waipapa Point** *headland* South Island, NZ 46.39S 168.51E
193 I18 **Waipara** Canterbury, South Island, NZ 43.03S 172.44E
192 N12 **Waipawa** Hawke's Bay, North Island, NZ 39.57S 176.35E
192 K4 **Waipu** Northland, North Island, NZ 35.58S 174.25E
192 N12 **Waipukurau** Hawke's Bay, North Island, NZ 40.01S 176.34E
176 Vv13 **Wair** Pulau Kai Besar, E Indonesia 5.16S 133.09E
Wairakai *see* Wairakei
192 N9 **Wairakei** *var.* Wairakai. Waikato, North Island, NZ 38.37S 176.05E
193 M14 **Wairarapa, Lake** North Island, NZ
193 J15 **Wairau** South Island, NZ
192 P10 **Wairoa** Hawke's Bay, North Island, NZ 39.03S 105.25E
192 P10 **Wairoa** North Island, NZ
192 J4 **Wairoa** North Island, NZ
192 N9 **Waitahanui** Waikato, North Island, NZ 38.48S 176.04E
192 M6 **Waitakaruru** Waikato, North Island, NZ 37.14S 175.22E
193 F21 **Waitaki** South Island, NZ
192 K10 **Waitara** Taranaki, North Island, NZ 39.01S 174.14E
192 M7 **Waitoa** Waikato, North Island, NZ 37.36S 175.37E
192 L8 **Waitomo Caves** Waikato, North Island, NZ 38.17S 175.06E
192 L11 **Waitotara** Taranaki, North Island, NZ 39.49S 174.43E
192 L11 **Waitotara** North Island, NZ
34 L10 **Waitsburg** Washington, NW USA 46.16N 118.09W
Waitzen *see* Vác
192 L6 **Waiuku** Auckland, North Island, NZ 37.15S 174.44E
171 J12 **Wajima** *var.* Wazima. Ishikawa, Honshū, SW Japan 37.21N 136.53E
83 K17 **Wajir** North Eastern, NE Kenya 1.43N 40.04E
83 I14 **Waka** Southern, SW Ethiopia 7.12N 37.19E
81 J17 **Waka** Equateur, NW Dem. Rep. Congo (Zaire) 1.04N 20.11E
12 D9 **Wakami Lake** Ontario, S Canada
170 G13 **Wakasa** Tottori, Honshū, SW Japan 35.18N 134.25E
171 H13 **Wakasa-wan** *bay* C Japan
193 C22 **Wakatipu, Lake** South Island, NZ
9 T15 **Wakaw** Saskatchewan, S Canada 52.40N 105.45W
197 I14 **Wakaya** *island* C Fiji
170 Ff15 **Wakayama** Wakayama, Honshū, SW Japan 34.12N 135.09E
170 G16 **Wakayama** *off.* Wakayama-ken. *prefecture* Honshū, SW Japan
28 K4 **Wa Keeney** Kansas, C USA 39.01N 99.52W
193 I14 **Wakefield** Tasman, South Island, NZ 41.24S 173.03E
99 M17 **Wakefield** N England, UK 53.42N 1.28W
29 O4 **Wakefield** Kansas, C USA 39.12N 97.00W
32 L4 **Wakefield** Michigan, N USA 46.27N 89.55W
23 U9 **Wake Forest** North Carolina, SE USA 35.58N 78.30W
Wakeham Bay *see* Kangiqsujuaq
201 Y11 **Wake Island** ◇ *US unincorporated territory* NW Pacific Ocean
201 Y12 **Wake Island** ✕ NW Pacific Ocean
201 Y12 **Wake Island** *atoll* NW Pacific Ocean
201 X12 **Wake Lagoon** *lagoon* Wake Island, NW Pacific Ocean
177 Ff9 **Wakema** Irrawaddy, SW Burma 16.36N 95.10E
Wakhan *see* Khandūd
170 Ff15 **Waki** Tokushima, Shikoku, SW Japan 34.04N 134.10E
172 N8 **Wakinosawa** Aomori, Honshū, C Japan 41.08N 140.47E
172 Pp1 **Wakkanai** Hokkaidō, NE Japan 45.24N 141.39E
85 K22 **Wakkerstroom** Mpumalanga, E South Africa 27.21S 30.10E
12 C10 **Wakomata Lake** Ontario, S Canada
191 N10 **Wakool** New South Wales, SE Australia 35.30S 144.22E
Wakra *see* Al Wakrah
Waku Kungo *see* Uaco Cungo
195 S12 **Wakunai** Bougainville Island, NE PNG 5.52S 155.13E
Walachei/Walachia *see* Wallachia
175 Pp12 **Walanae, Sungai** Sulawesi, C Indonesia
161 K26 **Walawe Ganga** S Sri Lanka
113 F15 **Wałbrzych** *Ger.* Waldenburg, Waldenburg in Schlesien. Dolnośląskie, SW Poland 50.44N 16.19E
191 T6 **Walcha** New South Wales, SE Australia 31.01S 151.38E
103 K24 **Walchensee** SE Germany
101 D14 **Walcheren** *island* SW Netherlands
31 Z14 **Walcott** Iowa, C USA 41.34N 90.46W
35 W16 **Walcott** Wyoming, C USA 41.46N 106.46W
101 G21 **Walcourt** Namur, S Belgium 50.15N 4.26E
112 G9 **Wałcz** *Ger.* Deutsch Krone. Zachodniopomorskie, NW Poland 53.16N 16.28E
110 H7 **Wald** Zürich, N Switzerland 47.16N 8.54E
111 U3 **Waldaist** N Austria
188 I9 **Waldburg Range** ▲ Western Australia
39 R3 **Walden** Colorado, C USA 40.43N 106.16W
20 K13 **Walden** New York, NE USA 41.35N 74.09W
Waldenburg/Waldenburg in Schlesien *see* Wałbrzych
9 T15 **Waldheim** Saskatchewan, S Canada 52.38N 106.35W
Waldia *see* Weldiya
103 M23 **Waldkraiburg** Bayern, SE Germany 48.10N 12.23E
29 T14 **Waldo** Arkansas, C USA 33.21N 93.18W
25 V9 **Waldo** Florida, SE USA 29.47N 82.07W
21 R7 **Waldoboro** Maine, NE USA 44.06N 69.22W
23 W4 **Waldorf** Maryland, NE USA 38.36N 76.54W
34 F12 **Waldport** Oregon, NW USA 44.25N 124.04W
29 S11 **Waldron** Arkansas, C USA 34.54N 94.05W
205 Y13 **Waldron, Cape** *headland* Antarctica 66.08S 116.00E
103 F24 **Waldshut-Tiengen** Baden-Württemberg, S Germany 47.37N 8.13E
175 Qq9 **Walea, Selat** *strait* Sulawesi, C Indonesia
Wałeckie Międzyrzecze *see* Valašské Meziříčí
110 H8 **Walensee** NW Switzerland
40 L8 **Wales** Alaska, USA 65.36N 168.02W
99 J20 **Wales** *Wel.* Cymru. *national region* UK
15 Ll3 **Wales Island** *island* Nunavut, NE Canada
79 P14 **Walewale** N Ghana 10.21N 0.48W
101 M24 **Walferdange** Luxembourg, C Luxembourg 49.39N 6.07E
191 Q5 **Walgett** New South Wales, SE Australia 30.02S 148.13E
204 K10 **Walgreen Coast** *physical region* Antarctica
31 Q2 **Walhalla** North Dakota, N USA 48.55N 97.55W
23 O11 **Walhalla** South Carolina, SE USA 34.45N 83.03W
81 O19 **Walikale** Nord Kivu, E Dem. Rep. Congo (Zaire) 1.28S 28.04E
194 G9 **Walis Island** *island* NW PNG
Walk *see* Valga, Estonia
Walk *see* Valka, Latvia
31 U5 **Walker** Minnesota, N USA 47.06N 94.35W
13 V4 **Walker, Lac** Quebec, SE Canada
37 S7 **Walker Lake** Nevada, W USA
37 R6 **Walker River** Nevada, W USA
30 K10 **Wall** South Dakota, N USA 43.58N 102.12W
181 U9 **Wallaby Plateau** *undersea feature* E Indian Ocean
35 N8 **Wallace** Idaho, NW USA 47.28N 115.55W
23 V11 **Wallace** North Carolina, SE USA 34.42N 77.59W
12 D17 **Wallaceburg** Ontario, S Canada 42.36N 82.22W
24 F5 **Wallace Lake** Louisiana, S USA
9 P13 **Wallace Mountain** ▲ Alberta, W Canada 54.50N 115.57W
118 J14 **Wallachia** *var.* Walachia, *Ger.* Walachei, *Rom.* Valachia. *cultural region* S Romania
Wallachisch-Meseritsch *see* Valašské Meziříčí
191 U4 **Wallangarra** New South Wales, SE Australia 28.56S 151.57E
190 I8 **Wallaroo** South Australia 33.56S 137.38E
34 L10 **Walla Walla** Washington, NW USA 46.03N 118.20W
47 V9 **Wallblake** ✕ (The Valley) C Anguilla 18.12N 63.02W
103 H19 **Walldürn** Baden-Württemberg, SW Germany 49.34N 9.22E
102 F12 **Wallenhorst** Niedersachsen, NW Germany 52.21N 8.01E
Wallenthal *see* Haţeg
111 S4 **Wallern** Oberösterreich, N Austria 48.13N 13.58E
Wallern *see* Wallern im Burgenland
111 Z5 **Wallern im Burgenland** *var.* Wallern. Burgenland, E Austria 47.43N 16.56E
20 M9 **Wallingford** Vermont, NE USA 43.27N 72.56W
27 V11 **Wallis** Texas, SW USA 29.37N 96.04W
Wallis *see* Valais
199 Jj10 **Wallis and Futuna** *Fr.* Territoire de Wallis et Futuna. ◇ *French overseas territory* C Pacific Ocean
110 G7 **Wallisellen** Zürich, N Switzerland 47.27N 8.33E
202 H11 **Wallis, Îles** *island group* N Wallis and Futuna
101 H19 **Wallon Brabant** *province* C Belgium
33 Q5 **Walloon Lake** Michigan, N USA
34 K10 **Wallula** Washington, NW USA 46.03N 118.54W
34 K10 **Wallula, Lake** Washington, NW USA
23 S8 **Walnut Cove** North Carolina, SE USA 36.18N 80.08W
37 N8 **Walnut Creek** California, W USA 37.52N 122.04W
28 K5 **Walnut Creek** Kansas, C USA
29 W9 **Walnut Ridge** Arkansas, C USA 36.06N 90.56W
27 S7 **Walnut Springs** Texas, SW USA 32.05N 97.42W
190 L10 **Walpeup** Victoria, SE Australia 35.09S 142.01E
197 L7 **Walpole, Île** *island* SE New Caledonia
41 N13 **Walrus Islands** *island group* Alaska, USA
99 L19 **Walsall** C England, UK 52.34N 1.58W
39 T7 **Walsenburg** Colorado, C USA 37.37N 104.46W
9 S17 **Walsh** Alberta, SW Canada 49.58N 110.03W
39 W7 **Walsh** Colorado, C USA 37.20N 102.17W
102 I11 **Walsrode** Niedersachsen, NW Germany 52.52N 9.36E
Waltenberg *see* Zalău
23 R14 **Walterboro** South Carolina, SE USA 32.54N 80.40W
Walter F. George Lake *see* Walter F. George Reservoir
25 R6 **Walter F. George Reservoir** *var.* Walter F. George Lake. Alabama/Georgia, SE USA
28 M12 **Walters** Oklahoma, C USA 34.21N 98.18W
103 J16 **Waltershausen** Thüringen, C Germany 50.53N 10.33E
181 N10 **Walters Shoal** *var.* Walters Shoals. *reef* S Madagascar
Walters Shoals *see* Walters Shoal
24 M3 **Walthall** Mississippi, S USA 33.36N 89.16W
22 M4 **Walton** Kentucky, S USA 38.52N 84.36W
20 J11 **Walton** New York, NE USA 42.10N 75.07W
81 O20 **Walungu** Sud Kivu, E Dem. Rep. Congo (Zaire) 2.40S 28.37E
Walvisbaai *see* Walvis Bay
85 C19 **Walvis Bay** *Afr.* Walvisbaai. Erongo, NW Namibia 22.59S 14.33E
85 B19 **Walvis Bay** *bay* NW Namibia
Walvish Ridge *see* Walvis Ridge
67 O17 **Walvis Ridge** *var.* Walvish Ridge. *undersea feature* E Atlantic Ocean
176 Yy15 **Wamal** Irian Jaya, E Indonesia 8.00S 139.06E
176 W13 **Wamar, Pulau** *island* Kepulauan Aru, E Indonesia
79 V15 **Wamba** Nassarawa, C Nigeria 8.57N 8.35E
81 O17 **Wamba** Orientale, NE Dem. Rep. Congo (Zaire) 2.10N 27.58E
81 H22 **Wamba** *var.* Uamba. Angola/Dem. Rep. Congo (Zaire)
29 P4 **Wamego** Kansas, C USA 39.12N 96.18W
20 I10 **Wampsville** New York, NE USA 43.03N 75.40W
44 K6 **Wampú, Río** E Honduras
176 Xx16 **Wan** Irian Jaya, E Indonesia 8.15S 138.00E
Wan *see* Anhui
191 N4 **Wanaaring** New South Wales, SE Australia 29.42S 144.07E
193 D21 **Wanaka** Otago, South Island, NZ 44.42S 169.09E
193 D20 **Wanaka, Lake** South Island, NZ
176 Ww12 **Wanapiri** Irian Jaya, E Indonesia 4.21S 135.52E
12 F9 **Wanapitei** Ontario, S Canada
12 F10 **Wanapitei Lake** Ontario, S Canada
20 K14 **Wanaque** New Jersey, NE USA 41.02N 74.17W
176 V9 **Wanau** Irian Jaya, E Indonesia 1.20S 132.40E
193 F22 **Wanbrow, Cape** *headland* South Island, NZ 45.07S 170.59E
Wanchuan *see* Zhangjiakou
176 X11 **Wandai** *var.* Komeyo. Irian Jaya, E Indonesia 3.35S 136.15E
169 Z8 **Wanda Shan** ▲ NE China
207 R11 **Wandel Sea** *sea* Arctic Ocean
166 D13 **Wanding** *var.* Wandingzhen. Yunnan, SW China 24.12N 98.05E
Wandingzhen *see* Wanding
176 Z14 **Wandip** Irian Jaya, E Indonesia 6.08S 140.47E
101 H20 **Wanfercée-Baulet** Hainaut, S Belgium 50.27N 4.37E
192 L12 **Wanganui** Manawatu-Wanganui, North Island, NZ 39.56S 175.02E
192 L11 **Wanganui** North Island, NZ
191 P11 **Wangaratta** Victoria, SE Australia 36.22S 146.16E
166 J8 **Wangcang** *prev.* Fengjiaba. Sichuan, C China 32.15N 106.16E
Wangda *see* Zogang
103 I24 **Wangen im Allgäu** Baden-Württemberg, S Germany 47.40N 9.49E
Wangerin *see* Węgorzyno
102 F9 **Wangerooge** *island* NW Germany
176 Ww11 **Wanggar** Irian Jaya, E Indonesia 3.22S 135.15E
166 J13 **Wangmo** *var.* Fuxing. Guizhou, S China 25.10N 106.07E
Wangolodougou *see* Ouangolodougou
167 S9 **Wangpan Yang** *sea* E China
169 Y10 **Wangqing** Jilin, NE China 43.19N 129.42E
178 I9 **Wang Saphung** Loei, C Thailand 17.18N 101.45E
178 H6 **Wan Hsa-la** Shan State, E Burma 20.27N 98.39E
57 W9 **Wanica** *district* N Surinam
81 M18 **Wanie-Rukula** Orientale, C Dem. Rep. Congo (Zaire) 0.12N 25.31E
Wankie *see* Hwange
Wanki, Río *see* Coco, Río
83 N17 **Wanlaweyn** *var.* Wanle Weyn, *It.* Uanle Uen. Shabeellaha Hoose, SW Somalia 2.36N 44.47E
Wanle Weyn *see* Wanlaweyn
188 I12 **Wanneroo** Western Australia 31.37S 115.43E
166 L17 **Wanning** Hainan, S China 18.55N 110.27E
178 Ii8 **Wanon Niwat** Sakon Nakhon, E Thailand 17.39N 103.45E
161 H16 **Wanparti** Andhra Pradesh, C India 16.19N 78.06E
Wansen *see* Wiązów
166 L11 **Wanshan** Guizhou, S China 27.45N 109.12E
101 M14 **Wanssum** Limburg, SE Netherlands 51.31N 6.04E
192 N12 **Wanstead** Hawke's Bay, North Island, NZ 40.09S 176.31E
166 K9 **Wanxian** Chongqing Shi, C China 30.48N 108.21E
196 F16 **Wanyaan** Yap, Micronesia
166 K8 **Wanyuan** Sichuan, C China 32.04N 108.07E
167 O11 **Wanzai** Jiangxi, S China 28.06N 114.27E
101 J20 **Wanze** Liège, E Belgium 50.32N 5.16E
33 R12 **Wapakoneta** Ohio, N USA 40.34N 84.11W
10 D7 **Wapaseese** Ontario, C Canada
34 I10 **Wapato** Washington, NW USA 46.27N 120.25W
31 Y15 **Wapello** Iowa, C USA 41.10N 91.13W
194 H12 **Wapenamanda** Enga, W PNG 5.36S 143.51E
9 N13 **Wapiti** Alberta/British Columbia, SW Canada
29 X7 **Wappapello Lake** Missouri, C USA
20 K13 **Wappingers Falls** New York, NE USA 41.36N 73.54W
31 X13 **Wapsipinicon River** Iowa, C USA
194 G14 **Wapumba Island** *island* SW PNG
12 L9 **Wapus** Quebec, SE Canada
166 H7 **Waqên** Sichuan, C China 33.04N 102.41E
23 Q7 **War** West Virginia, NE USA 37.18N 81.39W
82 D13 **Warab** Warab, SW Sudan 8.13N 28.52E
83 D14 **Warab** *state* SW Sudan
161 J15 **Warangal** Andhra Pradesh, C India 18.00N 79.35E
Warasdin *see* Varaždin
191 O16 **Waratah** Tasmania, SE Australia 41.28S 145.34E
191 O14 **Waratah Bay** *bay* Victoria, SE Australia
103 H15 **Warburg** Nordrhein-Westfalen, W Germany 51.30N 9.10E

◆ Country ● Country Capital ◇ Dependent Territory ○ Dependent Territory Capital Administrative Region ✕ International Airport ▲ Mountain ▲ Mountain Range Volcano River Lake Reservoir

Warburton – West Columbia

188 M9 **Warburton** Western Australia 26.17S 126.18E
190 I1 **Warburton Creek** seasonal river South Australia 101 M20
Warche ≈ E Belgium
155 P5 **Wardag** var. Wardak, Per. Vardak. ◐ province E Afghanistan
Wardak see Wardag
34 K9 **Warden** Washington, NW USA 46.58N 119.02W
160 I12 **Wardha** Mahārāshtra, W India 20.40N 78.40E
194 L14 **Ward Hunt, Cape** headland S PNG 8.03S 148.15E
195 N16 **Ward Hunt Strait** strait S PNG
123 J16 **Wardija, Ras il-** var. Wardija Point. headland Gozo, NW Malta 36.03N 14.11E
145 P3 **Wardiyah** N Iraq 36.18N 41.45E
193 E19 **Ward, Mount** ▲ South Island, NZ 43.49S 169.54E
176 Ww9 **Wardo** Irian Jaya, E Indonesia 0.54S 135.52E
8 L11 **Ware** British Columbia, W Canada 57.25N 125.40W
101 D18 **Waregem** var. Waereghem. West-Vlaanderen, W Belgium 50.52N 3.25E
101 J19 **Waremme** Liège, E Belgium 50.40N 5.15E
102 N10 **Waren** Mecklenburg-Vorpommern, NE Germany 53.31N 12.42E
176 X10 **Waren** Irian Jaya, E Indonesia 2.13S 136.21E
103 F14 **Warendorf** Nordrhein-Westfalen, W Germany 51.57N 8.00E
23 P12 **Ware Shoals** South Carolina, SE USA 34.24N 82.15W
100 N4 **Warffum** Groningen, NE Netherlands 53.22N 6.34E
83 O15 **Wargalo** Mudug, E Somalia 6.06N 47.40E
152 M12 **Warganza** Rus. Varganzi. Qashqadaryo Wiloyati, S Uzbekistan 39.18N 66.00E
Wargla see Ouargla
194 K14 **Waria** ≈ S PNG
191 T4 **Warialda** New South Wales, SE Australia 29.34S 150.35E
160 F13 **Wāri Godri** Mahārāshtra, C India 19.28N 75.43E
176 W11 **Warika** Irian Jaya, E Indonesia 3.45S 134.16E
176 W13 **Warilau** Pulau Warilau, E Indonesia 5.19S 134.33E
176 Ww13 **Warilau, Pulau** island Kepulauan Aru, E Indonesia
178 J10 **Warin Chamrap** Ubon Ratchathani, E Thailand 15.10N 104.51E
27 R11 **Waring** Texas, SW USA 29.56N 98.48W
41 O8 **Waring Mountains** ▲▲ Alaska, USA
112 M12 **Warka** Mazowieckie, E Poland 51.45N 21.12E
192 L5 **Warkworth** Auckland, North Island, NZ 36.24S 174.39E
176 V8 **Warmandi** Irian Jaya, E Indonesia 0.21S 132.38E
85 E22 **Warmbad** Karas, S Namibia 28.28S 18.40E
100 H8 **Warmenhuizen** Noord-Holland, NW Netherlands 52.43N 4.45E
112 L8 **Warmińsko-Mazurskie** ◐ province NW Poland
99 L22 **Warminster** S England, UK 51.13N 2.12W
20 I15 **Warminster** Pennsylvania, NE USA 40.11N 75.04W
37 V8 **Warm Springs** Nevada, W USA 38.10N 116.21W
34 H12 **Warm Springs** Oregon, NW USA 44.51N 121.24W
23 S5 **Warm Springs** Virginia, NE USA 38.02N 79.46W
102 M8 **Warnemünde** Mecklenburg-Vorpommern, NE Germany 54.10N 12.03E
29 Q10 **Warner** Oklahoma, C USA 35.29N 95.18W
37 Q2 **Warner Mountains** ▲▲ California, W USA
25 T5 **Warner Robins** Georgia, SE USA 32.38N 83.38W
59 N18 **Warnes** Santa Cruz, C Bolivia 17.30S 63.07W
102 M9 **Warnow** ≈ NE Germany
Warnsdorf see Varnsdorf
100 M11 **Warnsveld** Gelderland, E Netherlands 52.07N 6.13E
176 Uu10 **Waromge, Teluk** bay Irian Jaya, E Indonesia
160 I13 **Warora** Mahārāshtra, C India 20.12N 79.01E
190 L11 **Warracknabeal** Victoria, SE Australia 36.17S 142.26E
191 O13 **Warragul** Victoria, SE Australia 38.10S 145.55E
191 O4 **Warrego River** seasonal river New South Wales/Queensland, E Australia
191 Q6 **Warren** New South Wales, SE Australia 31.41S 147.51E
9 X16 **Warren** Manitoba, S Canada 50.05N 97.33W
29 V14 **Warren** Arkansas, C USA 33.36N 92.03W
33 S10 **Warren** Michigan, N USA 42.28N 83.01W
31 R3 **Warren** Minnesota, N USA 48.12N 96.46W
33 U11 **Warren** Ohio, N USA 41.14N 80.49W
20 D12 **Warren** Pennsylvania, NE USA 41.52N 79.09W
27 X10 **Warren** Texas, SW USA 30.33N 94.24W
99 G16 **Warrenpoint** Ir. An Pointe. SE Northern Ireland, UK 54.07N 6.15W
29 S4 **Warrensburg** Missouri, C USA 38.45N 93.44W
85 H22 **Warrenton** Northern Cape, N South Africa 28.06S 24.49E
25 U4 **Warrenton** Georgia, SE USA 33.24N 82.39W
29 W4 **Warrenton** Missouri, C USA 38.48N 91.08W
23 V8 **Warrenton** North Carolina, SE USA 36.22N 78.09W
23 V4 **Warrenton** Virginia, NE USA 38.42N 77.48W
79 U17 **Warri** Delta, S Nigeria 5.26N 5.34E
99 L18 **Warrington** C England, UK 53.24N 2.37W
25 O9 **Warrington** Florida, SE USA 30.22N 87.16W
25 P3 **Warrior** Alabama, S USA 33.49N 86.49W
190 L13 **Warrnambool** Victoria, SE Australia 38.22S 142.30E
31 T2 **Warroad** Minnesota, N USA 48.55N 95.18W
191 S6 **Warrumbungle Range** ▲▲ New South Wales, SE Australia
160 J12 **Wārsa** Mahārāshtra, C India 20.42N 79.58E
33 P11 **Warsaw** Indiana, N USA 41.13N 85.52W
22 L4 **Warsaw** Kentucky, S USA 38.45N 84.51W
29 T5 **Warsaw** Missouri, C USA 38.14N 93.22W
20 E10 **Warsaw** New York, NE USA 42.44N 78.06W
23 V10 **Warsaw** North Carolina, SE USA 35.00N 78.05W
23 X5 **Warsaw** Virginia, NE USA 37.57N 76.45W
Warsaw/Warschau see Warszawa
83 N17 **Warshiikh** Shabeellaha Dhexe, C Somalia 2.22N 45.52E
103 G15 **Warstein** Nordrhein-Westfalen, W Germany 51.27N 8.21E
112 M11 **Warszawa** Eng. Warsaw, Ger. Warschau, Rus. Varshava. ● (Poland) Mazowieckie, C Poland 52.15N 21.00E
112 J13 **Warta** Sieradz, C Poland 51.43N 18.37E
112 D11 **Warta** Ger. Warthe. ≈ W Poland
Wartberg see Senec
22 M9 **Wartburg** Tennessee, S USA 36.06N 84.34W
110 J7 **Warth** Vorarlberg, NW Austria 47.16N 10.11E
Warthe see Warta
175 O9 **Waru** Borneo, C Indonesia 1.24S 116.37E
176 Uu11 **Waru** Pulau Seram, E Indonesia 3.24S 130.38E
145 N6 **Wa'r, Wādī al** dry watercourse E Syria
191 U3 **Warwick** Queensland, E Australia 28.12S 152.00E
13 Q11 **Warwick** Quebec, SE Canada 45.55N 72.00W
99 M20 **Warwick** C England, UK 52.16N 1.34W
20 K13 **Warwick** New York, NE USA 41.15N 74.21W
31 P4 **Warwick** North Dakota, N USA 47.49N 98.42W
21 O12 **Warwick** Rhode Island, NE USA 41.40N 71.21W
99 L20 **Warwickshire** cultural region C England, UK
12 G14 **Wasaga Beach** Ontario, S Canada 44.30N 80.00W
79 U13 **Wasagu** Kebbi, NW Nigeria 11.25N 5.48E
38 M2 **Wasatch Range** ▲▲ W USA
37 R12 **Wasco** California, W USA 35.34N 119.20W
31 V10 **Waseca** Minnesota, N USA 44.04N 93.30W
12 H13 **Washago** Ontario, S Canada 44.46N 79.48W
21 S2 **Washburn** Maine, NE USA 46.46N 68.08W
30 M5 **Washburn** North Dakota, N USA 47.15N 101.02W
32 K3 **Washburn** Wisconsin, N USA 46.40N 90.52W
33 S14 **Washburn Hill** hill Ohio, N USA 39.10N 83.25W
160 H13 **Wāshīm** Mahārāshtra, C India 20.06N 77.08E
99 M14 **Washington** NE England, UK 54.54N 1.31W
25 U3 **Washington** Georgia, SE USA 33.44N 82.44W
32 L12 **Washington** Illinois, N USA 40.42N 89.24W
33 N15 **Washington** Indiana, N USA 38.40N 87.10W
31 X15 **Washington** Iowa, C USA 41.18N 91.41W
29 O3 **Washington** Kansas, C USA 39.46N 97.03W
29 W5 **Washington** Missouri, C USA 38.31N 91.01W
23 X9 **Washington** North Carolina, SE USA 35.33N 77.03W
20 B15 **Washington** Pennsylvania, NE USA 40.10N 80.16W
27 V10 **Washington** Texas, SW USA 30.18N 96.08W
38 J8 **Washington** Utah, W USA 37.07N 113.30W
23 V4 **Washington** Virginia, NE USA 38.40N 78.10W
34 I9 **Washington** off. State of Washington; also known as Chinook State, Evergreen State. ◐ state NW USA
Washington see Washington Court House
33 S14 **Washington Court House** var. Washington. Ohio, NE USA 39.31N 83.25W
23 W4 **Washington DC** ● (USA) District of Columbia, NE USA 38.54N 77.02W
33 O5 **Washington Island** island Wisconsin, N USA
Washington Island see Teraina
21 O7 **Washington, Mount** ▲ New Hampshire, NE USA 44.16N 71.18W
28 M11 **Washita River** ≈ Oklahoma/Texas, C USA
99 O18 **Wash, The** inlet E England, UK
34 L9 **Washtucna** Washington, NW USA 46.44N 118.19W
Wasiliszki see Vasilishki
112 P9 **Wasilków** Podlaskie, NE Poland 53.12N 23.15E
41 R11 **Wasilla** Alaska, USA 61.34N 149.26W
57 U9 **Wasjabo** Sipaliwini, NW Surinam 5.09N 57.09W
9 X11 **Waskaiowaka Lake** ◎ Manitoba, C Canada
9 T14 **Waskesiu Lake** Saskatchewan, C Canada 53.55N 106.04W
27 X7 **Waskom** Texas, SW USA 32.28N 94.03W
112 G13 **Wąsosz** Dolnośląskie, SW Poland 51.36N 16.30E
44 M6 **Waspam** var. Waspán. Región Autónoma Atlántico Norte, NE Nicaragua 14.40N 84.04W
Waspán see Waspam
172 P4 **Wassamu** Hokkaidō, NE Japan 44.01N 142.25E
110 G9 **Wassen** Uri, C Switzerland 46.42N 8.34E
100 G11 **Wassenaar** Zuid-Holland, W Netherlands 52.07N 4.24E
101 N24 **Wasserbillig** Grevenmacher, E Luxembourg 49.43N 6.30E
Wasserburg see Wasserburg am Inn
103 M23 **Wasserburg am Inn** var. Wasserburg. Bayern, SE Germany 48.02N 12.12E
103 I17 **Wasserkuppe** ▲ C Germany 50.30N 9.55E
105 R5 **Wassy** Haute-Marne, N France 48.32N 4.54E
175 Pp12 **Watampone** var. Bone. Sulawesi, C Indonesia 4.31S 120.15E
175 Ss11 **Watawa** Pulau Buru, E Indonesia 3.36S 127.13E
Watenstedt-Salzgitter see Salzgitter
20 M13 **Waterbury** Connecticut, NE USA 41.33N 73.01W
23 R11 **Wateree Lake** ⊠ South Carolina, SE USA
23 R12 **Wateree River** ≈ South Carolina, SE USA
99 E20 **Waterford** Ir. Port Láirge. S Ireland 52.15N 7.07W
33 S9 **Waterford** Michigan, N USA 42.42N 83.24W
99 E20 **Waterford** Ir. Port Láirge. cultural region S Ireland
99 E21 **Waterford Harbour** Ir. Cuan Phort Láirge. inlet S Ireland
100 G12 **Wateringen** Zuid-Holland, W Netherlands 52.01N 4.16E
101 G19 **Waterloo** Wallon Brabant, C Belgium 50.43N 4.24E
12 F16 **Waterloo** Ontario, S Canada 43.28N 80.31W
13 P12 **Waterloo** Quebec, SE Canada 45.20N 72.28W
32 K16 **Waterloo** Illinois, N USA 38.20N 90.09W
31 X13 **Waterloo** Iowa, C USA 42.31N 92.16W
20 G10 **Waterloo** New York, NE USA 42.54N 76.51W
32 L4 **Watersmeet** Michigan, N USA 46.16N 89.10W
25 V9 **Watertown** Florida, SE USA 30.11N 82.36W
20 I8 **Watertown** New York, NE USA 43.37N 75.55W
31 R9 **Watertown** South Dakota, N USA 44.54N 97.06W
32 M8 **Watertown** Wisconsin, N USA 43.12N 88.44W
24 L3 **Water Valley** Mississippi, S USA 34.09N 89.37W
29 O3 **Waterville** Kansas, C USA 39.41N 96.45W
19 Ss4 **Waterville** Maine, NE USA 44.34N 69.40W
31 V10 **Waterville** Minnesota, N USA 44.13N 93.34W
20 I10 **Waterville** New York, NE USA 42.55N 75.18W
12 E16 **Watford** Ontario, S Canada 42.57N 81.51W
99 N21 **Watford** SE England, UK 51.39N 0.24W
30 K4 **Watford City** North Dakota, N USA 47.48N 103.16W
147 X12 **Wāṭif** S Oman 18.34N 56.31E
20 G11 **Watkins Glen** New York, NE USA 42.22N 76.52W
Watlings Island see San Salvador
176 V13 **Watnil** Pulau Kai Kecil, E Indonesia 5.45S 132.39E
28 M10 **Watonga** Oklahoma, C USA 35.50N 98.24W
9 T16 **Watrous** Saskatchewan, S Canada 51.40N 105.28W
39 T10 **Watrous** New Mexico, SW USA 35.48N 104.58W
81 P16 **Watsa** Orientale, NE Dem. Rep. Congo (Zaire) 3.00N 29.31E
33 N12 **Watseka** Illinois, N USA 40.46N 87.44W
81 J19 **Watsikengo** Equateur, C Dem. Rep. Congo (Zaire) 0.49S 20.34E
190 C5 **Watson** South Australia 30.32S 131.28E
9 U15 **Watson** Saskatchewan, S Canada 52.13N 104.30W
205 O10 **Watson Escarpment** ▲▲ Antarctica
8 K9 **Watson Lake** Yukon Territory, W Canada 60.04N 128.46W
37 N10 **Watsonville** California, W USA 36.53N 121.43W
178 I8 **Wattay** ✕ (Vientiane) Viangchan, C Laos 18.03N 102.36E
111 N7 **Wattens** Tirol, W Austria 47.18N 11.37E
22 M9 **Watts Bar Lake** ⊠ Tennessee, S USA
110 H7 **Wattwil** Sankt Gallen, NE Switzerland 47.19N 9.04E
176 Uu12 **Watubela, Kepulauan** island group E Indonesia
103 N24 **Watzmann** ▲ SE Germany 47.32N 12.56E
194 J13 **Wau** Morobe, C PNG 7.18S 146.38E
83 D14 **Wau** var. Wāw. Western Bahr el Ghazal, S Sudan 7.43N 28.01E
31 Q8 **Waubay** South Dakota, N USA 45.19N 97.18W
31 Q8 **Waubay Lake** ◎ South Dakota, N USA
191 U7 **Wauchope** New South Wales, SE Australia 31.30S 152.46E
25 W13 **Wauchula** Florida, SE USA 27.33N 81.48W
32 M10 **Wauconda** Illinois, N USA 42.15N 88.08W
190 J7 **Waukaringa** South Australia 32.19S 139.27E
33 N10 **Waukegan** Illinois, N USA 42.21N 87.50W
32 M9 **Waukesha** Wisconsin, N USA 43.01N 88.13W
31 X11 **Waukon** Iowa, C USA 43.16N 91.28W
32 L8 **Waunakee** Wisconsin, N USA 43.13N 89.28W
32 L7 **Waupaca** Wisconsin, N USA 44.22N 89.04W
32 M8 **Waupun** Wisconsin, N USA 43.40N 88.43W
28 M13 **Waurika** Oklahoma, C USA 34.10N 98.00W
28 M12 **Waurika Lake** ⊠ Oklahoma, C USA
32 L6 **Wausau** Wisconsin, N USA 44.58N 89.40W
33 R11 **Wauseon** Ohio, N USA 41.33N 84.08W
32 L7 **Wautoma** Wisconsin, N USA 44.04N 89.16W
32 M9 **Wauwatosa** Wisconsin, N USA 43.03N 88.03W
24 L9 **Waveland** Mississippi, S USA 30.17N 89.22W
99 Q20 **Waveney** ≈ E England, UK
192 L11 **Waverley** Taranaki, North Island, NZ 39.46S 174.37E
31 W12 **Waverly** Iowa, C USA 42.43N 92.28W
29 T4 **Waverly** Missouri, C USA 39.12N 93.31W
31 R15 **Waverly** Nebraska, C USA 40.56N 96.27W
20 G12 **Waverly** New York, NE USA 42.00N 76.33W
22 H8 **Waverly** Tennessee, S USA 36.04N 87.47W
23 W7 **Waverly** Virginia, NE USA 37.02N 77.06W
101 H19 **Wavre** Walloon Brabant, C Belgium 50.43N 4.37E
177 G8 **Waw** Pegu, SW Burma 17.25N 96.40E
Wāw see Wau
12 B7 **Wawa** Ontario, S Canada 47.59N 84.43W
79 T14 **Wawa** Niger, W Nigeria 9.52N 4.33E
77 Q11 **Wāw al Kabīr** S Libya 25.21N 16.40E
45 N7 **Wawa, Río** var. Rio Huahua. ≈ NE Nicaragua
194 G13 **Wawoi** ≈ SW PNG
Wawosungu, Teluk see Staring, Teluk
27 T7 **Waxahachie** Texas, SW USA 32.23N 96.51W
164 L9 **Waxxari** Xinjiang Uygur Zizhiqu, NW China 38.43N 87.11E
197 H14 **Waya** island Yasawa Group, NW Fiji
25 V7 **Waycross** Georgia, SE USA 31.12N 82.21W
188 K10 **Way, Lake** ◎ Western Australia
33 P9 **Wayland** Michigan, N USA 42.40N 85.38W
31 R13 **Wayne** Nebraska, C USA 42.13N 97.01W
20 K14 **Wayne** New Jersey, NE USA 40.57N 74.16W
23 P5 **Wayne** West Virginia, NE USA 38.13N 82.26W
25 V4 **Waynesboro** Georgia, SE USA 33.04N 82.01W
24 M7 **Waynesboro** Mississippi, S USA 31.40N 88.39W
22 H10 **Waynesboro** Tennessee, S USA 35.19N 87.45W
23 U5 **Waynesboro** Virginia, NE USA 38.04N 78.53W
20 B16 **Waynesburg** Pennsylvania, NE USA 39.51N 80.10W
29 U6 **Waynesville** Missouri, C USA 37.49N 92.12W
23 O10 **Waynesville** North Carolina, SE USA 35.29N 82.59W
28 L8 **Waynoka** Oklahoma, C USA 36.36N 98.53W
Wazan see Ouazzane
Wazima see Wajima
155 V7 **Wazīrābād** Punjab, NE Pakistan 32.28N 74.04E
Wazzan see Ouazzane
112 I8 **Wda** var. Czarna Woda, Ger. Schwarzwasser. ≈ N Poland
197 K6 **Wé** Province des Îles Loyauté, E New Caledonia 20.55S 167.15E
99 O23 **Weald, The** lowlands SE England, UK
194 E15 **Weam** Western, SW PNG 8.33S 141.10E
99 L15 **Wear** ≈ N England, UK
Wearmouth see Sunderland
28 L10 **Weatherford** Oklahoma, C USA 35.31N 98.42W
27 S6 **Weatherford** Texas, SW USA 32.45N 97.48W
36 M3 **Weaverville** California, W USA 40.42N 122.57W
29 R7 **Webb City** Missouri, C USA 37.07N 94.28W
198 G9 **Weber Basin** undersea feature S Ceram Sea
Webfoot State see Oregon
20 F9 **Webster** New York, NE USA 43.12N 77.25W
31 Q8 **Webster** South Dakota, N USA 45.19N 97.31W
31 V13 **Webster City** Iowa, C USA 42.28N 93.49W
29 X5 **Webster Groves** Missouri, C USA 38.32N 90.20W
23 S4 **Webster Springs** var. Addison. West Virginia, NE USA 38.27N 80.24W
175 T8 **Weda, Teluk** bay Pulau Halmahera, E Indonesia
67 B25 **Weddell Island** var. Isla San Jose. island W Falkland Islands
67 K22 **Weddell Plain** undersea feature SW Atlantic Ocean
67 K23 **Weddell Sea** sea SW Atlantic Ocean
67 B25 **Weddell Settlement** Weddell Island, W Falkland Islands 52.52S 60.54W
190 M11 **Wedderburn** Victoria, SE Australia 36.26S 143.37E
102 I9 **Wedel** Schleswig-Holstein, N Germany 53.35N 9.42E
94 N3 **Wedel Jarlsberg Land** physical region SW Svalbard
102 I12 **Wedemark** Niedersachsen, NW Germany 52.33N 9.43E
8 M17 **Wedge Mountain** ▲ British Columbia, SW Canada 50.10N 122.43W
25 R4 **Wedowee** Alabama, S USA 33.16N 85.28W
176 Vv13 **Weduar** Pulau Kai Besar, E Indonesia 5.55S 132.51E
176 Vv14 **Weduar, Tanjung** headland Pulau Kai Besar, SE Indonesia 5.58S 132.49E
37 N2 **Weed** California, W USA 41.26N 122.24W
13 Q12 **Weedon Centre** Quebec, SE Canada 45.40N 71.28W
20 E13 **Weedville** Pennsylvania, NE USA 41.15N 78.28W
102 F10 **Weener** Niedersachsen, NW Germany 53.09N 7.19E
31 S16 **Weeping Water** Nebraska, C USA 40.52N 96.08W
101 L16 **Weert** Limburg, SE Netherlands 51.15N 5.43E
100 I10 **Weesp** Noord-Holland, C Netherlands 52.18N 5.03E
191 S5 **Wee Waa** New South Wales, SE Australia 30.16S 149.27E
112 N7 **Węgorzewo** Ger. Angerburg. Warmińsko-Mazurskie, NE Poland 54.12N 21.49E
112 E9 **Węgorzyno** Ger. Wangerin. Zachodniopomorskie, NW Poland 53.34N 15.35E
112 N11 **Węgrów** Ger. Bingerau. Mazowieckie, E Poland 52.22N 22.00E
100 N5 **Wehe-Den Hoorn** Groningen, NE Netherlands 53.20N 6.29E
100 M12 **Wehl** Gelderland, E Netherlands 51.58N 6.13E
Wehlau see Znamensk
173 E2 **Weh, Pulau** island NW Indonesia
Wei see Weifang
167 P1 **Weichang** prev. Zhuizishan. Hebei, E China 41.55N 117.45E
Weichsel see Wisła
103 M16 **Weida** Thüringen, C Germany 50.46N 12.05E
Weiden see Weiden in der Oberpfalz
103 M19 **Weiden in der Oberpfalz** var. Weiden. Bayern, SE Germany 49.40N 12.10E
167 Q4 **Weifang** var. Wei, Wei-fang; prev. Weihsien. Shandong, E China 36.43N 119.10E
167 S4 **Weihai** Shandong, E China 37.30N 122.04E
166 K6 **Wei He** ≈ C China
Weihsien see Weifang
103 G17 **Weilburg** Hessen, W Germany 50.31N 8.18E
103 K24 **Weilheim** Bayern, SE Germany 47.50N 11.09E
191 P4 **Weilmoringle** New South Wales, SE Australia 29.13S 146.51E
103 L16 **Weimar** Thüringen, C Germany 50.58N 11.19E
27 U11 **Weimar** Texas, SW USA 29.42N 96.46W
166 L6 **Weinan** Shaanxi, C China 34.30N 109.30E
110 H6 **Weinfelden** Thurgau, NE Switzerland 47.33N 9.09E
103 I24 **Weingarten** Baden-Württemberg, S Germany 47.49N 9.37E
103 G20 **Weinheim** Baden-Württemberg, SW Germany 49.33N 8.40E
166 H11 **Weining** var. Weining Yizu Huizu Miaozu Zizhixian. Guizhou, S China 26.51N 104.16E
Weining Yizu Huizu Miaozu Zizhixian see Weining
189 V2 **Weipa** Queensland, NE Australia 12.43S 142.01E
9 Y11 **Weir River** Manitoba, C Canada 56.44N 94.06W
23 R1 **Weirton** West Virginia, NE USA 40.25N 80.35W
34 M13 **Weiser** Idaho, NW USA 44.15N 116.58W
166 F12 **Weishan** Yunnan, SW China 25.22N 100.19E
167 P6 **Weishan Hu** ◎ E China
103 M15 **Weisse Elster** Eng. White Elster. ≈ Czech Republic/Germany
Weisse Körös/Weisse Kreisch see Crişul Alb
110 L7 **Weissenbach am Lech** Tirol, W Austria 47.27N 10.39E
103 K21 **Weissenburg** Bayern, SE Germany 49.02N 10.58E
Weissenburg see Wissembourg, France
Weissenburg see Alba Iulia, Romania
103 M15 **Weissenfels** var. Weißenfels. Sachsen-Anhalt, C Germany 51.12N 11.58E
111 R9 **Weissensee** ◎ S Austria
Weissenstein see Paide
110 E11 **Weisshorn** var. Flüela Wisshorn. ▲ SW Switzerland 46.06N 7.43E
Weisskirchen see Bela Crkva
25 R3 **Weiss Lake** ⊠ Alabama, S USA
103 Q14 **Weisswasser** Lus. Běla Woda. Sachsen, E Germany 51.30N 14.37E
101 M22 **Weiswampach** Diekirch, N Luxembourg 50.07N 6.04E
111 U2 **Weitra** Niederösterreich, N Austria 48.41N 14.54E
167 O4 **Weixian** var. Wei Xian. Hebei, E China 36.58N 115.15E
165 V11 **Weiyuan** Gansu, C China 35.07N 104.12E
166 F14 **Weiyuan Jiang** ≈ SW China
111 W7 **Weiz** Steiermark, SE Austria 47.13N 15.37E
166 K16 **Weizhou Dao** island S China
112 I6 **Wejherowo** Pomorskie, NW Poland 54.36N 18.12E
29 Q8 **Welch** Oklahoma, C USA 36.52N 95.06W
26 M6 **Welch** Texas, SW USA 32.52N 102.06W
23 Q6 **Welch** West Virginia, NE USA 37.25N 81.34W
47 O14 **Welchman Hall** C Barbados 13.10N 59.34W
82 J11 **Weldiya** var. Waldia, It. Valdia. Amhara, N Ethiopia 11.45N 39.39E
23 W8 **Weldon** North Carolina, SE USA 36.25N 77.36W
27 V9 **Weldon** Texas, SW USA 31.00N 95.33W
101 M19 **Welkenraedt** Liège, E Belgium 50.40N 5.58E
199 L2 **Welker Seamount** undersea feature N Pacific Ocean 55.07N 140.18W
85 I22 **Welkom** Free State, C South Africa 27.58S 26.43E
12 H16 **Welland** Ontario, S Canada 43.58N 79.13W
12 G16 **Welland** ≈ Ontario, S Canada
99 O19 **Welland** ≈ C England, UK
12 H17 **Welland Canal** canal Ontario, S Canada
161 K25 **Wellawaya** Uva Province, SE Sri Lanka 6.43N 81.07E
Welle see Uele
189 T4 **Wellesley Islands** island group Queensland, N Australia
101 J22 **Wellin** Luxembourg, SE Belgium 50.06N 5.05E
99 N20 **Wellingborough** C England, UK 52.19N 0.42W
191 R7 **Wellington** New South Wales, SE Australia 32.34S 148.55E
12 J15 **Wellington** Ontario, SE Canada 43.57N 77.24W
193 L14 **Wellington** ● (NZ) Wellington, North Island, NZ 41.16S 174.46E
85 E26 **Wellington** Western Cape, SW South Africa 33.39S 19.00E
39 T2 **Wellington** Colorado, C USA 40.42N 105.00W
29 N7 **Wellington** Kansas, C USA 37.16N 97.22W
37 R7 **Wellington** Nevada, W USA 38.45N 119.22W
33 T11 **Wellington** Ohio, N USA 41.10N 82.13W
27 P3 **Wellington** Texas, SW USA 34.51N 100.12W
38 M4 **Wellington** Utah, W USA 39.31N 110.45W
193 M14 **Wellington** off. Wellington Region. ◐ region North Island, NZ
193 L14 **Wellington** ✕ Wellington, North Island, NZ 41.19S 174.48E
Wellington see Wellington, Isla
65 F22 **Wellington, Isla** var. Wellington. island S Chile
191 P12 **Wellington, Lake** ◎ Victoria, SE Australia
31 X14 **Wellman** Iowa, C USA 41.27N 91.50W
26 M6 **Wellman** Texas, SW USA 33.03N 102.25W
99 K22 **Wells** SW England, UK 51.13N 2.39W
31 V11 **Wells** Minnesota, N USA 43.45N 93.43W
37 X2 **Wells** Nevada, W USA 41.06N 114.57W
27 W8 **Wells** Texas, SW USA 31.28N 94.54W
20 F12 **Wellsboro** Pennsylvania, NE USA 41.43N 77.39W
23 R1 **Wellsburg** West Virginia, NE USA 40.16N 80.36W
192 K4 **Wellsford** Auckland, North Island, NZ 36.17S 174.30E
188 L9 **Wells, Lake** ◎ Western Australia
189 N4 **Wells, Mount** ▲ Western Australia 17.39S 127.08E
99 P18 **Wells-next-the-Sea** E England, UK 52.58N 0.48E
33 T15 **Wellston** Ohio, N USA 39.07N 82.31W
29 O10 **Wellston** Oklahoma, C USA 35.41N 97.03W
20 E11 **Wellsville** New York, NE USA 42.06N 77.55W
33 V12 **Wellsville** Ohio, N USA 40.36N 80.39W
38 L1 **Wellsville** Utah, W USA 41.38N 111.55W
38 I14 **Wellton** Arizona, SW USA 32.40N 114.09W
111 S4 **Wels** anc. Ovilava. Oberösterreich, N Austria 48.10N 14.01E
101 K15 **Welschap** ✕ (Eindhoven) Noord-Brabant, S Netherlands 51.27N 5.22E
102 P10 **Welse** ≈ NE Germany
24 H9 **Welsh** Louisiana, S USA 30.12N 92.49W
99 K19 **Welshpool** Wel. Y Trallwng. E Wales, UK 52.38N 3.06W
99 O21 **Welwyn Garden City** SE England, UK 51.48N 0.13W
81 K18 **Wema** Equateur, NW Dem. Rep. Congo (Zaire) 0.25S 21.33E
83 G21 **Wembere** ≈ C Tanzania
9 N13 **Wembley** Alberta, W Canada 55.07N 119.12W
10 I9 **Wemindji** prev. Nouveau-Comptoir, Paint Hills. Quebec, C Canada 53.00N 78.42W
101 G18 **Wemmel** Vlaams Brabant, C Belgium 50.54N 4.18E
34 J8 **Wenatchee** Washington, NW USA 47.49N 120.48W
166 M17 **Wenchang** Hainan, S China 19.34N 110.46E
167 R11 **Wencheng** prev. Daxue. Zhejiang, SE China 27.48N 120.01E
79 P16 **Wenchi** W Ghana 7.45N 2.01W
Wen-chou/Wenchow see Wenzhou
166 H8 **Wenchuan** prev. Weizhou. Sichuan, C China 31.29N 103.39E
Wendau see Võnnu
Wenden see Cēsis
167 S4 **Wendeng** Shandong, E China 37.14N 122.06E
83 J14 **Wendo** Southern, S Ethiopia 6.34N 38.28E
38 J2 **Wendover** Utah, W USA 40.41N 114.00W
12 D9 **Wenebegon** ≈ Ontario, S Canada
12 D8 **Wenebegon Lake** ◎ Ontario, S Canada
110 E9 **Wengen** Bern, W Switzerland 46.38N 7.57E
167 O13 **Wengyuan** prev. Longxian. Guangdong, S China 24.22N 114.06E
201 P15 **Weno** prev. Moen. Chuuk, C Micronesia
201 V12 **Weno** prev. Moen. atoll Chuuk Islands, C Micronesia
164 N13 **Wenquan** Qinghai, C China 33.16N 91.43E
165 H4 **Wenquan** var. Arixang. Xinjiang Uygur Zizhiqu, NW China 45.00N 81.02E
166 H14 **Wenshan** Yunnan, SW China 23.22N 104.21E
164 H6 **Wensu** Xinjiang Uygur Zizhiqu, W China 41.15N 80.10E
190 L8 **Wentworth** New South Wales, SE Australia 34.04S 141.53E
29 W4 **Wentzville** Missouri, C USA 38.48N 90.51W
165 V12 **Wenxian** var. Wen Xian. Gansu, C China 32.57N 104.42E
167 S10 **Wenzhou** var. Wen-chou, Wenchow. Zhejiang, SE China 28.02N 120.36E
36 L4 **Weott** California, W USA 40.19N 123.57W
101 I20 **Wépion** Namur, SE Belgium 50.24N 4.53E
102 O11 **Werbellinsee** ◎ NE Germany
101 L21 **Werbomont** Liège, E Belgium 50.22N 5.43E
85 G20 **Werda** Kgalagadi, S Botswana 25.13S 23.16E
Werder see Virtsu
83 N14 **Werdēr** Somali, E Ethiopia 6.59N 45.20E
Werenów see Voranava
176 V11 **Weri** Irian Jaya, E Indonesia 3.10S 132.39E
100 I13 **Werkendam** Noord-Brabant, S Netherlands 51.48N 4.54E
103 M20 **Wernberg-Köblitz** Bayern, SE Germany 49.31N 12.10E
103 J18 **Werneck** Bayern, C Germany 50.00N 10.06E
103 K14 **Wernigerode** Sachsen-Anhalt, C Germany 51.51N 10.48E
Werowitz see Virovitica
103 J16 **Werra** ≈ C Germany
191 N12 **Werribee** Victoria, SE Australia 37.55S 144.39E
191 T6 **Werris Creek** New South Wales, SE Australia 31.22S 150.40E
Werro see Võru
Werschetz see Vršac
103 K23 **Wertach** ≈ S Germany
103 I19 **Wertheim** Baden-Württemberg, SW Germany 49.45N 9.31E
100 J8 **Wervershoof** Noord-Holland, NW Netherlands 52.43N 5.09E
Wervicq see Wervik
101 C18 **Wervik** var. Wervicq, Werwick. West-Vlaanderen, W Belgium 50.46N 3.03E
Werwick see Wervik
103 D14 **Wesel** Nordrhein-Westfalen, W Germany 51.40N 6.37E
Weseli an der Lainsitz see Veselí nad Lužnicí
Wesenberg see Rakvere
102 H12 **Weser** ≈ NW Germany
Wes-Kaap see Western Cape
27 S17 **Weslaco** Texas, SW USA 26.09N 97.59W
12 J13 **Weslemkoon Lake** ◎ Ontario, SE Canada
189 R1 **Wessel Islands** island group Northern Territory, N Australia
31 P9 **Wessington** South Dakota, N USA 44.27N 98.40W
31 P10 **Wessington Springs** South Dakota, N USA 44.02N 98.33W
27 T8 **West** Texas, SW USA 31.48N 97.05W
West see Ouest
32 M9 **West Allis** Wisconsin, N USA 43.01N 88.00W
190 E8 **Westall, Point** headland South Australia 32.54S 134.04E
West Antarctica see Lesser Antarctica
12 G11 **West Arm** Ontario, S Canada 46.16N 80.25W
West Azerbaijan see Āzarbāyjān-e Gharbī
144 F10 **West Bank** disputed region SW Asia
9 N17 **Westbank** British Columbia, SW Canada 49.50N 119.37W
12 E11 **West Bay** Manitoulin Island, Ontario, S Canada 45.48N 82.09W
24 I11 **West Bay** bay Louisiana, S USA
32 M8 **West Bend** Wisconsin, N USA 43.25N 88.13W
159 R16 **West Bengal** ◐ state NE India
West Borneo see Kalimantan Barat
31 Y14 **West Branch** Iowa, C USA 41.40N 91.21W
33 R7 **West Branch** Michigan, N USA 44.16N 84.13W
20 F13 **West Branch Susquehanna River** ≈ Pennsylvania, NE USA
99 L20 **West Bromwich** C England, UK 52.28N 1.59W
21 P8 **Westbrook** Maine, NE USA 43.42N 70.21W
31 T10 **Westbrook** Minnesota, N USA 44.02N 95.26W
31 Y15 **West Burlington** Iowa, C USA 40.49N 91.09W
98 L2 **West Burra** island NE Scotland, UK
32 J8 **Westby** Wisconsin, N USA 43.39N 90.52W
46 L6 **West Caicos** island W Turks and Caicos Islands
193 A24 **West Cape** headland South Island, NZ 45.51S 166.26E
182 L4 **West Caroline Basin** undersea feature SW Pacific Ocean
20 I16 **West Chester** Pennsylvania, NE USA 39.56N 75.35W
193 E18 **West Coast** off. West Coast Region. ◐ region South Island, NZ
27 V12 **West Columbia** Texas, SW USA 29.08N 95.39W

◆ Country
● Country Capital
◇ Dependent Territory
○ Dependent Territory Capital
◐ Administrative Region
✕ International Airport
▲ Mountain
▲▲ Mountain Range
Volcano
≈ River
◎ Lake
⊠ Reservoir

West Concord – Windhoek

31 W10 **West Concord** Minnesota, N USA *44.09N 92.54W*
31 V14 **West Des Moines** Iowa, C USA *41.33N 93.42W*
39 Q6 **West Elk Peak** ▲ Colorado, C USA *38.43N 107.12W*
46 F1 **West End** Grand Bahama Island, N Bahamas *26.36N 78.55W*
46 F1 **West End Point** *headland* Grand Bahama Island, N Bahamas *26.40N 78.58W*
100 O7 **Westerbork** Drenthe, NE Netherlands *52.49N 6.36E*
100 N3 **Westereems** *strait* Germany/Netherlands
100 O9 **Westerhaar-Vriezenveensewijk** Overijssel, E Netherlands *52.28N 6.38E*
102 G6 **Westerland** Schleswig-Holstein, N Germany *54.54N 8.19E*
101 I17 **Westerlo** Antwerpen, N Belgium *51.05N 4.55E*
21 N13 **Westerly** Rhode Island, NE USA *41.22N 71.45W*
83 G18 **Western** ◈ *province* W Kenya
159 N11 **Western** ◈ *zone* C Nepal
194 E14 **Western** ◈ *province* SW PNG
195 T14 **Western** *off.* Western Province. ◈ *province* NW Solomon Islands
85 G15 **Western** ◈ *province* SW Zambia
188 K8 **Western Australia** ◈ *state* W Australia
82 A13 **Western Bahr el Ghazal** ◈ *state* SW Sudan
Western Bug *see* Bug
85 F25 **Western Cape** *off.* Western Cape Province, *Afr.* Wes-Kaap. ◈ *province* SW South Africa
82 A11 **Western Darfur** ◈ *state* W Sudan
Western Desert *see* Sahara el Gharbîya
120 G9 **Western Dvina** *Bel.* Dzvina, *Ger.* Düna, *Latv.* Daugava, *Rus.* Zapadnaya Dvina. ≈ W Europe
83 D15 **Western Equatoria** ◈ *state* SW Sudan
161 E16 **Western Ghats** ▲▲ SW India
194 G12 **Western Highlands** ◈ *province* C PNG
Western Isles *see* Outer Hebrides
82 C12 **Western Kordofan** ◈ *state* C Sudan
23 T3 **Westernport** Maryland, NE USA *39.29N 79.03W*
161 J26 **Western Province** ◈ *province* SW Sri Lanka
76 B10 **Western Sahara** ◇ *disputed territory* N Africa
Western Samoa *see* Samoa
Western Sayans *see* Zapadnyy Sayan
Western Scheldt *see* Westerschelde
Western Sierra Madre *see* Madre Occidental, Sierra
101 E15 **Westerschelde** *Eng.* Western Scheldt; *prev.* Honte. *inlet* S North Sea
33 S13 **Westerville** Ohio, N USA *40.07N 82.55W*
103 F17 **Westerwald** ▲▲ W Germany
67 C25 **West Falkland** *var.* Gran Malvina, Isla Gran Malvina. *island* W Falkland Islands
31 R5 **West Fargo** North Dakota, N USA *46.49N 96.51W*
196 M15 **West Fayu Atoll** *atoll* Caroline Islands, C Micronesia
20 C11 **Westfield** New York, NE USA *42.18N 79.34W*
32 L7 **Westfield** Wisconsin, N USA *43.56N 89.31W*
West Flanders *see* West-Vlaanderen
29 S10 **West Fork** Arkansas, C USA *35.55N 94.11W*
31 P16 **West Fork Big Blue River** ≈ Nebraska, C USA
31 U12 **West Fork Des Moines River** ≈ Iowa/Minnesota, C USA
27 S5 **West Fork Trinity River** ≈ Texas, SW USA
32 L16 **West Frankfort** Illinois, N USA *37.54N 88.55W*
100 I8 **West-Friesland** *physical region* NW Netherlands
West Frisian Islands *see* Waddeneilanden
21 T5 **West Grand Lake** ◎ Maine, NE USA
20 M12 **West Hartford** Connecticut, NE USA *41.44N 72.45W*
20 M13 **West Haven** Connecticut, NE USA *41.16N 72.57W*
29 X12 **West Helena** Arkansas, C USA *34.33N 90.38W*
30 M2 **Westhope** North Dakota, N USA *48.54N 101.01W*
205 Y8 **West Ice Shelf** *ice shelf* Antarctica
49 R2 **West Indies** *island group* SE North America
West Irian *see* Irian Jaya
West Java *see* Jawa Barat
38 L3 **West Jordan** Utah, W USA *40.37N 111.55W*
West Kalimantan *see* Kalimantan Barat
101 D14 **Westkapelle** Zeeland, SW Netherlands *51.32N 3.26E*
33 O13 **West Lafayette** Indiana, N USA *40.24N 86.54W*
33 T13 **West Lafayette** Ohio, N USA *40.16N 81.45W*
West Lake *see* Kagera
31 Y14 **West Liberty** Iowa, C USA *41.34N 91.15W*
23 O5 **West Liberty** Kentucky, S USA *38.04N 83.22W*
Westliche Morava *see* Zapadna Morava
15 I13 **Westlock** Alberta, SW Canada *54.12N 113.49W*
12 E17 **West Lorne** Ontario, S Canada *42.36N 81.34W*
98 J12 **West Lothian** *cultural region* S Scotland, UK
101 H16 **Westmalle** Antwerpen, N Belgium *51.18N 4.40E*
199 H6 **West Mariana Basin** *var.* Perece Vela Basin. *undersea feature* W Pacific Ocean
99 E17 **Westmeath** *Ir.* An Iarmhí, Na h-Iarmhidhe. *cultural region* C Ireland
29 Y11 **West Memphis** Arkansas, C USA *35.09N 90.11W*
23 W2 **Westminster** Maryland, NE USA *39.34N 77.00W*
23 O11 **Westminster** South Carolina, SE USA *34.39N 83.06W*
24 I5 **West Monroe** Louisiana, S USA *32.31N 92.09W*
20 D15 **Westmont** Pennsylvania, NE USA *40.16N 78.55W*
29 O3 **Westmoreland** Kansas, C USA *39.23N 96.30W*
37 W17 **Westmorland** California, W USA *33.02N 115.37W*
194 L11 **West New Britain** ◈ *province* E PNG
West New Guinea *see* Irian Jaya
85 K18 **West Nicholson** Matabeleland South, S Zimbabwe *21.06S 29.23E*
31 T14 **West Nishnabotna River** ≈ Iowa, C USA
183 P11 **West Norfolk Ridge** *undersea feature* W Pacific Ocean
27 P12 **West Nueces River** ≈ Texas, SW USA
West Nusa Tenggara *see* Nusa Tenggara Barat
31 T11 **West Okoboji Lake** ◎ Iowa, C USA
35 R16 **Weston** Idaho, NW USA *42.01N 119.29W*
23 R4 **Weston** West Virginia, NE USA *39.02N 80.28W*
99 J22 **Weston-super-Mare** SW England, UK *51.21N 2.58W*
25 Z14 **West Palm Beach** Florida, SE USA *26.43N 80.03W*
West Papua *see* Irian Jaya
196 E9 **West Passage** *passage* Babeldaob, N Palau
25 O9 **West Pensacola** Florida, SE USA *30.25N 87.16W*
29 V8 **West Plains** Missouri, C USA *36.43N 91.51W*
37 P7 **West Point** California, W USA *38.21N 120.33W*
25 R5 **West Point** Georgia, SE USA *32.52N 85.10W*
24 M3 **West Point** Mississippi, S USA *33.36N 88.39W*
31 R14 **West Point** Nebraska, C USA *41.50N 96.42W*
23 X6 **West Point** Virginia, NE USA *37.31N 76.48W*
190 G10 **West Point** *headland* South Australia *35.01S 135.58E*
67 B24 **Westpoint Island Settlement** Westpoint Island, NW Falkland Islands *51.21S 60.40W*
25 R4 **West Point Lake** ⊠ Alabama/Georgia, SE USA
99 B16 **Westport** *Ir.* Cathair na Mart. W Ireland *53.48N 9.31W*
193 G15 **Westport** West Coast, South Island, NZ *41.46S 171.37E*
34 F10 **Westport** Oregon, NW USA *46.07N 123.22W*
34 F9 **Westport** Washington, NW USA *46.53N 124.06W*
33 S15 **West Portsmouth** Ohio, N USA *38.45N 83.01W*
West Punjab *see* Punjab
9 V14 **Westray** Manitoba, C Canada *53.30N 101.19W*
98 J4 **Westray** *island* NE Scotland, UK
12 F9 **Westree** Ontario, S Canada *47.25N 81.32W*
99 L16 **West Riding** *cultural region* N England, UK
West River *see* Xi Jiang
32 J7 **West Salem** Wisconsin, N USA *43.54N 91.04W*
67 H21 **West Scotia Ridge** *undersea feature* W Scotia Sea
West Sepik *see* Sandaun
181 N4 **West Sheba Ridge** *undersea feature* W Indian Ocean
West Siberian Plain *see* Zapadno-Sibirskaya Ravnina
33 S11 **West Sister Island** *island* Ohio, N USA
West-Skylge *see* West-Terschelling
West Sumatra *see* Sumatera Barat
100 J5 **West-Terschelling** *Fris.* West-Skylge. Friesland, N Netherlands *53.22N 5.13E*
66 J7 **West Thulean Rise** *undersea feature* N Atlantic Ocean
31 X12 **West Union** Iowa, C USA *42.57N 91.48W*
33 R15 **West Union** Ohio, N USA *38.47N 83.33W*
23 R3 **West Union** West Virginia, NE USA *39.18N 80.46W*
33 N13 **Westville** Illinois, N USA *40.02N 87.38W*
23 R3 **West Virginia** *off.* State of West Virginia; also known as The Mountain State. ◈ *state* NE USA
101 A17 **West-Vlaanderen** *Eng.* West Flanders. ◈ *province* W Belgium
37 R7 **West Walker River** ≈ California/Nevada, W USA
37 P4 **Westwood** California, W USA *40.18N 121.02W*
191 P9 **West Wyalong** New South Wales, SE Australia *33.56S 147.10E*
179 N14 **West York Island** *island* N Spratly Islands
175 S15 **Wetar, Pulau** *island* Kepulauan Damar, E Indonesia
175 S16 **Wetar, Selat** *var.* Wetar Strait. *strait* Nusa Tenggara, S Indonesia
Wetar Strait *see* Wetar, Selat
9 Q15 **Wetaskiwin** Alberta, SW Canada *52.57N 113.19W*
83 K21 **Wete** Pemba, E Tanzania *5.03S 39.40E*
177 G4 **Wetlet** Sagaing, C Burma *22.21N 95.49E*
39 T6 **Wet Mountains** ▲▲ Colorado, C USA
103 E15 **Wetter** Nordrhein-Westfalen, W Germany *51.22N 7.24E*
103 H17 **Wetter** ≈ W Germany
101 F17 **Wetteren** Oost-Vlaanderen, NW Belgium *51.06N 3.58E*
110 F7 **Wettingen** Aargau, N Switzerland *47.30N 8.14E*
29 P11 **Wetumka** Oklahoma, C USA *35.14N 96.14W*
25 Q5 **Wetumpka** Alabama, S USA *32.32N 86.12W*
110 G7 **Wetzikon** Zürich, N Switzerland *47.19N 8.48E*
103 G17 **Wetzlar** Hessen, W Germany *50.33N 8.30E*
101 C18 **Wevelgem** West-Vlaanderen, W Belgium *50.48N 3.12E*
40 M6 **Wevok** *var.* Wewuk. Alaska, USA *68.52N 166.05W*
25 R9 **Wewahitchka** Florida, SE USA *30.06N 85.12W*
194 G10 **Wewak** East Sepik, NW PNG *3.32S 143.36E*
29 O11 **Wewoka** Oklahoma, C USA *35.09N 96.29W*
Wewuk *see* Wevok
99 F20 **Wexford** *Ir.* Loch Garman. SE Ireland *52.21N 6.31W*
99 F20 **Wexford** *Ir.* Loch Garman. *cultural region* SE Ireland
32 L7 **Weyauwega** Wisconsin, N USA *44.16N 88.54W*
9 U17 **Weyburn** Saskatchewan, S Canada *49.39N 103.51W*
Weyer *see* Weyer Markt
111 U5 **Weyer Markt** *var.* Weyer. Oberösterreich, N Austria *47.52N 14.39E*
102 H11 **Weyhe** Niedersachsen, NW Germany *53.00N 8.52E*
99 L24 **Weymouth** S England, UK *50.36N 2.28W*
21 P11 **Weymouth** Massachusetts, NE USA *42.13N 70.56W*
101 H18 **Wezembeek-Oppem** Vlaams Brabant, C Belgium *50.51N 4.28E*
100 M9 **Wezep** Gelderland, E Netherlands *52.28N 6.00E*
192 M9 **Whakamaru** Waikato, North Island, NZ *38.27S 175.48E*
192 O8 **Whakatane** Bay of Plenty, North Island, NZ *37.58S 105.00E*
192 O8 **Whakatane** ≈ North Island, NZ
15 L7 **Whale Cove** Nunavut, C Canada *62.13N 92.10W*
98 M2 **Whalsay** *island* NE Scotland, UK
192 L11 **Whangaehu** ≈ North Island, NZ
192 M6 **Whangamata** Waikato, North Island, NZ *37.13S 175.51E*
192 Q9 **Whangara** Gisborne, North Island, NZ *38.34S 178.12E*
192 K3 **Whangarei** Northland, North Island, NZ *35.44S 174.18E*
192 K3 **Whangaruru Harbour** *inlet* North Island, NZ
27 V12 **Wharton** Texas, SW USA *29.19N 96.08W*
181 U8 **Wharton Basin** *var.* West Australian Basin. *undersea feature* E Indian Ocean
193 E18 **Whataroa** West Coast, South Island, NZ *43.16S 170.19E*
15 Hh7 **Wha Ti** *prev.* Lac La Martre. Northwest Territories, W Canada *63.10N 117.12W*
192 K6 **Whatipu** Auckland, North Island, NZ *37.17S 174.44E*
35 Y16 **Wheatland** Wyoming, C USA *42.03N 104.57W*
12 D18 **Wheatley** Ontario, S Canada *42.06N 82.27W*
32 M10 **Wheaton** Illinois, N USA *41.52N 88.06W*
31 R7 **Wheaton** Minnesota, N USA *45.48N 96.30W*
39 T4 **Wheat Ridge** Colorado, C USA *39.44N 105.06W*
27 P2 **Wheeler** Texas, SW USA *35.26N 100.16W*
25 O2 **Wheeler Lake** ⊠ Alabama, S USA
37 Y6 **Wheeler Peak** ▲ Nevada, W USA *39.00N 114.17W*
39 T9 **Wheeler Peak** ▲ New Mexico, SW USA *36.34N 105.25W*
33 S15 **Wheelersburg** Ohio, N USA *38.43N 82.51W*
23 R2 **Wheeling** West Virginia, NE USA *40.03N 80.43W*
99 L16 **Whernside** ▲ N England, UK *54.13N 2.27W*
190 F9 **Whidbey, Point** *headland* South Australia *34.36S 135.08E*
188 I7 **Whim Creek** Western Australia *20.51S 117.54E*
8 L17 **Whistler** British Columbia, SW Canada *50.07N 122.57W*
23 W8 **Whitakers** North Carolina, SE USA *36.06N 77.43W*
12 H15 **Whitby** Ontario, S Canada *43.53N 78.54W*
99 N15 **Whitby** N England, UK *54.28N 0.37W*
8 G6 **White** ≈ Yukon Territory, W Canada
11 T11 **White Bay** *bay* Newfoundland, E Canada
22 I8 **White Bluff** Tennessee, S USA *36.06N 87.13W*
30 J6 **White Butte** ▲ North Dakota, N USA *46.23N 103.18W*
21 R5 **White Cap Mountain** ▲ Maine, NE USA *45.33N 69.15W*
24 J9 **White Castle** Louisiana, S USA *30.10N 91.09W*
190 M5 **White Cliffs** New South Wales, SE Australia *30.52S 143.04E*
33 P8 **White Cloud** Michigan, N USA *43.34N 85.46W*
9 P14 **Whitecourt** Alberta, SW Canada *54.10N 115.37W*
27 O2 **White Deer** Texas, SW USA *35.26N 101.10W*
White Elster *see* Weisse Elster
26 M5 **Whiteface** Texas, SW USA *33.36N 102.36W*
20 K7 **Whiteface Mountain** ▲ New York, NE USA *44.22N 73.54W*
31 W5 **Whiteface Reservoir** ⊠ Minnesota, N USA
35 O7 **Whitefish** Montana, NW USA *48.24N 114.20W*
33 N9 **Whitefish Bay** Wisconsin, N USA *43.09N 87.54W*
33 Q3 **Whitefish Bay** *lake bay* Canada/USA
12 E11 **Whitefish Falls** Ontario, S Canada *46.06N 81.42W*
12 B7 **Whitefish Lake** ◎ Ontario, S Canada
31 U6 **Whitefish Lake** ◎ Minnesota, C USA
33 Q3 **Whitefish Point** *headland* Michigan, N USA *46.46N 84.57W*
33 O4 **Whitefish River** ≈ Michigan, N USA
27 O4 **Whiteflat** Texas, SW USA *34.06N 100.55W*
29 V12 **White Hall** Arkansas, C USA *34.18N 92.05W*
32 K14 **White Hall** Illinois, N USA *39.26N 90.24W*
33 O8 **Whitehall** Michigan, N USA *43.24N 86.21W*
20 L9 **Whitehall** New York, NE USA *43.33N 73.24W*
33 S13 **Whitehall** Ohio, N USA *39.58N 82.53W*
32 J7 **Whitehall** Wisconsin, N USA *44.22N 91.19W*
99 J15 **Whitehaven** NW England, UK *54.33N 3.34W*
8 I8 **Whitehorse** *territory capital* Yukon Territory, W Canada *60.40N 135.07W*
192 O7 **White Island** *island* NE NZ
12 K13 **White Lake** ◎ Ontario, SE Canada
24 H10 **White Lake** ◎ Louisiana, S USA
195 N12 **Whiteman Range** ▲▲ New Britain, E PNG
191 Q15 **Whitemark** Tasmania, SE Australia *40.10S 148.01E*
37 S9 **White Mountains** ▲▲ California/Nevada, W USA
21 N7 **White Mountains** ▲▲ Maine/New Hampshire, NE USA
82 F11 **White Nile** ◈ *state* C Sudan
69 U7 **White Nile** *var.* Bahr el Jebel. ≈ S Sudan
83 E14 **White Nile** *Ar.* Al Baḥr al Abyaḍ, An Nīl al Abyaḍ, Bahr el Jebel. ≈ SE Sudan
27 W5 **White Oak Creek** ≈ Texas, SW USA
8 H9 **White Pass** *pass* Canada/USA *59.35N 135.05W*
34 I9 **White Pass** *pass* Washington, NW USA *46.38N 121.23W*
23 O9 **White Pine** Tennessee, S USA *36.06N 83.17W*
20 K14 **White Plains** New York, NE USA *41.01N 73.45W*
27 O5 **White River** ≈ Texas, SW USA
30 M11 **White River** South Dakota, N USA *43.34N 100.45W*
29 W12 **White River** ≈ Arkansas, SE USA
39 P3 **White River** ≈ Colorado/Utah, C USA
33 N15 **White River** ≈ Indiana, N USA
33 O8 **White River** ≈ Michigan, N USA
30 K11 **White River** ≈ South Dakota, N USA
20 M8 **White River** ≈ Vermont, NE USA
39 N13 **Whiteriver** Arizona, SW USA *33.50N 109.57W*
27 O5 **White River Lake** ⊠ Texas, SW USA
34 H11 **White Salmon** Washington, NW USA *45.43N 121.29W*
20 I10 **Whitesboro** New York, NE USA *43.07N 75.17W*
27 T5 **Whitesboro** Texas, SW USA *33.39N 96.54W*
23 O7 **Whitesburg** Kentucky, S USA *37.16N 82.55W*
White Sea *see* Beloye More
White Sea-Baltic Canal/White Sea Canal *see* Belomorsko-Baltiyskiy Kanal
65 I25 **Whiteside, Canal** *channel* S Chile
35 S10 **White Sulphur Springs** Montana, NW USA *46.33N 110.54W*
23 R6 **White Sulphur Springs** West Virginia, NE USA *37.48N 80.18W*
22 J6 **Whitesville** Kentucky, S USA *37.40N 86.48W*
34 I10 **White Swan** Washington, NW USA *46.22N 120.46W*
23 U12 **Whiteville** North Carolina, SE USA *34.20N 78.42W*
22 F10 **Whiteville** Tennessee, S USA *35.19N 89.09W*
79 Q13 **White Volta** *var.* Nakambé, *Fr.* Volta Blanche. ≈ Burkina/Ghana
32 M9 **Whitewater** Wisconsin, N USA *42.51N 88.43W*
39 P14 **Whitewater Baldy** ▲ New Mexico, SW USA *33.19N 108.38W*
25 X17 **Whitewater Bay** *bay* Florida, SE USA
33 Q14 **Whitewater River** ≈ Indiana/Ohio, N USA
9 V16 **Whitewood** Saskatchewan, S Canada *50.19N 102.16W*
30 J9 **Whitewood** South Dakota, N USA *44.27N 103.38W*
27 U5 **Whitewright** Texas, SW USA *33.30N 96.23W*
99 I15 **Whithorn** S Scotland, UK *54.43N 4.26W*
192 M6 **Whitianga** Waikato, North Island, NZ *36.49S 175.42E*
21 N11 **Whitinsville** Massachusetts, NE USA *42.06N 71.40W*
22 M8 **Whitley City** Kentucky, S USA *36.40N 84.28W*
23 Q11 **Whitmire** South Carolina, SE USA *34.30N 81.36W*
33 R10 **Whitmore Lake** Michigan, N USA *42.26N 83.44W*
205 N9 **Whitmore Mountains** ▲▲ Antarctica
12 I12 **Whitney** Ontario, SE Canada *45.29N 78.11W*
27 T8 **Whitney** Texas, SW USA *31.56N 97.20W*
27 S8 **Whitney, Lake** ⊠ Texas, SW USA
37 S11 **Whitney, Mount** ▲ California, W USA *37.45N 119.55W*
189 Y6 **Whitsunday Group** *island group* Queensland, E Australia
27 S6 **Whitt** Texas, SW USA *32.55N 98.01W*
31 U12 **Whittemore** Iowa, C USA *43.03N 94.25W*
41 R12 **Whittier** Alaska, USA *60.46N 148.40W*
37 T15 **Whittier** California, W USA *33.58N 118.01W*
85 I25 **Whittlesea** Eastern Cape, S South Africa *32.08S 26.51E*
22 K10 **Whitwell** Tennessee, S USA *35.12N 85.31W*
15 J9 **Wholdaia Lake** ◎ Northwest Territories, NW Canada
190 H7 **Whyalla** South Australia *33.04S 137.34E*
Whydah *see* Ouidah
12 F13 **Wiarton** Ontario, S Canada *44.44N 81.09W*
175 Q11 **Wiau** Sulawesi, C Indonesia *3.08S 121.22E*
113 H15 **Wiązów** *Ger.* Wansen. Dolnośląskie, SW Poland *50.49N 17.13E*
35 Y8 **Wibaux** Montana, NW USA *46.57N 104.11W*
29 N6 **Wichita** Kansas, C USA *37.42N 97.20W*
27 R5 **Wichita Falls** Texas, SW USA *33.54N 98.29W*
28 L11 **Wichita Mountains** ▲▲ Oklahoma, C USA
27 R5 **Wichita River** ≈ Texas, SW USA
98 K6 **Wick** N Scotland, UK *58.25N 3.06W*
38 K13 **Wickenburg** Arizona, SW USA *33.57N 112.41W*
26 L8 **Wickett** Texas, SW USA *31.34N 103.00W*
188 I7 **Wickham** Western Australia *20.40S 117.11E*
190 M14 **Wickham, Cape** *headland* Tasmania, SE Australia *39.36S 143.55E*
22 G7 **Wickliffe** Kentucky, S USA *37.14N 89.16W*
99 G19 **Wicklow** *Ir.* Cill Mhantáin. E Ireland *52.58N 6.03W*
99 F19 **Wicklow** *Ir.* Cill Mhantáin. *cultural region* E Ireland
99 G19 **Wicklow Head** *Ir.* Ceann Chill Mhantáin. *headland* E Ireland *52.57N 6.00W*
99 F18 **Wicklow Mountains** *Ir.* Sléibhte Chill Mhantáin. ▲▲ E Ireland
12 H10 **Wicksteed Lake** ◎ Ontario, S Canada
Wida *see* Ouidah
67 G15 **Wideawake Airfield** ✕ (Georgetown) SW Ascension Island
195 P11 **Wide Bay** *bay* New Britain, PNG
175 Tt9 **Widi, Kepulauan** *island group* E Indonesia
99 K18 **Widnes** C England, UK *53.22N 2.43W*
112 H9 **Więcbork** *Ger.* Vandsburg. Kujawsko-pomorskie, C Poland *53.21N 17.31E*
103 E17 **Wied** ≈ W Germany
103 F16 **Wiehl** Nordrhein-Westfalen, W Germany *50.57N 7.33E*
113 L17 **Wieliczka** Małopolskie, S Poland *50.00N 20.02E*
112 G12 **Wielkopolskie** ◈ *province* C Poland
113 J14 **Wieluń** Sieradz, C Poland *51.13N 18.33E*
111 X4 **Wien** *Eng.* Vienna, *Hung.* Bécs, *Slvk.* Vídeň, *Slvn.* Dunaj; *anc.* Vindobona. ● (Austria) Wien, NE Austria *48.13N 16.22E*
111 X4 **Wien** *off.* Land Wien, *Eng.* Vienna. ◈ *state* NE Austria
111 X5 **Wiener Neustadt** Niederösterreich, E Austria *47.49N 16.07E*
112 G7 **Wieprza** *Ger.* Wipper. ≈ NW Poland
100 O10 **Wierden** Overijssel, E Netherlands *52.22N 6.34E*
100 I7 **Wieringerwerf** Noord-Holland, NW Netherlands *52.51N 5.01E*
Wieruschow *see* Wieruszów
113 I14 **Wieruszów** *Ger.* Wieruschow. Łódzkie, C Poland *51.18N 18.09E*
111 V9 **Wies** Steiermark, SE Austria *46.40N 15.16E*
Wiesbachhorn *see* Grosses Wiesbachhorn
103 G18 **Wiesbaden** Hessen, W Germany *50.06N 8.13E*
Wieselburg and Ungarisch-Altenburg/Wieselburg-Ungarisch-Altenburg *see* Mosonmagyaróvár
Wiesenhof *see* Ostrołęka
103 G20 **Wiesloch** Baden-Württemberg, SW Germany *49.18N 8.42E*
102 F10 **Wiesmoor** Niedersachsen, NW Germany *53.22N 7.46E*
112 I7 **Wieżyca** *Ger.* Turmberg. *hill* Pomorskie, N Poland *54.13N 18.06E*
99 L17 **Wigan** NW England, UK *53.33N 2.37W*
39 U3 **Wiggins** Colorado, C USA *40.11N 104.03W*
24 M8 **Wiggins** Mississippi, S USA *30.50N 89.09W*
Wigorna Ceaster *see* Worcester
99 I14 **Wigtown** S Scotland, UK *54.52N 4.26W*
99 H14 **Wigtown** *cultural region* SW Scotland, UK
99 I15 **Wigtown Bay** *bay* SW Scotland, UK
100 L13 **Wijchen** Gelderland, SE Netherlands *51.48N 5.43E*
94 N1 **Wijdefjorden** *fjord* NW Svalbard
100 M10 **Wijhe** Overijssel, E Netherlands *52.22N 6.07E*
100 J12 **Wijk bij Duurstede** Utrecht, C Netherlands *51.58N 5.21E*
100 J13 **Wijk en Aalburg** Noord-Brabant, S Netherlands *51.46N 5.06E*
101 H16 **Wijnegem** Antwerpen, N Belgium *51.13N 4.31E*
12 E11 **Wikwemikong** Manitoulin Island, Ontario, S Canada *45.46N 81.43W*
110 H7 **Wil** Sankt Gallen, NE Switzerland *47.28N 9.03E*
31 R16 **Wilber** Nebraska, C USA *40.28N 96.57W*
34 K8 **Wilbur** Washington, NW USA *47.45N 118.42W*
29 Q11 **Wilburton** Oklahoma, C USA *34.55N 95.18W*
190 M6 **Wilcannia** New South Wales, SE Australia *31.34S 143.23E*
20 D12 **Wilcox** Pennsylvania, NE USA *41.34N 78.40W*
Wilczek Land *see* Vil'cheka, Zemlya
111 U6 **Wildalpen** Steiermark, E Austria *47.40N 14.54E*
33 O13 **Wildcat Creek** ≈ Indiana, N USA
110 L9 **Wilde Kreuzspitze** *It.* Picco di Croce. ▲ Austria/Italy *46.53N 10.51E*
Wildenschwert *see* Ústí nad Orlicí
100 O6 **Wildervank** Groningen, NE Netherlands *53.04N 6.52E*
102 G11 **Wildeshausen** Niedersachsen, NW Germany *52.54N 8.26E*
110 D10 **Wildhorn** ▲ SW Switzerland *46.21N 7.22E*
9 R17 **Wild Horse** Alberta, SW Canada *49.00N 110.19W*
29 N12 **Wildhorse Creek** ≈ Oklahoma, C USA
30 L14 **Wild Horse Hill** ▲ Nebraska, C USA *41.52N 101.56W*
111 W8 **Wildon** Steiermark, SE Austria *46.53N 15.29E*
26 M2 **Wildorado** Texas, SW USA *35.12N 102.10W*
31 R6 **Wild Rice River** ≈ Minnesota/North Dakota, N USA
Wilejka *see* Vileyka
205 Y9 **Wilhelm II Coast** *physical region* Antarctica
205 X9 **Wilhelm II Land** *physical region* Antarctica
57 U11 **Wilhelmina Gebergte** ▲▲ C Surinam
20 B13 **Wilhelm, Lake** ⊠ Pennsylvania, NE USA
194 I12 **Wilhelm, Mount** ▲ C PNG *5.51S 147.25E*
94 O2 **Wilhelmøya** *island* C Svalbard
Wilhelm-Pieck-Stadt *see* Guben
111 W4 **Wilhelmsburg** Niederösterreich, E Austria *48.07N 15.36E*
102 G10 **Wilhelmshaven** Niedersachsen, NW Germany *53.31N 8.07E*
Wilia/Wilja *see* Neris
20 H13 **Wilkes Barre** Pennsylvania, NE USA *41.15N 75.49W*
23 R9 **Wilkesboro** North Carolina, SE USA *36.09N 81.09W*
205 W15 **Wilkes Coast** *physical region* Antarctica
201 W12 **Wilkes Island** *island* N Wake Island
205 X12 **Wilkes Land** *physical region* Antarctica
9 S15 **Wilkie** Saskatchewan, S Canada *52.27N 108.42W*
204 I6 **Wilkins Ice Shelf** *ice shelf* Antarctica
190 D4 **Wilkinsons Lakes** *salt lake* South Australia
Wiłkomierz *see* Ukmergė
190 K11 **Willalooka** South Australia *36.24S 140.20E*
34 G11 **Willamette River** ≈ Oregon, NW USA
191 O8 **Willandra Billabong Creek** *seasonal river* New South Wales, SE Australia
34 F9 **Willapa Bay** *inlet* Washington, NW USA
29 T7 **Willard** Missouri, C USA *37.18N 93.25W*
39 S12 **Willard** New Mexico, SW USA *34.36N 106.01W*
33 S12 **Willard** Ohio, N USA *41.03N 82.43W*
38 L1 **Willard** Utah, W USA *41.23N 112.01W*
195 N11 **Willaumez Peninsula** *headland* New Britain, E PNG *5.03S 150.04E*
39 N15 **Willcox** Arizona, SW USA *32.13N 109.49W*
39 N16 **Willcox Playa** *salt flat* Arizona, SW USA
101 G17 **Willebroek** Antwerpen, C Belgium *51.04N 4.22E*
47 P16 **Willemstad** ○ (Netherlands Antilles) Curaçao, Netherlands Antilles *12.06N 68.54W*
101 G14 **Willemstad** Noord-Brabant, S Netherlands *51.40N 4.27E*
9 S11 **William** ≈ Saskatchewan, C Canada
25 O6 **William "Bill" Dannelly Reservoir** ⊠ Alabama, S USA
190 G3 **William Creek** South Australia *28.55S 136.23E*
189 T15 **William, Mount** ▲ South Australia
38 K11 **Williams** Arizona, SW USA *35.15N 112.11W*
31 X14 **Williamsburg** Iowa, C USA *41.39N 92.00W*
22 M8 **Williamsburg** Kentucky, S USA *36.43N 84.06W*
33 R15 **Williamsburg** Ohio, N USA *39.00N 84.02W*
23 X6 **Williamsburg** Virginia, NE USA *37.16N 76.41W*
8 M15 **Williams Lake** British Columbia, SW Canada *52.07N 122.09W*
23 P6 **Williamson** West Virginia, NE USA *37.40N 82.16W*
33 N13 **Williamsport** Indiana, N USA *40.18N 87.18W*
20 G13 **Williamsport** Pennsylvania, NE USA *41.13N 76.59W*
23 W9 **Williamston** North Carolina, SE USA *35.51N 77.03W*
23 P11 **Williamston** South Carolina, SE USA *34.37N 82.28W*
22 M4 **Williamstown** Kentucky, S USA *38.38N 84.33W*
20 L10 **Williamstown** Massachusetts, NE USA *42.41N 73.11W*
20 J16 **Willingboro** New Jersey, NE USA *40.01N 74.52W*
9 Q14 **Willingdon** Alberta, SW Canada *53.49N 112.08W*
27 W10 **Willis** Texas, SW USA *30.25N 95.28W*
110 F8 **Willisau** Luzern, W Switzerland *47.07N 8.00E*
85 F24 **Williston** Northern Cape, W South Africa *31.19S 20.52E*
25 V10 **Williston** Florida, SE USA *29.23N 82.27W*
30 J3 **Williston** North Dakota, N USA *48.07N 103.37W*
23 Q13 **Williston** South Carolina, SE USA *33.24N 81.25W*
8 L12 **Williston Lake** ⊠ British Columbia, W Canada
36 L5 **Willits** California, W USA *39.24N 123.22W*
31 T8 **Willmar** Minnesota, N USA *45.07N 95.02W*
8 K11 **Will, Mount** ▲ British Columbia, W Canada *57.31N 128.48W*
33 T11 **Willoughby** Ohio, N USA *41.38N 81.24W*
9 U17 **Willow Bunch** Saskatchewan, S Canada *49.30N 105.40W*
34 J11 **Willow Creek** ≈ Oregon, NW USA
41 R11 **Willow Lake** Alaska, USA *61.44N 150.02W*
15 H7 **Willowlake** ≈ Northwest Territories, NW Canada
85 H25 **Willowmore** Eastern Cape, S South Africa *33.18S 23.30E*
32 L5 **Willow Reservoir** ⊠ Wisconsin, N USA
37 N5 **Willows** California, W USA *39.28N 122.12W*
29 V7 **Willow Springs** Missouri, C USA *36.59N 91.58W*
190 I7 **Wilmington** South Australia *32.42S 138.08E*
23 Y2 **Wilmington** Delaware, NE USA *39.45N 75.33W*
23 V12 **Wilmington** North Carolina, SE USA *34.13N 77.57W*
33 R14 **Wilmington** Ohio, N USA *39.27N 83.49W*
22 M6 **Wilmore** Kentucky, S USA *37.51N 84.39W*
31 R8 **Wilmot** South Dakota, N USA *45.24N 96.51W*
Wilna/Wilno *see* Vilnius
103 G16 **Wilnsdorf** Nordrhein-Westfalen, W Germany *50.49N 8.06E*
101 G16 **Wilrijk** Antwerpen, N Belgium *51.10N 4.24E*
102 I10 **Wilseder Berg** *hill* NW Germany *53.10N 9.56E*
69 Z12 **Wilshaw Ridge** *undersea feature* W Indian Ocean
23 V9 **Wilson** North Carolina, SE USA *35.42N 77.54W*
27 N5 **Wilson** Texas, SW USA *33.21N 101.44W*
190 A7 **Wilson Bluff** *headland* South Australia/Western Australia *31.41S 129.01E*
37 Y7 **Wilson Creek Range** ▲▲ Nevada, W USA
25 O1 **Wilson Lake** ⊠ Alabama, S USA
28 M4 **Wilson Lake** ⊠ Kansas, SE USA
39 P7 **Wilson, Mount** ▲ Colorado, C USA *37.50N 107.59W*
191 P13 **Wilsons Promontory** *peninsula* Victoria, SE Australia
31 Y14 **Wilton** Iowa, C USA *41.35N 91.01W*
21 P7 **Wilton** Maine, NE USA *44.35N 70.15W*
30 M5 **Wilton** North Dakota, N USA *47.09N 100.46W*
99 L22 **Wiltshire** *cultural region* S England, UK
101 M23 **Wiltz** Diekirch, NW Luxembourg *49.58N 5.55E*
188 K9 **Wiluna** Western Australia *26.34S 120.14E*
101 M23 **Wilwerwiltz** Diekirch, NE Luxembourg *49.59N 6.00E*
31 P5 **Wimbledon** North Dakota, N USA *47.08N 98.25W*
44 K7 **Wina** *var.* Güina. Jinotega, N Nicaragua *13.58N 85.14W*
33 O12 **Winamac** Indiana, N USA *41.03N 86.37W*
83 G19 **Winam Gulf** *var.* Kavirondo Gulf. *gulf* SW Kenya
85 I22 **Winburg** Free State, C South Africa *28.31S 27.01E*
21 N10 **Winchendon** Massachusetts, NE USA *42.41N 72.01W*
12 M13 **Winchester** Ontario, SE Canada *45.07N 75.19W*
99 M23 **Winchester** *hist.* Wintanceaster, *Lat.* Venta Belgarum. S England, UK *51.04N 1.19W*
34 M10 **Winchester** Idaho, NW USA *46.13N 116.35W*
32 J14 **Winchester** Illinois, N USA *39.37N 90.28W*
33 Q13 **Winchester** Indiana, N USA *40.09N 84.58W*
22 M5 **Winchester** Kentucky, S USA *37.59N 84.10W*
20 M10 **Winchester** New Hampshire, NE USA *42.46N 72.21W*
22 K10 **Winchester** Tennessee, S USA *35.11N 86.06W*
23 V3 **Winchester** Virginia, NE USA *39.11N 78.09W*
101 L22 **Wincrange** Diekirch, NW Luxembourg *50.03N 5.55E*
8 I5 **Wind** ≈ Yukon Territory, NW Canada
191 S8 **Windamere, Lake** ◎ New South Wales, SE Australia
Windau *see* Ventspils, Latvia
Windau *see* Venta, Latvia/Lithuania
20 D15 **Windber** Pennsylvania, NE USA *40.12N 78.47W*
25 T3 **Winder** Georgia, SE USA *33.59N 83.43W*
99 K15 **Windermere** NW England, UK *54.24N 2.54W*
12 C7 **Windermere Lake** ◎ Ontario, S Canada
33 U11 **Windham** Ohio, N USA *41.14N 81.03W*
85 D19 **Windhoek** *Ger.* Windhuk. ● (Namibia) Khomas, C Namibia *22.34S 17.06E*

◆ Country ● Country Capital ◇ Dependent Territory ○ Dependent Territory Capital ◈ Administrative Region ✕ International Airport ▲ Mountain ▲▲ Mountain Range ⚠ Volcano ≈ River ◎ Lake ⊠ Reservoir

◆ COUNTRY   ◇ DEPENDENT TERRITORY   ◆ ADMINISTRATIVE REGION   ▲ MOUNTAIN   ℞ VOLCANO   ◎ LAKE
● COUNTRY CAPITAL   ○ DEPENDENT TERRITORY CAPITAL   ✈ INTERNATIONAL AIRPORT   ▲ MOUNTAIN RANGE   ✍ RIVER   ☑ RESERVOIR

Xicoténcatl – Yenisei Bay

43 P11 **Xicoténcatl** Tamaulipas, C Mexico 22.59N 98.54W
Xieng Khouang see Pèk
Xieng Ngeun see Muong Xiang Ngeun
165 X10 **Xifeng** Gansu, C China 35.46N 107.35E
166 J11 **Xifeng** Guizhou, S China 27.15N 106.44E
Xigang see Helan
164 L16 **Xigazê** var. Jih-k'a-tse, Shigatse, Xigaze. Xizang Zizhiqu, W China 29.18N 88.49E
166 I8 **Xi He** ≈ C China
165 W11 **Xihe** Gansu, C China 34.00N 105.24E
Xihuachi see Heshui
165 Q7 **Xijan Quan** spring NW China 40.52N 96.31E
165 W10 **Xiji** Ningxia, N China 36.02N 105.33E
166 M14 **Xi Jiang** var. Hsi Chiang, Eng. West River. ≈ S China
166 K15 **Xijin Shuiku** ⊡ S China
Xilaganí see Xylaganí
166 I13 **Xilin** prev. Bada. Guangxi Zhuangzu Zizhiqu, S China 24.30N 105.00E
169 Q10 **Xilinhot** var. Silinhot. Nei Mongol Zizhiqu, N China 43.58N 116.06E
Xilokastro see Xylókastro
Xin see Xinjiang Uygur Zizhiqu
167 R10 **Xin'anjiang Shuiku** ⊡ SE China
Xin'anzhen see Xinyi
169 Q7 **Xin Barag Youqi** var. Altan Emel. Nei Mongol Zizhiqu, N China 48.37N 116.40E
169 R7 **Xin Barag Zuoqi** var. Amgalang. Nei Mongol Zizhiqu, N China 48.12N 118.15E
169 W12 **Xinbin** Liaoning, NE China 41.39N 125.04E
167 O7 **Xincai** Henan, C China 32.46N 114.54E
165 V8 **Xincheng** var. Yinchuanzhan. Ningxia, N China 38.27N 106.04E
167 O13 **Xinfeng** Jiangxi, S China 25.30N 114.52E
Xinfengjiang Shuiku ⊡ S China
169 T13 **Xingcheng** Liaoning, NE China 40.38N 120.47E
84 E11 **Xinge** Lunda Norte, NE Angola 9.44S 19.10E
167 P12 **Xingguo** Jiangxi, S China 26.25N 115.22E
165 S11 **Xinghai** Qinghai, C China 35.12N 102.28E
167 R7 **Xinghua** Jiangsu, E China 32.54N 119.48E
Xingkai Hu see Khanka, Lake
167 P13 **Xingning** Guangdong, S China 24.13N 115.38E
166 I13 **Xingren** Guizhou, S China 25.25N 105.07E
167 O4 **Xingtai** Hebei, E China 37.07N 114.28E
61 J14 **Xingu, Rio** ≈ C Brazil
165 P6 **Xingxingxia** Xinjiang Uygur Zizhiqu, NW China 41.48N 95.01E
166 I13 **Xingyi** Guizhou, S China 25.04N 104.51E
164 I6 **Xinhe** var. Toksu. Xinjiang Uygur Zizhiqu, NW China 41.34N 82.30E
Xin Hot see Abag Qi
165 T10 **Xining** var. Hsining, Hsi-ning, Sining. province capital Qinghai, C China 36.37N 101.46E
167 O4 **Xinji** prev. Shulu. Hebei, E China 37.55N 115.14E
167 P10 **Xinjian** Jiangxi, S China 28.42N 115.43E
Xinjiang see Xinjiang Uygur Zizhiqu
168 D8 **Xinjiang Uygur Zizhiqu** var. Sinkiang, Sinkiang Uighur Autonomous Region, Xin, Xinjiang. ◐ autonomous region NW China
166 H9 **Xinjin** Sichuan, C China 30.24N 103.48E
Xinjin see Pulandian
169 U12 **Xinmin** Liaoning, NE China 41.58N 122.51E
166 M12 **Xinning** Hunan, S China 26.34N 110.57E
Xinpu see Lianyungang
167 P5 **Xinwen** prev. Suncun. Shandong, E China 35.49N 117.36E
Xin Xian see Xinzhou
167 N6 **Xinxiang** Henan, C China 35.13N 113.48E
167 O8 **Xinyang** var. Hsin-yang, Sinyang. Henan, C China 32.09N 114.04E
167 Q6 **Xinyi** var. Xin'anzhen. Jiangsu, E China 34.25N 118.19E
167 Q6 **Xinyi He** ≈ E China
167 O11 **Xinyu** Jiangxi, S China 27.51N 115.00E
164 I5 **Xinyuan** var. Künes. Xinjiang Uygur Zizhiqu, NW China 43.25N 83.12E
Xinyuan see Tianjun
168 M14 **Xinzhao Shan** ▲ N China 39.37N 107.51E
167 N3 **Xinzhou** var. Xin Xian. Shanxi, C China 38.24N 112.43E
106 H4 **Xinzo de Limia** Galicia, NW Spain 42.04N 7.45W
Xions see Książ Wielkopolski
167 O7 **Xiping** Henan, C China 33.22N 114.00E
165 T11 **Xiqing Shan** ▲▲ C China
61 N16 **Xique-Xique** Bahia, E Brazil 10.46S 42.43W
117 E14 **Xirovoúni** ▲ N Greece 40.31N 21.58E
Xishanzui see Urad Qianqi
166 J11 **Xishui** Guizhou, S China 28.24N 106.09E
167 O9 **Xishui** Hubei, C China 30.29N 115.13E
169 R10 **Xi Ujimqin Qi** var. Bayan Ul Hot. Nei Mongol Zizhiqu, N China 44.31N 117.36E
166 K11 **Xiushan** Sichuan, C China 28.23N 108.52E
167 O10 **Xiu Shui** ≈ S China
164 J16 **Xixabangma Feng** ▲ W China 28.25N 85.47E
166 M7 **Xixia** Henan, C China 33.19N 111.25E
Xixón see Gijón
Xixona see Jijona
Xizang see Xizang Zizhiqu
Xizang Gaoyuan see Qingzang Gaoyuan
166 E9 **Xizang Zizhiqu** var. Thibet, Tibetan Autonomous Region, Xizang, Eng. Tibet. ◐ autonomous region W China
169 U14 **Xizhong Dao** island N China
Xolotlán see Managua, Lago de
165 N9 **Xorkol** Xinjiang Uygur Zizhiqu, NW China 38.45N 91.07E
43 X14 **Xpujil** Quintana Roo, E Mexico 18.30N 89.24W
Xuancheng see Xuanzhou
178 Jj9 **Xuân Đuc** Quang Binh, C Vietnam 17.19N 106.38E
166 L9 **Xuan'en** Hubei, C China 30.03N 109.26E
166 K8 **Xuanhan** Sichuan, C China 31.25N 107.41E
167 O2 **Xuanhua** Hebei, E China 40.37N 115.04E
167 P4 **Xuanhui He** ≈ E China
167 Q8 **Xuanzhou** var. Xuancheng. Anhui, E China 30.59N 118.43E
167 N7 **Xuchang** Henan, C China 34.03N 113.48E
143 X10 **Xudat** Rus. Khudat. NE Azerbaijan 41.37N 48.39E
83 M16 **Xuddur** var. Hudur, It. Oddur. Bakool, SW Somalia 4.06N 43.47E
82 O13 **Xudun** Nugaal, N Somalia 9.12N 47.34E
166 L11 **Xuefeng Shan** ▲▲ S China
44 F2 **Xunantunich** ruins Cayo, W Belize 17.06N 89.10W
169 W6 **Xun He** ≈ NE China
166 L7 **Xun He** ≈ C China
166 L14 **Xun Jiang** ≈ S China
169 W5 **Xunke** Heilongjiang, NE China 49.36N 128.25E
167 P13 **Xunwu** Jiangxi, S China 24.58N 115.37E
167 O3 **Xushui** Hebei, E China 39.01N 115.37E
166 L16 **Xuwen** Guangdong, S China 20.20N 110.09E
166 I11 **Xuyong** var. Yongning. Sichuan, C China 28.16N 105.21E
167 P6 **Xuzhou** var. Hsu-chou, Suchow, Tongshan; prev. T'ung-shan. Jiangsu, E China 34.16N 117.09E
116 K13 **Xylaganí** var. Xilaganí. Anatolikí Makedonía kai Thráki, NE Greece 40.58N 25.27E
117 F19 **Xylókastro** var. Xilokastro. Pelopónnisos, S Greece 38.04N 22.36E

Y

166 H9 **Ya'an** var. Yaan. Sichuan, C China 30.00N 102.57E
190 L10 **Yaapeet** Victoria, SE Australia 35.48S 142.03E
81 D15 **Yabassi** Littoral, W Cameroon 4.30N 9.58E
83 J15 **Yabēlo** Oromo, C Ethiopia 4.53N 38.00E
172 Pp5 **Yabetsu-gawa** var. Yûbetsu-gawa. ≈ Hokkaidō, NE Japan
116 H9 **Yablanitsa** Lovech Oblast, W Bulgaria 43.02N 24.04E
45 N7 **Yablis** Región Autónoma Atlántico Norte, NE Nicaragua 14.02N 83.44W
126 Kk16 **Yablonovyy Khrebet** ▲▲ S Russian Federation
168 J14 **Yabrai Shan** ▲▲ NE China
47 U6 **Yabucoa** E Puerto Rico 18.03N 65.52W
197 K14 **Yacata** island Lau Group, E Fiji
167 J11 **Yachi He** ≈ S China
34 H10 **Yacolt** Washington, NW USA 45.49N 122.22W
56 M10 **Yacuaray** Amazonas, S Venezuela 4.12N 66.30W
59 M22 **Yacuiba** Tarija, S Bolivia 22.03S 63.40W
59 K16 **Yacuma, Río** ≈ C Bolivia
161 H16 **Yādgīr** Karnātaka, C India 16.46N 77.09E
23 R8 **Yadkin River** ≈ North Carolina, SE USA
23 R9 **Yadkinville** North Carolina, SE USA 36.07N 80.39W
131 P3 **Yadrin** Chuvashskaya Respublika, W Russian Federation 55.55N 46.10E
197 I13 **Yadua** prev. Yandua. island NW Fiji
172 Oo17 **Yaeyama-shotō** var. Yaegama-shotō. island group SW Japan
77 O8 **Yafran** NW Libya 32.04N 12.31E
197 L15 **Yagasa Cluster** island group Lau Group, E Fiji
172 Oo3 **Yagashiri-tō** island NE Japan
67 H21 **Yaghan Basin** undersea feature SE Pacific Ocean
127 Nn9 **Yagodnoye** Magadanskaya Oblast', E Russian Federation 62.37N 149.18E
Yagotin see Yahotyn
80 G12 **Yagoua** Extrême-Nord, NE Cameroon 10.22N 15.13E
165 Q11 **Yagradagzê Shan** ▲ C China 35.06N 95.41E
Yaguachi see Yaguachi Nuevo
58 B7 **Yaguachi Nuevo** var. Yaguachi. Guayas, W Ecuador 2.06S 79.43W
Yaguarón, Río see Jaguarão, Rio
171 I16 **Yahagi-gawa** ≈ Honshū, SW Japan
119 Q11 **Yahorlyts'kyy Lyman** bay S Ukraine
119 Q5 **Yahotyn** Rus. Yagotin. Kyyivs'ka Oblast', N Ukraine 50.15N 31.48E
42 L12 **Yahualica** Jalisco, SW Mexico 21.12N 102.52W
81 L17 **Yahuma** Orientale, N Dem. Rep. Congo (Zaire) 1.12N 23.00E
142 K15 **Yahyalı** Kayseri, C Turkey 38.07N 35.22E
178 Gg15 **Yai, Khao** ▲ SW Thailand 8.45N 99.32E
171 Kk15 **Yaita** Tochigi, Honshū, S Japan 36.47N 139.54E
171 Ii17 **Yaizu** Shizuoka, Honshū, S Japan 34.52N 138.19E
166 G9 **Yajiang** Sichuan, C China 30.05N 100.57E
121 O14 **Yakawlyevichi** Rus. Yakovlevichi. Vitsyebskaya Voblasts', NE Belarus 54.21N 30.29E
169 S6 **Yakeshi** Nei Mongol Zizhiqu, N China 49.16N 120.42E
34 I9 **Yakima** Washington, NW USA 46.36N 120.30W
34 J10 **Yakima River** ≈ Washington, NW USA
116 G7 **Yakimovo** Montana, NW Bulgaria 43.39N 23.21E
Yakkabag see Yakkabogh
153 N12 **Yakkabogh** Rus. Yakkabag. Qashqadaryo Wiloyati, S Uzbekistan 38.57N 66.35E
154 L12 **Yakmach** Baluchistān, SW Pakistan 28.48N 63.48E
79 O12 **Yako** W Burkina 12.58N 2.15W
41 W13 **Yakobi Island** island Alexander Archipelago, Alaska, USA
81 K15 **Yakoma** Equateur, N Dem. Rep. Congo (Zaire) 4.04N 22.22E
116 H11 **Yakoruda** Blagoevgrad, SW Bulgaria 42.01N 23.40E
Yakovlevichi see Yakawlyevichi
131 T2 **Yakshur-Bod'ya** Udmurtskaya Respublika, NW Russian Federation 57.10N 53.10E
172 N6 **Yakumo** Hokkaidō, NE Japan 42.18N 140.15E
170 B17 **Yaku-shima** island Nansei-shotō, SW Japan
41 V12 **Yakutat** Alaska, USA 59.33N 139.43W
41 U12 **Yakutat Bay** inlet Alaska, USA
Yakutia/Yakutiya/Yakutiya, Respublika see Sakha (Yakutiya), Respublika
126 Mm11 **Yakutsk** Respublika Sakha (Yakutiya), NE Russian Federation 62.10N 129.49E
178 Hh17 **Yala** Yala, SW Thailand 6.31N 101.19E
190 D6 **Yalata** South Australia 31.30S 131.53E
33 S9 **Yale** Michigan, N USA 43.07N 82.45W
188 I11 **Yalgoo** Western Australia 28.23S 116.43E
116 O12 **Yalıköy** İstanbul, NW Turkey 41.29N 28.19E
81 L14 **Yalinga** Haute-Kotto, C Central African Republic 6.47N 23.09E
121 M17 **Yalizava** Rus. Yelizovo. Mahilyowskaya Voblasts', E Belarus 53.24N 29.01E
46 L13 **Yallahs Hill** ▲ E Jamaica 17.53N 76.31W
24 L3 **Yalobusha River** ≈ Mississippi, S USA
81 H15 **Yaloké** Ombella-Mpoko, W Central African Republic 5.15N 17.12E
166 E7 **Yalong Jiang** ≈ C China
142 E11 **Yalova** Yalova, NW Turkey 40.40N 29.16E
142 E11 **Yalova** ◐ province NW Turkey
Yaloveny see Ialoveni
Yalpug see Ialpug
Yalpug, Ozero see Yalpuh, Ozero
119 N12 **Yalpuh, Ozero** Rus. Ozero Yalpug. ◎ SW Ukraine
119 T14 **Yalta** Respublika Krym, S Ukraine 44.30N 34.09E
169 W12 **Yalu** Chin. Yalu Jiang, Jap. Oryokko, Kor. Amnok-kang. ≈ China/North Korea
Yalu Jiang see Yalu
125 F12 **Yalutorovsk** Tyumenskaya Oblast', C Russian Federation 56.36N 66.09E
142 F14 **Yalvaç** Isparta, SW Turkey 38.16N 31.09E
172 N12 **Yamada** Iwate, Honshū, C Japan 39.27N 141.56E
170 Cc14 **Yamaga** Kumamoto, Kyūshū, SW Japan 33.01N 130.42E
171 L12 **Yamagata** Yamagata, Honshū, C Japan 38.15N 140.19E
171 Ll12 **Yamagata** off. Yamagata-ken. ◐ prefecture Honshū, C Japan
170 Bb16 **Yamagawa** Kagoshima, Kyūshū, SW Japan 31.12N 130.37E
170 Dd12 **Yamaguchi** var. Yamaguti. Yamaguchi, Honshū, SW Japan 34.10N 131.26E
170 Dd12 **Yamaguchi** off. Yamaguchi-ken, var. Yamaguti. ◐ prefecture Honshū, SW Japan
Yamaguti see Yamaguchi
129 X5 **Yamalo-Nenetskiy Avtonomnyy Okrug** ◐ autonomous district N Russian Federation
126 Gg5 **Yamal, Poluostrov** peninsula N Russian Federation
171 J16 **Yamanashi** off. Yamanashi-ken, var. Yamanasi. ◐ prefecture Honshū, S Japan
Yamanasi see Yamanashi
Yamaniyah, Al Jumhūrīyah al see Yemen
131 W5 **Yamantau** ▲ W Russian Federation 53.11N 57.30E
126 K15 **Yamarovka** Chitinskaya Oblast', S Russian Federation 50.36N 110.25E
Yamasaki see Yamazaki
13 P12 **Yamaska** ≈ Quebec, SE Canada
171 Jj17 **Yamato** Kanagawa, Honshū, S Japan 35.30N 139.25E
199 Gg4 **Yamato Ridge** undersea feature S Sea of Japan
170 G14 **Yamazaki** var. Yamasaki. Hyōgo, Honshū, SW Japan 35.00N 134.31E
191 V5 **Yamba** New South Wales, SE Australia 29.28S 153.22E
83 D15 **Yambio** var. Yambiyo. Western Equatoria, S Sudan 4.34N 28.21E
Yambiyo see Yambio
116 L10 **Yambol** Turk. Yanboli. Yambol, E Bulgaria 42.28N 26.30E
116 M11 **Yambol** ◐ province E Bulgaria
81 M17 **Yambuya** Orientale, N Dem. Rep. Congo (Zaire) 1.22N 24.21E
176 Uu15 **Yamdena, Pulau** prev. Jamdena. island Kepulauan Tanimbar, E Indonesia
170 Cc13 **Yame** Fukuoka, Kyūshū, SW Japan 33.12N 130.31E
177 G6 **Yamethin** Mandalay, C Burma 20.25N 96.08E
194 G11 **Yaminbot** East Sepik, NW PNG 4.30S 143.44E
171 L15 **Yamizo-san** ▲ Honshū, C Japan 36.56N 140.14E
189 U9 **Yamma Yamma, Lake** ◎ Queensland, C Australia
78 M16 **Yamoussoukro** ● (Ivory Coast) C Ivory Coast 6.51N 5.21W
39 P3 **Yampa River** ≈ Colorado, C USA
119 S2 **Yampil'** Sums'ka Oblast', NE Ukraine 51.57N 33.49E
118 M8 **Yampil'** Vinnyts'ka Oblast', C Ukraine 48.15N 28.18E
127 Oo10 **Yamsk** Magadanskaya Oblast', E Russian Federation 59.33N 154.04E
158 J8 **Yamuna** prev. Jumna. ≈ N India
158 I9 **Yamunānagar** Haryāna, N India 30.07N 77.16E
Yamundá see Nhamundá, Rio
151 U8 **Yamyshevo** Pavlodar, NE Kazakhstan 51.49N 77.28E
165 N16 **Yamzho Yumco** ◎ W China
126 Ll6 **Yana** ≈ NE Russian Federation
195 P15 **Yanaba Island** island SE PNG
170 C13 **Yanagawa** Fukuoka, Kyūshū, SW Japan 33.08N 130.23E
170 E13 **Yanai** Yamaguchi, Honshū, SW Japan 33.56N 132.05E
161 L16 **Yanam** var. Yanaon. Pondicherry, E India 16.45N 82.16E
166 L5 **Yan'an** var. Yanan. Shaanxi, C China 36.34N 109.26E
Yanaon see Yanam
131 U3 **Yanaul** Respublika Bashkortostan, W Russian Federation 56.15N 54.57E
120 O12 **Yanavichy** Rus. Yanovichi. Vitsyebskaya Voblasts', NE Belarus 55.16N 30.42E
Yanboli see Yambol
146 K8 **Yanbu' al Baḩr** Al Madīnah, W Saudi Arabia 24.06N 38.03E
23 T8 **Yanceyville** North Carolina, SE USA 36.24N 79.20W
167 R7 **Yancheng** Jiangsu, E China 33.27N 120.10E
165 W8 **Yanchi** Ningxia, N China 37.49N 107.24E
166 L5 **Yanchuan** Shaanxi, C China 36.54N 110.04E
191 O10 **Yanco Creek** seasonal river New South Wales, SE Australia
191 O6 **Yanda Creek** seasonal river New South Wales, SE Australia
190 K4 **Yandama Creek** seasonal river New South Wales/South Australia
167 S11 **Yandang Shan** ▲▲ SE China
197 G5 **Yandé, Île** island Îles Belep, W New Caledonia
Yandua see Yadua
165 O6 **Yandun** Xinjiang Uygur Zizhiqu, W China 42.24N 94.07E
78 L13 **Yanfolila** Sikasso, SW Mali 11.08N 8.12W
81 M18 **Yangambi** Orientale, N Dem. Rep. Congo (Zaire) 0.46N 24.24E
164 M15 **Yangbajain** Xizang Zizhiqu, W China 30.04N 90.34E
Yangchow see Yangzhou
166 M15 **Yangchun** Guangdong, S China 22.16N 111.49E
167 N2 **Yanggao** Shanxi, C China 40.24N 113.51E
Yanggeta see Yaqeta
Yangiabad see Yangiobod
Yangibazar see Dzhany-Bazar, Kyrgyzstan
Yangi-Bazar see Kofarnihon, Tajikistan
Yangikishlak see Yangiqishloq
152 M13 **Yangi-Nishon** Rus. Yang-Nishan. Qashqadaryo Wiloyati, S Uzbekistan 38.37N 65.39E
153 Q9 **Yangiobod** Rus. Yangiabad. Toshkent Wiloyati, E Uzbekistan 41.10N 70.10E
153 O10 **Yangiqishloq** Rus. Yangikishlak. Jizzakh Wiloyati, C Uzbekistan 40.27N 67.06E
153 P11 **Yangiyer** Sirdaryo Wiloyati, E Uzbekistan 40.19N 68.48E
153 P9 **Yangiyŭl** Rus. Yangiyul'. Toshkent Wiloyati, E Uzbekistan 41.12N 69.05E
166 M15 **Yangjiang** Guangdong, S China 21.52N 111.55E
Yangku see Taiyuan
Yang-Nishan see Yangi-Nishon
177 G9 **Yangon** Eng. Rangoon. ● (Burma) Yangon, S Burma 16.49N 96.10E
177 G8 **Yangon** Eng. Rangoon. ◐ division SW Burma
166 K17 **Yangpu Gang** harbour Hainan, S China
167 N4 **Yangquan** Shanxi, C China 37.52N 113.28E
167 N13 **Yangshan** Guangdong, S China 24.32N 112.36E
178 Kk13 **Yang Sin, Chu** ▲ S Vietnam 12.23N 108.25E
Yangtze see Chang Jiang, C China
Yangtze Kiang see Chang Jiang
167 R7 **Yangzhou** var. Yangchow. Jiangsu, E China 32.22N 119.22E
166 L5 **Yan He** ≈ C China
169 Y10 **Yanji** Jilin, NE China 42.53N 129.31E
Yanji see Longjing
31 Q12 **Yankton** South Dakota, N USA 42.52N 97.24W
Yannina see Ioánnina
126 M6 **Yano-Indigirskaya Nizmennost'** plain NE Russian Federation
Yanovichi see Yanavichy
161 K24 **Yan Oya** ≈ N Sri Lanka
164 K6 **Yanqi** var. Yanqi Huizu Zizhixian. Xinjiang Uygur Zizhiqu, NW China 42.04N 86.32E
Yanqi Huizu Zizhixian see Yanqi
167 P2 **Yan Shan** ▲▲ E China
167 Q10 **Yanshan** Jiangxi, S China 28.17N 117.47E
166 H14 **Yanshan** prev. Hekou. Yunnan, SW China 23.36N 104.20E
169 X8 **Yanshou** Heilongjiang, NE China 45.27N 128.19E
126 Ll6 **Yanskiy Zaliv** bay N Russian Federation
191 O4 **Yantabulla** New South Wales, SE Australia 29.22S 145.00E
167 R4 **Yantai** var. Yan-t'ai; prev. Chefoo, Chih-fu. Shandong, E China 37.30N 121.22E
120 A13 **Yantarnyy** Ger. Palmnicken. Kaliningradskaya Oblast', W Russian Federation 54.53N 19.59E
116 J9 **Yantra** Gabrovo, N Bulgaria 42.58N 25.19E
116 K9 **Yantra** ≈ N Bulgaria
166 G11 **Yanyuan** Sichuan, C China 27.30N 101.22E
167 P5 **Yanzhou** Shandong, E China 35.34N 116.52E
81 E16 **Yaoundé** var. Yaunde. ● (Cameroon) Centre, S Cameroon 3.51N 11.31E
196 I14 **Yap** ◐ state W Micronesia
196 F16 **Yap** island Caroline Islands, W Micronesia
59 M18 **Yapacani, Río** ≈ C Bolivia
176 Ww12 **Yapa Kopra** Irian Jaya, E Indonesia 4.18S 135.05E
Yapan see Yapen, Selat
Yapanskoye More see Japan, Sea of
79 P15 **Yapei** N Ghana 9.10N 1.08W
10 M10 **Yapeitso, Mont** ▲ Quebec, E Canada 52.18N 70.24W
176 X10 **Yapen, Pulau** prev. Japen. island E Indonesia
176 X9 **Yapen, Selat** var. Yapan. strait Irian Jaya, E Indonesia
63 E15 **Yapeyú** Corrientes, NE Argentina 29.28S 56.49W
142 I11 **Yapraklı** Çankırı, N Turkey 40.45N 33.46E
182 M3 **Yap Trench** var. Yap Trough. undersea feature SE Philippine Sea
Yap Trough see Yap Trench
Yapurá see Caquetá, Río, Brazil/Colombia
Yapurá see Japurá, Rio, Brazil/Colombia
176 U11 **Yaputih** Pulau Seram, E Indonesia 3.16S 129.29E
197 I13 **Yaqaga** island N Fiji
197 H13 **Yaqeta** prev. Yanggeta. island Yasawa Group, NW Fiji
42 G6 **Yaqui** Sonora, NW Mexico 27.21N 109.59W
34 E12 **Yaquina Bay** bay Oregon, NW USA
42 G6 **Yaqui, Río** ≈ NW Mexico
176 Y14 **Yar** channel Irian Jaya, E Indonesia
56 K5 **Yaracuy** off. Estado Yaracuy. ◐ state NW Venezuela
152 E13 **Yaradzhi** Turkm. Yarajy. Akhalskiy Velayat, C Turkmenistan 38.12N 57.40E
Yarajy see Yaradzhi
129 Q15 **Yaransk** Kirovskaya Oblast', NW Russian Federation 57.18N 47.52E
142 F17 **Yardımcı Burnu** headland SW Turkey 36.10N 30.25E
99 Q19 **Yare** ≈ E England, UK
129 S9 **Yarega** Respublika Komi, NW Russian Federation 63.27N 53.28E
118 I7 **Yaremcha** Ivano-Frankivs'ka Oblast', W Ukraine 48.27N 24.34E
201 Q9 **Yaren** SW Nauru 0.33S 166.54E
129 Q10 **Yarensk** Arkhangel'skaya Oblast', NW Russian Federation 62.09N 49.03E
161 F16 **Yargatti** Karnātaka, W India 16.07N 75.11E
171 Ii14 **Yariga-take** ▲ Honshū, S Japan 36.20N 137.38E
147 O15 **Yarīm** W Yemen 14.15N 44.22E
56 F14 **Yarí, Río** ≈ SW Colombia
56 K5 **Yaritagua** Yaracuy, N Venezuela 10.04N 69.07W
Yarkand see Yarkant He
Yarkant see Shache
164 E9 **Yarkant He** var. Yarkand. ≈ NW China
155 U3 **Yarkhūn** ≈ NW Pakistan
Yarlung Zangbo Jiang see Brahmaputra
118 L6 **Yarmolyntsi** Khmel'nyts'ka Oblast', W Ukraine 49.13N 26.53E
169 T11 **Yar Moron** ≈ N China
11 O16 **Yarmouth** Nova Scotia, SE Canada 43.53N 66.08W
Yarmouth see Great Yarmouth
Yaroslav see Jarosław
128 L15 **Yaroslavl'** Yaroslavskaya Oblast', W Russian Federation 57.38N 39.52E
128 K14 **Yaroslavskaya Oblast'** ◐ province W Russian Federation
126 Kk12 **Yaroslavskiy** Respublika Sakha (Yakutiya), NE Russian Federation 60.10N 114.12E
191 P13 **Yarram** Victoria, SE Australia 38.36S 146.40E
191 O11 **Yarrawonga** Victoria, SE Australia 36.04S 145.58E
190 L4 **Yarriarraburra Swamp** wetland New South Wales, SE Australia
126 Gg8 **Yar-Sale** Yamalo-Nenetskiy Avtonomnyy Okrug, N Russian Federation 66.52N 70.42E
126 I12 **Yartsevo** Krasnoyarskiy Kray, C Russian Federation 60.15N 90.09E
130 I4 **Yartsevo** Smolenskaya Oblast', W Russian Federation 55.03N 32.46E
56 E8 **Yarumal** Antioquia, NW Colombia 6.58N 75.25W
197 H13 **Yasawa Group** island group NW Fiji
79 V12 **Yashi** Katsina, N Nigeria 12.21N 7.56E
79 S14 **Yashikera** Kwara, W Nigeria 9.40N 3.19E
153 T10 **Yashilkŭl** Rus. Ozero Yashil'kul'. ◎ SE Tajikistan
Yashil'kul', Ozero see Yashilkŭl
171 Ll11 **Yashima** Akita, Honshū, C Japan 39.10N 140.10E
170 Dd14 **Ya-shima** island SW Japan
170 E14 **Yashiro-jima** island SW Japan
131 P13 **Yashkul'** Respublika Kalmykiya, SW Russian Federation 46.09N 45.22E
152 F13 **Yashlyk** Akhalskiy Velayat, C Turkmenistan 37.46N 58.51E
Yasinovataya see Yasynuvata
116 N10 **Yasna Polyana** Burgas, SE Bulgaria 42.18N 27.35E
126 M14 **Yasnyy** Amurskaya Oblast', SE Russian Federation 53.03N 127.52E
178 I10 **Yasothon** Yasothon, E Thailand 15.46N 104.12E
191 R10 **Yass** New South Wales, SE Australia 34.52S 148.55E
Yassy see Iaşi
170 Ff12 **Yasugi** Shimane, Honshū, SW Japan 35.25N 133.14E
149 N10 **Yāsūj** var. Yesuj; prev. Tal-e Khosravī. Kohkīlūyeh va Būyer Aḩmadī, C Iran 30.40N 51.34E
142 M11 **Yasun Burnu** headland N Turkey 41.07N 37.40E
119 X8 **Yasynuvata** Rus. Yasinovataya. Donets'ka Oblast', SE Ukraine 48.04N 37.56E
142 C15 **Yatağan** Muğla, SW Turkey 37.22N 28.07E
171 M9 **Yatate-tōge** pass Honshū, C Japan 40.25N 140.36E
197 J7 **Yaté** Province Sud, S New Caledonia 22.10S 166.56E
29 P6 **Yates Center** Kansas, C USA 37.52N 95.43W
193 B21 **Yates Point** headland South Island, NZ 44.30S 167.49E
15 Kk7 **Yathkyed Lake** ◎ Nunavut, NE Canada
176 U15 **Yatoke** Pulau Babar, E Indonesia 7.51S 129.49E
81 M18 **Yatolema** Orientale, N Dem. Rep. Congo (Zaire) 0.25N 24.36E
171 J15 **Yatsuga-take** ▲ Honshū, S Japan 35.58N 138.22E
170 C14 **Yatsushiro** var. Yatusiro. Kumamoto, Kyūshū, SW Japan 32.30N 130.34E
170 C15 **Yatsushiro-kai** bay SW Japan
144 F11 **Yatta** var. Yuta. S West Bank 31.29N 35.10E
83 J20 **Yatta Plateau** plateau SE Kenya
Yatusiro see Yatsushiro
59 F17 **Yauca, Río** ≈ SW Peru
47 S6 **Yauco** W Puerto Rico 18.02N 66.51W
176 Xx9 **Yauke** Irian Jaya, E Indonesia 1.34S 137.56E
Yaunde see Yaoundé
Yavan see Yovon
Yavarí see Javari, Rio
58 G9 **Yavari Mirim, Río** ≈ NE Peru
42 G7 **Yavaros** Sonora, NW Mexico 26.40N 109.32W
160 I13 **Yavatmāl** Mahārāshtra, C India 20.22N 78.10E
56 M9 **Yaví, Cerro** ▲ C Venezuela 5.43N 65.51W
45 W16 **Yaviza** Darién, SE Panama 8.09N 77.40W
144 F10 **Yavne** Central, W Israel 31.52N 34.45E
118 H5 **Yavoriv** Pol. Jaworów, Rus. Yavorov. L'vivs'ka Oblast', NW Ukraine 49.57N 23.21E
Yavorov see Yavoriv
170 F15 **Yawatahama** Ehime, Shikoku, SW Japan 33.27N 132.24E
Ya Xian see Sanya
142 L17 **Yayladaği** Hatay, S Turkey 35.55N 36.03E
129 V13 **Yayva** Permskaya Oblast', NW Russian Federation 59.19N 57.15E
129 V12 **Yayva** ≈ NW Russian Federation
149 Q9 **Yazd** var. Yezd. Yazd, C Iran 31.55N 54.22E
149 Q8 **Yazd** off. Ostān-e Yazd, var. Yezd. ◐ province C Iran
Yazgulemskiy Khrebet see Yazgulom, Qatorkŭhi
153 S13 **Yazgulom, Qatorkŭhi** Rus. Yazgulemskiy Khrebet. ▲▲ S Tajikistan
24 K5 **Yazoo City** Mississippi, S USA 32.51N 90.24W
24 K5 **Yazoo River** ≈ Mississippi, S USA
131 Q5 **Yazykovo** Ul'yanovskaya Oblast', W Russian Federation 54.19N 47.22E
111 U4 **Ybbs** Niederösterreich, NE Austria 48.10N 15.03E
111 U4 **Ybbs** ≈ C Austria
97 G22 **Yding Skovhøj** hill C Denmark
117 G20 **Ýdra** var. Ídhra, Idra. Ýdra, S Greece 37.20N 23.27E
117 G21 **Ýdra** var. Ídhra. island S Greece
117 G20 **Ýdras, Kólpos** strait S Greece
178 Gg10 **Ye** Mon State, S Burma 15.15N 97.49E
191 O12 **Yea** Victoria, SE Australia 37.15S 145.27E
80 I5 **Yebbi-Bou** Borkou-Ennedi-Tibesti, N Chad 21.12N 17.55E
164 F9 **Yecheng** var. Kargilik. Xinjiang Uygur Zizhiqu, NW China 37.54N 77.25E
107 R11 **Yecla** Murcia, SE Spain 38.36N 1.07W
42 H6 **Yécora** Sonora, NW Mexico 28.20N 108.55W
Yedintsy see Edineţ
128 I13 **Yefimovskiy** Leningradskaya Oblast', NW Russian Federation 59.32N 34.34E
176 Uu9 **Yeflio** Irian Jaya, E Indonesia 1.01S 131.17E
130 K6 **Yefremov** Tul'skaya Oblast', W Russian Federation 53.09N 38.02E
Yégainnyin see Henan
143 U12 **Yeghegis** Rus. Yekhegis. ≈ C Armenia
151 T10 **Yegindybulak** Kaz. Egindibulaq. Karaganda, C Kazakhstan 49.45N 75.45E
130 L4 **Yegor'yevsk** Moskovskaya Oblast', W Russian Federation 55.29N 39.03E
Yehuda, Haré see Judaean Hills
83 E15 **Yei** ≈ S Sudan
167 P8 **Yeji** var. Yejiaji. Anhui, E China 31.52N 115.58E
Yejiaji see Yeji
125 Ee11 **Yekaterinburg** prev. Sverdlovsk. Sverdlovskaya Oblast', C Russian Federation 56.52N 60.34E
Yekaterinodar see Krasnodar
Yekaterinoslav see Dnipropetrovs'k
126 Mm15 **Yekaterinoslavka** Amurskaya Oblast', SE Russian Federation 50.23N 129.03E
131 O7 **Yekaterinovka** Saratovskaya Oblast', W Russian Federation 52.01N 44.11E
78 K16 **Yekepa** NE Liberia 7.34N 8.31W
131 T3 **Yelabuga** Respublika Tatarstan, W Russian Federation 55.46N 52.07E
Yela Island see Rossel Island
131 O8 **Yelan'** Volgogradskaya Oblast', SW Russian Federation 51.00N 43.40E
119 Q9 **Yelanets'** Rus. Yelanets. Mykolayivs'ka Oblast', S Ukraine 47.40N 31.51E
125 G13 **Yelanka** Novosibirskaya Oblast', C Russian Federation 55.38N 75.23E
127 Nn15 **Yel'ban'** Khabarovskiy Kray, E Russian Federation 50.03N 136.34E
130 L7 **Yelets** Lipetskaya Oblast', W Russian Federation 52.37N 38.29E
129 W4 **Yeletskiy** Respublika Komi, NW Russian Federation 67.03N 64.05E
78 J11 **Yélimané** Kayes, W Mali 15.06N 10.43W
Yelisavetpol see Gäncä
Yelizavetgrad see Kirovohrad
127 O13 **Yelizavety, Mys** headland SE Russian Federation 54.20N 142.39E
127 Pp11 **Yelizovo** Kamchatskaya Oblast', E Russian Federation 53.12N 158.18E
Yelizovo see Yalizava
131 S5 **Yelkhovka** Samarskaya Oblast', W Russian Federation 53.51N 50.16E
98 M1 **Yell** island NE Scotland, UK
161 E17 **Yellāpur** Karnātaka, W India 15.06N 74.50E
9 U17 **Yellow Grass** Saskatchewan, S Canada 49.51N 104.09W
Yellowhammer State see Alabama
9 O15 **Yellowhead Pass** pass Alberta/British Columbia, SW Canada 52.54N 118.44W
15 Hh8 **Yellowknife** territory capital Northwest Territories, W Canada 62.30N 114.28W
15 I7 **Yellowknife** ≈ Northwest Territories, NW Canada
194 F10 **Yellow River** ≈ NW PNG
25 P8 **Yellow River** ≈ Alabama/Florida, S USA
32 I4 **Yellow River** ≈ Wisconsin, N USA
32 J6 **Yellow River** ≈ Wisconsin, N USA
32 K7 **Yellow River** ≈ Wisconsin, N USA
Yellow River see Huang He
163 V8 **Yellow Sea** Chin. Huang Hai, Kor. Hwang-Hae. sea E Asia
35 S13 **Yellowstone Lake** ◎ Wyoming, C USA
35 T13 **Yellowstone National Park** national park Wyoming, NW USA
35 Y8 **Yellowstone River** ≈ Montana/Wyoming, NW USA
98 L1 **Yell Sound** strait N Scotland, UK
29 U9 **Yellville** Arkansas, C USA 36.13N 92.40W
126 Hh11 **Yeloguy** ≈ C Russian Federation
152 J14 **Yëloten** prev. Iolotan', Turkm. Yolöten. Maryyskiy Velayat, S Turkmenistan 37.15N 62.18E
121 M20 **Yel'sk** Rus. Yel'sk. Homyel'skaya Voblasts', SE Belarus 51.49N 29.09E
79 T13 **Yelwa** Kebbi, W Nigeria 10.52N 4.46E
125 Ee12 **Yemanzhelinsk** Chelyabinskaya Oblast', C Russian Federation 54.43N 61.08E
23 R15 **Yemassee** South Carolina, SE USA 32.41N 80.51W
147 O15 **Yemen** off. Republic of Yemen, Ar. Al Jumhūrīyah al Yamanīyah, Al Yaman. ◆ republic SW Asia
118 M4 **Yemil'chyne** Zhytomyrs'ka Oblast', N Ukraine 50.51N 27.49E
128 M10 **Yemtsa** Arkhangel'skaya Oblast', NW Russian Federation 63.04N 40.18E
128 M10 **Yemtsa** ≈ NW Russian Federation
129 R10 **Yemva** prev. Zheleznodorozhnyy. Respublika Komi, NW Russian Federation 62.38N 50.58E
79 U17 **Yenagoa** Bayelsa, S Nigeria 4.58N 6.16E
119 X7 **Yenakiyeve** Rus. Yenakiyevo; prev. Ordzhonikidze, Rykovo. Donets'ka Oblast', E Ukraine 48.13N 38.13E
Yenakiyevo see Yenakiyeve
177 Ff6 **Yenangyaung** Magwe, W Burma 20.28N 94.54E
178 Jj5 **Yên Bai** Yên Bai, N Vietnam 21.43N 104.54E
191 P9 **Yenda** New South Wales, SE Australia 34.16S 146.15E
176 W10 **Yende** Irian Jaya, E Indonesia 2.19S 134.34E
79 Q14 **Yendi** NE Ghana 9.23N 0.02W
164 E8 **Yengisar** Xinjiang Uygur Zizhiqu, NW China 38.50N 76.10E
124 O3 **Yenibogaziçi** var. Ayios Seryios, Gk. Ágios Sérgios. E Cyprus 35.10N 33.53E
124 Oo2 **Yenierenköy** var. Yialousa, Gk. Agialoúsa. NE Cyprus 35.32N 34.12E
Yenipazar see Novi Pazar
142 E12 **Yenişehir** Bursa, NW Turkey 40.16N 29.36E
Yenisei Bay see Yeniseyskiy Zaliv

◆ Country ● Country Capital ◇ Dependent Territory ○ Dependent Territory Capital ◐ Administrative Region ✈ International Airport ▲ Mountain ▲▲ Mountain Range Volcano ≈ River ◎ Lake ⊡ Reservoir

YENISEY – ZAKOPANE

126 *Hh8* **Yenisey** ≈ Mongolia/Russian Federation
126 *I13* **Yeniseysk** Krasnoyarskiy Kray, C Russian Federation *58.23N 92.06E*
207 *W10* **Yeniseyskiy Zaliv** *var.* Yenisei Bay. *bay* N Russian Federation
131 *Q12* **Yenotayevka** Astrakhanskaya Oblast', SW Russian Federation *47.16N 47.01E*
128 *L4* **Yenozero, Ozero** ◎ NW Russian Federation
Yenping *see* Nanping
41 *Q11* **Yentna River** ≈ Alaska, USA
188 *M10* **Yeo, Lake** *salt lake* Western Australia
191 *R7* **Yeoval** New South Wales, SE Australia *32.45S 148.39E*
99 *K23* **Yeovil** SW England, UK *50.57N 2.39W*
42 *H6* **Yepachic** Chihuahua, N Mexico *28.27N 108.25W*
189 *Y8* **Yeppoon** Queensland, E Australia *23.04S 150.42E*
130 *M5* **Yeraktur** Ryazanskaya Oblast', W Russian Federation *54.45N 41.09E*
Yeraliyev *see* Kuryk
152 *F12* **Yerbent** Akhalskiy Velayat, C Turkmenistan *39.19N 58.34E*
126 *Jj12* **Yerbogachen** Irkutskaya Oblast', C Russian Federation *61.07N 108.03E*
143 *T12* **Yerevan** *Eng.* Erivan. ● (Armenia) C Armenia *40.12N 44.31E*
143 *U12* **Yerevan** ✕ C Armenia *40.07N 44.34E*
151 *R9* **Yereymentau** *var.* Jermentau, Yermentau, *Kaz.* Ereymentaū. Akmola, C Kazakhstan *51.37N 73.10E*
131 *O12* **Yergeni** *hill range* SW Russian Federation
Yeriho *see* Jericho
37 *R6* **Yerington** Nevada, W USA *38.58N 119.10W*
142 *J13* **Yerköy** Yozgat, C Turkey *39.39N 34.28E*
116 *L13* **Yerlisu** Edirne, NW Turkey *40.45N 26.38E*
Yermak *see* Aksu
151 *R9* **Yermenytau** *Kaz.* Ereymentaū, Jermentau. Akmola, C Kazakhstan *51.37N 73.10E*
151 *R9* **Yermenytau, Gory** ▲▲ C Kazakhstan
129 *R5* **Yermitsa** Respublika Komi, NW Russian Federation *66.57N 52.15E*
37 *V14* **Yermo** California, W USA *34.54N 116.49W*
126 *Ll14* **Yerofey Pavlovich** Amurskaya Oblast', SE Russian Federation *53.58N 121.49E*
101 *F15* **Yerseke** Zeeland, SW Netherlands *51.30N 4.03E*
131 *Q8* **Yershov** Saratovskaya Oblast', W Russian Federation *51.18N 48.16E*
129 *P9* **Yërtom** Respublika Komi, NW Russian Federation *63.27N 47.52E*
58 *D13* **Yerupaja, Nevado** ▲ C Peru *10.23S 76.58W*
Yerushalayim *see* Jerusalem
107 *R4* **Yesa, Embalse de** ⊠ NE Spain
151 *V15* **Yesik** *Kaz.* Esik; *prev.* Issyk. Almaty, SE Kazakhstan *43.23N 77.31E*
151 *O8* **Yesil'** *Kaz.* Esil. Akmola, C Kazakhstan *51.58N 66.22E*
142 *K15* **Yeşilhisar** Kayseri, C Turkey *38.22N 35.07E*
142 *L11* **Yeşilırmak** *anc.* Iris. ≈ N Turkey
39 *U12* **Yeso** New Mexico, SW USA *34.25N 104.36W*
Yeso *see* Hokkaidō
131 *N15* **Yessentuki** Stavropol'skiy Kray, SW Russian Federation *44.06N 42.51E*
126 *J9* **Yessey** Evenkiyskiy Avtonomnyy Okrug, N Russian Federation *68.18N 101.49E*
107 *P12* **Yeste** Castilla-La Mancha, C Spain *38.21N 2.18W*
Yesuj *see* Yāsūj
191 *T4* **Yetman** New South Wales, SE Australia *28.56S 150.47E*
78 *L4* **Yetti** *physical region* N Mauritania
177 *G4* **Ye-u** Sagaing, C Burma *22.49N 95.25E*
104 *H9* **Yeu, Île d'** *island* NW France
Yevlakh *see* Yevlax
143 *W11* **Yevlax** *Rus.* Yevlakh. C Azerbaijan *40.36N 47.09E*
119 *S13* **Yevpatoriya** Respublika Krym, S Ukraine *45.12N 33.22E*
125 *B17* **Yevreyskaya Avtonomnaya Oblast'** *Eng.* Jewish Autonomous Oblast. ◐ *autonomous province* SE Russian Federation
130 *K12* **Yeya** ≈ SW Russian Federation
164 *I10* **Yeyik** Xinjiang Uygur Zizhiqu, W China *36.43N 83.13E*
130 *K12* **Yeysk** Krasnodarskiy Kray, SW Russian Federation *46.41N 38.15E*
Yezd *see* Yazd
Yezerishche *see* Yezyaryshcha
Yezo *see* Hokkaidō
120 *N11* **Yezyaryshcha** *Rus.* Yezerishche. Vitsyebskaya Voblasts', NE Belarus *55.49N 29.58E*
Yialí *see* Gyalí
Yialousa *see* Yenierenköy
169 *V7* **Yi'an** Heilongjiang, NE China *47.52N 125.13E*
Yiannitsá *see* Giannitsá
166 *I10* **Yibin** Sichuan, C China *28.47N 104.36E*
164 *K13* **Yibug Caka** ◎ W China
166 *M9* **Yichang** Hubei, C China *30.37N 111.02E*
166 *L5* **Yichuan** Shaanxi, C China *36.05N 110.02E*
163 *W3* **Yichun** Heilongjiang, NE China *47.40N 129.10E*
169 *X6* **Yichun** *var.* I-ch'un. Heilongjiang, NE China *47.39N 128.54E*
167 *O11* **Yichun** Jiangxi, S China *27.45N 114.22E*
Yidu *see* Qingzhou
196 *C15* **Yigo** NE Guam *13.33N 144.52E*
167 *Q5* **Yi He** ≈ E China
169 *X8* **Yilan** Heilongjiang, NE China *46.18N 129.36E*
142 *C9* **Yıldız Dağları** ▲▲ NW Turkey
142 *L13* **Yıldızeli** Sivas, N Turkey *39.52N 36.37E*
169 *U4* **Yilehuli Shan** ▲▲ NE China
169 *S7* **Yimin He** ≈ NE China
165 *W8* **Yinchuan** *var.* Yinch'uan, Yin-ch'uan, Yinchwan. Ningxia, N China *38.30N 106.19E*
Yinchuanzhan *see* Xincheng
Yinchwan *see* Yinchuan
Yindu He *see* Indus
167 *N14* **Yingde** Guangdong, S China *24.08N 113.21E*
167 *O7* **Ying He** ≈ C China
169 *U13* **Yingkou** *var.* Ying-k'ou, Yingkow; *prev.* Newchwang, Niuchwang. Liaoning, NE China *40.38N 122.17E*
Yingkow *see* Yingkou
167 *P9* **Yingshan** Hubei, C China *30.45N 115.41E*
Yingshan *see* Guangshui
167 *Q10* **Yingtan** Jiangxi, S China *28.17N 117.03E*
Yin-hsien *see* Ningbo
164 *H5* **Yining** *var.* I-ning, *Uigh.* Gulja, Kuldja. Xinjiang Uygur Zizhiqu, NW China *43.53N 81.18E*
166 *K11* **Yinjiang** Guizhou, S China *28.22N 108.07E*
177 *Ff4* **Yinmabin** Sagaing, C Burma *22.04N 94.57E*
169 *N13* **Yin Shan** ▲▲ N China
Yin-tu Ho *see* Indus
165 *P15* **Yi'ong Zangbo** ≈ W China
Yioúra *see* Gyáros
83 *J14* **Yirga 'Alem** *It.* Irgalem. Southern, S Ethiopia *6.43N 38.24E*
63 *E19* **Yí, Río** ≈ C Uruguay
83 *E14* **Yirol** El Buhayrat, S Sudan *6.34N 30.33E*
Yirshi *see* Yirxie
169 *S8* **Yirxie** *prev.* Yirshi. Nei Mongol Zizhiqu, N China *47.16N 119.51E*
167 *Q5* **Yishui** Shandong, E China *35.49N 118.39E*
Yisrael/Yisra'el *see* Israel
Yíthion *see* Gýtheio
Yitiaoshan *see* Jingtai
169 *W10* **Yitong** Jilin, NE China *43.22N 125.19E*
165 *P5* **Yiwu** *var.* Aratürük. Xinjiang Uygur Zizhiqu, NW China *43.16N 94.38E*
169 *U12* **Yiwulü Shan** ▲▲ N China
169 *T12* **Yi Xian** Liaoning, NE China *41.29N 121.21E*
167 *N10* **Yiyang** Hunan, S China *28.39N 112.19E*
167 *Q10* **Yiyang** Jiangxi, S China *28.23N 117.24E*
167 *N13* **Yizhang** Hunan, S China *25.24N 112.55E*
95 *K19* **Yläne** Länsi-Suomi, W Finland *60.50N 22.25E*
95 *L14* **Yli-Ii** Oulu, C Finland *65.21N 25.55E*
95 *L14* **Ylikiiminki** Oulu, C Finland *65.00N 26.10E*
94 *N13* **Yli-Kitka** ◎ NE Finland
95 *K17* **Ylistaro** Länsi-Suomi, W Finland *62.58N 22.30E*
94 *K13* **Ylitornio** Lappi, NW Finland *66.16N 23.39E*
95 *L15* **Ylivieska** Oulu, W Finland *64.04N 24.30E*
95 *L18* **Ylöjärvi** Länsi-Suomi, W Finland *61.31N 23.37E*
97 *N17* **Yngaren** ◎ C Sweden
27 *T12* **Yoakum** Texas, SW USA *29.17N 97.09W*
79 *X13* **Yobe** ◐ *state* NE Nigeria
172 *Nn4* **Yobetsu-dake** ▲ Hokkaidō, NE Japan *43.15N 140.27E*
176 *Xx10* **Yobi** Irian Jaya, E Indonesia *1.42S 138.09E*
82 *L11* **Yoboki** C Djibouti *11.30N 42.04E*
170 *C12* **Yobuko** Saga, Kyūshū, SW Japan *33.31N 129.50E*
24 *M4* **Yockanookany River** ≈ Mississippi, S USA
24 *L2* **Yocona River** ≈ Mississippi, S USA
176 *Yy15* **Yodom** Irian Jaya, E Indonesia *7.12S 139.24E*
174 *Kk15* **Yogyakarta** *prev.* Djokjakarta, Jogjakarta, Jokyakarta. Jawa, C Indonesia *7.48S 110.24E*
174 *Kk16* **Yogyakarta** *off.* Daerah Istimewa Yogyakarta, *var.* Djokjakarta, Jogjakarta, Jokyakarta. ◐ *autonomous district* S Indonesia
172 *O5* **Yoichi** Hokkaidō, NE Japan *43.11N 140.45E*
44 *G6* **Yojoa, Lago de** ◎ NW Honduras
81 *G16* **Yokadouma** Est, SE Cameroon *3.25N 15.06E*
171 *H15* **Yōkaichi** *var.* Yôkaiti. Shiga, Honshū, SW Japan *35.07N 136.10E*
Yôkaiti *see* Yōkaichi
171 *H15* **Yokkaichi** *var.* Yokkaiti. Mie, Honshū, SW Japan *34.58N 136.36E*
Yokkaiti *see* Yokkaichi
81 *E15* **Yoko** Centre, C Cameroon *5.28N 12.19E*
172 *Qq12* **Yokoate-jima** *island* Nansei-shotō, SW Japan
172 *N9* **Yokohama** Aomori, Honshū, C Japan *41.04N 141.14E*
171 *Jj16* **Yokohama** Kanagawa, Honshū, S Japan *35.26N 139.37E*
171 *Jj17* **Yokosuka** Kanagawa, Honshū, S Japan *35.15N 139.39E*
170 *F12* **Yokota** Shimane, Honshū, SW Japan *35.10N 133.03E*
171 *M11* **Yokote** Akita, Honshū, C Japan *39.19N 140.33E*
172 *Nn7* **Yokotsu-dake** ▲ Hokkaidō, NE Japan *41.54N 140.48E*
79 *Y14* **Yola** Adamawa, E Nigeria *9.07N 12.24E*
81 *L19* **Yolombo** Equateur, C Dem. Rep. Congo (Zaire) *1.36S 23.13E*
Yolöten *see* Yëloten
176 *W10* **Yomber** Irian Jaya, E Indonesia *2.04S 134.22E*
172 *T16* **Yome-jima** *island* Ogasawara-shotō, SE Japan
78 *K16* **Yomou** Guinée-Forestière, SE Guinea *7.30N 9.13W*
176 *Y15* **Yomuka** Irian Jaya, E Indonesia *7.25S 138.36E*
196 *C16* **Yona** E Guam *13.24N 144.46E*
170 *Ff12* **Yonago** Tottori, Honshū, SW Japan *35.30N 134.15E*
172 *O17* **Yonaguni** Okinawa, SW Japan *24.29N 123.00E*
172 *Nn16* **Yonaguni-jima** *island* Nansei-shotō, SW Japan
172 *Pp14* **Yonaha-dake** ▲ Okinawa, SW Japan *26.43N 128.13E*
169 *X14* **Yonan** SW North Korea *37.50N 126.15E*
171 *L13* **Yonezawa** Yamagata, Honshū, C Japan *37.54N 140.06E*
167 *Q12* **Yong'an** *var.* Yongan. Fujian, SE China *25.58N 117.25E*
165 *T9* **Yongchang** Gansu, N China *38.15N 101.55E*
167 *P7* **Yongcheng** Henan, C China *33.55N 116.21E*
169 *Z15* **Yŏngch'ŏn** *Jap.* Eisen. SE South Korea *35.56N 128.55E*
166 *J10* **Yongchuan** Chongqing Shi, C China *29.27N 105.56E*
165 *U10* **Yongdeng** Gansu, C China *35.58N 103.27E*
133 *W9* **Yongding He** ≈ E China
167 *P11* **Yongfeng** Jiangxi, S China *27.19N 115.22E*
164 *L5* **Yongfengqu** Xinjiang Uygur Zizhiqu, W China *43.28N 87.09E*
166 *L13* **Yongfu** Guangxi Zhuangzu Ziziqu, S China *24.57 109.59E*
169 *X13* **Yŏnghŭng** E North Korea *39.30N 127.13E*
165 *U10* **Yongjing** Gansu, C China *36.00N 103.30E*
169 *Y15* **Yŏngju** *Jap.* Eishū. C South Korea *36.48N 128.37E*
Yongning *see* Xuyong
166 *E12* **Yongping** Yunnan, SW China *25.30N 99.28E*
166 *G12* **Yongren** Yunnan, SW China *26.11N 101.49E*
166 *L10* **Yongshun** *var.* Lingxi. Hunan, S China *29.01N 109.48E*
167 *P10* **Yongxiu** *var.* Tujiabu. Jiangxi, S China *29.08N 115.47E*
166 *M12* **Yongzhou** Hunan, S China *26.12N 111.36E*
20 *K14* **Yonkers** New York, NE USA *40.56N 73.51W*
105 *Q7* **Yonne** ◐ *department* C France
105 *P6* **Yonne** ≈ C France
56 *H9* **Yopal** *var.* El Yopal. Casanare, C Colombia *5.19N 72.19W*
164 *E8* **Yopurga** *var.* Yukuriawat. Xinjiang Uygur Zizhiqu, NW China *39.13N 76.44E*
188 *J12* **York** Western Australia *31.55S 116.52E*
99 *M16* **York** *anc.* Eboracum, Eburacum. N England, UK *53.58N 1.04W*
25 *N5* **York** Alabama, S USA *32.29N 88.18W*
31 *Q15* **York** Nebraska, C USA *40.52N 97.35W*
20 *G16* **York** Pennsylvania, NE USA *39.55N 76.42W*
23 *R11* **York** South Carolina, SE USA *34.59N 81.14W*
12 *J13* **York** ≈ Ontario, SE Canada
13 *X6* **York** ≈ Quebec, SE Canada
189 *V1* **York, Cape** *headland* Queensland, NE Australia *10.40S 142.36E*
190 *I9* **Yorke Peninsula** *peninsula* South Australia
190 *I9* **Yorketown** South Australia *35.01S 137.38E*
21 *P9* **York Harbor** Maine, NE USA *43.10N 70.37W*
23 *X6* **York River** ≈ Virginia, NE USA
99 *M16* **Yorkshire** *cultural region* N England, UK
99 *L16* **Yorkshire Dales** *physical region* N England, UK
9 *V16* **Yorkton** Saskatchewan, S Canada *51.12N 102.28W*
27 *T12* **Yorktown** Texas, SW USA *28.58N 97.30W*
23 *X6* **Yorktown** Virginia, NE USA *37.13N 76.29W*
32 *M11* **Yorkville** Illinois, N USA *41.38N 88.27W*
44 *I5* **Yoro** Yoro, C Honduras *15.06N 87.09W*
44 *H5* **Yoro** ◐ *department* N Honduras
172 *Pp14* **Yoron-jima** *island* Nansei-shotō, SW Japan
79 *N13* **Yorosso** Sikasso, S Mali *12.18N 4.44W*
37 *R8* **Yosemite National Park** *national park* California, W USA
170 *Ff14* **Yoshii-gawa** ≈ Honshū, SW Japan
170 *Ff15* **Yoshino-gawa** *var.* Yosino Gawa. ≈ Shikoku, SW Japan
131 *Q3* **Yoshkar-Ola** Respublika Mariy El, W Russian Federation *56.37N 47.53E*
Yosino Gawa *see* Yoshino-gawa
176 *Y15* **Yos Sudarso, Pulau** *var.* Pulau Dolak, Pulau Kolepom; *prev.* Jos Sudarso. *island* E Indonesia
176 *Z10* **Yos Sudarso, Teluk** *bay* Irian Jaya, E Indonesia
169 *Y17* **Yŏsu** *Jap.* Reisui. S South Korea *34.45N 127.40E*
172 *Nn5* **Yotei-zan** ▲ Hokkaidō, NE Japan *42.50N 140.46E*
99 *D21* **Youghal** *Ir.* Eochaill. S Ireland *51.57N 7.49W*
99 *D21* **Youghal Bay** *Ir.* Cuan Eochaille. *inlet* S Ireland
20 *C15* **Youghiogheny River** ≈ Pennsylvania, NE USA
166 *K14* **You Jiang** ≈ S China
191 *Q9* **Young** New South Wales, SE Australia *34.19S 148.19E*
9 *T15* **Young** Saskatchewan, S Canada *51.44N 105.44W*
63 *E18* **Young** Río Negro, W Uruguay *32.43S 57.36W*
190 *G5* **Younghusband, Lake** *salt lake* South Australia
190 *J10* **Younghusband Peninsula** *peninsula* South Australia
192 *Q10* **Young Nicks Head** *headland* North Island, NZ *39.38S 105.03E*
193 *D20* **Young Range** ▲▲ South Island, NZ
203 *Q15* **Young's Rock** *island* Pitcairn Island, Pitcairn Islands
9 *R16* **Youngstown** Alberta, SW Canada *51.31N 111.12W*
33 *V12* **Youngstown** Ohio, N USA *41.06N 80.39W*
165 *N9* **Youshashan** Qinghai, C China *38.12N 90.58E*
Youth, Isle of *see* Juventud, Isla de la
79 *N11* **Youvarou** Mopti, C Mali *15.19N 4.15W*
166 *K10* **Youyang** Sichuan, C China *28.48N 108.48E*
169 *Y7* **Youyi** Heilongjiang, NE China *46.51N 131.54E*
153 *P13* **Yovon** *Rus.* Yavan. SW Tajikistan *38.19N 69.02E*
142 *J13* **Yozgat** Yozgat, C Turkey *39.49N 34.48E*
142 *K13* **Yozgat** ◐ *province* C Turkey
64 *O6* **Ypacaraí** *var.* Ypacaray. Central, S Paraguay *25.22S 57.16W*
Ypacaray *see* Ypacaraí
64 *P5* **Ypané, Río** ≈ C Paraguay
Ypres *see* Ieper
116 *I13* **Ypsário** *var.* Ipsario. ▲ Thásos, E Greece *40.43N 24.39E*
33 *R10* **Ypsilanti** Michigan, N USA *42.12N 83.36W*
36 *M1* **Yreka** California, W USA *41.43N 122.38W*
Yrendagüé *see* General Eugenio A. Garay
195 *N8* **Ysabel Channel** *channel* N PNG
12 *K8* **Yser, Lac** ◎ Quebec, SE Canada
153 *Y8* **Yshtyk** Issyk-Kul'skaya Oblast', E Kyrgyzstan *41.34N 78.21E*
Yssel *see* IJssel
105 *Q12* **Yssingeaux** Haute-Loire, C France *45.09N 4.07E*
97 *K23* **Ystad** Skåne, S Sweden *55.25N 13.51E*
Ysyk-Köl *see* Balykchy, Kyrgyzstan
Ysyk-Köl *see* Issyk-Kul', Ozero, Kyrgyzstan
Ysyk-Köl Oblasty *see* Issyk-Kul'skaya Oblast'
98 *L8* **Ythan** ≈ NE Scotland, UK
Y Trallwng *see* Welshpool
96 *C13* **Ytre Arna** Hordaland, S Norway *60.28N 5.25E*
96 *B12* **Ytre Sula** *island* S Norway
95 *G17* **Ytterhogdal** Jämtland, C Sweden *62.10N 14.55E*
126 *M10* **Ytyk-Kyuyel'** Respublika Sakha (Yakutiya), NE Russian Federation *62.22N 133.37E*
Yu *see* Henan
Yuan Jiang *see* Red River
167 *S13* **Yüanlin** *Jap.* Inrin. C Taiwan *23.57N 120.33E*
167 *N3* **Yuanping** Shanxi, C China *38.26N 112.42E*
167 *O11* **Yuan Shui** ≈ S China
170 *G16* **Yuasa** Wakayama, Honshū, SW Japan *34.00N 135.08E*
194 *H10* **Yuat** ≈ N PNG
37 *O6* **Yuba City** California, W USA *39.07N 121.40W*
172 *Oo6* **Yūbari** Hokkaidō, NE Japan *43.09N 141.00E*
172 *P6* **Yūbari-sanchi** ▲▲ Hokkaidō, NE Japan
37 *O6* **Yuba River** ≈ California, W USA
82 *H13* **Yubdo** Oromo, C Ethiopia *9.05N 35.28E*
172 *Q5* **Yūbetsu** Hokkaidō, NE Japan *44.12N 143.34E*
Yūbetsu-gawa *see* Yabetsu-gawa
43 *X12* **Yucatán** ◐ *state* SE Mexico
49 *O3* **Yucatan Basin** *var.* Yucatan Deep. *undersea feature* N Caribbean Sea
Yucatán, Canal de *see* Yucatan Channel
43 *Y10* **Yucatan Channel** *Sp.* Canal de Yucatán. *channel* Cuba/Mexico
Yucatan Deep *see* Yucatan Basin
Yucatan Peninsula *see* Yucatán, Península de
43 *X13* **Yucatán, Península de** *Eng.* Yucatan Peninsula. *peninsula* Guatemala/Mexico
38 *I11* **Yucca** Arizona, SW USA *34.49N 114.06W*
37 *V15* **Yucca Valley** California, W USA *34.06N 116.30W*
167 *P4* **Yucheng** Shandong, E China *37.01N 116.37E*
167 *N4* **Yuci** Shanxi, C China *37.34N 112.45E*
133 *X5* **Yudoma** ≈ E Russian Federation
167 *P12* **Yudu** Jiangxi, C China *26.02N 115.24E*
Yue *see* Guangdong
166 *M12* **Yuecheng Ling** ▲▲ S China
189 *P7* **Yuendumu** Northern Territory, N Australia *22.19S 131.51E*
166 *H10* **Yuexi** Sichuan, C China *28.50N 102.36E*
167 *N10* **Yueyang** Hunan, S China *29.24N 113.08E*
129 *U14* **Yug** Permskaya Oblast', NW Russian Federation *57.49N 56.08E*
129 *P13* **Yug** ≈ NW Russian Federation
127 *N11* **Yugorenok** Respublika Sakha (Yakutiya), NE Russian Federation *59.46N 137.36E*
125 *F10* **Yugorsk** Khanty-Mansiyskiy Avtonomnyy Okrug, C Russian Federation *61.17N 63.25E*
125 *G6* **Yugorskiy Poluostrov** *peninsula* NW Russian Federation
114 *M13* **Yugoslavia** *off.* Federal Republic of Yugoslavia, *SCr.* Jugoslavija, Savezna Republika Jugoslavija. ◆ *federal republic* SE Europe
152 *K14* **Yugo-Vostochnyye Garagumy** *prev.* Yugo-Vostochnyye Karakumy. *desert* E Turkmenistan
Yugo-Vostochnyye Karakumy *see* Yugo-Vostochnyye Garagumy
167 *S10* **Yuhuan Dao** *island* SE China
166 *L14* **Yu Jiang** ≈ S China
127 *Nn7* **Yukagirskoye Ploskogor'ye** *plateau* NE Russian Federation
120 *L11* **Yukhavichy** *Rus.* Yukhovichi. Vitsyebskaya Voblasts', N Belarus *56.02N 28.39E*
130 *J4* **Yukhnov** Kaluzhskaya Oblast', W Russian Federation *54.43N 35.15E*
Yukhovichi *see* Yukhavichy
81 *J20* **Yuki** *var.* Yuki Kengunda. Bandundu, W Dem. Rep. Congo (Zaire) *3.52S 19.32E*
Yuki Kengunda *see* Yuki
28 *M10* **Yukon** Oklahoma, C USA *35.30N 97.45W*
(0) *F4* **Yukon** ≈ Canada/USA
Yukon *see* Yukon Territory
41 *S7* **Yukon Flats** *salt flat* Alaska, USA
14 *F5* **Yukon Territory** *var.* Yukon, *Fr.* Territoire du Yukon. ◐ *territory* NW Canada
143 *T16* **Yüksekova** Hakkâri, SE Turkey *37.34N 44.16E*
126 *Jj11* **Yukta** Evenkiyskiy Avtonomnyy Okrug, C Russian Federation *63.16N 106.04E*
170 *Dd13* **Yukuhashi** *var.* Yukuhasi. Fukuoka, Kyūshū, SW Japan *33.41N 131.00E*
Yukuhasi *see* Yukuhashi
Yukuriawat *see* Yopurga
129 *O9* **Yula** ≈ NW Russian Federation
189 *P8* **Yulara** Northern Territory, N Australia *25.15S 130.57E*
131 *W6* **Yuldybayevo** Respublika Bashkortostan, W Russian Federation *52.22N 57.55E*
25 *W8* **Yulee** Florida, SE USA *30.37N 81.36W*
164 *K7* **Yuli** *var.* Lopnur. Xinjiang Uygur Zizhiqu, NW China *41.24N 86.12E*
167 *T14* **Yüli** C Taiwan *23.23N 121.18E*
166 *L15* **Yulin** Guangxi Zhuangzu Zizhiqu, S China *22.37N 110.07E*
166 *L4* **Yulin** Shaanxi, C China *38.22N 109.47E*
167 *T14* **Yüli Shan** ▲ E Taiwan *23.22N 121.13E*
166 *F11* **Yulongxue Shan** ▲ SW China *27.09N 100.10E*
38 *H14* **Yuma** Arizona, SW USA *32.40N 114.38W*
39 *W3* **Yuma** Colorado, C USA *40.07N 102.43W*
56 *K5* **Yumare** Yaracuy, N Venezuela *10.37N 68.40W*
65 *G14* **Yumbel** Bío Bío, C Chile *37.07S 72.33W*
81 *N19* **Yumbi** Maniema, E Dem. Rep. Congo (Zaire) *1.13S 26.13E*
165 *R8* **Yumen** *var.* Laojunmiao, Yümen. Gansu, N China *39.49N 97.46E*
165 *Q7* **Yumenzhen** Gansu, N China *40.15N 97.03E*
164 *J3* **Yumin** Xinjiang Uygur Zizhiqu, NW China *46.14N 82.52E*
Yun *see* Yunnan
142 *G14* **Yunak** Konya, W Turkey *38.49N 31.42E*
47 *O8* **Yuna, Río** ≈ E Dominican Republic
40 *I17* **Yunaska Island** *island* Aleutian Islands, Alaska, USA
166 *M6* **Yuncheng** Shanxi, C China *35.07N 110.45E*
59 *L18* **Yungas** *physical region* E Bolivia
Yungki *see* Jilin
Yung-ning *see* Nanning
166 *I12* **Yun Gui Gaoyuan** *plateau* SW China
Yunjinghong *see* Jinghong
166 *M15* **Yunkai Dashan** ▲▲ S China
Yunki *see* Jilin
166 *E11* **Yun Ling** ▲▲ SW China
167 *N9* **Yunmeng** Hubei, C China *30.59N 113.44E*
163 *N14* **Yunnan** *var.* Yun, Yunnan Sheng, Yünnan, Yun-nan. ◐ *province* SW China
Yunnan *see* Kunming
Yunnan Sheng *see* Yunnan
170 *Cc15* **Yunomae** Kumamoto, Kyūshū, SW Japan *32.16N 131.00E*
167 *N8* **Yun Shui** ≈ C China
190 *J7* **Yunta** South Australia *32.37S 139.33E*
167 *Q14* **Yunxiao** Fujian, SE China *23.56N 117.16E*
166 *K9* **Yunyang** Sichuan, C China *31.03N 109.43E*
200 *Nn10* **Yupanqui Basin** *undersea feature* E Pacific Ocean
Yuratishki *see* Yuratsishki
121 *I15* **Yuratsishki** *Pol.* Juraciszki, *Rus.* Yuratishki. Hrodzyenskaya Voblasts', W Belarus *54.01N 25.55E*
Yurev *see* Tartu
126 *H14* **Yurga** Kemerovskaya Oblast', S Russian Federation *55.42N 84.59E*
58 *E10* **Yurimaguas** Loreto, N Peru *5.54S 76.07W*
131 *P3* **Yurino** Respublika Mariy El, W Russian Federation *56.19N 46.15E*
43 *N13* **Yuriria** Guanajuato, C Mexico *20.12N 101.09W*
129 *T13* **Yurla** Komi-Permyatskiy Avtonomnyy Okrug, NW Russian Federation *59.18N 54.19E*
Yuruá, Río *see* Juruá, Rio
116 *M13* **Yürük** Tekirdağ, NW Turkey *40.58N 27.09E*
164 *G10* **Yurungkax He** ≈ W China
129 *Q14* **Yur'ya** *var.* Jarja. Kirovskaya Oblast', NW Russian Federation *59.01N 49.22E*
Yur'yev *see* Tartu
129 *N16* **Yur'yevets** Ivanovskaya Oblast', W Russian Federation *57.19N 43.01E*
130 *M3* **Yur'yev-Pol'skiy** Vladimirskaya Oblast', W Russian Federation *56.28N 39.39E*
119 *V7* **Yur"yivka** Dnipropetrovs'ka Oblast', E Ukraine *48.45N 36.01E*
126 *K6* **Yuryung-Khaya** Respublika Sakha (Yakutiya), NE Russian Federation *72.45N 113.32E*
44 *I7* **Yuscarán** El Paraíso, S Honduras *13.58N 86.48W*
167 *P12* **Yu Shan** ▲ S China
128 *I7* **Yushkozero** Respublika Kareliya, NW Russian Federation *64.46N 32.13E*
165 *R13* **Yushu** Qinghai, C China *33.03N 97.00E*
131 *P12* **Yusta** Respublika Kalmykiya, SW Russian Federation *47.06N 46.16E*
128 *I10* **Yustozero** Respublika Kareliya, NW Russian Federation *62.44N 33.31E*
143 *Q11* **Yusufeli** Artvin, NE Turkey *40.49N 41.31E*
170 *E15* **Yusuhara** Kōchi, Shikoku, SW Japan *33.22N 132.52E*
129 *T14* **Yus'va** Permskaya Oblast', NW Russian Federation *58.48N 54.59E*
Yuta *see* Yatta
167 *P2* **Yutian** Hebei, E China *39.52N 117.43E*
164 *H10* **Yutian** *var.* Keriya. Xinjiang Uygur Zizhiqu, NW China *36.49N 81.31E*
64 *K5* **Yuto** Jujuy, NW Argentina *23.35S 64.28W*
64 *P7* **Yuty** Caazapá, S Paraguay *26.28S 56.11W*
166 *G13* **Yuxi** Yunnan, SW China *24.22N 102.28E*
167 *O2* **Yuxian** *prev.* Yu Xian. Hebei, E China *39.50N 114.33E*
171 *M11* **Yuzawa** Akita, Honshū, C Japan *39.11N 140.29E*
129 *N16* **Yuzha** Ivanovskaya Oblast', W Russian Federation *56.34N 42.00E*
Yuzhno-Alichurskiy Khrebet *see* Alichuri Janubí, Qatorkŭhi
Yuzhno-Kazakhstanskaya Oblast' *see* Yuzhnyy Kazakhstan
127 *Oo15* **Yuzhno-Sakhalinsk** *Jap.* Toyohara; *prev.* Vladimirovka. Ostrov Sakhalin, Sakhalinskaya Oblast', SE Russian Federation *46.58N 142.45E*
131 *P14* **Yuzhno-Sukhokumsk** Respublika Dagestan, SW Russian Federation *44.43N 45.32E*
125 *Ee12* **Yuzhnoural'sk** Chelyabinskaya Oblast', C Russian Federation *54.28N 61.13E*
126 *I13* **Yuzhno-Yeniseyskiy** Krasnoyarskiy Kray, C Russian Federation *58.40N 94.49E*
151 *Z10* **Yuzhnyy Altay, Khrebet** ▲▲ E Kazakhstan
Yuzhnyy Bug *see* Pivdennyy Buh
151 *O15* **Yuzhnyy Kazakhstan** *off.* Yuzhno-Kazakhstanskaya Oblast', *Eng.* South Kazakhstan, *Kaz.* Ongtüstik Qazaqstan Oblysy; *prev.* Chimkentskaya Oblast'. ◐ *province* S Kazakhstan
127 *Oo10* **Yuzhnyy, Mys** *headland* E Russian Federation *57.44N 156.49E*
131 *W6* **Yuzhnyy Ural** *var.* Southern Urals. ▲▲ W Russian Federation
165 *V10* **Yuzhong** Gansu, C China *35.52N 104.09E*
Yuzhou *see* Chongqing
105 *N5* **Yvelines** ◐ *department* N France
110 *B9* **Yverdon** *var.* Yverdon-les-Bains, *Ger.* Iferten; *anc.* Eborodunum. Vaud, W Switzerland *46.46N 6.37E*
Yverdon-les-Bains *see* Yverdon
104 *M3* **Yvetot** Seine-Maritime, N France *49.37N 0.48E*
Yylanly *see* Il'yaly

Z

153 *T12* **Zaalayskiy Khrebet** *Taj.* Qatorkŭhi Pasi Oloy. ▲▲ Kyrgyzstan/Tajikistan
Zaamin *see* Zomin
Zaandam *see* Zaanstad
100 *I10* **Zaanstad** *prev.* Zaandam. Noord-Holland, C Netherlands *52.27N 4.49E*
Zabadani *see* Az Zabdānī
121 *L18* **Zabalatstsye** *Rus.* Zabolot'ye. Homyel'skaya Voblasts', SE Belarus *52.38N 28.35E*
114 *L9* **Žabalj** *Ger.* Josefsdorf, *Hung.* Zsablya; *prev.* Józseffalva;. Serbia, N Yugoslavia *45.22N 20.01E*
Zāb aş Şaghīr, Nahraz *see* Little Zab
126 *L16* **Zabaykal'sk** Chitinskaya Oblast', S Russian Federation *49.37N 117.19E*
Zāb-e Kūchek, Rūdkhāneh-ye *see* Little Zab
Zabeln *see* Sabile
Zabéré *see* Zabré
Zabern *see* Saverne
147 *N16* **Zabīd** W Yemen *14.00N 43.00E*
147 *O16* **Zabīd, Wādī** *dry watercourse* SW Yemen
Żabinka *see* Zhabinka
Ząbkowice *see* Ząbkowice Śląskie
113 *G15* **Ząbkowice Śląskie** *var.* Ząbkowice, *Ger.* Frankenstein, Frankenstein in Schlesien. Dolnośląskie, SW Poland *50.34N 16.48E*
112 *P10* **Zabłudów** Podlaskie, NE Poland *53.00N 23.21E*
114 *D8* **Zabok** Krapina-Zagorje, N Croatia *46.00N 15.48E*
149 *W9* **Zābol** *var.* Shahr-i-Zabul, Zabul; *prev.* Nasratabad. Sīstān va Balūchestān, E Iran *31.00N 61.32E*
Zābol *see* Zābul
149 *W13* **Zāboli** Sīstān va Balūchestān, SE Iran *27.09N 61.31E*
Zabolot'ye *see* Zabalatstsye
79 *Q13* **Zabré** *var.* Zabéré. S Burkina *11.13N 0.34W*
113 *G17* **Zábřeh** *Ger.* Hohenstadt. Olomoucký Kraj, E Czech Republic *49.52N 16.52E*
113 *J16* **Zabrze** *Ger.* Hindenburg, Hindenburg in Oberschlesien. Śląskie, S Poland *50.19N 18.52E*
155 *O7* **Zābul** *Per.* Zābol. ◐ *province* SE Afghanistan
Zabul *see* Zābol
44 *E6* **Zacapa** Zacapa, E Guatemala *14.59N 89.32W*
44 *A3* **Zacapa** *off.* Departamento de Zacapa. ◐ *department* E Guatemala
42 *M14* **Zacapú** Michoacán de Ocampo, SW Mexico *19.49N 101.52W*
43 *V14* **Zacatal** Campeche, SE Mexico *18.37N 91.52W*
42 *M11* **Zacatecas** Zacatecas, C Mexico *22.45N 102.33W*
42 *L10* **Zacatecas** ◐ *state* C Mexico
44 *F8* **Zacatecoluca** La Paz, S El Salvador *13.28N 88.51W*
43 *P15* **Zacatepec** Morelos, S Mexico *18.40N 99.11W*
43 *Q13* **Zacatlán** Puebla, S Mexico *19.54N 97.59W*
150 *F8* **Zachagansk** Zapadnyy Kazakhstan, NW Kazakhstan *51.04N 51.13E*
117 *D20* **Zacháro** *var.* Zaharo, Zakháro. Dytikí Ellás, S Greece *37.28N 21.40E*
24 *J8* **Zachary** Louisiana, S USA *30.39N 91.09W*
119 *U6* **Zachepylivka** Kharkivs'ka Oblast', E Ukraine *49.13N 35.15E*
Zachist'ye *see* Zachystsye
112 *E9* **Zachodniopomorskie** ◐ *province* NW Poland
121 *L14* **Zachystsye** *Rus.* Zachist'ye. Minskaya Voblasts', NW Belarus *54.24N 28.45E*
42 *L13* **Zacoalco** *var.* Zacoalco de Torres. Jalisco, SW Mexico *20.12N 103.31W*
Zacoalco de Torres *see* Zacoalco
43 *P13* **Zacualtipán** Hidalgo, C Mexico *20.39N 98.42W*
114 *C12* **Zadar** *It.* Zara; *anc.* Iader. Zadar, W Croatia *44.06N 15.14E*
114 *C12* **Zadar** *off.* Zadarsko-Kninska Županija *prev.* Zadar-Knin. ◐ *province* SW Croatia
Zadar-Knin *see* Zadar
177 *G14* **Zadetkyi Kyun** *var.* St. Matthew's Island. *island* Mergui Archipelago, S Burma
69 *Q9* **Zadié** *var.* Djadié. ≈ NE Gabon
165 *Q13* **Zadoi** Qinghai, C China *32.56N 95.21E*
130 *L7* **Zadonsk** Lipetskaya Oblast', W Russian Federation *52.25N 38.55E*
77 *X8* **Za'farâna** E Egypt *29.06N 32.34E*
155 *W7* **Zafarwāl** Punjab, E Pakistan *32.19N 74.52E*
124 *P1* **Zafer Burnu** *var.* Cape Andreas, Cape Apostolas Andreas, *Gk.* Akrotíri Apostólou Andréa. *headland* NE Cyprus *35.42N 34.34E*
109 *J23* **Zafferano, Capo** *headland* Sicilia, Italy, C Mediterranean Sea *38.06N 13.31E*
116 *M7* **Zafirovo** Silistra, NE Bulgaria *44.00N 26.51E*
117 *L23* **Zaforá** *island* Kykládes, Greece, Aegean Sea
106 *J12* **Zafra** Extremadura, W Spain *38.25N 6.27W*
112 *E13* **Żagań** *var.* Zagań, Żegań, *Ger.* Sagan. Lubuskie, W Poland *51.37N 15.18E*
120 *F10* **Žagarė** *Pol.* Žagory. Joniškis, N Lithuania *56.22N 23.16E*
77 *W7* **Zagazig** *var.* Az Zaqāzīq. N Egypt *30.35N 31.31E*
76 *M5* **Zaghouan** *var.* Zaghwān. NE Tunisia *36.26N 10.05E*
Zaghwān *see* Zaghouan
117 *G16* **Zagorá** Thessalía, C Greece *39.27N 23.06E*
Zagorod'ye *see* Zaharoddzye
Żagory *see* Žagarė
Zágráb *see* Zagreb
114 *E8* **Zagreb** *Ger.* Agram, *Hung.* Zágráb. ● (Croatia) Zagreb, N Croatia *45.48N 15.57E*
114 *E8* **Zagreb** *prev.* Grad Zagreb. ◐ *province* NC Croatia
148 *L7* **Zāgros, Kūhhā-ye** *Eng.* Zagros Mountains. ▲▲ W Iran
Zagros Mountains *see* Zāgros, Kūhhā-ye
114 *O12* **Žagubica** Serbia, E Yugoslavia *44.13N 21.47E*
113 *L22* **Zagyva** ≈ N Hungary
Zaharo *see* Zacháro
121 *G19* **Zaharoddzye** *Rus.* Zagorod'ye. *physical region* SW Belarus
149 *W11* **Zāhedān** *var.* Zahidan; *prev.* Duzdab. Sīstān va Balūchestān, SE Iran *29.31N 60.51E*
Zahidan *see* Zāhedān
Zaḩlah *see* Zahlé
144 *H7* **Zahlé** *var.* Zaḩlah. C Lebanon *33.51N 35.54E*
Zähmet *see* Zakhmet
113 *O20* **Záhony** Szabolcs-Szatmár-Bereg, NE Hungary *48.26N 22.10E*
147 *N13* **Zahrān** 'Asīr, S Saudi Arabia *17.47N 43.27E*
145 *R12* **Zahrat al Baţn** *hill range* S Iraq
123 *I12* **Zahrez Chergui** *var.* Zahrez Chergúi. *marsh* N Algeria
131 *S4* **Zainsk** Respublika Tatarstan, W Russian Federation *55.12N 52.01E*
84 *A10* **Zaire** *prev.* Congo. ◐ *province* NW Angola
Zaire *see* Congo (Democratic Republic of)
Zaire *see* Congo (river)
114 *P13* **Zaječar** Serbia, E Yugoslavia *43.54N 22.16E*
85 *L18* **Zaka** Masvingo, E Zimbabwe *20.19S 31.27E*
126 *J16* **Zakamensk** Respublika Buryatiya, S Russian Federation *50.18N 102.57E*
118 *G7* **Zakarpats'ka Oblast'** *Eng.* Transcarpathian Oblast, *Rus.* Zakarpatskaya Oblast'. ◐ *province* W Ukraine
Zakarpatskaya Oblast' *see* Zakarpats'ka Oblast'
Zakataly *see* Zaqatala
Zakháro *see* Zacháro
Zakhidnyy Buh/Zakhodni Buh *see* Bug
152 *J14* **Zakhmet** *Turkm.* Zähmet. Maryyskiy Velayat, C Turkmenistan *37.48N 62.33E*
145 *Q1* **Zākhō** *var.* Zākhū. N Iraq *37.09N 42.40E*
Zākhū *see* Zākhō
Zákinthos *see* Zákynthos
113 *L18* **Zakopane** Małopolskie, S Poland *49.17N 19.57E*

◆ Country
● Country Capital
◇ Dependent Territory
○ Dependent Territory Capital
◐ Administrative Region
✕ International Airport
▲ Mountain
▲▲ Mountain Range
▲ Volcano
≈ River
◎ Lake
⊠ Reservoir

ZAKOUMA – ZITÁCUARO

80 J12 **Zakouma** Salamat, S Chad 10.47N 19.51E
117 L25 **Zákros** Kríti, Greece, E Mediterranean Sea 35.06N 26.12E
117 C19 **Zákynthos** var. Zákinthos. Zákynthos, W Greece 37.46N 20.54E
117 C20 **Zákynthos** var. Zákinthos, It. Zante. island Iónioi Nísoi, Greece, C Mediterranean Sea
117 C19 **Zakýnthou, Porthmós** strait SW Greece
113 G24 **Zala** off. Zala Megye. ◆ county W Hungary
113 G24 **Zala** ∽ W Hungary
144 M4 **Zalābiyah** Dayr az Zawr, C Syria 35.39N 39.51E
113 G24 **Zalaegerszeg** Zala, W Hungary 46.51N 16.49E
106 K11 **Zalamea de la Serena** Extremadura, W Spain 38.38N 5.37W
106 J13 **Zalamea la Real** Andalucía, S Spain 37.40N 6.40W
169 U7 **Zalantun** var. Butha Qi. Nei Mongol Zizhiqu, N China 47.57N 122.43E
126 J15 **Zalari** Irkutskaya Oblast', S Russian Federation 53.31N 102.10E
113 G23 **Zalaszentgrót** Zala, SW Hungary 46.57N 17.04E
Zalatna see Zlatna
118 G9 **Zalău** Ger. Waltenberg, Hung. Zilah; prev. Ger. Zillenmarkt. Sălaj, NW Romania 47.10N 23.03E
111 V10 **Žalec** Ger. Sachsenfeld. C Slovenia 46.15N 15.08E
119 S9 **Zalenodol's'k** Dnipropetrovs'ka Oblast', E Ukraine 47.31N 33.56E
112 K8 **Zalewo** Ger. Saalfeld. Warmińsko-Mazurskie, NE Poland 53.54N 19.39E
147 N9 **Ẓalim** Makkah, W Saudi Arabia 22.46N 42.12E
82 A11 **Zalingei** var. Zalinje. Western Darfur, W Sudan 12.51N 23.28E
Zalinje see Zalingei
118 K7 **Zalishchyky** Ternopil's'ka Oblast', W Ukraine 48.40N 25.43E
Zallah see Zillah
100 J13 **Zaltbommel** Gelderland, C Netherlands 51.49N 5.15E
128 H15 **Zaluch'ye** Novgorodskaya Oblast', NW Russian Federation 57.40N 31.45E
Zamak see Zamakh
147 Q14 **Zamakh** var. Zamak. N Yemen 16.25N 47.35E
142 K15 **Zamantı Irmağı** ∽ C Turkey
Zambesi/Zambeze see Zambezi
85 G14 **Zambezi** North Western, W Zambia 13.33S 23.07E
85 K15 **Zambezi** var. Zambesi, Port. Zambeze. ∽ S Africa
85 O15 **Zambézia** off. Província da Zambézia. ◆ province C Mozambique
85 I14 **Zambia** off. Republic of Zambia; prev. Northern Rhodesia. ◆ republic S Africa
179 Q16 **Zamboanga** off. Zamboanga City. Mindanao, S Philippines 6.56N 122.03E
56 E5 **Zambrano** Bolívar, N Colombia 9.45N 74.49W
112 N10 **Zambrów** Łomża, E Poland 52.59N 22.14E
85 L14 **Zambué** Tete, NW Mozambique 15.03S 30.49E
79 T13 **Zamfara** ∽ NW Nigeria
58 C9 **Zamora** Zamora Chinchipe, S Ecuador 4.05S 78.58W
106 K6 **Zamora** Castilla-León, NW Spain 41.30N 5.45W
106 K5 **Zamora** ◆ province Castilla-León, NW Spain
Zamora see Barinas
58 A13 **Zamora Chinchipe** ◆ province S Ecuador
42 M13 **Zamora de Hidalgo** Michoacán de Ocampo, SW Mexico 20.00N 102.18W
113 P15 **Zamość** Rus. Zamoste. Lubelskie, E Poland 50.43N 23.16E
Zamoste see Zamość
166 G7 **Zamtang** prev. Gamda. Sichuan, C China 32.19N 100.55E
77 O8 **Zamzam, Wādī** dry watercourse NW Libya
81 F20 **Zanaga** La Lékoumou, S Congo 2.49S 13.52E
43 T16 **Zanatepec** Oaxaca, SE Mexico 16.28N 94.24W
107 P9 **Záncara** ∽ C Spain
Zancle see Messina
164 G14 **Zanda** Xizang Zizhiqu, W China 31.28N 79.49E
100 H10 **Zandvoort** Noord-Holland, W Netherlands 52.22N 4.31E
41 P8 **Zane Hills** hill range Alaska, USA
33 T13 **Zanesville** Ohio, N USA 39.55N 82.01W
Zanga see Hrazdan
148 L4 **Zanjān** var. Zenjan, Zinjan. Zanjān, NW Iran 36.40N 48.30E
148 L4 **Zanjān** off. Ostān-e Zanjān, var. Zenjan, Zinjan. ◆ province NW Iran
Zante see Zákynthos
83 J22 **Zanzibar** Zanzibar, E Tanzania 6.10S 39.12E
83 J22 **Zanzibar** ◆ region E Tanzania
83 J22 **Zanzibar** Swa. Unguja. island E Tanzania
83 J22 **Zanzibar Channel** channel E Tanzania
171 Ll13 **Zaō-san** ▲ Honshū, C Japan 38.06N 140.27E
167 N8 **Zaoyang** Hubei, C China 32.11N 112.42E
126 I14 **Zaozernyy** Krasnoyarskiy Kray, S Russian Federation 55.53N 94.37E
167 Q6 **Zaozhuang** Shandong, E China 34.52N 117.37E
30 L4 **Zap** North Dakota, N USA 47.18N 101.55W
114 L13 **Zapadna Morava** Ger. Westliche Morava. ∽ C Yugoslavia
128 H16 **Zapadnaya Dvina** Tverskaya Oblast', W Russian Federation 56.16N 32.03E
Zapadnaya Dvina see Western Dvina
126 H10 **Zapadno-Sibirskaya Ravnina** Eng. West Siberian Plain. plain C Russian Federation
Zapadnyy Bug see Bug
150 E9 **Zapadnyy Kazakhstan** off. Zapadno-Kazakhstanskaya Oblast', Eng. West Kazakhstan, Kaz. Batys Qazaqstan Oblysy; prev. Ural'skaya Oblast'. ◆ province NW Kazakhstan
126 Hh15 **Zapadnyy Sayan** Eng. Western Sayans. ▲▲ S Russian Federation
65 H15 **Zapala** Neuquén, W Argentina 38.54S 70.06W
64 I4 **Zapaleri, Cerro** var. Cerro Sapaleri. ▲ N Chile 22.51S 67.10W
27 Q16 **Zapata** Texas, SW USA 26.54N 99.16W
46 D5 **Zapata, Península de** peninsula W Cuba
63 G19 **Zapicán** Lavalleja, S Uruguay 33.31S 54.55W
67 J19 **Zapiola Ridge** undersea feature SW Atlantic Ocean
67 L19 **Zapiola Seamount** undersea feature S Atlantic Ocean 38.15S 26.15W
128 I2 **Zapolyarnyy** Murmanskaya Oblast', NW Russian Federation 69.24N 30.53E
119 U8 **Zaporizhzhya** Rus. Zaporozh'ye; prev. Aleksandrovsk. Zaporiz'ka Oblast', SE Ukraine 47.46N 35.12E
Zaporizhzhya see Zaporiz'ka Oblast'
119 U9 **Zaporiz'ka Oblast'** var. Zaporizhzhya, Rus. Zaporozhskaya Oblast'. ◆ province SE Ukraine
Zaporozhskaya Oblast' see Zaporiz'ka Oblast'
Zaporozh'ye see Zaporizhzhya
42 L14 **Zapotiltic** Jalisco, SW Mexico 19.35N 103.25W
164 G13 **Zapug** Xizang Zizhiqu, W China
143 V10 **Zaqatala** Rus. Zakataly. NW Azerbaijan 41.38N 46.37E
165 P13 **Zaqên** Qinghai, W China 33.22N 94.31E
165 Q13 **Za Qu** ∽ C China
142 M13 **Zara** Sivas, C Turkey 39.55N 37.43E
Zara see Zadar
Zarafshan see Zarafshon
153 P12 **Zarafshon** Rus. Zeravshan. W Tajikistan 39.12N 68.36E
152 L9 **Zarafshon** Rus. Zarafshan. Nawoiy Wiloyati, N Uzbekistan 41.33N 64.09E
Zarafshon see Zeravshan
153 O12 **Zarafshon, Qatorkŭhi** Rus. Zeravshanskiy Khrebet, Uzb. Zarafshon Tizmasi. ▲▲ Tajikistan/Uzbekistan
Zarafshon Tizmasi see Zarafshon, Qatorkŭhi
56 E7 **Zaragoza** Antioquia, N Colombia 7.30N 74.52W
42 I5 **Zaragoza** Chihuahua, N Mexico 29.36N 107.41W
43 N6 **Zaragoza** Coahuila de Zaragoza, NE Mexico 28.30N 100.52W
43 O10 **Zaragoza** Nuevo León, NE Mexico 23.59N 99.49W
107 R5 **Zaragoza** Eng. Saragossa; anc. Caesaraugusta, Salduba. Aragón, NE Spain 41.39N 0.54W
107 R6 **Zaragoza** ◆ province Aragón, NE Spain
107 R5 **Zaragoza** ✕ Aragón, NE Spain 41.37N 0.52W
149 S10 **Zarand** Kermān, C Iran 30.49N 56.34E
154 J9 **Zaranj** Nīmrūz, SW Afghanistan 30.59N 61.54E
120 I11 **Zarasai** Zarasai, E Lithuania 55.44N 26.17E
64 N12 **Zárate** prev. General José F.Uriburu. Buenos Aires, E Argentina 34.06S 59.03W
107 Q2 **Zarautz** var. Zarauz. País Vasco, N Spain 43.16N 2.10W
Zarauz see Zarautz
Zaravecchia see Biograd na Moru
Zarāyīn see Zarēn
130 L4 **Zaraysk** Moskovskaya Oblast', W Russian Federation 54.48N 38.54E
57 N6 **Zaraza** Guárico, N Venezuela 9.21N 65.19W
Zarbdar see Zarbdor
153 P11 **Zarbdor** Rus. Zarbdar. Jizzakh Wiloyati, C Uzbekistan 40.04N 68.10E
148 M8 **Zard Kūh** ▲ SW Iran 32.19N 50.03E
128 I5 **Zarechensk** Murmanskaya Oblast', NW Russian Federation 66.39N 31.27E
155 Q7 **Zareh Sharan** Paktīkā, E Afghanistan 33.07N 68.46E
41 Y14 **Zarembo Island** island Alexander Archipelago, Alaska, USA
145 V4 **Zarēn** var. Zarāyīn. E Iraq 35.16N 45.43E
155 Q7 **Zarghūn Shahr** var. Katawaz. Paktīkā, SE Afghanistan 32.40N 68.19E
79 V13 **Zaria** Kaduna, C Nigeria 11.06N 7.42E
118 K2 **Zarichne** Rivnens'ka Oblast', NW Ukraine 51.49N 26.09E
126 H14 **Zarinsk** Altayskiy Kray, S Russian Federation 53.34N 85.22E
118 J12 **Zărnești** Hung. Zernest. Brașov, C Romania 45.34N 25.18E
117 J25 **Zarós** Kríti, Greece, E Mediterranean Sea 35.07N 24.54E
102 O9 **Zarow** ∽ NE Germany
Zarqa/Zarqā', Muḩāfaẓat az see Az Zarqā'
113 G20 **Záruby** ▲ W Slovakia 48.30N 17.24E
58 B8 **Zaruma** El Oro, SW Ecuador 3.41S 79.32W
112 E13 **Żary** Ger. Sorau, Sorau in der Niederlausitz. Lubuskie, W Poland 51.43N 15.09E
56 D10 **Zarzal** Valle del Cauca, W Colombia 4.22N 76.03W
44 I7 **Zarzalar, Cerro** ▲ S Honduras 14.15N 86.49W
158 I5 **Zāskār** ∽ NE India
158 I5 **Zāskār Range** ▲▲ NE India
121 K15 **Zaslawye** Minskaya Voblasts', C Belarus 54.01N 27.16E
118 K7 **Zastavna** Chernivets'ka Oblast', W Ukraine 48.30N 25.51E
113 B16 **Žatec** Ger. Saaz. Ústecký Kraj, NW Czech Republic 50.19N 13.32E
Zaumgarten see Chrzanów
152 G10 **Zaunguzskiye Garagumy** Turkm. Üngüz Angyrsyndaky Garagum. desert N Turkmenistan
27 X9 **Zavalla** Texas, SW USA 31.09N 94.25W
101 H18 **Zaventem** Vlaams Brabant, C Belgium 50.52N 4.28E
101 H18 **Zaventem** ✕ (Brussel/Bruxelles) Vlaams Brabant, C Belgium 50.55N 4.28E
Zavertse see Zawiercie
116 L7 **Zavet** Razgrad, NE Bulgaria 43.46N 26.40E
131 O12 **Zavetnoye** Rostovskaya Oblast', SW Russian Federation 47.10N 43.54E
162 M3 **Zavhan Gol** ∽ W Mongolia
114 H12 **Zavidovići** Federacija Bosna I Hercegovina, N Bosnia and Herzegovina 44.26N 18.07E
126 Mm16 **Zavitinsk** Amurskaya Oblast', SE Russian Federation 50.23N 128.57E
125 F12 **Zavodoukovsk** Tyumenskaya Oblast', C Russian Federation 56.27N 66.37E
Zawia see Az Zāwiyah
113 K15 **Zawiercie** Rus. Zavertse. Śląskie, S Poland 50.28N 19.24E
77 P11 **Zawīlah** var. Zuwaylah, It. Zueila. C Libya 26.10N 15.07E
144 I4 **Zāwiyah, Jabal az** ▲▲ NW Syria
111 Y3 **Zaya** ∽ NE Austria
177 G8 **Zayatkyi** Pegu, C Burma 17.48N 96.27E
151 Y11 **Zaysan** Vostochnyy Kazakhstan, E Kazakhstan 47.28N 84.48E
Zaysan Köl see Zaysan, Ozero
151 Y11 **Zaysan, Ozero** Kaz. Zaysan Köl. ◎ E Kazakhstan
165 R16 **Zayü** var. Gyigang. Xizang Zizhiqu, W China 28.36N 97.25E
Zayyq see Ural
46 F6 **Zaza** ∽ C Cuba
118 K5 **Zbarazh** Ternopil's'ka Oblast', W Ukraine 49.40N 25.47E
118 J5 **Zboriv** Ternopil's'ka Oblast', W Ukraine 49.40N 25.07E
113 F18 **Zbraslav** Brněnský Kraj, SE Czech Republic 49.13N 16.19E
118 K6 **Zbruch** ∽ W Ukraine
Žďár see Žďár nad Sázavou
113 F17 **Žďár nad Sázavou** Ger. Saar in Mähren; prev. Žďár. Jihlavský Kraj, C Czech Republic 49.34N 15.55E
118 K4 **Zdolbuniv** Pol. Zdołbunów, Rus. Zdolbunov. Rivnens'ka Oblast', NW Ukraine 50.33N 26.15E
Zdolbunov/Zdołbunów see Zdolbuniv
112 J13 **Zduńska Wola** Sieradz, C Poland 51.37N 18.57E
119 O4 **Zdvizh** ∽ N Ukraine
Zdzięciół see Dzyatlava
113 I16 **Zdzieszowice** Ger. Odertal. Opolskie, S Poland 50.24N 18.06E
Zealand see Sjælland
196 K6 **Zealandia Bank** undersea feature C Pacific Ocean
65 H20 **Zeballos, Monte** ▲ S Argentina 47.04S 71.32W
85 K20 **Zebediela** Northern, NE South Africa 24.16S 29.21E
115 L18 **Zebë, Mal** var. Mali i Zebës. ▲ NE Albania 41.57N 20.16E
Zebës, Mali i see Zebë, Mal
23 V9 **Zebulon** North Carolina, SE USA 35.49N 78.19W
114 K8 **Žednik** Hung. Bácsjózseffalva. Serbia, N Yugoslavia 45.58N 19.40E
101 C15 **Zeebrugge** West-Vlaanderen, NW Belgium 51.19N 3.13E
191 N16 **Zeehan** Tasmania, SE Australia 41.54S 145.19E
101 L14 **Zeeland** Noord-Brabant, SE Netherlands 51.42N 5.40E
31 N7 **Zeeland** North Dakota, N USA 45.57N 99.49W
101 E14 **Zeeland** ◆ province SW Netherlands
85 I21 **Zeerust** North-West, N South Africa 25.33S 26.04E
100 K10 **Zeewolde** Flevoland, C Netherlands 52.19N 5.31E
144 G8 **Ẓefat** var. Safed, Tsefat, Ar. Safad. Northern, N Israel 32.57N 35.27E
Zegań see Żagań
Zehden see Cedynia
102 O11 **Zehdenick** Brandenburg, NE Germany 52.58N 13.19E
Zē-i Bādīnān see Great Zab
Zeiden see Codlea
152 M14 **Zeidskoye Vodokhranilishche** ⊠ E Turkmenistan
Zē-i Kōya see Little Zab
189 P7 **Zeil, Mount** ▲ Northern Territory, C Australia 23.31S 132.41E
100 J12 **Zeist** Utrecht, C Netherlands 52.04N 5.15E
103 M16 **Zeitz** Sachsen-Anhalt, E Germany 51.03N 12.07E
165 T11 **Zêkog** Qinghai, C China 35.03N 101.30E
Zelaya Norte see Atlántico Norte, Región Autónoma
Zelaya Sur see Atlántico Sur, Región Autónoma
101 F17 **Zele** Oost-Vlaanderen, NW Belgium 51.04N 4.01E
112 N12 **Żelechów** Lubelskie, E Poland 51.49N 21.57E
115 H14 **Zelena Glava** ▲ SE Bosnia and Herzegovina 43.32N 17.55E
115 I14 **Zelengora** ▲▲ S Bosnia and Herzegovina
128 I5 **Zelenoborskiy** Murmanskaya Oblast', NW Russian Federation 66.52N 32.25E
131 R3 **Zelenodol'sk** Respublika Tatarstan, W Russian Federation 55.52N 48.49E
128 G12 **Zelenogorsk** Fin. Terijoki. Leningradskaya Oblast', NW Russian Federation 60.08N 30.06E
130 K3 **Zelenograd** Moskovskaya Oblast', W Russian Federation 56.02N 37.08E
120 B13 **Zelenogradsk** Ger. Cranz, Kranz. Kaliningradskaya Oblast', W Russian Federation 54.57N 20.30E
131 O15 **Zelenokumsk** Stavropol'skiy Kray, SW Russian Federation 44.22N 43.48E
172 Rr7 **Zelënyy, Ostrov** var. Shibotsu-jima. island NE Russian Federation
Železna Kapela see Eisenkappel
Železna Vrata see Demir Kapija
114 L11 **Železniki** Serbia, N Yugoslavia 44.45N 20.23E
100 N12 **Zelhem** Gelderland, E Netherlands 52.00N 6.21E
115 N18 **Želino** NW FYR Macedonia 42.00N 21.06E
115 M14 **Željin** ▲▲ C Yugoslavia
103 K17 **Zella-Mehlis** Thüringen, C Germany 50.40N 10.40E
111 P7 **Zell am See** var. Zell-am-See. Salzburg, S Austria 47.19N 12.48E
111 N7 **Zell am Ziller** Tirol, W Austria 47.13N 11.52E
Zelle see Celle
111 W2 **Zellerndorf** Niederösterreich, NE Austria 48.40N 15.57E
111 U7 **Zeltweg** Steiermark, S Austria 47.10N 14.43E
121 G17 **Zel'va** Pol. Zelwa. Hrodzyenskaya Voblasts', W Belarus 53.09N 24.49E
120 H13 **Želva** Ukmergė, C Lithuania 55.13N 25.07E
Zelwa see Zel'va
101 E16 **Zelzate** var. Selzaete. Oost-Vlaanderen, NW Belgium 51.12N 3.49E
120 E11 **Žemaičių Aukštumas** physical region W Lithuania
120 C12 **Žemaičių Naumiestis** Šilutė, SW Lithuania 55.22N 21.39E
Zembin see Zyembin
131 N6 **Zemetchino** Penzenskaya Oblast', W Russian Federation 53.31N 42.35E
81 M15 **Zémio** Haut-Mbomou, E Central African Republic 5.04N 25.07E
43 R16 **Zempoaltepec, Cerro** ▲ SE Mexico 17.04N 95.54W
101 G17 **Zemst** Vlaams Brabant, C Belgium 50.59N 4.28E
114 L11 **Zemun** Serbia, N Yugoslavia 44.51N 20.24E
Zendajan see Zendeh Jan
154 J5 **Zendeh Jan** var. Zendajan, Zindajān. Herāt, NW Afghanistan 34.55N 61.53E
Zengg see Senj
114 H12 **Zenica** Federacija Bosna I Hercegovina, C Bosnia and Herzegovina 44.12N 17.52E
Zenjan see Zanjān
Zen'kov see Zin'kiv
Zenshū see Chŏnju
Zenta see Senta
170 Ff14 **Zentsūji** var. Zentûzi. Kagawa, Shikoku, SW Japan 34.13N 133.45E
Zentûzi see Zentsūji
84 B11 **Zenza do Itombe** Cuanza Norte, NW Angola 9.22S 14.10E
114 H12 **Žepče** Federacija Bosna I Hercegovina, N Bosnia and Herzegovina 44.26N 18.00E
25 W12 **Zephyrhills** Florida, SE USA 28.13N 82.10W
199 J10 **Zephyr Reef** reef Pacific Ocean
164 F9 **Zepu** var. Poskam. Xinjiang Uygur Zizhiqu, NW China 38.10N 77.18E
153 Q12 **Zeravshan** Taj./Uzb. Zarafshon. ∽ Tajikistan/Uzbekistan
Zeravshan see Zarafshon
Zeravshanskiy Khrebet see Zarafshon, Qatorkŭhi
103 M14 **Zerbst** Sachsen-Anhalt, E Germany 51.57N 12.05E
151 P8 **Zerenda** Severnyy Kazakhstan, N Kazakhstan 52.55N 69.09E
112 H12 **Żerków** Wielkopolskie, C Poland 52.03N 17.33E
110 E11 **Zermatt** Valais, SW Switzerland 46.00N 7.44E
Zernest see Zărnești
110 J9 **Zernez** Graubünden, SE Switzerland 46.42N 10.06E
130 L12 **Zernograd** Rostovskaya Oblast', SW Russian Federation 46.52N 40.13E
Zestafoni see Zestap'oni
143 S9 **Zestap'oni** Rus. Zestafoni. C Georgia 42.09N 43.00E
100 H12 **Zestienhoven** ✕ (Rotterdam) Zuid-Holland, SW Netherlands 51.57N 4.30E
115 J16 **Zeta** ∽ SW Yugoslavia
15 J2 **Zeta Lake** ◎ Victoria Island, Nunavut, N Canada
100 L12 **Zetten** Gelderland, SE Netherlands 51.55N 5.43E
103 M17 **Zeulenroda** Thüringen, C Germany 50.40N 11.58E
102 H10 **Zeven** Niedersachsen, NW Germany 53.17N 9.16E
100 M12 **Zevenaar** Gelderland, SE Netherlands 51.55N 6.04E
101 H14 **Zevenbergen** Noord-Brabant, S Netherlands 51.39N 4.36E
126 M14 **Zeya** Amurskaya Oblast', SE Russian Federation 53.43N 127.14E
133 X6 **Zeya** ∽ SE Russian Federation
Zeya Reservoir see Zeyskoye Vodokhranilishche
149 T11 **Zeynalābād** Kermān, C Iran 29.55N 57.28E
126 M14 **Zeyskoye Vodokhranilishche** Eng. Zeya Reservoir. ⊠ SE Russian Federation
106 H8 **Zêzere, Rio** ∽ C Portugal
Zgerzh see Zgierz
144 H6 **Zgharta** N Lebanon 34.24N 35.54E
112 K12 **Zgierz** Ger. Neuhof, Rus. Zgerzh. Łódź, C Poland 51.55N 19.19E
113 E14 **Zgorzelec** Ger. Görlitz. Dolnośląskie, SW Poland 51.10N 15.00E
Zhabdün see Zhongba
121 F19 **Zhabinka** Pol. Żabinka, Rus. Zhabinka. Brestskaya Voblasts', SW Belarus 52.12N 24.01E
Zhaggo see Luhuo
165 R15 **Zhag'yab** Xizang Zizhiqu, W China 30.42N 97.33E
150 L9 **Zhailma** Kaz. Zhayylma. Kostanay, N Kazakhstan 51.34N 61.39E
151 V16 **Zhalanash** Almaty, SE Kazakhstan 43.07N 78.40E
Zhalashash see Dzhalagash
151 S7 **Zhalauly, Ozero** ◎ NE Kazakhstan
150 E9 **Zhalpaktal** prev. Furmanovo. Zapadnyy Kazakhstan, W Kazakhstan 49.40N 49.27E
121 G16 **Zhaludok** Rus. Zheludok. Hrodzyenskaya Voblasts', W Belarus 53.36N 24.58E
Zhaman-Akkol', Ozero see Akkol', Ozero
Zhambyl see Taraz
151 Q14 **Zhambyl** off. Zhambylskaya Oblast', Kaz. Zhambyl Oblysy; prev. Dzhambulskaya Oblast'. ◆ province S Kazakhstan
Zhambyl Oblysy/Zhambylskaya Oblast' see Zhambyl
Zhamo see Bomi
151 S12 **Zhamshy** ∽ C Kazakhstan
150 M15 **Zhanadar'ya** Kzylorda, S Kazakhstan 44.41N 64.39E
151 O15 **Zhanakorgan** Kaz. Zhangaqorghan. Kzylorda, S Kazakhstan 43.57N 67.14E
165 N16 **Zhanang** Xizang Zizhiqu, W China 29.15N 91.19E
151 T12 **Zhanaortalyk** Zhezkazgan, C Kazakhstan 47.31N 75.42E
150 F15 **Zhanaozen** Kaz. Zhangaözen, prev. Novyy Uzen'. Mangistau, W Kazakhstan 43.21N 52.50E
151 Q16 **Zhanatas** Zhambyl, S Kazakhstan 43.33N 69.40E
Zhangaözen see Zhanaozen
Zhangaqazaly see Ayteke Bi
Zhangaqorghan see Zhanakorgan
167 O2 **Zhangbei** Hebei, E China 41.13N 114.43E
Zhangdian see Zibo
169 X9 **Zhangguangcai Ling** ▲▲ NE China
151 W10 **Zhangiztobe** Vostochnyy Kazakhstan, E Kazakhstan 49.16N 81.16E
165 W11 **Zhangjiachuan** Gansu, N China 34.55N 106.25E
166 L10 **Zhangjiajie** var. Dayong. Hunan, S China 29.10N 110.22E
167 O2 **Zhangjiakou** var. Changkiakow, Zhang-chia-k'ou, Eng. Kalgan; prev. Wanchuan. Hebei, E China 40.48N 114.51E
167 Q13 **Zhangping** Fujian, SE China 25.21N 117.29E
167 Q13 **Zhangpu** Fujian, SE China 24.07N 117.36E
169 U11 **Zhangwu** Liaoning, NE China 42.21N 122.32E
165 S8 **Zhangye** Gansu, N China 38.59N 100.27E
167 Q13 **Zhangzhou** Fujian, SE China 24.31N 117.40E
169 W6 **Zhan He** ∽ NE China
Zhānibek see Dzhanybek
166 L16 **Zhanjiang** var. Chanchiang, Chan-chiang, Cant. Tsamkong, Fr. Fort-Bayard. Guangdong, S China 21.10N 110.19E
Zhansügirov see Dzhansugurov
169 V8 **Zhaodong** Heilongjiang, NE China 46.03N 125.58E
Zhaoge see Qixian
166 H11 **Zhaojue** Sichuan, C China 28.03N 102.50E
167 N14 **Zhaoqing** Guangdong, S China 23.07N 112.26E
164 H5 **Zhaosu** var. Mongolküre. Xinjiang Uygur Zizhiqu, NW China 43.09N 81.07E
166 H11 **Zhaotong** Yunnan, SW China 27.17N 103.42E
169 V9 **Zhaoyuan** Heilongjiang, NE China 45.30N 125.04E
169 V9 **Zhaozhou** Heilongjiang, NE China 45.40N 125.16E
151 X13 **Zharbulak** Vostochnyy Kazakhstan, E Kazakhstan 46.05N 82.06E
164 J15 **Zhari Namco** ◎ W China
150 I12 **Zharkamys** Kaz. Zharqamys. Aktyubinsk, W Kazakhstan 47.58N 56.33E
151 W15 **Zharkent** prev. Panfilov. Almaty, SE Kazakhstan 44.10N 80.01E
128 H17 **Zharkovskiy** Tverskaya Oblast', W Russian Federation 55.51N 32.19E
151 W11 **Zharma** Vostochnyy Kazakhstan, E Kazakhstan 48.48N 80.55E
150 F14 **Zharmysh** Mangistau, SW Kazakhstan 44.12N 52.27E
Zharqamys see Zharkamys
120 L13 **Zhary** Rus. Zhary. Vitsyebskaya Voblasts', N Belarus 55.04N 28.40E
Zhaslyk see Jasliq
126 Ll11 **Zhatay** Respublika Sakha (Yakutiya), NE Russian Federation 62.07N 129.42E
164 J14 **Zhaxi Co** ◎ W China
Zhayylma see Zhailma
Zhdanov see Beyläqan, Azerbaijan
Zhdanov see Mariupol', Ukraine
Zhe see Zhejiang
167 R10 **Zhejiang** var. Che-chiang, Chekiang, Zhe, Zhejiang Sheng. ◆ province SE China
Zhejiang Sheng see Zhejiang
151 S7 **Zhelezinka** Pavlodar, N Kazakhstan 53.35N 75.16E
121 C14 **Zheleznodorozhnyy** Ger. Gerdauen. Kaliningradskaya Oblast', W Russian Federation 54.21N 21.17E
126 J13 **Zheleznodorozhnyy** Irkutskaya Oblast', C Russian Federation 57.54N 102.40E
Zheleznodorozhnyy see Yemva
130 J7 **Zheleznogorsk** Kurskaya Oblast', W Russian Federation 52.22N 35.21E
126 Jj14 **Zheleznogorsk-Ilimskiy** Irkutskaya Oblast', S Russian Federation 56.38N 103.53E
131 N15 **Zheleznovodsk** Stavropol'skiy Kray, SW Russian Federation 44.12N 43.01E
Zhëltyye Vody see Zhovti Vody
Zheludok see Zhaludok
Zhem see Emba
166 K7 **Zhenba** Shaanxi, C China 32.42N 107.55E
166 I13 **Zhenfeng** Guizhou, S China 25.27N 105.38E
Zhengjiatun see Shuangliao
165 X10 **Zhengning** Gansu, N China 35.28N 108.21E
169 Q12 **Zhengxiangbai Qi** Nei Mongol Zizhiqu, N China 42.10N 114.57E
167 N6 **Zhengzhou** var. Ch'eng-chou, Chengchow; prev. Chenghsien. Henan, C China 34.45N 113.37E
167 R8 **Zhenjiang** var. Chenkiang. Jiangsu, E China 32.12N 119.30E
169 U9 **Zhenlai** Jilin, NE China 45.52N 123.11E
166 I11 **Zhenxiong** Yunnan, SW China 27.31N 104.52E
166 K11 **Zhenyuan** prev. Wuyang. Guizhou, S China 27.07N 108.33E
167 R11 **Zherong** Fujian, SE China 27.16N 119.54E
Zhetiqara see Dzhetygara
150 F15 **Zhetybay** Mangistau, SW Kazakhstan 43.30N 52.09E
151 P17 **Zhetysay** var. Dzhetysay. Yuzhnyy Kazakhstan 40.45N 68.18E
166 M11 **Zhexi Shuiku** ⊠ C China
151 O12 **Zhezdy** Zhezkazgan, C Kazakhstan 48.06N 67.01E
151 O12 **Zhezkazgan** Kaz. Zhezqazghan; prev. Dzhezkazgan. Zhezkazgan, C Kazakhstan 47.48N 67.43E
Zhezqazghan see Zhezkazgan
166 M9 **Zhicheng** Hubei, C China 30.21N 111.27E
Zhidachov see Zhydachiv
165 Q12 **Zhidoi** Qinghai, C China 33.55N 95.39E
126 Jj15 **Zhigalovo** Irkutskaya Oblast', S Russian Federation 54.47N 105.00E
126 L9 **Zhigansk** Respublika Sakha (Yakutiya), NE Russian Federation 66.45N 123.20E
131 R6 **Zhigulevsk** Samarskaya Oblast', W Russian Federation 53.24N 49.30E
120 D13 **Zhilino** Ger. Schillen. Kaliningradskaya Oblast', W Russian Federation 54.55N 21.54E
131 O8 **Zhirnovsk** Volgogradskaya Oblast', SW Russian Federation 51.01N 44.49E
Zhitarovo see Vetren
Zhitkovichi see Zhytkavichy
131 P10 **Zhitkur** Volgogradskaya Oblast', SW Russian Federation 49.00N 46.16E
Zhitomir see Zhytomyr
Zhitomirskaya Oblast' see Zhytomyrs'ka Oblast'
130 J5 **Zhizdra** Kaluzhskaya Oblast', W Russian Federation 53.38N 34.39E
121 N18 **Zhlobin** Homyel'skaya Voblasts', SE Belarus 52.52N 30.01E
Zhmerinka see Zhmerynka
118 M7 **Zhmerynka** Rus. Zhmerinka. Vinnyts'ka Oblast', C Ukraine 49.01N 28.01E
155 R9 **Zhob** var. Fort Sandeman. Baluchistān, SW Pakistan 31.22N 69.25E
155 R8 **Zhob** ∽ C Pakistan
150 I10 **Zhobda** prev. Novoalekseyevka. Aktyubinsk, W Kazakhstan 50.10N 55.39E
Zhodino see Zhodzina
121 L15 **Zhodzina** Rus. Zhodino. Minskaya Voblasts', C Belarus 54.05N 28.19E
126 Mm3 **Zhokhova, Ostrov** island Novosibirskiye Ostrova, NE Russian Federation
Zholkev/Zholkva see Zhovkva
Zholsaly see Dzhusaly
Zhondor see Jondor
164 I15 **Zhongba** var. Zhabdün. Xizang Zizhiqu, W China 29.37N 84.11E
166 F11 **Zhongdian** Yunnan, SW China 27.48N 99.40E
Zhonghua Renmin Gongheguo see China
165 V9 **Zhongning** Ningxia, N China 37.25N 105.40E
167 N15 **Zhongshan** Guangdong, S China 22.30N 113.19E
205 X7 **Zhongshan** Chinese research station Antarctica 69.23S 76.34E
166 M6 **Zhongtiao Shan** ▲▲ C China
165 V9 **Zhongwei** Ningxia, N China 37.31N 105.10E
166 K9 **Zhongxian** var. Zhong Xian. Chongqing Shi, C China 30.16N 108.03E
167 N9 **Zhongxiang** Hubei, C China 31.12N 112.35E
167 O7 **Zhoukou** var. Zhoukouzhen. Henan, C China 33.37N 114.34E
Zhoukouzhen see Zhoukou
167 S9 **Zhoushan** Zhejiang, S China
167 S9 **Zhoushan Qundao** Eng. Zhoushan Islands. island group SE China
118 I5 **Zhovkva** Pol. Żółkiew, Rus. Zholkev, Zholkva; prev. Nesterov. L'vivs'ka Oblast', NW Ukraine 50.03N 24.00E
119 S7 **Zhovti Vody** Rus. Zhëltyye Vody. Dnipropetrovs'ka Oblast', E Ukraine 48.24N 33.30E
119 Q10 **Zhovtneve** Rus. Zhovtnevoye. Mykolayivs'ka Oblast', S Ukraine 46.50N 32.00E
Zhovtnevoye see Zhovtneve
116 K9 **Zhrebchevo, Yazovir** ⊠ C Bulgaria
169 V13 **Zhuanghe** Liaoning, NE China 39.43N 122.57E
165 W11 **Zhuanglang** Gansu, N China 35.06N 106.21E
151 P15 **Zhuantobe** Kaz. Zhūantöbe. Yuzhnyy Kazakhstan, S Kazakhstan 44.45N 68.50E
167 Q5 **Zhucheng** Shandong, E China 35.58N 119.24E
165 V12 **Zhugqu** Gansu, C China 33.51N 104.14E
167 N15 **Zhuhai** Guangdong, S China 22.16N 113.30E
Zhuizishan see Weichang
Zhuji see Shangqiu
130 I5 **Zhukovka** Bryanskaya Oblast', W Russian Federation 53.33N 33.48E
167 O3 **Zhuozhou** prev. Zhuo Xian. Hebei, E China 39.22N 115.40E
168 L14 **Zhuozi Shan** ▲ N China 39.28N 106.58E
Zhuravichi see Zhuravichy
121 O17 **Zhuravichy** Rus. Zhuravichi. Homyel'skaya Voblasts', SE Belarus 53.15N 30.29E
151 Q8 **Zhuravlevka** Akmola, N Kazakhstan 51.56N 69.56E
119 Q4 **Zhurivka** Kyyivs'ka Oblast', N Ukraine 50.28N 31.48E
150 J11 **Zhuryn** Aktyubinsk, W Kazakhstan 49.13N 57.36E
151 T15 **Zhusandala, Step'** grassland SE Kazakhstan
166 L8 **Zhushan** Hubei, C China 32.11N 110.05E
167 N11 **Zhuzhou** Hunan, S China 27.52N 112.52E
118 I6 **Zhydachiv** Pol. Żydaczów, Rus. Zhidachov. L'vivs'ka Oblast', NW Ukraine 49.22N 24.09E
Zhympity see Dzhambeyty
121 K19 **Zhytkavichy** Rus. Zhitkovichi. Homyel'skaya Voblasts', SE Belarus 52.13N 27.52E
119 N4 **Zhytomyr** Rus. Zhitomir. Zhytomyrs'ka Oblast', NW Ukraine 50.17N 28.39E
Zhytomyr see Zhytomyrs'ka Oblast'
118 M4 **Zhytomyrs'ka Oblast'** var. Zhytomyr, Rus. Zhitomirskaya Oblast'. ◆ province N Ukraine
159 U15 **Zia** ✕ (Dhaka) Dhaka, C Bangladesh
113 J20 **Žiar nad Hronom** var. Svätý Kríž nad Hronom, Ger. Heiligenkreuz, Hung. Garamszentkereszt. Banskobystrický Kraj, C Slovakia 48.36N 18.52E
167 Q4 **Zibo** var. Zhangdian. Shandong, E China 36.51N 118.01E
166 L4 **Zichang** prev. Wayaobu. Shaanxi, C China 37.08N 109.40E
Zichenau see Ciechanów
113 G15 **Ziębice** Ger. Münsterberg in Schlesien. Dolnośląskie, SW Poland 50.37N 17.01E
Ziebingen see Cybinka
Ziegenhais see Głuchołazy
112 E12 **Zielona Góra** Ger. Grünberg, Grünberg in Schlesien, Grüneberg. Lubuskie, W Poland 51.55N 15.30E
101 F14 **Zierikzee** Zeeland, SW Netherlands 51.39N 3.55E
166 I10 **Zigong** var. Tzekung. Sichuan, C China 29.19N 104.48E
78 G12 **Ziguinchor** SW Senegal 12.33N 16.19W
43 N16 **Zihuatanejo** Guerrero, S Mexico 17.39N 101.33W
Zilah see Zalău
131 W7 **Zilair** Respublika Bashkortostan, W Russian Federation 52.12N 57.15E
142 L12 **Zile** Tokat, N Turkey 40.18N 35.52E
113 J18 **Žilina** Ger. Sillein, Hung. Zsolna. Žilinský Kraj, N Slovakia 49.13N 18.43E
113 J19 **Žilinský Kraj** ◆ region N Slovakia
77 Q9 **Zillah** var. Zallah. C Libya 28.30N 17.33E
Zillenmarkt see Zalău
111 N7 **Ziller** ∽ W Austria
Zillertal Alps see Zillertaler Alpen
111 N8 **Zillertaler Alpen** Eng. Zillertal Alps, It. Alpi Aurine. ▲▲ Austria/Italy
120 K10 **Zilupe** Ger. Rosenhof. Ludza, E Latvia 56.10N 28.06E
126 J15 **Zima** Irkutskaya Oblast', S Russian Federation 53.57N 101.57E
43 O13 **Zimapán** Hidalgo, C Mexico 20.42N 99.23W
85 I16 **Zimba** Southern, S Zambia 17.16S 26.10E
85 J17 **Zimbabwe** off. Republic of Zimbabwe; prev. Rhodesia. ◆ republic S Africa
118 H10 **Zimbor** Hung. Magyarzsombor. Sălaj, NW Romania 47.00N 23.16E
Zimmerbude see Svetlyy
118 J15 **Zimnicea** Teleorman, S Romania 43.39N 25.21E
116 L9 **Zimnitsa** Yambol, E Bulgaria 42.34N 26.37E
131 N12 **Zimovniki** Rostovskaya Oblast', SW Russian Federation 47.07N 42.28E
Zindajān see Zendeh Jan
79 V12 **Zinder** Zinder, S Niger 13.46N 9.01E
79 W11 **Zinder** ◆ department S Niger
79 P12 **Ziniaré** C Burkina 12.35N 1.21W
Zinjan see Zanjān
147 P16 **Zinjibār** SW Yemen 13.07N 45.22E
119 T4 **Zin'kiv** var. Zen'kov. Poltavs'ka Oblast', NE Ukraine 50.11N 34.21E
Zinov'yevsk see Kirovohrad
Zintenhof see Sindi
33 N10 **Zion** Illinois, N USA 42.27N 87.49W
56 F10 **Zipaquirá** Cundinamarca, C Colombia 5.03N 74.01W
Zipser Neudorf see Spišská Nová Ves
113 H23 **Zirc** Veszprém, W Hungary 47.16N 17.52E
115 D14 **Žirje** It. Zuri. island S Croatia
Zirknitz see Cerknica
110 M7 **Zirl** Tirol, W Austria 47.16N 11.16E
103 K20 **Zirndorf** Bayern, SE Germany 49.27N 10.57E
166 M11 **Zi Shui** ∽ C China
111 Y3 **Zistersdorf** Niederösterreich, NE Austria 48.31N 16.45E
43 O14 **Zitácuaro** Michoacán de Ocampo, SW Mexico 19.28N 100.21W

◆ Country ● Country Capital ◇ Dependent Territory ○ Dependent Territory Capital ◆ Administrative Region ✕ International Airport ▲ Mountain ▲▲ Mountain Range ♠ Volcano ∽ River ◎ Lake ⊠ Reservoir

PICTURE CREDITS

DORLING KINDERSLEY would like to express their thanks to the following individuals, companies and institutions for their help in preparing this Atlas.

Earth Resources Mapping Ltd., *Egham, Surrey*
Brian Groombridge, World Conservation Monitoring Centre, *Cambridge*
The British Library, *London*
British Library of Political and Economic Science, *London*
The British Museum, *London*
The City Business Library, *London*
King's College, *London*
National Meteorological Library and Archive, *Bracknell, Berkshire*
The Printed Word, *London*
The Royal Geographical Society, *London*
University of London Library
Paul Beardmore
Philip Boyes
Hayley Crockford
Alistair Dougal
Nick Drake
Reg Grant
Louise Keane
Zoe Livesley
Laura Porter
Jeff Eidenshink
Chris Hornby
Rachelle Smith
Ray Pinchard
Robert Meisner
Fiona Strawbridge
Wim Jenkins

T = top, B = bottom, A=above, L = left, R = right, C = centre

Every effort has been made to trace the copyright holders and we apologize in advance for any unintentional omissions. We would be pleased to insert the appropriate acknowledgement in any subsequent edition of this publication.

Adams Picture Library: 88CLA; **G Andrews:** 194CR; **Ardea London Ltd:** K Andrews 154TL; M Iljima 140TC; R Waller 154TR; **Aspect Picture Library:** P Carmichael 137CRB, 166TR; G Tompkinson 202TRB; **Axiom:** C Bradley 154CA, 165CA; J Holmes xivCRA, xxivBCR, xxviiCIRB, 156TCR, 172BC, 172TL, J Morris 77TL, 77CRB, J Spaull 134BL; **Bridgeman Art Library, London / New York:** Collection of the Earl of Pembroke, Wilton House xxvBC; **The J. Allan Cash Photolibrary:** xIBR, xliiCLA, xlivCL, 8BC, 62CL, 71CLB, 72CL, 74CLB, 77BR, 78BC, 89BL, 111BR, 144BCL, 147TL, 160CR, 186BR, 189TR; **Bruce Coleman Ltd:** 88BC, 100CL, 102TC; S Alden 198BR; Atlantide xxviTCR, 144BR; E Bjurstrom 147BR; S Bond 98CRB; T Buchholz xvCL, 96TR, 130TCL; J Burton xxiiiC; J Cancalosi 189TRB; B J Coates xxvBL, 198BC; B Coleman 65TL; B Coleman 2TR, 38CB; A Compost xxiiiCBR; Dr S Coyne 47TL; G Cubitt xviTCL, 173BCL, 186TR, 192TR; P Davey xviiiCLB, 123BL; N Devore 201CBL; S J Doylee xxiiCRR; H Flygare xviiCRA; M P L Fogden 17CB; Jeff Foott Productions xxiiiCRB, 9CRA; M Freeman 93BRA; P van Gaalen 88TR; G Gualco 146C; B Henderson 200CR; Dr C Henneghien 71C; HPH Photography, H Van den Berg 71CR; C Hughes 71BCL; C James xxxixTC; J Johnson 41CR, 207TR; J Jurka 93CA; S C Kaufman 30C; S J Krasemann 35TR; H Lange 8TRB, 70CA; C Lockwood 34BC; L C Marigo xxiiBC, xxviiiCLA, 51CRA, 61BR; M McCoy 195TR; D Meredith 3CR; J Murray xvCR, 187BR; Orion Press 172TTR; Orion Services & Trading Co. Inc. 171TR; C Ott 18BL; Dr E Pott 14C, 42CL, 89C, 95TL, 204CLB; F Prenzel 197C, 200CB; M Read 44BR, 45CRB; H Reinhard xxiiCR, xxviiTR, 204BR; L Lee Rue III 157BCL; J Shaw xixTL; L N Swenson 204BC; P Terry 117CR; N Tomalin 56BCL; P Ward 80TC; S Widstrand 59TR; K Wothe 93C, 181TCL; J T Wright 131BR; **Colorific:** Black Star / L Mulvehil 162CLL; Black Star / R Rogers 59BR; Black Star / J Rupp 167BCR; Camera Tres / C. Meyer 61BRA; R Caputo / Matrix 80CL; J. Hill 119CLB; M Koene 57TR; G Satterley xliiCLAR; Y Yamashita 162BL, 179CA; **Comstock:** 110CRB; **D Cousens:** 153 CRA; **Sue Cunningham Photography:** 53CR; **James Davis Travel Photography:** xviiTCB, xxxviiTR, xxxviCL, xxxiii CRA; 11CA, 21LB, 51TLB, 58BCR, 59CLA, 63BL, 95BC, 96TC, 104TR, 122CB, 164BCL, 187CRA, 203BR; **G Dunnet:** 128CA; **Environmental Picture Library:** Chris Westwood 130C; **Eye Ubiquitous:** xCA; Marcus Störie xxxiii tr; L. Fordyce 10CLA; J Johnstone 6CRA, 30BLA, 32CB; S. Miller xivCLA; M Southern 75BLA; **Chris Fairclough Colour Library:** xIiBR; **Ffotograff:** C Aithie 137CL, N. Tapsell 166TC; **Geoscience Features:** xliiiBR, 104CL, 112CB, 127BR; Solar Film 66TC; **Robert Harding Picture Library:** xviiTC, xxivCR, xxxC, xxxivTC, Gavin Heller xxxiii cl; 2TLB, 3CA, 13CRB, 13CR, 39BC, 40CRA, 52BL, 97BR, 101CR, 116CR, 126BL, 138CLA, 148CB, 149TL, 153TR, 162TR, 173CA, 177BR; P G. Adam 11TCB; D Atchison-Jones 72BLA; J Bayne 74BC; B Schuster 82CR; C Bowman 52BR, 55CA, 64CL, 72CRL;

C Campbell xxiiBC; G Corrigan 165CRB, 167CRB; P Craven xxxvBL; R Cundy 71BR; Delu 81BC; A Durand 113BR; Financial Times 148BR; R Frerck 53BL; T Gervis 3BCL, 7CR; J Griffiths xxxCL, 79TL; T Hall 177CRA; D Harney 148CA; S Harris xliiiBCL; G Hellier xivCRB, 135BL; F Jackson 143BCR; Jacobs xxxviiTL; P Koch 145TR; F Joseph Land 125TR; Y Marcoux 16BR; S Massif xivBC; A Mills 90CLB; L Murray 116TR; R Rainford xlivBL; G Renner 76CB, 204C; C Rennie 50CL, 118BR; R Richardson 120CL; P Van Riel 50BR; E Rooney 123TR; Sassoon xxivCL, 154CLB; P Scholey 184TR; M Short 143TL; E Simanor xxviiCR; V Southwell 145CR; ' Strachan 44TR, 113BL, 136BCR; C Tokeley 140CLA; C Waltham 167C; T Waltham xviiiBL, xxiiCLLL, 144CRB; Westlight 39CR; N Wheeler 145BL; A Williams xxxviiiBR, xlTR; A Woolfitt 97BRA; **Paul Harris:** 126TR, 174TC; **Hutchison Library:** 6BL, 140BCL; P Collomb 143CR; C Dodwell 139TR; S Errington 72BCL; P. Hellyer 148BC; J. Horner xxxiTC; R. Ian Lloyd 134CRA; N. Durrell McKenna xxviBCR; J.Nowell 135CLB, 149TC; A Zvoznikov xxiiiCL; **Image Bank:** 89BR; J Banagan 202BCA; A Becker xxivBCL; F Hendrie 174BC; M Isy-Schwart 200C, 203CL; M Khansa 124BR; K Forest 169TR; Lomeo xxivTCR; T Madison 167CC; C Molyneux xxiiiCRRR; K Mori 200TC; C Navajas xviiiTR; Ocean Images Inc. 138BR; J van Os xviiTCR; S Proehl 6CL; T Rakke xixTC, 66CL; M Reitz 206CA; R Romanelli 177BL; G A Rossi 157BCR, 184BLS; B Roussel 111TL; S Satushek xviiiBR; Stock Photos / J M Spielman xxivTRL; **Images Colour Library:** xxiiCLL, xxxixTR, xliCR, xliiiPLL, 3BR, 21BR, 39TL, 46TL, 64TL, 93BR, 104CLB, 105CR, 156CL, 171CL, 172TRB, 188CA; **Impact Photos:** J S Andrews 194BL; C. Bluntzer 162BR; Cosmos / G. Buthaud 67BC; S Franklin 130BL; A. le Garsmeur 172CRB; A Macintyre xviiiTC; C Jones xxxiCB, 72BR; V. Nemirousky 143BR; J Nicholl 78TCR; C. Penn 1973R; G Sweeney xviiiBR; 206CB, 206TR; **JVZ Picture Library:** T Nilson 135TC; **Frank Lane Picture Agency:** xxiTCR, xxiiiBL, 95TR; A Christiansen 64TC; J Holmes xivBL; S. McCutcheon 3C; Silvestris 181TCR; D Smith xxiiiBCL; W Wisniewski 126TL, 205BR; **Leeds Castle Foundation:** xxxviiBC; **Magnum:** Abbas 85CR, 142CA; S Franklin 134CRB; D Hurn 4BCL; P. Jones-Griffiths 203BL; H Kubota xviBCL, 162CLB; F Maver xviBL; S McCurry 75CL, 144TBR; G. Rodger 76TR; C Steele Perkins 74BL; **Mountain Camera / John Cleare:** 159TR; C Monteath 159CR; **Nature Photographers:** E.A. Janes 114CL; **Natural Science Photos:** M Andera 112C; **Network Photographers:** C Sappa / Rapho 201CL; P Chesley 193BCL, 179BC; W Clay 32BL, 33CRA; J Cornish 98BL, 109TL; C Condina 43CB; T Craddock xxivTTR; P Deggirger 38CLB; Demetrio 5BR; N DeVore xxivBC; A Diesendruck 62BR; S Egan 89CRA, 98BR; R Elliot xxiiBCR; S Elmore 21C; R Frerck 122TR; J Garrett 75CR; S Grandadam 12BR; R Grosskopf 30BL; D Hanson 106BC; C Harvey 71TL; G Hellier 112BL, 172CR; S Huber 105CRB; D Hughs xxxiBR; A Husmo 93TR; G Irvine 33BC; J Jangoux 60CL; P Koskas xviTR; J Lamb 98CRA; J Lawrence 5L Lefkowitz 7CA; M Lewis 48TCA; J Neibauer xviTL; R Nosing xxxiiCBL, 9TL, 207BR; D Simonson 59C; Survival Anglia / C Catton 143TR; R Towse xxxiiiBR; K Wothe xxiBL, xviiCLA; **Panos Pictures:** B Aris 147C; P Barker xxxixTR; J-L Dugast 177CB, 178BC; J Hartley 75CA, 92CL; J Holmes 155BC; J Morris

78CLB; M Rose 152TR; D Sansoni 161CL; C Stowers 169TL; **Edward Parker:** 51TL, 51CLB; **Pictor International:** xivBR, xvBRA, xixTCL, xxCL, 3CLA, 19BR, 22TR, 22CRB, 25BCA, 25CL, 28CB, 29BC, 32CA, 35TRB, 36BC, 36BR, 36CR, 40CLB, 40CL, 45CL, 65BR, 67TC, 84CL, 85CLB, 101BR, 109CLA, 177TCR, 178BR, 179CR, 188CLB, 193TL; **Pictures Colour Library:** xxiBCL, xxiiiBR, xxviiBCL, 6BR, 13TR. 14TC, 17TR, 21TL, 22BL, 26C, 26CLA, 29TR, 34TRB, 38BC, 43CA, 45CRA, 70BL, 92TCB, 96BL, 101BL, 108CA, 109CLB, 109CR, 109BR, 119BL, 170BC, 171BR, 198CL; **Planet Earth Pictures:** 200BL; D Barrett 154CB, 192CA; R Coomber 173CL; G Douwma 180BR; E Edmonds 181BR; HC Heap 124TR; J Lythgoe 236BL; A Mounter 137BCR, 180CR; M Potts 6CA; P Scoones xxTR; J Walencik 112TR; J Waters 55BCL; **Popperfoto:** Reuters / J Drake xxxiCLA; **Rex Features:** 170CR; Antelope xxxiiCLB; M Friedel xxiCR; I McIlgorm xxxCBR; J Shelley xxxCR; Sipa Press xxxCR; Sipa Press / Alix xxxCBL; Sipa Press / Chamussy 184BL; **Russia & Republics Photolibrary:** M Wadlow 120CR, 121CL, 128BC, 128CL, 129TL, 129BR, 130TCR; **Science Photo Library:** CNES, 1990 Distribution Spot Image 137BL; Earth Satellite Corporation xixTRB, xxxiCR, 51BCL; F Gohier xixCR; J Heseltine xviTCB; K Kent xvBLA; P Menzell xvBL; N.A.S.A. xBR; D Parker xivBC; University of Cambridge Collection Air Pictures 89CLB; RJ Wainscoat / P Arnold, Inc. xiBC; D Weintraub xiBL; **South American Pictures:** 59BL, 64TR; R Francis 54BL; Guyana Space Centre 52TR; T Morrison 51CRB, 51BL, 52CR, 54TR, 56TR, 62BL, 63C; **Southampton Oceanography: Sovofoto / Eastfoto:** xxxiiiCBR; **Spectrum Colour Library:** 52BC, 166BC; J King 151BR; **Frank Spooner Pictures / Gamma:** 28CRB; E. Baitel xxxiiBC; Bernstein xxxiCL; Contrast 114CR; Diard / Photo News 115CL; Liaison / C. Hires xxxiiTCB; Liaison / Nickelsberg xxxiiTR; Liaison / Vogel 140BL; Marleen 115TL; Novosti 118CA; P. Piel xxxCA; N Quidu 115CL; H Stucke 196CLB, 202CA; Torrengo / Figaro 80BR; A Zamur 115BL; **Still Pictures:** C Caldicott 79TC; A Crump 201CL; M & C Denis-Huot xxiiA, 80CR, 83BL; M Edwards xxiCRL, 55BL, 66CR, 71BLA, 161BR; J Frebet 55CLB; H Giradet 55TC; M Gunther 123BC; E Parker 54CL; R Seitre 137CA, 138BL, 138TL; **Tony Stone Images:** xxviTR, 4CA, 7BL, 7CL, 11CRB, 41BR, 60C, 90BG, 103BR, 108TR, 111CL, 111CRB, 141BR, 170CLB, 171C,188CB, 189BR, 196BC, 198TR; G Allison 20TR, 33CRB, 195CRB; D Armand 12TCB; D Austen 188TR, 194CL, 195CL; J Beatty 76CL; O Benn xxviBR; K Biggs xxiTL; R Bradbury 46BR; R A Butcher xxviTL; J Callahan xxviiCRA; P Chesley 193CL, 109TL; J Dennis 24BL; Dinodia 160CL; Eye Ubiquitous / L Fordyce 2CLB; A Gasson 155CR; W Jacobs 45TL, 56BL, 185BC, 186CLA, 193BCR, 197BL; P Kingsbury 114C; K Knight 185BR; V Kolpakov 153BL; T Noorits 89TL, 121BR, 152CL; R Power 43TR; N Ray 176CA; C Rennie 118CLB; V Sidoropolev 151TR; E Smith 191BC, 191TL; **Woodfin Camp & Associates:** 94BLR; **World Pictures:** xvCRA, xviiCRA, 16CRB, 24CL, 25BC, 26BL, 37BL, 42TR, 53TR, 73BR, 82TCR, 84TR, 85BL, 88BCR, 98TC, 100BL, 102CR, 103CR, 105BC, 107TC, 123CB, 124BL, 163BL, 167BCL, 168CLB, 180CLB, 180BC, 187BL, 190CB, 191C, 192CL, 193CRC; **Zefa Picture Library:** xviBLR, xviiiCL, 3CL, 11BC, 12TC, 17CA, 23TL, 24CRB, 27BL, 34TCR, 38BCR, 61BCL, 67TCL, 71CLA, 81TL, 83BR, 89CRB, 94C, 100C, 101TL, 102BL, 109TR, 120CRB, 122BL, 126CB, 128CLA, 170CA, 191TR; Anatol 115BR; Barone 116BL; Brandenburg 5CL; A J Brown 46TR; H J Clauss 57CLB; Damm 73BC; Evert 94BL; W Felger 3BL; J Fields 201CRA; R Frerck 4BL; G Heil 58BR; K Heibig 117BR; Heilman 30BC; Hunter 8C; Kitchen 8TR, 14CL, 14BL, 16TR; Dr H Kramarz 7BLA, 127CRA; Mehlio 161BL; J F Raga 267BR; Rossenbach 107BR, 122CA; Streichan 91TL; T Stewart 11TR, 21CR; Sunak 56BR, 168TR; D H Teuffen 97TL; B Zaunders 42BC; **Additional Photography:** Geoff Dann; Rob Reichenfeld; H Taylor; Jerry Young.

◆ COUNTRY ◇ DEPENDENT TERRITORY ◈ ADMINISTRATIVE REGION ▲ MOUNTAIN ▨ VOLCANO ◇ LAKE
● COUNTRY CAPITAL ○ DEPENDENT TERRITORY CAPITAL ✕ INTERNATIONAL AIRPORT ▲▲ MOUNTAIN RANGE ◆ RIVER ▨ RESERVOIR

Abyssal plain A broad plain found in the depths of the ocean, more than 10,000 ft (3000 m) below sea level.

Air mass A huge, homogeneous mass of air, within which horizontal patterns of temperature and humidity are consistent. Air masses are separated by fronts.

Alluvial fan Large fan-shaped deposit of fine *sediments* deposited by a river as it emerges from a narrow, mountain valley onto a broad, open plain.

Alluvium Material deposited by rivers. Nowadays usually only applied to finer particles of silt and clay.

Anticline A geological fold which forms an arch shape, curving upwards in the rock strata.

Aquifer A body of rock which can absorb water. .

Arête A thin, jagged mountain ridge which divides two adjacent cirques, found in regions where *glaciation* has occurred.

Artesian well A naturally occurring source of underground water, stored in an *aquifer*.

Atoll A ring-shaped island or coral reef often enclosing a lagoon of sea water.

Badlands A landscape that has been heavily *eroded* and dissected by rainwater, and which has little or no vegetation.

Back slope The gentler windward slope of a sand dune or gentler slope of a *cuesta*.

Bajos An *alluvial fan* deposited by a river at the base of mountains and hills that encircle desert areas.

Bar, coastal An offshore strip of sand or shingle, either above or below the water. Usually parallel to the shore but sometimes crescent-shaped or at an oblique angle.

Barchan A crescent-shaped sand dune, formed where wind direction is very consistent. The horns of the crescent point downwind and where there is enough sand the barchan is mobile.

Base level The level below which flowing water cannot erode the land.

Basement rock A mass of ancient rock often of *Pre-Cambrian* age, covered by a layer of more recent *sedimentary rocks*. Commonly associated with *shield* areas.

Bedrock Solid, consolidated and relatively unweathered rock, found on the surface of the land or just below a layer of soil or weathered rock.

Bluff The steep bank of a meander, formed by the erosive action of a river.

Breccia A type of rock composed of sharp fragments, cemented by a fine-grained material such as clay.

Butte An isolated, flat-topped hill with steep or vertical sides, buttes are the eroded remnants of a former land surface.

Calcite Hexagonal crystals of calcium carbonate.

Caldera A huge volcanic vent, often containing a number of smaller vents, and sometimes a crater lake.

Carbonation Process whereby rocks are broken down by carbonic acid. Carbon dioxide in the air dissolves in rainwater, forming carbonic acid.

Castle kopje Hill or rock outcrop, especially in southern Africa, where steep sides, and a summit composed of blocks, give a castle-like appearance.

Cataracts A series of stepped waterfalls created as a river flows over a band of hard, resistant rock.

Chernozem A fertile soil, also known as 'black earth' consisting of a layer of dark topsoil, rich in decaying vegetation, overlying a lighter chalky layer.

Confluence The point at which two rivers meet.

Continental drift The theory that the continents of today are fragments of one or more prehistoric *supercontinents* which have moved across the Earth's surface, creating ocean basins.

Continental shelf An area of the continental *crust*, below sea level, which slopes gently.

Continental slope A steep slope running from the edge of the continental shelf to the ocean floor.

Core The centre of the Earth, consisting of a dense mass of iron and nickel.

Coulées A US / Canadian term for a ravine formed by river *erosion*.

Craton A large block of the Earth's *crust* which has remained stable for a long period of geological time. It is made up of ancient *shield* rocks.

Cretaceous A period of geological time beginning about 145 million years ago and lasting until c. 65 million years ago.

Crevasse A deep crack in a *glacier*.

Crust The hard, thin outer shell of the Earth. It floats on the *mantle*, which is softer and more dense.

Crystalline rock Rocks formed when molten *magma* crystallizes (*igneous rocks*) or when heat or pressure cause re-crystallization (*metamorphic rocks*).

Cuesta A hill which rises into a steep slope on one side but has a gentler gradient on its other slope.

Delta Low-lying, fan-shaped area at a river mouth, formed by the *deposition* of successive layers of *sediment*.

Denudation The combined effect of *weathering*, *erosion*, and mass movement, which, over long periods, exposes underlying rocks.

Deposition The laying down of material that has accumulated: after being eroded and then transported by wind, ice, or water; as organic remains, such as coal and coral; as the result of evaporation and chemical *precipitation*.

Depression 1 In climatic terms it is a large low pressure system; 2 a complex fold, producing a large valley, which incorporates both a *syncline* and an *anticline*.

Detritus Piles of rock deposited by an erosive agent such as a river or *glacier*.

Distributary A minor branch of a river, which does not rejoin the main stream, common at *deltas*.

Divide A US term describing the area of high ground separating two *drainage basins*.

Donga A steep-sided gully, resulting from *erosion* by a river or by floods.

Drainage basin The area drained by a single river system, its boundary is marked by a *watershed* or *divide*.

Drumlin A long, streamlined hillock composed of material deposited by a *glacier*. They often occur in groups known as swarms.

Earthflow The rapid movement of soil and other loose surface material down a slope, when saturated by water.

Ephemeral A non-permanent feature, often used in connection with seasonal rivers or lakes in dry areas.

Epicentre The point on the Earth's surface directly above the underground origin or focus of an earthquake.

Erg An extensive area of sand dunes, particularly in the Sahara.

Erosion The processes which wear away the surface of the land. *Glaciers*, wind, rivers, waves and currents all carry debris that causes erosion.

Escarpment A steep slope at the margin of a level, upland surface. In a landscape created by folding, escarpments (or scarps) frequently lie behind a more gentle backward slope.

Esker A narrow, winding ridge of sand and gravel deposited by streams of water flowing beneath or at the edge of a *glacier*.

Erratic A rock transported by a *glacier* and deposited some distance from its place of origin.

Eustacy A world-wide fall or rise in ocean levels.

Exfoliation A kind of *weathering* whereby scale-like flakes of rock are peeled or broken off by the development of salt crystals in water within the rocks.

Extrusive rock *Igneous rock* formed when molten material (*magma*) pours forth at the Earth's surface and cools rapidly. It usually has a glassy texture.

Fault A fracture or crack in rock, where strains (*tectonic* movement) have caused blocks to move, vertically or laterally, relative to each other.

Ferrel cell A component in the global pattern of air circulation, which rises in the colder *latitudes* (60° N and S) and descends in warmer latitudes (30° N and S).

Fissure A deep crack in a rock or a *glacier*.

Fjord A deep, narrow inlet, created when the sea inundates the *U-shaped valley* created by a *glacier*.

Flash flood A sudden, short-lived rise in the water level of a river or stream, or surge of water down a dry river channel, or wadi, caused by heavy rainfall.

Flood plain The broad, flat part of a river valley, adjacent to the river itself, formed by *sediment* deposited during flooding.

Fold A bend in the rock strata of the Earth's *crust*, resulting from compression.

Frost shattering A form of *weathering* where water freezes in cracks, causing expansion. As temperatures fluctuate and the ice melts and refreezes, it eventually causes the rocks to shatter.

Geosyncline A concave fold (*syncline*) or large depression in the Earth's *crust*, extending hundreds of kilometres.

Geothermal energy Heat derived from hot rocks within the Earth's *crust* and resulting in hot springs, steam, or hot rocks at the surface.

Geyser A jet of steam and hot water that intermittently erupts from vents in the ground in areas that are, or were, volcanic.

Glaciation The growth of *glaciers* and *ice sheets*, and their impact on the landscape.

Glacier A body of ice moving downslope under the influence of gravity and consisting of compacted and frozen snow.

Glacio-eustacy A worldwide change in the level of the oceans, caused when the formation of *ice sheets* takes up water or when their melting returns water to the ocean.

Glaciofluvial To do with glacial *meltwater*, the landforms it creates and its processes; *erosion*, transportation and *deposition*.

Glacis A gentle slope or pediment.

Gondwanaland The *supercontinent* thought to have existed over 200 million years ago in the southern hemisphere.

Graben A block of rock let down between two parallel faults. Where the graben occurs within a valley, the structure is known as a *rift valley*.

Grease ice Slicks of ice that form in Antarctic seas, when ice crystals are bonded together by wind and wave action.

Groundwater Water that has seeped into the pores, cavities, and cracks of rocks or into soil and water held in an *aquifer*.

Gully A deep, narrow channel eroded in the landscape by ephemeral streams.

Guyot A small, flat-topped submarine mountain, formed as a result of subsidence which occurs during *sea-floor spreading*.

Hadley cell A large-scale component in the global pattern of air circulation. Warm air rises over the Equator and blows at high altitude toward the poles, sinking in subtropical regions (30° N and 30° S) and creating high pressure. The air then flows at the surface towards the Equator in the form of trade winds.

Hamada An Arabic word for a plateau of bare rock in a desert.

Hanging valley A tributary valley that ends suddenly, high above the bed of the main valley.

Headwards The action of a river eroding back upstream, as opposed to the normal process of downstream *erosion*. Headwards erosion is often associated with gullying.

Hoodos Pinnacles of rock which have been worn away by *weathering* in semi-arid regions.

Horst A block of the Earth's crust that has been left upstanding by the sinking of adjoining blocks along fault lines.

Hot spot A region of the Earth's *crust* where high thermal activity occurs, often leading to volcanic eruptions.

Hydrolysis The chemical breakdown of rocks in reaction with water, forming new compounds.

Ice Age A period in the Earth's history when surface temperatures in the temperate *latitudes* were much lower and ice sheets expanded considerably. There have been ice ages from *Pre-Cambrian* times onwards.

Ice cap A permanent dome of ice in highland areas.

Ice floe A large, flat mass of ice floating free on the ocean surface. It is usually formed after the break-up of winter ice by heavy storms.

Ice sheet A continuous, very thick layer of ice and snow. The term is usually used of ice masses which are continental in extent.

Ice shelf A floating mass of ice attached to the edge of a coast. The seaward edge is usually a sheer cliff up to 100 ft (30 m) high.

Ice wedge Massive blocks of ice up to 6.5 ft (2 m) wide at the top and extending 32 ft (10 m) deep.

Iceberg A large mass of ice in a lake or a sea, which has broken off from a floating ice sheet (an *ice shelf*) or from a *glacier*.

Igneous rock Rock formed when molten material, *magma*, from the hot, lower layers of the Earth's crust, cools, solidifies, and crystallizes, either within the Earth's *crust* (intrusive) or on the surface (extrusive).

Inselberg An isolated, steep-sided hill, rising from a low plain in semi-arid and savannah landscapes.

Interglacial A period of global climate, between two *ice ages*, when temperatures rise and *ice sheets* and *glaciers* retreat.

Intraplate volcano A volcano that lies in the centre of one of the Earth's *tectonic plates*, rather than, as is more common, at its edge.

Intrusion (intrusive *igneous rock*) Rock formed when molten material, *magma*, penetrates existing rocks below the Earth's surface before cooling and solidifying.

Isostasy The state of equilibrium that the Earth's *crust* maintains as its lighter and heavier parts float on the denser underlying *mantle*.

Isthmus A narrow strip of land connecting two larger landmasses or islands.

Joint A crack in a rock, formed where blocks of rock have not shifted relative to each other, as is the case with a *fault*. Joints are created by folding; by shrinkage in *igneous rock* as it cools or *sedimentary rock* as it dries out; and by the release of pressure in a rock mass when overlying materials are removed by *erosion*.

Kame A mound of stratified sand and gravel with steep sides, deposited in a *crevasse* by *meltwater* running over a *glacier*. When the ice retreats, this forms an undulating terrain of hummocks.

Karst A barren limestone landscape created by carbonic acid in streams and rainwater, in areas where limestone is close to the surface.

Kettle hole A round hollow formed in a glacial deposit by a detached block of glacial ice, which later melted. They can fill with water to form kettle-lakes.

Lagoon A shallow stretch of coastal salt-water behind a partial barrier such as a sandbank or coral reef. Also used to describe the water encircled by an *atoll*.

Laterite A hard red deposit left by chemical *weathering* in tropical conditions, and consisting mainly of oxides of iron and aluminium.

Latitude The angular distance from the Equator, to a given point on the Earth's surface. Imaginary lines of latitude running parallel to the Equator encircle the Earth, and are measured in degrees north or south of the Equator. The Equator is 0°, the poles 90° South and North respectively. Also called parallels.

Laurasia In the theory of *continental drift*, the northern part of the great *supercontinent* of Pangaea. Laurasia is said to consist of North America, Greenland and all of Eurasia north of the Indian subcontinent.

Lava The molten rock, *magma*, which erupts onto the Earth's surface through a volcano, or through a *fault* or crack in the Earth's *crust*.

Leaching The process whereby water dissolves minerals and moves them down through layers of soil or rock.

Levée A raised bank alongside the channel of a river. Levées are either man-made or formed in times of flood when the river overflows its channel, slows and *deposits* much of its *sediment* load.

Lithosphere The rigid, upper layer of the Earth, comprising the *crust* and the upper part of the *mantle*.

Loess Fertile, fine-grained, yellow deposits of unstratified silts and sands.

Longitude A division of the Earth which pinpoints how far east or west a given place is from the Prime Meridian (0°) which runs through the Royal Observatory at Greenwich, England (UK). Imaginary lines of longitude are drawn around the world from pole to pole. The world is divided into 360 degrees.

Longshore drift The movement of sand and silt along the coast, carried by waves hitting the beach at an angle.

Magma Underground, molten rock, which is very hot and highly charged with gas. It is generated at great pressure, at depths 10 miles (16 km) or more below the Earth's surface.

Mantle The layer of the Earth between the *crust* and the *core*. It is about 1800 miles (2900 km) thick.

Massif A single very large mountain or an area of mountains with uniform characteristics and clearly defined boundaries.

Meltwater Water resulting from the melting of a *glacier* or *ice sheet*.

Mesa A broad, flat-topped hill, characteristic of arid regions.

Metamorphic rocks Rocks which have been altered from their original form, in terms of texture, composition and structure by intense heat, pressure or by the introduction of new chemical substances – or a combination of more than one of these.

Milankovitch hypothesis A theory suggesting that there are a series of cycles that slightly alter the Earth's position when rotating about the Sun.

Mistral A strong, dry, cold northerly or north-westerly wind, which blows from the Massif Central of France to the Mediterranean Sea.

Mohorovičić discontinuity (Moho) The structural divide at the margin between the Earth's *crust* and the *mantle*. On average it is 20 miles (35 km) below the continents and 6 miles (10 km) below the oceans.

Monsoon A wind which changes direction bi-annually. The change is caused by the reversal of pressure over landmasses and the adjacent oceans. Because the inflowing moist winds bring rain, the term monsoon is also used to refer to the rains themselves.

Moraine Debris, transported and deposited by a *glacier* or *ice sheet* in unstratified, mixed, piles of rock, boulders, pebbles and clay.

Mountain-building The formation of fold mountains by tectonic activity. Also known as orogeny, mountain-building often occurs on the margin where two *tectonic plates* collide.

Nappe A mass of rocks which has been overfolded by repeated thrust faulting.

Oasis A fertile area in the midst of a desert, usually watered by an underground *aquifer*.

Oceanic ridge A mid-ocean ridge formed, according to the theory of plate tectonics, when plates drift apart and hot *magma* pours through to form new oceanic crust.

Onion-skin weathering The weathering away or exfoliation of a rock or outcrop by the peeling off of surface layers.

Outwash plain Glaciofluvial material (typically clay, sand and gravel) carried beyond an *ice sheet* by *meltwater* streams, forming a broad, flat deposit.

Oxbow lake A crescent-shaped lake formed on a river *flood plain* when a river erodes the outside bend of a meander, making the neck of the meander narrower until the river cuts across the neck. The meander is cut off and is dammed off with *sediment*, creating an oxbow lake.

Oxidation A form of chemical *weathering* where oxygen dissolved in water reacts with minerals in rocks – particularly iron to form oxides.

Pack ice Ice masses more than 10 ft (3 m) thick that form on the sea surface and are not attached to a landmass.

Pancake ice Thin discs of ice, up to 8 ft (2.4 m) wide which form when slicks of *grease ice* are tossed together by winds and stormy seas.

Pangaea In the theory of *continental drift*, Pangaea is the original great land mass which, about 190 million years ago, began to split into Gondwanaland in the south and Laurasia in the north, separated by the Tethys Sea.

Pediment A gently sloping ramp of bedrock below a steeper slope, often found at mountain edges in desert areas, but also in other climatic zones. Pediments may include depositional elements such as *alluvial fans*.

Periglacial Regions on the edges of *ice sheets* or *glaciers* or, more commonly, cold regions experiencing intense frost action, permafrost or both.

Permafrost Permanently frozen ground, typical of Arctic regions.

Permeable rocks Rocks through which water can seep, because they are either porous or cracked.

Phreatic eruption A volcanic eruption which occurs when lava combines with groundwater, superheating the water and causing a sudden emission of steam at the surface.

Pingo A dome of earth with a core of ice, found in tundra regions. Pingos are formed either when groundwater freezes and expands, pushing up the land surface, or when trapped, freezing water in a lake expands and pushes up lake sediments to form the pingo dome.

Placer A belt of mineral-bearing rock strata lying at or close to the Earth's surface, from which minerals can be easily extracted.

Plate, plate tectonics The study of tectonic plates, that helps to explain *continental drift*, mountain formation and volcanic activity. The movement of tectonic plates may be explained by the currents of rock rising and falling from within the Earth's *mantle*, as it heats up and then cools. The boundaries of the plates are known as plate margins and most mountains, earthquakes and volcanoes occur at these margins. Constructive margins are moving apart; destructive margins are crunching together and conservative margins are sliding past one another.

Pleistocene A period of geological time spanning from about 5.2 million years ago to 1.6 million years ago.

Plutonic rock Igneous rocks found deep below the surface. They are coarse-grained because they cooled and solidified slowly.

Polje A long, broad depression found in karst (limestone) regions.

Polygonal patterning Typical ground patterning, found in areas where the soil is subject to severe frost action, often in *periglacial* regions.

Porosity A measure of how much water can be held within a rock or a soil.

Pre-Cambrian The earliest period of geological time dating from over 570 million years ago.

Precipitation The fall of moisture from the atmosphere onto the surface of the Earth, whether as dew, hail, rain, sleet or snow.

Pyramidal peak A steep, isolated mountain summit, formed when the back walls of three or more cirques are cut back and move towards each other. The cliffs around such a horned peak, or horn, are divided by sharp *arêtes*.

Pyroclasts Fragments of rock ejected during volcanic eruptions.

Quaternary The current period of geological time, which started about 1.6 million years ago.

Reg A large area of stony desert, where tightly-packed gravel lies on top of clayey sand. A reg is formed where the wind blows away the finer sand.

Resistance The capacity of a rock to resist denudation, by processes such as *weathering* and *erosion*.

Ria A flooded *V-shaped river valley* or estuary, flooded by a rise in sea level (eustacy) or sinking land. It is shorter than a fjord and gets deeper as it meets the sea.

Rift valley A long, narrow depression in the Earth's crust, formed by the sinking of rocks between two faults.

Roche moutonée A rock found in a glaciated valley. The side facing the flow of the glacier has been smoothed and rounded, while the other side has been left more rugged because the *glacier*, as it flows over it, has plucked out frozen fragments and carried them away.

Runoff Water draining from a land surface by flowing across it.

Sabkha The floor of an isolated depression that occurs in an arid environment – usually covered by salt deposits and devoid of vegetation.

Salt plug A rounded hill produced by the upward doming of rock strata caused by the movement of salt or other evaporite deposits under intense pressure.

Sastrugi Ice ridges formed by wind action. They lie parallel to the direction of the wind.

Scree Piles of rock fragments beneath a cliff or rock face, caused by mechanical *weathering*, especially *frost shattering*, where the expansion and contraction of freezing and thawing water within the rock, gradually breaks it up.

Sea-floor spreading The process whereby *tectonic plates* move apart, allowing hot magma to erupt and solidify.

Seamount An isolated, submarine mountain or hill, probably of volcanic origin.

Sediment Grains of rock transported and deposited by rivers, sea, ice or wind.

Sedimentary rocks Rocks formed from the debris of pre-existing rocks or of organic material. They are found in many environments on the ocean floor, on beaches, rivers and deserts.

Seif A sand dune which lies parallel to the direction of the prevailing wind. Seifs form steep-sided ridges, sometimes extending for miles.

Selva A region of wet forest found in the Amazon Basin.

Shale (marine shale) A compacted *sedimentary rock*, with fine-grained particles. Marine shale is formed on the seabed. Fuel such as oil may be extracted from it.

Sheetwash Water that runs downhill in thin sheets without forming channels. It can cause *sheet erosion*.

Sheet erosion The washing away of soil by a thin film or sheet of water, known as *sheetwash*.

Shield A vast stable block of the Earth's *crust*, which has experienced little or no mountain-building.

Sinkhole A circular depression in a limestone region. They are formed by the collapse of an underground cave system or the chemical *weathering* of the limestone.

Slip face The steep leeward side of a sand dune or slope. Opposite side to a back slope.

Soil creep The very gradual downslope movement of rock debris and soil, under the influence of gravity. This is a type of mass movement.

Solifluction A kind of soil creep, where water in the surface layer has saturated the soil and rock debris which slips slowly downhill. It often happens where frozen top-layer deposits thaw, leaving frozen layers below them.

Spit A thin linear deposit of sand or shingle extending from the sea shore.

Stack A tall, isolated pillar of rock near a coastline, created as wave action erodes away the adjacent rock.

Strike-slip fault Occurs where plates move sideways past each other and blocks of rocks move horizontally in relation to each other, not up or down as in normal faults.

Subduction zone A region where two *tectonic plates* collide, forcing one beneath the other.

Submarine fan Deposits of silt and alluvium, carried by large rivers forming great fan-shaped deposits on the ocean floor.

Supercontinent A large continent that breaks up to form smaller continents or that forms when smaller continents merge.

Syncline A basin-shaped downfold in rock strata, created when the strata are compressed, for example where *tectonic plates* collide.

Tableland A highland area with a flat or gently undulating surface.

Tectonic plates Plates, or tectonic plates, are the rigid slabs which form the Earth's outer shell, the *lithosphere*. Eight big plates and several smaller ones have been identified.

Thermokarst Subsidence created by the thawing of ground ice in *periglacial* areas, creating depressions.

Till Unstratified glacial deposits or drift left by a *glacier* or *ice sheet*. Includes mixtures of clay, sand, gravel and boulders.

Topography The typical shape and features of a given area such as land height and terrain.

Tombolo A large sand spit which attaches part of the mainland to an island.

Transform fault In *plate tectonics*, a fault of continental scale, occurring where two plates slide past each other, staying close together for example, the San Andreas Fault. The jerky, uneven movement creates earthquakes but does not destroy or add to the Earth's *crust*

Trench (oceanic trench) A long, deep trough in the ocean floor, formed, according to the theory of *plate tectonics*, when two plates collide and one dives under the other, creating a *subduction zone*.

Tropic of Cancer A line of *latitude* or imaginary circle round the Earth, lying at 23° 28' N.

Tropic of Capricorn A line of *latitude* or imaginary circle round the Earth, lying at 23° 28' S.

U-shaped valley A river valley that has been deepened and widened by a *glacier*. They are characteristically flat-bottomed and steep-sided and generally much deeper than river valleys.

V-shaped valley A typical valley eroded by a river in its upper course.

Wadi The dry bed left by a torrent of water. Also classified as a ephemeral stream, found in arid and semi-arid regions, which are subject to sudden and often severe *flash flooding*.

Watershed The dividing line between one *drainage basin* an area where all streams flow into a single river system – and another. In the US, watershed also means the whole drainage basin of a single river system – its catchment area.

Waterspout A rotating column of water in the form of cloud, mist and spray which form on open water. Often has the appearance of a small tornado.

Weathering The decay and break-up of rocks at or near the Earth's surface, caused by water, wind, heat, or ice, organic material or the atmosphere. Physical weathering includes the effects of frost and temperature changes. Biological weathering includes the effects of plant roots, burrowing animals and the acids produced by animals, especially as they decay after death. Carbonation and hydrolysis are among many kinds of chemical weathering.

NORTH AMERICA

CANADA
PAGES 8–16

UNITED STATES OF AMERICA
PAGES 17–41

MEXICO
PAGES 42–43

BELIZE
PAGES 44–45

COSTA RICA
PAGES 44–45

EL SALVADOR
PAGES 44–45

GUATEMALA
PAGES 44–45

HONDURAS
PAGES 44–45

SOUTH AMERICA

GRENADA
PAGES 46–47

HAITI
PAGES 46–47

JAMAICA
PAGES 46–47

ST KITTS & NEVIS
PAGES 46–47

ST LUCIA
PAGES 46–47

ST VINCENT & THE GRENADINES
PAGES 46–47

TRINIDAD & TOBAGO
PAGES 46–47

COLOMBIA
PAGES 56–57

AFRICA

URUGUAY
PAGES 62–63

CHILE
PAGES 64–65

PARAGUAY
PAGES 64–65

ALGERIA
PAGES 76–77

EGYPT
PAGES 76–77

LIBYA
PAGES 76–77

MOROCCO
PAGES 76–77

TUNISIA
PAGES 76–77

LIBERIA
PAGES 78–79

MALI
PAGES 78–79

MAURITANIA
PAGES 78–79

NIGER
PAGES 78–79

NIGERIA
PAGES 78–79

SENEGAL
PAGES 78–79

SIERRA LEONE
PAGES 78–79

TOGO
PAGES 78–79

BURUNDI
PAGES 82–83

DJIBOUTI
PAGES 82–83

ERITREA
PAGES 82–83

ETHIOPIA
PAGES 82–83

KENYA
PAGES 82–83

RWANDA
PAGES 82–83

SOMALIA
PAGES 82–83

SUDAN
PAGES 82–83

EUROPE

SOUTH AFRICA
PAGES 84–85

SWAZILAND
PAGES 84–85

ZAMBIA
PAGES 84–85

ZIMBABWE
PAGES 84–85

DENMARK
PAGES 94–97

FINLAND
PAGES 94–95

ICELAND
PAGES 94–95

NORWAY
PAGES 94–97

MONACO
PAGES 104–105

ANDORRA
PAGES 106–107

PORTUGAL
PAGES 106–107

SPAIN
PAGES 106–107

ITALY
PAGES 108–109

SAN MARINO
PAGES 108–109

VATICAN CITY
PAGES 108–109

AUSTRIA
PAGES 110–111

BOSNIA & HERZEGOVINA
PAGES 114–115

CROATIA
PAGES 114–115

MACEDONIA
PAGES 114–115

YUGOSLAVIA
PAGES 114–115

BULGARIA
PAGES 116–117

GREECE
PAGES 116–117

MOLDOVA
PAGES 118–119

ROMANIA
PAGES 118–119

ASIA

ARMENIA
PAGES 142–143

AZERBAIJAN
PAGES 142–143

GEORGIA
PAGES 142–143

TURKEY
PAGES 142–143/116–117

IRAQ
PAGES 144–145

ISRAEL
PAGES 144–145

JORDAN
PAGES 144–145

LEBANON
PAGES 144–145

IRAN
PAGES 148–149

KAZAKHSTAN
PAGES 150–151

KYRGYZSTAN
PAGES 152–153

TAJIKISTAN
PAGES 152–153

TURKMENISTAN
PAGES 152–153

UZBEKISTAN
PAGES 152–153

AFGHANISTAN
PAGES 154–155

PAKISTAN
PAGES 154–157

SOUTH KOREA
PAGES 162–163/168–169

TAIWAN
PAGES 166–167

JAPAN
PAGES 170–172

BRUNEI
PAGES 173–176

INDONESIA
PAGES 173–176

MALAYSIA
PAGES 173–176

SINGAPORE
PAGES 173–176

BURMA
PAGES 177–179

AUSTRALASIA & OCEANIA

MAURITIUS
PAGES 180–181

SEYCHELLES
PAGES 180–181

AUSTRALIA
PAGES 188–191

NEW ZEALAND
PAGES 192–193

PAPUA NEW GUINEA
PAGES 194–195

SOLOMON ISLANDS
PAGES 194–195

MARSHALL ISLANDS
PAGES 196/201

MICRONESIA
PAGES 196/201

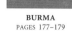